Who's Who in the West®

Biographical Titles Currently Published by Marquis Who's Who

Who's Who in America
Who's Who in America Junior & Senior High School Version
Who Was Who in America
  Historical Volume (1607–1896)
  Volume I (1897–1942)
  Volume II (1943–1950)
  Volume III (1951–1960)
  Volume IV (1961–1968)
  Volume V (1969–1973)
  Volume VI (1974–1976)
  Volume VII (1977–1981)
  Volume VIII (1982–1985)
  Volume IX (1985–1989)
  Volume X (1989–1993)
  Index Volume (1607–1993)
Who's Who in the World
Who's Who in the East
Who's Who in the Midwest
Who's Who in the South and Southwest
Who's Who in the West
Who's Who in American Education
Who's Who in American Law
Who's Who in American Nursing
Who's Who of American Women
Who's Who of Emerging Leaders in America
Who's Who in Entertainment
Who's Who in Finance and Industry
Who's Who in Religion
Who's Who in Science and Engineering
Index to Who's Who Books
The *Official* ABMS Directory of Board Certified Medical Specialists

Who's Who in the West®

Including Alaska, Arizona, California, Colorado, Hawaii, Idaho, Montana, Nevada, New Mexico, Oregon, Utah, Washington, and Wyoming; and in Canada, the provinces of Alberta, British Columbia, and Saskatchewan, and the Northwest and Yukon Territories.

24th Edition
1994-1995

121 Chanlon Road
New Providence, NJ 07974 U.S.A

Marquis Who'sWho
Who'sWho in the West

Published by Marquis Who's Who, A Reed Reference Publishing Company.

Library of Congress Catalog Card Number 49-48186
International Standard Book Number 0-8379-0924-4 (Classic Edition)
0-8379-0925-2 (Deluxe Edition)

Manufactured in the United States of America

Table of Contents

Preface

The twenty-fourth edition of Marquis *Who's Who in the West* is a current compilation of biographical information on men and women of distinction whose influence is concentrated in the western sector of North America. Such individuals are of decided reference interest locally and, in many instances, nationally.

The volume contains approximately 23,500 names from the western region of the United States including Alaska, Arizona, California, Colorado, Hawaii, Idaho, Montana, Nevada, New Mexico, Oregon, Utah, Washington, and Wyoming. Also included are the Canadian provinces of Alberta, British Columbia, and Saskatchewan, and the Northwest and Yukon Territories. Reviewed, revised, and amended, the twenty-fourth edition offers up-to-date coverage of a broad range of Westerners based on position or individual achievement.

The persons sketched in this volume represent virtually every important field of endeavor. Included are executives and officials in government, business, education, religion, the press, civic affairs, the arts, cultural activities, law, and other fields. This edition also includes significant contributors to such fields as contemporary art, music, and science.

Selection of a name for inclusion in Marquis *Who's Who in the West* is based on reference value. Some individuals achieve eligibility for listing through professional position, while others have distinguished themselves through notable achievements in their fields. Biographees are persons who are of reference importance to colleagues, librarians, researchers, scholars, the press, historians, biographers, participants in business and civic affairs, and others with specific or general inquiry needs. Many of these individuals are nationally recognized as well as of regional or local importance.

In the editorial evaluation that resulted in the ultimate selection of the names in this directory, an individual's desire to be listed was not sufficient reason for inclusion. Only occupational stature or achievement in a field within the western region of North America influenced selection.

Each candidate is invited to submit biographical data about his or her life and business career. Submitted information is reviewed by the Marquis editorial staff before being written in sketch form, and a prepublicaton proof of the composed sketch is sent to potential Biographees for verification. Every verified sketch returned by a candidate and accepted by the editorial staff is written in the final Marquis Who's Who format. This process ensures a high degree of accuracy.

In the event that individuals of significant reference interest fail to submit biographical data, the Marquis staff compiles the information through independent research. Brief key information is provided in the sketches of selected individuals, new to this edition, who did not submit data. Such sketches are denoted by an asterisk.

Marquis Who's Who editors exercise the utmost care in preparing each biographical sketch for publication. Occasionally, however, errors do appear. Users of this directory are requested to draw to the attention of the publisher any errors found so that corrections can be made in a subsequent edition.

Board of Advisors

Marquis Who's Who gratefully acknowledges the following distinguished individuals who have made themselves available for review, evaluation, and general comment with regard to the publication of the twenty-fourth edition of Marquis *Who's Who in the West*. The advisors have enhanced the reference value of this edition by the nomination of outstanding individuals for inclusion. However, the Board of Advisors, either collectively or individually, is in no way responsible for the final selection of names, or for the accuracy or comprehensiveness of the biographical information or other material contained herein.

John David Alexander
Trustees Professor
Pomona College
Claremont, California

Duncan Ferguson Cameron
Director Emeritus
Glenbow-Alberta Institute
Calgary, Alberta

Edward W. Carter
Chair of the Board Emeritus
Carter Hawley Hale Stores, Inc.
Los Angeles, California

Marion Irvine Lederer
Cultural Administrator
Los Angeles, California

James A. Mason
Dean
College of Fine Arts and Communications
Brigham Young University
Provo, Utah

William A. Nierenberg
Director Emeritus
Scripps Institution of Oceanography
La Jolla, California

Jerold D. Ottley
Music Director
Salt Lake Mormon Tabernacle Choir
Salt Lake City, Utah

Margaret W. Owings
Conservationist, Artist
Big Sur, California

Russell Ritter
Mayor
Helena, Montana
Vice President for College Relations
Carroll College
Helena, Montana

Board of Nominators

Marquis Who's Who gratefully acknowledges the following distinguished individuals who have made themselves available for review, evaluation, and general comment with regard to the publication of the twenty-fourth edition of Marquis *Who's Who in the West*. The nominators have enhanced the reference value of this edition by the nomination of outstanding individuals for inclusion. However, the Board of Nominators, either collectively or individually, is in no way responsible for the final selection of names, or for the accuracy or comprehensiveness of the biographical information or other material contained herein.

Terri L. Cole
President
Greater Albuquerque Chamber of Commerce
Albuquerque, New Mexico

Allan B. Hughes
Executive Director
Anaheim Chamber of Commerce
Anaheim, California

Art Pick
Executive Vice President
Greater Riverside Chambers of Commerce
Riverside, California

Ray Remy
President
Los Angeles Area Chamber of Commerce
Los Angeles, California

Harry L. York
Executive Vice President
Concord Chamber of Commerce
Concord, California

Standards of Admission

The foremost consideration in selecting Biographees for Marquis *Who's Who in the West* is the extent of an individual's reference interest. Such reference interest is judged on either of two factors: (1) the position of responsibility held, or (2) the level of achievement attained by the individual.

Admissions based on the factor of position include:

Members of the U.S. Congress

Federal judges

Governors of states covered by this volume

Premiers of Canadian provinces covered by this volume

State attorneys general

Judges of state and territorial courts of highest appellate jurisdiction

Mayors of major cities

Heads of major universities and colleges

Heads of leading philanthropic, educational, cultural, and scientific institutions and associations

Chief ecclesiastics of the principal religious denominations

Principal officers of national and international business

Others chosen because of incumbency or membership

Admission for individual achievement is based on objective qualitative criteria. To be selected, a person must have attained conspicuous achievement.

Key to Information

[1] ASHTON, HARDY AMES, [2] lawyer; **[3]** b. Topeka, Aug. 3, 1934; **[4]** s. Samuel Taylor and Barbara (Hanson) A.; **[5]** m. Nancy Richardson, June 20, 1955; **[6]** children: Marilyn Ashton Heim, Barbara Anne, William Marc. **[7]** BA, Pa. State U., 1955; JD, Syracuse U., 1960. **[8]** Bar: Calif. 1960, U.S. Supreme Ct. 1968. **[9]** Assoc. Prine, Belden & Coates, Sacramento, 1960-67; mem. Johnson, Randolph, Sikes and Bord, Sacramento, 1967—, ptnr., 1969-74, sr. ptnr., 1974—; **[10]** legal cons. Sacramento Urban League. **[11]** Author: Urban Renewal and the Law, 1975, Changes in California Zoning Laws: A Perspective, Enterprise Zones: A New Perspective, 1993. **[12]** Commr. Sutter County Park Dist., 1971-78; mem. planning com. Arroyo Seco Redevel. Project, Sacramento, 1980; bd. dirs. Hargrave Inst., 1985—. **[13]** Served with U.S. Army, 1956-57. **[14]** Named Man of Yr., Sacramento C. of C., 1986. **[15]** Mem. ABA, Calif. Bar Assn., Sacramento Bar Assn., Am. Judicature Soc., Order of Coif, Twelve Trees Country Club, Tuesday Luncheon Club, Lions (Sacramento). **[16]** Democrat. **[17]** Episcopalian. **[18]** Home: 3080 Grant St Sacramento CA 95814 **[19]** Office: Johnson Randolph Sikes and Bord 10 Saint Paul Ave Sacramento CA 95822

KEY

[1] Name
[2] Occupation
[3] Vital statistics
[4] Parents
[5] Marriage
[6] Children
[7] Education
[8] Professional certifications
[9] Career
[10] Career related
[11] Writings and creative works
[12] Civic and political activities
[13] Military
[14] Awards and fellowships
[15] Professional and association memberships, clubs and lodges
[16] Political affiliation
[17] Religion
[18] Home address
[19] Office address

Table of Abbreviations

The following abbreviations and symbols are frequently used in this book.

*An asterisk following a sketch indicates that it was researched by the Marquis Who's Who editorial staff and has not been verified by the Biographee.

A Associate (used with academic degrees only)
AA, A.A. Associate in Arts, Associate of Arts
AAAL American Academy of Arts and Letters
AAAS American Association for the Advancement of Science
AACD American Association for Counseling and Development
AACN American Association of Critical Care Nurses
AAHA American Academy of Health Administrators
AAHP American Association of Hospital Planners
AAHPERD American Alliance for Health, Physical Education, Recreation, and Dance
AAS Associate of Applied Science
AASL American Association of School Librarians
AASPA American Association of School Personnel Administrators
AAU Amateur Athletic Union
AAUP American Association of University Professors
AAUW American Association of University Women
AB, A.B. Arts, Bachelor of
AB Alberta
ABA American Bar Association
ABC American Broadcasting Company
AC Air Corps
acad. academy, academic
acct. accountant
acctg. accounting
ACDA Arms Control and Disarmament Agency
ACHA American College of Hospital Administrators
ACLS Advanced Cardiac Life Support
ACLU American Civil Liberties Union
ACOG American College of Ob-Gyn
ACP American College of Physicians
ACS American College of Surgeons
ADA American Dental Association
a.d.c. aide-de-camp
adj. adjunct, adjutant
adj. gen. adjutant general
adm. admiral
adminstr. administrator
adminstrn. administration
adminstrv. administrative
ADN Associate's Degree in Nursing
ADP Automatic Data Processing
adv. advocate, advisory
advt. advertising
AE, A.E. Agricultural Engineer
A.E. and P. Ambassador Extraordinary and Plenipotentiary
AEC Atomic Energy Commission
aero. aeronautical, aeronautic
aerodyn. aerodynamic
AFB Air Force Base
AFL-CIO American Federation of Labor and Congress of Industrial Organizations
AFTRA American Federation of TV and Radio Artists
AFSCME American Federation of State, County and Municipal Employees
agr. agriculture
agrl. agricultural
agt. agent
AGVA American Guild of Variety Artists
agy. agency
A&I Agricultural and Industrial
AIA American Institute of Architects
AIAA American Institute of Aeronautics and Astronautics
AICE American Institute of Chemical Engineers
AICPA American Institute of Certified Public Accountants
AID Agency for International Development
AIDS Acquired Immune Deficiency Syndrome
AIEE American Institute of Electrical Engineers
AIM American Institute of Management
AIME American Institute of Mining, Metallurgy, and Petroleum Engineers
AK Alaska
AL Alabama
ALA American Library Association
Ala. Alabama
alt. alternate
Alta. Alberta
A&M Agricultural and Mechanical
AM, A.M. Arts, Master of
Am. American, America
AMA American Medical Association
amb. ambassador
A.M.E. African Methodist Episcopal
Amtrak National Railroad Passenger Corporation
AMVETS American Veterans of World War II, Korea, Vietnam
ANA American Nurses Association
anat. anatomical
ANCC American Nurses Credentialing Center
ann. annual
ANTA American National Theatre and Academy
anthrop. anthropological
AP Associated Press
APA American Psychological Association
APGA American Personnel Guidance Association
APHA American Public Health Association
APO Army Post Office
apptd. appointed
Apr. April
apt. apartment
AR Arkansas
ARC American Red Cross
archeol. archeological
archtl. architectural
Ariz. Arizona
Ark. Arkansas
ArtsD, ArtsD. Arts, Doctor of
arty. artillery
AS American Samoa
AS Associate in Science
ASCAP American Society of Composers, Authors and Publishers
ASCD Association for Supervision and Curriculum Development
ASCE American Society of Civil Engineers
ASHRAE American Society of Heating, Refrigeration, and Air Conditioning Engineers
ASME American Society of Mechanical Engineers
ASNSA American Society for Nursing Service Administrators
ASPA American Society for Public Administration
ASPCA American Society for the Prevention of Cruelty to Animals
assn. association
assoc. associate
asst. assistant
ASTD American Society for Training and Development
ASTM American Society for Testing and Materials
astron. astronomical
astrophys. astrophysical
ATSC Air Technical Service Command
AT&T American Telephone & Telegraph Company
atty. attorney
Aug. August
AUS Army of the United States
aux. auxiliary
Ave. Avenue
AVMA American Veterinary Medical Association
AZ Arizona
AWHONN Association of Women's Health Obstetric and Neonatal Nurses

B. Bachelor
b. born
BA, B.A. Bachelor of Arts
BAgr, B.Agr. Bachelor of Agriculture
Balt. Baltimore
Bapt. Baptist
BArch, B.Arch. Bachelor of Architecture
BAS, B.A.S. Bachelor of Agricultural Science
BBA, B.B.A. Bachelor of Business Administration
BBC British Broadcasting Corporation
BC, B.C. British Columbia
BCE, B.C.E. Bachelor of Civil Engineering

BChir, B.Chir. Bachelor of Surgery
BCL, B.C.L. Bachelor of Civil Law
BCLS Basic Cardiac Life Support
BCS, B.C.S. Bachelor of Commercial Science
BD, B.D. Bachelor of Divinity
bd. board
BE, B.E. Bachelor of Education
BEE, B.E.E. Bachelor of Electrical Engineering
BFA, B.F.A. Bachelor of Fine Arts
bibl. biblical
bibliog. bibliographical
biog. biographical
biol. biological
BJ, B.J. Bachelor of Journalism
Bklyn. Brooklyn
BL, B.L. Bachelor of Letters
bldg. building
BLS, B.L.S. Bachelor of Library Science
BLS Basic Life Support
Blvd. Boulevard
BMI Broadcast Music, Inc.
BMW Bavarian Motor Works (Bayerische Motoren Werke)
bn. battalion
B.&O.R.R. Baltimore & Ohio Railroad
bot. botanical
BPE, B.P.E. Bachelor of Physical Education
BPhil, B.Phil. Bachelor of Philosophy
br. branch
BRE, B.R.E. Bachelor of Religious Education
brig. gen. brigadier general
Brit. British, Brittanica
Bros. Brothers
BS, B.S. Bachelor of Science
BSA, B.S.A. Bachelor of Agricultural Science
BSBA Bachelor of Science in Business Administration
BSChemE Bachelor of Science in Chemical Engineering
BSD, B.S.D. Bachelor of Didactic Science
BSEE Bachelor of Science in Electrical Engineering
BSN Bachelor of Science in Nursing
BST, B.S.T. Bachelor of Sacred Theology
BTh, B.Th. Bachelor of Theology
bull. bulletin
bur. bureau
bus. business
B.W.I. British West Indies

CA California
CAA Civil Aeronautics Administration
CAB Civil Aeronautics Board
CAD-CAM Computer Aided Design-Computer Aided Model
Calif. California
C.Am. Central America
Can. Canada, Canadian
CAP Civil Air Patrol
capt. captain
CARE Cooperative American Relief Everywhere
Cath. Catholic
cav. cavalry
CBC Canadian Broadcasting Company
CBI China, Burma, India Theatre of Operations
CBS Columbia Broadcasting Company
C.C. Community College
CCC Commodity Credit Corporation
CCNY City College of New York
CCRN Critical Care Registered Nurse
CCU Cardiac Care Unit
CD Civil Defense
CE, C.E. Corps of Engineers, Civil Engineer
CEN Certified Emergency Nurse
CENTO Central Treaty Organization
CEO chief executive officer
CERN European Organization of Nuclear Research
cert. certificate, certification, certified
CETA Comprehensive Employment Training Act
CFA Chartered Financial Analyst
CFL Canadian Football League
CFO chief financial officer
CFP Certified Financial Planner
ch. church
ChD, Ch.D. Doctor of Chemistry
chem. chemical
ChemE, Chem.E. Chemical Engineer
ChFC Chartered Financial Consultant
Chgo. Chicago
chirurg. chirurgical
chmn. chairman
chpt. chapter
CIA Central Intelligence Agency
Cin. Cincinnati
cir. circuit
Cleve. Cleveland
climatol. climatological
clin. clinical
clk. clerk
C.L.U. Chartered Life Underwriter
CM, C.M. Master in Surgery
CM Northern Mariana Islands
CMA Certified Medical Assistant
CNA Certified Nurse's Aide
CNOR Certified Nurse (Operating Room)
C.&N.W.Ry. Chicago & North Western Railway
CO Colorado
Co. Company
COF Catholic Order of Foresters
C. of C. Chamber of Commerce
col. colonel
coll. college
Colo. Colorado
com. committee
comd. commanded
comdg. commanding
comdr. commander
comdt. commandant
comm. communications
commd. commissioned
comml. commercial
commn. commission
commr. commissioner
compt. comptroller
condr. conductor
Conf. Conference
Congl. Congregational, Congressional
Conglist. Congregationalist
Conn. Connecticut
cons. consultant, consulting
consol. consolidated
constl. constitutional
constn. constitution
constrn. construction
contbd. contributed
contbg. contributing
contbn. contribution
contbr. contributor
contr. controller
Conv. Convention
COO chief operating officer
coop. cooperative
coord. coordinator
CORDS Civil Operations and Revolutionary Development Support
CORE Congress of Racial Equality
corp. corporation, corporate
corr. correspondent, corresponding, correspondence
C.&O.Ry. Chesapeake & Ohio Railway
coun. council
CPA Certified Public Accountant
CPCU Chartered Property and Casualty Underwriter
CPH, C.P.H. Certificate of Public Health
cpl. corporal
CPR Cardio-Pulmonary Resuscitation
C.P.Ry. Canadian Pacific Railway
CRT Cathode Ray Terminal
C.S. Christian Science
CSB, C.S.B. Bachelor of Christian Science
C.S.C. Civil Service Commission
CT Connecticut
ct. court
ctr. center
ctrl. central
CWS Chemical Warfare Service
C.Z. Canal Zone

D. Doctor
d. daughter
DAgr, D.Agr. Doctor of Agriculture
DAR Daughters of the American Revolution
dau. daughter
DAV Disabled American Veterans
DC, D.C. District of Columbia
DCL, D.C.L. Doctor of Civil Law
DCS, D.C.S. Doctor of Commercial Science
DD, D.D. Doctor of Divinity
DDS, D.D.S. Doctor of Dental Surgery
DE Delaware
Dec. December
dec. deceased
def. defense
Del. Delaware

del. delegate, delegation
Dem. Democrat, Democratic
DEng, D.Eng. Doctor of Engineering
denom. denomination, denominational
dep. deputy
dept. department
dermatol. dermatological
desc. descendant
devel. development, developmental
DFA, D.F.A. Doctor of Fine Arts
D.F.C. Distinguished Flying Cross
DHL, D.H.L. Doctor of Hebrew Literature
dir. director
dist. district
distbg. distributing
distbn. distribution
distbr. distributor
disting. distinguished
div. division, divinity, divorce
DLitt, D.Litt. Doctor of Literature
DMD, D.M.D. Doctor of Dental Medicine
DMS, D.M.S. Doctor of Medical Science
DO, D.O. Doctor of Osteopathy
DON Director of Nursing
DPH, D.P.H. Diploma in Public Health
DPhil, D.Phil. Doctor of Philosophy
D.R. Daughters of the Revolution
Dr. Drive, Doctor
DRE, D.R.E. Doctor of Religious Education
DrPH, Dr.P.H. Doctor of Public Health, Doctor of Public Hygiene
D.S.C. Distinguished Service Cross
DSc, D.Sc. Doctor of Science
DSChemE Doctor of Science in Chemical Engineering
D.S.M. Distinguished Service Medal
DST, D.S.T. Doctor of Sacred Theology
DTM, D.T.M. Doctor of Tropical Medicine
DVM, D.V.M. Doctor of Veterinary Medicine
DVS, D.V.S. Doctor of Veterinary Surgery

E, E. East
ea. eastern
E. and P. Extraordinary and Plenipotentiary
Eccles. Ecclesiastical
ecol. ecological
econ. economic
ECOSOC Economic and Social Council (of the UN)
ED, E.D. Doctor of Engineering
ed. educated
EdB, Ed.B. Bachelor of Education
EdD, Ed.D. Doctor of Education
edit. edition
EdM, Ed.M. Master of Education
edn. education
ednl. educational
EDP Electronic Data Processing
EdS, Ed.S. Specialist in Education
EE, E.E. Electrical Engineer
E.E. and M.P. Envoy Extraordinary and Minister Plenipotentiary
EEC European Economic Community
EEG Electroencephalogram
EEO Equal Employment Opportunity
EEOC Equal Employment Opportunity Commission
E.Ger. German Democratic Republic
EKG Electrocardiogram
elec. electrical
electrochem. electrochemical
electrophys. electrophysical
elem. elementary
EM, E.M. Engineer of Mines
EMT Emergency Medical Technician
ency. encyclopedia
Eng. England
engr. engineer
engring. engineering
entomol. entomological
environ. environmental
EPA Environmental Protection Agency
epidemiol. epidemiological
Episc. Episcopalian
ERA Equal Rights Amendment
ERDA Energy Research and Development Administration
ESEA Elementary and Secondary Education Act
ESL English as Second Language
ESPN Entertainment and Sports Programming Network
ESSA Environmental Science Services Administration
ethnol. ethnological
ETO European Theatre of Operations
Evang. Evangelical
exam. examination, examining
Exch. Exchange
exec. executive
exhbn. exhibition
expdn. expedition
expn. exposition
expt. experiment
exptl. experimental
Expy. Expressway
Ext. Extension

F.A. Field Artillery
FAA Federal Aviation Administration
FAO Food and Agriculture Organization (of the UN)
FBI Federal Bureau of Investigation
FCA Farm Credit Administration
FCC Federal Communications Commission
FCDA Federal Civil Defense Administration
FDA Food and Drug Administration
FDIA Federal Deposit Insurance Administration
FDIC Federal Deposit Insurance Corporation
FE, F.E. Forest Engineer
FEA Federal Energy Administration
Feb. February
fed. federal
fedn. federation
FERC Federal Energy Regulatory Commission
fgn. foreign
FHA Federal Housing Administration
fin. financial, finance
FL Florida
Fl. Floor
Fla. Florida
FMC Federal Maritime Commission
FNP Family Nurse Practitioner
FOA Foreign Operations Administration
found. foundation
FPC Federal Power Commission
FPO Fleet Post Office
frat. fraternity
FRS Federal Reserve System
FSA Federal Security Agency
Ft. Fort
FTC Federal Trade Commission
Fwy. Freeway

G-1 (or other number) Division of General Staff
GA, Ga. Georgia
GAO General Accounting Office
gastroent. gastroenterological
GATE Gifted and Talented Educators
GATT General Agreement on Tariffs and Trade
GE General Electric Company
gen. general
geneal. genealogical
geod. geodetic
geog. geographic, geographical
geol. geological
geophys. geophysical
gerontol. gerontological
G.H.Q. General Headquarters
GM General Motors Corporation
GMAC General Motors Acceptance Corporation
G.N.Ry. Great Northern Railway
gov. governor
govt. government
govtl. governmental
GPO Government Printing Office
grad. graduate, graduated
GSA General Services Administration
Gt. Great
GTE General Telephone and Electric Company
GU Guam
gynecol. gynecological

HBO Home Box Office
hdqs. headquarters
HEW Department of Health, Education and Welfare
HHD, H.H.D. Doctor of Humanities
HHFA Housing and Home Finance Agency
HHS Department of Health and Human Services
HI Hawaii

hist. historical, historic
HM, H.M. Master of Humanities
HMO Health Maintenance Organization
homeo. homeopathic
hon. honorary, honorable
Ho. of Dels. House of Delegates
Ho. of Reps. House of Representatives
hort. horticultural
hosp. hospital
HUD Department of Housing and Urban Development
Hwy. Highway
hydrog. hydrographic

IA Iowa
IAEA International Atomic Energy Agency
IATSE International Alliance of Theatrical and Stage Employees and Moving Picture Operators of the United States and Canada
IBM International Business Machines Corporation
IBRD International Bank for Reconstruction and Development
ICA International Cooperation Administration
ICC Interstate Commerce Commission
ICCE International Council for Computers in Education
ICU Intensive Care Unit
ID Idaho
IEEE Institute of Electrical and Electronics Engineers
IFC International Finance Corporation
IGY International Geophysical Year
IL Illinois
Ill. Illinois
illus. illustrated
ILO International Labor Organization
IMF International Monetary Fund
IN Indiana
Inc. Incorporated
Ind. Indiana
ind. independent
Indpls. Indianapolis
indsl. industrial
inf. infantry
info. information
ins. insurance
insp. inspector
insp. gen. inspector general
inst. institute
instl. institutional
instn. institution
instr. instructor
instrn. instruction
instrnl. instructional
internat. international
intro. introduction
IRE Institute of Radio Engineers
IRS Internal Revenue Service
ITT International Telephone & Telegraph Corporation

JAG Judge Advocate General
JAGC Judge Advocate General Corps
Jan. January
Jaycees Junior Chamber of Commerce
JB, J.B. Jurum Baccalaureus
JCB, J.C.B. Juris Canoni Baccalaureus
JCD, J.C.D. Juris Canonici Doctor, Juris Civilis Doctor
JCL, J.C.L. Juris Canonici Licentiatus
JD, J.D. Juris Doctor
jg. junior grade
jour. journal
jr. junior
JSD, J.S.D. Juris Scientiae Doctor
JUD, J.U.D. Juris Utriusque Doctor
jud. judicial

Kans. Kansas
K.C. Knights of Columbus
K.P. Knights of Pythias
KS Kansas
K.T. Knight Templar
KY, Ky. Kentucky

LA, La. Louisiana
L.A. Los Angeles
lab. laboratory
L.Am. Latin America
lang. language
laryngol. laryngological
LB Labrador
LDS Latter Day Saints
LDS Church Church of Jesus Christ of Latter Day Saints
lectr. lecturer
legis. legislation, legislative
LHD, L.H.D. Doctor of Humane Letters
L.I. Long Island
libr. librarian, library
lic. licensed, license
L.I.R.R. Long Island Railroad
lit. literature
LittB, Litt.B. Bachelor of Letters
LittD, Litt.D. Doctor of Letters
LLB, LL.B. Bachelor of Laws
LLD, L.L.D. Doctor of Laws
LLM, L.L.M. Master of Laws
Ln. Lane
L.&N.R.R. Louisville & Nashville Railroad
LPGA Ladies Professional Golf Association
LPN Licensed Practical Nurse
LS, L.S. Library Science (in degree)
lt. lieutenant
Ltd. Limited
Luth. Lutheran
LWV League of Women Voters

M. Master
m. married
MA, M.A. Master of Arts
MA Massachusetts
MADD Mothers Against Drunk Driving
mag. magazine
MAgr, M.Agr. Master of Agriculture
maj. major
Man. Manitoba
Mar. March
MArch, M.Arch. Master in Architecture
Mass. Massachusetts
math. mathematics, mathematical
MATS Military Air Transport Service
MB, M.B. Bachelor of Medicine
MB Manitoba
MBA, M.B.A. Master of Business Administration
MBS Mutual Broadcasting System
M.C. Medical Corps
MCE, M.C.E. Master of Civil Engineering
mcht. merchant
mcpl. municipal
MCS, M.C.S. Master of Commercial Science
MD, M.D. Doctor of Medicine
MD, Md. Maryland
MDiv Master of Divinity
MDip, M.Dip. Master in Diplomacy
mdse. merchandise
MDV, M.D.V. Doctor of Veterinary Medicine
ME, M.E. Mechanical Engineer
ME Maine
M.E.Ch. Methodist Episcopal Church
mech. mechanical
MEd., M.Ed. Master of Education
med. medical
MEE, M.E.E. Master of Electrical Engineering
mem. member
meml. memorial
merc. mercantile
met. metropolitan
metall. metallurgical
MetE, Met.E. Metallurgical Engineer
meteorol. meteorological
Meth. Methodist
Mex. Mexico
MF, M.F. Master of Forestry
MFA, M.F.A. Master of Fine Arts
mfg. manufacturing
mfr. manufacturer
mgmt. management
mgr. manager
MHA, M.H.A. Master of Hospital Administration
M.I. Military Intelligence
MI Michigan
Mich. Michigan
micros. microscopic, microscopical
mid. middle
mil. military
Milw. Milwaukee
Min. Minister
mineral. mineralogical
Minn. Minnesota
MIS Management Information Systems
Miss. Mississippi
MIT Massachusetts Institute of Technology
mktg. marketing
ML, M.L. Master of Laws
MLA Modern Language Association

M.L.D. Magister Legnum Diplomatic
MLitt, M.Litt. Master of Literature, Master of Letters
MLS, M.L.S. Master of Library Science
MME, M.M.E. Master of Mechanical Engineering
MN Minnesota
mng. managing
MO, Mo. Missouri
moblzn. mobilization
Mont. Montana
MP Northern Mariana Islands
M.P. Member of Parliament
MPA Master of Public Administration
MPE, M.P.E. Master of Physical Education
MPH, M.P.H. Master of Public Health
MPhil, M.Phil. Master of Philosophy
MPL, M.P.L. Master of Patent Law
Mpls. Minneapolis
MRE, M.R.E. Master of Religious Education
MS, M.S. Master of Science
MS, Ms. Mississippi
MSc, M.Sc. Master of Science
MSChemE Master of Science in Chemical Engineering
MSEE Master of Science in Electrical Engineering
MSF, M.S.F. Master of Science of Forestry
MSN Master of Science in Nursing
MST, M.S.T. Master of Sacred Theology
MSW, M.S.W. Master of Social Work
MT Montana
Mt. Mount
MTO Mediterranean Theatre of Operation
MTV Music Television
mus. museum, musical
MusB, Mus.B. Bachelor of Music
MusD, Mus.D. Doctor of Music
MusM, Mus.M. Master of Music
mut. mutual
mycol. mycological

N. North
NAACOG Nurses Association of the American College of Obstetricians and Gynecologists
NAACP National Association for the Advancement of Colored People
NACA National Advisory Committee for Aeronautics
NACU National Association of Colleges and Universities
NAD National Academy of Design
NAE National Academy of Engineering, National Association of Educators
NAESP National Association of Elementary School Principals
NAFE National Association of Female Executives
N.Am. North America
NAM National Association of Manufacturers
NAMH National Association for Mental Health
NAPA National Association of Performing Artists
NARAS National Academy of Recording Arts and Sciences
NAREB National Association of Real Estate Boards
NARS National Archives and Record Service
NAS National Academy of Sciences
NASA National Aeronautics and Space Administration
NASP National Association of School Psychologists
NASW National Association of Social Workers
nat. national
NATAS National Academy of Television Arts and Sciences
NATO North Atlantic Treaty Organization
NATOUSA North African Theatre of Operations, United States Army
nav. navigation
NB, N.B. New Brunswick
NBA National Basketball Association
NBC National Broadcasting Company
NC, N.C. North Carolina
NCAA National College Athletic Association
NCCJ National Conference of Christians and Jews
ND, N.D. North Dakota
NDEA National Defense Education Act
NE Nebraska
NE, N.E. Northeast
NEA National Education Association
Nebr. Nebraska
NEH National Endowment for Humanities
neurol. neurological
Nev. Nevada
NF Newfoundland
NFL National Football League
Nfld. Newfoundland
NG National Guard
NH, N.H. New Hampshire
NHL National Hockey League
NIH National Institutes of Health
NIMH National Institute of Mental Health
NJ, N.J. New Jersey
NLRB National Labor Relations Board
NM New Mexico
N.Mex. New Mexico
No. Northern
NOAA National Oceanographic and Atmospheric Administration
NORAD North America Air Defense
Nov. November
NOW National Organization for Women
N.P.Ry. Northern Pacific Railway
nr. near
NRA National Rifle Association
NRC National Research Council
NS, N.S. Nova Scotia
NSC National Security Council
NSF National Science Foundation
NSTA National Science Teachers Association
NSW New South Wales
N.T. New Testament
NT Northwest Territories
numis. numismatic
NV Nevada
NW, N.W. Northwest
N.W.T. Northwest Territories
NY, N.Y. New York
N.Y.C. New York City
NYU New York University
N.Z. New Zealand

OAS Organization of American States
ob-gyn obstetrics-gynecology
obs. observatory
obstet. obstetrical
Oct. October
OD, O.D. Doctor of Optometry
OECD Organization of European Cooperation and Development
OEEC Organization of European Economic Cooperation
OEO Office of Economic Opportunity
ofcl. official
OH Ohio
OK Oklahoma
Okla. Oklahoma
ON Ontario
Ont. Ontario
oper. operating
ophthal. ophthalmological
ops. operations
OR Oregon
orch. orchestra
Oreg. Oregon
orgn. organization
orgnl. organizational
ornithol. ornithological
OSHA Occupational Safety and Health Administration
OSRD Office of Scientific Research and Development
OSS Office of Strategic Services
osteo. osteopathic
otol. otological
otolaryn. otolaryngological

PA, Pa. Pennsylvania
P.A. Professional Association
paleontol. paleontological
path. pathological
PBS Public Broadcasting System
P.C. Professional Corporation
PE Prince Edward Island
P.E.I. Prince Edward Island
PEN Poets, Playwrights, Editors, Essayists and Novelists (international association)
penol. penological
P.E.O. women's organization (full name not disclosed)
pers. personnel
pfc. private first class
PGA Professional Golfers' Association of America
PHA Public Housing Administration

pharm. pharmaceutical
PharmD, Pharm.D. Doctor of Pharmacy
PharmM, Pharm.M. Master of Pharmacy
PhB, Ph.B. Bachelor of Philosophy
PhD, Ph.D. Doctor of Philosophy
PhDChemE Doctor of Science in Chemical Engineering
PhM, Ph.M. Master of Philosophy
Phila. Philadelphia
philharm. philharmonic
philol. philological
philos. philosophical
photog. photographic
phys. physical
physiol. physiological
Pitts. Pittsburgh
Pk. Park
Pky. Parkway
Pl. Place
P.&L.E.R.R. Pittsburgh & Lake Erie Railroad
Plz. Plaza
PNP Pediatric Nurse Practitioner
P.O. Post Office
PO Box Post Office Box
polit. political
poly. polytechnic, polytechnical
PQ Province of Quebec
PR, P.R. Puerto Rico
prep. preparatory
pres. president
Presbyn. Presbyterian
presdl. presidential
prin. principal
procs. proceedings
prod. produced (play production)
prodn. production
prodr. producer
prof. professor
profl. professional
prog. progressive
propr. proprietor
pros. atty. prosecuting attorney
pro tem. pro tempore
PSRO Professional Services Review Organization
psychiat. psychiatric
psychol. psychological
PTA Parent-Teachers Association
ptnr. partner
PTO Pacific Theatre of Operations, Parent Teacher Organization
pub. publisher, publishing, published
pub. public
publ. publication
pvt. private

quar. quarterly
qm. quartermaster
Q.M.C. Quartermaster Corps
Que. Quebec

radiol. radiological
RAF Royal Air Force
RCA Radio Corporation of America
RCAF Royal Canadian Air Force
RD Rural Delivery
Rd. Road
R&D Research & Development
REA Rural Electrification Administration
rec. recording
ref. reformed
regt. regiment
regtl. regimental
rehab. rehabilitation
rels. relations
Rep. Republican
rep. representative
Res. Reserve
ret. retired
Rev. Reverend
rev. review, revised
RFC Reconstruction Finance Corporation
RFD Rural Free Delivery
rhinol. rhinological
RI, R.I. Rhode Island
RISD Rhode Island School of Design
Rlwy. Railway
Rm. Room
RN, R.N. Registered Nurse
roentgenol. roentgenological
ROTC Reserve Officers Training Corps
RR Rural Route
R.R. Railroad
rsch. research
rschr. researcher
Rt. Route

S. South
s. son
SAC Strategic Air Command
SAG Screen Actors Guild
SALT Strategic Arms Limitation Talks
S.Am. South America
san. sanitary
SAR Sons of the American Revolution
Sask. Saskatchewan
savs. savings
SB, S.B. Bachelor of Science
SBA Small Business Administration
SC, S.C. South Carolina
SCAP Supreme Command Allies Pacific
ScB, Sc.B. Bachelor of Science
SCD, S.C.D. Doctor of Commercial Science
ScD, Sc.D. Doctor of Science
sch. school
sci. science, scientific
SCLC Southern Christian Leadership Conference
SCV Sons of Confederate Veterans
SD, S.D. South Dakota
SE, S.E. Southeast
SEATO Southeast Asia Treaty Organization
SEC Securities and Exchange Commission
sec. secretary
sect. section
seismol. seismological
sem. seminary
Sept. September
s.g. senior grade
sgt. sergeant
SHAEF Supreme Headquarters Allied Expeditionary Forces
SHAPE Supreme Headquarters Allied Powers in Europe
S.I. Staten Island
S.J. Society of Jesus (Jesuit)
SJD Scientiae Juridicae Doctor
SK Saskatchewan
SM, S.M. Master of Science
SNP Society of Nursing Professionals
So. Southern
soc. society
sociol. sociological
S.P.Co. Southern Pacific Company
spl. special
splty. specialty
Sq. Square
S.R. Sons of the Revolution
sr. senior
SS Steamship
SSS Selective Service System
St. Saint, Street
sta. station
stats. statistics
statis. statistical
STB, S.T.B. Bachelor of Sacred Theology
stblzn. stabilization
STD, S.T.D. Doctor of Sacred Theology
std. standard
Ste. Suite
subs. subsidiary
SUNY State University of New York
supr. supervisor
supt. superintendent
surg. surgical
svc. service
SW, S.W. Southwest

TAPPI Technical Association of the Pulp and Paper Industry
tb. tuberculosis
tchr. teacher
tech. technical, technology
technol. technological
tel. telephone
Tel. & Tel. Telephone & Telegraph
telecom. telecommunications
temp. temporary
Tenn. Tennessee
Ter. Territory
Ter. Terrace
Tex. Texas
ThD, Th.D. Doctor of Theology
theol. theological
ThM, Th.M. Master of Theology
TN Tennessee
tng. training
topog. topographical
trans. transaction, transferred
transl. translation, translated
transp. transportation

treas. treasurer
TT Trust Territory
TV television
TVA Tennessee Valley Authority
TWA Trans World Airlines
twp. township
TX Texas
typog. typographical

U. University
UAW United Auto Workers
UCLA University of California at Los Angeles
UDC United Daughters of the Confederacy
U.K. United Kingdom
UN United Nations
UNESCO United Nations Educational, Scientific and Cultural Organization
UNICEF United Nations International Children's Emergency Fund
univ. university
UNRRA United Nations Relief and Rehabilitation Administration
UPI United Press International
U.P.R.R. United Pacific Railroad
urol. urological
U.S. United States
U.S.A. United States of America
USAAF United States Army Air Force
USAF United States Air Force
USAFR United States Air Force Reserve
USAR United States Army Reserve
USCG United States Coast Guard
USCGR United States Coast Guard Reserve
USES United States Employment Service
USIA United States Information Agency
USMC United States Marine Corps
USMCR United States Marine Corps Reserve
USN United States Navy
USNG United States National Guard
USNR United States Naval Reserve
USO United Service Organizations
USPHS United States Public Health Service
USS United States Ship
USSR Union of the Soviet Socialist Republics
USTA United States Tennis Association
USV United States Volunteers
UT Utah

VA Veterans Administration
VA, Va. Virginia
vet. veteran, veterinary
VFW Veterans of Foreign Wars
VI, V.I. Virgin Islands
vice pres. vice president
vis. visiting
VISTA Volunteers in Service to America
VITA Volunteers in Technical Assistance
vocat. vocational
vol. volunteer, volume
v.p. vice president
vs. versus
VT, Vt. Vermont

W, W. West
WA Washington (state)
WAC Women's Army Corps
Wash. Washington (state)
WATS Wide Area Telecommunications Service
WAVES Women's Reserve, US Naval Reserve
WCTU Women's Christian Temperance Union
we. western
W. Ger. Germany, Federal Republic of
WHO World Health Organization
WI Wisconsin
W.I. West Indies
Wis. Wisconsin
WSB Wage Stabilization Board
WV West Virginia
W.Va. West Virginia
WY Wyoming
Wyo. Wyoming

YK Yukon Territory
YMCA Young Men's Christian Association
YMHA Young Men's Hebrew Association
YM & YWHA Young Men's and Young Women's Hebrew Association
yr. year
YT, Y.T. Yukon Territory
YWCA Young Women's Christian Association

zool. zoological

Alphabetical Practices

Names are arranged alphabetically according to the surnames, and under identical surnames according to the first given name. If both surname and first given name are identical, names are arranged alphabetically according to the second given name.

Surnames beginning with De, Des, Du, however capitalized or spaced, are recorded with the prefix preceding the surname and arranged alphabetically under the letter D.

Surnames beginning with Mac and Mc are arranged alphabetically under M.

Surnames beginning with Saint or St. appear after names that begin Sains, and are arranged according to the second part of the name, e.g. St. Clair before Saint Dennis.

Surnames beginning with Van, Von, or von are arranged alphabetically under letter V.

Compound hyphenated surnames are arranged according to the first member of the compound. Compound unhyphenated surnames are treated as hyphenated names.

Many hyphenated Arabic names begin Al-, El-, or al-. These names are alphabetized according to each Biographee's designation of last name. Thus Al-Bahar, Mohammed may be listed either under Al- or under Bahar, depending on the preference of the listee.

Parentheses used in connection with a name indicate which part of the full name is usually deleted in common usage. Hence Abbott, W(illiam) Lewis indicates that the usual form of the given name is W. Lewis. In such a case, the parentheses are ignored in alphabetizing and the name would be arranged as Abbott, William Lewis. However, if the name is recorded Abbott, (William) Lewis, signifying that the entire name William is not commonly used, the alphabetizing would be arranged as though the name were Abbott, Lewis. If an entire middle or last name is enclosed in parentheses, that portion of the name is used in the alphabetical arrangement. Hence Abbott, William (Lewis) would be arranged as Abbott, William Lewis.

Who'sWho in the West®

Biographies

AADAHL, JORG, business executive; b. Trondheim, Norway, June 16, 1937; came to U.S., 1966; s. Ottar P. and Gurli (Lockra) A.; MS in Mech. Engring., Tech. U. Norway, 1961; MBA, U. San Francisco, 1973; m. Inger R. Holst, July 13, 1973; children: Erik, Nina. Research fellow Tech. U. Norway, Trondheim, 1961-62; mgr. arc welding devel. NAG, Oslo, 1964-66; mfg. engr. Varian Assocs., Palo Alto, Calif., 1966-67; bus. mgr. United Airlines, San Francisco, 1974-75, sr. systems analyst, 1977-81; strategic planning specialist Magnex Corp., San Jose, 1981-82; cons. in mgmt., 1982-84; founder, pres. Safeware, Inc., San Mateo, Calif., 1984—; dir. Safeware Sys.Ltd., U.K., 1990—. Developer Safechem Hazardous Chem. Mgmt. System. Recipient Cert. of Honor, San Francisco Bd. Suprs., 1973. Mem. Leif Erikson League (pres. 1973), Norwegian Soc. Profl. Engrs. Club: Young Scandinavians (v.p. 1971), Environment and Safety Data Exch. (founding mem., dir.). Author: Strength Analysis, Welded Structures, 1967; contbr. articles in various fields to profl. jours.; editor Nordic Highlights, 1972. Office: Safeware Inc 999 Baker Way San Mateo CA 94404-1568

AALTO, MADELEINE, library administrator. BA, Wellesley Coll., 1964; BLS, U. Toronto, 1967. Clerical asst. Toronto Pub. Libr., 1964-66, children's libr. Parkdale br., 1968-69, collection libr. Spaced Out libr., 1969-73, br. head Annette St. br., 1973-74, coord. adult svcs., 1974-75; chief libr. East York Pub. Libr., 1975-84, Greater Victoria Pub. Libr., 1984-88; dir. Vancouver (B.C.) Pub. Libr., Can., 1988—. Contbr. intro. to A Geography for Children (Philippe du Fresnoy), 1968. Recipient Commerative medal 125th Anniversary Confederation Can., 1993. Mem. B.C. Libr. Assn. Office: Vancouver Pub Lib, 750 Burrard St, Vancouver, BC Canada V6Z 1X5*

AARON, BUD, systems analyst; b. White Sulphur Springs, Mont., Apr. 27, 1927; m. Dina Aaron, Jan. 10, 1960; children: Alex, Roy, Erica, Bill. Owner Microkits, 1963-67; prodn. mgr. Ednl. Computer Products, 1967-68, mfg. rep., 1968-69; instr. Control Data Inst., 1969-70; supr. ICL, Kidsgrove, England, 1970-73; tech. writer Philips Small Computers, Fontenay aux Rose, France, 1973-74; designer, developer computer programs Hughes, JPL. Lawrence Livermore Labs. and others, 1974-76; programmer, mgr., sales BusinessMaster, Carlsbad, Calif., 1976-86; mgr., writer, programmer The Aaron Group, Oceanside, Calif., 1986—.

AARON, ROY HENRY, entertainment company executive, lawyer; b. Los Angeles, Apr. 8, 1929; s. Samuel Arthur and Natalie (Krakauer) A.; m. Theresa Gesas, Dec. 20, 1953; 1 child, Jill. BA, U. Calif.-Berkeley, 1951; LLB, U. So. Calif., 1956. Bar: Calif. 1957. Mem. Pacht, Ross, Warne, Bernhard & Sears, Inc., Los Angeles, 1957-79, of counsel, 1979-83; sr. v.p., gen. counsel Plitt Theatres, Inc. and Plitt Theatre Holdings, Inc., Los Angeles, 1978-80, pres., chief operating officer, 1980-85; pres. Plitt Entertainment Group, Inc., Los Angeles, 1985—; pres., chief exec. officer Showscan Corp., Los Angeles, 1985-93; lectr. Calif. Continuing Edn. of Bar; lectr. continuing legal edn. Loyola U. Law Sch., Los Angeles. Mem. editorial bd. U. So. Calif. Law Rev., 1954-56. Trustee, mem. exec. com. Vista Del Mar Child-Care Service, 1968-80, Reiss-Davis Child Study Center, 1977-80; bd. dirs. Jewish Fedn. Council Greater Los Angeles, 1970-75; vice chmn. lawyers div. United Crusade Campaigns, 1971, 72; mem. adv. bd. dirs. Rape Treatment Ctr. of Santa Monica Hosp.; pres. Royce Two Seventy, 1986-88. With USAF, 1951-53. Fellow Am. Bar Found. (life), L.A. County Bar Found. (life); mem. ABA, State Bar Calif., L.A. County Bar Assn. (trustee 1977-83, v.p. 1979-80, pres. 1982-83), Beverly Hills Bar Assn., UCLA Found. (bd. dirs., trustee), U. So. Calif. Law Alumni Assn., Legion Lex, Found. Motion Picture Pioneers (bd. dirs.), Am. Judicature Soc., Order of Coif, Chancery Club L.A. Office: Showscan Corp Ste 1225 1801 Century Park E Los Angeles CA 90067-2314

AARON, SHIRLEY MAE, tax consultant; b. Covington, La., Feb. 28, 1935; d. Morgan and Pearl (Jenkins) King; m. Richard L. King, Feb. 16, 1952 (div. Feb. 1965); children: Deborah, Richard, Roberta, Keely; m. Michael A. Aaron, Nov. 27, 1976 (dec. July 1987). Adminstrv. asst. South Central Bell, Covington, La., 1954-62; acct. Brown & Root, Inc., Houston, 1962-75; timekeeper Alyeska Pipeline Co., Fairbanks, Alaska, 1975-77; adminstrv. asst. Boeing Co., Seattle, 1979-93; pres. Aaron Enterprises, Seattle, 1977—. Bd. dirs. Burien 146 Homeowners Assn., Seattle, 1979—, pres., 1980-83. Mem. NAFE. Avocation: singing. Home: 131 Gerard St Mandeville LA 70448

AASE, JON MORTON, dysmorphologist, pediatrics educator; b. Eau Claire, Wis., July 15, 1936; s. Maurice Ferdinand and Lorraine (Moe) A.; m. Kathleen Frances Doherty, July 17, 1982; children: Lara Kirsten, Nicholas Edward Jonathan, Caitlin Mariele. BA, Pomona Coll., 1958; MD, Yale U., 1962. Diplomate Am. Bd. Pediatrics. Straight pediatric intern U. Minn. Hosps., Mpls., 1962-63; resident U. Wash. Sch. Medicine, Seattle, 1963-65, sr. fellow dysmorphology unit dept. pediatrics, 1967-69, clin. instr., 1969-74; chief resident Children's Orthopedic Hosp., Seattle, 1964; pvt. practice, Anchorage, 1969-74; asst. prof. U. N.Mex. Sch. Medicine, Albuquerque, 1974-77, assoc. prof., dir. div. dysmorphology, 1977-90, mem. faculty senate sch. medicine, 1978-80; pvt. practice Albuquerque, 1990—; dep. dir. Wash.-Alaska Regional Med. Program, Anchorage, 1969-71; cons. Alaska Native Svc., USPHS, 1969-74, Indian Health Svc., 1979—; assoc. in med. sci. Wash.-Alaska-Mont.-Idaho program U. Alaska, Fairbanks, 1971-74; med. cons. Alaska satellite biomed. communication project Lister Hill Ctr. for Biomed. Communications, Bethesda, Md., 1972-74; program dir. Alaska March of Dimes Svc. Project, Anchorage, 1972-74; vis. prof. Fitzsimons Army Med. Ctr., 1988, U. Hawaii, 1989, also others. Author: Diagnostic Dysmorphology: An approach to the child with congenital abnormalities, 1990; also articles. Acting surgeon USPHS, 1965-67. Recipient William C. and Katherine K. Adamson Scholars award Inst. for Child Devel., Hackensack (N.J.) Med. Ctr., 1990; grantee Nat. Found., 1972-74, 75-78, 80-82, Regional Med. Program Health Care Delivery grantee, 1974-75, Nat. Arthritis, Metabolism and Digestive Diseases, 1978-82, Maternal Child Health, 1985-89, Ctrs. for Disease Control, 1991—. Fellow Am. Acad. Pediatrics; mem. Teratology Soc., Internat. Dermatoglyphics Assn., Western Soc. for Pediatric Rsch., Mountain States Regional Genetic Svcs. Network (steering com.), Alpha Omega Alpha. Office: 201 Cedar St SE Ste 609 Albuquerque NM 87106-4924

AASEN, EUGENE NELS, workers' compensation underwriting manager; b. Seattle, Nov. 28, 1952; s. Paul Holden and Pearl Mathilda (Lanson) A.; m. Alison Hedquist, Aug. 30, 1983 (div. Jan. 23, 1985); 1 child, Daniel Erik. BS in Econs. and Bus. Adminstrn., Idaho State U., 1982. Office mgr. N.Y. Life Ins. Co., Colorado Springs, 1977-85, Phoenix Mut. Life Ins. Co., Denver, 1985-86; workers compensation underwriting mgr. Farmers Ins. Group, L.A., 1986—; loaned exec. United Way, Colorado Springs, 1987-88; project bus. cons. Jr. Achievement, Colorado Springs, 1984-85. Home: 5577 Cochran St #179 Simi Valley CA 93063 Office: Farmers Ins Group 4700 Wilshire Blvd Los Angeles CA 90010

ABARBANEL, JUDITH EDNA, marketing executive; b. N.Y.C., Jan. 26, 1956; d. Albert Brandt and Dorothy Irene (Fennell) A.; m. Christopher George Lucas, June 17, 1984. BA, UCLA, 1977; MBA, MA, Ohio State U., 1980. Accredited pub. relations profl., 1988. Sales mgr. Columbus Magic, Ohio, 1979; account mgr. Mktg. Centre, St. Petersburg, Fla., 1980-82; asst. mktg. dir. MBI, Inc., Golden, Colo., 1983; dir. mktg. Colo. Outward Bound. Sch., Denver, 1983—; owner A Sporting Proposition, Boulder, Colo., 1984—; western region sales promotion mgr. Hinckley & Schmitt, Inc., L.A., 1991—; sr. v.p. Caldirola Prodns., 1992—. Mem. Pub. Rels. Soc. Am. Avocations: mountain biking, race organizing, teaching.

ABBOTT, FRANK CURTIS, educational administrator, consultant; b. Newtonville, Mass., Dec. 12, 1920; s. Clark Daniel and Erma Frances (Richardson) A.; m. Lois Ann Bergen, Dec. 20, 1948; children: Curtis, Jane, Paul, Ken, Alison. BA, Cornell U., 1942, MPA, 1949; PhD, Harvard U., 1956. Account clk. Fed. Pub. Housing Authority, Washington, 1942-43; asst. to provost and pres. Cornell U., Ithaca, N.Y., 1946-49; staff assoc. Am. Coun. on Edn., Washington, 1951-58; asst. dean of univ. Bucknell U., Lewisburg, Pa., 1958-60; acad. v.p. U. Mont., Missoula, 1961-65; exec. dir. Colo. Commn. on Higher Edn., Denver, 1965-76; asst. commr. for professions N.Y. State Edn. Dept., Albany, 1976-84; sr. program dir. Western Interstate Commn. for Higher Edn., Boulder, Colo., 1984-92, coordinating cons., 1992—; cons. Midwestern Higher Edn. Commn., 1991—; staff dir. Regents Comm. Higher Edn. Univ. State of New York, 1992-93. Author: (monograph) The Cambridge City Manager, 1951; Government Policy and Higher Edn., 1958; editor: (monograph) International Programs and Centers for Instruction, Research, and Public Srvice, 1986, 2d edit., 1989; also numerous articles. Bd. dirs. Denver Urban Coalition, 1969-75; pub. mem. coun. on optometric edn. Am. Optometric Assn., St. Louis, 1990—; bd. overseers Regents Coll., U. State N.Y., Albany, 1986—. Lt. USNR, 1943-46. Mem. Am. Assn. for Higher Edn. (life). Democrat. Unitarian.

ABBOTT, JOHN RODGER, electrical engineer; b. L.A., Aug. 2, 1933; s. Carl Raymond and Helen Catherine (Roche) A.; m. Theresa Andrea McQuaide, Apr. 20, 1968. BS with honors, UCLA, 1955; MSEE, U. So. Calif., 1957. Registered profl. engr., Calif. Advanced study engr. Lockheed Missile Systems, L.A., 1955-56; radar systems engr. Hughes Aircraft Co., L.A., 1956-59; devel. engr. Garrett Airesearch Co., L.A., 1959-63, instr. inplant tng. program, 1962-63; asst. project engr. Litton Industries, L.A., 1963; space power systems engr. TRW Systems, L.A., 1963-65; engr. specialist L.A. Dept. Water and Power, 1965-92; engr. specialist Abtronix, 1992—; frequency coordination chmn. Region X, Utilities Telecommunications Coun., 1977-79, sec.-treas. Utilities Telecommunication Coun., 1979-80; instr. amateur radio course L.A. City Schs., Birmingham High Sch., Van Nuys, Calif., 1965-66, Los Feliz Elem. Sch., Hollywood, Calif., 1990—. Contbr. articles to profl. jours. Mem. IEEE, Am. Radio Relay League (Pub. Svc. award 1971), Tau Beta Pi. Office: Abtronix PO Box 220066 Santa Clarita CA 91322-0066

ABBOTT, MARLENE LOUISE, nursing agency administrator; b. Hornell, N.Y., Aug. 11, 1935; d. George Wilfred and Eloise Lois (Simpson) Little; m. Robert Leroy, Mar. 16, 1953; children: Valarie, Kimberley, Steven, Tracey. AAS in Nursing, Corning Community Coll., 1968; BSN, Ariz. State U., 1984. Registered psychiatric community mental health nurse. R.N. ICU-CCU Arnot-Ogden Hosp., Elmira, N.Y., 1968-70, Good Samaritan Hosp., Phoenix, 1972-73; R.N. Scottsdale (Ariz.) Meml. Hosp., 1973-74; inservice dir. Mohave Gen. Hosp., Kingman, Ariz., 1974-75; school nurse Manzanita Elem. Sch., Kingman, 1975-77; R.N. staff surgical VA Med. Ctr., Phoenix, 1979-83; R.N. med., surgical Humana Hosp., Phoenix, 1983-84; R.N. psychiatric staff Camelback Hosp., Phoenix, 1984-86; owner, adminstr. Tri-Nursing, Inc., Phoenix, 1986—; bd. dirs. Career One/Ariz. Coll., Phoenix, 1987-89. Precinct committeewoman Dem. Party, Phoenix, 1987-92, state committeewoman, 1990—; candidate Ariz. State Senate, 1990; mem. Phoenix Community Coun. Mem. ANA, Ariz. Assn. Health Care Agencies (pres. 1988-89), Phoenix C. of C. Office: Tri Nursing Inc 1901 W Earll Dr # 1 Phoenix AZ 85015-6041

ABBOTT, PATTI MARIE, educator; b. Lewistown, Mont., Mar. 15, 1942; d. Vernal Hall and Marquerite (Cowen) A. BS, Eastern Mont. Coll., 1963, MS, 1968; postgrad. in adminstrn., Mont. State U., 1980. Tchr. Sch. Dist. No. 1, Glendive, Mont., 1964; tchr. Billings (Mont.) Pub. Schs., 1964—, pub. rels. rep., 1983-87. Contbr. articles to profl. jours. Resource person Girl Scouts U.S.A., Billings, 1973—, cadet leader, 1976-79; resource person Campfire Girls, Billings, 1978—; vol. Heart Fund, Am. Cancer Soc., Birth Defects Found., 1976—. Named Tchr. of Yr., Masonic Order, Billings, 1985, 86. Mem. NEA, Am. Bus. Womens Assn. (pres. Billings 1980-82, Woman of Yr. award 1980), AAUW (sec. Billings 1985-87, scholar 1987, essay chair 1992-93), Sweet Adlines (v.p. Billings 1981-83), Alpha Delta Kappa (internat. exec. bd., grand historian, grand v.p. 1983-87, grand pres.-elect 1991-93, grand pres. 1993—), Harmony Club (pres. 1986-87), Rebeccas, Eagles. Home: 701 Torch Dr Billings MT 59102-5925 Office: Lewis and Clark Jr High 1315 Lewis Ave Billings MT 59102-4237

ABBOTT, RICHARD ALLEN, training center administrator, auditor; b. Ft. Worth, July 9, 1943; s. Melvin Earl and Elizabeth Jo (Staup) A.; m. Zelia Elizabeth Moran, Sept. 8, 1984; 1 child, Andrew Allen. AA in Police Sci., North Seattle C.C., 1973; BPA, U. Puget Sound, 1975, MPA, 1977. Machinist Boeing Co., Seattle, 1964-70; police officer Lynwood, Mercer Island, Wash., 1968-78; supr. RCA Svc. Co., Seattle, 1978-80, dir., 1980-82; dir. Intelcom Edn. Svcs., Seattle, 1982-85; dir. ednl. svcs. Mgmt. and Tng. Corp., Clearfield, Utah, 1987-91; dep. ctr. dir. Mgmt. and Tng. Corp., Albany, Ga., 1985-87; ctr. dir. Mgmt. and Tng. Corp., Reno, 1991—; auditor Mgmt. and Tng. Coprp., Clearfield, 1987-91. Author: (tng. manual) Police Recruits, 1977. Bd. dirs. Liberty House for Battered Women, Albany, 1986-87; fin. chmn. Children's Clinic, Albany, 1986-87. With Naval Air Corps, 1962-64, Japan. Named Police Office of Yr., Mercer Island C. of C., 1971, City of Mercer Island, 1972. Mem. Reno C. of C., Sparks C. of C. Republican. Roman Catholic. Home: 5810 Shadow Park Dr Reno NV 89523

ABBOTT, ROBERT CARL, management company executive; b. Riverside, Calif., Oct. 20, 1955; s. Orville Hancock and Erna Adella (Sparber) Whitney; m. Diane Alicia Sallstrom, Aug. 5, 1978; children: Ryan Christian, Aaron Matthew, Kalen James. Ordained to ministry Calvary Grace Christian, 1976; firefighter, Wash., Emergency Med. Tech., first aid instr. and survival instr. Affirmative action officer State of Wash., Spokane, Wash., 1976-77; personnel supr. Key Tronic Corp., Spokane, 1977-80; personnel mgr. ISC Systems Corp., Spokane, 1980-84; fire chief Millwood Fire Dept., Millwood, Wash., 1982-88; pres. and chief exec. officer Total Mgmt. Systems, Inc., Millwood, 1984-88; gen. mgr. Ptarmigan Village, Whitefish, Mont., 1988-91, Unitech Composites, Inc., Hayden Lake, Idaho, 1991-93; CEO Total Mgmt Sys., Rathdrum, Idaho, 1993—; bd. dirs. Jans Touch, Hayden Lake, Idaho; cons. Total Mgmt. Systems, Spokane. Mem. Gov.'s Com. of Vet. Bus., Washington, 1983-84; chmn. Whitefish Fire Svcs. Area Commn., 1989-91; mem. CAP. Named Most Influential for the Year, Millwood Fire Dept., 1984. Mem. Millwood Fire Assn., Inland Empire Emergency Svcs. Assn. (pres.). Christian. Home: 719 Crenshaw Rathdrum ID 83858 Office: Total Mgmt Sys 719 Crenshaw Rathdrum ID 83858

ABBOTT, RUSSELL J., computer science educator; b. Bklyn., Mar. 1, 1942; s. Samuel and Lillian (Ginsberg) A.; m. Gail Ann Whitley, May 6, 1981; children: Michael Cole, Julian Carey, Danielle Lynn. BA, Columbia U., 1962; MA, Harvard U., 1963; PhD, U. So. Calif., 1973. Researcher The Aerospace Corp., El Segundo, Calif., 1978-84, 87—; prof. computer sci. Calif. State U.-Northridge, 1973-84, Calif. State U.-L.A., 1987—; chief scientist Silogic, Inc., L.A., 1984-87. Author: An Integrated Approach to Software Development, 1986; contbr. articles to profl. jours. Mem. ACM. Office: Calif State U Dept Math & Computer Sci 5151 State University Dr Los Angeles CA 90032-4221

ABBOTT, STEPHANIE LYNN, counselor; b. Shanghai, China, July 7, 1934; came to U.S., 1936; d. Howard Joseph and Constance (Kennedy) A.; m. Thomas B. Leary, Dec. 18, 1954; children: Thomas A. Leary, David A. Leary, Alison Leary Estep. BA, Boston U., 1957; MA, Oakland U., 1975. Cert. alcoholism counselor. Founding dir. family program Brighton (Mich.) Hosp., 1975-86; editor/columnist Alcoholism & Addiction Mag., Seattle, 1980-87, Lifeline Mag., Seattle, 1988; pvt. practice Seattle, 1987—, freelance writer, 1980—; instr. Seattle U., 1989—; cons. Community Alcohol Svcs., Everett, Wash., 1988—; co-host radio program Straight Talk KEZX. Author: Family Album, 1988, Codependency: Second Hand Life, 1985, Forgiveness, 1989; contbr. articles to profl. jours. Mem. Nat. Assn. Alcoholism and Drug Counselors (adv. bd.), Nat. Found. Alcoholism Communications (pres. 1980—), Wash. State Coun. on Alcoholism (bd. dirs.), King County Coun. on Substance Abuse Svcs. (bd. dirs.), Nat. Assn. Children of Alcoholics (chmn. edit. adv. bd. 1992—, editor network newsletter 1993—). Republican. Episcopalian. Home and Office: 352 Halladay St Seattle WA 98109-2030

ABBRUZZESE, CARLO ENRICO, physician, writer, educator; b. Rome, Italy, May 28, 1923; came to U.S., 1951, naturalized, 1959; s. Aurelio and Maria (Sbriccoli) A.; children: Marco A., Carlo M., Eric L., Christopher E., Romana S. Liceo-Ginnasio, Dante Alighieri, Roma, 1935-43; Facoltà di Medicina e Chirurgia, Università di Roma, 1943-49. Resident in tropical subtropical diseases U. Rome, 1950-51; intern Woman's and Highland Park Gen. hosps., Detroit, 1951-53; resident in family practice Saratoga Gen. Hosp., Detroit, Columbus Hosp., Newark, 1953-57; gen. practice occupational and sport medicine Rome, 1949-51, Oakland, Calif., 1958-75, Santa Ana, Calif., 1975-84; dir. emergency and outpatient depts. Drs. Hosp. Santa Ana, Calif., 1975-77; dir. North Bristol Family Med. Clinic, Rsch. and Diagnostic Lab. Author: Storia della Psicologia, 1949, Roma, L'ascoltazione Stetoscopica Tetoscopica del curoe, RCA italiana, 1953, L'ascoltazione stetoscopica, 1955, 56, 83, 86, Roma, 1986, Esercitazioni di diagnostics ascoltatoria, 1983, 86; founder, pub., editor-in-chief ESDNA, Rome, 1983, ESDI, Rome, 1986; pub. Med. Newsletter, 1987; contbr. articles to profl. jours. Founder, leader polit. youth movements, Rome, 1943-47; co-founder, nat. chmn. U.S. divorce reforms orgns., 1975; UN rep. on domestic human rights, 1977. . Decorated Commendatore di Merito, 1950; Fulbright fellow, 1951-53. Fellow Am. Acad. Family Physicians; mem. AMA, Am. Acad. Gen. Practice, Ordine dei Medici di Roma Società Italiana di Chirurgia, Am. Coll. Emergency Physicians, Union Am. Physicians, Am. Acad. Family Practice (co-founder). Office: 316 N Bristol St Santa Ana CA 92703-3811

ABDUL, CORINNA GAY, software engineer, consultant; b. Honolulu, Aug. 10, 1961; d. Daniel Lawrence and Katherine Yoshie (Kanada) A. BS in Computer Sci., U. Hawaii, 1984. With computer support for adminstrv. and fiscal svcs. U. Hawaii, Honolulu, 1982-84; mem. tech. staff II test systems and software engr. dept. of Space & Tech. Group TRW Inc., Redondo Beach, Calif., 1985-89; systems software engr. II, Sierra On-Line, Inc., Oakhurst, Calif., 1989-90; sr. programmer, analyst Decision Rsch. Corp., Honolulu, 1990-92; ind. computer cons. Honolulu, Hawaii, 1992—. Home: 1825 Anapuni St Apt 201 Honolulu HI 96822

ABDUL-JABBAR, KAREEM (LEWIS FERDINAND ALCINDOR), former professional basketball player; b. N.Y.C., Apr. 16, 1947; s. Ferdinand Lewis and Cora Alcindor; m. Habiba (Janice Brown), 1971 (div. 1973); children: Habiba, Kareem, Sultana, Amir. B.A., UCLA, 1969. Basketball player with Milw. Bucks, 1969-75, Los Angeles Lakers, 1975-89. Became NBA all-time leading scorer, 1984; appeared on TV in episodes of Mannix, The Man from Atlantis, Diff'rent Strokes, Tales from the Darkside, Pryor's Place, The ABC Afterschool Spl.; appeared in movies: The Fish that Saved Pittsburgh, 1979, Airplane, 1980, Fletch, 1985; author: (with Peter Knobler) Giant Steps: An Autobiography of Kareem Abdul-Jabbar, 1983, (with Mignon McCarthy) Kareem, 1990. Named Rookie of Year NBA, 1970; recipient Maurice Podoloff Cup; named Most Valuable Player NBA, 1971, 72, 74, 76, 77, 80; player NBA All-Star game, 1970-87, 89; named to NBA 35th Anniversary All-Time Team, 1980; NBA Playoff Most Valuable Player, 1971, 85; mem. NBA Championship Team, 1971, 80, 82, 85, 87, 88, NCAA Championship Team, 1967, 68, 69; named NCAA Tournament Most Outstanding Player, 1967, 68, 69. Muslim. Office: care Los Angeles Lakers The Forum PO Box 10 Inglewood CA 90306-0010

ABE, GREGORY, microbiologist; b. L.A., Nov. 25, 1954; s. Mabel (Tsumori) A. AA, L.A. Valley Coll., 1978; PharmD, Calif. State U., L.A., 1988, BS, 1990. Men's asst. tennis coach, Calif. State U., L.A., 1990—. Mem. Am. Soc. Microbiology, So. Calif. Soc. Microbiology, Calif. Faculty Assn., Intercollegiate Tennis Coaches Assn. Office: Calif State U 5151 State University Dr Los Angeles CA 90032-4221

ABEDON, STEPHEN TOBIAS, microbiology researcher; b. Providence, July 20, 1961; s. Michael Stein and Deanne (Tobias) A. Student, West Conn. State U., 1980-82; BS, U. Mass., Amherst, 1984; PhD, U. Ariz., 1990. Predoctoral fellow dept. microbiology and immunology U. Ariz., Tucson, 1985-86, pre-doctoral Nat. Cancer Inst., 1986-90, rsch. asst. dept. microbiology & immunology, 1990-91, rsch. assoc. dept. microbiology & immunology, 1990-93; post-doctoral Nat. Insts. of Health, 1993—. Author: (computer programs) Bacteriophage Growth Dude, Memory Dude; contbr. articles to profl. jours. Mem. N.Y. Acad. Sci., AAAS, Phi Beta Kappa.

ABEL, JONATHAN STUART, applied mathematician; b. Sarasota, Fla., Dec. 29, 1960; s. Harvey J. and Marcia Helen (Koplin) A.; m. Barbara Joan Lamb, July 3, 1989. BS in Elec. Enging and Computer Sci., MIT, 1982; MS in Elec. Engring, Stanford U., 1984, PhD, 1989. V.p. Am. Computer Techs., Sarasota, Fla., 1979-82; staff engr. MIT Lincoln (Mass.) Labs., 1982; publisher MacLine, Inc., Menlo Park, Calif., 1984-85; rsch. engr. Systems Control Tech., Palo Alto, Calif., 1985-88; lectr. Yale U., New Haven, Conn., 1988-89; v.p. Tetra Systems Inc., Palo Alto, Calif., 1989-93; prin. Abel Innovations, Palo Alto, 1993—; cons. Apple Computer, Cupertino, Calif., 1984, Saxpy Computer Corp. Sunnyvale, Calif., 1987-88, Systems Control Tech., Palo Alto, Calif., 1988—. Contbr. articles in signal processing, detection-estimation and information theory to profl. jours. Treas. Fla. Teenage Reps., 1977-78. Winner MIT Guillemin award, 1982. Mem. IEEE, Soc. Indsl. and Applied Mathematicians, Inst. Navigation. Jewish. Office: Abel Innovations 184 Tennyson Ave Palo Alto CA 94301-3758

ABELES, KIM VICTORIA, artist; b. Richmond Heights, Mo., Aug. 28, 1952; d. Burton Noel Wright and Frances Elizabeth (Sander) Hoffman. B.F.A. in Painting, Ohio U., 1974; M.F.A. in Studio Art, U. Calif.-Irvine, 1980. Free-lance artist, Los Angeles, 1975—; lectr. various schs. and art ctrs., 1980—; vis. disting. artist Calif. State U., Fullerton, 1985-87. Author, illustrator: Crafts, Cookery and Country Living, 1976. Author, photographer: Impressions, 1979. Work featured in Artery, 1979, Pacific Poetry and Fiction Review, 1980, Fiction Internat., 1985. One-woman shows include U. Calif.-Irvine, 1979, 80, Mcpl. Art Gallery, L.A., 1981, L.A. City Hall, 1982, Phyllis Kind Gallery, Chgo., 1983, Karl Bornstein Gallery, Santa Monica, Calif., 1983, 85, 87, Pepperdine U., Malibu, Calif., 1985, A.I.R. Gallery, N.Y.C., 1986, Chapman Coll., Orange, Calif., 1986, Mount St. Mary's Coll., Los Angeles, 1987, Atlanta Pavilion, 1990, Calif. Mus. of Sci. and Industry, L.A., 1991, Laguna Art Mus. Satellite Gallery, Costa Mesa, Calif., 1991, Turner-Krull Gallery, L.A., 1992, Lawrence Miller Gallery, N.Y.C., 1992, Santa Monica Mus. of Art (15 yr. survey), L.A., 1993.

Honored for outstanding student research and creative achievement, U. Calif.-Irvine, 1979; recipient U.S. Steel award Exhibition of the Associated Artists of Pitts., 1977; Hand Hollow Found. fellow, 1984; grantee Pollock-Krasner Found., 1990. Art; commn. grantee Calif. Arts coun., 1990; grantee L.A. Cultural Affairs, 1991; recipient Clean Air award Air Quality Mgmt. Dist., Calif., 1992; fellow, J. Paul Getty Trust Fund for the Visual Arts, 1993, Design Team, Panorama City Libr., Calif., 1992-93. Address: 2401 Santa Fe #100 Los Angeles CA 90058

ABELLA, ALEX, writer, journalist; b. Havana, Cuba, Nov. 8, 1950; came to U.S., 1961; s. Lorenzo and Elvira (Alvarez) A.; m. Armeen Kathleen Abella, June, 1985; 1 child, Veronica Lee. BA, Columbia U., 1972. Freelance reporter N.Y.C., San Francisco, 1972-77; reporter San Francisco Chronicle, 1977; reporter and newswriter Sta. KTVU-TV, Oakland, Calif., 1978-84; interpreter L.A. Superior Ct., 1985—. Author: The Killing of the Saints, 1991 (N.Y. Times Notable Book of Yr.). Named Pulitzer scholar, Columbia U., N.Y.C., 1968-72, Emmy nominee, NATAS, Calif., 1983. Mem. Calif. Ct. Interpreters Assn. (Greater L.A. chpt.). Democrat. Episcopalian.

ABELMANN, WILLIAM WELDON, real estate consultant; b. Elgin, Ill., Feb. 11, 1915; s. William H. and Mathilda (Meyer) A.; divorced; children: Carole, William; m. Theo F. Frick, Sept. 14, 1974. BS in Speech, Northwestern U., 1938; M (hon.), Western States U., 1984, PhD (hon.), 1985. Owner William W. Abelmann Assocs., La Canada, Calif., 1939—; lectr. real estate valuation various U.S. univs. and instns. throughout world; pres. Chgo. chpt. Soc. Real Estate Appraisers, 1972, pres. L.A. chpt., 1967; pres. Inst. Real Estate Valuers, Scottsdale, Ariz. Mem. Appraisal Inst., Inst. Real Estate Mgmt., Kiwanis (v.p. 1957), Masons, Lambda Alpha. Presbyterian. Office: William W Abelmann Assocs PO Box 1035 La Canada CA 91012

ABELS, ROBERT FREDERICK, tax consultant; b. West Palm Beach, Fla., Nov. 18, 1926; s. John Frederick and Nelly (Bulfin) A.; m. Shirley Mae Larsen, May 31, 1953; children: Robert Frederick, Steven John, Richard Alan. BS, U.S. Naval Postgrad. Sch., 1965; MBA in Finance, U. West Fla., 1971. Enlisted USN, 1944, commd. ensign, 1949, advanced through grades to comdr., 1963, aviator in Korea and Vietnam; dir. Naval Officer Candidate Sch. USN, Pensacola, Fla., 1966-68; ret. USN, 1969; tchr. math. and bus. Skyline High Sch., Lemon Grove, Calif., 1971-83; tax counselor, real estate salesman. Decorated Bronze Star, Air medal, Commendation medal; Vietnamese Cross Gallantry. Mem. Nat. Assn. Enrolled Agts., Inland Soc. Tax. Cons., Nat. Assn. Tax Consultors. Republican. Lutheran. Office: 20411 N Wintergreen Dr Sun City West AZ 85375-5458

ABEND, JOSHUA C., business executive, product innovation consultant; b. N.Y., May 26, 1924; s. Joseph and Frieda (Friefield) A.; student basic engring. Loyola U., Calif., 1943; architecture certificate Cooper Union, 1949; B.S. in Product Design, Stanford, 1950; postgrad. Creative Edn. Found., 1972, Syracuse U.; m. Arlene R. Achiron, Oct. 3, 1953 (div. 1984); children: Les, Tema. Jr. designer Norman Bel Geddes, N.Y.C., 1942-43; design engr. Gen. Motors, Detroit, 1950-51; design project leader Paxton-Krueger Assocs., N.Y.C., 1951-53; chief designer Braun-Crystal Mfg., Long Island City, N.Y., 1953-54; cons. c. Joshua Abend Assos., N.Y.C., 1954-58; human factors design mgr. Dunlap & Assos. Cons., Darien, Conn., 1958-61; v.p., indsl. design SCM Corp., Syracuse, 1961-76; pres., founder Innovation Am., Inc., 1976-85; mgr. innovation programs SRI Internat., Technology and Innovation Mgmt. Ctr. Menlo Park, Calif., 1985-89; cons. tech. mgmt.; pres. Innovation Rsch. of Calif. Innovation engring. Systems and Mgmt.; mem. organizing com. Design in Americas Congress, Mexico City, 1972; mem. com. on disaster research Nat. Acad. Sci. Served with US Army Combat Engrs., 1943-46; ETO. Mem. Indsl. Designers Soc. Am. (v.p. 1974-76, dir.), Human Factors Soc. (pres. Western N.Y. chpt. 1970), Product Devel. and Mgmt. Assn., Am. Assn. Small Research Cos., Am. Soc. Tng. and Devel. Contbr. articles to profl. jours.; patentee in field. Home: 854 Fremont St Menlo Park CA 94025 Office: 335 Bryant St Palo Alto CA 94301

ABENDROTH, KENT ALLEN, broadcast engineer, electronic engineer; b. Portland, Oreg., May 18, 1943; s. Telore William and Dorothy Hellen (Moorhead) A.; m. Irene A. Brady, July 9, 1963 (div. Jan. 1969); m. Sandra Ann Jensen, June 10, 1972; children: Crystal Kay, Amy Lynn. Assoc. in Gen. Studies with honors, Everett Community Coll., 1981. Lic. FCC gen. radiotelephone. Engr./announcer KIHR Radio, Hood River, Oreg., 1963-65; electronics technician Rodgers Organ Co., Hillsboro, Oreg., 1972-73; tech. svcs. mgr. WR Communications, Seattle, 1974-79; ptnr. Cascade Computerware Co., Everett, Wash., 1979-84; sr. mfg. engr. John Fluke Mfg. Co., Everett, Wash., 1979-84; network dir. World Radio Network, McAllen, Tex., 1984-88; dir. engring. Enterprise Network, Billings, Mont., 1988—; owner Electronics Unltd., Billings, 1992—. Developer electronic device; contbr. articles to profl. jours. Founding mem. Bellingham (Wash.) Christian Singles, 1970-71; spl. rep. HCJB World Radio, Colorado Springs, Colo., 1979—; mem. Yellowstone Creationism Com., Billings, 1991-92. With USN, 1965-71. Recipient Outstanding Communications award Civil Air Patrol, 1973; cited in book Mount Hood-Complete History, 1975. Mem. Soc. Broadcast Engrs., Civil Air Patrol (comdr. 1989—, Commendation 1991), Yellowstone Amateur Radio Club, Beartooth Mountain Rescue Unit. Republican. Evangelical. Home: 839 Lynch Dr Billings MT 59105 Office: Enterprise Network PO Box 30455 Billings MT 59107

ABERBACH, JOEL DAVID, political science educator, author; b. New York City, June 19, 1940; s. Isidore and Miriam (Meltzer) A.; m. Joan F. Gross, June 17, 1962; Children: Ian Mark, Amy Joyce, Matthew Daniel, Rachel Ann. AB, Cornell U., 1961; MA, Ohio State U., 1963, Yale U., 1965; PhD, Yale U., 1967. Asst. prof. U. Mich., Ann Arbor, 1967-72; research scientist U. Mich., 1967-88, assoc. prof., 1972-78, prof., 1978-88; sr. fellow Brookings Inst., Washington, 1977-80; dir. Ctr. for Am. Politics and Pub. Policy, UCLA, 1988; prof. UCLA, 1986—; cons. Commn. on the Op. of the Senate, Washington, 1976, U.S. Office of Pers. Mgmt., Washington, 1983, Nat. Pub. Radio, Washington, 1983-84, U.S. Gen. Acctg. Office, 1990—. Author: Keeping a Watchful Eye, 1990; co-author: Race in the City, 1973, Bureaucrats and Politicians in Western Democracies, 1981. Del. Mich. Dem. Conv., Detroit, 1972; editorial bd. Congress and the Presidency, Washington, 1981—, Governance, Oxford, Eng., 1987—. Research grantee Nat. Sci. Found., Washington, 1969-73, 1978-81, 1986-89. Fellow Brookings Inst., Ctr. for Advanced Study in Behavioral Scis.; mem. Am. Polit. Sci. Assn., Am. Sociol. Assn. Rsch. Com. on Structure and Orgn. Govt. of Internat. Polit. Sci. Assn. (exec. bd., co-chmn. 1986—, structure and orgn. govt. rsch. com.), Phi Beta Kappa. Jewish. Home: 10453 Colina Way Los Angeles CA 90077-2041 Office: UCLA 4289 Bunche Hall Los Angeles CA 90024

ABERCROMBIE, JOE WAYNE, rental agent; b. Beaumont, Tex., May 16, 1956; s. James Wayne and Ouida (Hebert) A.; m. Katherine Agnes Abercrombie, May 17, 1986; children: Tracy, Kimberly, Tucker. Grad. high sch., Beaumont. Salesman Leones Cycle Shop, Beaumont, 1974-78; transp. agt. Port Arthur Steamship Agy., Nederland, Tex., 1978-80, Astral Internat., New Orleans, 1981-83; salesman Champion Chevrolet, Manhattan Beach, Calif., 1985, Magruder Chevrolet, Palm Springs, Calif., 1985-86; owner JWA Rentals, Cathedral City, Calif., 1986—. Mem. Cathedral City C. of C., Rotary (sgt. at arms Palm Desert club 1992—). Republican. Roman Catholic. Office: JWA Rentals 36510 Cathedral Canyon Dr Cathedral City CA 92234-7273

ABERCROMBIE, NEIL, congressman; s. G. Don and Vera June (Giersdorf) A.; m. Nancie Ellen Caraway, July 18, 1981; BA Union Coll., 1959, MA U. Hawaii, 1964, PhD in Am. Studies, 1974; Mem. Hawaii state legislature, 1974-86; elected to U.S. Congress, 1986, 91—, mem. armed svcs., interior and aging coms., natural resources com.; mem. Honolulu City Coun., 1988-90. Democrat. Address: US Ho of Reps 1440 Longworth Washington DC 20515-1101*

ABERLE, DAVID FRIEND, anthropologist, educator; b. St. Paul, Nov. 23, 1918; s. David Winfield and Lisette (Friend) A.; m. Eleanor Kathleen Gough, Sept. 5, 1955 (dec. Sept. 1990); 1 son. A.B. summa cum laude, Harvard U., 1940; Ph.D. in Anthropology, Columbia U., 1950; postgrad., U. N.Mex., summers 1938-40, No. Ariz. U., summers 1971, 73, Harvard U., 1946-47. Instr. dept. social rels. Harvard U., Cambridge, Mass., 1947-50, rsch. assoc. Sch. Pub. Health, 1948-50; vis. assoc. prof. Page Sch., Johns Hopkins U., Balt., 1950-52; assoc. prof., then prof. dept. sociology and dept. anthropology U. Mich., Ann Arbor, 1952-60; fellow Ctr. Advanced Study in Behavioral Scis., Stanford, Calif., 1955-56; Simon vis. prof. and hon. research assoc. dept. social anthropology Manchester U., Eng., 1960-61; prof., chmn. dept. anthropology Brandeis U., Waltham, Mass., 1961-63; prof. dept. anthropology U. Oreg., Eugene, 1963-67; prof. dept. anthropology and sociology U. B.C., Vancouver, Can., 1967-83, prof. emeritus, 1983—; cons. Inst. Devel. Anthropology, Inc., Binghamton, N.Y., 1978-79; cons. to attys. Navajo Tribe, 1976-77; disting. lectr. at ann. meeting Am. Anthrop. Assn., 1986. Author: The Peyote Religion Among the Navaho, 1966, (with Isidore Dyen) Lexical Reconstruction, the Case of the Proto-Athapaskan Kinship System, 1974; contbr. articles on anthropological theory and Navajo Indians to scholarly jours.; rev. editor: Am. Anthropologist, 1952-55. Served with U.S. Army, 1942-46. Recipient Social Sci. Research Council Demobilization award, 1946; Harvard U. Nat. scholar; NIMH grantee; USPHS grantee; Wenner-Gren Found. grantee, 1954-63; NSF grantee, 1965-72; Can. Council grantee, 1969-77; Social Scis. and Humanities Research Council Can., 1978-80, 84-86. Fellow Royal Soc. Can., Am. Anthrop. Assn. (mem. panel on Navajo-Hopi land dispute 1973—); mem. Royal Anthrop. Inst. Gt. Britain and Ireland, Am. Sociol. Assn., Soc. Applied Anthropology, Am. Ethnol. Assn., Can. Anthropology Soc., Can. Sociology and Anthropology Assn., Assn. Social Anthropologists of the Commonwealth, Phi Beta Kappa. Jewish. Office: U BC Dept Anthropology, 6303 NW Marine Dr, Vancouver, BC Canada V6T 2B2

ABERNETHY, ROBERT JOHN, real estate developer; b. Indpls., Feb. 28, 1940; s. George Lawrence and Helen Sarah (McLandress) A. BA, John Hopkins U., 1962; MBA, Harvard U., 1968; cert. in Real Estate and Constrn., UCLA, 1974. Asst. to chief scientist Phoenix missile program Hughes Aircraft Co., L.A., 1968-69, asst. program mgr. Iroquois night fighter and night tracker program, 1969-71, asst. to contr. space and communication group, 1971-72, contr. tech. div., 1972-74; pres. Am. Standard Devel. Co., L.A., 1974—; bd. dirs. Storage Equities, Glendale, Calif., Marathon Nat. Bank, L.A., L.A. Bancorp, Met. Water Dist., L.A.; pres. Self Svc. Storage Assn., San Francisco, 1978-83. Asst. to dep. campaign mgr. Humphrey for Pres., Washington, 1968; commr. L.A. Planning Commn., 1984-88, L.A. Telecommunications Commn., 1992—; vice chmn. L.A. Econ. Devel. Coun., 1988—; chmn. Ctr. for the Study Democratic Inst., Santa Barbara, Calif., 1986—; adv. bd. Peabody Conservatory, 1992—, Nitse Sch. of Advanced Internat. Studies, 1993—; bd. dirs. L.A. Theatre Ctr., 1986-92; trustee Johns Hopkins U., 1991— Lt. USNR, 1962-66. Mem. So. Calif. Planning Congress (bd. dirs.), Parker Found. (bd. dirs.), Californian Club, St. Francis Yacht Club, Jonathan Club, Calif. Yacht Club, Alpha Lambda. Home: 5800 W Century Blvd Los Angeles CA 90009 Office: Am Standard Devel Co 5221 W 102d St Los Angeles CA 90045

ABERNETHY, RONALD HAYES, lawyer; b. Corning, Calif., Aug. 6, 1948; s. W. C. and Wilma (Peter) A. BA, Sacramento State Coll., 1970; JD, U. Calif., San Francisco, 1974. Bar: Calif., 1985. Dep. pub. defender San Joaquin County Office of the Pub. Defender, Stockton, Calif., 1975-80, asst. pub. defender, 1980-90; assoc. Harris, Perisho & Woodson, Stockton, 1990—; Mem. judicial coun. Adv. Com. on Change of Venue, 1988; mem. law enforcement com. Gov.'s Coun. on Drug and Alcohol Abuse, 1989-90; instr. Modelnetics, 1988-90, U. of the Pacific, Stockton, 1990. Bd. dirs. Ctr. for Positive Prevention Alternatives, 1976-87; mem. San Joaquin County Inter-Agy. Gang Violence Task Force, 1983-90. Mem. ABA (program of assistance and review cons. 1991—), Calif. State Bar Assn. (chmn. standing com. on lawyer referral svcs. 1987, Larry Long award 1990). Office: Harris Perisho & Woodson 3031 W March Ln Ste 210 W Stockton CA 95219

ABEYTA, JOSE REYNATO, retired pharmacist, state legislator, cattle rancher; b. Blanco, N.Mex., July 18, 1927; s. Jose Porfirio and Carmen (Sandoval) A.; m. Margarita M. Ledoux, Nov. 24, 1950; children: Carolyn, Georgean, Gary, Diana. BS in Pharmacy, U. N.Mex., 1951. Registered pharmacist. Staff pharmacist Western Drug Co., Las Vegas, N.Mex., 1951-53, Duran Ctrl. Drug, Albuquerque, 1953-63, Linder Drug, Springer, N.Mex., 1981-82, Springer Drug, 1985-90, Walgreen Drug Co., Las Vegas, 1990-92; owner, mgr. Best Drug Co., Albuquerque, 1963-80; chief pharmacist Northeastern Regional Hosp., Las Vegas, 1982-85; ret., 1992; mem. N.Mex. Ho. of Reps., 1992—; vice-chmn. Bernalillo Alcohol Treatment Bd., 1972-74. Mem. Albuquerque City Coun., 1974-80. With U.S. Army, 1945-47. Mem. Nat. Assn. Retail Druggists, N.Mex. Pharm. Assn., Am. Soc. Hosp. Pharmacists, Elks. Democrat. Roman Catholic. Home: PO Box 147 Wagon Mound NM 87752

ABILDGAARD, CHARLES FREDERICK, pediatrician; b. Winfield, Kans., Aug. 10, 1930; s. Fred William Jr. and Edna Mildred (Snyder) A.; m. Helen Klevickis, Sept. 1953 (div. 1981); children: Mark, Noel, Adam; m. Nancy Abildgaard, Mar. 7, 1982. Student, San Jose (Calif.) State Coll., 1947-50; AB, Stanford U., 1952, MD, 1955. Asst. prof., prof. pediatrics U. Ill. Coll. Medicine, Chgo., 1961-68; prof. pediatrics Sch. Medicine U. Calif., Davis, 1968-93. Contbr. articles to profl. jours. Fellow Am. Acad. Pediatrics; mem. Am. Pediatric Soc., Am. Physiological Soc., Am. Soc. Hematology, Soc. for Pediatric Rsch., Hemophilia Rsch. Soc. (interim dir. 1989-90).

ABLAD, BJORN ERIC BERTIL, executive; b. Vasteras, Sweden, July 4, 1945; came to U.S., 1982; s. Bertil Eric Gunnar and Ellen Inga Lill Asta (Sigroth) A.; m. Siv Elisabeth Hallsmar, Aug. 13, 1976 (div. Apr. 1984); 1 child, Andreas; m. Judith Ann Rose, June 22, 1985; children: Eric, Rebecca. Zimmermanska skolan, Vasteras, Sweden, 1970; Student, U. Stockholm, 1971-72. Export mgr. Nord Transmission AB, Sala, Sweden, 1973-79; mng. dir. Kungsors Pressprodukter AB, Kugsor, Sweden, 1980-81; chief exec. officer BH/SALA Inc., Salt Lake City, 1982-85; pres. AROS, Inc., Salt Lake City, 1986—; sec., bd. dirs. BH/SALA, Inc., Salt Lake City, 1982-85, Hornell Speedglas, Inc., Twinsburg, Ohio, 1986-89, AROS, Inc., Salt Lake City, 1986—, Swedish/Am. C. of C., Salt Lake City, 1990—. Mem. YMCA, Vasteras, Sweden, 1960-82; player Swedish Nat. Basketball Team, Stockholm, 1972-75; mem. Swedish Heritage Soc., Salt Lake City, 1989—. Corp. Swedish Air Force, 1965-66. Named Hon. Tex. Citizen, 1963, Hon. Asst. Atty. Gen., State of Tex., 1963. Office: AROS Inc 883 S 200 E Salt Lake City UT 84111-4202

ABRAHAM, ALBERT DAVID, retired railroad official; b. Baghdad, Iraq, Feb. 15, 1924; came to U.S., 1967; s. David and Mariam (Shawootha) A.; m. Lily John David, Jan. 12, 1958 (div. Dec. 1978); children: Peter, Paul. BA in English, San Francisco State U., 1975; BA in Law, Blackstone, 1976. Translator Basrah Petroleum Co., Basrah, 1947-54; chief translator Brit. Bank of the Middle East, Baghdad, 1958-67; claims investigator So. Pacific Transp. Co., San Francisco, 1967-86, ret., 1986; translator, interpreter U.S. and Brit. Armed Forces, Basrah, Iraq, 1942-45; hort., gardening con. The Home Depot, San Leandro, Calif., 1988-92. Mem. Elks, Moose, Optimist (pres. 1988-89, Outstanding Svc. award). Democrat. Home: 1090 Hyde St San Leandro CA 94577-3723

ABRAHAM, CAROL JEANNE, artist, photography educator; b. Phila., Jan. 14, 1949; d. Hans Alfred and Lillian Elizabeth (Fredericks) A. BS in Edn., Tufts U., 1971; MFA, Rochester Inst. Tech., 1973; diploma, Brooks Inst. Photography, 1988. Cert. tchr. Calif. Tchr. Framingham (Mass.) Pub. Sch., 1970, Boston Pilot Sch. (Harvard Project), 1970, Boston State Coll., 1971; asst. prof. Rochester (N.Y.) Inst. Tech., 1972-73, Southern Utah State U., Cedar City, 1975-77; tchr. El Camino Coll., Torrance, Calif., 1980-81, Ventura (Calif.) Community Coll., 1982-84, Brooks Inst. Photography, Santa Barbara, Calif., 1989—; curator Western States Mus. of Photography, Santa Barbara, 1985-88; colections Mus. Ceramics, Italy, Internat. Acad. Ceramics, Can., Nova Inst. Ceramics, Italy, Smithsonian Inst., Washington. Artist (book) Ceramics: A Potters Handbook, 1978, 84, Contempory International Ceramics, 1980, Porcelain: Traditions and New Visions, 1981; author: (photography) Egypt, Images and Adventures, 1988. Bd. dirs. United Boys & Girls Club, Santa Barbara, 1991—. Nat. Park Assn. grantee, 1974.

ABRAHAM, MARY ANN, police academy instructor; b. Glendive, Mont., Sept. 17, 1955; d. Glenn E. and Annabelle E. (Erhart) Stucky; divorced; children: Apryl, Autumn. Grad., Mont. Law Enforcement Acad., 1988. Instr. Mont. Law Enforcement Acad., Bozeman, 1986—. Vol. Battered Women's Network, Bozeman, 1986-87, bd. dirs., adv., 1986—, liaison, 1987—; pres. Prevention of Child Abuse, Bozeman, 1989-90. Recipient Victim's Adv. award Atty. Gen. of Mont., 1989, Christy Svc. awards Mont. State U., 1989, 90; named Outstanding Young Women Am., 1988. Democrat. Roman Catholic. Home: 506 W Central Ave Apt 3A Belgrade MT 59714-3407 Office: Mont Law Enforcement Acad 620 S 16th Ave Bozeman MT 59715-4198

ABRAHAM, WILLIAM ISRAEL, economist, statistician, international advisor; b. Phila., Mar. 3, 1919; s. Benjamin Abraham and Mary Shenker; m. Janet Elizabeth Margaret Cole, May 29, 1945; children: Stephen Benjamin, Roger Douglas, Susan Edith, Charles Raymond. BA, U. Pa., 1940; MBA, U. Chgo., 1942; PhD, Columbia U., 1953. Statistician UN Secretariat, N.Y.C., 1946-61; prof. econs. NYU, N.Y.C., 1961-74; vis. prof. Yale U., New Haven, 1965; Ford Found. vis. advisor U. Singapore, 1970; econ. advisor, inst. assoc. Harvard Inst. for Internat. Devel., Cambridge, Mass. and overseas; fgn. advisor, cons., project mgr. various counties in Latin Am., Asia, Africa, Bangladesh, 1983-85, Bolivia, 1987, Sri Lanka, 1987-88, People's Rep. China, 1988, Malaysia, 1989; cons. AID, 1962-67, Nat. Planning Assn., 1963-65, U.S. Census Bur., 1967, World Bank, UN, UN Devel. Prog., Asian Devel. Bank. Author: Annual Budgeting and Devel. Planning, 1965, National Income and Economic Accounting, 1969; co-editor: Structural Interrdependence and Economic Development, 1963; contbr. articles to profl. jours., chpt. to book. With Signal Corp, AUS, 1943-45, ETO. Mem. Internat. Assn. for Rsch. in Income and Wealth, Assn. Former Internat. Civil Servants (west coast corr.), Highlands Country Club (membership com. 1990, 91), Commonwealth Club Calif., City Commons Club Berkeley (pres.-elect 1993). Home: 6333 Longcroft Dr Piedmont CA 94611-2521

ABRAHAMS, SIDNEY CYRIL, physicist, crystallographer; b. London, May 28, 1924; arrived in U.S., 1948; s. Aaron Harry and Freda (Cohen) A.; m. Rhoda Banks, May 1, 1950; children: David Mark, Peter Brian, Jennifer Anne. BSc, U. Glasgow, Scotland, 1946; PhD, U. Glasgow, 1949, DSc, 1957; Fil. Dr. (hon.), U. Uppsala, Sweden, 1981. Rsch. fellow U. Minn., Mpls., 1949-50; mem. staff MIT, Cambridge, 1950-54; rsch. fellow U. Glasgow, 1954-57; mem. tech. staff Bell Labs., Murray Hill, N.J., 1957-82; disting. mem. tech. staff AT&T Bell Labs., Murray Hill, 1982-88; Humboldt sr. scientist Inst. Crystallography, U. Tübingen, Fed. Republic Germany, 1989-90; guest scientist, Brookhaven Nat. Lab., Upton, N.Y., 1957—; vis. prof., U. Bordeaux, France, 1979, 90; adj. prof. physics dept. So. Oreg. State Coll., 1990—. Mem. editorial bd., Rev. Sci. Instruments, 1963-65; co-editor, Anomalous Scattering, 1975; editor, World Directory of Crystallographers, 1977, Acta Crystallographica, 1978-87; book rev. editor, Ferroelectrics, 1975—. Recipient Sr. U.S. Scientist award, Alexander von Humboldt Found., 1989-90. Fellow AAAS, Am. Phys. Soc.; mem. Am. Crystallographic Assn. (pres. 1968, mng. editor 1965—), Royal Soc. Chemistry, Am. Inst. Physics (chmn. pub. policy com. 1981-91), Internat. Union Crystallography (chmn. commn. on crystallographic apparatus 1972-75, commn. on jours. 1978-87, commn. on crystallographic nomenclature 1978—), Sigma Xi. Home: 2995 Nova Dr Ashland OR 97520-1493 Office: So Oreg State Coll Physics Dept Ashland OR 97520

ABRAHAMSON, MARK COURTNEY, photographer, dentist; b. Seattle, June 28, 1944; s. Courtney H. and Marguerite L. (Anderson) A.; divorced; 1 child, Page; m. Carey A. Christensen, Sept. 24, 1983; 1 child, Elizabeth. BA in Chemistry, Whitman Coll., 1966; DDS, U. Wash., 1970. Pvt. practice dentistry Seattle, 1972—; ind. photographer Stanwood, Wash., 1976—; juror numerous art exhbns.; cons. various orgns. One-man shows include Erica Williams Gallery, Seattle, 1977, Carnegie Art Ctr., Walla Walla, Wash., 1982, Coast House Gallery, Monterey, Calif., 1983, Westwood Ctr. for Arts, L.A., 1983, Chongqing People's Cultural Palace, China, 1984, Mind's Eye Gallery, Idaho State U., 1985, Frye Art Mus., Seattle, 1987, Sichuan Inst. Fine Arts, China, 1987, Silver Image Gallery, Seattle, 1988, Arts Ctr., Everett, Wash., 1990, Columbia (Mo.) Coll., 1991, Benham Gallery, Seattle, 1991, 55 Mercer St. Gallery, N.Y.C., 1991, Shoreline coll. Gallery, Seattle, 1992, Eleven East Ashland, Phoenix, Ariz., 1992, U. Calif., San Francisco, 1992, Viridian Gallery, N.Y.C., 1993, Bush Barn Art Ctr., Salem, Oreg., 1993, PACCAR, Bellevue, Wash., 1993; exhibited in numerous group shows including Sheehan Gallery, Whitman Coll., Walla Walla, Wash. 1978, Lightworks III, Seattle, 1981, The Print Club, 58th Internat. Exhbn., Phila., 1982, Tex. Fine Arts Assoc. Annual Exhbn., Austin, 1982, 83, Newport (R.I.) Nat. Photography Exhbn., 1983, U. Tex. Arlington, 1985, Photography West Gallery, Carmel, Calif., 1986, San Diego Art Inst., 1987, Laguna Gloria Art Mus., Austin, Tex. 1988, N.J. Ctr for Visual Arts, Summit, 1989, Art Works for AIDS, Seattle, 1990, Chautauqua Nat. Exhbn. Am. Art, 1991, The Bowery Gallery, N.Y.C., 1991, Wetherholt Galleries, Washington, 1992, U. Oreg., Eugene, 1992, Pleiades Gallery, N.Y.C., 1992, Amos Eno Gallery, N.Y.C., 1992, viridian Gallery, N.Y.C., 1992, Ctr. for Photography at Woodstock, N.Y., 1993, Limner Gallery, N.Y.C., 1993, Bromfield Gallery, Boston, 1993, ARC Gallery, Chgo., 1993, Lever House, N.Y.C., 1993. Pres. Kayak Point Citizens Group, Stanwood, 1983—; bd. dirs. Wing Luke Asian Mus., Seattle, 1984-90, Seattle/Chongqing Sister City Assn., 1985-91, Stillaguamish Watershed Plan, Everett, 1987—. Capt. USAF, 1970-72. Grantee Artist Trust, Seattle, 1991. Mem. Seattle Art Mus., Friends of Photography, N.W. Ctr. for Arts, Harrisburg Art Assn., Warm Beach Precision Lawnmower Drill Team, Wash. State Grange. Democrat. Home and Studio: 17002 Marine Dr Stanwood WA 98292

ABRAM, DONALD EUGENE, U.S. magistrate judge; b. Des Moines, Feb. 8, 1935; s. Irwin and Freda Phyllis (Gibson) A.; m. Frances Jennette Cooley, Apr. 22, 1962; children: Karen Lynn, Susan Ann, Scott Alan, Diane Jennette. BS in Bus., U. Col., 1957, JD, 1963. Ptnr. Phelps, Fonda, Hays, Abram and Shaw (now Peterson & Fonda, PC), Pueblo, Colo., 1963-75; dist. judge Colo. 10th Jud. Dist., Pueblo, 1975-81; chief U.S. magistrate judge U.S. Dist. Ct. State of Colo., 1981—; lectr. law in criminal procedure U. Denver Sch. of Law, 1983-90; adj. prof. sociology, instr. bus. law U. So. Colo., Pueblo, 1977-81. Mng. editor, bd. dir. Colo. Law Review, 1961-63. Vice chmn. Pueblo County Rep. Party, 1973-75; city councilman Pueblo, 1970-73; pres. Pueblo city coun., 1972-73, Pueblo Goodwill Industries, 1965, Pueblo United Fund, 1968; chmn. consolidation planning com. Pueblo County Sch. Dists. 60, 70, 1968-70; mem. gov's. milit. affairs adv. com., 1975-78; mem. gov's. commn. children and families, 1978-80. Lt. (j.g.) USN, 1957-60, capt. Res. ret. Recipient Disting. Svc. award Colo. Jaycee, 1970, Disting. Citizen Svc. award, Pueblo Rotary, 1975. Mem. Fed. Magistrate Judges Assn. (pres. 1990-91), Pueblo C. of C.(bd. dirs. 1972, chmn. edn. com. 1970-71), Colo. Bar Assn. (1st v.p. 1975-76), Nat. Coun. U. S. Magistrates (dir., officer 1984-89), Juvenile Judges Assn. Colo. (chmn. 1979-80), Colo. Navy League (state pres. 1976-78). Presbyterian. Office: US Dist Ct US Courthouse C-316 1929 Stout St Denver CO 80294-3576

ABRAMOVITZ, MOSES, economist, educator; b. Bklyn., Jan. 1, 1912; s. Nathan and Betty (Goldenberg) A.; m. Carrie Glasser, June 23, 1937; 1 son, Joel Nathan. A.B., Harvard U., 1932; Ph.D., Columbia U., 1939; Ph.D. (hon.), Uppsala U., Sweden, 1985, U. Ancona, Italy, 1992. Instr. Harvard U., 1936-38; mem. research staff Nat. Bur. Econ. Research, 1938-69; lectr. Columbia U., 1940-42, 46-48; prof. econs. Stanford U., 1948—, Coe prof. Am. econ. history, exec. head dept. econs., 1963-65, 71-74; vis. prof. U. Pa., 1955; prin. economist WPB, 1942, OSS, 1943-44; econ. adviser to U.S. rep. on Allied Commn. on Reparations, 1945-46; econ. adviser to sec.-gen. Orgn. for Econ. Coop. and Devel., 1962-63; vis. fellow All Souls Coll., Oxford, Eng., 1968. Author: Price Theory for a Changing Economy, 1939, Inventories and Business Cycles, 1950, The Growth of Public Employment in Great Britain, 1957, (with Vera Eliasberg) Thinking About Growth, 1989; also articles.; editor: Capital Formation and Economic Growth, 1955; mng. editor Jour. Econ. Lit., 1981-85. Served as lt. AUS, 1944-45. Recipient Nitti prize Accademia Nazionale Dei Lincei, Rome, 1990. Fellow Am. Acad. Arts and Scis., Am. Econ. Assn. (disting. (pres. 1980), Am. Statis. Assn.; mem. Am. Econ. History Assn. (pres. 1991-92), Western Econ. Assn. (pres. 1988), Accademia Nazionale dei Lincei (fgn.), Phi Beta Kappa. Home: 762 Dolores St Palo Alto CA 94305-8428 Office: Stanford Univ Stanford CA 94305

ABRAMS, FREDRICK RALPH, physician, clinical ethicist; b. N.Y.C., June 18, 1928; s. David and Jane R. (Rein) A.; m. Alice Marilyn Engelhard, Nov. 25, 1949; children: Reid, Glenn, Hal. BA, Cornell U., 1950, MD, 1954. Diplomate Am. Bd. Ob-Gyn. Intern Letterman Army Hosp., San Francisco, 1954-55; pvt. practice gynecology Denver, 1962—; resident Fitzsimons Army Hosp., Denver, 1956-59; prof. U. Colo. Grad. Sch. Pub. Affairs, Denver, 1987—; dir. biomed. ethics Ctr. for Health Ethics and Policy, U. Colo., 1987—; exec. dir. Govs. Commn. on Life and the Law, State of Colo., 1991—; founder Ctr. for Applied Biomed. Ethics Rose Med. Ctr., Denver, 1982-87; lectr. for pub. edn. in med. ethics. Contbr. chpts. to book and articles to profl. jours. Maj. U.S. Army, 1955-62. Grantee Robert Wood Johnson, 1988-89, Colo. Trust, 1987-90, Rose Found., 1982-87. Mem. Internat. Soc. for Advancement of Humanistic Studies in Gynecology (past pres.), Denver Med. Soc. (past v.p.), Colo. Med. Soc., Am. Coll. Ob-Gyn. (past chmn. ethics com.). Office: 2530 S Parker Rd Aurora CO 80014

ABRAMS, HELAYNE JOAN, preschool educator; b. Chgo., Apr. 15, 1937; d. Isidore and Fanny (Weinberg) Kremen; divorced; children: Lisa, Leda Abrams Miller, Lenore Abrams DeSpain. BA in Elem. Edn. with distinction, U. N.Mex., 1975. Lic. tchr., N.Mex. Tchr., dir. Albuquerque Pre-Sch. Coop., 1966—; multi-cultural and anti-bias curriculum workshop presenter, N.Mex., 1988—. Author:: Learning the Rainbow: A Multi-Cultural, Anti-Bias Activity Book for Teachers, 1992. Founding mem., bd. dirs. Living Through Cancer, 1984-87; bd. dirs. Albuquerque Ctr. for Peace and Justice, 1989-90, developer children's peace mus., 1990. Recipient Peace award Albuquerque Ctr. for Peace and Justice, 1990; grantee Mary Ann Binford Found., 1989, 90. Mem. Nat. Assn. for Edn. Young Children, N.Mex. Assn. for Edn. Young Children. Home: 4715 Grand Ave NE Albuquerque NM 87108

ABRAMS, JEANNE ESTHER, historian, archivist; b. Stockholm, Apr. 2, 1951; came to U.S., 1951; d. I. Edward and Gilda (Zielona) Lichtman; m. Lewis H. Abrams, Aug. 29, 1971; children: Yehudah, Chaim, Avraham, Yocheved. BA, Yeshiva U., 1972; MA, U. Colo., 1978, PhD, 1983. Dir. Rocky Mountain Hist. Soc./Beck Archives U. Denver, 1982—. Author: (monograph) Blazing The Tuberculosis Trail, 1990, (booklet) Historic Jewish Denver, 1983; contbr. articles to profl. jours. V.p. Jewish Women's League of Denver, 1988—; pres. Yeshiva Toras Chaim High Sch. PTA, 1989-91. N.Y. State Regent's scholar, 1968-72, scholar Am. Jewish Hist. Soc., 1988; grantee Colo. Endowment for Humanities, 1989, 92. Mem. Am. Jewish Hist. Soc. (acad. coun.), Soc. Am. Archivists. Democrat. Office: U Denver 2199 S University Blvd Denver CO 80208-0001

ABRAMS, RICHARD LEE, physicist; b. Cleve., Apr. 20, 1941; s. Morris S. and Corinne (Tobias) A.; m. Jane Shack, Aug. 12, 1962; children: Elizabeth, Laura. B. Engring. Physics, Cornell U., Ithaca, N.Y., 1964, Ph.D., 1968. Mem. tech. staff Bell Telephone Labs., Whippany, N.J., 1968-71; sect. head Hughes Research Labs., Malibu, Calif., 1971-75, dept. mgr., 1975-83; chief scientist Space and Communications group Hughes Aircraft Co., El Segundo, Calif., 1983-89; chief scientist Hughes Rsch. Labs., Malibu, Calif., 1989—; program co-chmn. Conf. on Laser Engring. and Applications, Washington, 1979; chmn. Conf. on Lasers and Electro-Optics, Phoenix, 1982. Assoc. editor: Optics Letters, 1979-82; patentee in field. Fellow IEEE (assoc. editor Jour. Quantum Electronics 1980-83, bd. editors Proc. 1987-89, Centennial medal 1989), Optical Soc. Am. (bd. dirs. 1982-85, v.p. 1988, pres. 1990); mem. IEEE Quantum Electronics and Applications Soc. (adminstrve. com. 1980-83, v.p. 1982, pres. 1983), Tau Beta Pi, Phi Kappa Phi. Club: Riviera Country (Pacific Palisades, Calif.). Home: 922 Enchanted Way Pacific Palisades CA 90272-2823 also: Hughes Aircraft Co Rsch Lab 3011 Malibu Canyon Rd Malibu CA 90265

ABRAMSON, ALBERT, television historian, consultant; b. Chgo., June 9, 1922; s. Joseph David and Minnie Lillian (Edelstein) A.; m. Arlene Betty Corin, Jan. 8, 1950; children: Jay Allen, Susan Marie. BA, U. So. Calif., 1950. Tchr. L.A. City Schs., 1950-52; TV engr. CBS-TV, Hollywood, Calif., 1952-87; hist. cons. RCA, Princeton, N.J., Ampex Mus., Redwood City, Calif., UCLA/ATAS TV Archives, L.A. Author: Electronic Motion Pictures, 1955, The History of Television, 1880-1941, 1987; contbr. articles to profl. jours; patentee three dimensional TV without glasses, super high brightness TV projector. With U.S. Army Air Forces. Mem. IEEE, Royal TV Soc. London, Brit. Kinematagraph, Sound and TV Soc., LeComité d'histoire de la Télévision, ATAS, SMPTE. Democrat. Jewish. Home: 6223 1/2 Randi Ave Woodland Hills CA 91367

ABRAMSON, MARK JOSEPH, county official, data processing executive, consultant; b. Torrance, Calif., July 13, 1949; s. Harvey Stanley and Gladys (Kaufman) A.; m. Ilene Marcia Simons, Aug. 5, 1977; children: Elizabeth Jane, Daniel Kevin. BS, Calif. Inst. Tech., 1971; MEng, UCLA, 1984. Programmer Jet Propulsion Labs, Pasadena, Calif., 1971-72; systems analyst Bio Sci Labs, Van Nuys, Calif., 1972-77; sr. programmer and analyst Meml. Med. Ctr., Long Beach, Calif., 1977-84, mgr. systems applications, 1984-86; applications specialist Health Data Scis., San Bernardino, Calif., 1986-87; data processing specialist Los Angeles County, Downey, Calif., 1987—; cons. Control Data Inst. L.A., 1979-86, Tandem Computers, Cupertino, Calif., 1986, Sci. Applications Internat., San Diego, 1987-89, Automated Case Mgmt. Systems Inc., L.A., 1989-93, Abramson Consulting, Encino, Calif., 1993—. Mem. Mumps Users Group, Calif. Inst. Tech. Alumni Assn., Braemer Country Club (Tarzana). Office: Abramson Consulting Data Processing Dept PO Box 260414 Encino CA 91426-2402

ABRAMSON, MASON HARRY, pediatrician; b. Portland, Oreg., May 31, 1916; s. Philip and Sara (Tobias) A.; m. Beatric Aronson, June 10, 1939 (dec. 1956); m. Yvonne E. Stowell, June 17, 1956; children: Gerry, Mason, Elesa, David, Donald, Christopher, Joni, Marc. BA with distinction, Stanford (Calif.) U., 1937, MD, 1942. Intern Stanford Hosps., 1941-42, asst. resident in pediatrics, 1942-43; resident in communicable diseases San Francisco, 1943-44; pvt. practice Redwood City, Calif., 1946—; chmn. utilization rev. com. Sequoia Hosp., 1978—. Contbr. articles to profl. jours. Capt. U.S. Army, 1944-46. Mem. San Mateo County Med. Soc., Calif. Med. Assn., Am. Pediatrics, Am. Acad. Pediatrics, Phi Beta Kappa, Alpha Omega Alpha, Sigma Xi. Democrat. Home: 3765 Country Club Dr Redwood City CA 94061-1109 Office: 155 Birch St Redwood City CA 94062-1306

ABRAVANEL, ALLAN RAY, lawyer; b. N.Y.C., Mar. 11, 1947; s. Leon and Sydelle (Berenson) A.; m. Susan Ava Paikin, Dec. 28, 1971; children: Karen, David. BA magna cum laude, Yale U., 1968; JD cum laude, Harvard U., 1971. Bar: N.Y. 1972, Oreg. 1976. Assoc. Paul, Weiss, Rifkind, Wharton & Garrison, N.Y.C., 1971-72, 74-76; fellow Internat. Legal Ctr., Lima, Peru, 1972-74; from assoc. to ptnr. Stoel, Rives, Boley, Fraser & Wyse, Portland, Oreg., 1976-83; ptnr. Perkins Coie, Portland, 1983—. Editor, pub. Abravanel Family Newsletter. Mem. ABA, Inter-Am. Bar Assn., Phi Beta Kappa. Office: Perkins Coie 111 SW 5th Ave Portland OR 97204-3604

ABRAVANEL, MAURICE, musical director; b. Salonica, Greece, Jan. 6, 1903; came to U.S., 1936; s. Edouard and Rachel (Bitty) A.; m. Lucy Carasso, 1947 (dec. 1985); m. Carolyn Firmage, 1987. Student, Gymnasium, Lausanne, Switzerland, 1917-19, U. Lausanne, 1919-21, U. Zurich, 1921-22; PhD (hon.), Cleve. Music Inst.; LLD, U. Utah, State U., Westminster Coll. mem. music panel Nat. Endowment for Arts, 1968-70, 89—; mem. Nat. Coun. for Arts, 1970-76. Began as orch. condr., 1924, has conducted leading symphony orchs. in U.S., Europe, Australia, condr. Met. Opera, N.Y.; Kurt Weill premieres Seven Deadly Sins, 1933; Knickerbocker Holiday, 1938, Lady in the Dark, 1940, One Touch of Venus, 1943, Street Scene, 1946, Marc Blitzstein's Regina, 1949, Utah Symphony Orch., 1947-79, music dir. Acad. of the West, Santa Barbara, Calif., acting music dir. Berkshire Music Ctr., Tanglewood, Mass., 1982, permanent artist-in-residence, Berkshire Music Ctr., Tanglewood, Mass.; condr. numerous rec. premieres: 1st studio recs. Mahler—Symphony #7 and #8; condr. complete orchestral works of Mahler, Brahms, Tchaikovsky and Grieg, complete symphonies of Sibelius. Recipient Antoinette Perry award, 1950, Kilenyi Mahler medal, 1965, Ditson Condr.'s award, 1971, Gold Baton award Am. Symphony Orch. League, 1981, Nat. medal of Arts Pres. and Mrs. Bush, 1991, Theodor Thomas award Condrs. Guild, 1992; 4 concert halls named in his honor. Mem. Internat. Gustav Mahler Soc. (hon.). Home: 1235 S 7th S Salt Lake City UT 84102-3214

ABREU, MARKUS SANTIAGO, data processing executive; b. Bklyn., Oct. 13, 1961; s. Frank and Gloria (Cuevas) Zarragoitia. Cert. Completion, Canterbury Bus. Sch., Levittown, N.Y., 1981. Lead word processing operator Allied Stores Mktg. Corp., N.Y.C., 1981-82; asst. supr. Mfrs. Hanover Trust, N.Y.C., 1982-83; supr. Touche Ross & Co., N.Y.C., 1983-84; systems cons. Wang Labs., Inc., N.Y.C., 1984-87; sr. instr. Wang Labs., Inc., L.A., 1987-88; MIS dir. Playright Sports, Newport Beach, Calif., 1988-89; instr. Travel & Trade Career Inst., Garden Grove, Calif., 1989-90, New Horizons Learning Ctr., Santa Ana, Calif., 1990-91; owner Act for the Future, Santa Ana, Calif., 1991—. Designer/programmer: Landscape Purchasing System, 1991, Purchase and Sales Memo System, 1992. Mem. Nat. Fedn. Ind. Bus. Office: Act for the Future 2740 S Harbor Blvd #G Santa Ana CA 92704

ABRUMS, JOHN DENISE, internist; b. Trinidad, Colo., Sept. 20, 1923; s. Horatio Ely and Clara (Apfel) A.; m. Annie Louise Manning, June 15, 1947; children: Louanne C. Abrums Sargent, John Ely. BA, U. Colo., 1944; MD, U. Colo., Denver, 1947. Diplomate Am. Bd. Internal Medicine. Intern Wisc. Gen. Hosp., Madison, 1947-48; resident in internal medicine VA Hosp., Albuquerque, 1949-52, attending physician, 1956-80; mem. staff Presbyn. Hosp. Ctr., Albuquerque; cons. staff physician St. Joseph Hosp., Albuquerque, 1957-85; attending physician U. N.Mex. Hosp. (formerly Bernalillo County Med. Ctr.), Albuquerque, 1954-86; cons. physician A.T. & S.F. Meml. Hosp., Albuquerque, 1957-83; clin. assoc. in medicine U. N.Mex.; mem. N.Mex. Bd. of Med. Examiners. Bd. dirs. Blue Cross/Blue Shield, 1962-76. Brig. gen. M.C., U.S. Army, ret., N.Mex. Nat. Guard. Fellow ACP (life), AMA, Am. Soc. Internal Medicine (trustee 1976-82, pres. 1983-84), N.Mex. Soc. Internal Medicine (pres. 1962-64), N.Mex. Med. Soc. (pres. 1980-81), Nat. Acads. Practice (disting. practitioner), Albuquerque and Bernalillo County Med. Assn. (bd. govs. 1959-61, chmn. pub. rels. com. 1959-61), Am. Geriatric Soc., 1992—. Brig. gen. M.C., U.S. Army, ret. Republican. Episcopalian. Office: N Mex Med Group PC 717 Encino Pl NE Encino Medical Pla Albuquerque NM 87102

ABRUNZO, VICTOR DANIEL, JR., lawyer, state-court receiver; b. Teaneck, N.J., Dec. 28, 1946; s. Victor Daniel and Jane Aline (Bates) A. BS, Fairfield U., 1970; MBA, Golden Gate U., 1972; postgrad., U. San Francisco, 1976; JD, Golden Gate U., 1980. Bar: Calif. 1982, U.S. Dist. Ct. (no. dist.) Calif. 1982, U.S. Dist. Ct. (cen. dist.) Calif. 1990. Sch. adminstr. Fairfield-Suisun U. San Diego, 1972-78; intern Calif. State Senate, Sacramento, 1980; estate adminstr. bankruptcy U.S. Cts., Oakland, Calif., 1982-83; bankruptcy analyst Dept. of Justice State of N.Y., N.Y.C, 1983-85, asst. U.S. trustee Dept. of Justice, 1985-87; group v.p. Mfrs. Hanover Fin. Mgmt. Systems, Santa Ana, Calif., 1987-89; pres., CEO Estate and Adminstrv. Svcs., Inc., Encino, Calif., 1989—; lectr. Golden Gate U., San Francisco,1 976-79; speaker Small Bus. Assn., N.Y.C., 1984-85; mem. Fed. Exec. Bd., N.Y.C., 1985-86; moot ct. judge Fordham U. Sch. Law, N.Y.C., 1985-87. Pres. Assist A Grad. Scholarship Found., Fairfield, Calif., 1976. With USAF, 1968-72. Mem. ABA, Calif. Bar Assn., Nat. Assn. Bankruptcy Trustee (editor com. 1988), N.Y.C. Bankruptcy Bar, Santa Ana C. of C., Fairfield C. of C. Republican. Roman Catholic. Office: Estate and Adminstrv Svcs 16633 Ventura Blvd Ste 530 Encino CA 91436-1861

ABUL-HAJ, SULEIMAN KAHIL, pathologist; b. Jordan, Apr. 20, 1925; s. Sheik Khalil and S. Buteina (Oda) Abul-H.; B.S., U. Calif. at Berkeley, 1949; M.S., U. Calif. at San Francisco, 1951, M.D., 1955; m. Elizabeth Abood, Feb. 11, 1948; children—Charles, Alan, Cary; came to U.S., 1946, naturalized, 1955. Intern, Cook County Hosp., Chgo., 1955-56; resident U. Calif. Hosp., San Francisco, 1949, Brooke Gen. Hosp., 1957-59; chief clin. and anatomic pathology Walter Reed Army Hosp., Washington, 1959-62; assoc. prof. U. So. Calif. Sch. Medicine, Los Angeles, 1963—; sr. surg. pathologist Los Angeles County Gen. Hosp., 1963; dir. dept. pathology Community Meml. Hosp., Ventura, Calif., 1964-80, Gen. Hosp. Ventura County, 1966-74; dir. Pathology Service Med. Group, 1970—; cons. Calif. Tumor Tissue Registry, 1962—, Camarillo State Hosp., 1964-70, Tripler Gen. Hosp., Hawaii, 1963-67, Armed Forces Inst. Pathology, 1960—. Bd. dirs. Tri-Counties Blood Bank, Am. Cancer Soc. Served to maj., M.C., U.S. Army, 1956-62. Recipient Borden award Calif. Honor Soc., 1949; Achievement cert. Surgeon Gen. Army, 1962. Fellow Am. Soc. Clin. Pathologists, Coll. Am. Pathologists; mem. Internat. Coll. Surgeons, World Affairs Council, Jonathan Club. Contbr. articles to profl. jours. Research in cardiovascular disease, endocrine, renal, skin diseases, also cancer. Home and Office: 105 Encinal Way Ventura CA 93001-3317

ACHEN, DOROTHY KAREN THOMPSON, professional society administrator; b. Washington, Dec. 21, 1944; d. John Murray and Dorothy (Doggette) Thompson; m. James Richard Achen Sr., June 17, 1966; children: James Richard Jr., Eric Christopher. BA, U. N.Mex., Albuquerque, 1969. Writer E.V.C.O. Instructional Texts, Albuquerque, 1966-67; real estate assoc. Roger Cox & Assoc., Albuquerque, 1977-79; substitute tchr. Albuquerque Pub. Schs., 1982-83; color cons. Beauty for All Seasons, 1983-85; coord. grand opening N.Mex. Mus. Natural History, 1985-86, pub. info. officer, 1986-87; exec. dir. N.Mex. Psychol. Assn., 1990—. Mem. Mayor's Beautification Com., Albuquerque, 1975-76; mediator Met. Ct., Albuquerque, 1989—; com. chmn. Albuquerque Acad. PTA, 1983-84, treas., 1988-89; mem. adv. bd. U. N.Mex. Cancer Ctr., 1991-93. Mem. N.Mex. Mediation Assn., Jr. League of Albuquerque (asst. treas. 1979-80, treas. 1980-81, chair devl. for vol. ctr. 1984-85, chair planning and by-laws com. 1982-83). Methodist. Office: 2425 San Pedro Dr NE Ste D Albuquerque NM 87110-4101

ACHEN, MARK KENNEDY, city manager; b. Vancouver, Wash., Apr. 13, 1943; s. George Ben and Marjorie Beth (Pierson) A.; m. Mary Ann Uzzell, Aug. 14, 1971; children: Wyndi Marie, Kara Lynn. BA, U. Wash., 1967; MA, U. Mo., 1981. Asst. to city mgr. City of Ferguson, Mo., 1972-74; city adminstr. City of Mounds View, Minn., 1974-79; city mgr. City of Gladstone, Mo., 1979-84, City of Grand Junction, Colo., 1984—; cons. U.S. Nat. Fire Acad., Emmitsburg, Md., 1990-91, adj. faculty, 1991—. Recipient J.F. Kennedy Sch. Govt. fellow Gates Found., 1987. Mem. ASPA (Kans. chpt. Adminstr. of Yr. 1983), Colo. City Mgmt. Assn. (pres. 1988-89, bd. dirs. 1985-91), Internat. City Mgmt. Assn. (chmn. 1988, internat. conf. planning com.), Rotary (pres. 1983-84, bd. dirs. 1989-90, 92-93, Paul HArris fellow 1991). Home: 3344 Northridge Dr Grand Junction CO 81506 Office: City of Grand Junction 250 N Fifth St Grand Junction CO 81501

ACHESON, ALICE BREWEN, publicist; b. Indiana, Pa., July 26, 1936; d. Stewart F. and Anna M.J. (Mohr) Brewen; m. Donald H. Acheson, Dec. 12, 1970 (dec.); m. Edward B. Greub, Sept. 8, 1990. AB, Bucknell U., 1958; MA, CUNY, 1963. Tchr. English and Spanish, Mt. Vernon (N.Y.) High Sch., 1958-69; exec. sec., then exec. asst. Media Medica, Inc., N.Y.C., 1969-71; with McGraw Hill Book Co., N.Y.C., 1971-78, assoc. editor, 1971-76, publicity assoc., 1977-78; assoc. publicity dir. Simon & Schuster, N.Y.C., 1979-80, Crown Pubs., Inc., N.Y.C., 1980-81; ind. publicist, prin. Alice B. Acheson, N.Y.C., 1981-88, San Francisco, 1988—; mem. faculty Willamette Writers' Conf., 1981, Folio Pub. Week, 1983, 84, Face to Face Pub. Conf. and Expn., 1977, 79, 81, Howard U. Press Book Pub. Inst., 1984, NYU Pub. Inst., 1985, Nat. Writers Union seminar, 1985, Small Press Expo, 1987, 88, Pubs. Mktg. Assn., 1990-93, Tucson Book Pubs. Assn., 1991-92; mem. publishing bd. Aperture Found., 1987-89. Recipient Ptnr.-in-Edn. award N.Y.C. Bd. Edn., 1977, 78. Mem. NAFE, Pubs. Publicity Assn. (program com. 1979-83), No. Calif. Book Publicists Assn. (bd. dirs. 1989-92), Pubs. Mktg. Assn. (bd. dirs. 1991-92). Offices: 3362 Laguna St San Francisco CA 94123-2208

ACHTEL, ROBERT ANDREW, pediatric cardiologist; b. Bklyn., May 5, 1941; s. Murray and Amelia (Ellian) A.; m. Erica Noel Woods, Mar. 10, 1063; children: Bergen Alison, Roland Hugh. BA, Adelphi U., 1963; MD, U. Cin., 1967. Diplomate Am. Bd. Pediatric Cardiology. Intern, Cin. Children's Hosp., 1967-68; resident in pediatrics Yale U., 1968-69, fellow in pediatric cardiology, 1969-71; clin. instr. pediatrics U. Calif.-Davis, 1972-73, clin. asst. prof., 1977-83; asst. prof. pediatrics, U. Ky., 1973-76; dir. pediatric ICU, Sutter Meml. Hosp., Sacramento, 1977-85, dir. pediatric Cardiology, 1982—, chmn. instl. rev. com., 1981-85; chmn. dept. pediatrics Mercy Hosp., Sacramento, 1981-83, vice chmn. pediatrics, 1983-85; dir. pediatric ICU, 1982-83; dir. Laurel Hills Devel. Ctr., 1985-89.; chmn. rsch com. Sutter Inst. for Med. Rsch., 1989—; trustee, mem. exec. com. Sutler Hosps. Found., vice chmn., 1992—. Contbr. articles in cardiovascular research. Bd. dirs. Sutter Meml. Hosp. Found., 1986—; bd. dirs. Sutter Found., 1989, trustee, 1989—. Maj. M.C., USAF, 1971-73. Recipient grants from Heart Assn., U. Ky. Tobacco and Health Research Found. Mem. Am. Heart Assn. (dir. Sacramento chpt., mem. councils congenital heart disease and atherosclerosis and cardiovascular surgery), Am. Coll. Chest Physicians, Am. Acad Pediatrics, SW Pediatric Cardiology Soc., So. Soc. Pediatric Research. Office: Pediatric Cardiology Assocs 5609 J St Ste A Sacramento CA 95819-3992

ACHTENHAGEN, STEPHEN H., education educator; b. Oberlin, Ohio, June 11, 1929; s. Oscar Fisher and Gladys Emmie Christine (Huntley) A.; m. Yvonne Leveque, Dec. 31, 1956 (div.); m. 2d. Mary Alice Yackey, Dec. 31, 1967 (div.); children: Karen, Erica, Gudrun, Kurt. BSME, U. Colo., 1952, BS in Bus. Adminstrn., 1952; PhD in Bus., Stanford U., 1974. Registered indsl. engr., Calif. Engr. manpower rep. Lockheed Aircraft, Burbank, Calif., 1952-53; owner RCA Distbrs., San Diego, 1955-57; asst. to tech. dir. Ramo Wooldridge, Denver, 1957-60; economist Stanford Rsch. Inst., Menlo Pk., Calif., 1960-61; market analyst, controller, indsl. engr., gen. sales mgr. Gen. Brewing Corp., San Francisco, 1961-64, asst. v.p. mktg., v.p. corp. planning, 1964-65, 65-68; prof. Calif. State U., San Jose, Calif., 1974—; dir. McNeil Money Market Fund, San Mateo, Calif., 1978—, Mapes Industries, Palo Alto, 1976—; cons. Corp. Strategy Assocs., Palo Alto, 1974—. Mil. specialist AUS, 1953-54. Recipient Calif. State U. Meritorious Performance and Profl. Promise award, 1987. Mem. IEEE, Am. Mktg. Assn. (pres. Santa Clara chpt. 1980-82), Corp. Planners Assn., San Francisco (pres. 1976), P.S. Mktg. Assn. (pres. 1963, 65), Elks, Nat. Assn. Corp. Dirs. Republican. Presbyterian. Home: 4150 Thain Way Palo Alto CA 94306

ACKER, JOAN ELISE ROBINSON, sociology educator; b. Springfield, Ill., Mar. 18, 1924; d. Harold D. Robinson and Frieda (Steinman) Ellsworth; children: Michael, David, Steven. BA, Hunter Coll., 1946; MA, U. Chgo., 1948; PhD, U. Oreg., 1967. Med. social worker N.Y. Hosp., N.Y.C., 1948-56; instr. U. Calif., Berkeley, 1956-58; dir. Ctr. for the Sociol. Study of Women, U. Oreg., Eugene, 1973-81, Ctr. for the Study of Women in Soc., U. Oreg., Eugene, 1982-86; from asst. prof. to prof. U. Oreg., Eugene, 1966-80; rsch. prof. Swedish Ctr. for Working Life, Stockholm, 1987-89; disting. vi. prof. Ont. Inst. for Studies in Edn., Toronto, Can., 1990; cons. Ont. Pay Equity Commn., Toronto, 1990, Equality Commn., Helsinki, Finland, 1988-89, Inst. for Social Sci. Rsch., Oslo, Norway, 1988-89. Author: Doing Comparable Worth, 1989; editor Econ. & Indsl. Democracy, 1982, Internat. Jour. Sociology, 1976; contbr. articles to profl. jours. Task force mem. Pay Equity, State of Oreg., Salem, 1983-85; chairperson Women's Studies Coun., U. Oreg., Eugene, 1979-81; bd. dirs. Nat. Coun. for Rsch. on Women, N.Y.C., 1983-86. Ford Found. fellow, 1965. Mem. Am. Sociol. Assn. (chair sex and gender sect. 1979-80, coun. 1992-95, Jessie Bernard award 1989, Career of Disting. Scholarships award 1993), Internat. Sociol. Assn., Pacific Sociol. Assn. (v.p. 1975), Sociologists for Women in Soc., Phi Beta Kappa. Office: U Oreg Dept Sociology Eugene OR 97403

ACKERLEY, BARRY, professional basketball team executive, communications company executive. Student, U. Iowa, 1956. Exec. v.p. Advan, Inc.; owner Golden West Outdoor Advt., 1968-75; chmn., CEO Ackerley Comm., Inc., 1975—; owner, chmn. bd. dirs. Seattle SuperSonics, 1984—. Office: Seattle SuperSonics PO Box C-900911 190 Queen Anne Ave N Seattle WA 98109-9711 also: Ackerley Communications Inc 800 Fifth Ave Seattle WA 98104

ACKERMAN, JOHN TRYON, utility company executive; b. Cleve., Aug. 12, 1941; s. William Tryon and Lillian Edith (Lancaster) A.; B.S. in Engring. (Harry and Mabel F. Leonard Tuition scholar), U. N.Mex., 1968; M.S. in Utility Mgmt. (Electric Utility Mgmt. Program fellow), N.Mex. State U., 1971; m. Katherine Murphy Pooler, May 1, 1965; children: Joseph Daniel, William Clay, Michael Eric. Design and devel. engr. Gen. Electric Co., Binghamton, N.Y., 1968-71; with Pub. Service Co. N.Mex., Albuquerque, 1971—, asst. to pres., 1976-78, dist. v.p. 1978-81, v.p. div. ops., 1981-83, sr. v.p., 1983-85, pres., ceo gas ops., 1985-90, now chmn., CEO, pres., 1991—; mem. N.Mex. Multiple Use Adv. Bd., Bur. Land Mgmt., 1975-77. V.p. bd. dirs. Albuquerque Assn. Children with Learning Disabilities, 1976-77, pres. bd., 1978; nat. assoc. Boys' Clubs Am., 1981-85; corp. chmn. United Way of Greater Albuquerque, 1978, bd. dirs. exec. com., 1979, v.p. bd. dirs., 1980, pres., 1981, 82; bd. dirs. 1st Interstate Bank, 1985-90, Albuquerque Community Found., 1984-90, Presbyn. Healthcare Services, 1986-90, U. N.Mex. Sch. of Mgmt., 1986-89. Served with USN, 1960-64. Registered profl. engr., N.Mex. Mem. Nat. Soc. Profl. Engrs., IEEE, Eta Kappa Nu (life). Republican. Office: Pub Svc Co NMex Alvarado Sq Albuquerque NM 87158

ACKERMAN, LILLIAN ALICE, anthropologist; b. Detroit, Apr. 14, 1928; d. John and Marie (Eurenjian) Hanjian; m. Robert Edwin Ackerman, Mar. 30, 1952; children: Laura Lynn, Gail Ellen, James Eric. BA in Anthropology, U. Mich., 1950, MA in Anthropology, 1951; PhD in Anthropology, Wash. State U., 1982. Russian translator Arctic Inst. of N.Am., Toronto, Ont., Can., 1960-62; instr. in anthropology Wash. State U., Pullman, 1963-65, Wenatchee Valley Coll., Nespelem, Wash., 1979; researcher in anthropology Wash. State U., Pullman, 1982—; adj. asst. prof. Wash. State U., Pullman, 1991—; cons. in anthropology, Pullman, 1982—; researcher, cons. U.S. Census, Washington, 1989-90. Contbr. articles to profl. jurs. Chairperson Developmental Disabilities Bd., Whitman County, Wash., 1969—. Woodrow Wilson fellowship, 1979; fellowship AAUW, 1979; grantee Phillips Fund of Am. Philos. Soc., 1979, 88. Mem. Am. Anthropol. Assn., Am. Ethnol. Soc., Alaska Anthropol. Assn., Sigma Xi (grantee 1978). Democrat. Office: Dept Anthropology Wash State U Pullman WA 99163

ACKERMAN, LINDA DIANE, manufacturing executive; b. Portland, Oreg., May 4, 1964; d. David Gilbert and Diane (Sause) A. BA in Econs., U. Wash., 1991. Office mgr. Hawaii Wood Preserving Co., Kahului, 1984-85, v.p., 1987—; with inventory control dept. Monarch Bldg. Supply, Kahului, 1986-87. Adminstrv. asst. I Have A Dream Program, Kahului, 1990-91; mem. area com. Spl. Olympics Maui County, 1993. Mem. Am. Wood Preservers Assn., Chi Omega (pres. Phi chpt. 1985). Republican. Mem. Christian Ch. Home: 43 Nonohe Pl Paia HI 96779 Office: Hawaii Wood Preserving Co 356 Hanakai St Kahului HI 96732-2407

ACKERMAN, MARK ROBERT, scientist; b. New Ulm, Minn., Oct. 7, 1959; s. Elmer Frederick and Joanne Marie (Olson) A.; m. Judith Elizabeth Chavez, July 31, 1987; 1 child, Edward Robert. BS, USAF Acad., 1981; MS, U. N.Mex., 1983. Commd. 2d lt. USAF, 1981, advanced through grades to capt., 1985, resigned, 1990; sr. mem. tech. staff Sandia Nat. Labs., Albuquerque, 1990—. Grantee Def. Nuclear Agy., 1992. Mem. NRA. Republican. Roman Catholic. Office: Sandia Nat Labs Dept 2271 PO Box 5800 Albuquerque NM 87105

ACKLAND, LEN, journalist, educator; b. Washington, June 2, 1944; s. Jack F. and Eleanor L. (Yoder) A.; m. Carol S. Stutzman, July 28, 1972; children: Seth, John, Sarah. BA, U. Colo., 1966; exch. student, U. Bonn, Germany, 1964-65; MA, Johns Hopkins U., 1970; DHL (hon.), Meadville Lombard Theol. Sch., Chgo., 1988. Tchr., refugee worker Internat. Vol. Svcs., Vietnam, 1967-68; rschr. RAND Corp.; rsch. asst. The Brookings Instn., Washington, 1969-71; asst. editor Dispatch News Svc., Washington, 1971-72; reporter Capital Ledger Mag., Denver, 1972-73, Cervi's Rocky Mountain Jour., Denver, 1973-75, Des Moines Register, 1975-78, Chgo. Tribune, 1978-84; editor Bull. of the Atomic Scientists, Chgo., 1984-91; assoc. prof. journalism U. Colo., Boulder, 1991—. Author: Credibility Gap: A Digest of the Pentagon Papers, 1972; editor: Why Are We Still in Vietnam?, 1970; co-editor: Assessing the Nuclear Age, 1986. Bd. dirs., chmn. 3d Unitarian Ch., Chgo., 1984-87; mem. bd. Global Outlook, Palo Alto, Calif., 1991—. Rsch. and writing grantee MacArthur Found., 1990, Davenport fellow in econs., U. Mo., 1976. Mem. Soc. Environ. Journalists, Investigative Reporters and Editors. Home: 920 Crescent Dr Boulder CO 80303 Office: Univ of Colo Campus Box 287 Boulder CO 80309-0287

ACKLES, JANICE VOGEL, fundraising executive, writer; b. Pasadena, Calif.; d. Roy George August and Genevieve Irene (Hunter) Vogel; m. David Thomas Ackles, Dec. 9, 1972; 1 child, George Arthur Vogel. BA in Art History, Calif. State U., L.A.; postgrad., U. So. Calif. Free-lance writer, 1972—; asst. editor Am. Jour. Physiology, L.A., 1980-84; dir. devel. rsch. World Vision, Monrovia, 1985-88; v.p. major gifts and rsch. Childrens Hosp., L.A., 1988-93; principal Ackles Communications, Tujunga, Calif., 1993—. Contbr. articles to nat. mags. and newspapers. Vol. researcher L.A. County Mus. Art, 1973-75; mem. Assistance League So. Calif., L.A., East African Wildlife Soc., Mus. Contemporary Art, L.A., Greater L.A. Zoo Assn., Natural History Mus. Mem. Am. Prospect Rsch. Assn., Nat. Soc.

Fund Raising Execs. (bd. dirs., cert.), Assn. for Hosp. Philanthropy, Ind. Writers So. Calif., Calif. Press Women, Inc. (bd. dirs.). Democrat.

ACKLEY, MARJORIE ROSE, health educator; b. Shanghai, China, Nov. 15, 1922; came to U.S., 1926; d. Millard Charles Ackley and Luella Alice (Williams) Scharffenberg; m. Donald Wilton Oswald, Sept. 24, 1942 (div. 1955); children: Donald Theodore Oswald, Jaclyn Rae Hoiland. AS, Grossmont Coll., 1977; BS in Allied Health Professions, Loma Linda U., 1987, MPH, 1988. RN, registered dietitian, fitness instr.; lic. M/V operator. Adminstrv. grant sec. Palo Alto (Calif.) Med. Research Found., 1962-67; devel. dir. San Francisco Eye and Ear Hosp., 1967-70; fin. planner Robert W. P. Holstrom Co., San Francisco, 1971-74; health educator San Francisco, 1972-74; registered nurse Groves Registry, San Francisco, 1977-88, Humana Hosp., Anchorage, 1983-85; owner, dir. Profl. Health Svcs., 1984-93; registered nurse Providence Hosp., Anchorage, 1983-85, 90-93, MedPro Nurses Registry, San Diego, 1984-89; cardiac rehabilitation Providence Hosp., Anchorage, 1990-93; health educator Anchorage, 1983-93; med. coord. Canvasback Mission, Inc., Benecia, Calif., 1988-93; health educator, Sch. of Pub. Health, Loma Linda, Calif., 1988, Seventh-Day Adventist Ch., San Francisco, 1973, Health Expo, Yucaipa, Calif., 1988; health edn. lectr. 1990-93. Author of numerous articles in field. Vol. Health Expo, Alaska, 1988. Mem. Am. Dietetic Assn. (Eleanor Mitchell Meml. award 1986), Alaska Dietetic Assn., Seventh-Day Adventist Dietetic Assn., Am. Pub. Health Assn., Inst. for Advancement of Health. Republican. Seventh-Day Adventist. Home: 3225 Boniface Pky Anchorage AK 99504-3741

ACOB, NORMA DENISE, transportation executive, consultant; b. Hilo, Hawaii, June 7, 1952; d. Arsento Albano Acob, Sr. and Evelyn Tarsila (Arsenio) Dismaya. BA in Physical Edn., San Diego State U., 1973. Recreation dir. YWCA San Diego, 1968-72; med. lab. technician Clinical Lab 4th St, San Diego, 1972-75; ops. mgr. Hawaii Anth. Coop., Hilo, 1976-80; freight dir. Commodity Forwarders, Inc., Hawaii, 1980-87, freight dir., ptnr., 1987—. Mem. Hilo Florist & Shippers Assn. (bd. dirs.), Kanoelehua Indsl. Area Assn. (bd. dirs. 1986-88, v.p. 1988-92), Hawaii Anthurium Product Promotion Assn., Hawaii Air Transport Assn., Hawaii Island C. of C. Democrat. Roman Catholic. Home: 34 E Kawili St Apt 12 Hilo HI 46720 Office: Commodity Forwarders Inc PO Box 4565 Hilo HI 96721

ACORD-SKELTON, BARBARA BURROWS, counselor, educator, artist; b. L.A., Dec. 26, 1928; d. Harry and Sophia (Dittman) Burrows; m. Benjamin Raddatz, June 11, 1949 (div. Dec. 1970); children: Randolph, Marjorie, Thomas, Deborah; m. William A. Acord, Feb. 26, 1974 (dec.); m. Gerald Skelton, 1989. AA, Riverside City Coll., 1956; BA, Calif. State U., San Bernardino, 1970; MA, Pacific Oaks Coll., 1974; postgrad., Claremont Coll., 1976-91. Lic. marriage, family and child counselor, Calif., 1974. Dir. pvt. nursery sch. Headstart, Riverside, Calif., 1964-66; career devel., coord. Riverside County Head Start and Corono Norco Sch. Dist., Riverside, 1966-72; instr. Chaffey Community Coll., Alta Loma, Calif., 1971-82; class room coord., family counselor Casa Colina Hosp., Pomona, Calif., 1973-79; counselor LaVerne (Calif.) Ctr. for Edn. Counseling, 1976-82; social worker III San Andreas Regional Ctr., Salinas, Calif., 1984-87; pvt. practice family and individual counseling Medford, 1987-92; cons. Pomona U. Sch. Dist., Calif., 1973-80, San Gabriel Valley Regional Ctr., Covina, Calif., 1976-82, Nat. Council Alcoholism, Covina, 1980-82; instr. U. LaVerne, 1976-82. Author: On Learning and Growing, 1974; co-author: Parent Advocacy Training, 1977, Creative Competency, 1978. Vol. Day Springs Hospice, Medford, 1987—; bd. dirs. Gold Coast Arab Horse Assn., Santa Clara County, Calif., 1983-85. Riverside County Headstart scholar, 1967, Ednl. Profl. Devel. Act scholar, 1971-74. Mem. Am. Assn. Marriage and Family Therapists, Calif. Assn. Marriage and Family Therapists, Upper Rogue Art Assn., Arab Horse Assn. (So. Oreg. bd. dirs. 1988, pres. 1989), Women Artists Cascades Mountains, Region III Arab Horse Assn. (bd. dirs. 1983-85), GRA, WSO, WACM. Home: 13856 Weowna Way White City OR 97503-9572

ACOSTA, NELSON JOHN, civil engineer; b. Newark, N.J., July 8, 1947; s. Pedro Nelson and Bertha Maud (Williams) A.; m. Twyla Liasine Flaherty, June 19, 1970; children: Jeffrey Thomas, Stephen Patrick, Bryan Edward. BCE, Ga. Inst. Tech., 1969, MSCE, 1970. Registered profl. engr., Ill. Design engr. Chgo. Bridge and Iron Co., Birmingham, Ala., 1970-73; sales estimator Chgo. Bridge and Iron Co., Oak Brook, Ill., 1973-74; contracting engr. Chgo. Bridge and Iron Co., Atlanta, 1975-79, CBI Constructors, Ltd., London, 1979-80, Arabian CBI Ltd., Al Khobar, Saudi Arabia, 1980-84, CBI Na-Con, Inc., Fontana, Calif., 1984-88; mgr. spl. projects and estimating HMT, Inc., Cerritos, Calif., 1989—. Recipient traineeship NSF, Atlanta, 1969. Mem. ASCE. Republican. Roman Catholic. Office: HMT Inc 13921 Artesia Blvd Cerritos CA 90701

ACOSTA, PAMELA ANN, head teller; b. Cheyenne, Wyo., Aug. 29, 1955; d. Hubert S. and Alice G. (Thompson) Norfleet; m. Leo F. Wilson, June 28, 1975 (div. Nov. 1983); m. Michael Acosta, Feb. 14, 1988; children: Jeffrey S., Daniel S., Amy S. AAS, Laramie County Community Coll., 1987. Teller Equality State Bank, Cheyenne, 1983-88; head teller Key Bank of Wyo., Cheyenne, 1988—. Dir. fashion show Miss Wyo. Com., Cheyenne, 1983; mem. ticket com. Cheyenne Frontier Days. Mem. Am. Legion Aux. (dept. chmn., past unit pres., Wyo. Girls State 1972), Key Club, Order of Eastern Star, Jaycees (Cheyenne past pres. parley 1990, named Oustanding Young Woman of Am. 1984). Republican. Presbyterian. Office: Key Bank of Wyo 18th & Carey Ave Cheyenne WY 82001

ACOSTA, PATRICIA, marketing consultant; b. South Gate, Calif., July 21, 1961; d. Ramon and Carlota (Melendez) A. BA, UCLA, 1984; cert. mgmt., U. So. Calif., 1991. Lic. Spanish translator and interpretor. Project coord. Community & Human Resources, Inc., L.A., 1982-84; mktg. cons. Vitro Fibras, S.A., Mexico City, 1984-86; projects dir. Exec. Industries, L.A., 1986-87; legis. cons. Calif. State Legislature, L.A., 1987-88; adminstrv. asst. Calif. State Senator Art Torres, L.A., 1988-89; nat. account exec. Del Valle and Assocs., L.A., 1989; mktg. cons. Sebastian Internat., L.A., 1989—, Soc. Hispanic Profl. Engrs., L.A., 1991—, Am. Inst. Graphic Arts, L.A., 1991—; pub. policy specialist AIDS Project L.A., 1993—; project dir. Oldtimers Found., L.A., 1992—. Candidate State Assembly, Calif., 1992; commr. L.A. County Planning Commn., 1992; del. Ctrl. Dem. Com., L.A., 1992; bd. mem., v.p. ARC, 1989-90; bd. mem. Multinat. Health Edn.; treas. S.E. Voter Registration Project, 1991-92. Named Outstanding Vol. L.A. County Children Svcs., 1988; recipient Dedicated Svc. award 33d Senatorial Dist., Calif. Senate, 1988, Community Svc. awards Lt. Gov. Leo McCarthy, Calif. Legislature, 1989, 55th Assembly Dist. Calif. Assembly, 1990. Mem. Comision Femenil, Hispanic Womens Coun., Mexican Am. Polit. Assn. (v.p. 1992), Mexican C. of C. Roman Catholic. Home: 10012 Otis St South Gate CA 90280 Office: AIDS Project LA 1313 N Vine St Los Angeles CA 90028

ACQUAFRESCA, STEVEN JOSEPH, fruitgrower, consultant, state legislator; b. Calif., Jan. 4, 1951; children: Marcy Ann, Carey Lane, Phillip Todd. Student, Mesa State Coll., 1972-74; BS in Agr., Colo. State U., 1976. Fruitgrower Acquafresca Orchards, Cedaridge, Colo.; mem. Colo. Ho. of Reps., 1990—, mem. adv. com. C.C. and Occupational Edn. System, vice chmn. agr., livestock and natural resources com., 1993—, mem. edn. com., 1993—; agrl. advisor; mem. tech. adv. com. CCCOES; bd. dirs. Apple Adminstrv. Com. Mem. Nat. Assn. Ind. Ag Cons., Colo. Farm Bur., Wash. State Hort. Assn., We. Colo. Hort. Soc., Colo. Agrl. Leadership Alumni Assn., Colo. State U. Alumni Assn., South Am. Explorers Club, Tree Bd. Republican. Roman Catholic. Office: House of Representatives 2290 Rd S Cedaredge CO 81413

ACREE, MICHAEL COY, psychology educator; b. Terre Haute, Ind., May 6, 1946; s. Coy Ray and Roberta Ann (Shank) A.; m. Harriet Roberts O'Neal, Oct. 5, 1985 (div. Dec. 1986). BA, Oberlin Coll., 1968; MA, Clark U., 1973, PhD, 1978. Asst. prof. U. Nebr., Lincoln, 1978-79; rsch. psychologist Ctr. on Deafness U. Calif., San Francisco, 1980-85; asst. prof. Pacific Grad. Sch. Psychology, Palo Alto, Calif., 1985-90; assoc. prof. Calif. Inst. Integral Studies, San Francisco, 1991—; statistician Ctr. for AIDS Prevention Studies, U. Calif., San Francisco, 1991—. Grantee Nat. Inst. Handicapped Rsch. 1984, Chapman Rsch. Fund 1986. Home: 859 45th Ave San Francisco CA 94121 Office: Calif Inst Integral Studies 765 Ashbury St San Francisco CA 94117

ACTON, EDWARD MCINTOSH, medicinal chemist; b. Morgan Hill, Calif., May 30, 1930; s. John Edward and Margaret (McIntosh) A. BS, Stanford (Calif.) U., 1951; PhD, MIT, 1957. Chemist Merck & Co., Rahway, N.J., 1951-53; organic chemist SRI Internat., Menlo Park, Calif., 1957-75, program mgr., 1975-85; prof. medicinal chemistry U. Tex. M.D. Anderson Hosp. and Cancer Inst., Houston, 1985-87; dep. br. chief, expert Nat. Cancer Inst., Bethesda, Md., 1987-91; cons. Menlo Park, 1991—. Editorial bd. Cancer Chemotherapy and Pharmacology, 1981-87, Am. Cancer Soc., Adv. Com. on Clin. Invest II--Chemotherapy and Hematology, 1984-87, Nat. Cancer Inst., Devel. Therapeutics Contracts Rev. Com., 1983-86; contbr. numerous articles to profl. jours. Numerous grants Nat. Cancer Inst., 1976-87. Mem. AAAS, Am. Chem. Soc., Royal Soc. of Chemistry. Republican. Congregationalist. Home and Office: 281 Arlington Way Menlo Park CA 94025

ADACHI, DEREK KASUMI, pharmacist, computer programmer; b. Seattle, Aug. 2, 1961; s. Seiichi and Yoko (Horita) A. BS in Pharmacy, U. Wash., 1985; MS in Pharmacology, Wash. State U., 1989; MS in Computer Sci., Pacific Luth. U., 1992. Registered pharmacist. Clin. pharmacist Puyallup Tribal Health Authority, Tacoma, Wash., 1985-87, 89-92; microcomputer cons. Pacific Luth. U., Tacoma, 1989-92; clin. pharmicist, health care systems analyst, mgr. pharmacy Caremark Inc., Redmond, Wash., 1992—. Contbr. articles to profl. jours. Mem. IEEE, Am. Pharm. Assn., Assn. for Computing Machinery, Wash. State Pharmacists Assn. Mem. United Ch. Christ. Home: 19223 34th Ave S Seatac WA 98188-5313 Office: Caremark 6645 185th Ave NE Ste 151 Redmond WA 98052

ADAIR, JAMES ALLEN, Canadian provincial government official; b. Edmonton, Alta., Can., May 13, 1929; s. James Wilfred and Beatrice (Shewfelt) A.; m. Joyce Helen Johnson, Oct. 31, 1960; children: Richard, Catherine, Robert. Student pub. schs., Edmonton. Feed mill operator Searle Grain Co., St. Paul, 1948-49, grain buyer, 1949; seed buyer Peace Milling Co. Ltd., Peace River, Alta., 1953-59; catering supr. Fortier & Assocs., Peace River, 1960-64; salesman, sports dir. Sta. CKYL, Peace River, 1964-71, ptnr., 1971—; mem. Legis. Assembly for Peace River, 1971—; cabinet minister Alta. Provincial Govt., Edmonton, 1971—. Progressive Conservative. Anglican. Home: 9634 83d Ave, Peace River, AB Canada T8S 1A4 Office: Minister Transp & Utilities, Legislature Bldg Rm 208, Edmonton, AB Canada T5K 2B6

ADAM, CORNEL See LENGYEL, CORNEL ADAM

ADAM, RODNEY DEAN, physician, researcher, educator; b. Holdrege, Nebr., Aug. 18, 1954; s. Robert Henry and Delores Ann (Lienemann) A.; m. Mary Beth Saufferer, Apr. 20, 1980; children: Jennifer, Benjamin, Sara. BA in Math., Chemistry & Biology, Trinity Coll., 1976; MD, U. Ill., 1981. Diplomate Am. Bd. Internal Medicine, Am. Bd. Infectious Diseases. Intern, then resident in medicine U. Ariz., Tucson, 1981-84, infectious disease fellow, 1984-85; med. staff fellow NIH, Bethesda, Md., 1985-88; asst. prof. Coll. of Medicine, Univ. Ariz., Tucson, 1988—. Mem. First Evang. Free Ch., Tucson, 1989—. Fellow ACP; mem. Am. Soc. Tropical Medicine and Hygiene, Am. Soc. for Microbiology, Infectious Disease Soc. Am. (assoc.), Christian Med. and Dental Soc. Republican. Office: U Ariz Coll of Medicine 1501 N Campbell Ave Tucson AZ 85724-0001

ADAM, WALLACE BURNS, project manager, engineering educator; b. Hyannis, Nebr., Oct. 14, 1933; s. G. Donald and Marcella (Shackelford) A.; m. Dorothy Constance Ford, July 27, 1962; children: Bradley Dwain, Steven Charles. MS in Aero. Engring., Air Force Inst. Tech., 1968; BSME, U. Nebr., 1958. Registered profl. engr., Colo. Commd. 2d lt. USAF, 1958, advanced through grades to lt. col., command pilot, 1974; asst. prof. aero. engring. USAF Acad., Colorado Springs, Colo., 1969-73; devel. plans engr. USAF Systems Command Hdqrs., Andrews AFB, Md., 1973-76; dir. test track 6585th Test Group Armanent Test Group, Holloman AFB, N.Mex., 1976-81; mgr. elec. sect. land/air div. DynCorp, Holloman AFB, N.Mex., 1981-85; dept. mgr. radar backscatter div. DynCorp, 1985-87, project mgr. radar svcs. div., 1987-90, gen. mgr. radar svcs. and land-air divsns., 1992—. Life mem. Rep. Presdl. Task Force, Washington, 1981. Decorated Bronze Star (Republic of Vietnam). Mem. AIAA (sr., chmn. sect. 1971-72, 85-86, regional coun. 1986-87), Air Force Assn. (life), Am. Def. Preparedness Assn., Assn. U.S. Army (v.p. pubs. 1992-93), Nat. Contracts Mgmt. Assn. (treas. 1992-93), Am. Assn. Ret. Persons, Masons (master). Republican. Office: DynCorp Land-Air Divsn PO Box 1206 Holloman Air Force Base NM 88330-1206

ADAMICH, SUSAN JO ANN, educator; b. L.A., Jan. 2, 1959; d. Frank Joseph and Elizabeth (Moore) A. Student, Ventura Coll., 1977-79; BA in Psychology, Pepperdine U., 1982; teaching credential, Calif. State U., Northridge, 1988, MA in Ednl. Psychology, 1991. Youth minister Youth for Christ/Mil. Community Youth Ministries, Berlin, 1982-85; substitute tchr. Ventura (Calif.) Unified Sch. Dist., 1987-90; tutorial program dir. Ventura Unified Sch. Dist., De Anza Mid. Sch., 1990-92, study skills instr., 1992—. Chair pastor nominating com. Community Presbyn. Ch., Ventura, 1990-91. Home: 352 Hamilton Ave Ventura CA 93003 Office: De Anza Mid Sch 2060 Cameron St Ventura CA 93001

ADAMS, ALAN LEONARD, retired air force officer, meteorologist; b. Atlanta, June 15, 1949; s. Seldon Leonard and Mary Hazel (Britt) A.; m. Carol Ann Hanson, Mar. 1970 (div. 1973); m. Cinthia Lee Preg, Nov. 9, 1974; children: Scott Alan, Christopher Patrick. B in Aerospace Engring., Ga. Inst. Tech., 1971; BS in Engring. Sci., U. Tex., 1972; MS in Meteorology, MIT, 1976. Wing weather officer 5th Weather Wing Detachment 75, Hurlburt Field, Fla., 1972-74, 1st Weather Wing Detachment 4, Hickam AFB, Hawaii, 1976-80; weather staff officer Air Force Global Weather Cen., Offutt AFB, Nebr., 1980-83; comdr. 31st Weather Squadron Detachment 11, Spangdahlem Air Base, Fed. Republic Germany, 1983-86; lt. col., air weather svc. liaison Defense Meteorol. Satellite Program Air Force Systems Command, L.A. AFB, 1986-91; ret. USAF, 1991; mem. tech. support staff bd Systems, Inc., Torrance, Calif., 1992—. Mem. Ga. Tech. Alumni Assn., Lions. Baptist. Home: 5026 Carmelynn St Torrance CA 90503-1902 Office: Bd Systems 385 Van Ness Ave Ste 200 Torrance CA 90501-1483

ADAMS, ANN LOUISE, publisher; b. Palestine, Tex., Nov. 17, 1934; d. Henry George and Ola Monteel (Goodin) Beard; m. J.G. Price, Mar. 15, 1956 (div. 1973); m. Mark Adams, May 12, 1979. BA, U. Tex., Austin, 1957. Proofreader Austin (Tex.) Am.-Statesman, 1960-67; typesetter Tulsa World, 1967-68, San Antonio Express-Light, 1970-73, Austin Am.-Statesman, 1973-77, Albuquerque Jour., 1977-78, Everett (Wash.) Herald, 1978-80; editor U. Okla. Press, Norman, Okla., 1968-70; freelance editor Everett and Oak Harbor, Wash., 1981--; pub. Packrat Press, Oak Harbor, 1981--; pub. cons. Wash. Pub. Utility Dists. Assn., Seattle, 1987-88; news clk. Whidbey News-Times, 1989—. Editor: The Clay Pedestal (Wash. Gov.'s award), 1981, Public and Private Letters of Franklin Jones, Sr. (4 vols.), 1982-89; author: Travels With A Donkey, 1982; contbr. articles to various publs. Mem. Com. of Corr., Pandorans. Home and Office: Packrat Press 4366 N Hamilton Dr Oak Harbor WA 98277

ADAMS, BERNARD LEROY, computer consulting company executive; b. Sidney, Mont., Oct. 11, 1954; s. Faye Emmett and Kathleen (Blanc) A.; m. Paulette Vee Weisbeck, Oct. 9, 1982; children: Belinda Kay, Bradley George. BS in Computer Sci., Mont. State U., 1976. Computer programmer Idaho Power & Light, Boise, 1976-77; programmer, analyst State of Mont., Helena, 1977-80; ind. cons. Adams Computer Cons., Helena, 1980—; prin. cons. Applied Mgmt. Corp., Helena, 1982—; cons. Met. Airports Commn., Mpls., 1989—, State of Mont. Dept. of Revenue, 1980-82, Amtech Corp., Dallas, 1992—, 3M Corp., St. Paul, 1989-90, Westinghouse Electric Corp., 1992—. Mem. Helena Area Crimestoppers, 1992-93. Office: Applied Mgmt Corp 636 Logan Helena MT 59601

ADAMS, CHARLES RICHARD, manufacturing executive; b. Frederick, Okla., Sept. 4, 1927; s. Oran Bailey and Corin Lucille (Adkins) A.; m. Katie Hennen, Apr. 23, 1949 (dec. Jan. 17, 1989); children: Patrick, Molly Ewing, Cynthia Lawson; m. Janice Marie Whelan, Sept. 22, 1990. Student, Tex. A&M U., 1944-45; BA, Baylor U., 1950. Sales Endo Labs., Dallas, 1951-53; sales Riker Labs., Northridge, Calif., 1953-55, dist. mgr., 1955-59, sales mgr., 1959-61, v.p. mktg., 1961-66, pres., 1966-80; chmn., pres., CEO Chad Therapeutics, Inc., Chatsworth, Calif., 1982—. With USN, 1945-47. Mem. Health Industry Mfg. Assn., Pharm. Mfg. Assn. (dir. 1970-80). Republican. Methodist. Office: Chad Therapeutics Inc 9441 DeSoto Ave Chatsworth CA 91311

ADAMS, CLINTON, painter, historian; b. Glendale, Calif., Dec. 11, 1918; s. Merritt Cooley and Effie (Mackenzie) A.; m. Mary Elizabeth Atchison, Jan. 9, 1943; 1 child, Michael Gerald. Ed.B., UCLA, 1940, M.A., 1942. Instr. art UCLA, 1946-48, asst. prof., 1948-54; prof. art, head dept. U. Ky.; also dir. Art Gallery, 1954-57; prof. art, head dept. U. Fla., 1957-61; dean Coll. Fine Arts U. N.Mex., Albuquerque, 1961-76, asso. provost, dean faculties, 1976-77; dir. Tamarind Inst., 1970-85; asso. dir. Tamarind Lithography Workshop, Los Angeles, 1960-61, program cons., 1961-70. Represented in permanent collections Bklyn. Mus., Art. Inst. Chgo., Australian Nat. Gallery, Grunwald Center Graphic Arts, Mus. Modern Art, Los Angeles County Art Mus., and others; author: (with Garo Antreasian) The Tamarind Book of Lithography: Art and Techniques, 1970, Fritz Scholder: Lithographs, 1975, American Lithographers, 1900-1960: The Artists and Their Printers, 1983, (with others) Lasting Impressions: Lithography As Art, 1988, Printmaking in New Mexico, 1880-1990, 1991, Crayonstone: The Life and Work of Bolton Brown, 1993; editor The Tamarind Papers, 1974-90; subject: bibliography Clinton Adams: Paintings and Watercolors 1945-87; exhbn. catalogue Albuquerque: University of New Mexico Art Mus., 1987; biography A Spectrum of Innovation: Color in American Printmaking, 1890-1990, 1990. Recipient Gov.'s award for outstanding contbns. to arts of N.Mex., 1985. Mem. NAD (academician), Coll. Art Assn. (program chmn. 1963), Nat. Coun. Fine Arts Deans (chmn. 1965-67), Mid-Am. Coll. Art Assn. (pres. 1973). Home: 1917 Morningside Dr NE Albuquerque NM 87110-4927

ADAMS, DAVID BENNION, psychologist; b. Salt Lake City, May 21, 1945; s. Ferrell Harrison and Maurine (Bennion) A. B.A., U. Utah, 1968, M.S. (Kappa Sigma fellow), 1972, Ph.D. in Psychology cum laude, 1976. Staff psychologist Granite Mental Health Ctr., 1972-74; dir. Juvenile Alcohol Program, 1974-75; clin. supr. Adolescent Residential Treatment Ctr., 1974-79; pvt. practice clin. psychology, Salt Lake City, 1976—, also clin. dir. Am. Community Youth Services, 1979-82, Intermountain Youth Care, 1982-90, Interstate Youth Svcs., 1992—; instr. U. Utah, Brigham Young U.; program coord. Children's div. Charter Summit Hosp. Local dist. Dem. del., 1972. Served with USAR, 1963-71. Lic. and cert. psychologist, Utah; cert. marriage and family counselor, Utah. Mem. Am. Psychol. Assn., Utah Psychol. Assn., Utah Psychologists in Pvt. Practice, Zero Population Growth, Nat. Register for Health Service Providers in Psychology, Sierra Club, Utah Assn. Juvenile and Adult Corrections, Kappa Sigma. Contbr. articles to profl. jours. Home: 1036 Countrylane Rd Salt Lake City UT 84117-4158 Office: 7138 Highland Dr Ste 105 Salt Lake City UT 84121-3755

ADAMS, DAVID CHRISTOPHER, writer, filmmaker; b. Bryn Mawr, Pa., Apr. 17, 1967; s. Paul K. Adams and Linn (Chapel) Schulte. BA, U. Denver, 1989; MFA, U. So. Calif., 1993. Asst. producer Sta. KMGH-TV/McGraw Hill Broadcasting, Denver, 1986; freelance writer Suburban Pubs., Wayne, Pa., 1987, 88; writer Morgan Industries, Phila., 1989-90; freelance writer L.A., 1990—; tchr. ESL Linguex Lang. Ctr., Denver, 1989-90, 90; writer, researcher Rich Clarkson ans Assocs., Denver, 1989-90; tchr. English Colo. Acad., Denver, 1989-90; booking agt. Crew Connection, Inc., Denver, 1990-91; founder Tomato Soup Films-Freelance Production Co. Contbr. articles, poem to profl. jours., mags.; author screenplays for ednl. videos and feature treatments. Mem. Lambda Chi Alpha. Home: 16 Thornton Ave Apt 100A Venice CA 90291-2557

ADAMS, DAVID JOHN, elementary school educator, art historian; b. Ft. Wayne, Ind., Feb. 8, 1949; s. Vernon John and Barbara Jean (Morton) A.; m. Jane Murrell Johnson, June 9, 1979 (div. 1983); m. Janet Olive, Dec. 4, 1987. BA, New Coll. Sarasota, 1971; postgrad., Met. State Coll., Denver, 1973, Waldorf Inst., Detroit, 1975-76; PhD, Union Inst. Grad. Sch., Cin., 1978. Cert. tchr., Colo. Utilization rsch. analyst Blue Cross & Blue Shield Mich., Detroit, 1977, 78-79; instr., exhbn. curator Found. Yr. Adult Edn. Program, Spring Valley, N.Y., 1980-81; gen. mgr. J & R Lamb Studios, Philmont, N.Y., 1980-83; indexer Art Index, Bronx, N.Y., 1985-86; instr., adminstr. Threefold Painting Sch., Spring Valley, N.Y., 1983-86; asst. prof. art history U. Minn., Morris, 1987-88, Calif. State U., Fresno, 1988-89, U. Nev., Reno, 1989-90; class tchr. Portland (Oreg.) Waldorf Sch., 1991-92, Mariposa Waldorf Sch., Cedar Ridge, Calif., 1992—; instr. Interior Design Inst., Woodcliff Lake, N.J., 1985-86; vis. asst. prof. art history U. Mont., Missoula, 1986-87; dir. Ctr. for Archtl. & Design Rsch., Spring Valley; bd. govs. The Census of Stained Glass Windows in Am. 1940-1940, Worcester, Mass., 1980—. Contbr. articles to books and profl. jours.; publisher exhbn. catalogs. Mem. adv. com. City of Reno Hist. Mem. Coll. Art Assn., Soc. Archtl. Historians, Am. Assn. Mus., Anthrop. Soc. in Am., The Greens.

ADAMS, DEANNA SUE DUNCAN, health care educator; b. Chattanooga, Mar. 1, 1942; d. William Quentin and Mamie (Rogers) Duncan; children: Amanda Foree, Amelia Fine; m. Ivan C. Adams, Jr., 1989. Nursing diploma, Johns Hopkins Hosp., 1963; BS, Athens (Ala.) State Coll., 1978; MEd, Ala. A&M, 1980; postgrad., Fla. Inst. Tech., 1988-89, Weber State U., 1992—. RN, Md., Ala.; cert. diabetes educator. Staff nurse Johns Hopkins Hosp., Balt., 1963, George Washington U. Hosp., Washington, 1964-66; staff nurse, supr. Colbert County Hosp., Sheffield, Ala., 1966-67; supr. nursing Crestwood Hosp., Huntsville, Ala., 1967; staff nurse, instr. U.S. Army Hosp., Redstone Arsenal, Ala., 1969-72; insvc. coord. 5th Ave. Hosp., Huntsville, 1972-74; instr. Huntsville Hosp., 1974-76, dir. edn., 1976-89; health cons., North Ogden, Utah, 1989—; outpatient instr. for diabetes, case mgr. continuing care St. Benedict's Hosp., Ogden, Utah, 1990—; mem. affiliate faculty Am. Heart Assn., Birmingham, 1976—. Contbr. articles to profl. jours. Mem. Plantation South Condo Assn., Huntsville, 1987—; instr. standard first aid Bonneville chpt. ARC. Recipient 2d Pl. Life Saver award Ala. Cancer Soc., 1987. Mem. Am. Assn. Diabetes Educators, Am. Diabetes Assn. (subcom. on edn. Utah div.), Johns Hopkins U. Alumni Assn., Plantation South Condominium Assn., Altrusa (bd. dirs. 1987-89, 92—, treas. 1987-89, corr. sec. 1991), Sigma Theta Tau (charter, sec. Nu Nu chpt. 1992—). Episcopalian.

ADAMS, GLEN CAMERON, publisher; b. Trent, Wash., June 19, 1912; s. Otto Ulysses and Mae (Cameron) A.; m. Nina Lenore Finch, Apr. 30, 1936 (div. June 1939); 1 child, Robert Glen; m. Jean Pierie Evers, June 29, 1946. BA, Ea. Wash. U., 1938; LittD (hon.), Gonzaga U., 1990. Prin. Burbank (Wash.) Sch. Dist., 1938-39; livestock breeder Fairfield, Wash., 1939-51; postmaster Fairfield Post Office, 1951-72; printer, pub. Ye Galleon Press, Fairfield, 1972—; hon. prof. history Eastern Wash. U., Cheney, 1983. Mayor Town of Fairfield, 1974-78. Named to Wash. State Hall of Honor, Washington State Hist. Soc., Tacoma, 1983. Democrat. Presbyterian. Home: 103 Brewster St Fairfield WA 99012 Office: 103 E Main St Fairfield WA 99012

ADAMS, JACK, film company executive, screenwriter, educator; b. Lakehurst, N.J., Sept. 15, 1952; s. John Carey and Dorothy Jeanne (Conover) A.; m. Shirley Janulewicz, June 28, 1975; children: Carey Miller, Chanine Angelina, Mikael Walter, Jozef Conover. MusB in Music Edn., U. Del., 1974. Pres. Koala Studio, Valencia, Calif., 1977—; v.p. devel. Unifilms, Inc., North Hollywood, Calif., 1984—; instr. film, TV writing and script analysis Coll. of Canyons, Valencia, 1988—, L.A. City Coll., 1989—, EveryWoman's Village, Van Nuys, Calif., 1990—, Info. Exch., L.A., 1990—, Learning Tree U., Chatsworth, Calif., 1990—, U. Wis., Madison, 1991—, U. Hawaii, 1992—, USIA, Washington, 1991—, Info. Network, South Pasadena, Calif., 1990—, Moorpark Coll., 1991—, Oxnard Coll., 1991—, Northwestern U., Evanston, Ill., 1991—, Glendale (Calif.) Community Coll., 1991—, U. Wis., Milw., 1993, Johnson County C.C., 1993; co-founder ScripTip, 1990, Classes Unlimited, 1992—, Johnson County Community Coll., Kansas City, 1993, Univ. Wis., Milwaukee, 1993; script cons. Wis. Screenwriters Forum; mem. KNX Speakers Bur., CBS Radio, 1989—, Story Bd. Devel. Group, Paramount Studios, 1989—; pres. NBC Writers Workshop; mem. Larry Wilson Devel. Workshop, Paramount Studios, Le Group, Paramount Studios; founding mem., officer, bd. dirs. L.A. Filmmakers Workshop, 1989-91; founder Santa Clarita Scriptwriters Workshop; pres. Entertainment Writers' Workshop, 1990; mem. Ind. Feature Project West.

Composer (film) Eat, 1980 (Filmex award 1981, best short film award Cinemagic mag. 1981); writer, co-creator sitcom pilot Lola, Universal Studios, 1991; writer, developer sitcom pilot Fat Farm; writer, producer, dir. sitcom pilot Box # 22; line producer sitcom pilots Zebra, It's Not My Fault; TV editor Freelance Screenwriters' Forum Newsletter; columnist ScreenWrite Now mag.; creator (audiotape) Top 50 Script Marketing Tips. Mem. Indian Guides/Princesses Program, chief Apache tribe YMCA, 1990—. Mem. Am. Film Inst. (alumni assn. writers workshop), Scriptwriters Network (bd. advisors), Film Artists Network, Ind. Writers So. Calif. Scriptwriters Caucus, Assn. Info. Systems Profls. (bd. dirs. 1983), Freelance Screenwriter's Forum (founding), Comedy Writers Co-op (founding ABC), Wis. Screenwriters Forum (advisor 1989—). Home and Office: 22931 Sycamore Creek Dr Santa Clarita CA 91354-2050

ADAMS, JAMES DAVID, pharmacology and toxicology educator; b. Provo, Utah, May 28, 1954; s. James David and Nadine (Holley) A.; m. Linda Jean Mei, Aug. 23, 1975; 1 child, Elliott Trevor. AB, U. Calif., Riverside, 1975; PhD, U. Calif., San Francisco, 1981. Postdoctoral fellow Baylor Coll. Medicine, Houston, 1981-83; staff fellow NIH, Bethesda, Md., 1983-85; asst. prof. pharmacology and toxicology Wash. State U., Pullman, 1985-87, U. So. Calif., L.A., 1987—; speaker Calif. Biomed. Rsch. Assn., L.A., 1990, Mensa, L.A., 1992. Contbr. articles to sci. jours. Named Prof. of Yr., U. So. Calif. Coll. Pharmacy, 1990; grantee NIH, 1987, 92. Mem. Soc. for Neurosci., Oxygen Soc. Democrat. Office: U So Calif Sch Pharmacy 1985 Zonal Ave Los Angeles CA 90033

ADAMS, JAMES FREDERICK, psychologist, educational administrator; b. Andong, Korea, Dec. 27, 1927; s. Benjamin Nyce and Phyllis Irene (Taylor) A.; m. Carol Ann Wagner, Jan. 17, 1980; children—James Edward, Dorothy Lee Adams Vanderhorst, Robert Benjamin. B.A. In Psychology, U. Calif.-Berkeley, 1950; Ed.M. in Counseling and Psychology, Temple U., 1951; Ph.D. in Exptl. Psychology, Wash. State U., 1959. Cert. psychologist, Wash., Pa.; lic. psychologist, Pa. Psychometrician Measurement and Research Ctr., Temple U., Phila., 1951-52; asst. prof. psychology Whitworth Coll., Spokane, Wash., 1952-55; teaching and research asst. State U. Wash., 1955-57; research assoc. Miami U., Oxford, Ohio, 1957-59; asst. prof. psychology Coll. Liberal Arts, Temple U., 1959-62, assoc. prof., 1962-66, prof., 1966-80, chmn. dept. counseling psychology, 1969-72; vis. prof. psychology Coll. Soc. Scis., U. P.R., Rio Piedras, 1963-64, Coll. Scis., Cath. U., Ponce, P.R., 1971-72; chmn. dept. counseling psychology Coll. Edn., Temple U., 1973-77, coordinator div. ednl. psychology, 1974-76; grad. dean, prof. psychology Grad. Coll., U. Nev., Las Vegas, 1980-85; acad. (sr.) v.p. Longwood Coll., Farmville, Va., 1985-86. Author: Problems in Counseling: A Case Study Approach, 1962, Instructors Manual for Understanding Adolescence, 1969; (exhbn. catalogue with J. D. Selig) Colonial Spanish Art of the Americas, 1976; (comml. pamphlet with C. L. Davis) The Use of the Vu-graph as an Instructional Aid, 1960; editor: Counseling and Guidance: A Summary View, 1965, Understanding Adolescence: Current Developments in Adolescent Psychology, 1968, 4th edit., 1980, Human Behavior in a Changing Society, 1973, Songs that had to be Sung (by B. N. Adams), 1979; contbr. chpts., articles, tests and book revs. to profl. publs. Served to cpl. USMC, 1945-46. Recipient Alexander Meiklejohn award AAUP, 1984; James McKean Cattell research fund grantee Miami U., Oxford, Ohio, 1958, Bolton fund research grantee Temple U., 1960, 62, faculty research grantee Temple U., 1961, 63, Commonwealth of Pa. research grantee Temple U., 1969, 70, 71, 72, summer research fellow Temple U., 1979; recipient scholarship U. Munich, 1955. Fellow Am. Psychol. Assn. (divs. 26, 17); mem. Eastern Psychol. Assn., Western Psychol. Assn., Interam. Soc. Psychology, Sigma Xi, Psi Chi. Home: 130 Palacio Rd Corrales NM 87048-9648

ADAMS, JAMES JAY, minister, district youth director; b. Encino, Calif., July 9, 1955; s. John Gordon and Georgina Alfreda (Copeland) A.; m. Lori Tuttle Adams, Nov. 4, 1978; children: Alissa Marie, Amanda Reneé. BA, Life Bible Coll., 1977. Ordained to ministry Internat. Ch. of Foursquare Gospel, 1977. Youth pastor Burbank (Calif.) Foursquare Ch., 1977-79; tchr. Heritage Jr./Sr. High Sch., Glendale, Calif., 1979-81; ch. adminstr., youth pastor Valley View Foursquare Ch., Canoga Park, Calif., 1981-90; dist. youth dir. Western Dist. Foursquare Chs., Modesto, Calif., 1990—; camp dir. Old Oak Ranch, Sonora, Calif., 1990—; mem. camp staff, coord. Camp Cedar Crest, So. CAlif., 1981—; cons., speaker in field. Res. officer, chaplain West Valley div. L.A. Police Dept., Canoga Park, 1985-90. Recipient Cert. of Recognition, County of L.A., 1989, City of L.A., 1989, Calif. State Assembly, 1989, Calif. State Senate, 1989. Republican. Office: Youthwest/Western Dist Foursquare Chs PO Box 3008 Modesto CA 95353-3008

ADAMS, JAMES RUSSELL, semiconductor electronics company executive; b. North Platte, Nebr., Apr. 10, 1945; s. George Howard and Verle Margaret (Kinnan) A.; m. Judy Ann Killham, June 18, 1967; 1 child, Janelle. BSEE, U. Nebr., 1967, MSEE, 1969, PhD in Elec. Engring., 1974. Mem. tech. staff Sandia Nat. Labs., Albuquerque, 1969-79; mgr. product tech. devel. Inmos Corp., Colorado Springs, Colo., 1979-83, v.p. quality and reliability, 1983-85; v.p. R & D Triad Semiconductors, BV, Colorado Springs, 1985-86; dir. advanced tech. devel. Monolithic Memories, Inc., Santa Clara, Calif., 1986-87; mgr. tech. programs United Techs. Microelectronics, Colorado Springs, 1987-88, dir. strategic planning, 1988—. Contbr. 24 articles to profl. jours.; 4 patents in field. Recipient TOBIE award for Best R & D Achievement Electronics-UK, 1981. Mem. IEEE (sr., best paper award GOMAC conf. 1978), Electrochem. Soc., Sigma Xi, Eta Kappa Nu, Sigma Tau.

ADAMS, JIMMIE VICK, retired military officer; b. Prichard, Ala., May 1, 1936; s. Anthony J. and Verlie (Adams) Antonidis; m. Ouida Bumpers, Dec. 27, 1955; children: Vickie, Lisa Floyd. BS in Mech. Engring., Auburn U., 1957; MME, U. Tex., 1963; grad., Squadron Officer Sch., 1964, Indsl. Coll. Armed Forces, 1978, Joint Flag Officer Warfighting Course, 1987. Commd. USAF, 1958, advanced through ranks to gen., 1957, various flying and staff positions, 1958-85; dep. chief of staff Requirements HQTAC USAF, Langley AFB, Va., 1985-87; comdr. 1st Air Force USAF, Langley AFB, 1987-88, vice comdr. Tactical Air Command, 1988-89; former dep. chief of staff Plans and Ops. USAF, Washington, 1989; comdr. in chief Pacific Air Forces Hickam AFB, Hawaii, 1993. Mem. AF Assn., Daedalians. Office: Pacific Air Forces Office Comdr in Chief Hickam AFB Honolulu HI 96853-5001

ADAMS, JO-ANN MARIE, data processing executive; b. L.A., May 27, 1949; d. Joseph John and Georgia S. (Wein) A.; AA, Pasadena City Coll., 1968; BA, Pomona Coll., 1970; MA, Calif. State U., L.A., 1971; MBA, Pacific Luth. U., 1983. Secondary tchr. South Pasadena (Calif.) Unified Schs., 1970-71; appraiser Riverside County (Calif.) Assessor's Office, 1972-74; systems and procedures analyst Riverside County Data Processing Dept., 1974-76, supervising systems analyst, 1976-79; systems analyst computer Boeing Computer Svcs. Co., Seattle, 1979-81; sr. systems analyst Thurston County Central Svcs., Olympia, Wash., 1981-83, data processing systems mgr., 1983-84; data processing systems engr. IBM Corp., 1984-87; realtor-assoc., Dower Realty, 1987-92; corp. sales rep. UniGlobe Met. Travel, 1988-89; project mgr. Servco Pacific, 1989-90, Scott Software Systems, 1990-91; systems analyst Dept. Atty. Gen., 1991—; instr. Riverside City Coll., 1977-79. Chairperson legis. task force Riverside/San Bernardino chpt. NOW, 1975-76, chpt. co-chairperson, 1978; mem. ethics com. Calif. NOW Inc., 1978; alt. del. Calif Dem. Caucus, 1978. Mem. Data Processing Mgmt. Assn., NAFE, Nat. Assn. Computing Machinery, Pomona Coll. Alumni Assn. Home: 2200 Round Top Dr Honolulu HI 96822-0269 Office: Dept Atty Gen 425 Queen St Honolulu HI 96813

ADAMS, JOHN M., library director; b. Chicago, Ill., June 10, 1950; s. Merlin J. and Esther (Bohn) A.; m. Nancy Ileen Coultas, June 12, 1970; 1 child, Arwen Lee. B.A. in English, U. Ill., 1972, M.L.S., 1973. Grad. asst. U. Ill. Libr., Urbana, 1972-73; libr.-reference Sherman Oaks Libr., L.A., 1973-75; libr. philosophy dept. L.A. Pub. Libr., 1975-77, head gen. reading svc., 1977-78; dir. Moline Pub. Libr., Ill., 1978-83, Tampa (Fla.)-Hillsborough County Pub. Libr. System, 1983-91; dir., county librarian Orange County (Calif.) Public Library System, 1991—; dir. Tampa Bay Libr. Consortium, Fla., 1983-91, Santiago Libr. System, 1991—; mem. adv. com. on pub. librs. OCLC, 1992—. Contbr. articles to profl. jours. Bd. dirs. Planned Parenthood of Tampa, 1984. Recipient Frontier award ALA Mag., 1981; named Outstanding Young Man, Moline Jaycees, 1983. Mem. ALA (J.C. Dana award 1982, 93), Calif. Libr. Assn., Calif. County Librs. Assn., Orange County C. of C. Office: Orange County Pub Libr Office of the Librarian 1501 E St Andrew Pl Santa Ana CA 92705

ADAMS, JOHN PHILLIPS, JR., economics educator, forensic economics consultant; b. Dothan, Ala., June 29, 1920; s. John Phillips Sr. and Lucile (Brown) A.; m. Flavienne Marcelle David, Dec. 5, 1946; children: Gilles David, Sidney Michel. Student Ga. Sch. Tech., 1939-43, U. S.C., 1964-65; M.A., Claremont Grad. Sch., 1968, Ph.D., 1972. Commd. 2d lt. U.S. Army, 1943, advanced through grades to lt. col., 1963, ret., 1963; lectr. econs. Calif. State Poly. U., Pomona, 1968-70; prof. econs., Calif. Poly. State U., San Luis Obispo, 1970-90; prof. emeritus, 1990—; trustee Calif. Council on Econ. Edn., 1972-78; forensic econs. cons., San Luis Obispo, 1976—. Pres. Calif. Cen. Coast chpt. Mended Hearts, Inc., Arroyo Grande, 1983-84. Mem. Am. Econ. Assn., Am. Rehab. Econs. Assn. (exec. bd. dirs. 1992—), Western Econ. Assn. Internat., Atlantic Econ. Soc., Western Soc. Scis. Assn., Nat. Assn. Forensic Economists (charter mem., West regional dir. 1986-87, v.p. 1988-92), Nat. Acad. Econ. Arbitrators (charter mem., bd. dirs. 1989—), Nat. Assn. Uniform Svcs. (life), Am. Acad. Econ. and Fin. Experts, Ret. Officers Assn. (life), White Sands Pioneer Group (life), Aircraft Owners and Pilots Assn., Omicron Delta Epsilon, Delta Sigma Pi, Alpha Tau Omega. Home: 2000 Wilding Ln San Luis Obispo CA 93401-3049 Office: Calif Poly State U Dept Econs San Luis Obispo CA 93407

ADAMS, JOHN SHEPARD, financial planner; b. Seattle, Apr. 28, 1961; s. John Bright and Carol (DeLima) A.; m. Andrea L. Halleck; 1 child, Karen Elaine. BA, Evergreen State Coll., 1982; CLU, Chartered Fin. Cons., Am. Coll., 1989. Cert. fin. planner. Registered rep. The Prudential, Olympia, Wash., 1982—; CEO Emerald Benefits Group, Olympia and Seattle, 1990—; moderator advanced sales cours Am. Assn. Life Underwriters, Olympia, 1989-90. Contbr. articles on investments and employee benefit plans to bus. publs. Vol. local polit. campaign. Mem. Am. Soc. CLU/Chartered Fin. Cons., Am. Assn. Life Underwriters (membership chmn. Southwest Wash. unit 1990-91), Southwest Wash. Estate Planning Coun. (bd. dirs. 1989-90), Amnesty Internat. Office: Emerald Benefits Group Ste # 3500 1201 Third Ave Seattle WA 98101

ADAMS, JON MICHAEL, marketing executive, consultant; b. Eglin AFB, Fla., May 14, 1956; s. James Winston and Mabel June (Hocum) A.; m. Darlene Anne Christensen, June 5, 19765; children: Michelle, Jessica, Celeste, Desirae, Daniel, Aaron. AAS, Ricks Coll., Rexburg, Idaho, 1977; BA in Bus. Adminstrn., N.C. Wesleyan Coll., 1985; MEd in Occupational Tng., Idaho State U., 1992. Program dir. Boy Scouts Am., Ogden, Utah, 1985-91; program adminstr., cons. EG&G, Idaho Inc., Idaho Falls, 1991-92; mktg. dir. Exec. Tng. Resources, Idaho Falls, 1992—. Editor: Leadership Institute for Exployers, 1988. Scoutmaster Boy Scouts Am., Shelley, Idaho, 1977—. With USAF, 1978-85. Mem. ASTD, Am. Vocat. Assn., Nat. Eagle Scout Assn., Rotary (membership bd. Layton, Utah 1989), Order of Arrow (advisor Wolverine dist.). Mem. LDS Ch. Home: 610 Bluebird Ave Shelley ID 83274 Office: Exec Tng Resources 2300 N Yellowstone Ste 113 Idaho Falls ID 83401

ADAMS, L(EON) ASHBY, III, actor, scientific research consultant; b. Phila., Jan. 31, 1951; s. Leon Ashby and Jean Crichton (Davis) A. BA in Biology, Lafayette Coll., 1973; MS in Physiology, Rutgers U., 1975. Lab. instr. cellular and intro. physiology Rutgers U., New Brunswick, N.J., 1974-75; rsch. scientist FACS Cell Sorter Applications and Support Group, Becton Dickinson, Research Triangle Park, N.C., 1976-79; lab. instr. comparative vertebrate anatomy, embryology and histology Lafayette Coll., Easton, Pa., 1972-73; rsch. technician Rutgers U., New Brunswick, 1974-75. Actor (TV shows) The Doctors, 1981, Santa Barbara, 1985, (guest star) As the World Turns, 1981, All My Children, 1982, Loving, 1984, Simon & Simon, 1986, FBI Untold Stories, 1992, Silk Stalkings, 1992, (radio shows) Discovery, Calif. Artists Radio Theatre; (comml. performer) Ford Motor Corp., Lincoln Mercury, GE, Pactell. Voice Recordings of math. textbooks Braille Inst., L.A., 1992. Mem. SAG, AFTRA, AAAS, Analytical Psychology Club of L.A., Astron. Soc. of the Desert. Episcopalian. Home: Apt D 3012 Riverside Dr Burbank CA 91505

ADAMS, MARK, artist; b. Ft. Plain, N.Y., Oct. 27, 1925; s. Earl D. and Edith (Wohlgemuth) A.; m. Beth Van Hoesen, Sept. 12, 1953. Student, Syracuse U., 1943-46, Hans Hofmann Sch. Fine Arts, 1946, 48, Jean Lurcat, 1955. Instr. San Francisco Art Inst., 1961; panelist Internat. Symposium on Tapestry, San Francisco, 1976; disting. vis. prof. U. Calif. at Davis, 1978; painter in residence Am. Acad. in Rome, 1963. Book: Mark Adams, 1985; one-man shows include deYoung Mus., San Francisco, 1959, Portland (Oreg.) Mus., 1961, Calif. Palace of Legion of Honor, San Francisco, 1961, retrospective, 1970, San Francisco Mus. Modern Art, 1962, French & Co., N.Y.C., 1964, John Berggruen Gallery, San Francisco, 1978, 80, 82, 83, 85, 87, 90, Graham Modern, N.Y.C., 1981, 84, Jane Haslem Salon, Washington, 1989, Palo Alto (Calif.) Cultural Ctr., 1990; exhibited in numerous group shows including Mus. Contemporary Crafts, N.Y.C., 1957, 58, 62, 65, Dallas Mus., 1958, Internat. Biennial of Tapestry, Lausanne, Switzerland, 1962, 65, St. Louis Art Mus., 1964, Norfolk Mus., 1966; represented in permanent collections San Francisco Mus. Modern Art, Dallas Mus. Fine Arts, Chase Manhattan Bank, N.Y.C., San Francisco Pub. Library, Legion of Honor Mus., San Francisco; maj. archtl. commns. include tapestries, Bank of Calif., San Francisco, Weyerhauser Co., Tacoma, Wash., Fairmont Hotel, Dallas, San Francisco Internat. Airport, Luth. Brotherhood, Mpls., stained glass, Temple Emanu-el, San Francisco, St. Thomas More Cath. Ch., San Francisco, St. Andrews Episcopal Ch., Saratoga, Calif. Address: care John Berggruen Gallery 228 Grant Ave San Francisco CA 94108

ADAMS, MICHAEL CURTIS, geochemist; b. Somerville, N.J., Nov. 11, 1953; s. William and Bonnie (Connell) A.; m. Leslie Peterson, June 14, 1986; 1 child, Christopher Michael. BS, U. Utah, 1978, MS, 1983. Geochemist U. Utah Rsch. Inst., Salt Lake City, 1978—; cons. Italian Elec. Agy. (ENEL), Pisa, 1990, Internat. Atomic Energy Agy., Vienna, Austria, 1990—, Guatamala Elec. (INDE), 1989—, United Nations, 1992—. Contbr. articles to profl. jours. Mem. Geochem. Assn., Internat. Geothermal Assn., Geothermal Resources Coun. Democrat. Home: 375 3rd Ave Salt Lake City UT 84103 Office: Univ Utah Rsch Inst Ste C 391 Chipeta Way Salt Lake City UT 84108

ADAMS, NORMAN JOSEPH, economist, corporate mergers broker; b. Los Angeles, Feb. 21, 1930; s. Joseph O'Neil and Florence Mary (Michalek) A.; B.S., U. So. Calif., 1951; M.A. Oxford U., 1953; postgrad. Harvard U., 1956; Ph.D., U. Karachi (Pakistan), 1958; diploma London's Sch. Accountancy and N.Y. Inst. Fin.; m. Julia Jewell, Oct. 16, 1960; children: Darlene, Janet. Pres., Adams & Co., mergers and aquisitions, Newport Beach, Calif., 1960—. Recipient 11 fellowships; Fulbright scholar.

ADAMS, PAUL DOUGLAS, journalism educator; b. Stockton, Calif., Oct. 26, 1942; s. Loy and Lillian Nagdeline (Spiva) A.; m. Patricia Marie Egger, Nov. 2, 1968; children: Jennifer Marie, John Douglas. BA, U. Okla., 1964; MA, U Tex., 1971, PhD, 1974. Mag. writer Dept. Wildlife Conservation, Oklahoma City, 1965-66; newspaper reporter Lawton (Okla.) Constn., 1966-67; info. officer CIA, Washington, 1967-69; instr. journalism U. Tex., Austin, 1971; asst. prof. journalism Baylor U., Waco, Tex., 1974-76; features editor The Oregonian, Portland, 1976-84; assoc. prof. communications U. Portland, Oreg., 1984-85; asso. prof. journalism La. State U., Baton Rouge, 1985-87; prof. journalism Calif. State U., Fresno, 1987—. Contbr. chpts. to books, articles to profl. jours. Sec., Calif. Faculty Union, Fresno, 1990-91. Mem. Assn. for Edn. in Journalism, Calif. Newspaper Pubs. Assn. Home: 916 E Chennault Ave Fresno CA 93720 Office: Calif State U Fresno CA 93740-0010

ADAMS, PHILIP, lawyer; b. Los Angeles, July 18, 1905; s. Thaddeus Lafayette and Lena (Kelly) A.; m. Alice Rahman, 1933; children: Stephen, Judith, Deborah, Kate; m. Elaine Margaret Anderson, 1968. Student, Pomona Coll., 1924-27; JD, Hastings Coll. Law, U. Calif., 1938; LLD (hon.), Ch. Div. Sch. of Pacific, Berkeley, Calif., 1965. Bar: Calif. 1938. Purser Panama Mail S.S. Line, 1928-29; profl. investigator, 1930-38; individual practice law San Francisco, 1938—; atty. U.S. Govt., 1942-46; instr. domestic relations Golden Gate Law Sch., 1971-72. Author: Adoption Practice in California, 1956. Dir. Children's Protective Soc., 1939-44, United Cerebral Palsy Assn., San Francisco, 1952-72, Assn. Mental Health, 1952—, United Bay Area Crusade, 1955-61, United Community Fund, San Francisco,1 957-62, San Francisco State Coll., 1964-69; trustee Ch. Divinity Sch. of Pacific, 1951-76; nat. v.p. Episcopal Evang. Fellowship, 1952-61; chancellor Episcopal Diocese Calif., 1960-67; dep. Episcopal Gen. Conv., 1946-70; trustee Grad. Theol. Union, Berkeley, 1959-66, pres. bd., 1963-66. Fellow Am. Acad. Matrimonial Lawyers (dir. No. Calif. chpt. 1968—), Acad. Calif. Adoption Lawyers (dir. 1988—); mem. ABA (chmn. com. on adoption, family law sect. 1959-60), Calif., San Francisco Bar Assn., Lawyers Club San Francisco (gov. 1956), San Francisco Symphony Assn., Chamber Soloists San Francisco (dir. 1985—), Soc. Genealogists (London). Clubs: Villa Taverna, Commonwealth. Home: 2170 Jackson St San Francisco CA 94115-1550 Office: 220 Montgomery St San Francisco CA 94104

ADAMS, PHILIP JAMES, insurance company executive, consultant; b. Bangor, Maine, July 25, 1920; s. Benjamin Franklin and Grace Easter (Russell) A.; m. Dorothy Elinor Claire, May 5, 1945; children: Philip James, Dean E., Dorothy Mary. B.S., Maine Maritime Acad., 1943. Master mariner Am. Export Lines, N.Y.C., 1943-46; with Aetna Life & Casualty, Hartford, Conn., 1946—, v.p., 1983—; cons. in field. Chmn. Democratic Town Com., Avon, Conn., 1970-78. Mem. Nat. Assn. Life Underwriters, Gen. Agts. and Mgrs. Assn. (pres. N.H. 1963), Am. Soc. C.L.U.s, Am. Cons. League. Roman Catholic. Home: 2659 Mossy Oak Dr Danville CA 94506-2115

ADAMS, RICHARD ARTHUR, air force officer; b. New Hampton, Iowa, Dec. 12, 1951; s. Ralph William and Constance Jean (Crowe) A.; m. Heather Margaret Olds, Aug. 20, 1983; children: Karen Jean, Jennifer Margaret. BS, Iowa State U., 1974; MS, Air Force Inst. Tech., 1979; BA, U. Md., Heidelberg, Germany, 1983; PhD, U. Ill., 1986. Computer systems analyst HQ Strategic Air Command, Omaha, 1974-77, HQ U.S.European Command, Stuttgart, Germany, 1979-83; asst. prof. U.S. Naval Postgrad. Sch., Monterey, Calif., 1986-88; computer systems analyst Air Force Studies and Analyses Agy., Washington, 1988-92; commd. 2d lt. USAF, 1991, advanced through grades to lt. col., 1991; squadron comdr. 21st Space System Squadron, Denver, 1992—; adj. prof. George Washington U., Washington, 1988-89. Recipient ROTC Gold Medal Honor award Armed Forces Comms. and Electronics Assn., 1974. Mem. Assn. for Computing Machinery, Air Force Assn., Officers' Christian Fellowship. Methodist. Home: 11752 E Adriatic Pl Aurora CO 80014

ADAMS, RICHARD MAXWELL, English educator; b. Merton Park, Surrey, United Kingdom, June 13, 1938; came to U.S., 1985; s. Ernest Maxwell and Beatrice Gladys (Barker) A. BA, U. Oxford, Eng., 1961, MA, 1965, M of Letters, 1965; spl. diploma in edn. studies with distn., 1985. Asst. tutor (English) St. Catherine's Coll., Oxford U., Oxford, United Kingdom, 1962-70; tchr., adminstr. Lord William's Sch., Thame, Oxfordshire, United Kingdom, 1965-84; lectr. San Jose (Calif.) State U., 1986; asst. prof. Calif. State U., Sacramento, 1986-90; assoc. prof., 1990—; examiner, awarder, Oxford U. delegacy of local exams., 1962-88; U.S. Affiliate, Shakespeare and Sch., U. Cambridge, 1985—; dir. Calif. Lit. Project, 1988—. Author: Teaching Shakespeare, 1985, A Book of British Music Festivals, 1986; gen. editor: Longman Study Texts, 1983-89; editor: Shakespeare: Richard III, 1974, Shakespeare: Richard II, 1975, Shakespeare: Antony and Cleopatra, 1984, Critical Study of Conrad's Heart of Darkness, 1991. With Royal Air Force, 1956-58, United Kingdom. Recipient Meritorious Performance awards, Calif. State U., Sacramento, 1988-89, Classroom Excellence award, Calif. Assn. Tchrs. of English, 1989. Mem. Soc. of Authors, Calif. Faculty Assn., Nat. Council Tchrs. of English. Anglican/Episcopalian. Home: 9417 Cedarview Way Elk Grove CA 95758 Office: Calif State U Dept of English 6000 J St Sacramento CA 95819-6075

ADAMS, RICK ALAN, biologist, educator; b. Bethesda, Md., Jan. 18, 1956; s. Henry Lewis and Josephine Vince (Bredice) A. BA, U. Colo., 1985, MA, 1989, PhD, 1992. Teaching asst. U. Colo., Boulder, 1984-92; prin. investigator Nat. Park Svc., Fruita, Colo., 1989-90, Colo. Div. Wildlife, Denver, 1990; instr., resch. assoc. U. Colo. Mus., Boulder, 1992; asst. prof. biology U. Wis., Whitewater, 1993—. Contbr. articles to profl. jours. Mem. Colo. Bat Soc. (pres., founder 1990—). Home: 777 Juniper Ave Boulder CO 80304 Office: U Colo Mus Boulder CO 80309-0315

ADAMS, ROBERT GRANVILLE, marketing professional; b. Indpls., July 2, 1927; s. Jack and Iris (Trippeer) A.; m. Marilyn Howe (div.); m. Ilona Molnar; children: Lynn, Victoria, Amy. BS, Ind. U., 1953. Capt. USAF, 1945-65; horse rancher Am. Quarter Horse Assn., Scottsdale, Ariz., 1965-88; wholesaler Nat. Home Furnishings Assn., Scottsdale, 1988—; pres. Sunrise Bakery Inc., Mesa, Ariz., 1987, Adams Mktg., Inc., Scottsdale, 1980—. Mem. Desert Caballeros, Wickenburg Ariz. Club, Rancheros Visitadores, Santa Barbara, Calif. Club., Sigma Chi. Home: 5817 E Crocus Dr Scottsdale AZ 85254-5551 Office: PO Box 1747 Scottsdale AZ 85252-1747

ADAMS, RUSSELL FRANCIS, computer company executive, consultant; b. San Diego, May 17, 1955; s. Robert E. Adams and Marjorie Lois (Reece) Omer; m. Rosa Lee Andrews, June 23, 1984. AAS, Nat. U., San Diego, 1983, BBA magna cum laude, 1990. Analyst Home Fed. Savs. & Loan, San Diego, 1979-83; analyst, programmer Nat. Steel and Shipbuilding, San Diego, 1983-85; cons. Am. Fin. Systems, Detroit, 1985; pres. Russell F. Adams, Inc., San Diego, 1986—; cons. Soc. Bank N.A., Cleve., 1985-87, 90-93, Australia and New Zealand Bank, 1993—, IBM Employees Fed. Credit Union, Poukeepsie, N.Y., 1988-90, Automated Mgmt. Systems, Detroit, 1986—. Mem. Mercedes Benz Club Am., Internat. 190 SL Group. Republican. Home and Office: 405 W Washington St Ste 206 San Diego CA 92103-1994

ADAMS, SARAH VIRCINIA, family counselor; b. San Francisco, Oct. 23, 1955; d. Marco Tulio and Helen (Jorge) Zea; m. Glenn Richard Adams, Mar 22, 1980; children: Mark Vincent, Elena Giselle, Johnathan Richard. BA, Calif. State U., Long Beach, 1978, MS, 1980; postgrad., Fuller Theological Sem., Pasadena, 1990—. Lic. marriage, family, child counseling. Tutor math. and sci. Montebello, Calif., 1979-82; behavioral specialist Cross Cultural Psychol. Corp., L.A., 1979-80; psychol. asst. Legal Psychology, L.A., 1980-82, Eisner Psychol. Assocs., L.A., 1982-83; assoc. dir. Legal Psychodiagnosis and Forensic Psychology, L.A., 1982-83; adminstrv. dir. Diagnostic Clinic, Calif., 1983-85; dir. Diagnostic Clinic of West Covina, Calif., 1985-87; owner Adams Family Counseling Inc., Calif., 1987—; tchr. piano, Montebello, 1973-84; ins. agent Am. Mut. Life Ins., Des Moines, 1982-84. Fellow Am. Assn. Marriage and Family Therapists, Am. Psychol. Assn.; mem. NAFE, Calif. Assn. Marriage and Family Therapists, Calif. State Psychol. Assn., Calif. Soc. Indsl. Medicine and Surgery, Western Psychol. Assn., Psi Chi, Pi Delta Phi. Republican. Roman Catholic. Office: Adams Family Counseling Inc 260 S Glendora Ave # 101 West Covina CA 91790-3041

ADAMS, TODD DEAN, water resources engineer, computer consultant; b. Pocatello, Idaho, May 15, 1966; s. Virgil Dean and Joyce Ann (Young) A.; m. Melinda Seamons, Aug. 5, 1989. BS, Utah State U., 1988, MS, 1990. Rsch. assoc. Internat. Environ. Inc., Salt Lake City, 1982; heavy equipment operator Mohr Constrn. Co., Logan, Utah, 1984-85; lab. asst. Ctr. for Elec. Power, Tenn. Tech. U., Cookeville, 1986; lab. asst. Utah State U., Logan, 1987, grad. rsch. asst., 1988-90; engr. State of Utah, Div. Water Resources, Salt Lake City, 1990—. Contbr. articles to profl. jours. Named to Outstanding Young Men of Am. Mem. ASCE, Am. Chem. Soc. (div. environ. chemistry).

ADAMS, WARREN DALE, fundraising administrator; b. Twin Falls, Idaho, Dec. 11, 1949; s. Dale Lewis and Fern Louella (Ebersole) A.; m. Lucille Fern Bertram, June 20, 1970. BA in English, Coll. of Idaho, 1972. Reporter Idaho Press Tribune, Nampa, 1972-77, city editor, 1977-79; mng. editor Herald and News, Klamath Falls, Oreg., 1979-86; v.p. campaign United Way/Benton & Franklin Counties, Kennewick, Wash., 1986—; participant Nat. Acad. Voluntarism, Stanford (Calif.) U., 1988, 93; trainer United Way Am., Alexandria, Va., 1986-89; cons. Lake County Examiner, Lakeview, Oreg., 1984-85; advisor Dirs. of Vols. in Agys., Tri-Cities, Wash., 1986-93. Vol. dep. sheriff Owyhee County Sheriff's Office, Murphy, Idaho, 1972-77; chair tourism com. Klamath Falls C. of C., 1984-85; vol. chair gen. campaign United Way of Klamath Basin, Klamath Falls, 1985; fundraising cons. Tri-City Corp. Coun. for Arts, 1992, 93; adminstrv. dir., co-founder Columbia River Music Festival, 1991; vol. fundraising cons. Goodwill

Games Tri-Cities, 1990; fundraiser Tri-Cities Econ. Devel. Coun. Renaissance, 1989. Mem. Nat. Mgmt. Assn. (charter, sec. 1988, 92-93, pres. 1989, bd. dirs., Outstanding Chpt. award 1989), Columbia Basin Area Coun. (bd. dirs., pres. 1990—, Mgr. of yr. 1992), Wash. State U. (Tri-Cities br. campus curriculum com. 1988), Mid-Columbia Symphony Soc. (bd. dirs., sec. 1990-92), Kiwanis. Home: 5201 W 16th Ct Kennewick WA 99337-1734 Office: United Way Benton & Franklin Counties PO Box 2870 Tri-Cities WA 99302-2870

ADAMS, WILLIAM HAMPTON, archaeologist; b. Bloomington, Ind., Nov. 23, 1948; s. William Richard and Margaret Mary (Kime) A. AB in Anthropology, Ind. U., 1970; MA in Anthropology, Wash. State U., 1972, PhD in Anthropology, 1976. Asst. prof. anthropology Wash. State U., Pullman, 1976-77; vis. asst. prof. U. Ky., Lexington, 1977-78; sr. archaeologist Resource Analysts, Bloomington, 1978-81; asst. research scientist U. Fla., Gainesville, 1981-87; sr. staff archaeologist Colonial Williamsburg, Va., 1983-84; lectr. Lamar U., 1986-87; assoc. prof. Ctrl. Wash. U., 1987-88, Oreg. State U., 1988—; mem. adv. council on remote sensing in archaeology NASA, Slidell, La., 1984—. Author: Silcott, Washington, 1977; with others Bay Springs Mill Community, 1980; author, editor: Waverly Plantation, 1987. Mem. Soc. Hist. Archaeology (pres. 1983-85), Am. Anthrop. Assn., Soc. Am. Archaeology, Soc. Post-Medieval Archaeology, Sierra Club, Sigma Xi. Office: Oreg State U Dept Anthropology Waldo Hall 238 Corvallis OR 97331 also: Adams & Assocs PO Box 1177 Philomath OR 97370

ADAMS, WILLIAM LEE, financial consultant; b. Monterey Park, Calif., Sept. 4, 1945; s. Edward William and Mildred Jeniece (Oakes) A.; m. Lucie Anne Staples, Oct. 17, 1971; children: Randall J., Anthony S., Timothy W., Daisha L. AA in Edn., Chaffey Coll., 1975; BSBA with honors, U. Redlands, 1980. Calif. community coll. (life) credential. Chaplain dir. The Quiet Hour Prison Min., Redlands, Calif.; chaplain, commdr. San Bernardino (Calif.) County Sheriff; paralegal super Michael J. Hemming Atty., Diamond Bar, Calif.; tchr. Clackamas Community Coll., Oregon City, Oreg.; pres. Action Credit Cons., Beavercreek, Oreg.; bd. dirs. Redlands Jr. Acad., 1980-81, Someone Cares Prison Ministry. Author: (manual) How To Collect Your Money Thet's Due You, 1978. Bd. dirs. Kiwanis Internat., Loma Linda, Calif., 1978; vol. Calif. Dept. Corrections, Norco, Calif., 1982-86, Riverside (Calif.) Police Dept., 1971-74; reserve deputy San Bernardino County Sheriff, 1983-86. Recipient award of Merit, Soc. Magicians, Hollywood, Calif., 1967. Mem. Magic Castle Inc.

ADAMS, WILLIAM TAYLOR, small business owner; b. Phoenix, Jan. 23, 1957; s. John William and Dora Jean (Coe) A. AA, Glendale (Ariz.) C.C., 1978; BA, Ariz. State U., 1982. Cert. tchr., Ariz. Resident asst. Ariz. State U., Tempe, 1981-82, asst. resident ops., 1982-84, dir. resident hall, 1984-86; mgr. Tinder Box Internat. Ltd., Scottsdale, Ariz., 1986-87; proprietary cons. Synoptic Resources, Phoenix, 1986—; gen. mgr. Tinder Box Internat. Ltd., Phoenix, 1987-92; mfr.'s rep. Smithway Enterprises, Sun City, Ariz., 1992—; gen. ptnr. Neptune's Galley, Phoenix, 1992—; cons. WaterCo. Ltd., Phoenix, 1989-90, Pillar Fin. Group, Phoenix, 1989-90, Kinko's Copy Ctr., Paradise Valley, 1992, Citiwide Chiropractic, Phoenix, 1992. Editor Infocopygram newsletter, 1992. Trainer Goodwill Industries Ariz., Phoenix, 1991; program dir. Promoting Animal Welfare, Phoenix, 1992. Mem. ASPCA, Popular Rotorcraft Assn., Nat. Eagle Scout Assn., Caledonian Soc. Ariz., Soc. for Creative Anachronism, Retail Tobacco Dealers Assn., The Universal Coteric of Pipe Smokers. Democrat. Home: 8235 N 15th Dr Phoenix AZ 85021-5407 Office: Neptune's Galley 20003 N 23d Ave Ste 338 Phoenix AZ 85027

ADAMSON, ARTHUR WILSON, chemistry educator; b. Shanghai, China, Aug. 15, 1919; s. Arthur Quintin and Ethel (Rhoda) A.; m. Virginia Louise Dillman, Mar. 24, 1942; children—Carol Ann, Janet Louise, Jean Elizabeth. B.S. with honors, U. Calif.-Berkeley, 1940; Ph.D. in Phys. Chemistry, U. Chgo., 1944. Research assoc. Manhattan Project, Oak Ridge, 1944-46; asst. prof. U. So. Calif., 1946-49, assoc. prof., 1949-53, prof., 1953-89, prof. emeritus, 1989—, chmn. dept. chemistry, 1972-75; Foster lectr. U. Buffalo, 1970; Venable lectr. U. N.C., 1975; Bikerman lectr. Case Western U., 1982; Reilly lectr. Notre Dame U., 1984. Author: Concepts of Inorganic Photochemistry, 1975, Understanding Physical Chemistry, 1980, Textbook of Physical Chemistry, 1986, Physical Chemistry of Surfaces, 1990; editor Langmuir Am. Chem. Soc., 1984-89; editor emeritus, 1990—; contbr. articles to profl. jours. Recipient Creative Scholarship and rsch. award U. So. Calif., 1971, Excellence in Teaching award, 1979, Raubenheimer award, 1984, Disting. Emeritus award, 1991; Alexander von Humboldt Sr. Scientist award, 1971, others. Fellow Am. Inst. Chemists; mem. Am. Chem. Soc. (councillor So. Calif. sect. 1964-80, chmn. 1964, Tolman award 1967, Kendall award 1979, Langmuir lectr. 1981, Disting. Svc. in Inorganic Chemistry award 1982, Chem. Edn. award 1984, Agnes Ann Green Disting. Svc. award 1989, Harry and Carol Mosher award 1990, Arthur W. Adamson Award for Disting. Svc. in Advancement of Surface Chemistry established in his honor 1992). Republican. Club: Palos Verdes Tennis. Office: U So Calif Dept of Chemistry U Park Los Angeles CA 90089

ADAMSON, GEOFFREY DAVID, reproductive endocrinologist, surgeon; b. Ottawa, Ont., Can., Sept. 16, 1946; came to U.S., 1978, naturalized, 1986; s. Geoffrey Peter Adamson and Anne Marian Allan; m. Rosemary C. Oddie, Apr. 28, 1973; children: Stephanie, Rebecca, Eric. BSc with honors, Trinity Coll., Toronto, Can., 1969; MD, U. Toronto, 1973. Diplomate Am. Bd. Ob-Gyn., Am. Bd. Laser Surgery; cert. Bd. Reproductive Endocrinology. Resident in ob-gyn. Toronto Gen. Hosp., 1973-77, fellow in ob-gyn., 1977-78; fellow reproductive endocrinology Stanford (Calif.) U. Med. Ctr., 1978-80; practice medicine specializing in infertility Los Gatos, Calif., 1980-84; instr. Sch. Medicine Stanford (Calif.) U., Stanford Univ., Calif., 1984-92, clin. asst. prof., 1992; clin. assoc. prof. Stanford (Calif.) U., San Francisco, 1992—; assoc. clin. prof. Sch. Medicine U. Calif., San Francisco, 1992—. Mem. editorial adv. bd. Can. Doctor mag., 1977-83; contbr. numerous articles to sci. jours. Ontario Ministry of Health fellow, 1977-78. Fellow ACS, Royal Coll. Surgeons Can., Am. Coll. Ob-Gyns.; mem. AAAS, AMA, Am. Fertility Soc., Soc. Reproductive Endocrinologists (charter), Soc. Reproductive Surgeons (charter), Soc. Assisted Reproductive Tech., Pacific Coast Fertility Soc. (dir.), Pacific Coast Ob-Gyn. Soc., San Francisco Ob-Gyn. Soc, Bay Area Reproductive Endocrinologists Soc. (founding pres.), Am. Assn. Gynecol. Laparoscopists, Gynecol. Laser Soc., N.Y. Acad. Scis., Shufelt Gynecol. Soc., Peninsula Gynecol. Soc. (past pres.), Calif. Med. Assn., San Mateo County Med. Assn., Santa Clara County Med. Assn., Am. Fedn. Clin. Rsch., Nat. Resolve (bd. dirs.), Can. Assn. Internes and Residents (hon. life, pres. 1977-79, bd. dirs. 1974-79, rep. AMA resident physician sect. 1978-79, rep. Can. Med. Protective Assn. 1975-78, rep. Can. Med. Assn. 1975-78, Disting. Svc. award 1980), Profl. Assn. Interns and Residents Ont. (bd. dirs. 1973-76, v.p. 1974-75, pres. 1975-76), Royal Coll. Physician and Surgeons Can. (com. exams. 1977-80), Ont. Med. Assn. (sec. internes and residents sect. 1973-74). Home: 16520 S Kennedy Rd Los Gatos CA 95032-6440 Office: 540 University Ave # 200 Palo Alto CA 94301-1912

ADAMSON, MARY ANNE, geographer, systems engineer; b. Berkeley, Calif., June 25, 1954; d. Arthur Frank and Frances Isobel (Key) A.; m. Richard John Harrington, Sept. 20, 1974. BA with highest honors and great distinction U. Calif., Berkeley, 1975, MA, 1976, postgrad., 1976-78. Cert. tchr. earth scis., Calif.; cert. cave rescue ops. and mgmt., Calif.; lic. emergency med. technician, Contra Costa (Calif.) County, 1983. Teaching asst. dept. geography U. Calif., Berkeley, 1976; geographer, environ. and fgn. area analyst Lawrence Livermore Nat. Lab., Livermore, Calif., 1978-83, cons., 1983-86; systems engr. ESL, Sunnyvale, Calif., 1986-90; rsch. analyst, rsch. devel. and analysis P.G. & E., San Francisco, 1990-93; admin. asst. Internal Audit Dept., 1993—. Contbr. articles to profl. jours. Lt. Comdr. USNR, 1983—. Recipient Navy Achievement medal, 1992. Staff mem. ARC/Am. Trauma Soc/Sierra Club Urgent Care and Mountain Medicine seminars, 1983—. Asst. editor Vulcan's Voice, 1982. Mem. Assn. Am. Geographers (life), Assn. Pacific Coast Geographers, Nat. Speleol. Soc. (geology, geography sects., sec., editor newsletter Diablo Grotto chpt. 1982-86), Toastmasters Internat. Club (adminstrv. v.p. Blue Monday Club 1991), Commonwealth Club, Sierra Club (life), Nature Conservancy (life), U. Calif. Alumnae Assn., Phi Beta Kappa. Home: 4603 Lakewood St Pleasanton CA 94588-4342 Office: PG&E Internal Auditing 50 Fremont St San Francisco CA 94106-0001

ADASKAVEG, JAMES ELLIOTT, mycologist, plant pathologist, educator; b. Waterbury, Conn., Feb. 27, 1960; s. Alexander Peter and Fannie (Venditto) A.; m. Peggy Ann Mauk, June 15, 1990. BS, U. Conn., 1982; MS, U. Ariz., 1984, PhD, 1986. Postdoctoral rsch. dept. plant pathology U. Calif., Davis, 1987-90, rsch. plant pathologist, 1990-92, lectr. mycology dept. botany, 1990-91. Mem. Am. Phytopath. Soc., Mycol. Soc. Am., Brit. Mycol. Soc. Office: U Calif Dept Plant Pathology Davis CA 95616

ADDAMS, ROBERT JEAN, business and financial consultant; b. Salt Lake City, Sept. 24, 1942; s. Harvey J. and Virginia (Dutson) A.; m. Mary A. Watkins, Feb. 10, 1973; children—Ryan, Kelley, Amy, Michael. B.S., U. Utah, 1968, M.B.A., 1969. Fin. analyst Western Airlines, Inc., Los Angeles, 1969-72, mgr. budgets and cost control, 1972-74, controller mktg. div., 1974-76, dir. budgets and cost control, 1976-80; v.p., gen. mgr. Ball Bros., Inc., Everette, Wash., and Anchorage, 1980-82; pres., cons. Addams & Assocs., Redmond, Wash., 1982—. Author: Care and Handling of Wetsalted Cod Fish, 1984; also articles on budgeting and business plans to monthly newsletter. Scoutmaster, Explorer advisor Gt. Salt Lake and Los Angeles councils Boy Scouts Am., 1973-75; served 2-yr. mission for Ch. Jesus Christ Latter-day Saints, 1962-64. Served with U.S. Army, 1961-62. Named Outstanding Grad., Coll. Bus., 1968, Beehive Honor Soc., 1969. Mem. U. Utah Alumni Assn. (pres. So. Calif. chpt. 1976-80), U. Utah Coll. of Bus. Alumni (pres. So. Calif. group 1978-79), Alpha Kappa Psi. Republican. Home and Office: Addams & Assocs 17003 NE 136th Pl Redmond WA 98052-1714

ADDEO, JON, electrical engineer; b. N.Y.C., Feb. 16, 1947; s. Alfred and Phyllippa Pearl (Sparks) A. Aviation Fundamental & Electronic Tech., USN, 1966; BSEE, N.Y.S. I.B.E.W., 1971. Field engr. Citicorp I.B.E.W., N.Y.C., 1976-77; field engring. cons. Kerr McGee, Calif., 1977-78; field engr. Dept. of Def., Nev., 1978-83; elec. tech. engr. Tropicana, Las Vegas, 1983-84; hi tech. optics engr. Wall St. and Banking Firms, N.Y.C., 1985-88; systems engr. Mfg. Hanover Trust, N.Y.C., 1989—; fiber optics surveillance systems internat. cons. Author: L.A.S.E.R., 1985, Sandpie Kingdom, 1975, Ships of Sea and Men, 1976. With USN, 1966-70. Mem. D.A.V. Comds. Club, Merchant Marine 6466. Home: 618 E Carson #111 Las Vegas NV 89101

ADDIE, HARVEY WOODWARD, retired educator, music director; b. Birmingham, Ala., June 14, 1930; s. LeRoy and Frances (Driscoll) A.; m. Gwendolyn Marie Mendes, June 5, 1955; children: Cynthia Marie Mendes, June 5, 1955; children: Cynthia Marie Corra, Julie Ann Lorch, Mary Elizabeth Dunaway. MusB, Coll. Pacific, 1959; MusM, U. Pacific, 1970. Cert. life music tchr., Calif. Mgr. dept. S.H. Kress and Co., Santa Monica and Stockton, Calif., 1953-55; head produce, mgr. area Safeway Stores Inc., Lodi, Stockton, Calif., 1955-61; tchr. music Manteca (Calif.) Elem. Sch. Dist., 1959-61, San Joaquin County Sch. Music Office, Stockton, 1961-71; mgr. store Bill's Music Sales, Stockton, 1971-73; dir. music El Dorado High Sch., Placerville, Calif., 1973, Stockton Unified Sch. Dist., 1973-89; pres. San. Joaquin County Band Dirs. Assn., Stockton, 1984-86, Stagg High Sch. Faculty Assn., 1984-85. 1st. v.p. San Joaquin Concert Ballet Assn., Stockton, 1966; bd. dirs. Stockton opera Assn., 1968, Stockton Concert Band Assn., 1986-88. Served to cpl. U.S. Army, 1951-53, Korea. Mem. Assn. Jazz Edn., Calif. Music Educators Assn. (bd. dirs. 1983-87), Stockton Tchrs. Assn. (treas. 1986-87, 88-89), Am. Fedn. Musicians (life mem., bd. dirs., sec.-treas. 1992—), Calif. Tchrs. Assn. (state coun. 1986-89), Noble Grand Fraternal Order of Odd Fellows. Democrat. Methodist. Home: 1426 W Euclid Ave Stockton CA 95204-2903 Office: Stockton Musicians' Assn 33 W Alpine Ave Stockton CA 95204

ADDIS, RICHARD BARTON, lawyer; b. Columbus, Ohio, Apr. 9, 1929; s. Wilbur Jennings and Leila Olive (Grant) A.; m. Marguerite C. Christjohn, Feb. 9, 1957; children: Jacqueline Carol, Barton David. BA, Ohio State U., 1954, JD, 1955. Bar: Ohio 1956, U.S. Dist. Ct. (no. dist.) Ohio 1957, N.Mex. 1963, U.S. Dist. Ct. N.Mex. 1963, Laguna Pueblo (N.Mex.) Tribal Ct. 1986. Pvt. practice, Canton, Ohio, 1956-63, Albuquerque, 1963—, Laguna Pueblo, Navajo Nation, 1986—. Counsel N.Mex. Cultural Arts Ctr. at Angel Fire, 1990. With USMC, 1946-48, 50-52. Mem. Ohio Bar Assn., N.Mex. Bar Assn., Am. Arbitration Assn. (arbitrator 1968—), Soc. Mining Engrs. Office: 5111 San Mateo Blvd NE Albuquerque NM 87109-2483

ADDIS, THOMAS HOMER, III, professional golfer; b. San Diego, Nov. 30, 1945; s. Thomas H. and Martha J. (Edwards) A.; student Foothill Jr. Coll., 1963, Grossmont Jr. Coll., 1965; m. Susan Tera Buckley, June 13, 1966; children: Thomas Homer IV, Bryan Michael. Head golf profl., mgr. Sun Valley Golf Course, La Mesa, Calif., 1966-67; head golf profl., dir. golf ops. Singing Hills Country Club and Lodge, 1969—; gen. chmn. Nat. Jr. Golf championship U.S. Golf Assn., 1973, 89; lectr.; owner Golf Cons. & Design, Rocky Mountain Chocolate Factory, Mammoth. Pres. Calif. State Open, 1980-84; chmn. Nat. Com. Liaison for Physically Challenged, 1984-88. Recipient Retailer award Golf Industry mag., 1985; named to Lady Aztec San Diego State U. Hall of Fame. Mem. PGA (pres. San Diego chpt. 1978-79; pres. sect. 1980-82, bd. dirs. sect. 1974-90, speaker, chmn. mem. svc. com. 1986-87, bd. dirs. San Diego sect. 1974-90, assn. coord. bus. schs. and seminars, named Profl. of Yr. So. Calif. sect. 1979, 89, Nat. Golf Day Contbn. Leader, So. Calif. sect. 1973-76, 79, Horton Smith award So. Calif. sect. 1980-81, 89, PGA Golf Profl. of Yr. 1989, Nat. Horton Smith award 1981, Resort Merchandiser of Yr., So. Calif. sect. 1978, 83, ofcl. del. nat. annual meeting 1978-90, mem. nat. bd. control 1978-85, chmn. nat. bd. control 1991-92, membership com. 1978, 89-90, nat. edn. com. 1980-85, 89-90, long-range planning com. 1983-85, nat. bd. dirs., 1986-88, rules com. 1986-90, championship com. 1986—, hon. life mem. So. Calif. sect., sec. PGA Am. 1991, 92, v.p. PGA Am. 1993—), Nat. Golf Found. (Joe Graffis award, 1988) Nat. Amputee Golf Assn. (hon. mem.), San Diego Jr. Golf Assn. (dir.), Assn. Golf Educators, Golf Collector's Soc., Singing Hills Tennis Club, Rotary. Author articles. Office: Singing Hills Golf Course 3007 Dehesa Rd El Cajon CA 92019-2808

ADDISON, ANITA LOUISE, health services planner, clinic official; b. L.A., Aug. 9, 1953; d. Edward Thurman and Carolyn Elizabeth (Boddie) A. BA in Sociology, Stanford U., 1975; M City Planning, U. Calif., Berkeley, 1978, MPH, 1979. Planning analyst Spanish Speaking Unity Coun., Oakland, Calif., 1979-81, sr. planner, 1981-82, program devel. dir., 1988-89; planner William F. Ryan Community Health Ctr., N.Y.C., 1982-86, dir. planning and devel., 1986-88; dir. planning and devel. La Clinica de la Raza, Oakland, 1989—. Bd. dirs. Support Svcs. for Srs., Hayward, Calif., 1989-90. Scholar State of Calif., 1971-75. Mem. Nat. Women's Health Network, Planned Parenthood, Sierra Club, Soka Gakkai Internat.-USA, Am., Stanford U. Alumni Assn. Democrat. Buddhist. Home: 5919 Howell St Oakland CA 94609

ADDISON, J. BRUCE, bank executive; b. Portland, Oreg., Feb. 18, 1953; s. James Douglas and Marian H. (Woodworth) A.; m. Andra E. Marhefka, June 2, 1990. BA in Polit. Sci., Wash. State U., 1975. Legis. asst. U.S. Ho. of Reps., Washington, 1976-78; state rep. Wash. State Ho. of Reps., Olympia, 1979-87; asst. v.p. Wash. Mut. Savs. Bank, Seattle, 1986—. Pres. South Seattle Community Coll. Found., 1990; bd. dirs. West Seattle YMCA, 1980-86. Republican. Lutheran. Home: 4509 SW Holgate St Seattle WA 98116-1933 Office: Wash Mut Savs Bank 1201 3rd Ave Seattle WA 98101-3000

ADDISON, JOHN ROBERT, counselor; b. Northfield, Mass., Aug. 4, 1927; s. Warren Grant and Mildred Elizabeth (Vorce) A.; m. Emily Loveland Kirk, Jan. 3, 1953; children: Karen Louise, David Martin. BA, U. Mass., 1950; MA, U. Colo., 1963, postgrad., 1964-87. Tchr. Jeffco Pub. Schs., Arvada, Colo., 1956-64; counselor Jeffco Pub. Schs., Arvada Sr. High Sch., Arvada, Colo., 1964-91; mem. Jeffco Area Vocat. Sch. Adv. Coun., 1990-91; mem. Cooperative Occupational Adv. Bd., 1976-91; mem. various adv. coms. Warren Occupational Tng. Ctr., 1970-91. Coach Arvada Soccer Assn., 1971-76; chmn., trustee Arvada Pub. Libr.; active charter rev. com. City of Arvada; admissions counselor Red Rocks C.C., Golden, Colo., 1991-93. With U.S. Army, 1945-47; 1st lt. USAF, 1950-55. Decorated Air medal. Mem. NEA, Jefferson County Edn. Assn. (pres. salary com.), Jeffco Counselors Assn. (pres.), Colo. Edn. Assn., Colo. Guidance Counselors Assn. Home: 6066 Lewis Ct Arvada CO 80004-4928

ADEGBOLA, SIKIRU KOLAWOLE, aerospace engineer, educator; b. Ibadan, Nigeria, Jan. 21, 1949; came to U.S., 1971; s. Lasisi and Moriamo Abeke (Akinyemi) A. BSME, Calif. State U., Fullerton, 1974; MBA, Calif. State U., Dominguez Hills, 1988; MSME, U. Ariz., 1975; MS in Applied Mechanics, U. So. Calif., 1977; PhD in Engring., Calif. Coast U., 1983. Registered profl. mech. engr., Calif., Ariz. Rsch. engr. Jet Propulsion Lab., Pasadena, Calif., 1976-78; stress analyst Bechtel Power Corp., Norwalk, Calif., 1978-87; engring. mem. tech. staff structural analysis dept. Space Systems div. Rockwell Internat., Downey, Calif., 1987—; prof. engring. Calif. State U., Fullerton, 1984—. Leopold Schepp Found. fellowship, 1972-74. Mem. ASME, NSPE, Calif. Soc. Profl. Engrs., Nat. Mgmt. Assn. Home: PO Box 345 Downey CA 90241-0345 Office: Rockwell Internat Corp Space Systems Divsn 12214 Lakewood Blvd Downey CA 90242-2693

ADELMAN, IRMA GLICMAN, economics educator; b. Cernowitz, Rumania, Mar. 14, 1930; came to U.S., 1949, naturalized, 1955; d. Jacob Max and Raissa (Ettinger) Glicman; m. Frank L. Adelman, Aug. 16, 1950 (div. 1979); 1 son, Alexander. B.S., U. Calif., Berkeley, 1950, M.A., 1951, Ph.D., 1955. Teaching assoc. U. Calif., Berkeley, 1955-56; instr. U. Calif., 1956-57, lectr. with rank asst. prof., 1957-58; vis. asst. prof. Mills Coll., 1958-59; acting asst. prof. Stanford, 1959-61, asst. prof., 1961-62; assoc. prof. Johns Hopkins, Balt., 1962-65; prof. econs. Northwestern U., Evanston, Ill., 1966-72, U. Md., 1972-78; prof. econs. and agrl. econs. U. Calif. at Berkeley, 1979—; cons. div. indsl. devel. UN, 1962-63, AID, U.S. Dept. State, Washington, 1963—, Internat. Bank Reconstrn. and Devel., 1968—, ILO, Geneva, 1973—. Author: Theories of Economic Growth and Development, 1961, (with A. Pepelasis and L. Mears) Economic Development: Analysis and Case Studies, 1961, (with Eric Thorbecke) The Theory and Design of Economic Development, 1966, (with C.T. Morris) Society, Politics and Economic Development—A Quantitative Approach, 1967, Practical Approaches to Development Planning-Korea's Second Five Year Plan, 1969, (with C.T. Morris) Economic Development and Social Equity in Developing Countries, 1973, (with Sherman Robinson) Planning for Income Distribution, 1977-78, (with C. T. Morris) Comparative Patterns of Economic Growth, 1850-1914, 1987. Fellow Center Advanced Study Behavioral Scis., 1970-71. Fellow Am. Acad. Arts and Scis., Econometric Soc., Royal Soc. Encouragement Arts, Manufactures & Commerce, 1990—; mem. Am. Econ. Assn. (mem. exec. com., v.p. 1969-71), Social Sci. Research Council (dir.-at-large), Comparative Econ. Assn. (exec. com.), Am. Statis. Assn. Office: Univ Calif Dept Agr & Natural Resources Berkeley CA 94720

ADELMAN, JONATHAN REUBEN, political science educator, consultant; b. Washington, Oct. 30, 1948; s. Benjamin and Kitty (Sandler) A.; m. Dora Zhu, Aug. 12, 1988; 1 child, David Shanghai. BA, Columbia U., 1969, MA, 1972, M in Philosophy, 1974, PhD, 1976. Vis. asst. prof. Columbia U., N.Y.C., 1977; vis. asst. prof. U. Ala., Tuscaloosa, 1977-78; asst. prof. Grad. Sch. Internat. Studies U. Denver, 1978-85, assoc. prof., 1985-92, prof. polit. sci., 1992—; sr. rsch. analyst Sci. Applications, Inc., Denver, 1981-87; cons. 1988-89; Lady Davis vis. assoc. prof. Hebrew U. Jerusalem, 1986; vis. fellow Soviet Acad. Scis., 1989, 90, Chinese Inst. Contemporary Internat. Rels., Beijing, 1988, People's U., Beijing, 1990, 93; vis. prof. Beijing U., 1989, U. Haifa, Israel, 1990; vis. speaker Soviet Acad. Scis., 1990, Barcelona (Spain) U. and Complutense U., 1990, Cambridge U., England, 1991, Tel Aviv U., 1993; vis. lectr. Japan, India, Hong Kong, Yugoslavia, Spain, 1990, 91, Germany, 1991, Bulgaria, 1991; vis. speaker Conf. for Study of European Ideas, Aalborg U., Denmark, 1992; vis. prof. People's U., Beijing, 1990, Janus Pannonius U., Pecs, Hungary, 1991. Author: The Revolutionary Armies, 1980, Revolution, Armies and War, 1986, Prelude to the Cold War: Tsarist, Soviet and U.S. Armies in Two World Wars, 1988; co-author: The Dynamics of Soviet Foreign Policy, 1988; editor: Communist Armies in Politics, 1982, Terror and Communist Politics, 1984, Superpowers and Revolution, 1986; co-editor: Contemporary Soviet Military Affairs: The Legacy World War II, 1989; contbr. numerous articles in field to profl. jours. Charles Phelps Taft fellow U. Cin., 1976-77; Am. Philos. Soc. grantee, 1980. Mem. Am. Polit. Sci. Assn., Am. Assn. Advancement Slavic Studies. Democrat. Jewish. Office: U Denver Grad Sch Internat Studies Denver CO 80208

ADELMAN, RICK, professional basketball coach; b. June 16, 1946; m. Mary Kay Adelman; children: Kathryn Mary, Laura, R.J., David. Master's, Loyola Marymount U. Profl. basketball player San Diego, 1968-70; profl. basketball player Portland (Oreg.) Trail Blazers, 1970-73, asst. coach, 1983-89, head coach, 1989—; basketball player Chgo., New Orleans, Kansas City, and Omaha, 1973-75; head coach Chemeketa Community Coll., Salem, Oreg., 1975-83. Office: Portland Trail Blazers 700 NE Multnomah St Portland OR 97232-2131*

ADELMAN, WILLIAM JAMES, information systems analyst, musician, songwriter; b. Sacramento, Sept. 28, 1954; s. Gordon Phillip and Carol Ann (Popesco) A.; m. Judith Lynn Carerra, Aug. 21, 1983; children: Linda Marie, Lennon Michael. Student, Calif. State U., Sacramento, 1973, 80-81, Charles J.T. Schulte Sch. Performing Arts, Anaheim, Calif., 1976. Vol. Kibbutz Ein Harod, Gilboa, Israel, 1973-74; actor, theater technician, 1974-78, musician,, 1978-84; program technician Calif. Dept. Motor Vehicles, Sacramento, 1981-84, supr., 1984-86, info. systems analyst, 1986—, safety coord. emergency response team, 1988-92; space planner Calif. Div. EDP Svc., Sacramento, 1986—, systems adminstr. CAD Svcs., Sacramento, 1989—. Author, performer record albums Folk Wave Music, 1979, One World, One People, 1987, Sweet Alibi, 1992, Let's Dance, 1993. Umpire, coach Northridge Little League, Fair Oaks, Calif., 1991, 92. Recipient dir.'s quality svc. award Calif. Dept. Motor Vehicles, 1987, employee safety award Gov. of Calif., 1990. Mem. Intercap Graphics Users Soc., Inter Works-Hewlett-Packard Group. Jewish. Office: Calif DMV 2415 1st Ave Sacramento CA 95818

ADELSON, MERVYN LEE, entertainment and communication industry executive; b. Los Angeles, Oct. 23, 1929; s. Nathan and Pearl (Schwarzman) A.; m. Barbara Walters, May 10, 1986; children from previous marriage: Ellen, Gary, Andrew. Student, Menlo Park Jr. Coll. Pres. Markettown Supermarket and Builders Emporium, Las Vegas, 1953-63; mng. ptnr. Paradise Devel., Las Vegas, 1958—; pres. Realty Holdings, 1962—, La Costa, Inc., 1963-87; chmn. bd. dirs. Lorimar Inc., Culver City, Calif., 1969-86; chmn. bd. dirs., chief exec. officer Lorimar Telepictures Corp., Culver City, 1986-89; vice chmn. Warner Communications, 1989—; chmn. East-West Capital Assocs., Inc., 1989—; bd. dirs. Time-Warner Inc. Co-founder Nathan Adelson Hospice Found. Recipient Sherill Corwin Human Relations award Am. Jewish Com., 1987. Mem. Am. Film Inst. (trustee), Am. Mus. of Moving Images (trustee), Entertainment Industries Council (trustee), Acad. Motion Pictures Arts and Scis., Acad. TV Arts and Sciences, Nat. Acad. Cable Programming, Alliance for Capital Access (bd. dirs.), Com. Publicly Owned Cos. (bd. dirs.).

ADELSTEIN, ROBERT MILTON, social worker; b. Sioux City, Iowa, Dec. 8, 1934; s. Morris and Bertha (Greenburg) A.; m. Joanie Greintz, Aug. 26, 1956 (div. Nov., 1972); children: Deborah Kay Adelstein Morrison, Dana Jo Adelstein Schwartz, David Aaron; m. Sheila Greenberg, Sept. 18, 1986. BA, Met. State Coll., Denver, 1971; MSW, U. Denver, 1975. Lic. social worker II, Colo. Equipment mgr. Northwestern Engring. Co., Denver, 1957-69, corp. sec., 1969-91; pvt. practice psychiat. social work and family therapy Denver, 1975--. Trustee Allied Jewish Fedn., Denver, 1979-90; bd. dirs. Coun. Jewish Fedns., N.Y., 1988-89; Jewish Telegraphic Agy., N.Y.C., 1981—, v.p., 1993—; nat. commr. B'nai B'rith Hillel, Washington, 1986-91; pres. Hillel Coun. Colo., 1987-89, trustee, 1989—. Mem. Acad. Cert. Social Workers, Am. Assn. Marriage and Family Therapists, Nat. Assn. Social Workers (diplomate in clin. social work, cert. IMAGO therapist). Republican. Office: 3601 S Clarkson St Ste 540 Englewood CO 80220

ADENIRAN, DIXIE DARLENE, library administrator; b. L.A., May 26, 1943; d. Alfred and Madge (Clare) Harvey. BA, U. Calif., Santa Barbara, 1965; MA, Mich. State U., 1968; MLS, U. Mich., 1970. Libr. Free Libr. of Phila., 1970-72, Coll. Sci. and Tech., Port Harcourt, Nigeria, 1972-73; libr. Ventura (Calif.) County Libr. Svcs. Agy., 1974-79, libr. dir., 1979—. Pres. Ventura County Master Chorale and Opera Assn., 1985. Mem. ALA, Calif. Libr. Assn., Calif. County Librs'. Assn. (pres. 1988), Soroptimists (pres. Ventura club 1984). Home: 5548 Rainier St Ventura CA 93003-1135 Office: Ventura County Libr Svcs 4274 Telegraph Rd Ventura CA 93003-3706

ADICOFF, ARNOLD, cardiologist, consultant; b. Bronx, N.Y., July 8, 1927; s. Samson and Esther (Brown) A.; m. Ruth Kahn, Mar., 1954; children: Carrie Susan, Samuel David, Ann Rebecca. Student, NYU, 1945, BA in Psychology, 1950; MD, Chgo. Med. Sch., 1954. Diplomate Am. Bd. Internal Medicine. Chief of admissions VA Med. Ctr., Mpls., 1958-60, staff physician, 1960-67, cons. cardiologist, 1967-87; dir. cardiac catherization lab. Met. Mt. Sinai Med. Ctr., Mpls., 1967-90, intervention cardiology cons., 1990—; former asst. prof. medicine U. Minn.; clin. asst. prof. medicine U. Calif., Davis, 1991—. Contbr. articles to profl. jours. With USN, 1945-47. Fellow ACP, Am. Coll. Cardiology, Am. Coll. Chest Physicians, Soc. for Cardiac Angiography Interventions, Coun. on Clin. Cardiology of Am. Heart Assn., ; mem. Minn. Med. Assn., Flying Physicians Assn., Air Lifeline. Home: 13952 Collier Rd Grass Valley CA 95945-9340

ADKINS, BEN FRANK, management and engineering consultant; b. West Liberty, Ky., Mar. 6, 1938; s. Stuart Kendall Adkins and Dorothy Elizabeth (Shaver) Indes; m. Judith Ann Williams, Mar. 14, 1959; children: Michelle Rene, Lori Lee. BS in Indsl. Engring., Ariz. State U., 1964; MBA, Western New Eng. Coll., Springfield, Mass., 1971; MS in Systems Mgmt., U. So. Calif., 1983. Registered profl. engr. Enlisted USAF, 1955, commd. 2d lt., 1964, advanced through grades to maj., 1975, ret., 1979; internal cons., mgr. State of Wash., Olympia, 1979-87; mgmt. and engring. cons. Olympia, 1987-88; sr. rsch. sci. Battelle Pacific N.W. Labs., Richland, Wash., 1988-89; mng. prin. Ben Adkins & Assocs., Olympia, 1989—. Decorated Bronze star USAF. Mem. Inst. Indsl. Engrs. (sr. mem., bd. dirs. Puget Sound chpt. 1984-86, asst. dir. and dir. govt. div. 1979-83, v.p. Washington chpt. 1969-76). Home: 6606 Miner Dr SW Olympia WA 98512-7257 Office: Ben Adkins & Assocs PO Box 7613 Olympia WA 98507-7613

ADLAI, RICHARD SALVATORE, financial and management executive; b. Los Angeles; s. Al and Hadia Adlai. Student, U. So. Calif., 1966-67; BS, NYU, 1975; MBA, Pepperdine U., 1982. Writer, tech. dir. Paramount Pictures Corp., Hollywood, Calif., 1967-71; writer, film producer Hollywood Cinema Center Inc., 1971-78; bus. exec. IME, Inc., Beverly Hills, Calif., 1978—, The Hilton Group, Inc., Beverly Hills, 1980—; CEO Royal Fin. Group; bd. dirs. Hilton Fin. Group, Hilton Mgmt. Group, CMA, M. Margani, Inc., Hollywood Cinema Ctr., Inc., Calif. Beverage Corp., Chateau Madeleine, Baron du Bordeaux, Hilton Creative Agy. Author: King Tarick, 1965, Winternude, 1980; plays 22 Miles To Bagdad, 1966, Hassan & Hanna, 1967, By Love Defiant, 1968. Mem. Pepperdine U. Assocs., Export Mgrs. Assn. (bd. dirs. 1978-83), Toluca Lake C. of C. (bd. dirs., exec. v.p. 1974-78, world affair coun. 1978-87). Republican. Lodge: Rotary (pres. Toluca Lake, Calif. 1982-83, bd. dirs., exec. v.p., chmn. internat. relations). Home and Office: Hilton Group Inc PO Box 2026 Toluca Lake CA 91610-0026

ADLER, CHARLES SPENCER, psychiatrist; b. N.Y.C., Nov. 27, 1941; s. Benjamin H. and Anne (Greenfield) A.; m. Sheila Noel Morrissey, Oct. 8, 1966 (dec.); m. Peggy Dolan Bean, Feb. 23, 1991. BA, Cornell U., 1962; MD, Duke U., 1966. Diplomate Nat. Bd. Med. Examiners, Am. Bd. Psychiatry and Neurology. Intern Tucson Hosps. Med. Edn. Program, 1966-67; psychiat. resident U. Colo. Med. Sch., Denver, 1967-70; pvt. practice medicine specializing in psychiatry and psychosomatic medicine Denver, 1970—; chief div. psychiatry Rose Med. Ctr., 1982-87; co-founder Applied Biofeedback Inst., Denver, 1972-75; prof. pro tempore Cleve. Clinic, 1977; asst. clin. prof. psychiatry U. Colo. Med. Ctr., 1986—, chief of psychiatry and psychophysiology Colo. Neurology and Headache Ctr., 1988—. Author: (with Gene Stanford and Sheila M. Adler) We Are But a Moment's Sunlight, 1976, (with Sheila M. Adler and Russell Packard) Psychiatric Aspects of Headache, 1987; contbr. (with S. Adler) sect. biofeedback med. and health ann. Ency. Britannica, 1986; chpts. to books, articles to profl. jours.; mem. editorial bd. Cephalalgia: an Internat. Jour. of Headache, Headache Quar. Emeritus mem. Citizen's Adv Bd. Duke U. Ctr. Aging and Human Devel. Recipient Award of Recognition, Nat. Migraine Found., 1981; N.Y. State regents scholar, 1958-62. Fellow Am. Psychiat. Assn.; mem. AAAS (rep. of AAPB to med. sect. com.), Am. Assn. Study Headache, Internat. Headache Soc. (chmn. subcom. on classifying psychiat. headaches), Am. Acad. Psychoanalysis (sci. assoc.), Colo. Psychiat. Soc., Biofeedback Soc. Colo. (pres. 1977-78), Assn. for Applied Psychophysiology and Biofeedback (rep. to AAAS, chmn. ethics com. 1983-87, bd. dirs. 1990-93, Sheila M. Adler cert. honor 1988). Jewish. Office: 955 Eudora St Ste 1605 Denver CO 80220

ADLER, DONALD JAMES, JR., real estate investment and accounting executive; b. Trenton, Mich., June 16, 1958; s. Donald James and Rowena (Himes) A. BS, Wayne State U., 1981. CFO Muntz Electronics, Inc., 1986-90; pres. R.D.H. Mgmt., Inc., West Hollywood, Calif., 1990—. Republican. Office: 7985 Santa Monica Blvd # 109-92 West Hollywood CA 90046

ADLER, ERWIN ELLERY, lawyer; b. Flint, Mich., July 22, 1941; s. Ben and Helen M. (Schwartz) A.; m. Stephanie Ruskin, June 8, 1967; children: Lauren, Michael, Jonathan. B.A., U. Mich., 1963, LL.M., 1967; J.D., Harvard U., 1966. Bar: Mich. 1966, Calif. 1967. Assoc. Pillsbury, Madison & Sutro, San Francisco, 1967-73; assoc. Lawler, Felix & Hall, L.A., 1973-76, ptnr., 1977-80; ptnr. Rogers & Wells, L.A., 1981-83, Richards, Watson & Gershon, L.A., 1983—. Bd. dirs. Hollywood Civic Opera Assn., 1975-76, Children's Scholarships Inc., 1979-80. Mem. ABA (vice chmn. appellate advocacy com. 1982-87), Calif. Bar Assn., Phi Beta Kappa, Phi Kappa Phi. Jewish. Office: Richards Watson & Gershon 333 S Hope St Bldg 38 Los Angeles CA 90071-3003

ADLER, LAUREL ANN, educational administrator, consultant; b. Cleve., Sept. 6, 1948; d. Clarence Linsley and Margaret Ann (Roberts) Wheeler; m. Thomas Jay Johnson, June 6, 1981; children: David, Anthony, Jennifer. BA, U. Calif.-Irvine, 1968; MA, UCLA, 1972; EdD, U. La Verne, 1980. Adult Edn. adminstr. Hacienda La Puente Unified Sch. Dist., 1972-79; dir. career and vocat. edn. El Monte Union High Sch. Dist., 1979-83; supt. East San Gabriel Valley Regional Occupational Ctr., West Covina, Calif., 1984—; instr. Calif. State U.-L.A., 1979-81; instr. UCLA, 1989—; cons. Trust Ty. Pacific Islands, 1979—, L.A. Community Colls, 1993—. Recipient Nat. Vol. Action award 1974; Calif. Consortium Ind. Study Recognition award of Outstanding Ednl. Program, 1983, Calif. Sch. Adminstrs. award, 1981, Woman Achievement award YWCA, 1991; named Citizen of Yr., La Puente C. of C., 1977, Outstanding Vocat. Educator, Hoffman Ednl. Systems, 1983. Mem. Assn. Calif. Sch. Adminstrs., Internat. Reading Assn., Assn. Supervision and Curriculum Devel., Calif. Consortium Ind. Study, Phi Delta Kappa. Author: A Self Evaluation Model for Micronesian Education Programs, 1987, Poor Readers, What Do They Really See on the Page?, 1987, Shedding Light on Reading Disabilities, 1989, How Students and Programs Benefit From Business/Education Partnerships, 1993; pub. Essential English for Micronesians, Beginning, 1980; Essential English for Micronesians, 1980; Reading Exercises for Micronesians, 1980; contbr. articles to profl. jours. Home: 3366 S Garden Terrace Ln La Puente CA 91745-6244 Office: E San Gabriel Valley Regional Occupational Ctr 1024 W Workman Ave West Covina CA 91790-1755

ADLER, MARK, physicist; b. Miami, Fla., Apr. 3, 1959; s. David James and Bertha (Brucker) A.; 1 child, Joshua Hod. BA in Math., U. Fla., 1981, MSEE, 1985; PhD in Physics, Calif. Inst. Tech., 1990. Systems analyst U. Fla., Gainesville, 1981-85; staff physicist Hughes Aircraft Co., L.A., 1985-92; mem. tech. staff Jet Propulsion Lab. Calif. Inst. Tech., Pasadena, 1992—. Contbg. author: Fast Chemical Kinetics, 1982. Reader Recording for the Blind, Hollywood, Calif. Named Silver Knight Miami Herald, 1977. Mem. Am. Phys. Soc. Democrat. Home: PO Box 92795 Pasadena CA 91109 Office: Jet Propulsion Lab Mail Stop 301 170K 4800 Oak Grove Dr Pasadena CA 91109

ADLER, PATRICIA ANN, sociologist, educator; b. N.Y.C., Sept. 7, 1951; d. Benjamin Theodore and Judith Ann (Goldhill) Heller; m. Peter Adler, Aug. 20, 1972; children: Jori Ann, Brye Jacob. AB in Sociology summa cum laude, Washington U., St. Louis, 1973; MA in Sociol. Sci., U. Chgo., 1974; PhD in Sociology, U. Calif., San Diego, 1984. Instr. Tulsa Jr. Coll., 1981-83; rsch. assoc. U. Tulsa, 1983-84; asst. prof., 1984-85; asst. prof. sociology Okla. State U., Stillwater, 1985-86; asst. prof. U. Colo., Boulder, 1987—; vis. asst. prof. sociology Washington U., St. Louis, 1986-87. Author: Wheeling and Dealing, 1985, (with others) The Social Dynamics of Financial Markets, 1984, The Sociologies of Everyday Life, 1980, Membership Roles in Field Research, 1987, Backboards and Blackboards, 1991, Constructions of Deviance, 1993; editor Jour. Contemporary Ethnography, 1986—, (ann. series) Sociol. Studies of Child Devel., 1984-92; assoc. editor Social Problems Jour., 1984-87, Jour. Urban Life, 1982—, Administrative Science Quarterly, 1989—; contbr. articles to profl. jours. Mem. Am. Sociol. Assn. (com. regulation rsch. 1992-95, chair alcohol and drug sect. 1993-94), Soc. for Study Social Problems, Am. Soc. Criminology, Sociologists for Women in Soc., Soc. for Study of Symbolic Interaction (publ. com. 1985-88, program chmn. 1984, 86), Midwest Sociol. Soc. (bd. dirs. 1993-95), Pacific Sociol. Assn. (pub. com. 1991-94, com. on coms. 1992-95), Phi Beta Kappa. Avocations: aerobics, travel, photography, skiing. Office: Dept Sociology CB 327 U Colo Boulder CO 80309

ADLER, STEVEN VALENTINE, lawyer; b. L.A., May 20, 1947; s. Denis Csiklay Adler and Patricia Rae (Valentine) Adler Ingram; m. Diva Clair, Dec. 1977 (div. 1988). BA, UCLA, 1969; JD, U. So. Calif., 1973. Bar: Calif. 1973. Dep. atty. gen. Criminal div. Calif. Dept. of Justice, San Diego, 1973-78, supervising dep. atty. gen. Criminal div., 1978-84, chief Maj. Fraud unit, 1984-89; chief Bur. of Medi-Cal Fraud, Calif. Dept. Justice, Sacramento, 1989-92; sr. litigation counsel Price Co., San Diego, 1992-93; sr. dept. atty. gen. Health Quality Enforcement, San Diego, 1993—. Mem. Calif. Bar, Calif. Dist. Atty.'s Assn., San Diego County Bar Assn. Office: Office of Atty Gen PO Box 85266 110 W A St Ste 700 San Diego CA 92186-5266

ADOLPH, DALE DENNIS, agricultural executive; b. Roundup, Mont., Apr. 28, 1948; s. Albert Jake and Lillian (Schaefer) A.; m. Victoria Marie Clark, 1967; 1 child, Steven Daniel. BS in Agrl. Bus. and Econs., Mont. State U., 1968. Field dept. mgr. Lamb Weston, Inc., Connell, Wash., 1970-75; procurement mgr. R.T. French Co., Shelley, Idaho, 1975-79; gen. mgr. Dave Kingston Produce, Inc., Ucon, Idaho, 1979—. V.p. Connell (Wash.) C. of C., 1972-73. Mem. Exchange Club (v.p. 1979-80, pres. 1980-81), Idaho Leadership Agri. Republican. Lutheran. Home: 1836 Malibu Dr Idaho Falls ID 83404-6446 Office: Dave Kingston Produce Inc PO Box 158 Ucon ID 83454-0158

ADOLPH, MARY ROSENQUIST, financial executive; b. Springfield, Mass., Oct. 7, 1949; d. Jesse Woodson and Doris May (Marquette) Rosenquist; m. Earl Anthony Soares, Mar. 18, 1972 (div. 1982); m. Joseph Edward Adolph, Oct. 3, 1986. Student San Domenico Sch., 1966-68, Dominican Coll., San Rafael, 1967-69, Calif., San Francisco Conservatory of Music, 1968-70; A.A., Coll. of Marin, 1969. Asst. v.p. Western Travelers Life Ins. Co./Putnam Fin. Services, San Rafael, 1970-80; v.p. Unimarc, Ltd., Novato, Calif., 1980-83; v.p. mktg. Western States Monetary Planning Services, Inc., Newhall, Calif., 1983-88; asst. to pres. Fed. Inventory Wholesale, Inc., 1988-90; v.p. E.W. Richardson & Assocs. Inc., 1991—. Mem. exec. com. San Marin Valley Homeowners Assn., 1979-81. Mem. Internat. Assn. Fin. Planners, Life Underwriters Assn. Democrat. Roman Catholic. Home: 909 Las Pavadas Ave San Rafael CA 94903 Office: E W Richardson & Assocs RENET Fin-Newhall 24325 Arcadia St Newhall CA 91321

ADSIT, JOHN MICHAEL, lawyer; b. Ft. Atkinson, Wis., May 25, 1961; s. John Miley and Nancy Belle (Philbin) A. BA, U. Mich., 1983; JD, George Washington U., 1987. Bar: Calif. 1988. Legal asst. World Bank, Washington, 1986-87; assoc. Zobrist & McCullough, L.A., 1988, Carlsmith, Wichman, L.A., 1989-90; mng. ptnr. Ko & Adsit, Attys. at Law, L.A., 1991, v.p., 1992—. Mem. ABA, L.A. County Bar, Beverly Hills Bar Assn. Republican. Congregationalist. Home: 2509 Hines Dr Los Angeles CA 90065 Office: Ko & Adsit Attys at Law 5750 Wilshire Blvd Ste 572 Los Angeles CA 90036

ADY, RICHARD NORMAN, clergyman, humanitarian aid institute executive; b. Elmer, Okla., June 22, 1931; s. George Matthew and Christine (Howell) A.; m. Maudine Foster, June 2, 1955; children: Deborah June Ady Henry, Richard Norman II. BA, Abilene Christian U., 1956, MS, 1957; DMin, San Francisco Theol. Sem., San Anselmo, Calif., 1983. Min. of edn. Ayers St. Ch. of Christ, Corpus Christi, 1957-61; dir. Bible chair Del Mar Coll., Corpus Christi, 1957-61; min. Netherwood Park Ch. of Christ, Albuquerque, 1961-64; missionary, founder C.C.C. Sch. Bibl. Studies, Taipei, Taiwan, 1968-69, 72-74; instr., lectr. Columbia Christian Coll., Portland, Oreg., 1964-76; min. Ctrl. Ch. of Christ, Portland, 1964-76, Sonoma Ave. Ch. of Christ, Santa Rosa, Calif., 1976-87; co-founder, supr. World English Sch., Santa Rosa, 1987-89; pres., founder World English Inst., Gresham, Oreg., 1989—; co-founder, moderator Friends of Refugees, Santa Rosa, 1980-81; bd. dirs. Indochinese Am. Coun., Santa Rosa, 1981-85; chair Sonoma County Refugee Forum, Santa Rosa, 1982-84. Author: International English Course, Books 1, 2, 3, 1991, International Bible Course, Books 1, 2, 3, 1990; co-author: Nguyen thi Long An/The Vietnam Experience in America, 1992; contbr. articles to profl. jours. Elder, Metro Ch. of Christ, Gresham, 1990—. Named Minister of Yr., Pacific Christian Acad., 1983. Republican. Home: 1625 SE Paloma Ct Gresham OR 97080 Office: World English Inst 1525 NW Division Gresham OR 97030

AFFLECK, JULIE KARLEEN, accountant; b. Upland, Calif., Dec. 23, 1944; d. Karl W. and Juliette O. (Oppegaard) Hall; m. William J. Affleck, Aug. 29, 1964; children: Stephen, Tamara. BS in Bus., U. Colo., 1967; MBA, U. Denver, 1972. CPA, Colo. Cost acct. IBM, Boulder, Colo., 1967-71; audit supr. Ernst & Young, Denver, 1972-79, Rosemary E. Weiss & Co., Denver, 1979-80; ptnr. Affleck, Melaragno, Gilman & Co., Denver, 1980—; tchr. Colo. Soc. CPA's., U. Denver; dir., corp. sec. Better-Way Electric, Inc. Treas., bd. dirs. Bal Swan Children's Ctr. for Handicapped, Broomfield, Colo. Mem. Am. Inst. CPA's., Colo. Soc. CPA's., Am. Soc. Women Accts. (pres. chpt. 1980-81), Nat. Assn. Women Bus. Owners (treas., dir., pres. 1988-89). Republican. Lutheran. Home: 1055 Hemlock Way Broomfield CO 80020-1858

AFFLECK-ASCH, WILLIAM CHRISTOPHER SETH, software systems analyst and designer; b. San Antonio, Feb. 18, 1960; s. Anthony Gair Asch and Rosamond Jean (Affleck) Lowe; m. Carla Lynne Holley, Mar. 8, 1960 (div. May 1992); 1 child, Ian Whitesell. Diploma gen. studies, Capilano Coll., North Vancouver, B.C. Can., 1988, cert. bus. mgmt., 1988; cert. data resource mgmt., U. Wash., 1993. DC power asst. operator Cominco Ltd., Trail, B.C., 1980-82; programmer, analyst Century 21 Real Estate Can. Ltd., Richmond, B.C., 1988-89; personal computer adminstr. WOSCA Shippers Coop., Seattle, 1989-90; systems analyst Analysts Internat. Corp., Seattle, 1990; tech. support contractor Neo Rx Corp., Seattle, 1990; software systems analyst on contract at PEMCO Corp., Excell Data Corp., Seattle, 1990—; owner, designer Omicron Galactic Clouds, Trail, 1980-84; co-chmn., translator Can. Sci. Fiction Conv., Vancouver, 1985-89; treas., gaming coord. Western Regional Sci. Fiction Conv., Vancouver, 1991. Author: (plays) The Grenouille Tales, 1988, L'entrevue avec les anciens, 1986; editor C.F. Machiavelli mag., 1982-84; author, designer CAMPFIRE, freeware for feminists, DBMS, software for polit. candidates; contbr. articles to mag. Active Babble-17, 1989—; founding, contact mem. Utne Reader Neighborhood Salon, Seattle, 1991—; bd. dirs. NOW, Seattle, 1991—, Wash. State, 1992—. Sgt. Can. Armed Forces, 1982-88, mem. Res. Mem. Clipper Users Group Seattle. Democrat. Home: 524 N 47th St Seattle WA 98103-6448

AFLATOONI, ARFA, sociology educator; b. Kerman, Iran, Nov. 3, 1955; came to U.S., 1979; s. Ahmad and Bahieh Aflatooni. BA, Idaho State U., 1981, MA, 1985; PhD, Wash. State U., 1990. Counselor Sierra Nevada Job Corps, Reno, 1983-85; teaching asst. Wash. State U., Pullman, 1985-90; vis. asst. prof. sociology Wash. State U., Vancouver, 1990-92, Whitman Coll., Walla Walla, Wash., 1992—. Contbr. articles, book reviews to profl. jours. Mem. Bahai Faith. Office: Sociology Dept Whitman Coll Walla Walla WA 99362

AFSARI, KHOSROW, physician, consultant, internist; b. Babol, Mazandoran, Iran, Apr. 26, 1941; came to U.S., 1970; s. Abraham and Afsar (Shahgholi) A.; m. Susan Mahshid Abedi, June 21, 1970; children: Peter, Mary, Bobby, Michael. BA, U. Shiraz, Iran, 1963; MD, Shiraz Med. Sch., 1969. Diplomate Am. Bd. of Internal Medicine. Rotating intern U. Hosp. of Shiraz Med. Sch., 1969-70; intern in internal medicine Balt. City Hosp., 1970-71; fellow dept. medicine and infectious disease Johns Hopkins Med. Sch. and Hosp., Balt., 1970-73; asst. resident Balt. City Hosp., 1971-72, sr. resident in medicine, 1972-73; sr. resident in medicine U. Ill., Chgo., 1973-74; mem. staff Abraham Lincoln Med. Sch. U. Hosp., 1974-75; pvt. practice Lombard, Ill., 1974-75; mem. staff Elmhurst (Ill.) Hosp., 1974-75; asst. prof. medicne U. of Shiraz Med. Sch., 1975-76; pvt. practice internal medicine, cons. infectious diseases San Pablo, Calif., 1977—; mem. staff, cons. Brookside Hosp., San Pablo, 1977—, chmn. antibiotic com., mem. infectious control com., 1978—, chmn. dept. medicine, 1982-84, pres. med. staff, 1987; mem. staff, cons. infectious diseases Dr.'s Hosp. of Pinole, Calif., 1977—, mem. infectious control com., 1988—. Fellow ACP; mem. AMA, ACCMA, CMA. Home: 909 Raintree Pl Lafayette CA 94549-4815 Office: 2089 Yale Rd #21 San Pablo CA 94806

AFSARMANESH, HAMIDEH, computer science educator, research scientist; b. Tehran, Iran, Aug. 23, 1953; came to U.S., 1977; d. Esmail Afsarmanesh and Mehrangiz Hoveida; m. Farhad Arbab, Mar. 8, 1977; children: Taraneh, Mandana. BBA, Tehran Bus. Sch., 1975; MS, Aryamehr Tech. U., Tehran, 1977; MSc, UCLA, 1980; PhD, U. So. Calif., 1985. Rsch. scientist SDC (now subs. Unisys), L.A., 1985-86; assoc. prof. dept. computer sci. Calif. State U., Dominguez Hills, 1986—; vis. rsch. prof. U. Amsterdam, 1990—; cons. dept. elec. engring. U. So. Calif., 1987—. Contbr. chpts. to books. Rsch., Scholarship and Creative Activities Program fellow Calif. State U., 1989. Mem. IEEE (chairperson various confs. 1988—), Assn. Computing Machinery, Sigma Xi.

AFSARY, CYRUS, artist; b. Oct. 18, 1940; s. Merabon and Mehrbonoo (Jamasbi) A.; m. Gohar Jamzedeh, Apr. 1, 1978 (div. Apr. 1980); 1 child, Anohita Mehrbonoo; m. Kathy Ricker, Jan. 26, 1988 (div. June 1990), 1 child, Jacqueline Mitra. BA in Art, U. Tehran, 1962, BA in Interior Design, 1971. Resident artist Grand Gallery, Las Vegas, Nev., 1975-80; free lance artist Las Vegas, 1980-88, Scottsdale, Ariz., 1988—; art tchr., Middle East, 1967-68; participant Artists of Am., 1988, 92. Works featured in Southwest Art, 1987, Midwest Art, 1988, Arts of the West, 1988. Recipient Exceptional Award Pastel Soc. Am., 1986; named Best of Show, C.M. Russell Show, 1985, Best Oil, Amarillo Rotary Club Art Show, 1991, chosen Official Poster Artist, 1991. Mem. Nat. Acad. Western Art (gold medal 1987, Robert Lougheed gold medal 198, silver medal 1989), N.W. Renedzvous Art (merit award 1987). Studio: PO Box 3217 Scottsdale AZ 85271

AGEE, DAVID ANTHONY, military officer; b. Roanoke, Va., Sept. 27, 1949; s. Joseph Rudolph and Gladys Christine (Huddle) A.; m. Susan Gay Coester, Mar. 19, 1983. BA in Sec. Edn., U. Md., 1972; MS in Space Ops., A.F. Inst. Tech., 1984. Math. instr. Blue Ridge Mid. Sch., Purcellville, Va., 1972; commd. 2d lt. USAF, 1972, advanced through grades to lt. col., 1988; student navigator Mather AFB, Calif., 1972-73; navigator 6th Mil. Airlift Squadron, McGuire AFB, N.J., 1973-79; instr. navigator 1st Mil. Airlift Squadron, Andrews AFB, Md., 1979-83; grad. student A.F. Inst. Tech., Wright-Patterson AFB, Ohio, 1983-84; space surveillance contr. U.S. Space Command, Peterson AFB, Colo., 1984-87; comdr. detachment 4 1st Space WG, British Indian Ocean, 1987-88; comdr. 1st Command & Control Squadron, Cheyenne Mtn. AFB, Colo., 1988-91; chief sensor operations divsn. 1st Space Wing, Peterson AFB, Colo., 1991-92; comdr. Air Force ROTC det. 752 Wilkes U., Wilkes-Barre, Pa., 1992—. Mem. A.F. Assn., Ret. Officer Assn., Am. Legion, Omicron Delta Kappa.

AGEE, WILLIAM J., transportation, engineering and construction company executive; b. Boise, Idaho, Jan. 5, 1938; s. Harold J. and Suzanne (McReynolds) A.; m. Mary Cunningham, June 5, 1982; children: Mary Alana, William N. AA, Boise Jr. Coll., 1958; BS with high honors, U. Idaho, 1960; MBA with distinction, Harvard U., 1963; DSc in Indsl. Mgmt. (hon.), Lawrence Inst. Tech., 1977, Nathaniel Hawthorne Coll., 1977; D.C.S., Eastern Mich. U., 1978; LLD (hon.), U. Detroit, 1980; DBA (hon.), Bryant Coll., 1980, Cleary Coll., 1980. Various positions Boise Cascade Corp., 1963-69, sr. v.p., chief fin. officer, 1969-72; exec. v.p., chief fin. officer Bendix Corp., Southfield, Mich., 1972-76, pres., 1976-79, chief oper. officer, 1976-77, chmn. bd., 1977-83; chmn., chief exec. officer Semper Enterprises, Inc., Osterville, Mass., from 1983; chmn. bd., chief exec. officer Morrison Knudsen Corp., Boise, 1988—, also bd. dirs.; bd. dirs. Dow Jones & Co., Key Corp.; chmn. data processing and office automation Grace Commn., 1981-82; presdl. appointee U.S. Quadrennial Commn., 1988. Chmn. Gov.'s Higher Edn. Capital Investment Adv. Com., 1979; mem. adv. coun. Japan-U.S. Econ. Relations, 1982-84. Named Disting. Alumnus Boise State U. (formerly Boise Jr. Coll.), 1972; recipient Alumni Achievement Award Harvard U. Bus. Sch., 1977; named to U. Idaho Hall of Fame, 1978. Mem. AICPA, Idaho Soc. CPAs, Mich. Assn. CPAs, Coun. on Fgn. Rels., Brit-N.Am. Com., Conf. Bd., Bus. Roundtable, Harvard Bus. Sch. Assocs., Phi Kappa Phi, Arid Club Boise, Economic Club, Hillcrest Country Club, Oyster Harbors Club (Osterville, Mass.). Republican. Roman Catholic. Office: Morrison Knudsen Corp Morrison-Knudsen Pla PO Box 73 Boise ID 83707

AGERBEK, SVEN, mechanical engineer; b. Soerabaya, Dutch Indies, Aug. 2, 1926; came to U.S., 1958, naturalized, 1964; s. Niels Magnus and Else Heidam (Nielsen) Agerbek-Poulsen; m. Helen Hadsbjerg Gerup, May 30, 1963; 1 child, Jesper. MSME, Tech. U., Denmark, 1952; LLB, LaSalle Estension U., 1967; postgrad., UCLA, 1969. Registered profl. engr., Calif., Ohio, Fla. With Danish Refrigeration Research Inst., Copenhagen, 1952; engr. B.P. Oil Co., Copenhagen, 1952-54; refrigeration insp. J. Lauritzen, Copenhagen, 1954-56; engr. Danish-Am. Gulf Oil Co., Copenhagen, 1956-58; instr. Ohio U., Athens, 1958-60; asst. prof. Calif. State Poly. U., San Luis Obispo, 1960-62; prin. engr., environment dept. Ralph M. Parsons Co., Los Angeles, 1962-73; engring. supr. Bechtel Power Co., Norwalk, Calif., 1973-85; pres., owner Woodcraft Cabinets, Inc., Rancho Cordova, Calif., 1985-90; owner Acrebrook Cons., Fair Oaks, Calif., 1990—. Past mem. Luth. Ch. council, pres. Luth. Sch. bd. Served with Danish underground movement, World War II. Mem. ASHRAE (mem. tech. com., author Guide on Air Conditioning of Nuclear Power Plants), Danish Engring. Soc. Home and Office: Acrebrook Consulting 5201 Vista Del Oro Way Fair Oaks CA 95628-4148

AGLER, DAVID, conductor; b. South Bend, Ind., Apr. 12, 1947; s. Wave Bloom and Doris (Sheeler) A. B.Music, Westminister Choir Coll., Princeton, N.J., 1965-70; postgrad., Phila. Coll. Performing Arts, 1973-75. Mem. faculty Westminster Choir Coll., 1970-72, Acad. Vocal Arts, Phila., 1970-72, Phila. Coll. Performing Arts, 1973-75; adminstrv. dir. Spoleto Festival, 1974-75, gen. mgr., asso. music dir., 1975-76; mem. faculty San Francisco Conservatory Music, 1980-82; dir. Am. Opera Project.; music dir. Syracuse Opera Theatre, 1978-79; music supr., resident condr. San Francisco Opera, 1979-84; prin. condr. Australian Opera, 1986—. Named Exxon Arts-Endowment condr., 1979. Office: Australian Opera, PO Box 291, Strawberry Hills NSW 2012, Australia also: Vancouver Opera, 1132 Hamilton St, Vancouver, BC Canada V6B 2S2

AGLER, VICKIE LYN, state legislator; b. St. Joseph, Mo., July 14, 1946; d. Harry Ernest and Fern Dorothy (Hart) Kerr; m. Rex Duane Agler, June 7, 1968; children: Kristen Michelle, Stephanie Dianne. Assoc. degree, Mo. Western Jr. Coll., St. Joseph, 1966; BS in Edn., U. Mo., 1968. Secondary sch. tchr. Topeka (Kans.) Pub. Sch., 1968-70; paralegal Dan Moran, Atty. at Law, Huntsville, Ala., 1970-76; stained glass artist Agler's Arts & Glass, Littleton, Colo., 1980-86; planning commr. Jefferson Co. Planning Commn., Littleton, 1983-87; staff asst. Congressman Joel Hefley, Littleton, 1987-90; state rep. Colo. Gen. Assembly, Denver, 1990—; coun. mem., v.p. Arapahoe C.C. Coun., 1989-92. Mem. Colo. Fedn. Rep. Women, Littleton, Am. Legis. Exchange Coun., Washington, So. Jefferson County Rep. Club, Littleton, Rep. Leadership Program, Colo.; dir. Foothills Found. Bd.; bd. mem., legis. liaison Chatfield P.T.S.A., 1989-92; del., v.p. Coun. Homeowners for Planned Environment, 1984-89. Named Woman of Yr., Sentinal Newspaper, Jefferson County, Colo., 1984, Outstanding Legislator, Colo. Counties, 1992. Mem. West C. of C. (Community Svc. award 1992), Beta Sigma Phi. Methodist. Home: 10289 W Burgundy Ave Littleton CO 80127 Office: Colo Gen Assembly State Capital Denver CO 80203

AGNEW, EDWARD CHARLES, JR., business executive; b. Chgo., May 12, 1939; s. Edward Charles Sr. and Adelaide (Brost) A.; m. Ann Louise Meyer, June 14, 1961; chilren: Daniel Charles, Christine Agnew Christon, Brian Patrick, Ellen Bridgid. BBA, U. Notre Dame, 1961; MBA, U. Chgo., 1974. Trainee, store mgr. Jewel Food Stores, Inc., Melrose Park, Ill., 1961-66, div. produce mgr., 1966-72, grocery merchandiser, 1972-75, dist. mgr.,

1975-77, dir. grocery merchandising, 1977-80, v.p. distbn. and mfg., 1980-85, sr. v.p., gen. mgr., 1985-87; pres., chief oper. officer Buttrey Food and Drug Stores Co., Great Falls, Mont., 1987-90; pres., CEO Buttrey Food and Drug Co., Great Falls, Mont., 1990-92, chmn., CEO, 1993—; bd. dir. Shurfine-Cen., Inc., Northlake, Ill. Mem. pres.'s coun. Coll. Great Falls, 1990—; mem. adv. coun. U. Mont. Sch. of Bus., Missoula, 1991—; trustee Columbus Hosp. Great Falls, 1991—. Mem. Mont. C. of C. (bd. dirs. 1992—), Food Mktg. Ins. (distgn. com. 1981-84, chmn. distbn. com. Washington chpt. 1985), Rotary Internat. Republican. Roman Catholic. Office: Buttrey Food & Drug Stores Co PO Box 5008 Great Falls MT 59403-5008

AGNEW, ROBERT DANA, sculptor; b. Altadena, Calif., Dec. 18, 1937; s. Thomas Leon and Alice Marie (Voettiner) A.; m. Janice Louise Rosenberg, July 7, 1963; children: Jeffrey Dean, Dianne Marie. AA, Pasadena City Coll., 1957; BA, Whittier (Calif.) Coll., 1959; postgrad., Long Beach State, 1962-63, Fullerton State, 1961, 64, Rancho Santiago Coll., 1987-88, 92-93. Dep. probation officer County of Orange, Calif., 1959-90; owner-originator Agnew's String Art, Orange, Calif., 1968-76; string art designer Spinnerin Yarn Co. Inc., N.Y.C., 1971-76; sculptor Bob Agnew-Wood Sculptor, Orange, 1982—. Orginator string art hobby kit, 1968; designer 30 Spinnerin string art kits, 1971-76; wood sculptor abstract curvilinear sculptures in avocado and walnut woods, 1982—. Recipient Juror's award La Mirada (Calif.) Festival of Arts, 1987, Grumbacher award Arts Colony La Mirada, 1993.

AGNEW, THOMAS EDWARD, communications executive; b. Spokane, Wash., Feb. 26, 1950; s. Edward John and Mary Ann (Schroeder) A.; m. Stephanie Stone, Sept. 3, 1977; children: Anna Maria, Julia Jean, Therese Alexandria. BA in Polit. Sci., U. Wash., 1972, postgrad., 1972-73. Asst. dir. Seattle Dept. Human Resources, 1972-74; mgmt. cons. Toner & Assocs., Seattle, 1974-76; sales mgr. Sta. KAOI Radio, Wailuku, Maui, Hawaii, 1976-81, Sta. KXLY News Radio, Spokane, Wash., 1981-82, Sta. KAYU TV, Spokane, 1982-86; gen. mgr. Sta. KXLY AM-FM, Spokane, 1986—; guest lectr. Maui Community Coll, 1979-80; mem. Spokane Community Coll. Radio Broadcasting Adv. Com., 1988. Pres. exec. bd. St. Mary's Sch., Spokane, 1987-88, bd. dirs. Maui Jr. Achievement, 1984-85, Kihei (Maui) Aloha Assn.; v.p. Liberty Lake (Wash.) Property Owners' Assn., 1988-89. Mem. Nat. Assn. Broadcasters, Radio Advt. Bur., Spokane Area Radio Broadcasters, Spokane Executive Assn. Roman Catholic. Office: KXLY AM-FM 500 W Boone Ave Spokane WA 99201-2497

AGOGINO, GEORGE ALLEN, anthropologist, educator; b. West Palm Beach, Fla., Nov. 18, 1920; s. Andrew and Beulah Mae A.; m. Mercedes Merner, Dec. 1, 1952; children: Alice, Karen. BA, U. N.Mex., 1948, MA, 1951; PhD, Syracuse U., 1958; postgrad., Harvard U., 1962-63. Asst. prof. anthropology Syracuse U., N.Y., 1956-58; asst. prof. anthropology, acting dir. mus. U. S.D., Vermillion, 1958-59; asst. prof. anthropology U. Wyo., Laramie, 1959-61; Wenner-Gren postdoctoral fellow Harvard U., Cambridge, Mass., 1961-62; assoc. prof. Baylor U., Waco, Tex., 1962-63; assoc. prof. anthropology Ea. N.Mex. U., Portales, 1963-68, prof., 1968-85, Disting. rsch. prof. anthropology, 1985-91, emeritus Disting. rsch. prof. anthropology, 1991—, dir. Paleo-Indian Inst., 1963—, founding dir. Anthropology Mus., Blackwater Draw Mus., Miles Mus., 1967-86, chmn. dept. anthropology, 1963-80, dir. spl. programs, 1972-73, dir. humanities div., 1973-74; cons. forensic phys. anthropology U. S. Bur. Reclamation, 1984—. Author monographs in field including (with C.V. Haynes) Smithsonian Contributions in Anthropology, No. 32; contbr. over 395 articles on Mexican anthropology, primitive religion and folklore to profl. jours.; cons. to mags. Am. Antiquity, Plains Anthropologist, Nat. Geographic, Pursuit, Smithsonian. Signal Corps, U.S. Army, 1942-46. Recipient Pres.'s award Eastern N.Mex. U., 1971, numerous rsch. grants; proclaimed Ofcl. Eminent Scholar by State of N.Mex. Fellow Explorers Club Am., Am. Anthrop. Assn., AAAS, Instituto Interamericana. Republican. Home: 1600 S Main Ave Portales NM 88130-7331 Office: Eastern NMex U Paleo-Indian Inst PO Box 2154 Portales NM 88130-2154

AGONIA, BARBARA ANN, retired English language educator, communications consultant; b. St. Louis, June 11, 1934; d. Robert Lewis and Suzanne (Carter) Klinefelter; m. Robert James Agonia, Mar. 25, 1972. Student, U. Exeter, Devon, Eng., 1954-55; BA, Hanover Coll., 1957; MA, U. Nev., Las Vegas, 1971; postgrad., U. Nev., Reno, 1983—. Tchr. Carrollton (Ill.) Community Unit High Sch., 1955-56, 59-61, White Hall (Ill.) Community Unit High Sch., 1957-59; tchr., chmn. dept. English ROVA Community Unit High Sch., Oneida, Ill., 1961-69; prof. English Clark County Community Coll., North Las Vegas, Nev., 1971-89, chmn. dept., 1972-75, 87-89, dir. re-entry ctr., 1980-83; speaker in field, Ind., Ill., Nev., Eng., 1952—. Author poems. Vol. Opportunity Village, Las Vegas, Nev., 1985—; bd. dirs. Friends of Nev. Wilderness, Las Vegas, 1985—. Mem. Western Lit. Assn. (Golden award 1984), Shakespeare Assn. Am., Coll. Conf. Composition and Communication (exec. com.), Nev. State Edn. Assn. (exec. bd. 1975-79), League United Latin Am. Citizens (nat. parliamentarian 1978-82), Internat. Platform Assn., Soroptimists Internat. (parliamentarian Las Vegas 1984—, pres.-elect 1986-87, pres. 1987-88, Women Helping Women award 1983, Woman of Distinction 1986), Order of Eastern Star (Worthy Matron 1960-61). Methodist. Home and Office: 3411 Frontier St Las Vegas NV 89102-8158

AGOSTINO, MICHAEL N., software engineer; b. San Jose, Calif., Jan. 28, 1968; s. Norman R. and Elena J. (Cinelli) A. BS, Calif. Poly., San Luis Obispo, 1990. Mem. programming staff X Soft (a Xerox Co.), Palo Alto, Calif., 1990-92; software engr. Go Corp., Foster City, Calif., 1992—.

AGOSTON, MAX KARL, computer science educator; b. Stockerau, Austria, Mar. 25, 1941; s. George Anton Agoston and Grete (Mihokovic) Broadwell. BA, Reed Coll., 1962; MS, Yale U., 1964, PhD, 1967; MS in Computer Sci., Stanford U., 1977. Lectr. Wesleyan U., Middletown, Conn., 1966-67, asst. prof., 1967-75; lectr. San Jose (Calif.) State U., 1976-77, asst. prof., 1977-80, assoc. prof., 1980—; vis. lectr. Heidelberg U., Germany, 1970-71; vis. fellow U. Auckland, New Zealand, 1973-74. Author: Albebraic Topology: A First Course, 1976; contbr. articles to profl. jours. Mem. Assn. Computing Machinery, Am. Math. Soc., Computer Soc. IEEE, Spl. Interest Group in Computer Graphics of ACM. Office: San Jose State U Dept Math and Computer Sci San Jose CA 95192

AGRAWAL, DIVYAKANT, computer science educator; b. Indore, India, Dec. 1, 1958; came to U.S., 1982; s. Lavkush Prasad and Prabha (Gupta) A.; m. Shubra Gupta, Dec. 28, 1986; 1 child, Meha. BE with honors, BITS, Pilani, India, 1980; MS, SUNY, Stony Brook, 1984, PhD, 1987. Software engr. Tata Burroughs Ltd., Bombay, 1980-82; asst. prof. U. Calif., Santa Barbara, 1987—. Author: (with others) Database Transaction Model, 1992; contbr. articles to profl. jours. Grantee NSF, 1988, 90, 91. Mem. IEEE, Assn. of Computing Machinery. Office: Univ Calif Dept Computer Sci Santa Barbara CA 93106

AGRESTI, JACK JOSEPH, construction company executive; b. San Francisco, 1937. Grad., San Jose State U., 1959. Pres., COO Guy F. Atkinson Co., South San Francisco. Mem. Constrn. Industry Inst., Soc. Am. Mil. Engrs., Am. Arbitration Assn. Office: Guy F Atkinson Co 10 W Orange Ave South San Francisco CA 94080-3399

AGTHE, DALE ROBERT, lawyer, editor; b. Buffalo, Sept. 28, 1953; s. Richard Erwin and Jilene Inez (Werner) A. BA in Polit. Sci., SUNY, Buffalo, 1975, JD, 1978. Bar: N.Y. 1979. Editor Lawyers Coop. Pub. Co., Rochester, N.Y., 1979-83; freelance legal researcher Las Cruces, N.Mex., 1983-85; sr. editor Shepard's/McGraw Hill, Colorado Springs, CO1985—. Editor law texts, treatises; contbr. articles to legal publs. Mem. N.Y. State Bar Assn., Phi Beta Kappa. Republican. Baptist. Home: 1123 Royale Dr Colorado Springs CO 80910-2017 Office: Shepards McGraw Hill 555 Middle Creek Pkwy PO Box 35300 Colorado Springs CO 80935-3530

AGUAYO, JOSÉ, museum administrator; b. Sedgwick, Colo., Nov. 18, 1941; s. Marciano and Jovita (Ortega) A.; m. Magdalena M. Arellano, May 28, 1966; children: Marisa, Lucia. AA, Colo. Inst. Art, 1964; BA with distinction, Loretto Heights Coll., 1983; MA in Mus. Studies, Anthropology, U. Denver, 1990. Staff designer J.R. Riddle & Assocs., Denver, 1964-67, Designers West, Denver, 1967-68; ptnr., designer Unit 1, Inc., Denver, 1968-75; owner Aguayo Design, Denver, 1975-85; mgr. copr. I.D. and allied businesses Adolph Coors Co., Golden, Colo., 1985-88; dir. design Colo. Hist. Soc., Denver, 1988-92; exec. dir. Museo de Las Americas, Denver, 1992—. Dist. capt. Dem. Party, Arvada, Colo., 1976. With U.S. Army, 1959-62. Mem. Am. Assn. Mus. (councilor-at-large nat. coun., bd. dirs. 1990-93), Am. Anthropol. Assn. Roman Catholic.

AGUILAR, MARGARET HOPE, lawyer; b. Wilmette, Ill., Aug. 13, 1951; d. Gabriel and Nona May (Linton) A. BSBA in Fin., U. So. Calif., 1979; JD, Loyola U., L.A., 1985. Bar: Calif. 1986, U.S. Dist. Ct. (cen. dist.) Calif. 1986. Intern TRW Def. & Space Systems, Redondo Beach, Calif., 1978; trader fgn. exch. Citibank, N.Y.C., 1979-80; corp. banker Security Pacific Bank, L.A., 1980-85, Calif. Fed. Savs. & Loan, Santa Monica, Calif., 1985-86; pvt. practice corp. law Century City, Calif., 1986-87; bankruptcy, securities lawyer Petillon & Davidoff, L.A., 1987-90; corp. bankruptcy lawyer Broad, Schulz, Larson & Wineberg, 1990—. Vol. Nat. Counsel of Jewish Women. Mem. ABA, L.A. County Bar Assn., Century City Bar Assn., Beverly Hills Bar Assn., Women Lawyers of L.A., L.A. and Orange County Bankruptcy Forum. Office: Broad Schulz Larson & Wineberg 10390 Santa Monica Blvd 4th Flr Los Angeles CA 90025-5058

AGUILAR, RAUL ABRAHAM, adult school administrator; b. L.A., Feb. 12, 1954; s. Arturo Joseph and Angie (Sierra) A.; m. Ofelia G. Vasquez, 1990; children: Julio, Angie. BA in English, Calif. State U., L.A., 1979; MS in Edn., Mount St. Mary's Coll., 1985. Tchr. Met. High Sch. L.A.U.S.D., L.A., 1980-85; in-house dean W. Hollywood Opportunity Ctr., L.A., 1985-87; prin. John Hope High Sch. L.A.U.S.D., L.A., 1987-89, Highland Park High Sch. L.A.U.S.D., L.A., 1989-91; asst. prin. Pacoima Skills Ctr. L.A. Unified Sch. Dist., 1991-92; asst. prin. L.A. Community Adult Sch., 1992—; tchr., adv. Belmont Community Adult Sch., L.A., 1988-91; mem. adv. com. Mount St. Mary's Coll., L.A., 1987-90. Mem. Calif. Continuing Edn. Assn. (v.p. 1990-91, sec. 1989-90, Jerry Dean Medallion award 1984), Associated Adminstrs. L.A., Coun. Mex.-Am. Adminstrs., Calif. Assn. Regional Occupational Programs/Ctrs., Assn. Calif. Sch. Adminstrs., Aussi Toastmasters (cert. toastmaster 1989), The Cousteau Soc., Ctr. Marine Conservation. Democrat. Home: 1855 Yosemite Dr # 6 Los Angeles CA 90041 Office: LA Community Adult Sch 4650 W Olympic Blvd Los Angeles CA 90019

AGUILAR, ROBERT P., federal judge; b. Madera, Calif., Apr. 15, 1931. B.A., U. Calif., Berkeley, 1954; J.D., Hastings Coll. Law, San Francisco, 1958. Bar: Calif. 1960, U.S. Supreme Ct. 1966. Partner Aguilar & Edwards, San Jose, Calif., from 1960; judge U.S. Dist. Ct., No. Dist. Calif., San Francisco, 1980—; Mem. Regional Criminal Justice Planning Bd., from 1974; chmn. Santa Clara County (Calif.) Juvenile Justice Commn., 1975; mem. Santa Clara County Drug Abuse Task Force, 1974. Mem. Calif. Trial Lawyers Assn., Santa Clara County Criminal Trial Lawyers Assn., Am. Bar Assn., Calif. Bar Assn., Santa Clara County Bar Assn. (pres. 1972). Office: US Dist Ct 280 S 1st St San Jose CA 95113-3002

AGUILERA, DONNA CONANT, psychologist, researcher; b. Kinmundy, Ill.; d. Charles E. and Daisy L. (Frost) Conant; m. George Limon Aguilera; children: Bruce Allen, Craig Steven. B.S., UCLA, 1963, M.S., 1965; Ph.D., U. So. Calif., 1974. Teaching asst. UCLA, 1965, grad. rsch. asst., 1965-66; prof. Calif. State U., L.A., 1966-81; cons. crisis intervention Didi Hirsch Community Mental Health Ctr., L.A., 1967-82; mem. Def. Adv. Com. Women in the Services, 1978-82; originator, project dir. Project Link Lab. U. Author: Crisis Intervention: Theory and Methodology, 1974, 7th edit. 1993, pub. in seven langs., braille and tapes, Review of Psychiatric Nursing, 1977, 7th edit. 1978; Crisis Intervention: Therapy for Psychological Emergencies, 1983. contbr. articles to profl. publs. Docent Huntington Libr. San Marino, Calif. 1991—. NIH fellow, 1972-75. Fellow Am. Acad. Nursing (sec. 1976-77, pres. 1977-78), Acad. Psychiat. Nurse Specialists, Internat. Acad. Eclectic Psychotherapists (pres. 1987-89); mem. Am. Nurses Assn., Faculty Women's Assn., Am. Psychol. Assn., Calif. Psychol. Assn., AAUP, Alpha Tau Delta, Sigma Theta Tau. Home: 3924 Dixie Canyon Ave Sherman Oaks CA 91423-4830 Office: 450 North Bedford Suite 210 Beverly Hills CA 90210

AGUINSKY, RICHARD DANIEL, electronics engineer; b. Buenos Aires, Dec. 26, 1958; s. Elias Lorenzo and Rosa Isabel (Grille) A. Electronics Engr., Univ. Tech. Nacional, Avellaneda, 1984; MS in Elec. Engring. San Jose State U., 1991. Serial prodn. technician Norman S.A., Buenos Aires, 1978-80; electronics lab. technician Univ. Technologica Nacional, Avellaneda, 1980-84; engring. sub mgr. Northern Telecom, Buenos Aires, 1983-86; project engr. No. Telecom, Santa Clara, Calif., 1986—. Instr. digital technics Univ. Tech. Nacional, Avellaneda, 1985; mentor adelante program San Jose City Coll. Contbr. articles to Revista Telegrafica Electronica, No. Telecom, Am. Nat. Standard Telecommunications. Lodge: Kiwanis Internat. Avocations: travel, camping, windsurfing, skiing, sky diving. Office: No Telecom 2305 Mission College Blvd Santa Clara CA 95054-1591

AGURTO, MARTIN, human services professional; b. Loma Linda, Calif., Nov. 11, 1952; s. Wilfrido and Angelica (Guerra) A. AA in Psychology, San Bernardino Valley Coll., 1973; BA in Psychology, U. Calif., Riverside, 1976; MPA in Healthcare Adminstrn., Golden Gate U., 1989. Cert. tchr., Calif. Eligibility worker Dept. Pub. Social Svcs., Riverside, Calif., 1975-77; social worker Dept. Pub. Social Svcs., San Bernardino, Calif., 1977-79; child protection social worker Dept. Social Svcs., Riverside, 1979-80; mental health clinician San Bernardino County Mental Health Dept., 1980-82, mental heath clinician, conservatorship investigator, 1982-84, coord. drug program, 1984-86; asst. to dir., drug program adminstr. San Benito County Mental Health Dept., Hollister, Calif., 1986-87; div. mgr. alcohol and drug programs Fresno (Calif.) County Mental Health Dept., 1988-89; mental health program specialist Dept. Mental Health, Sacramento, 1989-91; victim svcs. specialist Calif. Dept. Corrections, Sacramento, 1991-93; liaison gov.'s policy coun. on alcohol, drug abuse Dept. Alcohol and Drug Programs, Sacramento, 1992—; alcohol and drug program analyst. Home: 4200 Dymic Way Sacramento CA 95838 Office: Dept Alcohol and Drug Programs 1700 K St Sacramento CA 95814

AGUZZI-BARBAGLI, DANILO LORENZO, literature educator; b. Arezzo, Italy, Aug. 1, 1924; came to U.S., 1950; s. Guglielmo and Marianna (Barbagli) Aguzzi-B. Dottore in Lettere, U. Florence (Italy), 1949; Ph.D., Columbia U., 1959. Instr., asst. U. Chgo., 1959-64; assoc. prof. Tulane U., New Orleans, 1964-71; prof. U. B.C., Vancouver, 1971-90; Mem. Fulbright-Hayes final scholarship com., 1970—; adviser on scholarship application Can. Council, 1972-75. Author: Critical Edition of Della Poetica of Francesco Patrizi, 3 vols., 1969, 70, 71, 72, Critical Edition of Francesco Patrizi's Lettere ed Opuscoli inediti, 1975, Critical Edition of Pellegrino Prisciani's Spectacula, 1992; contbg. author: L'unamesimo in Istria, 1983, Contemporaries of Erasmus, 1985, Renaissance Humanism, Foundations, Forms and Legacy, 1988; contbr. articles to profl. jours. Newberry Library fellow Chgo., 1974; Folger Shakespeare Library fellow Washington, 1975. Fellow Am. Philos. Soc.; mem. AAUP, Newberry Libr. Assocs., Dante Soc. Am., Italian Honor Soc. (regional rep.), Accademia Petrarca, Medieval Soc. Am., Renaissance Soc., Am., Modern Lang. Assn., Am. Assn. Tchrs. Italian. Address: 1260 Nelson St Ste 1902, Vancouver, BC Canada V6E 1J7

AHAD, RAFIUL, software architect; b. Rangoon, Burma, Sept. 30, 1950; came to U.S., 1980; s. Nurul and Sobeh Aktar (Khatoon) A.; m. frances Gutierrez Kasala, Jan. 1, 1981; children: Raphael N.K. Ahad, Alexander K. Ahad. BS in Physics, Arts and Scis. U., Rangoon, 1973, MS in Computer Sci., 1975; MS in Computer Applications, Asian Inst. of Tech., Bangkok, 1980; PhD in Computer Sci., U. So. Calif., L.A., 1985. Systems programmer, analyst Universities' Computer Ctr., Rangoon, 1976-78; asst. prof. U. Md., College Park, 1985-89; software design engr. Hewlett-Packard, Cupertino, Calif., 1989-92, chief architect Open ODB program, 1992—; cons. STX Corp., Greenbelt, Md., 1988. Contbr. articles to profl. jours. Sec. track and field subcom. Rangoon U., 1972; trip officer student union Asian Inst. of Tech., Bangkok, 1980; sec. Burmese Assn. of Capital Area, Md., 1987-89. Scholarship Royal Thai Govt., 1979. Mem. IEEE, Assn. for Computing Machinery, Sigma Xi. Office: Hewlett-Packard Co MS 44 UT 19111 Pruneridge Ave Cupertino CA 95014

AHERN, ARLEEN FLEMING, retired librarian; b. Mt. Harris, Colo., Oct. 15, 1922; d. John R. and Josephine (Vidmar) Fleming; m. George Irving Ahern, June 14, 1944; 1 child, George Irving. BA, U. Utah, 1943; MA, U. Denver, 1962; postgrad. U. Colo., 1967. Library asst. Army Air Force Library, Salt Lake City, 1943-44; library asst. Colo. Women's Coll. Library (now U. Denver/CWC Campus), 1952-60, acquisitions librarian, 1960—, rep. Adult Edn. Council Denver, 1960-90, reference librarian Penrose Library, WEC librarian, assoc. prof. librarianship through 1987. Committeewoman, Republican Com., Denver, 1958-59; vol., Opera Colo. Guild, Denver Lyric Opera, U. Denver Women's Libr. Assn., bd. dirs., 1992-93, Samaritan House Guild, Jeanne Jugan (Little Sisters Poor) Aux., Colo. Symphony Guild, Cinema Study Club Colo., Carson Brierly Dance Libr., bd. dirs. Mem. AAUP, ALA, Mountain Plains Library Assn., Colo. (1st v.p., pres. 1969-70, dir. 1971—), Library Assn., Altrusa Club of Denver (2d v.p. 1968-69, dir. 1971-74, 76, 78), Soc. Am. Archivists, Mountain Plains Adult Edn. Assn., Denver Botanic Gardens. Home: 746 Monaco Pky Denver CO 80220-6041 Office: U Denver Penrose Libr Denver CO 80208

AHLERS, GUENTER, physicist, educator; b. Bremen, Germany, Mar. 28, 1934; came to U.S., 1951; s. William Carl and Ida Pauline (Cornelson) A.; m. June Bly, Aug. 24, 1964. BS, U. Calif., Riverside, 1958; PhD, U. Calif., Berkeley, 1963. Mem. tech. staff Bell Labs., Murray Hill, N.J., 1963-79; prof. physics U. Calif.-Santa Barbara, 1979—. Contbr. numerous articles to profl. jours. Recipient Fritz London award in low temperature physics, 1978. Fellow AAAS, Am. Phys. Soc.; mem. NAS. Home: 523 Carriage Hill Ct Santa Barbara CA 93110 Office: U Calif Dept of Physics Santa Barbara CA 93106

AHLGREN, GIBSON-TAYLOR, real estate broker; b. Memphis, Sept. 7, 1940; s. Frank Richard and Nona Elizabeth (Alley) A. B.S., U. Md., 1967; J.D., Western State U., San Diego, 1978. Legis. clk. U.S. Senate, Washington, 1963-67, spl. asst., 1970-71; legis. rep. Associated Gen. Contractors, Washington, 1971-73, San Diego, 1973-74; campaign dir. Brown for Gov. Calif., 1974; mgmt. cons. Ahlgren, Peters & Assocs., La Jolla, Calif., 1975-77; v.p., dir. pub. affairs Gt. Am. First Savs. Bank, San Diego, 1977-84; polit. cons., 1984-85; real estate broker, 1986—. Served to lt. USN, 1967-70; Vietnam. Mem. Pi Kappa Alpha.

AHLSTRAND, CHARLES THOMAS, administrative director; b. Greeley, Colo., Aug. 19, 1942; s. Charles Thomas Ahlstrand and Ruth Edith (Siegmann) Johnston; m. Sandra Jean Winslow, Feb. 1962 (div. 1970); 1 child, Ruthe Michelle; m. Faith Ross Permenter, Apr. 10, 1975; 1 stepchild, Elizabeth Hope Reed; 1 child, Christine Ross. BS, Mid. Tenn. State U., 1967, MEd, 1980; PhD, So. Ill. U., 1988. Rsch. analyst CIA, McLean, Va., 1968-71; pers. cons. John Paisios and Assocs., Nashville, 1972-74; dir. internat. staffing Hosp. Corp. Am., Nashville, 1974-80; program coord. So. Ill. U., Carbondale, 1981-83, adj. asst. prof. aviation mgmt., 1983-89; career ctr. dir. Embry-Riddle Aero. U., Prescott, Ariz., 1989—. Bd. dirs Ctr. for Adult Day Care, Prescott, 1991—; pres. Cherry Grove Precinct Rep. Party, Myrtle Beach, S.C., 1986. With USAF, 1961-66. Mem. Am. Assn. Airport Execs., Univ. Aviation Assn. (com. chmn. 1992—), Assn. Former Intelligence Officers, Coll. Placement Coun., Coop. Edn. Assns., Rocky Mountain Coll. Placement Assn. Home: 4541 Donna Dr Prescott AZ 86301 Office: Embry-Riddle Aero U 3200 Willow Creek Rd Prescott AZ 86301

AHLSTROM, JOHN KEITH, computer infosystem engineer, educator; b. Jamestown, N.Y., July 1, 1942; s. Paul A. and Ruth M. (Conner) A.; m. Anne D. Pemberton, Dec. 15, 1964 (div. June 1976); m. Janice Tribe, June 17, 1982; 1 child, Elizabeth. BA in Internat. Relations, Am. U., Washington, 1964, MA in Internat. Relations, 1968. Founder, systems mgr. Data Resources Inc., Lexington, Mass., 1969-74; operating systems programmer Burroughs Corp., Goleta, Calif., 1974-76; computer micro architect Data Gen. Corp., Mass. and Calif., 1976-78; mgr. software devel. Olivetti Corp., Cupertino, Calif., 1978-79; founder CompuShop Inc., Dallas, 1976-85; mgr. systems architecture Bell-No. Research, Mountain View, Calif., 1979-82; founder, dir. systems engring. DAVID Systems, Sunnyvale, Calif., 1982-86; adj. prof. computer sci. San Francisco State U., 1976-86, assoc. prof. computer sci., 1986-87; architect network systems Avant-Grade Computings, 1988-89, Boole & Babbage, 1990—. Inventor in field. Mem. Assn. Computing Machinery, Computer Soc. of IEEE (affiliate).

AHLUWALIA, HARJIT SINGH, physicist; b. Bombay, May 13, 1934; came to U.S., 1968; s. Sewa Singh and Jaswant Kaur A.; m. Manjit Kaur Pal, Nov. 29, 1964; children: Suvinder Singh, Davinder Singh. BSc with honors, Panjab U., Hoshiarpur, India, 1953, MSc, 1954; PhD (Univ. Merit scholar), Gujarat U., Ahmedabad, India, 1960. Sr. rsch. fellow Phys. Rsch. Lab., Ahmedabad, 1954-62; tech. assistance expert UNESCO, Paris, 1962-63; rsch. assoc. S.W. Ctr. Advanced Studies, Dallas, 1963-64; vis. prof. IAEA, Vienna, Austria, 1965-67; sci. dir. Lab de Fisica Cosmica, La Paz, Bolivia, 1965-67; vis. prof. Pan Am. Union, Washington, 1967-68; assoc. prof. physics U. N.Mex., 1968-73, prof., 1973—; nat. rep. of Bolivia on profl. groups, 1966-69; rapporteur XIV Internat. Conf. Cosmic Rays, Munich, 1975; gen. sec. High Energy Cosmic Ray Group, Solar Traveling Interplanetary Phenomena subcom. Internat. Coun. Sci. Unions, 1976-86; vis. sr. scientist Office of Space Sci. and Applications NASA, Washington, 1987-88. Contbr. numerous articles to profl. jours. Panjab U. Merit scholar, 1948-53; NSF grantee, 1963-65, 68-81; USAF grantee, 1962-68; Sandia Corp. grantee, 1969-72; NASA grantee, 1972-77, 88—. Mem. AAAS, AAUP, IEEE, Am. Astron. Soc., Am. Geophys. Union, Am. Meteorol. Soc., Am. Phys. Soc., Calcutta Math. Soc., Internat. Astron. Union, Sigma Xi. Democrat. Sikh. Home: 13000 Cedar Brook Ave NE Albuquerque NM 87111-3018 Office: U NMex Dept Physics & Astronomy Albuquerque NM 87131-1156

AHMED, IQBAL, psychiatrist, consultant; b. Tumkur, Karnataka, India, Aug. 23, 1951; came to U.S., 1976; s. Rahimuddin Ahmed and Arifa (Banu) Rahimuddin; m. Lisa Suzanne Rose, Oct. 9, 1983; children: Yasmin, Jihan. BS, MB, St. John's Med. Coll., Bangalore, India, 1975. Diplomate in gen. psychiatry and geriatric psychiatry Am. Bd. Psychiatry and Neurology. Intern St. Martha's Hosp., Bangalore, India, 1974-75; resident in psychiatry U. Nebr. Med. Ctr., Omaha, 1976-79; fellowship in consultation Boston U. Sch. Medicine, 1979-81; staff psychiatrist in consultation liaison psychiatry Boston City Hosp., 1981-87, staff psychiatrist, geriatric psychiatry, 1983-85, dir. geriatric neuropsychiatry unit, 1985-87, dir. geriatric psychiatry, 1988-92; assoc. dir. consultation liaison psychiatry New England Med. Ctr., Boston, 1989-92; chief spl. svc. Hawaii State Hosp., 1992—; asst. prof. psychiatry Sch. Medicine, Boston U., 1981-87, Sch. Medicine, Tufts U., Boston, 1987-92; dir. med. student edn. in psychiatry Boston City Hosp., 1981-87; chief spl. svcs. Hawaii State Hosp., 1992—; assoc. prof. John A. Burn's Sch. Medicine, U. Hawaii, 1992—. Contbr. articles to profl. jours. Mem. Mass. State Dem. Party Minority Caucus, Boston, 1983. Mem. AMA, Am. Psychiat. Assn., Am. Neuropsychiatry Assn., Royal Coll. Psychiatrists, Acad. Psychosomatic Medicine, Am. Acad. Geriatric Psychiatry. Democrat. Office: Hawaii State Hosp 45-710 Keaahala Rd Kaneohe HI 96744

AHRENS, ERICK KARL FREDERICK, computer software executive; b. Detroit, Feb. 22, 1949; s. Herman Frederick Ahrens and Evelyn (Metcalf) Finch; m. Dorothy Ann Swiercz, June 22, 1972. AA in Math., Coll. San Mateo, Calif., 1975; BS in Engring. Math., U. Calif., Berkeley, Calif., 1980; MBA in Bus. Analysis, San Francisco State U., 1987. Applications analyst Victor Comptometer Corp., South San Francisco, Calif., 1975; research and devel. engr. Earl and Wright Consulting Engrs., San Francisco, 1976-83; v.p. product engring. Molecular Design, Ltd., San Leandro, Calif., 1984—. Contbr.to profl. jours. With USN, 1969-73, Vietnam. Mem. IEEE Computer Sc., Assn. Computing Machinery, Am. Chem. Soc., Marin Power Squadron (past comdr.), Corinthian Yacht Club (Tiburon, Calif.). Home: PO Box 20984 Castro Valley CA 94546-8984 Office: Molecular Design Ltd 2132 Farallon Dr San Leandro CA 94577-6604

AHRENS, ERNST H., geological engineer; b. Alliance, Nebr., June 24, 1929; s. Ernst Henry and Lora (Moore) A.; m. Mariana Helene Rafish, Dec. 30, 1951; children: Brandon, Lori, Steven, Susan. BS, U. Calif., Berkeley, 1951. Engr. geologist Anaconda Mining Co., Butte, Mont., 1961-68; engr. geologist U.S.S.R., Salt Lake City, 1968, Vanadium, N.Mex., 1969-79; engr. geologist Home Stake Mining Co., Calusa, Calif., 1979-80; chief geologist Lakeshore Mine Noranda Mining Co., Casa Grande, Ariz., 1980-87, Cypress Mining Co., Casa Grande, 1987-90; with Sandia Corp., Albuquerque, 1990—. Patentee in field. Pres. B'nai Brith, Butte, 1962-64; v.p. Little League, Bayard, N.Mex., 1970-75. Mem. AIME, Active Club (v.p. 1956—). Republican. Jewish.

AHSANULLAH, OMAR FARUK, product administrator, consultant; b. Suri, India, Feb. 20, 1964; came to U.S., 1981; s. Mohammad and Masuda (Gowas) A.; m. Angela Rahim, August 4, 1991. BS, Rensselaer Poly. Inst., 1986, MS in Computer Systems Engring., 1987. Coop. student IBM, Atlanta, 1984-85; coop. student Factron, Latham, N.Y., 1985-87, design engr., 1987-88; lead design engr. Schlumberger, Simi Valley, Calif., 1988-90, new product introduction project mgr., 1990-92, product mgr. diagnostic systems, 1992-93, product mgr. diagnostic systems and well svcs., 1993—; con. Omega Rsch. & Applications, Valencia, Calif., 1989—; instr. Calif. Luth. U., 1991—. Recipient scholarship Rensselaer Poly. Inst., 1981-85, Nat. Honor Soc., 1981. Mem. Am. Prodn. and Inventory Control Soc., World Affairs Coun., Eta Kappa Nu. Office: Schlumberger Techs 85 Moreland Rd Simi Valley CA 93065-1662

AIELLO, LOUIS PETER, interior designer; b. Wappingers Falls, N.Y., July 14, 1932; s. Peter Joseph and Edith (Catenzaro) A.; m. Penelope Anne Heilman, Sept. 7, 1985; children: Colette, Tyler, Antonio. Degree in interior design, Parsons Sch. Design, N.Y.C., 1959. Designer Morris, Lapidus, Harle, Liebman, N.Y.C., 1959-61, W. J. Sloane, N.Y.C., 1961-62. Projects include Westin Hotel, Denver, Vail (Colo.) Athletic Club, Embassy Suites, Denver, Palace Sta. Hotel and Casino, Las Vegas, Nev., Pointe Hilton, Phoenix, Ariz., others; contbr. design articles to nat. publs. With USAF, 1951-55. Mem. Am. Soc. Interior Designers. Home: Penthouse 1443 Wazee St Denver CO 80202 Office: Aiello Assocs Inc 1441 Wazee St Denver CO 80202-1343

AIELLO, NENO JOSEPH, social worker, consultant; b. Pitts., Dec. 12, 1928; s. Guiseppe and Angielina (Russo) A.; m. Geneva Parkhill, May 22, 1965 (div. Feb. 1972); children: Kathleen, Sarah, Margaret; m. Carlene K. Frank, Apr. 10, 1987; children: Suzanne, Diane. AA, Sacramento Coll., 1948; BA, Sacramento State U., 1960; MSW, Washington U., 1962. Cert. tchr. lifetime, Calif. Group supr. Calif. Youth Authority, San Andreas, 1956-58; sociologist Calif. Dept. Corrections, Vacaville, 1960-61; social work supr. Santa Clara County, San Jose, Calif., 1963—; tchr. Gavilan Coll., Gilroy, Calif., 1967-82; cons. Master Plan City of Milpitas, Calif., 1968-72, City of San Jose Mayors Conf., 1988-89; presentor Youth Law Ctr., Oakland, Calif., 1989. Co-author: (booklet) State Guide for Public Schools, 1958; contbr. articles to profl. jours. Bd. dirs. Vol. Ctr., San Jose, 1965-85; vol. various community orgns. including March of Dimes, Family Ctr., Martha's Kitchen, Girl Scouts U.S.A., Dental Soc., KRON-TV, San Jose Pub. Schs.; judge speech and interview Academic Decathalon; mem. sch. attendance rev. bd. Oak Grove Sch. Dist. With U.S. Army, 1950-52, Korea. Recipient Govs. award for Creative Citizenship State of Calif., Sacramento, 1968, Vol. Recognition Head Start, 1975, For Those Who Care award (first recipient) Sta. KRON-TV, 1983; named Citizen of Month Kiwanis, 1982. Mem. Nat. Assn. Social Workers, Italian-Am. Heritage Found., Assn. Vol. Action Scholars. Democrat.

AIKAWA, JERRY KAZUO, physician, educator; b. Stockton, Calif., Aug. 24, 1921; s. Genmatsu and Shizuko (Yamamoto) A.; m. Chitose Aihara, Sept. 20, 1944; 1 son, Ronald K. A.B., U. Calif., 1942; M.D., Wake Forest Coll., 1945. Intern, asst. resident N.C. Baptist Hosp., 1945-47; NRC fellow in med. scis. U. Calif. Med. Sch., 1947-48; NRC, AEC postdoctoral fellow in med. scis. Bowman Gray Sch. Medicine, 1948-50, instr. internal medicine, 1950-53, asst. prof., 1953; established investigator Am. Heart Assn., 1952-58; exec. officer lab. service Univ. Hosps., 1958-61, dir. lab. services, 1961-83, dir. allied health program, 1969—, assoc. dean allied health program, 1983—, pres. med. bd.; assoc. dean clin. affairs asst. prof. U. Colo. Sch. Medicine, 1953- 60, asso. prof. medicine, 1960-67, prof., 1967—, prof. biometrics, 1974—, assoc. dean clin. affairs, 1974—; Pres. Med. bd. Univ. Hosps. Fellow ACP, Am. Coll. Nutrition; mem. Western Soc. Clin. Research, So. Soc. Clin. Research, Soc. Exptl. Biology and Medicine, Am. Fedn. Clin. Research, AAAS, Central Soc. Clin. Research, AMA, Assn. Am. Med. Colls., Phi Beta Kappa, Sigma Xi, Alpha Omega Alpha. Home: # 115 7222 E Gainey Ranch Rd Scottsdale AZ 85258-1530 Office: U Colo Sch Medicine 4200 E 9th Ave Denver CO 80262-0001

AIKEN, JOHN WALLACE, physician; b. Marceline, Mo., Apr. 25, 1947; s. Donald Neal Aiken and Martha Jean (Vissering) Quatto; m. Agnes Maria Hooper, June 24, 1967 (div. 1982); children: Alicia Lynnette, Lara Elizabeth. MD, U. Mich., 1971. Diplomate Am. Bd. Ob-Gyn. Pvt. practice Ventura, Calif., 1976-80, Taos, N.Mex., 1980-83, Ventura, Calif., 1983-86; health educator Tri-County AIDS Project Santa Barbara (Calif) Health Dept., 1986-87; asst. prof. UCLA Sch. of Medicine, 1987—; ptv. practice Granada Med. Group, Granada Hills, Calif., 1991—; bd. dirs. Olive View Med. Ctr. Found., Sylmar, Calif., 1988—. Maj. USAF, 1974-76. Fellow Am. Coll. Ob-Gyn. Bahai. Office: Granada Med Group 10660 White Oak Ave Granada Hills CA 91344

AIKEN, PHIL LUND, chiropractic physician; b. Mitchell, Nebr., Aug. 22, 1924; s. Evan L. and Ruth L. (Lund) A.; m. Lorena M. Mason, Apr. 17, 1951; children: Miriam, Laura Aiken Conners. D Chiropractic, Lincoln Chiropractic Coll., Indpls., 1949. Diplomate Am. Bd. Chiropractic Orthopedics. Pvt. practice Provo, Utah, 1951—. With USN, 1943-45. Mem. Am. Chiropractic Assn. (pres. 1978, v.p. 1977, pres. Coun. State dels. 1976), Utah Chiropractic Assn. (bd. dirs.), Coun. on Chiropractic Orthopedics of ACA(treas. 1985, pres. 1984, v.p. 1983), Nat. Chiropractic Mutual Ins. Co. (bd. dirs.). Home: 190 E 100 S Provo UT 84606-4691

AIKENS, C(LYDE) MELVIN, anthropology educator, archaeologist; b. Ogden, Utah, July 13, 1938; s. Clyde Walter and Claudia Elena (Brown) A.; m. Alice Hiroko Endo, Mar. 23, 1963; children: Barton Hiroyuki, Quinn Yoshihisa. A.S., Weber Coll., 1958; B.A., U. Utah, 1960; M.A., U. Chgo., 1962, Ph.D., 1966. Curator U. Utah Mus. Anthropology, Salt Lake City, 1963-66; asst. prof. U. Nev.-Reno, 1966-68; asst. prof. U. Oreg., Eugene, 1968-72, assoc. prof., 1972-78, prof. anthropology, 1978—. Author: Fremont Relationships, 1966, Hogup Cave, 1970, Great Basin Archaeology, 1978, The Last 10,000 Years in Japan and Eastern North America, 1981, From Asia to America: The First Peopling of the New World, 1990; co-author: Prehistory of Japan, 1982, Great Basin Numic Prehistory, 1986, Early Human Occupation in Far Western North America, 1988; editor: Archaeological Studies Willamette Valley, 1975; co-editor: Prehistoric Hunter-Gatherers in Japan, 1986, Pacific Northeast Asia in Prehistory, 1992. NSF research grantee, 1970, 73, 78-80, 84; NSF Sci. Faculty fellow Kyoto U., Japan, 1971-72; Japan Found. research fellow Kyoto U., 1977-78, Tokyo U., 1986. Fellow Am. Anthrop. Assn., AAAS; mem. Soc. for Am. Archaeology. Home: 3470 Mcmillan St Eugene OR 97405-3317 Office: U Oreg Dept Anthropology Eugene OR 97403

AILOR, KAREN TANA, magazine writer, proposal consultant; b. Seattle, June 1, 1943; d. Dale Ingram and Neva Gail (Houck) A. Student, U. Calif., Berkeley, 1961-63; BA in Journalism, U. Oreg., 1992. Copy editor Physical Review Letters, Brookhaven, N.Y., 1963-65; proposal writer TRW Def. Systems, L.A., 1965-73; mktg. support mgr. TRW Electronics, L.A., 1973-79; proposal cons. TRW, Hughes, Northrop and others, L.A., 1980-93; contbg. writer Old Oreg. Mag., Eugene, 1991—. Mem. Phi Beta Kappa (award 1992), Kappa Tau Alpha (award 1991). Democrat. Home and Office: 1800 W 25th Ave Eugene OR 97405

AILSHIE, ROGER ALLEN, auditor, accountant; b. Hutchinson, Kans., Sept. 27, 1962; s. Roger Howard and Jeanette Ray (McCall) A. BS in Acctg., Baker U., 1987. Staff acct. Lindberg & Vogel, Hutchinson, 1987-88; sr. auditor Def. Contract Audit Agy., Mountain View, Calif., 1989—. Wayne P. Randall Found. grantee, 1986. Mem. Sunshine Club (pres. Mountain View chpt. 1990—), Zeta Chi (pres. 1986-87). Methodist. Home: 168 Woodland Way Milpitas CA 95035-6246 Office: Def Contract Audit Agy 321 Castro St Mountain View CA 94041-1205

AINSLEY, STUART MARTIN, lawyer; b. Levittown, N.Y., Feb. 2, 1956; s. Herbert William and Margaret Isis (Megalli) A. m. Shannon Dea Gillen; children: Zachary Tyler, Samantha Lauren. BS in Fgn. Svc., Georgetown U., 1978, JD, 1982. Bar: Wash. 1982, U.S. Dist. Ct. (we. dist.) Wash., U.S. Ct. Appeals (9th cir.). Assoc. Ferguson & Burdell, Seattle, 1982-88, Montgomery Purdue Blankinship & Austin, Seattle, 1988-92, MacDonald, Houge and Bayless, Seattle, 1992—; atty. Puget Sound Engrs. Ctr., Seattle, 1989-90. Author: Title Insurance, 1988. Mem. ABA, Wash. State Bar Assn., Meadowmoor Golf and Country Club. Episcopalian. Office: Montgomery Purdue Blankinship & Austin 701 5th Ave Ste 5800 Seattle WA 98104-7096

AINSWORTH, DAVID VINCENT, lawyer; b. Holland, Mich., Feb. 10, 1940; s. William Earl and Carmen Sylvia (Vincent) A.; m. Judy Gail Harman, Sept. 15, 1962 (div. 1972); children: Gray Harman, Erin Judith; m. Carol Ann Bradford, Oct. 15, 1983. BA, U. Kans., 1962; JD, Golden Gate U., 1972. Bar: Calif. 1972. Ops. supr. Matson Nav. Co., San Francisco, 1965-68; supt. Matson Terminals, Inc., San Francisco, 1968-72; counsel Matson Nav. Co., San Francisco, 1972-75, sr. counsel, 1975-78; sr. counsel Am. Pres. Lines, Ltd., Oakland, Calif., 1978-82; asst. gen. counsel Am. Pres. Lines, Ltd., Oakland, 1982-89, v.p., gen. counsel, 1989—; bd. dirs. Matson Fed. Credit Union, San Francisco, 1976-78. Author: A Legislative Proposal Concerning California Small Claims Courts, Golden Gate U. law review, 1971, Murphy's Law: The Pan Am Corollary, 1980, editor, 1971-72, Cal Law - Trends and Developments, 1970. Chmn. Planning Commn., San Anselmo, Calif., 1976, mem. 1973-75. Capt. USMC, 1962-68. Mem. ABA, Am. Corp. Counsel Assn., Maritime Law Assn. (Carriage Goods com., Multimodal com. 1979—), Transp. Lawyers Assn., Assn. Transp. Practitioners. Democrat. Home: 55 Crest Ave San Anselmo CA 94960-2560 Office: Am Pres Lines LTD 1111 Broadway Oakland CA 94607-4021

AIRAUDI, RICHARD ALLAN, health care executive; b. San Francisco, Mar. 11, 1947; s. Claud James and Winnifred (Patch) A.; m. Theresa Marie Hart, Aug. 15, 1970; children: Jon, David, Michael. BA, U. San Francisco, 1969; MA, San Francisco State U., 1971; MBA, Pepperdine U., 1978; Exec. MBA, Stanford U., 1991. Life rep. Safeco Ins. Co., Burlingame, Calif., 1972; dist. mgr. Calif. Assn. Employers, San Jose, 1973-78; mgr. labor rels. Blue Cross Calif., Oakland, 1978-80, dir. human resources div., 1980-82, v.p. corp. mgmt. systems, 1982-87; dir. ops. support svcs. The Permanente Med. Group, Oakland, 1987—. 2d lt. U.S. Army, 1969-71. Office: The Permanente Med Group 1950 Franklin St 18th Fl Oakland CA 94612

AIRY, WILLIAM W., cable television executive; b. Albuquerque, Sept. 14, 1954; s. Frederic W. and Helen (Lichens) A.; m. Linda Koury, Dec. 20, 1977; children: Michelle, Jennifer, William, Rebecca, Sarah. BBA, Fort Lewis Coll., 1975; MIM, Thunderbird Grad. Sch., Glendale, Ariz., 1976. V.p. Airy Advt., Inc., Albuquerque, 1976-83, pres., 1983-89; pres. Visn Group, Inc., Denver, 1989—. Campaign mgr. Becht for Gov., Albuquerque, 1984. Mem. Nat. Cable TV Assn., Women in Cable. Republican. Presbyterian.

AITKEN, JOHN EAKIN, JR., controller; b. Denver, July 30, 1941; s. John Eakin Sr. and Bernadette (Lacy) A.; m. Maureen Elizabeth Evans, June 11, 1966; children: Kimberly S., Wendy L., Eric J. BSBA, Colo. State U., 1964; postgrad., Va. Commonwealth U., 1968-69. CPA, Colo. Acct. Greyhound at the World's Fair, Flushing Meadows, N.Y., 1964-65; budget coord. Clairol, Inc., Stamford, Conn., 1965-66; sr. acct. Price Waterhouse, Denver, 1969-73; controller Ridgewood Realty, Inc., Lakewood, Colo., 1973—; bd. dirs. College Park Water & Sanitation Dist., Golden, Colo., 1st Nat. Bank of Arapahoe County, Aurora, Colo. Chmn. bd. Rocky Mountain chpt. Nat. Arthritis Found., Denver, 1984-86, audit chmn., Atlanta, 1987-89, chmn. fin. com., Atlanta, 1992—. 1st lt. U.S. Army, 1966-69. Mem. AICPA, Colo. Soc. CPA's (chpt. bd. dirs. 1984-86). Office: Ridgewood Realty Inc 143 Union Blvd Ste 110 Lakewood CO 80228-1825

AJAWARA, AUGUSTUS CHIEDOZIE, engineering company executive; b. Umuowa, Imo, Nigeria, Aug. 8, 1953; came to U.S., 1974; s. Innocent Onyemekara and Patricia Nwamgbede (Ekpeogu) A.; m. Lettie Louise Tolbert, May 1, 1977; children: Augdosha Ijeoma, Christiana Chinwendu, Serenity Nkechinyere, James Patrick Okechukwu, Silvarious Stamlilaus. BS in Civil and Transp. Engring., Calif. Polytech. State U., 1982; MPA, Golden Gate U., 1983. Registered profl. engr. Traffic engring. asst. Calif. Dept. Transp., San Luis Obispo, 1977-79; jr. civil engr. Calif. Dept. Transp., San Francisco, 1979-80; staff engr. Dept. Pub. Works City of Austin, Tex., 1983-84, engr. assoc. Land Devel. Svcs., 1984-85, engr. assoc., program mgr. Transp. Systems Mgmt., 1985, engr. assoc., program mgr. traffic safety Dept. Pub. Service/Transp., 1985-86; project mgr. Oji Internat., Pomona, Calif., 1987; v.p., prin. Oji Internat., Pomona, 1988—, also bd. dirs.; cons. transp. engr. Pub. Works/Redevel. Agy., City of Compton, Calif., 1988—; prin. engr., dist. div. mgr. BSI Cons., 1990-91. Contbr. articles to profl. jours. Campaign worker Brown for Pres., San Francisco, 1979-80, Jackson for Pres., 1984, Barientos for Sen., Austin, 1984; campaign coordinator Jackson for Pres., Pomona, 1988. Mem. ASCE (assoc., transp. tech. group. Orange County), Inst. Tranps. Engrs. (tech. coun. 1986, com. mem. 1986-88), Am. Soc. Pub. Adminstrn., Toastmasters (adminstrv. v.p.), Knight of Peter Claver (comdr. jr. knight 1986-88). Democrat. Roman Catholic. Home: 23295 Via Bahia San Juan Capistrano CA 92691-2113 Office: BSI Cons 2001 E 1st St Santa Ana CA 92705-4020

AKAKA, DANIEL KAHIKINA, senator; b. Honolulu, Sept. 11, 1924; s. Kahikina and Annie (Kahoa) A.; m. Mary Mildred Chong, May 22, 1948; children: Millannie, Daniel, Gerard, Alan, Nicholas. BEdn, U. Hawaii, 1952, MEdn, 1966. Tchr. schs. in Hawaii, 1953-60; vice prin., then prin. Ewa Beach Elem. Sch., Honolulu, 1960-64; prin. Pohakea Elem. Sch., 1964-65, Kaneohe Elem. Sch., 1965-68; program specialist Hawaii Compensatory Edn., 1978-79, from 1985; dir. Hawaii OEO, 1971-74; spl. asst. human resources Office Gov. Hawaii, 1975-76; mem. 95th-101st Congresses from 2d Dist., Hawaii, 1977-90; U.S. senator from Hawaii, 1990—; chmn. Hawaii Principals' Conf. Bd. dirs. Hanahauoli Sch.; mem. Act 4 Ednl. Adv. Council, Library Adv. Council.; Trustee Kawaiahao Congl. Ch. Served with U.S. Army, 1945-47. Mem. NEA, Musicians Assn. Hawaii. Democrat. Office: US Senate 720 Senate Hart Bldg Washington DC 20510-1103*

AKAKA, ELLEN L., nursing educator, women's health nurse; m. W. Hinano Akaka, Mar. 3, 1962; children: W. Hinano II, Puanani C., Andy Gardiner. AA, Santa Rosa (Calif.) Jr. Coll. Sch. Nursing, 1958, diploma, 1959; AA in Liberal Arts, Windward Community Coll., Kaneohe, Hawaii, 1981; BS with high honors, U. Hawaii, Honolulu, 1983, MS, 1986. RN, Hawaii. Staff nurse various locations; tutor adolescent pregnancy Honolulu Dept. of Edn.; pvt. practice childbirth educator Kaneohe; asst. prof. Hawaii Loa campus Hawaii Pacific U., Kaneohe. Fellow Am. Coll. Childbirth Educators; mem. Am. Women's Health, Obstetric and Neonatal Nurses, Hawaii Childbirth Edn. Assn., Hawaii Wholistic Nurses Assn., Sigma Theta Tau (Gamma Psi chpt.).

AKASOFU, SYUN-ICHI, geophysicist; b. Nagano-Ken, Japan, Dec. 4, 1930; came to U.S., 1958, naturalized, 1986; s. Shigenori and Kumiko (Koike) A.; m. Emiko Endo, Sept. 25, 1961; children: Ken-Ichi, Keiko. B.S., Tohoku U., 1953, M.S., 1957; Ph.D., U. Alaska, 1961. Sr. research asst. Nagasaki U., 1953-55; research asst. Geophys. Inst., U. Alaska, Fairbanks, 1958-61, mem. faculty, 1961—, prof. geophysics, 1964—, dir. Geophys. Inst., 1986—. Author: Polar and Magnetospheric Substorms (Russian edit. 1971), 1968, The Aurora: A Discharge Phenomenon Surrounding the Earth (in Japanese), 1975, Physics of Magnetospheric Substorms, 1977, Aurora Borealis: The Amazing Northern Lights (Japanese edit. 1981), 1979; co-author: Sydney Chapman, Eighty, 1968, Solar-Terrestrial Physics (Russian edit. 1974); editor: Dynamics of the Magnetosphere, 1979; co-editor: Physics of Auroral Arc Formation, 1980—, The Solar Wind and the Earth, 1987; editorial bd.: Planet and Earth Sci; co-editor: Space Sci. Revs. Recipient Chapman medal Royal Astron. Soc., 1976, award Japan Acad., 1977; named Disting. Alumnus U. Alaska, 1980, Centennial Alumnus Nat. Assn. State Univs. and Land Grant Colls., 1987. Fellow Am. Geophys. Union (John Adam Fleming medal 1977); mem. AAAS, Sigma Xi.

AKAU, RONALD LEIALOHA, mechanical engineer; b. Honolulu, May 30, 1955; s. Samuel Kawehi and Agnes Kealohaokalani (Kamakawiwoole) A.; m. Laurie Ann Misako Shirai, Aug. 16, 1980; children: Melanie, Stephanie, Christen. BS in Engring., Loyola Marymount U., 1977; MS in Mech. Engring., Purdue U., 1980, PhD, 1983. Jr. engr. WED Enterprises, L.A., 1977; rschr. Westinghouse, West Lafayette, Ind., 1980; sr. mem. tech. staff Sandia Nat. Labs., Albuquerque, 1984—. Welding Found. award, 1981. Mem. AIAA, ASME, Inst. Environ. Scis. Office: Sandia Nat Labs PO Box 5800 Div 1513 Albuquerque NM 87185

AKBARIAN, S.R., management consultant; b. Abadan, Khuzestan, Iran, May 20, 1953; came to U.S., 1969; s. Ramezan and Mahin (Gachpazany) A.; m. Joni Louise Stump, Nov. 1, 1980; 1 child, Katayun Alexandra. BA, Westminster Coll., 1976, BS, 1977; M of Internat. Mgmt., Am. Grad. Sch. Internat. Mgmt., Glendale, Ariz., 1980. Account exec. Bonneville Rsch., Salt Lake City, 1980-84; prin. Pendar Internat., Salt Lake City, 1984—; bd. dirs. Sports Am, Salt Lake City, 1980—. Contbr. articles to profl. jours. and editor of pub. Mem. adv. bd. U. Utah Internat. Ctr., 1992—; mem. exec. coun. Westminster Coll. Alumni Assn., 1993—. Mem. Inst. Indsl. Engrs. Salt Lake City, Assn. MBA Execs.

AKELLA, JAGANNADHAM, geochemist, materials science investigator; b. Kakinada, Andhra, India, Sept. 13, 1937; came to U.S., 1965; s. Visweswara Rao and Balatripura Sundari (Gollakota) A.; m. Lalita-Vemparala, July 14, 1967; children: Anita Sundari, Sadhana Sri, Mamata Kumari. BS with honors, U. Coll. Andhra U., Vizag (A.P.), India, 1957; MS, Andhra U., 1958; PhD, Indian Inst. Tech., Kharagpur (W.B.), India, 1962. Cert. tchr., Calif. Univ. System. Sr. lectr. dept. geology Rajastan U., Udaipur, Raj, India, 1962-63; acad. exchange scholar U. Göttingen (Fed. Republic of Germany), 1963-65; rsch. assoc. UCLA, 1965-66, 67-71; fellow Geophys. Lab. Carnegie Instn., Washington, 1971-74; sr. resident rsch. assoc. NASA Johnson Space Ctr., Houston, 1974-77; sr. scientist Lawrence Livermore (Calif.) Nat. Lab. U. Calif., 1977—; petrology group leader Lawrence Livermore Nat. Lab. Earth Scis., Livermore, 1979-82; adj. prof. Calif. State U., Hayward, 1983, Chabo Coll. Valley Campus, Livermore, 1984; advisor high pressure rsch. UN Devel. Program, Nat. Geophys. Rsch. Inst. Hyderabad, India, 1986. Contbr. numerous articles to profl. jours. Treas. Hindu Community Cultural Ctr., Livermore, 1987-90, bd. dirs., 1990-93, pres., 1992-93. Named German Acad. Exchange scholar, 1963-65, sr. rsch. fellow NAS and NRC, 1974-77. Fellow Indian Mineral. Soc., Mineral. Soc. Am., Carnegie Instn. Geophys. Lab.; mem. Am. Geophys. Union. Democrat. Hindu. Home: 2667 Chateau Way Livermore CA 94550-5735 Office: U Calif Lawrence Livermore Nat Lab Livermore CA 94550

AKIBA, LORRAINE HIROKO, lawyer; b. Honolulu, Dec. 28, 1956; d. Lawrence H. and Florence K. (Iwasa) Katsuyama. BS with honors, U. Calif., Berkeley, 1977; JD, U. Calif., San Francisco, 1981. Bar: Hawaii 1981, U.S. Dist. Ct. Hawaii 1981, U.S. Ct. Appeals (9th cir.) 1981, U.S. Supreme Ct. 1986. Ptnr. Cades, Schutte, Fleming & Wright, Honolulu, 1981—; lawyer rep. 9th Cir. Jud. Conf., 1991—; mem. past treas. Hawaii Inst. for Continuing Legal Edn., Honolulu, 1987—. Chair attys. divsn. Aloha United Way, Honolulu, 1991; mem. State of Hawaii Environ. Coun., Honolulu, 1990—, chair 1992. Named one of Outstanding Young Women Am., 1985. Mem. ABA, Hawaii Bar Assn., Hawaii Women Lawyers Assn., Hawaii Women Lawyers Found. (pres. 1988-92), Phi Beta Kappa. Club: Honolulu. Office: Cades Schutte Fleming & Wright 1000 Bishop St Fl 12 Honolulu HI 96813-4212

AKIMA, HIROSHI, electronic engineer; b. Tokyo, Nov. 20, 1925; came to U.S., 1965; s. Yoshio and Chiyo (Sato) A.; m. Mieko Miyasawa, Dec. 15, 1955; children: Kiyoshi Akima, Hiroko Akima. B in Engring., Tokyo U., 1947, Dr. of Engring., 1961. Rsch. official Radio Rsch. Labs. Ministry of Posts and Telecomm., Tokyo, 1947-65; electronic engr. Boulder (Colo.) Labs., U.S. Dept. Commerce, 1965—. Author: (Japanese) America: 200 Key Words, 1991; contbr. articles to profl. jours. Mem. IEEE (sr. mem.). Home: 2880 20th St Boulder CO 80304 Office: Dept Commerce 325 Broadway ITS.N4 Boulder CO 80303

AKINS, CHIP, electronics engineer; b. Miami, Fla., Sept. 21, 1952; s. Charles Garvis and Mildred Kathryn (Bierman) A.; m. Jerri Lynn Dunnam, July 15, 1973; children: Charlton Kent, April Nicole. Avionics technician Federal Express, Little Rock, 1974-75; maint. supr. Channel 4 TV, Little Rock, 1975-76; chief engr. Ark. Radio Network, Little Rock, 1976-77; cons. various radio stas., Tex., 1977-78; chief engr. CSC Telephone, Longview, Tex., 1978-79; dir. ops. KTYL Radio, Tyler, Tex., 1980-82; dir. rsch. and devel. J.G. Assocs., Big Sandy, Tex., 1982-83; dept. supr. Ambassador Coll., Big Sandy, 1983-86; dir. electronic engring. ATC Flight Simulators, Santa Monica, Calif., 1988-90; flight simulation engr., proprietor Emulation Systems, Culver City, Calif., 1990—. Patentee in operator services, electronics and software to assist in telecommunication for the deaf. Capt. Civil Air Patrol, Little Rock, 1977; bd. dirs. Woodvale Sch., Big Sandy, Tex., 1986.

AKINS, GEORGE CHARLES, accountant; b. Willits, Calif., Feb. 22, 1917; s. Guy Brookins and Eugenie (Swan) A.; A.A., Sacramento City Coll., 1941; m. Jane Babcock, Mar. 27, 1945. Accountant, auditor Calif. Bd. Equalization, Dept. Finance, Sacramento, 1940-44; controller-treas. DeVons Jewelers, Sacramento, 1944-73, v.p., controller, 1973-80, v.p., chief fin. officer, dir., 1980-84; individual accounting and tax practice, Sacramento, 1944—. Accountant, cons. Mercy Children's Hosp. Guild, Sacramento, 1957-77. Served with USAAF, 1942. Mem. Soc. Calif. Pioneers, Nat. Soc. Pub. Accountants, U.S. Navy League, Calif. Hist. Soc., Drake Navigators Guild, Internat. Platform Assn., Mendocino County Hist. Soc. (life), Sacramento County Hist. Soc. (life), Crocker Art Mus. (life). Republican. Roman Catholic. Clubs: Commonwealth of Calif., Comstock. Contbg. author: Portfolio of Accounting Systems for Small and Medium-Sized Business, 1968, rev., 1977. Home and Office: 96 S Humboldt St Willits CA 95490-3539

AKIYAMA, CAROL LYNN, motion picture industry executive; b. Chgo., Dec. 5, 1946; d. Makio M. Akiyama and Mary (Uyeda) Maruyama; m. Peter Richard Bierstedt, Aug. 23, 1980. BA magna cum laude, U. So. Calif., 1968, JD, 1971. Bar: Calif. Atty. NLRB, Los Angeles, 1971-75, ABC-TV, Hollywood, Calif., 1975-79, So. Calif. Edison, Rosemead, 1980-81; asst. gen. atty. CBS Inc., Los Angeles, 1981-82; sr. v.p. Alliance of Motion Picture and TV Producers, Sherman Oaks, Calif., 1982-88; ind. producer and writer TV and motion pictures Sherman Oaks, 1988—. Mem. Los Angeles County Bar Assn. (chmn. labor law sect. 1981-82, exec. com. 1975-85), Phi Kappa Phi, Phi Beta Kappa.

AKOI, ROBERT, JR, cultural organization executive; b. Hilo, Hawaii, July 4, 1953; s. Robert Sr. and Rhea K. Josephine (Enos) A.; m. Hiromi Ikeda, July 4, 1978; children: Neil, Mikilani, Allen, Keilani. BS in Travel Mgmt., Brigham Young U., Laie, Hawaii, 1980, BS in Elem. Edn. with highest honors, 1985; M of Sci. Adminstrn., Cen. Mich. U., Honolulu, 1988. Music resource tchr. Keaukaha Elem. Sch., Hilo, Hawaii, 1982-83; Hawaiian village sponsor Polynesian Cultural Ctr., Laie, 1983-84, village asst. mgr., 1984-85, guest svcs. mgr., 1985-86, staff asst. to v.p., 1986-91, ops. analyst, 1991-92, mgr. eastbound guides, 1992—. Choer dir. Brigham Young Hawaii Japanese Choir, 1976-90; treas. Windward Oahu Dist PTSA, Laie, 1984-85; statistician Nat. Athletic Intercollegiat Assn., Laie, 1989-90; missionary LDS Ch., Saporro, Japan, 1973-75, bishopric, 1990. Named Best Choral Dir. Brigham Young U., 1976, 77, 84, 85, one of Outstanding Young Men Am., 1988; travel mgmt. scholar Laie Travel, 1977. Mem. Laie Community Assn., Hui Kapono Puna Aloha, Sigma Iota Epsilon. Home and Office: 55-670 B Naniloa Loop Laie HI 96762

AKSOY, ERCUMENT GALIP, economics educator; b. Nigde, Turkey, Jan. 29, 1952; came to U.S., 1978; s. Semsettin and Nezahat (Tartanoglu) A.; m. Guven Asuman, Oct. 18, 1976; children: Can Aksoy, Sinan Aksoy. BS, Middle East T.U., Ankara, Turkey, 1976; MS, Ea. Mich. U., 1980; PhD, Mich. State U., 1988. Chief of fgn. exch. The Cen. Bank, Ankara, 1976-78; instr. U. Mich., Flint, 1985, GMI Engring. and Mgmt. Inst., Flint, 1986-87; instr. Calif. State U., Pomona, 1987-88; instr. Calif. State U., Fullerton, 1988-89, lectr., 1989—. Author: The Problem of Multiple Interpretation of Ricardo, 1991; contbr. articles to profl. jours. Mem. History of Econs. Soc., Am. Econs. Assn., Western Econs. Assn. Home: 2841 N Mountain Ave Claremont CA 91711 Office: Calif State Fullerton Dept Econs Fullerton CA 93635

AKUTAGAWA, DONALD, psychologist, educator; b. Grace, Idaho, June 7, 1923; s. Fred T. and Shizue (Oyama) A.; children: Trina Bortko, Murray, Doran. MA, U. Chgo., 1951; PhD, U. Pitts., 1956. Group counselor Orthogenic Sch., U. Chgo., 1951-52; clin. psychologist Inst. Pa. Hosp., Phila., 1959-67; pvt. practice Phila., 1957—, Bellevue, Wash., 1968—; chief community services Eastside Community Mental Health Center, Bellevue, 1968-72; clin. prof. psychology U. Wash., Seattle, 1974-90. Served with

AUS, 1944-46. Fellow Am. Orthopsychiat. Assn. Office: Family Treatment Ctr 10845 Main St Bellevue WA 98004-6397

ALAMEDA, RUSSELL RAYMOND, JR., radiologic technologist; b. San Jose, Calif., Oct. 13, 1945; s. Russell Raymond and Rose Margaret (Manzone) A.; m. Gayle Evileen Allison, Feb. 16, 1969 (div. 1975); children: Lynda Rae, Anthony David. Student San Jose City Coll., 1963-65. Served with U.S. Navy, 1966-75; x-ray technician VA Hosp., Palo Alto, Calif., 1975-78; office mgr., radiologic technologist, responsible safety officer, orthopedic surgery Mountain View (Calif.), 1978—; owner, operator Ren-Tech, San Jose, 1982-87; radiologic technologist San Jose (Calif.) Med. Clinic, 1982-93. Mem. DeFrank Community Ctr. Recipient Mallinckrodt Outstanding Achievement award Mallinckrodt Corp., 1971. Mem. DAV (life), ACLU, Am. Registry of Radiologic Technologists, United We Stand Am. (formerly BAYMEC), Calif. Soc. Radiologic Technologists, N.Mex. Registry Radiologic Technologists, Am. Soc. Radiologic Technologist. Republican. Lutheran. Home: 165 Blossom Hill Rd # 76sp San Jose CA 95123-5938 Office: Orthopedic Surgery 2500 Hospital Dr Ste 7 Mountain View CA 94040

ALAN DALE, FLETCHER, operations specialist, consultant; b. Ventura, Calif., Oct. 6, 1954; s. Dale Eugene Fletcher and Clara Angie (Tyler) Lane; m. Jana Dené Barnes, Dec. 16, 1978; children: Javai Nicole, Brittany Danyel, Colby Dené. BA, U. Calif., Santa Barbara, 1976. Meat cutter M & F Packing, Carpinteria, Calif., 1976-78; dep. harbormaster Ventura Port Dist., Ventura, 1978-81; programmer Bus. Info. Systems, Ventura, 1981-86; br. mgr. Contel Bus. Systems, Ventura, 1986-88; dir. ops. Nexxus Products Co., Santa Barbara, 1988—; cons. Ojai, Calif., 1988—. Treas. PTA, Meiners Oaks, 1991, v.p., 1992. Mem. MENSA. Republican. Home: 856 Quail St Ojai CA 93023 Office: Nexxus Products Co PO Box 1274 Santa Barbara CA 93116

ALANIZ, MIGUEL JOSÉ CASTAÑEDA, library director; b. L.A., Oct. 21, 1944; s. Francisco and Amalia (Castañeda) A.; m. Mercedes P., June 7, 1980. AA, Chabot C.C., 1972; BA in Child/Human Devel., Calif. State U., Hayward, 1974; MS in Library Sci., Calif. State U., Fullerton, 1975; MS Pub. Admnstrn., Calif. State U., San Bernardino, 1988. Spanish svcs. libr. Alameda County Libr., Hayward, 1975-77; branch mgr. San Jose Pub. Libr., 1977-78, Santa Ana (Calif.) Pub. Libr., 1978-79; divsn. chief, tech. process San Bernardino (Calif.) County Libr., 1979-84; city libr. Azusa City (Calif.) Libr., 1984-92; libr. dir. Inglewood Pub. (Calif.) Libr., 1992—. With U.S. Army, 1965-71. Recipient Grad. Rsch. Fellow Clf. State U., 1974. Mem. ALA, Calif. Libr. Assn., Reforma. Office: City of Inglewood Public Library 101 W Manchester Blvd Inglewood CA 90301

ALARCON, ARTHUR LAWRENCE, federal judge; b. Los Angeles, Aug. 14, 1925; s. Lorenzo Marques and Margaret (Sais) A.; m. Sandra D. Paterson, Sept. 1, 1979; children—Jan Marie, Gregory, Lance. B.A. in Polit. Sci., U. So. Calif., 1949, J.D., 1951. Bar: Calif. 1952. Dep. dist. atty. Los Angeles County, Los Angeles, 1952-61; exec. asst. to Gov. Pat Brown State of Calif., Sacramento, 1962-64, legal adv. to gov., 1961-62; judge Los Angeles Superior Ct., 1964-78; assoc. justice Calif. Ct. Appeals, Los Angeles, 1978-79; judge U.S. Ct. Appeals for 9th Circuit, Los Angeles, 1979—. Served with U.S. Army, 1943-46, ETO. Office: US Ct Appeals 9th Cir 312 N Spring St Los Angeles CA 90012-4701

ALARCÓN, FRANCISCO XAVIER, poet, educator; b. L.A., Feb. 21, 1954; s. Jesus Pastor and Consuelo (Vargas) A. Student, East L.A. Coll., 1973-74; BA, Calif. State U., Long Beach, 1977; MA, Stanford U., 1979. Rsch. asst. Mex.-Am. Studies, Calif. State U., Long Beach, 1976-77; summer youth counselor Horizons Unltd., San Francisco, 1981; program dir. Milagro Books, Oakland, Calif., 1981-82; translator Computer Curriculum Corp., Palo Alto, Calif., 1984; Spanish tchr. San Francisco U. High Sch., 1984; lectr. U. Calif., Santa Cruz, 1985-92, Davis, 1992—; pres. Aztlán Cultural/Centro Chicano de Escritores, Oakland, 1985—. Author: (poetry) Tattoos, 1985, Quake Poems, 1989, Body in Flames, 1990, Loma Prieta, 1990, Of Dark Love, 1992, Poemas Zurdos, 1992, Snake Poems, 1992, No Golden Gate for Us, 1993, (with others) Ya vas, carnal, 1985; co-editor Chicanas y Chicanos en diálogo, 1989. Bd. dirs. La Raza/Galería Posada, Sacramento, 1993, Familia Ctr., Santa Cruz, 1990-92, Mission Cultural Ctr., San Francisco, 1986—, San Francisco Poetry Ctr., 1988—. Recipient Am. Book award, 1993, PEN Oakland Josephine Miles Lit. award, 1993, Writer's fellowship Calif. Arts Coun., 1989-90, Fulbright fellowship, 1982-83, Dorothy Danforth Compton Dissertation fellowship Stanford U., 1983; recipient First Prize 10th Ann. Chicano Lit. prize U. Calif., 1984, Palabra Nueva 2d prize U. Calif., 1983. Mem. Nat. Poetry Assn. (bd. dirs.). Home: 1712 Albion Pl Davis CA 95616 Office: U Calif Dept Spanish Davis CA 95616

ALARID, ALBERT JOSEPH, judge; b. Albuquerque, Sept. 4, 1948; s. Albert Joseph and Evelyn Sylvia (Torres) A. BA, U. N.Mex., 1970; JD, Georgetown U., 1973. Bar: N.Mex. 1973, U.S. Dist. Ct. N.Mex. 1973, U.S. Supreme Ct. 1977. Civil rights atty. U.S. Dept. Justice, Washington, 1973-74; legis. counsel to U.S. Senator Joseph Montoya, Washington, 1974-77; asst. atty. gen. Office of N.Mex. Atty. Gen., Santa Fe, 1977-80; judge. Met. Ct., Albuquerque, 1980-81; 2d Jud. Dist., Albuquerque, 1981-83, N.Mex. Ct. Appeals, Santa Fe, 1984—, chief judge, 1990-93; adj. prof. U. N.Mex. Sch. Pub. Adminstrn., Albuquerque, 1980-81; summer legal instr. U. NM, 1992; chmn. Jud. Performance Evaluation Com., 1990—. Mem. Gov.'s Com. on Disting. Svc., Santa Fe, 1984; bd. dirs. N.Mex. Coun. on Crime and Delinquency, Albuquerque, 1983-84, Albuquerque Civic Light Opera, 1989-93; mem. adv. bd. N.Mex. Law Related Edn. Project. Mem. N.Mex. Jud. Conf. (chmn. 1983-84), U. N.Mex. Alumni (bd. dirs. 1981-84, mem. appellate and dist. ct. jud. nominating commns.), Delta Theta Phi. Democrat. Roman Catholic. Office: N Mex Ct of Appeals PO Box 2008 Santa Fe NM 87504-2008

ALBANO, ANDRES, JR., real estate developer, real estate broker, engineer; b. Honolulu, Apr. 16, 1941; s. Andres Pacis and Florence (Paglinawan) A.; m. Sandra Kam Mee Ymas, Nov. 29, 1961; children: Cheryl Ann, Denise Lynn. BEE, U. Hawaii, 1965, MBA, 1972. Engr. nuclear power USN, 1965-67; elec. engr. U.S. Aviation Adminstrn., Honolulu, 1967-69, Honolulu Bd. Water Supply, 1969-79; exec. v.p. MidPac Devel. Ltd., Honolulu, 1979-84; pres. Albano & Assocs., Honolulu, 1984—. Mem. NSPE, Hawaii Soc. Profl. Engrs. (pres. 1979-80), Devel. Assn. Hawaii (pres. 1992-93), Nat. Assn. Realtors, Hawaii Developers' Coun., Rotary, Beta Gamma Sigma. Roman Catholic. Home: 748 Kokomo Pl Honolulu HI 96825-1603 Office: Albano & Assocs Inc 3322 Campbell Ave Honolulu HI 96815-3856

ALBAUM, GERALD SHERWIN, marketing educator; b. L.A., Nov. 2, 1933; s. Leslie and Edith (Elster) A.; m. Carol Joan Weinstein, Oct. 10, 1954; children: Marc, Lisa, Daniel. BA, U. Wash., 1954, MBA, 1958; PhD, U. Wis., 1962. Instr. U. Wis., Madison, 1960-62; asst. prof. U. Pitts., 1962-64; assoc. prof. U. Ariz., Tucson, 1964-67, U. Mass., Amherst, 1967-69; vis. assoc. prof. U. Hawaii, Honolulu, 1968-69; prof. U. Oreg., Eugene, 1969—. Co-author: International Marketing and Export Management, 1989, Research for Marketing Decisions, 1988; contbr. numerous articles to profl. jours. With U.S. Army, 1954-56. Fellow Acad. of Mktg. Sci. (sr., bd. dirs. 1990—); mem. Am. Mktg. Assn., Acad. Internat. Bus., Soc. for Consumer Psychology, Assn. for Consumer Rsch. Home: 720 Fair Oaks Dr Eugene OR 97401 Office: U Oreg Coll of Bus Adminstrn Eugene OR 97403

AL-BAYATI, MOHAMMED A. SULTAN, pathologist, toxicologist; b. Iraq, July 1, 1951; came to U.S. 1978; s. Sultan and Zahra (Jawad) Al-B.; m. Boshra Al-Bayati, Dec. 24, 1987; 1 child, Basma. DVM, U. Baghdad, Iraq, 1975; MVSc, U. Cairo, 1978; PhD in Comparative Pathology, U. Calif., Davis, 1989. Staff rsch. assoc. II and IV U. Calif., Davis, 1979-90, asst. rsch. toxicologist and Hammarskjold House faculty adv., 1991—; teaching asst. pathology dept. Vet. Med. Coll., U. Cairo, 1976-78; lectr. in field. Contbr. numerous articles to profl. jours.; toxicology editorial bd. Bull. Environ. Contamination and Toxicology, 1992—; patentee in field. Mem. AAAS, Am. Lung Assn., Am. Chem. Soc. Home: 150 Bloom Dr Dixon CA 95620 Office: Univ of Calif Dept ITEH Davis CA 95616

ALBEE, ARDEN LEROY, geologist, educator; b. Port Huron, Mich., May 28, 1928; s. Emery A. and Mildred (Tool) A.; m. Charleen H. Ettenheim, 1978; children: Janet, Margaret, Carol, Kathy, James, Ginger, Mary, George. B.A., Harvard, 1950, M.A., 1951, Ph.D., 1957. Geologist U.S. Geol. Survey, 1950-59; prof. geology Calif. Inst. Tech., 1959—; chief scientist Jet Propulsion Lab., 1978-84, dean grad. studies, 1984—, project scientist Mars Observer Mission, 1978—; cons. in field, 1950; chmn. lunar sci. rev. panel NASA, 1972-77, mem. space sci. adv. com., 1976-84. Assoc. editor Jour. Geophys. Rsch., 1976-82, Ann. Rev. Earth Space Scis., 1978—; contbr. numerous articles to profl. jours. Mem. bd. regents L.A. Chiropractic Coll., 1990—. Recipient Exceptional Sci. Achievement medal NASA, 1976. Fellow Mineral Soc. Am. (assoc. editor Am. Mineralogist 1972-76), Geol. Soc. Am. (assoc. editor bull. 1972-89, councilor 1989-92), Am. Geophys. Union. Office: Calif Inst Tech Mail Code 02 31 Pasadena CA 91125

ALBERT, MICHAEL ROBERT, advertising executive; b. N.Y.C., Apr. 23, 1946; s. Edward Albert and Evelyn Katheryn (Purcell) A.; m. Christina Ellen Misiura, Aug. 17, 1968 (dec. Feb. 1969); children: Rachael Anne, Max Samuel Nikolaij. BA magna cum laude in Psychology, CCNY, 1972. Sales mgr. Crestline Inc., N.Y.C., 1974-77; advt. account exec. Fairchild Publs., N.Y.C., 1977-79; account dir. Austin Knight Advt., N.Y.C., 1979-88, v.p., 1982—; bus. devel. mgr. McFrank & Williams Advt., N.Y.C., 1978-79; adj. prof. Fordham U., N.Y.C., 1983—; v.p. Davis and Dorand Advt., 1988-89, BSA Advt., 1989-91; dir. bus. devel. thompson Recruitment Advt., 1992-93; dir. mktg. Bicycle Club Casino, 1993—. Active Am. Mus. Natural History, N.Y.C., 1982—. Served to lance cpl. USMC, 1966-67. Recipient Athena Creativity award Newspaper Advt. Bur., 1983. Mem. Soc. Human Resources Mgmt., Employment Mgmt. Assn., Profl. and Ind. Rels. Assn., Western Coll. Placement Assn., CCNY Alumni Assn., Wayfarers Chapel (bd. dirs.). Home: 1816 Speyer Ln Apt 1 Redondo Beach CA 90278-4847 Office: Bicycle Club Casino 7301 Eastern Ave Bell Gardens CA 90201

ALBERT, STEPHEN F., podiatrist; b. Elk City, Okla., Mar. 20, 1950; s. Ned Frederick and Wilma Faye A. BS, Calif. Coll. Podiatric Med, San Francisco, 1973, DPM, 1975. Diplomate Am. Bd. Podiatric Surgery, Orthopedics. Pvt. practice Arvada, Colo., 1977-78, Denver, 1980-87; chief podiatric sect. Dept. Vets. Affairs Med. Ctr., Denver, 1978—; asst. clin. prof. podiatric sect. dept. surgery Sch. Medicine, U. Colo. Health Scis. Ctr., Denver, 1993—; bd. dirs. Am. Bd. Podiatric Orthopedics, Orange, Calif, 1990—. Co-guest editor: Clinics in Podiatric Medicine and Surgery, Vol. 8, 1991; contbr. articles to profl. jours. Geriatrics ednl. grantee Dept. Vets. Affairs, Washington, 1983, rehab. R&D merit rev. grantee Dept. Vets. Affairs, Washington, 1990. Mem. Am. Podiatric Med. Assn. (ednl. grant 1984), Fed. Svcs. Podiatric Med. Assn., Wound Healing Soc., Pi Delta. Office: Dept Vets Affairs Med Ctr 1055 Clermont St Denver CO 80220

ALBERT, WILLIAM CHARLES, human resource development trainer, consultant; b. Great Falls, Mont., June 17, 1941; s. William Merrill and Eva Rose (Cooper) A.; m. Bertha May Wurl, June 9, 1963; children: Jon, Lisa. BA, Ea. Washington State Coll., 1963; MSW, U. Washington, 1966; D of Social Work, U. So. Calif., 1976. Tchr. Richland (Wash.) Sch. Dist., 1963-64; social worker State of Wash., Spokane, 1964-68; asst. prof. Ea. Wash. State Coll., Cheney, 1968-70, Va. Commonwealth U., Richland, 1973-75, U. So. Calif., L.A., 1975-78; assoc. prof. Ariz. State U., Tempe, 1978-80; owner Human Svc. Assocs., Mesa, Ariz., 1980—. Author: (chtp. in book) Readings in Aging and Dealth, 1978, From Both Sides of the Desk, 1990. Mem. Mesa Leadership Tng. and Devel., 1983. Rsch. grantee Nat. Inst. of Child Health and Human Devel., 1975. Mem. Nat. Speakers Assn., Acad. of Cert. Social Workers, Am. Soc. Tng. and Devel.

ALBERTS, DAVID, mime artist; b. Akron, Ohio, Nov. 14, 1946; married (div. 1972); 1 child, Morgan Elizabeth; married (div. 1992); children: Sarah Aimee, Samantha Kaitlin Wynne. BA in Music, Kent State U., 1972; MA in Theatre, West Va. U., 1978; PhD in Theatre, Bowling Green State U., 1989. Instr. Akron (Ohio) U., 1970-71, W.Va. U., 1978, Va. Commonwealth U., Richmond, 1979-81, Calif. State U., Turlock, Calif., 1981-83, Kent (Ohio) State U., 1986-87, Bowling Green (Ohio) State U., 1987-89, San Diego Job Corps Ctr., 1991-92, S.D. Jr. Theatre, 1992—; mime artist in field. Author: Pantomime: Exercises and Elements, 1971, Guide to Mime, 1993, (play) Death By Arrangement, 1981; contbr. articles to profl. jours. Recipient Founders award Internat. Thespian Soc., 1972, Directing award Am. Coll. Theatre Festival, 1982. Mem. Internat. Mimes and Pantomimes, Assn. for Theatre in Higher Edn., Speech Comms. Assn.

ALBERTSEN, HAROLD LAWRENCE, land use consultant, retired appraiser; b. Port Chicago, Calif., July 9, 1931; s. Richard Hans Christian and Theresa Mary (Maglio) A.; m. Patricia Katherine Herrick, Feb. 4, 1951 (div. 1975); m. Judith Anne McCormick, July 10, 1982; children: Michael, Daniel, Kevin, Kelly. AA, Diablo Valley Jr. Coll., Pleasant Hill, Calif., 1963. Advanced appraisal cert., Calif. Svc. engr. Pacific Tel. & Telegaph, Walnut Creek, Calif., 1955-57; adminstrv. asst. Aerojet Gen. Nucleonics, San Ramon, Calif., 1957-67; sr. appraiser Contra Costa County, Martinez, Calif., 1967-89; ret., 1989; land use cons. A. G. Spanos, Stockton, Calif., 1990—; founder, pres. Single Hearts Inc., Danville, Calif., 1984-88. Author: One Man's Opinion, 1993; patentee quick fence, roll-a-wall. Mem. Vine Hill Sch. Bd., Martinez, 1958-59. With USN, 1951-55. Scholar U. San Francisco, 1949-50. Mem. Navy League, World of Poetry, Lions. Republican. Roman Catholic. Home and Office: 1290 Monument Pl Newcastle CA 95658

ALBIN, RANDY CLARK, record company executive; b. Pasadena, Calif., Sept. 25, 1957; s. Clark Eugene and Aileen Mary (Vrooman) A. AA, Foothill Coll., Los Altos Hills, Calif., 1983; student, Stanford U., 1984; BA, Menlo Coll., 1985. With Recreation Tennis, Inc., Stanford, Calif., 1986, Roberta's Personnel Agy., Palo Alto, Calif., 1988, Wollborg-Michelson Personnel, Palo Alto, Calif., 1988; pres., chief exec. officer Randall Record Co., Los Altos, Calif., 1988—. Mem. Foothill Coll. Alumni Assn. (bd. dirs. 1986—), Menlo Coll. Alumni Assn. (treas. 1988). Home and Office: PO Box 920 Los Altos CA 94023-0920

ALBINO, JUDITH E. N., university president; b. Jackson, Tenn.; m. Salvatore Albino; children: Austin, Adrian. BJ, U. Tex., 1967, PhD, 1973. Mem. faculty sch. dental medicine SUNY, Buffalo, 1972-90, assoc. provost, 1984-87, dean sch. arch. and planning, 1987-89, dean grad. sch., 1989-90; v.p. acad. affairs and rsch, dean system grad. sch. U. Colo., Boulder, 1990-91, pres., 1991—. Contbr. articles to profl. jours. Acad. Adminstrn. fellow Am. Coun. on Edn., 1983; grantee NIH. Fellow APA (treas., bd. dirs.); mem. Behavioral Scientists in Dental Rsch. (past pres.), Am. Assn. Dental Rsch. (bd. dirs.). Office: U Colo Office of President 914 Broadway Boulder CO 80309

ALBRECHT, ALBERT PEARSON, electronics engineer, consultant; b. Bakersfield, Calif., Aug. 23, 1920; s. Albert Waldo and Elva (Shuck) A.; m. Muriel Elizabeth Grenell, June 15, 1942 (dec. Apr. 1943); m. Edith J. Dorner, July 18, 1944. BSEE, Calif. Inst. Tech., 1942; MSEE, U. So. Calif., L.A., 1947. Registered profl. engr., Calif. Rsch. assoc. radiation lab. MIT, Cambridge, Mass., 1942-43; chief engr. Gilfillan Bros., L.A., 1943-58; v.p. Space Gen. Corp., El Monte, Calif., 1958-68; exec. v.p. Telluran Cons., Santa Monica, Calif., 1968-72; dir. systems evaluation Office of Asst. Sec. of Def. for Intelligence, Washington, 1972-76; assoc. adminstr. FAA, Washington, 1976-86; cons., prin. AP Albrecht-Cons., Alexandria, Va., 1986—; mem. exec. bd. RADIO Tech. Commn. for Aeronautics, Washington, 1980-86; mem. aeronautics adv. com. NASA, Washington, 1980-90. Co-author: Electronic Designers Handbook-Design Compendium, 1957, 2d edit., 1974. Fellow AIAA (adv. com. Aerospace Am. 1984—), IEEE (Engr. Mgr. of the Yr. 1989). Home and Office: 243 Garden Bellingham WA 98225

ALBRECHT, ALEXANDER JOSEPH, development executive; b. West New York, N.J., Apr. 14, 1946; s. Alexander J. and Helen E. (Kilventon) A. BA, Cornell U., 1968; MBA, Fairleigh Dickinson U., 1972. Project devel. mgr. Boise (Idaho) Cascade Corp., 1980-89, Bechtel Group, San Francisco, 1990—; v.p., dir. Missisquoi Assocs., Brattleboro, Vt., 1988-90. Ltjg. USNR, 1968-70. Home: 3524 Broderick St San Francisco CA 94123 Office: Bechtel Group 50 Beale St San Francisco CA 94105

ALBRECHT, DUANE TAYLOR, veterinarian; b. Sioux City, Iowa, Nov. 7, 1927; s. Carl Frederick Albrecht and Mildred Ida (Taylor) Chapin; m. Elinor Gaylord, Mar. 22, 1952; children: Steven Gaylord, Stanley Taylor, Susan Elaine Albrecht O'Neil, Duane Taylor Jr. DVM, Iowa State U., 1950. Intern Angell Meml. Animal Hosp., Boston, 1950-51; instr. Iowa State U., Ames, 1951-52; founding pres. Aspenwood Animal Hosp., P.C., Denver, 1952—; sec. Colo. State Bd. Vet. Medicine, 1970-80; pres. Am. Assn. Vet. State Bds., 1975-76; mem. Nat. Bd. Vet. Medicine, 1973-87, chmn. com. 1980-81; mem. Ednl. Commn. Fgn. Vet. Grads.; bd. dirs. Citizens Bank of Glendale. Designer Aspenwood Animal Hosp., P.C., 1976 (Design Merit award Vet. Econs. Jour.); contbr. articles to profl. jours. Sponsor Vet. Explorer Scout Post Boy Scouts Am.; endowment fund bd. dirs. Colo. State U. Coll. Vet. Medicine and Biomed. Scis., 1985-88; alumni advisor Beta Theta Pi, U. Denver, 1955-56. Recipient Stange award meritorius svc. vet. medicine Iowa State U., 1982, Disting. Svc. award Ohio Vet. Med. Assn., 1984, Centennial Merit award U. Pa. Sch. Vet. Medicine, 1984. Mem. Nat. Acad. Practice in Vet. Medicine (Disting. Practitioner 1986—), AVMA (dist. IX rep., exec. bd. 1978-82, pres. 1983-84), Colo. Vet. Med. Assn. (rep. bd. control 1958-60, named Vet. of Yr. 1980), Denver Area Vet. Med. Soc. (life, pres. 1956-57), Am. Animal Hosp. Assn. (Outstanding Svc. award region IV 1980), Flying Vets Assn. Am. Vet. Dental Soc., Iowa State U. Alumni Assn. (pres. 1957, Svc. award 1958), Shriners, Rotary, Denver Athletic Club, Cherry Hills Country Club, Phi Zeta. Republican. Presbyterian. Home: 9 Huntwick Ln Englewood CO 80110-7110 Office: Aspenwood Animal Hosp PC 1290 S Colorado Blvd Denver CO 80222-2904

ALBRECHT, MAUREEN ANN, coroner, funeral director; b. Neptune, N.J., Nov. 7, 1952; d. David Ring and Geraldine Ruth (Pritchard) A.; m. Richard David Johnson, Oct. 31, 1986; 1 stepchild, Michelle Dolan Johnson. AS, Mercer County Community Coll., 1982; BS, Calif. State U., L.A., 1989. Funeral dir., embalmer Turner Stevens Mortuary, Pasadena, Calif., 1983-85; forensic technician Orange County Sheriff Coroner, Santa Ana, Calif., 1985-88, dep. coroner, 1988—; rec. sec. Coast Guard Aux., Sierra Madre, Calif., 1985-86, Animal Hosp. Asst. Assn., Newark, 1972-74; animal technician Millar Animal Hosp., Deal, N.J., 1968-78; pharmacy technician Parkwarner Drugs, Neptune, 1971-76; apprientice emblamer Johnson Funeral Home, Wall, N.J., 1980-82. Block parent Block Watch, Arcadia, Calif., 1985; recorder election bd., Arcadia, 1988. Roman Catholic. Office: Orange County Sheriff Coroner 1071 W Santa Ana Blvd Santa Ana CA 92703-3927

ALBRIGHT, LOIS, operetta company executive director; b. Elwood, Ind., May 17, 1904. Student, Chgo. Musical Coll., Berlin Conservatory (scholar), Vienna Conservatory. Concertmaster Nashville Symphony; 1st violinist Gary String Ensemble, 1935; condr. Opera in the Parks, Chgo., Harding U. Choir, South Music Festival, Chgo. Music Festival, Phoenix Symphonic Choir, Phoenix Opera Assn., 1948-53, Ariz. Music Drama Guild, 1954, others; tchr. voice Glendale Community Coll., Phoenix, 1964-72; chmn. music dept. Harding U., Ark., 1935-40; founder, artistic dir. Phoenix Opera Assn., Inc.; exec. dir. Phoenix Oratorio, Opera Singers; lectr. on Hopi lore throughout U.S. to museums, univs., high schs., others; pianist, first concert at age four; concerts in Midwest; soloist with mem. Chgo. Symphony Orch. Hall; tours throughout U.S.; violinist, concerts throughout Midwest; played many chamber music concerts throughout Midwest and East coast; mem. Chgo. Women's Symphony; compositions include Psalm 99, S.A.T.B. with soprano obbligato, Psalm 136, S.A.T.B. with piano, Isaiah 62, S.A.T.B. tenor, mezzo and soprano solos with piano, Revelation 22, S.A.T.B. soprano, tenor mezzo and soprano solos with piano, Psalm 45, soprano or tenor solo, with piano, others; coach Opera for Chgo. Opera Co.; tchr. voice Chgo., Los Angeles, Phoenix, N.Y.C.; founder, artistic dir. Phoenix Opera Assn., Inc.; exec. dir. Phoenix Oratorio/Opera Singers; founder, exec. dir., Viennese Operetta Co. of N.Y., Inc., N.Y.C., 1975—, pres., condr. at Sun Dial, Sun City, Ariz, 1990; pres. Viennese Operetta Co. Am., Inc., 1989—, condr. in Sun City, 1990; condr. all performances Lincoln Ctr., toured West Coast, 1982, East Coast, 1983. Author: Saul and the Medium, 1965; composed: Hopitu, folk opera, 1955; presented: Three Opuses, 1987; condr. six performances of Viennase Operetta Co., Phoenix, Sun City, Ariz., 1992, tchr. artist students Met. Opera, N.Y.C., N.Y. C. Opera, 1991-92. Recipient award Internat. Robert Stolz Soc. of Vienna. Mem. N.Y. Singing Tchrs. Assn. (rec. sec. 1959-60), Sun City Symphony Assn. (bd. dirs.). Home and Office: 207 W Clarendon Ave Apt 10G Phoenix AZ 85013-3435

ALBRIGHT, ROBERT JAMES, electrical engineering educator; b. Silverton, Oreg., Mar. 6, 1941; s. William A. and Clara (DeConinck) A.; m. Libbi J. Gerber, Aug. 11, 1979; children: Mary Ann, Anna Marie. BSEE, Oreg. State U., 1963, MSEE, 1965; PhD in Electrical Engring., U. Wash., 1971. Registered profl. engr., Oreg. Asst. prof. electrical engring. U. Portland, Oreg., 1970-75, assoc. prof. electrical engring., 1975-81, prof. electrical engring., 1981—; chmn. elec. engring U. Portland, Oreg., 1971-86, 88-90, acting dean of engring., 1976-77; elec. engr. U.S. Army Corps of Engrs., Portland, 1978, 79, 80, Bonneville Power Adminstrn. U.S. Dept. Energy, Portland, 1991, 92. Contbr. articles to profl. jours. Mem. IEEE (exec. com. Portland sect. 1970-76), Am. Soc. Engring. Edn. Roman Catholic. Home: 3925 N Willamette Blvd Portland OR 97217-5164 Office: Univ of Portland 5000 N Willamette Blvd Portland OR 97203-5750

ALBRIGHT, WILLIAM ALEXANDER, JR., pharmaceutical company executive; b. Baton Rouge, May 3, 1957; s. William Alexander and Mary (Holeman) A.; m. Jeryl Lynn Hilleman, Mar. 19, 1988; children: Colin Maurice, Evan Minter. BS in Biology, Stanford U., 1979, MS in Biology, 1981; MBA, Harvard Bus. Sch., 1986. Rsch. asst. Crosby, Heafey, Roach & May, Oakland, Calif., 1980-81; sales rep., region mgr. GCA/Precision Scientific, Chgo., 1981-83, OEM prodn. mgr., 1983-84; bus. planning assoc. Eli Lilly and Co., Indpls., 1985; mgr. strategic planning IVAC, Div. of Eli Lilly and Co., San Diego, 1986-87, product mgr. disposables, 1987-89; dir. bus. devel. and fin. Genta Inc., San Diego, 1989—. Mem. Commonwealth Club Calif. Home: 645 Center Dr Palo Alto CA 94301 Office: Genta Inc 3550 General Atomics Ct San Diego CA 92121

ALCORN, GEORGE BENNETT, agricultural economics and administration consultant; b. Englewood, Colo., Apr. 12, 1910; s. Charles and Anna Victoria (Oberg) A.; m. Ragnhild Christine Johnson, July 29, 1932 (dec. Oct. 1959); children: James Leigh, David George; m. Marie Olivia Johnson, Dec. 6, 1963. BS, U. Calif., Berkeley, 1936, MS, 1937; DPA, Harvard U., 1955. Agrl. economist Agrl. Extension U. Calif., Berkeley, 1937-56, dir., 1956-75; chmn. Walnut Control Bd., San Mateo, Calif., 1966-83; cons. A.I.D., Washington, 1973—, World Bank, Washington, 1976—. Mem. Commonwealth Club Calif., Rotary. Republican. Presbyterian. Home: 4653 Malabar Ave Castro Valley CA 94546-2311

ALDANA, CARL, artist, film design, illustration; b. Guatemala, Guatemala, Sept. 26, 1938; came to U.S. 1944.; s. Bertha (Carillo) L.; m. Susan Ann finch, Dec. 13, 1973; children: Davis, Casy Dare. Designer free lance, San Diego, 1966-73, San Francisco, 1966-68; freelance designer L.A., 1966—; univ./coll. Calif. State U. Long Beach, Fullerton, Calif., 1974-78; art dir./illustrator Feature Motion Pictures, Hollywood, 1977—; guest lecturer Calif. State U. Long Beach, Santa Monica Coll., Local Sch. Dist., 1980—. Exhibitor of fine paintings San Diego Mus. Art. Recipient Gold Medal, Award of Merit, Second Place, Soc. of Illus., N.Y.. Mem. Acad. Motion Picture Arts and Sci., I.A.T.S.E. #790 Illus., Navy Combat Artist Inactive, Air Force Artist Inactive, Soc. of Illus., L.A. Inactive.

ALDER, DOUGLAS DEXTER, college president, historian; b. Salt Lake City, Nov. 10, 1932; s. Linden Benson and Georgia (Payzant) A.; m. Elaine Reiser, Dec. 20, 1958; children: Scott, Elise, Nathan, Linden. BA, U. Utah, 1957, MA, 1959; PhD, U. Oreg., 1966. Instr., asst. prof., assoc. prof. history Utah State U., Logan, 1963-70, prof., 1970-86, dir. NDEA History Inst., 1965-67, dir. experienced tchr. fellowship program, 1967-70, assoc. dir. for instrnl. devel., 1969-74, dir. honors program, 1974-86; pres. Dixie Coll., St. George, Utah, 1986-93, prof. history, 1993—; Danforth assoc., 1971-83; mem. nat. adv. bd. History Tchr., 1976-85; former mem. coms. Nat. Coun. for Social Studies; former mem. task groups Social Sci. Edn. Consortium, Boulder, Colo, now mem. bd. dirs.; mem. accrediation teams Nat. Coun. for Accrediating Tchr. Edn. Mem. bd. editors Dialogue: Jour. Mormon Thought, 1967-70, 83-93; contbr. numerous articles to profl. publs. Chmn. for Logan City, U.S. Bicentennial, 1976; bd. dirs. Utah Endowment for Humanities, Salt Lake City, 1981—, vice chmn., 1982-83, chmn., 1984-86. Named Prof. of Yr., Utah State U., 1967; recipient Outstanding Faculty award Assoc. Students Utah State U., 1981, gov.'s award in humanities State of Utah, 1991; Fulbright scholar U. Vienna, Austria, 1962-63, U. Bonn, Germany, 1980. Mem. Utah Hist. Soc. (bd. dirs.), Western Assn. for German Studies (awards com. 1981), Mormon History Assn. (pres. 1977-78, chmn. awards com. 1981-84). Republican. Mem. LDS Ch. Office: Office of Pres Dixie Coll Saint George UT 84770

ALDER, HENRY LUDWIG, mathematics educator; b. Duisburg, Fed. Republic Germany, Mar. 26, 1922; came to U.S., 1941; s. Ludwig and Otti (Gottschalk) A.; m. Benne B. Daniel, Apr. 8, 1963; 1 child, Lawrence J. AB in Chemistry and Math., U. Calif., Berkeley, 1942, PhD in Math., 1947. Instr. U. Calif., Berkeley, 1947-48; instr. U. Calif., Davis, 1948-49, asst. prof., 1949-55, assoc. prof., 1955-65, prof. math., 1965—, chmn. dept. math., 1992—; mem. Calif. State Bd. Edn., Sacramento, 1982-85. Author: (with Edward B. Roessler) Introduction to Probability and Statistics, 1960; contbr. articles to profl. jours. Served with USAF, 1944-45. Recipient Cert. of Merit, Nat. Council Tchrs. Maths., 1975. Mem. Math. Assn. Am. (sec. 1960-75, pres. 1977-78, Lester R. Ford award 1970, Disting. Svc. to Math. award 1980), Am. Math. Soc., Coun. Sci. Soc. Pres.'s (chmn. 1980), Mu Alpha Theta (pres. 1956-59, Internat. Disting. Svc. award 1965). Home: 724 Elmwood Dr Davis CA 95616-3517 Office: U Calif Dept Math Davis CA 95616

ALDERETTE, ROBERT, painter, art educator; b. L.A., July 19, 1943. BA, Calif. State U., Long Beach, 1968; MA, MFA, Claremont Grad. Sch., 1971. Painting and drawing prof. Golden West Coll., Huntington Beach, Calif., 1971-84; assoc. prof. painting U. So. Calif., L.A., 1984—. Painting award NEA, 1984.

ALDERMAN, MINNIS AMELIA, psychologist, educator, small business owner; b. Douglas, Ga., Oct. 14, 1928; d. Louis Cleveland Sr. and Minnis Amelia (Wooten) A. AB in Music, Speech and Drama, Ga. State Coll., Milledgeville, 1949; MA in Supervision and Counseling Psychology, Murray State U., 1960; postgrad. Columbia Pacific U., 1987—. Tchr. music Lake County Sch. Dist., Umatilla, Fla., 1949-50; instr. vocal and instrumental music, dir. band, orch. and choral Fulton County Sch. Dist., Atlanta, 1950-54; instr. English, speech, debate, vocal and instrumental music, dir. drama, band, choral and orch. Elko County Sch. Dist., Wells, Nev., 1954-59; tchr. English and social studies Christian County Sch. Dist., Hopkinsville, Ky., 1960; instr. psychology, counselor critic prof. Murray (Ky.) State U., 1961-63, U. Nev., Reno, 1963-67; owner Minisizer Exercising Salon, Ely, Nev., 1969-71, Knit Knook, Ely, 1969—, Minimimeo, Ely, 1969—, Gift Gamut, Ely, 1977—; prof. dept. fine arts Wassuk Coll., Ely, 1986-91, assoc. dean, 1986-87, dean, 1987-90; counselor White Pine County Sch. Dist., Ely, 1960-68; dir. Child and Family Ctr., Ely Indian Tribe, 1988—, Family and Community Ctr., Ely Shoshone Indian Tribe, 1989—; adv. Ely Shoshone Tribal Youth Coun., 1990—, Budge Stanton Meml. Scholarship, 1991—, Budge Stanton Meml. Living Mus. and Cultural Ctr., 1991—; fin. aid contracting officer Ely Shoshone Tribe, 1990—; supr. testing Ednl. Testing Svc., Princeton, N.J., 1960-68, Am. Coll. Testing Program, Iowa, 1960-68, U. Nev., Reno, 1960-68; chmn. bd. White Pine Sch. Dist. Employees Fed. Credit Union, Ely, 1961-69; psychologist mental hygiene div. Nev. Pers., Ely, 1969-75, dept. employment security, 1975-80; sec.-treas. bd. dirs. Gt. Basin Enterprises, Ely, 1969-71; speaker at confs. Pvt. instr. piano, violin, voice and organ, Ely, 1981—; bd. dirs. band Sacred Heart Sch., Ely, 1982—. Author various news articles, feature stories, pamphlets, handbooks and grants in field. Pres. White Pine County Mental Health Assn., 1960-63, 78—; mem. Gov.'s Mental Health State Commn., 1963-65, Ely Shoshone Tribal Youth Camp, 1991-92, Elys Shoshone Tribal Unity Conf., 1991-92, Tribal Parenting Skills Coord., 1991; bd. dirs. White Pine County Sch. Employees Fed. Credit Union, 1961-68, pres., 1963-68; 2d v.p. White Pine Community Concert Assn., 1965-67, pres., 1967, 85—, treas., 1975-79, dr. chmn., 1981-85; chmn. of bd., 1984; bd. dirs. White Pine chpt. ARC, 1978-82; mem. Nev. Hwy. Safety Leaders Bd., 1979-82; mem. Gov.'s Commn. on Status Women, 1968-74, Gov.'s Nevada State Juvenile Justice Adv. Commn., 1992—, White Pine Overall Econ. Devel. Plan Coun., 1992—; sec.-treas. White Pine Rehab. Tng. Ctr. for Retarded Persons, 1973-75; mem. Gov.'s Commn. on Hwy. Safety, 1979-81, Gov's. Juvenile Justice Program, White Pine County Juvenile Problems Cabinet; dir. Ret. Sr. Vol. Program, 1973-74; vice chmn. Gt. Basin Health Coun., 1973-75, Home Extension Adv. Bd., 1977-80; sec.-treas. Great Basin chpt. Nev. Employees Assn.; bd. dirs. United Way, 1970-76; vice chmn. White Pine Coun. on Alcoholism and Drug Abuse, 1975-76, chmn., 1976-77; grants author 3 yrs. Indian Child Welfare Act, originator Community Tng. Ctr. for Retarded People, 1972, Ret. Sr. Vol. Program, 1974, Nutrition Program for Sr. Citizens, 1974, Sr. Citizens Ctr., 1974, Home Repairs for Sr. Citizens, 1974, Sr. Citizens Home Assistance Program, 1977, Creative Crafters Assns., 1976, Inst. Current World Affairs, 1989, Victims of Crime, 1990-92; bd. dirs. Family coalition, 1990-92, Sacred Heart Parochial Sch., 1982—, dir. band, 1982—; candidate for diaconal ministry, 1982—; dir. White Pine Community Choir, 1962—, Ely Meth. Ch. Choir, 1960-84; choir dir., organist Sacred Heart Ch., 1984—. Precinct reporter ABC News 1966; speaker U.S. Atty. Gen. Conf. Bringing Nev. Together. Fellow Am. Coll. Musicians, Nat. Guild Piano Tchrs.; mem. NEA (life), Nat. Fedn. Ind. Bus. (dist. chair 1971-85, nat. guardian coun. 1985—, state guardian coun.ells br. 1957-58, pres. White Pine br. 1965-66, 86-87, 89-91, bd. dirs. 1965-87, rep. edn. 1965-67, implementation chair 1967-69, area advisor 1969-73, 89-91), Nat. Fedn. Bus. and Profl. Women (1st v.p. Ely chpt. 1965-66, pres. Ely chpt. 1966-68, 74-76, 85—, bd. dirs. Nev. chpt. 1966—, 1st v.p. Nev. Fedn. 1970-71, pres. Nev. chpt. 1972-73, nat. bd. dirs. 1972-73), Mensa (supr. testing 1965—), Delta Kappa Gamma (br. pres. 1968-72, state bd. 1967—, chpt. parliamentarian 1974-78, state 1st v.p. 1967-69, state pres. 1969-71, nat. bd. 1969-71, state parliamentarian 1971-73), White Pine Knife and Fork Club (1st v.p. 1969-70, pres. 1970-71, bd. dirs. 1979—). Home: 945 Avenue H PO Box 150457 East Ely NV 89315-0457 Office: Ely Shoshone Tribe 16 Shoshone Cir Ely NV 89301-2055 also: 1280 Avenue F East Ely NV 89315

ALDERSON, JAMES MICHAEL, social worker; b. Englewood, Calif., Feb. 8, 1947; s. James Raymond and Maltrude Marie (Medchior) A.; m. Barbara Gwyn Cloyd, Sept. 7, 1968 (div. 1993); children: James H., Peter David. BS in Social Work, Mt. Angel Coll., 1970; MSW, U. Utah, 1972. Lic. clin. social worker, Oreg. Pvt. practice clin. social worker Salem, Oreg., 1980—. Contbr. articles to Man! mag., 1991, to book The Best Man, 1992. Chair Marion County Mental Health Bd., Salem, 1977-79; chair social work region I, Nat. Assn. Mental Deficiency, 1980-83. Mem. NASW, Pi Kappa Alpha. Home: PO Box 2166 Salem OR 97308 Office: 910 Capitol St NE Salem OR 97701

ALDERSON, RICHARD LYNN, professional baseball team executive; b. Seattle, Nov. 22, 1947; s. John Lester and Gwenny (Parry) A.; m. Linda Lee Huff, Dec. 20, 1969; children: Catrin Gwennan, Bryn Garreth. B.A., Dartmouth Coll., 1969; J.D., Harvard U., 1976. Assoc. Farella, Braun & Martel, San Francisco, 1976-81; gen. counsel Oakland Athletics, Calif., 1981-83, v.p. baseball ops., 1983-93, pres., gen. mgr., 1993—; dir. Major League Scouting Bur., Newport Beach, Calif. Served to lt. USMC, 1969-73, Vietnam. Office: Oakland Athletics Oakland Coliseum Oakland CA 94621

ALDOUS, DUANE LEO, pharmacist; b. Albuquerque, Nov. 2, 1930; s. Clarence Moroni and Sarah Eunice (Robinson) A.; m. Barbara K. Kekauoha, July 21, 1955; children: Keith, Valerie, Jeffrey, Melanie, Wade. BS in Pharmacy, U. N.Mex., 1953, PhD in Chemistry, 1961, postgrad., 1962. Registered pharmacist, N.Mex. Postdoctoral fellow U. N.Mex., Albuquerque, 1961-62; rsch. chemist E.I. duPont de Nemours & Co., Inc., Kinston, N.C., 1962-68; asst. prof. pharm. chemistry Xavier U. of La., New Orleans, 1968-71, assoc. prof., 1971-80, dean Coll. of Pharmacy, 1973-79; rsch. assoc. Nat. Ctr. for Health Svcs. Rsch., Silver Spring, Md., 1979-80; prof. pharm. chemistry Xavier U. of La., New Orleans, 1980-90; dir. Nu Skin Labs., Provo, Utah, 1990—. Contbr. to book: Pyridazines, 1972. Bishop LDS Ch., Metairie, La., 1978-87. With U.S. Army, 1953-56. Named Outstanding Educator Ciba-Geigy Pharm. Co., New Orleans, 1988. Mem. Soc. Cosmetic Chemists, Am. Chem. Soc., Sigma Xi. Office: Nu Skin Internat Inc 1 Nu Skin Plaza Provo UT 84601

ALDRETE, LORI JOHNSON, communications and public relations executive, television director; b. Portland, Oreg., Apr. 20, 1946; d. Carlock E. and Helen A. (Hatz) J.; m. Al Aldrete, May 14, 1977; children: Al, Michelle. BA in Mass Communications, Mich. State U., 1968; MBA, Calif. State U., 1983. News talent Sta. KHBV-TV, Las Vegas, Nev., 1968; producer, dir. Sta. WTVN-TV, Columbus, Ohio, 1968-72, Sta. KTVK-TV, Phoenix, 1972-73, Sta. KGTV-TV, San Diego, 1973-76; staff dir. Sta. KNBC-TV, Burbank, Calif., 1976-77; cooperative mgr. Davis (Calif.) Community Cable Cooperative, 1983-86; dir. mktg., devel. Sutter Davis (Calif.) Hosp., 1986-89; v.p. communications Calif. Assn. of Hosps. and Health Systems, 1989-91, v.p. pub. affairs, 1991—; Bd. dirs Davis Community TV, 1988—. Mem. Davis Sch. Arts Found., 1986, 87, City of Davis Econ. Devel. Study Com., 1986, Mental Health Assn. of Yolo County, 1987. Recipient Silver Halo award So. Calif. Motion Picture Council, 1977, Gold Achievement award Acad. for Health Svcs. Mktg. Mem. Nat. Acad. TV Arts and Scis., Dirs. Guild Am., Am. Coll. Healthcare Mktg., Am. Hosp. Assn. Pub. Rels. Execs., Internat. Assn. Bus. Communicators, Radio & TV News Dirs. Assn., Calif. Newspaper Pubs. Assn., No. Calif. Soc. for Healthcare Pub. Relations and Mktg., Am. Soc. Health Care Mktg. and Pub. Relations, Pub. Relations Soc. Am., Davis C. of C. (chmn. health com. 1987-89), Sacramento Press Club.

ALDRICH, DANIEL EUGENE, small business owner; b. Colony, Kans., May 26, 1954; s. Harold Eugene and Dorothy May (Connor) A.; m. Sandra May Lindsay, Aug. 16, 1972 (div. 1976); children: Latisha Ilean, Blain Dean, Paula L., Amber Dove; m. Donna L. Audet, Mar. 15, 1977 (div. Apr. 1979). AA, Big Bend C.C., 1979; student, Ea. Wash. U., 1981-83. With Bunker Hill Mines, Kellogg, Idaho, 1972-74; prin. Aldrich Inc., South Beach, Oreg., 1988—. Vol. Lincoln County Food Share, Newport, Oreg., 1988-90. With U.S. Army, 1974-76. Mem. ABATE of Oreg. Republican. Methodist. Home and Office: 11628 SE Birch St South Beach OR 97366

ALDRICH, DAVID LAWRENCE, public relations executive; b. Lakehurst Naval Air Sta., N.J., Feb. 21, 1948; s. Clarence Edward and Sarah Stiles (Andrews) A.; m. Benita Susan Massler, Mar. 17, 1974. BA in Communications, Calif. State U.-Dominguez Hills, 1976. Pub. info. technician City of Carson (Calif.), 1973-77; pub. rels. dir./adminstrv. asst. Calif. Fed. Savs., L.A., 1977-78; v.p., group supr. Hill & Knowlton, L.A., 1978-81; v.p., mgr. Ayer Pub. Rels. western div. N.W. Ayer, L.A., 1981-84; pres. Aldrich and Assocs. Inc., L.A., 1984—; bd. dirs. Drum Corps Internat. With USAF, 1968-72. Mem. L.A. Athletic Club. Democrat. Home: 25 15th Pl Unit 704 Long Beach CA 90802-6061 Office: Aldrich & Assocs 110 Pine Ave Ste 510 Long Beach CA 90802-4422

ALDRICH, J. WINTHROP, engineering educator, consultant; b. Woodbury, Conn., Sept. 26, 1944; s. John W. and Dorothy (Dizney) A.; m. Carole A. Mehlig, June 17, 1967; 1 child, Elliott Fournier. BSME, Rensselaer Poly. Inst., 1966; MS in Engring., Brown U., 1968, PhD, 1971. Registered profl. engr., Mass. Asst. prof. coll. engring. Boston U., 1969-73; sr. rsch. engr. Am. Optical Corp., Southbridge, Mass., 1973-76; prin. engr. sesame divsn. Polaroid Corp., Norwood, Mass., 1976-78, engring. mgr. sesame divsn., 1978-82, plant mgr. sesame divsn., 1982-89; assoc. prof. Oreg. Inst. Tech., Klamath Falls, 1989-90, chair dept., 1990-91; assoc. prof. Calif. Poly. Inst., Pomona, 1991—. Co-contbr. articles to profl. jours. Advanced Rsch. Project Agy. fellow U.S. Dept. Def., 1966-68; Rsch. fellow NSF, 1968-69. Mem. Am. Soc. for Materials, Soc. for Advancement of Materials and Process Engring., Sigma Xi. Home: 1215 N Indian Hill Blvd Claremont CA 91711-3852 Office: Calif Poly Inst 13-219 3801 W Temple Ave Pomona CA 91768-4069

ALDRICH, MICHAEL RAY, organization executive; b. Vermillion, S.D., Feb. 7, 1942; s. Ray J. and Lucile W. (Hamm) A.; AB, Princeton, 1964; MA, U. S.D., 1965; PhD, SUNY, 1970; m. Michelle Cauble, Dec. 26, 1977. Fulbright tutor Govt. Arts and Commerce Coll., Indore, Madhya Pradesh, India, 1965-66; founder Lemar Internat., 1966-71; mem. faculty Sch. Critical Studies, Calif. Inst. Arts, Valencia, 1970-72; workshop leader Esalen Inst., San Francisco, 1972; co-founder AMORPHIA, Inc., The Cannabis Coop., Mill Valley, Calif., 1969-74; curator Fitz Hugh Ludlow Meml. Libr., San Francisco, 1974—. Freelance writer, photographer, lectr., cons. on drug rsch., and sociolegal reform specializing in drug laws and history to various colls., drug confs., publishers, svc. groups; cons. Commn. of Inquiry into Non-Med. Use of Drugs, Ottawa, Ont., 1973; rsch. aide, select com. on control marijuana Calif. Senate, 1974. Bd. dirs. Ethno-Pharmacology Soc., 1976-83. Calif. Marijuana Initiative, 1971-74; mem. nat. adv. bd. Nat. Orgn. for Reform of Marijuana Laws, 1976—; mem. Princeton working group Future of Drug Policy, 1990—; asst. dir. Nat. Inst. on Drug Abuse AIDS Project Menu Youth Environment Study, San Francisco, 1987-88; project adminstr. YES Tng. Ctr., 1989, program coord. Calif. AIDS Intervention Tng. Ctr., 1990—. Author: The Dope Chronicles 1850-1950, 1979, Coricancha, The Golden Enclosure, 1983; co-author: High Times Ency. of Recreational Drugs, 1978, Fiscal Costs of California Marijuana Law Enforcement, 1986, YES Tng. Manual, 1989, Methods of Estimating Needle Users at Risk for AIDS, 1990; editor: Marijuana Review, 1968-74, Ludlow Library Newsletter, 1974—; contbg. author Cocaine Handbook, 1981, 2d edit., 1987; mem. editorial rev. bd. Jour. Psychoactive Drugs, 1981—, marijuana theme issue editor, 1988; research photographer Life mag., 1984; contbg. editor High Times, 1979-85; contbr. articles to profl. publs. Office: PO Box 640346 San Francisco CA 94164-0346

ALDRIDGE, DONALD O'NEAL, military officer; b. Solo, Mo., July 22, 1932. BA in History, U. Nebr.-Omaha, 1974; postgrad. Creighton U., 1975. Commd. 2d lt. U.S. Air Force, 1958, advanced through grades to lt. gen., 1988; asst. dir. plans U.S. Air Force, Washington, 1978-79; spl. asst. to dir. Joint Chiefs of Staff, Washington, 1979-80; dep. dir. Def. Mapping Agy., Washington, 1980-81; dep. U.S. rep. NATO Mil. Com., Brussels, Belgium, 1981-83; rep. Joint Chiefs of Staff, Geneva, Switzerland, 1983-86; comdr. 1st Strat. Aerospace div. Vandenberg AFB, Calif., 1986-88; vice-CINC Strategic Air Command, Offutt AFB, Nebr., 1988-91; mgmt. cons. Sacramento, Calif., 1991—. Office: Aldridge Assocs 159 Orange Blossom Cir Folsom CA 95630

ALDRIDGE, NOEL HENRY, radiologist; b. Durban, South Africa, Dec. 19, 1924; s. Percy Verey and Isaleine (Wilson) A.; came to U.S., 1955, naturalized, 1967; M.B., Ch.B., U. Cape Town (S.Africa), 1951; D.M.R.D., Roy Coll., London, 1955; L.M.C.C., Royal Coll. Can., 1958, m. Theresa Horton, Dec. 19, 1981; children by previous marriage—Anthony Mark, Andrea Marie. Intern, Groote Schuur Hosp., Cape Town, 1951-52; asst. govt. pathologist, Cape Town, 1952-53; sr. house officer Leeds (Eng.) Gen. Hosp., 1953-55; postgrad. tng. Karolinska Sjukhusset, Stockholm, 1955; fellow Johns Hopkins Hosp., 1955, instr. radiology, 1956; asso. radiologist, instr. Victoria Hosp.-U. Western Ont., 1956-59; clin. fellow in radiology Mass. Gen. Hosp. and Harvard Med. Sch., 1960-61, assoc. radiologist, 1961-62; radiologist with pvt. group, Seattle, 1962-63; dir. dept. radiology Stevens Meml. Hosp., Edmonds, Wash., 1963—; pres. Stevens Radiologists, Inc. Diplomate Am. Bd. Radiology. Fellow Royal Coll. Physicians Can., Am. Coll. Radiology; mem. AMA, Canadian, Brit., Wash. State med. assns., King County Med. Soc., Am. Coll. Radiology, Royal Coll. Radiologists (London), Brit. Inst. Radiology, Canadian Assn. Radiologists, Johns Hopkins Radiologic Alumni Assn., Wash. State Radiologic Assn., Coll. Physicians and Surgeons of B.C., Coll. Physicians and Surgeons of Ont., Aircraft Owners and Pilots Assn., Wash. Pilots Assn., Am. Forestry Assn., Wildlife Fedn., Les Amis du Vin. Episcopalian. Club: Elks. Contbr. articles to profl. jours. Office: Stevens Meml Hosp Dept Radiology Edmonds WA 98020

ALENIKOV, VLADIMIR, motion picture director and writer; b. Leningard, Russia, Aug. 7, 1948; came to U.S., 1990; s. Michael and Stella (Alenikova) Volkenshtein; 1 child, Philip; m. Tamara Karpovitch; 1 child, Anastassia. Student, Leningrad State U., 1965-67, Leningrad Inst. Theatre, 1967-69, Moscow State U., 1969-72. Tchr. Russian lit. and french, dep. prin. Secondary Sch. 2, Moscow, 1969-72; dir. Gorky Film Studios, Moscow, 1974-78, 88-89, Odessa Film Studio, 1982-84; dir. music Ekran TV Studio, Moscow, 1979-81, dir., 1985-87; dir., pres. Aquilon Co., Moscow, 1989—; dir., owner Destiny Films, L.A., 1992—; lectr. at film showsing; mem. 1st Soviet del. of cinematographers, Cyprus, Greece. Author: The White Page, 1972, The Mysteries of a Women's Heart, 1975, also articles, poems and short stories; Dir. and writer of feature films: The Garden, 1973, The Composer Comitas, 1974, The Room of Laughter, 1975, What a Mess, 1976, There Lived a Piano-Tuner, 1979, The Adventures of Petrov and Vasechkin, Ordinary and Extraordinary, 1982, The Hooligan, 1983, The Knight, 1983, Unique, 1986, Valuable Friends, 1987, The Drayman and the King, 1989, The Time of Darkness, 1991, The Awakening, 1991, Monique, 1993; Dir. and writer of stage plays: The Locals, 1976, The Adventures of d'Artagnan, 1986, (with David Wolcomb), Peace Child, 1985, The Hooligan is Coming, 1986, The Tale of the Warrior, 1987, The Tower, 1988, White Mercedes, 1992; Screen plays include: August Weather Forecast, 1984, A Night Story, 1985, To Kill and be Alive, 1990, The Incredible Adventures of Ricky Plim, 1992, Without Past, 1993, War of Princess, 1993. Pres. Russian-Am. Art Ctr., L.A., 1992—. Recipient 1st prize for best TV film 22d Internat. Festival Children and Youth Films Gijon Spain 1984, award for best film dir.'s debut Internat. Festival TV Films Montreux Switzerland 1979, Danube prize 8th Internat. Festival Childrens' TV Films Bratislava Czechoslovakia 1985, Grand Prix Soviet Nat. Festival Youth-83 1983, Grand Prix First Moscow Film Festival of Children's Scetches 1987, prize for funniest movie 10th Internat. Festival Children's Films Moscow 1987, AFI Film Internat. Festival award L.A. 1990, Jerusalem Film Festival award 1990, Toronto Festival of Festivals diploma 1990, Moscow Internat. Film Festival award 1991; also others. Mem. Russian Film Makers, Russian Guild Scriptwriters, Russian Guild Dir., Moscow Guild Diirs., L.A. Press Club. Jewish. Home and Office: 1308 9th St Apt 8 Santa Monica CA 90401

ALEVY, DANIEL I., clinical psychologist; b. Long Beach, N.Y., May 29, 1929; s. Gabriel Moshe and Marie (Raphael) A.; children: Michael, Jonathan, Adam. BA, CCNY, 1954; PhD, Ind. U., 1960. Diplomate Am. Bd. Profl. Psychologists; lic. psychologist, Calif., Conn., N.Y. Field selection officer Peace Corps, Washington, 1964-70; psychology cons. New Haven (Conn.) Police Dept., 1969-78; chief psychologist Elmcrest Psychiat. Inst., Portland, Conn., 1979-81; asst. clin. prof. Yale U. Med. Sch., New Haven, 1969—; dir. Psychology Intern Tng., Santa Barbara, Calif., 1991—; chmn. Human Resources Ctr. Conn., New Haven, 1968. Contbr. articles to profl. jours. Bd. dirs. New Haven Halfway House, 1973-76; unit commr. Quinnipiac coun. Boy Scouts Am., Hamden, Conn., 1985-86; bd. dirs. Big Bros./Big Sisters, South Cen. Conn., New Haven, 1985-86. With U.S. Army, 1950-52, Korea, Japan. USPHS fellow Ind. U., 1955-56. Mem. APA, Sigma Xi. Home: PO Box 1745 Santa Ynez CA 93460-1745 Office: Santa Barbara County Mental Health Svcs 4444 Calle Real Santa Barbara CA 93110

ALEXANDER, BARTON, consumer products company manager; b. Toledo, Dec. 8, 1951; s. Barton and Marian (Gordon) A. BA magna cum laude, Harvard U., 1973; MSc, London Sch. Econs., 1975. Exec. dir. Toledo Coalition, 1970; policy analyst U.S. Dept. HEW, 1971-72; spl. asst. Mass. Dept. Mental Health, 1973-74; analyst/sr. policy budget analyst Colo. Gov. Office, 1975-77; acting dir. Adams Co. (Colo.) Dept Social Svcs., 1978-79, asst. dir., 1977-80, dir. program devel., 1980-83; dep. dir. to acting exec. dir. Colo. Dept. Labor and Employment, 1983-87; dep. dir. Colo. Dept. Local Affairs Govs. Econ. Devel. Offices, 1987-88; exec. dir. Jobs for Colorado's Future, Denver, 1988-89; mgr. alcohol issues Coors Brewing Co., Golden, Colo., 1990—; bd. dirs. Bacchus, Beer Inst. Alcohol Issues Working Group; cons. in field. Bd. dirs. Capital Hill Community Svcs.; mem. human resources com. St. thomas Episcopal Ch. Gates Found. Pub. Leadership fellow, 1986, Rotary Internat. fellow. Mem. London Sch. Econs. Soc. Democrat. Home: 7 Ogden St Denver CO 80218-3868

ALEXANDER, CATHARINE COLEMAN, college administrator; b. Memphis, June 23, 1934; d. John Breen and Janie Elizabeth (Cobb) Coleman; m. John David Alexander, Aug. 26, 1956; children: Catharine McKinnon, John David III, Julia Mary. BA with distinction, Rhodes Coll., 1955. Coordinator spl. events Pomona Coll., Claremont, Calif., 1969-91. Mem. Foothill Philharmonic Com., Claremont, Calif., 1969—; bd. dirs. Planned Parenthood L.A., 1986-92. Mem. Curtain Raisers Claremont Colls., KCET Women's Coun., LWV, Rembrandt Club (life), Town Club, Phi Beta Kappa. Democratic. Presbyterian. Home: 807 N College Ave Claremont CA 91711-3923

ALEXANDER, GEORGE DAVID, life insurance broker; b. Conn.; s. Nicholas M. and Penny (Angelides) A.; m. Lisa C. Alexander; 1 child, Elizabeth E. BA, U. Calif., Santa Barbara, 1981. CLU; ChFC. Ins. broker Con. Mutual, San Diego, 1982—. Mem. Am. Soc. CLU and ChFC, Nat. Assn. Life Underwriters, MIT Enterprise Forum, San Diego Bus. Venture Group, Million Dollar Round Table, Kearny Mesa Rotary Club. Office: 3333 Camino del Rio S #300 San Diego CA 92108

ALEXANDER, GEORGE JONATHON, legal educator, former dean; b. Berlin, Germany, Mar. 8, 1931; s. Walter and Sylvia (Grill) A.; m. Katharine Violet Sziklai, Sept. 6, 1958; children: Susan Katina, George Jonathon II. A.B. with maj. honors, U. Pa., 1953, J.D. cum laude, 1969; LL.M., Yale U., 1965, J.S.D., 1969. Bar: Ill. 1960, N.Y. 1961, Calif. 1974. Instr. law, Bigelow fellow U. Chgo., 1959-60; instr. internat. relations Naval Res. Officers Sch., Forrest Park, Ill., 1959-60; prof. law Syracuse U. Coll. Law, 1960-70, assoc. dean, 1968-69; vis. prof. law U. So. Calif., 1963; prof. law U. Santa Clara (Calif.) Law Sch., 1970—, dean, 1970-85; vis. scholar Stanford Law Sch., 1985-86, 92; dir. Inst. Internat. and Comparative Law, 1986—; cons. in field. Author: Civil Rights, U.S.A., Public Schools, 1963, Honesty and Competition, 1967, Jury Instructing on Medical Issues, 1966, Cases and Materials on Space Law, 1971, The Aged and the Need for Surrogate Management, 1972, Commercial Torts, 1973, 2d edit. 1988, U.S. Antitrust Laws, 1980, Writing A Living Will: Using a Durable Power of Attorney, 1988; author, editor: International Perspectives on Aging, 1992; also articles, chpts. in books, one film. Dir. Domestic and Internat. Bus. Problems Honors Clinic, Syracuse U., 1966-69, Regulations in Space Project, 1968-70; ednl. cons. Comptroller Gen. U.S., 1977—; mem. Nat. Sr. Citizens Law Ctr., 1983-89, pres., 1986-90; co-founder Am. Assn. Abolition Involuntary Mental Hospitalization, 1970, dir., 1970-83. With USN, 1953-56. U.S. Navy scholar U. Pa., 1949-52; Law Boards scholar, 1956-59; Sterling fellow Yale, 1964-65; recipient Ralph E. Kharas Civil Liberties award, 1970, Owens award as Alumnus of Yr., 1984. Mem. Calif. Bar Assn. (first chmn. com. legal problems of aging), Assn. Am. Law Schs., Soc. Am. Law Tchrs. (dir., pres. 1979), AAUP (chpt. pres. 1962), N.Y. Civil Liberties Union (chpt. pres. 1965, dir., v.p. 1966-70), Am. Acad. Polit. and Social Sci., Order of Coif, Justinian Honor Soc., Phi Alpha Delta (chpt. faculty adviser 1967-70). Home: 11600 Summit Wood Ct Los Altos CA 94022-4500 Office: U Santa Clara Santa Clara CA 95053

ALEXANDER, HAROLD EDWIN, JR., psychiatrist; b. Austin, Tex., Mar. 27, 1949; s. Harold Edwin and Elizabeth Ann (Rowe) A.; m. Doreene Mary Ward, Mar. 25, 1978; 1 child, Allyson Kendall. BS in Chemistry, U. Tex., El Paso, 1971; MD, U. Tex., San Antonio, 1977. Diplomate Am. Bd. Psychiatry and Neurology. Internship U. Tex. Health Sci. Ctr., San Antonio, 1977-78, resident, 1978-81; analytical chemist Phelps Dodge Refining Corp., El Paso, 1972-73; asst. prof. psychiatry U. Tex. Med. Sch., San Antonio, 1981-84; pvt. practice Las Cruces, N.Mex., 1984—; med. dir. S.W. Counseling Ctr., Las Cruces, 1984-87; clin. dir. Mesilla Valley Hosp., Las Cruces, 1987-91, med dir., 1992—. Contbr. articles to med. jours. Ohio State U. fellow, 1971. Mem. AMA, Am. Psychiat Assn., Am. Soc. for Adolescent Psychiatry, Am. Acad. Clin. Psychiatrists, Beta Beta Beta, Alpha Ci. Methodist. Office: 570 W Griggs Ave Las Cruces NM 88005

ALEXANDER, HENRY ALAN, academic administrator; b. Berkeley, Calif., Aug. 24, 1953; s. Ernest and Frances (Connelley) A.; m. Shelley Tornheim, Aug. 24, 1975; children: Aliza, Yonina, Yehuda. AB in Philosophy summa cum laude, UCLA, 1976; BA in Philosophies of Judaism, U. Judaism, 1977; MA in Judaic Studies, The Jewish Theol. Sem. Am., 1982; EdS in Evaluation Studies, Stanford U., 1982, PhD in Edn. and Humanities, 1985. Ordained rabbi, 1982. Instr. philosophy and edn. U. Judaism, L.A., 1983-85, asst. prof., 1985-88, assoc. prof. philosophy and edn., 1988—, from acad. coord. to dean Lee Coll., 1984—, dean acad. affairs, 1990—, v.p. acad. affairs, 1992—; program dir. Camp Young Judaea, St. Helena, Calif., summer 1973; ednl. activities coord. Hashachar/Young Judaea, L.A., 1972-74; dir. informal edn. Herzl High Sch., L.A., 1976-77; day camp dir. Encino, Calif., summer 1976; staff tng. coord. Camp Ramah in the Berkshires, summer 1981; dir. leadership devel. The Jewish Theol. Sem. Am., 1980-82; prof. edn. in residence, dir. Mador Leadership Tng. Program Camp Ramah in Calif., summers 1984, 85, prof. in residence, summers 1986, 87; vis. scholar The Hebrew U. of Jerusalem, 1982-83; vis. scholar, lectr. Sch. Edn. UCLA, 1989—; dir. Lee Coll. U. Judaism, 1986-89; editor: Religious Education, 1991—. Reviewer jour. Curriculum Inquiry, 1989, The Jour. of Moral Edn., 1987-88; editor Religious Edn., 1991—; mem. editorial bd. Educational Theory; contbr. chpts. to books and articles to profl. jours. Rsch. cons.

Commn. on Jewish Edn. in N.Am., 1989, Commn. Jewish Future Jewish Fedn. Coun., L.A., 1988-89; curriculum cons. Wexner Found. Project Stanford U., 1989; trustee Jewish Educators Assembly, 1989—; ednl. dir. Congregation Beth Sholom, San Francisco, 1978-80; chair leadership devel. program Temple Beth Am. L.A., 1986—; evaluation cons. Hollywood Temple Beth El, L.A., 1985, Bur. Jewish Edn., Sacramento, 1985. Scholar-in-residence Australian Inst. for Jewish Affairs Outlook Conf., 1991, Australian Union Jewish Students, 1992. Mem. ASCD, Am. Conf. Acad. Deans, Am. Ednl. Rsch. Assn., Am. Assn. Higher Edn., Am. Phils. Assn., Assn. Philosophy Education, Assn. Jewish Studies, Calif. Assn. Philosophy Edn. (pres. 1989-91), Farwestern Philosophy Edn. Soc., Moral Edn. Assn., Coalition for Advancement of Jewish Edn., Jewish Edn. Rsch. Network, Jewish Educators Assembly, Nat. Soc. for Study of Edn., Philosophy Edn. Soc. (program chair 1991—), Rabbinical Assembly. Office: U Judaism 15600 Mulholland Dr Los Angeles CA 90077-1599

ALEXANDER, JACK DUDLEY, III, natural resources consultant; b. Nashville, Apr. 8, 1962; s. Jack Dudley II and Linda Lee (Shackleford) A. BS, Texas A&M U., 1984; MS, Mont. State U., 1989. Ranch mgr. Caldwell Estate, McKinney, Tex., 1986-89; extension mgr. U. Nebr., Scottsbluff, 1989-90; natural resources cons. Resource Concepts, Inc., Carson City, Nev., 1990—. Editor: Drought Mgmt. Handbook, 1990; contbr. articles to jours. Mem. Soc. Range Mgmt. Home: PO Box 2408 Carson City NV 89702-2408 Office: Resource Concepts, Inc. 340 N Minnesota St Carson City NV 89703

ALEXANDER, JOHN CHARLES, editor, writer; b. Lincoln, Nebr., Jan. 25, 1915; s. John Merriam Alexander and Helen (Abbott) Boggs; m. Ruth Edna McLane, Aug. 20, 1955. Student, U. Nebr., 1933-37, Chouinard Art Inst./Ben Bard Playhouse Sch., L.A., 1937-38, Pasadena Playhouse, 1939-42, UCLA, 1945-47. Aircraft assembler N. Am. aviation, Inglewood, Calif., 1941-42; engring. writer Lockheed-Vega Aircraft, Burbank, Calif., 1942-45; prodn. mgr/actor Gryphon Playhouse, Laguna Beach, Calif., 1947-49; asst. producer/writer Young & Rubicam/ABC, Hollywood, Calif., 1949-51; editor-in-chief Grand Cen. Aircraft, Tucson, 1952-53; sr. writer/editor various cos., Calif., 1953-60; sr. editor/writer, sec. Sci. Guidance Rsch. Coun. Stanford Rsch. Inst., U.S. Army Combat Devel. Command, Menlo Park, Calif., 1962-66; editor-in-chief Litton Sci. Support Lab. USACDC, Fort Ord, Calif., 1966-70; editorial dir./sec. The Nelson Co., Film and Video Prodn., Tarzana, Calif., 1971—; editorial cons., dir. Human Resources Rsch. Office, George Washington U., The Presidio, Monterey, Calif., 1960-62; book editor The Dryden Press, Hinsdale, Ill., 1971-72; book editor/adaptor Gen. Learning Press, Silver Burdette Co., Morristown, N.J., 1972-74; contbg. editor West Coast Writers Conspiracy mag., Hollywood, Calif., 1975-77; contbg. editor/book reviewer Santa Ynez Valley Times, Solvang, Calif., 1976-77; editorial cons. to author of Strangers in Their Land: CBR Bombardier, 1939-45; participant Santa Barbara Writers Conf., Montecito, Calif., 1974, 75. Author TV play: Michael Has Company for Coffee, 1948; author radio drama: The Couple Next Door, 1951; co-author nine films for U.S. Dept. Justice: Under the Law, Parts I and II, 1973; co-author 10 films for Walt Disney Ednl. Media Co.: Lessons in Learning, Parts I and II, 1978-81; author: (with others) The American West Anthology, 1971; editorial cons. Strangers in Their Land: CBI Bombardier, 1939-45, 1990-92. Recipient award for short story, Writer's Digest, 1960, 61, Gold award, The Festival of the Americas, Houston Internat. Film Festival, 1977. Mem. Nat. Cowboy Hall of Fam, Nat. Geog. Soc., Nat. Soc. Lit. and Arts, Am. Film Inst., Western Hist. Soc., Calif. Acad. Sci., Nat. Air and Space Mus., Smithsonian Instn., Woodrow Wilson Internat. Ctr. for Scholars, Aircraft Owners and Pilots Assn., Air Force Assn., Sigma Nu, Alpha Phi Omega. Home: 23123 Village 23 Camarillo CA 93012-7602

ALEXANDER, JOHN DAVID, JR., college administrator; b. Springfield, Tenn., Oct. 18, 1932; s. John David and Mary Agnes (McKinnon) A.; m. Catharine Coleman, Aug. 26, 1956; children: Catharine McKinnon, John David III, Julia Mary. BA, Southwestern at Memphis, 1953; student, Louisville Presbyn. Theol. Sem., 1953-54; DPhil (Rhodes Scholar), Oxford (Eng.) U., 1957; LLD, U. So. Calif., Occidental Coll., 1970, Centre Coll. of Ky., 1971, Pepperdine U., 1991, Albertson Coll. Idaho, 1992; LHD, Loyola Marymount U., 1983; LittD, Rhodes Coll., 1986; LLD, Pepperdine U., 1991, Albertson Coll. Idaho, 1992. Assoc. prof. San Francisco Theol. Sem., 1957-65; pres. Southwestern at Memphis, 1965-69; pres. Pomona Coll., Claremont, Calif., 1969-91, trustees prof., 1991; Am. sec. Rhodes Scholarship Trust, 1981—; mem. commn. liberal learning Assn. Am. Colls., 1966-69, mem. commn. instl. affairs, 1971-74; mem. commn. colls. So. Assn. Colls. and Schs., 1966-69; mem. Nat. Commn. Acad. Tenure, 1971-72; dir. Am. Coun. on Edn., 1981-84, Nat. Assn. Ind. Coll. and Univs.; bd. dirs. Gt. Western Fin. Corp.; trustee Tchrs. Inst. and Annuity Assn., 1970—, Woodrow Wilson Nat. Fellowship Found., 1978—, Seaver Inst., 1992—; bd. overseers Huntington Libr., 1991—. Mem. Soc. Bib. Lit., Soc. Religion in Higher Edn., Phi Beta Kappa Alumni in So. Calif. (pres. 1974-76), Century Club, Calif. Club, Bohemian Club, Phi Beta Kappa, Omicron Delta Kappa, Sigma Nu. Office: Pomona Coll Office Am Sec Rhodes Scholarship Trust 333 College Way Claremont CA 91711

ALEXANDER, JOHN HEALY, university administrator, consultant; b. Joliet, Ill., Oct. 11, 1942; s. John H. and Mary (Pell) A.; m. Sally Ann Farnsworth, Mar. 26, 1965; children: John, James, Susan. BS, Lewis U., 1965. Dist. exec. Boy Scouts Am., Joliet, 1966-67; v.p. devel. & pub. rels. Lewis U., Lockport, Ill., 1967-71; dir. corp. rels. DePaul U., Chgo., 1971-73; v.p. devel. & pub. rels. North Cen. Coll., Naperville, Ill., 1973-79, Regis U., Denver, 1979-87; v.p. univ. rels. Loyola Marymount U., L.A., 1987—; cons. various non-profit orgns., 1980—; faculty mem. various seminars & workshops, 1980—. Contbr. articles to profl. jours. Mem. Coun. for Advancement and Support of Edn., Nat. Soc. Fund Raising Execs., Colo. Assn. Fund Raisers (pres.), Jesuit Advancement Adminstrs. (pres.). Episcopalian. Home: 2417 Elm Ave Manhattan Beach CA 90266 Office: Loyola Marymount U 7101 W 80th St Los Angeles CA 90045

ALEXANDER, KENNETH SIDNEY, mathematics educator, researcher; b. Seattle, Mar. 3, 1958; s. Stuart Murray and Elspeth (Dautoff) A.; m. Crystal Czarnecki, Aug. 21, 1982; 1 child, Glenn. BS in Maths., U. Wash., 1979; PhD in Maths., MIT, 1982. Mem. Math. Scis. Rsch. Inst., Berkeley, Calif., 1982-83; postdoctoral fellow U. Wash., Seattle, 1983-86; asst. prof. U. So. Calif., L.A., 1986-90, assoc. prof., 1990—. Editor: Spatial Stochastic Processes, 1991; assoc. editor Probability Theory and Related Fields, 1987—; contbr. numerous articles to profl. jours. Fellow Inst. Math. Statis.; mem. Am. Math. Soc., Phi Beta Kappa. Office: U So Calif Dept Math DRB-155 Los Angeles CA 90089-1113

ALEXANDER, MICHAEL K., writer, editor; b. Indpls., Apr. 10, 1961; s. David K. Alexander and Judith A. (Stich) Ralston. AS with honors, Cerritos Coll., 1991; student, Long Beach State U., 1992—. Contbg. editor DAV News, Santa Fe Springs, Calif., 1991—. Active Surfrider Found., Huntington Beach; participant Citizens Against Govt. Waste, Washington. With USMC, 1982-86. Mem. 1st Marine Divsn. Assn. Home: 8351 Littlefield St Long Beach CA 90808 Office: DAV News 5901 E 7th St Long Beach CA 90822

ALEXANDER, ROBB SMITH, JR., academic program director; b. Salt Lake City, Mar. 13, 1955; s. Robb Smith and Jane (Felt) A.; m. Cami Blau, Apr. 26, 1985; children: Nathan Spencer, Parker Thomas. BA, Weber State U., 1978. Ter. mgr. Burroughs Corp., Salt Lake City, 1978-81; dir. advt. and pub. rels. A&K Railroad Materials, Inc., Salt Lake City, 1981-84; asst. dir. devel. Weber State U., Ogden, Utah, 1984-92, dir. donor rels., 1992—. Recipient Outstanding Alumni award Weber State U., 1983. Mem. Utah Soc. Fund Raisers (bd. dirs. 1986-87), Coun. for Support and Advancement Edn., Athletic Fundraisers Am., Ogden/Weber C. of C. (pub. rels. adv. com. 1990-92), Ogden Breakfast Exch. Club, Mt. Ogden Rotary Club. Office: Weber State U Devel Office Ogden UT 84408-1008

ALEXANDER, TESSA ELIZABETH, telecommunications specialist; b. Port-of-Spain, W.I., Trinidad, Apr. 20, 1954; came to U.S., 1975; d. Wallace E. and Phyllis Theresa (Jadunath) A.; m. Mervyn A. DeFour, Oct. 17, 1974 (div. Apr. 1987); children: Duane, Sean. AS, Community Coll. of Denver, 1979; BSBA, U. Colo., 1987, M in Bus., 1992, postgrad., 1992—. Bank teller Capital Fed. Savs. & Loan, Denver, 1984-86; advt. intern U.S. West Communications, Denver, 1987; advt. cons. Hamilton Sweeney Ad Agy., Denver, 1987-88, sales mgr., 1987-89, product mgr., 1989-90, regulatory mgr., 1990—, mgr. switched svcs.; exec. v.p., founding mem. Chi Rho Mktg. Fraternity, Denver, 1987. Vol. friend Denver Girls, 1990—; team capt. March of Dimes Phonathon, Denver, 1988; polit. mktg. analyst lt. gov.'s campaign, Denver, 1986; amb. U. Colo., Denver, 1989—; chair Met. Youth Mktg. Adv. Bd., Denver, 1990—; bus. community rep. collaborative decision making com. Metro Youth Edn. Ctr. Mem. U.S. West Ski Club (pres. 1990—), Golden Key. Office: US West Communication 1801 California St Ste 2160 Denver CO 80202-2621

ALEXANDER, THERON, psychologist, writer; s. Theron and Mary Helen (Jones) A.; m. Marie Bailey; children: Thomas, Mary. B.A., Maryville Coll., 1935; M.A., U. Tenn., 1939; postgrad. Naval tng., Princeton U., 1943, Harvard U., 1944; Ph.D., U. Chgo., 1949. Asst. prof. psychology Fla. State U., 1949-54; dir. Mental Health Clinic, 1954-57; assoc. prof. psychology in pediatrics U. Iowa, to 1965; prof. psychology in pediatrics U. Miami (Fla.), 1965-66; research prof. Community Studies Ctr. of Temple U., Phila., 1966-68; dir. Child Devel. Research Ctr., 1966-69; prof. human devel., 1966-80; pres. Alexander Assocs., 1980-86; vis. scholar Hoover Instn., Stanford U., 1987—; dir. study tour human devel. programs, facilties and rsch. in govt., industry and univs. Temple U., Holland, France, Switzerland, Italy, Yugoslavia, Germany, England, Sweden, Denmark, 1969, univ. study leave for travel and writing, England, 1972, study tour in Soviet Union, 1974. Author: Psychotherapy in Our Society, 1963, Children and Adolescents, 1969, Human Development in an Urban Age, 1973, El Desarrollo Humano en la Epoca del Urbanismo, 1978, (with others) Developmental Psychology, 1980; sr. author: Psicologia evolutiva, 1984; contbr. articles to Ency. of Psychology; rsch. paper Stanford Sch. Medicine, 1989, 93. Staff of commdr. USN, World War II, PTO. Recipient cert. Gov. State of Sao Paulo (Brazil), 1977; Legion of Honor, 1979. Mem. APA (cert. disting. contbn. clin. div. 186), Am. Psychol. Soc. (charter fellow). Address: 350 Sharon Park Dr C3 Menlo Park CA 94025

ALFARO, ARMANDO JOFFROY, plastic surgeon; b. Tucson, Sept. 18, 1950; s. Armando J. and Yolanda (Joffroy) A.; m. Jill Heinrich, May 21, 1983; children: Karina, Janella, Brittany, Briana. BS in Zoology, Ariz. State U., 1972; MD, U. Ariz., 1976. Cert. Am. Bd. Plastic Surgeons; diplomate Am. Bd. Plastic Surgeons, Am. Coll. Surgeons. Intern Emory U. Affiliated Hosps., Atlanta, 1976-77, resident gen. surgery, 1976-81; resident plastic surgery U. Rochester (N.Y.), 1981-83; pvt. practice plastic surgery Tucson, 1983—; assoc. prof. surgery Med. Sch. U. Ariz., Tucson, 1983—; chmn. plastic surgery Tucson Med. Ctr., St. Mary's Hosp., Tucson, St. Joseph's Hosp., Tucson. Mem. AMA, Plastic Surg. Ednl. Found., Tucson Hand Surg. Soc., Am. Soc. Plastic & Reconstructive Surgeons, Rocky Mountain Assn.-Plastic Surgeons, Pima County Med. Assn. Republican. Roman Catholic. Office: 2304 N Rosemont Blvd Tucson AZ 85712-2139

ALFARO, FELIX BENJAMIN, physician; b. Managua, Nicaragua, Oct. 22, 1939; came to U.S., 1945, naturalized, 1962; s. Agustin Jose and Amanda Julieta (Barillas) A.; student (State scholar) U. San Francisco, 1958-59, 61-62; M.D., Creighton U., 1967; m. Carmen Heide Meyer, Aug. 14, 1965; children—Felix Benjamin, Mark. Clk., Pacific Gas & Electric Co., San Francisco, 1960-61; intern St. Mary's Hosp., San Francisco, 1967; resident Scenic Gen. Hosp., Modesto, Calif., 1970; practice family medicine, Watsonville, Calif., 1971—; active staff Watsonville Community Hosp., 1971—. Served to capt., M.C., U.S. Army, 1968-69. Lic. physician, Nebr., La., Calif. Diplomate Am. Bd. Family Practice. Fellow Am. Acad. Family Practice; mem. AMA, Calif. Med. Assn., Santa Cruz County Med. Soc., 38th Parrallel Med. Soc. of Korea, Nat Rifle Assn., VFW. Republican. Roman Catholic. Office: 30 Brennan St Watsonville CA 95016

ALFRED, LINDBERGH DAVIS, government official, lawyer; b. Tuba City, Ariz., Jan. 20, 1948; s. Johnnie D. and Lucille (Davis) A.; m. Della Jim, Nov. 23, 1985; children: Michelle, Melissa, Derrick, Dedrick. AS in Police Sci., Contra Costa Coll., San Pablo, Calif., 1968; BSPA in Law Enforcement Adminstrn., U. Ariz., 1971; JD, Antioch Sch. Law, 1976. Officer Navajo Police Dept., Tuba City, Ariz., 1971-72; hwy. patrolman Ariz. Dept. Pub. Safety, Phoenix, 1972-77; criminal investigator Bur. Indian Affairs, Tuba City, 1977-78; supervisory criminal investigator Bur. Indian Affairs, Chinle, Ariz., 1978-80, Valentine, Ariz., 1980-82, Red Lake, Minn., 1982, Window Rock, Ariz., 1982-90; special agt. U.S. Dept. Agr. OIG/I, Phoenix, Ariz., 1990—; acting dir. Indian Police Acad., Marana, Ariz., 1984. Recipient Disting. Expert award Ariz. Dept. Pub. Safety, 1972, Superior Performance award Bur. Indian Affairs, 1984. Mem. Internat. Assn. Chiefs Police, Ariz. Law Enforcement Assn., Four Corners Police Assn., Federal Law Enforcement Officers Assn., Federal Criminal Investigators Assn. Republican. Roman Catholic. Home: 16426 N 47th Ave Glendale AZ 85306-2002 Office: US Dept of Agr Office of Insp Gen-Investigations 522 N Central Ave Phoenix AZ 85004-2168

ALFREY, THOMAS NEVILLE, lawyer; b. New Braunfels, Tex., Oct. 30, 1944; s. Clarence Powhattan and Lilla Carlton (Beadel) A.; m. Rebecca Ann Fruland, June 22, 1979; children: Kimberly, Jessica. BA, Tex. Christian U., 1967; JD, U. Tex., Austin, 1970. Bar: Colo. 1970, U.S. Dist. Ct. Colo. 1970, U.S. Ct. Appeals (10th cir.) 1970. Dep. dist. atty. State of Colo., Denver, 1971-72; asst. dist. atty. 9th jud. dist. State of Colo., Aspen, 1973-74; dir. organized crime strike force Colo. Atty. Gen., Denver, 1974-75; asst. U.S. atty. Dept. Justice, Denver, 1975; assoc. Hall & Evans, Denver, 1975, ptnr., 1976—; cons. Tex. Organized Crime Strike Force, Austin, 1975; lectr. various profl. groups; mem. faculty, Nat. Inst. Trial Advocacy, Denver, 1987-88. 1st lt. U.S. Army, 1970. Mem. ABA, Colo. Bar Assn., Colo. Def. Lawyers Assn., Internat. Assn. Def. Counsel, Denver Partnership, Glenmoor Country Club (bd. govs.). Office: Treece Alfrey Musat PC 999 18th St # 1600 Denver CO 80202

ALFVÉN, HANNES OLOF GOSTA, physicist; b. May 30, 1908. Ph.D., U. Uppsala, 1934. Prof. theory of electricity Royal Inst. Tech., Stockholm, 1940-45, prof. electronics, 1945-63, prof. plasma physics, 1963-73; prof. dept. applied physics, electrical engring. and info. sci. U. Calif., San Diego, 1967—; mem. Swedish Sci. Adv. Council, 1963-67; past mem. Swedish AEC; past gov. Swedish Def. Research Inst., Swedish Atomic Energy Co.; past sci. adv. Swedish Govt.; pres. Pugwash Confs. on Sci. and World Affairs, 1970-75; mem. panel on comets and asteroids NASA. Author: Cosmical Electrodynamics, 1950; On the Origin of the Solar System, 1954; Cosmical Electrodynamics: Fundamental Principles, 1963; Worlds-Antiworlds, 1966; The Tale of the Big Computer, 1968; Atom, Man and the Universe, 1969; Living on the Third Planet, 1972; Evolution of the Solar System, 1976; Cosmic Plasma, 1981. Recipient Nobel prize for physics, 1970; Lomonsov gold medal USSR Acad. Scis., 1971; Franklin medal, 1971, Bowie Gold medal Am. Geophysical Union, 1987. Fellow Royal Soc. (Eng.); mem. Swedish Acad. Scis., Akademia NAUK (USSR), NAS (fgn. assoc.), others. Office: Royal Inst Tech, Alfvén Lab Dept Plasma Physics, S-100-44 Stockholm 70, Sweden

ALGER, DAVID TOWNLEY, religious organization director; b. Warsaw, N.Y., June 4, 1945; s. Clifton and Dorothy (Townley) A.; m. Sarah Ileene Alger, Aug. 17, 1968; 1 child, Hannah Ileene. BA, Coll. of Wooster, 1967; MSW, U. Ill., Chgo., 1971; MDiv, McCormick Theol. Sem., Chgo., 1971. Ordained to ministry Presbyn. Ch. (U.S.A.). Assoc. pastor 1st Presbyn. Ch., Grand Forks, N.D., 1971-75; pastor Riverside Presbyn. Ch., Clinton, Iowa, 1975-79; exec. dir. Associated Ministries, Tacoma, 1980—; mem. Adv. Coun. on Ch. and Soc., United Presbyn. Ch. in U.S.A., 1976-82, mem. Coun. on Ch. and Race, 1981-82; chair mission strategy and evangelism com. Olympia (Wash.) Presbytery, 1982-88; accredited visitor World Coun. of Chs., 1983; del., planner Pacific Ecumenical Forum, Hilo, Hawaii, 1990. Mem. Clinton City Coun., 1978-80; pres. Tacoma Community House Bd., 1980-88; vice-chair Tacoma Housing Com., 1991—. Recipient key to city City of Clinton, 1979, St. Francis award Franciscan Found., 1989, Disting. Citizen award Tacoma chpt. Rotary, 1989. Mem. Presbyn. Health, Edn. and Welfare Assn., Nat. Assn. Ecumenical Staff, Wash. Assn. Chs. (bd. dirs. 1980—, treas. 1991—). Democrat. Home: 4759-15th Ave NE Seattle WA 98105 Office: Associated Ministries 1224 S I St Tacoma WA 98405-5021

ALGRA, RONALD JAMES, dermatologist; b. Artesia, Calif., Feb. 23, 1949; s. Cornelius and Helena Joyce (De Boom) A.; m. Phyllis Ann Brandsma, July 31, 1970; children: Brian David, Stephanie Ann. BS in Chemistry, Calvin Coll., 1971; MD, Baylor Coll. Medicine, 1974; MBA, Pepperdine U., 1989. Diplomate Am. Bd. Dermatology. Intern Gen. Hosp. Ventura County, Ventura, Calif., 1974-75; resident in dermatology Baylor Coll. Medicine, Houston, 1975-78; pvt. practice Hawthorne, Calif., 1978-88; asst. med. dir. FHP, Inc., Fountain Valley, 1988-89, assoc. med. dir., 1990-91, med. dir., 1991-93, sr. med. dir., 1993—. Fellow Am. Acad. Dermatology; mem. Am. Coll. Physician Executives, Alpha Omega Alpha. Republican. Mem. Christian Reformed Ch. Office: FHP Inc Regional Exec Offices 18000 Studebaker Rd Cerritos CA 90701

ALHADEFF, DAVID ALBERT, economics educator; b. Seattle, Mar. 22, 1923; s. Albert David and Pearl (Taranto) A.; m. Charlotte Pechman, Aug. 1, 1948. B.A., U. Wash., 1944; M.A., Harvard U., 1948, Ph.D., 1950. Faculty U. Calif.-Berkeley, 1949-87, prof. bus. adminstrn., 1959-87, prof. emeritus, 1987—, assoc. dean Sch. Bus. Adminstrn., 1980-82, 85-86. Author: Monopoly and Competition in Banking, 1954, Competition and Controls in Banking, 1968, Microeconomics and Human Behavior, 1982; Contbr. articles to profl. jours., chpts. to books. Served with AUS, 1943-46. Recipient The Berkeley Citation U. Calif.-Berkeley, 1987. Mem. Am., Western econ. assns., Am. Finance Assn. Home: 2101 Shoreline Dr Apt 456 Alameda CA 94501-6209 Office: U Calif Barrows Hall Berkeley CA 94720

ALINDER, MARY STREET, writer; b. Bowling Green, Ohio, Sept. 23, 1946; d. Scott Winfield and McDonna Matlock (Sitterle) Street; m. James Gilbert Alinder, Dec. 17, 1965; children: Jasmine, Jesse, Zachary. Student, U. Mich., 1964-65, U. N.Mex., 1966-68; BA, U. Nebr., 1976. Mgr. The Weston Gallery, Carmel, Calif., 1978-79; chief asst. Ansel Adams, Carmel, 1979-84; exec. editor, bus. mgr. The Ansel Adams Pub. Rights Trust, Carmel, 1984-88; freelance writer, lectr., curator, Gualala, Calif., 1989—; ptnr. The Alinder Gallery, Gualala, 1990—; selector and writer biographies Focal Press Ency., 3d edit., 1993; curator Ansel Adams: 80th Birthday Retrospective, Friends of Photography, Carmel, Acad. Sci., San Francisco, Denver Mus. Natural History; co-curator One With Beauty, M.H. deYoung Meml. Mus., 1987, Ansel Adams: American Artist, The Ansel Adams Ctr., San Francisco; lectr. Nat. Gallery Art, Barbican Ctr., M.H. deYoung Meml. Mus., Stanford U., L.A. County Mus., U. Mich. Author: Picturing Yosemite (Places), 1990, The Limits of Reality: Ansel Adams and Group, 1992; co-author: Ansel Adams: An Aubobiography, 1985; co-editor: Ansel Adams: Letters and Images, 1988; contbr. articles to jours. Office: Alinder Gallery PO Box 1146 Gualala CA 95445-1146

ALISHETTI, BHOOMAIAH, engineer; b. Hyderabad, Andhra, India, Apr. 3, 1948; came to U.S., 1984; s. Kistaiah and Sattamma (Boju) A.; m. Bramaramba Jetty, June 10, 1981; 1 child, Shudhanshu. M in Tech., Indian Inst. of Tech., Kanpur, India, 1979; MS in Computer Sci., U.S.C., 1988, MS in Computer Engring., 1990, PhD, 1990. Nuclear design engr. Nuclear Power Corp., Bombay, India, 1971-84; software engr. Structural Rsch. and Analysis, L.A., Calif., 1984-90; sr. software engr. McNeal-Schwendler Corp., L.A., 1990—. Contbr. articles to profl. jours. Named David Wilson scholar U.S.C., 1981, Merit scholar Osmania U., India, 1970. Mem. Am. Soc. Mech. Engring., Associated Computing Machinery. Home: 1720 Ellincourt Dr # 7 South Pasadena CA 91030

ALISKY, MARVIN HOWARD, political science educator; b. Kansas City, Mo., Mar. 12, 1923; s. Joseph and Bess June (Capp) A.; m. Beverly Kay, June 10, 1955; children: Sander Michael, Joseph. BA, U. Tex., 1946, MA, 1947, PhD, 1953; cert., Instituto Tecnologico, Monterey, Mex., 1951. News corr. S.W. and Latin Am. NBC, 1947-49, news corr. Midwest, 1954-56; news corr. NBC and Christian Sci. Monitor, Latin Am., 1957-72; asst. prof. Ind. U., 1953-57; assoc. prof. journalism and polit. sci. Ariz. State U., Tempe, 1957-60; prof. polit. sci. Ariz. State U., 1960—, founding chmn. dept. mass communication (now Sch. Journalism and Telecommunications), 1957-65, founding dir. Ctr. Latin Am. Studies, 1965-72; vis. fellow Princeton U., 1963-64, Hoover Inst., Stanford, 1978; Fulbright prof. Cath. U., Lima, Peru, 1958, U. Nicaragua, 1960; researcher U.S.-Mex. Interparliamentary Conf., Baja, Calif., 1965, Latin Am. Inst., Chinese Acad. Social Scis., Beijing, 1986, European Inst. Def. and Strategic Studies, London, 1985, Politics Inst., Copenhagen, Denmark, 1987, U. So. Calif., 1982—; U.S. del. UNESCO Conf., Quito, Ecuador, 1960; dir. Gov.'s Ariz.-Mex. Commn., 1975—; U.S. State Dept. lectr., Costa Rica, Peru, Argentina, Chile, 1983, 88; bd. dirs. Goldwater Inst. Pub. Policy Rsch., 1989—. Author: Governors of Mexico, 1965, Uruguay: Contemporary Survey, 1969, The Foreign Press, 1964, 70, Who's Who in Mexican Government, 1969, Political Forces in Latin America, 1970, Government in Nuevo Leon, 1971, Government in Sonora, 1971, Peruvian Political Perspective, 1975, Historical Dictionary of Peru, 1979, Historical Dictionary of Mexico, 1981, Latin American Media: Guidance and Censorship, 1981, Global Journalism, 1983; co-author: Political Systems of Latin America, 1970, Political Parties of the Americas, 1982, Yucatan: A World Apart, 1980, (with J.E. Katz) Arms Production in Developing Nations, 1984, Mexico: Country in Crisis, 1986, (with Phil Rosen) International Handbook of Broadcasting Systems, 1988, Dictionary Latin American Political Leaders, 1988, (with W.C. Soderlund) Mass Media and the Caribbean, 1990; contbr. numerous articles to profl. jours. and mags. Bd. dirs. Phoenix Com. on Fgn. Res., 1975—, Ariz. Acad. Town Hall, 1981, Tempe Pub. Libr., 1974-80; mem. U.S. Bd. Fgn. Scholarships, 1984—, Acad. Coun. Goldwater Inst. of Pub. Policy, 1989—. Served as ensign USNR, 1944-45. NSF grantee, 1984; Ariz. State U. rsch. grantee, 1962, 65, 70; Southwestern Studies Ctr. rsch. grantee, 1983; Latin Am. rsch. in China grantee, 1986, World Media rsch. in Soviet Union grantee, 1989, rsch. grantee, London, 1992. Fellow Hispanic Soc. Am.; mem. Am. Polit. Sci. Assn., Western Polit. Sci. Assn., Latin Am. Studies Assn., Pacific Coast Coun. Latin Am. Studies (dir.), Inter-Am. Press Assn., Inter-Am. Broadcasters Assn. (rsch. assoc.), Assocs. Liga de Municipios de Sonora, Friends of Mex. Art, Southwestern Polit. Sci. Assn. (chmn. 1976-77), Nat. Assn. Scholars, Tempe Rep. Men's Club, Knights of Sq. Roundtable, Sigma Delta Chi. Home: 44 W Palmdale Dr Tempe AZ 85282-2139 Office: Ariz State U Dept Polit Sci Tempe AZ 85287-2001

ALKANA, RONALD LEE, neuropsychopharmacologist, psychobiologist; b. Los Angeles, Oct. 17, 1945; s. Sam Alkana and Madelyn Jane Davis; student UCLA, 1963-66; Pharm.D., U. So. Calif., 1970; Ph.D., U. Calif., Irvine, 1975; m. Linda Anne Kelly, Sept. 12, 1970; children: Alexander Philippe Kelly, Lorna Jane Kelly. Postdoctoral fellow Nat. Inst. Alcohol Abuse and Alcoholism, U. Calif., Irvine, 1974-76; resident asst. dir. div. neurochemistry, dept. psychiatry and human behavior U. Calif., Irvine, 1976; asst. prof. pharmacy (pharmacology) U. So. Calif., Los Angeles, 1976-82, assoc. prof. pharmacy (pharmacology and toxicology), 1982-89, prof., 1989—. Editorial bd. Alcoholism: Clinical and Experimental Research, 1989—; contbr. chpts. to books, articles to profl. jours. Recipient various scholarships and grants. Mem. Soc. Neurosci., Am. Coll. Clin. Pharmacology, Am. Soc. Pharmacology and Exptl. Therapeutics, Internat. Soc. Biomed. Research on Alcoholism, Research Soc. Alcoholism, Internat. Brain Rsch. Organizational World Fedn. Neuroscientists, Western Pharmacology Soc., AAAS, Sigma Xi, Phi Delta Chi. Office: Sch Pharmacy U So Calif Dept Molecular Pharmacolgy Toxicology 1985 Zonal Ave Los Angeles CA 90033-1058

ALKER, BRUCE BRADLEY, engineering research company executive; b. New Orleans, Jan. 30, 1945; s. Albert Raymond and Winifred Emily (Lilley) A.; m. Carol Jean Nelson, Mar. 3, 1966; children: Kenneth, Wendy C., Amy. AA, Santa Monica City Coll., Calif., 1964; student, UCLA, 1965-66; BS in Nuclear Engring., Calif. State U., Northridge, 1967. Tech. writer Bunker Ramo, Inc., Westlake Village, Calif., 1966-68; sr. field engr. Bunker Ramo, Inc., Westlake Village, 1968-72, applications engr., 1972-73, sr. design engr., 1973-75, engring. specialist, 1975-80, staff systems engr., 1980-81; co founder, v.p. advanced planning Alpharel Inc., Camarillo, Calif., 1981-86; chief engr. Image Engring., Thousand Oaks, Calif., 1991—; pres., founder, CEO Vista Computers Systems, Inc., Westlake Village, Calif., 1986—; cons. Autologic, Inc. Newbury Park, Calif., 1980, advisor to bd. Alpharel, Inc., Camarillo, Calif., 1982-86, chmn. of bd. Vista Computer Systems, Inc., Westlake Village, Calif., 1986—. Co-inventor: Front End Comm Processor, 1977 (Engr. Merit award 1977); inventor: Refined Mill 188-C Driver, 1978, Computer Based Drawing Mgmt. System, 1985. Cub scout leader, Boy Scouts Am., Thousand Oaks, 1975-76, asst. scout master, 1977-82. Recipient grant U.S. Navy, 1976. Mem. IEEE, Soc. for Exptl. Stress Analysis (Winner Ca. State Lab Contest 1966).

ALLAN, ROBERT MOFFAT, JR., corporate executive, educator; b. Detroit, Dec. 8, 1920; s. Robert M. and Jane (Christman) A.; m. Harriet Spicer, Nov. 28, 1942; children: Robert M. III, Scott, David, Marilee. B.S., Stanford U., 1941; postgrad. Stanford Grad. Sch. Bus., 1941-42; M.S., UCLA, 1943; postgrad. Loyola Law Sch., 1947-50. Economist research dept. Security First Nat. Bank, 1942; exec. Marine Ins., 1946-53; asst. to pres., work mgr. Zinsco Elec. Products, 1953-55, v.p., dir., 1956-59; asst. to pres. The Times-Mirror Corp., 1959-60, corp. v.p., 1961-64; pres., dir. Cyprus Mines Corp., 1964-67; pres. Litton Internat., 1967-69; pres. U.S. Naval Postgrad. Sch. Found., prof. internat. mgmt. 1969-85. Bd. dirs., advisor U.S. Naval Acad.; trustee Boys Republic, Pomona Grad. Sch., Claremont Grad. Sch., Del Monte Forest Homeowners; vis. prof. of internat. mgmt. grad. schs. of bus. MBA Stanford, Harvard, U. of Chgo., UCLA, USA and Internat. Inst. Fgn. Studies, Monterey. Served with USAF, 1942-45. Recipient award Helms Athletic Found., 1947, 49, Cross of Merit, 1976, Plaque of Merit USCG, 1990, Medal for Heroism, 1990; named Outstanding Businessman of Yr., L.A., Nat. Assn. Accts., 1966; elected to Sailing Hall of Fame, 1969; named Monterey Inst. Fgn. Studies trustee and sr. fellow, 1976. Mem. Mchts. and Mfrs. Assn. (dir.), Intercollegiate Yachting Assn. (regional dir. 1940-55), Phi Gamma Delta, Phi Delta Phi. Clubs: Newport Harbor Yacht (commodore 1962), Trans-Pacific Yacht, Carmel Valley Country. Home: 7026 Valley Greens Cir # 11 Carmel CA 93923-9520

ALLARD, ROBERT WAYNE, geneticist, educator; b. L.A., Sept. 3, 1919; s. Glenn A. and Alma A. (Roose) A.; m. Ann Catherine Wilson, June 16, 1944; children: Susan, Thomas, Jane, Gillian, Stacie. B.S., U. Calif., Davis, 1941; Ph.D., U. Wis., 1946. From asst. to assoc. prof. U. Calif., Davis, 1946—, prof. genetics, 1955—. Author books; contbr. articles to profl. jours. Served to lt. USNR. Recipient Crop Sci. award Am. Soc. Agronomy, 1964, DeKalb Disting. Career award Crop Sci. Soc. Am., 1983; Guggenheim fellow, 1954, 60; Fulbright fellow, 1955. Mem. Nat. Acad. Scis., Am. Acad. Arts and Scis., Am. Soc. Naturalists (pres. 1974-75), Genetics Soc. Am. (pres. 1983-84), Am. Genetics Assn. (pres. 1989), Phi Beta Kappa, Sigma Xi, Alpha Gamma Rho, Alpha Zeta. Democrat. Unitarian. Home: PO Box 185 Bodega Bay CA 94923 Office: U Calif Davis 133 Hunt Davis CA 95616-2322

ALLARD, THURMAN J., electrical engineer; b. U.S. Canal Zone, Nov. 15, 1959; s. George W. and Martha Cynthia (Rapp) A.; m. Heather Lorelei Ingham, Aug. 12, 1983; children: Chase Kehr, Duncan G. BSEE, U. N.Mex., 1981; MSEE, Purdue U., 1982. With Sandia Nat. Labs., Albuquerque, 1977-80, mem. tech. staff, 1980—, dept. mgr., 1990—. Mem. IEEE. Republican. Home: 13617 Crested Butte NE Albuquerque NM 87112 Office: Sandia Nat Labs PO Box 5800 Albuquerque NM 87185-5800

ALLARD, WAYNE A., veterinarian; b. Ft. Collins, Colo., Dec. 12, 1943; m. Joan Malcolm, Mar. 23, 1967; children: Cheryl, Christie. D.V.M., Colo. State U., 1968. Veterinarian, Allard Animal Hosp.; mem. Colo. State Senate, from 1982, chmn. health, environment and instn. com., chmn. senate majority caucus; mem. 102nd-103rd Congresses from 4th dist., Colo., 1991—; health officer Loveland, Colo.; mem. regional adv. council on vet. medicine Western Interstate Commn. Higher Edn.; mem. Colo. Low-level Radioactive Waste Adv. Com. Chmn. United Way; active 4-H Found. Mem. Loveland C. of C., AVMA, Colo. Vet. Medicine Assn., Latimer County Vet. Medicine Assn. (past pres.), Bd. Vet. Practitioners (charter mem.), Am. Animal Hosp. Assn., Nat. Conf. State Legislatures (vice chmn. human resources com. 1987—, healthcare cost containment com.). Republican. Methodist. Home: 1203 Jennifer Dr Loveland CO 80537-6753 Office: US House of Reps Offices of House Members Washington DC 20515

ALLAWAY, WILLIAM HARRIS, university adminstrator; b. Oak Park, Ill., Mar. 31, 1924; s. William Horsford and Helen Margaret (Harris) A.; m. Olivia Woodhull Foster, June 28, 1952; children: William Harris Jr., Ben Foster, Eve Olivia. BS, U. Ill., 1949; postgrad., U. Grenoble, France, 1950-51; MA, U. Ill., 1951; EdD, U. Denver, 1957. Traveling sec. World Student Svc. Fund, 1947-48; spl. asst. to chmn. U.S. Nat. Commn. for UNESCO, 1949; asst. to field dir. World U. Svc. attached to Internat. Refugee Orgn., Salzburg, Austria, 1951; field rep. Inst.of Internat. Edn., Chgo. and Denver, 1952-54; gen. sec. U. Kans. YMCA, 1954-57; asst. dean of men and dir. Wilbur Hall Stanford (Calif.) U., 1957-61; dir. edn. abroad program U. Calif., Santa Barbara, 1961-89, spl. asst. to chancellor, 1990—; cons. and lectr. in field; mem. ednl. assoc. adv. com. Inst. Internat. Edn., 1984-87; mem. Pres.'s Coun. for Internat. Youth Exch., 1982-85; mem. U.S. Del. to conf. on ednl. exch. between U.S. and U.K., 1970, 1974. Co-chair Peace and Justice Com., Goleta Presbyn. Ch., chair steering com. PAX 2100; mem. Nuclear Age Peace Found., Santa Barbara, Internat. Peace Rsch. Assn., Yellow Springs, Ohio; mem. Coun. on Internat. Ednl. Exch., 1961—, chmn. bd. dirs. 1978-83; past bd. dirs., hon. trustee Am. Ctr. for Students and Artists, Paris; bd. advisors Hariri Found., 1987—; exec. sec. Internat. Com. for Study of Edn. Exch., 1970—; exec. com. Inter-U. Centre Postgrad. Studies, Dubrovnik, 1988—. With USAAF, 1943-46. Hon. DHC, U. Sussex, Eng., 1992; PhD h.c. U. Bergen, Norway, 1990; DHC, U. Bordeaux, France, 1988; Hon. Dr. of U. of Stirling, Scotland, 1981; recipient Scroll of Appreciation Leningrad State U., 1989, Award for Svc. to Internat. Ednl. Exch. Council on Internat. Ednl. Exch., 1989, Silver medal U. Lund, Sweden, 1990, Alumni Achievement award Coll. Liberal Arts and Sci. Alumni Assn. U. Ill., 1990, Gold Medal of Honor of the Complutense U. of Madrid, Spain, 1991. Mem. NAFSAS, Assn. Internat. Educators (hon. life mem.), Comparative and Internat. Edn. Soc., European Assn. for Internat. Edn., La Cumbre Golf and Country Club. Democrat. Presbyterian. Home: 724 Calle de Los Amigos Santa Barbara CA 93105

ALLBEE, CARLYNNE MARIE, horsebreeder, consultant; b. Dayton, Ohio, July 1, 1947; d. Robert Gordon and Mary Louise (Thompson) Harvey. AA in Acctg., Grossmont Coll., El Cajon, Calif., 1968; BS in Acctg., San Diego State U., 1971; MBA in Govt. Relations, Nat. U., San Diego, 1980. Owner, trainer championship miniature horses Just Samwise Baggins & Parks Tonto miniature Pinto stallions, Calif., 1980—; acctg. cons. Paxton, Shreve & Hays, Inc., San Diego, 1988—; adj. prof. acctg. S D Mesa Community Coll., 1981—. Editor (newsletter) ABCSD, 1986-87; contbr. articles to profl. sports publs. elected official, bd. dirs. Lakeside Fire Protection Dist., 1981, re-elected, 1986; parade equestrianne Parades throughout So. Calif. Recipient numerous scholarships, San Diego, 1965-70. Mem. Am. Paint Horse Assn. (life), Pinto Horse Assn. Am. (life, nat. com. mem. 1986—, Horse of Yr. awards), Nat. Assn. Accts. (most valuable mem. award), Toastmasters Club (most valuable mem. award). Office: Middle Earth Acres PO Box 454 La Mesa CA 91944-0454

ALLBEE, CHARLES EUGENE, college professor; b. Holly, Colo., Nov. 18, 1937; s. Claudius Evan and Cora Ellen (Gillispie) A.; m. Nancy Jo Aughenbaugh, Dec. 23, 1961; children: Brian Dean, Janet Lynn. BA, Adams State Coll., Alamosa, Colo., 1960, MA, 1961; ArtsD, U. N. Colo., Greeley, 1979. Instr. Adams State Coll., 1961-64, asst. prof., 1965-80, assoc. prof., 1980-84; prof. English Met. State Coll., Denver, 1984—; pres. Faculty Senate Met. State Coll., 1986-88. Mem. Nat. Council Tchrs. English, Conf. on Coll. Composition and Communication. Democrat. Home: 6824 Urban St Arvada CO 80004-2339

ALLBEE, SANDRA MOLL, real estate broker; b. Reading, Pa., July 15, 1947; d. Charles Lewars and Isabel May (Ackerman) Frederici; m. Thomas J. Allbee, Oct. 18, 1975 (div. 1987). Exec. sec. Hamburg (Pa.) State Sch. and Hosp., 1965-73; regional mgr. Am. Bus. Service Corp., Newport Beach, Calif., 1973-78; v.p. T.A.S.A., Inc., Long Beach, Calif., 1978-86; realtor Very Important Properties, Inc., Rolling Hills Estates, Calif., 1986-90, Re/Max Palos Verdes Realty, Rolling Hills Estates, Calif., 1990—. Bd. dirs. Nat. Council on Alcoholism, Torrance, Calif., 1987—; pres. Rollingwood Homeowners Assn., Rolling Hills Estates, Calif., 1985-92. Mem. Palos Verdes Rep. Women's Club (bd. dirs. 1989—). Office: Re/Max Palos Verdes Realty 4030 Palos Verdes Dr N Ste 104 Rolling Hills Estates CA 90274

ALLDREDGE, RENDEL BURDETTE, volunteer, retired government official; b. Portland, Oreg., Jan. 2, 1920; s. Joseph Melvin and Elda (Vollentine) A.; m. Edna Blanche Swannell, June 25, 1949 (div. June 1977); 1 child, Marguerite Beryl. BS, U. Oreg., 1942; postgrad., Stanford U., 1946-49. Instr. in econs. Stanford U., Palo Alto, Calif., 1946-49; asst. prof. econs. Tex. Tech U., Lubbock, 1950-52; economist U.S. Nat. Park Svc., Washington, 1952-53, chief statistician, 1956-66, policy officer, 1970-73; econ. advisor Govt. of Eritrea U.S. Internat. Coop. Adminstrn, Asmara, Ethiopia, 1954-56; mem. high commrs. cabinet program and budget Trust Terr. of Pacific Islands, Saipan, M.I., 1967-70; chief crude oil prodn. ERA U.S. Dept. Energy, Washington, 1973-80; pres., v.p. Atkinson Meml. Ch., Oregon City, Oreg., 1984-93; pvt. practice cons., Oregon City, 1980-83. Contbr. articles to profl. jours. Capt. U.S. Army, 1944-46, PTo. Recipient Silver medal Dept. Interio, Washington, 1967; superior achievement award, Dept. Energy, Washington, 1980; named Hon. Sen., Congress Micronesia, 1969. Home and Office: 14114 S Livesay Rd Oregon City OR 97045-9013

ALLDRIN, DORIS REED, orchard management company executive; b. Stockton, Calif., June 5, 1930; d. Leslie Wilmer and Winnie Myrtle (Olson) Reed; m. Caleb Nathaniel Alldrin, Oct. 1, 1967; children: Jeffery, Laura; stepchildren: Victoria, Stephen, Kenfield. Student, U. Pacific, Stockton, Calif., 1948, 49. Bus. office supr. Pacific Telephone Co., Stockton, 1949-59; owner, corp. sec. Montpelier Orchard Mgmt. Co., Modesto, Calif., 1985—. Bd. dirs., sponsor Family Svc. Agy., Modesto; mem. Yosemite Deanery Commn. on Alcohol and Drug Abuse for Episcopal Ch., Modesto and Fresno. Republican. Office: Montpelier Orchard Mgmt Co 1131 12th St Modesto CA 95354-0813

ALLEN, BONNIE LYNN, pension actuary; b. L.A., Oct. 2, 1957; d. David and Lucille M. (Scott) A. B.A. summa cum laude, UCLA, 1979. Math. tutor, L.A., 1971—; reader math. dept. UCLA, 1977-79; pension actuary Martin E. Segal Co., L.A., 1980-92. Author short stories and poetry. Active mentor program UCLA Alumni Assn., 1978-79, bd. dirs. Westside Bruins. Mem. Math. Assn. Am., Am. Math. Soc., L.A. Film Tchrs'. Assn., Acad. Sci. Fiction, Fantasy and Horror Films, UCLA Alumni Assn. (life), Westside Bruin Club (bd. dirs.), L.A. Actuarial Club, Phi Beta Kappa.

ALLEN, CHRISTOPHER JAMES, material facilities specialist; b. Mount Clemens, Mich., Mar. 19, 1964; s. James Brabham and Barbara Joyce (Smith) A. AA, Antelope Valley Coll., 1985. Materiel locator operator 6510 Test Wing and 650 Supply Squadron, Edwards AFB, Calif., 1989, materiel facilities specialist, 1989—; local purchase monitor 6510 Test Wing and 650 Supply Squadron, Edwards AFB, 1991-93, functional check monitor, 1991—, sample inventory monitor, 1991—. Author: (computer software) Post post Log, 1990, Sample Inventory Generator, 1991; SHIPADDS, 1990. Referee U.S. Soccer Fedn., 1986—, Am. Youth Soccer Orgn., 1987—, referee adminstr. region 789, California City, 1992—. Mem. Assn. for Computing Machinery, Role-Playing Game Assn. Home: 21200 94th St California City CA 93505 Office: 650 Supply Squadron 120 N Rosamond Blvd Edwards AFB CA 93524-8680

ALLEN, CHUCK, football team executive. V.p. football ops. Seattle Seahawks. Office: Seattle Seahawks 11220 NE 53rd St Kirkland WA 98033

ALLEN, CONSTANCE OLLEEN, artist, jewelry designer; b. Camphill, Ala., June 10, 1923; d. Alonza Evans and Sara Alvesta (Jones) Adcock; m. Byron Benjamin Webb, Oct. 12, 1947 (dec. Jan. 1975); children: Martha Ellen, Alan James, Deana Olleen; m. Walton Stanley Allen, Mar. 11, 1976. Student George Washington U., 1942-44, Gemological Inst. Am., 1984-87. Pvt. tchr., Chickasha, Okla., 1969-74; instr. art U. Sci. and Arts Okla., Chickasha, 1974-75; owner, dir. The Studio Gallery, Chickasha, 1979—, Green Valley, Ariz., 1983—. One woman shows: Pima Club, Green Valley, 1985; group shows include: Santa Cruz Valley Art Assn. Show, Tubac, Ariz., 1985, Santa Rita Art League Show, Green Valley (second place award 1986, 87), Nogales, Ariz., 1987, Festival of Arts, Tubac, 1987, juried show, 1987, 88, 89, 91, 92. Recipient 1st place watercolor Lawton-Fort Sill Art League, 1978, second place award Pastel Spring Atr Exhibit, Canoa Gallery, Green Valley, Ariz., 1992; Merit award Nat. Miniature Sch., 1976; first place awards for watercolors, 1987. Mem. Santa Rita Art League (pres. 1984-85), Santa Cruz Valley Art Assn., Arts and Crafts Club of Green Valley (v.p. 1986-88), Nat. League Am. Pen Women (Sonora Desert br. pres. 1988-90). Democrat. Baptist. Club: Fortnighters (sec. 1977-78, pres. 1978-79). Avocations: gemology, lapidary, reading, traveling, sewing.

ALLEN, D. SCOTT, pastor; b. Portland, Oreg., Nov. 22, 1953; s. Marney L. and Margaret E. (Herndon) A.; m. Laurel A. Allen, Feb. 14, 1992; children: Anna E., Sarah E. BS, Willamette U., 1976; MDiv., DMin., Sch. Theology at Claremont, 1991. Mgr. Camp Sturtevant United Meth. Ch., Pasadena, Calif., 1978-84; youth min. First United Meth. Ch., Riverside, Calif., 1984-87; assoc. pastor Boise (Idaho) First United Meth. Ch., 1987-90; pastor Jerome (Idaho) United Meth. Ch., 1990—. Elder United Meth. Ch. Office: Jerome United Meth Ch PO Box 90 Jerome ID 83338

ALLEN, DANA RAYMOND, software company executive; b. San Francisco, July 11, 1953; s. Raymond Dana and Rowena V. (Fink) A. BA in Geology, Calif. State U., Chico, 1976. Asst. mgr. Irving Auto Supply, San Francisco, 1968-78; pres. DARP, Burlingame, Calif., 1979, H and A Auto Supply, San Bruno, Calif., 1980-81; pvt. practice as contractor Burlingame, 1982-83; mfg. equipment fabricator Micro Miniture Refrigeration, Mountain View, Calif., 1983; product mgr. catalog divsn. Triad Systems, Sunnyvale, Calif., 1984; data devel. mgr. electronic catalog Triad Systems, Livermore, Calif., 1985-87; pres., chmn. Sequoia Data Corp., Burlingame, 1987—. Patentee in field. Pres. Ams. Competition Media, Challenge, Calif., 1982-84. Recipient Product of Yr. award Imaging Mag., 1993. Mem. OCR/Scanner/FAX Assn. (founding), Software Entrepreneurs Forum, Assn. Info. and Image Mgmt. Republican. Office: Sequoia Data Corp 433 Airport Blvd Burlingame CA 94010

ALLEN, DAVID CHARLES, educator; b. Syracuse, N.Y., Jan. 15, 1944; s. Charles Robert and Jane Loretta (Doolittle) A.; m. Mary Ann Stanke, June 15, 1968; children: Meredith Rae, Amelia Kathrine, Carl James. B.Tech. Edn., Nat. U., San Diego, 1983, MA in Human Behavior, 1984. Dir. retail sales Nat. U. Alumni Assn., 1981-83; audiovisual technician Grossmont Union High Sch. Dist., La Mesa, Calif., 1983-84; spl. project instr. San Diego Community Coll., 1985-91; instr. Coleman Coll., 1991. Mem. Presdl. Task Force; mem. Congl. Adv. Com. on Vets. Benefits for congressmen 44th. With USN, 1961-81. Mem. DAV, VFW, Am. Legion, Vietnam Vets. Am., Fleet Reservation Assn., Nat. U. Student and Alumni Assn., Am. Tech. Edn. Assn., Beta Sigma Phi (hon.), K.C. Republican. Roman Catholic. Home: 9860 Dale Ave # D10 Spring Valley CA 91977-2432 Office: Coleman Coll Computer Tech 7380 Parkway Dr La Mesa CA 91942-1500

ALLEN, DAVID HARLOW, educator, consultant; b. Lynn, Mass., May 26, 1930; s. Donald H. and Miriam Ellsworth (Harlow) A.; m. Roberta Arlene Miller, July 15, 1952; children: Donald Bruce, Richard Leroy, William David. BS in Gen. Edn., U. Nebr., Omaha, 1967; MBA, N.Mex. Highlands U., 1978. Cert. profl. logistician, cert. cost analyst. Commd. 2d lt. USAF, 1955, advanced through grades to lt. col., 1970; aircraft maintenance, staff, prodn. control officer, squadron comdr., wing asst. dep. comdr. maintenance SAC, 1948-74; dir. aircraft maintenance, dir. materiel Air Force Inspection and Safety Ctr., San Bernardino, Calif., 1969-72; dep. dir. logistics Air Force Test and Evaluation Ctr., Albuquerque, 1974-78; ret., 1978; sr. systems analyst, space systems project leader Arinc Rsch. Corp., 1978-84; dep. program mgr. for logistics, mgr. logistics project Ventura div. Northrop Corp., Newbury Park, Calif., 1984-91; sr. lectr. Coll. Bus. and Mgmt., West Coast U., L.A., 1988—, asst. dean, 1988-90, mem. faculty senate, acquisitions and contract mgmt., curricula com., 1991—; com. chmn. So. Calif. Logistics Conf. and Workshop, 1989, 91, 92, 93, Annual Internat. Logistics Symposium, 1994, 29th Internat. Logistics Conf. and Tech. Expn. Contbr. articles to profl. publs. Mem. state and nat. Rep. orgns., 1978—; mem. Ventura County-Santa Barbara County Planning Com. for Nat. Engring. Week, 1990—. Decorated Bronze Star. Mem. Nat. Contract Mgmt. Assn., Soc. Logistics Engrs. (chmn. chpt. 1988-90), Inst. Cost Analysis, Configuration and Data Mgmt. Assn. (chmn. fin. com. 1989), Am. Mgmt. Assn., Air Force Assn., Phi Kappa Phi. Home and Office: 428 Moondance St Thousand Oaks CA 91360-1209

ALLEN, DEAN ELLIS, correctional institution administrator; b. Caldwell, Idaho, May 13, 1950; s. Perry George and Laura Ella (Ford) A.; m. Carletta Jean Midby, June 27, 1975; children: Nancy Rose, Annette Elizabeth. BS, Boise State U., 1974; MEd., Coll. of Idaho, 1978. Cert. social worker, prof. cert. secondary edn.; lic. pvt. counselor. Pvt. tutor Ebronix Learning Ctrs., Boise, Idaho, 1969-72; child care counselor Warm Springs Ctr., Boise, 1972-74; jr. high tchr. Meridian (Idaho) Jt. Sch. Dist., 1974-76; correctional officer Idaho Dept. of Corrections, Boise, 1976-78, counselor/social worker, 1978-79; social worker Idaho Dept. of Corrections, Cottonwood, 1979-85; dep. warden of inst. Idaho Dept. Corrections, Cottonwood, 1985—; pvt. counselor St. Mary's Hosp., Cottonwood, 1982—. City councilman Garden City, Idaho, 1975-79; mem. coun. St. Mary's Hosp. Devel., Cottonwood, 1982-88; technician Emergency Med. Technician, Cottonwood, 1982—. Mem. Am. Correctional Assn., Idaho Correctional Assn. (Outstanding Contbns. in Adult Correction 1987), Idaho Assn. for Councilors. Nazarene. Office: North Idaho Correctional Inst HC 3 Box 147 Cottonwood ID 83522-9499

ALLEN, DONALD PHILLIP, corporate executive; b. L.A., Oct. 23, 1928; s. Isador Richard and Marion (Cohen) A.; m. Teresa Ann Durland, Feb. 19, 1952 (div. 1964); children: Paul David, Leslie Ann Platner, Curtis Martin; m. Mary Alice Hughes, June 19, 1964; children: Michael Richard, Phillip Hughes. BS in Mech. Engring., U. Calif., Berkeley, 1950; MS, Stanford U., 1958. Registered profl. engr., Calif. Engr. Ampex Corp., Redwood City, Calif., 1955-58, mktg. mgr., 1958-62; adminstrv. dir. Internat. Found. for Advanced Study, Menlo Park, Calif., 1962-65; product mktg. mgr. Vidar Corp., Mountain View, Calif., 1966-71; v.p. mktg. Trendar Automation Corp., Mountain View, 1971-78; pres., chief exec. officer Amtel Systems Corp., Sunnyvale, Calif., 1978-85; mng. dir. Noetic Systems, Los Altos, Calif., 1985—; bd. dirs. Stellar GPS Corp., San Jose, Calif., Anamet Systems, Inc., Hayward, Calif. Contbr. articles to profl. jours. Fundraiser Keystone and Cornerstone Stanford U., 1983—. 1st lt. USAF, 1952-54. Mem. IEEE (sr.), Instrument Soc. Am. (sr.). Office: Noetic Systems 900 N San Antonio Rd Los Altos CA 94022

ALLEN, DONALD VAIL, author, classical musician, investment executive; b. South Bend, Ind., Aug. 1, 1928; s. Frank Eugene and Vera Irene (Vail) A.; m. Betty Dunn, Nov. 17, 1956. BA magna cum laude, UCLA, 1972, MA, 1973, D (hon.), 1973. Developer major comml. properties Cambridge Investment Corp.; music editor and critic Times-Herald, Washington; music critic L.A. Times; lectr. George Washington U., Am. U., Washington, Pasadena City Coll. Transl. works of Ezra Pound from Italian into English; author of papers on the musical motifs in the writings of James Joyce; mem. Steinway Roster of Concert Artists; specialist in works of Beethoven, Chopin, Debussy and Liszt; premiere performances of worls by Paul Creston, Norman dello Joio, Ross Lee Finney, appearances in N.Y., L.A., Washington; represented by William Matthews Concert Agy., N.Y.C. Pres. Funds for Needy Children, 1974-76. Mem. Am. Mgmt. Assn., Nat. Assn. Securities Dealers, Am. Guild of Organists, Chamber Music Soc. Republican. Congregationalist. Home: 3371 Celinda Dr Carlsbad CA 92008-2073

ALLEN, DONALD WAYNE, accountant, educator; b. Billings, Mont., Apr. 9, 1936; s. D. Wayne and Olga Carmen (Ferguson) A.; m. Judith Marie Johnson, Dec. 28, 1959; children: Brian Kieth, Brendan Kirk. BS in Bus. Adminstrn., U. Denver, 1958. CPA, Mont., Wyo. Staff acct. Pan Am. Petroleum Corp., Casper, Wyo., 1958-61, Raab, Roush & Gaymon CPAs, Casper, 1961-64; office mgr. Sumatra Oil Corp., Billings, 1964-68; treas., dir. Oil Resources, Inc., Billings, 1968-73; ptnr. Smith, Birkeland, Mangis, Allen & Deming, Billings, 1973-78; pres. Allen & Nelson CPAs P.C., Billings, 1978-88, Donald W. Allen, CPA, P.C., Billings, 1988—; instr. Ea. Mont. Coll., Billings, 1983-85. Treas. Billings Jaycees, 1965; pres. Yellowstone Kiwanis, Billings, 1971; bd. dirs. J.K. Ralston Found., Billings, 1988-91, Billings Symphony Orch., 1990-92, treas., 1991-92. Mem. AICPA, Mon. Soc. CPAs (dir. 1968-71, instr., 1982-85, Outstanding Com. Chmn. 1984), Wyo. Soc. CPAs, Billings Rotary. Home: 3221 Country Club Cir Billings MT 59102-0609 Office: 490 N 31st Ste 206 Billings MT 59101-1256

ALLEN, DORIS, state legislator; b. Mo., May 26, 1936. Student, U. Wyo., Long Beach C.C., Golden West Coll. Lic. real estate agent. Mem. Calif. State Assembly, 1982—, mem. various coms.; mem. Calif. Planning Coun. Mental Health Master Plan, 1990. Active Orange County Commn. Status Women, Met. Water Dist. Speakers' Bur., West Orange County Consortium Spl. Edn.; founder, dir. Orange County Bus-Bloc, 1978; mem. adv. bd. Casa de Bienvenidos; bd. dirs. Coastline C.C. Found., Huntington Beach Conf. and Visitors Bur.; trustee Huntington Beach Union High Sch., 1976-81, pres., 1980. Recipient Spl. Recognition, Calif. Assn. Work Experience Educators, 1987, Nat. Coalition Marine Conservation, 1987, 90, Soc. Preservation Bighorn Sheep, 1988, Calif. Spl. Edn. Local Planning Area Adminstrs., 1989, Order of Jassid, Sierra Pacific Flyfisher, 1988, Project Workability award State Dept. Edn., 1988, Conservation award Internat. Game Fish Assn., 1992; named Legislator of Yr., Sportsmen's Coun. Ctrl. Calif., 1986, Calif. Bus. Educators Assn., 1987, 91, Calif. Indsl. and Tech. Edn. Assn., Inc., 1989, Pacific region Nat. Coalition Marine Conservation, 1989, Pub. Ofcl. of Yr., Orange County chpt. Am. Soc. Pub. Adminstrn., 1987, Woman of Distinction, Westminster Soroptimist Internat., 1987, Personality of Yr., Hunting and Fishing News, 1989, Nat. Legislator of Yr., Am. Fishing Tackle Mfrs. Assn., 1991. Mem. Am. Bus. Women's Assn., Calif. Elected Women;s Assn. Edn. and Rsch., L.A. Rod and Reel Club (hon.). Address: 4133 Larwin Ave Cypress CA 90630

ALLEN, DOUGLAS BRUCE, management consultant educator; b. Tulare, Calif., Feb. 5, 1955; s. Dwight William and Carole Jeannine (Swall) A.; m. Ginny Gregg, Sept. 27, 1980; children: Lindsay Dana, Sydnay Alissa. BSc in Sociology, U. Zimbabwe, 1977; MBA, Harvard U., 1982; PhD of Bus. Adminstrn., U. Mich., 1991. Sta. mgr. Good Hope Industries, Springfield, Mass., 1978; internat. placement cons. Baha'i Nat. Ctr., Wilmette, Ill., 1978-80; human resource mgmt. specialist Chrysler Corp., Highland Park, Mich., 1982-84; rsch. asst. U. Mich., Ann Arbor, 1984-89; asst. prof. U. Denver, 1989—; cons. Martin Marietta, Denver, 1989, Honeywell, Mpls., 1990—, GE, Crotonville, N.Y., 1986-88. Co-author: (chpt. in book) North America, 1988. chair Bear Canyon Sch. Accountability Com., Highlands Ranch, Colo., 1990—. Mem. Acad. Mgmt., World Future Soc., World Assn. Case Rsch. and Application. Mem. Baha'i faith. Office: U Denver Dept Mgmt 2020 S Race Denver CO 80208

ALLEN, EDGAR BURNS, records management professional; b. L.A., Sept. 1, 1929; s. Harry James and Hela Ruth (Graham) A.; m. Eleanor Angela Gregory, July 24, 1960; children: Linda Marie, Lisa Ann. AA, L.A. City Coll., 1958; student, Calif. State U., L.A., 1958, 81; BS, UCLA, 1985. Supr. records ctr. L.A. Dept. Water and Power, 1958-67, records mgr., 1967-76; records mgmt. officer City of L.A., 1976-85; records mgmt. cons. L.A., 1985—; profl. creator records mgmt. systems, tax preparer, L.A., 1990—. Chmn. Leimert Pk. Community Assn., L.A., 1972-75. Mem. Assn. Records Mgrs. and Adminstrs. (bd. dirs. 1975-76), Soc. Calif. Archivists, All Yr. Figure Skating Club (bd. dirs. 1970-79). Democrat. Roman Catholic.

ALLEN, EDWARD RAYMOND, educator, accountant; b. Indpls., Sept. 30, 1913; s. Edward L. and Emmeline (Rice) A.; B.S. in Commerce, Drake U., 1950, M.A. in Accounting, 1951; m. Norma D. M. Brennan, May 10, 1941. Asst. prof. bus. adminstrn. Parsons Coll., Fairfield, Iowa, 1952-56; faculty Coll. of Idaho, Caldwell, 1956— , prof. bus. adminstrn., 1956-73, head dept., 1962-70, chmn. dept., 1970-73, emeritus, 1973—, vis. lectr., 1973-74; practicing CPA, Caldwell, 1958-92; ret. Contbr. articles to profl. jours. Served to capt. AUS, 1942-46; lt. col. Res. ret. Decorated Bronze Star with 1 palm; CPA, Iowa, Idaho. Mem. AICPA, Idaho Soc. CPAs (dir., regional v.p. 1958-61, mem. standards of practice com. 1974-83, chmn. com. 1980-83, chmn. relations with ednl. instns. com. 1984-86, mem. 1991—), AAUP (past pres. Coll. of Idaho chpt.), C. of C., Elks, Pi Kappa Phi. Home: PO Box 336 Caldwell ID 83606-0336

ALLEN, GAIL COOPER, air force officer, management educator; b. Denver, Oct. 23, 1960; d. Donald Sylvester and Patty Jean (Ruppert) Cooper; m. William Michael Allen, Aug. 10, 1985; children: Joshua Michael, Jonathan Daniel. BS in Mgmt., USAF Acad., 1982; MS in Engring. Mgmt., U. Mo., Rolla, 1983. Commd. 2d lt. USAF, 1982; acquisition contracting officer spl. projects USAF, L.A., 1984-89, chief ground systems contracting div., 1987-88; asst. prof. dept. mgmt. USAF Acad. USAF, Colorado Springs, Colo., 1989—. Bd. dirs. Assn. Grads. USAF Acad., 1991—, mem. fin. com., 1991—. Winner tennis and running awards USAF. Mem. Nat. Contract Mgmt. Assn., Decision Scis. Inst. Republican. Home: 830 Towne Ct

Monument CO 80132 Office: DFM USAF Acad Colorado Springs CO 80840 also: Air Command and Staff Coll Maxwell AFB 1553 Pine Ridge Rd Montgomery AL 36109

ALLEN, HEATHER WILD, psychologist; b. Royal Oak, Mich., June 28, 1959; d. Robert Gardner and Vivian Lucille (Markley) Wild; m. Steven Earle Allen, Dec. 30, 1989. BA, Berry Coll., Mt. Berry, Ga., 1981; MS, U. Ga., 1982, PhD, 1985. Engring. psychologist U.S. Naval Air Devel. Ctr., Warminster, Pa., 1985-87; psychologist, sr. mem. tech. staff Sandia Nat. Labs., Albuquerque, 1987—. Contbr. articles to profl. jours. Elder Immanuel Presbyn. Ch., Albuquerque, 1988—. Mem. Human Factors Soc., IEEE, N.Mex. Network for Women in Sci. and Engring., N.Mex. Chpt. Performance and Instrn., Sigma Xi, Psi Chi. Republican. Home: 11420 Ranchitos Ave NE Albuquerque NM 87122 Office: Sandia Nat Labs Dept 323 PO Box 5800 Albuquerque NM 87185

ALLEN, HOWARD NORMAN, cardiologist, educator; b. Chgo., Nov. 19, 1936; s. Herman and Ida Gertrude (Weinstein) A.; children: Michael Daniel, Jeffrey Scott. BS, U. Ill., Chgo., 1958, MD, 1960. Diplomate Am. Bd. Internal Medicine, Am. Bd. Cardiovascular Disease, Nat. Bd. Med. Examiners. Intern Los Angeles County Gen. Hosp., L.A., 1960-61; resident in internal medicine Wadsworth VA Med. Ctr., L.A., 1961, 64-66; fellow in cardiology Cedars-Sinai Med. Ctr., L.A., 1966-67, dir. cardiac care unit Cedars of Lebanon Hosp. div., 1968-74, dir. Pacemaker Evaluation Ctr., 1968-89, dir. Cardiac Noninvasive Lab., 1972-88; Markus Found. fellow in cardiology St. George's Hosp., London, 1967-68; attending physician cardiology svc. Sepulveda (Calif.) VA Med. Ctr., 1972-86; pvt. practice Beverly Hills, Calif., 1988—; asst. prof. medicine UCLA, 1970-76, assoc. prof., 1976-84, adj. prof., 1984-88, clin. prof., 1988—; cons. Sutherland Learning Assocs., Inc., L.A., 1970-75; cardiology cons. Occidental Life Ins. Co., L.A., 1972-86. Contbr. articles to med. jours., chpts. to books. Commr. L.A. County Emergency Med. Svcs., 1989-91. Capt. M.C., U.S. Army, 1962-63, Korea. Fellow NSF, 1958, NIH, 1966-67. Fellow ACP, Am. Coll. Cardiology; mem. Am. Heart Assn. (fellow coun. on clin. cardiology, pres. Greater L.A. affiliate 1987-88, bd. dirs. 1979—), U. Ill. Alumni Assn. (life), Big Ten Club So. Calif., Alpha Omega Alpha, Pi Kappa Epsilon. Office: 414 N Camden Dr Ste 1100 Beverly Hills CA 90210-4532

ALLEN, HOWARD PFEIFFER, electric utility executive, lawyer; b. Upland, Calif., Oct. 7, 1925; s. Howard Clinton and Emma Maud (Pfeiffer) A.; m. Dixie Mae Illa, May 14, 1948; 1 child, Alisa Cary. AA, Chaffey Jr. Coll., 1946; BA in Econs. cum laude, Pomona Coll., 1948; JD, Stanford U., 1951. Bar: Calif. 1951, U.S. Supreme Ct. Asst. prof. law, asst. dean law sch. Stanford (Calif.) U., 1951-54; with So. Calif. Edison Co., Rosemead, Calif., 1954—; v.p. So. Calif. Edison Co., Rosemead, 1962-71, sr. v.p., 1971-73, exec. v.p., 1973-80, pres., dir., 1980-84; chmn., chief exec. officer So. Calif. Edison Co., Rosemead, Calif., 1984-90, chmn. exec. com., 1990—; also bd. dirs. So. Calif. Edison Co.; bd. dirs. AMR Corp., Am. Airlines, Inc., Computer Scis. Corp., PS Group, Inc., Trust Co. of the West, The Parsons Corp., The Ralph M. Parsons Co., The Presley Cos. Mem. Bus. Coun.; mem. comdr. coun. Salvation Army; trustee Los Angeles County Mus. Art; hon. trustee Pomona Coll.; bd. dirs. Los Angeles County Fair Assn., LAOC Amateur Athletic Found.; former fin. chmn. Watts Summer Games, 1982; chmn. Ann. Awards Dinner, Black Bus. Assn. L.A., 1988. Recipient Whitney M. Young, Jr. award L.A. Urban League, 1985, Outstanding Pub. Svc. Recognition awards State of Calif., County of L.A., City of L.A., Carrie Chapman Catt award LWV, 1985, Human Rels. award Am. Jewish Com., 1986, Am. Spirit award Coun. Energy Resource Tribes, 1987, Spl. award Improvment for Sci. Edn. Calif. State Dept. Edn., 1988; named Industrialist of Yr. Calif. Mus. Sci. and Industry, 1989. Mem. ABA, NCCJ (nat. Protestant co-chmn. 1983-87, Brotherhood award 1988), Am. Judicature Soc., Pacific Coast Elec. Assn. (pres. 1984-85, bd. dirs.), Inst. for Resource Mgmt. (chmn. bd.), Sundance Inst., Assn. Edison Illuminating Cos. (bd. dirs.), Electric Power Rsch. Inst. (bd. dirs.), Calif. C. of C. (Outstanding Community Svc. Merit award 1982, bd. dirs.), Calif. Club (L.A.), Pacific Union Club (San Francisco), Bohemian Club (San Francisco), L.A. Country Club, La Quinta Hotel Golf Club, PGA West Golf Club, Mission Hills Country Club, 100 Club (exec. com.), Sunset Club, Phi Beta Kappa. Office: So Calif Edison Co 2244 Walnut Grove Ave Rosemead CA 91770-3714

ALLEN, JEANETTE MARY, secondary education educator; b. Reno, Apr. 4, 1958; d. Richard Joseph and Jeanne Louise (McGrath) A. BS in Secondary Edn., U. Nev., 1986. Cert. tchr., Nev. Patient rep. St. Mary's Regional Med. Ctr., Reno, 1980-82; tchr. St. Albert Elem. Sch., Reno, 1986-91; asst. mgr., formalwear cons. Gingiss Formalwear, Reno, 1984-90; high sch. tchr. Washoe High Sch., Reno, 1990-91; tchr. drama, English, dir. drama. Sparks (Nev.) High Sch., 1991—. Cast mem. Up With People, Inc., Tucson, 1980. Named Outstanding Young Women of Am., 1985, 91. Mem. Up With People Internat. Alumni Assn. (vice chmn. edn. and programs com. 1988-90, admissions rep. 1988—). Home: 2602 Fanto Ct Sparks NV 89431

ALLEN, JEANIE UNTERSINGER, sales representative; b. Ogden, Utah, Jan. 28, 1963; d. Clyde Roberts and Margaret (Peterson) Untersinger; m. Stan Russell Allen, Apr. 30, 1982; children: Taralyn Allen, Parker Allen. BS, Weber State U., 1984. Dental hygienist Dr. DuWayne Swenson, Bountiful, Utah, 1984-86, Dr. Robert Hazen, Bountiful, 1985-87; sales rep. Scherer Labs., Dallas, 1987-90; dental hygienist Dr. Roger Green, Centerville, Utah, 1986-88, Dr. Ted Green, Kaysville, Utah, 1988-89; pharm. sales rep. Colgate-Hoyt, Canton, Mass., 1990-91; account rep. Ciba Corning Diagnostics, Medfield, Mass., 1992—. Vol. Farmington Elem., 1990-92, Arthritis Found., 1991-92. Recipient Best Clinician award Utah Dental Hygiene Assn., 1984. Mem. Am. Dental Hygiene Assn., Phi Kappa Phi, Sigma Phi Alpha. Republican. Mem. LDS Church. Home: 511 S 450 E Farmington UT 84025

ALLEN, JOHN DAVID, sales executive; b. Lima, Ohio, Jan. 12, 1957; s. Darrell and Margaret (Dumm) A.; m. Denice Hana Knezovich, May 28, 1983; children: Adrienne Yvonne, Alana Nadyne. BA in Internat. Affairs, Ohio U., 1979; M Internat. Mgmt., Am. Grad. Sch. Internat. Mgmt., Glendale, Ariz., 1981. Latin Am. dir. LeRoi div. Dresser Industries, Sidney, Ohio, 1981-82; v.p. sales & mktg. Wilden Pump & Engring., Grand Terrace, Calif., 1982—. Mem. Orthodox Ch. Home: 7185 Rockspring Ln Highland CA 92346 Office: Wilden Pump & Engring 22069 Van Buren Grand Terrace CA 92324

ALLEN, JOHN KELSEY, operations executive; b. Sacramento, Calif., Dec. 6, 1950; s. Kirke Monroe and Elizabeth Mitchell (Newman) A.; m. Mary Margaret Duffield, Jan. 21, 1979. BS, U. Calif., Berkeley, 1973, PhC, 1975, cert., 1991. Staff rsch. assoc. Bodega Marine Lab. U. Calif., Bodega Bay, 1974-77; teaching assoc. U. Calif., Berkeley, 1977-80; supr. Airport Parking Mgmt., San Francisco, 1980-91; sr. supr. Ampco Parking, San Francisco, 1991—. Contbr. articles to profl. jours. Regents fellow U. Calif., 1973-74, Earle C. Anthony fellow, 1974-75, Edwin Pauley fellow, 1975-76; Henry Luce Found. scholar, 1978-79. Mem. Sierra Club, Nature Conservancy, Wilderness Soc., Sigma Xi (assoc.). Democrat. Home: 298 Glorietta Blvd Orinda CA 94563-3253 Office: Ampco Parking PO Box 281441 San Francisco CA 94128-1441

ALLEN, LEW, JR., laboratory executive, former air force officer; b. Miami, Fla., Sept. 30, 1925; s. Lew and Zella (Holman) A.; m. Barbara Frink Hatch, Aug. 19, 1949; children: Barbara Allen Miller, Lew III, Marjorie Allen Dauster, Christie Allen Jameson, James Allen. BS, U.S. Mil. Acad., 1946; MS, U. Ill., 1952, PhD in Physics, 1954. Commd. 2d lt. USAAF, 1946; advanced through grades to gen. USAF, 1977, ret., 1982; physicist test div. AEC, Los Alamos, N.Mex., 1954-57; sci. advisor Air Force Spl. Weapons Lab., Kirtland, N.Mex., 1957-61; with office of spl. tech. Sec. of Def., Washington, 1961-65; from dir. spl. projects to dep. dir. adv. plans Air Force Space Program, 1965-72; dir. Nat. Security Agy., Ft. Meade, Md., 1973-77; comdr. Air Force Systems Command, 1977-78; vice chief of staff USAF, Washington, 1978, chief of staff, 1978-82; dir. Jet Propulsion Lab., Calif. Inst. Tech., Pasadena, Calif., 1982-90; chmn. bd. Draper Lab, Boston, 1991—. Decorated Def. D.S.M. with two clusters, Air Force D.S.M. with one cluster, Nat. Intelligence D.S.M., NASA D.S.M., Legion of Merit with two oak leaf clusters. Fellow Am. Phys. Soc.; mem. Am. Geophys. Union, Nat. Acad. Engring., Coun. on Fgn. Rels., Sigma Xi, Sunset Club (L.A.), Alfalfa Club (Washington). Republican. Episcopalian.

ALLEN, LINDA KAY, administrative secretary; b. Nampa, Idaho, May 4, 1944; d. Harold O. and Maxine E. (Jack) Stewart.; m. Harry C. Allen, Feb. 5, 1965. BA, Boise State U., 1971. Registration clk. Dept. Law Enforcement, Boise, Idaho, 1963-70; Exec. Sec. Loomix, Inc., Boise, 1978-79; tech. records specialist Dept. Employment Interstate, Boise, 1982-85; claims interviewer Dept. Employment Job Svc. Appeals Bur., Boise, Idaho, 1985-86; sec., office coord. Boise State U. Libr., 1986-88; adminstrv. sec. Boise State U. Honors, 1990-91; pres. Past Assn. Leaders, Boise, 1990-91. Mem. Visions City of Boise, 1990—. Mem. Idaho Assn. Office Pers. (chair person, 1990—), Boise State U. Assn. Office Pers. (pres., 1989-90, membership and bosses breakfast chair), Nat. Collegiate Honors Coun. (membership com., workshop presentor), Western Regional Honors Coun. (workshop presentor), Assn. Classified Employees of Boise State U. (senator 1991—). Office: Boise State U Honors Program 1910 University Dr # 408lg Boise ID 83725-0001

ALLEN, MARCUS, professional football player; b. San Diego, Mar. 26, 1960. Student, U. So. Calif. Running back with Los Angeles Raiders, NFL, El Segundo, Calif., 1982-92; with Kansas City Chiefs, NFL, 1993—; established NFL season record for most combined yards, 1985; played in NFL championship game, 1984; Pro Bowl, 1983, 85, 86, 88; co-owner, Pro Ball Beverage Corp. Recipient Heisman Trophy Downtown Athletic Club of N.Y.C., 1981; named The Sporting News NFL Rookie of Yr., 1982, Player of Yr., 1985. Office: care Kansas City Chiefs One Arrowhead Dr Kansas City MO 64129

ALLEN, MERRILL JAMES, marine biologist; b. Brady, Tex., July 16, 1945; s. Clarence Francis and Sara Barbara (Finlay) A. BA, U. Calif., Santa Barbara, 1967; MA, UCLA, 1970; PhD, U. Calif., San Diego, 1982. Cert. jr. coll. tchr., Calif. Asst. environ. specialist So. Calif. Coastal Water Rsch. Project, El Segundo, 1971-77; postdoctoral assoc. Nat. Rsch. Coun., Seattle, 1982-84; oceanographer Nat. Marine Fisheries Svc., Seattle, 1984-86; sr. scientist MBC Applied Environ. Scis., Costa Mesa, Calif., 1986-93; prin. scientist So. Calif. Coastal Water Rsch. Project, Long Beach, Calif., 1993—; tech. adv. com. Santa Monica Bay Restoration Project, Monterey Park, Calif., 1989—; affiliate asst. prof. sch. fisheries U. Wash., Seattle, 1985-89. Mem. AAAS, Am. Inst. Fisheries Rsch. Biologists (dir. So. Calif. dist. 1991—), Am. Fisheries Soc., Am. Soc. Ichthyologists and Herpetologists. Office: So Calif Coastal Water Rsch Project 7171 Fenwick Ln Westminster CA 92683

ALLEN, MICHAEL ROBERT, hotel/resort executive; b. Daytona Beach, Fla., July 21, 1945; s. Robert Finch and Ellen Henrietta (Haldeman) A.; m. Terri Jean Begley, Oct. 4, 1985; children: Rebecca Rachel, Courtney Ashton and Cayleigh Anne (twins). Student, NCMC Jr. Coll., Petoskey, Mich., 1968-69, Western Mich. U., 1970-71, U. Calif., Chico, 1980-83. Chef, kitchen mgr. Alex's Hole in the Wall Italian Restaurant, Lahaina, Hawaii, 1983-86; asst. club mgr., food and beverage mgr. Ojai (Calif.) Valley Raquet Club, 1986-88; food and beverage mgr. Rippling River Resort, Welches, Oreg., 1988-90; gen. mgr. Breakwater Inn, Inc., Juneau, Alaska, 1990-93; asst. gen. mgr., food and beverage dir. Westmark Juneau Hotel, 1993—. Mem. draft bd., Emmet County, Mich., 1970-71. Mem. C. of C. (com. chair), Visitor and Conv. Bur. (bd. dirs.), Gull Cove Condo Assn. (bd. dirs.). Office: Westmark Juneau Hotel Egan Dr Juneau AK 99801

ALLEN, MICHAEL WAYNE, oil company executive; b. Spokane, Sept. 23, 1958; s. Harry H. and Shirley A. (Hembree) A.; m. Lynette M. Biegler, Nov. 25, 1989. BS in Edn., No. Mont. Coll., 1981; postgrad., Carroll Coll., 1981-82. Gen. mgr. Allen Oil Co., Helena, Mont., 1971—; now pres. Allen's Inc., Helena, Mont. Pres. Helena Jaycees, 1983-84, 92—; sec. Jr. Achievement, Helena, 1985-89; bd. dirs. Leadership Helena, 1991—; regional dir. Montana Jaycees, Helena, 1984-85; alumni dir. No. Mont. Coll., Havre, Mont., 1982—. Named Senator Montana/U.S. Jaycees, 1990. Mem. Western Petroleum Marketers (bd. dirs. 1987—), Montana Shriners (Algeria shrine). Office: Allens Inc 1131 Phoenix Ave Helena MT 59601

ALLEN, PATRICK MICHAEL, legislative aide; b. Portland, Oreg., Dec. 2, 1962; s. Robert L.M. and Constance J. (Winandy) A.; m. Joan M. Bodyfelt, Dec. 29, 1984. BS in Econs., Oreg. State U., 1985. Loan officer U.S. Bank of Oreg., Madras, 1985-86; comml. loan officer U.S. Bank of Oreg., Albany, 1986-87; loss prevention mgr. U.S. Bank of Oreg., Salem, 1987-89, direct credit mgr., 1988-89; asst. v.p., comml. consumer loan mgr. First Security Bank of Oreg., Salem, 1989-91; field rep. U.S. Rep. Mike Kopetski, Oregon City, Oreg., 1991-92; dist. field dir. U.S. Rep. Mike Kopetski, Salem, 1992—. Mem. Mayor's Task Force on Cruising, Albany, 1987, agr. and natural resources com. Albany Area C. of C., 1986-87; vol. Kopetski for Congress, Salem, 1990. Mem. Oreg. Banker's Assn. (chairperson comml./consumer credit com. 1990-91), Salem Area C. of C. (bd. dirs. 1990-91, chmn. legis. affairs com. 1993—), Kiwanis (2d v.p. Salem chpt. 1989-90, 1st v.p. 1990-91). Democrat. Roman Catholic.

ALLEN, PAUL, computer executive, professional sports team owner. Student, Wash. State U. Co-founder Microsoft Corp., Redmond, Wash., 1975, exec. v.p., 1975-83; pres. Asymetrix Corp., Bellevue, Wash., 1985—; owner, chmn. bd. Portland (Oreg.) Trail Blazers, 1988—; bd. dirs. Egghead Discount Software, Layered, Inc. Office: care Portland Trail Blazers 1630 SW Morrison St # 110 Portland OR 97205-1815 also: Asymetrix Corp 110 110th NE Bellevue WA 98004*

ALLEN, PENNY, marketing professional; b. Norfolk, Va., Oct. 15, 1947; d. George Erety Grieb and Susan (Pouch) Burns; m. David Russell Allen, Aug. 27, 1966; children: Todd Michael, Travis Ethan. Student, UCLA, 1965-67. V.p., gen. mgr. Delphi Industries, Inc., San Diego, 1985-87; owner Allen & Co., San Diego, 1987—; co-owner The Phone Bank, San Diego, 1990—. Past chair South Bay Family YMCA; chair Chula Vista, Calif., 1990—, Econ. Devel. Commn., Chula Vista, 1991—, Calif. State Coastal Conservancy, 1991—. Recipient Red Triangle award YMCA, San Diego, 1985, Golden Triangle award YMCA, San Diego, 1991, Disting. Svc. award Chula Vista Jaycees, Outstanding Community Svc. award Jaycee Women. Mem. Downtown San Diego Rotary Club (bd. dirs.). Republican.

ALLEN, RICHARD, physician; b. Portland, Oreg., Feb. 16, 1937; s. Jack and Lois Florene (Mower) A.; m. Patricia Elaine MacDonald, Oct. 3, 1959; children: Mark C., Rebecca L., Scott M. BA, U. Oreg., 1958; MA, U. Calif., Los Angeles, 1961; MD, N.Y. Med. Coll., 1965. Diplomate Am. Bd. OB-Gyn. Intern. Emanual Hosp., Portland, Oreg., 1965; resident Emanual Hosp., Portland, 1966-69; physician Portland (Oreg.) Ob-Gyn. Clin., 1965-66; clin. assoc. prof. Oreg. Health Scis. Univ., Portland, 1979—; pvt. practice Portland, 1969-93; program dir. St. Joseph Hosp., Denver, Colo., 1993—; adj. prof. Oreg. Health Scis. Univ., 1989-93. Contbg. author: How To Choose A Medical Specialist, 1986; contbr. articles to profl. jours. Mem. Office of Health Policy, State of Oreg., Salem, 1989, Gov's. Commn. on Health Care, Salem, 1988, Pub. Health Adv. Bd., State of Oreg., Salem, 1990; bd. dirs. Univ. Oreg. Alumni Assn., Eugene, 1990; pres. Oreg. Club of Portland, 1980-81, Mt. Hood Ski Patrol, Portland, 1979-81. With USAR, 1959-60. Fellow Am. Coll. Ob-Gyn.; mem. AMA (del. 1989, residency rev. comm. 1989), Oreg. Med. Assn. (pres. 1988-89), Pacific N.W. Ob-Gyn. Assn. (pres. 1987-88), Pacific Coast Ob-Gyn. Assn. Oreg. Ob-Gyn. Soc. (pres. 1980-81), Multnomah County Med. Soc. (pres. 1984-85), Am. Coll. Obstetricians and Gynecologists, A.C.G.M.E. (residency rev. com. for ob-gyn. 1989), Sigma Phi Epsilon, Cor Et Manus. Democrat. Office: St Joseph Hosp OB-GYN 1835 Franklin St Denver CO 80218

ALLEN, RICHARD DEAN, cell biology educator, researcher; b. Dallas Center, Iowa, Sept. 20, 1935; s. Deane Curtis and Lemira Inez (Packard) A.; m. Marilyn Grace Switzer, June 28, 1958 (dec. June 1987); children: Lorna Marie Allen Wilfong, Steven Richard, William Scott. Student, Messiah Coll., Grantham, Pa., 1953-55; AB, Greenville (Ill.) Coll., 1957; MS, U. Ill., 1960; PhD, Iowa State U., 1964. Instr. Greenville Coll., 1960-61; postdoctoral fellow Harvard U., Cambridge, Mass., 1964-65, lectr., dir. Electron Microscope Svc. Lab., 1968-69; asst. prof. Messiah Coll., 1965-68; assoc. prof. microbiology U. Hawaii, Honolulu, 1969-75, prof., 1975—, mem. grad. faculty dept. tropical medicine, 1977—, dir. biol. electron microscope facility, 1985—, mem. grad. faculty cell, molecular and neuroscis., 1988—; vis. prof. U. Colo., Boulder, 1975-76. Editor: Protoplasma, 1990—; mem. editorial bd. Jour. Protozoology, Jour. Histochemistry and Cytochemistry, European Jour. Cell Biology, 1975-86; contbr. numerous articles and abstracts to profl. jours., also chpts. to books. Rsch. grantee NIH, 1972-78, 80-82, Am. Heart Assn., 1976-78, NSF, 1979-93. Fellow AAAS; mem. Soc. Protozoologists (pres. 1981-82, Hutner prize 1978), Am. Soc. for Cell Biology, Sigma Xi. Office: U Hawaii 2538 The Mall Honolulu HI 96822-2233

ALLEN, RICHARD EUGENE, college administrator, educator; b. Portland, Oreg., Oct. 21, 1938; s. George M. and L. Vernal (Admire) A.; m. Flora M. Todd, Aug. 19, 1961; children: Michael T., Gregory P. BS in Phys. Edn., Seattle Pacific Coll., 1961; MS in Phys. Edn., U. Oreg., 1968. Cert. tchr. Elem. tchr. Seattle (Wash.) Pub. Schs., 1961-62; various positions including tchr. and coach Salem (Oreg.) Acad., 1962-69; tchr., coach, adminstr. George Fox Coll., Newberg, Oreg., 1969—; assoc. dir. dept. continuing studies George Fox Coll., Newberg, 1987—; speaker Pacific U. Track Coaching Clinic, 1977. Contbr. chpts. to book. Mem. Nat. Assn. Intercollegiate Athletics (dist. II track and cross country coaches 1969-87, dist. II exec. com., games com. nat. championship track and field meet 1987, dist. II cross country coach of yr. 1977, track coach of yr. 1978, 79, 80, coach of yr. all sports 1978, coaches hall of fame 1981). Free Methodist. Office: George Fox College 414 N Meridien Newberg OR 97132

ALLEN, RICK (FREDERICK ALLEN KLYCINSKI), magician, advertising and publicity consultant; b. Detroit, Nov. 4, 1941; s. Chester Bruno and Johana Jean (Guzdzial) Klycinski; m. Marie DeLeon, Nov. 2, 1965 (div. Mar. 1985); children: John Paul, Marie Louise, Diane Lynn, Mark Frederick. AA, Pasadena Coll., 1961. Account exec. Knight Ridder Newspapers, Long Beach, Calif., 1966-68, advt. mgr., 1969-71; advt. mgr. Copley Newspapers, Torrance, Calif., 1972-73; cons. Scripps Newspapers, Napa, Calif., 1974-75; founder, owner, mgr. Creative Advt. Svc., Vallejo, Calif., 1976—; dir. mail advt. cons. Vallejo, 1980—; profl. magician for fund-raising orgns., 1976—. Author: Public Relations and Publicity for Entertainers, 1978; editor: Stick to the Cash Register, 1970; contbr. articles to various publs. Creator Anto-Grafitti Task Force. Named top fund raiser United Way, L.A., Long Beach, 1971; recipient awards for creative advt. Calif. Advt. Assn., Calif. Pubs. Assn., Am. Assn. Advt. Agys. Mem. Soc. Am. Magicians, Internat. Brotherhood Magicians, Pacfic Coast Assn. Magicians, Lions. Home and Office: 122 Clearview Dr Vallejo CA 94591

ALLEN, ROBERT EUGENE BARTON, lawyer; b. Bloomington, Ind., Mar. 16, 1940; s. Robert Eugene Barton and Berth R. A.; m. Cecelia Ward Dooley, Sept. 23, 1960 (div. 1971); children: Victoria, Elizabeth, Robert; m. Judith Elaine Hecht, May 27, 1979 (div. 1989). B.S., Columbia U., 1962; LL.B., Harvard U., 1965. Bar: Ariz. 1965, U.S. Dist. Ct. Ariz. 1965, U.S. Tax Ct., 1965, U.S. Supreme Ct. 1970, U.S. Ct. Customs and Patent Appeals 1971, U.S. Dist. Ct. D.C. 1972, U.S. Ct. Appeals (9th cir.) 1974, U.S. Ct. Appeals (10th, and D.C. cirs.) 1984, U.S. Dist. Ct. N.Mex., U.S. Dist. Ct. (no. dist.) Calif., U.S. Ct. Appeals (fed. cir.) 1992. Ptnr., dir. Streich, Lang, Weeks and Cardon, Phoenix, 1965-83; ptnr., dir. Brown & Bain, Phoenix, Tucson, Palo Alto (Calif.), 1983—; spl. asst. atty. gen. pro tem Ariz. Ct. Appeals, atty. gen. pro-tem, 1978, 84, 92. Nat. pres. Young Dems. Clubs Am., 1971-73; mem. exec. com. Dem. Nat. Com., 1972-73; mem. Ariz. Gov.'s Kitchen Cabinet working on wide range of state projects; bd. dirs. Phoenix Bapt. Hosp. and Health Systems, Phoenix and Valley of the Sun Conv. and Visitors Bur., United Cerebral Palsy Ariz., 1984-89, Planned Parenthood of Cen. and No. Ariz., 1984-90; mem. Ariz. Aviation Futures Task Force; chmn. Ariz. Airport Devel. Criteria. Subcom.; mem. Apache Junction Airport Rev. Com., former mem Vestry and Sunday Sch. Tchr. Trinity Episcopal Cathedral; Am. rep. exec. bd. Atlantic Alliance of Young Polit. Leaders, 1973-77, 1977-80; trustee Am. Counsel of Young Polit. Leaders, 1971-76, 1981-85, mem. Am. delegations to Germany, 1971, 72, 76, 79, USSR, 1971, 76, 88, France, 1974, 79, Belgium, 1974, 77, Can., 1974, Eng., 1975, 79, Norway, 1975, Denmark, 1976, Yugoslavia and Hungary, 1985; Am. observer European Parliamentary elections, Eng., France, Germany, Belgium, 1979, Moscow Congressional, Journalist delegation, 1989, NAFTA Trade Conf., Mexico City, 1993. Speaker seminars and profl. assns.; contbr. articles on comml. litigation to profl. jours. Mem. ABA, Ariz. Bar Assn., Maricopa County Bar Assn., N. Mex. State Bar, D.C. Bar Assn., Am. Judicature Soc., Fed. Bar Assn., Am. Arbitration Assn., Phi Beta Kappa. Democrat. Episcopalian (lay reader). Club: Harvard (Phoenix). Office: Brown & Bain 2901 N Central Ave # 2000 Phoenix AZ 85012

ALLEN, ROGER KAY, psychologist, management consultant; b. Heber, Utah, Aug. 28, 1951; s. C. Kay and Doris (Brady) A.; m. Judy Bickmore, Aug. 15, 1975; children: Melinda, Jonathan, Cheryl-Lynn. BS, Brigham Young U., 1975; PhD, U. Minn., 1980. Lic. psychologist. Pres. Human Devel. Inst., Denver, 1981—; v.p. human resources KeyTronic Corp., Spokane, Wash., 1990-91; assoc., cons. Belgard, Fisher, Rayner, Portland, Oreg., 1992—. Author: The Team Book, 1992, (workbook) Mastery, 1990, (audio tapes) Making Things Happen, 1989. Recipient Community Svc. award Brigham Young U. Alumni Assn., 1991. Mem. APA, ASTD, ACA, Am. Mgmt. Assn. Mem. LDS Ch. Office: Human Devel Inst 6909 S Holly Cir # 203 Englewood CO 80112

ALLEN, RONALD CARL, computer consulting executive, visual artist; b. Salt Lake City, Mar. 25, 1953; s. Carl Franklin and Mary Jean (Benson) A.; m. Delia Ann Fordham, Nov. 15, 1974; children: Lisa, Cindy, Jeffrey. BS in Acctg., U. Utah, 1980. Owner, bus. mgr. Alinco Mfg., Salt Lake City, 1977-79; owner, pres. Comics Utah Bookstores, Salt Lake City, 1984-86; adminstrv. supr. Am. Stores, Salt Lake City, 1978-89; v.p. Anamatrix, Layton, Utah, 1989; pres. Cons. Svcs., Salt Lake City, 1989—; pres. Intermountain EDP Trainers, Salt Lake City, 1984-86. Author: Step-by-Step Computer Books. Chmn. legis. dist. 47 Dem. Cen. Com., Taylorsville, Utah, 1982-84; chmn., chief North Tooele County (Utah) Fire Dept., 1987—. Recipient over 30 awards for visual arts, 1981—. Mem. LDS Ch. Office: Cons Svcs 835 Lakeview Tooele UT 84074-9676

ALLEN, ROY VERL, life insurance company executive; b. Hyrum, Utah, Aug. 3, 1933; s. Winfrd A. and Sarah Ann (Nielsen) A.; m. Judith Green, Aug. 11, 1961; children: Ann Marie Allen Webb, Michael R., Blair J. BS, Utah State U., 1958. CLU, Chartered Fin. Cons. Mgr. employee benefits Thiokol Chem. Corp., Brigham City, Utah, 1959-61; employment interviewer Hercules, Salt Lake City, 1962-63; agy. mgr. Standard Ins. Co., Salt Lake City, 1963—. Maj. U.S. Army Res., 1962-79. Mem. CLUs (bd. mem. 1973-75), Estate Planning Coun. (bd. mem. 1979-81), Utah Gen. Agts. and Mgrs. (sec., v.p., pres. 1979-83), Utah Assn. Life Underwrtiers (pres. 1988-89), Exchange Club. Republican. Mormon. Home: 2526 Olympus Dr Salt Lake City UT 84124-2916 Office: Standard Ins Co 525 E 3d St S Salt Lake City UT 84102

ALLEN, RUSSELL PLOWMAN, symphony orchestra executive; b. Washington, Dec. 30, 1951; s. Gale Wilson and Anne (Plowman) A. BA, Macalester Coll., 1974. Gen. mgr. Shreveport (La.) Symphony Orchestra, 1979-80; mgr. Houston Symphony Orchestra, 1980-84, San Antonio Symphony Orchestra, 1984-86; gen. mgr. Phoenix Symphony Orchestra, 1986—; cons. N.Mex. Symphony Orchestra, Albuquerque, 1986, Chattanooga (Tenn.) Symphony Orchestra, 1986. Mem. grants rev. panel Ariz. Commn. on Arts, Phoenix, 1987-90, Phoenix Arts Commn., 1987; program chmn. Phoenix Symphony Coun., 1986—; mem. mktg. com. Downtown Phoenix Partnership Class XIII, Valley Leadership; mem. Heritage Sq. Adv. Bd., 1991—. Mem. Am. Symphony Orchestra League, Phoenix City Club. Home: 1528 E Colter St # 235 Phoenix AZ 85014-3027 Office: Phoenix Symphony Orch 3707 N 7th St Ste 107 Phoenix AZ 85014-5094

ALLEN, SALLY ROTHFUS, editor; b. Pitts., Sept. 5, 1941; d. Elmer Arthur and Olive Corrine (Thompson) Rothfus; m. Arthur William Allen Jr., Dec. 27, 1964 (div. Oct. 1983); 1 child, Rebecca Rothfus Allen. BA, U. Mich., 1963; MBA, Golden Gate U., 1985. Writer, editor various newspapers, univs., 1964-69; with investment dept. investor rels. Homestead Savs., Burlingame, Calif., 1986-88; securities analyst Fisher Investments Inc., Woodside, Calif., 1988-93; sr. editor rsch. dept. Robertson, Stephens & Co., San Francisco, 1993—. Mem. Nat. Investor Rels. Inst., San Francisco, 1987-88; mem. coun. Soc. for Encouragement Contemporary Art, San Francisco Mus. Modern Art, 1984-89; mem. Northern Calif. coun. Nat. Mus. for Women in the Arts, 1992—; bd. dirs. San Francisco Cinematheque, 1989-92. Mem. Security Analysts of San Francisco. Republican. Presbyterian. Office: Robertson Stephens & Co 555 California St San Francisco CA 94104

ALLEN, SAM RAYMOND, training manager; b. Cody, Wyo., Oct. 6, 1953; s. Robert Sam and Jerrine (Cross) A.; m. Melinda Jo Daniels, Oct. 23, 1979; children: Eric Samuel, Andrew William. BS, U. Wyo., 1976, MBA, 1986; postgrad., George Washington U., 1977-79, Hastings Coll., Nebr., 1972-74. Accredited pub. rels. cert. Teller Bank of Va., Rosslyn, Va., 1978-79; legis. asst. U.S. Senate/Alan K. Simpson, Washington, 1979-81; bus. mgr. Coors Brewing Co., Golden, Colo., 1986-87; vol. prog. mgr. Coors Brewing Co., 1987-90, tng. mgr., 1990—. Editor V.I.C.E. Activity Guide newsletter, 1987-90. Bus. advisor Jr. Achievement, Denver, 1988-90; corp. mem. Assn. for Vol. Adminstrn., Boulder, 1987-90; elder Shepherd of the Hills Presbyn. Ch., 1986-89. Named Outstanding Corp. Coord., Adopt-A-School, Denver, 1987. Mem. ASTD, U. Wyo. Alumni Assn., Pub. Rels. Soc. Am., Rotary (community svc. dir. 1989), Alpha Kappa Psi. Republican. Presbyterian. Home: 11636 W 74th Way Arvada CO 80005-3274 Office: Coors Brewing Co 311 10th St Golden CO 80401-1087

ALLEN, SCOTT, institute administrator; b. St. Paul, Nov. 24, 1933; s. Edward Martin and Anne (Bizjak) A.; m. Barbara Virginia Wilcox, 1953 (div.); m. Barbra Ann Couse, Aug. 25, 1973; children: Douglas Andrew, Susan Denise, Kathleen Elizabeth; stepchildren: Ralph K. Hipps, Freda E. Hipps. AB, George Washington U., 1955; MA in Polit. Sci., U. Hawaii, 1973, PhD, 1976. Commd. ensign U.S. Navy, 1955, advanced through grades to lt. comdr., 1965; intelligence officer U.S. Navy, various locations, 1955-76; assoc. dir. Law of the Sea Inst., U. Hawaii, Honolulu, 1977-92, acting dir., 1992—; instr. polit. sci. Chaminade U. Honolulu, 1976-83, U. Hawaii, 1983-86. Co-editor: Alternatives in Deep Seabed Mining, 1979, Ocean Development in Pacific Basin, 1983, New Developments in Marine Science and Technology, 1989; contbr. articles to profl. jours. Bd. dirs. Moiliili Community Assn., Honolulu, 1973-83. Decorated Joint Svc. Commendation medal, Vietnam Svc. medal, Vietnam Campaign medal. Mem. Am. Statis. Assn., U.S. Naval Inst., Law of the Sea Inst. (life), Am. Radio Relay League, Masons. Home: 1457 Aunauna St Kailua HI 96734

ALLEN, STEPHEN D., management consultant; b. Amsterdam, N.Y., Apr. 20, 1953; s. Roger E. and Marilyn (Geiselman) A.; m. Stasia Stachura, July 19, 1980; children: Christopher Elliott, Thomas Charles. BSCE, Cornell U., 1975. Staff engr. Stewart Engrs., Santa Barbara, Calif., 1975-76; founder SPC Co., Inc., Wallington, N.J., 1976-78; import and prodn. mgr. Otto Roth & Co., Inc., Moonachie, N.J., 1978-82; pres. Esty Co., Santa Monica, Calif., 1982-83; ops. mgr. Gen. Foods Corp., San Francisco, 1983-86; mgmt. cons., prin. Stephen D. Allen, Montara, Calif., 1986-89; pres. Allen Assocs., University Place, Wash., 1989—; cons. Gen. Foods, 1986, Dorman Roth Foods, 1987—. Sec.-treas. University Place Parks, 1991—. Mem. Am. Mgmt. Assn., Astron. Soc. of Pacific, Mensa. Office: Allen Assocs 2902 Soundview Dr W University Place WA 98466-1711

ALLEN, SUSAN MACALL, librarian; b. Detroit, Nov. 4, 1944; d. Edward and Barbara E. (Johnson) M.; m. William Barclay Allen, Oct. 14, 1969; children: Danielle, B. Marc. BA, U. Wis., 1967, MALS, 1968; MA, St. John's Coll., Santa Fe, N.M., 1989. Lic. life jr. coll. tchr., Calif. Asst. dir., librarian Coll. Student Personnel Inst., Claremont, Calif., 1968-70; abstracter Higher Edn Abstracts, Claremont, Calif., 1972-73, assoc. editor, 1973-78; master Webb Sch. Calif., Claremont, Calif., 1979-81; reference librarian Libraries of Claremont Colls., Claremont, Calif., 1981-87; asst. to dir., acting head Spl. Coll. Libraries, Claremont, Calif., 1987-90; head Spl. Coll. Librs., Claremont, Calif., 1990—; founder Oldtown Press, Claremont, 1984—; mem. adv. bd. Am. Antiquarian Soc. Program in the History of the Book, Worcester, Mass., 1988--. Contbr. articles in field to profl. jours. Mem. Calif. Rep. Cen. Com., 1987-88. Mem. ALA, Am. Coll. and Rsch. Librs. (mem. security com. 1988—, rare books and manuscripts sect. ethical standards rev. com. 1990—). Office: Honnold/Mudd Libr 800 N Dartmouth Ave Claremont CA 91711-3991

ALLEN, THOMAS LAVERN, university development administrator; b. St. Louis, June 24, 1947; s. Ottis Lavern and Lillian Wanda A.; m. Sharon Marie Kuntzman, June 6, 1969; children: Nathaniel Thomas, Rebekah Sarah. BJ, U. Mo., 1969. Vol. tchr. U.S. Peace Corps, Bondoukou, Ivory Coast, 1969-71; editor Meramec Valley Transcript, Pacific, Mo., 1972-73; asst. dir. fund raising Midwestern Area Office ARC, St. Louis, 1973-77; dir. pub. relations, fin. devel. Epworth Children's Home, Webster Groves, Mo., 1977-83; v.p. Welch Assocs., St. Louis, 1983-85; dir. devel. St. Louis Mercantile Libr. Assn., 1985-86; devel. cons. Mt. W. Ctr. for Regional Studies, Logan, Utah, 1986-89; exec. dir. of devel. Utah State U., Logan, 1989—. Active Nat. Com. Planned Giving, Coun. Advancement and Support of Edn., Utah Planned Giving Roundtable. Named Ky. Col., Gov. Commonwealth of Ky., 1974; recipient Presdl. citation, Religious Pub. Rels. Coun., 1986. Mem. Nat. Soc. Fund Raising Execs. (cert. fund raising exec., nat. bd. dirs. 1984, 85, 1st v.p. St. Louis 1984, 85), Utah Soc. Fund Raisers (v.p. professionalism and edn. 1992-93), Am. Long Rifle Assn. (western partisan 1989-90). Methodist. Home: 140 E 200 N PO Box # 138 Millville UT 84326-0138 Office: Utah State Univ Old Main 101 Logan UT 84322-1420

ALLEN, TIMOTHY BURBANK, recreational company executive; b. Burlington, Vt., Feb. 12, 1956; s. George Wyman and Helen Louise (Hamilton) A.; m. Karen Ann Sprague, Sept. 28, 1991; 1 child, Kristen Alison. Owner, operator Windsurf Del Valle, Livermore, Calif., 1980—; windsurfing instr. Internat. Windsurf Sailing Schs., Vt., 1978—. Appeared as clown on skis, juggler on skis for Spl. Olympics, ABC Sports, 1979-80; co-author: Family Windsurfing, 1983. Celebrity ski instr. Celebrity Pro-Am, Heavenly Valley Tahoe, 1979-80, 80-81. Company named Largest Windsurfing Sch. in the U.S.A., 1984. Mem. Profl. Ski. Instrs. Am. (alpine ski instr. 1978—), Am. Windsurf Industries Assn. (Sch. of Yr. 1990, bd. dirs. 1991—).

ALLENBAUGH, G. ERIC, organization development consulting company owner; b. San Fernando, Calif., Aug. 8, 1944; s. Donald Hoyt and Wilhelmina (Jordan) A.; m. Kay M. (Studebaker), Nov. 7, 1987; children: Peter, Timothy, Rick, David. BA, U. Calif., Northridge, 1966; MPH, UCLA, 1968; PhD, U. Oreg., 1981. Asst. adminstr. Valley Presbyn. Hosp., Van Nuys, Calif., 1968-71, Sacred Heart Gen. Hosp., Eugene, Oreg., 1971-79; pres. Allenbaugh Assocs., Inc., Lake Oswego, Oreg., 1979--. Author: Wake-up Calls: You Don't Have to Sleepwalk Through Your Life, Love, or Career, 1992. Recipient Walter S. Hilborne Human Relations award, 1962; Hosp. Council of So. Calif. Performance award, 1971; Ky. Colonel 1988. Fellow Am. Coll. Hosp. Adminstrs. Home and Office: 17545 Kelok Rd Lake Oswego OR 97034-6653

ALLERHEILIGEN, ROBERT PAUL, marketing educator; b. Denver, Dec. 23, 1944; s. Paul William and Helen Idris (Hodges) A.; m. Sandra Jeanne Lee, June 17, 1967 (div. 1982); children: Laura, Brad. BA, Colo. State U., 1967, MBA, 1974; PhD, U. So. Calif., 1986. Asst. prof. U. No. Colo., Greeley, 1974-75; instr. U. So. Calif., L.A., 1979-85; coord. spl. programs Colo. State U., Ft. Collins, 1975-79, asst. prof. mktg., 1985—, dir. internat. programs Coll. of Bus., 1991—; officer JMN Enterprises, Inc., L.A., 1980—; prof. Exec. Devel. Inst., Ft. Collins, 1985-90, Exec. MBA, Denver, 1990—; prof. MBA program Mind Ext. U. Cable V, 1990—; cons. in field. Contbr. articles to profl. jours. Capt. USMC, 1967-70. Mem. Internat. Agribus. Mgmt. Assn., Japan Am. Soc., Australian-Am. C. of C., Internat. Trade Assn. Colo., Colo. Internat. Edn. Assn., Am. Mktg. Assn., Internat. Bus. Assn. Rockies (bd. dirs. no. Colo.-Wyo. chpt.), Sertoma (bd. dirs.). Republican. Home: 1201 Solstice Ln Fort Collins CO 80525-1225 Office: Colo State U Mktg Dept Clark Bldg Fort Collins CO 80523

ALLERY, KENNETH EDWARD, air force officer; b. Holyoke, Mass., Mar. 3, 1925; s. Alfred Edward and Anne (Millen) A.; m. Constance DuFresne, June 22, 1946; children—Katherine Ann, Kenneth Scott, Bryan Keith, David Edward. B.A., Park Coll., 1965; M.S., George Washington U., 1969; grad., Air Command and Staff Coll., 1961, Nat. War Coll., 1969. Commd. 2d lt. U.S. Army Air Force, 1944; advanced through grades to brig. gen. U.S. Air Force, 1972; insp. with Insp. Gen. Team 17th Air Force; exec. officer, ops. officer 526th Fighter Interceptor Squadron, Ramstein Air Base, Germany, 1961; sr. Air Force adviser Oreg. Air N.G., Portland Internat. Airport, 1965-67; dir. ops. and tng. 1st Air Force, Stewart AFB, N.Y., 1967-68; mem. N.Am. br. Directorate Plans and Programs, Orgn. Joint Chiefs of Staff, 1969-71; asst. dep. chief of staff for plans Aerospace Def. Command, Ent AFB, Colo., 1971-72; asst. dep. chief of staff for plans N.Am. Air Def. Command/Continental Air Def. Command, 1972-73, asst. dep. chief of staff for ops., 1973-74; also dep. chief of staff for ops. Aerospace Def. Command; command insp. gen. NORAD/CONAD/ADC, 1974-76; ret.; asst. to v.p. Syscon Corp., Colorado Springs, 1976-85; bus. devel. mgr. Litton Computer Services, Colorado Springs, 1985—; bd. govs. Nat. Coll., Colorado Springs, 1993—. Decorated D.S.M., D.F.C., Air medal with 4 oak leaf clusters, Meritorious Service medal with oak leaf cluster, Air Force Commendation medal. Home: 1320 Rangely Dr Colorado Springs CO 80921-2692 Office: Litton Computer Svcs 985 Space Center Dr Ste 204 Colorado Springs CO 80915-3627

ALLGAIER, ALLISON E., systems development manager; b. Princeton, N.J., Aug. 18, 1965; d. Glen Robert and Cynthia Margaret (Campbell) A. BS in Bus. Mgmt., Brigham Young U., 1991. Cons. Computer Cons. Ctr., Provo, Utah, 1989-91; contracts mgr. Pacific Physician Svcs., Redlands, Calif., 1991-92, systems development mgr., 1992—. Treas. Habitat for Humanity, San Bernardino, Calif., 1992, v.p. fiscal svcs., 1992—. Republican. Mem. Ch. Jesus Christ of Latter-day Saints. Home: 1336 E Pennsylvania Ave Redlands CA 92374 Office: Pacific Physician Svcs 1826 Orange Tree Ln Redlands CA 92374

ALLGOWER, EUGENE LEO, mathematics educator; b. Chgo., Aug. 11, 1935; s. Eugene and Martha (Kettner) A.; m. Solveig Allgower, Aug. 30, 1958; 1 child, Chris. BS in Math., Ill. Inst. Tech., 1957, MS in Math., 1959, PhD in Math., 1964. Prof. math. Colo. State U., Fort Collins, 1966--. Co-author: (with K. Georg) Numerical Continuation Methods, 1990; editor: (with H. O. Peitgen) Numerical Solution of Nonlinear Equations, 1981, (with K. Georg) Computational Solution of Nonlinear Systems, 1990 (with K. Bohmer and M. Golubitsky) Bifurcation and Symmetry, 1992; contbg. writer to SIAM Review. Alexander V. Humboldt Found. sr. fellowship, Bonn, Germany, 1988-89. Mem. Am. Math. Soc., Soc. for Indsl. and Applied Math. Office: Colo State Univ Dept Math Fort Collins CO 80523

ALLIN, ROBERT CAMERON, obstetrician and gynecologist; b. Evanston, Ill., Sept. 29, 1938; s. Frank Cameron and June Barber A.; m. Joann Elaine Spencer, Sept. 20, 1969; children: Blake Cameron, Kimberly June. BA, Northwestern, 1960, MD, 1964. Diplomate Am. Bd. of Obstetrics and Gynecology. Intern Highland Gen. Hosp., Oakland, Calif., 1964-65; resident Santa Clara Valley Med. Ctr., San Jose, Calif., 1967-70; med. staff Hawaii Permanente Med. Group, Honolulu, 1970-82; pvt. practice Honolulu, 1982—. Capt. USMC, 1965-67, Vietnam. Mem. Am. Coll. Obstetrics and Gynecology, Hawaii Med. Assn., Hawaii County Med. Assn. Republican. Club: Outrigger Canoe. Home: 1452 Kamole St Honolulu HI 96821-1422

ALLISON, DAVID LORD, lawyer; b. Washington, Dec. 2, 1942; s. Robert Thomas and Patricia Ellen (Lord) A. BA, Marian Coll., Indpls., 1964; JD, Ind. U., 1968; LLM in Marine Affairs, U. Wash., 1990. Bar: Ind. 1968, Alaska. 1982. Pvt. practice Indpls., 1968-69, 73-79; ptnr. Allison & Barnhart, Attys., Indpls., 1969-73; policy analyst Office of Gov., State of Alaska, Juneau, 1979-82; ptnr. George & Allison, P.C., Juneau, 1982-84; pvt. practice Juneau, 1984—; bd. dirs. Alaska Power Authority, 1983-88, Alaska Environ. Lobby, 1983—; U.S. adviser, Internat. North Pacific Fisheries Commn., Vancouver, B.C., Can., 1983—; pres. Alaska Environ. Polit. Action Com., Juneau, 1987-89; environ. adviser U.S. Dept. State, Washington and Tokyo, 1988-91. Contbr. articles to pub. affairs and legal publs. Elected to Ind. Ho. of Reps., Indpls., 1969, 70; vol. coord., Hammond for Gov., Anchorage, 1978; regional campaign mgr., Sheffield for Gov., Juneau, 1984. Mem. Am. Judicature Soc., Alaska Bar Assn., Phi Alpha Delta. Democrat. Roman Catholic. Home and Office: PO Box 20229 Juneau AK 99802-0229

ALLISON, LAIRD BURL, business educator; b. St. Marys, W.Va., Nov. 7, 1917; s. Joseph Alexander and Opal Marie (Robinson) A.; m. Katherine Louise Hunt, Nov. 25, 1943 (div. 1947); 1 child, William Lee; m. Genevieve Nora Elmore, Feb. 1, 1957. BS in Personnel and Indsl. Relations magna cum laude, U. So. Calif., 1956; MBA, UCLA, 1958. Chief petty officer USN, 1936-51, PTO; asst. prof. to prof. mgmt. Calif. State U., L.A., 1956-83; asst. dean Calif. State U. Sch. Bus. and Econs., L.A., 1971-72, assoc. dean, 1973-83, emeritus prof. mgmt., 1983—; vis. asst. prof. mgmt. Calif. State U., Fullerton, 1970. Co-authored the Bachelors degree program in mgmt. sci. at Calif. State U., 1963. Mem. U.S. Naval Inst., Navy League U.S. Ford Found. fellow, 1960. Mem. Acad. Mgmt., Inst. Mgmt. Sci., Western Econs. Assn. Internat., World Future Soc., Am. Acad. Polit. Social Sci., Calif. State U. Assn. Emeriti Profs., Calif. State U. L.A. Emeriti Assn. (program v.p. 1986-87, v.p. adminstrn. 1987-88, pres. 1988-89, exec. com. 1990-91, treas. 1991-93), Am. Assn. Individual Investors, Am. Assn. Ret. Persons, Ret. Pub. Employees Assn. Calif. (chpt. sec. 1984-88, v.p. 1989, pres. 1990-92), Am. Legion, Phi Kappa Phi, Beta Gamma Sigma, Alpha Kappa Psi. Home: 2176 E Bellbrook St Covina CA 91724-2346 Office: Calif State U Dept Mgmt 5151 State University Dr Los Angeles CA 90032-4221

ALLISON, SAMUEL DUDLESTON, retired dermatologist; b. Eureka, Utah, May 10, 1911; s. Samuel and Mable Louise (Dudleston) A.; m. Cecil Belle McCready, Sept. 8, 1937; 1 child, Kathryn Lynn Allison Foster. Student Northwestern U., 1930-31; BA, Gooding Coll., 1932; MD, U. Oreg., 1936; MPH, Johns Hopkins U., 1941; cert. in dermatology, NYU-Bellevue Hosp., 1948. Intern, Multnomah County Hosp., Portland, Oreg., 1936-37; dermatol. fellow U. Oreg. Hosps., Portland, 1937-38; venereal disease control officer Oreg. Bd. Health, 1938-42; dir. bur. venereal diseases Honolulu Dept. Health, 1942-45, acting asst. health exec., 1945-46, dir. div. preventive medicine, 1946-47; practice medicine specializing in dermatology, Honolulu, 1948-86; former assoc. clin. prof. dermatology U. Hawaii; med. cons. WHO, Western Pacific Area, 1952; former mem. staffs Queens, Children's St. Francis Hosps., Honolulu; mem. adv. bd. cancer rsch. ctr. Hawaii U. Hawaii, 1987-89, chmn. 1989. Author: (with June Johnson) VD Manual for Teachers, 1946; contbr. articles to profl. jours. Pres., Hawaii Mental Hygiene Soc., 1959. Fellow ACP, AAAS, Royal Soc. Health; mem. AMA, Am. Cancer Soc. (chmn. exec. com. Hawaii div. 1966-67, pres. Hawaii div. 1967, rep. dir. 1968-70), Hawaii Med. Assn. (pres. 1964-65), Honolulu County Med. Soc., Hawaii Dermatol. Assn. (past pres.), Am. Acad. Dermatology, Pacific Dermatologic Soc., Rotary (past pres.), Adventurers Club, Alpha Omega Alpha. Republican. Home: 4240 Kaikoo Pl Honolulu HI 96816-4824

ALLISON, THOMAS JAY, ironworker, clergyman; b. Phoenix, Aug. 16, 1959; s. William Clyde Allison and Gloria Lee (McCintic) Daumau; m. Nitaya Chansaub, May 19, 1985. Student, Bethany Bible Coll., Scotts Valley, Calif., 1984, Berean Sch. of Bible, Springfield, Mo., 1983—. Lic. minister Assemblies of God, 1986; ordained Anchor Bay Evang. Assn., 1991. Journeyman ironworker Ironworkers Apprenticeship, Santa Clara, Calif., 1983, Ironworkers Local 377, San Francisco, 1980—; foreman Wickman Steel Co., Santa Clara, 1988—; pastor S.E. Asian Assembly of God, San Jose, 1987—. Contbr. articles to profl. jours. Children and youth dir. S.E. Asian Assembly of San Jose, 1984-87; chaplain Royal Rangers, Bethel Ch., San Jose, 1985-86. Named to Outstanding Young Men of Am., 1988. Republican. Home: 829 Leigh Ave # 3 San Jose CA 95128 Office: SE Asian Assembly San Jose 1201 S Winchester Blvd San Jose CA 95128

ALLISON, WILLIAM ROBERT, management consultant; b. Newport, Vt., Feb. 4, 1941; s. William Hugh and Eva Marie (Herbert) A.; m. Linda Kay Jarrett, Aug. 13, 1962 (div. Nov. 1974); children: Cherie Louise Allison Coughlin, William Robert Jr.; m. Joan Marie Lisowski, Aug. 4, 1979; 1 child, Donna Marie. BS in Bus. and Psychology, La Roche Coll., 1981. Foreman RCA Computer Systems, Palm Beach Gardens, Fla., 1965-67; mgr. tng. and adminstrn. RCA Computer Systems, Marlboro, Mass., 1967-72; dir. tng. Fruehauf Corp., Detroit, 1972-73; mgr. tng. and edn.automotive ops. Rockwell Internat., Troy, Mich.; 1973-76, mgr. personnel adminstrn., 1977-79; mgr. mgmt. succession planning corp. Rockwell Internat., Pitts., 1979-81, dir. exec. resources, 1981-82, dir. orgn. planning, 1982-85; dir. mgmt. and orgn. planning Rockwell Internat., El Segundo, Calif., 1985-88, v.p. orgn. and human resources planning, 1988-91; mgmt. cons. William Allison & Assocs., Rancho Palos Verdes, Calif., 1991—; corp. bd. advisors Nat. Coun. of La Raza, Washington, 1988-91; bd. advisors MESA, Berkeley, Calif., 1989-91; bd. dirs. Seismic Control Systems, Inc., Anaheim, Calif.; bd. dirs. Cons. Roundtable of So. Calif., 1992—. Served with USAF, 1961-65. Mem. N.Am. Coun. on Mgmt. and Orgn. (conf. bd.), Am. Soc. Human Resources Mgmt., Human Resources Planning Soc., Va. Country Club of Long Beach, Calif. (bd. dirs. 1991—). Republican. Roman Catholic.

ALLMAN, CLESSON DALE, air force officer; b. Erie, Pa., Feb. 27, 1952; s. Frank C. and Josephine N. (Nye) A.; m. Laura L. Mathews Dec. 31, 1983 (div. 1992). Cert. hotel adminstr. Commd. 2d lt. USAF, 1974; advanced through grades to lt. col., 1991; ops. officer N.E. Commissary Complex, Air Force Commissary Svc., Hanscom AFB, Mass., 1979-80; strategic missile flight comdr. 742d Strategic Missile Squadron, Minot AFB, N.D., 1980-82; wing self-inspection program mgr. 91st Strategic Missile Wing, Minot AFB, 1982-84; food svc. officer 437th Svcs. Squadron, Charleston AFB, S.C., 1984-85; comdr. 43d Svcs. Squadron, Andersen AFB, Guam, 1985-87; dir. resource mgmt. Pacific region HQ Air Force Commissary Svc., Hickam AFB, Hawaii, 1987-89; exec. officer HQ Air Force Commissary Svc., Kelly AFB, Tex., 1989-91; subsistence dir. HQ U.S. Ctrl. Command Air Forces, Riyadh, Saudi Arabia, 1990-91; comdr. 3415th Morale, Welfare, Recreation and Svcs. Squadron, Lowry AFB, Colo., 1991—. Decorated Bronze Star. Mem. VFW, Am. Legion, Air Force Assn., St. Andrew Soc. Colo., Air Force Acad. Quarterback Club. Presbyterian. Home: 1872 S Walden Way Aurora CO 80017 Office: 3415 Morale Welfare Rec and Svcs Squadron 3415 MWRS/CC Lowry AFB CO 80230

ALLNUTT, ALVIN HOWARD, real estate associate; b. Okla. City, Aug. 19, 1932; s. Alvin Matthew and Loretta Janetta (Zimmerman) A.; m. Kathryn Ann Miller, Dec. 19, 1953; 1 child, Wesley Howard. BS in Econs., Okla. City U., 1955; MBA, U. Mich., 1965. Commd. ensign USN, 1956, advanced through grades to capt., 1978, ret., 1987; logistics mgr. western region Systems Engring. Assocs. Corp., Bremerton, Wash., 1987-90; comml. real estate sales assoc. Coldwell Banker, Port Orchard, Wash., 1990-93, Herb Loop & Assoc., Port Orchard, Wash., 1993—. Task force dir. Flagship 88, 89, 90, 91, Bremerton. Mem. Soc. Logistics Engrs., Rotary (mem. chmn. 1988), Navy League (sec., treas. 1991). Republican. Home: 6289 Gleneagle Ave SW Port Orchard WA 98366-9184 Office: Herb Loop & Assocs 2501 Mile Hill Dr Port Orchard WA 98366

ALLRED, C. KEITH, lawyer. BA magna cum laude, Brigham Young U.; JD, U. Chgo. Bar: Wash. 1976, U.S. Dist. Ct. (ea. and we. dists.) Wash. 1976, U.S. Ct. Appeals (9th cir.). Ptnr. Davis Wright Tremaine, Seattle; vis. prof. law J. Reuben Clark Sch. Brigham Young U., 1991; lectr. in field. Office: Davis Wright Tremaine 2600 Century Sq 1501 4th Ave Seattle WA 98101

ALLRED, EUGENE LYLE, physician, educator, small business owner; b. Glendale, Calif., Dec. 29, 1949; s. Linville H. and Earlene (Campbell) A.; m. Margaret C. Petersen, Sept. 2, 1973; children: Ryan, Jason, Kyle. BA summa cum laude, U. Calif., Santa Barbara, 1972; MD, U. So. Calif., L.A., 1976. Emergency physician Siskiyou Hosp., Yreka, Calif., 1979—; owner Adventure Whitewater, Ashland, Oreg., 1981—; dir. Mountain Med. Seminars, Ashland, 1982—. Lt. USPHS, 1976-78. Mem. Wilderness Med. Soc. (founder), Audubon Soc. (founder Marble Mountain chpt. 1982), Phi Beta Kappa. Republican. Home: 352 Terrace St Ashland OR 97520-3002 Office: Mountain Med Seminars PO Box 321 Yreka CA 96097-0321

ALLSWANG, JOHN MYERS, computer science educator, historian; b. Chgo., Jan. 16, 1937; s. Eugene Allen and Katherine (Myers) A.; m. Suzanne Menzel, Dec. 19, 1964; children: Eden, Yael. BA, U. Ill., 1959; MA, U. Iowa, 1960; PhD, U. Pitts., 1967. Instr. No. Ill. U., Dekalb, 1965-66; asst. prof. No. Mich. U., Marquette, 1966-68; prof. Calif. State U., Los Angeles, 1968—, chair, 1992—; vis. prof. Hebrew U., Jerusalem, 1971-72, U. Leiden, The Netherlands, 1977-78. Author: California Initiatives and Referendums, 1912-1990, 1992, Bosses, Machines and Urban Voters, 1986, Physician's Guide to Computers, 1985, New Deal and American Politics, 1978, House for All Peoples, 1972. Dir. Calif. Direct Democracy Project. IBM fellow, 1968; recipient Merit award Calif. State U., Los Angeles, 1985, 86, 87, 88, 89. Mem. Orgn. Am. Historians, Am. Hist. Assn. Democrat. Jewish. Home: 2438 La Condesa Dr Los Angeles CA 90049-1222 Office: Calif State U 5151 State University Dr Los Angeles CA 90032

ALLUMBAUGH, BYRON, grocery company executive. Student, Long Beach, Calif., City Coll. Dir. meat ops. Ralph's Grocery Co., Compton, Calif., from 1958, v.p. store ops., 1967-69, exec. v.p., then pres.; chmn., ceo Ralph's Grocery Co., 1976—. Office: Ralph's Grocery Co 1100 W Artesia Blvd Compton CA 90220-5186

ALMGREN, PETER ERIC, aerospace industry executive; b. Everett, Wash., Oct. 10, 1948; s. Peter Edward A. and Gayle Zoe (Gustufson) Schroeder; m. Diane Kay Jenft, Dec. 20, 1975; children: John Peter, Nathaniel Eric, Karl David, Kristen Diane. Student, Everett Coll., 1967-71. Millright Pubs. Forest Products, Everett, 1970-72; dept. mgr. Ayr-Way Stores, Middletown, Ohio, 1972-73; truck driver Almgren Trucking, Mukilteo, Wash., 1973-75; auto salesperson Everett Datsun, 1976-77; lumber grader Quadra-Tech, Arlington, Wash., 1977-78; tool maker Boeing, Seattle, 1978-83, 84-85, cost estimator, 1985—; truck driver John Kooy Trucking, Lynnwood, Wash., 1983-84. Firefighter Mukilteo Fire Dept., 1977-87; den leader Cub Scout Pack 16, Mukilteo, 1989. Mem. Edmonds Yacht Club (rear commodore 1990-91, vice commodore 1991-92, commodore 1992-93, Boating Family of Yr. 1989, Lifesaving award 1989, Commodore's award 1990). Democrat. Congregationalist. Home: 1320 Goat Trail Rd Mukilteo WA 98275-2201

ALMONTE, PATRICIA KILLELEA, writer; b. Leominster, Mass., Feb. 5, 1952; d. John Francis and Mary Catherine (Canzio) Killelea; m. Robert H. Boudreau, Sept. 1973 (div. 1978); m. Ronald Wayne Almonte, Mar. 22, 1986. BA, U. Hawaii, Manoa, 1990. Rsch. asst. Oceanic Inst., Waimanalo, Hawaii, 1990—; contbg. writer Trade Pub. Co., Honolulu, 1991—. Home: 575 C Keolu Dr 1 Kailua HI 96734 Office: Oceanic Inst Makapuu Point Waimanalo HI 96795

ALMQUIST, HERMAN JAMES, research and development executive; b. Helena, Mont., Mar. 3, 1903; s. Harry and Mary (Ericson) A.; m. Viola Dorothy Pimentel, Oct. 7, 1935; children: Alan James, Eric John. BS, Mont. State U., 1925; PhD, U. Calif., 1932; DSc (hon.), Mont. State U., 1952. Instr. to asst. prof. to assoc. prof. U. Calif., Berkeley, 1932-44; dir. rsch. F.E. Bouth Co., San Francisco, 1944-48; v.p., dir. rsch. The Grange Co., Modesto, Calif., 1948-68; ret. The Grange Co., Modesto, 1968; Editorial bd. Ann. Rev. Biochemistry, 1942-50, bd. dirs., 1942-73. Co-discoverer of vitamin K; research in isolation, identification and synthesis of vitamin K. 1st lt. Mont. Nat. Guard, 1927-30. Recipient Citation Calif. Legis., 1967, Borden award, Borden Co., 1939. Fellow AAAS, Am. Inst. Nutrition, Poultry Sci. Assn.; mem. Masons. Republican. Home: 5231 Mississippi Bar Dr Orangevale CA 95662-5716

ALONZO, R. GREGORY, professional speaker; b. San Bernardino, Calif., Apr. 9, 1954; s. Rudy and Remi (Vicente) A. BA, Pitzer Coll., Claremont, Calif., 1980. Dir. programs P.T. Bina, Jakarta, Indonesia, 1980-84; v.p. sales PacTel, Cypress, Calif., 1984-89; prof. sales trainer Success Unltd., Brea, Calif., 1989—. Mem. Nat. Speakers Assn., Profl. Speakers Network, Internat. Platform Assn., Toastmasters Internat. Democrat. Roman Catholic. Office: R Gregory Unlimited 101 W Central Ave Ste 111B Brea CA 92621-3364

ALOOT, MARIANO DANIEL, business management consultant; b. Covina, Calif., Dec. 2, 1947; s. Mariano DeVera and Louise Ruby (Rundle) A.; children: John Daniel, Michael David. BA, San Jose State U., 1969. Asst. exec. dir. Mental Health Assn., Santa Clara, Calif., 1968-71; project dir. Op. Share, San Jose, Calif., 1971-73; asst. to v.p. Calif. State U., Hayward, 1973-80; exec. dir. Merit Shop Tng. Ctr., Dublin, Calif., 1980-82; v.p. bus. devel. San Jose Devel. Corp., 1985-87; prin. Mariano Group, San Jose, 1982—; pres., chmn. bd. Profl. Tng. Ctr., Inc., San Jose, 1987-91; dir. Silicon Valley/San Mateo County Small Bus. Devel. Ctr., San Jose, Calif., 1991—. Mem. Filipino-Am. C. of C., San Jose C. of C. Republican. Lutheran. Office: Small Bus Devel Ctr 111 N Market St Ste 150 San Jose CA 95131-1806

ALPERS, JOHN HARDESTY, JR., financial planning executive, retired military officer; b. Richmond, Va., Sept. 7, 1939; s. John Hardesty and Laura Elizabeth (Gaylor) A.; m. Sharon Kay Kurrle, May 1, 1971; 1 child, John Hardesty III. BS, U. Colo., 1963; MBA, InterAm. U., 1969; postgrad. USAF Squadron Officers Sch., 1968-69, USAF Command and Staff Coll., 1976-78, USAF Air War Coll., 1978-79, Coll. of Fin. Planning, 1989. CFP; registered investment adv. svc. exec. Commd. 2d lt. U.S. Air Force, 1964, advanced through grades to lt. col., 1979; SAC B-52 navigator, select radar bombardier, P.R., 1967-70; squadron weapon systems officer Ubon RTAFB, Thailand, 1970-71, radar strike officer Linebacker II strike plans officer, 1972; prisoner of war, Hanoi, N. Vietnam, 1972-73; asst. wing weapons officer Seymour-Johnson AFB, N.C., 1971-72, wing command post controller, 1973-74; asst. prof. aerospace studies AFROTC, U. Ariz., Tucson, 1974-78; asst. div. chief aviation sci. USAF Acad., Colorado Springs, 1978-79, spl. asst. to commandant, 1979-80, div. chief plans, policy and standardization/evaluation, 1980-83; ret., 1983; rep. Waddell & Reed, Inc., 1986-90; v.p. Fin. Planning & Mgmt., Inc. Boulder, Colo., 1990—; rep., Fin. Network Investment Corp; lectr., speaker in field. POW/MIA Activist. With USCG, 1961-63. Decorated Legion of Merit, D.F.C. (2), Bronze Star, Air Medal (9), Air Force Commendation medal (2), Purple Heart (2), Vietnamese Cross of Gallantry; recipient ceremonial sabre U.S. Air Force Acad. Cadet Corps, 1983. Mem. Air Force Assn., Ret. Officers Assn., U.S. Strategic Inst., Am. Def. Inst., Red River Valley Fighter Pilots Assn., Arnold Air Soc., Nam-POWS, Inc., Inst. CFPs, Internat. Assn. Fin. Planning, Internat. Bd. Standards & Practices Cert. Fin. Planners, Internat. Platform Assn., Pi Kappa Alpha. Republican. Home: JSR Boulder Heights 189 Overlook Ln Boulder CO 80302 Office: Fin Planning & Mgmt Inc 2995 Center Green Ct South Boulder CO 80301

ALPERS, ROBERT CHRISTOPHER, engineer; b. Lansing, Mich., Mar. 14, 1949; s. Robert Joseph and Elizabeth (Carroll) A.; m. Barbara Colleen Porter, June 9, 1973; children: Rhiannon, Julia, Nicholas. BS in Engring., Ohio State U., 1972. Registered profl. engr., Colo. Sales engr. Nelson Div. TRW, Columbus, Ohio, 1973-74; sr. sales engr. MCC Powers Regulator, Denver, 1974-79; project adminstr. RMH Group Cons., Lakewood, Colo., 1979-83; gen. mgr. Staefa Control Systems Inc., Denver, 1983—; instr. Tech Sch., Denver Pub. Sch., Emily Griffith, Denver, 1976-79; guest speaker Climitization, Madrid, 1989. Pres. St. Vincent DePaul Parish Council, Denver, 1984-86. Capt. USAR, 1972-80. Mem. ASHRAE. Republican. Roman Catholic. Home: 1134 S Williams St Denver CO 80210-1822 Office: Staefa Control System Inc Ste 200 1205 S Platte River Dr Denver CO 80223

ALPERSTEIN, DONALD WAYNE, lawyer; b. Denver, June 25, 1951; s. Arnold and Pearl (Greenblot) A.; m. Jean Margaret Herzberger, May 12, 1979. BA, Whitman Coll., 1973; JD, Harvard U., 1976. Bar: Colo. 1976, U.S. Dist. Ct. Colo. 1976, U.S. Ct. Appeals (10th cir.) 1979. Law clk. to Hon. Aurel M. Kelly Colo. Ct. Appeals, Denver, 1976-77; pvt. practice Denver, 1977-79; instr. Denver Paralegal Inst., 1978; assoc. Arnold Alperstein, Atty. at Law, Denver, 1979-81; prin. Alperstein, Alperstein & Forman, P.C., Denver, 1981-83; ptnr. Dominick, Covell & Stern, P.C., Denver, 1983-85; prin. Alperstein & Covell, P.C., Denver, 1985—; chmn. legal fee arbitration com., Denver Bar Assn., 1990—; speaker Nat. Bus. Inst., Denver, 1991, 92, Continuing Legal Edn. of Colo., Inc., Denver, 1991, 93. Pres. Colo. Manufactured Housing Licensing Bd., 1991—; active U.S. Fencing Assn., Olympic Tng. Ctr. Colorado Springs, Colo., 1990—; literary tutor Adult Learning Source, Denver, 1987—; vol. atty. Thursday Night Bar Assn. Recipient Pro Bono award Colo. Bar Assn., 1985, 86. Mem. ABA, AME Arbitration Assn. (panel arbitrator 1992—), Am. Trial Lawyers Assn., Colo. Bar Assn., Denver Bar Assn., U.S. Fencing Assn. (bd. dirs. 1986—, exec. com. 1992—), Planetary Soc. Democrat. Office: Alperstein & Covell P C 1600 Broadway Ste 2000 Denver CO 80202-4920

ALPERT, BURT MORRIS, social worker, retired; b. N.Y.C., May 26, 1926; s. Herman and Pauline (Kameny) A.; m. Elizabeth Freeman, Mar. 21, 1950 (div. 1978); children: Peter, David, Joshua White. BS in Psychology, CCNY, 1947; postgrad., Columbia U., 1947-48. Machinist various cos., N.Y.C., 1949-56; social worker King County Dept. Social Svcs., Seattle, 1956-58; instr. Berkeley (Calif.) Free U., 1967, Antioch Coll. West, San Francisco, 1972; social worker San Francisco Dept. Social Svcs., 1958-80; rsch. asst. Am. Inst. for Psychical Rsch., N.Y.C., 1946, CCNY, 1946. Author: Inversions, 1972, Organizing, 1974, Book of R, 1983, Mother of Waters, 1989; author (play) Parabhagavadgita, 1991; satirical essayist March of Labor mag., 1954-55; movie reviewer Liberation mag., 1977. R&D, Ideas for Action, N.Y.C., 1946-48; organizer Progressive Party Am., Bronx, N.Y., 1948; pres. San Francisco Social Svc. Employees Union, 1969. With USN, 1944-46. Green. Home: 877 26th Ave San Francisco CA 94121

ALPS, GLEN EARL, printmaker, educator; b. Loveland, Colo., June 20, 1914. B.A., U. No. Colo.; M.F.A., U. Wash.; postgrad., U. Iowa. prof. art emeritus U. Wash. Author: works included in numerous art and print books. The Collagraph; Work represented in permanent collections, Mus. Modern Art, N.Y.C., Phila. Art Mus., Chgo. Art Inst., Los Angeles County Art Mus., Library of Congress, others; sculpture includes panels, Seattle Public Library, 1960, fountains, Seattle Mcpl. Bldg., 1961, First Christian Ch, Greeley, Colo., 1962, others; numerous exhbns. prints. Tamarind fellow; Ford Found. fellow; recipient Wash. Gov.'s award, U. No. Colo. Trail Blazer Alumnus award, 1985, Hall of Fame award U. No. Colo. Alumni, 1989. Mem. NW Printmakers (pres. 1951-53, 62-64). Address: 6523 40th Ave NE Seattle WA 98115

AL-QAZZAZ, AYAD, sociology educator; b. Baghdad, Iraq, Aug. 23, 1941; s. Ali and Sharifa (Ahmad) Al-Q.; m. Samira Zara (div. 1975); 1 child, Mayada. BA, U. Baghdad, 1962; MA, U. Calif., Berkeley, 1966; PhD, U. Calif., 1970. Rsch. asst. U. Calif., Berkeley, 1967; teaching asst. U. Calif., summer 1968, asst. prof. sociology, summer 1970; assoc. prof. Chapman Coll., Sacramento, 1976; asst. prof. sociology Calif. State U., Sacramento, 1969-75; assoc. prof. sociology Calif. State U., 1975-80, prof. sociology, 1980—. Author: Women in the Middle East and North Africa, 1977, Transnational Links Between the Arab Community in the U.S. and the Arab World, 1978; co-author: The Arab World--Handbook for Teachers; co-editor: The Arab World Notebook, 1989; contbr. articles to profl. jours. Iraqi Govt. fellow, 1963-65, U. Calif. grantee, 1966-69, others. Mem. Assn. Arab-Am. Univ. Grads. (pres. 1990), Iraqi Sociol. Assn. (bd. dirs. 1978—), Mid. East Studies Assn., World Affairs Coun. (bd. dirs.), Calif. Coun. Social Studies, Nat. Coun. Social Studies. Democrat. Islam. Home: 3501 Detuch Way Carmichael CA 95608 Office: California State Univ 6000 J St Sacramento CA 95819-2605

ALQUIST, ALFRED E., state senator; b. Memphis; m. Elaine Alquist; 1 son, Alan. Educated Southwestern U. Former mem. Calif. State Assembly; mem. Calif. State Senate, 1966—, chmn. fin. com., mem. govt. orgn. and energy and pub. utilities coms. Candidate for lt. gov. State of Calif., 1970; mem. Little Hoover Commn.; mem. Calif. Seismic Safety Commn., Com. Sci. and Tech.; trustee Good Samaritan Hosp. Served with Air-Sea Emergency Rescue Service, USAAF, 1942-44. Mem. Nat. Conf. State Legislators, Am. Legion. Democrat. Clubs: Commonwealth, Elks. Home: 100 Paseo De San Antonio San Jose CA 95113-1402 Office: Office of State Senate 100 Paseo de San Antonio #209 San Jose CA 95113

ALQUIST, LEWIS RUSSELL, art educator; b. Glen Cove, N.Y., Sept. 27, 1946; s. Russell Edward and Marie (Lewis) A. AS, Broward Community Coll., 1966; BFA, Fla. Atlantic U., 1968; MFA, Cranbrook Acad. Art, 1972. Asst. prof. Edinboro (Pa.) State U., 1973-80; vis. artist Sch. of Art Inst. of Chgo., 1980-84; assoc. prof. Ariz. State U., Tempe, 1984—; artist-in-residence The Exploratorium, San Francisco, 1985-86; cons. Phoenix Arts Commn., 1990, Ariz. Commn. on the Arts, Phoenix, 1988. One-man shows include Weber State U., Ogden, 1990, U. Tex., El Paso, 1989, Randolph State Gallery, Chgo., 1982; curator group exhibition Name Gallery, Chgo., 1982. Visual artist fellowship Ariz. Commn. Arts, 1988, Nat. Endowment for Arts, 1986, Ill. Arts Coun., 1985; artists material grant Contemporary Forum, Phoenix Art Mus., 1988. Office: Sch of Art Ariz State U Tempe AZ 85287

ALSAKER, ROBERT JOHN, information systems specialist; b. Los Angeles, June 15, 1945; s. Lauris Ronald and Hazel Mildred (Danz) A.; m. Cynthia Ann Gillesvog, Feb. 25, 1984; children: Troy R., Erik G., Karlee A. AA, Fullerton (Calif.) Jr. Coll., 1966; BS, Moorhead (Minn.) State Coll., 1970. Project mgr. Jet Propulsion Lab., Pasadena, Calif., 1970-80; mgr. mgmt. info. systems Kroy Inc., Scottsdale, Ariz., 1980-85; adminstr. City of Pasadena, 1985-86; mgr. tech. cons. U.S. West Info. Systems, Phoenix, 1986-88; v.p., mgmt. info. systems ACB Cos. Inc., Phoenix, 1988—; bd. dirs. ACB Cos. Inc., Phoenix, Toby House Inc. Served in U.S. Army, 1968-69, Vietnam. Republican. Lutheran. Office: 714 E Van Buren St Phoenix AZ 85006-3399

ALSCHULER, GEORGE ARTHUR, lawyer; b. Aurora, Ill., Apr. 17, 1935; s. Jacob Edward and Carolyn Amelia (Strauss) A.; m. Mary Ann Yuen, July 1, 1983; 1 child, Erik Benjamin. AA, Menlo Coll., 1955; BA in Polit. Sci., Stanford U., 1957, JD, 196l. Bar: Calif. 1967; cert. p.o.s.t. police officer, Calif. Assoc. Hardin Fletcher Cook & Hayes, Oakland, Calif., 1968, Schofield & Cunningham, Oakland, 1968-70; ptnr. Vendt, Johnson & Alschuler, Berkeley, Calif., 1970-72; pvt. practice Oakland, 1972-77; ptnr. specializing in arbitration and dispute resolution Curran & Alschuler P.C., Oakland, 1977—; pro tem judge Berkeley Mcpl. Ct., Oakland Mcpl. Ct.; arbitrator Alameda County Superior Ct., Am. Artibration Assn.; past sec., trustee Legal Aide Soc. Alameda County, Oakland, 1983-88; with Alameda County Bar Judicial Qualification Com. Res. police officer Berkeley Police Dept., 1975—; sec., trustee East Bay Zoo Soc., Oakland, 1984-93. Mem. Calif. State Bar, Alameda County Bar Assn., Acad. Model Aeros. Democrat. Jewish. Office: 166 Santa Clara Ave Oakland CA 94610

ALSOP, ROGER CLARK, biochemist, chemist, researcher; b. Burbank, Calif., Mar. 19, 1957; s. John Disney and Marion Ann (Sullivan) A.; m. Edith Zaplan, Aug. 8, 1992. AA in Liberal Arts, Mt. San Antonio Coll., 1977; BS in Biology, Calif. State Polytech. U., Pomona, 1982, postgrad., 1982-84. Clin. lab. asst. CLMG Clin. Lab., L.A., 1984-85; rsch. asst. Rsch. Ednl. Inst., Torrance, Calif., 1985-86; prodn. chemist D.P.C., L.A., 1986-88; scientist Alpha Therapeutics, L.A., 1988-91; rsch. scientist II Baxter Biotech, 1991—. Mem. ACS, N.Y. Acad. Sci., Protein Soc. Home: 8534 Hyacinth St Rancho Cucamonga CA 91730

ALSPACH, BRIAN ROGER, educator; b. Minot, N.D., May 29, 1938; s. Eugene Victor A. and Dolores Elaine (Barke) Kennedy; m. Linda Jo Nelson, June 14, 1978 (div.); children: Alina Rae, Mark Cameron; m. Katherine Anne Heinrich, Jan. 1, 1980. BA, U. Wash., 1961; MA, U. Calif., Santa Barbara, 1964, PhD, 1966. Asst. prof. Simon Fraser U., Burnaby, B.C., Can., 1966-73, assoc. prof., 1973-80, prof. math., 1980—; bd. editors Jour. Graph Theory, Discrete Math., Amsterdam, The Netherlands, Ars Combinatoria, Winnipeg, Man., Can., TREK, Vancouver, B.C., Can.; cons. Glan Cooper & Assocs., Vancouver, 1989—. Editor: Algorithmic Aspects of Combinatorics, 1977, Cycles in Graphs, 1985; contbr. articles to profl. jours. Natural Scis. Engring Rsch. Coun. Can. grnatee, 1966—. Mem. Am. Math. Soc., Math. Assn. Am., Can. Math. Soc., Combinatorics Math. Soc. Australasia. Office: Simon Fraser U, Dept Math, Burnaby, BC Canada V5A 1S6

ALSPACH, DONALD STUART, land use planner; b. Akron, Ohio, May 31, 1944; s. H. Stuart and Louise Anita (Loughman) A.; m. Donna Jean Wyler, May 26, 1967; 1 child, Garrette Ann. BS in Edn., U. Akron, 1968. Assoc. planner Greater Anchorage Area Borough, 1974-75, platting officer, 1975-79; mgr. zoning and platting Municipality of Anchorage, 1979-88, dep. dir., 1988—. Vice chair Alaska Pub. TV, Anchorage, 1990-91, treas., 1988-90. With U.S. Air Force, 1969-73. Mem. Am. Planning Assn. Methodist. Home: 2101 Dawnlight Ct Anchorage AK 99501 Office: Municipality of Anchorage Dept Community Planning & Devel PO Box 1996650 Anchorage AK 99519-6650

ALSPACH, PHILIP HALLIDAY, manufacturing company executive; b. Buffalo, Apr. 19, 1923; s. Walter L. and Jean E. (Halliday) A.; m. Jean Edwards, Dec. 20, 1947; children—Philip Clough, Bruce Edwards, David Christopher; m. Loretta M. Hildebrand, Aug. 1982. B.Engring. in Mech. Engring, Tulane U., 1944. Registered profl. engr., Mass., Wis., La. With Gen. Electric Co., 1945-64, mgr. indsl. electronics div. planning, 1961-64; v.p., gen. mgr. constrn. machinery div. Allis Chalmers Mfg. Co., Milw., 1964-68; exec. v.p., dir., mem. exec. com. Jeffrey Galion, Inc., 1968-69; v.p. I.T.E. Imperial Corp., Springhouse, Pa., 1969-75; pres. E.W. Bliss div. Gulf & Western Mfg. Co., Southfield, Mich., 1975-79; group v.p. Katy Industries, Inc., Elgin, Ill., 1979-85; pres. Intercon Inc., Irvine, Calif., 1985—; bd. dirs. Intercon. Inc., Jandy Ind., Inc., Data-Design Labs., Pansini Corp., Savoy Corp., Carr-Grif, Inc., Fortifiber Corp. Author: Swiss-Bernese Oberland, 1992; papers in field. Mem. pres.'s coun. Tulane U., 1982-90. Mem. Soc. Automotive Engrs. (sr.), IEEE, Soc. Mfg. Engrs., Internat. Fedn. Corp. Dirs., Inst. Dirs. (U.K.), Am. Mgmt. Assn. Clubs: Canadian (N.Y.C.), Met. (N.Y.C.). Home: 23 Alejo Irvine CA 92715-2913 Office: Intercon Inc 2500 Michelson Dr Ste 410 Irvine CA 92715-1548

ALSTON, LELA, state senator; b. Phoenix, June 26, 1942; d. Virgil Lee and Frances Mae Koonse Mulkey; B.S., U. Ariz., 1967; M.S., Ariz. State U., 1971; children—Brenda Susan, Charles William. Tchr. high sch., 1968—; mem. Ariz. State Senate, 1977—. Named Disting. Citizen, U. Ariz. Alumni Assn., 1978. Mem. NEA, Ariz. Edn. Assn., Am. Home Econs. Assn., Ariz. Home Econs. Assn., Am. Vocat. Assn. Methodist. Office: State Senate 1700 W Washington Rd Phoenix AZ 85007

ALSTON, ROBERTA T(HERESA), medical technologist; b. Washburn, Wis., Jan. 19, 1923; d. Thomas Harkness and Theresa (Sullivan) Pratt; m. Henry Farrell Alston, Feb. 6, 1947 (dec. Sept. 1978); children: Joseph, Thomas, Jane; m. Leonard Beverson Farrell, Feb. 26, 1983. BS, U. Calif., Berkeley, 1947. Lic. clin. lab. technologist. Rsch. chemist Scripps Metabolic Clinic, La Jolla, Calif., 1947-48; med. technologist Sloan Kettering Meml. Hosp., N.Y.C., 1949-50, Letterman Army Med. Ctr., San Francisco, 1973-76; supr. chemistry and hematology U.S. Naval Hosp., Long Beach, Calif., 1976—. Treas. Orange County Crippled Children, 1966, PTO, 1967; past scout leader Boy Scouts Am., Girl Scouts Am. Mem. Am. Soc. for Med. Tech., Calif. Assn. for Med. Lab. Tech. Home: 18193 Blue Ridge Dr Santa Ana CA 92705

ALTAMIRANO, BEN D., merchant, insurance agent, state senator; b. Silver City, N.Mex., Oct. 17, 1930; s. Ramon and Eloisa P. (Davila) A.; student Western N.Mex. U.; m. Nina Melendrez, July 24, 1949; children—Yolanda, Benjamin, Paul. Owner, operator Benny's Market Baskets, Silver City, 1949-78, C.H. Pennington Fashions, 1971-84, Nina's Guys N Gals; ins. agt. TBA Ins. Co., Dallas; founder, chmn. bd. Silver City Savs. & Loan Assn.; mem. N.Mex. Senate, 1970—. Mem. City Council Silver City; county commr. Served with U.S. Army, 1946-48. Democrat. Roman Catholic. Home: 1123 N Santa Rita St Silver City NM 88061-5156

ALTAMURA, MICHAEL VICTOR, physician; b. Bklyn., Sept. 28, 1923; s. Frank and Theresa (Inganamorte) A.; m. Emily Catherine Wandell, Sept. 21, 1948; children: Michael Victor, Robert Frank. BS, LIU, 1949; MA, Columbia U., 1951; DO, Kirksville Coll., 1961; MD, Calif. Coll. Medicine, 1962. Diplomate Am. Bd. Family Practice. Intern Los Angeles County Gen. Hosp., 1961-62; practice medicine specializing in family practice Sunnyvale, Calif., 1962—; staff El Camino Hosp., chief family practice dept., 1972-73; preceptor family practice Stanford Sch. Medicine, 1972-73, clin. asst. prof., 1974-81, clin. assoc. prof., 1982—; assoc. prof. family medicine Calif. Coll. Osteopathic Medicine, 1985—; preceptor family practice Davis (Calif.) Sch. Medicine, 1974-75. Author: (with Mary Falconer and Helen Behnke) Aging Patients: A Guide for Their Care. Served to 1st lt. AUS, 1942-45, 51-53; ETO. Recipient Order of Golden Sword, Am. Cancer Soc., 1973. Fellow Am. Acad. Family Physicians (pres. Santa Clara County chpt. 1972-73, Calif. del. Santa Clara chpt. 1991), Calif. Acad. of Family Physicians (bd. dirs. 1987-90), Royal Soc. Health, Am. Geriatric Soc.; mem. AMA, Calif., Santa Clara County socs., Internat. Platform Assn. Republican. Lutheran. Office: 500 E Remington Dr Sunnyvale CA 94087-2657

ALTER, EDWARD T., state treasurer; b. Glen Ridge, N.J., July 26, 1941; s. E. Irving and Norma (Fisher) A.; m. Patricia R. Olsen, 1975; children: Christina Lyn, Ashly Ann, Darci Lee. B.A., U. Utah., 1966; M.B.A., U. Utah, 1967. C.P.A., Calif., Utah. Sr. acct. Touche Ross & Co., Los Angeles, 1967-72; asst. treas. U. Utah, Salt Lake City, 1972-80; treas. State of Utah, Salt Lake City, 1981—; pres. Nat. Assn. State Treas., 1987-88. Bd. dirs. Utah Housing Fin. Agy., Utah State Retirement Bd., pres., 1984-93; mem. Utah State Rep. Ctrl. Com., 1981—, Anthony Com. on Pub. Fin., 1988—. Sgt. USAR, 1958-66. Named to All-pro Govt. Team, City and State Mag., 1988; recipient Jesse M. Uhruh Award for Svc. to State Treas.', 1989. Mem. Am. Inst. CPAs, Nat. Assn. State Treas. (past sr. v.p., pres. 1987), Delta Sigma Pi, Delta Phi Kappa. Club: Utah Bond (pres. 1981-82). Office: State Capitol 215 State Capital Salt Lake City UT 84114

ALTERMAN, DEAN N., lawyer; b. Portland, Oreg., Mar. 15, 1960; s. Clifford B. and Charlotte E. (Horner) A. AB, Harvard U., 1981; JD, Lewis & Clark Coll., 1989. Bar: Oreg. 1989. Assoc. Craig Cooley & Co., Portland, 1981-89; with Stan Wiley, Inc., Portland, 1989; assoc. Kell, Alterman and Runstein, Portland, Oreg., 1989—; bd. dirs. Bank of Vancouver; cons. in field, Portland, 1981-89. Author: Friend Family of West Virginia, 1985; mng. editor Environ. Law, 1987-88; contbr. articles to profl. jours. Mem. Multnomah County Planning Commn., Portland, 1983-91, chmn., 1984-86; bd. dirs. Portland Opportunites Industrialization Ctr., 1986—; ann. fund chmn. Catlin Gabel Sch., Portland, 1987-89; pres., trustee Friend Family Assn. Am. Inc., 1988-92. Mem. Catlin Gabel Alumni Assn., (pres. 1989-92), Harvard U. Club Oreg. (treas. 1984-92, v.p. 1986-89, pres. 1989-92). Democrat. Home: 2935 SE 35th Ave Portland OR 97202-1801 Office: Kell Alterman & Runstein 1001 SW 5th Ave Ste 1800 Portland OR 97204-1194

ALTERMAN, ERIC ROSS, author, journalist; b. Queens, N.Y., Jan. 14, 1960; s. Carl J. and Ruth N. (Weitzman) A.; m. Patricia Ann Caplan, Aug. 10, 1992. BA, Cornell U., 1982; MA, Yale U., 1986; AB, Stanford U., 1993. Assoc. for pub. policy Bus. Execs. for Nat. Security, Washington, 1983-84; sr. fellow World Policy Inst., N.Y.C., 1985—; peace studies fellow Stanford (Calif.) U., 1992; critic-at-large World Policy Jour., Stanford, 1992—. Author: Sound and Fury: The Washington Punditocracy and the Collapse of American Politics, 1992; columnist Mother Jones, 1992—. Home and Office: 7C Abrams Ct Stanford CA 94305

ALTERSITZ, JANET KINAHAN, principal; b. Orange, N.J., May 19, 1951; d. Patrick Joseph and Ida (Ciamillio) K.; 1 child, Jacob. AA, County Coll. Morris, 1971; BA, Glassboro State Coll., 1973; MEd, Ariz. State U., 1980. Educator Washington (N.J.) Twp. Mid. Sch., 1974-77, Deer Valley Sch. Dist., Phoenix, 1977-82; asst. prin. Desert Sky Mid. Sch., Glendale, Ariz., 1983-86, prin., 1986—; cons. and presenter in field. Mem. ASCD, NAASP, Nat. Mid. Sch. Assn., Western Regional Mid. Level. Assn. (program chmn. 1992), Ariz. Sch. Adminstrs. (sec., treas. 1989—), Cen. Ariz. Mid. Level. Assn. (bd. dirs. 1989—), P.O.K. Democrat. Roman Catholic. Home: 4642 W Villa Rita Dr Glendale AZ 85308-1520 Office: Desert Sky Mid Sch 5130 W Grovers Ave Glendale AZ 85308-1300

ALTHEIMER, BRIAN P. See TUTASHINDA, KWELI

ALTMAN, ADELE ROSENHAIN, radiologist; b. Tel Aviv, Israel, June 4, 1924; came to U.S., 1933, naturalized, 1939; d. Bruno and Salla (Silberzweig) Rosenhain; m. Emmett Altman, Sept. 3, 1944; children: Brian R., Alan L., Karen D. Diplomate Am. Bd. Radiology. Intern Queens Gen. Hosp., N.Y.C., 1949-51; resident Hosp. for Joint Diseases, N.Y.C., 1951-52, Roosevelt Hosp., N.Y.C., 1955-57; clin. instr. radiology Downstate Med. Ctr., SUNY, Bklyn., 1957-61; asst. prof. radiology N.Y. Med. Coll., N.Y.C., 1961-65, assoc. prof., 1965-68; assoc. prof. radiology U. Okla. Health Sci. Ctr., Oklahoma City, 1968-78; assoc. prof. dept. radiology U. N.Mex. Sch. Medicine, Albuquerque, 1978-85. Author: Radiology of the Respiratory System: A Basic Review, 1978; contbr. articles to profl. jours. Fellow Am. Coll. Angiology, N.Y. Acad. Medicine; mem. Am. Coll. Radiology, Am. Roentgen Ray Soc., Assn. Univ. Radiologists, Radiol. Soc. N.Am., B'nai B'rith Anti-Defamation League (bd. dirs. N.Mex. state bd.), Hadassah Club.

ALTMAN, IRWIN, psychology educator; b. N.Y.C., July 16, 1930; s. Louis L. and Ethel (Schonberg) A.; m. Gloria Seckler, Jan. 2, 1953; children: David Gary, William Michael. B.A., N.Y.U., 1951; M.A., U. Md., 1954, Ph.D., 1957. Asst. prof. Am. U., Washington, 1957-58; sr. research scientist, asso. prof. Am. U., 1960-62, adj. prof., 1962-69; research scientist human scis. research Arlington, Va., 1958-60; research psychologist Naval Med. Research Inst., Bethesda, Md., 1962-69; adj. prof. U. Md., 1968-69; prof., chmn. psychology dept. U. Utah, Salt Lake City, 1969-76; prof. U. Utah, 1976-79, dean Coll. Social and Behavioral Scis., 1979-83, v.p. for acad. affairs, 1983-87, disting. prof., 1987—. Author: (with J.E. McGrath) Small Groups, 1966, (with D.A. Taylor) Social Penetration, 1973, Environment and Social Behavior, 1975, (with M.Chemers) Culture and Environment, 1980, (with J. Wohlwill) Human Behavior and Environment: Vol. I, 1976, Vol. II, 1977, Vol. III, 1978, Vol. IV, 1980, Vol. V, 1981, Vol. VI, 1983, Vol. VII, 1984, (with C. Werner) Vol. VIII, 1985, (with A. Wandersman) Vol. IX, 1987, (with E. Zube) Vol. X, 1989, (with K. Christensen) Vol. XI, 1990, (with S. Low) Vol. XII, 1992, (with D. Stokols) Handbook of Environmental Psychology, Vols. I & II, 1987; mem. editorial bds.: Small Groups, 1970-79, Man-Environment Systems, 1969-73, Jour. Applied Social Psychology, 1973-85, Sociometry, 1973-76, Environment and Behavior, 1975, Jour. Personality and Social Psychology, 1974-83, Contemporary Psychology, 1975-86, Environ. Psychology and Nonverbal Behavior, Psychology, 1976-90, Am. Jour. Community Psychology, 1978-81, Population and Environment, 1979, Jour. Environ. Psychology, 1982, Computers and Human Behavior, 1985, Internat. Jour. Applied Social Psychology, 1984, Communication Monographs, 1992; assoc. editor Am. Jour. Community Psychology, 1988-92; co-editor Jour. of Eviron. Psychology, 1990—; contbr. articles to profl. jours. Served to 1st lt. Adj. Gen. Corps. AUS, 1954-56. Mem. Am. Psychol. Assn. (pres. div. population and environment), AAAS, Soc. Exptl. Social Psychology, Soc. Psychol. Study Social Issues, Soc. Personality and Social Psychology (pres.), Environ. Design Rsch. Assn., Am. Psychol. Soc.

ALTMAN, JACK, plant pathologist, educator. BS in Plant Pathology, Rutgers U., 1954, PhD, 1957. Grad. rsch. fellow Squibb Inst. Rutgers U., 1954-57; asst. prof., plant pathologist Colo. State U., 1957-63, assoc. prof., plant pathologist, 1963-70, prof., plant pathologist, 1970—; head symposium sect. on soil fumigation Internat. Congress Soil Disinfestation, Brussels, 1973; leader Plant Pathology Delegation., Peoples Rep. China, 1986, Internat. Plant Pathology Delegation, Sweden, Russia, Yugoslavia, Germany, 1989; head plant pathology lab. Dier Allah Expt. Sat., Jordan, 1987. Author, editor: Pesticide Interactions in Crop Production: Beneficial and Deleterious Effects, 1993; contbr. articles to sci. jours.; rsch. in interaction of pesticides in plant disease complexes. Recipient Sr. U.S. Scientist Alexander von Humboldt award Hannover Tech. U., 1977-78, 1983; Peoples Rep. China Disting. Exch. Progam scholar NAS, 1981; Sr. Rural Agrl. fellow Res. Bank Australia., 1988. Mem. Am. Phytopathological Soc., Soc. for Plant Pathology (APS com. for internat. coop. 1992—), Soc. Nematologists, Sigma Xi. Office: Colo State U Dept Plant Path & Weed Science Colorado State University CO 80523

ALTMAN, MORTON IRVING, podiatrist; b. Chgo., June 27, 1942; s. Melvin Altman and Shirley Hill; m. Nancy S. Davis, Jan. 18, 1992; children: Jeffrey, Kenneth, Kindra, Kimberly, Tanya. AA, U. Fla., 1962, BS in Chemistry, 1964; BS, Calif. Coll. Podiatric Med., San Francisco, 1965, DPM, 1968. Diplomate Am. Bd. Podiatric Surgery, Am. Bd. Podiatric Orthopedics. Podiatrist in pvt. practice Miami, Fla., 1969-81; chief podiatry sect. VA Med. Ctr., Albuquerque, 1981—. Editor: Modern Therapeutic Approaches to Foot Problems, 1973. Recipient numerous rsch. grants, 1975—. Mem. Am. Podiatric Med. Assn. (Stickels Silver award 1969, Recognition award 1990), Fed. Svcs. Podiatric Med. Assn., Assn. Mil. Surgeons. Office: VA Med Ctr 2100 Ridgecrest Dr SE Albuquerque NM 87108

ALTMAN, SHELDON, veterinarian; b. Denver, May 15, 1937; s. Sam Bernard and Bessie (Radetsky) A.; BS in Biol. Sci., Colo. State U., 1959, DVM, 1961; m. Arlene Barbara Heller, Aug. 23, 1959; children: Susan Wendy, Howard William, Eden Debra. With Newmark Animal Hosp., 1961-62, Lockhart Animal Hosp., 1964; founder, operator Universal City Pet Clinic, North Hollywood, Calif, 1965-70, merged with M.S. Animal Hosps., Inc., Burbank, 1970—, v.p., 1970—; dir. vet. rsch. and cons. acupuncture rsch. project, pain control unit UCLA, 1975-80; hon. prof. Chinese Medicine U. Oriental Studies, Sch. Chinese Medicine, Los Angeles; mem. faculty Internat. Vet. Acupuncture Soc. Ctr. for Chinese Medicine. Author: An Introduction to Acupuncture for Animals; mem. editorial adv. bd. Calif.

Veterinarian, Internat. Jour. Chinese Medicine; contbr. articles on vet. acupuncture to vet. jours.; contbg. author Veterinary Internal Medicine, 3d edit. Bd. dirs. Emek Hebrew Acad. Served with AUS, 1962-64. Mem. AVMA (conv. speaker 1982), So. Calif., Calif. (co-chmn. com. on alternative therapies) vet. med. assns., Am. Animal Hosp. Assn., Am. Veterinarians for Israel (chpt. pres. 1972-73), Assn. Orthodox Jewish Scientists, Internat. Vet. Acupuncture Soc. (dir.), Ctr. for Chinese Medicine, Internat. Congress Chinese Medicine, Acupuncture Rsch. Inst., Colo. State U. Alumni Assn., Nat. Assn. Vet. Acupuncture (dir. rsch.), Phi Kappa Phi, Phi Zeta, Beta Beta Beta. Jewish (pres. congregation 70-71, dir. 1964—). Home: 5647 Wilkinson Ave North Hollywood CA 91607-1629 Office: 2723 W Olive St Burbank CA 91505

ALTON, COLLEEN EDNA, educator; b. Ventura, Calif., Mar. 17, 1959; d. Donald F. and Edna E. Mills; m. David S. Alton, Sept. 29, 1984; 1 child, Matthew C. BA, U. Calif., Irvine, 1981; diploma, Goldwest Police Acad., 1981; credential, U. Calif., Irvine, 1985. Community svc. officer Irvine Police Dept., 1979-81, police officer, 1981-88; tchr. Chino (Calif.) Unified Sch. Dist., 1989—. Vol. Spl. Olympics, Ventura County, 1974-77, Orange County, 1977-85; vol. rape crisis counselor Irvine Police Dept., 1981-85; coach Chino Youth Softball, 1989-90; mem. PTA Chino, 1991—; libr. PTA-Butterfield Ranch Sch. Mem. Job's Daus. (queen 1977). Republican. Office: Chino Unified Sch Dist 5130 Riverside Dr Chino CA 91710-4130

ALTSCHUL, DAVID EDWIN, record company executive, lawyer; b. N.Y.C., Apr. 8, 1947; s. Norbert and Grace (Aderer) A.; m. Margaret Berne, July 4, 1969; children: Jonathan, Jared, Eric, Emily. BA summa cum laude, Amherst Coll., 1969; JD, Yale U., 1974. Bar: Calif. 1974. Law clerk U.S. Dist. Ct. Conn., Hartford, 1974-75; assoc. Tuttle & Taylor, Los Angeles, 1975-76, Pryor, Cashman, Sherman & Flynn, Beverly Hills, Calif., 1976-77, Hardee, Barovick, Konecky & Braun, Beverly Hills, 1977-79; prin. Rosenfeld, Kassoy & Kraus, Beverly Hills, 1979-80; dir. bus. affairs Warner Bros. Records, Inc., Burbank, Calif., 1980-83, v.p. bus. and legal affairs, 1983-88, sr. v.p. bus. and legal affairs, 1988—. Bd. dirs. Los Encinos Sch., Encino, Calif., 1986—, treas., 1986-87, pres., 1987-92; bd. dirs. People for the Am. Way, 1991—, San Fernando Valley Neighborhood Legal Svcs., Inc., 1989-90. Mem. Phi Beta Kappa. Democrat. Jewish. Office: Warner Bros Records Inc 3300 W Warner Blvd Burbank CA 91505-4694

ALTSHILLER, ARTHUR LEONARD, physics educator; b. N.Y.C., Aug. 12, 1942; s. Samuel Martin and Betty Rose (Lepson) A.; m. Gloria Silvern, Nov. 23, 1970 (div. 1975); m. Carol Heiser, Aug. 16, 1980. BS in Physics, U. Okla., 1963; MS in Physics, Calif. State U., Northridge, 1971. Elec. engr. Garrett Corp., Torrance, Calif., 1963-64, Volt Tech. Corp., Phoenix, 1965; engr., physicist Aerojet Gen. Corp., Azusa, Calif., 1966-68; elec. engr. Magnavox Rsch. Labs., Torrance, 1968-69; sr. engr. Litton Guidance & Control, Canoga Park, Calif., 1969; physics tchr. L.A. Unified Sch. Dist./Van Nuys Math/Sci. Magnet High Sch., 1971—; math. instr. Valley Coll., Van Nuys, Calif., 1986—; part-time physics/chemistry tchr. West Coast Talmudical Sem., L.A., 1978-88. Mesa Club sponsor Math.-Engring. Sci. Achievement L.A. High Sch. and U. So. Calif., 1984-87. Recipient Cert. of Honor Westinghouse Sci. Talent Search, 1990. Mem. AAAS, Am. Assn. Physics Tchrs., Nat. Coun. Tchrs. of Math., So. Calif. Striders. Democrat. Jewish. Home: 6776 Vickiview Dr Canoga Park CA 91307-2751 Office: Van Nuys High Sch 6535 Cedros Ave Van Nuys CA 91411-1599

ALVERNAZ, BIL, software company executive; b. Oakland, Calif., July 15, 1947; s. Alvin and Dorothy (Harris) A.; m. Diana Brinkerhoff, July 11, 1970; 1 child, Ian W. BA in Journalism, Calif. State U., Fresno, 1974. Exec. v.p. Santa Barbara (Calif.) Bd., 1975-80; pres. Computer Resources, Livingston, Calif., 1980—; bd. dirs. Calif. Real Estate Task Force, Sacramento, 1982-85. Author: Expanding Your IBM PC, 1984; (software) Ventura Boulevard, 1988, Open Door Operating System, 1989. With USAF, 1967-71. Office: Computer Resources PO Box 426 Livingston CA 95334-0426

ALVERSON, DALE CLARK, physician, researcher, educator; b. Detroit, June 29, 1945; s. Glenn W. and Edna V. (Chadwick) A.; m. Mary H. Morrison (div. Sept. 1985); children: Melissa E., Dale H., Heather M., Jessica S., Arianna C.; m. Jennifer J. Bean, May 24, 1986. MD, U. Mich., 1974. Diplomate Am. Bd. Pediatrics and Neonatal-Perinatal Medicine. Intern in pediatrics Butterworth Hosp., Grand Rapids, Mich.; resident U. Colo., Denver; pvt. practice pediatrician Marquette, Mich., 1977-80; fellow in neonatalogy U. Mich., Ann Arbor, 1980-81, U. N.Mex., Albuquerque, 1981-82; asst. clin. prof. Mich. State U., East Lansing, 1979-81; with U. N.Mex., Albuquerque, 1982—; tenured assoc. prof. pediatrics, 1986—; assoc. dir. Gen. Clin. Rsch. Ctr. U. N.Mex., Albuquerque, 1986-90, dir. div. neonatology Sch. Medicine, 1988—; host KOB-TV Channel 4 med. segment, "4 Your Family's Health", 1990—. Contbr. articles to profl. jours. Chair rsch. com., pres. N.Mex. sect. Am. Heart Assn., 1991-92. Fellow Am. Acad. Pediatrics; mem. Am. Inst. Ultrasound in Medicine, Am. Acad. Pediatrics (perinatal pediatrics sect.), Soc. Critical Care Medicine, Soc. for Pediatric Rsch., Western Soc. for Pediatric Rsch., N.Mex. Pediatric Soc., Am. Heart Assn. (pres. N.Mex. affiliate 1991-92). Home: 312 Laguna Blvd SW Albuquerque NM 87104-1113 Office: U NMex Sch of Medicine Dept Pediatrics ACC-3-W Albuquerque NM 87131

AMADO, PATRICIA ANN, management and human resource professional; b. Tucson, Nov. 10, 1960; d. Hector Gustelum Jr. and Betty Louise (Stull) A. BFA, U. Ariz., 1982, MBA. Asst. mgr. US. Shoe Corp., Houston, 1982-83; asst. mgr. to mgr. Mathews, Inc. Accessory Lady, Houston, 1983-84; mgr. to regional mgr. Decor Corp., Houston, 1984-87; dir. mktg. lab. Tucson Med. Ctr. Health Enterprises, 1988; freelance tech. writer, 1987-90; S.W. exec. recruiter The Gap, Inc., 1987-91; ind. mgmt. & pers. cons. Tucson, 1991—; polit. campaign cons., speechwriter Washington and, Ariz., 1992—. State del. Ariz. Dem. Conv., 1980, campaign speechwriter and cons. 1980-82. Mem. Sierra, Greenpeace, 20/30 Club, Gamma Phi Beta (corp. bd. 1987-89). Democrat. Roman Catholic. Club: Smithsonian (Washington). Home: PO Box 40836 Tucson AZ 85717-0836

AMALFI, FREDERICK ANTHONY, limnologist; b. Rochester, N.Y., Feb. 8, 1950; s. Fred and Elizabeth Virginia (Biorde) A.; 1 child, James Anthony. BS in Biology, St. John Fisher Coll., Rochester, 1972; MS in Biology, U. Ariz., 1974; PhD in Botany, Ariz. State U., 1988. Sr. chemist Pima County Wastewater Mgmt., Tucson, 1977-78; sr. pretreatment engr. Planning Rsch. Corp., Yuma, Ariz., 1979-81; lab. dir. North Am. Labs., Tempe, Ariz., 1981-82, Western Tech., Inc., Phoenix, 1982-84; teaching asst. Ariz. State U., Tempe, 1984-88; lab. dir. Aquatic Cons. & Testing, Inc., Tempe, 1988—; faculty assoc. Ariz. State U., Tempe, 1987-91; advisor Ariz. Lab. Adv. Com., 1992, tech. adv. State Ariz. Water Reuse Com. Contbr. articles to profl. jours. Soccer coach Tempe YMCA, 1978-88, cert. lake mgr. N. Am. Lake Mgmt. Soc. Recipient Award for Coll. Scientists ARCS Found., 1987; grantee Ariz. Water Resources Rsch. Ctr., 1991, Ariz. Disease Control, 1988. Mem. Water Environ. Fedn., Am. Water Wks. Assn., North Am. Lake Mgmt. Soc., Am. Water Resources Assn., Fla. Aquatic Lake Mgmt. Soc., Ariz.-Nev. Acad. Scis., Sigma Xi. Home: 4710 S LaRosa Dr Tempe AZ 85282 Office: Aquatic Cons & Testing Inc 1555 W University Dr #103 Tempe AZ 85282

AMAN, REINHOLD ALBERT, philologist, publisher; b. Fuerstenzell, Bavaria, Apr. 8, 1936; came to U.S., 1959, naturalized, 1963; s. Ludwig and Anna Margarete (Waindinger) A.; m. Shirley Ann Beischel, Apr. 9, 1960 (div. 1990); 1 child, Susan. Student, Chem. Engring. Inst., Augsburg, Germany, 1953-54; B.S. with high honors, U. Wis., 1965; Ph.D., U. Tex., 1968. Chem. engr. Munich and Frankfurt, Ger., 1954-57; petroleum chemist Shell Oil Co., Montreal, Que., Can., 1957-59; chem. analyst A. O. Smith Corp., Milw., 1959-62; prof. German U. Wis., Milw., 1968-74; editor, pub. Maledicta Jour., Maledicta Press Publs., Santa Rosa, Calif., 1976—; pres. Maledicta Press, Santa Rosa, 1976—; dir. Internat. Maledicta Archives, Santa Rosa, 1975—. Author: Der Kampf in Wolframs Parzival, 1968, Bayrisch-oesterreichisches Schimpfwoerterbuch, 1973, 86; gen. editor Mammoth Cod (Mark Twain), 1976, Dictionary of International Slurs (A. Roback), 1979, Graffiti (A. Read), 1977; editor Maledicta: The Internat. Jour. Verbal Aggression, 1977—, Maledicta Monitor, 1990—; contbr. articles to profl. jours. U. Wis. scholar, 1963-65; U. Wis. research grantee, 1973, 74; NDEA Title IV fellow, 1965-68. Mem. Internat. Maledicta Soc. (pres.), Am. Dialect Soc., Am. Name Soc., Dictionary Soc. N.Am. Home and Office: PO Box 14123 Santa Rosa CA 95402-6123

AMARAT, ISSARIYAPORN CHULAJATA, diplomat; b. Bangkok, Thailand, Apr. 29, 1961; came to U.S., 1990; d. Air Marshall Issara and Sophia Chulajata; m. Apichart Amarat, Sept. 1, 1985; children; Klungploy (Nancy), Ratcharhak (Duke). MS in Econs., Nat. Inst. Devel. Adminstrn., Thailand; MBA, Woodbury U. Second sec. Ministry of Fgn. Affairs, Bangkok, 1985-90; consul Royal Thai Consulate Gen., L.A., 1990—. Mem. Royal Bangkok Sports Club. Buddhist. Office: Royal Thai Consulate Gen 801 N La Brea Los Angeles CA 90038

AMATO, CAROL JOY, anthropologist, technical publications consulting company executive, writer; b. Portland, Oreg., Apr. 9, 1944; d. Sam Lawrence and Lena Dorothy (Dindia) A.; m. Neville Stanley Motts, Aug. 26, 1967 (div. 1978); children: Tracy, Damon. BA, U. Portland, 1966; MA, Calif. State U., 1986. Freelance writer, Westminster, Calif., 1969—; human factor cons. Design Sci. Corp., L.A., 1979—; dir. software documentation Trans-Ed Communications, Westminster, 1980-84, pres. Advanced Profl. Software, Inc., Westminster, 1984-86, Systems Rsch. Analysis, Inc., Westminster, 1986—. Author: The Earth, 1992, Astronomy, 1992, The Human Body, 1992, Inventions, 1992, Inside Out: The Wonders of Modern Technologies Explained, 1992, 50 Nifty Science Fair Projects, 1993; editor, Cultural Futuristics, 1975-80, CICS Essentials for Developers and Programmers; author 6 books on sci and related topics, numerous articles and short stories; participant in numerous radio and TV interviews. Sec. bd. dirs. Am. Space Meml. Found., L.A., 1986-87; bd. dirs. Orange County Acad. Decathalon. Mem. Ind. Writers of So. Calif., Writers' Club of Whittier, Inc., Internat. Pen. Home: 10151 Heather Ct Westminster CA 92683-5754

AMATO, FRANK CHARLES, financial and investment company executive; b. Bklyn., Dec. 30, 1941; s. Frank Charles and Sarina (Anacreonte) A.; m. Regina Cichy, July 10, 1965; children—Jeffrey, David. B.S., U. Vt., 1963; M.B.A., U. Mass., 1967. Product controller IBM, Burlington, Vt., 1967-69; cons. Ernst & Young, Boston, 1969-70; co-founder, chmn. Amherst Assocs., Walnut Creek, Calif., 1970-85, Mobile Tech. Inc., Walnut Creek, 1983-92; dir. Golden West Tech. Services, Sunnyvale, Calif., John Muir Med. Ctr. Walnut Creek Little League, 1983-84. Served to 1st lt. U.S. Army, 1964-65. Mem. Healthcare Fin. Mgmt. Assn. (bd. dirs. 1981-84, W. Follmer Merit award 1980), Am. Hosp. Assn., Calif. Hosp. Assn., Assn. Venture Founders, Office: Shell Ridge Capital 1333 N California Blvd # 545 Walnut Creek CA 94596

AMATORI, MICHAEL LOUIS, radio production manager, consultant, performer; b. San Francisco, Jan. 26, 1951; s. Fred and Ana Dolores (Espitia) A. BA, San Francisco State U., 1974. Cert. Community Coll. instr., Calif. Announcer Sta. KCSM-FM, KCSM-TV, San Mateo (Calif.), 1969-71, Sta. KFOG-FM Kaiser Broadcasting Co., San Francisco, 1972, Sta. KRON-FM Chronicle Broadcasting Co., San Francisco, 1972; engr., producer Sta. KSFO Golden West Broadcasters, San Francisco, 1973-83; sports producer, prodn. dir. for prodn. mgr. Sta. KSFO/KYA King Broadcasting Co., San Francisco, 1983-92; prodr., announcer Sta. KQED-FM, San Francisco, 1992—; owner, founder Creative Matrix Prodns., San Mateo, Calif., 1988—; instr. broadcasting Coll. of San Mateo, 1983-92, program cons., 1975; prodn. cons. Salem Comm., San Francisco, 1987, Champion Prodns., San Francisco, 1991, Publicity Express, Berkeley, Calif., 1990-91; network comml. announcer Oakland (Calif.) Athletics, 1987-91; network voice S.N.P. Radio Network, Mill Valley, Calif., 1992—; narrator, TechNation, Ams. and Tech. for Mogo Tech Media, San Francisco, 1992—. Cons. Childrens Fund for Adoption of Black Children, San Francisco, 1987; mem. Broadcast Industry Adv. Panel, San Mateo (Calif.) Community Coll. Dist., 1990—. Recipient Paul Romagna award Coll. of San Mateo, 1971, Best Radio Entry award Nat. Assn. Consumer Adminstrs., 1988, Creative Media award Ad Week Mag., 1989. Democrat. Roman Catholic. Office: Creative Matrix Prodns 50 N San Mateo Dr Ste 215 San Mateo CA 94401

AMBLER, JOHN RICHARD, retired archaeology educator; b. Denver, Jan. 23, 1934; s. John Vernon Ambler and Mary Louise (Sterling) Williamson; divorced; children: Susan Kelly, George Michael, Bridget Meghan. BA, U. Colo., 1958, PhD, 1966; MA, U. Ariz., 1961. Archaeologist U. Utah, Salt Lake City, 1958-60, Mus. N.Mex., Santa Fe, 1960-61, Mus. No. Ariz., Flagstaff, 1961-63; exec. dir. Tex. archaeol. salvage program U. Tex., Austin, 1965-67; assoc. prof. anthropology No. Ariz. U., Flagstaff, 1957-84, prof., 1984-86, univ. archaeologist, 1968-86, prof. emeritus, 1986—. Co-author: Survey and Excavation of Caves in Hidalgo County, Nex Mexico, 1961, Survey and Excavation of North and East at Navajo Mountain, Utah, 1968; author: Caldwell Village, 1966, The Anasazi, 1977, 2d edit., 1986. Chmn. Ft. Valley Fire Dist., Flagstaff, 1980-85. Mem. ACLU (bd. dirs. 1982-92), Soc. for Am. Archaeology. Home: 6510 N Bader Rd Flagstaff AZ 86001-9310

AMBROSE, THOMAS CLEARY, communications executive; b. Kalispell, Mont., Mar. 6, 1932; s. William Patrick and Anne Marie (Cleary) A.; m. Joyce Leona Demco, Aug. 13, 1960; children: Thomas Neal, John Alan, Bridget Sharon. BA in Journalism, U. Mont., 1952. Editor Choteau (Mont.) Acantha, 1952; reporter Daily Chronicle, Spokane, Wash., 1954-57, bus. editor, 1957-64; rep., mgr. media rels. Weyerhaeuser Co., Tacoma, 1964-74, dir. external communications, 1974-91; prin. Ambrose & Assocs., Seattle, 1991—. Author, editor: Where The Future Grows, 1989. Pres. Spokane Editorial Soc., 1963-64, Spokane Press Club, 1959-60; dir. Federal Way C. of C., 1968-71. 1st lt. U.S. Army, 1952-54, Korea.

AMDAHL, GENE MYRON, computer company executive; b. Flandreau, S.D., Nov. 16, 1922; s. Anton E. and Inga (Brendsel) A.; m. Marian Quissell, June 23, 1946; children: Carlton Gene, Beth Delaine, Andrea Leigh. BSEE, S.D. State U., 1948, DEng (hon.), 1974; PhD, U. Wis., 1952, DSc (hon.), 1979; D.Sc. (hon.), Luther Coll., 1980, Augustana Coll., 1984. Project mgr. IBM Corp., Poughkeepsie, N.Y., 1952-55; group head Ramo-Wooldridge Corp., L.A., 1956; mgr. systems design Aeronutronics, L.A., 1956-60; mgr. systems design advanced data processing systems IBM Corp., N.Y.C., Los Gatos, Calif., Menlo Park, Calif., 1960-70; founder, chmn. Amdahl Corp., Sunnyvale, Calif., 1970-80; founder, chief exec. officer Trilogy Systems Corp., Cupertino, Calif., 1980-87; chmn. bd. Elxsi (name changed from Trilogy Systems Corp.), San Jose, Calif., 1987-89; founder, pres., chief exec. officer Andor Internat. Ltd., Cupertino, 1987—, also bd. dirs. Patentee in field. With USN, 1942-44. Recipient Disting. Alumnus award S.D. State U., 1973, Data Processing Man of Yr. award Data Processing Mgmt. Assn., 1976, Disting. Svc. citation U. Wis., 1976, Michelson-Morley award Case-Western Res. U., 1977, Harry Goode Meml. award for outstanding contbns. to design and manufacture of large, high-performance computers, 1983 and Eckert-Mauchly award, 1987, Am. Fedn. Info. Processing Socs., Centennial Alumnus award S.D. State U., 1987, Good Samaritan award City Team Ministries, San Jose, 1991, Man of Achievement award Computer Weekly mag., 1991; named to Info. Processing Hall of Fame, Infomart, Tex., 1985; named one of 1000 Makers of 20th Century London Times, 1991; IBM fellow, 1965. Fellow IEEE, Brit. Computer Soc. (disting.); mem. Nat. Acad. Engring., IEEE (profl. group, W.W. McDowell award 1976), Quadrato della Radio, Pontecchio Marcon. Presbyterian. Club: Los Altos (Calif.) Country. Home: 165 Patricia Dr Menlo Park CA 94027-3922 Office: Andor Internat Ltd 10131 Bubb Rd Cupertino CA 95014-4133

AMELIO, GILBERT FRANK, electronics company executive; b. N.Y.C., Mar. 1, 1943; s. Anthony and Elizabeth (DeAngelis) A.; m. Glenda Charlene Amelio; children: Anthony Todd, Tracy Elizabeth, Andrew Ryan; stepchildren: Brent Paul Chappell, Tina LaRae Chappell. B.S. in Physics, Ga. Inst. Tech., 1965, M.S. in Physics, 1967, Ph.D. in Physics, 1968. Tech. dir., cofounder Info. Sci., Atlanta, 1962-65; mem. tech. staff Bell Telephone Labs., Murray Hill, N.J., 1968-71; div. v.p., gen. mgr. Fairchild, Mountain View, Calif., 1971-83; pres. semiconductor products div. Rockwell Internat., Newport Beach, Calif., 1983-88; pres. communication systems Rockwell Internat., Dallas, 1988-91; pres., chief exec. officer Nat. Semicondr. Corp., Santa Clara, Calif., 1991—; dir. Ga. Inst. Tech. Nat. Adv. Bd., Atlanta, 1981-87, Ga. Inst. Tech. Research Inst., Atlanta, 1982-89, Sematech, Chiron Corp., Everyville, Calif., 1992—; dir., chmn. Recticon, Pottstown, Pa., 1983-87. Patentee in field. Mem. chief exec. roundtable Univ. Calif., Irvine, 1985-89. Fellow IEEE (chmn. subcom. 1974-81, Masaru Ibuka Consumer Electronics award 1991); mem. Semicondr. Industry Assn. (bd. dirs. 1983—, vice chmn. 1992, chmn. 1993), Bus. Higher Edn. Forum. Republican. Roman Catholic. Home: 13416 Middle Fork Ln Los Altos CA 94022-2420 Office: National Semiconductor Corp PO Box 58090 Santa Clara CA 95052

AMEMIYA, TAKESHI, economist, statistician; b. Tokyo, Mar. 29, 1935; s. Kenji and Shizuko A.; m. Yoshiko Miyaki, May 5, 1969; children: Naoko, Kentaro. B.A., Internat. Christian U., 1958; M.A. in Econs., Am. U., 1961; Ph.D., Johns Hopkins U., 1964. Mem. faculty Stanford U., (Calif.), 1964-66, 68—, prof. econs., 1974-86, Edward Ames Edmonds prof. econs., 1986—; lectr. Inst. Econ. Research, Hitotsubashi U., Tokyo, 1966-68; cons. Author articles; editorial profl. jours. Recipient U.S. Sr. Scientist award Alexander von Humboldt Found., Fed. Republic Germany, 1988; Ford Found. fellow, 1963; Guggenheim fellow, 1975; NSF grantee; fellow Japan Soc. for Promotion of Sci., 1989. Fellow Econometric Soc., Am. Acad. Arts and Scis., Am. Statis. Assn.; mem. Internat. Statis. Inst., Am. Econ. Assn., Inst. Math. Stats., Phi Beta Kappa. Home: 923 Casanueva Pl Stanford CA 94305-1001 Office: Stanford Univ Dept of Econs Stanford CA 94305

AMER, KENNETH BENJAMIN, helicopter engineer; b. Bklyn., Mar. 23, 1924; s. Harry and Rose (Wolkow) Am; m. Hedie Ankle, Dec. 25, 1946; children: Harold, Les. B Aero. Engring., NYU, 1944; MS in Aero. Engring., MIT, 1947. Rsch. engr. NACA, Langley Field, Va., 1947-53; rsch. engr. Hughes Helicopters, L.A., 1953-60, mgr. tech. dept., 1960-85; chief scientist McDonnell Douglas Helicopter Co., L.A., 1985-86; helicopter cons. Rand Corp, Santa Monica, Calif., 1987—. Contbr. articles on helicopters to profl. jours.; patentee helicopter field. McDonnell Douglas Corp. engring. and rsch. fellow, 1986. Fellow Am. Helicopter Soc. (hon., Alexander Klemin award 1976). Home: 8025 Alverstone Ave Los Angeles CA 90045-1436

AMERMAN, JOHN W., toy company executive; b. 1932; married. BA, Dartmouth Coll., 1953, MBA, 1954. With Colgate-Palmolive Co., 1958-64, Warner-Lambert Co., 1965-80; v.p. Du Barry Cosmetics, 1971-72, v.p. internat. group, 1972-77, v.p. Am. Chicle div., 1977-79, pres. Am. Chicle div., 1979-80; pres. Mattel Internat., from 1980; chmn., chief exec. officer Mattel Inc., El Segundo, Calif., 1987—; also bd. dirs. Mattel Inc., Hawthorne, Calif.; bd. dirs. Unocal Corp. Served with U.S. Army, 1954-57. Office: Mattel Inc 333 Continental Blvd El Segundo CA 90245-5012*

AMERMAN, MONIQUE GABRIELLE, academic administrator, consultant; b. Beirut, June 26, 1934; came to U.S., 1954; d. Raymond and Gabrielle (Pierrat) Hestin; m. Eugene Carl Amerman, Aug. 21, 1954; children: Anne-Marie, Daniel, Michael. BA, Colo. Coll., 1963, MA, 1964; PhD, U. Colo., 1977; postgrad., Harvard U., 1989. From instr. to prof. U. So. Colo., Pueblo, 1964-80; dean arts and sci. Pikes Peak Community Coll., Colorado Springs, Colo., 1980-81, v.p. instrn., 1981-86, interim pres., 1984-85; v.p. instrn. Pueblo Community Coll., 1986—. Bd. dirs. Colo. Endowment for the Humanities, Denver, 1982-87. Mem. Colo. Internat. Edn. Assn. (pres. 1984—), Zonta Internat. Club (pres. 1982-84, lt. gov. Dist. XII 1984-86, gov. Dist. XII 1986-88, internat. bd. dirs. Chgo. chpt. 1984-88, chmn. long-range planning com. 1986-90, by-laws com. 1988-90), Colo. Women Forum. Home: 4026 Hillside Dr Pueblo CO 81008-1703 Office: Pueblo Community Coll 900 W Orman Ave Pueblo CO 81004-1499

AMES, BRUCE N(ATHAN), biochemist, geneticist; b. N.Y.C., Dec. 16, 1928; s. Maurice U. and Dorothy (Andres) A.; m. Giovanna Ferro-Luzzi, Aug. 26, 1960; children: Sofia, Matteo. BA, Cornell U., 1950; PhD, Calif. Inst. Tech., 1953. Chief sect. microbial genetics NIH, Bethesda, Md., 1953-68; prof. biochemistry and molecular biology U. Calif., Berkeley, 1968—, chmn. biochemistry dept., 1983-89; mem. Nat. Cancer Adv. Bd., 1976-82. Research, publs. on bacterial molecular biology, histidine biosynthesis and its control, aging, mutagenesis, detection of environ. mutagens and carcinogens, genetic toxicology, oxygen radicals and disease. Recipient Flemming award, 1966, Rosenstiel award, 1976, Fedn. Am. Soc. Exptl. Biology award, 1976, Felix Wankel award, 1978, John Scott medal, 1979, Corson medal, 1980, N.B. lectureship Am. Soc. Microbiology, 1980, Mott prize GM Cancer Rsch. Found., 1983, Gairdner award, 1983, Tyler prize Environ. Achievement, 1985, Gold medal Am. Inst. Chemists, 1991. Fellow Am. Acad. Microbiology, Gerontol. Soc. of Am. (Glenn Found. award, 1992), Acad. of Toxilogical Scis.; mem. NAS, Am. Soc. Biol. Chemists, Am. Soc. Microbiology, Environ. Mutagen Soc. (award 1977), Genetics Soc., Am. Assn. Cancer Rsch., Soc. Toxicology, Am. Chem. Soc. (Eli Lilly award 1964), Royal Swedish Acad. Scis., Am. Acad. Arts and Scis. Home: 1324 Spruce St Berkeley CA 94709-1435 Office: U Calif 401 Barker Hall Berkeley CA 94720

AMES, LAWRENCE COFFIN, JR., investment counsellor; b. Oakland, Calif., July 27, 1925; s. Lawrence Coffin and Helen (Rodolph) A.; m. Beatrice Feer, Dec. 9, 1959 (div. 1971); children: Lawrence III, Catherine, Philip; m. Betty Mitchell, Aug. 1, 1973. BS, Stanford U., 1947. Investment counsellor Turrell & Dahl, San Francisco, 1962-68, Bank of Calif., San Francisco, 1968-71, Ames & Co., Piedmont, Calif., 1971—. Served to 1st lt. USAF, 1951-52. Club: Bohemian (San Francisco). Home and Office: PO Box 11277 Piedmont CA 94611-0277

AMES, MICHAEL MCCLEAN, university museum director, anthropology educator; b. Vancouver, B.C., Can, June 19, 1933; s. Ernest Oliver Francis and Elsie A.; children: Daniel J., Kristin Julia. BA with honors, U. B.C., 1956; PhD, Harvard U., 1961. Asst. prof. sociology McMaster U., Hamilton, Can., 1962-64; asst. prof. to full prof. of anthropology U. B.C., Vancouver, 1964—, dir. Mus. Anthropology, 1974—. Author: Museums, The Public and Anthropology, 1986, Cannibal Tours and Glass Boxes: The Anthropology of Museums, 1992; co-editor: Man-like Monsters on Trial, 1980; contbr. articles to profl. jours. Guggenheim fellow, 1970-71; Nat. Mus. Can. grantee, 1976—. Fellow Royal Soc. Can., Am. Anthrop. Soc., Can. Anthropology Soc.; mem. Indian sociol. Assn., Internat. Coun. Mus. Office: U BC Mus Anthropology, 6393 NW Marine Dr, Vancouver, BC Canada V6T 1Z2

AMES, NORMA HARRIET, wildlife consultant, writer; b. Buffalo, Aug. 17, 1920; d. Robert Martin and Flora Mary (Wiener) Knipple; m. Donald Fairbanks Ames, July 8, 1944 (div. 1956); 1 child, Karyn Roberta; m. Richard Allen Rasmussen, Dec. 20, 1991. BA, Smith Coll., 1942; postgrad., Wellesley Coll., 1942, U. Colo., 1964. Asst. chief game mgmt. N.Mex. Dept Game and Fish, Santa Fe, 1956-76, asst. chief pub. affairs, 1976-82; leader Mex. wolf recovery team U.S. Fish and Wildlife Service, 1979-91; wildlife cons. Santa Fe, 1982-87, Colville, Wash., 1988—; wolf breeder and researcher Rancho Ma'ii-tsoh, Santa Fe, 1971-87. Author: My Path Belated, 1970, Whisper in the Forest, 1971, (book revs.) Science Books and Films, 1970—; author/illustrator booklets, 1960-82; author/editor: New Mexico Wildlife Management, 1967 (conservation edn. award 1968);. Named Conservationist of Yr., Sta. KOB TV and Radio, Albuquerque, 1980; recipient Leopold Conservation award The Nature Conservancy, 1983. Mem. AAAS, The Nature Conservancy, World Wildlife Fund, Defenders of Wildlife, Can. Nature Fedn., Nat. Wildlife Fedn., Am. Minor Breeds Conservancy, Inland Empire Pub. Lands Coun., N.W. Rivers Coun., AK Wildlife Alliance, The Wildlife Soc. (cert.), Am. Soc. Mammalogists, Sierra Club (lectr.), Nat. Audubon Soc. (lectr.), Phi Beta Kappa, Sigma Xi. Home and Office: Raven Spirit Ranch 2509 Aladdin Rd Colville WA 99114-9158

AMES, WILLIAM CLARK, academic administrator; b. Macomb, Ill., July 11, 1950; s. Clark Earl and Betty Amelia (Hegstrom) A. BA, Knox Coll., 1972; MS, Western Ill. U., 1974; postgrad., Ariz. State U., 1974. Asst. to dean students, instr. human interaction Knox Coll., Galesburg, Ill., 1974-75; instr. human interaction, counselor edn. Western Ill. U., Macomb, 1974-75; resident area coord. Western Carolina U., Cullowhee, N.C., 1975-77; dir. Sahuaro Complex Ariz. State U., Tempe, 1977-78, dir. housing office vending programs, 1978-79, asst. dir. housing-adminstrn., 1979-80, grad. assoc. for student leadership programs, 1980-81, rsch. assoc., office of pres., 1981-82; asst. to chancellor Maricopa C.C., Phoenix, 1982-84, dir. mgmt. and budget, 1984—. Contbr. articles to profl. jours. Mem. funding panel Phoenix United Way, 1988, Western Carolina coun. on Alcohol and Use and Abuse, 1975-77. Am. Coun. Edn. fellow, 1989-90; NSF grantee, 1970-72; recipient Leadership award Elks Ill., 1968; Robert Cunningham Taylor Jr. scholar, 1968-72. Mem. Nat. Assn. student Pers. Adminstrs., Am. Pers. and Guidance Assn., Am. Coll. Pers. Assn., Am. Coun. Univ. Housing Officers,

Southeastern Assn. Housing Officers, Smithsonian Inst. (asso.), Knox Coll., Western Ill. U. Alumni Assn. Home: 1321 W Lynwood St Phoenix AZ 85007-1918

AMES-URIE, PATRICIA YVONNE, aerospace, systems engineer; b. Norfolk, Va., Aug. 31, 1946; d. George Spencer Ames and Olive Marvil (Carraway) Thompson; 1 child, Lara Ellen. BA, Va. Poly. Inst., 1970; MS in Edn., U. Va., 1973. Sci. and math. instr. Commonwealth of Va., 1970-76; project dir. Dept. Health, Edn. and Welfare, 1976-79; mgr. project and systems engring. Lockheed Aero. Systems Co., Burbank, Calif., 1979-90; advanced systems engr. Lockheed Missiles & Space Co., Sunnyvale, Calif., 1990—.

AMICO, CHARLES WILLIAM, management consultant; b. Boston, May 6, 1942; s. William Charles and Marie Josephine (Nicholas) A. Assoc. in Engring., Franklin Inst., 1962; BS, Suffolk U., 1968. Jr. chem. technician Avco Corp., Lowell, Mass., 1963-64; advanced vacuum tech. technician Nat. Rsch. Corp., Newton, Mass., 1964-68; semicondr. engr. IBM, Essex Junction, Vt., 1968-72, semicondr. mfg. engring. mgr., 1972-76, mgmt. devel. cons., 1976-86; founder, pres., CEO Creative Directions, Inc., San Francisco, Burlington, Vt., 1982—; bd. dirs. Holiday Project, 1987-88. State chmn. Vt. Hugh O'Brian Youth Leadership Seminar; bd. dirs. Vt. Hugh O'Brian Youth Seminars, Inc., chief exec officer, 1984-85. Recipient Hugh O'Brian Outstanding State Chmn. in Nation award, 1984, 85. Office: Creative Directions Inc 2932 Pierce St San Francisco CA 94123-3825

AMICO, DAVID MICHAEL, artist; b. Rochester, N.Y., Sept. 24, 1951; s. Michael Angelo and Mary Nancy (Salvatore) A. BA, Calif. State U., Fullerton, 1974; postgrad., Hunter Coll., 1975. One-man shows include Newspace Gallery, L.A., 1976, 78, Jancar/Kuhlenschmidt Gallery, L.A., 1980-81, Ulrike Kantor Gallery, L.A., 1983, Irit Krygier Contemporary Art, L.A., 1985, Carnegie Mellon U. Gallery, Pitts., 1986, Ace Contemporary Exhbns., 1987, 90, Marc Jancou Galerie, Zürich, Switzerland, 1990; exhibited in group shows at Newspace Gallery, 1976, 88, Vanguard Gallery, 1979, 80, Madison (Wis.) Art Ctr., 1981, Milw. Art Mus., 1982, Mus. Contemporary Art, L.A., 1983, Santa Barbara Mus. Art, 1984, U. Art Mus., 1985, Ace Gallery, 1992, others. Cartier Found. scholar, Paris, France, 1990. Office: 443 S San Pedro St # 503 Los Angeles CA 90013-2131

AMIEL, DAVID, orthopaedic surgery educator; b. Alexandria, Egypt, Oct. 25, 1938; came to U.S., 1962; s. Eli and Inez (Bokey) A.; m. Nancy Joy Lyons, Nov. 27, 1966; 1 child, Michael Eli. B Math., Lycee Francais, Alexandria, 1955; PhD in Chem. Engring., U. Brussels, Belgium, 1962. Chem. engr. Polymers Lab. Boeing Aeorspace, Renton, Wash., 1962-63; assoc. in orthopaedics U. Wash., Seattle, 1964-66; chief chemist Laucks Testing Lab., Seattle, 1966-68; assoc. orthopaedic specialist U. Calif., La Jolla, 1968-75, orthopaedic specialist, 1975-83, from asst. prof. to assoc. prof. surgery, 1983-91, prof. orthopaedics, 1992—, mem. exec. com. sch. medicine, 1990-91; dept. head biochemistry M&D Coutts Inst., San Diego, 1984—; bd. dirs. Am. Coll. Sports Medicine, Indpls., 1989-92. Reviewer Am. J. Physiol., 1989-92, JBJS, JOR; contbr. chpts. to books and articles to profl. jours. Grant reviewer Arthritis Soc. Can. Recipient Award Excellence Basic Sci. Rsch., Am. Orthopaedic Soc. Sports Medicine, 1983, 86, Merit award NIH, 1989-99. Grant revewier Arthritis Soc. Can.

AMIOKA, WALLACE SHUZO, retired petroleum company executive, public affairs consultant; b. Honolulu, June 28, 1914; s. Tsurumatsu and Reye (Yoshimura) A.; B.A., U. Hawaii, 1966, M.B.A., 1968; m. Ellen Misao Honda, Aug. 9, 1942; children—Carol L. Amioka Price, Joanne M. Amioka Chikuma. With Shell Oil Co., 1931-77, fin. svcs. mgr., Honolulu, 1973-77; pub. affairs cons., Honolulu, 1977-87; gen. ptnr. Pub. Affairs Cons. Hawaii, 1988—; lectr. econs. U. Hawaii, 1969-79. Mem. Honolulu Police Commn., 1965-73, vice chmn., 1966, 68, chmn., 1971; U.S. civil adm. Ryuku Islands, 1950-52. Mem. City and County of Honolulu Charter Commn., 1981-82; bd. dirs. Honolulu Symphony Soc., 1968. Served with M.I., AUS, 1944-48. Mem. M.I. Service Vets. (pres. 1981-82), Hawaii C. of C. (chmn. edn. com. 1963-64, chmn. pub. health com. 1966-67), Hui 31 Club, Hui Aikane Club, Honolulu Police Old Timers Club, Phi Beta Kappa, Phi Kappa Phi. Home: 4844 Matsonia Dr Honolulu HI 96816-4014 Office: Pub Affairs Cons-Hawaii 1411 S King St Honolulu HI 96814-2506

AMISTAD, GLENN REPIEDAD, tax manager; b. Tamuning, Guam, Mar. 22, 1955; s. Felino Borbon and Polly (Repiedad) A. BBA in Acctg., Chaminade U., 1977; MBA in Real Estate, Golden Gate U., 1987. CPA, Hawaii. Tax preparer Beneficial Fin. & Loan Co., Union City, Calif., 1978-79; staff acct. Maisel & Bohn, CPAs, Hayward, Calif., 1980-81, Donald H. Seiler & Co., CPAs, Redwood City, Calif., 1981-82; internal auditor Polly's House of Fabrics, Agana, Guam, 1983-84; br. auditor Bank of Guam, San Francisco, 1984-90; tax mgr. Loomis Armored, Inc., Oakland, Calif., 1990—. Mem. AICPAs, Nat. Assn. Accts. (bd. dirs. local chpt. 1983-84, bd. dirs. rels. com. 1984-85), Alameda Owners Assn., Golden Gate U. Alumni Assn. (steering com. 1989), Chaminade U. Alumni Assn. (pres. Bay Area chpt. 1988-89). Republican. Roman Catholic. Home: 44201 Arapaho Ave Fremont CA 94539-6556 Office: Loomis Armored Inc One Kaiser Pla Ste #901 Oakland CA 94612

AMME, ROBERT C., physics educator; b. Ames, Iowa, May 15, 1930; s. Lewis Earnest and Kathryn Pearl (Swartz) A.; m. Janice E. Fausch, June 23, 1951; children: Amy, David. BS in Physics, Iowa State U., 1953, MS in Physics, 1956, PhD in Physics, 1958. Grad. asst. Iowa State Engring. Experiment Sta., Ames, 1953-57; rsch. engr. Exxon Prodn. Rsch. Ctr., Houston, 1958-59; rsch. physicist Denver Rsch. Inst. U. Denver, 1959-65; asst. prof. physics dept. U. Denver, 1961-65, assoc. prof. physics dept., 1965-68, prof., sr. rsch. physicist, 1968—, chmn. physics dept., 1980-85; assoc. dean Coll. Arts. & Scis. U. Denver, 1973-75, acting dean, 1975-76; dean, dir. acad. rsch. Grad. Sch. Arts & Scis. U. Denver, 1976-80. Author: Excited State in Chemical Physics, 1975; contbr. ency. of physics, 1975; contbr. numerous sci. paper to profl. jours. Mem. Govs. Task Force on Sci. Edn., 1983. Grantee NSF, USAF Office Sci. Rsch., U.S. Army Rsch. Office; internat. travel grantee NSF, NAS. Fellow Am. Phys. Soc.; mem. Soc. Automotive Engrs., Am. Assn. Physics Tchrs., Acoustical Soc. Am., Phi Beta Kappa, Sigma Xi (pres. Denver chpt. 1986-88), Pi Mu Epsilon, Sigma Pi Sigma. Office: U Denver Physics Dept Space Scis Denver CO 80208

AMMERMAN, CALVIN P., minister; b. Richmond, Ind., Oct. 2, 1924; s. Frank Parker and Ula Oliva (Beeson) A.; m. Rigel Jane, Rise Leisle Ammerman-Moody, Ravel Fisher-Ammerman. BA, Cin. Bible Sem., 1950, U. Denver, 1953; ThM, Iliff Sch. Theology, 1957, ThD, 1962. Family life counsellor Augustanta Luth. Ch., Denver, 1962-83, sr., social, health ministry, 1983—; coord. material and prodn. Samsonite, Denver, 1977-83; editorial bd. Luth. Ptnrs., Luth. Ch. in Am., N.Y.C., 1986-88; contbg. editor Rocky Mountain Luth., Golden, Colo., 1986-90. Mem. Govs. Coun. for Health Edn. Gov. Richard Lamm and Gov. Roy Romer; mem. Mayor's Commn. on Aging Mayor Frederico Pena and Mayor Wellington Webb, 1990-92; treas. Cen. Denver Community Svc., 1988. Mem. Am. Assn. for Marriage and Family Therapy (clin. mem.). Office: Augustana Luth Ch 5000 E Alameda Ave Denver CO 80222

AMOR, SIMEON, JR., photographer, historian; b. Lahaina, Hawaii, Apr. 24, 1924; s. Simeon and Victoria Amor. Grad. high sch., Hilo, Hawaii. Post commdr. Engrs. Post #22, Am. Legion, Honolulu, 1952-53; approp. acct. Hawaii Air Nat. Guard, Honolulu, 1953-64; prodn. control supr. Svc. Bur. Corp., Honolulu, 1964-73; prodn. control computer ops. Bank of Hawaii, Honolulu, 1973-86; owner, propreitor Image Engring., Honolulu, 1986—; historian VFW Dept. Hawaii, Honolulu, 1987-90, First Filipino Infantry Regiment Hawaii Connection; treas. DAV Dept. Hawaii, Honolulu. Cpl. U.S. Infantry, 1943-46, master sgt. USNG, 1952-64. Mem. Am. Photographer's Internat. Home: 1634 Kino St Honolulu HI 96819 Office: Disabled Am Vets 2685 N Nimitz Hwy Honolulu HI 96819

AMORY, THOMAS CARHART, management consultant; b. N.Y.C., Oct. 29, 1933; s. George Sullivan and Marion Renee (Carhart) A.; m. Elisabeth Andrews Jackson, June, 1956 (div. Mar. 1969); children: Renee Elizabeth, Caroline Carhart, Gillian Brookman; m. Carolyn Marie Pesnell, May 10, 1969 (div. Nov. 1987) ; m. Doris Ruth Mack, Mar. 18, 1989. A.B., Harvard U., 1956. Comml. mgr. N.Y. Telephone Co., N.Y.C., 1957-60; sales mgr. Royce Chem. Co., East Rutherford, N.J., 1960-62; asst. to chmn. Seatrain Lines, Inc., Edgewater, N.J., 1963-65; mgmt. cons. Booz Allen & Hamilton, N.Y.C., 1966-67; ptnr. William H. Clark Assocs., Inc., N.Y.C., 1967-75, pres., 1975-79, chmn., 1979-88; mgmt. cons. Montecito, Calif., 1989—. Trustee Mus. City, N.Y., 1971-92, Santa Barbara mus. of Art, 1990—, Santa Barbara Chamber Orch., 1991—. Mem. River Club, Tuxedo Club, Nantucket Yacht Club, Clove Valley Rod and Gun Club, Santa Barbara Club, Birnam Wood Golf Club. Republican. Roman Catholic. Office: Ste 1-210 1187 Coast Village Rd Santa Barbara CA 93108

AMOS, GEORGE HENRY, III, real estate company executive; b. Colorado Springs, Colo., Aug. 6, 1959; s. George Henry Jr. and Barbara Joanna (Hicks) A.; m. Theresa Marie McCready, Oct. 24, 1987. BSBA, U. Ariz., 1981. Salesperson Tucson Realty & Trust Co., 1981-87, exec. v.p., 1988-89, pres., 1989—, chmn., 1991—; dir. Pima County Real Estate Rsch. Coun., Tucson. Mem. bus. adv. coun. Tucson Unified Sch. Dist., 1989-90; trustee, pres. Found. for St. Joseph's Hosp., Tucson, 1990-92; civil svc. commn. City of Tucson, 1992—; co-chmn. fin. com. Gov. Fife Symington, So. Ariz., 1990—; bd. dirs. Jr. Achievement, Tucson, Big Bros. & Big Sisters of Tucson. Named Big Brother of the Yr., Big Bros. & Big Sisters of Tucson, 1989. Mem. Nat. Bd. Realtors, Ariz. Assn. Realtors, Tucson Bd. Realtors, Tucson Broker Roundtable, Young Pres.'s Orgn., Comml. Network, Estates Club, Tucson Country Club. Republican. Roman Catholic. Office: Tucson Realty & Trust Co 1890 E River Rd Tucson AZ 85718-5838

AMOS, PAUL DENVER, ship pilot; b. Denton, Tex., Aug. 30, 1951; s. George Denver and Mary Jo (Watkins) A.; m. Debbie Annette Wilburn, Mar. 16, 1973 (div. Dec. 1981); chilren: Juliet Ann, Joshua Denver; m. Della Marie Anholt, Aug. 27, 1988; 1 child, Benjamin Joseph. Grad., Denton High Sch., 1969. Federally cert. 1st class pilot Columbia River, Snake River, Willamette River. Deckhand Knappton Corp. (now Brix Maritime), Portland, Oreg., 1974-80, capt., 1980-90; pilot Columbia River Pilots, Portland, 1990—; treas. Marine Transp. Picnic Com., Portland, 1992—. Baptist. Office: Columbia River Pilots 13225 N Lombard Portland OR 97203

AMUNDSON, EVA DONALDA, civic worker; b. Langdon, N.D., Apr. 23, 1911; d. Elmer Fritjof and Alma Julia (Nelson) Hultin; m. Leif Amundson, Mar. 1, 1929 (dec. 1974); children: Constance, Eleanor, Ardis, Priscilla. Bd. dirs. Opportunity Workshop, Missoula, Mont., 1950—, Rockmont Group Homes, Missoula, 1976—, Bethany L'Arche (group home for girls), 1976—; sec. bd. dirs. Opportunity Industries, 1990-91, pres. 1991—; mem. Missoula Sr. Citizen's Ctr., 1980-82, 88—, pres., 1982-85, bd. dirs., 1988—; tchr. Norwegian cooking and baking, 1954-56, Norweigan Rosemaling, 1975-79; treas. Sacakawea Homemakers Club, 1979-81; mem. Am. Luth. Ch. Women St. Pauls' Lutheran Ch., 1951—; active Easter Seal Program, Heart Fund, March of Dimes, United Way, Campfire Girls; mem. adv. council Area Agy. on Aging, Missoula, 1984—. Recipient Outstanding Sr. award Missoula Jr. C. of C., 1984. Mem. Sons. of Norway (sec. 1989—), Orchard Homes Country Club (mem. art judging com.), Order of Eastern Star, Elks. Avocations: rosemaling, oil painting, poetry. Home: 324 Kensington Ave Missoula MT 59801-5726

AMUR-UMARJEE, SHASHI GURURAJ, neurobiologist, researcher; b. India, Mar. 14, 1955; came to U.S., 1981; d. Gururaj Shyamacharya and Shanta Gururaj Amur; m. Dheerendra Madhwarao Umarjee, Feb. 2, 1987; 1 chld, Sphoorti Dheerendra Umarjee. BSc, S. B. Coll., Aurangabad, Maharashtra, India, 1973; MSc, Marathwada U., Aurangabad, Maharashtra, India, 1975; PhD in Biochemistry, Indian Inst. Sci., Bangalore, India, 1981. Post-doctoral rschr. Temple U., Phila., 1981-84; pool officer Indian Inst. Sci., 1985-88; postgrad. rschr. UCLA, 1988-90, sr. rsch. assoc. I, 1991-92, sr. rsch. assoc. III, 1992—; sci. coord. UCLA, 1992—. Univ. Grant Commn. scholar, 1973, rsch. fellow, 1975-76; BRSG grantee NPI, UCLA, 1988-89. Mem. Am. Soc. Neurochemistry. Office: UCLA 760 Westwood Plz Los Angeles CA 90024

ANAND, SURESH CHANDRA, physician; b. Mathura, India, Sept. 13, 1931; came to U.S., 1957, naturalized, 1971; s. Satchit and Sumaran (Bai) A. m. Wiltrud, Jan. 29, 1966; children: Miriam, Michael. MB, BS, King George's Coll., U. Lucknow (India), 1954; MS in Medicine, U. Colo., 1962. Diplomate Am. Bd. Allergy and Immunology. Fellow pulmonary diseases Nat. Jewish Hosp., Denver, 1957-58, resident in chest medicine, 1958-59, chief resident allergy-asthma, 1960-62; intern Mt. Sinai Hosp., Toronto, Ont., Can., 1962-63, resident in medicine, 1963-64, chief resident, 1964-65, demonstrator clin. technique, 1963-64, U. Toronto fellow in medicine, 1964-65; rsch. assoc. asthma-allergy Nat. Jewish Hosp., Denver, 1967-69; clin. instr. medicine U. Colo., Denver, 1967-69; internist Ft. Logan Mental Health Ctr., Denver, 1968-69; pres. Allergy Assocs. & Lab., Ltd., Phoenix, 1974—; mem. staff Phoenix Bapt. Hosp., chmn. med. records com., 1987; mem. staff St. Joseph's Hosp., St. Luke's Hosp., Humana Hosp., Chandler Regional Hosp., Valley Luth. Hosp., John C. Lincoln Hosp., Good Samaritan Hosp., Phoenix Children's Hosp., Tempe St. Luke Hosp., Desert Samaritan Hosp., Mesa Luth. Hosp., Scottsdale Meml. Hosp., Phoenix Meml. Hosp.; pres. NJH Fed. Credit Union, 1967-68. Contbr. articles to profl. jours. Mem. Camelback Hosp. Mental Health Ctr. Citizens Adv. Bd., Scottsdale, Ariz., 1974-80; mem. Phoenix Symphony Coun., 1973-90; mem. Ariz. Opera Co., Boyce Thmpson Southwestern Arboretum; mem. Ariz. Hist. Soc., Phoenix Arts. Mus., Smithsonian Inst. Fellow ACP, Am. Coll. Chest Physicians (critical care com.), Am. Acad. Allergy, Am. Assn. Cert. Allergists, Am. Coll. Allergy and Immunology (aerobiology com., internat. com., pub. edn. com.); mem. AAAS, AMA, Ariz. Med. Assn., Ariz. Allergy Soc. (v.p. 1988-90, pres. 1990-91), Maricopa County Med. Soc., West Coast Soc. Allergy and Immunology, Greater Phoenix Allergy Soc (v.p. 1984-86, pres. 1986-88), Phoenix Zoo, N.Y. Acad. Scis., World Med. Assn., Internat. Assn. Asthmology, Assn. Care of Asthma, Ariz. Thoracic Soc., Nat. Geographic Soc., Village Tennis Club, Ariz. Club, Ariz. Wild Life Assn. Office: 1006 E Guadalupe Rd Tempe AZ 85283-3044 also: 6641 Baywood Ave Mesa AZ 85206 also: Ste 350 7331 E Osborn Dr Scottsdale AZ 85253

ANAST, DAVID GEORGE, editor, publishing executive; b. Joliet, Ill., Oct. 9, 1955; s. George F. and Athey (Kusunis) A. Student, Ariz. State U., 1973-74; B. in Pub. Adminstrn., Calif. State U., Bakersfield, 1975-79, M. in Pub. Adminstrn., 1979. Corr. The Bakersfield Californian Daily Newspaper, 1975-79; mktg. and publs. mgr. U. So. Calif., L.A., 1979; assoc. editor Calif. Good Life mag., Van Nuys, Calif., 1979-80, Worldwide Meetings & Incentives mag., Encino, Calif., 1980-81; from assoc. editor to mng. editor Contemporary Dialysis & Nephrology mag., Encino, 1980-85, editor, assoc. pub., 1985-86; exec. editor, pub. Nephrology News & Issues mag., Huntington Beach, Calif., 1986-89; dir. publs. Biomed. Bus. Internat., Santa Ana, Calif., 1989-90; pub. cons. Costa Mesa, Calif., 1990-91; founder, pub. Biomed. Market Newsletter Inc., Costa Mesa, Calif., 1991—; with Dir. Med. Industry Exec. Search Firms and Recruiters, Dir. Med. Publs., FDA 510(k) Approval Addresses on Mail Labels/Data Bases, Med. Industry Conf. Calendar, Med. Industry Directory So. Calif. Companies. Author: (chpt.) Clinical Vascular Surgery, 1988; contbr. articles to profl. jours. Bd. dirs. NOW, San Fernando Valley, Calif., 1984, publs. advisor, 1984; bd. dirs. Orange County Venture Forum, 1991—. Recipient Pub. Service award Nat. Kidney Found., 1984, 88. Mem. Western Publs. Assn. (Maggie awards judge 1983-85, 92), Hellenic of U. Club of So. Calif. (sec. 1985-87). Greek Orthodox. Office: Biomedical Market Newsletter 3237 Idaho Pl Costa Mesa CA 92626-2207

ANAWALT, PATRICIA RIEFF, anthropologist; b. Ripon, Calif., Mar. 10, 1924; d. Edmund Lee and Anita Esto (Capps) Rieff; m. Richard Lee Anawalt, June 8, 1945; children: David, Katherine Anawalt Arnoldi, Harmon Fred. BA in Anthropology, UCLA, 1957, MA in Anthropology, 1971, PhD in Anthropology, 1975. Cons. curator costumes and textiles Mus. Cultural History UCLA, 1975-90, dir. Ctr. for Study Regional Dress, Fowler Mus. Cultural History, 1990—; trustee S.W. Mus., L.A., 1978-92, rsch. assoc., 1981—; rsch. assoc. San Diego Mus. of Man, 1981—; dir. Ctr. Study Regional Dress Fowler Mus. Cultural History U. Calif., L.A., 1990—; traveling lectr. Archaeol. Inst. Am., U.S., Can., 1975-86, trustee, 1983—; cons. Nat. Geog. Soc., 1980-82, Denver Mus. Natural History, 1992-93; apptd. by U.S. Pres. to Cultural Property Adv. Com., Washington, 1984-93; vis. lectr. various mus., univs. 1975-93; fieldwork Guatemala, 1961, 70, 72, Spain 1975, Sierra Norte de Puebla, Mex., 1983, 85, 88, 89, 91; spkr. in field, 1973-93. Author: Indian Clothing Before Cortés: Mesoamerican Costumes from the Codices, 1981, paperback edit., 1990; co-author: The Codex Mendoza, 4 vols., 1992; contbr. articles to scholarly publs. Adv. com. Textile Mus. Washington, 1983-87, Pres'. Cultural Property, 1984—; trustee Southwest Mus. Highland Park, L.A., 1979-89. Guggenheim fellow, 1988-89; Nat. Geog. Soc. grantee, 1983, 85, 88, 89, 91—. Fellow Am. Anthrop. Assn., L.A. County Mus. Natural History; mem. Am. Ethnol. Soc., Soc. Am. Archaeology, Soc. Women Geographers, Textile Soc. Am., Pres.'s Patrons Cir. L.A. County Mus. Art, So. Calif. Soc. (pres.), Archael. Inst. Am. (trustee 1983—).

ANAWATI, JOSEPH SOLIMAN, pharmacist; b. Alexandria, Egypt, Dec. 25, 1941; came to U.S., 1979; became U.S. citizen, 1985; s. Soliman Youssef and Rosine (Naif) A.; m. Fernande Doummar; children: Kevin Joseph, Caroline Jo. Degree in Pharmacy, U. Alexandria, 1966, MPharm, 1968; MBA, City Exec. Coll., 1985. Med. rep. Eli Lilly Co. Indpls., Cairo and Libya, 1966-71; surp. sales and mktg., dist. mgr., then area mgr. Upjohn Co. Kalamazoo, Middle East and Africa, 1971-79; group area mgr. Allergan Pharm.-Irvine (Calif.), Middle East, Africa and Europe, 1979-82; prodn. and plant mgr., dir. internat. export MD Pharm., Santa Ana, Calif., 1983—; pres., IMS Consulting, Fountain Valley, Calif., 1983—. Recipient Mayor's Cert. of Appreciation, City of L.A., Cert. of Merit Internat. Biographical Ctr., Cambridge, Eng. Mem. Cairo Bd. Pharmacy, Art and Antiques Orgn. Can., World Trade Ctr. Assn., Am. Mktg. Assn., Los Caballeros Club Orange County. Greek Orthodox. Home and Office: 25651 Minoa Dr Mission Viejo CA 92691-4655

ANCELL, JUDITH ANNE, gemologist, small business owner; b. Coldwater, Mich., Feb. 20, 1943; d. Frederick Hall and Beatrice Marguerite (Cornell) Weeks; m. William Joseph Ancell, Oct. 1, 1961; children: William Joseph II, Brian Eugene, Mark Edward. Various certs., Gemol. Inst. Am., Santa Monica, Calif. Owner Turquoise Mesa, 1974-79; salesperson various jewelry stores, 1979-85; owner Judith A. Ancell Fine Jewelry, Boise, Idaho, 1985—, Geneal. & Hist. Book Source, Boise, Idaho, 1992—. Mem. Idaho Soc. Profl. Engrs. Aux. (pres. S.W. chpt. 1989), Am. Bus. Women's Assn., Idaho State Geneological Soc. (bd. dirs. 1992), Huguenot Soc. State of Idaho (v.p. 1992). Office: PO Box 6443 Boise ID 83707

ANCHELL, MELVIN, physician, psychoanalyst, educator; b. Balt., Aug. 23, 1919; s. Robert and Nettie (Snyder) A.; m. Janice Ruth Levick, July 6, 1948; children: Wendy, Marilyn, Steve, Douglas, James. BS, U. Md., 1941, MD, 1944. Diplomate Am. Bd. Family Physicians (charter); cert. psychoanalyst; cert. in rsch., sci. and mental health Nat. Assn. for Advancement of Psychoanalysis. Intern Sinai Hosp., Balt., 1945-46; intern in neuropsychiatry Columbia Neuropsychiat. Inst., N.Y.C., 1946-47; resident in internal medicine Cornell U., N.Y.C., 1947; pvt. practice Houston, 1948-64, L.A., 1964-85; ret., 1985; lectr. in field; expert witness in obscenity and pornography trials, 1968—; expert witness Presdl. Commn. on Pornography and Obscenity. Author numerous books on medicine and human sexuality, 1964-90; contbr. articles to mags. and profl. jours. Capt. AUS, 1945-47, PTO. Fellow Am. Acad. Family Physicians (charter), Am. Acad. Psychosomatic Medicine (life), Am. Soc. Psychoanalytic Physicians; mem. Pan Am. Med. Assn. (counsel mem., sect. psychiatry 1971—), Calif. Med. Assn., Orange County Med. Assn., Los Angeles County Med. Assn. (ethics com.). Home: 28255 Las Casas Mission Viejo CA 92692

ANCOLI-ISRAEL, SONIA, psychologist, researcher; b. Tel Aviv, Israel, Dec. 25, 1951; came to U.S., 1955; m. Andrew G. Israel; 2 children. BA, SUNY, Stony Brook, 1972; MA, Calif. State U., Long Beach, 1974; PhD, U. Calif., San Francisco, 1979. Lic. psychologist, Calif. Staff psychologist U. Calif. San Diego, La Jolla, 1979-84, asst. adj. prof., 1984-88, assoc. prof., 1988—; assoc. dir. Sleep Disorders Ctr., VA Med. Ctr., San Diego, 1981-92, dir., 1992—. Contbr. numerous articles to profl. jours. Bd. mgrs. Jewish Community Ctr., La Jolla, 1985-91. Recipient Robert E. Harris Meml. award, U. Calif. San Francisco, 1978. Mem. AAAS, Sleep Rsch. Soc., Am. Sleep Disorders Assn., Gerontol. Soc. Am., Biofeedback Soc. Am. (mem. program com. 1978, 87, chairperson, 1989, mem. cert. subcom. of profl. affairs com. 1979-80, mem. nominating com. 1985—), Biofeedback Soc. Calif. (bd. dirs. 1977-80,. chairperson cert. com. 1978-80, chairperson fin. com. 1977, cert. examiner 1977-80), Soc. for Psychophysiol. Rsch., N.Y. Acad. Sci.

ANCONA, GEORGE EPHRAIM, photographer, film producer, author; b. N.Y.C., Dec. 4, 1929; s. Ephraim Jose and Emma Graziana (Diaz) A.; m. Helga Von Sydow, July 20, 1968; children: Lisa, Gina, Tomas, Isabel, Marina, Pablo. Student, Academia de San Carlos, Mexico, 1949, Art Students League, 1950, Cooper Union Sch. Design, 1950. Art dir. Esquire Inc., N.Y.C., 1951-53, Seventeen mag., N.Y.C., 1953-54, Grey Advt. Agy., N.Y.C., 1954-58, Daniel & Charles Advt. Agy., N.Y.C., 1958-60; free lance photographer, film producer N.Y.C., 1960—; lectr. graphic design, photography Rockland Community Coll., 1973—, Parsons Sch. Design, 1974—, Sch. Visual Arts, 1978—. Author: Handtalk, 1974, Monsters on Wheels, 1974, What Do You Do?, 1976, I Feel, 1977, Growing Older, 1978, It's A Baby!, 1979, Dancing Is, 1981, Bananas, from Manolo to Margie, Team Work, 1983, Monster Movers, Sheepdog, Helping Out, Freighters, 1985, Handtalk Birthday, 1986 (N.Y. Times 10 Best Illustrated Children's Books of Yr.), Turtle Watch, 1987, The American Family Farm, 1989, Handtalk Zoo, 1989, Riverkeeper,1990, Harry's Helicopter, 1990, Handtalk School, 1991, The Aquarium Book, 1991, Man and Mustang, 1992, Pow Wow, 1992, My Camera, 1992, Pablo Remembers, 1993; designer, photographer over 75 books. Address: Rte 10 Box 94G Rd Santa Fe NM 87501

ANDARY, THOMAS JOSEPH, biochemist; b. Sault Sainte Marie, Mich., Oct. 8, 1942; s. Joseph Boula and Marion (Schwifetti) A. BS, No. Mich. U., 1966, MA, 1968; PhD, Wayne State U., 1974. Instr. biology No. Mich. U., Marquette, 1967-69; rsch. assoc. physiology Wayne State U., Detroit, 1973-76; sr. rsch. scientist, mgr. coagulation research Hyland Labs., Costa Mesa, Calif., 1976-83; dir. quality control Hyland Therapeutics, Glendale, Calif., 1983-90; dir. quality assurance and regulatory affairs Baxter/Hyland Div., Glendale, 1990-91; v.p. quality assurance and regulatory affairs, 1991—; lectr. in field. Mem. Parenteral Drug Assn. NDEA fellow, 1969-72. Mem. Am. Chem. Soc., N.Y. Acad. Sci., Internat. Assn. Biol. Standardization, Sigma Xi (Rsch. award 1973). Roman Catholic. Contbr. over 25 articles to profl. publs. Home: 531 N Canyon Blvd Monrovia CA 91016-1707 Office: 550 N Brand Blvd Glendale CA 91203

ANDERBERG, ROBERT JOHN, biological researcher; b. Spokane, Wash., Feb. 16, 1967; s. Merlyn Leslie and Gretchen Jean (Reim) A. BS in Microbiology, Wash. State U., 1989, MS in Plant Physiology, 1992. Rsch. intern Pacific NW Labs., Richland, Wash., 1988; rsch. technician USDA, Pullman, Wash., 1989-92, Seattle Biomed. Rsch. Inst., 1992—. Mem. Delta Sigma Phi. Lutheran. Home: 3210 26th Ave W Seattle WA 98199

ANDERBERG, ROY ANTHONY, journalist; b. Camden, N.J., Mar. 30, 1921; s. Arthur R. and Mary V. (McHugh) A.; m. Louise M. Brooks, Feb. 5, 1953; children: Roy, Mary. AA, Diablo Valley Coll., 1975. Enlisted USN, 1942, commd. officer, 1960, ret., 1970; waterfront columnist Pacific Daily News, Agana, Guam, 1966-67; pub. rels. officer Naval Forces, Mariana Islands, 1967; travel editor Contra Costa (Calif.) Times, 1968-69; entertainment and restaurant editor Concord (Calif.) Transcript, 1971-75; entertainment editor Contra Costa Advertiser, 1975-76; dining editor Rossmoor News, Walnut Creek, Calif., 1977-78; free-lance non-fiction journalist, 1976—. Recipient Best Feature Story award Guam Press Assoc., 1966. Mem. VFW, DAV, U.S. Power Squadron, Ret. Officers Assn., Am. Legion, U.S. Submarine Vets. World War II (state comdr., regional dir., nat. 2d v.p.), Naval Submarine League, Martinez Yacht Club, Rossmoor Yacht Club, Toastmasters. Democrat. Home: 1840-2228 Tice Creek Dr Walnut Creek CA 94595-2400 Office: Box 52 Concord CA 94522

ANDERMAN, GEORGE GIBBS, geologist; b. Albuquerque, Oct. 17, 1926; s. George Royal and Maud Burleson (Rodney) A.; m. Joan Evans, Apr. 10, 1953; children: Ellen, George Taylor, Evan Rodney. BA, Princeton U., 1950, PhD, 1955. Geologist Ohio Oil (now Marathon Oil), 1952-54, Gulf Oil Corp., 1954-56; chmn. bd., pres. Anderman/Smith Operating Co., Denver, 1957—. Bd. dirs. Opera Colo., Denver, Music Assocs. of Aspen, Colo., Verde Valley Sch., Sedona, Ariz. Fellow Geol. Soc. Am.; mem. Am. Assn.

Petroleum Geologists, Wyo. Geol. Soc., Ind. Petroleum Assn. Am., Ind. Petroleum Assn. of Mountain States (Wildcatter of Yr. 1992). Democrat. Episcopalian. Home: 4999 S Birch St Littleton CO 80121 Office: Anderman/Smith Operating Co 1776 Lincoln St Ste 500 Denver CO 80110

ANDERS, PATRICIA LEE, reading educator; b. Mason, Mich., Mar. 11, 1948; d. Howard R. and Ruth C.(Webb) Smith; m. Clare Anders, June 21, 1969, (div. Mar. 10, 1974), m. Joel Stout, Mar. 19, 1979, (dec.); 1 child, Paul; stepchildren: Karen, Joel. Student, Adrian (Mich.) Coll., 1966-69; BS, U. Wis., 1970, MS, 1972, PhD, 1976. Tchr. Madison (Wis.) Pub. Schs., 1970-72; reading specialist Racine (Wis.) Pub. Schs., 1972-76; from asst. to assoc. prof. reading edn. U. Ariz., 1976-90, prof. reading edn., 1990—; cons. Ctr. for Expansion of Lang. and Thinking, Tucson, 1981—; dir. Nat. Reading Conf. 1981-83, treas., 1985-89. Author: Understanding Readers' Understanding, 1987; contbr. articles to profl. jours. Bd. dirs. Pima County Literacy Coalition, Tucson, 1987-89. Office of Edn. rsch. grantee, 1987, 1988. Mem. Internat. Reading Assn., Nat. Coun. Tchrs. English, Nat. Conf. Rsch. on English, Ariz. Reading Assn. (bd. dirs. 1980-82). Democrat. Unitarian-Universalist. Home: 5635 E Burns St Tucson AZ 85711-3264 Office: U Ariz Coll Edn Tucson AZ 85721

ANDERS, ROBERT LEE, nursing administrator, educator; b. Delta, Colo., Feb. 8, 1947; s. Robert D. and Eva JoAnn (Brew) A.; children: Eric, Andrew. BS, Union Coll., Lincoln, Nebr., 1970; MS, U. Hawaii, 1975, DrPH, 1990. RN, Hawaii; cert. advanced nurse adminstr., Hawaii. Commd. 2d lt. U.S. Army, 1968, advanced through grades to maj., 1979; resigned, 1980; lt. col. USAR, 1980—; pres. Hale Nui, Inc., Denver, 1982-87; asst. prof. nursing U. Hawaii, Honolulu, 1987—; chief dept. nursing Hawaii State Hosp., Honolulu, 1990—, pres. faculty senate Sch. Nursing, 1990-91; presneter in field, 1980—; commun. reviewer Hawaii Mental Health Div., Honolulu, 1988—; expert on Japanese health care systems. Producer audiovisual tapes How to Interview a Terminal Patient, 1973, Interview with a Terminal Patient, 1973, The States of Death and Dying, 1975, Death-Grief-Life Beyond, 1977; procuder interactive video disks on health assessment, 1992; contbr. articles to profl. jours. Named Nurse of Yr. for Dist. I, Tex. Nurses Assn., 1980; grantee U. Hawaii, 1990—, Office of Info. Tech. and Dept. Health, State of Hawaii, 1990, 91, 92. Mem. ANA, APHA, Am. Orgn. Nurse Execs., Hawaii Pub. Health Assn., Healthcare Forum, Hawaii Nurses Assn. (by-laws com. 1974, conv. del. 1976, nominating com. dist. 1, 1989—), Sigma Theta Tau, Phi Kappa Phi. Home: 2439 Kapiolani Blvd # 603 Honolulu HI 96826-4657 Office: Hawaii State Hosp 45-710 Keaahala Rd Kaneohe HI 96744

ANDERS, WILLIAM ALISON, aerospace and diversified manufacturing company executive, former astronaut, former ambassador; b. Hong Kong, Oct. 17, 1933; s. Arthur Ferdinand and Muriel Florence (Adams) A.; m. Valerie Elizabeth Hoard, June 26, 1955; children: Alan Frank, Glen Thomas, Gayle Alison, Gregory Michael, Eric William, Diana Elizabeth. BS, U.S. Naval Acad., Annapolis, 1955; MS in Naval Engring., U.S. Inst. Tech., Wright-Patterson AFB, 1962. Commnd. 2d lt. U.S. Air Force, 1955, pilot, engr., 1955-69; astronaut NASA-Johnson Space Ctr., Houston, 1963-69, Apollo 8, 1st lunar flight, 1968; exec. sec. Nat. Aero. and Space Council, Washington, 1963-72; commr. AEC, Washington, 1973-74; chmn. Nuclear Regulatory Commn., Washington, 1975-76; U.S. Ambassador to Norway, 1976-77; v.p., gen. mgr. nuclear energy products div. Gen. Electric Co., 1977-80; v.p., gen. mgr. aircraft equipment div. Gen. Electric Co., DeWitt, N.Y., 1980-84; sr. exec., v.p. ops. Textron Inc., Providence, R.I., 1984-89; vice chmn. Gen. Dynamics, St. Louis, 1990-91; chmn., CEO Gen. Dynamics, 1991-93, chmn. bd. dirs., 1993—; bd. dirs. Enron Corp. Trustee Battell Meml. Inst., Washington U., St. Louis. Maj. gen. USAFR, 1983-88. Decorated various mil. awards; recipient Wright, Collier, Goddard and Arnold flight awards; co-holder several world flight records. Mem. Soc. Exptl. Test Pilots , Nat. Acad. Engring., Tau Beta Pi. Office: PO Box 1618 Eastsound WA 98245-1618

ANDERSEN, CAROL ANN, family therapist; b. Ft. Wayne, Ind., Sept. 9, 1946; d. Oren and Mary Ann (Lamb) Culver; m. Patrick McGregor, June 15, 1968 (div. July 1978); m. Robert T. Dorris Sr., Dec. 13, 1986 (dec. Oct. 1991); 1 child, Jeffrey Klein; m. Steven Craig Andersen, May 21, 1992. BA, Ind. U., 1968; MBA, Fordham U., 1977; MA in Counseling Psychology, Loyola Marymount U., L.A., 1985. Instr. Title I Carteret (N.J.) Bd. Edn., 1968-73; fin. analyst Technitron, Inc., N.Y.C., 1973-75; tech. cons. On-Line Systems, N.Y.C., 1975-78; fin. cons. Wilshire Assocs., Santa Monica, Calif., 1979-80; tng. cons. GTE, Thousand Oaks, Calif., 1980-86; owner Carol Dorris Cons., L.A., 1987—; treas. P.A.L.M., Thousand Oaks, 1990-91. Named Woman of the Yr., L.A. YWCA, 1989, 90. Mem. L.A. Consumer Credit Counselors (bd. dirs. 1987—). Mem. LDS Ch. Home: 3523 Chief Cir Thousand Oaks CA 91360 Office: Carol Dorris Cons 9607 National Blvd Los Angeles CA 91360

ANDERSEN, DORIS EVELYN, real estate broker; b. Christian County, Ky., Oct. 30, 1923; d. William Earl and Blanche Elma (Withers) Johnston; m. Roger Lewis Shirk, July 9, 1944 (div. 1946); 1 child, Vicki Lee Shirk Sanderson; m. DeLaire Andersen, July 6, 1946; children: Craig Bryant, Karen Rae, Kent DeLaire, Chris Jay, Mardi Lynn. Diploma, South Bend Coll. Commerce, 1942; diploma in banking, Notre Dame U., 1946; student, Ind. U., 1942-44. Tng. dir. Portland, Oreg., 1963-69; assoc. broker Stan Wiley, Inc., Portland, 1969-79; prin. Doris Andersen & Assocs., Portland, 1979-91; sales mgr. VanVleet & Assocs. Real Estate, Ashland, Oreg., 1991-93; real estate appraiser Andersen and Assocs., 1993—; co-owner ServiceMaster of the Cascades; tchr. media spokesperson courses; speaker at seminars; mem. Gov.'s Task Force Coun. on Housing, Salem, Oreg., 1985-86; mem. Oreg. Real Estate Bd., 1992—. Contbr. articles to profl. jours. Regional dir. Dale & Dorothy Carnegie Courses for Women Ind. Inst. Leadership Tng., 1954-56; gov.'s appointee Oreg. Real Estate Bd., 1992-94; mem. task force Oreg. Dept. Energy, Salem, 1984-85. Mem. Nat. Assn. Realtors (bd. dirs. 1983—, regional v.p. Northwest region 1988), Oreg. Assn. Realtors (dir. 1979—, pres. 1986—), Portland Bd. Realtors (pres. 1982), Women's Council Realtors (local pres. 1977, state pres. 1978, gov. nat. orgn. 1979), Internat. Platform Assn., Internat. Biog. Assn. Home: PO Box 1169 Shady Cove OR 97539-1169

ANDERSEN, ERNEST CHRISTOPHER, lawyer; b. Minden, Nebr., Sept. 10, 1909; s. Dines Peter and Marie (Jensen) A.; m. Audrey Etta Robertson, Sept. 10, 1954; 1 dau., Elaine Carolyn Andersen Smith; 1 stepson, Albert Henry Whitaker. J.D., U. Denver, 1952, B.S. in Bus. Adminstrn., 1956. Bar: Colo. 1954, U.S. Supreme Ct. 1960. With U.S. Treasury Dept., Denver, 1935-39; accountant, Denver, 1939-41; with Civilian Prodn. Adminstrn., Denver, 1946-49; dep. state auditor Colo., 1949-51; with U.S. Commerce Dept., Denver, 1951-52; mgmt. cons., Denver, 1953-54; sole practice law, Denver, 1955-56, 69-75; asst. dir. GAO, Los Angeles, 1957-58, Denver, 1959, Washington, 1960-69, cons., 1969-75; sole practice law, Cedaredge, Colo., 1975-86; owner Cedar Crest Farm, 1983—, Stand Sure Press (later Christopher Pub. Co.), 1977—; mem. faculty U. Denver, 1948-56; mcpl. judge Cedaredge, 1977-86; exec. in residence Tulane U., spring 1973. Bd. dirs. Delta Montrose Electric Assn., 1976-84, Colo.-Ute Electric Assn., 1980-84. Served to lt. col. U.S. Army, 1941-46. Recipient Meritorious Service award GAO, 1968. Republican. Presbyterian. Clubs: Masons, Shriners. Home: 1856 Rd 2375 Cedaredge CO 81413 Office: PO Box 747 Cedaredge CO 81413-0747

ANDERSEN, JAMES A., state supreme court chief justice; b. Auburn, Wash., Sept. 21, 1924; s. James A. and Margaret Cecelia (Norgaard) A.; children: James Blair, Tia Louise. BA, U. Wash., 1949, JD, 1951. Bar: Wash. 1952, U.S. Dist. Ct. (we. dist.) Wash. 1957, U.S. Ct. Appeals 1957. Dep. pros. atty. King County, Seattle, 1953-57; assoc. Lycette, Diamond & Sylvester, Seattle, 1957-61; ptnr. Clinton, Andersen, Fleck & Glein, Seattle, 1961-75; judge Wash. State Ct. of Appeals, Seattle, 1975-84; justice Wash. State Supreme Ct., Olympia, 1984-92, acting chief justice, 1992—. Mem. Wash. State Ho. of Reps., 1958-67, Wash. State Senate, 1967-72. Served with U.S. Army, 1943-45, ETO. Decorated Purple Heart. Mem. ABA, Wash. State Bar Assn., Am. Judicature Soc. Office: Wash State Supreme Ct Temple of Justice PO Box 40929 Olympia WA 98504-0929

ANDERSEN, MICHAEL PAUL, goverment agency payroll manager; b. Denver, Oct. 13, 1946; s. Donald Paul and Betty Jean (Webber) A.; m. Carolyn Ann Antolini, Dec. 29, 1966; children: Andrew, Dawn. BS in Psychology, Colo. State U., Ft. Collins, 1968. Pers. specialist U.S. Army Ft. Carson, Colorado Springs, Colo., 1968-70, U.S. Civil Svc. Commn., Denver, 1970-71; area mgr. U.S. Civil Svc. Commn., Providence, 1972-73; adminstrv. officer Action Region 8, Denver, 1973-75; program mgr. Office of Pers. Mgmt., Denver, 1975-81; owner, mgr. Ski N Sport Ltd., Arvada, Colo., 1979-82; mgmt. cons. Denver Bur. Reclamation, 1981-82, program mgr., 1983—; aide White House Fellows, Denver and Washington, 1980-81. Mem. Fed. Exec. Coun., Providence, 1972-73; cons. ARC, Denver, 1973-75, City of Denver Auditor's Office, 1989. Recipient Gubenatorial Citation Gov. of R.I., 1973. Mem. Devel. Plus Inc. (assoc.), Pres.'s Coun. Mgmt. Improvement (Excellence award 1990). Republican. Home: 2592 S Independence St Denver CO 80227-2846 Office: Adminstrv Svc Ctr 7201 W Mansfield Denver CO 80235

ANDERSEN, SHEREE HILTON, research analyst, educator; b. Provo, Utah, Aug. 28, 1954; d. Lynn Mathers and Annalee Hope (Averall) Hilton; m. Blaine Perkes Andersen, Sept. 19, 1979; children: Ashlee Brynn, Reghan Yael, Jamie Coy, Eryn Mellree. BS, Brigham Young U., 1975; MS, U. Utah, 1980. Assoc. systems analyst ITEL Corp., Salt Lake City, 1977-78; programmer analyst State of Utah, Salt Lake City, 1980-81; research analyst Ford Motor Co., Dearborn, Mich., 1982-88; pvt. practice computer cons. Bloomfield, Mich., 1988-89, Logan, Utah, 1989—; adj. instr. Madonna Coll., Livonia, Mich., 1986-88, Utah State U., Logan, 1989-90; systems cons. Young & Rubicam, Detroit, 1986-90; system trainer Ford Motor Co., Detroit, 1991—, speaker, Dearborn, Mich., 1986; system cons., instr. R.L. Polk & Co., Detroit, 1987-88. asst. dir. Multi-Congl. Youth Program, Southeast Mich., 1984-85; troop leader Girl Scouts U.S., 1986-88; mem. cen. com. Bush for Pres., Utah, 1979-80; staff Headlee for Gov., Mich., 1982. Nat. Merit scholar, 1972, Deseret Newspaper Sterling scholar 1972. Mem. SAS Users Group Internat., Detroit SAS Users Group, Am. Statis. Assn. (speaker 1986). Republican. Mormon. Home: 1530 Deerhaven Dr Logan UT 84321-2185 Office: 500 E 1300 N # 260 Logan UT 84321-2471

ANDERSEN, TORBEN BRENDER, optical researcher, astronomer; b. Naestved, Denmark, May 17, 1954; came to U.S., 1983; s. Bjarne and Anna Margrethe (Brender) A.; m. Alice Louise Palmer, Nov. 3, 1990. PhD, Copenhagen U., Denmark, 1979. Rsch. fellow Copenhagen U., 1980-82, sr. rsch. fellow, 1982-85; optical cons. Nordic Optical Telescope Assn., Roskilde, Denmark, 1985; optical systems analyst Telos Corp., Santa Clara, Calif., 1985-88; rsch. scientist Lockheed Missiles and Space Co., Palo Alto, Calif., 1988—; vis. scholar Optical Scis. Ctr., U. Ariz., Tucson, 1983-85. Editor: Astronomical Papers Dedicated to Bengt Strömgren, 1978; contbr. articles to Jour. Quantitative Spectroscopy Radiation Transfer, Applied Optics, Astronomische Nachrichten. Mem. Optical Soc. Am., Internat. Astron. Union, Soc. Photo-Optical Instrumentation Engrs. Office: Lockheed Rsch Labs O/97-20 3251 Hanover St # 254G Palo Alto CA 94304-1191

ANDERSEN, WILLEM HENDRIK JAN, physicist; b. Pontianak, Indonesia, Feb. 27, 1941; came to the U.S., 1969; s. Willem D.J. and Christina (Reinders) A.; m. Trijntje DeHaan, Sept. 11, 1964 (div. 1987); children: Willem P. J. Adriaan, Jan Bart, Jan Hein; m. Rosalie E.M. Schmalen, Nov. 20, 1987. PhD, Tech. U. Delft, Netherlands, 1965; AMP, Harvard U., 1984. Asst. prof. Tech. U. Delft, 1965-69; assoc. prof. Cornell U., Ithaca, N.Y., 1969-70; bus. unit mgr. N.V. Philips, Eindhoven, Netherlands, 1970-76, mng. dir. subsystems, 1984-86; v.p. mktg. and engring. Simmonds Precision, Netherlands, 1976-78; sr. mgr. V.D. Heem Electronics, Netherlands, 1978-84; CEO Laser Magnetic Storage, Colo. Springs, 1986-92, Comlinear Corp., Ft. Collins, Colo., 1992—; bd. dirs. Ctr. for Entrepreneurship, Colo. Springs. Contbr. articles to profl. jours.; patentee in field.

ANDERSON, ALDON J., judge; b. Salt Lake City, Jan. 3, 1917; s. Aldon J. and Minnie (Egan) A.; m. Virginia Barbara Weilenmann, Nov. 5, 1943; children—Jeffrey Lance, Aldon Scott, Craig W., Paul Christian, Kevin E., Rebecca C., Douglas K. B.A., U. Utah, 1939, J.D., 1943. Bar: Utah 1943. Ptnr. King, Anderson & Durham, King, Anderson & Brown, 1943-57; dist. atty. 3d dist. Dist. Ct. of Utah, 1953-57; judge state dist. ct. State of Utah, 1957-71; judge U.S. Dist. Ct. Utah, 1971—, chief judge, from 1978, now sr. judge; vice chmn. State Bar Com. on Uniform Cts., Utah, 1970, chmn.; subcom. on Jud. Improvement, Jud. Adminstrv. Conf., 1979—; vice chmn. State Bar Com. on Compiling State Rules of Evidence; past chmn. ad hoc com. of judicial conf. Am. Inns of Ct.; past chmn. Am. Inns of Ct. Found. Active Mormon Ch. Named Judge of Yr. Utah Bar Assn., 1980, 85. Mem. ABA, Am. Bar Found. (past pres.), Dist. Attys. Assn. Utah, U.S. Dist. Judges Assn. (past pres. 10th cir.), Order of Coif (hon.), Pi Kappa Alpha, Phi Delta Phi. Office: US Dist Ct 110 US Courthouse 324 S State St Ste 105 Salt Lake City UT 84111-2321

ANDERSON, ALICE MARIE, psychologist, counselor; b. Coleridge, Nebr., Dec. 5, 1931; d. George Edwin and Marie Haines; m. John Edward Berry, July 8, 1951 (div. 1975); children: David Paul, Alice Kathleen McKellar, Pamela Jeanne Jeffery, Daniel Mark; m. Leroy Frank Weed, Aug. 6, 1988. MA in Psychology, Calif. State U., Chico, 1971. Counselor, psychologist Anderson (Calif.) Union High Sch. Dist., 1971-87; pvt. practice lic. ednl. psychologist Redding, Calif., 1986—; counselor Shasta Community Coll., Redding, 1986-92; marriage, family, and child counselor intern Covenant Counseling Ctr., Redding, 1990—. Mem. AACD, Nat. Assn. Sch. Psychologists, Calif. Assn. Sch. Psychologists, Calif. Assn. Marriage and Family Therapists, Shasta County Psychol. Assn. Mem. United Church of Christ. Home: 8973 Brentwood Way Redding CA 96002

ANDERSON, ANN, state legislator; b. Yakima, Wash., 1952; married Eric Anderson; 1 child, Cori. Former tchr., mem. Wash. State Senate, majority whip. Republican. Home: 2718 McLeod Rd Bellingham WA 98225 Office: 205 Institutions Bldg Olympia WA 98504-0001

ANDERSON, ARTHUR ROLAND, engineering company executive, civil engineer; b. Tacoma, Mar. 11, 1910; s. Eivind and Aslaug (Axness) A.; BS, U. Wash., 1934; MS, MIT, 1935, DSc, 1938; LLD (hon.), Gonzaga U., 1983; m. Barbara Hinman Beck, June 5, 1938; children: Martha Anderson Nelson, Karl, Richard, Elisabeth Anderson Zerzan, Deborah Anderson Ray. Mem. staff MIT, Cambridge, 1936-38, 39-41; design engr. Klonne Steel Co., Dortmund, Germany, 1938-39; head tech. dept. Cramp Shipyard, USN Bur. Ships, Phila., 1941-46; pvt. practice cons. civil engr., Stamford, Conn., 1946-51; co-founder Concrete Tech. Corp., Tacoma, 1951, sr. v.p., 1956—; pres. Anderson Enterprises Corp., Tacoma, 1957-87; vis. lectr. U. Wash., 1954-55; chmn. bd. Anderson, Birkeland, Anderson & Mast, Engrs., Inc. (now ABAM Engrs. Inc.), Tacoma, 1951-77. Pres. Puget Sound (Wash.) Sci. Fair, 1954-58; mem. Tacoma Pub. Utility Bd., 1954-69, chmn., 1968-69; mem. ednl. council MIT, 1954-86, vis. com., 1960-70; mem. Pacific Luth. U. Collegium, 1976—; mem. vis. com. U. Wash.; mem. Wash. State Coun. for Post-Secondary Edn., 1977-84. Registered profl. engr., Wash.; named Alumnus Summa Laude Dignatus, U. Wash., 1980. Mem. Am. Concrete Inst. (hon. mem., dir. 1962-69, pres. 1966-67, Constrn. Practice award 1962, Alfred E. Lindau medal 1970, Roger Corbetta award 1974, Charles S. Whitney award 1975, Turner medal 1977, Arthur J. Boase award 1979), ASCE (hon., life mem., mem. tech. com. 1963-66, T.Y. Lin award 1971), Soc. Exptl. Stress Analysis (charter), ASTM, Nat. Soc. Profl. Engrs., Soc. Naval Architects and Marine Engrs., Internat. Assn. Bridge and Structural Engrs. (hon.), Prestressed Concrete Inst. (pres. 1970-71), N.E. Coast Shipbuilders and Engrs., Japan Concrete Inst. (hon.), Fedn. Internat. de la Precontrainte (F.I.P. medal 1974), Comité European de Beton, Nat. Acad. Engring., Sigma Xi, Chi Epsilon, Beta Gamma Sigma, Tau Beta Pi. Contbr. numerous articles in tech. of concrete and research on welded steel ships to profl. jours.; patentee in field. Home: 502 Tacoma Ave N Tacoma WA 98403-2741 Office: 1123 Port Of Tacoma Rd Tacoma WA 98421-3799

ANDERSON, ARTHUR SALZNER, publishing company executive, marketing executive; b. Boise, Idaho, Jan. 17, 1923; s. Howard Ballantyne and Mildred Ina (Salzner) A.; m. Janice Virginia Jacobsen, June 21, 1948; children: Roger Bruce, Gregory Bryan, Julie Janice Olsen, Lane Jacobsen, Margaret Virginia Ence, Heidi Gail Eldredge, Steven Jacobsen. B.A., U. Utah, 1947. Sales promotion asst. Internat. Harvester Co., 1947-48, zone mgr., 1948-51; sr. v.p., dir., chmn. exec. com. Evans Communications, Inc., Salt Lake City, 1977-84, dir., chmn. exec. com., 1984-87, pres., 1984-87; chmn. bd. Panoram Prodns., 1977-82; pres. Deseret Book Co., 1975-80, dir., 1975-92; pres., chief exec. officer Anderson Mktg. Inc., Salt Lake City, 1987—. Author: By Example, 1961. Vice-pres. Salt Lake Area United Fund, 1977-80; mem. governing bd. Primary Children's Med. Ctr., 1975—, vice chmn., 1981-83, chmn., 1983-92; bd. dirs. Osmond Found., 1982-83. Served with AUS, 1943-46. Mem. Utah Advt. Fedn. (pres. 1967-68), Sales and Mktg. Execs. Utah (pres. 1965-66). Mem. LDS Ch. Home: 334 W 4620 N Provo UT 84604 Office: Anderson Mktg Inc Graystone Office Plz 1174 E 2700 S # 19 Salt Lake City UT 84106-2673

ANDERSON, BARBARA LOUISE, library director; b. San Diego, Jan. 5, 1933; d. Lorenzo and Louise (Morgan) A.; 1 child, Sean Allen. BS, San Diego State U., 1954; MLS, Kans. State Teachers Coll., 1955. Br. librarian L.A. Pub. Library, 1956-59; br. librarian, reference, young adult librarian San Diego Pub. Library, 1959-64; librarian U.S. Army, Europe, 1964-69; coordinator Serra Reference Project, Serra Regional Library System, San Diego, 1969-71; head readers services Riverside (Calif.) City and County Pub. Library, 1972-74; county librarian San Bernardino County (Calif.) Library, 1974—; del. White House Conf. on Libraries and Info. Services, 1979. Bd. dirs. Inland Empire Symphony, 1982-84, Riverside Mental Health Assn., 1975-79; mem. citizens adv. bd. San Bernardino YWCA, 1988-89. Mem. ALA, Calif. Library Assn., Black Caucus of Calif. Library Assn., Congress of Pub. Library Systems (pres. 1984), Calif. County Librarians Assn., Calif. Soc. Librarians (pres. 1974-75, mem. OCLC Users Council 1984-88), AAUW (pres. Riverside Br. 1976-77), NAACP, Bus. and Profl. Women San Bernardino. Democrat. Baptist. Contbr. articles to publs. in field. Office: San Bernardino County Libr 104 W 4th St San Bernardino CA 92415*

ANDERSON, BRADFORD WILLIAM, food company sales executive; b. Redlands, Calif., Feb. 17, 1956; s. B.W. and Helen Louise (Wisel) A.; m. Diane Elizabeth Hutt, Aug. 22, 1981; 1 child, David B. BS in Mgmt., U. Redlands, 1978; MBA in Mktg. Mgmt., Calif. State U., 1982. Cert. instr. in bus. edn., Calif. Store mgr. Fringer's Market, Redlands, Calif., 1978-80; ter. mgr. Carnation Co., Fullerton, Calif., 1980-82, sr. ter. mgr., trainer, 1982-84, dist. sales coord., 1984-85; nat. mgr. sales planning Carnation Co., L.A., 1985-91; nat. mgr. sales tech. Nestle Food Co., Glendale, Calif., 1991—; implementation coord. Carnation Co., L.A., 1984; nat. mgr. sales tech. Nestle Food Co., Glendale, Calif., 1991—; instr. Chaffey Coll., Alta Loma, Calif., 1984-87. Mem. Muckenthaler Cultural Ctr. and Theater, 1987—, Friends of Santa Ana Zoo, 1988, Diamond Bar Improvement Assn., Diamond Bar Ranch Festival, L.A. Zoo Friends and Support, 1990—, Diamond Bar Children's Ctr. Parent Aux.; trustee Diamond Bar Congl. Ch. Named one of Outstanding Young Men in Am., Jaycees, 1984; recipient P. Pat Patterson Meml. Award, Santa Fe Fed. Savs., 1978; Harris Meml. scholar Harris Dept. Stores, 1978. Mem. Am. Mgmt. Assn., Food Industry Sales Club, Alumni Assn. San Bernardino, Calif., Young Alumni Com. U. Redlands, Alpha Gamma Nu. Republican. Home: 24442 E Rosegate Pl Diamond Bar CA 91765-1465 Office: Nestlé Food Co 800 N Brand Blvd Glendale CA 91203-1244

ANDERSON, BRADLEY CLARK, management consultant; b. Corvallis, Oreg., July 19, 1961; s. Merlin Frank and Elaine Miriam (Peterson) A.; m. Ida Marie Milano; Aug. 5, 1983; children: Devin, Katy, Tyson. BS, Brigham Young U., 1985. CPA, Ariz. Mgr. auditing svcs. Deloitte & Touche, Phoenix, 1985—; instr. econs. Junior Achievement, Phoenix, 1988-89. Mem. allocation com. Valley of the Sun United Way, Phoenix, 1985-89. Mem. AICPA, Ariz. Soc. CPAs, Brigham Young U. Mgmt. Soc. Republican. Mem. LDS Ch. Office: Deloitte & Touche 2901 N Central Ave Ste 1200 Phoenix AZ 85012-2799

ANDERSON, BRUCE CARL, orthopedic medicine physician; b. San Diego, Nov. 3, 1949; s. Earl Woodrow and Eva (Allison) A.; m. Sherry Poole, June 10, 1979 (div. June 1980); 1 child, Jennifer Elizabeth; m. Gwendolyn Joy, May 6, 1987; children: Jeremy, Ryan. BS in Chemistry, San Diego State U., 1972; MD, UCLA, 1976. Resident Providence Hosp., Portland, Oreg., 1976-79; physician Kaiser Sunnyside Hosp., Clackamas, Oreg., 1980—; orthopedic medicine dept. dir. Kaiser Sunnyside Hosp., Clackamas, 1986—. Author: Office Orthopedics for Primary Care, 1992; contbr. articles to profl. jours.

ANDERSON, BRUCE MACLEOD, magazine editor; b. Hollister, Calif., Oct. 6, 1956; s. George Howard and Dawn Viola (Page) A. BA, Stanford U., 1979. Reporter The Miami Herald, West Palm Beach, 1979-80, Sports Illustrated, N.Y.C., 1980-85; writer, reporter Sports Illustrated, L.A., 1985-90; freelance writer San Francisco, 1990; editor Stanford (Calif.) Mag., 1991—. Recipient Robert Sibley award Coun. for Advancement and Support of Edn., Washington, 1992. Office: Stanford Mag Bowman Alumni House Stanford CA 94305-4005

ANDERSON, BRUCE MORGAN, computer scientist; b. Battle Creek, Mich., Oct. 8, 1941; s. James Albert and Beverly Jane (Morgan) A.; m. Jeannie Marie Hignight, May 24, 1975; children: Ronald, Michael, Valerie, John, Carolyn. BEE, Northwestern U., 1964; MEE, Purdue U., 1966; PhD in Elec. Engring., Northwestern U., 1973. Rsch. engr. Zenith Radio Corp., Chgo., 1965-66; assoc. engr. Ill. Inst. Tech. Rsch. Inst., Chgo., 1966-68; sr. electronics engr. Rockwell Internat., Downers Grove, Ill., 1973-75; computer scientist Argonne (Ill.) Nat. Lab., 1975-77; mem. group tech. staff Tex. Instruments, Dallas, 1977-88; sr. scientist BBN Systems and Techs., Cambridge, Mass., 1988-90; sr. systems engr. Martin Marietta, Denver, 1990—; lectr. computer sci. U. Tex.-Arlington and Dallas; adj. prof. computer sci. N. Tex. State U.; vis. indsl. prof. So. Meth. U.; computer systems cons. Info. Internat., Culver City, Calif., HCM Graphic Systems, Gt. Neck, N.Y.; computer cons. depts. geography, transp., econs., sociology and computer sci. Northwestern U., also instr. computer sci.; expert witness for firm Burleson, Pate and Gibson. Contbr. articles to tech. jours. NASA fellow Northwestern U., 1973. Mem. IEEE Computer Soc. (chmn. Dallas 1984-85), Am. Assn. Artificial Intelligence, Assn. Computing Machinery (publs. chmn. 1986 fall joint computer conf. IEEE and Assn. Computing Machinery), Toastmasters Internat., Sigma Xi, Eta Kappa Nu, Theta Delta Chi. Home: 3473 E Euclid Ave Littleton CO 80121-3663 Office: Martin Marietta Mail Stop XL4370 700 W Mineral Ave Littleton CO 80120-4511

ANDERSON, BRUCE NILS, psychiatrist; b. L.A., May 26, 1939; s. Charles Landis and Elizabeth (Caviness) A.; m. Audrey A. Thompson, Dec. 30, 1962; children: Steven, Elizabeth, John. BA, Pacific Union Coll., 1960; MD, Loma Linda U., 1964; MS, Ohio State U., 1969. Diplomate Am. Bd. Psychiatry and Neurology. Intern, resident in medicine Stanford U. Hosps., Palo Alto, Calif., 1964-65; resident in psychiatry Harding Hosp., Worthington, Ohio, 1967-70; fellow in child psychiatry Ohio State U. Hosps., Columbus, 1969; pvt. practice, Hinsdale, Ill., 1970-78, Deer Park, Calif., 1978—; med. dir. mental health programs St. Helena Hosp., Deer Park, 1986—, chief staff, 1986. Chmn. Walter Utt Endowment Com., 1986—. Capt. M.C., U.S. Army, 1965-67. Mem. Am. Psychiat. Assn., Napa County Med. Soc., Am. Judo and Jujitsu Fedn. (black belt), Alpha Omega Alpha. Republican. Adventist. Office: Silverado Psychiat Ctr PO Box 508 Deer Park CA 94576-1508

ANDERSON, BYRON FLOYD, business and political consultant; b. Plentywood, Mont., May 4, 1953; s. Byron L. and Betty Jo (White) A.; m. Sheri L. Wessman, Aug. 11, 1982 (div. 1988); 1 child, Lindsie Ni. AAS, Weber State U., 1987, postgrad., 1988—. Brakeman/condr. CMSP&P RR, Three Forks, Mont., 1971-78; timeshare sales rep. Island Park Village, Macks Inn, Idaho, 1978-80; mng. ptnr. ComCo, Missoula, Mont., 1980-81; mktg. specialist Camelot Mktg., Ogden, Utah, 1981; new car sales rep. Whetton Buick, Ogden, 1982-84; real estate project mgr. Ivory Homes, Ogden, 1986-88; new home sales agt. Woodside Homes, Ogden, 1989; pvt. bus. and polit. cons. Ogden, 1989—; chmn. bd. dirs. Avatar, Inc., Ogden. Mem. Utah Ho. of Reps., 1991—; sec. Utah State Dem. Party, 1993—. Mem. Sigma Alpha Epsilon (founding mem., Order of Phoenix award 1992), Phi Kappa Phi, Delta Epsilon Chi (past pres. WSU). Democrat. Mem. LDS Ch. Home: 5648 S 1150 W # 6 Riverdale UT 84405

ANDERSON, C. LEONARD, librarian; b. Spokane, Wash., Jan. 13, 1946; s. Charles Arthur and Elsa Alida (Ericsson) A.; m. Shirley Rae Bacon, June 16, 1967; children: Douglas Arthur, Eric Bror. BA in Edn., Ea. Wash. State Coll., 1968; MLS, U. Oreg., 1972. Library asst. Spokane Pub. Library, 1962-68; with Portland Pub. Schs., 1968—, mid. sch. librarian, 1978-80, high sch.

librarian, 1986—; pres. Portland Assn. Tchrs., 1977-78, 82-86; mem. Nat. Bd. Profl. Teaching Standards, Nat. Edn. Goals Panel Resource Group; mem. bd. examiners Nat. Coun. for Accreditation Tchr. Edn., 1987—; chmn. Oreg. Tchr. Standards and Practice Commn., 1981-86. Mem. Oreg. Rep. Tchrs. Adv. Commn., Beaverton, 1985—; appointee del. Rep. Nat. Conv., Dallas, 1984; mem., chmn. Beaverton Libr. Bd., 1983-89; bd. dirs. Nat. Found. for Improvement of Edn., Washington, 1981-84. Mem. NEA (bd. dirs. 1987—, chmn. instrn. and profl. devel. com. 1988-91), ALA, Oreg. Edn. Assn. (bd. dirs., v.p. 1975—). Presbyterian. Home: 5595 SW Chestnut Ave Beaverton OR 97005-4250 Office: Grant High Sch 2245 NE 36th Ave Portland OR 97212-5299

ANDERSON, CAROL RUTH, secondary school educator; b. Conewango, N.Y., Aug. 24, 1926; d. Maynard William and Hila Martha (Kent) Phillips; m. George Boyer, Mar. 27, 1948 (div. July 1967); children: Gregory, Gail, Martha; m. Donald Anderson, Jan. 13, 1978 (div. Jan. 1981). Assoc. BS, Jamestown (N.Y.) Community Coll., 1962; BEd, U. Buffalo, 1966; MS in Edn., SUNY, Fredonia, 1971; postgrad., Ariz. State U., 1980-81. Cert. secondary tchr., N.Y., Ariz. Sec. Jamestown Metal Corp., 1957-61; sec. to judge Cattaraugus County, Little Valley, N.Y., 1961-66; bus. educator Jamestown High Sch., 1966-82, Phoenix Union High Sch. Dist., 1982-88; ret., 1988. Rep. committeewoman Cattaraugus County, 1960-62. Mem. N.Y. State Ret. Tchr.'s Assn., U. of Buffalo Alumni Assn., NEA, Jamestown High Sch. Tchrs. Club (sec., treas. 1967-82), Ariz. State Ret. Tchrs. Assn., Am. Legion, VFW, Women of Moose. Republican. Methodist.

ANDERSON, CARSON ANTHONY, historic preservation consultant; b. L.A., Aug. 8, 1951; s. Fred Arthur and Julia Alicia (Washington) A. Student, Pomona Coll., 1972; BA, U. Calif., Berkeley, 1974; MA, U. Va., 1983. Planning asst. L.A. County Reg. Planning Dept., 1974-77; archtl. historian Vt. State Div. for Hist. Preservation, Montpelier, 1979-81; asst. planner City Beverly Hills, Calif., 1981-84; pvt. practice as hist. preservation cons. L.A., 1985; community planner U.S. Army Corps Engrs., L.A., 1986-87; sr. city planner cultural resources City Pasadena, 1987-90; hist. preservation cons. L.A. Community Redevelopment Agy., 1990—; hist. preservation cons. W. Adams Heritage Assn., L.A., 1987—; archtl. annotator Da Camera Soc., L.A., 1987—. Mem. citizens adv. panel Downtown L.A. Redevel. Plan; docent L.A. Conservancy, 1987-90, mem. cultural resources com., 1981-90; mem. peace and justice commn. Episcopal Diocese of L.A., 1992. Mem. Soc. Archtl. Historians, Nat. Trust for Hist. Preservation, Calif. Preservation Found. (So. Calif. chpt.), ACLU. Democrat. Episcopalian. Home: The Vista Montoya 1119 Albany St Apt 227 Los Angeles CA 90015-2069 Office: PO Box 86222 Los Angeles CA 90086-0222

ANDERSON, CHARLES MICHAEL, accountant; b. Londonderry, N. Ireland, England, July 15, 1944; came to U.S., 1946; s. Albert and Elizabeth (McDaid) A.; m. Terri Lynn Good, Oct. 6, 1981; children: Sean Michael, Kevin Patrick, Kelli Marie. BS, Northern Ill. U., 1966; MBA, U. Southern Calif., 1970. CPA. Staff acct. Price Waterhouse Co., Chgo., 1966-69; mgmt. cons. Price Waterhouse Co., L.A., 1970-72, pvt practice, Manahttan Beach, Calif., 1972-73; mgr. corp. budgets Great Southwest Corp., L.A., 1973-76; dir. internal audit Standard Brands Paint, Torrance, Calif., 1976-86; dir. control systems Standard Brands Paint, 1986-87; chief fin. officer One-Day Paint & Body, Torrance, 1988-89; ptnr. Anderson & Assocs., Manhattan Beach, 1989—. Contbr. articles to profl. jours. Chmn. city budget review com. Torrance Area C of C, 1990—; pres. Joie De Vive Homeowners Assn., Manhattan Beach, 1979-82, treas., 1985—; pres., chmn. Calif. Museum Sci. & Industry, L.A., 1975-78; mem. Cath. Big Bros., Torrance, 1973-84 (Ten Yr. award 1984). Fellow AICPA, Calif. Soc. CPA's, Am. Inst. Profl. Bookkeepers; mem. Irish Network Southern Calif, Le Tip Internat. (treas. 1991—), Rotary (bd. dirs. 1989—). Democrat. Roman Catholic. Home: 1155 11th St Unit 1 Manhattan Beach CA 90266-6054

ANDERSON, CHARLES ROSS, civil engineer; b. N.Y.C., Oct. 4, 1937; s. Biard Eclare and Melva (Smith) A.; m. Susan Breinholt, Aug. 29, 1961; children: Loralee, Brian, Craig, Thomas, David. BSCE, U. Utah, 1961; MBA, Harvard U., 1963. Registered profl. engr.; cert. land surveyor. Owner, operator AAA Engring. and Drafting, Inc., Salt Lake City, 1960—; mem. acad. adv. com. U. Utah, 1990-91. Mayoral appointee Housing Devel. Com., Salt Lake City, 1981-86; bd. dirs., cons. Met. Water Dist., Salt Lake City, 1985—; bd. dirs., pres., v.p., sec. bd. Utah Mus. Natural History, Salt Lake City, 1980-92; asst. dist. commr. Sunrise Dist. Boy Scouts Am., Salt Lake City, 1985-86; fundraising coord. architects and engrs. United Fund; mem. Sunstone Nat. Adv. Bd., 1980-88; bd. dirs. Provo River Water Users Assn., 1986—. Fellow Am. Gen. Contractors, Salt Lake City, 1960; recipient Hamilton Watch award, 1961. Mem. ASCE, Am. Congress on Surveying and Mapping, U. Utah Alumni Assn. (bd. dirs. 1989-92), Harvard U. Bus. Sch. Club (pres. 1970-72), The Country Club, Bonneville Knife and Fork Club, Rotary (v.p. 1990-91, chmn. election com. 1980-81, vice chmn. and chmn. membership com. 1988-90), Pi Kappa Alpha (internat. pres. 1972-74, trustee endowment fund 1974-80, Outstanding Alumnus 1967, 72), Phi Eta Sigma, Chi Epsilon, Tau Beta Pi. Home: 2689 Comanche Dr Salt Lake City UT 84108-2846 Office: AAA Engring & Drafting Inc 1865 S Main St Salt Lake City UT 84115-2045

ANDERSON, CLIFTON EINAR, editor, writer; b. Frederic, Wis., Dec. 17, 1923; s. Andrew John and Ida Louise (Johnson) A.; m. Phyllis Mary Nolan, Oct. 5, 1943; children: Kristine, Craig. BS, U. Wis., 1947; MA, U. Calif., Berkeley, 1954. News editor Chgo. Daily Drover's Jour., 1943-45; asst. editor The Progressive, Madison, Wis., 1946-47; dir. publs. Am. Press, Beirut, 1948-53; mgr. rural programs Houston C. of C., 1957-62; faculty Tex. A&M U., College Station, 1962-65; rsch. fellow U. Tex., Austin, 1965-68; faculty Southwestern Okla. U., Weatherford, 1968-72; extension editor U. Idaho, Moscow, 1972—; speaker John Macmurray Centennial Conf., Marquette U., 1991, Nat. Conf. on Peacemaking and Conflict Resolution, 1993. Editor: The Horse Interlude, 1976; author: (with others) Ways Out: The Book of Changes for Peace, 1988, The Future: Opportunity Not Destiny, 1989; contbr. articles to profl. jours. and mags. Treas. Moscow Sister City Assn., 1986—; founding mem. Coalition for Cen. Am., Moscow, 1986; chmn. U. Idaho Affirmative Action Com., 1990; writer campaign staff Senator R.M. La Follette, Jr., Madison, Wis., 1946, on the senatorial campaign staff of Hubert H. Humphrey, Mpls., 1948; chmn. Borah Found. for the Outlawry of War, U. Idaho, 1986-87, chmn. Borah Symposium, 1986-87. Recipient Rsch. award The Fund for Adult Edn., 1954-55, U.S. Office Edn., 1965-68, 1st prize in newswriting competition Assn. Am. Agrl. Coll. Editors, 1976. Mem. World Future Soc. (speaker 6th gen. assembly 1989, 7th gen. assembly 1993), Agr., Food and Social Values Soc., Agrl. Communicators in Edn., Am. Acad. Religion, Profs. World Peace Acad., Martin Inst. for Peace Studies and Conflict Resolution (Moscow, adv. com.), Nat. Assn. Mediation in Edn. Democrat. Home: 234 N Washington St Moscow ID 83843-2757 Office: U Idaho Agrl Communications Ctr Moscow ID 83843

ANDERSON, CRAIG JAMES, probation officer; b. Billings, Mont., Sept. 9, 1952; s. James R. and Pat (Schultz) A. BA, U. Mont., 1975. Spl. events coord. Mont. Easter Seal Soc., Billings, 1977-78; dep. probation officer 4th Jud. Dist., Polson, Mont., 1978-79; chief probation officer 7th Jud. Dist., Glendive, Mont., 1979—. Bd. dirs. Mont. Bd. Crime Control, Helena, 1985—, Mont. Bd. of Crime Youth Justice Coun., Helena, 1982—, Glendive Med. Ctr., 1992; chmn. Big Brother/Big Sister, Glendive and Miles City, Mont., 1987-88. Recipient numerous grants for juvenile justice, 1982—. Mem. Mont. Probation Officers Assn. (pres. 1986-87, 88-89). Office: Youth Ct Probation 207 W Bell Glendive MT 59330

ANDERSON, DANA ALAN, law enforcement officer; b. Pensacola, Fla., Nov. 27, 1945; s. Daniel Jonah Anderson and Francis Elizabeth (Flinn) Allen.; m. Carol Ann Fogarty, June 20, 1970; children: Drew, Brett, Devon. AA in Bus. Adminstrn., Harrisburg Area Community Coll., 1976; BS in Adminstrn. of Justice, U. Wyo., 1987. Cert. profl. peace officer. Law enforcement officer Laramie County Sheriff's Dept., Cheyenne, Wyo., 1981—; instr. peace officer standards and tng., Cheyenne, 1988—. Chmn. Brthers Vietnam, Cheyenne, 1991—. Mem. Hostage Negotiators Am., Masons (jr. deacon 1992—), Scottish Rite. Republican. Home: 2416 Sitting Bull Rd Cheyenne WY 82009-9623 Office: Laramie County Sheriff's Dept 1910 Pioneer Ave Cheyenne WY 82001-3605

ANDERSON, DANA DEWITT, psychologist, educator; b. Huntsville, Ala., Mar. 10, 1948; s. Oscar Morring Jr. and Alyce (Baldridge) A.; m. Linda Mary Johnstone, Nov. 14, 1980; 1 child, Benjamin Blake Johnstone-Anderson. BA, Antioch Coll., 1971; MA, Ohio State U., 1974, PhD, 1981. Intern U. Fla., Gainesville, 1979; instr. psychology Pa. State U., Erie, 1978-81, asst. prof., 1981-84; asst. prof. Pacific Luth. U., Tacoma, 1984-89, assoc. prof., 1989—, chmn. psychology dept., 1989-90; cons. Office Human Devel., City of Tacoma, 1986, Pvt. Industry Coun., Tacoma, 1989-91. Contbr. articles and papers to profl. jours. and confs. Recipient rsch. grant Office Human Devel., Tacoma, 1985. Mem. Psi Chi. Democrat. Office: Pacific Luth U Tacoma WA 98447

ANDERSON, DARLENE YVONNE, public administrator; b. Fresno, Calif., Dec. 23, 1953; d. Calvin Carroll Coolidge and Gonvella (Parrish) A.; 1 child, Shakibria Shauntae. BA, U. Wash., 1978, MPA, 1987. Cert. secondary tchr., 1978. Adminstrv. asst. Head Start Program, Seattle, 1981-82; bus. tchr. Seattle and Renton, Wash., 1983-84; bus. edn. instr. Seattle Cen. Community Coll., 1984-86; grad. teaching asst. U. Wash., Seattle, 1985-87; program specialist Wash. State Office of Minority and Women's Bus. Enterprises, Olympia, 1987-89; exec. dir. Operational Emergency Ctr., Seattle, 1989-93; dir. Ctrl. Area Youth Assn., Seattle, 1993—; legis. asst. Seattle City Council, 1984. Dep. dir. Mondale-Ferraro Presdl. campaign, Seattle, 1984; mem. Seattle Mcpl. League, 1986; guest speaker, mem. con. panel polit. action forums; mem. World Affairs Coun., Seattle; mem. St. Therese Sch. Bd., 1989, Seattle King County Pvt. Industry Coun., 1990—; U.S. del. Seattle Goodwill Games Women's Conf., 1990; USSR/U.S./G.B./ Ireland/Japan Internat. Women's Forum in Soviet Union; mem. Dem. Nat. Com., 1992—. Mem. Nat. Women's Politic Caucus (honored as Wash. state woman leader 1989), Alpha Kappa Alpha. Democrat. Baptist.

ANDERSON, DAVID CHARLES, librarian, writer; b. Oakland, Calif., Apr. 27, 1931; s. Charles Emil Sr. and Alice P. (Smith) A.; m. Jean Lynn Hess; children: Alan R., David Christian, Gregory L., Brad R., Lisa L. BA, U. Calif., Berkeley, 1952, BLS, 1953. Libr. local planning office State of Calif., Sacramento, 1956-62; libr. Calif. State Dept. of Fin., Sacramento, 1959-62; libr. serials cataloger U. Calif., Davis, 1962-68, head tech. svcs. dept. Carlson Health Sci. Libr., 1968-91. Editor: Veterinary Serials, A Union List, 2d edit., The InterActions Bibliography (quar. resource jour.); author poetry; contbr. articles to profl. jours. Mem. Med. Libr. Assn. (chair vet. med. librs. sect. 1988-89), No. Calif. Med. Libr. Group, Spl. Librs. Assn., Internat. Soc. for Anthrozoology, Delta Soc.

ANDERSON, DAVID E., zoological park administrator. Student, Pfeiffer Coll., 1964-65; BS in Zoology/Psychology, Duke U., 1972, postgrad., 1973. Colony supervisor Primate Ctr. Duke U., Durham, N.C., 1972-77, asst. dir. Primate Ctr., 1977-78; curator of mammals San Francisco Zool. Gardens, 1978-81, gen. curator, 1981-87, assoc. dir., gen. curator, 1987-90, dir., 1990—; tech. advisor Nature Conservancy La., 1987-90; animal tech. cons., mem. advisement com. La. State U.; mem. animal care com. Tulane U.; chmn. steering com. Madagascar Fauna Captive Propagation Group. Revs. editor Zoo Biology, 1982-88; contbr. articles to profl. pubis. With USMC, 1965-69, Vietnam. Mem. Am. Assn. Zool. Parks and Aquariums (grad. mgmt. sch. 1982, ethics com., long range planning com., accreditation com., program chmn. Nat. Conf. 1981, others), Internat. Union Dirs. Zool. Gardens (captive breeding specialist group). Office: San Francisco Zool Gardens 1 Zoo Rd San Francisco CA 94132-1098

ANDERSON, DAVID ELLIOTT, aeronautical engineer; b. Portland, Oreg., Apr. 24, 1964; s. Richard Harold and Barbara Janet (Elliott) A. BS in Aero. and Astronautical Engring., MIT, 1986, MS, 1988. Rsch. asst. MIT Space Systems Lab., Cambridge, Mass., 1986-88; sr. engr./scientist McDonnell Douglas Space Systems Co., Huntington Beach, Calif., 1988—. Mem. Pacific Chorale, Orange County, Calif., 1988—. Mem. AIAA (mem. robotics tech. com.), Sigma Xi. Republican. Episcopalian. Office: McDonnell Douglas Space Systems 5301 Bolsa Ave Huntington Beach CA 92647-2099

ANDERSON, DAVID MELVIN, mechanical engineer, educator; b. Berkeley, Calif., July 2, 1944; s. Oscar Melvin and Helen Odessa (Haaland) A. BS, U. Calif., Berkeley, 1967, MS, 1969, DEng, 1972. Registered mech. and mfg. engr., Calif., mech. and indsl. engr., Oreg. Asst. research engr. U. Calif., Berkeley, 1968-74; design engr. MB Assocs., San Ramon, Calif., 1974; project engr. DiGiorgio Corp., Reno, 1974-77; pres. Anderson Automation, Inc., Pleasanton, Calif., 1977-84; mgr. flexible mfg. Intel Corp., Hillsboro, Oreg., 1984-89; pvt. practice cons. on competitive mfg., lectr. on design for mfg. Lafayette, Calif., 1989—; instr. new product devel. Univ. Calif. Berkeley Grad. Sch. Bus., 1993—; adj. prof. U. Portland, Oreg., 1988-89; instr. design for manufacturability course, new product devel. course U. Calif., Berkeley Extension; cons. Anderson Automation, Inc., 1977-84; lectr. pvt. seminars on design for manufacturability. Patentee universal wheelchair, 1973, peach pitting machine, 1977; author: Design for Manufacturability, Optimizing Cost, Quality and Time-to-Market, 1990; contbr. articles to profl. jours. Served to capt. U.S. Army, 1972-75. Mem. Soc. Mfg. Engrs. (sr.), Robotics Internat. (charter), ASME, Calif. Alumni. Republican. Office: PO Box 1082 Lafayette CA 94549

ANDERSON, DENNIS LESTER, provincial official; b. Edmonton, Alta., Can., Aug. 16, 1949; m. Barbara Lynne Lupasko, Aug. 21, 1971. Mem. Legis. Assembly, Calgary, Alta., 1979—; chmn. health facilities rev. com., house strategy com. Legis. Assembly, 1982, vice chmn. Calgary caucus, 1982, chmn. spl. select com. on senate reform, 1983, minister of culture, minister responsible for women's issues, 1986, minister of culture and multiculturalism, 1987, minister consumer and corp. affairs, 1989—, chmn. legis. rev. com. Office: Minister of Cons & Corp Affairs, Legislature Bldg Rm 229, Edmonton, AB Canada T5K 2B6

ANDERSON, DONALD BERNARD, oil company executive; b. Chgo., Apr. 6, 1919; s. Hugo August and Hilda (Nelson) A.; m. Patricia Gaylord, 1945 (dec. 1978); m. Sarah Midgette, 1980. BS in Mech. Engring, Purdue U., 1942. Vice pres. Hondo Oil & Gas Co. (formerly Malco Refineries, Inc.), Roswell, N.Mex.; vice pres. Hondo Oil & Gas Co. and subs. corps., Roswell, N.Mex., 1946-63; pres. Anderson Oil Co., Roswell, 1963—; pres. Cotter Corp., 1966-70, chmn. bd., 1966-74; founder, pres. Anderson Drilling Co., Denver, 1974-77; chmn. bd. Anderson Drilling Co., 1977-85. Curator fine arts, mem. acquisitions com. Roswell Mus. and Art Center, 1949-56, trustee, 1956-85, pres. bd., 1960-85, 87—, trustee, pres. 1987-90; bd. dirs. Sch. Am. Rsch., Santa Fe, chmn. bd., 1985-88, bd. dirs. 1989—; bd. dirs. Jargon Soc., Penland, N.C.; regent Ea. N.Mex. U., 1966-72; commr. Smithsonian Instn., Nat. Mus. Am. Art, 1980-88. Lt. USNR, 1942-46. Office: PO Box 1 Roswell NM 88202-0001

ANDERSON, DONALD LLOYD, consultant; b. Stoughton, Wis., Sept. 19, 1921; s. Carl Gustave and Bessie (Cook) A.; m. Augusta Neidermeier, Sept. 10, 1948; children: Anita Briggs, Catarine Krakower, Christine Robertson. Student, U. Niagara, Niagara Falls, N.Y., 1960, U. Md., Sembaen, Germany, 1963-64, City Coll., Riverside, Calif., 1971-72. Commd. USAF, 1940, advanced through grades to chief master sgt., 1963, supply supt., 1940-71; weapon systems specialist Dynalectron Corp., Norco, Calif., 1971-88, VSE Corona (Calif.), Inc., 1988-89; weapon systems specialist Dyncorp, Norco, Calif., 1989-92, cons., 1992—; tutor Myra Linn Sch., Riverside, Calif., 1991—. Author: (tng. manual) Standard Missile Data Processing Manual, 1989, 92. Vol. info. specialist Parkview Hosp., Riverside, 1992—; staff mem., vol. NCO Acad., March AFB, Calif., 1991—. Decorated Bronze Star medal, Meritorious Svc. medal, Vietnam Gallantry Cross with gold palm. Mem. DAV, VFW, NCOAC (life), Bomard Soc., Phoenix Club (life).

ANDERSON, DONALD NORTON, JR., retired electrical engineer; b. Chgo., Aug. 15, 1928; s. Donald Norton and Helen Dorothy (Lehmann) A.; B.S., Purdue U., 1950, M.S., 1952. With Hughes Aircraft Co., Culver City and El Segundo, Calif., 1952-84, sect. head, sr. project engr., 1960-65, tech. mgr. Apollo program, 1965-66, mgr. visible systems dept., 1966-69, 70-73, project mgr., 1969-70, mgr. space sensors lab., 1973-79, mgr. space electro-optical systems labs., 1979-80, mgr. space electro-optical systems labs., 1980-84, ret., 1984. Recipient Apollo Achievement award, 1970; Robert J. Collier Landsat award, 1974. Mem. Research Soc. Am., Nat. Speleological Soc., Am. Theatre Organ Soc., Sigma XI (sec. Hughes Labs. br. 1974-75), Eta Kappa Nu, Sierra Club. Home: 2625 Topanga Skyline Dr Topanga CA 90290-9543

ANDERSON, DOROTHY FISHER, social worker, psychotherapist; b. Funchal, Madeira, May 31, 1924; d. Lewis Mann Anker and Edna (Gilbert) Fisher (adoptive father David Henry Fisher); m. Theodore W. Anderson, July 8, 1950; children: Robert Lewis, Janet Anderson Yang, Jeanne Elizabeth. BA, Queens Coll., Flushing, N.Y., 1945; AM, U. Chgo., 1947. Diplomate Am. Bd. Examiners in Clin. Social Work; lic. clin. social worker, Calif.; registered cert. social worker, N.Y.;. Intern Cook County (Ill.) Bur. Pub. Welfare, Chgo., 1945-46, Ill. Neuropsychiat. Inst., Chgo., 1946; clin. caseworker, Neurol. Inst. Presbyn. Hosp., N.Y.C., 1947; therapist, Mental Hygiene Clinic VA, N.Y.C., 1947-50; therapist, Child Guidance Clinic Pub. Elem. Sch. 42, N.Y.C., 1950-53; social worker, counselor Cedarhurst (N.Y.) Family Service Agy., 1954-55; psychotherapist, counselor Family Service of the Midpeninsula, Palo Alto, Calif., 1971-73, 79-86, George Hexter, M.D., Inc., 1972-83; clin. social worker Tavistock Clinic, London, 1974-75, El Camino Hosp., Mountain View, Calif., 1979; pvt. practice clin. social work, 1978-92, ret., 1992; cons. Human Resource Services, Sunnyvale, Calif., 1981-86. Hannah G. Solomon scholar U. Chgo., 1945-46; Commonwealth fellow U. Chgo., 1946-47. Fellow Soc. Clin. Social Work (Continuing Edn. Recognition award 1980-83); mem. Nat. Assn. Social Workers (diplomate in clin. social work).

ANDERSON, EDWARD V., lawyer; b. San Francisco, Oct. 17, 1953; s. Virgil P and Edna Pauline (Pedersen) A.; m. Kathleen Helen Dunbar, Sept. 3, 1983; children: Elizabeth D., Hilary J. AB in Econs., Stanford U., 1975, JD, 1978. Bar: Calif. 1978. Assoc. Pillsbury Madison & Sutro, San Francisco, 1978—, ptnr., 1987—. Bd. editors Antitrust Law Development, 1983-86. Trustee Lick-Wilmerding High Sch., San Francisco, 1980—, pres. Mem. ABA, Calif. Bar Assn., San Francisco Bar Assn., Santa Clara Bar Assn. (counsel), City Club San Francisco, Stanford Golf Club, Phi Beta Kappa. Republican. Episcopal. Home: 45 Dorantes Ave San Francisco CA 94116-1430 Office: Pillsbury Madison & Sutro 225 Bush St San Francisco CA 94104-4207

ANDERSON, EVANS LELAND, clinical psychologist, retired educator; b. Upsala, Minn., Sept. 26, 1914; s. Carl Martin and Agda Otelia (Ryberg) A.; m. Virginia Elaine Anderson, Mar. 7, 1944 (dec. Apr. 1983); 1 child, Anita Elaine; m. Irene Victoria Jones, Jan. 5, 1985. BA, Gustavus Adolphus Coll., 1938; MA, U. Minn., 1939; EdD, U. Denver, 1951. Lic. psychologist, Calif. Tchr. Upsala Consol. Sch., 1935-37; dir. tchr. edn. Waldorf Coll., Forest City, Iowa, 1939-42; prof. psychology, counselor St. Cloud (Minn.) State U., 1946-50, 51-54; prof. San Diego State U., 1954-84; pvt. practice, San Diego, 1960—; cons. various pub. schs., San Diego County, 1960-80; teaching fellow U. Denver, 1950-51. Author: Successful Teaching: A Problem-Solving Approach, 1964, Self Help for Good Mental Health, 1992. With AUS, 1942-46, PTO. Scholar Gustavus Adolphus Coll., 1932. Mem. Calif. State Employees Assn. (chpt. v.p.), Am. Legion (pub. rels. chmn. 1949-53), Phi Delta Kappa (pres. San Diego chpt. 1975-76), Pi Kappa Delta, Kappa Delta Pi, Pi Gamma Mu, Psi Chi.

ANDERSON, GEORGE ALLAN, retired foreign service officer; b. Newman Grove, Nebr., Mar. 11, 1930; s. Clarence Emil and Wyllma Ruth (Knapp) A.; m. Eleanor Fay Pohl, Aug. 14, 1952; children: Travis Knapp, Miles Scott, Greta Marie, Jon Warren, Grant Allan. BA, Mo. U., 1952; cert. polit. econs., U. Copenhagen, 1953; postgrad., Am. U., 1962-63; MS, U. So. Calif., 1973. Fgn. svc. officer U.S. Dept. State, Washington, 1957-80; v.p. United Technologies Corp. Europe, Brussels, 1980-83; pres. Widcom Internat., Brussels, 1984-87. Chmn. indsl. policy group, EC com. Am. C. of C., Brussels, 1980-85. Lt. USN, 1948-56. Scholar U.S. Fulbright Found., 1952; recipient Curator's medal Bd. Curators Mo. U., 1952. Mem. Phi Beta Kappa. Republican. Home: 1065 E Jensen St Mesa AZ 85203

ANDERSON, GEORGE EDWARD, financial services company executive; b. Denver, Nov. 24, 1938; s. George Francis and Bernice Rose (Tartaglio) A.; m. Patricia Maxine Martinez, Dec. 6, 1957; children: Gregory George, Annette Marie. Student, Southwestern Coll., Chula Vista, Calif., 1963-69. Area v.p. Transam. Fin. Svcs., L.A., 1958-77; gen. mgr. La Mesa Recreational Products, Westminster, Calif., 1977-8l; v.p. O'Rielly Recreational Products, Tucson, 1981-84; exec. v.p., pres. Transamerica Fin. Svcs., L.A., 1984—; exec. v.p. Transam. Fin. Svcs., L.A., 1990—. Pres. Tempe Jaycees, 197l-76; mem. Nice Guys, Inc., San Diego, 1988. Mem. Am. Fin. Svcs. Assn. (bd. dirs. 1988—), Nat. Second Mortgage Assn., Calif. Fin. Svcs. Assn. (bd. dirs. 1985—), San Diego C. of C., Hon. Dep. Sheriffs Assn. (capt. San Diego), Jaycees Internat. Senate (life), Harbor Island Yacht Club. Republican. Lutheran. Office: Transam Fin 1150 S Olive St Bldg 2000 Los Angeles CA 90015-2234

ANDERSON, GERALD VERNE, aerospace company executive; b. Long Beach, Calif., Oct. 25, 1931; s. Gordon Valentine and Aletha Marian (Parkins) A.; m. Judith B. Marx, May 14, 1992; children by previous marriage: Lori Jean Anderson Fronk, Gregory Verne, David Harman, Lynn Elaine Anderson Lee, Brian Earl, Michael Gordon. AA, Long Beach City Coll., 1952; BS, U. Calif., Berkeley, 1958. Registered profl. engr., Calif. Tech. specialist N. Am. Aviation Co., L.A., 1958-65; tech. specialist McDonnell Douglas Astronautics, Huntington Beach, Calif., 1965-84; mgr. McDonnell Douglas Astronautics, Huntington Beach, 1984-87; sr. mgr. McDonnell Douglas Aerospace, Huntington Beach, 1987—; cons. Mitsubishi Heavy Industries, Nagoya, Japan, 1972-73, Aeritalia, Turin, Italy, 1975-76. Patentee, portable vacuum chamber, electron beam welding device. Mem. Westminster (Calif.) Planning Com., 1974, Huntington Beach Citizens Adv. Com., 1975, Westminster Bicentennial Com., 1976, L.A. Classical Ballet Guild, 1992—. Mem. Soc. Mfg. Engrs., Soc. Automotive Engrs., Aerospace Industries Assn., AIAA. Republican. Home: 3452 Falcon Ave Long Beach CA 90807-4814 Office: McDonnell Douglas Aerospace 5301 Bolsa Ave Huntington Beach CA 92647-2099

ANDERSON, GLEN CLARK, judge; b. Glendale, Calif., Nov. 26, 1944; s. O. Kenneth and Rhoda S. (Putzig) A.; m. Diane L. Decker, Aug. 26, 1967 (div. 1978); 1 child, Kenneth Paul; m. Yvonne Iryne Owens, Jan. 2, 1983. BS, Colo. State U., 1967, MA, 1970; JD, Willamette U., 1974. Bar: Alaska 1974, U.S. Dist. Ct. Alaska 1976, U.S. Ct. Appeals (9th cir.) 1976. Tchr. Cheyenne (Wyo.) Pub. Schs., 1967-68, Richland (Wash.) Pub. Schs., 1968-71; law clk. to hon. justice Robert Erwin Alaska Supreme Ct., Anchorage, 1974-75; asst. dist. atty. Alaska Dept. of Law, Anchorage, 1975-77, asst. atty. gen., 1977-78; judge State of Alaska Dist. Ct., Anchorage, 1978-91, State of Alaska Superior Ct., Valdez, 1991—. Mem. ABA (jud. adminstrn. div.), Alaska Bar Assn. Methodist. Office: Superior Ct Box 127 Valdez AK 99686-0127

ANDERSON, GORDON EARL, university administrator, consultant; b. Hobart, Ind., Apr. 12, 1940; s. Harvey Carl Anderson and Thelma L (Cook) Edwards. BS, Ball State U., Muncie, Ind., 1966; MS, Southern Ill. U., Edwardsville, 1975; EdD, U. Ark., Fayetteville, 1986. Pres. Am. Ednl. Counseling Svc., L.A., 1985—; v.p., chief fin. officer West Coast U., L.A., 1990—; mem. exec. com., trustee Mt. Senario Coll., Ladysmith, Wis., 1990—. Author: A Guide to U.S. Colleges and Universities for the Foreign Student, 1991. Mem. Rep. Nat. Com. Mem. Nat. Assn. Coll. & Univ. Bus. Officers, Nat. Assn. Scholars, Seven Seas Cruising Assn., Phi Epsilon Kappa, Sigma Tau Gamma. Home: 13967 Marquesas Way Slip 38 Marina Del Rey CA 90292

ANDERSON, GRANT ALLAN, spacecraft engineer; b. Alexandria, Va., Apr. 10, 1963; s. George Allan and Eleanor Fay (Pohl) A.; m. Inés Josefina Lahiff, Aug. 4, 1990. BS, Stanford U., 1985, MS, 1986; postgrad., Internat. Space U., 1991. Contr. Banfe Group Inc., Palo Alto, Calif., 1983-88; assoc. engr. Lockheed Missiles & Space Co., Sunnyvale, Calif., 1986-87, sr. assoc. engr., 1987-89, design engr., 1989-91, sr. design engr., 1991—; design project leader Space Sta. Freedom Solar Arrays. Charles Lee Powell scholar, 1985. Mem. AIAA (sec. nat. stds. design engring. com. 1989-91), Toastmasters (cert.). Office: Lockheed Missiles & Space B/551 0/7412 1111 Lockheed Way Sunnyvale CA 94089-1212

ANDERSON, HAROLD PAUL, historian, archivist, bank executive; b. Darby, Pa., Oct. 4, 1946; s. Harold P. and Mary Ann A.; B.A., Villanova U., 1968; M.A., Ohio State U., 1969, Ph.D., 1978. Teaching and research fellow Stanford U., 1973-75; archives and library specialist Hoover Instn., Stanford, Calif., 1975-77; asst. archivist dept. history Wells Fargo Bank, N.A., San Francisco, 1977-79, pub. relations officer and corp. archivist dept. history, 1979, asst. v.p. and corp. archivist dept. history, 1979—, v.p. dept. history, 1984—; v.p. and divsn. mgr., corp. mktg. and adv., 1992—; lectr. Stanford U., 1981; bd. dirs. Nat. Council on Pub. History, 1981-83. Mem. Am. Hist. Assn., Orgn. Am. Historians, Soc. Am. Archivists. Office: Wells Fargo Bank 420 Montgomery St San Francisco CA 94163-0001

ANDERSON, HENRY LEE NORMAN, academic administrator; b. Ogeechee, Ga., May 23, 1934; s. Lee and Louise Anderson; m. Agnes A. Fox, 1961; 3 children. BSEd, U. Pa., 1957; EdD, UCLA, 1972; MAR, Yale U., 1973. Lic. marriage, family, child counsellor. Tchr. L.A. County Schs., 1961-66; instr., adminstr. L.A. Unified Schs. Dist., 1967-68; assoc. dir. Dept. Special Edn. Program UCLA, 1968-69; dir. Evaluations & Mgmt. Internat., Inc., 1970, HELP, Inc.; prin. Worldwide Trading Co.; v.p. Windsor U., L.A., 1973-75; chancellor City U. L.A., 1974—; pres. Bakersfield Sch. Law, City U. Sch. Law; asst. prof. Grad. Sch. Edn., Loyola U. and Calif. State U., L.A., 1968-72; cons. in field; real estate developer; internat. commodities broker/cons. Author: You & Race: A Christian Reflects, 1960, No Use Cryn, 1961, Revolutionary Urban Teaching, 1973, Helping Hand: 8-Day Diet Programs, 1986, Helping Hand: A Guide to Health Living, 1990, 8-Day Diet Programs (Japanese edit.) 1992, Wellness Guide Book (German edit.), 1992, Anderson Small Books series: Fountain of Youth Discovered, What Vegetarians Should Know About Wellness, others; hosts weekly talk radio and wellness TV series (1991 Renaissance award as best talk show); lectr. in field. Founder, chancellor Martin Luther King Meml. Urban Core Multi-Versity; founder Youth Internat. Entrepreneurs in Wellness, Organic Wellness Network, The H.O.L.I.S.T.I.C. Group, Youth Employment Svcs., Organic Wellness Crusade, Imahe Wellness Village. Mem. NAACP (life), Nat. Speakers' Assn., Wilshire C. of C., UCLA Alumni Assn., Cheyney Alumni Assn., Yale Club Soc. Calif., World Fedn., Million Dollar Club. Republican. Episcopalian. Office: City Univ Los Angeles 3960 Wilshire Blvd Ste 501 Los Angeles CA 90010-3324

ANDERSON, HERSCHEL VINCENT, librarian; b. Charlotte, N.C., Mar. 14, 1932; s. Paul Kemper and Lillian (Johnson) A. B.A., Duke U., 1954; M.S., Columbia U., 1959. Library asst. Bklyn. Public Library, 1954-59; asst. bookmobile librarian King County Public Library, Seattle, 1959-62; asst. librarian Longview (Wash.) Public Library, 1962-63; librarian N.C. Mus. Art, Raleigh, 1963-64; audio-visual cons. N.C. State Library, Raleigh, 1964-68; dir. Sandhill Regional Library, Rockingham, N.C., 1968-70; asso. state librarian Tenn. State Library and Archives, Nashville, 1970-72; unit dir. Colo. State Library, Denver, 1972-73; state librarian S.D. State Library, Pierre, 1973-80; dir. Mesa (Ariz.) Public Library, 1980—; dir. Bibliographical Ctr. for Rsch., Denver, 1974-80, v.p. 1977; mem. Western Coun. State Librs., 1975-80, v.p., 1978, pres., 1979; mem. Ariz. State Libr., Adv. Coun., 1981-84, pres., 1982-83, Ariz. Libr. Devel. Coun., 1991—; mem. libr. technician tng. adv. com. Mesa C.C., 1982-85, mem. planning task force East Mesa campus, 1990-93, mem. task force for excellence in edn., 1993—; chmn. Serials On-Line in Ariz. Consortia, 1985-86. Jr. warden St. Mark's Episcopal Ch., Mesa, 1985-87, vestryman, 1987-90; del. Ann. Conv. Diocese of Ariz., 1989-92, mem. archives com., 1990—; mem. Maricopa County Libr. Coun., 1981—, treas., 1981—, pres., 1983, 93; mem. govt. com. Valley Citizens League, 1991-93. With AUS, 1955-57. Recipient Emeritus Honors Ariz. Library Friends, 1987. Mem. ALA, S.D. Libr. Assn. (Libr. of Yr. 1977, hon. life 1980), Mountain Plains Libr. Assn. (pres. 1974, dir. 1974-77, 86-87, Intellectual Freedom award 1979), Ariz. State Libr. Assn. (exec. com. 1986-87), Chief Officers of State Libr. Agys. (dir. 1974-76), Kiwanis (dir. Mesa Club 1981-86, v.p. 1983, pres. 1985-86), Phi Kappa Psi. Office: Mesa Pub Libr 64 E 1st St Mesa AZ 85201-6768

ANDERSON, HOLLY GEIS, medical clinic executive, radio personality; b. Waukesha, Wis., Oct. 23, 1946; d. Henry H. and Hulda (Sebroff) Geis; m. Richard Kent Anderson, June 6, 1969. BA, Azusa Pacific U., 1970. CEO Oak Tree Antiques, San Gabriel, Calif., 1975-82; pres., founder, CEO Premenstrual Syndrome Treatment Clinic, Arcadia, Calif., 1982—, Hormonal Treatment Ctrs., Inc., Arcadia, Calif., 1992—; Lectr. radio and TV shows, L.A.; on-air radio personality PMS Clinic with Holly Anderson, 1990—. Author: What Every Woman Needs to Know About PMS (audio cassette), 1987, The PMS Treatment Program (video cassette), 1989, PMS Talk (audio cassette), 1989. Mem. NAFE, The Dalton Soc. Republican. Office: PMS Treatment Clinic 150 N Santa Anita Ave Ste 755 Arcadia CA 91006-3113

ANDERSON, IRIS ANITA, retired educator; b. Forks, Wash., Aug. 18, 1930; d. James Adolphus and Alma Elizabeth (Haase) Gilbreath; m. Donald Rene Anderson, 1951; children: Karen Christine, Susan Adele, Gayle Lynne, Brian Dale. BA in Teaching, U. Wash., 1969; MA in English, Seattle U., 1972. Cert. English tchr., adminstr., Calif. Tchr. Issaquah (Wash.) Sr. High Sch., 1969-77, L.A. Sr. High Sch., 1977-79. Nutrition vol. Santa Monica (Calif.) Hosp. Aux., Jules Stein Eye Inst., L.A.; mem. Desert Beautiful, Palm Springs Panhellenic; mem. Rancho Mirage Reps., Desert Four Reps. W-Key activities scholar U. Wash. Mem. NEA, DAR (vice regent Palm Springs), AAUW, LWV, Wash. Speech Assn., Nat. Thespians, Bob Hope Cultural Ctr., Palm Springs Press Women, Coachella Valley Hist. Soc., Palm Desert Women's Club, Calif. Ret. Tchrs. Assn., CPA Wives Club, Desert Celebrities, Rancho Mirage Women's Club. Republican.

ANDERSON, JACK JOE, communications executive; b. Lipan, Tex., Oct. 22, 1928; s. William Amon and Tommie Lucille (Roberts) A.; B.A., San Jose State U., 1965, M.A., 1967; postgrad. in bus. adminstrn. Pepperdine U., Los Angeles; m. Maria I. Kamantauskas, Mar. 13, 1976; children—Mark, Douglas, Craig. Asst. mgr. edn. systems Lockheed Missiles & Space Co., Sunnyvale, Calif., 1966-69; v.p. Learning Achievement Corp., San Jose, Calif., 1969-74; mgr. instrnl. systems Ford Aerospace & Communications Corp., Pasadena, Calif., 1974-83; pres. Anderson & Assocs., Alta Loma, Calif., 1983—; cons. tng. programs and systems, 1969—. Served with USAF, 1946-66. Recipient Nat. award for tng. program design Indsl. TV Assn., 1974. Mem. Am. Mgmt. Assn., Am. Soc. Tng. and Devel. Contbr. tech. and gen. instrnl. materials in field. Office: Anderson & Assocs 9155 Carrari Ct Alta Loma CA 91737-1557

ANDERSON, JAMES MICHAEL, editor; b. Milw., July 22, 1944; s. Arvid Walter and Valberg Lucille (Mickelson) A.; m. Marilyn Kay Alexander, Aug. 25, 1973; 1 child, David James. BA, U. Colo., 1976. Editor Petroleum Info. Corp., Littleton, Colo., 1976—. With U.S. Army, 1965-69. Office: Petroleum Info Corp 4100 E Dry Creek Rd Littleton CO 80122-3757

ANDERSON, JANEEN DRENÉ WILLIAMS, computer software development company executive; b. Ft. Meade, Md., July 10, 1964; d. George Leon Williams and Jacqueline Willa Swain; m. Glyn Harold Anderson, Oct. 6, 1984; 1 child, Ian Michael. Student, Calif. Inst. Tech., 1982-84; BS in Engring., U. Calif., Berkeley, 1987. Design engr. Synaptics, Inc., San Jose, Calif., 1988-93; v.p. ABALONE, Fremont, Calif., 1993—. Patentee for synaptic elements and arrays, CMOS device for long-term learning, CMOS amplifiers with offset adaptation, CMOS current mirror with offset adaptation. Mem. Commonwealth Club Calif. Home: 40801 Stockton Way Fremont CA 94538

ANDERSON, JANET ALM, librarian; b. Lafayette, Ind., Dec. 20, 1952; d. Charles Henry and Lenore Elaine Alm; m. Jay Allan Anderson, May 21, 1983. BS, Bemidji State U., 1975; MA, Western Ky. U., 1981, MSLS in Libr. Sci., 1982; postgrad., Utah State U. Cert. elem. tchr., sch. libr. and media specialist. Storyteller, puppeteer North Country Arts Coun., Bemidji, Minn., 1975-76; head children's libr. Bemidji State U., 1976-77; mid. sch. libr. Custer County Sch. Dist., Miles City, Mont., 1977-79; tchr. of gifted and talented Custer County Sch. Dist., Miles City, 1979-80; folklore archivist Western Ky. U., Bowling Green, 1981-83; head children's and young adults' svcs. Bowling Green Pub. Libr., 1983-85; head of serials Utah State U., Logan, 1986-91, campus svcs. libr., 1991—, chmn. adv. bd. Women's Ctr., 1988-92; adj. instr. Miles Community Coll., 1978-80; cons. to various Am. outdoor museums; speaker Utah Endowment for the Humanities Speakers Bur., Salt Lake City, 1987—. Author: Old Fred, 1972, A Taste of Kentucky, 1986 (Ky. State Book Fair award), Bounty, 1990; (with others) Advances in Serials Management, Vol. 3, 1989, Vendors and Library Acquistions, 1991; contbr. to Ency. of Am. Popular Belifes and Superstitions, articles on folklore, librarianship and museology to mags. and periodicals; delivered radio and TV presentations on folklore and librarianship. Co-founder and past pres. Rosebud chpt. Nat. Audubon Soc., Miles City, Mont., 1978-80; invited author Ky. State Book Fair, 1986, Utah Arts Festival, 1991. Recipient Exhibit and Program Grant Nat. Endowment for the Arts, Bowling Green, Ky., 1984-85. Mem. ALA, Utah Libr. Assn., N.Am. Serials Interest Group, Mt.-Plains Libr. Assn., Consortium of Utah Women in Higher Edn. (campus coord. 1989-91), Bridgerland Bus. and Profl. Women (bd. dirs., pub. chairperson Logan chpt. 1986-90), Ky. Coun. on Archives, Am. Folklore Soc., Utah Folklore Soc., Assn. Living Hist. Farms and Agrl. Mus., Visitor Studies Assn., Am. Assn. Mus., Assn. Coll. and Rsch. Librs. Democrat. Lutheran. Home: 1090 S 400 E Providence UT 84332-9461 Office: Utah State U Merrill Libr Logan UT 84322-3000

ANDERSON, JANET ELISABETH PETTIT, adult education educator; b. Rock Island, Ill., June 30, 1929; d. Royce Edgar Sr. and Dorothy Clark (Wait) Pettit; m. Forrest Melcher Anderson, Jan. 20, 1952 (div. 1974); children: Lorraine Anderson Dunlap, J. Spencer, Erik Anderson. AB, Augustana Coll., Rock Island, Ill., 1952; MA, Ariz. State U., Tempe, 1981. Cert. tchr., Ariz. Elem. tchr. Villa de Chantal, Rock Island, 1970-71; elem. and jr. high tchr. Tempe Elem. Sch. Dist. 3, 1973-91; jr. high tchr. Esso Elem. Sch., Marsa el Brega, Libya, 1978-80; high sch. tchr. The Columbus Sch., Medellin, Colombia, 1989-90; ESL tchr. adult Rio Salado Coll., Phoenix, 1992—. Editor: (tng. manual) United Bank of Arizona, 1984; editor, reporter monthly newsletter Am. Sch. of Madrid, 1968-69. Mem. bd., fund drive chmn. Am. Lung Assn., Rock Island, 1955-60, ARC, Rock Island chpt., 1954-59; founder, pres. Roc-Mer chpt. Mentally Handicapped, Reynolds, Ill., 1963-64; pres. Reynolds Mother's Club, 1963-64. Lutheran.

ANDERSON, JEAN BLANCHE, fiction writer; b. St. Louis, Sept. 13, 1940; d. Clifford George and Blanche Jean (Pell) Schulze; m. Donald Wyckliffe Anderson; children: Thomas, Laura. AA, Harris Tchrs. Coll., 1960; student, U. Mo., 1965-66; BA, U. Alaska, 1977, MFA, 1980. Lectr. in English U. Alaska, Fairbanks, 1980-85, 88-89, vis. asst. prof., 1990-91; book reviewer Fairbanks Daily News-Miner, Heartland, Alaska, 1985-88; poet in the schs. Fairbanks Arts Assn., 1981-82; faculty mem. Midnight Sun Writers' Conf., Fairbanks, 1990, 91, 92. Author: In Extremis and Other Alaskan Stories, 1989; co-editor Inroads: Alaska's Twenty-Seven Fellowship Writers, 1988; contbr. short stories, poems and essays to periodicals. Fellowship Alaska State Coun. on Arts, 1982; recipient PEN Syndicated Fiction award PEN Am. Ctr., 1985. Mem. Poets and Writers Inc. Home: 509 Aquila St Fairbanks AK 99712-1320

ANDERSON, JOHN ALBERT, protective services official; b. Shenandoah, Iowa, June 30, 1943; s. Albert Roscoe and Margaret Jane (Craft) A.; m. Deborah P. Kraft, July 26, 1985; children: Philip J., Ingrid A., Thomas J. BS, U. San Francisco, 1980. Cert. community coll. tchr., Calif. Police officer U. Calif. Police, Berkeley, 1969-73, sgt., 1973-78; lt. U. Calif. Police, San Francisco, 1978-82; asst. chief of police U. Calif. Police, San Diego, 1982-85, chief of police, 1985—; coord. police svcs. U. Calif. Police, Oakland, 1991—. Trustee San Diego Regional Fire and Emergency Svcs. Found., 1988—; mem. exec. com. San Diego Crime Stoppers, Inc., 1992; bd. dirs. Boys Club San Diego, 1983-89. Sgt. USMC, 1964-69, Vietnam. Mem. Internat. Assn. Chiefs of Police, Internat. Assn. Campus Law Enforcement Adminstrs., Calif. Peace Officers Assn. (life), San Diego County Police Chiefs and Sheriff's Assn. (exec. com. 1990—), Old Mission Beach Athletic Club, Masons, Shriners. Home: 8153 La Jolla Shores Dr La Jolla CA 92037 Office: U Calif 9500 Gilman Dr 0017 La Jolla CA 92093

ANDERSON, JOHN RICHARD, entomologist, educator; b. Fargo, N.D., May 5, 1931; s. John Raymond and Mary Ann (Beaulieu) A.; m. Shereen V. Erickson, Mar. 26, 1955; children: Scott F., Lisa K., Steven F. BS, Utah State U., 1957; MS, U. Wis., 1958, PhD, 1960. Asst. prof. entomology U. Calif.-Berkeley, 1961-66, assoc. prof., 1967-70, prof., 1970—, chmn. div. parasitology Coll. Natural Resources,, 1970-71, assoc. dean research, 1979-85; Trustee, past chmn. Alameda County (Calif.) Mosquito Abatement Dist., 1961-73, 79—. Editoral bd.: Jour. Med. Entomology, 1968-72, Jour. Econ. Entomology, 1977-81, Thomas Say Found, 1968-72. Served with USN, 1950-54. Research grantee. Fellow AAAS, Royal Entomol. Soc. (London); mem. Entomol. Soc. Am. (governing bd. 1987-90, C. W. Woodworth award Pacific br. 1988), Can. Entomol. Soc., Pacific Coast Entomol. Soc., Am., Calif. mosquito control assns., Calif. Acad. Sci., N.Y. Acad. Sci., No. Calif. Parasitologists, Oakland Mus. Assn., Soc. Vector Ecologists, Nature Conservancy. Home: 2881 Shasta Rd Berkeley CA 94708-2049 Office: U Calif Berkeley CA 94720

ANDERSON, JONPATRICK SCHUYLER, minister, financial consultant, archivist; b. Chgo., July 20, 1951; s. Ralph Anderson and Helena Hilda (Robinson) Hardy; children: André, Mary, David. AA, L.A. Trade Tech. Coll., 1978; BA, UCLA, 1979; postgrad., SUNY, Albany, 1983, Govs. State U., 1985; MRE, DMin., PhD, Internat. Sem. (in coop. with Unification Theol. Sem. N.Y.), 1989. Clerical supr. VA, L.A., 1976-80; fin. adminstr. Antioch Primitive Bapt. Ch., L.A., 1979-80; pres., exec. dir. All-Around Prodns., L.A., 1980-83; assoc. minister St. Stephen Ch., San Diego, Calif., 1983-87; stadium mgr. San Diego Jack Murphy Stadium, 1985-87; mgr. Horton Plaza Shopping Ctr., San Diego, 1985-86; exec. dir. Christ-Immanuel Ministerial Assn., San Diego, 1983—; acting supr. psychiatry dept. VA Mental Health Clinic, San Diego, 1991—; pvt. investigator Merit Protective Svcs., L.A., 1972-74; adminstrv. asst. Dept. Def., 1981; cons. pvt. practice mgmt., cons. comptr., San Diego, 1981-82; cons. writer All-Around Music divsn. Broadcast Music, Inc., San Diego, 1980—; instr. San Diego Community Coll. Dist., 1984; libr. asst. San Diego State U., 1982-83; chaplain of the Day U. Calif., San Diego, 1984-85; archives technician Nat. Archives & Records Adminstrn., Laguna Niguel, Calif., 1988; mem. Nat. Conf. Ministry Armed Forces. Mem. Am. Freedom Coalition, Washington, 1988, Causa, USA, Washington, 1985-87. With USAR, 1979-80. Grammy nominee NARAS, 1980; recipient Personal award former Pres. Ronald Reagan, L.A., 1988. Mem. NAACP (life), NARAS, AFTRA, AGVA, Assn. MBA Execs. (Bus. award 1980), UCLA Alumni Assn. (life, interviewing com. adv. and scholarship program 1988—, bd. dirs. scholarship chmn. 1991—), Res. Officers Assn. of U.S. (life), UCLA Black Alumni Assn. (life, bd. dirs., scholarship chmn.), N.G. Assn. Calif. (life), Nat. Conf. Ministry to Armed Forces, VFW (life), DAV (life), AMVETS, Am. Legion, Ret. Officers Assn. U.S., Am. Assn. Religious Counselors. Democrat. Mem. Ch. of God. Office: Christ-Immanuel Ministries PO Box 1202 San Diego CA 92112-1202

ANDERSON, JOSEPHINE MARGARET, university enrollment management associate director; b. Pocatello, Idaho, Mar. 1, 1959; d. David R. and Barbara J. Anderson. BA in Journalism, Idaho State U., 1982, BBA, 1982; postgrad., Utah State U. Pub. rels. devel. dir. Silver Sage Coun. Girl Scouts U.S., Boise, Idaho, 1982-85; asst. pub. rels. dir. Treasure Valley Community Coll., Ontario, Oreg., 1986-87; assoc. dir. enrollment mgmt. Idaho State U., Pocatello, 1987—. Asst. coach Pocatello Spl. Olympics, 1990. Mem. P.E.O., Alpha Chi Omega.

ANDERSON, JUDSON TRUETT, psychiatrist; b. Durham, N.C., Oct. 23, 1933; s. Henry Brown and Grace Elizabeth (Ganzert) A.; m. Evelyn Marie Hunt, June 17, 1955; 1 child, David Brian. BS, Wake Forest Coll., 1955; MD, Bowman Gray Med. Sch., 1959. Diplomate Am. Bd. Psychiatry and Neurology. Intern Fitzsimmons Gen. Hosp., Denver, 1959-60; flight surgeon USAF, 1960-63; resident in psychiatry U. Colo., Denver, 1963-66; chief of psychiatry USAF Acad. Hosp., Colo., 1966-71; pvt. practice Colorado Springs, Colo., 1971-73; psychiatrist Psychiat. Assocs., P.C., Colorado Springs, 1973—; mem. staff Meml. Hosp., Colorado Springs, 1971—; mem. courtesy staff Penrose-St. Francis Health Care System, Colorado Springs, 1971—, Cedar Springs Psychiat. Ctr., Colorado Springs, 1971—; med. cons. Div. of Vocat. Rehab., Colorado Springs, 1976—. Lt. col. USAF, 1959-71, ETO. Mem. Colo. Med. Soc., Colorado Springs Psychiat. Soc., El Paso County Med. Soc., Phi Beta Kappa. Baptist. Office: Psychiat Assocs PC 1622 Rainier Dr Colorado Springs CO 80910-2099

ANDERSON, KARL RICHARD, aerospace engineer, consultant; b. Vinita, Okla., Sept. 27, 1917; s. Axel Richard and Hildred Audrey (Marshall) A.; B.S., Calif. Western U., 1964, M.A., 1966; Ph.D., U.S. Internat. U., 1970; m. Jane Shigeko Hiratsuka, June 20, 1953; 1 son, Karl Richard. Engr. personnel subsystems Atlas Missile Program, Gen. Dynamics, San Diego, 1960-63; design engr. Solar div. Internat. Harvester, San Diego, 1964-66, sr. design engr., 1967-69, project engr., 1970-74, product safety specialist, 1975-78; aerospace engring. cons., 1979-86; cons. engring., 1979—; lectr. Am. Indian Sci. and Engring. Soc. Served to maj. USAF, 1936-60. Recipient Spl. Commendation San Diego County Bd. Supervisors, 1985, Spl. Commendation San Diego City Council, 1985. Registered profl. engr., Calif. Republican. Episcopalian. Home: 5886 Scripps St San Diego CA 92122-3212

ANDERSON, KATHLEEN GAY, investigator, mediator, arbitrator, educator; b. Cin., July 27, 1950; d. Harold B. and Trudi L. (Chambers) Briggs; m. J.R. Carr, July 4, 1988; 1 child, Jesse J. Anderson. Student, U. Cin., 1971-72, Antioch Coll., 1973-74; cert., Nat. Jud. Coll., U. Nev., Reno, 1987, Inst. Applied Law, 1987, Acad. Family Mediators, 1991. Cert. Am. Arbitration Assn., Lemmon Mediation Inst. Paralegal Lauer & Lauer, Santa Fe, 1976-79, Wilkinson, Cragun & Barker, Anchorage, 1981-82; employment law paralegal specialist Hughes, Thorsness, Gantz, Powell & Brundin, Anchorage, 1983-91; investigator, mediator Alaska State Commn. Human Rights, 1992-93; mediator, arbitrator The Arbitration Group, Anchorage, 1987—; mem. faculty Nat. Jud. coll., U. Nev., Reno, 1988-89; adj. prof. U. Alaska, Anchorage, 1985—, Alaska Pacific U., 1990—, Chapman U., 1990; mem. Alaska Supreme Ct. Mediation Task Force, 1991—. Author, editor: Professional Responsibility Handbook for Legal Assistants and Paralegals, 1986; contbr. articles to profl. jours. Lectr. Alaska Bar Assn., 1989—, NLRB, Anchorage, 1986, Alaska Assn. Bus. and Profl. Women, 1988—, Coun. on Edn. and Mgmt., 1993—, various employers and bus. groups. Mem. Alaska Assn. Legal Assts. (pres. 1988-89, chmn. ethics com. 1985-91), Nat. Fedn. Paralegal Assn. (edn. task force coord. 1988-89, adminstrv. v.p. 1988-91), Alaska Bar Assn. (employment, alternative dispute resolution, family law sects.), Am. Soc. Human Resource Mgmt., Anchorage Soc. Human Resource Mgmt., Acad. Family Mediators (cert.), Alaska Dispute Settlement Assn. (v.p. 1992—). Home: PO Box 100098 Anchorage AK 99510-0098 Office: PO Box 240783 Anchorage AK 99524

ANDERSON, KELLY ELIZABETH, marketing professional; b. Oakland, Calif., June 7, 1957; d. Frank Stoakes Anderson and Emily Elizabeth (Wright) Kimlinger. BA in Math., BA in Environ. Studies, U. Calif., Santa Cruz, 1979, BA in Sci. Communications, 1980; grad. exec. challenge program, San Diego State U., 1989, postgrad., 1991—. Staff writer Charlotte (N.C.) Observer, 1980; sci. writer, editor Frank Porter Graham Child Devel Ctr., U. N.C., Chapel Hill, 1980-81; coordinator communications Sea Grant Coll. Program, U. Calif., San Diego, 1981-84; mgr. tech. publs. Loral Instrumentation, San Diego, 1984-87, mgr. mktg. communications, 1987-90; corp. mgr. mktg. ops. Wavetek Corp., San Diego, 1990; mgr. corp. mktg. communications ORINCON Corp., San Diego, 1990-91, mgr. corp. devel., 1991-93; mgr. pub. relations Jazzercise, Inc., Carlsbad, Calif., 1993—; owner People Pictures, portrait photography co., 1985—; acting dir. tech. svcs. Loral Instrumentation, San Diego, 1986. Contbr. more than 200 articles to profl. jours. Mem. Desktop Pub. Adv. Com., Grossmont Coll., San Diego, 1986-90; pres. Toastmasters Internat., 1983. AAAS fellow, 1980; recipient Excellence in Writing award Internat. Assn. Bus. Communicators, 1981, Council for Advancement and Support of Edn., 1984. Mem. Nat. Mgmt. Assn. (v.p. 1986), Soc. Tech. Comm. (awards of Excellence and Achievement 1981-84), Computer and Electronics Mktg. Assn. (officer 1987-89), Assn. Interim Execs. (bd. dirs. 1991-93), FASTTRAX: Women in Bus. (officer 1991-93). Office: Jazzercise Inc 2808 Roosevelt St Carlsbad CA 92008

ANDERSON, KENNETH JEFFERY, family wealth planner, accountant, lawyer; b. Daytona Beach, Fla., May 7, 1954; s. Kenneth E. and Petronella G. (Jeffer) A.; m. Susan Wagner, Aug. 19, 1978; children: Melissa, Kiersten. BSBA, Valparaiso U., 1976, JD, 1979. CPA, Ill. Prof. staff, mgr. Arthur Andersen & Co., Chgo., 1979-84; mgr. Arthur Andersen & Co., L.A., 1984-90, ptnr., 1990—, dir. individual taxed fin. svcs., western region. Gov., treas. Idyllwild (Calif.) Sch. Music and the Arts, 1990; mem. Assocs. Bd. Chgo. Lung Assn., 1980-84; vol. Hospice of the North Shore, Winnetka, 1981. Mem. AICPA, Fla. Bar Assn., Ill. Bar Assn., Ill. CPA Soc., Calif. CPA Soc. (apptd. to state com. on personal fin. planning), Soc. CPA-Fin. Planners (bd. dirs. 1987-89), Sports Lawyers Assn., Calif. Club. Republican. Home: 28 Cinch Rd Bell Canyon CA 91307-1003 Office: Arthur Andersen & Co 633 W 5th St Fl 32D Los Angeles CA 90071-2005

ANDERSON, LARRY ERNEST, biochemist; b. Corvallis, Oreg., Jan. 30, 1943; s. Ernest Clifford and Idon Anderson; m. Sally Anne Bond, June 12, 1967; children: Nicol, Todd, Kevin, Trevor, Jared, Mark, Brittney, Bradley, Tyrelle. BSc, Brigham Young U., 1968; PhD, U. Ill., 1973. Post-doctoral fellow U. Wash., Seattle, 1973-77; rsch. assoc. Battelle N.W., Richland, Wash., 1977-79, rsch. scientist, 1979-81, sr. rsch. scientist, 1981-85, staff scientist, 1985—, program mgr., 1985—; chmn. Hanford Life Scis. Symposium, Richland, Wash., 1984; U.S. del. US/USSR Coop. Agreement on Health, 1985—; plenary leader NIOSH Com. on Electromagnetics, 1990; com. mem. nonionizing radiation WHO Working Group, 1985-89., Nat. Coun. Radiation Protection, extremely low frequency electric and magnetic fields. Editor: Extremely Low Frequency Electromagnetic Fields: The Question of Cancer, 1990, Interaction of Biological Systems with Static and ELF Electric and Magnetic Fields, 1987; contbr. articles to profl. jours. Exec. bd. Blue Mountain Coun. Boy Scouts Am., Kennewick, Wash., 1982—. Mem. Bioelectromagetics Soc. (bd. dirs. 1986-88, v.p. 1988-89, pres. 1989-90), Soc. for Neuroscience, Sigma Xi. Republican. Mormon. Office: Battelle NW Labs Battelle Blvd PO Box 999 Richland WA 99352-0999

ANDERSON, LAWRENCE KEITH, electrical engineer; b. Toronto, Ont., Can., Oct. 2, 1935; came to U.S., 1957; s. Wallace Ray and Irene Margaret (Linn) A.; m. Katherine Florence Drechsler, Sept. 21, 1963; children—Susan Barbara, Robert Keith. B. in Engring. Physics, McGill U., 1957; PhDEE, Stanford U., 1962. With Bell Labs., 1961-85; dir. electronic components and Subsystems lab. Bell Labs., Allentown, Pa., 1981-85; v.p. component devel. Sandia Nat. Labs., Albuquerque, 1985-88; exec. dir. AT&T Bell Labs. Interconnection and Power Tech. Div., Parsippany, NJ, 1988-89; prof., dir. Alliance for Photonic Tech., Albuquerque, 1990-91; dir. Colo. Inst. Tech. Transfer and Implementation, U. Colo., Colorado Springs, 1991—. Fellow IEEE (pres. Electron Devices Soc. 1976-77, dir. 1979-80). Home: 2545 Karamy Ct Colorado Springs CO 80919 Office: UCCS/CITTI PO Box 7150 Colorado Springs CO 80933

ANDERSON, LLOYD VINCENT, lawyer; b. Eau Claire, Wis., Apr. 5, 1943; s. Lloyd V. and Marion (Benner) A.; m. Mary Sue Wilson, June 19, 1965; children: Matthew, Kirsten, Sam. B.Mgmt.Engring., Rensselaer Poly. Inst., 1965; J.D., Georgetown U., 1969. Bar: Va. 1969, Alaska 1970, Minn. 1972, U.S. Ct. Appeals 1972, U.S. Dist. Ct. Minn. and Alaska 1972, Trust Ter. Pacific Islands 1972, D.C. 1969, U.S. Patent Office 1969. Law clk. Alaska Supreme Ct., Juneau, 1969-70; asst. U.S. atty. Dept. Justice, Agana, Guam, 1970-72; atty. Gray Plant Mooty & Anderson, Mpls., 1972-74; shareholder, dir. Birch Horton Bittner Pestinger & Anderson, Anchorage, 1974-89; pvt. practice, Anchorage, 1989—; bd. dirs. Arrow Leasing, Anchorage. Mem. Anchorage Park Bd., 1976. Mem. ABA, Alaska Bar Assn., Am. Trial Lawyers Assn., Wash. Athletic Club (Seattle) Office: 370 Oceanview Dr Anchorage AK 99515-3752

ANDERSON, LOUISE STOUT, crime analyst; b. Wellsville, N.Y., Aug. 11, 1952; d. Carlton C. and Mary (Gasdik) Stout; m. Leonard M. Anderson, June 2, 1973. BA in German Lit., Polit. Sci., Mt. Holyoke Coll., 1974; MA in Polit. Sci., San Diego State U., 1977; MS Human Resources and Organizational Devel., 1993. Cert. C.C. tchr., Calif. Statistician Grossmont Coll., El Cajon, Calif., 1976-78; crime analyst San Diego Police Dept., 1978-80; crime analyst Career Criminal Apprehension Program, Marin County Sheriff's Office, San Rafael, Calif., 1980-83; crime analyst CCAP Unit, Sonoma County Sheriff's Office, Santa Rosa, Calif., 1983-85; mgr. mktg. svcs. Command Data Systems, Dublin, Calif., 1985-87, client svcs. mgr., 1988-92; contracts mgr. Tiburon Inc., 1992—; cons. Search Group Inc. for Automated Crime Analysis. Contbr. articles in field. Owner Acacia Assocs., public safety cons. and training orgn. Mem. Antioch Police Commn.; alumna recruiter Mt. Holyoke Club No. Calif., 1981—. Named Outstanding Young Woman of Am., 1986. Mem. Am. Polit. Sci. Assn., Assn. Police Planners Research Officers, Calif. Women in Govt., Nat. Assn. Criminal Justice Stats. Assn., U.S. West Pres.'s Club. Office: Acacia Assocs 1931 Acacia Ave Antioch CA 94509

ANDERSON, MARC RICHARD, power and light specialist; b. Lubbock, Tex., July 13, 1954; s. Richard Henry Anderson and Patricia Mae (Stewart) Burgess; m. Connie Lynn Harnish, Aug. 29, 1977; children: Eric, Dane. BA in Journalism cum laude, Wash. State U., 1976. Asst. editor Grant County Jour., Ephrata, Wash., 1976-77; staff writer The Columbian, Vancouver, Wash., 1977-80; claims rep. Royal Ins., Portland, Oreg., 1980-83; sr. claims agt. Pacific Power & Light, Portland, 1983-90; regional staff asst. Pacific Power & Light, Yakima, Wash., 1990—. Author: Vancouver: A Pictorial History, 1983. Mem. Oreg. Casualty Adjusters. Mem. Christian Ch. Home: 106 N 77th Ave Yakima WA 98908-1510 Office: Pacific Power & Light 3800 Summitview Ave Yakima WA 98902-2715

ANDERSON, MARGARET ALLYN, carpet showroom manager; b. Meeker, Okla., Aug. 1, 1922; d. Edgar Allen and Maggie May (Smith) Martin; m. Ralph Carlos Huffman, Dec. 23, 1939 (div. Dec. 1954); children: Ronald Carlos, Darrell Duane; m. Walter Monroe Anderson, June 4, 1956. Student, San Antonio Jr. Coll., 1950-51. Clk. stenographer Sinclair Oil Co., Tulsa, 1947-48; clk. stenographer to sec. U.S. Govt. Civil Svc., San Antonio, 1948-56, Denver, 1956-57, Boise, Idaho, 1957-64; co-owner, sec./treas. Anthane, Inc., Boise, Idaho, 1964-87; co-owner, showroom mgr., sec. Anthane, Inc., San Francisco, 1987—. Mem. Am. Bus. Womens Assn. Democrat. Mem. Christian Ch. Office: Anthane Inc 6 S Linden Ave # 10 San Francisco CA 94080-6408

ANDERSON, MARILYN NELLE, elementary educator, librarian, counselor; b. Las Animas, Colo., May 5, 1942; d. Mason Hadley Moore and Alice Carrie (Dwyer) Coates; m. George Robert Anderson, Sept. 4, 1974; children: Lisa Lynn, Edward Alan, Justin Patrick. BEd magna cum laude, Adams State Coll., 1962, postgrad., 1965; MEd, Ariz. State U., 1967; postgrad., Idaho State U., 1971, 86, Columbia Pacific U., 1991—. Cert. elem. tchr., K-12 sch. counselor. Tchr. Wendell (Idaho) Sch. Dist. 232, 1962-66, Union-Endicott (N.Y.) Sch. Dist., 1967-68; counselor, librarian West Yuma (Colo.) Sch. Dist., 1968-69; elem. sch. counselor Am. Falls (Idaho) Sch. Dist. 381, 1969-73; project dir. Gooding County (Idaho) Sr. Citizens Orgn., 1974-75; tchr. Castleford (Idaho) Sch. Dist. 417, 1982-92; placement specialist, referral counselor Idaho Child Care Program S. Cen. Idaho Community Action Agy., Twin Falls, 1992—; mem. Castleford Schs. Merit Pay Devel. program, 1983-84, Accreditation Evaluation com., 1984-85, Math. Curriculum Devel. com., 1985-86. Leader Brownie Scouts, Endicott, 1967-68; chmn. fundraising com. Am. Falls Kindergarten, 1971-73; leader Gooding County 4-H Council, Wendell, 1983—. Recipient Leader's award Nat. 4-H Conservation Natural Resources Program, 1984. Mem. NEA, Idaho Edn. Assn., Idaho Coun. Internat. Reading Assn., Magic Valley Reading Assn., Internat. Platform Assn., Idaho Coun. Tchrs. of English. Republican. Baptist. Home: RR 1 Box 293 Wendell ID 83355-9801 Office: S Ctrl Idaho Community Action Agy Twin Falls ID 83301

ANDERSON, MARK ALEXANDER, lawyer; b. Santa Monica, Calif., Nov. 15, 1953; s. William Alexander and Christina (Murray) A.; m. Rosalie Louise Movius, Nov. 28, 1986; 1 child, Morgan Anderson Movius. AB, U. So. Calif., 1974; JD, Yale U., 1978. Bar: Calif. 1979, U.S. Dist. Ct. (no. dist.) Calif. 1979, U.S. Ct. Appeals (9th cir.) 1979, Oreg. 1982, U.S. Dist. Ct. Oreg. 1982, Wash. 1985, U.S. Dist. Ct. (we. dist.) Wash. 1986, U.S. Supreme Ct. 1989. Law clk. U.S. Ct. Appeals (9th cir.), San Francisco, 1978-79, U.S. Dist. Ct. Oreg., Portland, 1980-82; atty. Miller, Nash, Wiener, Hager & Carlsen, Portland, 1983-92; gen. counsel Dark Horse Comics, Inc., Milwaukie, Oreg., 1992—. Chair Raleigh Hills-Garden Home Citizen Participation Orgn., 1992-93. Mem. ABA, N.W. Lawyers and Artists (pres. 1988-90), State Bar Calif., Wash. State Bar Assn., Oreg. State Bar (chair antitrust, trade regulation and unfair bus. practices sect. 1991-92), U.S. Dist. Ct. Oreg. Hist. Soc., City Club of Portland (chair arts and culture standing com. 1990-92). Home: PO Box 8154 Portland OR 97207-8154 Office: Dark Horse Comics Inc 10956 SE Main Milwaukie OR 97222

ANDERSON, MARK EUGENE, specialized truck driver, safety inspector; b. Richland Center, Wis., Oct. 9, 1952; s. Harold Eugene and Laila Marie (Jacobson) A.; m. Marilyn Jones, June 22, 1972 (div. 1984); children: Michael, Kenneth, Thomas; m. Georgina Therese Scinta, Sept. 29, 1984. Enlisted U.S. Army, 1970, ret., 1977; mgr. Taco Bell, Farmington, N.Mex., 1977-78; truck driver Farmington Meat Processors, 1978-80, Nobel/Sysco, Albuquerque, 1980-89; specialized truck driver transuranic nuclear waste Dawn Enterprises Inc., Farmington, 1989—; truck driver, cert. safety inspector Comml. Vehicle Safety Alliance, Oreg., 1991; truck driver transp. safeguards div. U.S. Dept. Energy, Albuquerque, 1989. Named N.Mex. State Truck Driving Champion N.Mex. Motor Carriers, 1988. Home: 5201 Chuckwagon Trail NW Albuquerque NM 87120 Office: Dawn Enterprises Inc PO Box 204 Farmington NM 87499-0204

ANDERSON, MARK ROBERT, data processing executive, biochemist; b. Oak Park, Ill., Aug. 11, 1951; s. Robert Hugo and Marilyn Pettee (Johnson) A.; m. Mary Jane Helsell, June 6, 1980; children: Berit Bracken, Evan Robert. BS, Stanford U., 1972; MS, Stanford U., Hopkins Marine Sta., 1973; postgrad., U. Brit. Columbia, Vancouver, 1973. Publisher Potlatch Press, Friday Harbor, Wash., 1974-77; assoc. prof. Western Wash. U., Bellingham, 1977, Harvard U., Boston, 1978; chief scientist Ocean Research & End. Soc., Boston, 1978; v.p. Moclips Cetological Soc., Friday Harbor, 1979-81; founder, dir. The Whale Mus., Friday Harbor, 1979-81; pres. The Oikos Co., Friday Harbor, 1980—, San Juan Software, Friday Harbor, 1983-84, Island Tech. Inc., Friday Harbor, 1984—; also bd. dirs. Island Tech. Inc.; bd. dirs. Worldesign; bd. advisors HIT Lab., U. Wash., 1991—. Author: Nineteen Fathers, 1971, (software) The Agent's Advantage, 1983; producer TV film Survivors, 1980; editor, founder Jour. Cetus, 1981; discoverer Resonance Theory, 1981. Founder San Juan Musicians Guild, 1974-78, Anti-Spray Coalition, 1977. Mem. Wash. Software Assn. (chair pres.' group), Database Standards Com., Am. Electronics Assn.

ANDERSON, MARTIN CARL, economist; b. Lowell, Mass., Aug. 5, 1936; s. Ralph and Evelyn (Anderson) A.; m. Annelise Graebner, Sept. 25, 1965. AB summa cum laude, Dartmouth Coll., 1957, MS in Engring., MSBA; PhD in Indsl. Mgmt., MIT, 1962. Asst. to dean, instr. engring. Thayer Sch. Engring. Dartmouth Coll., Hanover, N.H., 1959; research fellow Joint Ctr. for Urban Studies MIT and Harvard U., Cambridge, 1961-62; asst. prof. fin. Grad. Sch. Bus. Columbia U., N.Y.C., 1962-65, assoc. prof. bus., 1965-68; sr. fellow Hoover Inst. on War, Revolution and Peace Stanford (Calif.) U., 1971—; spl. asst. to Pres. of U.S. The White House, 1969-70, spl. cons. for systems analysis, 1970-71, asst. for policy devel., 1981-82; syndicated columnist Scripps Howard News Svc., 1993—; mem. Pres.' Fgn. Intelligence Adv. Bd., 1982-85, Pres.' Econ. Policy Adv. Bd., 1982-88, Pres.' Gen. Adv. Com. on Arms Control and Disarmament, 1987—; pub. interest dir. Fed. Home Loan Bank San Francisco, 1972-79; mem Commn. on Crucial Choices for Ams., 1973-75, Def. Manpower Commn., 1975-76, Com. on the Present Danger, 1977—. Author: The Federal Bulldozer: A Critical Analysis of Urban Renewal, 1949-62, 1964, Conscription: A Select and Annotated Bibliography, 1976, Welfare: The Political Economy of Welfare Reform in the U.S., 1978, Registration and the Draft, 1982, The Military Draft, 1982, Revolution, 1988, Impostors in the Temple, 1992; columnist Scripps-Howard News Svc. Dir. research Nixon presdl. campaign, 1968; issues adviser Reagan presdl. campaign, 1976, 80; trustee Ronald Reagan Presdl. Found., 1985-88. 2d lt. AUS, 1958-59. Mem. Am. Econ. Assn., Mont Pelerin Soc., Phi Beta Kappa. Club: Bohemian. Office: Hoover Instn Stanford Univ Stanford CA 94305-6010

ANDERSON, MARY ANN, nurse, consultant; b. Tremonton, Utah, Jan. 20, 1946; d. Merlin J. and Margrette (Marble) Romer; m. Gary L. Anderson, Feb. 2, 1968 (dec. July 1976); 1 child, Emily Anderson. Diploma in nursing, St. Benedict's Sch. Nursing, 1967; BSN, U. Utah, 1973, MSN, 1984; student, U. Colo. Staff nurse St. Benedict's Hosp., Ogden, Utah, 1967-69; edn. coord. Weber County Hosp., Roy, Utah, 1969-79; instr. Weber State Coll., Ogden, 1981-86, C.C. nursing home partnership project coord., 1986-93; nursing faculty Weber State Univ., Ogden, 1993—; cons. Utah State Health Dept., 1976-78, Cath. Relief Svc., West Bank, Israel, 1985, Utah State Bd. Edn., Salt Lake City, 1989; delegation leader People-to People, People's Republic of China, 1989-90; instr. rural Korea, 1993. Editor (textbook) The Nursing Assistant Training Manual, 1988, Taking Charge, 1992, Gerontological Nursing for the LPN, 1994. Recipient Woman of Achievement award Utah Bus. and Profl. Women, 1990. Mem. ANA, Utah Nurses Assn. (exec. v.p. 1988-90), Nat. Gerontological Nursing Assn. (bd. dirs. 1992—), Nat. League of Nursing, Sigma Theta Tau (historian, editorial bd. Geriatric Nursing). Office: Weber State U 3750 Harrison Blvd Ogden UT 84408-3903

ANDERSON, MARY R., historian, educator; b. Escanaba, Mich., Apr. 4, 1937; d. Renold Walfred and Alice (Fox) A. BA summa cum laude, Holy Names Coll., Oakland, Calif., 1959; PhD, U. Calif., 1979. Prof. history Holy Names Coll., Oakland, Calif. Author: Art in a Desacralized World, 1984. Grantee Nat. Endowment for the Humanities, 1984. Mem. Am. Hist. Assn., Western Assn. of Women Historians, Inst. for Hist. Study. Democrat. Roman Catholic. Office: Holy Names Coll 3500 Mountain Blvd Oakland CA 94619

ANDERSON, MICHAEL GEORGE, marketing and advertising executive; b. Boulder, Colo., Aug. 3, 1951; s. George Martin and Annette Elizabeth (Girmann) A.; m. Susan Elliott, Mar. 19, 1977; children: Gregory Michael, Richard Charles. BS in Aero. Engring., U. Colo., 1973, MBA in Fin., 1978. Design engr. Beech Aircraft, Boulder, 1976-78, liaison engr., 1978-79; mech. engr. Dieterich Standard, Boulder, 1979-80, mgr. engring. design, 1980-84, quality assurance mgr., 1984-87, mgr. advt., mktg. strategic planning and quality assurance, 1987-90, mktg. regional mktg., advt. mgr., 1990—. Author (computer software) Tektronix Header Program, 1982. Vice-pres. Luth. Ch. Coun., 1988-91; asst. scoutmaster Troop 161 Boys Scouts Am. Recipient NPT Stamp and Cert., ASME, Boulder, 1986. Mem. Am. Mgmt. Assn., Boulder Flycasters Club, U. Colo. Alumni Assn. (bd. dirs. 1985-87, v.p. bd. dirs. Boulder chpt. 1985-86), Buff Club (v.p., bd. dirs., 1985-87, pres. 1988-90), Moose. Republican. Home: 7400 Mt Meeker Rd Longmont CO 80503-8679 Office: Dieterich Standard PO Box 9000 Boulder CO 80301-9000

ANDERSON, MICHAEL ROBERT, marketing representative; b. Mpls., Nov. 3, 1953; s. Arthur Robert Anderson and Patricia Roberta Carlson; m. Rebecca Ellan Pierce, June 6, 1981; children: Jenna Courtney, Evan Brendan. BSEE, U. Minn., 1976; MS in Systems Mgmt., U. So. Calif., 1981. Microelectronics engr. Hughes Aircraft Co., Fullerton, Calif., 1977; mktg. rep. Hewlett Packard, Orange County, Calif., 1977-81; regional mgr. Group III Elec., Orange County, 1981-85; mktg. rep. Lisp Machines Inc., Los Angeles, 1985-87, SUN Microsystems, Inc., Orange, Calif., 1987-91; mktg.rep. Auspex Systems, Inc., Santa Clara, Calif., 1992—. Big Brother, Big Bros. Inc., Orange, Calif., 1979-81. Fellow mem. AAAS, Am. Assn. Artificial Intelligence, Planetary Soc. Home: 703 Avenida Azor San Clemente CA 92672-5673 Office: Auspex 3601 Aviation Blvd Manhattan Beach CA 90266

ANDERSON, MILDRED WHITE, writer, artist; b. Berkeley, Calif., Sept. 28, 1922; d. Halsted Guilford and Auda Belle (Chaney) White; m. Frederick W. Anderson, Apr. 3, 1946; children—Susan Dey Anderson Cohen; Noreene Anderson. A.A., U. Calif.-Berkeley, 1943. Asst. to editor King Publs., San Francisco, 1945; asst. to traffic engr. Gen. Telephone, Santa Monica, Calif., 1948-49; mathematician Space Tech. Lab., El Segundo, Calif., 1957-60; tech. illustrator Aerospace Lab., El Segundo, 1960-61; writer, artist, Manhattan Beach, 1961—; founder, pres., chmn. bd. Manhattan Beach Sr. Housing Found., 1983-93. Author articles and short stories; producer and host (cable-TV program) Senior Lifestyle, 1990—. Recipient Cert. of Recognition, Beach Cities Council Aging, 1978, Community Service award County Los Angeles Com. Aging, 1979, Outstanding Sr. Citizens Leadership award City of L.A., 1992. Mem. Soc. Women Engrs. (assoc. life mem., publicity chmn. 1959), Nurse Healers-Profl. Assn., Inc., Shipmates Club (program chmn. 1980). Republican.

ANDERSON, MITCHELL, chiropractor; b. L.A., Aug. 9, 1963; s. Charles Terry and Anita Louise (Rose) A.; m. Patricia Elaine Evora, June 10, 1989. AA, Cerritos Coll., 1983; BS, Cleveland Chiropractic Coll., L.A., 1985; D of Chiropractic, Cleveland Chiropractic Coll., 1987; sports cert., L.A. Chiropractic Coll., 1988. Cert. chiropractor Nat. Bd. Chiropractic Examiners; lic. chiropractor, Calif., Hawaii. Massage therapist/owner Body Work by Mitch, Downey, Calif., 1983-87; chiropractor Anderson Chiropractic Ctr., Los Alamitos, Calif., 1987—; referal doctor/owner Anderson Worker's Referal Svc., Orange, Calif., 1991—; physician Rossmor Atletic Club, Seal Beach, Calif., 1987—, Bretheren Christian High Sch., Cypress, Calif., 1988—. Co-author: (book) Back to Basics, 1991. Mem. Am. Chiropractic Assn. (sports cert. 1989, coun. sports injuries 1988—), Fed. Internat. Chiropractic Sportive, Calif. Chiropractic Assn., Rotary, Masons (3 degree), Scottish Rite (32 degree). Republican. Baptist. Home: 5570 Camino de Bryant Yorba Linda CA 92686 Office: Anderson Chiropractic Ctr 3958 Cerritos Ave Los Alamitos CA 90720-2454

ANDERSON, N. CHRISTIAN, III, newspaper executive; b. Montpelier, Idaho, Aug. 4, 1950; s. Nelson C. and Esther Barbara (Yackley) A.; m. Sara Ann Coffenberry, Dec. 11, 1971 (div.); children—Ryan, Erica; m. Aletha Ann Yurewicz, May 3, 1986; children: Paul, Amanda. BA in Liberal Studies with honors, Oreg. State U., 1972. Asst. city editor, city editor Albany Democrat-Herald, Oreg., 1972-75; mng. editor Walla Walla Union-Bull., Wash., 1975-77; assoc. mng. editor Seattle Times, 1977-80, editor, 1980-89, v.p., 1989-92; exec. v.p., assoc. pub. The Orange County (Calif.) Register, 1992—; instr. Calif. State U.-Fullerton, 1983, 87; Pulitzer prize juror, 1987, 88; exec. editor Freedom Newspapers, Inc., Irvine, Calif., 1990—; exec. v.p., c.e.o. Golden West Pub., Inc., Irvine, 1991—. Bd. dirs. Santa Ana Rotary Found., 1984. Named Nat. Newspaper Editor of Yr., 1989; recipient George D. Beveridge award Nat. Press Found. Mem. AP Mng. Editors, Soc. Profl. Journalists (Barney Kilgore Finalist award 1971), Am. Soc. Newspaper Editors (bd. dirs. 1991—), Calif. Soc. Newspaper Editors (bd. dirs. 1984-89, v.p. 1985, pres. 1986-87), Soc. Newspaper Design (steering com. 1978), New Directions for News (bd. dirs. 1987-91, vice-chmn. 1987-88, chmn. 1988-90). Roman Catholic. Office: Orange County Register 625 N Grand Ave Santa Ana CA 92701-4397

ANDERSON, NED, SR., Apache tribal chairman; b. Bylas, Ariz., Jan. 18, 1943; s. Paul and Maggie (Rope) A.; m. Delphina Hinton; children—Therese Kay, Linette Mae, Magdalene Gail, Ned, Sean. AA, Ea. Ariz. Coll., 1964, AAS in computer sci., 1989; BS, U. Ariz., 1967, JD, 1973. Field dir. Nat. Study Indian Edn., dept. anthropology U. Ariz., Tucson, 1968-70; tech. asst. Project Head Start, Ariz. State U., Tempe, 1970; ethnographer Smithsonian Instn., Washington, 1970-73; dir. Jojoba Project, Office of Arid Land Studies, U. Ariz. Tucson, 1973-76; with Jojoba devel. project San Carlos Apache Tribe, Ariz., 1976-78, tribal councilman, 1976-78, 93—, tribal chmn., 1978-86, gen. mgr. spl. housing projects, 1991—. Contbr. articles to profl.jours. Bd. dirs. Southwestern Indian Devel., Inc., 1971; mem. affirmative action com. City of Tucson, 1975-76; bd. dirs. Indian Enterprise Devel. Corp., 1976-78; mem. study panel NAS, 1975-77; pres. Inter-Tribal Coun. Ariz., 1979—; mem. supervisory bd. Ariz. Justice Planning Commn., 1978—, Indian adv. bd. Intergovtl. Personnel Program, 1978—; pres. bd. Ft. Thomas High Sch. Unified Dist., 1987—, clk. bd., 1989—; trustee Bacone Coll., 1986—; mem. adv. bd. Am. Indian Registry for Performing Arts, 1985—, San Carlos Fish and Game Commn., 1975—, chmn., 1976—; mem. exec. com. San Carlos Apache Tribal Coun., 1976-78, budget, fin. com., 1976—, constn. and ordinance com. 1976-78, chmn. law and order com., 1976-78; adv. bd. Gila Pueblo Community Coll. extension Ea. Ariz. Coll., 1979—; mem. sch. bd. Ft. Thomas High Sch. Unified Dist., 1977—, clk., 1987—, pres. sch. bd., 1992—; mem. County Govt. Study Commn. State Ariz., 1981-84; adv. bd. Indian Edn., Ariz. State U., Tempe, 1978—, U. Ariz., Tucson, 1978— . Recipient Outstanding Community Coll. Alumni award Ariz. Community Coll. Bd./Ea. Ariz. Coll., 1982, Outstanding Cooperation award U.S. Secret Svc., 1984, A.T. Anderson Meml. scholarship, 1989, Univ. Rels. award AT&T, 1989. Mem. Nat. Tribal Chmn.'s Assn. (bd. edn. 1978—, adv. bd. 1978—), Ariz. Acad., Globe C. of C., Phi Theta Kappa.

ANDERSON, PAUL NATHANIEL, oncologist; b. Omaha, May 30, 1937; s. Nels Paul E. and Doris Marie (Chesnut) A.; BA, U. Colo., 1959, MD, 1963; m. Dee Ann Hipps, June 27, 1965; children: Mary Kathleen, Anne Christen; Diplomate Am. Bd. internal Medicine, Am. Bd. Med. Mgmt. Intern Johns Hopkins Hosp., 1963-64, resident in internal medicine, 1964-65; rsch. asso., staff assoc. NIH, Bethesda, Md., 1965-70; fellow in oncology Johns Hopkins Hosp., 1970-72, asst. prof. medicine, oncology Johns Hopkins U. Sch. Medicine, 1972-76; attending physician Balt. City Hosps., Johns Hopkins Hosp., 1972-76; dir. dept. med. oncology Penrose Cancer Hosp., Colorado Springs, Colo., 1976-86; clin. asst. prof. dept. medicine U. Colo. Sch. Medicine, 1976-90, clin. assoc. prof., 1990—; dir. Penrose Cancer Hosp., 1979-86, chief dept. medicine, 1985-86; founding dir. Cancer Ctr. of Colorado Springs, 1986—; med. dir. So. Colo. Cancer Program, 1979-86; pres., chmn. bd. dirs. Preferred Physicians, Inc., 1986-92; mem. Colo. Found. for Med. Care Health Standards Com., 1985, sec., exec. com., 1990, bd. dirs., pres. 1992-93; mem., chmn. treatment com. Colo. Cancer Control and Rsch. Panel, 1980-83; prin. investigator Cancer Info. Svc. of Colo., 1981-87. Editor Advances in Cancer Control; editorial bd. Journal of Cancer Progam Management, 1987-92, Health Care Management Review, 1988—. Mem. Colo. Gov.'s Rocky Flats Employee Health Assessment Group, 1983-84; mem. Gov.'s Breast Cancer Control Commn. Colo., 1984—; pres., founder Oncology Mgmt. Network, Inc., 1985—; founder, bd. dirs. Timberline Med. Assocs., 1986-87; founder, dir. So. Colo. AIDS project 1986-91; mem. adv. bd. Colo. State Bd. Health Tumor Registry, 1984—; chmn., bd. dirs. Preferred Physicians, Inc., 1986-92; bd. dirs. Share Devel. Co. of Colo. Share Health Plan of Colo., 1986-90, vice chmn., 1989-91; bd. dirs., chmn. Preferred Health Care, Inc., 1991-92; mem. health care standards com., trustee Colo. Found. for Med. Care (PRO); mem. nat. bd. med. dirs. Fox Chase Cancer Ctr. Network, Phila., 1987-89; mem. tech. expert panel Harvard Resource-Based Relatives Value Scale Study for Hematology/Oncology, 1991-92. Served with USPHS, 1965-70. Diplomate Am. Bd. Internal Medicine, Am. Bd. Med. Oncology. Mem. Am. Soc. Clin. Oncology (chmn. subcom. on oncology clin. practice standards, mem. clin. practice com., rep. to AMA 1991—, mem. healthcare svcs. rsch. com., chmn. clin. guidelines subcom.), Am. Assn. Cancer Rsch., Am. Assn. Cancer Insts. (liaison mem. bd. trustees 1980-92), Am. Coll. Physician Execs., Am. Hospice Assn., Am. Soc. Internal Medicine, Nat. Cancer Inst. (com. for community hosp. oncology program evaluation 1982-83), Colo. Soc. Internal Medicine, Assn. Community Cancer Ctrs. (chmn. membership com. 1980—, chmn. clin. rsch. com. 1983-85, sec. 1983-84, pres.-elect 1984-85, pres. 1986-87, trustee 1981-88), AAAS, N.Y. Acad. Scis., Johns Hopkins Med. Soc., AMA, Colo. Med. Soc., Am. Mgmt. Assn., Am. Assn. Profl. Cons., Am. Soc. for Quality Control, Am. Acad. Med. Dirs., Am. Coll. Physician Execs., El Paso County Med. Soc., Rocky Mountain Oncology Soc. (chmn. clin. practice com. 1989—, pres.-elect 1990, pres. 1993-95), Acad. Hospice Physicians, Coalition for Cancer, Colo. Springs Clin. Club, Alpha Omega Alpha. Contbr. articles to med. jours. Office: Cancer Ctr Colorado Springs 320 E Fontanero St Ste 100 Colorado Springs CO 80907-7537 also: 32 Sanford Rd Colorado Springs CO 80906

ANDERSON, POLLY GORDON, insurance rehabilitation nurse; b. Quincy, Mass., Dec. 18, 1934; d. Manson Lewis and Jean Nourse (Morrison) Gordon; m. Brooke Hamilton Anderson, Nov. 5, 1955; children: Wendy, Kimberley, Scott, Peter; m. R. Trent Coleman, Sept. 15, 1984. Grad., Mass. Gen. Hosp. Sch. Nursing, Boston, 1955. RN, Mass., Calif.; cert. ins. rehab. specialist, Workers' Compensation Claims Adminstrn. Clin. teaching intern Mass. Gen. Hosp., 1955-56; staff nurse Bataan Meml. Hosp., Albuquerque, 1962-64; sr. indsl. nurse San Pedro (Calif.) Inds. Clinic, 1965-75; rehab nurse Argonaut Ins., L.A., 1975-77; regional rehab. coord. Chubb & Sons, L.A., 1977-84; v.p. RTC Cons. Svcs. Inc., Escondido, Calif., 1984-92; rehab. nurse CNA Ins., Brea, Calif., 1992—; vocat. rehab. cons. Calif. Workers' Compensation System. Campaign mgr. for city coun. candidate, San Marcos, Calif., 1987. Mem. Nat. Assn. Rehab. Profls. in Pvt. Sector (standards and compliance rev. bd. 1986-87), Rehab. Nurses Soc., So. Calif. Rehab. Exch., Assn. Indsl. Rehab. Reps., Rehab. Nurses Coords. Network (bd. dirs.-at-large 1987, 3dn. and program chmn. 1987—, ethics chmn. 1992).

ANDERSON, RAYMOND HARTWELL, JR., metallurgical engineer; b. Staunton, Va., Feb. 25, 1932; s. Raymond Hartwell and Virginia Boatwright (Moseley) A.; m. Dana Bratton Wilson, Sept. 5, 1959; children: Kathryn, Margaret, Susan. BS in Ceramic and Metall. Engring., Va. Poly. Inst. and State U., 1957, MSMetE, 1959. Registered profl. engr. Asst. prof. metall. engring. Va. Poly. Inst. and State U., Blacksburg, 1957-59; metall. engr. Gen. Dynamics Corp., Ft. Worth, 1959-61; sr. engr. Babcock & Wilcox Co., Lynchburg, Va., 1961-65; tech. specialist McDonnell Douglas Astronautics Co., Huntington Beach, Calif., 1965-88, sr. engring. specialist space sta. div., 1988—; tchr. materials sci. and chemistry U. Calif., Irvine, Calif., 1990—; cons. in field Los Angeles Area, 1967-71. Author, patentee Roll Diffusion Bonding of Beryllium, 1970-71, Increased Ductility of Beryllium, 1971-72. Served to 1st lt. U.S. Army, 1954-56. Mem. Am. Soc. Metals (lectr. 1968-70), Nat. Soc. Corrosion Engrs., Bolting Tech. Coun., Am. Ceramic Soc., Am. Welding Soc. (space welding adv. bd. 1991—). Republican. Home: 1672 Kenneth Dr Santa Ana CA 92705-3429 Office: McDonnell Douglas Space System Co Space Sta Div 5301 Bolsa Ave Huntington Beach CA 92647-2099

ANDERSON, RICHARD ERNEST, energy and chemical research and development company executive, rancher; b. North Little Rock, Ark., Mar. 8, 1926; s. Victor Ernest and Lillian Josephine (Griffin) A.; m. Mary Ann Fitch, July 18, 1953; children: Vicki Lynn, Lucia Anita. BSCE, U. Ark., 1949; MSE, U. Mich., 1959. Registered profl. engr., Mich., Va., Tex., Mont. Commd. ensign USN, 1952, advanced through grades to capt., 1968, ret., 1974; v.p. Ocean Resources, Inc., Houston, 1974-77; mgr. maintenance and ops. Holmes & Narver, Inc., Orange, Calif., 1977-78; pres. No. Resources, Inc., Billings, Mont., 1978-81; v.p. Holmes & Narver, Inc., Orange, Calif., 1981-82; owner, operator Anderson Ranches, registered Arabian horses and comml. Murray Grey cows, Pony, Mont., 1982—; pres., dir. Carbon Resources Inc., Butte, Mont., 1983-88, Agri Resources, Inc., Butte, Mont., 1988—. Trustee Lake Barcroft-Virginia Watershed Improvement Dist., 1973-74; pres. Lake Barcroft-Virginia Recreation Center, Inc., 1972-73. With USAAF, 1944-45. Decorated Silver Star, Legion of Merit with Combat V (2), Navy Marine Corps medal, Bronze Star with Combat V, Meritorious Service medal, Purple Heart; Anderson Peninsula in Antarctica named in his honor. Mem. ASCE, Soc. Am. Mil. Engrs. (Morrell medal 1965). Republican. Methodist. Home: PO Box 266 Pony MT 59747-0266 Office: Agri Resources Inc 305 W Mercury St Butte MT 59701-1692

ANDERSON, RICHARD ERNEST, electrical engineer; b. Princeton, Ind., Mar. 7, 1945; s. Brice and Anna Rae (Beal) A.; m. Carolyn Ann Brock-Jones, June 10, 1967; children: David Richard, James Brock, Sarah Louise. BS, U. Ill, 1967, MS, 1970, PhD, 1974. Mem. tech. staff Sandia Nat. Labs., Albuquerque, 1974-81, supr., 1981-92, mgr., 1992—. Contbr. articles to profl. jours. Office: Sandia Nat Labs Dept 2275 Albuquerque NM 87185-5800

ANDERSON, RICHARD NORMAN, actor, film producer; b. Long Branch, N.J., Aug. 8, 1926; s. Henry and Olga (Lurie) A.; m. Katherine Thalberg, Oct. 30, 1961 (div. Aug. 1973); children: Ashley, Brooke Dominique, Deva Justine. Grad. high sch., West Los Angeles, Calif. Actor Metro Goldwyn Mayer Studios, Culver City, Calif., 1950-56, 20th Century Fox Film Corp., Beverly Hills, Calif., 1961-62, 83-84, CBS, Hollywood, Calif., 1964-65, Quinn Martin Prodns., Hollywood, 1967-68, Universal/MCA, Universal City, Calif., 1973-78; pres. Richard Anderson Film Co., 1977—; TV spokesman Kiplinger Washington Letter, 1985—. Film actor, prin. films include Escape from Fort Bravo, Long Hot Summer, Paths of Glory, Compulsion, Tora, Tora, Tora, Scaramouche, The Magnificent Yankee, Seven Days in May, Wackiest Ship in the Army, Doctors Wives, Seconds; numerous TV appearances including Fall Guy, Whiz Kids, Fantasy Island, Love Boat, Condominium, The Immigrants, Big Valley, Gunsmoke, The Rifleman, Playhouse 90, The Eighty Yard Run; regular actor on Bus Stop, 1960, Perry Mason, 1961, Dan August, 1969, as Oscar Goldman in Six Million Dollar Man, 1972-77, Bionic Woman, 1974-77, Cover-Up, 1984; additional TV appearances include Perry Mason Returns, 1985, The A Team, 1986, Simon and Simon, 1986, Hardcastle and McCormick, 1986, Dynasty, 1986-87, Return of the Six Million Dollar Man and Bionic Woman, 1987, Stepford Children, 1987, Hoover Vs. Kennedys, 1987, Eminent Domain, 1987, Danger Bay, 1987, Kane and Abel, 1987, Return of the Six Million Dollar Man and the Bionic Woman II, 1988, (pilot series) The New Six Million Dollar Man/Bionic Woman, 1988, (2 hr. movie series) Bionics, 1989, Return of the Six Million Dollar Man and Bionic Woman III, 1993, Alfred Hitchcock series, 1989, (miniseries) Lucky Chances, 1990, Killer

Angels, 1993, Kung Fu: The Legend Continues, 1993; appeared on Broadway in The Highest Tree; appeared in summer stock, Lobero Theatre, Santa Barbara, Calif., Laguna Beach (Calif.) Playhouse. Served with AUS, 1944-46. Recipient Emmy nomination Acad. TV Arts and Scis., 1976, 77. Mem. SAG, Acad. Motion Picture Arts and Scis., Actors Equity Assn., Friars Club. Office: Lewis and Joffe 10880 Wilshire Blvd # 2006 Los Angeles CA 90024-4199

ANDERSON, RICK GARY, newspaper columnist; b. Aberdeen, Wash., Sept. 14, 1941; s. Richard C. and Elinor V. (Eddy) A.; m. Burgene J. Burgon, Oct. 26, 1963; children: Erik, Erin, Kristen, Darcy. Student, Grays Harbor Coll., Aberdeen, 1960-61. Copy boy Seattle Post-Intelligencer, 1961-62, reporter, columnist, 1969-77; sports editor Skagit Valley Herald, Mt. Vernon, Wash., 1962-63, Daily Olympian, Olympia, Wash., 1963-65; sports writer Daily Rev., Hayward, Calif., 1965-66, The Chronicle, San Francisco, 1967-68, Tri-City Herald, Kennewick, Wash., 1968-69; columnist Seattle Times, 1977—. Recipient Haywood Broun award Newspaper Guild, 1986. Office: The Seattle Times Fairview Ave N & John St PO Box 70 Seattle WA 98111-0070

ANDERSON, ROBERT, retired manufacturing company executive; b. Columbus, Nebr., Nov. 2, 1920; s. Robert and Lillian (Devlin) A.; m. Constance Dahlun Severy, Oct. 2, 1942 (div.); children: Robert, Kathleen D.; m. Diane Clark Lowe, Nov. 2, 1973. BS in Mech. Engring, Colo. State U., 1943, LLD (hon.), 1966; M Automotive Engring., Chrysler Inst. Engring., 1948; DHL (hon.), U. Neb., 1985; JD (hon.), Pepperdine U., 1986; D of Engring. (hon.), Milw. Sch. Engring., 1987. With Chrysler Corp., 1946-68, v.p. corp., gen. mgr. Chrysler-Plymouth div., 1965-67; with Rockwell Internat., 1968-93, pres. comml. products group, 1968-69, v.p. corp., 1968-69, exec. v.p., 1969-70, pres., chief oper. officer, 1970-74, pres., 1974-79, chief exec. officer, 1974-88, chmn., 1979-88, chmn. exec. com., 1988-90, chmn. emeritus, 1990-93; bd. dirs. Timken Co., Canton, Ohio, Optical Data Systems, Richardson, Tex., Gulfstream Aerospace Corp., Savannah, Ga., Found Health Corp., Rancho Cordova, Calif. Trustee Calif. Inst. Tech.; chmn. bus.-higher edn. forum Am. Coun. on Edn., 1982-84; chmn. We. Hwy. Inst., 1983-84; trustee, bd. visitors John E. Anderson Grad. Sch. Mgmt. UCLA. Capt. F.A., U.S. Army, 1943-46. Named Exec. of Yr. Nat. Mgmt. Assn., 1980. Mem. Phi Kappa Phi, Tau Beta Pi, Sigma Nu. Office: Rockwell Internat Corp PO Box 92098 Los Angeles CA 90009-2098

ANDERSON, ROBERT, environmental specialist, physician; b. Ft. Sill, Okla., May 22, 1944. MD, George Washington U., 1970; MPH, U. Tex., 1974. Chief med. svcs. TWA, Kansas City, Kans., 1976-81; med. dir. Air Can., Montreal, Que., 1981-82; corp. med. dir. Manville Corp., Denver, 1982-87, v.p. health, safety and environ., 1987-89, v.p. sci. and tech., 1989-90, sr. v.p. sci. and tech., 1990—. Bd. dirs. Rocky Mountain Multiple Sclerosis Ctr., Denver, 1991. Maj. USAF, 1971-76. Mem. AMA, Am. Occupational Health Assn., Am. Coll. Preventive Medicine, Aerospace Med. Assn. Office: Manville Corp PO Box 5108 Denver CO 80217-5108

ANDERSON, ROBERT BRUCE, oil company executive; b. Roswell, N.Mex., Oct. 26, 1946; s. Robert O. and Barbara (Phelps) A.; m. Susan Nelson, Sept. 16, 1972; children: Nelson, Benjamin, Lauren. BS, Cornell U., 1969; postgrad., U. N.Mex., 1972-73. Pres., dir. Diamond A. Cattle Co. and subsidiaries, Roswell, N.Mex., 1973-76, Lincoln County Land & Cattle Co., Roswell, N.Mex., 1976-86; v.p., dir. The Hondo Co., Roswell, N.Mex., 1986—; exec. v.p., CFO Hondo Oil & Gas Co., Roswell, N.Mex., 1986-91, also bd. dirs.; also bd. dirs. Rio Magdalena Co., Albuquerque; bd. dirs. United N.Mex. Fin. Corp., Albuquerque, 1979—. Mem. bd. dirs. Lovelace Med. Ctr., Albuquerque, 1976-91, Am. Farmland Trust, Washington, 1987—, Anderson Schs. of Mgmt. Found., U. N.Mex., 1989—, Lovelace Anderson Endowment Found., 1988—, Sch. of Am. Rsch., Santa Fe, 1991—, Winrock Internat. Inst. for Agrl. Devel., Morrilton, Ark., 1988—. Republican. Episcopalian. Office: 3700 Rio Grand Blvd NW Ste 4 Albuquerque NM 87107-3042

ANDERSON, ROBERT ERNEST, safety consultant; b. Heavener, Okla., July 30, 1926; s. Ernest L. and Dewey M. (Vaught) A., m. Eleanor Jeanne Mauzy, Sept. 15, 1948; children: Robert, Sarah, David, Hans. BS, Okla. State U., 1949, MS, 1950. Registered profl. engr., Calif.; cert. safety profl. Instr. Okla. State U. Agr. and Applied Sci., Stillwater, 1950-51, asst. prof., 1951-52; with Mine Safety Appliances Co., Beaumont, Tex., Gary, Ind., and Little Rock, 1952-63; mgr. safety products MSA Internat., Pitts., 1963-67; mgr. intermountain dist. MSA, Salt Lake City, 1967-87; pvt. practice safety engring. cons. Salt Lake City, 1987—; adj. asst. prof. safety engring. U. Utah., 1988—; cons. Indsl. Health Inc. With USNR, 1944-46. Mem. AIME, Am. Indsl. Hygiene Assn., Am. Soc. Safety Engrs. (v.p. region II 1986-87, Safety Profl. of Yr. Utah chpt. 1993), Masons. Democrat. Methodist. Home and Office: 3372 Pioneer St Salt Lake City UT 84109-3048

ANDERSON, ROBERT FLOYD, entrepreneur, pastor; b. Ishpeming, Mich., Sept. 5, 1938; s. Oscar and Doris (Holder) Pelki; m. Berta J. Ozeran, Dec. 13, 1974; children: Kimball, Rebecca. BS, U. Nev., 1967; MDiv, Golden Gate Sem., 1977; PhD, Vision Christian U., 1991. Pastor Rock of the Comstock, Reno, Nev., 1977-79; pres. Evange-Lion Inc., Reno, 1979—. Author poetry. Member Sr. Olympics, Reno, 1989-91. 2d lt. U.S. Army, 1959-61. Fellow Pi Mu Epsilon. Republican. Home and Office: 1025B Baywood Dr Sparks NV 89434-1603

ANDERSON, ROBERT NILS, publisher; b. Marietta, Ohio, Jan. 6, 1936; s. Robert Frederick and Helen (West) A.; m. Beverlee Ann Byler, Sept. 2, 1966. BA, Ohio State U., 1958. Salesman Ronald Press, N.Y.C., 1964-67, Richard D. Irwin, Inc., Homewood, Ill., 1968-75; v.p. Grid Pub., Inc., Columbus, Ohio, 1976-86; pres. Pub. Horizons, Inc., Columbus, now Scottsdale, Ariz., 1987—. Home: 6645 N 78th Pl Scottsdale AZ 85250 Office: Pub Horizons Inc F 400 8233 Via Paseo del Norte Scottsdale AZ 85258

ANDERSON, ROBERT ORVILLE, oil and gas company executive; b. Chgo., Apr. 13, 1917; s. Hugo A. and Hilda (Nelson) A.; m. Barbara Phelps, Aug. 25, 1939; children: Katherine, Julia, Maria, Robert Bruce, Barbara Burton, William Phelps, Beverley. B.A., U. Chgo., 1939. With Am. Mineral Spirits Co., Chgo., 1939-41; pres. Malco Refineries, Inc., Roswell, N.Mex., 1941-63; with Atlantic Richfield Co., Los Angeles, retired chmn. bd., chief exec. officer; pres. Hondo Oil and Gas Co., Roswell; mem. Com. Econ. Devel., Washington. Hon. chmn. Aspen Inst.; chmn. Lovelace Med. Found.; trustee Calif. Inst. Tech., U. Chgo. Mem. Nat. Petroleum Council, Am. Petroleum Inst. Clubs: Century (N.Y.C.); California (Los Angeles); Pacific-Union (San Francisco). Office: Hondo Oil & Gas Co PO Box 2208 Roswell NM 88202

ANDERSON, ROBERT WAYNE, oil company financial officer; b. Brigham, Utah, July 16, 1951; s. Everett Carl and Margaret (Hatch) A.; m. Brenda Bingham, Dec. 1, 1971; children: Carl Arch, Mary-Esther, Hollyanna, Rex, Kirk, Trent. BS, Utah State U., 1975. CPA, Utah. Auditor Haskins and Sells, Salt Lake City, 1975-79; dir. internal auditing Browning Co., Mountain Green, Utah, 1979-80; internal auditor Thiokol Corp., Brighmam, 1980-83; dir. internal auditing, chief fin. officer Flying J Inc., Brighmam, 1983—. Baseball coach Little League, Corinne, Utah, 1983-85; scouting coordinator Boy Scouts Am., Corinne, 1986-87. Republican. Mormon. Office: Flying J Inc 50 W 990 S Brigham City UT 84302-3121

ANDERSON, ROSCOE ODELL (DALE), retired personnel officer; b. Snowville, Utah, Aug. 15, 1913; s. Roscoe Joseph and Diantha Jane (Robbins) A.; m. Elizabeth Jeanne Neil, June 4, 1939; 1 child, Dale Neil. BS, U. Utah, 1937, MS, 1943; postgrad., Cornell U., 1965, U. San Francisco, 1972. Cert. tchr. and adminstr. in secondary edn. Employee relations officer Utah Gen. Depot, Ogden, 1943-48; dir. civilian personnel Sharpe Army Depot, Lathrop, Calif., 1948-52, Aberdeen Proving Ground U.S. Army, Aberdeen, Md., 1952-55; field rep. Office Civilian Personnel Dep. Chief Staff Personnel, San Francisco, 1955-60; chief employee mgmt. div. Office Civilian Personnel Dep. Chief Staff Personnel, Washington, 1960-66; dir. civilian personnel 6th U.S. Army, Presidio, San Francisco, 1966-73; zone IV coord. U.S. Dept. Defense, San Francisco, 1973-76; cons. Defense Supply Agy., GSA, 1977-80; nat. v.p. Soc. for personnel Adminstrn., 1962, charter mem., pres. No. Calif., 1967, charter mem., pres., Hartford County, Md., 1955; guest lectr. U. San Francisco, 1969; chmn. Fed. Personnel Coun./No. Calif., San Francisco, 1967-68. Mem. Marin coun. ARC, Marin County, Calif., 1975-80; sec. Ogden City Svc. Baseball League, 1944-47; chmn. fed. employee div. Community Chest Drive, San Joaquin County, Calif., 1952, dep. chmn., Aberdeen Proving Ground, 1955. Recipient Meritorious Civilian Svc. award Dept. Army, Sec. Def., 1966, Meritorious Civilian Svc. award with Bronze Laurel Leaf Cluster, Dept. Army, 1972, Meritorious Civil Svc. award Sec. of Def., 1972. Mem. Army Civilian Personnel Alumni Assn., Nat. Assn. Ret. Fed. Employees, Am. Assn. Ret. Persons, Wilderness Soc., Audubon Soc., Sierra Club, Utah Golf Assn., Crimson Club U. Utah, Coun. Fgn. Rels. Mormon.

ANDERSON, ROSS CARL, lawyer; b. Logan, Utah, Sept. 9, 1951; s. E. LeRoy and Grace (Rasmussen) A.; 1 child, Lucas Craig Arment. BS in Philosophy magna cum laude, U. Utah, 1973; JD with honors, George Washington U., 1978. Bar: U.S. Dist. Ct. Utah 1978. Assoc. Berman & Giauque, Salt Lake City, 1978-80; v.p., ptnr. Berman & Anderson, Rooker Larsen Kimball & Parr, Salt Lake City, 1980-82; ptnr., sec. Berman & Anderson, Salt Lake City, 1982-85; ptnr., v.p. Hansen & Anderson, Salt Lake City, 1986-89, Anderson & Watkins, Salt Lake City, 1989-92; pres. Anderson & Karrenberg, Salt Lake City, 1992—. Pres. bd. dirs. Citizens for Penal Reform, 1991—, Guadalupe Ednl. Programs, Salt Lake City, 1985-91, ACLU of Utah, 1980-85; bd. dirs. Common Cause of Utah, 1987-89, Planned Parenthood of Utah, 1979-83; mem. Salt Lake Com. on Fgn. Rels., 1983—. Mem. Utah State Bar Assn., Assn. Trial Lawyers Am. Democrat. Home: 1015 S 1400 E Salt Lake City UT 84105-1616 Office: Anderson & Karrenberg 50 W Broadway Ste 700 Salt Lake City UT 84101-2006

ANDERSON, ROYAL JOHN, advertising agency executive; b. Portland, Oreg., Sept. 12, 1914; s. John Alfred and Martha Marie (Jacobsen) A.; m. Leticia G. Anderson; children: Michael, Johnny, Dora Kay, Mark Roy, Stan Ray, Ruth Gay, Janelle A., Jennifer T., Joseph, Daisy, Dina; 1 adopted dau., Muoi-Muoi. BA, Albany Coll., 1939; postgrad., U. Oreg., 1939-41, Oreg. Inst. Tech., 1940-41. Corp. cons. Dupont Corp., Beverly Hills, Calif., 1967-68; editor-pub. Nev. State Dem., Carson City, 1967-68, Nev. State Pub. Observer, Carson City, 1967-68, Nev. State Congl. Assn., Carson City, 1962-78; pres. Allied-Western Produce Co., Yuma, Ariz., 1962-78, Nev. Dem. Corp., 1966-78, Western Restaurant Corp., 1978-81, Nev. State Sage Co., 1979—, Midway Advt. Co., 1979—, Environ. Research Corp., 1983—, Mid-City Advt. Agy., 1983—, Nat. Newspaper Found., 1969, 71-76, The Gt. North Banks Seafood Co., 1984—, Food Services Corp., 1985—, Sterling Cruise Lines, 1986—, No-Tow Mfg. Inc., 1986—, Manela Mortgage Co., 1991—; pres. Trident Toothpaste Mfg., 1992-93, chmn. bd., pres., 1993—; chmn bd. Press/Register Daily Newspapers, Foster Mortgage Co., 1983—. Inventor No-Tow, 1988 worldwide.; designer prefabricated milk carton container, 1933, well water locating under-stream device, 1938, no-tow automotive product under fgn. mfrs. for world destruction. Bishop Ch. of Palms, Mexico; pres. Ch. of the Palms Found. Corp.; dep. registrar voters Washoe County, Nev., 1966; mem. Clark County Econ. Opportunity Bd., 1988-91; v.p. Trident Toothpaste Found., 1991-92, pres. 1990-93, chmn. bd. 1992-93. Recipient Heroism award for rescue, 1933; Research fellow, Alaska, 1936. Mem. Am. Hort. Soc., Nev. State C. of C. (pres.), Sparks C. of C. (pres. 1970-93), U.S. C. of C., Chatso Farm Assn. (pres. 1962-88), Smithsonian Assocs., N.Am. C. of C. Execs., Nat. Geog. Soc., Am. Newspaper Alliance (v.p. 1976), Millionare Club, Kiwanis, Elks, Lions. Home: PO Box 4349 North Las Vegas NV 89036-4349 Home: 5600 Sundance Ave Las Vegas NV 89110-3825

ANDERSON, SALLY JANE, artist; b. Rockford, Ill., Feb. 5, 1942; d. James Edward and Jane (Purnell) Moriarty; m. Charles Edward Anderson, Aug. 28, 1964; children: Erika Elizabeth, Seth Charles. Student, Inst. Allende, San Miguel de Allende, Mex., 1963; BA in Art, Beloit Coll., 1964; postgrad. in art, U. Wis., Milw., 1966. One-woman shows, 1964—, including Roswell (N.Mex) Mus. and Art Ctr., 1970, Jane Haslem Gallery, Washington, 1970, Gallery One, Albuquerque, 1975, Mariposa Gallery, Albuquerque, 1978, Gargoyle Gallery, Aspen, Colo., 1978, Suzanne Brown Gallery, Scottsdale, Ariz., 1980, Putney Gallery, Aspen, Colo., 1981, C.G. Rein Gallery, Santa Fe, 1982, 84, C.G. Rein Gallery, Edina, Minn., 1984, Works II Gallery, Southampton, N.Y., 1985; exhibited in numerous group shows, 1967—, including N.Mex. State U., Las Cruces, 1974, Carnegie Inst., Pitts., 1976, Albuquerque Mus., 1977, 79, Phoenix Art Mus., 1979, Los Angeles Craft and Folk Art Mus., 1980, C.G. Rein Gallery, Scottsdale, Ariz., 1984, Salon des nations, Paris, 1985; represented in permanent collections Bundy Mus., Stowe, Vt., Numerous Cos., banks; represented by C.G. Rein Galleries, Windsors Gallery, Miamia, Fla., Works II. Recipient 1st prize N.Mex. Crafts Biennial; Nat. Endowment for Arts grantee, also purchase prize. Home: 7522 Bear Canyon Rd NE Albuquerque NM 87109-3847

ANDERSON, SCOTT DAVID, clarinetist, soloist, chamber musician, educator; b. Mpls., Oct. 11, 1957; s. Ronald Leslie and Marion Shaw (Mitchell) A. MusB with high distinction, U. Rochester, 1980; postgrad., Northwestern U., 1980-81; studies with, Rosario Mazzeo, 1984-88. Founder, clarinetist Amabile Chamber Players, Mpls., 1976-79; clarinetist Spoleto (Italy) Festival, 1978; prin. clarinetist Hedelberg (Fed. Republic Germany) Opera Orch., 1980; clarinetist Orquesta Sinfônica del Estado de Mex., Toluca, 1981; assoc. prin. Orquesta Sinfônica de Xalapa, Vera Cruz, Mex., 1981-84; prin. clarinetist Oakland (Calif.) Symphony Orch., 1984-88, Grand Rapids (Mich.) Symphony Orch., 1988-89; clarinetist L.A. Chamber Orch., 1989-90; prin. clarinetist Honolulu Symphony, 1990—. Mem. Musicians Assn. Hawaii (orch. com. 1991). Office: Honolulu Symphony Orch 1441 Kapiolani Blvd Honolulu HI 96814-4401

ANDERSON, STANLEY EDWARD, JR., lawyer; b. Chgo., Oct. 11, 1940; s. Stanley Edward and Margaret Mary (Turner) A.; m. Louise Ann Perko, July 12, 1968; 1 child, Stephanie Elizabeth. BA, Northwestern U., 1962, MBA, 1964; MS, U. Del., 1966; JD, Am. U., 1972. Bar: Va. 1973, D.C. 1973, Ill. 1973, Calif. 1976; registered patent atty. 1973. Chemist E.I. duPont de Nemours & Co., Inc., Wilmington, Del., 1966-67; patent advisor Office of Naval Rsch., Arlington, Va., 73-74; patent atty. Merck & Co., Inc., Rahway, N.J., 1974-76, Harris, Kern, Wallin & Tinsley, L.A., 1977-78; pvt. practice law Thousand Oaks, Calif., 1978—; prof. law So. Calif. Inst. Law, Ventura. With USN, 1958-64. USPHS rsch. fellow, 1965; recipient Book Awards in Agy. and Creditors Rights, Am. U., 1972. Mem. Ill. Bar Assn., D.C. Bar Assn., Va. Bar Assn., State Bar of Calif. Republican. Roman Catholic. Home and Office: 1529 Lynnmere Dr Thousand Oaks CA 91360-1948

ANDERSON, STEPHEN HALE, federal judge; b. 1932; m. Shirlee G. Anderson. Student, Eastern Oreg. Coll. Edn., Brigham Young U.; LLB, U. Utah, 1960. Bar: Utah 1960, U.S. Claims Ct. 1963, U.S. Tax Ct. 1967, U.S. Ct. Appeals (10th cir.) 1970, U.S. Supreme Ct. 1971, U.S. Ct. Appeals (9th cir.) 1972, various U.S. Dist. Cts. Tchr. South High Sch., Salt Lake City, 1956-57; trial atty. tax div. U.S. Dept. Justice, 1960-64; ptnr. Ray, Quinney & Nebeker, 1964-85; judge U.S. Ct. Appeals (10th cir.), Salt Lake City, 1985—; spl. counsel Salt Lake County Grand Jury, 1975. Editor in chief Utah Law Rev. Cpl. U.S. Army, 1953-55. Mem. Utah State Bar (pres. 1983-84, various offices), Salt Lake County Bar Assn. (pres. 1977-78), Am. Bar Found., Salt Lake Area C. of C. (bd. govs. 1984), U. Utah Coll. Law Alumni Assn. (trustee 1979-83, pres. 1982-83), Order of Coif. Office: US Ct Appeals 4201 Fed Bldg 125 S State Salt Lake City UT 84138-1102

ANDERSON, SUSAN LYNNE, sales engineer; b. Pitts., Dec. 21, 1964; d. James Edward and Marianne (Meininger) A. BSEE, Iowa State U., 1987. Tech. sales rep. Tex. Instruments Inc., San Jose, Calif., 1988-93, dist. sales mgr., 1993—. Shelter vol. Family Living Ctr., Santa Clara, 1989-92. Democrat. Lutheran. Office: Tex Instruments Inc 2825 N 1st St Ste 200 San Jose CA 95134

ANDERSON, THOMAS LEIF, physician, researcher; b. New Orleans; s. Maurice John and Kitty Thordis (Thomstad) A.; m. Charlotte Ann Hull, Oct. 11, 1980; children: Laurel Emelia, Timothy Leif. BA, Denison U., 1971; MD, Yale U., 1975. Diplomate Am. Bd. Pschiatry and Neurology. Intern in medicine U. Fla. Hosps., Gainesville, 1975-76; resident Harbor-UCLA Med. Ctr., Torrance, 1976-79; fellow Barnes Hosp., St. Louis, 1979-80, staff physician, 1980—; mem. med. adv. com. L.A. County Muscular Dystrophy Assn., 1982—. Mem. Am. Acad. Neurology. Presbyterian. Office: Harbor-UCLA Med Ctr 1000 W Carson St Torrance CA 90502-2004

ANDERSON, WILLIAM, retail company executive, business education educator; b. L.A., May 21, 1923; s. William Bert and Marie (Novotney) A.; m. Margaret Lillian Phillips, Aug. 16, 1951; children: Margaret Gwen, Deborah Kay, William Keven, Denise Marie. BA in Econs., UCLA, 1948, MEd, 1957. Cert. secondary tchr. (life), Calif. Tchr. bus. edn. Big Bear Lake (Calif.) High Sch., 1949-52, Ventura (Calif.) Unified Sch. Dist. Buena High Sch., 1952-89; chief exec. officer Day's Aircraft Inc., Santa Paula, Calif., 1967—; cons. micro computers Calif. State Dept. Edn., 1983-85; pres. "Dollars for Schollars", Ventura. Crew chief Olympic Games basketball stats., 1984, basketball stats. World Games for the Deaf, 1985, U.S. Olympic Festival, 1991; vol. Calif. Police Olympics, 1989. With USAAF, 1943-45, PTO. Mem. NEA (life), Calif. Bus. Edn. Assn. (pres. So. sect. 1959-60, state sec. 1960-61, hon. life 1991), Internat. Soc. Bus. Edn. (voting del. to Soc. Internat. Pour l'Enseignemer Comml., Western rep. 1988-89, apptd. historian 1991), Am. Aviation Hist. Soc., Calif. Assn. Work Experience Educators (life), Air Force Assn. (life), So. Calif. Badminton Assn. (past bd. dirs.), Phi Delta Kappa, Delta Pi Epsilon (hon. life). Democrat. Lutheran. Home: 334 Manzanita Ave Ventura CA 93001-2227 Office: Day's Aircraft Co Inc PO Box 511 Santa Paula CA 93061-0511

ANDERSON, WILLIAM SCOVIL, classics educator; b. Brookline, Mass., Sept. 16, 1927; s. Edgar Weston and Katrina (Brewster) A.; m. Lorna Candee Bassette, June 12, 1954 (dec. Dec. 1977); children: Judith, Blythe, Heather, Meredith, Keith; m. Deirdre Burt, May 28, 1983. B.A., Yale U., 1950, Ph.D., 1954; A.B., Cambridge U., (Eng.), 1952; M.A., Cambridge U., 1955. Prix de Rome fellow Am. Acad. in Rome, 1954-55; instr. classics Yale U., 1955-59; resident in Rome, Morse fellow, 1959-60; mem. faculty U. Calif., Berkeley, 1960—, prof. Latin and comparative lit., 1966—, prof. charge Intercollegiate Ctr. Classical Studies, 1967-68, chmn. classics, 1970-73; rsch. prof. U. Melbourne, 1984; Robson lectr. Victoria Coll., Toronto, 1987; Blegen rsch. prof. Vassar Coll., 1989-90, vice-chair comparative lit., 1990—. Author: The Art of the Aeneid, 1969, Ovid, Metamorphoses, Critical Text, 1977, Essays on Roman Satire, 1982; mem. editorial bd.: Classical Jour., Vergilius, Satire newsletter; contbr. articles to profl. jours. Served with AUS, 1946-48, Korea. NEH sr. fellow, 1973-74. Mem. Am. Philol. Assn. (pres. 1977), Danforth Assocs., Soc. Religion. Episcopalian. Office: Univ Calif Dept Classics Berkeley CA 94720

ANDERSON-PIMES, CAROL, association executive; b. Red Bank, N.J., July 30, 1948; d. John Walters Wandling and Elaine Lucille (Bower) Bertolette; m. Steven G. Anderson, Aug. 31, 1971 (div. Oct. 1978); 1 child, Scott James; m. Jeffrey A. Pimes, Dec. 31, 1992. Student, Long Beach (Calif.) City Coll., 1968-73. Supr. communications ctr. McDonnell Douglas/Douglas Aircraft Co., Long Beach, 1967-76; data communications specialist 1st Interstate Svcs., El Segundo, Calif., 1977-79; realtor-assoc. Tiffany Real Estate, Huntington Beach, Calif., 1979-83; network analyst 20th Century Fox Film Corp., Beverly Hills, Calif., 1983-85; sr. network communications analyst B2 div. Northrop Corp., Pico Rivera, Calif., 1985-88; mgr. adminstrv. svcs. Tele-Communications Assn., Covina, Calif., 1988-92; dir. adminstrn. Xplor Internat., Palos Verdes Estates, Calif., 1992—. Mem. Am. Soc. Assn. Execs., So. Calif. Soc. Assn. Execs., Tele-Comm. Assn. Republican. Office: Xplor Internat 24238 Hawthorne Blvd Torrance CA 90505-6505

ANDICH, BRUCE ROBERT, physician; b. Davenport, Iowa, July 1, 1945; s. Hyman M. and Esther F. (Williamson) A.; m. m. Anne Elise Thal, 1969 (div. 1971); m. Cassandra Clune Hughes, Apr. 15, 1984; children: Molly, Krystal. BA in Biology, U. Chgo., 1967, MD, 1971. Diplomate Am. Bd. Internal Medicine. Epidemiologist World Health Orgn., Dacca, Bangladesh, 1974; pvt. practice physician Willits, Calif., 1976—; bd. dirs. Community Care Mgmt. Corp., Ukiah, Calif., Found. for Med. Care, Ukiah. Mem. AMA, Calif. Med. Assn., Am. Soc. Internal Medicine, Mendocino-Lake County Med. Soc. (pres. 1987-88). Office: 88 Madrone Willits CA 95490

ANDRADE, JOE RUSSELL, lumber company executive, artist; b. San Antonio, Oct. 17, 1947; s. Joe Nieto Andrade and Norma (Gonzales) Tindall; m. Diana Miller, July 7, 1983; 1 child, Noah Russell. MA, Calif. State U., Northridge, 1979. Pres. Pacific West Designs, Venice, Calif., 1979-83; v.p. Tradewest Hardwood Co., Rancho Dominguez, Calif., 1983-91; pres., gen. mgr. All City Milling Svcs. and Forestal Industries, Los Angeles, 1991—; fine artist Santa Monica, Calif., 1979—. Proponent of post modernist art movement Conjuntivism. Pres. Assn. Venice Artists, 1975. Cpl. USMC, 1968-70, Vietnam. Santa Monica City Coll. scholar, 1976. Mem. Mus. Contemporary Art, L.A. County Mus. Art. Democrat. Roman Catholic. Home: 236 S Westgate Ave Los Angeles CA 90049 Office: All City Milling Svcs and Forestal Industries 115 E 58th St Los Angeles CA 90011-5313

ANDRADE, NANCY LEE (BALL ANDRADE), realtor, jeweler; b. Seattle, Nov. 17, 1937; d. Hans Peter Marcher and Hilda Dorothy (Baisch) Middleton; m. Allan L. Andrade, Mar. 15, 1971 (div. 1980). Cert. travel agt., Cannon Bus. Coll., Honolulu, 1965; cert., Erhardt Seminar Tng., Honolulu, 1980; student, U. Hawaii, 1968-71; cert. real estate broker, Stapleton Sch. Real Estate, Honolulu, 1985. Cert. notary pub. Model Kathleen Peck Modeling Agy., Seattle, 1956-60; communications mgr. RCA Communicaions, Royal Hawaiian Hotel, Honolulu, 1960-62; TV and fashion specialist Careers Unltd., Honolulu, 1960-65; travel agt. Waters Travel, Kailua, Hawaii, 1965—; realtor assoc., property mgr. various realty firms, Honolulu, 1967-74; property mgr. Nancy Andrade Property Mgmt., Honolulu, 1974-85; realtor, broker, property mgr. Nancy Andrade Realty, Honolulu and Kaneohe, 1985—; jeweler, goldsmith Nancy Andrade Jewelry Design, 1974—; mfg. Koala Prodns., Hawaii and Australia, 1987—, Nancy Andrade Enterprises, Honolulu and Kaneohe, 1987—. Active Waikiki Residence Assn., 1978—, Neighborhood Bd., Honolulu, 1980; mem. Save Internat. Market Pl. Com. Mem. Nat. Assn. Realtors, Nat. Notary Assn. (cert.), Small Bus. Hawaii, Honolulu Bd. Realtors, Waikiki Improvement Assn., Australian-Am. C. of C., Lani-Kailua Outdoor Circle Club, Ala Wai Plaza Club, Makani Kai Marina Yacht Club, Beta Sigma Phi (v.p. Oahu coun. 1987—, v.p. Preceptor Delta 1988—, Preceptor degree 1980, Xi Zeta Exemplar degree 1969, Internat. Order Rose degree 1976, 25 Yr. Silver Circle award 1987, Alpha Chpt. Woman of Yr. 1965, Xi Zeta Chpt. Woman of Yr. 1977). Republican.

ANDRASIC, STANLEY, computer systems analyst; b. Bradford, Yorkshire, Eng., May 23, 1953; came to U.S. 1987; s. Stanislaw and Florence (Norton) A. BS in Biophysics, Kings Coll./London U., London, 1975; MS in Computer Sci., Bradford U., 1976. Supr. devel. engr. Gen. Electric Corp. Telecommunications, Ltd., Coventry, Eng., 1976-82; systems analyst programmer Documented Cirs., Inc., Kingston, Ont., Can., 1982-83, Difracto Ltd., Windsor, Ont., Can., 1985-86; cons. analyst programmer So. Pacific Pipelines, L.A., 1987; systems analyst programmer Restaurant Enterprises, Inc., Irvine, Calif., 1988-90; contract cons. systems analyst Hamilton Test Systems, Tucson, Ariz., 1990; contract cons. systems analyst Intel Corp., Albuquerque, 1991-92, Chandler, Ariz., 1992—. Mem. IEEE, IEEE Computer Soc., Assn. Computing Machinery, DEC User Group, Am. Contract Bridge League. Office: SAAS 92 Corporate Pk Ste #C321 Irvine CA 92714

ANDRE, CURT A., optometrist; b. Turlock, Calif., Nov. 5, 1953; s. Clarence A. and Marvelina (Almeida) A.; m. Julie A. Tiernan, Sept. 15, 1984; children: Meredith, Morgan. BS, U. Calif., Davis, 1974; OD, U. Calif., Berkeley, 1977. Pvt. practice Turlock, 1977—. Mayor City of Turlock, 1990—, planning commn. chair, 1979-90. Mem. Am. Optometric Assn., Active 20-30 Club of Turlock, C. of C. Office: 607 E Olive Turlock CA 95380

ANDRE, MICHAEL PAUL, physicist, educator; b. Des Moines, Apr. 25, 1951; s. Paul Leo and Pauline (Vermie) A.; m. Janice Joan Hanecak, Mar. 12, 1988. BA, Cen. U. Iowa, 1972; postgrad., U. Ariz., 1972-73; MS, UCLA, 1975, PhD, 1980. Assoc. engr. North Island Naval Air Sta., San Diego, 1970-71; rsch. assoc. Inst. Atmospheric Physics, Tucson, Ariz., 1972-73; mem. tech. staff Hughes Aircraft Co., L.A., 1973-74; postgrad. researcher UCLA, 1974-77; cons. L.A., 1975-84; med. radiologic physicist LACO/UCLA Olive View, L.A., 1977-81; sr. radiation physicist Cedars-Sinai Med.

Ctr., L.A., 1979-84; chief med. physicist Dept. Vet. Affairs, San Diego, 1981—; prof. radiology, chief divsn.Physics and Engring, sch. medicine U. Calif., La Jolla, 1981—; qualified expert Calif. Radiol. Health Dept., Berkeley, 1979—; pub. spokesman Radiol. Soc., San Diego, 1987—; chmn. Nat. Physics Conf., San Diego, 1984-89. Editor: Physics and Biology of Radiology, 1988, Investigative Radiology, 1990—; contbr. articles to profl. jours. Mountain guide Sierra Club, L.A., 1977-80; dir. Ariz. PIRG, Tucson, 1973; jury foreman San Diego Dist. Ct., 1990; mountain guide Am. Alpine Inst., Peru, 1987. Rsch. grantee U. Calif. San Diego Found., 1989—, NIH, Cancer Inst. 1986—, Dept. Vet. Affairs, 1989—. Mem. Am. Assn. Physicists in Medicine, Am. Inst. Ultrasound in Medicine, San Diego Radiol. Soc., Am. Inst. Physics, Soc. Photo-Optical Inst. Engrs. Office: U Calif Dept Radiology 9114 La Jolla CA 92093

ANDREOPOULOS, SPYROS GEORGE, writer; b. Athens, Greece, Feb. 12, 1929; came to U.S., 1953, naturalized, 1962; s. George S. and Anne (Levas) A.; m. Christiane Loesch Loriaux, June 6, 1958; 1 child, Sophie. AB, Wichita State U., 1957. Pub. info. specialist USIA, Salonica, Greece, 1951-53; asst. editorial page editor Wichita (Kans.) Beacon, 1955-59; asst. dir. info. svcs., editor The Menninger Quar., The Menninger Found., Topeka, 1959-63;; info. officer Stanford U. Med. Ctr., 1963-83; dir. comm., editor Stanford Medicine, 1983-93, dir. emeritus comm., editor emeritus, 1993—; editor Sun Valley Forum on Nat. Health, Inc. (Idaho), 1972-83, 85—. Co-author, editor: Medical Cure and Medical Care, 1972, Primary Care: Where Medicine Fails, 1974, National Health Insurance: Can We Learn from Canada? 1975, Heart Beat, 1978, Health Care for an Aging Society, 1989; contbr. articles to profl. jours. With Royal Hellenic Air Force, 1949-50. Mem. AAAS, Assn. Am. Med. Colls., Nat. Assn. Sci. Writers, Am. Med. Writers Assn., Am. Hosp. Assn., Am. Soc. Hosp. Mktg. and Pub. Rels., Coun. for Advancement and Support of Edn. Home: 1012 Vernier Pl Palo Alto CA 94305-1027

ANDREW, JANE HAYES, ballet company executive; b. Phila., Jan. 1, 1947; d. David Powell and Vivian Muriel (Saeger) Hayes; m. Brian David Andrew, June 14, 1977; 1 child, Kevin Hayes. AB, Barnard Coll., 1968, grad., Harvard Arts Administrn. Instit., 1972; MBA, U. Wash., 1992—. Mgr. theater Minor Latham Playhouse, Barnard Coll., N.Y.C., 1970-74; co. mgr. Houston Ballet, 1974-77, Ballet West, Salt Lake City, 1978-83; gen. mgr. Pacific N.W. Ballet, Seattle, 1983-87; organizer non-profit consortium nat. ballet cos. and nat. presenting orgns., 1987; pres., exec. dir. Ballet/America, 1988-91; ind. cons. arts mgmt., 1991—; panelist NEA Dance Program Presentors, 1987-88, 88-89, 89-90, Seattle Arts Commn. dance grants, 1989, 90; cons. Ariz. Arts Commn., Phoenix, 1985-86; com. mem. 25th Anniversary of World's Fair, Seattle, 1986-87; panelist NEA Local Programs, 1987. Editor (directory) Philadelphia Cultural Orgns., 1977. Bd. dirs. Good Shepherd Adv. Bd., Seattle, 1985-87. Recipient Dorothy D. Spivack award Barnard Coll., N.Y.C., 1972. Mem. Dance/USA (chmn. Mgrs. Coun. 1986). Home and Office: 7706 146th Ave NW Redmond WA 98052

ANDREW, JOHN-CHRISTIAN, artist; b. Oct. 9, 1952; s. Eugene Edward Kosin and Joan Lou (Dawn) Rafie. BA, U. Calif., Davis, 1979; postgrad., U. Calif., Berkeley, 1981-82. prof. art Exptl. Coll., U. Calif., Davis, 1977, 78; adult art instr. Susun Gallery & Art Sch., Santa Cruz, Calif., 1990; elem. art instr. Soquel (Calif.) Elem. Sch., 1990, 91. Shows include Vorpal Gallery, San Francisco, 1986, Susun Gallery, Santa Cruz, Calif., 1990; one-man shows include Great Western Savings Plaza, Sacramento, 1979, High on the Hog, Carmel, Calif., 1989. Exec. dir. Art for AIDS, San Francisco, 1986. Recipient grants U. Calif., Davis, 1977-79, Calif. State scholarships, 1977-79. Mem. Turquoise Trail Bus. Assn. Democrat. Christian Scientist. Home: PO Box 169 Cerrillos NM 87010-0169

ANDREWS, ANDREW EDWARD, nuclear engineer; b. Sheboygan, Wis., July 29, 1942; s. Francis Jerome and Ruth Janet (Rohde) A.; m. Maria Del Socorro Hernandez, Aug. 5, 1967; children: Marissa G., Margo A., Michelle J., Matthew L. BS, U.S. Mil. Acad., 1964; MS in Nuclear Engring., U. Calif., Berkeley, 1966; M. Mil. Arts and Sci., U.S. Army Command/Gen. Staff, 1973; MBA, L.I. U., 1951. Electromagnetic pulse staff officer Def. Nuclear Agy., Washington, 1970-72; commd. U.S. Army, 1964, advanced through grades to lt. col.; sec. of the gen. staff 32d Army Air Def. Command, Darmstadt, Germany, 1975-76; exec. officer dept. mil. instrn. U.S. Mil. Acad., West Point, 1976-79; mil. rsch. assoc. Los Alamos (N.Mex.) Nat. Lab., 1979-81; air def. officer Supreme HQ Allied Powers Europe, Shape, Belgium, 1981-84; staff mem. Mil. Systems Group, Los Alamos Nat. Lab., 1984-87; group leader cognitive systems engring. Los Alamos Nat. Lab., 1987-90, staff mem. mil. systems analysis and simulation, 1990—. Contbr. articles to profl. jours. Coach Los Alamos Mustangs Adv. Soccer Club, 1989-91; pres. Los Alamos Aquatomics, 1988-89. Decorated Bronze Star. Mem. Am. Coun. for Distance Edn. and Tng. (gov. 1991-92), Am. Cons. League, Am. Def. Preparedness Assn., Assn. of Grads. U.S. Mil. Acad., Shape Officers Assn., Mensa, Internat. Brotherhood of Magicians, Soc. Am. Magicians. Home: 350 Valle Del Sol Los Alamos NM 87544 Office: Los Alamos Nat Lab PO Box 1663 Los Alamos NM 87545

ANDREWS, CANDACE LOU, radio executive; b. Larson AFB, Wash., Apr. 20, 1957; d. Louis Warren Wilson and Lucie Halley Andrews. BA in Psychology, U. Tex., 1979, BBA in Mgmt., 1979. Sales and svc. rep. GranTree Furniture Rental, Austin, Tex., 1979-83, asst. sales and mktg. mgr., 1983; asst. sales and mktg. mgr. GranTree Furniture Rental, Denver, 1983-84; sales and mktg. mgr. GranTree Furniture Rental, Inland Empire, Calif., 1984-86; underwriting coord. Shepherd Communications (doing bus. as KLRD-FM Radio), Yucaipa, Calif., 1986-88, dir. devel., 1988; ops. mgr. Shepherd Communications, Yucaipa, 1988-92, CFO, gen. mgr., 1993—. Asst. fin. sec. Faith Bible Ch., San Bernardino, 1989-91, fin. sec., 1991; chums dir. AWANA Club Faith Bible Ch., San Bernardino, 1987-90, co-comdr., 1990-91; vol. Friends of Turkey, Grand Junction, Colo., 1987—; deaconess Faith Bible Ch., 1993. Mem. Gospel Music Assn., Nat. Religious Broadcasters, Nat. Assn. Broadcasters, Longhorn Assocs. (charter), Tex. Exes Alumni Assn. (life mem.), Fellowship of Christian Athletes, Christian Mgmt. Assn., Friends of Libr., Women's Sports Found. Republican. Office: Shepherd Communications 35225 Ave A Ste 204 PO Box 1000 Yucaipa CA 92399

ANDREWS, COLMAN ROBERT, writer; b. Santa Monica, Feb. 18, 1945; s. Robert Hardy and Irene (Colman) A.; m. Leslie Allyson Ward, May 26, 1979 (div. Sept. 1988); m. Paula Susan Fritz, Nov. 4, 1989; children: Madeleine Cartwright, Isabelle Scott. BA in History, UCLA, 1970, BA in Philosophy, 1970. Editor-in-chief Coast Mag., Beverly Hills, Calif., 1972-75; sr. editor New West Mag., Beverly Hills, 1978-79; writer, editor L.A. and Santa Monica, 1980—; editor Traveling in Style L.A. Times, 1991—. Author: Catalan Cuisine, 1988, Everything on the Table: Plain Talk About Food and Wine, 1992; contbg. editor L.A. Mag., 1979-91, Met. Home, 1981—; contbr. numerous articles to popular mags. and profl. pubs., 1968—. Mem. Chelsea Arts Club (London). Roman Catholic. Office: 2428 Santa Monica Blvd Ph 512 Santa Monica CA 90404-2045

ANDREWS, GARTH E., public relations executive; b. Bakersfield, Calif., Mar. 5, 1943; s. Milton Dale and F. Janice (Schermerhorn) A.; m. Lennie May Husen, Dec. 22, 1964; children: Corinna, Heather. BA in Radio-TV, East Wash. U., Cheney, 1967. Accreditated pub. rels. Reporter, photographer King Broadcasting, Seattle, Spokane, Wash., 1967-68; reporter, anchorman, exec. producer KBOI/KBCI Radio/TV, Boise, Idaho, 1968-75; adminstrn. pub. info. Idaho Pub. Utilities Commn., Boise, 1975-78; sr. pub. rels. assoc. P. R. Mallory & Co. Inc., Indpls., 1978-79; communications rep. S.W. Gas Corp., Las Vegas, Nev., 1979-81, dir. pub. info., 1981-83; dir. communications S.W. Gas Corp., Tucson, Ariz., 1983-87, Phoenix, 1987—. Mem. publicity steering com. Fiesta Bowl, Phoenix, 1987-88; publicity chmn. Fiesta Bowl Hot Air Balloon Classic, Phoenix, 1988-89; trustee Ariz. Mus. Sci. and Tech., Phoenix, 1987—; mem. Pima County Energy Commn., Tucson, 1984-87. With USNR, 1962-64, PTO. Mem. Pub. Rels. Soc. Am. (pres. 1993). Republican. Presbyterian. Office: SW Gas Corp 10851 N Black Canyon Hwy Phoenix AZ 85029-4755

ANDREWS, JAMES WHITMORE, JR., theatrical producer, director; b. New Haven, Sept. 30, 1950; s. James Whitmore Andrews and Nancy Lee (Peery) Levin; m. Sharon Gray Mills, Nov. 6, 1971; 1 child, Jesse Leigh. Student, U. N.C., 1968-71. Mng. dir. Homestead Arts Inc., Colorado Springs, Colo., 1970-73; producing dir. Theatreworks, Colorado Springs, 1977—; bd. dirs. Theatreworks Shakespeare Festival, Colorado Springs; founder, dir. Playwrights Forum awards, Colorado Springs, 1981—; mem. selection com. Gov.'s Awards for the Arts, 1989-90. Mem. Pike's Peak Arts Coun., Colorado Springs, 1983—, Leadership 2000, Citizens' Goals Colorado Springs; mem. grant rev. panels Colo. Coun. on Arts and Humanities, 1987-88. Mem. Am. Arts Alliance, Colo. Found. for the Arts, Colo. Citizens for the Arts, Colo. Theatre Producer's Guild, Rocky Mountain Theatre Guild. Democrat. Home: 436 N Franklin St Colorado Springs CO 80903-3011 Office: U Colo PO Box 7150 Colorado Springs CO 80933-7150

ANDREWS, JOHN KNEELAND, youth worker; b. Winchester, Mass., May 29, 1920; s. George Angell and Frances (Kneeland) A.; m. Marianne Hutchinson, Mar. 21, 1943 (dec. July 1978); children: John. K. Jr., James H., Eleanor Andrews Keasey, Sally Andrews Griego; m. Mary Folds, Feb. 14, 1979. BA, Principia, Elsah, Ill., 1942. Mgr. Fennville (Mich.) Milling Co., 1945-48; asst. traffic mgr. Mich. Fruit Canners, Fennville, 1948-50; food broker Rosen Brokerage Co., St. Louis, 1950-53; alumni sec., asst. to treas. The Principia, St. Louis, 1953-55; exec. dir. Sky Valley Ranch, Inc., Buena Vista, Colo., 1955-60; chief exec. officer, chmn. bd. dirs. Adventure Unltd., Englewood, Colo., 1960-83; chmn. emeritus Adventure Unltd., Englewood, 1983—; sole practice youth worker Denver, 1983—. Lt. Submarine Svc., USNR, 1942-45, PTO. Decorated Silver Star. Mem. Briarwood Country Club (Sun City West, Ariz.), Cherry Hills Country Club (Englewood), Rotary (bd. dirs. Denver chpt. 1983-85). Republican. Christian Scientist. Home and Office: 8505 E Temple Dr Unit 464 Denver CO 80237

ANDREWS, RICHARD OTIS, museum director; b. L.A., Nov. 8, 1949; s. Robert and Theodora (Hammond) A.; m. Colleen Chartier, Jan. 3, 1976; 1 child, Bryce. BA, Occidental Coll., L.A., 1971; BFA, U. Wash., 1973, MFA, 1975. Project mgr. Art in Pub. Places, Seattle Arts Commn., 1978-80, coord., 1980-84; dir. visual arts program Nat. Endowment for Arts, Washington, D.C., 1985-87; dir. Henry Art Gallery, U. Wash., Seattle, 1987—; co-curator Art Into Life: Russian Constructivism 1914-1932; cons. pub. art program devel., 1982-84. Author: Insights/On Sites, 1984, James Turrell: Sensing Space, 1992; editor Artwork/Network, 1984; contbg. editor Going Public, 1988. Office: Henry Art Gallery U Wash DE 15 Seattle WA 98195

ANDREWS, WILLIAM MITCHELL, education administrator; b. Marshalltown, Iowa, Oct. 20, 1946; s. Donald Virgil and Edith (Weller) A.; m. Jean Louise Cooper, Jan. 20, 1968; children: Allyson Marie, Amy Louise (twins). BA in English, U. No. Iowa, 1968, MALS, 1972, MA in Edn., 1976; EdD, N.Mex. State U., 1990. English tchr. Grundy Center (Iowa) High Sch., 1968-70, audiovisual specialist, 1971-72; head of media svcs. Waterloo (Iowa) Community Sch. Dist., 1972-74; media dept. head Hawkeye Inst. of Tech., Waterloo, 1974-76; dir. of learning resources U. Minn., Waseca, 1976-81; dir. of learning resources El Paso (Tex.) C.C. Dist., 1981-89, dir. instnl. rsch., 1989-90; dir. planning R&D Saddleback C.C. Dist., Mission Viejo, Calif., 1991—. Mem. Commn. on the Future, Rsch. and Planning Group for Calif. C.C., Orange County Labor Market Consortium, Calif. Assn. for Instl. Rsch., Nat. Coun. for Resource Devel., Nat. Coun. for Rsch. and Planning, Assn. for Instl. Rsch., Phi Kappa Phi. Republican. Office: Saddleback CC Dist 28000 Marguerite Pkwy Mission Viejo CA 92692

ANDRIE, EUGENE STEVEN, musician, educator; b. Grand Rapids, Mich., Aug. 23, 1914; s. Stephen Frank and Lucy (Kieras) A.; m. Lorraine Evelyn Kloskey, 1937 (dec. 1985); 1 child, Karen. BS, Western Mich. U., 1941; postgrad., U. Mich., 1941; MA, U. Wash., 1951. Prof. music U. Mont., Missoula, 1946-76, prof. emeritus, 1976—; vis. prof. Brigham Young U., Provo, Utah, 1948, U. B.C., Vancouver, Can., 1960; condr. Kalamazoo Jr. Symphony, 1938-41, Mont. All-State Orch., Missoula and Great Falls, 1950-70, Missoula Symphony Orch., 1952-76, Curry Del Norte Chamber Orch., Smith River, Calif., 1989-92; guest condr. Great Falls Symphony Orch., 1965; vol. Friends of Music, South Coast Fisherman STEP Program, 1985—; tchr. Suzuki Inst., Rocky Mt. Coll., Billings, Mont., 1989. Author: Violin Student's Source Book, 1980; contbr. to profl. publs. With USN, 1943-46. Recipient Gov.'s Award for Arts, Mont., 1981. Home: 98005 Olsen Ln PO Box 2909 Harbor OR 97415

ANDRING, RONALD PAUL, protective services official; b. Yakima, Wash., Apr. 17, 1953; s. Richard Joseph and JeRene Estelle (Krienke) A.; m. Margaret Anne Yount, Jan. 13, 1978; children: Margaret Ann, Ronald Paul Jr. BA in Criminal Justice, Ea. Wash. U., 1990, postgrad. Enforcement officer Wash. State Patrol, Kennewick, 1975-78, Walla Walla (Wash.) Police Dept., 1978-79; correctional officer Wash. State Penitentiary, Walla Walla, 1979-89, adminstrv. asst., 1990-91, correctional sgt., 1991—; mem. regional adv. com. Dept. Corrections, Olympia, Wash., 1991-93, trainer, 1988-91. Contbr. articles to profl. jours. and mags. Organizer Jr. Achievement awards, Walla Walla, 1991-93, Kid's Classic Fun Run, Walla Walla, 1991-93; candidate 14th legis. dist. Dem. Cen. Com., Wash., 1972; vol. Friends and Families of Violent Crime Victims, 1989-92; chair publs. com. Blue Ridge PTA, 1989-91. Mem. Wash. Correctional Assn. (exec. bd. 1989-93), Am. Correctional Assn. (adv. com. 1991-93), Western Correctional Assn., Am. Criminological Soc., Masons (master 1992-93). Congregationalist. Home: 502 W Chestnut St Walla Walla WA 99362 Office: Washington State Penitentiary PO Box 520 Walla Walla WA 99362

ANDROS, STEPHEN JOHN, architect; b. Joliet, Ill., July 21, 1955; s. Stephen Benedict and Jacquelyn M. (Schoob) A.; m. Vicki Lee McCaffery, June 24, 1978; children: Jeffrey Kenneth, Christopher John. BArch cum laude, Ariz. State U., 1978. Registered architect, Ariz.; cert. constrn. specifier. Project architect, specifier, contract adminstr. Cornoyer-Hedrick Architect and Planners Inc., Phoenix, 1978-83; ptnr. Perrell-Andros Cons. Architects, Scottsdale, Ariz., 1983-85; dir. specifications Haver, Nunn and Collamer Inc., Phoenix, 1985-86; faculty assoc. coll. architecture Ariz. State U., 1988; dir. specifications and quality control Gilleland, Hunt, Rehse, Ltd. Architects, Phoenix, 1986-88; prin. Stephen Andros Specification Cons., Phoenix, 1988—; instr. Phoenix Inst. Tech., 1983-84; guest lectr. materials Ariz. State U., Tempe, 1984; mem. ad hoc contracting com. City of Phoenix, 1982. Prin. works include Banking and Revenue Bldg. State of Ariz., Phoenix, F-16 Squadron Ops., Luke AFB, Ariz., Scottsdale (Ariz.) Horseman's Park, McDonnell-Douglas Helicopter Co. Mesa (Ariz.) Facility, Spl. Mgmt. Unit for Ariz. Dept. Corrections, Papago High Sch. BIA, San Simeon, Ariz., Student Activities Ctr. No. Ariz. U., Flagstaff, Remodel of Terminal 2 Sky Harbor Internat. Airport, Phoenix, Tempe Minicomputer Maintenance Ops. Ctr., Cen. One Thomas High Rise, Phoenix, Valley Nat. Bank, Phoenix. Mem. Osborn Sch. Dist. bond program, Glendale Union High Sch. Dist. bond program, Page Mid. Sch., ASU West Phase II Expansion, ADOT Frwy. Mgmt. Control Bldg., Am. West Arena, Gilbert High Sch. #2, Chase Credit Card Ops. Ctr.; charter orgn. rep. Cub Scout Pack #5, Boy Scouts Am. Recipient Cert. Recognition Copper Devel. Assn., 1977. Mem. AIA (profl. Cen. Ariz. chpt.), Constrn. Specifications Inst. (profl. Phoenix chpt., moderator Pres.'s forum, 1985, leader cert. workshop S.W. region, 1986, rep. to Constrn. Industry Council Ariz., 1981-84, chmn. Phoenix chpt. program, 1979-80, sec. Phoenix chpt., 1980-81, 1st v.p. Phoenix chpt., 1981-82, pres. Phoenix chpt., 1982-83, 83-84, treas. Phoenix chpt., 1987-88, program chmn. S.W. region conf., 1985, mem. inst. cert. com., 1984-87, chmn., 1986-87, jury of fellow 1987-90, practice subcom. 1990-91, S.W. region conf. chmn. 1991—), Specifications Cons. in Ind. Practice (corr., nat. v.p., 1984-85, editor newsletter, 1983-85, nat. sec. 1990—), Profl. Svcs. Mgmt. Assn. (rational conv. com.), Ariz. Masonry Guild (tech. com.), Am. Concrete Inst. (Ariz. chpt. edn. com. chmn.). Republican. Methodist. Home: 7321 N 19th Dr Phoenix AZ 85021-7805

ANDRUS, ALAN RICHARD, computer services executive; b. Bklyn., Sept. 10, 1943; s. Richard and Sophie Helen (Gruntmeyer) A.; m. Jeanne Anne Theis, July 20, 1968; children: Karen, Tracy, Ross, Amy. BS, Fordham U., 1965; postgrad. mgmt., U. So. Calif., 1968-70. Programmer Met. Life Ins. Co., 1965-66; engr., sect. head Automated Telemetry Sta., Grumman Data Systems, Calverton, N.Y., 1970-74, mgr. Calverton Computing Ctr., 1975-77, dir. electronic systems maintenance, Bethpage, N.Y., 1977-82; pres. Systems Support Corp., Woodbury, N.Y., 1983-87; sr. v.p. svc. and support ComputerLand Corp., Pleasanton, Calif., 1988—. Chmn. community adv. com. Connetquot Sch. Dist., 1978-79. Served with U.S. Army, 1966-70. N.Y. State Regents scholar, 1965-70. Mem. Assn. for Svcs. Mgmt. Internat. (mem. internat. bd. dirs., chmn. & pres. 1990, v.p. Ams. and Pacific 1989, N.Y. regional v.p., pres. N.Y.-N.J. Met. chpt., treas. 1988-89), Nat. Computer Service Network (past pres., past chmn. bd. dirs), Mensa, Oakdale Sportsman's Club, Blackhawk Country Club.

ANDRUS, CECIL DALE, governor; b. Hood River, Oreg., Aug. 25, 1931; s. Hal Stephen and Dorothy (Johnson) A.; m. Carol Mae May, Aug. 27, 1949; children: Tana Lee, Tracy Sue, Kelly Kay. Student, Oreg. State U., 1948-49; LLD (hon.), Gonzaga U., U. Idaho, U. N.Mex., Coll. Idaho. State gen. mgr. Paul Revere Life Ins. Co., 1969-70; gov. State of Idaho, 1971-77, 87—; sec. of interior, 1977-81; dir. Albertson's, Inc., 1985-87; mem. Idaho Senate, 1961-66, 69-70; mem. exec. com. Nat. Gov.'s Conf., 1971-72, chmn., 1976; chmn. Fedn. Rocky Mountain States, 1971-72. Chmn. bd. trustees Coll. of Idaho, 1985-89; bd. dirs. Sch. Forestry, Duke U. With USN, 1951-55. Recipient Disting. Citizen award Oreg. State U., 1980, Collier County Conservancy medal, 1979, Torch of Liberty award B'nai Brith, 1991; named Conservationist of Yr., Nat. Wildlife Fedn., 1980, Idaho Wildlife Fedn., 1972, Man of Yr., VFW, 1959. Mem. VFW, Idaho Taxpayers Assn. (bd. dirs. 1964-66). Democrat. Office: Office of Gov State Capitol Boise ID 83720

ANEMA, DURLYNN CAROL, communications and education professor, consultant, columnist, author, advocate; b. San Diego, Dec. 23, 1935; d. Durlin L. Flagg and Carolyn L. (Janeck) Owen; m. Charles Jay Anema, May 6, 1955 (dec. Sept. 1986); children: Charlynn Raimundi, Charles Jay Jr., Richard F. Student, Stanford U., 1953-55; BA, Calif. State U., Hayward, 1968, MS, 1977; EdD, U. of the Pacific, 1984. Cert. secondary edn. tchr., Calif. Columnist, reporter San Leandro (Calif.) Morning News, 1960-62; adult tchr. Hayward Unified Sch. Dist., 1969, tchr. secondary edn., 1972-75, vice prin., 1975-77; tchr. secondary edn. San Leandro Unified Sch. Dist., 1970-72; vice prin. Lodi (Calif.) Unified Sch. Dist., 1977-80; rsch. dir. Ctr. for Econ. Edn., U. of the Pacific, Stockton, Calif., 1980-81; dir. lifelong learning U. of the Pacific, Stockton, 1984-89, prof., 1984-89; columnist Stockton Record, 1984-89; cons. in field. Author: Don't Get Fired, 1978, Get Hired, 1979, Sharing An Apartment, 1981, Designing Effective Brochures and Newsletters, 1987, Late Life, 1988, I'm Not Alone in All This Crap That's Happening, 1993, Customs & Courtesies, 1993; (with others) California Yesterday and Today, 1983, Options, 1992. Pres., bd. dirs. Bd. of Library Trustees, San Leandro, 1970-75; elder Grace Presbyn. Ch., Lodi, 1985-87; pres., bd. dirs. Valley Community Counseling, Stockton, 1986-89; mem. Commn. on Children, San Joaquin County, Calif., 1986-92; hon. life mem. Monroe PTA, 1965. Recipient Susan B. Anthony award Commn. on Women, 1989. Mem. AAUW, Investigative Editors and Reporters, Soc. Profl. Journalists, Stanford U. Alumni Assn., Phi Kappa Phi, Delta Kappa Gamma, Phi Delta Kappa. Home: 401 Oak Ridge Ct Valley Springs CA 95252

ANGEL, ARMANDO CARLOS, internist; b. Las Vegas, N.Mex., Mar. 25, 1940; s. Edmundo Clemente and Pauline Teresa (Flores) Sanchez A.; m. Judith Lee Weedin, Aug. 5, 1961; children: Stephanie, Renee. BA, San Jose State U., 1963; MS, U. Ariz., 1970, PhD, 1971, M.D., 1977. Chemist Tracerlab, Inc., Richmond, Calif., 1963-67; prof. chemistry Pima Coll., Tucson, Ariz., 1971-74; intern U. N.Mex., Albuquerque, 1977-78, resident, 1978-80; resident VA Hosp., Lovelace Med. Ctr., Albuquerque, 1978-80; practice medicine specializing in internal medicine, Las Cruces, N.Mex., 1980-88; pvt. practice, El Paso, Tex., 1990—; dir. pain program Rio Vista Rehab. Hosp., 1992; cons. minority biomed. sci. project NIH, Washington, 1970-74, Ednl. Assocs., Tucson, 1971-74. Author: Llevve Tlaloc No. 2, 1973. Treas. Nat. Chicano Health Orgn., Los Angeles, 1974-75; v.p. Mexican-Am. Educators, Tucson, 1973-74; pres. N.Mex. affiliate Am. Diabetes Assn., Albuquerque, 1983-85. Fellow U. Ariz., 1988-90. Fellow Am. Coll. Rheumatology; mem. AMA, Tex. Med. Soc., El Paso County Medical Soc., Am. Diabetes Assn., ACP, Dona Ana County Med. Soc. (pres. 1983), Am. Coll. Rheumatology, Am. Assn. Internal Medicine, Alpha Chi Sigma.

ANGELE, ALFRED ROBERT, police labor union executive; b. N.Y.C., Dec. 9, 1940; s. Alfred Otto and Alma Margaret (Branda) A.; m. Barbara Ann Chavez, Sept. 30, 1961; children: Cynthia Lynn, Lynda Renee. AA, L.A. Valley Coll., 1968. Cert. tchr. community coll. police adminstrn. Patrolman Burbank (Calif.) Police Dept., 1963-67, detective, 1967-74, sgt., dept. self def. instr., 1974-78; gen. mgr. Calif. Orgn. Police and Sheriffs, Sacramento, 1978-89, exec. dir., 1989—; internat. sec./treas. Internat. Union Police Assns. AFL-CIO, Alexandria, Va., 1985-90; internat. sec./treas. emeritus Internat. Union Police Assns. AFL-CIO, Alexandria, 1990—; Govt. appt. commr. on Peace Officer Standards/Tng., Sacramento, 1979-84; mem. AFL-CIO observer team sent to Nicaragua to monitor presdl. election, 1990, Police Adv. Coun. on Car Clubs, 1967-70; mem. exch. progrm with German Police Union, 1987. Contbr. articles to profl. jours. including USA Today. Mem. L.A. Host committee for nat. tour Bill of Rights, 1991. Recipient Mike Maggiora Meml. Humanitarian award Maggiora family, 1980, Commendations, Letters of Appreciation Burbank Bar Assn., Elks, Calif. Hwy. Patrol, Mayor's Drug and Alcohol Abuse Com., L.A. County Dist. Atty.'s Office, Houston Police Patrolmans Union, Calif. Dept. Corrections, Mayor of L.A., numerous others; named 1st Officer of the Month Jaycees, 1977. Mem. Burbank Police Officers Assn. (pres. 1976-81, named dir. of yr. 1972, commendation award), Internat. Union Police Assns. AFL-CIO (sec.-treas. 1985—, dir. 1981-85, named law enforcement editor of the yr. 1987), Calif. Narcotics Officers Assn., Calif. Orgn. Police/Sheriffs (gen. mgr. 1978—, sec. 1976-78, commendation award), Calif. Narcotics Info. Network. Democrat. Roman Catholic. Office: 175 E Olive Ave Ste 400 Burbank CA 91502

ANGELES, PETER ADAM, philosophy educator, playwright; b. Ambridge, Pa., Feb. 21, 1931; s. Adam P. and Kalliope K. (Moschos) A.; m. Elizabeth F. McConnaughy, June 7, 1951 (dec. Nov. 1977); children: Beth Angeles Basham, Jane Angeles McKay, Adam; m. Darlene Elaine Jures, Aug. 12, 1987 (dec. Apr. 1993). BA, Columbia U., 1952, MA, 1954, PhD, 1956. Prof. philosophy U. Western Ont., London, Ont., Can., 1956-70; vis. prof. Albert Schweitzer Coll., Switzerland, 1963-66, U. Calif., Santa Barbara, 1968-69; prof. and chairperson dept. philosophy Santa Barbara (Calif.) City Coll., 1970-90; prof. Yavapai Coll., Clarkdale, Ariz., 1990—, U. Phoenix, Ariz., 1990—. Author: Introduction to Sentential Logic, 1976, The Problem of God, 1976, The Possible Dream: Toward Understanding the Black Experience, 1971, Dictionary of Philosophy. 1981, Dictionary of Christian Theology, 1986, Children's Storytime Radio Show, 1986 (Golden Mike award 1986-87, Heart of Am. award 1991), Mind Plays 1989, When Blind Eyes Pierce the Darkness, 1989. Home: 365 Foothills Dr Sedona AZ 86336-5027

ANGELOV, GEORGE ANGEL, pediatrician; b. Bulgaria, May 12, 1925; came to U.S., 1978; s. Angel Christov and Maria Steru (Sarambelieva) A.; m. Olga Valerie Minkova, Dec. 21, 1952; 1 child, Angel. MD, Sch. of Medicine, Sofia, Bulgaria, 1952. Pediatrician Distric Hosp., Bulgaria, 1952-53; asst. prof. Sch. of Medicine, Sofia, Bulgaria, 1953-64; prof. anatomy and anthropology Sch. of Biology, Sofia, Bulgaria, 1964-77; mgr. reproductive toxicology Lederle Labs., Pearl River, N.Y., 1979-89; cons. reproductive toxicology pvt. practice, Laguna Niguel, Calif., 1989—; assoc. dean Sch. of Biology, Sofia, 1970-72; vis. scientist Sch. of Medicine, Geneva, 1971, 74. Author: (textbook) Anatomy, 1970; mem. glossary com. Teratology Glossary, 1987-89; reviewer several sci. jours.; contbr. 49 sci. publs. to profl. jours. Mem. Teratology Soc. USA, European Teratology Soc., Human Biology Coun. USA, Free Union of Univ. Profs. of Anatomy. East Orthodox. Home: 29712 Michelis St Laguna Niguel CA 92677

ANGEVIN, ROBERT PERKINS BROWN, real estate development executive; b. Lake Forest, Ill., June 16, 1963; s. John Jay Angevin and Stella (Brown) Kenly. BA, Williams Coll., 1985; M Real Estate, U. So. Calif., 1992. Assoc. Continental Ill., Chgo., 1985-87; devel. mgr. JMB Realty Co., L.A., 1987-92; supervised loan specialist Bank of Calif., L.A., 1992—; bd. dirs. The Keystone-Garret Corp., Houston. Founder, The Food Network, L.A.

ANGLE, LISA ALISON, forester; b. Fort Dix, N.J., June 6, 1953; d. Frank Lee and Helen E. (Bonney) Vito; m. James Marcus Angle, Oct. 1, 1988; 1 child, Scott M. Vito. BS in Forest Mgmt., No. Ariz. U., 1975. Forestry aide U.S. Forest Service, Williams, Ariz., 1973; forestry tech. U.S. Forest

Service, Pagosa Springs, Colo., 1974, Hebo, Oreg., 1975-78; forester U.S. Forest Service, Sierra Vista, Ariz., 1978-81, Safford, Ariz., 1981—. Republican. Methodist. Office: USFS Safford Ranger Dist PO Box 709 504 5th Ave Safford AZ 85548

ANGLEMIRE, KENNETH NORTON, retired publishing company executive, writer, environmentalist, lawyer; b. Chgo.; s. Fred Rutherford and Isabel (Alguire) A.; m. Anne Hayes. (dec.); m. Geraldine Payne. Student, Northwestern U.; B.S., U. Ill., Urbana; LL.B., J.D., Chgo.-Kent Coll. Law, Ill. Inst. Tech. Bar: Ill. Pvt. practice of law, to 1936; atty. Chgo. Title and Trust Co., 1936-42; chief acct., office mgr. Graphic Arts Displays, Inc., Chgo., 1942-50; comptroller Marshall Industries, Chgo., 1950-59, Marquis-Who's Who, Inc., Chgo., 1953-59; v.p. Marquis-Who's Who, Inc., 1958-59, exec. v.p., chief ops. officer, 1959-69, chmn. bd., pub., 1969-70; pres., dir. A.N. Marquis Co., Inc., Chgo., 1964-69; Mem. Ill. State Scholarship Commn., 1966-69; charter mem. Bus. Adv. Council, Chgo. Urban League; hon. mem. staff N.Mex. Atty. Gen., 1971-74; mem. Adult Edn. Council Greater Chgo., bd. dirs., 1968-70. Writer articles on music, natural history and conservation, mountain adventure. Mem. ACLU, Ill. Audubon Soc. (v.p. fin., dir. 1961-65), Greater North Michigan Ave. Assn. (dir. 1966-70), Dickens Fellowship, Santa Fe Opera Guild, Internat. Alban Berg Soc., Sangre de Cristo Audubon Soc. N.Mex. (founder, pres. 1972-73, dir. 1972-75), Friends of Santa Fe (N.Mex.) Public Library, Historic Santa Fe Found., Wilderness Study Com. N.Mex., Santa Fe Concert Assn., Bus. Execs. Move for Peace in Viet Nam, Ridges Sanctuary, Bailey's Harbor, Wis., Armory for the Arts, Guadalupe Hist. Found., Santa Fe. Trail Assn. (End of the Trail chpt.), Pi Kappa Alpha, Delta Theta Phi, Sierra Club (founder, chmn. Great Lakes chpt. 1959-61, 64-66, exec. com. 1959-69, Rio Grande chpt., N.Mex.). Club: N.Mex. Mountain.

ANGLESIO, FRANCO J., hotel executive; b. Turin, Italy, Sept. 14, 1943; s. Cesare and Alma (Cattaneo) A.; m. Mary C. Bartlett, Aug. 22, 1970; children: Marco P., Michael S. Cert. in bus. adminstrn., Bishop's, 1982. Gen. mgr. Hotel Beau Sejour, Moncton, Can., 1972-78, Hotel MacDonald, Edmonton, Can., 1978-80, Chateau Laurier, Ottawa, Can., 1980-83, Hotel Vancouver, Can., 1983-86; v.p. ops. Coast Hotels & Resorts, Vancouver, 1986-91, exec. v.p., 1991-92, pres., 1992—; bd. dirs. Coast Hotels & Resorts Ltd., Vancouver, Okabe N.Am. Inc., Vancouver. Mem. Skal Club, Chaine des Rotisseurs. Roman Catholic. Home: 1278 Bracknell Pl, North Vancouver, BC Canada V7R1V5 Office: Coast Hotels & Resorts, 900-1090 W Georgia St, Vancouver, BC Canada V6E 3V7

ANGORA, ANNE LOUISE, small business owner, calligrapher; b. Cleve., May 24, 1947; d. Thomas Louis and Ruth Louise (Gilchrist) Zehe; m. Thomas James Beck, July 23, 1966 (div. 1984); children: Lisa, Laura, Sheryl; m. Richard Angora, Dec. 5, 1987. Student, Cuyahoga Community Coll., Parma, Ohio, 1967; studies with Michael Gullick, Las Vegas, 1985, studies with Roy Purcell, 1986; student, U. Nev., Las Vegas, 1987. Sales person Dick Blick Co., Henderson, Nev., 1983-91, animal veterinary products mgr., 1984-87, art class coord., 1988-91, instr. airbrush, 1989-91, asst. store mgr., 1988-90, store mgr., 1990-91; pres., owner AZA Prodns., Henderson, 1991—; instr. Reed Whipple Cultural Ctr., Las Vegas, 1988, Craftmart, Las Vegas, 1988, Civic Ctr., Henderson, 1988-89, Silversprings Ctr., Henderson, 1989; instr. calligraphy Boulder City Pk. & Recreation, 1991-92. Author: (with others) Shades of Herself, 1975; Herself Portrait, 1976; author (with others), illustrator: Her Echo, 1975; author numerous poems, calligraphic art, (judges choice 1986); designer Rainbow Casino, Henderson, 1992. Hon. vol. St. Rose De Lima Hosp., Henderson, 1989; mem. Las Vegas Art Mus. Mem. Nev. Watercolor Soc. (assoc.), Henderson C. of C. Roman Catholic. Office: AZA Prodns 542 Chelsea Dr Henderson NV 89014

ANGOTTI, ANTONIO MARIO, international merchant, banker; b. Whittier, Calif., Jan. 15, 1958; s. O.A. and Anna Maria (Massei) A. BA, U. Calif., Berkeley, 1981; postgrad., Cambridge U., Eng., 1981-82. With Paul H. Nitze Sch. Advanced Internat. Studies, Johns Hopkins U., 1982-84; assoc. Citicorp Investment Bank, N.Y.C., 1984-85; v.p. Bear Stearns & Co., Inc., N.Y.C., 1985-87; v.p., dir. sovereign debt Security Pacific Mcht. Bank, N.Y.C., 1987-89; White House fellow, spl. asst to dep. sec. of state U.S. Dept. State, Washington, 1989-90; chmn. bd. Calif. World Trade Ctrs., Inc., Long Beach, 1991—; pres. Grand Slam Softball Parks, Inc., 1992—; mem. adv. bd. Bologna Ctr., Johns Hopkins, Washington, coll. letters and sci. U. Calif. Mem. Fgn. Policy Assn., 1987; co-chair U. Calif. Berkeley, N.Y.C. campaing com., Coun. of 1000, Nat. Italian Am. Found., The Asia Found., Friends of the Philippines; Orange County Renaissance, Robert Scalapino Scholarship Fund; Leadership So. Calif., 1993; presdl. appt. The White House, 1989. Walter Haas Meml. scholar, 1980-81; named Brit.-Am. Successor Generation, 1990, U.S.-Italy Next Generation Leaders, 1988. Mem. Acad. Polit. Sci., U. Calif. Alumni Assn. N.Y.C., Johns Hopkins U. Alumni Assn. N.Y.C., No. Calif. World Affairs Coun., L.A. World Affairs Coun., Commonwealth Club Calif., Town Hall of L.A. Roman Catholic. Office: Calif World Trade Ctrs Inc One World Trade Ctr Ste 800 Long Beach CA 90831

ANGUS, RONALD G., systems engineer, civilian military employee; b. Hartford, Conn., Jan. 28, 1933; s. Alexander and Jane (Holgate) A.; m. Evlyn Northington Farris, Aug. 17, 1956; children: Jane, Diann, Ronald G. Jr. BS, Rensselaer U., 1954; MS, U. So. Calif., 1968. Registered profl. engr.; lic. comml. pilot. Commd. 2nd lt. USAF, 1954, advanced through grades to maj., ret., 1974; chief of safety 1st Combat Evaluation Group, Shreveport, La., 1974-88; sr. systems engr. Air Force Safety Ctr., Norton AFB, Calif., 1988—; mgr. automated hazard abatement program, mgr. occupational safety and health program USAF, 1988—; chmn. Ark.-La.-Tex. Fed. Safety Coun., Shreveport, 1980-82. Author: Motivating for Safety, 1966. Mem. Am. Soc. Safety Engrs. (profl.), Soc. Am. Mil. Engrs. (chpt. pres. 1966), Soc. Hazard Control Mgrs. (cert.), Internat. Soc. Air Safety Investigators, Assn. Fed. Safety and Health Profls., Shriners, Masons, Am. Trapshooting Assn. (life), Phi Kappa Phi, Sigma Chi (life). Office: Air Force Safety Ctr AFISC/SEGO Norton AFB CA 92409-7001

ANISMAN, JENIFER JILL, artist, graphic designer, filmmaker; b. Montreal, Que., Can., Mar. 24, 1964; d. Allan Lyon and Roselyn (Aberman) A. Cert. fine arts, Vanier Coll., Montreal, 1983; BFA, Concordia U., Montreal, 1987; MFA, Calif. Inst. Arts, 1990. Ind. filmmaker Montreal, 1980—; video-editor J. Walter Thompson, L.A., 1987-89; laserdisc prodr. Voyager Co., Santa Monica, Calif., 1990-91; scenic painter Crown Internat. Pictures-Feature Films, L.A., 1988; graphic designer, exhibit preparer James Acret Law Corp., Santa Monica, 1991—; cons. student filmmakers, L.A., 1991—; ind. artist oils, fabric & clothing, L.A., 1987—. Editor (feature film) Mindgames, 1991; prodn. asst. (film) Darkwind, 1991; dir. (film) The Art of Don Kottmann, 1987; keyboardist, songwriter, 1978—. Soup kitchen vol. Eglise Notre Dame, Montreal, 1989; women's shelter vol. Salvation Army, Montreal, 1989; mem. Nat. Gallery. Grantee Banff (Alta.) Ctr. for Arts, 1986, Calif. Inst. Arts, 1988; recipient Ahmanson scholarship awards William Ahmanson Found., 1989, 90. Mem. Women Artists, World Wildlife Fedn., Smithsonian Instn., Nat. Geog. Soc. Office: James Acret Law Corp 100 Wilshire Blvd Ste 800 Santa Monica CA 90401

ANNIS, JAMES TIMOTHY, astrophysicist; b. Billings, Mont., Nov. 30, 1961; s. Alan Robert and Esther (Frey) A. BS in Physics and Astronomy, U. Wash., 1986; MS in Astronomy, U. Hawaii, 1988; postgrad., Inst. for Astronomy, 1986—. Mem. tech. staff Jet Propulsion Lab., Pasadena, Calif., 1986-87; rsch. asst. Inst. for Astronomy, Honolulu, 1988—. Contbr. articles to profl. jours. Treas. Wash. State Citizens for Space, Seattle, 1984. Grantee NSF, 1989, Sigma Xi, 1991; NASA fellow, 1991—. Mem. Am. Astron. Soc., Astron. Soc. Pacific, Internat. Soc. for Optical Engring. Lutheran.

ANSBACHER, CHARLES ALEXANDER, conductor, musician; b. Providence, Oct. 5, 1942; s. Heinz L. and Rowena (Ripin) A.; m. Swanee Hunt, 1986; 1 son, Henry Lloyd. B.A., Brown U., 1965; M.Music, U. Cin., 1968, D.M.A., 1979. nat. adv. bd. Avery Fisher awards music, 1974—; mem. Colo. State Festival Council for Centennial-Bicentennial Commn., 1974-76; chmn. White House Fellows Regional Selection Com. Asst. condr., Kingsport (Tenn.) Symphony Orch., 1965-66, condr., mus. dir., Middletown (Ohio) Symphony Orch., 1967-70, Colorado Springs Symphony Orch., 1970-89 , condr. laureate, Colorado Springs Symphony Orch., 1989—, music dir., Rockefeller Found., Apprentice Musicians Program, Cin. Playhouse in Park, 1967, guest condr., Cin. Symphony Orch., Denver Symphony Orch., Frysk Orkest in Leeuwarden, Holland, Indpls. Symphony, Omaha Symphony, Ft. Worth Symphony, San Jose Symphony, Seoul Philharm., Young Musicians Symphony Orch. of London, 1985; condr., music dir., Young Artists Orch. Denver, 1980-84. White House fellow, 1976-77. Mem. Urban League Pike's Peak Region (treas.), Pike's Peak Musicians Assn. (v.p. 1974-76), Condrs. Guild of Am. Symphony Orch. League (chmn. 1979-81, pres. 1986—), Am. Symphony Orch. League (dir. 1979-81), Colo. Council Arts and Humanities (1978-84, chmn. 1987—), Colo. Pub. Edn. Partnership (1984—), Pub. Edn. Coalition of the Pikes Peak Region (co-pres. 1984—), Music Educators Nat. Conf., World Affairs Council Colorado Springs (pres. 1980-84, chmn. design constrn. subcom.), Pikes Peak Ctr. (founding bd. mem. charter fund), Conr.'s Guild, Inc. (pres. 1986—), Pub. Edn. Coalition Pikes Peak Region (bd. dirs. Colo. pub. edn. partnership, co-pres. 1985-86, chmn. design and constrn. subcom. Pikes Peak Ctr., founding bd. mem. charter fund). Clubs: Rotary, El Paso. Office: Colorado Springs Symphony PO Box 1692 Colorado Springs CO 80901-1692

ANSCHUTZ, PHILLIP F., diversified company executive; b. 1939. BS, Univ. Kansas, 1961. Former pres. Anschutz Corp., now chmn. bd., also dir.; chmn. bd. So. Pacific Transp. Co., San Francisco. Office: Southern Pacific Transportation Rm 859 1 Market Plaza San Francisco CA 94105

ANSELL, GEORGE STEPHEN, metallurgical engineering educator, academic administrator; b. Akron, Ohio, Apr. 1, 1934; s. Frederick Jesse and Fanny (Soletsky) A.; m. Marjorie Boris, Dec. 18, 1960; children: Frederick Stuart, Laura Ruth, Benjamin Jesse. B. in Metall. Engring., Rensselaer Poly. Inst., 1954, M. in Metall. Engring., 1955, PhD, 1960. Physical metallurgist USN Research Lab., Washington, 1957-58; mem. faculty Rensselaer Poly. Inst., Troy, N.Y., 1960-84, Robert W. Hunt prof., 1965-84, chmn. materials div., 1969-74, dean engring., 1974-84; pres. Colo. Sch. Mines, Golden, 1984—, now pres., chancellor; bd. dirs. Norwest Bank, Cyprus Minerals Co. Editor books; patentee in field; contbr. over 100 articles to profl. jours. Served with USN, 1955-58. Recipient Hardy Gold Medal AIME, 1961, Curtis W. McGraw award Am. Soc. Engring. Edn., 1971, Souzandrade Gold Medal of Univ. Merit Fed. U. Maranhao, 1986. Fellow Metall. Soc. (pres. 1986-87), Am. Soc. Metals (Alfred H. Geisler award 1964, Bradley Stoughton award 1968); mem. NSPE, Am. Soc. Engring. Edn. (Curtis W. McGraw award 1971), Sigma Xi, Tau Beta Pi, Phi Lambda Upsilon. Club: Denver. Office: Colo Sch of Mines 1500 Illinois St Golden CO 80401-1887

ANSEN, DAVID B., critic, writer; b. Los Angeles, Apr. 21, 1945; s. Joseph and Dorothy (Blum) A. BA, Harvard U., 1967. Film critic, editor Real Paper, Cambridge, Mass., 1975-77; film critic, sr. writer Newsweek, N.Y.C., 1977—; host, writer cable TV show Bravo International Film Show, 1983-87. Writer documentaries include The Divine Garbo, 1990, The One The Only...Groucho, 1991. Recipient Page One award Newspaper Guild N.Y., 1983, Headliner award, 1984, Page One award, 1986, 88. Mem. N.Y. Film Critics Circle, Nat. Society Film Critics. Office: Newsweek 11835 W Olympic Blvd Los Angeles CA 90064-5001

ANSON, FRED COLVIG, chemistry educator; b. Los Angeles, Feb. 17, 1933; m. Roxana Anson; children: Alison, Eric. BS, Calif. Inst. Tech., 1954; MS, Harvard U., 1955, PhD, 1957. Instr. chemistry Calif. Inst. Tech., Pasadena, 1957-58, asst. prof., 1958-62, assoc. prof., 1962-68, prof. chemistry, 1968—, chmn. div. chemistry and chem. engr., 1984—. Contbr. numerous articles to profl. jours. Fellow J.S. Guggenheim Found. U. Brussels, 1964, Alfred P. Sloan Found., 1965-69; scholar Fulbright-Hays Found. U. Florence, Italy, 1972, A. von Humboldt Found. Fritz Haber Inst., Berlin, 1984-86. Mem. AAAS, Nat. Acad. Sci., Am. Chem. Soc., Am. Electrochem. Soc., Internat. Soc. Electrochemistry, Soc. Electroanalytical Chemistry, Tau Beta Pi. Office: Calif Inst Tech Div Chemistry & Chem Eng MS 127-72 Pasadena CA 91125

ANSON, MICHAEL A., magazine publisher; b. San Diego, Dec. 11, 1946; s. C.A. and E.R. Anson; m. Viki Nolan; 1 child, Rory Michael. BA in Journalism, Calif. State U., 1969. Assoc. editor Car Life mag., Newport Beach, Calif., 1969-70; test editor Rd. & Track mag., Newport Beach, 1970-72; dir. advt. Interpart Corp., El Segundo, Calif., 1972-73; editor Petersen's 4 Wheel & Off-Rd. mag., L.A., 1978-79, pub., from 1979; pub. Pickup, Van & 4 Wheel Drive mag., L.A., from 1982; now editor Motor Trend mag., West Hollywood, Calif. Author: How to Customize Your Pickup Truck, 1977, also TV scripts, 1976-77; contbr. articles to mags. Office: Motor Trend Mag 8490 W Sunset Blvd Ste 600 West Hollywood CA 90069-1946

ANSPACH, DENNY SYKES, radiologist; b. Chgo., Feb. 5, 1934; s. William Earl and Rachel Mae (Sykes) A.; m. Carol Audrey Jacobs, June 22, 1958 and May 14, 1988; children: David Denny, Carolyn Margaret Anspach Smith; m. Polly Dakin Anspach, Jan. 2, 1981 (div. Oct. 1987). BA, Stanford U., 1956, MD, 1960. Diplomate Am. Bd. Radiology. Intern Mary Fletcher Hosp., Burlington, Vt., 1960-61; diagnostic radiology resident Stanford (Calif.) U., 1964; radiologist Radiol. Assocs. Sacramento, 1966-81; chief radiology Sutter Community Hosps., Sacramento, 1974-78, dir. radiology, 1978-80; radiologist Green Mountain Radiology, Montpelier, Vt., 1981-87; chief radiology Cen. Vt. Hosp., Barre, 1984-86; pvt. practice radiol. cons. Sacramento, 1987-90; staff radiologist, asst. prof. U. Calif.-Davis Med. Ctr., Sacramento, 1974-77, 90—; prop. Mammographia, Sacramento, 1991—; pres. Vt. Radiol. Soc., 1984-86. Founder,, bd. dirs., pres. Sacramento Trust for Hist. Preservation; co-founder Calif. State RR Mus., Sacramento, 1969—. Capt. U.S. Army, 1964-66. Recipient award of merit Calif. Resources Agy., 1978. Fellow Am. Coll. Radiology (councilor 1979-81, 86-87); mem. AMA, Sacramento-El Dorado Med. Soc. chmn. peer rev. com. 1972-81, 89—), Calif. Radiol. Soc. (exec. com. 1978-81), Northam County Radiol. Soc. (pres. elect 1993—), Ry. and Locomotive Hist. Soc. (bd. dirs. Pacific Coast chpt. 1961-93), Antique and Classic Boat Soc. (bd. dirs. 1988-91), Sutter Club (bd. dirs. 1978-81). Republican. Presbyterian. Home: 710 Coronado Blvd Sacramento CA 95864-5210 Office: Mammographia 920 29th St # J Sacramento CA 95816-4306

ANTHES, CLIFFORD CHARLES, retired mechanical engineer, consultant; b. Buffalo, Aug. 2, 1907; s. Edward Charles and Ethel Elmira (Cliff) A.; m. Theresa Roselyn Bischof, Sept. 2, 1931 (dec. Dec. 1982); children: Carol Louise, Clifford Charles Jr.; m. Ursula Elizabeth O'Leary, Apr. 7, 1984. Student, U. Buffalo, 1928-32, Newark Coll. Engring., 1934-39. Technician Linde div. apparatus devel. lab. Union Carbide Corp., Tonawanda, N.Y., 1928-33; project engr. Union Carbide Corp., Newark, 1933-64; sr. project engr. Union Carbide Corp., Florence, S.C., 1964-70; cons. Union Carbide Corp., Piscataway Twp., N.J., 1970-76; cons. So. Meth. U., Dallas, 1973, Gray Corp., Dallas, 1973, Brown & Brown Architects, Tucson, 1977, CF&I Steel Corp., Pueblo, Colo., 1982. Patentee in field; contbr. articles to profl. jours. and tech. papers to profl. soc. Vol. Civil Def., Union, N.J., 1939-42; com. mem., explorer, advisor Boy Scouts Am., Union, 1940s; trustee, mem. exec. bd. Florence Mus., 1960s. Mem. Eastern Fedn. Gem and Mineral Soc. (pres. 1967, citation for advancement of earth scis. 1972), Newark Gem and Mineral Soc. (pres. 1960s), Tucson Mineral Soc., Masons (Master 1949). Republican. Lutheran. Home: 5711 W Rafter Cir Tucson AZ 85713-4444

ANTHONY (ANTHONY EMMANUEL GERGIANNAKIS), bishop; b. Heraklion, Crete, Mar. 2, 1935. Degree in theology, Theol. Sch., Halki, Constantinople, 1960; MDiv, Yale U., 1964; postgrad., U. Chgo., U. Wis. Ordained deacon Greek Orthodox Ch., 1958, ordained priest, 1960. Priest Holy Trinity Ch., Ansonia, Conn., 1961-64; priest Assumption Ch., Chicago Heights, Ill., 1964-69, Madison, Wis., 1969-73; dean St. George Cathedral, Montreal, 1974-78; elevated to bishop, 1978; titular bishop Ammissos, Denver, 1978-79; bishop San Francisco, 1979—; pres. Archdiocesan Council of Dept. of Edn.; founder St. Nicholas Ranch and Retreat Ctr., Dunlop Calif., northwest Orthodox Found. Retreat Facilities, Tacoma, Wash. Office: Greek Orthodox Diocese 372 Santa Clara Ave San Francisco CA 94127-2090

ANTHONY, BRUCE, management executive, consultant; b. Long Beach, Calif., Sept. 26, 1931; m. Sharon M. Blackmun, Dec. 2, 1978. AB, Calif. State U., San Diego, 1957; MSW(C), Calif. State U., Fresno, 1968; JD, U. Calif., Davis, 1971. Pres. Mgmt. Counsel Inc., Salem, Oreg., 1961—, Anthony Enterprises Inc., Salem, Oreg., 1991—. Mem. Inst. Mgmt. Cons., Rotary (bd. dirs. 1985, Paul Harris fellow), Calif. Soc. Profl. Engrs. (hon. life). Home: 4638 Independence Dr SE Salem OR 97302 Office: Mgmt Counsel Inc 441 Union St NE Salem OR 97301

ANTHONY, ELAINE MARGARET, real estate executive, interior designer; b. Mpls., Apr. 23, 1932; d. Jerome Pius and Adeline (Shea) Clarkin; m. Ronald Carl Anthony, Aug 28, 1954 (div. 1977); children: Richard, Lisa, Laura. Student, U. Minn., 1950-51; AA, Diablo Valley Coll., 1978; postgrad., San Jose (Calif.) State U., 1979, U. Calif., Berkeley, 1983-91. Agt., broker Sycamore Realty, Danville, Calif., 1972-75; broker, project sales mgr. Crocker Homes, Dublin, Calif., 1975-80; exec. v.p. BlackHawk Properties, Danville, 1980-82; broker, project sales mgr. Harold W. Smith Co., Walnut Creek, Calif., 1982-86; pres. Elaine Anthony & Assocs., Inc., San Francisco, 1986—. Mem. vol. coun. San Francisco Symphony, 1986. Mem. Bldg. Industry Assn. (Outstanding Sales Person of Yr. No. Calif. chtp. 1983), Nat. Assn. Home Builders, Inst. Residential Mktg., Commonwealth Club Calif., Calif. Assn. Realtors, San Mateo/Burlingame Bd. Realtors, Bellevue Athletic Club Alameda County. Republican. Roman Catholic. Home and Office: 601 Van Ness Ave # 506 San Francisco CA 94102

ANTHONY, JOHN PETER, college official; b. Watford City, N.D., Aug. 20, 1941; s. John B. and Violet (Holt) A.; m. MaryAnn McClure, Oct. 9, 1966; children: Leslie Ann, Joelle Lynn. PhB, U. N.D., 1967, MS, 1968. Cert. psychol. counselor I and II, vocat. counselor, N.D. Psychiat. social worker U.S. Army, Phoenixville, Pa., 1964-66; counselor Project Talent Search, Devils Lake, N.D., 1968-70; counselor, instr. Lake Region Jr. Coll., Devils Lake, 1970-75, dir. off-campus, 1975-79, dean students, 1970-79; coll. coord. Ea. Wyo. Coll., Douglas, asst. dean, 1979—; evaluator North Cen. Assn., Torrington, Wyo., 1985; dir. Douglas Teaching Ctr., 1986—, Small Bus. Svcs., Douglas, 1986-88. Contbr. articles to profl. publs. Bd. dirs. Converse County Small Bus. Incubator, Douglas, 1985-92, Svc. Corps Of Ret. Execs./Active Corps Execs., Converse County, 1988—. Named Tchr. of Yr., Lake Region Jr. Coll., 1975. Mem. Nat. Community Edn. Assn., Wyo. Adult and Continuing Edn. Assn. (pres. 1991-92), Mountain Plains Adult Edn. Assn. (bd. dirs. 1986-89), Wyo. Alliance for Literacy, Am. Legion, Douglas C. of C. (bd. dirs. 1985-88, spl. svcs. bus. award 1984), Elks. Republican. Lutheran. Office: Ea Wyo Coll 203 N 6th St Douglas WY 82633

ANTIOCO, JOHN F., convenience store chain executive. Sr. v.p. store ops. Southland Corp; COO Pearle Vision, Dallas, 1990; pres., COO Circle K Corp, Phoenix, Ariz., 1991—. Office: The Circle K Corp Box 52084 1601 N 7th Ave Phoenix AZ 85006*

ANTIPA, GREGORY ALEXIS, biology educator, researcher; b. San Francisco, Aug. 9, 1941; s. August Alexander and Amanda (Kockos) A.; m. Sharon Dianne Haughee, Dec. 18, 1966 (dec. 1984); children: Alexander Thomas, Christopher Alexis. AB in Zoology, U. Calif., Berkeley, 1963; MA in Biology, San Francisco State U., 1966; PhD in Zoology, U. Ill., 1970. Postdoctoral fellow U. Chgo., 1970-71, Argonne (Ill.) Nat. Lab., 1971-74; prof. biology Wayne State U., Detroit, 1974-78; prof. biology San Francisco State U., 1978—, acting dir. research, 1986-89. Contbr. numerous articles to profl. jours. NIH Fellow U. Chgo., 1970; Atomic Energy Commn. fellow Argonne Nat. Lab., 1971-74; NSF research grantee, 1978-82. Mem. Am. Soc. Cell Biology, Soc. Protozoologists, Microscopy Soc. Am., Am. Soc. Zoologists, San Francisco Microscopical Soc. (pres. 1986-88). Office: San Francisco State U Dept Biology San Francisco CA 94132

ANTOCH, ZDENEK VINCENT, electrical engineering educator; b. Prague, Czechoslovakia, Oct. 16, 1943; came to U.S., 1950; s. Zdenek Antoch and Marta (Smidova) Frank; m. Maureen O. Shaw, June 24, 1968; 1 child, Anna Marie. BS, Portland State U., 1971, postgrad. in Engring., 1971-73, postgrad. in Physics, 1973-75, MS, 1989, postgrad., 1989—. Research asst. Portland (Oreg.) State U., 1972-75; electronics instr. Portland (Oreg.) Community Coll., 1975-80, 81—; part time instr. Portland (Oreg.) State U., 1989—. Mem. IEEE, Am. Soc. Engring. Edn. Democrat. Office: Portland Community Coll 12000 SW 49th Ave Portland OR 97219-7197

ANTON, WILLIAM R., school system administrator. Supt. of schools Los Angeles Public Schools, 1991—. Office: LA Unified School District Rm 223 A 450 N Grand Ave Los Angeles CA 90012-2100

ANTONE, STEVE, state legislator, farmer; b. Burley, Idaho, Nov. 17, 1921; s. Andrew and Diane (Glover) A.; m. Helen McKevitt, June 15, 1950 (dec. May 27, 1975); 1 child, Steven K.; Diane Meacham, Sept. 16, 1977; 1 child, Jill. State rep., legislature State of Idaho, 1968-94. Named Statesman of the Yr. Pi Sigma Alpha, Pocatello, Idaho, 1983, Dist. Citizen Idaho Statesman News, Boise, Idaho, 1986; recipient Boyd Martin award Assn. of Idaho Cities, Moscow, 1984. Republican. Methodist. Home: 1141 Link St Rupert ID 83350

ANTONINI, MICHAEL JOSEPH, dentist; b. Livermore, Calif., Apr. 21, 1946; s. Joseph and Doris Carolyn (Grana) A.; m. Linda Mae Madigan, May 12, 1973; children: John Michael, Peter Patrick, Gina Marie. BA, Santa Clara U., 1968; DDS, U. Pacific, 1972. Gen. practice dentistry San Francisco, 1972—; mem. exam. com. Calif. State Bd. Dental Examiners, 1986—. Coach baseball St. Brendan Sch., San Francisco, 1988, coach basketball, 1987—; 1st v.p. St. Brendans Men's Club, 1991-92, pres., 1992-93; active St. Ignatius Father's Club, 1992—. Mem. ADA, Calif. Dental Assn. (Best Editorial Newsletter award 1983, 84), San Francisco Dental Soc. (editor newsletter, 1982-84, v.p. 1984-85, pres. 1986-87), Olympic Club. Republican. Roman Catholic. Home: 110 Broadmoor Dr San Francisco CA 94132-2011 Office: Michael J Antonini DDS Inc 2827 Franklin St San Francisco CA 94123-3107

ANTONOVICH, MICHAEL DENNIS, county government official; b. L.A., Aug. 12, 1939; s. Michael and Francis Ann (McColm) A. BA, Calif. State U., L.A., 1963, MA, 1967; postgrad., Hoover Inst., 1968-70, Harvard U., 1984, 87. Govt. and history instr. L.A. Unified Sch. Dist., 1966-72; assemblyman State of Calif., 1972-78; supr. County of L.A., 1980—, chmn. bd. suprs., 1983, 87, 91; instr. Pepperdine U., 1979, Calif. State U., L.A., 1979, 85; Rep. whip Calif. State Assembly, 1976-78; active Pres. Commn. on Privatization, 1987-88, Atty. Gen.'s Missing Children's Adv. Bd., 1987-88, Pres.' U.S.-Japan Adv. Commn., 1984, Commn. of White House Fellowships Regional Panel, 1981-86, governing bd. South Coast Air Quality Mgmt. Dist., L.A. Coliseum Commn., mem., 1981, chmn. 1988; White House apptd. mem. U.S. Del. to UN Internat. Conf. on Indo-Chinese Refugees, Geneva, 1989; appointed by Pres. to Fulbright Scholarship Bd., 1991-93; bd. dirs. Pacific Data Mgmt. Co.; chmn. County-wide Criminal Justice Coordinating Com., 1983, 87, 90-91; charter mem. White House Intergovernmental Sci., Engring., and Tech. Coun., 1993—. Active Tournament of Roses Com., L.A. Zoo Assn., Good Shepherd Luth. Home for Retarded Children, South Pasadena Police Dept. Res.; bd. govs. Glendale (Calif.) Symphony; bd. trustees L.A. C.C., 1969-73; chmn. L.A. County Transp. Comm., 1992; bd. dirs. Boy Scouts Am., San Gabriel Valley Coun. With USNG, 1957-58, USAR. Named Alumnus of Yr. Calif. State U., 1977, Disting. Alumnus of Yr. John Marshall High Sch., 1984, Pub. Ofcl. of Yr. Nat. Fedn. Indian-Ams., 1989; recipient Good Scout award, 1987, Valley Shelter award, 1987, San Fernando Valley Interfaith Coun. award, 1983, Leadership award United Way, 1983, 87, 91, Brotherhood Crusade award, 1983, 87, 91, Didi Hirsch Community Mental Health award, 1984, Award for Caring Foster Parents Assn., 1987, Award of Merit Calif. State U., 1987, Wildlife Way Sta. award, 1984, Nat. Taxpayers Union award, 1984, L.A. Taxpayers Assn. award, 1981, L.A. Dep. Sheriffs Victims of Violent Crimes Found. award, 1981, Topanga C. of C. award, 1983, Menachim Begin medal of achievement Bar-Ilan U., 1983, Outstanding Am. award Nisei VFW, 1985, Thomas Jefferson Rsch. Ctr. Responsible Am. award, 1990, Commitment to Youth award MADD, 1992, Hon. Svc. award PTA, 1992, Award of Appreciation Antelope Valley Social Ctr. Mental Health Assn., 1991, Assn. Community Mental Health Assn., 1991, L.A. chpt. Soc. Hispanic Profl. Engrs., 1992; honored by bd. dirs. San Gabriel Valley Coun. Boy Scouts Am., 1992. Mem. County Suprs. Assn. Calif. (bd. dirs.), Native Sons of Golden West, Phila. Soc., Glendale C. of C., So. Calif. Assn. Govts. (pres.), Elks, Shomrim Soc. So. Calif. (hon.), Sigma Nu. Lutheran. Home: 3023 San Gabriel Ave Glendale CA 91208-1701

Office: County of LA Hall of Adminstrn 500 W Temple St Rm 869 Los Angeles CA 90012-2761

ANTONSON, JOAN MARGARET, historian; b. Mpls., Dec. 1, 1951; d. Lyman Theodore and Gladys (Korzan) A.; m. Donald Ernest Mohr Jr., Oct. 15, 1977 (div.); 1 child, Justin Thomas. BA in History and Secondary Edn., U. Minn., 1973; MA in History, U. Oregon, 1975. Cert. secondary tchr., Alaska. Historian, rsch. assoc. State of Alaska Div. Parks, Anchorage, 1975-79, state historian, 1986—; historian U.S. Bur. Land Mgmt., Anchorage, 1980-81, State of Alaska Hist. Commn., Anchorage, 1981-86; instr. U. Alaska, 1977—. Author: (with W.S. Hanable) Alaska's Heritage, 1986; Administrative History of Sitka National Park, History of the Anchorage Museum of History and Art, 1993; editor Heritage newsletter, 1986—. Bd. dirs. race com. Alaska Women's Run, 1986-90; bd. dirs., sec. Friends of Ind. Mine, Anchorage, 1986-88; bd. dirs., sec., pres. Cook Inlet Hist. Soc., 1979-85. U. Minn. scholar, 1973. Mem. Alaska Hist. Soc. (bd. dirs. 1983-86, assoc. editor jour. Alaska History 1984—, Beaver Log Pres.'s award 1985, 90, 91), Western History Assn., Am. Assn. for State and Local History (awards chmn. 1990—, membership chmn. 1982-87, cert. commendation 1988), Totally Fit Running Team (capt. 1988-91), Anchorage Running Club (bd. dirs. 1987-90). Home: 1026 Barrow St Anchorage AK 99501-3647 Office: Office of History and Arch PO Box 107001 Anchorage AK 99510-7001

ANTREASIAN, GARO ZAREH, painter, lithographer, art educator; b. Indpls., Feb. 16, 1922; s. Zareh Minas and Takouhie (Daniell) A.; m. Jeanne Glascock, May 2, 1947; children: David Garo, Thomas Berj. B.F.A., Herron Sch. Art, 1948; D.F.A. (hon.), Ind. U.-Purdue U. at Indpls., 1972. Instr. Herron Sch. Art, 1948-64; tech. dir. Tamarind Lithography Workshop, Los Angeles, 1960-61; prof. art U. N.Mex., 1964-87, chmn. dept. art, 1981-84; tech. dir. Tamarind Inst., U. N.Mex., 1970-72; vis. lectr., artist numerous univs.; Bd. dirs. Albuquerque Mus., 1980-90. Prin. author: The Tamarind Book of Lithography: Art and Techniques, 1970; one-man shows include Malvina Miller Gallery, San Francisco, 1971, Marjorie Kauffman Gallery, Houston, 1975-79, 84, 86, U. Colo., Boulder, 1972, Calif. Coll. Arts & Crafts, Oakland, 1973, Miami U., Oxford, Ohio, 1973, Kans. State U., 1973, Atlanta Coll. Art, 1974, U. Ga., Athens, 1974, Alice Simsar Gallery, Ann Arbor, 1977-79, Elaine Horwich Gallery, Santa Fe, 1977-79, Mus. of N.Mex., Santa Fe, 1979, Robischon Gallery, Denver, 1984, 86, 90, Moss-Chumley Gallery, Dallas, 1987, Rettig-Martinez Gallery, Santa Fe, 1988, 91, 92, U. N.Mex. Art Mus., 1988, Albuquerque Mus., 1988, Louis Newman Gallery, L.A., 1989, Expositum Gallery, Mexico City, 1989, State U. Coll., Cortland, N.Y., 1991, Mus. Art, U. Ariz., Tucson, 1991; exhibited group shows Phila. Print Club, 1960-63, Ind. Artists, 1947-63, White House, 1966, Nat. Lithographic Exhbn. Fla. State U., 1965, Library Congress, 1961-66, Bklyn. Mus., 1958-68, 76, U.S. Pavilion Venice Biennale, 1970, Internat. Biennial, Bradford, Eng., 1972-74, Internat. Biennial, Tokyo, 1972, City Mus. Hong Kong, 1972, Tamarind UCLA, 1985, Roswell Mus., 1989, Pace Gallery, 1990, Worcester (Mass.) Art Mus., 1990, Amon Carter Mus., Ft. Worth, 1990, Albuquerque Mus., 1991, 92, Art Mus. U. N.Mex., 1991, 92; represented in permanent collections: Bklyn. Mus., Guggenheim Mus., N.Y.C., Cin. Mus., Chgo. Art Inst., Ind. State Mus., Mus. Modern Art, N.Y.C., Library of Congress, Met. Mus., N.Y.C., also, Boston, Indpls., Seattle, Phila., San Diego, Dallas, Worcester art museums, Los Angeles County Mus., murals, Ind. U., Butler U., Ind. State Office Bldg. Fulbright vis. lectr. U. São Paulo and Found. Armando Alvares Penteado, Brazil, 1985. Combat artist with USCGR, World War II, PTO. Recipient Distinguished Alumni award Herron Sch. Art, 1972, N.Mex. Annual Gov.'s award, 1987; Grantee Nat. Endowment for Arts, 1983. Mem. World Print Council (dir. 1980-87), Nat. Print Council Am. (co-pres. 1980-82), Coll. Art Assn. Am. (dir. 1977-80). Home: 6512 Katson Ave NE Albuquerque NM 87109

ANUTA, KARL FREDERICK, lawyer; b. Menominee, Mich., May 16, 1935; s. Michael J. and Marianne (Strelic) A.; m. Barbara L. Olds Anuta, June 23, 1956; children: Karl Gregory Anuta, Natasha Louise Anuta. BA, Macalester Coll., 1957; LLB, U. Colo. Sch. Law, 1960. Bar: U.S. Supreme Ct., U.S. Dist. Ct., U.S. Ct. Appeals (D.C. and 10th cirs.). Staff atty. Office of Regional Solicitor U.S. Dept. Interior, Denver, 1960-63; staff atty. Frontier Refining Co., Denver, 1963-67, gen. counsel, 1967-68; sr. atty. Husky Oil Co., Denver, 1968-79, chief regional atty., 1979-83, gen. counsel, 1983-84; counsel Duncan, Weinberg & Miller, Denver, 1985-87; atty. pvt. practice, Boulder, Colo., 1987—. Pres. Interfaith Coun. Boulder, 1964, Hist. Boulder, Inc., 1980; mem. City Boulder Landmarks Bd., 1981-91; v.p. Colo. Chautauqua Assn., 1982, v.p. Boulder Hist. Soc., 1992; chmn. Boulder Coun. Internat. Visitors, 1986-88; bd. dirs. Spl. Transit System Boulder County, 1988—; mem. County Hist. Preservation Adv. Bd., 1992—. Mem. ABA, Colo. Bar Assn. Republican. Presbyterian. Office: 1720 14th St PO Box 1001 Boulder CO 80306

AOKI, JOHN H., hotel chain executive; b. 1931. With Aoki Corp., Tokyo, 1954—; chmn. Westin Hotel Co., Seattle, 1988—. Office: Westin Hotels & Resorts The Westin Bldg 2001 6th Ave Seattle WA 98121-2522

AOKI, MASANAO, economics educator; b. Hiroshima, Japan, May 14, 1931; came to U.S. 1956; BS, U. Tokyo, 1953, MS, 1955; PhD, UCLA, 1960; DSc, Tokyo Inst. Tech., 1966. Prof. elec. engring. and econs. UCLA, 1963-73, 75-81, 85-92; prof. U. Ill., 1973-75, U. Osaka, Japan, 1981-85. Author: Optimization of Stochastic Systems, 1967, 2d edit., 1989, State Space Modeling of Time Series, 1987, 2d edit., 1990, also 5 others. Mem. Econometric Soc., IEEE Control Sys. Soc., Am. Econ. Assn., Am. Statis. Assn., Soc. of Econ. Dynamics & Control (pres. 1982-83). Office: UCLA Dept Econs 405 Hilgard Ave Los Angeles CA 90024-1477

AOUDE, IBRAHIM GEORGES, ethnic studies educator; b. Jaffa, Palestine, Jan. 7, 1945; came to U.S., 1970; s. Jiryes Ibrahim and Sophie (Hanania) A.; m. Liana Mary Meyer Petranek, Sept. 20, 1976. BBA, U. Hawaii, 1974, PhD, 1980; MBA, Calif. State U., L.A., 1976. Lectr. ethnic studies and polit. sci. depts. U. Hawaii, Honolulu, 1981-85, academic advisor liberal studies program, 1986-89, assoc. prof. ethnic studies, 1990—. Author: (alias B.J. Odeh) Lebanon: Dynamics of Conflict, 1985). Pres. Am. for Impartiality in the Mid. East, Honolulu, 1992—; bd. dirs. People's Fund Bd., Honolulu, 1992—, Rainbow Peace Fund Bd., Honolulu, 1992—. Mem. Assn. Asian Am. Studies, Western Polit. Sci. Assn. Office: U Hawaii Ethnic Studies East-West Rd 4 4D Honolulu HI 96822

APATOFF, MICHAEL JOHN, finance executive; b. Harvey, Ill., June 12, 1955; s. William and Frances (Brown) A. BA, Reed Coll., 1980. Chief legis. asst. to U.S. Congressman Al Ullman, Chmn. Ways and Means Com., Washington, 1978-80; spl. asst. to U.S. Congressman Tom Foley, Majority Whip, Washington, 1981-85; exec. v.p., COO Chgo. Merc. Exch., 1986-90; exec. v.p., COO, prin. RCM Capital Mgmt., San Francisco, 1991—. Mem. World Affairs Coun., Com. on Fgn. Affairs, Japan Am. Soc. Democrat. Home: 2400 Pacific Ave Apt 710 San Francisco CA 94115-1229 Office: RCM Capital Mgmt Four Embarcadero San Francisco CA 94111

APFEL, GARY, lawyer; b. N.Y.C., June 2, 1952; s. Willy and Jenny (Last) A.; m. Serena Jakobovits, June 16, 1980; children: Alyssa J., I. Michael, Alanna J., Stephen J. BA, NYU magna cum laude, 1973; JD, Columbia U., 1976. Bar: N.Y. 1977, Calif. 1988, U.S. Dist. Ct. (so. and ea. dists.) N.Y. 1977, U.S. Dist. Ct. (cen. dist.) Calif. 1988, U.S. Ct. Appeals (9th cir.) 1988. Assoc. Sullivan & Cromwell, N.Y.C., 1976-80; assoc. LeBoeuf, Lamb, Leiby & MacRae, N.Y.C., 1980-84, ptnr., 1985-88; ptnr. Kaye, Scholer, Fierman, Hays & Handler, L.A., 1988—. Kent scholar Columbia U., 1976. Mem. ABA, Calif. State Bar Assn. (bus. law sect. corps. com.), Phi Beta Kappa. Office: Kaye Scholer Fierman et al 1999 Avenue Of The Stars Los Angeles CA 90067-6022

APGAR, DAVID ALLEN, clinical pharmacist; b. Plainfield, N.J., June 8, 1945; s. Allen Wood and Dorothy (Brennan) A. BS in Pharmacy, U. R.I., 1967; PharmD, U. Mich., 1968. Cert. pharmacist practioner; cert. physician asst. Staff pharmacist USPHS Indian Health Svc., Phoenix Indian Med. Ctr., 1969-71, 72-74, coord. pharmacy rsch./edn., 1974-76; staff pharmacist St. Joseph Hosp., Tucson, 1971; clin. instr. U. of Ariz. Coll. of Pharmacy, Tucson, 1971-72; dir. pharmacist practitioner tng. program USPHS Clin. Support Ctr., Phoenix Indian Med. Ctr., 1971; asst. chief Clin. Pharmacy Svcs., Phoenix Indian Med. Ctr., 1978-88; pharmacist cons. Federated States of Micronesia, USPHS and NHSC, Pohnpei, 1988-91; spl. asst. to dir. Indian Health Svc. Clin. Support Ctr., Phoenix, 1991-92; asst. prof. and mgr. clin. pharm. svcs. U. Ariz. Coll. of Pharmacy and Kino Community Hosp., Tucson, 1992—; speaker numerous health profl. groups. Mem. Am. Soc. Hosp. Pharmacists, Am. Pharm. Assn., USPHS Commd. Officers Assn., Internat. Pharmacy Fedn. Home: 4381 W Camino de Venias Tucson AZ 85745 Office: Kino Community Hosp Pharm 2800 E Ajo Way Tucson AZ 85713

APKER, BURTON MARCELLUS, JR., lawyer; b. Chetek, Wis., Aug. 26, 1924; s. Burton Marcellus Sr. and Mary C. (Farrington) A.; m. Geraldine F. Apker, Sept. 23, 1950; children: David B., Gerrie Apker Kurtz, Carolyn A. Thompson, Thomas P. JD magna cum laude, U. Notre Dame, 1948. Bar: Wis. 1949, Ariz. 1961, U.S. Supreme Ct. 1970, U.S. Ct. Appeals (9th cir.) 1972, U.S. Ct. Appeals (10th cir.) 1978. Pvt. practice law Chetek, 1949-59; assoc. counsel Phoenix Title and Trust, Tucson, 1959-61; officer, dir. Evans, Kitchel & Jenckes, P.C., Phoenix, Ariz., 1961-85; of counsel Kaufman, Apker & Nearhood, P.C., Phoenix, 1985-87; pres., bd. dirs. Apker, Apker, Haggard & Kurtz, P.C., 1987—; judge pro tem Maricopa County Superior Ct., Phoenix, 1982—, Ariz. Ct. Appeals, Phoenix, 1986—; arbitrator Am. Arbitration Assn. Note editor U. Notre Dame Law Rev., 1947. Chmn. Phoenix Adjustment Bd. #1, 1964-67. With USN, 1943-46, PTO. Mem. Assn. Trial Lawyers Am. Office: Apker Apker Haggard & Kurtz PC 2111 E Highland Ave Ste 230 Phoenix AZ 85016-4733

APODACA, ROBERT ANTHONY, military officer; b. Laredo, Tex., Jan. 27, 1964; s. Victor Joe Jr. and Rosalind (Alexander) Cain; m. Dora Annette Boyd, Aug. 18, 1984 (div. June 1985); m. Laura Meredith Ray, May 9, 1992. Student, USAF Acad., 1981-82; BSEE, U. Ala., 1986. Commd. 2d lt. USAF, 1986, advanced through grades to capt., 1990; satellite ops. officer 2d Satellite Control Squadron, Falcon AFB, Colo., 1986, ground systems engring. analyst, 1986-89, sr. satellite command & control systems engr., 1989-91; comdr. GPS Satellite Ops. Crew, 1991; flight test engr. Phillips Lab. Lasers and Imaging Directorate, Kirtland AFB, N.Mex., 1991-93, comdr. mission operations, 1993—. CPR and 1st aid instr. ARC, Patterson AFB, Colo., 1989-91, Kirtland AFB, 1991—; bd. dirs. Nat. League of Families, 1990-92. Mem. IEEE, Air Force Assn., Capstone Engring. Soc. (bd. dirs. 1990—). Home: 1017-B 24th Loop SE Albuquerque NM 87116-1122 Office: Phillips Lab Flight Test Br Kirtland A F B NM 87117

APODACA, RUDY SAMUEL, judge; b. Las Cruces, N.Mex., Aug. 8, 1939; s. Raymond and Elisa (Alvarez) A.; m. Bunny N. Gray, Nov. 1958 (div. 1963); m. Nancy R. Apodaca, Jan. 16, 1967; children: Cheryl Ann, Carla Renee, Cynthia Lynn, Rudy Samuel. BS, N.Mex. State U., 1961; JD, Georgetown U., 1964. Bar: N.Mex. 1964, U.S. Dist. Ct. N. Mex. 1965, U.S. Ct. Appeals (10th cir.) 1965, U.S. Supreme Ct. 1971. Pvt. practice Las Cruces, 1964-86; appellate judge N. Mex. Ct. Appeals, Santa Fe, 1987—; real estate broker, Las Cruces, 1984-86; gen. counsel Citizens Bank Las Cruces, 1976-86. Author: The Waxen Image, 1977; author screenplay: A Rare Thing, 1987. Bd. regents N.Mex. State U., 1975-83; mem. Coord. Coun. for Higher Edn., Santa Fe, 1975-78; pres. Assocs. N.Mex. State U., Las Cruces, 1982-84; bd. dirs. Am. S.W. Theatre Co., Las Cruces, 1984-86. Capt. U.S. Army, 1964-66. Mem. Inst. Jud. Adminstrn., N.Mex. Bar Assn., Poets and Writers, Phi Kappa Phi, Am. Mensa, Intertel, Pen Ctr. USA West, Pen N.Mex. Democrat. Home: 829 Canterbury Arc Las Cruces NM 88005-3715 Office: New Mexico Ct of Appeals 180 W Amador Ave Las Cruces NM 88005

APONTÉ, CHRISTOPHER BENNEDETTEY, artistic director, choreographer, educator; b. N.Y.C., May 4, 1950; s. German and Anna (Perez) A. Diploma, Nat. Acad. Ballet and Theatre Arts, 1978. Prin. dancer Harkness Ballet, N.Y.C., 1968-74, Alvin Ailey Co., N.Y.C., 1974-75, Am. Ballet Theatre, N.Y.C., 1975-76, Ballet de Marseille Rolland Petite, Marseille, France, 1976-77, Balleto Reggio Emillia, Italy, 1978-79, numerous European dance cos., France, Italy, Fed. Republic of Germany, 1978-80; with Cleve. Ballet, 1981-82, Boston Ballet, 1982-85; dir. Spokane (Wash.) Ballet Co., 1986—; instr., choreographer Spokane Ballet, 1986—; producer Tours to the Orient, 1980-86. Creator 33 ballets since 1986 including Stravinsky's Violen Concerto, Lady Macbeth, Eau de Koln, Song of the Earth, Rhapsody in Blue. Democrat. Catholic. Office: Spokane Ballet W 820 Sprague Spokane WA 99204

APPEL, JACOB J., information services technology executive; b. N.Y.C., Sept. 2, 1940; s. Gustav and Hilda A.; m. Anne M. Liuzzo, Feb. 1, 1962. BEE, Cooper Union, N.Y.C., 1961; MSEE, UCLA, 1963; ScD in Elec. Engring., Columbia U., 1970; Degree in Advanced Mgmt., Harvard U., 1992. Mem. tech. staff Hughes Aircraft, Culver City, Calif., 1961-65; with Bell Labs., various cities, N.J., 1965-83; asst. v.p. Bell Communications Rsch., various cities in N.J., 1984-86; asst. v.p. tech. planning Pacific Bell, San Ramon, Calif., 1986-88; v.p. tech. ops. Pacific Bell Info. Svcs., San Ramon, 1988—. Contbr. articles to profl. jours. Sci. adv. coun. Mills Coll., Oakland, Calif., 1986—. Hughes Aircraft fellow; doctoral fellowship Bell Labs. Mem. IEEE (chmn. COMSOC com. network ops. and mgmt.), IEEE Communications Soc., IEEE Computer Soc. Home: 1364 Virginia St Danville CA 94526-1243

APPEL, JUDITH ANN, interior decorator; b. Hollywood, Calif., Apr. 28, 1939; d. Paul Sayre and Wilma (Paul) Carnes; m. Cyril William Appel, June 30, 1965 (div. 1990); 1 child, Elizabeth Suzanne. BS, U. Calif., Santa Barbara, 1961. Elem. tchr. Anne Arundel (Md.) Sch. Dist., 1961-63, U.S. Army Dependent Schs., Heidelberg and Munich, Germany, 1963-66, Monterey Sch. Dist., Marina, Calif., 1967-68; owner Decorating Den, Monterey and Salinas, Calif., 1979—. Named Franchise Owner of Yr., First Calif. Divisional Conf., 1989. Mem. Salinas Steinbeck Rotary. Republican. Home and Office: 140F Casentini St Salinas CA 93907

APPELBAUM, BRUCE DAVID, physician; b. Lincroft, N.J., Apr. 24, 1957; s. John S. and Shirley B. (Wolfson) A. BS in pharmacy, Rutgers Coll., 1980; MS in pharmacology, Emory U., 1983, PhD in pharmacology, 1985; MD, Medical Coll. Ga., 1989. Diplomate Nat. Bd. Med. Examiners. Rsch. assoc. Emory U. Dept. Pharmacology, Atlanta, 1985; resident physician U. Calif. Dept. Psychiatry, Irvine, Calif., 1989—; cons. Avalon Med. Group, Garden Grove, Calif, 1990—; com. mem. quality assurance, Fountainblue Nursing Facility, Anaheim, Calif., 1990—. Contbr. articles to profl. jours. Recipient Nat. Rsch. Svc. award Nat. Inst. Health, 1982-83, Eastern Student Rsch. Forum U. Miami Medical Sch., 1984, Nat. Student Rsch. Forum, 1987. Mem. Am. Medical Assn., Am. Psychiatric Assn., Orange County Psychiatric Soc., Sigma Xi. Democrat. Jewish. Home: 18602 Creek Ln Huntington Beach CA 92648-1629 Office: U Calif Irvine Medical Ctr 101 City Dr South Orange CA

APPELBAUM, MATTHEW ARON, computer scientist; b. Bklyn., Nov. 30, 1951; s. Harold and Blanche (Reiner) A.; m. Katharine J. Teter, Aug. 14, 1982. BS in Math., CUNY, 1973; MS in Computer Sci., U. Wis., 1975. Mgr. tng. and cons. Netwise, Inc., Boulder, 1988-91; computer cons. Boulder, 1991—. City councilman City of Boulder, 1988-91, dep. mayor, 1991—; bd. dirs. Denver Regional Coun. of Govts., Denver, 1990—; co-chair, bd. dirs. PLAN-Boulder County, 1984-87; mem. Parks and Recreation Adv. Bd., Boulder, 1984-86. Mem. Assn. for Computing Machinery. Democrat. Home: 200 Pawnee Dr Boulder CO 80303 Office: City of Boulder PO Box 791 Boulder CO 80306

APPENZELLER, OTTO, neurologist, researcher; b. Czernowitz, Romania, Dec. 11, 1927; came to U.S., 1963; s. Emmanuel Adam and Josephine (Metsch) A.; m. Judith Bryce, Dec. 11, 1956; children: Timothy, Martin, Peter. MBBS, Sydney U., Australia, 1957, MD, 1966; PhD, U. London, Eng., 1963. Diplomate Am. Bd. Psychiatry and Neurology. Prof. U. N. Mex., Albuquerque, 1970-90; vis. prof. McGill U., Montreal, 1977; hon. rsch. fellow U. London, Eng., 1983; vis. scientist Oxygen Transport Program Lovelace Med. Found., Albuquerque, 1990-92; pres. N.Mex. Health Enhancement and Marathon Clinics Rsch. Found., Albuquerque, 1992—; U.S.-India exch. scientist NSF, 1992; Fogarty internat. exch. scientist, Kiev, Ukraine, 1993; mem. rsch. com. UNESCO Internat. Coun. Sports and Phys. Edn., 1978—; ref. Med. Rsch. Coun. New Zealand, 1986—, reviewer, 1988—; mem. editorial bd. numerous peer reviewed med. jours. Author: The Autonomic Nervous System, 4th edit., 1990; co-author: Headache, 1984; editor: Pathogenesis and Management of Headache, 1976, Health Aspects of Endurance Training, 1978, Sports Medicine, 3d edit., 1988, Jour. Headache, 1975-77, Annals of Sports Medicine, 1984-88; translator: Neurologic Differential Diagnosis (M. Mumentaler), 1992. Grantee Diabetes Rsch. and Edn. Found., 1988, individual health scientist exch. program Fogarty Internat. Ctr., Nat. Insts. Health to A. A. Bogomoletz Inst. Physiology, Kiev, Ukraine, 1993. Fellow ACP, Am. Acad. Neurology.

APPLE, DANIEL BRYCE, finance company executive, financial planner; b. Nevada City, Calif., June 30, 1951; s. Stanley Bryce and Bonnie Ruth (Kelley) A. BA, Chico (Calif.) State U., 1973. Engring. technician Clendenen & Assoc., Auburn, Calif., 1976-77; field engr. Pacific Gas & Electric Co., Sacramento, 1974-76, United Engrs. & Contractors, Richland, Wash., 1977-81; civil and structural engr. Bechtel Corp., Richland, 1981-84; rep. Fin. Network Investment Corp., Grass Valley, Calif., 1984-89, br. mgr., 1984—, prin., 1989—. Mem. Inst. Cert. Fin. Planners, Gold Country Estate Planning Coun. (charter, treas. Grass Valley chpt. 1989—). Republican. Office: Fin Network Investment Corp 350 Crown Point Cir Ste 200 Grass Valley CA 95945-9089

APPLE, STEVEN ANTHONY, city official; b. Los Angeles, Dec. 27, 1954; s. Nick P. and Joanne (Wilkin) A.; m. Rebecca McCorkle, Aug. 9, 1980. BA in Anthropology, Ohio State U., 1977; M in City Planning, San Diego State U., 1983. Freelance environ. cons. San Diego, 1979-80; environ. planner MSA, Inc., San Diego, 1981-82; land use planner New Horizons Planning Cons., San Diego, 1982-84, County San Diego, 1984-86; dir. community devel. City of Solana Beach (Calif.), 1986--; guest lectr., San Diego State U. 1984. Environ. chmn. Torrey Pines Community Planning Group, Del Mar, Calif., 1985-89. Univ. scholar, San Diego State U., 1983. Mem. Am. Planning Assn., San Diego County Archeol. Soc. (libr. 1979-80), Eagle Scout Alumni Assn. (exec. com. San Diego 1985), Mensa. Office: City of Solana Beach 380 Stevens Ave Ste 120 Solana Beach CA 92075-2068

APPLEBERRY, WALTER THOMAS, aerospace engineering project executive; b. Wilmington, N.C., Mar. 8, 1926; s. William Pembroke and Carroll Ernesteen (Shingleton) A.; m. Mae Magdalene Bozeman, Feb. 21, 1953; children: Thomas Kent, Robert William, Rebecca Jean. BS in Mech. Engring., Calif. State U., Long Beach, 1974. Facilities engr. Douglas Aircraft, Long Beach, 1942-50; missionary Mormon Ch., Salt Lake City, 1950-53; supr. engring. test McDonnell Douglas, Huntington Beach, Calif., 1953-74; adv. engring. project mgr. Rockwell Internat., Downey, Calif., 1974—. Patentee in field. Mem. Pi Tau Sigma. Republican. Mormon. Home: 3440 Val Verde Ave Long Beach CA 90808 Office: Rockwell Internat 12214 Lakewood Blvd Downey CA 90242-2693

APPLEGATE, ARTHUR DAVID, computer software developer, consultant; b. Glendale, Calif., May 23, 1965; s. Howard Cornell Applegate and Mary Alice Keenan. BS in Computer Sci. with distinction, U. Sydney, Australia, 1985. Pres. Crystal Script, Sydney, 1983-85; sr. computer scientist Inference Corp., L.A., 1986-90; software engr. Wall Data Inc., Redmond, Wash., 1990-91; pres. Applegate Software, Redmond, Wash., 1991—. Author computer software FastData, 1991, OptiMem for Windows, 1991, SmartHeap, 1992. Mem. Wash. Software Assn. (speaker 1992). Office: Applegate Software 4317 264th Ave NE Redmond WA 98053-8730

APPLETON, ELAINE, alcohol and drug dependency therapist; b. Pasadena, Calif., Aug. 31, 1942; d. Eldredge and Margaret (Dumont) Appleton; m. Duane H. Denfeld, July 21, 1962 (div. 1974); children: Dennis, René, Charles Denfeld, Michael, Nichole Appleton. Student, Portland State U., 1960-62, 72-73, Portland State U., 1976-78. Cert. in alcoholism counseling, Oreg. Tchr. Head Start, Portland, 1978; human resources asst. Multnomah County, Portland, 1979-80; alcoholism counselor Kaiser Permanente, Portland, 1980-83, team leader, 1983-88, alcohol-drug therapist, 1988—; lectr. Kaiser Permanente, 1988—, cons. labor and delivery, 1989-92; lectr. in field. Democrat. Office: Kaiser Permanente 3414 N Kaiser Center Dr Portland OR 97227

APPLETON, JAMES ROBERT, university president, educator; b. North Tonawanda, N.Y., Jan. 20, 1937; s. Robert Martin and Emma (Mollnow) A.; m. Carol Koelsch, Aug. 8, 1959; children: Steven, Jon, Jennifer. AB in Social Sci., Wheaton Coll., 1958; MA, PhD, Mich. State U., 1965. Lectr. Mich. State U., East Lansing, 1969-72; assoc. dean students Oakland U., Rochester, Mich., 1965-68, dean student life, 1968-72, assoc. prof. behavioral scis., 1969-72, v.p., 1969-72; v.p. student affairs U. So. Calif., L.A., 1972-82, v.p. devel., 1982-87; pres., Univ. prof. U. Redlands, Calif., 1987—. Author: (with others) Pieces of Eight: Rights, Roles & Styles of the Dean: guest editor Nat. Assn. Student Personnel Adminstrs. Jour., 1971; contbr. articles to profl. jours. Bd. dirs. So. Calif. Ind. Colls., Assn. Ind. Calif. Colls. and Univs., Inland Action; trustee San Francisco Presbyn. Sem. 1st lt. U.S. Army, 1958-60. Named One of 100 Emerging Young Leaders in Higher Edn., Am. Council Edn./Change, 1978; recipient Fred Turner award Nat. Assn. Student Personnel Adminstrs., 1980. Mem. AAUP, NCAA (mem. pres.'s commn.), Am. Assn. Higher Edn., Western Coll. Assn. (pres.). Home: 1861 Rossmont Dr Redlands CA 92373-7219 Office: U of Redlands 1200 E Colton Ave PO Box 3080 Redlands CA 92373-0999

APPLETON, PETER ARTHUR, motion picture editor and cameraman; b. Denver, June 10, 1941; s. David Olof and Dorothea Virginia (Smith) A.; m. Wanda Hoskins, Apr. 10, 1964; 1 child, Claire Palmer Brown. BA in Journalism, U. Denver, 1963; MA in Comm., U. Pa., 1964. Freelance film and video editor, cameraman, L.A., 1964-89, Portland, Oreg., 1990—; instr. cinematography Columbia Coll., Hollywood, Calif., 1980. Film editor Buffalo Bill, 1975 (1st Pl. Berlin Film Festival), The Late Show, 1977, Rainy Day Friends, 1984, The Passage, 1987, Iron Heart, 1991; sound editor My Own Private Idaho, 1991, Even Cowgirls Get the Blues, 1993; editor, dir. photography When I Am King, 1981; dir. photography TV series The Optimist, 1982, also numerous others; photographs exhibited Am. Imprint photographic exhbn., L.A., 1989, Portland, Oreg., 1990. Recipient award Indsl. Film Producers Assn., 1973, cert. Chgo. Internat. Film Festival, 1973, CINE Golden Eagle award Coun. on Non-Theatrical Events, 1978. Mem. Internat. Alliance Motion Picture and Theatrical Stage Employees, Internat. Underwater Explorers Soc. (life), Phi Beta Kappa. Democrat. Home: 1335 SE Morrison St Portland OR 97214-2422

APT, KENNETH ELLIS, arms control and verification analyst; b. Bellingham, Wash., Apr. 27, 1945; s. William H. Jr. and Clara R. (Dahlke) A.; children: Aimee C., Julie R. BA cum laude, Western Wash. U., 1967; PhD, MIT, 1971. Internat. nuclear safeguards insp. IAEA, Vienna, Austria, 1978-80; staff mem. Los Alamos (N.Mex.) Nat. Lab., 1971-78, asst. assoc. dir., 1980-84, assoc. chemistry div. leader, 1984-88, staff mem. Ctr. for Nat. Security Studies, 1988-91, program mgr. for arms reduction verification, 1991—; tech. analyst and cons. U.S. Dept. Energy, U.S. Dept. Def., Washington, 1988—. Contbr. articles to profl. jours. NSF grad. trainee, 1970. Mem. AAAS, Am. Chem. Soc. (div. Nuclear Chemistry and Tech.). Office: Los Alamos Nat Lab PO Box 1663 Los Alamos NM 87545-0001

APTHEKER, BETTINA FAY, women's studies educator; b. Ft. Bragg, N.C., Sept. 2, 1944; d. Herbert and Fay P. Aptheker; m. Jack H. Kurzweil, Aug. 29, 1965 (div. Jan. 1979); children: Joshua, Jennifer. BA, U. Calif., Berkeley, 1967; MA, San Jose State U., 1976; PhD, U. Calif., Santa Cruz, 1983. Lectr. San Jose State U., San Jose, Calif., 1976-79; adj. lectr. U. Calif., Santa Cruz, 1980-87, asst. prof., 1987-89, assoc. prof., 1989—. Author: The Morning Breaks: The Trial of Angela Davis, 1975, Woman's Legacy: Essays on Race, Class and Sex in American History, 1982, Tapestries of Life: Women's Work, Women's Consciousness and the Meaning of Daily Experience, 1989. Mem. Nat. Women's Studies Assn., Assn. Black Women Historians, Lesbian Alliance, Monterey Bay Zen Ctr. Jewish. Office: Dept Womens Studies Kresge Coll U Calif Santa Cruz CA 95064

APURON, ANTHONY SABLAN, archbishop; b. Agana, Guam, Nov. 1, 1945; s. Manuel Taijito and Ana Santos (Sablan) P. BA, St. Anthony Coll., 1969; MDiv, Maryknoll Sem., 1972, M Theology, 1973; MA in Liturgy, Notre Dame U., 1974. Ordained priest Roman Catholic ch., 1972, ordained bishop, 1984, installed archbishop, 1986. Chmn. Diocesan Liturgical Commn., Agana, 1974-86; vice chmn. Chamorro Lang. Commn., Agana,

1984-86; aux. bishop Archdiocese of Agana, 1984-85, archbishop, 1986—; chmn. Interfaith Vols. Caregivers, Agana, 1984—; mem. Civilian Adv. com., Agana, 1986—; pres. Cath. Bishops' Conf. of Pacific, 1990—; v.p. Cath. Bishops' Conf. of Aceania, 1990—. Author: A Structural Analysis of the Content of Myth in the Thought of Mircea Eliade, 1973. Chmn. Cath. Ednl. Radio. Named Most Outstanding Young Man, Jaycees of Guam, 1984. Office: Archbishop's Office Cuesta San Ramon Agana GU 96910

APYAN, ROSEANNE LUCILLE, nurse; b. Kenosha, Wis., Jan. 25, 1949; d. Sarkis and Angel (Hovigimian) A. Diploma, Decatur Meml. Hosp. Sch. Nursing, 1972; BS, Millikin U., 1972; instr.'s credential, Calif. Community Colls., 1977. RN, Calif., Ill. Med./surg. nurse St. Joseph's Med. Ctr., Burbank, Calif., 1972-74, critical care nurse ICU, 1974-78, asst. head nurse ICU, 1978-80, head nurse ICU, 1980-82; vascular nurse specialist Drs. Dulawa, Andros, Harris, Oblath and Schneider, Burbank, 1982-93. Contbr. articles to profl. jours. Active health enhancement adv. coun. MidValley YWCA, Van Nuys, Calif., 1985-90; vol. L.A. Marathon, 1989, Spl. Olympics, 1990, 91, 92. Mem. AACCN (San Fernando Valley, Calif. chpt.), Soc. for Peripheral Vascular Nurses (nat. bd. trustees 1989-93, chairperson local interest groups 1990-92), Single Ski Club (L.A., sec. 1977-78, membership chmn. 1982-83). Republican. Home: 330 N Maple St Apt G Burbank CA 91505-3450

ARABE, MICHAEL DON, publishing company executive; b. El Dorado, Ark., Jan. 29, 1947; s. Fred John and Evelyne (Nelson) A.; m. Laurie Elaine Donaldson, Oct. 6, 1984; children: David Nelson, William Christopher. BS in Econs., La. State U., 1972, postgrad., 1973. Project leader Gulf South Rsch. Inst., Baton Rouge, 1973-77; planning coord. Dept. Culture, Recreation and Tourism, Baton Rouge, 1976-77; sr. planner U.S. Dept. Interior, Denver, 1977-82; founder, pres. Michael Dean Inc., Denver, 1982-87; dir. franchise support CelluLand Inc., San Diego, 1987-89; chief exec. officer COMPS Inc., San Diego, 1989—. Contbr. articles to profl. jours. Recipient Golden Antenna award, CelluLand, 1988, Champion's award, Leadership Mgmt., Inc., 1984, Cert of Merit, La. Gov. Edwin Edwards, 1977, others. Office: COMPS Inc 5414 Oberlin Dr Ste 300 San Diego CA 92121-4745

ARABIAN, ARMAND, state supreme court justice; b. N.Y.C., Dec. 12, 1934; s. John and Aghavnie (Yalian) A.; m. Nancy Arabian, Aug. 26, 1962; children: Allison Ann, Robert Armand. BSBA, Boston U., 1956, JD, 1961; LLM, U. So. Calif., L.A., 1970; LLD (hon.), Southwestern Sch. Law, 1990, Pepperdine U., 1990. Bar: Calif. 1962, U.S. Supreme Ct. 1966. Dep. dist. atty. L.A. County, 1962-63; pvt. practice law Van Nuys, Calif., 1963-72; judge Mcpl. Ct., L.A., 1972-73, Superior Ct., L.A., 1973-83; assoc. justice U.S. Ct. Appeals Calif., L.A., 1983-90, U.S. Supreme Ct. Calif., San Francisco, 1990—. 1st lt. U.S. Army, 1956-58. Recipient Stanley Litz Meml. award San Fernando Valley Bar Assn., 1986, Lifetime Achievement award San Fernando Valley Bar Assn., 1993/. Mem. Calif. Judges Assn., San Fernando Criminal Cts. Bar Assn. Republican. Office: US Supreme Ct Calif 9th Fl 303 2ns St San Francisco CA 94107

ARAGON, JANICE LYNN, association executive; b. Fresno, Calif., Aug. 3, 1954; d. Herbert (McRoy) and Beverly Jeanne (Weisman) Verdugo; m. Vincent Ernest Aragon, Sept. 8, 1979 (div. May 1988); children: Tara Jeanne, Eric Vincent. Student, Cerritos Coll., 1972-73, Calif. State U., Long Beach, 1973-75. Contest dir. Nat. Scholastic Surfing Assn., Huntington Beach, Calif., 1986-89, exec. dir., 1989—; scholarship cons. U.S. Surfing Fedn., Long Beach, 1991-92. Author: (newsletter) Surflines. Exploring advisor Boy Scouts Am., Costa Mesa, Calif., 1989—. Recipient Exploring Award of Merit Boy Scouts Am., 1992; named 1984 World Amateur Surfing Champion, Internat. Surfing Assn. Home: 21342 Yarmouth Huntington Beach CA 92646 Office: Nat Scholastic Surfing Assn PO Box 495 Huntington Beach CA 92648

ARAUZ, CARLOS GASPAR, city official; b. Havana, Cuba, Jan. 6, 1949; came to U.S., 1960, naturalized, 1974; s. Agnelio Alejandro and Mariana (Rodriguez) A.; BS, Loyola U., Los Angeles, 1970; MS, Ga. Inst. Tech., 1975, postgrad., 1975—. Bacteriologist, Emory U. Hosp., Atlanta, 1970-72; rsch. psychologist Atlanta Regional Commn., 1973-74; dir. personnel City of College Park (Ga.), 1974-75; indsl. psychology cons. Lockheed Ga. Co., Marietta, 1976; asst. dir. human resources City of Miami, 1976-81, spl. asst. to city mgr., 1981-82; bur. chief labor rels./personnel adminstrn. City of Orlando, Fla., 1982-85; dir. personnel and labor relations City of Corpus Christi, Tex., 1985-86; dir. personnel City of Phoenix, 1986—; cons. govt. and industry. Bd. dirs. Valle del Sol, Inc., Ariz. Govt. Tng. Svc. Mem. Internat. Personnel Mgmt. Assn. (young personnel profl. award N. Ga. 1975; pres. N. Ga. chpt. 1976, S. Fla. chpt. 1978, pres. So. region 1980-81, exec. coun. 1990-92, pres.-elect 1992), Soc. Human Resource Mgmt., Metro Phoenix Human Resource Mgmt. Assn., Internat. City Mgmt. Assn., Nat. Pub. Employer Labor Rels. Assn., Rocky Mountain Pub. Employer Labor Rels. Assn. (pres. 1989-91), Sigma Xi. Roman Catholic. Club: Lake Arrowhead Yacht and Country. Office: City of Phoenix 135 N 2nd Ave Phoenix AZ 85003-2018

ARCADI, JOHN ALBERT, urologist; b. Whittier, Calif., Oct. 23, 1924; s. Antonio and Josephine (Ramirez) A; m. Doris M. Bohanan, Apr. 11, 1951; children: Patrick, Michael, Judith, Timothy, Margaret, William, Catherine. BS cum laude, U. Notre Dame, 1947; MD, Johns Hopkins U., 1950. Diplomate Am. Bd. Urology. Intern The Johns Hopkins Hosp., Balt., 1950-51, resident, 1951-52, 53-55; instr. urology Johns Hopkins U., Balt., Md., 1953-55, U. So. Calif., Los Angeles, 1955-60; research assoc. Whittier (Calif.) Coll., 1957-70, research prof., 1970—; staff mem. urology sect. Presbyn. Hosp., Whittier, 1960—. Fellow AAAS, Am. Coll. Surgeons; mem. Endocrine Soc., Am. Urology Assn., Am. Soc. Cell Biology, Am. Micro Soc., Internat. Urol. Soc., Am. Assn. Clin. Anatomy, Am. Assn. Anatomists, Soc. for Basic Urologic Rsch., Soc for Invertebrate Pathology. Republican. Roman Catholic. Home: 6202 Washington Ave Whittier CA 90601-3640 Office: 1313 Hadley St Whittier CA 90601 Mailing Address: PO Box 9220 Whittier CA 90608-9220

ARCHDEACON, JOHN ROBERT, orthopedic surgeon; b. N.Y.C., Aug. 1, 1919; s. Thomas Francis and Mary (O'Connor) A.; m. Molly Taylor Sinclair, Sept. 18, 1948; children—Patricia Archdeacon Holland, Douglas, John, Richard, Moira, Kenneth. Student Fordham U., 1939-41; MD, NYU, 1950. Diplomate Am. Bd. Orthopedic Surgery Am. Bd. Preventive Medicine. Commd. 1st lt. USAF, 1952, advanced through grades to col., 1965; intern St. Lukes Hosp., N.Y.C., 1950-51; resident orthopedic surgery N.Y. U.-Bellevue Med. Ctr., 1955-59; chief orthopedic surgery Carswell AFB Hosp., Ft. Worth, 1959-61; dir. orthopedic pathology course Armed Forces Inst. Pathology, 1963-64; chief of surgery, cons. to surgeon gen. Maxwell Air Force Hosp., Ala., 1964-66; chief profl. svcs., sr. med. adviser Air Evacuation System, USAF Hosp., Clark Hosp., Philippines, 1966-68, hosp. comdr., 1967-68; hosp. comdr. 78th USAF Hosp., Hamilton AFB, Calif., 1968-69; ret., 1969; pvt. practice medicine specializing in orthopedic surgery, Los Gatos-Saratoga, Calif., 1969—. Decorated D.F.C., Air medal with 3 oak leaf clusters, Air Force Commendation medal, Legion of Merit. Fellow ACS, Am. Acad. Orthopedic Surgeons, Am. Coll. Preventive Medicine; mem. AMA, Santa Clara County Med. Assn., Calif. Med. Assn. Office: 800 Pollard Rd Los Gatos CA 95030-1415

ARCHER, CHRIS JAMES, technical manager; b. Norwich, Norfolk, England, Dec. 2, 1948; came to U.S., 1986; s. Neil John and Dallas Constance (Pratt) A.; m. Dorothy Ann Mehringer, Sept. 4, 1982; children: Aimee Ann Archer, Gina Marie Archer. Norwich City Coll., England, 1970, City of Norwich Sch., England, 1965. City and Guilds of London Basic and Advanced Lithographic Printing. Lithographic printing apprentice Jarrold and Sons, Norwich, England, 1965-70, lithographic printer, 1970-74; disc jockey pvt. practice, Norwich, England, 1974-78; tech. sales rep. Horsell Graphic Industries, Morley, Leeds, England, 1978-80; tech. svcs. rep. Howson-Algraphy, Leeds, England, 1980-84, sr. tech. svcs. rep., 1984-86; tech. mgr. Howson-Algraphy, Wayne, N.J., 1986-89; sr. tech. mgr. E.I. Dupont Imaging Systems, Wilmington, Del., 1989—. Home: 3259 Oakshire Ln Chino Hills CA 91709-2400 Office: DuPont Printing and Publishing 18500 Von Karman Ave Ste 750 Irvine CA 92715-0504

ARCHER, DOUGLAS ROBERT, mayor, insurance services executive; b. Winnipeg, Man., Can., Mar. 23, 1948; s. Robert Clive and Annette Diane (Brabant) A.; m. Gloria Jean Knight, Feb. 28, 1976; children: James, Lindsey, Tracy. BA in Econs., U. Sask., Saskatoon, Can., 1970. Civil servant Govt. Sask., Regina, 1971-83; ptnr. Knight Archer Ins. Svcs., Regina, 1983—; mayor City of Regina, 1988—; chair City Coun., Regina Bd. Police Commrs., Wascana Centre Authority, Mayor's Bd. of Inquiry into Hunger in Regina. Mem. Regina Econ. Devel. Authority, Mayor's Task Force on Women, Sherwood-Regina Dist. Planning Commn.; chair Mayor's Task Force on Accessibility; past pres. Regina Open Door Soc., Sask. Fedn. Community Clinics. Mem. Fedn. Can. Municipalities (bd. dirs.), Regina Exhbn. Assn. Office: Office of Mayor, 2476 Victoria Ave, Regina, SK Canada S4P 3C8

ARCHER, HARRY RANDALL, personal financial advisor; b. Cambridge, July 3, 1947; s. Ronald and Mary Annabelle (Bates) A.; m. Soledad Macenas, July 20, 1979; children: Maria Divina, Randall Ronald, Michael. AA, Phoenix Coll., 1968; BSME, Ariz. State U., 1972; MS of Systems Mgmt., U. So. Calif., 1979. Commd. 2d. lt. U.S. Army, 1972, advanced through grades to capt., 1976, resigned, 1987; maj. Desert Storm U.S. Army, Yuma, Ariz., 1991; personal fin. advisor Killeen, Tex., 1987-90, Cottonwood, Ariz., 1991—; substitute tchr. Verde Valley Schs., 1991—. With USAR, 1987—. Office: PO Box 1976 Cottonwood AZ 86326

ARCHER, STEPHEN HUNT, economist, educator; b. Fargo, N.D., Nov. 30, 1928; s. Clifford Paul and Myrtle Mona (Blair) A.; m. Carol Rosa Mohr, Dec. 29, 1951 (div. Feb. 1971); children—Stephen Paul, Timothy William, David Conrad; m. Lana Jo Urban, Sept. 23, 1972. B.A., U. Minn., 1949, M.S., 1953, Ph.D., 1958; postdoctoral student (Ford Found. grantee), U. Calif. at Los Angeles, 1959-60. Mgr. trader J.M. Dain Co., Mpls., 1950; account exec. J.M. Dain Co., 1952-53; instr. econs. U. Minn., Mpls., 1954-56; asst. prof. fin. U. Wash., Seattle, 1956-60; assoc. prof. U. Wash., 1960-65, prof., 1965-73, chmn. dept. fin., bus. econs. and quantitative methods, 1966-70; dean Grad. Sch. Adminstrn. Willamette U., Salem, Oreg., 1973-76, 83-85; prof. Willamette U., 1976-79, Guy F. Atkinson prof., 1979—; Fulbright sr. lectr. Bocconi U., Milan, Italy, 1982; v.p. Hinton, Jones & Co., Inc. (investment brokers), Seattle, 1969-70; cons. Wash. Bankers Assn., 1971-72, Weyerhaeuser Co., 1971, Bus.-Econs. Adv. & Research Inc., 1969-77, State of Oreg., 1984, 86, 88, 91; vis. prof. Manchester Bus. Sch., Manchester, Eng., 1990-91. Author: Introduction to Mathematics for Business Analysis, 1960, Business Finance: Theory and Mgmt, 1966, revised edit., 1972, The Theory of Business Finance, 1967, 2d revised edit., 1983, Portfolio Analysis, 1971, revised edit., 1979, Introduction to Financial Management, 1979, revised edit., 1983, Cases and Readings in Corporate Finance, 1988; editor Jour. Fin. and Quantitative Analysis, 1966-70, Economic Perspectives, Economica Aziendale, Jour. Bus. and Entrepreneurship. Served with USNR, 1950-52. Mem. Fin. Mgmt. Assn. (pres. 1973-74), Western Fin. Assn., Acad. Internat. Bus., Am. Fin. Assn., Phi Beta Kappa. Home: 5171 Woodscape Dr SE Salem OR 97306-1004

ARCHERD, ARMY (ARMAND ARCHERD), columnist, tv commentator; b. N.Y.C., Jan. 13. Grad., UCLA, 1941, U.S. Naval Acad. Postgrad. Sch., 1943. With Hollywood bur. AP, from 1945; columnist Herald-Express, Daily Variety, from 1953; master of ceremonies numerous Hollywood premieres, Acad. Awards shows; co-host People's Choice Awards shows. Served to lt. USN. Recipient awards Masquers, L.A. Press Club, Hollywood Fgn. Press Club, Newsman of Yr. award Publicists Guild, 1970. Mem. Hollywood Press Club (founder). Office: Daily Variety # 120 5700 Wilshire Blvd Los Angeles CA 90036

ARCHIBALD, RAE WILLIAM, research company executive, educator; b. Modesto, Calif., Nov. 19, 1941; s. Hedley Chester and Martha Jane (Ashton) A.; m. Barbara Jean Sanders, June 15, 1963; 1 child, Christopher Rae. BArch, U. Calif., Berkeley, 1964, M City Planning, 1966, PhD in Planning, 1973. Sr. staff N.Y.C. City RAND Inst., 1968-71; dep. fire commr. City of N.Y., 1971-73; dep. dir. health ins. study RAND Corp., Santa Monica, Calif., 1973-79, compt., 1979-80, v.p., chief fin. officer, 1980—, pub. RAND Jour. of Econs., 1984—; faculty RAND Grad. Sch. of Policy Studies, Santa Monica, 1980—. Contbr. chpts. to books. Bd. dirs. Pier Restoration Corp., Santa Monica, 1985—, Ocean Pk. Community Ctr., Santa Monica, 1983—, Santa Monica Coll. Assocs., 1985—, St. John's Hosp. and Health Ctr., Santa Monica, 1989—. Mem. ASPA, Ops. Rsch. Soc. Am., Nat. Contract Mgmt. Assn., Mountain Gate Country Club. Office: RAND 1700 Main St PO Box 2138 Santa Monica CA 90407-2138

ARCINIEGA, TOMAS ABEL, university president; b. El Paso, Tex., Aug. 5, 1937; s. Tomas Hilario and Judith G. (Zozaya) A.; m. M. Concha Ochotorena, Aug. 10, 1957; children: Wendy, Lisa, Judy, Laura. B.S., N. Mex. State U., 1960; M.A., U. N. Mex., 1966, Ph.D., 1970; postdoctoral, Inst. for Ednl. Mgmt., Harvard U., 1989. Asst. dean Grad. Sch. U. Tex.-El Paso, 1972-73; co-dir. Southwestern Schs. Study, U. Tex.-El Paso, 1970-73; dean Coll. Edn. San Diego State U., 1973-80; v.p. acad. affairs. Calif. State U., Fresno, 1980-83; pres. Calif. State U., Bakersfield, 1983—; prof. ednl. adminstrn. and supervision U. N. Mex., U. Tex.-El Paso, San Diego State U., Calif. State U., Fresno, Calif. State U., Bakersfield; cons. in edn. to state and fed. agys., instrns.; dep. chief party U. N. Mex. AID Project, Colombia, 1969-70. Author: Public Education's Response to the Mexican-American, 1971, Preparing Teachers of Mexican Americans: A Sociocultural and Political Issue, 1977; co-author: Chicanos and Native Americans: The Territorial Minorities, 1973; guest editor: Calif. Jour. Tchr. Edn., 1981; editor Commn. on Hispanic Underrepresentation Reports, Hispanic Underrepresentation: A Call for Reinvestment and Innovation, 1985, 88. Trustee emeritus Carnegie Corp. N.Y.; trustee Ednl. Testing Svc., Princeton, J.J., The Aspen Inst.; bd. dirs. Math., Engring., Sci. Achievement, Berkeley, Calif. Lt. inf. U.S. Army, 1961-63. Recipient Legis. commendation for higher edn. Calif. Legislature, 1975-78, Meritorious Service award Am. Assn. Colls. Tchr. Edn., 1978, Meritorious Service award League United Latin Am. Citizens, 1983; named to Top 100 Acad. Leaders in Higher Edn. Change Mag., 1978. Mem. Am. Ednl. Rsch. Assn. (editorial com. 1979-82), Assn. Mexican Am. Educators (various commendations), Am. Assn. Higher Edn. (instl. rep.), Am. Coun. on Edn. (sec.). Democrat. Roman Catholic. Home: 2213 Sully Ct Bakersfield CA 93311-1506 Office: Calif State U Bakersfield 9001 Stockdale Hwy Bakersfield CA 93311-1022

ARDLEY, HARRY MOUNTCASTLE (MIKE ARDLEY), mathematical statistician, operations research consultant; b. Oakland, Calif., Jan. 22, 1926; s. Harry Mountcastle and Anne Alvina (Meyer) A.; m. Jane Partridge, June 24, 1948; children: David Michael, Douglas Mountcastle, Mary Elizabeth. AB, U. Calif., Berkeley, 1950, postgrad., 1950-51, 58-59, 62-63. Econ. statistician U.S. Dept. Commerce, Washington, 1951-53; math. statistician Pacific Telephone Co., San Francisco, 1953-59; gen. statistician San Diego, 1959-63; supr. math. and statis. research San Francisco, 1963-83; pvt. practice cons., 1984—. Active citizens com. to establish Foothill Coll., 1957-58, San Francisco Symphony Assn.; exec. com. Santa Clara County Dem. Council, 1957-59; pres. Palo Alto-Stanford Dem. Club, 1965; pres. Greenmeadow Community Assn., 1969. Served with USAAF, 1943-46. Mem. Am. Statis. Assn. (pres. San Francisco Bay area chpt. 1981-82), Ops. Research Soc. Am., Inst. Mgmt. Sci., Sierra Club, Western Wheelers Club. Home and Office: 352 Parkside Dr Palo Alto CA 94306-4532

ARDREY, ROSS JAMES, management consultant; b. N.Y.C., Jan. 4, 1943; s. Robert and Helen (Johnson) A.; m. Janet Kathleen Leslie, June 20, 1970; children: Robert Thornton, Janet Elizabeth. AB, U. Chgo., 1963; MA, U. Wash., 1966, JD, 1970. Mgmt. cons. Harry J. Prior/Martech Assoc., Bellevue, Wash., 1972-91, Howard John & Co., Seattle, 1991—. Bd. trustees Villa Acad., 1986-90, Friends of Seattle Pub. Libr., 1985—; pres. Pacific N.W. chpt. Inst. Mgmt. Cons., 1990—; mem. Mcpl. League of Seattle and King County, Wash., 1976—; mem. nat. fund bd. U. Chgo., Ill., 1973—; mem. strategic planning task force Inst. Mgmt. Cons., 1990, mem. exec. com. , regional v.p. Inst., 1991—. Mem. Inst. Mgmt. Cons., Pacific N.W. Pers. Mgmt. Assn. Office: 1111 Third Ave Bldg Ste # 1700 Seattle WA 98101

ARDREY, STEPHANIE DIONNE, marketing and promotions company executive; b. Berkeley, Calif., Aug. 26, 1965; d. Joel F. and Shirley A. (Lackey) A. Cert., U. Calif., Berkeley, 1984; AA, FIDM, San Francisco, 1985; BS, Golden Gate U., 1989; postgrad., St. Mary's Coll. Pres. S.D. Ardrey Enterprises, Oakland, Calif., 1983-85; jr. exec. Saks Fifth Ave., San Francisco, 1985-87; dir. promotions KDIA Radio Sta., Oakland, 1989—; pres. Ardrey Assocs. Internat., Oakland, 1987—; cons. Y.E.S., Oakland, 1987—, Oakland Youth Enterprises, 1986-87; bd. dirs. Oakland Unified Sch. Dist., Black MBA's Assn., San Francisco. Bd. Dirs. Sen. Diane Watson's Polit. Campaign, Sacramento, 1989; cons./advisor Youth Entrepreneurial Svcs., Intenat., Oakland, 1990. Mem. NAFE, Nat. Assn. Black MBA's, Common Wealth Club, Oakland C. of C. (sm. bus. com.). Office: Ardrey Assocs Internat 505 S Beverly Dr #742 Beverly Hills CA 90212

AREIAS, JOHN RUSTY, agriculturist, state legislator; b. Los Banos, Calif., Sept. 12, 1949; s. John A. BAS, Ca. State U., Chico, 1973. Mng. ptnr. Areias Dairy Farms, Los Banos, Calif., 1975—; mem. Calif. Assembly, 1982—. Democrat. Roman Catholic. Office: Calif State Capitol PO Box 942849 Sacramento CA 94249

ARELLANES, AUDREY SPENCER, society administrator; b. Lance Creek, Wyo., Feb. 23, 1920; d. William Sidney and Edith Catherine (Hall) Spencer; m. Lane James Thomas III, Nov. 13, 1943 (div. 1946); m. Lester Glenn Arellanes, Sept. 28, 1946 (div. Oct. 1978); 1 child, Denetia Ynez. Student, UCLA, 1944. Sec. to claims mgr. Calif. Physicians Svc., L.A., 1946-54; asst. editor house organ and sec. to v.p. Calcor, Whittier, Calif., 1954-58; rsch. asst. biokinetics lab. Calif. Coll. Medicine, L.A., 1958-62; human resources employee benefits Avery Internat., Pasadena, Calif., 1963-85; ret.; pub. pvt. press Bookworm Press, Alhambra. Author: Bookplates: A Selected Annotated Bibliography of the Periodical Literature, 1971; editor: Bookplates in the News: 1970-85, 1985, Year Book. Mem. Am. Soc. Bookplate Collectors & Designers (dir. 1970—, editor Year Book, Bookplates in the News quar.), Rounce and Coffin Club, The Book Collectors, Miniature Book Soc., Manuscript Soc. (nat. exec. sec. 1975-80, local treas., award of distinction 1980), Huntington Corral of Westerners Internat. (posse mem. 1980-86, trail boss 1984, registrar marks and brands 1982-83, keeper of chips 1985-86). Home and Office: Am Soc Bookplate Collectors and Designers 605 N Stoneman Ave # F Alhambra CA 91801-1406

ARENA, ALAN JOSEPH, manufacturing executive; b. Chgo., June 23, 1950; s. Joseph James and Madelyn Adele (Castrovillari) A.; m. Mary Ann Guglielmo, Nov. 26, 1972 (dec.); 1 child, Monica Kristen. BS in Mech. and Aerospace Engring., Ill. Inst. Tech., 1972; MME, Calif. State U., Los Angeles, 1984. Research and devel. engr. Fiat-Allis CMI, Deerfield, Ill., 1973-80; sr. project engr. Signet Sci. Co., El Monte, Calif., 1980-83; project mgr. def. electronics ops. Autonetics Strategic Systems div. Rockwell Internat., Anaheim, Calif., 1983-87, 89-93; dir. engring. Ride and Show Engring., Inc., San Dimas, Calif., 1987-89, Automotive Testing & Devel. Svcs., Inc., Ontario, Calif., 1993—; Instr. Calif. Poly. Inst., Pomona, 1983—. Patentee in field. Roman Catholic. Home: 12515 Sterling Pl Chino CA 91710-6230 Office: Automotive Testing & Devel Svcs Inc 400 S Etiwanda Ontario CA 91761

ARENBERG, JONATHAN WILLIAM, engineer; b. Denver, Jan. 6, 1961; s. Sheldon Ira and Janet Estelle (Rubin) A. BS in Physics, UCLA, 1983, MS in Engring., 1985, PhD in Engring., 1987. Cons. Pan Heuristics, Marina del Rey, Calif., 1985-87; staff physicist Hughes Aircraft Co., El Segundo, Calif., 1982-89; sr. mem. tech. staff TRW Space and Tech., Redondo Beach, Calif., 1989—. Patentee in field; contbr. articles to profl. jours. Founding dir. Santa Monica (Calif.) High Sch. Alumni Assn., 1989—; bd. dirs., vice-chmn. Friends of the Santa Monica Pub. Libr., 1989—; com. mem., past chmn. UCLA Alumni Scholarship, Dist. III-1, 1988—. Edward Dickson scholar, UCLA Alumni Assn., 1979, Regents scholar, UCLA, 1979; recipient Hughes Aircraft Masters and Doctoral fellowship, Hughes Aircraft Co., L.A., 1983, 85. Mem. IEEE, Sigma Pi Sigma (v.p. 1982-83), Eta Kappa Nu, Sigma Xi.

AREND, ROBERT LEE, English language educator, writer; b. Bridgman, Mich., Aug. 30, 1944; s. Delbert Lee and Dorothy (Martin) A.; m. Joanne Prince Arend, June 4, 1977; children: Brett, Julie, Joshua. BA, Moody Bible Inst., 1968, Western Mich. U., 1968; MA, Trinity Sem., 1970, Northwestern U., Evanston, Ill., 1971; postgrad., Purdue U., 1974—. Asst. prof. English Grace Coll., Winona Lake, Ind., 1971-76; prof. English Christian Heritage Coll., El Cajon, Calif., 1976-90, Miramar Coll., San Diego, 1990—; instr. in English Palomar Coll., San Marcos, Calif., 1972—; & Cuyamaca Coll., El Cajon, Calif., 1982--;; freelance tutor, Cardiff, Calif., 1982—. Author: (textbook) Fundamentals of Oral Communications, English Workbook for the Christian Student, Poetry in the Key of David; contbr. numerous articles to profl. jours. Precinct coord. Rep. Party, 1982—. Named Internat. Man of Yr., 1993. Mem. Nat. Coun. Tchrs. of English, Modern Lang. Assn., Shakespeare Assn., Internat. Platform Assn., Sigma Tau Honor Soc. Baptist. Office: Miramar College 10440 Black Mountain Rd San Diego CA 92126-2999

ARENDS, MARK PAUL, editor, consultant; b. Chico, Calif., Oct. 29, 1966; s. Paul William Arends and Donna (Graves) Moore. Editor Moon Publs. Inc., Chico, 1990—. Editor: Micronesia Handbook, 1992, South Pacific Handbook, 1992; indexer: Nepal Handbook, 1991; author book revs. Home: PO Box 4070 Chico CA 95927

ARENOWITZ, ALBERT HAROLD, psychiatrist; b. N.Y.C., Jan. 12, 1925; s. Louis Isaac and Lena Helen (Skovron) A.; m. Betty Jane Wiener, Oct. 11, 1953; children: Frederick Stuart, Diane Helen. BA with honors, U. Wis., 1948; MD, U. Va., 1951. Diplomate Am. Bd. Psychiatry, Am. Bd. Child Psychiatry. Intern Kings County Gen. Hosp., Bklyn., 1951-52; resident in psychiatry Bronx (N.Y.) VA Hosp., 1952-55; postdoctoral fellow Youth Guidance Ctr., Worcester, Mass., 1955-57; dir. Ctr. for Child Guidance, Phila., 1962-65, Hahnemann Med. Service Eastern State Sch. and Hosp., Trevose, Pa., 1965-68; dir., tng. dir. Child and Adolescent Psychiat. Clinic, Phila. Gen. Hosp., 1965-67; asst. clin. prof. psychiatry Jefferson Med. Coll., Phila., 1974-76; exec. dir. Child Guidance and Mental Health Clinics, Media, Pa., 1967-74; med. dir. Intercommunity Child Guidance Ctr., Whittier, Calif., 1976—; cons. Madison Pub. Schs., 1957-60, Dane County Child Guidance Ctr., Madison, 1957-62, Juvenile Ct., Madison, 1957-62; clin. asst. prof. child psychiatry Hahnemann Med. Coll., Phila., 1966-74; asst. clin. prof. psychiatry U. Wis., Madison, 1960-62, clin. asst. prof. psychiatry, behavioral scis. and family medicine U. So. Calif., L.A., 1976—; mem. med. staff Presbyn. Intercommunity Hosp., Whittier, 1976—. Pres. Whittier Area Coordinating Coun., 1978-80; chmn. ethics com. Presbyn. Intercommunity Hosp. Flight officer, navigator USAF, 1943-45. Decorated Air medal, POW medal. Fellow Am. Psychiat. Assn., Am. Acad. Child Psychiatry; mem. AAAS, Los Angeles County Med. Assn., So. Calif. Psychiat. Soc., So. Calif. Soc. Child Psychiatry, Phila. Soc. Adolescent Psychiatry (pres. 1967-68). Office: Intercommunity Child Guidance Ctr 8106 Broadway Ave Whittier CA 90606-3118

ARENSON, BARBARA LEVINE, educator; b. N.Y.C., Apr. 22, 1947; d. Abraham and Rebecca Levine; m. Paul Arenson, June 6, 1971; children: Adam, Aliza. BA in Sociology, U. Calif.-Berkeley, 1969; MA, San Francisco State U., 1970. Cert. elem., learning handicapped, severely handicapped tchr., adminstr., Calif. Spl. edn. tchr. Contra Costa County Pub. Schs., Alamo, Calif., 1970-72; spl. edn. diagnostic tchr. Children's Hosp., Boston, 1972-73; spl. edn. tchr. San Diego City Schs., 1973-76, spl. project tchr., 1976-78, resource tchr., 1978-82, mainstream project resource tchr., 1982-84, spl. edn. infant tchr., 1984—. Co-author: Hand in Hand--A Teacher's Guide to Preschool Mainstreaming, 1983. Mem. Assn. for Retarded Citizens, Phi Beta Kappa. Office: Alcott School 4680 Hidalgo Ave San Diego CA 92117-2503

ARENTZ, DICK, photographer; b. Detroit, May 19, 1935; s. Ewald and Hermina (Auner) A.; children: Paul, James, Pamela. DSc, U. Mich., 1959, MS, 1964. One-man shows include G. Ray Hawkins Gallery, L.A., 1987, Etherton Gallery, Tucson, 1987, U. Mo., St. Louis, 1988, Galerie Stockeregg, Zurich, 1989, Houston Ctr.for Photography, 1989, Huntington Mus. of Art, 1990, U. of Ky., 1991, Phoenix Art Mus. Triennial, 1990; represented in permanent collections Mus. Moderan Art, George Eastman House, Corcoran Gallery, Can. Ctr. for architecture, Amon Carter Mus. Western Art, Oaklan Art Mus., Nat. Mus. Am. Art. Capt. USAF, 1959-61. Isaac W. Bernheim fellow, 1988; grantee NEA, 1990. Mem. Soc. Photographic Edn., Phi Kappa Phi. Home and Office: 1640 Spyglass Way Flagstaff AZ 86004-7382

ARENTZEN, CHARLES, metallurgist, consultant; b. Grand Forks, N.D., Oct. 12, 1919; s. Karl Albert and Caroline (Larsen) A.; m. Margueritte Elizabeth Kane, July 14, 1951. BS in Metallurgy, Mont. Sch. of Mines, 1950; MetE (hon.), Mont. Coll. of Mineral Sci., 1970. Metall. engr. Galigher Co., Salt Lake City, 1950-51; asst. research engr., research engr. Anaconda Co., Mont., 1951-68; various positions to mgr. processs evaluation Anaconda Co., Tucson, 1968-84; metall. cons. Arentzen & Assocs., Tucson, 1984—. Contbr. articles to profl. jours.; 5 patents in field. Chief petty officer USN, 1938-46. Mem. Metall. Soc., AIME, Toastmasters Club. Home and Office: 7811 E Camino Bavispe Tucson AZ 85715-3709

ARGENTERI, LAETITIA, history educator; b. Milano, Lombardy, Italy, May 2, 1950; came to U.S., 1974; d. Antonio and Giacomina (Milesi) A. Doctorate, U. Milano, 1973; PhD in History, UCLA, 1989. Teaching assoc. UCLA, 1983-85; editor The J. Paul Getty Ctr., Santa Monica, Calif., 1985-90; asst. prof. dept. history U. San Diego, Calif., 1991—; vis. lectr. Bosphorus U., Istanbul, Turkey, 1980-81. Author: King Victor Emmanuel III of Savoy, 1992. Paul Harris fellow Rotary, Pavia, Italy, 1989; grantee Italian Embassy, Washington, 1986-88; recipient jr. fellowship Soc. of Fellows, Harvard U., 1988. Mem. Am. Hist. Assn., Am. Italian Hist. Assn., Friends of Teatro Alla Scala (Milano), Western Assn. Women Historians, Phi Beta Kappa (grantee 1985). Home: 1270-N Cleveland Ave #114 San Diego CA 92103 Office: Univ San Diego Dept History Alcala Park San Diego CA 92110

ARGERIS, GEORGE JOHN, lawyer; b. Ten Sleep, Wyo., May 12, 1931; s. John Brown and Martha (Wilsonoff) A. BA, U. Colo., 1954; JD, U. Wyo., 1959. Bar: Wyo. 1959, U.S. Dist. Ct. Wyo. 1959, U.S. Supreme Ct. 1968. Asst. atty. gen. State of Wyo., Cheyenne, 1960-63; supervisory atty. Fgn. Claims Commn. U.S., Washington, 1963-68; dep. gen. counsel U.S. Info. Agy., Washington, 1972-74; ptnr. Guy, Williams, White & Argeris, Cheyenne, 1974—. Assoc. editor U. Wyo. Law Rev., 1957-58. Mem. ABA, Assn. Def. Trial Lawyers, Wyo. Def. Lawyers Assn., Wyo. Trial Lawyers Assn., Omicron Delta Kappa, Chi Gamma Iota. Home: 3619 Carey Ave Cheyenne WY 82001 Office: Guy Williams White Argeris 1600 Van Lennen Ave Cheyenne WY 82001-4636

ARGUE, JOHN CLIFFORD, lawyer; b. Glendale, Calif., Jan. 25, 1932; s. J. Clifford and Catherine Emily (Clements) A.; m. Leah Elizabeth Moore, June 29, 1963; children: Elizabeth Anne, John Michael. AB in Commerce and Fin., Occidental Coll., 1953, LLD (hon.), 1987; LLB, U. So. Calif., 1956. Bar: Calif. 1957. Since practiced in Los Angeles; mem. firm Argue & Argue, 1958-59, Flint & MacKay, 1960-72, Argue, Pearson, Harbison & Myers, 1972—; bd. dirs. Avery Dennison, Cal Mat Inc.; mem. adv. bd. LAACO, Ltd., Rose Hills Meml. Park Assn., TCW/DW Mutl Funds, TCW Funds. Pres. So. Calif. Com. Olympic Games, 1972—; founding chmn. L.A. Olympic Organizing Com., 1978-79; bd. dirs. Amateur Athletic Found. L.A.; trustee, vice chmn. Pomona Coll, U. So. Calif., Occidental Coll., Mus. Sci. and Industry, U.S. Olympic Tng. Ctr., Criminal Justice Found.; chmn. bd. Greater L.A. affiliate Am. Heart Assn., 1982, chmn. adv. bd., 1985—; chmn. Verdugo Hills Hosp., 1979, chmn. adv. bd., 1983—; pres. Town Hall of Calif., 1985, U. So. Calif. Assocs., 1988—; chmn. PGA Championship, 1983, L.A. Sports Coun., 1986—, Magic Johnson's Golf Classic; vice chmn., sec. L.A. 2000 Com., 1991 Olympic Sports Festival, 1993, 1994 Superbowl Worldcup; chmn. Rose Hills Meml. Park Assn. Mem. L.A. Bar Assn., Calif. Bar Assn., Southern Calif. Golf Assn. (pres. 1979), Calif. Golf Assn. (v.p. 1979), L.A. Area C. of C. (bd. dirs., chmn. 1989), Chancery Club (pres. 1985-86), Calif. Club (pres. 1983-84), L.A. Athletic Club, Riviera Country Club, Oakmont Country Club (pres. 1972), L.A. Country Club, Flint Canyon Tennis Club, Calif. State Srs. Golf Assn., Rotary, Phi Delta Phi, Alpha Tau Omega. Home: 1314 Descanso Dr La Canada Flintridge CA 91011-3149 Office: 801 S Flower St Ste 5000 Los Angeles CA 90017-4699

ARIELI, ADI, aerospace company executive; b. Bucharest, Romania, Apr. 15, 1947; came to U.S., 1978; s. David and Rebecca (Greenberg) A.; m. Mihaela Popescu, July 31, 1969; 1 child, Robert Philip. Diploma engring., Polytech Inst., 1970; MS, Technion, 1976; PhD, U. Calif., Davis, 1979. Supr. metals tech. Israel Aircraft Inds., Lod, 1971-78; rsch. assoc. U. Calif., Davis, 1978-80; sr. scientist Olin Corp., New Haven, Conn., 1980-81; mgr. Northrop Corp., Hawthorne, Calif., 1981—; mem. bd. advisors dept. mech., aero. and materials engring. U. Calif., Davis, 1989—, mem. mfg. engring. adv. bd., UCLA, 1986—. Contbr. scientific and tech. articles to profl. jours. Mem. SAE (chmn. aerospace mfg. activity 1990—, vice chmn. 1988-90), ASM (mem. materials, synthesis and processing coms. 1987—). Home: 120 S Fuller Ave Los Angeles CA 90036 Office: Northrop Corp 1 Northrop Ave Hawthorne CA 90250

ARIO, JOEL SCOTT, organization executive, lawyer; b. Mpls., July 11, 1953; s. Frank Leroy and Georgette Frances (Lones) A. BA, St. Olaf Coll., Northfield, Minn., 1975; MDiv cum laude, Harvard U., 1978, JD cum laude, 1981. Bar: Mass. Atty. Legal Svcs. Inst., Jamaica Plain, Mass., 1980-81; consumer adv., legal counsel Mass. Pub. Interest Rsch. Group, Boston, 1981-86; founder, exec. dir. Wis. Pub. Interest Rsch. Group, Madison, 1986-87; exec. dir. Oreg. State-Student Pub. Interest Rsch. Group, Portland, 1987—; legal counsel, cons. Fund for Pub. Interest Rsch., Boston, 1982—; founder, exec. dir. Nat. Student Campaign Against Hunger, Boston, 1985—. Campaign chmn. Consumers for Recycling (Yes or No), Portland, 1990. Mem. Consumer Fedn. Am. (bd. dirs. 1987—), Portland City Club, Phi Beta Kappa. Office: Oreg Pub Interest Rsch Group 1536 SE 11th St Portland OR 97214

ARION, DOUGLAS NORMAN, physicist; b. N.Y.C., Jan. 27, 1957; s. Gilbert Roger and Barbara Diane (Swinkin) A.; m. Doreen Ella McMahon, Apr. 25, 1982 (div. 1989); m. Teresa Ann Sandoval, July 12, 1990. AB, Dartmouth Coll., 1978; MS, U. Md., 1980, PhD, 1984. Physicist U.S. Army Cold Regions Rsch. Engring. Lab., Hanover, N.H., 1978-79; grad. rsch. fellow NASA-Goddard Space Flight Ctr., Greenbelt, Md., 1982-84; sr. scientist Sci. Applications Internat. Corp., McLean, Va., 1984-89; div. mgr. Sci. Applications Internat. Corp., Albuquerque, 1989-93, asst. v.p., 1993—. Contbr. articles to profl. jours. Mem. Am. Phys. Soc., U.S. Cycling Fedn. Republican. Office: SAIC 2109 Airpark Rd SE Albuquerque NM 87106-3258

ARISS, DAVID WILLIAM, real estate developer; b. Toronto, Ont., Can., Nov. 29, 1939; s. William H. and Joyce Ethel (Oddy) A.; m. Lillie, Jan. 26, 1962 (div. 1989); children: Katherine Joyce, David William. BA, Claremont Men's Coll., 1961. Lic. real estate broker. Real estate broker Coldwell Banker, Torrance, Calif., 1971-75; v.p. The Lusk Co., Irvine, Calif., 1975-77; pres. DAL Devel. Co., Corona, Calif., 1977-84; mng. dir. Calif. Commerce Ctr. at Ontario, Ontario, Calif., 1984—. Chair Inland Empire Economic Coun., Ontario, Calif., 1991-92; pres. comml./indsl. coun. Baldy View chpt., Bldg. Industry Assn., San Bernardino County, Calif., 1987-88; pres., adv. com., Chaffey Coll., Ontario, 1989—. Maj. USMC, 1961-70, Vietnam. Decorated Silver Star, Disting. Flying Cross, two Purple Hearts, numerous Air medals. Mem. Urban Land Inst., Nat. Assn. Fgn. Trade Zone, Nat. Assn. Indsl. and Office Parks. Republican. Office: Calif Commerce Ctr 9580 Commerce Center Dr Rancho Cucamonga CA 91730-5828

ARITA, GEORGE SHIRO, biology educator; b. Honolulu, Oct. 9, 1940; s. Ichimatsu and Natsu (Kimoto) A.; m. Harriet Yooko Ide, Dec. 26, 1964; children: Laurie Reiko, Daren Shizuo. BA, U. Hawaii, 1962, MS, 1964; MS, U. B.C., Vancouver, 1967; postgrad., U. Calif., Santa Barbara, 1967-71. Cert. community coll. tchr., Calif. Prof. biology Ventura (Calif.) Coll., 1971—, curator fish collection, 1976—, head dept. biology, 1989—. Author: (with others, lab. manual) Basic Concepts in Biology, 1981, Study Guide to Accompany Biology: Today and Tomorrow, 2d edit., 1984; contbr. articles on ichthyology to profl. jours. Fushiminomiya Meml. scholar U. Hawaii, 1961-62, Fisheries Assn. B.C. scholar U. B.C., 1964-65; NSF grad. trainee U. Calif. Santa Barbara, 1969-71. Mem. AAAS, Am. Soc. Ichthyologists and Herpetologists, Western Soc. Naturalists, Sigma Xi. Home: 94 Howard Ave Oak View CA 93022-9524 Office: Ventura Coll Dept Biology Ventura CA 93003

ARIYOSHI, GEORGE RYOICHI, lawyer, business consultant, former governor Hawaii; b. Honolulu, Mar. 12, 1926; s. Ryozo and Mitsue (Yoshikawa) A.; m. Jean Miya Hayashi, Feb. 5, 1955; children: Lynn Miye, Todd Ryozo, Donn Ryoji. Student, U. Hawaii, 1944-45, 47; B.A., Mich. State U., 1949, LL.D. (hon.), 1979; J.D., U. Mich., 1952; LL.D. (hon.), U. Philippines, 1975, U. Guam, 1975; H.H.D. (hon.), U. Visayas, Philippines, 1977, U. Hawaii, 1986. Bar: Hawaii 1953. Sole practice Honolulu, 1953-70; mem. Ter. of Hawaii Ho. of Reps., 1954-58; mem. State of Hawaii Senate, 1959-70, chmn. ways and means com., 1963-64, majority leader, 1965-66, majority floor leader, 1969-70; lt. gov. State of Hawaii, 1970-73, acting gov., 1973-74, gov., 1974-86; of counsel Kobayashi, Watanabe, Sugita, Kawashima & Goda, Honolulu, 1986-90, Watanabe, Ing and Kawashima, Honolulu, 1990—; ptnr. Cole, Gilburn, Goldhaber & Ariyoshi Mgmt. Inc.; mnging. ptnr. Ariyoshi, Mills & Assocs.; chmn. Western Govs. Conf., 1977-78; chmn. Western Govs. Assn., 1984-85; dir. Hawaiian Ins. & Guaranty, Ltd., 1966-70, First Hawaiian Bank, 1962-70, Honolulu Gas Co., Ltd. (Pacific Resources, Inc.), 1964-70; bus. cons.; pres., ceo Hawaii Cultured Pearls, Inc.; pres. Aina Kamalii Corp.; co-chmn. Asia-Pacific Cons. Group; pres. Ctr. Internat. Comml. Dispute Resolution; bd. dirs. Pacific Internat. Ctr. for High Tech. Rsch.; mem. Japan-Hawaii Econ. Coun. Chmn. small bus. div. Community Chest, 1963; mem. adv. bd. Japan Found. Ctr. for Global Partnership; fund raiser pub. employees div. Aloha United Fund, 1971-72; exec. bd. Aloha council Boy Scouts Am., 1970-72; chmn. Citizenship Day Com., 1971; pres. Pacific Basin Devel. Council, 1980-81; bd. mgrs. YMCA, 1955-57; chmn., treas. Earth Consultants Inc.; hon. co-chmn. Japanese-Am. Nat. Mus.; bd. trustees Japanese-Am. Inst. Mgmt. Sci., bd. dirs. Bishop Mus.; bd. govs. Japanese Cultural Ctr. Hawaii; nat. committeeman Dem. Party of Hawaii. Served with M.I. Service AUS, 1945-46. Recipient Distinguished Alumni awards U. Hawaii, 1975, Distinguished Alumni awards Mich. State U., 1975, Japan's Order of Sacred Treasure 1st class, 1985, Emperor's Silver Cup award, 1986. Mem. ABA (ho. dels. 1969—), Hawaii Bar Assn. (pres. 1969), Hawaii Bar Found. (charter, pres. 1969—). Democrat. Club: Military Intelligence Service Vets (pres. 1968-69).

ARMENTROUT, STEVEN ALEXANDER, oncologist; b. Morgantown, W.Va., Aug. 22, 1933; s. Walter W. and Dorothy (Gasch) A.; m. Johanna Ruszkay; children—Marc, Susan, Sandra, Nancy. A.B., U. Chgo., 1953, M.D., 1959. Intern U. Hosp., Cleve., 1959-60; resident in medicine, fellow Am. Cancer Soc. Western Res. U. Hosp., 1960-63; project dir. USPHS, 1963-65; asst. prof. Case Western Res. U. Med. Sch., 1965-71; mem. faculty U. Calif. Med. Sch., Irvine, 1971—; prof. medicine, chief div. hematology-oncology U. Calif. Med. Sch., 1978—, also dir. program in oncology.; pres. med. staff U. Calif.-Irvine Med. Ctr., 1983-85; researcher in multiple sclerosis. Mem. Am. Assn. Cancer Research, AAUP, A.C.P., Am. Cancer Soc. (chmn. bd. 1973, pres. Orange County chpt. 1985-86), AMA, Am. Soc. Clin. Oncology, Am. Soc. Hematology, Orange County Med. Assn., Am. Soc. Internal Medicine, Calif. Med. Assn., Cen. Soc. Clin. Research, Leukemia Soc. Am., Orange County Chief of Staff Council. Office: 101 City Blvd W Orange CA 92668-2901

ARMEY, DOUGLAS RICHARD, minister; b. Fresno, Calif., Oct. 23, 1948; s. Wilbur Rutter and Mildred (Broadbent) A.; m. Jennifer Louise Armey, Sept. 23, 1972; children: Laura Elizabeth, Andrew Douglas. AA, Fresno (Calif.) City Coll., 1969; Bs summa cum laude, Calif. State U., Fresno, 1971; MA, Mennonite Brethren Sem., Fresno, 1976. Ordained to ministry, Ch. of Brethren, 1973. Intern pastor The Peoples Ch. of Fresno, 1972-73; founding chaplain Fresno County Juvenile Hall, 1973; pres. Precision Parts Distbrs., Inc., Fresno, 1973-80, Rutter Armey Engine Co., Inc., Bakersfield, Calif., 1980-88; sr. pastor Fresno Ch. of the Brethren, 1988—; radio broadcaster Fresno Fellowship of Christian Athletes/KIRV Radio, 1987—. Contbr. articles to profl. jours. and mags. Bd. dirs. Fresno Youth for Christ, 1985-87. With Calif. Air N.G., 1968-74. Mem. Nat. Assn. Evangelicals, Sigma Alpha Epsilon, Sunnyside Country Club. Republican. Ch. of the Brethren. Office: 3901 E Clinton Ave Fresno CA 93703-2599

ARMIJO, JACQULYN DORIS, interior designer; b. Gilmer, Tex., July 2, 1938; d. Jack King and Iris Adele (Cook) Smith; children—John, Christy, Mike; m. Chet Wigton. Student North Tex. State Coll., U. N.Mex. Profl. model, 1961-75; sec. State Farm Ins., Albuquerque, 1965-71; life ins. agt. Mountain States, Albuquerque, 1980; owner Interiors by Jacqulyn, Albuquerque, 1961—; cons., lectr. in field. Mem. Alby Little Theatre, Friends of Little Theatre, Symphony Women; fund raiser for Old Town Hist. Com., Arthritis Fund. Mem. Am. Soc. Interior Design (chmn. historic restoration Albuquerque), Internat. Soc. Interior Design, Internat. Platform Assn., Civil War Club (pres. local chpt.) Republican. Roman Catholic. Clubs: Albuquerque Jr. Women's, Los Amapolas Garden. Home and Office: 509 Chamiso Ln NW Albuquerque NM 87107-6601

ARMINANA, RUBEN, university administrator, educator; b. Santa Clara, Cuba, May 15, 1947; came to U.S., 1961; s. Aurelio Ruben and Olga Petrona (Nart) A.; m. Marne Olson, July 6, 1957; children: Cesar A. Martino, Maria G. Arminana. AA, Hill Jr. Coll., 1966; BA, U. Tex., 1968, MA, 1970; PhD, U. New Orleans, 1983; postgrad. Inst. of Applied Behavioral Scis., Nat. Tng. Labs., 1971. Nat. assoc. dir. Phi Theta Kappa, Canton, Miss., 1968-69; dir. ops. and tng. Inter-Am. Ctr., Loyola U., New Orleans, 1969-71; administrv. analyst City of New Orleans, 1972, adminstrv. analyst and organizational devel. and tng. cons., 1972-78; anchor and reporter part time STA. WWL-TV, New Orleans, 1973-81; v.p. Commerce Internat. Corp., New Orleans, 1978-83; exec. asst. to sr. v.p. Tulane U., New Orleans, 1983-85, assoc. exec. v.p., 1985-87, v.p., asst. to pres., 1987-88; v.p. fin. and devel. Calif. State Poly U., Pomona, 1988—; pres, Sonoma State U., 1992—; TV news cons., New Orleans, 1981-88; lectr. Internat. Trade Mart, New Orleans, 1983-89, U.S. Dept. Commerce, New Orleans. Co-author: Hemisphere West-El Futuro, 1968; co-editor: Colloquium on Central America-A Time for Understanding, Background Readings, 1985. Bd. dirs. Com. on Alcoholism and Substance Abuse, 1978-79, SER, Jobs for Progress, Inc., 1974-82, Citizens United for Responsive Broadcasting, Latin Am. Festival Com; dir., bd. advisors Sta. WDSU-TV, 1974-77; mem. Bus. Govt. Rsch., 1987-88, Coun. Advancment of Support to Edn.; mem. League of United Latin Am. Citizens, Mayor's Latin Am. Adv. Com., Citizens to Preserve the Charter, Met. Area Com., Mayor's Com. on Crime. Kiwanis scholar, 1966, Books scholar, 1966. Mem. Assn. U. Related Rsch. Prks., L.A. Higher Edn. Roundtable, Soc. Coll. and U. Planning, Nat. Assn. Coll. and U. Bus. Officers Cou., Am. Econ. Assn., Assn. of Evolutionary Econs., Am. Polit. Sci. Assn., AAUP, Latin Am. C. of C. (founding dir. New Orleans and River Region 1976-83), Cuban Profl. Club, Phi Theta Kappa, Omicron Delta Epsilon, Sigma Delta Pi, Delta Sigma Pi. Democrat. Roman Catholic. Avocation: mask collecting. Office: Sonoma State U Office of President Rohnert Park CA 94928

ARMITAGE, CARINTHIA URBANETTE, realtor; b. Honolulu, Aug. 27, 1954; d. Urban Edward and Salome Lilinoe (Needham) Kunewa; children: Marvel K.O., George K. III, Daven W.H.K., Keoni A.U., Chanelle B.K., Michelle C.W. AA in Liberal Arts, U. Hawaii, 1990, BA in Psychology, 1993, BA in Bus. Adminstrn., 1993. Tax preparer certs. H&R Block, Waianae, Hawaii, 1987-90; realtor assoc. Debra and Co., Aiea, Hawaii, 1986—. Mem. Women in Transition, Leeward Coll., 1987—. Mem. Nat. Bd. Realtors, Honolulu Bd. Realtors. Home: 86-263 Alamihi St Waianae HI 96792

ARMOUR, GORDON CHARLES, technology and contract manager; b. Denver, June 1, 1929; s. Gordon Thomas and Doris Hilda (Stoker) A.; m. Margaret Christine Graney, Sept. 22, 1951; children: Doris C., Thomas S. BS, UCLA, 1953, MBA, 1957, PhD, 196l. Registered profl. engr., Calif. Sr. indsl. engr. Johns-Manville Co., Long Beach, Calif., 1957-59; asst. prof. Grad. Sch. Bus., Ind. U., Bloomington, 196l-64; mgmt. systems specialist N.Am. Aviation Co., Anaheim, Calif., 1964-68; chief mgmt. systems and planning N.Am. Rockwell, Anaheim, Calif., 1968-69; exec. advisor N.Am. Rockwell, Anaheim, 1969-73; indsl. planning specialist Rockwell Internat., Anaheim, 1973-79, exec. advisor for computers, 1979-8l, mgr. telecommunications and computer tech., 198l-83, specialist for emerging tech., 1983-92; vis. prof. UCLA, 1963; cons. Gen. Water Heater Co., Burbank, Calif., 1960. Contbr. articles to profl. publs. Mem. selection panel for data procesing mgr. City of Anaheim, 1980. With USMC, 1953-55. Jo Downing scholar, 1953; Ford Found. fellow, 1959-6l, 63-64, Ind. U. rsch. fellow, 1962. Home: 128l2 Bubbling Well Rd Santa Ana CA 92705 Office: Rockwell Internat 3370 Mira Loma Ave AE12 Anaheim CA 92803

ARMS, RICHARD WOODWORTH, JR., money manager; b. Weymouth, Mass., Jan. 12, 1935; s. Richard W. and Ruth (Adams) A.; m. June Norma Arter, June 20, 1934; children: Allison, Richard III. With E.F. Hutton & Co., prior to 1984; analyst Prin./E.G.T., Albuquerque, 1984-91; pres. The Arms Cos., Albuquerque, 1991—. Author: Profits in Volume, 1972, Volume Cycles in the Stock Market, 1982, The Arms Index, 1990; developer The Arms Index, 1968, Equivolume Charting, 1972; contbr. articles to industry jours. With U.S. Army, 1958-66. Mem. Market Technician's Assn., Internat. Fedn. Tech. Analysts, Can. Soc. Tech. Analysts, Mensa, Toastmasters. Home: 800 Wagon Train Dr SE Albuquerque NM 87123-4140

ARMSTEAD, ROBERT LOUIS, physics educator; b. Blair, Nebr., Nov. 5, 1936; s. Louis Clifford and Florence (Curtis) A.; m. Mary Richards, Aug. 12, 1961; children: Karen, Janet. BS in Physics, U. Rochester, 1958; PhD in Physics, U. Calif., Berkeley, 1965. Asst. prof. Naval Postgrad. Sch., Monterey, Calif., 1964-70, assoc. prof., 1970—, assoc. chmn. for instrn. physics dept., 1986—. Treas., bd. dirs. Carmel (Calif.) Music Soc., 1984-89. Mem. Am. Phys. Soc., Am. Assn. Physics Tchrs., Sigma Xi. Home: PO Box 6491 Carmel CA 93921-6491 Office: Naval Postgrad Sch Physics Dept Monterey CA 93943

ARMSTRONG, ANNA DAWN, marketing professional, writer; b. San Francisco, Jan. 28, 1943. BBA, U. Portland, Oreg., 1964. Mktg. asst. Food Giant Markets, L.A., 1964-65; copywriter Young & Rubicam Advt., L.A., 1965-67; creative dir. Capitol Direct Mktg. Corp., Hollywood, Calif., 1967-70; ptnr. Harrison Assocs., L.A., 1970-73; mktg. officer Security Pacific Bank, L.A., 1973-76; creative cons. Dawn Armstrong, L.A., 1976-78; v.p., creative dir. Mktg. and Fin. Mgmt. Enterprises, Inc., Encino, Calif., 1978-81, Direct Mktg. Corp. Am., L.A., 1981-83; pres., creative dir. A Creative Group, Sebastopol and Lake Tahoe, Calif., 1983—; v.p. Mktg. Concepts and Mgmt., Lake Tahoe, Nev., 1991—; v.p., creative dir. Membership Clubs Internat., Century City, Calif., 1978-81, Direct Mktg. Internat., Australia, Can., France, U.K., 1981-83. Author: (7 book-series) Direct Marketing, 1988; contbr. articles to profl. jours. Exec. dir. South Lake Tahoe (Calif.) Humane Soc. and Lake Tahoe Humane Soc. (Nev.), 1991—; tutor State of Calif. Literacy Program, South Lake Tahoe, 1991—. Mem. Lake Tahoe Press Club (charter). Office: A Creative Group PO Box 612006 South Lake Tahoe CA 96152

ARMSTRONG, DAVID MICHAEL, biology educator; b. Louisville, July 31, 1944; s. John D. and Elizabeth Ann (Horine) A.; children: John D., Laura C. BS, Colo. State U., 1966; MA in Teaching, Harvard U., 1967; PhD, U. Kans., 1971. From asst. prof. natural sci. to full prof. U. Colo., Boulder, 1971—; sr. scientist Rocky Mountain Biol. Lab., Gothic, Colo., 1977, 79; resident naturalist Sylvan Dale Ranch, Loveland, Colo., 1984—; acting dir. Univ. Mus., 1987-88, dir., 1989—; cons. ecologist. Author: Distribution of Mammals in Colorado, 1972, Rocky Mountain Mammals, 1975, 87, Mammals of the Canyon Country, 1982; co-author: Mammals of the Northern Great Plains, Mammals of the Plains States. Mem. non-game adv. council Colo. Div. Wildlife, 1972-76, Colo. Natural Areas Council, 1975-80. Mem. Am. Soc. Mammalogists (editor 1981-87), Southwestern Assn. Naturalists (editor 1976-80), Rocky Mountain Biol. Lab. (trustee 1979-83), Sigma Xi. Office: U Colo Dept EPO Biology Box 334 Boulder CO 80309-0218

ARMSTRONG, DICKWIN DILL, chamber of commerce executive; b. Muncie, Ind., Aug. 18, 1934; s. Colby Cooler and Elizabeth A. (Houck) A.; m. Janice A. Flora, June 2, 1957; children—Brent D., Stacey J. BS in Gen. Bus, Ind. U., 1956. Chief exec. officer Madison C. of C., Ind., 1959-61; chief exec. officer Frankfort C. of C., Ind., 1961-63, Marion C. of C., Ind., 1963-66, Lakeland C. of C., Fla., 1966-80; chief exec. officer Portland C. of C., Oreg., 1980-86, treas. polit. action com.; pres. Bellevue C. of C., Wash., 1987—. Served to capt. AUS, 1957-59. Mem. Am. C. of C. Execs. (cert. chamber exec., past officer), U.S. C. of C., Oreg. Chamber Execs. (dir., com. chmn.), Washington C. of C. Execs. (former pres.), Rotary, Masons, Shriners, Sigma Alpha Epsilon. Republican. Presbyterian. Office: Bellevue C of C 10500 NE 8th Ste 212 Bellevue WA 98004

ARMSTRONG, F(REDRIC) MICHAEL, insurance company executive; b. Wichita, Kans., Dec. 20, 1942; s. Frederick Dale and Virginia Pauline A.; m. Patricia R. Latif, Dec. 13, 1976. B.S. in Elec. Engring., MIT, 1964; M.B.A., Stanford U., 1966. Mgr. capital appropriations Trans World Airlines, N.Y.C., 1966-69; corp. planner Transam. Corp., San Francisco, 1969-70; v.p. Transam. Film Service, Salt Lake City, 1970-73, also bd. dir.; v.p. fin. Europe Transam. Airlines, Madrid, 1973-75, v.p. planning and info. svcs., Oakland, Calif., 1975-77; exec. v.p. fin. Budget Rent a Car Corp., Chgo., 1977-83, also bd. dir.; exec. v.p., chief adminstrv. officer Transam. Ins. Group, Los Angeles, 1983—, also bd. dir.; bd. dirs. Melia Internat. Hotels, Panama, The Canadian Surety Co., Ins. Value Added Network Service, River Thames Ins. Co., London, Fairmont Fin. Inc., Mason-McDuffie Ins. Svc., Inc., The Completion Bond Co. Mem. adv. coun. Pierce Coll. Office: Transam Ins Group 6300 Canoga Ave Woodland Hills CA 91367-2555

ARMSTRONG, GENE LEE, retired aerospace company executive; b. Clinton, Ill., Mar. 9, 1922; s. George Dewey and Ruby Imald (Dickerson) A. m. Lael Jeanne Baker, Apr. 3, 1946; children—Susan Lael, Roberta Lynn, Gene Lee. BS with high honors, U. Ill., 1948, MS, 1951. registered profl. engr., Calif. With Boeing Aircraft, 1948-50, 51-52; chief engr. astronautics div., corp. dir. Gen. Dynamics, 1954-65; chief engr. Def. Systems Group TRW, Redondo Beach, Calif., 1956-86; pvt. cons. systems engring. Def. Systems Group TRW, 1986—; Mem. NASA Research Adv. Com. on Control, Guidance & Navigation, 1959-62. Contbr. chpts. to books, articles to profl. publs. Served to 1st lt. USAAF, 1942-45. Decorated Air medal; recipient alumni awards U. Ill., 1965, 77;. Mem. Am. Math. Soc., AIAA, Nat. Mgmt. Assn., Am. Def. Preparedness Assn., Masons. Home: 5242 Bryant Cir Westminster CA 92683-1713 Office: Armstrong Systems Engring Co PO Box 86 Westminster CA 92684-0086

ARMSTRONG, GLENN GARNETT, artist, retired postal executive; b. Nashville, May 19, 1916; s. Garnett and Frances Elizabeth (Hawkins) A.; m. Mary Jule Zito, July 5, 1960; children: Barbara Lynn, Elizabeth Marie, Rebecca Ann, Glenn Garnett Jr. Student, U. N.Mex., 1934-36; studied art with Carl Von Hassler, 1946-48; student, U. Ga., 1960, Northwestern U., 1962. Clk. U.S. Postal Svc., Albuquerque, 1936-47, foreman, 1947-50, asst. supt. mails, 1950-55, dist. mgr., 1955-59; regional mgr. U.S. Postal Svc., Atlanta, 1959-71; real estate broker Atlanta, 1971-80; ind. artist Albuquerque, 1980—; chief nat. staffing survey team U.S. Postal Svc., Washington, 1966; speaker in field. One-man shows include Mus. N.Mex., Santa Fe, 1952, Botts Meml. Gallery, Albuquerque, 1953; oil paintings represented in Gov.'s Gallery, Santa Fe, 1993 and permanent collections, nationwide. Mem. City Planning Bd., Albuquerque, 1950. With U.S. Army, 1943-45, ETO. Mem. N.Mex. Art League, Albuquerque United Artists, Albuquerque Arts Alliance. Republican. Roman Catholic. Home and Office: 1501 Park Ave SW Albuquerque NM 87104

ARMSTRONG, JUDITH ANN, university official; b. St. Louis, Dec. 12, 1946; d. Rudolph J. and Jessie N. (Brown) Blome; m. Halsey C. Armstrong, Aug. 20, 1983. BA, Ea. N.Mex. U., Portales, 1968, MA, 1969; postgrad., U. N.Mex. Tchr. English and speech Syracuse (Kans.) High Sch., 1969-71; tchr. English, High Sch. Equivalency Program, Roswell, N.Mex., 1971-81; asst. dir. Roswell Pub. Libr., 1981-83; instr. Ea. N.Mex. U., Roswell, 1983-87, dir. devel. studies, 1987-88, asst. dean instrnl. support, 1988—; weekly columnist Libr. Topics, Roswell Daily Record, 1982—, theatre reviewer, 1989—. Mem., officer Roswell Symphony Guild, 1983—; mem. Reach 2000-Ednl. Resource, Roswell, 1989—; bd. dirs. N.Mex. Coalition for Literacy, 1989-92, Friends of Libr., Roswell, 1982—; mem., officer Nat. Inst. for Leadership Devel., Phoenix, 1991-92; trustee First United Meth. Ch., Roswell, 1989, staff parish rels. com., 1992—. Recipient Celebrate Literacy award and State Literacy award Internat. Reading Assn., 1993, Gov.'s award for Outstanding Women N.Mex., 1993. Mem. Am. Bus. Women's Assn. (officer Roswell, 1979—, Woman of Yr. award 1986), Altrusa (offficer, dist. editor Roswell 1982—), Delta Kappa Gamma (v.p. Roswell 1984—). Republican. Home: PO Box 178 Roswell NM 88202-0178 Office: Ea NMex U PO Box 6000 Roswell NM 88202-6000

ARMSTRONG, KENNETH, lawyer; b. Chgo., Mar. 25, 1949. BS in Bus. Adminstrn., Sussex (Eng.) U., 1971; JD with distinction, Pacific Coast U., 1989. Cert. real estate appraiser, Nat. Assn. Real Estate Appraisers; cert.

review appraiser, Nat. Assn. Review Appraisers; registered locksmith, Nat. Assn. Associated Locksmiths Am. Pvt. practice Mt. Shasta, Calif.; mem. redevel. com. PAC, Long Beach, 1982; legal cons. student body Calif. State U., Long Beach, 1991. Contbr. articles to profl. jours. Mem. City of Long Beach Downtown; performing mem. Magic Castle, Hollywood, Calif., 1989—. Mem. ABA, Calif. State Bar, Long Beach Bar Assn., L.A. County Bar Assn., L.A. Trial Lawyers Assn., Calif. Trial Lawyers Assn., Siskiyou County Bar Assn., Cow Counties Bar Assn. Office: 415 N Mt Shasta Blvd Ste 4 Mount Shasta CA 96067

ARMSTRONG, MICHAEL C., aerospace executive; b. 1939. BS, Miami U. With Internat. Bus. Machines Corp., 1961-92; chmn. bd., CEO Hughes Aircraft Co., 1992—. Address: Hughes Aircraft Co PO Box 45066 Los Angeles CA 90045

ARMSTRONG, MOE, disability rights advocate, public radio broadcaster, educator; b. Keokuk, Iowa, June 25, 1944; s. Dale E. and Esther (Frischknecht) A.; m. Chalee Trainor, Jan. BBA, Coll. of Santa Fe, 1987, BA in Lit., MBA, 1990; MA, Webster U., 1991. Announcer Sta. KUNM; bd. dirs. vet. affairs Coll. of Sante Fe, 1985-89; moderator radio debate Sta. KUNM, 1990—; state consumer coun. pres. NAMI N.M. Author of selected poems. Co-chmn. Congl. Task Force Vets. Affairs, Santa Fe, 1986-89; co-coord. Raices Radio Collectives. With USN, 1962-66, Vietnam. Recipient Human Rights award City of Albuquerque. Mem. Nat. Alliance Mentally Ill (pres. N.Mex. state consumer coun., Grass Seeds grantee for mental health project in N.Mex.), N.Mex. Coalition for Disability (sec.). Roman Catholic. Home: Tierra W Estates No 158 12550 Central Ave SW Albuquerque NM 87121-7730

ARMSTRONG, ORVILLE, lawyer; b. Austin, Tex., Jan. 21, 1929; s. Orville Alexander and Velma Lucille (Reed) A.; m. Mary Dean Macfarlane. BBA, U. Tex., Austin, 1953; LLB, U. So. Calif., 1956. Bar: Calif., 1957, U.S. Ct. Appeals (9th cir.) 1958, U.S. Supreme Ct. 1980. Ptnr., Gray, Binkley & Pfaelzer, 1956-61, Pfaelzer, Robertson, Armstrong & Woodard, L.A., 1961-66, Armstrong & Lloyd, L.A., 1966-74, Macdonald, Halsted & Laybourne, L.A., 1975-88, Baker & McKenzie, 1988-90; judge Superior Ct. State of Calif., 1991-92, assoc. justice ct. appeal State of Calif., 1993—; lectr. Calif. Continuing Edn. of Bar. Served with USAF, 1946-49. Fellow ABA, Am. Coll. Trial Lawyers; mem. State Bar Calif. (gov. 1983-87, pres. 1986-87), L.A. County Bar Assn. (trustee 1971-72), Am. Judicature Soc., Chancery Club (pres. 1988), Assn. Bus. Trial Lawyers, Am. Arbitration Assn., Calif. Club. Baptist. Home: 2385 Coniston Pl San Marino CA 91108-2102 Office: 300 S Spring St Los Angeles CA 90013

ARMSTRONG, R(OBERT) DEAN, entertainer; b. Serena, Ill., July 2, 1923; s. Francis Robert and Viola D. (Thompson) A.; m. Ardith Roberta Taylor, Jan. 10, 1943; 1 child, Larry Dean. Grad. high sch., Serena, Ill.; student, Joliet (Ill.) Conservatory of Music, 1942. Host Dean Armstrong Show Sta. KOLD-TV, Tucson, 1953-75; leader, owner Ariz. Dance Hands, Tucson, 1946—. Served with U.S. Mil., 1943-45, ETO, PTO. Recipient Jefferson award for pub. svc., 1992. Mem. Tucson Musicians Assn. (meritorious svc. award 1981), VFW, Western Music Assn. (charter mem.), Profl. Western Music Assn. Democrat. Methodist. Lodges: Elks, Eagles. Home and Office: 4265 Avenida del Cazador Tucson AZ 85718

ARMSTRONG, ROBERT STILLMAN, insurance company executive; b. Chgo., Apr. 30, 1949; s. James Sinclair Armstrong and Elizabeth (Stillman) Upham; 1 child, James. BS, NYU, 1975; MBA, Calif. Luth. U., 1993. Acct. exec. Prudential Ins. Co. Am., L.A., 1975-93. With U.S. Army, 1967-71. Home and Office: 3362 Hidden Creek Ave Thousand Oaks CA 91360

ARMSTRONG, SAUNDRA BROWN, federal judge; b. Oakland, Calif., Mar. 23, 1947; d. Coolidge Logan and Pauline Marquette (Bearden) Brown; m. George Walter Armstrong, Apr. 18, 1982. B.A., Calif. State U.-Fresno, 1969; J.D., U. San Francisco, 1977. Bar: Calif. 1977, U.S. Supreme Ct. 1984. Policewoman Oakland Police Dept., 1970-77; prosecutor, dep. dist. atty. Alameda County Dist. Atty., Oakland, 1978-79, 80-82; staff atty. Calif. Legis. Assembly Com. on Criminal Justice, Sacramento, 1979-80; trial atty. Dept. Justice, Washington, 1982-83; vice chmn. U.S. Consumer Product Safety Commn., Washington, 1984-86; commr. U.S. Parole Commn., Washington, 1986-89; judge Alameda Superior Ct., 1989-91, U.S. Dist. Ct. (no. dist.) Calif., San Francisco, 1991—. Recipient commendation Calif. Assembly, 1980. Mem. Nat. Bar Assn., ABA, Calif. Bar Assn., Charles Houston Bar Assn., Black C. of C., Phi Alpha Delta. Democrat. Baptist. Office: US District Ct PO Box 36060 San Francisco CA 94102

ARMSTRONG, WALLACE DOWAN, JR., data processor; b. Los Angeles, Feb. 9, 1926; s. Wallace Dowan and Vina Edith (Kreinbring) A.; B.S. cum laude, U. So. Calif., 1951; postgrad. U. Oslo (Norway), 1955; 1 son, Erik Bentung. Supr. accounting Ramo Wooldridge Corp., 1955-60; mgr. programmers, systems analyst Aerospace Corp., El Segundo, Calif., 1960-80, mgr. bus. systems, 1980—. Mem. Common Cause, Handgun Control, Inc. With USMCR, 1944-46, 51. Mem. Data Processing Mgmt. Assn. Home: 25713 Crest Rd Torrance CA 90505-7022 Office: Aerospace Corp 2350 E El Segundo Blvd El Segundo CA 90245-4691

ARNDT, MICHAEL PAUL, financial consulting executive; b. Mt. Vernon, N.Y., Aug. 30, 1930; s. Stanley Morris Arndt and Helen Lucille (Wood) Arndt. BA, Pomona Coll., 1952; MBA, Harvard U., 1954. Analyst investment dept. N.Y. Life, San Francisco, 1954-56; v.p. fin. control TRW, Inc., L.A., 1956-86; pres. TOWR Assocs., L.A., 1987—, also bd. dirs. Pres. Pomona Coll. Assocs., Claremont, Calif., 1983-87; trustee Pomona Coll., Claremont, 1985-87; bd. dirs., treas. L.A. unit Rec. for the Blind. Am. Chem. Soc. scholar, 1947. Mem. Fin. Analyst Assn., Fin. Exec. Inst., Phi Beta Kappa, Phi Delta (pres. 1952, bd. dirs. 1960-75), Mar de Cortez (La Paz, Mex., bd. dirs. 1963-78). Republican. Home: 251 S Barrington Ave Los Angeles CA 90049-3303 Office: TOWR Assocs 1253 7th St Santa Monica CA 90401

ARNE, KENNETH GEORGE, mining executive, mineral consultant; b. Prairie City, Oreg., Feb. 5, 1942; s. John Ralph Arne and Mary Louise (Roland) Noud; m. Elizabeth Andre Spodnick, Mar. 23, 1968 (div. June 1992); children: Christopher L., Melissa A. BS in Engring., Mont. Tech., Butte, 1964; MBA, Stanford U., 1969. Registered profl. engr., Ariz., Colo. Petroleum engr. Amoco, Inc., Denver, 1964-67; dir. uranium mktg. Conoco, Inc., Stamford, Conn., 1969-79; 2d v.p. Continental Ill. Bank, Chgo., 1979-82; gen. mgr. Can-Am Corp., Tucson, 1982-88; fin. analyst Minorco, U.S.A. and affiliates, Denver, 1988-92; mineral cons. in pvt. practice Denver, 1992—; cons. Econ. Adv. Project, Republic of Georgia, 1992. Mem. AIME, Can. Inst. Mining and Metallurgy, Colo. Mining Assn. (bd. dirs. 1990-92), Denver Rep. Club, Rotary Club Evergreen, Theta Tau. Roman Catholic. Home: 1 Emmerson Pl # 4P Boston MA 02114 Office: 8330 E Quincy J-301 Denver CO 80237

ARNELL, ROBERT EDWARD, technical writer; b. Juneau, Alaska, Dec. 26, 1941; s. Edward Lloyd and Mary Ellen (Speanburg) A.; m. Kathleen Elizabeth Moehlman, July 27, 1967 (div. 1983); 1 child, Rebecca Ann. Seattle U., 1972. Tech. writer Western Gear Corp., Everett, Wash., 1968-70; communications specialist Milmanco Corp., Rento, Wash., 1972-74; engring. writer Honeywell Marine Systems, Seattle, 1974-76; pub., cons. Dynacom II, Inc., Seattle, 1976-79; sr. tech. writer Talley Corp., Kent, Wash., 1979-80; tech. publs. engring. Sundstrand Data Control Corp., Redmond, Wash., 1980-81; tech. publs. supr. Tacoma (Wash.) Boatbuilding, Inc., 1981-82; tech. publs. engr., logistics analysts, supr. Lockheed Corp., Seattle and Lompoc, 1982-86; tech. instr. Computer Sci. Corp., Lompoc, Calif., 1987-88; tech. writer Spar Communications Group, Spar Aerospace Corp., Santa Maria, Calif., 1988—; cons. Delco, Gen. Motors Corp., Goleta, Calif., 1988, Grumman Corp., Point Magu, Calif., 1988, Data Designs Co., Goleta, 1990—. Author: (brochure) Alaska: Investment in Tomorrow, 1972, (manual Wash. State Dept. Hwys.) Highway Maintenance, 1973/74, (manual for USN) Sonar Acoustic Target Source, 1974/75, (manual for SEDCO 445) Automatic Station Keeping System, 1975, (comml. manuals) Series T3000 Line Printer, 1979, Head-Up Display Computer, 1980/81, an many others; publisher, editor: (monthly periodical) Dinner's Almanac, 1976-79. Capt. U.S. Army, 1964-73. Mem. Soc. for Tech. Communication, Ctrl. Coast Calif. Arabian Horse Assn. (affiliate mem., treas. 1989-92). Republican. Roman Catholic. Home: 37 W Pine Ave #5 Lompoc CA 93436 Office: Spar Communications Group 2811 Airpark Dr Santa Maria CA 93455

ARNELL, WALTER JAMES WILLIAM, engineering educator, consultant; b. Farnborough, Eng., Jan. 9, 1924; came to U.S., 1953, naturalized, 1960; s. James Albert and Daisy (Payne) A.; m. Patricia Catherine Cannon, Nov. 12, 1955; children—Sean Paul, Victoria Clare, Sarah Michele Arnell. Aero. Engr., Royal Aircraft Establishment, 1946; BSc, U. London, 1953, PhD, 1967; MA, Occidental Coll., Los Angeles, 1956; MS, U. So. Calif., 1958. Lectr. Poly. and Northampton Coll. Advance Tech., London, 1948-53; instr. U. So. Calif., Los Angeles, 1954-59; asst. prof. mech. engring. Calif. State U., Long Beach, 1959-62, assoc. prof., 1962-66, prof., 1966-71, chmn. dept. mech. engring., 1964-65, acting chmn. div. engring., 1964-66, dean engring., 1967-69, researcher Ctr. Engring. Research; affiliate faculty dept. ocean engring. U. Hawaii, 1970-74; adj. prof. systems and insdl. engring. U. Ariz., 1981—; pres. Lenra Assocs. Ltd., 1973—; chmn., project mgr. Hawaii Environ. Simulation Lab., 1971-72. Contbr. articles to profl. jours. Trustee Rehab. Hosp. of the Pacific, 1975-78. Mem. Royal Aero. Soc., AIAA, IEEE Systems Man and Cybernetics Soc., AAUP, Am. Psychol. Assn., Soc. Engring., Psychology, Human Factors Soc., Ergonomics Soc., Psi Chi, Alpha Pi Mu, Tau Beta Pi, Phi Kappa Phi, Pi Tau Sigma. Home: 4491 E Ft Lowell Rd Tucson AZ 85712-1106

ARNEY, WILLIAM RAY, sociologist, educator; b. Charlotte, N.C., Sept. 18, 1950; s. John Wilson and Grace (Kuhn) A.; m. Deborah Henderson, Jan. 2, 1972; 1 child: John Arthur. BA with distinction, U. Colo., 1971, MA, 1972; PhD, 1974. Asst. prof. then assoc. prof. Dartmouth Coll., Hanover, N.H., 1974-81; dir. edn. and evaluation Vt.-N.H. Regional Perinatal Program, Hanover, N.H., 1978-80; mem. of the faculty Evergreen State Coll., Olympia, Wash., 1981—. Author: Power and the Profession of Obstetrics, 1982, Medicine and the Management of Living (with others), 1984, Understanding Statistics in the Social Sciences, 1990, Experts in the Age of Systems, 1991. NEH fellow, 1986; Rockefeller Found. resident Bellagio (Italy) Study and Conf. Ctr., 1988. Mem. Am. Statis. Assn., Am. Sociol. Assn. Mem. Disciples of Christ Church. Home: 2353 Crestline Blvd NW Olympia WA 98502-4323 Office: Evergreen State Coll Lab II Olympia WA 98505

ARNOLD, JAMES RICHARD, chemist, educator; b. New Brunswick, N.J., May 5, 1923; s. Abraham Samuel and Julia (Jacobs) A.; m. Louise Clark, Oct. 11, 1952; children: Robert C., Theodore J., Kenneth C. A.B., Princeton U., 1943, M.A., 1945, Ph.D., 1946. Postdoctoral fellow Inst. Nuclear Studies, U. Chgo., 1946-47, mem. faculty, 1948-55; NRC fellow Harvard U., 1947-48; mem. faculty chemistry Princeton U., 1955-58; assoc. prof. chemistry U. Calif., San Diego, 1958-60; prof. U. Calif., 1960-92, Harold C. Urey prof., 1983-92, chmn. dept. chemistry, 1960-63; asso. Manhattan Project, 1943-46; dir. Calif. Space Inst., 1980-89; mem. various bds. NASA, 1959—; mem. space sci. bd. Nat. Acad. Sci., 1970-74, mem. com. on sci. and public policy, 1973-77. Mem. editorial bd.: Ann. Rev. Nuclear Chemistry, 1972; asso. editor: Revs. Geophysics and Space Physics, 1972-75, Moon, 1972—; contbr. articles to profl. jours. Pres. Torrey Pines Elem. Sch. PTA, 1964-65; pres. La Jolla Democratic Club, 1965-66; mem. nat. council World Federalists-U.S.A., 1970-72. Recipient E.O. Lawrence medal AEC, 1968; Leonard medal Meteoritical Soc., 1976; asteroid 2143 named Jimarnold in his honor, 1980; Guggenheim fellow India, 1972-73. Mem. Nat. Acad. Sci., Am. Acad. Arts and Scis., Internat. Acad. Astronautics, Am. Chem. Soc., AAAS, Fedn. Am. Scientists, World Federalist Assn. Office: U Calif San Diego Dept Chemistry Code 0317 La Jolla CA 92093

ARNOLD, JAMES TRACY, physicist; b. Taiyuanfu, Shansi, China, Oct. 23, 1920; s. Roger David and Eleanor (Tracy) A.; m. Marna Craig, Aug. 17, 1957; children: Erica, Laura, David, Andrew. BA, Oberlin Coll., 1942; grad., USN Test Pilot Sch., 1946; PhD, Stanford U., 1954. Cert. jr. coll. tchr. Instr. Oberlin (Ohio) Coll., 1947-48; grad. asst. Stanford (Calif.) U., 1948-54, rsch. assoc., 1955-57; spl. asst. to dir. European Ctr. for Nuclear Rsch., Geneva, 1954-55; asst. prof. Oreg. State U., Corvallis, 1957-58; engr. Varian Assocs., Palo Alto, Calif., 1958-62, sr. scientist, 1962—. Author: Simplified Digital Automation With Microprocessors, 1976; contbr. articles to profl. jours. Active St. Andrews Sch. Bd., Saratoga, Calif., 1960-72. With USN, 1942-47, comdr. Res., 1950-72. Republican. Episcopalian. Office: Varian Assocs 3075 Hansen Way Palo Alto CA 94304-1025

ARNOLD, KENNETH JAMES, lawyer, publishing company executive; b. Brighton, Colo., Sept. 10, 1927; s. Kenneth Wilburt and Frances Irene (Lloyd) A. BA, U. Calif., Berkeley, 1949; JD, U. Calif., San Francisco, 1958. Bar: Calif. 1959. Pvt. practice law San Francisco, 1959-60, 63—, Sacramento, 1960-62; owner Law Book Svc. Co., San Francisco, 1969—; rsch. atty. Calif. Supreme Ct., Sacramento, 1960-62, Calif. Ct. Appeals for 1st Appelate Dist., San Francisco, 1958-60; asst. sr. editor-in-chief Matthew Bender & Co., San Francisco, 1963-81, staff author, 1981-87, sr. staff author, 1987-92; lectr. in field, 1972-81; cons. Calif. State Jud. Coun., 1970-75, Calif. Ctr. Jud. Edn. and Rsch., 1974—, Calif. Coll. Trial Judges, 1975, McGeorge Coll. Law, U. Pacific, 1975-80; mem. Calif. Legal Forms Com., 1971-73. Author: California Courts and Judges Handbook, 1968, 5th rev. edit., 1988, 6th rev. edit., 1993; California Justice Court Manual, 1971 supplement; (with others) California Points and Authorities, 23 vols., 1964-92, California Forms of Pleadings and Practice, 55 vols., 1966-92, California Legal Forms, 25 vols., 1967-69; Commencing Civil Actions in California, 1975, and supplements; (with others) California Family Law Practice, 6 vols., 1977-78, California Civil Actions, 5 vols., 1982-92; other manuals and handbooks; feature writer Barclays Law Monthly, 1979-82; editor-in-chief Vector Mag., 1965-67. Bd. dirs. Soc. for Individual Rights, 1965-67, PRIDE Found., San Francisco, 1974-77. With U.S. Army, 1952-55. Mem. State Bar Calif., U. Calif. Hastings Alumni Assn., Calif. Supreme Ct. Hist. Soc., 9th Jud. Dist. Hist. Soc., VFW, Am. Legion. Home and Office: 369 Harvard St San Francisco CA 94134-1345

ARNOLD, LEONARD J., construction executive; b. San Diego, Mar. 17, 1947; s. William W. and Thelma C. (Cook) A.; m. Judy Lynn Keeton, Aug. 30, 1969; children: Alyssa Noelle, Lorienne Eve. BS in Constrn. Mgmt., Colo. State U., 1970. V.p. G. E. Johnson Constrn., Colorado Springs, Colo., 1970-76; pres. Wyoming Johnson Inc., Casper, 1976-79; v.p. Hensel Phelps Constrn. Co., Greeley, Colo., 1979-88, Phelps, Inc., 1988-89, Hensel Phelps Constrn. Co., Greeley, Colo., 1989—. Chmn. Weld County Econ. Devel., Greeley, 1986-88. Mem. Urban Land Inst., Associated Gen. Contractors Am., Soc. Am. Mil. Engrs., U.S. Space Found., Colo. Assn. Sch. Bds., Sigma Lambda Chi. Republican. Club: Greeley Country. Home: 1309 42d Ave Greeley CO 80634 Office: Hensel Phelps Constrn Co 420 6th Ave Greeley CO 80631-2332

ARNOLD, MICHAEL JAMES, naval officer, aerospace engineer; b. Guatemala City, Guatemala, Jan. 8, 1946; s. James Elliott and Roberta Elaine (Anderson) A.; m. Michelle Lee Connelly, Feb. 1, 1969; children: Reenie Lee, Tige, Donovan. BS in Mech. Engring., U. Idaho, 1969; MS in Aero. Engring. with distinction, Naval Postgrad. Sch., 1978. Commd. ensign USN, 1969, advanced through grades to comdr., 1984; helicopter flight tng. Pensacola, Fla., 1969-70; pilot search and rescue Kingsville, Tex., 1970-72; pilot antisubmarine warfare (HS-4) San Diego, 1972-76; with USS Tarawa, San Diego, 1979-81, Antisubmarine Warefare Wing Pacific Fleet, San Diego, 1981-84, Naval Air Systems Command, Washington, 1984-88; dep. dir. Cruise Missiles Prog. Western Region, San Diego, 1988-91, dir., 1991-92; ret., 1992. Mem. Assn. Old Crows, Navy Helicopter Assn., Apple Programmers and Developers Assn. (ind.), Sigma Xi (assoc.). Roman Catholic.

ARNOLD, MICHAEL NEAL, real property appraiser, consultant; b. Madera, Calif., June 6, 1947; s. John Patrick and Patricia (Neal) A.; m. Suzanne Elizabeth Badal, Aug. 31, 1968; children: C. Matthew Neal Arnold, Nathaniel T. Badal Arnold, Andrew T. White Arnold, Thomas A. Badal Arnold. BA in Geography, U. Calif., Santa Barbara, 1974. Cert. appraiser. Assoc. R.W. Raymond & Co., Santa Barbara, 1974; appraiser Madera County Assessor Office, 1975; assoc. Pickthorne & Assocs., San Bruno, Calif., 1975-76; ptnr. Hammock, Arnold, Smith, Santa Barbara, 1976—; instr. Santa Barbara City Coll., 1980-85. Contbr. articles to profl. jours. Coach AYSO, Santa Barbara, 1978—; cub master Boy Scouts Am., Santa Barbara, 1985. Mem. Vieja Valley Site Coun., Santa Barbara Coun. Real Estate Appraisers (sec., speaker bur.), Appraisal Inst. (instr. 1990—, grader, com. chair, officer), Amateurs Club, Tennis Club of Santa Barbara, Santa Barbara Club, Santa Barbara City Coll. (adv. coun. mem.). Episcopalian. Home: 2325 Santa Barbara St Santa Barbara CA 93105-3547 Office: Hammock Arnold Smith & Co Spencer House 200 W Victoria St Santa Barbara CA 93101-3627

ARNOLD, RALPH LEO, III, valuation analyst, consultant; b. Butte, Mont., Oct. 22, 1949; s. Ralph L. Jr. and Annie B. (Baker) A. BS in Acctg., Calif. State U., Hayward, 1973. Auditor Calif. State Controller's Office, San Francisco, 1973-76, chief auditor, 1976-79; assoc. Holton Accountancy Corp., San Francisco, 1979-83; sr. valuation analyst Willamette Mgmt. Assocs., Portland, Oreg., 1983-92; valuation cons. Ralph Arnold Assocs., Portland, 1992—; instr. Portland State U., 1986-87. Contbr. chpt. to book, articles to profl. jours. Mem. Am. Soc. Appraisers (accredited sr. appraiser, pres. 1987-88), Am. Arbitration Assn. (panel), Fin. Analysts Fedn., Nat. Assn. Accts. Office: Ralph Arnold Assocs. 610 SW Alder St Ste 1001 Portland OR 97205

ARNOLD, ROBERT WAYNE, aerospace engineer; b. San Luis Obispo, Calif., Apr. 23, 1959; s. Robert William and Willa Pearl (Key) A.; m. Donna Marie Reid, Dec. 22, 1984; children: LaJuanda Marie, Bernadette Pearl. BS in Aerospace Engring., U. Colo., 1982. Engring. asst. Airborne div. Parker Hannifin, Longmont, Colo., 1982; prodn. lead E-Max Instruments, Inc., Denver, 1982-84; test engr. Gen. Dynamics, San Diego, 1984-85; sr. test engr. Martin Marietta Astronautics Group, Denver, 1985-90; sr. project engr. Honeywell, Inc., Glendale, Ariz., 1990—. Mem. Ariz. Coun. Black Engrs. and Scientists. Home: 1307 E Taro Ln Phoenix AZ 85024 Office: Honeywell Inc 19019 N 59th Ave Glendale AZ 85308

ARNOLD, RONALD HENRI, non-profit organization executive, consultant; b. Houston, Aug. 8, 1937; s. John Andrew and Carrie Virginia (Henri) A.; m. Phoebe Anne Trogdon, Oct. 12, 1963 (dec. Feb. 1974); 1 child, Andrea; m. Janet Ann Parkhurst, Aug. 8, 1974; stepchildren: Andrea Wright, Rosalyn Wright. Tech. publ. Boeing Co., Seattle, 1961-71; cons. Northwoods Studio, Bellevue, Wash., 1971—; exec. v.p. Ctr. for Def. of Free Enterprise, Bellevue, 1984—; Advisor Nat. Fed. Lands Conf., 1988—. Author: James Watt and the Environment, 1981, Ecology Wars, 1987, The Grand Prairie Years, 1987, (with Alan Gottlieb) Trashing the Economy, 1993; editor: Stealing The National Parks, 1987; contbg. editor Logging Mgmt. mag., 1978-81, Western Conservation Jour., 1974-81. Recipient Editorial Achievement award Am. Bus. Press, 1981. Mem. AFTRA, Forest History Soc. Republican. Home: 12605 N E 2d St Bellevue WA 98005

ARNOLD, SHEILA, former state legislator; b. N.Y.C., Jan. 15, 1929; d. Michael and Eileen (Lynch) Keddy; coll. courses; m. George Longan Arnold, Nov. 12, 1960; 1 child, Peter; 1 child by previous marriage, Michael C. Young; stepchildren: Drew, George Longan, Joe. Mem. Wyo. Ho. of Reps., 1978-93, mem. Laramie Regional Airport Bd.; mem. adv. bd. First Interstate Bank of Wyo., Laramie Br. Former mem., sec. Wyo. Land Use Adv. Coms.; past pres. Dem. Women's Club, Laramie; past vice-chmn. Albany County Dem. Cen. Com.; past mem. Dem. State Com.; mem. adv. bd. Wyo. Home Health Care; former mem. Nat. Conf. State Legislatures Com. on Fiscal Affairs and Oversight Com. Recipient Spl. Recognition award from Developmentally Disabled Citizens of Wyo., 1985. Mem. Laramie Area C. of C. (pres. 1982; Top Hand award 1977), LWV (Laramie bd. dirs.), Internat. Platform Assn., Faculty Women's Club (past pres.), VFW Ladies Aux. (jr. v.p. Post 2221), Zonta, Laramie Women's Club, Cowboy Joe Club.

ARNOLD PEDERSON, JULIE LOREE, real estate broker; b. Newcastle, Wyo., Dec. 2, 1966; d. Tom Lee and Marilyn Lorraine (Rawhouser) Arnold; m. Jim Edward Pederson, Dec. 24, 1991. Part-owner Spur Ranch, Four Corners, Wyo., 1981—; sales assoc. Arnold Realty-United Nat., Newcastle, Wyo., 1990-92, broker, assoc., 1992—. Timer Weston County Jr. Rodeo, Newcastle, 1987—; vol. Make-A-Wish Found., Casper, Wyo., 1989-91; vol. reporter KASL Radio, Newcastle, 1990-91. Mem. Nat. Assn. Realtors, Miss Rodeo Weston County Assn. (queen 1989), Newcastle C. of C., Fellowship Christian Cowboys. Republican. Home: Spur Ranch Four Corners WY 82715 Office: Arnold Realty-United Nat Box 98 Newcastle WY 82701

ARNST, ALBERT, editor, forester; b. Portland, Oreg., July 9, 1909; s. David and Alwina (Lorenz) A. BS in Forestry, Oreg. State U., 1931; m. Della Coleen Irwin, May 1, 1939; children: Audrey Karen, Robert Craig, Rosemary. Forester, Forest Svc., U.S. Dept. Agr., Portland, Oreg., 1931-35, Medford, Oreg., 1935-36, Lakeview, Oreg., 1937, pub. info. officer, Washington, 1962-75, with Soil Conservation Svcs., Dayton, Spokane and Sedro-Woolley, (all in Wash.), 1937-45, Corvallis and Portland, Oreg., 1941-43; sales rep Skagit Steel & Iron Works, Sedro-Woolley, 1945-46; pub. info. rep. Weyerhaeuer Co., Tacoma, 1946-52; editor Timberman mag., Portland, 1952-53; editor Miller Freeman Publs., Portland, 1954-62; mng. editor Western Conservation Jour., Portland, 1975-82. Contbr. articles on forestry to profl. jours. Fellow Soc. Am. Foresters; mem. Soil Conservation Soc. Am. (charter), Oreg. Logging Conf. (hon. life), Oreg. Soc. Am. Foresters (Lifetime Achievement award 1989), Internat. Assn. Bus. Communicators (Rodney Adair Meml. award 1978, pres. 1962, 71, 79, named Communicator of Yr. 1966 nat. Pres.'s award 1983), Foggy Bottom Club (Washington) (pres. 1971), Lions. Democrat. Address: 25200 SE Stark Apt 307 Gresham OR 97030

ARO, GLENN SCOTT, environmental and safety executive; b. Balt., Jan. 18, 1948; s. Raymond Charles Sr. and Elizabeth Virginia (Coppage) A.; m. Marlene Rose Lefler, Jan. 8, 1972 (div. June 1987); children: Vincent Wade, Marlena Irene. BS in Mech. Engring., Gen. Motors Inst., Flint, Mich., 1972; MBA in Fin., Wayne State U., 1980. Registered environmental assessor, Calif. From engr. to supr. GM, Detroit, Balt., L.A., 1966-84; environ. specialist New United Motor, Fremont, Calif., 1984-86; environ. engring. mgr. Def. Systems FMC Corp., San Jose, Calif., 1986-89; cons./exec. sales rep. Gaia Systems, Menlo Park, Calif., 1990; corp. environ. & safety mgr. Ampex Corp., Redwood City, Calif., 1990-92; audit programs mgr. Hughes Environ. Systems, Manhattan Beach, Calif., 1992—; lectr. colls. and seminars Environ. Regulatory Issues, 1988—. Author: Developing a National Environmental Policy in a Global Market, 1989; contbd. articles to profl. jours. Panel mem. Toxics Awareness Project, San Francisco, 1989—; com. mem. Environ. Working Group, Sacramento, 1986-88. Mem. Peninsula Indsl. & Bus. Assn. (bd. dirs., v.p. 1988-91). Republican. Roman Catholic. Home: 2836 Palos Verdes Dr W Palos Verdes Estates CA 90274

ARONI, SAMUEL, architecture and urban planning educator; b. Kishinew, Romania, May 26, 1927; came to U.S., 1963; s. David and Haia (Apoteker) Aharoni; m. Malca Corenfeld, Nov. 11, 1956; children: Ruth, Miriam. BS in Civil Engring., U. Melbourne, Victoria, Australia, 1954; MS, PhD, U. Calif., Berkeley, 1965. Lectr. in civil engring. U. Melbourne, Victoria, 1955-63; teaching fellow in structural engring. U. Calif., Berkeley, 1963-66; assoc. prof. San Francisco State Coll., 1966-67; rsch. engr. Am. Cement Corp., Riverside, Calif., 1967-70; prof. architecture and urban planning Grad. Sch. Architecture and Urban Planning, UCLA, 1970-91; prof. emeritus, 1991—, dir. spl. acad. cooperative projects, internat. studies, 1991—; acting dean Grad. Sch. Architecture and Urban Planning, UCLA, 1974-75, 83-85. Contbr. articles to profl. publs. Mem. adv. com. NSF, Washington, 1985-89, mem. panel reviewers applied sci. and rsch., 1979—; v.p. Archtl. Rsch. Ctrs. Consortium, Washington, 1985-86; bd. dirs. Urban Innovations Group, Westwood, Calif., 1983-85; bd. of govs. Ben-Gurion U. of Negev, Beer-Sheva, Israel, 1983—. Recipient Inst. prize Australian Town Planning Inst., 1955, Hon. Founder award Ben-Gurion U., 1984. Mem. ASCE (sec. com. 1970-71, J. James R. Cross Gold medal 1981), Am. Concrete Inst. (chmn. subcom. 1967-70), RILEM (membership com.), Sigma Xi. Jewish. Office: GSAUP UCLA Los Angeles CA 90024

ARONSON, FREDERICK RUPP, physician; b. N.Y.C., Nov. 5, 1953; s. Morton Jerome and Margaret (Rupp) A.; m. Jennifer Ann Goldfarb; 1 child, Jonathan George. BA, Johns Hopkins U., Baltimore, 1975; MPH, Yale U., New Haven, 1980, MD, 1980. Resident R.I. Hosp., Providence, 1980-83; clinical fellow New Eng. Med. Ctr., Boston, 1983-84; research fellow New England Medical Ctr., Boston, 1984-86; asst. professor of medicine Tufts U. Sch. Medicine, Boston, 1986-88; rsch. fellow The Med. Found., Inc., Boston, 1986-88; asst. clin. prof. U. Calif., San Francisco, 1988-93; dir. Biol.

REsponse Modifiers Program, U. Calif., San Francisco, 1988-93; vis. prof. Dalian Med. Coll., Shenyang Tunmor Hosp. and Inst., People's Republic of China, 1992; assoc. clin. prof. U. Vermont Sch. Medicine, 1993—; cons. in field. Contbr. chapters to various books, articles to profl. jours. Co-chmn. edn. com. Regional Cancer Found., San Francisco, 1989-91. Recipient Nat. Rsch. Svc. award Nat. Cancer Inst.; NIH grantee. Fellow ACP, Am. Fedn. Clin. Rsch., Am. Soc. Clin. Oncology, Am. Assn. Cancer Rsch. Democrat. Jewish.

ARONSON, JONATHAN DAVID, international relations educator; b. St. Louis, Oct. 28, 1949; s. Adam and Judith (Spector) A.; m. Joan Abrahamson, May 28, 1984; children: Adam Brody, Zachary Alden, James Dillon. BA, Harvard U., 1971; MA in Polit. Sci., Stanford U., 1973, MA in Applied Econs., 1975, PhD in Polit. Sci., 1977. Asst. prof. internat. relations U. So. Calif., Los Angeles, 1976-82; internat. economist rep. Office of U.S. Trade, Washington, 1982-83; assoc. prof. Sch. of Internat. Relations U. So. Calif., 1982-88, prof., 1988. Author: Money and Power, 1977; editor: Debt and the Less Developed Countries, 1979; author (with others): Trade Talks, 1986, When Countries Talk, 1988, Managing the World Economy, 1993. Fellow Ctr. Internat. Affairs; mem. Coun. Fgn. Rels. Jewish. Office: U So Calif Sch Internat Rels Los Angeles CA 90089-0043

AROS, JESSE RICHARD, psychologist, counselor. BS in Psychology, Brigham Young U., 1985; MA in Counseling, NYU, 1987; postgrad., Tex. A&M U., U. N.D. Counseling cons. Utah Migrant Coun., 1984; tutor NYU, N.Y.C., 1986-87; drop-out prevention counselor Bushwick High Sch./NYU Ctr., 1986-87; bilingual counselor Leeway Ednl. Therapy Ctr., L.A., 1987-88; measurement/design cons. Woodrow Wilson Internat. Ctr. for Scholars, Washington, 1989; contract seminar lectr. L.A. City Dept. of Aging, 1989-90; counselor L.A. City Coll., 1989-90; therapist psychol. svcs. St. Mary's Hosp., 1990-91; rsch. analyst San Pedro, Calif., 1990—. Recipient Physically Challenged Athletic scholarship U. So. Calif., 1990, Samerika Minority scholarship Samerika, Inc., 1990, Mexican Am. scholarship U. So. Calif. 1990, others; named to Outstanding Young Men of Am., 1988. Mem. Am. Psychol. Assn., Am. Assn. Counseling and Devel., Calif. Community Coll. Extended Opportunity Programs and Svcs. Assn.

ARREGUIN, ESTEBAN JOSE, aerospace company executive; b. Celaya, Mex., Aug. 31, 1958; came to U.S., 1964.; s. Agustin Montoya and Juana (Cacique) A.; m. Catharine Ann Barnett, Dec. 19, 1981; children: Christopher, Rachael, Michael. BME, UCLA, 1981; MME, U. So. Calif., 1984, MPA, 1991. Mem. tech. staff Aerospace Corp., El Segundo, Calif., 1981-85; engr. Aerojet Techsystems Co., Sacramento, Calif., 1985-86, mem. mgmt. tng. program, 1986-88; program supr. Aerojet Techsystems Co., Sacramento, 1988-90, project engr. aerojet propulsion div., 1990—; community adv. bd. U. Calif. Med. Ctr. Mem. River City Rep. Assembly, Sacramento, 1987; field coord. Sacramento Adult Soccer Assn., 1987. Aerospace Corp. fellow, 1984. Mem. Soc. Hispanic Profl. Engrs. (chmn. com. 1988), Sacramento C. of C. (mem. leadership Sacramento program 1987), League of United Latin Am. Citizens Club. Republican. Baptist. Office: Aerojet Propulsion Div PO Box 13222 Sacramento CA 95813-6000

ARRINGTON, HARRIET ANN, historian, writer; b. Salt Lake City, June 22, 1924; d. Lyman Merrill and Myrtle (Swainston) Horne; m. Frederick C. Sorensen, Dec. 22, 1943 (div. Dec. 1954); children: Annette S. Rogers, Frederick Christian, Heidi S. Swinton; m. Gordon B. Moody, July 26, 1958 (div. Aug. 1963); 1 child, Stephen Horne; m. Leonard James Arrington, Nov. 19, 1983. BS in Edn., U. Utah, 1957. Cert. tchr., Utah, Ga. Supr. surg. secs. Latter-day Sts. Hosp., Salt Lake City, 1954-58; tchr. Salt Lake City Schs., 1954-57, Glynn County Schs., Brunswick, Ga., 1958-59; from med. sec. to office mgr. Dr. Horne, Salt Lake City, 1962-83; tchr. Carden Sch., Salt Lake City, 1973-74, women's history rschr., tchr.; mem. Utah Women's Legis. Coun. Author: Heritage of Faith, 1988; contbr. articles to profl. jours. and confs. Dist. chmn. Utah Rep. Com., 1972-76; mem. art com. Salt Lake City Bd. Edn.; chmn. art exhibit Utah Women's Conf., 1986-87; active LDS Women's Relief Soc.; chmn. Utah Women Artists' Exhibition, 1986-87. Recipient Vol. Action award Utah Women Artists' Exhbn., 1987, resolution of appreciation Utah Arts Coun., 1989. Mem. AAUW (Utah state cultural refinement chmn., cert. of appreciation 1988), DAR (Utah Am. history chmn.), Old Main Soc. Utah State U., Chi Omega (past pres. alumni chpt.). Home and Office: 2236 S 2200 E Salt Lake City UT 84109-1135

ARRINGTON, JOHN N., educational administrator; b. Laurel, Miss., Oct. 22, 1939; s. Nathan and Lurelia (Sampson)) A.; m. Bernice Milton, Nov. 29, 1982; children: Pamela, Darryl, Restine, Jonathan. BS, Tuskegee U., 1963; MA, San Diego State U., 1974; PhD, U.S. Internat. U., San Diego, 1977; postgrad., U.C.S.D., UCLA, Howard U. Tchr. D.C. Pub. Schs., Washington, 1967-69; tchr., counselor, dist. counselor San Diego Unified Sch. Dist., 1969-73, tchr. on spl. assignment, 1973-77, adminstrv. intern, 1977-78, v.p. meml., 1978-87; v.p. Twain Jr.-Sr. High Sch., 1987-91, prin., 1991—. Author: Guide To Teaching English, 1970, (play) Strange Generation, 1976, Collected Poems, 1976. Mem. San Diego County Dem. Cen. Com.; del. Dem. Nat. Conv.; mem. Highland Park Ch.; mem. Parent Adv. Task Force, San Diego, 1986—, Booker T. Washington Plan Commn., San Diego, 1989-90; pres. bd. trustees Brooks-Bethone Pre-sch. With U.S. Army, 1963-66. Named Vol. of Yr. award San Diego Unified Sch. Dist., 1987. Mem. Assn. Calif. Sch. Adminstrs., Adminstrs. Assn., Vice Prins. Coun., Continuing Edn. Assn., Kiwanis (v.p. 1989, pres. San Diego 1990), Omega Psi Phi (basileus 1986-88, vice basileus 1988-91, Omega Man of Yr. award 1988, cert. of appreciation 12th dist. 1990), Assn. African Am. Educators (pres.). Baptist. Home: 1711 Alaquinas Dr San Ysidro CA 92173-1513 Office: 6402 Linda Vista Rd San Diego CA 92111-7398

ARRINGTON, STEVE, oil company executive; b. Muskogee, Okla., Feb. 17, 1951; s. Mark and Charlene (McElreath) A.; m. Diane Lynn Ewing, Aug. 28, 1971; children: Lauren Andrea, Mark Branton. BS with high honors, U. Wyo., 1973. Agt. State Farm Ins. Co., Farmington, N.Mex., 1974-78; dir. edn. and tng. State Farm Ins. Co., Tempe, Ariz., 1978-79; v.p. Cinarron, Inc., Billings, Mont., 1979-83; pres. Border Fuel Supply Corp., Denver, 1983—. Office: Border Fuel Supply Corp Ste 800 6400 S Fiddlers Green Cir Englewood CO 80111-4956

ARROW, KENNETH JOSEPH, economist, educator; b. N.Y.C., N.Y., Aug. 23, 1921; s. Harry I. and Lillian (Greenberg) A.; m. Selma Schweitzer, Aug. 31, 1947; children: David Michael, Andrew. B.S. in Social Sci., CCNY, 1940; M.A., Columbia U., 1941, Ph.D., 1951, DSc (hon.), 1973; LL.D. (hon.), U. Chgo., 1967, City U. N.Y., 1972, Hebrew U. Jerusalem, 1975, U. Pa., 1976, Washington U., St. Louis, 1989; D.Social and Econ. Scis. (hon.), U. Vienna, Austria, 1971; LL.D. (hon.), Ben-Gurion U. of the Negev, 1992; D.Social Scis. (hon.), Yale, 1974; Doctor (hon.), Université René Descartes, Paris, 1974, U. Aix-Marseille III, 1985; Dr.Pol., U. Helsinki, 1976; M.A. (hon.), Harvard U., 1968; D.Litt., Cambridge U., 1985. Research assoc. Cowles Commn. for Research in Econs., 1947-49; asst. prof. econs. U. Chgo., 1948-49; acting asst. prof. econs. and stats. Stanford, 1949-50, assoc. prof., 1950-53, prof. econs., statistics and ops. research, 1953-68; prof. econs. Harvard, 1968-74, James Bryant Conant univ. prof., 1974-79; exec. head dept. econs. Stanford U., 1954-56, acting exec. head dept., 1962-63, Joan Kenney prof. econs. and prof. ops. research, 1979-91, prof. emeritus, 1991—; economist Council Econ. Advisers, U.S. Govt., 1962; cons. RAND Corp. Author: Social Choice and Individual Values, 1951, Essays in the Theory of Risk Bearing, 1971, The Limits of Organization, 1974, Collected Papers, Vols. I-VI, 1983-85; co-author: Mathematical Studies in Inventory and Production, 1958, Studies in Linear and Nonlinear Programming, 1958, Time Series Analysis of Inter-industry Demands, 1959, Public Investment, The Rate of Return and Optimal Fiscal Policy, 1971, General Competitive Analysis, 1971, Studies in Resource Allocation Processes, 1977, Social Choice and Multicriterion Decision Making, 1985. Served as capt. AUS, 1942-46. Social Sci. Research fellow, 1952; fellow Center for Advanced Study in the Behavioral Scis., 1956-57; fellow Churchill Coll., Cambridge, Eng., 1963-64, 70, 73, 86; Guggenheim fellow, 1972-73; Recipient John Bates Clark medal Am. Econ. Assn., 1957; Alfred Nobel Meml. prize in econ. scis., 1972, von Neumann prize, 1986. Fellow AAAS (chmn. sect. K. 1983), Am. Acad. Arts and Scis. (v.p. 1979-81, 91-93), Econometric Soc. (v.p. 1955, pres. 1956), Am. Stats. Assn., Inst. Math. Stats., Am. Econ. Assn. (exec. com. 1967-69, pres. 1973), Internat. Soc. Inventory Rsch. (pres. 1983-90); mem. NAS (mem. coun. 1990-93), Internat. Econs. Assn. (pres. 1983-86), Am. Philos. Soc., Inst. Mgmt. Scis. (pres. 1963, chmn. coun. 1964, Finnish Acad. Scis. (fgn. hon.), Brit. Acad. (corr.), Western Econ. Assn. (pres. 1980-81), Soc. Social Choice and Welfare (pres. 1991-93). Office: Dept Econs Stanford U Stanford CA 94305-6072

ARROW, RICHARD STEWART, county official, auditor, controller; b. L.A., Aug. 26, 1947; s. Leon and Trude (Newstein) A.; m. Anne-Marie I. Gee, Apr. 17, 1990; children: Candice, Matthew. AA, Coll. of Marin, Kentfield, Calif., 1969; BA, Calif. State U., San Francisco, 1971; postgrad., Pepperdine U., 1978. CPA, Calif. Staff acct. Coopers & Lybrand, San Francisco, 1973-74; dep. auditor County of Marin, San Rafael, 1974-84, asst. auditor-contr., 1984-88, auditor-contr., 1988—. Bd. dirs. Marin br. ARC, Marin Suicide Prevention Ctr.; bd. mgrs. Marin YMCA, also mem. phys. edn. subcom. With USNR, 1965-71. Mem. AICPA, Calif. Soc. CPA's, State Assn. County Auditors, Calif. Community Redevel. Assn., Marin C. of C. (bd. dirs.), San Rafael C. of C., Sierra Club, Marin Rod and Gun Club, Rotary (bd. dirs. Terra Linda chpt.), Elks, B'nai B'rith. Office: County of Marin Civic Ctr San Rafael CA 94903

ARROYO, JACQUELINE, clinical psychologist; b. Santurce, P.R., Dec. 15, 1960; d. Jorge Luis and Aida (Roldan) Arroyo; m. John Christopher Brock, Dec. 2, 1989. Student, Valparaiso U., 1978-80; BA, San Francisco State U., 1982; MA, PhD, Calif. Sch. Profl. Psychology, 1988. Lic. psychologist, Calif. Psychology intern Mission Mental Health Ctr., San Francisco, 1983-84, Marin Community Client Svc., San Rafael, Calif., 1984-85, U. San Francisco Counseling Ctr., 1985-86; relief counselor Children's Home Soc., San Mateo, Calif., 1984-87; personal counselor San Jose State U. Counseling Ctr., 1987-88; family therapist U. Calif., San Francisco, 1986-88; clin. psychologist Adult and Child Guidance Ctr., San Jose, 1988—. Youth Opportunities Found. scholar, 1983-84, 85-86, 87-88, Calif. Sch. Profl. Psychology scholar, 1982-86, League of United Latin Am. Citizens nat. scholar, 1982-84; Calif. Grad fellow, Calif. Student Aid Commn., 1982-86. Home: 38260 Redwood Ter Fremont CA 94536 Office: Adult & Child Guidance Ctr 950 W Julian St San Jose CA 95126

ARSENAULT, RICHARD JOSEPH, video producer; b. Morristown, N.J., June 17, 1964; s. Robert and Margaret (Robideau) A.; m. Jennifer Saman, Nov. 9, 1991; children: Benjamin, Jonathan. BA in Film, U. So. Calif., L.A., 1986. Producer Triad Artists, L.A., 1987-91, Ready Reference Press, L.A., 1991—; pres. Pacific Pictures, Castaic, Calif., 1986—. Producer numerous programs including The Guidance Club for Kids, 1991, The Guidance Club for Teens, 1992. Democrat. Home: 31922 Gelding Rd Castaic CA 91384

ARSHAM, GARY, medical educator; b. Cleve., 1941; s. Sanford Ronald and Florence A.; m. Diana Silver, 1971. AB cum laude, Harvard U., 1963; MD, Case-Western Res. U., 1967; PhD, U. Ill., 1971. Fellow in med. edn. U. Ill., Chgo., 1968-71; asst. then assoc. dean curriculum devel., asst. prof. medicine and health scis. communication SUNY, 1971-72; assoc. prof., prof. health professions edn. U. of Pacific, San Francisco, 1972-79; chmn. Council on Edn. Pacific Med. Ctr., San Francisco, 1976-81; v.p. Arsham Cons., Inc., San Francisco, 1981—; adminstr. Pacific Vision Found., 1977-84, dir. edn., 1983—; mem. nat. adv. bd. John Muir Hosp. Med. Film Festival, 1981—; mem. task force on interdisciplinary edn. Nat. Joint Practice Commn., 1973-74; bd. dirs. U.S.-China Ednl. Inst., 1980—, sec., 1986-88. Co-author: Diabetes: A Guide To Living Well, 1989, 2d edit. 1992; chief editor Family Medicine Reports, San Francisco, 1983. Fellow ACP; mem. Am. Assn. Individual Investors (chpt. bd. dirs. 1984-88), Am. Ednl. Rsch. Assn., Assn. Am. Med. Colls., Assn. Study Med. Edn., Assn. Hosp. Med. Edn. (past exec. com., sec.-treas.), Am. Diabetes Assn. (chpt. bd. dirs. 1984—, pres. 1990-91, v.p. Calif. affiliate 1992—), Am. Assn. Diabetes Educators (assoc. editor 1985-92), Calif. Med. Assn., San Francisco Med. Soc., Harvard Club San Francisco (bd. dirs., past pres.), Lane Med. Soc., Tech. Security Analysts Assn. San Francisco. Office: Arsham Cons Inc PO Box 15608 San Francisco CA 94115-0608

ARSURA, EDWARD LOUIS, physician, educator; b. N.Y.C., June 28, 1950; s. Louis and Edith (Cagnoni) A.; m. Donna Ross, Sept. 7, 1983; children: Alexandra, Edward. BS, St. John's U., N.Y.C., 1972; MD, U. Bologna (Italy), 1978. Diplomate Am. Bd. Internal Medicine, Am. Bd. Critical Care Medicine. Intern Maimonides Med. Ctr., Bklyn., 1979, resident, 1979-81, asst. physician depts. community medicine and health svcs., 1981-82, asst. attending physician, asst. dir. dept. med. & med. edn., 1983-84, assoc. attending physic-- ı, then attending physician, 1984-88, dir. div. gen. internal medicine and gerontology, 1986-88; attending physician dept. internal medicine St. Vincent's Hoep. and Med. Ctr., 1988-89, chief residency tng., 1988-89; program dir. dept. medicine Kern Med. Ctr., Bakersfield, Calif., 1989—, chmn. dept. medicine, 1989—. Reviewer Am. Hosp. Formulary, Svc. Drug Info., 1990.; author numerous manuscripts, abstracts, presentations. Mem. Myasthenia Gravis Found., 1988—. Fellow ACP; mem. Am. Fedn. Clin. Rsch., Assn. Program Dirs. Internal Medicine, N.Y. Acad. Scis., Am. Heart Assn., Soc. Gen. Internal Medicine. Roman Catholic. Office: Kern Med Ctr 1830 Flower St Bakersfield CA 93305-4197

ARTAUD-WILD, SABINE MARIE, research dietitian; b. Marseille, France, Jan. 25, 1928; came to U.S., 1953; d. Charles Marie and Jane Virginie (Millaud) Artaud; divorced Sept. 1981; children: Anne Wild Mozell, Phillip Charles, Paul James. BS in Pharmacy, U. Aix-Marseille, 1950, BS in Dietetic, 1958. Lic. dietitian; registered Am. Dietetic Assn. Pharmacist Ciotat, France, 1950-52; rsch. dietitian Inst. Gustave Roussy, Villejuif, France, 1952-53; adminstrv. dietitian Children's Hosp., Iowa City, 1954-55; cons. dietitian Weight Mgmt., Portland, Oreg., 1985—, Health Mgmt. Resources, Portland, 1987-91; rsch. dietitian Lipid Atherosclerosis Oreg. Health Scis. U.-Lab., Portland, 1977-92. Editor: Simply Nutritious, 1985; contbr. articles to profl. jours. Pres. Reed Coll. Women Com., Portland, 1974-75; docent Portland Art Mus., 1971-77, Oreg. Hist. Soc., Portland, 1976-78; sec. Alliance Francaise, Portland, 1986; mem. City Club of Portland, 1983—; mem. program com. Native Am. Art Coun. of Portland Art Mus., 1992—; mem. house of dels. Am. Dietetic Assn., 1992—. Mem. Oreg. Dietetic Assn. (pres. 1989-90, newsletter editor 1986-87, historian 1992, career guidance 1985). Home: 111 SW Harrison # 21A Portland OR 97201 Office: Oreg Health Scis U 3181 SW Sam Jackson Portland OR 97201

ARTHUR, PAUL KEITH, electronic engineer; b. Kansas City, Mo., Jan. 14, 1931; s. Walter B. and Frieda J. (Burckhardt) A.; m. Joy N. Lim, Apr. 26, 1958; children: Gregory V., Lia F. Student Ohio No. U., 1947, Taylor U., Upland, Ind., 1948-49; BSEE, Purdue U., 1956; postgrad. N.Mex. State U., 1957-78. Registered profl. engr., N.Mex. With White Sands Missile Range, N.Mex., 1956—, electronic engr. field engring. group missile flight surveillance office, 1956-60, chief field engring. group, 1960-62, project engr. Pershing weapon system Army Missile Test and Evaluation Directorate, 1962-74, chief high altitude air def. projects br., 1974-82, chief air def. materiel test div., 1982-91, dep. dir. Materiel Test Directorate, 1991—, career program mgr. for engrs. and scientists, past pres. missile range pioneer group; bd. dirs. Dagupan Electric Corp. of the Philippines. Chmn. adminstrv. bd. Meth. Ch. Served with USN, 1949-53, USNR, 1954-87, rear adm. and, sr. engring. duty officer, 1984-87. Decorated Legion of Merit, Meritorious Svc. medal, Navy Achievement medal, Mil. Order St. Barbara, others. Mem. Am. Def. Preparedness Assn. (past pres.), AIAA (past vice chmn.), Assn. Old Crows, Naval Res. Assn., Res. Officers Assn. (pres. 1983-85), United Vets. Council (chmn. 1984-85), Am. Soc. Naval Engrs., Naval Inst., Navy League, Surface Navy Assn., Assn. U.S. Army, Purdue Alumni Assn. (past pres.), N.Mex. State U. Alumni Assn., Sierra Club, Mesilla Valley Track Club, Bujutsukan Acad. Martial Arts. Author numerous plans and reports on weapon systems test and evaluation and topics in naval engring. Home: 2050 San Acacio St Las Cruces NM 88001-1570 Office: STEWS-MTD White Sands Missile Range NM 88002

ARTHUR, RANDY LEE, lawyer, social worker; b. Sullivan, Ind., Feb. 19, 1955; s. Allen Warren and Ruth Lillian (Shirton) A.; m. Katie Gordon, May 16, 1992. AB, Occidental Coll., 1977; MSW, U. Calif., Berkeley, 1983; JD with distinction, Hofstra Law Sch., Hempstead, N.Y., 1985. Bar: Oreg. 1985, U.S. Dist. Ct. Oreg. 1986, U.S. Ct. Appeals (9th cir.) 1990. Child devel. specialist, psychol. examiner Portland (Oreg.) Pub. Schs., 1977-79, 90; social worker San Francisco Sr. Ctr., 1979-80; ins. claims examiner Nationwide Ins. Co., Portland, 1980-81; social worker Oakland (Calif.) Catholic Charities, 1982-83; law intern to judge and magistrate U.S. Dist. Ct. (ea. dist.) N.Y., Uniondale, 1984, 85; assoc. Bullivant, Houser, Bailey, Pendergrass & Hoffman, Portland, 1985-91, spl. counsel, 1991—. Editor and Co-Producer (video) Social Welfare Education, 1983; articles editor, contbr. Hofstra Labor Law Jour., 1985; contbr. articles to numerous profl. jours. Vol. atty. Sr. Law Project, Portland, 1987-88, St. Andrew's Legal Clinic, Portland, 1989—; chair Community Law Week com. MBA/YLS, 1919, chair pub. svc. com., 1991-92, bd. dirs., 1991-92; dir., sec. MBA Vol. Lawyer's Project, 1993—. Legal Rsch. fellow Hofstra U., 1984. Mem. ABA, NASW, Oreg. State Bar Assn., Def. Rsch. Inst., Multnomah County Bar Assn., Multnomah Athletic Club, City Club Portland (mem. standing com. on energy and the environment, mem. membership com. 1989—). Mem. Ch. of the Nazarene. Home: 3130 NE 142nd Portland OR 97230 Office: Bullivant Houser Bailey Pendergrass & Hoffman 888 SW 5th Ave Ste 300 Portland OR 97204-2089

ARTHUR, WILLIAM LYNN, environmental advocate; b. Spokane, Wash., May 22, 1954; s. Robert Cyril and Mabel Mildred (Collison) A.; m. Debora Lee Donovan, Feb. 2, 1975; children: Kathleen, Jonathan. BA in Econs., Wash. State U., 1976, postgrad., 1982-83. Rsch. asst. Wash. State U., 1976-77; project mgr. Ctr. Environ. Understanding, Cheney, Wash., 1977-78; program dir. Wash. Energy Extension Svc., Spokane, 1978-79; econs. instr. Spokane Falls Community Coll., 1977-81; economist, cons. Biosystems Analysis Inc., Spokane, 1983; assoc. N.W. rep. Sierra Club, Seattle, 1983-87, N.W. rep., 1987-91, N.W. regional dir., 1992—; chmn. bd. N.W. Conservation Act Coalition, Seattle, 1982-83, bd. dirs., 1988—; adv. com. N.W. Renewable Resources Ctr., Seattle, 1987-91, bd. dirs., 1992—; cons. energy workshops N.W. Regional Found., Spokane, 1982; mem. exec. com. Save Our Wild Salmon Coalition, 1991—; mem. adv. com. Inland Empire Pub. Lands Coun., 1990—. Chmn., mem. city commn. Environ. Quality Commn., Pullman, Wash., 1976-77; bd. dirs. Ryegrass Sch., Spokane, 1978-81; conservation rep. Internat. Mountain Caribou Tech. Com., 1978-81; bd. dirs. Wash. Citizens for Recycling, Seattle, 1980-82; chair Washington State Environmentalists for Clinton/Gore Com., 1992; environ. rep. Northwest Forest Conf. convened & chaired by Pres. Clinton, Apr. 2, 1993. Office: Sierra Club NW Office 1516 Melrose Ave Seattle WA 98122-3608

ARTIST, EVERETTE WARD, brokerage house executive; b. Greeley, Colo., Sept. 13, 1954; s. Elmer Jacob and Ava Justine (Sutton) A.; m. Lori Ann Slabozewski, Oct. 17, 1987. BS in Bus., U. No. Colo., 1977. Registered rep. I.D.S., Phoenix, 1978-80; account exec. Thomson McKinnon, Scottsdale, Ariz., 1980-82, E.F. Hutton, Tempe, Ariz., 1982-84; 2d v.p. Shearson Lehman Bros., Scottsdale, Ariz., 1984-87; v.p. The Miller Group, Phoenix, 1987—; cons. CenPac Securities, Phoenix. Producer (TV Program) Wall St. Awareness Series FNN, 1987. Fund Raiser Ariz. Arthritis Found., Phoenix, 1988. Mem. Anglers United, Scottsdale Racquet Club, Dueks Unltd., Elks. Republican. Home: 3603 E Tano Ct Phoenix AZ 85044-3869

ARVIZU, OSCAR BECERRA, artist, illustrator; b. L.A., Aug. 11, 1971; s. Ismael Ledezma and Maria (Becerra) A. AA, Coll. Ea. Utah, 1992. Designer various schools and businesses, Price, Utah, 1988—; ceramic tile installer Tile Plus, Price, 1990-92; mus. artist Coll. Ea. Utah Prehistoric Mus., Price, 1990—. Exhibited in group shows at Utah State Fair, Salt Lake City, 1991-92, Carbon County Home Arts Show, Helper, Utah, 1991-92, C.E.U. Student Art Show, Price, Utah, 1991-92, Springville (Utah) Art Show, 1990, Utah State Univ., Logan, 1992-93. Sec. SOCIO Youth Group, 1986-87; patrol leader Boy Scout Troop 282. Southeastern Utah Sterling Scholar in Visual Art, 1990. Roman Catholic.

ARZUBE, JUAN ALFREDO, bishop; b. Guayaquil, Ecuador, June 1, 1918; came to U.S., 1944, naturalized, 1961; s. Juan Bautista and Maria (Jaramillo) A. B.S. in Civil Enging, Rensselaer Poly. Inst., 1942; B.A., St. John's Sem., 1954. Ordained priest Roman Catholic Ch., 1954; asso. pastor St. Agnes Ch., Los Angeles, Resurrection Ch., Los Angeles, Ascension Ch., Los Angeles, Our Lady of Guadalupe Ch., El Monte, Calif.; aux. bishop, vicar gen. Diocese L.A., Los Angeles, 1971—; episcopal vicar for Spanish speaking Los Angeles, 1973—; mem. nat. bishops coms. Ad Hoc Com. for Spanish Speaking; chmn. Com. for Latin Am. Recipient Humanitarian award Mexican Am. Opportunity Found., 1978, John Anson Ford award Los Angeles County Commn. Human Relations, 1979. Home: 3149 Sunset Hill Dr West Covina CA 91791 Office: San Gabriel Region 16009 E Cypress Ave Irwindale CA 91706*

ASAHARA, STELLA L. T., academic administrator; b. Honolulu. BA, U. Hawaii, 1973, MEd, 1975. Fin. aid officer Leeward Community Coll., Pearl City, Hawaii, 1975-81; student svcs. coord. W. Oahu Coll., Pearl City, 1981-90; dean of student svcs. U. Hawaii-West Oahu, Pearl City, 1990—. Mem. Western Interstate Commn. for Higher Edn., Boulder, Colo., 1984-92. Mem. Am. Assn. Collegiate Registrars and Admissions Officers, Phi Beta Kappa. Office: U Hawaii West Oahu 96-043 Ala Ike Pearl City HI 96782

ASAY, KAY HARRIS, research geneticist; b. Lovell, Wyo., Nov. 20, 1933; s. Orson Vern and Ella Fay Asay; m. Barbara Bennion, Sept. 4, 1953 (widowed); children: Larry, Shelley, Ross, Julie; m. Tamra Welling, Sept. 14, 1983; children: Cathie, Reese, Susan. BS, U. Wyo., 1957, MS, 1959; PhD, Iowa State U., 1965. Rsch. assoc. Iowa State U., Ames, 1961-65; asst. prof. then assoc. prof. U. Mo., Columbia, 1965-74; rsch. geneticist USDA Agrl. Rsch. Svc., Utah State U., Logan, 1974—. Mem. editorial bd. Jour. Crop Sci., Internat. Grassland Congress; contbr. numerous articles to profl. jours. Recipient Scientist of Yr. award USDA-ARS, 1988. Fellow Am. Soc. Agronomy, Crop Soc. Am.; mem. N.Am. Grass Breeders (pres. 1983-84, chmn. crop adv. com. grasses 1984-91), Soc. Range Mgmt., Sigma Xi. Mormon. Home: 1655 N 1560 E Logan UT 84321-2111 Office: USDA-ARS Forage Range Rsch Utah State U Logan UT 84322-6300

ASBURY, CHRIS MERLIN, surveyor, consultant; b. Salt Lake City, Dec. 31, 1952; s. Norman Paul and Karolyn Joy (Jensen); m. Marsha Ellin Brekke, May 28, 1977; children: Rachel Erika, Sara Elizabeth. AS, Casper Coll., 1975. lic. land surveyor, Wyo. Surveyor Am. Nuclear Corp., Casper, Wyo., 1976-82; v.p., ptnr. Forysyth-Asbury Surveying, Inc., Casper, 1978-83; county surveyor Natrona County Surveyors Office, Casper, 1983—; cons. Horton Engring., Casper, ,1983-88, Am. Nuclear Corp., 1985-86. Bd. dirs. Community Action, Referral and Emergency Svc., 1972, Wyo. Pub. Works Coun., 1991—; pres. Especially for Children Manor Heights Sch., Casper, 1989-90. Mem. Am. Congress of Surveying and Mapping, Nat. Soc. Profl. Surveyors, Profl. Land Surveyors of Wyo. Republican. Methodist. Home: 3830 E 20th St Casper WY 82609-3622 Office: Natrona County Surveyors Office Drawer 848 Mills WY 82644

ASBURY, EARL EVANS, retired newspaper executive, stockbroker; b. O'Fallon, Ill., May 31, 1924; s. Earl E. and Josephine (Lienesch) A.; m. Sara Carstens, Dec. 24, 1945; 1 child, Timothy. BS, Northwestern U., 1945; BA in Journalism, U. Ill., 1946. Ptnr., editor Bent County Democrat Weekly Newspaper, Las Animas, Colo., 1952-68; stockbroker, v.p. Boettcher & Co., Colorado Springs, Colo., 1968-91; ret. 2nd Lt. USMC, 1943-46. Named Outstanding Colo. Editor Colo. U., 1961. Mem. Las Animas C. of C. (pres. 1958), Kiwanis (pres. 1966), Men's Thurs. Evening Study Club (pres. 1965). Republican. Home: 3101B Broadmoor Valley Rd Colorado Springs CO 80906

ASCHAFFENBURG, WALTER EUGENE, composer, music educator; b. Essen, Germany, May 20, 1927; came to U.S., 1938, naturalized, 1944; s. William Arthur and Margarete (Herz) A.; m. Nancy Dandridge Cooper, Aug. 14, 1951 (div.); children: Ruth Margareta, Katherine Elizabeth; m. Rayna Klatzkin Barroll, Aug. 5, 1987. Diploma, Hartford Sch. Music, 1945; B.A., Oberlin Coll., 1951; M.A., Eastman Sch. Music, 1952. Prof. composition and music theory, former chmn. composition dept. Oberlin (Ohio) Coll. Conservatory of Music, prof. emeritus, 1987—, also former chmn. dept. music theory., 1952-87. Composer: Ozymandias-Symphonic Reflections for Orch., 1952, Cello Sonata, 1953, Sonata for Solo Violin, 1954, Piano Sonatina, 1954, String Quartet, 1955, Bartleby-opera, 1962, Elegy for Strings, 1961, Three Dances for Orch., 1966, Three Shakespeare Sonnets, 1967, Quintet for Winds, 1967, Proem for Brass and Percussion, 1969, Duo for Violin and Cello, 1971, Conversations-Six Pieces for Piano, 1973, Libertatem Appellant for Tenor, Baritone and Orch., 1976, Carrousel—24 Pieces for Piano, 1980, Concertino for Violin, Ten Winds and Contrabass,

1982, Laughing Time for Mixed Chorus, 1983, Concerto for Oboe and Orch., 1985, From South Mountain for Brass Quintet, 1988, Coalescence for Oboe and Cello, 1989, Sonata for the Fortepiano or Pianoforte, 1990, Parings for Clarinet and Piano, 1993. Served with AUS, 1945-47. Recipient award Fromm Music Found., 1953; Nat. Inst. Arts and Letters award, 1966; Cleve. arts prize, 1980; Guggenheim fellow, 1955-56, 73-74. Mem. ASCAP, Soc. Composers, Am. Music Ctr., Soc. Music Theory. Home: 4639 E Monte Way Phoenix AZ 85044-7517

ASCHENBRENNER, FRANK ALOYSIOUS, former diversified manufacturing company executive; b. Ellis, Kans., June 26, 1924; s. Philip A. and Rose E. Aschenbrenner; m. Gertrude Wilhelmina DeBie, Nov. 15, 1946; children: Richard David, Robert Wayne, Mary Lynne. BS with high honors, Kans. State U., 1950; PhD in Physics, M.I.T., 1954. Mgr. physics and math. Gen. Electric, Cin., 1958-61; asst. dir. space div. Rockwell Internat., Downey, Calif., 1961-69; corp. dir. tech. Rockwell Internat., Pitts., 1969-71; v.p., gen. mgr. div. yarn machinery Rockwell Internat., Charlotte, N.C., 1971-75; pres. COR, Inc., Charlotte, 1975-77; v.p. research and devel. and engring. Ball Corp., Muncie, Ind., 1977-86; pvt. bus. cons. Poway, Calif., 1986—; chmn. bd. RAMZ Corp., Dunkirk, Ind., 1985—; nat. bd. advisors Rose-Hulman Inst., Terre Haute, Ind., 1984—, U. Tenn. Space Inst., Tullahoma, 1982—. Served with USN, 1943-47. Mem. AIAA, Am. Phys. Soc., Naval Res. Assn., San Diego Venture Group. Home and Office: 14258 Palisades Dr Poway CA 92064-6443

ASCHLIMAN, PAT TANNER, health facility adminstrator; b. Idaho Falls, Idaho, Aug. 12, 1944; s. Nels Rullen Aschliman and Thelma Marie (Tanner) Green; m. Estelle VanDerVeer, May 17, 1969; children: Eldora Marie Dell, Jeff, Teresa. Grad. high sch., Idaho Falls. Cert. residential care adminstr. Mgr. Samo's Electric and Plumbing, Salt Lake City, 1969-76; owner, operator Aschliman Living Ctr., Shelley, Idaho, 1976—. With USAF, 1962-66. Mem. Nat. Assn. Residential Care (bd. dirs. 1986-89), Idaho Assn. Residential Care (pres. 1987-88), Kiwanis (2d v.p. 1992). Republican. Home and Office: 326 N State St Shelley ID 83274-1141

ASH, JAMES MATHEW, purchasing executive; b. Ft. Stewart, Ga., Aug. 25, 1958; s. Frederick Charles and Joyce Jean (Kumm) A. BS in Prodn. Mgmt., U. Colo., 1988. Gen. mdse. mgr. Safeway Stores, Colorado Springs, Colo., 1982-84; buyer Hewlett Packard Co., Colorado Springs, 1985-90, strategic buyer, 1991—. With USN, 1977-81. Mem. Am. Prodn. and Inventory Control Soc. Republican. Lutheran. Home: 6353 Turret Dr Colorado Springs CO 80918 Office: Hewlett Packard Co 1900 Garden Of The Gods Rd Colorado Springs CO 80907-3483

ASH, WALTER BRINKER, lawyer; b. Wichita, Kans., June 8, 1932; s. Walter Bonsall and Gladys Elvira (Brinker) A.; m. Fern Ostrom, Sept. 16, 1986; children: Paul B., Allison L., Carolyn A. BA, U. Kans., 1955, BL, 1957. Bar: Kans. 1957, Colo. 1959. Personal asst. to Solicitor Gen. U.S. Dept. Justice, Washington, 1957-58, trial atty., 1958-59; assoc. Davis, Graham & Stubbs, Denver, 1959-63, ptnr., 1964-82; ptnr. Wade Ash Woods Hill & Guthery P.C., Denver, 1982-91, Wade Ash Woods & Hill P.C., Denver, 1991-93, Wade Ash Woods Hill & Farley, P.C., Denver, 1993—. Fellow Am. Coll. Trust and Estate Counsel; mem. ABA, Colo. Bar Assn., Denver Bar Assn., Internat. Acad. Estate and Trust Law. Home: 6814 N Trailway Cir Parker CO 80134-6200 Office: Wade Ash Woods Hill & Farley 360 S Monroe St Ste 400 Denver CO 80209-3709

ASHBY, LAURA LEE, maintenance company executive; b. Santa Monica, Calif., Jan. 13, 1954; d. Gordon Bruce Ashby and Norma Mary (Withers) Devincenzi. Student, Los Angeles Valley Coll., Van Nuys, Calif., 1971-72; cert. bus. mgmt., UCLA, 1989; pediatric radiologic technologist cert., Children's Hosp., L.A., 1975. X-ray technician Univ. Hosp., San Diego, 1975-76; radiol. tech. X-Ray Assocs., San Diego, 1976-77, Kaiser Lahaina Clinic, Maui, Hawaii, 1977-79; ptnr., gen. mgr. Ashby's White Glove, L.A., 1980—. Sec.-treas. Catharsis, Sherman Oaks, Calif., 1986—; adminstrv. asst. non-profit program Children of the Night, 1981-83. Mem. Am. Soc. Radiologic Tech., Hawaiian Soc. Radiologic Technologists, Am. Registry Radiologic Technologists, Calif. Soc. Radiologic Technologists, Nat. Assn. Women in Constrn., Pioneer Skippers Assn. Marina Del Rey (bd. dirs.), Marina Del Rey C. of C. (chair 1984). Republican.

ASHBY, LUCIUS ANTONE, financial consultant; b. Des Moines, Feb. 1, 1944; s. Ruth Moore A.; m. Penny Ware (div.); children: Felecia, Wind; m. Victoria Lacy, Nov. 1, 1984; 1 child, Armand. BS, U. Colo., 1969; grad. owner/pres. mgmt. program, Harvard U., 1985. Sr. acct. Arthur Andersen & Co., Denver, 1969-72; managing ptnr. Ashby, Armstrong & Co., Denver, 1973-91; pvt. cons. Denver, 1991—. Bd. dirs. Salvation Army, Denver, 1988—, Red Shield Community Ctr., Denver, 1988—; mem. Minority Bus. Adv. Council, Denver, 1988—. With U.S. Army, 1961-64. Recipient Barney Ford Award for Bus. Achievement Eastside Action Movement, Denver, 1975, Entrepreneur award United Negro Coll. Fund, Denver, 1980. Mem. Colo. Soc. CPA's, Colo. State Bd. of Accountancy (pres. 1984), Nat. Assn. Black Accts. (Achievement award 1979). Democrat. Baptist. Office: 1380 Lawrence St Ste 640 Denver CO 80204

ASHCROFT, RICHARD THOMAS, computer company executive; b. Utica, N.Y., Nov. 9, 1934; s. Edwin William and Ann Catherine (Bogan) A.; m. Beverly Rita Trimm, July 6, 1957. BEE, Clarkson U., 1956; postgrad., U. Rochester, 1963-64. Instrument engr. E.I. du Pont, Niagara Falls, N.Y., 1956-57, power engr., 1957-60; engr., product mgr. Gen. Dynamics/Electronics, Rochester, N.Y., 1960-61, mktg. mgr., 1962-68; v.p. mktg. Aydin Energy Systems, Palo Alto, Calif., 1968-74; v.p. internat. Stanford Technology Corp., Sunnyvale, Calif., 1975-79; pres., CEO Internat. Imaging Systems, Milpitas, Calif., 1979—; instr. signal sch. U.S. Army Signal Corps., Ft. Monmouth, N.J., 1957. Active electronic div. campaign com. United Way, Santa Clara County, Calif., 1984-87. Capt. U.S. Army, 1961-62. Recipient Disting. Alumni award Clarkson U., 1991. Mem. Am. Electronics Assn. (bd. dirs. 1989-92), Electronics Assn. Calif. (bd. dirs. 1984-87), Santa Clara County Family Svcs. Assn. (bd. dirs., 1992—). Office: Internat Imaging Systems Inc 1500 Buckeye Dr Milpitas CA 95035-7484

ASHDOWN, FRANKLIN DONALD, physician, composer; b. Logan, Utah, May 2, 1942; s. Donald and Theresa Marie (Hill) A. BA, Tex. Tech. U., 1963; MD, U. Tex., 1967. Chief of med. Holloman Air Force Base, New Mexico, 1971-73; chief of staff Gerald Champion Mem. Hosp., Alamogordo, N.M., 1976, 91, 92; pres. Otero County Concerts Assn., Alamogordo, 1985-92, Otero County Med. Soc., Alamogordo, 1986; cons. New Mexico Sch. for Visually Handicapped, Alamogordo, 1973-76. Composer of more than 25 published and recorded works. Bd. dir. Otero County Mental Health Assn., Alamogordo, 1973-77; bd. trustees Gerlad Champion Meml. Hosp., 1992. Mem. Gerald Champion Mem. Hosp., N.M. Med. Soc., Am. Soc. Internal Med., ASCAP. Republican. Home: 1435 Rockwood Alamogordo NM 88310-3920 Office: 1301 Cuba Ave Alamogordo NM 88310-5797

ASHE, ANDREW MUNRO, naval officer, civil engineer; b. Brookline, Mass., May 27, 1959; s. Harry Joseph and Carole Celine (MacIntyre) A. BS in Civil Engring., U. N.H., 1982; MS in Civil Engring., U. Wash., 1988. Profl. engr., Calif. Commd. ensign USN, 1982, advanced through grades to lt. comdr., 1986; resident officer in charge of constrn. USN, Pearl Harbor, Hawaii, 1983-85, civil engr. U.S. naval submarine base, 1985-87; co. comdr. U.S. Naval Mobile Constrn. Bn. 4, Port Hueneme, Calif., also Okinawa, Cuba, Saudi Arabia, 1988-91; pub. works officer U.S. Naval Facility Centerville Beach, Ferndale, Calif., 1991—. Sec./treas. Civil Engr. Corp. Orgn., Pearl Harbor, 1983-85. Mem. ASCE, Soc. Am. Mil. Engrs., VFW. Democrat. Office: Naval Facility Centerville Beach Pub Works Dept Ferndale CA 95536

ASHE, JOHN HERMAN, scientist, neuroscience and physiological educator; b. Phila., Mar. 27, 1944; s. John Herman Ashe Sr. and Gloria (Jones) Faison; 1 child from previous marriage, John Miles. BA in Physiological Psychology with highest honors, U. Calif., Riverside, 1972; PhD in Biol. Sci., U. Calif., Irvine, 1977. Asst. rsch. physiologist U. Calif., San Francisco, 1979-80; asst. prof. U. Calif., Riverside, 1980-84, assoc. prof., 1984-90, prof., 1990—; mem. Ctr. for the Neurobiology of Learning and Memory U. Calif., Irvine, 1984—. Contbr. articles to profl. jours. Mem. div. rsch. grants, behavirol and neuroscis. study sect. 1985-88; mem. panel on mental and neurol. disorders/diseases Ariz. Disease Control Rsch. Commn., 1986—; mem. adv. panel in neural mechanisms of behavior NSF, 1990—. Mem. AAAS, Am. Soc. for Cell Biology, Am. Physiol. Soc., Soc. for Neurosci., Internat. Brain Rsch. Orgn., N.Y. Acad. Scis. Office: U Calif Depts Neurosci & Psychology Riverside CA 92521

ASHENDEN, WILLIAM JOSEPH, broadcast executive; b. Evanston, Ill., Feb. 6, 1957; s. James Fredrick Jr. and Mary Jane (Hummel) A.; m. Beverly Joan Bruns, Aug. 25, 1984. BA, U. Portland, 1980. Acct. exec. Sta. KCYX, McMinnville, Oreg., 1980-82, Sta. KEX/KQFM, Portland, Oreg., 1982-83, Sta. KYTE/KRCK, Portland, 1983-85; acct. exec. Sta. KKRZ, Portland, 1985-87, mgr. local sales, 1987-88, mgr. gen. sales, 1988-91, gen. mgr., 1991—. Bd. dirs. MDA, Portland, 1991—; mem. mktg. comm. com. United Way, 1992-93. Mem. Advertising Golf Assn., Portland Advertising Fedn., Portland Area Radio Coun. (v.p., pres.-elect 1993). Office: Station KKRZ-FM 4949 SW Macadam Ave Portland OR 97201

ASHER, JAMES EDWARD, forestry consultant, engineer, arborist; b. L.A., July 22, 1931; s. John Edward and Dorothy (Ingraham) A.; student Pasadena City Coll., 1949-50; BS, Oreg. State U., 1954; Cert. continuing forestry edn. Soc. of Am. Foresters, 1979; m. Marilyn Lee Struebing, Dec. 28, 1953; children: Lynne Marie, Laure Ann. With U.S. Forest Svc., San Bernardino (Calif.) Nat. Forest, summers 1950-53, forester, 1956-57; prin. James E. Asher, ACF, Cons. Forester, 1957—; capt., bn. chief, asst. chief, fire prevention officer Crest Forest Fire Protection Dist., Crestline, Calif., 1960-69, chief, 1969-71; forester Big Bear div. Golden State Bldg. Products, Redlands, 1972, timber mgr., 1972-74; mem. profl. foresters exam. com. Calif. Bd. Forestry, 1978-90, vice chmn., 1982-90; mem. Calif. Integrated Hardwood, Calif. Forest Pest Control Action Coun.; mem. Forest Adv. Com., 1982—, Mountaintop Adv. Com., 1991—; chmn. Profl. Foresters Ad Hoc Task Force, 1983-90. Vol. firewarden State of Calif., 1967—; mem. adv. com. Range Mgmt. Program, 1986-90, Greywater Reuse Tech. San Bernardino County, 1991—; chmn. Tree Conservation Subcom., First Dist. Suprs. Ad Hoc Com. on Soil Erosion and Sediment Control, County of San Bernardino, 1984—. With AUS, 1954-56. Recipient Certificate of Merit Nat. Fire Protection Assn., San Bernardino Mountains Assn.; Resolution of Commendation, County Bd. Suprs.; Forester of Year award So. Calif. sect. Soc. Am. Foresters, 1977; others. Registered profl. forester, registered profl. engr., Calif.; lic. pest control advisor, pest control operator, Calif. Mem. Internat. Soc. Arboriculture (cert. arborist western chpt. 1988—), Am. Forestry Assn., So. Calif. Assn. Foresters and Fire Wardens, Soc. Am. Foresters (cert., chmn. licensing and ethics com. So. Calif. sect., chmn. So. Calif. 1983), Assn. Cons. Foresters, Internat. Soc. Arboriculture, Sierra-Cascade Logging Conf., Calif. Urban Forests Coun., Calif. Agrl. Prodn. Cons. Assn., Pesticide Applicators Profl. Assn., Masons, Tau Kappa Epsilon. Presbyterian. Author: (with others) A Technical Guide for Community and Urban Forestry in Washington, Oregon and California. Contbr. articles to profl. Office: PO Box 2326 Lake Arrowhead CA 92352-2326

ASHER, JEFFERSON WILLIAM, JR., venture capitalist; b. Los Angeles, Sept. 6, 1924; s. Jefferson William and Emily Gertrude (Pinter) A.; m. Mary Frances Neville, Sept. 1, 1944; children—Susan Emily, Catherine Louise, Jefferson William. A.B. in Polit. Sci., UCLA, 1946; M.B.A. with distinction, Harvard U., 1948. Sales mgr. Sweet Sue Candy Co., Los Angeles, 1948-49; staff analyst Am. Research & Devel. Corp., Boston, 1949-51; gen. mgr., treas. Colter Corp., Palacios, Tex., 1951-52; mgmt. cons. Robert Heller & Assocs., Cleve., 1952-57; div. mgr. fittings div. Parker Aircraft Co., Los Angeles, 1957-58; controller, bus. mgr. Kirk Douglas & Related Entities, Beverly Hills, Calif., 1959-61; v.p. West Coast ops. Boston Capital Corp., Los Angeles, 1961-69; venture capitalist, mgmt. cons., Los Angeles, 1969—; dir., chmn. audit com. Baldor Electric Co., Ft. Smith, Ark., 1973—. Mem. task force for adminstrv. reorgn. of U.S. Dept. State, Washington, 1953-54. Served to lt. USNR, 1942-46; PTO. Decorated Purple Heart. Mem. Am. Arbitration Assn. (arbitrator 1979—), Phi Beta Kappa. Republican. Episcopalian.

ASHFORD, EVELYN, track and field athlete; M. Ray Washington; 1 child, Rana. Student, UCLA. Track and field athlete, 1976—. Competed in 1976 Olympics; winner 2 Gold medals, 1984 Olympics (Women's 100 Meters, Women's 4x100-Meter); winner Gold medal, 1988 Olympics (Women's 4x100-Meter); recipient Flo Hyman award Women's Sport Found., 1989; winner Gold medal, 1992 Olympics, Barcelona, Spain (4x100-Meter). Address: 818 Plantation Ln Walnut CA 91789

ASHLAND, CALVIN KOLLE, federal judge; b. Mason City, Iowa, Feb. 22, 1933; m. Ilse Doerr, 1957. BS, Iowa State U., 1957; JD, George Washington U., 1963. Bar: Calif. 1973, D.C. 1964, Md. 1968. Credit mgr. GE, Laurel, Md., 1957-67; atty. Law firm of David S. Rubenstein, Bethesda, Md., 1967-72, Sulmeyer Kupetz Baumann and Rothman, L.A., 1972-76; judge U.S. Bankruptcy Ct., L.A., 1976—, 9th Cir. Bankruptcy Appellate Panel, L.A., 1982—; chief bankruptcy judge Cen. Dist. Calif., 1991—; treas. Fin. Lawyers Conf., L.A., 1987—. With U.S. Army, 1954-56. Fellow Am. Coll. Bankruptcy; mem. ABA, L.A. County Bar Assn., Comm. Law League, Am. Bankruptcy Inst. Office: US Bankruptcy Ct 255 E Temple St # 1634 Los Angeles CA 90012-3308

ASHLEY, MICHAEL HAROLD, systems engineer; b. New Castle, Ind., Dec. 7, 1956; s. Richard Harold and Nancy Helen (Hueston) A. BSBA, U. Fla., 1978. Cost analyst Gen. Foods Corp., Dover, Del., 1978-80; sr. rsch. engr. Gen. Dynamics Corp., Pomona, Calif., 1984-86; project engr. Northrop B-2 Div., Pico Rivera, Calif., 1986—. Lt. USN, 1980-84, Res. Mem. Naval Res. Assn., Northrop B-2 Div. Mgmt. Club. Home: 960 E Bonita Ave # 83 Pomona CA 91767 Office: Northrop B-2 Div 8900 E Washington Blvd Pico Rivera CA 90660

ASHLEY, PAULA CLAIRE, engineer; b. Pasadena, Calif., Oct. 23, 1939; d. Pierre Marcel and Mabel Claire (Brown) Honnell; m. Paul Edward Ashley, Dec. 27, 1962 (div. 1986); children: Steven Lane (dec. Aug. 1991), Loren Kendall. BA, Vassar Coll., 1961; MS, Ariz. State U., 1979. Mathematician Lawrence Radiation Lab., Livermore, Calif., 1961-64; scientific programmer Goodyear Aerospace, Litchfield Park, Ariz., 1976-80; mem. tech. staff Automatic Electric Labs. GTE, Phoenix, 1980-82; sr. software engr. Digital Equipment Corp., Phoenix, 1982-84; systems software engr. comml. flight systems Sperry, Phoenix, 1984-86; prin. engr. comml. flight systems Honeywell Inc., Phoenix, 1986-88, engring. sect. head air transport systems div., 1988—. Mem. IEEE, Ariz. State U. West Alumni Assn. (bd. dirs.). Methodist. Office: Honeywell Air Transport Systems Div PO Box 21111 Phoenix AZ 85036-1111

ASHLEY, ROSALIND MINOR, writer; b. Chgo., Oct. 10, 1923; d. Jack and Frances (Wasser) Minor; m. Charles Ashley, Mar. 1, 1941; children: Stephen David, Richard Arthur. Grad., Moser Bus. Coll., Chgo., 1940; BS in Edn., Northwestern U., 1963; postgrad., Nat. Coll. Edn., 1968. Sec. Platt Luggage, Inc., 1944; Chgo. producer, performer Story Book Ladies WEAW, Evanston, Ill., 1954-55; elem. tchr. Sch. Dist. No. 65, Evanston, 1962-63, Sch. Dist. No. 39, Wilmette, Ill., 1964-70; assoc. editor Scott, Foresman & Co., Inc., Glenview, Ill., 1970-72; weekly humor columnist Citizen, Del Mar Citizen and La Costan, Solana Beach, Calif., 1986-87; freelance writer San Diego edit. L.A. Times and Citizen, 1987—; cons. Carlsbad (Calif.) Unified Sch., 1986-87. Author: Successful Techniques for Teaching Elementary Language Arts, 1970, paperback edit., 1981, Activities for Motivating and Teaching Bright Children, 1973, Simplified Teaching Techniques and Materials for Flexible Group Instruction, 1976, Portfolio of Daily Classroom Activities with Model Lesson Plans, 1979; editor: Language and How to Use It, 1970; contbr. articles to profl. and popular publs. Vol. Recs. for Blind, Chgo.; publicity chmn. Rancho Santa Fe (Calif.) Community Concerts Assn., 1986-88; play judge Assoc. Community Theatres. Recipient grand prize for poetry Sta. KFAC-FM, L.A., 1984. Mem. AAUW, Welcome Wagon Club. Democrat. Jewish. Home: 260 Via Tavira Encinitas CA 92024-5324

ASHLEY, SHARON ANITA, pediatric anesthesiologist; b. Goulds, Fla., Dec. 28, 1948; d. John H. Ashley and Johnnie Mae (Everett) Ashley-Mitchell; m. Clifford K. Sessions, Sept. 1977 (div. 1985); children: Cecili, Nicole, Erika. BA, Lincoln U., 1970; postgrad., Pomona Coll., 1971; MD, Hahnemann Med. Sch., Phila., 1976. Diplomate Am. Bd. Pain Mgmt. Intern pediatrics Martin Luther King Hosp., L.A., 1976-77, resident pediatrics, 1977-78, resident anesthesiology, 1978-80, mem. staff, 1981—. Named Outstanding Tchr. of Yr., King Drew Med. Ctr., Dept. Anesthesia, 1989, Outstanding Faculty of Yr., 1991. Mem. Am. Soc. Anesthesiologists, Calif. Med. Assn., L.A. County Med. Soc., Soc. Regional Anesthesia, Soc. Pediatric Anesthesia. Democrat. Baptist. Office: Martin Luther King Hosp 12021 Wilmington Ave Los Angeles CA 90059-3099

ASHLEY-FARRAND, MARGALO, lawyer, mediator, family law specialist; b. N.Y.C., July 26, 1944; d. Joel Thomas and Margalo (Wilson) Ashley; m. Marvin H. Bennett, Mar. 5, 1964 (div. June 1974),; children: Marc, Aliza; m. Thomas Ashley-Farrand, Dec. 11, 1981. Student, UCLA, 1962-63, U. Pitts., 1972-74; BA, NYU, 1978; JD, Southwestern U., 1980. Bar: D.C. 1981, Md. 1981, Calif. 1983, U.S. Dist. Ct. (cen. and no. dists.) Calif. 1984; cert. family law specialist. Legal asst to Sylvia Roberts, atty., 1973-74; paralegal, office mgr. Fly, Shuebruck, Blume, Gaquine, Boros & Shulkind, 1976; asst. to mgr. editorials WCBS-TV, 1977-78; pvt. practice law Washington, 1981-82; ptnr. Ashley-Farrand & Smith, Glendale, Calif., 1983-87; pvt. practice law Glendale, 1987—; judge pro tem L.A. Mcpl. Ct., 1989—, settlement officer, 1990—; judge pro tem L.A. Mcpl. Ct., 1989—, L.A. Superior Ct., 1993—; mcpl. ct. settlement officer, 1990—. Active La Leche League, 1967-71; convenor, pres., NOW East Hills chpt., 1972-74, mem. Pa. State bd., 1972-74, pres. Hollywood chpt., 1974-75, mem. bd. N.Y.C. chpt., 1975-78; convenor, coord. L.A. Women's Coalition for Better Broadcasting, 1974-75. Themis soc. scholar, 1980; named one of Outstanding Young Women of Am., 1980. Mem. ACLU, LWV, AAUW, NOW, NWPC, Calif. Women Lawyers, Women Lawyers Assn. L.A., Los Angeles County Bar Assn., San Fernando Valley Bar Assn. Office: 100 N Brand Blvd Ste 200 Glendale CA 91203-2614

ASHMAN, WILLIAM ALFRED, JR., manufacturing research institute executive; b. Highland Park, Mich., Sept. 21, 1954; s. William A. and Leila Ann (Wilson) A. Student, Whittier Coll., 1972-74; BA, Pepperdine U., 1978, MBA, 1983. Contracts adminstr. Computer Communications, Inc., Torrance, Calif., 1978-79; bus. mgr. Hughes Aircraft Co., L.A., 1979-84; asst. dean, dir. Mgmt. Inst., Pepperdine U. Sch. Bus. and Mgmt., Malibu, Calif., 1984-85; cons. Ashman & Assocs., Lakewood, Calif., 1986-90; asst. to exec. dir., chief fin. and chief adminstrv. officer Inst. for Mfg. and Automation Rsch., Brea, Calif., 1990—; nat. and internat. cons. to med. cos., small bus., univs., rsch. orgns., and fgn. mfrs., 1984—; mem. statewide com. evaluation and review curriculum, Calif. Community Colls., 1991—. Vol. golf coach Mayfair High Sch., Lakewood, 1989-90. Mem. Skylinks Golf Club. Home: 25622 Calabria Dr Moreno Valley Ranch CA 92388

ASHMEAD, ALLEZ MORRILL, speech-hearing-language pathologist, orofacial myologist, consultant; b. Provo, Utah, Dec. 18, 1916; d. Laban Rupert and Zella May (Miller) M.; m. Harve DeWayne, Sheryl Mae Harames, Zeltha Janeel Henderson, Emma Allez Broadfoot. BS, Utah State U., 1938; MS summa cum laude, U. Utah, 1952, PhD summa cum laude, 1970; postgrad., Idaho State U., Oreg. State Coll., U. Denver, U. Utah, Brigham Young U., Utah State U., U. Washington, U. No. Colo. Cert. secondary edn., remedial reading, spl. edn., learning disabilities; cert. clin. competence speech pathology and audiology; profl. cert. in orofacial myology. Tchr. pub. schs. Utah, Idaho, 1938-43; speech and hearing pathologist Bushnell Hosp., Brigham City, Utah, 1943-45; sr. speech correctionist Utah State Dept. Health, Salt Lake City, 1945-52; dir. speech and hearing dept. Davis County Sch. Dist., Farmington, Utah, 1952-65; clin., field supr. U. Utah, Salt Lake City, 1965-70, 75-78; speech pathologist Box Elder Sch. Dist., Brigham City, 1970-75, 78-84; teaching specialist Brigham Young U., Provo, 1970-73; speech pathologist Primary Children's Med. Ctr., Salt Lake City, 1975-77; pvt. practice speech pathology and orofacial myology, 1970-88; del. USSR Profl. Speech Pathology seminar, 1984, 86; participant numerous internat. seminars. Author: Physical Facilities for Handicapped Children, 1957, A Guide for Training Public School Speech and Hearing Clinicians, 1965, A Guide for Public School Speech Hearing Programs, 1959, Impact of Orofacial Myofunctional Treatment on Orthodontic Correction, 1982, Meeting Needs of Handicapped Children, 1975, Relationship of Trace Minerals to Disease, 1972, Macro and Trace Minerals in Human Metabolism, 1971, Electromotive Potential Differences Between Stutterers and Non-stutterers, 1970, Learning Disability, An Educational Adventure, 1969, New Horizons in Special Education, 1969, Developing Speech and Language in the Exceptional Child, 1961, Parent Teacher Guidance in Primary Stuttering, 1951, numerous others; contbr. research articles to profl. jours. Student Placement chair Am. Field Service, Kaysville, Utah, 1962-66; ednl. del. Women's State Legis. Council, Salt Lake City, 1958-70; chairwoman fund raising Utah Symphony Orch., Salt Lake City, 1970-71; sec., treas. Utah chpt. U.S. Council for Exceptional Children, 1958-62, membership com. chair, 1962-66, program com. chair, 1966-68. Recipient Scholarship award for Higher Edn. U. Utah, Salt Lake City, 1969; Delta Kappa Gamma scholar, 1968; rsch. grantee Utah Dept. Edn., 1962. Mem. NEA, Utah Ednl. Assn., Am. Speech, Lang. Hearing Assn. (life, continuing edn. com. 1985, Ace award for Continuing Edn. 1984), Western Speech Assn., Internat. Assn. Orofacial Myology (life, bd. examiners, Sci. Contribution award 1982), Utah Speech, Hearing and Lang. Assn. (life, sec., treas. 1956-60), AAUW (Utah state bd. chair status of women 1959-62, Kaysville br. 1957-60, bd. dirs. Kaysville-Davis br. 1987-92, chair internat. rels. 1987-91, chair cultural interests Kaysville-Davis br. 1991-92), Delta Kappa Gamma (state scholarship award 1968, del. Woman's State Legis. Coun. 1958-70, profl. affairs chair 1963-67, tchr. of yr. award 1978), AAUW (bd. dirs. internat. rels. Kaysville-Davis br., 1988-91), Sigma Alpha Eta, Theta Alpha Phi, Psi Chi, Zeta Phi Eta, Phi Kappa Phi. Republican. Mormon. Lodges: Daus. Utah Pioneers (parlimentarian Kaysville chpt. 1980-92, historian 1975-80, lesson leader 1992—), Soroptimist Internat. (charter mem. 1954, bd. dirs. 1954-56, pres. Davis County chpt. 1965-69, treas. 1956-54, Rocky Mountain regional bd. dirs. 1965-70, community service award 1968, pub. service award 1970). Home: 719 E Center St Kaysville UT 84037-2138

ASHMEAD, HARVE DEWAYNE, nutritionist, executive, educator; b. Brigham City, Utah, June 6, 1944; s. Harvey Harold and Allez (Morrill) A.; m. Eugele Baird, June 24, 1966; children: Stephen, Jilane, Brett, Angelique, Heidi. BS, Weber State Coll., 1969; PhD, Pacific Inst., 1970; PhD magna cum laude, Donsbach U., 1981. Cert. nutritional cons. With Ch. Jesus Christ of Latter Day Saints, Paris, 1963-66; v.p. Albion Labs., Ogden, Utah, 1966-71, exec. v.p., Clearfield, Utah, 1971-82, pres., 1982—, also bd. dirs.; pres. Albion Internat.; adj. prof. Weber State Coll., also adv. council; former advisor Weber County Sch. Dist.; bd. dirs. Albion Internat., Zions Bank, Albion Labs., Inc., Unilabco, Inc., Albion Middle East, Albion Europe, Rhondell Labs.; guest lectr. Adv. Fruit Heights City (Utah); pres. PTA. Fellow Am. Coll. Nutrition; mem. Am. Soc. Animal Sci., Am. Assn. Nutrition and Dietary Cons., Internat. Acad. Nutritional Cons., Am. Assn. Nutritional Cons., Am. Acad. Applied Health Sci., AAAS, Am. Biographical Inst. (bd. govs.), Clearfield C. of C. (bd. dirs.), Delta Sigma Pi. Mormon. Author: Chelated Mineral Nutrition, 1981, Mineral Absorption Mechanisms, 1981, Chelated Mineral Nutrition in Plants, Animals and Man, 1982, A New Era in Plant Nutrition, 1982, Intestinal Absorption of Metal Ions and Chelates, 1985, Foliar Feeding of Plants with Amino Acid Chelates, 1986, In Search of a Rainbow, 1988, Amino Acids in Animal Nutrition, 1991; Conversations on Chelation and Mineral Nutrition, 1989, The Roles of Amino Acid Creates in Animal Nutrition, 1993; contbr. numerous articles to profl. jours. Office: Albion Labs 101 N Main St Clearfield UT 84015-2243

ASHTON, ALAN C., computer software company executive. Pres. WordPerfect Corp., Orem, Utah. Office: Wordperfect Corp 1555 N Technology Way Orem UT 84057-2399

ASHTON, ARTHUR BENNER, business educator, consultant; b. Alliance, Ohio, Jan. 27, 1941; s. Arthur E. and Mary (Riddle) A.; m. Diane J. Jelinek, Aug. 9, 1988; children: Amy, Angela. BS, Am. U., 1967, MBA, 1972; PhD, U. Ariz., 1983. Dir. budget, rsch. Colo. Commn. on Higher Edn., Denver, 1972-75; dir. fiscal affairs W. Va. State Coll., Charleston, 1975-79; spl. asst. strategic planning Ariz. Bd. Regents, Phoenix, 1981—; Ariz. rep. Western Interstate Commn. on Higher Edn., Telecom. Coop.; chmn. oper. com. Ariz. Telecom. Coop. Mem. Ariz. Strategic Planning for Econ. Devel. Mem. Soc. Coll. and Univ. Planners (publ. com.), Toastmasters. Home: 5601 E Calle

Del Paisano Phoenix AZ 85018 Office: Ariz Bd Regents 2020 N Central Ave Phoenix AZ 85004

ASHTON, GERALD, international human resources and personnel consultant; b. Guayaquil, Guayas, Ecuador, June 30, 1931; s. Alexander Hawkes and Ines Mercedes (Arosemena) A.; m. Christina Julia Allen, Aug. 28, 1954; 1 child, Nina Mercedes. BA, Wash. State U., 1953, MA, 1954. Trainee, safety adminstr. Caribbean, pers. mgr. Aluminum Co. of Am., L.A, Bauxite, Ark., Pitts, Suriname, Dominican Republic, 1956-64; pers. mgr., internat. pers. mgr. Standard Fruit Co. (now Dole Co.), San Francisco, Calif., Honduras, 1965-75; pers. dir. Bio-Rad Labs., Richmond, Calif., 1975-76; internat. pers. mgr., pers. dir. for Latin Am. Syntex Corp., Palo Alto, Calif., 1976-83; prin. Gerald Ashton & Assocs., San Mateo, Calif., 1983—. Chmn., mem. pers. bd. City of San Mateo, 1986—. Republican. Office: Gerald Ashton and Assocs 4009 Kingridge Dr San Mateo CA 94403

ASHTON, JOHN PETER, lawyer; b. Provo, Utah, Jan. 13, 1945; s. Preston E. and Eleanor (Lowe) A.; m. Neena Duimenti, Aug. 17, 1974; children: Alexander, Anthony, Sophia. BA, Stanford U., 1967; JD, U. Utah, 1971. Bar: Utah 1971, D.C. 1972, U.S. Ct. Appeals (10th cir.) 1972, U.S. Tax Ct. 1982, U.S. Dist. Ct. (no. dist.) Ill. 1984, U.S. Ct. Appeals (3d cir.) 1984, U.S. Dist. Ct. (no. dist.) Ga. 1985, U.S. Ct. Appeals (11th cir.) 1987, U.S. Supreme Ct. 1988. Atty. U.S. Dept. Justice, Washington, 1971-73; assoc. Prince, Yeates & Geldzahter, Salt Lake City, 1973-76, ptnr., 1976—. Assoc. editor U. Utah Law Rev., 1970-71. Bd. dirs. Utah Arts Festival, 1986-90, chmn. bd. trustees, 1987-88; bd. dirs. Utah Citizens for Arts, Salt Lake City, 1982-90. Mem. ABA, Utah State Bar, D.C. Bar Assn., Stanford Club of Utah (pres. 1974), U. Utah Law Sch. Alumni Assn. (pres. 1989, trustee 1986-91), Sutherland Inns of Ct. (pres. 1993—). Office: Prince Yeates & Geldzahler 175 E 400 S Ste 900 Salt Lake City UT 84111-2314

ASHTON, RICK JAMES, librarian; b. Middletown, Ohio, Sept. 18, 1945; s. Ralph James and Lydia Marie (Thornbery) A.; m. Marcia K. Zuroweste, Dec. 23, 1966; children: Jonathan Paul, David Andrew. AB, Harvard U., 1967; MA, Northwestern U., 1969, PhD, 1973; MA, U. Chgo., 1976. Instr., asst. prof. history Northwestern U., Evanston, Ill., 1972-74; curator local and family history Newberry Library, Chgo., 1974-77; asst. dir. Allen County Pub. Library, Ft. Wayne, Ind., 1977-80, dir., 1980-85; city librarian Denver Pub. Library, 1985—; mem. Ind. Coop Library Services Authority, 1980-85, pres., 1984-85; mem. Ft. Wayne Cable TV Adv. Council, 1982-85; cons. Nat. Endowment Humanities, Nat. Ctr. Edn. Stats., Northwestern U. Office Estate Planning. Author: The Life of Henry Ruiter, 1742-1819, 1974, The Genealogy Beginner's Manual: A New Edition, 1977, Stuntz, Fuller, Kennard and Cheadle Ancestors, 1987 (with others) Trends in Urban Library Management, 1989. Bd. dirs. Community Coordinated Child Care, Evanston, 1972-74, Three Rivers Montessori Sch., Ft. Wayne, 1977-80; bd. dirs., sec. Allen County-Ft. Wayne Hist. Soc., 1977-83; active Denver Mcpl. Access Cable TV Policy Bd. Conscientious objector. Recipient Nat. Merit scholar, 1963-67, Old City Hall Hist. Service award, 1985; NDEA fellow, 1967-69; Woodrow Wilson fellow, 1971-72. Mem. ALA, Colo. Libr. Assn., Colo. Alliance Rsch. Librs. (pres. 1987-88), Rotary. Home: 2974 S Verbena Way Denver CO 80231-4219 Office: Denver Pub Libr 1357 Broadway Denver CO 80203-2165

ASHWOOD, ANDREW MARK, radio station executive; b. Milw., Feb. 28, 1957; s. Loren Frisk and Helen Elizabeth (Passmore) A. Student, Albion (Mich.) Coll., 1975-79. Program, music dir. Sta. WGBF-AM, Evansville, Ind., 1980-81, Sta. WKTI-FM, Milw., 1981-82; asst. program dir. Sta. WABX-FM, Detroit, 1983; on-air personality Sta. KOPA-AM/FM, Phoenix, 1983-85; ops. mgr. Sta. KOOL-AM/FM, Phoenix, 1985-90; v.p. programming Adams Communications, Phoenix, 1990—; pres., gen. mgr.WAQQ/WAQS Adams Communications, 1991—; OM/PD WVRI, Paxson Broadcasting, Orlando, Fla., 1992—; cons. Satellite Music Network, Dallas, 1986—. Named Outstanding Citizen, Kelly Svcs., Ariz., 1985, Outstanding Young Men of Am., 1988. Methodist. Office: KOOL Radio 2196 E Camelback Rd Phoenix AZ 85016-4752

ASHWORTH, ALAN A., human resources professional; b. Wichita, Kans., Sept. 23, 1929; s. Arthur Albert and Oma Marie (Swindell) A.; m. Rose Elaine Edwards, Aug. 22, 1953; children: Randall M. Durant, Jay A. Ashworth, Dan A. Ashworth, Candace J. Hulse. Student, Wichita State U., 1956, 62-63, Cornell U., 1975. Owner, mgr. Dairy Queen franchise, Augusta, Kans., 1950-53; illustrator, planner depts. mfg., engring. Boeing Corp., Wichita and Seattle, 1952-59; supr. various factory, flight line and field assignments Boeing Corp., Wichita, Phila., Seattle, 1959-65; tech. assist team mgr. mfg. and human resource depts. Boeing Corp., Seattle, 1965-77, Spain, 1975-76; dir. human resources fabrication div. Boeing Corp., Seattle and Macon, Ga., 1978-85; dir. human resources Boeing Support Svcs., Seattle, 1985—; Boeing Corp. rep. Presdl. Com. for Employment of People With Disabilities, Washington, 1989—, Puget Sound Transit Com., Seattle, 1989—. Adult leader Boy Scouts Am., Kirkland, Wash., 1965-70; officer, coach Little League Baseball, Kirkland, 1965-71; mem. citizen adv. com. Lake Washington Sch. Dist., Kirkland, 1967-70. With U.S. Army, 1954-56. Home: 11507 Holmes Point Dr Kirkland WA 98034 Office: Boeing Support Svcs Div MS 6U-16 MS 3W-EW PO Box 3707 Seattle WA 98124

ASIA, DANIEL ISAAC, composer, conductor; b. Seattle, June 27, 1953; s. Benjamin Samuel and Hilda Fay (Aronson) A.; m. Caroli Thompson, July, 1979; children: Shoshana, Reuben, Eve. BA, Hampshire Coll., 1975; MusM, Yale U., 1977. Asst. prof. Oberlin (Ohio) Conservatory of Music, 1980-86; visiting lectr. City U., London, 1986-88; assoc. prof. U. Ariz., Tucson, 1988—; music dir. Musical Elements, N.Y.C., 1977—; composer in residence Meet the Composer, Phoenix Symphony Orch., 1991—. Composer Symphony Number 1, 1987, Piano Quartet, 1989, Black Light, 1990, Symphony Number 2, 1990, Symphony Number 3, 1992, Symphony Number 4, 1993. Recipient Piano Set II award Gaudeamus Festival,1 979, BMI prize Young Composers Sand II, 1979; grantee Martha Baird Rockefeller Found., 1979, Nat. Endowment Arts, 1978-79, 81-82, 86-87, 92—, DAAD-Fulbright Found., 1979-81; U.K. Fulbright Arts fellow, 1986-87, Guggenheim fellow, 1987-88. Jewish.

ASKIN, RICHARD HENRY, JR., entertainment company executive; b. Flushing, N.Y., Feb. 11, 1947; s. Richard H. and Anne Margaret A.; children: Jennifer Leigh, Michael Richard. BA in Econs., Rutgers U., 1969; MA in Communications, U. Tex., 1971; MBA in Fin., Fordham U., 1976. Sales rep. Proctor & Gamble Distbg. Co., Jericho, N.Y., 1969; account exec. CableRep, Inc., N.Y.C., 1973-74, WNBC-TV Nat. Broadcasting Co., N.Y.C., 1974-75, NBC-TV, NBC, N.Y.C., 1975-76, sales mgr. KNBC-TV, Los Angeles, 1976-79, dir. sales, 1979-85; v.p. domestic sales Fries Distbn. Co., Los Angeles, 1985-86, sr. v.p. distbn., 1986-87; pres. TV, The Samuel Goldwyn Co., Los Angeles; pres. The Breckford Group, Inc. Served to 1st lt. Adj. Gen. Corps, U.S. Army, 1971-73. Decorated Army Commendation medal; Alcoa fellow, 1969-70. Mem. Hollywood Radio and TV Soc., Advt. Industry Emergency Fund (pres., bd. dirs.), Acad. of TV, Arts and Scis., Sierra Club, Alpha Rho Alumni Assn., Chi Psi. Republican. Home: 1520 Aldercreek Pl Thousand Oaks CA 91362-4211 Office: Samuel Goldwyn Co 10780 Santa Monica Blvd Los Angeles CA 90067

ASMONAS, VLADAS, career officer, retired; b. Marijampole, Lithuania, Oct. 23, 1910; came to U.S., 1961; s. Jonas and Elizabeth (Galeckas) A.; m. Ona Kacergius, Mar. 29, 1937; children: Arvydas, Lina. Grad. gymnasium, Marijampole, 1930; grad. mil. coll., Lithuania, 1932. Commd. 2d lt. Lithuanian army, 1932, infantry platoon comdr., 1932-36, infantry co. comdr., 1938-40, retired, 1976; sport instruction, nursing sick people. Contbr. articles to profl. jours. Mem. AAAS, N.Y. Acad. Scis. Home: 986 Jasmine Dr Salt Lake City UT 84123-3341

ASSMANN, DAVID OSWALD, paper company executive; b. Southport, Eng., Feb. 3, 1952; s. Oswald Johann and Marianne Eva (Levenbach) A.; m. Robyn Ann Yale, Sept. 21, 1991. BS in Physics, U. Waterloo, Ont., Can., 1974. Sta. mgr. CKMS-FM, Waterloo, 1975-83; adminstr. Jour. Cote de Neiges, Montreal, 1983-84; bus. mgr. Heyday Books, Berkeley, Calif., 1984-85; bus. dir. Mother Jones Mag., San Francisco, 1985-86, circulation dir., 1986-87, assoc. pubr., 1987-88, pubr., 1988-90; v.p. Conservatree Paper Co., San Francisco, 1990—; mem. mkt. devel. com. Nat. Recycling Coalition, Washington, 1991—; adv. bd. Paper Stock Report, Cleve., 1992—; legis. com. Calif. Resource Recovery Assn., San Jose, 1991—. Editor newsletter Environmentally Sound Paper News, 1990—; contbr. articles to profl. jours., chpts. to books. Chair sta. adv. bd. KPFA-FM, Berkeley, Calif., 1991—; adv. bd. Arrowsmith Acad., Berkeley, 1991—; bd. dirs. Found. for Nat. Progress, San Francisco, 1988-90. Recipient Silver award circulation direct mktg. Mag. Pub. Congress, 1989. Home: 1067 Filbert San Francisco CA 94133 Office: Conservatree Paper 10 Lombard # 250 San Francisco CA 94111

ASTLEY, EUGENE ROY, seamless tube manufacturing executive; b. Alameda, Calif., Dec. 5, 1926; s. Frank Robert Astley and Mary Grace (Barr) Pease; m. Peggy Lund, June 27, 1948; children: Clifford Andrew, Michael J., William Lawrence. BS in Physics and Math., U. Oreg., 1948; MS in Physics and Math., Oreg. State U., 1950. Physicist GE, Schenectady, N.Y. and, Richland, Wash., 1950-65; dir., inventor Fast Flux Test Facility Battelle Northwest, Richland, 1965-69; dir. Systems Electronics & Econs. Battelle Northwest, Richland, 1969-71; v.p. New Projects & Products Exxon Nuclear Co., Bellevue, Wash., 1971-79; v.p., bd. dirs. Mfg. Facilities-U.S. & Germany, Exxon Nuclear Co., Richland, 1979-83; pres., chief exec. officer, bd. dirs. Sandvik Spl. Metals Corp., Kennewick, Wash., 1983—; bd. dirs. Sandvik Rhenium Alloys Inc., Elyria, Ohio; chmn. bd. Astley Enterprises Inc., 1990—. Contbr. articles to profl. jours.; inventor, patentee in field. Pres. Blue Mountain coun. Boy Scouts Am., Kennewick, 1987-89, v.p. at large, 1989—. Recipient Boy Scouts Am. Disting. Eagle Scout award, 1990. Mem. Nat. Assn. Corp. Dirs., U.S. Coun. for Energy Awareness, Am. Nuclear Soc. (Appreciation award 1958). Republican. Unitarian. Home: 2414 Harris Ave Richland WA 99352-1636 Office: Sandvik Spl Metals Corp PO Box 6027 Kennewick WA 99336-0027

ASTRIAB, STEVEN MICHAEL, army officer; b. Pitts., Mar. 10, 1952; s. Steven Leonard and Anna (Popivchak) a.; m. BettyLou Elaine Gimmi, Dec. 27, 1975 (div. Sept. 1991). BA in Psychology, Washington and Jefferson Coll., 1974; MS in Manpower Planning, W.Va. U., 1976. Commd. 2d lt. U.S. Army, 1974, advanced through grades to lt. col., 1992; div. social work officer 1st Cav. Div., Ft. Hood, Tex., 1976-77, med. platoon leader, then med. co. comdr. 15th med. bn., 1977-79; med. ops. officer 1st Cav. Div. Hdqs., Ft. Hood, Tex., 1979-81; chief M.C. procurement Office Army Surgeon Gen., Washington, 1982-85; chief combat medicine Office Project Mgr., Saudi Arabian Nat. Guard, Riyadh, 1985-88; pers. officer 62 Med. Group, Ft. Lewis, Wash., 1988-90; asst. chief staff for med. civil and mil. ops. 3d U.S. Army (Army Cen. Command), Riyadh, 1990-91; med. ops. officer Hdqrs. I Corps, Ft. Lewis, 1991-93; med. plans officer HQs 3d U.S. Army, Atlanta, 1993—. Decorated Bronze Star medal. Republican. Baptist. Home: PO Box 90745 Atlanta GA 30364-0745

ASTURIAS, JOSEPH LOUIS, priest, foundation administrator; b. Guatemala, May 18, 1908; came to U.S., 1910; s. Manuel Francisco and Rosa (Coblentz) A. Student, St. Thomas Coll., 1927-30; BA, BD, St. Albert's Sem., 1939. Parish priest Dominican Order, Seattle, 1930-35, San Francisco, 1935-40; missionary Dominican Order, Western U.S., 1940-58, Alaska, 1958-63, Mex., 1963-70; dir. Dominican Mission Found., San Francisco, 1971—. Author monthly bull. Missionaries in Action, 1979—. Home: 2390 Bush St San Francisco CA 94115 Office: Dominican Mission Found 2506 Pine St San Francisco CA 94115

ATAIE, ATA JENNATI, oil products marketing executive; b. Mashad, Iran, Mar. 15, 1934; s. Hamid Jennati and Mohtaram (Momeni) A.; came to U.S., 1957, naturalized, 1969; B.S. in Agr., Fresno (Calif.) State U., 1964; B.A. in Econs., San Francisco State U., 1966; m. Judith Garrett Bush, Oct. 7, 1961; children—Ata Jennati, Andrew J. Mktg. exec. Shell Oil Co., Oakland, Calif., 1966-75; pres. A.J. Ataie & Cos., Danville, Calif., 1975—; Am. Value Inc., 1976—. Served as 2d lt. Iranian Army, 1953. Mem. Nat. Petroleum Retailers Assn. Democrat.

ATCHESON, SUE HART, business educator; b. Dubuque, Iowa, Apr. 12; d. Oscar Raymond and Anna (Cook) Hart; m. Walter Clark Atcheson (div.); children: Christine A. Hischar, Moffet Zoe, Claye Williams. BBA, Mich. State U.; MBA, Calif. State Poly. U., Pomona, 1973. Cert. tchr. and adminstr. Instr. Mt. San Antonio Coll., Walnut, Calif., 1968-90; bd. dirs. faculty assn. Mt. San Antonio Coll.; mem. acad. senate Mt. San Antonio Coll.; originator vol. income tax assistance Mt. San Antonio Coll.; speaker in field. Author: Fractions and Equations on Your Own, 1975. Speaker Howard Ruff Nat. Conv., San Diego, 1983, Mike DeFalco Numismatics Seminar, Claremont, Calif., 1986; charter mem. Internat. Commn. on Monetary and Econ. Reform; panelist infrastructure funding reform, Freeport, Ill., 1989. Mem. Community Concert Assn. of Inland Empire (bd. dirs.), Scripps Coll. Fine Arts Found.

ATCHISON, CHARLES MARVIN, management systems consultant; b. Pasadena, Calif., Mar. 27, 1933; s. Clarence Murray Atchison and Louella May (Migendt) Key; m. Maxine Womack, Nov. 3, 1954; children: Kay Marie, Alexander Charles. Student, So. Calif. Bible Coll., Pasadena, 1949, Reed Coll., 1956-57; cert. in mgmt., U. Calif., Berkeley, 1969; MBA, Golden Gate U., 1979. Lab. technician, computer services coordinator Gen. Electric Co., Vallecitos Atomic Labs, San Jose, Calif., 1957-59; computer ops. mgr. Control Data Corp., Palo Alto, Calif., 1959-62; programmer, ops. cons. Lockheed Missles and Space Co., Sunnyvale, Calif., 1962-65; supr. jobsite computing Bechtel Corp., San Francisco, 1966-69; dir. systems and computing Esco Corp., Portland, Oreg., 1970-73; field procurement mgr. Bechtel Corp., 1973-78, mgr. systems and planning, 1978-79; mgr. decentralization Fairchild Semiconductor, Mt. View, Calif., 1979-83; pres., chief exec. officer Alcinous Internat. Ltd., Palo Alto, 1983—; instr. mgmt. Golden Gate U., Los Altos, Calif., 1984-86, City U., Bellevue, Wash., 1986-88, chair Calif. adv. bd., 1988. Bd. dirs. Calif. Youth Symphony, Palo Alto, 1977-78; referee, commr. Am. Youth Soccer Orgn., Palo Alto, 1978-85. Served with USN, 1952-56. Mem. Assn. for Computing Machinery (chpt. chmn. 1968), Assn. for Systems Mgmt., Planning Execs. Inst. (chpt. pres. 1985-86), World Future Soc., Cert. Systems Profls., MENSA. Republican. Office: Alcinous Global PO Box 10538 Palo Alto CA 94309-0538

ATCHISON, OLIVER CROMWELL, retired accountant; b. Berkeley, Calif., Jan. 19, 1918; s. Frederick Charles and Lillie Louise (Chapman) A. Student, Am. Inst. Banking, San Francisco, 1936-38. Asst. cashier Bank Am. NT&SA, San Francisco, Oakland, Calif., 1936-41; sr. warehouse acct. Alltrans Express USA Inc., San Francisco, 1953-82; ret., 1982. Editor The Dispatcher, 1984-92 (silver award 1985, silver and bronze awards 1986, bronze award 1987). With USNR, 1941-45. Recipient silver medal Chgo. Philatelic Soc., 1989. Fellow Am. Topical Assn. (treas., editor Casey Jones R.R. unit 1984—), Am. Philatelic Soc. Office: Am Topical Assn Casey Jones RR Unit PO Box 31631 San Francisco CA 94131-0631

ATENCIO, J(OSEPH) ANDREW, computer systems official, computer designer; b. Canon City, Colo., May 26, 1965; s. Joseph Andrew Atencio and Carol Lynn (Gordon) Pross; m. Kimberly Ann Maritz, Aug. 8, 1992. AS in Applied Techs., Phoenix Inst. Tech., 1988. Cert. AUTOCAD technician. Designer, drafter Fine Line Designs, Tempe, Ariz., 1987-89; tchr. Phoenix Inst. Tech., 1989-90; computer aided designer, computer system mgr. PRC Environ. Mgmt., Inc., Denver, 1990-91; mgr. computer systems RUST Environment and Infrastructure (formerly SEC Donohue), Englewood, Colo., 1991-92, regional info. systems mgr., 1992—; computer aided drafter Greeley & Hansen Engrs., Phoenix, 1988-90; owner, designer, cons. Midnight Wind Design Svcs., Phoenix and Denver, 1990—. Mem. Am. Design Drafting Assn. Democrat. Office: SEC Donohue 6143 S Willow Dr Ste 200 Englewood CO 80111

ATHERLY, DARST BARNARD, lawyer; b. Kalamazoo, Mich., Nov. 4, 1930; s. Harold James and Dorothy Lucille (Barnard) A.; m. Helen Calesta Bure, Sept. 2, 1956 (dec. 1982); children: DArst M., Benjamin H., Adam J. BBA, Western Mich. U., 1956; JD, U. Mich., 1956. Bar: Oreg. 1959. Ptnr. Thwing, Atherly, Butler, Eugene, Oreg., 1961-81, Atherly, Butler, Burgout, Eugene, 1981—. Capt. USAF, 1951-56. Fellow Am. Coll. Trial Lawyers. Republican. Episcopalian. Home: 477 W 27th Ave Eugene OR 97405

ATHERTON, ALEXANDER SIMPSON, newspaper executive; b. Honolulu, Mar. 29, 1913; s. Frank Cooke and Eleanore Alice (Simpson) A.; m. LeBurta Marie Gates, Oct. 8, 1941; children—Burta Lee, Frank Cooke II, Marjory Gates. Grad., Tabor Acad., Marion, Mass., 1931; B.A., Dartmouth, 1936. With Hawaiian Trust Co., Honolulu, 1954-66; asst. v.p. Hawaiian Trust Co., 1958-66. Past campaign chmn. Honolulu Community Chest; trustee Atherton Family Found.; bd. dirs. Africare, Inc. Mem. Pacific Club, Adventurers Club, Waialae Country Club, Oahu Country Club, Collectors Club, Outrigger Canoe Club, Theta Delta Chi. Republican. Mem. United Ch. of Christ. Home: 2150 Puualii Pl Honolulu HI 96822-2053

ATKIN, ARLO KAY, systems analyst, consultant; b. Bakersfield, Calif., July 5, 1956; s. Levi Kay and Beverly Jean (Kinghorn) A.; m. Myrna Jarvis, Nov. 17, 1978 (div. Jan. 1991); children: Tyson, Cameron, Bryce, Austin, Taylor; m. Edna Kay Pepera, July 5, 1991; 1 child, Steven. BA, Brigham Young U., 1980. Customer svc. rep. D. H. I., Provo, Utah, 1978-80; asst. mgr. Area Processing Ctrs., Provo, 1980-82, mgr., 1982-84; asst. dir. St. Luke's Hosp., Phoenix, 1984-86; sr. analyst Ariz. State U., Tempe, 1986-90; sr. cons. Bus. Info. Tech., Concord, Calif., 1990-91; owner, operator Comstar Computers, Ventura, Calif., 1991—. Bishop Ch. of Jesus LDS, Chandler, Ariz., 1986-89; v.p. Boy Scouts Am., Phoenix, 1988-89; acting dir. Ariz. State U., 1989. Mem. Human Resource Systems Profls. Republican. Office: Comstar Computers 4255-6 E Main St Ventura CA 93009

ATKIN, RUTH, social worker; b. Urbana, Ill., Jan. 30, 1958; d. J. Myron and Ann (Spiegel) A. BA cum laude, Brandeis U., 1979; MSW, Yeshiva U., 1982. Program coord. Jewish Community Ctr. Greater Boston, Boston, Brookline, Mass., 1980-81; community worker Elizabeth Peabody House, Somerville, Mass., 1981-82; day camp dir. Albert L. Schultz Jewish Community Ctr., Palo Alto, Calif., 1983; caseworker Jewish Home for Aged, San Francisco, 1984; program coord. Berkeley (Calif.)/Richmond Jewish Community Ctr., 1984-85; vol. dir. Jewish Family Svc. of Greater East Bay, Oakland, Calif., 1985-87; dir. in-home svcs. registry Bay Area Community Svcs., Oakland, 1986-88; sr. info. and referral coord. Contra Costa County Office on Aging, Martinez, Calif., 1988-92; ambulatory care social worker VA No. Calif. System Clinics, 1992—; bd. dirs. Support Svcs. Srs. of Alameda County, Hayward, Calif., 1985-89, Pacific Ctr., Berkeley, v.p., 1991—; bd. dirs. West County Sr. Svcs. Network, 1989—. Editor: (periodicals) Genesis 2, 1979-82; co-founder, editor: Jewish Women's Newsletter, 1985-89, BRIDGES, 1989—. Recipient Steve Berman Social Action award Congregation Ahavat Shalom, 1987. Mem. NASW. Jewish. Office: VA Outpatient Clinic 150 Muir Rd Martinez CA 94553

ATKINS, ROSEMARY BARNES, civic worker; b. N.Y.C., Aug. 16, 1912; d. Roderic Barbour Barnes and Rose Marie (Naething) Barnes Holden; m. Ernest Alan Atkins, June 24, 1932 (dec. Dec. 1990); children: Eleanore Atkins Hartz, Paul V., Katherine Atkins Kirk. Student, Bryn Mawr Coll., 1929-31; BA with honors, U. Calif., Berkeley, 1965, postgrad., 1965-67. Former bookkeeper, acct., office mgr., saleswoman. Pres. St. Anne's Svc. League, St. Paul's Ch., San Rafael, Calif., 1974-75; jr. warden St. Clare's Episcopal Ch., Arnold, Calif., 1984-88; coord. Stamp Club Calavaras County, Arnold, 1986-88; mem. Sun Health Aux., Sun City Symphony Guild. Travel fellow U. Calif., 1967. Mem. Order of St. Luke, Order of St Benedict, Sun City Art Assn., Sun City West Coin and Stamp Club, Phi Beta Kappa. Republican. Home: 13421 Countryside Dr Sun City West AZ 85375

ATKINSON, DAVID HERRING, electrical engineering educator; b. San Mateo, Calif., Nov. 13, 1955; s. Earl H. and Julia A. (Clarkson) A.; m. Donna M., June 24, 1984; children: Robert H., Michael E., Christa M. BA, Whitman Coll., 1977; BS, Wash. State U., 1980; MS, Stanford U., 1981; PhD, Wash. State U., 1989. Engr. NASA Ames Rsch. Ctr., Moffett Field, Calif., 1981-86; asst. prof. U Idaho, Moscow, 1989—; asst. dir. Idaho Space Grant Coll. and Fellowship Program, Moscow, 1990—. Recipient Superior Achievement award NASA, 1985; NASA Rsch. fellow, 1986-89; grantee, co-investigator, European Space Agy., 1991—. Mem. IEEE, Am. Geophys. Union, Am. Astron. Soc. Div. of Planetary Scis., Sigma Chi Frat., Sigma Xi. Office: U of Idaho Dept Elec Engring Moscow ID 83843

ATKINSON, DOROTHY GILLIS, academic administrator; b. Malden, Mass., Aug. 5, 1929; d. George Edward and Grace Margaret (Campagna) Gillis; m. Sterling K. Atkinson, June 25, 1950 (div.); children: Kim Leslie, Paul David. BA, Barnard Coll., N.Y.C., 1951; MA, U. Calif., Berkeley, 1953; PhD, Stanford (Calif.) U., 1971. Asst. prof. history Stanford U., 1973-82; exec. dir. Am. Assn. Advancement Slavic Studies, Stanford, 1981—; vis. assoc. prof. U. Calif., Berkeley, 1985; mem. adv. com. on Soviet and East European studies U.S. Dept. State; exec. officer Nat. Coun. Area Studies; exec. com. Internat. Coun. for East European Studies. Author: The End of the Russian Land Commune, 1983; co-editor: Women in Russia, 1977; contbr. articles to profl. jours. and newspapers. Recipient fellowships Stanford U., 1972, Hoover Instn., 1971-72; grantee Fulbright-Hays, 1978-79, Ford Found., 1976, Mellon Found., 1977, Internat. Rsch. Exchs. Bd., 1978-79, Stanford-Ford, 1970; recipient Pulitzer scholarship, 1947-51, Cory scholarship, 1968-69. Mem. Am. Assn. Advancement Slavic Studies, Nat. Coun. Area Studies Assns., Am. Hist. Assn., Am. Coun. Learned Socs. Home: 525 W Crescent Dr Palo Alto CA 94301-3110 Office: Stanford U Am Assn Advancement Slavic Studies Jordan Quad/Acacia Stanford CA 94305-4130

ATKINSON, ELSIE ANN, sculptor, ecclesiastical artist; b. Cambridge, Iowa, Jan. 29, 1922; d. Elias J. and Anna Martha (Lee) Hemmingson; m. Daniel Edward Atkinson, Sept. 14, 1948; children: Kristine Ruth, Owen Rolf, Joyce Elaine, Ellen Lee, David Eric. BA, St. Olaf Coll., 1943; MS, Iowa State U., 1949. Chemist Tenn. Eastman Corp., Kingsport, 1943-46; rsch. assoc. embryology Calif. Inst. Tech., Pasadena, 1949-50; sculptor props & models for motion pictures Saul Bass, Herb Yager & Assocs., L.A., 1982-87; ind. sculptor & ecclesiastical artist L.A., 1973—. Designer, prod. paraments & banners for churches, L.A. area, 1981—; solo exhbns. include Westwood Ctr. of Arts, L.A., 1983, Victoria's Gallery, Malibu, Calif., 1989; exhibited in group shows at Pasadena (Calif.) Festival of Arts Invitational Sculpture Show, 1977, Quorum Art Gallery, Laguna Beach, Calif., 1979-84, Crestwood Hills Park, Brentwood, Calif., 1982, 2d Ann. Sculpture Show, Long Beach Art Assn., 1985, Earth Day Art Invitational Exhibit, Audubon Soc., 1990; participant Nat. Small Sculptures and Drawing Competition, Westwood Ctr. of Arts, 1981; sculptures represented in corp. & pvt. collections in U.S., Japan, Eng. Treas., exhbn. chair Westwood Ctr. of Arts, L.A., 1980-84. Mem. Internat. Sculpture Ctr., Nat. Mus. Women in the Arts, UCLA Art Coun. Home: 3123 Malcolm Ave Los Angeles CA 90034

ATKINSON, JOHN CHRISTOPHER, magazine editor, critic, writer; b. Hitchin, Eng., June 12, 1948; came to U.S., 1987; s. Harry Archer and Jacqueline Ellen (Elliott) A.; m. Maree Froy, Dec. 12, 1970 (div. 1981); m. Pamela Margaret Edwards, June 19, 1982 (div. 1987); 1 child, Heather Louise; m. Laura Jean LoVecchio, Nov. 28, 1987; children; Henry Joseph, Emily Claire. BSc in Chemistry and Physics, U. London, 1972; grad. cert. in edn., 1974. Sci. officer Warren Spring Lab., Stevenage, Eng., 1969-72; free-lance bass guitarist, London, 1972-76; news editor Hi-Fi News and Record Rev. mag., Croydon, Surrey, Eng., 1976-78, dep. editor, 1978-82, editor, 1982-86; internat. editor Stereophile UK Ltd., London, 1986-87; editor Stereophile mag., Santa Fe, 1987—. Prodn. compact discs Hi-Fi News Test Disc, 1985, Poem (flute/piano music), 1989, Stereophile Test Disc, 1990, Intermezzo (Brahms piano music), 1991, Stereophile Test CD 2, 1992, Concert (piano recital), 1993; contbr. numerous articles and rev. of hi-fidelity components to music mags. Office: 208 Delgado St Santa Fe NM 87501-2728

ATKINSON, RICHARD CHATHAM, university chancellor, cognitive psychologist, educator; b. Oak Park, Ill., Mar. 19, 1929; s. Herbert and Margaret (Feuerbach) A.; m. Rita Loyd, Aug. 20, 1952; 1 dau., Lynn Loyd. Ph.B., U. Chgo., 1948; Ph.D., Ind. U., 1955. Lectr. applied math. and stats. Stanford (Calif.) U., 1956-57, assoc. prof. psychology, 1961-64, prof. psychology, 1964-80; asst. prof. psychology UCLA, 1957-61; dep. dir. NSF, 1975-76, acting dir., 1976, dir., 1976-80; chancellor U. Calif., San Diego, 1980—; dep. dir. NSF, 1975-76, acting dir., 1976, dir., 1976-80; chancellor U. Calif. at San Diego, 1980—. Author: (with Atkinson, Smith and Bem) Introduction to Psychology, 11th edit, 1993, Computer Assisted Instruction, 1969, An Introduction to Mathematical Learning Theory, 1965,

Studies in Mathematical Psychology, 1964, Contemporary Developments in Mathematical Psychology, 1974, Mind and Behavior, 1980, Stevens' Handbook of Experimental Psychology, 1988. Served with AUS, 1954-56. Guggenheim fellow, 1967; fellow Ctr. for Advanced Study in Behavioral Scis., 1963; recipient Distinguished Research award Social Sci. Research Council, 1962. Fellow APA (pres. exptl. div. 1974, Disting. Sci. Contbn. award 1977, Thorndike award 1980), AAAS (pres. 1989-90), Am. Psychol. Soc. (William James fellow 1985), Am. Acad. Arts and Scis.; mem. Soc. Exptl. Psychologists, Nat. Acad. Scis., Am. Philos. Soc., Nat. Acad. Edn., Inst. of Medicine, Psychonomic Soc., Cognitive Sci. Soc., Cosmos Club (Washington), Explorer's Club (N.Y.C.). Home: 9630 La Jolla Farms Rd La Jolla CA 92037-1131 Office: U Calif at San Diego Office of Chancellor La Jolla CA 92093*

ATKINSON, RICK MILTON, manufacturing executive; b. Boise, Idaho, Feb. 4, 1959; s. Robert Milton and Hope Caroline (Bowen) A.; m. Michelle Marie Kinzer, June 19, 1986; children: Alexis Michelle, Oliver Warren. BBA, Boise State U., 1981. CPA, Idaho. Systems cons. mgmt. info. Arthur Andersen and Co., Denver, 1981-82; controller Aluma-Glass Ind., Inc., Nampa, Idaho, 1982-86, v.p. info., 1986—, also bd. dirs. Com. mem. Fundsy Civic Auction, Boise, 1990. Mem. Bronco Athletic Assn. (bd. dirs. 1986-87). Republican. Roman Catholic. Office: Aluma Glass Ind Inc 16265 Star Rd Nampa ID 83687

ATKINSON, SHERIDAN EARLE, lawyer; b. Oakland, Calif., Feb. 14, 1945; s. Arthur Sheridan and Esther Louise (Johnson) A.; m. Margie Ann Lehtin, Aug. 13, 1966. 1 son, Ian Sheridan. BS, U. Calif.-Berkeley, 1966, MBA, 1971; JD, U. San Francisco, 1969. Bar: Calif. 1970. Prin. Atkinson & Assocs., fin. and mgmt. cons., corp. and bus. valuations, San Francisco, 1968—; assoc. Charles O. Morgan, Jr., San Francisco, 1972-76; pvt. practice, San Francisco Bay Area,1976—. With USAR, 1970-76. Mem. Calif. Bar Assn. Republican.

ATLAS, JAY DAVID, philosopher, consultant, linguist; b. Houston, Tex., Feb. 1, 1945; s. Jacob Henry and Babette Fancile (Friedman) A. AB summa cum laude, Amherst (Mass.) Coll., 1966; PhD, Princeton (N.J.) U., 1976. Mem. common rm. Wolfson Coll., Oxford, Eng., 1978, 80; vis. fellow Princeton U., 1979; rsch. assoc. Inst. for Advanced Study, Princeton, 1982-84; vis. lectr. U. Hong Kong, 1986; vis. assoc. prof. UCLA, 1988, vis. prof., 1989-93; prof. Pomona Coll., Claremont, Calif., 1989—; sr. assoc. Jurecon, Inc., L.A.; lectr. 2nd European Summer Sch. in Logic, Lang. and Info., Leuven, Belgium, 1990. Author: Philosophy Without Ambiguity, 1989; contbr. articles to profl. jours. Mem. Am. Philos. Assn., Linguistic Soc. Am. Home: 1360 N Oxford Ave # 8 Claremont CA 91711-3460 Office: Pomona Coll 551 North College Ave Claremont CA 91711-6355

ATTEBERY, LOUIE WAYNE, English educator, folklorist; b. Weiser, Idaho, Aug. 14, 1927; s. John Thomas Attebery and Tressie Mae (Blevins) Miller; m. Barbara Phyllis Olson, Dec. 31, 1947; children: Bobby Lou, Brian Leonard. B.A., Coll. of Idaho, 1950; M.A., U. Mont., 1951; Ph.D., U. Denver, 1961. Tchr., Middleton High Sch., Idaho, 1949-50, Payette High Sch., Idaho, 1951-52, Nyssa High Sch., Oreg., 1952-55, East High Sch., Denver, 1955-61; prof. English, Coll. of Idaho, Caldwell, 1961—, Eyck-Berringer chair English, 1987—, acting acad. v.p., 1983-84. Author: The College of Idaho 1891-1991: A Centennial History, 1991, Sheep May Safely Graze: A Personal Essay on Tradition and A Contemporary Sheep Ranch, 1993; editor: Idaho Folklife: Homesteads to Headstones, 1985; editor Northwest Folklore, 1985-91; gen. editor U. Idaho Northwest Folklife series, 1991—. Trustee Idaho Hist. Soc., 1984-91. Served with USN, 1945-46. Bruern fellow U. Leeds, Eng., 1971-72. Mem. Am. Folklore Soc., Western Lit. Assn. (exec. council 1964-65), Rocky Mountain MLA. Methodist. Office: Albertson Coll Idaho 2112 Cleveland Blvd Caldwell ID 83605-4494

ATTIG, JOHN CLARE, history educator, consultant; b. Chgo., Apr. 2, 1936; s. Clare McKinley and Elsie Bertha (Nagel) A.; m. Harriet Jane Rinehart, June 13, 1959; children: Laura, Victoria. BA, DePauw U., 1958; MA, U. Chgo., 1961. Cert. tchr., Calif. Social studies tchr. Lyons Twp. High Sch., LaGrange, Ill., 1961-65, Henry Gunn High Sch., Palo Alto, Calif., 1965-72, 78—; univ. faculty assoc. Simon Fraser U., Burnaby, Canada, 1972-73; social studies tchr. Jordan Jr. High Sch., Palo Alto, 1973-75, Cubberley Sr. High Sch., Palo Alto, 1975-78; lectr., demonstrator simulation games for classes in history and govt. various univs. and sch. dists. in U.S. and Canada. Contbr. numerous articles to profl. jours.; author numerous simulation games. With USAR, 1958-64. NEH fellow, 1983, 87, 89. Mem. NEH (project dir. Masterworks Seminar, 1991), Santa Clara County Coun. for Social Studies (pres. 1971-72), Calif. Coun. for Social Studies, Western History Assn., Ednl. Excellence Network. Methodist. Office: Henry Gunn Sr High Sch 780 Arastradero Rd Palo Alto CA 94306

ATWATER, JULIE DEMERS, critical care nurse; b. Santa Maria, Calif., Aug. 29, 1945; d. Julian G. and Luella M. (Drown) Demers; m. Roy Michael Atwater, Jan. 29, 1977; children: Michael J. Kawecki, Joel M. LPN, Fanny Allen Sch. for Practical Nursing, Winooski, Vt., 1967; ADN, Weber State Coll., Ogden, Utah, 1982, BS in Allied Health, 1987, BSN, 1989. Lic. practical nurse, Vt., Mass., N.H.; RN, Utah, Wyo. Practical nurse Brattleboro (Vt.) Meml. Hosp.; practical nurse ICU, Cooley Dickerson Hosp., Northampton, Mass., Cheshire Meml. Hosp., Keene, N.H.; clin. nurse ICU/CCU Evanston (Wyo.) Regional Hosp., 1978-87; critical care nurse ladder IV McKay Dee Hosp., Ogden, Utah, 1987-92, clinical head nurse ICU, 1992—; 1st chmn. organ donor com. 1990—; com. mem. ICU and Heart Right Group. Mem. AACN (CCRN 1981, mem.-at-large 1983—, v.p. No. Utah chpt.1983-84, bd. dirs. 1984—, NUAACN, Utah critical care nurse of Yr. 1991-92), Utah Nurses Assn. (bd. dirs. 1992-93). Home: 3191 S 3500 W Hooper UT 84315-9624

ATWATER, STEPHEN DENNIS, professional football player; b. Chicago, Oct. 28, 1966. BS in Bus. Adminstrn., U. Ark., 1989. Safety Denver Broncos, 1989—. Office: Denver Broncos 13655 Broncos Pkwy Englewood CO 80112

ATWOOD, KELLY PALMER, insurance agency executive; b. Portland, Oreg., Jan. 7, 1946; s. Baird Ewing and Lelia Claire (Donham) McNeese A.; m. Regina Louise Hamilton, July 30, 1983; children: Derek, Lynn, Jason, Beri, Courtney. Student, U. Oreg., 1964-66, Chemeketa Community Coll., 1976-78. Pres., chief exec. officer Group Ins. Mktg., Inc., Salem, Oreg., 1970-85, Contractors Ins. Svcs. Inc., Lake Oswego, Oreg., 1985—; also bd. dirs. Metro Ins. Agy., Inc., Lake Oswego, Oreg. Contbr. articles on ins. to profl. jours. Former mem. Reagan Task Force, Washington, 1985-86, Denny Smith Task Force on Crime, Salem, 1988. Served with USN, 1967-69. Named Sr. Agt. of Yr. Salem Life Underwriters Assn., 1980, 81. Mem. Nat. Assn. Life Underwriters, Nat. Assn. Home Builders, Oreg. State Home Builders Assn., Home Builders Assn. Met. Portland (bd. dirs. 1985—). Republican. Office: Contractors Ins Svcs Inc PO Box 2267 Lake Oswego OR 97035-0071

ATWOOD, MARY SANFORD, writer; b. Mt. Pleasant, Mich., Jan. 27, 1935; d. Burton Jay and Lillian Belle (Sampson) Sanford; B.S., U. Miami, 1957; m. John C. Atwood, III, Mar. 23, 1957. Author: A Taste of India, 1969. Mem. San Francisco/N. Peninsula Opera Action, Hillsborough-Burlingame Newcomers, Suicide Prevention and Crisis Center, DeYoung Art Mus., Internat. Hospitality Center, Peninsula Symphony, San Francisco Art Mus., World Affairs Council, Mills Hosp. Assos. Mem. AAUW, Suicide Prevention Aux. Republican. Club: St. Francis Yacht. Office: 40 Knightwood Ln Hillsborough CA 94010

ATWOOD, ROBERT BRUCE, publisher; b. Chgo., Mar. 31, 1907; s. Burton H. and Mary Beach (Stevenson) A.; m. Evangeline Rasmuson, Apr. 2, 1932; children: Marilyn A. Odom, Sara Elaine. A.B., Clark U., 1929; Litt.D. (hon.), Alaska Meth. U., 1967; D.Journalism (hon.), U. Alaska, 1979. Reporter Worcester (Mass.) Telegram, 1926-29, 34-35, Ill. State Jour., Springfield, 1929-34; pres. and pub. Anchorage Times, 1935-89, pub. emeritus, 1989-92; dir. Alaska Sales and Svc., Inc., Anchorage, 1991—. Author pamphlets, articles, editorials pub. in various jours. Chmn. Alaska Statehood Com., 1949-59; hon. Norwegian consul at Anchorage, 1960-86; mem. civilian affairs bd. Alaskan Air Command, 1962—, now chmn.; chmn. Chancellor's Circle U. Alaska; bd. dirs. Commonwealth North; founder Atwood Found. Decorated knight of first rank Order of St. Olaf, 1976; Alaska commr. to Expo '88, Australia. Mem. Am. Soc. Newspaper Editors, Am. Polar Soc. (bd. govs.), C. of C. (pres. 1944, 48), Soc. Profl. Journalists. Republican. Presbyterian. Clubs: Explorers, Nat. Press. Lodges: Sons of Norway, Rotary, Elks, Masons, Pioneers of Alaska. Home and Office: 2000 Atwood Dr Anchorage AK 99517-1333

AU, MARY WAI-YIN, accountant; b. Kowloon, Hong Kong; d. Waiman and Enid (Tang) Au. BA, MusB, MusM, MBA, U. So. Calif., 1987, MBA, 1987; Assoc., Royal Coll. of Music, Eng.; Licentiate, recital diploma, Royal Acad. Music, Eng. CPA, Calif. Property mgr. Charles Dunn Co., L.A.; concert pianist, accompanist, music coach L.A.; acct., audito, corp. fin. assoc., valuation cons. Deloitte & Touche, L.A., 1987-91; pvt. practice bus. cons., 1992—. Treas. Mu Nu chpt. Mu Phi Epsilon, L.A.; mem. dean's adv. bd. U. So. Calif., L.A.; panelist MBA & You, L.A.; vol. L.A. Marathon, 1990, 92, 93; advisor Jr. Achievment project, 1989. Named one of Outstanding Young Women of Am., Mu Phi Epsilon Alumni scholar; recipient Albert Quon scholarship, 1986, Albert Quon Svc. award, 1987. Mem. AICPA.

AUBIN, RICHARD THOMAS, II, broker, business consultant; b. Colorado Springs, Colo., Aug. 11, 1946; s. Richard T. Aubin and Harriet (Bozeman) Leber; m. Sheelagh Murray, Nov. 14, 1980 (div. Jan. 1983); m. Denise Maltz, Aug. 7, 1983; children: Corine, Danielle. AA in Arts and Music, Coll. of Marin, 1975; BA in Creative Arts, San Francisco State U., 1976. Lic. elec. contractor, real estate broker. Pres. Electric/Light Constrn., San Rafael, Calif., 1978-84; owner Spl. Projects, Woodacre, Calif., 1985—; pres. Profit Line, Inc., Woodacre, 1990—; owner Array Bus. Investments, Woodacre, 1990—. Republican. Home and Office: 35 Sylvan Way Woodacre CA 94973

AUER, BENEDICT LEROY, education educator, college official, priest; b. Chgo., Nov. 4, 1939; s. William F. and Marcelline D. (Boudreau) A. BS in Humanities, Loyola U., Chgo., 1962; MA in History, Creighton U., 1964; MDiv, St. Meinrad Sch. Theology, Ind., 1980; HHD (hon.), London Inst. for Applied Rsch., 1991; D in Ministry, San Francisco Theol. Sem., 1993. Joined Order St. Benedict, 1976, Roman Cath. Ch., ordained priest, 1980. Teaching fellow and scholar Creighton U., Omaha, 1963-64; instr. history Marymount Coll., Salina, Kans., 1964-65; chmn. English dept. Jr. Mil. Acad., Chgo., 1965-67; chmn. humanities Univ. Sch. Milw., 1967-71; tchr. history and English, St. Viator High Sch., Arlington Heights, Ill., 1972-76; chmn. English dept., assoc. coll. counselor, dir. admissions Marmion Mil. Acad., Aurora, Ill., 1980-88; dir. campus ministry St. Martin's Coll., Lacey, Wash., 1988—, asst. prof. edn., 1991—; various pastoral assignments Diocese of Rockford, Ill., 1980-88; assoc. pastor St. Joseph Parish, Aurora, 1981-88; textbook editor social studies div. Laidlaw Bros., Ill., 1971-72. Author: (poetry) Touching Fingers with God, 1986, Priestless People, 1990, From Chicago to Canterbury: A Poetic Pilgrimage, 1991, Godspeak: Thirteen Characters in Search of an Author, 1991; contbr. articles to profl. jours., poetry to numerous mags. Recipient Poem of Yr. award Jubilee Press, 1987; scholar St. Meinrad Sch. Theology, 1977-80. Mem. Internat. Parliament for Peace and Safety, Acad. Midi, Pi Gamma Mu, Phi Alpha Theta. Home: St Martin's Abbey Lacey WA 98503 Office: St Martin's Coll 5300 Pacific Ave SE Lacey WA 98503

AUERBACH, BRADFORD CARLTON, lawyer; b. Bethesda, Md., Apr. 17, 1957; s. Richard Carlton and Rita (Argen) A.; m. Jane Donnan Irwin, Apr. 30, 1988. BA, Hamilton Coll., 1979; JD, Boston Coll., 1982. Bar: Calif. 1984, U.S. Dist. Ct. (so., cen. and no. dists.) Calif. 1984, U.S. Ct. Appeals (9th cir.) 1985. Assoc. Law Offices of Peter J. Sullivan, Marina del Rey, Calif., 1984-89; atty. home video legal and bus. affairs Walt Disney Studios, Burbank, Calif., 1989-92; v.p. legal and bus. affairs, gen. counsel Philips Interactive Media of Am., L.A., 1992—. Arts correspondent various Am. and Brit. arts pubs. Mem. ABA, Assn. Trial Lawyers Am., L.A. County Bar Assn., Beverly Hills Bar Assn., Paladins of Temerity (head 1985-93). Republican. Episcopalian.

AUERBACH, BRYAN NEIL, pediatrician; b. Chgo., May 6, 1946; s. Max R. and Jennie (Helman) A.; m. Angela Grace Anzalone, Apr. 14, 1973; children: Kimberly, Suzanne, David. BS, U. Mich., 1968; MD, U. Ill., Chgo., 1972. Diplomate Am. Bd. Pediatrics, Nat. Bd. Med. Examiners. Intern, resident pediatrics U. Ariz. Med. Ctr., 1972-75; pvt. practice, South Lake Tahoe, Calif., 1975-81, Tucson, 1981—. Fellow Am. Acad. Pediatrics. Office: 2222 N Craycroft Tucson AZ 85712

AUERBACH, EVALINE JONES, English language educator, editor, writing consultant; b. Frankfort, Kans., Jan. 7, 1943; d. Owen Robert and Faye Opal (Lucas) Jones; m. Abraham E. Auerbach, Dec. 20, 1980; 1 child, David Owen. BA, Kans. State U., 1964, MA, 1967; EdS, U. Iowa, 1972, PhD, 1989. Tchr. English, Washington (Kans.) High Sch., 1964-65, Luckey High Sch., Manhattan, 1965-67; instr. Indian Hills C.C., Centerville, Iowa, 1967-76; prof. English Cen. Ariz. Coll., Winkelman, 1976—, chmn. div. arts and scis., 1989-92, project dir. League for Innovation, 1992-93. Founder, dir. theater group (now SPATS), 1977; pres. Oracle (Ariz.) Hist. Soc., 1977-79, 91-92. Mem. AAUW (founder Centerville), Nat. Coun. Tchrs. English, Assn. Ednl. Communication and Tech., Ariz. English Tchrs. Assn., Computer Users in Edn. Democrat. Methodist. Office: Cen Ariz Coll Aravaipa Campus Star Rt Box 97 Winkelman AZ 85292

AUERBACK, SANDRA JEAN, social worker; b. San Francisco, Feb. 21, 1946; d. Alfred and Molly Loy (Friedman) A. BA, U. Calif., Berkeley, 1967; MSW, Hunter Sch. Social Work, 1972. Diplomate clin. social work. Clin. social worker Jewish Family Services, Bklyn., 1972-73; clin. social worker Jewish Family Services, Hackensack, N.J., 1973-78; pvt. practice psychotherapy San Francisco, 1978—; dir. intake adult day care Jewish Home for the Aged, San Francisco, 1979-91. Mem. NASW (cert., bd. dirs. Bay Area Referral Svc. 1983-87, chmn. referral svc. 1984-87, state practice com. 1987-91, regional treas. 1989-91, rep. to Calif. Coun. Psychiatry, Psychology, Social Work and Nursing 1987—, chmn. 1989, 93, v.p. community svcs. 1991-93), Mental Health Assn. San Francisco (trustee 1987—), Am. Group Psychotherapy Assn. Home: 1100 Gough St Apt 8C San Francisco CA 94109-6638 Office: 450 Sutter St San Francisco CA 94108-3903

AUGSBURGER, ROBERT RAY, management educator; b. Canton, Ohio, Aug. 24, 1926; s. Clyde and Frances (Russell) A.; m. Jean Ann Holes, Sept. 2, 1950; children: David, John, Jane. Student, Purdue U., 1943-44, 46-47; BS, Northwestern U., 1948; JD, Case Western Res. U., 1950. Bar: Ohio 1950, CFA. Treas. Floyd A. Holes Co., Bedford, Ohio, 1950-53; dir. fin. rels. Glidden Co., Cleve., 1953-63; exec. v.p. Donaldson, Lufkin & Jeurette, Inc., N.Y.C., 1963-70; v.p. bus. and fin. Stanford (Calif.) U., 1971-77; exec. dir. Peninsula Open Space Trust, Menlo Park, Calif., 1977-86; lectr. Grad. Sch. Bus. Stanford (Calif.) U., 1986—; bd. dirs. Tab Products Co., Palo Alto, Calif., 1976—, Stanford U. Bookstore, Inc., 1992—; chair bd. dirs. Land Trust Alliance, Washington, 1982-87. Bd. dirs. Children's Health Coun., Palo Alto, 1975-85, pres. bd., 1981-83; trustee Trust for Hidden Villa, Los Altos Hills, Calif., 1988-92. With USN, 1944-46. Mem. Assn. for Investment Mgmt. and Rsch., Acad. Mgmt., Stanford Assocs., Fin. Execs. Inst.,. Republican. Office: Stanford U Grad Sch Bus Stanford CA 94305

AUGUSTINE, KATHY MARIE, state legislator, primary school educator; b. L.A., Calif., May 29, 1956; d. Philip Blase and Katherine Alice (Thompson) A.; m. Charles Francis Augustine, July 22, 1988; children: Andrea, Greg, Larry, Dallas. AB, Occidental Coll., 1977; MPA, Calif. State U., Long Beach, 1983. Flight attendant Continental Airlines, Houston, 1978-83; crew scheduler Delta Airlines, L.A., 1983-88; tchr. Diocese of Reno/Las Vegas, 1990-92; assemblywoman Nev. State Legislature, Carson City, 1992—. Mem. Active Rep. Women's Club, Las Vegas, Nev., 1992-93. Recipient Achievement award Bank of Am., Calif., 1974, Achievement Medallion Am. Legion, 1974, Congressional Internship grantee, Washington, 1975. Mem. AAUP (v.p. programs), Am. Legislative Exchg. Coun. (transportation com.), Nat. Conf. of State Legislators (arts & tourism com.), Nev. Dance Theater Guild, Jr. League of Las Vegas (sr. legis. rep.), Clark County Panhellenic Assn. (treas.), Italian-Am. Club of Las Vegas, Women Legislator's Lobby. Republican. Roman Catholic. Home: 1400 Maria Elena Dr Las Vegas NV 89104

AULD-LOUIE, MARGARET ELIZABETH, computer consultant, desktop publisher; b. New Haven, Conn., Sept. 9, 1958; d. Benjamin Franklin and Elinor James Auld; m. Russell Jay Louie, June 3, 1989. BA in Biology, Colo. Coll., 1980. Office mgr. Viking Resources Corp., Denver, 1981-88; ptnr. Computer Ptnrs., Golden, Colo., 1990—; co-dir. Creative Light Ctr, 1989—, minister, 1992—. Rec. sec. Colo. Mountain Club Found., Denver, 1986-88; vol. naturalist Lookout Mountain Open Space Nature Ctr., Golden, 1990—. Mem. Golden Bus. and Profl. Women's Club (newsletter editor 1991-93, rec. sec. 1991-92, treas. 1992—), Golden C. of C., PC Users Group of Colo. (corr. sec. 1992—), Mile-High Computer Resource Orn. (PCUG liaison 1992—), Microsoft Windows Cons. Group. Democrat. Episcopalian. Home and Office: Computer Ptnrs 416 Plateau Pkwy Golden CO 80403-1533

AULT, PHILLIP H., author, editor; b. Maywood, Ill., Apr. 26, 1914; s. Frank W. and Bernda (Halliday) A.; m. Karoline Byberg, June 5, 1943 (dec. Jan. 1990); children: Frank, Ingrid, Bruce; m. Jane Born, May 1, 1993. AB, DePauw U., 1935. Reporter LaGrange (Ill.) Citizen, 1935-37; corr. editor UPI, Chgo., N.Y.C., Iceland, Norht Africa, London, 1938-48; bur. chief UPI, London, 1944-45; asst. mng. editor, dir. editorial page Times-Mirror Co., L.A., 1948; editorial page editor L.A. Mirror-News, 1948-57; exec. editor Associated Desert Newspapers, 1958-68; assoc. editor South Bend (Ind.) Tribune, 1968-79, cons. editor, 1979—. Author: This is the Desert, 1959, News Around the Clock, 1960, How to Live in California, 1961, Home Book of Western Humor, 1967, Wonders of the Mosquito World, 1970, These Are The Great Lakes, 1972, Wires West, 1974, All Aboard, 1976, By the Seat of Their Pants, 1978, Whistles Round the Bend, 1982; co-author: Springboard to Berlin, 1943, Reporting and Writing the News, 1983, Introduction to Mass Communications, 1960, Public Relations: Strategies and Tactics, 1986; editor: Santa Maria Historical Photo Album, 1987. Mem. Am. Soc. Newspaper Editors, Assn. Edn. in Journalism, Western Writers Am. (Spur award 1977), Sigma Nu. Home: 21408 157th Dr Sun City West AZ 85375

AULTMAN, WILLIAM ROBERT, U.S. army officer; b. Ft. Benning, Ga., July 15, 1953; s. William Wilmer and Kazuko Suzie (Sano) A.; m. Barbara Ellen Tison, Dec. 22, 1979; children: Sara Alexandra, Nicholas Christian. BS in Engring, U.S. Military Acad., 1975; student, U.S. Army Intelligence Sch., Ft. Huachucha, Ariz., 1979; MSSM, USC, 1987. Commd. 2nd. lt. U.S. Army, 1975, advanced through grades to lt. col., 1992; platoon leader 3rd infantry div. U.S. Army, Aschaffenburg, Fed. Republic Germany, 1975-78; tactical reconnaissance officer 82nd Airborne Div., Ft. Bragg, N.C., 1980-81; co. commdr. 1st Mil. Intelligence Battalion, Ft. Bragg, 1981-82; ops. officer Ft. Shafter, HI, 1982-85; plans officer Defense Intelligence Agy., Washington, 1985-88; chief intelligence collection mgmt. Combined Field Army, Camp Red Cloud, Korea, 1988-89; chief ADP applications Intelligence Ctr. Pacific, Camp Smith, Hawaii, 1989-91; VII Corps G2 Collection mgr. Operation Desert Storm, Persian Gulf, 1991; chief logistics mgmt. Joint Intelligence Ctr., Pacific, Pearl Harbor, Hawaii, 1992-93; chief resource mgmt. U.S. Army info. systems command Pentagon, Arlington, Va., 1993—. Decorated with Bronze Star, U.S. Army, Saudi Arabia; selected for Army Acquisition Corps. Mem. Retired Officers Assn., Assn. Grads. U.S. Military Acad. Baptist. Home: 8811 Telegraph Crossing Ct Lorton VA 22079 Office: US Army Info Systems Command Pentagon Washington DC 20310

AUMAND, ERNEST JAMES, III, purchasing professional; b. Bellows Falls, Vt., Sept. 2; s. Ernest James Jr. and Sophie Rose (Rachiski) A.; m. Linda Miranda; children: Brandon Joseph, Justin Miranda. BSBA, Nichols Coll., 1978; postgrad., U. Calif., Santa Barbara, 1988-90. Purchasing agt. RCA Entgerprises, Walpole, N.H., 1978-81, 83-84, Familian Corp., Van Nuys, Calif., 1981-83; purchasing mgr. Appropriate Tech., Brattleboro, Vt., 1984-86, Westmont Coll., Santa Barbara, Calif., 1987-92; buyer County of Santa Barbara, Calif., 1992-93; purchasing agt. R. P. Richards, Goleta, Calif., 1993—; sr. comdr. Royal Ranger Boys Orgn., Santa Maria, Calif., 1982—; instr. Royal Ranger Men's Leadership, Costa Mesa, Calif., 1988—; cons. Smokelin Industries, Santa Maria, 1983—; speaker in field. Author: Walking What We Talk, 1986, Devotions on Righteousness, 1988, God, Family and Work, 1991; contbr. articles to pubis. Disaster team mgr. Santa maria unit ARC, 1988—; pres. Parent-Tchr. Fellowship, Christian Heritage, Brattleboro, 1986-87; food svc. leader Good Samaritan Homeless Shelter, Santa Maria, 1990-92; pres. Men's Ministries, Assembly of God, Santa Maria, 1990—. With U.S. Army, 1971-74, Vietnam. Mem. Am. Security Coun. Found., Santa Barbara Purchasing Assn. (bd. dirs. 1988-92), Nat. Assn. Purchasing Mgmt., Nat. Assn. Ednl. Buyers, Frontiersmen Camping Fellowship, Am. Legion, Elks. Republican. Home: 1644 B So McClelland St Santa Maria CA 93454 Office: R P Richards 5949 Hollister Ave Goleta CA 93117

AURAND, CHARLES HENRY, JR., music educator; b. Battle Creek, Mich., Sept. 6, 1932; s. Charles Henry and Elisabeth Dirk (Hoekstra) A.; m. Donna Mae Erb, June 19, 1954; children: Janice, Cheryl, Sandra, Charles III, William. MusB, Mich. State U., 1954, MusM, 1958; PhD, U. Mich., 1971. Cert. tchr., Mich., Ohio. Asst. prof. music Hiram Coll., Ohio, 1958-60; dean, prof. music Youngstown State U., 1960-73; dean No. Ariz. U., Flagstaff, 1973-88, prof. music, 1988—; chmn. Ariz. Alliance for Arts Edn., 1974-77; solo clarinetist Flagstaff Symphony; solo, chamber music and orch. musician, 1973-86; fine arts cons. Miami U. of Ohio, 1982. Author: Selected Solos, Methods, 1963. Elder Presbyterian Ch., 1965; chmn. Boy Scouts Am., Coconino dist., 1974-78; bd. dirs. Ariz. Com. Arts for the Handicapped, 1982-88, Flagstaff Symphony Orch., 1973-85, Flagstaff Festival of Arts, 1973-89; bd. dirs. Sedona Chamber Mus. Soc., 1989—; conf. dir. Internat. Clarinet Soc., 1991. Served to 1st lt. USAF, 1955-57. Recipient award of merit Boy Scouts Am., 1977; cert. appreciation John F. Kennedy Ctr. Performing Arts, 1985. Mem. Am. Assn. Higher Edn., Ariz. Humanities Assn., Music Educators Nat. Conf., State Adminstrs. of Music Schs. (chmn. 1971-73), Internat. Clarinet Soc./ClariNetwork Internat. (conf. dir. 1991). Republican. Presbyterian. Lodge: Kiwanis (pres. 1984-85). Home: 140 Fairway Oaks Ln Sedona AZ 86336-8835 Office: No Ariz U Box 6040 Flagstaff AZ 86011

AURINGER, AMOS LEWIS, defense agency administrator; b. Onieda, N.Y., Oct. 30, 1963; s. Paul Lewis Auringer and Margorie (Harrington) Bellinger; m. Rhonda Kay Brannon, July 18, 1987; 1 child, Corey Lee. Student, U. Alaska, 1983-84, U. N.Mex., 1984-85, Champman Coll., 1989-90, U. Phoenix, 1992—. Enlisted USAF, 1981; communication adminstr. Cryptologic Support Ctr., San Antonio, 1982-83; resource mgr. Air Wing, King Salmon, Ark., 1983-84; ops. adminstr. Nuclear Weapons Sch., Albuquerque, 1984-89; divsn. adminstr. Def. Nuclear Agy., Albuquerque, 1989—; mem. satellite commn. Air Wing, King Salmon, Ark., 1983-84. Author: Information Brochure, 1988. Mem. Sandia Mountain Ranger Dist., Albuquerque; coach YAFL, Albuquerque, Kirtland Basketball, Albuquerque. Decorated Air Force Achievement medal, Air Force Commendation medal, Joint Svc. Commendation medal, Good Conduct medal. Mem. Automated Data Processing Com., Quality Mgmt. Bd. (facilitator), Enlisted Adv. Coun. (rep.), Squadron Fund Account (recorder), Nat. Geog. Sco. Home: 6117 Montano Pointe NW Albuquerque NM 87120 Office: Def Nuclear Agy Tex Blvd Kirtland A F B NM 87117

AURNER, ROBERT RAY, corporate executive, author; b. Adel, Iowa, Aug. 20, 1898; s. Clarence Ray and Nellie (Slayton) A.; m. Kathryn Dayton, June 16, 1921; 1 son, Robert Ray II. B.A. summa cum laude, U. Iowa, 1919, M.A., 1920, Ph.D., 1922. Dir. customer relations, new bus. The State Bank, Madison, Wis., 1925-28; research dir. Walker Co., 1925-30; established Aurner and Assocs., Cons. to Mgmt., bus. adminstrn., market distbn. and human relations, pres., chmn., chief exec. officer, 1938—, pres., 1988—; v.p., dir. Pacific Futures, Inc., 1962—; dir., chmn. bus adv. com. VNA Corp., 1959-62; fin. cons., dir. Carmel Savs. & Loan Assn., Calif., 1960-71; lectr. NBC Station WTMJ, 1929-30; state commr. Wis. Library Certification Bd., 1931-38; pres. Am. Bus. Communication Assn., 1939-40; mem. faculty, adminstrv. staff U. Wis., 1925-48, ranking research prof. bus. adminstrn., chmn. adminstrn. and mgmt. div., mem. univ. lectr. bur., 1930-48; vis. prof. bus. mgmt. U. Pitts., 1934, 36, 39; vis. research prof. Rare Book Rm., Huntington Library, San Marino, Calif., 1941; adminstrv. cons. Internat.

Cellucotton Products Co., Chgo., 1947-52; cons., dir. Communications Div., Fox River Paper Corp., Appleton, Wis., 1947-60; v.p., gen. cons., dir. Scott, Inc., Milw. and Carmel, 1949—; cons. U.S. Naval Postgrad. Sch., Mgmt. Sch. Div., Dept. Navy, Dept. Def., 1957—, Jahn & Ollier Corp., Morris, Schenker, Roth, Inc., First Nat. Bank, Chgo., Library Research Service, New Haven, Nat. Assn. Real Estate Bds., N.Y.C., Allis-Chalmers Corp., Milw.; ltd. partner Salinas-Peninsula Investment Co., 1963-72; cons. Wis. Div. Vital Statistics, 1930-48; Dean Coll. of Commerce, Biarritz Am. U., France, U.S. Army Univ. Center No. 2, ETO, 1945-46; attached U.S. Army, USFET, I. and E. Div., Field Grade, rank of col., 1945-46; spl. lectr. Netherlands Sch. Econs., Rotterdam, 1945; U.S. State Dept. rep. Dutch-Am. Conf., The Hague, Holland, 1945; mem. nat. adv. com. Conf. Am. Small Business Orgns., 1947—; Dir. SAE Corp., Evanston, Ill., 1943-53, pres., chmn. bd., chief exec. officer, 1951-53, Eminent Supreme Archon; mem. nat. adv. counsel Atlantic Union, Inc., 1949—. Author: Specialized Field Approach, 1963, Language Control for Business, 1965, Success Factors in Executive Development, 1967, Effective English for Colleges, 6th edit., 1980, Effective English for Business Communication, 8th edit., 1982, Effective Communication in Business with Management Emphasis, 8th edit., 1988; contbg. editor: Am. Ency. Social Scis.; co-author, contbg. editor, American Business Practice (4 vols.). Trustee Levere Meml. Found., Chgo., 1943-53, pres., chmn. bd., chief exec. officer, 1951-53; chmn. bd., pres., chief exec. officer Carmel Found., Calif., 1981-85, v.p., 1977-81, dir., past chmn. fin. com., past chmn. meml. policy com. mem. internal trusteeship com., exec. com., 1954-83; mem. bd. investment mgmt. Hazeltine Fund Calif., 1963-83; adv. gov., bd. dirs. Monterey Fund Edn., 1965—; dir., chmn. com. endowments York Sch., 1966-69; bd. dirs. Wis. div. AAA, 1936-47. Recipient Disting. Service award with gold medal Sigma Alpha Epsilon, 1967; Championship Gold Medal award N.O.L. Big Ten Univ. Debate Competition, 1919. Fellow Assn. Bus. Communication (hon.); mem. Am. Mktg. Assn., Nat. Assn. Mktg. (v.p. 1931), Smithsonian Instn. Nat. Assos., Wis. Acad. Scis., Arts and Letters, State Hist. Soc. Iowa, Phi Beta Kappa, Delta Sigma Rho, Alpha Kappa Psi (vice chmn. com. profl. programs, exec. group 1955—), Sigma Alpha Epsilon (supreme council 1943-53, nat. pres. 1951-53). Clubs: Continental (Chgo.); Highlands (Monterey Peninsula), Decemvir (Monterey Peninsula), Convivium (Monterey Peninsula); Statesman's (Los Angeles); The Group (Pebble Beach, Calif.). Home: San Antonio and Inspiration Aves Carmel Point PO Box 3434 Carmel-by-the Sea CA 93921 Office: PO Box 3434 Carmel CA 93921-3434 also: PO Box 240 Beach Haven NJ 08008 also: Bristlecone Trading and Devel Corp 908 Long Beach Blvd Surf City NJ 08008

AURNHAMMER, THOMAS WALTER, fire marshal; b. Summit, N.J., Jan. 18, 1958; s. Douglas Robert and Helen Jean (Buchholz) A.; m. Lori Kay Uselman, Jan. 9, 1988; children: Robert Wayne, Shaylee Jean. Grad. exec. fire officer program, Nat. Fire Acad., Emmitsburg, Md., 1992. Cert. fire investigator. Paid-on-call firefighter Millburn (N.J.) Fire Dept., 1976-80; aux. firefighter Newark Fire Dept., 1977-80; career firefighter Farmington (N.Mex.) Fire Dept., 1980-82, fire engr., 1982-84, fire capt., 1984-88, fire marshal, 1988—. Contbr. articles to profl. jours. Mem. Nat. Fire Protection Assn., Internat. Assn. Fire Chiefs, Fire Marshals Assn., N.Am. Internat. Assn. Arson Investigators (pres. N.Mex. chpt. 1993—). Democrat. Roman Catholic. Office: Farmington Fire Dept 301 N Auburn Ave Farmington NM 87401-5894

AUSTEN, HALLIE IGLEHART, author; b. N.Y.C., Nov. 4, 1947; d. Francis Nash and Harriet Austen (Stokes) Iglehart. AB, Brown U., 1969; student, Union Grad. Sch., Columbus, Ohio, 1983-86. instr. Nat. Women's Studies Assn. Rutgers U., Camden, N.J., 1984, Graduate Theol. Union, Berkeley, Calif., 1984; lectr. UN Non-Govtl. Orgns, Women's Conf., Copenhagen, 1980, U. Calif., Santa Cruz, Calif., 1978, Berkeley, Calif., 1975-76, 86, 88, Feminist Therapy Ctr. Conf., Malibu, Calif., 1980, Heartwood Coll., Santa Cruz. 1981, Ancient Ways Festival, Harbin, Calif. 1984, Welcome Home Conf., San Francisco State U., 1985, Long Beach Woman spirit, 1988, John F. Kennedy U., Orinda, Calif., 1988, The Spotted Fawn Gallery, Pt. Reyes, 1988. Mem. Museum of Modern Art, San Francisco, 1978, Glyptotek Museum, Copenhagen, 1980, Damon Studio, N.Y.C., 1980, Cerridwen Salon, N.Y.C., 1980, Esalen Inst., Big Sur, Calif., 1981, U. Calif., L.A., 1985; dir., instr. Women In Spiritual Edn., Berkeley, Point Reyes, Calif., 1975—; instr. Nat. Women's Studies Assn. Rutgers U., Camden, N.J., 1984; lectr. U. Calif., Berkeley, 1975-76, 86, 88, Santa Cruz, 1978, Feminist Therapy Ctr. Conf., Malibu, Calif., 1980, UN N.G.O. Women's Conf., Copenhagen, 1980, San Jose State U., 1980, Heartwood Coll., Santa Cruz, 1981, San Francisco State U., 1985, Women's Alliance, Nevada City, Calif., 1985-86, Long Beach Womanspirit, 1988, U. Calif., 1988, John F. Kennedy U., Orinda, Calif., 1988, Calif. Sch. of Herbal Studies, Guerneville, Calif., 1978-80, 83-84, 87-88. Appeared in Take Back the Night, 1978, Presence of the Goddess (Balcorman Films), 1985; author: Womanspirit: A Guide to Women's Wisdom, 1983, The Heart of the Goddess: Art, Myth and Meditations of the World's Sacred Feminine, 1990, Quest: A Feminist Quarterly, 1977; contbr. numerous articles to books, newspapers and mags. Counselor San Francisco Women's Switchboard, 1973-74; instr. Am. Friends Svcs. Com., San Francisco, 1974; workshop leader Nat. Conf. on Violence Against Women, San Francisco, 1977; mem. Nat. Caucus of Women and the Arts, San Francisco, 1982, San Francisco Art Inst., 1982, Nat. Film Bd. of Can., 1985. Mem. San Francisco Women's Found. (assoc. 1983—), Point Reyes Dzog Chen, San Francisco Sonar, Druid Heights Artists Retreat (v.p. 1988—). Democrat. Office: Women In Spiritual Edn PO Box 697 Point Reyes Station CA 94956-0697

AUSTEN, SHELLI, political media consultant, writer; b. Tulsa, Sept. 8, 1954; m. Fred Chris Sorenson, Dec. 31, 1984 (div. Oct. 1988); 1 child, Kristen Amara. BA, U. Calif., Santa Barbara, 1974. Exec. officer Calif. Bd. Real Estate, Ojai, 1975-80; news dir. Sta. KMVI, Maui, Hawaii, 1980-83; v.p. Bill Baker Advt., Honolulu, 1983-85; advt. dir. Ground Swell Mag., Haleiwa, 1985-87; prodr., reporter, anchor Sta. KHVH, Honolulu, 1987-92; dir. adv. Beachcomber Mag., 1992—; media cons. Rep. Party of Hawaii, Honolulu, 1987—. Contbr. articles to profl. jours. Media coord. Merimed found., Honolulu, 1988; del. Rep. Party, Honolulu, 1989, mem. presdl. task force, Honolulu, 1989-90. Mem. Platform Assn., Surfrider Found. Episcopalian. Home: 58-032 Kapuai Pl Haleiwa HI 96712

AUSTERMANN, KURT, public information officer, writer, photographer; b. Peterborough, N.H., Jan. 8, 1937; s. George Simon and Eleanor (Shattuck) A.; m. Valerie Miller, June 23, 1961; children: Kyle, Kirstin (dec.), Kevin. BS in Journalism, Boston U., 1962. News dir. KOTI-TV, Klamath Falls, Oreg., 1962-66; assoc. news dir. KATU-TV, Portland, Oreg., 1966-67; news dir. KOTI-TV, Klamath Falls, 1967-72; corr. The Oregonian newspaper, Klamath Falls, 1963-73; pub. info. officer USDA Forest Svc., Portland, 1972-83, Bur. of Land Mgmt., USDI, Medford, Oreg., 1983—. Pres. Washington County (Oreg.) Planning Orgn., 1977-89; bd. dirs. United Way of Jackson County, Medford, 1986—, pres., 1988, sec., 1991—. Named Fed. Employee of Yr., Rogue Valley Fed. Exec. Assn., 1986. Mem. Soc. Am. Foresters, Rotary. Home: 1525 Angelcrest Dr Medford OR 97504 Office: BLM Medford Dist 3040 Biddle Rd Medford OR 97504

AUSTIN, CARL FULTON, SR., geologist, researcher, mining engineer; b. Oakland, Calif., July 18, 1932; s. Ward Hunting and Miriam (Fulton) A.; m. Barbara Ann Vest, Sept. 18, 1953; children: Miriam Louise, Carl Fulton Jr., Richard Randall. AA, Coll.of Marin, 1952; BS, U. Utah, 1954, MS, 1955, PhD, 1958. Registered profl. geologist, Calif. Mining engr. N.Mex. Bur. of Mines, Socorro, 1958-61; rsch. geologist Naval Ordnance Test Sta., China Lake, Calif., 1961-76; supr. geologist Naval Weapons Ctr., China Lake, 1976-90, rsch. scientist, 1990-91; cons. geologist, weapons scientist; co-owner Cedarsage Farm, Oakley, Idaho, 1973—, Golden Jubilee Mining, Oakley, 1980—; expert witness on mining scams and explosives incidents. Mem. AIME, RESA, Geothermal Resources Coun., Rotary (past pres. China Lake chpt.). LDS. Home: PO Box 93 Oakley ID 83346

AUSTIN, DANIEL LYNN, insurance association manager; b. Holyoke, Colo., Dec. 29, 1952; s. Frank and Delores (Fisbeck) A.; m. Deborah L. Ocken, Sept. 7, 1974; children: Jordan K., Lindsey L. Bachelor degree, Colo. State U., 1975. Fraternal ins. counselor. Loan officer Fed. Land Bank, Denver, 1975-76, Greeley, Colo., 1976-78; credit officer Fed. Land Bank, Wichita, Kans., 1978-79; br. mgr. Fed. Land Bank, Colorado Springs, Colo., 1979-82; chief exec. officer Fed. Land Bank, Denver, 1982-86; adminstr. and mgmt. Farm Credit Svcs., Greeley, 1986-87; dist. rep. Aid Assn. for Lutherans, Greeley, 1987--. Mem. pres. cabinet Aid Assn. Lutherans, 1988, 89, 90, 91. Named Nat. 4-H Winner, 1972, Lion of the Yr., Lions Club, 1982. Fellow Life Underwriters Tng. Coun.; mem. Million Dollar Round Table, Greeley Centennial Rotary (sec. 1988-90, dir. 1990—). Republican. Lutheran. Home and Office: Aid Assn for Luths 1414 41st Ave Greeley CO 80634-2732

AUSTIN, DAVID FLETCHER, physician, surgeon; b. Wellman, Iowa, Apr. 24, 1927; s. Marvin Fletcher and Pauline (LaRue) A.; m. Sally Jo Anderson, Dec. 20, 1953 (div. 1969); children: Andrew, Stephanie, James, John, Lisa; m. Linda Conley, June 20, 1969; 1 child, Christopher C. BS, Northwestern U., Evanston, Ill., 1949; MD, Northwestern U., Chgo., 1953. Diplomate Am. Bd. Otolaryngologists, Am. Bd. Surgery. Ptnr. Shea Clinic, Memphis, 1959-64; owner Austin Otologic Ctr., Chgo., 1964-89, Idaho ENT P.A., Idaho Falls, 1989—; assoc. prof. otolaryngology U. Ill., Chgo., 1970-78, Rush Med. Sch., Chgo., 1980—. Contbr. articles to profl. jours., chpts. to books. Bd. dirs. Old Town Sch. Folk Music, Chgo., 1972-88. Rawson scholar, 1951. Fellow ACS; mem. AMA, Am. Otologic Soc., Triologic Soc. (coun. mem. 1984-89), Chgo. Larngologic and Otologic Soc., Am. Acad. Otolaryngology and Head and Neck Surgeons, Am. Neurotology Soc., Politzer Soc. (bd. dirs. 1976—), Idaho Falls C. of C. Home: 125 W 16th St Idaho Falls ID 83402-4232 Office: Idaho ENT 2860 Channing Way Idaho Falls ID 83404-7531

AUSTIN, JAMES ALBERT, healthcare executive, obstetrician-gynecologist; b. Phoenix, Sept. 23, 1931; s. Albert Morris and Martha Lupkin (Mercer) A.; m. Margaret Jeanne Arnold, July 26, 1952 (div. 1978); children: Cynthia Milee Ludgin, Lauri Jeanne Fuller, Wendy Patrice Rhea; m. Sandra Lee Marsh, Jan. 3, 1979 (div. 1992). BA, U. So. Calif., 1952; MD, George Wash. U., 1956; MBA, Pepperdine U., 1991. Diplomate Am. Bd. Ob-Gyn., Am. Bd. Med. Mgmt. Intern U.S. Naval Hosp., Bethesda, Md., 1956-57, resident in ob-gyn, 1957-60; ob-gyn. Washington Gynecologists, Washington, 1966-69; pres. Ariz. Obstetrics and Gynecology Ltd., Phoenix, 1969-79; chmn. dept. ob-gyn. USN, Agana Hgts., Guam, 1979-81; ob-gyn. Sanger Med. Group, Coronado, Calif., 1981-83; chmn. ob-gyn. FHP Corp., Salt Lake City, 1983-84, assoc. med. dir., 1984-85; hosp. med. dir. FHP Corp., Fountain Valley, Calif., 1985-86; assoc. v.p. med. affairs FHP Corp., Fountain Valley, 1987-90; chief exec. officer Ultra Link Nationwide HMO Network, Costa Mesa, Calif., 1990-93; clin. prof. ob-gyn. George Wash. U., Georgetown, Washington, 1966-69; asst. clin. prof. U. Calif. San Diego, 1981-83, U. Utah, Salt Lake City, 1983-85. Rear adm. USNR, 1956-88. Fellow Am. Coll. Ob-Gyn.; mem. AMA, Am. Acad. Med. Dir., Ariz. Med. Assn. (bd. dirs. 1978), Am. coll. Physician Execs. Republican. Presbyterian. Home: 16811 S Pacific Ave Sunset Beach CA 90742-1477 Office: 11500 Brookshire Ave Downey CA 90241-7010

AUSTIN, L. KATHLEEN, executive assistant; b. Corona, Calif., Aug. 1, 1949; d. Gilbert Edward Austin and Lorna Nadine (Powell) Lockwood; m. Donald G. Reiff II, Sept. 17, 1970 (div. May 1983); children: Donald G. III, Michele D. AA, Chabot Coll., 1970. Dir. edn. Palo Alto (Calif.) Med. Found., 1982-85; conf. mgr. Contemporary Forums, Danville, Calif., 1985-89; dir. meetings & convs. Prestige Accommodations, Irvine, Calif., 1989—. Bd. dirs. Am. Cancer Soc., Santa Clara, Calif.; ex offico mem. Palo Alto Child Care Task Force, 1986; core com. mem. Joint Planning Com. Lifeskills Program, Palo Alto, 1985-86. Mem. Am. Soc. Assn. Execs., Meeting Planners Internat., Profl. Conv. Mgmt. Assn. Republican. Presbyterian. Home: 350 St Tropez Ct Laguna Beach CA 92651-4433 Office: Prestige Accommodations 2603 Main St Ste 690 Irvine CA 92714-6232

AUSTIN, ROBERT CLARKE, naval officer; b. Cleve., Sept. 5, 1931; s. Clarke Albert and Margaret Jane (Richardson) A.; m. Joyce Ann Bisese, Apr. 22, 1957; children—Susan Lynn, James Holden, Robert Clarke, Cecelia Ann. B.S., U.S. Naval Acad., 1954; M.S. in Physics, Naval Postgrad. Sch., 1963. Enlisted U.S. Navy, 1948, commd. ensign, 1954, advanced through grades to rear adm., 1980; comdg. officer USS Finback, 1968-72; comdr. Submarine Devel. Group Two, 1974-76; comdg. officer Naval Submarine Sch., 1976-78; chief of staff submarine force U.S. Atlantic Fleet, 1979-80; dep. dir. for internat. negotiations for Plans and Policy Directorate, Joint Chiefs of Staff, Pentagon, Washington, 1981-82; chief naval tech. tng., 1982-86; supt. Naval Postgrad. Sch., 1986-89; ret. USN, 1989; pres. Austin Assocs., Inc., Alexandria, Va., 1989—. Decorated Def. Superior Service Medal, Legion of Merit with 4 gold stars, Meritorious Service medal, others. Mem. Sigma Xi. Episcopalian.

AUSTIN-LAZARUS, PHYLLIS CHAPPELL, electrical engineer; b. Rockledge, Fla., Oct. 26, 1962; d. Nicholas Sean and Elizabeth Bechtal (Coleman) Austin; m. Kenneth Alan Lazarus, Dec. 1, 1984. BSEE, Boston U., 1983; MSEE, U. South Fla., 1988. Engr. GE, Utica, N.Y., 1983-84, ECI div. E-Systems, St. Petersburg, Fla., 1984-89, Repco, Orlando, Fla., 1989-90; mem. tech. staff Hughes Network Systems, San Diego, 1990—. Contbr. articles to profl. jours. Office: Hughes Network Systems 10450 Pacific Ctr Ct San Diego CA 92121

AUTH, ROBERT RALPH, art educator; b. Bloomington, Ill., Oct. 27, 1926; s. Phillip C. and Frances E. BFA, Ill. Wesleyan U., Bloomington, 1953; MFA, Wash. State U., Pullman, Ill., 1963. Artist Burley, ID, 1959; artist Boise Ind. Sch. Dist., Boise, ID, 1960-81, art supr., 1981-87. Author: ID State Humanities Curriculum Guide, 1985. community svc. Adv. to Boise's Jr. League, mem. Allied Arts Coun., Boise Gallery of Art Bd. of Dir., Boise Edn. Assn., Alliance for Arts in Edn. Recipient Allied Arts Coun. Artist of the Year Award, 1972, Nat. Art Edn. Award, 1979, ID Hist. Soc. Hon. Curator of Military Hist. Award, 1983, Gov. of ID Medal for Excellence in the Arts, 1988, The ID Statesman's Distinguished Citizen, 1988, Phi Delta Kappa Friend of Edn. Award, 1989. Roman Catholic. Home: PO Box 91 Yellow Pine ID 83677

AUTRY, GENE (ORVON GENE AUTRY), actor, radio entertainer, broadcasting executive, baseball team executive; b. Tioga, Tex., Sept. 29, 1907; s. Delbert and Elnora (Ozmont) A.; m. Ina Mae Spivey, Apr. 1, 1932; m. Jacqueline Ellam, 1981. Grad., Tioga (Tex.) High Sch., 1925. R.R. telegraph operator Sapulpa, Okla., 1925; owner, chmn. bd. Calif. Angels; pres. Flying A Prodns.; owner Sta. KMPC AM & KLITE FM, Hollywood, Calif., Stas. KVI & KPLZ Radio, Seattle, Golden West Broadcasters; pres. several music and publ. cos. Made first phonograph record of cowboy songs, 1929; radio artist Sta. WLS, Chgo., 1930-34; motion picture actor, 1934-53, including In Old Santa Fe; starred in 88 musical Western feature pictures, 91 half-hour TV pictures 1950-55; has written or co-written over 200 songs including That Silver-Haired Daddy of Mine, 1931, You're the Only Star in My Blue Heaven, 1938, Dust, 1938, Tears On My Pillow, 1941, Be Honest With Me, 1941, Tweedle O'Twill, 1942, Here Comes Santa Claus, 1948; host Melody Ranch Theater Nashville Network, 1987, 88. Served with USAAF, 1942-45. Recipient: D.W. Griffith award, 1991. Mem. Internat. Footprinters. Clubs: Masons (33 degree), Shriners, Elks. Address: PO Box 710 Los Angeles CA 90078 Office: care Calif Angels PO Box 2000 Anaheim CA 92803-2000

AVAKOFF, JOSEPH CARNEGIE, plastic surgeon; b. Fairbanks, Alaska, July 15, 1936; s. Harry B. and Margaret (Adams) A.; m. Teddy I. Law, May 7, 1966; children: Caroline, Joey, John. AA, U. Calif., Berkeley, 1955, AB, 1957; MD, U. Calif., San Francisco, 1961; JD, Santa Clara U., 1985. Bar: Calif. 1987; diplomate Am. Bd. Surgery, Am. Bd. Plastic Surgery. Physicist U.S. Naval Radiol. Def. Lab., San Francisco, 1957, 59; intern So. Pacific Gen. Hosp., San Francisco, 1961-62; resident in surgery Kaiser Found. Hosp., San Francisco, 1962-66; resident in plastic surgery U. Tex. Sch. Medicine, San Antonio, 1970-72; pvt. practice specializing in surgery Sacramento, 1966-70; pvt. practice specializing in plastic surgery Los Gatos and San Jose, Calif., 1972—; clin. instr. surgery Sch. Medicine U. Calif., Davis, 1967-70; chief dept. surgery Mission Oaks Hosp., Los Gatos, 1988-90, chief div. plastic surgery Good Samaritan Hosp., San Jose, 1989-91; presenter numerous med. orgns. Contbr. numerous articles to med. jours. Mem. San Jose Adv. Commn. on Health, 1975-82; bd. govs. San Jose YMCA, 1977-80. Mem. AMA, Calif. Med. Assn., Santa Clara County Bar Assn., Santa Clara County Med. Assn., Union Am. Physicians and Dentists, Phi Beta Kappa, Phi Eta Sigma. Republican. Presbyterian. Home: 6832 Rockview Ct San Jose CA 95120-5607 Office: 15899 Los Gatos Almaden Rd Los Gatos CA 95032-3739

AVEDIAN, LEONARD V., physician; b. Fresno, Calif., July 21, 1934; s. George M. and Lily (Tarpinian) A.; m. Bonny Lou Krause; children: Kristen Elizabeth, Gabrielle Suzanne. AB, Calif. State U., Fresno, 1956; MD, U. Wis., 1970. Diplomate Am. Bd. Plastic Surgery. Practice medicine specializing in plastic surgery Newport Beach, Calif., 1970—. Served with USAF, 1957-59. Fellow ACS; mem. Am. Soc. Plastic and Reconstructive Surgery, Am. Soc. Aesthetic Plastic Surgery. Republican. Mem. Ch. Assemblies of God. Office: 1441 Avocado Ave Ste 602 Newport Beach CA 92660-7707

AVERILL, MARILYN, lawyer; b. St. Louis, Nov. 30, 1946. BA, Wellesley Coll., 1968; MA, U. Colo., 1973, JD, 1988. Bar: Colo. 1988, U.S. Dist. Ct. Colo. 1991. Jud. law clk. to Chief Justice Joseph R. Quinn Colo. Supreme Ct., Denver, 1988-89; atty. Kobayashi & Assocs., Denver, 1989-91; atty. Office of Solicitor Rocky Mountain Region U.S. Dept. Interior, Golden, Colo., 1991—; instr. U. Denver Coll. Law, 1991-93. Articles editor U. Colo. Law Rev., 1987-88. Mem. ABA, Colo. Bar Assn., Colo. Women's Bar Assn., Denver Bar Assn. Office: US Dept Interior Office of Solicitor PO Box 25007 Denver Fed Ctr Denver CO 80225

AVERY, BRYCE DAVID, electronic engineer; b. Downey, Calif., Feb. 21, 1965; s. David Ray and Elizabeth Ann (Hill) A.; m. Annette Hales, Dec. 10, 1988; children: Daniel, Katherine. BSEE, Brigham Young U., 1986, BA in German, 1986; MS in Engring., Calif. State Poly. U., Pomona, 1992. Tech. writer Hughes Aircraft Co., Buena Park, Calif., 1985; metrology engr. U.S. Naval Warfare Assessment Ctr., Corona, Calif., 1988-92; supr. tech. documentation Naval Air Warfare Ctr., Patuxent River, Md., 1992—. Contbr. articles, column to Chess Corr., 1983—. Mem. Nat. Eagle Scout Assn., Corr. Chess League Am. (bd. dirs. 1990—).

AVERY, RICHARD EUGENE, retired instrumentation engineer; b. Newcastle, Pa., Oct. 21, 1935; s. Francis William and Thelma Marie (Inman) A.; m. Diane Marie Carter, Dec. 3, 1954; children: Richard William, Cynthia Ann. Student, U. Minn., 1956; AS, Pierce-Moorpark Coll., 1964. Rocket engr. test leadman Rocketdyne div. Rockwell Internat., Canoga Park, Calif., 1957-60, reactor operator, 196l, engring. assoc. instrumentman, 1962-68; sr. instrument engr. Rockwell Internat., El Segundo, Calif., 1970-85; sr. instrument engr. Rockwell Internat., Canoga Park, 1985-91, retired, 1991; sr. mfg. engr. Zerox Corp., El Segundo, 1968-70. Tenor Simi Valley (Calif.) Chorale, 1964; scoutmaster Simi Valley area Boy Scouts Am., 1968-72; bd. dirs. Citizens Against Govt. Waste Ventura County; sec. treas. waters road domestic Water Assn. Inc. Sgt. USAF, 1953-57. Mem. Simi Valley Hist. Soc., U.S. Power Squadron. Republican. Lutheran. Home: 8469 Waters Rd Moorpark CA 93021-9759

AVERY, SUSAN KATHRYN, electrical engineering educator, researcher; b. Detroit, Jan. 5, 1950; d. Theodore Peter and Alice Jane (Greene) Rykala; m. James Paul Avery, Aug. 12, 1972; 1 child, Christopher Scott. BS in Physics, Mich. State U., 1972; MS in Physics, U. Ill., 1974, PhD in Atmospheric Sci., 1978. adv. com. chair Elec. and Communications Systems Div. NSF, Washington, 1991—; working group ionosphere, thermosphere, mesosphere NASA, Washington, 1991—; mem.-at-large USNC/URSI NRC, Washington, 1991—, com. on solar terrestrial rsch., 1987-90; trustee Univ. Corp. for Atmospheric Rsch., 1991—, vice chair bd. trustees. Asst. prof. elec. engring. U. Ill., Urbana, 1978-83; fellow CIRES U. Colo., Boulder, 1982—, assoc. prof. elec. engring., 1985-92, assoc. dean rsch. and grad. edn. Coll. Engring., 1989-92, prof. elec. engring., 1992—; adv. com. chair Elec. and Communications Div. NSF, Washington, 1991—, adv. panel atmospheric scis. program, 1985-88, steering com. CEDAR program, 1986-87, adv. com. engring. directorate, 1991—, vis. professorship, 1982-83; working group ionosphere, thermosphere, mesosphere NASA, Washington, 1991—; mem.-at-large USNC/URSI NRC, Washington, 1991—, com. on solar-terrestrial rsch., 1987-90; trustee Univ. Corp. for Atmospheric Rsch., 1991—, sci. programs evaluation com., 1989-91; working group on tides in mesosphere and lower thermosphere Internat. Commn. Meteorology of Upper Atmosphere, 1981-86; mesosphere-lower thermosphere network steering com. Internat. STEP Program, 1989—, equatorial mid. atmosphere dynamics steering com., 1990—. Contbr. articles to Radio Sci., Adv. Space Rsch., Jour. Atmosphere Terrestrial Physics, Jour. Geophys. Rsch., others. Recipient Faculty Award for Women, NSF, 1991, Outstanding Publication award NCAR, 1990; vis. fellow Coop. Inst. for Rsch. in Environ. Scis., 1982-83. Mem. IEEE, Am. Meteorol. Soc. (com. on mid. atmosphere 1990—), Am. Geophys. Union (com. edn and human resources 1988—), Am. Soc. Engring. Edn., Sigma Xi. Office: U Colo Engring Rsch Ctr CB 423 Boulder CO 80309-0425

AVIEL, JO ANN B. FAGOT, political science educator; b. Mpls., May 15, 1942; d. Joseph B. and Joyce B. (Cawley) Fagot; m. S. David Aviel; children: Rebecca, Sara. BA, Lone Mt. Coll., 1964; MA, Fletcher Sch. Law and Diplomacy, 1965, MALD, 1966, PhD, 1971. Asst. prof. social studies U. Costa Rica, San Jose, 1966-68; asst. prof. polit. sci. Humboldt State U., Arcata, Calif., 1968-70; prof. internat. rels. dept. San Francisco State U., 1970—; bd. advisors Internat. Pub. Policy Inst. in N.Y.; vis. fellow Leonard Davis Inst. for Internat. Rels. Hebrew U., Jerusalem, 1975; vis. prof. Diplomatic Acad. Peru, 1984. Author: Resource Shortages and World Politics, 1979; reviewer Western Polit. Quarterly, The Jour. of Developing Areas, Westview Press; contbr. articles to profl. jours. Mem. Am. Polit. Sci. Assn., Western Polit. Sci. Assn., N. Calif. Polit. Sci. Assn., Women's Caucus for Polit. Sci. (nat. pres. 1973-74), Internat. Studies Assn., Latin Am. Studies Assn., Pacific Coast Coun. for Latin Am. Studies (mem. pres.' adv. coun., bd. govs.), U.N. Assn. San Francisco (bd. dirs.), World Affairs Coun. No. Calif. (guest lectr.). Home: 868 Overlook Ct San Mateo CA 94403-3860 Office: San Francisco State U Dept Internat Rels 1600 Holloway Ave San Francisco CA 94132-1722

AVILA, RAUL, real estate investor; b. L.A., June 24, 1959; s. Jesse and Lupe (Jordan) A.; m. Miriam Escobar, June 2, 1990; children: Cynthia, Christine. AS, Don Bosco Tech, 1979. Ptnr. Diversified Investments, L.A., 1979-84, Avila & Co., Monterey Park, Calif., 1984-86; pres. Avila Fin. Group, L.A., 1986-90, A.F.G. Capital Corp., Montebello, Calif., 1990—; chmn. Avcorp Fin. Group, Montebello, Calif., 1991—. Bd. dirs. Fair Housing Coun., San Gabriel Valley, Calif., 1990—; mem. Greater L.A. Apt. Assn., 1992; pres. Belvedere Rotary Club, L.A., 1983-84; commr. City of Monterey Park, 1984-86; elected mem. Dem. County Ctrl. Com., 59th assembly, L.A., 1985-87; field rep. congressman Matthew Martinez, L.A., 1984-87; fin. chmn. after class scouting Boy Scouts Am., 1984; bd. mgrs. L.A. YMCA, 1984-88; police res. officer, Monterey Park. Mem. Latin Bus. Assn., ARC (chmn. bd. dirs. 1991-93), Montebello C. of C., Don Bosco Alumni Assn. (bd. dirs. 1983-84). Democrat. Roman Catholic.

AVNET, JOHN BENJAMIN, data processing consultant; b. Bklyn., June 8, 1933; s. George and Nanette (Kaplan) A.; m. Roslyn Mandel, Oct. 2, 1961 (div. 1974); 1 child, Stephanie L.; m. Jo Anne Wolfe, Oct. 15, 1978. BS, NYU, 1959. Programmer System Devel. Corp., Santa Monica, Calif., 1959-60; support mgr. Burroughs Corp., L.A., 1960-63; owner, mgr. Bus. Computer Svcs., L.A., 1963-67; western regional mgr. Control Data Corp., Mpls., 1967-86; owner, mgr. John B. Avnet & Assocs., Sherman Oaks, Calif., 1986—. Cons. Ctr. for Non-Profit Mgmt., L.A., 1987—. Sgt. USAF, 1952-56, Korea. Offfice: 4005 Woodman Ave Sherman Oaks CA 91423

AVOLIO, WENDY FREEDMAN, speech and language pathologist; b. Phila., Feb. 24, 1953; d. Harold Stanley and Phyllis Maxine (Broodno) Freedman; m. Michael Howard Strauss, Aug. 31, 1975 (div. 1981); children: Nicole Erin, Mallary Blair; m. Mark Richard Avolio, Mar. 24, 1985. BS, Bradley U., 1973; MA, No. Ill. U., 1975. Speech-lang. pathologist Bartlett (Ill.) Sch. Dist., 1975-76, Proviso Area for Exceptional Children, Maywood, Ill., 1976-77, Cen. Reading and Speech Clinic, Mt. Prospect, Ill., 1977-78, Tucson Unified Sch. Dist., 1978-79, Handmaker Jewish Geriatric Ctr., Tucson, 1981; mgr. speech-lang. therapy program Dept. Econ. Security/Div. Devel. Disabilities, Tucson, 1981-86, So. Ariz. Spl. Edn. Coop., Vail, 1986-92, Amphitheater Sch. Dist., 1992—; cons. speech-lang. Parent Support Group, Tucson, 1981-87, Ariz. Adv. Com. For Deaf-Blind, Tucson, 1983-87; lang. cons. Community Outreach Program for Deaf, Tucson, 1983. Active youth and children com. Jewish Community Ctr., Tucson, 1986-88, Tucson Classics, 1989—. Mem. Am. Speech Lang. and Hearing Assn. (cert.), Ariz. Speech and Lang. Assn. Home: 3532 N Fiesta Del Sol Tucson AZ 85715-2013 Office: 701 W Wetmore Tucson AZ 85705

AVRAMIS, TOM PETER, priest; b. Tucson, July 15, 1955; s. Christopher and Toula (Troupis) A.; m. Alicia Lorraine Ott, Jan. 6, 1979; children: Alethea, Stefan. BA, U. Ariz., 1977; MDiv, Holy Cross Coll., 1981; MS, Calif. State U., Hayward, 1989. Ordained priest Greek Orthodox Ch., 1981. Priest Holy Trinity Cathedral, Phoenix, 1981-83, Resurrection Ch., Castro Valley, Calif., 1983-91; CEO Guadalupe Homes for Children, Colton, Calif., 1991—; v.p. bd. dirs. Guadalupe Homes, 1984-91. Author: Sacrament of Holy Communion, 1986. Recipient Youth Leadership medal Western States Youth Coun., Oakland, 1985. Office: Guadalupe Homes 1470 Cooley Dr Colton CA 92324

AVRIL, JACK JOSEPH, ceramic engineer, forensic scientist; b. Tacoma, Wash., Jan. 17, 1932; S. Charles Walter (Jack) and Madge Lorena (Hall) A.; m. Janice A. Hardison, Aug. 23, 1958; children: Susan, Michael, Margaret. BS in Ceramic Engring., U. Wash., 1959. Registereed profl. engr., Calif. Sr. scientist, owner Ind. Forensics, Inc., Tacoma, Wash., 1980—. Active in 28th Dist. Dem. Orgn., Lakewood, Wash., 1980—; bd. dirs. YMCA Tacoma, 1984-92, Lakewood United, 1988—. Mem. Interna. Assn. Arson Investigators (cert. fire investigator, 1st v.p. Wash. chpt. 1991-92, pres. 1992—), Nat. Assn. Fire Investigators (cert. fire and explosion investigator), Nat. Fire Protection Assn. Baptist. Office: Ind Forensics Inc PO Box 97192 Tacoma WA 98497

AXELRAD, STEPHEN, interactive video artist, consultant; b. Washington, Sept. 12, 1943; s. Irving Irmas and Harriet (Levene) A.; m. Pamela Berg, June 1971 (div. 1977); 1 child, Joshua Berg; m. Sylvia Impert, Dec. 18, 1982. BA in English, U. Calif., Berkeley, 1965; JD, U. Chgo., 1969; MD in Art, Photography, Calif. State U., Fullerton, 1979. Lawyer Mass. Defenders Com., 1969-71; pvt. law practice Calif., 1971-73, 76-80; prin. Stephen Alexrad Photography, Calif., 1971-80; lawyer Nat. Health Law Program, 1973-76; adminstrv. law judge Calif. Agrl. Labor Rels. Bd., 1977-78; lawyer Legal Aid Soc. Orange County, Calif., 1981-87; computer/interactive video cons. Visions of Naples, Long Beach, Calif., 1987—; law instr. Calif. State U., Northridge, 1974-76, UCLA, 1975-76, Western State U. Sch. Law, 1977-79; video instr. Alt. Sch. L.A. City Sch. Dist., 1980; instr. photography Harbor Coll. and Long Beach City Coll., 1981, Irvine Valley Coll., 1988-89; computer instr. Inacomp Corp., 1985, Met. Tech. Coll., 1989; instr. society, tech. and the arts Calif. State U., 1986; interactive multimedia instr. UCLA Ext., Irvine Valley Coll., Orange Coast Coll., 1989—; instr. computer/videodisc workshops L.A. Ctr. for Photographic Studies, 1984, San Francisco City Coll., 1989; cons. L.A. Ctr. for Photographic Studies, 1982, Olympics videodisc exhbn. proposal, 1984; community TV prodr. Mcpl. Usage Corp., Los Alamitos and Sta. KYOU-TV, Santa Ana, 1984-86; speaker several symposiums; lectr. in field. Prodr. community TV program, 1984-86; creator interactive videos; exhibited in group and solo photography shows U. Colo., Boulder, 1985, Emmanuel Gallery, Denver, 1984, Ithaca Coll., 1984, L.A. Ctr. for Photographic Studies, 1983, Albuquerque United Artists, 1983, Ohio U., 1983, Stone Gallery, Hays, Kans., 1982, Santa Barbara (Calif.) Mus. Art, 1982 (purchase award), Mills House, Garden Grove, Calif., 1981, Mcpl. Art Gallery, Barnsdale Park, Calif., 1981, Seigfred Gallery, Ohio U., Athens, 1980, others. Bd. dirs. Long Beach Mus. Art, 1991-92, chair Media Arts Coun. Grantee Calif. Mus. Photography, 1988, 91, Tech 200 Mus., 1989; purchase award Kansas City Art Inst., 1979; cash award James Madison U., 1980. Mem. Internat. Interactive Communications Soc., SIGGRAPH. Home and Office: 293 Ravenna Dr Long Beach CA 90803

AXELROD, STEPHEN LEE, physician; b. Detroit, June 23, 1951; s. Reuben and Selma Josia (Kazanoff) A.; m. Paula Evans, May 24, 1986. BS, U. Mich., 1972; MD, Wayne State U., 1977. Diplomate Am. Bd. Emergency Medicine. Intern Presbyn.-Denver Med. Ctr., 1977-78; emergency physician Emergency Cons. Inc., Petoskey, Mich., 1978-80, Colo. Emergency Med. Assocs., Thornton, 1980-87; physician, med. dir. Med. Ctrs. Colo., Denver, 1980-89; med. dir. Coors Brewing Co., Denver, 1990—; clin. instr. Okla. Coll. Medicine and Surgery, Tulsa, 1982-87; chmn. credential com. Humana Hosp., Thornton, 1984-88; mem. editorial adv. bd. Medictr. Mgmt. jour., 1985-87. Mgmt. jour., 1985-87; editorial adv. bd. Medicenter Mgmt. jour., 1986-89. Physician Family Builders by Adoption- Fun Run, Denver, 1985-86, Community Home Health Care-Greek Marathon, Seattle, 1984; physician advisor Broomfield (Colo.) Vol. Ambulance Svc., 1980-83; corp. sponsor fin. com. Allied Jewish Fedn., Denver, 1987. Fellow Am. Coll. Emergency Physicians; mem. Colo. Med. Soc., Nat. Assn. Ambulatory Care (bd. dirs. 1984-86, cert. of recognition 1985), Am. Coll. Physician Execs., Am. Coll. Occupational Medicine. Avocations: skiing, travel, squash. Home: 45 S Dexter St Denver CO 80222-1050 Office: Med First Inc 1200 17th St Ste 1000 Denver CO 80202-5810

AXELSON, JOSEPH ALLEN, professional athletics executive; b. Peoria, Dec. 25, 1927; s. Joseph Victor Axelson and Florence (Ealen) Massey; m. Malcolm Rae Smith, Oct. 7, 1950; children: David Allen, Mark Stephen, Linda Rae. B.S., Northwestern U., 1949. Sports info. dir. Ga. So. U., Statesboro, 1957-60, Nat. Assn. Intercollegiate Athletics, Kansas City, Mo., 1961-62; tournament dir. Bowling Proprs. Assn. Am., Park Ridge, Ill., 1963-64; asst. exec. sec. Nat. Assn. Intercollegiate Athletics, Kansas City, Mo., 1964-68; exec. v.p., gen. mgr. Cin. Royals Profl. Basketball Team, Cin., 1969-72; mgr. Cin. Gardens, 1970-72; pres., gen. mgr. Kansas City Kings Profl. Basketball Team, Kansas City, Mo., 1972-79, 82-85; pres., gen. mgr. Sacramento Kings Profl. Basketball Team, 1985-88, exec. v.p., 1988-90; pres. Arco Arena, Sacramento, 1985-88; exec. v.p. Sacramento Sports Assn., Arco Sports Complex, 1988-90, Profl. Team Publs., Inc., Stamford, Conn., 1991-93; exec. v.p. ops. NBA, N.Y.C., 1979-82, chmn. competition and rules com., 1975-79; trustee Naismith Basketball Hall of Fame. Author: Basketball Basics, 1987. Mem. Emil Verban Meml. Soc., Washington. Capt. Signal Corps. AUS, 1949-54. Named Nat. Basketball Exec. of Yr. The Sporting News, St. Louis, 1973; recipient Annual Dirs. award Downtown, Inc., Kansas City, Mo., 1979, Nat. Assn. Intercollegiate Athletics Frank Cramer Nat. Svc. award, 1983, Man of Yr. award Sacramento (Calif.) C. of C., 1986; named to Ga. So. U. Sports Hall of Fame, 1990. Mem. Am. Philatelic Soc., Phi Kappa Psi. Republican. Presbyterian. Office: 1112 1st St Ste 139 Coronado CA 92118-1499

AYA, RODERICK HONEYMAN, retired corporate tax executive; b. Portland, Oreg., Sept. 17, 1916; s. Alfred Anthony and Grace Myrtle (Honeyman) A.; student U. Oreg., 1935-36, Internat. Accts. Soc., 1937-39, LaSalle Extension U., 1940-42, Walton Sch. Commerce, 1942, U. Calif. Extension, 1945, Nat. Grad. U., 1973; m. Helen Marjorie Riddle, June 16, 1945 (dec. Dec. 1983); children: Roderick Riddle, Deborah Aya Reynolds, Ronald Honeyman; m. Kathryn Rehnstrom Chatalas, June 22, 1986; stepchildren: John Todd, Paul Seth, Elizabeth Kate. Chief statistician Hotel Employers Assn., San Francisco, 1939-42; acct. Pacific Tel. & Tel. Co., San Francisco, 1942-52, spl. acct., 1952-63; tax acct., 1963-65; spl. acct. AT&T, N.Y.C., 1965-68, mgr. tax studies, 1968-73, div. mgr. tax rsch. and planning, 1973-80; pub. acct., San Francisco, 1940-90; music tchr., 1959—; v.p., treas., dir. Snell Rsch. Assocs., Inc., 1974-79; guest lectr. on taxes Westchester County (N.Y.) Adult Edn. Program. Committeeman, Marin County (Calif.) coun. Boy Scouts Am., 1959-60, com. chmn., 1959-61; mem. Marin County Sheriffs' Reserve, 1962-65; law enforcement liaison com. on Juvenile Control; sec. Am. Nat. Standards Inst. Z90 Com. on Protective Headgear, 1967-80. V.p., treas., bd. dirs. Snell Meml. Found., 1957-80, dir. emeritus, 1990—; trustee Snell Meml. Found. (U.K.), Ltd., 1972-88; mem. chmn.'s com. U.S. Senatorial Bus. Adv. Bd.; mem. Rep. Presdl. Task Force. Author: The Legacy of Pete Snell, 1965, Determination of Corporate Earnings and Profits for Federal Income Tax Purposes, 2 vols., 1966. Fin. com. Seaside (Oreg.) United Meth. Ch.; dir., past pres. Stuart Highlanders Pipe Band of San Francisco. Recipient Wisdom award of honor Wisdom Soc., 1970; Winston Churchill Medal of Wisdom, 1989; Pres.'s Medal of Merit, 1981; Eminent Wisdom fellow Hall of Fame, 1989, Eminent Churchill fellow Winston Churchill Medal of Wisdom Soc., 1989. Fellow Anglo Am. Soc. (hon.); mem. Nat. Soc. Pub. Accts., St. Andrews Soc. San Francisco, Telephone Pioneers Am., Soc. for Ethnomusicology (contbr. to jour.), U.S. Naval Inst., Corinthian Yacht Club (Tiburon, Calif.), Astoria (Oreg.) Golf & Country Club, Sports Car Club of Am. (San Francisco region chief safety inspector, 1955-56, treas. 1957-58, dir. 1957-59), U.S. Yacht Racing Union, Phi Chi, Sigma Nu. Home: PO Box 668 Seaside OR 97138-0668

AYALA, JOHN, librarian, dean; b. Long Beach, Calif., Aug. 28, 1943; s. Francisco and Angelina (Rodriguez) A.; m. Patricia Marie Dozier, July 11, 1987; children: Juan, Sara. BA in History, Calif. State U., Long Beach, 1970, MPA, 1981; MLS, Immaculate Heart Coll., L.A., 1971. Library paraprofl. Long Beach Pub. Library, 1963-70; librarian L.A. County Pub. Libr., 1971-72; librarian Long Beach City Coll., 1972-90, assoc. prof., 1972-90, pres. acad. senate, 1985-87; dean, Learning Resources Fullerton (Calif.) Coll., 1990—; chmn. L.A. County Com. to Recruit Mexican-Am. Librarians, 1973-74; mem. acad. senate Calif. Community Colls., 1985. Editor Calif. Librarian, 1971. Served with USAF, 1966-68, Vietnam. U.S. Office Edn. fellow for library sci., 1970-71. Mem. ALA (com. mem. 1971-85), Calif. Libr. Assn., Nat. Assn. to Promote Spanish Speaking Libr. Svc. (v.p., pres. 1973-76, founding mem.). Democrat. Roman Catholic. Office: Fullerton College Library 321 E Chapman Ave Fullerton CA 92632-2095

AYALA, REYNALDO, geography educator; b. Saltillo, Mex., Sept. 28, 1934; came to U.S., 1952; s. Francisco and Maria (Vallejo) A.; m. Marta Stiefel, June 8, 1958; children: Carlos Cuahutemoc, Guadalupe Xochitl, Emiliano Cuitlahuac. BA in Geography, U. Minn., 1960; MA in Geography, So. Ill. U., 1964, PhD in Geography, 1971; MLS, Tex. Woman's U., 1983. Teaching asst., asst. dir. Latin Am. Inst., So. Ill. U., Carbondale, 1961-66; instr. in geography U. N.Mex., Albuquerque, 1966-69; assoc. prof. San Diego State U., Calexico, Calif., 1969-82, prof., 1986—, libr. dir., 1986—; teaching asst. libr. sch. Tex. Woman's U., Denton, 1982-83; cons. libr. OAS, Washington, 1983-84; dir. Inst. Border Studies San Diego State U., Calexico, 1984—; cons. Libr. of Congress, Washington, 1983—; cons. tchr. OAS, 1983-84. Contbr. articles to profl. publs. Pres. bd. dirs. Kiki Camarena Libr., Calexico, 1990—; pres. sch. bd. Calexico Unified Sch. Dist., 1990—; mem. Calexico Planning Commn., 1978-79; bd. dirs. Neighborhood Ho., Calexico, 1976-90, pres. 1987-88. Grantee Calif. State Libr., 1985, 86, S.H. Cowell Found., 1986. Mem. ALA (internat. rels. com. U.S.-Mex. subcom. 1990—), Ethnic Materials Info. Exchange (chmn. edn. com. 1989—), Reforma (chmn. edn. com. 1988—), Sem Acqui Latin Am. Libr. Materials (chmn. edn. com. 1987—), Pacific Coast Coun. Latin Am. Studies (pres. 1988, sec. 1991—). Democrat. Home: 848 Heber Ave Calexico CA 92231-2410 Office: 720 Heber Ave Calexico CA 92231-2480

AYALA, RUBEN SAMUEL, state senator; b. Chino, Calif., Mar. 6, 1922; s. Mauricio R. and Erminia (Martínez) A.; student Pomona Jr. Coll., 1941-42; grad. Nat. Electronic Inst. Los Angeles, 1948; m. Irene Morales, July 22, 1945; children: Bud, Maurice Edward, Gary. Mem. sch. bd. Chino (Calif.), 1955-62; councilman City of Chino, 1962-64, mayor, 1964-66; bd. suprs., 1966-73; chmn. San Bernardino County Bd. Suprs., 1968-72; mem. Calif. Senate from 34th dist., 1974—, vice chair coms. on rules, agriculture and water resources, local govt., mem. bus. and professions, transportation, vets. affaurs coms., mem. joint legis. audit com., com. fairs allocations. Mem. Chino Sch. Bd., 1955-62; chmn. San Bernardino County Health Com., 1968-72, Chino Police Commn., 1964-66, Chino Parks and Recreation Commn., 1962-64; mem. Nat. Alliance of Businessmen Com., Washington, 1970; chmn. West Valley Planning Agy., 1968-72; mem. steering com. County Hwy. Safety Orgn., 1968-72; bd. dirs. Pomona Freeway Assn., 1968; life mem. PTA, Chino. Served with USMC, World War II; PTO. Recipient Outstanding Civil Leaders of Am. award, 1967; Citizen of Year award Chino Valley C. of C., 1970, VFW of San Bernardino County, Mex. Am. Polit. Assn., Disting. Citizens award Claf. Inland Empire council Boy Scouts Am., 1985; named Calif. Legislator of Yr. Democrats United, 1982; named Citizen of Yr. Assn. Calif. Water Agys. and Am. Public Works Assn., San-Bernardino-Riverside branch, hon. City of Pomona, 1971, 80; parks named in his honor, Chino and Bloomington, Calif.; Chino Sch. Dist. high sch. named in his honor, 1986. Mem. Assn. Calif. Water Agys., Assn. Calif. Engrs., Am. Legion, Native Sons of Golden West. Club: Kiwanis. Office: Office of State Senate 9620 Center Ave #100 Rancho Cucamonga CA 91730 also: Office of State Senate State Capitol Sacramento CA 95814

AYER, FREDERICK, physicist, retired; b. N.Y.C., Dec. 29, 1908; s. James Cook Ayer and May Hancock; m. Betty Jenney, Sept. 20, 1930; children James, Anthony, Frederick III; m. Marcella Flood, June 25, 1946 (dec. 1956); m. Rosa Hahn, June 25, 1966. BS, Harvard Coll., 1931; MS, NYU, 1952. Guest physicist Brookhaven Nat. Lab., Upton, N.Y., 1947-62; lectr. NYU, N.Y.C., 1961-62; physicist U. Colo., Boulder, 1962-69; UFO investigator, U. Colo., 1968-69. Contbg. author: Scientific Study of Unidentified Flying Objects, 1969. Bd. dirs. Masters & Johnson Inst. Mem. AAAS, N.Y. Acad. Scis. Home: The Highlands Seattle WA 98177-5001

AYERS, EVERETTE LEE, highway patrol director; b. Bowling Green, Va., Dec. 20, 1940; s. Everette L. and Hauzie (Rouse) A.; m. Donna Rae Rose, Aug. 24, 1961; children: Jeff, Shelley. Student, Laramie County Community Coll., 1976-77. Patrolman Wyo. Hwy. Patrol, Wheatland, 1964-72; sgt. Wyo. Hwy. Patrol, Rawlins, 1972-76; sgt. Wyo. Hwy. Patrol, Laramie, 1976-78, lt., 1978-81; maj. Wyo. Hwy. Patrol, Cheyenne, 1982-85, col., 1985—. Served with USAF, 1959-63. Mem. Peace Officer's Standards Tng. Commn., Internat. Assn. Chiefs of Police, Am. Assn. Motor Vehicle Adminstrs., Wyo. Hwy. Patrol Assn. Methodist. Lodge: Odd Fellows. Office: Wyo Hwy Patrol 5300 Bishop Blvd PO Box 1708 Cheyenne WY 82002-9019

AYERS, STEPHEN M., lawyer; b. Oakland, Calif., Oct. 7, 1946; s. John Martin Ayers and Marica Crosby (McLean) Ogle; m. Mary Frances Petrin, Dec. 7, 1979; children: Douglas, David. BS, U. Idaho, 1969, JD, 1974. Bar: Idaho, 1974, U.S. Dist. Ct. Idaho 1976. Law clerk to Hon. Fred M. Taylor U.S. Dist. Ct., Boise, Idaho, 1974-76; pvt. practice Coeur d'Alene, Idaho, 1976—; magistrate judge U.S. Dist. Ct., Coeur d'Alene, 1977-92. Bd. dirs. Idaho Spl. Olympics, Boise, 1988-91, legal com., 1991—; trustee Cooper Charitable Found., Coeur d'Alene, 1990—. 1st lt. U.S. Army, 1968-70. Mem. Idaho Bar Assn., First Dist. Bar Assn. Office: 1034 N 3rd Coeur D Alene ID 83814

AYLER, MAYNARD FRANKLIN, mining consultant; b. Tacoma, Wash., Oct. 15, 1922; s. Thomas Frank and Edith Agusta (Sivear) A.; m. Marjory Annabelle Loyd, Aug. 25, 1945; children: Corliss Ann, David Franklin. Engr. of Mining, Colo. Sch. Mines, Golden, 1945; MS, Colo. Sch. Mines, 1963. Registered profl. engr., Colo. Geologist U.S. Bur. Reclamation, Denver, 1945-47; petroleum geologist Calif. Co., Denver, 1947-52; mining engr. Bur. of Mines, Denver, 1961-64, 66-77; faculty Colo. Sch. Mines, Golden, 1958-63; chief Libyan Geol. Survey, Tripoli, 1964-66; faculty U. Md. Overseas, Tripoli, 1965-66; mining cons. Golden, 1952—; pres. Oil Mining Corp., Golden, 1986—. Patentee in field. Playing mem. Jefferson Symphony, Golden, 1956-75, playing mem., bd. dirs. Brico Symphony, Denver, 1958-85; founder, playing mem. Mostly Strauss Orch., Denver, 1980—. Mem. Am. Def. preparedness Assn. (dir. 1982—). Home: 1315 Normandy Rd Golden CO 80401-4124

AYLING, HENRY FAITHFUL, editorial director, consultant; b. Bklyn., Dec. 30, 1931; s. Albert Edward John and Mina Campbell McCurdy (Lindsay) A.; m. Julia Corinne Gornto, 1954; children: Campbell, Eben, Corey, Harry, Faith. BA, Grinnel Coll., 1953; MA, Columbia U., 1958, Calif. State U., Carson, 1984; 2 grad. teaching certs., Calif. State U., Carson, 1985. Asst to registrar Columbia U., N.Y.C., 1958-59; shift supr. crew scheduling Pan Am World Airways, Jamaica, N.Y., 1959-62, supr. payload control, 1963-65; mgr. crew scheduling Seabd. World Airlines, Jamaica, 1962-63, 65-68, mgr. system control, 1968-80; mgr. ops. control Flying Tiger Line, 1980-84; instr. English, ESL Long Beach (Calif.) City Coll., 1984-85; mng. editor IEEE Expert, IEEE Computing Futures IEEE Computer Soc., Los Alamitos, Calif., 1985-90, editorial dir. Computer Soc. Press, 1990—. Mem. editorial bd. Expert Mag., 1986-90, CamAm Programming Inc., 1987-88; columnist Mag. Design and Prodn. mag., 1988-89; contbr. articles to profl. mags. and tech. books; contbr. poetry to various mags. and anthologies. Bd. dirs. Playa Serena Home Owners Assn., Playa Del Rey, Calif., 1983-85. Recipient Maggie awards Western Publs. Assn., 1988-89. Home: 8828 Pershing Dr Ste 120 Play Del Rey CA 92093 Office: IEEE Computer Soc 10662 Los Vaqueros Cir Los Alamitos CA 90720

AYLWARD, J. PATRICK, lawyer; b. Walla Walla, Wash., Aug. 20, 1951; s. James F. and Mary Jane (Little) A.; m. Peggy D. Deobald, Feb. 13, 1982; children: Alana Nicole, Sean Patrick. BA, Stanford U., 1973; JD, U. Wash., 1976. Bar: Wash. 1976, U.S. Dist. Ct. (ea. dist.) Wash. 1980, U.S. Tax Ct. 1984, U.S. Ct. Appeals (9th cir.) 1984, U.S. Dist. Ct. (we. dist.) 1987. Assoc. Hughes, Jeffers and Danielson, Wenatchee, Wash., 1976-81; ptnr., prin. Jeffers, Danielson, Sonn and Aylward, P.S., Wenatchee, 1981—; mem. Ltd. Practice Bd., Olympia, Wash., 1985-90; tchr., panel mem. Continuing Edn. Seminars for Attys. and Ltd. Practice Officers, 1981—. Vol. Wash. State Centennial Games, Wenatchee, 1989. Mem. ABA (real property, probate & trust sect.), Wash. State Bar Assn. (exec. com. real property, probate & trust sect. 1991-93, litigation sect., 1976—, legis. com. 1988—), Chelan-Couglas County Bar Assn. (pres. 1990-91, v.p. 1988-90, past sec., participant legal aid and edn. programs 1976—), Aircraft Owners and Pilots Assn., Exch. Club. Office: Jeffers Danielson et al 317 N Mission Ave Wenatchee WA 98801-2005

AYRES, JANICE RUTH, social service executive; b. Idaho Falls, Idaho, Jan. 23, 1930; d. Low Ray and Frances Mae (Salem) Mason; m. Thomas Woodrow Ayres, Nov. 27, 1953 (dec. 1966); 1 child, Thomas Woodrow Jr. (dec.). MBA, U. So. Calif., 1952, M in Mass Comms., 1953. Asst. mktg. dir. Disneyland, Inc., Anaheim, Calif., 1954-59; gen. mgr. Tamasha Town & Country Club, Anaheim, Calif., 1959-65; dir. mktg. Am. Heart Assn., Santa Ana, Calif., 1966-69; state exec. dir. Nev. Assn. Mental Health, Las Vegas, 1969-71; exec. dir. Clark Co. Easter Seal Treatment Ctr., Las Vegas, 1971-73; mktg. dir., fin devel. officer So. Nev. Drug Abuse Coun., Las Vegas, 1973-74; exec. dir. Nev. Assn. Retarded Citizens, Las Vegas, 1974-75; assoc., cons. Don Luke & Assocs., Phoenix, 1976-77; program dir. Inter-Tribal Coun. Nev., Reno, 1977-79; exec. dir. Ret. Sr. Vol. Program, Carson City, Nev., 1979—; conductor workshops in field. Elected to bd. suprs. Carson City, Nev., 1992—. Named Woman of Distinction, Soroptimist Club, 1988, Outstanding Dir. of Excellence, Gov. State of Nev., 1989, Outstanding Dir., Vol. Action Ctr., J.C. Penney Co. Mem. AAUW, Am. Mktg. Assn., Internat. Platform Assn., Nat. Pub. Rels. Soc. Am. (chpt. pres.), Women Radio & TV, Nat. Soc. Fund Raising Execs., Nev. Fair & Rodeo Assn. (pres.). Home: 1624 Karin Dr Carson City NV 89706-2626 Office: Ret Sr Vol Program 801 N Division St Carson City NV 89703-3925

AZARLOZA, ARMANDO E., political consultant; b. Caracas, Venezuela, Mar. 12, 1965; came to U.S., 1967; s. Jose Ramon and Elsa (Otero) A. BA in Polit. Sci., UCLA, 1988. Field dep. Jack Kemp for Pres., L.A., 1987-88; advance rep. First Lady Nancy Regan, L.A., 1985-88; acct. exec. Dantona and Assoc., Simi Valley, Calif., 1988-90; dir. media rels. Patrick Media Group, L.A., 1990-92; prin. The Capitol Group, North Hills, Calif., 1990—; mem. L.A. Police Dept. Hispanic Outreach Com., 1991—, United Way Hispanic Advancement Com., 1990—, L.A. County Rep. Ctrl. Com., 1990—; vice chmn. Calif. Rep. Hispanic Assembly, L.A., 1987-89. Writer: (essay) Media Mix, 1991, Options Plus, 1992. Cons. Buck McKeon for Congress, Santa Clarita, Calif., 1992, Tom Campbell of U.S. Senate, L.A., 1992, Tony Trias for Sch. Bd., L.A., 1990. Named Outstanding Young Man of Am., 1988, 89; recipient Pub. Affairs MVP award Patrick Media Group, Inc., 1991. Mem. Am. Assn. Polit. Consultants, Pub. Affairs Officers Assn., L.A. Press Club, KC. Republican. Roman Catholic. Home: 16034 Plummer St North Hills CA 91343

AZARNOFF, DANIEL LESTER, pharmaceutical company consultant; b. Bklyn., Aug. 4, 1926; s. Samuel J. and Kate (Asarnow) A.; m. Joanne Stokes, Dec. 26, 1951; children: Rachel, Richard, Martin. BS, Rutgers U., 1947, MS, 1948; MD, U. Kans., 1955. Asst. instr. anatomy U. Kans. Med. Sch., 1949-50, research fellow, 1950-52, intern, 1955-56, resident, Nat. Heart Inst. research fellow, 1956-58, asst. prof. medicine, 1962-64, assoc. prof., 1964-68, dir. clin. pharmacology study unit, 1964-68, assoc. prof. pharmacology, 1965-68, prof. medicine and pharmacology, 1968, dir. Clin. Pharmacology-Toxicology Ctr., 1967-78, Disting. prof., 1973-78, also prof. medicine, 1965-67, pres. Sigma Xi Club, 1966-69, clin. prof. medicine, 1982—; Nat. Inst. Neurol. Diseases and Blindness spl. trainee Washington U. Sch. Medicine, St. Louis, 1958-60; asst. prof. medicine St. Louis U. Sch. Medicine, 1960-62; vis. scientist, Fulbright scholar Karolinska Inst., Stockholm, Sweden, 1968; sr. v.p. worldwide research and devel. G.D. Searle & Co., Skokie, 1978; pres. Searle Research and Devel., Skokie, Ill., 1979-85, Azarnoff Assocs., Inc., Evanston, Ill., 1987—, D.L. Azarnoff Assocs., So. San Francisco, 1986—; prof. pathology, clin. prof. pharmacology Northwestern U. Med. Sch., 1978-85; commr. Nat. Commn. on Orphan Diseases, 1985-87; chmn. bd. dirs. Alpha RX Corp., South San Francisco, Calif., 1992—; professorial lectr. U. Chgo., 1978; dir. Second Workshop on Prins. Drug Evaluation in Man, 1970; chmn. com. on problems of drug safety NRC-Nat. Acad. Sci., 1972-76; cons. numerous govtl. agys. Editor: Devel. of Drug Interactions, 1974-77, Yearbook of Drug Therapy, 1977-79; series editor: Monographs in Clin. Pharmacology, 1977-84; mem. editorial bd. Drug Investigation, 1989—, others. Served with U.S. Army, 1945-46. Recipient Ginsburg award in phys. diagnosis U. Kans. Med. Center, 1953, Outstanding Intern award, 1956, Ciba award for gerontol. research, 1958; Rectors medal U. Helsinki, 1968; John and Mary R. Markle scholar, 1962, Burroughs Wellcome scholar, 1964, William N. Creasy vis. prof. clin. pharmacology Med. Coll. Va., 1975; Bruce Hall Meml. lectr. St. Vincents Hosp., Sydney, 1976, 7th Sir Henry Hallett Dale lectr. Johns Hopkins U. Med. Sch., 1978. Fellow ACP, N.Y. Acad. Scis., Am. Assn. Pharm. Scientistss; mem. Am. Soc. Clin. Nutrition, Am. Nutrition Instn., Am. Soc. Pharmacology and Exptl. Therapeutics (chmn. clin. pharmacology div. 1969-71, mem. exec. com. 1966-73, 78-81, del. 1975-78, bd. publ. trustees), Am. Soc. Clin. Pharmacology and Therapeutics, Am. Fedn. Clin. Research, Brit. Pharmacol. Soc., AMA (vice chmn. council on drugs 1971-72, editorial bd. Jour.), Central Soc. Clin. Research, Royal Soc. for Promotion Health, Inst. Medicine of Nat. Acad. Scis., Soc. Exptl. Biology and Medicine (councillor 1976-80), Internat. Union Pharmacologists (sec. clin. pharmacology sect. 1975-81, internat. adv. com. Paris Congress 1978, GPIA (blue ribbon com. on generic medicine 1990), Sigma Xi.

AZCUE, PEDRO ARTURO, marketing professional; b. Mexico City, Sept. 12, 1955; s. Pedro P. and Lilly (Aderman) A.; m. Ana Attolini, Dec. 21, 1979; children: pedro, Derrick, Axel. BS in Indsl. Engring., U. Iberoamericana, Mexico City, 1977; MBA, Stanford U., 1981. Profl. indsl. engr., Mexico. Investments officer Banco de Mexico, Mexico City, 1977-79; mktg. officer Credit Suisse First Boston, London, 1980; fin. mgr. La Salle Ptnrs., Chgo., 1981-84; v.p., devel. group La Salle Ptnrs., Dallas, 1984-88; v.p., corp. relocation La Salle Ptnrs., L.A., 1988-92; sr. v.p., dir. gen. LaSalle Ptnrs.-Mex., 1992—; mktg. dir. Santa Fe hdqrs. Hewlett Packard, Mexico City, 1992—; project dir. relocation of Mayor Brown Platt's L.A. office, 1988-90, Alexander & Alexander's L.A. office, 1988-90, AT&T Mex. office, 1991-92, Bank of Am. Recipient Best Student of Mexico award Pres. of Republic of Mexico, 1977, hon. mention award U. Iberoamerican, 1977. Mem. U.S.-Mexico C. of C., Jonathan Club, Las Colinas Sports Club. Roman Catholic. Home: 24939 Alicante Dr Calabasas CA 91302-3026 Office: La Salle Ptnrs 355 S Grand Ave Los Angeles CA 90071-1560

AZEVEDO, KATHERINE ANN, agricultural pest control advisor; b. Turlock, Calif., Apr. 5, 1956; d. George John and Mary Lou (Morris) a. AS, Modesto (Calif.) Jr. Coll., 1978; BS, Calif. Poly. State U., 1985, MS, 1988. Lic. to recommend pesticides to farmer, Calif. Cons. Modesto, 1988—. Fellow Calif. Agrl. Prodn. Cons. Assn.; mem. Am. Soc. Agronomy, Soil Sci. Soc. of Am. Democrat. Roman Catholic. Home and Office: 1117 Main St Modesto CA 95351

AZUMANO, GEORGE ICHIRO, travel agent; b. Portland, Oreg., June 9, 1918; s. Hatsutaro and Satsuki (Kinouchi) A.; m. Ise, Nov. 18, 1943 (dec. 1974); children: Loen, Bette-Jo-Jim; m. Nobuko, Mar. 21, 1976. BS, U. Oreg., 1940. Owner grocery store, 1940-41, 42; owner Azumano Ins. Agy., Portland, 1946—, Azumano Travel Svc., Inc., Portland, 1949—, Overseas Courier Svc., Portland, 1976—. Trustee Oreg. Mus. Sci. & Industry, 1991, Willamette U., Salem, 1988—; mem. adv. bd. St. Vincent Hosp., 1991. Recipient Fourth Class Order of the Rising Sun, Gov. Japan, Portland, 1982, Outstanding Contbn. award to travel and tourism industries, Portland, 1985. Mem. Am. Soc. Travel Agts., Rotary (bd. dirs. 1980-82). Republican. Methodist. Home: 2802 SE Moreland Ln Portland OR 97202-8121 Office: Azumano Travel Svc Inc 320 SW Stark St # 600 Portland OR 97204-2692

BAARS, BERNARD JOSEPH, cognitive scientist, psychologist; b. Amsterdam, Netherlands, Mar. 21, 1946; came to U.S., 1958; s. Louis Jacques and Engeltje (Roselaar) B. BA, UCLA, 1970, PhD, 1977; MA, Calif. State U., L.A., 1973. Fellow Ctr. for Rsch. in Human Learning, U. Minn., Mpls., 1974-75; asst. prof. psychology SUNY, Stony Brook, 1977-85; cognitive sci. fellow Ctr. Human Info. Processing, U. Calif., San Diego, 1979-80; vis. scientist conscious and unconscious mental devel. Langley Porter Psychiat.

Inst., U. Calif., San Francisco, 1985-86; assoc. prof. psychology Wright Inst., Berkeley, Calif., 1986—; co-chair Soc. Cognition and Brain Theory, 1980-83; assoc. Behavioral and Brain Scis., 1988—. Author: The Cognitive Revolution in Psychology, 1986, A Cognitive Theory of Consciousness, 1988; editor: Experimental Slips and Human Error: Exploring the Architecture of Volition, 1992; founding editor: Consciousness and Cognition: An Internat. Jour., 1990—; editorial bd. Jour. Psycholinguistic Rsch., 1991—; contbr. articles to profl. jours. Mem. Am. Psychol. Assn., Assn. Psychol. Sci., Soc. Psychonomic Sci., Cognitive Sci. Soc. Office: Wright Inst 2728 Durant Ave Berkeley CA 94704

BAAS, JACQUELYNN, art historian, museum administrator; b. Grand Rapids, Mich., Feb. 14, 1948. BA in History of Art, Mich. State U.; Ph.D. in History of Art, U. Mich. Registrar U. Mich. Mus. Art, Ann Arbor, 1974-78, asst. dir., 1978-82; editor Bull. Museums of Art and Archaeology, U. Mich., 1976-82; chief curator Hood Mus. Art, Dartmouth Coll., Hanover, N.H., 1982-84, dir., 1985-89; dir. Univ. Art Mus. and Pacific Film Archive, Berkeley, Calif., 1989—. Contbr. articles to jours. and catalogues. NEH fellow, 1972-73; Nat. Endowment Arts fellow, 1973-74, 87-88. Mem. Coll. Art Assn. Am., Print Council Am., Am. Assn. Museums, Assn. Art Mus. Dirs.. Office: Univ Art Mus and Pacific Film Archive 2625 Durant Ave Berkeley CA 94720

BABAYANS, EMIL, financial planner; b. Tehran, Iran, Nov. 9, 1951; came to U.S., 1969; s. Hacob and Jenik (Khatchatourian) B.; m. Annie Ashjian. B.S., U. So. Calif., 1974, M.S., 1976; m. Annie Ashjian. Cert. fin. planner; chartered life underwriter, fin. cons. Pres. Babtech Internat., Inc., Sherman Oaks, Calif., 1975-85; sr. ptnr. Emil Babayans & Assocs., Woodland Hills, Calif., 1985—. Mem. Am. Mgmt. Assn., Nat. Assn. Life Underwriters, Inst. Cert. Fin. Planners, Internat. Assn. Fin. Planners, Am. Soc. CLU and Chartered Fin. Cons., Million Dollar Round Table. Armenian Orthodox. Office: 21700 Oxnard St Ste 1100 Woodland Hills CA 91367-7300

BABCOCK, HORACE, astronomer; b. Pasadena, Calif., Sept. 13, 1912; s. Harold Delos and Mary Geddie (Henderson) B.; children: Ann Lucille, Bruce Harold, Kenneth L. B.S., Calif. Inst. Tech., 1934; Ph.D., U. Calif., 1938; D.Sc. (hon.), U. Newcastle-upon-Tyne (Eng.), 1965. Asst. Lick Obs., Mt. Hamilton, Calif., 1938-39; instr. Yerkes and McDonald Obs., Williams Bay, Wis., Ft. Davis, Tex., 1939-41; with Radiation Lab., MIT, 1941-42, Rocket Project, Calif. Inst. Tech., 1942-45; staff mem. Mt. Wilson and Palomar Obs., Carnegie Instn. of Washington, Calif. Inst. Tech., Pasadena, 1946-80; dir. Mt. Wilson and Palomar Obs., 1964-78. Author sci. and tech. papers in profl. jours. Recipient USN Bur. Ordnance Devel. award, 1946, Draper medal NAS, 1957, Eddington medal Royal Astron. Soc., 1958, Bruce medal Astron. Soc. Pacific, 1969, Rank prize, 1993. Mem. NAS (councilor 1973-76), Royal Astron. Soc. (assoc.), Societé Royale des Sciences de Liege (corr. mem.), Am. Philos. Soc., Am. Acad. Arts and Scis., Am. Astron. Soc. (councilor 1956-58, Hale prize 1992), Astron. Soc. Pacific, Internat. Astron. Union. Home: 2189 N Altadena Dr Altadena CA 91001-3533 Office: Obs of Carnegie Instn Washington 813 Santa Barbara St Pasadena CA 91101-1232

BABCOCK, LEWIS THORNTON, judge; b. 1943. BA cum laude, U. Denver, 1965, JD, 1968; LLM, U. Va., 1968. Ptnr. Mitchell and Babcock, Rocky Ford, Colo., 1968-76; atty. City Las Animas, Colo., 1969-74, City Rocky Ford, 1970-76; asst. dist. atty. 11th Jud. Cir., La Junta, Colo., 1973-76, dist. judge, 1978-83; judge Colo. Ct. Appeals, 1983-88, U.S. Dist. Ct. Colo., Denver, 1988—; escrow and loan closing agt. FHA, Rocky Ford, 1973-76. Bd. dirs. Colo. Rural Legal Svcs. Inc., 1974-76. With Colo. N.G., 1968-74. Named to Order St. Ives. Mem. ABA, Colo. Bar Assn., Denver Bar Assn., Colo. Bar Found., North Ind. Dist. Bar Assn. Office: US Dist Ct 1929 Stout St Rm 246C Denver CO 80294-2900

BABEL, HENRY WOLFGANG, space station materials and processes manager; b. Chgo., Oct. 14, 1933; s. Willi Paul and Frieda Martha (Schultz) B.; m. Joyce Joan Smoda, Nov. 15, 1952(div. 1980); children: Lisa Leigh Babel Ruegg, Todd Henry, Kurt Allan, Karen Leigh Babel Espinoza, Paul Allen; m. Ryoko Nakagawa, Mar. 14, 1980; children: James Takashi, Michiko Lori. Student, Ill. Inst. Tech., 1951-52; BSME, U. Ill., 1955, MSME, 1957; PhD, Ohio State U., 1966. Asst. instr. U. Ill., Champaign-Urbana, 1955-57; metall. engr. Battelle Meml. Inst., Columbus, Ohio, 1957; instr. Ohio State U., Columbus, 1957-60; engring. mgr. McDonnell Douglas Astronautics, Huntington Beach, Calif., 1960—. Contbr. articles to profl. publs.; patentee in field. TV moderator, session organizer Major Econ. Issues Newport Found., Newport Beach, Calif., 1983—; pres. Home Owners Orgn., Huntington Beach, 1971-78, Homeowners Watch Program, Huntington Beach, 1977-78. Mem. Soc. Materials and Processes. Home: 6872 Loyola Dr Huntington Beach CA 92647-4054

BABINEC, GEORGE FREDERICK, bank executive; b. Bridgeport, Conn., Apr. 29, 1957; s. George and Jean Lois (Williams) B.; m. Janice Lynn Carlson, Oct. 25, 1982; children: Kathryn Jean, Margaret Ann, Todd Alfred. BA in Acctg., U. Bridgeport, Conn., 1979; postgrad., Ariz. State U., Tempe, 1987—; grad. bank adminstrn., U. Wis., 1988. CPA; chartered bank auditor, 1984; cert. internal auditor, 1986. Internal staff auditor Milton H. Friedberg, Smith and Co., CPA's, Bridgeport, 1978, People's Bank, Bridgeport, 1978-79; mgr. in audit dept. Union Trust Co., Stamford, Conn., 1980-83, Western Savs. and Loan Assn., Phoenix, 1983-90, Lincoln Savings, 1990-92; v.p., mgr. internal control Bank of Am., Phoenix, 1992—. Mem. Inst. Internal Auditors (bd. govs. Phoenix chpt. 1987—, pres. bd. govs. 1991-93), Bank Adminstrns. Inst. (v.p. Ariz. chpt. 1986-88, pres., bd. dirs. 1988-90). Republican. Episcopalian. Home: 4051 E Jicarilla St Phoenix AZ 85044-1501 Office: Bank of Am 1825 E Buckeye Rd Phoenix AZ 85034

BABST, DEAN VORIS, criminologist; b. Great Falls, Mont., Oct. 14, 1921; s. John H. and Amanda (Swanson) B.; m. Gail Wyone, Apr. 5, 1947; children: Beverly, Carol, Ronald, Gail. BA in Polit. Sci., U. Wash., 1947, MA in Sociology, 1950. Ops. analyst Johns Hopkins U., Chevy Chase, Md., 1952-53; social worker/county supr. Mont. State Dept. Pub. Welfare, 1954-56; statistician Mont. State Dept. Welfare, Helena, 1956-58; statis. analyst Wash. Dept. Welfare, Mental Health, Corrections, Olympia, 1958-61; social rsch. analyst for corrections Wis. Dept. Pub. Welfare, Madison, 1961-66; rsch. assoc. Joint Commn. on Correctional Manpower & Tng., Washington, 1966-67; rsch. scientist V Office of Drug Abuse Svcs., N.Y., 1967-77; cons. criminologist Am. Justice Inst., Sacramento, 1977-83; coordinator accidental war studies Nuclear Age Peace Found., Santa Barbara, Calif., 1983—; cons. in field. Reviewer Criminology, An Interdisciplinary Jour., 1977-80; contbr. articles to profl. jours.; patentee in field. With USAF, 1943-45. Mem. Arms Control Assn., Vets. for Peace, Ctr. for Def. Info., Internat. Physicians for Prevention of Nuclear War. Presbyterian. Home: 7915 Alma Mesa Way Citrus Heights CA 95610-3109 Office: Nuclear Age Peace Found Ste 123 1187 Coast Village Rd Santa Barbara CA 93108

BABULA, WILLIAM, university dean; b. Stamford, Conn., May 19, 1943; s. Benny F. and Lottie (Zajkowski) B.; m. Karen L. Gemi, June 19, 1965; children: Jared, Joelle. BA, Rutgers U., 1965; MA, U. Calif., Berkeley, 1967, PhD, 1969. Asst. prof. English U. Miami, Coral Gables, Fla., 1969-75; assoc. prof. U. Miami, Coral Gables, 1975-77, prof., 1977-81, chmn. dept. Eng., 1976-81; dean of arts and humanities Sonoma State U., Rohnert Park, Calif., 1981—. Author: Shakespeare and the Tragicomic Archetype, 1975, Shakespeare in Production, 1935-79, 1981; (short stories) Motorcycle, 1982, Quarterback Sneak, 1983, The First Edsel, 1983, Ransom, 1983, The Last Jogger in Virginia, 1983, The Orthodontist and the Rock Star, 1984, Greenearth, 1984, Football and Other Seasons, The Great American Basketball Shoot, 1984, Ms. Skywriter, Inc., 1987; (plays) The Fragging of Lt. Jones (1st prize Gualala Arts Competition, 1983), Creatures (1st prize Jacksonville U. competition 1987), The Winter of Mrs. Levy (Odyssey Stage Co., New Play Series 1988), Nat. Playwright's Showcase, 1988, Theatre Americana, 1990 (James Ellis award), Basketball Jones, Black Rep of Berkeley, 1988, West Coast Ensemble, Festival of One Acts, 1992, The Last Roundup, 1991 (Odyssey Stage Co.); (novels) The Bombing of Berkeley and Other Pranks (1st prize 24th Ann. Deep South Writers' Conf. 1984), St. John's Baptism, 1988, According to St. John, 1989, St. John and the Seven Veils, 1991; contbr. articles to profl. pubs. and short stories to lit. mags. Mem. Dramatists Guild, Authors League Am., Assoc. Writing Programs, Mystery Writers Am., Internat. Assn. Crime Writers, Phi Beta Kappa. Office: Sonoma State U Sch Arts and Humanities Rohnert Park CA 94928

BACA, JOSEPH FRANCIS, judge; b. Albuquerque, Oct. 1, 1936; s. Amado and Inez (Pino) B.; m. Dorothy Lee Burrow, June 28, 1969; children: Jolynn, Andrea, Anna Marie. BA in Edn., U. N.Mex., 1960; JD, George Washington U., 1964; LLM, U. Va., 1992. Asst. dist. atty. 1st Jud. Dist., Santa Fe, 1965-66; pvt. practice Albuquerque, 1966-72; dist. judge 2d Jud. Dist., Albuquerque, 1972-88; justice N.Mex. Supreme Ct., Santa Fe, 1989—; spl. asst. to atty. gen. Office of N.Mex. Atty. Gen., Albuquerque, 1966-71. Dem. precinct chmn., Albuquerque, 1968; del. N.Mex. Constl. Conv., Santa Fe, 1969. Recipient Judge of Yr. award Peoples Commn. for Criminal Justice, 1989, Quincentennial Commemoration Achievement award La Hispanidad Com., 1992. Mem. ABA (Recognition and Achievement Award 1992, commn. on Opportunities for Minorities in the Profession), Hispanic Nat. Bar Assn., N.Mex. Bar Assn., Albuquerque Bar Assn., U. N.Mex. Alumni Assn. (pres. 1980-81, Erna S. Ferguson Outstanding Alumnus award, Albuquerque chpt. 1990), Kiwanis (pres. Albuquerque chpt. 1984-85), KC (dep. grand knight 1968). Roman Catholic. Office: Supreme Ct NMex PO Box 848 Santa Fe NM 87504-0848

BACA, M. CARLOTA, grants administrator; b. Washington, Mar. 27, 1943; d. Fermin I. and Dixie (Sapp) B.; m. Ira S. Cohen, June 16, 1984 (dec. Dec., 1992). BA, U. N.Mex., 1966, MA, 1968; PhD, U. So. Calif., L.A., 1973. Instr. U. So. Calif., L.A., 1968-73; asst. provost SUNY, Buffalo, 1973-75, asst. to exec. v.p., 1975-80, asst. for internat. affairs, 1976-83, asst. to pres., 1980-83; dir. acad. liaison Coun. for Internat. Exchange of Scholars, Washington, 1984-90. Editor: Professional Ethics in University Adminstration, 1981, Ethical Principles in Higher Education, 1983, (jour.) The Fulbright Experience, 1986. Bd. dirs. Resource Theatre Co., Inc., Santa Fe, 1990—, Coun. on Internat. Rels., Santa Fe, 1991—, Santa Fe Community Found., 1993—. Named ACE fellow Am. Coun. on Edn., Washington, 1975-76; recipient cert. appreciation U.S. Info. Agy., Washington, 1989, Am. Studies Assn., Washington, 1989. Mem. The Nature Conservancy, Sierra Club, Wilderness Soc. Home: 686 La Viveza Ct Santa Fe NM 87501

BACA, PAUL ANTHONY, automobile dealership financial administrator; b. Belen, N.Mex., June 4, 1965; s. LeRoy O. and Sylvia (Sachs) B.; m. Loretta A. Gomez, Aug. 9, 1965. Bus. mgr. Baca Auto Sales, Inc., Belen, 1984—; owner U-Save Auto Rental Franchise; active implementation of Lodgers Tax Fund, Belen; bd. dirs. First Nat. Bank of Belen. Vice pres. U. N.Mex. BAS Bd., Belen, 1989; v.p. Belen Harvey House, 1989. Mem. Greater Belen C. of C. (pres. 1991), Rotary Cub (bd. dirs. 1991-92). Democrat. Christian. Home: 1613 Velta Dr Belen NM 87002 Office: Baca Auto Sales Inc 1301 S Main St Belen NM 87002

BACCIGALUPPI, ROGER JOHN, agricultural company executive; b. N.Y.C., Mar. 17, 1934; s. Harry and Ethel (Hutcheon) B.; m. Patricia Marie Wier, Feb. 6, 1960 (div. 1978); children: John, Elisabeth, Andrea; m. Iris Christine Walfridson, Feb. 3, 1979; 1 child, Jason. B.S., U. Calif., Berkeley, 1956; M.S., Columbia U., 1957. Asst. sales promotion mgr. Maco Mag. Corp., N.Y.C., 1956-57; merchandising asst. Honig, Cooper & Harrington, San Francisco and L.A., 1957-58, 1958-60; asst. dir. merchandising Honig, Cooper & Harrington, 1960-61; sales rep. Blue Diamond Growers (formerly Calif. Almond Growers Exch.), Sacramento, 1961-64, mgr. advt. and sales promotion, 1964-70; v.p. mktg. Blue Diamond Growers (formerly Calif. Almond Growers Exch.), 1970-73, sr. v.p. mktg., 1973-74, exec. v.p., 1974-75, pres., 1975-91; founder RB Internat, Sacramento, 1992—; bd. dirs. Nat. Coun. Farmer Coops., Grocery Mfrs. Am., Inc.; vice chmn., bd. dirs. Agrl. Coun. Calif., 1975-91; mem. consumer-producer com., adminstrn. com.; mem. U.S. adv. com. TRADE Policy and Negotiations, 1983—, U.S. adv. bd. Rabobank Nederlands, 1988-91; bd. dirs. Mad Rover Records, Inc.; mem. adv. coun. Nat. Ctr. for Food and Agriculture Policy Resources for Future, 1990—. Vice chmn. Calif. State R.R. Mus. Found.; active Los Rios Community Coll. Found.; mem. dean's adv. coun. U. Calif., Davis; vice chmn. Grad. Inst. Cooperative Leadership, 1986-87, chair, 1987-89. With AUS, 1957. Mem. Calif. C. of C. (chmn. internat. trade com. 1988—, bd. dirs. 1988—, vice chmn. bd. 1992—, Sacramento Host Com. 1987—), Calif. for Higher Edn., Grad. Inst. Coop. Leadership (chmn., trustee), Grocery Mfrs. Am., Inc. (bd. dirs. 1988-91), Sutter Club, Del Paso Country Club. Office: RB Internat 455 University Ave Ste 100 Sacramento CA 95825

BACCUS, JANET GLEE, genealogist, educator, community volunteer; b. Roy, Wash., Mar. 27, 1933; d. George Robert and Kathleen Madge (Hall) Nixon; m. Dwaine Curtiss Baccus, June 9, 1951; children: Richard D., James L., Ronald G. Grad., Roy High Sch., 1951. Lectr. genealogy orgns., Wash., Alaska, 1985—; tchr. genealogy courses. Author (family history) Ancestors and Descendants of George William Nixon 1848-1926, 1977; contbr. articles to geneal. publs. Panel mem. Community Youth Coun./Diversion Ct., Pierce County, Wash., 1975-77; Dem. precinct com. person, 1975-79, 88—; mem. local and state Ext. Homemaker orgn., 1964—; leader Cub Scouts Am., Boy Scouts Am., 1965-72; vol. Good Samaritan Hosp., 1990—. Mem. Tacoma-Pierce County Geneal. Soc. (pres. 1980, projects chmn. 1978—), Wash. State Geneal. Soc. (charter, charter sec. 1983-85), Coun. Genealogy Columnists (charter, Hon. Mention 1988). Evangelical Lutheran. Home and Office: Baccus Geneal Rsch 5817 144th St E Puyallup WA 98373-5221

BACH, MARTIN WAYNE, stockbroker, owner antique clock stores; b. Milw., Mar. 30, 1940; s. Jack Baer and Rose (Weiss) B.; m. Roberta Sklar, Aug. 19, 1962; children: David Louis, Emily Elizabeth. BA, U. Wis., 1963. Stockbroker J. Barth & Co., Oakland, Calif., 1966-72, v.p., 1970-72; sr. v.p., stockbroker Dean Witter & Co., Oakland, 1972—; founder The TimePeace, Carmel, Calif., 1972-83, San Francisco, 1975-83, La Jolla, 1977-83; instr. fin. San Leandro, Lafayette and Hayward (Calif.) Adult Sch., 1970—. Chmn. bd. dirs. Diablo Light Opera Co., 1985-87; bd. dirs. East Bay Hosp., 1985-90. 1st lt. U.S. Army, 1963-65. Mem. Calif. Thoroughbred Breeders Assn., Calif. Thoroughbred Assn., Nat. Assn. Clock and Watch Collectors, Am. Horse Coun., East Bay Brokers Club, Moraga Country Club, Dean Witter Chairmen's Club, B'nai B'rith. Home: 180 Sandringham S Moraga CA 94556-1931 Office: 1 Kaiser Pla Ste 1950 Oakland CA 94556

BACHER, ROSALIE WRIDE, educational administrator; b. L.A., May 25, 1925; d. Homer M. and Reine (Rogers) Wride; m. Archie O. Bacher, Jr., Mar. 30, 1963. AB, Occidental Coll., 1947, MA, 1949. Tchr. English, Latin, history David Starr Jordan High Sch., Long Beach, Calif., 1949-55, counselor, 1955-65; counselor Lakewood (Calif.) Sr. High Sch., Long Beach, 1965-66; rsch. asst., counselor Poly. High Sch., Long Beach, 1966-67; counselor, office occupational preparation, vocat. guidance sect. Long Beach Unified School Dist., Long Beach, 1967-68; vice prin. Washington Jr. High Sch., Long Beach, 1968-70; asst. prin. Lakewood Sr. High Sch., Long Beach, spring 1970; vice prin. Marshall Jr. High Sch., Long Beach, 1981-87, 1981-87; vice prin. Lindbergh Jr. High Sch., Long Beach, 1987—; counselor Millikan High Sch., Calif., 1988—, Hill Jr. High Sch., Calif., 1988-89; ret. Hill Jr. High Sch., 1989; chmn. vocat. guidance steering com. Long Beach Unified Sch. Dist., 1963—. Philanthropy com. Palos Verdes Women's Club. docent coun. sec. Palos Verdes Art Ctr., 1991-93, leader TOPS CA 471, 1992-93. Mem. AAUW, Internat. Platform Assn., Long Beach Pers. and Guidance Assn. (dir. 1958-60), Long Beach Sch. Counselors Assn. (sec. high sch. segment 1963-64), Phi Beta Kappa, Delta Kappa Gamma (pres. Delta Psi chpt., area dir.; Calif. profl. affairs com. chmn. 1972-74), Phi Delta Gamma (pres. chpt. 1977-78, 87-90, nat. chmn. bylaws com. 1980-91, 87-90, Nat. conv. com. 1987-88, nat. nominating com. 1989), Pi Lambda Theta (pres. chpt. 1974-76, v.p. So. Calif. coun. 1974-76, sec. 1991—), Phi Delta Kappa (sec. Long Beach chpt. 1977-80). Home: 265 Rocky Point Rd Palos Verdes Peninsula CA 90274-2621 also: 17721 Misty Ln Huntington Beach CA 92649

BACHMAN, BRIAN RICHARD, electronics executive; b. Aurora, Ill., Jan. 14, 1945. BS, U. Ill., 1967; MBA, U. Chgo., 1969. With Gen. Electric, Syracuse, N.Y., 1982-85; bus. dir. TRW, Schaumburg, Ill., 1985-87; pres. Gen. Semiconductor Industries, Tempe, Ariz., 1987-90; group gen. mgr. ITT Cannon, Santa Ana, Calif., 1990-91; v.p., group gen. mgr. Philips Semiconductor, Sunnyvale, Calif., 1991—. Office: Philips Semiconductors 811 E Argues Sunnyvale CA 94088

BACHTEL, ANN ELIZABETH, educational consultant, researcher, educator; b. Winnipeg, Man., Can., Dec. 12, 1928; d. John Wills and Margaret Agnes (Gray) Macleod; m. Richard Earl Bachtel, Dec. 19, 1947 (div.); children: Margaret Ann, John Macleod, Bradley Wills; m. Louis Philip Nash, June 30, 1978 (dec. 1987). AB, Occidental Coll., 1947; MA, Calif. State U.-L.A., 1976; PhD, U. So. Calif., 1988. Cert. life tchr., adminstr., Calif. Elem. tchr. pub. and pvt. schs. in Calif., 1947-50, 64-77; dir. Emergency Sch. Aid Act program, spl. projects, spl. arts State of Calif., 1977-80; leader, mem. program rev. team Calif. State Dept. Edn., 1981—; cons. Pasadena Unified Sch. Dist., 1981—; teaching asst., adj. prof. U. So. Calif.; cons. sch. dists., state depts. internat. edn.; presenter workshops/seminars; mem. legis. task forces. Chmn. resource allocation com. City of Pasadena, 1982-90, Pasadena-Mishima (Japan) Sister Cities Internat. Com., 1983-87; asst. chair Pasadena-Jarvenpaa, Finland, 1990-92, chair, 1992—; mem. L.A. World Affairs Coun., Bonita Unified Sch. Dist. Curriculum Coun., 1990, Dist. Task Force Fine Arts, 1990, Dist. Task Force Tech., 1990, Dist. Handwriting Task Force, 1993; docent coun. Pasadena Hist. Soc., Pasadena Philharm. Com., Women's Com. Pasadena Symphony Assn.; deacon Pasadena Presbyn. Ch., 1989-92. Emergency Sch. Aid Act grantee, 1977-81. Named to Hall of Fame Bonita Unified Sch. Dist., 1990-91. Mem. ASCD, World Coun. Gifted and Talented Children, Internat. Soc. Edn. Through Art, Coun. Exceptional Children, Am. Ednl. Rsch. Assn., Nat. Art Educators Assn. (dels. assembly 1988—), Calif. Art Educators Assn., Calif. Humanities Edn. Assn., Clan MacLeod Soc. (bd. dirs. So. Calif. chpt.), Phi Delta Kappa, Kappa Delta Pi, Pi Lambda Theta (Ella Victoria Dobbs Nat. award 1989, pres. L.A chpt. 1991—, nat. rsch. awards com. 1989-91, chair 1993-93), Assistance League of Pasadena. Contbr. articles to publs.; writer/editor: Arts for the Gifted and Talented, 1981; author Nat. Directory of Programs for Artistically Gifted and Talented Students, K-12.

BACHUS, BENSON FLOYD, mechanical engineer, consultant; b. LeRoy, Kans., Aug. 10, 1917; s. Perry Claude and Eva Marie (Benson) B.; m. Ruth Elizabeth Beck, May 31, 1942; children: Carol Jean Schueler, Bruce Floyd, Linda Ruth Gadway. Degree, Hemphill Diesel Sch., Chgo., 1937; student, Sterling Coll., 1937-39; BSME, Kans. State U., 1942; postgrad., Ohio State U., 1961, Stevens Inst., 1964; MBA, Creighton U., 1967. Registered profl. engr., Ariz., Ill., Nebr. Researcher, mech. engr. Naval Ordnance Rsch. Lab., Washington, 1942-43; jr. product engr. Western Electric Co., Inc., Chgo. and Eau Claire, Wis., 1944-46; sr. devel. engr. Western Electric Co., Inc., Chgo., 1946-56; devel. engr. Western Electric Co., Inc., Omaha, 1960-66; product engr. mgr. Century Electronics and Instruments, Inc., Tulsa, Okla., 1956-60; sr. staff engr. Western Electric Co. div. AT&T Techs., Phoenix, 1966-85; cons. in field, 1985-93; cons. in field, Phoenix, 1985—; chmn. energy conservation AT&T Techs., Inc., 1973-85; advisor to student engrs. Ariz. State U., 1967-87. Patentee in field. Trustee, Village of Westchester (Ill.), 1949-53; sec.-treas. Westchester Broadview Water Commn., 1949-53; Sunday Sch. supr. Westchester Community Ch., 1949-56; vol. campaign worker, precint committeeman Phoenix Rep. Party, 1986—. Named Westchester Family of Yr., Westchester Community Ch., 1952; recipient Centennial medal Am. Soc. Engrs., 1979. Fellow ASME (state legis. coord. 1985-86, 88-93, treas. Ariz. sect. 1971-72, sec. 1972-73, vice chmn. 1973-74, chmn. 1974-75, 50-Yr. Membership award, President's Dedicated Svc., Devotion, Leadership, Performance award 1992, Dedicated Svc. award 1993); mem. TAPPI, NSPE (Engr. of Yr. award 1979), Soc. Profl. Engrs. (editor mag. 1972-86), Ariz. Coun. Engring. and Sci. Assn., Am. Security Coun., Soc. Plastics Engrs., Weoma Sci. Club (pres. 1963-66), Tel. Pioneers Am., Order of Engrs., Elks. Home and Office: 5229 N 43d St Phoenix AZ 85018

BACIGALUPA, ANDREA, art gallery owner, writer, artist; b. Balt., May 26, 1923; s. Andrew Leo and Maria Laura (Merolla) B.; m. Ellen Wilcox Williams, Oct. 9, 1952; children: Gian Andrea, Pier Francesca, Ruan Saire, Chiara Domenica, Daria Concessa. BFA, Md. Inst. of Fine Arts, 1950; postgrad., Accademia di Belli Arti, Florence, Italy, 1950-51. Owner The Studio of Gian Andrea, Santa Fe, 1954—; cons. on interior sacred art and ch. design Diocese of Amarillo, Tex., 1974—, St. Thomas More Ch., Manhattan, Kans., 1987-90, Our Lady of the Rosary Ch., Albuquerque, 1990-92. Author: Journal of Itinerant Artist, 1977, A Good and Perfect Gift, 1978, Song of Guadalupana, 1979, Franco and Pirata, 1985, (column) The Santa Fe Reporter, 1989-92. Sgt. U.S. Army, 1943-46, ETO. Recipient 1st Prize City of Santa Fe, 1980. Mem. AIA (1st Prize 1975). Roman Catholic.

BACKE, PAMELA RENEE, casino executive; b. Marinette, Wis., Dec. 25, 1955; d. Wilbur Milton and Eulalia Ellen (Johnson) Mandigo; m. Stephen Allen Backe, June 15, 1974. AA, Truckee Meadows Community Coll., 1981, AAS in Data Processing, 1982; BS in Info. Systems, U. Nev., 1987; MBA, Pepperdine U., 1991. Proof operator Bank of Am., Watsonville, Calif., 1973-76; adminstrv. asst. Truckee Meadows Christian Ctr., Reno, 1976-82; mgr. info. systems Sierra Office Concepts, Reno, 1982-84; auditor electronic data processing Harrah's, No. Nev., 1984-86, sr. auditor electronic data processing, 1986-87, mgr. internal audit, 1987-88, mgr. strategic mktg. projects, 1988-90, svc. mktg. dir., 1990-92; slot svcs. mgr. Harrah's, Reno, 1992—. Mem. Am. Mktg. Assn. Republican. Club: Silver State Striders. Home: 12980 Broili Dr Reno NV 89511-9234 Office: Harrah's 300 E 2d St Reno NV 89502

BACKER, BRUCE EVERETT, trade show exhibit design, manufacturing executive; b. L.A., June 1, 1955; s. Thomas Griffin and Beverly Ann (Ulsh) B.; m. Vanessa Raffi Marootian, July 21, 1979; 1 child, Evan Everett. BS in Indsl. Design, San Jose State U., 1981. Constrn. inspector, various cities, Calif., 1974-77; designer Exhibits of Calif., Palo Alto, 1977-80; design cons. Giltspur Exhibits, San Francisco, 1980-81; sr. designer Dimensional Coordinates, Inc., San Diego, 1981-82; founder, chief exec. officer Exponents Inc., San Diego, 1982—. Inventor and patentee in field; designer of numerous exhibits. Office: Exponents Inc 3290 Kurtz St San Diego CA 92110-4426

BACKHAUS, RALPH ANDREW, botany educator, researcher; b. Elizabeth, N.J., Jan. 12, 1951; s. Rolf Richard and Suzanne (Sladek) B.; m. Balbir Singh Takher, Mar. 12, 1983; children: Jaclyn, Benjamin. BS, Rutgers U., 1973; MS, U. Calif., Davis, 1975, PhD, 1977. Asst. prof. div. agr. Ariz. State U., Tempe, 1977-82, assoc. prof., 1982-87, prof., 1987-88, prof. dept. botany, 1988—; rsch. scientist Western Regional Rsch. Lab., USDA, Albany, Calif., 1990. Mem. Am. Soc. for Advancement of Sci., Am. Soc. Plant Physiology, Am. Soc. Hort. Sci. Office: Ariz State U Dept Botany Tempe AZ 85287

BACKUS, CHARLES EDWARD, engineering educator, researcher; b. Wadestown, W.Va., Sept. 17, 1937; s. Clyde Harvey and Opal Daisy (Strader) B.; m. Judith Ann Clouston, Sept. 1, 1957; children: David, Elizabeth, Amy. B.S. in Mech. Engring., Ohio U., 1959; M.S., U. Ariz.-Tucson, 1961, Ph.D., 1965. Supr., system engr. Westinghouse Astronuclear, Pitts., 1965-68; asst. prof. engring. Ariz. State U., Tempe, 1968-71, assoc. prof., 1971-76, prof., 1976—, asst. dean research, 1979-90, assoc. dean research, 1990-91, dir. Ctr. for Research, 1980-91, interim dean Coll. Engring. and Applied Sci., 1991-92, assoc. dean Indsl. and Profl. Devel., 1992—. Contbr. chpts. to books, articles to profl. jours. Mem. Ariz. Solar Energy Commn., Phoenix, 1975-87. Fellow IEEE; mem. AAAS, Am. Nuclear Soc., ASME, Am. Soc. Engring. Edn., Mesa C. of C., Sigma Xi, Phi Mu Epsilon, Tau Beta Pi. Methodist. Lodge: Rotary. Office: Ariz State U Coll Engring & Applied Sci Ctr Rsch Tempe AZ 85287-5506

BACON, LEONARD ANTHONY, accounting educator; b. Santa Fe, June 10, 1931; s. Manuel R. and Maria (Chavez) Baca; m. Patricia Balzaretti; children—Bernadine M., Jerry A., Tiffany A. B.E., U. Nebr.-Omaha, 1965; M.B.A., U. of the Americas, Mexico City, 1969; Ph.D., U. Miss., 1971. CPA; cert. mgmt. acct., internal auditor. Commd. 2d lt. U.S. Army, 1951, advanced through grades to maj., 1964, served fin. and acctg. officer mainly Korea, Vietnam; ret., 1966; asst. prof. Delta State U., Cleveland, Miss., 1971-76; assoc. prof. West Tex. State U., Canyon, 1976-79; prof. acctg. Calif. State U., Bakersfield, 1979—; cons. Kershen Co. (now Atlantic Richfield Oil Co.), Canyon, 1979-80. Contbr. articles to profl. jours. U.S., Mex., Can., papers to profl. confs. Leader Delta area Boy Scouts Am., Cleveland, 1971-76; dir. United Campus Ministry, Canyon, 1976-79; min. Kern Youth Facility, Bakersfield, 1983—, Christians in Commerce, 1990—. Paratrooper Brazilian Army, 1955. Mem. Am. Acctg. Assn., Am. Inst. CPA's, Am. Assn. Spanish Speaking CPA's, Inst. Mgmt. Accts. (pres. Bakersfield chpt. 1981-82, Most Valuable Mem. award 1981), Am. Mgmt. Assn., Inst. Mgmt. Acctg., Calif. Faculty Assn., Acad. Internat. Bus., Inst. Internal Auditors, Inst. Cost Estimators and Analysts, Alpha Kappa Psi (Dedicated Service award 1979), Omicron Delta Epsilon, Beta Gamma Sigma. Clubs: Jockey (Rio de Janeiro).

Lodges: Lions (v.p. Cleveland 1971-73), Kiwanis (v.p. 1974-79, A Whale of a Guy award, Cleveland 1975). Office: Calif State U 9001 Stockdale Hwy Bakersfield CA 93311-1022

BACON, PAUL CALDWELL, training system company executive, aviation consultant, engineering test pilot; b. Camp Lejeune, N.C., Oct. 8, 1945; s. Franklin Camp and Marjorie Edna (Caldwell) B.; m. Carol Wetherell, June 7, 1967 (div. Oct. 1974); 1 child, Paul Caldwell Jr.; m. Martha Jean Court, Feb. 2, 1986; 1 child, Catherine Caldwell Bacon. BS in Aerospace Engring., U.S. Naval Acad., 1967; MS in Aerospace Engring., U.S. Air Force Test Pilot Sch., 1976; MS in Systems Mgmt., U. So. Calif., 1979. Commd. 2nd lt. USMC, 1967, advanced through grades to maj., 1978, ret., 1980; advanced through grades to lt. col. USMCR, 1980—; fighter pilot, maintenance mgr. USMC, Beaufort, S.C., 1969-70, Danang, Republic of Vietnam, 1970-71, Kaneohe, Hawaii, 1971-73; advanced flight instr. USMC, Meridian, Miss., 1973-75; exptl. test pilot 1st F18 USMC, Patuxent River, Md., 1977-80; engring. test pilot United Airlines, Denver, 1980-84; dir. systems implementation United Airlines Svcs. Corp., Lakewood, Colo., 1984-86; dir. product assurance, chief pilot United Airlines Svcs. Corp., Lakewood, 1986-90; mgr., tng. systems mktg. Hughes Aircraft Co., Manhattan Beach, Calif., 1990-91; program mgr. tng. systems Rockwell Internat., L.A., 1991—; cons. Nat. Traffic Safety Bd., FAA, NASA, USAF, Australian Aviation Agy., Time-Life Books, aircraft simulator mfrs., 1980—; info. officer U.S. Naval Acad., Denver. Decorated Air medal. Mem. Soc. Exptl. Text Pilots, Nat. Mgmt. Assn., U. So. Calif. Alumni Assn., U.S. Naval Acad. Alumni Assn., Hornet 100 Club. Republican. Presbyterian. Home: 331 Via El Chico Redondo Beach CA 90277-6608 Office: Rockwell Internat NAm Aircraft 201 Douglas St Los Angeles CA 90026-5630

BACON, RANDALL CLYDE, city official; b. Youngstown, Ohio, Oct. 2, 1937; s. Arthur and Audrey E. (Gross) B.; m. Mildred V. Rand, Jan. 1961 (div. Nov. 1968); children: Randy, Keith, Kevin. AA, L.A. City Coll., 1958; BS, Calif. State U., L.A., 1962; postgrad., U. So. Calif., 1962-64. Acct. County of Los Angeles, L.A., 1956-62, head acct., 1962-65, fiscal officer, 1965-68, chief dep. dir. parks and recreation, 1968-74, asst. div. chmn., chief adminstrv. officer, 1975-79; asst. chief adminstrv. officer County of San Diego, San Diego, 1979-81, dir. social svcs., 1981-87, dep. chief adminstrv. officer, 1987-88; gen. mgr. City of L.A., 1988—. Bdd. dirs. Afro-Am. Achievers Network, L.A., 1989-92, ARC, L.A., 1992. Recipient community svc. award Pan-Hellenic Coun., L.A., 1988. Mem. Am. Soc. Pub. Adminstrs. (v.p. 1992, Pub. Svc. award 1987), Western Govt. Rsch. Assn., Natt. Forum for Black Pub. Adminstrs. (pres. 1993—, achievement award 1990), Calif. State U. Alumni Assn. (life), Kappa Alpha Psi (nat. pres. 1985-88, achievement award 1979), Kappa Found. (pres. 1992—). Democrat. Methodist. Office: City of LA 200 N Main St Los Angeles CA 90012

BACON, VICKY LEE, lighting services executive; b. Oregon City, Oreg., Mar. 25, 1950; d. Herbert Kenneth and Lorean Betty (Boltz) Rushford; m. Dennis M. Bacon, Aug. 7, 1971; 1 child, Randene Tess. Student, Portland Community Coll., 1974-75, Mt. Hood Community Coll., 1976, Portland State Coll., 1979. With All Electric Constrn., Milwaukie, Oreg., 1968-70, Lighting Maintenance Co., Portland, Oreg., 1970-78; svc. mgr. GTE Sylvania Lighting Svcs., Portland, 1978-80, br. mgr., 1980-83; div. mgr. Christenson Electric Co. Inc., Portland, 1983-90, v.p. mktg. and lighting svcs., 1990-91, v.p. svc. ops. and mktg., 1991—. Mem. Illuminating Engring. Soc., Nat. Assn. Lighting Maintenance Contractors. Office: Christenson Electric Co Inc 111 SW Columbia St Ste 480 Portland OR 97201-5886

BACON, WALLACE ALGER, emeritus speech communications educator, author; b. Bad Axe, Mich., Jan. 27, 1914; s. Russell Alger and Mana (Wallace) B. A.B., Albion Coll., 1935, Litt. D., 1967; A.M., U. Mich., 1936, Ph.D., 1940; LL.D., Emerson Coll., 1975. Instr. English U. Mich., 1941-47; chmn. dept. interpretation Northwestern U., Evanston, Ill., 1947-79; asst. prof. English and speech Northwestern U., 1947-50, assoc. prof. English and speech, 1950-55, prof. speech, 1955-80, prof. emeritus, 1980—; Fulbright lectr., Philippines, 1961-62, Fulbright-Hays lectr., 1964-65; vis. prof. U. Calif.-Berkeley, U. Wash., Nihon U., Tokyo, U. N.C., Chapel Hill, N.Mex. State U., U. Philippines, Santo Tomas U., Philippines; mem. adv. bd. Inst. for Readers Theatre, 1974-85; mem. adv. bd. Harwood Found. of U. N.Mex., 1982-91, pres., 1984-87, 90-91, v.p. 1988-89. Author: verse play Savonarola, 1950 (Bishop Sheil award 1946), William Warner's Syrinx, 1950, (with Robert S. Breen) Literature as Experience, 1959, Literature for Interpretation, 1961, (with N. Crame-Rogers and C. V. Fonacier) Spoken English, 1962, (with C.V. Fonacier) The Art of Oral Interpretation, 1965; The Art of Interpretation, 1966, 3d edit., 1979, Oral Interpretation and the Teaching of Literature in Secondary Schools, 1974, also articles, poetry, monographs.; editor: Festschrift for Isabel Crouch: Essays on the Theory, Practice and Criticism of Performance, 1988; assoc. editor: Performance of Literature in Historical Perspectives, 1983; editor Text and Performance Quar., 1989-91, assoc. editor, 1992-94; assoc. editor Quar. Jour. Speech, 1957-59, 63-65, 75-77, Speech Monographs, 1966-71; adv. editor Lit. in Performance, 1980-82, assoc. editor, 1983-88. Served with AUS, 1942-46. Decorated Legion of Merit; Alfred Lloyd postdoctoral fellow U. Mich., 1940-41; Rockefeller fellow, 1948-49; Ford Found. fellow, 1954-55; recipient Hopwood Major award writing drama U. MIch., 1936; spl. citation U. Philippines, 1965, 70; spl. commendation Ednl. Found. Philippines, 1965; Disting. Alumnus award Albion Coll., 1986. Mem. Speech Communication Assn. (Golden Anniversary Prize Fund award 1965, 74, disting. service award 1983, awards com. 1967, 85, 2d v.p. 1975, 1st v.p. 1976, pres. 1977), Western States Communication Assn., Malone Soc., AAUP, Phi Beta Kappa, Delta Sigma Rho, Theta Alpha Phi, Zeta Phi Eta. Home: PO Box 2257 Taos NM 87571-2257

BADER, BARBARA CAROL JOANIS, research, consulting and training executive; b. Dowagiac, Mich., Jan. 17, 1945; d. Howard F. and M. Virginia (Collins) Joanis; 1 child, Scott Allen. BA with honors, Mich. State U., 1969; MSW, U. Mich., 1974, MA in Psychology, 1976, PhD in Community Psychology and Social Work, 1980. Pvt. practice psychotherapy Ann Arbor, Mich., 1970-82; asst. dir. Corrections Tng. Evaluation Rsch. Project, Ann Arbor, 1975-76; co-dir. Community Mental Health Rsch. Project, Detroit, 1976-77; faculty mem. Mental Health Exec. Devel. Project, Ann Arbor, 1978-81; dir. Monroe County Employer Labor Needs Study, Mich., 1982; founder, exec. dir. Community Systems, Bozeman, Mont., 1984—; founder, pres. Action Rsch. Assocs., Inc., Ann Arbor, 1977-83, Ctr. for Human Svcs. Rsch., Ann Arbor, 1977-83; clin. and rsch. intern Mental Health and Correction, Ann Arbor, 1973-75; rsch. assoc. Mont. State U., 1984; departmental assoc. Dept. Psychology U. Mich., 1978-80. Author, editor: Prevention in Mental Health, 1980, Board Leadership and Development: Enhancing the Effectiveness of Boards, Councils, and Committees, 1990, Get That Grant: Grantwriting From Conception to Completion, 1991, 5th edit., Planning: Essential Skills for Short-Range and Long-Range Strategic Planning, 1992, 3rd edit. V.p. bd. Citizens Adv. Coun. Ctr. for Forensic Psychiatry, Ypsilanti, Mich., 1978-82. C.E.W. scholar Ctr. for Continuing Edn. of Women, U. Mich., 1976-77; competitive grad. rsch. fellow U.S. Dept. Justice, 1977-78, Rackham Predoctoral fellow U. Mich., 1977-78, Rackham Grad. sch. Nontraditional fellow, 1975-76, fellow NIMH, 1974-75. Office: Community Systems PO Box 516 Bozeman MT 59771-0516

BADGLEY, JOHN ROY, architect; b. Huntington, W. Va., July 10, 1922; s. Roy Joseph and Fannie Myrtle (Limbaugh) B.; m. Janice Atwell, July 10, 1975; 1 son, Adam; children by previous marriage: Dan, Lisa, Holly, Marcus, Michael. AB, Occidental Coll., 1943; MArch, Harvard, 1949; postgrad., Centro Internazionale, Vincenza, Italy, 1959. Pvt. practice, San Luis Obispo, Calif., 1952-65; chief architect, planner Crocker Land Co., San Francisco, 1965-80; v.p. Cushman & Wakefield Inc., San Francisco, 1980-84; pvt. practice, San Rafael, Calif., 1984—; tchr. Calif. State U. at San Luis Obispo, 1952-65; bd. dirs. Ft. Mason Ctr., Angel Island Assn. Served with USCGR, 1942-46. Mem. AIA, Am. Arbitration Assn., Golden Gate Wine Soc. Home and Office: 1356 Idylberry Rd San Rafael CA 94903-1074

BADGLEY, JUDETH BIRDWELL, motivational learning consultant; b. Cheyenne, Wyo., Dec. 29, 1954; d. Weldon James and Patricia (Finnerty) Birdwell; m. Michael Benedict Badgley, Oct. 7, 1983; children: Sara Pat, Brian, Mark. BA in Edn., U. Mont., 1979; MA in Edn. Adminstrn., No. Ariz. U., 1986. Tchr. Crane Sch. Dist., Yuma, Ariz., 1979-86; adminstrv. intern Crane Sch. Dist., 1986-87; owner/cons. Success Express, Yuma, 1986—; prin. summer sch. Crane Sch. Dist., 1989; guest lectr. in field; instr. No. Ariz. U., Flagstaff, 1989—. Author: Teaching with Style, 1990, I'm Positive: Building Self-Esteem, 1987, It's About Time, 1989, Discipline with Dignity and Self Respect, 1990, Handling the Gulf War Crisis on the Homefront, 1991, S.T.E.P.S. Toward Success, 1992. Chmn. City of Yuma Task Force, 1990—; chmn. com. United Way, Yuma, 1988-90; mem. Friends of the Ballet, 1986—; coord. Girl Scouts U.S., Yuma, 1979-91. Mem. Assn. Supervision and Curriculum Devel., Nat. Staff Devel. Coun., Ariz. Sch. Adminstrs. Roman Catholic. Home: 1239 S 40th Dr Yuma AZ 85364-4079

BADHAM, ROBERT E., former congressman; b. Los Angeles, June 9, 1929; s. Byron J. and Bess (Kissinger) B.; m. Anne Carroll; children: Sharron, Robert, William, Phyllis, Jennifer Stewart. A.B., Stanford U., 1951. V.p., dir. Hoffman Hardware Co., L.A., 1955-69; mem. Calif. Assembly from 71st Dist., 1962-76, 95th-100th Congresses from 40th Calif. Dist., 1977-89; pres. The Badham Group, Polit. Cons., Sacramento, 1989—, Robert E. Badham Assocs., Govt. Rels., Newport Beach, Calif., 1989—. Author articles. Del. So. Pacific Dist. conv. Am. Luth. Ch., 1967, Nat. conv., 1968, bd. dirs. ch. com., Newport Harbor area; alt. del. Rep. Nat. Conv., 1964-68, del., 1980, 84, 88; mem. Calif. Rep. Central Com., 1962-88, Orange County Rep. Cen. Com., 1962-88. Lt. (j.g.) USNR, 1951-54. Mem. Am. Soc. Archtl. Hardware Cons., Orange Coast Assn., Am. Legion, NRA, Phi Gamma Delta. Office: 881 Dover Dr Ste 14 Newport Beach CA 92663-5979

BADISH, KENNETH MICHAEL, film executive; b. Baldwin, N.Y., Dec. 30, 1951; s. Alan W. and Adele Y. (Goodman) B.; m. Laurie Jean Halloway, May 1, 1985. BA in Psychology, U. Pa., 1973. Media dir. Benton & Bowles Inc., N.Y.C., 1973-77; dir. film acquisition Home Box Office, N.Y.C., 1978-81; pres., chief exec. officer Moviestore Entertainment, L.A., 1981—; educator UCLA, L.A., 1986-87. Office: Moviestore Entertainment Ste 1850 11111 Santa Monica Blvd Los Angeles CA 90025

BADOYEN, DEAN ANDREW, financial planner; b. Wailuku, Hawaii, Nov. 20, 1968; s. Andrew and Norma Ann (Ganialongo) B. BS, Boston Coll., 1990. Personal fin. planner IDS Fin. Svcs., Inc., Wailuku, 1990—; owner Access Cons., 1992—, Da Bruddah's Restaurant, 1993—; pres. Maui Sportcard Investments, Wailuku, 1991—. Group facilitator Alternatives to Violence, Wailuku, 1991—. Mem. Internat. Assn. Fin. Planning (practioner 1993—), Lotus Ltd., Hawaii Vintage Card Collectors Group. Office: IDS Fin Svcs Inc 1883 Wili Pa Lp # 2 Wailuku HI 96793

BADSTUEBNER, HANS ALEXANDER, electric company executive; b. Berlin, Feb. 26, 1916; came to U.S. 1960; s. Alexander and Emilie (Luechters) B.; m. Vera Ott, Jan. 9, 1939; 1 son, Stefan. Grad. E.E., Berlin, 1938, PhD, 1972. Asst. to gen. mgr. research, devel. depts. Telefunken G.M.B.H., Leubus and Berlin, 1942-45; con. efficiency engring. Berlin, 1945-52; owner Elba Electric Co., Burnaby, B.C., Can., 1952-60; v.p. prodn. engring. R.M. Hadley Co., Inc., L.A., 1960-64; sr. v.p. engring. Baum Electric Co., Inc., Garden Grove, Calif., 1964—; owner Hansera Co., Fullerton, Calif., 1969—; cons. Foster-Mathews Electric Co., 1981—. Inventor in various fields. Mem. Soc. Plastic Engrs., Am. Mensa Selection Agy., Triple Nine Soc., Cincinnatus High IQ Soc., Minerva High IQ Soc., Masons, Shriners. Home: 17222 Fern Ridge Rd SE Stayton OR 97383-9634

BAEHR, KARL JOSEPH, broadcasting executive; b. San Bernardino, Calif., Jan. 29, 1959. BA in Radio/TV/Film, Stephen F. Austin State U., Nacogdoches, Tex., 1981; postgrad., U. N.Mex., 1992—. News dir. Sta. KSKS FM, Houston, 1981-82; music dir. "Y99" Sta. KEYP FM, Tyler, Tex., 1982-85; program dir. Sta. KIVA FM, Albuquerque, 1985-87; West Coast regional mgr. Drake/Chenault, Albuquerque, 1987-88; program dir. Sta. KFMG FM, Albuquerque, 1988-89; pres. KBE "Broadcasting by Design", Albuquerque, 1989—; cons. Southwestern Entertainment Group, Lubbock, Tex., 1990—, Radio Tropico Internacional, 1990, Actual Radio Measurement, Albuquerque, "Addictions" Talk Show, Detroit, 1991-92. Author mag. column Uplink, 1992. Office: KBE Broadcasting By Design 8116 San Francisco NE Albuquerque NM 87109

BAENDER, MARGARET WOODRUFF, free-lance writer; b. Salt Lake City, Apr. 1, 1921; d. Russell Kimball and Margaret Angline (McIntyre) Woodruff; m. Phillip Albers Baender, Aug. 17, 1946 (dec.); children: Kristine Lynn, Charlene Anne, Michael Phillip, Russell Richard. BA, U. Utah, 1944. In clerical, personnel work various firms, San Francisco Bay area, 1970-75; reporter, columnist Valley Pioneer, Danville, Calif., 1975-77; editor Diablo (Calif.) Inferno, 1971-76; author Shifting Sands, 1981, Tail Waggings of Maggie, 1982. Fellow Internat. Biog. Assn.; mem. Nat. Writers Club, AAUW, Soc. Children's Book Writers, Am. Biog. Inst. (life, Raleigh, N.C.), Internat. Women's Writers Guild, Alpha Delta Pi. Republican. Episcopalian. Started a Pen-Pal svc. for children and young adults in Nyazura, Zimbabwe, 1986.

BAER, WILLIAM BRUCE, ophthalmologist; b. Louisville, Sept. 30, 1938; s. Louis and Miriam (Wile) B.; m. Joan Anita Teckler, Apr. 26, 1966 (dec. Oct. 1968); m. Sydney Ann Anker, Dec. 26, 1976; children: Allison, Louis. BSEE, MIT, 1960; BA, U. Louisville, 1961, MS in Pathology, MD cum laude, 1965. Diplomate Am. Bd. Ophthalmology. Intern, then resident SUNY Upstate Med. Ctr., Syracuse, 1965-67; resident in ophthalmology U. Oreg., Portland, 1969-72; pvt. practice, Portland, 1972—. Capt. USAF, 1967-69. Fellow Am. Acad. Ophthalmology; mem. AMA, Oreg. Med. Assn., Oreg. Acad. Ophthalmology, Multnomah County Med. Soc. (trustee 1988-90), Multnomah Athletic Club, Oswego Lake Country Club. Jewish. Office: 1130 NW 22d Ave Portland OR 97210

BAEZ, JOAN CHANDOS, folk singer; b. S.I., N.Y., Jan. 9, 1941; d. Albert V. and Joan (Bridge) B.; m. David Victor Harris, Mar. 1968 (div. 1973); 1 son, Gabriel Earl. Appeared in coffeehouses, Gate of Horn, Chgo., 1958, Ballad Room, Club 47, 1958-68, Newport (R.I.) Folk Festival, 1959-69, 85, 87, 90, extended tour to colls. and concert halls, 1960's, appeared Town Hall and Carnegie Hall, 1962, 67, 68, U.S. tours, 1970—, concert tours, Japan, 1966, 82, Europe, 1970-73, 80, 83-84, 87-90, 93, Australia, 1985; rec. artist for Vanguard Records, 1960-72, A&M, 1973-76, Portrait Records, 1977-80, Gold Castle Records, 1986-89, (awarded 8 gold albums, 1 gold single), Virgin Records, 1990—, European record albums, 1981, 83; other albums include: Play Me Backwards, 1992; author: Joan Baez Songbook, 1964, (biography) Daybreak, 1968, (with David Harris) Coming Out, 1971, And A Voice To Sing With, 1987, (songbook) And then I wrote, 1979; extensive TV appearances and speaking tours U.S. and Can. for anti-militarism, 1967-68; visit to war torn Bosnia-Herzegovina, 1993. Visit to Dem. Republic of Vietnam, 1972; founder, v.p. Inst. for Study Nonviolence (now Resource Ctr. for Nonviolence, Santa Cruz, Calif.), Palo Alto, Calif., 1965; mem. nat. adv. council Amnesty Internat., 1974-92; founder, pres. Humanitas/Internat. Human Rights Com., 1979-92, condr. fact-finding mission to refugee camps, S.E. Asia, Oct. 1979; began refusing payment of war taxes, 1964; arrested for civil disobedience opposing draft, Oct., Dec., 1967. Office: care Diamonds and Rust Prodns PO Box 1026 Menlo Park CA 94026-1026

BAGARRY, ALEXANDER ANTHONY, III, quality assurance professional; b. McAllen, Tex., Nov. 10, 1949; s. Edward Louis and Billie Jean (Hajee) B.; m. Susan Lynn King, Sept. 21, 1988; 1 child, Alexander Anthony IV. Degree Level II inspector, USN Tng. Sch., San Diego, 1973; degree Level III examiner, Bettis Atomic Power Lab., West Mifflin, Pa., 1976. Dimensional inspector Solar Turbines Internat., San Diego, 1979-81; nuclear power plant inspector Ametek-Straza Corp., El Cajon, Calif., 1981-82; chief inspector Astro-Cast Corp., Cucamonga, Calif., 1982-83; quality control mgr. Hemet Casting Co., Cucamonga, 1983-87, Vard Newport Co., Santa Ana, Calif., 1987-89; dir. quality control M.M.P. Quality Inspections, Inc., Long Beach, Calif., 1989—; Level III cons. in field, 1989—. with USN, 1971-79. Mem. Am. Soc. for Non-Destructive Testing, Am. Welding Soc., Pacific Energy Assn. Republican. Roman Catholic. Home: 4201 W 5th St Apt 109 Santa Ana CA 92703-3284 Office: MMP Quality Inspections Inc 3935 E Broadway # 397 Long Beach CA 90803-6192

BAGDASARIAN, ANDRANIK, biochemist; b. Tehran, Iran, Dec. 5, 1935; s. Mamegon and Satenik (Gregorian) B.; m. Vilma T. Rincon, Mar. 15, 1979; children: Patrick, Armen, Levon. PhD in Biochemistry, U. Louisville, 1967; D in Pharmacy, U. Tehran, Iran, 1962. Rsch. asst. prof. U. Pa., Phila., 1975-78; sr. rsch. scientist Hyland Therapeutics, Costa Mesa, Calif., 1978-80, rsch. mgr., Costa Mesa, 1980-83, assoc. dir. rsch., Duarte, Calif., 1983-85, mgr. spl. projects, 1985-88; with family bus., 1989-90; prin. scientist Alpha Therapeutics, L.A., 1991-92, sr. prin. scientist, 1992—. NIH grantee, 1975-78; Nat. Cancer Inst. grantee, 1975-78; Am. Cancer Soc. grantee, 1975-77. Mem. Am. Soc. Biol. Chemists, Sigma Xi. Republican. Mem. Armenian Apostolic Ch. Home: 1227 Calle Estrella San Dimas CA 91773-4081 Office: Alpha Therapeutics 5555 Valley Blvd Los Angeles CA 90032-3548

BAGDIKIAN, BEN HAIG, journalist, emeritus university educator; b. Marash, Turkey, Jan. 30, 1920; came to U.S., 1920, naturalized, 1926; s. Aram Theodore and Daisy (Uvezian) B.; m. Elizabeth Ogasapian, Oct. 2, 1942 (div. 1972); children: Christopher Ben, Frederick Haig; m. Betty L. Medsger, 1973 (div.); m. Marlene Griffith, 1983. A.B., Clark U., 1941, LittD, 1963; LHD, Brown U., 1961, U. R.I., 1992. Reporter Springfield (Mass.) Morning Union, 1941-42; assoc. editor Periodical House, Inc., N.Y.C., 1946; successively reporter, fgn. corr., chief Washington corr. Providence Jour., 1947-62; contbg. editor Sat. Eve. Post, 1963-67; project dir. study of future U.S. news media Rand Corp., 1967-69; asst. mng. editor for nat. news Washington Post, 1970-71, asst. mng. editor, 1971-72; nat. corr. Columbia Journalism Review, 1972-74; prof. Grad. Sch. Journalism, U. Calif., Berkeley, 1976-90, prof. emeritus, 1990—, dean, 1985-88. Author: In The Midst of Plenty: The Poor in America, 1964, The Information Machines: Their Impact on Men and the Media, 1971, The Shame of the Prisons, 1972, The Effete Conspiracy, 1972, Caged: Eight Prisoners and their Keepers, 1976, The Media Monopoly, 1983, rev. edit., 1987, 3d edit., 1990, 4th edit., 1992; also pamphlets.; Contbr.: The Kennedy Circle, 1961; Editor: Man's Contracting World in an Expanding Universe, 1959; bd. editors: Jour. Investigative Reporters and Editors, 1980—. Mem. steering com. Nat. Prison Project, 1974-82; trustee Clark U., 1964-76; bd. dirs. Nat. Capital Area Civil Liberties Union, 1964-66, Com. to Protect Journalists, 1981-88, Data Ctr., Oakland, Calif.; pres. Lowell Mellett Fund for Free and Responsible Press, 1965-76; acad. adv. bd. Nat. Citizens Com. for Broadcasting, 1978—. Recipient George Foster Peabody award, 1951, Sidney Hillman Found. award, 1956, Most Perceptive Critic citation Am. Soc. Journalism Adminstrs., 1978; fellow Ogden Reid Found., 1956, Guggenheim Found., 1961-62; named to R.I. Journalism Hall of Fame, 1992. Mem. ACLU. Home: 25 Stonewall Rd Berkeley CA 94705-1414

BAGGERLY, LEO LON, physicist; b. Wichita, Kans., Mar. 13, 1928; s. Isaac Edison and Elna Matilda B; m. Jean Louise Bickford, June 8, 1951 (div., Jan. 1966); children: Philip, Jennifer; m. Carole Christine Applewhite, Apr. 2, 1966; children: Keith, Derek, Christine. BS in Sci., Calif. Inst. Tech., 1951, MS in Physics, 1952, PhD, 1956. Sr. rsch. engr. Jet Propulsion Lab., Pasadena, Calif., 1955-56; Fulbright lectr. U. Ceylon, Colombo, 1956-59; asst. prof., assoc. prof., prof. Physics Tex. Christian U., Ft. Worth, 1959-69; program mgr. NSF, Washington, 1969-71; vis. fellow Cornell U., Ithaca, N.Y., 1971-72; prof. Physics Calif. State Coll., Bakersfield, 1972-75; vis. prof. Pomona Coll., Claremont, Calif., 1975-76, Harvey Mudd Coll., Claremont, Calif., 1976-77; sr. staff scientist Ballistics Missiles Div TRW, San Bernardino, Calif., 1977—; cons. Tex. Nuclear Corp. Austin, 1960-61, Milco Internat., Huntington Beach, Calif., 1975-77; cons. scientist LTV Rsch. Ctr., Grand Prairie, Tex., 1962-67. Contbr. articles to profl. jours. V.p. So. Calif. chpt. ACLU, 1955-56; treas. Am. Field Svc., Claremont, 1984--. With USN, 1946-48. Fellow Tex. Acad. Sci.; mem. AAAS, Am. Assn. Physics Tchrs. (pres. So. Calif. chpt. 1973-75), UN Assn. (treas. Pomona Valley chpt. 1979-86), Sigma Xi. Mem. Soc. of Friends. Home: 2218 Grand Ave Claremont CA 91711

BAGGETT, KELSEA KINDRICK, retired nurse; b. Pine Bluff, Ark., Nov. 19, 1937; s. Joe Layton and Mildred (Franks) B.; m. Roxanna Veronica Dixon, Jan. 5, 1963; children: Daniel Kenneth, Sheryl Angela, Noel Alexander, Douglas Anthony. Diploma nursing, L.A. County Gen. Hosp., 1964; AS, Cypress (Calif.) Coll., 1975; BS, Calif. State U., Fullerton, 1980. RN, Calif.; cert. correctional healthcare profl., Calif. Staff nurse Los Angeles County Sheriff's Dept., 1964-69, supr. nurse, 1969-75, dir. nursing sheriff med. services, 1975-86, head mgmt. services, 1986-93; ret., 1993. Chmn. Gifted and Talented Assn., Garden Grove Sch. Dist., 1986. Served with USAF, 1956-60. Mem. Am. Correctional Health Svcs. Assn. (pres. elect Calif. chpt. 1988-89, pres. 1989-90, immediate past pres. 1990-91, bd. dirs. 1981-87).

BAGGISH, JOY, actress, costume designer; b. Hartford, Conn., July 1, 1950; d. Samuel and Stefania (Wojcek) B. MS, Fla. State U., 1973; BFA, U. Conn., 1972. Freelance designer L.A., 1981-93; legal asst. Viacom Prodns., Universal City, Calif., 1985-86; supr. bus. affairs Viacom Prodns., Universal City, 1986—, Showtime Networks Inc., Universal City, 1990-92; costumer Middlesex Coll., Edison, N.J., 1975-79, U. Nev., 1979-80; costumer and visiting prof., U. Wis., 1980-81. Appeared in films: Best Defense, 1985, An American Summer, 1989, Whore, 1990; TV series: Divorce Court, 1987, Superior Court, 1988, Freddie's Nightmare, 1990; commls.: Clusters, 1989, VW, 1989; spokesperson (comml.) Jasco Department Stores, 1991—; designer for Nutmeg Summer Playhouse, 1972, Asolo State Theatre, 1972, PBS series Saga on Aging, 1980. Mem. AFTRA, SAG, Actors Equity Assn., Am. Women in Radio and Television, Costume Soc. of Victoria & Albert Mus., Actresses Helping Actresses,. Home: 7890 E Spring St # 2-0 Long Beach CA 90815 Office: Showtime Networks Inc 10 Universal City Plz Universal City CA 91608-1097

BAGHZOUZ, YAHIA, electrical engineering educator; b. Beri-Amrane, Bouira, Algeria, Aug. 13, 1956; came to U.S., 1976; s. Slimane and Zohra Baghzouz; m. Chanpheng Panyanouvong, Aug. 28, 1982; children: Lila, Mina. BSEE, La. State U., 1981, MSEE, 1982, PhD, 1986. Rsch. asst. La. State U., Baton Rouge, 1981-85, instr., 1985-86; asst. prof. U. Southwestern La., Lafayette, 1986-87; asst. prof. dept. elec. and computer engring. U. Nev., Las Vegas, 1987-91, assoc. prof. dept. elec. and computer engring., 1991—; cons. Western Area Power Adminstrn., Boulder City, Nev., 1989-90, Boulder City Pub. Works, 1990—. Contbr. articles to profl. jours. Rsch. grantee U. Nev.-Las Vegas, 1988, Western Area Power Adminstrn., 1989, Boulder City Pub. Works, 1990, Cray Rsch., 1991-93. Mem. IEEE (sr.), Power Engring. Soc. (Harmonics Working Group, reviewer tech. papers and NSF proposals 1988—). Home: 2821 High View Dr Henderson NV 89014 Office: U Nev Las Vegas Elec and Computer Engring Dept 4505 S Maryland Pky Las Vegas NV 89154-0002

BAGLEY, CONSTANCE ELIZABETH, lawyer, educator; b. Tucson, Dec. 18, 1952; d. Robert Porter Smith and Joanne Snow-Smith. AB in Polit. Sci. with distinction, with honors, Stanford U., 1974; JD magna cum laude, Harvard U., 1977. Bar: Calif. 1978, N.Y. 1978. Tchg. fellow Harvard U., 1975-77; assoc. Webster & Sheffield, N.Y.C., 1977-78, Heller, Ehrman, White & McAuliffe, San Francisco, 1978-79; assoc. McCutchen, Doyle, Brown & Enersen, San Francisco, 1979-84, ptnr., 1984-90; lectr. bus. law Stanford U., 1988-90, lectr. mgmt., 1990-91, lectr. law and mgmt., 1991—; also bd. dirs. exec. program Stanford (Calif.) U.; mem. exec. program for smaller cos.-Stanford exec. program; mem. corp. practice series adv. bd. Bur. Nat. Affairs, 1984—; lectr., mem. planning com. Calif. Continuing Edn. of Bar, L.A. and San Francisco, 1983, 85-87; lectr. So. Area Conf., Silverado, 1988, Young Pres. Orgn. Internat. U. for Pres., Hong Kong, 1988. Author: Mergers, Acquisitions and Tender Offers, 1983, Proxy Contests and Corporate Control, 1990, Managers and the Legal Environment: Strategies for the 21st Century, 1991; co-author: Negotiated Acquisitions, 1992, Cutting Edge Cases in the Legal Environment of Business, 1993. Vestry mem. Trinity Episcopal Ch., San Francisco, 1984-85; vol. Moffit Hosp. U. Calif., San Francisco, 1983-84. Mem. ABA, Acad. Legal Studies in Bus., Phi Beta Kappa. Republican. Office: Stanford U Grad Sch Bus Stanford CA 94305-5015

BAGLEY, JOHN NEFF, social worker, consultant; b. Murray, Utah, Apr. 21, 1944; s. Ben and Marie (Pearson) B.; m. Meggin Catmull, Nov. 18, 1981. BS, U. Utah, 1966, MSW, 1973. Lic. clin. social worker, marriage and family counselor, Utah. Sch. social worker Salt Lake City Bd. of Edn., 1973-74; psychiat. social worker Holy Cross Hosp., Salt Lake City, 1974-76; alcohol and drug counselor County of Salt Lake, 1976-78; dir. Salt Lake City Recovery Ctr., 1978-79; clin. social worker Richfield (Utah) Dept. Social Svcs., 1982—; mem. grad. faculty social work U. Utah, 1975-93, cons. Richfield Care Ctr., 1985-93, Richfield Hosp., 1986-93, Human Affairs, Ltd.,

Richfield, 1987-93, Gunnison (Utah) Hosp., 1988-93, New Horizons Crisis Ctr., Richfield, Utah, 1990-93, Sorenson's Ranch Sch., Koosharem, Utah, 1990-93. Capt. USAF, 1967-71, Vietnam. Home: 1109 N 2450 W Monroe UT 84754-3447 Office: Richfield Dept Social Svcs 500 N 201 E Richfield UT 84701

BAGRI, DURGADAS S., astronomer; b. Bikaner, India, Oct. 17, 1942; came to U.S. 1983; s. Shankerlal and J. Bagri; m. Vimala, June 3, 1967; 1 child, Anil. BE in Telecommunication, Poona (India) U., 1963; ME in Electronics, Rajasthan U., Jaipur, India, 1964; PhD in Physics, Bombay U., 1975. Rsch. assoc. Tata Inst. Fundamental Rsch., Bombay, 1964-70; fellow Tata Inst. Fundamental Rsch., 1971-75, rsch. scientist, 1978-83; electronic engr. Nat. Radio Astronomy Obs., Socorro, N.Mex., 1976-78; electronic engr. Nat. Radio Astronomy Obs., 1983-85, sys. engr., 1985—. J.C. Bose Meml. awardee, Inst. Electronics and Telecommunications Engrs., New Delhi, 1976. Mem. Internat. Astron. Union. Office: Nat Radio Astronomy Ob PO Box 0 Socorro NM 87801

BAHA, DANIEL SCOTT, lawyer; b. N.Y.C., Nov. 30, 1955; s. Douglas Scott and Robin (Von Hefflin) Mont Bahatten Berke. BA, Oklahoma State U., 1976; MBA, U. So. Calif., 1980; JD, Northrop U., 1985. Bar: Calif. 1985. Sole practice Redondo Beach, Calif., 1986—. Mem. ABA, Los Angeles County Bar, South Bay Bar. Republican. Office: 1840 S Elena Ave Redondo Beach CA 90277-5703

BAHLO, PETER, civil engineer; b. Bridgeport, Conn., Jan. 27, 1959; s. Klaus Wolfgang and Helga (Sahner) B. BSCE, U. Mass., 1983. Registered profl. engr., Calif. Staff sr. engr. L.A. County Bldg. and Safety Dept., 1983-86; staff engr. ICBO, Inc., Whittier, Calif., 1986—. Mem. Am. Concrete Inst., Structural Engrs. of So. Calif., Am. Soc. Civil Engrs., Nat. Soc. Profl. Engrs.

BAHN, GILBERT SCHUYLER, retired mechanical engineer, researcher; b. Syracuse, N.Y., Apr. 25, 1922; s. Chester Bert and Irene Eliza (Schuyler) B.; BS, Columbia U., 1943; MS in Mech. Engring., Rensselaer Poly. Inst., 1965; PhD in Engring., Columbia Pacific U., 1979; m. Iris Cummings Birch, Sept. 14, 1957 (dec.); 1 child, Gilbert Kennedy. Chem. engr. Gen. Electric Co., Pittsfield, Mass., 1946-48, devel. engr., Schenectady, 1948-53; sr. thermodynamics engr. Marquardt Co., Van Nuys, Calif., 1953-54, rsch. scientist, 1954-64, rsch. cons., 1964-70; engring. specialist LTV Aerospace Corp., Hampton, Va., 1970-88; ret.; freelance rsch. FDR at Nadir, 1988—. Mem. JANNAF Performance Standardization Working Group, 1966-83, thermochemistry working group, 1967-72; propr. Schuyler Tech. Libr., 1952—. Active Boy Scouts Am., 1958-78. Served to capt. USAAF, 1943-46. Recipient Silver Beaver award Boy Scouts Am., 1970. Registered profl. engr., N.Y., Calif. Mem. ASME, Combustion Inst. (sec. western states sect. 1957-71), Soc. for Preservation Book of Common Prayer. Episcopalian (vestryman 1968-70). Author: Reaction Rate Compilation for the H-O-N System, 1968; Blue and White and Evergreen: William Byron Mowery and His Novels, 1981; Oliver Norton Worden's Family, 1982; Studies in American Historical Demography to 1850, Vol. 1, 1987; Overall Population Trends, Age Profiles, and Settlement, Vol. 2, 1987; The Wordens, Representative of the Native Northern Population, 1987; The Ancient Worden Family in America: A Story of Growth and Migration, 1988. Founding editor Pyrodynamics, 1963-69; proceedings editor Kinetics, Equilibria and Performance of High Temperature Systems, 1960, 63, 67; contbr. articles to profl. jours.; discoverer free radical chem. species diboron monoxide, 1966. Home: 4519 N Ashtree St Moorpark CA 93021-2156 Office: 238 Encino Vista Dr Thousand Oaks CA 91362-2537

BAHR, EHRHARD, Germanic languages and literature educator; b. Kiel, Germany, Aug. 21, 1932; came to U.S., 1956; s. Klaus and Gisela (Badenhausen) B.; m. Diana Meyers, Nov. 21, 1973; stepchildren: Gary, Timothy, Christopher. Student, U. Heidelberg, Germany, 1952-53, U. Freiburg, Germany, 1953-56; M.S. Ed. (Fulbright scholar), U. Kans., 1956-58; postgrad., U. Cologne, 1959-61; Ph.D., U. Calif., Berkeley, 1968. Asst. prof. German UCLA, 1968-70, assoc. prof., 1970-72, prof., 1972—, chmn. dept. Germanic langs., 1981-84, 93—, chair grad. council, 1988-89. Author: Irony in the Late Works of Goethe, 1972, Georg Lukacs, 1970, Ernst Bloch, 1974, Nelly Sachs, 1980; edit. of Kant, What is Enlightenment, 1974, Goethe, Wilhelm Meister's Journeyman Years, 1982, History of German Lit., 3 vols., 1987-88; co-editor: The Revolution: German Reactions to the French Revolution, 1789-1989, 1992; commentary: Thomas Mann: Death in Venice, 1991; contbr. articles to profl. jours. Recipient Disting. Teaching award UCLA, 1970, Humanities Inst. award, 1972, summer stipend NEH, 1978. Mem. MLA, Am. Soc. 18th Century Studies, Am. Assn. Tchrs. German, Western Soc. 18th Century Studies, German Studies Assn., (pres. 1987-88), Philol. Assn. Pacific Coast, Lessing Soc., Goethe Soc. N.Am. (exec. sec. 1979-89, v.p. 1991—). Office: UCLA Dept Germanic Langs Los Angeles CA 90024-1539

BAHR, HOWARD MINER, sociologist, educator; b. Provo, Utah, Feb. 21, 1938; s. A. Francis and Louie Jean (Miner) B.; m. Rosemary Frances Smith, Aug. 28, 1961 (div. 1985); children: Bonnie Louise, Howard McKay, Rowena Ruth, Tanya Lavonne, Christopher J., Laura L., Stephen S., Rachel M.; m. Kathleen Slaugh, May 1, 1986; children: Alden Keith, Jonathan Andrew. B.A. with honors, Brigham Young U., 1962; M.A. in Sociology, U. Tex., 1964, Ph.D., 1965. Research asso. Columbia U., N.Y.C., 1965-68; vis. lectr., summer 1968; lectr. in sociology N.Y. U., 1967-68, Bklyn. Coll., City U. N.Y., 1967; asso. prof. sociology Wash. State U., Pullman, 1968-73; prof. Wash. State U., 1972-73, chmn. dept. rural sociology, 1971-73; prof. sociology Brigham Young U., Provo, Utah, 1973—; dir. Family Research Inst., 1977-83; fellow David M. Kennedy, 1992; vis. prof. sociology U. Va., 1976-77, 84-85. Author: Skid Row: An Introduction to Disaffiliation, 1973, Old Men Drunk and Sober, 1974, Women Alone: The Disaffiliation of Urban Females, 1976, American Ethnicity, 1979, Sunshine Widows: Adapting to Sudden Bereavement, 1980, Middletown Families, 1982, All Faithful People: Change and Continuity in Middletown's Religion, 1983, Life in Large Families, 1983, Divorce and Remarriage: Problems, Adaptations and Adjustments, 1983, Social Science Research Methods, 1984, Recent Social Trends in the United States 1960-90, 1991; contbr. articles to profl. jours.; asso. editor: Rural Sociology, 1978-83, Jour. Marriage and the Family, 1978-83. NIMH grantee, 1968-70, 71-73; NSF grantee, 1971-72, 76-80. Mem. Am. Sociol. Assn., Rural Sociol. Assn., Nat. Coun. Family Rels. Mem. LDS Ch. Office: Dept Sociology 842 SWKT Brigham Young U Provo UT 84602

BAHR, RICHARD GEORGE, electrical engineer; b. Lower Merion Twp., Pa., Feb. 25, 1954; s. George Richard and Theresa Ann (Dearing) B.; m. Molly Louise Dinan, June 4, 1988; children: Amelia Anne, Madeline Casey. BSEE, MIT, 1976, MSEE, 1978. Mem. tech. staff Hewlett Packard, Cupertino, Calif., 1978-80; design mgr. cen. processing unit Prime Computer, Framingham, Mass., 1980-84; sr. cons. engr. Apollo Computer, Chelmsford, Mass., 1984-89, HP/Apollo Computer, Chelmsford, Mass., 1989-91; dir. engring. supercomputing systems div. Silicon Graphics Computer, Mountain View, Calif., 1991—; bd. dirs. Cami Rsch., Arlington, Mass. Mem. IEEE (sr.). Roman Catholic. Home: 324 Concord Dr Menlo Park CA 94025-2904 Office: Silicon Graphics 2011 N Shoreline Blvd Mountain View CA 94039

BAHTI, MARK TOMAS, art appraiser; b. Tucson, Sept. 28, 1950; s. Thomas Neil and Margaret (Pack) B.; m. Ulla Lehtonen, June 1970 (div. Apr. 1981); m. Dolores Rivas, May 5, 1984; children: Kim Huong, Yuri Sakari, Santiago McFarland. Student, Prescott Coll., 1969-70, U. Ariz., 1970-71. Mgr. Bahti Indian Arts, Tucson, 1969-71, owner, 1972—; speaker in field. Author: Consumers Guide to S.W. Indian Arts and Crafts, 1975, S.W. Indian Jewelry, 1980, S.W. Indian Arts and Crafts, 1983, Pueblo Stories and Storytellers, 1987, Southwest Indian Design, 1993; co-author: Navaho Sandpainting Art, 1981; contbr. articles to profl. publs. Bd. dirs., mem. exec. com. Tucson Indian Ctr., 1976-81, 83—; bd. dirs. Tucson Citizen-Police Adv. Com.; mem. adv. bd. Ft. Lowell Hist. Dist., 1976-88, Ariz.-Sonora Desert Mus., Pio Decimo Neighborhood Ctr., 1984-85; bd. dirs. Local Alcohol Rehab. Ctr., 1978-80, Tucson Barrio Assn., 1982-84; mem. men's coun. Heard Mus., 1981-82; trustee Martha Graham Dance Co., 1985—; mem. Mayor and Coun. Downtown Preservation Ad-hoc Com., 1990—; mem. Pima County CETA Pvt. Industry Coun., 1980-82. Recipient Bus. Support for Arts-in-Edn. award Tucson Bus. Com. for Arts, 1990. Fellow Soc. for Applied Anthropology, Royal Anthropology Inst.; mem. Indian Arts and Crafts Assn. (charter mem., treas., v.p., pres., ethics and membership coms.), Soc. Applied Anthropology, Soc. Profl. Anthropologists (steering com. Tucson chpt.), S.W. Assn. Indian Affairs (bd. dirs.), World Archaeol. Coun., Latin Am. Indigenous Lit. Assn., Southwestern Anthropol. Assn., S.W. Ctr. Adv. Bd. Office: Bahti Indian Arts 4300 N Campbell Ave Tucson AZ 85718-6500

BAIKALOV, IGOR A., molecular biologist; b. Tomsk, Russia, Sept. 3, 1961; came to U.S., 1990; s. Alexander V. and Violetta P. (Dozoschuk) B. MS, Phys.-Technol. Inst., Moscow, 1985. Leading engr. Inst. of Protein Rsch., Moscow, 1985-90; staff rsch. assoc. UCLA, Molecular Biology Inst., 1990-91, grad. student, 1991—; dir. Ranet Ctr., Inc., Austin, 1990-91; cons. Atlantic Tharr, N.Y.C., 1991-92. Contbr. articles to profl. jours. Home: 11841 Mayfield Ave # 5 Los Angeles CA 90049 Office: UCLA Molecular Biology Inst 405 Hilgard Ave Los Angeles CA 90024

BAILEY, ALEX STUART, engineering executive; b. San Diego, June 23, 1952; s. Robert Earwood and Marcelle Adalyn (Groff) B.; m. Terri Anne Marsh, May 31, 1986; children: Kyle Alexander, Corinne Alexa. AA, Can. Coll., 1972; BA, U. Calif., Berkeley, 1974; MBA, Santa Clara U., 1982. Satellite ops. engr. Lockheed Missiles & Space Co., Sunnyvale, Calif., 1974-78, mgmt. devel. program participant, 1978-80, sr. rsch. engr., 1980-82; staff engr. Ultrasystems Def. & Space, Sunnyvale, 1982-85, program mgr., 1985-88; engring. mgr. GTE Govt. Systems, Mountain View, Calif., 1988—. Named one of Outstanding Young Men of Am., 1987. Mem. Smithsonian Instn. (assoc.), Calif. Scholarship Fedn., U.S. Fencing Assn., Bay Area Miniature Soc. Home: 1634 Juanita Ave San Jose CA 95125-3358 Office: GTE Govt Systems PO Box 7188 Mountain View CA 94039-7188

BAILEY, BRIAN DENNIS, management consultant, author, publisher; b. Tacoma, June 10, 1952; s. Hugh Charles and Elsie Denise (Hinds) B.; BBA, Pacific Luth. U., Tacoma, 1975; MBA, City U. Seattle, 1982; PhD in Bus. Adminstrn., Century U., Beverly Hills, Calif., 1985. Prin. Brian D. Bailey, Mgmt. Cons., Tacoma, 1975—; pres. and chief exec. officer Baico Industries Inc., Tacoma, 1975—; adj. instr. City U., Seattle, 1986—. Mem. corp. bd., pres. Victory Life Christian Fellowship, Tacoma. With USAF, 1971-73, with res. 1973-77. Mem. Full Gospel Businessmen's Fellowship Internat., World Bible Way Fellowship, Inc., Christian Writers Guild, Grange of Washington State. Office: Baico Industries Inc PO Box 44757 Tacoma WA 98444-0757

BAILEY, CHARLES-JAMES NICE, linguistics educator; b. Middlesborough, Ky., May 2, 1926; s. Charles Wise and Mary Elizabeth (Nice) B. A.B., Harvard Coll., 1950, M.Th., 1955; D.Min., Vanderbilt U., 1963; A.M., U. Chgo., 1967, Ph.D., 1969. Mem. faculty dept. linguistics U. Hawaii, Manoa, 1968-71, Georgetown U., 1971-73; prof. Technische U. Berlin, 1974-91, univ. prof. emeritus, 1991—; affiliate prof. U. Hawaii, Hilo; vis. prof. U. Mich., Ann Arbor, 1973, U. Witwatersrand, Johannesburg, 1976, U. Brunei, Darussalam, 1990; Forcheimer prof. U. Jerusalem, 1986; proprietor Orchid Land Publs. Fellow Netherlands Inst. Advanced Study (life); mem. European Acad. Arts, Scis. and Humanities (corr.), Linguistic Soc. Am., Internat. Phonetic Assn., Soc. Linguistica Europaea, Am. Dialect Soc., Am. Hort. Soc. Home: Orchid Land Dr PO Box 1416 Keaau HI 96749-1416

BAILEY, CLAYTON GEORGE, artist, educator; b. Antigo, Wis., Mar. 9, 1939; s. Clayton Pence and Mary (Pence) B.; m. Betty Graveen, Oct. 11, 1958; children: Kurt Douglas, Robin Lynn, George Gladstone. BS, U. Wis., 1961, MS, 1962. Asst. prof. U. Wis.-Whitewater, 1963-67; head ceramic dept. U. S.D., 1967-68; prof. Calif. State U.-Hayward, 1968—, chmn. dept. art, 1980-83. Exhibited in shows Mus. Contemporary Crafts, N.Y.C., Everson Mus. Art, Syracuse, Addison Gallery Am. Art, Andover, Mass., Milw. Art Ctr., Walker Art Ctr., Mpls., Art Inst. Chgo., San Francisco Art Inst., Richmond Art Mus., Renwick Gallery, Wash., Joseph Chowning Gallery, San Francisco, Natural History Mus., San Diego, U. Ariz. Mus. Art, Tucson, Am. Crafts Mus., Palm Springs Desert Mus. (Calif.), Triton Mus., Santa Clara, Calif., Exploratorium, San Francisco, Ctr. George Pompidou, Paris, others; represented in permanent collections U. Wis., Addison Gallery Am. Art, Brooks Meml. Gallery U. Okla., State U. Iowa, Fresno Art Mus., Milw. Art Ctr., Hokkoku Shinbun, Korinbo, Japan, Sacramento State Univ., Johnson Found., Racine, Wis., Laguna Art Museum, L.A. County Art Mus., Metromedia Collection, USIA, San Francisco Mus. Art., Mus. Contemporary Crafts, N.Y.C., Mus. Contemporary Art, Honolulu, L.A. County Mus., Redding (Calif.) Mus., Mills Coll., Oakland, Calif., USIA, Crocker Gallery, Sacramento, Oakland Mus., Asahi Shimbun, Japan, Karlstadt, W.Ger., others; founder, curator and ceramic sculptor Kaolithic curiosities Wonders of the World Mus., Port Costa, Calif.; patentee in field. Louis Comfort Tiffany Found. grantee, 1963; Am. Craftsmen's Council grantee, 1963; recipient George Gladstone award, 1970; Piltdown Found. grantee, 1972; Nobel Prize nominee in physics, 1976; NEA grantee, 1979, 90; Nat. Council for Edn. in Ceramic Arts fellow, 1982. Home: PO Box 69 Port Costa CA 94569-0069

BAILEY, DOUGLAS KENT, data processing executive; b. Pensacola, Fla., Mar. 16, 1949; s. Homer Dwight and Marjorie Louise (Shaw) B.; m. Wynette Lynn Kau, Apr. 26, 1986; children: Luisa Michelle, Brigita Nicole. BS cum laude, Wake Forest U., 1971; JD, Case Western Res. U., 1974. Bar: Ohio. Bus. analyst Union Carbide Corp., N.Y.C., 1974-76; legal analyst Fed. Jud. Ctr., Washington, 1976-81; court mgmt. analyst Jud. Coun. Calif., San Francisco, 1981-82, mgr. court mgmt. svcs. unit, 1982, mgr. data processing unit, 1982-87; gen. mgr. western regional office CMC Assocs., Inc., Alameda, Calif., 1987-91; systems coord. Alameda County Superior Ct., Oakland, Calif., 1991—. Home: 1434 St Charles St Alameda CA 94501-2312 Office: Alameda County Courthouse 1225 Fallon St Rm 205 Oakland CA 94612-4219

BAILEY, EXINE MARGARET ANDERSON, soprano, educator; b. Cottonwood, Minn., Jan. 4, 1922; d. Joseph Leonard and Exine Pearl (Robertson) Anderson; m. Arthur Albert Bailey, May 5, 1956. B.S., U. Minn., 1944; M.A., Columbia U., 1945; profl. diploma, 1951. Instr. Columbia U., 1947-51; faculty U. Oreg., Eugene, 1951—, prof. voice, 1966-87, coordinator voice instrn., 1969-87, prof. emeritus, 1987—; faculty dir. Salzburg, Austria, summer 1968, Europe, summer 1976; vis prof., head vocal instrn. Columbia U., summers 1952, 59; condr. master classes for singers, developer summer program study for high sch. students, U. Oreg. Sch. Music, 1988—. Profl. singer, N.Y.C.; appearances with NBC, ABC symphonies; solo artist appearing with Portland and Eugene (Oreg.) Symphonies, other groups in Wash., Calif., Mont., Idaho, also in concert; contbr. articles, book revs. to various mags. Del. fine arts program to Ea. Europe, People to People Internat. Mission for 1990. Recipient Young Artist award N.Y.C. Singing Tchrs., 1945, Music Fedn. Club (N.Y.C.) hon. award, 1951; Kathryn Long scholar Met. Opera, 1945. Mem. Nat. Assn. Tchrs. Singing (lt. gov. 1968-72), Oreg. Music Tchrs. Assn (pres. 1974-76), Music Tchrs. Nat. Assn. (nat. voice chmn. high sch. activities 1970-74, nat. chmn. voice 1973-75, 81-85, NW chmn. collegiate activities and artists competition 1978-80, editorial com. Am. Music Tchr. jour. 1987-89), AAUP, Internat. Platform Assn., Kappa Delta Pi, Sigma Alpha Iota, Pi Kappa Lambda. Home: 17 Westbrook Way Eugene OR 97405-2074 Office: U Oreg Sch Music Eugene OR 97403

BAILEY, GLENN MARTIN (MAX VOLUME), broadcast executive; b. Glendale, Calif., Feb. 19, 1956; s. Ralph Milburn and Jonita Lynn (Meyers) B.; m. Teresa Hilda Mace, Aug. 13, 1988; 1 child, John Patrick. Student, Truckee Meadows Community Coll, 1979-91. Lic. broadcaster FCC. Mgr. The Rock Shop, Reno, 1980-81; asst. program dir. Sta. KOZZ Radio, Reno, 1981-87; music dir. Sta. KRZQ Radio, Reno, 1987-90, 92—, program dir., 1990-92; cons. Whitesnake Inc., Reno, 1987—, Warrant Inc., L.A., 1988—, Nelson, Inc., L.A., 1992—. Democrat. Office: Sta KRZQ Radio 45600 Kietzke Ln D-136 Reno NV 89502

BAILEY, HARVEY ALAN, advertising executive; b. Chgo., Feb. 8, 1937; s. Joseph C. and Evelyn G. Bailey; m. Betsy Cohen; children: Jodie Claire, Robin Marianne, Dashiell Shapiro, Nathaniel Rex. BA, U. Mich., 1958. V.p., assoc. creative dir. Campbell Ewald Co., Detroit; v.p., group creative dir. Foote, Cone & Belding, Chgo.; creative dir. Tatham-Laird and Kudner, Chgo.; exec. v.p. Clinton E. Frank, Inc., Chgo., 1977-83; chmn., chief exec. officer, Bailey, Kepinger & Medrich, Ann Arbor, Mich. and San Francisco, 1983-92; chmn. The Bailey Group, 1992—; guest speaker, vis. advt. profl. Mich. State U. Contbr. articles to profl. jours. Recipient 9 Clio nominations for TV excellence; Gold and Silver medal winner (4) N.Y. Internat. Film Festival; Guttenberg award for The Power of Print. Mem. Adcraft Club (Detroit), Creative Advt. Club (Detroit), San Francisco Advt. Club, Admark. Office: The Bailey Group 41 Tunnel Rd Berkeley CA 94705-2499

BAILEY, HOWLAND HASKELL, physicist, consultant; b. Boston, Apr. 5, 1912; s. William Henry and Edith Stone (Haskell) B.; m. Anne Margaret Becchetti, Aug. 30, 1941; children: Bernadine Oberst, Barbara Ruth Kernochan. AB, Haverford Coll., 1932; student, Duke U., 1932-34; PhD, Calif. Inst. Tech., 1941. Tchr. Am. Coll., Tarsus, Turkey, 1934-36; grad. asst. Calif. Inst. Tech., Pasadena, 1936-40; asst. prof. U. Wyo., Laramie, 1940-41, U. Okla., Norman, 1941-43; staff mem., group leader Radiation Lab. MIT, Cambridge, 1943-45; mem. tech. staff Bell Telephone Labs., Whippany, N.J., 1945-53; mem. tech. staff, group leader Rand Corp., Santa Monica, Calif., 1953-87, cons., 1987-91; cons. Sci. Applications, Inc., La Jolla, Calif., 1977-81, Northrop Corp., Anahaeim, Calif., 1978-80, Pacific Sierra Rsch., Santa Monica, 1983. Contbr. articles to profl. jours. Mem. several Air Force Sci. Adv. Bd. Coms. Fellow Explorers Club; mem. Sierra Club (chpt. treas. 1980-82), Phi Beta Kappa. Home: 28791 Via Los Arboles San Juan Capistrano CA 92675-5510

BAILEY, IAN JAMES, electronics company official; b. Amesbury, Mass., Sept. 30, 1957; s. Alan Douglas and Catheryn May (McAuley) B. BA in Econs. cum laude, Harvard U., 1979; MBA, Dartmouth Coll., 1983. Country risk analyst Hartford (Conn.) Nat. Bank, 1979-80; fin. economist Pub. Svc. Co. N.Mex., Albuquerque, 1980-82; mgr. new products Digital Equipment, Albuquerque, 1982-85, supr. prodn. control, 1985-88, mgr. bus. planning, 1988—; pres. IJ Bailey & Assocs., Albuquerque, 1989—, PLZTech Inc., Albuquerque, 1992—; ptnr. Coronado Group, Albuquerque, 1990—. Tuck scholar Dartmouth Coll., 1983. Mem. Am. Prodn. and Inventory Control Soc. (cert.), Albuquerque C. of C., N.Mex. Entrepreneurs. Office: Digital Equipment PO Box 80 Albuquerque NM 87103-0080

BAILEY, JAMES ALLEN, wildlife biologist; b. Chgo., May 14, 1934; s. Leo Carl and Ella Maria (Voss) B.; m. Natalie Ann Jewett, June 13, 1959; children: Chistina Loren (Bailey) Hodges, Michael James. BSc in Forestry, Mich. Tech. U., 1956; MSc in Wildlife Biology, SUNY, Syracuse, 1958, PhD in Wildlife Biology, 1966. Rsch. biologist Ill. Natural History Survey, Urbana, 1964-68; instr. U. Mont., Missoula, 1968-69; prof. Colo. State U., Ft. Collins, 1969-91; cons. Fort Collins, Colo., 1991—. Editor, No. Wild Sheep and Goat Coun., 1982, 90; author: Principles of Wildlife Management, 1984; editor: Readings in Wildlife Conservation, 1974. With U.S. Army, 1960-62. Mem. The Wildlife Soc. Home and office: 2101 Sandstone Fort Collins CO 80524

BAILEY, JERRY WAYNE, municipal government official; b. Bellingham, Wash., Mar. 29, 1948; s. Loyd Herbert and Betty May (Blowers) B.; m. Nicki Lynn Husted, Sept. 18, 1982; children: Andrea Illona, Drew James. BA, Western Wash. U., 1973, MA, 1981. Capt. Bellingham Fire Dept., 1974—; co-owner Bailey & Assocs., Bellingham, 1983—; archaeol. field worker Western Wash. U., Bellingham; presenter in field. Mem. Soc. Am. Archaeology, Am. Acad. Forensic Scis., Internat. Assn. Arson Investigators. Presbyterian. Office: Bellingham Fire Dept 1800 Broadway Bellingham WA 98225-3133

BAILEY, JESSICA MARGOLIN, scientific business consultant; b. L.A., Apr. 19, 1962; d. N. Lionel Margolin and Carol Heifetz Neiman; m. Joseph Kent Bailey, June 1, 1985; 1 child, Nathaniel Karl. BA, U. Calif., Berkeley, 1985; MS, U. Minn., 1989, MBA, 1991. Pres., founder Sci. Communications, Albuquerque, 1991—; cons. to scientists. Mem. chpt. solid waste subcom. Audubon Soc., Mpls.-St. Paul, 1989-90. Mem. Sierra Club (editor Albuquerque chpt. 1991-92). Office: Sci Communications 4547 Oak Chase Way Eagan MN 55123

BAILEY, KATHERINE CHRISTINE, artist, writer; b. Glendale, Calif., Dec. 1, 1952; d. Carl Leonard and Anna Alice (Dzamka) Abrahamson; m. David Francis Bailey, Sept. 27, 1975. BA, Calif. State U., L.A., 1974, MA, 1975; PhD, U. N.Mex., 1982. Exhbns. include Miniature Painters Sculptors & Gravers Soc., Washington, Oil Pastel Assn., N.Y.C., Mont. Miniature Art Soc. Internat., many others; author: (novel) Brush With Death; also numerous short stories. Recipient tuition fellowship U. N.Mex., 1977. Mem. Oil Pastel Assn., Nat. Mus. Women in Arts, Mont. Miniature Art Soc., Phi Kappa Phi, Alpha Gamma Sigma. Home and Studio: PO Box 301 Daggett CA 92327

BAILEY, KERRY DOUGLAS, mathematician, computer scientist, educator; b. Pueblo, Colo., June 3, 1950; s. Herbert Armell and Ardith Mae (MacFarlane) B.; m. Janice Ann Groves, June 11, 1977; children: Matthew, Sara, Abby. AA, Southwestern Coll., Chula Vista, Calif., 1970; BA, San Diego State U., 1972; MA, U. Colo., 1974. Math. instr. Pikes Peak Community Coll., Colo. Springs, Colo., 1974-84, Laramie County Community Coll., Cheyenne, Wyo., 1984—. Inventor drafting device, 1978. Bd. dirs. Crisis Pregnancy Ctr. Cheyenne, treas., 1990, chmn., 1991-92; coord. Pack 219 Boy Scouts Am., Cheyenne, 1990. Mem. Am. Math. Assn. 2-Yr. Colls. (Wyo. del. 1985-88, 90—), Phi Kappa Phi (Phys. Sci. div. Excellence in Teaching award 1987, 88, 92). Office: Laramie County Comm Coll 1400 E College Dr Cheyenne WY 82007-3295

BAILEY, LEONARD LEE, surgeon; b. Takoma Park, Md., Aug. 28, 1942; s. Nelson Hulburt and Catherine Effie (Long) B.; m. Nancy Ann Schroeder, Aug. 21, 1966; children: Jonathan Brooks, Charles Connor. BS, Columbia Union Coll., 1960-64; postgrad., NIH, 1965; MD, Loma Linda U., 1969. Diplomate Am. Bd. Surgery, Am. Bd. Thoracic Surgery. Intern Loma Linda U. Med. Ctr., 1969-70, resident in surgery, 1970-73, resident in thoracic and cardiovascular surgery, 1973-74; resident in pediatric cardiovascular surgery Hosp. for Sick Children, Toronto, Ont., Can., 1974-75; resident in thoracic and cardiovascular surgery Loma Linda U. Med. Sch., 1975-76, asst. prof. surgery, 1976-86, prof. surgery, 1986—, dir. pediatric cardiac surgery, 1976—, chief div. cardiothoracic surgery, 1988, chair dept. surgery, 1992. Mem. AMA, ACS, AAAS, Calif. Med. Assn., San Bernadino County Med. Soc., Am. Coll. Cardiology, Tri-County Surg. Soc., Western Thoracic Surg. Assn., Soc. Thoracic Surgery, Western Soc. Pediatric Rsch., L.A. Transplant Soc., Internat. Soc. for Heart Transplantation, Lyman A. Brewer III Internat. Surg. Soc., Am. Heart Assn., Internat. Assn. for Cardiac Biol. Implants, Am. Soc. for Artificial Internal Organs, So. Calif. Transplant Soc., Pacific Coast Surg. Assn., Western Assn. Transplant Surgeons, Internat. Soc. for Cardiovascular Surgery, United Network for Organ Sharing, The Transplant Soc. Democrat. Seventh-day Adventist. Office: Loma Linda U Med Ctr Rm 2560 Loma Linda CA 92354

BAILEY, MICHAEL JOHN, computer scientist; b. Phila., Oct. 16, 1953; s. Theodore Warren and Anne (Pomeroy) B. BS in Mech. Engring., Purdue U., 1975, MS in Mech. Engring., 1976, PhD, 1979. Mem. tech. staff Sandia Nat. Labs., Albuquerque, 1979-81; prof. mech. engring. Purdue U., West Lafayette, Ind., 1981-85; dir. advanced devel. Megatek Corp., San Diego, 1985-89; mgr. sci. visualization San Diego Supercomputer Ctr., 1989—; freelance cons. in field, 1981—. Recipient Ralph Teetor Teaching award Soc. Automotive Engrs., 1983. Mem. Assn. Computing Machinery, Spl. Interest Group on Computer Graphics (chmn. courses 1984-85, 87-88, exec. com. 1986-90, conf. co-chair 1991), Nat. Computer Graphics Assn., ASME. Office: San Diego Supercomputer Ctr PO Box 85608 San Diego CA 92186-9784

BAILEY, PHILIP SIGMON, JR., academic dean, chemistry educator; b. Charlottesville, Va., Mar. 17, 1943; s. Philip Sigmon Bailey and Marie Jeanette (Schultz) Hatch; m. Christina Anne Wahl; children: Karl, Jennifer, Kristen, Michael. Student, Am. U., Cairo, 1961; BS in Chemistry, U. Tex., 1964; PhD, Purdue U., 1969. Asst. prof. chemistry Calif. Poly. State U., San Luis Obispo, 1969-73, prof., assoc. dean, 1973-83, prof. chemistry, dean Sch. Sci. and Math., 1983-89, v.p. acad. affairs, sr. v.p., 1989-90, dean, 1990—. Author: (lab. texts) Experimental Chemistry for Contemporary Times, 1975, Organic Chemistry, 1978, (textbook) Organic Chemistry, 1978, 4th edit., 1989. Mem. Am. Chem. Soc., Alpha Chi Sigma. Home: 1628 Royal Way

San Luis Obispo CA 93405 Office: Calif Poly State U Coll Sci and Math San Luis Obispo CA 93407

BAILEY, ROBERT C., opera company executive; b. Metropolis, Ill., Dec. 28, 1936; m. Sally McDermott, July 13, 1958. BA in Speech, U. Ill., 1958, MA in English, 1960; BM in Applied Voice, Eastman Sch. Music, 1965; MM in Applied Voice, New Eng. Conservatory Music, 1969. Music producer Nat. Pub. Radio, Washington, 1971-73, dir. cultural programming, 1973-75; mgr. Western Opera Theater, San Francisco, 1975-79; instr. arts mgmt. Golden Gate U., San Francisco, 1977-82; cons. arts mgmt., San Francisco, 1980-82; gen. dir. Portland Opera Assn., Oreg., 1982—; dir. Oreg. Advocates Arts, Portland, 1982—; cons. On-Site Program Nat. Endowment Arts, Washington, 1982—; judge Met. Opera Auditions, 1977—. Mem. Bohemian Club (San Francisco), City Club (Portland), University Club, Rotary. Office: Portland Opera Assn Inc 1516 SW Alder St Portland OR 97205-1899

BAILEY, ROBERT ROY, college dean; b. Portland, Oreg., Feb. 9, 1948; s. Gordon and Ruth (Chadwick) B.; m. Anita Lamb, Mar. 17, 1973; children: Benjamin, Christopher, Dustin, Katie. BS in Health Edn. and Phys. Edn., U. Oreg., 1970; MA, Talbot Sem., La Mirada, Calif., 1977. Phys. edn. specialist Eugene (Oreg.) Pub. Schs., 1970-72; program dir. Solid Rock Ministries, Soldotna, Alaska, 1973-74; instr. Biola U., La Mirada, 1975-77; youth dir. Youth for Christ, Eugene, 1978-80; dir. camping Green Oak Ranch, Vista, Calif., 1984-87; tchr. Portland Christian Schs., 1987-88, vice chmn. bd. trustees, 1988—; dean men Multnomah Sch. Bible, Portland, 1988—; cons. David C. Cook Pubs., Portland, 1980-84; bd. dirs. Christian Camping Internat., So. Calif., 1985-87. Developer Christian edn. curriculum, 1976. Bd. dirs. Tri-City Christian Sch., Vista, 1986-87. Office: Multnomah Sch Bible 8435 NE Glisan St Portland OR 97220

BAILEY, RONALD BRUCE, college dean; b. Mt. Pleasant, Iowa, Mar. 3, 1934; s. Bernard B. and Marjorie May (Donald) B.; m. Willa Jean McAndrew, Aug. 13, 1956; children: Jon M., Kristen Ann, James A. BS in Edn., N.E. Mo. State U., Kirksville, 1955; MA, U. No. Colo., 1966. Tchr. Jefferson County Schs., Wheat Ridge, Colo., 1955-56, Williamsburg (Iowa) pub. schs., 1958-60, Hobbs (N.Mex.) Mcpl. schs., 1960-67; theatre dir. Northeastern Jr. Coll., Sterling, Colo., 1967-81; dir. planning and devel. Northeastern Jr. Coll., 1981-87, dean of instruction, 1988—. Author children's plays, 1974-81. Mem. Bd. Pub. Wks., Sterling, Colo., 1987—; mem. personnel bd. Logan County Govt., Sterling. With U.S. Army, 1956-58. U. No. Colo. Little Theatre of Rockies grantee, 1962-66; U. Ill. Dirs. Symposium In Theatre grantee, 1979. Mem. Colo. Community Coll. Deans Assn., Nat. Coun. Instructional Adminstrs., Sterling Arts Coun. (bd. dirs. 1981-84), Elks. Democrat. Roman Catholic. Office: Northeastern Junior College 100 College Dr Sterling CO 80751-2344

BAILEY, THOMAS EVERETT, engineering company executive; b. Atlantic, Iowa, Mar. 30, 1936; s. Merritt E. and Clara May (Richardson) B.; m. Elizabeth Jane Taylor, Sept. 9, 1956; children: Thomas E., Douglas L., Steven W. BS, U. Iowa, 1959. Reg. profl. engr., environ. assessor, expert witness, arbitrator. Engr. Calif. Dept. Water Resources, Sacramento, 1960-67; sr. engr. Calif. Water Quality Control Bd., San Luis Obispo, 1967-72; asst. div. chief, dir. water quality planning State Water Resources Control Bd., Sacramento, 1972-75, chief div. planning rsch., 1975-77, chief tech. support br., 1977-79; sr. tech. advisor Yemen Arab Republic, Sana'a, 1979-81; chief Calif. superfund program Calif. Dept. Health Svcs., Sacramento, 1982-86; prin., v.p. Kleinfelder Inc., Walnut Creek, Calif., 1986-92; also bd. dirs. Kleinfelder Inc., Walnut Creek; pres. Bailey Environ., Sacramento, 1992—; cons. engr., arbitrator Calif. Hazardous Substance Cleanup Arbitration Panel. Contbr. articles to profl. jours. Mem. San Luis County Obispo Rep. Ctrl. Com., 1969-72, vice-chmn., 1970-71, chmn., 1971-72; vice-chmn. bd. trustees Meth. Ch., San Luis Obispo, 1970-72; mem. Contra Costa County Hazardous Materials Com., 1988-89, Calif. Remedial Action Group, co-chmn. 1991-92; With U.S. Army, 1959-60. Mem. ASCE, Cons. Engrs. and Land Surveyors of Calif. (chmn. hazardous waste mgmt. acad. 1992—), Am. Consulting Engrs. Coun., Hazardous Waste Action Coalition (chmn. bus. practices com. 1991-93, bd. dirs. 1992-93). Office: Bailey Environ Engring 7064 Riverside Blvd Sacramento CA 95831

BAILEY, VIRGINIA HURT, elementary school educator, poet; b. Constantine, Mich., July 30, 1937; d. John Henry and Eunice Leona (Hufstedler) Hurt; m. Jerry Dee Skaggs, June 17, 1961 (dec. May 4, 1969); 1 child, Susan Marie Skaggs Martinez; m. Elton Ray Bailey, Dec. 17, 1971; stepchildren: Michael, Marsha Smith, Ann Aviles. AB, William Jewell Coll., 1959; MA, N.Mex. State U., 1983; postgrad., U. N.Mex., 1989—; degree in elem. edn., y. Cert. elem. tchr., ESL endorsement, Ariz. Tchr. Window Rock (Ariz.) Dist. 8, 1959-61, 1969—; tchr. Liberty (Mo.) Pub. Schs., 1963-64, Kansas City (Mo.) Pub. Schs., 1964-67; civil svc. employee MECOM, St. Louis, 1967-69; instr. Navajo Community Coll., Window Rock, 1984-86; mem. career ladder steering com. Window Rock Dist. 8, Ft. Defiance, Ariz., 1984-85, 86-89; mem. child study team Window Rock Elem. Schs., 1985—, test adminstr. Gessell Devel. Test, 1986—. Author numerous poems, (Golden Poet award 1985, 86, 87, 88); contbr. articles to profl. jours. Mem. choir Presbyn. Ch. Ft. Defiance, 1974—, elder, lay reader, 1978—, clk. session, 1980-89. Mem. NEA (local pres. 1978-79, state del. 1979-81, local sec. 1980-82), ASCD, Internat. Assn. Cognitive Edn., Ariz. Assn. Bilingual Edn., Tchrs. ESL, Alpha Delta Kappa. Republican. Home: PO Box 40 Fort Defiance AZ 86504-0040 Office: Window Rock Elem Sch Drawer B Window Rock AZ 86515

BAILEY, WILLIAM RALPH, financial services company executive; b. Alpena, Mich., Sept. 10, 1937; s. Ralph George and Thelma Esther (Hansen) B.; m. Evelyn Margaret Hunter, Aug. 17, 1957 (div. Sept. 1982); children: Kevin M., Philip H., Cherie Lynn, David R. Student, Ariz. State U., 1955, U. Mich., 1956-57. Regional mgr. Besser Co., Alpena, 1960-70; regional v.p. Columbia Machine Co., Vancouver, Wash., 1970-80; v.p. Oak Tree Adminstrs., Westwood, Calif., 1980-84; founder, chair, CEO Fitzgerald-Bailey Corp., Beverly Hills, Calif., 1984—. Contbr. articles to profl. jours. and trade mags. Mem. Thalians, L.A., 1983, L.A. World Affairs Coun., 1991, L.A. Chamber Soc., 1991, Dorothy Chandler Music Ctr., 1989, Graphic Arts Coun. L.A., 1990, Starlight Found., 1990; bd. dirs., Jeffrey Found., 1993; founder, bd. dirs. Cabrito Found., L.A., 1972; bd. dirs. L.A. chpt. Nat. Coun. on Alcoholism, 1979. Mem. Beverly Hills Bankers Assn., Da Camera Soc., Beverly Hills C. of C. Home: 10701 Wilshire Blvd Los Angeles CA 90024 Office: Fitzgerald-Bailey Corp 409 N Camden Dr Beverly Hills CA 90210

BAILHE, JACQUES PIERRE, film producer; b. Norwalk, Ct., Feb. 2, 1952; s. Jack P. and Lois (Schwartz) B. BFA magna cum laude, Art Ctr. Coll. of Design, Pasadena, Calif., 1979. Dir. audio-visual Young & Rubicam, L.A., 1981-82; producer Kenyon & Eckhardt, L.A., 1982-83, McCann-Erickson, L.A., 1983-85; sr. producer, spl. cons. Ogilvy & Mather Worldwide, L.A., 1985-86; pres., exec. producer Trick Films, L.A., 1986-91; dir. advt. design and motion pictures San Francisco Acad. Art Coll., 1992—; faculty Art Ctr. Coll. of Design, 1982-91. Contbr. articles to profl. jours. Recipient Hugo, Cine Awards, 1981, Hugo, Chgo. Inst. Film Festival, 1981, Effy, Effy Awards, 1987, Clio, Clio Awards, 1988; Humanities grantee Hampshire Coll., 1972. Mem. Acad. TV Arts & Scis., Brit. Acad. Film & TV. Office: San Francisco Acad Art Coll 79 New Montgomery St San Francisco CA 94105

BAILLIE, PATRICIA ANN, military career officer; b. Sacramento, Nov. 10, 1952; d. Herbert Clarence and Dorothy Elizabeth (Lambrecht) B. BA in Phys. Edn., Calif. State U., Northridge, 1974, MA in Phys. Edn., 1976. Tchr. secondary edn. L.A. City Schs., San Fernando, 1974-79; enlisted USAF, 1978, 2d lt., 1979, advanced through grades to maj.; weapons dir. USAF, Phoenix and Fairbanks, Alaska, 1979-83; shuttle flight planner USAF/NASA, Houston, 1983-86; budget planner Pentagon USAF, Washington, 1986-88; space operator USAF, Sunnyvale, Calif., 1988-92; instr. spl. duty USAF, Monterey, Calif., 1992—. Mem. Diablo Valley Met. Community Ch., Concord, Calif., 1992—; vol. coord. Santa Cruz Community Ctr., Crisis Hotline, 1992—.

BAILY, DOUGLAS BOYD, lawyer; b. Evanston, Ill., Jan. 27, 1937; divorced; 3 children. BS in Geology, Beloit Coll., 1959; JD, U. Ill., 1964. Bar: Alaska 1965. Field geologist Pan Am. Petroleum Corp., United Geophys. Corp., Alaska, 1960-61; asst. atty. gen. Dept. Law, State of Alaska, Juneau and Fairbanks, 1964-67, state dist. atty. 3d jud. dist., 1968, 69; U.S. atty. State of Alaska, Anchorage, 1969-71; adminstrv. asst. to gov. State of Alaska, Juneau, 1975; atty. gen. State of Alaska, 1989-90; dir. Office External and Internat. Fisheries Affairs Alaska Dept. Fish and Game, 1988-89; ptnr. Baily & Mason, P.C., Anchorage, 1971-88; pvt. practice law Anchorage, 1991—; capt. charter fishing boat, Homer, Alaska, 1988. Lic. as master of passenger vessels to 50 tons, USCG; mem. ad hoc com. for creation of Chugach State Pk., Alaska, 1970-71. With U.S. Army, 1959-60, Res., 1960-66. Mem. ABA (Ho. of Dels. 1985-86), Anchorage Bar Assn. Home: 1130 W 6th Ave Anchorage AK 99501-5914

BAILY, EVERETT MINNICH, electrical engineer; b. Twin Falls, Idaho, June 9, 1938; s. Charles Levi Baily and Helen Louise (Minnich) Wall; m. Donna Rae Larson, Sept. 8, 1961; children: Susan Gayle, Brian Charles. BSEE, U. Idaho, 1961, MSEE, 1964; PhD, Stanford U., 1968. Asst. prof. U. Idaho, Moscow, 1965-71; assoc. prof. U. Idaho, 1971-74, prof., 1974; prodn. engr. Hewlett Packard Co., Boise, Idaho, 1974-75; devel. engr. Hewlett Packard Co., 1975-81, reliability engr., 1981-83, reliability engring. mgr., 1983-86, prodn. engring. mgr., 1986-89, sr. mfg. engr., 1990—; cons. researcher U. Idaho Rsch. Found., Moscow, 1971-73. Patentee in field. Recipient Dow Outstanding Young Faculty award, Am. Assn. Engring. Edn. Pacific Northwest sect, 1970. Mem. IEEE (Boise sect. chmn. 1979, numerous com. offices), Model A Ford Club Am., Lions. Home: 12080 Chinden Blvd Boise ID 83714-1035 Office: Hewlett Packard Co 11311 Chinden Blvd # 514 Boise ID 83714-1021

BAIMBRIDGE, GLORIA ANN, college administrator; b. Boise, Idaho, July 24, 1946; d. George Andrew and Lena Lee (Mitchell) Cameron; m. James Marlin Baimbridge, July 1, 1967; children: Kayleen Klundt, Ronda Agema, David. Student, Ozark Christian Coll., Joplin, Mo., 1964-65. Piano instr. Ozark Christian Coll., Joplin, Mo., 1964-65; piano tchr., 1967-85; optometric asst. Dr. Rod Porter, Worland, Wyo., 1977-78; bookkeeper B-C Diesel, Inc., Worland, 1978-79, Baimbridge Transport, Inc., Riverton, Wyo., 1979-83; bus. mgr. KTRZ Radio, Riverton, 1984-91, Boise Bible Coll., 1991—. Sec. Western Wyo. Christian Youth Camp, Riverton, Wyo., 1982-91; pres. Community Concert Assn., Riverton, 1985-86; mus. pianist Riverton High Sch., 1984-90, Ctrl. Wyo. Coll., Riverton, 1983-91; pianist, organist First Ch. of Christ/Castle Dr., Boise. Named Outstanding Musician Arts in Action, Riverton, 1985, 90. Republican. Office: Boise Bible Coll 8695 Marigold St Boise ID 83714

BAINS, LINDA JANE, software engineer, systems analyst; b. Columbia, Mo., Nov. 23, 1956; d. John M. and Geraldine (Swartz) Palmer; m. Suki S. Bains, July 5, 1985; 1 child, Christopher Andrew. B. in Bus., Aquinas, 1982; MBA, Xavier, 1990. Programmer, systems analyst Total Group Svcs., Grand Rapids, Mich., 1980-84, GE Aircraft Engring. (Contractor), Cin., 1984-85, Midwest Group of Funds, Cin., 1985; systems support analyst Prime Computer, Cin., 1985—; sr. on-site analyst to GE aircraft engine Prime Computer, Cin., 1985—. Campaign vol. Dem. Party, Grand Rapids, Mich., 1975; stewardship mem. Faith United Meth. Ch., Cin., 1988; charity fundraiser vol. Joy Junction, Albuquerque, 1991; cons. Encore/SBA, Albuquerque, 1991; children's libr. Ctrl. United Meth. Ch., Albuquerque, 1992. Office: Prime Computer 4273 Montgomery Ave NE Albuquerque NM 87109

BAINTON, DOROTHY FORD, pathology educator, researcher; b. Magnolia, Miss., June 18, 1933; d. Aubrey Ratcliff and Leta (Brumfield) Ford; m. Cedric R. Bainton, Nov. 28, 1959; children: Roland J., Bruce G., James H. BS, Millsaps Coll., 1955; MD, Tulane U. Sch. of Medicine, 1958; MS, U. Calif., San Francisco, 1966. Postdoctoral rsch. fellow U. Calif., San Francisco, 1963-66, postdoctoral rsch. pathologist, 1966-69, asst. prof. pathology, 1969-75, assoc. prof., 1975-81, prof. pathology, 1981—, chair pathology, 1987—; mem. Inst. of Medicine, NAS, 1990—. NIH grantee, 1978—. Mem. AAAS, Am. Soc. for Cell Biology, Am. Soc. Hematology, Am. Soc. Histochemists and Cytochemists, Am. Assn. of Pathologists. Democrat. Mem. Soc. of Friends. Office: U Calif Dept Pathology Box 0506 HSW-501 3rd and Parnassus San Francisco CA 94143

BAIRD, ALAN C., television producer, writer; b. Waterville, Maine, Jan. 5, 1951; s. Chester A. and Beverly E. (Gilbert) B. BA, Mich. State U., 1973. Pres. Souterrain Teeshirts, Nice, France, 1977-78; page NBC, N.Y.C., 1979-80; producer, dir. Random Prodns., Hollywood, Calif., 1981; writer, producer Preview STV, N.Y.C., 1982-83, Sta. KCOP-TV, Hollywood, 1983-84; writer Vidiom Prodns., Hollywood, 1985—. Author: ATS Operations, 1976, Writes of Passage, 1992; producer (TV script) Live at the Palomino, 1981; writer (TV scripts) Night Court, 1986, 20/60, 1986, Golden Girls, 1986, Family Ties, 1986, Max Headroom, 1987, (movie scripts) Trading Up, 1988, Merlinsky, 1989. Crisis counselor San Francisco Suicide Prevention, 1975; prodn. asst. March of Dimes Telethon, Hollywood, 1985. Recipient Harvard Book prize Harvard U., Cambridge, Mass., 1969.

BAIRD, DELPHA, state legislator; b. Brigham City, Utah, Dec. 13, 1930; m. Steven Baird; 9 children. BS, U. Utah, 1983. Treas. Holladay Cottonwood Community Coun., 1985—; sec., treas. Archl. Ornamentation Inc., 1985—; mem. Utah State Senate from 9th dist. Mem. Profl. Rep. Women, Utah Women's Legis. Coun. Republican. Mem. LDS Ch. Address: 2574 Kentucky Ave Salt Lake City UT 84117 Office: Utah House of Reps Office of House Mems Salt Lake City UT 84114

BAIRD, J. ERNEST, lawyer, state representative; b. Tempe, Ariz., Jan. 3, 1944; s. William Richard and Gertrude (Taylor) B.; m. Ginna Price, Oct. 14, 1972; children: Melissa, Dayne, Andrew, Brittany, Emily. Attended, Ariz. State U., 1962-63; BA, Brigham Young U., 1968; JD, Duke U., 1971. Assoc. atty. Shearman & Sterling, N.Y., 1971-72; capt. USAF, Calif., 1972-76, Eng., 1972-76; assoc. atty. Streich, Lang & Weeks, Phoenix, 1976-78; ptnr. Burton, Baird & Kries, Phoenix, 1978-79, Earl, Baird & Williams, Phoenix, 1983-90, Murphy & Posner, Phoenix, 1990—. dist. chmn. dist. 24 Ariz. Rep. Party, Phoenix, 1984-88, mem. state exec. com.; chmn. Trunk & Tusk, Phoenix, 1990; mem. Valley of the Sun Kiwanis, 1979-87; state rep. House of Reps., 1991—, chmn. house judiciary com. Mem. LDS Ch. Home: 3201 E Carol Ave Phoenix AZ 85028 Office: Ariz House of Reps 1700 E Washington Phoenix AZ 85007

BAIRD, JOHN JEFFERS, biology educator; b. North English, Iowa, Jan. 1, 1921; s. William Simon and Ruth Caroline (Jeffers) B.; m. Grace Geraldine Garner, Oct. 13, 1946; 1 child, Stephanie Lynn. BA in Sci., Iowa State Tchrs. Coll., 1948; MS in Zoology, U. Iowa, 1953, PhD, 1957. Cert. tchr., Iowa. Chief pilot M&T Aerial Spray Co., Cedar Falls, Iowa, 1948; tchr. Muscatine (Iowa) High Sch., 1948-54; from asst. prof. to prof. Calif. State U., Long Beach, 1956-67, dept. chmn., 1960-67; dep. dean, instr. Chancellors Office, Calif. State U., Long Beach, 1967-78; prof. biology Calif. State U., Long Beach, 1978—, prof. emeritus, 1984—. Mem., trustee Savanna Sch. Dist., anaheim, Calif., 1965-81; mem. of session 1st Presbyn. Ch., Anaheim, 1975-78, pres. 1985—; mem. Orange County Calif. Grand Jury, 1993—. Capt. USAFR, 1942-46, ETO, lt. col. Res. Named one of Outstanding Profs., Calif. State U. Associated Students, 1984; Recipient Mayfield award Calif. State U. Sch. of Nat. Scis., 1990. Fellow So. Calif. Acad. Sci.; mem. AAAS, Am. Soc. Zoologists, So. Calif. Acad. Sci. (pres. 1974-76, bd. dirs. 1968-81), Sigma Xi. Office: Calif State U 1250 N Bellflower Blvd Long Beach CA 90840-0001

BAIRD, LOURDES G., federal judge. BA with highest honors, UCLA, 1973, JD with honors, 1976. Asst. U.S. atty. U.S. Dist. Ct. (ctrl. dist.) Calif., L.A., 1977-83, U.S. atty., 1990-92; ptnr. Baird & Quadros, 1983-84, Baird, Munger & Myers, 1984-86; judge East L.A. Mcpl. Ct., 1986-87, L.A. Mcpl. Ct., 1987-88, L.A. Superior Ct., 1988-90, U.S. Dist. Ct. (ctrl. dist.) Calif., L.A., 1992—; faculty civil RICO program Practicing Law Inst., San Francisco, 1984-85, western regional program Nat. Inst. Trial Advocacy, Berkeley, Calif., 1987-88; adj. prof. trial advocacy Loyola U., L.A., 1987-90. Mem. Mexican-Am. Bar Assn., Calif. Women Lawyers, Hispanic Nat. Bar Assn., UCLA Sch. Law alumni Assn. (pres. 1984). Office: US Dist Ct Ctrl Dist Calif 255 E Temple St Ste 770 Los Angeles CA 90012

BAKEMAN, CAROL ANN, administrative services manager, singer; b. San Francisco, Oct. 27, 1934; d. Lars Hartvig and Gwendolyne Beatrice (Zimmer) Bergh; student UCLA, 1954-62; m. Delbert Clifton Bakeman, May 16, 1959; children: Laurie Ann, Deborah Ann. Singer, Roger Wagner Chorale, 1954-92, Los Angeles Master Chorale, 1964-86, The Wagner Ensemble, 1991—; librarian Hughes Aircraft Co., Culver City, Calif., 1954-61; head econs. library Planning Research Corp., L.A., 1961-63; corporate librarian Econ. Cons., Inc., Los Angeles, 1963-68; head econs. library Daniel, Mann, Johnson & Mendenhall, architects and engrs., L.A., 1969-71, corporate librarian, 1971-77, mgr. info. services, 1978-81, mgr. info. and office services, 1981-83, mgr. adminstrv. services, 1983—; pres., Creative Library Systems, Los Angeles, 1974-83; library cons. ArchiSystems, div. SUMMA Corp., Los Angeles, 1972-81, Property Rehab. Corp., Bell Gardens, Calif., 1974-75, VTN Corp., Irvine, Calif., 1974, William Pereira & Assos., 1975; mem. office systems and bus. edn. adv. bd. Calif. State U. Northridge, 1992—. Mem. Assistance League, So. Calif., 1956-86, mem. nat. auxilaries com. 1968-72, 75-78, mem. nat. by laws com. 1970-75, mem. asso. bd. dirs., 1966-76. Mem. AFTRA, SAG, Am. Guild Musical Artists, Adminstrv. Mgmt. Soc. (v.p. Los Angeles chpt. 1984-86, pres. 1986-88, internat. conf. chmn. 1988-89, internat. bd. dirs. 1988-90, internat. v.p. mgmt. edn. 1990-92), Los Angeles Master Chorale Assn. (bd. dirs. 1978-83), Internat. Office Mgmt. Assn. (charter 1993).

BAKER, ALTON FLETCHER, JR., newspaper editor; b. Cleve., Nov. 15, 1919; s. Alton Fletcher and Mildred (Moody) B.; m. Genevieve Mertzke, 1947 (div. 1975); m. Jeannette Workman Vollstedt, Feb. 14, 1976; children: Sue Baker Diamond, Alton Fletcher, III, Sarah Moody, Robin Baker O'Connor. A.B., Pomona Coll., 1942. Reporter Eugene (Oreg.) Register-Guard, 1946-50, mng. editor, 1950-54, editor, 1954—, pub., 1961-82, chmn. bd., 1982-87; chmn. Oreg. Press Conf., 1973. Chmn. fund drive United Way, Eugene, 1965, pres., 1966-67; bd. dirs., pres. YMCA, Eugene. Served to capt. USAAF, World War II. Mem. Oreg. Newspaper Pubs. Assn. (dir. 1965-70), Am. Soc. Newspaper Editors, Am. Newspaper Pubs. Assn. Republican. Clubs: Eugene Country, De Anza Country. Home: 2410 W 23rd Ave Eugene OR 97405-1404 Office: Guard Pub Co 975 High St PO Box 10188-2188 Eugene OR 97440

BAKER, BRIDGET DOWNEY, newspaper executive; b. Eugene, Oreg., Sept. 14, 1955; d. Edwin Moody and Patricia (Petersen) B.; m. Guy Dominique Wood, June 30, 1977 (div. Oct. 1981); m. Rayburn Keith Kincaid, June 27, 1987; stepchildren: Benjamin, Jacob. BA in English, French and Theatre, Lewis and Clark Coll., 1977; MA in Journalism, U. Oreg., 1985. Circulation dist. supr. The Register-Guard, Eugene, 1978-80, pub. relations coordinator, 1980-83, promotion dir., 1983-86, mktg. dir., 1986-88; corp. pub. rels. dir., 1989—; bd. dirs. Guard Pub. Co., Eugene. Bd. dirs. Wilani Coun. Camp Fire Girls, Eugene, 1982-88, pres. bd. dirs., 1986-88; bd. dirs. Lane County United Way, 1982-88, community info. com. chairperson, 1982-84; bd. dirs. Eugene Opera, 1988-91, pres. bd. dirs., 1990-91. Recipient 1st place advt. award Editor and Pub. Mag., N.Y.C., 1984, also 1st place TV promotion, 1st place newspaper rsch. award, 1988; Best Mktg. Idea/Campaign awrd Oreg. Newspaper Pub. Assn., 1984, 85. Mem. Internat. Mktg. Assn. (bd. dirs. Western region 1986-88, 8 1st Place Best in the West awards 1983-91), Pub. Rels. Soc. Am. (Spotlight award 1986), Eugene C. of C. (bd. dirs. 1989-92), U. Oreg. Alumni Assn. (bd. dirs. 1990-93), Downtown Athletic Club, Eugene Yacht Club, Zonta Internat. Republican. Office: Guard Pub Co 1065 High St Ste 1 Eugene OR 97401-3254

BAKER, CAMERON, lawyer; b. Chgo., Dec. 24, 1937; s. David Cameron and Marion (Fitzpatrick) B.; m. Katharine Julia Solari, Sept. 2, 1961; children: Cameron III, Ann, John. Student, U. Notre Dame, 1954-57; AB, Stanford U., 1958; LLB, U. Calif., Berkeley, 1961. Bar: Calif. 1962, U.S. Dist. Ct. (so. dist.) Calif. 1962, U.S. Dist. Ct. (no. dist.) Calif. 1963, U.S. Ct. Appeals (9th) 1963. Assoc. Adams, Duque & Hazeltine, Los Angeles, 1961-62; assoc. Pettit & Martin, San Francisco, 1962—, mng. ptnr., 1972-81, 84-87, mem. exec. com., 1971-82, 84-88; mayor City of Belvedere, Calif., 1978-79. Mem. Lawyers Com. for Civil Right San Francisco Bay Area, bd. dirs., 1975-83; bd. dirs. San Francisco Legal Aid Soc., 1971-72; dir. Lassen Volcanic Nat. Park Found., 1992—. Mem. ABA (sects. on bus. law and internat. law and practice), Union Internationale des Avocats, Calif. Bar Assn. (chmn. governing com. continuing edn. 1975), Bar Assn. San Francisco (bd. dirs. 1966, 72-73), Boalt Hall Alumni Assn. (dir. 1982-84), Bohemian Club, Tiburon Peninsula Club. Home: 38 Alcatraz Ave Belvedere CA 94920-2504 Office: Pettit & Martin 101 California St 35th Fl San Francisco CA 94111

BAKER, CHARLES DEWITT, research and development company executive; b. Dayton, Ohio, Jan. 5, 1932; s. Donald James and Lillian Mae (Pund) B.; m. June Thordis Tandberg, June 25, 1954; children: Charles, Robert, Thomas, Michael. AA in Electrical Engring., Long Beach City Coll., 1953; Boston U., 1954, Pacific Coast U., 1963, U. Utah, 1980. Registered profl. mfg. engr., Calif. Chemist Shell Oil, Torrance, Calif., 1957-60; materials and process engr. Northrop Corp., Hawthorne, Calif., 1960-63; packaging engr. Jet Propulsion Lab., Pasadena, Calif., 1963-71; med. design engr. Utah Biomed. Test Lab., Salt Lake City, 1971-78, sect. mgr., 1978-83; v.p. Tech. Rsch. Assocs., Salt Lake City, 1983-88, pres., 1988—; pres. Thordis Corp., 1980—. Contbr. articles to profl jours.; 20 patents in field. Com. mem. Heart and Lung Inst. Community Adv. Com., spl. study sect rev. NIH, Tech. Transfer Forum, U. Utah, 1984. Recipient Cost Reduction award NASA, 1969, New Tech. award, 1969, 71, 75. Mem. ASME, Soc. Mfg. Engrs., Utah Mfg. Assn., Acad. of Tech., Entrepreneurs and Innovators. Republican. Mormon. Office: Tech Rsch Assocs 2257 S 1100 E Salt Lake City UT 84106

BAKER, DANIAL EDWIN, director, consultant, pharmacy educator; b. Whitefish, Mont., May 25, 1955; s. Arby E. and Cathy Lee (Yarroll) B.; m. Patricia Samuelson, Aug. 28, 1976; 1 child, Kristin Nicole. B in Pharmacy, Wash. State U., 1978; PharmD, U. Minn., 1980. Lic. pharmacy, Idaho, Wash. Instr. in pharmacology for respiratory therapist St. Paul Tech. Vocat. Inst., 1980; asst. prof. U. Okla., 1980-83; asst. prof. Wash. State U., Spokane, 1983-88, dir. Drug Info. Ctr., 1983—, assoc. prof., 1988—; pharmacy cons. Moscow (Idaho) Care Ctr., 1985—; mem. drug formulatory adv. com. div. med. assistance Wash. Dept. Social and Health Svcs., Olympia, 1990, chmn., 1990-92; mem. cons. panel The UpJohn Co., Kalamazoo, 1990—; mem. adv. panel on drug info. sci. U.S. Pharmacopeial Conv., Inc., Rockville, Md., 1990—; mem. Inst. for Safe Medication Practices, Inc., Huntington Valley, Pa., 1990—, Inst. Rev. Bd., Spokane, 1992—, Wash. State U., 1993—. Named one of Outstanding Young Men of Am., 1982, 83. Fellow Am. Soc. Cons. Pharmacists, Am. Soc. Hosp. Pharmacists; mem. Am. Assn. Colls. Pharmacy, Am. Coll. Clin. Pharmacy, Am. Diabetes Assn., Am. Pharm. Assn., Am. Soc. Cons. Pharmacists, Am. Soc. Hosp. Pharmacists, Wash. Pharmacists Assn. (senator 1991—, continuing edn. com. 1988—, award com. 1989—, co-chairperson undergrad. affairs com. 1990-92, del. Quinquinnel conv. 1987—, Pharmacist of Yr. award 1992), Wash. Soc. Hosp. Pharmacists (coun. edn. and manpower 1989-92, chmn. 1990-92, bd. dirs. 1989—, pres. Spokane chpt. 1992—), Drug Info. Assn. Republican. Office: Wash State U 601 W 1st Ave Spokane WA 99204-0399

BAKER, DEBORAH ANN, business owner; b. Washington, May 12, 1956; d. Richard John and Shirley Ann (Jackson) Dunagan; m. Don Steven Baker, June 20, 1980; children: Adam Ross, Jason Richard, Natalie Rae. Grad. High Sch., Novato, Calif. Buyer, dept. mgr. Carithers. Dept. Store, Novato, Calif., 1975-77; mgr. books Baker Installations, Denver, 1977-79; mgr. Fashion Carpets, Englewood, Colo., 1979-83; owner, operator Baker Interiors, Inc., Englewood, 1983—, pres., 1991—. Office: Baker Interiors Inc 209 W Littleton Blvd Littleton CO 80120-2331

BAKER, DENYS MARIE, motel and restaurant executive; b. Payson, Utah, Jan. 7, 1948; d. Grant William Koyle and Shirley Jayne (Garbett) Schena; m. Alexander Ray Perea, Apr. 28, 1968 (div. 1979); children: Gary A., Dennis A.; m. John Dean Baker, Oct. 21, 1981; step-children: Christina, David, Craig, Tom. BA magna cum laude, U. Utah, 1970; postgrad., U. Calif.-Long Beach, 1976-77. Cert. tchr., Utah. Owner, mgr. Border Inn, Baker, Nev., 1977-81, 85—; instr. No. Nev. Community Coll., Ely, 1990—. Mem. Nev. Dem. Exec. Com., 1984, Nev. Dem. Ctrl. Com.; sec. Baker Town Adv. Bd., 1985-91, 93—; bd. dirs. White Pine County Libr., 1991—, chmn., 1992—. Recipient Gov.'s Tourism Devel. award, 1988. Mem. Nev. Cattlewomen's Assn. (officer local sect.), White Pine County C. of C. (bd. dirs.). Office: Border Inn Hwy 50 At Hwy # 6 Baker NV 89311

BAKER, DON ROBERT, chemist; b. Salt Lake City, Apr. 6, 1933; s. Ralph H. and Ruth Eve (Thalmann) B.; m. Shirley May Nelson, Nov. 20, 1954; children: Robert, David, George, Barbara. AA, Sacramento City Coll., 1953; AB, Calif. State U., Sacramento, 1955; PhD, U. Calif., Berkeley, 1959. Sr. rsch. chemist Stauffer Chem. Co., Richmond, Calif., 1958-72, rsch. assoc., 1970-74, supr., 1974-85; sr. rsch. assoc. ICI Ams. Inc. Zeneca Ag Products, Richmond, Calif., 1985—. Editor: California chemists Alert, 1986—, Synthesis and chemistry of Agrochemicals, 1987, 90, 92; contbr. articles to profl. jours.; patentee in field, 1990, 92. Mem. Am. Chem. Soc. (chmn. Calif. sect. 1973, councilor Calif. sect. 1971—, chmn. nat. div. profl. relations 1980, coordinating com. Calif. sects. 1970—, Walter Petersen award 1991), Plant Growth Regulator Soc. (vice chmn. agrochemical divsn. 1993, Fellow award 1992), Orchid Soc. Calif. (pres. 1979-80), Oakland Genealogy Library (librarian 1967—). Republican. Mormon. Home: 15 Muth Dr Orinda CA 94563-2805 Office: Zeneca Ag Products 1200 S 47th St Richmond CA 94804-4610

BAKER, DUSTY (JOHNNIE B. BAKER, JR.), professional baseball team manager; b. Riverside, Calif., June 15, 1949. Student, Am. River Coll. Player Atlanta Braves, 1968-75, L.A. Dodgers, 1976-83, San Francisco Giants, 1984, Oakland A's, 1985-86; coach San Francisco Giants, 1988-92, mgr., 1993—; mem. Nat. League All-Star Team, 1981-82. Recipient Silver Slugger award, 1980-81, Gold Glove, 1981; named to Sporting News All-Star Team, 1980. Office: San Francisco Giants Candlestick Park San Francisco CA 94124

BAKER, EDWIN MOODY, retired newspaper publisher; b. Cleve., Dec. 20, 1923; s. Alton Fletcher and Mildred Elizabeth (Moody) B.; m. Patricia Petersen, 1954 (dec. 1983); children: Bridget Baker Kincaid, Amanda Baker Barber, Jonathan; m. Marie Kottkamp Randall, 1984; children: Steven, Mark, Bruce Randall. B.S. in Bus. Adminstrn., U. Oreg., 1948. With Eugene (Oreg.) Register-Guard, 1948-88, successively advt. mgr., bus. mgr., gen. mgr., pub., pres., chmn. bd. Guard Pub. Co.; pres. Community Newspapers, Inc., Beaverton, Oreg., v.p. N.W. Web. Mem. exec. bd. Oreg. Trail Council, Boy Scouts Am., 1953—, pres. 1960-61, chmn. Region XI Area I (Northwest) 1971, pres., 1972, mem. nat. exec. bd., 1971-72, nat. adv. council, 1972-82; trustee U. Oreg. Found., 1975-90, Lane Community Coll.; bd. dirs. Oreg. Community Found., 1982-90; Oreg. Hist. Soc., 1988-92; trustee Eugene Arts Found., 1980-85; pres. Oreg. Pacific Econ. Devel. Corp., 1984-85; 2d v.p. Eugene Springfield Met. Ptnrship.; mem., chmn. Sister City com., 1986-88. Served with AUS, World War II. Decorated Bronze Star, Purple Heart; recipient Silver Beaver award, Boy Scouts Am., 1962, Silver Antelope, 1965, Pioneer award U. Oreg., 1982, Disting. Eagle Scout, 1982, Awbrey Watzig award Lewis and Clark Coll., 1988; named Eugene First Citizen, 1983. Mem. Am. Newspaper Pubs. Assn. (research inst. lab. com. 1978-79), Oreg. Newspaper Pubs. Assn. (dir. 1982-90, pres. 1988-89), U. Oreg. Pres. Assocs. , Rotary, Eugene Country Club. Home: 2121 Kimberly Cir Eugene OR 97405-5821 Office: Guard Pub Co PO Box 10188-2188 975 High St Eugene OR 97440

BAKER, EDWIN STUART, computer consultant; b. Ottumwa, Iowa, Feb. 14, 1944; s. Edwin Moore and Geraldine Vivian (Irby) B; m. Wilma Jeanne Parker, 1968 (div. 1970). Student, Whitman Coll., 1962-64; BS, Oreg. State U., 1978. Programmer agrl. engring. dept. Oreg. State U., Corvallis, 1977-78, rsch. asst., 1979-83, sr. rsch. asst., 1984-89; measurement standards specialist Oreg. Dept. Agr., Salem, 1990—; cons. in field. Mem. IEEE, Assn for Computing Machinery, Am. Legion, DAV, NRA, Nat. Intercollegiate Rodeo Assn., 59ers Svc. Club. Home: PO Box 68 Fairview OR 97024 Office: Oreg Dept Agr Measurements Standards Divsn Salem OR 97310

BAKER, EUGENE MANIGAULT, psychologist; b. Washington, Sept. 24, 1951; s. Eugene M. III and Rita (Bear) B.; m. Regina Brody, Aug. 25, 1991. BA, U. Colo., Boulder, 1973, MA, 1975, PhD, 1977. Lic. psychologist, Oreg. Assoc. psychologist Hutchings Psychiat. Ctr., Syracuse, N.Y., 1977-79; staff psychologist Linn County Mental Health, Albany, Oreg., 1979-82; pvt. practice Portland, Oreg., 1984—; tng. dir. Delaunay Mental Health Ctr., Portland, 1982-92; exec. dir. United Behavioral Systems, 1992—. Mem. Am. Psychol. Assn., Oreg. Psychol. Assn. (pres. 1989-90), Oreg. Acad. Profl. Psychologists (pres. 1987-88), Soc. Descriptive Psychology. Home: 1991 NW Walmer Dr Portland OR 97229-4252 Office: United Behavioral Systems 10163 SE Sunnyside Rd Ste 495 Portland OR 97015

BAKER, FRED GREENTREE, hydrogeologist; b. Chgo., July 26, 1950; s. Con James and Ethel M. (Skowbo) B.; m. Judith Ann Krill, 1972 (div. 1974); m. Hannah F. Pavlik, Apr. 26, 1976. BS in Geology, U. Wis., 1972, MS in Soil Sci., 1975; MS in Civil Engring., U. Colo., Boulder, 1981, PhD in Geology, 1985. Registered geologist, Calif.; registered profl. engr., Colo.; cert. engring. geologist, Calif. Rsch. specialist Wis. Geol. and Natural History Survey, Madison, 1973-76; rsch. assoc. dept. civil engring. Colo. State U., Fort Collins, 1977-78; hydrologist U.S. EPA, Denver, 1979-81; engring. geologist Charles C. Bowman Assocs., Inc., Boulder, Colo., 1982-85; sr. hydrogeologist Dames & Moore, Sacramento, 1985-88; dir. ops. On-Site Technologies, Inc., Sacramento, 1989; mgr. hydrogeologic svcs. Woodward-Clyde Cons., Denver, 1989-90; cons. engr., hydrogeologist Ebasco Environmental, Lakewood, Colo., 1990-91; pres. Baker Consultants, Inc., Golden, Colo., 1991—. Contbr. articles to profl. jours. Mem. ASCE, ASTM, Am. Geophys. Union, Soil Sci. Soc. Am., Am. Assn. Petroleum Geologists, Assn. Ground Water Scientists and Engrs., Sigma Xi. Office: Baker Consultants Inc 2970 Howell Rd Golden CO 80401

BAKER, GEORGE RUSSELL, environmental specialist; b. Suffern, NY, July 18, 1956; s. Joseph Eli Baker and Suzanne (Wilkenfeld) Dalrymple; m. Karen Kay Thomas, May 28, 1980. Student, U St. Andrews, Scotland, 1979-81; BA, Calif. State U., Chico, 80; postgrad., U. Calif., Riverside, 82-85. Assoc. hazardous materials specialist Calif. Dept Health Svcs., L.A., 1986-88; sr. hazardous materials specialist Calif. Dept Health Svcs., Long Beach, 1989—. Author: California Drum Recyclers Survey, 1988. Scholar Calif. State U., Scotland, 1979-81. Home: 7786 La Mona Cir Buena Park CA 90620 Office: Calif Dept Health Toxics Program 245 W Broadway Ste 350 Long Beach CA 90802

BAKER, GLADYS ELIZABETH, retired microbiologist, educator; b. Iowa City, Iowa, July 22, 1908; d. Richard Philip and Katherine (Riedelbauch) B. BA, U. Iowa, 1930, MS, 1932; PhD, Washington U., St. Louis, 1935. Biology instr. Hunter Coll., N.Y.C., 1936-40; instr., then asst. prof. Vassar Coll., Poughkeepsie, N.Y., 1940-45; assoc. prof., then prof., chmn. dept. plant scis. Vassar Coll., Poughkeepsie, 1945-61; prof. botany U. Hawaii, Honolulu, 1961-73; acting chmn. botany dept., U. Hawaii, 1965. Illustrator: The Myxomycetes, 1934; contbr. articles on mycology to profl., sci. jours. Recipient 3 research grants NSF, 1952-60, others. Fellow AAAS; mem. Mycol. Soc. Am., British Mycol. Soc., Med. Mycol. Soc. of the Ams. (charter). Episcopalian. Home: 158 Sierra Winds 17300 N 88th Ave Peoria AZ 85382

BAKER, HERBERT GEOFFREY, career officer; b. San Jose, Calif., Apr. 23, 1941; s. Herbert Alfred and Francis Constance (Knapton) B.; m. Dorinda Lee Peralta, May 10, 1964; children: Jonna Constance, Laura Gean. BA in English, Speech, San Jose State U., 1965, postgrad. in edn., 1966; student in indsl. mgmt., U. N.D., 1967-70; MA in Mass Comms., U. Denver, 1972. Cert. secondary education tchr. Commd. USAF, 1965, advanced through grades to col., 1987; chief, pub. affairs 36th Tactical Fighter Wing, Moody AFB, Ga., 1972-74, Bitburg AFB, Germany, 1974-77; chief, plans div. USAF in Europe, Pub. Affairs, Ramstein AB, Germany, 1977-80; dir. pub. affairs HQ Space Div., L.A. AFB, 1980-84; chief, media rels. Air Force Systems Comman, Andrews AFB, Md., 1984-87; asst. dir. print media plans and policy Dept. Def., Alexandria, Va., 1987-91; dir. pub. affairs U.S. Pacific Command, Hawaii, 1991-92. Editorial bd. Stars and Stripes newspapers. Mem. Soc. Profl. Journalists, Air Force Assn. (Excellence award 1984), Rotary.

BAKER, HERBERT GEORGE, botany educator; b. Brighton, Eng., Feb. 23, 1920; came to U.S., 1957; s. Herbert Reginald and Alice (Bambridge) B.; m. Irene Williams, Apr. 4, 1945; 1 dau., Ruth Elaine. B.S., U. London, 1941, Ph.D., 1945. Research chemist, asst. plant physiologist Hosa Research Labs., Sunbury-on-Thames, Eng., 1940-45; lectr. botany U. Leeds, Eng., 1945-54; research fellow Carnegie Instn., Washington, 1948-49; prof. botany U. Coll. Ghana, 1954-57; faculty U. Calif., Berkeley, 1957—, assoc. prof. botany, 1957-60, prof., 1960-90, prof. integrative biology emeritus, 1990—, dir. bot. garden, 1957-69. Author: Plants and Civilization, 1965, 70, 78 (translated into Spanish and Japanese); editor: (with G. L. Stebbins) Genetics of Colonizing Species, 1965; series editor: Bot. Monographs, 1971-84; contbr. articles to sci. jours. Fellow Assn. Tropical Biology, AAAS (past pres. Pacific div.); mem. Am. Acad. Arts and Sci., Am. Philos. Soc., Am. Inst. Biol. Sci., Brit. Ecol. Soc. (hon. mem.), Soc. Econ. Botany (Disting. mem. award), Internat. Assn. Botanic Gardens (past v.p.), Ecol. Soc. Am., Soc. for Study Evolution (past pres.), Bot. Soc. Am. (past pres.), Sigma Xi. Home: 635 Creston Rd Berkeley CA 94708-1239

BAKER, JANE ELAINE, municipal government official; b. Hamilton, Ohio, June 4, 1923; d. Ernst Andrew and Lillian (Schaub) Grimmer; m. Harris William Baker, Mar. 8, 1945; children: Cindi Marie, Bruce William. BS, Purdue U., 1944. Nutritionist Stokely-Van Camp Corp., Indpls., 1944-45, Cornell U., Ithaca, N.Y., 1945-46; dietitian U. Colo., Boulder, 1946; nutritionist Dairy Coun. of Indpls., 1947-48; performer Stas. KGO and KRON-TV, San Francisco, 1949-51, Sta. KNTV, San Jose, Calif., 1952; coun. member City of San Mateo, Calif., 1973—, mayor, 1975-76, 78-80, 82-83, 87-88, 92-93; mem. Met. Transp. Commn., Oakland, Calif., 1983—, chair, 1993—; mem. San Mateo County Transp. Agy., 1989—. Mem. State Job Tng. Coordinating Coun., Sacramento, 1984—; bd. dirs. League Calif. Cities, 1979-90, also past pres.; sec. Coyote Mus., 1975; bd. dirs. Nat. League of Cities, 1988-90, mem. adv. com., 1990—. Recipient Outstanding Alumnus award family and consumer sci. dept. Purdue U., 1986. Mem. AAUW (pres. San Mateo br. 1979), LWV. Republican. Presbyterian. Home: 1464 Woodberry Ave San Mateo CA 94403-3765 Office: City of San Mateo 330 W 20th Ave San Mateo CA 94403-1388

BAKER, JANE MARIE, human resources manager; b. Mpls., May 20, 1958; d. Kenneth Francis and Colleen Alta (Putnam) Mack; m. Phillip Joseph Baker, Apr. 28, 1984. AA in Bus., Mesa C.C., San Diego, 1979; BS in info. systems/bus. adminstrn., San Diego State U., 1981, MS in Counseling, 1993. Material coord. Linkabit Corp., San Diego, 1975-78, fin. analyst, 1978-82; adminstrn. compensation M/A-Com Govt. Systems, San Diego, 1982-86, mgr. compensation and benefits, 1986-90; mgr. human resources Titan Linkabit, San Diego, 1990—. Hotline operator Youth Devel. Inc., San Diego, 1989; vol. EEO Job Fairs, San Diego, 1989-92. Mem. Am. Compensation Assn., San Diego Compensation Practices (bd. dirs. 1989—), Am. Fertility Assn., Calif. Assn. Marriage and Family Therapists, Resolve Greater San Diego, Phi Kappa Phi. Office: Titan Corp 3033 Science Park Rd San Diego CA 92121

BAKER, JEANETTE SLEDGE, educational administrator; b. Atlanta, June 24, 1947; d. Jesse Alexander and Carolyn (Chapman) Sledge; m. Donald Todd Baker, Sept. 6, 1969. B.Mus., Fla. STate U., 1970; MEd, U. Ariz., 1980, PhD, 1983; student, U. Fla., 1965-67. Asst. admissions and fin. aid officer Columbia U., N.Y.C., 1970-72; degree cert. officer U. Ariz., Tucson, 1972-82, acad. advisor, 1982-84; asst. to v.p. No. Ariz. U., Flagstaff, 1984-87, asst. v.p., 1987-89, assoc. v.p., 1989—. Contbr. to book: At The Crossroads: General Education in Community Colleges, 1983. Vice chmn. Coconino County Silent Witness Bd., Flagstaff, 1987-93, chmn., 1990-93; pres. bd. dirs. Flagstaff Festival of Sci., 1992. Mem. NAFE, Flagstaff Festival Sci. (bd. dirs. 1993—), Flagstaff C. of C., We. States Govtl. Rels. Network. Office: No Ariz U PO Box 4115 Flagstaff AZ 86011-4115

BAKER, JOSEPH RODERICK, III, aviculturist; b. Middletown, Ohio, Sept. 26, 1947; s. Joseph Roderick and Lois Patricia (Barnhart) B. BS in Math., Rensselaer Poly. Tech., 1969. Systems rep. Burroughs Corp., Honolulu, 1973-80; mgr. data processing Kenault Inc., Honolulu, 1980-81; v.p. Software Solutions Inc., Honolulu, 1982-83; br. mgr. DataPhase Corp., Honolulu, 1983-88; pres. Birds of Paradise, Kurtistown, Hawaii, 1987—. Lt. (j.g.) USN, 1969-73. Mem. Am. Fedn. Aviculture, Nat. Cockatoo Soc., Macaw Soc. Am., Eclectus Soc., Am. Contract Bridge League, Pionus Breeders Assn., Amazona Soc.

BAKER, KATHLEEN ANN, student services counselor; b. Seattle, Oct. 6, 1935; d. Clifford A. and Inez E. (Clark) Duncan; m. David G. Baker, June 11, 1955; children: Mark Allen, Susan Baker Abyad. BS in Home Econs., UCLA, 1958, postgrad., 1959; MA in Human Devel., Pacific Oaks Coll., 1976. Calif. Community Coll. Teaching Credentials; cert. nursery sch. and presch. educator, community coll. supr. Teaching asst. UCLA, 1958-59; coll. instr. Fullerton (Calif.) Coll., 1959-61, 73-83; dir. Placentia (Calif.) Coop Nursery Sch., 1970-72; coll. counselor Fullerton Coll., 1983-85, dir. sch. and coll. rels., 1985-92, counselor, articulations officer, 1992—; pres. Pacific Oaks Coll. Alumni Assn., Pasadena, Calif., 1987-88, Faculty Senate, Fullerton Coll., 1981-82; del. Calif. C.C. Gt. Tchrs. Conf., Santa Barbara, 1982, Asilomar (Calif.) Leadership Skills Seminar, 1986. Editor: Fullerton College Guide to Majors, 1985—. Charter pres. AAUW, Placentia, Yorba Linda, Calif., 1967; trustee Yorba Linda Elem. Sch. Dist., 1973-76; mem. Orange County Child Care Task Force, Santa Ana, Calif., 1983. Named one of Outstanding Young Woman of Am., 1968, Outstanding Home Econs. for Rsch. and Leadership, 1977; recipient Cert. of Achievement, No. Orange County YWCA, 1986, Cert. of Appreciation, Calif. Articulation Number System, 1989. Mem. Nat. Assn. Women Deans, Adminstrs. & Counselors, Assn. of Psychol. Type, South Counties Women in Edn., UCLA and Pacific Oaks Coll. Alumni Assns., Calif. Tchrs. Assn., Calif. Community Coll. Counselors Assn., Am. Assn. Collegiate Registrars and Admissions Officers. Presbyterian. Office: Fullerton Coll 321 E Chapman Ave Fullerton CA 92632

BAKER, KEITH LORDEN, physician, surgeon; b. Portland, Oreg., Sept. 29, 1931; s. Harry Lorden and Stella (Bradshaw) B.; m. Ellen Irene Jensen, June 21, 1954; children: Deborah, Rebecca, David Lorden, Jennifer, Matthew Clyde, Julianna, Nancy, Laura, Kristi. AA, Antelope Valley Coll., 1957; MD, U. Calif., Irvine, 1963. Intern St. Mary's Long Beach (Calif.) Hosp., 1963-64; pvt. practice Simi Valley, Calif.; chief of staff Simi Valley Doctors Hosp., 1980-81; chmn. continuing med. edn. com. for physicians Simi Valley Doctors Hosp. Bishop LDS Ch., 1967-69, 1980-82, patriarch, 1969—. Fellow Am. Acad. Family Practice; mem. Ventura County Med. Assn. (mem. ethics com.). Republican. Home: 74 La Paz Ct Simi Valley CA 93065 Office: 2840 E Los Angeles Ave Simi Valley CA 93065

BAKER, KEITH MICHAEL, history educator; b. Swindon, Eng., Aug. 7, 1938; came to U.S., 1964; s. Raymond Eric and Winifred Evelyn (Shepherd) B.; m. Therese Louise Elzas, Oct. 25, 1961; children—Julian, Felix. B.A., Cambridge U., 1960, M.A., 1963; postgrad., Cornell U., 1960-61; Ph.D., Univ. Coll. U. London, 1964. Instr. history and humanities Reed Coll., 1964-65; asst. prof. European history U. Chgo., 1965-71, assoc. prof., 1971-76, prof., 1977-89, master collegiate div. social scis., 1975-78, assoc. dean coll., 1975-78, assoc. dean div. social scis., 1975-78, chmn. commn. grad. edn., 1980-82; chmn. Council Advanced Studies in Humanities and Social Scis., 1982-86; prof. European history Stanford U., 1989-92, J.E. Wallace Sterling prof. in humanities, 1992—; vis. assoc. prof. history Yale U., 1974; mem. Inst. Advanced Study, Princeton, N.J., 1979-80; vis. prof., dir. studies Ecole des Hautes Etudes en Scis. Sociales, Paris, 1982, 84, 91; fellow Ctr. for Advanced Study in Behavioral Scis., Stanford, Calif., 1986-87; vis. prof. UCLA, 1989; chair scholars com. Am. Com. on the French Revolution, 1989. Author: Condorcet: From Natural Philosophy to Social Mathematics, 1975, Inventing the French Revolution, 1990; prin. author: Report Commission on Graduate Education, U. Chgo., 1982; editor: Condorcet: Selected Writings, 1977, The Political Culture of the Old Regime, 1987, The Old Regime and the French Revolution, 1987; co-editor Jour. Modern History, 1980-89. Decorated chevalier Ordre des Palmes Académiques, 1988; NEH fellow, 1967-68, Am. Coun. Learned Soc. Study fellow, 1972-73, Guggenheim fellow, 1979. Fellow AAAS; mem. Am. Hist. Assn. (com. on coms. 1991—), Soc. French Hist. Studies. Office: Stanford U Dept History Stanford CA 94305

BAKER, KENNETH L., energy resource specialist, state official; b. Nebraska City, Nebr., Nov. 12, 1952; s. Merlin E. and Thelma M. (Miller) B.; m. Judith A. Walling, Nov. 25, 1981; children: Kendra Marks, Evan Marks, Justin Baker. BA in Psychology, U. Alaska, Anchorage, 1977; MArch, U. Idaho, 1982. Owner, designer Integrated Living Designs, Moscow, Idaho, 1982-86; energy resource specialist Idaho Dept. Water Resources, Boise, 1986—; chmn. Residential Gas Demonstration Devel. Com., Boise, 1988—, Idaho Energy-Code Edn. Com., Boise, 1990—. Author: The Soil-Cement Handbook, 1983. With U.S. Army, 1971-74. Recipient energy innovation program award U.S. Dept. Energy, 1990, State of Idaho, 1990. Office: Idaho Dept Water Resources Energy Div 1301 N Orchard Boise ID 83712

BAKER, KENT ALFRED, television news director; b. Sioux City, Iowa, Mar. 22, 1948; s. Carl Edmund Baker and Miriam M. (Hawthorn) Baker Nye. Student, Iowa State U., 1966-70. Editor Iowa State Daily, 1969-70; mem. U.S. Peace Corps., 1971-72; editor The Glidden (Iowa) Graphic, 1973-75; bureau chief The Waterloo (Iowa) Courier, Iowa, 1975; state editor The Des Moines Register, 1976-77; news dir. Sta. WQAD-TV, Moline, Ill., 1978; Sunday editor The Des Moines Sunday Register, 1979; news dir. Sta. KHON-TV, Honolulu, 1980—; chmn. Hawaii Freedom of Info. Coun., 1992. Mem. hist. Hawaii Assn., Honolulu; chmn. Hawaii Freedom of Info. Group. Recipient news writing awards Iowa Press Assn., 1973-74. Mem. Radio and TV News Dirs. Assn. (state coord.), Bishop Mus. Assn., East-West Ctr. Assn., Hoover Libr. Assn., Iowa State U. Alumni Assn. (state bd. dirs.). Lodge: Lions. Home: PO Box 23015 Honolulu HI 96823-3015 Office: Sta KHON-TV 1170 Auahi St Honolulu HI 96814-4975

BAKER, LARRY CURTIS, minister; b. L.A., Sept. 19, 1945; s. Charles Leonard and Genevee (Becker) B.; m. Mary Callicoat, Oct. 23, 1964; children: Christopher Daniel, Sarah Morgan. BA, Hardin-Simmons U., 1970; MDiv, Golden Gate Sem., 1975. Ordained to ministry So. Bapt. Conv., 1969. Pastor First Bapt. Ch., Maryneal, Tex., 1968-69, Cen. Bapt. Ch., Stamford, Tex., 1969-71, DeAnza Bapt. Ch., Cupertino, Calif., 1971-73; pub. rels. assoc. Golden Gate Bapt. Sem., Mill Valley, Calif., 1973-75; pastor First So. Bapt. Ch., Lodi, Calif., 1975-77, Ventura, Calif., 1977-81; v.p. communications Golden Gate Sem., Mill Valley, 1981-83; pastor Bethel Bapt. Ch., Concord, Calif., 1983—. Editor newspaper the HSU Brand, 1968-70; asst. pubr. newspaper Stamford Am., 1970-71. With USAF, 1963-67. Republican. Office: Bethel Bapt Ch 3578 Clayton Rd Concord CA 94519-2499

BAKER, LILLIAN L., author, historian, artist, lecturer; b. Yonkers, N.Y., Dec. 12, 1921; m. Roscoe A. Baker; children: Wanda Georgia, George Riley. Student, El Camino (Calif.) Coll., 1952, UCLA, 1968, 77. Continuity writer Sta. WINS, N.Y.C., 1945-46; columnist, free-lance writer, reviewer Gardena (Calif.) Valley News, 1964-76; free-lance writer, editor Gardena, 1971—; lectr. in field; founder, editor Internat. Club for Collectors of Hatpins and Hatpin Holders, monthly newsletter Points, ann. Pictorial Jour., 1977—, conv. and seminar coord., 1979, 82, 84, 87, 90, 92. Author: Collector's Encyclopedia of Hatpins and Hatpin Holders, 1976, third printing, 1993, 100 Years of Collectible Jewelry 1850-1950, 1978, rev. edit., 1986, 88, 89, 91, 92, Art Nouveau and Art Deco Jewelry, 1980, rev. edit. 1985, 87, 88, 90, 91, The Concentration Camp Conspiracy: A Second Pearl Harbor, 1981 (Scholarship Category award of Merit, Conf. of Calif. Hist. Socs. 1983), Hatpins and Hatpin Holders: An Illustrated Value Guide, 1983, rev. edit. 1988, 90, 91, Creative and Collectible Miniatures, 1984, rev., 1991, Fifty Years of Collectible Fashion Jewelry: 1925-1975, 1986, rev. edit., 1988, rev., 1991, Dishonoring America: The Collective Guilt of American Japanese, 1988, American and Japanese Relocation in World War II: Fact Fiction and Fallacy, 1989 (Pulitzer prize nomination, George Washington Honor medal Freedom Found., 1991), rev. edit., 1991, The Japanning of America: Redress and Reparations Demands by Japanese-Americans, 1991, 20th Century Fashionable Plastic Jewelry, 1992, The Common Doom, 1992; established The Lillian Baker Collection Hoover Archives, 1989; author poetry; contbg. author Vol. VII Time-Life Encyclopedia of Collectibles, 1979; numerous radio and TV appearances. Co-founder Ams. for Hist. Accuracy, 1972 (Inc. 1992), Com. for Equality for All Draftees, 1973; chair S. Bay election campaign S.I. Hayakawa, for U.S. Senator from Calif., 1976; witness U.S. Commn. Wartime Relocation, 1981, U.S. Senate Judiciary Com., 1983, U.S. Ho. Reps. Judiciary Com., 1986, U.S. Ho. Reps. Subcommittee on Appropriations, 1989; guest artist U.S. Olympics, 1984. Recipient award Freedoms Found., 1971, George Washington Honor medal, 1989, Ann. award Conf. Calif. Hist. Socs., 1983, monetary award Hoover Instn. Stanford (Calif.) U., 1985, award Pro-Am. Orgn., 1987, Golden Poet award Internat. Poets Soc., 1989. Fellow IBA (life); mem. Nat. League Am. Pen Women, Nat. Writers Club, Soc. Jewelry Historians USA, (charter), Art Students League N.Y. (life), Nat. Historic Soc. (founding), Nat. Trust Historic Preservation (founding), Ams. for Hist. Accuracy (co-founder), other orgns. Home and Office: 15237 Chanera Ave Gardena CA 90249-4042

BAKER, LISA RUTH, business adminstrator; b. Ft. Worth, Apr. 27, 1966; d. Alvin Wesley and Ruth (McKay) Wood; m. Richard E. Baker, June 7, 1986. BSBA, Grand Canyon Coll., 1988. Adminstrv. asst. Almassy Ins. and Fin. Svcs., Phoenix, 1988-90; new bus./electronics coord. The Acacia Group, Phoenix, 1990-91, client referral program coord., 1991-92; custom homes ops. mgr. Gary Gietz Master Builder, Phoenix, 1992—; adminstrv. dir. mktg. pub. relations Ariz. Baptist Retirement Ctrs. Inc., Youngtown, 1993—. Dir. tchr. tng. First So. Bapt. Ch., Phoenix, 1992, mem. pers. com., 1992, mem. strategic planning com., 1992; bd. dirs. Ariz. Bapt. Children's Svcs., Phoenix, 1992. Republican.

BAKER, LONNY, planetarium education coordinator; b. Buffalo, July 31, 1942; m. Todd C. Hansen, June 22, 1991. BS, U. Ariz., 1974. Rsch. asst. Lunar and Planetary Lab. U. Ariz., Tucson, 1970-78, asst. edn. dir. Flandrau Planetarium, 1978-87; edn. coord. Morrison Planetarium Calif. Acad. Scis., San Francisco, 1987—; astronomer Sitmar Cruise, 1986; astronomer, coord. eclipse trip, Oaxaca, Mex., 1991. Assoc. editor (jour. column) Planetarian jour., 1988-92; contbr. articles to profl. jours.; cons. to books in field. Treas. State Legis. Campaign, Tucson, 1984-86; commn. mem. City Magistrates Merit Selection Com., Tucson, 1982-87. Recipient Pub. Svc. Group Achievement Award NASA, 1974; named Profl. of Yr. Astronomical Assn. No. Calif., 1991. Fellow Internat. Planetarium Soc. (mem. exec. coun. 1990—, conf. coord. 1986, Planetarian of Yr. 1986), Pacific Planetarium Assn. (sec.-treas. 1987-91, pres. 1992—). Office: Calif Acad Scis Morrison Planetarium Golden Gate Park San Francisco CA 94118-4501

BAKER, MARIAN IRENE ARBAUGH, retail company executive; b. Indpls., Apr. 1, 1935; d. Olin Thomas Warren Logan and Vivian Catherine (Wiley) Arbaugh; divorced; children: Beth Ann, Amy Lynn, Meg Eileen, Jo Nan. BS in Edn., Ind. U., 1956; postgrad., U. No. Colo., 1975. Cert. tchr., Ind., Colo. Tchr. Indpls. Pub. Schs., 1956-58; tchr., tester St. Vrain Valley Pub. Schs., Longmont, Colo., 1975-78; with sales Ranch Wholesale, Longmont, 1978-80; lighting cons. Olde World Lighting, Boulder, Colo., 1980-82; mgr.-in-tng. K-Mart, Longmont, 1982-84; sports-auto mgr. K-Mart, Sterling, Colo., 1984-91, asst. mgr., 1987-91; self-employed artisan, 1991—; mem. Prairie Crossroads Artisans and Antique Coop., 1991—; lay adviser St. Vrain Valley Pub. Sch. Dist., 1969-79; tchr., tester pre-kindergarten screening, Longmont, 1975-78. Contbr. poems to profl. publs. Pres., chmn. bd. dirs. Santa Fe Jr. Women's Club, 1959-64; leader Camp Fire Girls, Albuquerque and Longmont, 1966-78. Recipient Comml. TV award Benton and Bowles Advt. Agy., 1962; award of merit Amherst Soc. Mem. AAUW (pres., mem. exec. bd. 1965—), NAFE, Internat. Platform Assn., Nat. Authors Registry, Am. Assn. Ret. Persons, Chi Omega Alumnae (pres. Santa Fe chpt. 1959—). Republican. Home: 416 S 3D Ave Sterling CO 80751

BAKER, PHILLIP WILSON, psychologist; b. Culver City, Calif., Mar. 5, 1942; s. Eugene F. and Bette Belle (Stewart) B.; m. Wendy Catherine Warren, Aug. 3, 1974; children: Ian, Colin. BS, San Jose State U., 1965, MBA, 1967; EdS, Vanderbilt U., 1978, EdD, 1982. Lic. clin. psychologist. Mgr., tng. and devel. Memorex Corp., Santa Clara, Calif., 1967-71; clin. supr. Island Counseling Ctr., Fairbanks, Alaska, 1971-74; instr. U. Alaska, Fairbanks, 1974-76; staff psychologist Manchester (N.H.) Mental Health Ctr., 1982-86; clin. supr., employee assistance program Human Affairs of Alaska, Anchorage, 1987-89; staff psychologist South Cen. Counseling Ctr., Anchorage, 1989; pvt. practice Anchorage, 1989—. Mem. APA, Alaska Psychol. Assn. (sec. 1990-91). Office: 4325 Laurel St Ste 215 Anchorage AK 99508-5338

BAKER, REGINALD RALPH, botany educator; b. Houston, Aug. 31, 1924; s. Reginald Ralph and Eleanora Margaret (Weiss) B.; m. Margaret

Katherine Whitaker, Aug. 15, 1952 (dec. 1961); children: Jock Maxwell, Kit Edmund, Jennifer Katherine; m. Eleanor Joann Damer, June 19, 1965 (dec. 1985); children: Sean Randal, Dawn Michelle, Nicole Diane. Student, Doane Coll., 1943-44; BS, Colo. State U., 1948, MS, 1950; PhD, U. Calif., Berkeley, 1954. Laborer Robin Hood Egg Farm, Houston, 1932-41; meter maintenance engr. Houston Lighting and Power Co., 1941-42; prof. Colo. State U., Ft. Collins, 1954—; visiting prof. U. Calif. Berkeley, 1962-63; NSF visiting prof. Cambridge U., Cambridge, Eng., 1968-69; cons. Mycogen, Inc., San Diego, 1980, AscoFlores, Bogota, Colombia, 1976-89; fellow Am. Phytopathological Soc., 1980. Author: Carnation Production, 1990; editor New Directions in Biological Control, 1990; sect. editor: Can. Jour. of Microbiology; prin. editor: Crop Protection; contbr. numerous articles to profl. jours. Lt. (j.g.) USN, 1943-46, PTO. Recipient Group Achievement award, NASA, 1976; named one of Outstanding Educators of Am., 1975. Home: 1216 Southridge Dr Fort Collins CO 80521-4433 Office: Colo State U Fort Collins CO 80523

BAKER, RICHARD EARL, business management educator; b. Inglewood, Calif., Sept. 22, 1928; s. Glyn Maynard and Ruth Elizabeth (Norton) B.; m. Dorotha Jean Mayo; children: Mary K. Walton, Thomas P., Kimberlee S. Tillman, Scott R. BS, U. So. Calif., L.A., 1951, MBA, 1956; postgrad., U. Calif., Berkeley, 1958-60. Various mgmt. positions AT&T Co., 1952-76; cons. Graves & Campbell, L.A., 1974-79; prof. U. LaVerne (Calif.), 1976-79, Calif. State Poly. U., Pomona, 1976-80; cons. Kingman, Ariz., 1980—; instr. Mohave Community Coll., Kingman, 1980—; bd. dirs. Profession Sales Gen. Motors Dealership, Kingman, 1987; adj. prof. Prescott (Ariz.) Coll., 1982—; sr. cons. Roberts & Heck Assocs., L.A., 1974-78; cons. Svc. Corps of Retired Execs. SBA, 1980—. Editor: Stress/Assertiveness, 1981; contbr. articles to profl. jours. Foster parent Foster Parent Assn., L.A., 1965-78; counselor Teenage Drug Rehab., L.A. 1970-78; coun. commr. Boy Scouts Am., L.A., 1975, scoutmaster, 1965-74; coord. Vocat. Adv. Coun., 1980-90. Lt. comdr. USN, 1945-48, PTO, 1950-52. Mem. Kingman C. of C., Kiwanis, Beta Gamma Sigma. Republican. Home: 4909 Scotty Dr Kingman AZ 86401-1077 Office: Mohave Community Coll 1971 Jagerson Ave Kingman AZ 86401-1299

BAKER, RICHARD W., structural and architectural engineer; b. Glendale, Calif., Aug. 16, 1945; s. Elwood V. and Eleanor J. (Vickers) B.; m. Judith K. Fields, July 5, 1969; children: Carrie A., Brian R. AA, Pasadena City Coll., 1965; BS in Archtl. Engring., Calif. State Poly. Coll., San Luis Obispo, 1968. Naval architect Long Beach (Calif.) Naval Shipyard, 1968-69; stress engr. Lockheed Aero. Systems Co., Burbank, Calif., 1969-73, 75-87, Rockwell Internat., Downey, Calif., 1974; group engr. Lockheed Aero. Systems Co., Burbank, Calif., 1987-89, project structures engr., 1989-90; dep. chief engr. Lockheed Aero. Devel. Co., Burbank, 1991—; archtl. cons., Cerritos, Calif., 1972--. Editor: Aircraft Stress Analysis, 1987. Mgr. Frontier Little League, Cerritos, 1985-92; coach City of Cerritos Parks & Recreation Dept., 1982-87. Mem. AIAA. Republican. Methodist. Home: 13518 La Jara St Cerritos CA 90701-6350 Office: Lockheed Advanced Devel Co Dept 72-02 Bldg 90-4 Plant A-1 PO Box 250 Sunland CA 91041

BAKER, ROBERT M. L., JR., university president; b. Los Angeles, Sept. 1, 1930; s. Robert M.L. and Martha (Harlan) B.; m. Bonnie Sue Vold, Nov. 14, 1964; children—Robert Randall, Robert M.L., Robin Michele Leslie. B.A., UCLA, 1954, M.A., 1956, Ph.D., 1958. Cons., Douglas Aircraft Co., Santa Monica, Calif., 1954-57; sr. scientist Aeronutronic, Newport Beach, Calif., 1957-60; head Lockheed Aircraft Research Center, West Los Angeles, 1961-64; assoc. mgr. Math. analysis Computer Scis. Corp., El Segundo, Calif., 1964-80; pres. West Coast U., Los Angeles, 1980—; faculty UCLA, 1958-72; dir. Internat. Info. Systems Corp., Pasadena, Calif., Transp. Scis. Corp., Los Angeles. Appointee Nat. Accreditation Adv. Com., U.S. Dept. Edn., 1987-90. Served to maj. USAF, 1960-61. Named Outstanding Young Man of Year, 1965; recipient Dirk Brouwer award, 1976. Fellow Am. Astro. Soc., Meteoritical Soc., Brit. Astro. Soc., AIAA; mem. Am. Phys. Soc., Phi Beta Kappa, Sigma Xi, Sigma Pi Sigma. Author: An Introduction to Astrodynamics, 1960; 2d edit., 1967; Astrodynamics-Advanced and Applied Topics, 1967, 87; editor: Jour. Astron. Scis., 1961-76.

BAKER, ROBERT WILLIAM, computer cable company executive; b. Phoenix, Sept. 15, 1946; s. Wiley Robert and Edna Lotie (Syler) B.; m. Marian Alice Carlson, Aug. 1, 1970; children: Bryann, Ashley. BS, Ariz. State U., 1973, MBA, 1975. Owner, mgr. Computer Cable Specialists, Phoenix, 1983—. Mem. Data Processing Mgrs. Assn. Office: Computer Cable Specialists 2436 E Indian School Rd Phoenix AZ 85016-6772

BAKER, RODNEY LEE, naval officer; b. Champaign, Ill., June 15, 1950; s. Claude William and Jean Madeline (Morrison) B.; m. Brenda Sue Siebert, Dec. 13, 1975; children: Deah, Jeffrey, Claire. BS in Edn., Southeast Mo. State U., 1975; student, Armed Forces Staff Coll., Norfolk, Va., 1988-89. Commd. ensign U.S. Navy, 1977, advanced through grades to comdr., 1992; Naval Aviation Trng. and Ops. Standardization officer VA-136 Electronic Warfare Squadron, U.S.S. Midway, 1979-82; administrv. officer VA-95 Attack Squadron, N Air Sta. Whidbey Island, Wash., 1985-88; maintenance officer VA95 Attack Squadron Naval Air Sta., Whidbey Island, Wash., 1990-92; safety officer Navavndepot, NAS Alameda, Calif., 1992—. Mem. Tail Hook Assn. Home: 521 E Sunrise Blvd Oak Harbor WA 98277-8916

BAKER, ROLAND JERALD, association executive; b. Pendleton, Oreg., Feb. 27, 1938; s. Roland E. and Theresa Helen (Forest) B.; m. Judy Lynn Murphy, Nov. 24, 1973; children: Kristen L., Kurt F., Brian H. B.A., Western Wash. U., 1961; M.B.A., U. Mich., 1968. Cert. purchasing mgr.; cert. profl. contract mgr. Asst. dir. purchasing and stores U. Wash., Seattle, 1970-75; mgr. purchasing and material control Foss Launch & Tug Co., Seattle, 1975-79; mem. faculty Shoreline Community Coll., 1972-79, Pacific Luth. U., 1977-79, Edmonds Community Coll., 1974-79; chmn. educators group Nat. Assn. Purchasing Mgmt., Tempe, Ariz., 1976-79, exec. v.p., 1979—; pres. Nat. Assn. Purchasing Mgmt. Svcs., Tempe, Ariz., 1989—; mem. faculty Ariz. State U., Tempe, 1988-91. Author: Purchasing Factomatic, 1977, Inventory System Factomatic, 1978, Policies and Procedures for Purchasing and Material Control, 1980, rev. edit., 1992. With USN, 1961-70, comdr. Res., 1969-91. U.S. Navy postgrad. fellow, 1967. Mem. Purchasing Mgmt. Assn. Wash. (pres. 1978-79), Nat. Minority Supplier Devel. Coun. (bd. dirs.), Am. Prodn. and Inventory Control Soc., Nat. Assn. Purchasing Mgmt. (exec. v.p. 1979—), Nat. Contract Mgmt. Assn., Internat. Fedn. Purchasing and Materials Mgmt. (exec. com. 1984-87, exec. adv. com. 1991—), Am. Soc. Assn. Execs. Office: Nat Assn Purchasing Mgmt PO Box 22160 Tempe AZ 85285-2160

BAKER, SALLY, television writer, producer; b. Chgo., Sept. 22, 1932; d. Harry and Lillian (La Viet) S.; m. Walter P. Baker; children: Kathleen Lynda, Kolleen Lynn. Student, UCLA, 1949, Woodbury Coll., 1950, Bradley U., 1960, U. So. Calif., since 1970. Producer, TV host Sta. WESH-TV, Daytona Beach, Fla., 1958-59, Sta. WLOF-TV, Orlando, Fla., 1959-60; producer, writer, TV host Sta. WTVH-TV, Peoria, Ill., 1960-62, Sta. KCHU-TV, San Bernardino, Calif., 1962-64, Sta. KTTV-TV, Hollywood, Calif., 1964-66; producer, writer Hartwest Prodns., N.Y.C., 1966-67, Sta. KCOP-TV, Hollywood, 1967-74, Sta. KHJ-TV, Hollywood, 1975-89; TV devel. producer Hanna-Barbera, Hollywood, 1976; writer, producer Sta. KNBC-TV, Burbank, Calif., 1977; co-producer Last Electric Knight ABC Network, 1985; co-producer Sidekicks Disney-Motown, ABC Network, Hollywood, 1985-87; writer. producer Salute to Hollywood/RKO, 1988; producer Secret Bodyguard, Disney Channel Cornerstone Prodn., 1990-91. Author: Color Me Love, 1978; producer: (TV show) Toyathon (nominated for Emmy, 1970), Hobo Kelly Show (nominated for Emmy, 1970, 71, 72), In Search of Reality (Emmy award, 1973), Secret Bodyguard, 1990; producer, writer: Salute to Hollywood, NBC Fall Preview, If I Should Die Before I Wake (nominated for Emmy, 1981), Our Small World, But Can She Type, A Whale of a Show (nominated for Emmy 1974), An Evening With Pat O'Brien, Sunday with Sally, Glamourama, The Magic Mirror, Knotts Berry Farm Spl., Election Show Central, Sidekicks, The Froozles (nominated for Emmy 1978); writer: (story) Highway to Heaven, "Another War Another Peace"; producer The Last Electric Knight. Recipient 8 Emmy award nominations, 1970, 71, 72, 73, 74, 78, 81. Mem. Women in Film (v.p. 1975-76, pres. 1976-77, Women in Govt. Women of the Yr. 1981), YWCA Leadership Luncheon Search Com. (Silver Achievement Merit award, 1983), So. Calif. Motion Picture Council 1977 (Golden Halo award, Film Adv. bd. Salute to Hollywood, prodn. award, 1987), Am. Women in TV, (1970 Merit award). Mem. Religious Science.

BAKER, SUSAN ELIZABETH, women's health nurse, lawyer; b. Huntsville, Ala., Sept. 12, 1954; d. Clyde Dilmus Baker and Caroline (Currin) B. BS in Nursing, U. Ala., Huntsville, 1978; JD, Jones Sch. Law, 1985. Bar: Ala. 1985, U.S. Dist. Ct. (no. dist.) Ala. 1988. RN Huntsville Hosp., 1978-81, Cooper Green Hosp., Birmingham, Ala., 1982-85, Carraway Meth. Med. Ctr., Birmingham, 1982-83; risk mgr. Cooper Green Hosp., Birmingham, 1985-87; claims specialist Mut. Assurance, Inc., Birmingham, 1987-88; assoc. Brinkley and Ford, Huntsville, 1988-89; reinsurance contract adminstr. Devonshire Svcs. Group, Inc., Santa Ana, Calif., 1989-90; obstet. nurse Nursing Registries, Huntington Beach, Calif., 1990-92; claims rep. Coop. of Am. Physicians, 1992-93; claims supr. So. Calif. Physicians Ins. Exch., Beverly Hills, 1993—. Mem. Ala. Bar Assn. Democrat. Ch. of Religious Sci. Office: Nursing Registries Ste 300 405 S Beverly Dr Beverly Hills CA 90212-4425

BAKER, SUSAN LEIGH, manufacturing company executive; b. Inglewood, Calif., Sept. 24, 1962; d. Richard Leigh and Betty Ann (Payne) B. BS, U. Calif., Irvine, 1990. Computer operator Screening Systems, Inc., Laguna Hills, Calif., 1980-85, systems analyst, 1985-87, acctg. supr., 1987, fin. mgr., 1987-90, corp. sec., 1989—, v.p. fin., 1991—. Republican. Office: Screening Systems Inc 7 Argonaut Laguna Hills CA 92656-1423

BAKER, TIMOTHY ALAN, healthcare administrator, educator, consultant; b. Myrtle Point, Oreg., July 30, 1954; s. Farris D. and Billie G. (Bradford) B.; 1 child, Amanda Susann. BS in Mgmt. with honors, Linfield Coll., McMinnville, Oreg., 1988; MPA in Health Adminstrn. with distinction, Portland State U., 1989, PhD in Pub. Adminstrn. and Policy, 1992. Registered emergency med. technician. Gen. mgr. Pennington's, Inc., Coos Bay, Oreg., 1974-83; dep. dir. Internat. Airport Projects Med. Svcs., Riyadh, Saudi Arabia, 1983-87; adminstrv. intern Kaiser Sunnyside Hosp., Portland, Oreg., 1988-89; grant mgr. Oreg. Health Sci. U., Portland, 1989-90; dir. health sci. program Linfield Coll., Portland, Oreg., 1992—; rsch. assoc. Portland State U., 1990—; instr. S.W. Oreg. C.C., Coos Bay, 1980-83; pres. Intermed. Inc., Portland, 1987—; sr. rschr. small area analysis Oreg. Health Sci. U., 1990, The Oreg. Helath Plann Project, 1990-91; developer, planner, prin. author trauma system devel. S.W. Wash. EMS and Trauma System, 1991-93; cons. ednl. defense Min. Civil Defense, Riyadh, Saudi Arabia, 1992. Contbr. articles to Jour. Family Practice. Planner mass disaster plan King Khaled Internat. Airport, 1983; EMS planner Emergency Med. Plan, Province of Cholburi, Thailand, 1985; bd. dirs. Coos County Kidney Assn., 1982, Coos Bay Kiwanis Club, 1979; regional adv. com. EMS and Trauma, State Wash. Dept. Health, 1990—. Recipient Pub. Svc. award Am. Radio and Relay League, 1969, Med. Excellence award KKIA Hosp., 1985; named Fireman of Yr. Eastside Fire Dept., 1982. Mem. Am. Soc. Pub. Asminstrn. (doctoral rep. to faculty senate 1990, Portland State U.), Am. Pub. Health Assn., Am. Coll. Healthcare Execs. Home: 12008 N Jantzen Beach Ave Portland OR 97217-8151 Office: Linfield Coll Portland Campus 2255 NW Northrup Portland OR 97210

BAKER, VICTOR RICHARD, geology researcher, educator, planetary sciences researcher; b. Waterbury, Conn., Feb. 19, 1945; s. Victor A. Baker and Doris Elizabeth (Day) MacGregor; m. Pauline Marie Heaton, June 10, 1967; children: Trent Heaton, Theodore William. BS, Rensselaer Poly. Inst., 1967; PhD, U. Colo., 1971. Geophysicist U.S. Geol. Survey, Denver, 1967-71; asst. prof. geology U. Tex., Austin, 1971-76, assoc. prof., 1976-81; prof. U. Ariz., Tucson, 1981—, Regents' prof., 1988—; cons. Lunar and Planetary Inst., Houston, 1983-86, Salt River Project, Phoenix, 1984-87, Argonne (Ill.) Nat. Lab., 1983—, Sandia (N.Mex.) Nat. Labs., 1991-92; com. mem. NRC, Washington, 1978—, NASA, 1978—; vis. fellow Nat. Inst. Hydrology, Roorkee, India, 1987-88, Deccan Coll., Pune, India, 1987-88, U. Adelaide, Australia, 1988. Author: The Channels of Mars, 1982, co-author: Surficial Geology, 1981; editor: Catastrophic Flooding, 1981, co-editor: The Channeled Scabland, 1978, Flood Geomorphology, 1988. Served to capt. U.S. Army, 1971-72. Fulbright sr. research fellow, 1979-80, vis. fellow Australian Nat. U., Canberra, 1979-80; research grantee NASA, 1975—, NSF, 1977—. Fellow AAAS (chmn. geol., geography sect. 1992-93, councilor 1993—), Geol. Soc. Am. (chmn. planetary geology div. 1986, Quaternary geology and geomorphology div. 1987, councilor 1990-93); mem. Am. Geophys. Union, Am. Quarternary Assn., Nat. Assn. Geology Tchrs., Soc. Sedimentary Geol., Sigma Xi. Office: U Ariz Dept Geoscis Tucson AZ 85721

BAKER, WALTER ROBERT, military analyst, columnist; b. Toledo, Aug. 13, 1951; s. Donald Leroy and Treva Rosemary (Hess) B.; m. Elizabeth Ann Noles, June 9, 1974; children: Kathleen, Kara, Robert, Christopher. BS in Govt., U. Md., Heidelberg, Fed. Republic of Germany, 1982. Intelligence analyst U.S. Army, Viet Nam, U.S., Fed. Republic of Germany, 1971-84; threat analyst Interstate Electronics Corp., Anaheim, Calif., 1984-89; sr. ops. specialist Northrop, Pico Rivera, Calif., 1989—. Author weekly column Anaheim Bull., 1988-92. Candidate City Coun., Anaheim, 1988, dem. cand. 41st Congl. Dist., 1992. Decorated Bronze Star, 1972. Mem. VFW, KC, Northrop Mgmt. Club. Democrat. Roman Catholic. Home: 401 N Deerfield St Anaheim CA 92807-2940 Office: Northrop 8900 Washington Blvd Pico Rivera CA 90660-3783

BAKER, WARREN J(OSEPH), university president; b. Fitchburg, Mass., Sept. 5, 1938; s. Preston A. and Grace F. (Jarvis) B.; m. Carol Ann Fitzsimons, Apr. 28, 1962; children: Carrie Ann, Kristin Robin, Christopher, Brian. B.S., U. Notre Dame, 1960, M.S., 1962; Ph.D., U. N.Mex., 1966. Research assoc., lectr. E. H. Wang Civil Engring. Research Facility, U. N.Mex., 1962-66; assoc. prof. civil engring. U. Detroit, 1966-71, prof., 1972-79, Chrysler prof., dean engring., 1973-78, acad. v.p., 1976-79; NSF faculty fellow M.I.T., 1971-72; pres. Calif. Poly. State U., San Luis Obispo, 1979—; mem. Bd. Internat. Food and Agr. Devel., 1983-86; mem. Nat. Sci. Bd., 1985—, Calif. Bus. Higher Edn. Forum, 1993; founding mem. Calif. Coun. on Sci. and Tech., 1989—; trustee Amigos of E.A.R.T.H. Coll., 1991—. Contbr. articles to profl. jours. Mem. Detroit Mayor's Mgmt. Adv. Com., 1975-76; mem. engring. adv. bd. U. Calif., Berkeley, 1984—; bd. dirs. Calif. Coun. for Environ. and Econ. Balance, 1980-85; trustee Nat. Coop. Edn. Assn.; chmn. bd. dirs. Civil Engring. Rsch. Found., 1989-91, bd. dirs., 1991—. Fellow Engring. Soc. Detroit; mem. ASCE (chmn. geotech. div. com. on reliability 1976-78, civil engring. edn. and rsch. policy com. 1985-89), NSPE (pres. Detroit chpt. 1976-77), Am. Soc. Engring. Edn., Am. Assn. State Colls. and Univs. (bd. dirs. 1982-84). Office: Calif Poly State U Office of Pres San Luis Obispo CA 93407

BAKER, WILLIAM P. (BILL BAKER), congressman; b. Oakland, Calif., June 14, 1940; m. Joanne Atack; children: Todd, Mary, Billy, Robby. Grad. in Bus. and Indsl. Mgmt., San Jose State Coll. Budget analyst State Dept. Fin., Calif.; assemblyman 15th dist. State of Calif., 1980-93; mem. 103rd Congress from 10th Calif. dist., 1993—; vice chmn. budget writing Ways and Means Com., 1984-91. Exec. v.p. Contra Costa Taxpayers Assn.; active Contra Costa County Farm Bur. With USCG, 1958-65. Republican. Office: House Of Represenatives Washington DC 20515

BAKER-LIEVANOS, NINA GILLSON, jewelry store executive; b. Boston, Dec. 19, 1950; d. Rev. John Robert and Patricia (Gillson) Baker; m. Jorge Alberto Lievanos, June 6, 1981; children: Jeremy John Baker, Wendy Mara Baker, Raoul Salvador Baker-Lievanos. Student, Mills Coll., 1969-70; grad. course in diamond grading, Gemology Inst. Am., 1983; student in diamondtology designation, Diamond Coun. Am., 1986—. Artist, tchr. Claremont, Calif., 1973-78; escrow officer Bank of Am., Claremont, 1978-81; retail salesman William Pitt Jewelers, Puente Hills, Montclair, Calif., 1981-83, asst. mgr., 1983; mgr. William Pitt Jewelers, Puente Hills, Santa Maria, Calif., 1983-91, corp. sales trainer, 1988-89; sales and design specialist Merksamer Jewelers, Santa Maria, 1991; mgr. Merksamer Jewelers, San Luis Obispo, Calif., 1991-92, Santa Maria, Calif., 1992—. Artist tapestry hanging Laguna Beach Mus. Art, 1974. Mem. Cen. Coast Pla. Adv. Bd., 1992. Recipient Cert. Merit Art Bank Am., 1968. Mem. NAFE, Internat. Platform Asn., Speaker's Bur., Santa Maria C. of C., Compassion Internat. Republican. Roman Catholic. Office: Merksamer Jewelers 141 Santa Maria Town Ctr Santa Maria CA 93454

BAKES, ROBERT ELDON, retired state supreme court justice; b. Boise, Idaho, Jan. 11, 1932; s. Warren H. and Oral Bakes; m. Lurleen M. Fisher; children: Juliann, Colleen, Diane, Rachel. Bar: Idaho 1956, U.S. Ct. Appeals (9th cir.) 1963. Instr. U. Ill., 1956-57; legal counsel Idaho State Tax Commn., Boise, 1959-61; asst. U.S. atty. Boise, 1961-66; sr. ptnr. Bakes, Ward & Bates, Boise, 1969-71; justice Supreme Ct. Idaho, Boise, 1971-93, chief justice, 1981-82, 89-93; ret., 1993. Office: Supreme Ct Idaho 451 W State St Boise ID 83720-0001

BAKHIET, NOUNA, microbiologist, researcher; b. Khartoum, Sudan, Apr. 9, 1956; d. Mukhtar and Amna (Kibeida) B. BS in Zoology, U. Al Fatah, Tripoli, Libya, 1977; BS in Microbiology, U. Iowa, 1981, MS in Microbiology, 1984, PhD in Microbiology, 1990. Rsch. asst. Min. of Health, Tripoli, 1977-78; teaching and rsch. asst. U. of Al Fatah, Tripoli, 1978-80; grad. teaching asst. U. Iowa, Iowa City, 1984-90, microbiology tutor, 1982-90; postdoctoral researcher U. Calif., Davis, 1990-91; rsch. assoc. Loma Linda U., 1991—. Contbr. articles to profl. jours. U. Iowa Grad. Student Scholar, 1981-84. Mem. Am. Soc. of Microbiology. Office: Loma Linda U Sch Medicine Alumni Hall Dept Microbiology Loma Linda CA 92350

BAKKEN, JOHN EDGAR, small business owner; b. Minot, N.D., Apr. 18, 1930; s. Elmaar Harald and Mary Lois (Chapel) B.; m. Hope Michel, Sept. 26, 1953 (div. 1975), m., Jan. 31, 1983; children: Kristopher Trulsen, Suzanna Wells, Andrew Skretteberg. AB, Hamilton Coll., Clinton, N.Y., 1952; MBA, Harvard U., 1954; postgrad., U. Colo., 1957-60, Met. State U., Denver, 1980-82. Staff jr. geophysicist The Tex. Co. now Texaco, Inc., Scott City, Kans., 1956-57; sect. chief, sr. engr. Martin-Marietta Corp., Denver, 1957-61; asst. controller Midwest Oil Corp., Denver, 1961-69; controller, v.p. Miller Internat. Inc., Denver, 1969-72; pres., owner Automatics Ltd., Englewood, Colo., 1972-74; treas., controller, chief fin. officer Oceanic Exploration Co., Denver, 1974-75; pres. Bus. Appraisal Assocs., Denver, 1975—; adj. instr. U. Colo., Boulder, 1984-85. Pub.: Business Valuation Review, 1982—, The Journal of Technical Valuation, 1987—. Sr. judge U.S. Yacht Racing Union, 1979-91; chmn. planning commn. City of Littleton, Colo., 1962-68; neighborhood commr. Boy Scouts Am., Littleton, 1959-68, scoutmaster, Castle Rock, Colo., 1969-74; pres. Holly Hills (Colo.) Water and Sanitation Dist., 1987—. With U.S. Army, 1954-56. Mem. Colo. Harvard Bus. Sch. Club (bd. dirs. 1978—, pres. 1977-78), Rocky Mountain Assn. Geologists, Colo. Mountain Club (climb leader 1975-91), Lake Granby Yacht Club, Sailing Assn. Intermountain Lakes (chmn. appeals 1980—, Colo. Sailor of Yr. 1986), Am. Soc. Appraisers (accredited appraiser, internat. sec. 1992-93, regional gov. 1985-89, internat. treas. 1993—), Inst. Cert. Computer Profls. (cert.), Nat. Assn. Rev. Appraisers and Mortgage Underwriters (cert.), Inst. Bus. Appraisers (cert. gen. appraiser state of Colo. 1991—), Rotary. Republican. Office: Bus Appraisal Assocs 2777 S Colorado Blvd Ste 200 Denver CO 80222-6615

BALAKRISHNAN, KRISHNA (BALKI BALAKRISHNAN), biotechnologist, corporate executive; b. Chelakkara, Kerala, India, June 30, 1955; came to U.S., 1977.; s. S. Krishna Iyer and C.K. Parvathy (Ammal); m. Sheela Kalyanakrishnan, Dec. 12, 1984; children: Karthik, Purnima. MS in Chem., Indian Inst. Tech., 1977; PhD in Biophysical Chem., Stanford U., 1982. Tchr., rsch. asst. dept. biophysical chem. Stanford U., Calif., 1977-82; staff sci. DNAX, Ltd., 1982-84; sr. sci. Biogenex, Inc., 1984-85; dir. hybridoma scis. Berkeley Antibody Co., Calif., 1985—, v.p. rsch. & devel., 1988—; guest lectr., sci. adv. biotech. program Contra Costa Coll., 1992—; indsl. ptrn. Stanford-NIH grad. tng. program biotech., 1992—. Contbr. articles to profl. jours.; speaker in field; patent applications. Mem. AAAS, Am. Chem. Soc. Office: Berkeley Antibody Co 4131 Lakeside Dr Ste B Richmond CA 94806-1965

BALASH, JEFFREY LINKE, investment banker; b. N.Y.C., Nov. 2, 1948; s. George Everett and Jeanne Marie (Linke) B.; m. Brenda Sue Coleman, Nov. 22, 1991; 1 stepchild, Blake. BA in Econs. summa cum laude, Princeton, 1970; MBA, Harvard U., 1974, JD cum laude, 1974. Bar: N.Y. 1974. Asst. to chmn. Louis-Dreyfus Corp., N.Y.C., 1974-76; dir. Avon Products, N.Y.C., 1976-79; mng. dir. Lehman Bros., N.Y.C., 1979-85, Drexel Burnham Lambert, Beverly Hills, Calif., 1985-90; founding ptnr. Anthem Ptnrs., L.A., 1991-92. Bd. dirs. Joffrey Ballet, N.Y.C. and L.A., 1986-89; mem. alumni coun. Harvard U. Bus. Sch., Boston, 1989-92. Baker scholar Harvard U. Sch. Bus. Adminstrn., 1974. Mem. Phi Beta Kappa. Republican. Roman Catholic. Home: 9430 Readcrest Dr Beverly Hills CA 90210-2552

BALCERZAK-DYER, JUDITH GENEVA, alcohol and drug program administrator; b. Grand Rapids, Mich., Dec. 23, 1949; d. Stanley Marvin and Hazel Marie (Mathis) Balcerzak; m. John Sinclair Dyer, June 2, 1984; stepchildren: John S. Dyer Jr., Kimberly Ann Dyer. BA in Psychology, Mich. State U., 1973; MSW, Wayne State U., 1977. Lic. clin. social worker, Calif.; community coll. credential-full, Calif.; cert. social worker, Mich. Coord. crisis svc. HELPLINE/Monroe County Drug Program, Monroe, Mich., 1974-77; psychotherapist alcohol program St. Lawrence Hosp., Lansing, Mich., 1977-80; social worker St. Barnabas Sr. Ctr., L.A., 1980-81; pvt. practice psychotherapist Ventura, Calif., 1982—; assoc. prof. social work Calif. State U., Long Beach, 1983-84; clin. social worker Raleigh Hills Hosp., Oxnard, Calif., 1984-85; instr. alcohol and drug studies Ventura Coll., 1983-90; clin. supr. Ventura County Alcohol Svc., Ventura, 1985-89; program adminstr. Ventura County Dept. Alcohol and Drug Programs, Ventura, 1989—; adv. bd. Ventural Colls. Alcohol and Drug Studies Adv. Bd., 1986—; cons., trainer Ventura County Mental Health, Ventura, 1988—. Contbr. articles to profl. jours. Deacon 1st Christian Ch., Ventura, 1988-91, presider, 1989—, elder, 1992—; mem. Channel Islands (Calif.) Photo Soc., 1986—, Channel Islands C. of C. Gull, Oxnard, 1983. Grantee-ednl. NIMH, Wayne State U., 1976-77; State of Mich. scholar-ednl. Mich. State U., 1969-73; recipient 2d place novice div. Channel Islands Underwater Photographic Soc., 1988. Mem. NASW, NASW Referral Svc., Ventura County Mgmt. Coun., Community Psychiat. Ctrs. Vista Del Mar Hosp./Allied Health Profls. Democrat. Mem. Christian Ch. Home: 2970 Windward Way Oxnard CA 93035-2474 Office: Ventura County Dept Alcohol and Drug Programs 4651 Telephone Rd # 210 Ventura CA 93003-5666

BALCH, GLENN MCCLAIN, JR., administrator, minister, former university president, author; b. Shattuck, Okla., Nov. 1, 1937; s. Glenn McClain and Marjorie (Daily) B.; student Panhandle State U., 1958-60, So. Meth. U., summers 1962-64; BA, S.W. State U. Okla., 1962; B.D., Phillips U., 1965; MA, Chapman Coll., 1973, MA in Edn., 1975, M.A. in Psychology, 1975; PhD, U.S. Internat. U., 1978; postgrad. Claremont Grad. Sch., 1968-70, U. Okla., 1965-66; m. Diana Gale Seeley, Oct. 15, 1970; children: Bryan, Gayle, Wesley, Johnny. Ordained to ministry Methodist Ch., 1962; sr. minister First Meth. Ch., Eakly, Okla., 1960-63, First Meth. Ch., Calumet, Okla., 1963-65, Goodrich Meml. Ch., Norman, Okla., 1965-66, First Meth. Ch., Barstow, Calif., 1966-70; asst. dean Chapman Coll., Orange, Calif., 1970-76; v.p. Pacific Christian Coll., Fullerton, Calif., 1976-79; pres. Newport U., Newport Beach, Calif., 1979-82; sr. pastor Brea United Meth. Ch., 1978-89; pres., chief exec. officer So. Calif. Inst., 1988—; edn. cons. USAF, 1974-75; mental health cons. U.S. Army, 1969. Mem. Community Adv. Bd. Minority Problems; Mayor's rep. to County Dependency Prevention Commn.; mem. Brea Econ. Devel. Com. With USMC, 1956-57. Recipient Eastern Star Religious Tng. award, 1963, 64; named Man of Year, Jr. C. of C., Barstow, 1969; Broadhurst fellow, 1963-65. Mem. Calif. Assn. Marriage and Family Therapists, Am. Assn. Marriage and Family Therapist, Rotary (pres. 1969-70, 83-84, dist. gov. 1987-88, 88-89), Masons, Shriners, Elks. Home: 1016 Steele Dr Brea CA 92621-2231 Office: So Calif Inst Ste 100 1717 S State College Blvd Anaheim CA 92806

BALCH, PAMELA MAE, education educator; b. Uniontown, Pa., June 4, 1950; d. James E. and Grace L. (Springer) Jubin; m. Patrick Eugene Balch, June 30, 1972; children: Paul James, Julie Lynn. BA in Edn., W.Va. Wesleyan Coll., 1971; MA in Edn., W.Va. U., 1973, EdD in Curriculum and Instrn., 1977. Elem. edn. tchr. Cen. Sch., Weston, W.Va., 1971-72; middle sch. tchr. Evansdale Elem., Morgantown, W.Va., 1972-78; asst. and assoc. prof. of edn. W.Va. Wesleyan Coll., Buckhannon, W.Va., 1978-85; assoc. and full prof. edn., dir. grad. program tchr. edn. W.Va. Wesleyan Coll., Buckhannon, 1985-88; assoc. and full prof. edn., dir. tchr. edn. Imperial Valley Campus San Diego State Univ., Calexico, Calif., 1988-91, assoc. dean acad. affairs Imperial Valley Campus, 1991—. Author: (textbook) The

Cooperative Teacher, 1987; contbr. articles to profl. jours. Mem. AAUW (bd. dirs., pres. 1992-93), Am. Assn. for Higher Edn., Phi Kappa Phi, Kappa Delta Pi, Phi Delta Kappa (v.p. Imperial Valley chpt. 1990—). Home: 2202 Desert Gardens Dr El Centro CA 92243-9404 Office: San Diego State Univ 720 Heber Ave Calexico CA 92231-2480

BALCIAR, GERALD GEORGE, artist; b. Medford, Wis., Aug. 28, 1942; s. George Paul and Bernice Gertrude (Schmidt) B.; m. Bonnie Kathryn Krohn, Aug. 30, 1963; children: Gerald Jr., John, Jackie. Recipient Ellin Speyer prize Nat. Acad. Design, 1986. Fellow Nat. Sculpture Soc. (Chilmark award 1989); mem. Nat. Acad. Western Art (People's Choice award, Silver medal 1990, Prix de West, Gold medal 1985), Allied Artists Am. (Marguerite Hexter award 1989), Soc. Animal Artists, Northwest Rendezvous Group. Home: 12501 Roundup Rd Parker CO 80134

BALCOM, GLORIA DARLEEN, marketing consultant; b. Porterville, Calif., July 23, 1939; d. Orel A. and Eunice E. Stadtmiller; AA, El Camino Coll., 1959; student computer sci. Harbor Coll., 1976-77; m. Orville R. Balcom, July 23, 1971; 1 stepchild, Cynthia Lou. Per. trainee AiResearch div. Garrett Corp., L.A., 1959-60, sales promotion adminstr., 1960-64; sales rep. Volt Temporary Svcs., El Segundo, Calif., 1965-69, mgr., Tarzana, Calif., 1969-71; co-owner, co-founder Brown Dog Engring., Lomita, Calif., 1972-77; pres., owner, cons. MicroSly Mktg., Lomita, 1977—. Mem. NAFE, Ind. Computer Cons. Assn., Am. Soc. Profl. and Exec. Women, Torrance Athletic, Direct Mktg. (So. Calif.). Home and Office: 24521 Walnut St Lomita CA 90717-1260

BALCOM, ORVILLE, engineer; b. Inglewood, Calif., Apr. 20, 1937; s. Orville R. and Rose Mae (Argo) B.; B.S. in Math., Calif. State U., Long Beach, 1958, postgrad., 1958-59; postgrad. UCLA, 1959-62; m. Gloria Stadtmiller, July 23, 1971; children—Cynthia, Steven. Engr., AiResearch Mfg. Co., 1959-62, 64-65; chief engr. Meditron, El Monte, Calif., 1962-64; chief engr. Astro Metrics, Burbank, Calif., 1965-67; chief engr., gen. mgr. Varadyne Power Systems, Van Nuys, Calif., 1968-71; owner, chief engr. Brown Dog Engring., Lomita, Calif., 1971—. Mem. IEEE Computer Group, Independent Computer Cons. Assn. Patentee in field. Club: Torrance Athletic. Home: 24521 Walnut St Lomita CA 90717-1260 Office: PO Box 427 Lomita CA 90717

BALCOMB, M. MICHELLE, scientific association executive, biologist, consultant; b. Colorado Springs, Colo., July 25, 1927; d. Paul and Gladys Mae (Petit) Michel; m. Kenneth Balcomb, Mar. 20, 1976; children: Laura Michelle Strong, Scott Petit Baker. BA, U. Colo., 1959, MA, 1961, PhD, 1964. Asst. prof. Adams State Coll., Alamosa, Colo., 1964-67; assoc. prof. U. Colo., Boulder, 1968-70; assoc. prof. biol. scis. Colo. Mountain Coll., Glenwood Springs, 1970-76, prof., 1976-83, trustee, 1985—; exec. dir. Southwestern and Rocky Mountain div. AAAS, Glenwood Springs, 1979—. Co-author: (manual) Biological Science, 1970; tech. editor: The Hohokam Village, 1988; contbr. numerous articles to profl. jours. Bd. dirs. Ctr. for Whale Rsch., Friday Harbor, Wash., 1987—, Glenwood Springs Arts Coun., 1990-92; precinct committeewoman Garfield County Reps., Glenwood Springs, 1984-88. Predoctoral fellow NIH, 1959-61, 61-64. Fellow AAAS (editor proc. Southwestern and Rocky Mountain div. 1984—, Pres.'s award 1988); mem. Nat. Assn. Biol. Tchrs., Am. Insts. Biol. Scis., Colo.-Wyo. Acad. Sci. (life), N.Mex. Acad. Sci. (life), Colo. Biology Tchrs. Assn. (life), Assn. Community Coll. Trustees (bd. dirs. 1989—), Phi Beta Kappa, Sigma Xi. Office: SWARM Div AAAS Colo Mountain Coll 215 9th St Glenwood Springs CO 81601-3307

BALDOCK, BOBBY RAY, federal judge; b. Rocky, Okla., Jan. 24, 1936; s. W. Jay and S. Golden (Farrell) B.; m. Mary Jane (Spunky) Holt, June 2, 1956; children: Robert Jennings, Christopher Guy. Grad., N.Mex. Mil. Inst., 1956; JD, U. Ariz., 1960. Bar: Ariz. 1960, N.Mex. 1961, U.S. Dist. Ct. N.Mex., 1965. Ptnr. Sanders, Bruin & Baldock, Roswell, N.Mex., 1960-83; adj. prof. Eastern N.Mex. U., 1962-81; judge U.S. Dist. Ct. N.Mex., Albuquerque, 1983-86, U.S. Ct. Appeals (10th cir.), 1986—. Mem. N.Mex. Bar Assn., Chaves County Bar Assn., Ariz. Bar Assn., Phi Alpha Delta. Office: US Ct Appeals PO Box 2388 Roswell NM 88202-2388*

BALDON, CLEO, interior designer; b. Leavenworth, Wash., June 1, 1927; d. Ernest Elsworth and Esther Jane (Hannan) Chute; m. Lewis Smith Baldon, Nov. 20, 1948 (div. July 1961); 1 child, Dirk; m. Ib Jørgen Melchior, Jan. 18, 1964; 1 stepson, Leif Melchior. BS, Woodbury Coll., 1948. Ptnr. Interior Designs Ltd., Los Angeles, 1948-50; freelance illustrator Los Angeles, 1952-54; prin. Cleo Baldon & Assocs., Los Angeles and Venice, Calif., 1954—; ptnr. Galper/Baldon Assocs., Venice, 1970—. Author: Steps and Stairways; contbr. articles to profl. jours.; patentee in field. Recipient City Beautification awards L.A., 1974-77, 80, 83, 85-90, 92, Beverly Hills, 1982, Calif. Landscape Contbr., 1975, 79, Pacifica award Resources Coun., CAlif., 1979. Home: 8228 Marmont Ln West Hollywood CA 90069-1624 Office: Galper/Baldon Assocs 723 Ocean Front Walk Venice CA 90291-3270

BALDWIN, BETTY JO, computer specialist; b. Fresno, Calif., May 28, 1925; d. Charles Monroe and Irma Blanche (Law) Inks; m. Barrett Stone Baldwin Jr.; two daughters. AB, U. Calif., Berkeley, 1945. With NASA Ames Rsch. Ctr., Moffett Field, Calif., 1951-53, math tech. 14' Wind Tunnel, 1954-55, math analyst 14' Wind Tunnel, 1956-63, supr. math analyst Structural Dynamics, 1963-68, supervisory computer programmer Structural Dynamics, 1968-71, computer programmer Theoretical Studies, 1971-82, adminstrv. specialist Astrophys. Experiments, 1982-85, computer specialist, resource mgr. Astrophysics br., 1985—; v.p. B&B Baldwin Farms, Bakersfield, Calif., 1978—. Mem. IEEE, Assn. for Computing Machinery, Am. Geophys. Union, Am. Bus. Womens Assn. (pres., v.p. 1967, one of Top 10 Women of Yr. 1971). Presbyterian. Office: NASA Ames Rsch Ctr Mail Stop 245-6 Moffett Field CA 94035-1000

BALDWIN, CARRIE MARIE, former data processing executive; b. Covina, Calif., Apr. 16, 1965; d. Richard Darrell Baldwin and Donna Kay (Goodson) Hyatt. Student, El Camino Coll., 1987-89; student, Mt. San Antonio Coll., 1991-92, Calif. Poly. U., Pomona, 1992—. Computer specialist Hugh Gibbs & Donald Gibbs Architects, Long Beach, Calif., 1984-86, Hayakawa Assocs., L.A., 1986-90. Mem. L.A. Conservancy, 1990-91. Mem. Constrn. Specifications Inst. Democrat. Home: 1033 E Nashport St La Verne CA 91750-2433

BALDWIN, CHARLENE MARIE, librarian; b. San Francisco, Jan. 12, 1946; d. Gale Warren and Lois (Ward) Hudkins; children: Christopher Ward, Anne Haynes, Sarah Isabella. BA, Calif. State U., Sacramento, 1970; MA, U. Chgo., 1973. Librarian Calif. Inst. Tech., Munger Library, Pasadena, 1974-75, Tetra Tech., Inc., Pasadena, 1976-81; chief reference librarian Lockheed-Calif. Co., Burbank, 1981-82; librarian Sci.-Engring. Library U. Ariz., Tucson, 1984-88; head map librarian U. Ariz., 1988—; tng. cons. Office of Arid Lands Studies U. Ariz., Tucson, 1986-87; free-lance info. specialist, Nigeria, 1975-76; field cons. sponsored devel. project U.S. Agy. Internat. Devel., Niamey, Niger, 1986; adj. librarian Office of Arid Lands Studies, U. Ariz., 1986—. Co-author: Yoruba of Southwestern Nigeria, 1976. Vice pres., founding mem. Friends of Calif. Inst. Tech. Librs.; founding mem. Internat. Librarianship Round Table, 1988; vol. U.S. Peace Corps Govt. Nigeria, Western State, 1966-68. Mem. Ariz. State Libr. Assn., Spl. Librs. Assn. (pres. Ariz. chpt. 1988-89, bd. dirs. 1991-93), Ariz. Online User Group (chmn. 1985-86). Office: U Ariz Libr Tucson AZ 85721

BALDWIN, GERALD ERWIN, airline pilot; b. Vandalia, Ill., Jan. 30, 1950; s. Hobart Erwin and Evelyn Violet (Wheatley) B.; m. Joan Beverly Koval, June 29, 1973. Student, Harris Community Coll., Houston, 1981, Prairie View A&M, 1981, U. Calif., San Diego, 1977-78; BS, U. Ill., 1972. Cert. naval aviator, airline transport pilot, flight engr. Houston dir. Corp. Campaign, Inc., 1980-81; pub. rels. spokesperson Continental Airlines master exec. coun. Air Line Pilots Assn., Houston, 1983-85; registered rep. 1st Am. Nat. Securities, Inc., Houston, 1983-88; div. mgr. A.L. Williams, Houston, 1983-88; pilot Tex. Internat. Airlines, Houston, 1979-81, Continental Airlines, Houston, 1981-85, United Airlines, Seattle, 1986—; vice chmn. pilots master exec. coun. United Airlines, Rosemont, Ill., 1992—. Del. Dem. State Conv., Dallas, 1984. Lt. USN, 1972-79. Mem. Air Line Pilots Assn. (del., com. chmn. 31st biennial bd. dirs. meeting 1988, sec.-treas. Coun. 27, 1987-91). Office: UAL-MEC 6400 Shafer Ct Ste 700 Rosemont IL 60618

BALDWIN, GLADYS JANE, retired community services administrator; b. Conde, S.D., Jan. 6, 1924; d. Ransom H. and Edna Inez (Cunningham) W.; m. Theron Scott Knapp, Apr. 21, 1945 (div. Sept. 1969); children: Terry S. Knapp, Betty J. Baker, Lois A. Thurber, Donna J. Akins (dec.), Cheryl Smith; m. Gilbert Ralph Baldwin, Feb. 14, 1974. AA, Highline Community Coll., 1978; B cum laude, Eastern Wash. U., 1981, MSW cum laude, 1985. Adminstrv. sec. Social and Health Services, Ephrata, Wash., 1960-62, clerical supr. 2, 1962-70; fin. supr. Social and Health Services, Seattle, 1970-72, fin. mgr., 1972-77; adminstr. Social and Health Services, Colfax, Wash., 1977-82; adminstr. Social and Health Services, Spokane, Wash., 1982-90, retired, 1990. Mem. Nat. Assn. Social Welfare, Wash. Assn. Social Work. Republican. Home: 13413 E 9th Ave Spokane WA 99216-0612

BALDWIN, GRANT KERMIT, management consultant; b. Redwood City, Calif., Oct. 23, 1953; s. William Francis and Bette Arlone (Darter) B.; m. Kathy Ann Reed, May 21, 1988; 1 child, Kelsy Rose. BA in Psychology, San Francisco State U., 1977; MS in Procurement and Contract Mgmt., Saint Mary's Coll., 1988. Cert. purchasing mgr. Purchasing mgr. DHL Worldwide Express, Redwood City, Calif., 1979-90; nat. purchasing dir. Grubb and Ellis, San Francisco, 1990-92; pres. G.K. Baldwin Assocs., Suisun City, Calif., 1993—; v.p. pub. affairs Bay Area Bus. Travel Assn., 1992—. Mem. Nat. Assn. Purchasing Mgmt., Bay Area Bus. Travel Assn. (v.p. pub. affairs 1992—). Home: 365 Silk Oak Dr Suisun City CA 94585-3820 Office: PO Box 356 Suisun City CA 94585

BALDWIN, JOHN DAVID, sociologist, educator; b. Cin., June 24, 1941; s. Herman Jackson and Helen Thomas (Scrivner) B.; m. Janice Irene Whiteside, Aug. 26, 1967. BA, Johns Hopkins U., 1963, PhD, 1967. From asst. to assoc. to prof. sociology U. Calif., Santa Barbara, 1967—. Author: Behavior Principles in Everyday Life, 1981, 2d rev. edit., 1986, Beyond Sociology, 1981, George Herbert Mead, 1986; contbr. numerous articles to profl. jours. Alfred Ludwig U. fellow, 1963-64. Mem. Am. Sociol. Assn., AAAS. Office: U Calif Sociology Dept Santa Barbara CA 93106

BALDWIN, LIONEL VERNON, university president; b. Beaumont, Tex., May 30, 1932; s. Eugene B. and Wanda (Wiley) B.; m. Kathleen Flanagan, Sept. 3, 1955; children: Brian, Michael, Diane, Daniel. BS, U. Notre Dame, 1954; SM, MIT, 1955; PhD, Case Inst. Tech., 1959. Rsch. engr. Nat. Adv. Com. Aeros., Ohio, 1957-59; unit head NASA, 1959-61; asso. prof. engring. Colo. State U., 1961-64; acting dean Coll. of Engring., 1964-65, dean, 1966-84; pres. Nat. Tech. U., Fort Collins, 1984—. Served to capt. USAF, 1955-57. Recipient award for plasma research NASA, 1964. Fellow AIAA, Am. Soc. Engring. Edn. (chmn. engring. deans coun.); mem. ASME, AICE, NSPE, Sigma Xi, Tau Beta Pi, Sigma Pi Sigma. Home: 1900 Sequoia St Fort Collins CO 80525-1540 Office: Nat Tech U 700 Centre Ave Fort Collins CO 80526-1842

BALDWIN, RICHARD EUGENE, real estate executive; b. Sona Bota, Belgian Congo, July 25, 1940; came to U.S., 1942.; s. Russell Eugene and Jesse Adele Baldwin; m. Margaret Alice Kearns, Aug. 11, 1962; 1 child, Robert Lanoue. BA, Northwestern U., 1962; MA, U. Calif., Berkeley, 1964, PhD, 1967. Asst. prof. English U. Wash., Seattle, 1967-74; sales assoc. Windermere Real Estate, Seattle, 1974-77; broker, pres. Windermere Real Estate/Capitol Hill, Inc., 1977—; v.p. Windermere-Wall St., 1983—. Editor: Neighborhood Coun. Newsletter, Seattle, 1977-81; contbr. articles to profl. jours. Chmn. steering com. Pike/Pine Project, 1989—. Mem. Seattle-King County Bd. Realtors, Capitol Hill C. of C. (pres. 1985-87). Office: Windermere Real Estate 1112 19th Ave E Seattle WA 98112-9908

BALE, STEVEN CHARLES, lawyer; b. Cleve., Apr. 22, 1957; s. James Russell and Edna Collins (Wright) B.; m. Lora Lee Baird, Dec. 18, 1982; children: Daniel V., Lora Marie. BS, Brigham Young U., 1981, MPA, 1985, JD, 1985. Bar: Nev. 1985, U.S. Tax Ct. 1991, U.S. Fed. Dist. Ct. 1986, U.S. Ct. Appeals (9th cir.) 1991. Clk. Nev. Supreme Ct., Carson City, 1985-86; assoc. Sheerin, Walsh & Keele, Minden, Nev., 1986-88, Anderson & Pearl, Reno, 1988-89; gen. counsel Ins. Sales Illustration Systems, Sparks, Nev., 1989-93. Mem. ABA, Nev. State Bar Assn., Washoe County Bar Assn. Office: 429 Marsh Ave Reno NV 89509

BALINT, JOSEPH PHILIP, medical products executive; b. Passaic, N.J., Mar. 24, 1948; s. Joseph and Margaret (Birish) B. BA, Rutgers U., 1970, PhD, 1977. Cert. med. technologist, Am. Soc. Clin. Pathology. Med. technologist N.J. Coll. Medicine and Dentistry, Newark, 1970-72; grad. student Rutgers U., New Brunswick, N.J., 1972-77; rsch. fellow Rsch. Inst. of Scripps Clinic, La Jolla, Calif., 1977-80; rsch. assoc. Baylor Coll. Medicine, Houston, 1980-82, rsch. instr., 1982; rsch. dir. Imré Corp., Seattle, 1983-89, v.p. product devel., 1989-92; dir. device devel. Imré Corp., seattle, 1993; cons. Imré Corp., 1982-83. Contbr. articles profl. jours., patentee in field. Recipient N.J. State scholarship, 1966-70, NIH rsch. grants, 1983, 84, Nat. Cancer Inst. grant, 1984. Home: 520 2d Ave W # 311 Seattle WA 98119 Office: Imré Corp 401 Queen Anne Ave N Seattle WA 98109-9838

BALL, BLAIR M, optometrist; b. Idaho Falls, Idaho, May 19, 1957; s. Arland Jay and Joyce (Monson) B.; m. Laurie Lyn Carlson, May 7, 1982; children: Meagan Laurie, Taylor Arland, Jeremy Blair, Dallin Carl. AAS, Ricks Coll., 1979; BS in Psychology, Brigham Young U., 1982; BS in Visual Sci., So. Calif. Coll. of Optometry, 1984, OD, 1986. Pvt. practice optometry Beaumont, Calif., 1986—. Com. mem. B.S.A., Beaumont, 1987-90, counselor bishopric LDS, Beaumont, 1987-90. Mem. Am. Optometric Assn., Calif. Optometric Assn., Cahuilla Optometric Soc. (sec.-treas. 1990-91, pres.-elect 1991-92, pres. 1992—), Beaumont C. of C. Office: Ste A 1659 E 6th St Beaumont CA 92223

BALL, DONALD EDMON, architect; b. Evansville, Ind., July 18, 1942; s. Harvey and Myrl (Norris) B. BA in Design, So. Ill. U., 1967. Registred architect Ariz., Calif., Colo.; cert. Nat. Coun. Archtl. Registration Bd. With design dept. Leo A. Daly Co., Architects and Engrs., Omaha, 1968; project mgr. Buetow & Assocs., St. Paul, 1969-70; ptnr. Comprehensive Design, Mpls., 1971-73; with Caudill Assocs., Aspen, Colo., 1973-76, Hagman Yaw, Ltd., Aspen, 1977; project mgr. Hauter Assocs., Aspen, 1978; pres. Jacobs, Ball & Assocs., Architects, Aspen and Denver, 1978-85; project mgr. Moshe Safdie & Assocs., Boston, 1985-87; dir. design Dwayne Lewis Architects, Inc., Phoenix, 1987-88; prin. Donald Ball and Assocs., Scottsdale, Ariz., 1988—. Mem. Aspen Bldg. Insp. Selection Com., 1982, Pitkin County Housing Authority Bd., Aspen, 1984. Mem. AIA (chmn. Colo. West chpt., documents com.), Ariz. Soc. Architects (profl. practice com.). Home: 7869 E Horseshoe Ln Scottsdale AZ 85250-4786 Office: 7201 E Camelback Rd Ste 345 Scottsdale AZ 85251-3318

BALL, GUY DAVID, electronic engineer, technical writer; b. Glen Ridge, N.J., Oct. 16, 1953; m. Linda A. Ball. Electronic engr. Hughes Aircraft Co., Newport Beach, Calif., 1983—. Author: Newsletter Production, 1991, Easy Desktop Publishing, 1991; co-author: Neighborhood Starter Kit, 1993, Neighborhood Organization, 1993; editor: Eye on Santa Ana Community Newsletter, 1989—. Mem. Santa Ana (Calif.) Housing Adv. Commn., 1990-93; co-chmn. Wilshire Square Neighborhood, Santa Ana, 1989; chmn. Neighborhood Linkage Com., 1993. Mem. Internat. Assn. Calculator Collectors (pres. 1990—, co-editor), Soc. for Tech. Comm., Leadership Santa Ana Alumni Assn., Toastmasters (pres. 1989-90, treas. 1990-92). Home: 1212 S Parton St Santa Ana CA 92707-1134

BALL, J. DONALD, III, software company executive, computer programmer; b. Van Nuys, Calif., Dec. 15, 1957; s. John Donald and Lenni (Weeks) B. Student, UCLA, San Jose State U. Machinist Lockheed Missles and Space Corp., Sunnyvale, Calif., 1979-80; programmer N.C. Labs., San Jose, Calif., 1981-85; owner Rapid Output Co., Hayward, Calif., 1985—. Office: Rapid Output Co 30995 San Benito St Hayward CA 94544

BALL, JAMES HERINGTON, lawyer; b. Kansas City, Mo., Sept. 20, 1942; s. James T. Jr. and Betty Sue (Herington) B.; m. Wendy Anne Wolfe, Dec. 28, 1964; children: James H., Steven Scott. AB, U. Mo., 1964; JD cum laude, St. Louis U., 1973. Bar: Mo. 1973. Asst. gen. counsel Anheuser-Busch, Inc., St. Louis, 1973-76; v.p., gen. counsel, sec. Stouffer Corp., Solon, Ohio, 1976-83; sr. v.p., gen. counsel Nestle Enterprises, Inc., Solon, 1983-91; gen. counsel, sr. v.p. Nestle USA, Inc., Glendale, Calif., 1991—. Editor-in-chief St. Louis U. Law Jour., 1972-73. Bd. dirs. Alliance for Children's Rights, L.A., 1992—. Served to lt. comdr. USN, 1964-70, Vietnam. Mem. Mo. Bar Assn. Office: Nestle USA Inc 800 N Brand Blvd Glendale CA 91203-1244

BALL, JO-ANNE MORELAND, public relations professional; b. Columbus, Ohio, Feb. 22, 1930; m. Donald E. Ball, July 22, 1946 (dec.); 2 children. BA in Music and Voice Performance, Otterbein Coll. bd. dirs. Marcus J. Lawrence Hosp. Found., Sedona Arts Ctr.; dir. devel. Cen. Ohio Assn. Builders and Contractors Inc., 1984-85. Pub. chmn. Orange PTA; mem. Worthington United Meth. Ch.; pub. rels. com. Project Passage; devel. fund steering com. Doctor's Hosp.; mem. Verde Valley Concert Choir; bd. dirs. Sedona Acad. Recipient Arbegast award in music, 1984. Mem. Pub. Rels. Soc. Am., Women in Communications Inc., Columbus C. of C. (pub. rels. com.), Worthington Civic Arts Assn. (co-founder), Worthington Women's Club, Worthington Music Club, Columbus Women's Music Club Inc., Olentangy Athletic Boosters, Orange Twp. Garden Club, Orange Twp. Vol. Fireman's Assn. Home: PO Box 10005 Sedona AZ 86339-8005

BALL, JON WINSTON, building construction executive; b. Libertyville, Ill., May 7, 1954; s. Malcolm Arthur and Nancy Karen (Longaker) B.; m. Paula Kay Adams, Mar. 24, 1979; 1 child, Kathleen Miran. BSCE, U. Ill., 1976. Registered profl. engr., Ill., Ind.; cert. to use high explosives. Level I quality control insp. Gust K. Newberg Constrn. Co., Braidwood, Ill., 1977; level II quality control engr. Gust K. Newberg Constrn. Co., New Washington, Ind., 1977-79, project engr., various positions, 1979-84; project engr. Hensel Phelps Constrn. Co., Santa Clara, Calif., 1984-85, project supt., 1985-86, project mgr., 1987-89; project mgr. Hensel Phelps Constrn. Co., Greeley, Colo., 1989-91, area mgr., 1991—. Mem. Rocky Mountain Vintage Racing Club. Office: Hensel Phelps Constrn Co 420 6th Ave Greeley CO 80632

BALL, KAREN ELAINE, marketing executive; b. Ames, Iowa, July 31, 1947; d. John Alfred and Arlene Elizabeth (Bergland) B.; m. Thomas Craig Carpenter, Aug. 26, 1967 (div. 1970); children: Carolyn, Gretchen. BA in English, U. No. Iowa, 1969; postgrad., U. Iowa, 1971-73; MS in Psychology, Calif. State U., Hayward, 1984. Urban planner United South End Settlements, Boston, 1974-79, Oakland (Calif.) Tree Task Force, 1979-81; mktg. mgr. Kaiser Engrs., Oakland, 1981-84, EQE Inc., San Francisco, 1984-88; mktg. dir. De Tienne Assocs., San Francisco, 1988-90, Geomatrix Consultants, Inc., San Francisco, 1990—; speaker RFP User Group, Chgo., 1992, SMPS Mktg. Coord. Workshop, San Francisco, 1990, 92. Author short story, poem. Aux. mem. A Friendly Place, Oakland, 1992; bd. dirs. AIDS Project of East Bay, Oakland, 1989-91; vol. A Safe Place, Oakland, 1980-85; sponsor Oreg. Shakespeare Festival, Ashland, Oreg., 1989, 92; founding mem. St. Paul AIDS Task Force, Oakland, 1987—; parish coun. mem. St. Paul Luth. Ch. Mem. AIA, Am. Planning Assn., Soc. for Mktg. Profl. Svcs. (steering com. 1991-92, nat. publ. 1988—), Oakland C. of C., Profl. Environ. Mktg. Assn., San Francisco Planning and Urban Rsch. Assn. Office: Geomatrix Consultants 10th Fl 100 Pine St San Francisco CA 94111

BALL, KAREN FISHER, non-profit agency administrator; b. Spokane, Wash., Jan. 31, 1958; d. Stanley Max and Beverly Jean (Hanley) F.; m. Kirk William Ball, Aug. 4, 1984; children: Kaelin Rene, Derek James. BS in Elem. Edn., Baylor U., 1981. Elem. sch. tchr. Klein Ind. Sch. Dist., Spring, Tex., 1981-85; pres. The Sturge-Weber Found., Denver, 1986—. Author: (booklet) A Laser Treatment for Port Wine Stains, 1991. Bd. dirs. March of Dimes of Greater Colo., Denver, 1991—; acting precinct chmn. Harris County Rep. Party, Houston, 1985. Recipient Betty Ford award, Mrs. Betty Ford and Com., 1990. Mem. Nat. Orgn. of Rare Disorders, Lets Face It. Methodist. Office: The Sturge-Weber Found PO Box 460931 Aurora CO 80046

BALL, LAWRENCE, physical scientist; b. Albion, N.Y., Aug. 10, 1933; s. Harold Witheral and Gladys (Gibbs) B.; m. Caroline Moran, June 21, 1957; children: Daniel Lawrence, Logan Edward, Stacey Laura Ball Lucero, Ryan Laird (dec.). Diploma, Williston Acad., 1952; BSME, Antioch Coll., 1957; MSc in Elec. Engring., Ohio State U., 1962. Engring. aid Wright Air Devel. Ctr., Dayton, Ohio, 1957-60; engr. Deco Electronics Inc., Boulder, Colo., 1962-66; sr. engr. Westinghouse Rsch. Labs., Boulder, 1966-73, Westinghouse Ocean Rsch. Lab., Annapolis, Md., 1973-74; program mgr. div. geothermal energy U.S. Dept. Energy, Washington, 1974-79; lab. dir. U.S. Dept. Energy, Grand Junction, Colo., 1979—; pres. Liberty Cons. Co., Grand Junction, 1984—. Co-inventor coal mine communications; contbr. articles to profl. jours. Mem. various vol. fire depts., 1954-79; mem., sr. patroller Nat. Ski Patrol System, Md., Colo., 1973-92; bd. dirs. Colo. Head Injury Found., chpt. pres., 1989-91. Named Profl. Govt. Employee of Yr., Western Colo. Fed. Exec. Assn., 1991. Mem. Soc. Exploration Geophysicists, Toastmasters Internat. (area gov. 1991-92, div. gov. 1992-93, Toastmaster of Yr. Western Colo. 1989), West Slope Wheelman (charter bd. dirs. 1992-93). Office: US Dept Energy Projects Office PO Box 2567 Grand Junction CO 81502

BALL, ROBERT EDWIN, engineering educator; b. Indpls., Aug. 2, 1935; s. Robert Raymond and Marjory May (McComb) B.; m. Rana Niola Applegate, Sept. 2, 1956; children: Robert Edwin Jr., Susan Marie Ball Culcasi. BSCE, Northwestern U., 1958, MSCE, 1959, PhD, 1962. Prof. dept. aeronautics and astronautics Naval Postgrad. Sch., Monterey, Calif., 1967—; pres. Aerospace Ednl. Svcs., Inc., Monterey, 1983—. Author: The Fundamentals of Aircraft Combat Survivability Analysis and Design, 1985. Fellow AIAA (chmn. survivability tech. com. 1989-92). Home: 642 Toyon Dr Monterey CA 93940-4225

BALL, WILLIAM PAUL, physicist, engineer; b. San Diego, Nov. 16, 1913; s. John and Mary (Kajla) B.; m. Edith Lucile March, June 28, 1941 (dec. 1976); children: Lura Irene Ball Raplee, Roy Ernest. AB, UCLA, 1940; PhD, U. Calif., Berkeley, 1952. Registered profl. engr. Calif. Projectionist, sound technician studios and theatres in Los Angeles, 1932-41; tchr. high sch. Montebello, Calif., 1941-42; instr. math. and physics Santa Ana (Calif.) Army Air Base, 1942-43; physicist U. Calif. Radiation Lab., Berkeley and Livermore, 1943-58; mem. tech. staff Ramo-Wooldridge Corp., Los Angeles, 1958-59; sr. scientist Hughes Aircraft Co., Culver City, Calif., 1959-64; sr. staff engr. TRW-Def. Systems Group, Redondo Beach, Calif., 1964-83, Hughes Aircraft Co., 1983-86; cons. Redondo Beach, 1986—. Contbr. articles to profl. jours.; patentee in field. Bd. dirs. So. Dist. Los Angeles chpt. ARC, 1979-86. Recipient Manhattan Project award for contbn. to 1st atomic bomb, 1945. Mem. AAAS, Am. Phys. Soc., Am. Nuclear Soc., N.Y. Acad. Scis., Torrance (Calif.) Area C. of C. (bd. dirs. 1978-84), Sigma Xi. Home and Office: 209 Via El Toro Redondo Beach CA 90277-6561

BALLAM, MICHAEL LYNN, opera singer, music educator; b. Logan, Utah, Aug. 21, 1951; s. Grant Lamb and Marianne (Fullmer) B.; m. Laurie Anne Israelsen, June 28, 1972; children: Christopher, Vanessa, Nicholas, Ester, Olivia, Benjamin. MusB, Utah State U., 1972; MusM, Ind. U., 1974, MusD with distinction, 1976. Artist in residence Ind. U., Bloomington, 1977; artist Chgo. Lyric Opera, 1979-81, San Francisco Opera, 1979-81, St. Louis Opera, 1983; artist in residence Music Acad. of West, Santa Barbara, Calif., 1980-82; guest prof. U. Utah, Salt Lake City, 1984; artist Santa Fe Opera, 1986, Dallas Opera, 1989; assoc. prof. Utah State U., Logan, 1987—; artist Utah Symphony, 1985, St. Paul Chamber Orch., 1986, Ky. Opera, 1982—, Pa. Opera Theater, 1979-87; music history lectr., U.S. & abroad. Author: History of Europe Through Music, 1975, Music the Divine Art, 1989, Language of Love, 1990, Musical First Aid Kit, 1991, I Was Am Hungered, 1991, Irving Berlin, 1991. Vol. Hospice, Logan, 1985—; artistic dir. Utah. Festival Opera Co. Performance grantee Opera Am. Mem. Am. Guild of Mus. Artists. Home: 53 Canterbury Ln Logan UT 84321

BALLANTINE, MORLEY COWLES (MRS. ARTHUR ATWOOD BALLANTINE), newspaper editor; b. Des Moines, May 21, 1925; d. John and Elizabeth (Bates) Cowles; m. Arthur Atwood Ballantine, July 26, 1947 (dec. 1975); children—Richard, Elizabeth Ballantine Leavitt, William, Helen Ballantine Healy. A.B., Ft. Lewis Coll., 1975; L.H.D. (hon.), Simpson Coll., Indianola, Iowa, 1980. Pub. Durango (Colo.) Herald, 1952-83, editor, pub., 1975-83, editor, chmn. bd., 1983—; dir. 1st Nat. Bank, Durango, 1976—,

Des Moines Register & Tribune, 1977-85, Cowles Media Co., 1982-86. Mem. Colo. Land Use Commn., 1975-81, Supreme Ct. Nominating Commn., 1984-90; mem. Colo. Forum, 1985—, Blueprint for Colo., 1985-92; pres. S.W. Colo. Mental Health Ctr., 1964-65, Four Corners Opera Assn., 1983-86; bd. dirs. Colo. Nat. Hist. Preservation Act, 1968-78; trustee Choate/Rosemary Hall, Wallingford, Conn., 1973-81, Simpson Coll., Indianola, Iowa, 1981—, U. Denver, 1984—, Fountain Valley Sch., Colorado Springs, 1976-89; mem. exec. com. Ft. Lewis Coll. Found., 1991—. Recipient 1st place award for editorial writing Nat. Fedn. Press Women, 1955, Outstanding Alumna award Rosemary Hall, Greenwich, Conn., 1969, Outstanding Journalism award U. Colo. Sch. Journalism, 1967, Distinguished Service award Ft. Lewis Coll., Durango, 1970; named to Colo. Community Journalism Hall of Fame, 1987; named Citizen of Yr. Durango Area Chamber Resort Assn., 1990. Mem. Nat. Soc. Colonial Dames, Colo. Press Assn. (bd. dirs. 1978-79), Colo. AP Assn. (chmn. 1966-67), Federated Women's Club Durango, Mill Reef Club (Antigua, W.I.) (bd. govs. 1985-91). Episcopalian. Address: care Herald PO Drawer A Durango CO 81302

BALLANTYNE, MICHAEL ALAN, legislator; b. Toronto, Ontario, Can., Feb. 27, 1945; s. Earnest Alan and Barbara Joyce (Stevens) B.; m. Penny Leanne Aumond, Aug. 2, 1987; Children: Erin, Alexandra, Nicholas. Attended, Carleton U., Ottawa, Ontario, 1966. With Giant Yellowknife Mines, 1976-79; alderman City of Yellowknife, 1976-79. Alderman City of Yellowknife. 1980-83, mayor 1980-83; MLA Yellowknife North (chmn. finance com. 1983-85, mem. special com. on housing); cabinet appointee (minister of housing 1985-87, minister of justice 1985-87); cabinet re-appointee (minister of justice 1987-91, minister of finance 1987-91, chair treasury bd. 1987-91, chair legislation and house planning com. 1987-91, govt. house leader 1987-91, minister responsible for pub. utilities bd. 1989-91, Aboriginal langs. 1989-90, chair of special com. on constitutional reform 1989-91); elected speaker legislative assembly of the NWT 1991— (chair mgmt. svcs. bd. 1991—). Office: Speaker/Legislative Assembly, PO Box 1320, Yellowknife, NT Canada X1A 2L9

BALLARD, CLARK TILTON, JR., psychiatrist, military officer, retired; b. Cin., Aug. 6, 1941; s. Clark Tilton Ballard and Mary Betty (Vanover) Schwettman; m. Nona Anne Christensen, Nov. 28, 1963; children: Nona, Bethany, Aryn, Samara. BS, U.S. Mil. Acad., West Point, N.Y., 1963; MS in Physics, Naval Postgraduate Sch., Monterey, Calif., 1967; postgrad., Tex. Tech U., 1972-73; MD, U. Tex., Galveston, 1977. Diplomate Am. Bd. Psychiatry and Neurology; lic. psychiatrist, Calif., N.Mex. Commd. 2d lt. U.S. Army, 1963, advanced through grades to col., 1983, asst. prof. physics U.S. Mil. Acad., 1968-71; exec. officer 36th Engr. Bn. U.S. Army, Vinh Long, Rep. Vietnam, 1971-72; intern Letterman Med. Ctr. U.S. Army, San Francisco, 1977-78, resident in psychiatry Letterman Med. Ctr., 1978-81; chief profl. svcs. U.S. Army Hosp. U.S. Army, Berlin, 1981-85; sr. med. officer VIIth Corps U.S. Army, Stuttgart, Fed. Rep. Germany, 1985-88; comdr. Raymond W. Bliss Army Community Hosp. U.S. Army, Ft. Huachuca, Ariz., 1988-90; pvt. practice psychiatry, co-med. dir. mental health svcs. Lea Regional Hosp., Hobbs, N.Mex., 1990—. Dir. Sierra Vista Chpt. Full Gospel Businessmen's Fellowship, Ariz., 1989-90. Decorated Legion of Merit, Bronze Star with one bronze oak leaf cluster. Mem. AMA, Am. Acad. Clin. Psychiatrists, Assn. Mil. Surgeons U.S., Am. Psychiat. Assn., Christian Med. and Dental Soc., Internat. Order of St. Luke the Physician. Home: 5002 N Ja Rob Ln Hobbs NM 88240-0928 Office: 5419 N Lovington Hwy Hobbs NM 88240-9131

BALLARD, JANE ELIZABETH, epidemiologist; b. Billings, Mont., Feb. 26, 1947; d. Floyd Hubert and Catherine Elizabeth (Fremgen) B. BS with honors, U. Mont., 1969; MS, U. Minn., 1971; PhD, U. Wash., 1989. Cert. specialist in microbiology. Rsch. scientist Ctrl. Pub. Health Lab., London, 1971-73; microbiology supr. Wash. State Health Dept., Seattle, 1974-78, epidemiologist, 1978-91; corp. epidemiologist The Boeing Co., Seattle, 1991—; mem. clin. faculty U. Wash., Seattle, 1990—; cons. Indian Health Svc., Seattle, 1991—. Contbr. articles to profl. jours. USPHS trainee, 1969-71. Mem. APHA, Soc. for Epidemiologic Rsch., Sigma Xi. Office: The Boeing Co PO Box 3707 MS7E-HP Seattle WA 98124

BALLARD, MELVIN RUSSELL, JR., church official; b. Salt Lake City, Oct. 8, 1928; s. Melvin Russell and Geraldine (Smith) B.; student U. Utah, 1946, 1950-52; m. Barbara Bowen, Aug. 28, 1951; children—Clark, Holly, Meleea, Tamara, Stacey, Brynn, Craig. Sales mgr. Ballard Motor Co., Salt Lake City, 1950-54; investment counselor, Salt Lake City, 1954-56; founder, owner, mgr. Russ Ballard Auto, Inc., Salt Lake City, 1956-58, Ballard-Wade Co., 1958-67; owner, mgr. Ballard & Co., Salt Lake City, 1962-72; gen. authority Ch. of Jesus Christ of Latter-day Saints, Salt Lake City, 1976—, now pres. 1st Quorum of the 70; dir. Foothill Thrift & Loan, Nate-Wade, Inc., Silver King Mines, Inc. (all Salt Lake City); gen. partner N & R Investment, Salt Lake City, 1958—, Ballard Investment Co., Salt Lake City, 1955—. Mem. bd. Salt Lake Jr. Achievement, 1978-80; bd. dirs. Freedoms Found., 1978—, David O. McKay Inst. Edn., 1979—; Served to 1st lt. USAR, 1950-57. Mem. Salt Lake Area C. of C. (gov. 1979—). Republican. Office: LDS Church 47 E South Temple St Salt Lake City UT 84150-0001

BALLARD, WILLIAM RALPH, mathematics educator; b. Yakima, Wash., Feb. 1, 1926; s. Edwin Robert and Frances Evelyn (White) B.; m. Lee Atwater Morgan, Sept. 20, 1952; children: Thomas, Henry, Martha. AB, Whitman Coll., Walla Walla, Wash., 1946; MS, U. Chgo., 1947, PhD, 1957. Instr. math. Wash. State U., Pullman, 1948-50; jr. mathematician Inst. for Air Weapons Rsch., U. Chgo., 1952-53; project officer Armament Lab., Wright-Patterson AFB, Dayton, Ohio, 1953-54; asst. prof. math. Air Force Inst. Tech., Dayton, 1954-57; math faculty, asst. prof. to prof. emeritus U. Mont., Missoula, 1957—. Author: Geometry, 1970. Mem. Dem. Cen. Com., Missoula County, 1975—; bd. dirs. United Way of Missoula County, 1984-90; mem. representing Missoula Cen. Labor Coun. of Bd. of Missoula Econ. Devel., 1984—; pres. Five Valleys Audubon Soc., 1988—. 1st lt. USAF, 1953-57. Mem. Math. Assn. Am., Am. Math. Soc. Democrat. Home: 5120 Larch Ave Missoula MT 59802-5248 Office: Univ Mont Dept of Math Scis Missoula MT 59812

BALLENTINE, LEE KENNEY, publishing company executive; b. Teaneck, N.J., Sept. 4, 1954; s. George Kenney and Veda Avis Maxine (Havens) B.; m. Jennifer Ursula Marie Moore, Aug. 20, 1983; 1 child, Philip Alden Emerson. Student, Harvey Mudd Coll., 1972-73; BS in Computer Sci., SUNY, Albany, 1976; postgrad., U. Colo., 1976-77, U. Calif., Berkeley, 1977-78. Software engr. Osborne & Assocs. Pubs., Berkeley, 1978-80, Triad Systems Corp., Sunnyvale, Calif., 1981-84; group leader, operating systems and communications Daisy Systems Corp., Sunnyvale, 1984-85; software applications engr. mgr. Fairchild Clipper Div., Palo Alto, Calif., 1985-87; cons. numerous electronic and pub. industry clients, 1987-88; pres. Ocean View Tech. Publs., Mountain View, Calif., 1989-91, Profl. Book Ctr., Denver, 1991—; pub. Ocean View Books, Denver, 1986—; seminar presenter Willamette Writer's Conf., Portland, Oreg., 1990; cons. Prentice-Hall Pub. Co., Englewood Cliffs, N.J., 1989-90, Amdahl Corp., Sunnyvale, 1988-90; mem. New Eng. Book Show, 1991. Author: Directional Information, 1981, Basements in the Music Box, 1986, Dream Protocols, 1992; editor: Poly: New Speculative Writing, 1989; pub. Phi Beta Kappa newsletter, San Francisco, 1987-89. Presenter Mount View Pub. Libr., 1990. Recipient Ednl. Explorations award Reader's Digest, 1975; Nat. Merit scholar, 1972. Mem. Sci. Fiction Writers of Am., Sci. Fiction Poetry Assn., USR Group Unix Profl. Assn., Book Builder's West (juried bookshow participant 1989), The Am. Booksellers Assn., Small Press Book Ctr., Poesis (advisory bd. 1993). Office: Profl Book Ctr Box 102650 Denver CO 80250

BALLENTINE, PAULA FISCAL, business development professional; b. San Antonio, Sept. 29, 1950; d. Jose and Paula (Calderon) Castillo; m. Jose Fiscal, Mar. 30, 1973 (div. 1978); 1 child, Jose Jr.; m. John Robert Ballentine, Apr. 25, 1993. Student, Whitewater State U., 1968-69, U. Wis., Milw., 1970-73, 84, San Mateo Community Coll., 1977-78, Calif. State U., San Francisco, 1979-80. Owner, mgr. Crystal by Candlelight, Milw., 1973-76; office adminstr. Southeast Wis. Housing Corp., Union Grove, 1969-70; edn. specialist U. Wis. Milw. Tech. Corps., 1970-73; dir. mktg. EMBA Prodns.-Fundraising, San Francisco, 1976-80; legis. and adminstrv. asst. to elected ofcl. San Francisco City/County Bd. Suprs., 1979-84; v.p. sales EMBA Security Investigations, San Francisco, 1980-84; co-owner, mgr. EMBA Advt.-Mktg., San Francisco, 1984-88; v.p. mktg. Security Tng. Inst., Sausalito, Calif., 1988—; pres. EMBA & Assocs., San Francisco, 1986—; gen. mgr. Vision of Am. at Peace, San Francisco, 1983-84; sales mgr. Fed. Employees Pub., San Francisco, 1985-87. Columnist El Bohemio News; author reference handbook, articles in field. Dir. Latin Drug Edn. Project, Milw., 1971-73, Hispanic Dem. Com., San Francisco, 1979-82, City Wide Alcoholism Commn.; del. Dem. Nat. Conv., N.Y.C., 1980, nat. co-chair ann. conv., 1984; vice-chair Mex.-Am. Polit. Assn., 1983; chair 6th Congl. dist. Dem. party. Recipient mktg. awards Elizabeth Arden, 1989; named Woman of Yr. Hispanic Dem. Com., San Francisco, 1980; recipient community svc. award Dorinda Moreno League, San Francisco, 1983. Mem. NAFE, Chicano/Latino Dem. Caucus, Hispanic C. of C., San Francisco C. of C., Am. Mktg. Assn., Soc. Govt. Meeting Planners, Nat. Assn. Latino Elected and Appointed Ofcls., Mex. Am. Polit. Assn. (pres.), Nat. Writers Union (local 3, UAW affiliate). Home: 150 Lombard # 309 San Francisco CA 94111 Office: 1255 Battery St # 300 San Francisco CA 94111

BALLESTEROS, DAVID, university dean; b. L.A., July 3, 1933; s. Leonardo and Rosa Ballesteros; m. Carol A. Williams, Mar. 25, 1966 (div. May 1979); children: Rita, Marra, Victoria; m. Dolores Ann Noffsinger, June 16, 1979. BA, U. Redlands, 1955; MA, Middlebury Coll., 1958; PhD, U. So. Calif., 1968. Tchr. Spanish, Helex High Sch., La Mesa, Calif., 1958-68; prof. modern langs. U. Okla., Norman, 1968-70; dir.. Tchr. Corps, U. Tex., Austin, 1970-72; dean arts and scis. Calif. State U., Sacramento, 1972-77; vice chancellor U. Colo., Colorado Springs, 1977-83; dean campus San Diego State U., Calexico, Calif., 1983—; cons. U.S. Dept. Edn., Washington, 1980—. Contbr. articles on lang. and multicultural edn. to profl. jours. Bd. dirs. Imperial County Arts Coun., v.p., 1988-89. Grantee Govt. of Spain, Madrid, 1957-58, Instr. for Edn. Mgmt. grantee Harvard U , summer 1986; fellow U.S. Office Edn., 1969-70. Mem. Rotary (pres. 1989-90), Phi Beta Delta (bd. dirs. San Diego State U.), Phi Delta Kappa (bd. dirs., v.p. Imperial County chpt. 1987—, Educator of Yr. award 1989). Home: 673 Calle de la Sierra El Cajon CA 92019 Office: San Diego State U 720 Heber Ave Calexico CA 92231

BALLHAUS, WILLIAM FRANCIS, JR., aerospace industry executive, research scientist; b. L.A., Jan. 28, 1945; s. William Francis Sr. and Edna A. (Dooley) B.; m. Jane Kerber; children from previous marriage: William Louis, Michael Frederick; stepchildren: Benjamin Joel, Jennifer Angela. BSME with honors, U. Calif., Berkeley, 1967, MS in Mech. Engring., 1968, PhD in Engring., 1971. Rsch. scientist U.S. Army Aviation R & D, Ames Rsch. Ctr., Moffett Field, Calif., 1971-79; chief applied computation aeronautics br. NASA-Ames Rsch. Ctr., Moffett Field, 1979-80, dir. astronautics, 1980-84, dir., 1984-89; acting assoc. adminstr. NASA Hdqrs., Washington, 1988-89; v.p. rsch. tech. Martin Marietta Astronautics Group, Denver, 1989-90, v.p., dir. Centaur program, 1990—; pres. Civil Space and Communications, Denver, 1990—. Contbr. articles on computational fluid dynamics to profl. jours. Mem. sci. and acad. adv. bd. U. Calif., 1987-92; mem. engring. adv. bd. U. Calif., Berkeley and Davis, San Jose State U.; chmn. govt. and edn. div. United Way of Santa Clara County, Calif., 1987. Capt USAR. Decorated Presdl. Rank of Disting. Exec., 1985; recipient H. Julian Allen award NASA-Ames Rsch. Ctr., 1977, Arthur S. Flemming award Jaycees, Washington, 1980, Disting. Profl. Engring. Sci. and Tech. award NSPE, 1986, Disting. Exec. Svc. award Sr. Execs. Assn., 1989, Disting. Svc. medal NASA, 1989, Disting. Engring. Alumnus award U. Calif., Berkeley, 1989. Fellow AIAA (pres. 1988-89, Lawrence Sperry award 1980), Royal Aero. Soc.; mem. NAE, Internat. Acad. Astronautics, Tau Beta Pi (named Eminent Engr. Berkeley chpt.). Roman Catholic. Office: Martin Marietta Civil Space and Communications Co PO Box 179 Denver CO 80201-0179

BALLINGER, CHARLES EDWIN, educational association executive; b. West Mansfield, Ohio, June 3, 1935; s. William E. and Mildred Arlene (Jester) B.; m. Venita Dee Riggs, June 12, 1982. BA, De Pauw U., 1957; MA, Ohio State U., 1958, PhD, 1971. Tchr. pub. schs., Ohio, 1958-62, Ohio State U. Lab. Sch., Columbus, 1962-63; asst. supt. North Canton (Ohio) City Schs., 1964-67; cons. Franklin County Schs., Columbus, 1967-70, Ohio Dept. Edn., Columbus, 1970-71; coord. San Diego County Office Edn., San Diego, 1971—; exec. dir. Nat. Assn. for Yr.-Round Edn., San Diego, 1980—. Contbr. numerous articles to profl. jours. Home: 4891 Jellett St San Diego CA 92110-2226 Office: Nat Assn for Yr-Round Edn 6401 Linda Vista Rd San Diego CA 92111-7399

BALLINGER, CHARLES KENNETH, information specialist; b. Johnstown, Pa., July 28, 1950; s. Delores Jean (Cool) B.; m. Deb C. Delger, Sept. 14, 1985. Programmer analyst Cowles Pub. Co., Spokane, Wash., 1975-78; systems analyst Old Nat. Bank, Spokane, 1978-82; software engr. ISC System, Spokane, 1982; micro computer analyst Acme Bus. Computers, Spokane, 1982-85; info. ctr. analyst Wash. Water Power Co., Spokane, 1985-92; office automation analyst EDS Corp., Spokane, 1992—; cons. IDP Co., Spokane, 1978—. Contbr. articles to profl. jours. Served with Signal Corps, U.S. Army, 1968-71. Mem. IEEE (assoc.), Spokane Health Users Group (pres. 1979-83). Home: S 3810 Havana Spokane WA 99223 Office: EDS-I/S Wash Water Power Co E 1411 Mission Spokane WA 99202

BALLINGER, JAMES K., art museum executive; b. Kansas City, Mo., July 7, 1949; s. Robert Eugene and Yvonne (Davidson) B.; m. Nina Lundgaard, Aug. 21, 1971; children—Erin, Cameron. B.A., U. Kans., 1972, M.A., 1974. Gallery coordinator Tucson Art Ctr., 1973; registrar U. Kans., Lawrence, 1973-74; curator collections Phoenix Art Mus., 1974-81, asst. dir., 1981, dir., 1982—. Author: (exhbn. catalogues) Beyond the Endless River, 1980, Visitors to Arizona 1846 to 1980, 1981, Peter Hurd, 1983, The Popular West, 1982, Thomas Moran, 1986, Frederick Remington, 1989. Bd. dirs. Balboa Art Conservation Ctr. Fellow Am. Assn. Mus. Dirs. (bd. dirs.), Western Assn. Art Museums; mem. Central Ariz. Mus. Assn. (v.p. 1983). Home: 5002 E Calle Tuberia Phoenix AZ 85018-4425 Office: Phoenix Art Mus 1625 N Central Ave Phoenix AZ 85004-1685

BALLINGER, PHILIP ALBERT, university administrator; b. Bordeaux, France, Feb. 9, 1957; came to U.S. 1959; s. Charles Minor and Michelle Jeanne (Tutor) B. BA in Philosophy, Coll. St. Pius X, Erlanger, Ky., 1979; BA in Religious Studies, U. Louvain, Belgium, 1980; MA, STB, U. Louvain, 1982, STL, 1984. Asst. dean admissions Gonzaga U., Spokane, Wash., 1987-89; assoc. dean admissions Gonzaga U., 1989-90, dean admissions, 1990-92, 1992—; adj. instr. Gonzaga U., 1986—. Office: Gonzaga U 502 E Boone Ave Spokane WA 99258-0001

BALLINGER, RUTH ANN, language professional, foreign language educator; b. Wailuku, Hawaii, Feb. 5, 1960; d. Donald Kenneth and Teruko Anne (Oka) B.; m. Richard John Duffy, June 30, 1984. AB, Harvard U., 1982; postgrad., Maui Community Coll., Kahului, Hawaii, 1987-90. Dir. audio-visual ctr. Kennedy Sch. Govt. Harvard U., Cambridge, Mass., 1982-84; exec. asst. Mass. Corp. Ednl. Telecommunications, Boston, 1984-86; rsch. asst. Brokton (Mass.) Vets. Adminstrn. Hosp., 1985-86; Japanese tour guide Trans Hawaiian, Kahului, Hawaii, 1988-89; Japanese language tchr. Maui Commmunity Coll, Kahului, Hawaii, 1990—; vegetable farmer, Kula, Hawaii, 1989—; founder Common Ground cons. firm, 1991—. Contbr. articles to profl. jours. Home: 113 Hapapa Rd Kula HI 96790

BALLOUE, JOHN EDWARD, artist; b. Richmond, Calif., Apr. 19, 1948; s. Mayburn Leo Balloue and Judy (Keeton) Laugesen; m. Connie Diane Philis, Mar. 7, 1978; children: Elizabeth Reneé, Rebecca Ann. BA in Art, Calif. State U., 1975. Waiter various restaurants, Hayward, Calif., 1975-91; free-lance artist Hayward, Calif., 1975—; vol. art instr. San Francisco Unified Sch. Dist., 1990-91; mem., artist Gallery-House Artist Coop., Palo Alto, Calif., 1976-78; art competition juror Chawse State Pk., Volcano, Calif., 1986, Calif. Native Am. Cultural Com., Volcano, 1986. Cover artist: People to Remember, 1992; artist: Reference Encyclopedia of the American Indian, 6th edit., 1992. Mem. PTA, Hayward, 1983—; art cons. Hayward Unified Sch. Dist., 1988—. With U.S. Army, 1968-69, Vietnam. Recipient Eureaka fellowship nominee Flieshhacker Found., 1992, numerous art competition awards. Mem. Indian Arts and Crafts Assn. (Artist of Yr. 1992), Am. Indian Traders Guild, Hayward Arts Coun., Am. Indian Contemporary Arts. Home: 26838 Grandview Ave Hayward CA 94542

BALL-SUNDINE, SANDRA JEAN, educator; b. Denver, July 7, 1963; d. Donald Ervin and Barbara Ellen (Koop) Ball; m. Brian James Sundine, June 30, 1990. BSE, Okla. Christian Coll., 1984; MA, U. Colo., Denver, 1991. Cert. tchr., Colo. Tchr. math. Cimarron Middle Sch., Edmond, Okla., 1984-86; tchr. of gifted and talented U. Denver, 1989-90; tchr. math., algebra West Middle Sch., Aurora, Colo., 1986-91; tchr. math Columbia Mid. Sch., Aurora, 1991—; asst. women's basketball coach Rangeview High Sch., Aurora, 1986-91, Littleton (Colo.) High Sch., 1991—; mem. North Cen. Steering Com., 1991; presenter at profl. confs. Mem. Nat. Coun. Tchrs. Math., Colo. Coun. Tchrs. Math., Women and Math. Edn., Women's Basketball Coaches Assn., Colo. Coaches Assn., Alpha Chi. Mem. Ch. of Christ. Home: 1518 S Elkhart St Aurora CO 80012-5712 Office: Columbia Middle Sch 17600 E Columbia Ave Aurora CO 80013-4401

BALOG, JAMES DENNIS, photographer; b. Danville, Pa., July 15, 1952; s. James and Alvina (Bartos) B.; m. Karen Mary Breunig, Nov. 28, 1982; 1 child, Simone Andrea. BA cum laude, Boston Coll., 1974; MA, U. Colo., 1977. Mountain climbing guide Colo. Outward Bound, Denver, 1976-80; owner, photographer James Balog Photography, Boulder, Colo., 1980—. Author: Wildlife Requiem, 1984, Survivors, 1990; major solo exhbns. include Calif. Mus. Photography, Riverside, 1985, Internat. Ctr. Photography, N.Y.C., 1985, 90, Mus. Contemporary Photography, Chgo., 1986, Canon Image Centre, Amsterdam, The Netherlands, 1990, Musee de l'Elysee, Laussane, Switzerland, 1990, Internat. Photography Expn., Perpignon, France, 1990, Internat. Mus. Photography at George Eastman House, Rochester, N.Y., 1990, Kathleen Ewing Gallery, Washington, 1990, Arvada Ctr. Arts and Humanities, Denver, 1991, Prescott (Ariz.) Fine Arts Assn., 1991, Ansel Adams Ctr., San Francisco, 1991, Centre Nat. de la Photographie, Paris, 1991, École Regionale des Beaux-Arts, Normandy, France, 1991, Museo Nacional de Ciencias Naturales, Madrid, 1991, Museo de Zoologia, Barcelona, Spain, 1991, Colorado Springs Fine Arts Ctr., 1991, Hamilton's Gallery, London, 1991, Halsted Gallery, Detroit, 1991, Robert Koch Gallery, San Fransisco, 1991, Robert Klein Gallery, Boston, 1991, Fahey/Klein, L.A., 1991, A Gallery for Fine Photography, New Orleans, 1991, Chrysler Mus., 1992, Norton Mus. Fine Arts, 1992, Woodson Mus., 1992, Centre Nationale d'Art Comtemporain, Grenoble, France, 1992; group shows NYU, 1981, Ronald Feldman Gallery, N.Y.C., 1983, Denver Art Mus., 1983, 87, 90, Colorado Springs Fine Arts Ctr., 1984, Nikon House, N.Y.C., 1986, 87, Corcoran Gallery, Washington, 1987, Orlando Mus. of Art, Fla., 1992, Centre Nationale de la Photographie, Paris, 1992; selected pub. collections Bklyn. Mus., Calif. Mus. Photography, Corcoran Gallery, Denver Art Mus., Forbes Collection, Internat. Ctr. Photography, Kaiser Permanente, Mountain Bell, Mus. Contemporary Photography, Chgo., Time, Inc., Orlando Mus. of Art, Fla., Mus. of Fine Arts, St. Petersburg, Fla., 1992; work included in: One Moment of the World, 3 edits., 1983-85, A Day in the Life of America, 1986, A Day in the Life of the Soviet Union, 1987, A Day in the Life of Spain, 1988; regular contbr. Nat. Geographic mags. Smithsonian Instn. Recipient Communications Arts award of excellence, 1984, 87, third pl. award, 2 awards of excellence Pictures of Yr. Competition Nat. Press Photographers, 1987, 89, 1st pl. award World Press Photo Competition, 1987, Leica Medal of Excellence for photographic books, 1990, Best of Show awards Graphics Mag., 1991; creative artists fellow Colo. Coun. Arts and Humanities, 1988; Kodak Photographic Arts grantee, 1988. Mem. Friends of Photography, Soc. Environ. Journalists. Home and Studio: 667 Walden Circle Boulder CO 80303

BALSIGER, DAVID WAYNE, television director, author, researcher, producer; b. Monroe, Wis., Dec. 14, 1945; s. Leon C. and Dorothy May (Meythaler) B.; m. Nancy Marie Dixon, Oct. 12, 1991; children from previous marriages: Jennifer Anne, Lisa Atalie, Lori Faith. Student, Pepperdine U., Malibu, Calif., 1964-66, Cypress Jr. Coll., 1966, Chapman Coll. World Campus Afloat, Orange, Calif., 1967-68, Internat. Coll., Copenhagen, 1968; BA, Nat. U., San Diego, 1977; LHD (hon.), Lincoln Meml. U., Harrogate, Tenn., 1978. Chief photographer, feature writer Anaheim (Calif.) Bull., 1968-69; pub., editor Money Doctor, consumer mag., Anaheim, 1969-70; media dir. World Evangelism, San Diego, 1970-72; dir. mktg. Logos Internat. Christian Book Pubs., Plainfield, N.J., 1972-73; pres., dir. Master Media, advt. agy., Costa Mesa, Calif., 1973-75; pres. Balsiger Lit. Svc., Costa Mesa, 1973-78; v.p. communications Donald S. Smith Assocs., Anaheim, Calif., 1975-78; dir. creative devel. Sunn Classic Pictures, L.A., Salt Lake City, 1976-78; owner Writeway Lit. Assocs., Costa Mesa, 1978—, Balsiger Enterprises, Costa Mesa, 1978-92, Bibl. News Svc., 1980-90; v.p. Donald S. Smith Assocs., Anaheim, 1982-86; owner BNS Publs., 1986-92; v.p. Am. Portrait Films Internat., Anaheim, 1990-91; chief rschr., field prodr., dir. Sun Internat. Pictures, Salt Lake City, 1992—; vis. prof. Nat. U., San Diego, 1977-80. Author: The Satan Seller, 1972, The Back Side of Satan, 1973, Noah's Ark: I Touched It, 1974, One More Time, 1974, It's Good to Know, 1975, In Search of Noah's Ark, 1976, The Lincoln Conspiracy, 1977, Beyond Defeat, 1978, On the Other Side, 1978, Mistah Abe, 1993, 8 Mini Guide Books (travel series), 1979, Presidential Biblical Scoreboard, 1980, 84, 88, Family Protection Scoreboard, South Africa, 1987, 88 (terorism), 89 (liberation theology), Candidates Biblical Scoreboard, 1986, Scoreboard Alert, 1989, Face in the Mirror, 1993, Ancient Secrets of the Bible, 1993, The Incredible Dicovery of Noah's Ark, 1993, Mistah Abe, 1993; director, field producer, writer, researcher: TV and motion pictures including Operation Thanks, 1965, The Life and Times of Grizzly Adams, 1976-77, In Search of Noah's Ark, 1976, The Lincoln Conspiracy, 1977, The Bermuda Triangle, 1977, In God We Trust: The Impact of Prayer on America, 1993, Mistah Abe, 1991; (CBS Network specials) Ancient Secrets of the Bible, 1992, The Incredible Discovery of Noah's Ark, 1993, Ancient Secrets of the Bible II, 1993, Ancient Mysteries of the World, 1993,; pub.-editor Christian Singles Connection, 1991-92; frequent debate page columnist USA Today, 1987—; author numerous law enforcement publs. Press agt. John G. Schmitz congl. campaign, 1972, Gordon Bishop supr. campaign, Orange County, 1970; press agt. asst. Ronald Reagan for Gov., statewide, 1966; statewide campaign mgr. James E. Johnson for U.S. Senate, 1974; campaign mgr. Dave Gubler Congl. campaign, 1974; candidate Costa Mesa City Coun., 1980; Rep. candidate for Congress from 38th Dist. Calif., 1978; mem. Calif. Rep. Assembly, 1975-78, 81-84, Rep. Assocs. Orange County, 1977-79; mem. World Affairs Coun. Orange County and San Diego, 1969-70; assoc. mem. Calif. Rep. Cen. Com., 1969-70; bd. dirs. Chapman Coll. World Campus Afloat, 1967, Chrisma Ministries, Orange, Calif., 1969-73; founder Ban the Soviets Coalition, 1983-84; exec. com. Anatole Fellowship, 1983-87; founder, pres. Nat. Citizens Action Network, 1984—; bd. dirs. Internat. Ch. Relief Fund, 1987-92. Recipient Vietnam appreciation citation Am. Soldiers in Vietnam, 1966, George Washington Honor medal Freedoms Found., 1978, 79, Religion in Media Angel trophy, 1981, 85, 87, 88, 89, 92; named Writer of Month Calif. Writer, 1967; grand winner Mercury award for Pub. Affairs, 1987, Gold Mercury award for Pub. Affairs Mag., 1987, Silver Mercury award for affairs video script, 1988; named to Lit. Hall of Fame, 1977; hon. tourism amb. Republic of South Africa, 1991. Mem. Nat. Univ. Pres. Assocs., Coun. on Nat. Policy, CamCrusade for Christ (com. on reference), Internat. Bible Reading Assn. (adv. bd.), Evang. Press Assn., Christian Action Network (adv. bd.). Office: Writeway Literary Assocs 1055 E 5800 S Ogden UT 84405-4919

BALSLEY, BEN BURTON, physicist; b. Santa Monica, Calif., Apr. 23, 1932; s. Floyd Lewis and Edna (Holmes) B.; m. Donna Elizabeth Holmes, Sept. 1, 1956; children—Christopher L., Tobin P., Debora E. B.Sc., Calif. State Poly. U., San Luis Obispo, 1957; M.Sc., U. Colo., 1964, Ph.D., 1967. Electronic engr., Nat. Bur. Standards, Boulder, Colo., 1957-59, Lima, Peru, 1960-63; physicist Jicamarca Radar Obs., Lima, 1966-69; physicist Aeronomy Lab., NOAA, Boulder, 1969-87, chief tropical dynamic and climate program area, 1987-90; sr. rsch. fellow coop. inst. for rsch. in environ. scis. U. Colo., Boulder, 1990—; res. prof. electrical and computer engring. dept. U. Boulder, 1991—; mem. Study Group on Internat. Equatorial Obs. Guest editor Jour. Atmospheric and Terrestrial Physics, 1976—. Contbr. articles to profl. jours. Served with USAF, 1949-52. Recipient gold medal U.S. Dept. Commerce, 1974; Outstanding Paper award, 1981; Disting. Alumnus award Calif. State Poly. U., 1975. Mem. Am. Meteorol. Soc., Am. Geophys. Union, Sci. Research Soc. Am., Sci. Radio Union, Soc. for Preservation and Encouragement, Barbershop Quartet Singing in Am. (pres. 1981-82). Home: 7240 Terrace Pl Boulder CO 80303-4638 Office: CIRES U Colo Boulder CO 80309-0216

BALTAKE, JOE, film critic; b. Camden, N.J., Sept. 16; s. Joseph John and Rose Clara (Bearint) B.; m. Susan Shapiro Hale. BA, Rutgers U., 1967. Film critic Gannett Newspapers (suburban), 1967-69, Phila. Daily News, 1970-86; movie editor Inside Phila., 1986—; film critic The Sacramento Bee,

1987—; leader criticism workshop Phila. Writer's Conf., 1977-79; film critic. Contbg. editor: Screen World, 1973-87 ; author: The Films of Jack Lemmon, 1977, updated, 1986; contbr. articles to Films in Rev., 1969—, broadcast criticism for Prism Cable TV, 1985; cons. Jack Lemmon: American Film Institute Life Achievemetn Award, 1987, Jack Lemmon: A Life in the Movies, 1990. Recipient Motion Picture Preview Group award for criticism, 1986, citation Phila. Mag., 1985. Mem. Nat. Soc. Film Critics. Office: Sacramento Bee 2100 Q St Sacramento CA 95816-6816

BALTICH, LINDA KAASE, metallurgical engineer; b. St. Paul, June 28, 1956; d. Roger C. and Janet L. (Tasler) Kaase; m. John F. Baltich, July 11, 1980; children: Elizabeth, Nathaniel. BS in Mineral Engring., U. Minn., 1978; postgrad., U. Utah, 1978-80. Project engr. AMAX R & D, Golden, Colo., 1980-90, Resource Devel. Inc., Wheat Ridge, Colo., 1990—. Contbr. articles to tech. publs. Me. Soc. Mining Engrs. of AIME.

BALUNI, ALICE, electronics company executive; b. Cairo, Dec. 10, 1945; came to U.S., 1975; s. Arthur Z. and Angele Baluni. M Physics of Semicondrs., Moscow State U., 1969; M Engring. Mgmt., Santa Clara U., 1981. Lectr. solid state physics Yerevan (Armenia) State U., 1969-75; engring. supr. Intel Co., Santa Clara, Calif., 1975-81; sr. design engr. Synertek Co., Santa Clara, 1981-82; product engring. mgr. Sygnetics Co., Sunnyvale, Calif., 1982-85; v.p. reliability and quality assurance Zilog Co., Campbell, Calif., 1985—. Mem. IEEE, Am. Soc. for Quality Control. Republican. Office: Zilog Co 210 Hacienda Ave Campbell CA 95008

BALYO, JOHN GABRIEL, minister, theology educator; b. Greenville, S.C., Jan. 18, 1920; s. John Gabor and Etta (Groce) B.; m. Betty Louise Lindstrand, Oct. 14, 1945; 1 son, John Michael. Student, Atlanta Law Sch., 1937-40; LL.B., Valparaiso U., 1945; student, Goshen Coll., 1945-46; A.B., Grace Theol. Sem., 1944, MDiv. magna cum laude, 1946; D.D., Grand Rapids Theol. Sem., 1960. Ordained to ministry Bible Bapt. Ch., 1950. Pastor Three Oaks, Mich., 1942-45, Elkhart, Ind., 1945-46, Kokomo, Ind., 1946-53; pastor Cedar Hill Bapt. Ch., Cleve., 1953-72; prof. Bible and practical theology Grand Rapids (Mich.) Bapt. Theol. Sem., 1972-80; chmn. council of ten Sunshine State Fellowship of Regular Bapt. Chs., Fla., 1980-81; pastor Sun Coast Bapt. Ch., New Port Richey, Fla., 1980-81; prof. theology and Bible Bapt. Bible Coll. and Sch. Theology, Clarks Summit, Pa., 1981-83; pres. Western Bapt. Coll., Salem, Oreg., 1983-91, chancellor, 1991—; mem. gen. council Bapt. Mid-Mission, 1954—, adminstrv. com., 1962-73, trustee, 1963-75, chmn. bd. trustees, 1968-75, chmn. council, 1966-68; mem. council 14 Gen. Assn. Regular Bapt. Chs., 1955-59, 60-64, sec. council, 1957-58, chmn. publs. com., 1956-60, 63-66, chmn. council 14, 1966-68, mem. finance com., 1968-69, publs. com., 1968-69, chmn. program com., 1968-69, chmn. edn. com., 1960-62, vice chmn. council, 1962-64, chmn., 1970-72, chmn. publs. com., 1972-73, chmn. council of 18, 1973-74, vice chmn. council of 18, 1983-86, chmn., 1986-87; exec. bd. dirs. Grand Rapids Bapt. Bible Coll. and Sem., 1961-72, chmn. curriculum com., 1963-66; missionary survey trips to, Europe and Africa, 1957-58, Ecuador, 1962, Peru, 1969, Brazil, 1975; bd. dirs. Hebrew Christian Soc., 1956-64; instr. pastor's seminar, Kiev, Ukraine, 1993. Author: Sunday sch. material for Regular Bapt. Press; also booklet Creation and Evolution. Active gen. coun. Bapt. Mid. Missions, 1954-88. Mem. Oreg. Ind. Colls. Assn. (exec. com. Portland chpt. 1990-91). Home: 5515 Springwood Ave SE Salem OR 97306-1673 Office: Western Bapt Coll 5000 Deer Park Dr SE Salem OR 97301-9330

BALZA, JOHN JOSEPH, research and development manager; b. Green Bay, Wis., Jan. 31, 1949; s. G. Tony and Grace M. (Angst) B.; m. Mary Margaret Grosche, July 17, 1976; children: Laura Marie, Mary Elizabeth. BS in Elec. Engring., Ill. Inst. Tech., 1971; MS in Elec. Engring., U. Wis., 1972; MBA, Colo. State U., 1985. Engr. Hewlett Packard Co., Loveland, Colo., 1972-76; project mgr. Hewlett Packard Co., Fort Collins, Colo., 1976-83; R&D section mgr. Hewlett Packard Co., Fort Collins, 1983-89, R&D lab. mgr., 1989—. Democrat. Roman Catholic. Home: 713 Hinsdale Dr Fort Collins CO 80526

BALZHISER, RICHARD EARL, research and development company executive; b. Wheaton, Ill., May 27, 1932; s. Frank E. and Esther K. (Merrill Werner) B.; m. Christine Karnuth, 1951; children: Gary, Robert, Patricia, Michelle. B.S. in Chem. Engring., U. Mich., 1955, M.S. in Nuclear Engring., 1956, Ph.D. in Chem. Engring., 1961. Mem. faculty U. Mich., Ann Arbor, 1961-67; White House fellow, spl. asst. to sec. Dept. Def., Washington, 1967-68; chmn. dept. chem. engring. U. Mich., 1970-71; assoc. dir. energy, environ. and natural resources White House Office of Sci. and Tech., Washington, 1971-73; dir. fossil fuel and advanced systems Electric Power Rsch. Inst., Palo Alto, Calif., 1973-79, sr. v.p. R&D, 1979-87, exec. v.p. R&D, 1987-88, pres., chief exec. officer, 1988—; chmn. U.S. Energy R&D Exch. with USSR, 1973-74; mem. EPCOT Ctr., Orlando, Fla., 1977-80, NAS acad. industry program, 1988—, U. Mich. Coll. Engring. nat. adv. com., 1989-92; energy rsch. adv. bd. U.S. Dept. Energy, 1988-89, mem. innovative control tech. adv. panel, 1989; adv. coun. U. Tex. Natural Sci. Found., Austin, 1990—; mem. NRC Energy Engring. Bd., 1991—; bd. dirs. Atlantic Coun. U.S., 1991—, Pres.'s Coun. Competitiveness, 1992; adv. bd. Woods Hole (Mass.) Oceanographic Instn., 1992—. Editorial bd.: Sci. mag., 1977—; co-author: Chemical Engineering Thermodynamics, 1972, Engineering Thermodynamics, 1977. Mem. Ann Arbor City Coun., 1965-67, mayor pro tem, 1967. Charles M. Schwab Meml. lectr. Am. Iron And Steel Inst., 1983. Mem. AAAS, ASME, Am. Inst. Chem. Engrs., Cosmos Club (Washington), Sigma Chi. Republican. Lutheran. Office: Electric Power Rsch Inst PO Box 10412 3412 Hillview Ave Palo Alto CA 94304-1395

BAMBA, JOSEPH GEORGE, senator, insurance executive; b. Tamuning, Guam, July 19, 1951; s. George Mariano and Cecilia (Cruz) B.; m. Joyce Claire Charfauros, Jan. 17, 1970; children: Brian, Tanya, Tara, George II. Student, U. Guam, Mangilao, 1969-71, U. Guam, La Salle, 1972. Ins. underwriter Bamba's Ins., Agana, Guam, 1972-75; pres. Bamba's Ins., Agana, 1983—; staff asst. Office of Guam Del. to U.S. Congress, Agana, 1975-78; spl. asst. to gov. Office of Gov., Agana, 1979-81, exec. asst. to gov., 1981-82; pres. J. Bamba & Assocs. Real Estate Brokers, Agana, 1983—; senator Guam Legislature, Agana, 1984—; bd. dirs. Guam Beauty Assn., Agana, 1986—; v.p., bd. dirs. Marianas Internat. Ins. Corp., Saipan, No. Marianas Islands, 1987—; mng. dir. MITA Travel (Guam), Inc., Agana, 1987—; minority leader, 1988-90; mem. 1992 NAS Land Transfer Task Force; chmn. econ. devel. & internat. trade Coun. State Govt. Western Legis. Conf. 1992—. Mem. cen. com. Rep. Party Guam, Agana, 1985—; mem. Guam Quincentennial Commn., 1991,Guam Tax Code Commn., 1990; mem. exec. com. Western Legis. Conf. Mem. Nat. Rep. Legis. Assn., Nat. Conf. State Legis., Paradise Jaycees (co-founder). Office: Guam Legislature Capitol Bldg 155 Hesler St Agana GU 96910-5004 also: 479 W O'Brien Dr Agana GU 96910

BAMFORD, NIGEL SIMON, pediatrician; b. St. Helens, Lancs., Eng., Oct. 15, 1960; came to U.S. 1968; s. Bernard and Olive (Williams) B. AAS, Salt Lake Community Coll., 1984; BSEE, U. Utah, 1986, MD, 1992. Electronic tech. Eaton Kenway, Bountiful, Utah, 1984-85; guitar performer Destiny, Salt Lake City, 1982-88; elec. engring. cons. Salt Lake City, 1985-92, WBK Controls, Salt Lake City, 1986-92; pediatric intern Columbia-Presbyn. Hosp., N.Y.C., 1992—. Mem. Utah Med. Assn Rural Health Com., Salt Lake City, 1991-92. Eagle Scout with Bronze Palm Boy Scouts Am., 1975; Salt Lake Community Coll. scholar, 1983-85, U. Utah Jr. Coll. Transfer scholar, 1985-87, Elec. Engring. scholar, 1987, Drew B. Meilstrup scholar, 1991. Home: 1908 S 775 E Bountiful UT 84010

BANAS, EMIL MIKE, physicist, educator; b. East Chicago, Ind., Dec. 5, 1921; s. John J. and Rose M. (Valcicak) B.; ed. Ill. Benedictine Coll., 1940-43; B.A. (U.S. Rubber fellow), U. Notre Dame, 1954, Ph.D., 1955; m. Margaret Fagyas, Oct. 9, 1948; children—Mary K., Barbara A. Instr. math. and physics Ill. Benedictine Coll., Lisle, 1946-48, adj. faculty mem., 1971-82, trustee, 1959-61; with Civil Service, State of Ind., Hammond, 1948-50; lectr. physics Purdue U., Hammond, 1955-60; staff research physicist Amoco Corp., Naperville, Ill., 1955-82; cons., 1983—. Served with USNR, 1943-46. Mem. Am. Philatelic Soc., Ill. Benedictine Coll. Alumni Assn. (dir. hon., named alumnus of yr., 1965, pres. 1959-60), U. Notre Dame Alumni Assn. (sec. grad. physics alumni), Am. Legion, Sigma Pi Sigma. Roman Catholic. Clubs: Soc. of Procopians. Contbr. articles to sci. jours. Home: SW 325 Clarkson Ct Apt 4 Pullman WA 99163

BANAUGH, ROBERT PETER, computer science educator; b. Los Angeles, Oct. 27, 1922; s. Rudolph Otto and Elizabeth (Mantz) B.; m. Catherine Haun, July 6, 1946; children: Elizabeth Anne, Catherine Marie, Robert George, Mary Louise, Laura Jean, Marjorie Theresa, John Gerard, Peter Andrew. AA, Pasadena Jr. Coll., 1942; BA, U. Calif., Berkeley, 1943, MA, 1952, PhD, 1962. Secondary sch. tchr. Richmond (Calif.) Jr. High Sch., 1947-50; instr. math. U. Calif., Berkeley, 1949-72, vis. prof., 1975-76; prof. computer sci. U. Mont., Missoula, 1964-75, 76—; vis. prof. U. Wollongong, Australia, 1985; physicist Boeing Aircraft, Seattle, 1966-72; applied mechanics scientist Appled Theory, Los Angeles, 1968-75; computer scientist U.S. Forest Service, Missoula, 1968-71, engr., 1972—. Contbr. numerous articles to profl. jours. Served to 1st lt. USAAF, 1943-45. Home: 9401 Upper Miller Creek Rd Missoula MT 59803-9801 Office: U Mont Dept Computer Sci Missoula MT 59812

BANDONG, PAUL ANTHONY, high-technology business consultant, investor; b. Ft. Carson, Colo., Apr. 21, 1956; s. Isidro Sevidal and Rosalia (Martinez) B. Grad., U.S. Mil. Acad., 1977. Pres., owner Mgmt. Cons. Svc., Menlo Park, 1978—; sr. assoc., staffing and mgmt. cons. Beckstead & Assocs., Santa Clara, Calif., 1978-81; v.p. bus. devel. and mktg. Ward Cons. Group, San Jose, 1981-82; exec. v.p. product devel., mktg., fin., ops. Advanced Custom Computer Engring. Labs., Santa Clara, 1982; exec. v.p. fin., ops. and product devel., mktg. Daystar Learning Corp., Palo Alto, Calif., 1983-84; v.p. fin., ops., bus. devel., product devel., mktg. Nat. Computer Tng. Inst., Fremont, Calif., 1984; pres., COO, CFO PCC/Systems, Inc., Menlo Park, Calif., 1985; group mgr. quality assurance/product devel. network products Apple Computer Inc., Cupertino, Calif., 1986-88; pres., owner Prosperity Art/Investment, Prosperity Pub., Prosperity Cons., Menlo Park, 1989—; founder, prin., mng. ptnr. Future Vision Investment Group I & II, Menlo Park, 1991—; lectr. seminars in leadership and mgmt., event organizer, author, free-lance writer. Mem. Nat. Right to Life Com., 1985—, Nat. Rep. Congl. Com., 1982—; deacon 1st Bapt. Ch., Menlo Park, 1982-83; mem. regional youth com. Am. Bapt. Chs. of West, 1983-84; charter mem. Grace Commn.; asst. coach Girls' Varsity Basketball Mountain View High Sch., 1987-91; head caoch bantam div. Pop Warner Football, 1980; asst. coach women's basketball De Anza Coll., 1987; asst. coach ASD/USA Women's Basketball Teams, Summer Internat. Champions, 1987-89. With U.S. Army, 1975-77. Mem. Smithsonian Instns., Profl. and Tech. Cons. Assn., NRA, Churchill Club, Commonwealth Club (San Francisco), Nat. Assn. for the Self-Employed, Art Collectors Circle. Home: 106 Marigold WAy Salinas CA 93905 Office: Management Cons Svc 1240 Hobart St Menlo Park CA 94025-5517

BANDT, PAUL DOUGLAS, physician; b. Milbank, S.D., June 22, 1938; s. Lester Herman and Edna Louella (Sogn) B.; m. Mary King, Aug. 26, 1962 (div. Feb. 1974); children: Douglas, Peggy; m. Inara Irene Von Rostas, Apr. 1, 1974; 1 child, Jennifer. BS in Edn. with distinction, U. Minn., 1960, BS in Medicine, 1966, D in Medicine, 1966. Diplomate Am. Bd. Diagnostic Radiology, Am. Bd. Nuclear Medicine. Intern U.S. Pub. Health Svc., San Francisco, 1966-68; physician U.S. Pub. Health Svc., Las Vegas, 1968-69; resident Stanford U., Palo Alto, Calif., 1969-72; physician Desert Radiologists, Las Vegas, 1972—; chmn. dept. of radiology Desert Springs Hosp., Las Vegas; immediate past chief of staff U. Med. Ctr. So. Nev., Las Vegas. Contbr. articles on diagnostic radiology to profl. jours. With USPHS, 1966-69. Mem. AMA, Am. Coll. Radiology, Am. Coll. Nuclear Medicine, Clark Med. Soc. Office: Desert Radiologists 2020 Palomino Ln Las Vegas NV 89106

BANDURRAGA, PETER LOUIS, museum director, historian; b. Los Angeles, Apr. 2, 1944; s. Luis Cipriano and E. Lillian (Slingsby) B.; m. Diane Elizabeth Nassir, Mar. 4 , 1979. B.A., Stanford U., 1966; M.A., U. Calif.-Santa Barbara, 1968; Ph.D., U. Calif.Santa Barbara, 1977. Instr. Chapman Coll., Orange, Calif., 1977-78; research librarian Ventura County Hist. Mus., Ventura, Calif., 1978-81; dir. Nev. Hist. Soc., Reno, 1981—; mem. Nev. State Adv. Council on Libraries, 1981-86, adv. bd. State Hist. Records, 1981—; adj. prof. U. Nev., Reno, 1981—. Co-author: Ventura County's Yesterdays today, 1980, Neon Nights, 1990. Mem. Am. Assn. State and Local History, Westerm Mus. Council, Soc. Calif. Archivists, Nev. Mus. Assn. Democrat. Methodist. Office: Nev Hist Soc 1650 N Virginia St Reno NV 89503-1799

BANERJEE, PRANAB KUMAR, computer systems analyst; b. Calcutta, India, Nov. 19, 1961; came to U.S., 1985; s. Kanty Pada and Anima (Anima) B. B. Tech., Indian Inst. Tech., Kharagpur, India, 1985; MS, Kansas State U., 1988. Computer rsch. programmer, analyst Crump Inst. Biological Imaging UCLA, 1989—. Contbr. articles to profl. jours. Home: 6209 Reseda Blvd # 208 Reseda CA 91335 Office: Crump Inst Biological Imaging UCLA Sch Medicine 10833 LeConte Ave B2-086 CHS Los Angeles CA 90024-1721

BANGARU, BABU RAJENDRA PRASAD, engineer; b. Palakol, India, Oct. 24, 1947; came to U.S., 1972; s. Raghavaiah and Sarojini Devi (Segu) B.; m. Jagadamba Narayanam, June 15, 1974; children: Sarojkamal, Vijay R., Sridevi. BS in Engring., Coll. Engring., Kakinada, India, 1968; MS in Engring., Coll. Engring., Trivandrum, India, 1971; MS, SUNY, Stony Brook, 1978, PhD, 1981. Lectr. Regional Engring. Coll., Calicut, India, 1971-72; research and tchng. asst. coll. engring. SUNY, Stony Brook, 1972-75; programmer NASA, N.Y.C. and Greenbelt, Md., 1975-78; sr. computer applications engr. EBASCO Services, Inc., N.Y.C., 1979-83; mem. tech. staff AT&T Bell Labs., Holmdel, N.J., 1983-87; sr. telecommunications engr. Boeing Computer Support Services, Huntsville, Ala., 1987-88; mem. tech. staff U.S. WEST Advanced Techs., Englewood, Colo., 1988—. Mem. IEEE, Assn. Computing Machinery, Toastmaster Internat. (Competent Toastmaster). Office: US West Advanced Techs 4001 Discovery Dr Boulder CO 80303-7816

BANGHAM, ROBERT ARTHUR, orthotist; b. San Antonio, Sept. 12, 1942; s. Robert Dave and Marguerite C. (Wyckoff) B.; m. Yvonne Janice Parminter, Sept. 23, 1961. Student, Northwestern U., 1965, 71, 76, NYU, 1969, Washtenaw Community Coll., Ann Arbor, Mich., 1971; misc. courses in field, various hosps, and med. orgns. Cert. orthotist; ordained to ministry Jehovah's Witness Ch., 1957. Orthotic resident J. R. Reets, Ann Arbor, Mich., 1960-65; orthotist Dreher-Jouett, Inc., Chgo., 1965-68; cert. orthotist U. Mich., 1968-75, Wright & Filipis, Inc., Alpena, Mich., 1975-78; mgr., orthotist Hittenbergers, Concord, Calif., 1978-81, 88-90; cert. orthotist Hittenbergers, Oakland, Calif., 1981-90; mgr., cert. orthotist Hittenbergers, Concord, Oakland, 1988-90; mktg. mgr. western region Nat. Orthotic Labs., Winter Haven, Fla., 1990; chief exec. officer Mobile Orthotic & Prosthetic Assocs., Antioch, Calif., 1990—; orthotics cons. Benchmark Med. Group, 1992—; cons. Health Careers Profl. Assn., Calif. State Dept. Edn., 1992—; mem.adv. com. ind. living svcs. program Los Medanos C.C.; presenter papers in field to profl. assns., hosps., govtl. bodies. Contbr. articles to profl. jours. Mem. Yosemite Park Assn., 1988; mem. adv. com. foster care edn. program Diablo Valley Community Coll., Concord, Calif., 1989—. Fellow Am. Back Soc. (internat. profl. rels. com., co-chair orthodontics divsn., vice chair orthotics com., AAOP liaison rep. to ABS), Am. Acad. Neurological and Orthopedic Surgeons (head dept. orthotics); mem. Am. Prosthetic Assn., Am. Acad. Orthotics and Prosthetists (nat. dir. 1988-91, pres. Calif. chpt. 1986-87, chpt. dir. 1989-91, sci. com. chmn., societies com., charter chmn. Spinal Orthotics Soc. 1991—, sec. lower extremity orthotics soc., bd. dirs. No. Calif. chpt., past pres. No. Calif. chpt., rep. Calif. coalition Allied Health Profls. No. Calif. chpt., co-chmn. sci. edn. com. No. Calif. chpt.), Am. Orthotics and Prosthetics Assn. (bd. dirs., chair NSF program), Internat. Soc. Orthotists and Prosthetists, Calif. Coalition Allied Health Professions (pres. 1989-90), Coun. of Growing Bus., Nat. Assn. for Self-Employed, Calif. State Foster Parents Assn. Contra Costa County, Assn. Children's Prosthetic-Orthotic Clinics, Yosemite Assn., Internat. Platform Assn. Home: PO Box 3016 Ste B Antioch CA 94531-3016 Office: PO Box 243 Antioch CA 94531-3016

BANGLE, RICHARD MORRIS, computer scientist; b. Chillicothe, Ohio, Apr. 23, 1941; s. Richard Sankey and Pauline (Saunders) B.; m. Sylvia Marie Manuel, Nov. 19, 1960; children: Richard Joseph, Charles Aaron, Thaddeus Wade. BS in Computer Sci., Wright State U., 1970. Design engr. Systems Rsch. Labs., Inc., Dayton, Ohio, 1965-72; project mgr. Electronic Arrays, Inc., Mountainview, Calif., 1972-76; test mgr. Monolithic Memories, Inc., Sunnyvale, Calif., 1976-79; project mgr. John Fluke Mfg. Co., Inc., Seattle, 1980-87; pres. Testar Corp., San Jose, 1987-91; dir. engring. ASA Systems, Inc., San Jose, 1991—; pres. Bangle TEC-Design, 1993—. With USNAF, 1959-63. Office: ASA Systems Inc 170 Nortech Pky San Jose CA 95134-2305

BANGS, CATE (CATHRYN MARGARET BANGS), motion picture art director, interior designer; b. Tacoma, Mar. 16, 1951; d. Henry Horan and Belva Virginia (Grandstaff) B.; m. Steve Bangs, Nov. 1, 1986. Student, Hammersmith Coll Art and Bldg., London, 1971; BA cum laude, Pitzer Coll., 1973; MFA, NYU, 1978. Owner Flying Pencil Design, Hollywood Hills, Calif., 1981—; art dir. Cobra, Warner Bros., 1985, Who Framed Roger Rabbit, 1986, A Year in the Life, Universal Studios, 1986, Beverly Hills Cop II, Paramount Studios, 1986-87, The Seventh Sign, 1987, Crime Story, 1987-88, Spies, Partners and Lovers, 1988, Far from Home, 1988, Hider in the House, 1988, Lock Up, Tri-Star, 1989, Die Harder, Fox, 1989-90, Air America, Carolco, 1990-91, RoboCop 3, (TV series) Mann and Machine, 1991-92, The Trapped Universal, 1992-93, The Birds II, Universal/Showtime, 1993-94. Prodn. designer Lucky Day, 1990. Bd. dirs. Hollywood Heights Assn., 1985-87, Cahuenga Pass Property Owners Assn.,1990; 1st v.p. Friends of the Highland-Camrose Bungalow Village, 1985—. Recipient Dramalogue Critics award, 1983. Mem. Soc. Motion Picture and TV Art Dirs., Set Designers and Model Makers (cert., exec. bd. 1980—, v.p. 1989—, pres. 1991—), United Scenic Artists. Democrat. Buddhist. Home: Angel Haven 3180 Oakshire Dr Hollywood CA 90068-1743

BANGS, JOHN WESLEY, III, law enforcement administrator; b. Phila., Dec. 26, 1941; s. John Wesley Jr. and Sarah Emily (Morcom) B.; m. Donna Louise McClanahan, June 1, 1963; children: Louis M., Terry M., John W. IV. AA summa cum laude, E. Los Angeles Coll., 1976. Calif. Commn. on Peace Officer Standards and Training: Basic, Intermediate, Advanced, Supervisory, Mgmt. Police officer Los Angeles Police Dept., 1964-70, sgt., 1970-74, lt., 1974-84; chief spl. officer I L.A. Dept. Airports Police, 1988—; lectr. U. So. Calif., 1978-79. Author: Narcotics Overview, 1983, Psychological Evaluation for Police Candidates, 1969. Cub master Cub Scouts Am., Ontario, Calif., 1968; scout master Boy Scouts Am., Ontario, 1971; explorer leader Explorer Scouts Am., Los Angeles, 1976; mem. Greater Los Angeles Scouting Council, 1976. Sgt. U.S. Army, 1959-62. Mem. Calif. Peace Officers Assn., Calif. Narcotic Officers, Los Angeles Police Protective League, Los Angeles Police Relief Assn., Lions Internat. Republican. Episcopalian. Office: Los Angeles Airport Police #1 World Way PO Box 92216 Los Angeles CA 90009-2216

BANGSUND, EDWARD LEE, aerospace company executive; b. Two Harbors, Minn., July 16, 1935; s. Ilo Henry and Hildur Margaret (Holter) B.; m. Caryl Ann Billingsley, Oct. 10, 1956; children: Julie Ann, Trina Lee, John Kirk, Edward Eric. BME, U. Wash., 1959. With Boeing Co., 1956-71; engr. Apollo program Boeing Co., Cape Kennedy, Fla., 1967-69, Houston, 1969-71; mgr. space vehicle design Space Systems div. Boeing Aerospace, Seattle, 1971-76, mgr. Inertial Upper Stage Futures, 1976-85, mgr. space transp., 1985-87, dir. strategic planning, 1987-90, dir. space mktg., 1990—. Contbr. articles to profl. publs.; patentee in field. Pres. Springbrook Parents Adv. Com., 1972-75; chmn. Citizens Budget Rev. Com., 1973-75, 76-78, Citizens Facility Planning Com., 1977-78, Citizens for Kent (Wash.) Schs. Levy, 1974, 76; bd. dirs. Kent Youth Ctr., 1980-83; pres. Kent Sch. Bd., 1978-84. Named to Apollo-Saturn Roll of Honor, NASA, 1969; recipient Golden Acorn award Wash. Congress PTA, 1977, Vol. of Yr. award Kent Sch. Dist., 1977, 78. Fellow AIAA (assoc., mem. space systems tech. com. 1985-87, dep. dir. region VI 1986-89, chmn. space transp. tech. com. 1987-90, pub. policy com. 1989—); mem. Internat. Acad. Astronautics, Internat. Astronautical Fedn. (chmn. space transp. exec. com. 1991—), Nat. Space Found., Aerospace Industries Assn. (mem. space com. 1987—, chmn. 1990—), Space Bus. Roundtable (pres. Seattle chpt., bd. dirs. 1988—), Boeing Mgmt. Assn. (vice chmn. 1990-91, chmn. 1993-94). Republican. Lutheran. Home: 9441 S 202nd St Kent WA 98031-1421 Office: Boeing Def and Space Group PO Box 3999 M/S 8C-22 Seattle WA 98124

BANKER, NANCY SIRMAY, healthcare executive, educator; b. Washington, Nov. 27, 1944; d. Maximillian Paul and Lillian (Steinkohl) Sirmay; m. Richard Banker, Sept. 10, 1969; 1 child, Sam. BA, Mills Coll., 1967; MA, San Francisco State U., 1970. Cert. tchr., Calif. 1970. Program mgr., edn. rsch. & devel. Far West Lab., San Francisco, 1972-80; regional mgr. Ctr. Resource Mgmt. Sopris West, San Francisco, 1980-82; v.p. Calif. Emergency Physicians Med. Group MedAm., Oakland, Calif., 1982-89; pres. Entremed, Oakland, 1989-93; adj. fac. Golden Gate U., Walnut Creek, Calif., 1989—, St. Mary's Coll., Moraga, Calif., 1990—, Calif. Coll. Podiatric Medicine, 1991—; sec., bd. dirs. Career Resources Devel. Ctr., San Francisco, 1989-93, vice chair, 1993—; fin. ptnr. Hermes Fund, Ltd., Oakland, 1989-93, presiding ptnr., 1993—; v.p. Levison Assocs., Inc., 1993—. Author: Experience-Based Career Education, 1976. Pres. Oakland/Piedmont JCC, 1980-82; bd. dirs. Jewish Fedn. of Greater East Bay, Oakland, 1980-86. Rsch. grantee Office Career Edn., Washington, 1978-79; fellow State of Calif., San Francisco, 1968-70, Inst. for Edn. Leadership, Washington, 1977-78; Mills Coll. scholar, 1963-67, Calif. State scholar, 1963-67. Mem. Health Care Execs. No. Calif., Women Health Care Execs., The Health Care Forum, Mills Coll. Alumnae Assn. (branch bd. dirs. 1990-92), R & R: The Physician Relations Group. Office: Levison Assocs 6039 Park Ave Richmond CA 94805

BANKETT, PAULA REGINA, law librarian; b. Travis AFB, Mar. 26, 1959; d. E.L. and Paulyne (P.) B. Student, Calif. U., Hayward; AB, Fisk U., Nashville, 1982; postgrad., Calif. State U. Libr. The Port of Oakland, Calif.; now sr. libr., archivist The State Bar of Calif., San Francisco. Mem. ARMA Internat., Nat. Assn. Govt. Archives and Records, Am. Assn. Law Librs., No. Calif. Assn. Law Librs., Calif. Supreme Ct. Hist. Soc. (bd. dirs. 1993—), Delta Sigma Theta. Democrat. Roman Catholic. Office: 555 Franklin St San Francisco CA 94102-4456

BANKHURST, ARTHUR DALE, medical educator, researcher; b. Cleve., July 21, 1937; s. John William and Daisy (Howard) B.; m. Lois Hull, Feb. 20, 1969; children: Anne, Claire, Benjamin, Noah. BS in Biochemistry, MIT, 1958; MD, Case Western Res. U., 1962. Diplomate Am. Bd. Medicine, Am. Bd. Rheumatology. Intern in medicine Univ. Hosp., Cleve., 1962-63, resident, fellow, 1965-69; rsch. fellow Walter & Eliza Hall Inst. Med. Rsch., Melbourne, Australia, 1969-71; sr. rsch. fellow rsch. unit U. Geneva WHO, 1971-73; asst. prof. Sch. of Medicine U. N.Mex., Albuquerque, 1973-77, assoc. prof. Sch. of Medicine, 1977-81, dir. dept. rheumatology Sch. of Medicine, 1979—, prof. medicine and microbiology Sch. of Medicine, 1981—; mem. fellowship com. Nat. Arthritis Found., Atlanta, 1977-81; chmn. ambulatory care rev. com. State of N.Mex., 1977-81. Assoc. editor Jour. of Immunology, 1984-87, Clin. Immunology & Immunopathology, 1988—; contbr. articles to profl. jours. Regional chmn. edn. coun. MIT, Albuquerque, 1988—. Decorated Knight, Republic of Liberia; NIH grantee, and numerous others. Fellow ACP, Am. Assn. Immunologists, Am. Coll. Rheumatology, Phi Lambda Epsilon; mem. Brit. Soc. Immunology, Western Soc. Clin. Investigation, Western Assn. Physicians. Office: U NMex Sch Medicine 7 S Albuquerque NM 87131

BANKS, CHERRY ANN MCGEE, educator; b. Benton Harbor, Mich., Oct. 11, 1945; d. Kelly and Geneva (Smith) McGee; m. James A. Banks, Feb. 15, 1969; children: Angela Marie, Patricia Ann. BS, Mich. State U., 1968; MA, Seattle U., 1977, EdD, 1991. Tchr. Benton Harbor Pub. Sch., 1968; staff assoc. Citizens Edn. Ctr. N.W., Seattle, 1984-85; edn. specialist Seattle Pub. Schs., Seattle, 1985-87; pres. Edn. Material and Svcs. Ctr., Edmonds, Wash., 1987—; asst. prof. edn. U. Wash., Bothell, 1992—; cons. Jackson (Miss.) Pub. Schs., 1988, Seattle Pub. Schs., 1988-90, Little Rock Pub. Schs., 1989, Scott Foresman Pub. Co., Glenview, Ill., 1992—; vis. asst. prof. Seattle U., 1991-92. Co-author: March Toward Freedom, 1978; co-editor Multicultural Education: Issues and Perspectives, 1989, rev. edit., 1993; contbr. chpts. to books. Mem. Jack and Jill Am., Seattle, 1978—, First AME Headstart Bd., Seattle, 1981-83; trustee Shoreline C.C., Seattle, 1983—; bd. dirs. King County Campfire, Seattle, 1985-88. Recipient Outstanding Commitment and Leadership of C.C. award Western Region Nat. Coun. on Black Am. Affairs, 1989. Mem. ASCD, Nat. Coun. for Social Studies Programs Com. (vice chair Carter G. Woodson Book award com. 1991-92, nominating com.), Am. Rsch. Assn., Phi Delta Kappa (founding mem. Seattle U. chpt.). Office: U Wash Edn Program 22011 26th Ave SE Bothell WA 98021

BANKS, ERNEST (ERNIE BANKS), business executive, former professional baseball player; b. Dallas, Jan. 31, 1931; s. Eddie B.; m. Eloyee Ector, Apr. 6, 1953. Grad. high sch.; student, Grad. Sch. Bus., Northwestern U. Player with Kansas City Monarchs (Negro Am. League), 1950-51, 53; shortstop, then 1st baseman Chgo. Cubs, 1953-71, mgr. group sales, to 1982; formerly co-owner, v.p. Bob Nelson-Ernie Banks Ford, Inc., Chgo.; with Associated Films Promotions, Los Angeles, 1982-84; with World Van Lines, Calif., 1984—. Author: (with Jim Enright) Mr. Cub. Past mem. bd. Chgo. Transit Authority; active Boy Scouts Am., YMCA. Served with AUS, 1951-53, Europe. Named most valuable player Nat. League, 1958, 59; recipient awards from Fans, 1969, awards from Press Club, 1969, awards from Jr. C. of C., 1971; inducted into Tex. Sports Hall Fame, 1971, Baseball Hall of Fame, 1977; mem. Nat. League All-Star Team, 1957-70; hold major league record for most career grand slam home runs. Office: New World Van Lines 14322 Commerce Dr Garden Grove CA 92643-4946

BANKS, PHILIP ALAN, environmental and agricultural consultant; b. Sentinel, Okla., Jan. 12, 1952; s. Jess and Melba Louise (Lankford) B. BS, Okla. State U., 1974, MS, 1976; PhD, Tex. A&M U., 1978. Instr. soil and crop sci. dept. Tex. A&M U., College Station, 1977-78; asst. prof. dept. agronomy U. Ga., Athens, 1979-84, assoc. prof., 1984-89, prof., 1989-90; pres. Marathon Agrl. and Environ. Cons., Inc., Las Cruces, N.Mex., 1990—; cons. Monsanto, St. Louis, 1989—, Sandoz, Des Plaines, Ill., 1992—, Ciba-Geigy, Greensboro, N.C., 1990—, Am. Cyanamid, Princeton, N.J., 1990—, Landec Labs. Inc., Menlo Park, Calif., 1990-93; vis. lectr. Ptnrs. of Ams., Pernambudo, Brazil, 1987. Contbr. to profl. publs. Vice-pres. Oconee County Little League, Watkinsville, Ga., 1985. Mem. Coun. Agrl. Sci. and Tech. (bd. dirs. 1990—), So. Weed Sci. Soc. (bd. dirs., v.p. 1992, pres. elect 1993, Outstanding Young Scientist award 1986), Weed Sci. Soc. Am. (Outstanding Young Scientist award 1988), Am. Soc. Agronomy, Sigma Xi. Office: Marathon Agrl/Environ Cons Inc 2649 Navajo Rd Las Cruces NM 88005-5227

BANKSON, DOUGLAS HENNECK, creative writing educator, playwright; b. Valley, Wash., May 13, 1920; s. Russell Arden and Ella Etna (Henneck) B.; m. Beverly Olga Carlson, June12, 1943; children: Jon Douglas, Daniel Duke, Barbro Sloan. B.A., U. Wash., 1943, M.A., 1949, Ph.D., 1954. Reporter, columnist Seattle Star, 1942-43, 46; account exec., copywriter Beatty Stevens Agy., Seattle, 1946-50; teaching fellow U. Washington, 1950-51; freelance advt. agt. Seattle, 1952-54; dir. research Frye Art Mus., Seattle, 1951-52; instr. English and humanities U. Idaho, 1955-57; asst. prof. English U. Mont., 1957-59, assoc. prof. drama, assoc. dir. theater, resident playwright, 1959-65; prof. playwriting U. B.C., Vancouver, 1965-85; prof. emeritus U. B.C., 1985—, head dept. creative writing, 1977-83; dir. Masquer Summer Theatre, Missoula, Mont., 1961-65. Author: (produced plays) Shellgame, 1960, Mr. Magoo, 1960, The Waterwitch, 1960, The Ball, 1961, Nature in the Raw is Seldom, 1962, Fallout, 1963, Shootup, 1963, Resthome, 1965, Lenore Nevermore, 1972, Signore Lizard, 1974, Whistle, 1977, The Schweinhuf Quartet, 1978, Ella, 1981, Felicity, 1982, Mr. Poe, 1985, (opera libretto) Poe, 1988,; co-author: (film) Nell, 1992; dir. numerous stage plays, 1959-75; sculptor, 1948—. Served as lt. (j.g.) USNR, 1943-46, ATO, ETO, PTO. Recipient Lifetime Achievement award Vancouver Profl. Theatre Alliance, 1983-84. Mem. Playwrights Union Can. Home: 3892 W 15th Ave, Vancouver, BC Canada V6R 2Z9

BANKSTON, MARY GAY, utility company executive; b. Lakeland, Fla., Nov. 27, 1952; d. Rex Lane and Frances (Williams) Gay; m. Clyde Perry Bankston, June 15, 1974. BA in Econs., Agnes Scott Coll., 1974. Asst. v.p. Citizens and So. Nat. Bank, Atlanta, 1974-79; v.p., area mgr. Lloyds Bank Calif., L.A., 1979-85; sr. v.p., dir. mktg. and planning First Interstate Bank of Calif., L.A., 1985-91; v.p. planning So. Calif. Gas Co., L.A., 1991—. Democrat. Office: So Calif Gas Co ML 29E1 555 W 5th St Los Angeles CA 90013-1011

BANNAN, JAN GUMPRECHT, freelance photographer and writer; b. West Salem, Ill., Oct. 2, 1931; d. Walter E. and Gladys A. (Smith) Giese; m. William H. Gumprecht, Sept. 14, 1952 (div. Oct. 1972); children: Linda S., Mark W., Diane M., Blake W.; m. Thomas Bannan, July 7, 1983 (div. May 1985). BS, U. Ill., 1953; PhD, U. Del., 1972. Organic chemist 3M Co., St. Paul, 1953-55; rsch. fellow, teaching asst. U. Del., Newark, 1968-72; rsch. fellow Harvard Med. Sch., Boston, 1972-74; coord. biochem. rsch. Redken Lab., Inc., Van Nuys, Calif., 1974-77, biochem. cons., 1977-78; rsch. biochemist UCLA, 1977-78, U. Wash., Seattle, 1989; editor, pub. ANCHOR, Port Orford, Oreg., 1983-84; freelance photographer, writer, real estate salesman, Port Orford, 1980-86; freelance photographer and writer, Waldport, Oreg., 1986—. Author, photographer: Sand Dunes, 1989; columnist, photographer Oreg. Coast mag., 1982-85; also numerous articles and photographs in popular mags. and newspapers; patentee hair cosmetic additive. Vol. Hatfield Marine Sci. Ctr., Newport, Oreg., 1990. Recipient 1st and 2d place photog. awards Multi-Image Show, Coos Bay, Oreg., 1983. Mem. Outdoor Writers Assn. Am., Iota Sigma Pi, Alpha Lambda Delta. Home and Office: PO Box 1209 Waldport OR 97394

BANNER, LARRY SHYRES, educator, athlete, consultant; b. L.A., June 4, 1936; s. Eldren Otho and Kathrine Gillette (LaVette) B.; m. Martha Estella Paulsen, Aug. 24, 1945; children: Eric Alexander, Bret Christian. BS, UCLA, Westwood, 1958; MA, Calif. State U., Long Beach, 1967; EdD, Ariz. State U., 1975. Tchr. various schs., Newhall, Calif., 1961-76, L.A., Calif., 1961-76, Newport Beach, Calif., 1961-76, Norwalk, Calif., 1961-76; asst. prof. Whittier (Calif.) Coll., 1976-81; founder, pres. Banner Learning Systems, Tustin, Calif., 1981-86; tchr. Turlock, Calif., 1986—; cons. Ariz. Migrant Edn. Lab., Phoenix, 1973-75; chief cons. Lopatin Prodns., Phila., 1980-81; sr. study performance counselor U. Calif., Irvine, 1984-85. Contbg. author: The Magic of Gymnastics, 1971; author various manuals; prodr. (video) The Art of Reading, 1981 (award N.Y. Critics, Best Ednl. Film award Am. Cine). Bd. dirs. Summer Clinic for Handicapped Athletes, L.A., 1973-75, Stanislaus County Task Force on Drug Abuse, Modesto, Calif., 1986-88; U.S.A. athlete Gymnastics Team, U.S. Olympic Team, 1960, capt., 1964. Gold medal Scandinavian champion (rings, parallel bars, saddle horse), 1962, European champion, 1963; inducted into U.S. Gymnastics Hall of Fame, 1993; named Stanislaus County Reading Tchr. of Yr., 1987. Mem. ASCD, Nat. Coun. Tchrs. English, Calif. Assn. Sch. Adminstrs., Internat. Reading Assn. (Orange County coun.).

BANNISTER, JOSEPH ANTHONY, computer engineer; b. Hanover, N.J., June 26, 1952; s. James Clarence and Maria Antonia (Visintini) B.; m. Pamela Marguerite Billings, Mar. 23, 1980. BA in Math. with high distinction, U. Va., 1977; MSEE, UCLA, 1980, MS in Computer Sci., 1984, PhD in Computer Sci., 1989. Engr. Xerox Corp., El Segundo, Calif., 1978-80; computer scientist Rsch. Triangle Inst., Research Triangle Park, N.C., 1980-82; network architect Sytek, Inc, Culver City, Calif., 1984-85; mgr. Unisys West Coast Rsch. Ctr., Santa Monica, 1985-88; computer scientist The Aerospace Corp., El Segundo, 1988—; v.p. PyBam, Inc., Hermosa Beach, Calif., 1990—. Contbr. articles to profl. jours. Mem. IEEE. Home: 754 26th St Manhattan Beach CA 90266

BANNISTER, LEE KENNETH, manufacturing executive, consultant; b. Pasadena, Calif., Apr. 28, 1939; s. Lee Robinson and Constance (Rosenquist) B.; m. Christina Louise Crawford, June 24, 1961; children: Lorinda Lee, Julieanne Marie, Cheryl Lynn. AA, Pasadena City Coll., 1960; cert. in photography, Pro Photos of Am., 1972. Sales mgr. Campbell Sales Co., Pasadena, 1961-72; pres. Larson Enterprises Inc., Fountain Valley, Calif., 1970-80, Debco Mfg. Co. Inc., Pasadena, 1989—; sales and mktg. mgr. Photic lab. of San Diego, 1991—; nat. sales mgr. Photic Color Lab., San Diego, 1991—. Mem. So. Calif. Studio Owners Assn. (pres. So. Calif. chpt. 1986-88), Profl. Photographers (bd. dirs. Orange County chpt. 1986-87, bd. dirs. L.A. chpt. 1985-87), Internat. Banana Club (pres., founder Altadena Internat. Hdqrs. 1972—), Rotary Internat., Kiwanis. Republican. Lutheran. Office: Internat Banana Club 2524 N El Molino Ave Altadena CA 91001-2318

BANOFF, HARRY, ophthalmology educator; b. Chgo., Mar. 31, 1915; s. Benjamin and Rose (Goldsmith) B.; m. Alice Young, Dec. 4, 1943 (dec. Aug. 1991); children: Barbara Ann, David Alan. BA, U. Ill., 1935; MA, NYU, 1939; MD, U. So. Calif., L.A., 1947. Diplomate Am. Bd. Ophthalmology. Resident ophthalmology L.A. County Gen. Hosp., L.A., 1948-50; pvt. practice ophthalmology Los Gatos, Calif., 1954-80; clin. instr. Sch. Medicine Stanford U., Palo Alto, Calif., 1954-84, clin. assoc. prof. ophthalmology Sch. Medicine, 1985—. Pres. Pacific Coast Unitarian Coun., Berkeley, Calif., 1959-62; v.p. Am. Unitarian Assn., Boston, 1961-62; treas. Los Gatos Homeowner's Assn., 1980-92. Capt. Med. Corps, U.S. Army, 1948-54. Fellow Am. Acad. Ophthalmology; mem. AMA, Santa Clara County Med. Soc., Calif. Med. Assn., Los Gatos Rotary Club (hon.), Phi Beta Kappa, Sigma Xi. Democrat. Home: 4042 Villa Vera Palo Alto CA 94306-3208

BANTA, ROBERT MASON, meteorologist; b. Neenah, Wis., Nov. 28, 1946; s. George Riddle III and Virginia (Jensen) B.; m. Connie Kelly, Aug. 21, 1976; children: Jared Robert, Lucas Adam. BS, Duke U., 1968; MS, Colo. State U., Ft. Collins, 1975, PhD, 1982. Grad. rsch. asst. dept. atmospheric sci. Colo. State U., Ft. Collins, 1972-82; rsch. physicist Air Force Geophysics Lab., Hanscom AFB, Mass., 1982-88; sr. rsch. meteorologist NOAA, Boulder, Colo., 1988—. Contbr. articles to sci. jours. Capt. USAF, 1968-72. mem. Am. Meteorol. Soc. (chair com. on mountain meteorology 1988-90), Sigma Xi. Home: 7390 Park Pl Boulder CO 80301 Office: NOAA ERL Wave Propagation Lab 325 Broadway Boulder CO 80303-3328

BANTHER, MICHAEL ROBERT, computer engineer; b. Kingfisher, Okla., Oct. 4, 1957; s. Robert L. and Lou Ann (Brown) B. BS, Wright State U., Dayton, Ohio, 1988. Programmer/analyst Cox Heart Inst., Dayton, 1980-81, Source Data Systems, Dayton, 1981-82; programmer/analyst Systems and Applied Scis. Corp., Dayton, 1982-84, systems analyst, 1984-86; computer engr. Hewlett-Packard Co., Cupertino, Calif., 1988-90, Boise, Idaho, 1990—; cons. in field. Joint venturer Cave Rsch. Found., Mammoth Cave, Ky., 1980-84; active Amnesty Internat., 1992—. Mem. ACM, IEEE, Tau Beta Omega, Order of the Engr. Office: Hewlett-Packard Co 11413 Chinden Blvd MS 470 Boise ID 83714-1023

BANUELOS, BETTY LOU, rehabilitation nurse; b. Vandergrift, Pa., Nov. 28, 1930; d. Archibald and Bella Irene (George) McKinney; m. Raul, Nov. 1, 1986; children: Patrice, Michael. Diploma, U. Pitts., 1951; cert., Loma Linda U., 1960. RN, Calif.; cert. chem. dependency nurse. Cons. occupational health svcs. Bd. Registered Nurses, 1984; charge nurse South Coast Med. Ctr., Laguna, Calif., 1985—; lectr., cons. in field. Recipient Scholarship U. Pitts. Mem. Dirs. of Nursing, Calif. Assn. Nurses in Substance Abuse. Home: 15 Oak Spring Ln Laguna Beach CA 92656-2980

BANUK, RONALD EDWARD, mechanical engineer; b. Brockton, Mass., Oct. 22, 1944; s. Joseph John and Leocadia Marilyn (Gusciora) B.; m. Patricia Audrey Ryan, July 4, 1969; children: Kim, Lance. BSME, Northeastern U., 1967; MSME, San Diego State U., 1971. Design and stress engr. in advanced systems Ryan Aero. Co., San Diego, 1967-76; sr. tech. specialist Northrop Corp., Pico Rivera, Calif., 1976-93, program mgr., 1987-89; structures tech. area mgr. Northrop Corp., Pico Rivera, 1991, prin. investigator in advanced structure and foam devel., 1986-93. Author: Design Considerations for Foam and Honeycomb Structure, 1993, On Saleem, 1993, Mary: Past, Present and Future. 1993. Mem. Soc. Adv. Material and Process Engrng. Republican. Home: 6441 Ringo Cir Huntington Beach CA 92647-3323 Office: Adv Structural Design & Devel T235/GK 8900 E Washington Blvd Pico Rivera CA 90660-3783

BAO, JOSEPH YUE-SE, orthopaedist, microsurgeon, educator; b. Shanghai, China, Feb. 20, 1937; s. George Zheng-En and Margaret Zhi-De (Wang) B.; m. Delia Way, Mar. 30, 1963; children: Alice, Angela. MD, Shanghai First Med. Coll., 1958. Intern affiliated hosps. Shanghai First. Med. Coll.; resident Shanghai Sixth People's Hosp., orthopaedist, 1958-78, orthopaedist-in-charge, 1978-79, vice chief orthopaedist, 1979-84; rsch. assoc. orthopaedic hosp. U. So. Calif., L.A., 1985-90, vis. clin. assoc. prof. dept. orthopaedics, 1986-89; coord. microvascular svcs. Orthopaedic Hosp., L.A., 1989-91; clin. assoc. prof. dept. orthopaedics U. So. Calif., L.A., 1989—; attending physician Los Angeles County and U. So. Calif. Med. Ctr., L.A., 1986, 90—; cons. Rancho Los Amigos Med. Ctr., Downey, Calif., 1986. Contbr. articles to profl. jours., chpts. to books. Mem. Internat. Microsurgical Soc., Am. Soc. for Reconstructive Microsurgery, Orthopaedic Rsch. Soc. Home: 17436 Terry Lyn Ln Cerritos CA 90701-4522 Office: LA County USC Med Ctr Dept Orthopaedics 2025 Zonal Ave COH 3900 Los Angeles CA 90033-4526

BAO, KATHERINE SUNG, pediatric cardiologist; b. Soochou, Kiangsu, China, Sept. 7, 1920; came to U.S., 1953; d. Yung H. Bao and Ming King; m. William S. Ting, May 2, 1948; children: Gordon K., Albert C. MD, Nat. Ctrl. Univ. Med. Coll., Nanking, China, 1944. Intern Mercer Hosp., Trenton, N.J., 1953; resident Children's Meml. Hosp. Northwestern U., Chgo., 1954-57; fellow in pediatric cardiology Children's Hosp. L.A., Calif., 1957-59; attending cardiologist Children's Hosp. L.A., Calif., 1960—; chief pediatric cardiology City of Hope Med. Ctr., Duarte, Calif., 1965-68; chief heart bd. L.A. Unified Sch. Dist. and PTA Specialty Health Clinics, L.A., 1968—; attending pediatrician, cardiologist Hollywood Presbyn. Med. Ctr., L.A., 1970—, UCLA, L.A., 1973—; pres.'s appointee Pres.'s Com. on Nat. Medal of Sci., 1983-85; adv. com. on health and med. care svcs. Dept. Health Svcs., Calif., 1988-90; pres. Chinese Physicians Soc. of So. Calif., 1969; speaker in field. Active Rep. Eagle, Rep. Presdl. Task Force, Rep. Presdl. Round Table. Named Rsch. Fellow Cardiologist, NIH, 1960-63; recipient Physician of Yr., Hon. Svc. award Calif. Congress of PTA, Inc., 1984. Fellow Am. Acad. Pediatrics; mem. AAAS, AMA, Calif. Med. Assn., L.A. County Med. Assn., Am. Heart Assn., Internat. Circle of L.A. World Affairs Coun., N.Y. Acad. Sci., Hollywood Acad. Medicine (coun.), Scripps Clinic La Jolla (coun.). Office: PO Box 10456 Beverly Hills CA 90213

BAPTISTA, LUIS FELIPE, ornithologist, educator, curator; b. Hong Kong, Aug. 9, 1941; s. Cezar Octoviano and Thelma Aurora (Rozario) B. BS in Biology, U. San Francisco, 1965, MS in Biology, 1968; PhD in Zoology, U. Calif., Berkeley, 1971. Curatorial asst. Mus. of Vertebrate Zoology U. Calif., Berkeley, 1967-70, asst. curator birds Mus. Vertebrate Zoology, 1971-72, acting asst. prof. zoology, 1971-72; NATO and Max Planck Gesellschaft postdoctoral fellow Max Planck Institut für Verhaltensphysiologie, Radolfzell, Fed. Republic of Germany, 1972-73; asst. prof. biology, curator Moore Lab. Zoology Occidental Coll., L.A., 1973-79, assoc. prof. biology, curator Moore Lab. of Zoology, 1979-80; chmn., assoc. curator ornithology and mammalogy Calif. Acad. Sci., San Francisco, 1980-86, chmn., curator ornithology and mammalogy, 1987—; chair Fulbright Scholar Exch. Program for Mex. and Caribbean, 1992—. Contbr. numerous articles to profl. jours. NATO fellow Fed. Republic of Germany, 1972, Max Planck Gesellschaft fellow, 1973; rsch. grantee NSF, 1978-80, 85-89, 89-93, NIH, 1982. Fellow Am. Ornithologists Union, Calif. Acad. Scis.; mem. Animal Behavior Soc., Deutsche Ornithology Gesellschaft (corr.), Wilson Ornithological Soc., Cooper Ornithological Soc., San Francisco Zool. Soc. (bd. dirs.), Coun. for Internat. Exch. Scholars (bd. dirs. 1992—). Office: Calif Acad Scis Dept Ornithology Golden Gate Park San Francisco CA 94118-4501

BAQAI, UDDIN AHMAD, geotechnical engineer; b. Punjab, Pakistan, Aug. 24, 1945; came to U.S., 1971; s. Mohammad Inamuddin and Jamila (Sultan) B.; m. Nanta Sonsee; children: Salma, Aisha. BSCE, U. Engring. and Tech., Lahore, Pakistan, 1968; MEE, Asian Inst. Tech., Bangkok, 1970; MBA, U. Calif., Riverside, 1984. Registered profl. engr., Calif. Chief envrion. engr. Polutec, Inc., El Monte, Calif., 1971-73; sr. engr. Calif. Regional Water Quality Control Bd., Riverside, 1973-87; mng. engr. Calif. Regional Water Quality Control Bd., Victorville, Calif., 1987—; adj. prof. San Bernardino (Calif.) Valley Coll., 1981—. Dir. High Desert Literacy Club, Victorville, 1991—. Fellow Southeast Asia Treaty Orgn., Bangkok, 1968, EPA, Washington, 1982-84. Mem. ASCE. Home: 14260 Meadow Grove Dr Victorville CA 92392 Office: Calif Regional Water Qual B 15428 Civic Dr Ste 100 Victorville CA 92392-2383

BARAB, MARVIN, financial consultant; b. Wilmington, Del., July 16, 1927; s. Jacob and Minnie (Press) B.; m. Gertrude Klein, June 13, 1951; children: Jordan, Neal, Caryn. BS with distinction, Ind. U., 1947, MBA, 1951. Dir. mktg. Edward Weiss & Co., Chgo., 1951-56; dir. bus. rsch. Parker Pen Co., Janesville, Wis., 1956-59; dir. mktg. rsch. packaging and graphics Mattel Co. Inc., Hawthorne, Calif., 1959-65; pres. Barcam Pub. Co., Rolling Hills Estates, Calif., 1959-70, Rajo Publs., Rolling Hills Estates, 1967-70, So. Calif. Coll. Med. & Dental Careers, Anaheim, 1970-81, Barbrook, Inc., Rolling Hills Estates, 1981—; cons. Marvin Barab & Assocs., Rolling Hills Estates, Calif., 1981—. Editor: Rand McNally Camping Guide, 1967-70; contbr. articles to various publs., 1982-87. Treas. Harbor Free Clinic, 1990-92; bd. dirs. So. Bay Contemporary Art Mus. Mem. Nat. Assn. Trade and Tech. Schs. (hon. life, sec. 1977-79, pres. 1979-81, bd. dirs.), Calif. Assn. Paramed. Schs. (pres. 1973-77). Office: Barbrook Inc 904 Silver Spur Rd Ste 110 Palos Verdes Peninsula CA 90274-3802

BARAD, JILL ELIKANN, toy company executive; b. N.Y.C., May 23, 1951; d. Lawrence Stanley and Corinne (Schuman) Elikann; m. Thomas Kenneth Barad, Jan., 28, 1979; children: Alexander David, Justin Harris. BA English and Psychology, Queens Coll., 1973. Asst. prod. mgr. mktg. Coty Cosmetics, N.Y.C., 1976-77, prod. mgr. mktg., 1977; account exec. Wells Rich Greene Advt. Agy., Los Angeles, 1978-79; product mgr. mktg. Mattel Toys, Inc., Los Angeles, 1981-82, dir. mktg., 1982-83, v.p. mktg., 1983-85, sr. v.p. mktg., 1985-86, sr. v.p. product devel., from 1986, exec. v.p. product design and devel., exec. v.p. mktg. and worldwide product devel., 1988-89; pres. girls and activity toys div. Mattel Toys, Inc. (name now Mattel Inc.), L.A., 1989-; pres. Mattel USA, 1990—, also bd. dirs.; bd. dirs. Arco Toys. Bd. dirs. Town Hall Big Sisters, L.A.; charter mem. Rainbow Guild/Amie Karen Cancer Fund, L.A., 1983, L.A. County Mus., 1985; trustee Queens Coll. Mem. Am. Film Inst. (charter). Office: Mattel Inc 333 Continental Blvd El Segundo CA 90245-5012

BARAM, TALLIE ZEEV, neurology and pediatrics practitioner, researcher, educator; b. Tel Aviv, Aug. 2, 1951; came to U.S., 1978; d. Zeev and Hassia (Amitai) B.; m. Craig Paul LaFrance, Sept. 10, 1992. PhD, Weiztmann Inst. Sci., Rehovoth, Israel, 1978; MD, U. Miami, 1980. Diplomate Am. Bd. Psychiatry and Neurology, Am. Bd. Pediatrics. Resident in pediatrics Baylor Coll. Medicine, Houston, 1980-82, resident in child neurology, 1982-85; asst. prof. neuro-oncology, neurology and pediatrics U. Tex. and M.D. Anderson Cancer Ctr., Houston, 1985-87; asst. prof. neurology and pediatrics U. So. Calif. and Childrens Hosp. L.A., 1987-92, assoc. prof., 1992—. Rsch. grantee NIH, 1987, 91, 92. Fellow Am. Acad. Pediatrics; mem. AAAS, Am. Acad. Neurology, Am. Epilepsy Soc. (sci. com. 1992—), Child Neurology Soc. (sci. com. 1991—), Soc. for Neurosci., Endocrine Soc., Internat. Soc. for Neuroendocrinology. Office: Childrens Hosp LA Neurology 82 4650 Sunset Blvd Los Angeles CA 90027

BARANEK, PAUL PETER, retired agriculturist; b. Wynn, Pa., Feb. 18, 1914; s. Joseph and Sophia (Koltas) B.; BS, U. Calif., Davis, 1936, cert. tchr., 1937, MEdn, 1946; m. Marie Agatha Herzog, Aug. 18, 1937 (dec. 1974); children: Jeanne Marie Baranek, Robert Paul, Barbara May Baranek Plaskett, John Peter. Dir. inst. vocat. agr. Escalon (Calif.) High Sch., 1937-42; mgr., operator Delta Dairy, Courtland, Calif., 1942-45; land use specialist Delta dist., Bur. Reclamation, Sacramento, Stockton, Calif., 1946-50; regional weed specialist Bur. Reclamation, Sacramento 1950-53; farm adviser Agrl. Extension Svc. U. Calif., Madera, 1953-74, agriculturist emeritus, 1974—; cons. rsch. com. Calif. Raisin Adv. Bd., 1958—, grading com. Fed. Raisin Adv. Bd., 1965—; ofcl. judge vine judging contest Future Farmers of Am., Fresno, Calif., 1955-84. Advancement chmn. Sequoia council Boy Scouts Am., 1953-62, counselor, 1953-62. Mem. Am. Soc. Enologists, Young Men's Inst., Alpha Gamma Rho, Alpha Zeta, Commonwealth Club. Democrat. Roman Catholic. Contbr. articles to profl. jours. Address: 511 Barsotti Ave Madera CA 93637

BARATH, PETER, cardiologist, educator; b. Zalaegerszeg, Zala, Hungary, Aug. 11, 1946; came to U.S., 1986; s. Ferenc Barath and Ilona Toth; m. Judith Barath, Dec. 7, 1981; 1 child, Barbara. D of Medicine, Semmelweis U., Hungary, 1970; PhD, Acad. Sci., Hungary, 1979. Cert. Internal Medicine Bd., Cardiology Bd., Hungary. Asst. prof. Semmelweis U., Biology Inst., Budapest, 1970-73; assoc. prof. Postgrad. Med. Sch., Budapest, 1976-86; rsch. scientist Cedars-Sinai Med. Ctr., L.A., 1986-89, dir. new device program, 1989—; asst. prof. med. sch. UCLA, 1989—; bd. dirs. Interventional Technologies, San Diego. Contbr. chpts. to books and articles to profl. jours. Inventor device for local drug delivery, cutting balloon for angioplasty. Grantee NIH, 1987, Am. Heart Assn., 1991. Office: Cedars-Sinai Med Ctr 8600 Beverly Blvd # 5316 Los Angeles CA 90048

BARBANO, FRANCES ELIZABETH, outdoor writer and photographer; b. Corry, Pa., May 28, 1944; d. Francis Joseph and Mercy Elizabeth (Quinn) Dufresne; m. Robert Lee Harkins, Nov. 11, 1967 (div. 1974); children: Matthew Scott, Sheila Marie; m. Duane Louis Barbano, Oct. 18, 1974; stepchildren: Terri Lyn, Jeffrey Scott. Student, Cecil Lawtor Real Estate Sch., Phoenix, 1973, Phoenix Union Area Vocat. Sch., 1977, N.Y. Inst. Photography. Cosmetologist, owner Carefree (Ariz.) Hair Designs, 1977-84; advt. dir. Ariz. Hunter mag., Cottonwood, 1985; supr. Boulders Club Restaurant, Carefree, 1985-87; editor U.S. Bass, Mesa, Ariz., 1988; freelance writer and photographer numerous nat. and regional publs., 1984—; owner, mgr. Profl. Images, Cave Creek Ariz., 19885—; feature writer Carefree Enterprise mag., Scottsdale, Ariz., 1987—; editor Lady Bass mag., West Monroe, La., 1989—; asst. mgr. Palo Verde Restaurant, Carefree, 1990. Mem. Outdoor Writers Assn. Am., Nat. Writers Club (profl.). Home and Office: PO Box 230 Cave Creek AZ 85331

BARBARICH, STANLEY JOSEPH, marketing executive; b. Indpls., June 13, 1945; m. Sonja J. West, Sept. 16, 1979. Student, Purdue U., 1968-71. Rsch. asst. Ind. U. Med. Ctr., Indpls., 1963-71; sales rep. G. D. Searle Labs., Skokie, Ill., 1971-73; tech. rep. United Med. Labs., Inc., Portland, Oreg., 1973-74; tech. sales rep. Howmedica, Inc., Rutherford, N.J., 1974-75; mktg. mgr. Synthes Ltd. (U.S.A.), Wayne, Pa., 1975-80; pres., founder MSI Mktg./Communications, Inc., Sausalito, Calif., 1980—; dir. mktg. Rainbow Group, Orinda, Calif., 1993—. Mem. editorial adv. bd. Computer Graphics World mag., 1983-84. CEO Harbor Equity Group, Inc., Sausalito, 1990—; chair pub. rels. com. Floating Homes Assn., Inc., Sausalito, 1990. Mem. Computer Soc. IEEE, Assn. for Computing Machinery (Spl. Interest Group on Computer Graphics), CEO Network. Office: MSI Mktg/Communications Inc 3 Main Dock Sausalito CA 94965-3152

BARBEE, ELIZABETH JOANN, mathematician, systems analyst; b. Oakboro, N.C., Dec. 27, 1940; d. Hubert R. and Ethel P. (Harris) B.; m. Donald L. Barnhardt, Aug. 5, 1962 (div. Aug. 1985); 1 child, Anthony Paul; m. Howard F. Derrickson, Sept. 21, 1985. BS, Appalachian State U., Boone, N.C., 1963; MS, Clemson U., 1967; PhD, U. Fla., 1975. Prof. math. U. Ark., Fayetteville, 1978-81; sci. programmer and analyst Computer Scis. Corp., Bay St. Louis, Miss., 1981-83; systems analyst Computer Scis. Corp., Ridgecrest, Calif., 1983-85; mathematician Naval Weapons Ctr., China Lake, Calif., 1985-89, Systems Analysis & Control, Ridgecrest, 1989—. Founder, treas. Loblolly Sch., Gainesville, Fla., 1974; mem. China Lake Mountain Rescue Group, 1985-89. Mem. Sigma Xi. Democrat. Office: Systems Analysis & Control 917 W Inyokern Rd Ridgecrest CA 93555-5602

BARBEE, JOE ED, lawyer; b. Pharr, Tex., Feb. 27, 1934; s. Archie Allen and Concha (Leal) B.; m. Yolanda Margaret Atonna, Feb. 17, 1962; children—Cynthia M., Adam A., Walter J. BSEE, U. Ariz., 1961; JD, Western New Eng. Coll., 1973. Bar: Mass. 1973, U.S. Patent Office 1973, U.S. Ct. Appeals (fed. cir.) 1982. Engr. Gen. Electric Co., Pittsfield, Mass., 1961-73; patent atty. Fort Wayne, Ind., 1973-75, Magnavox, Fort Wayne, 1975-76, Motorola, Inc., Phoenix, 1976—. Sgt. U.S. Army, 1953-56. Recipient Outstanding Performance award U.S. Civil Svc., 1960. Mem. ABA, Am. Patent Law Assn., Am. Intellectual Property Law Assn. Republican. Methodist. Home: 7611 N Mockingbird Ln Paradise Valley AZ 85253-3126 Office: Motorola Inc 8220 E Roosevelt B3 Scottsdale AZ 85257

BARBER, CLARENCE LYLE, economics educator; b. Wolseley, Sask., Can., May 5, 1917; s. Richard Edward and Lulu Pearl (Lyons) B.; m. Barbara Anne Patchet, May 10, 1947; children—Paul Edward, Richard Stephen, David Stuart, Alan Gordon. BA, U. Sask., 1939; MA, Clark U., 1941; postgrad., U. Minn., 1941-43, PhD, 1952; LLD (hon.), U. Guelph, 1988. With Stats. Can., 1945-48; mem. faculty McMaster U., 1948-49, U. Man., Winnipeg, Can., 1949-85; prof. econs. U. Man., 1956-85, disting. prof., 1982-85, emeritus, 1985—, head dept., 1963-72; vis. prof. Queen's U., 1954-55, McGill U., 1964-65; Commr. Royal Commn. on Farm Machinery, 1966-

71; spl. adviser on nat. income Phillipines Govt., 1959-60; commr. for study welfare policy in Man., 1972; mem. Nat. Commn. on Inflation, 1979, Royal Commn. Econ. Union and Devel. Prospects for Can., 1982-85. Author: Inventories and the Business Cycle, 1958, The Theory of Fiscal Policy as Applied to a Province, 1966, (with others) Inflation and Unemployment: The Canadian Experience, 1980, Controlling Inflation: Learning from Experience in Canada, Europe and Japan, 1982, False Promises: The Failure of Conservative Economics, 1993. Served with RCAF, 1943-45. Named Officer in Order of Can., 1987; Can. Coun. Profl. Leave fellow, 1970-71. Fellow Royal Soc. Can.; mem. Canadian Assn. U. Tchrs. (pres. 1958-59), Canadian Econ. Assn. (pres. 1971-72), Am. Econ. Assn., Royal Econ. Soc., Social Sci. Research Council Can. (mem. exec. 1972-73). Clubs: U. Vic. Faculty (Victoria). Home: 766 Richmond Ave, Victoria, BC Canada V8S 3Z1

BARBER, HERBERT BRADFORD, medical physicist; b. Worcester, Mass., Nov. 30, 1943; s. Clarence Edward and Virginia (Amidon) B.; m. Kathleen Ann Starks, Nov. 17, 1985. BS, Worcester Polytech. Inst., 1965; MS, U. Ariz., 1971, PhD, 1976. Research engr. Morgan Constrn. Co., Worcester, Mass., 1965; grad. teaching asst. U. Ariz., Tucson, 1968-69; physicist U. Calif. at Livermore, 1969; grad. research assoc. U. Ariz., 1971-75; assoc. faculty mem. Pima Community Coll., Tucson, 1975-79; research assoc. U. Ariz. Health Sci. Ctr., Tucson, 1976-80; rsch. assoc. sch. physics and astronomy U. Minn., Mpls., 1980-82; rsch. asst. prof. radiology U. Ariz. Health Sci. Ctr., 1982-90; rsch. assoc. prof. radiology and optical scis. Univ. Ariz. Health Sci. Ctr., 1990—. Patentee imaging probe and method. Dem. committeeperson, Tucson, 1986; vol. Victim Witness, Pima County, 1987—. Mem. AAAS, Am. Phys. Soc., Soc. Nuclear Medicine, Am. Astronomical Soc., Profl. Ski Instrs. Am., Sigma Xi. Democrat. Club: Tucson Soaring. Office: U Ariz Health Scis Ctr Div Nuclear Medicine Tucson AZ 85724

BARBER, KATHLEEN ANN STARKS, software developer, public relations consultant; b. Phoenix, Nov. 24, 1950; d. Ross Owen and Maribel Louise (Barnes) Starks; m. H. Bradford Barber, Nov. 17, 1984; 1 child. Student, Phoenix Coll., 1970; BS in Liberal Arts, U. Ariz., 1972, M.S., 1992. Retail worker Tucson, 1972-75, freelance pub. rels., 1972-78; from campaign mgr., legis. aide State Senator Morris Farr, Tucson, 1975-78; from consumer info. specialist to exec. dir. crime victim compensation program Office of Pima County Atty., Tucson, 1978-92; software developer Avalon Software, Inc., Tucson, 1992—. Sec. bd. dirs. Crime Prevention League, Tucson, 1987—; v.p. bd. dirs. Ariz.Consumers Coun., Phoenix, 1974—; exec. com. bd. dirs. Ariz. Coalition Victim Svcs., Phoenix, 1987-92; Dem. precinct committeeman, Pima County, 1974—, state committeeman, 1974—, state vice chair, Ariz.,1 978-80, Pima County, 1980-82; del. Dem. Nat. Conv., 1980. Mem. Nat. Assn. Crime Victim Compensation Bds., Nat. Orgn. Victim Assts., Nat. Women's Polit. Caucus (chpt. pres. state office 1974—), Assn. Computing Machinery, Soaring Assn. Am. Women's Soaring Pilots Assn., Ninety Nines, Ariz. Sonora Desert Mus. Home: 1545 W Calle Tiburon Tucson AZ 85704-1025 Office: Avalon Software Inc 3716 E Columbia St Tucson AZ 85714

BARBER, PUTNAM, association executive; b. Boston, Mar. 18, 1940; s. Cesar Lombardi and Elizabeth Duncan (Putnam) B.; m. Patricia Grace Holland, Sept. 1960 (div. Oct. 1970); children: Jonathan Holland, Lucy Grace; m. Valerie Ward Lynch, Oct. 17, 1973. BA, Haverford (Pa.) Coll., 1963; MA, U. Pa., 1966. Instr. sociology U. Mass., Amherst, 1966-71; asst. dir. policy and program devel. ACTION, Washington, 1971-74; dir. Office of Voluntary Action, Olympia, Wash., 1974-79, Wash. State OEO, Olympia, 1979-80; mgr. info. systems U.S. Community Svc. Adminstrn., Seattle, 1980-82; v.p. Coast Cons., Seattle, 1982-84; exec. sec. Wash. Centennial Commn., Olympia, 1984-90; pres. The Evergreen State Soc., Seattle, 1990—. Author: (with others) Fundamental Practices for Success of Non-Profit Boards, 1981. Bd. dirs. VOLUNTEER: The Nat. Ctr., Washington, 1978-88, Assn. Wash. Gens., Seattle, 1991. Mem. City Club (Seattle, bd. govs. 1984-90, 92—). Soc. of Friends. Office: The Evergreen State Soc 305 Harrison St # 201 Seattle WA 98109

BARBER, THEODORE FRANCIS, aircraft mechanic; b. Port Jervis, N.Y., Jan. 29, 1931; s. Theodore and Frances Mary (Gross) B.; m. Beverly Ann Horton, Mar. 15, 1961 (div. Dec. 1965); 1 child, Theodore Francis Barber, Jr. Student, Arlington Sch. Flight & Engring., Tillamook, Oreg., 1951-52. Lic. comml. eel fisherman, Pa. Laborer Erie RR, Port Jervis, N.Y., 1947-49; carpenter Erie R.R., Port Jervis, N.Y., 1950; mail handler Erie R.R., Jersey City, 1950-51; locomotive fireman Erie RR, Port Jervis, N.Y., 1951-59, locomotive engr., 1959-66; miniature golf course owner/operator Matamoras, Pa., 1963-65; lipstick moulder Kohmar Lab., Port Jervis, N.Y., 1965; interior installer Douglas Aircraft Co., Long Beach, Calif., 1966-67; field and svc. aircraft mechanic Douglas and McDonnell Douglas Aircraft Co., Long Beach, 1967—; structure assembly mechanic Northrop Corp., Anaheim, Calif., 1969-70; exptl. flight test mechanic McDonnell Douglas Aircraft Co., Long Beach, 1971, 77; systems mechanic Airco Cryogenics, Costa Mesa, Calif., 1977; co-owner C&B Sabot Fiberglass Boat Mfrs., 1976; mech. test technician Space Shuttle Arrowhead Products, Los Alamitos, Calif., 1976-77; B-1 bomber tool maker North Am. Rockwell, El Segundo, Calif., 1977; realtor Real Estate Store, Fullerton, Calif., 1976-79; metal fitter toolmaker F-18, Northrop, Hawthorn, Calif., 1978-79; toolmaker satellite and Space Shuttle div. North Am. Rockwell, Seal Beach, Calif., 1984; walnut orchard grower C & B Orchard, Fresno, Calif., 1982-83. With USAF, 1951-55. Mem. Am. Legion, Gold Wing Road Riders Assn., Moose. Democrat. Roman Catholic.

BARBEZAT, EUGENE LAVAR, systems engineer, retired air force officer; b. St. Johns, Ariz., Sept. 28, 1936; s. Fred Eugene Barbezat and Madge (Gibbons) Kindall; m. Karen Elizabeth Leichner, Dec. 22, 1970; children: Michele Lynn, Sean Michael. BS in Sociology, Brigham Young U., 1963; MA in Internat. Rels., U. So. Calif., 1980. Probation officer Ada County Probate Ct., Boise, Idaho, 1963-65; state probation officer 9th Dist. Ct., Ogden, Utah, 1965-66; commd. 2d lt. U.S. Air Force, 1966, advanced through grades to lt. col., 1981; chief Intelligence Report Ctr., 497th Reconaissance Tech. Group, Wiesbaden, Fed. Republic Germany, 1968-73; staff officer Def. Intelligence Agy., Washington, 1973-77, 84-85, Hdqrs. U.S. European Command, Vaihaingen, Fed. Republic Germany, 1977-80; chief Indications and Warning Ctr., Hdqrs. Mil. Airlift Command, Scott AFB, Ill., 1980-84; ret., 1985; staff integration and test software engr. Martin Marietta, Denver, 1985-92; documentation specialist Computer Data Systems Inc, Lakewood, Colo., 1992—; staff mem. com. on imagery and exploitation Dept. Def., 1975-77, mem. indications and warning study group, 1980-84. Commr., scoutmaster Boy Scouts Am., Denver, 1986-92; mem. Operation Santa Claus, Denver, 1987. Mem. Assn. Former Intelligence Officers, Air Force Assn., Denver Mus. Natural History, Denver Zool. Found., DAV (life), Order of Arrow. Republican. Mormon. Home: 8241 S Emerson Way Littleton CO 80122-4309 Office: Computer Data Systems Inc 165 S Union Blvd Lakewood CO 80228

BARBIERI, DAVID ARTHUR, company executive; b. Denver, Oct. 16, 1930; s. Alfred J. and Edna M. (Rowland) B.; m. Beatrice Beck, Apr. 23, 1953 (div.); children: Scott, Kurt; m. Karen Kai, Aug. 18, 1988; 1 child, Christopher. Student, U. Mo., 1948, Keio U., Tokyo, 1950, Coll. of San Mateo, 1952. Sales mgr. Lever Bros Co., N.Y.C., 1959-64; v.p. Sarvis Web Co., Tenafly, N.J., 1964-72, Security Market Group, Honolulu, 1972-75; pres. DABAR Co., Inc., Honolulu, 1975—; cons. Dryers of Hawaii, Honolulu, 1976-79, Contact Distbn., Honolulu, 1978-83. Author: Working with Brokers, 1962. Pres. United Cerebral Palsy Hawaii, 1985, bd. dirs. Staff sgt. USAF, 1948-51, Korea. Mem. Am. Logistic Assn. (v.p., bd. dirs. 1977), Sales and Mktg. Execs. (membership chair 1976), Assn. Apt. Owners (pres., bd. dirs. 1984), Oahu Country Club (2d v.p., bd. dirs. 1992). Republican. Roman Catholic. Office: Dabar Co Inc PO Box 10176 Honolulu HI 96816

BARBIERI, RONALD FRANCIS, wholesale firearms distributing company executive; b. Chgo., July 4, 1947; s. Victor O. and Alice M. (Zylowski) B.; m. Sandra P. Carlson, July 14, 1970; children: Raymond, Susan, Rhonda, Judy. BS, Ind. U. Lake County, 1970, MS, 1072. Pres., sr. exec. Pima Arms Co., Lake Havasu City, Ariz., 1974—. Staff sgt. U.S. Army, 1965-68, Vietnam. Mem. NRA, VFW, NADA, Am. Legion, Nat. Hot Rod Assn., Fraternal Order Police, Elks. Home: 3760 Sweetgrass Dr Lake Havasu City AZ 86403 Office: Pima Arms Co 2105 McCulloch Blvd Ste 3 Lake Havasu City AZ 86403

BARBOUR, ALTON BRADFORD, human communication studies educator; b. San Diego, Oct. 13, 1933; s. Ancel Baxter and Mary Jane (Fay) B.; m. Betty Sue Burch, Aug. 19, 1961 (div. 1991); children: Elizabeth, Christopher, Damon, Meagan. BA, U. No. Colo., 1956; MA, U. Denver, 1961, PhD, 1968; postdoctoral, Moreno Inst., 1976. Diplomate Am. Bd. Psychotherapy. Lectr. Colo. Sch. Mines, Golden, Colo., 1964-65; instr. U. Denver, Denver, 1965-68, asst. prof. Human Communication Studies, 1968-71, assoc. prof. Human Communication Studies, 1971-77, prof. Human Communication Studies, 1977—, chair dept. Human Communication Studies, 1980—; vis. lectr. Swiss Inst. for Group Psychotherapy, Switzerland, 1992. Co-author (books) Interpersonal Communication: Teaching Resources, 1972, Louder Than Words: Nonverbal Communication, 1974, Assessing Functional Communication, 1978; contbr. articles to profl. jours. With USN, 1956-58. Fellow Am. Soc. for Group Psychotherapy and Psychodrama, Am. Bd. of Med. Psychotherapists, Internat. Acad. of Behavioral Medicine, Counselling and Psychotherapy; mem. Am. Bd. Examiners in Group Psychotherapy (sec. 1983-93). Home: 1195 S Vine St Denver CO 80210 Office: Human Communication Studies U Denver Denver CO 80208

BARBUT, EROL, mathematics educator; b. Istanbul, Turkey, July 30, 1940; came to U.S. 1959; s. Mark and Margit (Herrman) B.; m. Ann Wilby, Apr. 23, 1963 (div. Aug. 1980); children: Eric, Sylvia; m. Alice Pope, Aug. 8, 1981; 1 child, Sarah. BA, U. Calif., Berkeley, 1963, MA, 1965; PhD, U. Calif., Riverside, 1967. From asst. prof. to assoc. prof. U. Idaho, Moscow, 1967-87, prof., 1988—. Contbr. articles to profl. jours. Mem. Math. Assn. Am., Am. Math. Soc. Office: U Idaho Moscow ID 83843

BARCA, GEORGE GINO, winery executive, financial investor; b. Sacramento, Jan. 28, 1937; s. Joseph and Annie (Muschetto) B.; m. Maria Sclafani, Nov. 19, 1960; children—Anna, Joseph, Gina and Nina (twins). A.A., Grant Jr. Coll.; student LaSalle U., 1963. With AeroJet Gen. Corp., Sacramento, 1958-65, United Vintners, Inc., San Francisco, 1960-73; pres., gen. mgr. Barcamerica U.S.A., Sacramento, 1963—; pres., gen. mgr. Barca Wine Cellars, Calif. Wine Cellars, U.S.A., Calif. Grape Growers, U.S.A., Calif. Vintage Wines, U.S.A., Am. Vintners, U.S.A.; cons. in field. Named Best Producer of Sales, United Vintners, Inc. Mem. Calif. Farm Bur., Met. C. of C., Better Bus. Bur., Roman Catholic. Club: KC. Developer wine trademarks.

BARCA, KATHLEEN, marketing executive; b. Burbank, Calif., July 26, 1946; d. Frank Allan and Blanch Irene (Griffith) Barnes; m. Gerald Albino Barca, Dec. 8, 1967; children: Patrick Gerald, Stacia Kathleen. Student, Pierce Coll., 1964; B in Bus., Hancock Coll., 1984. Teller Security Pacific Bank, Pasadena, Calif., 1968-69, Bank Am., Santa Maria, Calif., 1972-74; operator Gen. Telephone Co., Santa Maria, Calif., 1974-83, supr. operator, 1983-84; account exec. Sta. KRQK/KLLB Radio, Lompoc, Calif., 1984-85; owner Advt. Unltd., Orcutt, Calif., 1986-88; regional mgr. A.L. Williams Mktg. Co., Los Alamos, Calif., 1988-89; supr. Matol Botanical Internat., 1989-91; account exec. Santa Maria Times, 1989—. Author: numerous local TV and radio commercials, print advt. Activist Citizens Against Dumps in Residential Environments, Polit. Action Com., Orcutt and Santa Maria; chmn. Community Action Com., Santa Maria, Workshop EPA, Calif. Div., Dept. Health Svcs. State of Calif.; vice coord. Toughlove, Santa Maria, 1988-89; parent coord., mem. steering com. ASAP and Friends, 1988-89. Mem. NAFE, Womens Network-Santa Maria, Cen. Coast Ad (recipient numerous awards), Santa Maria C. of C. (ambassador representing Santa Maria Times 1990—). Democrat. Home: 509 Shaw St Los Alamos CA 93440-9999 Office: Santa Maria Times 3200 Skyway Dr Santa Maria CA 93455

BARCLAY, JOHN ALLEN, lawyer; b. L.A., Feb. 14, 1951; s. George H. and Shirley Iris (Handler) B. AA, L.A. Valley Coll., 1970; BA, U. Southern Calif., 1972, JD, 1975. Bar: Calif. 1975, U.S. Dist. Ct. (cen., ea., and no. dists.) Calif. 1976, U.S. Ct. Appeals (9th cir.) 1976, U.S. Tax Ct. 1976. Assoc. Karno & Fisher, Encino, Calif., 1975-78; prin. Barclay & Brestoff, Encino, 1978-80, Barclay & Moskatel, Beverly Hills, Calif., 1980-82, Barclay Law Corp., Newport Beach, Calif., 1982—; instr. U. Calif.-Irvine, 1985-87, UCLA, 1982-85, L.A. Valley Coll., Van Nuys, 1980-82. Author: Exchanging in the '80's, 1986, Accumulating Wealth, 1987, Insurance for Environmental Claims Against Bankruptcy Estates, 1992, (with others) Deducting Your Down Payment, 1984; contbr. articles to profl. jours. Active Dem. Found. Orange County (Calif.), 1986—. Mem. ABA, Orange County Bar Assn., Los Angeles County Bar Assn., Legion Lex (bd. dirs. Orange County chpt. 1987—, pres. 1992), Newport Harbor C. of C., Masons (master Hollywood chpt. 1982). Jewish. Office: Barclay Law Corp # 2900 5000 Birch St Newport Beach CA 92660

BARCUS, BENJAMIN FRANKLIN, lawyer; b. Tacoma, June 24, 1960; s. George Eldon Barcus and Gwendolyn (Evans) Johnson. BBA, U. Wash., 1982; JD, U. Puget Sound, 1985. Bar: Wash. 1986, U.S. Dist. Ct. (we. dist.) Wash. 1986, U.S. Ct. Appeals (9th cir.) 1986, U.S. Supreme Ct. 1991. Customer svc. rep. Tacoma News Tribune, 1979-80; claims rep., investigator Office Atty. Gen. State of Wash., Seattle, 1980-81; ind. svc. contractor Am. Express Co. Inc., Seattle, 1981-85; assoc. Talbot, Orlandini, Waldron & Hemmen, Tacoma, 1986-88; pvt. practice law Tacoma, 1989—. Precinct committeeman Wash. Dem. Com., Tacoma, 1982-88. Mem. ABA, Assn. Trial Lawyers Am., Wash. State Bar Assn., Wash. State Trial Lawyers Assn., Wash. Assn. Criminal Def. Lawyers, Tacoma-Pierce County Bar Assn., Mopars Unltd. (treas. Tacoma chpt. 1982-88), Ferrari Owner's Club, Ferrari Club Am. Mercedes Benz Club Am., Fircrest Golf Club. Congregational. Home: 2223 E Day Island Blvd W Tacoma WA 98466-1816 Office: 4041 N Ruston Way Ste 1B Tacoma WA 98402-5392

BARDACH, SHELDON GILBERT, lawyer; b. Holyoke, Mass., Sept. 4, 1937; s. Arthur Everett and Ruth (Goodstein) B.; m. Martha Robson, June 7, 1970; 1 child, Noah Arthur. AB, Bklyn. Coll., 1958; JD, UCLA, 1961. Bar: Calif. 1962. Pvt. practice Beverly Hills, Calif., 1962-67, Century City, Calif., 1967-85; sr. mem. Law Offices Sheldon G. Bardach, L.A., 1970—; bd. dirs. Mambo Films, Inc.; arbitrator L.A. Superior Ct., 1979—; mem. nat. panel arbitrators Am. Arbitration Assn. Bd. editors Law in Transition Quar., 1967; contbr. articles to profl. jours. Bd. govs. Studio Watts Workshop, 1963-71; founder, bd. dirs. UCLA Sch. Law, 1968. Recipient Lubin award Sch. Law UCLA, 1961, Bancroft-Whitney award UCLA Sch. Law, , 1961. Mem. ABA, Calif. Bar Assn., Beverly Hills Bar Assn. (bd. govs. barristers 1964-69), Am. Arbitration Assn. (nat. and internat. panels arbitrators), Century City Bar Assn., UCLA Law Sch. Alumni Assn. (bd. dirs. 1991), Los Angeles County Bar Assn., Assn. Trial Lawyers Am., Comml. Law League Am., Vikings of Scandia, Zeta Beta Tau, Phi Alpha Delta. Democrat. Jewish. Office: 12100 Wilshire Blvd Los Angeles CA 90025-7120

BARDON, DIANE MARIE, financial counselor, musician; b. Miles City, Mont., Sept. 24, 1949; d. Warren Franklin and Edith Roberta (Cridland) Brewer; m. Bruce Owen Bardon, June 3, 1967 (div. Apr. 1979); 1 child, Tamara Marie. BS in Rehab. Counseling with honors, Ea. Mont. Coll., 1984. Cert. fin. planner, Calif.; lic. ins. agt., Calif. Profl. musician, leader, mgr. Generation, Miles City, 1976-85, The Corvettes, San Diego, 1985—; rehab. counselor Mont. Dept. Social Svcs., Miles City, 1984-85, Community Svc. Ctr. for Disabled, San Diego, 1986-89; fin. counselor Hartman Fin. Group (name now Primerica Fin. Svcs.), San Diego, 1990—; mgr. br. office Excel Telecommunication, Inc., San Diego, 1990—; music therapist Custer County Convalescent Home, Miles City, 1984-85, Lemon Grove (Calif.) Convalescent Home, 1987. Author: (plays) Hatfields and McCoys, 1983, The Celebration, 1984, Rock Around the Clock, 1985. Vol. musician S.T.A.R., assn. for diabled, San Diego, 1986-89, spl. edn. dept. Grossmont Union High Sch., La Mesa, Calif., 1986-89. Recipient 3d place award Wrangler Country Showdown, 1983, 2d place, 1984. Mem. NAFE. Home: PO Box 3861 La Mesa CA 91944-3861

BARDWICK, DAVID ALAN, business owner; b. Elmhurst, Ill., Sept. 8, 1950; s. Howard Allen and Margaret Helene (Vandenberg) B.; m. Amita Grover, Mar. 9, 1984. BA, Ripon Coll., 1972. Owner Creative Carpentry & Woodworking, Solana Beach, Calif., 1979-89, ptnr., 1989—; pres. Cut & Dried Hardwood, Solana Beach, 1991—. Vol. Hunger Project, San Francisco, 1982-88, program coord., 1983-84; vol. Landmark Edn. Corp., San Francisco, 1991—; bd. dirs. Montessori Pub. Schs. Inc., San Francisco, 1990. Mem. Nature Conservancy, Sierra Club, Wilderness Soc. Home: 837 Passiflora Ave Leucadia CA 92024 Office: Cut & Dried Hardwood 241-C S Cedros Ave Solana Beach CA 92075

BARE, B. BRUCE, forest management and operations research educator; b. South Bend, Ind., Apr. 24, 1942; s. Clarence Evan and Barbara Louise (Bickel) B.; m. Ellenlee Throndsen, Mar. 26, 1971 (div. 1979); children: Daniel E., Jonathan T. BS in Forestry, Purdue U., 1964; MS, U. Minn., 1965; PhD, Purdue U., 1969. Instr. Purdue U., Lafayette, Ind., 1968-69; prof. U. Wash., Seattle, 1969—, chair Quantitative Ecology and Resource Mgmt. grad. program, 1990-92; cons. Sealaska Corp., Juneau, Alaska, 1988-89, 91-92. Contbr. articles to profl. publs. NDEA fellow, 1966-68. Office: U Wash Coll Forest Resources AR-10 Seattle WA 98195

BARELA, BERTHA CICCI, retired teacher, artist; b. McKeesport, Pa., June 13, 1913; d. James and Julia (Kolesar) Faix; m. John Slebodnik, June 23, 1934 (dec. Aug. 1967); children: Dolores S. Garvis, James, John, Judith Pavsek, Jane Minda, William, Cyrilla Lombardi, Rosemary Lewis, Martha Williams; m. Amerigo Cicci, May 25, 1974 (dec. Jan. 1975); m. Abran Barela, Dec. 8, 1984. BA, Seton Hill Coll., 1970. Elem. tchr. Blessed Sacrament Sch., Greensburg, Pa., 1967-74; ind. artist, clown Phoenix, 1985—; guest art tchr. various schs., 1980—. Formerly news and mag. writer; numerous commissioned art works. Dep. registrar Maricopa County, Phoenix, 1983-86, election bd. worker, 1980—; Dem. committeewoman, election worker, Pa., 1960-73, Phoenix, 1980—. Mem. Phoenix Art Guild, Women's Club St. Louis the King, Merrymakers Club, Washington Adult Ctr. Home: 10401 N Cavecreek Rd Apt 187 Phoenix AZ 85020

BARELA, ESMERLINDO JARAMILLO, infosystems specialist; b. Belen, N.Mex., Nov. 11, 1948; parents: Abelicio Baca and Beneranda (Jaramillo) B. AS in Electronics, Southeastern Signal Sch., Ft. Gordon, Ga., 1970. Asst. engr. GTE Lenkurt, Albuquerque, 1972-73, supr. quality control, 1973-75; successively computer technician, sr. computer technician, software specialist Pub. Service Co. N.Mex., Farmington, 1975-82, computer systems and process control data systems specialist III, 1982-92, sr. computer systems specialist, 1992—; tech. cons. Pub. Service Co. N.Mex., 1982-84. Mem. Sportmen Concerned N.Mex., Albuquerque, 1974. Served with U.S. Army, 1968-72, Vietnam. Mem. Nat. Rifle Assn. (life), Vietnam Vets. N.Mex., San Juan Fly Fishing Fedn. (pres. 1991—), Am. Legion, VFW (life), Ducks Unltd. (sponsor, bronze 92), N. Am. Hunting Club (life). Democrat. Roman Catholic. Home: 5705 Plaza Dr Farmington NM 87402-8213

BARENIS, PAT PEASTER, wholesale distribution company executive; b. Greenville, Miss., Sept. 7, 1951; d. Thomas Benjamin and Min (Young) Peaster; m. Uldis Atis Barenis, Nov. 13, 1975; children: Karl Alexander, Nicholas Benjamin. Mem. sales staff Nationwide Programming Co., Memphis, 1972-73; mktg. mgr. Nationwide Programming Co., Louisville, 1973-74; piano tchr. Deer Creek Acad., Arcola, Miss., 1977-80; pres., owner, chief exec. officer Barenis & Assocs., Vancouver, Wash., 1985—; cons., Security Products Group, Vancouver, 1987—. Bd. dirs. West Coast Life Safety and Communications, Inc., 1991-93; tutor coord. hosts program Felida Elem. Sch., Vancouver, 1985-91; mem. bd. exec. PTA, 1987-91. Mem. Salmon Creek Soccer Club (exec. bd. 1990-91), Lakeshore Athletic Club. Republican. Office: Barenis & Assocs 11703 NW 18th Ave Vancouver WA 98685-3725

BARFORD, LEE ALTON, computer scientist; b. Cheltenham, Pa., Oct. 14, 1961; s. Robert Alton and Frances Huber (Munz) B. AB summa cum laude, Temple U., 1982; MS, Cornell U., 1985, PhD, 1987. Cert. flight instr., FAA. Programmer TNR, Inc., Willow Grove, Pa., 1979-80; dir. software devel. Positioning Devices, Inc., Willow Grove, 1980-83; tech. staff mem. Hewlett-Packard Labs., Palo Alto, Calif., 1987—. Contbr. articles to profl. jours. Search & rescue pilot Civil Air Patrol, Palo Alto, 1987—, chief check pilot, 1992—; active Accident Prevention Coun., FAA. Mem. IEEE, Soc. Indsl. Applied Math., Palo Alto Flying Club (instr.), Phi Beta Kappa. Office: Hewlett-Packard Labs 3500 Deer Creek Rd Palo Alto CA 94304-1392

BARGABOS, SHEREE LYNN, manufacturing executive; b. Canastota, N.Y., Aug. 3, 1955; d. George Edward and Betty Jane (Holdridge) B. BS in Chemistry, McGill U., 1977; MBA, Babson Coll., 1986. Process engr. Owens-Corning Fiberglas, Ashton, R.I., 1977-79; sales rep. Owens-Corning Fiberglas, Braintree, Mass., 1979-83; market and product mgr. Owens-Corning Fiberglas, Toledo, 1983-88; dist. sales mgr. Owens-Corning Fiberglas, Santa Ana, Calif., 1988—; bd. dirs. SPI.

BARGE, JEFFREY THOMAS, publisher executive; b. Cleve., Dec. 13, 1957; s. Raymond H. and Nancy A. (Kolthoff) B. BA, Carleton Coll., 1979. Copy editor Twin Cities Reader, Mpls., 1981-84; editor Minn. Real Estate Jour., Mpls., 1984-85; pub. Minn. Lawyer, Mpls., 1985—, Ohio Law, Cleve., 1987—, Wash. Law, Seattle, 1990—. Mem. Calhoun Beach Club, Seattle Club.

BARGER, JAMES DANIEL, physician; b. Bismarck, N.C., May 17, 1917; s. Michael Thomas and Mayte (Donohue) B.; m. Susie Belle Helm, 1945 (dec. 1951); m. Josephine Steiner, 1952 (dec. 1971); m. Jane Ray Regan, Apr. 21, 1980 (dec. Feb. 1991); children: James Daniel, Mary Susan, Michael Thomas, Mary Elizabeth. Student, St. Mary's Coll., Winona, Minn., 1934-35; A.B., U. N.D., 1939, B.S., 1939; M.D., U. Pa., 1941; M.S. in Pathology, U. Minn., 1949. Diplomate Am. Bd. Pathology; registered quality engr., Calif. Intern. Milw. County Hosp., Wauwatosa, Wis., 1941-42; fellow in pathology Mayo Found., Rochester, Minn., 1941-49; pathologist Pima County Hosp., Tucson, 1949-50, Maricopa County Hosp., Phoenix, 1950-51; chmn. dept. pathology Good Samaritan Hosp., 1951-63; assoc. pathologist Sunrise Hosp., Las Vegas, Nev., 1964-69, chief pathology dept., 1969-81, sr. pathologist, 1981—; former med. dir. S.W. Blood Bank, Blood Services, Ariz., Blood Services Nev.; treas. Commn. for Lab. Assessment, 1988; emeritus clin. prof. pathology U. Nev. Sch. Medicine, 1988. Served to maj. AUS, 1942-46. Recipient Sioux award U. N.D. Alumni Assn., 1975; recipient disting. physician award NSMA, 1983; ASCP-CAP Disting. Service award, 1985. Mem. AAAS, AMA, Am. Assn. Pathologists, Am. Assn. Clin. Chemists, Am. Assn. History Medicine, Coll. Am. Pathologists (gov. 1966-72, sec.-treas. 1971-79, v.p. 1979-81, pres. 1980-81, historian 1988—, Pathologist of Yr. 1977), Nev. Soc. Pathologists (AMA del. 1990), Am. Assn. Blood Banks, Am. Soc. Quality Control (sr. mem.), Am. Mgmt. Assn., Soc. Advancement Mgmt., Am. Soc. Clin. Pathologists, Am. Cancer Soc. (nat. dir. 1974-80), Nat. Acad. Practice Medicine (dist. practitioner 1984—, del. AMA Ho. Dels. 1989—),others. Lodge: Knights of St. Lazarus (comdr. 1983). Home: 1307 Canosa Ave Las Vegas NV 89104-3132 Office: # 402 3196 S Maryland Pky Las Vegas NV 89109-2306

BARGER, STEPHEN RICHARD, diversified construction company executive; b. Palo Alto, Calif., Feb. 26, 1950; s. Richard Hugh and Doris Jean (Murphy) B.; m. Mary Constance Steinfeld, July 20, 1974; children: Sarah Murphy, Benjamin David. BA, Williams Coll., 1972; MBA, Harvard U., Boston, 1974. Assoc. cons. Cresap, McCormick & Paget, N.Y.C., 1974-76; sr. assoc. cons. Cresap, McCormick & Paget, San Francisco, 1976-77; brand mgr. Olympia Brewing Co., Olympia, Wash., 1977-83; nat. mktg. mgr. Nursery Products div. Weyerhaeuser, Tacoma, 1983-86; v.p., gen. mgr. Weyerhaeuser Specialty Plants, Tacoma, 1986-91; pres., chief exec. officer Container Integrity Corp., Tacoma, 1991-92; gen. mgr. N.W. Cascade, Inc., Puyallup, Wash., 1992—. Treas. Great Schs. Tacoma, 1987—; advisor Outward Bound, Portland, Oreg., 1988—; activities council Tacoma Art Mus., 1988—; chmn. Olympia Recycling Com., 1984-85. Mem. Assn. Landscape Contractors Am., Am. Assn. Nurserymen, Williams Coll. Alumni Assn. Wash. (pres. 1988—), City Club Tacoma, Tacoma Lawn Tennis Club. Episcopalian. Home: 2704 N Garfield Rd Tacoma WA 98403-2920

BARGHINI, SANDRA JEAN, curator; b. San Francisco, Dec. 3, 1951; d. Emo and Alice Barghini. BA, William Smith, 1974; MA, U. Ariz., 1976. Cons. museum Mission San Luis Obispo, San Luis Obispo, Calif., 1977-78; curator collections Chesapeake Bay Maritime Museum, St. Michaels, Md., 1979-84; curator Hearst Castle, San Simeon, Calif., 1984—. Editorial cons. (book) America's Hidden Corners, 1983; project dir. (exhibits) History

News, 1984, William R. Hearst, 1988. Fellow NEH, 1989. Mem. Am. Assn. Museums (panelist 1993 meeting), Archaeological Inst. Am. Office: Hearst San Simeon State Hist Monument 750 Hearst Castle Rd San Simeon CA 93452-9741

BARGREEN, MELINDA LUETH, music critic; b. Everett, Wash., Oct. 18, 1947; d. Richard Arthur and Doris Emily (Moxness) Lueth; m. Howard Judson Bargreen, Mar. 16, 1968; children: Owen, Maren. BA, U. Wash., Seattle, 1965, MA, 1969; PhD, U. Calif., Irvine, 1972. Music critic Seattle Times, 1977—; instr. Shoreline Community Coll., Seattle, 1973-74. Recipient Excellence in Journalism, Sigma Delta Chi, Wash., 1977-89, Arts Edn. Svc. award Kennedy Ctr., Washington, 1990. Mem. Music Critics Am. (Fellow summer inst., Saratoga, N.Y., 1977), Phi Beta Kappa. Office: Seattle Times PO Box 70 Fairview Ave N & John St Seattle WA 98109

BARHAM, ROBERT EDWARD, surgeon; b. Salt Lake City, Jan. 27, 1942; s. Tracy Robert and Margaret Ann (Rohrkemper) B.; children: Christopher, Kimberly; m. Lee Anne Zupan, June 14, 1989. BS, U. Utah, 1964, MD, 1969. Diplomate Am. Bd. Urology. Intern Providence Med. Ctr., Portland, Oreg., 1969-70; chmn. dept. surgery Providence Med. Ctr., Portland, 1984-87; resident in gen. surgery Ohio State U., Columbus, 1970-71; resident in urology U. Wash., Seattle, 1971-75, chief resident, instr., 1974-75; staff physician Urology Specialists, Portland, 1975—; asst. instr. depts. urology and family medicine Oreg. Health Scis. U. Mem. AMA, Oreg. Med. Assn., Multnomah County Med. Soc., Am. Urological Soc., N.W. Urological Assn., Western chpt. Am. Urological Assn., Oreg. Urological Assn. Office: Urology Specialists Ste 514 5050 NE Hoyt Portland OR 97213-2977

BARHAM HILL, BRENDA MARIE, college administrator; b. Oakland, Calif., Dec. 15, 1948; d. John Thomas and Frances Berneice (Spitler) B.; m. John Degelman Hill, May 10, 1980; children: Lauren Melissa, Adrienne Rebecca. AB, Occidental Coll., 1971; MA, Claremont U., 1972, PhD, 1979. Activities advisor Calif. State Coll., Bakersfield, Calif., 1972-74; asst. to v.p. for grad. studies, dir. summer sessions U. La Verne, Calif., 1974-79; asst. v.p. Claremont (Calif.) U. Ctr., 1979-83; sr. devel. officer grad. sch. Claremont U., 1983-86; v.p. planning and rsch. Scripps Coll., Claremont, 1986-93, dir. conf., 1992—; mem. accreditation team mem. Western Assn. Schs. and Colls., 1983-93. Vol. United Way of Mt. Baldy region, 1979-90, Girl Scouts U.S., Pomona Valley, 1987-93; bd. dirs. YWCA, Pomona Valley, 1982-86. Mem. Am. Assn. Higher Edn., Soc. Coll. and Univ. Planners, Calif. Assn. Instl. Rsch. (coll. rep. exec. com. 1987-88).

BARISAS, BERNARD GEORGE, JR., chemistry educator, immunology researcher; b. Shreveport, La., July 16, 1945; s. Bernard George and Edith (Bailey) B.; m. Judith Kathleen O'Rear, May 19, 1973 (div. Sept. 1978); m. Deborah Anne Roess, Aug. 6, 1981; 1 child, Derek Arthur George. BA, U. Kans., 1965; BA, Oxford (Eng.) U., 1967, MA, 1983; MPhil., Yale U., 1969, PhD, 1971. NIH postdoctoral trainee Yale U., New Haven, 1971-72, rsch. assoc., 1972; NIH postdoctoral fellow U. Colo., Boulder, 1973-75; asst. prof. biochemistry St. Louis U., 1975-80, assoc. prof., 1980-81; assoc. prof. chemistry and microbiology Colo. State U., Ft. Collins, 1981-87, prof., 1987—, assoc. dean Coll. Natural Scis., 1990—. Contbr. articles to tech. jours. Sec. Mo. Rhodes Scholarship Selection Com., 1976-81, mem. Colo. Selection Com., 1982-86, mem. Wyo. Selection Com., 1988-92. Rhodes scholar, 1965; Woodrow Wilson fellow, 1965, Fulbright sr. fellow, 1986; recipient Research Career Devel. award NIH, 1978. Mem. Am. Soc. Biol. Chemists, Am. Assn. Immunologists, Biophys. Soc., Am. Chem. Soc., AAAS, N.Y. Acad. Scis., Soc. Applied Spectroscopy, Phi Beta Kappa, Sigma Xi, Omicron Delta Kappa, Pi Mu Epsilon, Phi Lambda Upsilon, Delta Phi Alpha. Episcopalian. Clubs: Am. Alpine (N.Y.C.); Colo. Mountain (Denver); St. Louis Mountain (pres. 1976-77). Home: 1648 Collindale Dr Fort Collins CO 80525-2994 Office: Colo State U Dept Chemistry Fort Collins CO 80523

BARISH, JONAS ALEXANDER, English language educator; b. N.Y.C., Mar. 22, 1922; s. Philip H. and Mollie (Schaffer) B.; m. Mildred Ann Seaquist, July 26, 1964; children—Judith Rose, Rachel Alexandra. B.A., Harvard U., 1942, M.A., 1947, Ph.D., 1952. Instr. English Yale U., New Haven, 1953-54; asst. prof. English U. Calif., Berkeley, 1954-60, assoc. prof. English, 1960-66, prof. English, 1960-91, prof. English emeritus, 1991—. Author: Ben Jonson and the Language of Prose Comedy, 1960, The Antitheatrical Prejudice (Barnard Hewitt award for outstanding research in theater history 1982), 1981. Served with Signal Corps, U.S. Army, 1944-46. Fulbright research fellow, Paris, 1952-53, 61-62; Am. Council Learned Socs. fellow, 1961-62; NEH fellow, 1973-74, 86-87. Fellow Am. Acad. Arts and Scis., MLA, Malone Soc., Internat. Shakespeare Assn.; mem. Shakespeare Assn. Am. (trustee 1982-87, pres. 1984-85). Democrat. Jewish. Home: 107 Tamalpais Rd Berkeley CA 94708-1948 Office: U Calif Dept English Berkeley CA 94720

BARKER, CLAYTON GUINARD, mnaufacturing executive; b. Chgo.; s. Ray Samuel and Margaret (Guinard) B.; m. Shirley Nichols, May 21, 1923 (dec. Aug. 1985); children: Lynn Caruso, R. Steven; m. Patricia Dixon, July 16, 1989. Student, Northwestern U., 1940-42. Lic. coord. Armour Rsch. Found. Ill. Inst. Tech., Chgo., 1945-46; v.p. mktg. Magnecord, Inc., Chgo., 1946-54, Nat., Co., Malden, Mass., 1955-56, Filtors, Inc., East Northport, N.Y., 1957-65, Electro Materials, Inc., San Diego, 1966-69; pres. Cladan, Inc., San Diego, 1969-85, Crelco, Inc., San Diego, 1969-73; v.p. internat. Eagle Creek, San Marcos, Calif., 1986—; v.p., dir. mktg. Air/Space Am., San Diego, 1987-89; bd. dirs. Crelco, San Diego, Wallace Tech. Ceramics, San Diego. Mem. Dist. Export Coun., U.S. Dept. Commerce, San Diego, 1984—; vice chmn. San Diego (Calif.) County-Internat. Trade Commn., 1987. Sgt. U.S. Army, 1943-45. Mem. World Trade Assn. San Diego (pres. 1985-87, bd. mem. 1985—). Home: 1793 San Dablo Dr Lake San Marcos CA 92069 Office: Eagle Creek 1740 La Costa Meadows Dr San Marcos CA 92069

BARKER, JAMES EDWARD, JR., retired educator; b. Santa Barbara, Calif., Mar. 15, 1936; s. James Edward Sr. and Betty Cecelia (Babcock) B.; m. Gloria Teresina Fabbian, Dec. 6, 1964; children: Pamela, Corrine, Roberta. Teaching credential, UCLA, 1960; student, Santa Barbara Community Coll., 1961-62. Lic. contractors, Calif. Investor, rancher; contractor J E Barker, Santa Barbara, Calif.; dir. Channel Counties Trusts, Santa Barbara; tchr. Allan Hancock Coll., SAnta Maria, Calif. Republican. Roman Catholic. Home: 1933 Paquita Dr Carpinteria CA 93013-3026

BARKER, JAMES JOSEPH, chemical engineer, nuclear engineer; b. N.Y.C., Apr. 15, 1922; s. James Joseph Barker and Catherine Mildred (Walsh) Barker Richardson; m. Virginia Alice Casey, Dec. 26, 1945 (div. 1979); children: Kathleen Josephine Lyga, Robert James, Abbie Veronica Barker Dyer; m. Ollie Ione Thormodsgard, Oct. 6, 1979. B Chem. Engring., NYU, 1943, M Chem. Engring., 1950, D Engring. Sci. in Chem. Engring., 1959. Registered profl. engr., N.Y., Calif. In engring. positions with various firms N.Y.C., 1943-57; assoc. prof. dept. chem. engring NYU, N.Y.C., 1959-62; cons. engr. N.Y., Calif., 1959-79, 85-88; prof. physics, engring. C.W. Post Coll./L.I. U., Greenvale, N.Y., 1967-70; prof., dept. chair Manhattan Coll., N.Y.C., 1975-76; engring. specialist Air Rsch. Corp., Torrance, Calif., 1979-80, 83-85; prin. engr. ARCO Ventures, 1980-83; thermal engr. Lang Tech. Corp., Goleta, Calif., 1986-87; prin. engr. mech. engring. div., systems evaluations Westinghouse Hanford Co., Richland, Wash., 1989—; lectr. chem. engring. Calif. State U., Long Beach, 1986, San Jose (Calif.) State U., 1987-88. Author papers, reports, conf. procs. Supt. 1st Day Sch., Religious Soc. Friends, Jericho, 1950s and 60s. With U.S. Army, 1945-47. Mem. Am. Inst. Chem. Engrs., Am. Nuclear Soc., Am. Phys. Soc., Am. Chem. Soc., N.Y. Acad, Scis., Sigma Xi. Home: 1508 Arbor St Richland WA 99352-3963 Office: Westinghouse Hanford Co PO Box 1970 Richland WA 99352-0539

BARKER, JEFFREY DILLON, sales professional; b. Lincoln, Nebr., Mar. 14, 1959; s. Rodney Dillon Barker and Barbara (Rae) Johnston; m. Peri Kathleen Mechler, Nov. 28, 1981; children: Austin, Erin Marie. BBA, Tex. Tech U., 1981. Sales rep. Procter & Gamble, Cin., 1981-82; dist. field rep. Procter & Gamble, 1982, unit mgr., 1985-86, dist. sales mgr., 1986-91, div. mgr., 1991—. Mem. vestry Trinity Episcopal Ch., Orange, Calif., 1988—. Mem. Non-Foods Merchandising Assn., So. Calif. Grocers Assn., Kappa Alpha (pres. 1980-81). Republican. Home: 5725 Via Del Coyote Yorba Linda CA 92687-3543

BARKER, JOHN WILLIAM, agricultural property management; b. Oxnard, Calif., June 9, 1954; s. Robert Verne and Pauline Evelyn (Silveira) B.; m. Sharon Rose Richter, July 19, 1980; children: Teresa Marie, Daniel John, Marlena Dee. BS, Calif. State U., Northridge, 1991. Auditor Hyatt Hotels, Incline Village, Nev., 1975-77; oilwell driller Cal Pacific Drilling, Et Al, Camarillo, Calif., 1977-87; gen. ptnr. GGC Partnership, Camarillo, Calif., 1987—; trustee Manuel G. Silveria Trust, Camarillo, Calif., 1988—; gen. ptnr. Barker Farms, Camarillo, Calif., 1987—. treas. YMCA Indian Guides, 1992. Republican. Roman Catholic. Home: 220 Anacapa Dr Camarillo CA 93010 Office: Barker Farms 103 Alosta Dr Camarillo CA 93010

BARKER, NANCIE LYNNE, engineer; b. Berkeley, Calif., Apr. 25, 1942; d. Paul Thomas Marsh and Roberta Mildred (Wiggins) Brubaker; m. Loy Lee Barker, July 27, 1963; 1 child, Cindy Elizabeth. AS in Tool Design magna cum laude, De Anza Coll., 1979. Quality mgr. KRAS-West Corp., San Jose, Calif., 1977-82; quality engring. mgr. Siliconix, Santa Clara, Calif., 1982-87, package devel. engr., 1987-89, sr. engr. purchasing dept., 1989-91, mgr. supplier quality programs, 1991—; leader task force Semiconductor Equipment Materials Inst., Mountain View, Calif., 1989-91. Leader Camp Fire Girls, Cupertino, Calif., 1970-80; instr. in first aid ARC, San Jose and Los Gatos, Calif., 1970-84. Mem. Am. Soc. of Metals, Internat. Soc. Hybrid Mfg., Microelectronic Packaging and Processing Engrs. Office: Siliconix 2201 Laurelwood Rd Santa Clara CA 95054-1516

BARKER, ROBERT JEFFERY, financial executive; b. Glendale, Calif., Feb. 22, 1946; s. Albert and Margaret E. (Windle) B.; m. Ildiko Barker, Jan. 1, 1989; 1 child, Alexander A. BSEE, UCLA, 1968, MBA, 1970. Cert. mgmt. acctg. Cost analyst Lockheed, Sunnyvale, Calif., 1976-78; from cost acctg. supr. to fin. systems mgr. Monolithic Memories Inc., Sunnyvale, 1976-84; dir. fin. Waferscale Integration, Inc., Fremont, Calif., 1984-88, v.p. fin., chief fin. officer, 1988—; bd. dirs., treas. Am. Electronics Assn. Credit Union, Santa Clara, Calif., 1988—, bd. chmn., 1991; dir. Monolithic Memories Integration Fed. Credit Union, Sunnyvale, 1977-84, pres. 1983-84. Dir. Vets. Task Force, Palo Alto, Calif., 1980-87, pres. 1987. Capt. USAF, 1970-74. Mem. Nat. Assn. Accts., Fin. Execs. Inst., Toastmasters (pres. 1986-87). Republican. Methodist. Home: 1 Winchester Dr Atherton CA 94027

BARKER, WILEY FRANKLIN, surgeon, educator; b. Santa Fe, Oct. 16, 1919; s. Charles Burton and Bertha (Steed) B.; m. Nancy Ann Kerber, June 8, 1943; children: Robert Lawrence, Jonathan Steed, Christina Lee. B.S., Harvard, 1941, M.D., 1944. Diplomate: Am. Bd. Surgery (bd. dirs. 1964-70). Intern, then resident Peter Bent Brigham Hosp., Boston, 1944-46; Arthur Tracy Cabot fellow Harvard Med. Sch., 1948-49; asst. chief surg. service, then chief surg. sect. Wadsworth VA Hosp., Los Angeles, 1951-54; attending physician Wadsworth VA Hosp., 1951—; mem. faculty U. Calif. at Los Angeles Med. Sch., 1954—, prof. surgery, 1964-86, prof. emeritus, 1986—, chief div. gen. surgery, 1955-77; cons. Sepulveda VA Hosp., 1966-78, chief of staff, 1978-83; Mem. com. trauma NRC, 1964-68. Author: Surgical Treatment of Peripheral Vascular Disease, 1962, Peripheral Arterial Disease, 1966, 2d edit., 1976, Clio Chirugica: The Arteries, vols. I and II, 1992, , also papers, chpts. in books. Served as lt. (j.g.) M.C. USNR, 1946-47. Harvard Nat. scholar, 1937-44. Fellow ACS (2d v.p. 1986-87); mem. Am. Surg. Assn., Soc. Clin. Surgery (pres. 1972-74), Soc. Univ. Surgeons, Soc. Vascular Surgery (pres. 1972-73), Internat. Cardiovascular Soc. (v.p. N.Am. chpt. 1964-65, pres. 1979-80), So. Surg. Assn., Pacific Coast Surg. Assn. (pres. 1982-83), Pan Pacific Surg. Assn. (pres. 1986-88), Am., Calif., Los Angeles County med. assns., Phi Beta Kappa, Sigma Xi, Alpha Omega Alpha. Republican. Episcopalian. Mailing Address: 13216 Dobbins Pl Los Angeles CA 90049 Office: Dept Surgery Univ Calif Sch Medicine Los Angeles CA 90024

BARKER, WILLIAM CLYDE, financial management services executive, manufacturing executive; b. Bryantsville, Ky., Mar. 20, 1931; s. Isaac A. and Zelda (Onstott) B.; m. Irene Tomek, July 2, 1955; children: William, Charles, Stuart, Patricia. Cert., U. Md., Balt.; AS, Tampa Coll.; BS, Fullerton (Calif.) Coll., 1980; LLB, Blackstone Law Coll. Cert. internat. financier. Pres. fin. div. MCI, St. Petersburg, Fla., 1970-74; gen. foreman Marine Corps Depot, Yermo, Calif., 1977-83; regional v.p. A.L. Williams Fin. Services, Atlanta, 1983-88; chmn. Fin. Independence Clubs, Internat., Barstow, Calif., 1984-88; exec. dir. Millionaires Entrustment Assn., Europe, 1960-70; custodian Millionaires Library, Barstow, 1984-87; pub. relations rep. Future Millionaires Program, Phoenix, 1985. Past pres. Boy Scouts Am. Council, Fed. Republic Germany. Served as an officer with U.S. Army, 1948-70. Mem. Nat. Energy Specialists Assn. (charter), Masons. Home: 37142 Camarillo Ave Barstow CA 92311-1705 Office: Financial Clubs Internat PO Box 1701 Barstow CA 92312-1701

BARKHORDAR, PARVIZ, electronics engineer; b. Tehran, Iran; came to U.S., 1979; s. Aziz and Saltanat (Shamsi) B.; m. Forough Human, June 6, 1977 (div. 1978); 1 child, Shahram. BS in Electronic Engring., Technion U., Haifa, Israel, 1968. Test engr. Phillips TV Mfg., Tehran, 1974-76; shift mgr. Tehran Radio Sta., 1970-74; mr. ednl. dept. Parvahan Co., Tehran, 1974-78; test engr. Circon Co., Santa Barbara, Calif., 1980—. Jewish. Home: 7560 Cathedral Oaks Rd Apt 3 Santa Barbara CA 93117-1140

BARKHOUDARIAN, SARKIS, aerospace executive, engineer; b. Tehran, Iran, Feb. 12, 1938; s. Aram and Loussik (Abrahamian) B.; m. Sophia Bap Kazarian, Jan. 12, 1978; children: Garni, Melita. BEE, U. Detroit, 1962; MEE, Carnegie Mellon U., 1963, postgrad. in elec. engring., 1964. Project engr. Gen. Motors Mfg. Devel., Warren, Mich., 1964-67, Atomic Power Devel. Assn., Detroit, 1967-70, Bendix Rsch. Ctr., Southfield, Mich., 1970-73; project engr. Automotive Tech. Ctr., Rockwell Internat., Troy, Mich., 1973-76, mgr. instrumentation, 1976-80; mem. tech. staff Rocketdyne div. Rockwell Internat., Canoga Park, Calif., 1980-82, project engr., 1982-84, mgr. advanced instrn., 1984—; tchr. indsl. electronics U. Detroit. Contbr. over 20 articles to profl. publs.; holder over 10 U.S./Internat. patents. Fellow Instrument Soc. Am. (sr.); mem. AIAA (tech. panel on aerodynamic measurements), Soc. Automotive Engrs. (nat. chmn. condition monitoring com.). Home: 24415 Lemay St West Hills CA 91307-2735

BARKLEY, CHARLES WADE, professional basketball player; b. Leeds, Ala., Feb. 20, 1963. Student, Auburn U., 1981-84. mem. U.S. Olympic Basketball Team, 1992. With Phila. 76ers, 1984-92, Phoenix Suns, 1992—; mem. U.S. Olympic team, 1992. Author: (with Roy S. Johnson) Outrageous! The Fine Life and Flagrant Good Times of Basketball's Irresistible Force, 1992. Recipient NBA All-Star Game Most Valuable Player award, 1992, Schick Pivotal Player award, 1986-88, NBA Most Valuable Player Award, 1993; named to NBA All-Star team, 1987-93. Office: Phoenix Suns 2910 N Central Ave Phoenix AZ 85012

BARKLEY, THIERRY VINCENT, lawyer; b. Paris, Mar. 21, 1955; s. Jacques and Michéline Marié (Rossi) B.; came to U.S., 1967, naturalized, 1974; m. Mary Ellen Gamble, June 18, 1983; children: Richard A., Robert V., Marriah E., Christopher R. BA in Polit. Sci., UCLA, 1976; JD, Calif. Western Sch. Law, San Diego, 1979. Bar: Nev. 1980, U.S. Dist. Ct. Nev. 1982, U.S. Supreme Ct. 1986. Intern, Calif. Ct. Appeals 4th Circuit, San Diego, 1978-79; law clk. Nev. Dist. Ct., 7th Jud. Dist., Ely, 1979-81; assoc. firm C.E. Horton, Ely, 1982-83; asst. city atty. Ely, 1982-83; assoc. firm Barker, Gillock & Perry, Reno, 1983-87, Perry & Spann, 1987-89, ptnr., 1990—. Editor Internat. Law Jour., 1979. Mem. Internat. Moot Ct. Team, 1978; recipient Dean's award Calif. Western Sch. Law, 1979. Mem. Rep. Presdl. Task Force, 1990. Mem. Nev. Bar Assn., Washoe Bar Assn., U.S. Jaycees (past pres. White Pine, Nev.). Republican. Roman Catholic. Lodge: Elks (past treas. Ely club). Office: Perry & Spann 6130 Plumas St Reno NV 89509-6060

BARKS, RONALD EDWARD, federal laboratory executive; b. Paterson, N.J., July 6, 1938; s. Clarence Edward and Anna Ethel (Meyer) B.; m. Ruth Cosine, Aug. 27, 1960; children: James Harold, Jennine Ruth. BA in Geology, Princeton U., 1960; MA in Geochemistry, Rice U., 1962; PhD in Geochemistry, Pa. State U., 1966; postgrad. sch. indsl. mgmt., Worcester Poly. Inst., 1977. Sr. rsch. engr. Vitrified Products div. Norton Co., Worcester, Mass., 1968-74, asst. dir. rsch., 1974-75, dir. rsch. and devel., 1975-86; product mgr. Vitrified Bonds, Norton Co., 1980-81, exec. cons., 1986-88; dir. indsl. applications office Los Alamos (N.Mex.) Nat. Lab., 1988-92; prin. Ronald E. Barks Assocs., 1987—; condr. seminars on rsch. mgmt. Clark U., Worcester State Coll. Pres. Thompson (Conn.) Village Improvement Soc., 1970-72; vice chmn. regional adv. council Quinebaug Valley Community Coll., 1971-73, 83-86; chmn. Thompson Zoning Study Commn., 1972-74; with technol. transfer policy group Dept. Energy, 1988—. Capt. USAR, 1966-68, Vietnam. Fellow Am. Ceramic Soc. (v.p. 1992-93); mem. Assn. Fed. Tech. Transfer Execs., Licensing Execs. soc. (faculty mem.).

BARLOW, HAVEN J., state legislator, realtor; b. Clearfield, Utah, Jan. 4, 1922; s. Jesse and Asdora (Beck) B.; m. Bonnie Rae Ellison, Nov. 23, 1944; children: Jesselie Anderson, Heidi Harris, Rachel, Haven J., Stewart E., Duncan. BS, Utah State U., 1944, postgrad. U. Utah Law Sch., Harvard U. Sch. Bus. Sr. Senator State of Utah, 1957—, Utah Ho. of Reps., 1953-57; pres. Barlow Ins., Inc. 1950—; bd. dirs. Community 1st Bank (formerly Clearfield State Bank), Lockhart Corp. Past pres. Lake Bonniville council Boy Scouts Am.; bd. dirs. Utah State Symphony; trustee Humana Hosp. Davis North, Layton; mem. Davis County Pvt. Industry council, State Job Tng. Coordinating council. Served to lt. (j.g.) USN, 1942-44; PTO, ETO. Recipient Disting. Service award Utah State U., 1986, Humanitarian award Utah Vocat. Assn., Light of Learning award State Bd. Edn., Silver Beaver award Boy Scouts Am. Republican. Mormon. Home: 552 Elm St Layton UT 84041-4308

BARLOW, LOREN CALL, physician; b. St. Louis, Apr. 8, 1926; s. Loren Call adn Rachel Irene (Smith) B.; m. Margaret Wilson, Jan. 20, 1949 (dec. Dec. 1989); children: Stephen, David, Janet, John. BS, Northwestern U., Evanston, Ill., 1949; MD, Northwestern U., 1951. Diplomate Am. Bd. Internal Medicine. Intern Evanston (Ill.) Hosp., 1951-52; resident Mayo Clinic, Rochester, Minn., 1952-55; mem. Sacred Heart Hosp., Eugene, Oreg., 1955—, chief of internal medicine, 1964-69, chief of staff, 1971-73; pres. Patterson Internal Medinice, P.C., Eugene, 1976-88, Oreg. Med. Group, P.C., Eugene, 1988—; bd. dirs. Oreg. Med. Svcs. Orgn., Eugene, Select Care, Western Oreg. Health Svcs. Orgn., Eugene; pres., bd. dirs. Oreg. Med. Group, Eugene, 1988—. Bd. dirs. Sacred Heart Health Systems. Staff sgt. U.S. Army, 1944-46, PTO. Mem. AMA, ACP, North Pacific Soc. of Internal Medicine, Oreg. Med. Assn., Lane County Med. Soc. (pres. 1984-85). Home: 2810 Tomahawk Ln Eugene OR 97401-6406 Office: Oreg Med Group 495 Oakway Rd Eugene OR 97401

BARLOW, THOMAS MARTIN, mechanical engineer; b. Mpls., Aug. 13, 1935; s. Howard Walter and Eleanor Marian (Coreyell) B.; m. Patricia Carol Thomas, July 20, 1957 (div. Apr. 1977); m. Sandra Ruth Kvam, Dec. 31, 1985. BSME, Wash. State U., 1957; MBA in Mgmt., Golden Gate U., 1985. Engr. USAF, Ohio, 1957-60; mech. engr. Lawrence Livermore (Calif.) Nat. Lab., 1960-68, group leader, 1968-73, program Mgr., 1973-78, project mgr., 1978-81, resource mgr., 1981-86, program resource mgr., 1986-90, project engr., 1990—; rep. ASME, Sittard, The Netherlands, 1989-91. Patentee/inventor Cable Conector, 1975. Mem. ASME (chmn. advanced energy systems div., N.Y.C., 1987-88, mem. at large energy Resource bd., N.Y.C., 1987-91, region IX operating bd., N.Y.C., 1989—; gov. cert. 1988, 93, fellow, 1990, mem. at large Gen. Engr. Bd., 1992—; disting. svc. award 1991, v.p. Energy Resources 1993—), Tau Beta Pi, Sigma Tau, Phi Eta Sigma. Home: 1463 Wilton Rd Livermore CA 94550-1539 Office: Lawrence Livermore Nat Lab Mail Stop L-644 PO Box 808 Livermore CA 94551-0808

BARLOW, WILLIAM PUSEY, JR., accountant; b. Oakland, Calif., Feb. 11, 1934; s. William P. and Muriel (Block) B.; student Calif. Inst. Tech., 1952-54. AB in Econs., U. Calif.-Berkeley, 1956. CPA, Calif. Acct. Barlow, Davis & Wood, San Francisco, 1960-72, ptnr., 1964-72; ptnr., J.K. Lasser & Co., 1972-77, Touche Ross & Co., San Francisco, 1977-78; self employed acct., 1978-89; ptnr. Barlow & Hughan, 1990—. Co-author: Collectible Books: Some New Paths, 1979, The Grolier Club, 1884-1984, 1984; editor: Book Catalogues: Their Varieties and Uses, 2d edit., 1986; contbr. articles to profl. jours. Fellow Gleeson Libr. Assocs., 1969, pres., 1971-74; mem. Coun. Friends Bancroft Libr., 1971—, chmn., 1974-79; bd. dirs. Oakland Ballet, 1982—, pres. 1986-89. Recipient Sir Thomas More medal Gleeson Libr. Assocs., 1989; named to Water Ski Hall of Fame, 1993. Mem. Am. Water Ski Assn. (bd. dirs., regional chmn. 1959-63, pres. 1963-66, chmn. bd. 1966-69, 77-79, hon. v.p. 1969—), Internat. Water Ski Fedn. (exec. bd. 1961-71, 75-78), Bibliog. Soc. Am. (coun. 1986—, pres. 1992—), Grolier Club (N.Y.C.), Roxburghe Club (San Francisco), Book of Calif. Club (bd. dirs. 1963-76, pres. 1968-69, treas. 1971-83). Home: 1474 Hampel St Oakland CA 94602-1346 Office: 449 15th St Oakland CA 94612

BARMAN, ROBERT JOHN, home electronics company executive; b. Glendale, Calif.; s. Robert Grant and Geraldine (Howe) B.; m. Jean Ann Crane, June 19, 1965; children: John Robert, Jeffrey Wynn. BS in Mktg., Calif. State U., L.A., 1965. Sales coord. Teledyne Packard Bell, L.A., 1965-67; dist. mgr. Teledyne Packard Bell, Fresno, L.A., 1968-71; regional sales mgr. Teledyne Packard Bell, Boston, 1971-73; major accounts sales mgr. Quasar Co., L.A., 1973-75, regional sales mgr., 1975-76, sales mgr., 1976-77, zone mgr., 1985—; v.p., br. mgr. Quasar Co., Seattle, 1977-84; gen. mgr. Matsushita, L.A., 1985—; mem. mgmt. com. Matsushita Elec. Corp. of Am. West, Quasar Co., Chgo., mem. distbg. coun. Bd. dirs. Irvine (Calif.) Aquatics Swim Team, Bellevue (Wash.) Athletic Club Swim Team. Office: Quasar Co 1055 8th St Azusa CA 91702

BARMANN, BERNARD CHARLES, SR., lawyer; b. Maryville, Mo., Aug. 5, 1932; s. Charles Anselm and Veronica Rose (Fisher) B.; m. Beatrice Margaret Murphy, Sept. 27, 1965; children: Bernard Charles Jr., Brigit. PhD, Stanford U., 1966; JD, U. San Diego, 1974; MPA, Calif. State U., Bakersfield. Bar: Calif. 1974, U.S. Dist. Ct. (so. dist.) Calif. 1974, U.S. Dist. Ct. (ea. dist.) Calif. 1978, U.S. Ct. Appeals (9th cir.) 1984, U.S. Supreme Ct. Asst. prof. Ohio State U., Columbus, 1966-69, U. Toronto, Ont., Can., 1969-71; dep. county counsel Kern County, Bakersfield, Calif., 1974-85; county counsel Kern County, Bakersfield, 1985—; adj. prof. Calif. State U., Bakersfield, 1986—. Editor: The Bottom Line, 1991-93, contbr. articles to profl. jours. Mem. exec. bd. So. Sierra coun. Boy Scouts Am., Bakersfield, 1986—; bd. dirs. Kern County Acad. Decathlon, Bakersfield, 1988—. Danforth Found. fellow, 1963-65; grantee Fulbright Found., 1963-65. Mem. Calif. Bar Assn. (law practice mgmt. sect. exec. com.), County Counsel Assn. Calif. (bd. dirs. 1990—, chair 1993—), Rotary. Office: Kern County Office of County Counsel 1115 Truxtun Ave Bakersfield CA 93301-5222

BARNA, LILLIAN CARATTINI, superintendent of schools; b. N.Y.C., Jan. 18, 1929; d. Juan and Dolores Elsie Nieves (Alicea) Carattini; A.B. Hunter Coll. 1950; M.A. San Jose State U. 1970; m. Eugene Andrew Barna, July 1, 1951; children—Craig Andrew, Keith Andrew. Tchr., N.Y.C. Sch. Dist. 1950-52; tchr. Whittier (Calif.) Sch. Dist. 1952-54, tchr. high sch. 1954-56; tchr. presch. Long Beach and Los Gatos, Calif., 1958-67; supr. early childhood edn. San Jose (Calif.) Unified Sch. Dist. 1967-72, sch. adminstr., 1972-80, supt. schs., 1980-84; supt. schs. Albuquerque Pub. Schs., 1984-88, Tacoma Sch. Dist. 10, 1988-93; cons. in field. Recipient Soroptimist Internat. Woman of Yr. award 1980, Western Region Puertorican Council Achievement award 1980, Assn. Puertorican Profls. Achievement award 1981, Calif. State U. Outstanding Achievement in Edn. award 1982, Woman of Achievement award Santa Clara County Commn. on Status of Women/San Jose Mercury News, Disting. Alumni award San Jose State U. Mem. Nat. Assn. Edn. Young Children, Tchrs. English to Speakers of Other Langs., Women Leaders in Edn., Calif. Reading Assn., Calif. Assn. Women Adminstrs., Assn. Calif. Sch. Adminstrs., Phi Kappa Phi, Delta Zeta. Office: Tacoma School Dist # 10 Office of the Supt PO Box 1357 Tacoma WA 98401-1357

BARNARD, ANNETTE WILLIAMSON, elementary school educator; b. Phoenix, Nov. 29, 1948; d. Walter Albert and Geraldine (Dickman) Williamson; m. Richard W. Heinrich, Sept. 1969 (div.); 1 child, Jennifer Ann; m. Charles Jay Barnard, June 6, 1981. AA, Mesa C.C., 1979; BA in Spl. Edn., Elem. Edn., Ariz. State U., 1981, postgrad., 1989—. Cert. tchr., Ariz. Tchr. spl. edn. Tempe (Ariz.) Sch. Dist., 1981-83, tchr. Indian community, 1983-84; tchr. elem. sch. Kyrene Sch. Dist., Tempe, 1984-86, 90—; tchr. Chandler (Ariz.) Sch. Dist., 1986-89; chair profl. standards and cert. com. Ariz. Bd.

Edn., Phoenix, 1990—; chair, facilitator Kyrene Legis. Action Commmunity, 1991—; mentor Kyrene Sch. Dist., 1990—; commencement speaker Ariz. State U., 1981. Contbg. author: Environmental Education Compendium for Energy Resources, 1991, System of Personnel Development, 1989. Bd. dirs. Ariz. State Rep. Caucus, Phoenix, 1990—, precinct committeewoman, Tempe, 1990-92. Recipient Profl. Leadership award Kiwanis Club Am., Tempe, 1984; nominee to talent bank Coun. ow Women's Edn. Programs U.S. Dept. Edn., 1982. Mem. ASCD, Kyrene Edn. Assn. (chair legis. com. 1990—), Kappa Delta Pi, Phi Kappa Phi, Phi Theta Kappa, Pi Lambda Theta. Home: 3221 W Jasper Dr Chandler AZ 85226

BARNARD, MICHAEL DANA, orthopedic surgeon; b. Denver, Nov. 14, 1946; s. Rollin Dwight and Patricia Reynolds (Bierkamp) B.; m. Susan Carole Bondo, Aug. 3, 1969; children: Alison, Melissa. BA, Pomona Coll., 1968; MD, U. Colo., Denver, 1972. Diplomate Am. Bd. Orthopedic Surgery. Intern U. Oreg., Portland, 1972-73; resident U. Colo., Denver, 1973-77; practice medicine specializing in orthopedic surgery, Canon City, Colo., 1977-90, Shelton, Wash., 1990—; chief of staff St. Thomas More Hosp., Canon City, 1982-84. Fellow Am. Acad. Orthopedic Surgeons; mem. Canon City C. of C. (pres. 1982-83, dir. 1979-82), Shelton Mason County C. of C., Thurston Mason County Med. Soc., Fremont County Med. Soc. (pres. 1986-88), Rotary (pres. Canon City club 1983-84). Republican. Lutheran. Home: 382 SE Collier Rd Shelton WA 98584-9317 Office: 421 N 3d St Shelton WA 98584-1983

BARNARD, ROLLIN DWIGHT, retired financial executive; b. Denver, Apr. 14, 1922; s. George Cooper and Emma (Riggs) B.; m. Patricia Reynolds Bierkamp, Sept. 15, 1943; children: Michael Dana, Rebecca Susan (Mrs. Paul C. Wulfestieg), Laurie Beth (Mrs. Kenneth J. Kostelecky). B.A., Pomona Coll., 1943. Clk. Morey Merc. Co., Denver, 1937-40; ptnr George C. Barnard & Co. (gen. real estate and ins.), Denver, 1946-47; v.p. Foster & Barnard, Inc., 1947-53; instr. Denver U., 1949-53; dir. real estate U.S. P.O. Dept., Washington, 1953-55, dep. asst. postmaster gen., bur. facilities, 1955-59, asst. postmaster gen., 1959-61; pres., dir. Midland Fed. Savs. & Loan Assn., Denver, 1962-84; vice chmn. Bank Western Fed. Savs. Bank, 1984-87; vice chmn., pres. Western Capital Investment Corp., 1985-87. Mayor City of Greenwood Village, Colo., 1989—, chmn. Planning and Zoning Commn., 1969-73, mem. coun., 1975-77; pres. Denver Area coun. Boy Scouts Am., 1970-71, mem. exec. bd., 1962-73; mem. adv. bd. Denver Area coun. Boy Scouts Am., 1973—; mem. nat. coun. Pomona Coll., 1963—; bd. dirs. Downtown Denver Improvement Assn., pres., 1965; bd. dirs. Bethesda Found., Inc., 1973-82, Children's Hosp., 1979-84, treas., 1983-84; bd. dirs. Children's Health Corp., Inc., 1982—; trustee Mile High United Fund, 1969-72, Denver Symphony Assn., 1973-74; bd. dirs. Colo. Coun. Econ. Edn., 1971-80, chmn. 1971-76; trustee, v.p., treas. Morris Animal Found., 1969-81, pres., chmn. 1974-78, trustee emeritus, 1981—. Nominated One of Ten Outstanding Young Men in Am. U.S. Jaycees, 1955, 57; recipient Distinguished Service award Postmaster Gen. U.S., 1960; Silver Beaver award Boy Scouts Am., 1969; Outstanding Citizen of Year Sertoma, 1982; Colo. Citizen of Year Colo. Assn. Realtors, 1982. Mem. Greater Denver C. of C. (pres. 1966-67), U.S. League Savs. Instns. (bd. dirs. 1972-77, vice chmn. 1979-80, chmn. 1980-81, mem. nat. legis. com., exec. com. 1974-77), Savs. League Colo. (exec. com. 1969-73, pres. 1971-72), Colo. Assn. Commerce and Industry (dir. 1971-76), Fellowship Christian Athletes (Denver area dir. 1963-76), Western Stock Show Assn. (dir. 1971—, exec. com. 1982—, 1st v.p. 1985—), Mountain and Plains Appaloosa Horse Club (pres. 1970-71), Roundup Riders of the Rockies (bd. dirs. 1979—, treas. 1980-87, v.p. 1987-89, pres.-elect 1989-91, pres. 1991—), Met. Club, Nu Alpha Phi. Republican. Presbyterian. Home: 3151 E Long Rd Greenwood Village CO 80121-1716

BARNARD, WILLIAM CALVERT, retired news service executive; b. Corpus Christi, Tex., Feb. 25, 1914; s. W.C. and Eleanor (Erb) B.; m. Julia Lacy Salter, Mar. 25, 1961; children: William Cornell, Diana Eugenia. Student, Tex. Coll. Arts and Industries, Kingsville, 1933-35. Reporter-columnist Corpus Christi Caller-Times, 1935-40; feature editor San Antonio Express-News, 1941-42; writer, state editor AP, Dallas Bur., 1942-50; AP war corr. Korean War, Far East news editor, 1953-54; bur. chief AP, Dallas, 1954-62; gen. exec. AP, N.Y.C., 1962-71; gen. exec. for ten Western states AP, San Francisco, 1971-81; gen. exec. for 24 Western states AP, 1981-85. Recipient Journalism Forum award for coverage Korean War So. Meth. U., 1954. Presbyterian. Home: 1100 Village Dr # 30 Belmont CA 94002-3448

BARNARD, WILLIAM MARION, psychiatrist; b. Mt. Pleasant, Tex., Dec. 17, 1949; s. Marion Jaggers and Med (Cody) B. BA, Yale U., 1972; MD, Baylor U., 1976. Diplomate Am. Bd. Psychiatry and Neurology. Resident NYU/Bellevue Med. Ctr., 1976-79; fellow L.I. Jewish/Hillside Med. Ctr., 1979-80; chief, liaison, consultation psychiatrist Queens (N.Y.) Med. Ctr., 1980-83; liaison, consultation psychiatrist Mt. Sinai Med. Ctr., N.Y.C., 1983-84; clin. asst. prof., adminstrn. and emergency psychiatrist VA. Med. Ctr., NYU Med. Sch., N.Y.C., 1984-87; pvt. practice Pasadena, Calif., 1987—; chief psychiat. svc. Las Encinas Hosp., Pasadena, 1989, chief staff, 1990, med. dir. gen. adult. psychiat. svc., 1990-92, asst. med. dir., 1992; med. dir. CPC Alhambra Hosp., Rosemead, Calif., 1992—. Chmn. mental health com. All Saints AIDS Svc. Ctr., Pasadena, 1990—, bd. dirs., 1991—; bd. dirs. Pasadena Symphony, 1989—, Whiffenpoof Alumni, New Haven, 1991—. Wilson scholar Yale U., 1973. Mem. Am. Psychiat. Assn., NYU-Bellevue Psychiat. Assn., Am. Soc. Addiction Medicine, Amateur Comedy Club, Met. Opera Club, Yale Club N.Y.C. Republican. Episcopalian. Office: 2810 E Del Mar Blvd Pasadena CA 91107

BARNEA, URI N., music director, conductor, composer, violinist; b. Petah-Tikvah, Israel, May 29, 1943; came to U.S., 1971; s. Shimon and Miriam Burstein; m. Lizbeth A. Lund, Dec. 15, 1977; 2 children. Teaching cert., Oranim Music Inst., Israel, 1966; postgrad. Hebrew U., Israel, 1969-71; Mus.B., Rubin Acad. Music, Israel, 1971; M.A., U. Minn., 1974, Ph.D., 1977. Mus. dir. Jewish Community Ctr., Mpls. 1971-73; condr. Youval Chamber Orch., Mpls., 1971-73; asst. condr. U. Minn. Orchs., Mpls., 1972-77; music dir., condr. Unitarian Soc., Mpls., 1973-78, Kenwood Chamber Orch., Mpls., 1974-78, Knox-Galesburg Symphony, 1978-83, Billings Symphony Soc., Mont., 1984—; asst. prof. Knox Coll., Galesburg, Ill., 1978-83; violinist, violist Yellowstone Chamber players, Billings, 1984—; violist Tri-City Symphony, Quad-Cities, Ill., Iowa, 1983-84; condr. Cedar Arts Forum String Camp, Cedar Falls, Iowa, 1981, 82; European conducting debut, London, Eng., Neuchatel and Fribourg, Switzerland, 1986. Can. conducting debut No. Music Festival 1989, North Bay Ont., 1989; Violin Concerto, 1990; Russian conducting debut Symphony Orch. Kuzbass, Kemerovo, 1993; composer of numerous compositions including String Quartet (1st prize Aspen Composition Competition 1976), Sonata for Flute and Piano, 1975 (Diploma of Distinction 26th Viotti Internat. Competition, Italy 1975), Ruth A Ballet, 1974 (1st prize Oberhoffer Composition Contest 1976), Active in music adv. panel Ill. Arts Coun., 1980-83; v.p. Community Concert Assn., Galesburg, 1980-83; bd. dirs. Knox Coll. Credit Union, Galesburg, 1982-83, Sta. KEMC Pub. Radio, Billings, 1984—, Fox Theater Corp., Billings, 1984-86. Recipient Friend of Arts title Sigma Alpha Iota, 1982; Ill. Arts Coun. grantee, 1979; Hebrew U. Jerusalem scholar, 1972-74, Hebrew U. and Rubin Acad. Mus. scholar, 1969, 70; Individual Artist fellow Mont. Arts Coun., 1986. Mem. NEA (music adv. panel 1990—), ASCAP, Minn. Composers Forum, Conductors Guild, Am. String Tchrs. Assn. Office: Billings Symphony Soc PO Box 7055 Billings MT 59103-7055

BARNES, AUDRA GUYTON, nursing educator; b. Galveston, Tex., July 16, 1921; d. Emmett Edward Guyton and Margaret Beatrice (Wright) Guyton-Carter; m. John Berrel Barnes Sr., Apr., 1950; children: Audra Yvonne, John Jr. Diploma in Nursing, Meharry Med. Coll., 1941; BS in Home Econs., Tenn. State U., 1949; BS in Nursing, Calif. State U., L.A., 1973, MS in Nursing, 1975. RN, Calif., Tenn. Staff nurse Dept. of Health, N.Y.C., 1942-44, St. Joseph's Hosp., Ft. Worth, 1944-46; pvt. duty nurse L.A., 1956-58; nurse L.A. City Schs., 1963-66; from instr. to prof. nursing Compton Community Coll., Calif., 1976—. Fellow Am. Nurses Assn.; mem. Am. Fedn. Tchrs., Black Nurses Assn. (pres. 1985-89), Angel City Dental Soc. Aux., Alpha Kappa Alpha, Alpha Kappa Mu. Democrat. Methodist. Home: 3751 Cherrywood Ave Los Angeles CA 90018-4010 Office: Compton Community Coll 1111 E Artesia Blvd Compton CA 90221-5393

BARNES, DAVID ROBERT, JR., sales executive; b. Yonkers, N.Y., Sept. 8, 1952; s. David Robert Sr. and Marion C. (Boiling) B.; m. Deborah Furtado, June 15, 1981 (div. 1984); m. Paula Rose Wihongi, July 8, 1988. AA, Worcester Jr. Coll., 1972; BA, Worcester State Coll., 1975; MEd cum laude, U. Mass., 1976. Sales merchandiser Menley & James Labs., Worcester, Mass., 1977-79; area sales rep. Menley & James Labs., Springfield, Mass., 1979-81; unit mgr. SmithKline Corp., Springfield, 1981-83; terr. mgr. SmithKline Corp., Huntington Beach, Calif., 1983—; Pacific regional key accounts mgr., dist. mgr. Hills Pet Products, Topeka, 1990—; regional trainer Smith Kline Consumer Products, 1986-87, appointee pres.'s solid gold circle, 1968. Basketball coach Worchester Jr. Coll., 1974-75. Recipient Solid Gold Coin, Menley & James Labs., 1980, Solid Gold Sit. Democrat. Baptist.

BARNES, GERALD R., bishop; b. Phoenix, Ariz., June 22, 1945. Grad., St. Leonard Sem., Dayton, Ohio; student, Assumption-St. John's Sem., San Antonio. Ordained priest Roman Cath. Ch., 1975, titular bishop of Monte Fiascone. Aux. bishop San Bernardino, Calif., 1992—. Office: Chancery Office 1450 N D St San Bernardino CA 92405*

BARNES, JIM, fire protection designer; b. French Camp, Calif., Mar. 31, 1956; s. James Allen and Faye (Griffin) B.; m. Susan Kay Miller, June 4, 1983. Student, Antioch (Calif.) High Sch., 1974-75. Engr. in tng., Hawaii. Designer Lescure Co., Lafayette, Calif., 1983-84, Calif. Fire Protection, San Francisco, 1984-85; designer Grinnell Fire Protection, North Highlands, Calif., 1985-86, Honolulu, 1986-88; designer Automatic Sprinkler Corp., Waipahu, Hawaii, 1988-90; pvt. practice designer/drafter Hauula, Hawaii, 1990; designer Syntech Ltd. Cons. Engrs., Honolulu, 1990-91, FBS Hawaii (formerly Viking Fire Protection), Aiea, Hawaii, 1991-92. Author: Echoes in the Rain, 1992, (poem) Of Pride And ..., 1992. Jehovah's Witness. Home: PO Box 995 Mendocino CA 95460

BARNES, JOANNA, author, actress; b. Boston, Nov. 15, 1934; d. John Pindar and Alice Weston (Mutch) B. BA, Smith Coll., 1956. Actress appearing in motion pictures: Auntie Mame, 1958, B.S. I Love You, 1971, Spartacus, 1963, The Parent Trap, 1966, The War Wagon, 1971; TV appearances include What's My Line, The Tonight Show with Johnny Carson, Merv Griffin Show, Trials of O'Brien, Dateline: Hollywood, Murder She Wrote; book reviewer L. A. Times, syndicated columnist Chgo. Tribune, N.Y. News Syndicate, 1963-65; author: Starting from Scratch, 1968, The Deceivers, 1970, Who Is Carla Hart, 1973, Pastora, 1980, Silverwood, 1985. Mem. Phi Beta Kappa.

BARNES, JOHN FAYETTE, research scientist, educator; b. Santa Cruz, Calif., Jan. 28, 1930; s. John Fayette and Bertha Henrietta (Youngman) B.; m. Joanne Cecily Lyle, Aug. 28, 1955; children—John Fayette, David Lyle. B.A., U. Calif., Berkeley, 1951; M.S., U. Denver, 1952; Ph.D., U. N.Mex., 1963, M. Mgmt., 1981. Staff mem. Los Alamos (N.Mex.) Nat. Lab., 1953-91, asst. group leader, 1968-71, dep. group leader, 1971, group leader, 1971-76, asst. theoretical div. leader, 1976-77, assoc. theoretical div. leader, 1977-80, dep. theoretical div. leader, 1980-81, dep. assoc. dir. for energy programs, 1981-82, dep. assoc. dir. for physics and math., 1982-83, applied theoretical physics div. leader, 1983-85, research scientist, group leader, 1985-87, cons., 1987-91; mem. core faculty U. N.Mex., Los Alamos, 1987-91; part-time instr. Santa Fe Community Coll., 1991—; mathematician Research Directorate, Air Force Spl. Weapons Ctr., Albuquerque, 1956-57; mem. research adv. bd. Lab. for Laser Energetics U. Rochester, N.Y., 1980-88, chmn., 1981, 87; coord. math. and tech. programs U. N.Mex., Los Alamos, 1988-91. Contbr. articles to profl. jours.; originator of SESAME equation of state libr. Active Boy Scouts Am., Los Alamos, 1967-79; precinct chmn. Republican Party, 1968-85; del. state conv. 1972. Home: 2213 Calle Cacique Santa Fe NM 87505-4944 Office: Santa Fe Community Coll PO Box 87502 Santa Fe NM 87502

BARNES, KATHLEEN ADELE, artist; b. Red Bank, N.J., June 17, 1955; d. Anthony Lee and Mary Magdelene (De La Cruz) B.; m. Richard Alfred Morley, June 15, 1985; 1 child, Thomas Anthony. BA, W.Va. U., 1985. Art restorationist Garo Art Gallery, Morgantown, W.Va., 1983-85; tech. illustrator Corpus Christi (Tex.) Mus., 1986-87; art instr. Fuller Lodge Art Ctr., Los Alamos, N.Mex., 1987-89; artist, tchr. Las Vegas Art Mus., 1990—; adv. bd. Las Vegas Art Mus., 1991-92. Exhibited in group shows at U. Tex. Health Sci. Ctr., 1992, Marin County Civic Ctr., Calif., 1991, Las Vegas Art Mus., 1991, Nev. Watercolor Soc. Exhbns., 1991, Stanford Hist. Soc., 1991, Allied Arts Gallery, 1991, Black Crooke Theatre, 1991, Grandview Gallery, 1990, Fuller Lodge Art Ctr., 1990, N.Mex. State Fairgrounds Fine Arts Gallery, 1989, Coll. of Santa Fe Fine Arts Gallery, 1989, Los Alamos Women's Ctr., 1989, 90, and others. Mem. Soc. of Layerists in Multi-Media, Nev. Watercolor Soc. (pres.), Los Alamos Art Ctr. (bd. dirs.), Am. Watercolor Soc. (assoc.), Nat. Watercolor Soc. (assoc.), Phi Beta Kappa. Home: 2702 Karen Ave #2 Las Vegas NV 89121

BARNES, KEVIN J., insurance company executive; b. Pocatello, Idaho, Dec. 22, 1952; s. Stanley J. and Betty Mae (Owens) B.; m. Donna Marie Eaton, Jan. 24, 1975; children: Jay, Timothy, Michael, Lisa, Nathan, Matthew. BS, Brigham Young U., 1979. CLU. Ind. life agt. Beneficial Life Ins. Co., Salt Lake City, 1980, group sales rep., 1980-83; group sales rep. Pacific Heritage Assurance Co., Portland, Oreg., 1983-86; dir. group mktg. Educators Mut. Ins. Assn., Murray, Utah, 1986—. Scoutmaster, scout leader Boy Scouts Am., American Fork, Utah, 1977—, Second Miler award, 1987; leader local dist. Rep. Party, Utah County, Utah, 1978-82; asst. coach American Fork Recreation, 1986-91. Fellow Life Mgmt. Inst.; mem. Nat. Assn. Health Underwriters (v.p. Utah chpt. 1985-86). Mem. LDS Ch. Home: 755 N 350 W American Fork UT 84003-1160

BARNES, MICHAEL KEITH, transit marketing executive; b. N.Y.C., Apr. 22, 1942; s. Arthur M. and Roberta (Keith) B.; m. Ann T. Thomas, Feb. 11, 1967; children: Thomas, David. BA, U. Iowa, 1965, MA, 1969. Writer, editor, broadcaster Stas. KXIC and WSUI, Iowa City, Iowa, 1964-67; sr. publicist/account exec. Gen. Elec. Co., Chgo., 1970-73; news bureau mgr. So. Calif. Rapid Transit Dist., L.A., 1973-81, publ. and video programming mgr., 1983—; mktg. mgr. Orange County Transit Dist., Garden Grove, Calif., 1981-83; instr. reporting U. So. Calif., 1975-78. Active AFS, 1990—.With U.S. Army, 1967-69. Recipient 1st Pl award Am. Pub. Transit Assn., 1992. Republican. Office: MTA Dept 4400 425 S Main St Los Angeles CA 90013-1393

BARNES, PETER WILLIAM, marine geologist; b. Rochester, N.Y., Oct. 5, 1939; s. Arthur and Sidney Alice (Rosen) B.; m. Judith Carol Levine, Feb. 10, 1960 (div. 1980); children: David Michael, Kenneth Andrew, Deborah Ann, Laura Nicole; m. Nicole Summer, Oct. 27, 1984. BS, Antioch Coll., Yellow Springs, Ohio, 1962; PhD, U. So. Calif., 1970. Rsch. assoc. U. So. Calif., L.A., 1967-69; geologist U.S. Geol. Survey, Menlo Park, Calif., 1970—; cons./advisor fed., state and pvt. agencies. Rsch. on polar geologic processes, global change, coastal erosion (Alaska, Antartica, Gt. Lakes), ice rafting; expedition leader, sci. numerous polar studies. Vol. Alzheimers Assn., Palo Alto, Calif., 1990—. Alan Hancock fellow U. So. Calif., L.A., 1967-68. Mem. AAAS, Geol. Soc. Am., Soc. Econ. Mineralogists & Paleontologists, Union of Concerned Scientists, Electric Auto Assn., Sigma Xi. Office: US Geol Survey MS 999 345 Middlefield Rd Menlo Park CA 94025-3591

BARNES, RAYMOND EDWARD, fire department official; b. Denver, Colo., May 1, 1950; s. Carroll E. and Margaret A. (Minckler) B.; m. Katherine Michele Sanchez, Jan. 3, 1970; 1 child, Tamara Adrienne. BS in Aerospace Tech., Bus., Edn., Met. State Coll., 1971; postgrad., Red Rocks C.C., 1974-75, U. No. Colo., 1976; grad. exec. fire officer program, Nat. Fire Acad., 1990; MPA, U. Colo., 1991. With City of Aurora (Colo.) Fire Dept., 1971—, paramedic and rescue technician, 1976-79, lt., 1979-82, capt., 1982-85, battalion chief, suppression, 1985-87, dir. tng., 1987-91, fire chief, 1991—; adj. instr. Nat. Fire Acad., Md., 1987—; co-dir. Rocky Mountain Fire Acad.; metro co-chair Region VIII Tng. Resources and Data Exch. Active Aurora Gang Task Force; past committeeman, del. to county, state polit. assemblies;. Mem. Internat. Assn. Fire Chiefs, Internat. Assn. Metro Fire Chiefs, Internat. Soc. Fire Svc. Instrs., Internat. Assn. Firefighters (occupational safety and health com.), Soc. Nat. Fire Acad. Instrs., Soc. Exec. Fire Officers, Fire Dept. Safety Officers Orgn., State Fire Chiefs, Denver Metro Fire Chiefs, Aurora C. of C. (bd. dirs. leadership forum), Homeowners Assn. (past pres. bd. dirs.). Home: 10276 S Horizon View Dr Morrison CO 80465 Office: City of Aurora Fire Dept 1470 S Havana St Aurora CO 80012

BARNES, ROBERT E., bank executive; b. 1933. BA, Princeton U., 1955; grad., Am. Grad. Sch. of Internat. Mgmt., 1959. V.p. internat. dept. Chase Manhattan Bank, 1961-73; pres. Alaska State Bank, Anchorage, 1973-77; sr. exec. v.p. Bank of West, 1977-84; with Bay View Fed. Savings Bank, 1984-85, pres., CEO, 1985—; pres. Bay View Capital Corp., San Mateo, Calif., 1989—. Capt. USAF, 1956-58. Office: Bay View Capital Corp 2121 S El Camino Real San Mateo CA 94403*

BARNES, ROBERT HENRY, health facility administrator, psychiatrist; b. Worcester, Mass., Nov. 4, 1921; s. Harry Elmer and Grace (Stone) B.; m. Lois Starbuck, June, 1953 (div. 1967); m. Beverly Feingold, Sept. 30, 1967; children: Barton G., Mark G., Robin L. BS, Union Coll., 1943; MD, Duke U., 1948. Diplomate Am. Bd. Psychiatry and Neurology. Asst. prof. Duke U., Durham, N.C., 1953-56; assoc. clin. prof. U. Mo., Columbia, 1957-68; prof. Med. Sch. U. Tex., San Antonio, 1968-72; chief of staff, med. dir. St. Luke's Behavioral Ctr., Phoenix, 1972-82; pvt. practice Phoenix, 1974—; med. dir. Willow Creek Hosp., Scottsdale, Ariz., 1989-92; psychiat. cons. CODAMA, Phoenix, 1992—; exec. dir. Greater Kansas City (Mo.) Mental Health Found., 1958-68; med. dir. St. Luke's Pain Ctr., Phoenix, 1977-87; mem., chair Epidemiol. Study Sect. NIMH, Bethesda, Md., 1962-72; and others. Contbr. numerous articles to profl. jours. Fellow APA (life); mem. AMA, Am. Holistic Med. Soc. (founding mem. 1975), Am. Psychiat. Assn. (pres. we. Mo. chpt. 1962-63). Home: 5401 E Desert Jewel Dr Paradise Vly AZ 85253-2501 Office: CODAMA 1700 N 7th Ave Ste 250 Phoenix AZ 85007

BARNES, THOMAS AARON, SR., life and health insurance broker; b. Toledo, June 4, 1928; s. Paul Nash and Thelma Morita (Williams) B.; m. Margaret Ellen Muth, Dec. 26, 1951; 1 child, Thomas Aaron Jr. Grad. high sch., Bellefontaine, Ohio. Licensed life and health ins. agent, Ariz. Enlisted U.S. Army, 1946; advanced to maj. USAFR, 1968—; ret. maj. USAF, 1988; reporter Dun and Bradstreet, Inc., Dayton, Ohio, 1956-67; agent N.Y. Life Ins., Yuma, Ariz., 1968-73; owner Somerton (Ariz.) Trading Post, 1978-88; owner, mgr., insurance broker Tom Barnes & Assocs., Yuma, Somerton, 1973—. Mayor Somerton City Council, 1981-84; chmn. community action bd. Western Ariz. Council Govts., Yuma, 1978-84, 87-93; mem. The Salvation Army Adv. Bd., Yuma, 1974-93; co-chmn. Rep. Cen. Com., Yuma County, 1983-84. Recipient Montgomery Humanitarian award Ariz. State Council For Sr. Citizens, 1980, Citation For Outstanding Svc. Yuma Union High Sch. Dist., 1980; named to Life Membership Rep. Presdl. Task Force, 1988. Mem. VFW (post commdr. 1976-77), Am. Legion (Ariz. dist. comdr. 1987-88, Legionaire of the Yr., 1991-92), Masons, Shriners. Republican. Methodist. Home: 1449 W Jennifer Ln Yuma AZ 85365-9310

BARNES, VALERIE ELIZABETH, human factors psychologist; b. Everett, Wash., June 26, 1954; d. Robert John and Mona Elizabeth (Anderson) B.; children: Free, Kathryn, Stosh. BA, Whitman Coll., 1977; MS, U. Wash., 1982, PhD, 1985. Scientist Battelle HARC, Seattle, 1985-89, mgr., 1989-91; pres. Performance Safety & Health Assocs., Inc., Seattle, 1991—; cons. U.S. NRC, Rockville, Md., 1982—, U.S. Dept. Energy, Germantown, Md., 1989—. Author: Palo Verde Procedures Handbook, 1990 (Soc. for Tech. Comm. award 1991), Procedure Writing Principles and Practices, 1993; contbr. articles to profl. jours. Mem. Human Factors Soc., Judgment & Decision Making Soc. Home: 4767 NE 178th St Seattle WA 98155

BARNES, WILLIAM ANDERSON, real estate investor, developer; b. Cin., Mar. 11, 1944; s. Frederick Walter and Catherine Gardner (Bowden) B.; m. Sara Winkler, Dec. 13, 1980; children: Hanne, Tucker, Charlie. BA, Yale U., 1966; MBA, Harvard U., 1970. Adminstrv. asst. to pres. Boise Cascade Corp., Palo Alto, Calif., 1970-71; project gen. mgr. Boise Cascade Corp., Incline Village, Nev., 1971-73; sr. devel. dir. The Rouse Co., Columbia, Md., 1973-76; exec. dir. Pa. Ave. Devel. Corp., Washington, 1977-82; mng. dir. Edward Plant Co., San Francisco, 1982-87; pres. Broadacre Pacific Corp., San Francisco, 1987—; guest lectr. Harvard Bus. Sch., Cambridge, Mass.; faculty mem. Profl. Devel. Seminar; panelist Urban Land Inst; lectr. Smithsonian Instn. Trustee Navy Meml. Found., Brichard Properties Trust, Braun Programs Inc., Columbia Interfaith Housing Corp., 1974-76; mem. U.S./USSR Trade Mission, 1975, Bay Area Coun. Housing Action Task Force, 1983-85, Mill Valley City Gen. Plan Com.; treas. Yale U. Class of 1966. Recipient White House fellowship, Pres. of U.S., Washington, 1976, Presidential Design award, Pres. of U.S., 1988. Office: Broadacre Pacific Co Ste 300 60 E Sir Francis Drake Blvd Larkspur CA 94939-1714

BARNET, ROBERT JOSEPH, cardiologist; b. Port Huron, Mich., Apr. 27, 1929; s. John A. and Ruth Elizabeth (Wittliff) B.; m. Helen Kresoja, Dec. 8, 1969; children: Benedict, Maria, Antonia, Peter, Elizabeth, Rebecca, Christina, Jacqueline, Ann. Student, Port Huron Jr. Coll., summers 1947, 49; MD, Loyola U., Chgo., 1951; BS in Chemistry magna cum laude, U. Notre Dame, 1954; MA in History, U. of Nev., 1986; MA in Philosophy, U. Notre Dame, 1988. Diplomate: Nat. Bd. Med. Examiners, Am. Bd. Internal Medicine.; licensed physician Calif., Nev. Med. intern Boston City Hosp., 1954-55; rotating intern Mercy Hosp., Chgo., 1955; asst. resident in medicine Boston City Hosp., 1958-59; clin. and research fellow in cardiology Children's Med. Center and House of the Good Samaritan, Boston, 1959-60; cons. fellow in rheumatic fever pediatric service Boston City Hosp., 1959-60, Mass. State Rheumatic Fever Clinic, 1959-60; research fellow in pediatrics Harvard U., Boston, 1959-60; clin. fellow in cardiology Mass. Meml. Hosps., Boston, 1960-61; physician-in-charge St. Francis Mission Hosp., Solwezi, No. Rhodesia, 1961-62; vis. physician Solwezi Boma Rural Hosp., No. Rhodesia, 1961-62; dir. clinics, assoc. in medicine Stritch Sch. Medicine, Loyola U., Chgo., 1962-65; physician-in-charge Cardiac Clinic, Loyola U., Chgo., Fantus Outpatient dept. Cook County Hosp., Chgo., 1962-65, Hypertension Clinic, Fantus Outpatient dept. Cook County Hosp., 1962-65; lectr. in electrocardiography and cardiology Loyola U., Chgo., 1962-65; assoc. attending physician dept. medicine Cook County Hosp., 1962-63, attending physician, 1963-65; practice medicine specializing in cardiology Reno, 1965-87; med. staff Washoe Med. Center, 1965—, St. Mary's Hosp., 1965—; assoc. clin. prof. cardiology U. Nev.; also assoc. dir. Lab. Environ. Patho-Physiology, Desert Research Inst., U. Nev., Reno, 1965-68; dir. Cardiac Care unit Washoe Med. Center, 1965-83, exec. com., 1967-71, 73-77, vice chief dept. medicine, 1969, chief, 1970-71, 78, chief dept. emergency services, 1973-77; cons. cardiology Disability Determination unit State of Nev., 1966-87, Crippled Children's Svc., 1966-76; cons. in cardiology Reno VA Hosp., 1967-80; asst. clin. prof. med. edn. U. Utah, 1968-71; cons. Churchill Pub. Hosp., Fallon, Nev., 1969-87, Pershing Gen. Hosp., Lovelock, Nev., 1969-87, clin. assoc. U. Nev., Reno, 1971-72, assoc. clin. prof. medicine, 1973-77, prof., 1978—; vis. scholar U. Notre Dame, 1989-90. Contbr. articles to med. jours. Served with U.S. Army, 1955-58. Recipient Clin. Faculty Honor award for outstanding tchr. Loyola U., 1963-64. Fellow A.C.P. (bd. govs. 1980-85), Am. Coll. Cardiology (bd. govs. 1974-77), Am. Coll. Chest Physicians; mem. Nev., Washoe County med. socs., Am. Fedn. Clin. Research, Nev. Heart Assn. (bd. dirs., exec. com., pres. 1974-75). Home: 166 Greenridge Dr Reno NV 89509-3927

BARNETT, DAVID HUGHES, software engineer; b. Rockville Centre, N.Y., Oct. 9, 1947; s. Paul Wilson Jr. and Patricia (Hughes) B.; m. Rosemary Friday, July 9, 1979 (div. 1983). BA, Drew U., 1970. Program analyst So. Nev. Drug Abuse Coun., Las Vegas, 1974-75; project supr. Treatment Alternatives to Street Crime, Las Vegas, 1975-78; sr. project assoc. Helix Group, Berkeley, Calif., 1978-81; cons. Pacific Inst. for Rsch. and Evaluation, Berkeley, 1979-80; rsch. tech. Sonoma State U., Rohnert Park, Calif., 1981-82; system mgr. Database Minicomputers, San Francisco, 1982-84; cons. systems programmer Wells Fargo Bank, San Francisco, 1984-89; lead systems programmer Kaiser Permanente, Walnut Creek, Calif., 1989—. Contbr. articles to profl. jours. Mem. Info. Systems Security Assn., Am. Soc. for Quality Control.

BARNEY, KLINE PORTER, JR., engineering company executive, consultant; b. Dec. 16, 1934; s. Kline Porter and Doris (Nielsen) B.; m. Cheryl Kathleen Taylor, June 14, 1957; children: Peter, Suzanne, Cathleen, Patrick, Andrew. BS, U. Utah, 1957; MPA, San Diego State U , 1971. Registered profl. engr., 14 states. Asst. engr. Fallbrook (Calif.) Pub. Utility Dist., 1960-63; pres. Engring. Sci., Inc., Arcadia, Calif., 1963-85, Parsons Mcpl. Svcs., Inc., Pasadena, Calif., 1985-89; sr. v.p. Engrings. Sci., Inc., Pasadena, 1989—; presenter on field of privatization, 1983—; environ. cons. Contbr. articles to profl. jours. Mem. exec. bd. San Gabriel coun. Boy Scouts Am., 1981—. Capt. USMC, 1957-60. Mem. ASCE, NSPE, Am. Acad. Environ. Engrs. (diplomate), Am. Pub. Works Assn., Am. Waterworks Assn., Water Environ. Fedn., Cons. Engrs. Assn. Calif., Assn. Calif. Water Agys. (assoc.), L.A. C. of C. (water resources com.), Nat. Water Resources Assn., Watereuse, Tau Beta Pi, Chi Epsilon, Phi Eta Sigma. Republican. Mem. LDS Ch. Home: Po Box 3808 Arcadia CA 91066-3808 Office: Engring Sci Inc 100 W Walnut St Pasadena CA 91124

BARNHART, DAVID ALLAN, aerospace engineer; b. Scranton, Pa., June 26, 1961; s. Raymond Allan and Virginia Lynn (Moorehead) B. BS, Boston U., 1984; MS, Va. Poly. Inst. and State U., 1987. Resident asst. Boston U., 1982-84; propr. Epoch Internat., Blacksburg, Va., 1985-87; mgr. Computer Ctr. Va. Poly. Inst. and State U., Blacksburg, 1986-87; chief spacecraft design br. USAF space expts. Phillips Lab., Edwards, Calif., 1987—; spacecraft systems engring. rep. to Russia, Phillips Lab.-Strategic Def. Inst. Office, Washington, 1991—. Contbr. articles to profl. jours.; author computer programs Epoch, System XV. Pilot Am. Med. Flight Team, Van Nuys, Calif., 1990—; 1st lt. Kern County Search and Rescue, Rosamond, 1990—. Mem. AIAA, Nat. Assn. for Underwater Instrs.

BARNHILL, ROBERT E., university administrator, educator; b. Lawrence, Kans., Oct. 31, 1939; s. Ellis B. and Agnes L. (Ruskin) B.; m. Marigold L. Linton, Feb. 12, 1983; children: John E., Margaret S. BA with highest distinction, U. Kans., 1961; MA with honors, U. Wis., 1962, PhD, 1964. Asst. prof. math. U. Utah, Salt Lake City, 1964-67, assoc. prof., 1967-71, prof., 1971-86, adj. prof. computer sci., 1973-76, prof. computer sci., 1976-86; prof., chmn. dept. computer sci. Ariz. State U., Tempe, 1986-91, interim v.p. for rsch., 1991-93, v.p. for rsch., 1993—; vis. asst. prof. applied math. Brown U., Providence, 1966-67; assoc. rsch. prof. applied sci. George Washington U., 1971; Sci. Rsch. Coun. sr. vis. fellow Uxbridge (U.K.) U., 1971-72, Dundee (Scotland) U., 1974-75, Brunel U., Middlesex, U.K., 1979-80; cons. Hitachi Software Engring., 1977-78, U.S. Army Rsch. Office, Research Triangle Park, N.C., 1979-80, Sandia Labs., Livermore, Calif., 1979-80, Control Data Corp., Mpls., 1984-86, Mercedes, 1988, Environ. Systems Rsch., 1989-91, numerous others. Co-editor: Surfaces in Computer Aided Geometric Design, 1985; editor spl. issue Rocky Mountain Jour. Math., 1984; contbr. articles to profl. jours. Nat. Merit and Summerfield scholar, 1957-61; NSF and Woodrow Wilson fellow, 1961-62; U.S. Army Math. Rsch. Ctr. fellow, 1962-64. Mem. Soc. Indsl. and Applied Math. (chmn.), Assn. for Computing Machinery, Phi Beta Kappa, Sigma Xi. Office: Ariz State U Vice Pres for Rsch Tempe AZ 85287-2703

BARNUM, PAUL FREDERICK, communications manager; b. Portland, Oreg., Sept. 28, 1951; s. Fred L. and Pat C. (Aasen) B.; m. Sibyl M. Jones, Oct. 19, 1974; children: Lisa, Andrea, Claire. BS in English, U. Oreg., 1975, MA in Journalism, 1979. Dir. pub. info. Clatsop C.C., Astoria, Oreg., 1977-87; editor pub. affairs & devel. U. Oreg., Eugene, 1987-89; account exec. Cawood Comm., Eugene, 1989-90, dir. pub. rels., 1990-91; comm. mgr. Weyerhaeuser Co., Springfield, Oreg., 1991—. Editor: Steelheading for the Simple-Minded, 1987, Salmon Fishing for the Simple-Minded, 1988. Recipient Best Pub. Rels. Strategy award Am. Mktg. Assn. S.W. chpt., 1990, Spotlight award Columbia River chpt. Pub. Rels. Soc. Am., 1990, 91, Grand award & Apex awards for Publ. Excellence, 1991. Mem. U. Oreg. Alumni Assn. (v.p. comm. 1988-89), Rotary (bd. dirs. Eugene Delta club 1991-93). Republican. Mem. Nazarene Ch. Home: 658 Edgemont Way Springfield OR 97477 Office: Weyerhaeuser Co PO Box 275 Springfield OR 97477

BARNUM, WILLIAM LAIRD, pedodontist; b. Medford, Oreg., Nov. 12, 1916; s. William Henry and Jessie Amelia (Eifert) B.; m. Amy B. Elliott, June 20, 1937; children: William Laird, Robert Elliott. D.M.D., U. Oreg., 1940; postgrad. in Pedodontics, Coll. Physicians and Surgeons, San Francisco, 1946. Gen. practice dentistry Portland, Oreg., 1940-45; practice specializing in pedodontics Portland, 1945-64, Medford, 1964-80; mem. dental staff Rogue Valley Meml. Hosp., 1964-79; dir. Dental Health Program, Portland Pub. Schs., 1946-64; instr. pedodontics and dental hygiene U. Oreg. Dental Sch., Portland, 1945-60. Editor alumni publ. The Caementum, 1947-49. Pres. Adminstrs. and Suprs. Assn. for Portland Pub. Schs., 1958-59; chmn. health div. Portland Community Council, 1961-62. Fellow Internat. Coll. Dentists, Am. Coll. Dentists; mem. ADA (chmn. coun. on dental journalism 1952-56), Am. Soc. Dentistry for Children (pres. Oreg. unit 1952-53), Oreg. Dental Soc. (editor Oreg. Dental Jour. 1949-53), So. Oreg. Dental Soc. (pres. 1969-70), Am. Dental Interfraternity Coun. (pres. 1971-72, exec. sec. 1989-92), So. Oreg. Hist. Soc. (trustee 1985-87), Xi Psi Phi (supreme pres. 1965-67, supreme sec.-treas. 1970-91, editor Quar. 1953-58), Masons. Republican. Unitarian. Home: 245 Yale Dr Medford OR 97504-9736 Office: 832 E Main St # 13 Medford OR 97504-7153

BARNWELL, DAVID RAY, financial and computer systems analyst, computer programmer; b. Amarillo, Tex., Sept. 9, 1953; s. Jasper Clarence and Mary Evelyn (King) B.; m. Maria Milagrosa Bellido, July 7, 1975; 1 child, Miriam Louise. Student Army and Navy Acad., Carlsbad, Calif., 1971; AA in Bus. Adminstrn., Cerritos Coll., Norwalk, Calif., 1979, AA in Econs., 1986; BSBA, U. Redlands, 1981; MBA, 1990. tutor Cerritos Coll., 1977-79; adjuster Western Thrift and Loan Assn., Long Beach, Calif., 1978-80; prodn. cost analyst, space shuttle orbiter div. Rockwell Internat., Downey, Calif., 1980-85; mem. space shuttle speaker's bur., 1981-88, sr. cost analyst space shuttle orbiter div., 1985-86, sr. computer systems analyst, 1986-88, computer systems devel. specialist, 1988-92; sr. ops. bus. analyst of appraisal ops., Home Savings Am., Irwindale, Calif., 1993—; founder, pres. Bus. Electronics, 1985; . With USMC, 1970-76. Recipient First Shuttle Flight Achievement award, NASA, 1981; Alfred North Whitehead Leadership Soc. fellow U. Redlands (pres. 1992-93). Mem. AIAA, 1st Marine Div. Assn., Assn. for Computing Machinery, Am. Mgmt. Assn., Am. Legion, Mensa, Am. Philatelic Soc. Home: 8031 De Vries Ln La Palma CA 90623-2031 Office: Home Savings Am 4900 Rivergrade Rd Irwindale CA 91706

BAROFF, LYNN ELLIOTT, management consultant; b. Oklahoma City, Feb. 22, 1949; s. Phillip Dee and Estelle Claire (Reiss) B.; m. Beverly Ann Wolf, Mar. 21, 1970 (div. Dec. 1978); m. Janice Kazue Obita, Apr. 7, 1979; children: David Masanori, Steven Hideaki. BA in Mass Communications, Mundelein Coll., 1971. Producer, dir. Sta. WCIU-TV, Chgo., 1970-76; prodn. mgr. Sta. KWHY-TV, L.A., 1976-79; gen. mgr. Baroff Cons. Group, Inc., Santa Monica, Calif., 1979—; adj. prof. U. So. Calif. Internat. Tng. Trainers, L.A., 1985, 86, Antioch U. Grad. Sch., L.A., 1989—. Author poetry. Mem. adv. com. L.A. Valley Coll., 1977, Calif. State U., L.A., 1979-80, Antioch U., 1989—; v.p. Temple Shalom, West Covina, Calif. Recipient Honor Resolution, L.A. City Coun., 1976. Mem. Am. Soc. for Tng. and Devel. (v.p. 1983, pres. 1984, creator and developer HR 2000 conf. 1990), L.A. Orgn. Devel. Network, Delta Kappa Epsilon. Office: 3108 S Colima Rd # 432 Hacienda Heights CA 91745

BARON, MYRNA, state official; b. N.Y.C., Dec. 29, 1934; d. Joseph and Rose (Siegel) Orszag; m. Edmund Baron, June 10, 1956; children: Jeffrey, David. BA, Adelphi U., 1955. Program dir. B'nai B'rith Women, N.Y.C., 1975-78; project dir. CUNY, 1978-81; adminstr. N.Y.C. Bd. Edn., Bklyn., 1981-82; exec. dir. Reading Reform Found., N.Y.C., 1982-83; cons. Baron Assocs., Scottsdale, Ariz., 1983-85; evaluation specialist Ariz. Dept. Econ. Security, Phoenix, 1985-87, mgr. program devel. Aging and Adult Adminstrn., 1987—; mem. Ariz. Coalition on Aging, Phoenix, 1988—. Bd. dirs., v.p. women's div. Jewish Fedn. Greater Phoenix, 1987-89; bd. dirs. Ctr. Developing Older Adult Resources, 1988-89, v.p. 1989-90; mem. state Coun. Independent Living; bd. dirs., v.p. Ariz. Living Treasures Awards, 1988—. Mem. Am. Soc. on Aging, Nat. Coun. on Aging, Am. Evaluation Assn., Am. Pub. Welfare Assn., Jewish Bus. and Profl. Women (Pres. 1987-89), LWV (bd. dirs. N.Y.C. 1971-76, treas. Ariz. 1984—), Alzheimer's Assn. (bd. dirs. 1990—). Home: 5101 N Casa Blanca Dr Paradise Vly AZ 85253-6986 Office: Ariz Dept Econ Security Aging and Adult Adminstrn 1789 W Jefferson St # 950A Phoenix AZ 85007-3202

BARON, ROBERT CHARLES, publishing executive; b. L.A., Jan. 26, 1934; s. Leo Francis and Marietta (Schulze) B.; m. Faye Helen Rogers, Jan. 28, 1961 (div. 1984); m. Charlotte Rose Persinger, Nov. 29, 1986; stepchildren: Brett, Kristen. BS in Physics, St. Joseph's Coll., 1956. Registered profl. engr., Mass. Engr. RCA, Camden, N.J., 1955-57, Computer Control Co., Framingham, Mass., 1959-61; program mgr. Mariner II and IV space computers Computer Control Co., Framingham, 1961-65, engring. mgr., 1965-69; worldwide systems mgr. Honeywell Minicomputer, Framingham, 1970-71; founder, pres., CEO Prime Computer, Framingham, 1971-75; pvt. practice Boston, 1976-83; founder and pres. Fulcrum Pub., Golden, Colo., 1984—; dir. Prime Computer, Framingham, Mass., 1971-75, Alling-Lender, Cheshire, Conn.,1979-86, Starwood Pub., Washington, 1991—, Oxion, Hugoton, Kans., 1988—, FulcrumPub., Golden, Colo., 1984—. Author: (books) Digital Logic and Computer Operations, 1966, Micropower Electronics, 1970; editor (books) The Garden and Farm Books of Thomas Jefferson, 1987, Soul of America: Documenting our Past 1492-1974, 1989. Trustee Lincoln Filene Ctr., Tufts U., Medford, Mass., 1982-84; vice chmn. bd. dirs., Mass. Audubon Soc., Lincoln, 1980-85; dir. Rocky Mountain Women's Inst., Denver, 1987-90; v.p. and dir. Denver Pub. Libr. Friends Found., 1989—. Mem. Am. Antiquarian Soc., Internat. Wilderness Leadership Found., Thoreau Soc.,Mass. Hist. Soc. Office: Fulcrum Publishing 350 Indiana St #350 Golden CO 80401

BARR, A(LLAN) RALPH, retired entomologist; b. Ft. Worth, Aug. 13, 1926; s. William Christopher and Annie Lottie (Rose) B.; m. Sylvia Engel Weinstien, May 31, 1952. BSc, So. Meth. U., 1948; ScD, Johns Hopkins U., 1952. Instr. U. Minn., Mpls., 1952-55; asst. prof. U. Kans., Lawrence, 1955-58; supr. vector rsch. Calif. Dept. Pub. Health, Fresno, 1958-65; rsch. specialist II Sch. Pub. Health U. Calif., Berkeley, 1965-66, assoc. entomologist Sch. Pub. Health, 1966-67; from assoc. prof. to prof. emeritus UCLA, 1967—; vis. prof. faculty medicine U. Singapore, 1962-63; vis. scientist Inst. for Med. Rsch., Kuala Lumpur, Malaysia, 1975; vis. lectr. U. Philippines, Manila, 1979; cons. WHO, Geneva, 1964, 79-81, 90, NIH, Washington, 1973-77, 83, Walter Reed Army Inst. Rsch., Washington, 1977-81; mem. panel U.S.-Japan Coop. Med. Sci. Program, Washington, 1969-72; site visit team mem. Internat. Devel. Rsch. Ctr., Ottawa, Ont., Can., 1975. Author: Mosquitoes of Minnesota, 1958. With USN, 1944-46. Rsch. grantee NIH, 1968-86, Nat. Sci. Coun. Republic of China, 1983. Fellow Royal Entomol. Soc. London; mem. AAUP, Am. Soc. Tropical Medicine and Hygiene, Am. Com. of Med. Entomology (exec. com. 1985-87, chair 1992), Am. Mosquito Control Assn. (Meritorious Svc. award 1981, mem. various coms.), Entomol. Soc. Am. (mem. various coms. 1952-86, 88-92), Soc. Vector Ecology. Home: 3905 Malibu Vista Dr Malibu CA 90265 Office: U Calif Dept Epidemiology 405 Hilgard Ave Los Angeles CA 90024

BARR, JOHN TILMAN, IV, research and development executive; b. Newport, Ark., June 27, 1948; s. John Tilman III and Dorothy Lee (Cook) B.; m. Barbara Jane Hastreiter, Mar. 20, 1971; children: Jennifer Rebecca, Kathleen Marie. BSEE, Ga. Inst. Tech., 1971; MSEE, Stanford U., 1974, MS Engring. Mgmt., 1982. With Hewlett Packard, Palo Alto, Santa Rosa, Calif., 1971-81; R & D project mgr. Hewlett Packard, Santa Rosa, Calif., 1981-88, R & D program mgr., 1988-92, R & D sect. mgr., 1992—. Contbr. tech. articles, to profl. jours.; patentee in field. Active Gen. Plan Adv. Com., Santa Rosa, 1989. Mem. IEEE (sr., svc. award Redwood Subsect. 1985), Automatic RF Techniques Group (pres. 1987-89, chair 28th Conf. 1986, 36th Conf. 1990, Svc. award 1986, Best Paper award 1990, Disting. Svc. award 1990). Office: Hewlett Packard 1400 Fountain Grove Pky Santa Rosa CA 95403-1738

BARRAGAN, CHARLES J., III, human resources specialist; b. San Fernando, Calif., Nov. 6, 1958; s. Charles J. and Teresa (Lara) B. BA in Govt., U. San Francisco, 1980; postgrad., Hastings Coll. Law, 1981-85. Human resources specialist Feldman, Waldman & Kline, San Francisco, 1987—. Contbr. Bi Any Other Name, 1991, Lesbian and Gay Marriage, 1992. Writer, activist Amnesty Internat., San Francisco, 1984—. Democrat. Roman Catholic. Home: 23 Liberty St San Francisco CA 94110-2318 Office: Feldman Waldman & Kline 235 Montgomery St Ste 2700 San Francisco CA 94104-3160

BARRASS, STANLEY RUSSELL, electrical contractor; b. Bishop, Calif., Dec. 17, 1926; s. Russell Onslow and Iris Eula (Ayres) B.; m. Katherine Anne Spanyers, Feb. 14, 1954; children: Nancy Kathleen, Janet Gayle Garcia, Donna Elizabeth Hecker, Laurie Anne Adams. Tech. Deg., Calif. Poly., 1949; BSEE, Heald Engring., San Francisco, 1953. Elec. estimator ETS Hokin & Galvin, San Francisco, 1953-54, Coopman Elec., San Francisco, 1954-62; elec. contr. Northgate Elec., San Rafael, Calif., 1962-85, NBC Ventures, San Rafael, Calif., 1985-90; elec. cons. San Rafael, Calif., 1990—. Dir. Marin Bldrs. Exch., San Rafael, Calif., 1973-79, State of Calif. Apprenticeship Coun., Santa Rosa, 1964-73; elder, deacon Christ Presbyn. Ch., 1959—. Recipient Cert. of Meritorious Svc. State of Calif. Apprentice Coun., 1973. Mem. Terra Linda Rotary (pres. 1987-88, Rotarian of Yr. 1982-83, 85-86). Home: 25 Coast Oak Way San Rafael CA 94903

BARRATT, THOMAS KEATING, computer consultant; b. Wilcox, Pa., Sept. 11, 1927; s. Stanley and Margaret (Keating) B.; m. Joan Clare Anderson, Dec. 23, 1950; children: Thomas Whitford, Jennifer Lee. BS in Edn., Clarion State Coll., 1950; MEd, Pa. State U., 1954, EdD, 1964. Tchr. Coalport (Pa.) Schs., 1950-52; tchr., adminstr. Warren (Pa.) Pub. Schs., 1952-57; supt. of schs. Sheffield (Pa.) Area Schs., 1957-63; supt. Warren County Sch. Dist., 1966-69; prof. Edinboro (Pa.) State Coll., 1969-72; asst. supt. Gateway Schs., Monroeville, Pa., 1972-75; supt. Crawford Cen. Sch. Dist., Meadville, Pa., 1975-86; CEO GSG, 1990—; ptnr. Computer Based Svcs./Sales, Sun City, Ariz., 1992—; asst. to T.M. Cave Creek, Ariz., 1992—; participant summer seminar NEH, 1975, 81, 86; pres. Pa. Assn. Sch. Adminstrs., 1984-85, Pa. Assn. Dist. Supts., 1966-68; chmn. evaluation com. Middle State Assn. Schs. and Colls., 1966-80; pres. Com. on Higher Edn., Warren, 1969. Pres. Rotary Club, Sheffield, 1959, Edinboro, 1972, Meadville, 1979; bd. dirs. Libr. Bds. Sheffield and Meadville. I/D/E/A fellow Kettering Found. Mem. NEA (life), Pa. Assn. Ret. Sch. Employees (life), Am. Legion, VFW, Masons. Home: 10832 W Saratoga Cir Sun City AZ 85351-2140 Office: Computer Based Svcs/Sales PO Box 232 Sun City AZ 85372

BARRETO, CHARLTON BODENBERG, reliability engineer; b. Oakland, Calif., July 4, 1968; s. Dennis Lourenço and Amélia Roters (Bodenberg) B.; m. Maria Carmén Calara, May 16, 1992. BS in Stats., U. Calif., Berkeley, 1990, BS in Applied Math., 1990, BSBA, 1990. Registered profl. engr., Calif.; cert. quality engr., reliability engr. Intern in reliability engring. Hewlett-Packard, Palo Alto, Calif., 1987, Amdahl Corp., Sunnyvale, Calif., 1988, ESL Engring. Svcs., Inc., Martinez, Calif., 1989; assoc. cons. Coopers & Lybrand EC/RND Cons., San Francisco, 1990-92; sr. reliability engr. engring. div. Signetics Corp., Fremont, Calif., 1992—. Contbr. rsch. articles to profl. publs. Vol. Washington Hosp., Fremont, 1984-85, Big Bros., Fremont, 1988—. Golden Key scholar, 1986-90. Mem. IEEE, Am. Statis. Assn., Am. Soc. Quality Control, Inst. Math. Stats., Am. Mgmt. Assn., Japan Soc. No. Calif., Asian Bus. League, Beta Gamma Sigma. Home: 4419 Corto Monterey Union City CA 94587

BARRETT, BARBARA MCCONNELL, lawyer; b. Indiana County, Pa., Dec. 26, 1950; d. Robert Harvey and Betty (Dornheim) McC.; m. Craig R. Barrett, Jan. 19, 1985. BS, Ariz. State U., 1972, MPA, 1975, JD, 1978. Bar: Ariz. 1978, U.S. Dist. Ct. Ariz. 1979, U.S. Supreme Ct. Ariz. 1979. Atty. The Dial Corp., Phoenix, 1976-80; assoc. gen. counsel, asst. sec. Southwest Forest Industries, Inc., Phoenix, 1980-82; exec. asst. to chmn. CAB, Washington, 1982-83, mem., 1983-84, vice chmn., 1984-85; ptnr. Evans, Kitchel & Jenckes, P.C., Phoenix, 1985-88, 1989; dep. adminstr. FAA, Washington, 1988-89; pvt. practice internat. bus. and aviation law Paradise Valley, Ariz., 1989—; bd. dirs. Samaritan Health System, 1993—; mem. exec. com., vice chair career opportunities Subcom. U.S. Dept. Def., 1989-93; mem. adv. com. Gov.'s Regional Airport, Pres.'s Adv. Com. on Trade Negotiations; mem. Adminstrv. Con. U.S., 1982-85; chmn. Transp. Cluster Gov.'s Strategic Partnership for Econ. Devel., 1992—; mem. Ariz. Disease Control Rsch. Commn.; v.p. East Valley Partnership, 1992, Internat. Women's Forum, 1991—; mem. Phoenix Com. on Fgn. Rels., 1979—, Thunderbird Internat. Symposium Steering Com., 1992—. Chmn. Ariz. Dist. Export Coun., 1985-92, Ronald W. Reagan Scholarship Program, 1987-90, World Trade Ctr. Ariz., 1992—, Airshow Can. Symposium, 1989, 91; bd. dirs. Nat. Air and Space Mus. Smithsonian Inst., 1988-89, Palms Clinic & Hosp. Corp., 1985—; trustee Am. Grad. Sch. Internat. Mgmt., Glendale, Ariz., Embry-Riddle Aeronaut. U., Prescott, Ariz., Daytona Beach, Fla.; pres. World Affairs Ariz., 1987-88; named to Ariz. State U. Coll. Pub. Programs Hall of Fame, 1989; vice chmn. Kid's Voting, 1989—. Named Woman of Yr. Ariz. State U., 1971; Dubois scholar, 1977; recipient Disting. Achievement award Ariz. State U., 1987, Woman Who Made A Difference award Internat. Women's Forum, 1988. Mem. Am. Mgmt. Assn. (trustee, mem. exec. com.), Ariz. State Univ. Law Soc. (bd. govs. 1991—), Ariz. State Univ. Found., Ariz. Women in Internat. Trade (bd. dirs., mem. exec. com. 1992—), Plaza Club (bd. govs., mem. exec. com. 1989—), Phoenix C. of C. (bd. dirs. 1989—).

BARRETT, BRUCE RICHARD, physics educator; b. Kansas City, Kans., Aug. 19, 1939; s. Buford Russell and Miriam Aileen (Adams) B.; m. Gail Louise Geiger, Sept. 3, 1961 (div. Aug. 1969); m. Joan Frances Livermore, May 21, 1979. BS, U. Kans., 1961; postgrad., Swiss Poly., Zurich, 1961-62; MS, Stanford U., 1964, PhD, 1967. Research fellow Weizmann Inst. Sci., Rehovot, Israel, 1967-68; postdoctoral research fellow, research assoc. U. Pitts., 1968-70; asst. prof. physics U. Ariz., Tucson, 1970-72, assoc. prof., 1972-76, prof., 1976—, assoc. chmn. dept., 1977-83, mem. faculty senate, 1979-83, 88-90, 91—; program dir. theoretical physics NSF, 1985-87; chmn. adv. com. Internat. Scholars, Tucson, 1985—; chmn. rsch. policy com. U. Ariz. Faculty Senate, 1993—. Woodrow Wilson fellow, 1961-62; NSF fellow, 1962-66; Weizmann Inst. fellow, 1967-68; Andrew Mellon fellow, 1968-69; Alfred P. Sloan Found. research fellow, 1972-74; Alexander von Humboldt fellow, 1976-77; NSF grantee, 1971-85, 87—; Netherlands F.O.M. research fellow Groningen, 1980; recipient sr. U.S. scientist award (Humboldt prize) Alexander von Humboldt Found., 1983-85. Fellow Am. Phys. Soc. (mem. publs. com., mem. program com. 1993—, divsn. nuclear physics), Phi Beta Kappa (pres. Alpha ariz. chpt. 1992), Sigma Xi, Sigma Pi Sigma, Omicron Delta Kappa, Beta Theta Pi. Office: U Ariz Dept Physics Bldg 81 Tucson AZ 85721

BARRETT, CRAIG R., computer company executive; b. 1939. Assoc. prof. Stanford U., 1965-74; with Intel Corp., 1974—, v.p. components tech. and mfg. group, sr. v.p., gen. mgr. components tech. and mfg. group, exec. v.p., mgr. components tech., now exec. v.p., COO. Office: Intel Corp 2200 Mission College Blvd Santa Clara CA 95052

BARRETT, DONALD JOHN, library administrator; b. St. Paul, Sept. 30, 1927; s. Lawrence John and Pauline Catherine (Huth) B.; m. June Lorraine Medalen, Jan. 27, 1962; 1 child, Barbara Sue. BS, Coll. St. Thomas, 1950; MA, U. Minn., 1954. Reference librarian Coll. St. Thomas Library, St. Paul, 1950-54; librarian Electronic Supply Office, Great Lakes, Ill., 1954-55; reference librarian USAF Acad. Library, Denver, 1955-58; chief pub. svcs. div. USAF Acad. Library, Colorado Springs, 1959-69, asst. dir. pub. svcs., 1969—; library bldg. cons., 1975—. Contbr. articles to profl. jours. With U.S. Army, 1946-47. Mem. ALA, Assn. Coll. and Rsch. Librs., Colo. Libr. Assn. (Lifetime Achievement award 1990), Libr. Adminstrn. and Mgmt. Assn., Air Force Assn. Roman Catholic. Home: 2624 Flintridge Dr Colorado Springs CO 80918-4425 Office: USAF Acad Library USAF Academy CO 80840

BARRETT, JAMES E., federal judge; b. Lusk, Wyo., Apr. 8, 1922; s. Frank A. and Alice C. (Donoghue) B.; m. Carmel Ann Martinez, Oct. 8, 1949; children—Ann Catherine Barrett Sandahl, Richard James, John Donoghue. Student, U. Wyo., 1940-42, LL.B., 1949; student, St. Catherine's Coll., Oxford, Eng., 1945, Cath. U. Am., 1946. Bar: Wyo. 1949. Mem. firm Barrett and Barrett, Lusk, 1949-67; atty. gen. State of Wyo., 1967-71; judge U.S. Circuit Ct. Appeals (10th cir.), 1971—; county and pros. atty. Niobrara County, Wyo., 1951-62; atty. Town of Lusk, 1952-54, Niobrara Sch. Dist., 1950-64. Active Boy Scouts Am.; sec.-treas. Niobrara County Republican Central Com.; trustee St. Joseph's Children's Home, Torrington, Wyo., 1971-85. Served as cpl. AUS, 1942-45, ETO. Recipient Distinguished Alumni award U. Wyo., 1973. Mem. VFW, Am. Legion. Office: US Ct Appeals PO Box 1288 Cheyenne WY 82003-1288

BARRETT, JAMES JOSEPH, artist, technical consultant; b. Bklyn., July 19, 1956. Student, Orange County C.C. Freelance artist Calif., 1978—; tech. cons. Design Art Materials, Lewisburg, Tenn., 1991-92. Home and Office: 10362 San Pedro Pl Riverside CA 92505

BARRETT, JAMES PETER, realtor; b. Duluth, Minn., Dec. 17, 1924; s. James Sylvester and Susan (Pastoret) B.; m. Martha Miller, May 29, 1946; children: James Peter Jr., Steven John, Diane B. Knight, Lawrence Miller. Student, Loyola U., L.A., 1942-43, UCLA, 1943-46; cert. real estate, UCLA, 1965. Engr., supr. J.S. Barrett, Contractors, Newport Beach, Calif., 1946-63; owner Pete Barrett Realty, Newport Beach, 1963—. City Coun. City of Newport Beach, 1974-78; pres. Newport-Balboa Rotary, 1962-63. Mem. Bd. Realtors (pres. 1969), Calif. Assn. Realtors (v.p. dist. 32 1972), Newport Harbor Yacht Club, Balboa Bay Club, Newport Beach Nautical Mus. (pres. 1987-88). Republican. Roman Catholic. Home: 270 Cagney Ln Apt 307 Newport Beach CA 92663-2647

BARRETT, KIM ELAINE, medical educator; b. London, June 21, 1958; d. Peter William and Kathleen (McNally) B.; m. Philip Allan Bonomo, July 2, 1988. BSc, U. Coll., London, 1979, PhD, 1982. Vis. fellow NIH, Bethesda, Md., 1982-85; asst. rsch. immunologist U. Calif. at San Diego, La Jolla, 1985-88, asst. prof. medicine, 1988-92, assoc. prof., 1992—; curriculum cons. Valhalla High Sch., El Cajon, Calif., 1989-90. Contbr. articles to profl. jours. Fulbright scholarship, 1982; recipient First Rsch. award NIH, 1988-93. Fellow Am. Acad. Allergy and Immunology; mem. Am. Gastroent. Assn. (rsch. com. 1993—), Am. Assn. Immunologists, British Soc. for Immunology. Office: UCSD Med Ctr 8417 200 W Arbor Dr San Diego CA 92103-8417

BARRETT, LARRY LEON, housing and dining services administrator; b. Taft, Calif., July 5, 1940; m. Jean Orrison, Nov. 17, 1989. BS in Phys. Sci., Calif. State Poly., San Luis Obispo, 1964. Supr. trainee U. Calif., Santa Barbara, 1964-65, unit mgr., 1965-69, food svc. dir., 1969-72; dir. housing and dining svc. U. Calif., San Diego, 1972—. Contbr. articles to profl. jours. Recipient Food Svc. Operator of Yr. Silver Plate award Internat. Food Mfrs. Assn., 1981. Mem. Nat. Assn. of Coll. and Univ. Food Svc. (treas. 1979, pres. 1979-81, Theodore Minah Disting. Svc. 1990). Office: U Calif 0090 La Jolla CA 92093

BARRETT, LENORE HARDY, mining and investment consultant, state legislator; b. Newkirk, Okla., June 16, 1934; d. Floyd Jack and Minnie Bell (O'Dell) Hardy; m. Robert Sidney Cloud (div.); m. Robert Michael Barrett, 1964; 1 child, Michael Hardy. BS, Okla. Bapt. U., 1956. Pvt. practice Challis, Idaho; state legislator Ho. of Reps., Boise, Idaho, 1993. Active Idaho Farm Bureau Political Action Com., 1990-92; dir. Salmon River Electric Coop., Inc., Challis; police commr. Challis City Coun., 1984-89; mem. Assn. Idaho Cities Legis. Com., 2 yrs.; state committeewoman Custer County Rep. Ctrl. Com., Challis, 1982—. Mem. Nat. Inholder's Assn., Idaho Rep. Party, Ctrl. Idaho Mining Assn. (sec.), Custer County Farm Bureau, Grassroots for Multiple Use, Blue Ribbon Coalition, Order of Eastern Star (Grand Organist award Grand Chpt. Idaho 1985-86). Baptist. Home and Office: 143 W Pleasant Challis ID 83226

BARRETT, REGINALD HAUGHTON, wildlife management educator; b. San Francisco, June 11, 1942; s. Paul Hutchison and Mary Lambert (Hodgkin) B.; m. Katharine Lawrence Ditmars, July 15, 1967; children: Wade Lawrence, Heather Elizabeth. BS in Game Mgmt., Humboldt State U., 1965; MS in Wildlife Mgmt., U. Mich., 1966; PhD in Zoology, U. Calif., Berkeley, 1971. Rsch. biologist U. Calif., Berkeley, 1970-71, acting asst. prof., 1971-72; rsch. scientist div. wildlife rsch. Commonwealth Scientific and Indsl. Rsch. Orgn., Darwin, Australia, 1972-75; from asst. prof. to prof. U. Calif., Berkeley, 1975—; dir. Sagehen Creek Field Sta., Truckee, Calif., 1985—. Author: (with others) Report on the Use of Fire in National Parks and Reserves, 1977, Research and Management of Wild Hog Populations, Proceedings of a Symposium, 1977, Sitka Deer Symposium, 1979, Symposium on Ecology and Management of Barbary Sheep, 1980, Handbook of Census Methods for Birds and Mammals, 1981, Wildlife 2000: Modeling Habitat Relationships of Terrestrial Vertebrates, 1986, Translocation of Wild Animals, 1988, Wildlife 2001: Populations, 1992; contbr. articles, abstracts, reports to profl. jours. Recipient Outstanding Profl. Achievement award Humboldt State U. Alumni Assn., 1986, Bruce R. Dodd award, 1965, Howard M. Wight award, 1966; Undergrad. scholar Nat. Wildlife Fedn., 1964, NSF grad. fellow, 1965-70; Union found. Wildlife Rsch. grantee, 1968-70. Mem. The Wildlife Soc. (pres. Bay Area chpt. 1978-79, cert. wildlife biologist, R.F. Dasmann Profl. of Yr. award western sect. 1989), Am. Soc. Mammalogists (life), Soc. for Range Mgmt. (life), Ecol. Soc. Am. (life), Soc. Am. Foresters, Australian Mammal Soc., Am. Inst. Biol. Scis., AAAS, Calif. Acad. Scis., Internat. Union for the Conservation of Nature (life), Calif. Bot. Soc., Renewable Natural Resources Found., Internat. Assn. for Ecology, Orgn. Wildlife Planners, Sigma Xi, Xi Sigma Pi. Episcopalian. Office: U Calif 145 Mulford Hall Berkeley CA 94720

BARRETT, RICHARD HEWINS, oil company executive; b. Pitts., Dec. 5, 1949; s. Robert Hewins and Joan Lea (Mantler) B.; divorced; children: Robert, Jeffrey, Douglas; m. E. Paige Sexton, June 27, 1992; step-children: Fallon, Alisha. BS, Pa. State U., 1971, MBA, 1973. Lic. soccer referee 1988; cert. cash mgr., 1990. Ins./credit mgr. Perdue, Inc., Salisbury, Md., 1973-75, sales rep., 1975-76, dir. mgmt. analysis, 1976-77; sr. fin. analyst Gulf Oil Corp., Pitts., 1977-82, sr. cons., 1982-85; supr. sys. support Chevron Corp., San Francisco, 1985-86, sr. cash mgmt. analyst, 1986-87, mgr. banking ops., 1987-90, mgr. receivables, acctg., 1991-92; mgr. libricants bus. svcs. Chevron USA, San Francisco, 1992—; instr. Golden Gate U., San Francisco, 1987-90; adj. prof., Salisbury State Coll.,1975. Elder, trustee Sharon Community Presbyn. Ch., Coraopolis, Pa., 1981-84; treas., bd. dirs. Moon Area Soccer Assn., Coraopolis, 1983-85, Mustang Soccer League, Danville, Calif., 1988-91; youth soccer coach, 1980—. Mem. Nat. Corp. Cash Mgmt. Assn., Am Petroleum Inst. (treasury issues com. 1988-90). Republican. Home: 244 St Christopher Dr Danville CA 94526 Office: Chevron USA 575 Market St San Francisco CA 94105

BARRETT, ROBERT DAKER, arts center executive; b. Tulsa, Dec. 3, 1945; s. Charles and Alice (Daker) Lewis; m. Barbara Pilakowsky, Nov. 2, 1968; 1 son, Max. B.F.A. in Painting, Calif. Coll. Arts and Crafts, Oakland, 1968, M.F.A., 1972. Peace Corps vol. Saclepea, Liberia, 1969; visual arts supr. City of Long Beach, 1972-78; lectr. Calif. State U., Long Beach, 1976-78; cultural arts supr. City of Fresno, Calif., 1978-79; exec. dir. Fresno Arts Center, 1980—. Mem. Alliance for Arts (exec. bd.), Fresno City and County C. of C., Friends Meux House, Fresno City and County Hist. Soc. Club: Fresno Rotary. Office: Fresno Arts Ctr & Mus 2233 N 1st St Fresno CA 93703-2364

BARRETT, ROBERT MATTHEW, lawyer; b. Bronx, N.Y., Mar. 18, 1948; s. Harry and Rosalind B. AB summa cum laude, Georgetown U., 1976, MS in Fgn. Service, JD, 1980. Bar: Calif. 1981. Assoc. Latham & Watkins, L.A., 1980-82, Morgan, Lewis & Bockius, L.A., 1982-84, Skadden, Arps, Slate, Meagher & Flom, L.A., 1984-86, Shea & Gould, L.A., 1986-87, Donovan, Leisure, Newton & Irvine, L.A., 1988-90; ptnr. Barrett & Zipser, L.A., Calif., 1991-93; prof. law U. La Verne, L.A., 1993—. Mem. ABA, Los Angeles Bar Assn. (bd. advisors vols. in parole com. 1981—). Home: 13816 Bora Bora Way # 325A Marina Del Rey CA 90292-6883 Office: Barrett & Zipser Ste 1700 2121 Avenue Of The Stars Los Angeles CA 90067-5012

BARRETT, SHEILA ANN, educator; b. Sacramento, Oct. 7, 1966; d. Anthony James and Leah Lorraine (Cortelatzzi) B. BS, U. Calif., Davis, 1988, teaching credential, 1989; postgrad., Calif. Poly. State U., 1989—. Cert. tchr., Calif. Tchr. agr. Fullerton (Calif.) High Sch. Dist., 1989—; adviser Fullerton Future Farmers Am., 1989-92, Orange sect. Future Farmers Am., 1991-92. Writer, coord. course and curriculum materials. Com. mem. Fullerton Beautiful, 1990-92. Mem. Calif. Agr. Tchrs. Assn. (insvc. chair 1991—, vice-chair secondary unit 1992-93, sect. pres. 1992-93), So. Region Agr. Tchrs. (sales techniques presenter 1991-92), Calif. Tchrs. Assn., Nat. Vocat. Agr. tchrs.

BARRETT, WILLIAM OWEN, academic administrator; b. Hartford, Conn., Sept. 1, 1945; s. Fredric Deyoe and Elsie (Owen) B.; m. Diane Wyman Hamilton, Feb. 22, 1969; 1 child, Alexander Owen. BFA in Indsl. Design, R.I. Sch. of Design, 1967; MA in Edn., NYU, 1978. Asst. dir. admissions Parsons Sch. of Design, N.Y.C., 1970-73, dir. admissions, 1973-78, dean of students, 1978-80, asst. dean, 1980-81; dean Corcoran Sch. of Art, Washington, 1981-87; pres. San Francisco Art Inst., 1987—. Mem. design panel D.C. Commn. on Arts and Humanities, 1987; mem. adv. com. San Francisco High Sch. of the Arts, 1988-91; With U.S. Army, 1967-70, Korea. Mem. Nat. Assn. Schs. Art and Design (treas. 1986-89, v.p. 1989-90, pres. 1990—), Nat Coun. Arts Adminstrs. (treas. 1983-86), Alliance Ind. Colls. Art (v.p. 1989-91), Assn. Ind. Coll. Art and Design (bd. dirs. 1991—). Democrat. Office: San Francisco Art Inst 800 Chestnut St San Francisco CA 94133-2299

BARRIOS, ALFRED ANGEL, psychologist; b. N.Y.C., Oct. 1, 1933; s. Arthur Domingo and Carmen Maria (Vidal) B. BS, Calif. Inst. Tech., 1955; PhD, UCLA, 1969. Chem. engr. Mobil Oil Co., Torrance, Calif., 1955-57; instr. psychology East L.A. Coll., 1969-72, UCLA, 1972-73, Southwest Coll., L.A., 1973-74, Santa Monica (Calif.) Coll., 1975; psychologist Self-Programmed Control Ctr., L.A., 1972—, pres., 1975—. Author: Towards Greater Freedom and Happiness, 1978, The Stress Test, 1984, The Habit Buster, 1987; inventor Stress Control Biofeedback Card. Office: SPC Ctr 11949 Jefferson Blvd Ste 104 Culver City CA 90230-6336

BARRO, MARY HELEN, broadcast executive; b. Culver City, Calif., June 17, 1938; d. Manuel and Gloria (De La Mora) B. Student, UCLA, 1968; studied with Daws Butler, 1975-80. Community relations dir. Sta. KTLA-TV, Hollywood, Calif., 1972; producer/host Sta. KNXT-TV, Hollywood, 1972-73; advt. salesperson, community relations dir. Sta. KWKW, Hollywood, 1975-77; news reporter Sta. KTTV-TV, Hollywood, 1977-78; news anchor/reporter, producer/host, commentator Sta. KZLA-AM-FM, Hollywood, 1972-80; producer, host Am. Forces Radio and TV Services, Los Angeles, 1977-83; news anchor/producer/editor Sta. KRBK, Sacramento, 1982-83; Sacramento bur. chief Sta. KEZY, Anaheim, Calif., 1983; gen. mgr. Sta. KXEM, McFarland, Calif., 1983-84; sta. mgr. Sta. KRCX, Roseville, Calif., 1984-85; gen. mgr. King Videocable Co., Lodi, Calif., 1985-86; v.p. McGavren-Barro Broadcasting Corp., Bakersfield, Calif., 1987—; v.p./gen. mgr. Sta. KAFY, Bakersfield, 1987—; pres., bilingual media cons. Up Front Prodns., Citrus Heights, Calif., 1974—. Appeared in (TV shows) Eight is Enough, Marcus Welby (film) Am. Gigolo; ednl. films, commls. Adv. bd. mem. Bakersfield Coll. Chicano Ctr., 1987, Mexican Am. Opportunity Found., 1987, Girl Scouts, Joshua Tree Council, 1987, Centro Olin, 1987. Recipient legislative resolution, Los Angeles City Council, Calif. State Senate, commemorative resolution, Los Angeles County Fire Commn., Golden Mike award, 1972; named Mexican Am. Woman of Yr., Mexican Am. Opportunity Found., Kern County Bus. Woman of Yr. Hispanic C. of C., 1991. Mem. Calif. Assn. Latins in Broadcasting, U.S. Hispanic C. of C., U.S. Hispanic Women's C. of C. (bd. dirs. 1990—), Bus. and Profl. Women of Bakersfield, Women in Cable, Radio and TV News Dirs. Assn., Am. Hispanic Owned Radio Assn. (pres. 1991), Sacramento Press Club, Sundale Country Club Rio Bravo Country Club. Republican. Roman Catholic. Office: 230 Truxtun Ave Bakersfield CA 93301-5330

BARRON, CAROLINE, lawyer, editor; b. Orinda, Calif., Jan. 4, 1958; d. John Francis and Carolyn Patricia (Dunn) B. BA, Stanford U., 1978, JD, 1981. Bar: Calif. 1982, Ariz. 1983, D.C. 1990. Assoc. Brobeck, Phleger & Harrison, San Francisco, 1981-83, Beus, Gilbert, Wake & Morrill, Phoenix, 1983-88; editor Mead Ventures, Inc., Phoenix, 1983-92; assoc. Law Offices of Gerald North, 1988-89; ptnr. North & Barron, 1989—; bd. dirs. 1st Cen. Bank, Phoenix, 1983-88. Vol. Phoenix Art Mus. Contemporary Forum, 1985-88, Taliesin West, Frank Lloyd Wright Found., Phoenix, 1986-88, North Am. Soc. Interior Designers, Phoenix, 1985-88, Valley Leadership, 1986-87, Valley Citizens League, 1988—, also speaker AAA and NASD, arbitrator. Mem. ABA, Calif. Bar Assn., Ariz. Bar Assn., D.C. Bar Assn., Assn. Trial Lawyers Am. Office: North & Barron 3800 N Central Ave Ste 1600 Phoenix AZ 85012-1946

BARRON, MARTIN GEORGE, postal service clerk; b. Spokane, Wash., Jan. 17, 1963; s. Russell Allen and Cheryl Annette (Bowers) B. Cert. Data Processing, Griffin Coll., 1983. Food svc. supr. Maximilien's in the Market, Seattle, 1982-83; credit analyst The Bon/Allied Stores, Seattle, 1983; distbn. clk. U.S. Postal Svc., Seattle, 1983—; union steward Seattle Local Am. Postal Workers, 1985—, editor, 1985-86, clk. craft dir., 1986-90; clk. craft dir. of mail processing Greater Seattle Area Local, APWU, 1990—; various coms. Seattle Local APWU, contract arbitration adv., chief contract negotiator local negotiations. Author articles on stress mgmt. Mem. Freedom Day Com., Seattle, 1986; founder Union Mems. Against Discrimination, Seattle, 1987, ACT-UP (AIDS Coalition to Unleash Power), Seattle, 1990. Mem. Am. Postal Workers Union (various offices), Greater Seattle Area Local, Am. Postal Workers Union (clk. craft dir. of mail processing 1990—, other coms.). Office: Greater Seattle Area Local APWU 2450 6th Ave S PO Box 24206 Seattle WA 98124

BARRON, STEPHANIE, art museum curator; b. N.Y.C., Sept. 24, 1950; d. Manuel H. and Gloria (Pequignot) B.; m. Robert Gore Rifkind, Nov. 4, 1984; 1 child, Max Rifkind-Barron. AB, Barnard Coll., 1972; MA, Columbia U., 1973. Assoc. curator L.A. County Mus. Art, L.A., 1976-80; curator L.A. County Mus. Art, 1980—; curator The Avant-Garde in Russia: New Perspectives, 1980, German Expressionist Sculpture, 1983, German Expressionism: The Second Generation, 1988, David Hockney, 1988, "Degenerate Art": The Fate of the Avant-Garde in Nazi Germany, 1991. Recipient Order of Merit, First Class award Fed. Republic Germany, 1984; John J. McCloy Fellowship Am. Coun. on Germany, 1981, Nat. Endowment for the Arts Mus. Profl. Grant, 1986. Mem. Am. Assn. Mus., Com. Internat. Mus., Coll. Art Assn., Musées des Artes Moderne, Art Table. Office: LA County Mus of Art 5905 Wilshire Blvd Los Angeles CA 90036-4523

BARROW, THOMAS FRANCIS, artist, educator; b. Kansas City, Mo., Sept. 24, 1938; s. Luther Hopkins and Cleo Naomi (Francis) B.; m. Laurie Anderson, Nov. 30, 1974; children—Melissa, Timothy, Andrew. B.F.A., Kansas City Art Inst., 1963; M.S., Ill. Inst. Tech., 1965. With George Eastman House, Rochester, N.Y., 1966-72; asst. dir. George Eastman House, 1971-72; assoc. dir. Art Mus., U. N. Mex., Albuquerque, 1973-76; assoc. prof. U. N.Mex., 1976-81, prof., 1981—, Presdl. prof., 1985-90. Author: A Letter With Some Thoughts on Photographs Future, 1970, The Art of Photography, 1971, 600 Faces by Beaton, 1970; sr. editor: Reading Into Photography, 1982; contbr. to: Britannica Ency. Am. Art, 1973, A Hundred Years of Photographic History: Essays in Honor of Beaumont Newhall, 1975; foreward The Valiant Knights of Daguerre, 1978; one-man show include Light Gallery, N.Y.C., 1974-76, 79, 82, Amarillo Art Ctr., 1990, Andrew Smith Gallery, Santa Fe, 1992; group shows include Nat. Gallery Can., 1970, Pace Gallery, N.Y.C., 1973, Hudson River Mus., Yonkers, N.Y., 1973, Internat. Mus. Photography, Rochester, 1975, Seattle Art Mus., 1976, Mus. Fine Arts, Houston, 1977, Retrospective Exhbn. Los Angeles County Mus. of Art, 1987—; represented in permanent collections, Nat. Gallery Can., Mus. Modern Art, Fogg Art Mus., Cambridge. Nat. Endowment for Arts fellow, 1971, 78. Office: U NMex Dept Art Albuquerque NM 87131

BARROWS, ROBERT GUY, scriptwriter; b. Ft. Collins, Colo., Feb. 9, 1926; s. Barney M. and Marian Louise (Walker) B.; div.; children: Bret, Larry, David, Daniel, Josh, Grace; m. Georgia Jerilyn Harvey, June 30, 1989. BA, U. Colo., 1950; MA, UCLA, 1954. Freelance writer NBC-TV, CBS-TV, ABC-TV, MGM, 20th Century Fox, Universal, Paramount, Columbia, Warner Bros., various ind. TV and film prodn. cos.; faculty mem., theater, TV and film NYU, 1957-62, Am. Acad., N.Y.C., 1960-62, UCLA, 1964-70, Art Ctr., Pasadena, Calif., 1980-82; mem. faculty, theater, TV and film Loyola Marymount U., Los Angeles, 1981-82. Writer, producer, dir. (film) Bloodthirsty; writer (TV episodes) Bonanza, Ben Casey, Combat, Destry, Daniel Boone, The Bold Ones, The Big Valley, Empire, The Fugitive, The Green Hornet, Felony Squad, Ironside, Kraft Suspense Theater, The Man Who Never Was, Mission: Impossible, Run for Your Life, Wild, Wild West, The Virginian. Served to master sgt. U.S. Army, 1943-46. Recipient Samuel Goldwyn Creative Writing award. Mem. Writers Guild Am.

BARRUS, JOHN EVAN, lawyer; b. Salt Lake City, Dec. 1, 1954; s. George Stanton and Merlynn (Droubay) B.; m. Anna Leesa Stanley, June 9, 1978; children: Steven, Emily, Katherine, Kristina. BS, Brigham Young U., 1978, JD, 1985; MBA, U. Wash., 1979. Bar: Calif. 1985, Utah 1986; CPA, Wash. Owner Acctg. Svcs. Co., Seattle and Provo, Utah, 1977-80; acctg. supr. Hewlett Packard Co., Palo Alto, Calif., 1980-82; assoc. McCormick, Barstow, Fresno, Calif., 1985-87, Craig Christensen Law Office, Fresno, 1987-89; ptnr. Christensen & Barrus, Fresno, 1989—. Bd. dirs. Fresno/Madera Alzheimers Assn., Fresno, 1992; mem. bishopric LDS Ch., Fresno, 1988-92. Mem. Calif. Soc. CPAs, Wash. Soc. CPAs, Calif. State Bar, Utah State Bar. Republican.

BARRY, CAROLE JOYCE, physician, educator; b. Boston, Apr. 20, 1933; d. Nathan and Sadie (Rubin) B.; m. Marvin F. Atlas, Aug. 23, 1971; 1 child, Joshua J. BA, Brandeis U., 1954; MD, Ind. U., 1960; MPH, UCLA, 1964. Diplomate Am. Bd. Psychiatry and Neurology. Resident in psychiatry Strong Meml. Hosp., Rochester, N.Y., 1965-68, fellow in psychiatry, 1968-70; instr. U. Rochester, 1966-74; asst. prof. Emory U., Atlanta, 1970-71; clin. assoc. prof. U. N.Mex., Albuquerque, 1979—; pres. Carole J. Barry, MD, Albuquerque, 1980—, S.W. Psychiat. Assocs., Albuquerque, 1980—, The Therapeutic Alliance, Albuquerque, 1984—. Mem. Gov.'s Com. on Status of Women, Santa Fe, 1986—, Gov.'s Com. on Rape and Sexual Abuse, Santa Fe, 1988—. Mem. Am. Psychiat. Assn. (com. on women Washington chpt. 1987—), Am. Assn. Clin. Psychologists, Am. Assn. Psychiatry and the Law, AMA, Psychiat. Med. Assn. N.Mex. (chmn. Albuquerque chpt. 1988—), Greater Albuquerque Med. Assn. Home: 4900 Paseo Del Rey NW Albuquerque NM 87120-1033 Office: 8314 Kaseman Ct NE Albuquerque NM 87110-7639

BARRY, HENRY FORD, chemical company executive; b. Detroit, June 25, 1923; s. William H. and Antoinette (Griese) B.; m. Helen A. Sasso, Aug. 27, 1947 (dec. Dec. 1983); children: Henry F., John M., Robert C., Christine M., Elizabeth M., Catherine A. BS in Chemistry, Stanford U., Palo Alto, Calif., 1950; MS in Chem. Engring., U. Mich., 1952, MBA in Mktg., 1978. Registered profl. engr., Ind., Colo. Researcher Amoco Oil Co., Whiting, Ind., 1952-59; tech. dir. Haviland Products Co., Grand Rapids, Mich., 1960-62; supr. Climax Molybdenum Co., Detroit, 1962-66; mgr. chem. rsch. Climax Molybdenum Co., Ann Arbor, Mich., 1967-76, dir. chem. devel., 1977-82; v.p. tech. Shattuck Chem. Co., Denver, 1983—. Editor: Chemistry/Uses of Mo., Vol. III, 1979, Vol. IV, 1982. With U.S. Army, 1943-46. Mem. Am. Chem. Soc., Nat. Assn. Corrosion Engrs., Soc. Tribology and Lubrication Engrs. Home: 5337 W Iliff Dr Apt 101 Denver CO 80227-3991 Office: Shattuck Chem Co Inc 1805 S Bannock St Denver CO 80223-3699

BARRY, JAMES MICHAEL, property management company executive; b. Fontana, Calif., Dec. 22, 1956; s. Walter and Georgia Elizabeth (Spaeth) B.; m. Melanie Lynn Barry. BA in Econs., U. Colo., 1979. Sales rep. Proctor & Gamble, Denver, 1979-81; sales rep. Becton Dickinson, Orangeburg, N.Y., 1981-84; dist. mgr., new dealer devel. Control-O-Fax, Denver, 1984-85; dist. br. mgr. Norrell Health Care, Denver, 1985-87; prin., owner Innovative Mgmt. Svcs., Inc., Denver, 1987—. Treas. Delta Upsilon Corp. Colo., Boulder, 1980-87; pres. Chestnut Homeowners Assn., Littlton, Colo., 1984-87; chmn. Rep. State Sen. Dist., Denver, 1987—, Rep. State Rep. Dist., Denver, 1987—; bd. dirs. S.W. Mental Health Svcs., Denver, 1988—. Mem. Community Assn. Inst. Republican. Roman Catholic. Home: 4732 W 69th Westminster CO 80030 Office: Innovative Mgmt Svc Inc 4899 S Dudley St # 18A Littleton CO 80123-7603

BARRY, JAMES PAUL, consulting arborist, educator; b. Pasadena, Calif., Jan. 1, 1953; s. Donald J. and Jeanne S. (Wells) B. BS, Calif. State Poly. U., 1976; MS, Colo. State U., 1983. Cert. tchr., Calif. Prodn. mgr. Alta Loma (Calif.) Nursery, 1973-75; field rep. Wilbur-Ellis Co., Commerce, Calif., 1976-77; merchandise supr. K-Mart, Monrovia, Calif., 1977-78; field supt. Easyscape Co., San Jose, Calif., 1978-79; disturbed lands coord. Colo. State U., Ft. Collins, Colo., 1980-83; pvt. practice soil cons. Arcadia, Calif., 1984-85; instr. Mt. San Antonio Coll., Walnut, Calif., 1985, Calif. State Poly. U., Pomona, 1985-91, U. Calif., Irvine, 1990-93; pres. Barry Tree Care & Mobile Soil Labs., Fullerton, Calif., 1986-92, Barry Environ. Consulting, Orange, Calif., 1992—. Contbr. articles to profl. publs. Mem. Tree Soc. Orange County (bd. dirs. 1989, exec. v.p. 1990), Soc. Ecol. Restoration, Am. Soc. Surface Mining Reclamation, Soil and Water Conservation Assn., Am. Soc. Landscape Architects (affiliate), Alpha Zeta (life), Gamma Sigma Delta (life). Office: Barry Environ Consulting 4705 E Chapman Orange CA 92669

BARRY, JOHN WILLARD, biologist; b. Columbus, Ohio, July 18, 1934; s. George Willard and Sylvia Evelyn (Ward) B.; m. Patricia Ann Arends Barry, Dec. 29, 1956 (div. 1986); children: Cynthia Shawn Wilkinson, Sandra Sue Mills; m. Valerie Rubke Barry, May 30, 1987. BS, U. Cincinnati, 1956; postgrad., U. Utah, 1961-71, Brigham Young U., 1961-71. Test officer U.S. Army Dugway Proving Ground, Dugway, Utah, 1961-65; test dir. Deseret Test Ctr., Ft. Douglas, Utah, 1965-75; nat. pesticide application specialist USDA Forest Svc., Davis, Calif., 1975—; mgr. Program WIND joint and USDA and DOD program, Davis, 1982-87. Author: American Indian Pottery, 1981; contbr. to books on pesticide application and Am. Indian art and culture; co-developer aerial spray models, 1985—. Leader and organizer Am. SW Ethnology Tours, 1985—; pres., bd. dirs. Libr. Assocs. U. Calif., Davis, 1983-85; pres. Davis Art Ctr., 1986-90; mem. Mus. No. Ariz. Mem. Am. Soc. Agrl. Engring., Archaeol. Soc. N.Mex., Nature Conservancy, Ariz. Archaeol. and Hist. Soc. Democrat. Lutheran. Office: USDA Forest Svc 2121 2nd St # C Davis CA 95616-5472

BARRY, RICK (RICHARD FRANCIS DENNIS BARRY, III), former professional basketball player, broadcaster; b. Elizabeth, N.J., Mar. 28, 1944; s. Richard Francis and Alpha Monique (Stephanovich) B.; m. Pamela Hale, June 1965 (div.); children: Richard Francis IV, Jon Alan, Brent Robert, Drew William, Shannon Leigh; m. Pamela Stenesen, Sept. 1981 (div.); m. Lynn Norenberg. Student, U. Miami, 1961-65. Basketball player San Francisco Warriors, NBA, 1965-67, Oakland Oaks, Am. Basketball Assn., 1968-69, Washington, Am. Basketball Assn., 1969-70, N.Y. Nets, Am. Basketball Assn., 1970-72, Golden State Warriors, NBA, 1972-78, Houston Rockets, NBA, 1978-80; sports broadcaster, basketball analyst CBS Sports, 1974-81; NBA color analyst Turner Sports, 1984—. Mem. Am. Basketball Assn. All-Star Team, 1968-72, NBA All-Star Team, 1966-67, 73-78, NBA Championship Team, 1975; named Rookie of Yr., NBA, 1966, Most Valuable Player, 1966, Most Valuable Player Championship Series, 1975; inducted into Basketball Hall of Fame, 1987. Office: Turner Sports 1050 Techwood Dr NW Atlanta GA 30318-5695

BARS, ITZHAK, physics educator, researcher, consultant; b. Izmir, Turkey, Aug. 31, 1943; came to U.S., 1967; s. Albert Shemoel and Claire (Benshoam) Barsimantov; m. Paulette P. Navaro, Aug. 22, 1967 (div. 1993); children: Julie, Jamie. BS in Physics, Robert Coll., 1967; MPhil in Physics, Yale U., 1969, PhD in Physics, 1971. Asst. rsch. physicist U. Calif., Berkeley, 1971-73; asst. prof. Stanford (Calif.) U., 1973-75; asst. prof. Yale U., New Haven, 1975-79, assoc. prof., 1979-83; prof. U. So. Calif., L.A., 1983—; vis. asst. prof. Harvard U., Cambridge, Mass., 1978; mem. Inst. for Advanced Study, Princeton, N.J., 1979, 90. Editor: (book) Symmetries in Particle Physics, 1984; contbr. articles to profl. jours. Fulbright scholar Robert Coll., 1964-67; Gibbs fellow Yale U., 1967-69, grad. fellow IBM, 1969-71; A.P. Sloan Found. fellow, 1976-80; recipient 1st award Gravity Rsch. Found., 1988; named Outstanding Jr. Investigator U.S. Dept. Energy, 1983. Fellow Am. Phys. Soc., N.Y. Acad. Scis. Democrat. Jewish. Home: 1827 El Vista Cir Arcadia CA 91006

BARSAN, RICHARD EMIL, oral and maxillofacial surgeon; b. Selma, Ala., Dec. 18, 1945; s. Emil and Letitia (Dobrin) B.; m. Sandra Sherrick, June 22, 1974; children: Kelly Lynn, Robert Scott. BS in Chem. Engring., U. Cin., 1968; DDS, Ohio State U., 1979. Diplomate Am. Bd. Oral and Maxillofacial Surgeons. Chem. engr. various cos., 1968-76; resident VA Hosp., Sepulveda, Calif., 1979-80; resident in oral and maxillofacial surgery La. State U., New Orleans, 1980-84; pvt. practice, La Jolla and El Centro, Calif., 1985—. Chrysler scholar U. Cin., 1964. Fellow Am. Assn. Oral and Maxillofacial Surgeons; mem. ADA, Calif. Dental Assn., San Diego County Dental Soc. (bd. dirs. 1988-92), San Diego County Oral Surgeons (pres. 1990), So. Calif. Soc. Oral and Maxillofacial Surgeons, Paul Revere Study Club (pres. 1988), Toastmasters (pres. La Jolla chpt. 1988), Omicron Kappa Upsilon. Republican. Office: 470 Nautilus St Ste 212 La Jolla CA 92037 also: 1745 S Imperial Ave Ste 107 El Centro CA 92243

BARSDATE, MARY KATHRYN, educator; b. Windber, Pa., Apr. 28, 1933; d. Stephen and Kathryn (Shuster) Haschak; m. Robert John Barsdate, June 9, 1959; children: Lory Ann, Kelly Joan. BA, Allegheny Coll., 1955, MA, 1960. Cert. tchr., Pa. Tchr. pub. schs., Pa., 1955-62; sec. dept. linguistics U. Alaska, Fairbanks, 1966, lectr., 1966-67; instr. Ednl. Complex, Ft. Wainwright, Alaska, 1987-92; critic tchr. U. Pitts.,1960-62; tutor, Fairbanks, 1968—; ind. editor, Fairbanks, 1977—. Chmn. Alaska Gov.'s State Adv. Coun. on Librs., 1989-91; mem. Fairbanks North Star Borough Libr. Commn., 1983—, vice chmn., 1985-88, chmn., 1983-85; bd. dirs. Arts Alaska, Inc., Anchorage, 1983—, mem. exec. com., 1985—; bd. dirs. adv. coun. Sta. KUAC-TV-FM Pub. Broadcasting, Fairbanks, 1982-88, chmn., 1984-88; founder Fairbanks Montessori Assn., 1966-71; coord. Alaska State High Sch. Debate-Forensics Tournaments, 1984; trustee, sec.-treas. Libr. Found., Noel Wien Pub. Libr., Fairbanks, 1979—; sec. Weeks Field Park Assn., 1990-92. Recipient Gov.'s Award for Arts, 1986. Mem. Nat. Assn. Pub. TV Stas. (lay rep. bd. dels. 1984-88), Alaska State Coun. Arts (v.p. 1981-83), Assn. Alaska Sch. Bds. (v.p. 1977-78), Literacy Coun. Alaska (bd. dirs. 1978-86), Fairbanks Arts Assn. (sec. 1970-79), Phi Beta Kappa. Republican. Carpatho-Russian Orthodox. Home and Office: PO Box 80174 Fairbanks AK 99708-0174

BARSIS, EDWIN HOWARD, physicist; b. N.Y.C., June 28, 1940; s. Morris J. and Rose Barsis; children: James, Benjamin. BEP, Cornell U., 1963, MS, 1965, PhD, 1967. Mem. tech. staff Sandia Nat. Labs., Livermore, Calif., 1967-69; supr. applied physics Sandia Nat. Labs., Livermore, 1969-75, supr. advanced weapons div., 1975-77; mgr. electronic subsystems dept. Sandia Nat. Labs., Albuquerque, 1977-86, dir. computer scis. and math., 1986—, dir. engring. scis., 1989—; chmn. bd. dirs. Urologics, Inc., Albuquerque, 1984—. Contbr. articles to profl. jours. Capt. C.E., U.S. Army, 1967-69. Mem. Am. Phys. Soc. Home: 1538 Catron Ave SE Albuquerque NM 87123-4259 Office: Sandia Nat Labs PO Box 5800 Albuquerque NM 87185-5800

BARSKY, MARTIN, editor, publisher; b. Phila., Jan. 26, 1927; s. Philip and Mollie (Cohen) B.; children: Larry, Steve, Laura. Grad. high sch., Phila. Advt. mgr. Kiddie City Stores, Phila., 1954; sta. mgr., producer for various radio and TV stas. Pa., Mont., Calif., 1955-70; founder, editor, pub. So. Calif. Retailer, Los Angeles, 1971-81; owner, editor, pub. Retailer News, Anaheim, Calif., 1981-88; pres., pub. Video Software Dealer News, Los Angeles, 1984-86, Rental Dealer News, Orange, Calif., 1987-90; founder, editor, pub. Buying Group News mag. and Retailing News newspaper, Anaheim, 1990—. Producer Folk Music Theatre, 1967; contbr. articles to profl. jours. Bd. dirs. City of Hope Consumer Electronics, Los Angeles, 1987-88, pres., 1985-86. Served as sgt. USAAF, 1943-45. Recipient Cert. Appreciation Am. Legion, 1968, Outstanding Contributions award Associated Vol. Buyers, 1977, Outstanding Contributions award United Stores Inc., 1980. Mem. Soc. Profl. Journalists, Electronics Reps. Republican. Jewish. Home: 13490 Prospector Ct Victorville CA 92392-8849 Office: Buying Group News 2340 Plaza Del Amo Ste 225 Torrance CA 90501-3453

BARSTOW, LEON ELROY, health products executive; b. Union City, Pa., Dec. 14, 1940; s. George Arthur and Opal Pauline (Smith) B.; m. Nancy See Barstow, Aug. 15, 1959 (div. Feb. 1976); children: Brenda, Tanya; m. Kristie Ann Lurz, Oct. 16, 1982; children: Geoffrey, Brent, Katy. BS, Edinboro (Pa.) State Coll., 1962; PhD, Syracuse (N.Y.) U., 1967. Asst. prof. chemistry Roberts Coll., Istanbul, Turkey, 1966-69; rsch. assoc. U. Ariz., Tucson, 1969-71; postdoctoral fellow NIH, Bethesda, Md., 1971-72; pres., dir., chief exec. officer Vega Biotechs., Inc., Tucson, 1974-83; pres., dir., chief exec. officer Protein Techs., Inc., Tucson, 1985—, also bd. dirs.; adj. rsch. prof. U. Ariz., Tucson, 1972-84. Contbr. articles to profl. jours.; patentee amino acids/peptides. Mem. Breakfast Club. Republican. Office: Protein Techs Inc 1665 E 18th St Ste 106 Tucson AZ 85719-6808

BARTA, SHARYN LEVINE, legal assistant; b. N.Y.C., Feb. 10, 1952; d. William and Beatrice (Hirsch) Levine; m. Richard Schechter, Oct. 3, 1974 (div. 1984); children: Jade Schechter, Asha Schechter; m. Brian Barta, May 29, 1988. BA in Psychology and Edn., SUNY, Stony Brook, 1973. Tchr. Gresham (Oreg.) Sch., 1974-76; counselor Women's Health Clinic, Portland, Oreg., 1976-78; acctg. cons. Santa Rosa, CAlif., 1978-80; restaurant mgr. Fifth St. Cafe, Santa Rosa, 1980-85; in pub. rels. Verbatim Reporting Svc., Santa Rosa, 1985-87; legal asst. Alex Heckathorn, Esq., Santa Rosa, 1987—;

systems mgr. Barta Law Offices, Santa Rosa, 1992—. Recipient Math. Honor award State of N.Y., 1968.

BARTEL, ARTHUR GABRIEL, educational administrator, city official; b. San Francisco, Oct. 20, 1934; s. Irving Peter and Elian Leah (Barker) B.; m. Dottie Lu Smith, Dec. 14, 1963 (dec. Apr. 1972); children: Brian Blake, Scott Michael. Student, San Jose State Coll., 1952-54; BS, U. Calif., Berkeley, 1957; postgrad., U. So. Calif., 1968-70; MA, Pepperdine U., 1973. Cert. FAA air traffic controller, 1957-77, naval flight officer, 1965; lic. standard tchr., life standard service, life community coll. life chief coll. adminstrv. officer, life community coll. supr., life community coll. instr., Calif. Enlisted USMC, 1954, advanced through grades to sgt., 1967; comdg. officer VMFA-314 Fighter-Attack Squadron USMC, El Toro, Calif., 1970-72; ret. USMC, 1977; gen. mgr. Nieuport 17 Restaurant, Santa Ana, Calif., 1977-78; pres., chief exec. officer High Flight Inc., Hanford, San Diego, Calif., 1978-81; teaching vice prin. Armona (Calif.) Union Elem. Sch., 1982-84, tchr. sci. and lang. arts., 1981-84; curriculum cons. Kings County Office Edn., Hanford, 1984-86; program specialist Kings County Supt. Schs., Hanford, 1986-91; sch. site adminstr., edn. specialist Hanford Community Sch., 1992—; councilman City of Hanford, 1986-90, mayor, 1988-90; mem. adv. bd. San Joaquin Valley Writing Project, 1984-86, 92—. Vice chmn. Hanford Planning Commn., 1982-86; vice chmn. bd. trustees Sacred Heart Hosp., 1987-93; bd. dirs. Navy League, 1992—. Decorated Air medal, Vietnam Cross of Galantry with Palm Combat Action Ribbon. Fellow internat. writing project U. Calif., Irvine, 1985; mem. Assn. Calif. Sch. Adminstrs., Calif. Soc. Program Specialists, DAV (life), Retired Officers Assn., Hanford C. of C., Delta Upsilon (life). Office: Kings County Office Edn Kings Govt Ctr Hanford CA 93230

BARTH, DAVID VICTOR, computer systems designer; b. Tulsa, Sept. 23, 1942; s. Vincent David and Norma (Bell) B. BS summa cum laude, Met. State Coll., Denver, 1977; MS, U. No. Colo., 1982. Programming mgr. Am. Nat. Bank, Denver, 1967-72; cons. Colo. Farm Bur. Ins. Corp., Denver, 1972; systems analyst Mid-Continent Computer Services, Denver, 1972-73; programming mgr. Bayly Corp., Denver, 1973-75; project leader Cobe Labs. Inc., Denver, 1976-84; part-time tchr. Met. State Coll., 1982-83; systems analyst Affiliated Banks Service Co., Denver, 1985-87; real estate broker Van Schaack & Co., Denver, 1985; tech. supr. Affiliated Banks Svc. Co., Denver, 1987-89; software engr. Computer Data Systems, Inc., Aurora, Colo., 1990-91; sr. computer systems designer Martin Marietta Corp., Golden, Colo., 1991-92; computer systems designer and salesman Computer Shop, Lakewood, Colo., 1992—; freelance flight instr., 1977—. Vol. Am. Red Cross, 1987—; Served with USN, 1961-66. Mem. Soc. for Info. Mgmt. (editor newsletter 1983), Exptl. Aircraft Assn. (editor newsletter chpt. 660, 1989-91), Aircraft Owners and Pilots Assn., Flying Circus Skating Club. Republican. Home: 509 S Cody St Lakewood CO 80226-3047 Office: Computer Shop 6591 W Colfax Ave Space 2B Denver CO 80214-1803

BARTHOLOMEW, GRANT NEWMAN, social services administrator; b. Salt Lake City, Sept. 12, 1952; s. John Grant and Carol (Newman) B.; m. Paula Jane Wick, June 20, 1975; children: Christa, Camie, Angela, Kenneth. BS, Brigham Young U., 1976. Sch. social worker Nebo Sch. Dist., Spanish Fork, Utah, 1976-79; social svc. worker State of Utah Dept. Social Svcs., Brigham City, 1979-88, social svc. supr., 1988—, chairperson C.P.S. steering com., 1989—. Bishop LDS Ch., Brigham City, 1984-89. Recipient Finalist Commr.'s award U.S. Adminstrn. of Children, Youth, and Families, 1991. Office: Dept Human Svcs 1050 S 500 W Brigham City UT 84302

BARTHOLOMEW, JERRI LEE, microbiologist; b. Oxford, Pa., June 4, 1958; d. Ralph Eugene and Cleola Pearl (Wilson) B. BS in Biology, Pa. State U., 1980; MS in Fisheries, Oreg. State U., 1984, PhD in Microbiology, 1989. Fishery biologist U.S. Fish and Wildlife Svcs., Seattle, 1989-91, microbiologist, 1992—; rsch. assoc. Oreg. State U., Corvallis, 1991-92. Contbr. articles to profl. jours. Mem. Am. Fisheries Soc., Phi Kappa Phi, Sigma Xi. Office: US Fish and Wildlife Svc NFRC Bldg 204 Naval Sta Seattle WA 98115

BARTKUS, EDWARD ALFRED, paramedic educator; b. Pitts., Jan. 10, 1957; s. Edward Alfred and Dorothy Evelyn (Griffin) B.; m. Christine Louise Smith, Sept. 16, 1983 (div. Jan. 12, 1990); m. Cynthia Louise Stemper, Aug. 17, 1991. BS, Ea. Oreg. State Coll., 1989. Cert. EMT. Paramedic A-1 Ambulance Svc., Cheyenne, Wyo., 1977-79; neonatal emergency transport cons. Wyo. State Health Div., Cheyenne, 1979-80; chief EMS tng. officer Wyo. State EMS Office, Cheyenne, 1980-82; paramedic Cambell County Meml. Hosp., Gillette, Wyo., 1982, staff devel. coord., 1983-85; dep. sheriff Boulder (Colo.) County Sheriff's Dept., 1983; dir. of advanced paramedic tng. Oreg. Health Scis. U Sch. Medicine, Portland, 1985-91, asst. prof. of emergency medicine, 1991—. Co-author Pediatric Prehospital Guide, 1988, 91. Rsch. grant Emergency Medicine Found., 1992. Mem. Emergency Medicine Resident's Assn. (nat. bd. dirs.), Oreg. Health Scis. U. Sch. Medicine Curriculum Com., Oreg. State EMS Com. (chmn. 1990-91), Oreg. State Paramedic Assn. (v.p. 1987-89). Democrat. Roman Catholic. Home: 7436 SE 19th Ave Portland OR 97202 Office: Oreg Health Scis U Dept Emergency Medicine 3181 SW San Jackson Park Rd Portland OR 97201

BARTLETT, ALAN CLAYMORE, geneticist; b. Price, Utah, June 17, 1934; s. Rulon Ashley and Emily Bertha (Hunter) B.; m. Vanice Rae Baker, Mar. 16, 1956; children: Ravae Edith Johnson, Denice Alene Hardman, LeIsle Emily Jacobson, Trace Alan Bartlett. AA, Carbon Coll., 1954; BA, U. Utah, 1956, MS, 1957; PhD, Purdue U., 1962. Instr. Purdue U., West Lafayette, Ind., 1960-62; geneticist USDA, ARS, Boll Weevil Rsch. Lab., State College, Miss., 1962-67, USDA, ARS, We. Cotton Rsch. Lab., Phoenix, 1967—; adj. prof. Miss. State U., State Coll., 1964-67, Ariz. State U., Tempe, 1976-80. Author, editor: The Evolutionary Significance of Insect Polymorphism, 1982; contbr. articles to profl. jours. Pres. Tempe Assn. for Gifted Students, 1972-74. Recipient Outstanding Alumnus award Carbon Coll., 1993. Mem. Entomol. Soc. Am., Genetics Soc. Am., Sigma Xi (pres. local chb 1966). Mem. Ch. LDS. Office: USDA ARS Western Cotton Rsch Lab 4135 E Broadway Phoenix AZ 85040

BARTLETT, DAVID CARSON, state legislator; b. New London, Conn., Feb. 2, 1944; s. Neil Riley and Susan Marion (Carson) B.; m. Barbara Hunting, July 14, 1973 (div. 1974); m. Janice Anne Wezelman, Feb. 11, 1979; children: Daniel Wezelman, Elizabeth Anne. Student, Wesleyan U., Middletown, Conn., 1962-64; BA, U. Ariz., 1966, MA, 1970; JD, Georgetown U., 1976. Teaching asst. U. Ariz., Tucson, 1967-69; program analyst U.S. Dept. Labor, Washington, 1970-76; assoc. Snell & Wilmer, Tuscon, 1976-77; pvt. practice Tuscon, 1976-79; assoc. Davis, Eppstein & Hall, Tuscon, 1979-85; mem. Ariz. Ho. of Reps., Tuscon, 1983-88, Ariz. State Senate, Tuscon, 1989-92. Democrat. Home: 3236 E Via Palos Verdes Tucson AZ 85716-5854

BARTLETT, (HERBERT) HALL, motion picture producer, director; b. Kansas City, Mo., Nov. 27, 1929; s. Paul Dana and Alice (Hiestand) B.; m. Lupita Ferrer, Apr. 30, 1977 (div.); children: Cathy Bartlett Lynch, Laurie Bartlett Schrader. BA, Yale U., 1948. Owner, operator Hall Bartlett Prodn., L.A., 1960—; pres. Jonathan Livingston Seagull Mcht. Co.; bd. dirs. James Doolittle Theatre, Hollywood, Calif., founder Music Ctr., Los Angeles. Producer, dir. (films) Navajo, 1953, Crazylegs, 1958, Unchained, 1957, All the Young Men, 1961, Durango, 1959, Zero Hour, 1961, The Caretakers, 1963, A Global Affair, 1968, Changes, 1968, Sandpit Generals, 1971, Jonathan Livingston Seagull, 1973, The Children of Sanchez, 1979, Catch Me If You Can, 1988, The Search of Zubin Mehta, 1975, The Cleo Laine Story, 1978, Comeback, 1983; author: The Rest of Our Lives, 1987. mem. Friends of Library, L.A., Cinema Circulus; assoc. founder Pub. TV Music Ctr. Lt. USNr, 1949-51. Recipient 11 Acad. award nominations, Film Festival awards from Cannes, 1961, 63, Venice, 1959, 65, Edinburgh, 1952, San Sebastian, 1969, Moscow, 1971, NCCJ, 1955, Jimmy Stewart award for Career Achievement in Motion Pictures, 1992, Fgn. Press awards. Mem. Motion Picture Acad. Arts and Scis., Acad. TV Arts and Scis., Phi Beta Kappa. Republican. Presbyterian. Clubs: Bel-Air Country, Kansas City Country. Home and Office: 295 Strada Corta Rd Los Angeles CA 90073

BARTLETT, NEIL, chemist, educator; b. Newcastle-upon-Tyne, Eng., Sept. 15, 1932; s. Norman and Ann Willins (Vock) B.; m. Christina Isabel Cross, Dec. 26, 1957; children: Jeremy John, Jane Ann, Christopher, Robin. B.Sc., Kings Coll., U. Durham, Eng., 1954; Ph.D. in Inorganic Chemistry, Kings Coll., U. Durham, 1957; D.Sc. (hon.), U. Waterloo, Can., 1968, Colby Coll., 1972, U. Newcastle-upon-Tyne, 1981, McMaster U., Can., 1992; D.Univ. (hon.), U. Bordeaux, France, 1976, U. Ljubljana, Yugoslavia, 1989, U. Nantes, France, 1990; LLD, Simon Fraser U., Can., 1993. Lectr. chemistry U. B.C., Vancouver, Can., 1958-63; prof. U. B.C., 1963-66; prof. chemistry Princeton U., N.J., 1966-69, U. Calif., Berkeley, 1969—; mem. adv. bd. on inorganic reactions and methods Verlag Chemie, 1978—; mem. adv. panel Nat. Measurement Lab., Nat. Bur. Standards, 1974-80; E.W.R. Steacie Meml. fellow NRC, Can., 1964-66; Miller vis. prof. U. Calif., Berkeley, 1967-68; 20th G.N. Lewis Meml. lectr., 1973; William Lloyd Evans Meml. lectr. Ohio State U., 1966; A.D. Little lectr. Northeastern U., 1969; Phi Beta Upsilon lectr. U. Nebr., 1975; Henry Werner lectr. U. Kans., 1977; Jeremy Musher Meml. lectr., Israel, 1980, Randolph T. Major Meml. lectr. U. Conn., 1985, J.C. Karcher lectr. U. Okla., 1988; Brotherton vis. prof. U. Leeds, Eng., 1981; Erskine vis. lectr. U. Canterbury, New Zealand, 1983; Wilsmore fellow Melbourne U., Australia, 1983; vis. fellow All Souls Coll., Oxford U., 1984; Miller prof. U. Calif.-Berkeley, 1986-87. Bd. editors Inorganic Chemistry, 1967-78, Jour. Fluorine Chemistry, 1971-80, Synthetic Metals, Revue Chimie Minerale, Noveau Jour. de Chimie; mem. adv. bd. McGraw-Hill Ency. Sci. and Tech., Chemistry of Materials. Recipient Rsch. Corp. award; E.W.R. Steacie prize, 1965; Elliott Cresson medal Franklin Inst., 1968; Kirkwood medal Yale U. and Am. Chem. Soc. (New Haven sect.), 1969; Dannie-Heinemann prize The Gottingen acad. 1971; Robert A. Welch award in chemistry, 1987; Alexander von Humboldt Found. award, 1977; medal Jozef Stefan Inst., Slovenia, 1980; Moissan medal, 1986; Prix Moissan, Paris, 1988; fellow Alfred Pl. Sloan Found., 1964-66; Bonner Chemiepries, Bonn, 1991; Brekeley citation, 1993. Fellow Chem. Soc. London (Corday Morgan medal 1962), Royal Soc., Am. Acad. Arts and Scis., Royal Inst. Chemistry, Chem. Inst. Can. (1st Noranda lectr. 1963); mem. NAS (fgn. assoc.), Leopoldina Acad. (Halle, Salle), Akademie der Wissenschaften in Gottingen, Associé Etranger, Académie des Sciences, Institut de France, Am. Chem. Soc. (chmn. divs. fluorine chemistry 1972, inorganic chemistry 1977, award in inorganic chemistry 1970, W.H. Nichols award N.Y. sect. 1983, Pauling medal of Pacific N.W. sects. 1989, Disting. Svc. award 1989, award for Creative Work in Flourine Chemistry 1992), Phi Lambda Upsilon (hon.). Home: 6 Oak Dr Orinda CA 94563-3912 Office: U Calif Dept Chemistry Berkeley CA 94720

BARTLETT, RICHARD WRELTON, manufacturing executive; b. San Diego, Mar. 25, 1939; s. Richard L. Bartlett and Bernice (Clarke) Boyer; m. Brenda Kaye Reagan, Apr. 16, 1965 (div. Jan. 1987); children: Richard W. II, Bretley W.; m. Betty Ann Brewington Callaway, Dec. 29, 1990. BSME, Calif. State Poltechnic U., 1960; MBA, SUNY, Buffalo, 1972. Test engr. Aerojet-Gen., Sacramento, Calif., 1960-65; engr. mgr. Bell Aerospace, Niagara Falls, N.Y., 1965-73; controller Xerox Corp., Rochester, N.Y., 1973-84; controller, dir of Mgmt.Info. Svcs. Bendix Corp., Dayton, Ohio, 1984-87; v.p. controller Transp. Mfg. Corp., Roswell, N.Mex., 1987-90; v.p. fin., CFO R & G Sloane Mfg. Co., Inc., Sun Valley, Calif., Little Rock, 1991—; vol. cost acct. Grandview Hosp., Dayton, 1987. Capt. United Fund drive, Xerox, Rochester, 1983; mem. fin. com. Unitarian Ch., Rochester, 1982-83; capt. U.S. Savs. Bonds, 1988-90; bd. dirs. Roswell YMCA, 1989; corp. giving com. United Fund, Roswell, N.Mex., 1988. Mem. Am. Prodn. Inventory Control Soc., Roswell Running Club. Republican. Unitarian.

BARTLETT, ROBERT WATKINS, mining college dean, metallurgist; b. Salt Lake City, Jan. 8, 1933; s. Charles E. and Phyllis (Watkins) B.; m. Betty Cameron, Dec. 3, 1954; children: John C., Robin Parmley, Bruce R., Susanne. BS, U. Utah, 1953, PhD, 1961. Registered profl. engr., Calif. Scientist Ford Aerospace, 1961-64; group leader ceramics SRI Internat., Menlo Park, Calif., 1964-67; assoc. prof. metallurgy Stanford U., Palo Alto, Calif., 1967-74; mgr. hydrometallurgy Kennecott Minerals Co., Salt Lake City, 1974-77; dir. materials lab. SRI Internat., Menlo Park, Calif., 1977-80; v.p. research Anaconda Minerals Co., Tucson, 1980-85; mgr. materials tech. Idaho Sci. and Tech. Dept., Idaho Falls, 1985-87; dean Coll. Mines and Earth Resources, U. Idaho, Moscow, 1987—; dir. Idaho Geol. Survey, Moscow. Contbr. approx. 70 research publs. in metallurgy; 9 patents in field. Served to lt. (j.g.) USN, 1953-56. Recipient Turner award Electrochem. Soc., 1965, McConnell award AIME, 1985. Mem. Metall. Soc. (pres. 1989), Soc. Mining Engrs. (disting. mem.), Sigma Xi, Tau Beta Pi. Office: U Idaho Dept Metall & Mining Moscow ID 83844-3025

BARTLETT, STEVEN THADE, aerospace engineer; b. Glendale, Calif., Sept. 13, 1962; s. Ronald Thade Bartlett and Frances Mae (Bailey) Arrington. BS in Physics, Calif. State U., Long Beach, 1985, MS in Aerospace Engring., 1993. Retail salesman Tandy Corp., Beverly Hills, Calif., 1982-85; aerospace systems engr. McDonnell Douglas Corp., Huntington Beach, Calif., 1986—. Fellow Space Studies Inst.; mem. AIAA, Nat. Space Soc., Aircraft Owners and Pilots Assn., L.A. Sci. Fantasy Soc., World Future Soc., Nature Conservancy, Challenger Ctr. Libertarian. Office: McDonnell Douglas Space Co 5301 Bolsa Huntington Beach CA 92647

BARTLETT, THOMAS ALVA, educational administrator; b. Salem, Oreg., Aug. 20, 1930; s. Cleave Wines and Alma (Hanson) B.; m. Mary Louise Bixby, Mar. 20, 1954; children: Thomas Glenn, Richard A., Paul H. Student, Willamette U., 1947-49, DCL (hon.), 1986; A.B., Stanford U., 1951, Ph.D., 1959; M.A. (Rhodes scholar), Oxford U., 1953; L.H.D. (hon.), Colgate U., 1977, Mich. State U., 1978, Union Coll., 1979; D.C.L. (hon.), Pusan Nat. U., Korea, 1985, U. Ala., 1983. Mem. U.S. Permanent Mission to UN, 1956-63; advisor Gen. Assembly Dels., 1956-63; pres. Am. U., Cairo, 1963-69, Colgate U., Hamilton, N.Y., 1969-77, Assn. Am. Univs., Washington, 1977-82; chancellor U. Ala. System, 1982-89, Oreg. State System of Higher Edn. Office, Eugene, 1989—; mem. UAR-U.S. Ednl. Exch. Commn., 1966-69; mem. Task Force on Financing Higher Edn. in N.Y. State (Keppel Commn.), 1972-73; chmn. Commn. Ind. Colls. and Univs. N.Y., 1974-76; bd. dirs. Nat. Assn. Ind. Colls. and Univs., 1975-76; trustee Univs. Field Staff Internat., 1985-87; mem. NASA Comml. Space Adv. Com., 1988-90. Mem. nat. bd. examining Chaplains Episcopal Ch., 1978-91; trustee Gen. Theol. Sem., 1977-82, Am. U. in Cairo, 1978—, U.S.-Japan Found., 1988—. Mem. Coun. Fgn. Rels., Cosmos Club (Washington), Phi Beta Kappa. Home: 2237 Spring Blvd Eugene OR 97403-1897 Office: Oreg State System Higher Edn/Office of Chancellor PO Box 3175 Eugene OR 97403-0175

BARTLETT, THOMAS HENRY, chemist; b. Great Falls, Mont., Jan. 1, 1931; s. Thomas Henry and Sophia (Stenseth) B.; m. Alice Kay Lee, Dec. 29, 1959 (div. Feb. 1962); one child, Brady; m. Iris Elaine Cooper, Aug. 25, 1967; children: Karleen, Elaine. BS, Coll. Great Falls, 1952; postgrad., U. Wash., 1953, LaSalle Extension U., 1958-63. Chemist Anaconda Co., Grest Falls, 1954-57, Am. Chrome Co., Nye, Mont., 1957-61; chief chemist Western Nuclear Inc., Jeffery City, Wyo., 1962-67; gen. mgr. Chem. and Geol. Labs., Casper, Wyo., 1967-76; pres., chief exec. officer WAMCO Lab. Inc., Casper, 1977—. Chmn., pres. Winter Meml. Presbyn. Ch., Casper, 1982—. Mem. ASTM. Lodge: Elks. Home: 3301 E 12th St Casper WY 82609-3033 Office: WAMCO Lab Inc PO Box 2953 Casper WY 82602-2953

BARTLEY, MURRAY HILL, oral pathology educator and department chairman; b. Jamestown, N.Y., June 15, 1933; s. Merle Campbell and Doris Ann (Keller) B.; m. Anita Estelle Glatfelter, July 29, 1956; children: Todd L., Brian C., Kathleen A. Student, Lewis & Clark Coll., 1951-54; DMD, U. Oreg., 1958; PhD, U. Utah, 1968. Cert. in oral pathology. Teaching fellow U. Oreg. Dental Sch., Portland, 1961-64; assoc. dir. rsch. D.N. Sharp Hosp., San Diego, 1964-65; post-doctoral fellow dept. anatomy Sch. Medicine U. Utah, Salt Lake City, 1965-68; acting assoc. prof. oral biology and pathology UCLA, 1968-69; assoc. prof. oral pathology Dental Sch. U. Oreg., Portland, 1969-77; prof. oral pathology Sch. Dentistry Oreg. Health Sciences U., Portland, 1977—; chmn. oral pathology dept. Sch. Dentistry OHSU, Portland, 1972-76, 80—; cons. Wadsworth VA Hosp., Barnes VA Hosp., Vancouver, Wash., Portland Med. Ctr., 1968—, Coun. on Hosp. Dental Svcs., ADA, Chgo., 1970, Oreg. State Dental Assn. Biohazrds Com., Portland, 1976—, Oreg. Dept. Health AIDS Task Force, Portland, 1981-91, Project Hope-Stomatology Faculties, Peoples Republic of China, 1984, Mich. AMC. Contbr. sci. articles to profl. jours. Mem. com. ORE div., profl. edn. Am. Cancer Soc., Portland, 1974—; bd. dirs. Oreg. regional med. program O.C.C.P., Portland, 1973-81. Col. USAR, 1958—. USPHS Tchr.'s Tng. grantee NIH, Portland, 1961-64; Post-Doctoral Teaching fellow NIH, 1965-68; recipient Presdl. citation Oreg. Dental Assn., 1979, 89; decorated U.S. Army Meritorious Svc. medal, 1981. Mem. AAAS, ADA, Am. Acad. Oral Pathology, Soc. Mil. Surgeons, Sigma Xi, Omicron Kappa Upsilon (chpt. pres. 1988-89), Delta Sigma Delta. Episcopalian. Home: 6020 SW Arrow Wood Ln Portland OR 97223-7700 Office: OHSU Sch Dentistry Dept Oral Pathology 611 SW Campus Dr Portland OR 97201-3097

BARTLEY, OPELENE, actress, consultant; b. Chouteau, Okla., June 27, 1924; d. Leroy and Drucilla (Moore) Johnson; m. Paul Udell Bartley, Aug. 31, 1946 (dec. Feb. 1990). AA, L.A. Community Coll., 1985; stuent, U. So. Calif., L.A., 1986-87; student, Buffalo State Coll., 1962-63. Ordained to ministry, 1980. Actress appeared in (TV series) including White Shadow, Hill Street Blues, General Hosp., Redd Foxx, The Judge, L.A. Law, Amen, Superior Ct., (films) Let's Do It Again, Emergency Room, Falcon & The Snowman, Once Bitten, What's Hot, What's Not, The Blob, Let it Ride, (spl.) Roots II-Second Generation, (on stage) Raisin In the Sun, Happy Endings, Contribution, The Great White Hope, Black Girl, Something Cool, (comml.) Lee Jeans. Fundraiser Hunger & Homeless Coalition, 1987, 88, 90; donator Women Shelters Abused, Tenn., 1990—; owner Emotional People & Retardees, Detroit, 1968-72; bd. dirs. Jefferson Haven Forster Homes, Detroit, 1967. Recipient Community Svc. award L.A. Voter Edn. Project, 1977, Proclamation, City of L.A., 1987, Community Svc. award Sta. KTLA. Democrat. Home: PO Box 43723 Los Angeles CA 90043-0723 Office: Bartley and Assoc Unltd PO Box 43723 Los Angeles CA 90043-0723

BARTLEY, ROGER DAVID, former insurance company executive; b. Abingdon, Berkshire, Eng., Dec. 11, 1945; came to U.S., 1981; s. Percival and Kathleen (Wilkinson) B. BSc, U. Man., Winnipeg, Can., 1967. Various positions Gt.-West Life, Toronto, Ont., Can., 1968-77; mgr. underwriting Gt.-West Life, Winnipeg, 77-81; salesman Gt.-West Life, San Francisco, 1981-85; regional mgr. Gt.-West Life, Detroit, 1985-87, Denver, 1987-89; group v.p. John Hancock Life Ins. Co., San Francisco, 1989-90; disabled, 1990. Fellow Life Mgmt. Inst.; mem. Health Ins. Assn. Am. Home: 43 La Cuesta Orinda CA 94563

BARTLING, JUDD QUENTON, research corporation executive; b. Muncie, Ind., July 24, 1936; s. Hubert George and Hildagarde (Good) B.; m. Madeline Levesque, June 9, 1973 (div. 1989); stepchildren—Mary Johnson, Michael Johnson. BA, U. Calif., 1960, PhD, 1969; MS, Purdue U., 1964. Research asst. U. Calif., Riverside, 1965-69; cons. Dept. Def. Rsch., Azak Corp., Chatsworth, Calif., 1969-71, pres., 1971—. Served with U.S. Army, 1960-62. NSF grantee U. Fla., 1969. Research in bus., solid state physics, quantum electronics, electromagnetics and radar. Office: 21032 Devonshire St Ste 113 Chatsworth CA 91311

BARTOL, WALTER W., banker; b. Phoenix, June 24, 1931; s. Walter T. and Nora Mae (Trimble) B.; m. Betty Walker, Sept. 18, 1951; children: Thomas W., Nora Lisa, Walter Lynn. BS, U. Ariz., 1955. Mgr. Walker Feedyards, Glendale, Ariz., 1955-69; v.p. Valley Nat. Bank of Ariz., Phoenix, 1969-88; pres. Union Devel. Co., Inc., Phoenix, 1965—; ptnr. B&T Enterprises, 1981—. Treas. Am. Nat. Livestock Show, Phoenix, 1988-89. Sgt. USAF, 1951-52. Mem. Elks (past exalted ruler 1958-59). Republican. Office: Union Devel Co Inc 4546 N 17th Ave Phoenix AZ 85015-3809

BARTOLI, RENATO POMPEO, manufacturing executive; b. Foligno, Umbria, Italy, Dec. 16, 1946; came to U.S. 1974; s. Giuseppe and Emilia (Arcamone) B.; m. Anna V.A. Polesny, Aug. 7, 1976; children: Alena, Carlo, Antonia. BS, U. Perugia, 1968; MS, Rochester Inst. Tech., 1975; ScD, U. Perugia, 1972. Cert. quality engr. Adj. prof. Rochester (N.Y.) Inst. Tech., 1974-76; supr. raw material GAF Corp., Binghamton, N.Y., 1976-79; tech. dir. Xidex Corp., Holyoke, Mass., 1979-84; dir. ops. Xidex Corp., Sunnyvale, Calif., 1984-87; dir. quality assurance NCR Corp., Mountain View, Calif., 1987, dir. R&D, 1988-89; v.p. mfg. Micrographic Tech. Corp., Mountain View, Calif., 1989—; chmn. ANSI Std. Com., 1981-84. Editor: Microfilm Technology, 1983. Chmn. adv. bd. San Jose State U., 1990-92. Fulbright fellow, 1974. Fellow Am. Soc. Quality Control, Soc. for Imaging Sci. and Tech., Rotary. Home: 1029 Laurent St Santa Cruz CA 95060

BARTON, ANN ELIZABETH, financial executive; b. Long Lake, Mich., Sept. 8, 1923; d. John and Inez Mabel (Morse) Seaton; student Mt. San Antonio Coll., 1969-71, Adrian Coll., 1943, Citrus Coll., 1967, Golden Gate U., 1976, Coll. Fin. Planning, 1980-82; m. H. Kenneth Barton, Apr. 3, 1948; children: Michael, John, Nancy. Tax cons., real estate broker, Claremont, Calif., 1967-72, Newport Beach, Calif., 1972-74; v.p., officer Putney, Barton, Assos., Inc., Walnut Creek, Calif., 1975—; bd. dirs., officer Century Fin. Enterprises, Inc., Century Adv. Corp., Fin. Svc. Corp. Cert. fin. planner. Mem. Internat. Assn. Fin. Planners, (registered investment advisor), Calif. Soc. Enrolled Agts., Nat. Assn. Enrolled Agts., Nat. Soc. Public Accts., Inst. Cert. Fin. Planners. Office: Putney Barton Assocs Inc 1243 Alpine Rd Ste 219 Walnut Creek CA 94596-4431

BARTON, DAVID M., electronics engineer, consultant; b. Portland, Oreg., Jan. 23, 1939; s. Delwin Walter and Lillian (Strom) B.; m. Laura Schuette, June 1, 1962 (div. 1980); children: Kenneth Randall, Wesley Keith; m. Susan MIchelle Smith, Mar. 30, 1983. BA in Physics, Linfield Coll., 1961. Design engr. Field Emission Corp., McMinnville, Oreg., 1961-62, Tektronix, Inc, Beaverton, Oreg., 1962-64; sr. engr. Monsanto Co., St. Louis, 1964-66; mem. tech. staff Fairchild Instrumentation Div., Mountain View, Calif., 1966-69, Develco, Inc., Mountain View, 1969-72; sr. mem. tech. staff Litronix, Inc., Cupertino, Calif., 1972-76; product mktg. mgr. Litronix, Inc., Cupertino, 1976-80; sr. mem. tech. staff Victor Techs., Scotts Valley, Calif., 1980-84; engr. pvt. practice San Jose, Calif., 1984—; dir., bus. cons., Personal Tng. Systems, San Jose, 1986-91. Mem. No. Calif. DX Club (editor newsletter), Amateur Radio News Svc. (editor newsletter),. Republican. Home and Office: 14842 Nelson Way San Jose CA 95124

BARTON, GRANT ENNES, missionary training center administrator; b. Trementon, Utah, Aug. 14, 1940; s. Ray H. Jr. and Helen (Grant) B.; m. Marilyn Debenham, June 19, 1964; children: Grant Richard, Christine, Steven, Catherine, Heather. BA in Mgmt., U. Utah, 1966, MA in Ednl. Psychology, 1968; PhD in Ednl. Comms., U. Pitts., 1972. Instr. Inst. Religion, U. Utah, Salt Lake City, 1968-77; dir. C.C. Allegheny County, Pitts., 1968-70; asst. prof. ednl. psychology, asst. dir. instrnl. R & D, Brigham Young U., Provo, Utah, 1970-74; pres. wholesale and retail sales co., 1974-77; mgr. adult curriculum LDS Ch., Salt Lake City, 1977-82, 85-86; pres. Tex. Dallas Mission, LDS Ch., 1982-85; acting dir. pub. comm. LDS Ch., Salt Lake City, 1986-88; tng. dir. Missionary Tng. Ctr., Provo, 1988—; instr. religion, BYU. Author: Creating Instructional Objectives, 1975; co-author: Creating Valid Test Questions, 1976; also articles to instrnl., bus. and religious publs. Bd. dirs. Internat. Cultural Exch. Found., Salt Lake City, 1985-90; dist. advancement chmn. Boy Scouts Am., Provo. Mem. ASCD, ASTD, APA, Nat. Soc. Performance Instrn., Rotary (chmn. Polio Plus Salt Lake City 1987). Republican. Home: 1077 East 2500 North Provo UT 84604

BARTON, LAURENCE, crisis management educator, crisis consultant; b. Boston, Aug. 1, 1956; s. Paul and Lillian Barton; m. Judy Eicker, July 30, 1983. AB, Boston Coll., 1978, PhD, 1983; MA in Law and Diplomacy, Harvard U., 1981. Prof. Boston Coll., 1980-89, Harvard Bus. Sch., Boston, 1987-88, U. Nev., Las Vegas, 1989—; pvt. practice cons., Las Vegas, 1989—. Author: Crisis In Organizations, 1992; contbr. articles to profl. jours. Roman Catholic. Office: PO Box 71858 Las Vegas NV 89170

BARTON, PETER RICHARD, III, communications executive; b. Washington, Apr. 6, 1950; m. Laura Perry. BA, Columbia U., 1971, MS, 1972; postgrad., Harvard U., 1979, MBA, 1982. Mem. gov's staff State of N.Y., 1975-80; sr. v.p. Tele-Communications Inc., Englewood, Colo., 1982-86; pres. Cable Value Network, Mpls., 1986-88; sr. v.p. Tele-Communications Inc., Englewood, CO, 1988-90; pres. Liberty Media Corp, 1990—.

BARTON, STEPHEN HOWARD, broadcast executive; b. Coburg, Oreg., Nov. 1, 1951; s. Harold E.L. and Lois M. (Holloway) B.; m. Krysti L. Gorzny, Mar. 29, 1979. AS in Electronics Tech., Lane Community Coll., 1985. Owner Barton Electronics, Eugene, Oreg., 1975—; chief engr. KLCC/KCLO-FM, Eugene, 1977-87, gen. mgr., 1987—; certification sec. SBE

Local, Eugene, 1983-85; chmn. Consortium Pub. Radio Oreg., Inc., Eugene, 1988-92, sec., 1992—; bd. dirs. West Coast Pub. Radio, 1992—; chmn. Eugene Citizen Involvement Com., 1992—. Mem. Glenwood Refinement Planning Team, Eugene, 1987-90; sec. Glenwood Community Orgn., Eugene, 1990. Mem. Eugene Area Radio Stas., Mid Oreg. Ad Club. Home: 1655 Mississippi Ave Eugene OR 97403-2742 Office: KLCC/KLCO 4000 E 30th Ave Eugene OR 97405-0640

BARTON, WILLIAM HENRY, II, insurance executive; b. Portland, Oreg., May 24, 1921; s. William Henry and Louise Cardwell (Chalmers) B.; m. Mavis Fortier, Aug. 22, 1942; children: William Henry III, Steven John, Dana Barton Cress. BA, Oreg. State U., 1946. Broadcaster Sta. KBND, Bend, Oreg., 1942-51; broadcaster, mgr. sales Stas. KOIN-KALE Radio, Portland, Oreg., 1942-51; with Barton & Assocs., Portland, 1952—. Active Rehab. Inst., Friends of Timberline, Oreg. Hist. Soc., Japanese Garden Soc., Oreg. Zool. Soc., Oreg. Estate Planning Council; mem. bldg. com. Trinity Episc. Ch., Portland, chmn. canvas com.; vestry mem. various Episc. chs., Bend, Oreg. and Yakima, Wash.; bd. dirs. DePaul Treatment Ctr. Named Outstanding Jr. Citizen, Jr. C. of C., Bend, 1950; recipient Nat. Quality award. Mem. Nat. Assn. Life Underwriters, Oreg. Assn. Life Underwriters, Lincoln Nat. Pres.'s Club (mem. pres.'s cabinet), Alano Club. Home: 5274 SW Scholls Ferry Rd Portland OR 97225-1617 Office: Barton & Assocs 1221 SW Yamhill St # 100 Portland OR 97205-2195

BARUCH, RUTH-MARION EVELYN, photographer, writer; b. Berlin, Ger., June 15, 1922; d. Max and Bertha (Zweigenhaft) Baruch; m. Pirkle Jones, 1949. BA in Creative Writing, U. Mo., 1944, BJ, 1944; MFA in Photography, Ohio U., 1946; postgrad., Calif. Sch. Fine Arts, San Francisco, 1946-47. Grad. asst. Ohio U., 1944-46; tchr. workshops Home Studio, Mill Valley, Calif., 1969-71; guest artist San Francisco Art Inst., 1970, 85. Works in permanent collections at San Francisco Mus. Art, Oakland Mus. Art, Polaroid Corp., Cambridge, Mass., George Eastman House, Rochester, N.Y., Ctr. for Creative Photography (Ansel Adams Collection), U. Ariz., Tucson, Ariz. State U., Temple; author: The Vanguard: A Photographic Essay on the Black Panthers, 1970; included in Photography in the Twentieth Century, 1967, Photographers Ency. Internat., book and exhbn.: Family of Man, 1954; one person shows at San Francisco Mus. Modern Art, 1966, Carmel Photography Ctr., 1967, M.H. DeYoung Meml. Mus., San Francisco, 1968, Amon Carter Mus. Western Art, Ft. Worth, 1968, Focus Gallery, San Francisco, 1976, San Francisco Mus. Modern Art Rental Gallery, 1980; group shows include Mus. Modern Art, N.Y.C., 1954, Kongresshalla, Berlin, 1957, George Eastman House, 1960, DeCordova Mus., Lincoln, Mass., 1967, Focus Gallery, San Francisco, 1976, 80, Friends of Photography, Carmel, 1984, Monterey Peninsula Mus. Art, 1986. Home and Office: 663 Lovell Ave Mill Valley CA 94941-1086

BARUT, ASIM ORHAN, physicist, educator; b. Malatya, Turkey, June 24, 1926; came to U.S., 1953, naturalized, 1962; m. Pierrette Helene Gervaz, July 2, 1954. Diploma, Swiss Fed. Inst. Tech., 1949, Dr.Sc., 1952, Dr.h.c., 1982, 87. Mem. faculty U. Chgo., 1953-54, Reed Coll., Portland, Oreg., 1954-55, U. Montreal, 1955-56, Syracuse U., 1956-61, U. Calif., Berkeley, 1961-62; prof. physics U. Colo., Boulder, 1962—, Research lectr., 1982; lectr. in various countries; prof. physics U. Colo., Boulder, 1962—. Editor, editorial bd. Found. of Physics, Reports in Math. Physics, Hadronic Jour., Annales Fondat L. de Broglie, Com. Theor. Phys. Staff mem. Internat. Centre for Theoretical Physics, Trieste, Italy, 1964-65, 68-69, 72-73, 86-87; bd. dirs. NATO Advanced Study Insts., 1966, 67, 70, 72, 77, 83, 84, 89. Recipient Alexander von Humboldt award, 1974-75, 76, 85, medal of sci. (Turkey), 1982, Rsch. Lectureship award, 1983; faculty rsch. fellow, 1968, 72, 78, 85; Erskine fellow U. Canterbury, N.Z., 1970. Fellow Am. Phys. Soc. Office: U Colo at Boulder Dept Physics Box 390 Boulder CO 80309

BARVILLE, REBECCA PENELOPE, elementary school educator; b. Tulare, Calif., Nov. 7, 1936; m. David Leopold Barville, June 8, 1958; children: Mark, Becky, Curtis. BA, Simpson Coll., San Francisco, 1958; MA summa cum laude, Fresno State U., 1974. Cert. reading specialist, edn. adminstr., elem. tchr., Calif. Social worker Tulare County Welfare Dept., Porterville, Calif., 1961-63, San Bernadino Welfare, Ontario, Calif., 1963-65; tchr., reading specialist Pleasant View Sch., Porterville, 1969—; instr. Porterville Coll., 1993. Pres. PTA, Lindsay, Calif., 1966-67. Fellow Delta Kappa Gamma; mem. AAUW (bd. dirs. 1974-83), Calif. Reading Assn. (sec. 1974), Pleasant View Educators Assn. (past pres., sec. 1985—). Republican. Presbyterian. Club: P.E.O. (v.p. 1986-87).

BARZDUKAS, ROBERT CHARLES, social studies educator; b. Milw., Mar. 30, 1944; s. Albert Charles and Vivian Alice (Needham) B.; m. Elizabeth Anne McKirgan, Aug. 27, 1966; children: Sherri Anne, Shawna Lynn. BS in Edn., Western Ill. U., 1966; MA in Social Sci., U. No. Colo., 1972; postgrad., U. Colo., 1989, 90. Tchr. Poudre R-1 Schs., Ft. Collins, Colo., 1966-69, Lamar (Colo.) RE-2 Schs., 1969—. Author: Geographic Method of Study, 1989. Basketball ofcl. Internat. Assn. Approved Basketball Ofcls., Denver and Lamar, 1969-93; precint chair Prowers County Dem. Party, Lamar, 1980-91; swim ofcl. U.S. Swimming-Affiliated Colo. Swimming, Denver and Lamar, 1985-92. Recipient Lion award Southeast Colo. Uniserv Unit, LaJunta, 1987. Mem. NEA, Nat. Coun. Geographic Edn., Colo. Edn. Assn. (v.p. 1988-90), Colo. Coun. Social Studies, Lamar Edn. Assn. (pres. 1979-80, 91-92, Svc. award 1980, Tchr. of Yr. 1985). Democrat. Methodist. Office: Lamar High Sch 1900 S 11th St Lamar CO 81052-4061

BASCOM, EARL WESLEY, artist, writer; b. Vernal, Utah, June 19, 1906; s. John W. and Rachel C. (Lybbert) B.; m. Nadine Diffey, Dec. 20, 1939; children: Denise, Glen, Doris, John, Dona. BS, Brigham Young U., 1940, postgrad., 1965, 66; postgrad., U. Calif., Riverside, 1969. Profl. rodeo cowboy, 1918-40; producer 1st rodeo State of Miss., 1935, 36, 37; pres. Bascom and Wilkerson, 1947-51; owner Two Bar Qtr. Circle Ranch, 1951—; pres. High Desert Artists, Inc., 1964-65, Bascom Fine Arts, 1967—; owner Diamond B Ranch, 1975—; pres. Buckaroo Artists Am., 1978; tchr. art Barstow (Calif.) High Sch., 1966, 67, John F. Kennedy High Sch., 1966, 67; inventor rodeo equipment. Exhibited in group shows at Utah Artists, 1971, Cowboy Artists, 1972, Desert S.W. Artists, 1974, Mormon Festival of Arts, 1975, Cochise Mus., 1976, Wells Fargo Exhibit, 1976, Frank Tenney Johnson Invitational, 1979, Sun Valley, 1980, New Hibernia Exhibit, 1981, Santa Anita Nat. Horse Show, 1982, Cheyenne Frontier Days, 1983, Weighorst-Bascom Exhibit, 1984, Old Time Athletes, 1985, Golden Boot Exhibit, 1986, Nat. Salon, 1986, 87, 88, Internat. Art Exhibit, 1990, Equestrian Art Festival, 1991, Hollywood Park Exhibit, 1992, World Cup Exhibit (Las Vegas), 1993; represented in pvt. collections including Ronald Reagan, Roy Rogers, Gene Autrey, J.W. Marriott, Ezra Taft Benson, Louis L'Amour, Barry Goldwater, Charlton Heston; represented in permanent collections including Remington Mus. Art, Ogdensburg, N.Y., Nat. Cowboy Hall Fame Mus., Oklahoma City, N.Am. Cowboy Mus., Ft. Worth, Old West Mus., Cheyenne, Wyoming, Can. Rodeo Hall of Fame Mus., Calgary, Alberta, Can., U. Iowa Art Mus., Brigham Young U. Art Mus., Provo, Utah, Utah Mus. Fine Art, Salt Lake City, Whitney Mus. Art, Tucson Mus. Art; actor movie The Lawless Rider, 1954; appeared in commls. and documentarys; designed and made rodeo's first Hornless Bronc Saddle, 1922, also first One-Hand Bareback Rigging, 1924, Rodeo Chaps, 1926; invented Rodeo Exercizer, 1928; author, illustrator The History of Bareback Bronc Riding Western Horseman, 1990. Reserve champion, holder world record steer decorating N.Am. Championship, 1933; bareback, all-around champion, Lethbridge, Alb., Can., 1934; saddle bronc, steer decorating, all-around champion, Raymond, Alb., 1935, saddle bronc, bareback, all-around champion, 1940; all-around champion, Nephi, Utah, 1936; saddle bronc, bareback, bull riding, all-around champion, Pocatello, Idaho, 1937; bareback, bull riding, all-around champion, Portland, Oreg., 1938; inducted Can. Rodeo Hall Fame, 1984, Utah Sports Hall Fame, 1985, Raymond Sports Hall Fame, 1987; named honorary parade marshall, Cardston, Alb., 1982, Raymond, Alberta, 1984, Columbia, Miss., 1985, Vernal, Utah, 1989; honored as Legendary Cowboy various rodeo coms.; honored as Am. Hero U.S. Congl. Record, 1985; honored in resolutions various state and city govts.; named Outstanding Sr. Citizen Dept. Gerontology, 1987. Fellow Royal Soc. Arts (London); mem. Western Writers Am., Old Time Athletic Assn. (life), Profl. Rodeo Cowboys Assn. (hon. life), Nat. Outlaw and Lawman Assn. (life), Can. Rodeo Cowboys Assn. (hon. life), Can. Rodeo Hist. Assn. (founder), Pro Rodeo Hist. Soc. (life), Nat. Soc. Sons Utah Pioneers (life), U.S. Mormon Battalion Soc. (life), Assn. Latter-Day Media Artists, Old Timers Rodeo Assn., Cowboys Turtle Assn., Outlaw Trail History Assn., Brigham Young Univ. Emeritus Club (Spl. Recognition award 1992), Nat. Huguenot Soc., Basque Soc. Republican. Mormon. Office: Diamond B Ranch 15669 Stoddard Wells Rd Victorville CA 92392-2801

BASCONCILLO, LINDY, insurance and financial services company executive; b. Honolulu, Dec. 11, 1943; s. Catalino M. and Primitiva (Barientos) B.; children: Lisa M., Rod Alan. BA, Pacific Union Coll., 1965; MA, Azusa Pacific U., 1979. Chartered life underwriter, chartered fin. cons. Tchr., vice prin. Santa Monica (Calif.) Jr. Acad., 1965-68; tchr., coach Temple City (Calif.) Unified Sch. Dist., 1968-79; sales agent N.Y. Life Ins. Co., Eugene, Oreg., 1980-81, tng. mgr., 1981-87; sales mgr. MONY Fin. Svcs., Eugene, 1987-88; sr. mktg. cons. Prudential Ins. and Fin. Svcs., Woodland Hills, Calif., 1988-89; sales mgr. Prudential Ins. and Fin. Svcs., Sacramento, 1989-91; bus., estate, retirement specialist John Deere Life Ins. Co., Calif. and Nev., 1991—; mng. dir. Eute Consulting, Lincoln, Calif., 1993—; bus. cons. Jr. Achievement, Eugene, 1986; pres.-elect Eugene Life Underwriters Assn., 1988, v.p., 1987; chairperson Life Underwriter Tng. Coun., 1987, moderator, 1984-86. Mem. coun. for minority edn. U. Oreg., Eugene, 1986-88; mem. Lane County Tng. and Devel. Com., Eugene, 1985-87. Mem. Sacramento Chpt. CLU's, Sacramento Life Underwriters Assn. Home and Office: 1812 5th St Lincoln CA 95648-2328

BASDEN, BARBARA HOLZ, psychology educator; b. Coeur d'Alene, Idaho, Feb. 10, 1940; d. Albert R. and Carol (Utter) Holz; m.David R. Basden, May 25, 1962; children: Leslie H., Derin E. BA, Coll. Idaho, 1962; PhD, U. Calif., Santa Barbara, 1969. Asst. prof. psychology Calif. State U., Fresno, 1973-78, assoc. prof. psychology, 1978-82, prof. psychology, 1983—. Author: (study guide) Psychology, 1984, 2d edit., 1987, 3d edit., 1991, Implicit Memory & Aging, Memory & Hypnosis, 1987-93; contbr. articles to profl. jours. Mem. Psychonomic Soc., Am. Psychol. Assn., Am. Psychol. Soc., Western Psychol. Assn., Soc. Computer Psychology. Office: Calif State U Dept Psychology Fresno CA 93740

BASHIR, NAHEED, university administrator; b. Sibi, Pakistan, Aug. 4, 1937; came to U.S., 1959; d. Syed Mir Mohammad and Aquila (Bari) B.; m. Raza Aly, Sept. 24, 1958 (div. 1983); children: Hassan Aly, Tanya Aly. BA with honors, Kinnaird Coll., Lahore, Pakistan, 1956; MA in English Lit., Punjab U., Lahore, Pakistan, 1958; MA in Linguistics, U. Mich., 1961. Coll. instr. Quetta (Pakistan) Coll. for Women, 1958-59; lang. specialist Edn. Ministry, Pubjab Govt., Lahore, Pakistan, 1959-62; linguist English Lang. Inst. U. Mich., Ann Arbor, 1962-63, editor Bur. of Labor Rels., 1963-65; linguist Peace Corps, Ann Arbor, 1964; resource specialist Extension Div. U. Okla., Norman, 1965-67, extension specialist, 1967-69; asst. editor, cir. rsch. Am. Heart Assn., U. Calif., San Francisco, 1969-71; pub. info. officer Regional Med. Programs, U. Calif., San Francisco, 1971-72; sr. editor Pubs. Dept., U. Calif., San Francisco, 1972-73, dir., 1973—. Mng. editor Möbius, 1975; contbr. articles to profl. jours. Scholarship Ford Found., 1959. Mem. Coun. for Advancement and Support of Edn. (host recognition program 1992), U. and Coll. Designers Assn., Am. Inst. Graphic Designers. Democrat. Home: 510 Oak St San Francisco CA 94114 Office: U Calif MCB 630 San Francisco CA 94143-0828

BASICHIS, GORDON ALLEN, author, screenwriter; b. Phila., Aug. 23, 1947; s. Martin and Ruth (Gordon) B.; m. Marcia Hammond; 1 child, Casey James. BS, Temple U., 1969. Reporter Phila. Bull., 1969; writer, reporter Santa Fe News, 1971-72; with advt., pub. relations Jay Bernstein Pub. Relations, Los Angeles, 1978-80; screenwriter various studios, networks, Los Angeles, 1978-83; producer, dir. Big Sky, Inc., Sherman Oaks, Calif., 1980; screenwriter Metro Goldwyn Mayer Feature Films, Culver City, Calif., 1982-83; ind. writer, 1983—; pres. Moonlight, Inc., Los Angeles, 1982—; research cons. various pubs. Author: Beautiful Bad Girl: The Vicki Morgan Story, 1985, (novel) Constant Travelers, 1978; producer, dir. (video documentary) Jerry: One Man's Triumph, 1980; co-producer (TV series) Frank and Jesse; screenwriter (feature film) Return of the Jersey Devil, 1988, various other projects. Mem. Dem. Nat. Com. Mem. Writers Guild Am. West, Am. Film Inst., Simon Wiesenthal Inst., Nat. Rifle Assn., Statue of Liberty/Ellis Island Found. Office: PO Box 1511 Beverly Hills CA 90213-1511

BASILE, PAUL LOUIS, JR., lawyer; b. Oakland, Calif., Dec. 27, 1945; s. Paul Louis and Roma Florence (Paris) B.; m. Linda Lou Paige, June 20, 1970; m. 2d Diane Chierichetti, Sept. 2, 1977. BA, Occidental Coll., 1968; postgrad., U. Wash., 1969; JD, UCLA, 1971. Bar: Calif. 1972, U.S. Dist. Ct. (cen. dist.) Calif. 1972, U.S. Dist. Ct. (no. dist.) Calif. 1985, U.S. Ct. Appeals (9th cir.) 1972, U.S. Tax Ct. 1977, U.S. Ct. Claims. 1978, U.S. Customs Ct. 1979, U.S. Ct. Customs and Patent Appeals 1979, U.S. Ct. Internat. Trade 1981, U.S. Supreme Ct. 1977. Assoc. Parker, Milliken, Kohlmeier, Clark & O'Hara, L.A., 1971-72; corp. counsel TFI Cos., Inc., Irvine, Calif., 1972-73; pvt. practice L.A., 1973-80, 90—; mem. Basile & Siener, L.A., 1980-86, Clark & Trevithick, L.A., 1986-90; ptnr. Wolf, Rifkin & Shapiro, L.A., 1990, of counsel, 1990—; gen. counsel J.W. Brown, Inc., L.A., 1980—, asst. sec., 1984-92; sec., gen. counsel Souriau, Inc., Valencia, Calif., 1981-90; v.p., sec., dir., gen. counsel Pvt. Fin. Assocs., L.A., 1983—. Trustee, sec. Nat. Repertory Theatre Found., 1975—, mem. exec. com., 1976—, chmn. bd. dirs., 1991—; mem. fin. com., bd. dirs. Calif. Music Theatre, 1988-92; dir. March of Dimes Birth Defects Found., L.A. County, 1982-87, exec. com., 1983-86, sec., 1985-86; dist. fin. chmn. L.A. Area coun. Boy Scouts Am., 1982-83; trustee Occidental Coll., L.A., 1989—; active L.A. Olympic Organizing Com., Ketchum Downtown YMCA, Vols. Am. L.A., other orgns. Mem. ABA (taxation sect., corp. tax com., vice chmn. small bus. com. 1992—, chmn. subcom. on continuing legal edn. 1990-92, chmn. subcom. on estate planning 1992, bus. law sect., internat. bus. law com., real property sect., probate and trust law, spl. problems of bus. owners com.), Calif. State Bar Assn. (bus. law sect., nonprofit and unicorporated orgns. com., taxation sect., estate planning, trust and probate sect.), L.A. County Bar Assn. (taxation sect., com. on closely-held and pass-through entities, bus. and corps. law sect.), Can. Calif. C. of C. (dir. 1980-89, 2d v.p. 1983-84, 1st v.p. 1984-85, pres. 1985-87), French-Am. C. of C. (councilor 1979-84, v.p. 1980, 82-84), L.A. Area C. of C. (dir. 1980-81), Grand People (bd. dirs. 1985-92, chmn. bd. 1986-92), Rotary. Democrat. Baptist. Home: 3937 Beverly Glen Blvd Sherman Oaks CA 91423-4404 Office: 11400 W Olympic Blvd Fl 9 Los Angeles CA 90064-1507

BASILIO, ELEANOR VASCO, electronics and aerospace engineer; b. Manila, Philippines, Feb. 6, 1961; d. Sergio Rivera and Suerte (Ocampo) Vasco; m. Ralph Ramos Basilio, July 1, 1989. BA, UCLA, 1983; BS, Calif. State U., 1988. Electronics engr. Jet Propulsion Lab./Calif. Inst. Tech., Pasadena, 1987-89; spacecraft systems engr. Jet Propulsion Lab./Calif. Inst. Tech., 1989—. Calif. state scholar, 1978-82; recipient Award for Community Svc., County of L.A., 1978, achievement award NASA Guidance & Control Group, 1991, NASA group achievement award, 1992, 93. Mem. IEEE, Soc. Women Engrs., Engr. Honor Soc., Eta Kappa Nu. Roman Catholic. Home: 2055 Nordic Ave Chino Hills CA 91709 Office: Jet Propulsion Lab 4800 Oak Grove Dr Pasadena CA 91109-8099

BASINGER, RICHARD LEE, lawyer; b. Canton, Ohio, Nov. 24, 1941; s. Eldon R. and Alice M. (Bartholomew) B.; m. Rita Evelyn Gover, May 14, 1965; children: David A., Darron M. BA in Edn., Ariz. State U., 1963; postgrad. Macalester Coll., 1968-69; JD, U. Ariz., 1973. Bar: Ariz. 1973, U.S. Dist. Ct. Ariz. 1973, U.S. Tax Ct. 1977, U.S. Ct. Appeals (6th cir.) 1975, U.S. Ct. Appeals (9th cir.) 1976, U.S. Supreme Ct. 1977. Assoc. law offices, Phoenix, 1973-74; sole practice, Scottsdale, Ariz. 1974-75; pres. Basinger & Assocs., P.C., Scottsdale, 1975—, also bd. dirs. Contbr. articles to profl. jours. Bd. dirs. Masters Trail Ventures, Scottsdale, 1984-85, Here's Life, Ariz., Scottsdale, 1976—; precinct committeeman Republican Party, Phoenix, 1983—. NSF grantee, 1968-69. Mem. ABA, Ariz. Bar Assn., Maricopa County Bar Assn., Ariz. State Horseman's Assn. (bd. dirs. 1984-86, 1st v.p. 1986), Scottsdale Bar Assn., Western Saddle Club (bd. dirs. 1983-86, pres. 1985-86), Scottsdale Saddle Club, Saguaro Saddle Club. Baptist. Office: Basinger & Assocs PC 1184 N Tatum Blvd # P Phoenix AZ 85028-6116

BASKETT, JASON WELLS, healthcare management consulting company owner; b. Berkeley, Calif., Jan. 6, 1953; s. Charles Bennett and Eva Jane (Overstreet) B.; m. Lynn Ann Houston, Apr. 19, 1980; 1 child, Heather Marie. BS, U. Calif., Berkeley, Calif., 1974; MBA, Cornell U., 1978. Sr. v.p. Gerald Tracy Assocs., Oakland, Calif., 1978-86; mgr. The Peabody Group, San Francisco, 1987-88; acct. mgr. DKD & Co., Roseville, Calif., 1989; mng. dir., owner CMG Consulting, Inc., Berkeley, Calif., 1990—. Co-author: (book, manual) Resource Management Through Proudctivity Standards, 1984, 91. Mem. Healthcare Fin. Mgmt. Assn., Healthcare Execs. of Northern Calif. Democrat. Home: 744 Keeler Ave Berkeley CA 94708

BASLER, JOHN MICHELL, communications executive; b. Los Angeles, Oct. 25, 1926; s. Louis Adair and Caroline Mary (Michell) B.; m. Mary Ann Mohlengraft, Nov. 15, 1947; children: David Sutherland, Jon Edward. BS in Elec. Engring., U. So. Calif., 1947, MBA, 1961. Div. mgr. Pacific Telephone & Telegraph, Glendale, Calif., 1966-68; from dir. gen. employment to gen. program engr. Pacific Telephone & Telegraph, San Francisco, 1968-72; successively chief engr., asst. v.p., gen. mgr. Pacific Telephone & Telegraph, Los Angeles, 1972-75; asst. treas. AT&T, N.Y.C., 1975-76; network v.p. Pacific Telephone & Telegraph, Pasadena, Calif., 1976-78; v.p. support svcs. Pacific Bell, San Ramon, Calif., 1978-88; bd. dirs. Archimede's Circle U. So. Calif.; mem. adv. bd. Constrn. Industry Inst. U. Tex., Austin, 1986-88; chmn. exec. com. Western Council Constrn. Consumers, Calif., 1980-88; mem. Nat. Bus. Roundtable Constrn. Com., N.Y.C., 1986-88. Com. chmn., commission mem., Senate Adv. Commn. Cost Control State Govt., Sacramento, 1985-92; mem. Adv. Bd. Waste Mgmt., San Francisco, 1982-85; bd. dirs., San Francisco Opera Co., 1983-93. Sgt. USMC, 1952-54. Mem. Sigma Alpha Epsilon. Republican. Club: Engineer's (San Francisco), Commonwealth (San Francisco). Home: 46 Glenbrook Dr Hillsborough CA 94010-7410

BASLER, RICHARD ALAN, biomedical instruments manufacturer; b. San Francisco, Sept. 12, 1939; s. Henry Edwin and Margaret Henrietta (Cooper) B.; m. Carol Audrey Foster, Aug. 4, 1962; children: Rodney Giles, Eric Richard. BA, U. Calif., Berkeley, 1960; MBA, U. Phoenix, Irvine, Calif., 1983. Indsl. engr., prodn. supr. Standard Register, Oakland and Corcoran, Calif., 1967-72; knitting supt. Duplan Knits West, Carson, Calif., 1972-75; prodn. supr. Am. Edwards Labs., Irvine, 1976-78, chief indsl. engr., 1978-80, supr. mfg. engring., 1980-86, with engring. systems devel., 1986-87; mgr. quality assurance/quality control Cardiovascular Devices Inc., 1987-88; dir. quality assurance/quality control Applied Vascular Devices Inc., 1988-90, dir. compliance, 1990—; owner Internat. Numismatics, Irvine, 1974—. Editor Calif. Engr. mag., 1959; contbr. articles to mags. Bd. dirs. UNCAP, Inc., L.A., 1980-82; pres. Colonnade of History, 1990—. Lt. USN, 1960-67, Vietnam., with res. 1967-81. Recipient Kenneth Brainard Meml. Literary award, George Bennett Meml. Literary award. Mem. Am. Soc. Quality Control, U.S. Kerry Blue Terrier Club (gov. 1983-85), Gt. Western Terrier (bd. dirs. 1979-92). Republican. Office: Applied Vascular Devices Inc 26051 Merit Cir Laguna Beach CA 92653-7008

BASS, DAVID JASON, manufacturing engineer; b. Denver, July 8, 1954; s. Grover Terrell and Laura Annie (Whiting) B.; m. Debra Jean Meyer, Aug. 10, 1974; children: Jenell, Kevin, Kristyn, Staci. AS in Drafting Tech., Ea. Ariz. Coll., 1974; BS in Tech. Mgmt., Regis Coll., 1988. Electro-mech. designer govt. electronics group Motorola, Inc., Scottsdale, Ariz., 1974-79; mech. designer Motorola, Inc., Tempe, Ariz., 1979-80; mech. and tooling engr. Kustom Electronics, Chanute, Kans., 1980-81, liaison engr., 1981-82, mgr. mfg. engring., 1982-84; sr. design engr. Martin Marietta Co., Denver, 1984-87, sr. mfg. engr., 1987; supr. mfg. engring. Global-Wulfsberg, Prescott, Ariz., 1987—. Mem. curriculum adv. com. Ea. Ariz. Coll., Thatcher, 1976-80. Mem. Soc. Mfg. Engrs., Am. Prodn. and Inventory Control Soc. Republican. Home: 2090 Dineh Dr Prescott AZ 86301-3911 Office: Global-Wulfsberg 6400 Wilkinson Dr Prescott AZ 86301-6164

BASS, JAMES WILLIS, pediatrician, army officer, educator; b. Shreveport, La., May 25, 1930; s. Stewart Thomas Bass; m. Mary Beverley Smith, Sept. 13, 1951; children: Paulét McLellan, Brian Camille. BS, Tulane U. and Centenary Coll., 1952; postgrad., La. State U., Baton Rouge, 1952-53; MD, La. State U., New Orleans, 1957; MPH, Tulane U., 1968. Diplomate Am. Bd. Pediatrics, Am. Bd. Pediatric Infectious Disease. Commd. 2d lt. U.S. Army, 1956, advanced through grades to col., 1972; rotating and flexible intern Brooke Army Med. Ctr., San Antonio, 1957-58, resident in pediatrics, 1958-60; NIH fellow in pediatric infectious diseases Tulane U. Sch. Medicine, New Orleans, 1966-68; chief dept. pediatrics Walter Reed Army Med. Ctr., Washington, 1975-81; prof., chmn. dept. Uniformed Svcs. U. Health Scis., Bethesda, Md., 1976-81; prof. Tripler Army Med. Ctr. affiliate Uniformed Svcs. U. Health Scis., Honolulu, 1981—; chief dept. pediatrics Tripler Army Med. Ctr., 1981—; asst. clin. prof. U. Hawaii, 1968-70, assoc. clin. prof., 1970-73, clin. prof., 1970-75, 1981—; cons. in pediatrics to surgeon gen. U.S. Army, 1975-81; prof. Georgetown U. Sch. Medicine, Washington, 1976-81; clin. prof. Howard U. Sch. Medicine, Washington, 1976-81; assoc. clin. prof. U. So. Calif., L.A., 1972—; numerous presentations to med. confs., symposia, seminars; cons. Nat. Inst. Child Health and Human Devel., NIH, 1978-81; numerous vis. professorships. Mem. editorial bd. Pediatric Infectious Disease Jour., 1986; contbr. numerous articles and abstracts to med. jours. Recipient Lewis Aspey Malogne award for acad. excellence U.S. Army Surgeon Gen., 1990. Fellow ACP, Am. Acad. Pediatrics (exec. com. Hawaii chpt. 1983—), Infectious Disease Soc. Am.; mem. AMA, Honolulu Pediatric Soc., Hawaii Med. Assn., Am. Soc. Microbiology, Western Soc. Pediatric Rsch., Soc. Pediatric Rsch., So. Soc. Pediatric Rsch., Am. Pediatric Soc., Soc. Med. Cons. to Armed Forces (assoc.). Episcopalian. Home: 469 Ena Rd Apt 1901 Honolulu HI 96815 Office: Tripler Army Med Ctr Dept Pediatrics Honolulu HI 96859-5000

BASS, RICHARD SAMUEL, physician; b. July 18, 1938; m. Susan Schiffman; children: Deborah, Carolyn, Jennifer. BA, Rutgers Coll., 1960; MD, N.Y. Med. Coll., 1965. Diplomate Am. Bd. Psychiatry and Neurology. Intern San Francisco Gen. Hosp., 1965-66; resident U. Calif., San Francisco, 1966-69; pvt. practice, 1969—. Home: 435 Seneca St Palo Alto CA 94301-2227

BASS, RONALD, screenwriter. Screenplays include Code Name: Emerald, 1985, Black Widow, 1987, Gardens of Stone, 1987, Rainman, 1988 (Acad. award), Sleeping with the Enemy, 1991. Office: Creative Artists Agency 9830 Wilshire Blvd Beverly Hills CA 90212

BASSETT, ARTHUR RAY, humanities educator; b. St. Anthony, Idaho, Oct. 14, 1935; s. Thomas Myrthen and Henrietta (Minson) B.; m. Janet B. Peers, Sept. 1, 1959; children: Kedric A., Julene, Bevan P., Morgan J., Britany. BS, Brigham Young U., 1960, MRE, 1965; PhD, Syracuse U., 1975. Instr. Latter-Day Saints Ch. Edn. System, Heber City, Utah, 1960-63; curriculum writer Latter-day Saints Ch. Edn. System, Provo, Utah, 1963-67; instr. Latter-day Saints Ch. Edn. System, Salt Lake City, 1970-72; prof. humanities Brigham Young U., Provo, 1972—; chmn. Am. Studies Program, 1986-89. Recipient Karl G. Maeser Disting. Teaching award, 1985; named BYU Alcuin fellow, 1986-91. Mem. Am. Studies Assn., Nat. Assn. Humanities Educators, Phi Kappa Phi. Home: 35 W 1880 N Orem UT 84057-2111 Office: Brigham Young U 3010-G JKHB Provo UT 84602

BASSETT, BARBARA WIES, editor, publisher; b. Dec. 5, 1939; m. Norman W. Bassett. B.A., U. Conn., 1961; student, New Sch. for Social Research, 1961-62. Product devel. Fearn Soya, Melrose Park, Ill., 1973-75; product devel. Modern Products, Milw., 1973-75; editor, pub. Bestways Mag., Carson City, Nev., 1977-89; pub. The Healthy Gourmet Newsletter, 1989-91, Fine Wine-Good Food Newsletter, 1991—; owner Gualala (Calif.) Galleries, 1989-90; owner, operator cooking sch. Greensboro N.C. 1969-73. Author: Natural Cooking, 1968, Wok and Tempura, 1969, Japanese Home Cooking, 1970, The Wok, 1971, Super Soy, 1973, The Healthy Gourmet, 1981, International Healthy Gourmet, 1982; one-woman show paintings Dolphin Gallery, Gualala, Calif., 1990, 2-woman show, 1992, solo exhbn. Nev. Artists Assn. Gallery, 1993. Mem. Inst. Food Technologists, Pastel Soc. of the West Coast, Inst. Am. Culinary Profls.

BASSETT, H(ENRY) GORDON, petroleum company executive; b. Newton, Mass., Nov. 12, 1924; s. Harry and Phyllis Mildred (Proctor) B.; m. Marion Mae Griffiths, July 11, 1949; children—Alan, Beverly, James. B.Sc., McGill U., 1949, M.Sc., 1950; A.M., Princeton U., 1952, Ph.D., 1952. Registered profl. geologist, Can. Div. stratigrapher Shell Can. Ltd., Calgary and Edmonton, Alta., Can., 1952-72, head stratigraphic services, Houston, 1972-80; mgr. geologic tech. Sohio Petroleum Co., San Francisco, 1980-85; cons. geologist, 1986—. Served with RCAF, 1943-45. Recipient Pres.'s Gold medal

Can. Inst. Mining and Metallurgy, 1950. Fellow Geol. Assn. Can.; mem. Am. Assn. Petroleum Geologists, Can. Assn. Petroleum Geologists, Edmonton Geol. Soc. (pres. 1966). Republican. Home: 3320 Las Huertas Rd Lafayette CA 94549-5109

BASSIST, DONALD HERBERT, college president; b. Dallas, Oct. 28, 1923; s. Ellis and Adele (Gutz) B.; m. Norma Dale Andersen, Oct. 14, 1950; children: Matthew Perry, Bradford Beaumont. AB, Harvard U., 1948; MBA, Portland State U., 1975; grad., U.S. Army command and Gen. Staff Coll., 1967. Pres. Bassist Coll., Portland, Oreg., 1963—; chmn. ednl. adv. bd. pvt. vocat. schs., Salem, Oreg., 1972-78; active Oreg. Ednl. Coordinating Coun., 1970-73. Writer, dir. (film) Fashion: The Career of Fashion, 1969 (N.Y. Internat. Bronze award). Lt. A.C., U.S. Army, 1943-46. Mem. Nat. Assn. Scholars, Japanese Garden Soc. (bd. dirs. 1988—), Portland Advt. Fedn. (bd. dirs. 1969-72).

BASTIAN, BRUCE WAYNE, software company executive; b. Twin Falls, Idaho, Mar. 23, 1948; s. Arlon Lewis and Una (Davis) B.; m. Melanie Laycock, Apr. 17, 1976; children: C. Richard, Darren B., Jeffrey H., Robert A. BMus, Brigham Young U., 1975, MS in Computer Sci., 1978. Software engr. Eyring Research, Provo, Utah, 1978-79; software developer WordPerfect Corp., Orem, Utah, 1979-81; chmn. bd. Satellite Software, Orem, Utah, 1981—. Co-author Word Perfect computer program, 1979. Office: Wordperfect Corp 1555 N Technology Way Orem UT 84057-2399

BASTIAN, JANELLE ANNETTE, elementary education educator; b. Freeport, Ill., Aug. 15, 1955; d. Leonard Burdette and Janet Elaine (Baxter) B. BA, U. No. Iowa, Cedar Falls, 1976, MA in Edn., 1987. Cert. tchr., Iowa, Calif. Librarian, English tchr. Walnut Ridge Bapt. Acad., Waterloo, Iowa, 1977-78, tchr. 3d grade, 1978-88; tutor Grace Community Sch., Sun Valley, Calif., 1989—, tchr. 2d and 3d grades, 1989—; leader various seminars. Author: Honeycomb Tapestry, 1988; contbr. articles to profl. jours. Named to Outstanding Young Women of Am., 1991; Waterloo Women of Today reading grantee, 1987. Mem. Internat. Reading Assn. Republican. Home: 10831 Roycroft St # 50 Sun Valley CA 91352 Office: Grace Community Sch 13246 Roscoe Blvd Sun Valley CA 91352

BATARSE, ANTHONY ABRAHAM, JR., automobile executive; b. El Salvador, June 1, 1933; s. Antonio A. Sr. and Mirtha (Perla) B.; m. Esther Beltran, Nov. 27, 1953; children: Esther M., Rudy A., Mirtha C., Rocio L., Mark A., John A., James A. BS in Letters and Sci., Coll. Sci. and Letters, 1955; cert. in real estate fin. and law, Coll. San Mateo, 1969; cert. in bus. mgmt., Harvard U., 1987. Mgr. new car sales Hayward (Calif.) Ford, 1968-71; mgr. sales Lloyd A. Wise Oldsmobile, Oakland, Calif., 1971-75; pres., chief exec. officer Lloyd A. Wise, Inc., Oakland, 1975—. Bd. dirs. Oakland C. of C., 1992. Recipient Commendation City of Miami, 1985, Commendation City of San Leandro, 1987, Retailer Yr. award Oakland C. of C., 1989; ranked 14th largest bus. in U.S., Hispanic Bus. 500 Nat. Listing, 1992. Mem. Calif. Hispanic C. of C. (Bus. Man of Yr. 1987). Republican. Office: Lloyd A Wise Co 10550 E 14th St Oakland CA 94603-3804

BATCHELOR, JAMES KENT, lawyer; b. Long Beach, Calif., Oct. 4, 1934; s. Jack Morrell and Edith Marie (Ottinger) B.; m. Jeanette Lou Dyer, Mar. 27, 1959; children: John, Suzanne; m. Susan Mary Leonard, Dec. 4, 1976. AA, Sacramento City Coll., 1954; BA, Long Beach State Coll., 1956; JD, Hastings Coll. Law, U. Calif., 1959. Bar: Calif. 1960, U.S. Dist. Ct. (cen. dist.) Calif. 1960, U.S. Supreme Ct. 1968; cert. family law specialist Calif. Bd. Legal Specialization. Dep. dist. atty., Orange County, Calif., 1960-62; assoc. Miller, Nisson, Kogler & Wenke, Santa Ana, Calif., 1962-64; ptnr. Batchelor, Cohen & Oster, Santa Ana, 1964-67, Kurilich, Ballard, Batchelor, Fullerton, Calif., 1967-72; pres. James K. Batchelor, Inc., Santa Ana, 1972—; tchr. paralegal sect. Santa Ana City Coll.; judge pro-tem Superior Ct., 1974—; lectr. family law Calif. Continuing Edn. of Bar, 1973—. Contbr. articles to profl. jours. Fellow Am. Acad. Matrimonial Lawyers (pres. So. Calif. chpt. 1989-90); mem. ABA, Calif. Trial Lawyers Assn., Calif. State Bar (placque chmn. family law sect. 1975-76, advisor 1976-78), Orange County Barristers (founder, pres., placque 1963), Calif. State Barristers (placque 1965, v.p.), Orange County Bar Assn. (plaque sec. 1977, pres. family law sect. 1968-71). Republican. Methodist. Office: 820 N Parton St Ste 1A Santa Ana CA 92701-3324

BATDORF, SAMUEL B(URBRIDGE), physicist; b. Jung Hsien, China, Mar. 31, 1914; s. Charles William and Nellie (Burbridge) B.; m. Carol Catherine Schweiss, July 19, 1940; children: Samuel Charles, Laura Ann. A.B., U. Calif.-Berkeley, 1934, A.M., 1936, Ph.D., 1938. Assoc. prof. physics U. Nev., 1938-43; aero. rsch. scientist Langley Lab., NACA, 1943-51, chmn. advanced study com., 1946-51; mem. NACA subcom. on aircraft structural metals, 1946-51; dir. devel. Westinghouse Elec. Corp., Pitts., 1951-56; tech. dir. weapons systems Lockheed Missile & Space Co., Palo Alto, Calif., 1956-58; mgr. communication satellites Inst. Def. Analysis, Washington, 1958-59; dir. rsch. in physics, electronics and bionics Aeronutronic, Newport Beach, Calif., 1959-62; prin. staff scientist Aerospace Corp., El Segundo, Calif., 1962-77; Sigma Xi lectr. communication satellites; Disting. prof. Tsing Hua U., Republic of China, 1969; vis. scholar Va. Poly. Inst. and State U., 1984; adj. prof. engring. and applied sci. UCLA, 1973-86; mem. aeromechanics adv. com. Air Force Office Sci. Rsch., 1965-71, tech. assessment panel Engrs. Joint Coun., 1968-71. Contbr. articles to profl. jours. Fellow AIAA (edn., structures and materials coms.), ASME (hon., edn. materials and space structures coms., chmn. applied mechanics div. exec. com. materials and space structures com.), Am. Phys. Soc., Am. Acad. Mechanics (pres. 1982-83); mem. Aerospace Club, Rod and Gun Club, Academia Club, Engrs. Club of Va. Peninsula (pres. 1948), Phi Beta Kappa, Phi Kappa Phi. Republican. Presbyterian. Home: 5536 B Via La Mesa Laguna Hills CA 92653

BATEMAN, ANN CREIGHTON, minister; b. Blythe, Calif., June 7, 1943; d. William Stanley and Lucille Mildred (Beem) Creighton; m. Thomas Herbert Bateman, June 19, 1966; children: Mark Eric, Dale Kirk. BA, Whittier Coll., 1964; MAV, San Francisco Theol. Sem., 1981. Consecrated to diaconal ministry United Meth. Ch., 1972. Dir. Christian edn. Ch. of the Good Shepherd, Arcadia, Calif., 1965-67, Arlington United Meth. Ch., Riverside, Calif., 1970-74, First Unted Meth. Ch., Roseburg, Oreg., 1974-77; cons. Christian edn. Ch. Edn. Cons. Service, Salem, Oreg., 1977—; chair bd. diaconal ministry Oreg.-Idaho Ann. Conf., 1985-87, chair bd. higher edn. and campus ministry, 1992—; del. Western Jurisdictional Conf. United Meth. Ch., 1980, 84, 88, 92; mem. gen. bd. higher edn. and ministry United Meth. Ch., Nashville, 1988—. Author: Sermon Simulations, 1977, Doing the Bible, 1984; contbr. newsletter Tchr. Tng. Topics, 1983-86, Ch. Tchr. mag. Project leader 4-H, Salem, 1979-90, mem. state recognition and awards com., Corvallis, Oreg., 1985. Mem. United Meth. Women (life), Oreg.-Idaho Christian Educators Fellowship. Democrat. Office: Church Edn Cons Svc 595 Oregon Ave NE Salem OR 97301-4656

BATEMAN, JOHN L., government agency administrator; b. Whittier, Calif., Dec. 26, 1953; s. John William and Glenus (Redman) B. BA in Bus., U. of La Verne, 1976. Sales mgr. Conner Tours, Pasadena, Calif., 1976-84; dir. mktg. Corliss Tours, Monrovia, Calif., 1985; sales mgr. Trieloff Tours, Laguna Hills, Calif., 1985; dir. of tourism Govt. of British Columbia Ministry of Tourism, Irvine, Calif., 1985—. Mem. Am. Soc. Travel Agts., Paciic Area Travel Assn., Travel and Rsch. Assn. Republican. Mem. Soc. of Friends. Office: Tourism British Columbia 2600 Michelson Ste 1050 Irvine CA 90600

BATEMAN, ROBERT EARL, II, technology management consultant; b. Spokane, Wash., Apr. 4, 1958; s. Robert Earl and DeNai (McMullin) B.; m. Candace Elaine Harper, Dec. 17, 1979; children: Ronni, Robert August, Wilson Arthur, Kalli, Talya, Cecy. BS, Brigham Young U., 1981; M in Bus., Am. U., 1982. Staff intern Senate Banking Com., Washington, 1982; svc. mgr. Ken Garff Imports, Salt Lake City, 1982-85; adminstrv. officer U.S. State Dept., Washington, 1985-86; adminstrv. officer Am. Embassy, Riyadh, Saudi Arabia, 1986-88, San Jose, Costa Rica, 1988-90; pres. Integrated Systems Tech., Alpine, Utah, 1990—; guest lectr. Weber State U., Ogden, Utah, 1984—; cons. Lascasiana S.A., San Luis Potosi, Mex., 1991, Geneva Steel Corp., Provo, Utah, 1991-93, Technisar, Longmont, Colo., 1992, IOMEGA, Ogden, 1992; speaker in field. Contbr. articles to profl. jours. Scout leader Boy Scout Am., Alpine, 1992. Mem. Soc. Logistics Engrs., Internat. Assn. for Impact Assessment, World Devel. Coun., Inst. Indsl. Engrs. LDS. Office: Integrated Systems Tech 755 W 800 S Alpine UT 84004

BATEMAN, ROBERT EDWIN, aeronautical engineer; b. Butte, Mont., Apr. 11, 1923; s. Edwin Joseph and Katherine (Bronner) B.; m. Sarah Elizabeth Hayes, Mar. 2, 1947; children: Robert Eugene, Lucy Annette, Paul William. BS in Aero. Engring., Purdue U., 1946; ED (hon.), Purdue, 1992. Aero. staff Boeing Co., Seattle, 1946-59; devel. program mgr. Boeing Aerospace, Seattle, 1959-65, gen. mgr. turbine div., 1965-67, 747 program exec., 1967-71, v.p., mgr. Washington D.C. ops., 1971-75, v.p. gen. mgr. marine systems, 1975-85; v.p. govt. and internat. affairs Boeing Co., Seattle, 1985-88; chmn., bd. dirs. Mus. Flight, Seattle, 1989—. Bd. dirs. Naval War Coll., Newport, R.I., 1976—, Naval Meml. Found., 1983-88; pres. World Affairs Coun., Seattle, 1988—. Lt. comdr. USNR, 1946-66. Sec. Navy Meritorius Pub. Svc. award, 1968, Disting. Pub. Svc. award, 1972; named Disting. Engring. Alumnus Purdue U., 1974, Old Master award, 1988. Fellow (assoc.) AIAA; mem. Navy League U.S. (exec. com., nat. dir. 1965—, Disting. Svc. award 1986, Hall of Fame 1991). Home: 1645 E Boston Ter Seattle WA 98112-2831

BATEMAN, RONALD RAO, educational audiologist; b. Salt Lake City, May 20, 1947; s. Rao Henry and Phyllis Ruth (Parrish) B.; m. Beverly Rae Christiansen, Aug. 15, 1969; children: Jodi Kimball, Jonathan Rayo, Jana, Jeffrey Ronald. BS, Utah State U., 1971, MS, 1972, EdS, 1989. Cert. communicative disorders, hearing impaired edn. Audiologist, tchr. hearing impaired Granite Sch. Dist., Salt Lake City, 1972—; affiliate Bateman Cattle Ranch, Ibapah, Utah, 1972—; ops. employee Valley Bank and Trust, Salt Lake City, 1976-83; owner Bateman Enterprises, Granger, South Jordan, Utah, 1977—, Superior Printing, Granger, 1983; mem. ad hoc com. audiology cert. Utah State Bd. Edn., 1974-82; evaluation team Utah State U. EdS Program, 1982; presenter Am. Speech, Hearing and Lang. Assn., St. Louis, 1990; accreditation team Utah Sch. for the Deaf, Salt Lake City. Author: Deep Creek Reflections, 1984; compiler South Jordan City history book, 1993; contbr. articles to Utah History Ency., 1993. County and state del. Rep. Convs., Salt Lake City, 1976, 81; bishop LDS Ch., Granger, 1977-83; asst. and scoutmaster Boy Scouts Am., South Jordan, 1985—; youth leader 4-H Club, Ibapah, 1985—; mem. South Jordan (Utah) Hist. Preservation Com., 1990—. Named Outstanding Young Men of Am., 1984; recipient grant Utah State U., Logan, 1982-84, 89, Wood badge Boy Scouts Am., Grand Teton Coun., 1984. Mem. NEA, Utah Edn. Assn., Granite Edn. Assn. (faculty rep. 1970's). Home: 4049 Yorkshire Dr South Jordan UT 84065

BATES, CHARLES EMERSON, library administrator; b. Los Angeles, Dec. 1, 1946; s. Willard Emerson Bates and Erica (Schmidt) Bates Beckwith; m. Mary Joan Genz, Aug. 7, 1971; children—Christopher, Noah, Colin. BA, Valparaiso U., 1968; MEd, Loyola U., Chgo., 1970; MLS, Rosary Coll., 1973. Head of reference Decatur Pub. Libr., Ill., 1973-74; cons. Rolling Prairie Libr. System, Decatur, 1974-76; asst. dir. Fond du Lac Pub. Libr., Wis., 1976-81; dir. Pueblo Libr. Dist., Colo., 1981—. Bd. dirs. Pueblo United Way, 1982-86, Sangre de Cristo Arts and Conf. Ctr., Pueblo, 1990—; pres. bd. dirs. Rosemount Victorian House Mus., Pueblo, 1984—. Mem. ALA, Colo. Libr. Assn., Ark. Valley Libr. System (pres. 1984-85, 89-90), Mountain Plains Libr. Assn., Rotary (pres. bd. dirs. 1981—). Lutheran. Office: Pueblo Libr Dist McClelland Libr 100 E Abriendo Ave Pueblo CO 81004-4232

BATES, CHARLES WALTER, human resources executive, lawyer, politician; b. Detroit, June 28, 1953; s. E. Frederick and Virginia Marion (Nunneley) B. BA in Psychology and Econs. cum laude, Mich. State U., 1975, M in Labor and Indsl. Rels., 1977; postgrad. DePaul U., 1979-80; JD William Mitchell Coll. Law, 1984. Bar: Wash. 1990, U.S. Dist. Ct. (we. dist.) Washington, 1992. ; cert. sr. profl. in human resources, 1989. Vista vol., paralegal, Ventura County Legal Aid Assn. (now Channel Counties Legal Aid Assn.), Calif., 1975-76; job analyst Gen. Mills, Inc., Mpls., 1977-78, plant pers. asst. II, Chgo., 1978-80, asst. plant pers. mgr., Chgo., 1980-81, pers. mgr. consumer foods mktg., Mpls., 1981-82; pers. mgr. consumer foods mktg. divs. Saluto Pizza, Mpls., 1982-84; human resources mgr. Western div., Godfather's Pizza, Inc., Costa Mesa, Calif., 1984-85, human resources mgr. Western U.S., Can., Bellevue, Washington, 1985-91; dir. human resources. Royal Seafoods, Inc., Seattle, 1991-92, dir. human resources and employee rels. counsel, 1992—; instr. employee and labor rels., Lake Wash. Tech. Coll., 1992—. Contbr. articles and commentary to Bellevue Jour.-Am., Seattle Times, Seattle Post-Intelligencer; mem. editorial adv. bd. Recruitment Today mag., 1990-91. Candidate for lt. gov., 1982, Minn.; asst. scoutmaster Boy Scouts Am., 1971—, asst. advisor-activities Order of Arrow, 1989-92 (recipient Vigil Honor award, 1990); elected Sammamish Community Coun., Bellevue, 1989, councilman, 1990-93; mem. E. Bellevue Transp. Study Adv. Group, 1989-92. Rep. precinct com. officer, 1990—, 48th Legis. Dist. Republican Candidate Search Com, 1992. Recipient Scouter's Tng. award Boy Scouts Am., 1979, Dist. award of merit, 1991, Nat. Vantage Recruiting award, 1990. Mem. ABA (urban, state and local got. law, labor and employment), Nat. Eagle Scout Assn., Pacific NW Pers. Mgmt. Assn. (Seattle chpt.), Soc. for Human Resources Mgmt, Wash. State Bar Assn. (environ. and land use law), Fishing Industry Personnel Assn. Wash., Seattle-King County Bar Assn. (labor law, maritime and fisheries law), Mich. State U. Alumni Assn., Puget Sound Alumni Club, William Mitchell Coll. Law Alumni Assn. Home: 232 168th Ave NE Bellevue WA 98008-4522 Office: Royal Seafoods Inc PO Box 19032 Seattle WA 98109-1032

BATES, CRAIG DANA, ethnographer, curator, government official; b. Oakland, Calif., Aug. 2, 1952; s. Dana Raymond and June (Robinson) B.; m. Jennifer Dawn Bernido, May 12, 1973 (div. 1987); 1 child, Carson Dana. Park technician Nat. Park Svc., Yosemite National Park, Calif., 1973-76, Indian cultural specialist, 1976-80, asst. curator, 1980-82, curator ethnography, 1982—; rsch. assoc. Santa Barbara (Calif.) Mus. Natural History, 1983—; cons. Calif. Indian exhbn. SW Mus., L.A., 1985, Culin exhbn. Bklyn. Mus., 1988-89, Lowie Mus. Anthropology, U. Calif., Berkeley, 1990. Co-author: (with Martha Lee) Tradition and Innovation: A Basket History of the Indians of the Yosemite Mono Lake Area, 1990; contbr. more than 90 articles on Am. Indian culture to profl. jours. Office: Nat Park Svc Yosemite Mus PO Box 577 Yosemite National Park CA 95389-0577

BATES, DONALD LLOYD, civil engineer; b. Knightstown, Ind., Feb. 18, 1932; s. Edgar Richard and Lora Norinda (Miller) B.; m. Ngan Yeng, Sept. 3, 1983. BCE, U. Md., 1964; MBA, U. Ind., 1972; PhD, Columbia Pacific U., 1990. Registered profl. engr., Va., Wis., Ariz. Geologist Shell Oil Ltd., Brunei, North Borneo, 1964-66; materials engr. FHA U.S. Dept. Transp., Arlington, Va., 1966-88; quality control engr. Century Materials, Inc., Tempe, Ariz., 1988-91; civil engr. Centennial Civil Engring. Cons., Inc., Irvine, Calif., 1991—; engring. cons. Calif. Dept. Transp., Santa Ana, 1991—. Capt. U.S. Army, 1948-52. Mem. Nat. Soc. Profl. Engrs., ASCE (vice chmn. materials com. 1991-92), ASTM, Assn. Asphalt Paving Engrs., Am. Concrete Inst. Roman Catholic.

BATES, DWIGHT LEE, mechanical engineer; b. Miles City, Mont., Aug. 19, 1943; s. Edmond Russell and Verna Elizabeth (Johnson) B.; m. Diane Marie Seppi, Aug. 19, 1967. BSME, U. Wyo., 1966; MBA in Mktg., Seattle U., 1971. Registered profl. engr., Wash. Rsch. engr. comml. airplane div. Boeing Co., Seattle, 1966-70; product devel. engr. internat. mktg. div. Warn Industries, Seattle, 1972-73, 1972-73; prin. engr. Heath Tecna, Kent, Wash., 1973-74; mech. design engr. Puget sound naval shipyard U.S. Dept. Def., Bremerton, Wash., 1974-78; supervisory indsl. engr. Supship Seattle, 1978-85; sr. specialist engr. Comml. Airplane div. Boeing Co., Seattle, 1985—; cons. in field. Contbr. publs. in field. Pres. Melrose E. Condo Assn., Seattle, 1978-81; bus. adv. coun. Resource Ctr. for Handicapped. With USCG Aux. Recipient 2 letters of appreciation and 2 letters of commendation U.S. Dept. Def., award Am. Mktg. Assn., 1973. Mem. Resource Ctr. for Handicapped Bus. Adv. Coun. (4 letters of commendation), AIAA (pres. Laramie, Wyo. chpt. 1966), NSPE, Wash. State Profl. Engrs. Soc., Wash. State Power Squadron, Am. Inst. Indsl. Engrs., Seattle U. MBA Assn. Democrat. Lutheran. Home: 1912 E Mcgraw St Seattle WA 98112-2629 Office: Boeing Co PO Box 707 Seattle WA 98111-0707

BATES, GEORGE EDMONDS, bishop; b. Binghampton, N.Y., Aug. 11, 1933; m. Sue Onstott; children: Richard Howard, Katherine Bates Schey. BA in Sociology and English, Dartmouth Coll., 1955; MDiv, Episcopal Theol. Sem., 1958. ordained deacon, The Episcopal Ch., 1958, priest, 1959. Parish priest Ithaca and Syracuse, N.Y.; rector Ch. of the Redeemer, Pendleton, Oreg., 1970-83, St. Mark's-on-the-Mesa, Albuquerque, 1983-86; consecrated bishop Diocese of Utah, 1986. Chmn. bd. dirs. St. Mark's Hosp.; bd. dirs. Westminster Coll., Rowland Hall-St. Mark's Sch.; mem. Gov.'s Task Force on Health Care Costs, Utah Econ. Devel. Office: Diocese of Utah 231 E 1st S Salt Lake City UT 84111-1699

BATES, GRACE KAMP, civic volunteer; b. Manhattan, Mont., Apr. 26, 1917; d. John T. and Elizabeth (deRuig) Kamp; m. Avery Verne Bates, Apr. 16, 1939; children: Ronald, Virgil, Gary. Author: Alaska and Back, 1975, Gallatin County Places and Things, 1985, 100 Delegates-Montana Constitutional Convention 1972, 1989; author historic booklets, rsch. articles. Dem. precinct committeewoman, 1956-78; vice-chair Gallatin County Dem. Cen. Com., 1956-58, Mont. Dem. Cen. Com., 1959-61; pres. Gallatin County Dem. Women's Club, 1965-70; bd. dirs. Mont. Comprehensive Health Planning Coun., 1969-76, White House Conf. on Aging, 1971, County Comprehensive Health Planning Coun., 1971-75; del. Mont. Constl. Conv., 1971-72. Mem. LWV (chair local govt. publ. com. 1977), Federated Women's Club (sec. bd. dirs. 1966-86), Mont. Constl. Conv. Soc. of 1972 (sec. 1979-81), Gallatin County Hist. Soc. (co-founder 1977, bd. dirs. 1977-92, pres. bd. 1979-83, 85-92, coord. Lewis and Clark pageant 1980, 81, coord. county jail renovation project 1982), Bozeman Woman's Club, Mont. Hist. Soc., Lewis and Clark Trails. Home: 6800 Amsterdam Rd Manhattan MT 59741

BATES, KENNETH NORRIS, scientist; b. Dallas, June 15, 1949; s. Kenneth L. Bates and Lesta J. (Norris) Burt; m. Carmen Lorz, June 14, 1981; children: Kevin, Cassandra. BS, U. Tex., 1972; MS, Stanford (Calif.) U., 1975, PhD, 1982. Project mgr. Hewlett Packard, Palo Alto, Calif., 1979-82; prin. engr. Advanced Tech. Labs., Bothell, Wash., 1982-85; founder, v.p. engring. Ariel Electronics, Sunnyvale, Calif., 1985-89; sr. scientist KLA Instruments Corp., Springfield, Oreg., 1989-91; pres. Applied Concepts, Eugene, Oreg., 1991—; mem. tech. transfer com. U. Oreg. Contbr. articles on materials, signal processing, acoustics and ednl. aids to profl. jours.; inventor solar collector device. Mem. AAAS, IEEE, Internat. Soc. for Optical Engring. Office: Applied Concepts 575 Stonegate St Eugene OR 97401-5819

BATIUK, THOMAS MARTIN, cartoonist; b. Akron, Ohio, Mar. 14, 1947; s. Martin and Verna (Greskovics) B.; m. Catherine L. Wesemeyer, June 26, 1971. B.F.A., Kent (Ohio) State U., 1969, cert. edn., 1969. Tchr. art Eastern Heights Jr. High Sch., 1969-72. Cartoonist: comic strip Funky Winkerbean, Field Newspaper Syndicate, Chgo., 1972—, John Darling for Field Newspaper Syndicate, Calif., 1979—, Crankshaft for Creators Syndicate, 1987—; author, cartoonist: comic strip Funky Winkerbean, 1973, Funky Winkerbean, Play It Again Funky, 1975, Funky Winkerbean, Closed Out, 1977, Yearbook, 1979, You Know You'vr Got Trouble When Your Mascot is a Scapegoat, 1984, Football Fields are for Band Practice, 1986, Sunday Concert, 1987, Harry C. Dinkle-Live at Carnegie Hall, 1988. Mem. Nat. Cartoonists Soc., Newspaper Features Coun. Office: care Creators Syndicate 5777 W Century Blvd Ste 700 Los Angeles CA 90045-5677

BATSON, RAYMOND MILNER, research cartographer; b. Lincoln, Nebr., July 8, 1931; s. Avery A. and Margaret Elizabeth (Milner) B.; m. Rhoda May Meier, Aug. 31, 1955; children: Beverly Ann Batson White, Frederick Avery, Thomas Raymond. Student, U. Colo., 1953-57, BA, 1962. Field engr., photogrammetrist U.S. Geol. Survey, Denver, 1957-63; rsch. cartographer U.S. Geol. Survey, Flagstaff, Ariz., 1963—, chief planetary cartography, 1970-92; mem. planetary cartography working group NASA, Washington, 1978—, mem. planetary geol. and geophys. working group, 1982-92, expert mem. U.S./USSR joint working group for planetary data exch., 1988-92. Author, editor: Planetary Mapping, 1990. Staff sgt. USAF, 1951-52. Mem. Am. Soc. for Photogrammetry, Am. Soc. Photogrammetry (chmn. extraterrestrial sci. com. 1981-88), Astron. Soc. of the Pacific (hon.), Internat. Soc. Photogrammetry (chmn. working group 3 com. IV 1982-85), Internat. Astron. Union (working group for planetary system nomenclature com. 16 1991—). Office: US Geol Survey 2255 N Gemini Dr Flagstaff AZ 86001-1698

BATTAGLIA, RICHARD ANTHONY, sales executive; b. Phila., June 8, 1955; s. Anthony Joseph and Victoria Grace (LaSpada) B.; m. Robin Ann Piccone, July 11, 1987; children: Maximillian Anton, Luca James. Assoc., Community Coll. of Phila, 1974; BA in Theatre, Temple U., 1977. Nat. sales mgr. Piccone Apparel doing business as Body Glove Swimwear, L.A., 1986—; v.p. sales Robin Piccone Sportswear and Swimwear, L.A., 1991. Bd. dirs. Venice (Calif.) Canals Assn., 1988. Republican. Roman Catholic. Home: 144 N Norton Ave Los Angeles CA 90004-3913

BATTAGLIA, ROBERT KENNETH, entrepreneur; b. Buffalo, Feb. 15, 1939; s. Russell and Jennie (Barreca) B.; m. Colette Marie Coury, Sept. 29, 1984. BS, Bowling Green U., 1960. Ea. region mgr. Libbey Div., Owens-Ill., Inc., N.Y.C., 1960-67; v.p. Saber Internat., Inc., N.Y.C., 1967-69; mng. dir. Deba & Shea, Ltd., Hong Kong, 1969-73, Deba Internat., Ltd., Manila, 1973-77; v.p. mktg. Koracorp. Industries, Inc., San Francisco, 1978-79; pres. Snow Lion Internat., Emeryville, Calif., 1979-80, Fettuccine Bros., Inc., San Francisco, 1981-88, Fax & File Legal Svcs. Inc., San Francisco, 1988—. Republican.

BATTERMAN, ROBERT COLEMAN, cardiologist; b. N.Y.C., Apr. 12, 1911; s. Max and Rebecca (Silverman) B.; m. June Snyder, Feb. 27, 1947; children: Christie, Mark, Hollis. BS, NYU, 1931, MD, 1935. Diplomate Am. Bd. Internal Medicine. Intern, resident Bellevue Hosp., NYU Coll. Medicine, N.Y.C., 1936-39; fellow in therapeutics NYU U. Coll. Medicine, 1939-40, instr. in therapeutics, 1940-49, asst. prof. medicine, 1949-50; assoc. clin. prof. medicine N.Y. Med. Coll., 1951-55, assoc. prof. physiology and pharmacology, 1956-59; dir. Inst. Clin. Pharmacology and Med. Rsch., Berkeley, Calif., 1959-87; vis. physician Highland Hosp., Oakland, Calif., Harrick Meml. Hosp., Berkeley, 1959-86, St. Francis Meml. Hosp., San Francisco, 1964-66, Calif. State Dept. Correction, Vacaville; sr. vis. physician, past asst. chief medicine Mount Zion Hosp. and Rsch. Ctr., San Francisco. Contbr. articles, abstracts to profl. publs. Pres. Nat. Family Coun. of Drug Addiction Inc., 1956-65, Comprehensive Health Edn. Inc., 1969-71, City of Berkeley Commn. Health Adv. Com., 1971-73; mem. Alameda County Comprehensive Health Planning Hosp. and Facility Com., 1972-76; mem. Calif. Health Facilities Authority, 1981—. Fellow N.Y. Acad. Medicine, N.Y. Acad. Scis., Internat. Acad. Law and Sci. (2d v.p. 1966-67), Internat. Angiology (pres. 1967-69), Am. Inst. Chemists, ACP; mem. Alameda-Contra Costa Med. Assn., AAAS, Am. Soc. Clin. Pharmacology and Therapeutics, Am. Rheumatism Assn., No. Calif. Rheumatism Assn., Am. Soc. Clin. Investigation, Am. Soc. Pharmacol. and Explt. Therapeutics, Am. Therapeutic Soc., Drug Info. Assn., Soc. Comprehensive Medicine, Sigma Xi, numerous other med. orgns. Home: 5538 Taft Ave Oakland CA 94618-1519 Office: 2006 Dwight Way Rm 208 Berkeley CA 94704-2633

BATTEY, CHARLES W., gas industry executive; b. 1932; married. B.B.A., U. Nebr., 1954. With Continental Ill. Nat. Bank & Trust Co., Chgo., 1954-70; pres. Commerce Bank of Kansas City, 1970-73; sr. v.p. corp. relations United Telecommunications, Inc., Kansas City, Mo., 1973-75; sr. v.p. staff United Telecommunications, Inc., Kansas City, 1975-77, exec. v.p., 1977-79, exec. v.p. fin. and adminstrn. and chief fin. officer, 1979-81, pres., chief operating officer, dir., 1981-85, vice chmn., chief. fin. officer, 1985-88; chmn., chief exec. officer KN Energy Inc., Lakewood, Colo., 1989—; bd. dirs. Boatmen's Trust Co. of Kansas City., K N Energy Inc. Bd. dirs. Kansas City Crime Commn., Midwest Research Inst., Heart of Am. United Way, Council on Edn.; bd. dirs., past pres. Kansas City Public TV. Office: KN Energy Inc PO Box 281304 Lakewood CO 80228-8304 also: KN Energy Inc Ste 210 4200 Somerset Dr Prairie Village KS 66208

BATTIN, CYNTHIA ANN (CYNTHIA ANN PRICE), electrical engineer; b. Tucson, Aug. 29, 1957; d. Gene Price and Peggy Ann (Purcell) Eid; m. Richard Scott Battin, June 23, 1990. BSEE, San Diego State U., 1986. Office mgr. VA, San Diego, 1983-84; elec. engr. intern, tech. Alexander

Systems, San Diego, 1984-86; jr. engr. intern Naval Ocean Systems Ctr., San Diego, 1985-86; elec. engr. Arinc Res. Corp., San Diego, 1987—; attended coll. courses and seminars in telecom. and computer programming, 1992. With U.S. Navy, 1975-81. Mem. IEEE, Am. Soc. Quality Control (cert. quality auditor), Surface Mount Tech. Assn., Toastmasters (sec. 1988—, exec. v.p. 1989, pres. 1990, adminstrv. v.p., treas. 1991-92, asst. area V gov. 1990-91, Toastmaster of Yr. 1991, sgt.-at-arms 1992, newsletter editor 1993). Republican. Mem. Christian Ch. Office: Arinc Res Corp 4055 E Fountain Blvd Ste 100 Colorado Springs CO 80916

BATTIN, JAMES FRANKLIN, judge, former congressman; b. Wichita, Kans., Feb. 13, 1925; m. Barbara Choate; children: Loyce Battin Peterson, Patricia Battin Pfeiffer, James Franklin. J.D., George Washington U., 1951. Bar: D.C., Mont. Practice in Washington, 1951-52; now in Billings; past dep. county atty.; past sec.-counsel City-County Planning Bd.; past asst. city atty. Billings; then city atty.; mem. Mont. Ho. of Reps., 1958-59; mem. 87th-91st Congresses from 2d Mont. dist., Mont.; resigned when apptd. U.S. dist. judge Mont., 1969; chief judge U.S. Dist. Ct. Mont., Billings, 1978-90, sr. judge, 1990—. Served with USNR, World War II, 1990—. Mem. Am. Legion, DeMolay Legion of Honor. Presbyterian. Club: Mason (Shriner). Office: US Dist Ct 5319 Fed Bldg 316 N 26th St #1476 Billings MT 59101-1362

BATTJES, CARL ROBERT, electrical engineer; b. Grand Rapids, Mich., Dec. 30, 1929; s. Harold A. and Helen (Bolt) B.; m. Grace Lydia Battjes, Apr. 5, 1953 (div. 1979). BSEE, U. Mich., 1958; MSEE, Stanford U., 1960. Registered profl. engr., Oreg. Sr. engr. Sylvania Mt. View (Calif.) Labs., 1958-61; prin. engr. Tektronix, Inc., Beaverton, Oreg., 1961-83; pvt. practice Portland, Oreg., 1983—; vis. prof. U. Calif., Berkeley, 1974. Contbr. articles to profl. jours.; patentee in field. 1st lt. USAF, 1950-55. Home and Office: 8318 SW 41st Ave Portland OR 97219-3508

BATTLE, EDWARD GENE, geologist, engineer; b. Mont Belvieu, Tex., June 19, 1931; s. Paul E. and Annie-Mae B. B.S., Tex. A&M U., 1954. With Continental Oil Co., Tex., from 1954; evaluation engr. Medallion Petroleums, Ltd., 1957, v.p prodn., 1965, exec. v.p., 1966, pres., from 1973; pres., chief operating officer No. and Cen. Gas Corp., 1974-75; pres., chief exec. officer, dir. Norcen Energy Resources Ltd., Calgary, Alta., Can., 1975-91, chmn., dir., 1991—; bd. dirs. Hollinger, Inc., Liquid Carbonic Inc. Mem. Assn. Profl. Engrs., Geologists and Geophysicists Alta., Assn. Profl. Engrs. Ont., Soc. Petroleum Engrs., AIME. Clubs: Calgary Golf and Country, Rosedale Golf. Office: Norcen Energy Resources Ltd, 715 5th Ave SW, Calgary, AB Canada T2P 2X7

BATTLE, THOMAS HOWARD, human resources executive; b. Denver, Nov. 7, 1950; s. Louis and Zular (Bumpers) B.; m. Ella Louise Maye, Feb. 12, 1977; children: Kellie, Bryan. BBA, Loyola Marymount U., 1972; MBA, Pepperdine U., 1980. Compensation adminstr. Mattel Toy Co., Hawthorne, Calif., 1975-78; supr. compensation/benefits The Gillette Co., Santa Monica, Calif., 1978-80, supr. employment and affirmative action, 1980-82; territory sales rep. The Gillette Co., L.A., 1982-84; mgr. employment and tng. The Gillette Co., Santa Monica, 1984-86, mgr. employment tng., security and employee rels., 1986-89, div. mgr. human resources, 1989—. Pres. Neighborhood Block Club, Gardena, Calif., 1988. With U.S. Army, 1972-74. Decorated Army Commendation medal. Mem. Soc. for Human Resource Mgmt. Democrat. Methodist. Home: 14912 Van Buren Ave Gardena CA 90247 Office: The Gillette Co 1681 26th St Santa Monica CA 90404

BATTLES, GARY DENNIS, wine company executive; b. St. Louis, Aug. 8, 1950; s. Bert Lamar and Gloria May (Potts) B.; m. Anne Elizabeth Flanders, Dec. 27, 1975; 1 child, Bradley. BA in History, Creighton U., 1972; MA, Cen. Mich. U., 1976; grad., U.S. Army Command and Gen. Staff Coll., 1989. Unit mgr. Proctor & Gamble Distbg. Co., Omaha, 1978-80; gen. sales mgr. McKesson Wine & Spirits, Honolulu, 1985-87; N.W. div. mgr. E & J Gallo Winery, Seattle, 1980-85; gen. mgr. Valley Wine Co. E & J Gallo Winery, Portland, Oreg., 1987-90; western regional mgr. E & J Gallo Winery, Modesto, Calif., 1990—; co-chmn. Classic Wine Auction, Portland, 1988-90; instr. U.S. Army Command and Gen. Staff Coll., 1992—. Capt. U.S. Army, 1972-78; lt. comdr. USAR. Mem. Res. Officers Assn., Creighton U. Alumni Assn. (pres. 1988—). Republican. Roman Catholic. Home: 20450 NW Quail Hollow Dr Portland OR 97229-1083 Office: E & J Gallo Winery 5825 SW Arctic Dr Beaverton OR 97005

BATTLES, RONALD LEE, lawyer, consultant; b. Chgo., July 7, 1948; s. John Thomas and Juanita Viola (Snyder) B.; m. Jacqueline Ann Smid, Feb. 2, 1974; children: Christopher, Jonathan, Lauren. BSChemE, Ill. Inst. Tech., Chgo., 1970, MSChemE, MBA, 1972; JD, U. Denver, 1988. Bar: Colo. 1988, Ill. 1990. Rsch. microscopist W.M. McCrone Assocs., Chgo., 1971-72; project mgr. York Rsch., Stamford, Conn., 1972-76; prin. Battles Rsch. Corp., Denver, 1976-81; engring. dir. Manville Corp., Denver, 1981-90; program mgr. ENSR Corp., Chgo., 1990—. Contbg. author: The Particle Atlas, 1972; contbr. articles to particle physics jours. Mem. ABA, TAPPI, Am. Inst. Chem. Engrs., Air & Waste Mgmt. Assn. Republican. Roman Catholic. Office: Environ Mgmt Internat Ste 220 5995 Greenwood Pla Blv Englewood CO 80111

BATTS, MICHAEL STANLEY, German language educator; b. Mitcham, Eng., Aug. 2, 1929; s. Stanley George and Alixe Kathleen (Watson) B.; m. Misao Yoshida, Mar. 19, 1959; 1 dau., Anna. B.A. Gen., U. London, 1952, B.A. with honors, 1953, D.Litt., 1973; Dr. Phil., U. Freiburg, Germany, 1957; M.L.S., U. Toronto, 1974. Mem. faculty U. Mainz, Germany, 1953-54, U. Basel, Switzerland, 1954-56, U. Wurzburg, Germany, 1956-58; instr. German U. Calif., Berkeley, 1958-60; mem. faculty dept. German U. B.C., Can., 1960-91; prof. U. B.C., 1967-91, head dept., 1968-80. Author: Die Form der Aventiuren im Nibelungenlied, 1961, Bruder Hansens Marienlieder, 1964, Studien zu Bruder Hansens Marienliedern, 1964, Das hohe Mittelalter, 1969, Das Nibelungenlied-Synoptische Ausgabe, 1971, Gottfried von Strasburg, 1971, A Checklist of German Literature, 1945-75, 1977, The Bibliography of German Literature: An Historical and Critical Survey, 1978, A History of Histories of German Literature: Prolegomena, 1987; editor: Seminar, 1970-80. Served with Brit. Army, 1947-49. Alexander von Humboldt fellow, 1964-65, 83; Can. Council sr. fellow, 1964-65, 71-72; Killam fellow, 1981-82. Fellow Royal Soc. Can.; mem. Canadian Assn. Univ. Tchrs. German (pres. 1982-1984), Modern Humanities Research Assn., Alcuin Soc. (exec. v.p. 1972-79, pres. 1979-80), Internat. Assn. for Germanic Studies (pres. 1990—). Office: U Brit Columbia, German Dept, Vancouver, BC Canada V6T 1Z1

BATTY, HUGH KENWORTHY, physician; b. Kansas City, Kans.; s. James Jacob and Genevieve Adeline (Johnston) B.; m. Mercedes Aguirre, Mar. 17, 1979; 1 child, Henry Briton. BS in Zoology, U. Wash., 1970; PhD in Anatomy, U. Utah, 1974; MD, Ciudad Juárez, Mex., 1977. Intern, asst. resident St. Vincent's Med. Ctr., Bridgeport, Conn., 1977-78, resident, 1978-79, chief resident, 1979-80; pvt. practice Sheridan, Wyo., 1981—; chmn. dept. medicine Meml. Hosp. Sheridan, 1989-91. Contbr. articles to profl. jours. Eleanor Roosevelt Cancer Rsch. Found. grantee, 1972. Mem. ACP, Wyo. Med. Soc., Sheridan County Med. Soc. Office: 1260 1262 W 5th St Sheridan WY 82801

BAUCH, THOMAS JAY, lawyer, apparel company executive; b. Indpls., May 24, 1943; s. Thomas and Violet (Smith) B.; m. Ellen L. Burstein, Oct. 31, 1982; children: Chelsea Sara, Elizabeth Tree. BS with honors, U. Wis., 1964, JD with highest honors, 1966. Bar: Ill. 1966, Calif. 1978. Assoc. Lord, Bissell & Brook, Chgo., 1966-72; lawyer, asst. sec. Marcor-Montgomery Ward, Chgo., 1973-75; spl. asst. to solicitor Dept. Labor, Washington, 1975-77; dep. gen. counsel Levi Strauss & Co., San Francisco, 1977-81, sr. v.p., gen. counsel, 1981—; mem. U. Wis. Law Review, Madison, 1964-66. Bd. dirs. Urban Sch., San Francisco, 1986-91; bd. visitors U. Wis. Law Sch., 1991-93. Mem. Am. Assn. Corp. Counsel (bd. dirs. 1982-87), Commonwealth Club (bd. govs. 1991), Univ. Club, Villa Taverna Club, Racquet Club, Order of Coif. Office: Levi Strauss & Co Levi's Pla PO Box 7215 San Francisco CA 94120-7215

BAUCUS, MAX S., senator; b. Helena, Mont., Dec. 11, 1941; s. John and Jean (Sheriff) B.; m. Wanda Minge, Apr. 23, 1983. BA, Stanford U., 1964, LLB, 1967. Bar: D.C. 1969, Mont. 1972. Staff atty. CAB, Washington, 1967-68; lawyer SEC, Washington, 1968-71; legal asst. to chmn. SEC, 1970-71; sole practice Missoula, Mont., 1971-74; mem. Mont. Ho. of Reps., 1973-74; mem. 94th-95th congresses from 1st Dist. Mont., 1975-79, mem. com. appropriations; U.S. senator from Mont., 1979—; acting exec. dir., com. coordinator Mont. Constl. Conv., 1972. Office: US Senate 706 Hart Senate Bldg Washington DC 20510-2602*

BAUER, A(UGUST) ROBERT, JR., surgeon, educator; b. Phila., Dec. 23, 1928; s. A(ugust) Robert and Jessie Martha-Maynard (Monie) B.; BS, U. Mich., 1949, MS, 1950, MD, 1954; M Med. Sci.-Surgery, Ohio State U., 1960; m. Charmaine Louise Studer, June 28, 1957; children: Robert, John, William, Anne, Charles, James. Intern Walter Reed Army Med. Ctr., 1954-55; resident in surgery Univ. Hosp., Ohio State U., Columbus, also instr., 1957-61; pvt. practice medicine, specializing in surgery, Mt. Pleasant, Mich., 1962-74; chief surgery Ctrl. Mich. Community Hosp., Mt. Pleasant, 1964-65, vice chief of staff, 1967, chief of staff, 1968; clin. faculty Mich. State Med. Sch., East Lansing, 1974; mem. staff St. Mark's Hosp., Salt Lake City, 1974-91; pvt. practice surgery, Salt Lake City, 1974-91; clin. instr. surgery U. Utah, 1975-91. Trustee Rowland Hall, St. Mark's Sch., Salt Lake City, 1978-84; mem. Utah Health Planning Coun., 1979-81. Served with M.C., U.S. Army, 1954-57. Diplomate Am. Bd. Surgery. Fellow ACS, Southwestern Surg. Congress; mem. AMA, Salt Lake County Med. Soc., Utah Med. Assn. (various coms.), Utah Soc. Certified Surgeons, Salt Lake Surg. Soc., Pan Am. Med. Assn. (affiliate), AAAS (affiliate), Sigma Phi Epsilon, Phi Rho Sigma. Episcopalian. Club: Zollinger. Contbr. articles to profl. publs., researcher surg. immunology. Office: PO Box 17533 Salt Lake City UT 84117-0533

BAUER, BERNARD OSWALD, geography educator; b. Salmon Arm, B.C., Can., Feb. 7, 1957; s. Joseph and Gerda (Frisch) B. BSc. with honors, U. Toronto (Can.), 1980, MSc., 1982; PhD, Johns Hopkins U., 1988. Instr. U. Toronto, 1985-86; asst. prof. U. So. Calif., L.A., 1987-93; assoc. prof. U. So. Calif., 1993—; prin. GeoCan Cons., Toronto, 1985—. Author: (reference bibliography) Council of Planning Librarians, 1981, (lab. manual) Laboratory Exercises in Physical Geography, 1990; contbr. articles to profl. jours. Recipient J. Warren Nystrom award Assn. Am. Geographers, 1989, Hydrolab award Internat. Assn. for Great Lakes Rsch., 1986, Presdl. Young Investigator award Nat. Sci. Found., 1991; Postgrad. scholar Nat. Scis. and Engring. Coun., Ottawa, Can., 1981-85. Mem. Assn. Am. Geographers (bd. dirs. coastal and marine geography specialty group 1990-92, vice chair 1992-93, chair 1993-94). Office: U So Calif 3620 S Vermont Ave Los Angeles CA 90089-0255

BAUER, EARL WILLIAM, manufacturing company executive; b. Sturgis, S.D., Oct. 16, 1934; s. Claude Allen and Mabel (Sheel) B.; m. Ellie Feinblatt, Dec. 17, 1953; children: Robyn Cheryl Prud'homme-Bauer, Lawrence Michael, Eric William. BSBA, U. Denver, 1961; postgrad., Ohio State U., 1968-69, Fgn. Svc. Inst., Washington, 1979-80. Clk. United Airlines, Denver, 1953-55; comml. specialist Shell Oil Co., Denver, 1955-60; sr. analyst II statis. reporting svc. Colo. Dept. Agr., Denver, 1961-76; vol. Peace Corps, Rampur, Nepal, 1976-79; specialist USDA, Washington, 1979-80; cons., counsel Ministry Agr., Colo. State U., Yaounde, Cameroon, 1980-83; prin. owner, mgr. Alcora Marble, Clarkdale, Ariz., 1984—. Mem. Yavapai County (Ariz.) Pvt. Industry Coun., 1987—, chmn., 1989—; mem., chmn. legal element Verde River Corridor Planning Project, Clarkdale, 1990—. Mem. Clarkdale C. of C. (bd. dirs. 1985-90, pres. 1987, 89, 92). Office: Alcora Marble PO Box 555 Clarkdale AZ 86324-0555

BAUER, HENRY LELAND, lawyer; b. Portland, Oreg., June 7, 1928; s. Henry and Emma L. (Peterson) B.; m. Doris Jane Philbrick, Sept. 11, 1952 (dec.); children: Henry Stephen, Thomas Leland. BS in Bus., Oreg. State U., 1950; JD, U. Oreg., 1953. Bar: Oreg. 1953, U.S. Dist. Ct. Oreg., 1956; U.S. Ct. Appeals (9th cir.), 1960. Mem. Bauer & Bauer, Portland, Oreg., 1955-70, Bauer, Murphy, Bayless & Fundingsland, and successor firms, Portland, 1970-75; prin. Henry L. Bauer & Assocs. P.C., Portland. Past mem. adv. council Oreg. State U. Coll. Bus.; past bd. dirs., vice chmn. St. Vincent Hosp. and Med. Ctr.; mem., past pres. council of trustees St. Vincent Med. Found.; lifetime trustee Kappa Sigma Emdowment Fund; bd. dirs., past pres. Nat. Interfrat. Conf.; past pres. Columbia Pacific council Boy Scouts Am., mem. nat. com.; past pres. Portland Civic Theatre; bd. visitors U. Oreg. Sch. Law, 1979-83; trustee Oreg. State U. Found. 1st lt. USAF, 1953-55. Recipient Silver Antelope award Boy Scouts Am. Mem. ABA, Oreg. Bar Assn., Multnomah County Bar Assn., Am. Judicature Soc., Oreg. State U. Alumni Assn. (bd. dirs.), Delta Theta Phi, Kappa Sigma (past nat. pres.). Republican. Presbyterian. Clubs: Multnomah Athletic, Arlington, Masons, Rotary. Office: 25-3 NW 23d Pl Portland OR 97210

BAUER, HERBERT, physician; b. Vienna, Austria, Jan. 21, 1910; came to U.S., 1940; s. Fritz and Irma (Lindenfeld) B.; m. Hanna Goldsmith, 1939; children: Timothy, Christopher. MD, U. Vienna, Austria, 1936; MPH, U. Calif., Berkeley, 1948. Chief county physician San Luis Obispo County, San Luis Obispo, Calif., 1942-47; med. dir. Sacramento Health Dept., 1948-52; pub. and mental health dir. Yolo County, Calif., 1952-72; clin. prof. U. Calif., Davis, Calif., 1972-92. Recipient Liberty Bell award Bar Assn. Woodland, Calif., 1955, Peace and Justice award City of Davis, Calif., 1991. Mem. AMA, APHA, Am. Psychiat. Assn., Am. Acad. Child Psychiatry, Am. Acad. Psychiatry and Law, Calif. Med. Assn. Democrat. Unitarian. Home and Office: 831 Oeste Dr Davis CA 95616

BAUER, JEROME LEO, JR., chemical engineer; b. Pitts., Oct. 12, 1938; s. Jerome L. and Anna Mae (Tucker) B.; children from previous marriage: children: Lori, Trish, Jeff. BSChemE, U. Dayton, 1960; MSChemE, Pa. State U., 1963; postgrad., Ohio State U., 1969. Registered profl. engr., Ohio. Asst. prof. chem. engring. U. Dayton, Ohio, 1963-67; mgr. advanced composites dept. Ferro Corp., Cleve., 1967-72; engring. material and process specifications mgr. Lockheed Missiles & Space Co., Inc., Sunnyvale, Calif., 1972-74; gen. dynamics design specialist Convair Div., San Diego, 1974-76, project devel. engr., 1976-77; dir. research Furane div. M&T Chems. Inc., Glendale, Calif., 1980-82; mem. tech. staff Jet Propulsion Lab., Calif. Inst. Tech., Pasadena, Calif., 1977-80, 82-90; mem. tech. staff mfg. engring. The Aerospace Corp., El Segundo, Calif., 1990—. Editor: Materials Sciences for Future, 1986; contbr. articles to profl. jours. Jr. warden St. Luke Episcopal Ch., La Crescenta, Calif., 1980, sr. warden 1981. Mem. Am. Inst. Chem. Engrs. (founder, chmn. Dayton sect. 1964-66, spl. projects chmn. Cleve. sect. 1968-69), Soc. Advancement of Material Process Engring. (membership chmn. no. Calif. sect. 1973-74, sec. San Diego sect. 1974-75, vice chmn. 1975-76, chmn. 1976, chmn. Los Angeles sect. 1977, nat. treas. 1978-82, gen. chmn. 31st internat. symposium exhibition, Las Vegas, Nev., 1986, Meritiorous Achievement award 1983, internat. v.p. 1987-89, internat. pres. 1989-90), Internat. Electronics Packaging Soc. (pres. Los Angeles chpt. 1982), Phi Lambda Upsilon, Delta Sigma Epsilon. Republican. Home: PO Box 3298 El Segundo CA 90245-8398 Office: The Aerospace Corp 2350 E El Segundo Blvd El Segundo CA 90245-4691

BAUER, LOGAN PROBST, academic administrator; b. Grand Forks, N.D., Sept. 27, 1940; s. Ronald Cloyd and Ethel (Church) B.; m. Gloria Melluzzo, Dec. 7, 1989; children: Christl, Sean. BA, Trinity U., 1963; MA, World U., 1970; EdS, Ariz. State U., 1978; EdD, No. Ariz. U., 1984. Instr., councilor San Antonio State Hosp., 1965-67; instr. Glendale Union High Sch. Dist., Phoenix, 1970-76; program developer World U., Phoenix, 1976-78; exec. dean Western Internat. U., Phoenix, 1978-84; pres., founder Ariz. Inst. Bus. & Tech., Phoenix, 1984—; pres. Nat. Assn. PCA, Phoenix, 1990, Ariz. Temp. Employment Bur., Phoenix, 1989-90; founder Western Internat. U., Phoenix, 1978. Author: Administrative Career Training, 1978, Inservice Education for Administration, 1984. Lt. col. USAR, 1986—. Mem. NEA, Ariz. Pvt. Sch. Assn. (bd. dirs. 1984), Data Process Mgmt. Assn., Soc. Mfrs. Engrs., Am. Mgmt. Assn. Office: Ariz Inst Bus & Tech 2330 N 75th Ave Phoenix AZ 85035-1200

BAUER, LOUIS EDWARD, retail bookstore executive, educator; b. Chgo., Mar. 11, 1937; s. Hermann Martin and Louise Eva (Winckler) B.; m. Inez Marie Gugel, Aug. 26, 1961; children: Erik Nathan, Ethan Joel, Elizabeth Marie, Elena Louise. Student, Valparaiso U., 1955-56; BS, No. State U., Aberdeen, S.D., 1961; MEd, Idaho State U., Pocatello, 1969. Asst. dir. student union No. State U., 1961-62; program dir. student union Idaho State U., 1962-67, dir. student union, 1967-69; dir. union and recreation U. Calif., Davis, 1969-74; dir. Stony Brook Union SUNY, Stony Brook, 1974-77; mng. dir. student union San Francisco State U., 1977-79; dir. aux. svcs. No. State U., 1979-87; pres., gen. mgr. Portland (Oreg.) State Bookstore, 1987—; adj. instr. Faculty of Bus., No. State U., 1979-87; maj. prof. Accelerated Degree program Concordia Coll., Portland, 1990—. Bd. dirs. Luth. Campus Coun., Portland, 1989—. Mem. Optimists Internat. (lt. gov. 1985-86). Democrat. Lutheran. Home: 11845 NW Vaughan Ct Portland OR 97201 Office: Portland State U Bookstore 1880 SW 6th St Portland OR 97201

BAUER, MAX WILLIAM, manufacturing executive; b. La Mesa, Calif., Nov. 12, 1957; s. Max Harnish and Ruby Nell (Daily) B.; m. Karen Dee Lepker, Jan. 5, 1985. BS, Colo. State U., 1985, MS, 1987. Engr. Rohr Industries, Inc., Chula Vista, Calif., 1981-83, rsch. engr., 1988-92; asst. grad. teaching Colo. State U., Ft. Collins, Colo., 1986-87; mfg. mgr. Engring. Measurements Co., Longmont, Colo., 1992—. Author: American Production and Inventory Control Society, 1992. Soc. of Mfg. Engrs. scholar, 1983. Mem. Golden Key, Phi Kappa Phi. Republican. Office: Engring Measurements Co 600 Diagonal Hwy Longmont CO 80501

BAUER, NYLES JASON, electrical engineer; b. N.Y.C., Mar. 31, 1961; s. Elias and Dianne (Littlejohn) B. BSEE, U. Ariz., 1990. Polit. cons. Clinton Group, Washington, 1981-83; pres. Camel Adventures, Tucson, 1989—; tchr. U. Ariz., Tucson, 1989-90. Inventor computer peripherals. Candidate pres. of U.S., Tucson, 1988; cons. People for Ethical Treatment of Animals, Tucson, 1985-86. Named Man of the Yr., New Rochelle Humane Soc., 1983. Democrat. Home: PO Box 3738 Tucson AZ 85722-3738 Office: Camel Adventures PO Box 3738 Tucson AZ 85722-3738

BAUER, RALPH LEROY, business executive; b. Evansville, Ind., Dec. 19, 1925; s. John George and Elfrieda Louise (Gresser) Huber; m. Margaret Ellen Masters, Sept. 11, 1948 (div. 1975); children: Clinton L., Warren L., Brian E., Scott A.; m. Anna Mae Cooke, Nov. 9, 1984. BSEE, U. Evansville, 1950; postgrad., U. Calif., Riverside, 1956-58, UCLA, 1960-65, U. Mich., 1969. Ordnance engr. Internat. Harvester Co., Evansville, Ind., 1950-54; test & product design Naval Ordnance Lab., Silver Springs, Md., 1954-55; test engr. Naval Ordnance Lab., Carona, Calif., 1955-57, br. head, 1957-61, div. head, 1961-70; div. head Naval Weapons Ctr., China Lake, Calif., 1970-82, assoc. dept. head, 1982-83; pres. RB Assocs. Inc., Lake Arrowhead, Calif., 1983—; cons. in field. Inventor in field. With U.S. Army Air Corps, 1944-46. Mem. IEEE (life mem., sect. pres. 1968, sect. v.p. 1967, sect. sec.-treas. 1966), Am. Def. Preparedness Assn., Assn. Old Crows. Home: 987 LeMont Way Lake Arrowhead CA 92352 Office: RB Assocs Inc PO Box 2172 Arrowhead CA 92352

BAUER, RANDY MARK, management training firm executive; b. Cleve., Sept. 2, 1946; s. Ralph I. and Gloria P. Bauer; B.S. summa cum laude, Ohio State U., 1968; M.B.A., Kent State U., 1971; m. Sue Dellva, July 4, 1975; children—Sherri, Kevin. Mgmt. auditor Peat Marwick Mitchell & Co., Cleve., 1971-72; mgmt. devel. specialist GAO, Denver, 1972-80; adj. prof. mgmt. Columbia Coll., Denver, 1979—; pres. Leadership Tng. Assos., Denver, 1979—; condr. exec. devel. workshops U. Colo., Denver, 1979—. Recipient Best in 1976 award GAO. Mem. Am. Soc. for Tng. and Devel., Beta Gamma Sigma. Address: 10462 E Prentice Ave Englewood CO 80111

BAUER, STEVEN MICHAEL, cost containment engineer; b. Hemet, Calif., Nov. 8, 1949; s. Donald Richard and Jeanne Patricia (Lamont) B.; m. Myung-Hee Min, Sept. 10, 1983; children: Claudia Margaret, Monica Anne. BA in Physics, Calif. State U., San Bernardino, 1971, BS in Physics, 1984, cert. in acctg., 1980, cert. in computer programming, 1986; postgrad., U. Calif., 1974; post grad., Calif. State U., 1982, 87—; cert. in counseling skills, U. Calif. extension, 1991., cert. in alcohol and other drug studies, 1992. Registered engr. in tng., Calif., 1976. Asst. neuclear engr. So. Calif. Edison Co., Rosemead, 1973-76, assoc. nuclear engr., 1976-88, cost containment engr., 1988—; cons. rsch. dept. Jerry L. Pettis Meml. Vets. Hosp., 1978-79, Calif. State U., San Bernardino, 1983—; cons. planning San Bernardino County, 1975-76; cons. alumni rels. Calif. State U., San. Bernardino, 1989-90. Supporter St. Labre Indian Sch., 1984, Asian Relief Fund, 1985—, So. Poverty Law Ctr., Amnesty Internat., Freedom Writer, 1988; mem. Greenpeace, Wilderness Soc., Internat. Platform Assn.; supporter United Negro Coll. Fund., 1985, vol., 1988; vol. counselor San Bernardino Girl's Juvenile Hall, ARC, 1990—; fellow Casa Colina Hosp.; mem. L.A. County Mus. Art; campaign vol. Congressment George E. Brown, 1966; block capt. Neighborhood Watch, sec., bd. dirs., 1992—; chpt. sec. Sierra Club, 1992. Mem. Am. Nuclear Soc. (assoc.), Calif. State U. San Bernadino Alumni Assn. (sec. bd. 1979-80, rep. food com. 1980-82), Nat. Assn. Accts., Astron. Soc. Pacific, Assn. Computing Machinery (assoc.), Ams. for Energy Independence (bd. dirs. 1990—), K.C. (sec., recorder 1989, community dir., Outstanding Svcs. award 1989), Toastmasters, Numismatic Assn. So. Calif., UCLA Alumni (life), Calif. State U. Fullerton Computer Club, Sierra Club (sec. San Gargonio chpt. 1992—). Home and Office: 131 Monroe Ct San Bernardino CA 92408-4137

BAUERS, JOHN ALLEN, air traffic controller, minister, counselor; b. Tomahawk, Wis., May 31, 1950; s. Carl John and Glayds Henrietta (Brazelton) B.; m. Deborah Lynn Coates, Aug. 22, 1970; children: William Carl, Promise Rose, Tabitha Gabrielle. BA in Bibl. Edn., Alaska Bible Coll., 1973; postgrad., U. Alaska, 1980, Alaska Pacific U., 1985-86; MA in Psychology, Liberty U., 1990. Ordained to ministry Assemblies of God; cert. control tower operator. Air traffic controller FAA, Nome, Alaska, 1974-76, Deadhorse, Alaska, 1976, Anchorage, 1976-81; assoc. pastor Muldoon Community Assembly, Anchorage, 1976-86; sr. pastor Gateway Christian Fellowship, Sequim, Wash., 1986-88; pub. rels./lifeguard Sequim Acquatic Recreation Ctr., 1988; area supr. FAA, Aspen, Colo., 1990-91, air traffic controller, 1988—; therapist Therapeutic Christian Counseling, Glenwood Springs, Colo., 1988—; vice chmn. publicity Jimmy Swaggart Crusade, Anchorage, 1983; chmn. publicity Alaska Gov.'s Prayer Breakfast, Anchorage, 1983, Assembly of God Dist. Coun., Anchorage, 1984; contact chaplin Ft. Richardson Army Base, 1984-86, Elmendorf AFB, 1984-86. Mem. AACD, Glenwood Springs Ministerial Assn. Republican. Home and Office: 3900 Old Lodge Rd Apt 7B Glenwood Springs CO 81601-4564

BAUGH, L. DARRELL, financial executive; b. Prairie Grove, Ark., Oct. 7, 1930; s. Lacey D. and Mary Grace (Brown) B.; BBA, U. Ark., 1954; MBA, U. Colo., 1960; CLU, Am. Coll., 1967. Chartered fin. cons.; cert. estate planner. m. Wileeta Claire Gray, June 15, 1958; children: Adrienne Leigh Calvo, John Grayson. With Penn Mut. Life Ins. Co., 1961-71, gen. agt., Sacramento, 1968-71; pres. Nat. Estate Planning Inst., Boulder, Colo., 1974—; faculty estate planning seminars Colo. State U.; cons. U. Colo. Center for Confs. Mgmt./Tech. Programs, 1975-80; sponsor ednl. programs for profl. estate planners and estate owners. Bd. dirs. Boulder Men's Christian Fellowship. With U.S. Army, 1954-56. Mem. Boulder C. of C., Am. Soc. CLU's, Rocky Mountain CLU's (chmn. grad. studies programs), Boulder County Estate Planning Coun. (pres. 1972-73), Sacramento Estate Planning Coun., Family Firm Inst., Nat. Registry Fin. Planners (interview com.), Nat. Assn. Estate Planners (planners accreditation com., bd. dirs. student venture, mem. Denver study group), Student Venture (bd. dirs.), Nat. Assn. Estate Planners (accreditation com.), Family Firm Inst. Contbr. articles to profl. jours. Club: Flatirons Country. Home: 600 Manhattan Dr Boulder CO 80303-4021 Office: 75 Manhattan Dr Boulder CO 80303-4254

BAUGH, ROBERT FRANKLIN, biochemist, researcher; b. Albuquerque, June 23, 1942; s. John Louis and Clydena Beatrice (Kehler) B.; m. Joan Kay Gapter, Aug. 28, 1965 (div. July 1974); m. Sun Yong Cho, Aug. 26, 1984. BS, Colo. State U., 1964, MS, 1967; PhD, SUNY, Albany, 1973. NIH rsch. fellow Dept. Pathology U. Calif., La Jolla, 1974-76; asst. rsch. biochemist U. Calif., San Diego, 1977-81; biochem. cons. Arvada, Colo., 1982; dir. disposable rsch. devel. Hemotec, Inc., Englewood, Colo., 1982-83, dir. R&D, 1983-86, dir. rsch., 1986—; reviewer J. Lab. & Clin. Medicine; med. sch. adviser U. Calif., San Diego, 1980-81; lectr. U. Calif. Sch. Med. Pub. Affairs, 1980-81; mem. edn. com. Allied Health Professions, U. Calif., 1980-81. Contbr. articles to profl. jours; patentee gas flow test cartridge, collection medium for whole blood. Mem. San Diego High Sch. Sci. Fair Judge, 1981, Am. Heart Assn. Recipient Rsch. Career Devel. award NIH, 1976-81, Calif. Am. Heart Assn. award Calif. Affiliate of Am. Heart, 1978-

79; grant Am. Heart Assn., 1979-81; fellowship NIH, 1974-75; Regents scholarship, State of N.Y., 1960. Mem. AAAS, Am. Chem. Soc., N.Y. Acad. Scis., Internat. Soc. Thrombosis and Hemostasis, Sigma Xi. Republican. Home: 7926 E Windcrest Row Parker CO 80134-6347 Office: Hemotec Inc 7103 S Revere Pky Englewood CO 80112-3992

BAUGHCUM, STEVEN LEE, physical chemist; b. Atlanta, Dec. 18, 1950; s. George Lee and Henrietta (Stevens) B.; BS, Emory U., 1972; MA, Harvard U., 1973, PhD, 1978. Teaching fellow Harvard U., Cambridge, Mass., 1973-76; NRC rsch. assoc. Joint Inst. Lab. Astrophysics, U. Colo., Nat. Bur. Standards, Boulder, Colo., 1978-80; mem. staff Los Alamos Nat. Lab., N.Mex., 1980-87; prin. rsch. scientist, mgr. chem. physics, Spectra Tech., Bellevue, Wash., 1987-88; rsch. analyst atmospheric physics Boeing Co., Seattle, 1988—. Contbr. articles to profl. jours. 1st lt. USAF, 1976. NSF grad. fellow, 1972-75. Mem. AAAS, Am. Chem. Soc., Am. Phys. Soc., Combustion Inst., Am. Geophys. Union, Phi Beta Kappa, Sigma Xi. Home: 2215 185th Pl NE Redmond WA 98052-6020 Office: Boeing Co MS 6H-FC PO Box 3707 Seattle WA 98124

BAUGHN, ALFRED FAIRHURST, lawyer; b. Florence, Ariz., May 1, 1912; s. Otis James and Mary Holman (Fairhurst) B.; m. Barbara Hobbs, June 17, 1935; children: Brent F., Barbara E. AB, U. So. Calif., 1935, JD, 1938. Bar: Calif. 1938, U.S. Dist. Ct. (so. dist.) Calif. 1939, U.S. Ct. Appeals (9th cir.) 1945, U.S. Dist. Ct. Ariz. 1948, Ariz. 1959, U.S. Supreme Ct. 1967. With Title Guarantee & Trust, L.A., 1937-41; corp. counsel Pacific Western Oil Co., 1942-43; pvt. practice law, L.A. and Hollywood, Calif., 1943-56; Ariz. chief corp. counsel Garrett Corp., 1956-77, ret., 1977; pvt. practice law, Phoenix, 1977—; Ariz. Assn. Industries spl. counsel utility rate hearings Ariz. Corp. Commn., 1977-80; bd. dirs. EPI-HAB, Inc., 1974-90. Adopted by Hopi Indian Chief Seletstewa and Squaw (2d Mesa), 1967; Pres. scholar U. So. Calif., 1931-35. Mem. Calif. Bar Assn., Ariz. Bar Assn., L.A. Philanthropic Found. (life), Skull and Scales (U. So. Calif.), Phi Alpha Delta (chpt. pres. 1938), Kappa Sigma (pres. L.A. alumni 1945, pres. Phoenix Alumni 1960). Republican. Mem. Christian Ch. Clubs: Hollywood Exch. (pres. 1947); Kiwanis (Phoenix pres. club 1965); Kachina Klub (organizer, charter v.p. 1974), Hon. Order Ky. Cols. (pres. Phoenix chpt. 1980—), Phoenix Teocali of Order Quetzalcoatl (pres. 1984), Ariz. Bola Tie Soc., Masons (Master 1953), Shriners (Potentate 1971), Jesters (head Phoenix Ct. 1969), Internat. Gorillas (chief 1971—).

BAUGHN, WILLIAM HUBERT, former business educator and academic administrator; b. Marshall County, Ala., Aug. 27, 1918; s. J.W. and Beatrice (Jackson) B.; m. Mary Madiera Morris, Feb. 20, 1945; children: Charles Madiera, William Marsteller. BS, U. Ala., 1940; MA, U. Va, 1941, PhD, 1948. Instr. U. Va., 1942-43, asst. prof., 1946-48; assoc. prof., then prof. econs. and bus. adminstrn. La. State U., 1948-56; prof. U. Tex., 1956-62, chmn. fin. dept., 1958-60, assoc. dean Coll. Bus. Adminstrn., 1959-62; assoc. dir. Sch. Banking of South, 1952-66; dean Coll. Bus. and Pub. Adminstrn. U. Mo., 1962-64; dean Coll. Bus. and Adminstrn. U. Colo., 1964-84, pres., 1985, acting chancellor, 1986-87; pres. U. Colo. System, Boulder, 1990-91; pres. Am. Assembly Collegiate Schs. Bus., 1973-74; chmn. Big Eight Athletic Conf., 1970-71, 78-79, 86-87; dir. Stonier Grad. Sch. of Banking, Rutgers U., 1966-86; mem. council Nat. Collegiate Athletic Assn., 1983-86. Author: (with E.W. Walker) Financial Planning and Policy, 1961; editor: (with C.E. Walker) The Bankers' Handbook, 1966, (with C.E. Walker and T.I. Storrs) 3d rev. edit., 1988, (with D. R. Mandich) The International Banking Handbook, 1983. Served to 1st lt. USAAF, World War II; lt. col. Res. Home: 555 Baseline Rd Boulder CO 80302-7421 Office: U Colo System Boulder CO 80309

BAUM, CARL EDWARD, electromagnetic theorist; b. Binghamton, N.Y., Feb. 6, 1940; s. George Theodore and Evelyn Monica (Bliven) B. BS with honors, Calif. Inst. Tech., 1962, MS, 1963, PhD, 1969. Commd. 2d lt. USAF, 1962; advanced through grades to capt., 1967, resigned, 1971; project officer Phillips Lab. (formerly Air Force Weapons Lab.), Kirtland AFB, N.Mex., 1963-71, sr. scientist for electromagnetics, 1971—; pres. SUMMA Found.; U.S. del. to gen. assembly Internat. Union Radio Sci., Lima, Peru, 1975, Helsinki, Finland, 1978, Washington,1 981, Florence, Italy, 1984, Tel Aviv, 1987, Prague, Czechoslovakia, 1990; mem. Commn. B U.S. Nat. Com., 1975—, Commn. E, 1982—, Commn. A, 1990—. Author: (with others) Transient Electromagnetic Fields, 1976, Electromagnetic Scattering, 1978, Acoustic, Electromagnetic and Elastic Wave Scattering, 1980, Fast Electrical and Optical Measurements, 1986, EMP Interaction: Principles, Techniques and Reference Data, 1986, Lightning Electromagnetics, 1990, Modern Radio Science, 1990, Recent Advances in Electromagnetic Theory, 1990, Direct and Inverse Methods in Radar Polarimetry, 1992; co-author: (with A.P. Stone) Transient Lens Synthesis: Differential Geometry in Electromagnetic Theory, 1991; contbr. articles to profl. jours. Recipient award Honeywell Corp., 1962, R & D award USAF, 1970, Harold Brown award Air Force Systems Command, 1990; Electromagnetic pulse fellow. Fellow IEEE (Harry Diamond Meml. award, 1987, Richard R. Stoddart award, 1984); mem. Electromagnetics Soc. (pres. 1983-85), Electromagnetics Acad., Sigma Xi, Tau Beta Pi. Roman Catholic. Home: 5116 Eastern Ave SE Unit D Albuquerque NM 87108 Office: Phillips Lab/WSR Kirtland A F B NM 87117

BAUM, DEREK MICHAEL, small business owner; b. London, Jan. 21, 1935; s. Abraham Bernard and Charlotte (Fisher) Tarl B.; m. Ruth (div. 1986); m. Magdalena, May 8, 1987; children: Joshua Bernard, Gregory David. AAS in Mgmt., NYU, 1966. Pres. Kandy Lou of Calif., L.A., 1968-84; quality control mgr. Stylecraft, L.A., 1985-87; v.p. Cuckoo's Nest Inc., L.A., 1974-78; prodn. mgr. M&R Internat., L.A., 1987-88; owner Room With A View, Sylmar, Calif., 1988-90; gen. counsel Shadecrafters, L.A., 1992—; bd. dirs. Garment Contractor Assn. So. Calif., 1975-82. Mem. Sylmar C. of C. Jewish. Home: 13442 Almetz St Sylmar CA 91342

BAUM, DIRK SAWYERS, computer software developer; b. Provo, Utah, Aug. 6, 1956; s. H. Lowell and Linda Rae (Sawyers) B.; m. Daphne Ruf, July 5, 1978; children: Christina, Mandy, Aaron, Ian, Mathew, Jeremy, Annily. Student, Brigham Young U., 1975, 77-79. Software engr. DHI Computing Svc., Provo, 1979-83; lead project mgr. DHJ Computing Svc., Provo, 1983-88, exec. v.p., 1988—; instr. ednl. classes for software langs. and devel., Provo, 1990-92; lectr. computer workshops/seminars, 1987-92. Developer numerous computer software, 1990-92; contbr. articles to profl. jours. Mem. Assn. for Computing Machinery, Assn. for Info. and Image Mgmt., Info. Mgmt. Congress (del. 1990, 91). Mem. LDS Ch. Office: DHI Computing Svc 1525 W 820 N Provo UT 84601

BAUM, KERRY ROBERT, retired military officer; b. LaGrande, Oreg., May 25, 1939; s. Guy Hiatt B. and Niola (Anderson) Jones; m. Lynda Sue Christian, Dec. 18, 1964; children: Kerry Jr., Tatia D., Christian H., Buffy Jo, Patrick H., Britta Sue, Natalie A. BA in History, Brigham Young U., 1967; MBA in Mktg., Murray State U., 1978; postgrad., Webster Coll., St. Louis, 1979-80. Commd. 2d lt. U.S. Army, 1957, advanced through grades to col., 1990, ret., 1991; U.S. rep. to Major NATO Comdrs. Alert Conf., 1987-90; joint staff rep LIVE OAK, 1986-90. Author, editor: NATO Alert Procedures for Joint Staff, 1988, Transfer of U.S. Forces to NATO Command, 1990, Focal Point Procedures Manual, 1989. Bishop Mormon Ch., Hopkinsville, Ky., 1974-78, councilor, bishopric, Newport, R.I., 1985-86. Decorated Bronze Star, Army Commendation medal, Air Force Commendation medal, Defense Superior Service Medal. Mem. Res. Officer Assn., Ret. Officers Assn. Home: 10938 N 5870 W American Fork UT 84003-9487

BAUM, PHYLLIS GARDNER, travel management consultant; b. Ashtabula, Ohio, Dec. 13, 1930; d. Charles Edward Schneider and Stella Elizabeth (Schaefer) Gardner; m. Kenneth Walter Baum, Oct. 21, 1948 (div. July 1971); children: Deidre Adair, Cynthia Gail; m. Dennis Carl Marquardt, Sept. 22, 1979 (dec. 1991). Grad. high sch., Cleve. Am. Soc. Travel Agents. Travel cons. Fredo Travel Svc., Ashland, Ohio, 1960-66; sales mgr. Travelmart, Willoughby, Ohio, 1966-68; br. mgr. Travelmart, Mentor, Ohio, 1966-68, Diners Fugazy Travel, Sun City, Ariz., 1968-69; travel cons. Jarrett's Travel Svc., Phoenix, 1969-72; sr. cons. Loyal Travel, Phoenix, 1972-74; co-mgr. Phil Carr Travel, Sun City, 1974-77; tour ops. mgr. ASL Travel, Phoenix, 1978-79; owner, mgr. Travel Temporaries, Glendale, Ariz., 1979—; cons. and lectr. in field. Adv. bd. mem. Small Bus. Devel. Ctr., Phoenix, 1986—. Mem. Pacific Asia Travel Assn. Ariz. (bd. dirs. 1986—), Ariz. Women in Travel, NAFE, Altrusa. Republican. Home and Office: Travel Temporaries 10249 N 45th Ave Glendale AZ 85302-1901

BAUMAN, EARL WILLIAM, accountant, government official; b. Arcadia, Nebr., Jan. 30, 1916; s. William A. and Gracia M. (Jones) B.; m. Margaret E. Blackman, Oct. 21, 1940 (dec. 1984); children: Carol Ann Bauman Ammerman. Earl William Jr.; m. Jessie C. Morgan, Dec. 23, 1990. BS with honors, U. Wyo., 1938; postgrad. Northwestern U., 1938-39. Acct., Haselmire, Cordle & Co., Casper, Wyo., 1939-42; asst. dir. fin. VA, Chgo., 1946-49, chief acctg. group VA, Washington, 1949-52, supr. systems acctg. GAO, Washington, 1952-55; supervising auditor GAO, Washington, 1955-58; dir. finance, asst. dir. Directorate Acctg. and Fin. Policy, Office Asst. Sec. Def., Washington, 1958-63; tech. asst. to comdr. AF Acctg. and Fin. Ctr., Denver, 1963-73; mem. investigations staff Ho. of Reps. Appropriations Com., 1953-54; prof. acctg. Benjamin Franklin U., 1960-63; mem. exec. council Army Finance, 1963-64; dir. Real Estate Investment Corp., 1962-64; sr. ptnr. EMB Enterprises, 1973—; chmn. Acctg. Careers Council Colo., 1969-71. Chmn. Aurora Citizens Adv. Budget Com., 1975-76; chmn. fin. and taxation com. Denver Met. Study, 1976-78. Served with AUS, 1942-46; col. Res., now ret. CPA. Mem. AICPA, Wyo. Assn. CPAs, Fed. Govt. Accts. Assn. (nat. v.p. 1972-73, pres. Denver 1973-74), Army Finance Assn., Am. Soc. Mil. Comptrollers, Denver Am. Soc. Mil. Comptrollers (pres. 1968-69), Citizens Band Radio Assn. (pres. 1963), Nat. Assn. Ret. Fed. Employees (Aurora 1072 pres. 1986-87), Alpha Kappa Psi, Beta Alpha Psi, Phi Kappa Phi. Club: Columbine Sertoma (pres. 1975-76). Avocations: photography, tennis, collector cars. Home: 536 Newark Ct Aurora CO 80010-4728

BAUMAN, JEFFREY ALLEN, computer consultant; b. Amityville, N.Y., Aug. 28, 1955; s. Robert Poe and Edith Jane (Gerkin) B.; m. Shiaulin Jou, Apr. 10, 1982; children: Carina Eileen, Daniel Joseph. Student, Ala. Sch. Fine Arts, 1969-73; BA, U. Ala., Birmingham, 1980; MA, U. Ga., 1982. Dramatic artist in residence Jefferson County Bd. Edn., Fine Arts Dept., Birmingham, 1975-79; broadcast journalist ICRT, Taipei, Taiwan, 1983-84, news dir., 1984-86, spl. project dir., 1986-87; broadcast journalist, computer cons. Nat. Pub. Radio, KPLU-FM, Tacoma, 1988-90, computer resource mgr., 1991—. Author: (book) Nickels and Dimes: Song Lyrics from 1972-85, 1987.

BAUMAN, WILLIAM WINTER, financial company executive; b. Washington, July 30, 1961; s. Walter Winter Bauman and Helen Charles (Murrell) Smith; m. Elizabeth Anne Mitchell. BS in Fin. magna cum laude, Ariz. State U., 1983, MBA, 1985. Treasury analyst Greyhound Capital Corp., Phoenix, 1983-84; investment analyst Greyhound Capital Mgmt. Corp., Phoenix, 1984-86; dir. investment analysis Venture Capital Mgmt. Corp., Phoenix, 1986-88; mgr. acquisitions Bell Atlantic Systems Leasing, Internat., Phoenix, 1988-89, portfolio sales manager, 1989-90; gen. mgr. JLC Fin., Phoenix, 1990—. Republican. Presbyterian. Home: 5330 E Calle del Norte Phoenix AZ 85018 Office: JLC Fin 7878 N 16th St Phoenix AZ 85020-4402

BAUMANN, FREDERICK, management consultant; b. Los Angeles, Nov. 26, 1930; s. Christian Frederick and Marie (Tiemann) B.; m. Flora Jane Sick, May 5, 1962; children: David, Chris, Hilary. B.S., UCLA, 1952; Ph.D., U. Wis., 1956. Rsch. chemist Chevron Rsch. Corp., Richmond, Calif., 1956-65; tech. group leader Varian Instrument Group, Walnut Creek, Calif., 1965-70, rsch. and engring. mgr., 1970-80, mng. dir., Melbourne, Australia, 1980-81, tech. dir., Palo Alto, Calif., 1981-82, mgr. lab. data systems, Walnut Creek, 1983-89, mgr. tech. and strategic planning, 1989-91; cons., 1991—; mem. adv. bd. Analytical Chemistry, Washington, 1972-75; instr. U. Calif.-Berkeley, 1968-74. Contbr. articles to profl. jours. Mem. Am. Chem. Soc., Sigma Xi, Alpha Chi Sigma. Home and Office: 166 Rudgear Dr Walnut Creek CA 94596-6316

BAUMANN, RICHARD CHARLES, physician; b. Milw., June 10, 1935; s. Carl and Hazel (Shingen) B.; m. Barbara Guse, Jan. 25, 1958; children: Daniel, David, Mark, John, Jane, Alan, Mary, Ann. BSEE, Marquette U., 1957, MD, 1965. Intern. St. Joseph Hosp., Milw., 1965-66; resident Bernalillo County Med. Ctr., Albuquerque, 1968-70; fellow Med. Coll. Wis., Milw., 1970-71; pvt. practice specializing in allergy P & A Ltd., Albuquerque, 1971—. Capt. USAF, 1966-68. Recipient Physicians Recognition award AMA, 1993. Fellow Am. Acad. Allergy, Am. Acad. Pediatrics; mem. N.Mex. Allergy Soc. (sec. 1987-88). Office: P&A Ltd 2509 Virginia St NE Albuquerque NM 87110-4641

BAUMANN, THEODORE ROBERT, aerospace engineer, consultant, army officer; b. Bklyn., May 13, 1932; s. Emil Joseph and Sophie (Reiblein) B.; m. Patricia Louise Drake, Dec. 16, 1967; children: Veronica Ann, Robert Theodore, Joseph Edmund. B in Aerospace Engring., Poly. U., Bklyn., 1954; MS in Aerospace Engring., U. So. Calif., L.A., 1962; grad., US Army C&GS Coll., 1970, Indsl. Coll. of Armed Forces, 1970, US Army War Coll., 1979, Air War Coll., 1982. Structures engr. Glenn L. Martin Co., Balt., 1954-55; structural loads engr. N.Am. Rockwell, L.A., 1958-67; dynamics engr. TRW Systems Group, Redondo Beach, Calif., 1967-71, systems engr., 1971-75, project engr., 1975-84, sr. project engr., 1984-92; cons. SAAB-Scania Aerospace Div., Linkoping, Sweden, 1981-82; asst. dir. Dir. Weapons Systems, U.S. Army, Washington, 1981-85, staff officer Missile & Air Def. System div., 1975-81. Contbr. articles to Machine Design, tech. publs., tech. symposia. Asst. scoutmaster Boy Scouts Am., Downey, Calif., 1985—; instr. Venice Judo Boys Club, 1966-86. 1st. lt. U.S. Army, 1955-58, col. USAR. Decorated Legion of Merit. Mem. AIAA; mem. Soc. Am. Mil. Engrs (life), Am. Legion, Res. Officers Assn. (life), U.S. Judo Fedn., Nat. Rifle Assn. Republican. Roman Catholic. Office: Theodore R Baumann & Assoc 7732 Brunache St Downey CA 90242

BAUMGAERTEL, MARC WARREN, financial consultant. BA, U. Wash., Seattle, 1985. Sr. fin. cons. Merrill Lynch, Lynnwood, Wash., 1988—; regional mgr. Market Performance Group, Seattle, 1986-87; instr. Wash. Community Schs., Seattle, 1988—. Office: Merrill Lynch 3500 188th St SW # 121 Lynnwood WA 98037-4716

BAUMGARTEN, WILLARD FREDERICK, JR., insurance broker; b. Santa Barbara, Calif., Nov. 24, 1943; s. Willard Frederick Baumgarten and Marie Effie (McEckern) Hale; m. Diane Wilson, Nov. 12, 1965 (div. 1967); m. Dawna Gene Dishaw, Sept. 13, 1968; stepchildren: Troy, Shawn. Student, Foothill Coll., 1966-68. Ins. agt. Equitable of Iowa, San Jose, Calif., 1966-67, Continental Am., San Jose, 1967-68, Liberty Mut., San Jose, 1968-70; prin. Baumgarten Ins., San Jose, 1970-78; ptnr., broker Campus Ins. Svc., Inc., San Jose, 1978-80, pres., broker, 1980—; bd. dirs. Ind. Ins. Agts. Bd. San Jose, 1977-81, mem. pers. com. 1982-84, founder, chmn. young agts. com. 1975-78; pres. Ind. Ins. Agts. Assn., San Jose, 1980-81. Vol. Am. Heart Assn.; mem. Milpitas (Calif.) Jaycees, 1970-75, pres., 1973, 74; mem. Santa Cruz Jaycees, 1976. With USN, 1962-66. Mem. Am. Agts. Alliance, Santa Cruz Ind. Agts. Assn., San Jose Ind. Agts. Assn. Republican. Episcopalian. Home: 705 Navarra Dr Scotts Valley CA 95066 Office: Campus Ins Svc Inc 4340 Stevens Creek Blvd San Jose CA 95129

BAUMGARTNER, ANTON EDWARD, automotive sales professional; b. N.Y.C., May 18, 1948; s. Hans and Carmen Maria (Figueroa) B.; m. Brenda Lee Lemmon, May 24, 1969 (div. 1990); 1 child, Anton Nicholaus; m. Virginia Thiele, 1992; 1 child, Bree Alexandra. BS, Woodbury U., 1970. Sales mgr. Maywood Bell Ford, Bell, Calif., 1966-69, O.R. Haan, Inc., Santa Ana, Calif., 1969-72; pres. Parkinson Volkswagen, Placentia, Calif., 1972-77; exec. v.p. United Moped, Fountain Valley, Calif., 1975-82; pres. Automobili Intermeccanica, Fountain Valley, 1975-82; gen. mgr. Bishop (Calif.) Volkswagen-Bishop Motors, 1982-85, Beach Imports-Irvine Imports, Newport Beach, Calif., 1985-88; chmn. bd. Stan and Ollie Ins. Co., Santa Ana, Calif., 1989—; mem. faculty, Automotive World Congress, Detroit, 1980. Contbr. articles to weekly serial publs. Mem. Coachbuilders Assn. N.Am. (sec. 1975-78).

BAUMHOFF, WALTER HENRY, headmaster; b. N.Y.C., May 27, 1937; s. Joseph and Elli (Schillig) B. BA, Wagner Coll., 1959; MS, Ind. U., 1961; postgrad., Harvard U.; Stanford U. Asst. dir. scholarship and fin. aid Ind. U., Bloomington, 1960-61; dean of freshmen St. Lawrence U., Canton, N.Y., 1961-65; dean of students St. Lawrence U., Canton, 1965-71; faculty, dept. of psychiatry and behavioral scis. Stanford U., Palo Alto, Calif., 1973-74; headmaster The Buckley Sch., Sherman Oaks, Calif., 1978—. Mem. St. James Club. Republican. Office: The Buckley Sch 3900 Stansbury Ave Sherman Oaks CA 91423-4699

BAUMRIND, DIANA, research psychologist; b. N.Y.C., Aug. 23, 1927. A.B., Hunter Coll., 1948; M.A., U. Calif., Berkeley, 1951, Ph.D., 1955. Cert. and lic. psychologist, Calif. Project dir. psychology dept. U. Calif., Berkeley, 1955-58; project dir. Inst. of Human Devel., 1960—, also rsch. psychologist and prin. investigator family socialization and devel. competence project; lectr. and cons. in field; referee for rsch. proposals Grant Found., NIH, 1970—, NSF, 1970—. Contbr. numerous articles to profl. jours. and books; author 2 monographs; mem. editorial bd. Devel. Psychology, 1986—, Jour. Rsch. on Adolescence, 1990—. NIMH grantee, 1955-58, 60-66, rsch. scientist award, 1984-89; Nat. Inst. Child Health and Human Devel. grantee, 1967-74, MacArthur Found. grantee, Grant Found. grantee, 1967—. Fellow Am. Psychol. Assn., Am. Psychol. Soc. (G. Stanley Hall award 1988); mem. Soc. Research in Child Devel. Office: U Calif Inst of Human Devel 1203 Tolman Hall Berkeley CA 94720

BAUTISTA, ANTHONY HERNANDEZ, biomedical company executive; b. Palo Alto, Calif., Sept. 19, 1955; s. Anthony Hernandez and Velma Rose (Morinan) B.; m. Jill Davis, June 17, 1978; children: Evan Thomas, Laura Anne. AA in Electronic Tech., Coll. of San Mateo, 1976; BSEE, San Jose (Calif.) State U., 1992. Elec. engr. Hewlett Packard, Palo Alto, Calif., 1976-86; engring. mgr. Molecular Devices Corp., Menlo Park, Calif., 1986-91; ops. mgr. LJL Biosystems, Inc., Sunnyvale, Calif., 1991—. Mem. Toastmasters Internat. (adminstv. v.p. 1990).

BAVERSJO, CHARLOTTE ELIZABETH, missionary radio broadcaster; b. St. Paul, Jan. 25, 1959; d. Hugo Robert Nathaniel and Eleanor Elizabeth (Anderson) B. Bs, U. Minn., 1983; postgrad., Northwestern Coll., Roseville, Minn., 1987-90. Cert. vet. tech., animal behaviorist. With Birkeland's Bay Lake Lodge, Deerwood, Minn., 1975-80; vet. tech. Brighton Vet. Hosp., New Brighton, Minn., 1977-90; missionary Evang. Covenant Ch., Nome, Alaska, 1990—; obedience class instr. Brighton Vet. Hosp., 1987-90; part-time vet. tech. Nome Vet. Hosp., 1990—; dog musher/racer Doolittle Dog Farm, Nome, 1991—. Author/designer tng. pamphlets: ABC Animal Behavior Ctr., 1988. Active Nome Covenant Ch., 1990—. U. Minn. grantee, 1977-83. Mem. Minn. Assn. Vet. Tech., Nome Kennel Club. Home: 373 D St Nome AK 99762 Office: KICY Radio PO Box 820 Nome AK 99762

BAWDEN, GARTH LAWRY, museum director; b. Truro, Eng., Dec. 31, 1939; s. Richard Thomas and Susan Elizabeth Olga (Lawry) B.; m. Margaret Ruth Greet, Dec. 21, 1963 (div. Mar. 1978); children: Michael Greet, Teona Mary, Kerenza Elizabeth; m. Elaine Louise Comack, Oct. 26, 1978; children: Jonathan Richard, Rebecca Lawry. Diploma in phys. medicine, West Middlesex Sch. Phys. Medicine, Isleworth, Eng., 1961; BA in Art History, U. Oreg., 1970; PhD in Anthropology, Harvard U., 1977. Assoc. in archaeology Harvard U., Cambridge, Mass., 1977-81, instr., 1980-85, asst., acting dir. Peabody Mus., 1980-85; assoc. prof. U. N.Mex., Albuquerque, 1985—, dir. Maxwell Mus., 1985—; dir. field research project Harvard U., Galindo, Peru, 1971-74, dir. field survey Peabody Mus., Saudi Arabian Archaeol. Survey, 1978-80; field supr. Cuntisuyu Project, Moquegua, Peru, 1983-86; dir. U. N.Mex. Acheol. Project, So. Peru, 1985—. Author: (with G. Conrad) The Andean Heritage, 1982; contbr. articles on archaeology to profl. jours. Fellow Woodrow Wilson, U. Oreg., 1970, Tinker, Harvard U., 1983. Mem. Soc. Am. Archaeology, Assn. Field Archaeology, Assn. Sci. Mus. Dirs., Current Anthropology (assoc.), Phi Beta Kappa, Sigma Xi. Home: 6 Applewood Ln NW Albuquerque NM 87107-6404 Office: Maxwell Mus Anthropology University of New Mexico Albuquerque NM 87131

BAXTER, CAROL CAIRNS, computer scientist; b. Oakland, Calif., Dec. 24, 1940; d. Walter V. and Helen Cairns; m. William F. Baxter, Mar. 27, 1987; 1 child, Bernard Treanor. AB, Stanford U., 1962; MA, U. Calif., Berkeley, 1966, EdD, 1969. Systems engr. Internat. Bus. Machines, Oakland, Calif., 1962-64; rsch. specialist U. Calif., Berkeley, 1969-71; rsch. dir. Ctr. for Advanced Study, Stanford, Calif., 1972-81; dir. computer rsch. Am. Enterprise Inst., Washington, 1981-83; rsch. dir. Ctr. for Advanced Study, Stanford, Calif., 1983-93.

BAXTER, DUBY YVONNE, government official; b. El Campo, Tex., July 21, 1953; d. Ray Eugene and Hazel Evelyn (Roades) Allenson; m. Loran Richard Baxter, April 7, 1979. Student, Alvin Jr. Coll., 1971, Tex. Tech U., 1972; cert. legal sec., Alaska Bus. Coll., 1974; student, Alaska Pacific U., 1981, Anchorage Community Coll., 1981-85, U. Santa Clara, 1982-83; BBA in Mgmt. cum laude, U. Alaska, Anchorage, 1985. Sr. office assoc., legal sec. Municipality of Anchorage, 1975-78; exec. sec. Security Nat. Bank, Anchorage, 1978-80, Alaska Renewable Resources Corp., Anchorage, 1980-82; pers. mgmt. specialist Dept. of Army, Ft. Richardson, Alaska, 1986-87; pers. mgmt. specialist, position classification specialist 10th Mtn. Div. (Light) Civilian Pers. Office, Ft. Drum, N.Y., 1987-89; pers. mgmt. specialist U.S. Army C.E., Anchorage, 1989-90; position classification specialist Civilian Pers. Office, 6th Inf. Div. (Light)-USA Garrison, Ft. Richardson, Alaska, 1990-91; position mgmt. and classification specialist 11th AF Cen. Civilian Personnel Office, Elmendorf AFB, Alaska, 1991—; by-laws com. mem. spl. emphasis program Fed. Women's Program, Ft. Richardson, 1986-87; instr. Prevention of Sexual Harassment, Ft. Richardson, 1986-87. Contbr. Alaska Repertoire Theater, Anchorage, 1982-87; leader Awana Christian Youth Orgn., Anchorage, 1985-87. Mem. NAFE, Classification and Compensation Soc., Missions Bd., U. Alaska Alumni Assn., Bernese Mountain Dog Club, Safari Club Internat. Mem. Brethren Ch. Office: 3 MSSQ/MSCC 2900 9th St Elmendorf AFB AK 99506

BAXTER, KEVIN VICTOR, engineer; b. Whittier, Calif., Apr. 7, 1957; s. David Ernest and Elizabeth Anita (Lucas) B.; m. Marsha Faye Cook, June 2, 1984. Student, C.C. of Air Force, Maxwell AFB, Al., 1976-90. Field tech. Ford Aerospace Corp., Santa Maria, Calif., 1987-90; assoc. tng. rep. Loral Space & Range Systems, Sunnyvale, Calif., 1990-91; sr. field engr. Bendix Field Engring. Corp., Colorado Springs, Colo., 1991—. With USAF, 1976-86, USAFR, 1986-92. Decorated Air Force Commendation medals (2). Mem. Gold Prospectors Assn. of Am. Republican. Lutheran. Home: 830 Pulpit Rock Cir S Colorado Springs CO 80918-7049 Office: Bendix Field Engring Corp 1925 Aerotech Dr #200 Colorado Springs CO 80916

BAXTER, MARVIN R., state supreme court judge; b. Fowler, Calif., Jan. 9, 1940; m. Jane Pippert, June 22, 1963; children: Laura, Brent. BA in Econs., Calif. State U., 1962; JD, U. Calif.-Hasting Coll. Law, 1966. Dep. dist. atty. Fresno County, Calif., 1967-68; assoc. Andrews, Andrews, Thaxter & Jones, 1968-70, ptnr., 1971-82; prin. advisor to gov. Office of Gov., 1983-88; then assoc. justice U.S. Ct. Appeals (5th cir.), from 1988; now justice Supreme Ct. Calif., San Francisco. Mem. Fresno County Bar Assn. (bd. dirs. 1977-82, pres. 1981), Calif. Young Lawyers Assn. (bd. gov. 1973-76, sec.-treas. 1974-75), Fresno County Young Lawyers Assn. (pres. 1973-74), Fresno County Legal Svcs., Inc. (bd. dirs. 1973-74), U. Calif. Alumni Assn. (pres. 1970-71), Alumni Trust Coun. (pres. 1970-75). Office: Jud Coun of Calif Adminstrv Office Cts 303 2nd St San Francisco CA 94107-1366*

BAXTER, PAT ANN, accountant, educator; b. Oct. 17, 1929; d. Homer H. and Ada Irene (Dowell) Layman; m. Cecil William Baxter Jr., June 6, 1951; children: Cecil William, Michael Kent, Patrick Alan. BA, Kans. Wesleyan U., 1951; MA, U. Tex., 1970. Instr. Belleville (Kans.) High Sch., 1951-54; substitute instr. area high schs., Nevada, Mo., 1954-63; instr. Manpower Devel. & Tng., Nevada, Mo., 1963-64; chief acct. Multi-Svc. Ctr., Bothell, Wash., 1977-80. Com. chair Bothell United Meth. Ch., 1985-89, vice-chair women, 1988-89; mem. King County Libr. Bd., 1986-88. Mem. AAUW. Democrat. Home: 18726 56th Ave NE Seattle WA 98155-4430

BAXTER, RONALD JAMES, ecologist; b. L.A., Nov. 6, 1952; s. Clifford James and Esther Mary (Heemstra) B.; m. Patricia Lillian Van Buskirk, Sept. 9, 1972; children: Scott Ronald, Kyle James. BS in Environ. Biology, Calif. Poly., San Luis Obispo, 1979; MS in Biology, Calif. Poly., Pomona, 1987; postgrad., U. Calif., Riverside. Biologist Bur. of Land Mgmt., Las Vegas, 1982; assoc. prof. Allergan Pharms., Santa Ana, Calif., 1982-84; lectr. Calif.-Poly State U., Pomona, 1985-87; staff ecologist Michael Brandman Assocs., Santa Ana, Calif., 1989-90; owner, sr. ecologist Baxter Cons. Svcs., Lake

Mathews, Calif., 1990—. Contbr. articles to profl. jours. Mem. Biology com. Stephens Kangaroo Rat Habitat Conservation Plan, Riverside County, Calif., 1991-92. Mem. Ecol. Soc. of Am., Soc. for Conservation Biology, Am. Soc. of Naturalists, Soc. of Systematic Biology, Nat. Geographic Soc., Orgn. for Tropical Studies (assoc.), Epsilon Phi (pres. Beta Beta Beta chpt. 1978-79). Office: Baxter Cons Svcs 20350 Chalon Rd Lake Mathews CA 92570

BAY, RICHARD ANTHONY, data processing professional; b. Erie, Pa., Sept. 19, 1948; s. Roy A. and M. Alice (Musser) B.; m. Linda L. Breaux, June 30, 1984; stepchildren: Daniel A. Breaux, Jasen A. Christian. BA in Philosophy, Vanderbilt U., 1970. With L.K. Lloyd & Assocs., San Francisco, 1979-81; systems analyst L.K. Lloyd & Assocs., 1986-87, asst. mgr. systems and programming, 1987-90, sr. mgr. systems and programming, 1990, asst. v.p., 1987—; profl. musician, freelance graphic artist, Nashville, L.A. and San Francisco, 1970-79. Composer, lyricist over 90 songs. Vol. performer Bread & Roses, Marin County, Calif., 1989—. Grantee, Am. Film Inst., 1970. Mem. Computer Profls. for Social Responsibility, No. Calif. Pick Users Group, Amnesty Internat., Sierra Club. Democrat. Home: 21 Lorraine Ct Novato CA 94947-1927 Office: LK Lloyd & Assocs 160 Spear St San Francisco CA 94105-1542

BAYDA, EDWARD DMYTRO, judge; b. Alvena, Sask, Can., Sept. 9, 1931; s. Dmytro Andrew and Mary (Bilinski) B.; m. Marie-Thérèse Yvonne Gagné, May 28, 1953; children: Paula, Christopher, Margot, Marie-Therésè, Sheila, Kathryn. BA, U. Sask., 1951, LLB cum laude, 1953; LLD (hon.), 1989. Bar: Sask. 1954. Barrister, solicitor Regina, Sask., 1953-72; sr. ptnr. Bayda, Halvorson, Scheibel & Thompson, 1966-72; justice Ct. Queen's Bench for Sask., Regina, 1972-74, Ct. Appeal for Sask., Regina, 1974-81; chief justice Sask., Regina, 1981—. Mem. Assiniboia Club (past bd. dirs.). Roman Catholic. Home: 3000 Albert St, Regina, SK Canada S4S 3N7 Office: Ct Appeal Sask Courthouse, 2425 Victoria Ave, Regina, SK Canada S4P 3V7

BAYLIN, FRANK, physicist; b. Montreal, Quebec, Can., Mar. 10, 1947; s. Samuel and Rosalynd (Gold) B.; m. Karen Kuddos, June 1, 1991. BS, McGill U., Montreal, Can., 1968; MS, U. Pa., 1969; MBA, Wharton Sch. of Bus., 1977; PhD in Physics, U. Pa., 1975. Grad. teaching fellow U. Pa., Phila., 1973-76; postdoctoral fellow Monell Chem. Senses Ctr., Phila., 1975-76; lectr. statistics U. Pa., Phila., 1976-77; scientist Solar Energy Rsch. Inst., Golden, Colo., 1978-81; owner, pres. Satellite Store, 1984-86; pres. Baylin Publs., Boulder, Colo., 1985—, Consol Network, Inc., Boulder, Colo., 1981—; cons., trainer, lectr. in field. Author: Satellite Communication Fundamentals Video Series, World Satellite TV and Scrambling Methods, 2d edit., Ku-Band Satellite TV-Theory, Installation and Repair, 4th edit., Satellite and Cable TV-Scrambling and Descrambling, 2d edit., Satellite TV Installation and Troubleshooting Manual, 3rd edit., The Home Satellite TV Installation Video Tape, Satellites Today-The Complete Guide to Satellite TV System, 2d edit., World Satellite Yearly, 1993, Satellite Textbook Software, 1993; contbr. over 40 tech. publs. to profl. jours. Recipient Wharton Pub. Policy fellowship, 1977, Med. Rsch. Coun. of Can. grant, 1972-75, U. Pa. scholarship, 1968-71, McGill U. scholarship, 1964-68, Quebec Math. prize, 1963; named Woodrow Wilson fellow, 1968.

BAYLOR, ELGIN GAY, professional basketball team executive; b. Washington, Sept. 16, 1934; m. Elaine; 1 dau., Krystle. Ed., Coll. Idaho, Seattle U. Profl. basketball player Los Angeles (formerly Minneapolis) Lakers, 1958-72; asst. coach New Orleans Jazz, NBA, 1974-76, coach, 1976-79; exec. v.p., gen. mgr. Los Angeles Clippers, 1986—. Most Valuable Player, NCAA Tournament, 1958; mem. NBA All-Star Team, 1959-65, 67-70; Rookie of the Yr., NBA, 1959; co-Most Valuable Player, NBA All-Star Game, 1959; named to NBA 35th Anniversary All-Time Team, 1980. Office: Los Angeles Clippers 3939 S Figueroa St Los Angeles CA 90037-1207*

BAYNE, CHARLES LEE, JR., law enforcement officer; b. Laramie, Wyo., July 2, 1963; s. Charles L. Sr. and Mina A. (Liden) B.; 1 child, Charles L. Bayne III. Grad. high sch., Laramie. Cert. peace officer profl. Comm. officer Albany County Sheriff Dept., Laramie, 1981-83, patrol dep., 1983-84, 85-87, comm. sgt., 1984-85, sr. patrol dep., 1987-88; police officer Wheatland (Wyo.) Police Dept., 1988-89, police sgt., 1989-92, police lt., 1992—; guest lectr. Platte County Project S.A.F.E., Wheatland, 1991—; guest instr. Wyo. Law Enforcement Acad., Douglas, 1991. Mem., advisor Boy Scouts Am. Explorer Post #134, Laramie, 1979-84. J. Edgar Hoover scholarship J.E. Hoover Found., 1981; recipient Cert. of Appreciation VFW, 1991. Mem. Wyo. Peace Officer Assn., Wyo. Assn. Chiefs of Police, Wyo. Assn. of Sheriff's and Chiefs of Police. Office: Wheatland Police Dept 605 10th St Wheatland WY 82201

BAYO, EDUARDO, civil engineering educator; b. Madrid, Castille, Spain, Sept. 3, 1954; came to U.S., 1978; s. Candido and Ana Maria (Perez) B.; m. Elizabeth Anne Delgado, Sept. 25, 1982; children: Carolina, Eduardo, Joseph, Annelise, Christopher. BS in Civil Enging., Poly. U., Madrid, 1976; M. Engring. in Civil Engring., U. Calif., Berkeley, 1980, PhD in Civil Engring., 1983. Engr. Gibbs & Hill Española, Madrid, 1976-78; rsch. asst. U. Calif., Berkeley, 1980-83; rsch. supr. INITEC, Madrid, 1983-85; asst. prof. U. Calif., Santa Barbara, 1986-89, assoc. prof., 1989—; cons. EDO, Santa Barbara, 1988—, Computer & Structures, Inc., Berkeley, 1985—, Structural Analysis Programs, Inc., Berkeley, 1982—. Author: Inverse Dynamics and Kinematics of Flexible Manipulations and Multibody Systems; contbr. articles to profl. jours.; inventor inverse dynamics of flexible manipulators. With Spanish Air Force, 1973-74. Scholar Fundacion Instituto Nacional, 1978-80, Ford Motor Co., 1981-82; Regent's Jr. fellow U. Calif., 1988; grantee Spanish Govt., 1990-91. Mem. ASME, Am. Soc. Engring. Edn. Roman Catholic. Office: U Calif Mech Engring Dept Santa Barbara CA 93117

BAYS, ERIC, bishop; b. Portage La Prairie, Manitoba, Can., Aug. 10, 1932; s. Percy Clarence and Hilda (Harper) B.; m. Patricia Ann Earle, Dec. 28, 1967; children: Jonathan Edmund, Rebecca Jane. BS, U. Man., Winnipeg, Can., 1955; BA, U. Sask., Saskatoon, Can., 1959; L in Theology, U. Emmanuel Coll., Saskatoon, 1959, DD (hon.), 1987; M in Ministry, Christian Theol. Sem., Indpls., 1974. Ordained to ministry Anglican Ch., 1959. Asst. curate All Saints' Anglican Ch., Winnipeg, 1959-61; lectr. Emmanuel Coll., Saskatoon, 1961-62; mission priest Diocese Caledonia, B.C., 1962-64; novice in religion Community of the Resurrection, Mirfield, Eng., 1964-65; vicar St. Saviour's with St. Catherine Parish, Winnipeg, 1965-67; rector All Saints' Parish, Winnipeg, 1968-76; prof. Coll. Emmanuel/St. Chad, Saskatoon, 1976-81; vice-prin. Coll. of Emmanuel/St. Chad, Saskatoon, 1981-86; bishop Diocese Qu'Appelle, Regina, Sask., 1986—. With RCAF, 1955-59. Office: Diocese of Qu'Appelle, 1501 College Ave, Regina, SK Canada S4P 1B8

BEACH, ARTHUR O'NEAL, lawyer; b. Albuquerque, Feb. 8, 1945; s. William Pearce and Vivian Lucille (Kronig) B.; B.B.A., U. N.Mex., 1967, J.D., 1970; m. Alex Clark Doyle, Sept. 12, 1970; 1 son, Eric Kronig. Admitted to N.Mex. bar, 1970; assoc. firm Smith & Ransom, Albuquerque, 1970-74; assoc. firm Keleher & McLeod, Albuquerque, 1974-75, ptnr., 1976-78, shareholder firm Keleher & McLeod, P.A., Albuquerque, 1978—; teaching asst. U. N. Mex., 1970. Bd. editors Natural Resources Jour., 1968-70. Mem. State Bar N.Mex. (unauthorized practice of law com., adv. opinions com., med.-legal panel, legal-dental-osteo.-podiatry com., jud. selection com.), Am., Albuquerque (dir. 1978-82) bar assns., State Bar Specialization Bd. Democrat. Mem. Christian Sci. Ch. Home: 2015 Dietz Pl NW Albuquerque NM 87107-3240 Office: Keleher & McLeod PA PO Drawer AA Albuquerque NM 87103

BEACH, LEE ROY, psychologist, educator; b. Gallup, N.Mex., Feb. 29, 1936; s. Dearl and Lucile Ruth (Krumtum) B.; m. Barbara Ann Heinrich, Nov. 13, 1971. B.A., Ind. U., 1957; M.A., U. Colo., 1959, Ph.D., 1961. Aviation psychologist U.S. Sch. Aviation Medicine, Pensacola, Fla., 1961-63; human factors officer Office of Naval Research, Washington, 1963-64; postdoctoral research U. Mich., Ann Arbor, 1964-66; faculty dept. psychology U. Wash., Seattle, 1966-89; faculty mgmt. & policy, psychology U. Ariz., Tucson, 1990—, McClelland chair mgmt. & policy, 1989—. Contbr. articles to profl. jours. Recipient Feldman rsch. award, 1981, Disting. Tchr. award U. Wash., 1986, Prof. of Yr. award State of Wash., 1989, nat. teaching award Coun. for Advancement and Support Edn., 1989; fellow NIMH, 1964-66. Fellow Am. Psychol. Assn.; mem. Soc. for Orgnl. Behavior. Office: Univ Arizona Coll Bus and Pub Adminstrn Tucson AZ 85721

BEACH, ROGER C., oil company executive; b. Lincoln, Nebr., Dec. 5, 1936; s. Melvin C. and L. Mayme (Hoham) B.; m. Elaine M. Wilson, Oct. 1954 (div. 1972); children: Kristi, Mark, Anne; m. Karen Lynn Ogden, July 27, 1974. BS, Colo. Sch. Mines, 1961. Registered profl. petroleum refining engr., Calif. Mgr. spl. projects Unocal Corp., Los Angeles, 1976-77, dir. planning, 1977-80, v.p. crude supply, 1980-86, pres. refining and mktg., 1986-92, corp. sr. v.p., until 1992, pres., chief oper. officer, 1992—. Mem. Am. Petroleum Inst., U.S.-Korea Soc., Nat. Petroleum Refiner's Assn., Pres.'s Interchange Exec. Alumni Assn. Office: Unocal Refining & Mktg Div PO Box 7600 Los Angeles CA 90051*

BEAGLE, JOHN GORDON, real estate broker; b. Spokane, Wash., Dec. 31, 1943; s. Gordon Avril and Sylvia Alberta (Dobbs) B.; m. Shihoko Ledo, Nov. 14, 1964; children: James, Steven, Kevin, Melanie. BS, Mont. State U., 1970; GRI, Realtors Inst., Helena, Mont. Cert. real estate broker. Instr. Kalispell (Mont.) High Sch., 1970-71; gen. mgr. Equity Coop. Assn., Harlem, Mont., 1971-76; owner, operator Howards Pizza, Livingston, Mont., 1976-79; broker, owner ERA Beagle Properties, Sidney, Mont., 1979—. Mem. City Coun. City of Harlem, 1975. With USN, 1963-67. Mem. Mont. Assn. Realtors (v.p. ea. dist. 1982-84), Gateway Bd. Realtors (pres. 1987-88), Kiwanis, Lions. Republican. Mem. Ch. of Christ. Home: Holly and North Dr Sidney MT 59270 Office: ERA Beagle Properties 120 2D Ave SW Sidney MT 59270

BEAGRIE, GEORGE SIMPSON, dentist, educator, dean emeritus; b. Peterhead, Scotland, Sept. 14, 1925; emigrated to Can., 1968, naturalized, 1973; s. George and Eliza Lawson (Simpson) B.; m. Marjorie McVie, Sept. 30, 1950; children: Jennifer, Lesley, Ailsa, Elspeth. LDS, Royal Coll. Surgeons, Edinburgh, Scotland, 1947; DDS, U. Edinburgh, 1966, DDS (hon.), 1987; DSc (hon.), McGill U., Can., 1985, U. Montreal, Can., 1991. Prof., chmn. dept. restorative dentistry U. Edinburgh Dental Sch., 1963-68; prof., chmn. dept. clin. scis. U. Toronto Dental Sch., 1968-78, dir. postgrad. div., 1974-78; dean faculty dentistry U. B.C., Vancouver, Can., 1978-88, dean emeritus, 1989—; sci. officer grants com. dental scis. Med. Research Council Can., 1971-76, dir. dental tng. grants programme, 1971-78; mem. Nat. Dental Examining Bd. Can.; chmn. written exams. com. Nat. Dental Examining Bd., Can., 1984—; cons. in field. Contbr. over 100 articles to dental jours. Mem. United Ch. Can. Served to flight lt. RAF, 1948-50. Fellow Nuffield Found., 1957-58; grantee Med. Research Council U.K., 1962-64; grantee Med. Research Council Can., 1968; grantee Commonwealth Found., 1973. Fellow Royal Coll. Dentists Can. (pres. 1977-79), Am. Coll. Dentists, Internat. Coll. Dentists; fellow in dental surgery Royal Coll. Surgeons Edinburgh and Eng.; mem. ADA (hon.), Internat. Assn. Dental Research (pres. 1977-78), Fedn. Dentaire Internat. (chmn. commn. on dental edn. and practice 1981-87), Can. Dental Assn. (editor tape cassette program 1972-76), Brit. Dental Assn., Ont. Dental Assn., Canadian Acad. Periodontists, Brit., Ont. socs. periodontology, Omicron Kappa Upsilon. Office: Univ BC Faculty Dentistry, 345-2194 Health Scis Mall, Vancouver, BC Canada V6T 1W5

BEAKE, JOHN, professional football team executive; m. Marcia Beake; children: Jerilyn, Chip, Christopher. Grad., Trenton (N.J.) State Coll.; M degree, Pa. State U. Asst. coach Pa. State U., 1961-62, Kansas City Chiefs, NFL, 1968-74, New Orleans Saints, NFL, 1976-77; offensive coordinator Colo. State U., 1974-76; dir. profl. personnel Denver Broncos, NFL, 1979-83, dir. football ops., 1983-84, asst. gen. mgr., 1984-85, gen. mgr., 1985—. Office: Denver Broncos 13655 Broncos Pky Englewood CO 80112-4150 also: Denver Broncos 13665 E Dove Valley Pkwy Englewood CO 80112*

BEAL, ANDREW ALLEN, lawn care company executive; b. Tucson, July 23, 1953; s. Richard Sidney and Wilma Juhree (Gibbons) B.; m. Nancy Lynne Godemann, Jan. 8, 1977; children: Tyler Benjamin, Noelle Loy. BS in Philosophy, No. Ariz. U., 1976. Police officer No. Ariz. U., Flagstaff, 1975-76; asst. mgr. Pillow Kingdom, Denver, 1978-80; pres. Svc.Master Downtown, Denver, 1980-90, A.N.T.N., Denver, 1986—; chmn. Svc.Master Lawn Care, Memphis, 1990-91. Counselor Peak Adventures, Denver, 1987—; mem. choir Bear Valley Ch., Denver, 1991—. Mem. Colo. Assn. Lawn Care Profls. (v.p. 1991-92). Republican. Home: 7795 W Ottawa Dr Littleton CO 80123

BEALER, JONATHAN MILES, educator; b. San Jose, Calif., Nov. 12, 1946; s. John Leslie and Maxine (Rhoades) B.; m. Virginia Anderson Caretto, Dec. 20, 1969; children: Ian Marshall, Glynis Amanda. BA, U. Calif., Santa Barbara, 1969; M Natural Sci., Ariz. State U., 1979. Cert. standard secondary tchr., Ariz. Tchr. sci. Buena High Sch., Sierra Vista, Ariz., 1971—, chmn. dept., 1985—, computer coord., 1986—; state, regional and nat. conv. presenter in field; chmn. Ariz. Health Occupations Adv. Coun., 1985-86. Contbr. articles to profl. jours. Pres. Huachuca Audubon Soc., Sierra Vista, 1978, editor newsletter, 1989—. Recipient Golden Bell award Ariz. Sch. Bd. Assn., 1985; named Az. Teacher of Year, Ambassador of Excellence, 1985. Mem. NEA, NSTA, Nat. Assn. Biology Tchrs. (Outstanding Biology Tchr. award 1982), Nat. Audubon Soc., Sierra Vista Classroom Tchrs. Assn. (negotiations spokesman 1979), Health Occupations Educators Ariz. (bd. dirs. 1990, Tchr. of Yr. award 1985). Democrat. Home: 8143 Geoffrion St Hereford AZ 85615 Office: Buena High Sch 3555 Fry Blvd Sierra Vista AZ 85635

BEALL, CHARLES PORTER, political science educator; b. Ft. Wayne, Ind., May 13, 1924; s. Charles Giffen and Myrtle (Wilding) B.; m. Lynette Bradley, Dec. 31, 1946 (div. 1971); m. Gretchen H. Hieronymus, Nov. 7, 1976; children: Jacquelyn, C. Douglas, Marilyn. BA, De Pauw U., 1948; MA, Ind. U., 1949; diploma, U. Stockholm, Sweden, 1949; PhD, Ind. U., 1952. Instr. Ind. U., Bloomington, 1950-52; asst. prof. polit. sci. U. Wyo., Laramie, 1952-55, assoc. prof. polit. sci., 1956-63; prof., head. dept. polit. sci. Ea. Ill. U., Charleston, 1963-66; prof., chmn. dept. polit. sci. U. Denver, 1966-72, prof. polit. sci., 1972-82; prof. emeritus U. Denver, Longmont, Colo., 1982—; lectr. Adult Edn. Soc., Stockholm, 1948-49; vis. prof. polit. sci. U. Wyo., summer 1958, Colo. Coll., summer 1965, U. Nev., summer 1964, Alaska Meth. U., 1960-61; guest lectr. and vis. dir. Ea. Mont. State U., Billings, Summer Inst. Internat. Affairs, 1960; cons. USAF, 1954, St. Vrain Valley Schs., Longmont, 1990—, Wyo. State Dept. Edn., 1955, Princeton U. Conf., summer 1960; mem. adv. bd. Denver Jour. Internat. Law and Policy, 1971-82. Contbg. author: Western Politics, 1960; contbr. articles to profl. jours. Candidate Ind. State Legis., 1950; Dem. county chmn., Albany County, Wyo., 1954-58; Dem. State Cen. Com., Wyo., 1954-58; mem. platform com. State Dem. Conv., Wyo., 1954, credentials com., 1956; councilman Laramie City Coun., 1956-60; mem. zoning bd. adjustments City of Laramie, 1960-63, chmn., civil svc. commn., 1960-63; vice chmn. Wyo. Civil Rights Commn., 1962-63; adv. Colo. Coun. of Arts and Humanities, 1966-67; precinct committeeman Dem. Orgn., 1979-82. With USN, 1942-46. Recipient Svc. awards City Coun. of Laramie, 1963, Omicron Delta Kappa Disting. Faculty-Adminstrn. award U. Denver, 1979. Mem. Am. Polit. Sci. Assn., Western Polit. Sci. Assn., Internat. Studies Assn., Rocky Mountain Social Sci. Assn., Dobra Slovo, Pi Sigma Alpha. Democrat. Home: 37 Princeton Cir Longmont CO 80503

BEALL, DENNIS RAY, artist, educator; b. Chickasha, Okla., Mar. 13, 1929; s. Roy A. and Lois O. (Phillips) B.; 1 son, Garm. Musician,, Okla. City U., 1950-52; B.A., San Francisco State U., 1953, M.A., 1958. Registrar Oakland (Calif.) Art Mus., 1958; curator Achenbach Found. for Graphic Arts, Calif. Palace of the Legion of Honor, San Francisco, 1958-1965; asst. prof. art San Francisco State U., 1965-69, assoc. prof., 1969-76, prof. art, 1976-92; prof. emeritus, 1992—. Numerous one-man shows of prints, 1957—, including: Award Exhbn. of San Francisco Art Commn., Calif. Coll. Arts and Crafts, 1978, San Francisco U. Art Gallery, 1978, Los Robles Galleries, Palo Alto, Calif.; numerous group shows, 1960—, including, Mills Coll. Art Gallery, Oakland, Calif., Univ. Gallery of Calif. State U., Hayward, 1979, Marshall-Meyers Gallery, 1979, 80, Marin Civic Center Art Galleries, San Rafael, Calif., 1980, San Francisco Mus. Modern Art, 1985; touring exhibit U. Mont., 1987-91; represented in numerous permanent collections including, Library of Congress, Washington, Mus. Modern Art, N.Y.C., Nat. Library of Medicine, Washington, Phila. Mus., U.S. embassy collections, Tokyo, London and other major cities, Victoria and Albert Mus., London, Achenbach Found. for Graphic Arts, Calif. Palace of Legion of Honor, San Francisco, Oakland Art Mus., Phila. Free Library, Roanoke (Va.) Art Center, various colls. and univs. in U.S. Served with USN, 1947-50, PTO. Office: San Francisco State Univ Art Dept 1600 Holloway St San Francisco CA 94132

BEALL, DEWITT TALMADGE, interior designer; b. Ripley, W.Va., Apr. 10, 1940; s. DeWitt T.and Orpha Auline (Hartley) B.; m. Callista Marie Card, Sept. 15, 1973 (div. 1988); m. Elina Katsioula, Nov. 19, 1988; children: John Aaron, Olivia Simone. BA, Dartmouth Coll., 1965. Copywriter Leo Burnett, Chgo., 1965-66; freelance filmmaker Chgo., 1966-71, 73-75; producer, dir. Sta. WTTW-TV, Chgo., 1971-73; assoc. producer Goldsholl Assocs., Northfield, Ill., 1975-78; freelance designer, writer L.A., 1979-87; pres. The Kitchen Architect, L.A., 1988—. Author: Ravenswood, 1963; producer documentary and ednl. films. Founder, Found. Years., Chgo., 1968. Recipient Chgo. award Chgo. Internat. Film Festival, 1977, Cine Golden Eagle, 1969, 72, Silver medal Venice Film Festival, 1970; featured in cover story, Kitchen and Bath Design News, 1985, 88. Mem. Am. Soc. Interior Designers. Democrat. Methodist. Office: The Kitchen Architect 143 S Robertson Blvd West Hollywood CA 90048-3207

BEALL, DONALD RAY, multi-industry high-tech company executive; b. Beaumont, Calif., Nov. 29, 1938; s. Ray C. and Margaret (Murray) B. B.S., San Jose State Coll., 1960; M.B.A., U. Pitts., 1961; postgrad., UCLA. With Ford Motor Co., 1961-68; fin. mgmt. positions Newport Beach, Calif., 1961-66; mgr. corp. fin. planning and contracts Phila., 1966-67; controller Palo Alto, Calif., 1967-68; exec. dir. corp. fin. planning N.Am. Rockwell, El Segundo, Calif., 1968-69, exec. v.p. electronics group, 1969-71; exec. v.p. Collins Radio Co., Dallas, 1971-74; pres. Collins Radio Group, Rockwell Internat. Corp., Dallas, 1974-76; corp. v.p., pres. Electronic Ops., Dallas, 1976-77; exec. v.p. Rockwell Internat. Corp., Dallas, 1977-79; pres., chief operating officer Rockwell Internat. Corp., Pitts., 1979-88; chmn. bd., chief exec. officer Rockwell Internat. Corp., Seal Beach, Calif., 1988—; bd. overseers U. Calif., Irvine, 1988—; bd. dirs. Proctor & Gamble Co., Amoco Corp., Times-Mirror Corp., L.A. World Affairs Coun. Mem. Bus.-Higher Edn. Forum, Bus. Coun., Bus. Roundtable, SRI Adv. Coun., Coun. on Competitiveness. Recipient award of distinction San Jose State U. Sch. Engring., 1980. Mem. AIAA, Navy League U.S., Young Pres.'s Orgn., Sigma Alpha Epsilon, Beta Gamma Sigma. Office: Rockwell Internat Corp Box 4250 2201 Seal Beach Rd Seal Beach CA 90740*

BEALL, FRANK CARROLL, science director and educator; b. Balt., Oct. 3, 1933; s. Frederick Carroll Beall and Virginia Laura (Ogier) McNally; m. Mavis Lillian Holmes, Sep. 7, 1963; children: Amanda Jane Cysewski, Mark Walter Beall, Alyssa Joan Beall. BS, Pa. State U., 1964; MS, Syracuse U., 1966, PhD, 1968. Rsch. technologist U.S. Forest Products Lab., Madison, Wis., 1966-68; asst., then assoc. prof. Pa. State U., University Park, 1968-75; assoc. prof. U. Toronto, Can., 1975-77; scientist, mgr. Weyerhaeuser Co., Federal Way, Wash., 1977-88; prof., dir. U. Calif. Forest Products Lab., Richmond, 1988—. Contbr. numerous articles in wood and sci. tech.; patentee for wood forming method, method of measuring content of dielectric materials, vertical progressive lumber dryer, bond strength measurement of composite panel products, hybrid poltruded products and method for their manufacture. Mem. ASTM, Am. Soc. for Non-destructive Testing, Forest Products Soc., Soc. Wood Sci. and Tech. (pres. 1991-92), Acoustic Emission Working Group (sec.-treas. 1992—). Office: U Calif Forest Products Lab 1301 S 46th St Richmond CA 94804-4698

BEALL, JAMES CRICHTON, electronic engineer, aerodynamic engineer; b. Atlanta, June 11, 1942; s. Robert Marion and Patricia Jane (Crichton) B.; m. Joan Claire Theresa Rea, July 26, 1968 (div. Apr. 1988); children: Pamela Joan, James Michael, David Robert. Student, Embry-Riddle, 1979. Computer engr. IBM Corp., Armonk, N.Y., 1963-69; chief pilot part-time Cape Coral (Fla.)/Bimini Flying Svc., 1965-68; air traffic controller Fed. Aviation Agy., Washington, 1969-76; CEO Beall Videophone Corp., Ft. Myers, Fla., 1980-88, Beall-Jaquish Spacelines, Tucson, 1990—. Inventor rocket pressure pump, rocket air induction nozzle, hypersonic aerobraking, hypersonic wing design. Mem. vol. staff U.S. Senator Dennis DeConcini, Tucson, 1991; vol. restoration Pima Air and Space Mus., Tucson, 1991. With USN, 1959-63. Mem. Am. Hydrogen Assn., Tuscon Space Soc., Tucson Electric Vehicle Assn. (tech. com.), Nat. Space Soc., Aircraft Owners and Pilots Assn. Home: 280 N Carapan 216 Tucson AZ 85745 Office: Beall Jaquish Spacelines 2A W Greenock Dr Tucson AZ 85737

BEAM, WILLIAM WASHINGTON, III, data coordinator; b. L.A., Jan. 21, 1960; s. William Washington and Ada Frances (Towler) B. BS, UCLA, 1982; MA, U. Wash., 1985. Paralegal Arco, L.A., 1985-88, programmer, 1988-90, data coord., 1990—. Mem. Am. Econ. Assn. Office: Arco 515 S Flower St AP-4661 Los Angeles CA 90071

BEAMAN, JOHN DAVID, editor, consultant; b. Montclair, N.J., Aug. 10, 1965; s. Alden Gamaliel and Lucille Beatrice (Papenhusen) B.; m. Myrta Lynn Brown, Aug. 24, 1991. BA in Communications, Pub. Rels., Brigham Young U., 1991. Assoc. editor R.I. Families Assn., Princeton, Mass., 1989; media rels. rep. Bradley Agy., Provo, Utah, 1989-90; intern United Way Utah County, Provo, 1991-92; cons. Am. Rsch. Bur., Salt Lake City, 1992—, Teleconsulting Svcs. Inc., Salt Lake City, 1992—; cons. Family History Libr., Salt Lake City, 1991. Dist. leader Ch. of Jesus Christ of Latter-day Saints, Oakland, Calif., 1985, pres. elders' quorum, Provo, 1987, exec. sec., Provo, 1987. Home: 1926 SW Temple Salt Lake City UT 84115 Office: Teleconsulting Svcs Inc 635 W 5300 S Salt Lake City UT 84123

BEAMAN, WILLIAM CHARLES, magistrate, legal clerk; b. Cheyenne, Wyo., Oct. 25, 1945; s. Walter Frank and Genevieve Matilda (Clausen) B.; m. Carol Kay Childers, June 22, 1974 (div.). B.A., Ariz. State U., 1967; J.D., U. Wyo., 1971. Bar: Wyo. 1971, U.S. Dist. Ct. Wyo., 1971, U.S. Ct. Appeals (10th cir.) 1973. Law clk. to judge U.S. Dist. Ct. Wyo., 1971-73; mem. Beaman & Galeotos, Cheyenne, 1973-78; magistrate U.S. Dist. Ct. Wyo. 1975—, clk., 1978—. Mem. Cheyenne Bd. Adjustments, 1974-83, chmn., 1978; mem. Cheyenne Area Devel. Com., 1979-82; mem. Cheyenne Waste Mgmt. Study Group, 1982; mem. Wyo. Blood Services Adv. Council, 1982—. Served to staff sgt. Air. N.G., 1967-73. Mem. ABA, Wyo. State Bar Assn., Laramie County Bar Assn., Am. Judicature Soc., Wyo. Trial Lawyers Assn., Fed. Ct. Clk.'s Assn., Nat. Council U.S. Magistrates, Cheyenne C. of C. Episcopalian. Lodges: Rotary, Elks (Cheyenne). Office: PO Box 727 Cheyenne WY 82003-0606

BEAMER-PATTON, JUNE ELIZABETH, dermatologist; b. Martin's Ferry, Ohio, Mar. 9, 1944; d. Ralph Clark and Betty June (Sedgwick) Patton; m. Yancey Brintle, Aug. 20, 1967 (div. Dec. 1986). BS in Chemistry, Marshall U., 1965; MD, Med. Coll. Va., 1969. Diplomate Am. Bd. Dermatology; cert. Nat. Bd. Med. Examiners, Calif.; cert. Colo. Basic Sci., Colo., Utah; cert. X-ray Supr. and Operator, Calif. Intern Med. Coll. Va., Richmond, 1969-70, U. Calif., Irvine, 1970; resident in dermatology Long Beach (Calif.) Veteran's Hosp., 1970-73; with U. Calif. Med. Ctr., Irvine, 1970-82, Healthcare Med. Ctr. Tustin, 1988; pvt. practice Tustin, 1973—; clin. assoc. medicine dermatology, U. Calif., Irvine, 1972, clin. instr. medicine dermatology, 1973, asst. clin. prof. 1976, clin. prof. 1977-82. Contbr. articles profl. jours. Mem. Calvary Ch. Mem. AMA, Am. Med. Women's Assn., Calif. Med. Assn., Pacific Dermatologic Assn., Orange County Med. Assn., Orange County Dermatological Soc., Am. Acad. Dermatology, Am. Coun. Hosp. Staffs, Internat. Acad. Cosmetic Surgery, Cooperative of Am. Physicians, Inc., Am. Soc. Dermatology Surgery, Audio Enging. Soc., Am. Mgmt. Assn., Nat. Assn. Women Bus. Owners, Am. Soc. Profl. and Exec. Women, Tustin C. of C., Wings Club, Alpha Epsilon Delta, Chi Beta Phi, Phi Alpha Theta. Republican. Office: June E Beamer-Patton MD 13372 Newport Ave # A Tustin CA 92680-3426

BEAMON, LAUNA RAE, special education educator; b. Hamilton, Ohio, Mar. 8, 1955; d. Robert Don and Edna Maxine (Webb) Howard; m. John Wesley McKinzie Jr., June 13, 1975 (div. Apr. 1979); 1 child, John Wesley III; m. Willie C. Beamon, Feb. 14, 1990; 1 stepchild, Joshua Daniel. BS in Edn., Spl. Edn., Learning Disabilities/Behavioral Disorders, Miami U., 1982; postgrad., Calif. State U., 1992—. Rater, coder Ohio Casualty Ins. Co., Hamilton, 1975-79; cons., substitute tchr. Oxford (Ohio) Sch. Young Children, 1980-83; workshop specialist Butler County Bd. MR/DD, Hamilton,

1982-83; tchr. learning disabled Millcreek Psychiat. Ctr. Children, Cin., 1983-87; tchr. San Bernardino (Calif.) County Schs., 1987-88; program dir. Sierra Vista Rehab., Highland, Calif., 1988-91; tchr., resource specialist San Bernardino City Schs., 1991—; mem. resource adv. coun. San Bernardino City Schs., 1991—; presenter in field. Foster parent Hamilton County Dept. Human Svcs., 1985; bd. dirs. Oxford Sch. Young Children, 1983-86. Mem. NEA, Calif. Assn. Spl. Treatment Program Dirs. (charter mem., treas., 1988-91), Calif. Tchrs. Assn., Kappa Delta Pi. Home: 2680 E Highland #522 Highland CA 92346

BEAN, DONNA RAE, healthcare facility executive; b. Wichita, Kans., Dec. 31, 1950; d. Roy E. and Esther E. (Young) B. BS, Azusa (Calif.) Pacific U., 1972; MT, San Bernardino (Calif.) Hosp., 1974; MBA, Boise (Idaho) State U., 1984. Med. technologist Caldwell (Idaho) Health Ctr., 1975-77, supr. lab., 1978-80, clinic mgr., 1980-81; systems mgr. Payette (Idaho) Health Care, 1982-85; dir. material svcs. Holy Rosary Med. Ctr., Ontario, Calif., 1985—; lab. cons. State of Idaho, Boise, 1985—; systems cons. in field. Boise State U. scholar, 1982, 83, Whittenberger Found. scholar, 1983-84. Mem. Am. Soc. Clin. Pathologists, Healthcare Material Mgmt. Soc., NAFE. Republican. Methodist. Office: Holy Rosary Med Ctr 351 SW 9th St Ontario OR 97914-2693

BEAN, JAMES WOOLSON, JR., bank executive; b. Pasadena, Calif., Aug. 11, 1947; s. James Woolson and Mildred (Hand) B.; m. Linda Badi Bean, Oct. 18, 1978 (div. Dec. 1988); children: Linda Marie, Christina Suzanne. BA in Econs., Pomona Coll., 1969; MBA in Fin., Harvard U., 1971; postgrad., Claremont U., 1988—. CPA, Calif. Sr. mgr. Price Waterhouse, N.Y.C., 1971-84; div. contr. 1st Interstate Bank, L.A., 1984-85; contr. Glendale (Calif.) Fed. Bank, 1985—. Mem. com. Tournament of Roses, Pasadena, 1990. Mem. Fin. Execs. Inst., Fin. Mgrs. Soc. (pres. 1989-90), La Canada Country Club. Republican. Presbyterian. Home: 715 Lakewood Pl Pasadena CA 91106-3923 Office: Glendale Fed Bank 700 N Broad Blvd Glendale CA 91209

BEAN, WILLIAM JAMES, federal agency administrator; b. Pocatello, Idaho, Mar. 24, 1933; s. James Lynch and Katye (Archer) B.; m. Laurine Elizabeth Campbell, Jan. 22, 1964. BA, N.Mex. Western Coll., 1958; MS, Tex. Tech. U., 1960, PhD, 1967. Rehab. program specialist Rehab. Svcs. Adminstrn., U.S. Dept. Edn., Washington, 1967-83; regional commr. Rehab. Svcs. Adminstrn., U.S. Dept. Edn., Seattle, 1983-93. Home: 870 W Birch St Deming NM 88030

BEANS, DOANLD RING, acupuncture physician; b. Great Falls, Mont., Aug. 17, 1953; s. Robert Blandin Beans and Emma Louise (Ring) Raff. BSN, Mont. State U., 1978; PhD, U. Health Sci., 1989; DSc (hon.), Open Internat. U. Complimentary Medicine, Colombo, Sri Lanka, 1992. Nurse Mont. Deaconess Med. Ctr., Great Falls, 1978-79, St. Patrick Hosp., Missoula, Mont., 1979; pvt. practice Missoula, Mont., 1980-85, Big Fork, Mont., 1985—. Contbr. articles to profl. jours.; creator profl. and instrnl. video tapes. Mem. Am. Assn. Acupuncture and Oriental Medicine (chair ins. com.), Homeopathic Acad. Naturopathic Physicians, Nat. Ctr. for Homeopathy, Internat. Found. for Homeopathy, Mont. Assn. Acupuncture and Oriental Medicine (founding pres. 1985, acupuncture liason to Mont. Bd. Med. Examiners, 1992—), Bigfork C. of C. (pres. 1991-92). Office: The Health Clinic 245 Commerce St Bigfork MT 59911

BEAR, GREGORY DALE, writer, illustrator; b. San Diego, Aug. 20, 1951; s. Dale Franklin and Wilma (Merriman) B.; m. Christina Marie Nielsen, Jan. 11, 1975 (div. 1981); m. Astrid May Anderson, June 18, 1983; children: Erik William, Alexandra. AB in English, San Diego State U., 1973. Tech. writer, host Reuben H. Fleet Space Theater, 1973; freelance writer, 1975—. Author: Hegira, 1979; Psychlone, 1979, Beyond Heaven's River, 1980, Strength of Stones, 1981, The Wind from a Burning Woman, 1983, The Infinity Concerto, 1984, Blood Music, 1985, Eon, 1985, The Serpent Mage, 1986, The Forge of God, 1987, Eternity, 1988, Tangents, 1989, Heads, 1990, Queen of Angels, 1990, Anvil of Stars, 1992, Moving Mars, 1993; short stories: Blood Music (Hugo and Nebula awards), 1983, Hardfought (Nebula award), 1983, Tangents (Hugo and Nebula awards), 1987. Cons. Citizen's Adv. Council on Nat. Space Policy, Tarzana, Calif., 1983-84. Mem. Sci. Fiction Writers of Am. (editor Forum 1983-84, chmn. grievance com. 1985-86, v.p. 1987, pres. 1988-90). Home: 506 Lakeview Rd Lynnwood WA 98037-2141

BEAR, HERBERT STANLEY, JR., mathematics educator; b. Phila., Mar. 13, 1929; s. Herbert Stanley and Katharine (Schaeffer) B.; m. Jean I. Munro, May 30, 1951 (div. 1982); children: Katharine, John; m. Ruth E. Murashige Wong, June 30, 1984. BA, U. Calif.-Berkeley, 1950, PhD, 1957. Instr. U. Oreg., Eugene, 1955-56; vis. asst. prof. Princeton U., 1959-60; instr. to asst. prof. U. Wash., Seattle, 1957-59, 60-62; assoc. prof. math. U. Calif.-Santa Barbara, 1962-67; prof. math. N.Mex. State U., Las Cruces, 1967-69; vis. prof. math. U. Erlangen-Nurnberg, 1969, dept. chmn. math., 1969-74, grad. chmn., 1980-83; prof. math. U. Hawaii, Honolulu, 1969—. Contbr. articles to profl. jours. Trustee Math. Scis. Rsch. Inst., Berkeley, 1981-91. Office: U Hawaii Dept Math 2565 The Mall Honolulu HI 96822-2273

BEAR, JEFFREY WARREN, construction executive; b. Amittyville, N.Y., Mar. 18, 1945. BA, San Diego State U., 1972, MFA, 1975; postgrad., Harvard U., 1985; PhD with honors, Coll. of Edassea, Mararastra, India, 1978. Pres. Orion Fin. Fund, San Diego, 1972-83; bus. mgr. Matlines, Inc., San Diego, 1983-87; priest Good Samaritans, National City, Calif., 1978—; chief adminstrv. officer Phoenix Cos., San Diego, 1987—; chmn. Svc. Benefit Corp. of Am., San Diego, 1987—; cons. Arts Counsel, Reno, 1975—; bd. dirs. J. Christopher Enterprises, Reno. Author: American Contemporary Pottery, 1974; contbr. articles to profl. jours. Bd. dirs. Soc. St. Thomas, San Diego, 1978—; floor runner Dem. Conv., L.A., 1960. Mem. Am. Mgmt. Assn., Am. Bldg. Contractors, Assoc. Bldg. Contractor Assn., Internat. Assn. Concrete Repair Specialists (bd. dirs.), Nat. Restoration Contractors Assn. Eastern Catholic. Office: Phoenix Cos 3566 Nobel Dr San Diego CA 92122-1001

BEAR, WILLIAM EDWARD, educational technology consultant; b. Salem, Oreg., Mar. 24, 1931; s. Earl Charles and Agnes Alzina (Gillett) B.; m. Marylou Raggio, Aug. 3, 1957 (div. 1974); 1 child, Karen Louise; m. Joan Marie Crittenden, June 12, 1975. BS in Elem. Edn., Western Oreg. State Coll., 1955; MA in Elem. Sch. Adminstrn., U. No. Colo., 1959; postgrad., Hayward (Calif.) State U., 1962-63. Elementary tchr. Springfield (Oreg.) pub. schs., 1955-57, Fontana (Calif.) Unified Sch. Dist., 1957-59; elementary tchr. Monterey (Calif.) City Sch. Dist., 1959-63, tchr. jr. high, 1963-65; elementary sch. vice prin. Monterey Peninsula Unified Sch. Dist., 1965-68, elementary sch. prin., 1968-87, curriculum coord., 1987-89, ednl. tech. cons., 1989—; edn. instr. specialist IBM, Monterey, 1988-90; cons. Ednl. Support Sys., Hillsborough, Calif., 1989—. With U.S. Army, 1953-55. Recipient Adminstrv. Leadership award Calif. Media Libr. Educators Assn., 1984, Edn. Leadership awrd NAACP, 1981; Oreg. PTA scholar, 1950-54. Mem. Assn. Calif. Sch. Adminstrs., Sea and Tree Dance Club, Computer User Educators Assn., Phi Delta Kappa. Republican. Home and Office: 276 Waugh Ave Santa Cruz CA 95065-1136

BEARD, CONSTANCE RACHELLE, small business owner; b. Greeley, Colo., Jan. 12, 1949; d. Ralph Eugene and Nadine Luella (Onnen) Blackman; m. James Hanover Beard, Jr., July 9, 1976; children: Mark Eugene, Amy Christine, Jonathan Hanover. Student, U. No. Colo., 1967—. Intern clk. typist U. No. Colo., Greeley, 1971-76, sec., 1976-83, sr. acad. credential evaluator, AA/EO coord., 1983—; legal sec. William E. Shade, Atty., Greeley, 1985—; owner, operator Word Pro, Greeley, 1990—. Editor: Annotate Bibliography, 1990; editor Chorale Notes, 1989-91. Mem. Greeley Chorale, Inc., 1976—, sec., 1979-85, mem. sterring com. United Way. Democrat. Lutheran. Office: U No Colo Grad Sch Greeley CO 80639

BEARLEY, WILLIAM LEON, consulting company executive; b. Hays, Kans., June 6, 1938; s. William L. and Wilma M. (Sechrist) B.; BS, U. Wyo., 1969, MEd, 1964; EdD, U. La Verne, 1983; M.H.R.D., Univ. Assos. Grad. Sch. Human Resource Devel., 1980; also grad. Lab. Edn. Intern Program; m. Diane Lee Kiser, Dec. 15, 1967. Tchr. math. Baldwin Park Unified Sch. Dist., Baldwin Park, Calif., 1961-64, chmn. dept. math, 1962-64; chmn. math. dept. Citrus Coll., Azusa, Calif., 1965-69, chmn. data processing dept., 1969-80, dir. computing and info. systems, 1972-80; pres. Computer Info. Assocs., Inc., Pasadena, Calif., 1980-82; prof. Edn. Mgmt., U. LaVerne, 1982—; v.p. Organizational Universe Systems, Valley Ctr., Calif., 1985—; cons., trainer info. resource mgmt., 1981—. Mem. Data Processing Mgmt. Assn. (cert.), Am. Soc. Tng. and Devel., Orgn. Devel. Network, Assn. Computing Machinery, Assn. Systems Mgmt. (cert.), Phi Delta Kappa. Author/co-author computer software, books and articles in field. Home: 12665 Cumbres Rd Valley Center CA 92082-4023 Office: U La Verne 1950 3D St La Verne CA 91750

BEARWALD, JEAN HAYNES, company executive; b. San Francisco, Aug. 31, 1924; d. Joseph Robert and Edna Haynes (Goudey) Bearwald; m. William Henry Sherburn, Apr. 12, 1969 (dec. 1970); 1 child by previous marriage, David Richard Cross. BA, Stephens Coll., Columbia, Mo., 1945. Adminstrv. asst. Bearwald & Assocs., Sacramento, 1966-78; acct. Truck Parts Co., Sand City, Calif., 1979-80; pres., chief exec. officer Bearwald and Assocs., Fresno, Calif., 1980-89, Las Vegas, N.Mex., 1989-91; owner Bearwald and Assocs. dbs. A Touch of Class Party Planner, Santa Fe, N.Mex., 1991—; program dir. hosp. and institution State of Calif. Ann. Conf., Carmel, 1980-82. Republican. Episcopalian. Home and Office: 941 Calle Mejia # 1604 Santa Fe NM 87501

BEASLEY, BRUCE MILLER, sculptor; b. Los Angeles, May 20, 1939; s. Robert Seth and Bernice (Palmer) B.; m. Laurence Leaute, May 21, 1973; children: Julian Bernard, Celia Beranice. Student, Dartmouth Coll., 1957-59; B.A., U. Calif. at Berkeley, 1962. Sculptor in metal and plastic, one man shows at, Everett Ellin Gallery, Los Angeles, Kornblee Gallery, N.Y.C., Hansen-Fuller Gallery, San Francisco, David Stuart Gallery, Los Angeles, Andre Emmerich Gallery, N.Y.C., De Young Mus., San Francisco, Santa Barbara Mus. Art, Fine Arts Gallery, San Diego, Sonoma State U., Rhonert Park, Calif., Hooks-Epstein Gallery, Houston, Oakland (Calif.) Mus., Fresno (Calif.) Art Mus., John Natsoulas Gallery, Davis, Calif., Galerie Scheffel, Bad Homburg, Germany; exhibited in group shows at, Mus. Modern Art, N.Y.C., Guggenheim Mus., N.Y.C., Albright Knox Gallery, Buffalo, LaJolla (Calif.) Art Mus., Musée d'Art Modern, Paris, San Francisco Mus. Art, Krannert Art Mus. at U. Ill., Jewish Mus., N.Y.C., Luxembourg Gardens, Paris, Calif. Palace of Legion of Honor, De Young Mus., Middleheim (Fed. Republic of Germany) Sculpture Park, Yorkshire (Eng.) Sculpture Park, Santa Barbara Art Mus., others; represented in permanent collections, Mus. Modern Art, Guggenheim Mus., Musée d'Art Modern, Paris, Los Angeles County Art Mus., Univ. Art Mus., Berkeley, Oakland (Calif.) Mus., Wichita (Kans.) Art Mus., San Francisco Art Commn., Santa Barbara Art Mus., Dartmouth Coll., U. Nebr.-Lincoln, others; major sculpture commns. include State of Calif., 1967, Oakland Mus., 1972, City of San Francisco, 1976, U.S. govt., 1976, City of Eugene, Oreg., 1974, City of Salinas, Calif., 1977, Miami Internat. Airport, Fla., 1978, San Francisco Internat. Airport, 1981, Stanford U., 1982, City of Anchorage, Alaska, L.A. Olympic Stadium, 1984, Fed. Home Loan Bank, San Francisco, 1992. Recipient Andre Malraux purchase award Biennale de Paris, 1961. Mem. Nat. Mus. Am. Art, Crocker Art Mus. Home: 322 Lewis St Oakland CA 94607-1236

BEATHARD, BOBBY, professional football team executive; b. Zanesville, Ohio, Jan. 24, 1937; m. Christine Beathard; children: Kurt, Jeff, Casey, James. Student, Calif. Poly. Inst. Scout Kansas City Chiefs, Am. Football League, 1963-68, Atlanta Falcons, NFL, 1968-72; dir. player personnel Miami Dolphins, NFL, 1972-78; gen. mgr. Washington Redskins, NFL, 1978-89, San Diego Chargers, NFL, 1990—. Office: San Diego Chargers Jack Murphy Stadium PO Box 609609 San Diego CA 92160-0001*

BEATTIE, GEORGE CHAPIN, orthopaedic surgeon; b. Bowling Green, Ohio, Sept. 24, 1919; s. George Wilson and Mary Turner (Chapin) B.; m. Nancy U. Fant, Mar. 1, 1947; children: Michael, Suzanne, Eric. BA, Bowling Green U., 1939; MD, U. Chgo., 1943. Diplomate Am. Bd. Orthopaedic Surgery. Commd. lt. (j.g.) MC USN, 1943, advanced through grades to lt. comdr., 1951; med. officer, intern U.S. Naval Hosp., Great Lakes, Ill., 1943-44; resident, fellow in orthopaedic surgery Lahey Clinic, Boston, 1944; ward med. officer orthopaedic services Naval Hosp., Guam, 1944-46; sr. med. officer USN, Manus Island, Papua New Guinea, 1946; resident tng. in orthopaedic surgery U.S. Naval Hosp. St. Albans, N.Y.C., 1947-48; resident in orthopaedic surgery Children's Hosp., Boston, 1949; asst. chief orthopaedic surgery U.S. Naval Hosp. Oak Knoll, Oakland, Calif., 1950-52; comdg. officer med. co. 1st Marine Div. Med. Bn., Republic of Korea, 1952-53; chief orthopaedic service Dept. Phys. Medicine and Navy Amputee Ctr. U.S. Naval Hosp., Phila., 1954; resigned USN, 1954; practice medicine specializing in orthopaedic surgery San Francisco, 1954—; co-chmn. handicapping conditions com. Health Action Study San Mateo County, 1965; 1st chmn. orthopaedic sect. surg. dept. Peninsula Hosp. and Med. Ctr., Burlingame, Calif., 1967, chmn. rehab. service, 1967-71, chmn. phys. therapy and rehab. com., 1956—, vice chmn. orthopaedic dept., 1973-76, chmn., 1977-79; med. dir. research and rehab. ctr. San Mateo (Calif.) County Soc. Crippled Children and Adults, 1958-63; mem. exec. com. Harold D. Chope Community Hosp., San Mateo, 1971-76, chief, co-chmn. orthopaedic sect., 1971-76; chief orthopaedic surg. sect. Mills Meml. Hosp., San Mateo, 1976-78; others. Contbr. articles to profl. jours. Active Indian Guides, 1972-77; pres. Calif. Easter Seal Soc., 1969-71. Decorated Bronze Star. Fellow Am. Acad. Orthopaedic Surgeons (exhibit com. 1979-86); mem. AMA (Billings Bronze medal 1954), Western Orthopaedic Assn. (pres., bd. dirs. 1986), Leroy Abbott Orthopaedic Soc. U. Calif. San Francisco (assoc. clin. prof.), Alpha Omega Alpha. Office: 1828 El Camino Real Ste 606 Burlingame CA 94010-3120

BEATTY, HUGH TYRRELL, radiologist, naval officer; b. Wenatchee, Wash., Dec. 10, 1939; s. Donald Turner Beatty and Aileen Margurite (Tyrrell) Beatty Ramsey; m. Sara Ann Matthei, June 18, 1962 (div. Dec. 1968); children: Philip, Michael; m. Monty Lee Madsen, Dec. 21, 1968; children: D'Le Beatty Tobias, Todd, Terry, Michelle. B.S., U. Utah, 1965, M.D., 1968; postgrad. Sch. Submarine Medicine, Groton, Conn., 1969. Diplomate Nat. Bd. Med. Examiners. Commd. ensign USN, 1957, advanced through grades to comdr., 1975; intern Naval Hosp., Jacksonville, Fla., 1968-69; ship med. officer U.S.S. Patrick Henry, 1969-70; research med. officer, Naval Exptl. Diving Unit, Washington, 1970-72; resident in radiology Nat. Naval Med. Ctr., Bethesda, Md., 1972-75; chief radiology service Naval Hosp., Oak Harbor, Wash., 1975-81; med. officer Med. Clinic, Naval Submarine Base Bangor, Bremerton, Wash., 1981-82, sr. med. officer, 1984-85; ship's med. officer U.S.S. Ohio, 1982-84; radiol. cons. dysbaric osteonecrosis panel USN, Washington, 1972-85; pvt. practive cons., Stanwood, Wash., 1985—. Author monograph. Chmn. 4th of July Celebration Com., Oak Harbor, Wash., 1978; pres. Whidbey Playhouse, Oak Harbor, 1978-80. Mem. Underseas Med. Soc., Lions (pres. North Whidbey club). Republican. Mormon. Avocations: stamps, genealogy, backpacking. Home: 3135 N Robin Ln Oak Harbor WA 98277-8841 Office: 27500 102D NW Stanwood WA 98292

BEATTY, MARTHA NELL, travel agency owner; b. San Francisco, Oct. 29, 1933; d. Harold Miles Tucker and Audrey Martha (Kirkbride) Pinney; m. Alden R. Crow, Feb. 9, 1956 (dec. Oct. 1984); children: Alana Sims, Tucker (dec. 1984); m. Denis Beatty, Sept. 19, 1986. BA, Stanford U., 1955. Cert. travel counselor. Sales cons. Thomas Cook, San Francisco, 1955-56, Am. Express, San Francisco, 1963-64, Gulliver's Travel, San Francisco, 1964-66; pres., owner Unravel Travel, Inc., San Francisco, 1969—. Author: (guide book) San Francisco at a Glance, 1971; contbr. articles to profl. jour. Active community svcs. devel. com. Calif. Pacific Med. Ctr. Found., 1980—. Mem. Carriage Trade Assn. (pres. 1987-88), Am. Soc. Travel Agts., Pacific Area Travel Assn., Hamlin Sch. Alumni Assn. (sec. 1982—), Jr. League of San Francisco. Republican. Episcopalian. Home: 1709 Broderick St San Francisco CA 94115-2525 Office: Unravel Travel Inc 660 Market St San Francisco CA 94104-5005

BEATY, PAUL RICHARD, aquatic biologist; b. Ames, Iowa, June 2, 1946; s. Harold Huxford and Judith Helen (Skromme) B.; m. Sue Ann Weber, Sept. 7, 1968; children: Joel R., Christopher P., Michael A. BS in Edn., Ea. Ill. U., 1969; MS, U. Ill., 1976, PhD, 1979. Tchr. Unit 7 Schs., Tolono, Ill., 1969-73; tech. asst. Ill. Nat. History Survey, Urbana, 1974-78, asst. prof. scientist, 1978-80; dir. aquatic rsch. Coachella (Calif.) Valley Water Dist., 1980-86; prin., pres. Beaty & Assocs. S.W. Aquatics, Palm Desert, Calif., 1985—. Contbr. articles to profl. jours. Bd. dirs. Family YMCA of Desert, Palm Desert, 1984-86, Desert Youth Sports Assn., 1984—; player agt. Palm Desert Youth Sports Assn., 1984-85; pres. Riverside County Com. on Sch. Dist. Orgn., Palm Desert, 1986—; active Palm Desert Planning Commn., 1993—. Mem. Aquatic Plant Mgmt. Soc., Western Aquatic Plant Mgmt. Soc. (program chmn. 1983, 92, pres. 1993), North Am. Lake Mgmt. Soc. (program co-chmn. 1986—), Calif. Lake Mgmt. Soc. (bd. dirs. 1987-92), Am. Fisheries Soc., Optimists. Home: 75-686 Dolmar St Palm Desert CA 92260 Office: Paul R Beaty & Assocs PO Box 13212 Palm Desert CA 92255-3212

BEAUDET, ROBERT ARTHUR, chemistry educator; b. Woonsocket, R.I., Aug. 18, 1935; s. Ralph Edgar and Blanche L. (Pelchat) B.; m. Julia Marie Hughes, Sept. 14, 1957; children: Susan, Donna, Debra, Stephanie, Michelle, David, Nicole. BS, Worchester Poly. Inst., 1957; MA, Harvard U., 1960, PhD, 1962. Asst. prof. chemistry U. So. Calif., Los Angeles, 1963-66, assoc. prof., 1966-72, prof., 1972—. Served to lt. U.S. Army, 1961-63. Fellow NSF, 1957-61, A.P. Sloan Found., 1966-67, Humboldt, Cologne, Germany, 1974-75. Mem. Am. Chem. Soc., Am. Phys. Soc. Roman Catholic. Home: 887 Vallombrosa Dr Pasadena CA 91107-5642

BEAUDRY, JANIS STONIER, real estate company officer; b. Sacramento, Calif., Feb. 8, 1956; d. William Henry and Vivian June (Terril) Stonier. BA in Social Sci. and Sociology, Calif. State U., 1978. Lic. real estate broker. Asst. head cashier Toys R Us, Sacramento, Calif., 1974-78; banking svcs. officer Wells Fargo Bank, Sacramento, 1979-82; loan mgr. Western Community Savs. and Loan, Walnut Creek, Calif., 1982-84; real estate loan officer Sunrise Bank, Sacramento, 1984-85; dir. property mgmt. Mark III Mgmt., Inc., Sacramento, 1985-91; broker, owner Stonier Real Estate, Sacramento, 1992—; cons. self Resume writing and fin., 1986—. Co-producer The Show Below; exhibited painting in group shows, 1982-91. Crisis counselor, speaker Rape Crisis Ctr., Sacramento, 1982-84 (counseling award 1984); com. worker for assemblyman campaign, Sacramento, 1984; mem. Sacto Area Literacy Coalition, Sacramento, 1989. Mem. NAFE, Sacramento Valley Apt. Assn., Sacramento Women's Network, Backgammon Club, Lions (2d v.p. Sacramento chpt. 1988). Democrat. Baptist.

BEAUMONT, MONA, artist; b. Paris; d. Jacques Hippolyte and Elsie M. (Didisheim) Marx. m. William G. Beaumont; children: Garrett, Kevin. Postgrad., Harvard U., Fogg Mus., Cambridge, Mass. One-woman shows include Galeria Proteo, Mexico City, Gumps Gallery, San Francisco, Palace of Legion of Honor, San Francisco, L'Armitiere Gallery, Rouen, France, Hoover Gallery, San Francisco, San Francisco Mus. Modern Art, Galeria Van der Voort, San Francisco, William Sawyer Gallery, San Francisco, Palo Alto (Calif.) Cultural Ctr., Galerie Alexandre Monnet, Brussels, Honolulu Acad. Arts; group shows include San Francisco Mus. Modern Art, San Francisco Art Inst., DeYoung Meml. Mus., San Francisco, Grey Found. Tour of Asia, Bell Telephone Invitational, Chgo., Richmond Art Ctr., L.A. County Mus. Art, Galerie Zodiaque, Geneva, Galerie Le Manoir, La Chaux de Fonds, Switzerland, others; represented in permanent collections Oakland (Calif.) Mus. Art, City and County of San Francisco, Hoover Found., San Francisco, Grey Found., Washington, Bulart Found., San Francisco; also numerous pvt. collections. Mem. Soc. for Encouragement of Contemporary Art, Bay Area Graphic Art Coun., San Francisco Art Inst., San Francisco Mus. Modern Art, Capp Street Project, others. Recipient ann. painting award Jack London Square, 2 ann. awards San Francisco Women Artists, One-man Show award San Francisco Art Festival; purchase award Grey Found., San Francisco Women Artists (2), San Francisco Art Festival; included in Printworld Internat., Internat. Art Diary, Am. Artists, N.Y. Art Rev., Calif. Art Rev., Art in San Francisco Bay Area. Address: 1087 Upper Happy Valley Rd Lafayette CA 94549

BEAUPEURT, JOSEPH EUGENE, design engineer; b. St. Joseph, Mo., Jan. 23, 1912; s. Joseph Eugene and Nora (Smith) B.; m. Helene Frances Alexander, Aug. 2, 1941; children: Sharon Lynn, Debra Jo Beau-Schantz, Edward Lee. Student aircraft design, Finlay Engring. Sch., Kansas City, Mo., 1940-41; student modern bus., Alexander Hamilton U., N.Y.C., 1947-48; cert. in mech. engring., I.C.S., Scranton, Pa., 1952; postgrad., Wichita U., 1953. Registered profl. engr., Kans. Display artist Plymouth Clothing Co., St. Joseph, 1935-37, Lee's Studio, St. Joseph, 1937-40; design engr., engring. supr. Boeing Co., Wichita, 1941-57, human factors chief, 1957-69, product devel. engr., 1969-72; chief engr. S.V. Tool Co., Newton, Kans., 1973-74; pvt. practice Manitou Springs, Colo., 1976-83; pvt. practice, Safford, Ariz., 1983-91; prin. investigator, sponsor Office Naval Res., Washington, 1959-68. Election judge City of Manitou Springs, 1977-82; trustee Unity Ch., Wichita, 1956-59, pres. bd. trustees, 1959-60. Republican. Home: 525 Ponderosa Cir Parachute CO 81635-9517

BEBBER, DONNA GAYE, development director, research consultant; b. Statesville, N.C., June 14, 1956; d. Vance Carl and Mildred K. (Ruppe) B.; 1 child, Kylie. AA in Liberal Arts, Leeward C.C., Pearl City, Hawaii, 1986; BA in Social Scis., U. Hawaii, Pearl City, 1988. Patient svcs. coord. Muscular Dystrophy Assn., Mobile, Ala., 1988-89; evaluation asst. curriculum R & D group U. Hawaii, Honolulu, 1989-91; devel. officer Rehab. Hosp. of the Pacific, Honolulu, 1990-93; rsch. assoc. The Rsch. Corp., Honolulu, 1991—; dir. devel. Rehab. Hosp. of Pacific, Honolulu, 1993—; cons. various non-profit orgns., Honolulu, 1989—. Author: (tng. manual) USCG, 1986. Vol. adminstr. USCG-14th dist., Honolulu, 1986-87; project dir. LWV and KHON TV, Honolulu, 1986; bd. mem. LWV of Hawaii, Honolulu, 1989—; legis. advisor Rep. Duke Bainum, Honolulu, 1990—; dep. voter registrar State of Hawaii, Honolulu, 1990-91; mem. Neighborhood bd. dirs., 1993—. Recipient award of merit City and County of Honolulu, 1986, cert. of appreciation Dept. Transp., 1988; named Svc. Spouse of the Yr., C. of C. Hawaii, 1986. Mem. Nat. Soc. Fundraising Execs. (dir. Aloha chpt. 1992—), Assn. Healthcare Philanthropy, Healthcare Taskforce C. of C. Democrat. Office: Rehab Hosp of the Pacific 226 N Kuakini St Honolulu HI 96817

BEBOUT, ELI DANIEL, oil executive; b. Rawlings, Wyo., Oct. 14, 1946; s. Hugh and Debbie Bebout; m. Lorraine J. Tavares; children: Jordan, Jentry, Reagen, Taggert. BEE, U. Wyo., 1969. With U.S. Energy Co., Riverton, Wyo., 1972-75; field engr. Am. Bechtel Corp., Green River, Wyo., 1975-76; pres. NUPEC Resources, Inc., Riverton, 1976-83, Smith-Collins Pharm. Inc., Riverton, 1976-83; cons. Nucor Drilling, Inc., Riverton, 1984-87, v.p., 1987—; mem., issues whip Wyo. Ho. of Reps. Mem. Govt. Reorgn. Coun., Wyuo.; mem. Wyo. Mgmt. Audit Com., Select Water Com., Mgmt. Coun. Democrat. Office: Nucor Drilling PO Box 112 Riverton WY 82501-0112

BECCHETTI, JOHN JOSEPH, surgeon; b. Hibbing, Minn., Nov. 13, 1935; s. John Louis and Mary E. (Paciotti) B.; m. Mary Elizabeth Ness, Aug. 22, 1962; children: Gina, Teri. BS, Coll. of St. Thomas, 1958; MD, U. Minn., 1962. Pvt. practice gen. surgery Oakland, Calif., 1970—. Capt. USAF, 1963-66. Fellow ACS. Home: 2070 Pebble Dr Alamo CA 94507 Office: 3300 Webster St Ste 306 Oakland CA 94609

BECERRA, XAVIER, congressman, lawyer; b. Sacramento, Calif., Jan. 26, 1958; s. Manuel and Maria Teresa B.; m. Carolina Reyes, 1987. AB, Stanford U., 1980, JD, 1984. Atty., 1984—; dir. dist. office State Senator Art Torres, L.A.; dep. atty. gen. dept. justice, Calif., 1987-90; assemblyman, 59th dist. State of Calif., 1990-93; mem. 103rd Congress from 30th Calif. dist., 1993—; mem. com. edn. and labor, com. judiciary, com. sci., space and tech.; freshman Dem. whip; mem. Congl. Hispanic Caucus. Mexican-Am. Bar Assn., Calif. Bar Assn., Assn. Calif. State Attys and Admin. Law Judges. Democrat. Office: House of Representatives 1710 Longworth Bldg Washington DC 20515

BECHTEL, RILEY PEART, engineering company executive; s. Stephen Davison Bechtel, Jr. BA in Polit. Sci., Psychology, U. Calif., Davis, 1974; JD, MBA, Stanford U., 1979; 1979. Bar: Calif. 1979. With Bechtel Group, Inc., San Francisco, 1966-79, 81—, Thelen, Marrin, Johnson & Bridges, San Francisco, 1979-81; Bechtel Group Inc., San Francisco, 1966—; also bd. dirs. Bechtel Group Inc., pres., coo, 1989—, chmn. exec. com., ceo, 1990—; mem. Bus. Coun., Bus. Roundtable, Calif. Bus. Roundtable, J.P. Morgan Internat. Adv. Coun.; adv. coun. Stanford U. Grad. Sch. of Bus.; dean's adv. coun. Stanford Law Sch. Trustee Thacher Sch., Ojai, Calif. Mem. ABA, Calif. Bar Assn. Office: Bechtel Group Inc PO Box 193965 San Francisco CA 94119-3965

BECHTEL, STEPHEN DAVISON, JR., engineering company executive; b. Oakland, Calif., May 10, 1925; s. Stephen Davison and Laura (Peart) B.; m. Elizabeth Mead Hogan, June 5, 1946; 5 children. Student, U. Colo., 1943-44; BS, Purdue U., 1946, D. in Engring. (hon.), 1972; MBA, Stanford U., 1948; DSc (hon.), U. Colo., 1981. Registered profl. engr., N.Y., Mich., Alaska, Calif., Md., Hawaii, Ohio, D.C., Va., Ill. Engring. and mgmt. positions Bechtel Corp., San Francisco, 1941-60, pres., 1960-73, chmn. of cos. in Bechtel group, 1973-80; chmn. Bechtel Group, Inc., 1980-90, chmn. emeritus, 1990—; bd. dirs. IBM; former chmn., mem. bus. coun., life councillor, past chmn. conf. bd. Trustee, mem., past chmn. bldg. and grounds com. Calif. Inst. Tech.; mem. pres.'s coun. Purdue U.; adv. coun. Inst. Internat. Studies, bd. visitors, former charter mem., adv. coun. Stanford U. Grad. Sch. Bus. With USMC, 1943-46. Decorated officer French Legion of Honor; recipient Disting. Alumnus award Purdue U., 1964, U. Colo., 1978, Ernest C. Arbuckle Disting. Alumnus award Stanford Grad. Sch. Bus., 1974, Disting. Engring. Alumnus award 1979; named Man of Yr. Engring. News-Record, 1974, Outstanding Achievement in Constrn. award Moles, 1977, Chmn.'s award Am. Assn. Engring. Soc., 1982, Washington award Western Soc. Engrs., 1985, Nat. Medal Tech. from Pres. Bush, 1991, Golden Beaver award 1992, Herbert Hoover medal 1980. Fellow ASCE (Engring. Mgmt. award 1979, Pres. award 1985), AAAS, Instn. Chem. Engrs. (U.K., hon.); mem. AIME, NSPE (hon. chmn. Nat. Engrs. Week 1990), Nat. Acad. Engring. (past chmn.), Calif. Acad. Scis. (hon. trustee),Am. Soc. French Legion Honor (bd. dirs.), Am. Acad. Arts and Scis., Royal Acad. Engring. (U.K., fgn. mem.), Pacific Union Club, Bohemian Club, San Francisco Golf Club, Claremont Country Club, Cypress Point Club, Met. Club (Washington), Chi Epsilon, Tau Beta Pi. Office: Bechtel Group Inc PO Box 193965 San Francisco CA 94119-3965

BECHTELHEIMER, ROBERT RUSSELL, retired career officer, financial executive; b. Camden, Ark., May 13, 1932; s. Jesse Cletus and Margie (Launius) B.; m. Dottie Logan, Nov. 5, 1966; children: Russ, David, Lisa, John. BS, South Ark. U., 1954. Cert. internal auditor. Commd. ensign USN, 1954, advanced through grades to capt., 1975, ret., 1982; dir. West region Naval Audit Svc., San Diego, 1982-89; chief fin. officer Rockwell Fed. Credit Union, Downey, Calif., 1989-90; pres. RFCU Svcs., Inc., Downey, 1990-91, Rockwell Fed. Credit Union, Downey, 1991—. Mem. Kiwanis (sec. 1988-89, v.p. 1989-90, pres. 1990-91). Methodist.

BECHTLE, ROBERT ALAN, artist, educator; b. San Francisco, May 14, 1932; m. Nancy Elizabeth Dalton, 1963 (div. 1982); children: Max, Robert, Anne Elizabeth; m. Whitney Chadwick, 1982. B.A., Calif. Coll. Arts and Crafts, Oakland, 1954, M.F.A., 1958; postgrad., U. Calif.-Berkeley, 1960-61. Graphic designer Kaiser Industries, Oakland, 1956-59; instr. Calif. Coll. Arts and Crafts, 1957-61, assoc. prof. to prof.; lectr. U. Calif.-Berkeley, 1965-66; vis. artist U. Calif.-Davis, 1966-68; assoc. prof. San Francisco State U., 1968-76, prof., 1976—. One-man shows Mus. of Art, San Francisco, 1959, 64, Berkeley Gallery, 1965, Richmond Art Ctr. (Calif.), 1965, U. Calif.-Davis, 1967, O.K. Harris Gallery, N.Y.C., 1971, 74, 76, 81, 84, 87, Berggruen Gallery, San Francisco, 1972, E.B. Crocker Art Gallery, Sacramento, 1972, Univ. Art Mus., U. Calif.-Berkeley, 1979, Daniel Weinberg Gallery, Santa Monica, 1991, Gallery Paul Anglim, San Francisco, 1991, San Francisco Mus. Modern Art, 1991; exhibited in group shows San Francisco Art Inst., 1966, Whitney Mus. N.Y.C., 1967, Milw. Art Ctr., 1969, Mus. Contemporary Art, Chgo., 1971, Serpentine Gallery, London, 1973, Toledo Mus. Art, 1975, San Francisco Mus. Modern Art, 1976, Pushkin Fine Arts Mus., Moscow, 1978, Pa. Acad. Fine Arts, Phila., 1981, San Antonio Mus. Art, 1981, Pa. Acad. Fine Arts, Phila, 1981, Calif. Palace of Legion of Honor, San Francisco, 1983, Mus. Contemporary Art, L.A., 1984, San Francisco Mus. Modern Art, 1985, Univ. Art Mus., U. Calif., Berkeley, 1987; represented in permanent collections Achenbach Found. for Graphic Arts, San Francisco, Chase Manhattan Bank, N.Y.C., E.B. Crocker Art Gallery, Sacramento, Gibbes Art Gallery, High Mus. Art, Atlanta, Hunter Art Mus., Chattanooga, Library of Congress, Washington, Lowe Art Mus.-U. Miami, Coral Gables, Fla., Mills Coll., Oakland, Mus. Modern Art, N.Y.C., Met. Mus., N.Y.C., Neue Gal der Stadt Aachen, West Germany, Oakland Mus., San Francisco Mus. Modern Art, Univ. Art Mus.-U. Calif-Berkeley, U. Nebr.-Lincoln, Whitney Mus., N.Y.C., Guggenheim Mus., N.Y.C. Served with U.S. Army, 1954-56. Recipient James D. Phelan award, 1965; Nat. Endowment for Arts grantee, 1977, 83, 89; Guggenheim grantee, 1986. Office: San Francisco State U Dept Art San Francisco CA 94132

BECK, JEROME JOSEPH, health care administrator, biomedical technologist; b. Mesa, Ariz., Nov. 7, 1957; s. Robert Leon and Marie Margaret (Curry) B.; m. Catherine Elizabeth Williams, June 27, 1981; 1 child, John Robert. BSBA, U. Phoenix, 1989. Cert. hemodialysis technologist Bd. of Nephrology Examiners Nursing & Tech. Dialysis unit housekeeper Good Samaritan Hosp., Phoenix, 1976-78, dialysis equipment technician, 1978-81, dialysis sr. equipment technician, 1981-83, coord. tech. staff devel., 1983-88, mgr. dialysis tech. svcs., 1988-89; dir. tech. svcs. East Valley Dialysis Svcs., Mesa, 1989-91, program dir., 1991—; bd. dirs. Bd. Nephrology Examiners, Madison, Wis., 1990—; mem. renal disease and detoxification com. Assn. for the Advancement of Med. Instrumentation, 1989—; mem. technicians com. ESRD Network VI, Albuquerque, 1984-85. Contbr. articles to profl. jours. Mem. Nat. Assn. Nephrology Technologists (bd. dirs., western v.p. 1989-91). Republican. Office: East Valley Dialysis Svcs 952 E Baseline Ste 102 Mesa AZ 85204

BECK, JOHN CHRISTEN, sociologist, educator, businessman; b. Provo, Utah, Dec. 7, 1959; s. Jay Vern and Allida Faye (Ellison) B.; m. Martha Nibley, June 21, 1983; children: Katherine, Adam, Elizabeth. BA, Harvard U., 1983, MA, 1988, PhD, 1989. Pres. Asian Bus. Info., Provo, 1988—; asst. prof. Brigham Young U.; pres. Asian Bus. Info., Provo, 1988—. Author: Breaking the Cycle of Compulsive Behavior, 1990, The Change of a Lifetime, 1993; contbr. articles to profl. jours. Harvard Bus. Sch. grantee, 1988, fellow, 1984-89; recipient Hoopes Rsch. prize Harvard U., 1983; Rotary scholar, 1983-84. Mem. LDS Ch.

BECK, JOHN ROBERT, pathologist, information scientist; b. Cleve., Sept. 8, 1953; s. John Edward and Maralyn Janet (Smith) B.; m. Sharon Louise Dombkowski, Aug. 30, 1975; children: John Benjamin, Stefan Andrew, Meredith Louise. AB, Dartmouth Coll., 1974; MD, Johns Hopkins U., 1978. Diplomate Am. Bd. Pathology. Intern, then resident in pathology Dartmouth-Hitchcock Med. Ctr., Hanover, N.H., 1978-80; dir. clin. pathology Dartmouth-Hitchcock Med. Ctr., Hanover, 1987-89; fellow, clin. decision making New Eng. Med. Ctr., Boston, 1981; from asst. to assoc. prof. pathology Dartmouth Med. Sch., Hanover, 1982-89; prof., dir. biomed. info. communication ctr. Oreg. Health Scis. U., Portland, 1989-92; prof., v.p. info. tech. Baylor Coll. Medicine, Houston, 1992—; bloodbank dir. Dartmouth-Hitchcock Med. Ctr., Hanover, 1984-89; chmn. Health Outcome Technologies, Inc., Portland, 1991—; dir. Creative Multimedia Corp., Portland, 1989-92; cons. Nat. Libr. Medicine, Bethesda, Md., 1988-92. Editor-in-chief: Med. Decision Making, 1989—. Recipient Rsch. Career Devel. award Nat. Libr. Medicine, 1986. Fellow Am. Coll. Med. Informatics, Am. Soc. Clin. Pathologists (coun. chair 1991-93); mem. Soc. for Med. Decision Making (sec.-treas. 1985-87, v.p. 1987-88), Acad. Clin. Lab. Physicians & Scientists (exec. councilor 1989-91, Young Investigator award 1981), Am. Assn. Blood Banks (vice-chair, inspection and accreditation com. 1989-91), Phi Beta Kappa. Republican. Office: Baylor Coll of Medicine Information Technology One Baylor Plz Houston TX 77030

BECK, JOHN ROLAND, environmental consultant; b. Las Vegas, N.Mex., Feb. 26, 1929; s. Roland L. and Betty L. (Shrock) B.; m. Doris A. Olson, Feb. 9, 1951; children: Elizabeth J., Thomas R., Patricia L., John William. BS, Okla. A. & M. U., 1950; MS, Okla. State U., 1957; postgrad., U. Tex., 1954, George Washington U., 1965. Registered sanitarian, Ohio, Ariz.; cert. wildlife biologist. Wildlife researcher King Ranch, Kingsville, Tex., 1950-51; faculty Inst. Human Physiology U. Tenn., Martin, 1954-55; rsch. biologist FWS, USDI, Grangeville, Idaho, 1955-57; ctr. dir. Job Corps, OEO, Indiahoma, Okla., 1965-67; supr. animal control biology FWS, USDI, 1953-69; operating v.p. Bio-Svc. Corp., Troy, Mich., 1969-78; pres. BECS Ltd., Prescott, Ariz., 1981-85; spl. asst. USDA - APHIS, Washington, 1986-87; prin. cons. Biol. Environ. Cons. Svc. Inc., Phoenix, 1978—; faculty assoc. Ariz. State U., Tempe, 1980-89. Sr. author: Managing Service for Success, 1987, 2d edit., 1991; columnist mo. column on pest control in 2 mags., 1980-88; contbr. articles to profl. jours. Capt. USAR, 1950-62. Fellow Royal Soc. Health, N.Y. Explorers Soc.; mem. ASTM, Wildlife Soc., Wildlife Disease Assn., nat. Environ. Health Assn., Sigma Xi. Republican. Baptist. Office: PO Box 26482 Prescott Valley AZ 86312

BECK, KEITH LINDELL, small business owner; b. Ranger, Tex., Sept. 21, 1946; s. Corvis Lavon and Alta Ileane (Carney) B.; m. Cheryl Lynn Holmoe, May 8, 1976; children: Heather Aileen, Chelsey Nicole, Cameron David. BA, U. Redlands, 1969; postgrad., Calif. State U., Long Beach, 1974-76. Cert. tchr., Calif. Vol. U.S. Peace Corps, Ponape Island, Micronesia, 1969-70; mgmt. trainee J.C. Penney Co., Palm Springs, Calif., 1970-71; regional mgr. Fidelity Union Life Ins. Co., Dallas, 1971-72; corp. personnel mgr. Mervyn's Dept. Stores, Hayward, Calif., 1972-87; pres., owner Proforma Pacific Systems, Pleasanton, Calif., 1987--. Vol. admissions program U. Redlands; mem. coun. Trinity Luth. Ch. Named Western Regional adv. councilman Western Regional Franchise Owners, 1988; recipient Partner of the Yr. award Proforma, Inc., 1989, 1990. Mem. Bus. Forms Mgmt. Assn. (bd. dirs.), Nat. Bus. Forms Assn., Returned Peace Corps Vol. Home: 2646 Calle Alegre Pleasanton CA 94566-5863 Office: Proforma Pacific Systems 3958 Valley Ave Ste D Pleasanton CA 94566

BECK, LEWIS ALFRED, sales executive; b. Denver, July 13, 1919; s. Alfred and Lillie May (Groesbeck) B.; m. Priscilla May Ryder, Dec. 29, 1941; children: Lewis A. Jr., Georgina Lee Wadsworth. BSEE, U. Colo., 1941. Test engr. Gen. Electric Co., Schenectady, N.Y., 1941-42, control engr., 1942-47; sales engr. Peterson Co., Denver, 1947-54, v.p., 1955-69, pres., chief exec. officer, 1969-89, chmn., 1990—. Mem. IEEE (life), Elec. Equipment Reps. Assn. (pres. 1970-71, bd. dirs. 1963-72), Rocky Mountain Elec. League (pres. 1974--75, bd. dirs. 1963-76), Lakewood Country Club (bd. dirs. 1956-60), Garden of Gods Club. Home: 1851 Winfield Dr Lakewood CO 80215-2552

BECK, MARILYN MOHR, columnist; b. Chgo., Dec. 17, 1928; d. Max and Rose (Lieberman) Mohr; m. Roger Beck, Jan. 8, 1949 (div. 1974); children: Mark Elliott, Andrea; m. Arthur Levine, Oct. 12, 1980. AA, U. So. Calif., 1950. Free-lance writer nat. mags. and newspapers Hollywood, Calif., 1959-63; Hollywood columnist Valley Times and Citizen News, Hollywood, 1963-65; West Coast editor Sterling Mags., Hollywood, 1963-74; free-lance entertainment writer L.A. Times, 1965-67; Hollywood columnist Bell-McClure Syndicate, 1967-72; chief Bell-McClure Syndicate (West Coast bur.), 1967-72; Hollywood columnist NANA Syndicate, 1967-72; syndicated Hollywood columnist N.Y. Times Spl. Features, 1972-78, N.Y. Times Spl. Features (United Feature Syndicate), 1978-80, United Press abroad, 1978-80, Internat. Editors News and Features, Chgo. Tribune/N.Y. Daily News Syndicate, 1980—; Grapevine columnist TV Guide, 1989-92. Creator, host: Marilyn Beck's Hollywood Outtakes spls. NBC, 1977, 78; host: Marilyn Beck's Hollywood Hotline, Sta. KFI, L.A., 1975-77; Hollywood reporter: Eyewitness News Sta. KABC-TV, L.A., 1981; TV program PM Mag., 1983-88; author: (non-fiction) Marilyn Beck's Hollywood, 1973, (novel) Only Make Believe, 1988. Recipient Citation of Merit L.A. City Coun., 1973, Press award Pub. Guild Am., 1974, Bronze Halo award So. Calif. Motion Picture Coun., 1982. Office: PO Box 11079 Beverly Hills CA 90213-4579

BECK, MAXINE LOUISE, educator; b. Plainview, Tex., Feb. 1, 1917; d. Charles Lewis and Helen Louise (Thomas) Barrett; m. Paul Cris Beck, Oct. 13, 1940 (div.); children: Christine Louise, Thomas Paul. BA, Pomona Coll., 1938; MA in Edn., Claremont Grad. Sch., 1972. Cert. elem. tchr., counselor. Tchr. Calif. Pub. Schs., 1939-70, Foothill Country Day Sch., Claremont, Calif., 1956-64; headmistress Girls Collegiate Sch., Claremont, Calif., 1965-69; continuing edn. dir. counseling Claremont Grad. Sch., 1970-72; dir. Marlborough Lower Sch., L.A., 1972-74; instr. career devel. Foothill Community Coll., Los Altos, Calif., 1979-81; ednl. cons. San Mateo Found., Menlo Park, Calif., 1980-81. Author: poetry 1988. Mem. Towne Hall, Yakima, Wash., 1982-87; publicity chmn. Yakima Community Concert Assn., 1985-87; mem. Yakima Symphony Assn., 1983-88; coord., dir. Well-Elder program Peninsula Vols. Little House Sr. Ctr., Menlo Park, 1988—; mem. task force Spl. Com. on Shortage of RN's in Calif., 1989-90. Mem. AAUW (1st v.p. 1984-86), AARP (spokesperson women's initiative 1987—, mem. leadership coun. Calif. 1989-91, task force fifty plus for career action ctr. Palo Alto, Calif., subject of documentary on aging 1989, 91), Calif. Assn. Women Deans (vice prin. 1970-72), Alpha Iota. Republican. Home: 2282 Eastridge Ave Menlo Park CA 94025-6713

BECK, RODNEY ROY, professional baseball player; b. Burbank, Calif., Aug. 3, 1968. Pitcher San Francisco Giants, 1991—; mem. Nat. League All-Star Team, 1993. Office: San Francisco Giants Candlestick Park San Francisco CA 94124

BECK, THOMAS DAVIS, history educator; b. Los Angeles, June 4, 1943; s. Duane W. and Marcelline (Davis) B.; m. Martha Wakefield, Feb. 1, 1964; children—John, Kelly, Stacy, Eric, Alison. B.A., U. Calif.-Berkeley, 1965, M.A., 1966, Ph.D., 1972. Asst. prof. SUNY-Albany, 1973-80; vis. asst. prof. U. N.C., Chapel Hill, 1981; asst. prof. history Chapman Coll., Orange, Calif., 1981-83, assoc. prof., 1983—, asst. to pres., 1985-87, assoc. dean Sch. Bus. and Mgmt., 1987-88, assoc. v.p. for planning, 1988-90; dean Coll. Arts and Scis., Pacific U., 1991—. Author: French Legislators, 1800-1834, 1974, French Notables, 1987. Bd. dirs. Calif. Assn. for Gifted, 1984-85. NEH summer stipend, 1975; Am. Council Learned Socs. fellow, 1978; Am. Council on Edn. fellow, 1985-86. Mem. Am. Hist. Assn., Soc. for French Hist. Studies. Home: 39893 Blooming Fern Hill Rd Forest Grove OR 97116 Office: Pacific U 2043 College Way Forest Grove OR 97116

BECK, THOMAS EDWIN, furniture maker; b. Stockton, Calif., Dec. 31, 1946; s. Harold Marquis and Verna (Johnson) B.; m. Ellen Marie Hill, June 1, 1973; 1 child, Alexander Hill-Beck. Student, San Francisco City Coll., 1964-66, U. Calif., Berkeley, 1966-67, Coll. of the Desert, 1984-85, Calif. Poly. State U., 1985. Carpenter U.B.C. of Am., Portland, Oreg., 1972—; cabinetmaker apprentice Drago Dimitri/Furniture, Calgary, Alta., Can., 1976; owner, operator Thomas Beck Fine Furniture, Morongo Valley, Calif., 1981—; cons. San Bernardino County Regional Employment. Conscientious objector, Vietnam War. Recipient Best of Show award Bellevue Art Mus., 1990; Design in Wood award Calif. Expo., 1993. Home and Office: 52355 Altadena Dr Morongo Valley CA 92256-9671

BECK, TIMOTHY DANIEL, human resources specialist, consultant; b. Santa Monica, Calif., Mar. 21, 1953; s. James Daniel and Bettye June (Cisler) B.; m. Marcia Ann Smith, Jan. 16, 1977; children: Tracy Beth and Erica Brandy (twins), Jenna Michelle. AA, El Camino Community Coll., 1974; BA, Calif. State U., Northridge, 1979. Registered health underwriter, registered employee benefits cons. Candidate cert. employee benefit specialist, group claims supr. Prudential Ins. Co. Am., L.A., 1973-79; employee benefits cons. Olanie, Hurst & Hemrich, L.A., 1979-81; v.p. policyholder svc. dept. Health Maintenance Life Ins. Co., Fountain Valley, Calif., 1981; v.p. Robert E. French Ins. Svcs., Inc., Huntington Beach, Calif., 1981-85; v.p., mng. cons. employee benefits Warren, McVeigh & Griffin, Inc., Newport Beach, Calif., 1985-91; mng. cons. employee benefits A. Foster Higgins and Co., Inc., 1991—; mem. Kaiser Permanente Orange County Consumer Coun., 1987—; mem. pub. edn. com. Calif. Health Decision, 1988—; mem. bus. and health adv. panel Am. Health Pub.; speaker to confs. and profl. socs. Creator, contbg. editor Employee Benefits Mgmt. Letter, 1985-91; contbr. articles to profl. publs. Mem. Internat. Found. Employee Benefits, Nat. Assn. Health Underwriters, Calif. Assn. Health Underwriters (bd. dirs. 1992—), Employee Benefit Planning Assn. So. Calif., So. Calif. Assn. Benefit Plan Adminstrs., Orange County Assn. Health Underwriters (founder, 1st v.p. 1987-88), Orange County Employee Benefit Coun., Calif. State U. Northridge Alumni Assn.

BECKEL, CHARLES LEROY, physics educator; b. Phila., Feb. 7, 1928; s. Samuel Mercer and Katherine (Linsky) B.; m. Josephine Ann Beck, June 27, 1958; children: Amanda S., Sarah Beckel Lentz, Timothy C., Andrea C. BS, U. Scranton, 1948; PhD, Johns Hopkins U., 1954. Asst. prof. physics Georgetown U., 1953-59, assoc. prof., 1959-64; rsch. staff mem. Inst. for Defense Analyses, Arlington, Va., 1964-66; assoc. prof. physics U. N.Mex., 1966-69, prof., 1969—, asst. dean, 1971-72, acting v.p. rsch., 1972-73; acting dir. Inst. Social R&D, 1972; vis. prof. theoretical chemistry Oxford U., 1973; vis. prof. chemistry and molecular scis. U. Sussex, U.K., 1987; Fulbright lectr. U. Peshawar, Pakistan, 1957-58, Cheng Kung U., Tainan, Taiwan, 1963-64; cons. Ballistics Rsch. Lab., Aberdeen Proving Ground, Md., 1955-57, Dikewood Corp., Albuquerque, 1967-72, 74-80, Albuquerque Urban Obs., 1969-71, Inst. Def. Analyses, 1962-64, 66-69, U.S. ACDA, 1981-84; phys. sci. officer U.S. Arms Control and Disarmament Agy., 1980-81. Pres. Nat. Kidney Found. N.Mex. Inc., 1968-72, del. trustee, 1972-73, 76-80, exec. com., 1974-80, 83-86, v.p., 1982-83, bd. trustees, 1987—; bd. dirs. Nat. Capitol area Nat. Kidney Found., 1965-66, N.Mex. Combined Health Appeal, 1972-73; mem. edn. subcom. Navajo Sci. Com., 1975-82. Recipient Vol. award Nat. Kidney Found. of N.Mex., 1988, Frank J. O'Hara award for disting. achievement in sci. U. Scranton Nat. Alumni Soc., 1988, U.S. Dept. Energy award in solid state physics materials scis., 1988, Outstanding Teaching award Burlington Northern Found., 1989. Mem. Am. Phys. Soc., Bioelectromagnetics Soc., Nat. Eagle Scout Assn., Sigma Xi. Home: 7212 Dellwood Rd NE Albuquerque NM 87110-2207 Office: U NMex Dept Physics and Astronomy Albuquerque NM 87131

BECKER, FRED PAUL, real estate executive; b. Logan, Kans., Sept. 2, 1926; s. Fred P. and Emma (States) B.; m. Neta Faye Simpson, Mar. 25, 1954; children: Cynthia Diane, Jerry Lee, Patricia Ann, Frederick P. III. Cert. in real estate, UCLA, 1961. Mgr. Branham Realty, Burbank, Calif., 1947-60; v.p. PWC Realtors, Burbank, 1960-79; with sales dept. Merrill Lynch Realty, Burbank, 1979-85; prin. Fred Becker Realtor, Ventura, Calif., 1985—. With USAAF, 1943-45. Mem. Nat. Assn. Realtors (bd. dirs. 1976-85), Calif. Assn. Realtors (bd. dirs. 1960—, master instr. 1962—), Realtors Nat. Mktg. Inst. (bd. govs., sr. instr. 1968—), Comml. Investment Real Estate Inst., Ventura Bd. Realtors, Rotary (bd. dirs. 1965-66). Republican. Roman Catholic. Home: 912 Scenic Way Dr Ventura CA 93003-1435

BECKER, JOHN LIONEL, JR., insurance company executive; b. Staten Island, N.Y., Aug. 10, 1956; s. John L. and Marianne (Ziti) B.; m. Patricia Delaney, Nov. 8, 1977; children: Bridget, Benjamin, Robert. BS in Bus. Adminstrn., Portland State U., 1980. Field underwriter N.Y. Life, Portland, Oreg., 1980-86; v.p., sales mgr. Far West Ins. Svcs., Portland, 1986-87; mktg. v.p. United Pacific Life, Portland, 1987—. Pres. student body Portland State U., 1977-78; fin. chmn. Oreg. Rep. Orgn., 1980-81; chmn. bd. Counseling Intervention Programs, Portland, 1984-86; co-chmn. Oreg. prayer com. Nat. Day of Prayer, 1984; fundraiser St. Therese Cath. Sch., Portland, 1992; chmn. bd. Worldwide Seminarian Support, 1992. Named Outstanding Man of Yr. Oreg. Young Reps., 1980, 81, 83, 85, 87. Mem. K.C., NALU (Million Dollar Roundtable 1985), Oreg. Bankers Assn. (assoc.), N.W. Assn. Affiliated Agys. (assoc.), Portland States Pres.' Club, Portland State U. Alumni, 1620 Club (sec.-treas. 1992—), Nat. Eagle Scout Assn., Kappa Sigma. Home: 10651 NE Wasco Portland OR 97220 Office: United Pacific Life 11300 NE Halsey Ste 217 Portland OR 97220

BECKER, LARRY WAYNE, property and casualty insurance company official; b. Grand Rapids, Minn., Apr. 20, 1946; s. Carroll Robert and Evelyn Bernita (Schultz) B.; m. Katherine F. McFadden, Oct. 2, 1971; children: Heidi Katherine, Matthew Robert. BS in Fin., Portland State U., 1968. CPCU; cert. ins. counselor. Underwriter North Pacific Ins. Co., Portland, Oreg., 1969-72; personal lines mgr. North Pacific Ins. Co., Portland, 1972-77; br. mgr. North Pacific Ins. Co., Boise, Idaho, 1977-80; br. mgr. North Pacific Ins. Co., Portland, 1980-85, v.p. br. ops., 1985—, also bd. dirs.; bd. dirs. Idaho Survey and Rating Bur., Boise, 1988-93, chm. 1992-93; chmn. Oreg. Ins. Coun., Portland, 1988; mem. Bd. Bar Examiners, 1991—. Chmn. Oreg. Traffic Safety NOW, Salem, 1988-91. Sec. CPCU, Hon. Order Blue Goose (chmn. Portland 1985-87), Alpha Kappa Psi. Republican. Roman Catholic. Office: North Pacific Ins Co 1475 SW Marlow Ave Portland OR 97225

BECKER, LILLIE ELAINE, executive secretary; b. Salmon, Idaho, Aug. 15, 1950; d. Samuel Elmer Sims and Lillie Mae (Scoble) Newcomb; m. Rocford C. Becker, June 6, 1970 (div. 1984). Student, Boise State Coll., 1968-69, Coll. So. Idaho, 1972, Coll. Legal Arts, Portland, Oreg., 1988-89. Legal stenographer Gooding (Idaho) County Commrs., 1976-78; legal asst., sec., office mgr. Becker, Shaw and Stuart, Gooding, 1969-79; svc. rep. Mountain Bell Telephone, Gooding, 1979-83; legal sec. Nakamoto, Yoshioka and Okamoto, Hilo, Hawaii, 1985-89; pvt. sec. to mayor County of Hawaii, Hilo, 1989-91; exec. sec. Law Office of Christopher J. Yuen, Hilo, 1991—. Sec. Gooding County Rep. Cen. Com., 1980-84; bd. dirs. Hilo unit Am. Heart Assn. Mem. NAFE. Home: 180A Inia Ln Hilo HI 96720-2617

BECKER, MICHAEL, quality control administrator; b. Ramatgan, Israel, Oct. 10, 1948; came to U.S., 1953; s. Rolf and Lilli (Bender) B.; m. Anne Margaret Spitzer, Nov. 21, 1973; children: Miriam, Davina. BA in Geology, San Francisco State U., 1972. Ink technician Cal Ink Co., Berkeley, 1972-73; quality control profl. ICI Speciality Inks, Berkeley, 1973-92; ink supr. U.S. Printing Ink, San Leandro, Calif., 1992—. Pres. local unit PTA, South San Francisco, 1988, Hillel Local Unit, San Francisco, 1970. Democrat. Jewish. Home: 612 Stonegate Dr South San Francisco CA 94080 Office: US Printing Ink 14465 Griffith St San Leandro CA 94577

BECKER, ROGER VERN, legal educator; b. Omaha, Apr. 12, 1947; s. LaVern Herman and Doris Bessie (Smith) B.; m. D'Lea Bruaner; children: Lindsey Vern, Hannah Anna, Mary Sophia Rose, Christopher John Micah. Student, U. Nebr., 1965-67, JD, 1970; LLM, U. Wash., 1971; M in Library and Info. Sci., Ind. U., 1981. Dir. info. svcs. U. Va. Sch. Law, Charlottesville, 1971-73; dir. legal rsch. U. N.D. Sch. Law, Grand Forks, 1973-80; dir. tech. U. Ark. Sch. Law, Fayetteville, 1981-83; planner, systems strategist, dir. tech. U. Puget Sound Sch. Law, Tacoma, Wash., 1983—; bus. and mktg. advisor P.S. The Last Word in Personal Style, Mercer Island, Wash., 1984—. Producer various legal edn. video tapes; program designer various computer programs; author articles in field. Mem. Govs. Commn. on Libraries, N.D., 1974-76. Mem. Order of Coif, Beta Phi Mu. Home: 1710 Emerald St Milton WA 98354-9429 Office: U Puget Sound Sch Law 950 Broadway Tacoma WA 98402-4405

BECKER, STANLEY R., advertising executive. Past exec. v.p., exec. creative dir. Saatchi & Saatchi DFS, Inc., N.Y.C.; now vice chmn., chief creative officer Saatchi & Saatchi DFS, Inc. Office: Saatchi & Saatchi DFS/Pacific 3501 Sepulveda Blvd Torrance CA 90505-2538

BECKETT, RAY H(ERBERT), JR., director engineering activities, fundraiser for research and development; b. Ogden, Utah, Sept. 9, 1928; s. Ray Herbert Sr. and Rosalia Sophia (Nielsen) B.; m. Mary Geraldine Walker, July 20, 1954; children: Steven W., David R., Robert J. AA, L.A. City Coll., 1950; BS, Brigham Young U., 1954; MBA, U. So. Calif., L.A., 1963; PhD, U. Utah, 1973. Budget adminstr. engring. div. Aerospace Corp., El Segundo, Calif., 1960-68; dir. devel. and spl. products intermountain regional med. program U. Utah, Salt Lake City, 1968-74, dir. engring. network Coll. of Engring., 1989-92, dir. devel., adviser to dean Coll. Engring., 1988—, devel. adviser to the dean Coll. of Engring., 1988—; exec. v.p. Health Systems Rsch. Inst., Salt Lake City, 1975-77; exec. dir. S.W. Ctr. for Environ. Rsch. and Devel., Salt Lake City, 1990—; dir. econs., health sci. and social sci. div. Eyring Rsch. Inst., Provo, Utah, 1977-79; dir. devel. Coll. of Ea. Utah, Price, 1982-86; exec. dir. Utah Consortium of Community Colls., Orem, 1986-88; chief exec. officer, chmn. bd. Resource Bus. Inst., Salt Lake City, 1980—; program dir. S.W. Ctr. Environ. Rsch. and Policy, 1991—. Author: Facts and Falacies of Programs to Encourage Creativity in Industry, 1963, Planned Giving Programs in Higher Education, 1973. Del. State Polit. Conv., Utah, 1984—; scoutmaster Boy Scouts Am. Troop 694, Salt Lake City, 1970-82, dist. commr., 1978-82; bus. mgr. Mormon Youth Symphony & Chrous, Salt Lake City, 1985—; treas. Nat. Coun. for Resource Devel., 1985-86. Recipient Silver Beaver award Boy Scouts Am., 1982. Mem. Coun. for Advancement and Support of Edn., Intercollegiate Studies Inst., Silver Beaver Assn. Republican. LDS. Home: 4965 Pinehill Dr Salt Lake City UT 84107-5025 Office: U Utah Coll Engring Merrill Engring Bldg 2216 Salt Lake City UT 84112

BECKMAN, ARNOLD ORVILLE, analytical instrument manufacturing company executive; b. Cullom, Ill., Apr. 10, 1900; s. George W. and Elizabeth E. (Jewkes) B.; m. Mabel S. Meinzer, June 10, 1925; children: Gloria Patricia, Arnold Stone. BS, U. Ill., 1922, MS, 1923; PhD, Calif. Inst. Tech., 1928; DSc (hon.), Chapman Coll., 1965, Whittier Coll., 1971, Clarkson U., 1989, Rockefeller U., 1992; LLD (hon.), U. Calif., Riverside, 1966, Loyola U., L.A., 1969, U. Ill., 1982, Pepperdine U., 1977, Ill. Wesleyan U., 1991; DHL (hon.), Calif. State U., Fullerton, 1984, Ill. State U.,

1990. Rsch. assoc. Bell Tel. Labs., N.Y.C., 1924-26; chem. faculty Calif. Inst. Tech., 1926-39; v.p. Nat. Tech. Lab., Pasadena, Calif., 1935-39; pres. Nat. Tech. Lab., 1939-40, Helipot Corp., 1944-58, Arnold O. Beckman, Inc., South Pasadena, Calif., 1946-58; founder, chmn. Beckman Instruments, Inc., Fullerton, Calif., 1940-65, chmn. emeritus, 1988—; vice chmn. SmithKline Beckman Corp., 1984-86; bd. dirs. Security Pacific Nat. Bank, 1956-72, adv. dir., 1972-75; bd. dirs. Continental Airlines, 1956-71, adv. dir., 1971-73. Author articles in field; inventor; patentee in field. Mem. Pres.'s Air Quality Bd., 1970-74; chmn. System Devel. Found., 1970-88; chmn. bd. trustees emeritus Calif. Inst. Tech.; hon. trustee Calif. Mus. Found.; bd. overseers House Ear Inst., 1981—; trustee Scripps Clinic and Rsch. Found., 1971—; bd. dirs. Hoag Meml. Hosp.; co-founder, bd. dirs. Beckman Laser Inst. and Med. Clinic, 1982—; mem. bd. overseers U. Calif., Irvine, 1982—. With USMC, 1918-19. Benjamin Franklin fellow Royal Soc. Arts; named to Nat. Inventors Hall of Fame, 1987; recipient Nat. Medal Tech., 1988, Presdl. Citizens medal, 1989, Nat. Medal of Sci., 1989, Order of Lincoln award State of Ill., 1991, Bower award for Bus. Leadership, 1992. Fellow Assn. Clin. Scientists; mem. NAM, AAAS, Am. Acad. Arts and Scis., L.A. C. of C. (bd. dir. 1954-58, pres. 1956), Calif. C. of C. (dir., pres. 1967-68), Nat. Acad. Engring. (Disting. Honoree, 1986, Founders Award, 1987), Am. Inst. Chemists (Gold medal 1987), Instrument Soc. Am. (pres. 1952), Am. Chem. Soc., Social Sci. Rsch. Coun., Am. Assn. Clin. Chemistry (hon.), Newcomen Soc., Auto Club So. Calif. (bd. dirs. 1965-73, hon. dir. 1973—), Sigma Xi, Delta Upsilon, Alpha Chi Sigma, Phi Lambda Upsilon. Clubs: Newport Harbor Yacht, Pacific. Office: 100 Academy Dr Irvine CA 92715-3002

BECKMAN, JAMES WALLACE BIM, economist, marketing executive; b. Mpls., May 2, 1936; s. Wallace Gerald and Mary Louise (Frissell) B. BA, Princeton U., 1958; PhD, U. Calif., 1973. Pvt. practice econ. cons., Berkeley, Calif. 1962-67; cons. Calif. State Assembly, Sacramento, 1967-68; pvt. practice market rsch. and econs. cons., Laguna Beach, Calif., 1969-77; cons. Calif. State Gov.'s Office, Sacramento 1977-80; pvt. practice real estate cons., L.A. 1980-83; v.p. mktg. Gold-Well Investments, Inc., L.A. 1982-83; pres. Beckman Analytics Internat., econ. cons. to bus. and govt., L.A. and Lake Arrowhead, Calif., 1983—, East European Bus. and Govt., 1992—; adj. prof. Calif. State U. Sch. Bus., San Bernardino, 1989—, U. Redlands, 1992—; cons. E European. Contbr. articles on regional & internat. econ. devel. & social change to profl. jours. Maj. USMC 1958-67. NIMH fellow 1971-72. Fellow Soc. Applied Anthropology; mem. Am. Econs. Assn., Am. Statis. Assn., Am. Mktg. Assn. (officer), Nat. Assn. Bus. Economists (officer). Democrat. Presbyterian. Home: PO Box 1753 Lake Arrowhead CA 92352-1753

BECKMAN, JOHN COYLE, management consultant; b. Portland, Oreg., Dec. 15, 1919; s. John Joseph Beckman and Lelah Mildred (Coyle) Halton; m. Elizabeth Hurlbut, 1947 (div. 1979); children: Barbara Elizabeth, Wendy Joan; m. Patricia Jane Huckins, 1980. Student, U. Portland, 1938-39. Various tech. positions Aircraft and Shipbuilding Cos., Oreg. and Wash., 1940-42; pres. Beckman & Whitley, Portland, 1942-48, San Carlos, Calif., 1948-64; cons. pvt. practice San Francisco, 1964-82, Portland, 1982—; pres. Collector's Press, San Francisco, 1967-72, First San Francisco Fin. Corp., 1970-72; livestock owner (Herefords) Etna, Calif., 1967-77; bd. dirs. Hosts Corp., Vancouver, Wash., FEI Co. Inventor automatic film loader and phototimer. Trustee Oreg. Symphony Assn., Portland, 1983-89; chmn., trustee San Francisco Conservatory Music, 1971-78; bd. dirs. Calif. Nev. Hereford Assn., Madera, Calif., 1971-77; pres. Siskiyou County Farm Bur., Yreka, Calif., 1976-77; regent Univ. Portland, 1971—. Mem. Am. Meteorol. Soc. (Charles Franklin Brooks award 1966, chmn. planning commn. 1959-64, councillor 1962-65), Univ. Club. Republican. Home: 2800 NW Linmere Dr Portland OR 97229-3663

BECKMAN, KENNETH OREN, film and video specialist, researcher; b. Detroit, Nov. 26, 1948; s. Aron J. Beckman; m. Sally Tuttle, Sept. 9, 1963; children: Oren Rigel, Sienna Grace. BA in Theater, Mich. State U., 1970; MA in Film, San Francisco State U., 1982. Freelance producer, 1969-74; tech. dir. Center for Contemporary Music, Oakland, Calif., 1974-76; producer Optic Nerve, San Francisco, 1976-78; dir. video lab. Xerox/Parc, Palo Alto, Calif., 1978-86; founding ptnr. SIRIUS Communications Group, La Honda, Calif., 1984-90; mgr. video lab. Systems Rsch. Ctr. Systems Rsch. Ctr., Digital Equipment Corp., Palo Alto, 1986—; founder Foton Factory, La Honda, 1991; cons. Apple Computer, Multi-Media Group, Oceanic Inst. Dir. video art including A Man With an Idea, Reach Out, 1986, Clean Machine, 1987, Song of the Street of the Singing Chicken, 1982 (1st place award Santa Cruz Video Festival 1982, Am. Film Inst. Nat. Winner 1982); patentee in field. Recipient Hometown USA Video Festival award, Denver, 1984. Fellow Photon Factory (dir. 1984-87, Wave/Particle award 1986); mem. Music Video Dirs. Guild (dir. 1985-87, Deep Purple Music TV award 1985), Soc. Motion Picture TV Engrs. Office: Foton Factory PO Box 251 La Honda CA 94020-0251

BECKMANN, JANE MILUNA, acoustical company executive, consultant; b. Ostrava, Slezko, Czechoslovakia, Nov. 27, 1935; came to U.S., 1969; d. František Mašín and Miloslava (Pospíšilová) Mašínová; m. Raoul Beckmann; 1 child, Denisa Ann Rafalowski. BS in Structural Engring., Archtl. Tech. U. Prague, Czechoslovakia, 1955, MS in Structural Engring., 1958; postgrad. sch. cert., Electro-Engring. Tech. U. Prague, Czechoslovakia, 1962. Engr. Bldg. Isolation Inst., Prague, 1958-62, mgr., 1962-66; rsch. engr. Inst. Prefabricated Bldgs., Prague, 1966-68; acoustical cons. Bolt Beranek and Newman Inc., L.A., 1969-87; prin., treas. Acoustical Analysis Assocs. Inc., Canoga Park, Calif., 1987—. Mem. Acoustical Soc. Am. Republican. Roman Catholic. Office: Acoustical Analysis Assocs Inc 22148 Sherman Way Ste 206 Canoga Park CA 91303

BECKMANN, JON MICHAEL, publisher; b. N.Y.C., Oct. 24, 1936; s. John L. and Grace (Hazelton) B.; m. Barbara Ann Efting, June 26, 1965. BA, U. Pa., 1958; MA, NYU, 1961. Sr. editor Prentice-Hall Inc., Englewood Cliffs, N.J., 1964-68; v.p., editor Barre Pubs., Mass., 1970-73; pub. Sierra Club Books, San Francisco, 1973—. Contbr. articles, book revs., poetry to publs. Mem. Book Club of Calif. Home: 18185 7th St E Sonoma CA 95476-4701 Office: 100 Bush St San Francisco CA 94104-3902

BECKMEYER, DWIGHT CLARENCE, pianist; b. Glen Cove, N.Y., Apr. 11, 1962; s. Theodore and Claretta Joy (Erdman) B.; m. Susan Diane Olsen, Aug. 30, 1986. BA in Music, U. Wash., 1986, BMus in Piano Performance, 1986, MMusic, 1989, postgrad., 1989—. Choir dir., organist, pianist Christ the King Luth. Ch., Snohomish, Wash., 1977-90; piano tchr. Seattle, 1989—; organist St. Michael's Cath. Ch., Snohomish, 1978-89; asst. dir., worship and music. coord. Camp Lutherwood, Bellingham, Wash., 1986-87; pianist, accompanist Johannessen Internat. Sch. Arts, Victoria, B.C., Can., 1988-91; accompanist U. Wash. Sch. Music, Seattle, 1989-91, N.W. Girlchoir, Seattle, 1991—; pianist, soloist Everett (Wash.) Symphony Orch., 1989, N.W. Symphony Orch., Seattle, 1991-92, N.W. Sch. Internat. Chamber Orch., 1993. Composer New Song, 1980, We Have Faith in Christ the King, 1989. Pianist, Oreg. State U. Summer Piano Festival, Corvallis, 1989, Wash. Centenial Concert Series, Orcas Island, 1989. Mem. Mus. Poetical Soc., Am. Choir Dirs. Assn. Lutheran. Home: 2128 N 53d St Seattle WA 98103

BECKS, RONALD ARTHUR, film producer; b. N.Y.C., July 9, 1953; s. Wellington and Vivian (Newkirk) B. Student, York Coll., 1969-71; cert. for prodrs., Cintel Corp., 1974-75; cert., Ch. Religious Sc., 1975-77; D of Religious Communication (hon.), Temple Faith, 1974. Owner, pres., chmn. Ronald A. Becks Internat. Theatre Soc., N.Y.C., 1978-90; v.p. Miracle Prodns., N.Y.C., 1978-90; pres. Magic Circle Players, Australia and Hong Kong, Sodeko Films, Australia and Hong Kong; mktg. dir. V.R.B. Enterprises, Australia and Hong Kong, Multi-Media Svcs., Australia and Hong Kong; pres. Noduki Films, Australia and Hong Kong, 1990, Face Affair, Beverly Hills, Calif., 1991, Film Gods Prodns., Beverly Hills, 1991—. Author: The 3rd Testament, 1990, There's Only You, 1988; composer: You Bring Out the Best In Me, 1984 (top 40 song); inventor phone device. Dep. chmn. UN Assn., 1979, dep. amb., 1979, chmn. Song Quest, 1979; entertainment coord. Keep Australia Beautiful, 1980; prodr. children's show Consulate of Peru, 1979; prodr. and host Living Environment Found., N.Y.C., 1978. Mem. Prodrs. and Dirs. Guild, Producers Assn., Pen Internat., Journalists Club, Writers Guild, Masons. Home and Office: 642 N Plymouth Blvd Ste # 7 Los Angeles CA 90004

BECK-VON-PECCOZ, STEPHEN GEORGE WOLFGANG, artist; b. Munich, Oct. 18, 1933; came to U.S., 1937; s. Wolfgang Anna Marie and Martha Jeanette (Morse) Beck-von-P.; m. Dorothy Ann Freytag, June 16, 1956 (div. 1971); m. Michele Marie Perry, Feb. 8, 1972; children: Stephen Jr., David, Kenneth, Lisa. BEE, Cornell U., 1956; MA in Art, Calif. State U., San Diego, 1974. Electronic engr. Stromberg Carlson Co., San Diego, 1958-60; project mgr. Control Data Corp., San Diego, 1960-65, Digital Devel. Corp., San Diego, 1965-66; project engr. Stromberg Datagraphix, Inc., San Diego, 1966-69; project mgr. Digital Sci. Corp., San Diego, 1969-71; artist San Diego, 1974—; cons. elec. engring., San Diego, 1974-78. Served to 2d lt. USAF, 1956-58. Mem. Artists Equity Assn., Internat. Sculpture Ctr., Kappa Alpha Soc. Home and Studio: 636 Nardito Ln Solana Beach CA 92075

BEDERKA, STEPHEN EDWARD, management consultant; b. N.Y.C., July 6, 1930; s. Stephen and Emilia Rose (Toth) B.; m. Ann Sabina Canor, Nov. 29, 1952; children: Celeste Ann, Valerie Ann Bederka Collins. BS in Physics, St. Bernadine of Siena, 1952; postgrad., Stanford U., 1968. Radar design engr. GE, Utica, N.Y., 1952-55; communications system engr. Lockheed Missiles and Space Co., Sunnyvale, Calif., 1955-66, system engring. mgr., 1966-74, program mgr., 1974-91; founder, mgmt. and bus. cons. Toth Co., Los Gatos, Calif., 1991—; counselor Svc. Corps Ret. Execs., 1992—. Contbr. articles to profl. jours. and mags. Mem. IEEE (past officer San Francisco chpt.). Home: 15286 Via Palomino Los Gatos CA 95030-2238

BEDORE, MICHAEL PAUL, marketing company executive, consultant; b. Highland Park, Mich., July 30, 1956; s. Charles Dustay and Mary (Fuciu) B. BS in Psychology, Wayne State U., 1979. Asst. mgr. C&M Supermarket, Detroit, 1966-77; mktg. rsch. analyst GM, Detroit, 1977-79; credit authorizer Am. Express, Phoenix, 1979-81, Valley Nat. Bank, Phoenix, 1981-82; ins. coord. Marsh & McLennan Inc., Detroit, 1982; internat. coord. Ramada Inn, Phoenix, 1982-85; internat. franchise licensing adminstr. Armour Internat. Co., Phoenix, 1985-88; tax auditor Ariz. Dept. of Revenue, Phoenix, 1989; chief exec. officer Bedore Mktg. & Computer Enterprises, Phoenix, 1988—. Mem. Mecham Recall Com., Phoenix, 1987—; dep. registrar Maricopa County Elections Office, Phoenix, 1987—. Republican. Roman Catholic. Home and Office: 8129 N 35th Ave # 2267 Phoenix AZ 85051-5892

BEDRICK, JEFFREY KEITH, artist, commercial illustator; b. Providence, Oct. 4, 1960; s. Barry David and Ann Glenda (Rosenberg) B. Art student of Gage Taylor, Woodacre, Calif., 1978-80; student, Coll. of Marin, Kentfield, Calif., 1979-81, San Francisco State U., 1983. ind. comml. illustrator numerous pubs., including Doubleday Books, 1979—, San Francisco Opera Guild Wine and Travel Auction Mag., 1991, Magical Blend Mag., 1991—; prodn. and background artist and animator Colossal Pictures, San Francisco, 1982—; posters and art cards published by Pomegranate, 1979—, Visionary Pub., Inc., 1986—, Aquamarin Verlag, 1987—, The Queen's Cards, 1991—; designer EArth Flag merchandising enterprise Red Rose Collection, Burlingame, Calif. Illustrator: Weather (by Howard Smith), 1989, also numerous book covers; exhibited in numerous group shows, 1978—, latest being The Environment group exhibition Toyota Corp. hdqrs., Tokyo, 1991, Brandywine Fantacy Gallery, Chgo., 1991, Conacher Galleries, San Francisco, 1991, ARchitects & Heroes, 1992, Fine Arts Enterprises, 1992; represented in numerous pvt. and company collections; represented exclusively for Fine Art by Collectors Editions, Canoga Park, Calif., 1993—. Pell grantee, 1979. Mem. Artists in Print, Internat. Platform Assn., U.S. Hang Gliding Assn., Inc., San Francisco Soc. Illustrators, World Affairs Coun. Home and Office: 477 25th Ave Apt 6 San Francisco CA 94121-1945

BEEBE, ROBERT GARDNER, retired meteorologist; b. Auburn, Nebr., Feb. 24, 1915; s. Jared Gardner and Clara Lois (Smith) B.; m. Gertrude Viola Clifton, July 12, 1942; children: Robert Clifton, Carolyn Sue Beebe Dunn. AB, Nebr. Wesleyan, 1941; postgrad., U. Chgo., 1941-44. Meteorology instr. U. Chgo., 1942-44; airline forecaster Pan Am Airlines, Lima, Peru, 1944-45; aviation forecaster U.S. Weather Bur., Washington, 1945-48; rsch. meteorologist Atlanta Weather Bur., 1948-53; rsch. meteorologist severe storms Washington Weather Bur., 1953-54, Kansas City (Mo.) Weather Bur., 1954-58; consulting meteorologist Midwest Weather Svc., Kansas City, 1958-66; exec. meteorologist Nat. Weather Svc., Silver Spring, Md., 1966-70, Kansas City, 1970-73, Cheyenne, Wyo., 1973-85. Contbr. numerous articles to profl. jours. Recipient Silver medal U.S. Dept. Commerce, 1958. Fellow Am. Meteorol. Soc. (elected councilor 1958). Methodist. Home: 949 Shoshoni Cheyenne WY 82009

BEEBE, ROBERT R., retired mining industry executive; b. 1928. BSMetE, Mont. Sch. Mines, 1953, MSMetE, 1954. Rsch. assoc., project engr. U. Minn., 1964-66; with Marcona Corp., 1966-72, 73-76, v.p. devel.; chief exec. officer Carpco Rsch. and Engring., 1972-73; with Newmont Mining Corp., 1976-86, v.p. project devel.; sr. v.p. Homestake Mining Co., San Francisco, 1986-91; cons., 1991—. With U.S. Army, 1946-49. Mem. NAE. Office: PO Box 1739 Mendocino CA 95460

BEEBE, SANDRA E., English language educator, artist; b. March AFB, Calif., Nov. 10, 1934; d. Eugene H. and Margaret (Fox) B. AB in English & Speech, UCLA, 1956; MA in Sec. Edn., Calif. State U., Long Beach, 1957. English tchr. Garden Grove (Calif.) High Sch., 1957-93, attendance supr., 1976-83; ind. artist, 1964—. Contbr. articles to English Jour., chpt. to book; exhbns. include Okla. Watercolor Soc., Watercolor West, San Diego Internat., La. Watercolor Soc., San Diego Art Inst., Knickerbocker Artists N.Y., Midwest Watercolor Soc., Am. Watercolor Soc., Butler Inst. Am. Art, Youngstown, Ohio, Kings Art Ctr., Audubon Artists N.Y., B-Q Gallery, Long Beach; title page artist Exploring Painting, 1990, Understanding Watercolor, American Artist, 1991. Mem. Nat. Watercolor Soc., Midwest Watercolor Soc., Watercolor West, Nat. Arts Club, Knickerbocker Artists N.Y., Audubon Artists N.Y., West Coast Watercolor Soc., Rocky Mountain Nat. Watermedia Honor Soc., Soc. Layerists in Multi-Media, Salmagundi Club, Kappa Kappa Alumnae Assn. Republican. Home: 239 Mira Mar Ave Long Beach CA 90803-6153 Office: B-Q Gallery 3920 E 4th St Long Beach CA 90814

BEEKMAN, CAROL TSCHANNEN, public relations director. BA, Purdue U., 1968. Accredited in pub. rels. Tchr. various locations, 1968-79; pub. info. officer City of Brea, Calif., 1979-82; pub. rels. mgr. Pacific Mutual, Newport Beach, Calif., 1983-86; pub. rels. supr. Cochrane Chase, Livingston, Newport Beach, Calif., 1986-89; nat. dir. pub. rels. Coldwell Banker, Mission Viejo, Calif., 1990—. Mem. bldg. com. Laguna Beach (Calif.) Meth. Ch., 1988; literacy tutor South Orange County (Calif.) Literacy Coun., 1990. Mem. Pub. Rels. Soc. Am. (bd. dirs. 1987-89, treas. 1990-91). Office: Coldwell Banker Residential 27271 Las Ramblas Mission Viejo CA 92691

BEELER, LAUREL DANIELS, lawyer; b. Boston, Sept. 5, 1961; d. Ann (Haywood) B. AB cum laude, Bowdoin Coll., 1983; JD with honors, U. Wash., 1989. Bar: Wash. Staff atty., ct. law clerk, 9th cir. U.S. Ct. of Appeals, San Francisco, 1989-90, civil appeals, divsn. chief, 1990-92, law clerk, Hon. Cecil F. Poole, 1992—; lectr. CLE Program Wash. State Bar Assn., Seattle, 1988. mem. Community Impact, 1992—. Mem. Wash. State Bar Assn. Democrat. Office: US Ct Appeals 9th Cir 121 Spear St San Francisco CA 94105

BEEN, HANS HENRIK, finance executive; b. Copenhagen, Aug. 30, 1949; came to U.S., 1976; s. Borge and Tove (Hansen) B.; m. Helle Nymann Eriksen, Jan. 16, 1971; children: Louise, Henriette. BA in Econs., U. Copenhagen, 1970; MBA, Copenhagen Sch. Econs., 1973; MSc in Fin., Calif. State U., Northridge, 1979. Fin. planner Novo Pharms., Ltd., Copenhagen, 1972-74; asst. gen. mgr. Sadolin & Holmblad, Ltd., Copenhagen, 1974-76; comml. officer Danish Fgn. Svc., Royal Danish Consulate Gen., L.A., 1976-80; mgr. corp. banking Den Danske Bank, Copenhagen, 1980-81; mgr. proj. fin. Bank of Montreal, Toronto, Ont., 1981-85, N.Y.C., 1985-86; v.p. Bechtel Financing Svcs., Inc., San Francisco, 1986-89, Bechtel Enterprises, Inc., San Francisco, 1989—; lectr. fin. U. So. Calif., St. Mary's Coll., 1977-91. Mem. Danish-Am. C. of C., L.A., 1976-79. Recipient Pathfinder Leadership award Applied Energy Svcs., Washington, 1990. Mem. Nat. Assn. Securities Dealers (registered rep. 1989). Home: 1869 Countrywood Ct Walnut Creek CA 94598-1013 Office: Bechtel Enterprises Inc 50 Beale St San Francisco CA 94105-1813

BEER, JOSEPH ERNEST, telecommunications manager; b. Pasadena, Calif., June 5, 1959; s. Joseph Andrew and Pauline Sylvia (Micciche) B.; m. Amy Shun-Fong Wu, Oct. 13, 1984. BS in Internat. Bus., Calif. State U., L.A., 1982; MBA in Info. Tech. Mgmt., U. So. Calif., 1987. Asst. engr. ARCO-Electronics & Telecommunications, L.A., 1979-83, sr. coord., 1983-84, project engr., 1984-85, sr. project engr., 1985-87; sr. mgr. Ernst & Young, L.A., 1987-91; dir. telecommunications and network svcs. South Coast Air Quality Mgmt. Dist., L.A., 1991. Recipient scholarship, Ebell Found., L.A., 1981, Bank Am. scholarship, Bank Am. Found., 1981. Mem. Soc. Telecommunications Consultants, Project Mgmt. Inst. Republican. Home: 530 S Sandy Hook St West Covina CA 91790-3635 Office: SCAQMD 21865 Copley Dr Diamond Bar CA 91765

BEESEMYER, FRITZ TIMOTHY, radio executive; b. Santa Monica, Calif., Aug. 10, 1952; s. Richard Louis and Mary Wood (Tebbe) B. BA, UCLA, 1974. Account exec. Sta. KIIS, L.A., 1975-76; v.p., gen. sales Sta. KBBC, Phoenix, 1976-78; v.p., gen. mgr. Sta. WCZY, Detroit, 1978-80, Sta. K-101, San Francisco, 1980-83; pres., gen. mgr. Sta. KAIR- JYK, Tucson, Sta. KKFM, Colorado Springs, 1984—; pres. Citadel Communications Corp., Phoenix, 1984—. Republican. Roman Catholic. Office: Citadel Communications Corp 5221 N 24th St Ste 205 Phoenix AZ 85016

BEESLEY, DAVID, educator; b. Salt Lake City, Sept. 27, 1938; s. P. Gordon and Margaret (McHale) B.; m. Louise Lynne Roripaugh, Mar. 11, 1989; children: Brooks, Peter, Nathan, Sarah. BS, U. Utah, 1961, MA, 1964, PhD, 1968. Asst. prof. Tarleton State U., Stephenville, Tex., 1967-69; rsch. asst. Calif. State Coordinating Coun. for Higher Edn., Sacramento, 1969-70; prof. Sierra Coll., Rocklin, Calif., 1970—; vis. prof. Morehead (Minn.) State U., 1969. Contbr. articles to profl. jours. NDEA fellow U. Utah, 1965-67. Mem. Chinese Hist. Soc., Calif. Hist. Soc., Am. Soc. for Environ. History. Office: Sierra Coll 5000 Rocklin Rd Rocklin CA 95677-3337

BEESTON, JOSEPH MACK, metallurgist; b. Fillmore, Utah, Aug. 12, 1918; s. Joseph W. and Florence (Swallow) B.; m. Blanche Weight, Dec. 20, 1946; children: Miriam, Jolynn. BChEng, U. Utah, 1949; postgrad., Oreg. State U., 1949-50; PhD in Metall. Engring., U. Utah, 1953. Asst. prof. Wash. State U., Pullman, 1953-58; sr. metallurgist Phillips Pet Atomic Energy Div., Idaho Falls, Idaho, 1958-61, leader irr. material group, 1961-64; chief materials rsch. sect. Idaho Nuclear, Idaho Falls, 1964-71; chief irradiation material engring. Aerojeg Gen., Idaho Falls, 1971-78; sci. specialist EG&G Idaho Inc., Idaho Falls, 1978-85; cons. metallurgist Garrison, Utah, 1985—. Contbr. over 100 articles to profl. jours. With USAF, 1941-45. Mem. ASTM (com. nuclear tech. and applications), Am. Soc. Metals. Home and Office: 625 Circle Dr Garrison UT 84728-9702

BEETHAM, STANLEY WILLIAMS, international management consultant; b. Montpelier, Idaho, Nov. 2, 1933; s. Harry Stanley and Mary (Williams) B.; m. Barbara Burnham, June 20, 1987; 1 child, Lara Mary. BA, Wesleyan U., 1956; MA, U. Amsterdam, The Netherlands, 1957; postgrad., Harvard U., 1958-59, U. Wash., 1959-60. Internat. market mgr. U.S. Rubber/Uniroyal, N.Y.C., 1960-63; corp. mktg. cons. GE, N.Y.C., 1963-65; assoc. dir. Benton & Bowles, Inc., N.Y.C., 1965-67; dir. corp. planning Esmark, Chgo., 1967-72, Consol. Packaging Co., Chgo., 1972-74; sr. cons. Booz Allen Hamilton/Hay Assocs., N.Y.C. and Phila., 1975-80; sr. v.p. U.S. Tobacco Co., Greenwich, Conn., 1981-87; pres. S.W. Beetham & Co., Seattle, 1987—. Contbr. articles in field. Candidate for U.S. Congress from 13th Ill. Dist., 1972, 74; chmn. roundtable Westchester (Conn.) Planning Forum. Fulbright scholar, 1956, Marshall scholar, 1957; Woodrow Wilson fellow, 1958. Mem. N.Am. Soc. Corp. Planning, Nat. Assn. Bus. Economists, Coun. for Urban Econ. Devel., Internat. Soc. for Planing and Strategic Mgmt., Rainier Club, Phi Beta Kappa. Office: 202 W Olympic Pl Apt 301 Seattle WA 98119-3783

BEEVERS, HARRY, biologist; b. Shildon, Eng., Jan. 10, 1924; came to U.S., 1950, naturalized, 1958; s. Norman and Olive (Ayre) B.; m. Jean Sykes, Nov. 19, 1949; 1 child, Michael. BSc, U. Durham, Eng., 1945, PhD, 1947; DSc, U. Newcastle-on-Tyne, 1974, Purdue U., 1972, Nagoya U., 1986. Research fellow Oxford U., Eng., 1946-50; asst. to prof. Purdue U., West Lafayette, Ind., 1950-69; prof. biology U. Calif., Santa Cruz, 1969-90, prof. emeritus, 1990—; fellow Crown Coll. U. Calif., Santa Cruz, 1969—. Author: Respiratory Metabolism in Plants, 1961; contbr. articles to profl. jours. Recipient von Humboldt Sr. Scientist award, 1987. Mem. NAS, Am. Soc. Plant Physiologists (Stephen Hales award 1970, pres. 1960), Am. Soc. Biol. Chemists, Am. Acad. Arts and Scis, Accademia Nazionale dei Lincei, Deutsche Botanische Gesselschaft (hon.). Home: 46 S Circle Dr Santa Cruz CA 95060-1816 Office: U Calif Santa Cruz Dept Biology Santa Cruz CA 95064

BEEZER, ROBERT ARNOLD, mathematics educator; b. Seattle, Sept. 4, 1958; s. Robert Renaut and Hazlehurst Plant (Smith) B.; m. Patricia Ina Dorsey, Aug. 2, 1986; 1 child: David Ross. BS, Santa Clara U., 1978; MS, U. Ill., 1982, PhD, 1984. Asst. prof. U. Puget Sound, Tacoma, 1984-90, assoc. prof., 1990—. Contbr. articles to profl. jours. Martin Nelson Jr. Sabbatical fellow, 1988. Fellow Inst. Combinatorics and its Applications; mem. Am. Math. Soc., Math. Assn. Am., Coun. Undergraduate Rsch., Seattle Tennis Club, Phi Eta Sigma. Office: Univ Puget Sound Math Dept 1500 N Warner St Tacoma WA 98416-0001

BEEZER, ROBERT RENAUT, federal judge; b. Seattle, July 21, 1928; s. Arnold Roswell and Josephine (May) B.; m. Hazlehurst Plant Smith, June 15, 1957; children: Robert Arnold, John Leighton, Mary Allison. Student, U. Wash., 1946-48, 51; BA, U. Va., 1951, LLB, 1956. Bar: Wash. 1956, U.S. Supreme Ct. 1968. Ptnr. Schweppe, Krug, Tausend & Beezer, P.S., Seattle, 1956-84; judge U.S. Ct. Appeals (9th cir.), Seattle, 1984—; alt. mem. Wash. Jud. Qualifications Commn., Olympia, 1981-84. 1st lt. USMCR, 1951-53. Fellow Am. Coll. Trust and Estate Counsel, Am. Bar Found.; mem. ABA, Seattle-King County Bar Assn. (pres. 1975-76), Wash. Bar Assn. (bd. govs. 1980-83). Clubs: Rainier, Tennis (Seattle). Office: US Ct Appeals 802 US Courthouse 1010 5th Ave Seattle WA 98104-1130

BEEZLEY, LINDA D., state legislator. Supr. clin. lab. Samaritan Health Svcs., Phoenix, 1982-84, supr. adminstrv. support, compensation and benefits, 1984-91, spl. projects coord. human resources, 1991—; state rep. Ariz. Legis. Dist. 20, 1991—; mem. govt. ops., health com., human svcs. com. Legis. Dist. 20, 1991—; mem. Phoenix (Ariz.) Arts Commn., 1989, co-chair planning com. edn. and the arts, 1990, nomination com., 1991, advocacy com., 1991-92. Exec. com. mem. Boy Scouts Am., 1976-86; cub scouts leader Cub Scouts Am., 1976-84, weeblos leader, 1978-84; team mother, mgr. Catalina/Barcelona Little League, 1976-86, Pop Warner Football Assn., 1979-85; t-ball and soccer coach YMCA, 1976-80; active Alhambra Dist. Legis. Com., 1982—, Alhambra Dist. Liaison Com., 1986—; campaign worker and coord. United Way Campaign, 1984—; governing bd. mem. Alhambra Elem. Sch. Dist. No. 68, 1986—, governing bd. pres., 1989. Recipient Art Edn. Advocacy award Ariz. Art Edn. Assn., 1990, award of merit Ariz. Sch. Pub. Rels. Assn., 1990. Mem. Ariz. Sch. Bds. Assn., Maricopa County Sch. Bds. Assn. (exec. com. sec. 1989-90, founder, dir. mini-grants program 1989—, pres. 1990-91). Address: House of Representatives 1700 W Washington Phoenix AZ 85006

BEGGS, HARRY MARK, lawyer; b. Los Angeles, Nov. 15, 1941; s. John Edgar and Agnes (Kentro) B.; m. Sandra Lynne Mikal, May 25, 1963; children: Brendan, Sean, Corey, Michael. Student, Ariz. State U., 1959-61, Phoenix Coll., 1961; LL.B., U. Ariz., 1964. Bar: Ariz. 1964, U.S. Dist. Ct. Ariz. 1964, U.S. Ct. Appeals (9th cir.) 1973; U.S. Supreme Ct. 1991. Assoc. Carson Messinger, Elliott, Laughlin & Ragan, Phoenix, 1964-69, ptnr., 1969—. Mem. editorial bd. Ariz. Law Rev. 1963-64; contbr. articles to profl. jours. Recipient award for highest grade on state bar exam. Atty. Gen. Ariz., 1964; Fegtly Moot Ct. award, 1963, 64; Abner S. Lipscomb scholar U. Ariz. Law Sch., 1963. Fellow Ariz. Bar Found. (founder); mem. State Bar Ariz., Ariz. Acad., Maricopa County Bar Assn., Plaza Club. Office: PO Box 33907 Phoenix AZ 85067-3907

BEHAR, DAVID ALBERT, computer consultant; b. Seattle, Oct. 21, 1958; s. Albert David and Marilyn Diane (Edelson) B. BS in Computer Sci., U.

Wash., 1980; MBA, Seattle U., 1988, M of Software Engring., 1988. Programmer ENI Cos., Bellevue, Wash., 1979-80, programmer analyst, 1980-83; cons. Seattle, 1983—; acting dir. systems devel. Media Graphics, Inc., Seattle, 1985-86; acting dir. info. systems Catapult, Inc. (formerly Egghead U.), Bellevue, 1991-92. Advisor Jr. Achievement of Greater Puget Sound, Seattle, 1990-92, cons., 1991. Recipient Max Kaminoff Vol. of Yr. Stroum Jewish Community Ctr. of Greater Seattle, 1992. Mem. Assn. for Computing Machinery, Mensa.

BEHLER, ERNST HEITMAR, educator; b. Essen, West Germany, Sept. 4, 1928; came to U.S., 1963, naturalized, 1976; s. Philip and Elisabeth (Lammerskoetter) B.; m. Diana Elizabeth Ipsen, Nov. 24, 1967; children—Constantine, Sophia, Caroline. Ph.D., U. Munich, Germany, 1951; postgrad., Sorbonne, Paris, France, 1951-53; Habilitation, U. Bonn, Germany, 1961. Asst. prof. philosophy U. Bonn, 1961-63; prof. Germanics and comparative lit. Washington U., St. Louis, 1963-65; prof. U. Wash., 1965—, chmn. humanities council, 1972-78, chmn. dept. comparative lit., dir. program humanities, 1975—; hon. prof. U. B.C., Can., Vancouver, 1968-73. Author: Die Ewigkeit der Welt, 1965, Friedrich Schlegel, 1968, Japanese transl., 1974, Klassische Ironie, Romantische Ironie, Tragische Ironie, 1972; Editor: Critical Edit. of Friedrich Schlegel, 35 vols, 1958—; Contbr. numerous articles on romantic movement, history of Aristotelianism during Middle Ages, and on lit. criticism to profl. jours. Guggenheim fellow, 1967, 75-76; Am. Philos. Soc. grantee, 1969, 72; Am. Council Learned Socs. fellow, 1970; grantee, 1974. Mem. Am. Comparative Lit. Assn., Ovidianum Societas (Bucharest, Roumania) (honoris causa), Medieval Acad. Am., Am. Soc. Eighteenth Century Studies, Am. Lessing Soc., Modern Lang. Assn. Am. Home: 5525 NE Penrith Rd Seattle WA 98105-2844 Office: U of Washington Dept of Comparative Lit GN 32 Seattle WA 98195

BEHLMER, RUDY H., JR., writer, film educator; b. San Francisco, Oct. 13, 1926; s. Rudy H. and Helen Mae (McDonough) B.; 1 child by previous marriage, Curt; m. Stacey Endres, Oct. 1992. Student, Pasadena Playhouse Coll., 1946-49, Los Angeles City Coll., 1949-50. Dir. Sta. KLAC-TV, Hollywood, Calif., 1952-56; network TV dir. ABC-TV, Hollywood, 1956-57; TV comml. producer-dir., exec. Grant Advt., Hollywood, 1957-60; exec. producer-dir. Sta. KCOP-TV, Hollywood, 1960-63; v.p., TV comml. producer-dir. Hollywood office Leo Burnett USA, 1963-84; lectr. film Art Ctr. Coll. of Design, Pasadena, Calif., 1967-92, Calif. State U., Northridge, 1984-92, UCLA, 1988. Author: Memo from David O. Selznick, 1972, (with Tony Thomas) Hollywood's Hollywood, 1975, America's Favorite Movies-Behind the Scenes, 1982, Inside Warner Bros., 1985, Behind the Scenes: The Making of..., 1990, Memo From Darryl F. Zanuck, 1993; co-author: The Films of Errol Flynn, 1969; text on warner Bros. Fifty Years of Film Music, 1973; editor: The Adventures of Robin Hood, 1979, The Sea Hawk, 1982 (Wis./Warner Bros. screenplay series); contbr. articles on film history; writer and narrator for laserdiscs. Served with AC, USNR, 1944-46. Mem. Dirs. Guild Am.

BEHNEY, CHARLES AUGUSTUS, JR., veterinarian; b. Bryn Mawr, Pa., Nov. 30, 1929; s. Charles Augustus and Victoria Parks (Wythe) B.; B.S., U. Wyo., D.V.M., Colo. State U., 1961; m. Judith Ann Boggs, May 26, 1979; children—Charles Augustus III, Keenan F. Owner, Cochise Animal Hosp., Bisbee, Ariz., 1961—; veterinarian, dir. S.W. Traildust Zoo, Bisbee, 1966—; owner Kazam Arabians, Bisbee, 1969—; asso. prof. Cochise Coll. Chmn., Comprehensive Health Planning, Cochise County, Ariz., 1968. Mem. Am. Vet. Med. Assn., Soc. for Breeding Soundness, Internat. Platform Assn. Republican. Episcopalian. Rotarian, Elk. Patentee ultrasound device and eye cover for treating infections, apparatus to alter equine leg conformation, external vein clamp, equine sanitation instrument; developer ear implant instrumentation system. Home and Office: PO Box 4337 Bisbee AZ 85603-4337

BEHNKE, JOE MARTIN, bank executive; b. Roswell, N.Mex., June 23, 1950; s. Emil Martin and Grace Mary (Mullen) B.; m. Elizabeth Ann Sanchez, Jan. 3, 1970; children: Theresa, Sarah. AA, Ea. N.Mex. U., 1970. Lic. real estate appraiser, N.Mex. Staff nurse St. Joseph's Hosp., Albuquerque, 1971-72; staff mgr. Ky. Cen. Life Ins. Co., Roswell, 1972-76; loan adjuster 1st Nat. Bank Roswell, 1976-77, loan officer, 1978-81; mgr. trainee 1st Nat. Bank Albuquerque, 1978; asst. v.p. Chaves County Savs. & Loan, Roswell, 1981-82; v.p., mgr. consumer loans 1st Fed. Savs. Bank N.Mex., Roswell, 1982-91, sr. v.p., 1991—. Pres. Roswell Fireworks Com., 1984. Mem. KC (state sec. 1985-87, state dep. 1987-89), Pecos Valley Sertoma (pres. 1984). Republican. Roman Catholic. Office: 1st Savs Bank NMex 300 N Pennsylvania St Roswell NM 88202

BEHRENBRUCH, WILLIAM DAVID, filmmaker, educator; b. South Bend, Ind., July 23, 1946; s. Willard Herman and Mildred Kathleen (Steele) B.; m. Ingrid M. Neuschwander, Aug. 16, 1969 (div. 1975). Student, Ind. U., 1970-71; BA, Brooks Inst., 1974. Editor Rex Fleming Prodns., Santa Barbara, Calif., 1974-76, Golden Coast Films, Santa Barbara, 1976; pres. Visual Systems, Santa Barbara, 1976—; adj. instr. Brooks Inst., Santa Barbara, 1978—. Graphic designer (motion picture) Sweat, 1986; designer optical effects and titles Death Spa, 1986, War, 1986, Private Road, 1987, Blue Movies, 1987, Prime Suspect, 1988, Never Cry Devil, 1988, Ghosts Can't Do It, 1989, The Night Visitor, 1989, The Treasure, 1990, Grim Prairie Tales, 1990. Served to sgt. USAF, 1966-70. Mem. Soc. Motion Picture and TV Engrs., Assn. Ind. Video and Film Producers, Aircraft Owners and Pilots Assn. Club: Santa Barbara Flying. Office: Visual Systems 2050 Alameda Padre Serra Santa Barbara CA 93103-1761

BEHREND, DONALD FRASER, university administrator; b. Manchester, Conn., Aug. 30, 1931; s. Sherwood Martin and Margaret (Fraser) B.; m. Joan Belcher, Nov. 9, 1957; children: Andrew Fraser, Eric Hemingway, David William. BS with honors and distinction, U. Conn., 1958, MS, 1960; PhD in Forest Zoology, SUNY, Syracuse, 1966. Forest game mgmt. specialist Ohio Dept. Natural Resources, Athens, 1960; res. asst. Coll. Forestry, SUNY, Newcomb, 1960-63, res. assoc., 1963-67; dir. Adirondack ecol. ctr. Coll. Environ. Science and Forestry, SUNY, Newcomb, 1968-73; acting dean grad. studies Syracuse, 1973-74; asst. v.p. research programs, exec. dir. Inst. Environ. Program Affairs, 1974-79, v.p. acad. affairs, prof., 1979-85, prof. emeritus, 1987—; asst. prof. wildlife mgmt. U. Maine, Orono, 1967-68; provost, v.p. acad. affairs U. Alaska Statewide System, Fairbanks, 1985-87, exec. v.p., provost, 1988; chancellor U. Alaska, Anchorage, 1988—; mem. patent policy bd. SUNY, 1983-85, chmn. Res. Found. com. acad. res. devel., 1984-85; chmn. 6-Yr. planning com. U. Alaska, 1985-86; bd. dirs. Commonwealth North, 1991-92; mem. selection com. Harry S. Truman Scholarship Found.; mem. Pres.' Commn., NCAA, 1992. Contbr. numerous articles and papers to profl. jours. Mem. Newcomb Planning Bd., 1967-69; mem., pres. Bd. Edn. Newcomb Cent. Sch., 1967-73; chmn. governing bd. N.Y. Sea Grant Inst., 1984-85; trustee U. Alaska Found., 1990—. Served with USN, 1950-54. Mem. Wildlife Soc., Soc. Am. Foresters, AAAS, Phi Kappa Phi (hon.), Sigma Xi, Gamma Sigma Delta, Sigma Lambda Alpha (hon.). Lodges: Rotary (bd. dirs. Fairbanks club 1985-86), Lions (bd. dirs. Newcomb club 1966-67). Home: 333 M St # 403 Anchorage AK 99501 Office: U Alaska Anchorage Office of Chancellor Adm 214 3211 Providence Dr Anchorage AK 99508-4614

BEHRENS, JUNE ADELLE, writer; b. Maricopa, Calif., Apr. 25, 1925; d. Mark H. and Mattie Aline (Stafford) York; m. Henry William Behrens, Aug. 23, 1948; children: Terry Lynne, Denise Noel. BA, U. Calif., Santa Barbara, 1947; MA in Edn. Adminstrn., U. So. Calif., L.A., 1961; postgrad., UCLA, 1964-65, 73-74. Tchr. Hermosa Beach (Calif.) City Schs., 1947-48, Torrance (Calif.) Schs., 1950-54, 56-58, Am. Dependent Schs., Fed. Republic Germany, France, 1954-56; tchr., adminstr., reading specialist L.A. City Schs., 1958-80; reading specialist Carson (Calif.) Sch., 1968-74; with Park Western Pl. Sch., San Pedro, Calif., 1974-80; writer, 1962—. Author: Soo Ling Finds A Way, 1965, Who Am I?, 1968, Walk in Neighborhood, 1968, Earth is Home, 1971, Farm, 1971, Desert, 1973, Feast of Thanksgiving, 1974, Death Valley, 1980, The Manners Book, 1980, Whalewatch!, 1980, (biography) Ronald Reagon, 1981, Gung Hay Fat Choy, 1982, Hanukkah, 1983, Powwow, 1983, (biography) Sally Ride, 1984, ICan Be An Astronaut, 1984, I Can Be A Truck Driver, 1985, I Can Be A Pilot, 1985, Miss Liberty, First Lady, 1986, Samoans!, 1986, I Can Be A Nurse, 1986, Whales of the World, 1987, Passover, 1987, (biography) Juliette Low, 1988, (biography) George Bush, 1989, Dolphins!, 1989, Sharks!, 1989, (biography) Barbara Bush, 1990, Spanish California and the Mission Trail, 1993. Docent Museum of Natural History. Named Disting. Alumni of Yr., U. Calif. Santa Barbara, 1979. Mem. Internat. Reading Assn., So. Calif. Coun. on Lit.-Children & Young People, Soc. Children's Book Writers, Delta Kappa Gamma. Democrat. Home: 829 Mission Canyon Rd Santa Barbara CA 93105-2171

BEHRING, KENNETH E., professional sports team owner; b. Freeport, Ill., June 13, 1928; s. Elmer and Mae (Priewe) B.; m. Patricia Riffle, Oct. 16, 1949; children: Michael, Thomas, David, Jeffrey, Scott. Student, U. Wis., 1947. Owner Behring Motors, Monroe, Wis., 1953-56, Behring Corp., Ft. Lauderdale, Fla., 1956-72; owner Blackhawk Corp., Danville, Calif., 1972—, also chmn. bd. dirs.; owner Seattle Seahawks, NFL, 1988—; Calif. land developer; mem. policy adv. bd. real estate and urban econs. U. Calif., Berkeley.; chmn. bd. dirs. Behring-Hofmann Ednl. Inst., Inc. U. Calif. Trustee U. Calif., Berkeley; regent St. Mary's Coll., Moraga, Calif., Holy Name Coll., Oakland, Calif.; hon. trustee Mt. Diablo Hosp. Found., Concord, Calif.; hon. chmn. Seattle Art Mus., Am. Cancer Soc., Muscular Dystrophy, Silverado Concours. Named Man of Yr. Boys Town Italy, Entrepreneur of Yr. INC mag. Mem. Am. Acad. Achievement (honoree 1989), Assn. Wash. Bus., Seattle Master Builders Assn., Blackhawk Club, Vintage Club, Seattle Yacht Club, Wash. Athletic Club. Office: Blackhawk Corp PO Box 807 Danville CA 94526-0807 also: Seattle Seahawks 11220 NE 53rd St Kirkland WA 98033*

BEICHMAN, ARNOLD, political scientist, educator, writer; b. N.Y.C., May 17, 1913; s. Solomon and Mary Beichman; mm. Doris Modry (div. 1946); m. Carroll Aikins, Oct. 9, 1950; children: Charles, Janine, John, Anthony (dec.). BA in Polit. Sci., Columbia U., MA in Polit. Sci., PhD in Polit. Sci., 1973. Assoc. prof., polit. scientist U. Mass., 1970-78; assoc. prof. polit. sci. U. B.C., 1974-75, U. Calgary, Alta., Can.; 1977; adj. prof. polit. sci. Georgetown U.; mem. editorial adv. bd., columnist Washington Times; vis. scholar Hoover Instn., 1982—, rsch. fellow, 1988—. Author: The "Other" State Department, Herman Wouk: The Novelist as Social Historian, Nine Lies About America, (with others) Yuri Andropov: New Challenge to the West, The Long Pretense: Soviet Treaty Diplomacy from Lenin to Gorbachev, Anti-American Myths: Their Causes and Consequences; contbr. numerous articles to profl. jours. Founding mem. Consortium for the Study of Intelligence, Washington. Home: PO Box 37, Naramata, BC Canada V0H 1N0 Office: Hoover Instn Stanford U Stanford CA 94305

BEICKEL, SHARON LYNNE, psychologist; b. Hanford, Calif., Mar. 1, 1943; d. William Wayne and Kathleen (Haun) B.; m. Wilbur Oran Hutton, Aug. 8, 1964 (div. Aug. 1974); m. Roland G. Bomstad Jr., Sept. 1, 1991. BS, Ea. Oreg. State U., 1965; MS, U. Oreg., 1970, PhD, 1977. Lic. psychologist, Oreg., Ariz. With U. Oreg., Eugene, 1966-78, dir. Debusk counseling ctr., 1975-76, intern in psychology, 1976-77; psychologist Ariz. State U., Tempe, 1978-84; pvt. practice Tempe, 1978-84; psychologist Beickel and Assocs., Eugene, 1984—; clin. dir. Aslan House Counseling Ctr., Eugene, 1985-86; cons. Vocat. Rehab., Eugene, 1986—. Mem. APA, Oreg. Psychol. Assn. (bd. dirs. 1986-88, chair profl. affairs com. 1989-90), Lane County Psychol. Assn. (sec., treas. 1986-87, bd. dirs. 1986-90), Western Psychol. Assn., Ariz. Psychol. Assn., Zonta (bd. dirs. 1990-92). Home: 1678 Orchard St Eugene OR 97403-2034 Office: Beickel & Assocs 1244 Walnut Ste E Eugene OR 97403

BEILBY, ALVIN LESTER, chemistry educator; b. Watsonville, Calif., Sept. 17, 1932; s. Claud Eldred and Elma Fern (Hockabout) B.; m. Ruby Irene Nelson, June 21, 1958; children: Mark Alfred, Lorene Sigrid. BA, San Jose State U., 1954; postgrad., Harvard U., 1954-55; PhD, U. Wash., 1958. Instr. Pomona Coll., Claremont, Calif., 1958-60, asst. prof., 1960-66, assoc. prof., 1966-72, prof. chemistry, 1972—, chmn. dept. chemistry, 1972-85, chmn. sci. div., 1987-90; vis. scholar U. Ill., Urbana, 1964-65; guest worker, research chemist Nat. Bur. Standards, Gaithersburg, Md., 1971-72; guest worker Lockheed Research Lab., Palo Alto, Calif., 1979-80; guest prof. Uppsala U., Sweden, 1986-87. Co-author: Laboratory Manual for Chemistry: A Quantitative Approach, 1969; editor: Modern Classics in Analytical Chemistry, Vol. I, 1970, Vol. II, 1976; contbr. articles to profl. jours. Moderator Claremont United Ch. of Christ Congl., 1975-77; vice moderator, then moderator and bd. dirs. So. Calif. Conf., United Ch. of Christ, 1983-85; corp. mem. Congl. Homes, Inc., Pomona, Calif., 1986-92; bd. dirs. Calif. Christian Home (Christian Ch., Disciples of Christ), Rosemead, Calif., 1990—, treas., 1993—. Sci. Faculty Profl. Devel. award NSF, 1979-80; Standard Oil Co. Calif. fellow U. Wash., 1957-58. Mem. AAAS, Am. Chem. Soc. (Petroleum Rsch. Fund faculty award for advanced study 1964-65), Assn. Am. Med. Colls., Western Assn. Advisors for Health Professions, (lst chmn. 1970-71), Internat. Union Pure and Applied Chemistry (affiliate), Sigma Xi. Democrat. Home: 663 W Hood Dr Claremont CA 91711-3432 Office: Pomona Coll Seaver Chemistry Lab 645 N College Ave Claremont CA 91711-6338

BEILENSON, ANTHONY CHARLES, congressman; b. New Rochelle, N.Y., Oct. 26, 1932; s. Peter and Edna (Rudolph) B.; m. Dolores Martin, June 20, 1959; children: Peter, Dayna, Adam. B.A., Harvard Coll., 1954; LL.B., Harvard U., 1957. Bar: Calif. 1957. Mem. Calif. Assembly from 59th Dist., 1963-66, Calif. Senate from 22d Dist., 1967-76, 95th-103rd Congresses from 23rd (now 24th) Calif. Dist., 1977—. Democrat. Office: Ho of Reps 2465 Rayburn Bldg Washington DC 20515

BEKAVAC, NANCY YAVOR, college president, lawyer; b. Pitts., Aug. 28, 1947; d. Anthony Joseph and Elvira (Yavor) B. BA, Swarthmore Coll., 1969; JD, Yale U., 1973. Bar: Calif. 1974, U.S. Dist. Ct. (cen. dist.) 1974, (no. dist.) Calif. 1975, (so. dist.) Calif. 1976, U.S. Ct. Appeals (9th cir.) 1975, (8th cir.) 1981, U.S. Supreme Ct. 1979. Law clk. at large U.S. Ct. Appeals (D.C. cir.), Washington, 1973-74; assoc. Munger, Tolles & Rickershauser, L.A., 1974-79, ptnr., 1980-85; exec. dir. Thomas J. Watson Found., Providence, 1985-87, cons., 1987-88; counselor to pres. Dartmouth Coll., Hanover, N.H., 1988-90; pres. Scripps Coll., Claremont, Calif., 1990—; adj. prof. law UCLA Law Sch., 1982-83. Bd. mgrs. Swarthmore Coll., 1984-88, 90—; trustee Wenner-Gren Found. for Anthrop. Rsch., 1987—. Recipient Human Rights award L.A. County Commn. on Civil Rights, 1984; Woodrow Wilson fellow, Thomas J. Watson fellow, 1969. Mem. L.A. County Bar Assn. (trustee 1980-84, chair com. on individual rights and responsibilities 1984-85), Assn. Bus. Trial Lawyers (lectr. 1985). Office: Scripps Coll Office of President 10th & Columbus Claremont CA 91711*

BEKEY, GEORGE ALBERT, engineer, computer scientist, educator; b. Bratislava, Czechoslovakia, June 19, 1928; came to U.S., 1945, naturalized, 1956; s. Andrew and Elizabeth B.; m. Shirley White, June 10, 1951; children: Ronald Steven, Michelle Elaine. B.S. with honors, U. Calif., Berkeley, 1950; M.S., UCLA, 1952, Ph.D., 1962. Research engr. UCLA, 1950-54; mgr. computer center Beckman Instruments, Los Angeles and Berkeley, 1955-58; mem. sr. staff, dir. computer center TRW Systems Group, Redondo Beach, Calif., 1958-62; mem. faculty U. So. Calif., Los Angeles, 1962—, prof. elec. and biomed. engring. and computer sci., 1968-82, chmn. dept. elec. engring. systems, 1978-86; dir. Robotics Inst., chmn. computer sci. dept. U. So. Calif., L.A., 1984-89, dir. Ctr. for Mfg. and Automation Research, 1987—; chair computer sci. Gordon Marshall, 1990—; cons. to govt. agys. and indsl. orgns. Author: (with W.J. Karplus) Hybrid Computation, 1968; editor 3 books; mem. editorial bd. 3 profl. jours.; founding editor IEEE Trans. Robotics and Automation; contbr. over 140 articles to profl. jours.; patentee in field. Served with U.S. Army, 1954-56. Recipient Disting. Faculty award, 1977, Sch. Engring. and Service award U. So. Calif., 1990. Fellow AAAS, IEEE, Am. Inst. Med. and Biol. Engring.; mem. NAE, Am. Assn. for Artificial Intelligence, Assn. for Computing Machinery, Soc. for Computer Simulation, Neural Network Soc., Biomed. Engring. Soc., World Affairs Coun., Sigma Xi, Tau Beta Pi, Eta Kappa Nu. Office: U So Calif Dept Computer Sci Los Angeles CA 90089-0781

BEKEY, SHIRLEY WHITE, psychotherapist; b. L.A.; d. Lawrence Francis and Alice (King) White; m. George Albert Bekey, June 10, 1951; children: Ronald S., Michelle E. BA in Psychology, Occidental Coll., 1949; MSW in Psychiat. Social Work, UCLA, 1954; PhD in Edn. Psychology, U. So. Calif., 1980. Lic. social worker, Calif. Caseworker outpatient svcs. Calif. State Dept. Mental Health, Montebello; caseworker Lowman Sch. for Handicapped, L.A. Unified Sch. Dist., North Hollywood, Calif., 1971-72; psychotherapist Hofmann Psychiat. Clinic, Glendale (Calif.) Adventist Hosp., 1973-75; pvt. practice psychotherapy Encino, Calif., 1980—; mem. staff Woodview Calabasas (Calif.) Hosp., Van Nuys (Calif.) Hosp., Northridge (Calif.) Hosp. Mem. World Affairs Coun., L.A., 1960—. Fellow Soc. for Clin. Social Work; mem. NASW, Am. Psychol. Assn., Am. Ednl. Rsch. Assn., Nat. Assn. Gifted Children, Assn. Ednl. Therapists, Analytical Psychology Club L.A. Democrat. Office: 18075 Ventura Blvd Encino CA 91316-3521

BEKIR, NAGWA ESMAT, electrical engineer, educator, consultant; b. Cairo, Dec. 31, 1944; came to U.S., 1972; s. Mohammed Ragab Shalaby and Kamla (Abdel Megeed) Mahmood; m. Esmat Chibl, Sept. 23, 1971; children: Ahmad C., Badr E. BSEE, Cairo U., Egypt, 1966; MSEE, U. So. Calif., 1975, PhD in EE, 1978. Rsch. and hardware engr. Egyptian Indsl. Rsch. Inst., Cairo, 1966-69; quality control engr. Nat. Egyptian Co. for TV and Electronics, Cairo, 1969-72; mem. tech. staff Axiomatics, L.A., 1978, Hughes Aircraft Co., Canoga Park, Calif., 1978-80; assoc. prof. elec. and computer engring. dept. Calif. State U., Northridge, 1980-83, prof., 1984—; tech. staff ITT Gilfillan, Van Nuys, Calif., 1984; sr. staff engr. Hughes Aircraft Co., Canoga Park, Calif., 1985; cons. Aircraft div. Northrop Co., El Segundo, Calif., 1987; cons. Budlong & Assocs., Inc., Agoura Hills, Calif., 1992—. Contbr. articles to profl. jours. Mem. Calif. State U. Affirmative action com., 1986-88. Recipient Meritorious Performance and Profl. Promise award Calif. State U., Northridge, 1989, Outstanding Faculty awards Sch. of Engring. and Computer Sci., 1990. Mem. IEEE (sr.), Health and Tennis Corp. Am., Eta Kappa Nu, Tau Beta Pi. Office: Calif State U 18111 Nordhoff St Northridge CA 91330-0001

BELCHER, WILLIAM WALTER, JR., electronics company executive; b. Sayre, Pa., Oct. 22, 1943; s. William Walter Sr. and Mildred Rae (Smith) B.; m. Carole Jean Drake, June 12, 1965; children: Jon Christian, Katryna Dora. BE, Mansfield (Pa.) State Coll., 1964. Cert. tchr., Pa. Tchr. Galeton (Pa.) Pub. Schs., 1964-65, Susquehanna Valley Cen. Schs., Conklin, N.Y., 1965-66; quality engr. GE, Binghamton, N.Y., 1966-74, mgr. quality engring., 1974-75; mgr. reliability and quality assurance GE, Erie, Pa., 1975-79; mgr. x-ray tube mfg. GE, Milw., 1979-85; mgr. mfg. GE, Syracuse, N.Y., 1985-87; v.p. ops. NavCom Def. Electronics, Inc., El Monte, Calif., 1988—. Mem. adv. coun. Calif. State Poly. Inst., Pomona, Calif., 1988—, ind. adv. coun. El Monte Adult Edn.; chmn. com. Boy Scouts Am., Erie, 1978, Waukesha, Wis., 1983-85; mem. adminstrv. coun. Salem Meth. Ch., Waukesha, 1981; elder First Presbyn. Ch., Waukesha, 1985; mem. fin. com. United Meth. Ch., Glendora. Recipient Nat. Dir.'s award for outstanding achievement in labor rels. U.S. Dept. Labor, 1991. Mem. Armed Forces Communications and Electronics Assn. Republican. Home: 609 E Calle Santa Barbara San Dimas CA 91773-3949 Office: NavCom Def Electronics Inc 4323 N Arden Dr El Monte CA 91731-1997

BELDING, MELVIN EARL, internist, educator; b. Arvada, Colo., Aug. 8, 1938; s. Earl J. and Esther (Wertin) B.; m. Anita M. Kurzenberger, June 11, 1960; children: Mark A., Gregory A. MD, U. Colo., Denver, 1962. Diplomate Am. Bd. Internal Medicine, also sub-bds. Infectious Disease and Pulmonary Medicine. Intern Met. Gen. Hosp., Cleve., 1962-63; resident in internal medicine U. Wash., 1965-67, chief resident in medicine, 1969-70; fellow Rsch.Tng. unit U. Wash. Sch. Medicine, 1967-69, 70-71; asst. prof. medicine U. Wash., Seattle, 1970-72, clin. assoc. prof., 1976—; pvt. practice, Bremerton, Wash., 1972-93; med. dir. KPS Health Svcs., Bremerton, 1993—; co-chmn. Wash. State Drug Utilization Coun., Olympia, 1991—. Contbr. articles to med. jours. Bd. dirs. Harrison Meml. Hosp., Bremerton, 1991—. Capt. USAR. 1963-65. Boettcher scholar U. Colo., 1960-62. Fellow ACP, Am. Coll. Chest Physicians; mem. Infectious Disease Soc. Am., Am. Soc. for Microbiology, Wash. Thoracic Soc. (pres. 1985-87), Wash. Med. Assn. (liaison com. 1991—), Waring Honor Soc., Alpha Omega Alpha, Phi Sigma. Office: KPS Health Plans 400 Warren Ave Bremerton WA 98310

BELILLE, RONALD, safety and security coordinator; b. Portland, Nov. 22, 1947; s. Frank and Geraldine (Kron) B. AA in Law Enforcement, Portland Community Coll., 1970; student, Fed. Law Enforcement Tng. Ctr., Glynco, Ga., 1978; BS in Adminstrn. Justice, Portland State U., 1979; AA in Occupational Safety and Health, Mt. Hood Community Coll., 1985; grad., Police Reserve Acad., Oregon City, Oreg., 1985; grad. Intermediate Security Acad., Clackamas Community Coll., 1987; AA in Mgmt. and Supervisory Devel., Portland Community Coll., 1988; postgrad., Portland State U., 1985. Cert. emergency med. technician 1. Correctional officer State Penitentiary, Salem, Oreg., 1972; fed. protective officer Fed. Protective Svcs., Portland, 1978; safety/security officer Precision Castparts, Portland, 1979-83, security coordinator, 1983—; CPR instr., first aid instr., portable fire extinguishers instr. Precision Castparts, 1983-85; chmn. steering com. Intermediate Security Acad. Clackamas Community Coll., 1987. Vol. asst. counselor Multiple County Adult Probation/Parole, Portland, Oreg., 1975; vol. asst. recognizance Officer Multiple County Ct., Oreg., 1982; mem. police and law enforcement task force Citizen's Crime Commn., 1989—); vice chair Citizens Bur. Adv. Coordinating Com. City of Portland; mem. Portland bur. adv. com. Portland Police Bureau; bd. dirs. Ryles Med. Ctr. Evaluation and Treatment. With USAF, 1966-68. Mem. Am. Soc. for Indsl. Security (chmn. legis. com. 1989-90, treas. 1990-91), Am. Soc. Safety Engrs., Nat. Assn. Chiefs Police, Portland Police Athletic Assn., Masons, Elks, Phi Theta Kappa. Home: 1238 SE 47th Ave Portland OR 97215-2512

BELJAN, JOHN RICHARD, university administrator, medical educator; b. Detroit, May 26, 1930; s. Joseph and Margaret Anne (Brozovich) B.; m. Bernadette Marie Marenda, Feb. 2, 1952; children: Ann Marie, John Richard, Paul Eric. B.S., U. Mich., 1951, M.D., 1954. Diplomate: Am. Bd. Surgery. Intern U. Mich., Ann Arbor, 1954-55, resident in gen. surgery, 1955-59; dir. med. services Stuart div. Atlas Chem. Industries, Pasadena, Calif., 1965-66; from asst. prof. to assoc. prof. surgery U. Calif. Med. Sch., Davis, 1966-74, from asst. prof. to assoc. prof. engring., 1968-74, from asst. dean to assoc. dean, 1971-74; prof. surgery, prof. biol. engring. Wright State U., Dayton, Ohio, 1974-83, dean Sch. Medicine, 1974-81, vice provost, 1974-78, v.p. health affairs, 1978-81, provost, sr. v.p., 1981-83; prof. arts and scis., assoc. v.p. med. affairs Cen. State U., Wilberforce, Ohio, 1976-83; provost, v.p. acad. affairs, dean Sch. Medicine Hahnemann U., Phila., 1983-85, prof. surgery and biomed. engring., 1983-86, spl. adviser to pres., 1985-86; v.p. acad. affairs Calif. State U., Long Beach, 1986-89, prof. anat., physiology and biomed. engring., 1986-91, provost, 1989-91; pres. Northrop U., L.A., 1989-93, pres. emeritus, 1993—; trustee Cox Heart Inst., 1975-77, Drew Health Center, 1977-78, Wright State U. Found., 1975-83, CSULB Found., 1986-89—, 49er Athletic Found., 1986-89; trustee, regional v.p. Engring. and Sci. Inst. Hall of Fame, 1983—; bd. dirs. Miami Valley Health Systems Agy., 1975-82, UCI Ctr for Health Edn., 1987-90, Long Beach Rsch. Found., 1989—; cons. in field. Author articles, revs., chpts. in books. Served with M.C. USAF, 1955-65. Decorated Commendation medal; Braun fellow, 1949; grantee USPHS, 1967—, NASA, 1968—. Fellow A.C.S.; mem. Aerospace Med. Assn., AAUP, AMA (council on sci. affairs 1978-87), F.A. Coller Surg. Soc., Biomed. Engring. Soc., IEEE, Instrument Soc. Am., Calif. Med. Assn., Los Angeles County Med. Assn., Phi Beta Delta, Phi Beta Kappa, Alpha Omega Alpha, Phi Eta Sigma, Phi Kappa Phi, Alpha Kappa Kappa. Clubs: Mich. Alumni (Dayton) (Outstanding Alumnus award 1976), Oakwood Fur, Fin and Feather. Lodge: Rotary. Home: 6490 E Saddle Dr Long Beach CA 90815-4740 Office: Northrop U PO Box 45065 Los Angeles CA 90045-0065

BELK, JOHN BLANTON, educational and cultural organization executive; b. Orlando, Fla., Feb. 4, 1925; s. John Blanton and Jennie (Wannamaker) B.; m. Elizabeth Jane Wilkes, Dec. 11, 1954; children: Virginia Elizabeth, Katherine Wilkes. Student, Davidson Coll., 1943, U. N.C., 1943-45. With Moral Re-Armament (numerous locations), 1950-68, exec. dir., 1966-68; founder, chmn. bd., pres. Up With People, Tucson, 1968-91, chmn. exec. com., 1991—. Bd. dirs. Internat. Fund Sports Disabled, Arnhem, Netherlands; mem. Gov.'s Ariz.-Mexico Commn. Lt. (j.g.) USNR, 1943-45. Decorated officer Order Vasco Nunez de Balboa (Panama); officer Order of Leopold (Belgium). Mem. Zeta Psi. Clubs: Mountain Oyster; Guaymas Yacht (Mexico). Home: 2920 E Cerrado Los Palitos Tucson AZ 85718-4222 Office: Up With People 7070 N Oracle Rd Ste 260 Tucson AZ 85704-4339

BELKNAP, KATHY ANDRE, college adminstrator; b. El Paso, Feb. 11, 1954; d. H. William and Barbara J. (Melton) B.; m. Warren Joe Day, May

18, 1974 (div. 1983); children: Jennifer Day, Bill Day; m. Wallace G. Kay, Aug. 10, 1984. B of Gen. Studies, U. Idaho, 1978; MEd, U. South Miss., 1985. Asst. to dir. honors program Boise (Idaho) State U., 1972-84; counselor student support program, 1987-89; grad. asst. U. So. Miss., Hattiesburg, 1984-85, acad. advisor, 1985; acad. advisor Utah State U., Logan, 1986; asst. dir. U. Idaho Engring. in Boise, 1989—; pres. Western Regional Honors Coun., Boise, 1979-81. Recipient Meritorious Svc. award Phi Kappa Phi, 1984. Mem. N.W. Assn. Student Pers. Adminstrs., Nat. Collegiate Honors Coun. Office: U Idaho Engring in Boise Boise ID 83725

BELL, ALAN, lawyer, environmental health activist; b. N.Y.C., Aug. 13, 1954; s. Julius and Vivian B.; m. Joyce Karen Rago, Mar. 8, 1986; 1 child, Ashlee. BBA magna cum laude, U. Miami, 1976, JD, 1979. Bar: Fla. 1979, U.S. Dist. Ct. (so. dist.) Fla. 1980. Cert. legal intern felony and juvenile divs. Dade County State Atty. Office, Miami, Fla., 1978-79; asst. state atty. Broward County, Ft. Lauderdale, Fla., 1980-86; corp. counsel and atty. The Travelers Insur. Co., Ft. Lauderdale, Fla., 1986-89; lawyer pvt. practice, 1989-91; pres., founder The Found. for Environ. Health Rsch., Tucson, Ariz., 1992—. Chief justice Student Supreme Ct., U. Miami, 1976. Mem. Omicron Delta Kappa (hon., pres.). Home and Office: Alan Bell Esq Found Environ Health Rsch 4161 N Camino del Calador Tucson AZ 85718

BELL, CHAROLETTE RENEE, psychologist; b. St. Louis, Jan. 23, 1949. BA, Dillard U., New Orleans, 1970; MA, U. No. Colo., Greeley, 1973; EdD, U. No. Colo., 1976. Sch. psychologist Aurora (Colo.) Pub. Schs., 1974-76, Cherry Creek Schs., Englewood, Colo., 1976-78; psychologist Orangeburg (S.C.) Area Mental Health Ctr., 1978-79; prin. investigator 1890 research S.C. State Coll., 1979-83; private practice Columbia, S.C., 1983-87; research and program evaluator S.C. Inst. Poverty & Deprivation, 1987-88; rsch. and program evaluator coll. edn. U. S.C., 1988-89; cons. Calif. State U., San Marcos, 1989-90, assoc. prof. edn. Coll. of Edn., 1990—; founder, chairperson Citizens Against Sexual Assault, O'burg, S.C., Columbia Coalition Black Concerns, Cola, S.C., 1987—; exec. dir. Project Soaring, Cola, 1986-87. Co-author: Discipline and Classroom Management, 1980, Added Dimensions in Fitness, 1984. Sec. Dem. Precinct Ward, Columbia, 1988. Home: PO Box 2111 San Marcos CA 92079-2111

BELL, CHESTER GORDON, computer engineering company executive; b. Kirksville, Mo., Aug. 19, 1934; s. Roy Chester and Lola Dolph (Gordon) B.; m. Gwendolyn Kay Druyor, Jan. 3, 1959; children: Brigham Roy, Laura Louise. BSEE, MIT, 1956, MSEE, 1957; DEng (hon.), WPI, 1993. Engr. Speech Communication Lab., MIT, Cambridge, 1959-60; mgr. computer design Digital Equipment Corp., Maynard, Mass., 1960-66, v.p. engring., 1972-83; prof. computer sci. Carnegie-Mellon U., 1966-72; vice chmn. Encore Computer Corp., Marlboro, Mass., 1983-86; asst. dir. NSF, Washington, 1986-87; v.p. R & D Stardent Computer, Sunnyvale, Calif., 1987-89; bd. dirs. Inst. Rsch. and Coordination Acoustic Music, Cirrus Logic, Chronologic Simulation, The Bell-Mason Group, Univ. Video Comm., Visix Software, Velox; bd. dirs., trustee Computer Mus., 1982—. Author: (with Newell) Computer Structures, 1971, (with Grason, Newell) Designing Computers and Digital Systems, 1972, (with Mudge, McNamara) Computer Engineering, 1978, (with Siewiorek, Newell) Computer Structures, 1982, (with McNamara) High Tech Ventures, 1991. Recipient 6th Mellon Inst. award, 1972. Fellow IEEE (McDowell award 1975, Eckert-Mauchly award 1982), AAAS (von Neumann medal 1992, Nat. Medal of Tech. 1991, AEA award for greatest econ. contbn. to region 1993); mem. Nat. Acad. Engring., Assn. for Computing Machinery (editor Computer Structures sect. 1972-78), Eta Kappa Nu. Home: 450 Old Oak Ct Los Altos CA 94022-2634

BELL, DANIEL CARROLL, campground management consultant, ranch manager; b. Chgo., July 17, 1940; s. Daniel Gregory and Inez Margarite (Carroll) B.; m. Elaine Paula Rhody, Feb. 1, 1960; children: Tana Lou, Daniel Arden, Andrea Jane. Student, Colo. State U., 1958-62, Reisch Coll. Auctioneering, Mason City, Iowa, 1983. Mgr. ptnr. Three Bell Ranch, Ft. Collins, Colo., 1958-69; sales rep. Pacific Vegetable Oil Co., San Francisco, 1969-70; mng. dir. Paveocor A.G. subs. PVO Internat., Rotterdam, Netherlands, 1970-71; nat. sales mgr. PVO Internat., San Francisco, 1971-72; v.p. commodity trading San Pablo Mfg. Co. subs. PVO Internat., Manila, Philippines, 1972-74; v.p. Rothschild Brokerage Co., San Francisco, 1975-76; owner, prin. Feed, Etc., Harbor, Oreg., 1976-79; commodity specialist Shearson Loeb Rhodes, Medford, Oreg., 1979-80; exec. v.p., gen. mgr. Superior Credit Assocs., Inc., Medford, 1981-86; mng. ptnr. Three Bell Land Co., Pierce, Colo., 1986-88; ptnr. Legacy Transp. Co., 1986—; photography judge, 1989—. Mem. Medford (Oreg.) Planning Coun., 1981-84, Medford Sister Cities Commn., 1984; treas. Jackson County Rep. Cen. Com., Medford, 1982-84; arbitrator Better Bus. Bur., Medford and Ft. Collins, Colo., 1984—; candidate Oreg. Ho. Reps., 1984. With USAR, 1958-63, Colo. Air N.G., 1963-65. Mem. Profl. Photographers Am., Photographic Soc. Am., Wildlife Photographers Assn., Am. Legion, Eaton Country Club, Heather Ridge Country Club, Elks. Republican. Presbyterian. Office: 4700 E Main St # 870 Mesa AZ 85205-8609

BELL, DAVID LEE, lawyer; b. Ponca City, Okla., Apr. 25, 1953; s. Wayne D. Bell; m. Janet Bell. BArch, U. Okla., 1977; JD, Southwestern U., 1990. Bar: Calif., 1990. Sr. programmer Quotron Systems, Inc., L.A., 1982-85; systems analyst Lisp Machines, Inc., L.A., 1985-86; mem. tech. staff TRW, Redondo Beach, Calif., 1986-87; assoc. Moore, Sorensen & Horner, Beverly Hills, Calif., 1990—; with LaFollette, Johnson, DeHaas, Fesler & Ames, L.A.; pres. Micro Systems Rsch., Hermosa Beach, Calif., 1988—. Author computer software: Brief-It, 1992. Mem. State Bar Calif. (intellectual property sect., corp. and bus. law sect.), Pres.'s Ptnrs. U. Okla., Sierra Club.

BELL, DENISE LOUISE, newspaper editor; b. Washington, Nov. 27, 1967; d. Richard Keith Bell and Kay Lorraine (Southerland) Reynolds. Student, Inst. Adventiste du Salare, Collonges, France, 1988; BA in French, Loma Linda U., 1990. Yearbook editor Loma Linda U., La Sierra, Calif., 1989-90; desk technician Loma Linda U., Loma Linda, Calif., 1990-92; staff writer Inland Empire Community Newspapers, Colton, Calif., 1990-91; city editor Inland Empire Community Newspapers, San Bernardino, Calif., 1991—. Asst. leader Girl Scouts U.S., Walla Walla Wash., 1986; co-leader Girl Scouts Switzerland, Geneva, 1987, Girl Scouts U.S., Loma Linda, 1988—. Mem. Toastmasters, Lions Club (mem. pub. rels. com.). Home: 25421 Cole St Apt U Loma Linda CA 92354-3112

BELL, DON WAYNE, financial consultant; b. Albemarle, N.C., Aug. 23, 1945; s. John Caswell and Margaret Syloma (Shave) B.; m. Sandra G. Lee, Aug. 2, 1989. AA, Clark Community, Vancouver, Wash., 1968; BA, Evergreen State Coll., 1978; JD, Lewis & Clark U., 1983. Bar: Oreg. 1983, Wash. 1991; cert. fin. planner. Co-owner Linnton Plywood, Portland, Oreg., 1976-81; fin. planner Resource Fin. Planning, Portland, 1981-89, Integrated Planning Svcs., Silverdale, Wash., 1989-90; chief exec. officer, pres. Kitsap Fin. Svcs., Bremerton, Wash., 1990-93; church financing cons. Poulsbo, Wash., 1993—; investment advisor Fin. Network Investment Corp., 1993—. Finance chair Pacific NW dist. Unitarian Universalist Assn., 1988-91. Mem. Internat. Assn. for Fin. Planning (Oreg. chpt., ethics officer, conf. chair, v.p., pres., bd. dirs. 1983-89), Am. Arbitration Assn. (securities panel 1988—). Office: 26818 Edgewater Blvd Ste B Poulsbo WA 98370-9516

BELL, DONALD ROBERT, engineer; b. Santa Barbara, Calif., Aug. 30, 1928; s. Stanley Garfield Vanderick and Ellen Agnes (Hart) B.; m. June Laverne Emge, Jan. 20, 1952 (div. Feb. 1962); children: Diane Elizabeth, Donna June; m. Dorothea Alice Searle, Oct. 13, 1962. Student, U.S. Naval Acad., 1948-49, West Coast U., 1953-54, Santa Monica (Calif.) City Coll., 1965-66. Registered quality engr., Calif., profl. engr., Calif. Asst. foreman Hughes Aircraft Co., Culver City, Calif., 1954-59; supr. Transvaal Electronics, El Segundo, Calif., 1959-60; sr. engring. aide Litton Systems, Inc., Woodland Hills, Calif., 1960-65; systems engring. asst. Hughes Aircraft Co., Culver City, 1965-67; test facilities engr. Hughes Aircraft Co., 1967-74, program quality engr., 1974-77, sr. project engr., 1977-78; sr. quality engr. Hughes Aircraft Co., El Segundo, 1978-83; staff engr. Hughes Aircraft Co., 1983-86, sr. staff engr., 1986-89; sr. staff engr. Electro-Optical and Data Systems Group, El Segundo, 1983-89; ret., 1989. Served with USN, 1950-54, Korea. Mem. NRA (life), U.S. Naval Acad. Alumni Assn. (nat. chpt. L.A. chpt.), Naval Inst. (life), Am. Assn. Ret. Persons, So. Calif. Past Masters Assn., Calif. Rifle and Pistol Assn. (life), Golden State Mobile Home Owners League, Inc., Calif. Rsch. Lodge (life), Hughes Aircraft Co. Mgmt. Club (life), West L.A. Builder's Club, Santa Monica Bay Staff Club, Masons (past master, Hiram award, mem. homes endowment bd.), Order Demolay, Ind. Order Foresters, Order Eastern Star, Internat. Order Job's Daus. Democrat. Home: Sp 276 1065 Lomita Blvd Harbor City CA 90710-1922

BELL, DONALD WILLIAM, experimental psychologist; b. Los Angeles, Apr. 28, 1936; s. Samuel Chamblis and Betty M. (Welz) B. BA, U. So. Calif., 1959, MA, 1963, PhD, 1966. Research assoc. Subcom. on Noise Research Ctr., Los Angeles, 1962-66; postdoctoral fellow Stanford (Calif.) U., 1966-68; research psychologist SRI Internat., Menlo Park, Calif., 1968-76, sr. research psychologist, 1976-82, program mgr., 1982-83, dir. speech research program, 1983-89; dir., sensory sci. and tech. ctr., 1989—; pres. Digital Voice Corp., 1982—. Contbr. articles to profl. jours. Mem. planning commn. Town of Portola Valley, Calif. Mem. IEEE, Acoustical Soc. Am., Psychonomic Soc., Am. Voice I/O Soc. (dir.). Republican. Home: 15 Peak Ln Portola Valley CA 94028-7753 Office: SRI Internat 333 Ravenswood Ave Menlo Park CA 94025-3493

BELL, JOSEPH JAMES, lawyer; b. Kansas City, Mo., Sept. 30, 1947; s. James Joseph and Mary Beatrice (O'Rourke) B. BA in Polit. Sci., U. Nev., Reno, 1969; JD, New Coll. of Calif., San Francisco, 1979. Bar: Calif. 1980, U.S. Dist. Ct. (no.dist.) Calif. 1980, U.S. Dist. Ct. (ea. dist.) Calif. 1981, U.S. Dist. Ct. (ctrl. dist.) Calif. 1988, U.S. Ct. Appeals (9th cir.) 1988. Student extern Pub. Advocates, Inc., San Francisco, 1976-77; supervising atty. Nevada County Legal Assistance, Inc., Grass Valley, Calif., 1980-81; sole practice Grass Valley, 1982—; pro tem judge Nevada County Superior Ct., Nevada City, Calif., 1988-91, Nevada County Mcpl. Ct., 1989—. Bd. dirs. Legal Svcs. No. Calif., Inc., Sacramento, 1981-84; mem. Dem. Ctrl. Com., Nevada County, Calif., 1982-86; vol. firefighter Ophir Hill Fire Dept., pres., 1991-92, bd. dirs., 1993—. Recipient Pro Bono award State Bar Calif., 1982, 87-88. Mem. Nevada County Bar (pres. 1986-87, family law sect., pro tem judge fee arbitration com. 1988—), Sierra Club (Sierra Nevada Group, officer Mother Lode chpt., Conservationist award 1991). Democrat. Office: 131 S Auburn St Ste 201 Grass Valley CA 95945

BELL, LARRY STUART, artist; b. Chgo., Dec. 6, 1939; s. Hyman David and Rebecca Ann (Kriegmont) B.; three children. Student, Chouinard Art Inst., L.A., 1957-59. One man exhbns. include Stedelijk Mus., Amsterdam, 1967, Pasadena (Calif.) Art Mus., 1972, Oakland (Calif.) Mus., 1973, Ft. Worth Art Mus., 1975, Santa Barbara (Calif.) Mus. Art, 1976, Washington U., St. Louis, 1976, Art Mus. So. Tex., Corpus Christi, 1976, Erica Williams, Anne Johnson Gallery, Seattle, 1978, Hayden Gallery, MIT, Cambridge, Mass., 1977, Hudson River Mus., Yonkers, N.Y., 1981, Newport Harbor Art Mus., 1982, Marian Goodman Gallery, N.Y.C., 1982, Ruth S. Schaffner Gallery, Santa Barbara, Calif., Arco Ctr. Visual Arts, L.A., 1983, Unicorn Gallery, Aspen, Colo., 1983, Butler Inst. Am. Art, Youngstown, Ohio, 1984, Leigh Yawkey Woodson Art Mus., Wausau, Wis., 1984, Colorado Springs, Colo. Fine Arts Ctr., 1987, Cleve. Ctr. for Contemporary Art, Ohio, 1987, Mus. Contemporary Art, L.A., 1987, Am. Acad. and Inst. Arts and Letters, N.Y.C., 1987, Boise (Idaho) Gallery Art, 1987, Gilbert Brownstone Gallery, Paris, 1987, Braunstein/Quay Gallery, San Francisco, 1987, 89, Fine Arts Gallery, N.Mex. State Fairgrounds, 1987, Laguna Art Mus., Laguna Beach, Calif., 1987, High Mus. Art, Atlanta, 1988, Sena Galleries West, Santa Fe, 1989, Kiyo Higashi Gallery, L.A., 1989, Musee D'Art Contemporain, Lyon, France, 1989, Contemporary Art Ctr., Kansas City, Mo., 1989, San Antonio Art Inst., 1990, New Gallery, Houston, 1990, Braunstein/Quay Gallery, San Francisco, 1990, Galerie Rolf Ricke, Koln, Fed. Republic Germany, 1990, Galerie Montenay, Paris, 1990, Kiyo Higashi Gallery, L.A., 1990, The Works Gallery, L.A., 1990, Galerie Kammer, Hamburg, Germany, 1990, Tony Shafrazi Gallery, N.Y.C., 1991, Tucson Mus. Art, 1991, New Gallery, Houston, 1991, Janus Gallery, Santa Fe, 1992, Kiyo Higashi Gallery, L.A., 1992, 93, New Gallery, Houston, 1992, Tampa Mus. Art, 1992, Kiyo Higashi Gallery, L.A., 1993, New Directions Gallery, Taos, N.M., 1993; group exhbns. include Mus. Modern Art, N.Y.C., 1965, 79, Jewish Mus., N.Y.C., 1966, Whitney Mus. Am. Art, 1966, Guggenheim Mus., N.Y.C., 1967, Tate Gallery, London, 1970, Hayward Gallery, London, 1971, Detroit Inst. Arts, 1973, Nat. Collections Fine Arts, 1975, San Francisco Mus. Modern Art, 1976, Museo de Arte Contemporaneo de Caracas, Venezuela, 1978, Aspen Ctr. for Visual Arts, 1980, Fruit Market Gallery, Edinburgh, Scotland, 1980, Albuquerque Mus., 1980, Art Inst. Chgo., 1982, Santa Barbara Art Mus., 1984, The Rufino Tamayo Mus., Mexico City, 1985, Colorado Springs Fine Art Ctr., 1986, Mus. Comtemporary Art, 1986, AAAL, 1986, Ariz. State U., Tempe, 1987, Phoenix Art Mus., 1987, Braunstein/Quay Gallery, 1987, The Works Gallery, Long Beach, 1987, Davis/McClain Gallery, Houston, 1987, Basel (Switzerland) Art Fair, 1989, Galerie Joan Prats, Barcelona, Spain, 1989, Musee d'Art Contemporain, Lyon, 1989, Harcus Gallery, Boston, 1989, Colorado Springs Gallery Contemporary Art, 1990, Mus. Contemporary Art, L.A., 1990, Musee de Grenoble, France, 1990, L.A. County Mus. Art, 1991, U. So. Calif. Fisher Gallery, L.A., 1991, Espace Lyonnais d'Art Contemporain, France, 1991, Galerie Montenay, Paris, 1991, Galerie Rolf Ricke, Köln, Germany, 1991, Arolsen, Germany, 1992, Leedy/Voulkos Gallery, Kansas City, Musee du Palais du Luxembourge, Paris, 1993, Denver Art Mus., 1993, New Gallery, Houston, 1993, Leedy/Voulkos Gallery, Kansas City, Mo., 1993, Musee du Palais du Luxembourge, Paris, 1993, Denver Art Mus., 1993, New Gallery, Houston, 1993; represented in permanent collections including Nat. Collection Fine Arts, Musee de Art Contemporaine, Lyon, France, Mus. of Fine Arts, Santa Fe, N.Mex., Whitney Mus. Am. Art, N.Y.C., Tate Gallery, London, Gallery New South Wales, Australia, Albright-Knox Gallery, Buffalo, Art Inst. Chgo., Denver Art Mus., Dallas Mus. Fine Arts, Guggenheim Mus., Houston, L.A. County Mus., Victoria and Albert Mus., London, San Antonio Mus. Art, The Menil Collection, Houston, Mpls. Inst. Arts, Mus. Ludwig, Koln, Albuquerque Mus., Mpls. Inst. Arts, others; instr. sculpture, U. South Fla., Tampa, U. Calif., Berkeley, Irvine, 1970-73, So. Calif. Inst. of Architecture, 1988, Taos (N.Mex.) Inst. of Art, 1989-93. Copley Found. grantee, 1962; Guggenheim Found. fellow, 1970; Nat. Endowment Arts grantee, 1975; recipient Gov.'s award for excellence in visual arts, N.Mex., 1990. Office: PO Box 4101 Taos NM 87571-9998

BELL, LEO S., retired physician; b. Newark, Nov. 7, 1913; s. Alexander M. and Marie (Saxon) B.; AB, Syracuse U., 1934; MD, 1938; m. Edith Lewis, July 3, 1938; children: Jewyl Linn, David Alden. Intern, N.Y.C. Hosp., 1938, Bklyn. Hosp., 1939-40; resident in pediatrics Sea View Hosp., N.Y.C., 1940-41, N.Y.C. Hosp., 1941-42; practice medicine specializing in pediatrics, San Mateo, Calif., 1946-86; mem. staff Mills Meml. Hosp., San Mateo, Peninsula Hosp. & Med. Ctr., Burlingame, Children's Hosp., San Francisco; assoc. clin. prof. pediatrics U. Calif. Med Sch., prof. emeritus San Francisco, Stanford Med. Sch. Palo Alto; mem. curriculum & ednl. affairs comm. U. San Francisco Med. Sch., adminstv. coun.; med. columnist San Mateo Times. Bd. dirs. Mills Hosp. Found., San Mateo, U. Calif. San Francisco Hosp., San Mateo County Heart Assn., Hillsborough Schs. Found. (Calif.), 1980-83. Capt. as flight surgeon USAAF, 1942-46. Recipient bronze and silver medals Am. Heart Assn. Diplomate Am. Bd. Pediatrics. Fellow Am. Acad. Pediatrics, Am. Pub. Health Assn.; mem. Calif. Fedn. Pediatric Socs. (pres.), Am. Fedn. Pediatric Socs. (pres.), Calif. Med. Assn., Am. Pub. Health Assn., Air Force Assn., AMA (alt. del. to ho. of dels.), Calif. Med. Assn. (ho. of dels.), San Mateo County Med. Assn., Internat. Snuff Bottle Soc., Hong Kong Snuff Bottle Soc., San Francisco Gem and Mineral Soc., World Affairs Coun. San Francisco, U. San Francisco Med. Sch. Clin. Faculty Assn. (coun., pres.), Peninsula Golf and Country Club, Commonwealth Club. Contbr. articles to profl. jours. Home: 220 Roblar Ave Burlingame CA 94010-6846 Office: PO Box 1877 San Mateo CA 94401-0948

BELL, MAXINE TOOLSON, librarian, state legislator; b. Logan, Utah, Aug. 6, 1931; d. John Max and Norma (Watson) Toolson; m. H. Jack Bell, Oct. 26, 1949; children: Randy J. (dec.), Jeff M., Scott Alan (dec.). Assocs. in Libr. Sci., Coll. So. Idaho; CSI, Idaho State U., 1975. Librarian Sch. Dist. 261, Jerome, Idaho, 1975-88; mem. Idaho Ho. of Reps., 1988-. Bd. dirs. Idaho Farm Bureau, 1976-88; rep. western states Am. Farm Bureau Women, 1980-93, vice-chmn., 1993—; mem. Jerome County Rep. Precinct Com., 1980-88. Home: 194 S 300 E Jerome ID 83338-6532

BELL, NORMAN FRANCIS, journalist; b. Troy, N.Y., July 6, 1948; s. Marc E. Bell and Marjorie E. (Francis) Roy; m. Lisa Diane Hayner, Nov. 20, 1971. B. Commerce, McGill U., (Que.), 1970; MA in Am. Studies, Union Coll., 1990. Copy editor Troy Record, N.Y., 1970-73; city editor Knickerbocker News, Albany, N.Y., 1973-77; metro editor Detroit News, 1977-78; asst. managing editor Columbus Citizen Jour., Ohio, 1979-81; managing editor Albuquerque Tribune, 1981-85, Morning News Tribune, 1985-91; Mc Mahon Centennial prof. of news communication Univ. Okla., Norman, 1992—. Mem. N. Mex. Associated Press Managing Editors (pres. 1982-84). Office: Univ Oklahoma Copeland Hall Norman OK 73069

BELL, SHARON KAYE, small business owner; b. Lincoln, Nebr., Sept. 14, 1943; d. Edwin B. and Evelyn F. (Young) Czachurski; m. James P. Kittrell (div. Sept. 1974); children: Nathan James, Nona Kaye; m. Joseph S. Bell, June 5, 1976; stepchildren: Eugene, Patricia, Bobbie, Linda. Continuing edn./active tax preparer/interviewer assoc., H&R Block, Laguna Hills, 1987—. Various positions mgmt., bookkeeping, 1961-71; bookkeeper Internat. Harvester, Chesapeake, Va., 1971-73, Cheat'AH Engring., Santa Ana, Calif., 1973-74, Fre Del Engring., Santa Ana, Calif., 1974-75; bookkeeper/mgr. Tek Sheet Metal Co., Santa Ana, Calif., 1975-79; owner, bookkeeper Bell's Bookkeeping, Huntington Beach, Calif., 1979-86, Fountain Valley, Calif., 1986—, Laguna Hills, Calif., 1986—; tax preparer H.R. Block, 1989—. Mem. Inst. Mgmt. Accts. (bd. dirs. 1985-86, sec. 1986-87, v.p. 1987-90, dir. manuscripts 1990-91), Nat. Notary Assn., NAFE, Wives of Submarine Vets. World War II (v.p. L.A. chpt. 1986-87, treas. 1990-92), Nat. Soc. Pub. Accts., Internat. Platform Assn. Republican. Office: Bells Bookkeeping PO Box 2713 Laguna Beach CA 92654-2713

BELL, WAYNE STEVEN, lawyer; b. L.A., June 24, 1954; s. Joseph and Jane Barbara (Barsook) B.; m. M. Susan Modzelewski, Apr. 1, 1989. BA magna cum laude, UCLA, 1976; JD, Loyola U., L.A., 1979; postgrad., Rutgers U., 1992. Bar: Calif. 1980, U.S. Dist. Ct. (cen. dist.) 1981, U.S. Tax Ct. 1981, U.S. Ct. Appeals (9th cir.) 1981, U.S. Dist. Ct. (so. and no. dists.) Calif. 1983, U.S. Supreme Ct. 1984, D.C. 1986; lic. real estate broker, Calif. Intern office of gov. State of Calif., Sacramento, summer 1976; assoc. Levinson, Rowen, Miller, Jacobs & Kabrins, L.A., 1980-82; sr. assoc. Montgomery, Gascou, Gemmill & Thornton, L.A., 1982-84; counsel, project developer Thomas Safran & Assocs., L.A., 1984-85; of counsel Greenspan, Glasser & Medina, Santa Monica, Calif., 1984-86; assoc. gen. counsel Am. Diversified Cos., Costa Mesa, Calif., 1985-88; legal cons. Project Atty., L.A., 1988-89; assoc. counsel Ralphs Grocery Co., L.A., 1989—; judge pro tem Mcpl. Ct. South Bay Jud. Dist., 1987, L.A. Superior Ct., 1991; settlement officer L.A. Mcpl. Ct., Settlement Officer Program, 1990-92; spl. master State Bar of Calif., 1991-92. Chief note and comment editor Loyola U. Law Rev., 1978-79; contbr. articles to profl. jours. and gen. pubs. Vol. atty. Westside Legal Services, Santa Monica, 1982-87; legal ombudsman Olympics Ombudsman program L.A. County Bar Assn., 1984; gov. appointed mem. Calif. adv. council Legal Services Corp., 1982-88, Autism Soc. Am., Amnesty Internat.; contbg. mem. Dem. Nat. Com., So. Poverty Law Ctr.; charter mem. presdl. task force Ams. for Change; bd. dirs. Am. Theatre Arts, Hollywood, Calif., 1983-84; pres., mem. exec. com., bd. dirs. Programs for the Developmentally Handicapped, Inc., L.A., 1987-92; chmn. bd. appeals handicapped accommodations City of Manhattan Beach, 1986-88; sec., bd. dirs. The Foodbank of So. Calif., 1991—. Mem. Calif. Bar Assn. (legal svcs. sect. standing com. legal problems of aging 1983-86, chmn. legis. subcom. 1984-86, conf. dels. alternate 1987), D.C. Bar Assn. (real estate sect. com. on comml. real estate), L.A. County Bar Assn., Legal Assistance Assn. Calif. (bd. dirs., mem. exec. com., legis. strategy com. 1984-86), Loyola Law Sch. (advocate), Smithsonian Instn., UCLA Alumni Assn., Phi Beta Kappa, Pi Gamma Mu, Phi Sigma Alpha, Phi Alpha Delta. Democrat. Office: Ralphs Grocery Co PO Box 54143 Los Angeles CA 90054-0143

BELLAH, ROBERT NEELLY, sociologist, educator; b. Altus, Okla., Feb. 23, 1927; s. Luther Hutton and Lillian Lucille (Neelly); m. Melanie Hyman, Aug. 17, 1949; children: Jennifer, Harriet. B.A., Harvard U., 1950, Ph.D., 1955. Research assoc. Inst. Islamic Studies, McGill U., Montreal, Can., 1955-57; with Harvard U., Cambridge, Mass., 1957-67; prof. Harvard U., 1966-67; Elliott prof. sociology U. Calif., Berkeley, 1967—. Author: Tokugawa Religion, 1957, Beyond Belief, 1970, The Broken Covenant, 1975 (Sorokin award Am. Sociol. Assn. 1976), (with Charles Y. Glock) The New Religious Consciousness, 1976, (with Phillip E. Hammond) Varieties of Civil Religion, 1980, (with others) Habits of the Heart, 1985, (with others) The Good Society, 1991. Served with U.S. Army, 1945-46. Fulbright fellow, 1960-61; recipient Harbison award Danforth Found., 1971. Mem. Am. Acad. Arts and Scis., Assn. for Asian Studies, Am. Acad. Religion. Office: U Calif Dept Sociology Berkeley CA 94720

BELLAMY, JOHN CARY, civil engineer; b. Cheyenne, Wyo., Apr. 18, 1915; s. Benjamin Charles and Alice Elizabeth (Cary) B.; m. Josephine Eugenia Johnston, Sept. 21, 1940; children: John Cary, Agnes Louise, Charles Fulton, William Delaney, Mary Elizabeth. BCE, U. Wyo., 1936; PhM, U. Wis., 1938; PhD in Meteorology, Chgo. U., 1947. Registered profl. engr., Wyo. Ptnr. Bellamy & Sons Engrs., Lamont, Wyo., 1938-42; asst. prof. U. Chgo., 1942-47; assoc. dir. Cook Rsch. Labs., Chgo., 1947-60; dir. NRRI U. Wyo., Laramie, 1960-73; prof. civil engring. U. Wyo., 1973-81; prin. Bellamy & Sons Engrs., Laramie, 1981—; dir. Inst. Tropical Meteorology, U. P.R., 1943-44; spl. cons. U.S. Army Air Corps, Washington, 1944-45; mem. Western Interstate Nuclear Bd., Denver, 1964-75. Contbr. articles to profl. jours.; contbr. to books; patentee in field. Recipient Losey award, Inst. Aero. Sci., 1944, Medal of Freedom, Pres. U.S.A., 1946, Thurlow award Inst. Navigation, 1946. Fellow Am. Meteorol. Soc. (dir. 1948-52); mem. Wyo. Engring. Soc., Am. Geophys. Union, Inst. Navigation (pres. 1962), Nat. Soc. Profl. Engrs. (chpt. pres. 1976), Lions (chpt. pres. 1981, 84). Home and Office: 2308 Holliday Dr Laramie WY 82070-4847

BELLE, CHARLES EARL, investment manager; b. Chgo., Sept. 2, 1940; s. Charles Douglas and Ella (McGhee) B.; m. Rita Cummings, Aug. 23, 1980. BBA, Roosevelt U., 1963; MBA, Harvard U., 1973. Credit officer Wells Fargo Bank, San Francisco, 1963-68; stockbroker Shearson Hammill, San Francisco, 1968-72, Drexel, Burnham & Lambert, San Francisco, 1972-81, A.G. Edwards, San Francisco, 1981-84, Wedbush Securities, San Francisco, 1984-87, Prudential Securities, San Francisco, 1987—; syndicated columnist Nat. Newspaper Pubs. Assn., Washington, 1973—. Bd. dirs. Press. Com. for Disabled, Washington, 1975; pres. African Am. Cultural and Hist. Soc., San Francisco, 1976-78, NAACP, 1976-80; chmn. Mayor's Com. on Community Devel., 1983-88. Recipient Econ. for Journalists award, Brookings Instn., 1974, Journalist award NEH, 1976, Best Econ. Reporting award Lincoln Univ., 1976, Media Fellowship World Affairs Coun., 1986.

BELLER, GERALD STEPHEN, research analyst, former insurance company executive; b. Phila., Aug. 6, 1935; s. Nathan and Adelaide B. (Goldfarb) B.; m. Nancy R. Nelson, June 8, 1968; children: Fay A., Mark S., Royce W., Merrilee A., Marie A., Frank A. CLU, Am. Coll., Bryn Mawr, Pa., 1972. Spl. agt. Prudential Ins. Co., San Bernardino, Calif., 1959-62, div. mgr., 1962-66; agy. supr. Aetna Life & Casualty, L.A., 1966-69, gen. agt., 1969-77; rsch. analyst Investigative Svcs. Bur. San Bernardino County Sheriff's Dept., 1991—; capt. specialized svcs. bur. San Bernardino County Sheriff's Dept.; mem. Magician Magic Castle, Hollywood, Calif. mem. sheriff's coun. San Bernardino County Sheriff's Dept., Apple Valley sheriff's adv. bd. Served with USAF, 1953-57. Recipient Man of Year award, 1961; Manpower Builders award, 1966-69; Agy. Builders award, 1970-72; Pres.'s Trophy award, 1973-74. Mem. Life Underwriters Assn. L.A., Am. Soc. CLUs, Golden Key Soc., Internat. Exec. Svc. Corps. (vol.), Acad. Magical Arts, Internat. Brotherhood of Magicians (Outstanding Magic Lectr. of Yr. 1989-90, Aldini Meml. award 1990), Soc. Am. Magicians. Home: 20625 Tonawanda Rd Apple Valley CA 92307-5736 Office: Sheriffs Hdqs Narcotics Div 655 E 3d St San Bernardino CA 92415

BELLES, DONALD ARNOLD, pastoral therapist, mental health counselor; b. Sayre, Pa., Mar. 7, 1948; s. William and Alice (Arnold) B.; m. Linda Scheel, July 7, 1981. BA, St. Martin's U., 1973; MDiv, Fuller Theol. Sem., 1977; PhD, Calif. Grad. Sch. Theology, 1981; postgrad., U. Bellevue. Ordained to ministry Worldwide Congregational Fellowship, 1989; cert. community coll. tchr., Calif.; cert. mental health counselor, Wash., profl. stage hypnotist. Chaplain Vols. of Am., L.A., 1976-78; therapist Greater life Found., Seattle, 1979-81; industrial engr. commercial airplane divsn. Boeing, 1979-80, program planner aerospace divsn., 1980-86, sr., lead program planner electronics divsn., 1986-89, systems analyst, contract tech. mgr., software engring. practices process analyst, total quality improvement project mgr., 1989—; therapist, dir. clinic Creative Therapies, Seattle, 1982-83; clin. dir. Applied Hypnosis, Tacoma, 1984-87; dir. Active Therapy Assoc., Tacoma, 1988-89; dean of students Coll. Therapeutic Hypnosis, Puyallup, Wash., 1989-93; cons. theological issues, abduction rsch., psychic phenomena, paranormal events; adult edn. instr. Tacoma Community Coll., 1987-88, Pierce Coll., 1990-92; presenter, lectr. in field. Contbr. articles to profl. jours.; producer videos in field. Exec. dir. Nat. Assn. to Prevent and Eliminate Child Abuse, Tacoma, 1987-89. Maj. U.S. Army, 1969-75, USAR, 1975—. Fellow Am. Assn. Profl. Hypnotherapists; mem. Nat. Assn. Clergy Hypnotherapists (bd. dirs. 1987-88, editor jour. 1987), Mutual UFO Network, Wash. State Head Injury Found.

BELLIS, CARROLL JOSEPH, surgeon; b. Shreveport, La.; s. Joseph and Rose (Bloome) B.; m. Mildred Darmody, Dec. 26, 1939; children—Joseph, David. BS, U. Minn., 1930, MS in Physiology, 1932, PhD in Physiology, 1934, MD, 1936, PhD in Surgery, 1941. Diplomate Am. Bd. Surgery. Resident surgery U. Minn. Hosps., 1937-41; pvt. practice surgery Long Beach, Calif., 1945—; mem. staff St. Mary's, Community hosps., Long Beach; cons. surgery Long Beach Gen. Hosp.; prof., chmn. dept. surgery Calif. Coll. Medicine, 1962—; surgical cons. to Surgeon-Gen., U.S. Army. Author: Fundamentals of Human Physiology, 1935, A Critique of Reason, 1938, Lectures in Medical Physiology; contbr. numerous articles in field of surgery, physiology to profl. jours. Served to col. M.C. AUS, 1941-46. Nat. Cancer Inst. fellow, 1934; recipient Charles Lyman Green prize in physiology, 1934; prize Mpls. Surg. Soc., 1938; ann. award Mississippi Valley Med. Soc., 1955. Fellow ACS, Royal Soc. Medicine, Internat. Coll. Surgeons, Am. Coll. Gastroenterology, Am. Med. Writers Assn., Internat. Coll. Angiology (sci. council), Gerontol. Soc., Am. Soc. Abdominal Surgeons, Nat. Cancer Inst., Phlebology Soc. Am., Internat. Acad. Proctology, Peripheral Vascular Soc. Am. (founding); mem. AAAS, Am. Assn. Study Neoplastic Diseases, Mississippi Valley Med. Soc., N.Y. Acad. Scis., Hollywood Acad. Medicine, Am. Geriatrics Soc., Irish Med. Assn., Am. Assn. History Medicine, Pan Pacific Surgical Assn., Indsl. Med. Assn., L.A. Musicians Union (hon.), Pan Am. Med. Assn. (diplomate), Internat. Bd. Surgery (cert.), Internat. Bd. Proctology (cert.), Wisdom Soc. (wisdom award of honor), Sigma Xi, Phi Beta Kappa, Alpha Omega Alpha. Office: 904 Silver Spur Rd Ste 804 Rolling Hills Estates CA 90274

BELLISTON, EDWARD GLEN, medical facility administrator, consultant; b. Upland, Calif., Oct. 20, 1958; s. G. Howard and MaryAnn (Fitzgerald) B.; m. Kristine Marie Holmes, Aug. 12, 1981. BS, Brigham Young U., 1984, MHA, 1987. Cert. EMT. Admitting clk. Utah Valley Regional Med. Ctr., Provo, 1985; adminstrv. resident St. Benedict's Hosp., Holy Cross Health System, Ogden, Utah, 1986; fin. counselor Utah Valley Regional Med. Ctr., Provo, 1986, adminstrv. dir., 1986; regional clin. admministrv. coord. Intermountain Health Care-IHC Physicians Svcs., Salt Lake City, 1989; sr. phys. cons. Intermountain Health Care-IHC Physicians Svcs., Salt Lake, 1990—. Instr. gospel doctrine LDS Ch., Springville, Utah, 1989-91, bishopric Brigham Young U. 81st ward, 1991—, leader Boy Scouts Am., Springville, 1988. Mem. Med. Group Mgmt. Assn., Am. Coll. Healthcare Execs. Republican. Home: 363 W 1400 N American Fork UT 84003-2794 Office: Intermountain Health Care PO Box 57010 650 E 4500 S Ste # 340 Salt Lake City UT 84157-0010

BELLMYRE, CAROLE, publisher; b. Columbus, Ohio, Aug. 1; d. Ole Bellmyre and June (Wood) Thompson; children: Dean Philip D'Amato (dec.), Damon Christopher D'Amato. BA in Fine Arts, U. Miami (Fla.). Photographer L.A. and Las Vegas, Nev., 1974—; seminar dir. L.A. and Las Vegas, 1978—; pres. CareLine/Nat. Hotline Svc., Las Vegas, 1986—; guest speaker schs. and theatrical groups, L.A., 1978—; mem. comm. com. Nev. Gov.'s Conf. on Women, Las Vegas, 1990; mem. adv. bd. Women's Devel. Ctr., 1992—. Pub. Disting. Women in So. Nev., 1988-93 (1st pl. book award State Nev., Nat. Fedn. Press Women 1991); pub., photographer Romantic Visions, 1986; photographic art one-woman shows, 1978-86. mem. pub. rels. com. Am. Cancer Soc., 1993. Mem. NAFE, AFTRA, SAG, Profl. Photographers Am., Nat. Assn. Women Bus. Owners (nominating com. 1990-91, awards chair 1992), Nat. League Am. Pen Women (membership chair 1992—), Nat. Fedn. Press Women, Las Vegas C. of C. (women's coun., finalist Honored Woman of Achievement 1992), Allied Arts Coun., Women's Devel. Ctr. (adv. bd. 1992). Office: Disting Women in So Nev PO Box 12448 Las Vegas NV 89112-0448

BELLONI, ROBERT CLINTON, federal judge; b. Riverton, Oreg., Apr. 4, 1919; s. John Edward and Della (Clinton) B.; children: James L., Susan K. BA, U. Oreg., 1941, LLB, 1951. Bar: Oreg. 1951. Practiced in Coquille, Oreg., 1951-52, Myrtle Point, Oreg., 1952-57; judge Oreg. Circuit Ct., Coos and Curry Counties, Coquille, 1957-67; U.S. dist. judge Dist. Oreg., 1967—, chief judge, 1971-76. Councilman, Myrtle Point, 1953-57, mayor, 1957; chmn. Coos County Democratic Central Com., 1957; Hon. trustee Boys and Girls Aid Soc. Oreg., 1960. Served to 1st lt. AUS, 1942-46. Robert C. Belloni Boys Forest Ranch dedicated in his honor Coos County Bd. Commrs., 1969. Mem. ABA, Oreg. Bar Assn., Am. Judicature Soc., Oreg. Juvenile Ct. Judges Assn. (pres. 1963), Circuit Ct. Judges Assn. Oreg. (pres. 1966), 9th Circuit Dist. Judges Assn. (pres. 1980-81), Sigma Alpha Epsilon, Delta Theta Phi. Episcopalian. Office: US Dist Ct 708 US Courthouse 620 SW Main St Portland OR 97205-3023

BELLUOMINI, FRANK STEPHEN, accountant; b. Healdsburg, Calif., May 19, 1934; s. Francesco and Rose (Giorgi) B.; m. Alta Anita Gifford, Sept. 16, 1967; 1 child, Wendy Ann. AA, Santa Rosa Jr. Coll., 1954; BA with honors, San Jose State U., 1956. CPA, Calif. Staff acct. Hood, Gire & Co., CPA's, San Jose, Calif., 1956-60, ptnr., 1960-66; ptnr. Touche Ross & Co., CPA's, San Jose, 1967-89, ptnr.-in-charge San Jose office, 1971-85, sr. ptnr. San Jose office, 1985-89; ptnr. Deloitte & Touche, San Jose, 1989—. Mem. adv. bd. Salvation Army, San Jose, 1979-85, San Jose Children's Coun., 1982-89, citizens adv. coun. The Crippled Children's Soc. of Santa Clara County, 1989-92; trustee Santa Clara County (Calif.) United Way, 1979—, v.p. planning and allocations, 1981-83, vice chmn., 1985-87, chmn. 1987-89; bd. dirs. San Jose Mus. Art, 1984-86; mem. Presentation High Sch. Devel. Bd., 1989-92; mem. dean's adv. coun. San Jose State U. Bus. Sch., 1990—, mem. adv. bd. The Acad. of Fin., 1992—. Named Disting. Alumnus, San Jose State U. Sch. Bus., 1978. Mem. Santa Clara County Estate Planning Council (pres. 1979-80), Calif. Soc. CPA's (pres. chpt. 1968-69, state v.p. 1976-77), Am. Inst. CPA's (chmn. state and local govt. com. 1976-79), San Jose State Alumni Assn. (treas. 1960-61, dir. 1961-62, exec. com. 1961-62), San Jose State Acctg. Round Table (bd. dirs., treas. 1982-87), Beta Alpha Psi (San Jose State U. Outstanding Alumnus award 1986). Roman Catholic. Clubs: San Jose Rotary (dir. 1979-81, trustee and treas. San Jose Rotary Endowment 1976-83), Silicon Valley Capital. Office: 60 S Market St San Jose CA 95113-2300

BELLUS, RONALD JOSEPH, marketing and communications executive; b. Travis AFB, Calif., Feb. 25, 1951; s. Vincent Joseph and Katherine Venonica (Giudice) B.; m. Beth Ann Johnson, June 26, 1976 (div.); children: Veronica Lee, Joseph Vincent, Kenneth James.; m. Ginà Jean Prom, Aug. 9, 1990; 1 child, Anthony Taylor. BA in Communications, Brigham Young U., 1977. Lic. FCC radio telephone operator, 1979. Sports dir. Sta. KGUY-AM, Palm Desert, Calif., 1979; news, sports dir. Sta. KBLQ-AM/FM, Logan, Utah, 1979-80; gen. sales mgr. Sta. KSTM-FM/KVVA-AM, Phoenix, 1980-84, Sta. KLFF-AM/KMZK-FM, Phoenix, 1984-85; media cons. Mediacorp Planning & Buying, Phoenix, 1985-86; press sec. Gov. of Ariz., Phoenix, 1986-87; asst. dir. Ariz. Office of Tourism, Phoenix, 1987-88; media cons. Bellus Media, Phoenix, 1988—; ptnr. Desertwest Media Group, Inc., Phoenix, 1988—; v.p. Nat. Restaurant Group, Inc., Phoenix, 1990-91; media cons. Mecham for Gov. com., Glendale, Ariz., 1986; host cable TV show Arizona-Now and Then, Dimension Cable, 1990—; v.p. Infosystems, Tempe, 1991—, Green Valley Health Group, Phoenix, 1992—. Author: Mecham: Silence Cannot Be Misquoted, 1988, Ariz. Tourism Travel Planner, 1988. Comm. mem. Phoenix Boys Choir, 1988; precinct committeeman Rep. State Com., Phoenix, 1987-89, del., 1988; candidate for state senate, Phoenix, 1988. Named one of Outstanding Young Men Am., 1987. Mem. Phoenix Press Box Assn. (treas. 1984-85, exec. dir. 1985-86). Ch. of Latter Day Saints. Office: Bellus Media 5869 S Kyrene Rd Ste # 16 Tempe AZ 85283

BELMONT, LARRY MILLER, health association executive; b. Reno, Apr. 13, 1936; s. Miller Lawrence and Madeline (Echante) B.; m. Laureen Metzger, Aug. 14, 1966; children: Miller Lawrence, Rebecca Madeline, Amie Echante, Bradley August. BA in Psychology, U. Nev., 1962; MPH, U. Mich., 1968; cert. in environ. mgmt., U. So. Calif., 1978; M in Pub. Adminstrn., U. Idaho, 1979. Rep. on loan to city health depts. USPHS, Los Angeles and Long Beach, 1962-63; advisor pub. health on loan to Alaska dept. health and welfare USPHS, Anchorage, 1963-64, Juneau and Anchorage, 1964-67; dep. dir. Wash./Alaska Regional Med. Program, Spokane, Wash., 1968-71; dir. Panhandle Health Dist., Coeur d'Alene, Idaho, 1971—; mem. adj. faculty Whitworth Coll., Spokane; presenter papers nat., region, state confs., 1981-82; testifier congl. coms., Washington, 1973, 76, state legis. com., Idaho, 1972-82. Chmn. nominating com. Kootenai Econ. Devel. Council, Idaho, 1985, bd. dirs. 1981-86; mem. adv. com. Kootenai County Council Alcoholism, 1979-80; regional coordinator Gov.'s Com. Vol. Services, Idaho, 1979-80; chmn. Montessori Adv. Bd., Idaho, 1975-79; chmn. personnel com. North Idaho Hospice, 1985-88, bd. dirs. 1985-88; bd. dirs. North Idaho Spl. Services Agy., 1972-76; bd. dirs., vice chmn. Pub. Employees Credit Union, 1990—; bd. dirs. United Way of Kootenai County, Inc., 1990-91; mem. steering com. APEX/PH, 1987-91; active numerous other organizations. USPHS trainee U. Mich., 1967-68, EPA trainee U. So. Calif., 1978. Mem. Am. Pub. Health Assn., Nat. Assn. Home Health Agys. (chmn. legis. com. 1979-81, bd. dirs. 1978-81), Nat. Assn. County Health Officials (bd. dirs. 1986-88, registry com. 1990), Idaho Pub. Health Assn. (bd. dirs., treas. 1973-77), Idaho Forest Owners Assn., Kootenai County Environ. Alliance, Washington Pub. Health Assn., Idaho Conservation League, Ducks Ultd. Democrat.

BELNAP, DAVID FOSTER, journalist; b. Ogden, Utah, July 27, 1922; s. Hyrum Adolphus and Lois Ellen (Foster) B.; m. Barbara Virginia Carlberg, Jan. 17, 1947. Student, Weber Coll., Ogden, 1940. Asst. city editor Seattle Star, 1945-47; bur. chief UP Assns., Helena, Mont., 1947-50, Honolulu, 1950-52; regional exec. Pacific N.W., 1952-55, dir. Latin Am. services, 1955-67; Latin Am. corr. L.A. Times, 1967-80, asst. fgn. news editor, 1980—. Recipient Overseas Press Club Am. award for best article on Latin Am., 1970, Maria Moors Cabot prize, 1973. Mem. Overseas Press Club Am., Greater Los Angeles Press Club, Audiophile Soc. Clubs: Am. of Buenos Aires; Phoenix of Lima (Peru). Home: 1134 W Huntington Dr Arcadia CA 91007-6303 Office: Times Mirror Sq Los Angeles CA 90053

BELNAP, NORMA LEE MADSEN, musician; b. Tremonton, Utah, Dec. 2, 1927; d. Doyle Franklin and Cleo (Crawforth) Madsen; m. H. Austin Belnap, Jan. 19, 1980; 7 stepchildren. Student, Brigham Young U., summer 1947, San Francisco Conservatory of Music, summer 1949; B.S., U. Utah, 1951; postgrad., Aspen Inst. Music, 1953, Music Acad. of West, Santa Barbara, Calif., 1962. Sec.-treas., dir., mem. faculty Treasure Mountain Festival of Arts, 1965, 66; mem. nat. adv. com. Nat. Black Music Colloquium and Competition, 1979; lectr. U. Utah, 1951—, instr., 1965, adj. asst. prof. music, 1969-73, adj. assoc. prof., 1973-77, adj. prof., 1977—; exec. v.p. LOZO Pub. Co., 1991—. Violinist, Utah Symphony, 1944-94, asst. concert master, 1977-93, mem., Utah Opera Theatre Orch., 1951-54, Utah Ballet Theatre Orch., 1953—, Melody Maids, 4 violins and piano, 1943-49; active in chamber music circles, 1946-81, concert mistress, U. Utah Symphony, 1947-58, prin. violist, 1958-62, soloist, Utah Artist Series, 1964, mem., Treasure Mountain String Quartet, Park City, Utah, 1964, 65, 66; appeared as violin soloist, U. Utah Symphony and Ballet Theatre Orch., 1954, 56, 57, 82; 2d violinist (affiliated with Young Audiences, Inc.) Utah String Quartet, 1958-68; Quartet-in-residence U. Utah, 1968-81, Idaho State U., 1967; with Bach Festival Orch., Carmel, Calif., 1963, 69, Sunriver Festival Orch., summer 1988, Utah-ASTA Faculty Quartet, 1970-79, tour of Europe with, Utah Symphony, 1966, 77, 81, 86, S. and Cen. Am., 1971, Brit. Isles, 1975, Hawaii, 1979, concertizing throughout Western states, frequent festival adjudicator; numerous solo recitals. Recipient Tchr. Recognition award Music Tchrs. Nat. Assn., 1971, 72, 73. Mem. Music Educators Nat. Conf., Utah String Tchrs. Assn. (state membership chmn. 1969-73), Utah Music Tchrs. Assn. (state cert. bd. 1968—), Utah Fedn. Music Clubs (1st v.p.), Am. String Tchrs. Assn. (dir. Utah nat. string conf. ann. 1970-79), Mortar Bd., Mu Phi Epsilon (founder, 1st pres. U. Utah chpt. 1950, compiler Mu Phi Epsilon Composers and Their Works 1956, nat. v.p., music adv., province gov. 1954-58, chpt. honoree for 30 yrs. of dedicated svc. 1981), Alpha Lambda Delta, Phi Kappa Phi, Alpha Xi Delta, Lambda Delta Sigma. Mem. LDS Ch. Home: 3054 E Millcreek Rd Salt Lake City UT 84109-3100 Office: U Utah Music Hall Salt Lake City UT 84112 also: Lozo Pub Co 3054 E Millcreek Rd Salt Lake City UT 84109-3100

BELNAP, TIMOTHY GEORGE, insurance agency executive; b. Blackfoot, Idaho, May 26, 1960; s. Lyle E. and Shelda (Elison) B.; m. Lisa Joann Petersen, Nov. 29, 1985; children: Logan T., Tiana Jo, Stetson L., Parker L. A., Ricks Coll., 1982; student, Idaho State U., 1982-83. Cert. life underwriters tng. coun. fellow. Asst. mgr. Mercantile Stores Co., Blackfoot, Idaho, 1983-85; salesman Blackfoot Motor Co., Blackfoot, 1985-87; agt. Allstate Ins. Co., Idaho Falls, Idaho, 1987-88; agy. exec. Tandy & Wood, Inc., Idaho Falls, 1988—. Parade judge Blackfoot C. of C., 1991, Idaho Falls C. of C., 1992. Mem. Nat. Assn. Life Underwriters (legis. chmn. Idaho chpt. 1990—, pres. elect Ea. Idaho chpt. 1993), Life Underwriters Tng. Coun. (profl. growth moderator Idaho Falls 1991-92), Ea. Idaho Ind. Ins. Agts. (pres. 1990-92), Ea. Idaho Life Underwriters Assn. (bd. dirs. 1990—), Safeco Life Ins. Co. Dirs. Club, Lions Club Internat. (bd. dirs., v.p. 1985-87). Mem. LDS Church. Home: 3763 Michelle Idaho Falls ID 83401 Office: Tandy & Wood Inc 101 S Park Ave Idaho Falls ID 83402

BELOTE, ROBERT GARNET, III, human resource specialist; b. L.A., June 13, 1952; s. Robert Garnet Jr. and Julianne (Lemon) B.; m. Patricia Louise Douglas, July 17, 1982; children: Judith Eloise, Olivia Joy. BA in Speech, San Francisco State U., 1976, BA in Psychology, 1976; MA in Comm., U. Denver, 1978, PhD in Orgnl. Comm., 1989. Devel. specialist Bur. Land Mgmt., Dept. Interior, 1979-81; comm. instr. Arapahoe C.C., 1977-79, 81-86, Regis Coll., 1983-84; mktg. agt. Goldberg & Larson's Inc., 1984-86; employee devel. specialist City of Westminster, 1987-88; mgmt. specialist Poudre Valley Hosp., 1988-90; human resources devel. assoc. Leprino Foods, Denver, 1990—. Author: An Investigation into the Relationship Between Power Orientations and Compliance Gaining Strategies, 1989. Dir. Skyland Village Covenant Com.; mem. Colo. Voter Registration Coun. Mem. ASTD, ACLU, Nat. Soc. Performance Instrn., Am. Mgmt. Assn., Am. Soc. Quality, Speech Communication Assn., Amnesty Internat., Greenpeace, Sierra Club. Home: 4007 W 99th Pl Westminster CO 80030 Office: Leprino Foods 1830 W 38th Ave Denver CO 80211-2225

BELT, AUDREY EVON, social worker, consultant; b. New Orleans, June 23, 1948. BS in Social Work and Psychology, Grambling State U., 1970; MSW in Adminstrn. and Policy, U. Mich., 1972. Adult probation officer City/County San Francisco Hall of Justice, 1973-74; child welfare worker dept. social svcs. City/County San Francisco, 1974-79; rsch. and planning specialist City of Ann Arbor (Mich.) Model Cities Interdisciplinary Agy; cons. San Francisco; cons. in field. Grambling State U. scholar, 1966-70, U. Mich. scholar, 1971-72. Mem. ABA, Nat. Assn. Social Workers (edn. task force), Am. Orthopsychiat. Assn., Am. Humane Soc., Child Welfare League Am., Black Am. Polit. Assn. Calif. (legis. com.), Alpha Kappa Delta. Democrat. Roman Catholic. Home and Office: PO Box 424288 San Francisco CA 94142-4288

BELTRAMO, MICHAEL NORMAN, management consultant; b. L.A., Feb. 9, 1942; s. Blase and Violette (Murphy) B.; m. Susan Annette Lawton, Dec. 24, 1969 (div. 1980); m. Jane Sinden Spiegel, Apr. 21, 1984; children: Helen Weedon, Anna Sinden, Emily Murphy. AB, UCLA, 1964; MPA, U. So. Calif., 1967; PhD, Rand Grad. Inst., Santa Monica, Calif., 1983. Cert. cost estimator/analyst. Mem. tech. staff The RAND Corp., Santa Monica, 1969-75; dep. mgr. Sci. Applications Internat. Corp., L.A., 1975-80; pres. Beltramo and Assocs., L.A., 1980—. Author: LA County Economic Adjustment Strategy for Defense Reduction; contbr. articles to profl. publs. Named Ky. Col. Commonwealth of Ky., 1973. Mem. Soc. Cost Estimating and Analysis (cert., bd. dirs. 1987-88). Republican. Methodist. Home and Office: 13039 Sky Valley Rd Los Angeles CA 90049-1037

BELTRÁN, ANTHONY NATALICIO, military officer, deacon; b. Flagstaff, Ariz., Aug. 17, 1938; s. Natalicio Torres and Mary Mercedes (Sandoval) B.; m. Patricia Emily Cañez, Nov. 18, 1962; children: Geralyn P., Bernadette M., Albert A., Catherine M., Elizabeth R., Michael J., Theresa R., Christopher M. AA, Phoenix Jr. Coll., 1971, C.C. of Air Force, 1992; grad., Def. Equal Oppty. Mgmt. Inst., 1991. Gen. clk. Blue Cross Blue Shield, Phoenix, 1958-61; unit clk. Ariz. Air N.G., Phoenix, 1961, personnel technician, 1962-65, adminstrv. supr., 1965-81, support services supr., 1981-88, equal employment specialist, 1988—. Bd. dirs. Friendly House, Phoenix, 1982-86, mem. aux. bd., 1989—; mem. Alma de la Gente, Phoenix, 1982—, Chiefs Police Community Adv. Group, Phoenix, 1984-85, Mayor's Task Force on Juvenile Crime, Phoenix, 1979-81; pres. IMAGE de Phoenix, 1985-87. Staff sgt. USAF, 1961-62. Recipient Community Service award Phoenix C. of C., 1982. Mem. Fed. Exec. Assn. (sec., treas. Phoenix chpt. 1985-86, 1st v.p. 1987, pres. 1987-88, Community Svc. award 1986), Ariz. Hispanic Employment Program Mgrs. (treas. 1980-81, v.p. 1981-82, pres. 1982-84, named Outstanding Mem. of Yr. 1981, 83), Enlisted Assn. N.G. Ariz. (pres. Copperhead chpt. 1987-90), Non-Commd. Officers Acad. Grad. Assn. (chpt. 46 v.p. 1992—). Democrat. Home: 4109 W Monte Vista Rd Phoenix AZ 85009-2005 Office: NG Ariz Hdqrs Support Personnel Mgmt Office 5636 E Mcdowell Rd Phoenix AZ 85008-3495

BELZBERG, SAMUEL, business executive; b. Calgary, Alta., Can., June 26, 1928; s. Abraham and Hinda (Fishman) B.; m. Frances Cooper; children: Cheryl Rae, Marc David, Wendy Jay, Lisa. B.Comm., U. Alta., Edmonton, 1948. Pres. Bel-Fran Investments, Ltd., Vancouver, B.C., Can., 1968—, Balfour Holdings, Inc., 1992—; pres. First City Fin. Corp. Ltd., Vancouver, 1970-83, 86-91, chmn., 1983-91; pres. Balfour Holdings, Inc.; bd. dirs. Franklin Supply Co., Ltd. Home: 3711 Alexandra St, Vancouver, BC Canada V6J 4C3 Office: 1177 W Hastings St Ste 2000, Vancouver, BC Canada V6E 2K3

BEMIS, JAMES ERNEST SANFORD, religious organization administrator, massage therapist, musician; b. Santa Monica, Calif., Aug. 18, 1954; s. Charles Ernest Bemis and Corinne (Self) Bemis Jones; m. Vivian Sara Gilbert, Feb. 14, 1973 (div. 1975). Student, Phoenix Coll., 1974-77; lic. massage therapist, Ralston Sch., 1991. Ops. officer, purchasing agt. 1st Interstate Bank Nev., Reno, 1979-88; regional mgr. Robert Half Nev., Inc., Reno, 1986-88; mgr. adminstrn. Episcopal Diocese Nev., 1989-92; dir. music So. Reno United Meth. Ch., 1991—; pres., founder Massage Assocs., Inc., Reno, 1991—. Vol. Nev. AIDS Found., Reno, 1991—, Hospice of No. Nev., Reno, 1991—; treas. Reno Chamber Orch., 1982-83; organist Reno Philharmonic Orch., 1982-83. With USAF, 1973-74. Mem. Am. Guild of Organists (founding dean No. Nev. chpt. 1982-83), Nat. Assn. Accts. (bd. dirs. Reno area chpt. 1986-88), Reno Advt. Club (assoc. prodr. Sheep Dip Show 1990, dir. Sheep Dip Show 1991, Master of Sheep Dip award 1989, Dr. of Sheep Dip award 1992). Democrat. Episcopalian. Home: 11060 Fir Dr P O Box 6078 Reno NV 89513-6078 Office: Massage Assocs Inc 888 W Second St Ste 107 Reno NV 89503

BENACH, SHARON ANN, physician assistant; b. New Orleans, Aug. 28, 1944; d. Wilbur G. and Freda Helen (Klaas) Cherry; m. Richard Benach, Dec. 6, 1969 (div. Oct. 1976); children: Craig, Rachel. Degree, St. Louis U., 1978. Physician asst. VA Hosp., St. Louis, 1982-84, Maricopa County Health Svcs., Phoenix, 1984—. Served with USPHS, 1978-82. Recipient Outstanding Performance award HHS. Mem. Mensa. Jewish. Home: 5726 N 10th St No 5 Phoenix AZ 85014-2273

BEN-ASHER, M. DAVID, physician; b. Newark, June 18, 1931; s. Samuel Irving and Dora Ruth (Kagan)B.; m. Bryna S. Zeller, Nov. 22, 1956. BA, Syracuse U., 1952; postgrad., U. Buffalo Sch. Med., 1956. Intern E.J. Meyer Mem. Hosp., Buffalo, N.Y., 1956-57; resident Jersey City Med. Ctr., 1957-58; asst. chief med. service U.S. Army Hosp., Ft. McPherson, Ga., 1958-60; resident Madigan Mem. Hosp., Tacoma, Wash., 1960-62; chief gen. med. service Walson Army Hosp., Ft. Dix, N.Y., 1962-64; attending staff St. Mary's Hosp., Tucson, Ariz., 1964—; private practice Self Employed, Tucson, 1964—; mem. Ariz. State Bd. Med. Examiners, 1978-88. Bd. dirs. Tucson Symphony, 1971-73; mem. Ariz. State Bd. Med. Examiners, 1978-88; bd. trustees United Synagogue Am., 1981-87, nat. adv. bd., 1987-91. Mem. Pima County Med. Soc. (bd. dirs. 1971-77, pres. 1976), Ariz. Med. Assn., AMA, ACP. Democrat. Home: 3401 N Tanuri Dr Tucson AZ 85715-6735 Office: So Ariz Med Specialists 4711 N 1st Ave Tucson AZ 85718-5690

BENAVIDES, TOM R., state senator, realtor; b. Socorro, N.Mex., Jan. 6, 1939; s. Juan Sanchez and Neph P. (Pino) B.; m. Kathleen Jacobsen, June 22, 1962; children: Tomas Rey, Michael Rey, David Rey. BS-BA, U. Albuquerque, 1961; postgrad., U. N.Mex. State senator State of N.Mex., Albuquerque, 1966-70, 84—; real estate broker, investor Tom Benavides Realty, Albuquerque; owner, operator Tom Benavides Realty Co.; pres. Salamanca Prodns. Ltd.; justice of the peace, Albuquerque, 1959-60; appraiser for Bernalillo County assessor, Albuquerque, 1961; bd. dirs. Southwest Valley Area Coun., Albuquerque, Model Cities, Am. G.I. Form; state chmn. coll. Young Democrats, 1959-62. Author: (book) New Mexican, 1990. Dem. candidate for gov. State of N.Mex., 1986; bd. dirs. Model Cities, Albuquerque, S.W. Area Council. Roman Catholic. Office: Tom Benavides Realty Co 2821 Gun Club Rd SW Albuquerque NM 87105-6333

BENAVIDEZ, CELINA GARCIA, state legislator; b. Denver, Feb. 6, 1954; d. Robert Lee and Alice (Crespin) Garcia. BS in Bus., Pub. Adminstrn., U. Alberquerque, Denver, 1978. Civil rights investigator Colo. Civil Rights Divsn., Denver, 1979-80; program adminstr. human resources Colo. Dept. Transp., Denver, 1980-92; mem. Colo. Ho. Reps., 1992—. Bd. dirs. Auraria Community Ctr., Denver, 1986, chair 1988-89. Recipient Vol. of Yr. award Women In Community Svc., 1988, Colo. Social Worker award 1992. Mem. NOW, Vol. Women in Community Svc., Mexican-Am. Policy Inst. (bd. dirs., chair women's causes), Jane Jefferson Hispanic League. Democrat. Roman Catholic. Home: 2825 W 34th Ave Denver CO 80211 Office: State Capitol State Capitol Bldg Denver CO 80204

BENBOW, RICHARD ADDISON, psychological counselor; b. Las Vegas, Dec. 27, 1949; s. Jules Coleman and Bonnie Ray B. BBA, U. Nev. 1972, MS in Counseling, 1974; AAS in Bus. Mgmt. and Real Estate, Clark County Community Coll., 1980; PhD in Clin. Psychology, U. Humanistic Studies, 1986. Cert. tchr., Nev.; cert. clin. mental health counselor, secondary sch. counselor, Nev., substance abuse counselor, Nev., substance abuse program adminstr., Nev.; nat. cert. counselor. Pretrial program coord., 1982-88; jud. svcs. officer Mcpl. Ct., City of Las Vegas, 1988—, inmate classification technician Detention and Correctional Svcs., 1982-83; stress mgmt. cons. Mem. Biofeedback Soc. Am., Assn. Humanistic Psychology, Nat. Assn. Psychotherapists, Am. Counseling Assn., Am. Mental Health Counselors Assn., Am. Acad. Crisis Interveners, Jr. C. of C., U.S. Jaycees (presdl. award of honor 1978-79), Delta Sigma Phi. Democrat. Christian Scientist. Office: Mcpl Ct Jud Svcs City of Las Vegas 400 Stewart Ave Las Vegas NV 89101-2942

BENCH, JOHN REES, dentist; b. Provo, Utah, Feb. 20, 1927; s. Rees Edward and Georgia Eden (Christensen) B.; m. Iris Dawn Bigler, Apr. 9, 1954; children: John Bigler, Gretta, Ellen, Andrew Bigler, Jennifer. BA, Brigham Young U., 1952; DDS, Northwestern U., Chgo., 1958. Pvt. practice, Orem, Utah, 1958-93; mem. adv. com. Profl. Ins. Exch., Salt Lake City, 1984—. Dist. chmn. Orem Rep. Com. With USNR, 1945-46. Mem. ADA (life), Utah Dental Assn. (bd. dirs. 1968-70), Provo Dist. Dental Soc. (pres. 1966-67, bd. dirs. 1968-70). Mem. LDS Ch.

BENCHIMOL, ALBERTO, cardiologist, author; b. Belem, Para, Brazil, Apr. 26, 1932; s. Isaac I. and Nina (Siqueira) B.; came to U.S., 1957, naturalized, 1964; B.S., State Coll., Rio de Janeiro, Brazil, 1950; M.D., U. Brazil, 1956; m. Helena Lourdes Levy, Apr. 14, 1962; children—Nelson, Alex. Intern, U. Brazil Med. Center, Rio de Janeiro, 1956-57, resident in medicine, 1957; fellow in medicine U. Kans. Med. Center, Kansas City, 1958-60, Scripps Clinic, La Jolla, Calif., 1960-61; practice medicine specializing in cardiology, La Jolla, now Phoenix; research assoc. Inst. Cardiopulmonary Diseases, Scripps Clinic and Research Found., La Jolla, 1961-63, assoc., 1963-66; dir. Inst. Cardiovascular Diseases, Good Samaritan Med. Center, Phoenix, 1966-82; vis. prof. U. Brazil, 1966, Desert Hosp., Palm Springs, Calif., 1971; tutor U. Mo. Sch. Medicine, Kansas City, 1974-77, lectr., 1978-81; prof. in residence U. Oreg., Portland, 1975; vis. prof. Nagasaki U., Japan, 1970, Letterman Gen. Hosp., San Francisco, 1972. Haskell fellow in cardiology, 1957-59. Fellow ACP, Am. Coll. Cardiology, Am. Coll. Chest Physicians, Am. Coll. Angiology; mem. Am., Ariz. heart assns., Am. Physiol. Soc., Western Soc. Clin. Research, AMA, Biol. and Med. Scis. Research Club San Diego, Am. Fedn. Clin. Research. Author: Atlas of Vectorcardiography, 1971; Atlas of Phonocardiography, 1971; Vectorcardiography, 1973; Non-Invasive Diagnostic Techniques in Cardiology, 1977, 2d edit., 1981; Noninvasive Techniques in Cardiology for the Nurse and Technician, 1978; contbr. articles on cardiology and cardiography to profl. jours., chpts. to med. books; editorial bd. Am. Heart Jour., 1968-76, Am. Jour. Cardiology, 1969-76, Catheterization and Cardiovascular Diagnosis, 1974—, Chest, 1974; producer films on cardiography, 1962, 66. Home: 195 E Desert Park Ln Phoenix AZ 85020-4030

BENDELL, DONALD RAY, writer, director, poet; b. Akron, Ohio, Jan. 8, 1947; s. David Clyde Bendell and Alma Marguerite (Eby) Magenau; m. Linda Edith Liles, Apr. 13, 1968 (div. Oct. 1979); children: Jennifer Brooke, Brenna Alexandra, Justis Britton; m. Shirley Ann Ebert, Sept. 6, 1981; adopted children: Donald Ray Jr., Brent, Josh. Student, U.S. Armed Forces Inst., 1966-70, N.C. State U., Ft. Bragg, 1969-70, Pembroke State U., 1970-71, Akron State U., 1972. Disc. jockey, prodr. Sta. WAYN Inc., Rockingham, N.C., 1970-71; sr. sales exec. F.W. Means & Co., Inc., Akron, Cleve., 1972-74; instr. karate Karate Inst./Pro-Am Studios, Raeford, N.C., Akron, Ohio, 1972-75; prodr., dir., actor Am. Eagle Prodns., Akron, 1975-82; author, writer, dir. Don Bendell Inc./B.I.G./A.E.E., Inc., Cañon City, Colo., 1982—. Author: Crossbow, 1990, The B-52 Overture, 1992, Valley of Tears, 1993, Snake-Eater, 1993, Chief of Schout, 1993; (series) Tracker I-VI, 1990-91. Precinct chmn. Fremont County Rep. Party, Cañon City, 1984-87; state del. Colo. State Rep. Party, 1992. Capt. U.S. Army, 1966-70. Named Dist. Speak Up Champion, U.S. Jaycees, 1973; named to Internat. Karate Hall of Fame, 1992. Mem. VFW (post 4061), Am. Indian Registry for Performing Arts (nat. adv. bd. 1985—), Directory Am. Poets and Fiction Writers, World Martial Arts Coun. (midwest dir. 1980—, vice chair 1980—), Royal Gorge Rodeo Assn., Spl. Forces Assn. Mem. Christian Ch. Home and Office: PO Box 276 Canon City CO 81215

BENDER, BERT ARTHUR, American literature educator, fisherman; b. Cape Girardeau, Mo., Jan. 29, 1938; s. Walter William and Fern Evelyn (Stroud) B.; m. Roberta Burnett, June 1971 (di.); 1 child, Nathan Todd; m. Judith C. Darknall, Nov. 5, 1982. BA, U. Wash., Seattle, 1959; PhD in Lit. Theory, U. Calif., Irvine, 1973. Prof. Am. lit. dept. English Ariz. State U., Tempe, 1971—. Author: Sea-Brothers: The Tradition of American Sea Fiction from Moby Dick to the Present, 1988; contbr. articles to profl. jours. 1st lt. U.S. Army, 1960-62. Office: Ariz State U Dept of English Tempe AZ 85287

BENDER, BILL, artist, writer, historian; b. El Segundo, Calif., Jan. 5, 1919; s. Joseph Edward and Pauline (Beck) B.; m. Helen Lerma, Dec. 22, 1957. Grad. high sch., El Segundo. Freelance western artist, 1948—; dir. Death Valley (Calif.) Art Show, 1953-73; artist USAF, Vietnam, Thailand, Taiwan, 1963, USN, Pensacola, Fla., 1966. Illustrator: Beckoning Desert, 1962, Unnatural History of Death Valley, 1978; commd. to execute 16 murals Palisades Ranch Mus., 1991; group shows High Plains Heritage Mus., Spearfish, S.D., 1990, 91. Named hon. Tex. citizen State of Tex., 1966, hon. dep. sheriff Office of Sheriff, San Bernardino, 1988. Life mem. Cowboy Hall of Fame, Living Desert Mus., Mountain Oyster Club, Westerners (L.A., San Diego, San Dimas, Calif.), Death Valley 49ers (hon. bd. dirs. 1980). Republican. Home and Studio: 24887 National Trails Hwy Oro Grande CA 92368

BENDER, BOB GEORGE, consulting semiconductor packaging engineer; b. Watertown, S.D., June 10, 1925; s. George Almon and Ruby Belle (Duryee) B.; m. Amalia Gizella Nemeth, July 10, 1945 (div. July 1977); m. Grace Jadwiga Kowalski, Nov. 29, 1947; children: Bruce G., Carol S., Barbara G., Paul F., Holly M., Dean F. BS in Ceramic Engring., U. Ill., 1949. Mfg. engr. Owens-Ill. Glass Co., Toledo, 1949; chief ceramic engr. The Rauland Corp., Chgo., 1949-54; sr. glass technologist CBS-Hytron, Newburyport, Mass., 1954-56; mgr. microelectronics Hughes Aircraft Co., Newport Beach, Calif., 1956-67; mgr. packing engring. Rockwell Internat., Anaheim, Calif., 1967-77, mem. tech. staff, 1985-90; packaging engr. Silicon Systems, Irvine, Calif., 1977-79; cons. mem. engring. staff Xerox Corp., El Segundo, Calif., 1979-85; mgr. assembly engring. Silicon Gen., Garden Grove, Calif., 1985; cons. semicondr. packaging engr., Garden Grove, 1990—; cons. Bourns, Riverside, Calif., 1985, Densepak, Garden Grove, 1985, Semicoa, Costa Mesa, Calif., 1991—, Microsemi Corp., Santa Ana, Calif., 1992—; chmn. conf. tech. sessions. Contbr. articles to profl. jours.; patentee in field. Ward clk. LDS Ch., Garden Grove, 1989—. 2d lt. USAAF, 1943-45. Republican. Home: 11371 Homeway Dr Garden Grove CA 92641

BENDER, COLEMAN COALPORT, executive; b. Coalport, Pa., Mar. 30, 1921; s. Harry and Annie Bender; m. Pauline Evelyn, Apr. 12, 1948; children: Sue Ann, David. BA, Pa. State U., 1946, MA, 1947; PhD, U. Ill., 1955; AM (hon.), Emerson Coll., 1961. Instr. Pa. State U., State College, 1946-48, U. Ill., Champaign, 1948-50, USAF, Chanute, Ill., 1950-51; prof., chmn. Emerson Coll., Boston, 1951-69, dir. ednl. rsch., 1969-71, dir. orgn. rsch., 1969-82; prof. Am. Coll. of Greece, Athens, 1980-81; asst. prof. U. Hawaii, Honolulu, 1982-88; pres. C.C. Bender and Assocs., Honolulu, 1988—; cons. Aloha Airlines, Honolulu, 1982-87, Hawaii Electric, Honolulu, 1983-90, Dole Pineapple, Honolulu, 1983-90, U. Pa. Med. Sch., Phila., 1975-90. Author: Speaking is a Practical, 1968, Speech Communications, 1976, Words in Context, 1970. Staff sgt. USAF, 1942-46, PTO. McAllister scholar Pa. State U., State College, 1939; fellow in speech U. Ill., Champaign, 1950. Mem. Eastern Speech Assn. (exec. sect. 1965-68), Soc. for Inst. Tech. (v.p. 1967-69), Mass. Speech Assn. (pres. 1962-64, Speaker of Yr. 1970). Home: 3138 Waialae 436 Honolulu HI 96816-6000 Office: U Hawaii Manoa Campus Honolulu HI 96822

BENDER, ERWIN RADER, aerospace engineer, management consultant; b. Phila., Apr. 1, 1930; s. Wallace H. and Marian (Rader) B.; m. Beth Lois Deweese, Apr. 12, 1955 (div. July 1964); children: Erwin R. Jr., Elizabeth Ann; m. Katherine Verlee Lawson, Sept. 20, 1964. BSEE, Okla. State U., 1956. Engr. RCA, Moorestown, N.J., 1956-59; engr., sect. chief Martin Marietta Corp., Denver, 1959-75; mgr. TRW, Inc., Redondo Beach, Calif., 1975-92; also mgmt. cons., 1989-92, ret. Mem. Ltd. Growth Action Com., San Clemente, Calif., 1978-81. Lt. U.S. Army, 1948-57. Recipient awards NASA, 1975, 83. Mem. Elks (exalted ruler 1970-71). Home: 19341 Weymouth Ln Huntington Beach CA 92646

BENDER, FRANK NORCROSS, warehouse executive; b. Reno, Oct. 5, 1920; s. Edwin Samuel and Adele Cutts (Norcross) B.; m. Barbara Syble Weston, Dec. 6, 1944 (div. July 1977); children: Chris Norcross, Leslee; m. Terry Axtell Rooney, July 10, 1977. U. Calif., Berkeley, 1943. Ptnr. Bender Warehouse Co., Reno, 1946-60, pres., 1960-88, CEO, 1988—; dir. First Western Fin., Las Vegas, 1986—, First Western Bank, Las Vegas, 1984—, Am. Savs. & Loan Assn., Reno, 1965-84. Pres. Greater Reno C. of C., 1959-61; mem., bd. dirs. Nev. State Dept. Econ. Devel., Carson City, Nev., 1964-77; chmn. bd. Am. Warehouse Assn., Chgo., 1981-82; pres., founder U. Nev. Ctr. for Logistics, Reno, 1988. Lt. USNR, 1943-46. Named Reno Civic Leader of Yr., Reno C. of C., 1970, Nev. Ambassador, 1986; recipient Pres.'s medal U. Nev., 1990; named to Bus. Leader's Hall of Fame, Jr. Achievement, 1991. Mem. Prospectors Club (dir. 1969-70), Rotary Club of Reno (pres. 1969-70), Nev. Area Coun. Boy Scouts of Am. (v.p. 1971), Jr. Achievement (dir. 1970s), Nev. Roundtable Coun. of Logistics Mgmt. (pres. 1990-91). Republican. Episcopalian. Office: Bender Warehouse Co 345 Parr Circle PO Box 11430 Reno NV 89510

BENDIX, RICHARD CHARLES, marketing executive; b. Redlands, Calif., Sept. 20, 1948; s. Paul Alexander and Frances (Briscoe) B.; m. Deborah Devan, July 28, 1984; children: Richard Paul, Christopher David. BA, U. Calif., Riverside, 1975. Mng. ptnr. Lamb, Sexton, Bendix, Riverside, 1976-80; exec. v.p. Monterey Domes, Inc., Riverside, 1980-88; v.p. Lindal Cedar Homes, Seattle, 1988—; pres. NAHB Nat. Dome Coun., Washington, 1987-88; trustee Bldg. Systems Coun., Washington, 1987-88. Mem. Mktg. Comm. Execs. (sec.). Office: Lindal Cedar Homes PO Box 24426 Seattle WA 98124-0426

BENEDICT, BURTON, museum director, anthropology educator; b. Balt., May 20, 1923; s. Burton Eli Oppenheim and Helen Blanche (Deiches) B.; m. Marion MacColl Steuber, Sept. 23, 1950; children: Helen, Barbara MacVean. AB cum laude, Harvard U., 1949; PhD, U. London, 1954. Sr. rsch. fellow Inst. Islamic Studies, McGill U., Montreal, Que., Can., 1954-55; sociol. rsch. officer Colonial Office, London and Mauritius, 1955-58; sr. lectr. social anthropology London Sch. Econs., 1958-68; prof. anthropology U. Calif., Berkeley, 1968—, chmn. dept., 1970-71, dean social scis., 1971-74, dir. Hearst Mus. Anthropology, 1989—; prof. emeritus, 1991—; dir. U. Calif. Study Ctr. for U.K. and Ireland, London, 1986-88. Author: Indians in a Plural Society, 1961; author and editor: Problems of Smaller Territories, 1967, (with M. Benedict) Men, Women & Money in Seychelles, 1982, The Anthropology of World's Fairs, 1983; contbr. numerous articles to profl. jours. Sgt. USAF, 1942-46. Recipient Western Heritage award Nat. Cowboy Hall of Fame, 1984; rsch. fellow Colonial Office, 1955-58, 60, U. Calif., Berkeley, 1974-75; grantee NEH, 1981-83. Fellow Royal Anthrop. Inst. (mem. coun. 1962-65, 67-68, 86-89), Am. Anthrop. Assn.; mem. Assn. Social Anthropologists of Brit. Commonwealth, Athenaeum Club (London). Office: U Calif Berkeley Heart Mus Anthropology Berkeley CA 94720

BENEDICT, GARY FRANCIS, manufacturing executive, educator; b. Chgo., May 31, 1954; s. Courtney Smith and Elizabeth Dorothea (Lorentz) B.; m. Marilyn Henderson Brown, Aug. 13, 1977; children: Jason, Melinda, Cherie, John. BS in Mfg. Engring. Tech., Ariz. State U., 1977; M in Internat. Mgmt., Am. Grad. Sch. Internat. Mgmt., 1993. Mfg. engr. Allied-Signal Aerospace Co., Phoenix, 1977-81, sr. engr., 1981-84, project leader, 1984-86, sr. supr. axial-centrifugal compressor engine group, 1986-91; mfg. dir. CFE Co. (AlliedSignal Co. and GE), Phoenix, 1991—; assoc. prof. Ariz. State U., Tempe, 1978-91. Author: Nontraditional Manufacturing Processes, 1987; co-author 5 books; contbr. articles to profl. jours. and mags. in U.S., U.K. and France; patentee method and appratus for laser gear hardening and laser hardening of steel. Recipient award for excellence in oral presentation Soc. Automotive Engrs., 1980. Mem. Am. Mgmt. Assn., Soc. Mfg. Engrs. (Young Engr. of Yr. award 1987). Office: CFE Co PO Box 62332 111 S 34th St Phoenix AZ 85082-2332

BENEDICT, KENT, emergency physician, consultant; b. L.A., Nov. 30, 1941; s. Joseph and Kathryn (Kent) B.; m. Paula Carol Gomez; children: Karl Kent, Andrew Taylor, Alix. AB, U. Calif., Berkeley, 1963; MD, U. So. Calif., 1968. Diplomate Am. Bd. Emergency Medicine. Intern Kaiser Found. Hosp., San Francisco, 1968-69; resident Stanford U. Hosp., Palo Alto, 1969-71; emergency physician Emergency Med. Group, Watsonville, Calif., 1977—; clin. asst. prof. Med. Ctr. Stanford (Calif.) U., 1978—; comdr. U.S. Maritime Svc., 1979—; chief med. officer Calif. Maritime Acad., Vallejo, 1980—; med. dir. Emergency Med. Svcs., San Benito County, Calif., 1990—, Santa Cruz County, Calif., 1991—; med. cons. Project Piaxtla/Hesperian Found., Palo Alto, Calif., 1971-73, Santa Cruz and San Benito County Emergency Med. Svcs., 1985-90; spl. med. cons. to the Pres. Argentina, 1986. Contbg. author: Merchant Marine Officer's Handbook, 1989; cons.: Where There is No Doctor, 1974. Mem. Select Com. to Study Med. Edn., U. Calif., Santa Cruz, 1974, Emergency Med. Care Commn., Santa Cruz, 1979-89; chmn. Santa Cruz County Trauma Com., 1986-88. U. Calif. Alumni Assn. scholar, 1960; named Outstanding Resident in Pediatrics, Stanford U. Med. Ctr., 1971, Emergency Physician of Yr., County of Santa Cruz, 1988. Fellow Am. Coll. Emergency Phyisians; mem. Emergency Med. Svcs. Med. Dirs. Assn. Calif., Nat. Assn. Emergency Med. Svcs. Physicians. Office: Emergency Med Group 6800 Soquel Dr Aptos CA 95003

BENENSON, ABRAM SALMON, epidomiologist; b. Napanoch, N.Y., Jan. 22, 1914; s. Jacob and Sonia (Mekler) B.; m. Regina Van Aalten, May 20, 1939; children: Michael W., Thomas R., James S., Sonia A. BA, Cornell U., Ithaca, N.Y., 1933; MD, Cornell U., N.Y.C., 1937. Diplomate Am. Bd. Pathology, Preventive Medicine, Microbiology. Commanding officer Tropical Rsch. Med. Lab., San Juan, 1952-54; dir. exptl. medicine U.S. Army, Ft. Detrick, Md., 1954-55; dir. immunology div. Walter Reed Inst. Rsch., Washington, 1957-60, dir. communicable disease and immunology, 1960-62; dir. sci. adv. SEATO Cholera Rsch. Lab., Dacca, East Pakistan, 1962-66; prof. preventive medicine and microbiology Jefferson Med. Coll., Phila., 1966-69; prof., chmn. dept. of community medicine U. Ky. Coll. of Medicine, Lexington, 1969-77; dir. Gorgas Meml. Lab., Panama, 1977-81; prof. divsn. of epidemiology biostats. Grad. Sch. Pub. Health, San Diego State U., 1982-92, prof. emeritus, 1992—, head, 1982-90; dir. com. immunization, dir. subcom. disease control Armed Forces Epidemiol. Bd., Washington. Editor: Control of Communicable Diseases in Man, 1970, 75, 80, 85, 90; contbr. articles to profl. jours. Bd. dirs. Project Concern Internat. Task Force on AIDS, San Diego County. Col. U.S. Army, 1940-62. Recipient award for excellence APHA, 1991, John Snow award, 1992. Jewish. Home: 6619 Claremore Ave San Diego CA 92120-3121

BENES, ANDREW CHARLES, professional baseball player; b. Evansville, Ind., Aug. 20, 1967. With San Diego Padres, 1989—; mem. U.S. Olympic Baseball Team, 1988, Nat. League All-Star Team, 1993. Named Sporting News Rookie Pitcher of Yr., 1989. Office: San Diego Padres PO Box 2000 San Diego CA 92112

BENEŠ, NORMAN STANLEY, meteorologist; b. Detroit, July 1, 1921; s. Stanley and Cecelia (Sereneck) B.; m. Elinor Simson, May 5, 1945 (div. Feb. 1972); children: Gregory, Heather, Michelle, Francine; m. Celia Sereneck, Mar. 3, 1972. BS, U. Wash., 1949; postgrad., U. Calif., Davis, 1963, U. Mich., 1966. Chief meteorologist Hawthorne Sch. of Aero., Moultrie, Ga., 1951-55; meteorologist U.S. Weather Bur., Phoenix, 1955-57, 59-60; meteorologist in charge NSF, Hallett, Antarctica, 1958; sta. sci. leader NSF, Byrd, Antarctica, 1960-61; meteorologist Nat. Weather Service, Sacramento, Calif., 1962-84; mem. Exec. Com. Range Benes Peak, Antarctica. Contbr. articles to profl. jours. Pres. local chpt. PTA, 1965. With USN, 1943-46, PTO. Mem. AAAS, Am. Meteorol. Soc., Am. Geophys. Union, Nat. Weather Assn., Masons. Home: 3311 Holiday Ln Placerville CA 95667

BENGELSDORF, IRVING SWEM, science writer, consultant; b. Chgo., Oct. 23, 1922; s. Jacob and Frieda (Wiener) B.; m. Beverly Devorah Knapp, June 12, 1949; children: Ruth, Lea, Judith. BS in Chemistry with highest honors, U. Ill., 1943; student, Cornell U.; MS, U. Chgo., 1948, PhD, 1951. Mem. chemistry faculty UCLA, 1952-54; rsch. chemist Gen. Electric Rsch. Lab., Schenectady, N.Y., 1954-59; rsch. group leader Texaco-U.S. Rubber Rsch. Ctr., Parsippany, N.J., 1959-60; sr. scientist U.S. Borax Rsch. Corp., Anaheim, Calif., 1960-63; sci. editor L.A. Times, 1963-70; dir. sci. communication Calif. Inst. Tech., Pasadena, 1971-80; contbg. sci. columnist L.A. Herald-Examiner, 1978-86; tech. writer, specialist Jet Propulsion Lab., Calif. Inst. Tech., Pasadena, 1980-88; contb. sci. columnist Oceanside (Calif.) Blade-Citizen, 1992—; cons. Jet Propulsion Lab., 1988—; Disting. vis. prof. U. So. Calif., L.A., 1971-90; tchr. TV course in Russian lang. Gen. Electric Rsch. Lab., Schenectady, 1958; cons. NASA, 1979. Author: Spaceship Earth: People and Pollution, 1969; co-author: Biology: A Unique Science, 1978; contbr. chpts. to books, articles to profl. jours.; patentee in field. Participant 19th Pugwash Conf. on Sci. and World Affairs, Sochi, USSR, 1969; mem. cabinet U. Chgo. Alumni Cabinet, 1968-71; mem. U. Calif. Water Resources Ctr. ADv. Coun., Riverside, 1973—; mem. Mayor Bradley's Energy Policy Com., L.A., 1974. With USN, 1944-46. Recipient Claude Bernard Sci. Journalism award Nat. Soc. for Med. Rsch., 1968, Bicentennial Humanitarian award City of L.A., 1981. Mem. AAAS (Westinghouse Writing award 1967, 69), Am. Chem. Soc. (James T. Grady award 1967), Nat. Assn. Sci. Writers, U. Chgo. Alumni Club L.A. (Disting. Alumnus award 1975), Soc. for Tech. Communication (hon.), Sigma Xi. Home and Office: 3778 Via Las Villas Oceanside CA 92056-7258

BENGHIAT, JACQUES, computer science engineer, consultant; b. Apr. 23, 1955; s. Samuel and Celine (Gholam) B. BS, Imperial Coll., London, 1976; MS, U. Manchester, Eng., 1978, PhD, 1981. Engr. Marconi Space and Def., Eng., 1977, 78, OSM Computer Corp., Mountain View, Calif., 1982-84; v.p. engring. Synergistic Computers, Milpitas, Calif., 1988-91; engr., prin. Syscon Consulting, Cupertino, Calif., 1984—; pres. Northport Techs., Fremont, Calif., 1989—, Centerpointe Techs., Cupertino, 1990—, Syscon Devel. Corp., Cupertino, 1991—. Office: Syscon Devel Corp 22330 Homestead Rd # 201 Cupertino CA 95014

BENGISU, MURAT, materials engineer; b. Karlsruhe, Germany, Sept. 21, 1963; came to U.S., 1985; s. Ozdemir Latif and Nevin (Dincer) B.; m. Pelin Acar, May 21, 1988; children: Basak Sila, Beste Gizem. BSME, Dokuz Eylul U., Izmir, Turkey, 1984; MS Materials Engring., N.Mex. Inst. Mining & Tech., 1987, PhD in Materials Engring., 1992. Rsch. asst. N.Mex. Inst. Mining & Tech., Socorro, 1985-93. Contbr. articles to profl. jours. Mem. Am. Soc. Metals, Am. Ceramic Soc. Muslim. Office: New Mex Inst Mining & Tech Materials & Metallurgical Socorro NM 87801

BENGSON, STUART A., land reclamationist; b. Marquette, Mich., Aug. 20, 1943; s. Carl E. and Clara L. (Anderson) B.; m. Wendie J. McVay, Oct. 16, 1976. BS in Forestry, U. Ariz., 1970, MS in Nat. Resources Adminstrn., 1978. Cert. profl. soil erosion and sediment control specialist. Seasonal technician U.S. Forest Svc., U.S. Nat. Park Svc., Cave Creek and Tucson, Ariz., and Mapleton, Oreg., 1965-69; lab./field technician U. Ariz., Tucson, 1969-71; forester U.S. Forest Svc../St. Joe Nat. Forest, St. Maries, Idaho, 1971-73; agronomist Mission Complex, Sahuarita, Ariz., 1973—; cons. U.S. Bur. Reclamation, 1985-91, Cyprus, Magma, Phels-Dodge; prog. dir. Nat. Resource Conservation Workshop for Ariz. Youth, 1982-91; chmn. Pima Natural Resource Conservation Dist., 1984—. Contbr. articles to profl. jours. Vice chmn. BLM Safford Dist. Pub. Lands Adv. Coun., Ariz., 1978-88; mem. com. on the Ariz. Environement Adv. Coun., 1976—, Pima Assn. Govts. Environ. Planning Adv. Com., 1983—; apptd. by Gov. to Ariz. Environ. Edn. Task Force, 1990-92. Mem. Soc. Range Mgmt. (Ariz. sect. sec.-treas. 1978, Pres.'s award 1989, 91), Soil and Water Conservation Soc. (Ariz. chpt. pres. 1982, Conservationist of the Yr. award 1984), Soc. Mining Engrs. of AIME, Am. Soc. Surface Mining and Reclamation (chmn. internat. tailing reclamation tech. dir. 1985—), Ariz. Mining Assn. (chmn. pub. lands com. 1988—), United Four Wheel Drive Assn. (4-Wheeler of the Yr. 1986, land-use dir. 1986-86), others. Office: ASARCO Inc Mission Unit PO Box 111 Sahuarita AZ 85629-0111

BENGTSON, GAYLYNN SNIDER, dentistry office manager; b. Boise, Idaho, June 16, 1957; d. Paul Lawrence Clifford and Cathryn Marlene (Rhoades) Snider; married, Sept. 13, 1986; children: Erika Kaitlin, Adrienne Kayla. Grad., Boise State U., 1976; student, Lewis & Clark State Coll., 1977-79. Oper. rm. technician St. Joseph's Regional Med. Ctr., 1976-79; new accounts rep., pub. rels., mktg. & merchant svcs. rep. Twin River Nat. Bank, 1979-82; outside sales supr. classified advt. Lewiston (Idaho) Morning Tribune, 1983-84, retail advt. rep., 1984-86; territorial sales rep. Moore Bus. Forms, 1984; now office mgr., safety & health mgr., surg. asst. Implant & Gen. Dentistry of Idaho, Lewiston, 1986—; owner, children's couture clothing co. M.Bellish, Lewiston, Idaho, 1993—. Bd. dirs. Lewiston Svc. League, 1989—. Anne Bollinger Music scholar Lewis & Clark State Coll. Fellow Internat. Congress of Oral Implantologists. Office: Implant & Gen Dentistry 602 11th Ave Lewiston ID 83501

BENIRSCHKE, KURT, pathologist, educator; b. Glueckstadt, Germany, May 26, 1924; came to U.S., 1949, naturalized, 1955; s. Fritz Franz and Marie (Luebcke) B.; m. Marion Elizabeth Waldhausen, May 17, 1952; children: Stephen Kurt, Rolf Joachim, Ingrid Marie. Student, U. Hamburg, Germany, 1942, 45-48, U. Berlin, Germany, 1943, U. Wuerzburg, Germany, 1943-44; M.D., U. Hamburg, 1948. Resident Teaneck, N.J., 1950-51, Peter Bent Brigham Hosp., Boston, 1951-52, Boston Lying-in-Hosp., 1952-53, Free Hosp. for Women, Boston, 1953, Children's Hosp., Boston, 1953; pathologist Boston Lying-in-Hosp., 1955-60; teaching fellow, assoc. Med. Sch. Harvard, 1954-60; prof. pathology, chmn. dept. pathology Med. Sch. Dartmouth, Hanover, N.H., 1960-70; prof. reproductive medicine and pathology U. Calif. at San Diego, 1970—; chmn. dept. pathology U. Calif. at San Diego (Sch. Med.), La Jolla, 1976-79; dir. research San Diego Zoo, 1975-86, trustee, 1986—; cons. NIH, 1957-70. Served with German Army, 1942-45. Mem. Am. Soc. Pathology, Internat. Acad. Pathology, Am. Coll. Pathology, Teratol. Soc., Am. Soc. Zool. Veterinarians. Home: 8457 Prestwick Dr La Jolla CA 92037-2023 Office: U Calif at San Diego San Diego CA 92013-8321

BENJAMIN, DAVID JOEL, III, radio broadcasting executive; b. Kansas City, Mo., Jan. 3, 1947; s. David Joel II and Jeanne Louise (Lyon) B.; m. Laurie Melcher, Aug. 6, 1983; children: Elizabeth Melcher, David Theodore. BA, Yale U., 1969; MBA, Harvard U., 1971. Asst. pub. Fortune Mag., N.Y.C., 1971-72; pres., chief exec. officer Community Pacific Broadcasting Co. L.P., Salinas, Calif., 1974—. Former v.p. World Affairs Coun., Portland, Oreg., 1982; former pres. Richard D. Collins Cancer Wellness Ctr., Monterey, Calif., 1990; v.p. Yale Club of Monterey County, 1990; commr. Community and Cultural Commn., Carmel, Calif., 1990; mem. adv. bd. mem. Nat. Security Archive, Washington, 1990. Mem. Nat. Assn. Broadcasters (bd .dirs.), Calif. Assn. Broadcasters (bd. dirs.), Oreg. Assn. Broadcasters (former pres.), Beach and Tennis Club (Pebble Beach, Calif.), John Gardiner's Tennis Ranch Club, Old Capital Club (Monterey, Calif.). Jewish. Office: Community Pacific Broadcasting Co PO Box 80011 933 N Main St Ste A Salinas CA 93912

BENJAMIN, JEFFREY ROYCE, media executive; b. Lansing, Mich., Mar. 15, 1954; s. Royce M. and Ann Elizabeth (Wettlaufer) B. BA, U. Mich., 1978, MBA, 1980. Auditor Arthur Andersen & Co., Detroit, 1979; sr. auditor Arthur Young & Co., Los Angeles, 1980-83; controller, mgr. Los Angeles Olympic Organizing Com., 1983-85; treas., chief fin. officer Global Media, Ltd., Washington, 1986-88; dir. fin. and adminstrn. Sony Imagesoft Inc., L.A., 1988—; also mgr. for singer and songwriter Kenny Rankin; mgr. Kenny Rankin Music Prodns., L.A. Editor, author polit. commentary The Mackinac Spectator, 1988. 89. 90. Bd. dirs., treas. Live Aid Found., L.A., 1985—, Rock Against Drugs Found., 1986—. Mem. Beta Alpha Psi. Republican. Home: 839 N Hayworth Ave West Hollywood CA 90046-7106 Office: Sony Imagesoft Inc 9200 W Sunset Blvd Bldg 820 West Hollywood CA 90069-3603

BENJAMIN, KAREN JEAN, real estate broker; b. Biddeford, Maine, May 21, 1951; d. George and Rachel (Shevenell) Reggep; m. Christopher Mark Benjamin, Mar. 1, 1980; children: Matthew C., Michael T. Student, U. Maine, 1977, Ea. Ariz. Coll., 1990—. Proprietor Neptune's Landing Restaurant, Old Orchard Beach, Maine, 1977-78; agt. Star Valley Real Estate, Payson, Ariz., 1979-82; proprietor Benjamin Realty, Payson, 1982—. Vol. Payson Food Bank, 1987; mem. fin. com. Ponderosa Bapt. Ch., Payson, 1989, auditor, 1990, Sunday sch. tchr., 1992—; Payson coord. Phoenix Children's Hosp., 1988—; v.p., pres. Head Start, Payson, 1987-88; classroom vol. Payson Elem. Sch., 1988—; bd. dirs. PTA, Payson, 1989—; precinct committeeman, dist. sec., state committeeman, Phoenix, 1973. Named Outstanding Young Women in Am., 1987. Mem. Ctrl. Ariz. Bd. of Realtors (sec. Payson chpt. 1982-83, grievance com. 1988—, chair 1990-92, fin. com. 1990-91, bd. dirs. 1990-91). Republican. Home: 755 Ezell Rd Payson AZ 85541 Office: HCR PO Box 49aa Payson AZ 85547-0049

BENJAMIN, KARL STANLEY, artist; b. Chicago, Ill., Dec. 29, 1925; s. Eustace Lincoln and Marie (Klamsteiner) B.; m. Beverly Jean Paschke, Jan. 29, 1949; children: Beth Marie, Kris Ellen, Bruce Lincoln. Student, Northwestern U., 1943, 46; B.A., U. Redlands, 1949; M.A., Claremont Grad. Sch., 1960. Loren Barton Babcock Miller prof. of fine arts, artist in resident Pomona Coll. Traveling exhbns. include New Talent, Am. Fedn. Arts, 1959, 4 Abstract Classicists, Los Angeles and San Francisco museums, 1959-61, West Coast Hard Edge, Inst. Contemporary Arts, London, Eng., 1960, Purist Painting, Am. Fedn. Arts, 1960-61, Geometric Abstractions in Am, Whitney Mus., 1962, Paintings of the Pacific, U.S., Japan and Australia, 1961-63, Artists Environment, West Coast, Amon Carter Mus., Houston, 1962-63, Denver annual, 1965, Survey of Contemporary Art, Speed Mus., Louisville, 1965, The Colorists, San Francisco Mus., 1965, Art Across Am, Mead Corp., 1965-67, The Responsive Eye, Mus. Modern Art, 1965-66, 30th Biennial Exhbn. Am. Painting, Corcoran Gallery, 1967, 35th Biennial Exhbn. Am. Painting, 1977, Painting and Sculpture in California: The Modern Era, San Francisco Mus. Modern Art, 1976-77, Smithsonian Nat. Collection Fine Arts, Washington, 1976-77, Los Angeles Hard Edge: The Fifties and Seventies, Los Angeles County Mus. Art, 1977, Corcoran Gallery, Washington, Cheney Cowles Mus., Spokane, 1980, Calif. State U., Bakersfield, 1982, Henry Gallery, U. Wash., 1982, U. Calif., Santa Barbara, 1984, L.A. Mcpl. Art Galleries, Barnsdall Park, 1986, Turning the Tide: Early Los Angeles Modernists, Santa Barbara Mus. Art, Oakland Mus., others, 1989-91; rep. permanent collections, Whitney Mus., L.A. County Mus. Art, San Francisco Mus. Art, Santa Barbara (Calif.) Mus. Art, Pasadena (Calif.) Art Mus., Long Beach (Calif.) Mus. Art, La Jolla (Calif.) Mus. Art, Fine Arts Gallery San Diego, U. Redlands, Mus. Modern Art, Israel, Pomona Coll., Scripps Coll., Univ. Mus., Berkeley, Calif., Wadsworth Atheneum, Nat. Collection Fine

Arts, Seattle Mus. Modern Art, Newport Harbor Mus., U. N.Mex. Mus. Art, Wash. State U., L.A. Mus. Contemporary Art; retrospective exhbn. covering yrs. 1955-87 Calif State U. at Northridge, 1989. Served with USNR, 1943-46. Visual Arts grantee NEA, 1983, 89. Address: 675 W 8th St Claremont CA 91711 Office: Pomona Coll Dept Arts 333 N College Way Claremont CA 91711-6328

BENJAMIN, LORNA SMITH, psychologist; b. Rochester, N.Y., Jan. 7, 1934; d. Lloyd Albert and Esther (Tack) Smith; children—Laureen, Linda. A.B., Oberlin Coll., 1955; Ph.D., U. Wis., 1960. NIMH fellow dept. psychiatry U. Wis., 1958-62, clin. psychology intern, 1960-64, asst. prof., 1966-71, assoc. prof., 1971-77, prof. psychiatry, 1977-88; prof. psychology U. Utah, 1988—; research asso. Wis. Psychol. Inst., Madison, 1962-66. Contbr. articles to profl. jours. Mem. Am. Psychol. Assn., Soc. Psychotherapy Research, Phi Beta Kappa. Office: U Utah Dept Psychology Salt Lake City UT 84112

BENNER, DOROTHY SPURLOCK, educator; b. Greeley, Colo., Dec. 17, 1938; d. Lloyd Elsworth and Helen Rosalee (Pierce) Spurlock; m. Jerry Lee Benner, June 7, 1959; children: Shey Lee, Craig Lloyd. BA, Colo. State Coll., 1962, MA, 1968; EdS, U. No. Colo., 1978. Cert. tchr. elem. and bus. edn., spl. edn. and sch. psychology. Telephone operator Mountain Bell, Greeley, Colo., 1957; sec. Conn. Mut. Life, Greeley, Colo., 1960-61; substitute tchr. Sch. Dist. 6 and Outlying Dists., Greeley, Colo., 1962-67; tchr. Sch. Dist. 6, Greeley, Colo., 1968—; tchr. night sch. Aims Community Coll., 1989-93. Mem. NEA (life), Greeley Tchrs. Assn. (mem. negotiation team 1981—, sec. 1985-91, v.p. 1991-92, pres. elect 1992-93, pres. 1993—), Colo. Edn. Assn., Kappa Delta Pi, Delta Kappa Gamma (pres. 1980-81). Republican. Methodist. Home: 1839 26th St Greeley CO 80631-8115

BENNET, WILLIAM S(AMUEL), II, sales representative; b. L.A., July 26, 1952; s. William Samuel and Phyllis (Stay) B.; m. Denise Ann Raggi, Nov. 20, 1976. BS, Calif. Polytech. State U., 1974; MBA, Calif. State U., Fresno, 1990. Sales rep. Helena Chem. Co., Fresno, 1974-76, Nor-Am Agrl. Products, Chgo., 1976-79; mgr. United Agri. Products, Fresno, 1979-81; sales rep. Am. Cyanamid Co., Wayne, N.J., 1981—. Bd. dirs. Californians for Food Safety, Sacramento, 1990. Mem. Calif. Agrl. Prodn. Cons. Assn. (pres. 1990), NAMA (pres. Fresno chpt. 1988-89), Plant Protectors Golf Assn. (chmn. Fresno chpt. 1986). Home and Office: 3205 E Fremont Ave Fresno CA 93710-4907

BENNETT, BRADFORD CARL, research scientist; b. Dayton, Ohio, May 27, 1953; s. Carl Vernon and Norma June (Linkinhoker) B. BSME, U. Wis., 1975; MSME, Stanford U., 1976, PhD in ME, 1982. Staff engr. Acurex Corp., Mt. View, Calif., 1988; sr. rsch. scientist MCAT Inst., San Jose, 1988-93; dir. Somatic Learning Ctr., San Francisco, 1993—, co-coord. 1993 profl. tng. in Hanna Somatic Edn.; assoc. Novato Inst. for Somatic Rsch. and Tng., 1991—. Contbr. articles to profl. jours. Mem. AIAA, ASME, Trager Inst., Cloud Hands West Tai Chi Assn. (chmn.), Tai Chi Friends Reunion (chmn. 1991-93). Office: Somatic Learning Ctr 367 Joost Ave San Francisco CA 94131

BENNETT, BRIAN O'LEARY, utilities executive; b. Bklyn., Dec. 5, 1955; s. Robert Joseph and Barbara Ashton (Michael) B. BA in Econs., George Washington U., 1982; JD, Southwestern U., 1982. Legis. caseworker U.S. Sen. James L. Buckley, Washington, 1973-77; legis. asst. U.S. Congressman Bob Dornan, L.A., 1977-78; dist. field rep. State Congressman Bob Dornan, L.A., 1978-83; dir. comm. Calif. Dept. Housing & Community Devel., Sacramento, 1983-84; chief of staff U.S. Congressman R.K. Dornan, Washington, 1985-89; reg. affairs mgr. So. Calif. Edison Co., Santa Ana, 1989—. Contbr. articles to L.A. Times. Active organizing com. Calif. Bush for U.S. Pres., 1986-88; Calif. del. selection com., 1988, 92; campaign mgr. Dornan for U.S. Congress, 1984, 86, 88; mem. cen. com. Calif. State Rep. Party, mem. platform com., 1988; del. Rep. Nat. Conf., 1988, 92; mem. Orange County Pro-Life PAC; bd. dirs. Orange County Forum, Orange County Pub. Affairs Assn. Named one of Outstanding Young Men of Am., 1988. Mem. Orange County Pro Life Polit. Action Com., Orange County Pub. Affairs Assn. (bd. dirs.). Roman Catholic. Office: So Calif Edison 1325 S Grand Ave Santa Ana CA 92705-4499

BENNETT, BRUCE DAVID, educational administrator; b. Putnam, Conn., Aug. 3, 1948; s. Wilfred H. and Rita A. (Orlowski) B.; m. Karson Joy Brazee, May 22, 1976. BS, E. Conn. State Coll., 1971; MA, U. Conn., 1980; postgrad. U. Washington, 1989. Asst. dir. community edn. Ea. Conn. State Coll., Willimantic, 1968-71; tchr. Thompson (Conn.) Pub. Sch. System, 1971-72; asst. dir. community edn. Mohegan Community Coll., Norwich, Conn., 1972-74; dir. student activities/alumni affairs Mohegan Community Coll., Norwich, 1975-81, adj. faculty, 1974-81, dir. fin. aid, 1981-83; asst. dir. student service/ fin. aid officer Seattle Opportunities Indsl. Ctr., 1983-86; coord. student svcs. Continuing Edn. Div. U. Wash., Seattle, 1986—; edn. cons. Bennett and Assocs., Seattle, 1986—; adv. bd. North Seattle C.C., 1990—. Bd. dirs. King County Coun. Vocat. Edn., Settle, 1986-90; mem. Burns Soc. Seattle; aide to Soviet amb. Goodwill Games, 1990; exec. bd. Seattle Community Coun. Mem. Am. Coll. Pers. Assn., Nat. Acad. Advising Assn. (conf. planner and presentor 1988-92), Nat. Assn. Campus Activities (presentor-coord. numerous confs.), Nat. Assn. Student Pers. Adminstrs., Nat. Univ. Continuing Edn. Assn. (conf. planner and presentor 1987-91), Washington Assn. Profl. Counselors and Advisors (exec. bd. 1989-91), U. Wash. Profl. Staff Assn. (bd. dirs. 1993—). Home: 10718 38th Ave NE Seattle WA 98125-7906 Office: U Wash 5001 25th Ave NE Seattle WA 98195-0001

BENNETT, BRUCE MICHAEL, mathematics educator; b. N.Y.C., Mar. 25, 1941; s. Edwin P. and Frances (Neuschatz) B.; m. Bonnie Charley, Aug. 2, 1962 (div.); children: Raphael Sebastian, Kamala Sati. Student, Harvard U., 1958-61; BA, L.I. U., 1964; PhD, Columbia U., 1968. Asst. prof. in math. Harvard U., Cambridge, Mass., 1968-71, Stanford U., Palo Alto, Calif., 1971-74; assoc. prof. U. Calif., Irvine, 1974-88, prof., 1988—. Co-author: Observer Mechanics, 1989; contbr. articles to profl. publs. Bd. dirs. Trabuco Canyon (Calif.) Water Dist., 1979-85. Home: 1294 Star Rte Orange CA 92667 Office: U Calif Dept Math Irvine CA 92717

BENNETT, BRUCE WEBB, healthcare executive; b. Pasadena, Calif., Nov. 23, 1948; s. Ben and Elizabeth (Pedrini) B.; m. Merilee Ann Bennett, Aug. 31, 1968; children: Brian Timothy, Christopher Thomas. BA, U. Md., 1973. Interpreter U.S. Air Force, 1969-73; asst. adminstr. Community Convalescent Ctr., Riverside, Calif., 1973-75; adminstr. Community Convalescent Ctr., 1975-89; pres. Ben Bennett, Inc., Riverside, 1988—; guest lectr. U. Calif., Riverside, 1978-79, San Bernardino County Ombudsman Tng. prog., 1980-81, Loma Linda U./VA Hosp., 1982; mem. adv. com. Grad. Sch. Mgmt., U. Calif. Riverside; bd. dirs. Provident Savings Bank. Chmn. Riverside Arts Found., 1985-86, chmn. Mayor's ball for the arts, 1986-88; chmn. Cultural Heritage Bd., City of Riverside, 1980-81; treas. Children's Ctr. of Riverside, 1982-88; chmn. community adv. com. spl. edn. Riverside Unified Sch. Dist., 1986-88; chief fin. officer Riverside Community Hosp. Found., 1988, bd. dirs., 1986-87, vice chmn., 1991-93, chmn., 1993—; mem. City of Riverside Downtown Master Plan Com., 1980; bd. dirs. United Way of Riverside, 1984-86; vice chmn. Bus. Vols. for the Arts, 1989, others. Recipient Am. Coll. Health Care Adminstrs. 1987 Disting. Adminstr. award, So. Calif. Coun. of Activity Coordinators 1986 Outstanding Long Term Care Adminstr. award, Nat. Assn. Activity Profls. 1988 Adminstr. of Yr award. Mem. San Bernardino-Riverside Assn. Health Facilities (pres. 1980), Calif. Assn. Health Facilities (v.p. Region V 1986-87), Am. Health Care Assn. (facilities stds. com. 1987), Am. Coll. Health Care Adminstrs. (chpt. pres. 1981-82, REgion X gov. 1991-92), Young Pres. Orgn., Kiwanis Club (chmn. 1989). Episcopalian. Home: 2787 Rumsey Dr Riverside CA 92506-1448 Office: Ben Bennett Inc 6086 Brockton Ave Ste 4 Riverside CA 92506-2295

BENNETT, CARL MCGHIE, engineering company executive, consultant, army reserve and national guard officer; b. Salt Lake City, Sept. 11, 1933; s. M. Woodruff and Sybil L. (McGhie) B.; m. Ardel Krantz, Aug. 10, 1954; children: Carlene, Matt, Brent, Dale, Hugh, Caren, Teri. BS, U. Utah, 1956; postgrad., U.S. Army Engr. Sch., 1964; M, Command and Gen. Staff Coll., 1974; postgrad., Indsl. Coll. Armed Forces, 1976. Commd. 2d. lt. ROTC U.S. Army, 1953; treas. and office mgr. Hercules Inc. and Data Source Corp., Salt Lake City and Los Angeles, 1963-70; controller Boise Cascade, Los Angeles, 1970-72; corp. controller Griffin Devel. Co., Los Angeles, 1972-75; controller Dart Industries, Dart Resorts, Los Angeles, 1975-78; chief fin. officer Ford, Bacon & Davis, Salt Lake City, 1978-87; pres. B & Assocs., 1987—; cons. in field, 1985-89. Rep. County Del., 1992—. Served to lt. col. U.S. Army Res., 1953-79, col. Utah N.G., 1985—. Recipient Meritorious Service medal Pres. of the U.S., 1979. Mem. Controllers Council, Nat. Assn. Accts. (v.p., bd. dirs. 1979-85), Inst. Mgmt. Accts. Office: 8425 South 20th East C-5 Sandy UT 84093

BENNETT, CHARLES LEON, vocational and graphic arts educator; b. Salem, Oreg., Feb. 5, 1951; s. Theodore John and Cora Larena (Rowland) B.; m. Cynthia Alice Hostman, June 12, 1976 (div.); m. Lynn Marie Toland, Aug. 12, 1977 (div.); children: Mizzy Marie, Charles David; m. Christina M. Crawford, Dec. 19, 1987 (div.). AS in Vocat. Tchr. Edn., Clackamas Community Coll., 1977; AS in Gen. Studies, Linn Benton Community Coll., 1979; student Ea. Oreg. State Coll., 1989—. Tchr. printing Tongue Point Job Corps, Astoria, Oreg., 1979-80; tchr., dept. chmn. Portland (Oreg.) pub. schs., 1980—; owner, mgr. printing and pub. co., Portland, 1981-87. With AUS, 1970-72. Mem. Oreg. Vocat. Trade-Tech. Assn. (dept. chmn., pres. graphic arts div., Indsl. Educator of Year 1981-82), Oreg. Vocat. Assn. (Vocat. Tchr. of Yr. 1982-83), Graphic Arts Tech. Found., In-Plant Printing Mgmt. Assn., Internat. Graphic Arts Edn. Assn. (v.p. N.W. region VI), Oreg. Assn. Manpower Spl. Needs Personnel, Oreg. Indsl. Arts Assn., Nat. Rifle Assn., Internat. Platform Assn. Nat. Assn. Quick Printers, Am. Vocat. Assn., Inplant Printing Mgmt. Assn., Portland Club Lithographers and Printing House Craftsmen. Republican. Home: 20295 S Unger Rd Beavercreek OR 97004 Office: 8020 NE Tillamook St Portland OR 97213-6655

BENNETT, CHARLES TURNER, social welfare administrator; b. Egypt, Ark., June 17, 1932; s. Charley Clower and Lois LaJoy (Turner) B.; m. Ella Jane Fye, July 6, 1962; children: Rebeca Joy, Lisa Anne. Grad., Moody Bible Inst., Chgo., 1953; student, UCLA, 1970; MA, Fuller Theol. Seminary, Pasadena, Calif., 1972, Claremont (Calif.) Grad. Sch., 1983. Bush pilot Mission Aviation, Mexico, Mexico, 1955-68; dir. research Mission Aviation Fellowship, Fullerton, Calif., 1968-72; pres., chief exec. officer Mission Aviation Fellowship, Redlands, Calif., 1973-85; exec. dir. Presby. Ctr. for Mission Studies, Fullerton, 1972-73; exec. v.p. Food for the Hungry Internat., Geneva, Switzerland, 1985-88, Scottsdale, Ariz., 1988-91; pres. Ptnrs. Internat., San Jose, Calif., 1992—; bd. chmn. Air Serv. Internat. Redlands; bd. dirs. Evang. Fgn. Missions Assn., Washington, 1976-82; founder Redlands Aviation Corp., 1980; adv. bd. Presbyn. Ctr. for Mission Studies, 1983—. Author: Tinder in Tabasco, 1968, Pantano Ardiente, 1989, (with others) From Nairobi to Berkeley, 1967, God, Man and Church Growth, 1973. Chmn. world service Redlands Rotary Club., 1982-85. Named Alumnus of Yr. Fuller Theol. Seminary, 1985. Democrat. Home: 2395 Delaware-Sp 198 Santa Cruz CA 95060 Office: Ptnrs Internat 1470 4th St San Jose CA 95112

BENNETT, CHARLES WILLIAM, JR., sales executive; b. Atwater, Calif., Mar. 12, 1962; s. Charles William and Marion June (Hulsman) B.; 1 child, Austin Charles. Student, Ariz. State U., 1984. Engr. McQuay Svc., Phoenix, 1978—. Republican. Home: 8875 N 48th Dr Glendale AZ 85302-5126 Office: McQuay Svc 2330 W Mission Ln Phoenix AZ 85021

BENNETT, DOUGLAS, college official; b. Norfolk, Va., Jan. 8, 1955; s. William Oliver and Marilyn Alida (Leisk) B.; m. Mailei Cozy Mucha, Apr. 22, 1978; children: Tiffany Marie, Erika Annelise, Sarah Alida. BA, Calif. State U., Fullerton, 1977. Dir. pub. rels. Orange County Mental Health Assn., Santa Ana, Calif., 1978-80; asst. dir. devel. St. Joseph Hosp., Orange, Calif., 1981-85; found. dir. Orange Coast Coll., Costa Mesa, Calif., 1986—. Recipient Friend of Students award Assoc. Students Orange Coast Coll., 1989. Home: 14541 Hyannis Port Rd Tustin CA 92680-6728 Office: Orange Coast Coll 2701 Fairview Rd Costa Mesa CA 92626-5561

BENNETT, FRED LAWRENCE, engineering educator; b. Troy, N.Y., Apr. 4, 1939; s. Fred A. and Dorothy (Lee) B.; m. Margaret Ann Musgrave, Aug. 25, 1962; children: Matthew Lawrence, Andrew Lee. BCE, Rensselaer Poly. Inst., 1961; MS, Cornell U., 1963, PhD, 1965. Registered profl. engr., Alaska, Pa., N.H. Planning and scheduling engr. United Engrs. & Cons. Inc., Phila., 1965-68; assoc. prof. engring. mgmt. U. Alaska, Fairbanks, 1968-74, prof. engring. mgmt., 1974—, asst. to chancellor, 1977-79, vice chancellor acad. affairs, 1979-82, acting v.p. for acad. affairs, 1982-83, head dept. engring. and sci. mgmt., 1969-80, 83—; owner F. Lawrence Bennett, P.E., Engring. and Mgmt. Cons., 1969—; vis. prof. engring. Luleå, Sweden, 1992. Author: Critical Path Precedence Networks, 1977, (with others) Construction in Cold Regions, 1991; contbr. papers and articles on engring. mgmt. and cold regions constrn. to profl. publs. Mem. coun. exec. bd. Boy Scouts Am., Fairbanks, 1982—. Fellow ASCE; mem. NSPE, Am. Soc. Engring. Edn., Am. Soc. Engring. Mgmt., Project Mgmt. Inst., Soc. Logistics Engrs., Sigma Xi, Phi Kappa Phi, Tau Beta Pi, Chi Epsilon. Home: PO Box 83009 Fairbanks AK 99708-3009 Office: U Alaska 248 Duckering Bldg Fairbanks AK 99775

BENNETT, JACQUELINE BEEKMAN, school psychologist; b. Santa Paula, Calif., Sept. 4, 1946; d. Jack Edward and Margaret Blanche (MacPherson) Beekman.; m. Thomas LeRoy Bennett Jr., Aug. 5, 1972; children: Shannon, Brian, Laurie. BA, U. Calif., Davis, 1968; MS, Colo. State U., 1975, PhD, 1984. Histologist Sch. Veterinary Medicine, Davis, 1969-71; sch. psychologist Poudre Sch. Dist. R-1, Ft. Collins, Colo., 1983—. Mem. Colo. State Grievance Bd. Augment Panel, 1988-92; nominating chmn. United Presbyn. Women, Timnath, Colo., 1982, pres., 1986; com. mem. Women and the Ch. Com., Boulder Presbytery, Colo., 1985-86; elder Timnath Presbyn. Ch., 1985—. Mem. Colo. Soc. Sch. Psychologists (cert.), Nat. Assn. Sch. Psychologists (cert.), NEA, Am. Psychol. Assn., Ft. Collins Parents of Twins (pres. 1977-78), Sigma Xi, Phi Kappa Phi. Democrat. Club: Squaredusters (Ft. Collins) (v.p. 1977-78). Home: 213 Camino Real Fort Collins CO 80524-8907 Office: Poudre Sch Dist R-1 2407 La Porte Ave Fort Collins CO 80521-2297

BENNETT, JAMES CHESTER, computer consultant, real estate developer; b. Chico, Calif., May 14, 1932; s. George Clerk and Georgia Mae (James) B.; m. Grace M. Schutrum, Feb. 14, 1955 (div. 1967); children: Ronald, Becky Ann, Todd Bryant. BA in Bus., Calif. State U., Long Beach, 1965. Sgt. USAF, 1947-62; customer engr. IBM, L.A., 1962-70; mgr. computer systems Continental Airlines, L.A., 1970-82; instr. ITT Tech. Inst., Buena Park, Calif., 1982-84; dir. Ramasat Comm., LTD, Bangkok, Thailand, 1984-89; instr. ITT Tech. Inst., San Diego, 1989-90; computer cons. The Systems Group, Ramona, Calif., 1990—. Home: 1446 Cedar St Ramona CA 92065

BENNETT, JANET HUFF, legislative staff member; b. Portland, Oreg., Oct. 6, 1932; d. Stephen Loren and Melba Sperry (Stout) Huff; m. Gerald Randolph Petrey, Oct. 11, 1950 (div. 1968); m. Michael Jesse Bennett, Dec. 30, 1968; children: Mark Randall, Karee Meg Petrey Cannon, Creighton Loren; also stepchildren. Student, U. Wash. With ZCMI Dept. Store, Salt Lake City, 1975-77; office mgr. Promised Valley Theatre, Salt Lake City, 1977-79; asst. state dir. U.S. Sen. Orrin Hatch, Utah, Salt Lake City, 1979-92; dep. state dir. Senator Robert Bennett, 1993—. Chair Utah Women's Conf., Salt Lake City, 1985-92, Conf. for Srs., 1989-92; mem. task force Prevention Ritual Abuse, 1991-93, 3d Dist. Judicial Nominating Commn., 1992—, Gov's. Commn. on Women and Families, 1993—; co-chair legis. issues Women's Legis. Coun., 1989—; bd. chair Children's Mus. of Utah, Salt Lake City, 1989-90; bd. dirs. Utah Symphony, 1991—, Utah Coun. for Crime Prevention, 1989—; pres. Utah Symphony Guild, 1992-93. Mem. Profl. Rep. Women, Utah Fedn. Rep. Women. LDS. Office: Office of Senator R Bennett 4225 Bennett Federal Bldg Salt Lake City UT 84138

BENNETT, JOHN A., judge; b. Chgo., Apr. 14, 1937; s. John William and Iren (Durnovich) Bocskovits; m. Jeanine Delores Boomgarden, July 23, 1960; children: Martin John, Renea Jean, Denise Lynn, Michelle Ann. AA, Univ. State of N.Y. Regents Coll. Degree, 1975, BS, 1981; AS in Law Enforcement, Blue Mountain Community Coll., Pendleton, Oreg., 1976; LLB, La Salle Extension U., Chgo., 1976; postgrad., Nat. Judicial Coll., Reno, Nev., 1979. Enlisted chief warrant officer U.S. Army, 1955-75; ret., 1975; served intelligence agy., U.S. Army Intelligence Command, 1966-75; judge Mcpl. Ct., Hermiston, Oreg., 1978-91, Umatilla, Oreg., 1983—, Echo, Oreg., 1987—; discussion leader Nat. Jud. Coll., Reno, 1984; apptd. spl. ct. adv. com. Oreg. Supreme Ct. Bd. dirs. People to People Handicapped Group, Hermiston, Oreg., 1980-92; exec. dir. Hermiston Heritage Assn., 1982-92; bd. dirs. Oreg. Trail Tourism Council, Hermiston, 1983-92, Hist. Preservation League Oreg., 1985-87, Ft. Henrietta Found., 1987—; mem. Confederated Tribes of Umatilla Hist. Rsch. and Resources Com., 1989—; active Umatilla County Hist. Soc., 1983-92. Mem. Nat. Judges Assn. (pres. 1984-85, pub. quar. newspaper 1984, judicial career edn. achievement award, 1985, advanced achievement award in judicial edn., 1985), Oreg. Mcpl. Judges Assn. (bd. dirs. 1980-91, v.p. 1987, pres. 1987-89, editor quar. newspaper 1983-87, Meritorious Service award 1982). Roman Catholic. Home: 820 W Highland Ave Hermiston OR 97838-2234 Office: Mcpl Ct PO Box 130 Umatilla OR 97882-0130

BENNETT, JUNE NEWTON, interior designer; b. Windsor, Colo., June 17, 1926; d. Arthur Arnaud and Irma Mae (Wilkinson) Newton; m. Thomas Willard Bennett, Aug. 14, 1948; children: Polly Alison Bennett Wissing, Susan Jane Bennett Mallory. BA, U. Denver, 1948. Pvt. sec. to univ. dean Northwestern U., Evanston, Chgo., Ill., 1948-52; interior designer Bowling's Furniture, Ft. Collins, Colo., 1963-65; owner, designer Bennett-Raetzman Interior Design, Ft. Collins, 1965-67; owner, pres., designer June Newton Bennett Interior Design, Ft. Collins, 1967—. Sec., founder Ft. Collins Coun. Arts-Humanities, 1963; chairperson, founder Ft. Collins Hist. Landamrks Commn., 1968; project mgr. Avery House Restoration, 1974-79; mem. design com. Lincoln Ctr. for Performing Arts, Ft. Collins, 1982—; pres. bd. Ft. Collins Symphony, 1987-88; trustee Ft. Collins Symphony Orch., 1990—. Mem. Interior Design Guild (sec. 1986-88). Republican. Episcopalian.

BENNETT, LAWRENCE ALLEN, psychologist, criminal justice researcher; b. Selma, Calif., Jan. 4, 1923; s. Allen Walter and Eva Eleanor (Hall) B.; m. Beth J. Thompson, Aug. 14, 1948; 1 son, Glenn Livingston; 1 child, Yvonne Irene Solis. B.A., Fresno State Coll., 1949; M.A., Claremont Grad. Sch., 1954, Ph.D., 1968. Supervising psychologist Calif. med. facility Calif. Dept. Corrections, Vacaville, 1955-60, departmental supr. clin. psychology, Sacramento, 1960-67, chief of research, Sacramento, 1967-76; dir. Center for Study of Crime, Delinquency and Corrections, So. Ill. U., Carbondale, 1976-79; dir. Office of Program Evaluation, 1979-84; dir. Crime Prevention and Enforcement Div. Nat. Inst. of Justice, Washington, 1985-86; dir. Adjudication and Corrections Div., 1987-88; criminal justice cons., Sacramento, 1988—; practice clin. psychology, Sacramento, 1988—; mem. part-time faculty U. Calif., Davis, U. Calif., Berkeley, 1959-76, Calif. State U., Sacramento, 1988—; mem. bd. Calif. Crime Technol. Research Found., 1970-75; mem. Calif. State Interdepartmental Coordinating Council, 1967-76, chmn., 1970; bd. dirs. Am. Justice Inst., Sacramento, 1970-79, 88—, v.p., 1989-90, pres., 1991—; mem. juvenile adv. bd. State of Ill., 1977-79; commr. Calif. Blue Ribbon Commn. on Inmate Population Mgmt., 1988-90. Served with U.S. Army, 1942-45, 49-50. Decorated Bronze Star with oak leaf cluster. Mem. Acad. of Criminal Justice Scis., Am. Psychol. Assn., Am. Soc. Criminology, Am. Correctional Assn., Evaluation Research Soc., Assn. for Correctional Rsch. and Info. Mgmt. (pres. 1989-90). Unitarian. Author: (with Thomas S. Rosenbaum and Wayne R. McCollough) Counseling in Correctional Environments, 1978; contbr. articles in field to profl. jours. Home: 1129 Rivara Cir Sacramento CA 95864-3720 Office: Am Justice Inst 2717 Cottage Way Ste 15 Sacramento CA 95825

BENNETT, LESLIE ROBERT, radiological sciences educator, researcher; b. Denver, Feb. 13, 1918; s. Lester and Margaret E. (Gleason) B.; m. Vera Collier, Dec. 17, 1949; children: Robert Joe, Ann Bennett-Rogers, John C., Andrew C. BA, U. Calif., Berkeley, 1940; MD, U. Rochester, 1943; hon. degree, U. Uruguay, 1982. Asst. prof. radiol. scis. UCLA, 1949-54, assoc. prof., 1954-60, prof., 1960-87, prof. emeritus, 1987—; cons. HHS, L.A., 1952—, VA, L.A., 1968—. Contbr. over 100 articles on muclear medicine and cancer radiobiology to profl. publs. Lt. USN, 1944-46. Mem. AAAS, AMA, Am. Roentgen Ray Soc., Radiation Rsch. Soc., Soc. Nuclear Medicine, Radiol. Soc. N. Am., Mexican Soc. Nuclear Medicine (hon.) Cath. U. Faculty of Medicine of Chile.

BENNETT, LEWIS TILTON, JR., advertising and communications company executive, actor; b. Manchester, N.H, Jan. 14, 1940; s. Lewis Tilton and Elizabeth (Goodwin) B. BBA, Babson Inst., 1961; BA in Film, San Francisco State U., 1965. Pres. Bennett, Inc., San Francisco, 1967—, Luxembourg, 1967—; v.p. Europe United Films, Luxembourg, 1968—. actor in films: Petulia, Guess Who's Coming to Dinner, Bullitt, Zabriski Point, Strawberry Statement, Harold and Maude, Magnum Force, Towering Inferno, Time After Time, Over My Dead Body, Casualties of War, Final Analysis, Jagged Edge, Dead Pool, Presidio, also TV commls.; tchr. San Francisco Film Clinic, 1968-71, 74—; stand-in for film actor Steve McQueen, Richard Gere, Michael Douglas, Anthony Hopkins, Jack Warden in TV series Crazy Like A Fox; also photographer. Mem. San Francisco Symphony Found., 1967—; del. sponsor San Francisco Internat. Film Festival, 1967, 68, 69. Mem. SAR, SAG, Screen Extras Guild (adv. bd. 1986—). Clubs: Olympic, Lakeside Country, Carmel Beach, Commonwealth, West Coast Yacht, Racket, University, Europe United. Home (Summer): 20 rue des Roses, Luxembourg Luxembourg Office: 1348 Sacramento St San Francisco CA 94109-4263

BENNETT, MARTA DAWN, minister; b. Seattle, May 24, 1953; d. Manson O. and Lucile (Divine) B. BA, Lewis & Clark Coll., 1975; MDiv, Fuller Theol. Sem., 1982; postgrad., Seattle U., 1991—. Ordained to ministry, Presbyn. Ch., 1982. Co-dir. univ. ministry Univ. Presbyn. Ch., Seattle, 1977-79; acad. advisor, teaching asst. Fuller Theol. Sem., Pasadena, Calif., 1980-82; chapel asst. Occidental Coll., L.A., 1981-82; assoc. dir. campus ministries Seattle Pacific U., 1982-90, dir. campus ministries, 1990—; parish assoc. Univ. Presbyn. Ch., 1983—; team leader SPRINT to West Africa, Brazil and Jamaica, Seattle, 1987-90; adj. faculty mem. Seattle Pacific U., 1985—; vice moderator Synod of Alaska-Northwest, 1990-91; mem. Seattle Presbytery. Office: Seattle Pacific U Campus Ministries 3307 3d Ave W Seattle WA 98119

BENNETT, MICHAEL WILLIAM, museum and historical society director; b. Springfield, Mass., Jan. 29, 1947; s. Leonard William and Betty Ann (Milloglav) B.; m. Tracy Lee Joy, Oct. 8, 1977. AA, Am. River Coll.; BS, Calif. State U., Sacramento. Curator San Joaquin County Hist. Mus., Lodi, Calif., 1977-80, dir., 1980-84, dir. hist. soc. and mus., 1984—. Designer Newcastle exhibit works. Chmn. San Joaquin County Historic Records Commn., 1987-88; bd. dirs. Lodi Area Crime Stoppers, 1986—. With U.S. Army, 1967-70. Mem. Lodi Dist. C. of C. (bd. dirs. 1985—), Rotary (pres. Lodi/Tokay club 1987-88). Office: San Joaquin County Hist Mus PO Box 21 Lodi CA 95241-0021

BENNETT, NEVILLE HOUGH, electronics executive; b. Phoenix, Jan. 8, 1934; s. Carl Hough and Ann (Ellison) B.; m. Edith Umathum, Aug. 24, 1958 (div.); children: Susan, Mike. Student, UCLA, 1952-54; BSAE, N.Am. Inst., Downey, Calif., 1957; MBA, Calif. Western U., 1981; PhD, Xaverin U., 1984. Engr. Hewlett Packard, Palo Alto, Calif., 1955-57; sales engr. Dukane, St. Charles, Ill., 1959-65; v.p. Shrader Sound, Washington, 1965-69, Diamond Electronics, Lancaster, Ohio, 1969-76, Bosch GmbH, Salt Lake City, 1976-81, Video Tek, Parsippany, N.J., 1981-83; pres. Global Tek, Salt Lake City, 1983-87; v.p. Colo. Videc, Boulder, 1987-89, Pearpoint Inc., Palm Springs, Calif., 1989—; sec.-treas. Acad. Floral Design, Denver, 1987-89; chmn. Internat. Travel Inc., Salt Lake City, 1983-85. With U.S. Army, 1954-55, Korea. Recipient Bronze medal Carnegie Found., 1960. Office: Pearpoint Inc 1196 Montalvo Way # 1 Palm Springs CA 92262-5465

BENNETT, PAUL LESTER, producer; b. Jamaica, N.Y., Mar. 25, 1946; s. Frank and Frances (Katz) B. BA in Speech, Theater, L.I. U., 1970. Mgr. dir., producer New Artef Players, L.A., 1976-78, Actors Workshop & Repertory Co., West Palm Beach, Fla., 1982-83, Hippodrome State Theatre, Gainesville, Fla., 1983-84, East Coast Arts, New Rochelle, N.Y., 1986-87; mng. dir. Dupree Dance Acad., L.A., 1978-82; mng. dir., assoc. producer Two-Head Video Prodns., Gainesville, 1984-86; dir. mktg. Hesperia (Calif.) Incorporation Com., 1987-88; dir. promotions Comic Relief, L.A., 1988—; pres. Ain't Too Proud To Beg Prodns., L.A., 1992—; producer Laugh For Life, L.A., 1989, 90, 92; mng. cons. Fla. Theatre, Gainesville, 1985; mem. Gainesville Cultural Affairs Adv. Bd., 1985. Recipient Addy award, Golden Images award, Fla. Pub. Rels. Assn., 1984. Democrat. Jewish.

BENNETT, ROBERT, retired senator; b. Salt Lake City, Utah, 1933; s. Wallace F. Bennett; m. Joyce McKay; 6 children. BS, U. of Utah, 1957. Various staff positions U.S Ho. of Reps., U.S. Senate, Washington; CEO Franklin Quest, Salt Lake City, 1984-92; U.S. senator from Utah, 1993—; lobbyist various orgns., Washington; head Dept. Transp's. Congl. Liaison. Author: Gaining Control. Chmn. Education Strategic Planning Commn. Utah State Bd. Edn. (mem. Edn. Strategic Planning Com.). Recipient Light of Learning award for Outstanding Contbns. to Utah edn., 1989; named Entrepreneur of Yr. for Rocky Mtn. region INC. magazine, 1989. Republican. Office: US Senate Office of Senate Mems Washington DC 20510

BENNETT, ROBERT LOUIS, college administrator; b. Winnett, Mont., July 17, 1925; s. William and Florence B.; m. Jean Kathryn Pearson, Oct. 20, 1972; children: Mary, Jean, James, William, Stephen. B.A., Mont. State Coll., 1950; M.S., Eastern Mont. Coll., 1959; Ed.D., U. Calif.-Berkeley, 1967. Tchr., counselor, Billings, Mont., 1951-60; researcher in ednl. devel. San Mateo (Calif.) High Sch. Dist., 1961-67; prof., acad. counselor Coll. of San Mateo, 1984-92; coll. adminstr. in resource devel. San Mateo Community Coll. Dist.; project dir. Ford Found. Cooperative Edn. Program, Kellogg Found. Community Coll. Mgmt. by Objectives, U.S. Office Edn. Career Edn. Nat. Demonstration, High Tech. Bus. Tng. Ctr. Served with USN, 1945-46. Mem. Am. Soc. Tng. and Devel., Assn. Calif. Community Coll. Adminstrs. (charter), Internat. Platform Assn. Author: Identification of Curriculum Strengths and Weaknesses, 1967, An Improved Urban-Suburban Management Model for Community Colleges, 1977, Careers Through Cooperative Work Experience, 1978, Earning and Learning, 1980, Action Link Industrial Training Systems, 1986, Action Link Interactive Video Computer Learning Systems, 1989-92, Action Link automated prodn. system mgmt. quality control, team self-mgmt. Address: 53 Condon Ct San Mateo CA 94403

BENNETT, RONALD THOMAS, photojournalist; b. Portland, Oreg., Nov. 6, 1944; s. E.E. and Donna Mae (Thomas) B.; m. Gardina L. Wyckoff, Jan. 23, 1971 (div. 1982); children: Ronald Thomas, Gardina W. Student, Portland State U., 1964-67; student in photojournalism, U. Wash., 1965; student pre-law and bus. mgmt, Multnomah Coll., Portland, 1963-64. Lab. technician, photographer sta. KATU-TV, Portland, 1963-65; staff photographer Oreg. Jour., Portland, 1965-68, UPI Newspictures, Los Angeles, 1968-70; staff photojournalist UPI at White House, 1970-88; sr. photo editor The San Diego Union, 1988—; owner, chief exec. officer Capital TV; tchr. photojournalism Portland State U., 1967; past bd. dirs. Los Angeles Press Photographers; mem. standing com. U.S. Senate Press Photographer Gallery., 1980—, chmn., sec. treas. Photographer: Assassination, 1968; one-man shows Lake Oswego, Oreg., 1979, group exhbn. Library of Congress, 1971—. Served with USAFR, 1966-72. Recipient 1st prize World Press Photo Assn., 1969, Calif. Press Photographers, 1968, 69, Gold Seal competition, 1968, 69; nominated for Pulitzer prize, 1968, 76, 77, 78. Mem. White House News Photographers (bd. dirs. photo exhbn. com. 1974-78, 1st prize 1976, 77, 78, 80, 84, 86, 87), Nat. Headliner Club (1st prize 1969, 78), Nat. Press Photographers Assn. (1st prize 1972). Baptist. Home: 12907 La Tortola San Diego CA 92129-3057

BENNETT, WALTER SCOTT, JR., electrical engineer, consultant; b. Washington, Nov. 29, 1929; s. Walter Scott and Grace (Phillips) B.; m. Jean Gladys Drinkworth, Stpe. 14, 1959 (dec. 1984); children: Nancy Lee, Susan Jean, Walter Scott III. BEE, Syracuse U., 1963, MEE, 1965, PhD in Elec. Engring., 1967. Instr. elec. engring. Syracuse (N.Y.) U., 1965-67; asst. prof. elec. engring. Va. Polytech. Inst., Blacksburg, Va., 1967-70; staff engr. Burroughs Corp., City of Industry, Calif., 1970-74; mem. tech. staff Hewlett-Packard Co., Ft.Collins, Colo., 1974-90; pvt. cons. Loveland, Colo., 1990—. Contbr. numerous articles to publs.; patentee in field. 2d sgt. USAF, 1948-52. Mem. IEEE (sr., disting. lectr. 1988-90, transactions prize paper 1985).

BENNETT, WILLIAM ANDREW, computer market researcher; b. Cleve., Mar. 11, 1963; s. Andrew Jr. and Carol Ann (Pretz) Bubonic. BS in Bus. Adminstrn., Miami U., Oxford, Ohio, 1986; postgrad. U. Oreg., 1990—. Adminstrv. asst. sports info. Miami U., 1981-86; corp. staff mgmt. trainee Figgie Internat., Willoughby, Ohio, 1986-90; computer market researcher Internat. Bus. Machines, Eugene, Oreg., 1991—. Mem. Gilmour Acad. Alumni Assn., Miami U. Alumni Assn. Republican. Roman Catholic. Home: 372 W Broadway Apt 7 Eugene OR 97401-2879 Office: Internat Bus Machines 111 W 7th Ave Eugene OR 97401-2622

BENNETT, WILLIAM PAUL, JR., automotive marketing company executive; b. Verona, Pa., Feb. 23, 1942; s. William Paul and Florence Louise (Stevenson) B.; m. Roby Althea Anderson, Mar. 7, 1984 (div. June 1990); m. Mona Jeanne Roth, May 3, 1992; children: William Todd, Kimberly Anne, William III, Milisa Rae-Anne, Casey James. AA, USN Continuation Coll., 1960; AA in Bus. Adminstrn., L.A. City Coll., 1964; AA in Police Sci., East L.A. City Coll., 1966; LLB, Univ. Chicago, 1967; PhD, U. Pa., 1977. Dep. sheriff Los Angeles Co. Sheriff Dept., L.A., 1963-68; mktg. and sales mgr. Cutter Mgmt. Corp., L.A., 1968-85; pres., owner B&B Internationale Mgmt., L.A., 1984—; pres., owner M.J.B. Stables, Inc., Albany, Oreg., 1991—, Benson, Ariz., 1991—; numerous mgmt. and cons. contracts for mktg. and revamping dealership activities through Ford Motor Corp., Daihatsu, Isuzu, Toyota, Nissan, Chrysler, DeLoren, Electric Auto Corp. Contbr. numerous western short stories under nom de plume to mags. With USN, 1959-63. Presdl. citation from John F. Kennedy, 1962 (for inception of coded messages concerning placement of Russian Missiles into Cuba). Mem. Am. Mgmt. Assn., Ret. Police and Sheriffs Assn., Nat. Automobile Dealers Assn., Greater L.A. Press Club. Republican. Mem. LDS Ch. Home and Office: MJB Stables Inc 37710 Shady Bend Rd NE Albany OR 97321

BENNEWITT, LOI DENE, personnel director; b. Thermopolis, Wyo., Sept. 19, 1946; d. Lloyd Henry and Doratha Edith (Kimber) Groseclose; m. Robert L. Williams, Sept. 10, 1965 (div. Nov. 1985); m. Richard Bennewitt, Nov. 5, 1989; 1 child, Kendra Kathleen Williams. BA cum laude, U. Wyo., 1974. Various pers. positions Job Svc. of Wyo., Laramie, 1975-79, U. Wyo., Laramie, 1979-87; dir. pers. Ariz. Western Coll., Yuma, 1987—. Contbr. articles to profl. jours. Office: Ariz Western Coll Box 929 Yuma AZ 85366

BENNINGTON, LESLIE ORVILLE, JR., insurance agent; b. Sedalia, Mo., Dec. 29, 1946; s. Leslie Orville Sr. and Eunice May Marguerite (Cole) B.; m. Susan Frances Grotha, June 1, 1968; children: Leslie O. III, Jeremy Lawrence. BSME, U. Mo., Rolla, 1968; postgrad., U. Tenn. Space Inst., 1969; ChFC, Am. Coll., 1988. CLU; chartered fin. cons.; registered profl. engr., Wash., Wyo. Design engr. Arnold Research Orgn., Tullahoma, Tenn., 1968-70; engr. Pacific Power & Light, Glenrock, Wyo., 1973-75; agt., asst. gen. agt. Am. Nat. Ins. Co., Casper, Wyo., 1975-85; gen. agt. Ins. Sales, Glenrock, 1985—; pres. Cen.Wyo. Estate Planning Coun., Casper, 1985-86. Mem. Glenrock Vol. Fire Dept., 1973—, asst. chief, 1982, pres., 1993—; pres., v.p. Converse County Recreation Bd., Douglas, Wyo., 1980-90; judge dist. high sch. speech contests, Glenrock; bd. dirs. Converse County Sch. Dist. 2, 1976; bd. dirs. Greater Glenrock Recreation Dist., 1990—, pres., 1992—; guide Helluva Hunt for physically disabled hunters, 1986—, bd. dirs., 1991-93. Mem. Nat. Assn. Life Underwriters (Nat. Quality award, Health Ins. Quality award, Nat. Sales Achievement award), Cen. Wyo. Life Underwriters (pres. 1978-80), Wyo. Life Underwriters Assn. (chmn. membership com. 1985-87, nat. com. 1982-87, v.p. 1986-87, bd. dirs. 1980-90, Ins. Agt. of Yr., 1980, pres. 1988-89), West Cen. Wyo. CLUs (pres. 1986-88), Million Dollar Round Table, Nat. Pony Express Assn. (pres. Ea. Wyo. div. 1985-89, v.p. Wyo. div. 1989—), KC (grand knight, faithful navigator). Republican. Roman Catholic. Home: 6 Shannon Dr Glenrock WY 82637 Office: PO Box 2049 1260 US Hwy 20 26 87 Glenrock WY 82637

BENNION, BRUCE CARVER, librarian, educator; b. Ogden, Utah, Nov. 2, 1941; s. Vernon Palmer and Iris Elaine (Carver) B.; m. Ursula Irmgard Scherwinski, Aug. 23, 1973; children: Rebecca, Jonathan, Aaron, Eliot. BS, Brigham Young U., 1966; PhD, U. Utah, 1969; MS, Columbia U., 1974. Postdoctoral researcher Uppsala (Sweden) U., 1969-72; rsch. chemist Amalgamated Sugar Co., Ogden, 1972-73; asst. prof. U. So. Calif., L.A., 1973-80, assoc. prof., 1980—; vis. faculty U. Tex., Austin, 1984, UCLA, 1988, 89, 90, Emporia (Kans.) State U., 1991, San Jose (Calif.) State U., 1992. Contbr. articles to profl. jours. Recipient R.K. Dietrich award for scholastic excellencd Columbia U. Sch. Libr. Sci., N.Y.C., 1974. Mem. ALA, Am. Soc. for Info. Sci. (chpt. pres. 1979, Outstanding Chpt. Mem. of Yr., L.A. Chpt., 1983), Sigma Xi (chpt. sec.-treas. 1982—, del. to nat. orgn.). Republican. Home: 3421 Bentley Ave Los Angeles CA 90034 Office: Univ So Calif University Park Los Angeles CA 90089-0481

BENNION, JOHN EDWIN, telecommunications executive; b. Oakland, Calif., May 24, 1949; s. Donald Clark and Margaret Marie (Jacobsen) B.; m. Sondra Shumway, Apr. 24, 1974; children: Julie, Christine, Richard, Daniel, Mary, Matthew, Angela. BS in Math., Brigham Young U., 1973; MBA with distinction, Harvard U., 1977. Cons. Bain & Co., Boston, 1977-79; mgr. Bain & Co., Menlo Park, Calif., 1979-82; dir. strategic planning ICOT Corp., Mountain View, Calif., 1982-83; dir. mktg. ICOT Corp., Mountain View, 1983-85; mgr. corp. strategy Pacific Telesis, San Francisco, 1985-86; v.p. mktg./sales Mainstream Data, Salt Lake City, 1986-90, exec. v.p., 1990—; bd. dirs. Jacobsen Investment Co., Salt Lake City. Bishop Ch. LDS, Cupertino, Calif., 1985-86, Salt Lake City, 1991—. 1st lt. U.S. Army, 1973-75. Republican. Home: 2166 Parleys Terr Salt Lake City UT 84109 Office: Mainstream Data Inc 420 Chipeta Way Salt Lake City UT 84108

BENNION, JOHN WARREN, school system administrator; b. Salt Lake City, Nov. 25; s. M. Lynn and Katherine Bennion; m. Sylvia Lustig; children: Philip, Stanford, David, Bryan, Grant, Andrew. BS in Philosophy, English, U. Utah, 1961, MA in Edn. Adminstrn., 1962; PhD in Edn. Adminstrn., Ohio State U., 1966. Tchr. Granite High Sch., Salt Lake City, 1961-63; asst. instr. Ohio State U., Columbus, 1963-64, adminstrv. asst., 1965-66; adminstrv. intern Parma (Ohio) Sch. Dist., 1964-65; asst. supt. Elgin (Ill.) Pub. Schs., 1966-68; asst. prof. edn. adminstrn. Ind. U., Bloomington, 1968-69; supt. Brighton Cen. Schs., Rochester, N.Y., 1969-79, Bloomington (Minn.) Pub. Schs., 1979-80, Provo (Utah) Sch. Dist., 1980-85, Salt Lake City Schs., 1985—. Mem. Assn. Supervision and Curriculum Devel., Assn. Early Childhood Edn., Am. Assn. Sch. Adminstrs., Phi Delta Kappa, Rotary. Home: 1837 Harvard Ave Salt Lake City UT 84108-1804 Office: Salt Lake City Sch Dist Office of Supt of Schools 440 E 100 South Salt Lake City UT 84111-1898

BENNIS, WARREN GAMELIEL, business administration educator, author, consultant; b. N.Y.C., Mar. 8, 1925; s. Philip and Rachel (Landau) B.; m. Clurie Williams, Mar. 30, 1962 (div. 1983); children: Katharine, John Leslie, Will Martin; m. Mary Jane O'Donnell, Mar. 8, 1988 (div. 1991); m. Grace Gabe, Nov. 29, 1992. A.B., Antioch Coll., 1951; hon. cert. econs., London Sch. Econs., 1952; Ph.D., MIT, 1955; LL.D. (hon.), Xavier U., Cin., 1972, George Washington U., 1977; L.H.D. (hon.), Hebrew Union Coll., 1974, Kans. State U., 1979; D.Sc. (hon.), U. Louisville, 1977, Pacific Grad. Sch. Psychology, 1987, Gov.'s State U., 1991; LHD (hon.), Doan Coll., 1993. Diplomate Am. Bd. Profl. Psychology. Asst. prof. psychology MIT, Cambridge, 1953-56, prof., 1959-67; asst. prof. psychology and bus. Boston U., 1956-59; prof. Sloan Sch. Mgmt., 1959-67; provost SUNY-Buffalo, 1967-68, v.p. acad. devel., 1968-71; pres. U. Cin., 1971-77; U.S. prof. corps. and soc. Centre d'Etudes Industrielles, Geneva, Switzerland, 1978-79; exec.-in-residence Pepperdine U., 1978-79; George Miller Disting. prof.-in-residence U. Ill., Champaign-Urbana, 1978; Disting. prof. Bus. Adminstrn. Sch. Bus., U. So. Calif., L.A., 1980-88; univ. prof. U. So. Calif., L.A., 1988—; vis. lectr. Harvard U., 1958-59, Indian Mgmt. Inst., Calcutta; vis. prof. U. Lausanne (Switzerland), 1961-62, INSEAD, France, 1983; bd. dirs. The Foothill Group. Author: Planning of Change, 4th edit., 1985, Interpersonal Dynamics, 1963, 3d and 4th edits., 1975, Personal and Organizational Change, 1965, Changing Organizations, 1966, repub. in paperback as Beyond Bureaucracy, 1974, The Temporary Society, 1968, Organization Development, 1969, American Bureaucracy, 1970, Management of Change and Conflict, 1972, The Leaning Ivory Tower, 1973, The Unconscious Conspiracy: Why Leaders Can't Lead, 1976, Essays in Interpersonal Dynamics, 1979; (with B. Nanus): Leaders, 1985, On Becoming a Leader, 1989, (with I. Mitroff) The Unreality Industry, 1989, Why Leaders Can't Lead, 1989, Leaders on Leadership, 1992, An Invented Life: Reflections on Leadership and Change, 1993, Beyond Bureaucracy, 1993; assoc. editor Jour. Transpersonal Psychology, Community Psychology; cons. editor Jour. Creative Behavior, Jour. Higher Edn., Jour. Occupational Behavior, Ency. of Econs. and Bus., Jour. Humanistic Psychology, Calif. Mgmt. Rev., Mgmt. Series Jossey-Bass Pubs. Mem. Pres.' White House Task Force on Sci. Policy, 1969-70; mem. FAA study task force U.S. Dept. Transp., 1975; mem. adv. com. N.Y. State Joint Legis. Com. Higher Edn., 1970-71; mem. Ohio Gov.'s Bus. and Employment Council, 1972-74; mem. panel on alt. approaches to grad. edn. Council Grad. Schs. and Grad. Record-Exam Bd., 1971-73; chmn. Nat. Adv. Commn. on Higher Edn. for Police Officers, 1976-78; adv. bd. NIH, 1978-84; trustee Colo. Rocky Mountains Sch., 1978-82; bd. dirs. Am. Leadership Forum, 1984-89, Foothill Group; mem. vis. com. for humanities MIT, 1975-81; trustee Antioch Coll., Salk Inst., Claremont U. Ctr. Capt. AUS, World War II. Decorated Bronze Star, Purple Heart; recipient Dow Jones award, 1987, McKinsey Fedn. award, 1967, 68. Mem. Am. Acad. Arts and Scis. (co-chmn. policy coun. 1969-71), Am. Soc. Pub. Adminstrn. (nat. coun.), Am. Mgmt. Assn. (dr. 1974-77), U.S. C. of C. (adv. group scholars). Office: U So Calif Sch Bus University Park Los Angeles CA 90089-1421

BENO, CAROLYN ELIZABETH, pharmacist, marketing professional; b. Council Bluffs, Iowa, Sept. 2, 1953; d. Adolph Frank Jr. and Gertrude Marie Sophia (Spetman) B. BA, U. Nebr., 1975, BS in Pharmacy, 1976; MS, U. Iowa, 1978; postgrad., U. S.C., 1980—. Pharmacy intern Walgreens Gateway, Lincoln, Nebr., 1974-75; pharmacist Hushaw Drug Co., Council Bluffs, Iowa, 1976-77; grad. asst. U. Iowa, Iowa City, 1977-78; asst. prof. pharmacy Temple U., Phila., 1978-80; pharmacist Kroger and Springwood Lake Pharmacies, Columbia, S.C., 1982-84; sr. analyst U.S. pharm. and nutrition group Bristol Myers, Evansville, Ind., 1985-89; mgr. client svcs. Hosp. Data Svcs./Walsh Am., Scottsdale, Ariz., 1989-92; dir. data integrity Walsh Am./PMSI, Phoenix, Ariz., 1992—; chmn. drug edn. com. coll. pharmacy U. Nebr., Lincoln, 1973-74; vol. cons. Chem. Dependency Agy. S. W. Iowa, Council Bluffs, 1975-77; vol. pharmacist Iowa City (Iowa) Free Med. Clinic, 1977-78. Contbr. articles to profl. jours. Mem. Am. Pharm. Assn., Health Care Businesswomen's Assn., Alpha Mu Alpha, Kappa Epsilon (co-advisor 1983-84), Phi Lambda Sigma. Republican. Lutheran. Home: 5309 E Wallace Ave Scottsdale AZ 85254-1119 Office: Walsh Am 2394 E Camelback Rd Phoenix AZ 85016

BENSCH, KLAUS GEORGE, pathology educator; b. Miedar, Germany, Sept. 1, 1928; (married); 3 children. M.D., U. Erlangen, Germany, 1953. Diplomate: Am. Bd. Pathology. Intern U. Hosps. of Erlangen, 1953-54; resident in anat. pathology U. Tex. and; M.D. Anderson Hosp., Houston, 1954-56, Yale, 1956-57; instr. pathology Yale Med. Sch., 1958-61, asst. prof., 1961-64, assoc. prof., 1964-68; prof. pathology Stanford Med. Sch., 1968—, acting chmn. dept. pathology, 1984-85, chmn. dept. pathology, 1985—. Mem. Am. Assn. Pathology and Bacteriology. Office: Stanford U Med Sch Dept Pathology 300 Pasteur Dr Stanford CA 94305

BENSCHEIDT, STEVEN EUGENE, veterinarian; b. La Junta, Colo., Sept. 19, 1954; s. George N. and Charlotte J. (Reams) B.; 1 child, Nicole L. DVM, Colo. State U., 1980. Pvt. practice Modesto, Calif., 1980-81, Nelson Road Vet. Clinic, Longmont, Colo., 1983—; agrl. dir. Western Food Products, La Junta, 1981-83; also bd. dirs. Bd. dirs. Colo. Small Animal Comm., 1988—; treas. Longmont Humane Soc., 1990—. Mem. AVMA, Colo. Vet. Med. Assn. (bd. dirs. 1988—, dist. rep., chmn. small animal commn.), Nat. Food Processors (nat. agrl. com. 1982-83), Rotary (bd. dirs. Longmont Twin Peaks chpt. 1988-90). Republican. Mennonite.

BENSELER, ROLF WILHELM, biological sciences educator, researcher; b. San Jose, Calif., Sept. 24, 1932; s. Wilhelm August and Ella Karoline (Vaeth) B.; m. Donna Alyce Kirk, Dec. 16, 1961; children: William Paul, Mark Christian. Student, San Jose State Coll., 1951-53; BS in Forestry, U. Calif., Berkeley, 1955-57; MF in Forest Ecology and Silviculture, Yale U., 1958; PhD in Botany, U. Calif., Berkeley, 1968. Jr. specialist U. Calif. Agrl. Expt. Sta., 1958-61; instr. San Francisco City Coll., spring 1961, Modesto (Calif.) Jr. Coll., 1961-63; acting instr. U. Calif., Berkeley, 1966-67; lectr. San Jose (Calif.) State U., 1967-68; asst. prof. Calif. State U., Hayward, 1968-70, assoc. prof., 1970-75, prof., 1975—, chmn. dept. biol. scis., 1986-89, assoc. coord. liberal studies program, 1985—. Contbr. articles to profl. jours. With USNR, 1951-59. Mem. Soc. for Conservation Biology, Calif. Acad. Scis., Calif. Native Plant Soc. (bd. dirs. 1968-72), Calif. Bot. Soc. (corr. sec. 1973-75, 1st v.p. 1983-84, pres. 1984-85, ex officio, exec. coun. 1985-86), Bot. Soc. Am. (conservation com. 1979-81), Friends of Jepson Herbarium. Office: Calif State U Dept Biological Sci Hayward CA 94542

BENSINGER, LENORE COOPER, theater director; b. Washington, Sept. 10, 1943; d. J.D. and R.Z. (Zeidner) Cooper; m. Richard E. Bensinger, Dec. 14, 1968; children: Kenneth, Gregory. AB, Am. U., 1965; MA, Washington U., 1977; MFA, U. Wash., 1991. Legis. asst. U.S. Congress, Washington, 1962-68; policy analyst NIH Bethesda, Washington, 1968-70; policy planner U.S. Dept. Health and Human Svcs., Washington, 1970-73; intern Edison Theater, Wash. U., St. Louis, 1973-77; artistic intern Columbus Theater, San Francisco, 1977-78; dir. Rain City Theater, Seattle, 1988—; cons. Annex Theater, Seattle, 1988—. Author over 20 plays. Recipient King County Playwriting award King County Arts Commn., 1986, Seattle Arts award Seattle Arts Commn., 1987, Wash. State fellowship Wash. State Arts Commn., 1989. Office: Rain City Studio Theater 5263 17th Ave NE Seattle WA 98105

BENSKY, LAWRENCE MARTIN, journalist; b. Bklyn., May 1, 1937; s. Eli and Sarah (Davidson) B. BA, Yale U., 1958. Reporter Mpls. Star-Tribune, 1958-59; assoc. editor Random House Pub., N.Y.C., 1960-63; Paris editor Paris Rev., 1964-66; asst. editor N.Y. Times Book Rev., N.Y.C., 1966-68; mng. editor Ramparts mag., San Francisco, 1968; news reporter, anchor Sta. KSAN, San Francisco, 1969-70, 77-79; gen. mgr. Sta. KPFA, Berkeley, Calif., 1974-77; news dir. Sta. KBLX, Berkeley, 1981-82; mng. editor Calif. Pub. Radio, San Francisco, 1982-83; nat. affairs corr. Pacifica Radio, Washington, Berkeley, 1987—; co-founder, bd. dirs. Media Alliance, San Francisco, 1975—; vis. lectr. Stanford U., 1989, 91, 93, U. Calif., Berkeley, 1991—; lectr. Calif. State U., Hayward, 1992—. Bd. dirs. Am. Youth Hostels, San Francisco, 1991—. Recipient George Polk award L.I. U., 1987, Golden Gadfly award Media Alliance, 1988, Golden Reel award Nat. Fedn. Community Broadcasters, 1988, 91, 92, 93, Thomas M. Storke award World Affairs Coun., San Francisco, 1991. Office: PO Box 40247 San Francisco CA 94140

BENSON, ALFRED M., real estate appraiser, analyst; b. Jamaica, N.Y., Jan. 21, 1941; s. Peter Henry Benson and Susan (Maloney) Benson Alexander; m. Kathleen Mary Laffan, Feb. 8, 1964; children: Jonathan, Jennifer, Eileen. Student Brown U., 1958-62; B.Econs., C.W. Post Coll., 1963. Appraiser James Matthews, MAI, Mineola, N.Y., 1964-67; pres. Peter H. Benson, Inc., New Hyde Park, N.Y., 1967-76; asst. v.p. Seamen's Bank, N.Y.C., 1969-76; ptnr. Klafter and Benson, Tucson, 1976-81; prin. Burke, Hansen & Homan, Tucson, 1981-83, Alfred M. Benson, MAI, Tucson, 1983—; pres. Alfred M. Benson Co., real estate investment analysis, Tucson, 1984—. Mem. vestry Christ Episcopal Ch., Garden City, N.Y., 1973-76. Vice chmn. editorial bd. Appraisal Jour. Mem. Appraisal Inst. (pres. Ariz. chpt. 1984, mem. MAI examination subcom. 1986-90, mem. regional com. 1991), Ariz. Assn. Realtors (bd. dirs. 1984), Tucson Bd. Realtors, Soc. Real Estate Appraisers (pres. Tucson chpt. 1983), Am. Soc. Appraisers (v.p. Tucson chpt. 1983), Omega Tau Rho. Republican. Home: 3232 N Placita Brazos Tucson AZ 85715-2840 Office: Alfred M Benson Co 6115 E Grant Rd Tucson AZ 85712-5828

BENSON, ALVIN K., geophysicist, consultant, educator; b. Payson, Utah, Jan. 25, 1944; s. Carl William and Josephine Katherine (Wirthlin) B.; m. Connie Lynn Perry, June 17, 1966; children: Alauna Marie, Alisa Michelle, Alaura Dawn. BS, Brigham Young U., 1966, PhD in Physics, 1972. Cert. environmentalist. Nuclear group physicist Phillips Petroleum Co., Arco, Idaho, 1966; assoc. prof. physics Ind. U., New Albany, 1972-78, head physics dept., 1976-78; sr. rsch. geophysicist Conoco, Inc., Ponca City, Okla., 1978-81, supr. geophysical rsch., 1981-85; geophysics rsch. assoc. DuPont, Ponca City, 1985-86; prof. geophysics Brigham Young U., Provo, Utah, 1986—; cons. Dames and Moore Engring., Salt Lake city, 1987-88, DuPont, Ponca City, 1989-91, Kuwait U., 1991-92, Coleman Rsch., Laurel, Md., 1991, Centennial Mine, Boise, 1990-91, Certified Environ., Salt Lake City, 1991-92, EPA, Washington, 1992; developer vis. geoscientist program Bringham Young U. Author: Seismic Migration, 1986, Theory and Practice of Seismic Imaging, 1988; contbr. articles to over 90 publs. including Geophysics, Jour. Computational Physics, Geophys Prospecting, Engring. Geology. Bishop LDS Ch., New Albany, 1976-78, Stake High Coun., Tulsa, 1979-81; active polit. adv. com. Rep. Party, Provo, 1990; polit. cons. Guatemala, 1991-92. Recipient Hon. Sci. award Bausch and Lomb, Rochester, N.Y., 1966; geophysics grantee Rotary, Provo, 1987. Am. Assn. Petroleum Geologists, Tulsa, 1988, Geol. Soc. Am., Boulder, Colo., 1988. Mem. Am. Phys. Soc., Am. Geophys. Union, Soc. Exploration Geophysicists (referee 1980-93), Exploration Geophysicists (referee 1980-93), Utah Geol. Assn. Home: 249 W 1100 S Orem UT 84058-6709 Office: Brigham Young U University Hill Provo UT 84602

BENSON, ANNETTE JENKINS, association executive; b. Logan, Utah, May 2, 1939; d. Allan Henry and VeNeal Hannah (Jensen) Jenkins; m. Mark Keith Benson, June 26, 1959; children: Andrea Benson Davenport, Bryan Mark. Student, Utah State U., 1956-57. Asst. sec. and mgr. Am. Suffolk Sheep Soc., Logan, 1973-85; exec. sec. mgr. Am. Suffolk Sheep Soc., Logan and Newton, Utah, 1985-92. Mem. Cache County Bd. Mental Health, 1965, 71, Town Beautification Com. Newton Park, Newton, Utah, 1983-84; del. State Rep. Caucus, Ogden, Utah, 1992. Named Young Homemaker of Yr., North Cache Young Homemakers, 1974. LDS. Home: PO Box 194 Newton UT 84327

BENSON, BRADLEY DUANE, banker; b. La Mesa, Calif., Apr. 10, 1959; s. Robert Omer and Margere Anne (Cain) B.; m. Jill Theresa Jaramillo, Mar. 3, 1984; children: Ashley Laine, Patrick Rand. AA, Grossmont Coll., 1978; BSBA, Calif. State U., Sacramento, 1982; MS in Systems Mgmt., U. So. Calif., 1988. Credit authorizer Sears Roebuck & Co., Sacramento, 1980-82; auditor Inventory Auditors, Inc., Sacramento, 1982; br. mgr., asst. v.p. Seafirst Nat. Bank, Spokane, Wash., 1988—; sec.-treas. Hansen's Creamery, Spokane, 1992—. Vol. United Way Allocation Panel, 1990-93; vol. sportswriter Goodwill Games, 1988; bus. cons. Jr. Achievement, 1992; vol. counselor Consumer Credit Svc., 1988-90. Mem. Am. Inst. Banking, Air Force Assn. Republican. Baptist. Home: 8028 N Pamela St Spokane WA 99208-9659 Office: Seafirst Nat Bank N 804 Monroe Spokane WA 99201

BENSON, DAVID BERNARD, computer science educator; b. Seattle, Nov. 18, 1940; s. Allan I. and Martha (White) B.; BS in Engring., Calif. Inst. Tech., 1962, MSEE, 1963, PhD (NASA fellow), 1967; m. Nancy Elaine Dollahite, Sept. 17, 1962 (div. Aug. 1986); children: Megan, Bjorn, Nils, Amy, Kjell, Ingri. Rsch. engr. N. Am. Rockwell, Downey, Calif., 1963-64; asst. prof. U. N.C., Chapel Hill, 1967-70; vis. assoc. prof. U. Colo., Boulder, 1976-77; asst. prof. Wash. State U., Pullman, 1970-72, assoc. prof., 1972-79, prof. computer sci., 1979—; vis. computer scientist U. Edinburgh, Scotland, 1983, U. Sydney, Australia, 1990; pres. BENTEC, 1985-89. Contbr. over 30 articles to profl. jours. Precinct chmn. 72d Precinct, Whitman County, Wash., 1978-82; Whitman County Dem. Conv. del., 1972, 76. NSF grantee, 1969-89. Mem. Assn. Computing Machinery, Am. Math. Soc., AAAS, AAUP, Sigma Xi. Mem. Soc. of Friends. Home: 725 NE Illinois St Pullman WA 99163-3920 Office: Wash State U Sch Elec Engring & Computer Sci Pullman WA 99164-2752

BENSON, DEE VANCE, judge; b. Salt Lake City, Aug. 25, 1948; s. Gilbert and Beryl Butler (Despain) B.; m. Patricia Brown; children: Angela, Natalie, Lucas, Katherine. BA, Brigham Young U., 1973, JD, 1976. Bar: Utah 1976, U.S. Dist. Ct. Utah 1976, U.S. Ct. Appeals (10th cir.) 1976, U.S. Supreme Ct. 1984, U.S. Ct. Appeals (5th cir.) 1988. Ptnr. Snow, Christensen & Martineau, Salt Lake City, 1976-84; legal counsel Senate Judiciary Com., Washington, 1984-86; chief of staff Senator Orrin Hatch's Office, Washington, 1986-88; assoc. dep. atty. gen. U.S. Dept. Justice, Washington, 1988; U.S. atty. U.S. Dept. Justice, Salt Lake City, 1989-91; judge U.S. Dist. Ct., Salt Lake, 1991—; legal counsel Iran-Contra Congl. Investigating Com., Washington, 1987. Contbg. author univ. law rev. Mem. ABA, Utah State Bar (com. on cts. and judges), Salt Lake County Bar Assn., Phi Alpha Delta. Mem. LDS Ch. Office: US Dist Ct 350 S Main St Salt Lake City UT 84101

BENSON, EZRA TAFT, church executive, former secretary of agriculture; b. Whitney, Idaho, Aug. 4, 1899; s. George Taft and Sarah (Dunkley) B.; m. Flora Smith Amussen, Sept. 10, 1926; children: Reed, Mark, Barbara, Beverly, Bonnie, Flora Beth. Student, Utah State Agrl. Coll., Logan, 1918-

21; BS, Brigham Young U., 1926, Dr. Pub. Service (hon.), 1955; MS in Agrl. Econs., Iowa State Coll., 1927, D Agrl. (hon.), 1953; postgrad., U. Calif., 1937-38; HHD, Coll. Osteo. Physicians and Surgeons, 1951; LLD, U. Utah, 1953, Bowdoin Coll., 1955, U. Maine, 1956; D Agr. (hon.), Mich. State Coll., 1955; DSc (hon.), Rutgers U., 1955. Mission Ch. Jesus Christ Latter-day Saints, Brit. Isles and Europe; pres. Newcastle dist. Ch. Jesus Christ Latter-day Saints, 1921-23; farm operator, 1923-30; county agrl. agt. U. Idaho Extension Service, Preston, 1929-30; extension economist and mktg. specialist in charge econ. and mktg. work State of Idaho, 1930-38; organizer, sec. Idaho Coop. Council, 1933-38; exec. sec. Nat. Council Farmer Coops., 1939-44; mem. exec. com., bd. trustees Am. Inst. Co-op, 1942-52, vice chmn. bd. trustees, 1942-49, chmn., 1952; sec. agr. U.S., Washington, 1953-61; dir. Olson Bros., Inc.; bd. dirs. Farm Found., 1946-50; mem. Nat. Agrl. Adv. Com., World War II; mem. Nat. Farm Credit Com., 1940-43; U.S. del. 1st Internat. Conf. of Farm Orgns., London, 1946. Contbr. to agrl., coop. and church jours. Mem. nat. exec. bd. Boy Scouts Am., 1948-66, awarded Silver Antelope, 1951, Silver Buffalo award, 1954; mem. Boise Stake Presidency, Ch. of Jesus Christ of Latter-day Saints, Idaho, 1935-39, pres. Boise Stake, 1938-39; pres. Wash. Dist. Council, Eastern States Mission, 1939-40, Washington Stake, 1940-44; ordained apostle of Ch., mem. Council of Twelve, 1943, pres. European Mission, 1946, 63-65, mem. Gen. Ch. Bd. Edn.; pres. Ch. Jesus Christ Latter-day Saints, Salt Lake City, 1985—; br. trustees Brigham Young U. Recipient testimonial for disting. service to agr. U. Wis., 1952; scholarship Gamma Sigma Delta, hon. soc. agr. Iowa State Coll.; fellow U. Calif., Berkeley. Mem. Am. Mktg. Assn., Farm Econs. Assn., Delta Nu, Alpha Zeta. Office: LDS Ch 50 E North Temple Salt Lake City UT 84150

BENSON, JAMES BERNARD, JR., clinical hypnotherapist; b. Phila., May 8, 1930; s. James Bernard Benson and Elizabeth (Smeaton) Caswell; m. Hiroko Nakamura, Apr. 14, 1955. LLD (hon.), Nat. Law Enforcement Acad., 1968; BA in Police Sci., Pacific Coll., 1976; PhD (hon.), St. John's U., Springfield, La., 1988. Cert. behavioral therapist, Calif. Chief criminal investigator U.S. Marine Corps, 1947-66; corp. officer Bank of Am., L.A., 1966-85; pvt. practice Anaheim, Calif., 1985--. Editor: (poetry) Devotion in Blue, 1973, Lawman's Lament, 1974; contbr. articles to police mags. Fellow Am. Assn. Profl. Hypnotherapists; mem. Nat. Soc. Clin. Hypnotherapists. Republican. Home and Office: 1400 S Sunkist St Ste 199 Anaheim CA 92806

BENSON, JOAN ELLEN, dietetics educator, researcher; b. San Francisco, Aug. 26, 1954; d. Lloyd F. and Jean A. (Sullivan) B.; m. Dwight T. Hibdon, July 13, 1977. BS, U. Calif., Berkeley, 1977, registered dietician, 1978; MS, U. Utah, 1987. Cert. dietitian, Utah. Clin. dietitian Contra Costa County Med. Svcs., Martinez, Calif., 1978-85; nutrition cons. Cardiovascular Genetics, Salt Lake City, 1987-90; clin. instr. dietetics Coll. Health, U. Utah, Salt Lake City, 1987—, rsch. assoc. Sch. Medicine, 1991—; nutrition cons. Ctr. for Sports Medicine, St. Francis Hosp., San Francisco, 1984-87; vis. rsch. assoc. Inst. Rsch., Eidgenössische Sportschule, Magglingen, Switzerland, spring 1987; nutrition cons. Optifast progrm LDS Hosp., Salt Lake City, 1988-90; book reviewer Benjamin Cummings Pub. Co., Redwood City, Calif., 1989—, Mosby-Yearbook Pubs., St. Louis, 1990-91. Author: Coaches Guide to Nutrition, 1990; also articles, chpts. to books. Com. chmn. Am. Heart Assn., Salt Lake City, 1991-92. Calif. State scholar, 1975-77, Phoebe Hearst scholar, 1975-77; Spikes biomed. rsch. grantee U. Utah, 1986. Mem. Am. Dietetic Assn., Utah Dietetic Assn., Sports and Cardiovascular Nutritionists (state rep. 1990-91), Nat. Off-Road Biking Assn. (Utah Vet Mountain bike champion 1990, 92), Phi Kappa Phi. Democrat. Roman Catholic. Home: 4716 N Silver Meadows Park City UT 84060 Office: U Utah Family-Preventive Medicine 50 N Medical Dr Salt Lake City UT 84132

BENSON, JOHN ALEXANDER, JR., physician, educator; b. Manchester, Conn., July 23, 1921; s. John A. and Rachel (Patterson) B.; m. Irene Zucker, Sept. 29, 1947; children: Peter M., John Alexander III, Susan Leigh, Jeremy P. BA, Wesleyan U., 1943; MD, Harvard U., 1946. Diplomate Am. Bd. Internal Medicine (mem. bd. 1969-91, sec.-treas. 1972-75), and subsplty. bd. gastroenterology (mem. 1961-66, chmn. 1965-66). Intern Univ. Hosps., Cleve., 1946-47; resident Peter Bent Brigham Hosp., Boston, 1949-51; fellow Mass. Gen. Hosp., Boston, 1951-53; research asst. Mayo Clinic, Rochester, Minn., 1953-54; instr. medicine Harvard, 1956-59; prof. medicine U. Oreg., 1965—, head div. gastroenterology, 1959-75; pres. Am. Bd. Internal Medicine, 1975-91, pres. emeritus, 1991—; interim dean Sch. Medicine Oreg. Health Sci. U., 1991-93; cons. VA Hosps., Madigan Gen. Army Hosp. Editorial bd.: Am. Jour. Digestive Diseases, 1966-73; Contbr. articles to profl. jours. Mem. Oreg. Drug Adv. Council, 1965-73; Dir. Oreg. Med. Ednl. Found., 1967-73, pres., 1969-72. Served with USNR, 1947-49. Mem. AAS, AMA, ACP (master), Am. Gastroenterol. Assn. (sec. 1970-73, v.p. 1975-76, pres.-elect. 1976-77, pres. 1977-78), Am. Clin. and Climatol. Assn., Am. Soc. Internal Medicine, Western Assn. Physicians, North Pacific Soc. Internal Medicine, Am. Fedn. Clin. Rsch., Federated Coun. for Internal Medicine, Am. Assn. Study Liver Disease, Western Soc. Clin. Investigation, Soc. Health and Human Values, Assn. Health Svcs. Rsch., Inst. Medicine NAS (sr.), Phi Beta Kappa, Sigma Xi, Alpha Omega Alpha. Office: Am Bd Internal Medicine 200 SW Market St # 1950 Portland OR 97201

BENSON, KAREN A., nursing educator; b. Havre, Mont., Sept. 10, 1946; d. William Duncan and Norma Evelyn (Erickson) Ross; children: Alice, Evan, David, Marc. BSN, Mont. State U., 1968; MS in Biology, Wash. State U., 1978, PhD in Vet. Sci., 1983; MS in Nursing, Oreg. Health Scis. U., 1986. Lectr. Seattle U.; critical care nurse Northwest Hosp., Seattle. Contbr. articles to profl. publs. Dr. Lynn A. George scholar; Sigma Xi rsch. grantee. Mem. ANA, Wash. State Nurses Assn., Am. Holistic Nurses Assn., Sigma Theta Tau, Phi Kappa Phi. Home: 17103 25th Ave NE Seattle WA 98155-6124

BENSON, KENNETH PETER, forest industry executive; b. Vancouver, B.C., Can., Mar. 1, 1927; s. Lawrence and Clara (Peel) B.; m. Joyce Alice Heino, Nov. 4, 1949; children: David, Sally. Student, U. B.C., Vancouver, chartered acct., 1953. Asst. controller Powell River Co., Vancouver, 1955-62; with B.C. Forest Products Co. (now Fletcher Challenge Can., Ltd.), Vancouver, 1962, comptroller, 1962, v.p. fin., 1967, dir., 1970, exec. v.p. ops., 1972, sr. exec. v.p., 1974, pres., COO, 1976-79, pres., CEO, 1979-84, chmn., CEO, 1984-87, chmn., 1987-91; chmn., CEO Finlay Forest Industries Ltd., Vancouver, 1992—. Office: Finlay Forest Industries Ltd, 505 Burrard St Ste 680 Bentall 1, Vancouver, BC Canada V7X 1M4

BENSON, ROBERT SLATER, restaurant executive; b. South Bend, Ind., June 6, 1942; s. Ernest Birger and Ruth (Kenney) B.; m. Cynthia Carolyn Kappus, June 15, 1974; children: Erik, Kiersa. AB magna cum laude, Harvard U., 1964, MBA with high distinction, 1966. Asst. to compt. U.S. Dept. Def., Arlington, Va., 1966-68; dir. western region, then dir. nat. priorities project Nat. Urban Coalition, Washington, 1968-71; pres., bd. dirs. Children's World, Inc., Golden, Colo., 1971-87; pres. VICORP Restaurants, Inc., Denver, 1987—, also bd. dirs.; individual gen. ptnr. Boettcher Venture Capital Ptnrs., Denver, 1985—. Author: Counterbudget: A Blueprint for Changing National Priorities, 1971; contbr. articles to jours. Mem. adv. bd. Ill. Dept. Children & Family Svcs., Chgo., 1973-75; mem. Pres.'s Commn. on a Nat. Agenda for the Eighties, Washington, 1980-81; pres., bd. dirs. Nat. Repertory Orch., Evergreen, Colo., 1982-84; trustee Colo. Acad. Democrat. Home: 32177 Hwy 103 Evergreen CO 80439-9712

BENSON, SAM EDWARD, legal assistant; b. Upper Sandusky, Ohio, Nov. 29, 1957; s. Starling Edward and Clara Mae (Stansberry) B.; m. Didi Leah Chua, Nov. 9, 1979 (dec. 1983); children: Roxanne, Joseph, Cindy. Degree, S.J. Coll. Law, 1978, Profl. Career Devel. Inst., 1992. Ranch mgr. Arrow Farms, Inc., Kerman, Calif., 1969-76; fry cook, dishwasher Bob's Big Boy, Fresno, Calif., 1979-83; consumer advocate Stockton, Calif., 1986-90; legal asst. Stockton, 1992—. Editor: (newsletter) Voices for Justice, 1990. Active San Joaquin County Mental Health, Stockton, 1990. With U.S. Army, 1977-78. Mem. Nat. Head Injury Found., Inc., U.S. Marshall's Office Peace Officer Assn. Democrat. Mem. Assembly of God Ch. Home: 347 E Flora St # 37 Stockton CA 95202

BENSON, STEPHEN R., editorial cartoonist. Degree, Brigham Young U., 1978. With Nat. Rep. Com., 1978-80; cartoonist The Ariz. Republic, Phoenix, 1980-90, 91—, The Morning-News Tribune, Tacoma, Wash., 1990-91. Author: Fencin' with Benson, 1984, Evanly Days, 1988, Back at the Barb-B-Cue, 1991, Where Do You Draw the Line?, 1992. Recipient Nat. Headliner award, 1984, 1st Place Best of the West, 1991, 93, Pulitzer Prize finalist editorial cartooning, 1984, 89, 92, Pulitzer Prize for editorial cartooning, 1993. Office: The Arizona Republic Phoenix Newspapers Inc 120 E Van Buren St Phoenix AZ 85004

BENTLEY, JACK LOWELL, telecommunications executive; b. Freeport, Ill., Aug. 30, 1930; s. John and Frances (Foy) B.; m. Mary Jane Shumaker, May 15, 1954; 1 child, John. Grad. high sch., Freeport, Ill., 1948. Various positions, to plant acct. Northwestern Telephone Co., Freeport, 1946-57; asst. office mgr., asst. auditor Colo. River Telephone Co., Blythe, 1957-59; asst. auditor Mansfield (Ohio) Telephone Co., 1959-66; various positions, to gen. mgr. Mid-Rivers Telephone Coop., Circle, Mont., 1966-72; contr. Marvin R. Denning dba M&M Equipment, Bozeman, Mont., 1973-74; revenue requirements supr. Telephone & Data System, Madison, Wis., 1974-75; adminstrv. asst. contr. Delta County Tele-Comm, Inc., Paonia, Colo., 1975-77, gen. mgr., 1977-85; exec. v.p. Western N.Mex. Telephone Co., Silver City, 1985—. Mem. Nat. Rural Telecom Assn. (bd. dirs. 1985—), Western Rural Telephone Assn. (pres. 1991-92), Rural Telephone Bank (bd. dirs. 1992-93). Home: PO Box 173 Silver City NM 88062 Office: Western NMex Telephone Co PO Box 3079 Silver City NM 88062

BENTLY, DONALD EMERY, electrical engineer; b. Cleve., Oct. 18, 1924; s. Oliver E. Bently and Mary Evelyn (Conway) B.; m. Susan Lorraine Pumphrey, Sept. 1961 (div. Sept. 1982); 1 child, Christopher Paul. BSEE with distinction, State U. of Iowa, 1949; MSEE, Iowa State U., 1950; DS (hon.), U. Nev., 1987. Registered profl. engr., Calif., Nev. Pres. Bently Nev. Corp., Minden, 1961-85, chief exec. officer, 1985—; chief exec. officer Bently Rotor Dynamics and Research Corp., Minden, 1985—; also chmn. bd. dirs. Bently Nev. Corp., Minden; chief exec. officer Gibson Tool Co., Carson City, Nev., 1978—; bd. dirs. Sierra Pacific Resources, 1982-83. Contbr. articles to profl. jours.; developer electronic instruments for the observation of rotating machinery, and the algorithm for rotor fluid-induced instability; inventor in field. Served with USN, 1943-46, PTO. Named Inventor or Yr., State of Nev. Invention and Tech. Coun., 1983; recipient first Decade award Vibration Inst. Mem. ASME, Am. Petroleum Inst., Engrs. Club of San Francisco, St. Petersburg (Russian Fedn.) Acad. Engring., Sigma Xi, Eta Kappa Nu, Tau Beta Pi, Sigma Alpha Epsilon. Episcopalian. Office: Bently Nev Corp PO Box 157 Minden NV 89423-0157

BENTON, DEBRA ANN, management consultant; b. Quinter, Kans., Dec. 16, 1953; d. Fred Herman and Teresa Catherine (Feldt) B. BS, Colo. State U., 1974. With sales/mktg. Control Data Corp., Denver, 1974-76; owner Benton Mgmt. Resources, Denver, 1976—. Author: Lions Don't Need to Roar, 1992. Founder Nat. Assn. Bus. and Indsl. Saleswomen, Denver, 1980, Consultants Speakers Bur., Denver, 1983. Office: Benton Mgmt Resources 2221 W Lake St Fort Collins CO 80521

BENTON, FLETCHER, sculptor; b. Jackson, Ohio, 1931. BFA, Miami U., Oxford, Ohio, 1956, DFA (hon.), 1993. Mem. faculty Calif. Coll. Arts and Crafts, 1959, San Francisco Art Inst., 1964-67; asst. prof. art Calif. State U., San Jose, 1967-81; prof. Calif. State U., 1981-86. One-man shows include, San Francisco Mus. Modern Art, 1965, Albright-Knox Mus., Buffalo, 1970, Galeria Bonino, N.Y.C., 1969, Galerie Francoise Mayer, Brussels, San Francisco Mus. Modern Art, 1970, London Arts Gallery, Detroit, 1970, Galeria Bonino, Buenos Aires, Estudio Actual, Caracas, Venezuela, 1970, Landry-Bonino Gallery, N.Y.C., 1972, Phoenix Mus. Art, 1973, Galeria Bonino, Rio de Janiero, 1973, Calif. State U.-Berkeley, 1973, Neuberger Mus., N.Y., 1974, Hirshhorn Mus., 1974, Phila. Art Alliance, 1974, Elvehejem Mus. Art, Wis., 1976, San Francisco Modern Mus. Art, 1976, Huntsville Mus. Modern Art, Ala., 1977, Alrich Mus. Contemporary Art, Conn., John Berggruen Gallery, San Francisco, 1978, 84, 89, Am. Acad. and Inst. Arts and Letters, N.Y.C., 1979, Chgo. Arts Club, 1979, Milw. Art Ctr., 1980, Suermondt-Ludwig Mus., Asschen, Fed. Republic Germany, Klingspor Mus., Offenbach, Fed. Republic Germany, 1981, Kunsthandling Brigitte Haasner, Wiesbaden, Fed. Republic Germany, 1987, 92, Dorothy Goldeen Gallery, Santa Monica, Calif., 1988, Gallerie Simone Sterne, New Orleans, 1990, Riva Yares Gallery, Scottsdale, 1991, Miami U., Oxford, 1993; group shows include San Francisco Art Inst., 1964, San Francisco Modern Mus. Art, 1964, Calif. Pal. of Legion of Honor, 1964, Whitney Mus. Am. Art, N.Y.C., 1966, 68, Los Angeles County Mus., 1967, Phila. Art Mus., 1967, Walker Art Ctr., Mpls., 1968, Art Inst. Chgo., 1968, Internat. Mus. Fine Arts, Osaka, Japan, 1970, Hayward Gallery, London, 1970, Stanford (Calif.) Mus., 1971, Am. Acad. and Inst. Arts and Letters, N.Y.C., 1981, Amerika Haus, Frankfurt, 1981, Whitney Mus. Am. Art, N.Y.C., 1981, Oakland Mus., 1982, John Berggruen Gallery, 1983, Olympic Arts Festival, Los Angeles, France, Fed. Republic Germany, Eng., Norway, 1984, John Berggruen Gallery, 1985, 89, 92, Chapman Coll. (Calif.), 1985, The Adrich Mus. Contemporary Art, Conn., 1985, Centro de Arte Moderna, Lisbon, Portugal, 1986, Kleinewefers, Krefeld, Fed. Repbulic Germany, 1987, Kundsthandlung Brigitte Haasner, Wiesbaden, Fed. Republic Germany, 1987, 88, Dorothy Goldeen Gallery, Santa Monica, Calif., 1988, Andre Emmerich Gallery, 1991, 92, others; major collections Euroclear Hdqs. Brussels, Belgium, 1993, Edvard Munch Sculpture Garden, Oslo, 1993; subject of book, Fletcher Benton by Paul Karlstrom and Edward Lucie-Smith, 1990. Served with USN, 1949-50. Recipient award for disting. service to arts Am. Acad. and Inst. Arts and Letters, 1979; Pres.'s Scholar award San Jose State U., 1980. Office: 250 Dore St San Francisco CA 94103-4308

BENTON, GLADYS GAY, educator, musician; b. Fayette, Mo., Nov. 17, 1906; d. Benjamin Franklin and Celoa Alice (Perry) Hill; m. Robert Withrow, 1929; m. Charles B. Howell, July 12, 1939; children: Frances, Alice; m. Chester Roland Benton, July 7, 1951 (dec. 1989). BA in Edn., San Francisco State U., 1937; MA in Reading, U. Calif.-Northridge, 1979. Cert. Ryan reading specialist; Laubach tutor trainer; life cert. kindergarten, primary and elem. tchr., Calif. Tchr. Malen Burnett Sch. Music, San Francisco, 1925-30, Mendocino County, Solano, Santa Maria, Imperial, Ventura County Pub. Schs., Calif., 1929—; owner, tchr. Gladys Benton Music Studio and Reading Clinic, Ojai, Calif.; bd. dirs. Laubach Literacy Ctr., Ojai, Calif. bd. dirs. Laubach Literacy Ctr., Ojai, Calif.; piano accompanist for ch. svc. Victorian Retirement Home, 1992-93. Vol. ESL tchr., Ojai, Calif.; helper Little House, Ojai, 1978; docent Ojai Mus., 1984-85; tutor Topa Topa-Meiners Oaks Sch., Ojai, 1988-89; dir., organist, choir dir. Meth. Ch., Oak View, Calif., 1952; founder, organizer, trainer literacy ctrs., Ventura and Saticoy, Calif.; asst. leader Girl Scouts U.S.A.; vol. Boy Scout Camp, Meals on Wheels; accompianist various chs. Mem. Calif. Retired Tchrs. Assn., Am. Assn. Retired Persons, Legion Aux. (past pres.), Rural Carriers Aux., Music Tchrs. Assn. Woman's Club, Shakespeare Club, Bus. and Profl. Club (v.p.), Order Eastern Star (organist, sec.).

BENTON, HOMER GRABILL, business educator, consultant; b. Altoona, Pa., Oct. 11, 1926; s. Homer Soyster and Mary Elizabeth (Grabill) B.; m. Blanche Carolyn Saxe, Aug. 1947; children: Homer David, Stephen Richard, John Paul, Deborah Kay. BA, Wheaton Coll., 1947; ThM, Calif. Theol. Sem., 1955; MBA, Syracuse Grad. Sch. Mgmt., 1970; JD, Western State U., 1985. Ordained to ministry Ind. Chs. of Am., 1949. Pastor local chs., N.Y. and Calif., 1948-55; commd. lt. U.S. Army, 1955, advanced through grades to col., 1974; prof. U.S. Army Svc. Sch., 1970-74; comptr. U.S. Army European Hdqrs., 1974-77, dir. bookstore ops., 1974-77; part-time prof. Emory-Riddle U., Europe, 1976-77, ret., 1979; prof. Biola U., La Mirada, Calif., 1979-84; prof., chair bus. dept. Pacific Christian Coll., Fullerton, Calif., 1985—; cons. various profit and non-profit corps., Anaheim, Calif, 1988—, various small bus. corps., Anaheim, 1986—; newscaster Sta. KROP-AM, Brawley, Calif., 1951-53; book reviewer Voice Mag., Chgo., 1953-57; pres. So. Calif. Ind. Chs., L.A., 1956-59. Co-author: Pacific Coast Railways, 1960; editor So. Calif. Regional News, 1953-57; contbr. articles to profl. jours. Pres. Mission to Migrants, L.A., 1953-59; bd. dirs. Hosp. Chaplain's Assn., L.A., 1953-55, Am. Ice, Inc., Long Beach, Calif., 1982-85; trustee Christian Heritage Coll., El Cajon, Calif., 1983-85. Decorated Army Commendation medal, Meritorious Merit medal; recipient Freedom Found. awards, 1967, 70; named Chaplain of Yr., Ind. Chs., 1974. Mem. Railway and Locomotive Hist. Soc. (editorial bd. 1962-70), Johannes Schwalm Hist. Assn., Christian Bus. Faculty Assn., Western Coll. and Univ. Faculty Assn., Lancaster Mennonite Hist. Soc., Christian Mgmt. Assn., Western Pa. Gen. and Hist. Soc. Home: 12482 Madera St Victorville CA 92392-6746 Office: Pacific Christian Coll 2500 E Nutwood Ave Fullerton CA 92631-3104

BENTON, MARY ANNE, self esteem and wellness consultant; b. Charlotte, N.C., Dec. 31, 1952; d. William Pettigrew and Blanche Marilyn (Lampke) B.; m. Richard Michael Barr. BS, U. Calif., Berkeley, 1974. Cert. health/fitness instr. Am. Coll. Sports Medicine. Pres., owner Body Class, Santa Fe and Santa Cruz, 1982-92, Image-in, Santa Fe, 1992—; fitness trainer Japan Aerobic Fitness Assn., Tokyo, 1986-88; head wellness trainer various Am. Indian tribes, N.Mex., Colo., Ariz., Okla., Alaska, Maine, 1986—. Author: No Train, No Gain!, 1986, 30 Days to Body Esteem, 1990, (audio cassette program) Body Truths, 1990. Bd. dirs. Health Net N.Mex., Albuquerque, 1988-90; com. mem. Am. Coun. on Exercise, San Diego, 1992—; creator, dir. To Tell the Truth: Am. Speaks Out About Incest & Sexual Abuse, Santa Fe, 1992—. Mem. Am. Coll. Sports Medicine, Nat. Coun. on Self-Esteem. Office: Imáge-in PO Box 9323 Santa Fe NM 87504-9323

BENTON, ROBERT WILMER, educational administrator; b. Guthrie County, Iowa, Aug. 28, 1931; s. Howard Jasper and Nellie Mae (Gustin) B.; m. Beryl Edna Anderson, Aug. 20, 1955; children: Gregory R., Steven S., Sharon Coram, Linda Tomaio. BA, Northwestern Coll., 1955; ThM, Dallas Theol. Sem., 1959; ThD, Grace Theol. Sem., 1968; PhD, U. Nebr., 1983. Ordained to ministry Bapt. Ch., 1959. Pastor Martensdale (Iowa) Community Ch., 1959-64, Tippecanoe (Ind.) Community Ch., 1964-67; mem. faculty Grace Bible Inst. (now Grace Coll. of Bible), Omaha, 1967-71, pres., 1971-84; pres. Northeastern Bible Coll., Essex Falls, N.J., 1984-87; dir. devel. Northwestern Coll., St. Paul, 1988-89; pres. Ariz. Coll. of the Bible, Phoenix, 1989—. Contbr. articles to religious publs. Mem. Nat. Soc. Fund Raising Execs., Rotary Club. Republican. Baptist. Home: 4020 W Griswold Rd Phoenix AZ 85051-4636 Office: Ariz Coll of Bible 2045 W Northern Ave Phoenix AZ 85021-5197

BENVENISTE, DANIEL STEPHEN, psychotherapist, historian; b. Oakland, Calif., Mar. 10, 1954; s. Jacob and Lucie (Almeleh) B. BA in Psychology, San Francisco State U., 1976, MS in Clin. Psychology, 1979; PhD in Clin. Psychology, Calif. Sch. Profl. Psychology, Berkeley/Alameda, 1990. Lic. marriage, family and child counselor; lic. psychologist. Psychotherapist St. James Health Ctr., San Jose, Calif., 1988-90; postdoctoral intern Mt. Zion Community Crisis Clinic, San Francisco, 1989-91; ind. rschr., historian of psychoanalysis San Francisco, 1990—, pvt. practice, 1990—; adj. faculty San Francisco State U., 1991—; Bd. dirs. Friends of the San Francisco Psychoanalytic Inst., 1991—, mem. libr. com., 1991—. Contbr. articles to profl. jours. Sephardic. Office: 1939 Divisadero Ste # 3 San Francisco CA 94115

BENYO, RICHARD STEPHEN, magazine editor, writer; b. Palmerton, Pa., Apr. 20, 1946; s. Andrew Joseph and Dorothy Rita (Herman) B.; m. Jill Wapensky, Apr. 29, 1972 (div. 1979); m. Rhonda Provost, Nov. 16, 1985. B.A. in English Lit., Bloomsburg (Pa.) State U., 1968. Mng. editor Times-News, Lehighton, Pa., 1968-72; editor Stock Car Racing mag., Alexandria, Va., 1972-77; sr. editor Stock Car Racing mag., 1977—; exec. editor Runner's World mag., Mountain View, Calif., 1977-84; editorial dir. Skier's mag. and Fit mag., Mountain View, 1980-84, Anderson World Books, Mountain View, 1980-84, Strength Tng. for Beauty mag., 1983-84; editor Corporate Fitness Report, Mountain View, 1980-84, Nat. Health & Fitness Report, 1982-84, Runner's World Quar., 1982-84; v.p. J.R. Anderson Enterprizes, Inc., 1982-84; pres., pub. Specific Publs., Inc., 1983—; fitness columnist San Francisco Chronicle, 1985-91; columnist Sports Care and Fitness, 1988-90; editor Silver Sport Mag., Los Gatus, Calif., 1993—; program dir. PTVC-TV, Palmerton, Pa., 1969-72. Author: The Grand National Stars, 1975, The Book of Richard Petty, 1976, Superspeedway, 1977, Return to Running, 1978; (with Rhonda Provost) The Indoor ExerciseBook, 1980, Advanced Indoor Exercise Book, 1981, Feeling Fit in Your 40's, 1987; (with Kym Herrin) Sexercise, 1981; Masters of the Marathon, 1983; (with Elaine LaLanne) Fitness After 50, 1986, Dynastride!, 1988, Fitness After 50 Workout, 1989; The Exercise Fix, 1989, The Death Valley 300, 1991, (with Elaine LaLanne) Eating Right for a New You, 1992, Making the Marathon Your Event, 1992, (with Elaine LaLanne) Total Juicing, 1992; editor: The Complete Woman Runner, 1978, Running for Everybody, 1981. Mem. racing panel of experts Union 76; bd. dirs. Napa Valley Marathon; mem. The Athletic Congress, Pacific Assn. Ultramarathoning Grand Prix Com.; bd. dirs. E Clampus Vitus. Recipient 1st pl. award local column Pa. Newspaper Pubs. Assn., 1972; named Young Alumnus of Yr., Bloomsburg U., 1985. Mem. Am. Auto Racing Writers and Broadcasters Assn. (1st place award for tech. writing), Internat. Motor Press Assn., Athletic Congress, U.S. Ski Writers Assn., N.Y. Road Runners Club, Nat. Sportscasters and Sportswriters Assn., Track and Field Writers of Am., Internat. Sports Press Assn., Commonwealth Club (San Francisco). Democrat. Home and Office: 7050 Guisti Rd Forestville CA 95436-9637

BENZER, SEYMOUR, neurosciences educator; b. N.Y.C., Oct. 15, 1921; s. Mayer and Eva (Naidorf) B.; m. Dorothy Vlosky, Jan. 10, 1942 (dec. 1978); children: Barbara Ann Benzer Freidin, Martha Jane Benzer Goldberg; m. Carol A. Miller, May 11, 1980; 1 child, Alexander Robin. B.A., Bklyn. Coll., 1942; M.S., Purdue U., 1943, Ph.D., 1947, D.Sc. (hon.), 1968; D.Sc., Columbia U., 1974, Yale U., 1977, Brandeis U., 1978, CUNY, 1978, U. Paris, 1983, Rockefeller U., N.Y.C., 1993. Mem. faculty Purdue U., 1945-67, prof. biophysics, 1958-61, Stuart distinguished prof. biology, 1961-67; prof. biology Calif. Inst. Tech., 1967-75, Boswell prof. neurosci., 1975—; biophysicist Oak Ridge Nat. Lab., 1948-49; vis. asso. Calif. Inst. Tech., Pasadena, 1965-67. Contbr. articles to profl. jours. Rsch. fellow Calif. Inst. Tech., 1949-51; Fulbright rsch. fellow Pasteur Inst., Paris, 1951-52; sr. NSF postdoctoral fellow Cambridge, Eng., 1957-58; recipient Award of Honor Bklyn. Coll., 1956, Sigma Xi rsch. award Purdue U., 1957, Ricketts award U. Chgo., 1961, Gold medal N.Y. City Coll. Chemistry Alumni Assn., 1962, Gairdner award of merit, 1964, McCoy award Purdue U., 1965, Lasker award, 1971, T. Duckett Jones award, 1975, Prix Leopold Mayer French Acad. Scis., 1975, Louisa Gross Horwitz award, 1976, Harvey award Israel, 1977, Warren Triennial prize Mass. Gen. Hosp., 1977, Dickson award, 1978, Rosenstiel award, 1986, T.H. Morgan medal Genetics Soc. Am., 1986, Karl Spencer Lashley award, 1988, Gerard award Soc. Neurosci., 1989, Helmerich award, 1990, Wolf Prize, Israel, 1991, Bristol-Myers Squibb Neurosci. award, 1992, Crafoord prize Royal Swedish Acad. Scis., 1993. Fellow Indian Acad. Scis. (hon.); mem. Nat. Acad. Scis., Am. Acad. Arts and Scis., Am. Philos. Soc. (Lashley award 1988), Harvey Soc., N.Y. Acad. Scis., AAAS, Royal Soc. London (fgn. mem.). Home: 2075 Robin Rd San Marino CA 91108-2831

BENZING, DAVID WARREN, semiconductor equipment company executive; b. Perth Amboy, N.J., Feb. 11, 1953; s. Walter Charles and Ruth E. (McBride) B.; m. Pamela Jean Drummond, Dec. 28, 1972 (div. 1982); 1 child, Thor A.; m. Cathleen Lynn Hays, Sept. 12, 1985 (div. 1988); 1 child, Allison G. BSChemE, U. Calif., Berkeley, 1974; PhD in Chem. Engring., Princeton U., 1978. Sr. engr. Signetics Corp., Sunnyvale, Calif., 1978-81, Applied Materials, Inc., Santa Clara, Calif., 1981-82; dir. research and devel. Anelva Corp., San Jose, Calif., 1982-84; pres., founder Benzing Techs., Inc., Santa Clara, 1984—; bd. dirs. Direction Inc., Sunnyvale; lectr. Sci. and Tech. Inst., Mt. View, Calif., 1981-83; cons. Ube Industries, Ltd., Tokyo, 1984-87, Plasma System Corp., Tokyo, 1993—. Contbr. articles to profl. jours.; patentee in field. Mem. Electrochem. Soc., Thin Film Soc., Semiconductor Equipment and Materials Inst. Republican. Office: Benzing Techs Inc 3443 Edward Ave Santa Clara CA 95054-2310

BERAN, RUDOLF JAROSLAV VACLAV, statistics educator; b. Prague, Czechoslovakia, Sept. 12, 1943; s. Rudolf and Jirina (Chmel) B.; m. Carol Louise Viertel, Aug. 24, 1968; children: Rudolf K.F., Gregory J.O. BSc, U. Toronto, 1964, MA, 1965; PhD, Johns Hopkins U., 1968. Asst. prof. stats. U. Calif., Berkeley, 1968-73, assoc. prof., 1973-78, prof. stats., 1978—, chmn. dept., 1986-89; vis. assoc. prof. U. Toronto, 1982-83, vis. prof.,1 990; vis. prof. U. Heidelberg, Fed. Republic Germany, 1982, 86, 88-92, U. Paris-Sud, Orsay, France, 1985, U. Montreal, 1989, Nankai U., 1989; vis. fellow U. Melbourne, Australia, 1975, Australian Nat. U., 1990. Assoc. editor Annals of Statistics, 1977-82, 87-88; mem. editorial bd. Probability Theory and Related Fields, 1983-92, Annals Inst. Statis. Math., 1986—; contbr. rsch. papers to profl. jours. Research grantee NSF. Fellow Internat. Statis. Inst.,

Inst. Math. Stats., Am. Statis. Assn. Office: Univ of Calif Dept Stats Berkeley CA 94720

BERBERICH, GEORGE EDWARD, JR., educator; b. Cin.; s. George Edward Sr. and Elsie (Edwards) B. AA, St. Petersburg Jr. Coll., 1969; BA, U. South Fla., 1972; MA, Calif. State U., L.A., 1974; PhD, U. So. Calif., L.A., 1985. Waiter various restaurants and country clubs, Clearwater, Fla., 1967—; asst. to curators L.A. Mus. of Art, 1976-78; English tchr. L.A. and Glendale Schs., 1978-81; drama lit. lectr. U. So. Calif., L.A., 1979-84; spl. edn. tchr. L.A. Unified Schs., 1984—; asst. coach Acad. Decanthelon, L.A., 1990-91. Editor Studies in Comparative Communism, 1983; contbr. articles to profl. jours. Chair United Way Dr., L.A. 1970, 91. Recipient Appreciation award Secondary Schs. Assn., 1988. Mem. Mensa, Nat. Hist. Soc., Nat. Assn. for Lit. and the Arts, Nat. Piano Players Fraternity, Am. Philatelic Soc., Hallmark Ornament Collectors Club. Republican. Baptist.

BERCQ, ALEXIS CLAUDE, air force non-commissioned officer; b. Paris, Mar. 10, 1960; came to U.S., 1964; s. Jean Claude Bercq and Sandra Shahan; m. Laura Anne Moyer, Apr. 10, 1982 (div. 1982); m. Susan Gail Van Pelt, June 11, 1986 (div. 1989). Enlisted U.S. Air Force, 1979; aircraft maintenance specialist Nellis AFB, Nev., 1979-83; flight engr. Norton AFB, Calif., 1983-86; flight engr., NCO in charge safety, total quality mgmt. Spl. Air Missions detachment 1 89th Mil. Airlift Wing, Hickam AFB, Hawaii, 1986-92; flight engr., non-commd. officer in charge safety, manuals 65 Airlift Squadron, Hickam AFB, Hawaii, 1992-93; flight engr. 21 Airlift Squadron, Yokota Air Base, Japan, 1993—. Mem. NRA (life, benefactor), Calif. Rifle and Pistol Assn. (Gold Bear life), Tenn. State Rifle Assn. (Gold Ram, life), Nev. State Rifle and Pistol Assn. (Gold Ram, life), Hawaii Rifle Assn. (life), Ark. Rifle and Pistol Assn., Tex. State Rifle Assn. (life), Air Force Sgts. Assn. (life). Office: 21 Airlift Squadron APO AP 96326-5067

BERDELL, JAMES RUSSELL, venture capitalist, investment manager; b. Sellersville, Pa., Mar. 23, 1944; s. Russell Warren and Helen Dorothy (Schmidt) B.; m. Mary Cecilia Clark, Nov. 27, 1971; 1 child, Lauren Kimberly. BS in Engring., Drexel U., 1967; MS in Mgmt., MIT, 1969. Portfolio mgr. Hillsborough Capital Corp., San Francisco, 1969-71; fin. analyst Mitchum, Jones & Templeton, San Francisco, 1971-73; dir. of rsch. Schuman, Agnew & Co., San Francisco, 1973-75; ptnr. Montgomery Securities, San Francisco, 1975-82; pres. Berdell, Welling & Co., Menlo Park, Calif., 1982—. MIT grantee, 1967; Drexel U. scholar, 1962. Mem. San Francisco Soc. Security Analysts, West Coast Venture Capitalists Soc., Chartered Fin. Analysts, Commonwealth Club Calif., Univ. Club, Phi Kappa Phi, Sigma Rho. Republican. Lutheran. Office: Berdell Welling & Co 3000 Sandhill Rd # 3-125 Menlo Park CA 94025-7116

BERDROW, STANTON K., power company executive; b. Long Beach, Calif., Oct. 4, 1928; s. Earl Lester and Martha Ann B.; m. Rosa R. Rottger, Feb. 22, 1951; children: Nancy, John, Matthew. BS, Armstrong Coll., Berkeley, Calif., 1950; postgrad. Sch. Bus. Syracuse U., 1951-52. Dist. advt. and sales promotion mgr. The Pennzoil Co., Los Angeles, 1953-59; v.p., mgmt. supr. Batten, Barton, Durstine & Osborn, Inc., San Francisco, 1960-77; v.p., dir. acctg. services Commart Communications, Santa Clara, Calif., 1978-80; v.p. corp. comm. Sierra Pacific Resources and subs. Sierra Pacific Power Co. Reno, 1980—. Adminstr. Sierra Pacific Charitable Found., 1987—; chmn. bd. trustees PBS-TV, Reno. Served with U.S. Army, 1946-48. Mem. Pub. Relations Soc. Am. (past pres. Sierra Nev. chpt.), Utility Comm. Internat. (past pres. 1990-91), Reno Advt. Club, Newcomen Soc, Citizens for Pvt. Enterprise. Republican. Clubs: Rotary, Lakeridge Tennis. Contbr. articles to profl. jours. Home: 3925 Skyline Blvd Reno NV 89509-5661 Office: Sierra Pacific Power Co PO Box 10100 Reno NV 89520-0024

BEREK, JONATHAN SAMUEL, physician, surgeon; b. Sioux City, Iowa, Apr. 21, 1948; s. Samuel I. and Janet (Graetz) B.; m. Deborah L. Jones, June 6, 1970; children: Micah, James, Jessica. AB, Brown U., 1970, MMSc, 1973; MD, Johns Hopkins U., 1975; postgrad., Harvard U., 1979. Diplomate Am. Bd. Ob-Gyn. Intern and resident Brigham and Women's Hosp. Harvard U. Med. Sch., Boston, 1975-79; prof. UCLA Sch. Medicine, 1979-92, prof., vice chair dept. ob-gyn., 1992—. Author: Practical Gynecologic Oncology, 1989, Gynecologic Oncology: Rational Techniques, 1991; contbr. over 220 articles to profl. jours. Fellow Am. Coll. Ob-Gyn, Am. Coll. Surgeons; Cert. Gynecologic Oncology. Office: UCLA Sch Medicine CHS 24-127 Los Angeles CA 90024

BERESTYNSKI, ADAM S., architect, urban planner; b. Krakow, Poland, May 5, 1927; came to U.S., 1966; s. Adam and Kazimiera Berestynski; m. Magdalena Steinhagen, Oct. 4, 1957; 1 child, Peter. MSc in Architecture and City Planning, Poly. U., Krakow, 1951. Archtl. designer Archtl. Offices, Krakow, 1950-60; mgr. archtl. and planning dept. City of Krakow, 1960-64; archtl. and urban designer, planning cons. Royal Afghan Ministry of Public Works, Kabul, Afghanistan, 1964-66; sr. planner City of Oklahoma City, 1967-68; regional planner Leslie Properties, Inc., Redwood City, Calif., 1968-69; assoc. planner City of Fremont, Calif., 1969-70; urban designer VTN Consol., Inc., Irvine, 1970-76; asst. dir. planning Bein, Frost & Assoc., Newport Beach, 1976-81; urban design cons. Laguna Beach, Calif., 1981-82; mgr. planning & devel. control Saudi Arabian Parsons, Ltd., Yanbu, Saudi Arabia, 1982-89; ret., 1992. Contbr. articles to profl. jours. With Polish Underground Resistance Army, 1944-45. Recipient III Grade award Soc. Polish Architects, 1963, nat. philatelic awards. Mem. AIA (assoc.), Assn. Environ. Profls., Am. Inst. Planners (assoc.), Am. Planning Assn. (charter), Am. Philatelic Soc., Polonus Philatelic Soc., Am. Assn. Philatelic Exhibitors. Republican. Roman Catholic. Home: 2845 Chillon Way Laguna Beach CA 92651-2012

BERETTA, GIORDANO BRUNO, computer scientist, researcher; b. Brugg, Aargau, Switzerland, Apr. 14, 1951; came to U.S., 1984; PhD, ETH, Zurich, Switzerland, 1984. Mem. rsch. staff Xerox Palo Alto (Calif.) Rsch. Ctr., 1984-90; charter mem., sr. scientist Canon Info. Systems, Palo Alto, 1990—. Contbr. articles to profl. jours. Mem. IEEE, Assn. Computing Machinery, Soc. Imaging Sci. and Tech., Soc. Info. Display, Inter-Soc. Color Coun. Office: Canon Info Systems 4009 Miranda Ave Palo Alto CA 94304-1218

BERETZ, PAUL BASIL, financial executive; b. Washington, Oct. 15, 1938; s. O. Paul and Marthe (Szabo) B.; m. Jane Macmanus, Nov. 9, 1963; children: Charles, Melissa, John, Michele, Claudine. BBA, U. Notre Dame, 1960; MBA, Golden Gate U., 1974. Mgr. cen. credit Union Carbide Corp., Atlanta, San Francisco, N.Y.C., 1961-81; gen. mgr. Bayox/Almac Co., Oakland, Calif., 1981-83; asst. treas. Crown Zellerbach Corp., San Francisco, 1983-86; prin. P.B. Beretz and Co., Bus. Cons., San Francisco, 1986-91; mgr. fin. Applied Materials Inc., Santa Clara, Calif., 1991—; mem. faculty U. Calif., Berkeley, 1990-93. Author: Managing Commercial Credit, 1981; contbr. articles to profl. jours. Trustee Credit Rsch. Found., N.Y.C., 1983-86. Mem. U. Notre Dame Alumni Assn. (bd. dirs. 1983-86). Democrat. Roman Catholic. Home: 21 Sara Ln Alamo CA 94507 Office: Applied Materials Inc M/S 0932 2695 Augustine Dr Santa Clara CA 95054

BERFIELD, SUE ELLEN, systems coordinator; b. Williamsport, Pa., June 15, 1949; d. John Edward and Ruth Van Scoyic (Swartz) Watkins; m. Larry Edward Berfield, May 3, 1969; children: Timothy Alan, Todd Elliot. AAS, Clark County Community Coll., 1987; student, U. Nev., 1987-91. Cert. system mgr., cert. Novell adminstr. Clk. Clark County Justice's Cts., Las Vegas, 1979-82; jury svcs. asst. Eighth Jud. Dist. Ct., Las Vegas, 1982-85, sr. jury svc. asst., 1985-86, asst. jury commr., 1986-89, automated info. supr., 1987-89, ct. ops. supr., 1989-91, systems coord., 1991—; cons. in field; sponsor, advisor Regional Criminal History System, Las Vegas, 1992; chmn. Family Ct. Tech. Com., Las Vegas, 1992. Editor: Jury Svc. Handbook, 1989; author: Distributed Computing Handbook, 1991. Vol. J.C. Thompson Polit. Campaign, Las Vegas, 1982, 86, 92, Clark County Election Dept., Las Vegas, 1992; coord. United Blood Svcs., Las Vegas, 1989-92; campaign coord. United Way, Clark County, 1991. Mem. NAFE, Nev. Assn. Ct. Clks. and Adminstrs., Nat. Ctr. for State Cts., Math. Assn. Am., Toastmasters Internat. Office: 8th Jud Dist Ct 200 S Third St Las Vegas NV 89155-0001

BERG, CAROLYN NOURSE, research analyst; b. Des Moines, July 17, 1938; d. Archie B. and Katie Matilda (Taylor) Nourse; divorced; children: Christina Carole, Anna Lorraine. BA in History, U. Idaho, 1971; MBA, Ariz. State U., 1983. Sr. sec. U. Idaho, Moscow, 1972-74; owner, mgr. Something Different, Moscow, 1974-79, Inner Space, Moscow, 1979-81; coord. Moscow Downtown Assn., 1981-82; rsch. asst. Ariz. State U., Tempe, 1982-84; mgr. Door Store, Mesa, Ariz., 1984-86; rsch. analyst O'Neil Assocs., Tempe, 1986-89; faculty rsch. assoc. Ariz. State U., Tempe, 1989-90; adminstrv. coord. Maricopa County Dept. Pub. Health, Phoenix, 1990—. Home: 11202 S Mandan St Phoenix AZ 85044-1811

BERG, DAVE, television producer, writer; b. Hollywood, Calif., June 1, 1948; s. David Bernard and Beverly May (Sparks) B.; m. Mary Khourie, Sept. 24, 1983; children: Melissa, David. BA in Polit. Sci., Northwestern U., 1970; MS in Journalism, Kans. State U., 1974. Writer, producer Sta. KCUR-FM, Kansas City, Mo., 1971-73; anchor, reporter Sta. WFRV-TV, Green Bay, Wis., 1974-76; assignment mgr., anchor Sta. KTIV-TV, Sioux City, Iowa, 1976-78; assignment mgr., reporter Sta. KETV-TV, Omaha, 1978-80; exec. producer Sta. KOVR-TV, Sacramento, 1980-82; writer, producer NBC News-Burbank, 1982-89; bur. chief L.A. CNBC (cable div. NBC), Ft. Lee, N.J., 1989-92; segment producer The Tonight Show With Jay Leno, Burbank, Calif, 1992—. Songwriter: (country songs) Gonna Walk, 1990, Can't Make Up My Heart, 1990. Counselor prison inmates United Meth. Ch.-Valencia, Lake Hughes, Calif., 1988—, assoc. lay leader. NIMH fellow, 1973-74. Republican. Office: CNBC 3000 W Alameda Ave # 2190 Burbank CA 91523

BERG, HELEN MACDUFFEE, retired educator, statistician; b. Columbus, Ohio, July 15, 1932; d. Cyrus Colton and Mary Augusta (Bean) MacD.; m. Alan Ben Berg, June 6, 1981 (dec. July 1989); children: Christopher Clayton Ward, Ellen Elizabeth Ward Valachovic. BA, U. Wis., 1953; MS, Oreg. State U., 1973. Mathematician U.S. Naval Rsch. Lab., Madison, Wis., 1953-56; rsch. asst. Oreg. State U., Corvallis, 1963-72, project coord., 1975-86, dir. survery rsch. ctr., 1986-93, ret., 1993; rsch. assoc. U. Ill., Urbana, 1973-75. Contbr. articles to profl. jours. Pres. Corvallis City Coun., 1991—. Democrat. Home: 3645 NW Hayes Ave Corvallis OR 97330-1747

BERG, PAUL, biochemist, educator; b. N.Y.C., June 30, 1926; s. Harry and Sarah (Brodsky) B.; m. Mildred Levy, Sept. 13, 1947; 1 son, John. BS, Pa. State U., 1948; PhD (NIH fellow 1950-52), Western Res. U., 1952; DSc (hon.), U. Rochester, 1978, Yale U., 1978, Wash. U., St. Louis, 1986, Oreg. State U., 1989. Postdoctoral fellow Copenhagen (Denmark) U., 1952-53; postdoctoral fellow sch. medicine Washington U., St. Louis, 1953-54; Am. Cancer Soc. scholar cancer research dept. microbiology sch. medicine Washington U., 1954-57, from asst. to assoc. prof. microbiology sch. medicine, 1955-59; prof. biochemistry sch. medicine Stanford U., 1959—, Sam, Lula and Jack Willson prof. biochemistry sch. medicine, 1970, chmn. dept. sch. medicine, 1969-74; dir. Stanford U. Beckman Ctr. for Molecular and Genetic Medicine, 1985—; non-resident fellow Salk Inst., 1973-83; adv. bd. NIH, NSF, MIT; vis. com. dept. biochemistry and molecular biology Harvard U.; bd. sci. advisors Jane Coffin Childs Found. Med. Rsch., 1970-80; chmn. sci. adv. com. Whitehead Inst., 1984-90; internat. adv. bd. Basel Inst. Immunology; chmn. nat. adv. com. Human Genome Project, 1990-92. Contbr. profl. jours.; Editor: Biochem. and Biophys. Research Communications, 1959-68; editorial bd.: Molecular Biology, 1966-69. Trustee Rockefeller U., 1990-92. Served to lt. (j.g.) USNR, 1943-46. Recipient Eli Lilly prize biochemistry, 1959; V.D. Mattia award Roche Inst. Molecular Biology, 1972; Henry J. Kaiser award for excellence in teaching, 1974; Disting. Alumnus award Pa. State U., 1972; Sarasota Med. awards for achievement and excellence, 1979; Gairdner Found. annual award, 1980; Lasker Found. award, 1980; Nobel award in chemistry, 1980; N.Y. Acad. Sci. award, 1980; Sci. Freedom and Responsibility award AAAS, 1982; Nat. Medal of Sci., 1983; named Calif. Scientist of Yr. Calif. Museum Sci. and Industry, 1963; numerous disting. lectureships including Harvey lectr., 1972, Lynen lectr., 1977, Priestly lectrs. Pa. State U., 1978, Dreyfus Disting. lectrs. Northwestern U., 1979, Lawrence Livermore Dir.'s Disting. lectr., 1983. Fellow AAAS; mem. NAS, Inst. Medicine, Am. Acad. Arts and Scis., Am. Soc. Biol. Chemists (pres. 1974-75), Am. Soc. Microbiology, Am. Philos. Soc., Japan Biochem. Soc. (elected fgn. mem. 1978), French Acad. Sci. (elected fgn. mem. 1981), Royal Soc. (elected fgn. mem. 1992). Office: Stanford Sch Medicine Beckman Ctr B-062 Stanford CA 94305-5425

BERG, RICHARD ARCHIE, association executive, civil engineer; b. Kindred, N.D., Oct. 5, 1917; s. Morris C. and Julia Ottina (Rosendahl) B.; m. Shirley Foreman, Mar. 18, 1942; children: Melodie, Richard, Kevin, Chris. Student, Mont. State Coll, 1946-49. Registered profl. engr. and land surveyor. Brakeman No. Pacific R.R., Glendive, Mont., 1936-42; project engr. Mont. Dept. Hwys., Bozeman, 1949-55; office engr. Mont. Dept. Hwys., Gt. Falls, 1955-71; specifications engr. Mont. Dept. Hwys., Helena, 1971-76; exec. officer, sec. Winchester Arms Collectors Assn., Gt. Falls, 1983—. Scoutmaster area commr. Boy Scouts Am., Gt. Falls, 1961—. Served to sgt. U.S. Army, 1942-46. Recipient Silver Beaver award Boy Scouts Am., 1978, Virgil Honor award Order of the Arrow. Mem. DAV, VFW, Am. Legion (vice-commdr.), Mont. Arms Collectors Assn. (exec. sec./treas. 1976-83), Masons. Office: Winchester Arms Collectors Assn Inc PO Box 6754 Great Falls MT 59406

BERG, ROBERT CHARLES, neonatal respiratory therapist; b. Queens, N.Y., Oct. 17, 1944; s. Harrold and Lucy (Tronalon) B. AA, Rio Hondo Coll., 1979, AS in Respiratory Therapy, 1985. EMT-IA Ame Ambulance, Whittier, Calif., 1977; EMT/NA Norwalk (Calif.) Community Hosp., 1977-78; ICU/CCU tech. Whittier (Calif.) Hosp., 1978-80; pvt. practice instr. CPP and first aid Long Beach, Calif., 1980-83; respiratory therapist Hollywood Presbyn. Med. Ctr., L.A., 1984-86; neonatal ICU respiratory therapist St. Mary Med. Ctr., Long Beach, 1986-89, Cedar Sinai Med. Ctr., L.A., 1989-91; continuing edn. provider, Long Beach, 1991—. BCLS instr., advanced first aid instr., ARC; neonatal resucitation instr., ACLS instr. Am. Heart Assn. With USN, 1961-63, Vietnam. Mem. Am. Assn. Respiratory Care. Jewish. Home: 20516 Arline Ave Lakewood CA 90715

BERG, TOM, artist; b. Aberdeen, S.D., Feb. 10, 1943; s. Lloyd T. and Florence (Johnson) B.; m. Donna R. Berg, Aug. 25, 1965. BA, U. Wyo., 1966, MA, 1969, MFA, 1972. Artist-in-residence Wyo. Artists in Schs., 1973-76, U. Maine, Augusta, 1972-73, 87; vis. lectr. U. Okla., Norman, 1989, Okla. Arts Inst., Oklahoma City, 1989, N.Mex. State U., Las Cruces, 1989; works in permanent collections at Amoco, Denver and Houston, Chem. Bank, N.Y.C., Delta State U., Cleveland, Miss., El Paso Mus. Art, First Union Bank, Nashville, Frito Lay Collection, Chgo. and Dallas, Mus. Art, U. Okla., Mus. Art, U. Wyo., Mus. Fine Art, Santa Fe, Nat. Rsch. Libr., Ottawa, Can., Philip Morris Collection, N.Y.C., Whitney Mus. of Am. Art, N.Y.C., others. One-man shows include Heydt/Blair Gallery, Santa Fe, 1980, 81, Eason Gallery, 198, 83, Davis/McClain Gallery, Houston, 1984, Robischon Gallery, Denver, 1986, Wade Gallery, L.A., 1988, 90, Mus. Art, U. Okla., 1989, Linda Durham Gallery, Santa Fe, 1985, 86, 87, 89, Sangre de Cristo Art Ctr., Colo., 1990, Wade Wilson Gallery, Chgo., 1991, Janus Gallery, Santa, 1991, J. Cacciola Gallery, N.Y.C., 1992, Munson Gallery, Santa Fe, 1993—; group shows include Janus Gallery, 1984, 87, 89, 90, Chgo. Internat. Art Expo, 1986-89, L.A. Internat. Contemporary Art Fair, 1987-89, Linda Durham Gallery, 1988, numerous others. Visual Arts fellow, Western States Arts Found., 1976; recipient various purchase award. Mem. U.S. Ski Coaches Assn. (level III Nordic coach), Los Alamos Nordic Ski Team (head coach). Home and Office: RR 1 Box 171A Santa Fe NM 87501-9704

BERGAMO, RON, broadcasting company executive; b. Palm Springs, Calif., Nov. 26, 1943; s. Ralph and Dorothy (Johnson) B.; m. Jane E. Reed; children: Brad, Doug, Steve. BS, U. Ariz., 1965; MBA, Northwestern U., 1972. Pres., gen. mgr. Sta. KTSP-TV, Phoenix; with Leo Burnett, 1966-68, NBC Network, 1968-69, AVCO TV Sales, 1969-72, Eller Outdoor, 1972-74, Sta. KMBC-TV Sales, 1974-77, LSM Sta. WFAA-TV, 1977-80; gen. mgr. Sta. KFDM-TV, Beaumont, Tex., 1980-82, Sta. KWCH-TV, Wichita, Kans., 1983-88; pres., gen. mgr. Sta. KTSP-TV, Phoenix, 1988—; bd. CBS Affiliate. Bd. dirs. Phoenix Pride, Phoenix Art Mus. US Army Nat. Guard, 1965-71. Recipient Gen. Mgr. of Yr. award AWRT, 1990, Phoenix award PRSA, 1992; named Wichita Ad Person of Yr., 1985, Person of Yr. Phoenix Ad Club, 1993. Mem. Ariz. Broadcasters Assn. (pres. 1993), Phoenix C. of C. (bd. dirs.), U. Ariz. Alumni (bd. dirs.), Sigma Chi, Rotary. Republican. Methodist. Home: 5901 E Stella Ln Paradise Valley AZ 85253 Office: Sta KTSP-TV 511 W Adams St Phoenix AZ 85003-1638

BERGÉ, CAROL, author; b. N.Y.C., 1928; d. Albert and Molly Peppis; m. Jack Bergé, June 1955; 1 child, Peter. Asst. to pres. Pendray Public Relations, N.Y.C., 1955; disting. prof. lit. Thomas Jefferson Coll., Allendale, Mich., 1975-76; instr. adult degree program Goddard Coll. at Asilomar, 1976; tchr. fiction and poetry U. Calif. Extension Program, Berkeley, 1976-77; assoc. prof. U. So. Miss., Hattiesburg, 1977-78; vis. prof. Honors Ctr. and English dept. U. N.Mex., 1978-79, 87; vis. lectr. Wright State U., 1979, SUNY, Albany, 1980-81; tchr. Poets and Writers, Poets in the Schs. (N.Y. State Council on Arts), 1970-72, Poets in the Schs. (Conn. Commn. Arts); proprietor Blue Gate Gallery Art and Antiques, 1988—. Author: (fiction) The Unfolding, 1969, A Couple Called Moebius, 1972, Acts of Love: An American Novel, 1973 (N.Y. State Coun. on Arts CAPS award 1974), Timepieces, 1977, The Doppler Effect, 1979, Fierce Metronome, 1981, Secrets, Gossip and Slander, 1984, Zebras, or, Contour Lines, 1991; (poetry) The Vulnerable Island, 1964, Poems Made of Skin, 1968, The Chambers, 1969, Circles, as in the Eye, 1969, An American Romance, 1969, From a Soft Angle: Poems About Women, 1972, The Unexpected, 1976, Rituals and Gargoyles, 1976, A Song, A Chant, 1978, Alba Genesis, 1979, Alba Nemesis, 1979; editor: CENTER Mag., 1970-84, pub. 1991—; editor Miss. Rev., 1977-78, Subterraneans, 1975-76, Paper Branches, 1987; contbg. editor Woodstock Rev., 1977-81, Shearsman mag., 1980-82, S.W. Profile, 1981; editor, pub. CENTER Press, 1991—; pub. Medicine Journeys (Carl Ginsburg), Coastal Lives (Miriam Sagan), 1991; co-pub. Zebras (Carol Berge). Nat. Endowment Arts fellow, 1979-80. Mem. Authors' League, Poets and Writers, MacDowell Fellows Assn., Nat. Press Women. Home: 307 Johnson St Santa Fe NM 87501

BERGEMONT, ALBERT MICHEL, semiconductor scientist, consultant; b. Toulouse, France, Jan. 15, 1953; came to U.S., 1990; s. Raoul and Suzanne (Richou) B.; m. Bernadette DuBuis, Mar. 6, 1977; children: Sarah, Mickaël, Jimmy. Student, Nat. Inst. Applied Scis., Toulouse, 1975. Rsch. engr., physics engr. Nat. Ctr. Spatial Studies, Toulouse, 1975-77; process engr. CII Honeywell Bull, Paris, 1979-82, Harris Semicondr., Melbourne, Fla., 1982-83, Matra-Harris Semicondrs., Nantes, France, 1983-84; engring. mgr. Thomson-Eurotechnique, Rousset, France, 1984-88, SGS-Thomson Microelectronics, Grenoble, France, 1988-90, Nat. Semicondr., Santa Clara, Calif., 1990—; mem. Coll. Sci. Thomson, Paris, 1988-90. Contbr. articles to sci. jours.; numerous patents in field. Mem. IEEE (co-chmn. Internat. Electron Device Meeting conf. 1991, 92, Non Volatile Semicondr. Memory conf. 1992). Home: 5512 Castle Glen Ave San Jose CA 95129 Office: Nat Semicondr 2900 Semiconductor Dr Santa Clara CA 95052-8090

BERGEN, CHRISTOPHER BROOKE, opera company administrator, translator, editor; b. L.A., Jan. 11, 1949; s. Edward Grinnell Bergen and Alvina Ellen (Temple) Stevens; m. Tessa Jennifer von Grunebaum, May 7, 1972. BA, UCLA, 1971; MA, Yale U., 1977. Conf. officer IAEA, Vienna, Austria, 1973-75, data analyst, 1979-81; import mgr. COBEC Trading Corp., N.Y.C., 1978-79; assoc. Geissler Engring. Co., Oakland, Calif., 1982-83; dir. Yale Cons. Assocs., San Francisco, 1983-84; editor INPUT, Mountain View, Calif., 1984; adminstr. surtitles San Francisco Opera, 1985—. Editor profl. jours; translator operatic texts for projection during performances. Mem. Dolphin Swimming and Boating Club of San Francisco, Amnesty Internat., Sierra Club. Democrat. Home: 1450 Greenwich St # 604 San Francisco CA 94109-1466 Office: San Francisco Opera War Meml Opera House San Francisco CA 94102

BERGER, DIANE KLEIN, small business owner; b. Miami, Fla., Oct. 18, 1946; d. Bernard L. and Molly (Bear) Klein; m. Stephen E. Berger, Dec. 24, 1967; children: Michael Allen, Gary David. BE, U. Miami, 1968. Cert. elem. and early childhood tchr. Dir. Headstart Program Dade County Pub. Schs., Miami, 1968-69, tchr. 2d grade, 1970-71; dir. pre-kindergarten program Oxnard (Calif.) Sch. Dist., 1969-70; tchr. Green Valley Pres-Sch., San Pedro, Calif., 1973-76, Tuvia Pre-Sch., Redondo Beach, Calif., 1976-78; co-organizer Temple Eilat Pre-Sch., Mission Viejo, Calif., 1978; mgr. wallpaper dept. Frazee Paint and Wall Coverings, Mission Viejo, 1978—; owner Thing-a-majigs and Whatcha-ma-callits, El Toro, Calif., 1978—; mktg. rep. Discovery Toys, El Toro, 1980-87, Initial's Plus, El Toro, 1987-89, Accent on Elegence, El Toro, 1991—. Vice pres. B'nai B'rith Women, Torrance, Calif., 1971. Rsch. grantee U. Miami, 1968. Mem. Jewish Orgn. for Rahb. and Tng. Home: 24392 Mockingbird Pl Lake Forest CA 92630-1835

BERGER, EUGENIA HEPWORTH, sociology educator, author; b. Lawrence, Kans., Jan. 30, 1925; d. Richard Field and Gladys Fairchild (Henley) Hepworth; m. Glen Berger, June 18, 1946; children: Glen Richard, Debra Eugenia Berger McClave, John Hepworth. BME, U. Kans., 1946; MA, U. Denver, 1964, 66, PhD, 1968. Cert. tchr., Colo., family life educator. Tchr. Perry (Kans.) Consol. Schs., 1946-47, Burlingame (Kans.) Pub. Schs., 1947-48, Denver Pub. Schs., 1948-50; dir. parent edn. Arapahoe Sch. Dist. 6, Littleton, Colo., 1960-64; instr. U. Denver, 1966-68; prof. Met. State Coll. of Denver, 1968—; trainer Bldg. Family Strengths, Denver, 1986-93. Author: Parents as Partners in Education, 1981, 87, 91, Beyond the Classroom, 1983; contbr. chpt. in book. Bd. dirs., treas. Living Support Network, Denver, 1981-93. Recipient Foremost Mother award Littleton Ind. Newspaper, 1969. Mem. Am. Sociol. Assn., Assn. for Childhood Edn. Internat., Nat. Assn. for Edn. of Young Children, Nat. Coun. for Social Studies, Nat. Coun. on Family Rels. (sec., treas. affiliates 1990), Colo. Assn. for Childhood Edn. (bd. dirs. 1985-92), Rocky Mountain Coun. on Family Rels. (bd. dirs. 1982-92, acting pres. 1989-90). Office: Met State Coll Denver # 21 PO Box 173362 Denver CO 80217-3362

BERGER, GLENN WAYNE, geochronologist, researcher; b. Port Loring, Ont., Can., Dec. 23, 1945; came to U.S., 1986; s. Edmund Charles and Erna Melvina (Getz) B.; m. Wendy Maureen Beaman, Oct. 10, 1970 (div. Aug. 1984); 1 child, Michael Paul; m. Karla Dawn Kusmer, Sept. 24, 1988; 1 child, Carsen Lee. MSc, U. Toronto, Ont., 1970, PhD, 1973. Asst. prof. dept. geology U. Coimbra, Portugal, 1973-75; rsch. assoc. dept. physics U. Toronto, 1975-78, Simon Fraser U., Burnaby, B.C., Can., 1979-85; dir. TL lab. dept. geology Western Wash. U., Bellingham, 1986—; software cons. U. Cambridge Godwin Lab., Eng., 1982, U. Miami Dept. Geology, Coral Gables, Fla., 1981, adj. prof. 1983-86; vis. asst. prof. Simon Fraser U. Dept. Physics, Burnaby, 1981. Contbr. articles to profl. jours. Rsch. grantee U.S. NSF, 1986, 87, 90, 91, 93, U.S. Geol. Survey, 1987. Mem. Internat. Union for Quaternary Rsch. (inter-congress com. on tephrochronology, corr. mem. Internatl Loess Commn.), Am. Geophys. Union, Geol. Soc. Am. Office: Western Wash U Dept Geology Bellingham WA 98225-9080

BERGER, HOWARD MARTIN, industrial and service company executive; b. Jamestown, N.Y., Aug. 31, 1927; s. Frederick S. and Millicant (Petschau) B.; m. Barbara Diane Lubin, June 25, 1950; children: Teri Anne, Patricia Jeanne, Lisa Diane. BSE in Aeros. and Math., U. Mich., 1948; MS, Calif. Inst. Tech., 1949, PhD, 1954. Program dir. Inst. for Def. Analyses, Arlington, Va., 1961-66; dir. strategic forces div. Dept. Def., Arlington, 1966-69; mgr. strategic analysis Xerox Corp., Rochester, N.Y., 1969-75; sr. project mgr. Rand Corp., Santa Monica, Calif., 1975-76; asst. v.p. Sci. Applications Inc., El Segundo, Calif., 1976-77; pres. HMB Assocs., Palos Verdes, Calif., 1977-78; v.p. Analytical Assessments Corp., Marina del Rey, Calif., 1978-80, Logistics Tech. Internat., Torrance, Calif., 1980-81; pres., chmn. bd. Robotix Corp., Torrance, 1981—; bd. dirs., chief fin. officer Keats Manhattan, Inc., Torrance, 1980—, Justin-Time Svcs., Inc., Torrance, 1980—. Contbr. articles to profl. jours. With AUS, 1946-47. Recipient numerous scholarships and fellowships. Mem. Computer and Automated Systems Assn. of Soc. Mfg. Engrs. (sr., chmn. Greater L.A. chpt. 1987-88). Republican. Home: 2108 Via Fernandez Palos Verdes Peninsula CA 90274-2039 Office: Robotix Corp 23326 Hawthorne Blvd Ste 300 Torrance CA 90505-3732

BERGER, JAY VARI, executive recruiter, import company executive; b. San Francisco, Aug. 31, 1944; s. Jack Vari and Ruth (Wasserman) B.; m. Margareta Ahlberg, June 14, 1969; children: Karin Britta Margareta, John Vari Sten. BS, U. So. Calif., 1966, MS, 1967, PhD, 1971. Assoc. dean admissions U. So. Calif., L.A., 1969-76, dir. admissions, 1976-82, asst. v.p. devel., 1982-86; prin. ptnr. Morris & Berger, Pasadena, Calif., 1986—; chmn.

bd. Berger & Berger Internat., Pasadena, 1976—. Author: (juvenile) Willie the Worm, 1986; columnist Venture Connections, 1988. Pres. bd. dirs. The Sycamores, Pasadena, 1985—, Foothill Friends of Music, 1989-92; pres., trustee Chandler Sch., Pasadena, 1987-89; trustee Flintridge Preparatory Sch., 1992—. Mem. Calif. Exec. Recruiters Assn., Calif. Assn. Ind. Schs. (bd. trustees 1988-91), Annandale Golf Club, Valley Hunt Club, Rotary (bd. dirs. Pasadena chpt. 1988-92). Home: 412 Oaklawn Ave South Pasadena CA 91030-1833 Office: Morris & Berger Cons Exec Search 201 S Lake Ave Ste 700 Pasadena CA 91101-3019

BERGER, JOHN MILTON, state agency administrator; b. Marysville, Ohio, June 24, 1943; s. John Howard and Betty Louise (Mossbarger) B.; m. Joy Lynne Ansley, Dec. 29, 1969. BSBA, Franklin U., 1971; postgrad., Ohio State U., 1972. Cert. hazard control mgr., assoc. Ins. Inst. Am. risk mgmt. designation. Claims adjuster State Compensation Ins. Fund, Denver, 1974-78, loss control cons., 1978-84; adminstrv. officer Indsl. Commn., Denver, 1984-86; self-ins. adminstrn. Colo. Div. Labor, Denver, 1986-91; ins. complaince mgr. div. workers' compensation Colo. Dept. Labor and Employment, Denver, 1991—; mem. legis. com. Colo. Div. Ins., Denver, 1989-91; mem. self-ins. subcom. of Internat. Assn. Indsl. Accident Bds. and Commns. Author: Workers' Compensation Loss Prevention and Loss Control Manual, 1990. With USN, 1961-64. Recognized for Outstanding Svc. to State Govt., 1986. Mem. Colo. Self-Insurers Assn. Republican. Home: 675 Dudley St Lakewood CO 80215 Office: Colo Div Workers' Comp 1120 Lincoln St Denver CO 80203

BERGER, LELAND ROGER, lawyer; b. N.Y.C., Feb. 3, 1956; s. Albert and Audrey Sybil (Ellenbogen) B.; m. Lisa M. Burk, Feb. 15, 1987; 1 child, Robert Samson. Student, Am. U., 1977; BA, Dickinson Coll., 1978; JD, Lewis & Clark Coll., 1982. Bar: Oreg. 1983, U.S. Dist. Ct. Oreg. 1983, U.S. Ct. Appeals (9th cir.) 1990. Pvt. practice Portland, Oreg., 1983-84; assoc. Rieke, Geil & Savage, P.C., Portland, 1984—. Mem. Oreg. Bar Assn. (ad hoc com. to study multi-state bar exam. 1983-84, uniform criminal jury instrn. com. 1989-90, sec. 1990-91, criminal law sect.), Multnomah County Bar Assn. (corrections com. 1987), Oreg. Young Attys. Assn. (bd. dirs. 1983-84), Nat. Lawyers Guild (co-chair criminal justice com. Portland chpt. 1983-84), Oreg. Criminal Def. Lawyers Assn., Nat. Criminal Def. Lawyers Assn. Democrat. Jewish. Home: 2817 NE 12th Ave Portland OR 97212-3219 Office: Rieke Geil & Savage PC 820 SW 2d Ave Ste 200 Portland OR 97204

BERGER, NEWELL JAMES, JR., security professional; b. Pitts., Oct. 26, 1926; s. Newell James and Marjorie Ikler (Herndon) B.; m. Darlene Ingram, Sept. 6, 1950 (dec. Nov. 1990). BS, Mich. State U., 1958; grad., U.S. Army Command and Gen. Staff Coll., 1963, U.S. Army War Coll., 1972; MA, Webster U., 1993. Enlisted man U.S. Army, 1944, advanced through grades to staff sgt., 1948, commd. 2d lt., 1948, advanced through grades to col., 1970; chief corrections hdqrs. U.S. Army, Washington, 1970-72, dir. security Office Surgeon Gen., 1972-73; dir. security Health Svcs. Command U.S. Army, Ft. Sam Houston, Tex., 1973-78; ret. U.S. Army, 1978; security cons. Phoenix and San Diego, 1979-84; chief plant security Teledyne Ryan Aero. Co., San Diego, 1985-86; pers. security adminstr. GDE Systems, Inc., San Diego, 1986—. Decorated Legion of Merit with two oak leaf clusters. Mem. Internat. Assn. Chiefs Police, Am. Soc. for Indsl. Security (cert. protection profl.). Republican. Episcopalian. Home: 31961 Paseo Parallon Temecula CA 92592-1005 Office: GDE Systems Inc PO Box 1198 Poway CA 92074-1198

BERGER, PAT (PATRICIA EVE), artist, educator; b. N.Y.C., Mar. 17, 1929; d. Marion Sigmund and Florence (Hyman) Gardner; m. Jack Berger, Jan. 8, 1948 (div. 1971); children: Kenneth Steven, Russell Howard; m. Merlin Clarence Czoschke, Apr. 30, 1978. Student, Art Ctr. Sch. Design, L.A., 1947-48, UCLA, 1955-59, 63-66, UCLA, 1974-76. art unltd. chmn. Downey (Calif.) Mus. Art; muralist Millard Sheets, 1975-77; artist-in-residence Brandeis Inst., Simi Valley, Calif., 1961-65, 70; painting/drawing instr. L.A. Unified Sch. Dist., 1971—; permanent collections include Skirball Mus., L.A., Long Beach Mus. Art, San Diego Mus. Art, Springfield (Mo.) Art Mus., Polk County Bank, Mo., Palm Springs Desert Mus., Sodertalje Konstall, Sweden, City of La Mirada Collection, Calif., Hallmark Cards, West Publ. Co., St. Paul, many others. One woman shows at Mendenhall Gallery, Whittier Coll., 1982, Riverside Art Ctr. and Mus., 1983, Moosart Gallery, Miami, 1985, Bridge Gallery, L.A., 1986, Jewish Fedn. Galleries, L.A., 1988, West L.A. City Hall Gallery, 1990, U. Judaism, 1991, others; group shows include Valerie Miller Gallery, Palm Desert, 1988-93, Jewish Mus., 1989, 91, 93, Square House Mus., Tex., 1990, Long Beach Mus. Rental Gallery, 1990, Finegood Art Gallery, Calif., 1990, West '93 and the Law travelling exhibit, 1983, 84, 91, Biblical Art Ctr., Dallas, 1993, others. Mem. So. Calif. Women's Caucus for the Arts, Internat. Soc. for Edn. Through Art, Calif. Art Educators Art Assn., Artist Equity, Nat. Assn. Women Artists, Nat. Watercolor Soc. (past pres.), Watercolor USA Honor Soc. (bd. dirs.). Home: 2648 Anchor Ave Los Angeles CA 90064-4602

BERGER, PAUL ERIC, artist, photographer; b. The Dalles, Oreg., Jan. 20, 1948; s. Charles Glen and Virginia (Nunez) B. B.A., UCLA, 1970; M.F.A., SUNY-Buffalo, 1973. Vis. lectr. U. Ill., 1974-78; prof. art U. Wash.-Seattle, 1978—. Exhibited one-man shows, photographs, Art Inst. Chgo., 1975, Light Gallery, N.Y.C., 1977, Seattle Art Mus., 1980, Light Gallery, N.Y.C., 1982, Univ. Art Mus., Santa Barbara, Calif., 1984, Cliff Michel Gallery, 1989, Seattle Art Mus., 1990. NEA Photographer's fellow, 1979, NEA Visual Artist's fellow, 1986; recipient Artist's Commn., Wash. State Arts Commn., 1990. Mem. Soc. Photographic Edn. Office: U Wash Sch Art DM-10 Seattle WA 98195

BERGER, WOLFGANG H., oceanographer, marine geologist; b. Erlangen, Bavaria, Fed. Republic of Germany, Oct. 5, 1937; came to U.S., 1961; s. Helmut and Emilie Berger; m. Karen J. Thomas, June 9, 1966; children: Karl, Katrina. MS in Geology, U. Colo., 1963; PhD in Oceanography, U. Calif., San Diego, 1968. Wissensch. asst. Universität Kiel, Fed. Republic of Germany, 1969-71; rsch. asst. Scripps Inst. Oceanography U. Calif., La Jolla, 1963-68, asst. researcher, 1968-69, asst. prof., 1971-74, assoc. prof., 1974-80, prof. oceanography, 1980—; vis. prof. geology Universität Kiel, 1977, 80; guest researcher Universität Bremen, Fed. Republic of Germany, 1986—. Editor: Abrupt Climatic Change, 1987, Ocean Productivity, 1990. Mem. geology adv. bd. U. Colo., Boulder, 1989-92. Recipient Bigelow medal Woods Hole (Mass.) Oceanographic Inst., 1979, Huntsman medal Bedford Oceanographic Inst., Can., 1984, Humboldt award German Sci. Found., Bonn, Fed. Republic of Germany, 1986, Albert I medal, Paris, 1991. Fellow AAAS, Am. Geophysical Union (Ewing medal 1988), Geol. Soc. Am., European Geophysical Soc. Office: U Calif San Diego Scripps Inst Oceanography La Jolla CA 92093-0215

BERGESON, JOHN HENNING, denominational executive, theological educator; b. Ashland, Wis., May 10, 1919; s. Henning John and Lydia Roberta (Johnson) B.; m. Gladys Victoria Peterson, June 10, 1944; children: John Joel, Jane Ellen, Ruth Ann, Peter Lowell, Daniel Roger. BA, U. N.D., Grand Forks, 1943; BD, Bethel Theol. Sem., St. Paul, Minn., 1944; DD, Western Bapt. Sem., Portland, Oreg., 1983. Ordination by Baptist Gen. Conf. Pastor Alma Baptist Ch., Argyle, Minn., 1941-43, Eagle Point Baptist Ch., Stepen, Minn., 1941-43, Opstead Baptist Ch., Isle, Minn., 1944-53; exec. min. Platte Valley Baptist Conf., Gothenburg, Nebr., 1953-56, Rocky Mountain Baptist Conf., Denver, 1956-59; missions dir. Minn. Baptist Conf., St. Paul, Minn., 1959-70; exec. min. Columbia Baptist Conf., Seattle, 1970-85, British Columbia Bapt. Conf., Surrey, BC, Can., 1985-87; dir. of field edn. Bethel Theol. Sem., San Diego, 1987-92. Author: Churches Everywhere, 1978, Fourth Quarter, 1989. Named Moderator, Baptist Gen. Conf. Annual Meeting, Wheaton, Ill., 1973. Baptist. Home: 720 N 193rd Pl Seattle WA 98133-3942

BERGESON, MARIAN, state legislator; m. Garth Bergeson; children: Nancy, Garth Jr., Julie, James. Student UCLA; BA in Edn. Brigham Young U.; postgrad. UCLA. Pres., regional dir. Calif. Sch. Bds. Assn.; officer, dir. Orange County Sch. Bds. Assn.; mem. Newport Beach City Sch. Dist. Bd. Edn., 1964-65; mem. Newport-Mesa Unified Sch. Dist. Bd. Edn., 1965-77; mem. Calif. Assembly, 1978-82, Calif. Senate, 1984—. Past mem. Orange County Juvenile Justice Commn., Riles-Younger Task Force for Prevention of Crime and Violence in the Schs., Com. for Revision State Edn. Code, Joint Com. on Revision Penal Code; mem. Calif. YMCA Model Legislature/Ct.; mem. bd. advisors Calif. Elected Women's Assn. Edn. and Research; bd. dirs. Sta. KBIG Adv. Bd.; mem. govt. relations com. Orange County Arts Alliance. Recipient Marian Bergeson Community Services award Orange County Sch. Bds. Assn., 1975; Anchor award Newport Harbor C. of C., women's div., 1967; Community Services award AAUW, 1976; Disting. Women's award Irvine Soroptimists, 1981; Disting. Service award Brigham Young U., 1980-81; Woman of Achievement award Newport Harbor Zonta Club, 1981; Silver Medallion, YWCA, 1983; Pub. Service award Calif. Speech-Lang.-Hearing Assn., 1983; named Outstanding Pub. Ofcl., Orange County chpt. Am. Soc. Pub. Adminstrn., 1983, Woman of Yr., Anti Defamation League B'nai B'rith, 1987, So. Dist. Legislator of Yr., Calif. Assn. for Health., 1987. Office: Ste 120 140 Newport Center Dr Newport Beach CA 92660-6990 also: State Senate Offices PO Box 3151 Newport Beach CA 92663

BERGH, DAVID MORGAN, entrepreneur; b. Boise, Idaho, Aug. 8, 1947; s. Rolfe Roald and Margaret Rose (Morgan) B.; m. Jan R. Seda, May 17, 1975; children: Hillary Lauren, Benjamin Morgan, Salle Alberta. BS in Mgmt., U. Idaho, 1972. Chpt. cons., then dir. expansion, asst. exec. dir. Kappa Sigma Internat. Fraternity, Charlottesville, Va., 1972-75; propr. Morgan's Exchange, Boise, 1975-79, Strato Lanes, Mountain Home, Idaho, 1979—; concessionaire various recreational concerns, Alaska and Idaho; supr. com. P.F. Credit Union. Vice chmn. Cen. Dist. Health, Idaho, 1983—; pres. Mountain Home Mil. Affairs Com., 1985—; sec., treas. Silver City Hist. Soc. Mem. Idaho State Bowling Proprs., Bowling Proprs. Assn. Am., Nat. Restaurant and Beverage Assn., Kappa Sigma (dist. prs. 1975—), Elks. Republican. Roman Catholic. Home and Office: Drawer 9 Mountain Home ID 83647

BERGIN, ALLEN ERIC, clinical psychologist, educator; b. Spokane, Wash., Aug. 4, 1934; s. Bernard F. and Vivian Selma (Kullberg) B.; m. Marian Shafer, June 4, 1955; children: David, Sue, Cyndy, Kathy, Eric, Ben, Patrick, Daniel, Michael. BS, Brigham Young U., 1956, MS, 1957; PhD, Stanford U., 1960. Diplomate Am. Bd. Profl. Psychology. Postdoctoral fellow U. Wis., Madison, 1960-61; prof. psychology and edn. Tchrs. Coll., Columbia U., N.Y.C., 1961-72; prof. psychology Brigham Young U., Provo, Utah, 1972—, dir. Values Inst., 1976-78, dir. clin. psychology, 1989-93; sr. rsch. fellow Nat. Inst. Health Care Rsch., 1992—; assessment officer Peace Corps, Washington, 1961-66; cons. NIMH, Rockville, Md., 1969-75, 90. Co-author: Changing Frontiers in Psychotherapy, 1972; co-editor: Handbook of Psychotherapy, 1971, 4th edit., 1994 (citation classic 1979). Bishop, LDS Ch., Emerson, N.J., 1970-72, Provo, 1981-84, stake pres., 1992—; mem. steering com. Utah Gov.'s Conf. on Families, Salt Lake City, 1979-80. Recipient Biggs-Pine award AACD, 1986, Maeser rsch. award Brigham Young U. Alumni Assn., 1986. Fellow Am. Psychol. Assn. (Disting. Contbn. to Knowledge award 1989, William James award div. 36, 1990); mem. Soc. for Psychotherapy Integration (adv. bd.), Soc. for Sci. Study Religion, Soc. for Psychotherapy Rsch. (pres. 1974-75), Assn. Mormon Counselors (pres. 1979-80). Republican. Office: Brigham Young U 285 TLRB Provo UT 84602

BERGMAN, CHARLES CARROLL, mechanical engineer; b. Wheatland, Wyo., Apr. 6, 1932; s. Charles Edwin and Marjorie Elizabeth (Ankeny) B.; m. Dolores Ann Hermanson, July 6, 1968; children: Christopher C., Scott Carl. AA, N. Wyo. Community Coll., Sheridan, 1952; BSME, U. Wyo., 1955; MSME, U. Idaho, 1973. Registered profl. engr., Idaho. Mech. engr. various cos., Tex., Idaho and Oreg., 1955-82, Amalgamated Sugar Co., Twin Falls, Idaho, 1982—; instr. Frank Phillips Coll., Borger, Tex., 1958. Mem. ASME, NSPE. Home: Rte 2 3400 N Twin Falls ID 83301 Office: Amalgamated Sugar Co PO Box 127 Twin Falls ID 83303-0127

BERGMAN, ROBERT AARON, wholesale plumbing supply company executive; b. Phila., Apr. 8, 1928; s. Morris H. and Mollie (Chaiken) B.; m. Joan Hohenstein, Sept. 21, 1954; children: James, Allen, Julie. BA in Commerce, Fin., Pa. State U., 1950; acctg. grad., U. Pitts., 1952. Office mgr. Pennwood Numechron Co., Pitts., 1950-54, gen. mgr., 1954-61; salesman Smith Pipe & Steel Co., Tucson, 1962-68; pres. Cen. Pipe & Supply Co., Tucson, 1969—; bd. dirs. Pacific S.W. Distbrs.; chmn. Kasper-Hall Steel, Tucson, 1979-83; v.p. Bankers Resource, Tucson, 1990. Treas., v.p. Tucson Jewish Community Ctr.; v.p., chmn. affairs Tucson C. of C.; bd. dirs. Tucson Mus. Art, Caballeros Del Sol Intracity Com. C. of C. Named Young Man Yr., Tucson jewish Community Coun., 1970. Mem. Am. Inst. Petroleum and Mining Engrs., Ariz. Mining Industry Supplies Assn., Rotary, Old Pueblo Club, Nittany Lion Club, Wildcat Club, Skyline Country Club. Republican. Home: Paseo De El Encanto 588 N Country Club Rd Tucson AZ 85716 Office: Bankers Resource 440 S Williams Blvd Ste 202 Tucson AZ 85711-4403

BERGMAN, TERRIE, psychic consultant; b. Phila., Mar. 4, 1942; d. Harry Bernard and Berthe Rose (Simons) Goldberg; m. Clifford Coulston, May 4, 1960 (div. 1967); 1 child, Lori Coulston; m. Joel David Bergman, Dec. 22, 1979. B Metaphys. Sci., U. Metaphysics, 1979, D Metaphys. Counseling, 1982. Indsl. trainer, vocat. evaluator, mktg. mgr. Atlantic County Opportunity Ctr. for Handicapped, Atlantic City, N.J., 1971-74; job developer, vocat. evaluator, counselor Narcotics Addicts Rehab. Orgn., Atlantic City, 1974-75; psychic cons. Atlantic City & Las Vegas, 1973—; seminar facilitator on death and dying Las Vegas, 1990—; 1st, 2d, and 3d degree Reiki healer, Atlantic City and Las Vegas, 1984—. Appeared on TV programs, including People Are Talking, Hour Mag., others, 1974—; contbr. articles to mags. and newspapers. Vol. Nathan Adelson Hospice, 1989-92. Named 1 of 83 People to Watch, Atlantic City Mag., 1983; recipient Dynamics of Leadership cert. of achievement Human Factors, Inc., 1981, 82, 86. Mem. Network of Exec. Women in Hospitality, Women in Convention Sales. Home and Office: 208 Desert View Las Vegas NV 89107

BERGMANN, CHARLES ARNOLD, architect; b. Orange, N.J., Aug. 24, 1938; s. Charles Louis and Catherine (Arnold) B.; m. Hermine Marianne Visser, June 17, 1966; children: Susannah Marjan, Joslyn Andrea, Jonathan Bastiaan, Sarah Lenora. BS, Trinity Coll., Hartford, Conn., 1960; MArch, Columbia U., 1966. Registered architect, Wash. Architect, designer Burckhardt Architekten, Basel, Switzerland, 1967-68; sr. assoc. architect Ibsen Nelsen and Assocs., Seattle, 1969-75; prin. Charles Bergmann Architect, Seattle, 1976-77, 79—; designer, architect Erik Lopez Cordoza, Amsterdam, Holland, 1977-78; prin. St. Charles Hotel Bldg., Seattle, 1972-77; gen. ptnr. East Madison and 28th Project, Seattle, 1979—, 2711 East Madison Assocs., Seattle, 1984—; lectr. in design U. Wash., Seattle, 1989; ptnr. The Madisonian Bldg., Seattle, 1988—. Agt. Trinity Coll. Alumni Fund, Hartford, 1961-66; bd. dirs. Pioneer Square Assn., Seattle, 1972-75; vice chmn. Mus. Devel. Authority Seattle Art Mus., 1988—. With U.S. Army, 1960-62. William Kinne fellow Columbia U., 1965; Hist. Trust grantee State of Wash., 1975. Mem Nat. Trust for Hist. Preservation, Mountaineers, Am. Alpine Club, AIA. Office: 2812 E Madison St Seattle WA 98112-4863

BERGO, EDWARD ARTHUR, marketing research company executive; b. Evanston, Ill., Apr. 29, 1938; s. Arthur Conrad and Mary Margaret (Hunter) B.; m. Phyllis Elaine Dahlk, Aug. 29, 1959; children: Steven Edward, Mark Conrad. BA, St. Olaf Coll., Northfield, Minn., 1960; BS, U. Wis., Milw., 1966. With consumer rsch. dept. Johnson Wax Co., Racine, Wis., 1960-70; European market rsch. coord. Johnson Wax Co., Amsterdam, The Netherlands, 1970-72; with mktg. rsch. dept. Johnson Wax Co., Racine, 1972-74; pres. Wis. Rsch. Co., Green Bay, 1974-84, Sandia Mktg. Svcs., Albuquerque, 1978—, Bergo & Assocs., Mesa, Ariz., 1984—; prin. West Group Mktg. Rsch., Phoenix, 1989—. Mem. Mktg. Rsch. Assn. (bd. dirs. S.W. chpt. 1983-84, 88-90, nat. bd. dirs.), Am. Mktg. Assn. (treas. Phoenix chpt. 1988-89, pres.-elect 1990-91, pres. 1991-92). Republican. Office: 1948 W Main St Mesa AZ 85201-6914

BERG-RIDENOUR, SHERRYL LEE, sales executive; b. Brighton, Colo., May 9, 1963; d. Ron Carl and Linda Lou (Lewis) Berg; m. John Wayne Berg-Ridenour, June 1, 1985; 1 child, Samuel Alger. Student, Ft. Lewis Coll., 1981-84, El Camino Coll., 1987-90, Calif. State U., Carson, 1992—. Sta. agt. Aspen/United Airlines, Durango, Colo., 1979-81; travel agt. Discovery Travel, Durango, 1981-83; sta. agt. Am. West Airlines, Durango, 1983-84, Frontier Airlines, Durango, 1984-85; travel agt. Bergner's Travel, Rockford, Ill., 1985-87; sales exec. Dollar Systems, Inc., L.A., 1987—. Back-up counselor 1736 Crisis Ctr., Redondo Beach, Calif., 1988—; big sister YWCA, Rockford, 1986-87, L.A., 1987-89; ascension youth leader K-8 Ascension Luth. Ch. Sunday Sch., Torrance, Calif., 1990-91; mem. Planned Parenthood of L.A., 1989-92, Religious Coalition for Abortion Rights, 1990-92. Mem. L.A. Bus. Travel Assn., Sierra Club. Lutheran. Home: 6047 Gardenia Ave Long Beach CA 90805 Office: Dollar Systems Rent A Car 100 N Spv Blvd El Segundo CA 90245

BERGSMA, WILLIAM LAURENCE, composer; b. Oakland, Calif., Apr. 1, 1921; s. William Joseph and Helen Margaret (Doepfner) B.; m. Nancy Nickerson, 1946. Student, Stanford U., 1938-40; teaching fellow, Eastman Sch. Music, 1942-44; A.B., U. Rochester, 1942, Mus.M., 1943. Faculty Juilliard Sch. Music, N.Y.C., 1946-63, chmn. composition dept., also chmn. dept. lit. and materials of music, assoc. dean, 1961-63, prof., 1963-86; dir. Sch. Music, U. Wash., Seattle, 1963-71; vis. prof. Bklyn. Coll., CUNY, 1972-73. Composer: ballet Gold and the Señor Commandante, 1942, First Quartet, 1942, Symphony for Chamber Orchestra, 1942, Music on a Quiet Theme, 1943, Three Fantasies (piano solo), 1943, rev., 1983, Second Quartet, 1944, Six Songs, 1945, Suite from Children's Film, 1945, Symphony, 1949, string orch. The Fortunate Islands, 1947, rev. 1956, piano solo Tangents, 1951, Third Quartet, 1953, orch. A Carol on Twelfth Night, 1953, 3 act opera The Wife of Martin Guerre, 1955, rev. 1958, 3 choruses Riddle Me This, 1956, band March with Trumpets, 1957, Concerto for Woodwind Quintet, 1958, orch. Chameleon Variations, 1960, viola and piano Fantastic Variations, 1961, orch. In Celebration: Toccata for the Sixth Day, 1962, Confrontation from the Book of Job, orch. Documentary One, 1963, Serenade to Await the Moon, 1965, Concerto for Violin and Orchestra, 1966, for chorus, brass, percussion The Sun, The Soaring Eagle, The Turquoise Prince, The God, 1967; Orch. Documentary Two, 1967; clarinet, percussion Illegible Canons, 1969, 1969; Fourth Quartet, 1970, rev., 1974; solo woodwind quintet, harp, percussion, strings Changes, 1971; Changes for Seven, 1971; cello, percussion Clandestine Dialogues, 1972; two-act opera The Murder of Comrade Sharik, 1973; chorus, instruments Wishes, Wonders, Portents, Charms, 1974; soprano, instruments In Space, 1975; chorus and orch. Second Symphony: Voyages for Soloists, 1976; solo viola and orch. Sweet Was the Song the Virgin Sung/Tristan Revisited, 1977; trombone and percussion Blatent Hypotheses, 1977; 3 instruments, percussion Four All, 1979; Quintet for Flute and String Quartet, 1979, The Voice of the Coelacanth, 1980; oboe concertante, 2 bassoons and strings In Campo Aperto, 1981; medium voice, clarinet, bassoon and piano Four Songs, 1981; Fifth Quartet, 1982; Piano Variations, 1984, woodwind quintet Masquerade, 1986; four songs for voice and marimba I Toad You So, 1986, A Lick and a Promise for saxophone and chimes, 1988, Sixth Quartet, 1991. Recipient Town Hall commn. for Symphony for Chamber Orch., 1942; Bearns prize for String Quartet No. 1, 1943; Koussevitzky Found. commn., 1943-44; grant AAAL and Nat. Inst. Arts and Letters, 1945; award Soc. for Publ. Am. Music, 1945; Guggenheim fellow, 1946, 51; Collegiate Chorale commn., 1946; commn. from Carl Fischer, Inc., for 25th anniversary of League of Composers, 1947; Juilliard Found. commn., 1953, 62; Louisville commn., 1953; Elizabeth Sprague Coolidge commn., 1956; Collegiate Chorale of Ill. Wesleyan U. commn., 1956; 1st ann. Edwin Franco Goldman Meml. commn., 1957; Harvard Mus. Soc. commn., 1961; Portland Jr. Symphony commn., 1960; Mid-Am. Chorale commn., 1963; Mus. Arts Soc. La Jolla commn., 1965; Phi Beta commn., 1966; Am. Choral Dirs. Assn. commn., 1967; Kansas City Youth Symphony commn., 1967; U. Ala. for Cadek Quarter, 1970; Poncho and Brechemin Family Found. commn., 1971; New Dimensions in Music, 1972; Nat. Chorale and N.Y. State Council on Arts commn., 1974; Gt. Falls Symphony and Symphonic Choir, Mont. Bicentennial Adminstrn., 1975; Seattle Symphony Orch. commn., 1977; Chamber Music Soc. of Lincoln Center commn., 1980; Nat. Endowment Arts commn., 1979, Nat. Endowment Arts grantee, 1985; Wash. State Music Educators grantee, 1988. Mem. AAAL, Phi Beta Kappa, Phi Mu Alpha. Address: 2328 Delmar Dr E Seattle WA 98102

BERGSTROM, EDITH HARROD, artist; b. Denver, Aug. 19, 1941; S. William E. and Annabelle (Harrod) Youtsler; m. Erik E. Bergstrom, Mar. 22, 1964. BA in Applied Art, Pomona Coll., 1963; MA in Applied Art, Stanford U., 1964. Contbr. articles to profl. jours. Jury chairperson Nat. Watercolor Soc. 67th Annual Exhbn., 1987; juror Midwest Watercolor 9th Annual Open Juried Show, Tweed Mus., Soc. Western Artists, San Francisco, 1984, Alameda County Fair, Alameda, Calif., 1991; v.p. Erik E. and Edith H. Bergstrom Found., Inc., Palo Alto, Calif. Recipient acquisition award SW Mo. Mus. Assocs., 1987, acquisition award Achenbach Found. San Francisco Museums, 1987, Foothills Art Ctr. award Rocky Mt. Nat. Watermedia Exhbn., 1987, award of merit for watercolor Calif. State Fair, 1987. Mem. Am. Watercolor Soc., West Coast Watercolor Soc. (past pres.), Nat. Watercolor Soc., Rocky Mountain nat. Watermedia Soc., Watercolor USA Honor Soc. Republican. Christian Scientist. Home: 149 Hawthorn Dr Atherton CA 94027

BERITICH, MICHAEL LESTER, educator; b. Tacoma, May 28, 1960; s. Mitchell Charles and Roxie G. (Nicholson) B. AAS, Tacoma C.C., 1982; BA, U. Wash., 1985, secondary teaching cert., 1986. Cert. social studies, history, polit. sci. tchr., Wash. Substitute tchr. Tacoma Pub. Schs. Dist. 10, 1986-89, cadre tchr., 1989-91, contract tchr. Oakland Alternative High Sch., 1991—; tchr. alternative edn. Region V Learning Ctr., Tacoma, 1992—. Vol. Seattle Rep. Com., 1984. Mem. NEA, Wash. Edn. Assn., Tacoma Edn. Assn. (bldg. rep. 1990—), Tacoma Substitute Tchrs. (sec. 1990-91, v.p. 1991-92). Roman Catholic. Office: Region V Learning Ctr 1818 Tacoma Ave S Tacoma WA 98408

BERKES, LESLIE JOHN, psychologist; b. Simbach, Bavaria, Fed. Republic of Germany, Aug. 18, 1946; came to U.S., 1949; naturalized; s. Leslie Michael and Marie Gizella (Villanyi) B.; m. Cheryl Kaye Stelter, Dec. 28, 1968; children: Adrienne Villanyi, Andrew Stelter, Kathryn Fowlkes. BS, U. So. Calif., 1968; MS, U.S. Naval Portgrad. Sch., 1969; postgrad., Union coll., 1971, SUNY, 1971-72; PhD, U. Calif., 1976; postgrad., Wright State U., 1983. Lic. psychologist, Ohio, Calif. Mgmt. auditor U.S. Gen. Acctg. Office, L.A., 1972-73; asst. rsch. specialist Pub. Policy Rsch. Orgn. U. Calif., Irvine, 1974-76; faculty rsch. assoc. Program Study Crime and Delinquency Ohio State U., Columbus, 1980-82; asst. prof. mgmt. sci. Ohio State U., Columbus, 1976-82; clin. psychologist Psychol. Cons. Inc., Columbus, 1981-82; psychologist Mgmt. Health & Devel. Corp., Malibu, Calif., 1983-86; v.p., chief tech. officer Netmap Internat. Inc., San Francisco, 1986-90; pres. Mgmt. Tech. Inc., San Francisco, 1990—; adj. faculty Grad. Sch. Mgmt. U. Calif., Irvine, 1985-86, St. Mary's Coll. of Calif., 1987—; clin. assoc. prof. psychology Wright State U.; cons., presenter in field. Contbr. articles to profl. jours. Chair St. Monica's Town Hall, Moraga, Calif., 1988-89; mem. parish coun., St. Monica's, 1991—; co-dir. 7th grade edn. St. Monica's, 1988-89; police reserve officer, Columbus, 1979-81; reserve firefighter Moraga Fire Dist., 1991—; softball coach Lafayette Moraga Youth Assn., 1989—. With USN, 1968-72, Vietnam; with USNR Med. Svc. Corps, 1978-87. Mem. Acad. Mgmt., Am. Inst. Decision Scis., Am. Med. Joggers Assn., Am. Phychological Assn., Am. Soc. Pub. Adminstrn., Calif. Psychol. Assn., Internat. Assn. Applied Psychology, Soc. Indsl. and Orgnl. Psychology, Soc. Psychol. Study Social Issues, Beta Gamma Sigma. Democrat. Roman Catholic. Home: 292 Calle La Montana Moraga CA 94556-1642 Office: Human Resources Mgmt Group 600 Montgomery St Fl 35 San Francisco CA 94111-2702

BERKLEY, ROBERT JOHN, federal agency professional; b. Albion, Mich., Oct. 2, 1933; s. Paul Clifford and Ina Muriel (Burroughs) B.; m. Sharon Irene Haynes, Sept. 9, 1955 (div. 1965); children: Thomas Alan, Richard Jon, Luann Michele; m. Jacquelyn Jane (Lewis) Ballou, Jan. 14, 1966. AA, Jackson (Mich.) Jr. Coll., 1953; BS in Police Adminstrn., Calif. State U., L.A., 1962. Police officer City of Claremont, Calif., 1959-62, 63-66; investigator U.S. Civil Svc. Commn., Washington and L.A., 1962-63, 66-72; spl. agt. FAA, Seattle, 1972—, office mgr., 1973—. Local chmn. Selective Svc. Bd., Wash., 1981—. Sgt. USMC, 1953-56, Korea. Mem. SAR (chpt. pres. 1989-90, state sec. 1989-91, state pres. 1992, Patriots medal 1990, Law Enforcement medal 1991, 92), Am. Legion, Eastern Star (patron 1989-90), Masons (master 1984, life), Scottish Rite, Shriners. Home: 4403 192D Pl SE Issaquah WA 98027-9305 Office: FAA SEA-CASFO 1601 Lind Ave SW Rm 230 Renton WA 98055-4056

BERKLEY, STEPHEN MARK, computer peripherals manufacturing company executive; b. N.J., Apr. 19, 1944; s. Irving S. and Goldie A. (Karp) B.; student London Sch. Econs., 1964-65; BA in Econs., Colgate U., 1966; MBA, Harvard U., 1968; children: David, Michael.Mgmt. cons. Boston Cons. Group, 1968, 71-73; mgr. strategic planning Potlatch Corp., 1973-77; v.p. bus. devel. Qume Corp. subs. ITT, Hayward, Calif., 1977-80, v.p., gen. mgr. memory products div., 1980-81; v.p. mktg. Quantum Corp., Milpitas, Calif., 1981-83, chmn., CEO, 1987-92, chmn., 1992—; chmn. Coactive Computing Corp., 1993—; pres. Plus Devel. Corp. (Quantum subs.), 1983-87, chmn., chief exec. officer, 1987-92; pres., The Rosewood Found.; bd. dirs. Edify Corp., Coactive Computing Corp.; instr. bus. and econs. E. Carolina U., 1969-71. Served to lt. USNR, 1968-71. Mem. Corp. Planners Assn. (dir.), Harvard Bus. Sch. Club No. Calif., Phi Beta Kappa. Home: 7 Rosewood Dr Atherton CA 94027 Office: Quantum Corp 500 McCarthy Blvd Milpitas CA 95035-7908

BERKMAN, SUSAN C. JOSEPHS, association executive; b. L.A., Apr. 17, 1953; d. Fred and Alice Hodes Josephs; m. Donald W. Berkman Jr., Aug. 10, 1974; 1 child, Daniel. BA, U. Calif., Irvine, 1974; MA, UCLA, 1977, Calif. State U., Los Angeles, 1988. Cert. adult edn. tchr. Specialist personnel mgmt. U.S. Civil Svc. Commn., Washington, 1974-75; teaching asst. UCLA, 1976-77; rsch. editor Regensteiner Press, Sherman Oaks, Calif., 1977; dir. music Braille Inst., L.A., 1978-82, asst. dir. student tng., 1982-87, dir. spl. projects, 1987-89, dir. bus. svcs., 1989-91; instr. Coll. of the Desert, Rancho Mirage, Calif., 1991—; exec. dir. Sr. and Disabled Citizens Coalition, 1992—. Author: Teaching Music to the Blind, 1980, Teaching Music to the Visually Handicapped, 1982; (ednl. program) Just Like Me, 1983. Mem. Hermosa Beach (Calif.) Coordinating Coun., 1986; bd. dirs. Community Family Guidance Clinic, Cerritos, Calif., 1987-91; exec. dir. Sr. & Disabled Citizens Coalition, Riverside, Calif., 1992—. Travel grantee, UCLA, 1977; Calif. State scholar, 1970-73, William S. Schwartz Meml. scholar, 1974. Mem. AAUW, Assn. for Edn. and Rehab. of the Blind and Visually Impaired (v.p. So. Calif. chpt. 1987-88, pres. 1988-91), Calif. Transcribers and Eductors of the Blind and Visually Impaired, Soroptimist Internat., Kiwanis Internat., Kappa Delta Pi, Phi Kappa Phi. Baha'i. Home and Office: 43621 Vanda Cir Palm Desert CA 92260-2651

BERKSHIRE, STEVEN DAVID, hospital administrator; b. Fort Wayne, Ind., June 25, 1947; s. Harry George and Ludella (Droege) B.; m. Barbara Jean Billings, June 19, 1970; children: Marcus Jerome, David Alexander, Sarah Rebecca. Student, U. Alaska, 1965-67; BA in Polit. Sci., U. Colo., 1970; MHA, Ind. U. Sch. Medicine, Indpls., 1973; postgrad. in pub. adminstrn., Boise State U., 1975-79; postgrad. in doctoral program, Boston U./Alaska Pacific U., 1992—. Administrv. asst. to dean Ind. U. Sch. Medicine, Indpls., 1971-73; asst. dir. Idaho Hosp. Assn., Boise, 1973-75; asst. administr. St. Alphonsus Regional Med. Ctr., Boise, 1975-76; exec. dir. Idaho Coun. Devel. Disabilities, Boise, 1976-78; pres, chief exec. officer Greater Portland (Oreg.) Area Hosp. Coun., 1978-85; administr. Sitka (Alaska) Community Hosp., 1985; chief exec. officer Charter North Hosp., Anchorage, 1985-88, Charter Hosp. Denver, Lakewood, Colo., 1988-89, North Star Hosp., Anchorage, 1989—; prin. Steven D. Berkshire Assocs., 1992—; adj. instr. Chapman U. Alaska Acad. Ctr., 1991—; cons. numerous orgns.; speaker at presentations, workshops, seminars, various orgns. Contbr. articles to profl. jours.; editor monographs. Leader Boy Scouts Am., Anchorage; past bd. dirs. Anchorage Youth Symphony; coach Cook Inlet Soccer Assn., Anchorage. Recipient Dist. Award Merit, Boy Scouts Am., 1984, Eagle Scout, 1969. Mem. Am. Coll. Healthcare Execs., Commonwealth No. (program com., mem. urban/rural com.), Alaska Coun. Prevention Alcohol and Drug Abuse, Alaska Mental Health Assn., Rotary Internat., Elks, Anchorage C. of C., Alpha Phi Omega. Republican. Roman Catholic. Home: 1700 Stanford Dr Anchorage AK 99508-4453

BERKSON, BURTON MARTIN, physician, researcher; b. Chgo., Mar. 9, 1939; s. Milton and Fay Berkson; m. Ann Stern, Oct. 5, 1959; children: Arin Elizabeth, Arthur. BS, Roosevelt U., 1961; MS, Ea. Ill. U., 1964; PhD, U. Ill., 1968; MD, Autonomous U., Juarez, Mexico, 1977. Asst. prof. Rutgers U., Newark, 1968-72; assoc. prof. Chgo. State U., 1972-73; prof., student Autonomous U., Mexico, 1974-77; postgrad. physician Case Western Res. U., Cleve., 1977-79; pvt. practice medicine Lea County, N.Mex., 1979-86; emergency physician N.Mex., 1986-88; med. staff dir. Hunter Clinic, Wichita, Kans., 1988; med. cons., contractor U.S. Govt., White Sand Missile Range, N.Mex., 1989—; chief investigator hepatic growth factor/thiotic acid FDA, 1980—; mem. med.-legal commn. State of N.Mex., 1990—, Med. Health Profl. Bd., 1992—. Editor: Microbiology, 1975; author numerous papers on mycology & cell biology; editor various jours. Mem. AMA, N.Mex. Med. Soc. (assoc. editor 1990—, commn. mem.), White Sands Officers Club, Lions. Office: White Sands Missile Range McAfee Hosp White Sands Missle Range NM 88002-5520

BERKSON, WILLIAM CRAIG (BILL BERKSON), poet; b. N.Y.C., Aug. 30, 1939; s. Seymour and Eleanor (Lambert) B.; m. Lynn Blacker, July 17, 1975; children: Siobhan O'Hare, Moses Edwin Clay. Student, Brown U., Providence, 1957-59, The New Sch., N.Y.C., 1959-60, Columbia Coll., 1959-60. Editorial assoc. Art News, N.Y.C., 1960-63; assoc. producer WNDT-TV Art/New York, N.Y.C., 1964-65; instr. The New Sch., N.Y.C., 1964-69; reviewer Arts Mag., N.Y.C., 1965-66; vis. fellow Ezra Stiles Coll., Yale U., New Haven, 1969-70; editor/pubr. Big Sky, Bolinas, Calif., 1971-78; prof. San Francisco Art Inst., 1984—; reviewer Artforum, N.Y.C., 1985—; adj. prof. Southampton Coll., 1979-80; guest editor Mus. Modern Art, N.Y.C., 1964-69; instr. Poets in Schs., 1974-83; coord. Bay Area Consortium for Visual Arts, San Francisco, 1985-87; corr. editor Art in Am., N.Y.C., 1988—; lectr. in field; vis. artist and scholar Am. Acad. in Rome, 1991. Author: Saturday Night: Poems 1960-61, 1961, 2d edit., 1975, Shining Leaves, 1969, Recent Visitors, 1973, (with Frank O'Hara) Hymns of St. Bridget, 1975; Enigma Variations, 1975, Ants, 1975, (with Larry Fagin) Two Serious Poems and One Other, 1972; Lush Life, 1983, Start Over, 1983, Red Devil, 1983, Blue Is the Hero, 1976, also others; guest editor Art Jour., 1990; editor: (with Joe LeSueur) Homage to Frank O'Hara, 1978, Best and Company, 1969, also others; contbr. articles to profl. jours. Faculty rep. to bd. trustees San Francisco Art Inst., 1985-93. Recipient Dylan Thomas Meml. Poetry award New Sch. for Social Rsch., 1959, award for criticism Artspace, 1991; grantee Poets Found., 1968, Nat. Endowment of Arts Small Press, 1975, 77, also others; creative writing fellow Nat. Endowment for Arts, 1979, Yaddo fellow, 1968, Briarcombe fellow, 1983. Mem. Artists Equity Assn. (adv. bd.), Internat. Art Critics Assn., PEN. Home: PO Box 389 Bolinas CA 94924-0389 Office: San Francisco Art Inst 800 Chestnut St San Francisco CA 94133-2299

BERKUS, DAVID WILLIAM, computer company executive; b. Los Angeles, Mar. 23, 1941; s. Harry Jay and Clara S. (Widess) B.; m. Kathleen McGuire, Aug. 6, 1966; children: Eric, Matthew, Amy. BA, Occidental Coll., 1962. Pres. Custom Fidelity Inc., Hollywood, Calif., 1958-74, Berkus Compusystems Inc., Los Angeles, 1974-81; pres., chief exec. officer Computerized Lodging Systems Inc. and subs., Los Angeles, 1981-93; pres. Berkus Tech. Ventures (Venture Capital), L.A., 1983—. Author: (software) Hotel Compusystem, 1979; creator 1st artificial intelligence-based yield mgmt. system, 1987. Chmn. bd. Boy Scouts Am., San Gabriel Valley, 1986, mem. exec. com. Lt. USNR, 1963-72. Recipient Dist. award of merit Boy Scouts Am., 1986, INC. mag. 500 award, 1986, Silver Beaver award Boy Scouts Am., 1988. Mem. Am. Hotel-Motel Assn., Audio Engring. Soc. (chmn. Los Angeles sect. 1973-74). Office: Computerized Lodging Systems Inc 1430 Glencoe Dr Arcadia CA 91006-1909

BERLAD, ABRAHAM LEON, engineering educator, consultant; b. N.Y.C., Sept. 20, 1921; s. Harry and Celia B.; m. Alice Mae Halber, July 10, 1949; children: Glenda, Edward, Nancy. BA, Bklyn. Coll., 1943; PhD, Ohio State U., 1950. Rsch. scientist NASA, Cleve., 1951-56; sr. staff scientist Gen. Dynamics Corp., San Diego, 1956-64; rsch. scientist Gen. Rsch. Corp., Santa Barbara, Calif., 1964-66; chmn. dept. mech. engring. SUNY-Stony Brook, 1966-69, prof., 1966-84, prof. emeritus, 1984—; adj. prof. combustion sci. U. Calif.-San Diego, 1984—; chmn. combustion sci. working group NASA, 1980—; energy cons. U.S. Dept. Energy, 1973—, U.S. Nuclear Regulatory Commn., 1979—; vis. prof. U. Calif.-Berkeley, 1963, U. Calif.-San Diego, 1973, Hebrew U. Jerusalem, 1973. Author numerous tech. papers. Editorial adv. bd. Combustion and Flame, 1964—. Served with U.S. Army, 1943-46, PTO. Grantee NASA, U.S. Dept. Energy, NRC, U.S. Dept. Agr., Dept. Def., NSF, others. Mem. Internat. Combustion Inst. (bd. dirs. 1974-82), Am. Phys. Soc., Com. Space Research, Internat. Astronautical Fedn. (com. on microgravity experimentation 1986—) Jewish. Avocations: tennis, gardening. Office: U Calif La Jolla CA 92093

BERLO, ROBERT CHRISTOPHER, publications executive; b. San Francisco, Mar. 29, 1941; s. Ernest and Victoria (Schoenstein) B.; m. Juanita Maria Vogel, June 14, 1969; children: Mark Douglas, John Louis. BS, U. San Francisco, 1962; postgrad., MIT, 1962-65. Tech. journalist Am. Chem. Soc., Washington, 1966-68; tech. writer Lawrence Livermore (Calif.) Nat. Lab., 1968-78, editorial mgr., 1978-81, graphics mgr., 1981-85, prodn. mgr., 1985-87, dep. dept. head tech. info. dept., 1987—. Author: Ovulation (Billings) Method of Natural Family Planning 1976, (with others) The Scientific Report: A Guide for Authors. Nat. Merit scholar, 1958-62. Mem. Soc. Am. Baseball Rsch., Calif. Map Soc. Office: Lawrence Livermore Nat Lab PO Box 808 Livermore CA 94551-0808

BERMAN, BARUCH, electrical engineer; b. Israel, Nov. 10, 1925; s. Joseph and Sonia (Leoff) B.; m. Rose S. Goodman, Sept. 22, 1952; children: Sharon J., Orrie A. B.S.E.E., Israel Inst. Tech., 1947, diploma Ingenieur, 1948; M.S.E.E., Columbia U., 1957, postgrad., 1958-60. Chief engr., mgr. engring. and sect. head aerospace and indsl. firms, 1948-66; pres. Berman Engring., Palos Verdes Peninsula, Calif., 1966—; mgr. power systems and control advanced tech. div. and energy tech. div. TRW, Redondo Beach, Calif., 1966-74, 77-82; v.p., asst. gen. mgr. engineered magnetics div. Gulton Industries, Inc., Hawthorne, Calif., 1974-77; with Satellite and Space Electronics div. Rockwell Internat., Seal Beach, Calif., 1982-90, ret. Contbr. articles to profl. jours.; patentee transistorized regulators. Served with Brit. Coast Guard, 1944-45. Recipient Outstanding Engr. Merit award Inst. Advancement of Engring., 1987. Fellow IEEE (exec. com. region 6 1981, nat. ethics com., div. II pace coord, div. profl. leadership award 1990), Inst. for Advancement Engring.; mem. Nat. Soc. Profl. Engrs. (past nat. state govs. com.), Calif. Soc. Profl. Engrs. (past state chmn. profl. engr. in industry practice div.), Industry Application Soc. (mem. exec. com.), Indsl. Electronics and Control Instrumentation Soc., Magnetic Soc. Home and Office: Bemran Engring 28739 Trailriders Dr Palos Verdes Peninsula CA 90274-3051

BERMAN, DANIEL K(ATZEL), entrepreneur; b. Detroit, Nov. 17, 1954; s. Louis Arthur and Irene (Katzel) B. BS, Northwestern U., 1976, MS, 1977; AM, Harvard U., 1983; MA, U. Calif., Berkeley, 1984, PhD, 1991; cert. study, U. Paris, 1973, Peking (Peoples Rep. China) Normal U., 1981, Nat. Taiwan U., 1982. Subscription mgr. The N.Y. Times, 1983-84; editorial and rsch. asst. Inst. for Contemporary Studies, San Francisco, 1984-85; lang. cons. Berlitz Translation Svcs., San Francisco, 1986-89; v.p. Golden Gate Investment, San Francisco, 1985-87; lectr. St. Mary's Coll., Moraga, Calif., 1987; instr. U. Calif., Berkeley, 1984-90; chief exec. officer Pacific Fin. Svcs., San Francisco, 1987—; editor Credit Report Newsletter for Consumer Edn., San Francisco, 1989—; lectr. Calif. State U., Hayward, 1993—; sales and mktg. cons. The Deerwood Corp./MRI, San Ramon, Calif., 1989-91. Author: The Hottest Summer in Peking, 1982, The Credit Power Handbook for American Consumers, 1988, 89, Words Like Colored Glass: The Role of the Press in Taiwan's Democratization Process, 1992; editor, translator: The Butterfly's Revenge and Other Chinese Mystery Stories. Edn. scholar Rep. of China Ministry of Edn., 1979-82; rsch. grantee Pacific Cultural Found., 1981; fgn. lang. and area studies fellow in Chinese U. Calif., 1983-84. Fellow John F. Kennedy Libr. Found.; mem. The Harvard Club of San Francisco, Soc. of Profl. Journalists, The Acad. of Polit. Sci., Nat. Ctr. for Fin. Edn. (profl. sponsor), Kappa Tau Alpha (grantee). Jewish. Office: Pacific Fin Svcs PO Box 2006 Rohnert Park CA 94927

BERMAN, ELEANORE, artist; b. N.Y.C., Sept. 2, 1928; d. Isidor and Elsie (Goldstein) B.; children: Deborah Nicholas, Jan Nicholas, Tony Nicholas, David Lazarof. BA, UCLA, 1950. Mem. Nat. Assn Women Artists, Nat. Watercolor Soc., Coll. Art Assn., So. Calif. Women's Caucus Arts, Artists Equity Assn. (adv. bd. 1980-84), L.A. Printmaking Soc. Home: 718 N Maple Dr Beverly Hills CA 90210-3411

BERMAN, HOWARD LAWRENCE, congressman; b. Los Angeles, Apr. 15, 1941; s. Joseph M. and Eleanor (Schapiro) B.; m. Janis Schwartz, 1979; children: Brinley Ann, Lindsey Rose. BA, UCLA, 1962, LLB, 1965. Bar: Calif. 1966. Vol. VISTA, Balt., San Francisco, 1966-67; assoc. Levy, Van Bourg & Hackler, Los Angeles, 1967-72; mem. Calif. State Assembly from 43d dist., 1972-82 (majority leader), 98th-103rd Congresses from 26th Calif. dist.; freshman rep. steering & policy com. 98th-103rdCongresses from 26th Calif. dist., 1983, mem. judiciary com. econ. and comml. law; intellectual property and jud. adminstrn. 98th-103rd Congresses from 26th Calif. dist., adminstrv. law and gov. rels. subcom., mem. budget com., fgn. affairs com., chmn. internat. ops., internal security, internat. orgns. and human rights. Pres. Calif. Fedn. Young Democrats, 1967-69 (budget com.); mem. adv. bd. Jewish Fund for Justice, Valley Internat. Trade Assn. Office: Rayburn House Office Bldg Rm 2201 Washington DC 20515*

BERMAN, MARK LAURENCE, clinical psychologist; b. Los Angeles, Sept. 13, 1940; s. Joseph Erwin and Bernice (Levin) B.; m. Teresa Rose Davich, July 3, 1966; children: Alisa Ruth, Joseph Daniel. BA in Anthropology, UCLA, 1962; MA in Cultural Anthropology, Ariz. State U., 1964, PhD in Psychology, 1969. Lic. psychologist, Ariz. Asst. prof. Pa. State U., 1968-70; rsch. coord. U. Wash., 1970-72; pvt. practice psychology, Phoenix, 1973—; cons. in field. Author (with others): Essentials of Clothing Construction, 1971; editor, co-author: Motivation and Learning, 1971; contbr. articles to profl. jours., chpts. to books. Mem. Ariz. State Task on Elder Abuse; co-chmn. Hispanic-Jewish Coalition; mem. adv. bd. Hispanic Leadership Inst.; mem. exec. com. Community Rels. Council, Phoenix chpt. Am. Jewish Com.; mem. vol. task force Phoenix Union High Sch. Dist.; mem. exec. bd. Ariz. Citizens for Edn.; mem. Phoenix adv. coun. Conocimiento Project; commr. Aging Svcs. Commn., Phoenix; active Hispanic Rsch. Ctr., Ariz. State U., Community Documentation Project, Phoenix Dropout Prevention Coalition. Recipient Profl. Achievement award County Bar Assn., Profl. Achievement award Ariz. State Bar Assn.; grad. scholar Ariz. State U., 1963-68; Systems Devel. Corp. fellow, 1965; grantee Pa. State U., U.S. Office Edn., 1970-72. Mem. Maricopa Psychol. Soc. (pres. 1982), Ariz. State Psychol. Assn. (polit. action com. 1983—, Profl. Achievement award, ins. com.), Am. Psychol. Assn., Am. Assn. Family and Conciliation Cts., Ariz. Assn. Family and Conciliation Cts. Democrat. Jewish. Avocations: fishing, camping, traveling, reading, music. Home: 5714 N 21st St Phoenix AZ 85016-2738 Office: PO Box 44376 Phoenix AZ 85064-4376

BERMAN, SAUL J., strategic consultant; b. Phila., Jan. 1, 1946; s. Sherwood and Leona (Habelson) B.; m. S. Jann Gillen, June 6, 1980; 1 child, Ashley Scott. BS in Econs., U. Pa., 1967; MBA, Columbia U., 1969, PhD, 1973. Asst. prof. U. So. Calif., L.A., 1972-77; divisional v.p. Broadway Dept. Stores, L.A., 1977-82; case leader Boston Consulting Group, L.A., 1982-86; ptnr.-in-charge west region Price Waterhouse Strategic Cons. Group, L.A., 1986—; mem. Acad. Mgmt., L.A., 1972-77, Internat. Planning Forum, 1986. Bd. dirs. Love is Feeding Everyone, L.A., 1988-89; mem. L.A. County Beach Commn., 1978-80, Planning Forum, L.A., 1987—, Town Hall, L.A., 1987—. Mem. U. Pa. Alumni Club (bd. dirs. 1986-88, So. Calif. assoc. alumni trustee 1990—), Columbia Bus. Sch. Club of So. Calif. (bd. dirs. 1992—). Office: Price Waterhouse 1880 Century Park E Fl 16 Los Angeles CA 90067-1600

BERMAN, STEVE WILLIAM, lawyer, author; b. Chgo., Nov. 13, 1954; s. Mert E. and Lois Ann (Eliot) B.; m. Janet S. Friend, June 18, 1979; children: Eliot Michael, Jacob Paul. BS, U. Mich., 1976; JD, U. Chgo., 1980. Bar: Ill. 1980, Wash. 1982, U.S. Dist. Ct. Ill. 1980, U.S. Ct. Appeals (7th cir.) 1980, Wash. 1982, U.S. Dist. Ct. 1982, U.S. Ct. Appeals (3d and 9th cirs.), U.S. Supreme Ct. 1986. Assoc. Jenner & Block, Chgo., 1980-82, Shidler, McBroom & Gates, Seattle, 1982-85; resident ptnr. Bernstein, Litowitz, Berger & Grossman, Seattle, 1986-89; ptnr. Betts, Patterson & Mines, Seattle, 1989-92; mng. ptnr. Hagens & Berman, Seattle, 1993—; adj. prof. law U. Puget Sound, Tacoma, 1983-84; asst. coach Syracuse U., 1976. Author: A Tarnished Hero, 1988; contbr. articles to profl. jours. Mem. com. Juvenile Conf., Seattle, 1984; apptd. spl. counsel Wash. State Bar, 1988—. Mem. ABA (trial practice com., discovery com.), Nat. Assocs. Securities and Comml. Attys. (bd. dirs. 1991—), Lake Washington Rowing Club. Democrat. Jewish. Office: Hagen & Berman 2929 Rainer Tower 1301 Fifth Ave Ste 2929 Seattle WA 98101

BERMAN, STEVEN MARK, electrophysiologist; b. Syracuse, N.Y., Sept. 16, 1949; s. Bennet Herbert Berman and Roslyn (Ozur) Cantor: m. Deborah Rose Strichartz, Aug. 13, 1983; children: Juliet Alexandra, Serena Meredith. BS, Wayne State U., 1971; MS, CUNY, 1985, PhD, 1986. Lic. psychologist. Counselor Lane Ranch, Sebastopol, Calif., 1974-75; extern, neuropsychology Mt. Sinai Med. Ctr., N.Y.C., 1981-83; supr. Learning Disabilities Clinic/CCNY, N.Y.C., 1982-84, rsch. asst. psychology dept., 1979-86; head trauma cons. Inst. Rehab. Medicine, NYU Med. Ctr., N.Y.C., 1983-86; postdoctoral rsch. scientist Columbia U., N.Y.C., 1986-89; rsch. scientist N.Y. State Psychiat. Inst., N.Y.C., 1986-90; asst. researcher Alcohol Rsch. Ctr./UCLA, 1990—; adj. lectr. CCNY, 1981-86. Contbr. articles to profl. jours., publs. Freedom writer Amnesty Internat., 1988—; vol. sci. tchr. Peace Corps, Swaziland, Africa, 1975-77. Recipient Mich. Higher Edn. scholarship, 1967-71, grad. fellowship CCNY, 1980-81, Joseph E. Barmack Dissertation Rsch. award, 1986. Mem. Am. Psychol. Soc. (founding mem.), Soc. fo Psychophysiol. Rsch., N.Y. Acad. Scis., AAAS. Jewish. Office: Alcohol Rsch Ctr PO Box 11 760 Westwood Pl Los Angeles CA 90024

BERMAN, STEVEN RICHARD, computer systems analyst, research engineer; b. N.Y.C., Dec. 30, 1947; s. Harold and Norma (Bystock) B.; m. Susan Segall, Aug. 3, 1969; 1 child, Russell T. BS in Meteorology, CCNY, 1968; postgrad., U. Chgo., 1968-69; MS in Tech. Mgmt., Pepperdine U., 1993. Programmer, analyst Logicon, Inc., San Pedro, Calif., 1970-73, 75-78, Hughes Aircraft Co., Culver City, Calif., 1973-75; sr. analyst Argosystems, Inc., Sunnyvale, Calif., 1978-80; mgr. software support Ultrasystems, Inc., Irvine, Calif., 1981-86; sr. rsch. engr. Northrop, Inc., Hawthorne, Calif., 1986—. Author (computer programs) Recording Input-Output, 1983, Batch Jobs from Fortran, 1988, Marking Files No Backup, 1988. NDEA Title IV fellow, Chgo., 1968. Mem. Am. Contract Bridge League, Mensa. Home: 17336 Flame Tree Cir Fountain Valley CA 92708

BERMINGHAM, PETER, museum director; b. Buffalo, Nov. ; s. Donald Michael and Margaret Anne (Murphy) B.; m. Eleanor Joan Sigborn, Sept. 5, 1964; children: Christopher, Jason, Alexander, Noelle, Nicholas. B.A., U. Md., 1964, M.A., 1968; Ph.D. (Smithsonian Instn. fellow 1971-72), U. Mich., 1972. Teaching asst. U Mich., 1968-71; vis. prof. art history U. Cin., 1972-73; curator edn. Nat. Collection Fine Arts, Smithsonian Instn., 1973-78; dir., chief curator U. Ariz. Mus. Art, Tucson, 1978—; mem. mus. policy panel Nat. Endowment Arts. Author exhbn. catalogues. Served with USAF, 1956-60. Mus. tng. fellow Nat. Endowment Humanities, 1967-68. Mem. Western Assn. Art Museums, Coll. Art Assn. Roman Catholic. Home: 3585 E Thimble Peak Pl Tucson AZ 85718-2230 Office: U Ariz Mus Art Olive & Speedway Tucson AZ 85721

BERNAL, HARRIET JEAN DANIELS, real estate salesperson; b. Cin., Sept. 28, 1931; d. Ernest Richard and Amy Lillian (Jeffries) Daniels; m. Gil Bernal, July 9, 1950; children: Gil Jr., Lisa, Nicholas, Colette, Michelle. AA in Theatre Arts, Los Angeles City Coll., 1949-62; student, Kimballs Real Estate Sch., Burbank, Calif., 1974; AA in Humanities, Glendale Coll., 1982; BA in Polit. Sci. Pre-Law, Calif. State U., Los Angeles, 1987. Lic. real estate agt. Dancer, entertainer Greek Theatre, Los Angeles, 1949-50; travel, reservation agt. Iver's Dept. Store, Los Angeles, 1970-73, editor, dept. store news letters, 1972-73; sec. to area supt. and social chmn. Los Angeles Bd. Edn., 1973-74; exec. sec. CBS-TV City, Los Angeles, 1974; real estate salesperson, relocation mgr. Century 21 Realty, Los Angeles, Pasadena, Calif., San Marino, Calif., 1974-86; real estate salesperson Coldwell Banker Residential, Pasadena, Calif., 1986-89, Glendale, Calif., 1989—. Contbr. articles on sch. sci. ctrs., schs. in Russia, and schs. for the handicapped for local sch. paper, Ann. awards. Pres. San Pascual Elem. Sch. PTA, L.A., 1969-70, hon. life mem., 1970—; first soprano Consortium Angeli, 1991-92; fundraiser various groups to elect Mayor Tom Bradley, L.A.; wedding hostess Pasadena (Calif.) Ch. of Angels, 1980-88, also lic. lay minister. Mem. Pasadena Bd. Realtors (local govt. com., polit. affairs com.), Met. Player Guild. Democrat. Episcopalian. Home: 1075 Rutland Ave Los Angeles CA 90042-1536 Office: Jon Douglas Co 171 S Hudson Ave Pasadena CA 91101-2606

BERNAL, LYNDA EVELYN, video producer, writer; b. Detroit, July 9, 1959; d. Bernard and Joyce Lydia (Gunnett) Harris; m. Ronald Daniel Bernal, June 21, 1980 (div. Oct. 1985). BS in Health Sci., Ariz. State U., 1982. Audiovisual coord. Salt River Project, Phoenix, 1985-93; ind. writer/prodr. Phoenix, 1993—. Writer, dir.: (videotapes) Lake Powell: Heart of the Grand Circle, 1986 (Rocky Mountain Emmy award 1987, ITVA award 1986), The Wolf: A Howling in America's Parks, 1989 (CINDY award 1989). Media cons. YWCA of Maricopa County, Phoenix, 1986-90. Mem. Nat. Acad. TV Arts and Scis. Office: 16423 N 54th Ave Glendale AZ 85306

BERNARD, ALEXANDER, airport police official; b. L.A., Apr. 23, 1952; s. Louis and Hannah (Bergman) B.; m. Diana LoRee Winstead, Dec. 17, 1976; children: Michael Alexander, Andrew Alexander. AA magna cum laude, Los Angeles Valley Coll., 1976; BS summa cum laude, Calif. State U., L.A., 1989. Parking meter collector L.A. City Clk.'s Office, 1973-79; police officer L.A. Airport, 1979—. Contbr. articles to profl. jours. Active Boy Scouts Am. Mem. NRA (life), Internat. Police Assn., Indsl. Rels. Rsch. Assn. Calif. Peace Officers Assn., Los Angeles County Peace Officers Assn., Peace Officers Rsch. Assn. Calif. (chpt. pres. 1982-84, 85-87, state bd. dirs. 1984-85, 88—), L.A. Airport Peace Officers Assn. (pres. 1981-89, bd. dirs. 1992—), Calif. Rifle and Pistol Assn. (life), Golden Key (life), Phi Kappa Phi (life). Democrat. Mem. Assemblies of God Ch. Office: LA Airport Police Divsn 16461 Sherman Way Van Nuys CA 91406-3808

BERNARD, BRYCE ALLISON, accounting educator, management consultant; b. Kelso, Wash., July 23, 1960; s. Bernard Wayne and Dawn Maureen (Taylor) B.; m. Julie Ann Marlowe, July 11, 1981; children: Bryan Wayne, Jason Merritt, Carolyn Dawn. AA, Judson Bapt. Coll., Portland, Oreg., 1980; BS, Western Bapt. Coll., 1982; MBA, Oreg. State U., 1985. CPA, Oreg. Jr. auditor Aldrich, Kilbride & Tatone, CPAs, Salem, Oreg., 1984-85, sr. auditor, 1985-87, mgmt. cons., 1987—; prof. acctg. Western Bapt. Coll., Salem, Oreg., 1987—, bus. divsn. chmn., 1990—; chmn., bd. dirs. Sonshine Sch., Salem. Deacon First Bapt. ch., Salem, 1986-89, sec., bd. dirs., 1989, mem. pastoral search com., 1992. Mem. AICPA, Oreg. Soc. CPAs. Republican. Office: Western Bapt Coll 5000 Deer Park Dr SE Salem OR 97306

BERNARD, EDDIE NOLAN, oceanographer; b. Houston, Nov. 23, 1946; s. Edward Nolan and Geraldine Marie (Dempsey) B.; m. Shirley Ann Fielder, May 30, 1970; 1 child, Elizabeth Ann. B.S., Lamar U., 1969; M.S., Tex. A&M U., 1970, Ph.D., 1976. Geophysicist Pan Am. Petroleum Co., 1969; research asst. oceanographic research Tex. A&M U., College Station, Tex., 1969-70; researcher Nat. Oceanic and Atmospheric Adminstrn. (NOAA), 1970-73; dep. dir. NOAA Pacific Marine Environ. Lab., Seattle, 1980-82; researcher Joint Tsunami Research Effort, 1973-77; dir. Nat. Tsunami Warning Ctr., 1977-80; dir., Pacific Marine Environ. Lab., Seattle, 1982—; dir. NOAA hydrothermal vents program, fisheries oceanography program; mem. adminstrv. bd. Joint Inst. for Study of Atmosphere and Ocean, U. Wash., Seattle; mem. exec. com. Coop. Inst. for Marine Resource Studies Oreg. State U.; mem. adminstrv. bd. Joint Inst. Marine and Atmospheric Research, U. Hawaii; chmn. Internat. Union of Geodesy and Geophysics Tsunami Commn., 1987—; mem. Panel on Wind and Seismic Effects U.S.-Japan Coop. Program in Nat. Resources, 1981—; mem. Internat. Recruitment Investigations in the Subarctic Council, 1982—; mem. Washington Sea Grant Steering Com., 1987—; mem. sci. coun. Joint Inst. for Marine Observations, Scripps Instn. of Oceanography, 1992—, bd. dirs. Pacific Northwest Reg. Marine Rsch. Program, 1992—. Editor: Tsunami Hazard: A Practical Guide for Tsunami Hazard Reduction, 1991; mem. editorial adv. bd. Natural Hazards Jour.; contbr. articles to profl. jours. Recipient Best of New Generation 1984 Register award Esquire Mag., 1984. Mem. Internat. Union of Geodesy and Geophysics (chmn. Tsunami commn. 1987—), Am. Geophys. Union, Am. Meteorol. Soc., Marine Tech. Soc. Office: Pacific Marine Environ Lab 7600 Sand Point Way NE Seattle WA 98115-6349

BERNARD, JAMES WILLIAM, corporate executive; b. Brainerd, Minn., June 25, 1937; s. Paul Raymond and Maybelle Gertrude (Fynskov) B.; m. Maureen Day, Sept. 6, 1958; children: David, Kenneth, Kathleen. BS, U. Oreg., 1960. Trainee Univar Corp., San Francisco, 1960-61; resident mgr. Univar Corp., Honolulu, 1961-65; sales mgr. Univar Corp., San Francisco, 1965-67; v.p. Univar Corp., Phoenix, 1967-71; v.p. Univar Corp., San Francisco, 1971-74, corp. v.p., 1974-82; sr. v.p. Univar Corp., Seattle, 1982-83, exec. v.p., 1983-86; pres., chief exec. officer Univar Corp. (now Univar Van Waters & Rogers), Seattle, 1986—, also bd. dirs.; bd. dirs. VMR Corp., Bellevue, Wash., U.S. Bank of Washington. Bd. dirs. Jr. Achievement Greater Puget Sound, The Nature Conservancy Wash. chpt., Ctrl. Wash. U., Wash. Roundtable. Mem. Am. Chem. Soc., Chem. Mfgs. Assn. (bd. dirs.), Seattle C. of C., Columbia Tower Club, Rainier (Seattle) Club. Republican. Office: Univar Van Waters & Rogers PO Box 34325 Seattle WA 98124-1325*

BERNARD, PETER ALAN, federal agency executive; b. Detroit, Oct. 4, 1936; s. Felix J. and June (Odachowski) K.; m. Charlotte Smith, June 15, 1963; children: Cheryl, Susan, Kathleen. AB, John Carroll U., 1958; JD, U. Mich., 1961. Atty. Judge Advocate Gen. Corps, U.S. Army, 1962-65, AEC, Washington, 1965-72; counsel Joint Com. on Atomic Energy, U.S. Congress, Washington, 1973; chief counsel San Francisco Field Office Dept. Energy, Oakland, Calif., 1974—. Nat. Inst. Pub. Affairs fellow Stanford U., 1970-71. Mem. Mich. Bar Assn., D.C. Bar Assn. Office: US Dept Energy Rm 700 N 1301 Clay St 700 N Oakland CA 94612-5208

BERNARD, THELMA RENE, property management professional; b. Phila.; d. Michael John and Louise Thelma (Hoffman) Campione; m. Gene Bernard (div.). Sec. Penn. Mut. Life Ins. Co., Phila., Suffolk Franklin Savs. Bank, Boston, Holmes and Narver, Inc., Las Vegas; constrn. site office mgr. Miles R. Nay, Inc., Las Vegas; adminstrv. asst to pres. N.W.S. Constrn. Corp., Inc., Las Vegas, 1982-86, corp. sec., 1982-86; gen. mgr., corp. sec. D.A.P., Inc. property mgmt. com, Las Vegas, pres., 1991—. Author: Blue Marsh, 1972, Winds of Wakefield, 1972, Moonshadow Mansion, 1973, 2d edit., 1976, Spanish transl., 1974, German transl., 1977; contbr. articles to Doll Reader, Internat. Doll World, other mags.; past editor Cactus Courier; editor, pub. The Hoyer Enthusiastic Ladies Mail Assn., 1980-90, Friendly Tymes, 1991—; writer song lyrics. Mem. Nat. League Am. Pen Women (v.p. Red Rock Canyon br. 1986-88), Original Paper Doll Artists Guild, Am. Rose Soc., Heritage Rose Soc., Bookmark Collector Club. Office: PO Box 14002 Las Vegas NV 89114-4002

BERNARDEZ, GARY CHRISTOPHER, marketing executive; b. Oak Park, Ill., Feb. 28, 1963; s. Roger William and Kathryn Louise (Smegal) B.; m. Jeanne Marie Szimanski, Sept. 3, 1988; 1 child, Leanne Catherine. BS in Computer Sci., Bowling Green State U., 1985; MBA, Clemson U., 1991. Software designer and instr. McSoft Enterprises, Greenville, S.C., 1985; acctg. assoc. Daniel Constrn. Co., Greenville, 1985; dep. supr. Fluor Corp. subs. Am. Equipment Co., Greenville, 1986-88, div. adminstrv. mgr., 1988-89, bus. devel. mgr., 1989-91; mgr. mktg. Fluor Corp. subs. Am. Equipment Co., Irvine, Calif., 1991-92, mktg. assoc., 1993—. Mem. S.C. Internat. Trade Assn., World Future Soc. Home: 30 Alexandria Irvine CA 92714 Office: 3333 Michelson Dr Irvine CA 92714

BERNARDI, MARIO, conductor; b. Kirland Lake, Ont., Can., Aug. 20, 1930; s. Leone and Rina (Onisto) B.; m. Mona Kelly, May 12, 1962; 1 d., Julia. Ed., Coll. Piox, Treviso, Italy, Benedetto Marcello Conservatory, Venice, Italy, Mozarteum, Salzburg, Austria, Royal Conservatory, Toronto. Began career as pianist Italy; music dir. Sadler's Wells Opera Co., 1967-69; music dir., condr. Nat. Arts Centre, Ottawa, Ont., 1969-82; music dir. Calgary Philharm. Orch., 1984-93; prin. condr. CBC Vancouver Orch., 1982—; guest condr. with San Francisco Opera Assn., Vancouver Opera, Canadian Opera Co., Met. Opera, Chgo. Symphony, Washington Opera, Houston Symphony Orch.; prin. condr. with CBC, Vancouver Orch. Decorated companion Order of Can. Club: Savage. Office: Columbia Artists Mgmt Inc c/o Judie Janowski 165 W 57th St New York NY 10019

BERNEE, ANDREA LOREL, zookeeper, editor, operator; b. Chgo., May 30, 1960; d. Lewis Joseph and Rose (Eisenberg) B. BA, U. Ariz., 1981; MS, Bklyn. Coll., 1984. Tech. dir. KZAZ-TV, Tucson, 1982-83; camera operator Video Cen., Inc., N.Y.C., 1984-85; prodn. tech. Doyle, Dane, Advt., N.Y.C., 1985; editor Golden Gaters Prodns., Corte Madera, Calif., 1985-86; ops. supr. KSTS-TV, San Jose, 1986-87; master control operator KEYT-TV, Santa Barbara, Calif., 1987; video instr UniLex Coll., San Francisco, 1988; head tape operator West Coast Video Inc., Brisbane, Calif., 1987-88; editor Coastar Prodns., Monterey, Calif., 1988-89; asst. editor The Post Group, Hollywood, Calif., 1989, Modern Video Film, Hollywood, 1989-90; telecine asst. Starfax, L.A., 1990-91; zookeeper Cheyenne Mountain Zoo, Colorado Springs, Colo., 1992—; freelance video installer One Pass Film & Video, San Francisco, 1989. Vol. Woman Inc., San Francisco, 1988-89, Peace Corps, Fiji Islands, 1985. Mem. Broadcast Edn. Assn. Democrat. Jewish.

BERNEY, ROBERT EDWARD, economics educator, academic administrator; b. Walla Walla, Wash., Sept. 13, 1932; s. William E. and Dorothy A. (Smith) B.; m. Marilyn F. Trimble, Apr. 2, 1956 (div. Feb. 1987); children: Michael E, Peter W., Marybeth A., Timothy G. BA, Wash. State U., Pullman, 1954, MA, 1960; MS, U. Wis., 1962, PhD, 1963. Res. officer Royal Commn. on Taxation, Ottawa, Can., 1963; asst. prof. econs. Ariz. State U., Tempe, 1964-65; from asst. to assoc. prof. econs. Wash. State U., 1966-72, dir. grad. program, 1970-78, prof., 1972—; chmn. dept. econs., 1987—; sr. acad. resident in pub. fin. Adv. Commn. on Intergovtl. Rels., Washington, 1973-74; chief econs. U.S. SBA, Washington, 1978-80; vis. prof. econs. and fin. Ind. U., Bloomington, 1985-86; mem. exec. bd. Wash. Pub. Power Sypply System, Richland, 1983-86. Author: Tax Structure Variations in the State of Washington, 1970; contbr. articles to profl. jours. Mem. faculty senate steering com. Wash. State U., 1983-84, 88-92, chair grad. studies com., 1983-84, vice-chair, chair faculty senate, 1988-90. Mem. Nat. Tax Assn., Am. Econ. Assn., Beta Gamma Sigma. Office: Wash State U Dept Econs Pullman WA 99164-4860

BERNHAM, JOHN ALBERT, counselor; b. Spokane, Wash., Nov. 9, 1933; s. Alfred Max and Emily (Hasenkrug) B.; m. Dionne Gloria Tollefson, June 6, 1953 (dec. 1976); children: Lynn Griffith, Lori Sanders; m. Peggy Josephine Cordell, Sept. 10, 1977; 1 child, Jennifer Joy. BA, Cascade Coll., 1956; MEd, U. Oreg., 1960. Lic. profl. counselor, Oreg. Instr. Eugene (Oreg.) Bible Coll., 1956-58; tchr., dean of students Pleasant Hill (Oreg.) High Sch., 1958-62; tchr., counselor Eugene Pub. Schs., 1962-66; counselor Lane C.C., Eugene, 1966-78, dir. counseling, 1978-90; pres., owner Lane Counseling Svcs., Eugene, 1990—. Bd. dirs. Oreg. Counselors Polit. Action Com., 1989. Fellow U.S. Govt. 1963, 65. Mem. Am. Counseling Assn., Am. Mental Health Counselors Assn., Assn. (treas.), Assn. for Counselor Edn. and Supervision, Oreg. Coll. and Univ. Counseling Assn. (sec., Disting. Svc. award 1986), Oreg. Counseling Assn. (pres. 1988-89, presdl. liaison 1991, Disting. Svcs. award 1990), Oreg. Track Club. Home: PO Box 11905 Eugene OR 97440

BERNHARD, JON CASPER, architect, property manager; b. St. Paul, Feb. 10, 1961; s. James Casper and Jean Marie (Stougaard) B.; m. Teresa Ann Betting, Sept. 21, 1985. BS, N.D. State U., 1984, BArch, 1985. Draftsman Trice, Elson Assocs., Scottsdale, Ariz., 1985-86; architect, project mgr. Vernon Swaback Assocs., Scottsdale, 1986—; property mgr. Studio Garden Offices, Scottsdale, 1987—; co-owner, mgr. Style Hair Co., Phoenix, 1988—; v.p. Creative Hair, Inc., 1990—; advisor S.W. Acad. Tech. Prin. works include custom residences, chs., office bldgs. and interiors. Mem. Multiple Sclerosis Pancake Feed, Fargo, N.D., 1983-85, Meals on Wheels, Fargo, 1985, Nat. Trust Hist. Preservation. Mem. AIA, Smithsonian Nat. Inst. (hon.), Leadership in Design and Arts, Alpha Tau Omega. Lutheran. Home: 15240 E Alvarado Dr Fountain Hls AZ 85268-1700 Office: Vernon Swaback Assocs 7550 N Mcdonald Dr Scottsdale AZ 85250-6026

BERNHARDT, ROBERT, music director, conductor; m. Jennifer Bernhardt; children: Alexander, Charlotte. Grad. summa cum laude, Union Coll.; MMus with honors, U. So. Calif. Assoc. condr. Louisville Orch., 1981-87; music dir. Amarillo Symphony, 1985-88; music dir., condr. Tucson Symphony Orch., 1988—; prin. condr. Ky. Opera, 1991—; guest condr. Pitts. Symphony, Phoenix Symphony, Chattanooga Symphony, Seattle Symphony, Rochester Philharm., L.A. Chamber Orch., Denver Chamber Orch., Jacksonville Symphony, Nashville Opera, Birmingham Civic Opera, Chattanooga Opera, Louisville Ballet, Lone Star Ballet, others; recs. include for Vanguard, First Edit. Records. Mem. Phi Beta Kappa. Office: Tucson Symphony Orch 443 S Stone Ave Tucson AZ 85701-2399

BERNHARDT, ROGER, law educator, consultant; b. Cleve., May 27, 1934; s. Paul and Josephine (Harris) B.; m. Mary Louise Corner, Sept. 1, 1960 (dec. 1978); children: John Harlan, Jason Paul; m. Christine Toursarkissian, Dec. 27, 1991. AB, U Chgo., 1956; AM, U. Chgo., 1957, JD, 1960. Asst. prof. Golden Gate Coll., San Francisco, 1961-64; pvt. practice law San Francisco, 1964-69; prof. law Golden Gate U., San Francisco, 1969—. Author: Real Property in a Nutshell, 1975, Black Letter Law of Real Property, 1977, California Mortgage Practice, 1979, California Real Estate Finance Law, 1989, Bernhardt's California Real Estate Laws, 1993; editor Calif. Real Property Law Reporter. Chmn. San Francisco Relocation Appeals Bd., 1980-88. Office: Golden Gate U 536 Mission St San Francisco CA 94105-2967

BERNHEIMER, MARTIN, music critic; b. Munich, Germany, Sept. 28, 1936; came to U.S., 1940, naturalized, 1946; s. Paul Ernst and Louise (Nassauer) B.; m. Lucinda Pearson, Sept. 30, 1961 (div. Feb. 1989); children: Mark Richard, Nora Nicoll, Marina and Erika (twins); m. Linda Winer, Sept. 27, 1992. MusB with honors, Brown U., 1958; student, Munich Conservatory, 1958-59; MA in Musicology, NYU, 1961. Free-lance music critic, 1958—; contbg. critic N.Y. Herald Tribune, 1959-62; mem. music faculty NYU, 1959-62; contbg. editor Mus. Courier, 1961-64; temporary music critic N.Y. Post, 1961-65; N.Y. corr. for Brit. Publ. Opera, 1962-65, L.A. corr., 1965—; asst. to music editor Saturday Rev., 1962-65; mng. editor Philharmonic Hall Program, N.Y.C., 1962-65; music editor, chief critic L.A. Times, 1965—; mem. faculty U. So. Calif., 1966-71, music faculty UCLA, 1969-75, Calif. Inst. Arts, 1975-82, Calif. State U., Northridge, 1978-81, Rockefeller Program for Tng. of Music Critics; mem. Pulitzer Prize Music Jury, 1984, 86, 90; L.A. corr. for Swiss publ. Opernwelt, 1984—. Contbg. author New Groves Dictionary; contbr. liner notes for recordings; appearances on radio and TV, Met. Opera Broadcasts; contbr. articles to Vanity Fair, Music Quar., The Critic, Opera News, Mus. Am., others. Recipient Deems Taylor award ASCAP, 1974, 78, Headliners award, 1979, Pulitzer prize for disting. criticism, 1981. Mem. Nat. Opera Inst. (ind. selection com. 1980), Pi Kappa Lambda (hon.). Office: Los Angeles Times Times Mirror Sq Los Angeles CA 90012-3816

BERNHOFT, FRANKLIN OTTO, psychotherapist, psychologist. BA in English, N.D. State U., 1966; MA in Counseling Psychology, U. N.D., 1970; MA in English, Calif. State U., 1978; PhD in Counseling Psychology, Brigham Young U., 1985. Cert. therapist, hypnotherapist, counselor, secondary tchr.; lic. marriage, family and child counselor, ednl. psychologist. Instr. Chapman Coll., Brigham Young U., U. N.D., U.S. I.U.; staff trainer Sacramento (Calif.) County Office Edn.; therapist Lodi and Stockton, Calif.; therapist, family fitness trainer, master trainer systematic helping skills U. Pacific Behavioral Medicine Clinic; founder intervention project, Sacto County, 1977; presenter in field. Contbr. articles to profl. jours. Lt. U.S. Army, 1968-69. H.H. Kirk R. Askanase scholar; cert. achievement Ft. Carson; decorated Bronze star, combat med. badge Nat. Def. Svc. Vietnam. Mem. Am. Assn. Counseling and Devel., Children with Attention Deficit Disorders, Nat. Assn. Sch. Psychologists, Assn. Mormon Counselors and Psychotherapists, Calif. Assn. Marriage and Family Therapists,Sacramento Area Sch. Psychologists Assn., Calif. Continuation Edn. Assn. (past treas.), Calif. Assn. Lic. Edn. Psychologists, Mensa, Blue Key, Phi Eta Sigma. Office: Delta Ctr for Personal and Family Devel Ste E 317 3031 W March Ln Stockton CA 95207-6651 also: Creative Therapy 310 W Lockford Lodi CA 95240

BERNI, BETTY CATHERINE, actuary; b. Chgo., Feb. 2, 1942; d. James Gino and Helen M. (Gronkiewicz) B. BS, No. Ill. U., 1964, MS, 1968; postgrad., U. Ariz., 1968-70. Tchr. Proviso Twp. High Sch., Maywood, Ill., 1964-68; instr. U. Ariz., Tucson, 1969; actuarial asst. Wyatt Co., Washington, 1970, actuary, cons., San Francisco, 1970-80, actuary and mgr., Honolulu, 1980—. Fellow Soc. Actuaries, Conf. Consulting; mem. Am. Acad. Actuaries, Am. Math. Soc., San Francisco Actuarial Club (pres. 1979), Rotary. Roman Catholic. Home: 3551 Waakaua St Honolulu HI 96822-1173 Office: Wyatt Co 737 Bishop St Ste 2340 Honolulu HI 96813-3214

BERNIER, PAUL-EMILE, educator; b. St. Michel, Quebec, Can., Oct. 22, 1911; came to U.S., 1947; s. Phileas and Claire (Lagueux) B.; m. Isabelle Enrichetta Siracusa, June 20, 1940. BSc in Agr., Laval U., Quebec, 1932; student, McGill U., 1935-36; PhD, U. Calif., Berkeley, 1947. Lectr., asst. assoc. prof. Faculte d'Agriculture, La Pocatiere, Quebec, 1932-45; geneticist Can. Agr., Ottawa, Ontario, Can., 1945-47; assoc. prof. Oreg. State U., Corvallis, Oreg., 1947-55; prof. poultry genetics Oreg. State U., Corvallis, 1955-77, prof. emeritus, 1977—. Contbr. articles to profl. jours. Fellow AAAS; mem. Oreg. State Employees Assn. (pres., dist. dir., State Employee of Yr. award 1968), Poultry Sci. Assn. (Poultry Sci. Rsch. prize 1951), World's Poultry Sci. Assn., Genetics Soc. Am., Teratology Soc., Kiwanis (pres. Corvallis club. 1968-69). Democrat. Roman Catholic. Office: Oreg State U Animal Sci Dept Corvallis OR 97331-6702

BERNIERI, FRANK JOHN, social psychology educator; b. Bklyn., May 2, 1961; s. Gene J. and Rose (Autunnale) B.; divorced; 1 child, Jennifer. BA, U. Rochester, 1983; PhD, Harvard U., 1988. Asst. prof. Oreg. State U., Corvallis, 1988-93, assoc. prof., 1993—. Author: (with others) Coordinated Movement in Human Interaction, 1991; mem. editorial bd. Jour. Nonverbal Behavior, 1990—; contbr. articles to profl. jours. Fellow Harvard U., 1987; grantee NIH, 1988, Oreg. State U. Coll. Liberal Arts, 1990; NSF Young Investigator awardee, 1992. Mem. AAAS, APA, Am. Pschol. Soc., Soc. for Personality and Social Psychology. Democrat. Office: Oreg State Univ Dept Psychology Moreland Hall Corvallis OR 97331

BERNINGER, VIRGINIA WISE, psychologist, educator; b. Phila., Oct. 4, 1946; d. Oscar Sharpless and Lucille (Fike) Wise; m. Ronald William Berninger, Aug. 3, 1968. BA in Psychology, Elizabethtown (Pa.) Coll., 1967; MEd in Reading and Lang., U. Pitts., 1970; PhD in Psychology, Johns Hopkins U., 1981. Lic. psychologist, Wash. Educator Phila. Pub. Schs., 1967-68, Pitts. Pub. Schs., 1968, Baldwin-White Hall Pub. Schs., Pitts., 1969-72, Frederick (Md.) Pub. Schs., 1972-75, Balt. Pub. Schs., 1975-76; instr. Med. Sch. Harvard U., Boston, 1981-83; asst. prof. Sch. of Medicine Tufts U., Boston, 1983-86; asst. prof. Coll. Edn. U. Wash., Seattle, 1986-89, assoc. prof., 1989-93, prof., 1993—; mem. Ctr. for Study of Capable Youth, U. Wash., Seattle, 1989—; cons. grant rev. NICHD, 1990—, NIH, 1990—, others. Contbr. articles to profl. jours.; edited vols.; mem. editorial bds. NIMH fellow, 1978-80; U. Wash. Rsch. grantee, 1987-88, Inst. for Ethnic Studies in the U.S. Rsch. grantee, 1989-90, NIH Rsch. grantee, 1989—, Dept. Edn. grantee, 1993—. Mem. Am. Psychol. Assn., Am. Ednl. Rsch. Assn., Soc. for Rsch. on Child Devel., Nat. Assn. Sch. Psychologists, AAAS, N.Y. Acad. Sci. Office: U Wash 322J Miller Hall DQ-12 Seattle WA 98195

BERNOCO, DOMENICO, immunogeneticist, educator; b. Cherasco, Cuneo, Italy, Apr. 6, 1935; s. Giuseppe and Lucia (Merlo) D.; m. Marietta Magdelene von Diepow, July 20, 1972. DVM, U. Torino, Italy, 1959; lic. vet. medicine, Rome, 1961; Libera Docenza, Ministry Pub. Instrn., Rome, 1971. Asst. prof. med. genetics U. Torino, 1961-70; mem. staff Basel (Switzerland) Inst. Immunology, 1970-76; assoc. rsch. immunologist dept. surgery UCLA, 1977-81; assoc. prof. vet. medicine reproduction U. Calif., Davis, 1981—. Contbr. 98 articles to profl. jours. Fellow Italian Nat. Coun. Rsch., 1962-63, Italian Ministry for Pub. Instrn., 1963-64, fellow for fgn. countries NATO, 1967-68. Mem. Am. Assn. Immunologists, Internat. Soc. Animal Genetics, Am. Soc. Histocompatibility and Immunogenetics. Home: 1002 Deodara Ct Davis CA 95616-5037 Office: U Calif Sch Vet Medicine Dept Reproduction Davis CA 95616-8743

BERNSTEIN, BRUCE LAWRENCE, publisher, advertising executive; b. N.Y.C., Mar. 22, 1956; s. Alvin and Iris (Denton) B. BBA, Emory U., 1978. Bus. planning analyst CBS, Inc., N.Y.C., 1978-79; sales rep. Erving (Mass.) Paper Mills, 1981-85, Wis. Tissue Mills, Menasha, 1985-87; pres. Tel-A-Sale, Inc., Tampa, Fla., 1987-91; pub. Three Kings Pub., Taos, N.Mex., 1991—. Author: Tools for the 21st Century...The New Meditation, 1991. Home: 18 W 83rd St Apt 3B New York NY 10024 Office: Three Kings Pub Ste 404 216 Paseo del Pueblo N Taos NM 87571-5902

BERNSTEIN, CHARLES MARC, graphics software developer; b. Buffalo, July 19, 1952; s. M. Robert and Ethel-Rita Beverly (Rocklin) B.; m. Sandra M. Tompsett, Dec. 30, 1988; 1 child: Tammy Lynn. Tech. support supr. Bowling Green (Ohio) State U., 1972-79; sr. system programmer TRW, Cleve., 1979-80, Gould Ocean Systems, Cleve., 1980-82; systems cons. Systemation, Cleve., 1982-85; project engr. research and devel. Standard Oil Co., Cleve., 1985-88; sr. software designer Template Graphics Software, Inc., San Diego, Calif., 1988-91; sr. software engr. Ventura Software, Inc., San Diego, 1991-92; software engr. Excalibur Tech., Carlsbad, Calif., 1992—; tech. advisor Cleve. Planetarium, 1979-82. Mem. Digital Equipment Computer Users Soc. Home: 3354 Del Rio Ct Carlsbad CA 92009-7815

BERNSTEIN, GERALD WILLIAM, management consultant, researcher; b. Boston, Nov. 25, 1947; s. Alan Irwin and Anne (Fine) B.; m. Kathleen Ann Chaikin, Jan. 12, 1985. BS in Aero. Engring., Rensselaer Poly. Inst., 1969; MS in Engring., Stanford U., 1978. Transp. engr., dept. transp. State of N.Y., Albany, 1969-70; transp. planner Kennebec Regional Planning Com., Winslow, Me., 1974-77; dir. transp. dept. SRI Internat., Menlo Park, Calif., 1979—; session chmn. aviation workshop NSF, 1985, 91; profl. conf. chmn.; bd. dirs. GlobTran Corp., 1993—. Contbr. articles to profl. jours. Chmn. Transp. com. Glenn Park Neighborhood Assn., San Francisco, 1982-85; dir. Balboa Terrace Neighborhood Assn., San Francisco, 1986-88; trustee Congregation Beth Israel-Judea, 1991—. Served with U.S. Army, 1970-72. Recipient Cert. Appreciation City of Waterville, Maine, 1977. Mem. Transp. Research Bd. of Nat. Research Council. Democrat. Jewish. Club: Toastmasters (Menlo Park, pres. 1986). Office: SRI Internat Menlo Park CA 94025

BERNSTEIN, HARRIS, medical educator; b. N.Y.C., Dec. 12, 1934; s. Benjamin and Hannah B.; m. Carol Adelberg, June 7, 1962; children: Beryl, Golda, Benjamin. BS, Purdue U., 1956; PhD, Calif. Inst. Tech., 1961. Postdoctoral fellow Yale U., New Haven, 1961-63; asst. prof. U. Calif., Davis, 1963-68; assoc. prof. Coll. Medicine U. Ariz., Tucson, 1968-74, prof. dept. microbiology and immunology, 1974—. Author: Aging, Sex, and DNA Repair, 1991; contbr. more than 90 articles to profl. pubs. Grantee NSF, 1964-79, Am. Cancer Soc., 1975-93, Ariz. Disease Control Commn., 1986-93, NIH, 1979-87. Fellow Am. Acad. Mibrobiology; mem. AAAS, AAUP, Am. Soc. Microbiology, Genetics Soc. Am., Am. Soc. Biochemistry and Molecular Biology. Democrat. Jewish. Home: 2639 E 4th St Tucson AZ 85716-4417 Office: U Ariz Coll Medicine Dept Microbiology Tucson AZ 85724

BERNSTEIN, JONATHAN, public relations executive; b. Paris, Apr. 8, 1951; (parents Am. citizens); s. Joel and Merle Anne (Sloan) B.; m. Elaine Marie Larotonda, Sept. 27, 1980 (div. Sept. 1987); children: Erik Joel, Cara Michelle; m. Yvonne Robina Farrell, Jan. 17, 1988 (div. 1993); 1 child, Nathaniel James. BS magna cum laude, U. Md., 1977. Investigative reporter Columnist Jack Anderson, Washington, 1977-78; freelance writer Washington and L.A., 1978-82; mgr. corp. communications Playboy Enterprises, Inc., L.A., 1982; exec. dir. Redondo Beach (Calif.) C. of C., 1982-85; dir. pub. rels. The Blaine Group, L.A., 1985-86; account supr. Rowland Co., L.A., 1986-89; sr. v.p., dir. Crisis Communications Group & Mature Mktg. Group, Ruder Finn, Ruder Finn, L.A., 1989—; speaker U.S. League of Savings Instns., Ft. Myers, Fla., 1990, Nat. Assn. Home Builders, San Diego, 1990. Contbr. articles to profl. jours. Sgt. U.S. Army, 1972-77. Recipient Sage award Maturity Market Perspectives Mag., 1991, media award, 1992. Mem. Nat. Assn. for Sr. Living Industries (bd. dirs., nat. and regional pub. rels. chmn. 1989—, speaker 1990, 91, 92, 93, Disting. Svc. award 1990). Jewish. Office: Ruder Finn 16027 Ventura Blvd Ste 500 Encino CA 91436-2798

BERNSTEIN, SOL, cardiologist, medical services administrator; b. West New York, N.J., Feb. 3, 1927; s. Morris Irving and Rose (Leibowitz) B.; m. Suzi Maris Sommer, Sept. 15, 1963; 1 son, Paul. A.B. in Bacteriology, U. Southern Calif., 1952, M.D., 1956. Diplomate Am. Bd. Internal Medicine. Intern Los Angeles County Hosp., 1956-57, resident, 1957-60; practice medicine specializing in cardiology L.A., 1960—; staff physician dept. medicine Los Angeles County Hosp. U. So. Calif. Med. Center, L.A., 1960—, chief cardiology clinics, 1964, asst. dir. dept. medicine, 1965-72; chief profl. services Gen. Hosp., 1972-74; med. dir. Los Angeles County-U So. Calif. Med. Center, L.A., 1974—; med. dir. central region Los Angeles County, 1974-78; dir. Dept. Health Services, Los Angeles County, 1978; assoc. dean Sch. Medicine, U. So. Calif., L.A., 1986—, assoc. prof., 1968—; cons. Crippled Childrens Svc. Calif., 1965—. Contbr. articles on cardiac surgery, cardiology, diabetes and health care planning to med. jours. Served with AUS, 1946-47, 52-53. Fellow A.C.P., Am. Coll. Cardiology; mem. Am. Acad. Phys. Execs., Am. Fedn. Clin. Research, N.Y. Acad. Sci., Los Angeles, Am. heart assns., Los Angeles Soc. Internal Medicine, Los Angeles Acad. Medicine, Sigma Xi, Phi Beta Phi, Phi Eta Sigma, Alpha Omega Alpha. Home: 4966 Ambrose Ave Los Angeles CA 90027-1756 Office: 1200 N State St Los Angeles CA 90033-4525

BERNSTEIN, SUSAN LISA, corporate trainer, product specialist; b. New Hyde Park, N.Y., Oct. 20, 1965; d. Michael Harold and Judith (Sackser) B. BS in Mktg. and Econs., U. Ariz., 1987; MBA, U. Calif., Berkeley, 1992; hon. degree in Chinese studies, Chinese U. Hong Kong, 1989. Real estate analyst Drachman Inst., Tucson, 1986-87; mktg. cons. Founders Bank Ariz., Scottsdale, 1987-88; postgrad. U. Calif., Berkeley, 1992—; student advisor Inst. Internat. Edn., Wanchai, Hong Kong, 1989; corp. trainer Time Systems, Inc., Phoenix, 1989-92; coord. young entrepreneur program U. Calif., Berkeley, 1992—; owner workshop co. Study Buddy, Scottsdale, 1989-92. Author: Study Buddy, 1988; editor trade publ. Training Times; contbr. articles to newspapers. Mem. Taipei and Chengdu coms. Phoenix Sister Cities, 1989—; advisor Shapiro B'nai B'rith Girls, Scottsdale, 1989—. Rotary internat. grad. scholar Chines U. Hong Kong, 1988-89. Mem. Am. Soc. Tng. and Devel., Pacific Rim (adv. com.). Republican. Jewish. Home: 1771 Highland Pl # 2 Berkeley CA 94709 Office: Intel Corp Santa Clara CA

BERON, ALBERTO, mathematics educator, consultant, lecturer; b. Barranco, Lima, Peru, Nov. 26, 1940; came to U.S., 1962; s. Volf and Rosa (Ulfe) B.; m. Rachel K. Leggett, Dec. 19, 1981; children: Karina, Kristina. AA, L.A. City Coll., 1965; BS, Calif. State U., 1968; MA, Calif. State U., L.A., 1971. Math. specialist L.A. City Schs., 1968-71; prof. math. Moorpark (Calif.) Coll., 1971—; lectr. Calif. State U., Northridge, 1980—. Author: Mathematics Explained, 1980. Mem. Nat. Coun. Tchrs. Math., Calif. Math. Coun. Office: Moorpark Coll 7075 Campus Rd Moorpark CA 93021-1600

BERRIER, DAVID JEWELL, aerospace executive; b. Murphysboro, Ill., Mar. 20, 1934; s. Jewell Hilbourne and Thelma Irene (Walker) B.; m. Mary Rose Butcher, Dec. 26, 1954; children: James, Michael, Daniel. BSEE, U. Ill., 1957. Elec. project engr. GE, Ontario, Calif., 1960-65; engring. specialist McDonnell-Douglas Corp., Long Beach, Calif., 1965-67; test project engr. TRW Systems, Redondo Beach, Calif., 1967-70; program mgr. Hughes Aircraft Co., Fullerton, Calif., 1970-79; systems dir. Aerospace Corp., El Segundo, Calif., 1979—. Elder, Christian Ch., Upland, Calif., 1964-65, Huntington Beach, 1987-90. Lt. USN, 1957-63. Mem. AIAA, IEEE, Tech. Mktg. Soc. Am., Nat. Security Indsl. Assn. Republican. Home: 7071 Valentine Dr Huntington Beach CA 92647-3556

BERRY, CHARLES EUGENE (CHUCK BERRY), state legislator; b. Pitts., Kans., July 1, 1950; s. Paul A. and Margaret F. (Fortune) B.; m. Maria Garcia, June 18, 1988; children: Anne, Martha, James. BA magna cum laude, U. Colo., 1972, JD, 1975. Bar: Colo., 1975. Dep. dist. atty. 4th Judicial Dist. Colo., 1975-77; asst. county atty. El Paso County, Colo., 1978-80, county atty., 1981-84; mem. Colo. Ho. Reps., 1985—, asst. majority leader, 1986-90, speaker of house, 1991—; mem. tax. policy study com. 1985-86, legis. coun., 1987-90, joint review com. on econ. devel., 1988, commn. on uniform state laws, commn. on bicentennial of U.S. constitution; chair interim com. on criminal justice, 1989. Chmn., vice chmn., treas. El Paso County Young Reps.; chmn. 21st Dist. Rep. Ctrl. Com. Mem. Colo. Bar Assn., El Paso County Bar Assn. (treas. 1979), Colo. County Attys. Assn. (exec. com. 1981-83, treas. 1982-83), El Paso County Men's Club. Republican. Roman Catholic. Home: 314 Pine Ave Colorado Springs CO 80906 Office: Colo Gen Assembly 200 E Colfax Ave Denver CO 80203-1792

BERRY, CHARLES RICHARD, lawyer; b. Louisville, Apr. 19, 1948; s. Charles Russell and Lillie Juanita (Crady) B.; m. Joan Phyllis Rosenberg, Aug. 29, 1970; children: Kevin Charles, Ryan Andrew. BA, Northwestern U., 1970, JD, 1973. Bar: Ariz. 1973, U.S. Dist. Ct. Ariz. 1973, U.S. Ct. Appeals (9th cir.) 1983. Assoc. Snell & Wilmer, Phoenix, 1973-77; ptnr. Tilker, Burke & Berry, Scottsdale, Ariz., 1978-80, Norton, Berry, French & Perkins, P.C. and predecessor firm Norton, Burke, Berry & French, P.C., Phoenix, 1980-86; dir. Fennemore Craig, Phoenix, 1986-90; ptnr. Titus, Brueckner & Berry, Scottsdale, 1991. Mem. Unitarian Ch. Lodge: Rotary. Home: 6148 E Mountain View Rd Scottsdale AZ 85253-1807 Office: Titus Brueckner & Berry 7373 N Scottsdale Rd Ste B252 Scottsdale AZ 85253-3550

BERRY, DEBORAH, graphic designer, illustrator; b. Kentfield, Calif., Oct. 28, 1961; d. Derek and Indrid Gail (Ancevich) Cunninghame-Blank; m. Roy A. Berry, III, June 30, 1990; 1 child, Calvin. BA in Communications, Calif. State U., Chico, 1985. Freelance designer and illustrator, 1977, San Rafael, Calif., 1982-87; graphic designer Impulse mag., Chico, 1984, 88—; illustrator, design intern Chico News and Rev., 1984; graphic designer and illustrator Armstrong Image Group, Santa Rosa, Calif., 1985-88; graphic designer Anderson & Lembke, San Francisco, 1989-90; graphic designer/illustrator Michael Osborne Design, San Francisco, 1990; pres. Deborah Berry Design, San Francisco, 1991—. Vol. Marin Gen. Hosp., Kentfield, Calif., 1978. Recipient numerous awards in field including Gold award Crown Zellerbach Paper Co./Best Stationery Design, 1990, cert. of Design Excellence, Print Mag., 1987, 89, 90, 91, SADIE award for Best in Show, 1989, award of Merit for Illustration in Advt., The Sonoma County Ad Club, 1989, 91; finalist MAME Grand Award, 1987; First Pl. Illustration award; art scholar Fidelity Savs. and Loan, 1980, Achievement award Soc. Western Artists for Outstanding Graphic Design, 1980, others; label design selected for book on label designs, 1991,92, corporate identity selected for book of award-winning bus. systems, 1992, corp. capabilities brochure selected for publ. in Comm. Arts mag. illustration ann., 1993. Mem. Art Dirs. and Artists Club, San Francisco Art Dirs. Club. Republican. Episcopalian.

BERRY, EDWIN X., physicist; b. San Francisco, June 20, 1935; s. Edwin Flower and Frances Alice (Foley) B.; m. Carole Dianne Wallace, Sept. 4, 1957 (div. 1972); children: Kim Andrew, Jay Scott, Ingrid Minette. BSEE, Calif. Inst. Tech., 1957; MA in Physics, Dartmouth Coll., 1960; PhD in Physics, U. Nev., 1965. Rsch. assoc. Desert Rsch. Inst., Reno, Nev., 1965-72; program mgr. NSF, Washington, 1972-74, Burlingame, Calif., 1974-76; pres. Atmospheric Rsch. & Tech., Inc., Sacramento, 1976-86, Edwin X. Berry & Assocs., Sacramento, 1987—; cons. Naval Weapons Ctr., China Lake, Calif. 1965-72, Zond Systems, Tehachapi, Calif., 1981—, Calif. Energy Comn., 1979-84, Westinghouse, 1988—. Contbr. articles to profl. publs.; patentee in field. Mem. Am. Meteorol. Soc., Am. Wind Energy Assn., Am. Assn. for the Advancement Sci., Am. Geophys. Union.l. Republican. Office: Edwin X Berry & Assoc 6040 Verner Ave Sacramento CA 95841-2032

BERRY, JANICE RAE, printing company executive; b. Baker, Oreg., Dec. 6, 1937; d. Frank James and Lilly Fae (Kennedy) Colton; m. Larry Joe Berry, Aug. 25, 1956; children: Frank Joseph, Nancy Rae Clark, Ellen Marie McCowan, Jeffrey Allen. Typist Times Litho, Forest Grove, Oreg., 1970-72, prodn. coordinator, 1973-74, prodn. mgr., 1975-81, plant mgr., 1982-85, mfg. mgr., 1986, v.p. mfg., bd. dirs., 1987—. Mem. Graphic Arts Tech. Found. (cert.). Republican. Roman Catholic. Club: Portland Lithographers and Printing House Craftsmen. Office: Times Litho 1829 Pacific Ave Forest Grove OR 97116-2333

BERRY, JOHN CHARLES, clinical psychologist, educational administrator; b. Modesto, Calif., Nov. 29, 1938; s. John Wesley and Dorothy Evelyn (Harris) B.; A.B., Stanford, 1960; postgrad. Trinity Coll., Dublin, Ireland, 1960-61; Ph.D., Columbia, 1967; m. Arlene Ellen Sossin, Oct. 7, 1978; children—Elise, John Jordan, Kaitlyn. Research assoc. Judge Baker Guidance Center, Boston, 1965-66; psychology asso. Napa State Hosp., Imola, Calif., 1966-67, staff psychologist, 1967-75, program asst., 1975-76; program dir. Met. State Hosp., Norwalk, Calif., 1976-77; asst. supt. Empire Union Sch. Dist., Modesto, Calif., 1977—. Mem. Am. Psychol. Assn., Assn. Calif. Sch. Adminstrs., Sigma Xi. Contbg. author: Life History Research in Psychopathology, 1970. Home: 920 Eastridge Dr Modesto CA 95355-4672 Office: Empire Union Sch Dist 116 N Mcclure Rd Modesto CA 95354-9343

BERRY, PHILLIP SAMUEL, lawyer; b. Berkeley, Calif., Jan. 30, 1937; s. Samuel Harper and Jean Mobley (Kramer) B.; m. Michele Ann Perrault, Jan. 16, 1982; children: David, Douglas, Dylan, Shane, Matthew. AB, Stanford U., 1958, LLB, 1961. Bar: Calif. 1962. Ptnr., Berry, Davis & McInerney, Oakland, Calif., 1968-76; owner Berry & Berry, Oakland, 1976—, pres., 1977—. Mem. adv. com. coll. natural resources U. Calif., Berkeley; mem. Calif. State Bd. Forestry, 1974-86, vice-chmn., 1976-86; trustee So. Calif. Ctr. for Law in Pub. Interest, 1970-87, Sierra Club Legal Def. Fund, 1971-90, Pub. Advs., 1971-86, chmn. bd., 1980-82. Served with AUS, 1961-67. Mem. ABA, Calif. State Bar Assn., Sierra Club (nat. pres. 1969-71, 91-92, v.p. conservation law 1971—, v.p. polit. affairs 1983-85, John Muir award), Am. Alpine Club. Office: Berry & Berry 1300 Clay St 9th Flr Oakland CA 94612-1425

BERRY, ROBERT WORTH, lawyer, educator, retired army officer; b. Ryderwood, Wash., Mar. 2, 1926; s. John Franklin and Anita Louise (Worth) B. B.A. in Polit. Sci., Wash. State U., 1950; J.D., Harvard U., 1955; M.A., John Jay Coll. Criminal Justice, 1981. Bar: D.C. 1956, U.S. Ct. Mil. Appeals 1957, Pa. 1961, U.S. Supreme Ct. 1961, Calif. 1967, U.S. Ct. Claims 1975. Research assoc. Harvard U., 1955-56; atty. Office Gen. Counsel U.S. Dept. Def., Washington, 1956-60; staff counsel Philco Ford Co., Phila., 1960-63; dir. Washington office Litton Industries, 1967-71; gen. counsel U.S. Dept. Army, Washington, 1971-74, civilian aide to sec. army, 1975-77; col. U.S. Army, 1978-87; prof., head dept. law U.S. Mil. Acad., West Point, N.Y., 1978-86; retired brigadier gen. U.S. Mil. Acad., 1987; mil. asst. to asst. sec. of army, Manpower and Res. Affairs Dept. of Army, 1986-87; asst. gen. counsel pub. affairs Litton Industries, Beverly Hills, Calif., 1963-67; chair Coun. of Def. Space Industries Assns., 1968; resident ptnr. Quarles and Brady, Washington, 1974-78; dir., corp. sec., treas., gen. counsel G.A. Wright, Inc., Denver, 1987-92, dir., 1987—; pvt. practice law Fort Bragg, Calif., 1993—. Served with U.S. Army, 1944-46, 51-53, Korea. Decorated Bronze Star, Legion of Merit, Disting. Service Medal; recipient Disting. Civilian Service medal U.S. Dept. Army, 1973, 74, Outstanding Civilian Service medal, 1977. Mem. Fed. Bar Assn., Army-Navy Club, Army-Navy Country Club, Phi Beta Kappa, Phi Kappa Phi, Sigma Delta Chi, Lambda Chi Alpha. Methodist.

BERRY, THOMAS CLAYTON, marketing professional, consultant; b. Roswell, N.Mex., May 23, 1948; s. Homer C. and Betty J. (Cronic) B.; m. Bonnie L. Shamas, May 30, 1969; children: Lisa C., Joshua E. AA, N.Mex. Mil. Inst., 1969; Assoc. course in real estate, 1984, NASD DPP rep. and prin. courses, 1983. Farmer Berry Farms, Dexter, N.Mex., 1969-72; sec., dir. Victor & Assoc., Phoenix, 1972-74; dir., foreman Berry Land & Cattle, Dexter, 1974-82; v.p., dir. Trinity Investment Corp., Roswell, 1982-83; pres., dir. Jordache Investments, Roswell, 1982-83; v.p., dir. Diamond Braich Realtors, Roswell, 1982-83; v.p., dir. Tierra Fin. Group, Roswell, 1985-86, pres., dir., 1986-88; v.p., dir. Tierra Capital Corp., Roswell, 1984-86, pres., dir., 1986-88; pres., dir. Tierra Energy Corp., Roswell, 1987-88; pres. Petroleum Mktg. Cons., Roswell, 1989—. Chmn. bd. dirs. Christian Profl. Counseling Svcs., Inc., 1992—; deacon North Phoenix Bapt. Ch., 1973-74; bd. dirs. First Assembly of God Ch., Roswell, youth group sponsor, 1978-86; coach Roswell Youth Soccer, 1978-80. Named one of Outstanding Men of Am., 1982. Mem. Nat. Assn. Securities Dealers, Roswell Realtor Assn., N.Mex. Realtor Assn. Republican. Mem. Christ's Ch. Home and Office: Petroleum Mktg Cons Inc 2010 Brazos St Roswell NM 88201

BERRYESSA, RICHARD GREAVES, cardiovascular perfusion educator; b. Ogden, Utah, Feb. 9, 1947; s. Max Joseph and Janet Marion (Greaves) B.; m. Susan Reeder, Aug. 9, 1969; children: Shannon, Adrien, Lauren. Student, Brigham Young U., 1966, 70, U. Utah, 1971; BS, U. Tex., Houston, 1986. Surg. asst. Western Cardiovascular Assocs., Salt Lake City, 1973-74; chief perfusionist Western Cardiovascular Assocs., 1980-83; perfusionist Rumel Chest Clinic, 1974-79; assoc. dir. clin. perfusion tech. Tex. Heart Inst., Houston, 1983-84; regional mgr. PSICOR, Inc., San Diego, 1984-88; cons. continuing edn. PSICOR, Inc., 1988-90; examiner Am. Bd. Cardiovascular Perfusion, 1978-86; clin. instr. Sch. Medicine, U. Colo., Denver, 1986-88; instr. perfusion tech. prog. Grossmont Coll., San Diego, 1988; presenter in field. Manuscript editor Jour. Extracorporeal Tech., 1980-88; contbr. articles to profl. jours.; patentee in field. Fellow Am. Soc. Extracorporeal Tech.; mem. Am. Acad. Cardiovascular Perfusion. Mormon. Office: PSICOR Inc 16818 Via Del Campo Ct San Diego CA 92127-1799

BERRYHILL, STUART RANDALL, chemistry educator; b. Barnesville, Ohio, Sept. 13, 1951; s. Henry Lee and Louise Randall (Russell) B.; m. Lily Anne Lim, May 21, 1988; children: Heather Courtney Lim, Hayley Elizabeth Lim. BA in Chemistry, Williams Coll., 1973; PhD in Chemistry, U. Calif., Berkeley, 1978. Postdoctoral assoc. Brandeis U., Waltham, Mass., 1977-79; assoc. prof. chemistry U. des Scis. et Techniques du Languedoc, Montpellier, France, 1986-87; asst. prof. Calif. State U., Long Beach, 1979-83, assoc. prof., 1983-90; prof., 1990—; cons. Hewlett-Packard, Palo Alto, Calif., 1981-84. Contbr. articles to profl. jours. Rsch. Corp. grantee Atlantic Richfield Found., 1984. Mem. Am. Chem. Soc. (sec. So. Calif. sect. 1991—), Sierra Club, Phi Beta Kappa. Office: Calif State U 1250 N Bellflower Blvd Long Beach CA 90840-0001

BERRYMAN, DONALD CARROLL, cattle rancher; b. Cedarvale, N.Mex., Aug. 28, 1934; s. Benjamin Carroll and Jodie Lou (Harrel) B.; m. Sharron Lou Luster, May 31, 1968; children: Penny Jo, Robert Todd. Student, Portales U., 1952-54. Reg. bull producer. Co-owner, operator Berryman Ranch, Cebolla, N.Mex., 1954-56, owner, operator, 1960—; bd. dirs. Sunwest Bank, Espanola, N.Mex., Fed. Land Bank Assn. Alberquerque, 1967-85. Bd. dirs. Soil Conservation Agy., Chama, N.Mex., 1969-88. With U.S. Army, 1957-59. Recipient Excellence in Grazing award Soc. Range Mgmt., 1978. Republican. Office: Berryman Angus Ranch PO Box 188 Cebolla NM 87518

BERT, NORMAN ALLEN, educator, playwright; b. Upland, Calif., June 6, 1942; s. Eldon Franklin and Harriet (Bohen) B.; m. Barbara Ann Bayles, Aug. 15, 1964 (div. 1989); children: Tabitha Ann, Jeremy Bayles; m. Debbie DeAnne Enstrom, Sept. 1, 1990. BA, Upland Coll., 1964; BD, Assoc. Mennonite Sems., 1967; MA, Kans. State U., Manhattan, 1972; PhD, Ind. U., 1975. Pastor Nappanee (Ind.) Brethren in Christ, 1967-68; dep. headmaster Choma (Zambia) Secondary Sch., 1969-70; prof. of theatre Messiah Coll., Grantham, Pa., 1975-81; prof. of theatre Ea. Mont. Coll., Billings, 1981—, chair comm. art dept., 1991—; founder, editor Mont. Theatre Connection, Billings, 1983-89; playwriting chair Am. Coll. Theatre Festival, Region VII, Colo., Idaho, Mont., Utah and Wyo., 1984-87; mem. grants panel Idaho Commn. on Arts, Boise, 1986, 88, Mont. Arts Coun., Helena, 1990. Editor, author: (anthology) One-Act Plays for Acting Students, 1987, Theatre Alive!, 1991; editor: (with Deb Bert) Play It Again, 1993; editor: The Scene Book for Actors, 1990; playwright: Cowboy Serenade, 1989, The Montana Times, 1989, Dr. Dixie Duzzett's Delight, 1990. Recipient 1st prize Peace Play Competition, 1982, Faculty Achievement award for rsch. and creative endeavor Ea. Mont. Coll., 1992; fellow Pa. Coun. on Arts, 1979-80. Mem. Assn. for Theatre in Higher Edn., Mont. State Theatre Assn. (sec. 1987-89), Rocky Mountain Theatre Assn., Dramatists Guild (assoc.), AAUP. Democrat. Mem. Soc. of Friends. Home: 2936 Millice Ave Billings MT 59102-6642 Office: Ea Mont Coll 1500 N 30th St Billings MT 59101-0298

BERTAIN, G(EORGE) JOSEPH, JR., lawyer; b. Scotia, Calif., Mar. 9, 1929; s. George Joseph and Ellen Veronica (Canty) B.; m. Bernardine Joy Galli, May 11, 1957; 1 child, Joseph F. AB, St. Mary's Coll. Calif., 1951; JD, Cath. U. Am., 1955. Bar: Calif. 1957. Assoc. Hon. Joseph L. Alioto, San Francisco, 1955-57, 59-65; asst. U.S. Atty. No. Dist. Calif., 1957-59; pvt. practice of law San Francisco, 1966—. Editor-in-Chief, Law Rev. Cath. U. Am. (vol. 5), 1954-55. Mem. bd. regents St. Mary's Coll. Calif., 1980—; chmn. San Francisco Lawyers Com. for Ronald Reagan, 1966-78, San Francisco lawyers com. for elections of Gov./U.S. Pres. Ronald Reagan, 1966, 70, 80, 84; spl. confidential advisor to Gov. Reagan on jud. selection, San Francisco, 1967-74; chmn. San Francisco Lawyers for Better Govt., 1978—; confidential advisor to Senator Hayakawa on judicial selection, 1981-82, to Gov. Deukmejian, 1983-90, to Gov. Wilson, 1991-92. Recipient De La Salle medal St. Mary's Coll. Calif., 1951, Signum Fidei award, 1976. Mem. ABA, Calif. Bar Assn., Fed. Bar Assn. (del. to 9th cir. jud. conf. 1967-76), Am. Judicature Soc., St. Thomas More Soc. San Francisco, U.S. Supreme Ct. Hist. Soc., Assn. Former U.S. Attys and Asst. U.S. Attys. No. Calif. (past pres.), Commonwealth Club, Comml. Club, Wester Assn., Knights of Malta, KC. Republican. Roman Catholic. Office: One Maritime Pla Ste 1600 San Francisco CA 94111

BERTALAN, FRANK JOSEPH, retired academic administrator; b. Edwardsville, Ill., Sept. 18, 1914; s. Frank Joseph and Ida (Barthi) B.; m. Helen G. Scheck, Apr. 6, 1942; children: Edward, Mary, Patricia, Frank, Elaine, John, Joan. BEd, Ill. State U., 1938; BS in Libr. Sci., U. Ill., 1939, MS, 1945; PhD, Cath. U. Am., 1962. Head reference and bibliog. svcs. U.S. Office Edn. Libr., Washington, 1946-50; chief libr. svcs. div. Legis. LIbr. Svc. Libr. of Congress, Washington, 1950-55; head engring. info. br. Navy Bur. Aeros., Washington, 1955-58; exec. asst. for sci. info. Office Naval Rsch., Washington, 1958-62; chief emergency measures div. Office Emergency Planning Exec. Office of Pres., Washington, 1963-65; dir. U. Okla. Sch. Libr. Sci., Norman, 1965-74; dir. Sch. Libr. Sci. Tex. Women's U., Denton, 1974-80; ret., 1980; cons. Goddard Space Flight Ctr. Libr., NASA Hdqrs. Libr., comdt. USCG, U.S. Senate Fin. Com.; spl. rep. U.S. Book Exch., 1962-65. Author: Books for Junior Colleges, 1954, Provision of Federal Benefits for Veterans, 1955, Proposed Scope and Coverage of the Goddard Space Flight Center Library, 1963, The Junior College Library Collection, 1968, rev. 1970. Comdr. USNR, 1942-46, ETO. Mem. ALA (nat. chmn. libr. orgn. and mgmt. sect. 1968—), Assn. Am. Libr. Schs. (chmn. recruiting and pers. com. 1967—), Spl. Librs. Assn., Okla. Libr. Assn., Kappa Delta Pi, Kappa Mu Epsilon, Kappa Phi Kappa. Home: 12022 Ave Sivrita San Diego CA 92128

BERTEA, HYLA HOLMES, real estate investor; b. L.A., June 14, 1940; d. George Dawson Holmes and Beth (Bay) Maher; m. Richard Bertea, Mar. 15, 1964; children: Baret Bertea Walker, Alex, Blake, Bay. BS, U. So. Calif., 1962. Tchr. L.A. City Schs., 1962-65; realtor Dalebout Assn., Newport Beach, Calif., 1988-90, Grubb & Ellis, Newport Beach, 1990—; bd. dirs. Pacific Enterprises, L.A.; founding presiding ptnr. Women's Investments,. Co-commr. gymnastics L.A. Olympic Organizing Com., 1981-84; bd. dirs., co-chair U. So. Calif. Planning and Devel., Orange County. Recipient City of L.A. Commendation award U.S. Olympics, 1984. Republican. Presbyterian.

BERTERO, VITELMO VICTORIO, civil engineer. With U. Calif., Berkeley, 1959—; prof. civil engring. U. Calif., Berkeley, dir. Earthquake Engrng. Rsch. Ctr., 1988-90; cons. earthquake engring., Berkeley. Named ENR Man of Yr., 1990; recipient T. R. Higgins Lectureship Award, Am. Inst. Steel Constrn., 1990, Berkeley citation U. Calif., Berkeley, 1991, Nova award Cons. Innovation Forum, 1992. Fellow ASCE, Am. Concrete Inst. Office: U Calif EERC 1301 S 46th St Richmond CA 94804

BERTHELSDORF, SIEGFRIED, psychiatrist; b. Shannon County, Mo., June 16, 1911; s. Richard and Amalia (Morschenko) von Berthelsdorf; m. Mildred Friederich, May 13, 1945; children: Richard, Victor, Dianne. BA, U. Oreg., 1934, MA, MD, 1939. Lic. psychiatrist, psychoanalyst. Intern U.S. Marine Hosp., Staten Island, N.Y., 1939-40; psychiat. intern Bellevue Hosp., N.Y.C., 1940-41; psychiat. resident N.Y. State Psychiat. Hosp., N.Y.C., 1941-42; research assoc. Columbia U. Coll. Physicians and Surgeons, N.Y.C., 1942-43; asst. physician Presbyn. Hosp. and Vanderbilt Clinic, N.Y.C., 1942-51; supervising psychiatrist Manhattan (N.Y.) State Hosp., 1946-50; asst. adolescent psychiatrist Mt. Zion Hosp., N.Y.C., 1950-52; psychiat. cons. MacLaren Sch. for Boys, Woodburn, Oreg., 1952-84, Portland (Oreg.) Pub. Schs., 1952-67; clin. prof. U. Oreg. Health Scis. Ctr., 1956—'; tng. and supervising analyst Seattle Psychoanalytic Inst., 1970—. Author: Treatment of Drug Addiction in Psychoanalytic Study of the Child, Vol. 31, 1976, Ambivalence Towards Women in Chinese Characters and Its Implication for Feminism, American Imago, 1988, (with others) Psychiatrists Look at Aging, 1992. Bd. dirs., v.p. Portland Opera Assn., 1960-64, Portland Musical Theatre, 1987—; bd. dirs., pres. Portland Chamber Orch., 1964-70, 92—. Maj. USAF, 1943-46. Recipient Henry Waldo Coe award U. Oreg. Med. Sch., Portland, 1939, citation Parry Ctr. for Children, Portland, 1970. Fellow Am. Psychiat. Assn. (life), Am. Geriatrics Soc. (founding fellow); mem. Am. Psychoanalytic Assn. (life), Portland Psychiatrists in Pvt. Practice (charter, pres. 1958), Mental Health Assn. (bd. dirs., chmn. med. adv. com. 1952-60), Multnomah County Med. Soc. (pres.'s citation 1979), Oreg. Psychoanalytic Found. (founding mem.), Am. Rhododendron Soc. (bd. dirs., v.p. Portland chpt. 1956—, Bronze medal and citation 1974), Am. Rhododendron Species Found. (bd. dirs. 1960—), Phi Beta Kappa, Sigma Xi, Phi Sigma. Home and Office: 1125 SW St Clair Ave Portland OR 97205-1127

BERTINO, FRANK CHRISTEN, superintendent of schools; b. Culbertson, Mont., June 11, 1938; s. Frank Louis and Belvina (Williamson) B.; m. Memory Lee Robertson, Feb. 16, 1963; children: Shawna Estill, Lani Bertino. BS in Secondary Edn., Mont. State U., 1961, postgrad., 1976-84; ME in Sch. Adminstrn., U. Mont., 1965. Cert. tchr., Idaho; cert. adminstr. Band dir. Hinsdale (Mont.) Pub. Schs., 1961-62, Medicine Lake (Mont.) Pub. Schs., 1962-63; prin. Arlee (Mont.) Elem. Schs., 1963-67, Belgrade (Mont.) Elem. Schs., 1967-69; supt. Harrison (Mont.) Pub. Schs., 1969-72, Heart Butte (Mont.) Sch. Dist. #1, 1972-76; grad. asst. Mont. State U., Bozeman, 1976-78; asst. supt. Wallace (Idaho) Sch. Dist. #393, 1978-79, supt., 1979—; adj. instr. Lewis and Clark Coll., Lewiston, Idaho, 1962-84. Author poetry; contbr. articles to profl. jours. Chief organizer Heart Butte TV Translator Project, 1973; comptroller Water Users Assn., Heart Butte, 1974; mem. consol. task force State Dept. Edn., Boise, Idaho, 1988; mem. county census com., Wallace, 1982. Mem. Am. Assn. Sch. Adminstrs., Idaho Sch. Supts. Assn. (region I pres. 1983-85, bd. dirs. 1983-85), Phi Delta Kappa, Rotary (pres. 1985-88), Elks. Home: Box 768 Osburn ID 83849 Office: Wallace Sch Dist #393 401 River St Wallace ID 83873-2260

BERTOLAMI, CHARLES NICHOLAS, oral surgeon; b. Lorain, Ohio, Dec. 31, 1949; s. Salvatore Charles and Michela (Orlando) B.; m. Linda Silva, June 27, 1977; children: Michela, Joseph. AA, Lorain Community Coll., 1969; DDS, Ohio State U., 1974; DMedSci, Harvard U., 1979. Diplomate Am. Bd. Oral and Maxillofacial Surgery. Chief resident Mass. Gen. Hosp., Boston, 1979-80, asst. oral surgeon, 1983; asst. prof. U. Conn., 1980-83; asst. prof. Harvard Sch. Dental Medicine, Boston, 1983-89; assoc. prof. UCLA, 1989-90, prof. 1990—; chief dental svc. UCLA Med. Ctr., 1990—; chmn. sect. oral & maxillofacial surgery UCLA Sch. Dentistry, 1989—. Mem. editorial bd. Jour. Periodontal Research, 1985-87; mem. med. adv. bd. Ehlers-Danlos Nat. Found., mem. spol. grants review subcom.; chmn. Nat. Inst. Dental Rsch., 1990-91. Rsch. editor Jour. of Oral and Maxillofacial Surgery; contbr. articles to profl. jours. Recipient Callahan Meml. award Ohio Dental Assn., 1974, Fellow Am. Cancer Soc., 1984—, Am. Assn. Oral and Maxillofacial Surgery, 1975; grantee USPHS, 1983—. Fellow Am. Assn. Oral and Maxillofacial Surgeons (exec. com. 1983-84); mem. ADA, Internat. Assn. Dental Research (program chmn. 1984-85). Roman Catholic. Office: U of California Dept Oral Surgery 10833 LeConte Ave CHS 53-076 Los Angeles CA 90024

BERTONE, C. M. (BERT BERTONE), management consultant; b. Jersey City, July 12, 1930; s. Anthony Dominic and Dellora (Silvestri) B.; m. Stacey Ann Mueller, July 24, 1976; children: Kathleen, Victoria, Jenifer, Dana, Christopher, Amanda. BS, Seton Hall U., 1955; PhD, L.A. U., North Hollywood, Calif., 1972. Sr. social scientist The Rand Corp., Santa Monica, Calif., 1955-60; rsch. psychologist FAA, Pomona, N.J., 1960-62; sr. human factors engr. Lockheed Missile & Space Co., Sunnyvale, Calif., 1962-64; sr. scientist Bunker Ramo Corp., Canoga Park, Calif., 1964-72; pres. Bertone & Assocs., Calabasas, Calif., 1972-76; chief human factors engr. Sikorsky Aircraft, Stratford, Conn., 1976-86; mem. tech. staff McDonnell Douglas Helicopter Co., Mesa, Ariz., 1986-90; pres. The Phoenix Cons. Group, Fountain Hills, Ariz., 1990—; presenter 45 profl. meetings. Author: Soviet Psychology, 1968; contbr. 50 articles to profl. jours. Trustee Fountain Hills (Ariz.) Unified Rd. Dist., 1987-90. 1st sgt. USNG, 1947-57. Mem. Am. Assn. Profl. Hypnotists. Home: 15326 E Thistle Dr Fountain Hills AZ 85268

BERTRAM, EDWARD ARTHUR, mathematics educator, researcher; b. L.A., Dec. 9, 1939; s. Benjamin and Eleanor Julia (Cole) B.; m. Alice Lorena James, Oct. 4, 1961; children: Aaron, Miriam, Daniel, Benjamin. BA, UCLA, 1962, MA, 1964, PhD, 1968. Sr. statistician UCLA, 1967-68; from asst. to assoc. prof. math U. Hawaii-Manoa, Honolulu, 1968-92, prof., 1992—; statistics cons. Warner Bros., L.A., 1975-76, Altman & Vanairsdale, Honolulu, 1982, Dinman, Nakamura, Elisha et. al., 1988-89, 92—, Fujiyama, Duffy and Fujiyama, 1990. Contbr. articles to internat. math. jours. Bd. dirs. Hawaii Youth Symphony, Honolulu, 1979-82, Regency Park, Honolulu, 1988—. Mem. Am. Math. Soc., Math. Assn. Am. Office: U Hawaii-Manoa 2565 The Mall Math Dept Keller Hall Honolulu HI 96822

BERTRAM, JACK RENARD, infosystems specialist; b. Lincoln, Nebr., Nov. 20, 1943; s. John Lewis and Emma Louise (Doerr) B.; m. Ingrid Frieda Reschke, Feb. 14, 1975; children: Deborah Geniene, Kenneth Brian. BS, Stanford U., 1966, MA, 1971; MS, Santa Clara U., 1988; cert. mgr., James Madison U., 1988. Scientific programming specialist Lockheed Missles & Space Co., Sunnyvale, Calif., 1980-92; pres. HansaTech Internat., Redwood City, Calif., 1993—. Mem. AIAA, ACLU, IEEE Computer Soc., Am. Assn. for Artificial Intelligence, Am. Astronautical Soc., Assn.f or Computing Machinery, People for the Am. Way, Computer Profls. for Social Responsibility. Democrat. Home: 1580 Alameda De Las Pulgas Redwood City CA 94061-2404 Office: HansaTech Internat PO Box 554 Redwood City CA 94064-0554

BERTRAND, RALPH LEWIS, biology educator; b. Reno, Nev., Jan. 16, 1955; s. Leroy Joseph and Lydia (Garcia) B.; m. Dianne Marie Free, Aug. 20, 1977; children: Jacob Joseph, Zachary Lewis, Daniel Sage. BS in Biology, U. Nev., 1978, MS in Biology, 1982; PhD in Botany, U. Calif., 1987. Lectr. in biology U. Nev., Reno, 1982; rsch. asst. U. Calif., Riverside, 1982-87; rsch. assoc. U. Calif., Berkeley, 1987-91; asst. prof. Colo. Coll., Colorado Springs, 1991—; cons. Future Products Devel. Corp., Reno, 1978-80; plant physiologist Hesse Products Co., Reno, 1980-82. Author: (with others) A Laboratory Guide to Cell and Molecular Biology, 1991; contbr. articles to profl. jours. Coun. mem. Mount Diablo Sch. Dist., Concord, Calif., 1990-91; rep. Ednl. Adv. Com., Riverside, 1987-88. Recipient Postdoctoral Svc. award NIH, 1988, Pres. Postdoctoral fellowship U. Calif., 1988-91; scholar Nat. Hispanic Scholarship Found., 1986-87. Mem. Am. Bot. Soc., Soc. for Advancement of Chicanos and Native Ams. in Sci., Colo.-Wyo. Acad. Sci., Sigma Xi. Democrat. Office: Dept Biology Colo Coll 1040 N Nevada St Colorado Springs CO 80903

BERTSCH, HANS, marine biology educator; b. St. Louis, Nov. 2, 1944; s. Hugh Cecil and Olga Mary (Wolverson) B. BA, San Luis Rey (Calif.) Coll., 1967; BTh, Franciscan Sch. Theology, 1971; PhD, U. Calif., Berkeley, 1976. Asst. prof. Chaminade U., Honolulu, 1976-78; chmn., curator San Diego Natural History Mus., 1978-80; prof., investigator Ciencias Marinas Inst. Investigaciones Oceanologicas, U. Auto. Baja Calif., Ensenada, Mex., 1981-83; faculty Nat. U., San Diego and Irvine, 1983-93; assoc. prof., chair dept. math. and natural scis. Nat. U., San Diego, 1993—; rsch. assoc. Calif. Acad. Scis., San Francisco, 1972—, Natural History Mus., L.A., 1977—. Author: Hawaiian Nudibranchs, 1981; contbr. articles to profl. jours. Rsch. grants NSF, STRI, Ctr. for Field Rsch., CAS, others, 1974—. Mem. West Soc. of Malacologists (pres. 1988-89, editor ann. report 1986—), Calif. Malacolozool. Soc. (editorial bd. 1977—), Asociacion de Investigadores del Mar de Cortes, Profl. Assn. of Diving Instrs. Office: 4075 Camino del Rio South San Diego CA 92108

BERUEFY, ROBERT RYAN, retired chemist; b. Fort Worth, Tex., Mar. 16, 1914; s. Max and Wilhelmine (Goerte) B.; m. Edna Margaret Nelson, Feb. 21, 1948. BA, U. Colo., 1940; MA, Colo. Coll., 1944; PhD in Chemistry, St. Thomas U., 1948; PhD in Physiology, U. Nebr., 1956. Chemist U.S. Bur. of Stds., Washington, 1944-45, U.S. Dept. of Interior, Ketchikan, Alaska, 1945-47; head dept. chemistry Hartwick Coll., Oneanta, N.Y., 1949-52; prof. chemistry Omaha U., 1952-56; scientific dir. Lanpar Pharms., Dallas, 1956-57; pres. Bioassay Lab., Dallas and Seattle, 1957-87;

cons. Swedish Hosp., Seattle, 1967-72; assoc. Nat. Rsch. Coun., Washington, 1956—; Patentee in field. Fulbright prof., 1952. Mem. Phi Beta Kappa. Presbyterian. Home: 4861 Beach Dr Seattle WA 98116

BERZINS, VALDIS ANDRIS, computer science educator, researcher; b. N.Y.C., Mar. 24, 1951; s. Karlis and Lucija (Putnins) B.; m. Luqi Lu; 1 child, Katrina. BS in Physics, MSEE, Elec. Engr. degree, MIT, 1975, PhD in Computer Sci., 1979. Asst. prof. U. Tex., Dallas, 1979-80; asst. prof. U. Minn., Mpls., 1980-86, assoc. prof., 1986-89; assoc. prof. Naval Postgrad. Sch., Monterey, Calif., 1986-92, prof., 1992—; lab. asst. MIT, Cambridge, Mass., 1971-72, NSF fellow, 1972-75, rsch. asst., 1975-79; cons. Honeywell Corp., Mpls., 1984-86, Internat. Software Systems, Inc., Austin, Tex., 1988—; rsch. advisor NRC, Washington, 1990—; program evaluator Computer Sci. Accreditation Bd., N.Y.C., 1987—; reviewer NSF, 1984—, ACTA Informatica, 1986—. Author: Software Engineering with Abstractions, 1990; author specification langs. MSG84, SPEC, 1984, 90; contbr. numerous articles to profl. jours. Rsch. grantee, course devel. Micro Electronics & Info. Sci. Ctr., Mpls., 1981-83; rsch. grantee Micro Electronics & Info. Sci. Ctr., Honeywell, Sperry, Control Data Corp., Mpls., 1984-86, USN direct funding, Monterey, 1987—; travel grantee NSF, 1990—; grantee U.S. Army Rsch. Office, 1991—. Mem. IEEE (referee N.Y. 1978—, mag. ops. com. 1990—), Computer Soc. of IEEE, Assn. Computing Machinery (referee N.Y. 1978—, travel grant Mpls. 1983), Spl. Interest Groups on Software Engring, Design Automation, Documentation, Programming Langs. of Assn. Computing Machinery, Phi Beta Kappa, Sigma Xi. Office: Naval Postgrad Sch Code CS/Be Monterey CA 93943

BESHEARS, JOHN ROBERT, real estate developer; b. Phoenix, Feb. 16, 1959; s. Robert Gene and Doris Marie (Muchmore) B. BSBA, Ariz. State U., 1984, postgrad., 1987. Stockbroker RPR/Merrill Lynch, Phoenix, 1985-89; fin. planner Cigna, Phoenix, 1989-91; dir. investor rels. Stiteler Cos., Phoenix, 1991—. Active Human Rights Task Force, Phoenix, 1991—; event chmn. Compas, Phoenix, 1989—; chmn. Phoenix Young Reps., 1989-90. Mem. Univ. Club (bd. dirs. 1992—). Home: 3319 N 25th St Phoenix AZ 85016 Office: Stiteler Cos 3001 E Camelback Rd # 140 Phoenix AZ 85016

BESHIR, MOHAMMED JOHAR, electrical engineer; b. Asmara, Eritrea, Aug. 5, 1956; came to U.S., 1976; s. Johar and Sofia (Said) B.; m. Asia Mohammed Gidai, July 7, 1989; children: Fuad, Sarah. BAEE, Iowa State U., 1980; MSEE, U. So. Calif., 1982; MBA, Pepperdine U., 1988. Profl. engr., Calif. Elec. engr. Dept. Water & Power, L.A., 1980-83, sr. elec. engr., 1983—; chmn. Western Systems Coord. Coun.-Modeling Work Group, Salt Lake City, 1987—; advisor Electric Power Rsch. Inst. Palo Alto, Calif., 1989—. Contbr. articles to profl. jours. Bd. dirs. African Community Refugee Ctr., L.A., 1991-92. Mem. IEEE, L.A. Coun. Black Profl. Engrs., Amnesty Internat. Office: Dept Water & Power 111 N Hope St Rm 1129E Los Angeles CA 90012

BESHUR, JACQUELINE ELIZABETH, editor, periodical; b. Portland, Oreg., May 8, 1948; d. Charles Daniel and Mildred (Domreis) Beshears. BA, UCLA, 1970; MBA, Claremont Grad. Sch., 1980; postgrad., City U., Seattle, 1989-90. Dir. L.A. Ctr. for Photographic Studies, 1972-75; precious gem distbr. Douglas Group Holdings, Australia, 1976-78; small bus. owner Janitorial/Home Maintenance, Seattle, 1981-89. Author: Good Intentions Are Not Good Enough, 1992. Dir. County Citizens Against Incineration, Preston, Wash., 1987-92, Citizens for the Protection of Ames Lake, Redmond, Wash., 1989-92. Mem. Wash. Pot-bellied Pig Assn. (sec. 1992), Nature Conservancy, Wash. Wilderness Coaliton, Sierra Club, L.A. Ctr. for Photographic Studies. Republican. Fundamentalist. Office: Mr Pigs BeSure Tng PO Box 225 Carnation WA 98014

BESNETTE, FRANCIS HENRY (FRANK BESNETTE), state official, educator; b. N.Y.C., Jan. 6, 1939; s. Ulys Antoine and Evelyn Marie (Coullier) B.; m. Linda Sue Curton, Mar. 16, 1962; children: Carrie Anna, David Keith. BBA, Tex. Western Coll., 1962; MBA, Denver U., 1963; PhD in Bus. Adminstrn., Ariz. State U., 1970. Instr. bus. S.E. Mo. State Coll., Cape Girardeau, 1963-65; asst. prof. bus. No. Ariz. U., Flagstaff, 1967-69, assoc. dean, assoc. prof., 1969-73, prof., dean Coll. Bus. Adminstrn., 1973-80, v.p. adminstrn. and fin., 1980-88, exec. v.p., 1988-91; exec. dir. Ariz. Bd. Regents, Phoenix, 1992—; intern Office of Senator John McCain U.S. Senate, Washington, 1989. Contbr. articles to profl. jours. Bd. dirs. Flagstaff Health Mgmt. Corp., 1972-88; trustee Mus. No. Ariz., Flagstaff, 1984-89; founding dir. Flagstaff Leadership Program, 1990. Named Citizen of Yr. Ariz. Daily Sun, 1980. Mem. Flagstaff C. of C. (bd. dirs.). Republican. Methodist. Office: Ariz Bd Regents Ste 230 2020 N Central Ave Phoenix AZ 85004

BESS, HENRY DAVID, dean; b. New Haven, Conn., Apr. 15, 1939; s. Henry Alver and Ina Ozeal (Green) B.; m. Linda Lois Lyday, June 17, 1967; children: Tammy Loika, Cindy Loika. BS, U.S. Merchant Marine Acad., 1961; MBA, UCLA, 1964, PhD, 1967. Asst. prof., asst. dean of students U. Hawaii, Honolulu, 1967-70, assoc. prof., asst. dean of students, 1970-73, prof., assoc. dean coll. bus. adminstrn., 1974-80, prof., dean coll. bus. adminstrn., 1980—; vis. assoc. prof. U.S. Merchant Marine Acad., Kings Point, N.Y., 1973-74; vis. faculty Oreg. State U., 1992-93' vis. scholar UCLA, 1974; 2d officer Hawaiian Tug and Barge Co., Honolulu, 1961-63; bd. dirs. Pioneer Fed. Savs. Bank, Honolulu. Author: Marine Transportation, 1976, (with others) U.S. Maritime Policy: History and Prospects, 1981; contbr. articles to profl. jours. Bd. dirs. Hawaii Coun. Econ. Edn., Honolulu, 1982-89, Boy Scouts Am., Honolulu, 1984—, Japan-Am. Inst. Mgmt. Sci., Honolulu, 1988—, ARC, Honolulu, 1989—; trustee Grad. Mgmt. Admission Coun., 1992—. Lt. (j.g.) USN, 1961-68. Mem. C. of C. Hawaii, Hawaii Soc. Corp. Planners (bd. dirs. 1984-90), Am. Econ. Assn. (transp. and pub. utilities group), Rotary, Beta Gamma Sigma. Office: U Hawaii Coll Bus Adminstrn 2404 Maile Way Honolulu HI 96822-2282

BESSAC, FRANK BAGNALL, anthropology educator; b. Lodi, Calif., Jan. 13, 1922; s. Harry William and Nell (Hurd) B.; m. Susanne Leppmann, Sept. 9, 1951; children: Barbara Tracey, Andrea Maxeiner, Turan Albini, Joan Steelquist, Bret. BA in History, Coll. Pacific, 1946; postgrad., Fujen U., China, 1947-48; MA in Anthropology, U. Calif., Berkeley, 1957; PhD in Anthropology, U. Wis., 1963. Intelligence officer Office Strategic Svcs., Kunming, Beijing, China, 1945-47; exec. officer Paot'ou br. office, China Relief Mission Dept. State, 1948; dir. Mongol Project Econ. Cooperation Adminstrn., China, 1948; instr., asst. prof. Lawrence U., Appleton, Wis., 1959-65; assoc. prof. anthropology U. Mont., Missoula, 1965-69, prof., 1970—, prof. emeritus, 1989—, chair dept. anthropology, 1978-85; vis. lectr. U. Tex., Austin, 1958-59; adv. Asian Studies program U. Mont., 1974—, liberal arts degree program, 1980—; resource person Missoula County Schs., 1975-76; cons. various exhibits, gallery visual arts U. Mont., 1976, 77, 78; mem. Gov.'s Adv. Com. Forest Resources, 1981-84; mem. steering com. Mont. chpt. U.S.-Tibetan Resettlement Program, 1991—, Mont. Kazakh Exch. Program, 1991—; mem. various coms. U. Mont., 1967—; presenter state, nat., internat. confs. Author: (with Marshall, Marfvac, and Fuguitt) Population Estimates for Wisconsin Counties, 1957, (with others) The Archaeologist at Work, 1959, Culture Types of Northern and Western China, 1963, Peoples of Inner Asia, 1963; contbr. entry to Encyclopedia Britannica, 1974; contbr. articles to profl. jours. Judge behavioral and social scis. Sci. Fair, Mont., 1979-89. Sgt. U.S. Army, 1943-46. Recipient Rsch. award Agrl. Devel. Coun., 1964-65; Fulbright Student scholar, 1949-50, Ford grantee, 1955-56, Spl. Rsch. grantee NIMH, 1968-69. Fellow Am. Anthrop. Assn.; mem. Am. Ethnol. Soc., Ass. Asian Studies, N.W. Anthrop. Soc., Mont. Acad. Scis. (v.p., chair social scis. sect. 1967-68, bd. dirs. 1973-76) Mongolian Soc., Current Anthropology (assoc.),.

BESSE, ROBERT GALE, food technologist; b. Calgary, Alta., Can., Feb. 11, 1923 (parents Am. citizens); s. Rene A. and Doria (Bray) B.; student N.Mex. State Tchrs. Coll., 1941-42; B.S., Oreg. State Coll., 1948; m. Mary A. McKay, Sept. 11, 1948; children—Rene A., Madeleine E., Leon J., Alan G., Michele M., Marc P., Angelique C. Supt., also in quality control Alderman Farms Frozen Foods, Dayton, Oreg., 1948-50, plant supt., 1950-54; chief food technologist Kuner Empson Co., Brighton, Colo., 1954-60; food technologist Northwest Packing Co., Portland, Oreg., 1960-62; food technologist research and devel. Nat. Can Corp., San Francisco, 1962-67, mgr. Pacific Area tech. research service, 1967-70; mgr. tech. services Western Can Co., 1970-86 ; customer tech. services Continental Can Co., 1986-88; cons. to food and can industries, RGB Cons., 1988—; dir. Material Metrics. Pres. St. Gregory's Theatre Guild; vol. hunting safety instr. Calif. Fish and Game Dept., 1972—. Served with Signal Corps, AUS, 1942-45. Mem. Soc. Plastic Engrs., Pacific Fish Tech. (pres.), Inst. Food Technologists (emeritus, sec.-treas. Rocky Mountain sect.; exec. com. Oreg. sect.), Confraternity of Christian Doctrine Cath. (pres.), N.W. Canners and Packers, Packaging Inst. (profl. mem.), Nat. Canners Assn. (mem. Western lab. adv. com.), No. Calif. Metal Decorating Assn. (pres.), Western Packaging Assn.; Soc. Mfg. Engrs. Club: Elks. Home and Office: 264 Portola Dr San Mateo CA 94403-2327

BESSER, LES, electrical engineer; b. Budapest, Hungary, Aug. 27, 1936; came to U.S., 1956; s. Laszlo and Anna (Valkar) B.; m. Susan Wessrl; children: George, Nancy. BEE, U. Colo., 1966; MEE, Santa Clara U., 1973; PhD in Elec. Engring., Tech. U., Budapest, 1981. Project engr. Hewlett Packard, Palo Alto, Calif., 1966-70; engring. mgr. Fairchild Microwave, Palo Alto, 1970-72, Farinon Electric, San Carlos, Calif., 1972-76; pres. Compact Engring., Los Altos, Calif., 1976-80; sr. v.p., COO Comsat Gen., Palo Alto, 1980-85; pres. BAI, Los Altos, 1985—. Co-author: Analysis and Design of Circuits, 1988; author: (computer program) Compact, 1972; contbr. articles to profl. jours.; patentee in field. Recipient Application award IEEE Microwave Theory and Techniques Group, 1983, Carrier award IEEE Radio Frequencies Techniques Group, 1987. Fellow IEEE (chpt. chmn. 1973-74). Home: 1109 Russell Ave Los Altos CA 94024 Office: BAI 4600 El Camino Real Los Altos CA 94022

BEST, BARBARA, personal manager; b. San Diego, Dec. 2, 1921; d. Charles Lewis and Leila Harrison (Sanders) B. BA in Journalism, U. So. Calif., Los Angeles, 1943. Unit publicist 20th Century Fox Co., Los Angeles, 1943-50; reporter San Diego Jour., 1950; asst. to publicity dir. Stanley Kramer Co., Los Angeles, 1950-53; 0wner, mgr. Barbara Best & Assocs., Los Angeles, 1953-66; ptnr. Freeman and Best Pub. Rels., Los Angeles, 1967-75; owner, pres. Barbara Best, Inc., Pub. Relations, Los Angeles, 1975-87; personal mgr. Barbara Best Mgmt., Los Angeles, 1987--; exec. v.p. Maribar Prodns., Hollywood, Calif., 1986--. Co-founder, exec. dir. Vikki Carr Scholarship Found., Hollywood, 1971-82; pres. Publicists Fed. Credit Union, Hollywood, 1976-85. Mem. Hollywood Womens Press Club (past pres., bd. dirs.), Women in Film. Democrat. Episcopalian. Office: Barbara Best Mgmt 14159 Riverside Dr Sherman Oaks CA 91423-2362

BEST, GARY THORMAN, real estate broker; b. San Diego, Mar. 11, 1944; s. Roland Elmer and Mildred Mae (Thorman) B.; m. Hollyce Susan Hill, Feb. 22, 1967 (div. Mar. 1973); 1 child, Melissa Anne; m. Georgia Anne Flaherty, May 22, 1973; children: Roland Bryant, Heather Anne. AAS, Pima Community Coll., 1979. Cert. comml. investment mem. Sales Mohawk Data Scis. Corp, Tulsa, 1968-69; exec. v.p. Mid-Am. Mgmt. Corp., Tulsa, 1969-73; real estate sales Cragin Lang Free and Smythe, Cleve., 1973-74; land sales Coldwell Banker Comml., Tucson, 1975-80; mgr. sales Coldwell Banker Comml., Cin., Ohio, 1981; resident mgr. Coldwell Banker Comml., Nashville, 1982-83; investment sales Coldwell Banker Comml., Tucson, 1984-85; v.p. Del E. Webb Realty and Mgmt. Co., Tucson, 1986-87; pres. Best Comml. Real Estate, Tucson, 1987-93; sec./treas. Best Asset Mgmt. Svcs., Phoenix, 1993—; regional pres., regional 1st v.p. Comml. Investment Real Estate Inst., 1992-94; pres. So. Ariz. chpt. CCIM, Tucson, 1990; mem. New Am. Network, Tucson, 1987-93, mem. adv. bd., 1992-93. Mem. fin. com. Symington for Gov., Tucson, 1990, Kolbe for Congress, Tucson, 1988; adv. bd. Goodwill Industries of Tucson, Tucson Unified Sch. Dist. Recipient Pres. of Yr. award Civitan Internat., Ariz. dist., Tucson, 1979. Mem. Tucson Bd. Realtors (bd. dirs. 1988-91, v.p. 1992), Ariz. Assn. Realtors (bd. dirs. 1989-91, 92-94, exec. com. 1992), Tucson Econ. Devel. Corp. (bd. dirs., chmn. 1990), Greater Tucson Econ. Coun. (bd. dirs., exec. com. 1990-93), Tucson Met. C. of C. (bd. dirs., chmn. 1993-94, Small Bus. Leader of Yr. award 1989, chmn. 1993—), Breakfast Club, Rotary. Republican. Office: Best Asset Mgmt Svcs Inc 2633 E Indian Sch Ste 403 Phoenix AZ 85016 also: Best Comml Real Estate Inc 6339 E Speedway Blvd Ste 200 Tucson AZ 85710-1147

BEST, ROBERTA LOUISE, export company executive; b. Mpls., Apr. 8, 1941; d. Irving Wolfe and Beatrice Theresa (Marcus) Lichterman; m. Charles Patrick Best, Sept. 25, 1963 (div. Nov. 1966); 1 child, Bennett Thomas; m. Masaharu Ichino, May 29, 1977. AA, L.A. City Coll., 1962; paralegal cert., UCLA, 1974, postgrad. Internat. Bus., 1986—. Exec. legal sec. Litton Industries, Inc., Beverly Hills, Calif., 1967-73; life underwriter Conn. Mut. Life Ins. Co., L.A., 1976-80, Mut. Benefit Life Ins. Co., L.A., 1977-91; chief exec. officer Romac Export Mgmt. Corp., L.A., 1978—; owner, mgr. Canyon Gallery Two, L.A., 1978-82. Mem. steering com. Beverly Hills Dem. Club, 1972; bd. dirs. West Adams Heritage Assn., L.A., 1985, Ctr. for Creative Change, Newberry Park, Calif., 1987—; pres. West Adams Heights Neighborhood Assn., 1986—; apptd. adv. coun. Calif. Assembly Select Com. Small Bus., 1990, adv. bd. U.S. SBA Calif. Small Bus. Devel. Coun. for Export, 1991, U.S. Dept. Commerce So. Calif. Dist. Export Coun., 1992-96; mem. Nat. Women's Polit. Caucus. Named One of 100 largest Woman-owned bus. in L.A. City and County, 1990, 91, 92,93, Regional Exporter of Yr., SBA, 1990. Mem. Profl. Referral Orgn. (pres. 1980-81), Export Mgrs. Assn., Greater L.A. Trade Ctr. Assn., Nat. Assn. Women Bus. Owners, League of Women Voters, NOW, L.A. C. of C., Nat. Assn. Life Underwriters (women's leaders roundtable 1978), L.A. Natural History Mus., L.A. County Mus. Art (patron), Nat. Trust for Hist. Preservation, Huntington Libr., Rodale Inst., The Archaeol. Conservancy, Tree People, World Wildlife Fund, The Nature Conservancy, Greenpeace, Amnesty Internat., Alpha Pi Epsilon. Home and Office: Romac Export Mgmt Corp 2242 S Hobart Blvd Los Angeles CA 90018-2149

BEST, ROGER NORMAN, real estate investment manager; b. L.A., Apr. 16, 1949; s. Norman Frank and Muriel Noreen (Atkinson) B.; m. Sheri Lyn Kruyer, Oct. 16, 1982. BA, U. Wash., 1971. Lic. Real Estate Broker, Calif., 1985. Musician, entertainer, 1963-69; pres. Best Enterprises, L.A., 1969—; head electronic media svcs. Cedars-Sinai Med. Ctr., L.A., 1971-73; pres. Tazio Prodns., L.A., 1973-76; v.p. Video Disco & Assocs., L.A., 1975-76, DSL Constrn. Corp., L.A., 1977-85; v.p., chief operating officer Scott Properties, Inc., L.A., 1978-85; pres., chief exec. Tazio Properties, Inc., L.A., 1980—. Inventor correctable typewriter ribbon; creator original music videos concept with Visual Music, 1974; featured columnist Apt. Age Mag., L.A., 1989—. Mem. Van Nuys Airport Adv. Coun., 1987—. Citation of Appreciation, City of L.A., 1988, 89. Office: Tazio Properties, Inc. 3580 Wilshire Blvd 17th Fl Los Angeles CA 90010-2501

BETANCOURT, HECTOR MAINHARD, psychology scientist, educator; b. Chile, Sept. 1, 1949; came to U.S. 1979; s. Hector and Eleonora (Mainhard) B.; m. Bernardita Sahli; children: Paul, Daniel. BA, Cath. U., Santiago, Chile, 1976; MA, UCLA, 1981, PhD in Psychology, 1983. From asst. prof. to assoc. prof. psychology Cath. U., Santiago, Chile, 1977-79, 83-85; assoc. prof. psychology Loma Linda U., Riverside, Calif., 1985-91; prof. psychology, 1991-93; chmn., dept. psychology Loma Linda (Calif.) U., 1990-93, chmn. and coord. of Doctoral Programs in Psychology, 1993—. Editor Interam. Psychologist, 1962-86; mem. editorial bd. Jour. Community Psychology, 1986-89, Spanish Jour. Social Psychology, 1986—; contbr. articles to profl. jours. Recipient Rotary Found. award for Internat. Understanding, Rotary Internat., 1976-77; Fulbright fellow, UCLA, 1979-80. Mem. APA, Internat. Soc. Polit. Psychology, Internat. Soc. Cross-Cultural Psychology (exec. com. 1984-86), Interam. Soc. Psychology (sec. gen. 1983-87), Am. Psychol. Soc., Soc. for Psychol. Study Social Issues, Soc. Personality and Social Psychology. Office: Loma Linda U Grad Sch Loma Linda CA 92350

BETHUNE, ZINA, actress, dancer, singer, choreographer; b. N.Y., Feb. 17, 1950; d. William Charles and Ivy (Vigder) B.; m. Sean Feeley, Dec. 27, 1975. Grad. high sch., N.Y.C. Artistic dir., choreographer, performer Bethune Theatredanse, L.A., 1980—. Actress TV soap opera The Guiding Light, 1956, TV series The Nurses, 1964-67, film Who's That Knocking at My Door, 1969, Nutcracker: Money, Madness, Murder, 1987; dancer Broadway show Most Happy Fella, Nutcracker, N.Y.C., 1957, N.Y.C. Ballet, 1965-69, Royal Danish Symphony, Arhus, Denmark, 1979; singer, actress (stage) Carnival, Chgo., 1967; dancer, singer (stage) Sweet Charity, 1969-70; choreographer (stage) The Trials of Saint Joan, 1986, Mind's Eye-Year 2031, 1988; dance, choreograher (stage, video) The Rose, 1987; dirs., choreographer (video) Cradle of Fire, 1988; head sound technician, assoc. prodr. Paradigm Film, N.Y.C.; spl. invitation to teach and perform by the govt. of China; spl. invitation to dance at the White House, 1989; starring role (Broadway show) Grand Hotel-The Musical, 1991. Dance tchr. for disabled children Dance Outreach, L.A., 1983—. Recipient 2 citation awards Mayor of N.Y.C., 1965-69, 2 proclamation awards and an award from Mayor of L.A., 1985-89, Cece Robinson's Humanitarian award L.A., 1986, Community Svc. award Gov.'s Com. for Employment of Handicapped, Media Access award. Mem. SAG, AFTRA, Actors Equity Assn. Democrat. Office: Bethune Theatredanse 8033 W Sunset Blvd Ste 221 Los Angeles CA 90046-2427

BETTER, WILLIAM JOEL, utilities executive; b. Phoenix, Jan. 24, 1951; s. Julius Frank and Eleanor M. (Morgan) B.; m. Dona Bascom, Mar. 30, 1972; children: Rhonda, Jason Andrew, Joseph Earl, Elizabeth, Matthew John, Rebecca Anne. AA, Victor Valley Coll., 1971. Cert. pub. utilities operation and mgmt. Dist. storekeeper Contel Calif., Ridgecrest, 1973-74; employment ctr. rep. Contel Calif., 1974-75; state supply mgr. Contel NW, Silverton, Oreg., 1975-78; div. supply coord. Contel of the West, Phoenix, 1978-81; state supply mgr. Contel of the West, Lakeside, Ariz., 1981-83; engr. Contel of the West, Homedale, Idaho, 1983-84; material svcs. mgr. Citizens Utilities Co., Kingman, Ariz., 1984—. Cubmaster Boy Scouts Am., Show Low, Ariz., 1981-83, dist. scout leader., trainer, Caldwell, Idaho, 1983-84, fundraiser, Kingman, 1984—. Mem. Purchasing Mgmt. Assn. Ariz., Nat. Assn. Purchasing Mgmt., Ariz. Altos Users Group, Nat. Eagle Scout Assn. Home: 1420 Eastern St Kingman AZ 86401-5210 Office: Citizens Utilities Co 2202 Stockton Hill Rd Kingman AZ 86401-4663

BETTINGER, JAMES RICHARD, journalist; b. Oakland, Calif., May 4, 1947; s. Richard Vissing and Miriam Alice (Glines) B.; m. Katherine Pfister, June 16, 1968 (div. 1972); m. Dorothy Dean Lasater, Nov. 18, 1973; 1 child, Joshua Caleb. BA, U. Calif., Santa Barbara, 1969. Reporter, editorial writer, city editor Riverside (Calif.) Press-Ent., 1969-84; night city editor, city editor San Jose Mercury News, 1984-89; dep. dir. John S. Knight Fellowships for Profl. Journalists, Stanford, Calif., 1989—; lectr. Stanford U., 1991—; columnist San Jose Mercury News, 1990—; chmn. bd. Stanford Daily, 1990—. Stanford U. profl. journalism fellow, 1982-83. Home: 766 Garland Dr Palo Alto CA 94303 Office: Knight Fellowships Dept Comm Stanford CA 94305-2050

BETTIOL, MARIE E., school principal; b. Red Wing, Minn., Oct. 5, 1943; d. Harlan Edward and Ervila M. (Nelson) Sumner; m. Paul Bettiol, July 1, 1985. BS, St. Cloud U., 1964, MS, 1968; PhD, U. Wash., 1974; postdoctoral studies, U. Oreg., Portland State U. Tchr. Pub. Schs. of Minn. and Mont., 1964-71; teaching asst. U. Wash., Seattle, 1971-74; curriculum cons. Clackamas ESD, Marylhurst, Oreg., 1974-76; dir. West Linn (Oreg.) Sch.Dist., 1976-81; elem. prin. Springfield (Oreg.) Pub. Schs., 1981-84, Sch. Dist. 40, McMinnville, Oreg., 1984-91. Mem. Soroptimist (bd. dirs. 1987-89). Home: 137 NE 122d St Newport OR 97365

BETTIS, DENISE REED, sculptor, illustrator; b. Murfreesboro, Tenn., Dec. 16, 1955; d. Keith Kenyon and Lester Faye (Todd) Reed; m. David Earl Myers, Apr. 19, 1975 (dec. Mar. 1978); m. John Gregory Bettis, May 11, 1979. Student, Mid. Tenn. State U., 1973-75, 77-78, UCLA, 1981-82, Venice Sculpture Studio, 1983-85, Brucchion Sch. of Art, Culver City, Calif., 1987-90. Artist-in-residence Reed Studio and Gallery, Venice, Calif., 1990—; cons. Sweet Harmony Music, Sunset Beach, Calif., 1978-83, Bettis Paradise Music, Sunset Beach, 1978-85, John Bettis Music, L.A., 1983—, John Bettis Property Mgmt., L.A., 1986—. Sculptures, illustrations, home landscapings and pencil drawings exhibited in Calif., 1985—. Fundraiser Children's Hosp./Santa Monica Bay Aux., 1991, Nat. Acad. Songwriters, 1985, SEA Environ. Assn., Bonaventure Hotel, L.A., 1990, 91; mem. L.A. com. P.E.T.A. People for the Ethical Treatment of Animals, 1992. Office: Reed Studio and Gallery 1423 Abbot Kinney Blvd Venice CA 90291

BETTIS, JOHN GREGORY, songwriter; b. Long Beach, Calif., Oct. 24, 1946; s. Wayne Douglas and Nellie Jane (House) B.; m. Denise Reed, May 11, 1979. Songwriter, pub. Sperririo: Chappell Music, Beverly Hills, Calif., 1976-82, John Bettis Music, Santa Monica, Calif., 1982—. Composer: (songs) Yesterday Once More, 1973 (Gold Record), Top of the World, 1974 (Gold Record), Heartland, Can You Stop the Rain, 1991, (Grammy nominee 1991), Promise Me You'll Remember, 1990 (acad. awards nominee 1991), One Moment In Time, 1988 (Emmie 1989), Crazy for You, 1985 (Gold Record 1985), Slow Hand, 1981 (Gold Record 1985), Human Nature, 1983 (Grammy cert.-Album of Yr. 1984); composer songs for movies including Say Anything, Star Trek V, Cocktail, Nothing in Common, Godfather Part III; composer TV theme songs. Recipient Top TV Series award for Growing Pains, ASCAP, 1986, for Just the Ten of Us, ASCAP, 1987, for Empty Nest, ASCAP, 1990, 24 Gold Records, Recording Industry Assn. Am., 1970-90, 7 Platinum Records, Recording Industry Assn. Am., 1970-90, 30 Performance awards ASCAP, 1970-90. Mem. ASCAP (bd. of review 1982—), Nat. Acad. Songwriters (bd. dirs. 1980—, chmn. bd. dirs. 1983-85). Office: John Bettis Music PO Box 668 Sunset Beach CA 90742-0668

BETTISON, CYNTHIA ANN, museum director, archaeologist; b. St. Louis, Sept. 8, 1958; d. William Leslie and Barbara Ann (Yunker) B. BA in Anthropology and Biology, Pitzer Coll., 1980; MA in Anthropology, Eastern N.Mex. Univ., 1983; PhD in Anthropology, U. Calif., Santa Barbara, 1993. Asst. curator, Dept. Anthropology Univ. Calif., Santa Barbara, 1988-89, curator, Dept. Anthropology, 1990-91; dir. Western N.Mex. Univ. Mus., Silver City, N.Mex., 1991—; co-dir. Sta. WNMU Archaeol. Field Sch., 1992, 93; lectr. Western N.Mex. Univ., 1992—; assoc. Anthropology Univ. Calif., 1987-88, computer lab asst. dept. sociology, 1987-91, rsch. asst., 1988, statis. cons., 1987-88; various archaeol. positions, 1981—. Contbr. articles to profl. jours. Recipient Gila Nat. Forest grantee, 1992, 93, Mimbres Region Art Coun. Mini grantee, 1992, Silver City Lodger's Tax Bd. grantee, Andrew Isabell Meml. Fund grantee Dept. Anthropology Univ. Calif., 1990. Mem. Am. Assn. Mus., Am. Anthropological Assn., Am. Soc. Conservation Archaeol. N.Mex. Mus. Assn., Archaeol. Soc. N.Mex., N.Mex. Archaeol. Coun. (sec. 1993-94), Coun. Mus. Anthropology (sec. 1992-94), Mountain Plains Mus. Assn., Grant County Archaeol. Soc., Univ. Women's Club, Univ. Club, Optimist Club (sec. Silver City chpt.), Phi Kappa Phi. Office: Western NM Univ Mus 1000 W Coll Ave Silver City NM 88061

BETTS, BARBARA LANG (MRS. BERT A. BETTS), lawyer, rancher, realtor; b. Anaheim, Calif., Apr. 28, 1926; d. W. Harold and Helen (Thompson) Lang. BA magna cum laude, Stanford U., 1948; LLB, Balboa U., 1951; m. Roby F. Hayes, July 22, 1948 (dec.); children: John Chauncey IV, Frederick Prescott, Roby Francis II; m. Bert A. Betts, July 11, 1962; 1 child, Bruce Harold; stepchildren: Bert Alan, Randy W., Sally Betts Joynt, Terry Betts Marsteller, Linda Betts Hansen, LeAnn Betts Wilson. Bar: Calif. 1952, U.S. Supreme Ct. 1978; pvt. practice law, Oceanside, Calif., 1952-68, San Diego, 1960—, Sacramento, 1962—; ptnr. Roby F. Hayes & Barbara Lang Hayes, 1952-60; city atty., Carlsbad, Calif., 1959-63; v.p. Isle & Oceans Marinas, Inc., 1970-80, W. H. Lang Corp., 1964-69; sec. Internat. Prodn. Assos., 1968—, Margaret M. McCabe, M.D., Inc., 1977-88 . Chmn. Traveler's Aid, 1952-53; pres. Oceanside-Carlsbad Jr. Chambrettes, 1955-56; vice chmn. Carlsbad Planning Commn., 1959; mem. San Diego Planning Congress, 1959; v.p. Oceanside Diamond Jubilee Com., 1958. Candidate Calif. State Legislature, 7th Dist., 1954; mem. Calif. Dem. State Central Com., 1958-66; co-chmn. 28th Congl. Dist., Dem. State Central Com., 1960-62; alt. del. Dem. Nat. Conv., 1960. Named to Fullerton Union High Sch. Wall of Fame, 1986. Mem. Am. Judicature Soc., Nat. Inst. Mcpl. Officers, ABA, Calif. Bar Assn., San Diego County Bar Assn., Oceanside C. of C. (sec. 1957, v.p. 1958, dir. 1953-54, 57-59), AAUW (legis. com. 1958-59; local pres. 1959-60; asst. state legis. chmn. 1958-59), Heritage League (2d div. 8th Air Force), No. San Diego County Assn. Cs. of C. (sec.-treas.), Bus. and Profl. Women's Club (So. dist. legislation chmn. 1958-59), DAR (regent Oceanside chpt. 1960-61), San Diego C. of C., San Diego Hist. Soc., Fullerton Jr. Assistance League, Calif. Scholarship Fedn., Loyola Guild of Jesuit High Sch., Phi Beta Kappa. Clubs: Soroptimist Internat. (pres. Oceanside-Carlsbad 1958-59, sec. pub. affairs San Diego, Imperial Counties 1954; pres. of pres.'s council San Diego and Imperial counties and Mexico 1958-59), Barristers, Stanford (Sacramento), Stanford Mothers, Heritage League (2nd air divsn. USAAF). Author: (with Bert A. Betts) A Citizen Answers. Office: Betts Ranch PO Box 306 Elverta CA 95626-0306 also: 3119-A Howard Ave San Diego CA 92104

BETTS, BARBARA STOKE, artist, educator; b. Arlington, Mass., Apr. 19, 1924; d. Stuart and Barbara Lillian (Johnstone) Stoke; m. James William Betts, July 28, 1951; 1 child, Barbara Susan (dec.). BA, Mt. Holyoke Coll., 1946; MA, Columbia U., 1948. Cert. tchr., N.Y., Calif., Hawaii. Art tchr. Walton (N.Y.) Union Schs., 1947-48, Presidio Hill Sch., San Francisco, 1949-51; free-lance artist San Francisco, 1951; art tchr. Honolulu Acad. Arts, summer 1952, 59, 63, 85, spring 61, 64; libr. aide art rm. Libr. of Hawaii, Honolulu, 1959; art tchr. Hanahauoli Sch., Honolulu, 1961-62, Hawaii State Dept. Edn., Honolulu, 1958-59, 64-84; owner Ho'olaule'a Designs, Honolulu, 1973—. Illustrator: Cathedral Cooks, 1964, In Due Season, 1986; exhibited in Hawaii Pavilion Expo '90, Osaka, Japan, State Found. of Culture and Arts, group shows since 1964. Mem. Hawaii Watercolor Soc. (newsletter editor 1986-90), Nat. League Am. Pen Women (art chmn. 1990-92, sec. 1992—), Honolulu Printmakers (dir. 1986, 87), Assn. Hawaii Artists, Honolulu Printmaking Workshop. Republican. Episcopalian. Home: 1520 Ward Ave # 203 Honolulu HI 96822

BETTS, JAMES WILLIAM, JR., financial analyst, consultant; b. Montclair, N.J., Oct. 11, 1923; s. James William and Cora Anna (Banta) B.; m. Barbara Stoke, July 28, 1951; 1 child, Barbara Susan (dec.). BA, Rutgers U., 1946; MA, U. Hawaii, 1957. With Dun & Bradstreet, Inc., 1946-86, svc. cons., 1963-64, reporting and svc. mgr., 1964-65, sr. fin. analyst, Honolulu, 1965-86; owner, operator Portfolio Cons. of Hawaii, 1979—; cons. Saybrook Point Investments, Old Saybrook, Conn., 1979—. Contbr. articles to mag. Served with AUS, 1942-43. Mem. Am. Econ. Assn., Western Econ. Assn., Atlantic Econ. Soc. Republican. Episcopalian.

BETTY, LEWIS STAFFORD, religious studies educator, writer; b. Mobile, Ala., Dec. 31, 1942; s. Samuel Marks and Margaret Lillian; m. Lynette Anne Doyle, Aug. 15, 1981; children: Samuel DeWestfelt, Sage Campbell, Southey Faye Lewy, Louis Robert, Samuel Stafford. BS in Math. and English, Spring Hill Coll., 1964; MA in English, U. Detroit, 1966; PhD in Theology, Fordham U., 1975. From lectr. to prof. religious studies Calif. State U., Bakersfield, 1972—. Author: (scholarly) Vadiraja's Refutation of Sankara's Non-Dualism, 1978, (novel) The Rich Man, 1984, (adult fables) Sing Like the Whippoorwill, 1987, Sunlit Waters, 1990; contbr. articles to profl. jours. Bd. dirs. Mental Health Assn. Kern County, Bakersfield, 1982-84; chmn. project evaluation com. San Joaquin Valley Air Dist., 1992-93. 1st lt. U.S. Army, 1966-68. Recipient Clean Air award Kern County Lung Assn., 1990. Office: Calif State U Stockdale Hwy Bakersfield CA 93311

BETUNADA, ROSCO JULIO, consulting engineer; b. Buford, Wyo., Mar. 15, 1949; s. Pasquale X. and Miranda (Ruidoso) B.; m. Ruby N. Bulbous, Nov. 4, 1973 (div. Dec. 1974); m. Betty R. Luria, May 22, 1979; children: Rae, Garth. BS in Phys. Sci., Colo. State U., 1977; PhD, Inst. of Metamorphysics, Colchester, Yorkshire, Eng., 1973. Registered engr. in tng., Colo. V.p. sales BBSCO, 1966-68; dep. county assessor County of Gunnison, Colo., 1973-75; field engr. Schlumberger Well Svcs., Grand Junction, Colo., 1977-79; geophys. engr. Bendix Field Engrng., Grand Junction, 1979-86; cons. UNC Geotech, Grand Junction, 1987-90, ret., 1990. Conbr. articles Rocky Mountain Running mag., Rocky Mountain Sports and Fitness mag., 1980-87. Del. Rep. Party, Denver, 1974; v.p. Mesa-Monument (Colo.) Striders, 1982; asst. race dir. Gov.'s Cup 10K, Grand Junction, 1988; capt. Bendix Vol. Fire Team, Grand Junction, 1983-84. Home and Office: 2977 B 3/4 Rd Grand Junction CO 81503-2036

BETZA, BARBARA ANN, marketing executive; b. New Brunswick, N.J., Apr. 15, 1955; d. Frank James and Marjorie Ann (Kane) B. BSc in Pharmacy, Phila. Coll. Pharmacy & Sci., 1978. Registered pharmacist, Calif., Pa., N.J. Sr. staff pharmacist, IV pharmacy supr. Cooper Hosp./ Univ. Med. Ctr., Camden, N.J., 1978-83; profl. hosp. specialist products divsn. Abbott Labs.-Hosp., Abbott Park, Ill., 1983-91; clin. rsch. assoc. med. dept. products divsn. Abbott Labs., Mountain View, Calif., 1991-93; mktg. dir. Optioncare Home IV & Nutritional Svcs., Fairfield, Calif., 1993—; bd. dirs., co-owner Napa-Solano IV Co., Inc. dba: Optioncare Home IV & Nutritional Svcs., Fairfield, Calif., 1990—. Mem. Am. Soc. Hosp. Pharmacy, Calif. Soc. Hosp. Pharmacy, N.J. Soc. Hosp. Pharmacy (edn. coord. 1980-81, nat. del., 1981, 82, v.p. So. chpt. 1981-82, pres. So. chpt. 1982-83). Democrat. Episcopalian. Home: 1748 Gillespie Dr Fairfield CA 94533 Office: 2753 Clay Bank Rd Ste 11 Fairfield CA 94533

BEUMEL, WILFORD J., college president; b. Tell City, Ind., May 1, 1935; s. Wilford Clark and Frona Ann (Patmore) B.; m. Joyce Ann Castle, Jan. 31, 1955; children: Barry Kent, Bradley Clark, Brent Alan. BA, Ind. U., 1957, MA, 1960; EdD, Nova U., 1979; postgrad., Fla. Atlantic U., 1973-75. Mgr. Louden's Supermarket, Bloomington, Ind., 1955-57; coord. distributive edn. Columbus (Ind.) High Sch., 1957-63; dir. mid-mgmt. and summer sessions Manatee Community Coll., Bradenton, Fla., 1963-66; v.p. South Fla. Community Coll., Avon Park, Fla., 1966-87; dean coll. Palo Verde Coll., Blythe, Calif., 1987-88, pres., supt., 1988—; mem. accreditation teams So. Assn. Colls. and Schs., Atlanta, 1980-86, Western Assn. Schs. and Colls., Aptos, Calif., 1988. Mem. Juvenile Justice and Delinquency Prevention Commn., Riverside County, Calif., 1989—, Blythe Delinquency Prevention Network, 1989—; mem. adv. bd. Dean Mus. Decorative Arts, Riverside County, 1990—, Blythe Valley Resource Ctr., 1990—. Mem. Rotary (pres. Avon Park 1982, pres. Blythe 1992), Desert Horsemen's Assn. (pres., bd. dirs.). Home: 10170 N Broadway St Blythe CA 92225-1265 Office: Palo Verde Coll 811 W Chanslorway Blythe CA 92225

BEUS, STANLEY SPENCER, geology educator; b. Salt Lake City, July 31, 1930; s. Rulon Edwin and Hope (Spencer) B.; m. Carma Albrechtsen, Feb. 18, 1953; children: Rebecca, Marcia, Michele, Sterling, Jennifer. Student, Ricks Coll., 1948-50; BS, Utah State U., 1957, MS, 1958; PhD, UCLA, 1963. Geologist-explorer Mobil Oil Co., Alaska, 1958; asst. prof. geology No. Ariz. U., Flagstaff, 1962-65, assoc. prof., 1965-70, prof., 1970—, Regents prof., 1989—; rsch. assoc. Mus. No. Ariz., Flagstaff, 1962—; Regents prof. No. Ariz. U., 1989. Author, co-editor:Grand Canyon Geology; editor: Guidebook to Carboniferous Stratigraphy in the Grand Canyon Country; co-editor Soc. Econ. Paleontologists and Minerologists jour., 1974-80; contbr. articles to profl. jours. Served to sargeant U.S. Army, 1953-55, 1st lt., USAR, 1955-58. Recipient Outstanding Faculty award No. Ariz. U., 1976; Named Outstanding Alumni, Ricks Coll., 1983; Disting. Faculty scholar No. Ariz. U., 1979. Fellow Geol. Soc. Am.; mem. Ariz.-Nev. Acad. Sci., Paleontol. Soc. Republican. Mormon. Home: 3301 Little Dr Flagstaff AZ 86001-8950 Office: No Ariz U Dept Geology Box 4099 Flagstaff AZ 86011

BEUTLER, EARL BRYAN, software company executive; b. Milw., Sept. 4, 1954; s. Ernest and Bonnie (Fleisher) B.; m. Eve Resnik, June 16, 1984; children: Dahvia, Kiptyn, Bryce. BA, U. Calif., San Diego, 1975; MS, U. Calif., San Francisco, 1976. Software mgr. Diversified Electronics/Datatrak, Sunnyvale, Calif., 1976-80; gen. ptnr. Constrn. Computer Consulting, Sunnyvale, Calif., 1980-81; dir. software devel. Trade Svc. Corp., San Diego, 1981-86; pres., CEO Rsch. Info. Systems, Inc., Carlsbad, Calif., 1986—; bd. dirs. Rsch. Info. Systems, Carlsbad, Graph-Pad Software, San Diego; chmn. Scalex Corp., Carlsbad, 1992. Inventor Quick Scaler, 1982; developer (info. svc.) Reference Update, 1988.

BEUTLER, ERNEST, physician, research scientist; b. Berlin, Sept. 30, 1928; came to U.S., 1936, naturalized, 1943; s. Alfred David and Kaethe (Italiener) B.; m. Brondelle Fleisher, June 15, 1950; children: Steven Merrill, Earl Bryan, Bruce Alan, Deborah Ann. Ph.B., U. Chgo., 1946, B.S., 1948, M.D., 1950; PhD (hon.), Tel Aviv U., Israel, 1993. Intern U. Chgo. Clinics, 1950-51; resident in medicine 1951-53; asst. prof. U. Chgo., 1956-59; chmn. div. medicine City of Hope Med. Ctr., L.A., 1959-78; chmn. dept. clin. rsch. Scripps Clinic and Rsch. Found., La Jolla, Calif., 1978-82, chmn. dept. basic and clin. rsch., 1982-89, chmn. dept. molecular and exptl. medicine, 1989—; clin. prof. medicine U. So. Calif., 1964-79, U. Calif., San Diego, 1979—; mem. hematology study sect. NIH, 1970-74, 89—; Spinoza Chair U. Amsterdam, 1991. Author 8 books, numerous articles in med. jours.; mem. editorial bds. profl. jours. Adv. com. Blood Products FDA, 1984-88. Served with U.S. Army, 1953-55. Recipient Gairdner award, 1975, Blundell prize, 1985, Nat. Heart, Lung and Blood Inst. Merit award NIH, 1987, Nat. Acad. Clin. Biochemistry Lectureship award Kodak Instruments, 1990, Mayo Soley award Western Soc. Clin. Investigation, 1992, 5th Ann. Excellence award Gen. Clin. Rsch. Program NIH, 1993. Mem. NAS, Am. Acad. Arts and Scis., Assn. Am. Physicians, Am. Soc. Clin. Investigation, Western Assn. Physicians (pres. 1989), Am. Soc. Hematology (mem. exec. com. 1968-72, v.p. 1977, pres. 1979), Am. Soc. Human Genetics (mem. exec. com. 1968-72). Jewish. Home: 2707 Costebelle Dr La Jolla CA 92037-3518 Office: Scripps Clinic and Rsch Found 10666 N Torrey Pines Rd La Jolla CA 92037-1027

BEUZEKOM, RICHARD A., franchise consulting services executive; b. Balt., June 9, 1940; s. Richard and Jean (Monsma) B.; m. Joanne A. Sikkema, July 7, 1961; children: Tamara Jo, Michael Scott. Student, Calvin Coll., Grand Rapids, Mich., 1958-61. Area mgr. Olivetti Corp. Am., N.Y.C., 1961-73; gen. mgr. Redman Industries, Chandler, Ariz., 1973; western regional mgr. SCM, Phoenix, 1974; pres. Bus. Opportunities of Am., Phoenix, 1974-82, Franchise Brokerage Systems, Phoenix, 1982-85, Franchise Cons. Svcs., Tucson, 1985—. Contbr. articles to profl. jours. Mem. Sunbelt World Trade Assn. (v.p. 1993), Ariz. World Trade Ctr., Ariz. Licensor, Franchisor Assn. (bd. dirs.). Office: Franchise Cons Svcs Ste 302 PO Box 50306 Tucson AZ 85715

BEVERETT, ANDREW JACKSON, marketing executive; b. Midland City, Ala., Feb. 21, 1917; s. Andrew J. and Ella Levonia (Adams) B.; m. Martha Sophia Landgrebe, May 26, 1951; children: Andrew Jackson III, James Edmund, Faye A. BS, Samford U., 1940; MBA, Harvard U., 1942. Various exec. positions in corporate planning and mgmt. United Air Lines, Chgo., 1946-66; dir. aviation econs., sr. mktg. and econ. cons. Mgmt. and Econs. Research, Inc., Palo Alto, Calif., 1966-71; sr. economist Stanford Research Inst., Menlo Park, 1971-72; pres. Edy's on the Peninsula stores, 1973-78; real estate broker, fin. and tax cons., Saratoga and San Jose, Calif., 1979—. Ensign to lt. USNR, 1942-46. Mem. Nat. Assn. Enrolled Agts., Nat. Assn. Realtors, Pi Gamma Mu, Phi Kappa Phi. Home: 6325 Whaley Dr San Jose CA 95135

BEVERLEY, NICK, hockey team executive. Gen. mgr. Los Angeles Kings. Office: Los Angeles Kings 3900 West Manchester Blvd Los Angeles CA 90305

BEVERLY, ALAN CRAIG, landscape contractor, consultant; b. Fort Worth, Mar. 20, 1951; s. Bland Ray and Imogene (Autry) B.; m. Joan Kaplan, Sept. 22, 1984; 1 child, Lindsay Ann. BA, U. Calif., Santa Barbara, 1973; MSc, Calif. Poly., San Luis Obispo, 1979. With Peace Corps., Lesotho; owner Ecoscape Assocs., Santa Cruz, Calif., 1982—. Mem. Am. Soc. Hort. Sci., Pesticide Applicators Profl. Assn., Calif. Agr. Prodn. Cons. Assn., Calif. Landscape Contractors Assn. Home and Office: Ecoscape Assocs 424 National St Santa Cruz CA 95060

BEVERLY, NICK, sports team manager. Gen. mgr. L.A. Kings, 1992—. Office: Los Angeles Kings 3900 W Manchester Blvd Inglewood CA 90306*

BEVERLY, ROBERT GRAHAM, state senator, lawyer; b. Belmont, Mass., July 1, 1925; s. William James and Helen Lucille (Graham) B.; m. Elizabeth Louise Weisel, May 17, 1946; children: Barbara, William, Robert Jr., Brian. Student, UCLA, 1948; LLB, Loyola U., L.A., 1951. Ptnr. Richards, Watson & Gershon, L.A., 1954—; mem. Calif. State Assembly, Sacramento, 1967-76, Calif. Senate, Sacramento, 1976—; city atty. various Calif. cities, 1954-67. Mem. Manhattan Beach (Calif.) City Coun., 1958-67; mem. Manhattan Beach Planning Com., 1956-58; mem. Rep. State Cen. Com., 1967—. Cpl. USMC, 1943-46. Recipient Pub. Svc. award UCLA Alumni Assn., Outstanding Alumnus award Loyola U., L.A., 1990, Esteemed Alumnus award Loyola U. Sch. of Lw, 1974. Mem. Calif. State Bar Assn., L.A. County Bar Assn., So. Bay Bar Assn., Am. Legion. Office: Calif State Senate 1611 S Pacific Coast Hwy Redondo Beach CA 90277

BEVERLY, THERIA M., reading educator; b. Houston, May 20, 1931; d. Luther B. (dec.) and Essie (Coleman) Felder; children: Gayle B. Heiskell, Chester A. III. BA, Clark Atlanta U., Atlanta, 1951; MEd, U. Ariz., 1969; EdD, U. Sarasota (Fla.), 1990. Tchr. Grantville (Ga.) Tng. Sch., 1951-52, Dept. Def., USAFE, Ramstein, Ger., 1958-59, Dept. Army, Okinawa, Japan, 1964-67, Tucson Unified Sch. Dist., 1968-70; prof. reading/writing Cen. Ariz. Coll., Coolidge, 1972-75; lead faculty in reading Pima Community Coll., Tucson, 1975—; adminstrv. intern Pima Coll., 1988, chmn. multi-campus reading, 1989-90, mem. curriculum com., 1990. Contbr. articles to profl. jours. Bd. dirs. coms. Rincon United Ch. of Christ, Tucson, 1989, bd. worship.music, 1992—, bd. Christian edn., 1992—; bd. dirs., parliamentarian Planned Parenthood of So. Ariz.; hon. chmn. Pro Choice Ariz. Mem. Coll. Reading Learning Assn. (chmn. minority affairs 1984-85), Internat. Reading Assn. (internal. coms. bd. 1984-85), Tucson Urban League, NAACP, Heroines of Jericho, Parents without Partners (pres.), Sweet Adelines, Inc., Assn. for Supervision and Curriculum Devel., Coll. Reading and Learning Assn. (bd. dirs.), Phi Delta Kappa (pres., bd. dirs. 1986-90), Phi Theta Kappa (advisor), Alpha Kappa Alpha (v.p.). Home: PO Box 18529 Tucson AZ 85731-8529 Office: Pima Community Coll 1255 N Stone Ave Tucson AZ 85705-7335

BEWLEY, HARRISON JAMES, sales executive; b. St. Paul, May 11, 1957; s. Edward Lawrence Bewley and Dorothy Katherine Weisel Brown; m. Kathleen Ruth Toll, June 11, 1981 (div. 1985). BSEE, U. Iowa, 1981; MS in Nuclear Engrng., U. N.Mex., 1985; postgrad., Colo. State U., 1988-89. Staff engr. Applied Rsch. Assocs., S. Royalton, Vt., 1985-87; sr. engr. Applied Rsch. Assocs., Denver, 1987-89; ptnr. Aztec Ent., Salt Lake City, 1989—; bd. dirs. Aztec Ent., Denver, 1990—; USAF rep. Instrumentation Working Group, Washington, 1983-85. Contbr. articles to profl. jours. Mem. Archtl. Com. Bd., Eagle Ridge Community, Park City, Utah, 1990—; mem. Park City Community Coalition. Capt. USAF, 1981-85. Mem. IEEE, Instrument Soc. Am., Electronic Reps. Assn. Republican. Episcopalian. Home: 7440 Buckboard Dr Park City UT 84060-5366 Office: Aztec Ent 1817 S Main St # 17 Salt Lake City UT 84115-2036

BEYER, LEE LOUIS, public administrator; b. Norfolk, Nebr., June 4, 1948; s. Louis E. and Arlene (Henderson) B.; m. Elizabeth Terry Yates, July 26, 1969; children: Jonathan, Joshua, Megan. BS in Pub. Mgmt., U. Oreg., 1974. Exec. dir. Linn-Benton-Lincoln Manpower Consortium, Corvallis, Oreg., 1974-76; mgmt. analyst Oreg. State Exec. Dept., Salem, 1976-78; ops. mgr. Lane County Employment Tng. Dept., Eugene, Oreg., 1978-80; exec. dir. Eugene Pvt. Industry Coun., 1980-83; indsl. devel. mgr. City of Eugene, 1983—; mem., chair Lane C.C. Vocat. Edn. Commn., Eugene, 1978-79, 83—; bd. dirs. Eugene/Springfield Visitor and Conv. Bur., Eugene, Eugene/ Springfield Metro. Partnership, Eugene. Mem., chmn. Intergovtl. Met. Policy Com., Springfield, 1986—; pres., councilman City of Springfield, 1986—; mem., chair Springfield City Planning Commn., 1979-86, Springfield Budget Com., 1984—; Oreg. state rep., 1991—. With USAF, 1967-70. Democrat. Lutheran. Home: 1439 Lawnridge Ave Springfield OR 97477-2477

BEYERLEIN, DOUGLAS CRAIG, hydrologic engineer; b. Portland, Oreg., Sept. 23, 1950; s. R.W. and Marjorie Mae (Hovenden) B.; m. Marie Joan Cockrell, Apr. 26, 1975. BSCE, U. Wash., 1972, MSCE, 1973. Registered profl. engr., Wash. Hydrologist Hydrocomp, Inc., Palo Alto, Calif., 1973-79; sr. hydrologist Anderson-Nichols & Co., Inc., Palo Alto, 1979-85; v.p. Aqua Terra Cons., Mountain View, Calif., 1985-86; sr. hydrologic engr. Snohomish County Dept. Pub. Works, Everett, Wash., 1987-92; v.p. Aqua Terra Cons., Everett, 1992—. Author: Beyerlein Beginnings, 1989. Mem. Am. Inst. Hydrology, Am. Water Resources Assn., Puget Sound Cycling Club. Office: Aqua Terra Cons Ste 514 2930 Wetmore Ave Everett WA 98201-4044

BEYERS, ROBERT WEST, editor; b. N.Y.C., Oct. 10, 1931; s. Bernice West; m. Alice Mencher, Feb. 5, 1955; children: William W., Robert B., Amy Jane; m. Charlotte Kempner, June 20, 1971. BA in Sociology, Cornell U., 1953. Reporter Marshall (Tex.) News Messenger, 1953; brand asst. advt. dept. Procter and Gamble, Cin., 1954; dir. pub. rels. U.S. Nat. Student Assn., Phila., 1954-55; editor Reporter Newspaper, Saline, Mich., 1955-56; asst. mng. editor U. Mich. News Svc., Ann Arbor, 1956-61; dir. news svc. Stanford (Calif.) U., 1961-90; assoc. editor Pacific News Svc., San Francisco, 1990—; chmn. bd. trustees Editorial Projects in Edn., Washington, 1975—; communications cons. Oxford (Eng.) U., Harvard U., Cornell U., Calif. at Santa Cruz, U. So. Calif., Assn. Am. Univs., Colo. Coll., Carnegie Corp. N.Y., Robert Wood Johnson Found., Hewlett Found., U.S. Sec. of HEW. Co-founder newspapers Stanford Observer, 1966, Stanford Campus Report, 1968, Edn. Week, 1981, Tchr. mag., 1989, Youth Outlook, 1991. Dir. media and police rels. Coun. Federated Orgns., Miss. Freedom Project, Jackson, 1964; sr. staff mem. White House Conf. on Edn., Washington, 1965. Recipient Kenneth M. Cuthbertson award Stanford U., 1983. Mem. ACLU, Amnesty Internat., Soc. Profl. Journalists, Sigma Chi. Democrat. Unitarian. Home: 330 Santa Rita St Palo Alto CA 94301 Office: Pacific News Svc Ste 506 450 Market St San Francisco CA 94105-2526

BEYERS, WILLIAM BJORN, geography educator; b. Seattle, Mar. 24, 1940; s. William Abraham and Esther Jakobia (Svendsen) B.; m. Margaret Lyn Rice, July 28, 1968. B.A., U. Wash., 1962, Ph.D., 1967. Asst. prof. geography U. Wash., Seattle, 1968-74, assoc. prof., 1974-82, prof., 1982—, chmn. dept. geography, 1991—. Mem. Assn. Am. Geographers, Regional Sci. Assn., Am. Econs. Assn., Western Regional Sci. Assn. Home: 7159 Beach Dr SW Seattle WA 98136-2077 Office: U Wash Dept Geography DP 10 Seattle WA 98195

BEYLKIN, GREGORY, mathematician; b. St. Petersburg, USSR, Mar. 16, 1953; came to U.S., 1980; naturalized citizen, 1985; s. Jacob and Raya (Pripshtein) B.; m. Helen Simontov, 1974; children: Michael, Daniel. Diploma in Math., U. St. Petersburg, Leningrad, 1975; PhD in Math., NYU, 1982. Assoc. rsch. sci. NYU, 1982-83; mem. profl. staff Schlumberger-Doll Research, Ridgefield, Conn., 1983-91; prof. program in applied math. U. Colo., Boulder, 1991—. Contbr. articles to profl. jours. Mem. Am. Math. Soc., Soc. for Indsl. and Applied Math., Soc. Exptl. Geophysicists. Home: 2738 Winding Trail Pl Boulder CO 80304 Office: Program in Applied Math Univ Colo at Boulder University Of Colorado CO 80309-0526

BEZER, DAVID LEON, real estate appraiser; b. Phila., Nov. 25, 1943; s. Samuel and Frances (Rees) B.; m. Ellen Berkowitz, July 2, 1967; children: Daniel, Adam, Samara, John. Student, NYU, 1962-63, Temple U., 1969-70. Real estate salesman Magnus Internat. Inc., Camden, N.J., 1964-65; right of way agt. St. Davids, Pa., 1965-66; chief real estate appraiser Mfrs. Appraisal Co., Phila., 1966-70; exec. v.p. Enterprise Appraisal, Devon, Pa., 1971-75; pres. David L. Bezer & Co. Inc., Phila., 1975-86; v.p., treas. Valuation Network, Inc., N.Y.C., 1982-83, pres., 1983-84; pres. Valuation Network Inc. of So. Calif., San Diego, 1985-86; owner VNI Rainbow Appraisal Service, San Diego, 1986—. Mem. Am. Inst. Real Estate Appraisers, Am. Soc. Appraisers. Democrat. Jewish. Home: 2144 Belloc Ct San Diego CA 92109-1418 Office: VNI Rainbow Appraisal Service 2124 Garnet Ave San Diego CA 92109-3607

BHADA, ROHINTON KHURSHED, chemical engineering educator; b. Bombay, Mar. 23, 1935; s. Khurshed A. and Goola K. (Press) B.; m. Patricia Ann Bergman, Jan. 18, 1959; children: John, James, Sarah, Naomi, Jenny, Nikki. BS, U. Mich., 1955, MS, 1957, PhD, 1968; MBA, U. Akron, 1964. Registered profl. engr., Tex. Rsch. asst. U. Mich., Ann Arbor, 1955-59; rsch. engr. Babcock & Wilcox, Alliance, Ohio, 1959-64; group leader Babcock & Wilcox, 1964-72, sect. mgr., 1972-77, dept. mgr., 1977-88; assoc. dean, prof. N.Mex. State U., Las Cruces, 1988-92, prof., assoc. dean of engrng., 1992—; adj. prof. Youngstown (Ohio) State U., 1978-85; dir. Wast Edn. & Rsch. Consortium, Las Cruces, 1989—. Contbr. articles to profl. jours.; patentee in field. Local pres. Alliance Jaycees, 1964-65; state v.p. Ohio Jaycees, Marion, 1965-66; nat. dir. U.S. Jaycees, Tulsa, 1966-67; vice chair City Environment Com., Las Cruces, 1989—. Named Outstanding Pres. U.S. Jaycees, 1965, Outstanding Nat. Dir., 1967. Mem. AIChE (chmn. 1967-68), NSPE (Outstanding Engrng. Achievement award 1991), Am. Soc. Engrng. Edn., N.Mex. Soc. Profl. Engrs., Coun. for Chem. Rsch., Rio Grande Inst. Chem. Engrs. (sec. 1988-89), Phi Lambda Upsilon, Beta Gamma Sigma, Tau Beta Pi. Zorastrian. Home: 2228 Cimarron Dr Las Cruces NM 88001-8055 Office: N Mex State U Dept 3805 Dept WERO PO Box 30001 Las Cruces NM 88003-8001

BHAGWAN, SUDHIR, computer industry and research executive, consultant; b. Lahore, West Pakistan, Aug. 9, 1942; came to U.S., 1963; s. Vishan and Lakshmi Devi (Arora) B.; m. Sarita Bahl, Oct. 25, 1969; children: Sonia, Sunil. BSEE, Punjab Engrng. Coll., Chandigarh, India, 1963; MSEE, Stanford U., 1964; MBA with honors, Golden Gate U., 1977. Engr. Gaylor Products, North Hollywood, Calif., 1964-68, Burroughs Corp., Pasadena, Calif., 1968-70; engrng. mgr. Burroughs Corp., Santa Barbara, Calif., 1970-78; engrng. mgr. Intel Corp., Hillsboro, Oreg., 1978-81, chmn. strategic planning, 1981-82, gen. mgr., 1983-88; pres., exec. dir., bd. dirs. Oreg. Advanced Computing Inst., Beaverton, 1988-90; strategic bus. mgr. INTEL Corp., Hillsboro, Oreg., 1990-92, gen. mgr. bus. multimedia products, 1992—; speaker to high tech. industry, Oreg., 1988—; mem. organizing com. Distributed Memory Computing Conf., 1989-90, gen. chmn., 1990-91; chmn. computer tech. adv. bd. Oreg. Mus. Sci. and Industry, 1991—. Cons. Oreg. Econ. Devel. Dept., 1988—; bd. dirs. St. Mary's Acad., Portland, Oreg., 1989-92. Mem. Am. Electronics Assn. (higher edn. com. Oreg. chpt. 1989-90, exec. com. 1990). Home: 13940 NW Harvest Ln Portland OR 97229-3653 Office: INTEL Corp 5200 NE Elam Young Pky Hillsboro OR 97124-6497

BHAKTIPRANA, PRAVRAJIKA See THOMAS, GWENDOLYN JEANNE

BHALLA, DEEPAK KUMAR, cell biologist, toxicologist, educator; b. Kasauli, India, Aug. 31, 1946; s. Khazan Chand and Shyama Bhalla; m. Lilly Bhalla; 1 child, Neel. BS, Punjab U., India, 1968, MS, 1969; PhD, Howard U., Washington, 1976. Postdoctoral fellow Harvard U., Boston, 1976-79; asst. rsch. cell biologist U. Calif., San Francisco, 1979-82; asst. prof. U. Calif., Irvine, 1982-86, assoc. prof., 1986—; speaker in field. Contbr. articles and revs. to profl. jours. NIH grantee, 1985-88, 88—, Calif. Air Resources Bd. grantee, 1990—. Mem. AAAS, Am. Thoracic Soc., Am. Soc. for Cell Biology. Office: U Calif Community & Environ Medicine Irvine CA 92717

BHAMIDIPATY, KAMESWARA RAO, engineering educator, consultant; b. Vijayawada, Andhra, India, Aug. 23, 1955; came to U.S., 1982; s. Rama Krishna Rao and Subba Lakshmi (Viswanatha) B.; m. Vijay Lakshmi Mantravadi, Aug. 22, 1984; children: Gayatri, Keshava. B in Tech., REC, Warangal, India, 1977; ME, Indian Inst. Sci., Bangalore, India, 1982; PhD, U. Ill., 1986. Registered profl. engr., Idaho. Product engr. BHEL, India, 1977-80; postdoctoral fellow U. Ill., Chgo., 1986-88; asst. prof. engrng. Idaho State U., Pocatello, 1988—; examiner Graduate Record Examination. India Govt. scholar, 1972-77; recipient Disting. Engrng. Prof. award, 1993; named Grad. Record Examination examiner, 1991—. Mem. ASME, ANS, AIAA, NSPE, Am. Soc. Engrng. Edn., Internat. Solar Energy Soc., Soc. of Rheology, Combustion Inst., Instrument Soc. Am. Hindu. Office: Idaho State U Coll of Engrng Box 8060 Pocatello ID 83209

BHANDARI, ANIL KUMAR, cardiology educator; b. New Delhi, India, Jan. 26, 1953; came to U.S., 1977; s. Mukand Lal and Pushpa (Vij) B.; m. Eve-Marie Brindak, Mar. 29, 1980. Student, Panjab U., India, 1967-69; MB, BS, All India Inst. Med. Scis., New Delhi, 1975. Lic. physician, N.Y., Calif.; diplomate Am. Bd. Internal Medicine, Am. Bd. Cardiovascular Disease. Intern All India Inst. Med. Scis., New Delhi, 1975, resident in cardiology, 1976; intern in straight internal medicine SUNY, Stony Brook, 1977-78, resident in straight internal medicine, 1978-80; fellow in cardiology U. Rochester Med. Ctr., N.Y., 1980-82; fellow in clin. electrophysiology U. Calif. Med. Ctr., San Francisco, 1982-83; asst. prof. medicine U. So. Calif., 1983-87, assoc. prof., 1987—; staff physician Los Angeles County Med. Ctr. U. So. Calif., 1983—, dir. Electrophysiology Lab., 1985-89; dir. electrophysiology lab. Hosp. of the Good Samaritan, L.A., 1990—; presenter numerous seminars, studies to univs., hosps. and agys., 1981—. Assoc. editor Jour. of Electrocardiology, 1988—; contbr. articles and revs. to profl. jours., chpts. to books. Grantee Am. Heart Assn., 1982-83, Sandoz Labs., 1983-84, 84—, Riker Labs. 1985—; fellow NIH, 1981-82, Am. Heart Assn., 1982. Mem. AAAS, Am. Heart Assn. (Los Angeles chpt.), Am. Coll. Cardiology, N. Am. Soc. Pacing and Electrophysiology, Assn. Physicians of Los Angeles County Hosps., Greater Los Angeles Electrophysiology Soc. Home: 700 Warner Ave Los Angeles CA 90024-2500 Office: 1245 Wilshire Blvd Ste 606 Los Angeles CA 90017-4806

BHANU, BIR, computer information scientist, educator, director university program; b. Etah, India, Jan. 8, 1951; came to U.S., 1975; naturalized, 1987.; s. Rameshwar Dayal and Omwati Devi; m. Archana Bhanu Bhatnagar, Dec. 21, 1982; children: Shiv Bir, Ish Bir. BS with honors, Inst. Tech., Banaras Hindu U., Varanasi, India, 1972; M in Engring. with distinction, Birla Inst. Tech. and Sci., Pilani, India, 1974; SM and EE, MIT, 1975-77; PhD Image Processing Inst., U. So. Calif., 1981; MBA, U. Calif., Irvine, 1984; diploma in German, B.H.U., India, 1971. Lectr. in elec. engring. Birla Inst. Tech. and Sci., Pilani, 1974-75; acad. assoc. IBM Research Lab., San Jose, Calif., 1978; research fellow INRIA, Rocquencourt, France, 1980-81; engring. specialist Ford Aerospace and Communications Corp., Newport Beach, Calif., 1981-84; asst./assoc. prof. and dir. grad. admissions, dept. computer sci. U. Utah, Salt Lake City, 1984-87; staff scientist, Honeywell fellow Honeywell Systems and Rsch. Ctr., Mpls., 1986-91; prof. electrical engring., computer sci., program leader electrical engring., dir. Visualization and Intelligent Systems Lab. U. Calif., Riverside, 1991—; cons. U. Calif., Irvine, 1983-84, Evolving Tech. Inst., San Diego, 1983-85, Bonneville Sci. Co., Salt Lake City, 1985-86, TRW, L.A., 1991—; pres. Internat. Student Assn. U. So. Calif., 1976; prin. investigator grants from ARPA, NSF, NASA, Rockwell, Ford, others. Co-author Qualitative Motion Understanding, 1992, Genetic Learning for Adaptive Image Segmentation, 1993; assoc. editor Jour. Mathematical Imaging and Vision, Pattern Recognition Jour.; 5 patents in field; contbr. over 125 reviewed publications on subject of image processing, artificial intelligence, robotics. Recipient Iutstanding Paper award Pattern Recognition Soc., 1990, Honeywell Motec and Alpha team awards, 1989, Project award Outstanding contbn. IBM Corp., 1978. Mem. IEEE (sr., gen. chair workshop applications computer vision 1992), Am. Assn. Artificial Intelligence, Assn. Computing Machinery, Soc. Photo-Optical and Instrumentation Engrs., Pattern Recognition Soc., Sigma Xi. Home: 6733 Canyon Hill Dr Riverside CA 92506 Office: U Calif Coll Engring Riverside CA 92521

BHAT, BAL KRISHEN, geneticist, plant breeder; b. Srinagar, India, May 3, 1940; came to U.S. 1989; s. Justice Janki Nath and Dhanwati (Kaul) B.; m. Sarla Kaul, Sept. 23, 1966; children: Arun Bhat, Anupama Bhat. MSc, Indian Agrl. Rsch. Inst., New Delhi, 1963; PhD, I.A.R.I., New Delhi, 1967. Rsch. assoc. Rockefeller Found., New Delhi, 1967; plant breeder in charge of rsch. Birla Inst. of Sci. Rsch., Rupar, Punjab, India, 1967-68; scientist "C" Reg. Rsch. Lab. Coun. of Sci. and Indsl. Rsch., Srinagar, India, 1968-74, head, 1972-79, 87-89, scientist "E I", 1974-79, scientist "E II", 1981-85, scientist "F" (dep. dir.), 1985-89; v.p., dir. rsch. Bot. Resources, Inc., Independence, Oreg., 1989—; rsch. fellow U. Tasmania, Hobart, Australia, 1979-81, sr. rsch. fellow, 1981-86; cons. in field. Contbr. over 100 articles to profl. jours. Named Scientist of the Yr., Reg. Rsch. Lab., Srinagar, 1976. Fellow Indian Soc. Genetics and Plant Breeding; mem. Am. Soc. Agronomy, Crop Sci. Soc. Am., Soc. for Advancement of Breeding Rsch. in Asia and Oceania, Coun. for Agrl. Sci. and Tech. Office: Bot Resources Inc 5465 Halls Ferry Rd Independence OR 97351-9616

BHATIA, PETER K., editor, journalist; b. Pullman, Wash., May 22, 1953; s. Vishnu N. and Ursula Jean (Dawson) B.; m. Elizabeth M. Dahl, Sept. 27, 1981; children: Megan Jean, Jay Peter. B.A., Stanford U., 1975. Polit. reporter, asst. news editor Spokesman Rev., Spokane, Wash., 1975-77; news editor Dallas Times Herald, 1980-81; asst. news editor San Francisco Examiner, 1977-80, news editor, 1981-85, dep. mng. editor/news, 1985-87; mng. editor Dallas Times Herald, 1987-88; editor York Dispatch, York, Pa., 1988-89; mng. editor The Sacramento Bee, 1989—. editor-in-charge San Francisco Examiner's coverage of Philippines and fall of Marcos, 1986-87, pulitzer prize juror, 1992-93. Mem. Stanford U. Alumni Assn., Am. Soc. Newspaper Editors, AP Mng. Editors (bd. dirs. 1991), Sigma Delta Chi, Theta Delta Chi. Clubs: Stanford Buck, Stanford Cardinal. Office: Sacramento Bee PO Box 15779 21st and Q Sts Sacramento CA 95852-0779

BHAYANI, KIRAN LILACHAND, environmental engineer, programs manager; b. Bhavnagar, Gujarat, India, Dec. 2, 1944; came to U.S., 1968, naturalized; s. Lilachand Premchand and Rasila (Chhotalal Shah) B.; m. Chandra Vasantlal Gandhi, June 24, 1971; children: Nikhil K., Mihir K. B.Engring. with honors, U. Bombay, India, 1965, M.Engring., 1968; MS, U. R.I., 1970. Diplomate Am. Acad. Environ. Engrs.; registered profl. engr., Va., Ga., Utah. San. engr. Greeley & Hansen, N.Y.C., 1971-72, Hayes, Seay, Mattern & Mattern, Roanoke, Va., 1972-77; environ. engr. Hussey, Gay & Bell, Inc., Savannah, Ga., 1977-80; engring. mgr., Utah Div. Water Quality, Dept. Environ. Quality, Salt Lake City, 1980—; tech. transfer and sludge mgmt. coord., 1982—; mem. fair employment com. Dept. Health, Salt Lake City, 1982-90, adv. 1991—, chmn., 1988-89, cons., 1989-91; mem. Utah Engrs. Coun., 1989—, vice-chmn., 1992-93, chmn. 1993—; chmn. Engr's. Week, 1992; v.p. Gujarati Samaj of Utah. Reviewer (practice manual) Financing Sewer Projects, 1984; designer Municipal Wastewater Treatment Plants, 1990-91. Fellow ASCE (profl. coordination com. 1981-88, reviewer Jour. Environ. Engring. Div., Proceedings ASCE 1988—); mem. NSPE, Am. Acad. Environ. Engrs. (state chmn. 1988—), Am. Water Works Assn., Internat. Assn. Water Quality, Water and Environ. Fedn. (internat. com. 1984, mem. tech. rev. com. for manual of practice, 1990—), MATHCOUNTS (chmn. 1985-88, bd. govs. 1988—, regional coord. 1988—). Office: Utah Div Water Quality PO Box 144870 288 N 1460 W Salt Lake City UT 84114

BHUTANI, TONY, international marketing professional, consultant; b. India, Nov. 11, 1939; came to U.S., 1960; s. P. N. and Lila (Malik) B.; m. Rosemary Dorrien, Nov. 18, 1964; 1 child, Nina Anne. BA with honors, U. Delhi, India, 1959, MA, 1960; MBA, U. Calif., Berkeley, 1962. Bus. mgr. Westinghouse Electric, Tehran, Iran, 1974-78; bus. dir. Westinghouse Electric Corp., Pitts., 1978-79; area dir. Burns and Roe Inc., Oradell, N.J., 1979-81; area v.p. NPS Corp., Secacus, N.J., 1981-82; pres. NPST Inc., Taipei, Taiwan, 1982-85, Bhutani Assocs. Inc., Foster City, Calif., 1991—; cons. Westinghouse Electric Corp., various internat. locations, 1968-74. Mem. bd. edn., Tehran, 1975, Taipei, 1983. Fellow AMA. Republican. Office: Bhutani Assocs Inc PO Box 8254 Foster City CA 94404

BIAGI, SHIRLEY ANNE, journalism educator; b. San Francisco, June 21, 1944; d. Herbert Hamilton Rickey and Gerbina Mary (Biagi) Rickey; m. Victor J. Biondi, May 2, 1964; children: Paul and Tom (twins), David. BA, Calif. State U., Sacramento, 1967, MA, 1975. Prof. Calif. State U., Sacramento, 1975—, chmn. dept., 1987-92. Author: How to Write and Sell Magazine Articles, 1981, 2d rev. edit., 1989, Interviews That Work, 1986, 2d rev. edit., 1992, Media/Impact, 1988, 2d rev. edit., 1992, Media/Reader, 1990. Recipient teaching award Poynter Inst., 1983; Danforth fellow, 1981-86. Mem. Assn. for Edn. in Journalism and Mass Comm. (exec. bd. 1990—). Office: Calif State Univ 6000 J St Sacramento CA 95819

BIANCO, MICHAEL FABIUS PATRICK, financial executive; b. West Pittston, Pa., Dec. 27, 1940; s. Joseph Paul and Mary (Compitello) B., m. Marcia Ellen Schroeder, Apr. 27, 1968: children: Suzanne, Francesca, Michael Joseph. Student, Wilkes U., 1962, Georgetown U. Law Sch., 1963, U. Mich. 1968, Stanford U., 1992. Banking officer Chase Manhattan Bank, N.Y.C., 1968-72; pres., chief exec. officer Loeb Rhoades Securities Corp., N.Y.C., 1972-77; mng. dir. Security Pacific Leasing Corp., San Francisco, 1977-80, Internat. Bank, Washington, 1980-81; with Bank of Calif., San Francisco, 1981-82; v.p. Barclay's Bank, San Francisco, 1982-84; v.p., mgr. The Hibernia Bank, San Francisco, 1984-88; pres. Asia Pacific Capital Corp., 1988-91; mng. dir. Arthur Andersen & Co., San Francisco, 1991—. Bd. dirs. San Francisco Library Assn., 1986-88; speaker Bus. Week Exec. Programs, N.Y., 1987, The Planning Forum, San Francisco, 1988; mem. Pres.'s Univ. Coun. Wilkes U., 1990—. James A. Finnegan Found. fellowship, 1960-61. Mem. Calif. Coun. in Internat. Trade (bd. dirs. 1986—, treas. 1987-88), Assn. MBA Execs., Japan Soc. No. Calif., World Trade Assn., U. Mich. Alumni Assn., Stanford U. Alumni Assn., World Trade Club San Francisco, Fgn. Corrs. Club of Japan. Roman Catholic. Home: 1420 Oak Rim Dr Hillsborough CA 94010-7336 Office: Arthur Andersen & Co 1 Market Plz Ste 3500 San Francisco CA 94105-1019

BIANCO, NICOLE ANN, data processing executive; b. Allentown, Pa., Sept. 30, 1949; d. Welch Colleridge and Ruth Ellen (Sacher) Everman; m. William Joseph Bianco, Aug. 19, 1971. Cert., Pa. State U., 1967. Programmer RCA, Moorestown, N.J., 1967-69, Trenton (N.J.) Trust Co, 1969-71, Food Fair, Inc., Phila., 1971-73; data processing officer Provident Nat. Bank, Phila., 1973-77; grant coordinator Burlington County Coll., Pemberton, N.J., 1977-79; asst. v.p. Valley Nat. Bank, Phoenix, 1979-85; cons. in field Phoenix, 1985-87; dir. tech. services Trak-Tech, Inc., Phoenix, 1987-89; mgr. corp. mgmt. infosystems Motorola, Inc., Scottsdale, Ariz., 1989—; educator/tchr. Computer Systems Devel., Phoenix, 1985-87; adv. editor John Wiley & Sons, Inc., 1986--. Author: (textbooks) Introduction to Data Base, 1985, Data Communications, 1985, Advanced Project Management, 1986; author and devel.: (software) Parolee Tracking System, 1987. Mem. Profl. Software Programmers Assn. Home: 863 Happfield Dr Arlington Heights IL 60004 Office: Motorola Inc 1299 E Algonquin Rd Schaumburg IL 60196

BIASIN, GIAN-PAOLO, literature educator; b. Reggio Emilia, Italy, Nov. 7, 1933; s. Giovanni and Vittoria (Bedeschi) B.; m. Maria Rita Francia, Dec. 28, 1970; 1 child, Giovanni. Laurea Jurisprudence, U. Modena (Italy), 1956; MA in Polit. Sci., Syracuse U., 1958; PhD in Romance Lit., Johns Hopkins U., 1964. Asst. prof. Cornell U., Ithaca, N.Y., 1964-67, assoc. prof., 1967-73; prof. U. Tex., Austin, 1973-81, U. Calif., Berkeley, 1981—; chmn. comparative lit. U. Tex., Austin, 1974-75; chmn. Italian dept. U. Calif., Berkeley, 1983-88. Assoc. editor Forum Italicum, Stony Brook, N.Y., 1978—; author: The Smile of the Gods, 1968, Literary Diseases, 1975, Italian Literary Icons, 1983, Montale, Debussy, Modernism, 1989, The Flavors of Modernity, 1993. Mem. Coemit, Italian Govt. Com. on Emigration, San Francisco, 1987-90. Fulbright fellow Fulbright Commn., 1957-58,' 62-63, fellow Humanities Coun., Princeton U., 1992.; Univ. Rsch. grantee U. Tex., 1979; named Knight Officer in the Order of Merit of the Italian Republic, Rome, 1987; recipient Orio Vergani prize, 1992. Mem. Internat. Assn. Study Italian Lit., MLA, Am. Assn. Italian Studies, Am. Assn. Tchrs. Italian, Dante Soc. of Am., Accademia Italiana della Cucina. Roman Catholic. Office: U Calif Italian Dept Dwinelle 5205 Berkeley CA 94720

BIBLE, FRANCES LILLIAN, mezzo-soprano, educator; b. Sackets Harbor, N.Y.; d. Arthur and Lillian (Cooke) B. Student, Juilliard Sch. Music, 1939-47. Artist-in-residence Shepherd Sch. of Music Rice U., Houston, 1975-91. Appeared throughout U.S., Australia, Europe including Vienna Staatsoper, Karlsruhe Staatsoper, Dublin Opera Co., N.Y.C. Opera, NBC-TV Opera, San Francisco Opera, Glyndebourne Opera, San Antonio Opera Festival, New Orleans Opera, Houston Grand Opera, Miami Opera, Dallas Opera; appeared in concert with major symphonies. Mem. Am. Guild Mus. Artists (past 3d v.p., bd. dirs. 1989-91), Sigma Alpha Iota (hon.), Beta Sigma Pi (hon.). Republican. Episcopalian. Home: 2377 Thata Way Hemet CA 92544

BIBLER, TODD DOUGLAS, tentmaking company executive, mountain climber; b. St. Paul, Mar. 27, 1952; s. Nevin Neal and Maureen Rosilla (Cooley) B. Student, U. Wash., 1970-79. Owner, designer Bibler Tents, Boulder, Colo., 1977—; freelance profl. mountain climber, including 11 Himalayan expdns.; paraglider pilot, mem. U.S. team at World Championships, France, 1991. Mem. Am. Alpine Club, Am. Paragliding Assn. Office: Bibler Tents 5441-D Western Ave Boulder CO 80301

BICE, SCOTT HAAS, lawyer, educator; b. Los Angeles, Mar. 19, 1943; s. Fred Haas and Virginia M. (Scott) B.; m. Barbara Franks, Dec. 21, 1968. B.S., U. So. Calif., 1965, J.D., 1968. Bar: Calif. bar 1971. Law clk. to Chief Justice Earl Warren, 1968-69; successively asst. prof., assoc. prof., prof. law., Carl Mason Franklin prof. U. So. Calif., Los Angeles, 1969—; assoc. dean U. So. Calif., 1971-74, dean, 1980—; vis. prof. polit. sci. Calif. Inst. Tech., 1977; vis. prof. U. Va., 1978-79; bd. dirs. Western Mutual Ins. Co., Residence Mutual Ins. Co., Imagine Films Entertainment Co. Mem. editorial adv. bd. Calif. Lawyer, 1989—; contbr. articles to law jours. Bd. dirs. L.A. Family Housing Corp., 1989—, Extended Sch. Days Programs, 1988—. Affiliated scholar Am. Bar Found., 1972-74. Fellow Am. Bar Found.; mem. Am. Law Inst., Calif. Bar, Los Angeles County Bar Assn., Am. Judicature Soc. Club: Calif. Club, Chancery. Home: 787 S San Rafael Ave Pasadena CA 91105-2326 Office: U So Calif Law Ctr Univ Park Los Angeles CA 90089-0071

BICKEL, NANCY KRAMER, writer; b. Phoenix, Feb. 23, 1941; d. Sidney David and Miriam (Zales) Kramer; m. Peter John Bickel, Mar. 2, 1964; children: Amanda Sidney, Stephen Eliezer. BA with high honors, Swarthmore Coll., 1962; MA, U. Calif., Berkeley, 1965. Acting instr. English dept. U. Calif., Berkeley, 1974; bd. dirs., v.p., writer LWV, Berkeley, 1977-84; TV producer LWV, Oakland, Calif., 1978-86; writer, producer LWV, Calif., 1985—. Author and co-producer TV documentary Can I Drink the Water, 1986 (Silver Apple award 1987), Toxic Chemicals: Information is the Best Defense, 1 & 2, 1984 (Blue Ribbon award 1985); author, producer: Cleaning Up Toxics at Home and Cleaning Up Toxics in Business, 1990 (Bronze Apple award 1991), Teaming Up for the Bay and Delta, 1993. V.p., trustee Berkeley Pub. Lib., 1983-85; chair Cable TV Task Force, Berkeley, 1988-91, LWV. Woodrow Wilson fellow. Mem. Bay Area Video Coalition, Assn. Ind. Video & Filmmakers, Inc., Internat. TV Assn., Phi Beta Kappa. Home: 1522 Summit Rd Berkeley CA 94708-2217 Office: 926 J St Ste 1000 Sacramento CA 95814-2769

BICKERSTAFF, BERNIE LAVELLE, professional basketball team executive; b. Benham, Ky., Feb. 11, 1944; m. Eugenia Bickerstaff; children: Tim, Robin, Cyndi, Bernard, John. Student, U. San Diego. Formerly asst. coach U. San Diego; then asst. coach Washington Bullets, Nat. Basketball Assn., Landover, Md.; head coach Seattle SuperSonics, 1985-90, v.p. ops., 1990; gen. mgr. Denver Nuggests, 1990—. Office: care Denver Nuggets 1635 Clay St Denver CO 80204-1799*

BICKLE, MARIANNE CLAUDIA, retail executive, educator; b. Redford, Mich., Nov. 20, 1958; d. Gordon Earl and Melvina Mary (Bickle) Young. BS, Mich. State U., 1980, MS, 1982, PhD, 1990. Merchandising teaching asst. Mich. State U., East Lansing, 1980-82, teaching asst., 1984-85, rsch. asst., 1985-88; store mgr. NoName Stores, Inc., Sterling Heights, Mich., 1982; sales rep. Zip Mail Svcs., Inc., Detroit, 1983; asst. prof. Colo. State U., Fort Collins, 1989—, asst. prof., merchandising coord., 1991-93; cons. Mail-Order Retailers, 1990-91, Viodetex Retailers, 1989-90. Contbr. articles to profl. jours. Mem. Internat. Textile and Apparel Assn. (chair rsch./theory call for rsch. 1991), Sigma Xi, Kappa Omicron Nu. Office: Colo State U 302 Gifford DMCS Fort Collins CO 80523

BICKNELL, NADYNE C., civil official; b. Pontiac, Mich., Nov. 30, 1935; m. Joseph M. Bicknell. BA in Psychology, U. Mich., 1957, MA in Guidance and Counseling in Edn., 1959. Tchr. English and Psychology Wayne (Mich.) High Sch., 1957-61, testing dir., 1959-61; councillor dist. 7 Albuquerque, 1981-89; mem. Land Use, Planning and Zoning com., 1981-89, chmn. 1984-85, 87-89; mem. Albuquerque Charter Revision com., 1970, City Ad Hoc com. on Environ. Concerns, 1971, Albuquerque Environ. Planning Commn., 1972-78, Middle Rio Grande Coun. on Govs., 1974-89, vice chair 1987-88, Nat. Adv. Environ. Health Scis. Coun., 1975-80, 84-88, N.Mex. Mpcl. League Bd., 1983-89, pres. 1987-88, Nat. League Cities Transp. and Communications Steering com., 1984-89, chmn. 1987-88, Albuquerque/Bernalillo County Emergency Med. Svcs. Auth., 1989—; chmn. Urban Transp. Planning Policy Bd., 1982-84, 88-89; bd. dirs. First Interstate Bank. Mem. LWV, 1965—; bd. dirs. United Way, 1989—, sec./treas., 1993. Recipient N.Mex. Disting. Pub. Svc. award, 1980, YWCA Women on the Move award, 1991, Leadership Albuquerque Alumni Leadership award, 1992. Mem. Albuquerque C. of C. (vice chmn. 1990), Phi Lambda Theta. Home: 8721 La Sala Del Centro NE Albuquerque NM 87111-4521

BIDDLE, DONALD RAY, aerospace company executive; b. Alton, Mo., June 30, 1936; s. Ernest Everet and Dortha Marie (McGuire) B.; m. Nancy Ann Dunham, Mar. 13, 1955; children: Jeanne Kay Biddle Bednash, Mitchell Lee, Charles Alan. Student El Dorado (Kans.) Jr. Coll., 1953-55, Pratt (Kans.) Jr. Coll., 1955-56; BSME, Washington U., St. Louis, 1961; postgrad. computer sci. Pa. State U. Extension, 1963; cert. bus. mgmt. Alexander Hamilton Inst., 1958. Design group engr. Emerson Elec. Mfg., St. Louis, 1957-61; design specialist Boeing Vertol, Springfield, Pa., 1962; cons. engr. Ewing Tech. Design, Phila., 1962-66; chief engr. rotary wing Gates Learjet, Wichita, Kans., 1967-70; dir. engring./R & D BP Chems., Inc. Advanced Materials Div., Stockton, Calif., 1971-93; prin. Biddle & Assocs., Consulting Engrs., Stockton, 1993—. Guest lectr. on manrated structures various univs. and tech. socs. Cons. engr. Scoutmaster, counselor, instl. rep. Boy Scouts Am., St. Ann, Mo., 1958-61; mem. Springfield Sch. Bd., 1964. Mem. ASME, ASTM, AIAA, Am. Helicopter Soc. (sec.-treas. Wichita chpt. 1969), Am. Mgmt. Assn., Exptl. Pilots Assn., Soc. for Advancement of Metals and Process Engring. Republican. Methodist (trustee, chmn. 1974-76, 84-86, staff parish 1987—). Patentee landing gear designs, inflatable rescue system, glass retention systems, adjustable jack system, cold weather start fluorescent lamp, paper honeycomb core post-process systems. Home: 1140 Stanton Way Stockton CA 95207-2537 Office: Biddle & Assocs 1140 Stanton Way Stockton CA 95207

BIDWILL, WILLIAM V., professional football executive; S. Charles W. and Violet Bidwill; m. Nancy Bidwill; children: William Jr., Michael, Patrick, Timothy, Nicole. Grad., Georgetown U. Co-owner St. Louis Cardinals Football Team (now known as Phoenix Cardinals), 1962-72, owner, 1972—, also chmn., 1972—. Office: Phoenix Cardinals 9701 S Hardy Tempe AZ 85284 also: Phoenix Cardinals 8701 Hardy Dr Tempe AZ 85281*

BIE, JAMES EDWARD, nutritional research company executive, writer; b. Racine, Wis., Dec. 26, 1927; s. William Howard and Margaret Mary (Hanish) B.; m. Victoria Elizabeth Betts, Sept. 13, 1979; children: James Patrick, Garry Edward. BS in Journalism, U. Wis., 1950. Asst. exec. v.p. Assn. of Commerce, Milw., 1950-58; adminstrv. sec. U. Wis. Found., Madison, 1958-63; v.p. Marquette U., Milw., 1963-66; account exec. Hayden-Stone, Inc., La Jolla, Calif., 1966-69; v.p. San Diego Securities, Inc., 1969-78; pres. Nutrition 21, San Diego, 1978—. Editor: (fin.) La Jolla mag.; contbr. articles on health, nutrition and travel to numerous pubs. Chmn. La Jolla chpt. Am. Cancer Soc., 1969-71. Served to cpl. U.S. Army, 1946-48. Mem. (charter) Internat. Assn. Fin. Planners, Nat. Nutritional Foods Assn., (charter) Mutual Fund Council of Million Dollar Producers, Stock and Bond Club (pres. 1976), Wis. Indsl. Editors Assn. (pres. 1954), Mensa Soc. (pres. 1973), Wis. Alumni Club of San Diego (pres. 1974), Alpha Tau Omega. Republican. Home: 5930 La Jolla Hermosa Ave La Jolla CA 92037-7333 Office: Nutrition 21 1010 Turquoise St San Diego CA 92109-1259

BIEBER, (ADDA) LYNN, marriage, family and child counselor; b. San Diego, Oct. 14, 1928; d. William Vere and Hazel Frances (Robinett) Nall; m. Stanley Bieber, Feb. 22, 1952; children: Danny Vere, Robinett, Davi Lynn, William (dec.). BS in Home Econs., Okla. State U., 1950; MS, Calif. State U., Hayward, 1969. Designated pupil pers. svcs.; lic. marriage, family and child counselor. Buyer Kahn's Dept. Store, Oakland, Calif., 1950-52; sch. counselor Mendenhall Jr. High Sch., Livermore, Calif., 1969-72; pvt. practice psychotherapy Livermore and Pleasanton, Calif., 1972—; dir., founder The Alliance for Holographic Living, Pleasanton, 1991—; founder, pres. Earth Connection, Non-Profit, Pleasanton, 1992. Founder Anthropos Counseling Ctr., Livermore, 1975, Listening Project, 1978. Recipient Recogniton of Svcs. awards Ctr. for Edn. Infant Deaf, Berkeley, 1989, Buenas Vidas Youth Svcs., Livermore, 1990. Mem. Am. Assn. Family Therapists. Home: 5196 Oakdale Ct Pleasanton CA 94588

BIEDERMAN, DONALD ELLIS, lawyer; b. N.Y.C., Aug. 23, 1934; s. William and Sophye (Groll) B.; m. Marna M. Leerburger, Dec. 22, 1962; children: Charles Jefferson, Melissa Anne. AB, Cornell U., 1955; JD, Harvard U., 1958; LLM in Taxation, NYU, 1970. Bar: N.Y. 1959, Calif. 1977, U.S. Dist. Ct. (so. dist.) N.Y. 1967. Assoc. Hale, Russell & Stentzel, N.Y.C., 1962-66; asst. corp. counsel City of N.Y., 1966-68; assoc. Delson & Gordon, N.Y.C., 1968-69; ptnr. Roe, Carman, Clerke, Berkman & Berkman, Jamaica, N.Y., 1969-72; gen. atty. CBS Records, N.Y.C., 1972-76; sr. v.p. legal affairs and adminstrn. ABC Records, L.A., 1977-79; ptnr. Mitchell, Silberberg & Knupp, L.A., 1979-83; sr. v.p. gen. counsel, bus. affairs Warner Bros. Music (now Warner/Chappell Music Inc.), L.A., 1983—; adj. prof. law Southwestern U. Sch. Law, L.A., 1982—, Pepperdine U., Malibu, Calif., 1985-87, Loyola U., L.A., 1992; lectr. law UCLA Law Sch., 1993—, UCLA Anderson Sch. Mgmt., 1993—. Editor: Legal and Business Problems of the Music Industry, 1980; co-author: Law and Business of the Entertainment Industries, 1987, 2nd edit., 1991. Bd. dirs. Calif. Chamber Symphony Soc., L.A., 1981-92; co-chair USC Entertainment Law Inst., 1991-93. 1st lt. U.S. Army, 1959. Recipient Hon. Gold Record Recording Industry Assn. Am., 1974, Trendsetter award Billboard, 1976. Mem. N.Y. Bar Assn., Calif. Bar Assn., Riviera Country Club, Cornell Club. Democrat. Jewish. Home: 2406 Pesquera Dr Los Angeles CA 90049-1225 Office: Warner/Chappell Music Inc 10585 Santa Monica Blvd Los Angeles CA 90025

BIEN, DARL DEAN, business educator, consultant; b. Britton, S.D., July 12, 1940; s. Emil Otto and Clara Marie (Damgaard) B.; m. Bonnie Lee Thaden, Aug. 11, 1963 (div. 1980); children: Erik Neil, Christa Maren. BS, Huron Coll., S.D., 1962; MS, Case Western Res. U., 1966, PhD, 1970. Aerospace engr. Lewis Rsch. Ctr. NASA, Cleve., 1962-71; prof., dept. chair, assoc. dean to dean U. Denver, 1971—; cons. The Pullman Co., Chgo., 1977-79, Continental Oil Co., Houston, 1979-80, 86, TWA, N.Y.C., 1983-85; various law firms, Colo., N.Mex., Ill., Idaho, 1977-93. Author: Basic Programming, 1975; tech. editor: Decision Sciences, 1975-77; contbr. articles to profl. jours. Pub. rels. profl. Denver Symphony Orch., Colo., 1987; econ. devel. profl. Denver C. of C., 1988. Recipient Achievement award NASA, 1969, 70, Fulbright Hays Exch., Fulbright Found., Eng. 1975-76, Fulbright scholar, Thailand, 1988-89, Free Enterprise award United Bank Denver, 1987. Mem. Am. Statis. Assn., Decision Sci. Inst., Grad. Mgmt. Admission Coun., Am. Soc. for Quality Control, The Inst. Magmt. Sci. Democrat. Home: 2225 S Clayton St Denver CO 80210-4811 Office: U Denver 2020 S Race St Denver CO 80208-0001

BIENVENU, ROBERT CHARLES, lawyer; b. Milw., Dec. 3, 1922; s. Harold John and Nellie (Davidson) B.; AB, U. Calif., Berkeley, 1947; JD, U. Pacific, 1953. Bar: Calif. 1954. m. Martha Beard, Mar. 28, 1945 (dec. 1969); children: Susan Krestan, Nancy Simas, John; m. Joyce Marlene Holley, Aug. 13, 1971. State parole officer Dept. Corrections, Sacramento, 1947-54; mem. Hoover, Lacy & Bienvenu, Modesto, Calif., 1954-66; pvt. practice, 1966—. Pres., Stanislaus County Sch. Bds. Assn., 1968-69; mem. Modesto City Schs. Bd. Edn., 1961-81; mem. Calif. Rep. Cen.Com. 1960-70; bd. dirs. Modesto Symphony Orch., 1966-72, Retarded Children's Soc. Stanislaus County, 1965-70, Am. Cancer Soc., 1955-60. With AUS, 1942-45. Mem. ABA, State Bar Calif., Stanislaus County Bar Assn., Am. Trial Lawyers Assn. Home: 218 Brook Way Modesto CA 95354-1314 Office: 726 10th St Modesto CA 95354

BIER, JESSE, literature educator; b. Hoboken, N.J., July 18, 1925; s. Benjamin Arthur and Lenore (Greenberg) B.; m. Laure Victoria Darsa, July 21, 1950; children: Ethan, Leslie, Lilian. BA, Bucknell U., 1949; MA, Princeton U., 1952, PhD, 1956. From instr. to prof. lit. U. Mont., Missoula, 1955-90; Fulbright prof. U. Lyon and Clermont-Ferrand, France, 1957-58; vis. lectr. Bucknell U., Lewisburg, Pa., 1965-66; vis. prof. San Diego State Coll., 1971; chair in Am. lit. Université de Lausanne, Switzerland, 1971-72; cons. editor Bucknell U. Press, 1975-77; cons. Swiss Univ. System, Switzerland, 1978, U. Ottowa, Can., 1983. Author: The Rise and Fall of American Humor: Criticism, History, 1968, 81, Trial at Bannocock: Novels: 1963-64, A Hole in the Lead Apron, 1964, Year of the Cougar, 1976. Cpl. U.S. Army, 1943-45, ETO. Decorated Purple Heart. Home: Wildcat Rd Missoula MT 59802-5234 Office: U Mont Missoula MT 59812

BIERBAUM, JANITH MARIE, artist; b. Evanston, Ill., Jan. 14, 1927; d. Gerald Percy and Lillian (Sullivan) Turnbull; m. J. Armin Bierbaum, Apr. 17, 1948; children: Steve, Todd, Chad, Peter, Mark. BA, Northwestern U., 1948; postgrad., Mpls. Art Inst., 1964, St. Paul Art Inst., 1969-70. Rsch. asst. AMA, Chgo., 1948-49; tchr. Chgo. high schs., 1949-51; freelance artist Larkspur, Colo., 1951—. Exhibited in group shows at Foot Hills Art Ctr., 1985, 86, 87, Palmer Lake (Colo.) Art Assn., 1986-87, 88-89, Gov.'s Mansion, Bismarck, N.D., 1960; oil painting appeared in 1989 Women in Art Nat. calendar pub. by AAUW. Recipient 1st Place Purchase award U. Minn., Mpls., 1966, Coors Classic award Coors Beer, Golden, Colo., 1987. Mem. Colo. Artists Assn., Perry Park Country Club. Republican. Home and Office: 7787 S Perry Park Blvd Larkspur CO 80118-9005

BIERBAUM, PAUL MARTIN, JR., lawyer; b. Alton, Ill., Oct. 31, 1946; s. Paul Martin and Maryella (Godwin) B.; m. Kay Sheldon Edmunds, June 23, 1973; 1 child, Kim Elizabeth. BA, DePauw U., 1968; JD, U. Ill., 1972. Bar: Ill. 1972, Colo. 1973, U.S. Dist. Ct. Colo. 1973. Asst. prof. bus. and labor law Western Ill. U., Macomb, 1972-73; legal staff asst. II 20th Jud. Dist., Boulder, Colo., 1974-76; assoc. Johnson, Doty & Johnson, Boulder, 1976-78;

ptnr. Doty, Johnson & Bierbaum, Boulder, 1978-85, Doty, Johnson, Bierbaum & Shapiro, Boulder, 1985-88; pvt. practice law Boulder, 1988-89; ptnr. Bierbaum & Dalgoutte', Boulder, 1990-92; pvt. practice Boulder, 1993—; instr. bus. law U. Colo., Boulder, 1977-78; vol. atty. Boulder County Legal Svcs., 1978—, Boulder County Aids Project, 1992—. Charter atty. mem. Ctr. Human Rights Advocacy; bd. dirs. Boulder County Humane Soc., 1977-78; bd. dirs. Counseling Ctr., Inc., Boulder, 1977—, pres., 1978-87, 91—. Rector scholar, 1964-68. Mem. Ill. Bar Assn., Colo. Bar Assn., Boulder County Bar Assn. (chmn. corp., banking and bus. sect. 1986-88). Democrat. Office: 2010 14th St Ste 100 Boulder CO 80302-5315

BIERMAN, CHARLES WARREN, physician, educator; b. Ada, Ohio, May 27, 1924; s. Linn Carl and Margery (Warren) B.; m. Joan Wingate, May 15, 1952; children: Margot Ellen, Karen Linn, Charlotte Joane, Barbara Anne. MD, Harvard U., 1947. Diplomate: Am. Bd. Pediatrics, Am. Bd. Allergy and Immunology (dir. 1971-77). Intern Lankenau Hosp., Phila., 1947-48; resident in pediatrics Bellevue Hosp., N.Y.C., 1948-49, N.Y. Hosp., N.Y.C., 1949-50; fellow in neonatology N.Y. Hosp., 1950, Hosp. Enfants Malades, Paris, 1953-54; resident in allergy U. Wash., Seattle, 1965-67; pvt. practice medicine specializing in pediatric and adult allergy Seattle, 1967—; mem. staffs Children's Hosp. and Med. Ctr., Univ. Hosp., Harborview Hosp.; instr. pediatrics Cornell Med. Sch., 1949-50; clin. instr. pediatrics U. Wash., Seattle, 1958-59, clin. asst. prof., 1959-62, clin. assoc. prof., 1962-70, clin. prof., 1970—, chief div. allergy dept. pediatrics, 1967—; hon. rsch. fellow dept. pharmacology, hon. cons. respiratory disease Univ. Coll. London, 1978-79; cons. Wash. State Dept. Social and Health Svcs., 1979-87; gov. Am. Bd. Allergy and Immunology, 1970-78, mem., vice chmn. residency rev. com., 1982-90; vis. prof. pediatrics United Med. Dental Schs., Guy's Hosp., London, 1989. Editor: (with D.S. Pearlman) Allergic Diseases of Infancy, Childhood and Adolescence, 1980, Allergic Diseases from Infancy to Adulthood, 1988; mem. editorial bd. Pediatrics, 1972-76, Pediatrics in Review, 1977-82, Clin. Revs. in Allergy, 1981—, Jour. of Asthma, Annals of Allergy and Pediatric Allergy; contbr. articles to med. jours. With USN, 1944-46, 50-51, U.S. Army, 1951-52. Fellow Am. Acad. Allergy (exec. com. 1980-83), Am. Acad. Pediatrics (chmn. allergy sect. 1974-76); mem. AMA, Wash. State Med. Assn. (ho. of dels.), Wash. State Pediatrics Assn., Wash. State Allergy Soc., Puget Sound Allergy Soc., Seattle Pediatric Soc., Am. Pediatric Soc., Western Soc. for Pediatric Rsch., Brit. Soc. for Allergy and Clin. Immunology. Episcopalian. Home: 4524 E Laurel Dr NE Seattle WA 98105-3839 Office: 4540 Sand Point Way NE Seattle WA 98105-3941

BIERMAN, EDWIN LAWRENCE, physician, educator; b. N.Y.C., Sept. 17, 1930; s. J.M. and Bella (Smolens) B.; m. Marilyn Joan Soforan, July 1, 1956; children: Ellen M., David J. B.A., Bklyn. Coll., 1951; M.D. (Schepp, Shapiro, Grand St. Boys founds. scholar, Thorne Shaw scholar), Cornell U., 1955. Diplomate: Nat. Bd. Med. Examiners, Am. Bd. Internal Medicine. Intern N.Y. Hosp., N.Y.C., 1955-56; resident N.Y. Hosp., 1959-60; asst. Rockefeller Inst., N.Y.C., 1956-57; asst. prof. Rockefeller Inst., 1960-62; assoc. prof. medicine U. Wash. Med. Sch., Seattle, 1963-68; prof. medicine U. Wash. Med. Sch., 1968—; chief div. metabolism and gerontology VA Hosp., Seattle, 1967-75, head div. metabolism, endocrinology and nutrition, 1975—. Editor Arteriosclerosis, 1980-90; assoc. editor Diabetes, 1984-86; contbr. numerous articles to profl. jours. Served to capt. M.C. AUS, 1957-59. Mead Johnson postgrad. scholar A.C.P., 1959; Guggenheim fellow, 1972. Fellow ACP, AAAS; mem. AMA (Goldberger award 1988), Inst. Medicine (food and nutrition bd. 1989—), Am. Fedn. Clin. Rsch., Am. Diabetes Assn., Western Soc. for Clin. Investigation (Mayo Soley award 1993), Am. Soc. for Clin. Investigation, Assn. Am. Physicians, Endocrine Soc., Am. Physiology Soc., Am. Soc. Clin. Nutrition (Robert S. Herman award 1985, v.p. 1990-91, pres. 1991-92), Western Assn. Physicians (pres. 1980), Am. Heart Assn. (vice chmn. coun. on arteriosclerosis 1981-83, chmn. 1983-85, award of merit 1984, Gold Heart award 1990, Spl. Recognition award 1993, chmn. sci. adv. com. 1990-93). Home: 3517 E Olive St Seattle WA 98122-3427

BIERSTEDT, PETER RICHARD, lawyer, entertainment industry consultant; b. Rhinebeck, N.Y., Jan. 2, 1943; s. Robert Henry and Betty (MacIver) B.; m. Carol Lynn Akiyama, Aug. 23, 1980. AB, Columbia U., 1965, JD cum laude, 1969; cert., U. Sorbonne, Paris, 1966. Bar: N.Y. 1969, U.S. Supreme Ct. 1973, Calif. 1977. Atty. with firms in N.Y.C., 1969-74; pvt. practice cons. legal and entertainment industry, 1971, 75-76, 88—; with Avco Embassy Pictures Corp., L.A., 1977-83; v.p., gen. counsel Avco Embassy Pictures Corp., 1978-80, sr. v.p., 1980-83, dir., 1981-83; gen. counsel New World Entertainment (formerly New World Pictures), L.A., 1984-87, exec. v.p., 1985-87, sr. exec. v.p. Office of Chmn., 1987-88, also bd. dirs.; pres. subs. New World Prodns. and New World Advt. New World Pictures, 1985-88; guest lectr. U. Calif., Riverside, 1976-77, U. So. Calif., 1986, 91, UCLA, 1987; bd. dirs. New World Pictures (Australia), Ltd., FilmDallas Pictures, Inc., Cinedco, Inc. Exec. prodr. (home video series) The Comic Book Greats. Mem. Motion Picture Assn. Am. (dir. 1980-83), Acad. Motion Picture Arts and Scis. (exec. br.), Am. Film Inst., N.Y. State Bar Assn., L.A. County Bar Assn., ACLU. Democrat. Home and Office: 6201 Quebec Dr Los Angeles CA 90068-2219

BIETERMAN, MICHAEL BRADY, mathematician; b. Omaha, Dec. 5, 1952; s. Arthur L. and Florence C. (Pietryga) B.; m. Jillian Gould, June 7, 1986. BA, U. Nebr., 1975; MS, U. Md., 1977, PhD, 1982. Mathematician NIH, Bethesda, Md., 1976-82, staff fellow, 1982-84; analyst The Boeing Co., Seattle, 1984-91, sr. prin. scientist, 1991—. Contbr. articles to profl. jours. Mem. Soc. for Indsl. and Applied Math. Office: Boeing Computer Svcs PO Box 24346 MS 7L-21 Seattle WA 98124-0346

BIFFLE, RICHARD LEE, III, educator, researcher; b. Denver, Nov. 23, 1949; s. Richard Lee Jr. and Louise Sally (Hill) B.; m. Ana L. Cardenas, Dec. 31, 1977; 1 child, Maria L. BA, U. Calif., Riverside, 1971; MA, Ea. Mich. U., 1974; PhD in Edn., U. N.Mex., 1990. Youth counselor Calif. Youth Authority, Chino, 1971; mid-Atlantic regional youth dir. NAACP, Phila., 1971-72; youth ctr. dir. Holman Youth Ctr., Los Angeles, 1972-73; fellow, intern C.S. Mott Found. Nat. Ctr., Flint, Mich., 1973-74; elem. tchr. Val Verde Sch. Dist., Perris, Calif., 1974-76; assoc. prof., dir. community edn. ctr. U. of Redlands, Calif., 1976-80; supr., instr., reseach asst. U. N.Mex., Albuquerque, 1980-83; Pace instr. USN, San Diego, 1983-85; elem. resource tchr. San Diego Unified Sch. Dist., 1985-90; asst. prof. edn. Willamette U., Salem, Oreg., 1991—, coord. elem. edn.; commr., sec. Riverside (Calif.) County Juvenile Justice Delinquency Prevention Commn., 1977-80; pres. Nat. Alliance Black Community Educators, St. Louis, 1980; cons. U.S. Office Edn., Washington, 1977-81, Salem-Keizer Sch. Dist., Oreg. State Dept. Edn.; dir. Oreg. Gov.'s Sch. Citizen Leadership. Author: Intern Program Ethnic Studies, 1971, Comm Ed and School Desegregation, 1979. Bd. dirs. Calif. Community Edn. Assn., San Diego, 1977-80; v.p. Calif. Fedn. Black Leadership, Anaheim, 1977-80; chmn. budget com., chmn. multicultural edn. Salem-Keizer Sch. Dist. Recipient Mary McLeod Bethune award Nat. Coun. of Negro Women, San Diego, 1987, Spl. Recognition award Excel Tchr. Program, San Diego, 1988; nominated Tchr. of Yr. San Diego City Schs., 1986-87; Mott Found. fellow. Mem. Nat. Community Edn. Assn., NEA, Calif. Tchrs. Assn., Am. Assn. Polit. Sci., Am. School Curriculum Devel., Phi Kappa Phi (hon.), Alpha Phi Alpha, Phi Delta Kappa. Democrat. Office: Willamette U Dept Edn 900 State St Salem OR 97301

BIGATTI, MICHAEL MARSHALL, agricultural engineer; b. Torrance, Calif., Oct. 26, 1962; s. Osvaldo Omar and Margarita (Riba) B.; m. Maria Alejandra Leporati, Nov. 16, 1988. Grad. in Agrl. Engring., U. Nacional de Buenos Aires, 1989. Profl. agrl. engr.; lic. pest control advisor. Jour. editor Food & Agr. Orgn. Secretariat of Ad-Hoc Meat Group-Regional Office for Latin Am. & the Caribbean, Buenos Aires, 1987-88; written info. dissemination cons. Interam. Inst. for Cooperation to Agr., Buenos Aires, 1988-89; integrated pest mgmt. advisor El Modeno Gardens, Inc., Irvine, Calif., 1990-92, prodn. mgr., 1992-93; gen. mgr., 1993—. Mem. Calif. Agrl. Prodn. Cons. Assn., Club Univ. de Buenos Aires. Roman Catholic.

BIGBIE, SCOTT WOODSON, consulting engineering company executive; b. San Francisco, Oct. 5, 1946; s. Douglas Dillard and Claire (Condie) B.; m. Anne Croco, June 12, 1973 (div. 1981); 1 child, Claire; m. Constance Valerie Herig, Oct. 23, 1982. BSBA, U. So. Calif., L.A., 1968; M in Urban Planning, U. Wash., 1974. Dep. assessor County of Ventura, Calif., 1968-69; planner Murray-McCormick Environ. Group, Bellevue, Wash., 1974-75; dir. planning Triad Assocs., Kirkland, Wash., 1975-85, pres., 1985—. With U.S. Army, 1969-72, Vietnam. Mem. Profl. Svcs. Mgmt. Assn., Am. Civil Engrs. Coun., Am. Congress on Surveying and Mapping, Urban Land Inst., Bellevue Athletic Club, Theta Xi. Home: 9819 NE 32d St Bellevue WA 98004 Office: Triad Assocs 11415 NE 128th St Kirkland WA 98034-6399

BIGBIE, WANDA LOUISE, principal; b. Sherman, Tex., May 11, 1944; d. Roscoe Lewis and Wanda Naomi (Giles) Chadwick; m. Jerry Don Bigbie, Nov. 5, 1962; children: Donald Wesley, Charles Lewis. Student, Calif. State U., San Luis Obispo, 1963-64; BS in Edn., U. Alaska, 1965; MA, U. Calif., Riverside, 1970, postgrad., 1974-80. Cert. adminstr., pupil pers. svcs., gen. elem. tchr. Tchr. Anchorage Unified Sch. Dist., 1965-67; tchr. Moreno Valley (Calif.) Unified Sch. Dist., 1967-69, counselor, 1974-79, asst. prin., 1979-81, prin., 1981—; tchr. U. Calif., Riverside, 1979-81. Named Outstanding Adminstr. Coun. Exceptional Children, 1982, Woman of Achievement YWCA, Riverside, 1986; recipient Cert. of Recognition in Edn. Calif. Assembly, 1988, 89. Mem. Assn. Calif. Sch. Adminstrs. (del.), Western Riverside County Assn. Sch. Adminstrs. (past pres. membership 1989-90), Phi Delta Kappa (nat. del. 1987-90, area coord. 1990—, Outstanding Achievement award 1989, Trainer of Yr. 1991). Republican. Office: Moreno Valley Unified Schs 13911 Perris Blvd Moreno Valley CA 92553

BIGGS, JOEL GILSON, JR., planning, marketing and operations executive; b. Tucson, May 14, 1947; s. Joel Gilson Sr. and Alice Elizabeth (Briggman) B.; m. Anita Rita Cruz, Aug. 10, 1968 (div. Dec. 1981); children: Angela Lee, Jason Stanley; m. Marion A.F. Groom, Oct. 1, 1989. BS, U. Iowa, 1969, MS, 1981. Planner Dept. Land Mgmt. Govt. of Guam, Marianas Islands, 1969-70, Territorial Planning Commn., Guam, 1972-74; assoc. state planner Iowa State Office for Planning, Des Moines, 1974; econ. devel. specialist SE Iowa Regional Planning Commn., Keokuk, 1974-75; chief planner Bur. Planning, Guam, 1975-76; dir. Community Devel. Inst., Guam, 1977; asst. to pres. Guam Community Coll., 1978-81; dir. planning and rsch. Fontbonne Coll., St. Louis, 1981-84; product mgr. JonesMayer, Inc., St. Louis, 1984-88; v.p. planning and bus. devel. ETG Inc., Kansas City, Mo., 1988-89; mgr. strategic developer program Autodesk, Inc., Sausalito, Calif., 1989-90; ops. mgr. Archsoft Group, Sausalito, 1990-91; cons. Acad. Ednl. Devel., Washington, 1991—; lectr. various profl. confs.; instr. community devel. U. Guam, 1977; cons. Lincoln Mfg., St. Louis, 1987. Bd. dirs. Jr. Achievement of Guam, 1979-80; chmn. Territorial Seashore Protection Commn., Guam. 1979-80. Mem. Internat. Facilities Mgmt. Assn., Internat. Soc. Planning and Strategic Mgmt. (St. Louis chpt. pres. 1988-89). Home and Office: 50 Sonora Way Corte Madera CA 94925-2070

BIGGS, R.G., human resources professional; b. Dallas, July 14, 1935; s. Ralph Emerson and Grace Ruth (Butcher) B.; m. Nancy Kerr, 1958 (div. 1977); children: John, James, Nancy, Kristi; m. Lynn Rae Barnes, Oct. 9, 1981. BS, UCLA, 1960; MBA, Pepperdine U., 1972; postgrad., Southwestern Law Sch., L.A., 1965-66; cert., Antioch Sch. Law, 1982. Cert. tchr., Calif. Indsl. rels. GM Corp., Van Nuys, Calif., 1958-63; pers. mgr. Gaffers & Sattler Corp., L.A., 1963-66; indsl. rels. mgr. Internat. Rectifier, El Segundo, Calif., 1966-69, Rohr Industries, Riverside, Calif., 1970-76; dir. employee rels. Orange County Transit Dist., Santa Ana, Calif., 1976-78; sr. v.p. human resources Fedco Inc., Santa Fe Springs, Calif., 1978—. Contbr. articles to profl. jours. Pers. bd. City of Riverside, 1970-75, City of Santa Fe Springs, 1982—. With USAR. Mem. Personnel Industry Rels. Assn., Soc. Human Resource Mgmt, U.S. Golf Assn. Office: Fedco Inc 9300 Santa Fe Springs Rd Santa Fe Springs CA 90670

BIGGS, THOMAS WYLIE, chemical executive; b. Seattle, Oct. 28, 1950; s. Ray Wylie and Mildred Virginia (Ramsey) B.; m. Marcia Jean Holts, Aug. 4, 1973; children: Jennifer Tamar, Jordan Wylie. BA, U. Wash., 1972. Chemistry tchr. Samammish High Sch, Bellevue, Wash., 1972-74; sales rep. Litton Industries, Seattle, Wash., 1974-75; sales rep. Van Waters & Rogers (subs. Univar), Kent, Wash., 1975-80, area chem. mgr., 1988-90, br. mgr., 1990—, field sales mgr., 1980-85; sales mgr. Van Waters & Rogers (subs. Univar), South Bend, Ind., 1985-86; mgr. chem. dept. Van Waters & Rogers (subs. Univar), Indpls., 1986-88. 1st lt. USAR, 1973-80. Mem. Chgo. Drug and Chem. Assn., N.W. Paint and Coating Assn., Rotary (Kent), Kent C. of C. (bd. dirs.), The Lakes Club. Office: Van Waters and Rogers 8201 S 212th St Kent WA 98032-1994

BIGLER, ERIN DAVID, psychology educator; b. L.A., July 9, 1949; s. Erin Boley and Natalie (Webb) B.; m. Janet Beckstrom, June 22, 1990; children: Alicia Suzanne, Erin Daniel. BS, Brigham Young U., 1971, PhD, 1974. NIH postdoctoral fellow Barrow Neurol. Inst., St. Joseph's Hosp. and Med. Ctr., Phoenix, 1975-77; asst. to prof. of psychology U. Tex., Austin, 1977-90; prof. psychology Brigham Young U., Provo, Utah, 1990—. Author: Diagnostic Clinical Neuropsychology, 1984, 2d edit. 1988, Neuropsychological Function and Brain Imaging, 1989, Traumatic Brain Injury, 1990, Attention Deficit Disorder, 1990; assoc. editor: Archives of Clinical Neuropsychology, 1987—; cons. editor: Jour. of Learning Disabilities, 1987—, Neuropsychological Review, 1989—, Psychological Assessment, 1989—. Recipient Significant Contbrn. in Head Injury Rsch. and Treatment award Tex. Psychol. Assn. and Health Care Internat., Austin, 1990, grant NIH, Phoenix, 1975-77, grant Hogg Found. Univ. Tex., Austin, 1980-82. Fellow Nat. Acad. Neuropsychology (pres. 1989-90); mem. Am. Psychol. Assn., Soc. for Neuroscience, Internat. Neuropsychological Soc. Democrat. Mem. LDS Ch. Office: Dept Psychology 1086 SWKT Brigham Young U Provo UT 84602

BIGLIANI, GABRIELE, consular official; b. Rome, Feb. 27, 1952; s. Carlo and Licia (Giovannini) B.; m. Patricia Alagna, Sept. 7, 1985; 1 child, Veronica L.M. BA, La Sapienza Univ., Rome, 1978. Chancellor Ministry of Fgn. Affairs, Rome, 1984-90; consular official Consulate Gen. of Italy, San Francisco, 1990—; nat. mem., rep. Commissione Paritetica di Eleggibilità Per i Rifugiati (Joint Com. for Refugees), Rome, 1986-90. Author: Pittura Zen, 1982; contbr. articles Italian newspapers & mags. Office: Consulate General of Italy 2590 Webster St San Francisco CA 94115-1394

BIGOS, STANLEY JAMES, orthopaedic surgery spine specialist, educator; b. Grand Island, Nebr., Jan. 20, 1946; s. Stanley Joseph and Dorothy Marie (Krumel) B.; m. Karen Marie Hartnett Graybeal, Mar. 31, 1970 (div. Feb. 1988); children: Kristen Elizabeth (dec.), Jennifer Leah, John Bradley. AA, Fairbury (Nebr.) Coll., 1966; BS in Phys. Therapy, U. Mo., 1970, MD, 1975. Chief phys. therapist Johnson & Carroll County Hosp., Warrensburg and Carrollton, Mo., 1970-71; clin. instr. U. Mo. Phys. Therapy, Columbia, 1972-76; surg. intern U. Mo. Med. Ctr., Columbia, 1975-76; resident orthopaedics U. Utah, Salt Lake City, 1876-80; spine fellow Alf Nachemson, Gothenburg, Sweden, Seattle, 1980-81; from asst. prof. to assoc. prof. U. Wash., Seattle, 1982-91, prof. orthopaedics, 1991—; founder, dir. Spine Resource Clinic, Seattle, 1985—; chmn. panel guide Agy. for Health Care Policy Rsch., Rockville, Md., 1991—. Author: Musculoskeletal Guide, 1983; guest editor Seminars in Spine, 1992; contbr. chpt. to book and articles to profl. jours. Co-founder, mem. Patrons Cystic Fibrosis, Seattle, 1985; pres. 65 Roses Club, Seattle, 1986-88. Named Friend of Man Wash. Gens., 1988. Fellow Am. Acad. Orthopaedic Surgeons (occupational health/outcomes com. 1989—, Kappa Delta award 1991); mem. Am. Orthopaedic Assn., N.Am. Spine Soc., Western Orthopaedic Assn., Internat. Assn. Study of Pain, Internat. Soc. Study Lumber Spine (west coast rep. 1987-91), Patrons Cystic Fibrosis (v.p. 1985-86, award of merit 1987). Office: U Wash Dept Orthopaedics RK-10 Seattle WA 98195

BILBRAY, JAMES HUBERT, congressman, lawyer; b. Las Vegas, May 19, 1938; s. James A. and Ann E. (Miller) B.; m. Michaelene Mercer, Jan. 1960; children: Bridget, Kevin, Erin, Shannon. Student, Brigham Young U., 1957-58, U. Nev., Las Vegas, 1958-60; BA, Am. U., 1962; JD, Washington Coll. Law, 1964. Bar: Nev. 1965. Staff mem. Senator Howard Cannon U.S. Senate, 1960-64; dep. dist. atty. Clark County, Nev., 1965-68; mem. Lovell, Bilbray & Potter, Las Vegas, 1969-87; mem. Nev. Senate, 1980-86, chmn. taxation com., 1983-86, chmn. interim com. on pub. broadcasting, 1983; 100th-103d U.S. Congresses from 1st Nev. dist.; mem. 100th-103rd Congresses from 1st Nev. dist., 1987—; mem. fgn. affairs com., 1987-88, mem. house armed svs. com., subcom. procurement, mil. contracts, sea power, mem. small bus. com., chmn. procurement, taxation and tourism subcom., 1989—; mem. Spl. Panel on NATO and North Atlantic Alliance, fgn. affairs com., select com. on hunger, 1987-88, select com. on aging, 1988-93, subcoms. Africa, trade exports and tourism, select com. on intelligence, 1993—; alt. mcpl. judge city of Las Vegas, 1987-89; del. North Atlantic Alliance, 1989—. Bd. regents U. Nev. System, 1968-72; mem. Nat. Coun. State Govts. Commn. on Arts and Historic Preservation; mem. bd. visitors USAF Acad., 1991—. Named Outstanding Alumnus U. Nev., Las Vegas, 1979, Man of Yr. Am. Diabetes Assn., 1989, Man of Yr. Haddassah (Nev.), 1990. Mem. Nev. State Bar Assn., Clark county Bar Assn., U. Nev.-Las Vegas Alumni Assn. (pres. 1964-69, Humanitarian of Yr. 1984), Phi Alpha Delta, Sigma Chi, KC. Democrat. Roman Catholic. Lodges: Elks, Rotary. Office: House of Representatives Washington DC 20515

BILBY, RICHARD MANSFIELD, federal judge; b. Tucson, May 29, 1931; s. Ralph Willard and Marguerite (Mansfield) B.; m. Ann Louise Borchert, July 6, 1957; children: Claire Louise, Ellen M. Moore. B.S., U. Ariz., 1955; J.D., U. Mich., 1958. Bar: Ariz. 1959. Since practiced in Tucson; law clk. to Chief Judge Chambers, 9th Circuit Ct. Appeals, San Francisco, 1958-59; mem. firm Bilby, Thompson, Shoenhair & Warnock, 1959-79, partner, 1967-79; judge U.S. Dist. Ct., Dist. Ariz., Tucson, 1979—; chief judge U.S. Dist. Ct., Dist. Ariz., 1984-90; conscientious objector hearing officer Dept. Justice, 1959-62; chmn. Pima County Med.-Legal panel, 1968-70; Mem. Tucson Charter Revision Com., 1965-70. Chmn. United Fund Profl. Div., 1968; chmn. Spl. Gift Div., 1970, St. Joseph Hosp. Devel. Fund Drive, 1970; Republican state chmn. Vols. for Eisenhower, 1956; Rep. county chmn., Pima County, Ariz., 1972-74; Past pres. Tucson Conquistadores; bd. dirs. St. Josephs Hosp., 1969-77, chmn., 1972-75. Served with AUS, 1952-54. Fellow Am. Coll. Trial Lawyers; mem. Ariz. Acad., Town Hall (dir. 1976-79). Office: US Dist Ct US Courthouse Rm 426 44 E Broadway Blvd Tucson AZ 85701-1711

BILDERBACK, DIANE ELIZABETH, garden writer; b. Medford, Oreg., Apr. 13, 1951; d. Richard Middleton and Mary Lou (Harris) Letsom; m. David Earl Bilderback, June 27, 1970; children: Eric Leland, Christopher Brian. BS in Botany with honors, U. Mont., 1974. Calender columnist Rodale's Organic Gardening, Emmaus, Pa., 1984-87, regional advisor, 1987-88; student assistance coord. Univ. Coll. U. Mont., Missoula, 1989—; instrnl. aide Mt. Jumbo Elem. Sch., Missoula, Mont., 1987-88. Co-author: Garden Secrets, 1982, Backyard Fruits and Berries, 1984, The Harrowsmith's Book of Garden Secrets, 1991, The Gardener's Home Companion, 1991; contbr. various mags. including Nat. Gardening, Family Circle. Home: 5520 Larch Ln Missoula MT 59802-5242

BILEZIKJIAN, EDWARD ANDREW, architect; b. Los Angeles, Mar. 29, 1950; s. Andrew and Alice (Dardarian) B. BSArch, U. So. Calif., 1973, MArch, 1977. Registered architect, Calif. Project mgr. RMA Archtl. Group, Inc., Costa Mesa, Calif., 1977-78; dir. architecture Donald De Mars Assocs., Inc., Van Nuys, Calif., 1978-85; prin. architect EAB Architects, Sepulveda, Calif., 1985-87, Laguna Hills, Calif., 1988—; architect, planner III Trammell Crow Co., Irvine, Calif., 1986-88; prin. architect Fluor Daniel, Inc., Irvine, Calif., 1989—. Chmn. parish coun. Armenian Apostolic Ch. Newport Beach, 1988-91. Mem. AIA, Triple-X Fraternity of Calif. (corresponding sec. 1984-85), Nat. Coun. Archtl. Registration Bds. (cert.). Democrat. Mem. Armenia Apostolic Ch.

BILIMORIA, KARL DHUNJISHAW, aerospace engineer; b. Bombay, June 27, 1960; s. Dhun K. and Najoo D. (Motafram) B. BTech in Aero. Engring., Indian Inst. Tech., 1982; MS in Aero. Engring., Va. Poly. Inst. and State U., 1984, PhD in Aero. Engring., 1986. Grad. asst. Va. Poly. Inst. and State U., Blacksburg, 1982-86; asst. prof. Ariz. State U., Tempe, 1987-91, rsch. scientist, 1991—; referee Jour. Aircraft, Jour. Guidance, Control and Dynamics. Contbr. articles to profl. jours. Mem. AIAA (sr.), Sigma Gamma Tau. Office: Ariz State U Aero Rsch Ctr Tempe AZ 85287-8006

BILLHEIMER, STEPHANIE DANA, laboratory technologist; b. Fresno, Calif., July 25, 1955; d. Donald Howard and Rosemary Patricia (Lynch) Hester; m. Myles Edward Billheimer, Mar. 25, 1972; children: Amy Catherine, Heidi Marie. BS in Biology summa cum laude, Ea. Wash. U., 1985; diploma med. tech., Deaconess Sch. Med. Tech., Spokane, Wash., 1985-86. Cert. med. technologist Am. Soc. Clin. Pathologists. Med. technologist Watsonville (Calif.) Community Hosp., 1987-88; med. technologist, lab. mgr. Loma Vista Clin. Lab., San Jose, Calif., 1988—; tutor pvt. practice, Felton, Calif., 1988—. Vol. classroom parent Wash. schs., 1980-86; vol. visitor, music leader, Wash. and Calif. hosps., nursing homes. Recipient scholarship Rockwood Med. Clinic, Spokane, 1983. Mem. Calif. Assn. for Med. Lab. Tech. Republican. Presbyterian.

BILLINGS, JUDITH, state education official. Supt. public instrn. State of Washington. Office: Public Instruction Dept Old Capitol Bldg Mail Stop FG-11 Olympia WA 98504

BILLINGS, THOMAS NEAL, computer and publishing executive, management consultant; b. Milw., Mar. 2, 1931; s. Neal and Gladys Victoria (Lockard) B.; m. Barta Hope Chipman, June 12, 1954 (div. 1967); children: Bridget Ann, Bruce Neal; m. Marie Louise Farrell, Mar. 27, 1982. AB with honors, Harvard U., 1952, MBA, 1954. V.p. fin. and adminstrn. and technol. innovation Copley Newspapers Inc., La Jolla, Calif., 1957-70; group v.p., dir. tech. Harte-Hanks Comm. Inc., San Antonio, 1970-73; exec. v.p. United Media, Inc., Phoenix, 1973-75; asst. to pres., dir. corp. mgmt. systems Ramada Inns, Inc., Phoenix, 1975-76; exec. dir. NRA, Washington, 1976-77; pres. Ideation Inc., N.Y.C., 1977-81; chmn. Bergen-Billings Inc., N.Y.C., 1977-80; pres. The Assn. Svc. Corp, San Francisco, 1978-91; pres. Recorder Printing and Pub. Co. Inc., San Francisco, 1980-82; v.p. adminstrn. Victor Techs. Inc., Scotts Valley, Calif., 1982-84; mng. dir. Saga-Wilcox Computers Ltd., Wrexham, Wales, 1984-85; chmn. Thomas Billings & Assocs., Inc., Reno, 1978—, Intercontinental Travel Svc. Inc., Reno, 1983—, Oberon Optical Character Recognition, Ltd., Hemel-Hemstead, Eng., 1985-86; dir., chief exec. officer Insignia Software Solutions group, High Wycombe, England, Cupertino, Calif., 1986-89; v.p. Cromer Equipment Co., Oakland, Calif., 1989—; bd. dirs. Digital Broadcasting Corp., Mountain View, Calif., Lenny's Restaurants Inc., Wichita, Kans., Tymyndr Corp., Dover Del., Zzyzzyx Corp., Reno, Harrod's Hotel & Casino Corp., Las Vegas, Pandemonium Pictures, Inc., San Mateo, Calif., Bonanza Corp., Virginia City, Nev., Quillmill Ltd., London; speaker and seminar leader. Bd. dirs. Nat. Allergy Found., 1973—, The Wilderness Fund, 1978—, San Diego Civic Light Opera Assn., 1965-69; chmn. Intercontinental News Svc. Inc., London, and Alameda, Calif., 1989—; chief exec. San Diego 200th Anniversary Expn., 1969. Served with U.S. Army, 1955-57. Recipient Walter F. Carley Meml. award, 1966, 69. Fellow U.K. Inst. Dirs.; mem. Am. Newspaper Pubs. Assn., Inst. Execs. Inc. (dir.), Inst. Newspaper Fin. Officers, Sigma Delta Chi. Republican. Clubs: West Side Tennis, LaJolla Country; Washington Athletic; San Francisco Press; Harvard (N.Y.C.); Elks. Author: Creative Controllership, 1978, Our Credibility Crisis, 1983, Non-Euclidean Theology, 1987, Ruminations on Meta Mentality, 1990, Fixing our Broken System, 1992; editor: The Vice Presidents' Letter, 1978—; pub. The Microcomputer Letter, 1982—, Synthetic Hardware Update, 1987—; editor: Intercontinental News Svc., London, England, and Alameda Calif., 1985—. Address: PO Drawer I Alameda CA 94501-0262 Office: 4701 Oakport St Oakland CA 94601

BILLINGTON, PETER JAMES, management educator; b. New Bedford, Mass., June 18, 1948; s. George W. and Sophie H. (Fronczek) B.; m. Maryann I. Grusetskie, July 23, 1977; children: Drew, Alex. BSEE, Worcester Poly. Inst., 1970; MBA, Northeastern U., 1977; MS, Cornell U., 1980, PhD, 1983. Owner, pres. P.J. Billington Inc., Worcester, Mass., 1970-75; prof. Northeastern U., Boston, 1980-89; Martec prof. mgmt. U. So. Colo., Pueblo, 1989—; mgmt. cons., 1980—. Contbr. articles to profl. jours. Recipient Provost award U. So. Colo., 1991. Mem. Decision Scis. Inst. (v.p. publs. 1988), Inst. Mgmt. Sci., Am. Prodn. and Inventory Control Soc., Am. Soc. Quality Control. Home: 1955 Hunters Point Ln Colorado Springs CO 80919-3462 Office: U So Colo 2200 Bonforte Blvd Pueblo CO 81001-4990

BILLINTON, ROY, engineering educator; b. Leeds, Eng., Sept. 14, 1935; s. Edwin and Nettie (Billinton); m. Alice Joyce McKenna, July 21, 1956; children—Leslie, Kevin, Michael, Christopher, Jeffrey. B.Sc.E.E., U. Man., 1960, M.Sc., 1963; Ph.D., U. Sask., 1967, D.Sc., 1975. Journeyman electrician McCabe Electric, Winnipeg, Man., Can., 1956-60; mem. system operation dept. and system planning dept. Man. Hydro, from 1960; asst. prof. to prof., head dept. elec. engring. U. Sask., Saskatoon, 1964—; now assoc. dean pres. PowerComp Assocs., cons. Author: Power System Reliability Evaluation, 1970, (with R. J. Ringlee and A. J. Wood) Power System Reliability Calculations, 1973, (with C. Singh) System Reliability Modelling and Evaluation, 1977; (with R.N. Allan) Reliability Evaluation of Engineering Systems, 1983, Reliability Evaluation of Power Systems, 1984, (with R.N. Allan) Reliability of Large Electric Power Systems, 1988, (with R.N. Allan, L. Salvaderi) Applied Reliability Assessment in Electric Power Systems, 1990; also articles. Recipient Sir George Nelson award Engring. Inst. Can., 1965-67, Ross medal, 1972, Centennial Disting. Svc. award Can. Elect Assn., 1991. Fellow IEEE (Outstanding Power Engring. Educator award 1992), Royal Soc. Can., Engring. Inst. Can., U.K. Safety and Reliability Soc. Home: 3 McLean Crescent, Saskatoon, SK Canada S7J 2R6 Office: U Sask, Dept Elec Engring, Saskatoon, SK Canada S7N 0W0

BILOTTI-STARK, KATHRYN ELIZABETH, graphic designer; b. La Mesa, Calif., Aug. 6, 1950; d. Anthony D. Bilotti and Dorothy Helen (Moore) Marquet; m. Stephen E. Trombetta, 1971 (div. 1978); m. Michael F. Stark, Aug. 30, 1980. BA in Art, U. Calif. Santa Cruz, 1981; MA, Sch. of Design, Basel, Switzerland, 1987. Design and producton client and vendor liaison Aptos (Calif.) Press, 1981-82; freelance design prodn., 1982-84; sr. designer Jerry Takigawa Design, Pacific Grove, Calif., 1987-88; prin., creative dir. Kathryn B. Stark Graphic Design, Pacific Grove, Calif., 1988—; instr. U. Calif. Ext. Cert. Program in Graphic Design and Prodn., 1987—. Recipient Monterey Bay Ad Club-"Sammy's" award, 1989, Best of Show, 1 Gold and 2 Silver awards, 1990, 2 Silver and 3 Bronze awards, 1991, 1 Gold and 2 Bronze awards. Mem. Am. Inst. Graphic Arts, Montery Bay Ad Club, Western Art Dirs. Club, People in Comm. Arts (bd. dirs., sec. 1988, pres. 1989). Office: Kathryn B Stark Design 227 Forest Ave #8 Pacific Grove CA 93950

BILOW, STEVEN CRAIG, computer graphics specialist; b. L.A., July 10, 1960; s. Norman and Selma (Rifkin) B.; m. Patricia S. Crabb, Nov. 5, 1989. BFA in Music Composition, Calif. Inst. of the Arts, 1982; cert. logic design/theory, U. So. Calif., 1983. Cert. tchr. of movement expression, L.A., 1985. Mfg. engr. Hughes Aircraft EDSG, El Segundo, Calif., 1981-85; project engr. electro-optical test systems Hughes Aircraft EDSG, El Segundo, 1985-86; sr. systems analyst Tektronix, Info Display Group, Woodland Hills, Calif., 1986-88; software engr., math. surface representation Interactive Techs. div. Tektronix, Wilsonville, Oreg., 1988-91; sr. tech. support specialist Unix and X Window systems Interactive Techs. div. Tektronix, Wilsonville, Oreg., 1991—; cons. in graphics SCBA Software, Lake Oswego, Oreg., 1987—; cons. in music composition and ethnomusicology, Structured Perceptions Music, L.A., 1980-85; mem. ACM Spl. Interest Group in Computer Graphics, 1988—. Composer various electro-acoustic instrumental and choral works, 1978-83; author: (theater piece) Indra's Net, 1987; author, editor (book) Designing For Producibility, 1980; contbr. articles, columns and book revs. to profl. jours. Mem. Human/Dolphin Found., Malibu, Calif., 1977, Self-Realization Fellowship, L.A., 1985. Recipient Technical Excellence award, Tektronix, Inc., Wilsonville, 1988. Mem. Am. Musicol. Soc., Oreg. Master Gardner Assn., Am. Rose Soc., Assn. Computing Machinery, IEEE (tech. com. on computer graphics, 1985—, tech. com. on super computer applications, 1988), Am. Rose Soc., Oreg. Master Gardener Assn. Democrat. Office: Tektronix Interactive Tech PO Box 1000 Wilsonville OR 97070-1000

BIMSON, CARL ALFRED, bank executive; b. Berthoud, Colo., Mar. 15, 1900; s. Alfred George and Margaret (Eichman) B.; m. Irene M. Hildreth, Oct. 25, 1927 (dec. 1969). ME, Colo. A. & M. Coll., 1923. Dist. cashier, group mgr. Mt. States Tel. & Tel. Co., 1924-30; self-employed, 1930-33; with Valley Nat. Bank, Phoenix, 1933—; state mgr. fin. rels. State Ariz. Fed. Housing Administrn., 1934-36; mgr. installment loan dept. Valley Nat. Bank, 1936-39, asst. v.p., 1939-40, v.p., then sr. v.p., 1941-49, exec. v.p., 1949-53, pres., 1953-62, vice chmn. bd., chmn. exec. com., 1962-70, dir., 1941-70, vice chmn. emeritus, 1970—; pres. Concho Investment Co., Concho Life Ins. Co., 1965-76; mem. exec. com., asst. sec. Valley Nat. Ins. Co.; Dir. Sun Angel Found., Maricopa County Better Bus. Bur., past pres., Merchants & Mfrs. Assn. Phoenix, past pres., Internat. Retail Credit Men's Assn., Coun. Profit Sharing Inds.; mem. 1st bankers adv. com. Westinghouse Electric Co.; past pres. Municipal Indsl. Devel. Corp., Mchts. and Mfrs. Credit Bur., Maricopa County chpt. A.R.C., nat. v.p., Maricopa County chpt. March Dimes, Ariz. Evang. Council; v.p., dir., mem. adv. com. Phoenix YMCA; past pres. Phoenix Credit Bur.; mem. Phoenix Growth Com; chmn. finance com. Maricopa County Planning Com.; mem. adv. council Ariz. Bus.-Industry-Edn. Council; v.p., mem. bd. Jr. Achievement Met. Phoenix; mem. bd. exec. com. Phoenix Devel. Assn.; mem. dean's adv. council Ariz. State U. Sch. Bus.; mem. bd., treas. Christian Care, Inc.; elder, chmn. bd. trustees 1st Christian Ch., Phoenix; mem. bd. Tax Found., Inc. Contbr. articles trade jours. Founding dir., treas. Christian Care and Heritage Village, campus for the elderly, 1977-87; elder emeritus 1st Christian Ch. Phoenix. Recipient Hon. State Farmer award, Future Farmers of America; Significant Sig award Sigma Chi, 1963; Disting. Achievement award Ariz. State U. Coll. Bus. Adminstrn., 1977; citation honor 90th birthday from Gov. of Ariz. State, 1990, Merit award Colo. State U., 1965, Pub. Svc. award Ill. Bankers Assn., 1961, Honor award nat. com. 50th anniversary Consumer Credit in Banks, 1960; named Ky. by Col. Gov. Ky., 1960, Goodwill Amb. Savings Bond Program by Sec. Treas., 1960. Mem. Future Farmers Am. (v.p. 1959, pres. 1960, mgmt., adminstrv., govt. borrowing coms., Hon. Farmer of Yr. 1946), Ariz. Bankers Assn. (past pres., v.p. nat. bank divsn., past chmn. exec. com.), Am. Bankers Assn. (past pres., past consumer credit com., past small bus. credit com., past v.p., past administrv. com., past chmn. administrv. com., past ex-officio exec coun.), Am. Inst. Banking (life), Nat. Assn. Better Bus. Burs. (past mem. bd. govs., dist. gov. 11 western states), Financial Pub. Relations Assn. (3d v.p., past dir.), Phoenix Clearing House Assn. (past pres.), Nat. Retail Credit Men's Assn. (past dir.), Robert Morris Assos. (life), U.S. C. of C. (finance com., past chmn. subcom. credit unions), Phoenix C. of C. (past pres.), Phoenix Thunderbirds (life), Ariz. Club, Paradise Valley Country Club (founding dir.), Kiwanis (life), Sigma Chi, Beta Gamma Sigma (hon.). Home: 5221 N Saddle Rock Dr Phoenix AZ 85018-1829 Office: Valley Nat Bank Phoenix AZ 85036

BINA, MELVIN JOSEPH, engineer; b. Antigo, Wis., Oct. 28, 1931; s. Aloise Frank and Ann (Johanek) B.; m. La Donna Ann Tehan, Nov. 24, 1951; children: Denise Ann, David Louis. BS, U. Wis., 1953; MS, Air Force Inst. Tech., Dayton, Ohio, 1960; PhD, U. Ariz., 1972. Commd. 2nd lt. USAF, 1953, advanced through grades to lt. col., 1970, ret., 1975; sr. staff engr. Lockheed Missiles & Space Co., Sunnyvale, Calif., 1975—. Contbr. articles to profl. jorus.; patentee in field. Decorated 10 Air medals, 7 Vietnamese Svc. medals. Mem. Air Force Assn. (life), Sigma Pi Sigma. Republican. Home: 5811 E Paseo Busanic Tucson AZ 85715

BINDER, ERWIN, sculptor; b. Phila., Jan. 24, 1934; s. Albert and Betty (Kushner) B.; m. Diane Binder, Jan. 4, 1964; 1 child, Mark. Student, Temple U., 1951, Gemological Inst. Am., 1960, Otis Art Inst., 1962. bd. dirs. Base, Woodland Hills, Calif., Jovenes, Inc. Prin. works include Palm Springs Desert Mus., 1985, Butler Inst. Am. Art, Youngstown, Ohio, Johnny Carson Park, Burbank, Calif., 1988, Golda Meir Medallion, 1989, Art Gallery Internat., 1990, Fountain Valley (Calif.) Br. Libr., Lexington Hills Project, Santa Rosa Valley, Ventura, Calif., Givat Ram Campus, Jerusalem; author documentary film Binder the Sculptor, 1981. Bd. dirs. Arts of Mex. Exhibition 1991, Rockfeller Found., L.A. County Art. Mus., 1990-91, Fine Arts and Communication, LMU, L.A., 1989—, Bilingual Found. of the Arts, L.A., 1986-89, curator La Fiesta de los Mortas, 1989; curator Nearika, Myth & Magic Burbank Creative Arts Ctr., 1990. With USAF, 1952-55. Recipient Beautification award CIty of Brea, 1990. Mem. Burbank Fine Arts Fedn. (bd. dirs.). Jewish. Office: Topaz Universal 4632 W Magnolia Blvd Burbank CA 91505-2731

BINDER, GORDON M., health and medical products executive; b. St. Louis, 1935. Grad., Purdue U., 1957, Harvard U., 1962. Chmn., CEO Amgen, Inc. Office: Amgen Inc Amgen Ctr 1840 Dehavilland Dr Thousand Oaks CA 91320*

BINDER, JAMES KAUFFMAN, computer consultant; b. Reading, Pa., Nov. 20, 1920; s. Paul Burdette and Edna (Kauffman) B.; B.A., Lehigh U., 1941; M.A., Johns Hopkins U., 1952; profl. cert. in systems mgmt. U. Calif.-San Diego, 1976; A.S. in Data Processing, San Diego Evening Coll., 1979, A.A. in Fgn. Lang., 1979; A.A. in Spanish, Mira Costa Coll., Oceanside, Calif., 1981. Instr. English, Notre Dame U., South Bend, Ind., 1948-49; prof. English, Athens (Greece) Coll., 1950-51; CARE rep., Greece, 1951-52; reporter, staff writer Athens News, 1952-53; dir. lang. tng. World Council Chs. Refugee Service, Athens, 1953-54; co-editor Am. Overseas Guide, N.Y., West Berlin, 1957-58; lectr. English, U. Md. Overseas Program, European and Far East divs., 1958-66; successively supr. Cen. Info. Ctr., supt. documents, sr. systems analyst GA Techs., Inc., La Jolla, Calif., 1968-85. Recipient Williams Prize, Lehigh U., 1939, 41; Johns Hopkins U. Grad. Sch. Pres. scholar, 1945-48. Roman Catholic. Clubs: Tudor and Stuart, Automobile of So. Calif. Author: The Correct Comedy, 1951; contbg. translator Modern Scandinavian Poetry, 1948; editor: (with Erwin H. Tiebe) American Overseas Guide, 1958.

BINEGAR, GWENDOLYN ANN, social worker; b. Phoenix, Sept. 23, 1924; d. Glenn Marvin and Mary Lenore (Cartwright) Redington; B.S. in Sociology, Iowa State U., 1948; M. Social Svc., Bryn Mawr Coll., 1967; m. Lewis Albert Binegar, Nov. 2, 1951; children: Glen Albert, Birne Thomas, William Lewis, Alan Martin. Psychiat. social worker Child Study Inst., Bryn Mawr (Pa.) Coll., 1967-71; supervising counselor San Gabriel Valley Regional Ctr., Pomona, 1975-78, program mgr. six L.A. County Regional Ctrs' High Risk Infant Projects, 1978-79; chief case mgmt. svcs. San Diego Regional Ctr., 1981—, assoc. dir., 1988-91, cons., 1992—; v.p. Golden Years, Inc., Valley Ctr., Calif., 1987—. Lic. clin. social worker. Fellow Soc. Cert. Social Workers; mem. Am. Acad. Certified Social Workers, Am. Assn. on Mental Deficiency, Nat. Assn. Social Workers. Republican. Presbyterian. Home: 28809 Lilac Rd Valley Center CA 92082

BINÉT, BETSEY JAN, writer, editor; b. Missoula, Mont., Oct. 1, 1953; d. William Edward Binét and Betsey Louise (Sherburne) Stevens; m. Ronald Eugene Wolf, June 14, 1980 (div. Apr., 1990); 1 child, Christopher James Wolf. BA in English, Calif. State U., L.A., 1977. Dir. pubs. UCLA Med. Ctr., L.A., 1978-84; writer, editor, designer pvt. practice, Venice, Calif., 1984-86; mktg. writer, editor Churchill Films, L.A., 1986-89; sr. devel. writer UCLA, 1989—. Contbg. editor UCLA Mag., 1991—; multi-media composer. Contbr., sponsor Christian Children's Fund, 1977-91; activist Campaign for Nuclear Freeze, 1982; parliamentarian Farragut Sch. PTA, Culver City, 1991-92, legislation chair, 1993—, recording sec., 1992—; contbr. Naral Caral, 1992, People for the Am. Way, 1992. Named Woman of Yr. Intrafraternity Coun., Calif. State U., L.A., 1975; recipient Svc. award Community Coalition on Substance Abuse Prevention and Treatment, s. cen. L.A., 1992. Mem. NOW, Zero Population Growth. Democrat. Home: 4711 Maytime Ln Culver City CA 90230 Office: UCLA 405 Hilgard Ave Los Angeles CA 90024-1359

BING, RALPH SOL, advertising executive; b. Cleve., May 21, 1917; s. Sol Ralph and Helen (Einstein) B.; m. Barbara Cohen, Nov. 8, 1953; children: Aleta, Ralph Sam. Student, U. Ill., 1936-37; cert., John Huntington Poly., Cleve., 1939, Kent State U., 1966. Advt. copywriter The May Co., Cleve., 1938-41; advt. mgr. The Heights Press (now named Sun Newspapers), Cleve., 1941-42; ptnr. Bing and Haas Advt., Cleve., 1946-51; pres. Ralph Bing Advt. Co., Cleve., 1951—, Mktg. Assocs., Beachwood, Ohio, 1975-79; owner Ralph Bing Advt. Cons., San Diego, 1980-87; combat corr. 82nd Airborne div., The Stars and Stripes. Author: SMOKE DREAMS, 1950, History of the Temple, 1950; contbr. numerous articles to profl. jours., also radio and TV commls. Councilman City of Beachwood, 1965-79; pres. grouping of municipalities Coun. of Couns., Cleve., 1978-79; mem. Rancho Bernardo (Calif.) Pub. Utilities Commn., 1983-85; chmn. Community Alert Program Rancho Bernardo, 1986; mem., corr. sec., mem. exec. bd. Rancho Bernardo Community Coun., 1993—. Recipient Outstanding Citizen award Beachwood Civi League, 1980, Outstanding Service award United Appeal, 1950, 51, Appreciation plaque Ohio Bar Assn., 1975; Ralph S. Bing Days named in his honor Beachwood City Council, 1979, 80. Mem. Family Svc. Assn. (hon. life), Oakwood Club (Cleve., pub. newsletter 1946-80), Rancho Bernardo Press Club (exec. bd. 1991—), Woodcrafts Club, Masons, Kiwanis (pres. 1976). Republican. Clubs: Oakwood (Cleve.) (pub. newsletter 1946-80); Rancho Bernardo News; Woodcrafts. Lodges: Masons, Kiwanis (pres. 1976). Home and Office: 16109 Selva Dr San Diego CA 92128-3125

BINGAMAN, JEFF, senator; b. El Paso, Tex., Oct. 3, 1943; s. Jesse and Beth (Ball) B.; m. Anne Kovacovich, Sept. 13, 1968. BA Govt., Harvard U., 1965; JD, Stanford U., 1968. Bar: N.Mex. 1968. Asst. atty. gen., 1969; atty. Stephenson, Campbell & Olmsted, 1971-72; partner firm Campbell, Bingaman & Black, Santa Fe, 1972-78; atty. gen. State of N.Mex., from 1979; now U.S. senator from N.Mex. U.S. Army 1968-74. Democrat. Methodist. Home: PO Box 5775 Santa Fe NM 87502-5775 Office: US Senate 502 Hart Senate Bldg Washington DC 20510*

BINGHAM, PARIS EDWARD, JR., electrical engineer, computer consultant; b. Aurora, Colo., Sept. 26, 1957; s. Paris Edward and Shirley Ann (Blehm) B.; m. Laurie Sue Piersol, May 9, 1981 (div. Sept. 1987). BS in Elec. Engring. and Computer Sci., U. Colo., 1979. Mem. tech. staff Western Electric Co., Aurora, 1979-81, system engr., 1981; mem. electronic tech. staff Hughes Aircraft Co., Aurora, 1981-83, staff engr., 1983-86, sr. staff engr., 1986—; cons. RJM Assocs., Huntington, N.Y., 1987—; cons. Aurora, 1988—. Mem. AAAS, IEEE, Assn. for Computing Machinery, Math. Assn. Am. Republican. Presbyterian. Office: Hughes Aircraft Co 16800 E Centretech Pky Aurora CO 80011-9046

BINGHAM, ROBERT FREDERICK, communication company executive; b. N.Y.C., Dec. 30, 1962; s. Robert F. and Eileen (Wilson) B. BA, DePauw U. Market rep. IBM Corp., Cherry Hill, N.J., 1985-87; account exec. AT&T Data Systems, Chgo., 1987—; sales mgr. AT&T Info. Systems, Chgo., 1987-89; dist. staff mgr. AT&T Info. Systems, Parsippany, N.J., 1989-90; location mgr. AT&T Info. Systems, Southfield, Mich., 1990-91; v.p. Digital Systems Internat., Redmond, Wash., 1991—; ptnr. Southeastern Corp., Chgo., 1988—; leader coun. bd. dirs. AT&T Corp., N.Y.C. Mem. Am. Mgmt. Assn. Roman Catholic. Home: 2320 17th Ct Redmond WA 98052 Office: Digital Systems Internat 6464 185th Ave Redmond WA 98052-5032

BINI, DANTE NATALE, architect, industrial designer; b. Castelfranco Emilia, Modena, Italy, Apr. 22, 1932; came to U.S., 1981; s. Giovanni and Maria (Cavallini) B.; m. Adria Vittoria Moretti, June 27, 1963; children: Stefano Alec, Nicolo Guiseppe. Grad., L.S.A. Righi, Bologna, Italy, 1952; PhD in Architecture, U. Florence, 1962. Chmn. Societa' Anonima Immobiliare Castelfranco Emilia, Castelfranco Emilia, 1960-64, Vedova Bini, Castelfranco Emilia, 1960-64; founder, chmn. Unipack, Old Home, Bologna, 1961-65; founder, exec. v.p. Binishell Spa, Bologna, 1966-69; cons. Dept. Pub. Works New South Wales, Sydney, Australia, 1972-74, Jennings Industries Ltd., Melbourne, Australia, 1975-80; founder Bini Cons. Australia; founder, pres., chmn. Binistar, Inc., San Francisco, 1981—; external cons. Bechtel Nat., Inc., San Francisco, 1985-86; founder, pres., chmn. Pak-Home, Inc. (now Napa Valley Corp.), San Francisco, 1986—; cons. Shimizu Corp., Tokyo, 1989-93; spl. cons. to UN, Rome, 1968, Shimizu Tech. Ctr. Am., 1989, Shimizu Co., Tokyo, 1991-92; lectr. Moscow Expocenter, 1986; vis. lectr. NASA Ames Rsch. Ctr., 1989, vis. lectr. univs. Italy, Australia, U.S., Mex., Venezuela, Brazil, Argentina, Peru, Eng., USSR, Fed. Republic Germany. Contbr. articles and papers to profl. jours., also conf. procs.; patentee self-shaping structures for low-cost, sport and indsl./comml. bldgs., designer of a self-shaping mega-structure for a new city's infrastructure and framework, 1989; developer new automated constrn. system for multi-storied bldg.; co-researcher for self-shaping, self-sinking lunar habitat. Decorated Order of Commendatore Pres. Italian Republic, 1989; recipient Eurostar award European Inst. Packaging, 1964, Excellence in Engring. Design award Design News Mag., 1968, Best Idea of Yr. award European Design News Mag., 1968, Excellence in Indsl. Design award I.E.S. Australia, 1976. Mem. Bd. Architects Emilia e Romagna, Assn. Architects Bologna (co-founder 1963), Italian Assn. Indsl. Design, Italian Inst. Packaging Design (Oscar award 1961-63), Royal Australian Inst. Architects New South Wales, Am. Assn. Mil. Engrs. Roman Catholic.

BINING, AVTAR SINGH, energy, air quality specialist; b. Khera, Punjab, India, May 23, 1955; came to U.S., 1988; s. Sidhu Singh and Amar (Kaur) B.; m. Baljit Pannu, May 30, 1987. B in Agrl. Engring., U. India, 1978; M in Agrl. Engring., Punjab Agrl. U., Ludhiana, 1980; PhD in Engring., U. Calif., Davis, 1993. Cert. C.C. instr., Calif. Rsch. fellow energy Punjab Agrl. U., Ludhiana, India, 1980-82, asst. agrl. engr., 1982-85; air resources engr. alternate fuels Calif. Air Resources Bd., El Monte, 1990-91; assoc. energy industrial air quality specialist Calif. Energy Commn., Sacramento, 1991-93, energy comm. supr., 1993—. Contbr. articles to profl. jours. Mem. Air and Wast Mgmt. Assn. (curriculum devel. and rev. com. 1992—), Am. Soc. of Agrl. Engrs. (com. biomass energy and alternate products 1985), Sigma Xi. Home: 7720 Tea Berry Way Sacramento CA 95828 Office: Calif Energy Commn 1516 9th St MS-22 Sacramento CA 95814

BINKLEY, JOAN VIVIAN (JODY BINKLEY), artist, educator, gallery owner; b. Hanford, Calif., July 8, 1933; d. Albert Henry Lohse and Alice (Day) Romdall; m. Henry Alson Binkley, Sept. 20, 1958; children: Cameron, Brock, Clayton. Student, Colo. State U., 1951-53; studied with, Frederick Van Twente, Mary Ann Lohman, Larry Webster, Delbert Gish, Leslie B. Demille. Owner, instr. Studio West Galleries, Wheatridge, Colo., 1973-80; owner Studio West Galleries, Littleton, Colo., 1975-80; owner, instr. Country Lane Art Gallery, Lakewood, Colo., 1983-85, Lakewood Arts Studio Gallery, 1988—; workshop instr. Wheatridge Art Club, 1987, 89, 91. Exhbns. include Denver Cancer League Spring Benefit, 1989, 90, 91, 92, also Studio West Galleries, Wheatride and Littleton, Emily Ingram Galleries, Steamboat, Colo., 1984-92, Santa Fe Impressions, Littleton, 1987—, Gallery of Western Art, 1987—, Parade of Homes, 1988-89. Mem. Colo. Artist Assn., Lakewood Arts Coun., Foothills Art Ctr. Home: 12588 W 1st Pl Lakewood CO 80228 Studio: Lakewood Arts Studio 85 S Union Blvd Lakewood CO 80228

BINKLEY, NICHOLAS BURNS, banking executive; b. Pasadena, Calif., Oct. 31, 1945; s. John Thomas and Marijane (Tucker) B.; m. Diana Padelford Binkley, Aug. 3, 1974; children: Pepper Alexandra, Byron Jack. Student, Univrsite-d'Aix/Marseille, Aix-en-Privence, France, 1966-67; BS in Polit. Sci., Colo. Coll., 1968; MA in Internat. Studies, Johns Hopkins U., 1971. From London sr. credit analyst to middle-East asst. treas. of Petroleum div. Chase Manhattan Bank, N.Y.C., 1973-75; songwriter N.Y.C., 1975-77; from asst. v.p. to v.p., regional mgr. Security Pacific Nat. Bank, Los Angeles, 1977-83; 1st v.p. to exec. v.p., chmn., chief exec. officer fin. svc. Bank Am. Corp., San Diego, 1983—. Vol. Peace Corp., Tunisia, 1968-70; campaign mgr. U.S. COngl. Campaign, Pasadena, 1972—. Office: Bank America Corp 10124 Old Grove Rd San Diego CA 92131-1693

BINNIE, NANCY CATHERINE, nurse, educator; b. Sioux Falls, S.D., Jan. 28, 1937; d. Edward Grant and Jessie May (Martini) Larkin; m. Charles H. Binnie. Diploma, St. Joseph's Hosp. Sch. Nursing, Phoenix, 1965; BS in Nursing, Ariz. State U., 1970, MA, 1974. Intensive care charge nurse Scottsdale (Ariz.) Meml. Hosp., 1968-70, coordinator critical care, 1970-71; coordinator critical care John C. Lincoln Hosp., Phoenix, 1971-73; prof. nursing GateWay Community Coll., Phoenix, 1974—; coord. part-time evening nursing programs Gateway Community Coll., 1984—, interim dir. nursing, 1989, 91. Mem. Orgn. Advancement of Assoc. Degree Nursing. Office: Gateway C C 104 N 40th St Phoenix AZ 85034-1704

BIRCH, EDWARD ELTON, higher education executive; b. Medina, N.Y., July 8, 1938; s. Elton E. and Gertrude H. (Simonds) B.; m. Suzanne Arlene Pratt, Aug. 22, 1959; chldren: Yvette Suzanne, Michele Noel. BS, SUNY, 1960; MA, Ohio U., 1962; Phd, Mich. State U., 1969. Asst. dean students instr., human rels Ohio U., Athens, 1963-65; asst. vice chancellor Oakland U. (Mich. State U.), Rochester, Mich., 1965-70; v.p., assoc. prof. Ohio Wesleyan U., Delaware, 1970-76; vide chancellor student and isla vista affairs U. Calif., Santa Barbara, 1976-77, vice chancellor adminstrv. svcs. and student affairs, 1977-80, vice chancellor student and community affairs, 1980-88, vice chancellor instnl. advancement, 1988—; v.p. XXIIIrd Olympiad, L.A., 1984; dir. U. Calif. Santa Barbara Found., Alumni Assn. Dir. United Way, Santa Barbara, Santa Barbara C. of C., Santa Barbara Industry End. Coun., Santa Barbara Bank and Trust. Mem. Nat. Soc. Fund Raising Execs., Am. Coun. on Edn., Coun. for Advancement and Support of Edn., Nat. Assn. State U. and Land Grant Colls., LaCumbre Golf and Country Club. Episcopalian. Home: 4585 Vieja Dr Santa Barbara CA 93110 Office: U Calif Instnl Advancement Santa Barbara CA 93106-2030

BIRD, CHARLES ALBERT, lawyer; b. Stockton, Calif., July 1, 1947; s. Donald Gladstone and Elizabeth Clara (Jongeneel) B.; m. Charlotte Laura Soeters, June 28, 1969. BA, U. Calif.-Davis, 1969, JD, 1973. Bar: Calif. 1973, U.S. Dist. Ct. (so. dist.) 1975, U.S. Ct. Appeals (9th cir.) 1975, U.S. Supreme Ct. 1980, U.S. Dist. Ct. (cen. dist.) Calif. 1981. Tchr. Woodland Unified Sch. Dist. (Calif.), 1969-70; law clk. justice Supreme Ct. Alaska, Juneau, 1973-74; assoc. Luce, Forward, Hamilton & Scripps, San Diego, 1975-79, ptnr., 1980—. Contbr. articles to profl. publs. Bd. dirs. Defenders Orgn., San Diego, 1982-86, 87—, pres., 1990-92; founding dir. San Diego Vol. Lawyer Program, 1982-86. Mem. San Diego County Bar Assn. (legis chmn. 1980-81, bd. dirs. 1982-85, sec. 1984, v.p. 1985), State Bar Assn. Calif. (exec. com. real property sect. 1982-86, chmn. exec. com. 1985-86). Democrat. Episcopalian. Home: 4182 Ingalls St San Diego CA 92103-1354 Office: Luce Forward Hamilton 600 W Broadway Ste 2600 San Diego CA 92101

BIRD, DEBORAH KAY, biology and landscape educator; b. Toledo, Oct. 18, 1950; d. E.V. and Ruth Rose (York) Bird; m. Daniel Joseph Lenane IV, Oct. 14, 1972. BS, U. Ariz., 1979, MA, 1993. Rsch. asst. Office of Arid Lands, Tucson, 1979-83; instr. Pima C.C., Tucson, 1983—; job coach for mentally ill La Frontera-Herb's Etc., Tucson, 1991—; owner cons. bus. for environ. edn. Environ. Therapies, Tucson, 1992—. Mem. Greater Ariz. Bicycling Assn., Tucson, 1984—; mem. landscape adv. com. Pima Coll. Mem. Ariz. Native Plant Soc., Native Seed, Global ReLeaf (co-operator). Home and office: Environ Therapies 1214 N 6th Ave Tucson AZ 85705

BIRD, JOHN ERIC, electronic technician; b. St. Joseph, Mo., Oct. 7, 1958; s. William E. and Shirley (Waller) B.; m. Joyce E. Keller, Mar. 24, 1984; 1 child, Nicholas Alexander. Electronic technician CPT Corp., Hopkins, Minn., 1977-79, Electro Dynamics Corp., Overland Park, Kans., 1979-80, King Radio Corp., Overland Park, 1980-82, Tallgrass Tech. Corp., Overland Park, 1982-84, Structural Behavior Engring. Inc., Phoenix, 1984—. Contbr. design to profl. mag. Republican. Home: 10432 W Laurie Ln Peoria AZ 85345-7431 Office: Structural Behavior Engring 4236 N 39th Ave Phoenix AZ 85019-3511

BIRD, LESLEY ANN, computer engineer; b. Rome, N.Y., Nov. 10, 1963; d. Richard Andrew and Suzanne (Van Auken) B. BSEE, U. of the Pacific, Stockton, Calif., 1986; MSEE, U. Calif., Santa Barbara, 1990. Student engr. IBM Corp., San Jose, Calif., 1984-85; electronic design engr. Delco Electronics, Goleta, Calif., 1986-90; computer engr. Apple Computer, Cupertino, Calif., 1990—. Scholarship Soc. Women Engrs., 1984. Mem. IEEE, Eta Kappa Mu. Home: 2061 Foxhall Lp San Jose CA 95125 Office: Apple Computer 20705 Valley Green Dr Cupertino CA 95014

BIRD, PATRICIA COLEEN, business owner; b. Wolf Point, Mont., May 10, 1953; d. Harry Sidney and Pearl Rose (Firemoon) B. AA in Fine Arts, Haskell Indian JUCO, Lawrence, Kans., 1974; student, Kans. U., 1974-78; CDC Cert., Deaconess Hosp., Glasgow, Mont., 1990. Partnership bus. owner Blue Feather Indian Store, Wolf Point, Mont., 1980—; Indian arts steering com. mem. Mont. Arts Coun., Helena, 1991. First responder ambulance Trinity Hosp., Wolf Point, 1991-92; drug and alcohol facilitator Frazer (Mont.) Sch. Dist. 2-2B, 1990-91; acting sec. Frazer Community Coun., 1991-92; N.W. accrediting assn. mem. Poplar (Mont.) Sch., 1990-91; coord. "The Longest Walk", Davis, Calif., 1978, concert dir., 1978. Named Miss Nat. Congress of Am. Indians, 1975, The Modern Ms., 1975, Miss Haskell, 1974, Oil Discovery Celebration Pres., 1974, Oil Discovery Celebration Princess, 1973, 72, 71.

BIRD, RANDALL CHARLES, principal; b. Blackfoot, Idaho, Jan. 3, 1949; s. Blayne Duffin and Mary (Bohi) B.; m. Carla Aikele, Aug. 6, 1970; children: Erika, Angela, Meisha, Rachel, Michael, Scott. AA, Ricks Coll., Rexburg, Idaho, 1970; BS, Brigham Young U., 1973, MEd, 1980, postgrad., 1990—. Cert. tchr., Utah, Idaho. Seminary tchr. Mormon Ch., Driggs, Idaho, 1973-75; prin., tchr. Mormon Ch., Shelley, Idaho, 1975—; football coach Shelley High Sch., 1975—; track coach Teton High Sch., Driggs, 1973-

ptnr. Doty, Johnson & Bierbaum, Boulder, 1978-85, Doty, Johnson, Bierbaum & Shapiro, Boulder, 1985-88; pvt. practice law Boulder, 1988-89; ptnr. Bierbaum & Dalgoutte', Boulder, 1990-92; pvt. practice Boulder, 1993—; instr. bus. law U. Colo., Boulder, 1977-78; vol. atty. Boulder County Legal Svcs., 1978—, Boulder County Aids Project, 1992—. Charter atty. mem. Ctr. Human Rights Advocacy; bd. dirs. Boulder County Humane Soc., 1977-78; bd. dirs. Counseling Ctr., Inc., Boulder, 1977—, pres., 1978-87, 91—. Rector scholar, 1964-68. Mem. Ill. Bar Assn., Colo. Bar Assn., Boulder County Bar Assn. (chmn. corp., banking and bus. sect. 1986-88). Democrat. Office: 2010 14th St Ste 100 Boulder CO 80302-5315

BIERMAN, CHARLES WARREN, physician, educator; b. Ada, Ohio, May 27, 1924; s. Linn Carl and Margery (Warren) B.; m. Joan Wingate, May 15, 1952; children: Margot Ellen, Karen Linn, Charlotte Joane, Barbara Anne. MD, Harvard U., 1947. Diplomate: Am. Bd. Pediatrics, Am. Bd. Allergy and Immunology (dir. 1971-77). Intern Lankenau Hosp., Phila., 1947-48; resident in pediatrics Bellevue Hosp., N.Y.C., 1948-49, N.Y. Hosp., N.Y.C., 1949-50; fellow in neonatology N.Y. Hosp., 1950, Hosp. Enfants Malades, Paris, 1953-54; resident in allergy U. Wash., Seattle, 1965-67; pvt. practice medicine specializing in pediatric and adult allergy Seattle, 1967—; mem. staffs Children's Hosp. and Med. Ctr., Univ. Hosp., Harborview Hosp.; instr. pediatrics Cornell Med. Sch., 1949-50; clin. instr. pediatrics U. Wash., Seattle, 1958-59, clin. asst. prof., 1959-62, clin. assoc. prof., 1962-70, clin. prof., 1970—, chief div. allergy dept. pediatrics, 1967—; hon. rsch. fellow dept. pharmacology, hon. cons. respiratory disease Univ. Coll. London, 1978-79; cons. Wash. State Dept. Social and Health Svcs., 1979-87; gov. Am. Bd. Allergy and Immunology, 1970-78, mem., vice chmn. residency rev. com., 1982-90; vis. prof. pediatrics United Med. Dental Schs., Guy's Hosp., London, 1989. Editor: (with D.S. Pearlman) Allergic Diseases of Infancy, Childhood and Adolescence, 1980, Allergic Diseases from Infancy to Adulthood, 1988; mem. editorial bd. Pediatrics, 1972-76, Pediatrics in Review, 1977-82, Clin. Revs. in Allergy, 1981—, Jour. of Asthma, Annals of Allergy and Pediatric Allergy; contbr. articles to med. jours. With USN, 1944-46, 50-51, U.S. Army, 1951-52. Fellow Am. Acad. Allergy (exec. com. 1980-83), Am. Acad. Pediatrics (chmn. allergy sect. 1974-76); mem. AMA, Wash. State Med. Assn. (ho. of dels.), Wash. State Pediatrics Assn., Wash. State Allergy Soc., Puget Sound Allergy Soc., Seattle Pediatric Soc., Am. Pediatric Soc., Western Soc. for Pediatric Rsch., Brit. Soc. for Allergy and Clin. Immunology. Episcopalian. Home: 4524 E Laurel Dr NE Seattle WA 98105-3839 Office: 4540 Sand Point Way NE Seattle WA 98105-3941

BIERMAN, EDWIN LAWRENCE, physician, educator; b. N.Y.C., Sept. 17, 1930; s. J.M. and Bella (Smolens) B.; m. Marilyn Joan Soforan, July 1, 1956; children: Ellen M., David J. B.A., Bklyn. Coll., 1951; M.D. (Schepp, Shapiro, Grand St. Boys founds. scholar, Thorne Shaw scholar), Cornell U., 1955. Diplomate: Nat. Bd. Med. Examiners, Am. Bd. Internal Medicine. Intern N.Y. Hosp., N.Y.C., 1955-56; resident N.Y. Hosp., 1959-60; asst. Rockefeller Inst., N.Y.C., 1956-57; asst. prof. Rockefeller Inst., 1960-62; assoc. prof. medicine U. Wash. Med. Sch., Seattle, 1963-68; prof. medicine U. Wash. Med. Sch., 1968—; chief div. metabolism and gerontology VA Hosp., Seattle, 1967-75, head div. metabolism, endocrinology and nutrition, 1975—. Editor Arteriosclerosis, 1980-90; assoc. editor Diabetes, 1984-86; contbr. numerous articles to profl. jours. Served to capt. M.C. AUS, 1957-59. Mead Johnson postgrad. scholar A.C.P., 1959; Guggenheim fellow, 1972. Fellow ACP, AAAS; mem. AMA (Goldberger award 1988), Inst. Medicine (food and nutrition bd. 1989—), Am. Fedn. Clin. Rsch., Am. Diabetes Assn., Western Soc. for Clin. Investigation (Mayo Soley award 1993), Am. Soc. for Clin. Investigation, Assn. Am. Physicians, Endocrine Soc., Am. Physiology Soc., Am. Soc. Clin. Nutrition (Robert S. Herman award 1985, v.p. 1990-91, pres. 1991-92), Western Assn. Physicians (pres. 1980), Am. Heart Assn. (vice chmn. coun. on arteriosclerosis 1981-83, chmn. 1983-85, award of merit 1984, Gold Heart award 1990, Spl. Recognition award 1993, chmn. sci. adv. com. 1990-93). Home: 3517 E Olive St Seattle WA 98122-3427

BIERSTEDT, PETER RICHARD, lawyer, entertainment industry consultant; b. Rhinebeck, N.Y., Jan. 2, 1943; s. Robert Henry and Betty (MacIver) B.; m. Carol Lynn Akiyama, Aug. 23, 1980. AB, Columbia U., 1965, JD cum laude, 1969; cert., U. Sorbonne, Paris, 1966. Bar: N.Y. 1969, U.S. Supreme Ct. 1973, Calif. 1977. Atty. with firms in N.Y.C., 1969-74; pvt. practice cons. legal and entertainment industry, 1971, 75-76, 88—; with Avco Embassy Pictures Corp., L.A., 1977-83; v.p., gen. counsel Avco Embassy Pictures Corp., 1978-80, sr. v.p., 1980-83, dir., 1981-83; gen. counsel New World Entertainment (formerly New World Pictures), L.A., 1984-87, exec. v.p., 1985-87, sr. exec. v.p. Office of Chmn., 1987-88, also bd. dirs.; pres. subs. New World Prodns. and New World Advt. New World Pictures, 1985-88; guest lectr. U. Calif., Riverside, 1976-77, U. So. Calif., 1986, 91, UCLA, 1987; bd. dirs. New World Pictures (Australia), Ltd., FilmDallas Pictures, Inc., Cinedco, Inc. Exec. prodr. (home video series) The Comic Book Greats. Mem. Motion Picture Assn. Am. (dir. 1980-83), Acad. Motion Picture Arts and Scis. (exec. br.), Am. Film Inst., N.Y. State Bar Assn., L.A. County Bar Assn., ACLU. Democrat. Home and Office: 6201 Quebec Dr Los Angeles CA 90068-2219

BIETERMAN, MICHAEL BRADY, mathematician; b. Omaha, Dec. 5, 1952; s. Arthur L. and Florence C. (Pietryga) B.; m. Jillian Gould, June 7, 1986. BA, U. Nebr., 1975; MS, U. Md., 1977, PhD, 1982. Mathematician NIH, Bethesda, Md., 1976-82, staff fellow, 1982-84; analyst The Boeing Co., Seattle, 1984-91, sr. prin. scientist, 1991—. Contbr. articles to profl. jours. Mem. Soc. for Indsl. and Applied Math. Office: Boeing Computer Svcs PO Box 24346 MS 7L-21 Seattle WA 98124-0346

BIFFLE, RICHARD LEE, III, educator, researcher; b. Denver, Nov. 23, 1949; s. Richard Lee Jr. and Louise Sally (Hill) B.; m. Ana L. Cardenas, Dec. 31, 1977; 1 child, Maria L. BA, U. Calif., Riverside, 1971; MA, Ea. Mich. U., 1974; PhD in Edn., U. N.Mex., 1990. Youth counselor Calif. Youth Authority, Chino, 1971; mid-Atlantic regional youth dir. NAACP, Phila., 1971-72; youth ctr. dir. Holman Youth Ctr., Los Angeles, 1972-73; fellow, intern C.S. Mott Found. Nat. Ctr., Flint, Mich., 1973-74; elem. tchr. Val Verde Sch. Dist., Perris, Calif., 1974-76; assoc. prof., dir. community edn. ctr. U. of Redlands, Calif., 1976-80; supr., instr., reseach asst. U. N.Mex., Albuquerque, 1980-83; Pace instr. USN, San Diego, 1983-85; elem. resource tchr. San Diego Unified Sch. Dist., 1985-90; asst. prof. edn. Willamette U., Salem, Oreg., 1991—, coord. elem. edn.; commr., sec. Riverside (Calif.) County Juvenile Justice Delinquency Prevention Commn., 1977-80; pres. Nat. Alliance Black Community Educators, St. Louis, 1980; cons. U.S. Office Edn., Washington, 1977-81, Salem-Keizer Sch. Dist., Oreg. State Dept. Edn.; dir. Oreg. Gov.'s Sch. Citizen Leadership. Author: Intern Program Ethnic Studies, 1971, Comm Ed and School Desegregation, 1979. Bd. dirs. Calif. Community Edn. Assn., San Diego, 1977-80; v.p. Calif. Fedn. Black Leadership, Anaheim, 1977-80; chmn. budget com., chmn. multicultural edn. Salem-Keizer Sch. Dist. Recipient Mary McLeod Bethune award Nat. Coun. of Negro Women, San Diego, 1987, Spl. Recognition award Excel Tchr. Program, San Diego, 1988; nominated Tchr. of Yr. San Diego City Schs., 1986-87; Mott Found. fellow. Mem. Nat. Community Edn. Assn., NEA, Calif. Tchrs. Assn., Am. Assn. Polit. Sci., Am. School Curriculum Devel., Phi Kappa Phi (hon.), Alpha Phi Alpha, Phi Delta Kappa. Democrat. Office: Willamette U Dept Edn 900 State St Salem OR 97301

BIGATTI, MICHAEL MARSHALL, agricultural engineer; b. Torrance, Calif., Oct. 26, 1962; s. Osvaldo Omar and Margarita (Riba) B.; m. Maria Alejandra Leporati, Nov. 16, 1988. Grad. in Agrl. Engring., U. Nacional de Buenos Aires, 1989. Profl. agrl. engr.; lic. pest control advisor. Jour. editor Food & Agr. Orgn. Secretariat of Ad-Hoc Meat Group-Regional Office for Latin Am. & the Caribbean, Buenos Aires, 1987-88; written info. dissemination cons. Interam. Inst. for Cooperation to Agr., Buenos Aires, 1988-89; integrated pest mgmt. advisor El Modeno Gardens, Inc., Irvine, Calif., 1990-92, prodn. mgr., 1992-93; gen. mgr., 1993—. Mem. Calif. Agrl. Prodn. Cons. Assn., Club Univ. de Buenos Aires. Roman Catholic.

BIGBIE, SCOTT WOODSON, consulting engineering company executive; b. San Francisco, Oct. 5, 1946; s. Douglas Dillard and Claire (Condie) B.; m. Anne Croco, June 12, 1973 (div. 1981); 1 child, Claire; m. Constance Valerie Herig, Oct. 23, 1982. BSBA, U. So. Calif., L.A., 1968; M in Urban Planning, U. Wash., 1974. Dep. assessor County of Ventura, Calif., 1968-69; planner Murray-McCormick Environ. Group, Bellevue, Wash., 1974-75; dir. planning Triad Assocs., Kirkland, Wash., 1975-85, pres., 1985—. With U.S. Army, 1969-72, Vietnam. Mem. Profl. Svcs. Mgmt. Assn., Am. Civil Engrs. Coun., Am. Congress on Surveying and Mapping, Urban Land Inst., Bellevue Athletic Club, Theta Xi. Home: 9819 NE 32d St Bellevue WA 98004 Office: Triad Assocs 11415 NE 128th St Kirkland WA 98034-6399

BIGBIE, WANDA LOUISE, principal; b. Sherman, Tex., May 11, 1944; d. Roscoe Lewis and Wanda Naomi (Giles) Chadwick; m. Jerry Don Bigbie, Nov. 5, 1962; children: Donald Wesley, Charles Lewis. Student, Calif. State U., San Luis Obispo, 1963-64; BS in Edn., U. Alaska, 1965; MA, U. Calif., Riverside, 1970, postgrad., 1974-80. Cert. adminstr., pupil pers. svcs., gen. elem. tchr. Tchr. Anchorage Unified Sch. Dist., 1965-67; tchr. Moreno Valley (Calif.) Unified Sch. Dist., 1967-69, counselor, 1974-79, asst. prin., 1979-81, prin., 1981—; tchr. U. Calif., Riverside, 1979-81. Named Outstanding Adminstr. Coun. Exceptional Children, 1982, Woman of Achievement YWCA, Riverside, 1986; recipient Cert. of Recognition in Edn. Calif. Assembly, 1988, 89. Mem. Assn. Calif. Sch. Adminstrs. (del.), Western Riverside County Assn. Sch. Adminstrs. (past pres. membership 1989-90), Phi Delta Kappa (nat. del. 1987-90, area coord. 1990—, Outstanding Achievement award 1989, Trainer of Yr. 1991). Republican. Office: Moreno Valley Unified Schs 13911 Perris Blvd Moreno Valley CA 92553

BIGGS, JOEL GILSON, JR., planning, marketing and operations executive; b. Tucson, May 14, 1947; s. Joel Gilson Sr. and Alice Elizabeth (Briggman) B.; m. Anita Rita Cruz, Aug. 10, 1968 (div. Dec. 1981); children: Angela Lee, Jason Stanley; m. Marion A.F. Groom, Oct. 1, 1989. BS, U. Iowa, 1969, MS, 1981. Planner Dept. Land Mgmt. Govt. of Guam, Marianas Islands, 1969-70, Territorial Planning Commn., Guam, 1972-74; assoc. state planner Iowa State Office for Planning, Des Moines, 1974; econ. devel. specialist SE Iowa Regional Planning Commn., Keokuk, 1974-75; chief planner Bur. Planning, Guam, 1975-76; dir. Community Devel. Inst., Guam, 1977; asst. to pres. Guam Community Coll., 1978-81; dir. planning and rsch. Fontbonne Coll., St. Louis, 1981-84; product mgr. JonesMayer, Inc., St. Louis, 1984-88; v.p. planning and bus. devel. ETG Inc., Kansas City, Mo., 1988-89; mgr. strategic developer program Autodesk, Inc., Sausalito, Calif., 1989-90; ops. mgr. Archsoft Group, Sausalito, 1990-91; cons. Acad. Ednl. Devel., Washington, 1991—; lectr. various profl. confs.; instr. community devel. U. Guam, 1977; cons. Lincoln Mfg., St. Louis, 1987. Bd. dirs. Jr. Achievement of Guam, 1979-80; chmn. Territorial Seashore Protection Commn., Guam, 1979-80. Mem. Internat. Facilities Mgmt. Assn., Internat. Soc. Planning and Strategic Mgmt. (St. Louis chpt. pres. 1988-89). Home and Office: 50 Sonora Way Corte Madera CA 94925-2070

BIGGS, R.G., human resources professional; b. Dallas, July 14, 1935; s. Ralph Emerson and Grace Ruth (Butcher) B.; m. Nancy Kerr, 1958 (div. 1977); children: John, James, Nancy, Kristi; m. Lynn Rae Barnes, Oct. 9, 1981. BS, UCLA, 1960; MBA, Pepperdine U., 1972; postgrad., Southwestern Law Sch., L.A., 1965-66; cert., Antioch Sch. Law, 1982. Cert. tchr., Calif. Indsl. rels. GM Corp., Van Nuys, Calif., 1958-63; pers. mgr. Gaffers & Sattler Corp., L.A., 1963-66; indsl. rels. mgr. Internat. Rectifier, El Segundo, Calif., 1966-69, Rohr Industries, Riverside, Calif., 1970-76; dir. employee rels. Orange County Transit Dist., Santa Ana, Calif., 1976-78; sr. v.p. human resources Fedco Inc., Santa Fe Springs, Calif., 1978—. Contbr. articles to profl. jours. Pers. bd. City of Riverside, 1970-75, City of Santa Fe Springs, 1982—. With USAR. Mem. Personnel Industry Rels. Assn., Soc. Human Resource Mgmt, U.S. Golf Assn. Office: Fedco Inc 9300 Santa Fe Springs Rd Santa Fe Springs CA 90670

BIGGS, THOMAS WYLIE, chemical executive; b. Seattle, Oct. 28, 1950; s. Ray Wylie and Mildred Virginia (Ramsey) B.; m. Marcia Jean Holts, Aug. 4, 1973; children: Jennifer Tamar, Jordan Wylie. BA, U. Wash., 1972. Chemisty tchr. Samammish High Sch, Bellevue, Wash., 1972-74; sales rep. Litton Industries, Seattle, Wash., 1974-75; sales rep. Van Waters & Rogers (subs. Univar), Kent, Wash., 1975-80, area chem. mgr., 1988-90, br. mgr., 1990—, field sales mgr., 1980-85; sales mgr. Van Waters & Rogers (subs. Univar), South Bend, Ind., 1985-86; mgr. chem. dept. Van Waters & Rogers (subs. Univar), Indpls., 1986-88. 1st lt. USAR, 1973-80. Mem. Chgo. Drug and Chem. Assn., N.W. Paint and Coating Assn., Rotary (Kent), Kent C. of C. (bd. dirs.), The Lakes Club. Office: Van Waters and Rogers 8201 S 212th St Kent WA 98032-1994

BIGLER, ERIN DAVID, psychology educator; b. L.A., July 9, 1949; s. Erin Boley and Natalie (Webb) B.; m. Janet Beckstrom, June 22, 1990; children: Alicia Suzanne, Erin Daniel. BS, Brigham Young U., 1971, PhD, 1974. NIH postdoctoral fellow Barrow Neurol. Inst., St. Joseph's Hosp. and Med. Ctr., Phoenix, 1975-77; asst. to prof. of psychology U. Tex., Austin, 1977-90; prof. psychology Brigham Young U., Provo, Utah, 1990—. Author: Diagnostic Clinical Neuropsychology, 1984, 2d edit. 1988, Neuropsychological Function and Brain Imaging, 1989, Traumatic Brain Injury, 1990, Attention Deficit Disorder, 1990; assoc. editor: Archives of Clinical Neuropsychology, 1987—; cons. editor: Jour. of Learning Disabilities, 1987—, Neuropsychological Review, 1989—, Psychological Assessment, 1989—. Recipient Significant Contbrn. in Head Injury Rsch. and Treatment award Tex. Psychol. Assn. and Health Care Internat., Austin, 1990, grant NIH, Phoenix, 1975-77, grant Hogg Found. Univ. Tex., Austin, 1980-82. Fellow Nat. Acad. Neuropsychology (pres. 1989-90); mem. Am. Psychol. Assn., Soc. for Neuroscience, Internat. Neuropsychological Soc. Democrat. Mem. LDS Ch. Office: Dept Psychology 1086 SWKT Brigham Young U Provo UT 84602

BIGLIANI, GABRIELE, consular official; b. Rome, Feb. 27, 1952; s. Carlo and Licia (Giovannini) B.; m. Patricia Alagna, Sept. 7, 1985; 1 child, Veronica L.M. BA, La Sapienza Univ., Rome, 1978. Chancellor Ministry of Fgn. Affairs, Rome, 1984-90; consular official Consulate Gen. of Italy, San Francisco, 1990—; nat. mem., rep. Commissione Paritetica di Eleggibilità Per i Rifugiati (Joint Com. for Refugees), Rome, 1986-90. Author: Pittura Zen, 1982; contbr. articles Italian newspapers & mags. Office: Consulate General of Italy 2590 Webster St San Francisco CA 94115-1394

BIGOS, STANLEY JAMES, orthopaedic surgery spine specialist, educator; b. Grand Island, Nebr., Jan. 20, 1946; s. Stanley Joseph and Dorothy Marie (Krumel) B.; m. Karen Marie Hartnett Graybeal, Mar. 31, 1970 (div. Feb. 1988); children: Kristen Elizabeth (dec.), Jennifer Leah, John Bradley. AA, Fairbury (Nebr.) Coll., 1966; BS in Phys. Therapy, U. Mo., 1970, MD, 1975. Chief phys. therapist Johnson & Carroll County Hosp., Warrensburg and Carrollton, Mo., 1970-71; clin. instr. U. Mo. Phys. Therapy, Columbia, 1972-76; surg. intern U. Mo. Med. Ctr., Columbia, 1975-76; resident orthopaedics U. Utah, Salt Lake City, 1876-80; spine fellow Alf Nachemson, Gothenburg, Sweden, Seattle, 1980-81; from asst. prof. to assoc. prof. U. Wash., Seattle, 1982-91, prof. orthopaedics, 1991—; founder, dir. Spine Resource Clinic, Seattle, 1985—; chmn. panel guide Agy. for Health Care Policy Rsch., Rockville, Md., 1991—. Author: Musculoskeletal Guide, 1983; guest editor Seminars in Spine, 1992; contbr. chpt. to book and articles to profl. jours. Co-founder, mem. Patrons Cystic Fibrosis, Seattle, 1985; pres. 65 Roses Club, Seattle, 1986-88. Named Friend of Man Wash. Gens., 1988. Fellow Am. Acad. Orthopaedic Surgeons (occupational health/outcomes com. 1989—, Kappa Delta award 1991); mem. Am. Orthopaedic Assn., N.Am. Spine Soc., Western Orthopaedic Assn., Internat. Assn. Study of Pain, Internat. Soc. Study Lumber Spine (west coast rep. 1987-91), Patrons Cystic Fibrosis (v.p. 1985-86, award of merit 1987). Office: U Wash Dept Orthopaedics RK-10 Seattle WA 98195

BILBRAY, JAMES HUBERT, congressman, lawyer; b. Las Vegas, May 19, 1938; s. James A. and Ann E. (Miller) B.; m. Michaelene Mercer, Jan. 1960; children: Bridget, Kevin, Erin, Shannon. Student, Brigham Young U., 1957-58, U. Nev., Las Vegas, 1958-60; BA, Am. U., 1962; JD, Washington Coll. Law, 1964. Bar: Nev. 1965. Staff mem. Senator Howard Cannon U.S. Senate, 1960-64; dep. dist. atty. Clark County, Nev., 1965-68; mem. Lovell, Bilbray & Potter, Las Vegas, 1969-87; mem. Nev. Senate, 1980-86, chmn. taxation com., 1983-86, chmn. interim com. on pub. broadcasting, 1983; 100th-103d U.S. Congresses from 1st Nev. dist.; mem. 100th-103rd Congresses from 1st Nev. dist., 1987—; mem. fgn. affairs com., 1987-88, mem. house armed svs. com., subcom. procurement, mil. contracts, sea power, mem. small bus. com., chmn. procurement, taxation and tourism subcom., 1989—; mem. Spl. Panel on NATO and North Atlantic Alliance, fgn. affairs com., select com. on hunger, 1987-88, select com. on aging, 1988-93, subcoms. Africa, trade exports and tourism, select com. on intelligence, 1993—; alt. mcpl. judge city of Las Vegas, 1987-89; del. North Atlantic Alliance, 1989—. Bd. regents U. Nev. System, 1968-72; mem. Nat. Coun. State Govts. Commn. on Arts and Historic Preservation; mem. bd. visitors USAF Acad., 1991—. Named Outstanding Alumnus U. Nev., Las Vegas, 1979, Man of Yr. Am. Diabetes Assn., 1989, Man of Yr. Haddassah (Nev.), 1990. Mem. Nev. State Bar Assn., Clark county Bar Assn., U. Nev.-Las Vegas Alumni Assn. (pres. 1964-69, Humanitarian of Yr. 1984), Phi Alpha Delta, Sigma Chi, KC. Democrat. Roman Catholic. Lodges: Elks, Rotary. Office: House of Representatives Washington DC 20515

BILBY, RICHARD MANSFIELD, federal judge; b. Tucson, May 29, 1931; s. Ralph Willard and Marguerite (Mansfield) B.; m. Ann Louise Borchert, July 6, 1957; children: Claire Louise, Ellen M. Moore. B.S., U. Ariz., 1955; J.D., U. Mich., 1958. Bar: Ariz. 1959. Since practiced in Tucson; law clk. to Chief Judge Chambers, 9th Circuit Ct. Appeals, San Francisco, 1958-59; mem. firm Bilby, Thompson, Shoenhair & Warnock, 1959-79, partner, 1967-79; judge U.S. Dist. Ct., Dist. Ariz., Tucson, 1979—; chief judge U.S. Dist. Ct., Dist. Ariz., 1984-90; conscientious objector hearing officer Dept. Justice, 1959-62; chmn. Pima County Med.-Legal panel, 1968-70; Mem. Tucson Charter Revision Com., 1965-70. Chmn. United Fund Profl. Div., 1968; chmn. Spl. Gift Div., 1970, St. Joseph Hosp. Devel. Fund Drive, 1970; Republican state chmn. Vols. for Eisenhower, 1956; Rep. county chmn., Pima County, Ariz., 1972-74; Past pres. Tucson Conquistadores; bd. dirs. St. Josephs Hosp., 1969-77, chmn., 1972-75. Served with AUS, 1952-54. Fellow Am. Coll. Trial Lawyers; mem. Ariz. Acad., Town Hall (dir. 1976-79). Office: US Dist Ct US Courthouse Rm 426 44 E Broadway Blvd Tucson AZ 85701-1711

BILDERBACK, DIANE ELIZABETH, garden writer; b. Medford, Oreg., Apr. 13, 1951; d. Richard Middleton and Mary Lou (Harris) Letsom; m. David Earl Bilderback, June 27, 1970; children: Eric Leland, Christopher Brian. BS in Botany with honors, U. Mont., 1974. Calender columnist Rodale's Organic Gardening, Emmaus, Pa., 1984-87, regional advisor, 1987-88; student assistance coord. Univ. Coll. U. Mont., Missoula, 1989—; instrnl. aide Mt. Jumbo Elem. Sch., Missoula, Mont., 1987-88. Co-author: Garden Secrets, 1982, Backyard Fruits and Berries, 1984, The Harrowsmith's Book of Garden Secrets, 1991, The Gardener's Home Companion, 1991; contbr. various mags. including Nat. Gardening, Family Circle. Home: 5520 Larch Ln Missoula MT 59802-5242

BILEZIKJIAN, EDWARD ANDREW, architect; b. Los Angeles, Mar. 29, 1950; s. Andrew and Alice (Dardarian) B. BSArch, U. So. Calif., 1973, MArch, 1977. Registered architect, Calif. Project mgr. RMA Archtl. Group, Inc., Costa Mesa, Calif., 1977-78; dir. architecture Donald De Mars Assocs., Inc., Van Nuys, Calif., 1978-85; prin. architect EAB Architects, Sepulveda, Calif., 1985-87, Laguna Hills, Calif., 1988—; architect, planner III Trammell Crow Co., Irvine, Calif., 1986-88; prin. architect Fluor Daniel, Inc., Irvine, Calif., 1989—. Chmn. parish coun. Armenian Apostolic Ch. Newport Beach, 1988-91. Mem. AIA, Triple-X Fraternity of Calif. (corresponding sec. 1984-85), Nat. Coun. Archtl. Registration Bds. (cert.). Democrat. Mem. Armenia Apostolic Ch.

BILIMORIA, KARL DHUNJISHAW, aerospace engineer; b. Bombay, June 27, 1960; s. Dhun K. and Najoo D. (Motafram) B. BTech in Aero. Engring., Indian Inst. Tech., 1982; MS in Aero. Engring., Va. Poly. Inst. and State U., 1984, PhD in Aero. Engring., 1986. Grad. asst. Va. Poly. Inst. and State U., Blacksburg, 1982-86; asst. prof. Ariz. State U., Tempe, 1987-91, rsch. scientist, 1991—; referee Jour. Aircraft, Jour. Guidance, Control and Dynamics. Contbr. articles to profl. jours. Mem. AIAA (sr.), Sigma Gamma Tau. Office: Ariz State U Aero Rsch Ctr Tempe AZ 85287-8006

BILLHEIMER, STEPHANIE DANA, laboratory technologist; b. Fresno, Calif., July 25, 1955; d. Donald Howard and Rosemary Patricia (Lynch) Hester; m. Myles Edward Billheimer, Mar. 25, 1972; children: Amy Catherine, Heidi Marie. BS in Biology summa cum laude, Ea. Wash. U., 1985; diploma med. tech., Deaconess Sch. Med. Tech., Spokane, Wash., 1985-86. Cert. med. technologist Am. Soc. Clin. Pathologists. Med. technologist Watsonville (Calif.) Community Hosp., 1987-88; med. technologist, lab. mgr. Loma Vista Clin. Lab., San Jose, Calif., 1988—; tutor pvt. practice, Felton, Calif., 1988—. Vol. classroom parent Wash. schs., 1980-86; vol. visitor, music leader, Wash. and Calif. hosps., nursing homes. Recipient scholarship Rockwood Med. Clinic, Spokane, 1983. Mem. Calif. Assn. for Med. Lab. Tech. Republican. Presbyterian.

BILLINGS, JUDITH, state education official. Supt. public instrn. State of Washington. Office: Public Instruction Dept Old Capitol Bldg Mail Stop FG-11 Olympia WA 98504

BILLINGS, THOMAS NEAL, computer and publishing executive, management consultant; b. Milw., Mar. 2, 1931; s. Neal and Gladys Victoria (Lockard) B.; m. Barta Hope Chipman, June 12, 1954 (div. 1967); children: Bridget Ann, Bruce Neal; m. Marie Louise Farrell, Mar. 27, 1982. AB with honors, Harvard U., 1952, MBA, 1954. V.p. fin. and adminstrn. and technol. innovation Copley Newspapers Inc., La Jolla, Calif., 1957-70; group v.p., dir. tech. Harte-Hanks Comm. Inc., San Antonio, 1970-73; exec. v.p. United Media, Inc., Phoenix, 1973-75; asst. to pres., dir. corp. mgmt. systems Ramada Inns, Inc., Phoenix, 1975-76; exec. dir. NRA, Washington, 1976-77; pres. Ideation Inc., N.Y.C., 1977-81; chmn. Bergen-Billings Inc., N.Y.C., 1977-80; pres. The Assn. Svc. Corp, San Francisco, 1978-91; pres. Recorder Printing and Pub. Co. Inc., San Francisco, 1980-82; v.p. adminstrn. Victor Techs. Inc., Scotts Valley, Calif., 1982-84; mng. dir. Saga-Wilcox Computers Ltd., Wrexham, Wales, 1984-85; chmn. Thomas Billings & Assocs., Inc., Reno, 1978—, Intercontinental Travel Svc. Inc., Reno, 1983—, Oberon Optical Character Recognition, Ltd., Hemel-Hemstead, Eng., 1985-86; dir., chief exec. officer Insignia Software Solutions group, High Wycombe, England, Cupertino, Calif., 1986-89; v.p. Cromer Equipment Co., Oakland, Calif., 1989—; bd. dirs. Digital Broadcasting Corp., Mountain View, Calif., Lenny's Restaurants Inc., Wichita, Kans., Tymyndr Corp., Dover Del., Zzyzzyx Corp., Reno, Harrod's Hotel & Casino Corp., Las Vegas, Pandemonium Pictures, Inc., San Mateo, Calif., Bonanza Corp., Virginia City, Nev., Quillmill Ltd., London; speaker and seminar leader. Bd. dirs. Nat. Allergy Found., 1973—, The Wilderness Fund, 1978—, San Diego Civic Light Opera Assn., 1965-69; chmn. Intercontinental News Svc. Inc., London, and Alameda, Calif., 1989—; chief exec. San Diego 200th Anniversary Expn., 1969. Served with U.S. Army, 1955-57. Recipient Walter F. Carley Meml. award, 1966, 69. Fellow U.K. Inst. Dirs.; mem. Am. Newspaper Pubs. Assn., Inst. Execs. Inc. (dir.), Inst. Newspaper Fin. Officers, Sigma Delta Chi. Republican. Clubs: West Side Tennis, LaJolla Country; Washington Athletic; San Francisco Press; Harvard (N.Y.C.); Elks. Author: Creative Controllership, 1978, Our Credibility Crisis, 1983, Non-Euclidean Theology, 1987, Ruminations on Meta Mentality, 1990, Fixing our Broken System, 1992; editor: The Vice Presidents' Letter, 1978—; pub. The Microcomputer Letter, 1982—, Synthetic Hardware Update, 1987—; editor: Intercontinental News Svc., London, England, and Alameda Calif., 1985—. Address: PO Drawer I Alameda CA 94501-0262 Office: 4701 Oakport St Oakland CA 94601

BILLINGTON, PETER JAMES, management educator; b. New Bedford, Mass., June 18, 1948; s. George W. and Sophie H. (Fronczek) B.; m. Maryann I. Grusetskie, July 23, 1977; children: Drew, Alex. BSEE, Worcester Poly. Inst., 1970; MBA, Northeastern U., 1977; MS, Cornell U., 1980, PhD, 1983. Owner, pres. P.J. Billington Inc., Worcester, Mass., 1970-75; prof. Northeastern U., Boston, 1980-89; Martec prof. mgmt. U. So. Colo., Pueblo, 1989—; mgmt. cons., 1980—. Contbr. articles to profl. jours. Recipient Provost award U. So. Colo., 1991. Mem. Decision Scis. Inst. (v.p. publs. 1988), Inst. Mgmt. Sci., Am. Prodn. and Inventory Control Soc., Am. Soc. Quality Control. Home: 1955 Hunters Point Ln Colorado Springs CO 80919-3462 Office: U So Colo 2200 Bonforte Blvd Pueblo CO 81001-4901

BILLINTON, ROY, engineering educator; b. Leeds, Eng., Sept. 14, 1935; s. Edwin and Nettie (Billinton); m. Alice Joyce McKenna, July 21, 1956; children—Leslie, Kevin, Michael, Christopher, Jeffrey. B.Sc.E.E., U. Man., 1960, M.Sc., 1963; Ph.D., U. Sask., 1967, D.Sc., 1975. Journeyman electrician McCaine Electric, Winnipeg, Man., Can., 1956; mem. system operation dept. and system planning dept. Man. Hydro, from 1960; asst. prof. to prof., head dept. elec. engring. U. Sask., Saskatoon, 1964—; now assoc. dean pres. PowerComp Assocs., cons. Author: Power System Reliability Evaluation, 1970, (with R. J. Ringlee and A. J. Wood) Power System Reliability Calculations, 1973, (with C. Singh) System Reliability Modelling and Evaluation, 1977; (with R.N. Allan) Reliability Evaluation of Engineering Systems, 1983, Reliability Evaluation of Power Systems, 1984, (with R.N. Allan) Reliability of Large Electric Power Systems, 1988, (with R.N. Allan, L. Salvaderi) Applied Reliability Assessment in Electric Power Systems, 1990; also articles. Recipient Sir George Nelson award Engring. Inst. Can., 1965-67, Ross medal, 1972, Centennial Disting. Svc. award Can. Elect Assn., 1991. Fellow IEEE (Outstanding Power Engring. Educator award 1992), Royal Soc. Can., Engring. Inst. Can., U.K. Safety and Reliability Soc. Home: 3 McLean Crescent, Saskatoon, SK Canada S7J 2R6 Office: U Sask, Dept Elec Engring, Saskatoon, SK Canada S7N 0W0

BILOTTI-STARK, KATHRYN ELIZABETH, graphic designer; b. La Mesa, Calif., Aug. 6, 1950; d. Anthony D. Bilotti and Dorothy Helen (Moore) Marquet; m. Stephen E. Trombetta, 1971 (div. 1978); m. Michael F. Stark, Aug. 30, 1980. BA in Art, U. Calif. Santa Cruz, 1981; MA, Sch. of Design, Basel, Switzerland, 1987. Design and producton client and vendor liaison Aptos (Calif.) Press, 1981-82; freelance design prodn., 1982-84; sr. designer Jerry Takigawa Design, Pacific Grove, Calif., 1987-88; prin., creative dir. Kathryn B. Stark Graphic Design, Pacific Grove, Calif., 1988—; instr. U. Calif. Ext. Cert. Program in Graphic Design and Prodn., 1987—. Recipient Monterey Bay Ad Club-"Sammy's" award, 1989, Best of Show, 1 Gold and 2 Silver awards, 1990, 2 Silver and 3 Bronze awards, 1991, 1 Gold and 2 Bronze awards. Mem. Am. Inst. Graphic Arts, Montery Bay Ad Club, Western Art Dirs. Club, People in Comm. Arts (bd. dirs., sec. 1988, pres. 1989). Office: Kathryn B Stark Design 227 Forest Ave #8 Pacific Grove CA 93950

BILOW, STEVEN CRAIG, computer graphics specialist; b. L.A., July 10, 1960; s. Norman and Selma (Rifkin) B.; m. Patricia S. Crabb, Nov. 5, 1989. BFA in Music Composition, Calif. Inst. of the Arts, 1982; cert. logic design/theory, U. So. Calif., 1983. Cert. tchr. of movement expression, L.A., 1985. Mfg. engr. Hughes Aircraft EDSG, El Segundo, Calif., 1981-85; project engr. electro-optical test systems Hughes Aircraft EDSG, El Segundo, 1985-86; sr. systems analyst Tektronix, Info Display Group, Woodland Hills, Calif., 1986-88; software engr., math. surface representation Interactive Techs. div. Tektronix, Wilsonville, Oreg., 1988-91; sr. tech. support specialist Unix and X Window systems Interactive Techs. div. Tektronix, Wilsonville, Oreg., 1991—; cons. in graphics SCBA Software, Lake Oswego, Oreg., 1987—; cons. in music composition and ethnomusicology, Structured Perceptions Music, L.A., 1980-85; mem. ACM Spl. Interest Group in Computer Graphics, 1988—. Composer various electro-acoustic instrumental and choral works, 1978-83; author: (theater piece) Indra's Net, 1987; author, editor (book) Designing For Producibility, 1980; contbr. articles, columns and book revs. to profl. jours. Mem. Human/Dolphin Found., Malibu, Calif., 1977, Self-Realization Fellowship, L.A., 1985. Recipient Technical Excellence award, Tektronix, Inc., Wilsonville, 1988. Mem. Am. Musicol. Soc., Oreg. Master Gardner Assn., Am. Rose Soc., Assn. Computing Machinery, IEEE (tech. com. on computer graphics, 1985—, tech. com. on super computer applications, 1988), Am. Rose Soc., Oreg. Master Gardener Assn. Democrat. Office: Tektronix Interactive Tech PO Box 1000 Wilsonville OR 97070-1000

BIMSON, CARL ALFRED, bank executive; b. Berthoud, Colo., Mar. 15, 1900; s. Alfred George and Margaret (Eichman) B.; m. Irene M. Hildreth, Oct. 25, 1927 (dec. 1969). ME, Colo. A. & M. Coll., 1923. Dist. cashier, group mgr. Mt. States Tel. & Tel. Co., 1924-30; self-employed, 1930-33; with Valley Nat. Bank, Phoenix, 1933—; state mgr. fin. rels. State Ariz. Fed. Housing Administrn., 1934-36; mgr. installment loan dept. Valley Nat. Bank, 1936-39, asst. v.p., 1939-40, v.p., then sr. v.p., 1941-49, exec. v.p., 1949-53, pres., 1953-62, vice chmn. bd., chmn. exec. com., 1962-70, dir., 1941-70, vice chmn. emeritus, 1970—; pres. Concho Investment Co., Concho Life Ins. Co., 1965-76; mem. exec. com., asst. sec. Valley Nat. Ins. Co.; Dir. Sun Angel Found., Maricopa County Better Bus. Bur., past pres., Merchants & Mfrs. Assn. Phoenix, past pres., Internat. Retail Credit Men's Assn., Coun. Profit Sharing Inds.; mem. 1st bankers adv. com. Westinghouse Electric Co.; past pres. Municipal Indsl. Devel. Corp., Mchts. and Mfrs. Credit Bur., Maricopa County chpt. A.R.C., nat. v.p., Maricopa County chpt. March Dimes, Ariz. Evang. Council; v.p., dir., mem. adv. com. Phoenix YMCA; past pres. Phoenix Credit Bur.; mem. Phoenix Growth Com; chmn. finance com. Maricopa County Planning Com.; mem. adv. council Ariz. Bus.-Industry-Edn. Council; v.p., mem. bd. Jr. Achievement Met. Phoenix; mem. bd. exec. com. Phoenix Devel. Assn.; mem. dean's adv. council Ariz. State U. Sch. Bus.; mem. bd., treas. Christian Care, Inc.; elder, chmn. bd. trustees 1st Christian Ch., Phoenix; mem. bd. Tax Found., Inc. Contbr. articles trade jours. Founding dir., treas. Christian Care and Heritage Village, campus for the elderly, 1977-87; elder emeritus 1st Christian Ch. Phoenix. Recipient Hon. State Farmer award, Future Farmers of America; Significant Sig award Sigma Chi, 1963; Disting. Achievement award Ariz. State U. Coll. Bus. Adminstrn., 1977; citation honor 90th birthday from Gov. of Ariz. State, 1990, Merit award Colo. State U., 1965, Pub. Svc. award Ill. Bankers Assn., 1961, Honor award nat. com. 50th anniversary Consumer Credit in Banks, 1960; named Ky. by Col. Gov. Ky., 1960, Goodwill Amb. Savings Bond Program by Sec. Treas., 1960. Mem. Future Farmers Am. (v.p. 1959, pres. 1960, mgmt., adminstrv., govt. borrowing coms., Hon. Farmer of Yr. 1946), Ariz. Bankers Assn. (past pres., v.p. nat. bank divsn., past chmn. exec. com.), Am. Bankers Assn. (past pres., past consumer credit com., past small bus. credit com., past v.p., past administrv. com., past chmn. administrv. com., past ex-officio exec coun.), Am. Inst. Banking (life), Nat. Assn. Better Bus. Burs. (past mem. bd. govs., dist. gov. 11 western states), Financial Pub. Relations Assn. (3d v.p., past dir.), Phoenix Clearing House Assn. (past pres.), Nat. Retail Credit Men's Assn. (past dir.), Robert Morris Assos. (life), U.S. C. of C. (finance com., past chmn. subcom. credit unions), Phoenix C. of C. (past pres.), Phoenix Thunderbirds (life), Ariz. Club, Paradise Valley Country Club (founding dir.), Kiwanis (life), Sigma Chi, Beta Gamma Sigma (hon.). Home: 5221 N Saddle Rock Dr Phoenix AZ 85018-1829 Office: Valley Nat Bank Phoenix AZ 85036

BINA, MELVIN JOSEPH, engineer; b. Antigo, Wis., Oct. 28, 1931; s. Aloise Frank and Ann (Johanek) B.; m. La Donna Ann Tehan, Nov. 24, 1951; children: Denise Ann, David Louis. BS, U. Wis., 1953; MS, Air Force Inst. Tech., Dayton, Ohio, 1960; PhD, U. Ariz., 1972. Commd. 2nd lt. USAF, 1953, advanced through grades to lt. col., 1970, ret., 1975; sr. staff engr. Lockheed Missiles & Space Co., Sunnyvale, Calif., 1975—. Contbr. articles to profl. jorus.; patentee in field. Decorated 10 Air medals, 7 Vietnamese Svc. medals. Mem. Air Force Assn. (life), Sigma Pi Sigma. Republican. Home: 5811 E Paseo Busanic Tucson AZ 85715

BINDER, ERWIN, sculptor; b. Phila., Jan. 24, 1934; s. Albert and Betty (Kushner) B.; m. Diane Binder, Jan. 4, 1964; 1 child, Mark. Student, Temple U., 1951, Gemological Inst. Am., 1960, Otis Art Inst., 1962. bd. dirs. Base, Woodland Hills, Calif., Jovenes, Inc. Prin. works include Palm Springs Desert Mus., 1985, Butler Inst. Am. Art, Youngstown, Ohio, Johnny Carson Park, Burbank, Calif., 1988, Golda Meir Medallion, 1989, Art Gallery Internat., 1990, Fountain Valley (Calif.) Br. Libr., Lexington Hills Project, Santa Rosa Valley, Ventura, Calif., Givat Ram Campus, Jerusalem; author documentary film Binder the Sculptor, 1981. Bd. dirs. Arts of Mex. Exhibition 1991, Rockfeller Found., L.A. County Art. Mus., 1990-91, Fine Arts and Communication, LMU, L.A., 1989—, Bilingual Found. of the Arts, L.A., 1986-89, curator La Fiesta de los Mortas, 1989; curator Nearika, Myth & Magic Burbank Creative Arts Ctr., 1990. With USAF, 1952-55. Recipient Beautification award CIty of Brea, 1990. Mem. Burbank Fine Arts Fedn. (bd. dirs.). Jewish. Office: Topaz Universal 4632 W Magnolia Blvd Burbank CA 91505-2731

BINDER, GORDON M., health and medical products executive; b. St. Louis, 1935. Grad., Purdue U., 1957, Harvard U., 1962. Chmn., CEO Amgen, Inc. Office: Amgen Inc Amgen Ctr 1840 Dehavilland Dr Thousand Oaks CA 91320*

BINDER, JAMES KAUFFMAN, computer consultant; b. Reading, Pa., Nov. 20, 1920; s. Paul Burdette and Edna (Kauffman) B.; B.A., Lehigh U., 1941; M.A., Johns Hopkins U., 1952; profl. cert. in systems mgmt. U. Calif.-San Diego, 1976; A.S. in Data Processing, San Diego Evening Coll., 1979, A.A. in Fgn. Lang., 1979; A.A. in Spanish, Mira Costa Coll., Oceanside, Calif., 1981. Instr. English, Notre Dame U., South Bend, Ind., 1948-49; prof. English, Athens (Greece) Coll., 1950-51; CARE rep., Greece, 1951-52; reporter, staff writer Athens News, 1952-53; dir. lang. tng. World Council Chs. Refugee Service, Athens, 1953-54; co-editor Am. Overseas Guide, N.Y., West Berlin, 1957-58; lectr. English, U. Md. Overseas Program, European and Far East divs., 1958-66; successively supr. Cen. Info. Ctr., supt. documents, sr. systems analyst GA Techs., Inc., La Jolla, Calif., 1968-85. Recipient Williams Prize, Lehigh U., 1939, 41; Johns Hopkins U. Grad. Sch. Pres. scholar, 1945-48. Roman Catholic. Clubs: Tudor and Stuart, Automobile of So. Calif. Author: The Correct Comedy, 1951; contbg. translator Modern Scandinavian Poetry, 1948; editor: (with Erwin H. Tiebe) American Overseas Guide, 1958.

BINEGAR, GWENDOLYN ANN, social worker; b. Phoenix, Sept. 23, 1924; d. Glenn Marvin and Mary Lenore (Cartwright) Redington; B.S. in Sociology, Iowa State U., 1948; M. Social Svc., Bryn Mawr Coll., 1967; m. Lewis Albert Binegar, Nov. 2, 1951; children: Glen Albert, Birne Thomas, William Lewis, Alan Martin. Psychiat. social worker Child Study Inst., Bryn Mawr (Pa.) Coll., 1967-71; supervising counselor San Gabriel Valley Regional Ctr., Pomona, 1975-78, program mgr. six L.A. County Regional Ctrs' High Risk Infant Projects, 1978-79; chief case mgmt. svcs. San Diego Regional Ctr., 1981—, assoc. dir., 1988-91, cons., 1992—; v.p. Golden Years, Inc., Valley Ctr., Calif., 1987—. Lic. clin. social worker. Fellow Soc. Cert. Social Workers; mem. Am. Acad. Certified Social Workers, Am. Assn. on Mental Deficiency, Nat. Assn. Social Workers. Republican. Presbyterian. Home: 28809 Lilac Rd Valley Center CA 92082

BINÉT, BETSEY JAN, writer, editor; b. Missoula, Mont., Oct. 1, 1953; d. William Edward Binét and Betsey Louise (Sherburne) Stevens; m. Ronald Eugene Wolf, June 14, 1980 (div. Apr., 1990); 1 child, Christopher James Wolf. BA in English, Calif. State U., L.A., 1977. Dir. pubs. UCLA Med. Ctr., L.A., 1978-84; writer, editor, designer pvt. practice, Venice, Calif., 1984-86; mktg. writer, editor Churchill Films, L.A., 1986-89; sr. devel. writer UCLA, 1989—. Contbg. editor UCLA Mag., 1991—; multi-media composer. Contbr., sponsor Christian Children's Fund, 1977-91; activist Campaign for Nuclear Freeze, 1982; parliamentarian Farragut Sch. PTA, Culver City, 1991-92, legislation chair, 1993—, recording sec., 1992—; contbr. Naral Caral, 1992, People for the Am. Way, 1992. Named Woman of Yr. Intrafraternity Coun., Calif. State U., L.A., 1975; recipient Svc. award Community Coalition on Substance Abuse Prevention and Treatment, s. cen. L.A., 1992. Mem. NOW, Zero Population Growth. Democrat. Home: 4711 Maytime Ln Culver City CA 90230 Office: UCLA 405 Hilgard Ave Los Angeles CA 90024-1359

BING, RALPH SOL, advertising executive; b. Cleve., May 21, 1917; s. Sol Ralph and Helen (Einstein) B.; m. Barbara Cohen, Nov. 8, 1953; children: Aleta, Ralph Sam. Student, U. Ill., 1936-37; cert., John Huntington Poly., Cleve., 1939, Kent State U., 1966. Advt. copywriter The May Co., Cleve., 1938-41; advt. mgr. The Heights Press (now named Sun Newspapers), Cleve., 1941-42; ptnr. Bing and Haas Advt., Cleve., 1946-51; pres. Ralph Bing Advt. Co., Cleve., 1951—, Mktg. Assocs., Beachwood, Ohio, 1975-79; owner Ralph Bing Advt. Cons., San Diego, 1980-87; combat corr. 82nd Airborne div., The Stars and Stripes. Author: SMOKE DREAMS, 1950, History of the Temple, 1950; contbr. numerous articles to profl. jours., also radio and TV commls. Councilman City of Beachwood, 1965-79; pres. grouping of municipalities Coun. of Couns., Cleve., 1978-79; mem. Rancho Bernardo (Calif.) Pub. Utilities Commn., 1983-85; chmn. Community Alert Program Rancho Bernardo, 1986; mem., corr. sec., mem. exec. bd. Rancho Bernardo Community Coun., 1993—. Recipient Outstanding Citizen award Beachwood Civic League, 1980, Outstanding Service award United Appeal, 1950, 51, Appreciation plaque Ohio Bar Assn., 1975; Ralph S. Bing Days named in his honor Beachwood City Council, 1979, 80. Mem. Family Svc. Assn. (hon. life), Oakwood Club (Cleve., pub. newsletter 1946-80), Rancho Bernardo Press Club (exec. bd. 1991—), Woodcrafts Club, Masons, Kiwanis (pres. 1976). Republican. Clubs: Oakwood (Cleve.) (pub. newsletter 1946-80); Rancho Bernardo News; Woodcrafts. Lodges: Masons, Kiwanis (pres. 1976). Home and office: 16109 Selva Dr San Diego CA 92128-3125

BINGAMAN, JEFF, senator; b. El Paso, Tex., Oct. 3, 1943; s. Jesse and Beth (Ball) B.; m. Anne Kovacovich, Sept. 13, 1968. BA Govt., Harvard U., 1965; JD, Stanford U., 1968. Bar: N.Mex. 1968. Asst. atty. gen., 1969; atty. Stephenson, Campbell & Olmsted, 1971-72; partner firm Campbell, Bingaman & Black, Santa Fe, 1972-78; atty. gen. State of N.Mex., from 1979; now U.S. senator from N.Mex. U.S. Army 1968-74. Democrat. Methodist. Home: PO Box 5775 Santa Fe NM 87502-5775 Office: US Senate 502 Hart Senate Bldg Washington DC 20510*

BINGHAM, PARIS EDWARD, JR., electrical engineer, computer consultant; b. Aurora, Colo., Sept. 26, 1957; s. Paris Edward and Shirley Ann (Blehm) B.; m. Laurie Sue Piersol, May 9, 1981 (div. Sept. 1987). BS in Elec. Engring. and Computer Sci., U. Colo., 1979. Mem. tech. staff Western Electric Co., Aurora, 1979-81, system engr., 1981; mem. electronic tech. staff Hughes Aircraft Co., Aurora, 1981-83, staff engr., 1983-86, sr. staff engr., 1986—; cons. RJM Assocs., Huntington, N.Y., 1987—; cons. Aurora, 1988—. Mem. AAAS, IEEE, Assn. for Computing Machinery, Math. Assn. Am. Republican. Presbyterian. Office: Hughes Aircraft Co 16800 E Centretech Pky Aurora CO 80011-9046

BINGHAM, ROBERT FREDERICK, communication company executive; b. N.Y.C., Dec. 30, 1962; s. Robert F. and Eileen (Wilson) B. BA, DePauw U. Market rep. IBM Corp., Cherry Hill, N.J., 1985-87; account exec. AT&T Data Systems, Chgo., 1987—; sales mgr. AT&T Info. Systems, Chgo., 1987-89; dist. staff mgr. AT&T Info. Systems, Parsippany, N.J., 1989-90; location mgr. AT&T Info. Systems, Southfield, Mich., 1990-91; v.p. Digital Systems Internat., Redmond, Wash., 1991—; ptnr. Southeastern Corp., Chgo., 1988—; leader coun. bd. dirs. AT&T Corp., N.Y.C. Mem. Am. Mgmt. Assn. Roman Catholic. Home: 2320 17th Ct Redmond WA 98052 Office: Digital Systems Internat 6464 185th Ave Redmond WA 98052-5032

BINI, DANTE NATALE, architect, industrial designer; b. Castelfranco Emilia, Modena, Italy, Apr. 22, 1932; came to U.S., 1981; s. Giovanni and Maria (Cavallini) B.; m. Adria Vittoria Moretti, June 27, 1963; children: Stefano Alec, Nicolo Guiseppe. Grad., L.S.A. Righi, Bologna, Italy, 1952; PhD in Architecture, U. Florence, 1962. Chmn. Societa' Anonima Immobiliare Castelfranco Emilia, Castelfranco Emilia, 1960-64, Vedova Bini, Castelfranco Emilia, 1960-64; founder, chmn. Unipack, Old Home, Bologna, 1961-65; founder, exec. v.p. Binishell Spa, Bologna, 1966-69; cons. Dept. Pub. Works New South Wales, Sydney, Australia, 1972-74, Jennings Industries Ltd., Melbourne, Australia, 1975-80; founder Bini Cons. Australia; founder, pres., chmn. Binistar, Inc., San Francisco, 1981—; external cons. Bechtel Nat., Inc., San Francisco, 1985-86; founder, pres., chmn. Pak-Home, Inc. (now Napa Valley Corp.), San Francisco, 1986—; cons. Shimizu Corp., Tokyo, 1989-93; spl. cons. to UN, Rome, 1968, Shimizu Tech. Ctr. Am., 1989, Shimizu Co., Tokyo, 1991-92; lectr. Moscow Expocenter, 1986; vis. lectr. NASA Ames Rsch. Ctr., 1989, vis. lectr. univs. Italy, Australia, U.S., Mex., Venezuela, Brazil, Argentina, Peru, Eng., USSR, Fed. Republic Germany. Contbr. articles and papers to profl. jours., also conf. procs.; patentee self-shaping structures for low-cost, sport and indsl./comml. bldgs., designer of a self-shaping mega-structure for a new city's infrastructure and framework, 1989; developer new automated constrn. system for multi-storied bldg.; co-researcher for self-shaping, self-sinking lunar habitat. Decorated Order of Commendatore Pres. Italian Republic, 1989; recipient Eurostar award European Inst. Packaging, 1964, Excellence in Engring. Design award Design News Mag., 1968, Best Idea of Yr. award European Design News Mag., 1968, Excellence in Indsl. Design award I.E.S. Australia, 1976. Mem. Bd. Architects Emilia e Romagna, Assn. Architects Bologna (co-founder 1963), Italian Assn. Indsl. Design, Italian Inst. Packaging Design (Oscar award 1961-63), Royal Australian Inst. Architects New South Wales, Am. Assn. Mil. Engrs. Roman Catholic.

BINING, AVTAR SINGH, energy, air quality specialist; b. Khera, Punjab, India, May 23, 1955; came to U.S., 1988; s. Sidhu Singh and Amar (Kaur) B.; m. Baljit Pannu, May 30, 1987. B in Agrl. Engring., U. India, 1978; M in Agrl. Engring., Punjab Agrl. U., Ludhiana, 1980; PhD in Engring., U. Calif., Davis, 1993. Cert. C.C. instr., Calif. Rsch. fellow energy Punjab Agrl. U., Ludhiana, India, 1980-82, asst. agrl. engr., 1982-85; air resources engr. alternate fuels Calif. Air Resources Bd., El Monte, 1990-91; assoc. energy industrial air quality specialist Calif. Energy Commn., Sacramento, 1991-93, energy comm. supr., 1993—. Contbr. articles to profl. jours. Mem. Air and Wast Mgmt. Assn. (curriculum devel. and rev. com. 1992—), Am. Soc. of Agrl. Engrs. (com. biomass energy and alternate products 1985), Sigma Xi. Home: 7720 Tea Berry Way Sacramento CA 95828 Office: Calif Energy Commn 1516 9th St MS-22 Sacramento CA 95814

BINKLEY, JOAN VIVIAN (JODY BINKLEY), artist, educator, gallery owner; b. Hanford, Calif., July 8, 1933; d. Albert Henry Lohse and Alice (Day) Romdall; m. Henry Alson Binkley, Sept. 20, 1958; children: Cameron, Brock, Clayton. Student, Colo. State U., 1951-53; studied with, Frederick Van Twente, Mary Ann Lohman, Larry Webster, Delbert Gish, Leslie B. Demille. Owner, instr. Studio West Galleries, Wheatridge, Colo., 1973-80; owner Studio West Galleries, Littleton, Colo., 1975-80; owner, instr. Country Lane Art Gallery, Lakewood, Colo., 1983-85, Lakewood Arts Studio Gallery, 1988—; workshop instr. Wheatridge Art Club, 1987, 89, 91. Exhbns. include Denver Cancer League Spring Benefit, 1989, 90, 91, 92, also Studio West Galleries, Wheatride and Littleton, Emily Ingram Galleries, Steamboat, Colo., 1984-92, Santa Fe Impressions, Littleton, 1987—, Gallery of Western Art, 1987—, Parade of Homes, 1988-89. Mem. Colo. Artist Assn., Lakewood Arts Coun., Foothills Art Ctr. Home: 12588 W 1st Pl Lakewood CO 80228 Studio: Lakewood Arts Studio 85 S Union Blvd Lakewood CO 80228

BINKLEY, NICHOLAS BURNS, banking executive; b. Pasadena, Calif., Oct. 31, 1945; s. John Thomas and Marijane (Tucker) B.; m. Diana Padelford Binkley, Aug. 3, 1974; children: Pepper Alexandra, Byron Jack. Student, Univrsite-d'Aix/Marseille, Aix-en-Privence, France, 1966-67; BS in Polit. Sci., Colo. Coll., 1968; MA in Internat. Studies, Johns Hopkins U., 1971. From London sr. credit analyst to middle-East asst. treas. of Petroleum div. Chase Manhattan Bank, N.Y.C., 1973-75; songwriter N.Y.C., 1975-77; from asst. v.p. to v.p., regional mgr. Security Pacific Nat. Bank, Los Angeles, 1977-83; 1st v.p. to exec. v.p., chmn., chief exec. officer fin. svc. Bank Am. Corp., San Diego, 1983—. Vol. Peace Corp., Tunisia, 1968-70; campaign mgr. U.S. COngl. Campaign, Pasadena, 1972—. Office: Bank America Corp 10124 Old Grove Rd San Diego CA 92131-1693

BINNIE, NANCY CATHERINE, nurse, educator; b. Sioux Falls, S.D., Jan. 28, 1937; d. Edward Grant and Jessie May (Martini) Larkin; m. Charles H. Binnie. Diploma, St. Joseph's Hosp. Sch. Nursing, Phoenix, 1965; BS in Nursing, Ariz. State U., 1970, MA, 1974. Intensive care charge nurse Scottsdale (Ariz.) Meml. Hosp., 1968-70, coordinator critical care, 1970-71; coordinator critical care John C. Lincoln Hosp., Phoenix, 1971-73; prof. nursing GateWay Community Coll., Phoenix, 1974—; coord. part-time evening nursing programs Gateway Community Coll., 1984—, interim dir. nursing, 1989, 91. Mem. Orgn. Advancement of Assoc. Degree Nursing. Office: Gateway C C 104 N 40th St Phoenix AZ 85034-1704

BIRCH, EDWARD ELTON, higher education executive; b. Medina, N.Y., July 8, 1938; s. Elton E. and Gertrude H. (Simonds) B.; m. Suzanne Arlene Pratt, Aug. 22, 1959; children: Yvette Suzanne, Michele Noel. BS, SUNY, 1960; MA, Ohio U., 1962; Phd, Mich. State U., 1969. Asst. dean students instr., human rels Ohio U., Athens, 1963-65; asst. vice chancellor Oakland U. (Mich. State U.), Rochester, Mich., 1965-70; v.p., assoc. prof. Ohio Wesleyan U., Delaware, 1970-76; vide chancellor student and isla vista affairs U. Calif., Santa Barbara, 1976-77, vice chancellor adminstrv. svcs. and student affairs, 1977-80, vice chancellor student and community affairs, 1980-88, vice chancellor instnl. advancement, 1988—; v.p. XXIIIrd Olympiad, L.A., 1984; dir. U. Calif. Santa Barbara Found., Alumni Assn. Dir. United Way, Santa Barbara, Santa Barbara C. of C., Santa Barbara Industry End. Coun., Santa Barbara Bank and Trust. Mem. Nat. Soc. Fund Raising Execs., Am. Coun. on Edn., Coun. for Advancement and Support of Edn., Nat. Assn. State U. and Land Grant Colls., LaCumbre Golf and Country Club. Episcopalian. Home: 4585 Vieja Dr Santa Barbara CA 93110 Office: U Calif Instnl Advancement Santa Barbara CA 93106-2030

BIRD, CHARLES ALBERT, lawyer; b. Stockton, Calif., July 1, 1947; s. Donald Gladstone and Elizabeth Clara (Jongeneel) B.; m. Charlotte Laura Soeters, June 28, 1969. BA, U. Calif.-Davis, 1969, JD, 1973. Bar: Calif. 1973, U.S. Dist. Ct. (so. dist.) 1975, U.S. Ct. Appeals (9th cir.) 1975, U.S. Supreme Ct. 1980, U.S. Dist. Ct. (cen. dist.) Calif. 1981. Tchr. Woodland Unified Sch. Dist. (Calif.), 1969-70; law clk. justice Supreme Ct. Alaska, Juneau, 1973-74; assoc. Luce, Forward, Hamilton & Scripps, San Diego, 1975-79, ptnr., 1980—. Contbr. articles to profl. publs. Bd. dirs. Defenders Orgn., San Diego, 1982-86, 87—, pres., 1990-92; founding dir. San Diego Vol. Lawyer Program, 1982-86. Mem. San Diego County Bar Assn. (legis chmn. 1980-81, bd. dirs. 1982-85, sec. 1984, v.p. 1985), State Bar Assn. Calif. (exec. com. real property sect. 1982-86, chmn. exec. com. 1985-86). Democrat. Episcopalian. Home: 4182 Ingalls St San Diego CA 92103-1354 Office: Luce Forward Hamilton 600 W Broadway Ste 2600 San Diego CA 92101

BIRD, DEBORAH KAY, biology and landscape educator; b. Toledo, Oct. 18, 1950; d. E.V. and Ruth Rose (York) Bird; m. Daniel Joseph Lenane IV, Oct. 14, 1972. BS, U. Ariz., 1979, MA, 1993. Rsch. asst. Office of Arid Lands, Tucson, 1979-83; instr. Pima C.C., Tucson, 1983—; job coach for mentally ill La Frontera-Herb's Etc., Tucson, 1991—; owner cons. bus. for environ. edn. Environ. Therapies, Tucson, 1992—. Mem. Greater Ariz. Bicycling Assn., Tucson, 1984—; mem. landscape adv. com. Pima Coll. Mem. Ariz. Native Plant Soc., Native Seed, Global ReLeaf (co-operator). Home and office: Environ Therapies 1214 N 6th Ave Tucson AZ 85705

BIRD, JOHN ERIC, electronic technician; b. St. Joseph, Mo., Oct. 7, 1958; s. William E. and Shirley (Waller) B.; m. Joyce E. Keller, Mar. 24, 1984; 1 child, Nicholas Alexander. Electronic technician CPT Corp., Hopkins, Minn., 1977-79, Electro Dynamics Corp., Overland Park, Kans., 1979-80, King Radio Corp., Overland Park, 1980-82, Tallgrass Tech. Corp., Overland Park, 1982-84, Structural Behavior Engring. Inc., Phoenix, 1984—. Contbr. design to profl. mag. Republican. Home: 10432 W Laurie Ln Peoria AZ 85345-7431 Office: Structural Behavior Engring 4236 N 39th Ave Phoenix AZ 85019-3511

BIRD, LESLEY ANN, computer engineer; b. Rome, N.Y., Nov. 10, 1963; d. Richard Andrew and Suzanne (Van Auken) B. BSEE, U. of the Pacific, Stockton, Calif., 1986; MSEE, U. Calif., Santa Barbara, 1990. Student engr. IBM Corp., San Jose, Calif., 1984-85; electronic design engr. Delco Electronics, Goleta, Calif., 1986-90; computer engr. Apple Computer, Cupertino, Calif., 1990—. Scholarship Soc. Women Engrs., 1984. Mem. IEEE, Eta Kappa Mu. Home: 2061 Foxhall Lp San Jose CA 95125 Office: Apple Computer 20705 Valley Green Dr Cupertino CA 95014

BIRD, PATRICIA COLEEN, business owner; b. Wolf Point, Mont., May 10, 1953; d. Harry Sidney and Pearl Rose (Firemoon) B. AA in Fine Arts, Haskell Indian JUCO, Lawrence, Kans., 1974; student, Kans. U., 1974-78; CDC Cert., Deaconess Hosp., Glasgow, Mont., 1990. Partnership bus. owner Blue Feather Indian Store, Wolf Point, Mont., 1980—; Indian arts steering com. mem. Mont. Arts Coun., Helena, 1991. First responder ambulance Trinity Hosp., Wolf Point, 1991-92; drug and alcohol facilitator Frazer (Mont.) Sch. Dist. 2-2B, 1990-91; acting sec. Frazer Community Coun., 1991-92; N.W. accrediting assn. mem. Poplar (Mont.) Sch., 1990-91; coord. "The Longest Walk", Davis, Calif., 1978, concert dir., 1978. Named Miss Nat. Congress of Am. Indians, 1975, The Modern Ms., 1975, Miss Haskell, 1974, Oil Discovery Celebration Pres., 1974, Oil Discovery Celebration Princess, 1973, 72, 71.

BIRD, RANDALL CHARLES, principal; b. Blackfoot, Idaho, Jan. 3, 1949; s. Blayne Duffin and Mary (Bohi) B.; m. Carla Aikele, Aug. 6, 1970; children: Erika, Angela, Meisha, Rachel, Michael, Scott. AA, Ricks Coll., Rexburg, Idaho, 1970; BS, Brigham Young U., 1973, MEd, 1980, postgrad., 1990—. Cert. tchr., Utah, Idaho. Seminary tchr. Mormon Ch., Driggs, Idaho, 1973-75; prin., tchr. Mormon Ch., Shelley, Idaho, 1975—; football coach Shelley High Sch., 1975—; track coach Teton High Sch., Driggs, 1973-

75, Shelley High Sch., 1976-77; regional coord. Blackfoot Region Sem., Shelley, 1983-86; lectr. Brigham Young U., Provo, 1977-90, youth dir., 1976-90; mgr. seminary curriculum LDS. Author: High Fives and High Hopes, 1990, Sharing the Light, Finding the Light, Feeling Great, Doing Great. Active Com. to Teach AIDS in Schs., Shelley, 1990, Com. for Better Schs., Shelley, 1988; publicity chmn. bond for new high sch., Shelley, 1989. Hinckely scholar, 1973. Mem. Phi Kappa Phi. Home: 1200 Cherry Ln Layton UT 84040 Office: Latter Day Saints Seminary LDS Office Bldg 50 E N Temple 9th Flr Salt Lake City UT 84150

BIRDLEBOUGH, HAROLD, dentist; b. Yakima, Wash., May 4, 1928; s. Otis Theodore and Elizabeth (Brown) B.; D.D.S., U. Wash., 1959; m. Donna Mae Vensel, June 18, 1977; children: John Michael, Elizabeth, William Powers, Marcia; stepchildren: Steve Hassenfratz, Nancy Hassenfratz, Keith Fontel. Practice dentistry, Seattle, 1959-61, King County, Wash., 1961—; mem. dental adv. com. Blue Cross Ins. Co. Served with USNR, 1948-52. Mem. ADA, Wash. Dental Assn., Snohomish County Dental Soc., Gen. Acad. Dentistry, U. Wash. Dental Alumni, Soc. Preservation and Encouragement Barbershop Quartet Singing in Am., Delta Sigma Delta, Alpha Delta Phi (1st v.p. local alumni assn., del. nat. constl. conv. 1968). Republican. Episcopalian (sr. warden). Lodge: Elks. Office: 332 NW Richmond Beach Rd Seattle WA 98177-3120

BIRDSALL, DAVID LEE, molecular biophysicist; b. Bronx, N.Y., Sept. 27, 1954; s. Leonard W. B. and Mary A. (Banks) Johnson. BS cum laude, Lehman Coll., Bronx, 1978; MS, Purdue U., 1981, PhD, 1985. Postdoctoral fellow Harvard U., Cambridge, Mass., 1985-87; postdoctoral researcher U. Calif., Riverside, 1987-90; staff scientist Lawrence Livermore Nat. Lab., Calif., 1990—. Mem. AAAS, Am. Phys. Soc., Am. Crystallographic Assn., N.Y. Acad. Scis. Office: Lawrence Livermore Nat Lab Divsn Biomed Scis L-452 Livermore CA 94550

BIRKBY, WALTER HUDSON, physical anthropologist, curator; b. Gordon, Nebr., Feb. 28, 1931; s. Walter Levy and Margery Hazel (Moss) B.; m. Carmen Sue Gates, Aug. 18, 1955; children: Jeffrey Moss, Julianne. BA, U. Kans., 1961, MA, 1963; PhD, U. Ariz., 1973. Diplomate Am. Bd. Forensic Anthropology (pres. 1985-87, exec. com. 1980-87). Med. and X-ray technician Graham County (Kans.) Hosp., Hill City, 1955-58; phys. anthropologist Ariz. State Mus., Tucson, 1968-85; lectr. anthropology U. Ariz., Tucson, 1981-90, adj. rsch. prof. anthropology, 1990—; curator phys. anthropology Ariz. State Mus., Tucson, 1985—; forensic anthropologist Pima County Med. Examiner's Office, Tucson, 1981—, Recovery of Victims of Alfred G. Packer party (1874), Lake City, Colo., 1989; dental cons. USAF Hosp., Davis Monthan AFB, Tucson, 1984—; human osteologist U. Ariz.-Republic of Cyprus Archaeol. Expdn., 1984-87, Lugnano in Teverina (Italy) Expdn., 1990-91; dir. dept. anthropology masters program in forensic anthropology, 1984—; cons. to Chief Armed Svcs. Graves Registration Office U.S. Army, 1987—. Mem. editorial bd. (jour.) Cryptozoology, 1982—; bd. editors Am. Jour. Forensic Medicine and Pathology, 1992—; co-author video tng. film Identification of Human Remains, 1980; contbr. articles to profl. jours. Served as sgt. USMCR, 1951-52, Korea. NIH fellow U. Ariz., 1966-68; recipient Achievement medal for Meritorious Svc., Pima County Sheriff's Dept., 1992. Fellow Am. Acad. Forensic Scis. (exec. com. 1978-81, T. Dale Stewart award in anthropology 1991); mem. Am. Assn. Phys. Anthropologists, Calif. Assn. Criminalists, Ariz. Identification Coun. of the Internat. Assn. for Indentification, Ariz. Homicide Investigators Assn., Internat. Assn. Human Biologists, Sigma Xi (pres. local chpt. 1984-85). Democrat. Home: 7349 E 18th St Tucson AZ 85710-4904 Office: U Ariz Ariz State Mus Human Identification Lab Tucson AZ 85721

BIRKHEAD, JOHN ANDREW, political science educator; b. Anchorage, Jan. 10, 1954; s. Herbert Cecil and Eugenia Clarke (McChesney) B.; m. Kathryn Denise Birkhead, Nov. 28, 1980; children: Nathaniel Andrew, Colin Michael. BA, U. Colo., 1975; MA, U. Calif., Davis, 1984; PhD, Stanford U., 1993. Commd. 2d lt. USAF, 1975, advanced through grades to maj., 1987; navigator USAF, Little Rock, 1976-82; instr. polit. sci. USAF Acad., Colorado Springs, 1984-85; sr. navigator USAF, Okinawa, Japan, 1988-91; assoc. prof. USAF Acad., Colorado Springs, 1991—. Named Outstanding Young Men of Am., 1985. Mem. Pi Sigma Alpha. Democrat. Home: 1435 Spring Valley Dr Colorado Springs CO 80921 Office: USAF Academy Dept Polit Sci Colorado Springs CO 80840

BIRKINBINE, JOHN, II, philatelist; b. Chestnut Hill, Pa., Mar. 29, 1930; s. Olaf Weimer and Gertrude Marie (Tyson) B.; m. Ausencia Barrera Elen, Dec. 19, 1969; children: John III, Bayani Royd. Chmn., chief exec. officer Am. Philatelic Brokerages, Tucson, 1946—; chmn. bd. dirs. Ariz. Philatelic Rangers, Tucson, 1987—; bd. dirs. Confederate Stamp Alliance, 1987-88; bd. dirs. Postal History Found., 1991—. Chmn. bd. 1869 Pictorial Rsch. Assn., 1969, bd. dirs., 1970-76, chmn. Baha'i Faith Adminstrv. Body, Pima County, Ariz., 1977-81, 83-91; sheriff, chmn. Santa Catalina Corral of Westerners Internat., Tucson, 1986. Recipient Large Gold and Spl. award Spanish Soc. Internat., San Juan, P.R., 1982, New Zealand Soc. Internat., Aukland, 1990, Large Internat. Gold award Australian Soc. Internat., Melbourne. 1984, Swedish Soc. Internat., Stockholm, 1986, Internat. Gold award U.S. Soc. Internat., Chgo., 1986, Bulgarian Soc. Internat., Sofia, 1989. Mem. Am. Philatelic Soc. (U.S. Champion of Champions 1985), U.S. Philatelic Classics Soc., Am. Philatelic Congress (McCoy award 1969), Scandinavian Collectors Club, Collectors Club of N.Y., Western Cover Soc., Canal Zone Study Group,. Office: Am Philatelic Brokerages 7225 N Oracle Rd Tucson AZ 85704-6322

BIRMINGHAM, THOMAS EDWARD, hospital financial executive; b. Seattle, July 3, 1951; s. Joseph Eugene and Anitia (Loomis) B.; m. Linda T. Watanabe, June 24, 1977 (annulled Dec. 1985); m. Elizabeth Ann McCalley, Feb. 21, 1987; children: Michael Royce, Kristen Marie. BA, U. Wash., 1974; MS, Golden Gate U., Seattle, 1986. Cer. CPA, Wash. Auditor U.S. GAO, Seattle, 1975-83; mgmt. evaluator Insp. General VA, Seattle, 1983-86; asst. dir. fin. U. Wash. Hosps., Seattle, 1986-88; asst. adminstr. fin. U. Wash. Med. Ctr., Seattle, 1988-89; chief fin. officer, v.p. fin. St. Francis Community Hosp., Federal Way, Wash., 1989—. Organizer United Way, Seattle, 1990—. Mem. Assn. Govt. Accts. (pres. 1985-86), Hosp. Fin. Mgmt. Assn. (bd. dirs. 1990—), Am. Soc. CPAs, Wash. State CPAs (com. co-chmn. 1990—), Wash. State Acctg. Bd. (head proctor 1985—), Rotary (bd. dirs. 1991), Theta Delta Chi (pres. 1988-90). Roman Catholic. Home: 29411 4th Ave S Federal Way WA 98003-3666 Office: St Francis Community Hosp 34515 9th Ave S Federal Way WA 98003-6799

BIRNBAUM, MICHAEL HENRY, psychology educator; b. L.A., Mar. 10, 1946; s. Eugene David and Bessie (Holtzman) B.; m. Bonnie Gail Bruck, July 7, 1968; children: Melissa Anne, Kevin Michael. BA, UCLA, 1968, MA, 1969, PhD, 1972. Postdoctoral scholar NIMH, U. Calif., San Diego, 1972-73; asst. prof. psychology Kans. State U., Manhattan, 1973-74; from asst. to assoc. prof. U. Ill., Champaign, Ill., 1974-82; prof. U. Ill., Champaign, 1982-88, Calif. State U., Fullerton, 1986—; cons. RAND Corp., Santa Monica, Calif., 1980—. Contbr. articles to profl. jours. and chpts. to books. Mem. APA, Am. Psychol. Soc. (charter), Internat. Brotherhood Magicians (pres. Ring 236 1984-85), Judgment & Decision-Making Soc., Soc. Math. Psychology, Psychonomic Soc. Office: Calif State U Dept Psychology Fullerton CA 92634

BIRNBAUM, STEVAN ALLEN, investment company executive; b. L.A., Apr. 21, 1943; s. Eugene David and Bessie (Holtzman) B.; m. Barbara Patricia Ostroff, June 29, 1971 (div. Aug. 1991); children: Marc, Jill. BS in Engring., UCLA, 1965; MBA, Harvard U., 1967. Dir. advanced programs Whittaker Corp., L.A., 1967-69; v.p. Hohenberg & Assocs., Beverly Hills, Calif., 1969-74; dir. adminstrv. mgmt. Dames & Moore, L.A., 1974-77; prin. Xerox Venture Capital, L.A., 1977-81; venture capitalist, L.A., 1981-83; ptnr. Oxford Ptnrs., Santa Monica, Calif., 1983—; pres. Oxcal Venture Corp., Santa Monica, 1981—; founder, bd. dirs. Brentwood Savs. Bank, 1982; bd. dirs. Micro Gen. Corp., Santa Ana, Calif., Cogensys, La Jolla, Calif., Wangdat, Irvine, Calif., Quintar Corp., Torrance, Calif., Rexon Inc., Simi Valley, Calif. Republican. Jewish. Office: Oxford Ptnrs 16651 Cumbre Verde Ct Pacific Palisades CA 90272-1914

BIRR, TIMOTHY BLANE, public information director, consultant; b. Appleton, Wis., Apr. 13, 1953; s. Robert Frank and Julie Ann (Carlsen) B.; m. Mary Dana Crawford, Aug. 12, 1978; children: Meghan, Brendan. Student, U. Oreg., 1971-73, 74, 76, Lane C.C., Eugen, Oreg., 1970's, 1980's, Mt. Hood C.C., Gresham, Oreg., 1978. Health edn. asst. Lane County Health Dept., Eugene, 1973-74; firefighter, EMT Eugene (Oreg.) Fire Dept., 1975-80, fire lt., 1980-83, fire capt., 1983-84; acting pub. info. dir. City of Eugene, Oreg., 1984; pub. info. officer Eugene (Oreg.) Fire/Emergency Svcs. Dept., 1984-86, Eugene (Oreg.) Dept. Pub. Safety, 1986—; cons. Fed. Emergency Mgmt. Agy., Washington, 1980-82; lectr., cons. Misc. Govt. and Non-Profit Agys., 1980—. Editor: (mag.) Oreg. Fire Fighter Mag., 1982-87; corr. Western Fire Jour., 1982-84; contbr. articles to profl. jours. Mem. Lane County Fire Protection Adv. Com., Eugene, 1978-80; co-chair Meals on Wheels Fundraising Campaign, Eugene, 1990-92; mem. Oreg. State Fire Marshal/Pub. Edn. Adv. Com., Salem, Oreg., 1991—. Mem. Nat. Info. Officers Assn. (regional dir.), Internat. Assn. Firefighters (v.p. 1977-79), ARC (vol. Lane County chpt.), Eugene (Oreg.) City Club. Episcopalian. Office: Eugene Dept Pub Safety 777 Pearl St Eugene OR 97401

BIRTCHER, NORMAND HAROLD, lumber company executive; b. Phoenix, Jan. 6, 1955; s. Normand Franklin and Ida (Moffett) B.; m. Anna Begay, Dec. 12, 1992; children from a previous marriage: Michelle, Leona, Grant. BS in Forestry, No. Ariz. U., 1978. Dep. forest mgr. Navajo Forestry Dept., Ft. Defiance, Ariz., 1978-85; logging mgr. Navajo Forest Products, Navajo, N.Mex, 1985-88; plant ops. mgr. Navajo Forest Products, 1988—. Dir. Navajo N.Mex. Community Devel. Corp., 1990-91. Mem. Western Wood Products Assn. (resources and environ. com. 1990—, quality standards com. 1990—). Republican. Home: PO Box 1206 Navajo NM 87328-1206 Office: Navajo Forest Products Industries PO Box 1280 Navajo NM 87328-9998

BISCONE, JOSEPH GREGORY, investor; b. N.Y.C., May 12, 1950; s. Joseph Gregory and Eleanor Florence (Tomaszewski) B. BA in Psychology, San Diego State U., 1975; BSBA, U. Redlands, 1985. Pvt. practice as entrepreneur Escondido, Calif., 1975-81; pres., CEO Galleon Home Loan, Inc., San Diego, 1981-89; pvt. practice Escondido, 1989—. 1st lt. USMC, 1969-72. Republican. Home and Office: 1875 Glenridge Rd Escondido CA 92027

BISGAARD, EDWARD LAWRENCE, JR., financial services executive, accountant; b. El Cento, Calif., July 26, 1946; s. Edward Lawrence Sr. and Gail (Chambers) B.; m. Kathleen Susan Borenitsch; 1 child, Jackie. BS, Calif. Polytech. Coll., Pomona, 1971. CPA, Calif. Sr. auditor Arthur Young & Co., L.A., 1971-74; v.p. King Internat. Corp., Beverly Hills, Calif., 1975-78; v.p., mgr. fund ops. Capital Rsch. & Mgmt. Co., L.A., 1979-86; chief fin. officer Dunham & Greer, San Diego, 1987-89; v.p., treas. Atlas Securities, Atlas Assets, Oakland, Calif., 1989—. Mem. AICPAs, Calif. Soc. CPAs. Republican.

BISH, WILLIAM HOWARD, public relations executive; b. Des Moines, Sept. 29, 1957; s. Clarence Erwin and Margaret Martine (Sorter) B. BA in Pub. Rels. cum laude, Drake U., 1982. Pub. rels. specialist NRA Am., Washington; account exec. Madison Fielding Pub. Rels., North Hollywood, Calif.; exec. dir. CYCLELAW Law Offices of Brenner and Rostand, Van Nuys, Calif.; dir. mktg. and pub. rels. J. Russell Brown Jr., A Law Corp., L.A.; nat. dir. Bikers Against Manslaughter, L.A. Contbr. articles to newspapers and nat. mags. Sgt. USMC, 1976-79. Mem. Pub. Rels. Soc. Am. (award for profl. excellence 1984), Am. Brotherhood Aimed Toward Edn. of Calif. (chmn. bd. dirs.), Bipartisans Against Discriminatory Legislation.

BISHOP, BENJAMIN PIERCE, real estate development professional; b. Cleve., Aug. 8, 1953; s. Frank John and Irene Olga (Siebert) B.; 1 child, Emmett. BA in Art Hist., Case Western Res. U., 1977, MBA in Mgmt. Info. Systems, 1977. Mgmt. cons. Ritchie & Assocs., Beverly Hills, Calif., 1977-78; real estate devel. cons. Robert Siegel & Assocs., New Orleans, 1978-81; prin. Bishop Consultation Svc., Denver, 1981-86; instr. Outdoor Leadership Trng, Denver, 1987—; capt. U.S. Army Spl. Forces, 1988-93. Mem. Inst. Mgmt. Cons. Home and Office: Bishop Consultation Svc 374 Corona St Denver CO 80218-3940

BISHOP, BETTY JOSEPHINE, financial consultant; b. Seattle, Wash., Feb. 27, 1947; d. Arthur Joseph and Julia Teresa (Azzolina) Lovett; children: Deborah, Scott. BS, Wash. State U., 1969; postgrad., Ohio State U., 1983, Santa Barbara Coll. of Law, 1991—. Bar: Calif. Tchr. Seattle Sch. Dist., 1973-75; appraiser Pacific First Fed., Tacoma, 1977-78, asst. v.p., mgr., secondary market ops., 1978-82; regional exec. United Guaranty, Westlake Village, Calif., 1982-83; sr. v.p. comml. secondary mktg. FCA Am. Mortgage Corp./ Am. Savs., Santa Monica, Calif., 1983-85; v.p., mgr. secondary market ops. County Savs. Bank, Santa Barbara, Calif., 1985-88; pres., fin. cons. SMC Fin. Svcs., Montecito, Calif., 1988—; mem. conf. subcom., sec. mktg. com. Calif. Savs. and Loan League, L.A., 1985-88; document subcom., sec. mktg. subcom. U.S. Savs. and Loan League, Chgo., 1987-88; expert witness secondary mktg. and mortgage banking. Contbr. articles to profl. jours. Fund drive chmn. Easter Seal Soc., Olympia, 1972. Mem. L.A. Trial Lawyers Assn., Santa Barbara Bar Assn., S.B. Assocs., Univ. Club, Conejo Ski Club, Santa Barbara Ski Club (past pres., pres. L.A. coun.). Republican. Roman Catholic.

BISHOP, C. DIANE, state agency administrator, educator; b. Elmhurst, Ill., Nov. 23, 1943; d. Louis William and Constance Oleta (Mears) B. BS in Maths., U. Ariz., 1965, MS in Maths., MEd in Secondary Edn., 1972. Lic. secondary educator. Tchr. math. Tucson Unified Sch. Dist., 1966-86, mem. curriculum council, 1985-86, mem. maths. curriculum task teams, 1983-86; state supt. of pub. instrn. State of Ariz., 1987—; mem. assoc. faculty Pima C.C., Tucson, 1974-84; adj. lectr. U. Ariz., 1983, 85; mem. math. scis. edn. bd. NRC, 1987-90, mem. new standards project governing bd., 1991—; dir. adv. bd. sci. and engring. ednl. panel, NSF; mem. adv. bd. for arts edn. Nat. Endowment for Arts. Active Ariz. State Bd. Edn., 1984—, chmn. quality edn. commn., 1986-87, chmn. tchr. crt. subcom., 1984—, mem. outcomes based edn. adv. com., 1986-87, liaison bd. dirs. essential skills subcom., 1985-87, gifted edn. com. liaison, 1985—; mem. Ariz. State Bd. Regents, 1987—, mem. com. on preparing for U. Ariz., 1983, mem. high sch. task force, 1984-85; mem. bd. Ariz. State Community Coll., 1987—; mem. Ariz. Joint Legis. Com. on Revenues and Expenditures, 1989, Ariz. Joint Legis. Com. on Goals for Ednl. Excellence, 1987-89, Gov.'s Task Force on Ednl. Reform, 1991, Ariz. Bd. Regents Commn. on Higher Edn., 1992. Woodrow Wilson fellow Princeton U., summer 1984; recipient Presdl. Award for Excellence in Teaching of Maths., 1983, Ariz. Citation of Merit, 1984, Maths. Teaching award Nat. Sci. Research Soc., 1984, Distinction in Edn. award Flinn Found., 1986; named Maths. Tchr. of Yr. Ariz. Council of Engring. and Sci. Assns., 1984. Mem. AAUW, NEA, Nat. Coun. Tchrs. Math., Coun. Chief State Sch. Officers, Women Execs. in State Govt. (bd. dirs. 1993), Ariz. Assn. Tchrs. Math., Women Maths. Edn., Math. Assn. Am., Ednl. Commn. of the States (steering com.), Nat. Endowment Arts (adv. bd. for arts edn.), Nat. Forum Excellence Edn., Nat. Honors Workshop, Phi Delta Kappa. Democrat. Episcopalian. Office: Edn Svcs Dept 1535 W Jefferson Phoenix AZ 85007

BISHOP, CAROLYN BENKERT, public relations counselor; b. Monroe, Wis., Aug. 28, 1939; d. Arthur C. and Delphine (Heston) Benkert; m. Lloyd F. Bishop, June 15, 1963. BS, U. Wis., 1961; grad., Tobe-Coburn Sch., N.Y.C., 1962. Merchandising editor Co-Ed Mag., N.Y.C., 1962-63; advt. copywriter Woodward & Lothrop, Washington, 1963-65; home furnishings editor Co-Ed Mag., N.Y.C., 1965-68; editor Budget Decorating Mag., N.Y.C., 1968-69; home furnishings editor Family Cir. Mag., N.Y.C., 1969-75; v.p., pub., editorial dir. Scholastic, Inc., N.Y.C., 1975-80; owner Mesa Store Home Furnishings Co., Aspen, Colo., 1980-83; dir. pub. rels. Snowmass Resort Assn., Snowmass Village, Colo., 1983-86; pres. Bishop & Bishop Mktg. Communications, Aspen, 1986—; mem. media rels. com. Colo. Tourism Bd., Denver, 1987-90. Author: 25 Decorating Ideas Under $100, 1969; editor: Family Circle Special Home Decorating Guide, 1973. Bd. dirs. Aspen Camp Sch. for the Deaf, 1987-90. Recipient Dallas Market Editorial award Dallas Market Ctr., 1973, Dorothy Dawe award Chgo. Furniture Market, 1973, Guardian of Freedom award, Anti-Defamation League Appeal, 1974. Mem. Rocky Mountain Pub. Rels. Group (chmn.), Pub. Rels. Soc. Am. (accredited, small firms co-chair counselors acad. 1992—), Aspen Chamber Resort Assn., Aspen Writers' Found. (bd. dirs. 1991-93), NorthAm. Ski Journalist Assn. (corp. mem.), Aspen Womens Forum, Tobe-Coburn Alumni Assn., U. Wis. Alumni Assn. Democrat. Office: Bishop & Bishop Mktg Comm 312 AABC Ste B Aspen CO 81611

BISHOP, ERNEST MERRILL, physical scientist; b. Soquel, Calif., Mar. 6, 1927; s. Ernest S. and Ruth (Merrill) B.; m. Barbara Maggio, June 20, 1948 (div. 1985); children: Ruth, Kathy, Mark, Gail, Chris, Matt, Amy; m. Roberta Henley, Dec. 5, 1985. BS, U. Calif., Berkeley, 1950. Chemist Pabco Products, Emeryville, Calif., 1950-56, Stanford Research Inst., Menlo Park, Calif., 1956-59, Carad Chem., Palo Alto, Calif., 1959-63; materials engr. Sandia Corp., Livermore, Calif., 1963-66; research assoc. Hexcel Corp., Dublin, Calif., 1967—. Patentee in field. Scoutmaster Boy Scouts Am., 1956-67. Served to sgt. U.S. Army, 1945-47. Mem. AAAS, Materials Rsch. Soc. Democrat. Roman Catholic. Office: Hexcel Corp 11711 Dublin Blvd Dublin CA 94568-2898

BISHOP, JAMES ALLEN, wood products consultant; b. Bend, Oreg., Jan. 28, 1950; s. Leo Allen and Alice May (Nelson) B.; m. Ramona June Morris, Sept. 21, 1974; children: Cheryl, Tracee. BS, MS, Stanford U., 1973. Prodn. scheduler Brooks-Scanlon, Inc., Redmond, Oreg., 1974-80; real estate salesman United Properties, Redmond, 1980-82; mgr. quality assurance Contact Lumber, Prineville, Oreg., 1982-85; plant mgr. Contact Lumber, Hines, Oreg., 1985-91; wood products cons. Bishop Engring., Burns, Oreg., 1991—; chmn. bd. dirs. Harney County Fed. Credit Union, Burns, 1987-91; treas. The Oreg. Consortium (Job Tng. Partnership Act), Albany, 1990. Mem. Harney County Planning Commn., 1986-89. Scholar Bend Found., 1968-72. Mem. Harney County C. of C. (bd. dirs. 1985-89, Boss of Yr. award 1987, Man of Yr. award 1988, Lumberman of Yr. award 1989). Democrat. Presbyterian. Home: PO Box 428 Burns OR 97720-0428

BISHOP, JAY LYMAN, environmental chemist; b. Salt Lake City, July 7, 1932; s. Marvin James and Klar (Lyman) B.; m. Geneil True Walton, June 9, 1958; children: Peggy (dec.), Lynn, Janet, Nancy, Deanna, Linda, Michael, Stanley, Michelle. BS with honors, U. Utah, 1953, PhD, 1962. Lectr. U. Utah, Salt Lake City, 1960-62; rsch. assoc. Ariz. State U., Tempe, 1962-67, instr., 1964-67; sr. chemist Ciby-Geigy Corp., Summit, N.J., 1967-71; cons. Bishop Mfg. Co. and Western Cons., Bountiful, Utah, 1971—; chem. engr. civil svd. Tooele (Utah) Army Depot, 1982—; chemist Kennecott Copper Corp., Salt Lake City, 1972; chief chemist and metallurgist Assoc. Smelters Internat., 1973, United Refinery, 1973-75, Nat. Metals Inc., Salt Lake City, 1975-76; vis. lectr. Traveling Sci. Inst., Ariz. Acad. Sci., Tempe, 1962-66; historian, genealogist Western Cons., Bountiful, 1971—. Contbr. articles to profl. jours.; composer musical works; patentee in field. Missionary Ch. of Jesus Christ of Latter-Day Saints, East German Mission, 1953-56; mem. Salt Lake Mormon Tabernacle Choir, 1976-78, ch. organist, 1945—, other civic and religious activities. With U.S. Army, 1956-57. Mem. Sigma Xi. Republican. Office: 11 W 900 N Bountiful UT 84010-5919

BISHOP, JOHN MICHAEL, biomedical research scientist, educator; b. York, Pa., Feb. 22, 1936; married 1959. AB, Gettysburg Coll., 1957; MD, Harvard U., 1962. Intern in internal medicine Mass. Gen. Hosp., Boston, 1962-63, resident, 1963-64; rsch. assoc. virology NIH, Washington, 1964-66, sr. investigator, 1966-68; from asst. prof. to assoc. prof. U. Calif. Med. Ctr., San Francisco, 1968-72, prof. microbiology and immunology, 1972—, prof. biochemistry and biophysics, 1982—; dir. G.W. Hooper Rsch. Found., 1981—. Recipient Nobel prize in physiology or medicine, 1989, Biomed. Rsch. award Am. Assn. Med. Colls., 1981, Albert Lasker Basic Med. Rsch. award, 1981, Armand Hammer Cancer award, 1984, GM Found. Cancer Rsch. award, 1984, Gairdner Found. Internat. award, Can., 1984, Medal of Honor, Am. Cancer Soc., 1984; NIH grantee, 1968—. Fellow Salk Inst. (trustee 1991—); mem. NAS, Inst. Medicine. Office: U Calif Medical Ctr Dept Microbiology Box 0552 San Francisco CA 94143-0552

BISHOP, PHILIPPE CHARLES, physician; b. Las Vegas, Apr. 8, 1964; s. Simonne Jacqueline (Durci) B. BS in Biology, Loyola Marymount, L.A., 1985; MD, U. Nev. Sch. Medicine, 1993. Rsch. technician U. So. Calif., L.A., 1985-88; rsch. fellow U. Nev., Las Vegas, 1989-90; rsch. intern Bristol Myers Squibb, Princeton, N.J., 1991; commd. med. officer USPHS, Rockville, Md., 1992—. Contbr. articles to scientific jours. Chmn. Conf. on AIDS in Nev., 1989; mem. Student Teaching AIDS to Students, 1988-89; coord. Spl. Games for Handicap Chidlren, Loyola Marymount U., 1985. Rsch. scholar Howard Hughes Med. Inst., 1990-91; recipient Sandoz Med. Rsch. award Sandoz Pharm., 1989, Recognition award Loyola Marymount Spl. Games, 1985. Mem. AMA, Am. Med. Student Assn., Sigma Xi Rsch. Assn.

BISHOP, ROBERT CHARLES, architect, metals and minerals company executive; b. Butte, Mont., June 6, 1929; s. Lester Farragut and Helen Katherine (Bauman) B.; m. B. Jean Rausch, June 29, 1957; children: Desta Fawn Bishop O'Connor, Valerie Dawn. BS in Gen. Engring., Mont. State U., 1958, BArch., 1960. Assoc. architect various firms, Mont., 1960-64; owner, architect R.C. Bishop & Assocs., Butte, Great Falls and Missoula, Mont., 1965-69; owner, chief exec. officer Val-Desta 4M, Butte, 1980—, Val-Desta Mines and Minerals, Louisville, Ky., 1985—; prin. Archtl. Assocs., 1969—; chief exec. officer, pres. Cove-Lock Log Home Mfrs., Inc., Butte, 1968-72, Busy Beaver Enterprises, Great Falls, 1968-72, New Horizon Homes, Missoula, 1968-72; asst. contracts adminstr. Davy-McKee Constrn. Engrs., Butte, 1982-83. Develper 9 major and 2 minor algorithms for mineral prospecting, valid for over 100 areas in Mont. and Idaho; discoverer 100 to 300 million tons of high grade bull quartz and rock crystal, copper and molybdenum, potential world class deposits. Advisor, Kiwanis, Jaycees, Nat. Res., 1960-72, Am. Legion, 1976. With U.S. Army, 1953-55. Named One of 2,000 Men of Achievement Melrose Press, 1970, 73. Mem. Internat. Platform Assn., Nat. Hist. Soc. (founding assoc. 1971), Elk Bow Hunting Club (bugle tchr. 1970-84), Butte Mulitlist Club (real estate tchr. 1978-84), Nat. Coun. Archtl. Registeration Bds. (registered architect seismic design 1965—). Presbyterian. Home and Office: 1008 W Galena St Butte MT 59701-1420

BISHOP, TILMAN MALCOLM, state senator, college administrator; b. Colorado Springs, Jan. 1, 1933; B.A., M.A., U. No. Colo.; m. Pat Bishop, 1951; 1 son, Barry Alan. Adminstr., dir. student services Mesa State Coll., Grand Junction, Colo.; mem. Colo. Senate. World series com. Nat. Jr. Coll. Baseball. Served with U.S. Army. Mem. Am. Sch. Counselors Assn., Nat. Assn. for Counseling and Devel., Colo. Assn. for Counseling and Devel. Republican. Methodist. Lodges: Elks, Lions. Office: State Capitol Bldg Denver CO 80203 Home: 2697 G Rd Grand Junction CO 81506-8367

BISSELL, MICHAEL GILBERT, pathologist; b. Ridgecrest, Calif., Mar. 5, 1947; s. Henry Robert and Margaret Alberta (Encell) Benefiel; m. Sherrie L. Lyons, Mar. 27, 1977 (div. June 1990); children: Cassandra, Grahame; m. Lita A. Hill, Nov. 29, 1991. BS in Chemistry, U. Ariz., 1969, BS in Math., 1969; MD, Stanford U., 1975, PhD in Neurobiol., 1977; MPH, U. Calif., Berkeley, 1978. Diplomate Am. Bd. Pathology. Resident Martinez VA Med. Ctr. U. Calif., Davis, 1978-81; rsch. fellow NIMH, Bethesda, Md., 1981-84; asst. prof. pathology U. Chgo. Med. Ctr., 1984-88; dir. clin. pathology City of Hope Nat. Med. Ctr., Duarte, Calif., 1988-91; v.p./med. dir. Nichols Inst. Reference Lab., San Juan Capistrano, Calif., 1991-93; dir. lab. medicine, assoc. prof. pathology U. Texas, 1993—; ptnr. Biomed.-Environ. Cons., Richland, Wash., 1989—; speaker in field. Contbr. articles to profl. jours. Activist/lectr. Calif. Physicians Alliance, San Francisco, 1988—. Fellow Am. Soc. Clin. Pathologists (course dir. annual meeting), Coll. Am. Pathologists, mem. Nat. Com. Clin. Lab. Standards, Am. Assn. Clin. Chemistry, Clin. Lab. Mgmt. Assn. (treas.), Physicians for Nat. Health Program (activist, lectr.), Sierra Club, Sigma Xi. Democrat. Office: U Tex Med Branch 11th and Texas Ave Galveston TX 77555

BISSEN-NOBRIGA, SHERON LEIHUANANI, career counselor, consultant; b. Wailuku, Hawaii, Nov. 15, 1958; d. Richard Thomas Sr. and Edna Leinani (Nakoa) Bissen; m. James Jon Nobriga, June 29, 1985; children: Buddy James, Makana Aloha. AA, Maui C.C., 1979; BA in Journalism, U. Hawaii, 1983. Asst. dir. pub. rels. Hyatt Regency, Kaanapali, Hawaii; dir. pub. rels. Stouffer Wailea Beach Resort, Maui; dept. mgr. Maui Tropical Plantation; office mgr. Maui C. of C.; office clk. Hawaii Dept. Edn.; now career counselor Hawaii Dept. Labor and Indsl. Rels., Wailuku; presenter workshops on career devel. Adult mem. Maui unit Girl Scouts U.S.; lectr., song leader, mem. prayer group St. Anthony's Ch.,

Wailuku; past dir., producer Miss Maui Scholarship Pageant (former Miss Hawaii, 1979, Miss. Maui, 1979). Roman Catholic. Office: Baldwin High Sch 1650 Kaahumann Ave Wailuku HI 96793

BISTLINE, STEPHEN, state justice; b. Pocatello, Idaho, Mar. 12, 1921; s. Ray D. and Martha (Faber) B.; m. Sharon Mooney; children: Patrick, Claire, Susan, Shelley, Diana, Paul, Leslie, Arthur. LL.B., U. Idaho, 1949. Bar: Idaho 1949. Pvt. practice law Sandpoint, Idaho, 1950-76; justice Idaho Supreme Ct., Boise, 1976—. Served with USN, 1941-45. Office: Supreme Ct Idaho 451 W State St Boise ID 83720-0001

BITTENBENDER, BRAD JAMES, environmental safety and industrial hygiene manager; b. Kalamazoo, Dec. 4, 1948; s. Don J. and Thelma Lu (Bacon) B.; m. Patricia Stahl Hubbell, June, 1992. BS, Western Mich. U., 1972; Cert. Hazardous Material Mgmt., U. Calif., Irvine, 1987; Cert. Environ. Auditing, Calif. State U., Long Beach, 1992. Cert. safety profl. of the Ams.; cert. hazardous materials mgr. Supr. mfg. Am. Cyanamid, Kalamazoo, 1973-77; supr. mfg. Productol Chem. div. Ferro Corp., Santa Fe Springs, Calif., 1977-79, environ. adminstr., 1979-80; sr. environ. engr. Ferro Corp., Los Angeles, 1980-87, mgr. environ. safety and indsl. hygiene dept., 1988-91; mgr. environ. safety and indsl. hygiene dept. Structural Polymer Systems, Inc., Montedison, Calif., 1991—; bd. dirs., mem. adv. bd. safety and health extension program U. Calif. Irvine, 1985—. Bd. dirs. adv. com. hazardous materials Community Right to Know, Culver City, Calif., 1987—; mem. Calif. Mus. Found., L.A., 1985—, Mus. Contemporary Art, L.A., 1985—; founding sponsor Challenger Ctr. Mem. Am. Inst. Chem. Engrs., Nat. Assn. Environ. Mgmt., Acad. Cert. Hazardous Materials Mgrs., Suppliers of Advanced Composites Materials Assn. (mem. environ. health and safety com. 1989-92), Am. Indsl. Hygiene Assn., Am. Soc. Safety Engrs., Nat. Fire Protection Assn., Beta Beta Beta. Republican. Presbyterian. Office: Structural Polymer Systems Inc 5915 Rodeo Rd Los Angeles CA 90016-4381

BITTERMAN, MELVIN LEE, real estate developer; b. Yankton, S.D., Dec. 9, 1938; s. Edward Phillip and Amanda Bertha (Moke) B.; m. Constance Winfried Mann, Nov. 7, 1970; 1 child, Janet Amanda. BA, N. Tex. State U., 1967. Librarian City of Glendale, Calif., 1967-71; sales rep. Allstate Ins. Co., Glendale, 1971-86; property mgr./developer Glendale, 1986—. With U.S. Army, 1961-64. Mem. Rotary (sec. 1985), Alpha Beta Alpha. Republican. Roman Catholic. Address: 1400 Beaudry Blvd Glendale CA 91208-1708

BITTERMAN, MORTON EDWARD, psychologist, educator; b. N.Y.C., Jan. 19, 1921; s. Harry Michael and Stella (Weiss) B.; m. Mary Gayle Foley, June 26, 1967; children—Sarah Fleming, Joan, Ann. B.A., NYU, 1941; M.A., Columbia U., 1942; Ph.D., Cornell U., 1945. Asst. prof. Cornell U., Ithaca, N.Y., 1945-50; assoc. prof. U. Tex., Austin, 1950-55; mem. Inst. for Advanced Study, Princeton, N.J., 1955-57; prof. Bryn Mawr Coll., Pa., 1957-70, U. Hawaii, Honolulu, 1970—; dir. Békésy Lab. Neurobiology, Honolulu, 1991—. Author: (with others) Animal Learning, 1979; editor: Evolution of Brain and Behavior in Vertebrates, 1976; co-editor Am. Jour. Psychology, 1955-73; cons. editor jour. Animal Learning and Behavior, 1973-76, 85-88, Jour. of Comparative Psychology, 1988—. Recipient Humboldt prize Alexander von Humboldt Found., Bonn, W.Ger., 1981; Fulbright grantee; grantee NSF, Office Naval Research, NIMH, Air Force Office Sci. Research, Deutsche Forschungsgemeinschaft. Fellow Soc. Exptl. Psychologists, Am. Psychol. Assn., AAAS; mem. Psychonomic Soc. Home: 229 Kaalawai Pl Honolulu HI 96816-4435 Office: Univ Hawaii Bekesy Lab of Neurobiology 1993 East-West Rd Honolulu HI 96822

BITTERS, CONRAD LEE, biological sciences educator; b. Waco, Tex., Jan. 2, 1946; s. E. Conrad and Margaret Lee (Miles) B.; m. Karen Kay, May 1, 1970; children: Rebecca, Brian. BA, Calif. State U., Fresno, 1969. Life Credential, Biol./Phys. Sciences, Calif. Biology/zoology tchr. Clovis (Calif.) High Sch., 1970—, science dept. chmn., 1973-80, biology coordinator, 1980—; founder, sponsor Clovis (Calif.) High Ecology club, 1970—, Clovis High Foreign Studies Club, 1978-87, 92-93; jr. div. judge Cen. Valley Sci. Fair, Fresno, Calif., 1975—; vertebrate advisory com. Cen. Valley Sci. Fair, 1978—; coach-sr. div. Cen. Valley Sci. Fair, Fresno, 1972—; dist. rep. Jr. Sci. and Humanities Symposium, Berkeley, Calif., 1974—; Calif. Ednl. Initiatives Fund Grant Dir., 1986. Recipient Faculty award Eastman Kodak Co., 1980, Nat. Jr. Sci. and Humanities Symposium, 1985, 93, Merit award Rotary Club Fresno, 1985, 88, 93, Faculty Commendation Lawrence Hall of Sci., 1985, 87, John D. Isaacs Scholarship Com., 1985, Outstanding Sci. Tchrs. Fresno County Dow Chem. Co., 1986, Presdl. award in sci. teaching Calif. State Dept. Edn., 1986, Faculty Commendation Calif. Sci. Fair, 1988, commendation Internat. Sci. Engring. Fair, 1982, 93, Commendation for Dept. Energy award, 1993. Mem. Nat. Sci. Teachers' Assn. Republican. Church of Jesus Christ of Latter Day Saints. Home: 1330 Filbert Ave Clovis CA 93611 Office: Clovis High Sch 1055 Fowler Ave Clovis CA 93612-2099

BITTERWOLF, THOMAS EDWIN, chemistry educator; b. New Orleans, Jan. 19, 1947; s. Alvin John and Naomi Mae (Hendrix) B.; m. Caroline Elizabeth Means, May 25, 1968; children: Heidi Elizabeth, Katharine Naomi. BS, Centenary Coll., 1968; PhD, W.Va. U., 1976. Commd. ensign USN, 1973, advanced through grades to comdr., 1987; instr. Naval Nuclear Power Sch., Orlando, Fla., 1973-77, U.S. Naval Acad., Annapolis, Md., 1977-82; resigned USN, 1982; asst. prof. U.S. Naval Acad., Annapolis, Md., 1982-85, assoc. prof., 1985-88; assoc. prof. chemistry U. Idaho, Moscow, 1988-91, prof. chemistry, dir. teaching enhancement, 1991—. Contbr. articles to refereed jours. Mem. AAAS, Am. Chem. Soc., Royal Soc. Chemistry, Sigma Xi. Methodist. Home: PO Box 8188 Moscow ID 83843-0688 Office: U Idaho Dept Chemistry Moscow ID 63843

BITTON-SCHWARTZ, DENISE, curator, educational consultant; b. Morocco, Jan. 1, 1963; d. Yakov and Chana (Bitton) Bitton; m. Daniel Peter Schwartz, Aug. 4, 1991. BS in Counseling Edn., U. Haifa, Israel, 1989, BS in Comparative Lit., 1990. Comdr. Israeli Def. Forces, 1981-83; head counselor Perach Project/Israeli Govt., Haifa, 1987-89; ind. counseling edn. cons. La Jolla, Calif., 1989—; curator Hatikva Judaica Collection, La Jolla, 1991—. Author: Shirim Shelanu, 1991. Organizer Jerusalem Found., San Diego, 1991-92. Mem. Congregation Bethel Sisterhood (v.p. 1992). Jewish. Office: Hatikva Judaica Collection 8660 Gilman Dr La Jolla CA 92037

BIVINS, SUSAN STEINBACH, systems engineer; b. Chgo., June 5, 1941; d. Joseph Bernard and Eleanor Celeste (Mathes) S.; BS, Northwestern U., 1963; postgrad. U. Colo., 1964, U. Ill., 1965, UCLA, 1971; m. James Herbert Bivins, June 7, 1980. With IBM, 1967—, support mgr. East, White Plains, N.Y., 1977-78, systems support mgr., western region, L.A., 1978-81, br. market support mgr., 1981-84, mgr. IBM ops. and support L.A. Summer Olympics, 1984; mgr. IBM office supporting devel. FAA air traffic control system for 1990's, 1984-88, mgr. complex systems mktg., 1988-89, acct. devel. mgr. aerospace engring. and mfg., 1989-91, mgr. cons. and outsourcing indsl. sector trading area, 1991-92, cons. orgn. task forces, 1992—; pres. Jastech, 1986—. Vol. tchr. computer sci. Calif. Mentally Gifted Minor Programs; vol. L.A. Youth Motivation Task Force; dir. pub. rels. Lake of the Ozarks Jazz Festival, 1993. Mem. Systems Engring. Symposium, Pi Lambda Theta. Developed program to retrieve data via terminal and direct it to any appropriate hardcopy device, 1973. Office: 600 Anton 7th Fl Costa Mesa CA 92626

BIXLER, OTTO CHAUNCEY, management consultant; b. Morenci, Ariz., May 9, 1916; s. Otto C. and Marie Ophelia (Dominguez) B.; m. Annette Estelle Struck, Sept. 3, 1938; children: Otto C. Jr., Terry Roy. BSEE cum laude, U. So. Calif., 1937; MBA and PhD in Bus. Adminstrn., Kennedy Western U., 1985, PhDEE, 1986. Registered profl. engr., Calif. V.p. Wanlass Elec. Co., Santa Ana, Calif., 1966-67, Rexall Drug Co., Los Angeles, 1967-68, Corp. Exec. Services, Santa Ana, 1968-74; gen. mgr. Waimea (Hawaii) Dispensary & Clinic, 1974-84; adminstr. Hawaiian Eye Ctr., Wahiawa, 1984-85; pres. Comml. Ventures, Inc., Koloa, Hawaii, 1985-88; program mgr. QCM Rsch., Laguna Beach, Calif., 1990-92; mgr. group activity aeros. div. Ford Motor Co., Newport Beach, Calif., 1958-62, mgr. indsl. systems; asst. gen. mgr. Packard Bell Electronics Corp., Los Angeles, 1962-63, v.p. Univac div. Sperry Rand Corp., St. Paul, 1963-66. Author: Interpersonal Relationship Counseling Program, 1973; designer 1st modern magnetic tape recorder, tape recorder stereo system. Organizer Island of Kauai Elec. Rates Control com., 1978-82. Recipient Outstanding Service award Am. Lung Assn., 1979-85, Service award, 1976-84. Mem. Hawaii Med. Group Mgmt. Assn. (pres. 1978-79), Sigma Xi, Eta Kappa Nu, Tau Beta Pi. Republican. Presbyterian. Lodge: Rotary (pres. West Kauai club 1977-78). Home: 849 Promontory Dr W Newport Beach CA 92660 Office: QCM Research 2825 Laguna Canyon Rd Laguna Beach CA 92652

BJELLAND, HARLEY LEROY, writer; b. Erskine, Minn., Sept. 12, 1926; s. Even and Gina Emelie (Rud) B.; m. Delores Gabriel, Sept. 26, 1951 (div. 1977); children: Carol, David, Harley Jr., Darlene, Sandra; m. Doris Tokiko Onishi, Dec. 20, 1982. BSEE, Milw. Sch. Engring., 1951; postgrad., U. Okla., 1973-74. Sr. staff specialist various aerospace cos., L.A., 1951-82; sr. tech. writer IBM, Hughes Aircraft Co., TRW, Motorola, Northrop Co., various locations, 1982-86; freelance writer Springfield, Oreg., 1974—; owner, pres. Norway Books, Springfield, 1982—. Author: How to Sell Your Home, 1975, How to Buy the Right Home, 1980, Writing Better Technical Articles, 1990, The Write Stuff, 1991, Business Writing - The Modular Way, 1991, Using Online Scientific and Engineering Databases, 1992, Online Systems for Physicians and Medical Professionals, 1992, Outrageous DRDOS Batch Files, 1993. Staff sgt. U.S. Army, 1944-46. Republican. Lutheran. Home and Office: 2305 N 6th PO Box 676 Springfield OR 97477-0122

BJERGO, ALLEN CLIFFORD, agriculture specialist, consultant; b. Fergus Falls, Minn., Sept. 14, 1935; s. Adolph Christian and Alice Glenda (Hagen) B.; m. Norita LaVae Clark, Aug. 16, 1958 (div. Apr. 1973); children: Karl, Ann, Sunan, Orapin; m. Jacqueline Joan Jacks, Mar. 14, 1977; children: Erik, Kristi, Karen, Kelsey, Kyle. BS, N.D. State U., 1962; postgrad., Royal Agrl. Coll., Vollebekk, Norway, 1963; MA, N.Mex. State U., 1964; PhD, Cornell U., 1970. County ext. agt. Mont. Ext. Svc., Whitehall, 1964-66; dep. chief agr. U.S. AID, Can Tho, Vietnam, 1966-68; community devel. specialist Mont. Ext. Svc., Missoula, 1970-89, alternative agr. specialist, 1989—; cons. Can Tho U., Vietnam, 1989, U.N. Devel. Program, Dhakka, Bangladesh, 1990, Mont.-USSR Exch., Alma Ata, Kazakhstan, 1990, Citizens Democracy Corps, Plovdiv, Bulgaria, 1991. With U.S. Army, 1955-57. Grantee USDA 1989-92. Mem. Internat. Wildlife Film Festival (bd. dirs. 1991—), Nat. Ctr. for Appropriate Tech. (bd. dirs. 1989—), Inst. of Rockies (pres. 1988-90), Alternative Energy Resources Orgn. (bd. dirs. 1981—), Teller Wildlife Refuge (bd. dirs. 1989—), Great Northern Bots. Assn. (bd. dirs. 1985—), Mont. Land Reliance (pres. 1987-91). Home: 829 Weber Butte Trl Corvallis MT 59828

BJORKLUND, JANET VINSEN, speech pathologist; b. Seattle, July 31, 1947; d. Vernon Edward and Virginia Lea (Rogers) B.; m. Dan Robert Young, Dec. 04, 1971; children: Emery Allen, Alanna Vinsen, Marisa Rogers. Student, U. Vienna, Austria, 1966-67; BA, Pacific U., 1969; student, U. Wash., 1970-71; MA, San Francisco State U., 1977. Cert. clin. speech pathologist, audiologist. Speech pathologist, audiological cons. USN Hosp., Rota, Spain, 1972-75; traineeship in audiology VA Hosp., San Francisco, 1976; speech pathologist San Lorenzo (Calif.) Unified Schs., 1975-77, 78-81; dir. speech pathology St. Lukes Speech and Hearing Clinic, San Francisco, 1977-78; audiologist X.O. Barrios, M.D., San Francisco, 1977-81; cons. Visually Impaired Infant Program, Seattle, 1981-82; speech pathologist Everett (Wash.) Schs., 1982—; cons. Madison House, Kirkland, Wash., 1983-88, NW Devel. Therapists, Everett, 1985-87, Providence Hosp. Childrens Ctr., Everett, 1985—, Pacific Hearing and Speech, 1988—. Author: (with others) Screening for Bilingual Preschoolers, 1977, (TV script), Clinical Services in San Francisco, 1978, Developing Better Communication Skills, 1982. Coord. presch. Christian edn. Kirkland Congl. Ch., 1983-85; organizer Residents Against Speeding Drivers, Madison Park, Seattle, 1985-87; chmn. staff devel. com. Everett Schs., 1988-89; rep. Barrier Resolution Project, 1989-89; mem. Strategic Planning Com., 1989—. Mem. Am. Speech-Lang. and Hearing Assn., Wash. Speech and Hearing Assn. (regional rep. 1985-86, chair licensure task force 1986-88, rep. Birth to Six Project 1988-91, pres.-elect 1992, pres. 1993), Phi Lambda Omicron (pres. Pacific U. chpt. 1968). Congregationalist. Office: Everett Sch Dist 2 202 Alder St Everett WA 98203-3299

BJORKLUND, KATHARINE BROWNE, librarian; b. Los Alamos, N.Mex., Feb. 17, 1952; d. Philip Lincoln and Margaret (Powell) Browne; m. Eric Alan Bjorklund, June 30, 1973. BA, U. N.Mex., 1974; MLS, U. Wis., 1978. Info. desk staffer Meml. Library, U. Wis., Madison, 1976-78; circulation desk clk. Mesa Pub. Library, Los Alamos, 1978-79, circulation chief, 1979-80, head adult services div., 1980-86, head adult services sect., 1986-88, head reference and info. div., 1988-93, head reference sect., 1993—. Mem. ALA, N.Mex. Library Assn. Presbyterian. Office: Mesa Pub Libr 1742 Central Ave Los Alamos NM 87544-3094

BJORKMAN, OLLE ERIK, plant biologist, educator; b. Jonkoping, Sweden, July 29, 1933; came to U.S., 1964; s. Erik Gustaf and Dagmar Kristina (Svensson) B.; m. Monika Birgit Waldinger, Sept. 24, 1955; children: Thomas N.E., Per G.O. MS, U. Stockholm, 1957; PhD, U. Uppsala, 1960; DSc, U. Uppsala, Sweden, 1968. Asst. scientist dept. genetics and plant breeding U. Uppsala, 1956-61; rsch. fellow Swedish Natural Sci. Rsch. Coun., 1961-63; postdoctoral fellow Carnegie Instn. Wash., Stanford, Calif., 1964-65, mem. staff, 1966—; assoc. prof. biology by courtesy Stanford (Calif.) U., 1967-77, prof. biology by courtesy, 1977—; vis. fellow Australian Nat. U., Canberra, 1971-72, 78; advisor to pres. Desert Rsch. Inst., Nev., 1980-81; vis. sci. Australian Inst. Marine Sci., 1983; sci. advisor Kettering Found., 1976-77; mem. panel world food and nutrition study NRC, 1976; com. carbon dioxide effects Dept. Energy, 1977-82; competitive grants panel Dept. Agr., 1978; numerous other coms. and panels. Co-author: Experimental Studies of the Nature of Species V, 1971, Physiological Processes in Plant Ecology, 1980; mem. editorial bd. Planta, 1993—; contbr. articles to profl. publs. Recipient Linneus prize Royal Swedish Physiographic Soc., 1977. Fellow Am. Acad. Arts and Scis., AAAS; mem. Nat. Acad. Scis., Am. Soc. Plant Physiologists (Stephen Hales award 1986), Australian Acad. Sci. (Selby award 1987), Royal Swedish Acad. Scis. Home: 3040 Greer Rd Palo Alto CA 94303-4007 Office: Carnegie Inst Dept Plant Biology 290 Panama St Stanford CA 94305

BJORNDAHL, DAVID LEE, electrical engineer; b. Rock Island, Ill., June 19, 1927; s. Richard Gideon and Olive Muriel (Winter) B.; m. Clara Mae Buck, Feb. 16, 1952; children: William, Jay, Jan, Jill. PhD in Elec. Engring., Purdue U., 1956. Sr. engr. Litton Guidance & Control Systems, Beverly Hills, Calif., 1956-58; project engr. Litton Guidance & Control Systems, Woodland Hills, Calif., 1958-62, dir. advanced programs, 1962-66; mgr. Martin-Marietta, Denver, 1966-67; dir. advanced programs Litton Aero. Products, Woodland Hills, 1967-74; v.p. engring. Litton Aero. Products, Moorpark, Calif, 1974-86, chief scientist, 1986—. Contbr. articles to profl. jours. Mem. AIEE, Inst. Navigation, Simga Chi, Eta Kappa Nu. Republican. Office: Litton Aero Products 6101 Condor Dr Moorpark CA 93021-2605

BLACHER, JOAN HELEN, psychotherapist, educator; b. L.A., Aug. 10, 1928; d. Albert Scribner and Isabel (Marriott) Oakholt; m. Norman Blacher, July 27, 1973; stepchildren: Eric, Steven, Mark. BA, U. Calif., Berkeley, 1950; MEd, U. So. Calif., 1971, PhD, 1981. Lic. ednl. psychologist, Calif.; lic. marriage, family and child counselor, Calif. Elem. tchr. L.A. Unified Sch. Dist., 1962-71, sch. psychologist, 1971-72, 73-74; sch. psychologist Pasadena (Calif.) Unified Sch. Dist., 1972-73; sch. psychologist Ventura (Calif.) County Supt. Schs., 1974-79, prin., 1979-86; assoc. prof. sch. edn., head counseling and guidance program Calif. Luth. U., Thousand Oaks, 1987—; pvt. practice, Ventura, 1984—. Bd. dirs. Coalition Against Household Violence, Ventura, 1984-85. Mem. APA, Am. Counselors Assn., Am. Ednl. Rsch. Assn., Calif. Assn. Counselors, Educators, Supervisors (pres.-elect), Calif. Assn. Marriage & Family Therapists, Calif. Assn. Counseling Devel., Phi Delta Kappa. Republican.

BLACHER, ROBERT MICHAEL, sales executive; b. Chgo., Nov. 15, 1942; s. Louis Melvin and Dolores (Olshan) B.; m. Barbara Joy Zuckerman, July 4, 1966; children: Brian, Brett. BS in Communications, U. Ill., 1964. Sales devel. mgr. Chicago Tribune, 1970-72; account exec. Sta. WBBM-TV, Chgo., 1973-75; sales mgr. Sta. WTVJ-TV, Miami, Fla., 1975-91; gen. sales mgr. Sta. KGW-TV, Portland, Oreg., 1991—. Pres. Howard-Palmetto Khoury League, Miami, 1986-87, Palmetto Baseball Boosters Inc., 1989-90. Sgt. U.S. Army, 1964-70. Mem. Miami Advt. Fedn. (bd. dirs.), Ft. Lauderdale Advt. Fedn., Portland Advt. Fedn. Jewish. Home: 808 SW Regency Terr Portland OR 97225 Office: Sta KGW-TV 1501 SW Jefferson St Portland OR 97201

BLACK, CARLIN J., industrial marketing consultant; b. Toledo, Ohio, July 10, 1940; s. Charles T. and Dorothy Edna (Stokely) B.; m. Virginia Ann Hess, June 30, 1963 (div. Jan. 1991); children: Carlin Steven, Kevin James. BS in Chemistry, Stanford U., 1962, MBA, 1966. Chemist Aerojet Gen. Corp., Folsom, Calif., 1962-64; venture mgr. E.I. duPont de Nemours & Co., Wilmington, Del., 1966-71; flight svc. adminstrv. mgr. Pan Am. World Airways, N.Y.C., 1971-74, dir. capital budgets, 1974-76; orgn. analyst Interaction Analysts-Cons., N.Y.C., 1976-81; market devel. mgr. Allied Fibers & Plastics, Morristown, N.J., 1981-84; indsl. mktg. cons. CIMDI, N.Y.C., 1984-90, Carmichael, Calif., 1990—. Developer scientist inventions acrylic film mfg., 1975, wear resistant moldings, 1985. Bd. dirs. N.Y. Choral Soc., N.Y.C., 1985-88. Unitarian. Office: 2509 El Tonas Way Carmichael CA 95608

BLACK, COBEY, journalist, corporate executive; b. Washington, June 15, 1922; d. Elwood Alexander and Margaret (Beall) Cobey; m. Edwin F. Black; children: Star, Christopher, Noel, Nicholas, Brian, Bruce. BA, Wellesley Coll., 1944; postgrad., U. Hawaii. Exec. sec. to Irene, designer Metro-Goldwyn-Mayer, 1944; actress Fed. Republic Germany, 1945-46; women's editor Washington Daily News, 1947-50; columnist Honolulu Star Bull., 1954-65, Honolulu Advertiser, 1972-85; cons. HEW, Peace Corps; bd. dirs. Pacific and Asian Affairs Coun., 1986—, HonoluluCom. on Fgn. Rels., 1987—, Hawaii Internat. Film Festival, 1989—, Hawaii Army Mus., 1980—, Bishop Mus. Assn. Coun., 1988—; pres. Black & Black, Inc. Author: Birth of A Princess, 1962, Iolani Luahine, 1986; travel editor Bangkok World, 1968-69; publicist CBS-TV series Hawaii Five-O, 1978. Mem. Hawaii State Commn. on Status of Women, 1978-86. Mem. Nat. Press Club, Royal Bangkok Sports Club, Outrigger Canoe Club, Waialae Country Club, Garden Club of Honolulu. Democrat. Episcopalian. Office: Black & Black Inc 3081 La Pietra Cir Honolulu HI 96815-4736

BLACK, DAVID, writer, educator; b. Boston, Apr. 21, 1945; s. Henry Arnold and Zelda Edith (Hodosh) B.; m. Deborah Hughes Keehn, June 22, 1968; children: Susannah Haden, Tobiah Samuel McKee. BA cum laude, Amherst Coll., 1967; MFA, Columbia U., 1971. Free-lance writer, 1971—; writer-in-residence Mt. Holyoke Coll., South Hadley, Mass., 1982-86. Author: (novels) Minds, 1982, Like Father (Notable Book of Yr. N.Y. Times 1978, One of 7 Best Novels of Yr. Washington Post), 1978, Peep Show, 1986, (non-fiction) Ekstasy, 1975, The King of Fifth Avenue (Notable Book of Yr. N.Y. Times 1981), Murder at the Met, 1984, Medicine Man, 1985, The Plague Years, 1986, (play) An Impossible Life, 1990; contbr. articles and stories to various mags.; author screenplays for Disney, Michael Douglas, Martin Scorsese, Highgate, Paramount, Tristar, Aaron Russo Prodn., Largo, Universal/USA, miniseries for Chris-Rose/CBS/Viacom; writer teleplay Death and The Lady, others; author screenplay, exec. producer The Good Policeman, Legacy of Lies (winner Giorgi award Writers Found.); story editor Hill Street Blues, 1986-88, Miami Vice, 1987-88; producer The Lou Gossett Show, 1988; co-creator and supervising producer The Nasty Boys; supervising producer H.E.L.P., 1989-90, Law and Order, 1990-92 (Emmy nomination 1992); creator TV series including Heat, The Good Policeman; contbg. editor Rolling Stone, 1986-89. Recipient Atlantic Firsts award Atlantic Monthly, 1973, Playboy's Best Article of Yr. award Playboy mag., 1979; Nat. Assn. Sci. Writers award, 1985, hon. mention for Best Essay of Yr., 1986, Nat. Mag. award in reporting, 1986; Nat. Endowment Arts grantee, 1979; nominee for Best Episodic Drama of Yr. Writers Guild ann. awards, 1988. Mem. Mystery Writers Am. (nominated for Edgar-Best Fact Crime 1984, Edgar-Best 1 hour episodic series 1991), PEN, Authors Guild, Writers Guild East, Williams Club, Century Assn. Jewish/Unitarian. Office: care David Wirtschafter/ICM 8899 Beverly Blvd West Hollywood CA 90048-2412

BLACK, EILEEN MARY, elementary school educator; b. Bklyn., Sept. 20, 1944; d. Marvin Mize and Anne Joan (Salvia) B. Student, Grossmont Coll., El Cajon, Calif., 1964; BA, San Diego State U., 1967; postgrad., U. Calif., San Diego, Syracuse U. Cert. tchr., Calif. Tchr. La Mesa (Calif.)-Spring Valley Sch. Dist., 1967—. NDEA grantee Syracuse U., 1986; recipient 25 Yrs. Svc. award La Mesa-Spring Valley Sch. Dist., 1992. Mem. Calif. Tchrs. Assn., Calif. Young Reps. Roman Catholic. Home: 9320 Earl St Apt 15 La Mesa CA 91942-3846 Office: Northmont Elem Sch 9405 Gregory St La Mesa CA 91942-3811

BLACK, HUGH LAWRANCE, banker, lawyer; b. Cleve., Ohio, Mar. 8, 1942; s. Marion Eckert and Margaret Esther (Blaser) B. BA, Coll. Wooster, Ohio, 1964; JD, Case-Western Res. U., 1967. Bar: Ohio 1968, Fla. 1968, D.C. 1970, U.S. Supreme Ct. 1970. Asst. trust officer Cleve. Trust Co., 1968-70; trust officer, asst. v.p. Coconut Grove Bank, Miami, Fla., 1970-72; pvt. practice Miami and Palm Beach, Fla., 1972-76; mktg. specialist Wells Fargo Bank, Beverly Hills, Calif., 1976-80; asst. v.p., mgr. Lloyds Bank Calif., Newport Beach, 1980-84; v.p., regional mgr. personal trust and investment svcs. Union Bank, Irvine, Calif., 1984-92; v.p. corp. trust sales So. Calif. Union Bank, L.A., Calif., 1992—; lectr. Orange County Coll., Costa Mesa, Calif., 1980-85; adj. prof. law Pepperdine U., Malibu, Calif., 1977-84. Mem. endowment adv. com. Orange County Performing Arts Ctr., Costa Mesa, 1980—. Mem. ABA, Ohio Bar Assn., Fla. Bar Assn., D.C. Bar Assn., Orange County Trust Officers' Assn. (sec.-treas. 1986-87, pres. 1987-88), World Trade Ctr. Orange County, Am. Arbitration Assn., Newport Harbor C. of C. (chmn. bus. assistance and devel. com. 1980-83), Coconut Grove C. of C. (Disting. Citizen award 1972), Univ. Athletic Club, Breakers Beach Club. Presbyterian. Home: 900 Sea Ln Corona Del Mar CA 92625-1502 Office: Union Bank 445 S Figueron St 34th fl Los Angeles CA 90071

BLACK, KEITH CORYELL, radio news anchor, reporter; b. Kirkland, Wash., Aug. 11, 1959; s. John Coryell and Marian Olga (Edwardson) B.; m. Paula Kaye Stovall, July 18, 1987; 1 child, Andrew Coryell. BA in Comm., Wash. State U., 1981. Radio announcer Sta. KOZI, Chelan, Wash., 1980, Sta. KWSU, Pullman, Wash., 1981; news anchor, announcer Sta. KCMS/KCIS, Seattle, 1981—; radio program prodr. Sta. KZOK, Seattle, 1990-93; news anchor, reporter Mission Network News, Bainbridge Island, Wash., 1991—. Office: KCMS KCIS 19303 Fremont Ave N Seattle WA 98133

BLACK, KRISTINE MARY, physicist; b. St. Paul, July 11, 1953; d. Jaurd Oliver and Dorothy Helen (Amos) B. B in Physics, U. Minn., 1975, MS in Cell Biology, 1978, MS in Metallurgy and Materials Sci., 1981. Analytical physicist Cardiac Pacemakers, St. Paul, 1978, qualifications engr., 1978-81; biomaterials engr. St. Jude Med., Inc., St. Paul, 1981-83; mgr. quality assurance Unisys Semicondr. Ops., St. Paul, 1983-88; systems assurance sect. mgr. Unisys, 1988-90, quality assurance mgr. SMPO div., San Diego, 1990-91; mgr. reliability and quality assurance Carborundum Co., Phoenix, 1991-93; pvt. practice quality cons., Phoenix, 1993—. Contbr. articles to profl. jours. Mem. IEEE, Am. Soc. for Quality Control, Am. Soc. Metals, U. Minn. Inst. Tech. Alumni Soc. (dir. 1980-87, v.p. 1986-87, pres. 1987-88). Office: 16255 S 13th St Phoenix AZ 85044-9211

BLACK, LYDIA T., anthropologist, educator; b. Kiev, USSR, Dec. 16, 1925; came to U.S., 1950; m. Igor A. Black, Jan. 12, 1947 (dec. 1969); children: Anna Black Treiber, Maria Black McEvoy, Zoe M. Black Pierson, Elena. BS in History, Northeastern U., 1969; MA in Social Anthropology, Brandeis U., 1971; PhD in Social Anthropology, U. Mass., 1973. Asst. prof. to prof. anthropology Providence Coll., 1973-85; prof. anthropology U. Alaska, Fairbanks, 1985—; instr. anthropology U. Mass., 1972; vis. lectr. Am. Anthrop. Assn., 1974-76; cons. various orgns. Author: The Journals of Iakov Netsvetov-The Atkha Years, 1980, Aleut Art, 1982, Atkha-Ethnohistory of the Western Aleutians, 1983, The Journals of Iakov Netsvetov. The Yukon Years: 1845-1863, 1984, The Round the World Voyage of Hieromonk Gideon, 1803-1809, 1989, Glory Remembered: Wooden Headgear of Alaska Sea Hunters, 1991, Lovtsov's Atlas of the North Pacific Ocean, 1991; translator: Notes on the Islands of Unalaska District (by Ioann Veniaminov), 1984; contbr. numerous articles to profl. jours. Mem. Icon Preservation Task Force, Anchorage, 1986—. Eastern Orthodox. Office: U Alaska-Fairbanks Dept Anthropology Fairbanks AK 99775

BLACK, MAX C., insurance agent; b. Delta, Utah, July 2, 1936; s. William Ernst Black and Ella (Clark) B.; m. Clydene S. Black, June 29, 1961; children: Jeffrey, Gary, Wendi. BA in Bus., U. Utah, 1962. Underwriter Am. Agencies, Salt Lake City, 1962-67; field rep. USF&G Ins. Co., Boise, Idaho, 1967-75; agy. owner Black & Warr Ins. Agy., Boise, Idaho, 1975-91; pres. Boise Agents Assn., 1981, Idaho Profl. Agents, 1982 (bd. dirs. 1981-92, agent of the yr. 1981). Rep. House of Reps. State of Idaho, 1992—. Mem. Optomist Internat. Republican. Home: 3731 Buckingham Dr Boise ID 83704

BLACK, NOEL ANTHONY, television and film director; b. Chgo., June 30, 1937; s. Samuel Abraham and Susan (Quan) B.; m. Catherine Elizabeth Cownie, June 1, 1988; children: Marco Eugene, Nicole Alexandra, Carmen Elizabeth, Catherine Ellen. BA, UCLA, 1959, MA, 1964. Ind. fil, TV dir., 1966—; asst. prof. grad. program Inst. Film and TV, Tisch Sch. of Arts, NYU, 1992-93. Dir. (TV films) Trilogy: The American Boy, 1967 (Outstanding Young Dir. award Monte Carlo Internat. Festival of TV, Silver Dove award Internat. Cath. Soc. for Radio and TV), I'm a Fool, 1977, Mulligan's Stew, 1977, The Golden Honeymoon, 1979, The Electric Grandmother, 1981 (George Foster Peabody award 1982), The Other Victim, 1981, Prime Suspect, 1981, Happy Endings, 1982, Quarterback Princess, 1983, Deadly Intentions, 1985, Promises to Keep, 1985, A Time to Triumph, 1985, My Two Loves, 1986, Conspiracy of Love, 1987, The Town Bully, 1988, The Hollow Boy, 1991, (short films) Skaterdater, 1966 (Grand Prix award Cannes XX Film Festival, Grand Prix Tech. Cannes XX Internat. Film Festival, awards Cork Film Festival, Silver medal Moscow Internat. Film Festival, others), Riverboy, 1967 (Lion of St. Mark award Venice Internat. Film Festival, 1st prize Vancouver Internat. Film Festival), (feature films) Pretty Poison, 1968, Mirrors, 1974, A Man, a Woman and a Bank, 1978; screenwriter Mischief, 1984.. Mem. Writers Guild Am., Dirs. Guild Am., Acad. Motion Picture Arts and Scis., Acad. TV Arts and Scis. Office: Starfish Prodns 126 Wadsworth Ave Santa Monica CA 90405-3510

BLACK, PATRICIA EILEEN, French language educator; b. Amherst, Ohio, Apr. 25, 1955; d. William Marion and Virginia Eileen (Davidson) B.; m. Douglas Scott Henderson, Oct. 11, 1980; children: Anna Elene Henderson, Camille May Henderson. BA, Oberlin Coll., 1977; MA, Cornell U., 1980; Diplome d'Etudes Avancees, U. Poitiers, Poitiers, France, 1983; PhD, Cornell U., 1985. Prof. French SUNY, Potsdam, 1984-86; prof. French Calif. State U., Chico, 1986—, dir. internat. program in France, 1993—; Reviewer Holt Rinehart Winston, N.Y.C., 1987—, Olifant, U. Va.; asst. dir. Business in France Program, Chico, Calif., 1989, NEH Summer Inst., Potsdam, N.Y., 1985-87, Mt. Holyoke Coll., 1987; presenter in field to confs. and convs. Govt. Quebec Library grantee, 1989, Govt. Canada Faculty Enrichment grantee, 1988. Mem. Am. Coun. for Quebec Studies, N.Am. Catalan Soc., Modern Lang. Assn., Societe Guilhem IX, Rocky Mountain Medieval and Renaissance Soc., Societe Rencesvals (sec. 1991-93), Phi Beta Kappa. Office: Calif State University Dept Fgn Langs Chico CA 95929-0825

BLACK, PETE, state legislator, educator; b. Ansbach, Germany, Sept. 16, 1946; came to U.S., 1948; s. Howard and Kadi (Fietz) B.; m. Ronda Williams, July 12, 1970; 1 child, Darin. BS, Idaho State U., 1975; postgrad., 1991—. Cert. elem. tchr. Tchr. Pocatello (Idaho) Sch. Dist., 1975—; mem. Idaho Ho. Reps., Boise, 1983—, asst. minority leader, 1987—; mem. adv. coun. chpt. II ESEA. Bd. dirs. Arts for Idaho. With USNR, 1964. Mem. NEA, Idaho Edn. Assn., Idaho Libr. Assn. Democrat. Home: 2249 Cassia Pocatello ID 83201 Office: Idaho Ho Reps Statehouse Mail Boise ID 83720

BLACK, ROBERT JAMES, cabinetmaker, small business owner; b. Tioga, Pa., Apr. 13, 1955; s. Frank L. and Margaret (Reynolds) Blanchard; m. Alma Marie Solomon, Dec. 19, 1987; 1 child from previous marriage, Healther Louise. Lic. vocat. nurse, Calif. Shop foreman Wooden Nickel Furniture, Meadville, Pa., 1978-81; pres., owner Thoughts In Wood, San Diego and Vallejo, Calif., 1986—; bus. cons. Profl. Bus. Svcs., San Diego and Oakland, Calif., 1986—. Author: The Refrigerator Committed Suicide, 1983, Pigpiled, 1990. Leader 4-H Club Sunshine Riders, Akron, Ohio, 1975, Rep. canvasser, 1974. Served with USN, 1981-85. Mem. Assn. Surg. Technologists, Am. Legion, Glencannon Soc. Episcopalian.

BLACK, SHIRLEY NORMAN, lawyer, retired museum official, retired air force officer; b. Gardner, Mass., Sept. 26, 1916; s. Henry Warren and Ella (Thompson) B.; m. Kathryn Mary Linser, Mar. 19, 1947; 1 son, Peter Norman. B.S. in Commerce and Bus. Adminstrn., U. Ala., 1938; M.B.A. with distinction, Harvard U., 1954; postgrad. George Washington U., 1955; grad. Air U., 1959; J.D., Western State U., 1978. Commd. 2d lt., USAF, 1938, advanced through grades to col. U.S. Air Force, 1953; exec. dir. fin. Hdqrs., U.S. Air Force, 1951-52; dep. chief staff, comptroller hdqrs. Crew Tng., 1955-57; dir. acctg. and fin. Hdqrs. Air Tng. Command, 1957-58, Hdqrs. Pacific Air Force, 1959-60; dep. chief staff, comptroller Hdqrs. 5th Air Force, 1960-62; comptroller, asst. treas. Art Inst. Chgo., 1963-72, v.p. adminstrv. affairs, 1972-75; treas. Restaurant Food Buyers, Inc., 1972—, also dir.; pres. Restaurant Food Buyers Investment Co., 1972—. Commr. Far East Council Boy Scouts Am.; dir. Far East Little League, 1960-61. Decorated Bronze Star, Commendation medal with oak leaf cluster. Mem. ABA, VFW, Air Force Assn., Ret. Officers Assn., Am. Mgmt. Assn., Am. Soc. Mil. Comptrollers (outstanding achievement cert. 1959), Orange County Estate Planners (coun. 1988—), Orange County Bar Assn., Chgo. Assn. Commerce and Industry, Harvard Bus. Sch. Assn. So. Calif. Heroes of '76, Nat. Sojourners, Am. Legion. Clubs: Army Navy Country (Arlington, Va.); Yorba Linda Country; Toastmasters (pres. Scott AFB chpt. 1954). Lodges: Masons, Shriners. Home: 6151 Sandy Hill Ln Yorba Linda CA 92686-5836 Office: 810 E Commonwealth Ave Fullerton CA 92631

BLACK, WILFORD REX, JR., state senator; b. Salt Lake City, Jan. 31, 1920; s. Wilford Rex and Elsie Isabell (King) B.; m. Helen Shirley Frazer; children: Susan, Janet, Cindy, Joy, Peggy, Vanna, Gayle, Rex. Student schools in Utah. Locomotive engr. Rio Grande R.R., 1941-81; mem. Utah Senate, 1972—, speaker Third House, 1975-76, majority whip, 1977-78, minority leader, 1981-90; chmn., vice chmn. United Transp. Union, 1972-78; sec. Utah State Legis. Bd., United Transp. Chmn. bd. Rail Operators Credit Union, 1958-87; mission pres. Rose Park Stake Mormon Ch., high priest group leader Rose Park 9th Ward, 1980-83, mem. Rose Park Stake High Council, 1957-63. Served with U.S. Army, 1942-45. Recipient various awards r.r and legis. activities. Democrat. Office: 826 N 1300 W Salt Lake City UT 84116-3877

BLACK, WILLIAM REA, lawyer; b. N.Y.C., Nov. 4, 1952; s. Thomas Howard and Dorothy Chambers (Dailey) B.; m. Kathleen Jane Owen, June 24, 1978; children: William Ryan, Jonathan Wesley. BSBA, U. Denver, 1978, MBA, 1981; JD, Western State U., Fullerton, Calif., 1987. Bar: Calif., U.S. Ct. Appeals (fed. cir.); lic. real estate broker. Bus. mgr. Deere & Co., Moline, Ill., 1979-85; dir. Mgmt. Resource Svcs. Co., Chgo., 1985-86; sr. v.p. Geneva Corp., Irvine, Calif., 1986-91; pvt. practice Newport Beach, Calif., 1991—. Mng. editor Western State U. Law Rev., Fullerton, 1984-87. Instr. U.S. Judo Assn., Denver, 1975-80. Recipient Am. Jurisprudence award Bancroft-Whitney Co., 1984, 85, 86. Mem. Am. Soc. Appraisers, Inst. Bus. Appraisers, Assn. Productivity Specialists, Orange County Bar Assn., L.A. County Bar Assn., Mu Kappa Tau, Second Degree Black Belt Karate.

BLACKBURN, CHARLES EDWARD, chief executive officer; b. Detroit, June 19, 1939; s. Wallace Manders and Elva Jean (Beetham) B.; m. Rachel Burton, June 17, 1962 (div. June 1979); children: Michael, Thomas; m. Judith Ann Brady, June 30, 1979. BS, Baldwin-Wallace Coll., 1961; MBA, Pepperdine U., 1990. Assoc. rsch. chemist Parke-Davis and Co., Ann Arbor, Mich., 1963-71; mgr. Mallinckrodt Chem. Works, St. Louis, 1971-74; sr. product mgr. Packard Instrument Co., Downers Grove, Ill., 1974-77; product mktg. mgr. Beckman Instruments, Fullerton, Calif., 1977-80; gen. sales mgr. Wahl Instruments, Culver City, Calif., 1980-84; v.p. Signet Sci. Co., El Monte, Calif., 1984-91; chmn., chief exec. officer "C" Enterprises, San Marcos, Calif., 1991—. Contbr. articles to profl. jours. Mem. Rotary Internat. (sec. 1983, pres. 1984). Republican. Office: "C" Enterprises 310-110 Via Vera Cruz San Marcos CA 92069-1449

BLACKBURN, JOHN LEWIS, consulting engineer; b. Kansas City, Mo., Oct. 2, 1913; s. John Ealy and Lela (Garnett) B.; m. Margaret Bailey, Sept. 12, 1943; children: Susan T., Joan Blackburn Krist, Margaret A. Blackburn Jahns. BSEE with high honors, U. Ill., 1935. With Westinghouse Electric Corp., Newark, 1936-78, cons. engr., 1969-78; pvt. practice cons., Bothell, Wash., 1979—; adj. prof. Poly. Inst. N.Y., 1949-65, Poly. Inst. N.J., Newark, 1958-71; spl. lectr. IEEE Ednl. Activities, 1952—; affiliate prof. U. Wash., 1988; instr. North Seattle Community Coll., 1988—. Author, editor: Applied Protective Relaying, 1978; author: Protective Relaying Principles and Application, 1987, Symmetrical Components for Power Engring., 1993. Trustee, treas. Millington Bapt. Ch., N.J., 1952-69. Recipient Order of Merit award Westinghouse Electric Corp., 1971, Attwood Assocs. award U.S. Nat. Com. Internat. Conf. for Large High Voltage Electric Systems, 1986. Fellow IEEE (chmn. publ. dept. Power Engring. Soc. 1972-76, sec., 1977-79, chmn. power system relaying com. 1969-70, Disting. Service award 1978, Outstanding Service award IEEE ednl. bd. 1979, Centennial medal 1984); mem. China Stamp Soc. Inc. (pres. 1979—), Am. Soc. Polar Philatelists (bd. dirs., treas. 1967—), Sigma Xi, Tau Beta Pi, Eta Kappa Nu, Phi Kappa Phi. Home: 21816 8th Pl W Bothell WA 98021-8199

BLACKBURN, LOU JEAN, elementary school educator; b. Roy, Utah, Mar. 20, 1928; d. Lionel Earl and Mavis Fern (Johnston) Gibby; m. Oriel Dale Blackburn, June 10, 1949 (div. June 1964); children: Michael Dale, Diane Taylor, Terry Kent, Kirk Lee. Student, Weber State Coll., 1946-48, Utah State U., 1948-49; BS, Utah State U., 1964. Cert. elem. tchr. Tchr. Taylor Sch., Ogden, Utah, 1964-67, Grandview Sch., Ogden, 1967-84, Wasatch Sch., Ogden, 1984—; asst. prin. Wasatch Sch., Ogden, 1990-91; cons. Houghton Mifflin Math., 1983, Tchr. Acad. Weber State U., 1989-90. Del. Rep. State Conv., Ogden, 1969. Mem. NEA, Utah Edn. Assn., Utah Coun. Internat. Reading Assn. (treas. 1989-91, pres., named Reading Tchr. of Yr. 1990), Delta Kappa Gamma (state treas. 1985-87,Ogden treas. 1988-91, Ogden v.p. 1974-76, 78-80, 82-84, Ogden sec. 1972-73). Mormon.

BLACKBURN, THOMAS EARL, chemist; b. Flint, Mich., Oct. 10, 1951; s. Neal and Rosalyn (Gumm) B.; m. Lilly Chin, Apr. 24, 1993. BS in Chemistry with honors, U. Mich., Flint, 1978; MS, U. Mich., 1980, PhD, 1984. Atmospheric chemist NASA-Ames, Mountain View, Calif., 1984-88; environ. chemist IBM Corp., San Jose, Calif., 1988—; atmospheric rschr. Nat. Ctr. Atmospheric Rsch., Boulder, Colo., 1980; atmospheric support scientist NASA-Ames, Mountain View and Darwin, Australia, 1987. Instr. Aikido Yoshokai Assn. N.Am. Mem. Am. Geophys. Union, Am. Chem. Soc. Office: IBM Corp E41/110 5600 Cottle Rd San Jose CA 95193

BLACKFIELD, CECILIA MALIK, educator, civic volunteer; b. Oakland, Calif., Jan. 18, 1915; d. Benjamin Malik and Mollie Saak; m. William Blackfield, Dec. 25, 1941; children: Leland Gregory, Pamela Esther, Karen Ann. BA, U. Calif., Berkeley, 1936; MEdn., San Francisco State Tchrs Coll, 1937. cert. elem. tchr. Calif. (lifetime). Tchr. Albany (Calif.) Sch. Dist., 1938-43; rep. NEA, Alameda County, Calif., 1938-43. Pres. Calif. Tchrs. Assn., Alameda County, Calif., 1939; mem. (charter) Territorial Hosp. Aux., Kauikeolani Children's Hosp. (bd. dirs.); bd. dirs. Hastings Law Sch. Found., San Francisco, Calif., McCoy Pavilion Park, Honolulu, Hi., Daughters of the Nile, Honolulu, Temple Emmanuel; mem. Mayor's Citizen Advisory Com. for Diamond Head, Wakiki, Honolulu, Mayor's Adv. Com. for Community & Urban Renewal, Beautification Com., League of Women Voters; chmn. Hawaii Cancer Fund Crusade and many more; mem. master planning com. Vision for Waikiki 2020; mem. Preservation Rev. Com. Hist. Hawaii. Named Woman of the Year for Nat. Brotherhood Week, Honolulu, 1972. Mem. Nat. Assn. Home Builders (pres. Hawaii chpt. women's aux.), Outdoor Circle (pres.), Friends of Foster Gardens, Washington Palace State Capitol, Hadassah (past pres. Oakland chpt.), Women's Com. Brandeis U. (life mem.). Home: 901 Kealaolu Ave Honolulu HI 96816-5416

BLACKIE, JAMES RANDALL, educator; b. Pasadena, Calif., Jan. 4, 1958; s. Richard Allen and Anita Jean (Wehe) B.; m. Kelly Colleen Rhea, Aug. 20, 1988. AA, Orange Coast Coll., 1980; BA in Edn., BA in History cum laude, Christian Heritage Coll., 1983; MA in Edn. magna cum laude, Regent U., 1988. Cert. tchr., Calif. Youth intern Scott meml. Ch., El Cajon, Calif., 1981-83; tchr. Cornerstone Sch., Poway, Calif., 1983-84; tchr. Maranatha Acad., Santa Ana, Calif., 1984—, sci. specialist, 1987—; sci. instr. Community Achievement Svc., Fullerton, Calif., 1989—; art dir., curriculum coord. Camp Alandale, Idyllwild, Calif., 1985-90. Author: CBNU Model and Home Education, 1988. Mem. Calif. Edn. Assn. (pres. 1981-82), Christian Heritage Coll. Edn. Assn. (pres.), Sci. Club (founder, pres.). Home: 1117 S Van Ness Santa Ana CA 92707

BLACKLEDGE, SHERÍ DIONE, retail executive; b. Norwalk, Calif., July 23, 1968; d. John Edgar and Deborah Louise (Berry) B. BA in Psychology, U. Calif., Riverside, 1990; postgrad., Chapman Coll., 1991—. Retail territory mgr. Bradshaw Inc. South, Santa Fe Springs, Calif., 1988—; rsch. asst., Psychology Dept., U. Calif., Riverside, 1990—. Counselor Girl Scouts U.S., Orange County, 1987—; mem. Riverside Rape Crisis Advocate, 1990—; vol. Riverside Area Helpline, 1990. Recipient Riverside Kiwanis scholarship 1986, 1987, Am. Bus. Women's Assn. scholarship, San. Bernardino, Calif. 1988. Mem. Future Farmers Am. (reporter 1984, v.p. 1985-86), Riverside Hospice, Am. Cancer Soc. Democrat. Home: 3243 Arlington Ave # 140 Riverside CA 92506

BLACKMAN, DAVID IRA, health science administrator; b. L.A., Mar. 12, 1951; s. Soli and Erika Louise (Ullmann) B. BS, U. So. Calif., 1975; MS, U. LaVerne, 1986. Cert. tchr., Calif. Fin. specialist U. Calif. Med. Ctr., San Francisco, 1975-79; adminstrn. specialist U. Calif. Med. Ctr., Irvine, 1979-80; adminstr. Kaiser Found. Health Plan, L.A., 1980—; cons. health care DIB Group, Glendale, Calif., 1980—. Recipient Gold Achievement award United Way Campaigns, Los Angeles, 1984. Mem. Am. Guild Patient Acct. Mgrs., Health Care Fin. Mgmt. Assocs., Am. Mgmt. Assn., Am. Hosp. Assn., Nat. Right to Work Found., Assn. Western Hosps., Lake Mirage Country Club. Republican. Home: 5375 Crescent Cr Yorba Linda CA 92687

BLACKMAN, STEVE RALPH, management consultant; b. Vernon, Tex., Feb. 22, 1962; s. William Howard and Quincy Marie (Pomroy) B. BA summa cum laude, Calif. State U., Northridge, 1988; MS, Calif. Sch. Profl. Psychology, L.A., 1990, PhD, 1992. Supr. Genstar Mortgage Co., Glendale, Calif., 1985-86; mem. faculty Calif. State U., Northridge, 1987-88; data analyst U. So. Calif. Inst. Prevention Rsch., Pasadena, 1989-90; jr. cons. Mercer, Inc., L.A., 1990-91; orgn. devel. cons. Hughes Aircraft, L.A., 1990—; orgn. devel. cons., L.A., 1991—. Author: (tng. manuals) Leading Work Groups, 1989, Managing Organizational Change, 1990. Big Bro., pers. cons. Cath. Big Bros., L.A., 1984—. Mem. APA, Acad. Mgmt., L.A. Orgn. Devel. Network. Home: 17600 Covello St Van Nuys CA 91406 Office: Hughes Aircraft/HSC 909 N Sepulveda Los Angeles CA 90009

BLACKSTOCK, JAMES FIELDING, lawyer; b. L.A., Sept. 19, 1947; s. James Carne and Justine Fielding (Gibson) B.; m. Kathleen Ann Weigand, Dec. 12, 1969; children: Kristin Marie, James Fielding. AB, U. So. Calif., 1969; JD, 1976. Bar: Calif. 1976, U.S. Dist. Ct. (cen. dist.) Calif. 1977, U.S. Supreme Ct. 1980. Law clk. Hill Farrer Burrill, L.A., 1975-76, assoc., 1976-80; assoc. Zobrist, Garner, Garrett, L.A., 1980-83; ptnr. Zobrist & Vienna, L.A., 1983; v.p., gen. counsel Tatum Petroleum, La Habra, Calif., 1983; atty. Thorpe, Sullivan, Workman & Thorpe, 1984; ptnr. Sullivan, Workman & Dee, 1985-91; Profl. Law Corp., 1992—; prin. James F. Blackstock P.C., 1992; pres. Commerce Assocs., U. So. Calif., 1990-93. Mem. Town Hall, L.A., 1980-90. Served to lt. USN, 1969-73; comdr. USNR. Mem. ABA, L.A. County Bar Assn., U. So. Calif. Alumni Assn. (bd. govs. 1990-92), Pasadena Tournament Roses Assn., Saddle and Sirloin Club, Elks, Rancheros Visitadores. Republican. Roman Catholic. Home: 5316 Palm Dr La Canada Flintridge CA 91011 Office: James F Blackstock PLC 601 W 5th St 8th Flr Los Angeles CA 90071

BLACKSTOCK, JOSEPH ROBINSON, newspaper editor; b. L.A., Dec. 8, 1947; s. Joseph Richard McCall and Doris Louise (Robinson) B.; m. Nancy Ruth Frederiksen, Feb. 9, 1974; children: Miriam, Susan, Cynthia, Catherine. BA, Calif. State U., L.A., 1970, MA, 1977. Sports writer Monterey Park Californian, 1986-72; sports and news writer, mng. editor San Gabriel Valley Tribune, West Covina, Calif., 1972-89; exec. editor Pasadena (Calif.) Star-News, 1989-93; copy editor Riverside (Calif.) Press-Enterprise, 1993—. With USAR, 1970-78.

BLACKWELL, ANNA DERBY, public relations consultant; b. Honolulu, Aug. 12, 1932; d. Stephen Arthur and Dora (Cooke) Derby; m. Charles Hoffman Bond, Nov. 26, 1952 (div. Sept. 1970); children: Caroline Bond Dvojacki, Suzi, Boyd Davis, Sarah Bond Langan, Elizabeth; m. Robert Douglas Howe, Oct. 22, 1974 (dec. Apr. 1981); m. Jesse Eugene Blackwell, June 12, 1984. Student, Vassar Coll., 1950-52, U. Hawaii, 1952-53, U. Canterbury, New Zealand, 1985; BA, Hawaii Pacific U., 1991. Writer/reporter Waikiki Beach Press, Waihe'e, Hawaii, 1960-64; pub. rels. dir. YWCA of Oahu, Honolulu, 1966-72; first exec. dir. Moanalua Gardens Found., Honolulu, 1972-82; mng. editor Trade Pub. Co., Honolulu, 1987-88; pub. rels. and advt. coord. Chaney, Brooks and Co., Honolulu, 1988-89; account mgr. AdCorp Internat., Honolulu, 1989; cons. ANNAgram, Honolulu, 1965-92, Seattle, 1992—; asst. mgr. Cathedral Assocs. at St. Mark's, 1992—. Editor: Wilders of Waikiki, 1980. Choir mem. St. Andrew's Cathedral, Honolulu, 1946—; founder Women's Fund of Hawaii, Honolulu, 1989—; trustee, sec. Cooke Found., Ltd., Honolulu, 1989—. Mem. Pub. Rels. Soc. Am. (accredited), Women in Comm. Inc. Episcopalian.

BLACKWELL, GARLAND WAYNE, military officer; b. Roxboro, N.C., July 8, 1956; s. Garland and Mattie (Wright) B.; m. Joan Lelia Christensen, Mar. 12, 1984 (div. 1988); m. Sandra Luz Garcia, Feb. 9, 1991; 1 child, Brandi Alexis. BSBA, U. N.C., 1978; MBA, N.Mex. Highlands U., 1982. CPA. Commd. 2d lt. USAF, 1979, advanced through grades to major, 1990; dep. acctg. and fin. officer 1606 Air Base Wing USAF, Kirtland AFB, N.Mex., 1979-82; staff auditor Air Force Audit Agy., Vandenberg AFB, Calif., 1982-83, Torrejon AB, Spain, 1983-85; audit office chief Air Force Audit Agy., Castle AFB, Calif., 1985-89; audit mgr. Air Force Audit Agy., Norton AFB, Calif., 1989-92; comptroller 432 Fighter Wing USAF, Misawa AB, Japan, 1992—. Active Caring By Sharing Maranatha Community Ch., L.A., 1989-92; bd. dirs. project alpha March of Dimes, San Bernadino, Calif., 1990-91. Decorated Commendation medal; named one of Outstanding Young Men Am., 1984, 86, 89, Most Eligible Bachelor Ebony Mag., 1989. Mem. Inst. Internal Auditors, Am. Soc. Mil. Comptrollers (v.p. chmn. 1986-88), Nat. Black Masters in Bus. Adminstrn. Assn. (life), Air Force Assn., Tuskegee Airmen, Inc., Alpha Phi Alpha (chmn. v.p. 1981-82). Home: PO Box 4274 San Bernadino CA 92409 Office: 432 FW/FM Unit 5009 APO CA 96319-5000

BLACKWELL, TERRY LYNN, real estate and mortgage broker; b. Bend, Oreg., Dec. 4, 1947; s. Henry Branden and Gladys W. (Skeels) B.; m. Linda Sue Walkup, June 11, 1969; 1 child, Tyler. Student, Cen. Oreg. Community Coll., 1967-68, Portland State U., 1969. Broker, owner, agt. various coms., Bend, 1978-89; broker, owner Straford Realty, Bend, 1989—; owner Stratford Fin., Bend, 1988—. Mayor City of Bend, 1989-90, 91—, airport commn., 1989-90, mem. traffic safety com., 1989-90; mem. exec. bd. Your Community 2000, Bend, 1990; chair Bend Devel. Bd. Mem. Cen. Oreg. Bd. Realtors (Merit award 1990, comml. inv. dir. 1990, pres. Million Dollar Club 1984, exec. bd. Multiple Listing Svc. 1990-91, sec.-treas.). Republican. Baptist. Home: 2004 NE 8th St Bend OR 97701 Office: Stratford Realty 2150 NE Studio Rd Ste 1A Bend OR 97701-3640

BLADES, WILLIAM HOWARD, sales and management consultant, professional speaker; b. Salisbury, Md., Mar. 27, 1947; s. Nolan Edward and Anna (Kelly) B.; m. Kristyn Marie Ratlief; children: Stephanie, Billy. Student, U. Md., Princess Anne, 1969-71, Northwestern U., Evanston, Ill., 1985. Materials mgr. Allied Signal, Balt., 1971-72; regional sales mgr. Balt. Spice Co., Baltimore, Md., 1972-81; v.p. sales and mktg. Flavorite Labs., Inc., Memphis, Tenn., 1981-86; pres. William Blades & Assos., Phoenix, 1987—; mem. faculty Grad. Sch. Banking, Baton Rouge, 1989. Coauthor: Leadership Strategists, 1988; author cassette tapes: Professional Selling, 1986. Fin. chmn. Newt Gingrich, U.S. Congress, Atlanta, 1976. With U.S. Army, 1966-69, Korea. Mem. Sales and Mktg. Execs. (dir. 1981—), Memphis C. of C. Republican. Office: William Blades & Assocs 537 S 48th St Ste 103 Tempe AZ 85281

BLADON, RICHARD ANTHONY, speech professional; b. Leicester, U.K., Mar. 7, 1943; came to U.S., 1986; s. Leonard Harry and Barbara Irene (Jones) B.; m. Deborah McGerry, 1992. BA, U. Cambridge, Eng., 1965, MA, 1968; MPhil, U. Reading, Eng., 1969; DPhil, U. Oxford, Eng., 1985. Lectr. U. Ghent, Belgium, 1965-67; lectr. linguistics U. Coll. North Wales, Bangor, U.K., 1969-80; lectr. phonetics U. Oxford, 1980-88, fellow Wolfson Coll, 1980-90, assessor, 1983-84, curator Budleian Libr., 1983-84, chair Computing Teaching Ctr., 1984-88; assoc. prof. U. Calif., Santa Barbara, 1988, UCLA, 1989; sr. tech. mgr., dir. speech and platform software Digital Sound Corp., Santa Barbara, 1988-93; dir. engring. Voice Processing Corp., Santa Barbara, 1993—; rsch. scientist Infovox, A.B., Stockholm, 1986-88; bd. dels. Oxford U. Press., 1983-84. Contbr. articles to profl. jours.; patentee in field. Rsch. grantee U.K. Sci. and Engring. Rsch. Coun., U. Oxford, 1979-88, U.K. Social Sci. Rsch. Coun., U. Oxford, Royal Soc. Mem. The Philological Soc. (mem. coun. 1982-86), Internat. Phonetic Assn. (mem. coun. 1986-90, jour. editor 1986-89), Acoustical Soc. Am. Office: Voice Processing Corp 1 Main St Santa Barbara CA 02142

BLAETTLER, RICHARD BRUCE, school system administrator, educator; b. San Francisco, Sept. 3, 1938; s. Henry Walter and Veronica Jean (Smith) B.; m. Barbara Anne Crevier, June 1, 1968; children: Daniel Christopher, Derek Henry, Janelle Veronica. AA, City Coll. of San Francisco, 1959; BA, San Francisco State U., 1962, MA, 1964; EdD, U. LaVerne, Calif., 1991; grad., Bay Area Regional Adminstrv. Tng. Ctr., 1992, Supts. Acad., 1993. Cert. secondary adminstr., tchr., Calif. Tchr., coach San Francisco Unified Sch. Dist., 1964-65; asst. football coach Springfield (Mass.) Coll., 1965-66; tchr., coach San Lorenzo (Calif.) Unified Sch. Dist., 1966-70; tchr., coach Richmond (Calif.) Unified Sch. Dist., 1970-83, adminstr., 1983-90; adminstr. Richmond Adult Unified Sch. Dist., 1990-91; retired/CSM U.S. Army Spl. Forces, 1960-89; corrective therapist VA Hosp., Oakland, Calif., 1962-64; instr. in oil painting adult edn. div. Albany (Calif.) Unified Sch. Dist., 1980-85. Contbr. numerous articles to profl. jours. Mem. Vision 2020 Open Space, Fairfield, Calif., 1989-90, Cities Sounding Bd., Fairfield, 1990—; mem. Tolenas Farms Homeowners Assn., pres., 1985-86. Mem. Richmond Assn. Sch. Adminstrs., Ben Ali Shrine Club (pipe and drum unit 1988-92), Montezuma Shrine Club (pres.), Royal Arch, Masons. Republican. Home: 4424 Tolenas Rd Fairfield CA 94533-6613 Office: Richmond High Sch 1250 23d St Richmond CA 94804

BLAHA, KENNETH DAVID, mathematics and computer science educator; b. New Prague, Minn., Oct. 5, 1954; s. Christian Joseph and Verna Louis (Mecklenburg) B.; m. Barbara Jean Korando, Oct. 31, 1986; children: Seth, Alexander, Christian. BA with distinction, U. Minn., Morris, 1978; MS in Math., U. Oreg., 1981, MA in Computer Sci., 1984, PhD in Computer Sci., 1989. Instr. dept. math. U. Minn., Morris, 1978-79; grad. teaching fellow dept. math. U. Oreg., Eugene, 1979-83, grad. teaching fellow dept. computer sci., 1983-85, rsch. asst. dept. computer sci., 1985-89; asst. prof. dept. math. and computer sci. Pacific Luth. U., Tacoma, 1989—. Contbr. articles to profl. publs. Mem. Assn. for Computing Machinery, Am. Math. Soc., Spl. Interest Group Automatic and Computability Theory. Office: Pacific Luth U Dept Math and Computer Sci Tacoma WA 98447

BLAINE, DOROTHEA CONSTANCE RAGETTÉ, lawyer; b. N.Y.C., Sept. 23, 1930; d. Robert Raymond and Dorothea Ottilie Ragetté; BA, Barnard Coll., 1952; MA, Calif. State U., 1968; EdD, UCLA, 1978; JD, Western State U., 1981; postgrad. in taxation Golden Gate U. Bar: Calif. 1982, U.S. Dist. Ct. (ea., so. and cen. dists.) Calif., 1982. Mem. tech. staff Planning Rsch. Corp., L.A., 1964-67; assoc. scientist Holy Cross Hosp., Mission Hills, Calif., 1967-70; career devel. officer and affirmative action officer County of Orange, Santa Ana, Calif., 1970-74, sr. adminstrv. analyst, budget and program coord., 1974-78; spl. projects asst. CAO/Spl. Programs Office, 1978-80, sr. adminstrv. analyst, 1980-83; pvt. practice, 1982—; instr. Am. Coll. Law, Brea, Calif., 1987; judge pro tem Orange County Mcpl. Ct., 1988—. Bd. dirs. Deerfield Community Assn., 1975-78, Orange YMCA, 1975-77. Mem. ABA, ACLU, Trial Lawyers Am., Calif. Trial Lawyers Assn., Orange County Trial Lawyers Assn., Calif. Women Lawyers, Nat. Women's Polit. Caucus, Calif. Bar Assn., Orange County Bar Assn. (Orange County del. to Calif. State Bar Conv. 1985-92, bd. dirs. Orange County lawyers referral svc. 1988-92), Delta Theta Phi, Phi Delta Kappa. Office: 6 Hutton Center Dr Ste 845 Santa Ana CA 92707-5707

BLAIR, BILLIE, publisher; b. Tuscaloosa, Ala., June 20, 1945; d. John Lake and Mary Elizabeth (Shepherd) B.; m. Eugene Weisfeld; stepchildren. BA, U. Ala., Tuscaloosa, 1966, MA, 1967. Pub. The Taos (N.Mex.) News, 1989-90; assoc. pub. Santa Fe New Mexican, 1990—. Mem. N.Mex. Press Assn. (pres. 1991—). Democrat. Episcopalian. Office: Santa Fe New Mexican Box 2048 202 E Marcy St Santa Fe NM 87501

BLAIR, CAROL DEAN, microbiology educator, researcher, department adminstrator; b. Salt Lake City, Jan. 31, 1942; d. Doyle and Beulah (Bond) Blair; m. Patrick Joseph Brennan, Sept. 5, 1968; children: Deirdre, Niall, Justin. BA magna cum laude, U. Utah, 1964; PhD, U. Calif., Berkeley, 1968; MA juri officii, Dublin U., Ireland, 1974. Am. Cancer Soc. postdoctoral fellow Dublin U., 1968-70, lectr. microbiology, 1970-75; Internat. Union Against Cancer/Am. Cancer Soc. internat. fellow Baylor U. Coll. Medicine, Houston, 1972-73; asst.-assoc. prof. microbiology Colo. State U., Fort Collins, 1975-85, prof. microbiology, 1985—, asst. dean Coll. Vet. Medicine and Biomed. Scis., 1983-88, dept. head microbiology, 1988—. Contbr. articles to sci. jours. Fellow Woodrow Wilson Found., 1964, NSF, 1964, Damon Runyon Found., 1968. Mem. Am. Soc. Microbiology, Am. Soc. Virology, Soc. Gen. Microbiology, Am. Soc. Tropical Medicine and Hygiene, Phi Beta Kappa, Sigma Xi, Phi Kappa Phi, Gamma Sigma Delta. Home: 930 Breakwater Dr Fort Collins CO 80525-3345 Office: Colo State U Dept Microbiology Fort Collins CO 80523

BLAIR, FREDERICK DAVID, interior designer; b. Denver, June 15, 1946; s. Frederick Edward and Margaret (Whitely) B. BA, U. Colo., 1969; postgrad. in French, U. Denver, 1981-82. Interior designer The Denver, 1969-76, store mgr., 1976-80; v.p. Hartley House Interiors, Ltd., Denver, 1980-83; pvt. practice interior design Denver, 1983—; com. mem. Ice House Design Ctr., Denver, 1985-86, Design Directory Western Region, Denver, 1986; edn. com. for ASID Nat. Conf., Denver, 1991. Designs shown in various mags. Mem. Rep. Nat. Com.; bd. dirs. One Day orgn. for children with AIDS, Very Special Arts, 1993. Mem. Am. Soc. Interior Designers (co-chmn. com. profl. registration 1986, edn. com. nat. conf. 1991, bd. dirs. Colo. chpt. 1990—), Denver Art Mus., Nat. Trust Historic Preservation, Historic Denver, Inc. Christian Scientist.

BLAIR, GARY CHARLES, military officer; b. Iowa Falls, Iowa, Nov. 9, 1938; s. Gerald Willard and Ruth Virginia (Knox) B.; m. Rachel Margaret Gallagher, July 25, 1959; children: Laura K. Blair Linnell, Gary G., Chad R. AA, Ellsworth Coll., 1964; BS cum laude, Coll. of Great Falls, 1970; student, Squadron Officer Sch., 1972, Air Command and Staff Coll., 1976, Air War Coll. Assocs. Program, 1978, Indsl. Coll. Armed Forces, Ft Leslie T. McNair, Washington, 1982. Enlisted USAF, 1957, resigned, 1964; commd. 2d lt. Mont. Air Nat. Guard, 1964; with 64th fighter interceptor squadron DaNang, Vietnam, 1969; advanced through grades to maj. gen. Mont. Air Nat. Guard, 1989, comdr. 120th fighter interceptor group, 1985-89; adj. gen., dir. dept. mil. affairs Helena, 1989-93; ret., 1993. Decorated Legion of Merit, Air medal with two oak leaf clusters, Rep. of Vietnam Gallantry Cross with palm, others; recipient Hughes trophy USAF, 1985, Air Forcce Assn. Outstanding Unit award, 1986. Home: 2130 Highland St Helena MT 59601-5545

BLAIR, KAREN ELAINE, small business owner, social psychology researcher, psychiatric consultant; b. Salem, Ohio, Mar. 11, 1948; d. Kenneth Emmanuel and Ruth Annabelle (Niece) Schiller; m. Geroge LeRoy Blair, June 22, 1968 (dec. Mar. 1982); children: Princess Erin, Tiffany Alynn. BS in Psychology, Calif. Luth. U., 1986, postgrad., 1986—. Intern, asst. in med. records Baldwin Hills Hosp., Inglewood, Calif., 1968-69; freelance fashion model L.A. and Ventura, Calif., 1970-72; owner Conejo Bus. Machines, The Home Office, Thousand Oaks, Calif., 1970-74, Exactel Instrument Co., Oxnard, Calif., 1975-78, Sidewinder Aircraft, Thousand Oaks, 1977—; lab. asst. Neuropsychiat. Inst., UCLA, 1985-87. rsch. asst., psychiat. rehab. skills trainer and cons.; rsch. asst. UCLA-Camarillo (Calif.) State Hosp., 1989—; researcher treatment of stimulant abusing schizophrenics 1990-91, UCLA VA, Brentwood; program dir. The Life Adjustment Team, Culver City, Calif., 1991—; speaker on near-death experiences, 1987—; cons. psychiatric rehab., UCLA, Brentwood, 1993—. Author: Tie Your Own Heartstrings, 1983. Facilitator grief edn. and grant support groups Hospice, Camarillo, 1988-90; guest speaker Calif. Luth. U., Thousand Oaks, 1988—. Calif. Luth. U. scholar, 1983-86. Home: 1633 Old Castle Pl Westlake Village CA 91361

BLAIRE, STEPHEN E., bishop; b. L.A., Dec. 22, 1942. Grad., St. John's Sem., Camarillo, Calif. Ordained priest Roman Cath. Ch., 1967, titular bishop of Lamzella. Aux. bishop L.A., 1990—. Office: Chancery Office 1531 W 9th St Los Angeles CA 90015*

BLAKE, CRAIG THOMAS, college administrator; b. San Rafael, Calif., Nov. 2, 1946; s. Reinhart Joseph Blake and Grace Ann (Reid) Phillips; m. Maria Elena Rosales, Dec. 28, 1974; children: Matthew Joseph, Jeffrey Reinhart. BS, U. Calif., Berkeley, 1968, MBA, 1970; DPA, U. So. Calif., 1986. Cert. supr. community coll., Calif. Cons. A.T. Kearney & Co., Inc., San Francisco, 1971; sr. analyst U. Calif., Berkeley, 1972-77; asst. to pres. Aerojet Composites, Inc., San Rafael, Calif., 1977-78; budget dir. Oakland (Calif.) Unified Schs., 1978-82; bus. mgr. Orinda (Calif.) Union Schs., 1982-87; instr. Golden Gate U., Atwater, Calif., 1987; v.p. Merced (Calif.) Coll., 1987-92; assoc. chancellor San Mateo (Calif.) County C.C. Dist., 1992—; adj. faculty U. So. Calif., Sacramento, 1985-86; treas. Merced County Schs. Ins. Group, 1987—; chmn. bd. dirs. Valley Ins. Program, Fresno, 1988-90; pres. C.C. Chief Bus. Officers Coun., Sacramento, 1993-94; mem. U. Calif. Merced Steering Com., 198-9-92. Asst. editor: The Budget's New Clothes, 1970. Mem. Calif. Bus. Alumni, U. Calif. Alumni Assn. (scholarship com. 1989—), Merced C. of C. (chmn. edn. com. 1988-91), Nat. Coun. Instr. Adminstrs., Assn. Chief Bus. Ofcls. of Calif. Community Colls. (bd. dirs. 1989—), Leadership Merced. Republican. Roman Catholic. Home: 305 Eagle Trace Dr Half Moon Bay CA 94019 Office: San Mateo County CC Dist 3401 CSM Dr San Mateo CA 94402

BLAKE, DAN JONATHAN, advertising service company executive; b. Phila., Apr. 10, 1946; s. Carl James Keister and Dorothy Myrtle (Hill) Blake; m. Sheilla Louise Adkins, Jan. 13, 1969 (div. Nov. 1972); 1 child, Eric Christopher. Student, U. South Fla., 1969. Sales rep. Pfizer, Inc., Tampa, Fla., 1969-72; account exec. Perry Graf Advt., L.A., 1972-76, Nationwide Advt., San Francisco, 1976-80; sr. account exec. Backer & Spielvogel Advt., L.A., 1980-85; classified advt. mgr. Harte-Hanks Newspapers, Brea, Calif., 1985-89; owner, pres. Help Wanted Advt. Svc., San Dimas, Calif., 1989—. Commr. City of La Verne, Calif., 1991—; pres. Edgewater Homeowners Assn., 1989—; treas. Live Oake Homeowners Assn., 1992—. Bd. dirs. San Dimas C. of C.; mem. Rotary (pres. San Dimas 1992-93, editor weekly bull. 1992, Best in Dist. award 1992). Office: Help Wanted Advt Svc 120 W Bonita Ave Ste F San Dimas CA 91773-3085

BLAKE, J. PAUL, university public relations director; b. Neptune, N.J., Mar. 31, 1950; s. Joseph E. and Shirley T. (Jones) B. BA, Drake U., 1972. Pub. rels. writer Northwestern Bell Telephone Co., Mpls., 1973-75; pub. rels. mgr. Toro Co., Bloomington, Minn., 1975-76; asst. dir. univ. rels. U. Minn., Mpls., assoc. dir. univ. rels., asst. to v.p. for instnl. rels., asst. to v.p. for student affairs; pres. PANDAMONIUM, Mpls., 1986-89; asst. v.p. univ. relations and dir. pub. rels. Seattle U., 1989-93, inst. dept. comms., 1990—, asst. v.p., dir. pub. rels., 1993—. 1st v.p. First Hill Improvement Assn., Seattle, 1992-93. Recipient honorable mention media rels. Wash. Press Assn., 1991, gold award Puget Sound chpt. Pub. Rels. Soc. Am., 1991. Mem. Coun. for Advancement and Support of Edn. (bd. trustees 1981-83, 92—, silver award 1990, bronze award 1991). Roman Catholic. Home: 4021 S 154th St # C28 Tukwila WA 98188 Office: Seattle U Broadway and Madison Seattle WA 98122

BLAKE, MICHAEL HERBERT, resort facility executive; b. N.Y.C., Feb. 10, 1944; s. Ernest H. and Rhoda (Limburg) B.; m. Yvonne Deveaux, Nov. 17, 1967 (div. July 1981); children: Adriana, Alyda, Alexsis, Alejandro. BA, U. Denver, 1965, MBA, 1979. Asst. mgr. Taos Ski Valley (N.Mex.) Inc., 1965-72, mgr. ski area, 1972-91, pres., 1991—. 1st lt. U.S. Army, 1970-72. Office: Taos Ski Valley Inc 78 Sutton Taos Ski Valley NM 87525

BLAKE, PHILIP EDWARD, newspaper executive; b. Evanston, Ill., Nov. 7, 1944; s. Thomas Matthew and Louise Frances (Penning) B.; m. Katherine Ward Dower, Sept. 3, 1974; children: Matthew, Edward, Daniel. BA, Brown U., 1966; M in Fin., Northwestern U., 1979. Asst. controller Littelfuse Inc., Des Plaines, Ill., 1975-79; controller Madison (Wis.) Newspapers Inc., 1979-83, gen. mgr., 1983-86; pub. The Missoulian, Missoula, Mont., 1986—; group exec. Lee Enterprises Western Newspapers, 1990—; bd. dirs. Missoula Econ. Devel. Corp., Mont. Ambassadors; adv. bd. St. Patrick Hosp.; pres. Audience Info. Measurement Systems, Inc., 1986—. Served to lt. j.g. USN, 1966-69. Office: The Missoulian 500 S Higgins Ave Missoula MT 59801-2736

BLAKE, RICHARD RONALD, controller, Christian education specialist; b. Parkers Prairie, Minn., Mar. 7, 1930; s. John Paul and Marian Dorthy (Magnuson) B.; m. Thelma L. Barnes, Nov. 3, 1956; children: Richard Ronald Jr., Kenneth, James, Robert. BBA, Armstrong Coll., 1957; M of Christian Edn., Golden State Sch. Theology, Oakland, Calif., 1985, D of Ministry in Religious Edn., 1987. Regional contr. Boise Cascade Bldg., Hayward, Calif., 1968-75, Case Power and Equipment Sales and Svc. Co., San Leandro, Calif., 1974-80; owner Family Book Ctr., San Leandro, 1975—; contr. Carpet Craft, Inc., Hayward, 1989-91; bus. mgr. Redwood Chapel Community Ch., 1991—; customer advocate Nat. Tchr. Edn. Program, Durham, 1986—; cons., bd. dirs. Christian Edn. Leadership Svc., Los Gatos, Calif., 1987-90; founder, dir. Christian Edn. Resources, San Leandro, 1980—; mem. adv. bd. Follow Up Ministries, Inc., Castro Valley, Calif., 1987—; prof. Golden State Sch. Theology; instr. Evang. Tchr. Tng. Assn., Wheaton, Ill., 1989-92. Author: A Children's Church Curriculum; contbr. articles to The Ch. Tchr. mag., 1988. Program chmn. Bay Area Sunday Sch. Conv., Castro Valley, 1989—; active staff devel. and lay leadership Redwood Chapel Community Ch. Mem. ASCD, Nat. Mid. Sch. Assn., Christian Mgmt. Assn., Profl. Assn. Christian Educators (Ariz. chpt.), Assn. Child Edn. Internat., Christian Booksellers Assn., Writers Connection, Am. Legion. Home: 16630 Cowell St San Leandro CA 94578-1212

BLAKELY, EDWARD JAMES, economics educator; b. San Bernardino, Calif., Apr. 21, 1938; s. Edward Blakely and Josephine Elizabeth (Carter) Proctor; m. Maiike C. Vander Sleesen, July 1, 1971; children: Pieta C., Brette D. BA, U. Calif., Riverside, 1960; MA, U. Calif., Berkeley, 1964; MBA, Pasadena Nazerene Coll., 1967; EdD in Edn. and Mgmt., UCLA, 1971. Mgr. Pacific Telephone Co., Pasadena, Calif., 1960-65; exec. dir. Western Community Action Tng., Los Angeles, 1965-69; spl. asst. U.S. Dept. State, Washington, 1969-71; asst. chancellor, assoc. prof. U. Pitts., 1971-74; assoc. dean and prof. applied econs. and behavioral scis. U. Calif., Davis, 1974-77; asst. v.p. U. Calif., Berkeley, 1977-85, prof., chmn. dept. city and regional planning, 1985—; expert advisor Orgn. Econ. Cooperation and Devel., asst. to Mayor Elihu Harris, City of Oakland. Author: Rural Communities in Advanced Industrial Society, Community Development Research, Taking Local Development Initiative, Planning Local Economic Development SAGE, 1988, Separate Societies, 1992. Chmn. fin. com. Pvt. Industry Council of Oakland (Calif.), 1978-85; vice chmn. Ecole Bilingue Sch., Berkeley, 1982-85, chmn., 1988—; chmn. bd. Royce Sch., Oakland, Calif., 1988—; sec., treas. Econ. Devel. Corp., Oakland, 1983; expert advisor Orgn. Econ. Corp. and Devel., Paris, 1986. Served to 1st lt. USAF, 1961-63. Recipient San Francisco Found. award, 1991; fellow Urban Studies Australian Inst. Urban St., 1985, German Acad. Exch., 1984; Fulbright St. scholar Internat. Exch. of Scholars, 1986; named to Athlete Hall of Fame, U. Calif. Riverside Alumni Press, 1992, 125th Anniversary Prof. U. Calif. at Riverside for Berkeley Campus, 1992. Fellow Australian Inst. Urban Studies; mem. Community Devel. Soc. (bd. dirs. 1980-84, Service award 1983, Disting. Svc. award 1990), Calif. Local Econ. Devel. (mem. standing com. 1980-81), Am. Planning Assn. (mem. accreditation com.), Am. Assn. Collegiate Schs. of Planning, Nat. Assn. State and Land Grant Colls. (mem. exec. com. 1987), Phi Delta Kappa, Lambda Alpha. Club: Rueful Order. Home: 2709 Alida St Oakland CA 94602-3453 Office: Univ of Calif Coll of Environ Design Berkeley CA 94720

BLAKEMORE, PAUL HENRY, JR., retired publishing executive; b. Des Moines, Mar. 7, 1925; s. Paul Henry and Mabel (Evstace) B.; m. Barbara Jane Spargur, Oct. 24, 1952; chldren: Paul H. III, John E. BS, Drake U., 1950. Regional dir. First Fin. Group, Brookline, Mass., 1955-62; sr. v.p. TV/Radio Age, N.Y.C., 1963-87, cons., 1987—. Capt. USMC, 1943-47. Mem. Lions. Republican. Home: 4406 Cather Ave San Diego CA 92122-2614

BLAKEY, SCOTT CHALONER, journalist, writer; b. Nashua, N.H., Nov. 19, 1936; s. Elmer F. and Mildred Livingstone (Chaloner) B.; m. Lone Erting, July 18, 1970 (div.); 1 child, Nicholas Scott; m. Caroline M. Scarborough, June 28, 1985; children: Alexandra Scarborough; Susannah Chaloner. BA, U. N.H., 1960. Reporter, photographer Nashua (N.H.) Telegraph, 1960-62, polit. reporter, 1963-64; legis. asst. Congressman James C. Cleveland, Washington, 1963; mng. editor Concord (N.H.) Monitor, 1964-68; urban affairs corr. San Francisco Chronicle, 1968-70, reporter, asst. city editor, 1979-84, TV corr., 1985-87; corr., asst. news dir. KQED-TV, San Francisco, 1970-74; free-lance writer San Francisco, 1974-79; news editor KRON-TV (NBC), San Francisco, 1987-89; nationally syndicated columnist KidVid L.A. Times Syndicate, 1990—; sr. news rep. div. corp. communications Pacific Gas & Electric Co., San Francisco, 1991—. Writer, field producer TV documentary 2251 Days, 1973 (2 Emmy awards 1974); author (books) San Francisco, 1976, Prisoner at War, 1978; contbr. articles to profl. jours. Recipient Best Polit. Writing award New Eng. AP News Editors Assn., 1965, Dupont Columbia award, 1974. Mem. Authors Guild, Am. Air Mail Soc., Audubon Soc. Democrat. Home: 2626 Sutter St San Francisco CA 94115-2925 Office: Pacific Gas & Electric 77 Beale St Ste 2935A San Francisco CA 94106

BLANC, TARA ALISON, editor, writer; b. Jasper, Ind., Mar. 21, 1956; d. Ted Allen Shook and Mary Louise (Harling) Stewart; m. Gregory Lee Sessions, May 20, 1978 (div. Sept. 1985); m. Paul Le Blanc, June 6, 1986. BA in Journalism, Ariz. State U., 1978. Group mgr. Broadway Dept. Stores, Phoenix, 1978-80; account exec. Tempe (Ariz.) Daily News, 1980-81; mng. editor Ariz. State U. Alumni Assn., Tempe, 1981-83, editor, 1983-87, asst. dir., 1987-91, dir. communication and mktg., 1991-93; cons. Carte Blanc Comm., Tempe, 1993—. Editor (mags.) Ariz. State, 1990 (award of excellence Internat. Assn. Bus. Communicators/U.S. Dist. 5 1990, award of merit Internat. Assn. Bus. Communicators/U.S. Dist. 5 1991). Mem. Internat. Assn. Bus. Communicators (pres. Phoenix chpt. 1987, treas. U.S. Dist. 5, 1989-9, mem. chmn. 1991-92, sec. 1992—), Coun. for Advancement and Support Edn. Office: Carte Blanc Comm 21 E 7th St Tempe AZ 85281

BLANCH, ROY LAVERN, electrical engineer; b. Burley, Idaho, Nov. 5, 1946; s. James Donald and Georgia Elaine (Egan) B.; m. Garland Hill Smith, Jan. 23, 1982; children: Steven James, Edith Ann. BSEE, Brigham Young U., 1977. Elec. engr. asst. Burroughs Corp., San Diego, 1977-79, elec. engr., 1979-81; elec. engr. Burroughs Corp., Flemington, N.J., 1981-83, sr. elec. engr., 1983-84, project elec. engr., 1984-86; project elec. engr. Unisys, Flemington, 1986-89; staff engr. Unisys, San Jose, Calif., 1989—. Patentee in field. Sgt. USAF, 1970-74. Mormon. Office: Unisys Corp 2700 N 1st St M/S 18-004 San Jose CA 95134-2028

BLANCHARD, CHARLES ALAN, state senator; b. San Diego, Apr. 14, 1959; s. David Dean and Janet (Laxson) B. BS, Lewis & Clark Coll., 1981; M of Pub. Policy, Harvard U., 1985, JD, 1985. Bar: Ariz. 1987, U.S. Dist. Ct. Ariz. 1988, U.S. Ct. Appeals (D.C. cir.) 1988, U.S. Ct. Appeals (9th cir.) 1988. Law clk. to judge Harry T. Edwards Washington, 1985-86; law clk. to justice Sandra Day O'Connor U.S. Supreme Ct., Washington, 1986-87; assoc. ind. counsel Ind. Counsel James McKay, Washington, 1987-88; atty. Brown & Bain, P.A., Phoenix, 1988—; state senator State of Ariz., Phoenix, 1991—; chmn. Senate Judiciary Com., Phoenix, 1991-93. Contbr. articles to profl. jours. Bd. dirs. Florence (Ariz.) Immigrant and Refugee Rights Projects, 1990—, Homeless Legal Assistance Project, Phoenix, 1992—, Luth. Vol. Corps., Washington, 1986-88; state committeeman Ariz. Dem. Party, Phoenix, 1991—; chmn. Ariz. Dem. Leadership Coun., Inc., 1992—. Recipient Disting. Svc. award Ariz. Atty. Gen., 1992; Toll fellowship Coun. of State Govts., 1991; named Disting. Young Alumni Lewis and Clark Coll., 1987. Home: 315 W Cambridge Ave Phoenix AZ 85003 Office: Ariz State Senate 1700 W Washington Ave Phoenix AZ 85007

BLANCHARD, WILLIAM HENRY, psychologist; b. St. Paul, Mar. 25, 1922; s. Charles Edgar and Ethel Rachael (Gurney) B.; m. Martha Ida Lang, Aug. 11, 1947; children: Gregory Marcus, Mary Lisa. Diploma in Sci. Mason City Jr. Coll., 1942; BS in Chemistry, Iowa State U., 1944; PhD in Psychology, U. So. Calif., 1954. Lic. clin. psychologist, Calif. Shift chemist B.F. Goodrich Chem. Co., Port Neches, Tex., 1946-47; court psychologist L.A. County Gen. Hosp., 1954-55; psychologist, dir. rsch. So. Reception Ctr. and Clinic, Calif. Youth Authority, Norwalk, 1955-58; social scientist Rand Corp., 1958-60, System Devel. Corp., 1960-70; mem. faculty Calif. State U.-Northridge, L.A., 1970; assoc. prof. UCLA, 1971; faculty group leader urban semester U. So. Calif., L.A., 1971-75; sr. rsch. assoc. Office of Chancellor, Calif. State U., L.A., 1975-76; sr. rsch. fellow Planning Analysis and Rsch. Inst., Santa Monica, Calif., 1976—; pvt. practice psychologist, Calif., 1976—; clin. assoc. dept. psychology U. So. Calif., 1956-58. Author: Rousseau and the Spirit of Revolt, 1967; Aggression American Style, 1978; Revolutionary Morality, 1984. Contbr. articles to profl. jours. Mem. com. on mental health West Area Welfare Planning Council, L.A., 1960-61; bd. dirs. L.A. County Psychol. Assn., 1969; commr. Bd. Med. Examiners, Psychology Exam. Com., State of Calif., 1969; v.p. Parents and Friends of Mentally Ill Children, 1968—, pres., 1966-68, trustee, 1968—. Mem. Am. Psychol. Assn., Internat. Soc. Polit. Psychology, AAAS, Brit. Psychol. Assn. Home: 4307 Rosario Rd Woodland Hills CA 91364-5546

BLANCHE, JOE ADVINCULA, aerospace engineer; b. Rizal, Santa, Ilocos Sur, Philippines, Sept. 11, 1954; came to U.S. 1976; s. Emilio Peralta and Concepcion (Advincula) B.; m. Albine Selerio Lansangan, Oct. 9, 1982; children: Emmanuel Joseph, Earl Jordan. Cert. in mil. sci., U. Philippines, 1973; BS in Math., Adamson U., Manila, 1976; postgrad., Calif. State U., Long Beach, 1982-85; AAS in Avionics Systems Tech., Community Coll. Air Force, Maxwell AFB, Ala., 1990; cert. in mgmt., Cen. Tex. Coll., 1990; PhD in Mgmt., Pacific Western U., 1993. Lic. real estate broker, Calif.; registered tax preparer, Calif. Assoc. engr./scientist McDonnell Douglas Corp., Long Beach, Calif., 1981-84; engr./scientist McDonnell Douglas Corp., 1984-86, engr./scientist specialist, 1987-88, sr. engr./scientist, 1988—; lead aerospace engr. Sikorsky Aircraft-UTC, Stratford, Conn., 1986-87; avionics maint. inspector USAF, 1983-86, 87—. With USAF, 1976-80. Bur. Forestry grantee and scholar U. Philippines, 1971-73. Mem. AIAA, Nat. Notary Assn., NRA, So. Calif. Profl. Engrs. Assn., Corona-Norco Bd. Realtors, Internat. Soc. Allied Weight Engrs. (sr. mem.), Santanians USA Inc. (bd. dirs. 1984-87), Marinduque Assn So. Calif., Fil-Am. Assn. Corona (auditor). Republican. Roman Catholic. Home: 2179 Tehachapi Dr Corona CA 91719-1138 Office: McDonnell Douglas Corp 3855 N Lakewood Blvd Long Beach CA 90846-0001

BLANCHETTE, JAMES EDWARD, psychiatrist; b. Syracuse, N.Y., Aug. 28, 1924; s. Joseph M. and Margaret (Vincent) B.; m. Shirley Ruth Brisco, Sept. 1, 1948 (dec. May 1981). BA, Syracuse U., 1950; MD, SUNY-Syracuse Sch. Med., 1953. Diplomate Am. Bd. Med. Examiners, Am. Bd. Psychiatry and Neurology. Intern St. Vincent's Hosp., N.Y.C., 1953-54; resident Patton (Calif.) State Hosp., 1954-55, Met. State Hosp., Norwalk, Calif., 1957-59; pvt. practice psychiatry Redlands, Calif., 1959—; chief profl. edn. Patton State Hosp., 1960-64, teaching. cons., 1964-69; mem. staff San Bernardino Community Hosp., St. Bernadine Hosp. (both San Bernardino). With USAAF, 1945-47. Fellow Am. Psychiat. Assn. (life), AAAS, Pan.-Am. Med. Assn., Royal Soc. Health; mem. AMA, Calif. Med. Assn., San Bernardino Med. Soc., Internat. Platform Assn., So Calif. Psychiat. Soc. (pres. Inland chpt. 1963-64, pres. 1983-84), Am. Med. Soc. Vienna, Phi Mu Alpha Symphonia, Nu Sigma Nu. Home: 972 W Marshall Blvd San Bernardino CA 92405-2848 Office: 261 Cajon St Redlands CA 92373-5296

BLANCHETTE, STEPHEN, JR., software engineer; b. Bklyn., Mar. 16, 1964; s. Stephen Sr. and Roslyn (Katz) B.; m. Terri Sue Tossell, Sept. 28, 1991. BS in Computer Sci., Embry-Riddle Aero. U., 1986; postgrad., Ariz. State U., 1990—. With McDonnell Douglas Helicopter Co., Mesa, Ariz., 1987—. Mem. IEEE, AIAA, Am. Helicopter Soc., Assn. for Computing Machinery. Republican. Office: McDonnell Douglas 530/B347 5000 E McDowell Rd Mesa AZ 85205-9707

BLANCO, CATHERINE, software engineer; b. Stillwater, Okla., Nov. 18, 1961; d. Alfred Ted Zavodny and Shirley Mae Dawson; m. Maurice Blanco, Aug. 22, 1992. BA in Math., UCLA, 1984. Software engr. electro-optical and data systems group Hughes Aircraft, El Segundo, Calif., 1983-88; software engr. aircraft div. Northrop, Hawthorne, Calif., 1989-91; software engr. unigraphics div. EDS, Cypress, Calif., 1991; software engr. adv. tech. and design ctr. Northrop, Hawthorne, Calif., 1992—. Mem. IEEE Computer Soc., Assn. for Computing Machinery.

BLAND, JANEESE MYRA, editor; b. Evanston, Ill., Feb. 20, 1960; d. James Milton and Jeanette Malisa (Bryant) B. BA, U. Ark., 1980. Cert. tchr., Ark., Ill. Tutor counselor U. Ark., Pine Bluff, 1979; tchr. Pine Bluff High Sch., 1980, Chgo. Bd. Edn., 1981-84; editor, author, columnist Hollywood (Calif.) Gazette Newspaper, 1985—; VIP organizer People's Choice Awards, Beverly Hills, 1984—; exec. producer Sta. BH-TV, Beverly Hills, Calif; hostess The Janeese Bland Show. Proof editor: Nursing Rsch. Jour., 1989. Polit. vol. Rep. Party, Santa Monica, 1988—; vol. organizer Windfeather, Inc., Beverly Hills, 1983—, United Negro Coll. Fund, L.A., 1984—, Sickle Cell Disease Rsch. Found., L.A., 1985—. Recipient Image award Fred Hampton Scholarship Found., 1983. Republican. Baptist. Office: Sta BH-TV PO Box 16472 325 N Maple Dr Beverly Hills CA 90209-1472

BLANDFORD, ROGER DAVID, astronomy educator; b. Grantham, Eng., Aug. 28, 1949; s. Jack George and Janet Margaret (Evans) B.; m. Elizabeth Kellett, Aug. 5, 1972; children: Jonathan, Edward. BA, Magdalene Coll., Cambridge U., 1970; MA, PhD, Cambridge U., 1974. Rsch. fellow St. John's Coll., Cambridge U., 1973-76; asst. prof. astronomy Calif. Inst. Tech., Pasadena, 1976-79, prof., 1979-89, Richard Chace Tolman prof. theoretical astrophysics, 1989—; mem. Inst. Advanced Study, Princeton, 1974-75. Contbr. articles to profl. publs. W.B.R. King scholar, 1967-70; Charles Kingsley Bye fellow, 1972-73; Alfred P. Sloan research fellow, 1980, Guggenheim fellow, 1988—. Fellow Royal Soc., Royal Astron. Soc., Cambridge Philos. Soc.; mem. Am. Astron. Soc. (Warner prize 1982), Am. Acad. Arts and Scis. Office: Calif Inst Tech Dept Astrophysics Pasadena CA 91125

BLAND-SCHRICKER, LAUREL LE MIEUX, human resources executive, consultant; b. Spokane, Wash., Feb. 23, 1926; d. Alfred Theodore Le Mieux and Bernice Catherine (Lawrence) Alburty; m. Curtis Allen Bland, July 22, 1944 (div. June 1972); children: Laurel Kathleen Bland Eisinger, Daniel Matthew; m. Frank Hubert Schricker, Mar. 30, 1976. AA, Anchorage Community Coll., 1966; vis. student, Hebrew U., Jerusalem, 1968; BE cum laude, U. Alaska, 1968, MA, 1969; PhD, U. N.Mex., 1974. Tech. asst. Alaska Human Rights Commn., Anchorage, 1967; liaison 2d jud. dist. Alaska Legal Svcs., Nome, 1968; founder, CEO Human Environ. Resources Svcs., Inc., Alaska, 1969-78; instr. edn. and history of Alaska Natives Alaska Meth. Univ., Anchorage, 1969-73; asst. prof. U. Alaska, Fairbanks, 1974; prof. cross cultural edn. Sheldon Jackson Coll., Sitka, Ak., 1975; chief exec. officer Human Environ. Resources Svcs., Inc., Kennewick, Wash., 1976—; project dir. spl hist. and cultural inventory Imuruk Basin, Ak., 1969-73; founder Oquilluk Legacy Collection, U. Alaska-Fairbanks Archives, 1970; cons. manpower devel. and cultural heritage documentation and preservation various state and fed. agys., others.; primary contbr. to the Oquilluk Legacy Collection, 1970—; advisor, cons. to mem. groups Bering Straits Native Corp., 1971—. Author: Northern Eskimos of Alaska, 1972, (with William Oquilluk) People of Kauwerak, 1973, 2d edit., 1980, Alaska Native Population and Manpower, 1978, Careless Boy, 1980; contbr. articles on edn. and anthropology to profl. jours., 1969—. Appointee gov. adv. com. Office Minority and Women's Bus. Enterprises, Olympia, Wash., 1985-90; mem. apportionment panel United Way, Benton and Franklin Counties, Wash., 1988; participant seminar Future of Alaska, Brookings Inst., 1969. Teaching fellow Alaska Dept. Edn., 1968, 69. Roman Catholic. Home and Office: 1921 W 17th Ave Kennewick WA 99337-3432

BLANGY, ALAN BENNETT, theater company executive; b. Seattle, July 2, 1954; s. Harry and Jane (McClaren) B.; m. Margaret van Veen, Oct. 31, 1989. Theatre mgr. Seven Gables Theatres, Seattle, 1977-81, Landmark Theatre Corp., Seattle, 1982-87; dist. mgr. Landmark Theatre Corp., L.A.,

1987—; pres. Motion Picture Exhibitors, Washington, Alaska, Idaho, 1991-93. Producer: (short films) Daddy You Hit a Dog, 1975, Shirts, 1978 (Poetry Film Festival award 1978), Dial Your Prayer (Kodak Teenage award 1974). Office: Seven Gables Theatres 911 NE 50th St Seattle WA 98105

BLANK, LAWRENCE FRANCIS, computer consultant; b. Detroit, Oct. 4, 1932; s. Frank A. and Marcella A. (Pieper) B.; m. Carol Louise Mann, Oct. 12, 1963; children: Ann, Steven, Susan, Lori. BS, Xavier U., 1954. Asst. engr. Gen. Electric Co., Evendale, Ohio, 1956-60; research engr. Gen. Dynamics Corp., San Diego, 1960-62; mem. tech. staff Computer Scis. Corp., El Segundo, Calif., 1962-64; programming mgr. IBM, Los Angeles, 1964-69, Xerox Corp., El Segundo, 1969-74; ind. computer cons., 1974—. Mem. Assn. Computing Machinery, Ind. Computer Cons. Assn. Home and Office: 212 Via Eboli Newport Beach CA 92663-4604

BLANKENSHIP, DALE CLIFFORD, electrical engineer; b. Dayton, Ohio, Apr. 22, 1957; s. George Willard and Dordeen Harriet (Holland) B.; m. Patricia Mae Dory, Aug. 14, 1982; children: Dory Leigh, Timothy Paul. BSEE, Ariz. State U., 1981. Hardware engr. Phoenix Digital Corp., 1981-83; sr. engr. Lee Data Corp., Scottsdale, Ariz., 1983-87, Motorola Inc., Tempe, Ariz., 1987—.

BLANKENSHIP, EDWARD G., architect; b. Martin, Tenn., June 22, 1943; s. Edward G. and Martha Lucille (Baldridge) B. BArch, Columbia U., 1966, MSc in Architecture, 1967; MLitt in Arch., Cambridge U., U.K., 1971. Registered architect, N.Y., Calif. Sr. v.p. Thompson Cons. Internat., Los Angeles. Author: The Airport-Architecture, Urban Integration, Ecological Problems, 1974. William Kinne fellow, 1966; alt. Fulbright fellow to Eng., 1967. Mem. AIA. Episcopalian. Clubs: United Oxford and Cambridge U.; Meadow (Southampton), Am. Friends of Cambridge U. (sec. Los Angeles chpt.). Lodge: Rotary Internat. Home: 4225 Via Arbolada Villa # 543 Monterey Hills CA 90042 Office: 2250 N Hollywood Way Burbank CA 91505

BLANKFORT, LOWELL ARNOLD, newspaper publisher; b. N.Y.C., Apr. 29, 1926; s. Herbert and Gertrude (Butler) B.; m. April Pemberton; 1 child, Jonathan. BA in History and Polit. Sci., Rutgers U., 1946. Reporter, copy editor L.I. (N.Y.) Star-Jour., 1947-49; columnist London Daily Mail, Paris, 1949-50; copy editor The Stars & Stripes, Darmstadt, Germany, 1950-51, Wall St. Jour., N.Y.C., 1951; bus., labor editor Cowles Mags., N.Y.C., 1951-53; pub. Pacifica (Calif.) Tribune, 1954-59; free-lance writer, Europe, Asia, 1959-61; co-pub., editor Chula Vista (Calif.) Star-News, 1961-78; co-owner Paradise (Calif.) Post, 1977—, Monte Vista (Colo.) Jour., Ctr. (Colo.) Post-Dispatch, Del Norte (Colo.) Prospector, 1978—, Plainview (Minn.) News, St. Charles (Minn.) Press, Lewiston (Minn.) Jour., 1980—, Summit (Colo.) Sentinel, New Richmond (Wis.) News, 1981-87, Yuba City Valley Herald, Calif., 1982-85, TV Views, Monterey, Calif., 1982-87, Summit County Jour., Colo., 1982-87, Alpine (Calif.) Sun, 1987—. Columnist, contbr. articles on fgn. affairs to newspapers. Mem. Calif. Dem. Cen. Com., 1963. Named Outstanding Layman of Yr. Sweetwater Edn. Assn., 1966, Citizen of Yr. City of Chula Vista, 1976, Headliner of Yr. San Diego Press Club, 1980. Mem. ACLU (pres. San Diego chpt. 1970-71, nat. exec. bd. 1990-92), Calif. Newspaper Pubs. Assn., World Affairs Council San Diego (1st v.p. 1988-90), Ctr. Internat. Policy (bd. dirs. 1991—), Internat. Ctr. Devel. Policy (nat. bd. 1985-90), UN Assn. (pres. San Diego chpt. 1991-93, nat. coun. 1992—), World Federalist Assn. (nat. exec. bd., pres. San Diego chpt. 1984-86), Soc. Profl. Journalists Home: Old Orchard Ln Bonita CA 91902 Office: 315 4th Ave Ste S Chula Vista CA 91910-3873

BLANTON, JOHN ARTHUR, architect; b. Houston, Jan. 1, 1928; s. Arthur Alva and Caroline (Jeter) B.; m. Marietta Louise Newton, Apr. 10, 1953 (dec. 1976); children: Jill Blanton Lewis, Lynette Blanton Rowe, Elena Diane. BA, Rice U., 1948, BS in Architecture, 1949. With Richard J. Neutra, Los Angeles, 1950-64; pvt. practice architecture, Manhattan Beach, Calif., 1964—; lectr. UCLA Extension, 1967-76, 85, Harbor Coll., Los Angeles, 1970-72. Mem. Capital Improvements Com., Manhattan Beach, 1966, city commr. Bd. of Bldg. Code Appeals; mem. Bd. Zoning Adjustment, chmn., 1990. Served with Signal Corps, U.S. Army, 1951-53. Recipient Best House of Year award C. of C., 1969, 70, 71, 83, Preservation of Natural Site award, 1974, design award, 1975, 84. Mem. AIA (contbr. book revs. to jour. 1972-76, recipient Red Cedar Shingle/AIA nat. merit award 1979). Six bldgs. included in A Guide to the Architecture of Los Angeles and Southern California; works featured in L'architettura mag., 1988; design philosophy included in American Architects (Les Krantz), 1989. Office: 1456 12th St # 4 Manhattan Beach CA 90266-6113

BLASCHKE, JANET WINTER, technical director, cosmetic chemist; b. Inglewood, Calif., Jan. 2, 1959; d. Lowell William and Lota Ruth (Muffly) Winter; m. Rudy E. Blaschke, Apr. 20, 1985; 1 child, Robert Lowell. BA in Biology, U. Redlands, Calif., 1981. Chemist Dep Corp., L.A., 1981-83; labs. mgr. Dep Corp., Rancho Dominguez, Calif., 1983-87, tech. dir., 1987—; course coord. extension course cosmetic chemistry UCLA, 1983-86, guest lectr. microbiology, 1987-88. Mem. Soc. of Cosmetic Chemistry (chmn. Calif. chpt. 1988). Office: Dep Corp 2101 E Via Arado Compton CA 90220-6189

BLASDALE, ALLAN WALTER, organist, choirmaster, pianist; b. Berkeley, Calif., July 5, 1953; s. Herbert Halsey and Jean Bevans (Coolbaugh) B. BA in Music, U. Calif., Berkeley, 1976; postgrad., Ch. Div. Sch. of Pacific, 1980. Organist Centennial Presbyn. Ch., Oakland, Calif., 1971-72; organist, choirmaster North Congl. Ch., Berkeley, 1972-83; organist Ch. Div. Sch. of Pacific, Berkeley, 1978-80; dir. music Ch. of Advent of Christ the King, San Francisco, 1983-87, Holy Innocents Ch., San Francisco, 1987-88; min. music First Congl. Ch., San Francisco, 1988-91, St. Stephen's Episcopal Ch., Orinda, Calif., 1991—; dir. music Pilgrim Congl. Ch., Walnut Creek, Calif., 1976-92; with Nat. Park Svc., San Francisco, 1993—; concert organist, 1972—. Mem. Am. Guild Organists, Nat. Parks and Conservation Assn., Nat. Space Soc., Nat. Trust for Hist. Preservation, Yosemite Assn., Planetary Soc., Calif. History Soc. Democrat. Home: 1400 McAllister St # 17 San Francisco CA 94115

BLASOR-BERNHARDT, DONNA JO, screenwriter, poet, author; b. Pittsburg, Kans., May 8, 1944; d. Donald Archie and Bessie Beryl (Tatham) Blasor; m. Richard Wayne Bernhardt, Oct. 29, 1964 (dec. Feb. 1987); children: Erik Wayne, Katherine Elizabeth. Student, U. Alaska, Anchorage, 1963-64. Reporter, poet Mukluk News Paper, Tok, Alaska, 1977—; interior, coord., technical advisor Alaska Nitty Gritty Dirty Band Alcan Caravan, 1992—; interior coord. Up With People Internat. Show, 1992—; interior Alaska coord. and tech. advisor Nitty Gritty Dirt Band Alcan Caravan TV spl., 1992, Up With People Internat. Show, 1992. Author: (books) A Tent in Tok, 1980, More...A Tent in Tok, 1982, Friends of the Tent in Tok, 1987, (short story) K'hann Da G'hann, 1989 (1st pl. adult writing 1989), (book) Beyond the Tent in Tok, 1990, The Tent, 1991, Before the Tent in tok, 1992, Going to the End of the World, 1992, (audio tape musical drama) Gettysburg, Fields of Love & Honor, 1993; writer featured story (TV) Paul Harvey's News and Commentary, 1978; featured writer Alaska's S.W. Regional Newsletter, Juneau, 1985, Sta. WAMU Pub. Radio, 1990; featured profile writer Fairbanks (Alaska) Northland News, 1985; featured guest Senator Frank Murkowski's Show, 1988, CBS TV Night Watch, 1989, Tok Rider Fire Exhibit Dedication, 1992, Channel 11-TV News, Anchorage, 1992, KTVA-TV Norma Goodman Show, Anchorage, 1992, 20th Ann. show Highway Daze, 1992; featured profiles in various publs.; contbr. articles, short stories and poetry pub. in Anchorage Times, Anchorage News, Haiku Highlights, Copper River Jour., Delta News, Mukluk News, Fairbanks Northland News, State of Alaska Newsletter, Div. of Forestry, Country mag., Fireweed Jour., Bell's Alaska/Yukon Travel Guide, Alaska Mag., The S.C. Observer, Seattle Times, Santa Monica Daily Breeze, Ark. Dem. Gazette, Chgo. Daily News, Angoon Yearbook, Gettysburg Times. Tres. Tok Med. Clinic, 1982. Named Poet Laureate, 1990; winners of Alaska State Diving Championship, 1958-62, Internat. Biological Ctr. Internat. Woman of Yr., 1991-92; recipient 1st pl. Tok River Fire Writing Competition, 1990, 1st pl. Tok River Wildfire Photo Competition, 1990. Named Poet Laureate, 1990, IBC Internat. Woman of Yr., 1991-92; winners of Alaska State Diving Championship, 1958-62; recipient 1st pl. Tok River Fire WRiting Competition, 1990, 1st pl. Tok River Wildfire Photo Competition, 1990. Office: A Tent in Tok PO Box 110 Tok AK 99780-0110

BLATT, BEVERLY FAYE, biologist, consultant; b. Pitts., Mar. 17, 1944; d. Simon and Sadie (Skigen) B.; m. Marc Harry Lavietes, Aug. 13, 1966 (div. June 1987); children: Bryan Ross, Jonathan David; m. David Herman Filipek, Dec. 28, 1987. AB magna cum laude, Vassar Coll., 1965; PhD, Case Western Res. U., 1969; postdoctoral, NYU, 1969-70. Asst. prof. pathology Sch. Medicine NYU, 1971-80; asst. prof. medicine Sch. Medicine SUNY, Bklyn., 1980-84, Stony Brook, 1984-88; sect. head clin. immunology rsch. L.I. Jewish Med. Ctr., New Hyde Park, N.Y., 1986-88; cons. BFB Biocons., Alameda, Calif., 1988—; co-chair organizing com. Women in Bioscience: Opportunities in the Nineties, Stanford, 1993. Co-chair spl. gifts class of 1965 25th reunion Vassar Coll., 1988-89, 89-90, pres. Class of 1965, 1990-95; chmn. class gift com. Vassar 1965 25th Reunion, 1989-90; bd. dirs. Temple Israel, Alameda, Calif., 1990—, sec., 1990-91, v.p., 1991—. NSF fellow, 1967-69, Am. Cancer Soc. fellow, 1969-70, NIH fellow, 1970-71; N.Y. Arthritis Found. grantee SUNY, 1981-87, NIH grantee, 1971-77, 81-85. Mem. AAAS, Am. Soc. Cell Biology, Assn. for Women in Sci., Harvey Soc., N.Y. Acad. Scis. Office: BFB Biocons 3265 Central Ave Alameda CA 94501-3108

BLATT, DAVID HOWARD, anesthesiologist; b. L.A., June 10, 1956; s. Meyer and Rosalind Anne (Wallach) B.; m. Myra Jane Barnett, Oct. 9, 1988; children: Daniel Solomon, Diana Rebecca. BA, Pomona Coll., 1978; MD, U. Calif., Irvine, 1982. Diplomate Am. Bd. Anesthsiolgy. Intern U. Calif.-Irvine Med. Ctr., Orange, 1982-83, resident in anesthesiology, 1983-85; pvt. practice Intercommunity Med. Ctr., Covina, Calif., 1985—; clin. instr. dept. anesthesiology U. Calif.-Irvine Med. Ctr., 1985-87, asst. clin. prof., 1987—. Mem. Phi Beta Kappa.

BLATT, MELANIE JUDITH, professional speaker; b. Phila., Sept. 29, 1946; d. Jack and Rose (Ginsburg) Weinberger; children: Marnie, Keath, Lindsay. BA, Antioch U., 1980; MA, U. Phoenix, 1989. Cert. human service worker. Social worker Dept. Pub. Welfare Pa., Doylestown, 1977-80; mgr. customer service Qualidine Inc., Lansdale, Pa., 1980-81; sales rep. Sharp Products, Tempe, Ariz., 1982-83, Hobart Corp., Tempe, 1984-92; pres. Merit Enterprises, 1992—. Bd. dirs. Bucks County Jewish Family Service, Bucks City, 1982. Mem. Retail Grocers Assn. Ariz., U. Phoenix Alumni Network (bd. dirs.). Home: 14637 N Winston Ln Fountain Hls AZ 85268-2338 Office: Hobart Corp 929A S Hohokam Dr Tempe AZ 85281-5115

BLATT, MORTON BERNARD, medical illustrator; b. Chgo., Jan. 9, 1923; s. Arthur E. and Hazel B. Student Central YMCA Coll., 1940-42, U. Ill., 1943-46. Tchr., Ray-Vogue Art Schs., Chgo., 1946-51; med. illustrator VA Center, Wood, Wis., 1951-57, Swedish Covenant Hosp., Chgo., 1957-76; med. illustrator Laidlaw Bros., River Forest, Ill., 1956-59; cons., artist health textbooks, 1956-59; illustrator Standard Edn. Soc., Chgo., 1960; art editor Covenant Home Altar, 1972-83, Covenant Companion, 1958-82. Served with USAAF, 1943-44. Mem. Art Inst. Chgo. Club: Chgo. Press. Illustrator: Atlas and Demonstration Technique of the Central Nervous System, also numerous med. jours.; illustrator, designer Covenant Hymnal, books, record jackets. Address: PO Box 489 Mill Valley CA 94942

BLATTNER, MEERA MCCUAIG, educator; b. Chgo., Aug. 14, 1930; d. William D. McCuaig and Nina (Spertus) Klevs; m. Minao Kamegai, June 22 1985; children: Douglas, Robert, William. B.A., U. Chgo., 1952; M.S., U. So. Calif., 1966; Ph.D., UCLA, 1973 . Research fellow in computer sci. Harvard U., 1973-74; asst. prof. Rice U., 1974-80; assoc. prof. applied sci. U. Calif. at Davis, Livermore, 1980-91, prof. applied sci., 1991—; adj. prof. U. Tex., Houston, 1977-91; vis. prof. U. Paris, 1980; program dir. theoretical computer sci. NSF, Washington, 1979-80. Co-editor: (with R. Dannenberg) Multimedia Interface Design, 1992. NSF grantee, 1977-81, 93—. Mem. Soc. Women Engrs., Assn. Computing Machinery, IEEE Computer Soc. Contbr. articles to profl. jours. Office: U Calif Davis/Livermore Dept Applied Sci Livermore CA 94550

BLAUER, ROLAND EUGENE, petroleum engineer; b. Denver, May 8, 1947; s. Friend Frederick and Frances (Reddington) B.; m. Claudia Gancar, June 22, 1947 (div. 1978). Profl. Engr. Petroleum, Colo. Sch. Mines, 1969, MS, 1976. Registered profl. engr., Colo. Drilling and completions engr. Diamond Shamrock Corp., Casper, Wyo., 1969-71; pvt. cons., Denver, 1971-72; teaching asst. Colo. Sch. Mines, Golden, 1972-74; rsch. engr. Minerals Mgmt., Casper, 1973-75; mgr. spl. projects Sci. Software Corp., Denver, 1975-77; pres. Resource Svcs. Internat., Denver, 1977—. Contbr. articles to profl. jours.; inventor in foam fracturing and gold recovery fields. Mem. Soc. Petroleum Engrs. (various offices 1982-84), Am. Assn. Ind. Prodrs. Mem. Ch. of Religious Science. Office: Resource Svcs Internat 1580 Lincoln Ste 1110 Denver CO 80203

BLAUNER, BOB, sociologist; b. Chgo., May 18, 1929; s. Samuel and Esther (Shapiro) B.; m. Karina Epperlein; children—Marya, Jonathan. A.B., U. Chgo., 1948; M.A., U. Calif., Berkeley, 1950, Ph.D., 1962. Asst. prof. sociology San Francisco State U., 1961-62, U. Chgo., 1962-63; mem. faculty U. Calif., Berkeley, 1963—, prof. sociology, 1978—. Author: Alienation and Freedom, 1964, Racial Oppression in America, 1972, Black Lives, White Lives, 1989. Grantee Social Sci. Research Council; Grantee NIMH; Grantee Ford Found.; Grantee Rockefeller Found. Mem. Am. Sociol. Assn. Office: U Calif Dept Sociology Berkeley CA 94720

BLAWIE, JAMES LOUIS, law educator; b. Newark, Mar. 26, 1928; s. Louis Paul and Cecelia Ruth (Grish) B.; m. Marilyn June Beyerle, May 30, 1952; children: Elias J., Cecelia R., Christiana L. BA, U. Conn., 1950; AM, Boston U., 1951, PhD, 1959; JD, U. Chgo., 1955. Bar: Conn. 1956, Calif. 1965, U.S. Dist. Ct. (no. dist.) Calif. 1965, U.S. Ct. Appeals (9th cir.) 1967, U.S. Supreme Ct. 1968. Instr. polit. sci. Mich. State U., East Lansing, 1955; assoc. prof. U. Akron, Ohio, 1956-57, Kent State U., 1956-57; asst. prof. bus. law U. Calif., Berkeley, 1958-60; assoc. prof. law Santa Clara U., Calif., 1960-63, prof. law, 1963—; vis. prof. polit. sci. Calif. State U., Hayward, 1966-67; adminstrv. law judge U.S. Equal Employment Opportunity Commn., Washington, 1982-85; complaints examiner U.S. Equal Employment Opportunity Agy., Office Equal Employment Opportunity; cons. in field. Author: (handbook) The Michigan Township Board, 1957; contbr. articles to profl. jours. Mem. Citizen's Adv. Com. on Capital Improvements, 1962-65; bd. dirs. Washington Hosp., 1964-68. Maj. U.S. Army, 1963-74. Boston U. Faculty fellow, 1951-53; U. Chgo. Law Sch. scholar, 1953-55; grantee Mich. State U. grantee, 1955-56, Helsinki Govt. Ministry Edn. grantee, 1980-81. Mem. ABA, Fairfield County Bar Assn., Mensa. Republican. Home: 41752 Marigold Dr Fremont CA 94539-4716 also: PO Box 1102 Fremont CA 94538 Office: Santa Clara U Sch Law Santa Clara CA 95053

BLAZ, BEN, government official; b. Agana, Guam, Feb. 14, 1928; m. Ann Evers; children: Mike, Tom. BS, U. Notre Dame, 1951; MA, George Washington U., 1963; LLD (hon.), U. Guam, 1974. Commd. 2d lt. USMC, 1951, advanced through grades to brig. gen., ret., 1980; prof. U. Guam, Mangilao, 1983-84; del. from Guam to U.S. Congress, 1985—. Decorated Legion of Merit, Bronze star with Combat V, Vietnamese Cross of Gallantry; recipient Freedoms Found. Medal of Freedom, 1969, Disting. Alumnus award U. Notre Dame, 1988, Asian-Am. award for Pub. Svc., 1992. Republican. Office: 1130 Longworth Bldg Washington DC 20515

BLEIBERG, LEON WILLIAM, surgical podiatrist; b. Bklyn., June 9, 1932; s. Paul Pincus and Helen (Epstein) B.; m. Beth Daigle, June 7, 1970; children: Kristina Noel, Kelley Lynn, Kimberly Ann, Paul Joseph. Student, L.A. City Coll., 1950-51, U. So. Calif., 1951, Case Western Res. U., 1951-53; DSc with honors, Temple U., 1955; PhD, U. Beverly Hills, 1970. Served rotating internship various hosps., Phila., 1954-55; resident various hosps., Montebello, L.A., 1956-58; surg. podiatrist So. Calif. Podiatry Group, Westchester (Calif.), L.A., 1956-75; health care economist, researcher Drs. Home Health Care Svcs., 1976—; podiatric cons. U. So. Calif. Athletic Dept., Morningside and Inglewood (Calif.) High Schs., Internet Corp., Royal Naval Assn., Long Beach, Calif. Naval Sta.; lectr. in field; healthcare affiliate Internat. div. CARE/ASIA, 1987; pres. Medica, Totalcare, Cine-Medics Corp., and World-Wide Health Care Svcs.; exec. dir. Internat. Health Trust, developer Health Banking Program. Producer (films) The Gun Hawk, 1963, Terrified, Day of the Nightmare; contbr. articles to profl. jours. Hon. Sheriff Westchester 1962-64; commd. mem. Rep. Senatorial Inner Circle, 1984-86; co-chmn. Nat. Health Care Reform Com.-United We Stand Am. (Ross Perot orgn. chmn.), 1993; lt. comdr. med. svcs. corps Brit.-Am. Sea Cadet Corps, 1984—; track coach Westlake High Sch., Westlake Village, Calif. With USN, 1955-56. Recipient Medal of Merit, U.S. Presdl. Task Force. Mem. Philippine Hosp. Assn. (Cert. of Appreciation 1964, trophy for Outstanding Svc. 1979), Calif. Podiatry Assn. (hon.), Am. Podiatric Med. Assn. (hon.), Acad. TV Arts and Scis., Royal Soc. Health (Eng.), Western Foot Surgery Assn., Am. Coll. Foot Surgeons, Am. Coll. Podiatric Sports Medicine, Internat. Coll. Preventive Medicine, Hollywood Comedy Club, Sts. and Sinners Club, Westchester C. of C., Hall Und Beinbruch Ski Club, Beach Cities Ski Club, Orange County Stamp Club, Las Virgenes Track Club, Masons, Shriners. Home: 1675 Berkshire Dr Thousand Oaks CA 91362-1802

BLEISTEIN, CAROLE DENISE, artist; b. Nanaimo, B.C., Can., Apr. 19, 1950; came to U.S., 1952; d. Clifford Bradbury and Cecelia (Carroll) Bertram; m. Stephen Paul Bleistein, June 17, 1972; children: Laura, Vanessa. Student, Patricia Stevens Sch., Vancouver, B.C., 1969, U. Wash.; student of various established artists. Artist, working in collage, sumi ink, watercolor, and monoprinting. Exhibited works at Esvelt Gallery, Columbia Basin Coll., Vancouver, Wash., 1989, Gallery '76, Wenatchee (Wash.) Valley Coll., 1989, Kittredge Gallery, U. Puget Sound, Tacoma, 1989, Sarah Spurgeon Gallery, Ellensburg, Wash., 1990, Corbin Art Ctr., Spokane, 1990, Kirsten Marine Exhbn., Seattle and Redmond, 1991, Edmonds (Wash.) Arts Festival, 1992, Husted Gallery, Seattle, 1992, and others. Chair juried art show Rites of Autumn Festival, 1985; chmn. PTSA Reflections Program, Shoreline Sch. Dist., 1989-92, also juror, vol. docent. Recipient numerous art awards. Mem. North Coast Collage Soc. (bd. dirs. 1986-92, trustee 1992—, newsletter editor 1986-92), N.W. Watercolor Soc.

BLEIWEISS, MAX PHILLIP, physicist; b. Nogales, Ariz., June 23, 1944; s. Max Bleiweiss and Mildred (Fishler) Christensen; m. Gail Annette Siebenthal, Dec. 27, 1963; children: David Brian, Mark Daniel. BS, Calif. State Polytech. Coll., 1966; MS, Calif. State Coll., L.A., 1969. Physicist Naval Weapons Ctr. Corona Labs., Corona, Calif., 1966-70, Naval Ocean Systems Ctr., San Diego, Calif., 1970-77; v.p. Deseret Dental Supply, Salt Lake City, 1977-85; physicist U.S. Army Dugway (Utah) Proving Ground, Utah, 1985-89; with Measurements & Analysis div. U.S. Army Atmospheric Scis. Lab., N.Mex., 1989—. Scoutmaster Troop 13, 1st Bapt. Ch., Salt Lake City, 1982-85. Mem. Am. Astron. Soc. (pres. 1977), Am. Geophys. Union (pres. 1971), Sigma Pi Sigma. Home: 1215 Villita Loop Las Cruces NM 88005-6818 Office: US Army Atmospheric Scis Lab Field Assessment Br White Sands Missle Range NM 88002

BLEMKER, MARGARET RUTH, educator, world mission executive; b. New Bremen, Ohio, Apr. 2, 1915; d. Rudolf William and Lillian (Kohl) B. BA, Heidelberg Coll., Tiffin, Ohio, 1936, LHD (hon.), 1958; MEd, Syracuse U., 1942. Tchr. North Canton (Ohio) High Sch., 1936-39, Timken Voc. High Sch., Canton, 1939-40, Amerikan Kiz Koleji, Izmir, Turkey, 1945-48; dir. residences Univ. Hosps., Cleve., 1942-45; Near East exec. United Ch. Bd. for World Ministries, Boston, N.Y.C., 1949-80. Mem. AAUW, LWV. Democrat. Mem. United Church of Christ.

BLESSING, BUCK, real estate investment-management executive; b. Cin., Mar. 18, 1963; s. Norbert J. and Joan Claire (Thiel) B.; m. Michele Marie Hurt, July 21, 1990; children: Estelle Marie, Phoebe Michelle. BA, Colo. Coll., 1985. Lic. real estate broker, Colo.; cert. comml. investment mem.; cert. real estate brokerage mgr. Co-founder, dir., CEO Griffis/Blessing Inc., Colorado Springs, Colo., 1985—; cons. in field, 1986—; mem., chmn.-elect Colo. Coll. corp. and bus. adv. com., Colorado Springs, 1987—. Bd. dirs. Citizens for Downtown Action, Colorado Springs, 1988; chmn. Better Bus. Bur., Colorado Springs., 1989—; pres. Colo. Ctr. Contemporary Art & Craft, Colorado Springs., 1989—; mem. youth svcs. bd. YMCA, Colorado Springs, 1988-90; pres. Downtown Colorado Springs Inc., 1989-90; chmn. Community Devel. Adv. Bd., Colorado Springs, 1990—. Recipient Small Bus. Person of Yr. award C. of C., 1992, various awards for hist. preservation and archtl. achievements. Mem. Inst. Real Estate Mgmt., Phi Delta Theta. Office: Griffis/Blessing Inc 830 N Tejon St Colorado Springs CO 80903-4714

BLETHEN, FRANK A., newspaper publisher; b. Seattle, Apr. 20, 1945. B.S. in Bus., Ariz. State U.; P.M.D., Harvard U. Pub. Walla Walla Union-Bulletin, Wash., 1975-79; circulation mgr. Seattle Times, 1979-81, v.p. sales and mktg., 1982-85, pub., chief exec. officer, 1985—; chmn. Walla Walla Union-Bull., Yakima (Wash.) Herald Republic. Mem. adv. bd. Wash. State U. Mem. Am. Newspaper Pubs. Assn. (bd. dirs., chmn. telecomm. com.), Bellevue Athletic Club, Sigma Delta Chi. Office: Seattle Times Fairview Ave N & John St PO Box 70 Seattle WA 98111-0070

BLEVINS, WILLARD AHART, electrical engineer; b. Jonben, W.Va., Nov. 20, 1949; s. Oakley Cameron and Peggy Jane (Agee) B.; m. Nancy Phyllis Bailey, June 26, 1971; children: Maria Dawn, Teresa Lynn. AA in Elec. Tech. with honors, N.D. State Sch. Sci., 1974; BSEE with honors, Ariz. State U., 1988. Technician Sperry Flight Systems, Phoenix, 1974-88; engr. Sperry/Honeywell, Phoenix, 1988—. Patentee out of lock detector. With USAF, 1968-72. Named Parent of Yr., Phoenix Children's Chorus, 1985. Home: 15810 N 47th Ln Glendale AZ 85306 Office: Honeywell PO Box 21111 W33C5 Phoenix AZ 85036

BLEYL, ROBERT LINGREN, civil engineer; b. Salt Lake City, Mar. 25, 1936; s. Lorenzo A. and Alice (Lingren) B.; m. Merriam Fields, Mar. 20, 1961; children: Erik, Steven, Heidi, Katrine. BSCE, U. Utah, 1961, MS, 1962; Cert. Hwy. Transp., Yale U., 1964; PhD, Pa. State U., 1971. Registered profl. engr., N.Mex. Traffic engr. Utah Hwy. Dept., Salt Lake City, 1961-64; dep. state traffic engr. Utah Hwy. Dept., 1964-65; rsch. assoc. Yale U., 1965-68; pres. Bleyl Engring., Albuquerque, 1966—; instr. Pa. State U., University Park, 1968-71, asst. prof., 1971-72; assoc. prof. U. N.Mex., 1972-81. Fellow Nat. Acad. Forensic Engrs. (treas. 1991—, asst. treas. 1990-91); fellow Inst. Transp. Engrs.; mem. Inst. Traffic Engrs. (sect. pres. 1978-79, past pres. award 1968), Nat. Soc. Profl. Engrs., SAE, Southwestern Assn. Tech. Accident Investigators. Republican. Latter Day Saints. Office: Bleyl Engring 7816 Northridge Ave NE Albuquerque NM 87109-3014

BLIESNER, JAMES DOUGLAS, municipal/county official, consultant; b. Milw., Mar. 19, 1945; s. Milton Carl and Dorothy (St. George) B.; m. Phyllis Jean Byrd, June 15, 1966 (div. 1985); children: Tris, Cara. BA in Philosophy, Ea. Nazarene Coll., 1968; MA in Social Ethics, Andover, Newton Theol. Sch., 1973; postgrad., Boston U., 1969-70. Exec. dir. San Diego Youth and Community Svcs., 1974-78; cons., analyst San Diego Housing Commn., 1979-84; dir. San Diego City-County Reinvestment Task Force, 1984—; bd. dirs. Calif. Community Reinvestment Corp.; vice chmn. Calif. Reinvestment Com., 1989—; founder, chmn. City Heights Community Devel. Corp., San Diego, 1980-89; fin. com. chairperson Mid-City Revitalization Com., San Diego, 1988. Author monographs, 1979; contbr. articles to profl. jour. Coun. appointee City of San Diego Com. on Reapportionment, 1990, Com. on Growth and Devel., San Diego, 1989; gov. appointee Gov.'s Office of Neighborhoods, Calif., 1987; mem. City Heights Redevel. Project Com., San Diego, 1992. Recipient Award of Honor, Am. Planning Assn., 1987, Spl. Project award, 1987, Merit award, 1989; named Citizen of Yr., Mid-City C. of C., 1986. Mem. Urban Land Inst. Methodist. Home: 4106 Manzanita Dr San Diego CA 92105 Office: City County Reinvestment Task Force 1600 Pacific Hwy MS A6 San Diego CA 92101

BLINDER, JANET, art dealer; b. L.A., Sept. 21, 1953; d. Joseph and Margaret (Nadel) Weiss; m. Martin S. Blinder, Dec. 10, 1983. Founder Nationwide Baby Shops, Santa Monica, Calif., 1976-82; adminstr. Martin Lawrence Ltd. Editions, Van Nuys, Calif., 1982-90; art dealer L.A., 1990—. Mem. benefit com. AIDS Project L.A., 1988, prin. sponsor ann. fundraiser, 1990; mem. benefit com. Art Against AIDS, L.A., 1989; patron, sponsor Maryvale Orphanage, Rosemead, Calif., 1984—. Recipient Commendation for Philanthropic Efforts City of L.A. Mayor Tom Bradley, 1988. Mem. Mus. Modern Art, Whitney Mus. Am. Art, Guggenheim Mus., Palm Springs Mus. Art, Mus. of Contemporary Art (founder).

BLINDER, MARTIN S., publishing company executive; b. Bklyn., Nov. 18, 1946; s. Meyer and Lillian (Stein) B.; m. Janet Weiss, Dec. 10, 1983. BBA, Adelphi U., 1968. Account exec. Bruns, Nordeman & Co., N.Y.C., 1968-69; v.p. Blinder, Robinson & Co., Westbury, N.Y., 1969-73; treas. BHB Prodns.,

L.A., 1973-76; pres. Martin Lawrence Ltd. Edits., Van Nuys, Calif., 1976—, also chmn. bd. dirs.; pres., dir. Corp. Art Inc., Visual Artists Mgmt. Corp., Art Consultants Inc.; lectr. bus. symposia. Contbr. articles to mags. and newspapers; appeared on TV and radio. Mem. Dem. Nat. Com.; mem. benefit com. AIDS project, L.A., 1988; bd. dirs. Very Spl. Arts, 1989—, chmn. visual arts Internat. Very Spl. Arts Festival, 1989; patron Guggenheim Mus., N.Y.C., Mus. Modern Art, N.Y.C., L.A. County Mus. Art, L.A. Mus. Contemporary Art (hon. founder), Whitney Mus. Am. Art, Palm Springs Mus. Art, Hirschhorn Mus., Washington, Skirball Mus., L.A., Diabetes Found. of City of Hope, B'nai B'rith Anti-Defamation League, Very Spl. Arts; mem. Citizens for Common Sense; bd. dirs., pres. Rsch. Found. for Crohns Disease; mem. benefit com. Art Against AIDS, 1989; co-chair artists com. for Don't Bungle the Jungle Companions of Arts and Nature, 1989; prin. sponsor, ann. fundraiser AIDS Project, L.A., 1990. Read into Congl. Record, 1981, 83, 86, 88, 91; recipient resolution of commendation L.A. City Coun., 1983, State of Calif. resolution for contbn. to arts in Calif., 1983, Merit award Republic Haiti for contbn. to arts, 1985, U.S. Senate commendation, 1983, County of L.A. Bd. Suprs. resolution for Contbn. to arts in So. Calif., 1983, Gov. of R.I. resolution for contbns. to arts, 1985, commendation County of Los Angeles-Supr. Ed Edelman, 1991, commendation for contbns. to the arts and the healing arts City of L.A., 1991, commendation for contbns. to arts and philanthropy Mayor David Dinkins, N.Y.C., 1992; Nov. 18, 1985 declared Martin S. Blinder Day in L.A. in his honor by Mayor Tom Bradley. Mem. Fine Art Pub.'s Assn. (bd. dirs. 1990—), Med. Art Assn. at UCLA. Office: Martin Lawrence Ltd Edits 16250 Stagg St Van Nuys CA 91406-1726

BLISCHKE, WALLACE ROBERT, statistician; b. Oak Park, Ill., Apr. 20, 1934; s. Walter H. and Mabel E. (Schulz) B.; m. Rosemary A. Case, Sept. 10, 1960 (div. 1972); children: Elizabeth A., Scott D.; m. Beverly Blischke, Dec. 3, 1972 (dec.); 1 child, Michael Walter; stepchildren: Douglas P., Carol J. Satterblom. BS, Elmhurst (Ill.) Coll., 1956; MS, Cornell U., 1958, PhD, 1961. Rsch. fellow N.C. State U., Raleigh, 1961-62; mem. tech. staff TRW Sys., Redondo Beach, Calif., 1962-64; prin. statistician C-E-I-R/Control Data Corp., Beverly Hills, Calif., 1964-70; cons. in statistical analysis Van Nuys, Calif., 1970—; assoc. prof. dept. info. and ops. mgmt. U. So. Calif., L.A., 1972—; lectr. in field; cons. in field. Contbr. articles to profl. jours. Fellow Am. Statis Assn. (past pres. So. Calif. chpt., mem. nat. coun.); mem. AIAA, Inst. Mgmt. Scis., Inst. Math. Statistics, Biometric Soc., Sigma Xi., Phi Kappa Phi. Lutheran. Home: 5401 Katherine Ave Van Nuys CA 91401-4922 Office: Univ of So Calif Info and Ops Mgmt Los Angeles CA 90089-1421

BLISH, EUGENE SYLVESTER, trade association administrator; b. Denver, Oct. 9, 1912; s. George Joseph and Lillian Lenox (O'Neill) B.; m. Susan M. Monti, Feb. 21, 1950; children: Eugene A., Mary, Susan Blish Clarke, Julia. B.S.C., U. Notre Dame, 1934. Advt. dir. Colo. Milling and Elevator Co., Denver, 1934-45; advt. and mktg. cons., Denver, 1945-57; asst. exec. dir. Am. Sheep Producers Council, Denver, 1957-74; merchandising rep. Nat. Potato Bd., Denver, 1974-87. Mem. alumni bd. dirs. U. Notre Dame, 1947-49. Mem. Soc. Mayflower Desc., Barnstable Hist. Soc. (Mass.). Clubs: Denver Athletic, Mt. Vernon Country, Denver Notre Dame. Home and Office: 1370 Madison St Denver CO 80206-2613

BLISS, EDWIN CROSBY, business executive, consultant; b. Salt Lake City, Feb. 15, 1923; s. Edwin S. and Naomi (Crosby) B.; m. Mary Elizabeth Miller, Jan. 21, 1956; children: Rebecca, William, Roger, Kevin. BS, U. Utah, 1949, MS, 1958. Cert. speaking profl. Reporter Salt Lake Tribune, Salt Lake City, 1947-48; Sunday mag. editor Deseret News, Salt Lake City, 1948-52; asst. dir. pub. relations U. Utah, Salt Lake City, 1952-54; Sunday mag. editor Columbus (Ohio) Dispatch, 1954-55; exec. asst. Senator Wallace F. Bennett, Washington, 1955-63; pub. affairs dir. Nat. Assn. Mfrs., Washington, 1963-77; cons. Edwin C. Bliss and Assocs., Kingsburg, Calif., 1973—. Author: Getting Things Done, 1976, Doing It Now, 1983. Contbr. articles to profl. jours. Served to lt. col. U.S. Army, 1944-46. Mem. Nat. Assn. Parliamentarians, Am. Inst. Parliamentarians (adv. council 1984—). Home and Office: Edwin C Bliss & Assocs 2220 Carolyn St Kingsburg CA 93631-1427

BLITZ-WEISZ, SALLY, speech pathologist; b. Buffalo, Nov. 9, 1954; d. Isaac and Paula (Goldstein) Blitz; m. Andrew Weisz, Dec. 16, 1984. BA in Speech Pathology, Audiology, SUNY, Buffalo, 1976, MA in Speech Pathology, 1978; MS Sch Counseling, pupil pers credential, U. LaVerne, 1991. Lic. speech/lang. pathologist, Calif. Speech, lang. pathologist Lang. Devel. Program, Tonawanda, N.Y., 1978-82, Bailey and Drown Assocs., La Habra, Calif., 1982-83; speech, lang. specialist, cons. Pasadena (Calif.) Unified Schs., 1983—. Active Anti-Defamation League, San Fernando Valley, 1985-86; mem. 2d Generation Holocaust Survivors, Los Angeles, 1986—. Recipient Excellence in Studies award Temple Shaarey Zedek, Buffalo, 1968. Mem. Am. Speech-Lang.-Hearing Assn. Democrat. Club: Jewish Young Adults. Lodge: B'nai Brith. Home: 11671 Amigo Ave Northridge CA 91326-1849 Office: Pasadena Unified Sch Dist 351 S Hudson Ave Pasadena CA 91101-3599

BLIX, GLEN GARRY, preventive care educator; b. Central Butte, Can., Apr. 8, 1944; came to U.S., 1968; s. Rolf and Grace (Quigley) B.; m. Lorna Watts, Nov. 1963 (div. 1972); m. Arlene Jean Parrish; 1 child, Barton. BA, LaSierra U., 1970; MPH, Loma Linda U., 1984, DPH, 1987. Plant mgr. Loma Linda Foods, Mt. Vernon, Ohio, 1973-83; v.p. mfg. Loma Linda Foods, Riverside, Calif., 1983-86, v.p. rsch. and devel., 1986-87; dir. Loma Linda (Calif.) U., 1987-88, asst. prof. sch. of pub. health, 1988—; cons. Nutritia, Riverside, 1988—, Worthington (Ohio) Foods, 1990—. Supr. LaLoma Credit Union, Loma Linda, 1988—. Mem. Sch. Pub. Health Alumni Assn. (pres. 1990-91), Delta Omega. Home: 690 Temescal St Corona CA 91719 Office: Loma Linda U Sch of Public Health Loma Linda CA 92350

BLOCK, ALAN PETER, lawyer; b. New Haven, Nov. 29, 1964; s. Jacob and Harriet Barbara (Luft) B. BS, Cornell U., 1986; JD, UCLA, 1989. Bar: Calif. 1989, U.S. Dist. Ct. (cen. dist.) 1990, U.S. Ct. Appeals (9th cir.), 1989. Intern U.S. Nat Bur. Stds., Gaithersburg, Md., 1984, Compu-Mark U.S., Washington, 1985, W.R. Grace & Co., Columbia, Md., 1986; law clk. Frisenda, Morris & Nicholson, L.A., 1987-88, Sidley & Austin, L.A., 1988; assoc. Pretty, Schroeder, Brueggemann & Clark, L.A., 1989-91, Poms, Smith, Lande & Rose, L.A., 1991—. With USN, 1982-84. Mem. ABA, Calif. Bar Assn., Los Angeles County Bar Assn., L.A. Patent Bar Assn., Am. Intellectual Property Law Assn. Home: 9007 Norma Pl West Hollywood CA 90069-4820 Office: Poms Smith Lande & Rose Ste 1400 2121 Avenue Of The Stars Los Angeles CA 90067-5011

BLOCK, JAMES HAROLD, education educator; b. London, Sept. 24, 1945; came to U.S., 1946; s. Harold C. and Lilian (Ryan) B.; 1 child, William James. AB, U. Chgo., 1967, AM, 1968, PhD, 1970. Asst. prof. edn. U. Calif., Santa Barbara, 1971-75, assoc. prof., 1975-86, prof., 1986—. Co-author: Mastery Learning in Classroom Instruction, 1976, Building Effective Mastery Learning Schools, 1988; editor: Mastery Learning: Theory and Practice, 1971, Schools, Society and Mastery Learning, 1973; co-editor: School Play: A Source Book, 1987, Selecting and Integrating School Improvement Programs, 1993. Recipient John Smyth Meml. medal Victorian Inst. for Ednl. Rsch., Melbourne, Australia, 1977. Mem. ASCD, Am. Ednl. Rsch. Assn., Network of Outcome Based Schs. (bd. dirs. 1988—). Democrat. Office: U Calif Dept Edn Santa Barbara CA 93106

BLOCK, MICHAEL KENT, economics and law educator, public policy association executive, former government official; b. N.Y.C., Apr. 2, 1942; s. Philip and Roslyn (Klein) B.; m. Carole Arline Polansky, Aug. 30, 1964; children: Robert Justin, Tamara Nicole. A.B., Stanford U., 1964, A.M., 1969, Ph.D., 1972. Research analyst Bank of Am., San Francisco, 1965-66; research assoc. Planning Assocs., San Francisco, 1966-67; asst. prof. econs. U. Santa Clara, 1969-72; asst. prof. econs. dept. ops. research and adminstrv. sci. Naval Postgrad. Sch., Monterey, Calif., 1972-74, assoc. prof., 1974-76; research fellow Hoover Instn., Stanford U., 1975-76, sr. research fellow, 1976-87; dir. Center for Econometric Studies of Justice System, 1977-81; ptnr. Block & Nold, Cons., Palo Alto, Calif., 1980-81; assoc. prof. mgmt., econs. and law U. Ariz., Tucson, 1982-85, prof. econs. and law, 1989—; mem. U.S. Sentencing Commn., Washington, 1985-89; exec. v.p. Cybernomics, Tucson, 1991—; pres. Goldwater Inst. for Pub. Policy, Phoenix, Ariz., 1992—; cons. in field. Author: (with H.G. Demmert) Workbook and Programmed Guide to Economics, 1974, 77, 80, (with James M. Clabault) A Legal and Economic Analysis of Criminal Antitrust Indictments:, 1955-80; contbr. articles to profl. publs. Pes. Goldwater Inst. NSF fellow, 1965; Stanford U. fellow. Mem. Am. Econ. Assn., Soc. for Reform of Criminal Law, Phi Beta Kappa. Home: 2550 E Calle Los Altos Tucson AZ 85718-2062 Office: U Ariz Dept Econs Tucson AZ 85721

BLOCK, WALTER, economics educator, economist; B.A., Bklyn. Coll., 1964; Ph.D. in Econ., Columbia U., 1972. Earhart fellow Columbia U., 1966-68; from instr. to asst. prof. econ. dept. Rutgers U., Newark, N.J., 1968-71; asst. prof. Baruch Coll. CUNY, 1971-74; free lance cons. economist, 1974-76; asst. prof. Rutgers U., Newark, 1975-79; research fellow The Cato Inst., 1977-78, adj. scholar, 1982—; vis. fellow The Fraser Inst., 1979; sr. economist The Fraser Inst., Vancouver, B.C., Can., 1979-91; adj. scholar Ludwig von Mises Inst., Auburn U., 1983—, Coll. of Holy Cross, Mass., 1991—. Author: Defending the Undefendable, 1976, Focus on Economics and the Canadian Bishops, 1983; Amending the Combines Investigation Act, 1982, Employment Equity, 1985, Lexicon of Economic thought, 1989. Editor: Zoning: Its Costs and Relevance for the 1980s, 1980, Economics and the Environment: A Reconciliation, 1989, Economic Freedom: Toward a Theory of Measurement, 1991. Co-editor: (with Donald Shaw) Theology, Third World Development and Economic Justice, 1985; (with Irving Hexham) Religion, Economics and Social Thought, 1986; (with Geoffrey Brennan and Kenneth Elzinga) Morality of the Market: Religious and Economic Perspectives, 1985; (with Michael Walker) Taxation: An International Perspective, 1984, Discrimination, Affirmative Action and Equal Opportunity, 1982; (with Edgar Olsen) Rent Control: Myths and Realities, 1981. Frequent speaker to service and profl. organs. across Can.; regular columnist in various newspapers; contbr. articles to profl. jours. and chapters to books; editorial bd. The Jour. of Austrian Economics, The Jour. of Libertarian Studies, Reason Papers; assoc. editor The Jour. of Austrian Economics. Mem. adv. bd. Ctr. for Defense of Free Enterprise, Ideer om Frihet. Mem. British Columbia Assn. of Profl. Economists, Can. Econ. Assn., Am. Econ. Assn., Can. Assn. for Bus. Economists, Mont Pelerin Soc. Address: 3159 Dryden Way, North Vancouver, BC Canada V7K 2Y7 Office: Coll Holy Cross Econs Dept Worcester MA 01610

BLOCKER, ROBERT LEWIS, music school administrator, concert pianist; b. Charleston, S.C., Sept. 4, 1946; s. Lewis Albert and Frances (Bowen) B.; m. Delaney Mukley, Apr. 5, 1969; children: Brooke, Benjamin. BA, Furman U., 1968; M in Music, North Tex. State U., 1970, D Mus. Arts, 1972; cert., Harvard U. Inst. Ednl. Mgmt., 1986. Chmn. div. fine arts Western Tex. U., Snyder, 1973-74, Brevard (N.C.) Coll., 1974-76; chmn. sch. music Austin State U., Nacogdoches, Tex., 1976-81; dean sch. music. U. N.C., Greensboro, 1981-83, Baylor U., Waco, Tex., 1983-88, U. North Tex., Denton, 1988-91; dean sch. arts UCLA, 1991—; cons. various univs., and chs., U.S., 1976—; bd. dirs. Waco Symphony Orchestra. Concert pianist, approximately 75 performances throughout U.S. and Europe per year; contbr. articles to musical and art jours. Mem. music panel Tex. Commn. on Arts, Austin, Waco Chamber Cultural Affairs Com. Recipient Outstanding Faculty Mem. award Baylor U., 1986; Artist in Residence, S.C. Gov.'s Sch. for Arts, Greenville, 1986. Mem. Nat. Assn. Schs. (community/jr. sch. commn. 1984—), Internat. Council of Fine Arts Deans, Tex. Assn. Music Schs. (exec. dir. 1984—), Pi Kappa Lambda (nat. v.p.). Lodge: Rotary.

BLODGETT, ELSIE GRACE, association executive; b. Eldorado Springs, Mo., Aug. 2, 1921; d. Charles Ishmal and Naoma Florence (Worthington) Robison; m. Charles Davis Blodgett, Nov. 8, 1940; children: Carolyn Doyel, Charleen Bier, Lyndon Blodgett, Daryl (dec.). Student Warrensburg (Mo.) State Tchrs. Coll., 1939-40; BA, Fresno (Calif.) State Coll., 1953. Tchr. schs. in Mo. and Calif., 1940-42, 47-72; owner, mgr. rental units, 1965—; exec. dir. San Joaquin County (Calif.) Rental Property Assn., Stockton, 1970-81; prin. Delta Rental Property Owners and Assocs., 1981-82; propr. Crystal Springs Health World, Inc., Stockton, 1980-86; bd. dirs. Stockton Better Bus. Bur. Active local PTA, Girl Scouts U.S., Boy Scouts Am.; bd. dirs. Stockton Goodwill Industries; active Vols. in Police Svc., 1993. Named (with husband) Mr. and Mrs. Apt. Owner of San Joaquin County, 1977. Mem. Nat. Apt. Assn. (state treas. women's div. 1977-79), Calif. Ret. Tchrs. Assn. Republican. Methodist. Lodge: Stockton Zonta. Home and Office: 2285 W Mendocino Ave Stockton CA 95204-4005

BLODGETT, FORREST CLINTON, economics educator; b. Oregon City, Oreg., Oct. 6, 1927; s. Clinton Alexander and Mabel (Wells) B.; m. Beverley Janice Buchholz, Dec. 21, 1946; children: Cherine (Mrs. Jon R. Klein), Candis Melis, Clinton George. BS, U. Omaha, 1961; MA, U. Mo., 1969; PhD, Portland State U., 1979. Joined C.E. U.S. Army, 1946, commd. 2d lt., 1946, advanced through grades to lt. col., 1965, ret., 1968; engring. assignments U.S. Army, Japan, 1947-49, U.K., 1950-53, Korea, 1955-56, Alaska, 1958-60, Vietnam, 1963; staff engr. 2d Army Air Def. Region U.S. Army, Richards-Gebaur AFB, Mo., 1964-66; base engr. Def. Atomic Support Agy., Sandia Base, N.Mex., 1966-68; bus. mgr., trustee, asst. prof. econs. Linfield Coll., McMinnville, Oreg., 1968-73, assoc. prof., 1973-83, prof., 1983-90, emeritus prof. econs., 1990—; pres. Blodgett Enterprises, Inc., 1983-85; founder, dir. Valley Community Bank, 1980-86, vice chmn. bd. dirs., 1985-86. Commr., Housing Authority of Yamhill County (Oreg.), chmn., 1980-83; mem. Yamhill County Econ. Devel. Com., 1978-83; bd. dirs. Yamhill County Found., 1983-91. Decorated Army Commendation medal with oak leaf cluster; recipient Joint Service Commendation medal Dept. of Def. Mem. Soc. Am. Mil. Engrs. (pres. Albuquerque post 1968), Am. Econ. Assn., Western Econ. Assn. Internat., Nat. Retired Officers Assn., Res. Officers Assn. (pres. Marion chpt. 1976), SAR (pres. Oreg. soc. 1985-86, v.p. gen. Nat. Soc., 1991—), Urban Affairs Assn., Pi Sigma Epsilon, Pi Gamma Mu, Omicron Delta Epsilon (Pacific NW regional dir. 1978-88), Rotary (pres. McMinnville club 1983-84). Republican. Episcopalian. Office: Linfield Coll McMinnville OR 97128

BLODGETT, JULIAN ROBERT, small business owner; b. Honolulu, Nov. 21, 1919; s. Harry Hoagland and Esther Julia (Lyons) B.; m. Eleanor Anne Fischer, Nov. 4, 1941 (dec. 1983); children: Eric, Julie, Bryan, Paul. BA, UCLA, 1940. Stock clk. Northrop Aircraft Co., Hawthorne, Calif., 1941-42; spl. agt. FBI, Washington, 1942-44, 46-57, Standard Oil Calif., San Francisco, 1945-46; gen. mgr. Western Indsl. Security Co., L.A., 1961-63; chief bur. investigation L.A. Dist. Atty., 1957-61; owner, operator Julian R. Blodgett Investigations, L.A., 1961—. Chmn., commr. L.A. City Housing Authority, 1963-65. Mem. Former Agts. FBI. Office: PO Box 49658 Los Angeles CA 90049

BLOEDE, VICTOR CARL, lawyer, academic executive; b. Woodwardville, Md., July 17, 1917; s. Carl Schon and Eleanor (Eck) B.; m. Ellen Louise Miller, May 9, 1947; children—Karl Abbott, Pamela Elena. A.B., Dartmouth Coll., 1940; J.D. cum laude, U. Balt., 1950; LL.M. in Pub. Law, Georgetown U., 1967. Bar: Md. 1950, Fed. Hawaii 1958, U.S. Supreme Ct. 1971. Pvt. practice Balt., 1950-64; mem. Goldman & Bloede, Balt., 1959-64; counsel Seven-Up Bottling Co., Balt., 1958-64; dep. atty. gen. Pacific Trust Ter., Honolulu, 1952-53; asst. solicitor for ters. Office of Solicitor, U.S. Dept. Interior, Washington, 1953-54; atty. U.S. Justice, Honolulu, 1955-58; assoc. gen. counsel Dept. Navy, Washington, 1960-61, 63-64; spl. legal cons. Md. Legislature, Legis. Council, 1963-64, 66-67; assoc. prof. U. Hawaii, 1961-63, dir. property mgmt., 1964-67; house counsel, dir. contracts and grants U. Hawaii System, 1967-82; house counsel U. Hawaii Research Corp., 1970-82; legal counsel Law of Sea Inst., 1978-82; legal cons. Rsch. Corp. and grad. rsch. divsn. U. Hawaii, 1982—; spl. counsel to Holifield Congl. Commn. on Govt. Procurement, 1970-73. Author: Hawaii Legislative Manual, 1962, Maori Affairs, New Zealand, 1964, Oceanographic Research Vessel Operations, and Liabilities, 1972, Hawaiian Archipelago, Legal Effects of a 200 Mile Territorial Sea, 1973, Copyright-Guidelines to the 1976 Act, 1977, Forms Manual, Inventions: Policy, Law and Procedure, 1982; writer, contbr. Coll. Law Digest and other publs. on legislation and pub. law. Mem. Gov.'s Task Force Hawaii and The Sea, 1969, Citizens Housing Com. Balt., 1952-64; bd. govs. Balt. Community YMCA, 1954-64; bd. dirs. U. Hawaii Press, 1964-66, Coll. Housing Found., 1968-80; internat. rev. commn. Canada-France Hawaii Telescope Corp., 1973-82, chmn., 1973, 82; co-founder, incorporator First Unitarian Ch. Honolulu. Served to lt. comdr. USNR, 1942-45, PTO. Grantee ocean law studies NSF and NOAA, 1970-80. Mem. ABA, Balt. Bar Assn., Fed. Bar Assn., Am. Soc. Internat. Law, Nat. Assn. Univ. Attys. (founder & 1st chmn. patents & copyrights sect. 1974-76). Home: 635 Onaha St Honolulu HI 96816-4918

BLOMQUIST, CARL ARTHUR, medical trust company executive, insurance executive; b. L.A., Feb. 2, 1947; s. Carl Arthur and Delphine Marie (Forcier) B.; m. Diane Leslie Nunez, May 5, 1973 (div. Dec. 1979); 1 child, Kristin; m. Patricia Marie Johnson, Feb. 3, 1984 (div. Dec. 1988). BS, U. San Diego, 1969; MPH, UCLA, 1973. Auditor Naval Area Audit Svc., San Diego, 1969-71; trainee USPHS, Washhington, 1971; asst. adminstr. Northridge (Calif.) Hosp., 1973-76; asst. adminstr. fin. and facilities St. Vincent Med. Ctr., L.A., 1976-77; asst. v.p. 1st Interstate Mortgage, Pasadena, Calif., 1977-79; chief exec. officer Coop. Am. Physicians/Mut. Protection Trust, L.A., 1979—; spl. dep. Calif. ins. commr. Exec. Life Ins. Co., L.A., 1991—, acting CEO, 1991-92. Mem. Calif. Health Facilities Financing Authority, Sacramento, 1981—; co-chmn. Adv. Commn. on Malpractive Ins., Calif. Senate, Sacramento, 1984-92, mem. Commn. on Cost Containment in State Govt., 1984—; bd. dirs. Chaminade Coll. Prep. Sch., West Hills, Calif., 1988. Journalism grantee Helms Found., 1965. Mem. Am. Soc. Assn. Execs., Am. Coll. Healthcare Execs., Am. Hosp. Assn., President's Assn. of Am. Mgmt. Assn., Hosp. Coun. So. Calif., UCLA Health Care Mgmt. Alumni Assn. (bd. dirs. 1987—). Republican. Roman Catholic. Office: Coop Am Physicians/MPT 3550 Wilshire Blvd Ste 1800 Los Angeles CA 90010-2425

BLOMQUIST, THOMAS MELVILLE, physician; b. Redwood City, Calif., Feb. 18, 1957; s. William Groves and Barbara Gertrude (Anhalt) B.; m. Patricia Jan Baum, July 16, 1983; children: Alexandra Marie, Michael William. BS cum laude, Santa Clara U., 1979; MS, U. N.Mex., 1985, PhD, 1989, MD, 1993. Resident gen. surgery U. N.Mex., 1993—; Cons. D.H.C., subcontractor to Sandia Nat. Lab., Albuquerque, 1984-89. Contbr. numerous articles to sci. jours. Rsch. fellow Am. Heart Assn., 1978; grad. fellow U. N.Mex., 1983, 87. Mem. AMA, Am. Fedn. for Clin. Rsch., Am. Physiol. Soc., Am. Trauma Soc., Western Pharmacology Soc., Ducks Unltd., Quail Unltd., Alpha Omega Alpha, Sigma Xi. Roman Catholic. Home: 7509 Mayflower Rd NE Albuquerque NM 87109-5060

BLOMSTEDT, HERBERT THORSON, symphony director, conductor; b. Springfield, Mass., July 11, 1927; s. Adolphe and Alida Armintha (Thorson) B.; m. Waltraud Regina Petersen, May 29, 1955; children: Cecilia, Maria, Elisabet Vivianne, Kristina Ulrika. Diploma in music edn., Royal Acad. Music, Stockholm, 1948, diploma: organist, 1950, diploma: orch. condr., 1950; philosophy candidate, U. Uppsala, Sweden, 1952; MusD (hon.), Andrews U., Mich., 1978. Music dir. Norrköping Symphony, Sweden, 1954-61; prof. conducting Royal Acad. Music, Sweden, 1961-70; permanent condr. Oslo Philharm., Norway, 1962-68; music dir. Danish Radio Symphony, Copenhagen, 1967-77, Dresden Staatskapelle, German Dem. Republic, 1975-85, Swedish Radio Symphony, Stockholm, 1977-82, San Francisco Symphony, 1985—; condr. (hon.) NHK Symphony, Tokyo, 1986—. Author: Till Kännedomen om J.C. Bach's Symfonier, 1951; Lars Erik Larsson och hans Concertinor, 1957; contbr. articles to profl. jours.; editor: (mus. score) Franz Berwald: Sinfonie Singulière, 1965; 120 recordings. Jenny Lind scholar Royal Acad. Music, Stockholm, 1950; recipient Expressen Music prize, 1964, numerous rec. prizes; decorated Knight Royal Order North Star, King of Sweden, 1971; Knight Royal Order Dannebrogen, Queen of Denmark, 1978; Litteris et Artibus, Gold medal, King of Sweden, 1979. Seventh Day Adventist. Office: San Francisco Symphony Orch 201 Van Ness San Francisco CA 94102

BLOOM, FLOYD ELLIOTT, physician, research scientist; b. Mpls., Oct. 8, 1936; s. Jack Aaron and Frieda (Shochman) B.; m. D'Nell Bingham, Aug. 30, 1956 (dec. May 1973); children: Fl'Nell, Evan Russell; m. Jody Patricia Corey, Aug. 9, 1980. A.B. cum laude, So. Meth. U., 1956; M.D. cum laude, Washington U., St. Louis, 1960; D.Sc. (hon.), So. Meth. U., 1983, Hahnemann U., 1985, U. Rochester, 1985. Intern Barnes Hosp., St. Louis, 1960-61; resident internal medicine Barnes Hosp., 1961-62; research asso. NIMH, Washington, 1962-64; fellow depts. pharmacology, psychiatry and anatomy Yale Sch. Medicine, 1964-66, asst. prof., 1966-67, asso. prof., 1968; chief lab. neuropharmacology NIMH, Washington, 1968-75; acting dir. div. spl. mental health NIMH, 1973-75; commd. officer USPHS, 1974-75; dir. Arthur Vining Davis Center for Behavorial Neurobiology; prof. Salk Inst., La Jolla, Calif., 1975-83; dir. div. preclin. neurosci. and endocrinology Rsch. Inst. of Scripps Clinic, La Jolla, 1983-89, chmn. dept. neuropharmacology, 1989—; mem. Commn. on Alcoholism, 1980-81, Nat. Adv. Mental Health Coun., 1976-80; chmn. scientific adv. bd. Pharmavene, Inc.; bd. dirs. Alkermes, Inc., 1987—. Author: (with J.R. Cooper and R.H. Roth) Biochemical Basis of Neuropharmacology, 1971, 6th edit., 1991; (with Lazerson and Hofstadter) Brain, Mind, and Behavior, 1984 (with Lazerson) 2d edit., 1988 (with W. Young and Y. Kim) Brain Browser, 1989; editor: Peptides: Integrators of Cell and Tissue Function, 1980; co-editor: Regulatory Peptides, 1979-80, Funding Health Sciences Research, 1990. Recipient A. Cressy Morrison award N.Y. Acad. Scis., 1971, A.E. Bennett award for basic research Soc. Biol. Psychiatry, 1971, Arthur A. Fleming award Science mag., 1973, Mathilde Solowey award, 1973, Biol. Sci. award Washington Acad. Scis., 1975, Alumni Achievement citation Washington U., 1980, McAlpin Research Achievement award Mental Health Assn., 1980, Lectr.'s medal College de France, 1979, Steven Beering medal, 1985, Janssen award World Psychiat. Assn., 1989, Passerow Found. award, 1990, Herman von Helmholtz Award, 1991; Disting. fellow Am. Psychiatric Assn., 1986. Fellow AAAS (bd. dirs 1986-90), Am. Coll. Neuropsychopharmacology (mem. council 1976-78, chmn. program com. 1987, pres. 1988-89); mem. NAS (chmn. sect. neurobiology 1979-83), Inst. Medicine (mem. coun. 1986-89, 1993—), Am. Philos. Soc., Am. Acad. Arts and Scis., Soc. Neurosci. (sec. 1973-74, pres. 1976), Am. Soc. Pharmacology and Exptl. Therapeutics, Am. Soc. Cell Biology, Am. Physiol. Soc., Am. Assn. Anatomists, Rsch. Soc. Alcoholism (chmn. program com. 1985-87, pres. elect 1989-91, pres. 1991-93), Swedish Acad. Sci. (fgn. assoc. 1989). Home: 628 Pacific View Dr San Diego CA 92109-1768 Office: Scripps Rsch Inst Scripps Clinic 10666 N Torrey Pines Rd La Jolla CA 92037-1027

BLOOM, STEPHEN MICHAEL, lawyer, judge; b. San Francisco, June 10, 1948; s. Alan I. and Wilma (Morgan) B.; m. Rebecca J. Nelson, June 19, 1976; children: Benjamin Jacob, Molly Marie, John Robert. Student, Dartmouth Coll., 1966-68; BA in English, Stanford U., 1970; student, Calif. State U., Sacramento, 1973-74; JD, Willemette Coll. Law, 1977. Bar: Oreg. 1977, U.S. Dist. Ct. Oreg. 1979. Adminstrv. asst. Calif. Dept. Edn., Sacramento, 1973-74; atty. Joyce & Harding, Corvallis, Oreg., 1977-78; dep. dist. atty. Umatilla County, Pendleton, Oreg., 1978-79; atty. Morrison & Reynolds, Hermiston, Oreg., 1979-81, Kottkamp & O'Rourke, Pendleton, 1981—; appointed U.S. magistrate, 1988. Bd. dirs. Edn. Svc. Dist., Pendleton, 1982-89. Lt. (j.g.) USN, 1970-72. Mem. ABA, Oreg. Bar Assn., Rotary (pres. 1990-91, bd. dirs. 1991). Office: US Dist Ct PO Box 490 Pendleton OR 97801 also: Kottkamp & O'Rourke 331 SE 2nd St Pendleton OR 97801

BLOOMBERG, MARTY, librarian; b. Ft. Worth, Oct. 7, 1938; s. Alexander J. and Sarah (Shosid) B.; m. Leila Ann Manson, Aug. 25, 1963; children: Mark, Stacey. BA, Tex. Christian U., 1960; MA, U. Denver, 1961, U. Redlands, 1968. Libr. CIA, Langly, Va., 1961-62; libr. Calif. State U., Hayward, 1963-66, San Bernardino, 1966—. Author: Introduction to Public Services, 1985, Introduction to Technical Services, 1985, The Jewish Holocaust, 1991. Home: 16285 Whispering Spur Riverside CA 92504 Office: Calif State U at San Bernardino 5500 University Pkwy San Bernardino CA 92407-2397

BLOOMBERG, ROBERT JOSEPH, internist; b. Montreal, Que., Can., Dec. 2, 1947; came to U.S., 1980; s. William and Clara (Sederoff) B.; m. Kerri M. Zalasin, July 2, 1978; children: Joshua Z., Micah M., Leah R. BS in Biochemistry, Sir George Williams U., 1969; PhD in Biochemistry, U. Wyo., 1973; MD, McMaster U., Hamilton, Ont., 1976. mem. staff Desert Samaritan Hosp., Mesa, Ariz., chief of staff, 1992-93; mem. staff Mesa Luth. Hosp., Tempe St. Lukes Hosp.; cons. Drug Utilization Data Corp., Tempe, 1979—. Intern Georgetown U. Hosp., Washington, 1976-77, resident, 1977-79, chief med. resident, 1979-80; research asst. McGill U., Montreal, 1969-70; postdoctoral fellow Purdue U., Lafayette, Ind., 1973; practice medicine specializing in internal medicine Tempe, Ariz., 1980—; chief-of-staff Desert Samaritan Hosp., 1992-93; mem. Desert Samaritan Hosp, Mesa, Ariz., Mesa

Luth. Hosp., Valley Luth. Hosp., Mesa, Tempe St. Lukes Hosp.; cons. Drug Utilization Data Corp., Tempe, 1979—. Fellow Royal Coll. Physicians and Surgeons (Can.); mem. Assn., N.Y. Acad. Scis., Maricopa County Med. Soc., Ariz. Med. Assn. Home: 8527 S Willow Dr Tempe AZ 85284-2471 Office: 2501 E Southern Ave Ste 12 Tempe AZ 85282-7669

BLOOMER, WILLIAM ARTHUR, security industry executive; b. Bellaire, Kans., Jan. 23, 1933; s. James Charles and Nettie Alice (Baker) B.; m. Sharon Sue Vernon, May 30, 1954; children: Leigh Anne, Jeffrey Alan, Brenda Sue. BS in Edn., Emporia (Kans.) State U., 1955; MS in Mgmt., Rensselaer Poly. Inst., 1970. Commd. 2d lt. USMC, 1955, advanced through grades to brigadier gen., 1981, ret., 1986; sr. v.p. Am. Protective Svcs., Inc., Anaheim, Calif., 1986—; chmn. RNC Liquid Assets Fund, L.A. City councilman City of Irvine, Calif., 1990—, pub. safety commr., 1986-88; chmn. bd. govs. Rep. Assocs. Orange County, Calif., 1989; fin. commr. City of Irvine, 1989-90. Decorated 2 Legions of Merit, Disting. Flying Cross, Bronze star, 17 Air medals, Kuang Hua medal (Republic of China); named Disting. Alumnus Emporia State U., 1985. Mem. Soc. Experimental Test Pilots (assoc.), Am. Soc. Indsl. Security. Presbyterian. Home: 4 Pintail Irvine CA 92714-3634 Office: Am Protective Svcs Inc 421 N Brookhurst St Ste 222 Anaheim CA 92801-5619

BLOOMFIELD, JORDAN JAY, chemist, researcher; b. South Bend, Ind., Feb. 25, 1930; s. John Jacob and Edith (Gilman) B.; m. Elizabeth Helen Curtis, June 11, 1960 (div. Nov. 1982); children: Jaclyn Louise, Linda Joyce, Janet Lorene; m. Doris Joan Jameson, May 19, 1984. BS with highest honors, UCLA, 1952; PhD, MIT, 1958. Chemist E.I. DuPont, Waynesboro, Va., 1953; inst. U. Tex., Austin, 1957-60; post doctoral U. Ill., Urbana, 1960-61, U. Ariz., Tucson, 1961-62; asst. prof. to assoc. prof. U. Okla., Norman, 1962-66; sr. group leader, vis. prof. Monsanto Co., St. Louis, 1966-67, sr. research spl., 1967-81, fellow, 1981-85; v.p., research Organic Cons., Inc., Eugene, Oreg., 1987—; adj. assoc. prof., U. Mo., St. Louis, 1975-78, adj. prof., 1978-87; cons., vis. prof. U. Mich., Ann Arbor, 1985-86; presenter papers at numerous nat. and internat. meetings in field; mem. numerous profl. coms. and councils in field. Co-author: The Dieckmann Reaction, 1967, The Acyloin Reaction, 1976; contbr. articles to profl. jours.; patentee in field. With U.S. Army, 1953-55. Mem. Am. Chem. Soc. (chmn. St. Louis section, 1976, councilor, 1972-87, recipient St. Louis award, 1980), Royal Soc. Chem., AAAS, Am. Soc. Photobiology. Office: Organic Cons Inc 132 E Broadway Ste 107 Eugene OR 97401-3179

BLOOMQUIST, EDWARD ROBERT, anesthesiology educator, television producer, retired physician; b. Iowa City, Mar. 12, 1924; s. Edward William and Alice Katherine (Neal) B.; m. Lila Mae Skadsheim, Dec. 29, 1948; children: Carol Diane, Roger Edward, Donald Edward. BS, Andrews U., 1949; MD, Loma Linda U., 1949. Cert. Am. Bd. Anesthesiology, Nat. Bd. Med. Examiners. Intern White Meml. Hosp., L.A., 1948-49, resident anesthesiology, 1955-57; pvt. practice L.A., Upper Lake, Calif., 1949-51, Downey, Calif., 1953-55; assoc. clin. prof. anesthesiology Loma Linda (Calif.) U., 1956-68; pvt. practice anesthesiology Glendale, L.A., Calif., 1957-84; assoc. clin. prof. anesthesiology Sch. of Medicine U. So. Calif., 1966-92; lectr., vis. prof. dept. police sci. Calif. State Coll., 1968-74, lectr., vis. prof. dept. health and safety, 1965—; vis. prof. various colls., 1967—; cons. com. on radio and TV, AMA; script cons. and tech. advisor for TV shows and motion pictures. Author: Marijuana, 1968, Marijuana: The Second Trip, 1970; author (with others) books; inventor Bloomquist Y-Adapter, Bloomquist Infant Circle Absorber. Chmn. Calif. State Interagy. Coun. on Drug Abus, 1970-72; co-chmn. Com. on Dangerous Drug Edn. Mayors Com. on Drug Abuse City of L.A., 1971-72; mem. Rsch. Adv. Panel State of Calif., 1970-72; bd. dirs. Smart Set Internat., L.A., 1969-72. Recipient Honor award Am. Fedn. of Police, 1969, Meritorious Citation, Calif. Narcotics Officers Assn., 1968, 72, Cert. of Appreciation, Calif. State Juvenile Officers Assn., Internat. Narcotic Enforcement Assn., Am. Soc. Anesthesiologists, Cert. of Achievement, Nat. Dist. Attys. Assn., Cert. of Meritorious Svc. City of L.A., 1968. Fellow Am. Coll. Anesthesiologists, Royal Coll. Health (London); mem. L.A. County Med. Assn., Calif. Med. Assn., Am. Med. Writers Assn., N.Y. Acad. Scis., Internat. Narcotics Officers Assn. Home and Office: 1910 Niodrara Dr Glendale CA 91208-2647

BLOOMQUIST, RODNEY GORDON, geologist; b. Aberdeen, Wash., Feb. 3, 1943; s. Verner A. and Margaret E. (Olson) B.; m. Linda L. Lee, Dec. 19, 1964 (div. July 1968); m. Bente Brisson Jørgensen, Aug. 4, 1977; 1 child, Kira Brisson. BS in Geology, Portland State U., 1966; MS in Geology, U. Stockholm, 1970, PhD in Geology, 1977. Rschr. U. Stockholm, 1974-77; asst. prof. Oreg. Inst. Tech., Klamath Falls, 1978-80; geologist Wash. State Energy Office, Olympia, 1980—; vis. prof. Internat. Sch. Geothermics, Pisa, Italy, 1990—; cons. U.S. Dept. Energy, Washington, 1990, Govt. of Can., Asea-Stal Geoenergy, Lund, Sweden. Author: Regulatory Guide to Geothermics, 1990; mem. editorial bd. Geothermics, 1985-88; also numerous books and articles. Smitts fellow, Sweden, 1974, Royal Rsch. fellow, Sweden, 1975-77; rsch. grantee U. Stockholm, 1975-77. Mem. Geothermal Resources Coun. (bd. dirs. 1985—, pres. 1988, pres. Pacific N.W. sect. 1982-85), Internat. Geothermal Assn. (bd. dirs. 1989—, Western sect. 1990—), Internat. Dist. Heating and Cooling Assn., N.Am. Dist. Heating and Cooling Inst. (bd. dirs. 1986-88), Am. Blade Smith Soc. (bd. dirs. 1989—). Democrat. Lutheran. Office: Wash State Energy Office 925 Plum St Olympia WA 98504-3165

BLOTZER, TIMOTHY ROBERT, food products executive; b. Vallejo, Calif., July 9, 1952; s. Robert Stephen and Mary Josephine (Broderick) B.; children: Brian Timothy, Kevin Matthew. BS in personnel and indsl. relations, San Francisco State U., 1981; cert. of achievement, U. So. Calif., 1983, cert. in Mgmt. Devel. Program, 1988. Various positions Safeway Stores, Fremont, Calif., 1972-83, store mgr., 1983-85, dist. mgr., 1986-92; dist. mgr. MacFrugals Bargains & Closeouts, 1992—; speaker U. So. Calif. Food Industry Mgmt. Western Assn. Food Chains Conv., Hawaii, 1983; cons. Time and Attendance Group, Oakland, Calif., 1984-85. Mem. Smithsonian Instn., Commonwealth Club Calif., U. So. Calif. Alumni Assn.

BLOUKE, MILTON BAKER, lawyer; b. Chgo., Jan. 18, 1946; s. Pierre and Jessie (Scott) B.; m. Christine Hunt, Nov. 25, 1971; children: Scott M., Katie M. BS, U. Wash., 1970; JD, Lewis and Clark Law Sch., 1974; LLM in Taxation, Boston U., 1978. Bar: Oreg. 1974, U.S. Tax Ct. Atty. Dist. Counsel IRS, Boston, 1974-78, San Francisco, 1978-82; staff atty. Regional Counsel IRS, San Francisco, 1982-84; atty. Dist. Counsel IRS, San Jose, Calif., 1984-86; asst. dist. counsel Dist. Counsel IRS, San Jose, 1986-88, Seattle, 1988-91; atty. Dist. Counsel IRS, Las Vegas, Nev., 1991—. 1st lt. U.S. Army, 1966-69. Mem. ABA, Oreg. Bar Assn. Home: 2026 Grafton Ave Henderson NV 89014 Office: Dist Counsel IRS 4750 Oakey Blvd Las Vegas NV 89102

BLOUNT, HARRY NEIL, heavy equipment executive, marketing consultant; b. Blount, W.Va., Nov. 22, 1944; s. Harry and Stella Mae (Branard) B.; m. Dorothy Ann McDaniel, Oct. 1, 1965 (div. June 1977); children: Harry Neil II, Patricia Suzzette; m. Dolores Ruiz, Aug. 13, 1977. Student, W.Va. U., 1963-65, Hartnell Coll., 1974-77. Warranty adminstr. C.I. Walker Equipment Co., Charleston, W.Va., 1965-70; lt. Belle W.Va. Fire Dept., 1970-73; svc. advisor Quinn Co., Salinas, Calif., 1973-86; region sales mgr. Northwest Motor Welding, San Leandro, Calif., 1986-87; founder, pres. Parts World, Salinas, 1987—; ptnr. West World Mktg., Salinas, 1988—; account exec. Empire Tractor Co., Newark, Calif., 1988—; group advisor Equipment Explorers, Belle, 1970-73; cons. Indsl. Safety Club, Salinas, 1977-84. Author: Back Roads & Home, 1980; contbr. articles to publs. Mem. Big Buddy Program, Monterey County, Calif., 1981, Citizen's Traffic Com., Salinas, 1987, Friend's Outside, Monterey, 1988; asst. mgr. Community Recycle Program, Salinas, 1986; mem. Monterey County Grand Jury, 1991. Recipient Outstanding Svc. award State of W.Va., 1970, Vol. Achievement award Vol. Bur., Monterey County, 1984; named Bay Area Booster, KDON Radio, Salinas, 1981. Mem. Equipment Maintenence Suprs. Assn., Salinas C. of C., Lions (bd. dirs. Salinas Club 1984-86 spl. svc. award 1986). Republican. Methodist. Home: 1605 Siskiyou Dr Salinas CA 93906-2135 Office: Empire Tractor Co 38600 Cedar Blvd Newark CA 94560-4804

BLOUNT-PORTER, DAVID, jeweler, gemologist; b. Clovis, N.Mex., June 10, 1947; s. Shirley Davis and Lila Lee (Blount) Porter; m. Theda Diane Maxwell (div. Oct. 1988); children: Jessica Amber, Bonnii Allison. Student, U. Ala., Ala. A & M, Calif. State U., Hayward, Contra Costa Coll. Pres. Porter Ltd. of London dba David Porter Jewelery, Pinole, Calif., 1973—. With U.S. Army, 1969-71. Mem. Am. Gem Soc. (cert. gemologist appraiser), Gemological Inst. Am. Alumni Assn., Calif. Jewelers Assn., Retail Jewelers Am., Pinole C. of C. (pres. 1976, 90). Office: David Porter Jewelery 1552 Fitzgerald Dr Pinole CA 94564

BLOW, JOHN NEEDHAM, social services educator; b. Whitby, Ont., Can., Nov. 30, 1905; came to U.S., 1952; s. Ezekiel Richard and Edith May (Correll) B.; m. Emma Jane White, June 6, 1942; children: Carol Anne, Brenda Jane, Mary Roberta, Elizabeth Diane. BA, McMaster U., 1939; MSW, U. Toronto, Ont., 1948. Cert. elem. tchr., Toronto, community colls. instr., Calif. Exec. sec. Community Welfare Planning Council Ont., Toronto, 1948-52; exec. v.p. Motel Corp., Las Vegas, Nev., 1952-54; exec. dir. Nev. div. Am. Cancer Soc., 1954-56, assoc. exec. dir. Los Angeles County br., 1956-70; program assoc. Am. Heart Assn., Los Angeles, 1970-74; project dir., coordinator sr. community service employment program Orange County, Calif., 1974-75; instr. community service programs for adults North Orange County Community Coll. Dist. and Coastline Coll., 1976-79, Mira Costa and Palomar Community Colls., 1979-85. Author: (poems) New Frontiers, 1984. Vol. Arthritis Found.; asst. commr. tng. Boy Scouts Can., Ottawa, 1934-41; Chaplain Tri-City Coun. Navy League. Wing comdr. RCAF, 1941-46. Recipient Commendation for Outstanding Svc. to Srs., Orange County Sr. Citizens Coun., 1977, Gold award Orange County United Way, 1977, Golden Poet award, 1991, World of Poetry, 1989, 90. Mem. Nat. Assn. Social Workers, Acad. Cert. Social Workers, San Luis Rey Officers Club, Valley Sr. Ctr., North County Concert Assn., So. Calif. McMaster U. Alumni Assn. (past pres., inducted Alumni Gallery 1986), Can. Soc. Los Angeles (charter, past pres.), U. Toronto Alumni Assn. (exec. com., past pres. So. Calif. br.). Presbyterian. Lodge: Elks. Home: 3725 Sesame Way Oceanside CA 92057-8328

BLOYD, STEPHEN ROY, environmental manager; b. Alameda, Calif., Aug. 17, 1953; s. William Allen and Alice Louella (Scott) B. Grad. high sch., Reedley, Calif., 1971. Cert. environ. mgr., Nev.; registered hazardous substances profl. Reagent tech. Tenneco Corp., Gold Hill, Nev., 1982; environ. tech. Pierson Environ. Drilling, Modesto, Calif., 1982-84; pres. Bloyd and Assocs., Dayton, Nev., 1986—. Author: Hazardous Waste Site Operations for General Site Workers, 1992; editor: (newsletter) Pumper, 1991. Firefighter Dayton Vol. Fire Dept., 1975, capt., 1976-78, chief, 1978-83, tng. officer, 1984—; asst. prof. Dodd/Beals Fire Protection Tng. Acad. U. Nev., Reno, 1990—; instr. chemistry hazardous materials Nat. Fire Acad., Emmitsburg, Md., 1989—; mem. bylaw com. Dayton Regional Adv. Coun., 1989. Mem. Nev. State Firemens Assn. (1st v.p. 1992-93, 2d v.p. 1991-92, pres. 1993—, chmn. hazardous materials com. 1987-93, mem. legis. com. 1991, bylaws com. 1986), Nev. Fire Chiefs Assn., War on Regional Mis-Mgmt. (pres. 1991-92), Citizen Alert. Libertarian. Office: PO Box 152 Dayton NV 89403

BLUBAUGH, DANNY JAY, biochemistry educator; b. Wichita, Kans., Nov. 25, 1955; s. Felix Albert and Mary Elizabeth (Lewis) B.; m. Norma Marie Mann, Oct. 4, 1980; 1 child, Kathryn Rose. BA in Chemistry and Biology, Earlham Coll., Richmond, Ind., 1980; PhD in Cell Biology, U. Ill., 1987. Postdoctoral scholar U. Ky., Lexington, 1987-91; asst. prof. biochemistry Utah State U., Logan, 1991—. Contbr. articles to profl. jours. NIH-Dept. Health and Human Svcs. molecular and cellular biology traineeship, 1981-85. Mem. AAAS, Am. Chem. Soc., Am. Soc. Plant Physiologists, Sigma Xi. Baha'i faith. Office: Utah State Univ Dept Chemistry & Biochemistry Logan UT 84322-0300

BLUE, BUDDY See **SEIGAL, BERNARD ROBERT**

BLUE, JAMES GUTHRIE, veterinarian; b. Flora, Ind., Oct. 22, 1920; s. Van C. and Florence A. (Guthrie) B. AB, Wabash Coll., 1943; postgrad., Northwestern U., 1943; DVM, Ohio State U., 1950; AA, L.A. Trade Tech. Coll., 1989. Pvt. practice cons., 1950-80; field vet. City of L.A., 1980-92, acting chief vets., 1992, chief vets., 1992-93; rsch. project cons. Calif. State U., Northridge, 1980-87; negotiator AFSCME, L.A., 1983-93. Lt. comdr. USN, 1943-46. Mem. Am. Vet. Med. Assn., San Diego Vet. Med. Assn., So. Ariz. Vet. Med. Assn., Calif. Vet. Med Assn. (environ. and pub. health ecology com., 1986-89, state ethics com. 1986-93, wellness com. 1990-93), So. Calif. Vet. Med. Assn. (coun. mem., polit. action com., continuing edn. com. 1980-93). Democrat. Episcopalian. Home: 6116 Fulton Ave Apt 103 Van Nuys CA 91401-3127

BLUE, STEVEN JOSHUA, nutritional physiologist; b. Wichita, Kans., Aug. 5, 1945; s. Louis Edward and Lois Marie (Hull) Raymond. BA in Philosophy, Okla. U., 1967; postgrad., Denver U., 1970-72; sci. teaching cert., Ft. Lewis Coll., Durango, Colo., 1978; postgrad., Hawaii U. Manoa, 1982-83. Cert. neuro-linguistic programming practitioner. Educator Durango Bd. Edn., 1979-80, Hawaii Dept. Edn., Honolulu, 1980-89; salesman A.L. Williams, Honolulu, 1985-88; fin. cons. First Am. Nat. Sec., Honolulu, 1986-88; counselor Hawaii State Judiciary, Honolulu, 1984-85; founder Hawaiian Health Haven, Punalu'u, 1990-91; pres. Hawaiian Plantation Retreat, Kailua, 1991-92; researcher, educator Hawaiian Soils Rsch. Internat., Kailua, 1991—; presenter Gen. Semantics Tng., Honolulu, 1986; health cons. Hawaiian Health Haven and Hawaiian Plantation Retreat, Inc, I, Kailua, 1991; agr. cons. Sustainable Agriculture, Hilo, Hawaii, 1992. Inventor pers. ski equipment, 1978. Bd. chmn. Hian Ha Gliding Assn., Honolulu, 1982; coord. Hawaii Litter Campaign, Honolulu, 1981; presenter Ala Wai Community Garden, Honolulu, 1992; producer Community Access Cable TV, Honolulu, 1991-92. With U.S. Army, 1967-69, Korea. Mem. NRA, Gen. Semantics Inst., Am. Nat. Hygiene Tchrs. Orgn., Am. Assn. Nutrition and Dietary Cons., Phi Kappa Psi. Office: Hawaiian Soils Rsch Internat PO Box 757 Kailua HI 96734

BLUECHEL, ALAN, state senator, wood structural components manufacturing company executive; b. Edmonton, Alta., Can., Aug. 28, 1924; s. Joseph Harold and Edith (Daly) B.; m. Aylene Loughnan, Nov. 2, 1958; children: Gordon, Turner; m. Jeanne Ehrlichman, Aug. 8, 1981. BSc in Elec. Engring., BA, U. B.C.; postgrad. U. Wash.; diploma Harvard U., 1988. Vice pres. Loctwall Corp., Kirkland, Wash., 1948-64, pres., 1964—; pres. Crystal Mtn. Inn Co., developer condominiums, restaurants, hotels, swimming pools, 1968-80; mem. Wash. State Ho. of Reps., 1966-74; mem. Wash. Senate, 1974—, pres. pro tem, 1988-89, vice-chmn. rules com. 1988-89, Rep. whip, 1979-81, 83—, majority whip, 1981-83, mem. ways and means, 1988-89, pres. Pacific Northwest Econ. Region, 1989—, bd. dirs. Wash. State Inst. Pub. Policy, 1988—, v.p. pro-tem 1990-92, rep. pres. pro-tem 1993—; mem. exec. com. Western Legis. Conf., 1988-89, speaker various confs., convs., orgns. Mem. Wash. State Land Planning Commn., 1969-73, Wash. State Women's Council, 1976, Spl. Com. on Office State Actuary, 1983; chmn. Wash. State Winter Recreation Commn., 1983, Wash. State Commn. on Environ. Policy, 1983; mem. arts, tourism and cultural affairs com. Nat. Conf. of State Legis., 1976-897; mem. Juanita Citizens Devel. Council, 1975-79, King County Conservation Com., 1967-69, King County Flood Control Adv. Bd., 1968-70, Com. To Save Sch. Trust Lands, 1975—, Edwards Park Adv. Bd., 1977-79, Seattle Symphony Phonathon Fundraisers, 1980, 81, Gov.'s Council on Child Abuse and Neglect, 1983, Wash. State Expo '86 Commn., 1985-87; mem. conservation com. King County Environ. Devel. Commn., 1969-74, numerous other civic orgns. Recipient Outstanding Service award Lake Washington PTSA Council, 1982, Mountaineers Club, Sun Valley Ski Club, Forelaufer Ski Club.

BLUEMLE, PAUL EDWARD, college administrator; b. Springfield, Ohio, Sept. 9, 1926; s. Carl Henry and Mary Ann (Wolbert) B.; m. Helen Jean Smain, Sept. 13, 1958; children: Joy, Christine, Jude, Laura, Peter. BBA magna cum laude, Xavier U., 1951; MA, U. Oreg., 1953; postgrad., Mich. State U., 1957-63. Reporter Springfield Daily News, 1943-51; exec. sec. Young Christian Students, Chgo., 1952-54; dir. pub. relations Thomas More Coll., Covington, Ky., 1954-55; bus. mgr. Today mag., Chgo., 1955-56; instr. Mich. State U., East Lansing, 1956-59; editor univ. publs. Bowling Green (Ohio) State U., 1959-60; asst. prof., assoc. prof., exec. sec., asst. dean Monteith Coll., Wayne State U., Detroit, 1960-76; admissions dir., asst. dean U. Detroit, 1976-80; city clk. Pleasant Ridge, Mich., 1980-82; asst. to v.p. academics Northwood Inst., Midland, Mich., 1983; dir. admissions, rsch. and planning Holy Names Coll., Oakland, CA, 1983-90; retired, 1990—; bd. dirs. Chgo. Research Group Corp., 1956-73. Pres. sch. bd. St. Mary's Parish, Royal Oak, Mich., 1966; mem. Citizen's Adv. Commn., Ferndale (Mich.) Sch. Dist., 1972; chmn. com. on community Archdiocese of Detroit, 1972-74. Served with U.S. Army, 1945-46. Mem. Soc. Profl. Journalists, Am. Newspaper Guild (v.p. Springfield 1945), AAUP (sec. Wayne State U. chpt. 1971-72), Nat. Assn. Coll. Admission Counselors, Kappa Tau Alpha. Roman Catholic. Home: 2235 Lincoln Ave Apt 207 Alameda CA 94501-2946

BLUESTEIN, HAROLD ALAN, artist; b. Buffalo, Oct. 29, 1948; s. Robert William and Anne (Bacol) B.; m. Susan Janet Mathews, Oct. 1, 1979; children: David Robert, Katherine Marie, Daniel Marshall. BA, Kent State U., 1970. Gen. contractor Bluebird Constrn. Co., Boulder, Colo., 1971-76; golf profl. PGA, from 1976; asst. profl. at various country clubs Mo., N.Mex. and Oreg., 1976-80; head golf pro Rock Creek Country Club, Portland, 1981-83, Lewis River Golf Course, Woodland, Wash., 1983-85; men's golf coach Portland State U., 1981-86; artist Harold Bluestein Studio, Graphite Pencil Artist, Woodland, 1985—. Exhibited in group shows at Nat. Cooperstown (N.Y.) Art Competition, 1987, Salmagundi Club, N.Y.C., 1987, Haggin Mus., Stockton, Calif., 1988, Edmonds (Wash.) ARt Festival, 1987, 88, Beaverton (Wash.) Art Showcase, 1986, numerous others; works in pub. collections at World Golf Hall of Fame, Pinehurst, N.C., Gt. Am. Art Competition Permanent Collection, Houston; featured in mag. articles. Recipient numerous art awards. Home and Office: 40616 NW 9th Ave Woodland WA 98674

BLUM, BARRY, orthopedic surgeon; b. Bklyn., Nov. 21, 1940; s. Joseph and Jeanne (Masef) B.; m. Gloria Jeanne Itman, July 14, 1966; 1 child, Michelle Katie. AB, Columbia Coll., 1961; MD, U. Rochester, 1965. Diplomate Am. Bd. Orthopedic Surgery. Intern U. Minn. Hosps., Mpls., 1966; resident in orthopedics Stanford (Calif.) Med. Ctr., 1971; asst. to prof. Nuffield Orthopedic Ctr. Oxford U., 1972; pvt. practice Greenbrae, Calif., 1973-74, Larkspur, Calif., 1974-86, Kealakekua, Hawaii, 1986—; asst. chief orthopedics Stanford/V.A. Hosp., Palo Alto, Calif., 1973; edn. dir. Arthritis Found., Kailua-Kona, Hawaii, 1988—. Musical director: (music album) The Golden Gate Gypsy Orchestra of America and California Otherwise Known as the Travelling Jewish Wedding, 1988; editor, pub.: The Doctor's Directory. Pres. Aloha Performing Arts Ctr. Surgeon USPHS, 1966-68. Fellow Am. Acad. Orthopedic Surgeons; mem. Union Am. Physicians and Dentists, Western Orthopedic Assn., Hawaii Med. Assn. Office: PO Box S Kealakekua HI 96750-9017

BLUM, DAVID ARTHUR, computer company executive; b. Louisville, Aug. 10, 1962; s. Paul and Dorit (Korn) B. BA, Bellamine Coll., Louisville, 1985. Acctg. mgr. Internat. Color Svc., Inc., San Francisco, 1985-88; asst. controller Cut Flower Exchange, Inc., Sunnyvale, Calif., 1988-89; controller Future Packaging, Inc., Santa Clara, Calif., 1989-91; pres. Office Techs., Inc., Fremont, Calif., 1991—. Republican. Jewish. Home: 47112 Warm Springs Blvd Apt 228 Fremont CA 94539-7813

BLUM, DEBORAH, reporter. Sr. writer The Sacramento (Calif.) Bee; sci. writer in residence U. Wis., Madison, 1993. Recipient Pulitzer Prize, 1992. Mem. Nat. Assn. Sci. Writers (bd. dirs.), Sigma Xi. Office: Sacramento Bee PO Box 15779 Sacramento CA 95852

BLUM, FRED ANDREW, electronics company executive; b. Austin, Tex., Nov. 30, 1939; s. Freddie A. and Margaret E. (Stark) B.; children: Craig Houston, Karisa Laine; m. Diane F. Harbert, June 11, 1988. BS in Physics, U. Tex., 1962; MS in Physics, Calif. Inst. Tech., 1963, PhD, 1968. Rsch. scientist Gen. Dynamics, Ft. Worth, 1963-64; mem. tech. staff Hughes Rsch. Labs., Malibu, Calif., 1966-68, Lincoln Lab., MIT, Lexington, 1968-73; program mgr. Cen. Rsch. Labs., Tex. Instruments, Dallas, 1973-75; dir. solid state electronics Rockwell Internat., Thousand Oaks, Calif., 1975-79; v.p. Microelectronics R & D Ctr. Rockwell Internat., Anaheim, Calif., 1979-81; pres. GigaBit Logic, Newbury Park, Calif., 1981-86; chief exec. officer Sequel, Westlake Village, Calif., 1986—. Mem. editorial bd. Fiber Optics and Integrated Optics, 1977-83; contbr. numerous articles on solid state electronics to sci. jours. Chmn. local adv. coun. Am. Cancer Soc., 1980-81. NSF fellow, Howard Hughes fellow. Fellow IEEE; mem. AAAS, Am. Phys. Soc., Am. Mgmt. Assn., Phi Beta Kappa, Sigma Xi. Office: Sequel 2899 Agoura Rd Ste 347 Westlake Village CA 91361-3200

BLUM, JOHN ALAN, urologist, educator; b. Bklyn., Feb. 2, 1933; s. Louis J. and Pauline (Kushner) B.; m. Debra Merlin Ackerman, June 30, 1957; children: Louis Jeffrey, Alfred Merlin, Jacqueline. AB, Dartmouth, 1954; MD, NYU, 1958; MS, U. Minn., 1965. Diplomate Am. Bd. Urology. Intern, U. Minn. Hosp., Mpls., 1958-59, resident, 1959-64; practice medicine, specializing in urology, Chgo., 1964-66, Mpls., 1966-67, San Diego, 1969—; chmn. dept. urology Mt. Sinai Hosp., Chgo., 1965-66; asst. prof. urology U. Minn., Mpls., 1967; assoc. clin. prof. urology U. Calif., San Diego, 1969—; chief of staff Hillside Hosp., San Diego, 1989—; chmn. dept. surgery, div. urology Mercy Hosp., San Diego, 1991—; mem. staff Scripps Hosp., La Jolla, Calif., 1969—; adj. assoc. prof. uro-pathology Uniform Svcs. U. of Health Sci., Behtesda, Md., 1988—. Bd. dirs. Vietnam Vet. Leadership Program. Capt. USNR, 1967—, Vietnam. Fellow ACS; mem. Am., Calif. med. assns., Am. Urol. Assn., San Diego Urol. Soc. (pres. 1991—), San Diego Surg. Soc. (pres. 1977—), Phi Beta Kappa, Sigma Xi, Alpha Omega Alpha, San Diego Yacht Club. Research in devel. of silicone rubber for urinary tract. Home: 890 Cornish Dr San Diego CA 92107-4247 Office: 3415 6th Ave San Diego CA 92103-5084

BLUMBERG, NATHAN(IEL) BERNARD, journalist, educator, writer and publisher; b. Denver, Apr. 8, 1922; s. Abraham Moses and Jeannette Blumberg; m. Lynne Stout, June 1946 (div. Feb. 1970); children: Janet Leslie, Jenifer Lyn, Josephine Laura; m. Barbara Farquhar, July 1973. B.A., U. Colo., 1947, M.A., 1948; D.Phil. (Rhodes scholar), Oxford (Eng.) U., 1950. Reporter Denver Post, 1947-48; assoc. editor Lincoln (Nebr.) Star, 1950-53; asst. to editor Ashland (Nebr.) Gazette, 1954-55; asst. city editor Washington Post and Times Herald, 1956; from asst. prof. to assoc. prof. journalism U. Nebr., 1950-55; assoc. prof. journalism Mich. State U., 1955-56; dean, prof. Sch. Journalism, U. Mont., 1956-68, prof. journalism, 1968-78, prof. emeritus, 1978—; pub. Wood FIRE Ashes Press, 1981—; vis. prof. Pa. State U., 1964, Northwestern U., 1966-67, U. Calif., Berkeley, 1970; Dept. State specialist in Thailand, 1961, in Trinidad, Guyana, Surinam and Jamaica, 1964. Author: One-Party Press?, 1954; The Afternoon of March 30: A Contemporary Historical Novel, 1984, also articles in mags. and jours.; co-editor: A Century of Montana Journalism, 1971; editor: The Mansfield Lectures in International Relations, Vols. I and II, 1979; founder: Mont. Journalism Rev, 1958—; editor, pub. Treasure State Rev., 1991—. Served with arty. U.S. Army, 1943-46. Decorated Bronze Star medal. Mem. Assn. Am. Rhodes Scholars, Brasenose Soc., Kappa Tau Alpha (nat. pres. 1969-70). Home: PO Box 99 Bigfork MT 59911-0099

BLUMBERG, ROBERT LEE, manufacturing executive; b. Bklyn., Apr. 1, 1942; s. William T. and Hazel Blumberg; m. Joyce T. Yavner, Mar. 29, 1969; children: Matthew Y., Michael L. BS, MIT, 1964, MS, 1965; MBA, Harvard U., 1967. Assoc. J.H. Whitney & Co., N.Y.C., 1970-72; ptnr. Idanta Ptnrs., N.Y.C. and San Diego, 1972-80; pres., chief exec. Spectragraphics Corp., San Diego, 1981—; mem. vis. com. MIT Mech. Engring. Dept., Cambridge, 1986-92; regional chmn. MIT Ednl. Coun., San Diego, 1978-88; chmn. MIT Enterprise Forum San Diego, 1989-92, bd. dirs. 1992—; trustee Francis W. Parker Sch., 1984-89; bd. dirs. Pacific Communications Sci., Inc., San Diego, 1987-93. Served to lt. U.S. Army, 1967-69. Republican. Jewish. Office: Spectragraphics Corp 9707 Waples St San Diego CA 92121-2991

BLUME, BASIL WESTWOOD, auditor; b. Colorado Springs, Colo., June 30, 1965; s. Basil Edward Blume and Sharon Lee (Foster) Miller. BS in Bus. Fin., Colo. State U., 1987, MBA in Fin., 1991. Lic. real estate broker, Colo. Broker assoc., analyst Springs Assocs., Inc., Colorado Springs, 1987-88; account exec. ADP, Aurora, Colo., 1988, Lincor Properties, Englewood, Colo., 1988-89; comml. real estate appraiser Cushman & Wakefield, Inc., Denver, 1989-90; grad. teaching asst. Colo. State U., Ft. Collins, 1990-91; internal auditor Manville Corp., Denver, 1991—; owner, mgr. Basil W. Blume-Broker, fin. and real estate svcs., Denver, 1989-91. Mem. Fin. Mgmt. Assn., Am. Assn. Individual Investors, Wilderness Soc., Colo. Wildlife

Fedn., Golden Key. Home: 1321 S Gaylord St Denver CO 80210 Office: Manville Corp Dept 2-06 PO Box 5108 Denver CO 80217-5108

BLUME, JAMES BERYL, financial consultant; b. N.Y.C., Apr. 9, 1941; s. Philip Franklin Blume and Mary Kirschman Asch; m. Kathryn Weil Frank, Jan. 20, 1984; 1 child, Zachary Thomas Philip. BA, Williams Coll., Williamstown, Mass., 1963; MBA, Harvard U., Boston, 1966; M. Psychology, The Wright Inst., Berkeley, Calif., 1983, PhD in Philosophy, 1986. Security analyst Faulkner, Dawkins & Sullivan, N.Y.C., 1966-68; sr. v.p. Faulkner, Dawkins & Sullivan Securities, Inc., N.Y.C., 1968-73; ptnr. Omega Properties, N.Y.C., 1973-74; exec.v.p. Arthur M. Fischer, Inc., N.Y.C., 1974-77; psychotherapist in pvt. practice Berkeley, 1985-91, fin. cons., 1987—; bd. dirs. RHL/Golden State Pub. San Francisco, 1991-92. Bd. dirs. ACLU of No. Calif., San Francisco, 1988—, East Bay Clinic for Psychotherapy, Oakland, Calif., 1981-85, Marin Psychotherapy Inst., Mill Valley, Calif., 1986-87; bd. trustees The Wright Inst., 1981-85. Mem. Berkeley Tennis Club, Williams Club (bd. govs. 1968-72). Democrat. Jewish. Office: 1708 Shattuck Ave Berkeley CA 94709

BLUMENTHAL, RICHARD CARY, construction executive, consultant; b. Bklyn., Dec. 18, 1951; s. Mervin Harold and Barbara June (Engelson) B.; m. Ginnilyn Hawkins; children: Aaron Joseph, Meredith Taylor. BS, U. N.H., 1974. Planner RECON Assocs., Hamilton, Mont., 1976-77; project mgr. Grizzly Mfg., Hamilton, 1977-78; profl. carpenter Ed Brown Constrn., Bainbridge Island, Wash., 1978-79; pres. Richard Blumenthal Constrn., Inc., Bainbridge Island, 1979—; instr. Bainbridge Island Community Sch., 1993—. Mem. pk. bd. coun. City of Winslow, 1989-90; bd. dirs. Bainbridge Island Pub. Libr., 1992—; mem. Land Use Profls. Forum, 1992—; mem. advisory com. Bainbridge Band Park & Rec. Gymnastics Com., 1993—. Mem. Ind. Bus. Assn., C. of C. Home: 330 Nicholson Pl NW Bainbridge Is WA 98110-1702 Office: 10140 NE High School Rd Bainbridge Island WA 98110

BLUMHARDT, JON HOWARD, college administrator; b. Ft. Benning, Ga., Oct. 3, 1951; s. Howard Jerome and Joan (Tisdal) B.; m. Lisette Susan Vinet, Jan. 26, 1973; children: Matthew, Malia, Mark. BA in History, U. Hawaii, 1973, MA in Sociology, 1978, MEd, 1979; EdS, U Va., 1984. Media specialist U.S. Army JAG Sch., Charlottesville, Va., 1980-85; adminstr. officer OPM Fed. Exec. Inst., Charlottesville, 1985-86; chief resources mgmt. IRS Honolulu Dist., 1986-87; dir. Ednl. Media Svcs. Honolulu Community Coll., 1987—. Named one of Outstanding Young Men in Am., 1989, Eagle Scout, 1965; recipient Mahalo award Mayor of Honolulu, 1978, Cert. of Merit Aloha Coun. Boy Scouts Am., 1978, Scoutmaster award of Merit Nat. Eagle Scout Assn., 1990. Mem. DAV (life). Republican. Roman Catholic. Home: 1140 Lauloa St Kailua HI 96734-4065 Office: Honolulu Community Coll 874 Dillingham Blvd Honolulu HI 96817-4598

BLUMING, AVRUM ZVI, hematologist, oncologist, educator, researcher; b. N.Y.C., Apr. 10, 1940; s. Hy Charles and Mildred Goodblatt) B.; m. Martha Wolman, Sept. 1, 1963; children: Ariel, Adam. BA, Columbia U., 1961, MD, 1965. Diplomate Am. Bd. Internal Medicine, Am. Bd. Hematology, Am. Bd. Med. Oncology. Med. intern First Columbia Med. div. Bellevue Hosp., N.Y.C., 1965-66, resident in medicine, 1966-67; clin. assoc. Nat. Cancer Inst., Bethesda, Md., 1967-69, sr. investigator, 1969-71; dir. Lymphoma Treatment Ctr. Nat. Cancer Inst., Kampala, Uganda, 1970-71; asst. prof. medicine Tufts U., Boston, 1972-75; pvt. practice, Encino, Calif., 1975—; instr. Johns Hopkins U., Balt., 1968-69; sr. attending physician Los Angeles County-U. So. Calif. Med. Ctr., L.A., 1981—, clin. prof. medicine, 1981—; chief of staff Encino Hosp., 1984-85; chief of staff AMI Tarzana Regional Med. Ctr., L.A., 1991—, bd. dirs., 1989—; mem. cancer immunotherapy com. Nat. Cancer Inst., 1974-78; chmn. prof. edn. com. Am. Cancer Soc. San Fernando Valley, L.A., 1977-78. Contbg. author: Recent Results in Cancer Research, 1974, Manual of Endocrinology and Metabolism, 1986; creator cross-linked data base hist. calendar. Chmn. bd. H.O.P.E. Found., L.A., 1982—; mem. inst. com. Brandeis Camp, Simi Valley, Calif., 1982-86; mem. civic com. L.A. Music Ctr., 1983—. Recipient citation classic award Inst. for Sci. Info., 1984. Fellow ACP; mem. AAAS, Am. Assn. for Cancer Rsch., Am. Fedn. Clin. Rsch., Am. Soc. Clin. Oncology, Am. Soc. Hematology, N.Y. Acad. Scis., Alpha Omega Alpha. Jewish. Office: Hem-Onc Med Group San Fernando Valley 16311 Ventury Blvd Ste 780 Encino CA 91436

BLUMM, MICHAEL CHARLES, law educator; b. Detroit, Mar. 3, 1950; s. Charles F. and Margaret E. (Wilson) B. BA, Williams Coll., Williamstown, Mass., 1972; JD, George Washington U., Washington, D.C., 1976, LLM, 1979. Bar: Pa. 1976, D.C. 1977. Atty. Ctr. for Natural Areas, Washington, 1976-77, EPA, Washington, 1977-78; teaching fellow Nat. Resources Law Inst., Portland, Oreg., 1978-79; prof. of law Lewis and Clark Law Sch., Portland, 1979—; investigator Oreg. State Sea Grant Program, Corvallis, 1979-90; adv. com. mem. Northwest Power Planning Coun., Portland, 1981-83. Editor: (legal newsletter) Anadromous Fish Law Memo, 1979-90; contbr. articles to numerous profl. jours. Office: Lewis and Clark Law Sch 10015 SW Terwilliger Blvd Portland OR 97219-7799

BLUMMER, KATHLEEN ANN, counselor; b. Iowa Falls, Iowa, Apr. 17, 1945; d. Arthur G. and Julia C. (Ericson) Thorsbakken; m. Terry L. Blummer, Feb. 13, 1971 (dec. 1980); 1 child, Emily Erica. AA, Ellsworth Coll., Iowa Falls, 1965; BA, U. Iowa, 1967; postgrad., Northeastern Ill. U., 1969-70, U. N.Mex., 1980—; MA, Western N.Mex. U., 1973. Asst. buyer Marshall Field & Co., Chgo., 1967-68; social worker Cook County Dept. Pub. Aid, Chgo., 1968-69; tchr. Chgo. Pub. Schs., 1968-69; student fin. aid counselor Western N.Mex. U., Silver City, 1971-72; family social worker, counselor Southwestern N.Mex. Svcs. to Handicapped Children and Adults, Silver City, 1972-74; career edn. program specialist Galluo McKinley County (N.Mex.) Schs., 1974-76; dir. summer sch. Loving (N.Mex.) Mcpl. Schs., 1977; counselor, dept. chmn. Carlsbad (N.Mex.) Pub. Schs., 1977-82; counselor Albuquerque Pub. Schs., 1982—. Mem. AAUW (topic chmn. Carlsbad chpt., v.p. Albuquerque chpt.), N.Mex. Personnel and Guidance Assn., Theos Club, Highpoint Swim and Racquet Club (Albuquerque), Elks. Democrat. Lutheran.

BLUMRICH, JOSEF FRANZ, aerospace engineer; b. Steyr, Austria, Mar. 17, 1913; s. Franz and Maria Theresia (Mayr) B.; m. Hildegard Anna Schmidt-Elgers, Nov. 7, 1935; children: Michael Sebastian, Christoph, Stefan. BS in Aero. and Mech. Engring., Ingenieurschule Weimar (Germany), 1934. Engr., Gothaer Waggonfabrik A.G., Gotha, Germany, 1934-44; ct. interpreter U.S. Mil. Ct., Linz, Austria, 1946-51; dep. chief hydraulics dept. United Austrian Iron and Steel Works, Linz, 1951-59; structural design engr. Army Ballistic Missile Agy., Huntsville, Ala., 1959-61; chief structural engring. br. G.C. Marshall Space Flight Ctr., NASA, Huntsville, 1961-69, chief systems layout br., 1969-74; cons. in field, 1974—. Served with German Army, 1944-45. Recipient Apollo Achievement award NASA, 1969, Exceptional Service medal, 1972. Author: The Spaceships of Ezekiel, 1974; Kasskara, 1979; editorial cons. on space sci. and rocketry Scribner-Bantam English Dictionary, 1977; contbr. articles to profl. jours. Patentee in field. Home: PO Box 433 Estes Park CO 80517-0433

BLUNT, PETER HOWE, capital company executive, lawyer; b. Norwalk, Conn., Sept. 6, 1945; s. Robert Matteson and Jane Buros) B.; m. Mary Elizabeth Johnson, Aug. 29, 1967 (div. Aug. 1982); children: Martha, Carl, Melissa; m. Laurie Janet Anderson, Oct. 29, 1983 (div. May 1992); children: Katherine, Stephen. BA, Duke U., 1968; JD, U. Denver, 1972. Bar: Colo. 1973, U.S. Dist. Ct. Colo. 1973, Calif. 1991, U.S. Dist. Ct. (no. dist.) Calif. 1991, U.S. Ct. Appeals (9th cir.) 1991. Pvt. practice law Denver, 1973-76; house counsel Cinderella Cos., Denver, 1976-79; dir. devel. Confluence at Beaver Creek, Vail, Colo., 1979-88; editor Commerce Clearing House, San Rafael, Calif., 1988-90; pres. Retail Property Investments, San Francisco, 1990-93; gen. ptnr. Beaver Creek Capital, LP, Sausalito, Calif., 1993—; bd. dirs. Creative Design Inc., Phoenix. Contbr. articles to profl. jours. Bd. dirs. Greenwood Village (Colo.) HA Assn., 1978-80; participating contbr. Multiple Sclerosis Soc., 1990-91. Mem. San Francisco Yacht Bd. (sec. 1991), Phi Alpha Delta (pres. 1971-72). Republican. Methodist. Office: Beaver Creek Capital LP PO Box 1800 Sausalito CA 94966-1800

BLUNT, ROBERT MATTESON, pyrotechnics and ordnance researcher emeritus; b. Denver, Oct. 21, 1916; s. Laurence Calvin and Ruth Esther (Howe) B.; m. June Correan Romelle Buros, Sept. 9, 1939; children: Tona Louise, Robert Matteson, Peter Howe, Stephen Thomas, John Eric. Student, MIT, 1935-38; BSc, U. Denver, 1947, MSc, 1958. Registered profl. engr., Colo. Rsch. engr. Douglas Leigh Inc., N.Y.C., 1939; sr. ballistic engr. Denver Ordnance Plant, 1941-43; rsch. physicist Remington Arms Co., Bridgeport, Conn., 1943-46; rsch. physicist Labs. for Applied Mechanics U. Denver, Denver Rsch. Inst., 1948-80, sr. rsch. fellow, 1980-87; sr. rsch. fellow emeritus U. Denver Rsch. Inst. Labs. for Applied Mechanics, 1987—; founder, gen. chmn. Internat. Pyrotechnic Seminars, Denver, 1968-78, chmn. emeritus, 1980—. Mem. Internat. Pyrotechnics Soc. (founder, pres. 1980-84, life mem. 1984—), Masons, Sigma Xi, (pres. U. Denver chpt. 1975), Pi Delta Theta, Sigma Pi Sigma. Home: 2495 S Quebec St Unit 17 Denver CO 80231

BLUTE, JAMES FRANCIS, III, physician; b. Boston, Aug. 17, 1944; s. James F. Jr. and Rita M. (Sheridan) B.; m. Katherine L. Rolfe, Feb. 24, 1975 (div. 1991); children: Ryan P., Randall S., Alexandria L., Victoria M.; m. Karin Marie Frandsen, June 26, 1993. Student, Cornell U., 1962-64; BS, U. Ariz., 1967, MD, 1971. Diplomate Am. Bd. Obstetrics and Gynecology. Resident health scis. ctr. U. Ariz., Tucson, 1971-75; pvt. practice ob-gyn. Tucson, 1975—; clin. assoc. ob-gyn. U. Ariz., 1975—; trustee Tucson Med. Ctr., Tucson, 1986-90, chief of staff, 1988-90. Contbg. author (book) Currenty Therapy, 1975. Bd. dirs. Ariz. Theater Co., Tucson, 1992. Fellow ACOG; mem. AMA, ACP Execs., Am. Fertility Soc., Am. Assn. Gynecol. Laparoscopists. Republican. Roman Catholic. Office: 2375 N Wyatt Dr #107 Tucson AZ 85712

BLY, DAVID ALAN, computer services company executive; b. Kansas City, Mo., Nov. 9, 1953; s. Chauncey Goodrich and Ruth Madeline (Henion) B; m. Christine Elizabeth Bidle, Mar. 10, 1973; children: Sarah Christine, Adam David. Student, Boise State U., 1974-76; BA in Bus. Adminstrn., U. Wash., 1978; MBA, Pacific Luth. U., 1982. Fin. analyst Boeing Comml. Airplanes, Seattle, 1978-80; systems analyst and cons. Boeing Computer Svcs., Seattle, 1980-83; mgr. publs. and quality assurance Boeing Computer Svcs., 1983-85, mgr. strategic planning, 1985-86, mgr. customer support, 1986-89; mgr. fin. systems Boeing Def. and Space Group, 1989—; lectr. in field. Bd. dirs. Wash. Future Bus. Leaders of Am., 1986-91; mem. Teacher/Parent Adv. Com., Spring Glen Elem. Sch., 1991—. Mem. Puget Sound PC User Group (sec. 1985-86), Beta Gamma Sigma, Am. Legion, Kent Swim and Tennis Club (bd. dirs. 1992—). Home: 25712 119th Ave SE Kent WA 98031-8413

BOADO, RUBEN JOSE, biochemist; b. Buenos Aires, Argentina, Feb. 8, 1955; came to U.S., 1985; s. Osvaldo Ruben and Lucia B.; m. Adriana Graciela Swiecicki, Jan. 11, 1980; children: Augusto Ruben, Lucrecia Adriana. MS, U. Buenos Aires, 1979, Diploma in Biochemistry, 1980, PhD, 1982. Rsch. fellow endocrinology Nat. Coun. Scientific Rsch., Buenos Aires, 1979-81, postdoctoral rsch. fellow in endocrinology, 1981-83, established investigator, 1983-89; internat. fellow UCLA Sch. Medicine, 1985-88, asst. rsch. endocrinologist, 1988-91, asst. prof. medicine, 1991—. Author numerous scientific publs. Recipient Best Scientific Paper award Internat. Assn. Radiopharmacology, Chgo., 1981, Cross-Town Endocrine Soc., L.A., 1988. Mem. AAAS, Argentine Soc. Clin. Rsch., Am. Thyroid Assn. (travel award 1987), Endocrine Soc. (travel award 1984), Brain Rsch. Inst., Soc. Neurosci. Office: UCLA Dept Medicine/Endocrin Rsch Labs C-Lot Rm 104 Los Angeles CA 90024-1682

BOARDMAN, KAY IRENE, real estate executive; b. South Gate, Calif., Sept. 14, 1939; d. Lucian Harold and Geraldine Tine (Harper) Comer; m. David Charles; children: Steven Gerald, Kenneth Martin. AA in Industrial Rels., Long Beach City Coll., 1970. Mgr. Alkalie Music, Lakewood, Calif., 1958-82; realtor Guy Gagnon Century 21, Lakewood, 1978-88; gen. mgr. Guy Gagnon & Assocs. Realtors, Long Beach, Calif., 1988—; sec.-treas., bd. dirs. Lakewood (Calif.) Shopping Ctr., 1983-85. Columnist, 1982-85; contbr. articles to newspapers. Bd. govs. Com. of 300, Long Beach, 1990; coord. Friends of the Indians, 1969. Recipient Humanitarian award Exceptional Children's Home, Long Beach, 1960. Mem. Town Hall of Calif. Home: 4446 N Lakewood Blvd Long Beach CA 90808-1306 Office: Guy Gagnon & Assocs 1155 E San Antonio Dr Ste D Long Beach CA 90807-2372

BOARDMAN, ROSANNE VIRGINIA, logistics consultant; b. Twin Falls, Idaho, Oct. 4, 1946; d. Gordon Ross and Garnet Othalia (Peterson) Tobin; m. Lowell Jay Boardman, May 12, 1973; 1 child, Christina Garnet. BA cum laude, Occidental Coll., 1968; MA with honors, Columbia U., 1969; postgrad., U. Calif., Irvine, 1971-72, U. Calif., L.A. and Santa Barbara, 1969, 73-74. Cert. jr. coll. tchr., Calif., cert. secondary tchg., Calif. Instr. U. Calif., Irvine, 1971-72, Ventura (Calif.) Community Coll., 1973-77; tech. writer Raytheon Svc. Co., Ventura, 1977-78; engring. analyst John J. McMullen Co., Ventura, 1978-80; sr. logistics specialist Raytheon Co., Ventura, 1977-78, 80-83; civilian tech. writer, editor USN, Port Hueneme, Calif., 1983-84, civilian logistics mgr., 1984-88; cons. Support Mgmt. Systems, Oxnard, Calif., 1988—. Author numerous manuals and logistics guides. Internat. fellow Occidental Coll., 1967; recipient Outstanding Performance award Naval Ship Weapon Systems Engring. Sta., 1985, 86. Mem. Soc. Logistics Engrs., Phi Beta Kappa.

BOARINI, EDWARD JAMES, healthcare executive; b. Chgo., Sept. 26, 1949; s. Edward John and Celeste Mary (Butt) B.; m. Marla Bovar, Apr. 25, 1976; 1 child, David Vincent. BS in Biology, U. Ill., Chgo., 1975; MS in Tech. Mgmt., Pepperdine U., 1991. Prin. engr. Baxter Travenol, Round Lake, Ill., 1975-80; mgr. sect. Baxter Travenol, Round Lake, 1980-82, program mgr. parenteral products, 1982-84, program mgr. access products, 1984-86; mgr. sr. engring. Baxter Pharmaseal, Valencia, Calif., 1986-89, dir. med. R & D, 1989-91, dir. tech. svcs./ spl. bus., 1991-93; v.p. tech. ops. PS Med., Goleta, Calif., 1993—. Patentee in field. With USN, 1970-74. Office: PS Med 125 Cremona Dr Goleta CA 93117

BOARMAN, PATRICK MADIGAN, economics and business administration educator, public official; b. Buffalo, 1922; m. Shi Chun (Shane) Hu, Dec. 18, 1988; children by previous marriage: Thomas, Christopher, Jesse, Barbara. AB, Fordham U., 1943; MS, Columbia U., 1946; PhD in Econs., Grad. Inst. Internat. Studies, U. Geneva, 1965. Asst. to advt. mgr. Doubleday, N.Y.C., 1944-45; fgn. corr. CBS, Geneva, 1946-48; dir. office cultural affairs Nat. Catholic Welfare Conf., Bonn, W. Germany, 1951-55; asst. prof. econs. U. Wis.-Milw., 1956-62; assoc. prof. Bucknell U., Lewisburg, Pa., 1962-67; prof. L.I.U., Greenvale, N.Y., 1967-72; prof. internat. econs., dir. rsch. Ctr. Internat. Bus., Pepperdine U., L.A., 1972-75; prof. econs. Nat. U., San Diego, 1979-93; mgr. econ. research div. employee relations and mgmt. devel. Gen. Electric Co., N.Y.C., 1964-65; mgr. econ. reports div. econ. analysis AT&T, 1969; sr. economist cons. World Trade Inst., N.Y.C., 1971; pres. Patrick M. Boarman Assocs., Internat. Bus. Cons., 1975—; dir. rsch. Ho. Rep. Conf., Ho. of Reps., Washington, 1967-68; spl. cons. to Sec. Treasury, Washington, 1970; cons. Econ. Stblzn. Bd., Washington, 1971-72; guest lectr. U. Chgo., 1957, 64; Disting. vis. lectr. Denison U., 1959; vis. prof. econs. U. Geneva, 1965-66; supr. 3rd dist. San Diego County, Calif., 1983-85. Author: Union Monopolies and Antitrust Restraints, 1963, Germany's Economic Dilemma-Inflation and the Balance of Payments, 1964; editor: (with Hans Schollhammer) Multinational Corporations and Governments, 1975, Trade with China, 1974, (with David G. Tuerck) World Monetary Disorder, 1976; author monographs; author, contbr. numerous articles to profl. and popular jours. Served with U.S. Army, 1943. Decorated Disting. Service Cross, Order of Merit W. Germany; Fulbright fellow U. Amsterdam, 1949-50; Ford Found. fellow in econs. U. Mich., 1958; Gen. Electric Found fellow U. Va., 1965. Home: 6421 Caminito Estrellado San Diego CA 92120-3022

BOAT, RONALD ALLEN, business executive; b. Dayton, Ohio, Nov. 16, 1947; s. Robert Mallory and Elvetta June (Smith) B. Student, Naval Acad./ Army Sch. Music, Norfolk, Va., 1968-69, Ariz. State U., 1966-68. Pres. Prodn. Svcs., Phoenix, 1968—, Greek Specialties Corp., Phoenix, 1980—; v.p. Am. Baby Boomers, San Diego, 1984—; co-founder, v.p. Internat. Food Network, San Diego, 1985-90; founder, pres. AMC Food Svcs. Corp., 1991—; ind. prodr. Intel, Honeywell, Best Western, Sperry, Phoenix, 1985—; mem. Lund Team Real Estate Adv. Bd., 1991—; bd. dirs. Lund Real Estate Corp., 1990—. Mem. Lund Team Real Estate Adv. Bd., 1991—. With U.S. Army, 1968-71. With U.S. Army, 1968-71. Named Outstanding sales rep. Club Am., Dallas, 1972-73, Top Distbr. Club Am., Dallas, 1973; recipient Top Restaurant award Am. Heart Assn., Phoenix, 1988, Best of Phoenix restaurant award, 1991. Mem. Am. Radio Relay League, Internat. Platform Assn., Phi Mu Alpha Sinfonia. Republican. Office: P S A 14628 N 48th Way Scottsdale AZ 85254-2203

BOATMAN, DENNIS LEROY, social studies educator; b. Caldwell, Idaho, Aug. 1, 1952; s. Fred LeRoy and Leta Haroldeen (Tilton) B.; m. Georgia Ann Stevens, June 19, 1976; children: Kristopher LeRoy, Bryan Wayne, Mark Wesley. BS in Edn., U. Idaho, 1976, MEd, 1981. Cert. secondary sch. educator, ednl. adminstr., Idaho, Wash. Health educator Sch. Dist. No. 193, Mountain Home, Idaho, 1976-82, athletic adminstr., 1977-82, social studies educator, 1976—, athletic adminstr., 1988-92; track coach Sch. Dist. No. 193, 1976—; instr. coaching, athletic adminstr. certs. Nat. Fedn. Interscholastic Coaching Edn. Program, Champaign, Ill., 1991—. Co-author: Physical Education: A Program for All Seasons, 1981, Health Education: The Way I Am, 1980. State committeeman Idaho State Dem. Cen. Com., Boise, 1984-88, conv. del., 1980-88. Mem. NEA (local pres. 1981-83), Coaching Edn. Assn. U.S.A., Nat. Fedn. Interscholastic Coaches Assn., Athletic Congress, Idaho Coaches Assn., Nat. Interscholastic Athletic State Adminstrs. Assn. (liaison and standing com. 1989—), Idaho High Sch. Activities Assn. (reclassification and seeding coms. 1988—). Office: Mountain Home High Sch 300 S 11th E Mountain Home ID 83647-3255

BOBRICK, STEVEN AARON, property manager; b. Denver, Apr. 11, 1950; s. Samual Michael and Selma Gertrud (Birnbaum) B.; m. Maria Diane Boltz, Oct. 5, 1980. Attended, U. Colo., 1968-72. Registered apt. mgr. Owner Bobrick Constrn., Denver, 1969-72; with Bell Mtn. Sports, Aspen, Colo., 1972-75; mgr. Compass Imports, Denver, 1975-80, Aurora (Colo.) Bullion Exch., 1980-81; contr. Bobrich Constrn., Aurora, 1981-85; appraiser Aurora, 1985-89; property mgr. Aurora Community Mental Health, Aurora, 1989—; real estate cons. Aurora, 1989—. Co-author: Are You Paying Too Much in Property Taxes, 1990. Coun. mem. City of Aurora, 1981-89; chmn. Explore Commercial Opportunities, Aurora, 1986-89, bd. dirs.; bd. dirs. Adam County Econ. Devel. Commn., Northglenn, Colo., 1985-89; vice chair Aurora Urban Renewal Authority, 1982-89; chmn. Aurora Enterprise Zone Found., 1991—; bd. dirs. Aurora Community Med. Clinic, 1987-88. Office: Aurora Comm Mental Health 1523 Emporia Aurora CO 80010

BOBRY, HOWARD HALE, electronics industry executive; b. Rochester, N.Y., Feb. 29, 1948; s. Gerald and Rose (Wolfson) B.; m. Valerie J. Jarosz, May 20, 1984. BSEE, Case Western Res. U., 1971; MBA, Baldwin Wallace Coll., 1980. Registered profl. engr. Project engr. Western Res. Electronics, Twinsburg, Ohio, 1970-72; cons. engr. Cleve., 1972-75; project engr. Lorain (Ohio) Products Corp., 1975-77; engring.mgr. Lortec Power Systems, North Ridgeville, Ohio, 1977-83; pres. H.H. Bobry & Co., Shaker Heights, Ohio, 1983-87, Mill Creek, Wash., 1983-87; pres. Albar Inc., Lynnwood, Wash., 1987—; dir. Albar, Inc., BSA Inc., Lynnwood. Patentee in field (9 in electronics); contbr. articles to profl. jours. Mem. IEEE, Nature Conservancy, Mensa. Office: Albar Inc 19013 36th Ave W Lynnwood WA 98036

BOCCIA, MARIA LIBORIA, biologist; b. Bronx, Dec. 5, 1953; d. Silvio Mario and Emily (Russo) B. BA, SUNY, Geneseo, 1974; MS, U. Mass., 1979, PhD, 1981. Rsch. asst. dept. psychology U. Mass., Amherst, 1976-81; teaching asst. dept. zoology U. Mass., 1976-79, teaching assoc., 1979-81; postdoctoral fellow U. Denver, 1981-83; asst. prof. Okla. Bapt. U., Shawnee, 1983-86; rsch. assoc. psychiatry U. Colo. Health Scis. Ctr., Denver, 1986; asst. prof. psychiatry U. Colo. Health Scis. Ctr., 1986—; mem. spl. study sect. NIMH, Washington, 1988-89; outside reviewer NSF, 1988-90; reviewer various profl. jours. Editor Jour. Bibl. Equality, 1989—; contbr. articles to profl. jours. Bd. dirs. Front Range Christians for Bibl. Equality, Denver, 1989-93. SUNY Regents scholar, 1971-74. Mem. AAAS, Am. Psychol. Assn., Animal Behavior Soc., Am. Soc. Primatologists (prog. com. 1986-90, R&D com. 1990—), Devlopmental Psychobiology Rsch. Group (exec. com. 1989—). Office: UCHSC Campus Box C268-68 4200 E 9th Ave Denver CO 80262-0001

BOCK, FRED, music publisher, composer; b. Jamaica, N.Y., Mar. 30, 1939; s. Fred NMN and Louise Margaret (Popp) B.; m. Lois Elaine Dunham, Nov. 28, 1964; children: Stephen David, Jonathan Christopher. BS in Music Edn., Ithaca (N.Y.) Coll., 1960; M in Ch. Music, U. So. Calif., 1962; D in Musical Arts, Taylor U., Upland, Ind., 1986. Dir. publs. Word, Inc., L.A., 1964-71; pres. Fred Bock Music Co., Inc., L.A., 1970—; dir. music First Presbyn. CH., Hollywood, Calif., 1980—; condr., arranger Mrs. Miller nightclub and recording act, L.A., 1968-75; cons. Nazarene Publish House, Kansas City, Mo., 1971-77; commd. anthems for Am. Guild Organists Conv., San Francisco, 1984, Woodale Ch., Mpls., 1990. Dir. music TV show Storytime, 1959 (ASCAP award); author: Creating 4-part Harmony, 1989; compiler, editor (hymnal) Hymns for the Family of God, 1976. Recipient Telly award for TV commls., 1991. Mem. Am. Choral Dirs. Assn., Am. Soc. Composers, Authors, Pubs. Republican. Office: PO Box 570567 Tarzana CA 91357-0567

BOCK, JEFFREY WILLIAM, lawyer; b. Mpls., Mar. 26, 1950; s. Frederick Garland Bock and Vera (Lewer) Randall; m. Elaine Drinkwater, Dec. 5, 1976 (div. 1981). BA, Dartmouth Coll., 1972; JD, U. Chgo., 1975. Bar: Oreg. 1975. Assoc. Tonkon, Torp & Galen, Portland, Oreg., 1975-78, McEwen, Hanna & Gisvold, Portland, 1978-81; corp. counsel Thermo Electron, Waltham, Mass., 1981-83; of counsel Perkins Coie, Portland, 1983—. Mem. Univ. Club. Office: Perkins Coie US Bancorp Tower Ste 2500 111 SW 5th Ave Portland OR 97221

BOCK, RUSSELL SAMUEL, author; b. Spokane, Wash., Nov. 24, 1905; s. Alva and Elizabeth (Mellinger) B.; m. Suzanne Ray, Feb. 26, 1970; children: Beverly A. Bock Wunderlich, James Russell. B.B.A., U. Wash., 1929. Part-time instr. U. So. Calif., UCLA, 1942-50; with Ernst & Ernst, CPAs, Los Angeles, 1938, ptnr., 1951-69; cons. Ernst & Young, 1969—. Author: Guidebook to California Taxes, annually, 1950—, Taxes of Hawaii, annually, 1964—; also numerous articles. Dir., treas. Community TV So. Calif., 1964-74; dir., v.p., treas. So. Calif. Symphony-Hollywood Bowl Assn., 1964-70; trustee Internat. Center for Ednl. Devel., 1969-72, Claremont Men's Coll., 1964-70; bd. dirs. Community Arts Music Assn., 1974-76, 78-84, Santa Barbara Symphony Assn., 1976-78, Santa Barbara Boys and Girls Club, 1980-93, UCSB Affiliates, 1983-85. Mem. Am. Inst. C.P.A.s (council 1953-57, trial bd. 1955-58, v.p. 1959-60), Calif. Soc. C.P.A.s (past pres.), Los Angeles C. of C. (dir. 1957-65, v.p. 1963), Sigma Phi Epsilon, Beta Alpha Psi, Beta Gamma Sigma. Clubs: Birnam Wood Golf, Santa Barbara Yacht. Office: 300 Hot Springs Rd Apt 190 Santa Barbara CA 93108-2069

BODDIE, LEWIS FRANKLIN, obstetrics-gynecology educator; b. Forsyth, Ga., Apr. 4, 1913; s. William F. and Luetta T. (Sams) B.; m. Marian Bernice Claytor, Dec. 27, 1941; children: Roberta Boddie Miles, Lewis Jr., Bernice B. Jackson, Pamela, Kenneth, Fredda, Margaret. BA, Morehouse Coll., 1933; MD, Meharry Med. Sch., 1938. Diplomate Am. Bd. Ob-Gyn (proctor parti exam Los Angeles area 1955-63). Intern Homer-Phillips Hosp., St. Louis, 1938-39, resident in ob-gyn, 1939-42; mem. attending staff Grace Hosp., Detroit, 1944-48, Parkside Hosp., Detroit, 1944-48, Los Angeles County Gen. Hosp., 1952-79; sr. mem. attending staff Queen of Angels Hosp., Los Angeles, 1964-91, chmn. dept. ob-gyn, 1968-70; asst. prof. U. So. Calif. Sch. Medicine, L.A., 1953-79, asst. prof. emeritus, 1979—; assoc. prof. U. Calif., Irvine, 1956-81. vice chmn. bd. mgrs. 28th St. YMCA, Los Angeles 1960-75; steward African Meth. Episc. Ch., Los Angeles, 1949—. Fellow ACS (life), Am. Coll. Ob-Gyn (life), Los Angeles Ob-Gyn Soc. (life): mem. Los Angeles United Way (priorities and allocations coms., 1985—, standards com. 1987—, new admission com. 1988—), Children's Home Soc. (bd. dirs. 1952-89, , trustee 1989—, v.p. 1963-68, pres. 1968-70), Child Welfare League Am. (bd. dirs. 1969-76). Republican.

BODEN, DEIRDRE, sociology educator; b. San Francisco, May 8, 1940; d. Richard Eric and Mary Victoria (Roeder) B. AA, Parkland Coll., Champaign, Ill., 1976; BA, U. Calif., Santa Barbara, 1978, MA, 1981, PhD, 1984. Prodr. Ondatelerama Films, Rome, 1961-62; internat. prodr. Anglo-Scottish Pictures, London, 1962-65; chmn., mng. dir. Dede Boden and Assocs., London, 1965-75; NIMH postdoctoral fellow Stanford (Calif.) U., 1984-86; asst. prof. Washington U., St. Louis, 1986-91; Jean Monnet fellow European U. Inst., Florence, Italy, 1991-92; sr. lectr. sociology Lancaster (Eng.) U., 1992—. Author: The Business of Talk, 1993; editor: Talk and

Social Structure, 1991. Regents scholar U. Calif., 1976-78, Regents fellow, 1978-79. Fellow Sigma Xi; mem. Am. Sociol. Assn., Internat. Sociol. Assn., Midwest Sociology Soc. (state bd. dirs. 1988-91). Democrat. Roman Catholic. Office: Lancaster U, Dept Sociology, Lancaster England

BODENSIECK, ERNEST JUSTUS, mechanical engineer; b. Dubuque, Iowa, June 1, 1923; s. Julius Henry and Elma (Sommer) B.; BSME, Iowa State U., 1943; m. Margery Elenore Sande, Sept. 9, 1943; children: Elizabeth Bodensieck Eley, Stephen. Project engr. TRW Inc., Cleve., 1943-57; supr. rocket turbomachinery Rocketdyne div. Rockwell Internat., Canoga Park, Calif., 1957-60, supr. nuclear turbomachinery Rocketdyne div., 1964-70; advance gear engr. Gen. Electric Co., Lynn, 1960-64; asst. mgr. engine components Aerojet Nuclear Systems Co., Sacramento, 1970-71; gear and bearing cons. AiResearch div. Garrett Corp., Phoenix, 1971-81; transmission cons. Bodensieck Engrng. Co., Scottsdale, Ariz., 1981—. Registered profl. engr., Ariz. Mem. ASME, AIAA, Soc. Automotive Engrs. (various coms.), Aircraft Industries Assn. (various coms.), Am. Gear Mfrs. Assn. (mem. aerospace, gear rating and enclosed epicyclic coms.), Nat. Soc. Profl. Engrs., Pi Tau Sigma. Lutheran. Patentee in field. Home: 7133 N Via De Alegria Scottsdale AZ 85258-3812

BODERMAN, MARY LOU, music educator; b. Escalon, Calif., Dec. 29, 1953; d. Lee Roy and Mary Marguerite (Leach) Bayley; m. Donald Joseph Boderman, June 20, 1976; children: Nathan Kyle, Lindsay Diane, Adam Michael. BA, Columbia Christian Coll., Portland, Oreg., 1976, Warner Pacific Coll., 1976; MS in Teaching, Music, Portland State U., 1982. Cert. tchr., Oreg., concert band adjudicator, Oreg. Music specialist Rural Dell Elem. Sch., Molalla, Oreg., 1976-78; music specialist and band dir. Columbia Christian Schs., Portland, 1978-86; asst. prof. music Columbia Christian Coll., 1984-90; band dir. South Salem High Sch., 1990—; mem. adj. faculty Lewis and Clark Coll., Portland, 1989. Mem. Oreg. Band Dirs. Assn. (adjudicator 1983—, N.W. regional rep. 1987-92, pres.-elect 1992—), Oreg. Music Educators' Assn. (pvt. sch. rep. Dist. 1 1984—, instrumental chair 1985, pres. 1986-88), Music Educators' Nat. Conf. Republican. Ch. Christ.

BODETT, THOMAS EDWARD, writer, radio personality; b. Champaign, Ill., Feb. 23, 1955; s. Peter C. and Florence E. (De Paun) B.; m. Debi J. Hochstetler, Dec. 26, 1978; 1 child, Courtney H. Student, Mich. State U., 1973-75. Bldg. contractor Petersburg and Homer, Alaska, 1976-84; commentator All Things Considered Nat. Pub. Radio, Washington, 1984-87; author Addison-Wesley Pub., Boston, 1984—; radio spokesman Motel 6, Dallas, 1986—, The End of the Road, Dallas, 1988—; chmn. Kachemak Bay Broadcasting Inc., Pub. Radio Sta. KBBI, Homer, 1985—; host nationally syndicated radio show Bodett & Co., 1993—. Author: As Far As You Can Go Without A Passport, 1985, Small Comforts, 1987, The End of the Road, 1989, The Big Garage on Clean Shot, 1990, Growing Up, Growing Old and Going Fishing at the End of the Road, 1990, Exploded, 1992. Recipient Best Radio Commentary and Best Radio Feature awards Alaska Press Club, Anchorage, 1985, 86, 3 Motel 6 Clio awards, 1988, Mercury awards, 1992, Mobius awards, 1988, 89, 90, 91. Mem. AFTRA, Authors Guild. Home and Office: 3726 Lake St Homer AK 99603

BODEY, BELA, immuno-morphologist; b. Sofia, Bulgaria, Jan. 18, 1949; came to U.S. 1985; s. Joseph and Rossitza (Derebeeva) B.; m. Victoria Psenko, Aug. 29, 1979; children: Bela Jr., Vivian. MD, Med. Acad., Sofia, 1973; PhD, Bulgarian Acad. Sci., Sofia, 1977. Lic. physician Bulgaria, Hungary, embryologist, immuno-morphologist. Asst. prof. Semmelweis Med. U., Budapest, 1977-80; prof. Inst. Hematology, Budapest, 1980-83; rsch. assoc. Tufts U., Boston, 1985; rsch. fellow immuno-pathology Mass. Gen. Hosp./Harvard U., Boston, 1986; rsch. fellow Childrens Hosp. L.A., 1987-90, rsch. scientist, 1991-92; asst. prof. rsch. pathology, Sch. of Medicine Univ. Southern Calif., 1992—; tchr. Med. U., Sofia, 1973-77, Semmelweis Med. U., Budapest, 1977-80; vis. prof. von Humboldt Found., Ulm., Fed. Republic Germany, 1984. Mem. Am. Assn. Cancer Rsch., French Soc. Cell Biology, French Soc. Electronmic., Internat. Soc. Exptl. Hematology, Free Masons. Roman Catholic. Home: 15745 Saticoy St Van Nuys CA 91406 Office: U So Calif Sch Medicine Dept Pathology 2011 Zonal Ave Los Angeles CA 90033

BODIG, JOZSEF, engineering executive, consultant; b. Gonc, Hungary; came to U.S., 1959; s. Matyas and Maria (Markusz) B.; m. Verna Jean West, July 14, 1962; children: Ilona, Marcus, Peter. BS in Forestry, U. B.C., Vancouver, Can., 1959; MS in Forest Products, U. Wash., 1961, PhD in Forest Products, 1963; D (hon.), U. Sopron, Sopron, Hungary, 1991. Rsch. asst. U. Wash., Seattle, 1959-61, teaching asst., 1961-63; asst. prof. Colo. State U., Ft. Collins, 1963-66, assoc. prof., 1966-74, prof., 1974-89, prof. emeritus, 1989—; pres. Engrng. Data Mgmt., Ft. Collins, 1990—; treas. Engrng. Data Mgmt., 1982-90, chmn. bd., 1990—, bd. dirs.; cons. in field; vis. scientist U. Forestry, Sopron, Hungary, 1979; vis. lectr. Australian Inst. of Engrs., Sydney, 1985. Author: Mechanics of Wood, 1982, Reliability Based Design of Engineered Wood Structures, 1992. Referee Youth Soccer Assn., Ft. Collins, 1972-86; asst. coach Colo. State U., Ft. Collins, 1966-72, soccer coach, 1972-84; sec. Wild Goose Ranch Homeowners Assn., Ft. Collins, 1988—. A. H. Anderson fellow U. Wash., 1959-60. Fellow Internat. Acad. Wood Sci.; mem. ASTM, Am. Nat. Standards Inst., Forest Products Rsch. Soc. (sec. sec. 1970-73). Office: Engrng Data Mgmt Inc 4700 Mcmurray Ave Fort Collins CO 80525-5532

BODINSON, HOLT, conservationist; b. East Orange, N.J., Nov. 14, 1941; s. Earl Herdien and Hermoine (Holt) B. B.A., Harvard, 1963; m. Ilse Marie Maier, Feb. 29, 1970. Sr. asso. Am. Conservation Assn., Inc., N.Y.C., 1966-70; dir. Office of Policy Analysis, N.Y. State Dept. Environ. Conservation, Albany, 1970-71, dir. div. ednl. services, 1971-77; dir. Ariz.-Sonora Desert Mus., 1977-78; exec. dir. Safari Club Internat./Safari Club Internat. Conservation Fund, Tucson, 1980-89; conservation dir. Safari Club Internat., Tucson, 1991—; committeeman, Montgomery Twp. Conservation Commn., 1967-70; sec. N.Am. del. Conseil Internat. de la Chasse et de la Conservation du Gibier, 1988—; gen. sec. World Hunting and Conservation Congress, 1988; dir. Internat. Wildlife Mus., 1991—. Served with arty. AUS, 1964-66. Mem. Stony Brook-Millstone Watershed Assn. (dir.), Safari Club Internat. (dir. Ariz. chpt.), N.Y. Outdoor Edn. Assn. (dir.), Outdoor Writers Assn. of Am., N.Y. State Rifle and Pistol Assn. (dir.). Episcopalian. Club: Harvard of So. Ariz. (pres.). Author: (with Clepper and others) Leaders in American Conservation, 1971. Contbg. editor Jour. Environmental Edn., 1968—; dir. Conservationist mag. 1971-77, N.Y. State Environment newspaper, 1971-74. Home: 4525 N Hacienda Del Sol Tucson AZ 85718-6619 Office: 4800 W Gates Pass Rd Tucson AZ 85745

BODISCO, MICHAEL ANDREW, federal agency administrator; b. San Francisco, July 27, 1941; s. Andrew Michael Bodisco and Helen Dorothy (Jones) Dawson; m. Mary Joanne Higgins, Sept. 5, 1964; children: Andrew, Madeleine, Alexis, Ellen. BS in Polit. Sci., U. San Francisco, 1964, MA in Govt., 1972. Purchasing agt. Cath. Sch. Purchasing, San Francisco, 1968-69; insp. U.S. Bur. Alcohol, Tobacco & Firearms, San Francisco, 1969-75, coord. firearms and explosives, 1975-89, spl. insp., 1989-90; field ops. officer, 1990—. Capt. U.S. Army, 1964-67; lt. col. USAR, 1972-91. Mem. Assn. U.S. Army, Civil Affairs Assn., Res. Officers Assn., Ret. Officers Assn. Roman Catholic. Office: Bur Alcohol Tobacco 221 Main St 11th Fl San Francisco CA 94105

BODMAN-BUSTAMANTE, DENISE ANN, speech and language pathologist; b. Detroit, Dec. 7, 1951; d. Stephen Donald Bodman and Louella Lydia (Maj) Meagher; m. Raul Bracamonte Bustamante, Oct. 11, 1979; children: Bethany Lucia, R. Christopher. Student, U. N.Mex., 1969, U. Iowa, 1970, Mesa (Ariz.) Community Coll., 1970-71; BS, Ariz. State U., 1973, postgrad., 1985—; PhD, U. Ariz., 1993. Speech-lang. pathologist Community Speech & Hearing Ctr., Encino, Calif., 1976-78; founder, dir. Community Speech & Lang. Ctr., Tempe, Ariz., 1978-82; pvt. practice speech-lang. pathologist and cons. Ariz., 1982—; rsch. assoc. Ariz. State U., Tempe, 1985-88; founder, dir. Children's Activity Mus. Met. Phoenix, 1987—; assoc. faculty dept. family resources and human devel. Ariz. State U., Tempe, 1990—, bd. dirs. Contbr. articles to profl. jours. Vol. police officer Phoenix Police Dept., 1978-87. Mary E. Switzer fellow Nat. Inst. Handicapped Rsch., 1986; recipient Alex Mertens award Phoenix Police Dept., 1979, Life Sav. medal, 1984. Mem. Phi Kappa Phi. LDS. Home: 4605 W Gail Dr Chandler AZ 85226-8218

BODNEY, DAVID JEREMY, lawyer; b. Kansas City, Mo., July 15, 1954; s. Daniel F. and Retha (Silby) B.; m. J. Brooke Tesar, June 7, 1991. BA cum laude, Yale U., 1976; MA in Fgn. Affairs, U. Va., 1979, JD, 1979. Bar: Ariz. 1979, U.S. Dist Ct. Ariz. 1980, U.S. Ct. Appeals (9th cir.) 1980, U.S. Supreme Ct. 1983. Legis. asst., speechwriter U.S. Senator John V. Tunney, Washington, 1975-76; sr. editor Va. Jour. of Internat. Law, 1978-79; assoc. Brown and Bain PA, Phoenix, 1979-85, ptnr., 1985-90; gen. counsel New Times, Inc., Phoenix, 1990-92; ptnr. Steptoe & Johnson, Phoenix, 1992—; vis. prof. Ariz. State U., Tempe, 1985. Co-author: Libel Defense Resource Center: 50-State Survey, 1982-89. Bd. dirs. Ariz. chpt. ACLU, Phoenix, 1984-85, Ariz. Ctr. for Law in the Pub. Interest, Phoenix, 1983—, pres., 1989-90; chmn. Yale Alumni Schs. Com., Phoenix, 1984-87; vice chmn. City of Phoenix Solicitation Bd., 1986-88, chmn., 1988-89. Mem. ABA (forum com. on communication law 1984—, concerned correspondents network com. 1979—), Ariz. Bar Assn. Democrat. Clubs: Yale (bd. dirs. Phoenix club 1979—), Ariz. Acad. Office: Steptoe & Johnson 3300 N Central Ave Ste 1650 Phoenix AZ 85012

BOECK, LARRY JAMES, insurance agent; b. Portland, Oreg., Nov. 8, 1947; s. Elton Richard and Nancy Jane (DeYoung) B.; m. Regina Alice Burk, June 7, 1968; children: Andrea, Bradley Jason. BS, Oreg. State U., 1970. CLU, 1976, chartered fin. cons., 1985. Agt. Standard Ins. Co., Salem, Oreg., 1969-70, 72-74, asst. mgr., 1974-79; agy. mgr. Standard Ins. Co., Medford, Oreg., 1979-81; agt. Standard Ins. Co., Medford, 1981—; ptnr. Security Ins. Agy., Inc., Medford, 1981—; agts. adv. coun. Blue Cross/Blue Shield Oreg., Portland, 1987-89; bd. dirs. Health Masters of Oreg., Inc., Medford, Rogue Valley Physicians Svc., Medford. Pres., bd. dirs. Medford unit Am. Cancer Soc., 1979-89; bd. dirs. So. Oreg. Drug Awareness, Medford, 1988—, Rogue Vallely Transp. Dist., Medford, 1989-91. Lt. (j.g.) USN, 1970-72. Mem. Am. Soc. CLU, Rogue Valley Life Underwriters Assn. (pres. 1982-84), Oreg. Life Underwriters Assn. (pres. 1986-87), Nat. Assn. Life Underwriters (chmn. pub. svc. com. 1990—), Rotary, Rogue Valley Country Club, Million Dollar Roundtable. Republican. Home: 90 Fair Oaks Dr Medford OR 97504-7715 Office: Security Ins Agy Inc PO Box 4640 Medford OR 97501-0269

BOEDER, THOMAS L., lawyer; b. St. Cloud, Minn., Jan. 10, 1944; s. Oscar Morris and Eleanor (Gile) B.; m. Carol-Leigh Coombs, Apr. 6, 1968. BA, Yale U., 1965, LLB, 1968. Bar: Wash. 1970, U.S. Dist. Ct. (we. dist.) Wash. 1970, U.S. Dist. Ct. (ea. dist.) Wash. 1972, U.S. Ct. Appeals (9th cir.) 1970, U.S. Supreme Ct. 1974, U.S. Ct. Appeals (D.C. cir.) 1975. Litigation atty. Wash. State Atty. Gen., Seattle, 1970-72, antitrust div. head, 1972-76, chief, consumer protection and antitrust, 1976-78, also sr. asst. atty. gen. and criminal enforcement, 1979-81; ptnr. Perkins Coie, Seattle, 1981—. Served with U.S. Army, 1968-70, Vietnam. Mem. ABA (antitrust sect.), Wash. State Bar Assn. (antitrust sect.). Lutheran. Office: Perkins Coie 1201 3rd Ave Fl 40 Seattle WA 98101-3099

BOEHLKE, WILLIAM FREDRICK, public relations executive; b. Chgo., Dec. 16, 1946; s. William Fredrick and Cynthia Charlotte (Blackmore) B.; m. Christine Ann Chervenak, July 19, 1969. Student, Wharton Sch. Bus., Phila., 1965-69. Pres. and CEO Data Solve Corp., Chgo., 1981-84, Lati Corp. Inc., San Francisco, 1985-89; chmn. Phase Two Strategies Inc., San Francisco, 1989—. Contbr. articles to profl. jours. Mem. IEEE, USR/Group, Assn. Computing Machinery, San Francisco Bay Club. Office: Phase Two Strategies Inc 170 Columbus Ave San Francisco CA 94133-5148

BOEHM, FELIX HANS, physicist, educator; b. Basel, Switzerland, June 9, 1924; came to U.S., 1952, naturalized, 1964; s. Hans G. and Marguerite (Philippi) B.; m. Ruth Sommerhalder, Nov. 26, 1956; children: Marcus F., Claude N. M.S., Inst. Tech., Zurich, 1948, Ph.D., 1951. Research assoc. Inst. Tech., Zurich, Switzerland, 1949-52; Boese fellow Columbia U., 1952-53; faculty Calif. Inst. Tech., Pasadena, 1953—; prof. physics Calif. Inst. Tech., 1961—, William L. Valentine prof., 1985—; Sloan fellow, 1962-64, Niels Bohr Inst., Copenhagen, 1965-66, Cern, Geneva, 1971-72, Laue-Langevin Inst., 1980. Recipient Humboldt award, 1980. Fellow Am. Phys. Soc.; mem. Nat. Acad. Scis. Home: 2510 N Altadena Dr Altadena CA 91001-2836 Office: Calif Inst Tech Mail Code 161 33 Pasadena CA 91125

BOEHMER, CLIFFORD BERNARD, nuclear engineer, lawyer; b. St. Louis, Aug. 25, 1927; s. Arthur Herman and Pearl (Schmering) B.; m. Mary Frances Wilson, Aug. 19, 1950 (dec.); children: Richard, Robert, Terry, Sally; m. Joan Schweitzer Ashbrook, Sept. 5, 1981; m. Elaine Loeb Norman, May 18, 1985. BSEE, Washington U., 1952; MS in Physics, Drexel U., 1960; LLB, LaSalle Extension U., 1974. Bar: Calif. 1974, Fed. 1974, Ct. of Patent and Trademarks, 1978; registered profl. engr., Calif. Sr. engr. White Rodger Electric Co., St. Louis, 1953-56, Martin Co., Balt., 1956-61; supr. Westinghouse Electric Co., Pitts., 1961-64, 65-67; staff mem. Los Alamos Sci. Lab., Jackass Flats, Nev., 1964-65; sr. safety mgr. McDonnell Douglas Co., Huntington Beach, Calif., 1967—; pvt. practice law Mission Viejo, Calif., 1978—. Pres. Mission Viejo (Calif.) High Sch. Coun., 1970-71, Tustin (Calif.) Sch. Dist. Coun., 1971-72. 1st lt. U.S. Army, 1946-47, 52-53. Republican. Roman Catholic. Home: 25266 Pacifica Ave San Juan Capistrano CA 92691-3841 Office: 5301 Bolsa Ave Huntington Beach CA 92647-2099

BOEHMER, RONALD GLENN, financial executive; b. Detroit, Apr. 12, 1947; s. Harry Byron and Ollie Violet (Kumka) B.; m. Linda Dershow, July 10, 1977 (div. Nov. 1981); m. Valerie Jean Adams, Sept. 1, 1984; 1 child, Cathryn Megan. BS, Xavier U., Cin., 1969. Worker's compensation adjuster Liberty Mut. Ins. Co., Southfield, Mich., 1971-73; area mgr. Reed, Roberts Assocs., Southfield, 1973-79, Frick Co., Southfield, 1979-81; div. svc. mgr. Frick Co., Chgo., 1981-86; div. mgr. Frick Co., Thousand Oaks, Calif., 1986—; mem. labor adv. com. Mich. C. of C., 1979-81, Minn. Assn. Commerce and Industry, 1981-86, Ill. C. of C., 1981-86, Calif. C. of C., 1986—, Assn. Wash. Bus., 1986—. Mem. Young Friends of Art, Chgo., 1981-84. Capt. U.S. Army, 1969-71, Vietnam. Republican. Roman Catholic. Home: 1476 Calle Colina Thousand Oaks CA 91360-6815 Office: The Frick Co PO Box 9235 Van Nuys CA 91409-9235

BOEKELHEIDE, VIRGIL CARL, chemistry educator; b. Cheslea, S.D., July 28, 1919; s. Charles F. and Eleonor (Toennies) B.; m. Caroline Barrett, Apr. 7, 1924; children: Karl, Anne, Erich. AB magna cum laude, U. Minn., Mpls., 1939, PhD, 1943. Instr. U. Ill., Urbana, 1943-46; asst. prof. to prof. U. Rochester, 1946-60; prof. dept. chemistry U. Oreg., Eugene, 1960—. Contbr. articles to profl. jours. Recipient Disting. Achievement award U. Minn., 1967; recipient Alexander von Humboldt award W.Ger. Govt., 1974, 82, Centenary Lectureship Royal Soc. G.B., 1983, Coover award Iowa State U., 1981; Disting. scholar designate U.S.-China Acad. Sci., 1981; Fulbright Disting. prof. Yugoslavia, 1972. Mem. NAS, Pharm. Soc. Japan (hon.). Home: 2017 Elk Ave Eugene OR 97403-1788 Office: U Oreg Dept Chemistry Eugene OR 97403

BOERSMA, LAWRENCE ALLAN, animal welfare administrator; b. London, Ontario, Can., Apr. 24, 1932; s. Harry Albert and Valerie Kathryn (DeCordova) B.; m. Nancy Noble Jones, Aug. 16, 1952 (div. 1962) children: Juliana Jaye, Dirk John; m. June Elaine Schiefer McKim, Nov. 22, 1962; children: Kenneth Thomas McKim, Mark Rennie McKim. BA, U. Nebr., 1953, MS, 1955; PhD, Sussex U., 1972. Journalism tchr. Tech. High Sch., Omaha, Nebr., 1953-55; dir. pub. rels., chair journalism dept. Adams State Coll., Alamosa, Colo., 1955-59; advt. sales analyst, advt. salesman Better Homes and Gardens, Des Moines, N.Y.C., 1959-63; advt. account exec. This Week Mag., N.Y.C., 1963-66; eastern sales dir., mktg. dir. Ladies' Home Jour., N.Y.C., 1966-75; v.p. assoc. pub., v.p. pub. Saturday Evening Post and The Country Gentleman, N.Y.C., 1975; v.p., dir. mktg. and advt. sales Photo World Mag., N.Y.C., 1975-77; advt. mgr. LaJolla (Calif.) Light, 1977-80; owner, photographer Allan/The Animal Photographers, San Diego, 1980—; pres., CEO The Photographic Inst. Internat., 1982-86; dir. community rels. San Diego Humane Soc. and Soc. for the Prevention of Cruelty to Animals, 1985—; adj. asst. prof. Grad. Sch. of Bus., Pace U., N.Y.C., 1964-65; adj. instr. N.Y. Inst. of Advt., 1974-77; adj. prof. Sch. of Bus., Mesa Coll., San Diego, 1981-84, City Coll., San Diego, 1982-86; adj. prof. Coll. Bus. Adminstrn. U. LaVerne, San Diego, 1985; pres., CEO United Animal Welfare Found., San Diego, 1992—. Contbr. and photographer articles to mags. Spokesperson Coalition for Pet Population Control, San Diego, 1990, Com. Against Proposition C-Pound Animals for Med. Rsch., San Diego, 1990, Spay-Neuter Action Project, 1991, mem. steering com., 1991, bd. dirs., 1992-93; mem. evaluation subcom. County of San Diego Dept. Animal Control Adv. Com.; chair Feral Cat Coalition of San Diego County, 1992-93. Fellow Royal Photographic Soc. of Great Britain, Profl. Photographers of Calif.; mem. PRSA (chmn. So. Tier, N.Y. chpt. 1972), Al Bahr Shrine (pres. 1988, Businessmen's Club), Shriners, Masons, Soc. Animal Welfare Adminstrs., Nat. Soc. Fund Raising Execs. (bd. dirs. 1988-89, treas. San Diego chpt. 1990-91, mem. nat. faculty, 1992-93). Republican. Presbyterian. Home: 3503 Argonne St San Diego CA 92117-1009 Office: San Diego Human Soc/SPCA 887 Sherman St San Diego CA 92110-4088

BOETTGER, WILLIAM F., integrated information management executive; b. Ravenna, Ohio, Oct. 18, 1945; s. William Henry and Annabelle (Myers) B.; m. Patricia Ann Mackey, Aug. 25, 1972; children: Rebecca, Micki, Ella. BS in Math., U. Wash., 1971; BA, Ind. U., 1966. Tech. aide, propulsion staff Boeing Comml. Airplane Co., Everett, Wash., 1974-77, graphics operator, 1977-81, CAD-CAM systems analyst, 1977-83; prin. cons. Control Data Corp., Mpls., 1983-86; exec. cons. CAE and CIM implementations Control Data, Bellevue, Wash., 1986—. With USAF, 1965-68. Office: PO Box 628 Freeland WA 98249-0628

BOGARD, DAVID KENNETH, service executive; b. Peoria, Ill., Mar. 6, 1953; s. Dallas Kenneth and Emma Sue (Baker) B.; m. Candietta Ann Dominguez, May 7, 1976; children: Brittney Ann, Preston David, Breanna Sue. BA, So. Ill. U., 1974. Treas., v.p. Ken Bogard Remodeling, East Peoria, Ill., 1977-82; zone supr. Allright Houston, Inc., 1982-83; ops. auditor western div. Allright Auto Parks, Inc., Houston, 1983-84; city mgr. Allright San Francisco, 1984-86, Bay Park/Oakland, Calif., 1985-86; asst. regional mgr. no. Calif. and Nev. Allright Calif., Inc., 1986; regional mgr. no. Calif. Allright Sierra/ Nev., 1986-89; v.p. N.W. Parking Svcs. Inc., 1989; regional v.p. Allright Corp., Sacramento, 1990—. Republican. Office: Allright Corp 708 10th St Ste 140 Sacramento CA 95814-1806

BOGARD-REYNOLDS, CHRISTINE ELIZABETH, financial services executive; b. Aberdeen, Md., Apr. 15, 1954; d. Charles Francis and Donna June (Mosbaugh) Bogard; divorced; 1 child, Zachary Kagan; m. Cary Polevoy. Student, U. Colo., 1972-73. Adminstrv. asst. Lange Co., Broomfield, Colo., 1973-74; field sales and svc. rep. Bowman Products Div., Denver, 1974-75; cashier Regency Inn, Denver, 1975-76; gen. mgr., sec.-treas., Edison Agy. Inc., Denver, 1976-81; gen. mgr. Edison Press, Inc., Englewood, Colo., 1979-80, 81; advt. dir. Blinder, Robinson & Co., Englewood, 1981-89; v.p., sec.-treas. CBF Market Svcs. (named change to Comvest Corp.), Inc., 1989-91; owner Document Prep., Englewood, Colo., 1991—; corp. sec. Child Care Ctrs. North Am., Inc. Home: 5021 W Rowland Ave Littleton CO 80123 Office: Document Prep 7310 S Alton Way Englewood CO 80112-2317

BOGART, MARK HANKS, geneticist; b. Oakland, Calif., July 21, 1950; s. Tudo Misha and Luisa E. Bogart; 1 child, Ine L. AS, Southwestern U., Chula Vista, Calif., 1971; BA, U. Calif. at San Diego, LaJolla, 1973; PhD, U. Calif. at San Diego, 1988. Diplomate Am. Bd. Med. Genetics; cert. clin. cytogeneticist. Rsch. assoc. U. Calif. at San Diego, LaJolla, 1973-74, 80-83, assoc. specialist, 1983-89, rsch. geneticists, 1989—; rsch. technician San Diego Zoo, 1975-77, zoologist/primatologist, 1978-79; asst. dir. Med. Genetics, LaJolla, 1990—. Contbr. numerous articles to profl. jours.; inventor method of assessing placental dysfunction. Recipient Inventor of Yr. S.D. Patent Law Assn., 1989. Fellos Zool. Soc.; mem. Japanese Teratology Soc., Am. Soc. of Human Genetics, Clin. Ligand Assay Soc., Am. Soc. of Clin. Chemistry, N.Y. Acad. Scis. Home: U Calif at San Diego Med Genetics 0639 La Jolla CA 92093

BOGART, WANDA LEE, interior designer; b. Ashville, N.C., Feb. 26, 1939; d. Bob West and Virginia Elizbeth (Worley) McLemore-Snyder; m. Sterling X. Bogart, Feb. 12, 1962; children: Kevin Sterling, Kathleen Elizabeth. BA, San Jose (Calif.) State U., 1961. Tchr. Redondo Beach (Calif.) Sch. Dist., 1962-65; free-lance interior designer Ladera, Calif., 1970-75; designer MG Interior Design, Orange, Calif., 1975-80; prin., pres. Wanda Bogart Interior Design Inc., Orange, 1980—. Contbr. articles to profl. jours. Named on of Top 20 Interior Designers in So. Calif. Ranch and Coast Mag., 1987. Mem. Internat. Soc. Interior Design, Orange C. of C. Office: Wanda Bogart Interior Design Inc 1440 E Chapman Ave Orange CA 92666-2279

BOGDAN, JAMES THOMAS, secondary education educator, electronics researcher and developer; b. Kingston, Pa., Aug. 14, 1938; s. Fabian and Edna A. (Spray) B.; m. Carolyn Louetta Carpenter, May 5, 1961; 1 child, Thomas James. BS in Edn., Wilkes U., Wilkes-Barre, Pa., 1960. Cert. chemistry and physics tchr., Calif. Tchr. Forty Fort (Pa.) Sch. Dist., 1960-63; tchr., chmn. sci. dept. L.A. Unified Sch. Dist., 1963—; owner, mgr. Bogdan Electronic Rsch. & Devel., Lakewood, Calif., 1978—; cons. Lunar Electronics, San Diego, 1978-83, T.E. Systems, L.A., 1988-89. Author, pub. The VHF Reporter newsletter, 1967-76. Tng. officer L.A. County Disaster Communications, 1968-91, UHF & microwave systems staff officer, 1991—; pin chmn. Tournament of Roses Communications Group, Pasadena, Calif., 1985—. Republican. Office: PO Box 62 Lakewood CA 90714-0062

BOGEN, JOSEPH ELLIOT, neurosurgeon, educator; b. Cin., July 13, 1926; m. Glenda A. Miksch, 1955; children: Meriel, Mira. AB in Econs., Whittier Coll., 1949; postgrad., U. Cin., 1950, UCLA, 1951; MD, U. So. Calif., 1956. Lic. physician, Calif.; diplomate Am. Bd. Neurol. Surgery. Intern in surgery The N.Y. Hosp., 1956-57, asst. resident in surgery, 1957-58; resident in neurosurgery White Meml. Hosp., 1959-63; asst. in neurology Loma Linda U., 1963; asst. clin. prof. neurosurgery Calif. Coll. Medicine, 1964-68; cons. in neurosurgery Calif. Inst. Tech., 1968; assoc. clin. prof. U. So. Calif., 1973-77, clin. prof., 1977—; adj. prof. UCLA, 1984—. With USNR, 1944-46. Fellow ACS; mem. AAAS, L.A. Soc. Neurol. Psychiatry (bd. dirs. 1975, pres. 1983), So. Calif. Neurosurg. Soc. (pres. 1976), Am. Acad. Neurology, Am. Assn. Neurol. Surgeons, Soc. for Neurosci., Behavioral Neurol. Soc., Western Pain Soc., Am. Pain Soc., Calif. Neuropsychol. Soc., Internat. Neuropsychol. Soc., Acad. of Aphasia (bd. govs. 1976-80).

BOGER, DAN CALVIN, economics educator, statistical and economic consultant; b. Salisbury, N.C., July 9, 1946; s. Brady Cashwell and Gertrude Virginia (Hamilton) B.; m. Gail Lorraine Zivna, June 23, 1973; children: Gretchen Zivna, Gregory Zivna. B.S. in Mgmt. Sci., U. Rochester, 1968; M.S. in Mgmt. Sci., Naval Postgrad. Sch., Monterey, Calif., 1969; M.A. in Stats., U. Calif.-Berkeley, 1977, Ph.D. in Econs., 1979. Cert. cost analyst, profl. estimator. Research asst. U. Calif.-Berkeley, 1975-79; asst. prof. econs. Naval Postgrad. Sch., Monterey, Calif., 1979-85, assoc. prof., 1985-92, prof., 1992—; bd. dirs. Evan-Moor Corp., 1992—; cons. econs. and statis. legal matters CSX Corp, others, 1977—. Assoc. editor The Logistics and Transportation Rev., 1981-85, Jour. of Cost Analysis, 1989-92; mem. editorial rev. bd. Jour. Transp. Research Forum, 1987-91; contbr. articles to profl. jours. Served to lt. USN, 1968-75. Flood fellow Dept. Econs., U. Calif.-Berkeley, 1975-76; dissertation research grantee A.P. Sloan Found., 1978-79. Mem. Am. Econ. Assn., Am. Statis. Assn., Econometric Soc., Math. Assn. Am., Inst. Mgmt. Sci., Ops. Research Soc. Am. (sec., treas. mil. applications sect. 1987-91), Sigma Xi. Home: 61 Ave Maria Rd Monterey CA 93940-4407 Office: Naval Postgrad Sch Code AS/Bo Monterey CA 93943

BOGGIO, DENNIS RAY, architect; b. Detroit, Jan. 28, 1953; s. Michael Anthony and Esther Theresa Boggio; m. Meredith Coleen Ream, June 25, 1983. BArch, Ohio State U., 1975; MArch, U. Colo., 1977. Lic. architect, Colo., Wyo., Utah, N.M., Ga., Ariz., Nev., Calif., Okla., Minn. Ptnr. Lantz-Boggio Architects, Denver, 1980—; visiting critic Sch. Architecture, U. Colo., Denver, 1981—. Author: The Architecture of Assisted Living Residences, 1993. Recipient Design Excellence award USAF Acad., 1985. Mem. AIA, Nat. Assn. Sr. Living Industries, Assisted Living Facilities Assn. Am., Denver C. of C., Centennial C. of C., Rotary. Home: 8101 E Dartmouth Ave House 53 Denver CO 80231-4260 Office: Lantz-Boggio Architects 5200 Dtc Pky Ste 500 Englewood CO 80111-2720

BOGGS, CARL ELWOOD, JR., political scientist, writer; b. Long Beach, Calif., July 22, 1937; s. Carl Elwood and Harriet M. (Watts) B.; m. Ann Incaviglia, Nov. 20, 1961 (div. 1970). BA, U. Calif., Berkeley, 1963, MA,

1965, PhD, 1970. Prof. Wash. U., St. Louis, 1970-77, U. Calif., Irvine, 1977-78, UCLA, 1978-81, U. So. Calif., L.A., 1981-84, Capleton U., Ottawa, Can., 1984-85, Nat. U., L.A., 1986—. Author: The Two Revolutions, 1984, Gramsci's Marxism, 1976, The Impasse of European Communism, 1982, Social Movements and Political Power, 1986, Intellectuals and the Crisis of Modernity, 1993; contbg. writer L.A. Weekly/Village View, 1989—; mem. editorial bd. Theory and Soc., 1977—, Socialist Rev., 1971—, Humanities in Soc., 1981-83, Radical Am., 1977—, Democracy and Socialism, 1989—. Mem. Peace and Freedom Party, Calif., 1968; L.A. coord. Green's, 1988-91; radio programmer Sta. KPFK, L.A., 1981—. Ford Found. fellow, 1967, teaching award fellow Wash. U., 1972, Dean's Coun. award Carleton U., 1985. Home: 1251 Wellesley # 103 Los Angeles CA 90025 Office: Nat U 9920 S La Cienega Los Angeles CA 90301

BOGGS, DAVID WILLIAM, manufacturing engineer; b. Porland, Oreg., July 31, 1958; s. Harry Wayne and Avis Marlene (Morrow) B.; m. Deidra Lynn Brown, May 19, 1990; children: David William II, Daniel Wayne. BS in Chemistry, Portland State U., 1986. Process operator Tektronix, Inc., Beaverton, Oreg., 1978-79, process design technician, 1979-83, mfg. process engr., 1983—. Patentee for Method of Fabricating a Printed Circuit Board. Office: Tektronix Inc PO Box 500 Beaverton OR 97077

BOGGS, GEORGE EDWARD, JR., quality assurance executive; b. River Rouge, Mich., Sept. 23, 1946; s. George Edward and Elvira (Ponder) B.; m. Cheryl Ann Hamilton, Apr. 20, 1984; children: George Edward III, Jared Alan. BA, Eastern Mich. U., 1972; MBA, U. Phoenix, 1987. Supr. Ford Motor Co., Ypsilanti, Mich., 1970-77; inspector Dept. Def., Detroit, 1978-79; quality engr. Williams Internat., Walled Lake, Mich., 1979-81, Unidynamics Def. Systems, Goodyear, Ariz., 1981-84, Tiernay Turbines, inc., Phoenix, 1984-85; audit mgr. Motorola Govt. Electronics, Scottsdale, Ariz., 1985-90; compliance program mgr. Sundstrand Aerospace, Phoenix, 1990—. With U.S. Army, 1968-70, Vietnam. Decorated Bronze Star, Army Commendation medal with oak leaf. Mem. Am. Soc. Quality Control (sr. mem., cert. quality engr.), VFW. Democrat. Mem. Ch. of Christ. Home: 13229 S 48th St Phoenix AZ 85044

BOGGS, STEVEN EUGENE, lawyer; b. Santa Monica, Calif., Apr. 28, 1947; s. Eugene W. and Annie (Happe) B. BA in Econ., U. Calif., Santa Barbara, 1969; D of Chiropractic summa cum laude, Cleveland Chiropractic, L.A., 1974; PhD in Fin. Planning, Columbia Pacific U., 1986; JD in Law, U. So. Calif., 1990. Bar: Calif. 1990, U.S. Dist. Ct. (cen. dist.) Calif. 1990, Hawaii 1991, U.S. Ct. Appeals (9th cir.); CFP; lic. real estate salesman, Hawaii; lic. chiropractor Hawaii, Calif.; lic. radiography X-ray supr. and operator. Faculty mem. Cleveland Chiropractic Coll., 1972-74; pres. clinic dir. Hawaii Chiropratic Clinic, Inc., Aiea, 1974-87; pvt. practice Honolulu, 1991—; cons. in field; seminar presenter 1990—. Contbr. articles to profl. jours. Recipient Cert. Appreciation State of Hawaii, 1981-84. Fellow Internat. Coll. of Chiropractic; mem. ABA, Am. Trial Lawyers Assn., Am. Trial Lawyers Assn. of Hawaii, Am. Chriopractic Assn., Hawaii State Chiropractic Assn. (pres. 1978, 85, 86, v.p. 1977, sec. 1979-84, treas. 1976, other coms., Valuable Svc. award 1984, Cert. Appreciation 1986, Cert. Achievement 1986, Chiropractor of Yr. 1986, Outstanding Achievement award 1991). Democrat. Office: 804 Fort St Mall Honolulu HI 96813

BOGINIS, JAMES WILLIAM, aerospace executive; b. N.Y.C., Feb. 17, 1937; s. James Anthony Boginis and Estelle (Rosenbloom) Howard; m. Joanna Mildred Eberhart, Sept. 4, 1957; children: Patricia Annette Dolinger, John Charles, Thomas Herbert. BS, U. Ariz., 1958; MBA, Tulane U., New Orleans, 1967. Chemist E.I. duPont de Nemours & Co., Inc., Aiken, S.C., 1958-59; policy analyst U.S. Dept. Def., Washington, 1971-73, U.S. EPA, Washington, 1973-74; fin. mgr. CIA, Washington, 1974-87; aerospace exec. Martin Marietta Corp., Denver, 1987—; mem. naval studies bd. NSF; lectr. Nat. Security Agy., Ft. Meade, Md., 1977-87, CIA, Washington, 1977-87. Sr. warden St. James Episcopal Ch., Mt. Vernon, Va., 1973-81. With U.S. Army, 1959-71. Decorated Bronze Star; recipient Nat. Intelligence Disting. Svc. medal CIA, Washington, 1987. Mem. Armed Forces Communications and Electronics Assn. (mem. intelligence com. 1988—), Security Affairs Support Assn. Republican. Office: Martin Marietta PO Box 179 MS DC4010 Denver CO 80201

BOGNAR, CHARLES RALPH, marketing director; b. Phila., Feb. 2, 1926; s. Charles S. and Anna Bognar. Student Pa. State U., 1957-67; m. Bernadine L. Schantz, Oct. 2, 1948. Tool and model maker in machine shop Franklin Inst. Research Labs., Phila., 1949-55, sr. tech. assoc. friction lubrication div., 1955-70, sr. test engr. utilities svcs. group, 1970-73; mgr. test ops. and co-founder turbo exptl. div. Turbo Rsch., West Chester, Pa., 1973-75; co-founder Energy Tech., Inc., West Chester, 1975, v.p., dir. mktg., 1975-79; new bus. devel. mktg. spl. svcs. div. Ebasco Svcs., Inc., N.Y.C., 1979-80, mgr. project devel./mktg. for process indsl. div., Los Angeles, 1980-83, mgr. project devel./mktg. for indsl. bus. devel. for Pacific S.W. and Hawaii, 1983-86; regional sales mgr. Pall Well Tech. Corp. (subs. Pall Micro Trinity Corp.), 1986-89; regional mgr. bus. devel. UltraSystems Engrs. & Constructors div. Hadson Power Systems, Irvine, Calif., 1989-90, dir. of mktg., 1990-91; regional mgr. indsl. sales Mectron Industries, Inc. (subs. of Pall Corp.), 1991—. Mem. ASME, Soc. Petroleum Engrs., Am. Cogeneration Assn., Rsch. Engrs. Soc. Am., Sigma Xi. Home: 788 Park Shore Dr A-20 Naples FL 33940 Office: Mectron Industries Inc 6301 49th St N Pinellas Park FL 34665

BOGUS, SDIANE ADAMS, English language educator, poet, publisher; b. Chgo., Jan. 22, 1946; d. Lawrence and Florence B.; m. T. Nelson Gilbert, Apr. 1, 1989. BA, Stillman Coll., 1968; MA, Syracuse U., 1969; PhD, Miami U., Oxford, Ohio, 1988. Publisher Woman in The Moon Pub., Cuprtino, Calif., 1979—; prof. Am. lit. Calif. State U.-Stanislaus, Turlock, Calif., 1986-90; instr. composition DeAnza Coll., Cupertino, 1990—. Author: I'm Off to See the Goddamn Wizard, Alright!, 1971, Woman in The Moon, 1979, Sapphire's Sampler, 1982, Dykehands and Sutras Erotic & Lyric, 1989, The Chant of the Women of Magdalena, 1990, For the Love of Men, 1990. Active Christian Childrens Fund. Recipient award Art and Music Dept., Trenton Pub. Libr., 1983, named innovator of the Yr. 1992-93, Black Writers award Penninsula Book Club, 1992. Mem. Nat. Tchrs. English, Multicultural Pubs. Exchange, COSMP Indep. Pubs., Delta Sigma Theta. Democrat. Buddhist. Home: PO Box 2087 Cupertino CA 95015-2087

BOHANSKE, ROBERT THOMAS, psychologist; b. Amsterdam, N.Y., June 22, 1953; s. Thomas A. and Nadine K. (Grayson) B.; m. Jacquie C. Scholar, Apr. 20, 1980; children: Michael S., Jason A. BS, Ariz. State U., 1975; MS, U. So. Calif., 1977; PhD, U. Ariz., 1983. Lic. psychologist, Ariz., Calif. Resident Inst. Behavioral Medicine, Phoenix, 1982-83, postdoctoral fellow, 1983-84, asst. dir. out-patient services, 1985-87; chief psychologist Behavioral Health Inst. Mesa (Ariz.) Luth. Hosp., 1987-88; chief psychologist, clin. dir neurobehavioral program Meridian Pt. Rehab. Hosp., Scottsdale, Ariz., 1988-91; pvt. practice rehab. neuropsychology Mesa and Scottsdale, Ariz., 1991—; pres. MARC Behavioral Health Svcs., 1990—, Behavioral Edn. Inst., Mesa, 1992—. Mem. APA, Ariz. Psychol. Assn., Am. Congress of Rehab. Medicine. Jewish. Home: 5045 E Redfield Rd Scottsdale AZ 85254-2847 Office: 2058 S Dobson Rd Ste 3 Mesa AZ 85202-6455

BOHL, RANDALL JOSEPH, commercial photographer; b. South Bend, Ind., May 16, 1962. BS in Comms., Western Mich. U., 1984. 1st asst. Jim Powell Advt. Photography, Kalamazoo, Mich., 1984-88; owner Randall Bohl Photography, San Francisco, 1988-91, Scottsdale, Ariz., 1991—. Mem. Pro-Tip Inc. Home and Office: Randall Bohl Photography 6832 E Moreland St Scottsdale AZ 85257

BOHLIN, CAROL FRY, mathematics educator; b. Charlotte, N.C., Feb. 15, 1958; d. P. Allen and Carolyn J. (Sigmon) Fry.; married. BA, U. N.C., 1980, M of Human Devel. and Learning, 1982; PhD in Math. Edn. and Cognitive Neurosci., Ohio State U., 1987. Tchr. math. Quail Hollow Jr. High Sch., Charlotte, 1980-83; grad. teaching asst. Ohio State U., Columbus, 1983-87, asst. prof., 1987-88; asst. prof. math. edn. Ind. U., Bloomington, 1988-90; asst. prof. math. edn. Calif. State U., Fresno, 1990-93, assoc. prof., 1993—; dir. San Joaquin Valley Math. Project, Fresno, 1990—; cons. Fresno County Office Edn., 1990—; chmn. Mid. Sch. Math. Field Day, Fresno, 1990—. Editor: A Problem a Day for Primary People, 1990; also articles. Lowry Harding fellow Ohio State U., 1984; Calif. Jaycees Outstanding Young Educator award, 1992. Mem. ASCD, APA, Am. Ednl. Rsch. Assn., Sch. Sci. and Math. Assn. (fin. com. 1990—), Nat. Coun. Tchrs. Math. (life). Calif. Math. Coun. (cons. 1990—), Math. Assn. Am., Am. Coun. for Learning Disabilities, Mid-Western Ednl. Rsch. Assns., Am. Psychol. Soc. (charter), Internat. Soc. for Tech. in Edn., Internat. Group for Psychology Math. Edn., N.Am. Group for Psychology Math. Edn., Internat. Orgn. Women and Math. Edn., Learning Disabilities Assn. Am., Ohio Coun. Tchrs. Math., Ind. Coun. Tchrs. Math., Phi Beta Kappa. Republican. Lutheran. Office: Calif State U Sch Edn and Human Devel 5310 N Campus Dr Fresno CA 93740-0002

BOHLMANN, DANIEL ROBERT, financial planner, lawyer, real estate investor and broker; b. Portland, Oreg., Apr. 28, 1948; s. Walter Richard and Nora Laticia (DeCandido) B. AA with honors, Multnomah Jr. Coll., 1969; BSBA in Polit. Sci. and Bus. Adminstrn., Lewis & Clark Coll., 1970; JD, Northwestern U., 1974. Bar: Oreg. 1976, U.S. Dist. Ct. Oreg. 1976, U.S. Ct. Appeals (9th cir.) 1980, U.S. Supreme Ct. 1982. Supr. Bohlmann & Bohlmann Investment Trust, 1970—; pvt. practice Oreg., 1976—; chief exec. Atlas Internat. Investments, Ltd., 1981—; officer, co-owner, investor Investors Gen. Computer Software, Inc., 1981-89; investor, founder Rangefinder Petroleum, Ltd., Black Giant Mining & Petroleum; founder, owner Sun West Energy, Inc.; owner Gem-Con, Inc., 1979-81, Hopps Body and Paint Shop, Inc., 1976-80; owner Racquet Club Cove Hotel/Apts. Palm Springs; broker assoc. Century-21, Van Lizzen, Palm Springs Realtors; bd. dirs. Shakey's Pizza, Palm Springs, Unique Locations Internat., Creative Destinations Internat., Willamette Dem. Soc., 1976-81. Contbr. articles to fin. jours. Internat. fin. advisor U.S. Presdl. Task Force, 1981-84; mem. subcom. Oreg. Bd. Edn., 1973-75; alumni bd. Lewis & Clark Coll.; elected precinct committeeman, Oreg., 1976, 78, 80; mem. U.S. Senatorial Bus. Adv. Bd., 1981-83; mem. Oreg. Arts Found., Palm Springs Desert Mus., L.A. Bicentannial Coord. Com., 1975-76, Oreg. Environ. Coun. With USAR, 1967. Named one of Outstanding Young Men of Am. U.S. Jaycees, 1978-85. Mem. Assn. MBA Execs., Assn. Trial Lawyers Am., Oreg. Trial Lawyers Assn., Am. Judicature Soc., Am. Soc. Agrl. Engrs., Nat. Assn. Realtors, Calif. Assn. Realtors, Oreg.-U.S. and Palm Springs C. of C., Internat. Assn. Fin. Planners, Am. Soc. Travel Agts., Soc. Incentive Travel Execs., Assn. Retail Travel Agts., Assn. Meeting Industry Ski Enthusiasts, Travel Agy. Owners & Mgrs. Assn., U.S. Hist. Soc., Smithsonian Assocs., Am. Mgmt. Assn., Nat. Fedn. Ind. Businessmen, Nat. Life Underwriters Assn., Meeting Planners Internat., Hotels Sales and Meeting Assn., Internat. Soc. Meeting Planners, Meeting Cons. Network, U.S. Antique and Collectors Automobile Assn., Am. Legion, Palm Springs Bd. Realtors, Calif. Assn. Realtors, Nat. Assn. Realtors, Calif. Apt. Owners Assn., U.S. Restaurant Owners Assn., Internat. Assn. Travel Agts., Cruise Line Internat. Assn., Auto Body Craftsmen Assn., Variety Club, Columbia River Yacht Club, Desert Mus. Club, Living Desert Res. Club, Palm Springs Womens Press Club (hon. dir.), Rotary, Elks (Nat. Found. Outstanding Benefactor 1980), Phi Alpha Delta, Phi Theta Kappa. Republican. Lutheran. Office: Ste D-108 44489 Town Center Way Palm Desert CA 92260-2723

BOHM, KARL-HEINZ HERMANN, astrophysicist, educator; b. Hamburg, Germany, Sept. 27, 1923; came to U.S., 1968; s. Carl Hermann and Emma (Galonska) B.; m. Erika Helga Vitense, Sept. 19, 1953; children: Hans-Jurgen, Manfred, Helga, Eva. Physik-Diplom, U. Kiel, 1951, Ph.D., 1954. Research astronomer U. Calif., Berkeley, 1955, vis. prof., 1960-61, 63-64; asst. prof., then assoc. prof. U. Kiel, 1957-64; prof. theoretical astrophysics U. Heidelberg, 1964-67; prof. astronomy U. Wash., Seattle, 1968—; pres. commn. stellar atmospheres Internat. Astron. Union, 1964-67; Gauss prof. Goettingen (W. Ger.) Acad. Scis., 1976-77. Contbr. articles to profl. jours., books. Recipient Physics prize Goettingen Acad. Scis., 1958, Humboldt prize Fed. Republic Germany, 1974. Mem. Am. Astron. Soc., Astronomische Gesellschaft. Lutheran. Office: U Wash Astronomy Dept FM 20 Seattle WA 98195

BOHMAN, VERLE RUDOLPH, animal nutritionist; b. Peterson, Utah, Dec. 29, 1924; s. Victor Rudolph and Nancy A. (Fernelius) B.; m. Renee Jorgensen, June 22, 1945; children: Margaret Louise, Verle Duane, Jolene Renee, Van Reid, Gregory Nathan. BS, Utah State U., 1949, MS, 1951; PhD, Cornell U., 1952. Prof., researcher U. Nev., Reno, 1952-86; cons. Vet. Rsch. and Devel., Truckee, Calif., 1986—. Editor-in-chief: Jour. Animal Sci., 1970-72, sec. editor, 1968-70. With USN, 1944-46, PTO. Mem. Am. Soc. Animal Sci. (pres. 1974-75, pres. elect 1973-74). Mormon. Home and Office: 916 Sbragia Way Sparks NV 89431-2111

BOHN, DENNIS ALLEN, electrical engineer, consultant, writer; b. San Fernando, Calif., Oct. 5, 1942; s. Raymond Virgil and Iris Elouise (Johnson) B.; 1 dau., Kira Michelle; m. Patricia Tolle, Aug. 12, 1986. BSEE with honors, U. Calif., Berkeley, 1972, MSEE with honors, 1974. Engring. technician Gen. Electric Co., San Leandro, Calif., 1964-72; research and devel. engr. Hewlett-Packard Co., Santa Clara, Calif., 1973; application engr. Nat. Semicondr. Corp., Santa Clara, 1974-76; engring. mgr. Phase Linear Corp., Lynnwood, Wash., 1976-82; v.p. research and devel., ptnr. Rane Corp., Mukilteo, Wash., 1982—; founder Toleco Systems, Kingston, Wash., 1980. Suicide and crisis ctr. vol., Berkeley, 1972-74, Santa Clara, 1974-76. Served with USAF, 1960-64. Recipient Am. Spirit Honor medal USAF, 1961; Math. Achievement award Chem. Rubber Co., 1962-63. Editor: We Are Not Just Daffodils, 1975; contbr. poetry to Reason mag.; tech. editor Audio Handbook, 1976; contbr. articles to tech. jours.; columnist Polyphony mag., 1981-83; 2 patents in field. Mem. IEEE, Audio Engring. Soc., Tau Beta Pi. Office: Rane Corp 10802 47th Ave W Mukilteo WA 98275-5098

BOHN, HINRICH LORENZ, soil science educator; b. N.Y.C., Aug. 25, 1934; s. Julius T. and Maria Christina (Lorenzen) B.; m. Margaret Ann Johnson, Aug. 4, 1962; children: Kristina, Erika, Karl. BS, U. Calif., Berkeley, 1955, MS, 1957; PhD, Cornell U., 1963. Staff chemist Tenn. Valley Authority, Muscle Shoals, Ala., 1964-66; assoc. prof. soil sci. U. Ariz., Tucson, prof. Author: Soil Chemistry, 1979, 2nd edit., 1985. Recipient Sr. Scientist award A.V. Humboldt Found., Bonn, Fed. Republic of Germany, 1973. Fellow Soil Sci. Soc. Am. Office: Univ Ariz Dept Soil & Water Science 429 Shantz Bldg 38 Tucson AZ 85721

BOHN, PAUL BRADLEY, psychiatrist; b. Santa Monica, Calif., Apr. 11, 1957; s. John Moultrie and June Elizabeth (Bradley) B.; m. Pamela Honey Summit, Nov. 17, 1990. BA in Pharmacology, U. Calif., Santa Barbara, 1980; MD, U. Calif., Irvine, 1984. Diplomate Am. Bd. Psychiatry and Neurology. Psychiat. resident UCLA, 1984-88, assoc. dir. anxiety disorders clinic, 1989—, dir. social anxiety clinic, 1993—; fellow U. So. Calif., L.A., 1988-89; cons. in psychiatry Didi Hirsch Community Mental Health Ctr., Venice, Calif., 1986-88; substance abuse group co-leader Main St. Counseling Svcs., Venice, 1987-88; v.p. Pacific Psychopharmacology Rsch. Inst., Santa Monica, 1990—; pvt. practice psychiatry Santa Monica, 1988—; asst. clin. prof. UCLA, 1990—; candidate L.A. Psychoanalytic Inst., 1988—. Chm. polio com., Rotary Club, Santa Monica, 1992. Grantee Ciba-Geigy, Santa Monica, 1992. Mem. Am. Psychiat. Assn., So. Calif. Psychiat. Assn., Anxiety Disorders Assn. of Am., Obsessive Compulsive Found.. Office: 2730 Wilshire Blvd Ste 325 Santa Monica CA 90403

BOHN, RALPH CARL, education consultant, retired educator; b. Detroit, Feb. 19, 1930; s. Carl and Bertha (Abrams) B.; m. Adella Stanul, Sept. 2, 1950 (dec.); children: Cheryl Ann, Jeffrey Ralph; m. JoAnn Olvera Butler, Feb. 19, 1977 (div. 1990); stepchildren: Kathryn J., Kimberly J., Gregory E.; m. Mariko Tajima, Jan. 27, 1991; 1 child, Thomas Carl; 1 stepchild, Daichi Tajima. BS, Wayne State U., 1951, EdM, 1954, EdD, 1957. Instr. part-time Wayne State U., 1954-55, summer 1956; faculty San Jose (Calif.) State U., 1955-92, prof. div. tech., 1961-92, chmn. dept. indsl. studies, 1960-69, assoc. dean ednl. svc., 1968-70, dean continuing edn., 1970-92, prof. emeritus, 1992—; cons. Calif. State U. Sys., 1992—; cons. quality edn. sys. USAF, 1992—; guest summer faculty Colo. State Coll., 1963, Ariz. State U., 1966, U. P.R., 1967, 74, So. Ill. U., 1970, Oreg. State U., 1971, Utah State U., 1973, Va. Poly. Inst. & State U., 1973, U. Idaho, 1978; cons. U.S. Office of Edn., 1965-70, Calif. Pub. Schs., 1960, Nat. Assessment Ednl. Progress, 1968-79, ednl. div. Philco-Ford Corp., 1970-73, Am. Inst. Rsch., 1969-83, Far West Labs for Ednl. Rsch. Devel., 1971-86, Calif. State U. system, 1992—, USAF Quality Ednl. Sys., 1992—; mem. adv. bd. Ctr. for Vocat. and Tech. Edn., Ohio State U., 1968-74; dir. project Vocat. Edn. Act, 1965-67, NDEA, 1967, 68; co-dir. Project Edn. Profession Devel. Act, 1969, 70; mem. commn. coll. and univ. contracts Western Assn. Schs. and Colls, 1976-78, chmn. spl. com. on off-campus instrn. and continuing edn., 1978-88; chmn. continuing edn. accreditation visit U. Santa Clara, 1976; mem. accreditation team for Azusa Pacific Coll., 1975, Portland State U., 1975, Brigham Young U., 1976, 86, Columbia Coll., 1977, Western Wash. U., 1978, 88, Wash. State U., 1980, 90, Chapman Coll., 1980, Calif. State U., Fullerton, 1981, Westminster Coll., 1983, Columbia U., 1983, Boise State U., 1984, U. Hawaii, Hilo, 1984, U. Oreg., 1987, U. Mont., 1989, Calif. Poly. U., Ponona, 1990, North Island Naval Air Sta., USN, 1990, U. Calif., Irvine, 1991, Western Conservative Bapt. Sem., Oreg., 1992, US Naval Sta., Hawaii, 1992; vice chmn. accreditation team U. Guam, 1978, Pepperdine U., 1979, U. LaVerne, 1980, Azusa Pacific Coll., 1981, Nat. U., 1987, Loma Linda U., 1988, 91; chmn. accreditation team Azusa Pacific Coll, 1977, Calif. Coll. Podiatric Medicine, 1982, So. Ill. U., Carbondale, 1983, Northrup U., 1984, Cogswell Coll., 1986, spl. USAF visitation to George AFB, 1986, Calif. State U., Chico, 1987, Chapman Coll., 1987, Hawaii Loa Coll., 1990, Myrtle Beach Air Force Base, S.C., 1990, U. Hawaii, 1991, Homestead AFB, Fla., 1992, Nellis AFB, Nev., 1992, West Coast U., Calif., 1992, Langley AFB, 1992, Seymour Johnson AFB, N.C., 1992, Shaw AFB, S.C., 1993, Tustin Marine Corps Air Sta., Calif., 1993, El Toro Marine Corps Air Sta., Calif., 1993. Author: (with G.H. Silvius) Organizing Course Materials for Industrial Education, 1961, Planning and Organizing Instruction, 1976; (with A. MacDonald) Power-Mechanics of Energy Control, 1970, 2d edit., 1983, The McKnight Power Experimenter, 1970, (with A. MacDonald), Power and Energy Technology, 1989, (with A. MacDonald): Energy Technology: Power and Transportation, 1992; (with others) Basic Industrial Arts and Power Mechanics, 1978, Technology and Society: Interfaces with Industrial Arts, 1980, Fundamentals of Safety Education, 3d edit., 1981, (with others) Energy, Power and Transportation Technology, 1986, (with A. MacDonald) Energy Technology, Power and Transportation, 1991; editor (with Ralph Norman) Graduate Study in Industrial Arts, 1961; indsl. arts editor Am. Vocat. Jour., 1963-66; editor Jour. Indsl. Tchr. Edn., 1962-64. Lt. (j.g.) USCGR, 1951-53, capt. Res. ret. Recipient award Am. Legion, 1945; Wayne State U. scholar, 1953. Mem. NEA, Nat. Assn. Indsl. Tech. (bd. accreditation), Am. Indsl. Arts. Assn. (pres. 1967-68, Ship's citation 1971), Am. Coun. Indsl. Art Tchrs. Edn. (pres. 1964-66, Man of Yr. awar7), Nat. Univ. Continuing Edn. Assn. (chair accreditation com. 1988-91), Nat. Assn. Indsl. Tchr. Educators (past v.p.), Calif. Indsl. Edn. Assn. (State Ship's citation 1971), Am. Drive Edn. Assn., Nat. Fluid Power Soc., Am. Vocat. Assn. (svc. awards 1966, 67), N.Am. Assn. for Summer Sessions (v.p. western region 1976-78), Luth. Acad. Scholarship, Calif. Employees Assn. (pres. San Jose State Coll. chpt. 1966-67), Western Assn. Summer Session Adminstrs. (newsletter editor 1970-73, pres. 1974-75), Calif. C. of C. (edn. com 1969-77), Industry-Edn. Coun. Calif. (bd. dirs. 1974-80), Sci. and Human Values, Inc. (bd. dirs. 1974—, chmn. bd. 1976—), Tahoe Tavern (bd. dirs. 1987-91, chmn. bd. 1988-90), Seascape Lagoon Homeowners Assn. (bd. dirs. 1988—, chmn. 1989—). Home and Office: 105 Manresa Ct Aptos CA 95003-5722

BOHNENBERGER, DALE VINCENT, water utility executive, mayor pro tem; b. Avenal, Calif., Oct. 3, 1952; s. Ralph Vincent and Allie Mae (Goforth) B.; m. Myra Irene Cooper, Feb. 22, 1981; 1 child, Gregory Vincent. BSCE, Loyola U., 1974. Registered profl. engr., Calif. Domestic water engr. Coachella (Calif.) Valley Water Dist., 1974-84, asst. dep. chief engr., 1984-87, dep. chief engr., 1987-92, dir. engring., 1992—. Mayor pro tem City of La Quinta, Calif., 1984—. Mem. Assn. Calif. Water Agys., League of Calif. Cities, Am. Water Works Assn., La Quinta Rotary (v.p. 1987-88, bd. dirs. 1987-91). Republican. Home: 51-100 Calle Obispo La Quinta CA 92253 Office: Coachella Valley Water Dist PO Box 1058 Coachella CA 92236-1058

BOHNSTEDT, JOAN EMBICK, elementary bilingual educator; b. Van Nuys, Calif., Dec. 11, 1962; d. Edward Michael and Helen Sue (Teufel) Embick; m. Stephen Alan Bohnstedt, July 13, 1991. BA, Cal Luth. U., 1984; cert. tchr., San Diego State U., 1990. Cert. tchr., Calif. Food svc. mgr. Marriott Corp., San Diego, 1985-88; bilingual 2d grade tchr. Escondido (Calif.) Union Sch. Dist., 1990—. Leader Girl Scouts USA, San Diego, 1986-87; youth group advisor All Saints Episcopal Ch., Vista, Calif., 1988—. Mem. Kappa Delta Pi. Home: 11509 Poblado Rd San Diego CA 92127

BOHOR, BRUCE FORBES, geologist; b. Chgo., May 4, 1932; s. Rudolph Edward and Alexandria (Strain) B.; m. Barbara Ann Stegenga, Aug. 29, 1953 (div. 1974); children: Sue Ann, Jacquelin, Laura, Thomas; m. Leah Joan Barrier, June 19, 1983. BS magna cum laude, Beloit Coll., 1953; MA, Ind. U., 1955; PhD, U. Ill., 1959. Research geologist Continental Oil Co., Ponca City, Okla., 1957-65, Ill. Geol. Survey, Urbana, 1965-74, U.S. Geol. Survey, Denver, 1974—. Patentee in field. Fellow G.K. Gilbert, U.S. Geol. Survey, 1984-86, Ill. Clay Products, U. Ill., 1956-57. Mem. AAAS (fellow), Geochem. Soc., Meteoritical Soc., Clay Mineral Soc. (councilor 1981-83), Am. Geophysical Union, Sigma Xi. Office: US Geol Survey DFC MS 972 PO Box 25046 Denver CO 80225-0046

BOHRER, MARK W., electrical engineer; b. Chgo., Apr. 5, 1956; s. Mason L. and Marjorie A. (Proudfoot) B.; m. Jean A. Vrechek, May 17, 1978 (div. June 1985). BSEE, U. Ill., 1977, MSEE, 1982. Design engr. Nat. Semiconductor Corp., Santa Clara, Calif., 1978-79; sr. design engr. Advanced Micro Devices, Sunnyvale, Calif., 1979-84; engring. supr. Advanced Micro Devices, Sunnyvale, 1986-90; electronic design engr. Sequential Circuits, Inc., San Jose, Calif., 1984; staff engr. Precision Monolithics, Inc., Santa Clara, 1984-86; sr. staff engr. Chips & Technologies, Inc., San Jose, 1990-91; design engring. mgr. Micro Linear Corp., San Jose, 1991—. Inventor segmented waveform generator. Counselor for homeless Ultimate City Team, San Jose, 1991-92. Mem. IEEE. Office: Micro Linear Corp 2092 Concourse Dr San Jose CA 95131

BOICE, ROBERT MCINTOSH, JR., state banking administrator; b. Cheyenne, Wyo., May 27, 1958; s. Robert McIntosh and Jacqueline (Brimmer) B. BA, Yale U., 1980; MSc, London Sch. Econs. & Polit Sci, 1984. Credit analyst Manufactururer's Hanover Trust Co., N.Y., 1981-82; treasury analyst Fed. Home Loan Bank of San Francisco, 1985-88; sen. treasury analyst U.S. Leasing Internat., San Francisco, 1988-90; campaign coord. Republican Party, San Francisco, 1990-91; sr. dept. supt. of banks Calif. State Banking Dept., San Francisco, 1991—; prin. shareholder Boice Bros. Inc., Cheyenne, 1975—. Area chmn. San Francisco Republican Party, 1992. Mem. World Affairs Coun. No. Calif., Security Analysts of San Francisco, Univ. Club, Yale Club San Francisco (v.p. 1987-88), Lincoln Club No. Calif. Episcopalian. Home: 2131 Pierce St Apt 2 San Francisco CA 94115 Office: Calif State Banking Dept Ste 1100 111 Pine St San Francisco CA 94111

BOLAN, JAMES RUSSELL, real estate executive; b. Newark, Sept. 20, 1930; s. T. Leslie and Elizabeth (Raube) B.; m. Anne E. McConnell, June 8, 1957; children: Robert, Lynda, Jayme. BS, N.C. State U., 1966; BGS, U. Nebr., 1969. Commd. 2d lt. U.S. Army, 1951, advanced through grades to lt. col., 1966, served in Korea, Japan, Vietnam, Philippines, Taiwan, 1951-71; property mgr. Bishop Trust Co., Honolulu, 1971-72; systems analyst Computer Svcs. Corp., Saigon, Vietnam, 1973-75; property mgr. Airport Assocs., Honolulu, 1975—. Editor newsletter Coconut Wireless, 1979-92; contbr. articles to profl. jours. Decorated D.S.C., Silver Star, Legion of Merit. Mem. Bldg. Owners and Mgrs. Assn. (pres. 1983). Republican. Baptist. Home: 124 California Ave Wahiawa HI 96786 Office: Airport Assocs 3049 Valena St Ste 401 Honolulu HI 96819

BOLAS, GERALD DOUGLAS, art museum administrator, art history educator; b. Los Angeles, Nov. 1, 1949; s. Norman Theodore and Elizabeth Louise (Douglas) B.; m. Deborah Jean Wohletz, Nov. 25, 1978; children: Ellen Claire, John David. B.A., U. Calif.-Santa Barbara, 1972, M.A., 1975; postgrad. CUNY, 1984—. Teaching asst. U. Calif.-Santa Barbara, 1973-74; NEH mus. intern Yale U. Art Gallery, New Haven, 1975-76, asst. to dir., 1976-77; dir. Washington U. Gallery of Art, St. Louis, 1977-88; dir. Portland (Oreg.) Art Mus., 1988-92; adj. asst. prof. art history Washington U., 1982-88; advisor Mo. Arts Coun., St. Louis, 1981-82; field reviewer Inst. Mus. Svcs., Washington, 1980-83; panelist Nat. Endowment for Arts, 1989, NEH, 1990; bd. dirs. Asian Art Soc. of Washington U., 1983-88; mem. No. Calif. adv. com. Archives of Am. Art. Author: Illustrated Checklist of Washington University Collection, 1981; contbr. to (books): Paris in Japan: The Japanese

Encounter with European Painting, 1987; also contbr. articles to other publs.; numerous catalog forewords. Organizer numerous exhbns. Fellow Winterthur Mus. 1993, Smithsonian Instn., 1993. Mem. Coll. Art Assn., Am. Assn. Museums.

BOLDEN, MICHAEL GERONIA, finance company executive; b. Sumter, S.C., Nov. 26, 1953; s. Vermell Bolden. AA, Am. River Coll., Sacramento, Calif., 1978. Enlisted USAF, 1974; air traffic controller 1982d Communications Squadron, Travis AFB, Calif., 1974-82; resigned USAF, 1984; securities broker Robert Thomas Securities, Laguna Hills, Calif., 1980—; tax preparer Bolden Fin. Services Group Inc., Sacramento, Calif., 1980—; ins. agt. First Capital Life Ins., La Jolla, Calif., 1980-88; gen. ptnr. Bell & Assocs., Sacramento, 1986—, Entertainer Network Services, Sacramento, 1987—, Chanteclair Realty and Investments, Sacramento, 1987—. Bd. dirs. Celebration Arts Dance, Sacramento, 1986-88, LaSalle Thompson Kings for Kids, 1986-88, Brotherhood Crusade, 1988—; active Urban League, Concerned Black Men of Sacramento; mentor Grant Union High Sch., Sacramento, 1987-88. Named one of Outstanding Young Men of Am. U.S. Jaycees, 1985. Mem. NAACP, Sacramento C. of C., Sacramento Black C. of C., Sacramento Hispanic C. of C. Clubs: International Fitness, Price, Thunderbird; Tahoe Beach and Ski. Home and Office: BFSG Inc 648A Northfield Dr Ste 1 Sacramento CA 95833-2442

BOLDREY, EDWIN EASTLAND, retinal surgeon, educator; b. San Francisco, Dec. 8, 1941; s. Edwin Barkley and Helen Burns (Eastland) B.; m. Catherine Rose Oliphant, Oct. 20, 1973; children: Jennifer Elizabeth, Melissa Jeanne. BA with honors, De Pauw U., 1963; MD, Northwestern U., Chgo., 1967. Diplomate Am. Bd. Ophthalmology. Rotating intern U. Wash., Seattle, 1967-68; resident in gen. surgery U. Minn., Mpls., 1968-69; resident in ophthalmology U. Calif., San Francisco, 1971-74; Heed Found. fellow in retinal and vitreous surgery Washington U., St. Louis, 1974-75; mem. staff dept. ophthalmology Palo Alto (Calif.) Med. Clinic, 1975-91; dept. chmn., 1988-91; pvt. practice, San Jose, Mountain View, Calif., 1991—; clin. instr. Stanford (Calif.) U. Med. Sch., 1975-79, asst. clin. profl, 1979-87, assoc. clin. prof., 1987—; cons. VA Hosp., Palo Alto, Calif., 1976—. Contbr. articles to med. jours., chpt. to book. Lt. comdr. M.C., USNR, 1969-71. Recipient Asbury award dept. ophthalmology U. Calif., 1973. Fellow ACS, Am. Acad. Ophthalmology (honor award 1989); mem. AMA, Retina Soc., Vitreous Soc. (charter), Peninsula Eye Soc. (pres. 1987-88), Western Retina Study Club (charter, exec. sec.-treas. 1983—) also others. Office: Retina Vitreous Assocs Inc 2515 Samaritan Ct Ste A San Jose CA 95124

BOLEN, LYNNE N., art dealer, accountant, consultant; b. San Diego, Feb. 19, 1954; d. Leon R. and Maria N. (Ishida) Uyeda; m. John E. Bolen, July 25, 1976; children: James III, Katherine, Claire, Paul. BA, UCLA, 1976. Owner Bolen Pub., L.A., 1981-84; v.p. Bolen Gallery, Inc., Santa Monica, Calif., 1978-84; mgr. Carrington, Irvine, Calif., 1984-88; cons. acct. Huntington Beach, Calif., 1988—; art dealer John & Lynne Bolen Fine Arts, Huntington Beach, 1984—. Office: Bolen Fine Arts PO Box 5654 Huntington Beach CA 92615-5654

BOLEN, TERRY LEE, optometrist; b. Newark, Ohio, Sept. 16, 1945; s. Robert Howard and Mildred Irene (Hoover) B.; BS, Ohio U., 1968; postgrad. Youngstown State U., 1973; O.D., Ohio State U., 1978; m. Debbie Elaine Thompson, Mar. 23, 1985. Quality control inspector ITT Grinnell Corp., Warren, Ohio, 1973, jr. quality control engr., 1974; pvt. practice optometry, El Paso, Tex., 1978-80, Dallas, 1980-81, Waco, Tex., 1981-85, Hewitt, Tex., 1983-89; comdr. U.S. Pub. Health Svc., 1989—; bd. dirs. Am. Optometric Found., 1975-77; nat. pres. Am. Optometric Student Assn., 1977-78; pres. El Paso Optometric Soc., 1980. Vol. visual examiner, Juarez, Mex., 1979—; chmn. Westside Recreation Ctr. Adv. Com., El Paso, 1979, Lions Internat. Sight Conservation and Work With the Blind Chmn. award, 1989 . Served to lt. USN, 1969-72; capt. USAIRNG, 1987-89. Recipient pub. svc. award, City of El Paso, 1980. Mem. Am. Optometric Assn., Tex. Optometric Assn., Assn. Mil. Surgeons of U.S. (life, USPHS HSO liaison 1990—, edn. coord. optometry section, 1992), Reserve Officers Assn., Optometric Assn. (clin. assoc. Optometric Extension Program Found. 1978-89), Heart of Tex. Optometric Soc. (sec.-treas. 1984-85, pres.-elect 1986, pres. 1987), North Tex. Optometric Soc., USPHS (pres. No. Nev. chpt. Commd. Officers Assn. 1989-91), Epsilon Psi Epsilon (pres., 1977-78), Lions (3rd v.p. Coronado El Paso, svc. award, 1978, 79, Hewitt pres. 1985, v.p. W.Tex. Lions Eye Bank, 1980, 2d v.p. Cen. Tex. Lions Eye Bank, 1988, Hewitt Lion of Yr. 1987). Republican. Mem. Christian Ch. (Disciples of Christ). Home: 750 E Stillwater Ave # 173 Fallon NV 89406-4058

BOLES, DEBORAH ANN, medical/surgical nurse; b. Milw., July 1, 1953; d. William Bernard Sweeney Jr. and Ann (Hallead) Sweeney Nelson; children: Joanna, Catherine, Angeline, Elisabeth. BSN with distinction, Orvis Sch. Nursing, Reno, 1987. RN, Calif.; cert. med.-surg. nurse, cell saver. Staff nurse post surg. fl. St. Mary's Regional Med. Ctr., Reno, 1987-90; staff nurse med. fl. St. Francis Regional Med. Ctr., Santa Barbara, Calif., 1990-92, clin. nurse II, charge nurse transitional care unit, 1992—; instr. BCLS; mem. quality assurance com., models of care com. Former leader Sierra Nevada coun. Girl Scouts U.S.A., also del., neighborhood chmn., troop cookie chair Tres Condidos coun.; past pres. women's orgn. St. Albert's Ch. Mem. Orvis Honor Soc., Phi Kappa Phi. Home: 431 E Micheltorena St Santa Barbara CA 93101-1124

BOLIN, DARREN DWAYNE, budget analyst; b. Huntington Park, Calif., Mar. 11, 1966; s. Darrell Blaine and Marcella JoAnn (Shoulders) B. BBA, U. La Verne, Calif., 1990. Fin. assoc. Northrop Corp., Pico Rivera, Calif., 1988-90, budget analyst, 1990—. Mem. Northrop Employee Polit. Action Com., 1991. Home: 15516 Leibacher Ave Norwalk CA 90650 Office: 8900 E Washington Blvd Pico Rivera CA 90660

BOLIN, RICHARD LUDDINGTON, industrial development consultant; b. Burlington, Vt., May 13, 1923; s. Axel Birger and Eva Madora (Luddington) B.; m. Jeanne Marie Brown, Dec. 18, 1948; children: Richard Luddington, Jr., Douglas, Judith, Barbara, Elizabeth. BS in Chem. Engring., Tex. A&M U., 1947; MS in Chem. Engring., MIT, 1950. Jr. rsch. engr. Humble Oil & Refining Co., Baytown, Tex., 1947-49; staff mem. Arthur D. Little, Inc., Cambridge, Mass., 1950-56, Caribbean office mgr. San Juan, 1957-61, gen. mgr., Mex., 1961-72; pres. Internat. Parks, Inc., Flagstaff, Ariz., 1973—; dir. The Flagstaff Inst., 1976—, Parque Indsl. de Nogales, Nogales, Sonora, Mex.; dir. secretariat World Export Processing Zones Assn., 1985—. With U.S. Army, 1942-46. Mem. Univ. Club of Mex. Office: PO Box 986 Flagstaff AZ 86002

BOLIN, VERNON SPENCER, microbiologist, consultant; b. Parma, Idaho, July 9, 1913; s. Thadeus Howard Bolin and Jennie Bell Harm; m. Helen Epling, Jan. 5, 1948 (div. 1964); children—Rex, Janet, Mark; m. Barbara Sue Chase, Aug. 1965; children—Vladimir, Erik. B.S., U. Wash., 1942; M.S., U. Minn. 1949. Teaching asst. U. Minn.-Mpls., 1943-45; rsch. assoc. U. Utah, Salt Lake City, 1945-50, fellow in surgery, 1950-52; rsch. virologist Jensen-Salsbery Labs., Inc., Kansas City, Mo., 1952-57; rsch. assoc. Wistar Inst. U. Pa., 1957-58; rsch. virologist USPHS, 1958-61; founder Bolin Lab., 1959; dir. Bolin Labs., Inc., Phoenix. Contbr. articles to profl. jours. Served with U.S. Army, 1931-33. Mem. N.Y. Acad. Scis., Phi Mu Chi. Home: 302 West Wahalla Ln Phoenix AZ 85023-2114

BOLIN, VLADIMIR DUSTIN, chemist; b. Inglewood, Calif., Feb. 25, 1965; s. Vernon Spencer and Barbara Sue (Chase) B.; m. Elizabeth Lynne Boswood, May 18, 1985; children: Ragnar Spencer, Roark Morgan. BS, U. Ariz., 1987. Chemist, microbiologist Bolin Labs., Inc., Phoenix, 1987—, also bd. dirs., v.p. Mem. Am. Water Works Assn., Assn. Official Analytical Chemists, Am. Soc. Microbiology, Am. Chem. Soc., N.Y. Acad. Scis. Home: 1455 W Monona Dr Phoenix AZ 85027-3694 Office: Bolin Labs Inc 17631 N 25th Ave Phoenix AZ 85023-2192

BOLING, KAREN O'REILLY, chiropractor, wholistic practitioner; b. Montréal, Can., Apr. 10, 1961; m. Mark Alan Boling, Oct. 7, 1984. BA in Biology cum laude, Smith Coll., 1982; D Chiropractic cum laude, L.A. Coll. Chiropractic, 1986. With Whittier (Calif.) Health Ctr., 1985-86; pvt. practice, Glendale, Calif., 1986-89, Stanton, Calif., 1986-87, Santa Ana, Calif., 1987—. Acupuncture Soc. Am. fellow; recipient Reiki Mastership. Mem. Am. Chiropractic Assn., Calif. Chiropractic Assn., Internat. Found. Homeopathy Assn. Mental Health, Toastmasters, Delta Sigma. Office: 13122 Prospect Ave Santa Ana CA 92705-1944

BOLLÉ, FRANK KENNETH, real estate broker, business consultant; b. Amsterdam, The Netherlands, Nov. 21, 1935; came to U.S., 1955; s. Maarten Cornelus and Petronell Maria (Kramer) B.; children: Michelle Y., Frank Kenneth Jr. BA, U. San Francisco, 1971, BS, 1972, MBA, 1974. Lic. real estate broker, Calif. With McCall Corp., N.Y.C., 1961-71, Recorder Printing & Pub., San Francisco, 1971-85, Coldwell Banker, Capitola, Calif., 1985-91; broker Longacre Real Estate, Aptos, Calif., 1991—. Candidate for Santa Cruz County (Calif.) Bd. Edn., 1976; bd. dirs. Porter Meml. Libr., 1992—. Named Outstanding Bus. Person, Industry Edn. County, Santa Cruz County, 1988. Mem. Santa Cruz Assn. Realtors (bd. dirs. 1992—). Republican. Baptist. Home: PO Box 1525 Aptos CA 95001

BOLLES, RONALD KENT, music educator; b. El Paso, Dec. 29, 1948; s. Robert Benjamin and Audrey Nadine (Hawkins) B.; m. Terri Sue Alburger Aka Reina Marie, Apr. 7, 1979; children: Gina Marie, Heather Michelle. BA in Music, San Diego State U., 1971, MEd, 1975. Cert. secondary life tchr. Tchr. Castle Pk. Jr. High Sch., Chula Vista, Calif., 1972-74; dir. choir Pacific Beach United Meth., San Diego, 1973-75, All Hallows Cath. Ch., La Jolla, Calif., 1978-79, First Christian Ch., Chula Vista, 1980-87; tchr. Bonita Vista Jr. High Sch., Chula Vista, 1985—, Bonita Vista Sr. High Sch., Chula Vista, 1974—; dist. vocal music chmn. Sweetwater Union High Sch. Dist., Chula Vista, 1980-86; site div. chmn. Bonita Vista High Sch., 1975-77. Dir. high sch. show choir "The Music Machine," 1976—; author (with Terri Sue Bolles) Preparing an Awesome Musical Theater Audition, 1983. named Tchr. Yr. San Diego County, 1987, Bonita Vista High Sch., Chula Vista, 1983; recipient Alumnus of Yr. award San Diego State U. Sch. of Edn., 1989; named Citizen of Yr. Bonita Kiwanis, 1990. Mem. San Diego City/County Music Educators (hon., pres. 1983-88), Music Educators Nat. Conf., Calif. Music Educators Assn., Am. Choral Dirs. Assn., So. Calif. Vocal Assn. Office: Bonita Vista High Sch 1130 5th Ave Chula Vista CA 91911-2812

BOLOCOFSKY, DAVID N., psychology educator, lawyer; b. Hartford, Conn., Sept. 29, 1947; s. Samuel and Olga Bolocofsky. BA, Clark U., 1969; MS, Nova U., 1974, PhD, 1975; JD, U. Denver, 1988. Bar: Colo. 1988; cert. sch. psychologist, Colo., Fla., cert. counselor, Fla. Tchr. high sch. Univ. Sch., Ft. Lauderdale, Fla., 1972-73; ednl. coord. Living and Learning Ctr., Ft. Lauderdale, 1972-75; asst. prof. U. No. Colo., Greeley, 1975-79, assoc. prof., 1979-90, dir. sch. psychology program, 1979-82; assoc. Robert T. Hinds Jr. & Assocs., Littleton, Colo., 1988-93; hearing officer State of Colo., 1991—; pres. David N. Bolocofsky, P.C., Denver, 1993—; psychol. cons. Clin. Assocs., Englewood, Colo., 1978—. Author: Enhancing Personal Adjustment, 1986, (chpts. in books) Children and Obesity, 1987, Obtaining and Utilizing a Custody Evaluation, 1989; contbr. numerous articles to profl. jours. Mem. ABA (family law sect.), Douglas-Elbert Bar Assn., Arapahoe Bar Assn., 1st Jud. Dist. Bar Assn., Nat. Assn. Sch. Psychologists (ethics com. 1988-91), Colo. Soc. Sch. Psychologists (bd. dirs. 1978—, treas. 1993—), Interdisciplinary Commn. on Child Custody (pro bono com. 1988—), Colo. Bar Assn. (family law sect., sec. juvenile law sect. 1990-92), Nat. Assn. Counsel for Children, Colo. Soc. Behavioral Analysis Therapy (treas. 1990—). Home: 9848 E Maplewood Cir Englewood CO 80111-5401 Office: 5353 W Dartmouth Ave Ste 500 Denver CO 80227

BOLSTER, JILL ELAINE, health association administrator; b. Pasadena, Calif., Jan. 29, 1966; d. Merrill Frederick and Carol Jean (Mason) B.; m. James Moulton White, Oct. 5, 1991. BA in English, Calif. Poly. State U., 1990. Rehab. therapist Mental Health Assn., San Luis Obispo, Calif., 1990, program coord., 1990-91, exec. dir., 1992—; bd. dirs. Hotline, Inc., San Luis Obispo, 190—. Teen outreach worker Hotline, Inc., 1991, 92. Grantee Am. Horticulture Therapy Assn., 1992; recipient commendation San Luis Obispo County Bd. Suprs., 1992, Share award Alliance for Mentally Ill, San Luis Obispo, 1991. Mem. Calif. Landscape Contractors Assn., Calif. Assn. Nurserymen, Sierra Club (polit. action com. 1992). Democrat. Office: Mental Health Assn PO Box 100 San Luis Obispo CA 93406

BOLT, BRUCE ALAN, seismologist, educator; b. Largs, Australia, Feb. 15, 1930; came to U.S., 1963; s. Donald Frederick and Arlene (Stitt) B.; m. Beverley Bentley, Feb. 11, 1956; children: Gillian, Robert, Helen, Margaret. BS with honors, New Eng. U. Coll., 1952; MS, U. Sydney, Australia, 1954, PhD, 1959, DSc (hon.), 1972. Math. master Sydney (Australia) Boys' High Sch., 1953; lectr. U. Sydney, 1954-61, sr. lectr., 1961-62; research seismologist Columbia U., 1960; dir. seismographic stas. U. Calif., Berkeley, 1963-89, prof. seismology, 1963-93, prof. emeritus, 1993—, chmn. acad. senate, 1993—; mem. com. on seismology NAS, 1966-72, chmn. nat. earthquake obs. com., 1979-81; mem. earthquake and wind forces com. VA, 1971-75; mem. Calif. Seismic Safety Commn., 1978-93, chmn., 1984-86; earthquake studies adv. panel U.S. Geol. Survey, 1979-83, U.S. Geodynamics Com., 1979-84. Author, editor textbooks on applied math., earthquakes, geol. hazards and detection of underground nuclear explosions. Recipient H.O. Wood award in seismology, 1967, 72; Fulbright scholar, 1960; Churchill Coll. Cambridge overseas fellow, 1980, 91. Fellow Am. Geophys. Union (mem. geophys. monograph bd. 1971-78, chmn. 1976-78), Geol. Soc. Am., Calif. Acad. Scis. (trustee 1981-92, pres. 1982-85, Fellows medal 1989), Royal Astron. Soc. (assoc.); mem. NAE, (IDNDR com. 1992—), Seismol. Soc. Am. (editor bull. 1965-70, bd. dir. 1965-71, 73-76, pres. 1974-75), Internat. Assn. Seismology and Physics Earth's Interior (exec. com. 1964-67, v.p. 1975-79, pres. 1980-83), Earthquake Engring. Research Inst., Calif. Univs. Rsch. Earthquake Engring., (sec. 1988-91), Australian Math. Soc., Sigma Xi, Univ. Club, Chit Chat Club, Bohemian Club. Home: 1491 Greenwood Ter Berkeley CA 94708-1935

BOLTON, EARL CLINTON, lawyer, consultant; b. Los Angeles, Aug. 22, 1919; s. John R. and Hazel A. (Van Order) B.; m. Jean Studley, June 27, 1942; children—Barbara Bolton Poley, Elizabeth Ann Bolton Newell, William Earl. A.B. magna cum laude, U. So. Calif., 1941, J.D., 1948; LL.D. (hon.), U. San Diego, 1963. Bar: Calif. 1949, U.S. Supreme Ct. 1958. Staff, Coordinator Inter-Am. Affairs, N.Y.C., also Washington, 1941; v.p., treas. Nat. Public Discussions, Inc., N.Y.C., 1942; lectr. polit. sci. dept. U. So. Calif., 1946-48; asst. prof. U. So. Calif. (Coll. Liberal Arts and Sch. Commerce), 1948-50, asso. prof. law and v.p. planning, 1952-60; spl. asst. to pres. U. Calif., Berkeley, 1960-61; v.p. univ. relations U. Calif., 1962-64, v.p. adminstrn., 1964-66, v.p. govtl. relations, 1966-68, v.p. adminstrn., 1968-70; v.p. Booz, Allen & Hamilton, Inc., Chgo., 1970-79; of counsel firm Willis Butler & Scheifly, Los Angeles, 1979-81, Pepper, Hamilton & Scheetz, 1981-84, Earl C. Bolton & Assocs., 1984—. Mem. editorial bd. Law Rev., U. So. Calif., 1947-48. Mem. Calif. Gov.'s Mental Health Adv. Com., Citizens' Legis. Adv. Com.; past chmn., founding mem. Calif. Scholarship Com. Served to capt. USNR, 1942-46, 50-52. Mem. State Bar Calif., Order of Coif, Phi Beta Kappa, Phi Kappa Phi. Home: Marina View Towers Alameda CA 94501

BOLTON, MARTHA O., writer; b. Searcy, Ark., Sept. 1, 1951; d. Lonnie Leon and Eunice Dolores Ferren; m. Russell Norman Bolton, Apr. 17, 1970; children: Russell Norman II, Matthew David, Anthony Shane. Grad. high sch., Reseda, Calif. Freelance writer for various comedians, 1975-86; newspaper columnist Simi Valley Enterprise, Simi, Calif., 1979-87; staff writer Bob Hope, 1986—. Author: A Funny Thing Happened to Me on My Way Through the Bible, 1985, A View from the Pew, 1986, What's Growing Under Your Bed?, 1986, Tangled in the Tinsel, 1987, So, How'd I Get to be in Charge of the Program?, 1988, Humorous Monologues, 1989, Let My People Laugh, 1989, If Mr. Clean Calls Tell Him I'm Not In, 1989, Journey to the Center of the Stage, 1990, If You Can't Stand the Smoke, Get Out of My Kitchen, 1990, Home, Home on the Stage, 1991, TV Jokes and Riddles, 1991, These Truths Were Made For Walking, 1992, When the Meatloaf Explodes It's Done, 1993, Childhood Is A Stage, 1993. Pres. Vista Elem. Sch. PTA, Simi, 1980-81. Recipient Emmy award nomination for outstanding achievement in music and lyrics NATAS, 1988, Internat. Angel award, 1990, 91. Mem. Nat. League of Am. Pen Women (br. pres. 1984-86, Woman of Achievement award Simi Valley br. 1984), Writers Guild Am. West, ASCAP, Soc. Children's Book Writers, Acad. T.V. Arts and Scis. Office: PO Box 1212 Simi Valley CA 93062-1212

BOLTON, ROBERT FLOYD, construction executive; b. Dunlap, Iowa, Oct. 18, 1942; s. Russel J. And Mary Jane (Lacey) B.; m. Mary Louise Hartman, May 15, 1988. Lic. contractor. Sole practice farming Dunlap, Iowa, 1967-72; supr. Phillips Constrn. Co., Cottonwood, Ariz., 1972-84; contracto Bolton Bldg. and Devel. Co., Sedona, Ariz., 1984—; cons. in field. With U.S. Army, 1964-66. Mem. Nat. Assn. Home Builders, Am. Soc. Home Inspectors, C. of C., VFW, Meth. Mens Fellowship Club. Republican. Methodist. Home: 90 Evening Glow Pl Sedona AZ 86336-7912 Office: Bolton Bldg & Devel Co PO Box 754 Sedona AZ 86336-0754

BOMBERG, THOMAS JAMES, dental educator; b. Curtis, Nebr., May 31, 1928; s. Robert Joseph and Alpha Marie (Fairburn) B.; m. Arthurene Edens, Apr. 29, 1954; children—Bryan Craig, Scott Edens. B.S., U. Denver, 1951; D.D.S., U. Mo., Kansas City, 1961. Pvt. practice dentistry Colorado Springs, 1961-72; asst. prof. U. Ky. Coll. Dentistry, 1972-73; asso. prof. U. Okla. Coll. Dentistry, 1973-74; prof. U. Colo. Sch. Dentistry, Denver, 1974—; dean U. Colo. Sch. Dentistry, 1977-80, assoc. dean, 1988—. Contbr. articles to dental related jours. Bd. dirs. El Paso County (Colo.) Mental Health Assn., 1967-70. Served with USN, 1946-48; to 1st lt. USAF, 1951-56. Fellow Internat. Coll. Dentists, Am. Coll. Dentists; mem. Am. Dental Assn., Pierre Fauchard Acad., Am. Assn. Dental Schs., Am. Assn. for Dental Rsch. Republican. Episcopalian. Office: U Colo Sch Dentistry 4200 E 9th Ave Denver CO 80262-0001

BOMMER, TIMOTHY J., magistrate; b. Columbus, Ohio, Dec. 9, 1940; s. Thomas F. and Susan L. (Proper) B.; m. Sandra K. Bartlett, May 16, 1964; children: Breton J., Kevin A., Melissa K. BA, U. Wyo., 1963, JD, 1970. Bar: Wyo. 1970, Colo. 1970. Dep. county and pros. atty. Teton County Prosecutor's Office, Jackson, Wyo., 1970-74; ptnr. Ranck & Bommer, Jackson, 1970-77; magistrate U.S. Dist. Ct., Jackson, 1976—; sole practice Jackson, 1977—; regional dir. Govs.'s Planning Com. on Criminal Adminstrn., Wyo., 1973-74; pres. Western Assn. of State Depts. of Agriculture; bd. dirs. Nat. Assn. State Depts. of Agriculture. Served to capt. USAF, 1963-67. Mem. ABA, Assn. Trial Lawyers Am., Am. Bd. Trial Advocates, Wyo. Trial Lawyers Assn. (bd. dirs. 1976-79), Wyo. State Bar Ethics Com., Wyo. State Bar Fee Arbitration Com. (chmn. 1980-84), Wyo. Jud. Nominating Commn. Republican. Episcopalian. Office: PO Box 1728 172 Center St Jackson WY 83001

BOND, DOROTHY M., medical/surgical and geriatrics nurse; b. Hibbing, Minn., Nov. 13, 1927; d. Roydon Phillip and Lorena Ivadell (Williams) Showers; children: Cynthia Elizabeth Jones, Frances Lorena Jones Scott, Edward Lawrence Jones. Diploma, Adelphi U., 1948; BSN, U. Wash., 1962, postgrad., 1966-68. Cert. in pub. health nursing. Dir. nursing svcs. Linda Vista Care Ctr., Ashland, Oreg.; staff nurse, med. specialties unit Ballard Comprehensive Care for Integrated Health Svcs., Seattle; supplemental nursing, med.-surg. Favorite Nurses, Harborview Med. Ctr., Seattle. Mem. Sigma Theta Tau. Home: PO Box 30622 Seattle WA 98103-0622

BOND, EDWARD UNDERWOOD, educator, minister; b. Chanute, Kans., Nov. 11, 1959; s. Edward Underwood and Annie Elizabeth (Provorse) B.; m. Linda Jean Bertrand, Dec. 12, 1981; 1 child, Carissa Lynn. AB in Bible/Ministries, Manhattan Christian Coll., 1982; MA in Communication, U. No. Colo., 1989; postgrad., Ariz. State U., 1992—. Ordained to ministry Christian Ch./Church of Christ. Intern First Christian Ch., Medicine Lodge, Kans., 1980; asst. minister Greeley (Colo.) Christian Ch., 1982-86; founding pastor Christ's East Valley Ch., Mesa, Ariz., 1986-91; adj. faculty mem. Mesa C.C., 1990—; Gene Gallup grad. fellow svcs. mktg. Ariz. State U., 1992-93; bd. dirs. Ariz. Evangelistic Assn., Phoenix, 1989-91; mem. exec. com. Ariz. Christian Convention, Phoenix, 1988-91, United Christian Youth Camp, Prescott, Ariz., 1988-89; ch. growth assoc. Inst. for Am. Ch. Growth, Monrovia, Calif., 1986—; resident in new ch. planting Pacific Christian Coll., Fullerton, Calif., 1986-87. Campaign vol. Jack Londen for Gov., Mesa, 1988. Republican. Home: 721 S Sierra Mesa AZ 85204

BOND, LINDA JEAN BERTRAND, sign language educator; b. Oakley, Kans., Sept. 19, 1959; d. Richard Ernest and Elaine Loree (Kelling) Bertrand; m. Edward Underwood Bond III, Dec. 12, 1981; 1 child, Carissa Lynn. Student, Manhattan Christian Coll., 1977-82; BS in Theatre, Kans. State U., 1982; interpreter cert., Front Range C.C., Westminster, Colo., 1986; postgrad., Met. State Coll., 1985. Cert. interpreter quality assurance system. Interpreter for the deaf U. No. Colo. Lab. Sch., Greeley, Colo., 1982-85; freelance interpreter Valley Ctr. for the Deaf, Phoenix, 1986—, Ariz. Coun. for Hearing Impaired, 1986—, Statewide Interpreting Svcs., 1993—; ednl. interpreter Valley Ctr. for the Deaf, Phoenix, 1986—, Gilbert (Ariz.) High Sch., 1986-87; sign lang. interpreter for the deaf Mesa (Ariz.) C.C., 1986—; sign lang. interpreter for the deaf Ariz. State U., Tempe, 1986—, faculty assoc., 1987—; instr. Am. sign lang. Mesa C.C., 1988—; interpreter for the deaf Aurora Mime Theatre, Tempe, 1991—. Interpreter for the deaf Christ's East Valley Ch., Mesa, 1986-91, Bethany Community Ch., Tempe, 1992—; workshop leader/performer Phoenix Coll. "Students of Sign" Club, Phoenix, 1986, 87, 90, 92; new ch. planter Christ's East Valley Ch., 1986-91; sign choir dir., 1982-86; bd. dirs. Greeley (Colo.) Civic Theatre, 1982-86, No. Colo. Ctr. on Deafness, Greeley, 1985-86; play dir. Greeley Civic Theatre, 1982-86. Mem. The Registry of Interpreters for the Deaf, Inc., Interpreter Quality Assurance System (interpreter mem., level IV cert. 1986-89, level V cert. 1989—). Republican. Mem. Chs. of Christ. Home: 721 S Sierra Mesa AZ 85204 Office: Ariz State U Dept Speech and Hearing Sci Tempe AZ 85287-0102

BOND, RICHARD RANDOLPH, college administrator, legislator; b. Lost Creek, W.Va., Dec. 1, 1927; s. Harley Donovan and Marcella Randolph B.; m. Reva Stearns, Apr. 20, 1946; children: David, Philip, Josette, Michael. BS, Salem Coll., 1948, LHD (hon.), 1979; MS, W.Va. U., 1949; PhD, U. Wis., 1955; postdoctoral studies, U. Mich., 1958-59. Various teaching and fellowship positions, 1949-59; dean of faculty Elmira (N.Y.) Coll., 1959-63; dean coll. of Liberal Arts U. Liberia, Monrovia, 1963-64; chief of party Cornell U. Project in Liberia, Monrovia, 1964-66; v.p. acad. affairs Ill. State U., Normal, 1966-71; pres. U. No. Colo., Greeley, 1971-81, pres. emeritus, prof. zoology, 1981-89; state rep. Colo. Gen. Assembly, Denver, 1984-90; interim pres. Front Range Community Coll., Westminster, Colo., 1991; pres. Morgan Community Coll., Ft. Morgan, Colo., 1991—; founder Nat. Student Exch.; cons., examiner North Ctrl. Accrediting Assn., 1969-82; bd. dirs. Greeley Nat. Bank, 1971-81; founder, bd. dirs. First No. Savs. and Loan; bd. trustees Teiko Loretto Heights U. Author: Colorado Postsecondary Options Act., 1988; contbr. articles to profl. jours. Dir., chmn. Sunrise Community Health Ctr.; commr. Greeley Urban Renewal Assn.; founding mem. Dream Team on Dropout Prevention; Dem. candidate Colo. 4th Congl. Dist., 1990; co-founder Colo. chpt. Dem. Leadership Coun., 1991; co-chair Clinton cmapaign, Colo., 1992. Served with U.S. Army, 1945-47. Recipient Legislator of Yr. award DAV, 1988, Colo. Acad. Pediatrics, 1989; Mental Health award, 1990, Polit. Educator of Yr. award, Colo. Edn. Assn., 1991; fellow NSF, 1953-54, Am. Physiol. Soc., 1958, Carnegie Found., 1958-59. Mem. Am. Ornithologists Union, Am. Assn. Colls. and Univs. (bd. dirs. 1979-81), Colo. Assn. Colls. and Univs. (chmn. 1979-81), Rotary (bd. dirs. local chpt.), Sigma Xi. Democrat. Presbyterian. Home: 38 Paynter Pl Fort Morgan CO 80701

BOND, THOMAS ALDEN, university president; b. St. Louis, Mar. 23, 1938; s. Alden R. and Jean Elizabeth (Langen) B.; m. Judy Bess Borchardt, Sept. 2, 1961; children: Thomas A. Jr., Amy Elizabeth. Student, Washington U., 1956-58; A.B., U. Mo., 1961; M.S., U. Okla., 1963, Ph.D. (Humble Oil Co. fellow), 1966. Instr. U. Okla., Norman, 1964-65; geologist Okla. Geol. Survey, Norman, 1965-66; asst. prof. geology, acting chmn. dept. Ga. So. Coll., Statesboro, 1966-69, asso. prof., asst. dean Sch. Arts and Scis., 1969-70; asst. dean Coll. Liberal Arts, Idaho State U., Pocatello, 1970-73, chmn. dept. geology, dir. summer session, 1973-74, dean Coll. Liberal Arts, prof., 1974-76; v.p. for acad. affairs Midwestern State U., Wichita Falls, Tex., 1976-78; provost, v.p. acad. affairs Eastern Ill. U., 1978-80; pres. Clarion U. of Pa., 1980-89, Eastern N.Mex. U., Portales, 1989—. Contbr. articles to profl. jours. Chmn. United campaign Idaho State U., 1972; Alt. del. Idaho Democratic Conv., 1972. Fellow Okla. Acad. Sci.; mem. AAAS, Am. Assn. Petroleum Geologists, Soc. Econ. Paleontologists and Mineralogists, Geol. Soc. Am., Am. Assn. Stratigraphic Palynologists, Am. Assn. Quaternary Environment, Southeastern Geol. Soc., Palynological Soc. India, Ga. Geol.

Soc., Ga. Acad. Sci., Sigma Xi, Sigma Gamma Epsilon. Home: 1062 Willow Way Santa Fe NM 87501-9152

BOND, THOMAS MOORE, JR., labor mediation and arbitration executive; b. Louisville, Dec. 17, 1930; s. Thomas Moore and Louise Elleanor (Jones) B.; m. Kathryn Keith, Apr. 10, 1950 (dec.); children: Gilbert, Louise, Lela; m. Ethel Ayako Kuramitsu, Aug. 15, 1965; children: Richard, Jane, Julian Horace. BS in Econs., Ind. U., 1953. Bus. agt, organizer Hosp. Workers, San Francisco, 1961-65; internat. rep. organizer Svc. Employees' AFL-CIO, Louisville, 1965-70; exec. dir. Union Am. Physicians, San Francisco, 1973-78; owner Thomas Moore Bond & Assocs., Berkeley, Calif., 1979—; pvt. practice labor mediator and arbitrator, mgmt., labor cons., Berkeley, 1981—. Editor: The Negro Conservative, 1981. Bd. dirs. adv. com. for paralegal tng. Merritt Coll., Oakland, Calif., 1983; mem. labor commn. City of Berkeley, 1986-88, 91. 1st lt. inf., U.S. Army, 1946-50. Mem Indsl. Rels. Rsch. Assn., Soc. Fed. Labor Rels. Profls., Inst. Advanced Law Study. Republican. Congregationalist. Office: Thomas Moore Bond & Assocs 2123 1/2 5th St Berkeley CA 94710-2208

BOND, VINCENT EARL, public relations executive; b. Bethesda, Md., May 16, 1947; s. Norman Earl and Shirley Sybilla (Cavalier) B.; m. Betty Louise Huestis, Feb. 4, 1971; 1 child, Carolyn Anita. BA, Calif. State U., 1968; MBA, Nat. U., 1984. Supr. pub. info. Tucson Gen. Hosp, 1975; pub. info. officer Ariz. Dept. Transp., Phoenix, 1975-77; pub. affairs officer IRS, Phoenix, 1977-80; dir. communications Children's Hosp., San Diego, 1980-88; pub. affairs officer USN, San Diego, 1989-91, U.S. Customs Svcs., March AFB, Calif., 1991—. Mem. communications coun. March of Dimes, San Diego, 1990—. Capt. USAF, 1969-74. Recipient Excellence awards for best employee newsletter Ariz. Newspaper Assn., 1975, 76, Merit award for best mag. IABC, 1981, Excellence awards for best TV spot announcement and best print advertisement, 1986, Merit award for best print advertisement, 1986, Golden Advocate award So. Calif. Soc. for Hosp. Pub. Rels, 1982, Cert. of Excellence for best ann. report Am. Inst. Graphic Arts, 1983. Mem. Pub. Rels. Soc. Am. (publicity chmn. 1990-91, dir. at large 1990-91, profl. accreditation 1984). Democrat. Home: 2070 Basswood Ave Carlsbad CA 92008-1110 Office: USCS Aviations Ops Ctr West PO Box 6363 March AFB CA 92518

BONDI, BERT ROGER, accountant, financial planner; b. Portland, Oreg., Oct. 2, 1945; s. Gene L. and Elizabeth (Poynter) B. BBA, U. Notre Dame, 1967. CPA, Colo., Calif., Wyo. Sr. tax acct. Price Waterhouse, Los Angeles, 1970-73; ptnr. Valentine Adducci & Bondi, Denver, 1973-76; sr. ptnr. Bondi & Co., Englewood, Colo., 1977—; dir. Citizens Bank. Bd. govs. Met. State Coll. Found. Served with U.S. Army, 1968-70. Mem. C. of C., Community Assns. Inst., Govt. Fin. Officers Assn., Home Builders Assn., Am. Inst. CPAs, Colo. Soc. CPAs, Wyo. Soc. CPAs. Roman Catholic. Clubs: Notre Dame, Metropolitan (Denver); Castle Pines Country. Home: 49 Glenalla Pl Castle Rock CO 80104-9026 Office: Bondi & Co 44 Inverness Dr E Bldg B Englewood CO 80112-5410

BONDS, BARRY LAMAR, professional baseball player; b. Riverside, Calif., July 24, 1964. Student, Ariz. State U. With Pitts. Pirates, 1986-92, San Francisco Giants, 1992—. Named Most Valuable Player Baseball Writers' Assn. Am., 1990, 1992, Maj. League Player Yr. Sporting News, 1990, 1992, Nat. League Player Yr. Sporting News, 1990, 91, mem. Sporting News Coll. All-Am. team, 1985, mem. All-Star team, 1990, 1992-93; recipient Gold Glove award, 1990-92, Silver Slugger award, 1990-92. Office: San Francisco Giants Candlestick Park San Francisco CA 94124

BONDURANT, DAVID WILLIAM, marketing professional; b. Kirksville, Mo., June 8, 1948; s. William George and Leila Ruth (Mulford) B.; m. Judy Helen Rindahl, Mar. 17, 1973; children: Matthew David, Erik William. BSEE, U. Mo., Rolla, 1971; BS in Physics, Northeast Mo. State Coll., 1971. Registered profl. engr., Minn. Assoc. design engr. Control Data Corp., Arden Hills, Minn., 1971-72; sr. design engr. Sperry-Univac, Eagan, Minn., 1972-75; project engr. Robertshaw Controls Co., Richmond, Va., 1975-76; prin. design engr. Sperry-Univac, Eagan, 1976-80; mgr., systems applications Honywell Solid State, Electronics Div., Plymouth, Minn., 1980-84; com. bus. devel. mgr. Honywell Solid State, Electronics Div., Colorado Springs, Colo., 1984-88; dir. new bus. devel. Ramtron Corp., Colorado Springs, 1988—; ind. cons. Technomics Cons., Chgo., 1987. Contbr. articles to profl. jours. Mem. IEEE (pres., v.p., sec. 1977-79), Twin Cities Computer Soc., Country Club of Colo., Tau Beta Pi, Eta Kappa Nu, Phi Kappa Phi. Republican. Lutheran. Home: 4025 Becket Dr Colorado Springs CO 80906-4815 Office: Ramtron Corp 1850 Ramtron Dr Colorado Springs CO 80921-3695

BONE, ROBERT WILLIAM, writer, photojournalist; b. Gary, Ind., Sept. 15, 1932; s. Robert Ordway and Georgia Juanita (Clapp) B.; m. Sara Ann Cameron, Aug. 14, 1965; children: Christina Ann, David Robert. BS in Journalism, Bowling Green State U., 1954. Editor, tng. literature The Armor Sch., Ft. Knox, Ky., 1954-56; reporter, photographer Middletown (N.Y.) Daily Record, 1956-59, San Juan (Puerto Rico) Star, 1959-60; news editor Popular Photography Mag., N.Y.C., 1960-62; editor-in-chief Brazilian Bus. Mag., Rio de Janeiro, 1962-63; picture editor Time-Life Books, N.Y.C., 1963-68; sr. writer Fielding's Travel Guide to Europe, Mallorca, Spain, 1968-71; staff writer Honolulu Advertiser, 1971-84; free-lancer Honolulu, 1984—; stringer Time-Life News Svc., 1981-86. Author: Maverick Guide to Hawaii, 1977, Maverick Guide to Australia, 1979, Maverick Guide to New Zealand, 1981, Fielding's Alaska and the Yukon, 1989; travel editor Honolulu mag., 1985-88, R.S.V.P. mag., 1988-89; contbg. editor Recommend mag., 1986—. 1st lt., U.S. Army, 1954-56. Named to Journalism Hall Fame Bowling Green State U., 1990. Mem. Soc. of Am. Travel Writers (bd. dirs. western chpt. chmn. 1993—), Am. Soc. Magazine Photographers. Democrat. Home and Office: 1053 Lunaai St Kailua HI 96734-4633

BONELLI, JOSEPH EDWARD, physician, scientist; b. Denver, May 27, 1946; s. Edward F. and Sue B. (Shapard) B.; m. Jean Ann Koch, Mar. 13, 1970; children: Ryan Joseph, Damon Edward. BA in Chemistry, U. Colo., 1969; PhD in Analytical Chemistry, Colo. State U., 1980; MD, U. Miami, Coral Gables, Fla., 1984. Diplomate Nat. Bd. Med. Examiners, Am. Bd. Pathology (anatomic and clin.). Support scientist Nat. Ctr. Atmospheric Rsch., Boulder, Colo., 1969-74, 75-76; cons. environ. and applied earth scis. Dames & Moore, Denver, 1974-75; rsch. chemist, rsch. project chief water resources div. U.S. Geol. Survey, Denver, 1977-82; med. intern, resident in pathology Sch. of Medicine U. Colo., Denver, 1984-87, clin. fellow in dermatopathology, 1988; asst. prof. pathology, pathologist U. Ark., John L. McClellan Meml. Vets. Hosp., Little Rock, 1989; dir. clin. lab., continuing med. edn. Sterling (Colo.) Regional Med. Ctr., 1990—; chmn. Environ. Symposium Rocky Mountain Conf. on Analytic Chemistry Soc. Applied Spectroscopy, Denver, 1981, 82; clin. asst. prof. pathology Sch. of Medicine U. Colo., Denver, 1990—; cons. in occupational and environ. medicine, Boulder and Sterling, 1990—. Patentee in field; contbr. articles to profl. jours. Recipient Am. Cancer Soc. rsch. grants, Denver, 1988, Little Rock, 1989. Fellow Coll. Am. Pathologists (1st pl. clin. pathology resident's paper present award joint with Am. Soc. Clin. Pathologists 1988), Am. Soc. Clin. Pathologists; mem. AMA, Colo. Med. Soc., N.E. Colo. Med. Soc., Colo. Med. Soc. Coun. on Profl. Edn. Roman Catholic. Home: 552 Blackhawk Rd Boulder CO 80303-4008 Office: Dept Pathology 615 Fairhurst St Sterling CO 80751-4523

BONETTI, DAVID, art critic; b. Milford, Mass.; s. Albert and Lillian (FitzGerald) B. BA, Brandeis U., 1969. Boston correspondent ART News, N.Y.C., 1986-89; art critic Boston Phoenix, 1985-89, Art New England, Brighton, Mass., 1980—, San Francisco Examiner, 1989—; instr. art history Brown U., Providence, R.I., 1988, Boston Coll., 1988, U. Mass., Boston, 1987; curator Mass. Coll. Art, Boston, 1986. Recipient Mfrs. Hanover Trust Disting. Art World award, 1988, Critics Choice citation. Office: San Francisco Examiner PO Box 7260 San Francisco CA 94120

BONFIELD, ANDREW JOSEPH, tax practitioner; b. London, Jan. 26, 1924; s. George William and Elizabeth Agnes B.; came to U.S., 1946, naturalized, 1954; m. Eleanor Ackerman, Oct. 16, 1955; children—Bruce Ian, Sandra Karen. Gen. mgr. Am. Cushion Co., Los Angeles, 1948-50, Monson Calif. Co., Redwood City, 1951-58; mfrs. mktg. rep., San Francisco, 1958-62; tax practitioner, bus. cons., Redwood City, San Jose, Los Gatos, Calif., 1963—. Past treas., dir. Northwood Park Improvement Assn.; mem. exec. bd. Santa Clara County council Boy Scouts Am., 1971—, past council pres., mem. Nat. council; mem. Santa Clara County Parks and Recreation Commn., 1975-81, 82-86; mem. County Assessment Appeals Bd., 1978-86; mem. Hawaii Bd. Taxation Review, 1992. Served with Brit. Royal Navy, 1940-46. Decorated King George VI Silver Badge; recipient Silver Beaver award, Vigil honor award Boy Scouts Am.; enrolled to practice before IRS. Mem. Nat. Soc. Public Accts., Nat. Assn. Enrolled Agts., Calif. Soc. Enrolled Agts., Hawaii Assn. Pub. Accts., Hawaii Soc. Enrolled Agrs., Royal Can. Legion (past state parliamentarian, past state 1st vice comdr.). Club: Rotary (pres. San Jose E. 1977-78). Home: 760 S Kihei Rd Apt 215 Kihei HI 96753-7517

BONGE, NICHOLAS JAY, JR., biological engineering company executive; b. Harve de Grace, Md., Aug. 3, 1954; s. Nicholas Joseph Bonge and Marie Irene (Cile) Andree; m. Lisa Marie Thompson, Aug. 3, 1991. BSME, U. Colo., 1976; postgrad., So. Calif. Inst. Architecture, 1990-91. Rsch. assoc. Colo. Sch. Mines, Golden, 1976-80; chief engr. Vac Tec Systems, Boulder, Colo., 1980-83; chief engr. systems Innotech Group, Simi Valley, Calif., 1983-86; pres. Biol. Engring., Inc., Ventura, Calif., 1986—; bd. dirs. LMT Mktg., Inc., Ventura; guest speaker conf. on water jet tech., Golden, Colo., 1977-80. Patentee in field; contbr. articles to profl. jours. Recipient Rsch. grant U.S. Dept. Energy, 1977, U.S. Bur. Mines, 1978, U.S. office of Surface Mining, 1978, Dept. Army, 1980, South African Chamber of Mines, 1978. Mem. Am. Vacuum Soc. (guest speaker 1986—), Pet Industry Distbrs. Assn., Am. Pet Products Mfrs. Assn., Western World Pet Suppliers Assn. Office: Biol Engring Inc 2476 Palma Ave Ventura CA 93003

BONHAM, CHARLIE LEONARD, college official; b. Richmond, Calif., Sept. 26, 1939; s. Leonard Shelby and Lavern Luella (McKay) B.; m. Pamela Ann Prahl, Feb. 23, 1963; children: Stephen Shelby, Karen Elizebeth, Tracy Michelle. BS in Marine Engring., Calif. Maritime Acad., 1960; BA in Internat. Rels., Navy Postgrad. Sch., Monterey, Calif., 1970. Lic. engr. U.S. Mcht. Marine. 3d asst. engr. Mil. Sea Transport Svc., San Francisco, 1960; commd. ensign USN, 1961, advanced through grades to capt., 1982, comdr. 4 USN ships; ret., 1989; v.p. external affairs Calif. Maritime Acad., Vallejo, 1989—, pres. Calmaritime Acad. Found., 1990—. Mem. Propeller Club U.S. (pres. San Francisco 1989-91). Republican. Office: Calif Maritime Acad 200 Maritime Academy Dr Vallejo CA 94590-8181

BONHAM, CLIFFORD VERNON, social worker, educator; b. Paradise, Calif., July 11, 1921; s. Leon C. and Mary M. (Horn) B.; m. Vesta H. Williamson, May 4, 1956; children: William Robert Rohde (stepson), Larry Dean, Tami Marie. Student, San Francisco State U., 1948-49; B.A., U. Calif., Berkeley, 1951, M.S.W., 1953. Lic. clin. social worker, marriage and family counselor, Acad. Cert. Social Workers. Parole Agt. Calif. State Dept. Youth Authority, 1953-59, research interviewer, 1959-61, supervising parole agt., 1961-64; field instr. Grad. Sch. Social Work, Calif. State U., Fresno, 1964-67; assoc. prof. Grad. Sch. Social Work, Calif. State U., 1967-74, prof., 1974-91, prof. emeritus social work, 1991—, field sequence coordinator, 1971-80; counselor Suicide Prevention Program, Fresno, Calif., 1964-70; cons. Fresno County Domestic Relations, 1967-70, Fresno County Pub. Defenders' Office, 1986-88; commr. Fresno County Juvenile Justice Commn., 1971-81; (mem. state legislative com. on housing felons, 1980) social work cons. various hosps., Fresno, 1971-89; mem. Dept. Youth Authority Youth Justice Task Force, 1986—. Bd. dirs. Peidmont Pines Assn., Oakland, Calif., 1960-64; mem. Fresno County Emergency Housing Bd., 1970-72; mem. Adv. Com. on Correctional Edn., 1989—; mem Correctional Bd. Edn., 1991-92; mem. Madera County Mental Health Bd., 1991—. With USN, 1940-46. Mem. Nat. Assn. Social Workers, Calif. Probation and Parole Assn. (regional v.p. 1973-74), Soc. Clin. Social Workers, Assn. Advancement of Social Work with Groups. Democrat. Unitarian. Home: PO Box 1284 Oakhurst CA 93644-1284

BONHAM, HAROLD FLORIAN, research geologist; b. L.A., Sept. 1, 1928; s. Harold Florian and Viola Violet (Clopine) B.; m. Sally Mae Reimer, Sept. 6, 1952; children: Cynthia Jean Kimball, Douglas Craig, Gary Stephen. AA in Physics, U. Calif. Berkeley, 1951; BA in Geology, UCLA, 1954; MS in Geology, U. Nev., 1963. Geologist So. Pacific Co., 1955-61; mining geologist Nev. Bur. Mines and Geology, Reno, 1963-93, acting dir., state geologist; cons. UN, Can., Australia, Peowles, Republic of China, 1980-90; cons. in field. Contbr. articles to profl. jour. V.p. Palomino Valley Gen. Improvement Dist., Nev., 1986-88. With USN, 1946-49, PTO. Fellow Geol. Soc. Am., Soc. Econ. Geologist, Assn. Exploration Geochemists (councillor 1988—); mem. Geol. Soc. Nev. Republican. Home: 2100 Right Hand Canyon Rd Reno NV 89510-9300 Office: Nev Bur Mines & Geology Mail Stop 18 Reno NV 89557-0088

BONICELLI, JOANNE, professional model; b. Columbus, Ga., Oct. 26, 1951; d. Joseph Carl Tucker and Helga Erika (Hachnel) McClow; m. Silvio Joseph Bonicelli Jr., Mar. 21, 1971; children: Jennifer Christine, Julie Elizabeth. Student, U. So. Colo., 1969-71; student, Belt-El Coll. Nursing, 1990—. Asst. mgr. Gibson Girl, Inc., Colorado Springs, Colo., 1972-76; model Vannoy Talent Agy., Denver, 1983-87, Spring Talent, Inc., Colorado Springs, 1987-90, Looks, Inc., Colorado Springs, 1992—. Editor (newsletter) Heartstrings, 1987-88. Vice-pres. bd. dirs. The Pikes Peak Hospice, Inc., Colorado Springs, 1985-89; bd. dirs. Southern Colo. Accent on Kids, Inc., Colorado Springs, 1988-89; chmn. bd. dirs. Jr. League Colorado Springs, 1989-91; bd. dirs. Broadmoor Christian Women's Club, Colorado Springs, 1988. Mem. Country Club Colo., Phi Theta Kappa. Republican. Roman Catholic. Home: 130 Sierra Vista Dr Colorado Springs CO 80906-7227

BONNELL, VICTORIA EILEEN, sociologist; b. N.Y.C., June 15, 1942; d. Samuel S. and Frances (Nassau) B.; m. Gregory Freidin, May 4, 1971. B.A. Brandeis U., 1964; M.A., Harvard U., 1966, Ph.D., 1975. Lectr. politics U. Calif.-Santa Cruz, 1972-73, 74-76; asst. prof. sociology U. Calif.-Berkeley, 1976-82, assoc. prof., 1982-91, prof., 1991—. Recipient Heldt prize in Slavic women's studies, 1991; AAUW fellow, 1979; Regents faculty fellow, 1978; Fulbright Hays faculty fellow, 1977; Internat. Research and Exchanges Bd. fellow, 1977, 88; Stanford U. Hoover Instn. nat. fellow, 1973-74; Guggenheim fellow, 1985; fellow Ctr. for Advanced Study in Behavioral Scis., 1986-87; Pres.' Rsch. fellow in humanities, 1991-92; grantee Am. Philos. Soc., 1979, Am. Council Learned Socs., 1976, 90-91. Mem. Am. Sociol. Assn., Am. Assn. Advancement Slavic Studies. Am. Hist. Assn. Author: Roots of Rebellion: Workers' Politics and Organizations in St. Petersburg and Moscow, 1900-1914, 1983; editor: The Russian Worker: Life and Labor under the Tsarist Regime, 1983; contbr. articles to profl. jours. Office: U Calif Dept of Sociology Berkeley CA 94720

BONNEY, DONALD ERNEST, physician; b. Escondido, Calif., Sept. 21, 1952; s. Frederick Augustus and Eloise Blair (Duke) B.; m. Deborah Lynn Parries, Apr. 7, 1984. AA, Palomar Jr. Coll., 1973; BA in Social Work, San Diego State U., 1975; D in Chiropractic, Western State Coll., Portland, Oreg., 1985. Legis. asst. Calif. State Assembly, San Diego, 1975-76; adminstrv. asst. Calif. State Assembly, Sacramento, 1976, County of San Diego, 1976-77; carpenter numerous constrn. cos., Oreg., 1977-78; contractor Donald E. Bonney Constrn., Oreg., 1978-85; chiropractor Albuquerque Health Ctr., 1986, Accident & Pain Ctr., Corrales, N.Mex., 1986—. With USN, 1971-72, Vietnam. Recipient Declaration, San Diego County, 1977; Western States Chiropractic scholar, 1984, W.A. Budden scholar Western States Chiropractic, 1985. Mem. N.Mex. Chiropractic Assn., Ariz. Chiropractic Assn., Albuquerque Aerostat Ascension Assn., Corrales Hist. Soc., Rio Rancho C. of C., Western States Alumni Assn., N.Mex. Ski Touring Club, Rio Rancho TIPS Club (pres. 1991, bd. dirs. 1992-93). Office: Accident & Pain Ctr 10200 Box # 5 Corrales NM 87048

BONNEY, JOHN DENNIS, oil company executive; b. Blackpool, Eng., Dec. 22, 1930; s. John P. and Isabel (Evans) B.; four children from previous marriage; m. Elizabeth Shore-Wilson, Aug. 1986; two children. B.A., Hertford Coll., Oxford U., Eng., 1954, M.A., 1959; LL.M., U. Calif., Berkeley, 1956. Oil adviser Middle East, 1959-60; fgn. ops. adviser, asst. mgr., then mgr. Chevron Corp. (formerly Standard Oil Co. of Calif.), San Francisco, 1960-72, v.p., from 1972, vice chmn., 1987—, also dir.; bd. dirs. Am. Petroleum Inst. Clubs: Commonwealth; World Trade (San Francisco); Oxford and Cambridge (London). Office: Chevron Corp 225 Bush St San Francisco CA 94104-4207

BONNY, BLAINE MILAN, retired accountant; b. Midvale, Utah, Oct. 5, 1909; s. Frederick Fritz and Amelia (Poulson) B.; m. Helen Matilda Bolognese, Nov. 3, 1938 (dec. Nov. 18, 1988); 1 child, Brent G. Grad. West high sch., Salt Lake City. Corp. acct. Utah Pr. and Lt. Co., Salt Lake City, 1929-74; ret., 1974—. Patentee in field, 11 copyrights. Mem. Rep. N.H. Com., 1992. Mem. ASCAP, Copper Golf Club, Mason-Acacia Lodge #17, U.S. English, Inc. Home: 847 S 7th E Salt Lake City UT 84102

BONO, SONNY SALVATORE, singer, composer, former mayor; b. Detroit, Feb. 16, 1935; m. Donna Rankin; children: Christy, Santo, Jean; m. Cher LaPiere, Oct. 27, 1964 (div.); 1 child, Chastity; m. Susie Coehlo (div.); m. Mary Whitaker, Mar. 1986; 1 child, Chesare Elan. Songwriter, later artist and repertoire man for Speciality Records; singer with Cher as team Sonny and Cher, 1964-74, co-star The Sonny and Cher Show, 1976-77; now solo night club act; numerous recs., TV, concert and benefit appearances; has appeared on TV series The Love Boat; composer, lyricist, appearance in Good Times, 1966; films include: Escape to Athena, 1979, Airplane II-The Sequel, 1982, Hairspray, 1988; producer film: Chastity, 1969; composer: A Cowboy's Work is Never Done, I Got You, Babe, others; TV video Nitty Gritty Hour with Cher, 1992. Restaurateur; mayor Palm Springs, Calif., 1988-92; ran, defeated U.S. Senate, 1992. Office: care LaRocca Talent Group 3800 Barham Blvd Ste 105 Los Angeles CA 90068-1042 also: PO Box 1786 32 E Tahgutz-McCullum Way Palm Springs CA 92262

BONSER, QUENTIN, surgeon; b. Sedro Wooley, Wash., Nov. 1, 1920; s. George Wayne and Kathleen Imogene (Lynch) B.; BA in Zoology, UCLA, 1943; MD, U. Calif., San Francisco, 1947; m. Loellen Rocca, Oct. 20, 1945; children: Wayne, Gordon, Carol, Patricia (Mrs. Martin Sanford). Intern U. Calif. Hosp., San Francisco, 1947-49, resident gen. surgery, 1949-56; practice gen. surgery, Placerville, Calif., 1956—; ret.; surgeon King Faisal Splty. Hosp., Saudi Arabia, Sept.-Oct., 1984; vis. prof. surgery U. Calif., San Francisco, 1968. Capt. M.C., USAF, 1950-51. Vol. physician, tchr. surgery Vietnam, 1971, 72, 73. Diplomate Am. Bd. Surgery. Fellow A.C.S.; mem. H.C. Naffziger Surg. Soc. (pres. 1974-75). Home: 2590 Northridge Dr Placerville CA 95667-3416

BOOCHEVER, ROBERT, federal judge; b. N.Y.C., Oct. 2, 1917; s. Louis C. and Miriam (Cohen) B.; m. Lois Colleen Maddox, Apr. 22, 1943; children: Barbara K., Linda Lou, Ann Paula, Miriam Deon. AB, Cornell U., 1939, LLB, 1941; HD (hon.), U. Alaska, 1981. Bar: N.Y. 1944, Alaska 1947. Asst. U.S. atty. Juneau, 1946-47; partner firm Faulkner, Banfield, Boochever & Doogan, Juneau, 1947-72; asso. justice Alaska Supreme Ct., 1972-75, 78-80, chief justice, 1975-78; judge U.S. Ct. Appeals (9th cir.), 1980—; chmn. Alaska Jud. Coun., 1975-78; mem. appellate judges seminar NYU Sch. Law, 1975; mem. Conf. Chief Justices, 1975-79, vice chmn., 1978-79; mem. adv. bd. Nat Bank of Alaska, 1968-72; guest speaker Southwestern Law Sch. Disting. Lecture Series, 1992. Chmn. Juneau chpt. ARC, 1949-51, Juneau Planning Commn., 1956-61; mem. Alaska Devel. Bd., 1949-52, Alaska Jud. Qualification Commn., 1972-75; mem. adv. bd. Juneau-Douglas Community Coll. Served to capt. inf. AUS, 1941-45. Named Juneau Man of Year, Rotary, 1974; recipient Disting. Alumnus award Cornell U., 1989. Fellow Am. Coll. Trial Attys.; mem. ABA, Alaska Bar Assn. (pres. 1961-62), Juneau Bar Assn. (pres. 1971-72), Am. Judicature Soc. (dir. 1970-74), Am. Law Inst., Juneau C. of C. (pres. 1952, 55), Alaskans United (chmn. 1962). Clubs: Marine Meml, Wash. Athletic, Juneau Racket, Altadena Town and Country. Office: US Ct Appeals PO Box 91510 125 S Grand Ave Pasadena CA 91109-1510

BOOKMAN, PHILIP, newspaper editor; b. N.Y.C., July 11, 1936; s. Henry and Anne (Mandel) B.; children: Jonathan, Charles; m. H. Mary (Bookman,) Oct. 25, 1975. BA in English Lit., U. Buffalo, 1957. Assoc. editor Lebhar-Friedman Publs., N.Y.C., 1959-63; regional editor Evening Press, Binghamton, N.Y., 1964-71; asst. mng. editor Sun-Bull., Binghamton, 1971-74; mng. editor Camden (N.J.) Courier-Post, 1975-80; exec. editor The Record, Stockton, Calif., 1980—. Served with USANG, 1959, 1959-61. Mem. Calif. Freedom of Info. Com. (former chmn., exec. com.), Am. Soc. Newspaper Editors, Sigma Delta Chi. Office: Stockton Record 530 E Market St Stockton CA 95202-3097

BOOLOOTIAN, RICHARD ANDREW, communications executive; b. Fresno, Calif., Oct. 17, 1927; s. Vanig and Vivian (Ohannesian) B.; m. Mary Jo Blue, Oct. 20, 1945 (div. 1980); children: Mark, Alan, Craig; m. Yvonne Morse Daniels. BA, Calif. State U., Fresno, 1951, MA, 1953; PhD, Stanford U., 1957. Cert. tchr. (life) Calif. Assoc. prof. UCLA, 1957-67; cons. U. Colo., Boulder, 1967-68; pres. Sci. Software Systems Inc., Sherman Oaks, Calif., 1969—, Boolootian & Assocs., 1990—; cons. Morler Internat., Inc., Burbank, Calif., 1985-92; dir. sci. curriculum Mirman Sch. Gifted, L.A., 1974—, chmn. sci. dept., 1986—. Author 21 textbooks; contbr. articles to profl. jours. Fellow Lalor Found., 1963-64, NIH, 1965; nominee Excellence in Teaching Predl. award, 1991, 92. Fellow AAAS; mem. Challenger Soc. Office: Sci Software Systems Inc 3576 Woodcliff Rd Sherman Oaks CA 91403-5045

BOONE, JEFFREY LYNN, internist; b. Wichita, Kans., Aug. 1, 1951; s. Stewart and Joyce (Henkle) B.; m. Colette Marie Felgate, May 20, 1978; children: Tyler, Parker, Hunter, Mackenzie. BS, Southwestern Coll., 1973; MS, Kans. State U., 1975; MD, U. Iowa, 1983. Diplomate Am. Bd. Internal Medicine. Intern, resident in internal medicine Good Samaritan Hosp. and Med. Ctr., Portland, Oreg., 1983-86; phys. fitness specialist YMCA, Des Moines, 1974-79; assoc. med. dir., then med. dir. Nat. Ctr. Preventive and Stress Medicine, Phoenix, 1986-87; med. dir. Inst. Stress Medicine, Denver, 1987-90; dir. preventive medicine Swedish Med. Ctr., Englewood, Colo., 1990—; asst. clin. prof. medicine U. Colo., Denver, 1990—; dir. and founder Preventive and Stress Medicine Ctr. Excellence, 1992—. Contbg. author: Stress and Hypertension, 1991; guest editor: Primary Care: Clinics in Office Practice-Hypertension, 1991. Recipient award for innovations in disease prevention and health promotion HHS, 1986. Mem. Rotary Internat. Home: 5597 S Hillside St Englewood CO 80111 Office: Swedish Med Ctr 8200 E Belleview # 390 Englewood CO 80111

BOONE, LOIS RUTH, legislator; b. Vancouver, B.C., Can., Apr. 26, 1947; d. George Charles Bearne and Ruth (Lindberg) Chudley; ; children: Sonia, Tanis. Tchr.'s cert., Simon Fraser U., 1969. Tchr. Sch. Dist. 57, Prince George, B.C., 1969-71, Sch. Dist. 27, Williams Lake, B.C., 1971-72; office mgr. Prince George YM-YWCA, 1972-73; case aide worker Vancouver YWCA, 1973-74; adminstrv. asst. Gov. B.C., Prince George, 1978-86; mem. legis. assembly Gov. B.C., Victoria, 1986—. Trustee Sch. Dist. 57, Prince George, 1981-85. Mem. New Democratic Party. Office: Min Govt Svcs, Rm 103 Parliament Bldgs, Victoria, BC Canada V8V 1X4

BOONE, MARK PHILIP, manufacturing company official, consultant; b. Greensboro, N.C., Oct. 8, 1951; s. Philip Sidney and Julia Florence (Rippy) B.; m. Joanne Evelyn Rummell, Oct. 10, 1981; children: Geoffrey Philip, Johnathon Mark, Julianne Marie, Jameson David. BS, N.C. State U., 1974, MS, 1977; cert., Def. Systems Mgmt. Coll., Ft. Belvoir, Va., 1989. Cert. safety profl. Extension specialist indsl. extension svc. N.C. State U., Raleigh, 1977-79; scientist EG&G Idaho Inc., Idaho Falls, 1979-80; mgr. bus. devel. FMC Corp., San Jose, Calif., 1980—; human factors cons. Contbr. articles to profl. jours. Loaned exec. United Way Santa Clara County, San Jose, 1986, tng. chmn., 1987; co-chmn. auction, bd. dirs. Young Life San Jose, 1990; elder Westminster Presbyn. Ch., pres. corp., 1986-88, 92-94. Mem. Human Factors Soc. (chpt. v.p. 1978-79), Toastmasters (area bd. govs. 1985-86, Able Toastmaster award 1988). Republican. Home: 1394 Hanchett Ave San Jose CA 95126-2605 Office: FMC Corp 1105 Coleman PO Box 58123 Santa Clara CA 95052

BOONE, NORMAN MCKIEGHAN, financial planner; b. Inglewood, Calif., June 4, 1947; s. Elton D. and Barbara (Lombard) B.; m. Elisa A. Boone, May 31, 1982; children: Andrew, Anaelisa. BA in Polit. Sci., Stanford U., 1969; MBA, Harvard Bus. Sch., 1977. Cert. Fin. Planner, Registry Fin. Planner. Vol. VISTA, Price, Utah, 1969-71; asst. v.p. Wells Fargo Bank, San Francisco, 1977-80; CFO Henderson Group, Oakland, Calif., 1980-82; v.p. fin. adminstrn. D'Arcy, McManus, Masius, San Francisco, 1982-84; v.p. Hibernia Bank, San Francisco, 1984-87; fin. planner Associated Securities, San Francisco, 1987—. Contbr. articles to profl. jours. Lt. U.S. Army, 1972-75. Mem. Internat. Assn. for Fin. Planning, Rotary

Club, Estate Planning Coun. Office: Boone Assocs One Post St # 2750 San Francisco CA 94104-5231

BOOTH, JOHN LOUIS, service executive; b. Danville, Va., May 15, 1933; s. William Irvine and Melba (Harvey) B.; m. Ann Fennell, May 23, 1959; children: Mark, Robin. BA, U. Richmond, 1958; ThM, Dallas Theol. Sem., 1962, ThD, 1965; postgrad., Ariz. State U., 1972, 79. Pastor Skyway Bible Ch., Seattle, 1964-66, Mount Prospect (Ill.) Bible Ch., 1966-71, Camelback Bible Ch., Paradise Valley, Ariz., 1971-78; counselor Camelback Counseling Ctr., Phoenix, 1978-79; dir. Paradise Valley Counseling, Inc., Phoenix, 1980—; chmn. bd. Paradise Valley Counseling, Inc., 1980—; chmn. bd. Paradise Valley Counseling Found., Inc., Phoenix, 1982—; adj. prof. Grand Canyon U., 1981—, Southwestern Coll., Phoenix, 1979—, Talbott Theol. Sem. Phoenix Ext., 1983-85; seminar speaker frequent engagements, 1965—. Author: Understanding Today's Problems, 1980, Marriage by the Master Plan, 1980, Equipping for Effective Marriage, 1983, (tape series) Starting Over, 1982, Enjoying All God Intended, 1988, 91, 93. Precinct committeeman Rep. Party, Phoenix, 1983-84, 87-88, 90-91; chaplain Ariz. State Senate, Phoenix, 1973. Mem. Christian Assn. for Psychol. Studies, Am. Assn. Christian Counselors. Baptist. Office: Paradise Valley Counseling Inc Ste 211 10210 N 32d St Phoenix AZ 85028

BOOZE, THOMAS FRANKLIN, toxicologist; b. Denver, Mar. 4, 1955; s. Ralph Walker and Ann (McNatt) B.; m. Patricia Jude Bullock, Aug. 8, 1981; children: Heather N., Ian T. BS, U. Calif., Davis, 1978; MS, Kans. State U., 1981, PhD, 1985. Registered environ assessor, Calif. Asst. instr. Kans. State U., Manhattan, 1979-85; sr. consulting toxicologist Chevron Corp., Sacramento, 1985-92; sr. toxicologist Radian Corp., Sacramento, 1992—; cons. in field, Manhattan, Kans., 1981-83. contbr. articles to profl. jours. Vol. Amigos de las Americas, Marin County, Calif., 1973, Hospice Care, Manhattan, 1985. Mem. N.Y. Acad. Sci., Soc. Toxicology, Soc. for Risk Analysis, Sigma Xi. Home: 3918 Balverne Ct Sacramento CA 95842-5237 Office: Radian Corp 10389 Old Placerville Rd Sacramento CA 95827

BOQUIST, RONALD JAY, hazardous waste treatment consultant; b. International Falls, Minn., July 20, 1964; s. Alfred M. and Betty Boquist. AA, Bellevue Community Coll., 1985; BS, Ctrl. Washington U., 1987. Tech. ops. supr. N.W. EnviroSvc. Inc., Seattle, 1987—; cons., owner Chemquest Co., Tukwila, Wash., 1991—. Mem. Am. Chem. Soc., Rocky Mt. Elk Found. Home and Office: Chemquest PO Box 3874 Seattle WA 98124-3874

BORA, ALEXANDER, political party official; b. Snohomish County, Wash., Aug. 14, 1916; s. Feodor Boradzoff and Nadejda (Karaev) Boradzova. Student, Pomona Coll., 1934-36, U. So. Calif., L.A., 1936-37. Master Mariner Unlimited-4th Issue all tonnages, all oceans. With Merchant Marine, 1945-71; writer, 1971—; founder, nat. dir. New Federalist Polit. Party, 1975—. Author: On Freedom of the Seas, New Federalist Papers, 1988, On the Aristocracy, 1990, What is a Nation?, 1990. With USCG, 1941-45. Home: 760 Lillian Way Apt 6 Los Angeles CA 90038-3721

BORAH, BRETT A., lawyer; b. Los Angeles, 1950; s. A. Noah and Bernice (Zeidell) B.; m. Judy Nudler, May 1, 1983. AA, Glendale Jr. Coll., 1970; AB, U. Calif., Berkeley, 1972, JD, 1979. Bar: Calif., 1980, U.S. Ct. Appeals (9th cir.) 1980, U.S. Supreme Ct., 1983. Assoc. Scher & Bassett, Sunnyvale, Calif., 1980—; judge pro tem Santa Clara County Mcpl. Court, 1984—, Protem Santa Clara Superior Ct., 1987—; chmn. Saratoga City Pub. Safety Commn., 1989; foreman Santa Clara County Grand Jury, 1987-88. Chmn. Sunnyvale Parking Commn., 1982-83. Mem. Santa Clara County Bar Assn. (trustee 1981-84, 88, chmn. workers' compensation sect. 1989-90), Sunnyvale-Cupertino Bar Assn. (pres. 1988), Santa Clara County Barristers (trustee 1981-84), Sunnyvale C. of C. (pres. 1985-86). Office: Scher & Bassett 465 S Mathilda Ave Ste 210 Sunnyvale CA 94086-7606

BORBRIDGE, G., protective services official. Chief constable Calgary (Alta.) Police Svc., Can. Office: Calgary Police Service, PO Box 2100 Stn M, Calgary, AB Canada T2P 2M5*

BORCHERS, ROBERT REECE, physicist, laboratory administrator; b. Chgo., Apr. 4, 1936; s. Robert Harley and Rena Josephine (Reece) B.; m. Mary Bridget Hennessy, Nov. 26, 1960; children: Patrick Joseph, Anne Marie, Robert Edward. BS in Physics, U. Notre Dame, 1958; MS in Physics, Math., U. Wis., 1959, PhD in Nuclear Physics, 1961. Prof. physics U. Wis., Madison, 1961-76, vice chancellor, 1976-77; vice chancellor U. Colo., Boulder, 1977-79; dep. assoc. dir. MFE Program Lawrence Livermore (Calif.) Nat. Lab., 1979-83, assoc. dir. computation, 1983-91, asst. to dir. for univ. rels., 1991—, cons. laser fusion program, 1972-79; mem. com. NSF, Washington, 1973—, Nat. Acad. Sci., Washington, 1983—. Editor Computers in Physics jour., 1987-91, chmn. editorial bd., 1991—; contbr. numerous chpts. in books, articles on physics and computing. Mem. San Francisco Symphony Assn., 1984—. NSF postdoctoral fellow, 1964; A.J. Schmidt Found. fellow and scholar, 1954-60; Sloan Found. fellow, 1964-68; Guggenheim Found. fellow, 1970; recipient W.H. Kiekhofer Disting. Teaching award U. Wis., Madison, 1966; Centennial of Sci. Alumnus award U. Notre Dame, 1966. Fellow Am. Phys. Soc. Home: 2594 Chateau Way Livermore CA 94550-5729 Office: Lawrence Livermore Nat Lab Nat Lab 414 PO Box 808 Livermore CA 94551

BORDA, RICHARD JOSEPH, management consultant; b. San Francisco, Aug. 16, 1931; s. Joseph Clement and Ethel Cathleen (Donovan) B.; m. Judith Maxwell, Aug. 30, 1953; children: Michelle, Stephen Joseph. AB, Stanford U., 1953, MBA, 1957. With Wells Fargo Bank, San Francisco, 1957-70; mgr. Wells Fargo Bank, 1963-66, asst. v.p., 1966-67, v.p., 1967-70; exec. v.p. adminstrn. Wells Fargo Bank, San Francisco, 1973-85; asst. sec. Air Force Manpower Res. Affairs, Washington, 1970-73; vice chmn., chief fin. officer Nat. Life Ins. Co., Montpelier, Vt., 1985-90, also bd. dirs.; chmn., chief exec. officer Sentinal Group Funds, Inc., 1985-90, also bd. dirs.; mgmt. cons., 1990—. Pres. Air Force Aid Soc., Washington; trustee Scholarships for Children of Am. Mil. Pers., Monterey Inst. of Internat. Studies; bd. dirs. Monterray County Symphony. Served to lt. col. USMCR, 1953-55. Recipient Exceptional Civilian Service, 1973. Mem. USMC Res. Officers Assn., Air Force Assn., Army-Navy Club, Pilgrims Club, Bohemian Club, Monterey Peninsula Country Club, Old Capital Club, Phi Gamma Delta. Republican. Episcopalian.

BORDELON, SCOTT LEE, computer systems engineer; b. Fullerton, Calif., May 23, 1967; s. Sidney Augusten and Carolyn Ann (Dobsky) B. BSEE, U. Calif., 1989, MS in Computer Engring., 1990. Registered profl. engr., Calif. Analog crcts. designer Western Instrument Corp., Ventura, Calif., 1988; software engr. Rockwell Internat., Irvine, Calif., 1989; computer architecture rschr. UCSB Computer Architecture Lab., Goleta, Calif., 1988-90; systems design engr. Amdahl Corp., Sunnyvale, Calif., 1990—; networks cons. U. Calif., Santa Barbara, 1990-91. Inventor in field. Vol. homeless shelter Community Found. of Santa Clara, Calif., 1991-92. Mem. IEEE, Assn. Computing Machinery, Eta Kappa Nu. Unitarian. Office: MS 275 1250 E Arques Ave Sunnyvale CA 94088

BORDEN, RICHARD STANLEY, public relations professional; b. L.A., Feb. 3, 1962; s. Stanley Matthew and Evelyn (Phillips) B.; m. Felicia Cano Beeson, May 3, 1987; children: Theodore Cameron, Derek Matthew. BS in Journalism, Calif. State U., Northridge, 1983. Sr. account exec. Simon/McGarry Pub. Rels., L.A., 1984-86; gen. mgr. The Hamm Group, Westlake Village, Calif., 1986-89; mgr. mktg. communications Micom Communications Corp., Simi Valley, Calif., 1989—; pres. Borden & Assocs., Moorpark, Calif., 1989—; news anchor All Things Considered 1983. Dir., producer film Temporary Secretary, 1980; writer, actor tng. film Do-It Yourself Public Relations, 1989. Recipient Golden Mike award, 1983. Mem. Soc. Profl. Journalists (1st place award western region 1983), Toastmasters (pres. 1990-91, 1st place award Simi Valley 1990), Golden Key, Kappa Tau Alpha, Omicron Delta Kappa, Phi Kappa Phi. Home: 13578 Cedar Grove Ln Moorpark CA 93021-2867 Office: Micom Communications Corp 4100 E Los Angeles Ave Simi Valley CA 93063-3397

BORDEN, THOMAS ALLEN, urologist, educator; b. Richmond, Ind., Aug. 31, 1937; s. William C. and Mildred (Duffill) B.; m. Joan Mattmiller (div. 1988); married; children: Christopher, Catherine. BA, Earlham Coll., 1959; MS, U. Chgo., 1963, MD, 1963, cert., 1969. Chmn. Dept. of Urology, program dir. U. N.Mex., Albuquerque, 1973—; pres. N.Mex. Med. Found., 1985-88. Author: (textbook) Genitourinary Cancer Surgery, 1982; contbr. articles to profl. jours. Maj. USAF, 1969-71. Mem. AMA, Soc. Pediatric Urology, Am. Urology Assn. Republican. Office: U NMex Sch Medicine 2211 Lomas Blvd NE Albuquerque NM 87106-2745

BORDNER, GREGORY WILSON, environmental engineer; b. Buffalo, Aug. 16, 1959; s. Raymond Gordon and Nancy Lee (Immegart) B.; m. Margaret Patricia Toon, June 14, 1981; children: Eric Lawrence, Heather Rae. BS in Chem. Engring., Calif. State Poly. U., 1982; MS in Systems Mgmt., U. So. Calif., 1987. Commd. 2nd lt. USAF, 1983, advanced through grades to capt., 1987; engr., mgr. various air launched missile, anti-satellite and strategic def. initiative projects Air Force Rocket Propulsion Lab., Edwards AFB, Calif., 1983-86; asst. mgr. space transp. Air Force Astronautics Lab., Edwards AFB, 1986-87; chief small intercontinental ballistic missiles ordnance firing system br. Hdqrs. Ballistic Missile Orgn., San Bernardino, Calif., 1987-90; sr. plant environ. engr. Filtrol Corp./Akzo Chems. Inc., L.A., 1991-92; water/soils project engr. TABC, Inc., Long Beach, Calif., 1992—. Author: (manual) Pyrotechnic Transfer Line Evaluation, 1984, (with others) Rocket Motor Heat Transfer, 1984. Mem. Am. Inst. Chem. Engrs., Soc. for Advancement of Material and Process Engring. Home: 10841 Ring Ave Alta Loma CA 91737

BORDOW, ROBERT ALEXANDER, electrical engineer; b. N.Y.C., Nov. 7, 1954; s. Burton William and Norma Marta (DiBenedetto) B.; m. Joan M. Kernis, Sept. 28, 1972; children: Daisy Doe, Dandelion Kellie, Alissa Devi. AS in Electronic Technology, Santa Rosa (Calif.) Jr. Coll., 1979; BSEE, U. Calif., Berkeley, 1982, MSEE, 1983. Chief engr. Sta. KZST-FM, Santa Rosa, 1975-80; engring. tech. Datapoint Corp., Berkeley, Calif., 1981; head teaching asst. U. Calif., Berkeley, 1982-83; research assoc. Lawrence Berkeley Lab., 1981; design engr. Hewlett Packard Corp., Rohnert Park, Calif., 1983—; physics lectr. Sonoma State U., Rohnert Park, 1985-89; cons. Ice House Studio, San Rafael, 1982-83. Active World Runners, Santa Rosa, 1980—. Regents of U. Calif. Fellow, Berkeley, 1982, 83. Mem. Phi Beta Kappa. Democrat. Office: Hewlett Packard 1400 Fountaingrove Pkwy Santa Rosa CA 95403

BOREL, JAMES DAVID, anesthesiologist; b. Chgo., Nov. 15, 1951; s. James Albert and Nancy Ann (Sieverson) B. BS, U. Wis., 1973; MD, Med. Coll. of Wis., 1977. Diplomate Am. Bd. Anesthesiology, Nat. Bd. Med. Examiners, Am. Coll. Anesthesiologists. Research asst. McArdle Lab. for Cancer Research, Madison, Wis., 1972-73, Stanford U. and VA Hosp., Palo Alto, 1976-77; intern. The Cambridge (Mass.) Hosp., 1977-78; clin. fellow in medicine Harvard Med. Sch., Boston, 1977-78, clin. fellow in asaesthesia, 1978-80, clin. instr. in anaesthesia, 1980; resident in anesthesiology Peter Bent Brigham Hosp., Boston, 1978-80; anesthesiologist Mt. Auburn Hosp., Cambridge, 1980; fellow in anesthesiology Ariz. Health Scis. Ctr., Tucson, 1980-81; research assoc. U. Ariz. Coll. Medicine, Tucson, 1980-81, assoc. in anesthesiology, 1981—; active staff Mesa (Ariz.) Luth. Hosp., 1981—; courtesy staff Scottsdale (Ariz.) Meml. Hosp., 1982—; vis. anaesthetist St. Joseph's Hosp., Kingston, Jamaica, 1980. Contbr. numerous articles to profl. jours. Mem. AMA, AAAS, Mass. Anesthesia Council on Edn., Ariz. Anesthesia Alumni Assn., Ariz. Soc. Anesthesiologists, Am. Soc. Regional Anesthesia, Can. Anesthetists' Soc., Internat. Anesthesia Research Soc., Am. Soc. Anesthesiologists. Office: Valley Anesthesia Cons 2950 N 7th St Phoenix AZ 85014-5405

BOREN, KENNETH RAY, endocrinologist; b. Evansville, Ind., Dec. 31, 1945; s. Doyle Clifford and Jeannette (Koerner) B.; m. Rebecca Lane Wallace, Aug. 25, 1967; children: Jennifer, James, Michael, Peter, Nicklas, Benjamin. BS, Ariz. State U., 1967; MD, Ind. U., Indpls., 1972; MA, Ind. U., Bloomington, 1974. Diplomate Am. Bd. Endocrinology, Am. Bd. Nephrology. Intern in pathology Ind. U. Sch. Medicine, Indpls., 1972; intern in medicine Ind. U. Sch. Medicine, 1972-73, resident in medicine, 1975-77, fellow in endocrinology, 1977-79, fellow nephrology, 1979-80, instr., 1980; physician Renal and Endocrine Assocs., Mesa, Ariz., 1980—; chief medicine Mesa Luth Hosp., 1987-89, chief staff, 1990-91. Bd. dirs. Ariz. Kidney Found., Phoenix, 1984—. Lt. USN, 1973-75. Fellow ACP; mem. AMA, Maricopa County Med. Assn., Ariz. Med. Assn., Am. Soc. Nephrology, Internat. Soc. Nephrology, Am. Diabetes Assn. Republican. Latter Day Saints. Home: 4222 E Mclellan Rd # 10 Mesa AZ 85205-3119 Office: Renal and Endocrine Assocs 560 W Brown Rd Mesa AZ 85201-3221

BORESI, ARTHUR PETER, author, educator; b. Toluca, Ill.; s. John Peter and Eva (Grotti) B.; m. Clara Jean Gordon, Dec. 28, 1946; children—Jennifer Ann Boresi Hill, Annette Boresi Pueschel, Nancy Jean Boresi Broderick. Student, Kenyon Coll., 1943-44; BSEE, U. Ill., 1948, MS in Mechanics, 1949, PhD in Mechanics, 1953. Research engr. N. Am. Aviation, 1950; materials engr. Nat. Bur. Standards, 1951; mem. faculty U. Ill. at Urbana, 1953—, prof. theoretical and applied mechanics and nuclear engring., 1959-79; Disting. vis. prof. Clarkson Coll. Tech., Potsdam, N.Y., 1968-69; NAVSEA research prof. Naval Postgrad. Sch., Monterey, Calif., 1978-79; prof. civil engring. U. Wyo., Laramie, 1979—; head U. Wyo., 1980—; vis. prof. Naval Postgrad. Sch., Monterey, Calif., 1986-87.; cons. in field. Author: Engineering Mechanics, 1959, Elaasticity in Engineering Mechanics, 3d edit., 1987, Advanced Mechanics of Materials, 5th edit., 1993, Approximate Solution Methods in Engineering Mechanics, 1991; also articles. Served with USAAF, 1943-44; Served with AUS, 1944-46. Fellow ASME, ASCE; mem. Am. Soc. Engring. Edn., Am. Acad. Mechanics (founding, treas.), Soc. Exptl. Mechanics, Sigma Xi. Office: U Wyo Box 3295 Univ Station Laramie WY 82071

BORG, AXEL EDWIN, librarian, educator; b. Frankfurt/Main, Hesse, Germany, Sept. 22, 1953; naturalized citizen, 1961; s. Lavern Gerald and Jane Scott (Wood) B.; m. Myra Lynn Kitchens, Dec. 17, 1988; 1 child, Laura Jane. BA in History, Pomona Coll., 1976; MLS, U. Calif., Berkeley, 1984. Libr. Natural Resources Libr. U. Calif., Berkeley, 1984-86; reference libr. Sci. Libr. U. Calif., Santa Cruz, 1986-88; wine bibliographer Shields Libr. U. Calif., Davis, 1988—; vis. lectr. Libr. Sch., U. Calif., Berkeley, 1987-89, 92; instr. Sacramento City Coll., 1991—. Capt. U.S. Army, 1976-83. Mem. Calif. Hist. Soc., Book Club Calif., Sacramento Book Collectors Club, Sci. and Engring. Acad. Librs. Democrat. Methodist. Office: U Calif Shields Libr Davis CA 95616

BORGATTA, MARIE LENTINI, sociologist; b. N.Y.C., Apr. 17, 1925; d. Paul and Linda (Marco) Lentini; m. Edgar F. Borgatta, Oct. 5, 1946; children:Lynn, Kim, Lee. BS, Queens Coll., 1945; MA, NYU, 1961; PhD, CUNY, 1980. Biochemist Continental Baking Co., Jamaica, N.Y., 1945-47; rsch. asst. Sloan-Kettering Inst. Cancer Rsch., N.Y.C., 1947-50; instr. U. Wis., Madison, 1969; adj. lectr. Bklyn. Coll., 1972-74; rsch. asst. Grad. Ctr., CUNY, 1974-75, tng. fellow, 1976-79; project dir. Am. Found. for Blind, N.Y.C., 1979-80; lectr., rsch. assoc. U. Wash., Seattle, 1981—. Mng. editor Ency. of Sociology, 1987-91; co-editor: Marriage and the Family, 1969; contbr. articles to profl. jours. Mem. Am. Sociol. Assn., Am. Pub. Health Assn., Pacific Sociol. Assn., Internat. Inst. Sociology (congress coordinator 1984). Office: U Wash Mail Stop DK40 Seattle WA 98195

BORGES, CARLOS REGO, topology educator; b. Lomba da Fazenda, Azores, Portugal, Feb. 17, 1939; came to U.S., 1956; s. José Jacinto Rego and Maria do Nascimento (Borges) Borges; married; children: Mary Lou Freitas, Carlos F., Michael F. BS, Humboldt State Coll., 1960; MS, U. Wash., 1962, PhD, 1964. Asst. prof. U. Nev., Reno, 1964-65; asst. prof. U. Calif., Davis, 1965-68, assoc. prof., 1968-72, prof., 1972—. Contbr. articles to profl. jours. Republican. Roman Catholic. Office: U Calif Davis CA 95616

BORGES, WILLIAM, III, environmental analyst; b. Long Beach, Calif., Nov. 21, 1948; s. William Borges Jr. and Dorothy Mae (Raymond) Morris; m. Rosalind Denise Marye, Nov. 23, 1968; children: William IV, Blake Austin. BA in Geography, Calif. State U., Sonoma, 1973. Environ. planner Mendocino County Planning Dept., Ukiah, Calif., 1976; project mgr. Engring. Sci., Inc., Berkeley, Calif., 1976-79, Santa Clara County Planning Dept., San Jose, Calif., 1979-81, Internat. Tech. Corp., San Jose, 1985-88; mgr. sales ops. Adac Labs., Milpitas, Calif., 1983-85; prin. WT Environ. Cons., Phoenix, 1988-91; project mgr. Dynamac Corp., Newport Beach, Calif., 1991—. Contbr. photographs to various mags. Coord. pub. rels. Stellar Acad. for Dyslexics, Hayward, Calif., 1988. With M.I., U.S. Army, 1967-70. Democrat. Office: Dynamac Corp 1601 Dove St Newport Beach CA 92660

BORING, CHARLES MARION, credit manager; b. Ft. Knox, Ky., Jan. 14, 1943; s. William Lewis and Hilda Ethel (Crites) B.; m. Iris Marie Saueressig, June 3, 1967; children: Jennifer Lynn, Charles Darold. BS, U. Colo., 1972; MS, U. La Verne, 1981. Enlisted USAF, 1962, commd. 2d lt., 1972, advanced through grades to capt., 1982, ret., 1982, personnel officer, 1972-82; realtor Gallery of Homes, Anchorage, 1982-84, sales mgr., 1984-85; credit mgr. Anchorage Cold Storage, Anchorage, 1985—. Mem. supervisory com. Denali Fed. Credit Union, 1991—. Mem. Nat. Assn. Credit Mgmtm. (Anchorage Group chmn. 1992—). Lutheran. Office: Anchorage Cold Storage 240 W 1st Ave PO Box 100039 Anchorage AK 99501

BORINSTEIN, DENNIS IVAN, real estate investment company executive; b. Detroit, Feb. 1, 1949; s. Morris Z. and Dora (Denenberg) B.; m. Carole M. Haveman, June 22, 1973; 1 child, David Michael. BA, Mich. State U., 1970; AM, U. Chgo., 1972, PhD, 1976. Lic. real estate broker, Calif. Clin. practice psychology, Ill., 1973-75, N.Y., 1975-80; pres. MDI Systems, Inc., 1980—, Security Mortgage Co., 1988—; cons. in field. Contbr. articles to profl. jours. Mem. Am. Psychol. Assn., N.Y. State Psychol. Assn., Calif. State Psychol. Assn., Assn. Behavior Analysis. Office: 139 N La Peer Dr Beverly Hills CA 90211-1901

BORK, ALFRED, information and computer science educator; b. Jacksonville, Fla., Sept. 18, 1926. BS, Ga. Inst. Tech., 1947; MS, Brown U., 1950, PhD, 1953. Scholar Dublin Inst. for Advanced Studies, 1952-53; asst. to assoc. to prof. physics U. Alaska, 1953-62; staff physicist Commn. on Coll. Physics, 1963; cons. Harvard Project Physics, Harvard U., 1966-68; prof. physics Reed Coll., 1963-68; vice chair undergrad. studies, physics dept. U. Calif., Irvine, 1973-80, prof. info. and computer sci., 1968—; mem. internat. adv. bd. Internat. Conf. Series on Computer-Assisted Learning in Post-Secondary Edn. Author: FORTAN for Physics, 1967, Using the IBM 1130, 1968, Programmierund und Benutzung des Computersystems IBM 1130, 1970, Notions About Motion, 1970, 71, Computer Assisted Learning in Physics Education, 1980, Learning with Computers, 1981, Personal Computers for Education, 1985, (in Spanish) 1986, Learning With Personal Computers, 1986; (with A. Arons) Science and Ideas, 1964; editor: Science and Language, 1966, and others; contbg. editor Technol. Horizons in Edn. Jour., AEDS Monitor, Ednl. Computer Mag.; mem. editorial bd. Interactive Learning Internat., Jour. Ednl. Computing Rsch., Teaching Thinking & Problem Solving, Computer Grpahics '84 Daily, Jour. Interactive Instrn. Devel., Jour. Artificial Intelligence in Edn.; chair tech. com. on computers in edn. TCCE Newsletter; fgn. advisor Informatica Educativa; contbr. numerous articles to profl. jours. Rsch. fellow, Harvard U.; faculty fellow NSF, fellow Assn. for the Devel. of Computer Based Instructional Systems, 1986; recipient Millikan award Am. Assn. of Physics Tchrs., Rsch. award AEDS Outstanding Computer Educator, 1985. Office: Ednl Tech Ctr ICS U Calif Irvine CA 92717

BORN, STEVEN MURRAY, podiatrist; b. Chgo., Sept. 29, 1947; s. Victor Harry and Selma (Teplitz) B.; m. Janice Rochelle Aronesti, July 11, 1971; children: Jamie, Jordan. Bs, Eureka (Ill.) Coll., 1973; BS, DPM, Ill. Coll. Podiatric Medicine, Chgo., 1977. Diplomate Am. Bd. Quality Assurance Utilization Rev. Physician, Am. Acad. Pain Mgmt.; cert. Am. Coun. Cert. Podiatric Physicians & Surgeons. Surg. resident Henrotin Hosp., Chgo., 1977-78; pvt. practice specializing in podiatric medicine Phoenix; staff Good Samaritan Hosp., Phoenix Gen. hosp., Boswell Hosp., Del Webb Hosp., Valley of the Sun Rehab. Hosp. With U.S. Army, 1966-69. Mem. Am. Geriatric Soc., Ariz. Geriatric Soc., Acad. Ambulatory Foot Surgery, Am. Assn. Physicians and Podiatrists, Am. Assn. Podiatric Physicians and Surgeons, Am. Assn. Hosp. Podiatrists, Am. Pub. Health Assn., Am. Podiatric Circulatory Assn., Acad. Clin. Electrodynography. Office: 13660 N 94th Dr Ste 4A Peoria AZ 85381-4836

BORNEMAN, JOHN PAUL, pharmaceutical executive; b. Darby, Pa., Oct. 18, 1958; s. John A. III and Ann (Conway) B.; m. Anne Marie Albert, July 18, 1980; 1 child, Elizabeth Anne. BS in Chemistry, St. Joseph's U., Phila., 1980, MS in Chemistry, 1983, MBA in Fin., 1986. V.p. Boiron-Borneman Inc., Norwood, Pa., 1980-86; dir. mktg. Standard Homeopathic Co., L.A., 1986-89, v.p., 1989—; chmn. FDA liaison com. Am. Homeopathic Pharm. Assn., 1986—. Editor Homeopathic Pharmacopoeia U.S., 1983—; columnist Resonance mag., 1986—; contbr. articles to homeopathic jours. Bd. dirs. Internat. Found. for Homeopathy, 1986-92, Nat. Ctr. for Homeopathy, 1987—. Mem. Am. Chem. Soc., Am. Pharm. Assn., Sigma Xi. Office: Standard Homeopathic Co 210 W 131st St Box 61067 Los Angeles CA 90061

BORNS, DAVID JAMES, geologist; b. Phila., Feb. 10, 1950; s. William Joseph and Patricia (Flint) B. BA, Dartmouth Coll., 1972; MSc, U. Otago, Dunedin, New Zealand, 1975; PhD, U. Wash., 1980. Teaching, rsch. asst. U. Wash., Seattle, 1975-79, rsch. assoc., 1979-81; mem. tech. staff Sandia Nat. Labs., Albuquerque, 1981—. Contbr. articles to profl. jours. Suicide prevention counselor U. N.Mex. NSF grad. fellow, 1972, Fullbright fellow, 1972, Amoco Found. fellow, 1978. Mem. Geol. Soc. Am. Democrat. Unitarian. Home: 3615 Mackland Ave NE Albuquerque NM 87110-6121 Office: Sandia Nat Labs Org 6116 PO Box 5800 Albuquerque NM 87185-5800

BORNSTEIN, ELI, painter, sculptor; b. Milw., Dec. 28, 1922; naturalized, 1972; m. Christine; 2 children. BS, U. Wis., 1945, MS, 1954; student, Art Inst. Chgo., U. Chgo., 1943, Academie Montmartre of Fernand Leger, Paris, 1951, Academie Julian, 1952; DLitt (hon.), U. Sask., Can., 1990. Tchr. drawing, painting and sculpture Milw. Art Inst., 1943-47; tchr. design U. Wis., 1949; tchr. drawing, painting, sculpture, design and graphics U. Sask., Can., 1950-90; prof. U. Sask., 1963-90, prof. emeritus, 1990—, head art dept., 1963-71. Painted in France, 1951-52, Italy, 1957, Holland, 1958; exhibited widely, 1943—; retrospective exhbn. (works 1943-64), Mendel Art Gallery, Saskatoon, 1965, one man shows, Kazimir Gallery, Chgo., 1965, 67, Saskatoon Pub. Library, 1975, Can. Cultural Center, Paris, 1976, Glenbow-Alta. Inst. Art, Calgary, 1976, Mendel Art Gallery, Saskatoon, 1982, York U. Gallery, Toronto, 1983, Confedn. Ctr. Art Gallery, Charlottetown, P.E.I., 1983, Owens Art Gallery, Mt. Allison U., Sackville, N.B., 1984, Fine Arts Gallery, U. Wis.-Milw., 1984; represented in numerous pvt. collections; executed marble sculpture now in permanent collection, Walker Art Center, Mpls., 1947, aluminum constrn. for Sask. Tchrs. Fedn. Bldg., 1956, structurist relief in painted wood and aluminum for, Arts and Scis. Bldg., U. Sask., 1958, structurist relief in enamelled steel for, Internat. Air Terminal, Winnipeg, Man., Can., 1962, four-part constructed relief for, Wascana Pl., Wascana Ctr. Authority, Regina, Sask., 1983; also structurist reliefs exhibited, Mus. Contemporary Art, Chgo., Herron Mus. Art, Indpls., Cranbrook Acad. Art Galleries, Mich., High Mus., Atlanta, Can. House, Cultural Centre Gallery, London, 1983, Can. Cultural Ctr., Paris, 1983, Brussels, 1983, Milw. Art Mus., 1984, Bonn, 1985; model version of structurist relief in 5 parts, 1962, now in collection, Nat. Gallery, Ottawa, Ont., others in numerous collections.; Co-editor: periodical Structure, 1958; founder, editor: ann. publ. The Structurist, 1960—; Contbr. articles, principally on Structurist art to various publs. Recipient Allied Arts medal Royal Archtl. Inst. Can., 1968; honorable mention for 3 structurist reliefs 2d Biennial Internat. Art Exhbn., Colombia, S.Am., 1970. Address: Rural Route 5, Saskatoon, SK Canada S7K 3J8 Office: Box 378 Sub PO6, U Sask, Saskatoon, SK Canada S7N 0W0

BORNY, WALTER MICHAEL, lawyer, financial planner, general securities representative, real estate investment consultant; b. Bklyn., June 23, 1948; s. Walter S. and Dolores (Kaplon) B. Student, Clemson U., 1965-66; AA magna cum laude, County Coll. Morris, Randolph, N.J., 1973; BA magna cum laude, Rutgers U., 1975, JD, 1979. Bar: N.J. 1979; lic. gen. securities rep., real estate agt., life ins. agt., notary pub., Calif. Legal counsel, 2d v.p. Chase Manhattan Bank, Englewood Cliffs, N.J., 1981-83; legal counsel CIS Equipment Leasing Corp., San Francisco, 1983-84; pvt. practice law San Francisco, 1984-85, Borny & Assocs., Foster City, Calif., 1985—. Active March of Dimes Campaign for Healthier Babies. Sgt. U.S. Army Security Agy., Vietnam, 1968-69. Decorated Vietnam medal, Vietnamese Cross of Gallantry with Palm; Rutgers Honors Program sr. fellow. Mem. ABA, N.J.

State Bar Assn., Nat. Assn. Securities Dealers (cert. gen. securities rep.), Phi Beta Kappa, Phi Alpha Theta.. Home: 504 Cutwater Ln Foster City CA 94404 Office: Borny & Assocs Foster City CA 94404

BOROSKIN, ALAN, counselor, psychotherapist; b. Bklyn., Apr. 13, 1942; m. Judith Rostagno, Dec. 30, 1979; children: Aaron, Gina. BA, Calif. State U., Fullerton, 1967, MA, 1969, postgrad., 1977-79. Lic. psychotherapist, Calif. Rsch. asst. Fairview State Hosp., Costa Mesa, Calif., 1968-72; project dir. dept. psychiatry and mental retardation UCLA, 1972-77; dir. psychol. svcs. Ctr. for Dynamic Therapy, Westminster, Calif., 1977-79; sr. cons. Corp. Dynamics, Inc., Santa Ana, Calif., 1979-81; owner, dir. Alan Boroskin, M.A., Inc., Santa Ana, 1981—; owner, dir. ABA Evaluation Ctr., Santa Ana, 1982—; speaker Nat. Advt. Coun. Devel. Disabilities, Washington, 1974, 75, Pres.'s Com. on Mental Retardation, Utah, 1975. Contbr. articles to profl. jours. Mem. Nat. Rehab. Assn., Vocat. Evaluation and Work Adjustment Assn., So. Calif. Rehab. Exch. (1st v.p. 1990, pres. 1991, 92), Calif. Assn. Marriage and Family Therapists. Democrat. Jewish. Office: 1833 E 17th St Ste 227 Santa Ana CA 92701-6692

BOROVSKI, CONRAD, German and French languages educator; b. Prettin, Germany, Dec. 4, 1930; came to U.S. 1952; s. Jozef Lorenc and Anna (Truszis) B.; m. Catherine Angele Perrot, Apr. 10, 1962; 1 child, Julia Madeleine. BA, U. Calif., Berkeley, 1957, MA, 1958; PhD, U. Strasbourg, France, 1960. Asst. prof. German, French San Jose State U., 1962-72, assoc. prof., 1972-84, prof. German, French, 1984—. Author: Active German Idioms, 1972, 2d edit. 1978. With U.S. Army, 1952-54. Decorated Bronze Star medal. Mem. Am. Assn. Tchrs. German No. Calif. (pres. 1983-85), Am. Assn. Tchrs. French No. Calif. (fellow). Office: San Jose State U One Washington Sq San Jose CA 95192

BORREGO, JESUS GARCIA, engineer; b. El Paso, Tex., Nov. 12, 1953; s. Jesus F. and Maria Luisa (Garcia) B.; m. Maria Magdalena Ornelas, Dec. 18, 1972; children: Maria M., Cristina, Jesus Jr. BSEE, Calif. State U., Fullerton, 1984; BS in Computer Sci., Calif. State U., Dominguez Hills, 1987; MS in Computer Sci., Loyola Marymount, L.A., 1992. Cert. tchr., Calif. Enlisted USMC, 1972-83; mem. tech. staff Logicon, Inc., San Pedro, Calif., 1983-87; tech. lead Advanced Tech., Inc., El Segundo, Calif., 1987-88; staff engr. Hughes Aircraft, El Segundo, Calif., 1988-89; sr. prin. engr. Arinc Rsch. Corp., Fountain Valley, Calif., 1989—; adj. faculty El Camino Coll., Torrance, Calif., 1988—; cons. JMB Cons., Gardena, Calif., 1988—. Contbr. articles to profl. jours. With USMC Res., 1983-92. Mem. IEEE, IEEE Computer Soc., Assn. for Computer Machinery. Republican. Roman Catholic. Office: Arinc Rsch 11770 Warner Ave #210 Fountain Valley CA 92708

BORREL, ANDRE, corporate executive; b. Chambery, Savoie, France, June 5, 1936; m. Jacqueline Burdin, July 16, 1962; children: Herve, Florence, Jerome. Degree in math., Lycee St. Louis, Paris, 1957. Registered profl. telecomm. engr. R & D engr. in snias Toulouse, 1962-65, Cannes, 1965-67; mktg. engr. Semiconductor Products Sector Motorola, Inc., Phoenix, 1967-68; mktg. mgr. Motorola Semiconducteurs S.A., Toulouse, 1969-72, mgr. transistor and diode div., 1972-75, gen. mgr., pres., dir. gen., 1976-78; gen. mgr. Motorola European Semiconductors Group, Geneva, 1978-86; v.p. Motorola, Inc., 1979; sr. v.p., gen. mgr. Semiconductor Internat. Group Motorola, Inc., Phoenix, 1986—. Office: Motorola SPS CPSTG 5005 E McDowell Rd Phoenix AZ 85008

BORSCH, FREDERICK HOUK, bishop; b. Chgo., Sept. 13, 1935; s. Reuben A. and Pearl Irene (Houk) B.; m. Barbara Edgeley Sampson, June 25, 1960; children: Benjamin, Matthew, Stuart. AB, Princeton U., 1957; MA, Oxford U., 1959; STB, Gen. Theol. Sem., 1960; PhD, U. Birmingham, 1966; DD (hon.), Seabury Western Theol. Sem., 1978, Gen. Theol. Sem., 1988; STD (hon.), Ch. Div. Sch. of Pacific, 1981, Berk Div. Sch. Yale U., 1983. Ordained priest Episcopal Ch., 1960; curate Grace Episcopal Ch., Oak Park, Ill., 1960-63; tutor Queen's Coll., Birmingham, Eng., 1963-66; asst. prof. N.T. Seabury Western Theol. Sem., Evanston, Ill., 1966-69, assoc. prof. N.T., 1969-71; prof. N.T. Gen. Theol. Sem., N.Y.C., 1971-72; pres., dean Berk Div. Sch. Yale U., Berkeley, Calif., 1972-81; dean of chapel, prof. religion Princeton U., 1981-88; bishop Episc. Diocese, L.A., 1988—; rep. Faith and Order Commn., Nat. Coun. Chs., 1975-81; mem. exec. coun. Episc. Ch., 1981-88, Anglican Cons. Coun., 1984-88; chair bd. of govs. Trinity Press Internat., 1989—. Author: The Son of May in Myth and History, 1967, The Christian and Gnostic Son of Man, 1970, God's Parable, 1976, Introducing the Lessons of the Church Year, 1978, Coming Together in the Spirit, 1980, Power in Weakness, 1983, Anglicanism and the Bible, 1984, Jesus: The Human Life of God, 1987, Many Things in Parables, 1988, Christian Discipleship and Sexuality, 1992. Keasbey scholar, 1957-59. Fellow Soc. Arts, Religion and Contemporary Culture; mem. Am. Acad. Religion, Soc. Bibl. Lit., Studiorum Novi Testamenti Societas, Phi Beta Kappa. Home: 2930 Corda Ln Los Angeles CA 90049-1105 Office: Episcopal Diocese of LA PO Box 2164 Los Angeles CA 90051-0164

BORSON, DANIEL BENJAMIN, educator, inventor, researcher; b. Berkeley, Calif., Mar. 24, 1946; s. Harry J. and Josephine F. (Esterly) B.; m. Margaret Ann Rheinschmidt, May 22, 1974; children: Alexander Nathan, Galen Michael. BA, San Francisco State Coll., 1969; MA, U. Calif., Riverside, 1973; PhD, U. Calif., San Francisco, 1982. Lic. comml. pilot, flight instr. FAA. Musician Composer's Forum, Berkeley, San Francisco, 1961-70; flight instr. Buchanan Flying Club, Concord, Oakland, Calif., 1973-77, pres., 1975-77; lectr. dept. physiology U. Calif., San Francisco, 1984-92, asst. rsch. physiologist Cardiovascular Rsch. Inst., 1988-92; vis. scientist Genentech Inc., South San Francisco, 1990-92, Sch. Law U. San Francisco, 1992—; mem. spl. rev. com. NIH, Washington, 1991—; summer assoc. patent law firm Flehr, Hohbach, Test, Albritton & Herbert, 1993—. Contbr. articles, rev. chpts. and abstracts to profl. jours. and legal periodicals. Fellow NIH, 1976-84, grantee, 1988-93; fellow Cystic Fibrosis Found., 1985, grantee, 1989-91; fellow Parker B. Francis Found., 1985-87; grantee Am. Lung Assn., 1985-87. Mem. Am. Physiol. Soc. (editorial bd. Am. Jour. Physiology 1990—), Am. Soc. Cell Biology, Bay Flute Club (pres. 1978). Home: 146 San Aleso Ave San Francisco CA 94127 Office: 4 Embarcadero Center Ste 3400 San Francisco CA 94127

BORSON, ROBERT OLIVER, communication executive, consultant; b. Tyler, Minn., Oct. 5, 1938; s. Albert Oliver and Hazel Inga (Esping) B.; m. Elizabeth Jean Erickson, June 26, 1960 (div. Dec. 1976); children: Nathan Scott, Niklas Erik; m. Susan Arlene Haynes, June 15, 1984. BA, Concordia Coll., Moorhead, Minn., 1960. Writer, editor of employee publications Kemper Ins., Chgo., 1960-64; assoc. editor of VIP mag. HMH Publishing Co., Chgo., 1964-65; asst. editor of Sweden Now mag. Industria Press, Stockholm, 1965-68; foreign corr. Madrid, 1968-70; editor Pacific Bus. mag. Calif. C. of C., Sacramento, 1970-72; sr. communications officer BankAmerica Corp., San Francisco, 1972-79, chief speechwriter, 1979-82; prin. Borson Communications, Napa, Calif., 1982—; bd. dirs. Napa County Landmarks, Inc. Contbr. articles profl. jours. Mem. Napa County Landmarks, Inc., Napa Valley Opera House Assn. Club: Commonwealth Club of Calif.

BORSTING, JACK RAYMOND, university dean; b. Portland, Oreg., Jan. 31, 1929; s. John S. and Ruth (Nelson) B.; m. Peggy Anne Nygard, Mar. 22, 1953; children: Lynn Carol, Eric Jeffrey. B.A., Oreg. State U., 1951; M.A., U. Oreg., 1952, Ph.D., 1959. Instr. math. Western Wash. Coll., 1953-54; teaching fellow U. Oreg., 1956-59; mem. faculty Naval Postgrad. Sch., 1959-80, prof. ops. research, chmn. dept., 1964-73, provost, acad. dean, 1974-80; asst. sec. def. (comptroller) Washington, 1980-83; dean Sch. Bus. U. Miami, Fla., 1983-88; Robert Dockson prof. and dean bus. adminstrn. U. So. Calif., Los Angeles, 1988—; vis. prof. U. Colo., summers 1967, 69, 71; vis. disting. prof. Oreg. State U., summer 1968; bd. dirs. Delta Rsch., Northrup Corp.; bd. visitors Def. Systems Mgmt. Coll., 1985-91, chmn., 1988-91; mem. adv. bd. Naval Postgrad. Sch., 1982-86; bd. overseers Ctr. Naval Analysis, 1984—; trustee Aerospace Corp., 1986-92, Inst. Def. Analysis, 1990—. Contbr. to profl. jours. Mem. bd. visitors Def. Systems Mgmt. Coll., 1985-91, chmn., 1988-91; mem. adv. bd. Naval Postgrad. Sch., 1982-86; bd. overseers Ctr. Naval Analysis, 1984—; trustee Aerospace Corp., 1986-92, Inst. of Def. Analysis, 1990—, Orthopedic Hosp. L.A., 1992—, Rose Hills Assn., 1992—; gov. Town Hall of Calif. Recipient Disting. Pub. Service medal Dept. Def., 1980, 82. Fellow AAAS.; mem. Inst. Mgmt. Sci., Am. Statis. Soc., Ops. Rsch. Soc. Am.(mem. coun. 1969-79, sec. 1972-74, pres. 1975-76, Kimball medal 1982), Mil. Ops. Rsch. Soc. (bd. dirs. 1965-72, chmn. edn. com. 1968-69, pres. 1970-71), Internat. Fedn. Ops. Rsch. Socs. (treas. 1980-88), Rose Hills Assn. (bd. dirs. 1992—), Calif. Club, Sigma Xi, Pi Mu Epsilon, Beta Theta Pi. Episcopalian. Home: 2421 Century Hall Los Angeles CA 90067-3521 Office: U So Calif Sch of Bus Los Angeles CA 90089-1421

BORTHAKUR, DULAL, microbiologist, educator; b. Barua Bamun Gaon, Assam, India, Mar. 1, 1955; came to U.S., 1986; s. Jadav C. and Maijoni (Kondoli) B.; m. Pritty Bhattacharyya, Jan. 20, 1982; children: Rajsree D., Gitasree D. BSc in Agr., Assam Agrl. U., India, 1975; MSc, Punjab Agrl. U., India, 1977; PhD, U. East Anglia, Norwich, Eng., 1987. Sr. rsch. asst. Assam. Agrl. U., Jorhat, 1978-79, lectr., 1979-80, asst. prof., 1980-83; postdoctoral assoc. U. Chgo., 1986-89; asst. researcher, tchr. biotech. program U. Hawaii, Honolulu, 1989—. Contbr. articles to sci. jours. Grantee USDA, 1992. Mem. Am. Soc. Microbiology, Internat. Soc. Plant Microbe Interaction, Sigma Xi. Office: Univ Hawaii Gilmore 402 3050 Maile Way Honolulu HI 96822

BORTOLUSSI, MICHAEL RICHARD, aerospace human factors engineer; b. San Jose, Calif., Feb. 6, 1956; s. Giordano Antonio and Josephine Marie (Ferla) B. BS, Santa Clara (Calif.) U., 1980. Registered profl. engr., gen. contractor, Calif. Rsch. scientist Tufts U., Medford, Mass., 1980-82, Va. Poly. Inst. & State U., Blacksburg, 1982-83, Behavioral Inst. for Tech. and Sci., Inc., West Lafayette, Ind., 1983-86; chief exec. officer Western Aerospace Labs., Inc., Monte Sereno, Calif., 1986—; prin. scientist Western Aerospace Labs., Inc., 1986—. Contbr. articles to profl. jours. Mem. Assn. Aviation Psychologists, Bass Angulars Sportsman Soc. (life), Aircraft Owners and Pilots Assn. Republican. Roman Catholic. Home and Office: Western Aerospace Labs Inc 16111 Mays Ave Los Gatos CA 95030-4212

BORTON, GEORGE ROBERT, airline captain; b. Wichita Falls, Tex., Mar. 22, 1922; s. George Neat and Travis Lee (Jones) B.; m. Anne Louise Bowling, Feb. 5, 1944 (dec.); children: Trudie T., Robert B., Bruce M. AA, Hardin Coll., Wichita Falls, 1940. Cert. airline transport pilot, FAA flight examiner. Flight sch. operator Vallejo (Calif.) Sky Harbor, 1947-48; capt. S.W. Airways, San Francisco, 1948-55; check capt. Pacific Airlines, San Francisco, 1955-68, Hughes Air West, San Francisco, 1968-71; capt. N.W. Airlines, Mpls., 1971-82, ret., 1982. Col. (ret.) USAFR, 1943-73. Decorated Air medal. Mem. Airline Pilots Assn., Res. Officers Assn., Air Force Assn., Horseless Carriage Club, Model T of Am. Club (Phoenix). Republican. Congregationalist. Home: 4612 W Monte Cristo Ave Glendale AZ 85306-2724

BORUCHOWITZ, STEPHEN ALAN, state official; b. Plainfield, N.J., Sept. 24, 1952; s. Robert and Earla Louise (Sloat) B.; m. Linda Susan Grant, Sept. 16, 1989; 1 child, Grant Stephen. BA in Internat. Affairs, George Washington U., Washington, 1974; MA in Sci., Tech. and Pub. Policy, George Washington U., 1981. Food prog. specialist U.S. Food & Nutrition Svc., Washington, 1978-81; internat. affairs specialist Office Internat. Cooperation & Devel., Washington, 1981-87; legis. analyst Wash. State Senate, Olympia, 1986-89; project dir. Wash. 2000 Project, Olympia, 1989-92; health svcs. adminstr. Wash. State Dept. Health, Olympia, 1992—. Editor newsletter: Project Update, 1990-92. Study team mem. Gov.'s Efficiency Commn., 1990-91; com. mem. Coun. of State Govts. Strategic Planning Subcom., Lexington, Ky., 1990-92; chmn. Montclair Div. IV Neighborhood Assn., 1989-92, Shadywood Homeowners' Assn., 1992—; bd. dirs. Classical Music Supporters, Seattle, 1987-89. Recipient Superior Performance award, U.S. Dept. Agr., 1986. Mem. World Future Soc., Internat. Health Futures Network. Office: Washington State Dept Health PO Box 47851 Olympia WA 98504-7851

BORUNDA, PATRICK, management consultant; b. L.A., Nov. 25, 1947; s. Alfred and Margaret (Quesada) B. BA, Lewis & Clark Coll., 1968; MBA, U. Pa., 1978. Cert. mgmt. cons.. Mgmt. positions City of Portland (Oreg.), 1971-75; sr. cons. Deloitte, Haskins & Sells, Portland, 1978-80; mgr. MICD Authur Andersen & Co., Portland, 1980-83; prin. Navigator Group, Portland, 1983—; instr. Portland State U. MBA program, 1986-87, Lewis & Clark Coll. MPA program, 1985, Portland Community Coll., 1983-87; facilitator Youth Today, Portland, 1990. Contbr. articles to profl. jours. Rep. Oreg. Comm. Indian Svc., Salem, 1975-77; vice-chmn. Multnomah Econ. Devel. Comm., Portland, 1978-87; com. mem. Civic Index, Portland, 1990; trustee Boys and Girls Aid Soc. Oregon; bd. dirs. Kimiwa, 1993—. 1st lt. U.S. Army, 1969-71, Vietnam. Decorated Bronze Star; Gallantry Cross (Republic of Vietnam); Wharton Sch. Bus. Grad. Teaching fellow 1977-78. Mem. World Future Soc., Inst. Mgmt. Cons., Planning Exec. Inst. (sec. 1982), Planning Forum, City Club Portland (com. chmn., 1978-87). Office: Navigator Group 520 SW 6th Ave Portland OR 97204

BOS, JOHN ARTHUR, aircraft manufacturing executive; b. Holland, Mich., Nov. 6, 1933; s. John Arthur and Annabelle (Castelli) B.; m. Eileen Tempest, Feb. 15, 1974; children: John, James, William, Tiffany. BS in Acctg., Calif. State Coll., Long Beach, 1971. Officer 1st Nat. Bank, Holland, Mich., 1954-61; gen. mgr. fin. McDonnell Douglas, Long Beach, 1962—. Mem. Inst. Mgmt. Accts. (cert. mgmt. acct. 1979), Nat. Assn. Accts. Office: McDonnell Douglas Aircraft Co 3855 N Lakewood Blvd Long Beach CA 90846-0001

BOSCHÉ, ROBERT PAUL, JR., management executive; b. New Orleans, Dec. 12, 1951; s. Robert Paul Sr. and Lucille Mary (Calkins) B.; children: Giffin, Kerry, Lauren. BA, Thomas More Coll., 1974; MEd, Xavier U., 1976. Sr. underwriter ITT Hartford Ins Group, Cin., 1974-77; franchisee Baron Pers. Inc., Cin., 1977; gen. mgr. Clarke's Svcs. Inc., Cin., 1977-78; sr. analyst Great Am. Ins. Group, Cin., 1978-81; divsn. adminstrn. mgr. Great Am. Ins. Group, Orange, Calif., 1981-82; dir. Great Am. West Inc., Orange, Calif., 1982-85; prin. ACS/US Group, Costa Mesa, Calif., 1985-89; prin., pres. Bosché Mgmt. Group Inc., El Toro, Calif., 1985—; project mgr. So. Calif. Edison, San Onofre, Calif., 1986-87; program coord. Hughes Aircraft Co., L.A., 1987-92; project mgr. Bank of Am., Pasadena, Calif., 1993—. Pub. Effective By Design, 1987—. Chmn. Great Mason-Dixon Balloon Crossing, No. Ky., 1976-77, Neighborhood Support Program, Cin., 1978-79, Boy Scouts of Am., Lake Forest, Calif., 1988—; appointee Community Devel. Adv. Coun., Cin., 1979-81. Mem. Assn. Profl. Cons. (bd. dirs. 1987-92), Order of Ky. Colonels, Thomas More Coll. Alumni Assn. Office: Bosché Mgmt Group Inc 23268-2 Orange Ave El Toro CA 92630-4848

BOSE, ANJAN, electrical engineering educator, researcher, consultant; b. Calcutta, India, June 2, 1946; s. Amal Nath and Anima (Guha) B.; m. Frances Magdelen Pavlas, Oct. 30, 1976; children: Rajesh Paul, Shonali Marie, Jahar Robert. B Tech with honors, Indian Inst. Tech., Kharagpur, 1967; MS, U. Calif., Berkeley, 1968; PhD, Iowa State U., 1974. Systems planning engr. Con Edison Co., N.Y.C., 1968-70; instr., research assoc. Iowa State U., Ames, 1970-74; postdoctoral fellow IBM Sci. Ctr., Palo Alto, Calif., 1974-75; asst. prof. elec. engring. Clarkson U., Potsdam, N.Y., 1975-76; mgr. EMSD, Control Data Corp., Mpls., 1976-81; prof. elec. engring. Ariz. State U., Tempe, 1981—; v.p. Power Math Assocs., Tempe, 1981-84. Contbr. over 50 articles to engring. jours. Fellow IEEE.

BOSMAN, PAUL WRAY, wildlife artist; b. Glen, Republic of South Africa, Aug. 2, 1929; s. Ferdinand Hugo and Edith Cecilia Mary (Townshend) B.; m. Valerie Elaine Roos, July 7, 1956; children: Christopher Paul, Simon Villiers, Elizabeth Kate. Diploma, Johannesburg Art Sch., Republic of South Africa, 1950; postgrad., Cen. Sch. Art, London, 1951. Artist S.A. Litho Ltd., Johannesburg, 1952-53; visualiser Colman, Prentis & Varley Ltd., London, 1954-55; artist Bomac Ltd., Montreal, Que., Can., 1956-57, Afamal Advt. Ltd., Durban, Republic of South Africa, 1957-58; from art dir. to creative dir. Lindsay Smithers Advt. Ltd., Durban and Johannesburg, 1959-68; wildlife artist, owner Malapati Game Lodge, Rhodesia, 1969-75; wildlife artist Johannesburg, 1976-81, Phoenix, 1982-92; Sedona, Ariz., 1992—. Co-author; Elephants of Africa, 1986. Fellow Endangered Wildlife Trust So. Africa, Johannesburg, 1978—; advisor Rhino and Elephant Found., Johannesburg, 1986-92. Mem. Soc. Animal Artists. Home and Office: 55 Rock Top Rd Sedona AZ 86336 also: PO Box 20245 Village Of Oak Creek AZ 86341-0245

BOSSART, WILLIAM HAINES, philosophy educator; s. Herman E. and Ethel L. (Beer) B.; div. 1980; children: Suzanne, Louisa, Paul. BS in Polit. Sci., Northwestern U., 1952, MA in Philosophy, 1954, PhD in Philosophy, 1958; postgrad. studies (Fulbright scholar), U. Paris, 1955-56; cert. in German, U. Wien, Germany, 1956; postgrad., Ludwig-Maxmilian U., Munich, 1956-57. Acting instr. U. Wis., Madison, 1955 summer; acting instr. U. Calif., Davis, 1957-58, asst. prof. philosophy, 1959-65, assoc. prof., 1965-70, prof. of philosophy, 1970-92, emeritus prof., 1993—; chmn. Dept. Philosophy U. Calif., Davis, 1972-82, com. on History and Philosophy of Sci., U. Calif., Davis, 1981-85. Contbr. articles to profl. jours. Recipient scholarship Northwestern U., 1952, fellowship, 1954-55, Summer Faculty fellowship, U. Calif. Davis, 1964, Course Improvement fellowship summer, 1967, NEH Younger Scholar fellowship, 1969-70; named Fulbright scholar U. Paris, 1955-56. Mem. Am. Soc. for Aesthetics, Am. Philos. Assn. Home: 43358 Montgomery Ave Davis CA 95616 Office: U Calif Dept Philosophy Davis CA 95616

BOSSEN, DAVID AUGUST, electronics company executive; b. Clinton, Iowa, Jan. 9, 1927; s. August and Rose Faye (Nichols) B.; children: Alison, Amy, Julie, Laura; m. Darlene Phelps, Aug. 10, 1991. B.S. in Indsl. Mgmt, M.I.T., 1951. Indsl. engr. Alcoa, Davenport, Iowa, 1951; v.p. Indsl. Nucleonics Co., Columbus, Ohio, 1951-67; 1st pres. Measurex Corp., Cupertino, Calif., 1968—; chmn. bd. dirs. Santa Clara County Mfg. Group; mem. exec. com. Japan-Western States Assn.; mem. MIT Corp. Devel. Com. Bd. dirs. Bay Area Coun. Served with USMC, 1945-46. Mem. Paper Industry Mgmt. Assn., TAPPI, Beta Gamma Sigma, Sigma Alpha Epsilon. Office: Measurex Corp 1 Results Way Cupertino CA 95014-5991

BOSSERMAN, LORELEI, technical writer, screenwriter, literary editor; b. Berkeley, Calif., Apr. 14, 1964. BA, U. Calif., Santa Cruz, 1988. Editor-in-chief Shameless Hussy Press, Berkeley, Calif., 1984-88; intern The Sun, Santa Cruz, 1986-87; teaching asst. U. Calif., Santa Cruz, 1988; editing cons. Berkeley, 1989-91; tech. writer Chiron Corp., Emeryville, Calif., 1991-93; documentation specialist Systemix, Palo Alto, Calif., 1993—. Contbr.: The Before Columbus Foundation Poetry Anthology, 1992; author book revs.

BOST, THOMAS GLEN, lawyer; b. Oklahoma City, July 13, 1942; s. Burl John and Lorene Belle (Croka) B.; m. Sheila K. Pettigrew, Aug. 27, 1966; children: Amy Elizabeth, Stephen Luke, Emily Anne, Paul Alexander. BS in Acctg. summa cum laude, Abilene Christian U., 1964; JD, Vanderbilt U., 1967. Bar: Tenn. 1967, Calif. 1969. Instr. David Lipscomb Coll., Nashville, 1967; asst. prof. law Vanderbilt U., Nashville, 1967-68; ptnr. Latham & Watkins, Los Angeles, 1968—; lectr. on taxation subjects. Chmn. bd. regents, law sch. bd. visitors Pepperdine U., Malibu, Calif., 1980—. Mem. ABA (chmn. standards of tax practice com., sec. taxation 1988-90), State Bar of Calif., Los Angeles County Bar Assn. (chmn. taxation sect. 1981-82). Republican. Mem. Ch. of Christ. Club: Calif. (Los Angeles). Office: Latham & Watkins 633 W 5th St Ste 4000 Los Angeles CA 90071-2005

BOSTON, BETTY ROACH, realtor; b. Linton, Ind., May 16, 1926; d. Raleigh Owen and Pearl C. (Chaney) Roach; m. O.E. Boston, Oct. 11, 1952; children: Brian R., Kerry A. BS, Ind. State U., 1948. Cert. residential brokerage. Placement, employee relations adv. USAF, Dayton, Ohio, 1948-52; mgr. placement services CSC, Cin., 1953-56; substitue tchr. Pasco (Wash.) Sch. Dist., 1970-73; office and property mgr. Keith Adams & Assocs., Richland, Wash., 1973-81; assoc. broker, co-owner Boston Real Estate Assocs., Richland, 1981—. Civil Service commr. Franklin County, 1986—; precinct com. person Franklin County, 1972-76; active Franklin County Rep. Cen. Com., 1970-76. Mem. Wash. Assn. Realtors (bd. dirs. 1983-86, 90—, state chair fair housing/equal opportunity com. 1992), Columbia Basin Apt. Assn. (pres., bd. dirs. 1985—), Tri-City Bd. Realtors (v.p., sec.-treas., bd. dirs. 1982—, pres. 1990), Realtors Inst. (grad.), Altrusa Club (sec.), Franklin County Rep. Women's Club (pres.), Women of Rotary (pres. Richland chpt.). Home: 420 N Road 39 Pasco WA 99301-3160 Office: Boston Real Estate Assocs 118 N 5th Ave Pasco WA 99301

BOSTON, MARCIA ANN, elementary school educator; b. Akron, Ohio, Jan. 19, 1938; d. Mark Emmett and Mary Elizabeth (McMuldren) Henery; m. Roger Eugene Boston, Aug. 18, 1963; children: Mark Eugene, Craig Henery. BA, Grand Canyon U., 1960. Cert. elem. tchr., Ariz. Tchr. Glendale (Ariz.) Dist., 1960-64; sub. tchr. Itazuke (Japan) Air Base Sch., fall 1964, Washoe County, Reno, Nev., 1965-66, Albany (Oreg.) Sch. Dist., 1968-69; sub. tchr. Wash. Dist., Phoenix, 1970-71, tchr., 1972—. Mem. NEA, ASCD, Ariz. Edn. Assn., Wash. Dist. Edn. Assn., S.W. Marine Educator's Assn. Order of Ea. Star (organist Sunnyslope chpt. # 47 1962, 77, 78, 79, 81, 82), Glendale Mothers Club (pres. 1981), Order of Demolay (state pres. 1983-84). Republican. Episcopalian. Office: Orangewood Sch 7337 N 19th Ave Phoenix AZ 85021

BOSTWICK, ANGELINA CELESTE, technical writer; b. Longview, Wash., Nov. 6, 1969; d. Jonathan Wesley and Jenetta Ellen (Gray) Gain; m. Richard Brian Scott Bostwick, June 6, 1992. BA, San Jose State U., 1992. Adminstrv. asst. Biomed. Monitoring Systems, Campbell, Calif., 1987-90; layout editor The Writing Life, San Jose, Calif., 1991; prodn. mgr. Access Mag., San Jose, 1991; tech. writer AG Assocs., Sunnyvale, Calif., 1991—; freelance desktop pub., San Jose, 1987—. Counselor Los Gatos (Calif.) Christian Ch., 1988-90; voting inspector Santa Clara County, San Jose, 1990, Saratoga, Calif., 1992; poll clk. Alameda County, Fremont, Calif., 1992. Mem. Soc. for Tech. Communication, Reps. United Vol. Team.

BOSUSTOW, NICK ONSLOW, film producer; b. Los Angeles, Mar. 28, 1940; s. Stephen Reginald and Audrey Mildred (Stevenson) B.; m. Julienne Bosustow, Apr. 17, 1971; children: Nichole, Jeniffer. BS, Menlo (Calif.) Sch. of Bus. Adminstr., 1963. Pres. Bosustow Entertainment, Los Angeles, 1968—. Producer numerous TV spls. including Always Right To Be Right? (Acad. award 1971), Legend of John Henry (Acad. award nomination 1972), Incredible Book Escape (Emmy nomination 1981), Misunderstood Monsters, Tale of Four Wishes, Wrong Way Kid (Emmy award 1984), Haley Mills Story Book Series (Best Children's Series award Parents Mag. 1987). Served with U.S. Army. Mem. Acad. Motion Pictures Arts and Scis. (mem. short film exec. com.), Internat. Animated Film Assn. (bd. dirs., past pres.).

BOSWELL, CHRISTOPHER ORR, broadcast journalist; b. Milan, Oct. 4, 1957; came to U.S., 1958; s. William Osgood and Janine (Werner) B. BA in Broadcasting, U. Wyo., 1980, MA in Journalism, 1988. Press asst. Senator Malcolm Wallop, Washington, 1980-81; news dir. Sta. KUGR Radio, Green River, Wyo., 1981-83; freelance reporter Wagonwheel Broadcasting, Green River, 1983—; pres. Embassy Bar, Inc., Green River, 1985—. Interview judge Wyo. Acad. Decathlon, Laramie, 1986; chmn. Mayor's Com. on Tourism, 1988. Recipient Disting. Service award Sta. KUWR Radio, Laramie, Wyo., 1978-79, 79-80; named Broadcaster of Month, AP, Cheyenne, Wyo., 1982, 83. Mem. Soc. Profl. Journalists, Wyo. Assn. Broadcasters (bd. dirs. 1985-86). Democrat. Presbyterian. Home: 709 W 4th St N Green River WY 82935 Office: 77 E Railroad PO Box 272 Green River WY 82935-0272

BOSWORTH, BRUCE LEIGHTON, educator, consultant; b. Buffalo, Mar. 22, 1942; s. John Wayman and Alice Elizabeth Rodgers; children: David, Timothy, Paul. BA, U. Denver, 1964; MA, U. No. Colo., 1970; EdD, Walden U., 1984. Elem. tchr. Littleton (Colo.) Pub. Schs., 1964-67, 70-81; bldg. prin. East Smoky Sch. Div. 54, Valleyview, Alta., Can., 1967-70; pres., tchr. Chatfield Sch., Littleton, 1981—; mem. research bd. advisors Am. Biog. Inst.; adoption cons. hard-to-place children; ednl. cons. spl. needs children. Dir. Christian Edn.; mem. adminstrn. bd., mem. fin. com. Warren United Meth. Ch.;. Mem. Council Exceptional Children, Assn. Supervision and Curriculum Devel., Englewood C. of C. Republican. Methodist. Clubs: Masons, Shriners, York Rite. Home and Office: 3500 S Lowell Blvd # 207 Sheridan CO 80236

BOSWORTH, BRUCE LYNN, military officer, dentist; b. New Orleans, Oct. 7, 1943; s. Ralph Edward and Irma Caroline (Moskau) B.; m. Angelina Corpora, Nov. 25, 1965 (div. 1975); 1 child, Craig Stephen; m. Rosemary Jo Klaas, Jan. 17, 1976; 1 child, Patrick Timothy. DDS, Loyola U., New Orleans, 1967; cert. in Periodontics, U. Md., 1975; MA, George Washington U., 1988. Diplomate Am. Bd. Periodontology. Commd. lt. USN, 1967, advanced through grades to capt. periodontics specialty, 1975-85; resident U. Md., Balt., 1973-75; head Periodontal dept. Naval Regional Dental Ctr., Newport, R.I., 1975-79; pvt. practice Middletown, R.I., 1979-81; mem. Periodontics staff Naval Dental Clinic, Norfolk, Va., 1981-85; mem. Periodontics teaching staff Naval Dental Sch., Bethesda, Md., 1985-89; cons. in Periodontics Naval Dental Cntr., San Diego, 1989—; course dir. Periodontics Naval Dental Ctr., San Diego, 1989—, mem. rsch. com., 1989—, chmn. implant task force, 1991-92, dir. continuing edn., 1992—. Coach youth soccer, Virginia Beach, Va., 1981-85; mem. Citizens for a Better Herndon (Va.), 1988-89; v.p. Band Boosters Coronado (Calif.) High Sch., 1992. Mem. Am. Acad. of Periodontology (dist. sec. 1985-90, mem. com. 1985-88, profl. rels. com. 1988-91, bd. nominating com. 1988-91, dist. pres. 1990—, trustee 1990—).

BOSWORTH, THOMAS LAWRENCE, architect, educator; b. Oberlin, Ohio, June 15, 1930; s. Edward Franklin and Imogene (Rose) B.; m. Abigail Lumbard, Nov. 6, 1954 (div. Nov. 1974); children: Thomas Edward, Nathaniel David; m. Elaine R. Pedigo, Nov. 23, 1974. B.A., Oberlin Coll., 1952, M.A., 1954; postgrad., Princeton U., 1952-53, Harvard U., 1956-57; M.Arch., Yale U., 1960. Draftsman Gordon McMaster AIA, Cheshire, Conn., summer 1957-58; resident planner Tunnard & Harris Planning Cons., Newport, R.I., summer 1959; designer, field supr. Eero Saarinen & Assocs., Birmingham, Mich., 1960-61, Hamden, Conn., 1961-64; individual practice architecture Providence, 1964-68; asst. instr. architecture Yale U., 1962-65, vis. lectr., 1965-66; asst. prof. R.I. Sch. Design, 1964-66, asso. prof., head dept., 1966-68; prof. architecture U. Wash., Seattle, 1968—, chmn. dept., 1968-72; chief architecture Peace Corps Tng. Program, Tunisia, Brown U., summers 1965-66; archtl. cons., individual practice Seattle, 1972—; dir. multidisciplinary Rome Studies program U. Wash., Rome, Italy, 1984-86; vis. lectr. Kobe U., Japan, Oct. 1982, Nov. 1990; bd. dirs. N.W. Inst. for Arch. and Urban Studies, Italy, 1983-90, pres., 1983-85; mem. Seattle Model Cities Land Use Rev. Bd., 1969-70, Tech. Com. Site Selection Wash. Multi-Purpose Stadium, 1970; chmn. King County (Wash.) Environ. Devel. Commn., 1970-74; mem. Medina Planning Commn., 1972-74; chmn. King County Policy Devel. Commn., 1974-77; mem. steering adv. com. King County Stadium, 1972-74, others. Dir. Pilchuck Sch., Seattle, 1977-80, trustee, 1980-91. With U.S. Army, 1954-56. Winchester Traveling fellow Greece, 1960; assoc. fellow Ezra Stiles Coll. Yale U.; mid-career fellow in arch. Am. Acad. in Rome, 1980-81, vis. scholar, Spring 1988. Fellow AIA; mem. AAUP, Archtl. Inst. Japan, Soc. Archtl. Historians, Rainier Club, Monday Club, Tau Sigma Delta. Home: 4532 E Laurel Dr NE Seattle WA 98105-3839 Office: U Wash Dept Architecture JO-20 Seattle WA 98195

BOTELHO, BRUCE MANUEL, state official, mayor; b. Juneau, Alaska, Oct. 6, 1948; s. Emmett Manuel and Harriet Iowa (Tieszen) B.; m. Guadalupe Alvarez Breton, Sept. 23, 1988; 1 child, Alejandro Manuel. Student, U. Heidelberg, Federal Republic of Germany, 1970; BA, Willamette U., 1971, JD, 1976. Bar: Alaska 1976, U.S. Ct. Appeals (9th cir.), U.S. Supreme Ct. Asst. atty. gen. State of Alaska, Juneau, 1976-83, 1987—, dep. commr., acting commr. Dept. of Revenue, 1983-86; mayor City, Borough of Juneau, 1988-91, dep. atty. gen., 1991—. Editor: Willamette Law Jour., 1975-76; contbr. articles profl. jours. Assembly mem. City, Borough of Juneau, 1983-86; pres. Juneau Human Rights Commn., 1978-80; pres. SE Alaska Area Coun. Boy Scouts Am., 1991—; bd. dirs. Found. for Social Innovations, Alaska, 1990—. Democrat. Methodist. Home: 401 F St Douglas AK 99824-5353 Office: Alaska Dept Law PO Box K Juneau AK 99811-0300

BOTELLO, TROY JAMES, arts administrator, counselor; b. Long Beach, Calif., Sept. 2, 1953; s. Arthur P. and Jayme Alta (McBride) B. AA in Spl. Edn., Cerritos Coll., 1979; BA in Music Therapy, Calif. State U., Long Beach, 1984; postgrad., Calif. Polytech. Inst., Pomona, 1986—; cert. in arts adminstrn., U. So. Calif., Orange County, 1988. Cert. tchr., Calif. Asst. music dir. St. John Bosco High Sch., Bellflower, Calif., 1969-72; music dir. Bellflower Unified Schs., 1971-74; tchr. severely handicapped L.A. County Office of Edn., 1974-88; vocat. rehab. counselor Tesseler Counseling Group, Anaheim, Calif., 1988-91; dir. edn. Orange County Performing Arts Ctr., Costa Mesa, Calif., 1991—; exec. dir., founder Project: Arts in Motion, Bellflower, 1983—; ednl. cons. Edn. Div. Music Ctr., L.A., 1986—; vice chmn. La Mirada (Calif.) Community Concerts, 1976-79; v.p. grants Master Symphony Orch., Norwalk, Calif. Chairperson La Mirada Hist. Com., 1977-78; rep. Edn. Adv. Com., L.A., 1981; exec. prod., bd. dirs. Imagination Celebration of Orange County, 1991—; vice chmn. programs Anaheim Cultural Arts Found., 1993—; pres., bd. dirs Very Special Arts Calif., 1992—. Mem. Assn. for Music Therapy Profls., So. Calif. Band and Field Judges, Profl. Arts Mgmt. Inst., Calif. Assn. Rehab. Profls., Am. Assn. Orff Schwelrk, Young Composers of Am., Alumni of Drum Corps Internat. Home: 14216 Neargrove Rd La Mirada CA 90638-3854 Office: Orange County Performing Arts Ctr 600 Town Center Dr Costa Mesa CA 92626-1997

BOTIMER, ALLEN RAY, retired surgeon, retirement center administrator; b. Columbus, Miss., Jan. 30, 1930; s. Clare E. and Christel J. (Kalar) B.; m. Dorris LaJean, Aug. 17, 1950; children: Larry Alan, Gary David. BS, Walla Walla Coll., 1951; MD, Loma Linda U., 1955. Diplomate Am. Bd. Surgery. Intern U.S. Naval Hosp., San Diego, 1955-56, surg. resident, 1955-60; resident in surgery U.S. Naval Hosp., Guam, 1960-62; asst. chief surgery U.S. Naval Hosp., Bremerton, Wash., 1962-64; chief surgery Ballard Community Hosp., Seattle, 1970, chief of staff, 1972, chief surgery, 1986-87; pvt. practice Seattle, 1964-87; ret., 1987; ptnr. Heritage Retirement Ctr., Nampa, Idaho, 1972-82, owner, 1982—. Lt. comdr. USN, 1955-64. Fellow ACS, Seattle Surg. Soc.; mem. Wash. State Med. Soc., King County Med. Soc. Home and Office: 18419 17th Ave NW Seattle WA 98177-3315

BOTSKO, RONALD JOSEPH, business engineering consultant; b. Youngstown, Ohio, Sept. 4, 1937; s. Joseph and Lucile Marie (Donaldson) B.; m. Gayle A. Edwards, Feb. 14, 1991. BS in Engring., Case Inst. Tech., 1959. Registered profl. engr., Calif. Rsch. engr. Youngstown Sheet & Tube Co., 1959-60; sr. rsch./project engr. N. Am. Aviation, L.A., 1960-67; gen. mgr. Microwave Instruments Co., Corona del Mar, Calif., 1967-71; pres., chmn. bd. NDT Instruments, Inc., Huntington Beach, Calif., 1971-88; prin. cons. DuPont, NDT Instruments Div., Huntington Beach, 1988—; lectr. in field. Author (with others): Nondestructive Testing, 1986; author 2 booklets; contbr. over 50 articles to profl. jours. Fellow Am. Soc. for Nondestructive Testing (tech. achievement award 1968, gold medal 1983); mem. Am. Soc. Metals. Republican. Home: 50-1 Highland Greens Port Ludlow WA 98365

BOTTEL, HELEN ALFEA, columnist, writer; b. Beaumont, Calif.; d. Alpheus Russell and Mary Ellen (Alexander) Brigden; m. Robert E. Bottel; children: Robert Dennis, Rodger M., R. Kathryn Bottel Bernhardt, Suzanne V. Bottel Peppers. A.A., Riverside Coll. Calif.; student, Oreg. State U., 1958-59, So. Oreg. Coll., 1959. Editor Illinois Valley News, Cave Junction, Oreg.; writer Grants Pass (Oreg.) Courier, Portland Oregonian, Medford (Oreg.) Mail Tribune, 1952-58; daily columnist King Features Syndicate, N.Y.C., 1958-83; mem. adv. bd. Internat. Affairs Inst., N.Y.C. and Tokyo, 1986—; freelance mag. writer, author, lectr., 1956—. Author: To Teens with Love, 1969, Helen Help Us, 1970, Parents Survival Kit, 1979; contbg. editor, columnist Real World mag., 1978-84; weekly columnist Yomiuri Shimbun, Tokyo, 1982—; thrice weekly columnist Sacramento Union, 1986-88; syndicated newspaper and mag. columnist Look Who's Aging, 1992—; contbr. nonfiction to books and nat. mags.; video tape producer, 1991—. Staff mem. ACT Handicapped Children Games, Sacramento, 1986—; bd. dirs. Illinois Valley Med. Center, 1958-62, Childrens Center, Sacramento, 1969, Family Support Programs, Sacramento, 1991—; mem. Grants Pass br. Oreg. Juvenile Adv. Com., 1960-62, Students League Against Narcotics Temptation, 1968-70; charter patron Cosumnes River Coll., Sacramento, 1972—; mem. nat. adv. bd. Nat. Anorexic Aid Soc., 1977—; mem. Nat. Spina Bifida Assn.; scholarship com. judge Exec. Women Internat., 1985. Recipient Women's Svc. Cup Riverside Coll., citation for aid to U.s. servicemen in Vietnam Gov. Ga., 1967, Disting. Merit citation NCCJ, 1970, 1st place award for books Calif. Press Women, 1970, Sacramento Regional Arts Coun. Lit. Achievement award, 1974, Alumna of Yr. award Riverside Coll., 1987, Gold and Silver medals Calif. Sr. Games (tennis), 1990-91. Mem. Am. Soc. Journalists and Authors, Internat. Affairs Inst. (adv. bd. dirs. 1980—). Presbyterian. Clubs: Calif. Writers, Southgate Tennis. Home: 2060 56th Ave Sacramento CA 95822-4112

BOTTI, RICHARD CHARLES, association executive; b. Brockton, Mass., May 1, 1939; s. Alfred Benecchi and Elizabeth Savini; stepson Ernest Botti; student Pierce Jr. Coll., 1959, Orange Coast Coll., 1964; m. Gwen Botti; children—Randolph K., Douglas S., Richard II. Pres., Legis. Info. Services Hawaii, Inc., Honolulu, 1971—; exec. dir., profl. lobbyist Hawaii Food Industry Assn., Honolulu, Hawaii Automotive & Retail Gasoline Dealers Assn., Inc., Honolulu, Hawaii Bus. League, Retail Liquor Dealers Assn. Hawaii, Liquor Dispensers of Hawaii, Hawaii Pubs. Assn., Automotive Body and Painting Assn.; gen. mgr. Hawaii Fashion Industry Assn. Mem. Food Industry Assn. Execs., Am. Soc. Assn. Execs., Aloha Soc. Assn. Execs. (dir. Hawaii Foodbank). Address: Legis Info Services 677 Ala Moana Blvd Suite 815 Honolulu HI 96813

BOTTOMS, WILLIAM CLAY, JR., aviation and education company executive; b. Atlanta, June 13, 1946; s. William Clay and Alice Elizabeth (Walker) B.; m. Nancy Lou Snodgrass, Mar. 16, 1968 (div. 1991); children: Janet Elizabeth, Sharon Suzanne. B in Aerospace Engring., Ga. Inst. Tech., 1969. Aerodyn. engr. McDonnell Aircraft Co., St. Louis, 1969-73; dir. engring. and quality control Southern Airways, Atlanta, 1973-78; staff v.p. maintenance Tex. Internat. Airlines, Houston, 1978-80; v.p. tech. services N.Y. Air, N.Y.C., 1980-83; sr. v.p. ops. Rocky Mountain Airways, Denver, 1983-85; exec. dir. Colo. Aero Tech., Broomfield, 1985-89; group v.p. aviation UES, Broomfield, Colo., 1988-91; pres. Colo. Inst. of Art, 1991—; regional cons. Robert Jameson Assocs., Denver, 1985;. Pres. Golden Meadows Homeowners Assn., Morrison, Colo., 1983-87; del. Regional Homeowners Assn., Aspen Park, Colo., 1985-86; bd. dirs. Colo. Pvt. Sch. Assn., 1987—, pres.-elect, 1988-89, 91-92, pres., 1989-91; bd. dirs. Broomfield (Colo.) Econs. Devel. Corp., 1988-91; art edn. coun. Denver Pub. Sch., 1992—; bd. dirs. Temple Event Ctr. Mem. FAA (rule making adv. com. 1991), Colo. Tng. Assurance Found. (bd. dirs. 1987—), Aviation Tech. Edn. Coun. (bd. dirs. 1988-92, v.p. 1989-90, pres. 1991-92), Air Transport Assn. (maintenance tng. com. 1989-92), Nat. Coun. on Vocat. Edn. (aviation working group 1991). Republican. Baptist. Home: 8244 S Wagon Wheel Rd Morrison CO 80465-2471 Office: Colo Inst of Art 200 E 9th Ave Denver CO 80203-2983

BOTTORFF, C. W., marketing executive; b. Keokuk County, Iowa, May 8, 1941; s. Warren V. and Erma Lucille (Hollingsworth) B.; m. Karen F. Stall, 1962 (dec. 1976); 1 child, Kamarla Kae Bottorff-Welton; m. Holly A. Swanson, Oct. 10, 1981. DDS, U. Iowa, 1964. Pvt. dental practice Corvallis, Oreg., 1966-78; dir. mktg. PMS, Inc., Eugene, Oreg., 1978-80; CEO PMS of Calif., Sunnyvale, 1980-82; west regional mgr. Moore Bus. Systems, Pleasanton, Calif., 1982-87; dir. mktg. CMC ReSearch, Inc., Portland, Oreg., 1988-91, Aris Multimedia Entertainment, Marine del Rey, Calif., 1991—; bd. dirs. Citizens Info. Network, Ashland, Oreg. Author, pub. newsletter Oral Ecology, 1975. V.p., bd. dirs. Citizens Info. Network, Ashland, 1992. Capt. USAF, 1964-66.

BOUCHARD, PAUL EUGENE, artist; b. Providence, Sept. 26, 1946; s. Marcel Paul and Anna Theresa (Dullea) B., m. Ann Marie, Nov. 18, 1971 (div. 1976); 1 child Michael Paul. BFA, Calif. State U., Long Beach, 1978. bd. dir, Angeles Gate Cultural Ctr., San Pedro, Calif., 1983-85. Exhibited group shows at Coos Art Mus., Coos Bay, Oreg., 1989, Vietnam Vet.'s Art Exhibit, 1988, St. Andrew's Priory, Valyermo, Calif., Riverside (Calif.) Art Mus., Rental Gallery, 1987, Sixth Street Gallery, San Pedro, Calif., Aquarius Gallery, Cambria, Calif., 1986, Rental Gallery, L.A. County Mus. of Art, 1985, Rental Gallery, Oakland Mus., 1984, Grants Pass Mus. of Art, 1991, Eastern Wash. U., 1992, Dept. Vets. Affairs Hdqs., Sidney, Australia, 1992-93, Australian Nat. Gallery, Brisbane City Hall Gallery, others. Recipient Contribution to the Arts, City of Torrance, Calif., 1985; grantee Franklin Furnace, N.Y.C., 1989-90, Artist Space, N.Y.C., 1989-90. Home: 33140 Baldwin Blvd Lake Elsinore CA 92530-5954

BOUCHER, BILL ANTONIO, telecommunications consulting company executive; b. Nome, Alaska, Mar. 28, 1934; s. Wilfred Amade and Emily Pasqualina (Polet) B. Student in Engring., U. Va., 1952-54; student in Liberal Arts, U. Alaska, 1957-59. Installer, repairman Alaska Telephone & Telegraph, Nome, 1950-52; pvt. practice elec. contracting Nome, 1952-59; installer, asst. mgr. Fairbanks (Alaska) Mcpl. Utilities Svcs., 1959-73; contractor, cons. Digital Switching Assoc., Fairbanks, 1973-82; cons. Fairbanks and San Diego, 1985--; v.p. ops. Starnet, San Diego, 1982-85; mem. customer adv. panel ITT, Caracas, Venezuela, 1973. Sr. mem. CAP, Alaska, 1951--. With USAF, 1954-56. Mem. Soc. Mining Engrs., Aircraft Owners and Pilots Assn., Mooney Aircraft Pilots Assn., Alaska Airmens Assn. Home: Box 60174 2529 Clark St Fairbanks AK 99706-0174

BOUDART, MICHEL, chemist, chemical engineer; b. Belgium, June 18, 1924; came to U.S., 1947, naturalized, 1957; s. Francois and Marguerite (Swolfs) B.; m. Marina D'Haese, Dec. 27, 1948; children: Mark, Baudouin, Iris, Philip. BS, U. Louvain, Belgium, 1944, MS, 1947; PhD, Princeton U., 1950; D honoris causa, U. Liège, U. Notre Dame, U. Nancy, U. Ghent. Research asso. James Forrestal Research Ctr., Princeton, 1950-54; mem. faculty Princeton U., 1954-61; prof. chem. engring. U. Calif., Berkeley, 1961-64; prof. chem. engring. and chemistry Stanford U., 1964-80, Keck prof. engring., 1980—; cons. to industry, 1955—; co-founder Catalytica, Inc.; Humble Oil Co. lectr., 1958, Am. Inst. Chem. Engrs. lectr., 1961, Sigma Xi nat. lectr., 1965; chmn. Gordon Research Conf. Catalysis, 1962. Author: Kinetics of Chemical Processes, 1968, (with G. Djéga-Mariadassou) Kenetics of Heterogeneous Catalytic Reactions, 1983; editor: (with J.R. Anderson) Catalysis: Science and Technology, 1981, (with Marina Boudart and René Bryssinck) Modern Belgium, 1990; mem. adv. editorial bd. Jour. Internat. Chem. Engring., 1964—, Catalysis Rev., 1968—. Belgium-Am. Ednl. Found. fellow, 1948, Procter fellow, 1949; recipient Curtis-McGraw rsch. award Am. Soc. Engring. Edn., 1962, R.H. Wilhelm award in chem. reaction engring., 1974, Chem. Pioneer award Am. Inst. of Chemists, 1991. Fellow AAAS, Am. Acad. Arts. and Scis.; mem. NAS, NAE, Am. Chem. Soc. (Kendall award 1977, E.V. Murphee award in indsl. and engring. chemistry 1985), Catalysis Soc., Am. Inst. Chem. Engrs., Chem. Soc., Académie Royale de Belgique (fgn. assoc.). Home: 512 Gerona Rd Stanford CA 94305 Office: Stanford Univ Dept Chem Engring Stanford CA 94305

BOUDREAU, KATHRYN LYNDA SATTLER, alcoholism association administrator; b. San Diego, Sept. 28, 1947; d. James A. and Jane K. (Anderson) Sattler; married, June 24, 1974; children: Corey, Shane, Carly. BS, Wash. State U., 1969. Tchr. Wash. and Calif., 1969-80; vol. Probation Dept., 1980-88; exec. dir. Wash. State Coun. on Alcoholism, Drug Dependence, Bellevue, Wash., 1988—; sch. cons. for mentally gifted, Alameda, Calif., 1971-77. Recipient Calif. Gov.'s award, 1977. Mem. Nat. Edn. Assn., Nat. Coun. on Alcoholism and Drug Dependence, Wash. Edn. Assn., Employee Assistance Profls. Office: Wash State Coun on Alcohol 1050 140th Ave NE Bellevue WA 98005-2972

BOUDREAU, SUSAN KALMUS, science educator; b. Maidenhead, Berkshire, Eng., Mar. 8, 1960; came to U.S., 1987; d. George Ernest and Ann Christine (Harland) Kalmus; m. Phillip C. Boudreau, Apr. 18, 1992. BS in Zoology with honors, U. Bristol, Eng., 1981; cert. in Sci. Edn., U. Bath, Eng., 1984. Cert. life sci. tchr., Calif. Sci. tchr. Queen Elizabeth Sch., Crediton, Devon, Eng., 1984-87; elem. sci. tchr. Richmond (Calif.) Unified Sch. Dist., 1987-90; tchr., researcher U. Calif., Berkeley, 1990-92; tchr. sci. Orinda Intermediate Sch., Calif., 1992—. Author (curriculum) Kitchen Chemistry, 1988, Electricity, 1989. Home: 3819 Linden Ln El Sobrante CA 94803

BOUGHTON, WILLIAM HART, microbiologist; b. Cleve., Apr. 2, 1937; s. Ralph H. Boughton and Eloise C. (Graul) deWolfe; 1 child, Cindy. BS, Oreg. Stae U., 1964; MS, U. Ariz., 1965, PhD, 1969. Dir. microbiology San Diego Inst. of Pathology, 1972-74, 1983-84; dir. microbiology and immunology Pathology Assoc. Med. Lab., Honolulu, 1974-75, Kapiolani Children's Med. Ctr., Honolulu, 1975-81; co-dir. Anitbiotic Rsch. Lab., Honolulu, 1976-83; clin. lab. educator, vis. prof. Project Hope and USAID, Belize, Cen. Am., 1984-86; supr. microbiology Eisenhower Med. Ctr., Rancho Mirage, Calif., 1986-89; microbiologist Washoe Med. Ctr., Reno, 1990—; cons. Lab. Techniques, Rancho Mirage, 1986-89. Contbr. 20 articles to sci. jours. Mem. Am. Soc. for Microbiology, Sigma Xi. Home: 3983 S McCarran Blvd # 178 Reno NV 89502

BOUHOUTSOS, JACQUELINE COTCHER, clinical psychologist, educator; b. Phila.; d. David Jacob and Bertha (Blagman) Cotcher; m. Dimitri C. Bouhoutsos, June 11, 1948 (dec. 1983); 1 child, Elene Bouhoutsos Brown. BA cum laude, UCLA, 1944; MSW, U. Calif., Berkeley, 1950; PhD with highest honors, U. Innsbruck, Austria, 1956. Lic. psychologist, lic. clin. social worker, Calif.; diplomate Am. Bd. Examiners in Clin. Social Work; diplomate Internat. Acad. Behavioral Medicine, Counseling & Psychotherapy in profl. psychology, profl. counseling & behavioral medicine. Caseworker Alameda County Pub. Welfare, 1949-50, San Francisco City and County Pub. Welfare Dept., 1950-53; chief social work svcs. French and Am. zones of Austria, 1953-54; staff psychologist Toledo State Hosp., 1958-59, Toledo Mental Hygiene Clinic, 1959-60; dir. Calif. Family Guidance Ctr., 1964-67; dir. psychol. svcs. DePaulo Med. Group, 1974-77; pvt. practice clin. psychology Santa Monica, Calif., 1960—; mem. staff CPC Westwood Hosp., 1987—, St. John's Hosp. and Health Ctr., 1987—; mem. faculty Klinik Neurologie Psychiatrie, Innsbruck, 1954-56, Inst. Angewandte Psychologie Diagnostik, Innsbruck, 1954-55; asst. prof. Sch. Social Work UCLA, 1957-58, clin. prof. psychology, 1982—; adj. assoc. prof. community mental health, U. Wis., Green Bay, 1975-78; mem. faculty Calif. Sch. Profl. Psychology, 1974-81; cons. , rep. psychology mental health adv. bd. Los Angeles County Dept. Mental Health, 1968-74; cons. Motion Picture Assn. Am., 1969-74, Jerry L. Pettis Meml. Vets. Hosp., 1979, Masi Rsch. Cons., Inc., Washington, 1985—, others. Author: Sexual Intimacy Between Therapists and Patients (with K. Pope), 1986; contbr. chpts. to books, articles to profl. pubs.; cons. editor Profl. Psychology: Rsch. and Practice; editorial bd. Jour. of Imagination, Cognition and Personality; reviewer for Psychol. Abstracts, Am. Psychologist; guest TV and radio programs; producer documentary films. Chair Mental Health Info. Coord. Coun., 1968-69; mem. adv. com. Project Search, U. So. Calif., 1969-71, Allied Health Professions project, UCLA, 1969-71; chair acad. com. Modern Greek Studies Ctr., Loyola-Marymount U., 1979—; manpower adv. panel Calif. Dept. Mental Health, co-chair, 1980-85; mem. mental health adv. bd. County of Los Angeles, 1979-86; adv. bd. Psychologists for Social Responsibility, 1984—; chair Calif. State Senate Task Force on Sexual Involvement Therapists and Patients, 1986. Grantee John and Mary Markle Found., N.Y., 1981-82, 82-83, Ctr. Mental Health Initiatives, Washington, 1984, Simon Found., Beverly Hills, Calif., 1985, others; recipient Cine Golden Eagle award to TV documentary: A System in Shambles; recipient Outstanding Contbn. award City of L.A., Recognition award County of Los Angeles, others. Fellow APA (chair com. internat. rels. in psychology 1986, Champus peer reviewer 1980-84, cons. task force on impropriety 1991); mem. AAAS, Assn. for Media Psychology (exec. dir. 1986-88, bd. dirs. 1986-91), Calif. State Psychol. Assn. (chair ethics com. 1986-88, exec. coun. 1986—, pres. 1981), Los Angeles County Psychol. Assn. (pres. 1970), Psychol. Ctr. (bd. dirs. 1971-73, pres. 1973-74), Acad. Cert. Social Workers, Am. Orthopsychiat. Assn., Phi Beta Kappa. Office: 228 Santa Monica Blvd Ste 4 Santa Monica CA 90401-2200

BOUKIDIS, CONSTANTINE MICHAEL, lawyer; b. Burbank, Calif., Nov. 16, 1959; s. Michael A. and Frances (Mavros) B.; m. Eugenia Demetra Rodinos, May 17, 1987; children: Michael Constantine, Frances Anastasia. BA in Econs., Northwestern U., 1981; JD, Loyola Law Sch., L.A., 1984. Bar: Calif. 1985, U.S. Dist. Ct. (cen. dist.) Calif. 1985, U.S. Ct. Appeals (9th cir.), 1985. Investigator Harney & Moore, L.A., 1980-82; assoc. Law Offices of David M. Harney, L.A., 1985-92; pvt. practice, 1992—. Treas., chmn. cathedral planning com. St. Sophia Cathedral Orthodox Community, L.A., 1989. Mem. ABA, Assn. Trial Lawyers Am., Calif. Trial Lawyers Assn., L.A. County Bar Assn., Glendale (Calif.) Bar Assn., Phi Kappa Sigma (trea. 1980-81). Democrat. Home: 1641 Country Club Dr Glendale CA 91208-2038 Office: Law Office of Constantine Boukidis 144 N Glendale Ave Ste 101 Glendale CA 91206-4903

BOULDEN, JUDITH ANN, federal judge; b. Salt Lake City, Dec. 28, 1948; d. Douglas Lester and Emma Ruth (Robertson) Boulden; m. Alan Walter Barnes, Nov. 7, 1982; 1 child, Dorian Lisa. BA, U. Utah, 1971, JD, 1974. Bar: Utah 1974, U.S. Dist. Ct. Utah 1974. Law clk. to A. Sherman Christianson U.S. Cts., Salt Lake City, 1974; assoc. Roe & Fowler, Salt Lake City, 1975-81, McKay Burton Thurman & Coudie, Salt Lake City, 1982-83; Chpt. 7 trustee U.S. Trustee, Salt Lake City, 1976-82, Standing Chpt. 12 trustee, 1987-88, Standing Chpt. 13 trustee, 1988-89; sr. ptnr. Boulden & Gillman, Salt Lake City, 1983-88; U.S. Bankruptcy judge U.S. Cts., Salt Lake City, 1988—. Mem. Utah Bar Assn.

BOULDIN, DANNY LEE, electrical engineer; b. Fyffe, Ala., Oct. 31, 1953; s. Virgil Dee and Johnnie Mag (Gibson) B.; m. Brenda Gale Wooten, Apr. 13, 1974; children: Kelly, Stacey. BSEE, Auburn U., 1978; MSEE, Fla. Inst. Tech., 1983. Sr. engr. Harris Corp., Ft. Walton Beach, Fla., 1978-80, Martin Marietta Aerospace Div., Orlando, Fla., 1980-83, ITT Corp., Roanoke, Va., 1983-85; devel. engr. Hewlett Packard Corp., Palo Alto, Calif., 1985—. Republican. Home: PO Box 51477 Palo Alto CA 94303-0706 Office: Hewlett Packard Corp 370 W Trimble Rd San Jose CA 95131-1008

BOULET, ROGER HENRI, art gallery director, curator; b. Winnipeg, Man., Can., Feb. 15, 1944; s. Henri Elzear and Jeanne (Bourget) B. B.F.A. with honors, U. Man., 1970. Dir. Art Gallery of Greater Victoria, B.C., 1975-80; dir., curator Burnaby Art Gallery, B.C, 1981-87; dir. Edmonton Art Gallery, Alta., 1987-91; dir., curator Art Gallery of S. Okanagan, Penticton, B.C., 1993—. Author: F.M. Bell-Smith, 1978, The Silent Thunder, 1981, The Tranquility and the Turbulence, 1981, The Canadian Earth, 1982. Grantee Can. Coun., 1970.

BOULSE, GERALD LEE, secondary school educator; b. Pueblo, Colo., Aug. 27, 1950; s. Anthony Bede and Sally Hilda (Selensky) B.; m. Tommalee Minson, Aug. 5, 1972; children: Terra Lynn, Heather Ann, Craig Stephen. BS in Math., So. Colo. State Coll., 1972; MBA, U. So. Colo., 1990. Cert. tchr., Colo., administr., Colo. Prodn. mgr. CF&I Steel Corp., Pueblo, 1979-85; tchr. Pueblo Sch. Dist. #60, 1985—; cons. Aspen Badge & Nameplate Co., 1980—. Bd. dirs. Pueblo Edn. Assn., 1993—. Capt. U.S. Army, 1972-79. Mem. Pueblo Edn. Assn. (bd. dirs. 1992—), Minnequa U. Club (pres., bd. dirs. 1985-89), Pueblo Swim Club (bd. dirs. 1990-92), Elks. Office: Corwin Middle Sch 1500 Lakeview Ave Pueblo CO 81004-5699

BOULTON, LYNDIE MCHENRY, professional society administrator; b. Corvallis, Oreg.; d. W.B. Jim and Lillian (Hosken) McHenry; m. Roger Boulton. BA in Anthropology, U. Calif., Santa Barbara, 1974. Ops. mgr. C. Brent Scoh & Assocs., Sacramento, 1979-81; exec. dir. Am. Soc. Enology and Viticulture, Davis, Calif., 1981—; bd. dirs. Am. Vineyard Found., San Francisco. Mem. Nat. Assn. Expn. Mgrs., Am. Soc. Assn. Execs. Office: Am Soc Enology & Viticulture PO Box 1855 Davis CA 95617-1855

BOULWARE, RICHARD STARK, airport administrator; b. Chgo., Aug. 28, 1935; s. John Stark and Ellen Bradley (Bowlin) B.; m. Sylvia Grace Panaro, Sept. 17, 1960 (div. Jan. 1980); children: Susan Bradley, Robert Stark; M. Janice Gilliland Wells, Oct. 1, 1992. BFA, Art Ctr. Coll., 1967. Photographer Hughes Aircraft, Los Angeles, 1960-61; chief photographer U. Iowa, Iowa City, 1962-67; dir. audio/visual media TransWorld Airlines, N.Y.C., 1968-70; owner, mgr. RBA Prodns., Denver, 1970-80; dir. photography Colo. Inst. Art, Denver, 1980-84; dep. dir. aviation Stapleton Internat. Airport and Denver Internat. Airport, Denver, 1984—, Denver Internat. Airport, 1984—. Served with USN, 1954-58. Recipient Golden Eagle award CINE, 1976, award Bus. and Profl. Advt. Assn., Alfie award Denver Advt. Fedn., Christensen Meml. award Iowa Press Photographers Assn., award Art Dirs. Club Denver; named Nat. Photographer of Yr. U. Profl. Photographers Assn. Am., 1967. Mem. Pub. Relations Soc. Am. (award Colo. chpt.), Colo. Broadcasters Assn. Colo.Press Assn., Am. Assn. Airport Execs., Art Dirs Club Denver (v.p.). Home: 9112E E Amherst Dr Denver CO 80231-4040 Office: Terminal Bldg 433 Stapleton Internat Airport Denver CO 80207

BOUMANN, ROBERT LYLE, lawyer; b. Holdrege, Nebr., June 9, 1946; s. John G. and Loretta M. (Eckhardt) B. BS, U. Nebr., 1968, JD, 1974. Bar: Nebr. 1974, Colo. 1977. CPA, Nebr. Sr. acct. Peat, Marwick, Main and Co., Denver, 1968-71; atty., asst. sec. K N Energy, Inc., Lakewood, Colo., 1974—; bd. dirs. Consolidated Motor Freight, Inc., Hastings, Nebr. Treas. YMCA, Hastings, 1979-80. Mem. Nebr. Soc. CPAs, Nebr. State Bar Assn., Colo. State Bar Assn., ABA, Def. Rsch. Inst., Jaycees (treas. Hastings chpt. 1977-78), Phi Eta Sigma, Beta Gamma Sigma. Republican. Roman

Catholic. Office: K N Energy Inc PO Box 281304 Lakewood CO 80228-8304

BOUR, JEAN-ANTOINE, dean, French literature educator; b. Paris, Sept. 18, 1934; arrived in Can., 1975; s. Nicolas and Yvonne (Huntzinger) B.; m. Susan Allen, Aug. 3, 1963 (div. Dec. 1985); children: Suzanne, Christine, Nicolas, Jean-Paul; m. Jane Lewis Crowell, May 9, 1986; children: Christophe, Patrick. BA, U. Rochester, 1961, MA, 1962; MA, Princeton U., 1965, PhD, 1969; officier dans l'ordre des, Palmes Académiques. Instr. Eastman Sch. Music, Rochester, N.Y., 1958-59; lectr. Queens Coll., N.Y.C., 1962-63; asst. prof. Brown U., Providence, 1966-72; assoc. prof. Claremont (Calif.) Coll. and Grad. Sch., 1972-75; assoc. prof. Mt. Allison U., Sackville, N.B., Can., 1975-85, dean of arts, 1983-85; prof. French lit., dean U. Alta., Edmonton, 1985—. Author: (poetry) Evasions, 1970, Méandres, 1977; co-author: 15 Leçons de Francais, 1972. Sgt. U.S. Army, 1956-58. Mem. Assn. Canadienne d'Edn. de Langue Française, Assn. Francophone des Doyens et Directeurs d'Edn. du Can., Assn. Canadienne d'Edn., Réseau Francophone d'Enseignmement à distance (v.p. 1988-91), Revue des Sci. de l'Edn. (bd. dirs. 195—). Office: Fac St-Jean, Univ Alberta, 8406 - 91 St, Edmonton, AB Canada T6C 4G9

BOUREKIS, JAMES GEORGE, dentist; b. Warren, Ohio, Mar. 30, 1930; s. George and Maria B.; m. Katherine Barbas, Sept. 2, 1956; children: Maria Theresa, George James. DDS, Northwestern U., 1954. Pvt. practice, Warren, 1957-59, Spokane, Wash., 1960—; bd. dirs. Modern Electric Water Co., Spokane. Capt. USAF, 1954-56. Mem. ADA, Wash. State Dental Assn., Spokane Dist. Dental Soc., Rotary. Office: 20 S Pines Rd Spokane WA 99206-5390

BOURKE, LYLE JAMES, electronics company executive, small business owner; b. San Diego, May 28, 1963; s. Robert Victor and Virginia (Blackburn) B. Cert. in electronics, Southwestern Coll., San Diego, 1984; cert. in microelectronics, Burr Brown, Miramar, Calif., 1985; student, NACS, Scranton, Pa., 1988; AA in Econs., Cuyamaca Coll., 1991, postgrad., 1991-92; student, Wendelstedt Umpire Sch., 1992. Counselor Dept. Parks and Recreation City of Imperial Beach, Calif., 1979-80; warehouse worker Seafood Cannery, Cordova, Alaska, 1981, Nat. Beef Packing, Liberal, Kans., 1983; computer programmer ABC Heating and Air, San Diego, 1985; night mgr. Southland Corp., San Diego, 1983-85; tech. developer Unisys Corp., San Diego, 1985-92; founder Sparrells Ltd., 1992; instr. Harmonium Enrichment Program, 1993. Editor (handbook) College Policies, 1991; contbr. Cleanrooms mag., 1992; inventor Jacuzzi pillow. Vol. United Way, San Diego, 1987—; donor Imperial Beach Boys and Girls Club, 1988-93, Cal Farley's Boys Ranch, 1985-91, Assn. Handicapped Artists, 1988—, San Diego Jr. Theatre, 1992, Cabrillo Elem. Sch. Found., 1992; mem. Save the Earth Com., 1991—. Named Most Valuable Player Mex. Amateur Baseball League, San Diego-Tijuana, 1990. Mem. Am. Assn. Ret. Persons, Am. Mgmt. Assn. (charter), Prognosticators Club. Democrat. Office: Unisys 8011 Fairview Ave La Mesa CA 91941-6416

BOURQUE, LINDA ANNE BROOKOVER, public health educator; b. Indpls., Aug. 25, 1941; d. Wilbur Bone and Edna Mae (Eberhart) Brookover; m. Don Philippe Bourque, June 3, 1966 (div. Nov. 1974). BA, Ind. U., 1963; MA, Duke U., 1964, PhD, 1968. Postdoctoral researcher Duke U., Durham, N.C., 1968-69; asst. prof. sociology Calif. State U., Los Angeles, 1969-72; asst. prof. to assoc. prof. pub. health UCLA, 1972-86, prof. pub. health, 1986—, acting assoc. dir. Inst. for Social Sci. Research, 1981-82, vice chair dept. community health scis., 1991—. Author: Defining Rape, 1989, (with Virginia Clark) Processing Data: The Survey Example, 1992; contbr. articles to profl. jours. Violoncellist with Santa Monica (Calif.) Symphony Orch., 1978—, Los Angeles Doctors' Symphony, 1981—. Mem. AAAS, Am. Sociol. Assn. (mem. med. sociology sect. council 1975-78, co-chmn. com. freedom research and teaching, 1975-78, cert. recognition 1980), Pacific Sociol. Assn. (co-chmn. program com. 1982, v.p. 1983), Am. Pub. Health Assn. (mem. standing com. on status of women 1974-76), Sociologists for Women in Society, Am. Assn. Pub. Opinion Rsch., Assn. Rsch. in Vision and Ophthalmology, Delta Omega, Phi Alpha Theta. Office: UCLA Sch Pub Health 10833 Le Conte Ave Los Angeles CA 90024-1602

BOURRET, MARJORIE ANN, educational advocate, consultant; b. Denver, Sept. 9, 1925; d. Walter Brewster and Grace Helen (Thompson) Leaf; m. Raymond Roland Bourret, May 28, 1955; children: Robert B., Ronald P. BSEE, BS in Engring. Physics, U. Colo., 1947. Cons. for child advocacy and interagy. coordination San Benito-Santa Cruz Spl. Edn. Local Plan Agy., Aptos, Calif., 1991; cons. for Linkup to Learning Valley Resource Ctr., Ben Lomond, Calif., 1992—. Contbg. author: Board/Superintendent Roles, Responsibilities and relationships, 1980; prin. author: Citizens Guide to Scotts Valley, 1984; also articles. Trustee, pres. Scotts Valley (Calif.) Union Sch. Dist., 1970-81; mem., chmn. policy devel. com. San Benito-Santa Cruz Spl. Edn. Coordinating Agy., 1980-81; cons. on code sect. 7579, Calif. Adv. Commn. on Spl. Edn., Sacramento, 1984-89, chmn. legis. com., 1984, chmn. policy rev. com., 1987-89; mem. chmn. Hazardous Materials Adv. Commn., Santa Cruz, 1984-87; organizer, bd. dirs. Friends Long Marine Lab., U. Calif., Santa Cruz, 1979-84; bd. dirs. Group Home Soc., Santa Cruz, 1984-86; also others. Mem. Nat. Sch. Bds. Assn. (fed. rels. network 1977-81), Calif. Sch. Bds. Assn. (bd. dirs., com. chmn. 1977-81, mem. del. assembly 1974-81), LWV (pres. Santa Cruz County chpt. 1967-69). Home: 1160 Whispering Pines Dr Scotts Valley CA 95066

BOUSQUET, JOHN FREDERICK, security firm executive, desktop publishing executive; b. Washington, Nov. 19, 1948; s. Kenneth Joseph and Margaret Isabel (Sherrin) B. BSBA, Lehigh U., 1971; student, DeAnza Coll. Cert. profl locksmith. Staff asst. to gen. mgr. bank svcs. Yale Lock Co. Eaton Corp., Rye, N.Y., 1971; sales, installation, repairs alarms and electronic access controls Telcoa, Greenwich, Conn., 1971-73; from salesman to asst. mgr. Radio Shack, Stamford, Conn., 1973-74; sales rep. Electrolux, Stamford, 1974-75; pvt. practice locksmith contractor South San Francisco, 1975-85; locksmith NASA/Ames Rsch. Ctr. Smith Engring. & Contracting Svcs., Oakland, Calif., 1985-86, Bamsi Inc., Titusville, Fla., 1986-89, Quad S Co., Moffett Field, Calif., 1989—; prin. JFB Desktop Pub., South San Francisco; pres., CEO Computer Security Products, Inc., Am. Video Prodns., Inc.; dir. City Lock & Intercom., Inc., San Francisco, 1985-88; cons. NASA, Moffett Field, 1985—; spl. cons. Alcatraz Lock Renovation Project; asst. editor NASA Secutiry Awareness Bulletin, 1988; guest lectr. adminstrn. justice dept. DeAnza Coll., 1991. Mem. Associated Locksmiths Am., Calif. Locksmiths Assn. (Man of Yr. award San Francisco Bay Area chpt. 1983, cert. appreciation 1984), Door Hardware Inst., Nat. Classification Mgmt. Soc., Comm. Security Assn., Phi Theta Kappa (palimentarian Alpha Sigma Alpha chpt. 1992-93). Republican. Episcopalian. Home: 112 Eucalyptus Ave South San Francisco CA 94080-2447 Office: Quad S Co NASA Ames Rsch Ctr Moffett Field CA 94035-1000

BOUTELLE, SARA HOLMES, architectural historian, writer; b. Aberdeen, S.D.; d. John Horace and Marie Heloise (Adams) Holmes; m. William Eugene Boutelle, June 6, 1936 (dec. Jan. 1972); children: William Eugene, Jonathan Holmes, Christopher Curtis. BA with honors, Mt. Holyoke Coll., 1931. Head upper sch. The Brearley Sch., N.Y.C., 1946-74; researcher, pres. Julia Morgan Assn., Santa Cruz, Calif., 1974-84; vis. prof. U. Calif., Santa Cruz, 1980-84, 90, Williams Coll., Williamstown, Mass., 1990. Author: Julia Morgan Architect, 1988 (8 awards 1989-91); contbr. numerous articles to profl. jours. Mem. Hist. Preservation Commn., Santa Cruz, 1984—; bd. dirs., corr. sec. Santa Cruz County Hist. Trust. Mem. AIA (hon.), Soc. Archtl. Historians, Calif. Hist. Soc., Commonwealth Club of San Francisco, Phi Beta Kappa. Episcopalian.

BOUVIER, MARSHALL ANDRE, lawyer; b. Jacksonville, Fla., Sept. 30, 1923; s. Marshall and Helen Marion B.; m. Zepha Windle, July 11, 1938; children: Mark A., Marshall Andre III, Debra Bouvier Zanetti, Michael A., Jennifer Lynn, John A. Bouvier (dec.), Wendy Bouvier Clark, Suzanne. AB, Emory U., LLB, 1949. Bar: Ga. 1948, Nev. 1960. Commd. USN, 1949; naval aviator, judge advocate; ret., 1959; atty. State of Nevada, 1959-60; pvt. practice, Reno, 1960-82, 88—; dist. atty. County of Storey, Nev., 1982-88, spl. cons. to Nev.Dist. Atty., 1991—, Storey County Dist. Atty., 1991—; cons. on corp. securites problems. Mem. Judge Advocates Assn., Am. Bd. Hypnotherapy, Ancient and Honorable Order Quiet Birdmen, Rotary, E Clampus Vitus, Phi Delta Phi, Sigma Chi.

BOVERMAN, HAROLD, physician; b. San Francisco, June 19, 1927; m. Sue Randolph, Feb. 10, 1956; children: Daniel, Randolph, Joshua. AB, U. Calif., 1950; MD, U. Chgo., 1956. Clin. prof. psychiatry Health Scis. U. Oreg., Portland, 1981—. Office: 2250 NW Flanders St Portland OR 97210-3484

BOVEY, TERRY ROBINSON, insurance executive; b. Oregon, Ill., May 13, 1948; s. John Franklin and Frances (Robinson) B.; m. Diana Carmen Rodriguez, Aug. 29, 1970 (div. 1980); 1 child, Joshua; m. Kathy Jo Johnston, Sept. 14, 1985; children: Courtney, Taylor. Student, Ariz. Western Coll., 1966-68, Grand Canyon Coll., 1968-69; BBA, U. Ariz., 1972. Salesman All-Am. Dist. Co., Yuma, Ariz., 1972-76; dist. asst. mgr. Equitable Life Ins., Yuma, 1976-81; gen. sales mgr. Ins. Counselors, Yuma, 1981-83; mng. gen. agt. First Capital Life Ins. Co., Ariz., Calif., Nev., N.C., 1983-91; regional field dir. Southland Life Ins. Co. and Comml. Union Life Ins. Co., Tucson, 1991—; regional commnr. Ariz. Interscholastic Assn., Yuma, 1972-88. mem. Century Club, Boy's Club of Yuma. Mem. Million Dollar Round Table, Nat. Assn. Life Underwriters (numerous sales achievement awards, Nat. Quality awards), Life Underwriters Polit. Action Com., Tucson City Assn. Republican. Presbyterian.

BOWE, ROGER LEE, small business owner; b. Pueblo, Colo., Aug. 30, 1954; s. William Roy and Ruth Ann (Penn) B.; 1 child, Patrick William; m. Wendy C. Kempf, June 5, 1981. Grad. high sch., Denver. Mechanic Crest Motors, Denver, 1970-74; svc. mgr. Grand Prix Imports, Denver, 1974-76; line tech. Kerlin & Son, Denver, 1976-80; owner, operator Wheels of Fortune, Inc., Littleton, Colo., 1981—. Past mem. Vat. Fedn. Ind. Bus., 1988. Mem. Z Car Club Colo. (tech. advisor), Better Bus. Bur. Office: Wheels of Fortune Inc 2659 1/2 W Main St Littleton CO 80120-1914

BOWEN, 'ASTA, author; b. Chgo., Aug. 12, 1955. BA, St. Olaf Coll., 1977; MAT, Pacific U., 1993. Columnist Seattle Post-Intelligencer, 1988—. Author: The Huckleberry Book, 1988; contbr. articles to mags. Mem. Phi Beta Kappa. Address: 234 Old Hwy 93 Somers MT 59932

BOWEN, CLOTILDE DENT, retired army officer, psychiatrist; b. Chgo., Mar. 20, 1923; d. William Marion Dent and Clotilde (Tynes) D.; m. William N. Bowen, Dec. 29, 1945 (dec.). B.A., Ohio State U., 1943, M.D., 1947. Intern, Harlem Hosp., N.Y.C., 1947-48; resident and fellow in pulmonary diseases, Triboro Hosp., Jamaica, L.I., N.Y., 1948-50; resident in psychiatry VA Hosp., Albany, N.Y., 1959-62; pvt. practice, N.Y.C. 1950-55; chief pulmonary disease clinic, N.Y.C. 1950-55; asst. chief pulmonary disease svc., Valley Forge Army Hosp., Pa., 1956-59; chief psychiatry VA Hosp., Roseburg, Oreg., 1962-66, acting chief of staff, 1964-66; asst. chief neurology and psychiatry Tripler Gen. Hosp., Hawaii, 1966-68; psychiatr. cons. and chief Revv. Br., Office Civil Health and Med. Program, Uniform Svcs., 1968-70; commd. capt. U.S. Army, 1955, advanced through ranks to col., 1968; neuropsychiat. cons. U.S. Army Vietnam, 1970-71; chief dept. psychiatry Fitzsimons Army Med. Ctr., 1971-74; chief dept. psychiatry. Tripler Army Med. Ctr., 1974-75; comdr. Hawley Army Clinic, Ft. Benjamin, Harrison, Ind., 1977-78, chief dept. primary care and community medicine, 1978-83, chief psychiat. consultation svc., Fitzsimons Army Med. Ctr., 1983-85; chief psychiatry svc. med./regional office ctr. VA, Cheyenne, Wyo., 1987-90; staff psychiatrist Denver VA Satellite Clinic, Colorado Springs, Colo., 1990—; surveyor, Joint Commn. on Accreditation Healthcare Orgns., 1985-92; assoc. prof. psychiatry U. Colo. Med. Center, Denver, 1970-83. Decorated Legion of Merit, several other medals. Fellow Am. Psychiat. Assn. (life), Acad. Psychosomatic Medicine; mem. AMA, Menninger Found. (charter). Home: 1020 Tari Dr Colorado Springs CO 80921-2257

BOWEN, DEBRA LYNN, lawyer, state legislator; b. Rockford, Ill., Oct. 27, 1955; d. Robert Calvin and Marcia Ann (Crittenden) Bowen. B.A., Mich. State U., 1976; Rotary Internat. fellow Internat. Christian U., Tokyo, 1975; J.D., U. Va., 1979. Bar: Ill. 1979, Calif. 1983. Assoc., Winston & Strawn, Chgo., 1979-82, Washington, 1985-86, Hughes Hubbard & Reed, Los Angeles, 1982-84; sole practice, Los Angeles, 1984—; mem. Calif. State Assembly, 1992—; gen. counsel, State Employee's Retirement System Ill., Springfield, 1980-82; adj. prof. Watterson Coll. Sch. Paralegal Studies, 1985. Exec. editor Va. Jour. Internat. Law, 1977-78; contbr. articles to profl. jours. Mem. mental health law com. Chgo. Council Lawyers, 1980-82. Wigmore scholar Northwestern U. Sch. Law, Chgo., 1976; . Mem. ABA, Los Angeles County Bar Assn., Calif. Bar Assn. (exec. com. pub. law sect. 1990—), Phi Kappa Phi. Office: Dist Office 18411 Crenshaw Blvd Ste 280 Torrance CA 90504

BOWEN, EDWIN ANDERSON, television executive; b. Topeka, Jan. 19, 1932; s. Emery Jackson and Ruth Caroline (Anderson) B.; m. Joanne Longanecker, Apr. 4, 1953 (div. 1988); children: Sarah Denise, Rebecca Louise; m. Jane Wilkins, Oct. 19, 1988. BS, U. Kans., 1953; MBA, Harvard U., 1956. Analyst Amoco Prodn. Co., Tulsa, 1956-60, TWA/Hughes Tool Co., Kansas City, Mo., 1963-65; cons. McKinsey & Co., L.A., 1960-63; treas. Cyprus Mines Corp., L.A., 1965-72; sr. v.p. fin. and adminstrn. 20th Century Fox Film Corp., L.A., 1972-80; exec. v.p., CFO Knudsen Corp., L.A., 1980-82; ind. cons. Seattle, 1982-85; ptnr. Stanfill, Bowen & Co., L.A., 1985-91; exec. v.p., CFO MTM Entertainment, Inc., Studio City, Calif., 1991—. Mem. L.A. Yacht Club. Republican. Home: 890 Ronda Sevilla Apt Q Laguna Hills CA 92653 Office: MTM Entertainment Inc 4024 Radford Ave Studio City CA 91604

BOWEN, JAMES DAVID, accountant; b. L.A., Mar. 9, 1962; s. William Richard and Gloria (Frances) B.; m. Patricia Lynda Cocker, Jan. 1, 1988; children: Christopher West, Jessica Rose. BS in Acctg., Loyola U., L.A., 1984. CPA. Auditor Arthur Young & Co., Beverly Hills, Calif., 1984-85; experienced sr. auditor Arthur Andersen & Co., Las Vegas and L.A., 1985-89; dir. internal audit Dunes Hotel, Casino and Country Club, Las Vegas, 1989-91, controller, 1991; mgr. KPMG Peat Marwick, Las Vegas, 1991—. Treas. Alzheimer Disease Found., Las Vegas, 1991—. Mem. AICPA, Nev. Soc. CPAs, Inst. Internal Auditors (1st v.p. 1991, pres. 1992), Nat. Assn. Accts. (comm. dir. 1988-89, mem. dir. 1989-90, progs. dir. 1987-88). Republican. Mem. LDS Ch. Home: 6476 Lori Ct Las Vegas NV 89103-3241 Office: KPMG Peat Marwick 2300 W Sahara Ave Ste 300 Las Vegas NV 89102-4352

BOWEN, PETER GEOFFREY, real estate investment advisor; b. Iowa City, Iowa, July 10, 1939; s. Howard Rothmann and Lois Berntine (Schilling) B.; m. Shirley Johns Carlson, Sept. 14, 1968; children: Douglas Howard, Leslie Johns. B.A. in Govt. and Econs., Lawrence Coll., 1960; postgrad. U. Wis., 1960-61, U. Denver. cert. expert real estate witness, Denver Dist. Ct., 1987. Dir. devel. Mobile Home Communities, Denver, 1969-71; v.p. Perry & Butler, Denver, 1972-73; exec. v.p., dir. Little & Co., Denver, 1973; pres. Builders Agy. Ltd., Denver, 1974-75; pres. The Investment Mgmt. Group Ltd., Denver, 1975-87; independent investor, writer, Vail, Colo., 1987—; gen. ptnr. 8 real estate ltd. ptnrships.; lectr. on real estate syndications. Contbr. articles to profl. pubs. Mem. Colo. Coun. Econ. Devel., 1964-68; vice-chmn. Greenwood Village (Colo.) Planning and Zoning Commn., 1983-85; mem. Vail Planning and Environ. Commn., 1992—; elected mem. City Council Greenwood Village, 1985-86, also mayor pro tem, 1985-86; trustee Vail Mountain Sch. Found., 1987—; bd. dirs. Colo. Plan for Apportionment, 1966; speaker Forward Metro Denver, 1966-67. Mem. Rotary Club (bd. dirs. Vail chpt., named Rotarian of Yr. 1991-92), Lawrence U. Alumni Assn. (bd. dirs. 1966-72, 82-86). Home: 5047 Main Gore Dr Vail CO 81657-5440

BOWEN, RICHARD LEE, academic administrator, political science educator; b. Avoca, Iowa, Aug. 31, 1933; s. Howard L. and Donna (Milburn) B.; m. Connie Smith Bowen, 1976; children: James, Robert, Elizabeth, Christopher; children by previous marriage—Catherine, David, Thomas. B.A., Augustana Coll., 1957; M.A., Harvard, 1959, Ph.D., 1967. Fgn. service officer State Dept., 1959-60; research asst. to U.S. Senator Francis Case, 1960-62; legis. asst. to U.S. Senator Karl Mundt, 1962-65; minority cons. sub-com. exec. reorgn. U.S. Senate, 1966-67; asst. to pres., assoc. prof. polit. sci. U. S.D., Vermillion, 1967-69, pres., 1969-76; pres. Dakota State Coll., Madison, 1973-76; commr. higher edn. Bd. Regents State S.D., Pierre, 1976-80; Disting prof. polit. sci. U. S.D., 1980-85; pres. Idaho State U., Pocatello, 1985—. Served with USN, 1951-54. Recipient Outstanding Alumnus award Augustana Coll., 1970; Woodrow Wilson fellow, 1957, Congl. Staff fellow, 1965; Fulbright scholar, 1957. Office: Idaho State U Office of Pres Campus Box 8310 Pocatello ID 83209-0009

BOWEN, THOMAS EDWIN, cardiothoracic surgeon, army officer; b. Lackawanna, N.y., Dec. 16, 1934; m. Margaret Marie Harrington, 1959; children: Matthew, Mark, James, John, Thaddeus, Mary Cristine. BS, St. Bonaventure U., 1961; MD, Marquette U., 1965; diploma, U.S. Army War Coll., 1985. Diplomate Am. Bd. Surgery, Am. Bd. Thoracic Surgery, Nat. Bd. Med. Examiners. Commd. 2d lt. U.S. Army, 1961, advanced through grades to brig. gen., 1988; intern Tripler Army Gen. Hosp., Honolu, 1965-66, resident in gen. surgery, 1966-70; resident in gen. surgery Vietnam, 1970-71; resident in thoracic surgery Walter Reed Army Gen. Hosp., Washington, 1971-73; dep. dir. Profl. Svcs. Directorate Office of Surgeon Gen., Washington, 1985-87; comdr., surgeon 121st Evacuation Hosp., 1987-88; assoc. prof. dept. surgery Sch. Medicine Uniformed Svcs. U. of Health Scis., Bethesda, Md., 1981—; commanding gen. Fitzsimons Army Med. Ctr., Aurora, Colo., 1988; assoc. clin. prof. dept. surgery U. Colo. Sch. Medicine, Denver, 1989—. Contbr. articles to profl. pubis. Chmn. Combined Fed. Campaign, Denver, 1990. Decorated Legion of Merit with three oak leaf clusters, Bronze Star, Alfredo Lezcano Gomez medal for Svc. to Republic of Panama; recipient Raymond Franklin Metcalf award, 1971. Mem. Assn. Mil. Surgeons, Denver C. of C., Aurora C. of C., Rotary. Roman Catholic. Office: Fitzsimmons Army Med Ctr Office of Adminstr Aurora CO 80045

BOWEN, TRACEY SCOTT, physicist, researcher; b. St. Louis, June 18, 1961; s. William Francis and Beverley Jean (Wilkerson) B. BA in Physics, Northwestern U., 1983; MS in Physics, U. Texas, Dallas, 1987, PhD, 1988. Rsch. assoc. U. Tex., Dallas, 1985-88; founder, owner, pres. Novel Systems, Inc., Austin, Tex., 1985—; postdoctoral assoc. U.S. Army Ballistic Rsch. Lab., Aberdeen Proving Ground, Md., 1988-90; rsch. physicist Naval Weapons Ctr., China Lake, Calif., 1990-91, Phillips Lab., Kirtland AFB, N.Mex., 1991—. Contbr. articles to profl. jours. Postdoctoral assoc. NAS/Nat. Rsch. Coun., 1988-90. Mem. IEEE, Am. Phys. Soc., Optical Soc. Am., Laser and Electro-optics Soc., Electron Devices Soc., Beta Theta Pi. Roman Catholic. Office: Phillips Lab PL/WSM Kirtland A F B NM 87117-6008

BOWER, ALLAN MAXWELL, lawyer; b. Oak Park, Ill., May 21, 1936; s. David Robert and Frances Emily (Maxwell) B.; m. Deborah Ann Rottmayer, Dec. 28, 1959. BS, State U. Iowa, 1962; JD, U. Miami, Fla., 1968. Bar: Calif. 1969, U.S. Supreme Ct. 1979. Civil trial practice Los Angeles, 1969—; ptnr. Lane Powell Spears Lubersky, Los Angeles, 1990—. Contbr. articles to profl. pubis. Mem. Am., Los Angeles bar assns., Lawyer-Pilots Bar Assn., Am. Judicature Soc., Am. Trial Lawyers Assn., Am. Arbitration Assn. (nat. panel arbitrators), Alpha Tau Omega. Republican. Presbyterian. Home: 603 S Bundy Dr Los Angeles CA 90049-4037 Office: Lane Powell Spears Lubersky 333 S Hope St Ste 2400 Los Angeles CA 90071

BOWER, ANGUS BRUCE, aeronautical engineering consultant; b. Morganton, N.C., Oct. 6, 1927; s. Weldon Bruce and Hazel Pearl (Curry) B.; m. Ellen Darcus Everitt, June 20, 1954; children: Robert, William, Laura. BS in Physics, The Citadel, 1949; MS in Aero. Enginng., MIT, 1951. Registered profl. engr., Calif. Sr. aerodyns. engr. Chance Vought Aircraft, Dallas, 1951-54, Convair, San Diego, 1955-56; lead aerodyns. engr. Chance Vought Aircraft, Dallas, 1957-58; advanced design project mgr. Lockheed Aero. Systems Corp., Burbank, Calif., 1959-91; engring. cons. Frazier Park, Calif., 1991—. Bd. dirs. Lake of the Woods (Calif.) Mut. Water Co., 1992; vol. Ft. Tejon Hist. Soc., Lebec, Calif., 1992. Republican. Lutheran. Home: HC-1 Box 185 Frazier Park CA 93225

BOWER, DONALD EDWARD, author; b. Lockport, N.Y., July 19, 1920. BA, U. Nebr., 1942. D.E. Bower & Co., Inc., Denver, 1945-60; editor, pub. Arapahoe Tribune, 1960-62; editor Adams County Almanac, Adams County Dispatch, Jefferson County Herald, 1962-65; freelance staff Writer Fawcett Publs., 1962-64, lit. cons., 1962-67; editor, pub. Buyer's Showcase mag. and FURN Club News 1965-66; exec. editor Colo. mag., 1966-69; editor-in-chief, v.p., dir. Am. West Pub. Co., editor Am. West mag., 1970-74; pres. Colo. Authors League, 1975-76; dir. Nat. Writers Club, Denver, 1974-86; dir. Assoc. Bus. Writers Am., 1978-86, also pres. Assn. Hdqrs., 1978-86; editorial dir. Nat. Writers Press, 1982-86; lit. agent Don Bower Lit. Agy., 1991—. Author: Roaming the American West, 1970; Ghost Towns and Back Roads, 1972; intro. to The Magnificent Rockies, 1972; Fred Rosenstock: A Legend in Books and Art, 1976; The Professional Writers' Guide, 1984, rev. edition, 1990;Ten Keys to Writing Success, 1987, Sex and Espionage, 1990; also 4 paperback detective novels, 1960-64; editor: Living Water, Living Earth, 1971; Anasazi: Ancient People of the Rock, 1973; The Great Southwest, 1972; Edge of a Continent, 1970; The Mighty Sierra, 1972; The Magnificent Rockies, 1972; The Great Northwest, 1973; Gold and Silver in the West, 1973; Steinbeck Country, 1973; contbr. Western Writers Handbook, 1988, articles to mags. Mem. Authors Guild Am., Western Writers Assn. Am., Friends of Denver Pub. Libr., Sigma Delta Chi. Office: 3082 S Wheeling Way Apt 209 Aurora CO 80014-5611

BOWER, GREG HOLLIS, lawyer; b. Boise, Idaho, May 16, 1949; s. Jerry R. and Carol L. (Bancroft) B.; m. Janet Marie Sawaya, Sept. 7, 1973 (div. Feb. 1991); children: Lindsay, Leslie, Jeffrey; m. Linda Marie Hutchinson, July 17, 1992. BS in Fin., U. Idaho, 1971; JD, U. Utah, 1974. Dep. prosecutor Ada County Prosecutor, Boise, 1975-77, chief criminal div., 1977-83; pros. atty. Ada County, Boise, 1983—; mem. adv. bd. Am. Prosecutors Rsch. Inst., 1985—. Capt. U.S. Army Res., 1971-79. Mem. Idaho Bar Assn., Nat. Coll. Dist. Attys., Idaho Pros. Attys. Assn. (bd. dirs. 1983—, pres. 1986, 92). Republican. Methodist. Office: Ada County Prosecutor 602 W Idaho Boise ID 83702

BOWER, JEAN HELEN, civic volunteer; b. Seattle, June 12, 1933; d. Harold Elmer and Alice Josephine (Shiach) Lokken; m. Gene Alden Bower, Apr. 12, 1957; children: Gordon, Jeff, Sheryl. BA in Chemistry, U. Wash., 1956. Standard gen. cert. in edn. Vol. treas., Northshore Sch. Dist., Bothell, Wash., 1963-66, game chmn., 1969-70, health chmn., 1971-72, picture lady, 1973-74, hostess chmn., 1975-76, sr. party chmn., 1976, high sch. treas., 1977-79; treas. Northshore PTSA, Bothell, 1979-80, parent edn. chmn., 1980-81; sec. pastor seeking com., Inglewood Presbyn. Ch., Bothell, 1969, Sunday sch. tchr., 1970-75, 77, mem. adult edn. staff, 1986-88, deacon, 1985-88, elder, 1989-91; family interviewer, Kenmore (Wash.) C. of C., 1969; leader, Camp Fire Girls of Am., Seattle, 1970-75. Mem. AAUW (v.p. 1983-85, internat. rels. chmn. 1987-92, great decisions 1989-92, treas. 1992-93), Christian Women's Club (treas. 1982-85, contact advisor 1985-89, ticket chmn. 1988-90, book chmn. 1990-92), P.E.O. (program chmn. 1990-92, treas. 1993).

BOWER, PAUL GEORGE, lawyer; b. Chgo., Apr. 21, 1933; s. Chester L. and Retha (Dausmann) B.; m. Elreen L. Thurlow, June 23, 1962; children: Stephanie, Julienne, Aimee. B.A., Rice U., 1955; postgrad., Calif. Inst. Tech., 1959-60; LL.B., Stanford U., 1963. Bar: Calif. 1964, U.S. Sureme Ct. 1969. Assoc. Gibson, Dunn & Grutcher, Los Angeles, 1963-67, ptnr., 1970—. Asst. dir. Nat. Adv. Com. Civil Disorder, 1967-68; spl. asst. to dep. atty. gen. U.S. Dept. Justice, 1968-69, consumer counsel, 1969; bd. dirs. Legal Aid Found.; trustee Sierra Club Legal Def. Fund, 1982—; mem. legal svcs. Trust Fund Commn., 1990-93, chair 1993—. Served with U.S. Army, 1956-59. Mem. ABA, Calif. Bar Assn., Los Angeles County Bar Assn., Beverly Hills Bar Assn., Order of Coif. Democrat. Office: Gibson Dunn & Crutcher 2029 Century Park E Los Angeles CA 90067-2901 also: Gibson Dunn & Crutcher 333 S Grand Ave Los Angeles CA 90071

BOWER, WILLIAM DAVID, credit bureau firm executive; b. Atlanta, Jan. 22, 1964; s. Angus Bruce and Ellen (Everitt) B.; m. Sabrina Thai, June 20, 1984. BA in History, UCLA, 1988. Ptnr. Secret Svc. Limousine, Valencia, Calif., 1982-85; broker Prudential-Bache, Encino, Calif., 1985-87; pres., chief exec. officer Contemporary Info. Corp., Valencia, 1987—. Author: History of Darwin Days, 1985, Consumer's Guide to Credit, 1986. Nat. Rep. pollster, West L.A., 1985. Maj. U.S. Army Res., 1982—. Recipient Academic Scholarship U.S. Army, 1982. Mem. Valencia Ind. Assn. Santa Clarita C. of C., Santa Clarita Bruins (v.p. 1990—, pres. 1992—), UCLA Alumni San Juaquin, Sigma Chi. Lutheran. Office: Contemporary Info Corp Ste 110 25061 Avenue Stanford Santa Clarita CA 91355-3443

BOWERING, GEORGE HARRY, writer; b. Penticton, B.C., Can., Dec. 1, 1936; s. Ewart Harry and Pearl Patricia (Brinson) B.; m. Angela May Luoma, Dec. 14, 1962; 1 dau., Thea Claire. Student, Victoria Coll., 1953-54; B.A., U. B.C., 1960, M.A., 1963; postgrad., U. Western Ont., 1966-67. Asst. prof. Am. lit. U. Calgary, 1963-66; writer in residence Sir George Williams U., Montreal, Que., 1967-68; asst. prof. Sir George Williams U., 1968-71; prof. Simon Fraser U., Burnaby, B.C., 1972—. Author: Mirror on the Floor, 1967, Autobiology, 1972, Flycatcher and Other Stories, 1974, A Short Sad Book, 1977, Protective Footwear, 1978, Another Mouth, 1979, Burning Water, 1980, A Place to Die, 1983, Caprice, 1987, Harry's Fragments, 1990; poetry The Man in Yellow Boots, 1965, Rocky Mountain Foot, 1969, Touch, 1971, In the Flesh, 1973, The Catch, 1976, Particular Accidents: Selected Poems, 1981, Smoking Mirror, 1984, Kerrisdale Elegies, 1984, 71 Poems for People, 1985, Delayed Mercy, 1986, Sticks & Stones, 1989, Quarters, 1991, Urban Snow, 1992, George Bowering Selected, 1993; (essays) The Mask in Place, 1982, A Way with Words, 1982, Craft Slices, 1985, Errata, 1988, Imaginary Hand, 1988; editor Taking the Field: The best of baseball fiction, 1990, 92, Likely Stories: A Postmodern Sampler, 1992. Served with RCAF, 1954-57. Mem. Assn. Can. TV and Radio Artists. Home: 2499 W 37th Ave, Vancouver, BC Canada V6M 1P4

BOWERS, BOBBY EUGENE, metal products executive, small business owner; b. Bokosh, Okla., Apr. 12, 1933; s. Elmer Lefayet and Elizabeth (Hamilton) B.; m. Barbara Jean Baker, Feb. 2, 1952; children: Rory Eugene, Denise Lynn. Grad., Gemological Inst. Am., 1981, Revere Acad., 1985; postgrad., Trenton Sch. Jewelry Arts, 1985. Co-owner The Borrego Goldsmith, Borrego Springs, Calif., 1979—, B.O.S. Recording Studio, Borrego Springs, 1985—; lectr. gem mines of the world El Der Hostle, San Diego, 1992, Grossmont Coll., San Diego, 1992. Designer numerous signed works of fine jewelry. Mem. Masons. Home: 1470 Rango Way Borrego Springs CA 92004 Office: Borrego Goldsmith 563 Palm Canyon Dr Borrego Springs CA 92004

BOWERS, JACK (JOHN BURTON BOWERS, JR.), artist, real estate broker; b. Big Spring, Tex., Feb. 4, 1947; s. John Burton Bowers and Nola Mae Penny (Cuthberson) Reynolds; m. Victoria Barret Fuller, July 2, 1977 (div. 1982); m. Carol Ann Carbone, Oct. 11, 1985 (div. 1991); m. Patricia Lynn Veneman; 1 child, Carly Elizabeth. Student, N. Tex. State U., 1965-66; MFA, San Francisco Art Inst., 1984. Lic. real estate agt., Tex. Agy. sales mgr. The Penn Mutual Life Ins. Co., Dallas, 1967-74; mng. gen. ptnr. Bowers Enterprises, San Francisco, 1975—; nat. mgr. corp. real estate Werner Erhard & Assocs., San Francisco, 1986-89; dir. client svcs. Rapid, San Francisco, 1993—; Artist in residency, Moffet County High Sch., Craig, Colo., 1981. Represented in shows at Vallauris, France, 1988, N.Y.U., 1988, Boulder (Colo.) Art Ctr., 1987, Chgo. Internat. Art. Expo, Navy Pier, 1987, Dorothy Weiss Gallery, San Francisco, 1987, Berkeley (Calif.) Exhibition '87, 1st Internat. Ceramics Show, Aichi-ken Chusho Kigyo Ctr., Mino, Japan, 1986, Pro Arts Annual Exhibition, Pro Arts Galleries, Oakland, Calif., 1985, San Francisco Fine Arts Show, 1983, Aspen (Colo.) Mus. Art, Arvada Ctr. for the Arts, 1980, El Paso (Tex.) Mus. Fine Art, 1977, and numerous others; works include Space Case, Black Box, First Blond, Red and Black Box, Sally's Cenotaph, 2 Dozen Roaring Valleys, and numerous others; works reviewed in numerous mags. including The San Francisco Mag., 1988, San Francisco Chronicle, 1987, Oakland Tribune, 1987, Rocky Mtn. News, 1981, Westword, 1981, Art Space, 1981. Named Best of Show, Redding (Calif.) Mus., 1987, U. Ark., 1987, Aspen Mus. Art, 1980; recipient Honorable Mention, Mino, Japan, 1986, Purchase award, State of Colo., 1980, 81, Aspen Mall Competition, 1978, Juror's award, Aspen Mus. Art, 1979.

BOWERS, MICHAEL RAYMOND, clinical psychologist; b. Greenville, Ohio, Aug. 8, 1956; s. Marvin Thomas and Doris Irene (Benjamin) B.; m. Ann Therese Petrila, June 20, 1981; 1 child, Benjamin Petrila Bowers. BA, Otterbein Coll., 1978; D of Psychology, U. Denver, 1983. Lic. psychologist, Colo. Dir. weight mgmt. clinic Rose Med. Ctr., Denver, 1983-87; pvt. practice Denver, 1987—. Author: Eat, Drink and Be Wary: 1987. Mem. Colo. Psychol. Assn., Colo. Assn. of Behavior Analysts and Therapists, Eating Disorder Profls. of Colo. Office: Weight Choice 919 Jasmine St Denver CO 80220-4515

BOWERSOX, GLEN, Episcopal priest, foundation executive; b. York, Pa., Mar. 20, 1920; s. George Edward and Anna May (Hankey) Bowersox. BA, Gettysburg Coll., 1942; MS, Northeastern U., 1942-44; postgrad., Purdue U., 1944-45, U. Chgo., 1950-54; LHD, Gettysburg Coll., 1973. Ordained priest ch. Pakistan, 1973. Civilian specialist U.S. Army, Philippines, 1945-48; instr. Muhlenburg Coll., Allentown, Pa., 1948-50; field rep. Inst. Internat. Edn., Chgo., 1951-54, asst. dir., 1954-59; asst. rep. The Asia Found., N.Y.C., 1959-60; program officer The Asia Found., San Francisco, 1960-62; asst. rep. The Asia Found., Tokyo, Japan, 1962-66; program officer The Asia Found., San Francisco, 1966-68; rep. The Asia Found., Kabul, Afghanistan, 1968-73; priest assoc. Ch. of the Advent, San Francisco, 1973—; hon. canon Grace Cathedral, San Francisco, 1992—; fgn. study advisor U. Chgo., 1950-53; program officer The Asia Found., San Francisco, 1973-77; Luce Scholars coordinator The Asia Found., San Francisco, 1977-86. Home: 2484 Bush St San Francisco CA 94115-3106 Office: Ch of the Advent of Christ the King 162 Hickory St San Francisco CA 94102-5908

BOWES, FLORENCE (MRS. WILLIAM DAVID BOWES), writer; b. Salt Lake City, Nov. 19, 1925; d. John Albreckt Elias and Alma Wilhelmina (Jonasson) Norborg; student U. Utah, 1941-42, Columbia, 1945-46, N.Y. U., 1954-55; grad. N.Y. TV Workshop, 1950; m. Samuel Ellis Levine, July 15, 1944 (dec. July 1953); m. William David Bowes, Mar. 15, 1958 (dec. 1976); 1 son, Alan Richard. Actress, writer Hearst Radio Network, WINS, N.Y.C., 1944-45; personnel and adminstrv. exec. Mut. Broadcasting System, N.Y.C., 1946-49, free-lance editor, writer, 1948-49; freelance writer NBC and ABC, 1949-53; script editor, writer Robert A. Monroe Prodns., N.Y.C., Hollywood, Calif., 1953-56; script and comml. dir. KUTV-TV, Salt Lake City, 1956-58; spl. editor, writer pub. relations dept. U. Utah, Salt Lake City, 1966-68, editor, writer U. Utah Rev., 1968-75; author: Web of Solitude, 1979; The MacOrvan Curse, 1980; Interlude in Venice, 1981; Beauchamp, 1983. Mem. Beta Sigma Phi. Home: 338 K St Salt Lake City UT 84103-3562

BOWIE, PETER WENTWORTH, lawyer, educator; b. Alexandria, Va., Sept. 27, 1942; s. Beverley Munford and Louise Wentworth (Boynton) B.; m. Sarah Virginia Haught, Mar. 25, 1967; children—Heather, Gavin. B.A., Wake Forest Coll., 1964; J.D. magna cum laude, U. San Diego, 1971. Bar: Calif. 1972, D.C. 1972, U.S. Ct. Appeals D.C. Cir. 1972, U.S. Dist. Ct. D.C. 1972, U.S. Dist. Ct. Md. 1973, U.S. Ct. Appeals (9th cir.) 1974, U.S. Dist. Ct. (so. dist.) Calif. 1974, U.S. Supreme Ct. 1980. Trial atty. honors program Dept. Justice, Washington, 1971-74; asst. U.S. atty. U.S. Atty.'s Office, San Diego, 1974, asst. chief civil div., 1974-82, chief asst. U.S. atty., 1982—; lawyer rep. 9th Circuit Ct. Appeals Jud. Conf., 1977-78, 84-87; lectr. at law Calif. Western Sch. Law, 1979-83. Bd. dirs. Presidio Little League, San Diego, 1984; coach, 1983-84. Served to lt. USN, 1964-68; Vietnam. Mem. State Bar Calif. (hearing referee ct. 1982—), Fed. Bar Assn. (pres. San Diego chpt. 1981-83), San Diego County Bar Assn. (chmn. fed. ct. com. 1978-80, 83—), Phi Delta Phi. Republican. Unitarian. Home: 2205 La Callecita San Diego CA 92103-1112 Office: US Courthouse 940 Front St San Diego CA 92189

BOWKER, LEE HARRINGTON, academic administrator; b. Bethlehem, Pa., Dec. 19, 1940; s. Maurice H. Bowker and Blanche E. Heffner; m. Nancy Bachant, 1966 (div. 1973); 1 child, Kirsten Ruth; m. Dee C. Thomas, May 25, 1975; children: Jessica Lynn, Gwendolyn Alice. BA, Muhlenberg Coll., 1962; MA, U. Pa., 1965; PhD, Wash. State U., 1972. Instr. in Sociology Lebanon Valley Coll., Annville, Pa., 1965-66, Allbright Coll., Reading, Pa., 1966-67; assoc. prof. Whitman Coll., Walla Walla, Wash., 1967-77; prof., assoc. dean U. Wis., Milw., 1977-82; dean grad. sch. and research Ind. (Pa.) U. of Pa., 1982-85; provost, v.p. Augustana Coll., Sioux Falls, S.D., 1985-87; dean behavioral and social scis. Humboldt State U., 1987—; cons. various pubs., colls., univs. and state agys; expert witness. Author: Prison Victimization, 1980, Humanizing Institutions for the Aged, 1982, Ending the Violence, 1986, plus 13 other books; assoc. editor Pacific Sociol. Rev., 1975-78, Justice Quar., 1983-85, Criminal Justice Policy Rev., 1984—. Pres. Blue Mountain Action Coun., OEO, Walla Walla, 1969-71; dir. social therapy program, Wash. State penitentiary, Walla Walla, 1971-73; bd. dirs. Milw. Bur. Community Corrections, 1979-81, Sioux Falls Symphony, 1985, United Way of Humboldt County, 1988-91; expert witness in criminal and civil cases involving wife battering, rape and child abuse. Grantee NIMH 1973, 79, 81, Washington Arts Commn. 1972, Washington Office Community Devel. 1974, Fulbright Found. 1985, Nat. Retired Tchrs. Assn./Am. Assn. Retired Persons Andrus Found. 1980; Law Enforcement Assistance Adminstrn. co-grantee, 1978. Mem. AAUP, Am. Correctional Assn., Pacific Social. Assn., Am. Sociol. Assn. (staff mem., chmn. for teaching and adminstrv. workshops). Home: PO Box 208 Bayside CA 95524-0208 Office: Humboldt State U Dean Behavioral and Social Scis Arcata CA 95521

BOWKETT, GERALD EDSON, editorial consultant, writer; b. Sacramento, Sept. 6, 1926; s. Harry Stephen and Jessie (Fairbrother) B.; m. Norma Orel Swain, Jan. 1, 1953; children: Amanda Allyn, Laura Anne. B.A., San Francisco State Coll., 1952; postgrad., Georgetown U., 1954. Radio wire editor UP, Washington, 1956-57; reporter, columnist Anchorage Daily Times, 1957-64; spl. asst., press sec. to Gov. William A. Egan, 1964-66; pub. Alaska Newsletter, 1966-68; Juneau bur. chief Anchorage Daily News, 1967-68; editor S.E. Alaska Empire, Juneau, 1969-71; dir. info. svcs. U. Alaska, 1971-82. Author: Reaching for a Star: The Final Campaign for Alaska Statehood, 1989. Served with USMC, 1944-46, PTO. Cited for outstanding news and feature writing, editorial works Alaska Press Club. Mem. Alpha Phi Gamma. Home and Office: 2331 Innes Cir Anchorage AK 99515-4118

BOWLEN, PATRICK DENNIS, holding company executive, lawyer; b. Prairie du Chien, Wis., Feb. 18, 1944; s. Paul Dennis and Arvella (Woods) B. B.B.A., U. Okla., 1966, J.D., 1968. Bar: Alta. 1969. Read law Saucier, Jones, Calgary, Alta., Can., assoc., 1969-70; asst. to pres. Regent Drilling Ltd., 1970-71; pres. Batoni-Bowlen Enterprises Ltd., 1971-79, Bowlen Holdings Ltd., Edmonton, Alta., Can., 1979—; pres., chief exec. officer, owner Denver Broncos, 1984—. Mem. Law Soc. Alta., Can. Bar Assn., Young Presidents Orgn. Roman Catholic. Clubs: Mayfair Golf and Country; Edmonton Petroleum; Outrigger Canoe (Honolulu). Office: Denver Broncos 13655 Broncos Pkwy Denver CO 80216 also: Denver Broncos 13665 E Dove Valley Pkwy Englewood CO 80112*

BOWLER, JOSEPH LEGRAND, JR., Spanish language educator; b. St. George, Utah, Aug. 17, 1942; s. Joseph LeGrand Bowler and LaBerta (Woodbury) Altermatt; m. Dixie LaVern Taft, Sept. 15, 1962; children: Joseph III, Richard, Russell, Angela, Rochelle, Kimberly. BS, U. Utah, 1986; MA, No. Ariz. U., 1971; postgrad., U. Nev., Las Vegas. Lic. secondary sch. tchr./adminstr., Nev. Tchr. math. Booneville Jr. High Sch., Sandy, Utah, 1967-69; tchr. math./social scis. Sunset High Sch., Las Vegas, Nev., 1970-71; tchr. phys. edn., gen. sci., math., social sci. Burkholder Jr. High Sch., Henderson, Nev., 1969-79; tchr. econs., math., computer sci. Clark County Community Coll., 1978-85; tchr. Spanish, math., computer sci. Virgin Valley High Sch., Mesquite, Nev., 1979—; real estate broker Bowler Realty & Investment, Mesquite, Nev., 1973—. Chmn. Bunkerville (Nev.) Town Adv. Coun., 1980-84; mem. Paradise Adv. Coun., Las Vegas, 1978-79; pres. Quest, Las Vegas, 1976-78; mem. Clark County Dem. Cen. Com.; del. state and county convs.; active Boy Scouts Am. Mem. NEA, PTA, CCCTA, NSEA, Virgin Valley C. of C. (v.p. 1982-86). Home: PO Box 7209 Bunkerville NV 89007 Office: Bowler Realty & Investment PO Box 446 Mesquite NV 89024

BOWLES, THOMAS JOSEPH, nuclear physicist; b. Denver, June 27, 1950; s. Joseph Shipman and Mary Virginia (Belle) B.; m. Jeanne Marie Smith, May 30, 1987; 1 child, Kathleen Liana. BA, U. Colo., 1973; PhD, Princeton U., 1978. Postdoctoral fellow Argonne (Ill.) Nat. Lab., 1976-79; staff mem. Los Alamos (N.Mex.) Nat. Lab., 1979—; chmn. postdoctoral com. Los Alamos Nat. Lab., 1989-91; mem. tech. adv. panel LAMPF, Los Alamos; U.S. prin. investigator Soviet-Am. Gallium Experiment, Los Alamos and Baksan, Russia, 1987-92; speaker over 50 colloquia & confs. Contbr. over 20 articles to profl. jours. Mem. Am. Phys. Soc., World Tae Kwon Do Assn. Democrat. Roman Catholic. Office: Los Alamos Nat Lab MS D449 Los Alamos NM 87545

BOWLING, NINA RICHARDSON, dentist; b. Tokyo, Jan. 23, 1956; d. Donald McCuaig and Patricia Ann (Johnson) Richardson; m. Franklin L. Bowling Jr., Aug. 14, 1982; children: Patricia Ruth, Christopher Franklin. BS in Psychology, Coll. of William and Mary, 1976; DMD, Washington U., St. Louis, 1981. Assoc. dentist Dr. James Crandall, St. Louis, 1981-83; dentist, co-owner Broomfield (Colo.) Plaza Family Dentistry, 1983—. Am. Assn. Bus. Women grantee, 1978. Mem. ADA, Colo. Dental Assn., Boulder County Dental Soc., Delta Sigma Delta. Home: 2595 Outlook Trail Broomfield CO 80020-9686 Office: Broomfield Pla Family Dentistry 5015 W 120th Ave Broomfield CO 80020-5606

BOWLUS, DIANE MULLER, executive secretary; b. Erie, Pa., June 6, 1947; d. Meredith James and Ruth Cecelia (Hagaman) Muller; m. David Benjamin Bowlus, June 22, 1970. Grad. parochial high sch., Erie. Sec. to sales and engrng. dept. Union Iron Works subs. Riley Stoker Corp., Worcester, 1965-69; exec. sec. to v.p. sales and engring. Riley Stocker Corp., Worcester, 1969-83; exec. sec. to ops. mgr. Champion Internat., Seattle, 1984-85; exec. sec. to pres. Klopfensteins, Seattle, 1985-91; exec. sec. to regional ops. mgr. Hartmarx Retail Group, Seattle, 1991-92; exec. asst. to owner Car-Toys, Seattle, 1992—. Named Sec. of Yr., Profl. Secs., Worcester, Mass., 1980. Mem. English Speaking Union, Wash. Athletic Club. Republican. Lutheran. Home: 7 Crockett St Seattle WA 98109 Office: 307 Broad St Seattle WA 98121

BOWMAN, ARTHUR WAGNER, research company executive; b. San Diego, Aug. 18, 1938; s. Forest Bowman and Rachel Ball (Traylor) McDonald; m. Jaquelyn Sue Kelly, Dec. 13, 1961; children: Dona Marie Bowman Mayes, R. Steven, Michelle R. ASBA, Allen Hancock Coll., Santa Maria, Calif., 1975; BSBA, U. Redlands, 1980. Instr. U.S. Army Security Agy., Ft. Devers, Mass., 1961-64; sr. electronic tech. Bendix Field Engring., Pasadena, Calif., 1964-67; telemetry controller ITT/Fed. Electric Corp., Vandenburg AFB, Calif., 1967-74; mission controller, flight dir. JPL-Calif. Inst. Tech., Pasadena, 1975-79; sr. project engr. Aerospace Corp., El Sequndo, Calif., 1980-83; flight dir. Hughes Aircraft Co., El Segundo, 1983-84; sr. staff engr. Martin Marietta Astrountics, Denver, 1984-90; exec. dir. Colo. Inst. Risk Analysis, Littleton, 1990—; cons. Hughes Aircraft, El Segundo, 1984, A.W. Bowman & Assocs., Ventura, Calif., 1983-84. Author: A Guide to Risk, 1991, Risk Management, 1991; contbr. articles to profl. jours. Active loaned exec. program United Way, Denver, 1989. Recipient Voyager Achievement award NASA, 1980, Magellan Achievement award NASA, 1989. Fellow Brit. Interplanetary Soc.; mem. IEEE (sect. chmn. 1973-74, outstanding leadership award 1974), Soc. Risk Analysis, Am. Mgmt. Assn. Office: Colo Inst Risk Analysis PO Box 1087 Littleton CO 80160-1087

BOWMAN, BRUCE, writer, artist, educator; b. Dayton, Ohio, Nov. 23, 1938; s. Murray Edgar Bowman and Mildred May (Moler) Elleman; m. Julie Ann Gosselin, 1970 (div. 1980); 1 child, Carrie Lynn. AA, San Diego City Coll., 1962; BA, Calif. State U.-Los Angeles, 1964, MA, 1968. Tchr. art North Hollywood Adult Sch., Calif., 1966-68; instr. art Cypress Coll., Calif., 1976-78, West Los Angeles Coll., 1969—; tchr. art Los Angeles City Schs., 1966—; seminar leader So. Calif., 1986—. Author: Shaped Canvas, 1976; Toothpick Sculpture and Ice Cream Stick Art, 1976; Ideas: How to Get Them, 1985, (cassette tape) Develop Winning Willpower, 1986, Waikiki, 1988. Contbr. articles to profl. jours. One-man shows include Calif. State U.-Los Angeles, 1968, Pepperdine U., Malibu, Calif., 1978; exhibited in group shows McKenzie Gallery, Los Angeles, 1968, Trebor Gallery, Los Angeles, 1970, Cypress Coll., Calif., 1977, Design Recycled Gallery, Fullerton, Calif., 1977, Pierce Coll., Woodland Hills, Calif., 1978, Leopold/Gold Gallery, Santa Monica, Calif., 1980. Served with USN, 1957-61. Home: 28322 Rey De Copas Ln Malibu CA 90265-4463

BOWMAN, GARY MARTIN, social worker; b. Chatham, Ont., Can., July 13, 1943; came to U.S., 1960; s. John Martin and Hilda Ruth (Shaw) B.; m. Gwendolyn Yit-Wah Lee, July 3, 1970 (div. Dec. 1982); m. Jacqueline Custis Miller Lien, Mar. 17, 1984; 1 child, Alexander Stewart Bauman-Bowman. BA, Graceland Coll., 1965; MSW, U. Hawaii, 1972. Diplomate Clin. Social Work Am. Bd. Examiners. Pub. social service worker Linn County Dept. Social Svcs., Cedar Rapids, Iowa, 1965-67; dir. Joint Services Recreation Assn. for Handicapped, Honolulu, 1967-69, 71-72; social group worker Adolescent Unit Hawaii State Hosp., Kaneohe, 1970-73, 81-83; coordinator adolescent mental health svcs. St. Joseph's Hosp. Health Ctr., Syracuse, N.Y., 1973-74; community services coordinator Elmcrest Children's Svcs., Syracuse, 1974-75; psychiat. social worker Santa Rosa County Mental Health ctr., Milton, Fla., 1975-80, St. Francis Hosp. Health Care, Honolulu, 1980-81, Los Angeles County Coastal Community Mental Health Ctr., Carson, Calif., 1984-86, West-Cen. Family Mental Health Svcs., Los Angeles, 1986—; pvt. practice cons., therapy and tng. Burbank, 1986—; adj. faculty mem. U. Syracuse, Western Fla. U. at Pensacola, U. Hawaii, 1976-83; trainer crisis mgmt. Syracuse Police Dept., 1974; presentor Hawaii-Pacific Gerontology Conf., 1981, Happy Valley Singles Camp, Santa Cruz, Calif., 1984, Stas. KRLA-AM, KBZT-FM Separation/Divorce Trauma, Pasadena, Calif., 1986, Parenting By Men Cable TV, 1988, Buckhorn Women's Camp on Grief and Reconnection, Idlewild, Calif., 1988, Erie Beach Camp Families, Ont., Can., 1989, Nurturing Adolescent Nonconformists to Help Group, Van Nuys, Calif., 1989, Parents Without Ptnrs., Glendale, Calif., 1991, St. Luke's Hosp., Pasadena, 1991. Author: Joys, Fears, Tears, 1968; editor (newsletter) The Javelin, 1967-69; co-producer, dir. an interfaith gospel, country, western and contemporary music concert Spring Info Action - Reach Out for Excellence, Burbank, Calif., 1991; contbr. articles to mags. Bd. dirs., program chmn. Summer Action Vol. Youth Program, Honolulu, 1972-73, 80-83; pres. Friends of Libr. Santa Rosa County, Milton, 1979-80; founder singles separated divorced support group Reorganized Ch. Jesus Latter-day Saints, Burbank, Calif., 1985-92; founder Camp In Search Of, 1978-80; coord. Concert for Dr. Sharma-Candidate for Inglewood City Coun., 1993. Named Citizen for Day Sta. KGU, Honolulu, 1972; recipient Unheralded Humanitarianism, Dist. 1 Mental Health Bd., 1980. Mem. NASW (cert., steering con. region H&I Calif. 1983—, alt. dir. region H Calif. 1984-85, chmn. licensing com. 1979-80, mem. program and continuing edn. coms. 1980-83, Loyal and Dedicated Leadership award 1980), Assn. Labor Mgmt. Adminstrs. and Cons. on Alcoholism, Inc., Kiwanis (co-dir. Surrender Outreach Sports program 1991 Burbank club), Optimist (youth ctr. dir. Hiawatha, Iowa club 1966-67). Home: 4433 Sinova St Los Angeles CA 90032-1452

BOWMAN, GEORGE EDWARD, SR. (BUDDY BOWMAN), county official; b. Olympia, Wash., Apr. 17, 1926; s. David Edward and Ethel May (Young) B.; m. Maxine Patricia Hoerling, Oct 4, 1945 (dec. June 9, 1986); children: Diana Marie, Carolyn Jean, George Edward Jr., Janet Eileen. Student, Olympia High Sch. Spl. maintenance Thurston County Rd. Dept., Olympia, 1949-52; with Buchanan Lumber Co., Olympia, 1952-64, Ga. Pacific, Olympia, 1964-66; truck driver Thruston County Road Dept., Olympia, 1966-91. McLane vol., fireman, bn. chief Fire Dist. No. 9 Thurston County, 1956-91. With USN, 1944-46, PTO. Mem. VFW, Am. Legion, Wash. Assn. Retired Pub. Employees. Home: 4930 Cooper Pt Rd NW Olympia WA 98502-3620

BOWMAN, JEAN LOUISE, lawyer, civic worker; b. Albuquerque, Apr. 3, 1938; d. David Livingstone and Charlotte Louise (Smith) McArthur; student U. N.Mex., 1956-57, U. Pa., 1957-58, Rocky Mountain Coll., 1972-74; B.A. in Polit. Sci. with high honors, U. Mont., 1982, J.D., 1985; children—Carolyn Louise, Joan Emily, Amy Elizabeth, Eric Daniel. Dir. Christian edn. St. Luke's Episcopal Ch., 1979-80; law clk. to assoc. justice Mont. Supreme Ct., 1985-87; exec. v.p. St. Peter's Community Hospital Found., 1987-91; exec. dir. Harrison Hosp. Found., Bremerton, Wash., 1991-93, St. Patrick Hosp. and Health Found., 1993—; dir. 1st Bank West. Bd. trustees Rocky Mountain Coll., 1972-80; bd. dirs. Billings (Mont.) Area C. of C., 1977-80; mem. City-County Air Pollution Control Bd., 1969-74, chmn., 1970-71; del. Mont. State Constnl. Conv., 1971-72, sec. conv., 1971-72; chmn. County Local Govt. Study Commn., 1973-76; mem. Billings Sch. Dist. Long Range Planning Com., 1978-79; former pres. Billings LWV, dir., 1987-91, pres. Helena LWV, 2d v.p. Mont. LWV; former pres. Silver Run Ski Club. Named one of Billings' most influential citizens, Billings Gazette, 1977; Bertha Morton Scholar, 1982. Rotary. Republican. Home: 1911 E Broadway Missoula MT 59802

BOWMAN, JEFFREY R., protective services official; b. Akron, Ohio, Apr. 24, 1952; s. Roger Heath and Ruth Ann (Corrigan) B.; divorced; children: Katie, Andrew, Brian. BS in Orgnl. Behavior, U. San Francisco, 1986. Firefighter Anaheim (Calif.) Fire Dept., 1973-75, paramedic, 1975-79, capt., 1979-83, battalion chief, 1983-85, div. chief, 1985-86, fire chief, 1986—. Pres. bd. dirs. Anaheim Boys and Girls Club, 1988—; chmn. fundraising Boy Scouts Am., Anaheim, 1988. Mem. Internat. Assn. Fire Chiefs, Calif. Fire Chiefs Assn. Office: Anaheim Fire Dept 500 E Broadway Anaheim CA 92805-4099

BOWMAN, JON ROBERT, editor, film critic; b. Spokane, Wash., Nov. 9, 1954; s. Donald Ken and Carolyn Joyce (Crutchfield) B.; m. Geraldine Maria Jaramillo, Jan. 27, 1979 (div. Dec. 1985); m. Amy Farida Siswayanti, May 23, 1992. BA, U. N.Mex., 1976. Reporter, arts editor, news editor N.Mex. Daily Lobo, Albuquerque, 1972-76; film critic Albuquerque Jour., 1974-76; reporter Alamogordo (N.Mex.) Daily News, 1976; sci. writer, editor Los Alamos (N.Mex.) Monitor, 1976-81; reporter, arts editor New Mexican, Santa Fe, 1981-86, film critic, 1987—; editor New Mexico Mag., Santa Fe, 1986—; guest lectr. U. N.Mex., Coll. Santa Fe, 1976—. Author: (with others) Explore New Mexico, 1988, A New Mexico Scrapbook, 1990, Day Trip Discoveries: Selected New Mexico Excursions, 1993; contbr. articles to mags. and newspapers; author salutes for Greer Garson and John Huston for festivals honoring them. Vol. tchr. Albuquerque pub. schs., 1972-76; organizer film festivals Albuquerque and Santa Fe. 1972-91, benefits including Ctr. for Contemporary Arts, Santa Fe. Recipient Sci. Writing award AP, 1978, citation AP, 1979, others. Mem. Regional Pub. Assn., City and Regional Mag. Assn. Home: 2725 Camino Cimarron Santa Fe NM 87505-5805 Office: NMex Mag Lew Wallace Bldg 495 Old Santa Fe Trail Santa Fe NM 87503

BOWMAN, LARRY WAYNE, investigator; b. Mansfield, Ohio, Feb. 8, 1952; s. Ted L. Bowman and Mary Lou (Devore) Dessenberg. B in Criminal Justice, U. Md., 1978, M in Criminal Justice, 1980; MBA, So. Inst. Tech., 1987. Lic. pvt. investigator. Pvt. investigator Ohio and Mont., 1974—; security cons., 1974-92; drug awarness educator, 1974-92. Master sgt. USAF, 1970-74, with Res. ret. Named Outstanding Young Man of Am., 1988. Mem. VFW (life), NRA, Am. Legion, Lions, Optimist, Elks. Democrat. Presbyterian. Home: PO Box 6193 Great Falls MT 59406

BOWMAN, LESLIE GREENE, art museum curator; b. Springfield, Ohio, Nov. 9, 1956; d. Robert Hebblethwaite and Phyllis Jane (Weikart) Greene. B of Philosophy, Miami U., Oxford, Ohio, 1978; MA in Early Am. Culture, U. Del., 1980. Curatorial asst. L.A. County Mus. of Art, 1980-81, asst. curator, decorative arts and European sculpture, 1981-84, assoc. curator decorative arts, 1984-88, curator, dept. head decorative arts, 1989—; cons. curator Oakland Mus., 1986, Santa Barbara Mus. of Art, 1986-90; curatorial bd. dirs. Decorative Arts Study Ctr., San Juan Capistrano, Calif., 1990, adj. prof. U. So. Calif., 1988—, instr. UCLA, 1988—. Author: American Arts and Crafts: The Virtue in Design, 1990, American Rococo, 1750-1775: Elegance in Ornament, 1992, (with others) Silver in the Golden State, 1986, (with others) The Gilbert Collection of Gold and Silver, 1988; contbr. articles to profl. jours. Winterthur Mus. fellow, 1978-80, Crowninshield fellow, 1986-87, 87-88; Florence J. Gould Found. scholar, Friends of Vielles Maisons Françaises, 1989. Mem. Am. Ceramic Arts Soc., Am. Ceramic Circle, English Ceramic Circle, Furniture History Soc., French Porcelain Soc., Glass Circle, Nat. Early Am. Glass Club, Charles Rennie MacIntosh Soc. (Scotland), Soc. of Winterthur Grads., Soc. of Silver Collectors. Democrat. Office: LA County Mus of Art 5905 Wilshire Blvd Los Angeles CA 90036-4523

BOWMAN, RONALD LEE, design engineer; b. Dayton, Ohio, May 11, 1954; s. Robert Lee and Phyllis Jean (Roberts) B.; m. Deborah Ann Harrison, June 23, 1973 (div. June 1983); children: Kristie Ann, Beverly Sue. BA in Biology, Western State Coll., Gunnison, Colo., 1980. Water biologist Amax Metals, Crested Butte, Colo., 1980-84; prodn. engr. Headway Industries, Denver, 1985; design engr. Brass Smith Inc., Denver, 1985-89; design engr., co-founder Bowman Northey Co., Golden, Colo., 1986—; design engr., owner Bowman Contract Design, Golden, 1989—; founder Healing Energies Co., Golden, 1991—. Inventor, patentee locking clamping application; inventor polymer thermalset powder, artificial verdigris finish, anti-friction float slides; designer reversible glass support. Rsch. grantee Western State Coll., 1980; scholar Western State Coll., 1980; named as qualifier Mr. Am. Bodybuilding Championships, 1986.

BOWNE, MARTHA HOKE, magazine editor, consultant; b. Greeley, Colo., June 9, 1931; d. George Edwin and Krin (English) Hoke; children: Gretchen, William, Kay, Judith. BA, U. Mich., 1952; postgrad., Syracuse U., 1965. Tchr. Wayne (Mich.) Pub. Schs., 1953-54, East Syracuse and Minoa Cen. Schs., Minoa, N.Y., 1965-68; store mgr. Fabric Barn, Fayetteville, N.Y., 1969-77; store owner Fabric Fair, Oneida, N.Y., 1978-80; producer, owner Quilting by the Sound, Port Townsend, Wash., 1987—, Quilting by the Lake, Cazenovia, N.Y., 1981—; organizer symposium Am. Quilters Soc. Workshops, Paducah, 1984-93. Contbr. articles to profl. jours. Mem., pres. Minoa Library, 1960-75; mem. Onondaga County Library, Syracuse, 1968-71. Mem. Nat. Quilting Assn., Am. Quilters Soc. (editor Am. Quilter mag. 1985—), New Eng. Quilt Mus. Home: 12 Brook Bay Ln Mercer Island WA 98040

BOWYER, C(HARLES) STUART, astrophysicist, educator; b. Toledo, Aug. 2, 1934; s. Howard Douglas and Elizabeth (McEwen) B.; m. Jane Anne Baker, Feb. 27, 1957; children: William, Robert, Elizabeth. BA, Miami U., 1956; PhD, Cath. U., 1965; DSc (hon.), Miami U., 1985. Rsch. physicist Naval Rsch. Lab., Washington, 1959-67; prof. space scis. dept. Cath. Univ. Am., Washington, 1965-67; prof. astronomy dept. U. Calif., Berkeley, 1967—, dir. Ctr. Extreme Ultraviolet Astrophysics, 1989—; pres. Berkeley Photonics Inc., 1986—; cons. NASA, Washington, 1970—, NSF, Washington, 1970—, Israeli Space Agy., 1989—; vis. prof. Sci. Rsch. Coun., Eng., 1973; Humboldt Prize prof., Germany, 1982; Fulbright prof., 1983; Red Star prof. Centre National d'Etudes Spatiales, France, 1989. editor, co-editor 2 conf. proc.; contbr. over 400 articles to profl. jours. Miller Found. fellow U. Calif. Berkeley, 1978, Guggenheim fellow, 1992. Mem. Internat. Astron. Union, Am. Astron. Soc., Am. Inst. Astronautics and Aeronautics, Am. Geophysical Union, Internat. Acad. Astronautics, Optical Soc. Am., Astron. Soc. Pacific. Home: 147 Overhill Rd Orinda CA 94563-3110 Office: U Calif Ctr for Extreme Ultraviolet Astronomy Berkeley CA 94720

BOWYER, JANE BAKER, educator; b. Dayton, Ohio, Mar. 16, 1934; d. Homer Kenneth and Helen Elizabeth (Brown) Baker; m. Charles Stuart Bowyer, Feb. 27, 1957; children: William Stuart, Robert Baker, Elizabeth Ann. BA, Miami U., Oxford, Ohio, 1956; MA, U. Calif., Berkeley, 1972; PhD, U. Calif., 1974. Abbie Valley prof. Mills Coll., Oakland, Calif., 1975—, Abbie Valley head dept. edn., 1986—; cons. Lawrence Hall Sci., U. Calif., Berkeley, 1975—, Nat. Assn. Ednl. Progress, 1975-78, Utah State Bd. Edn., 1985-86; mem. Calif. Round Table's Math/Sci. Task Force, 1983-85; dir. ednl. research Industry Initiatives in Sci. and Math Edn., 1985-86, bd. dirs., 1985—; dir. Mills Coll./Oakland Unified Sch. Dist. Partnership, 1985—; dir. midcareer math. and sci. tchr. R&D, NSF, 1987—. Author: Science and Society, 1984, Science and Societies Activity Book, 1984; contbr. articles to profl. jours. Bd. dirs. Oakland Sci. and Art Sch., 1979-82, Eric Erickson Sch., San Francisco, 1983-85; prin. investigator Projects in Sci. Edn.; cons. UNESCO, Paris Div. Sci. Edn., 1989-90, 93. Fullbright Research fellow, 1982-83. Mem. Nat. Assn. Research in Sci. Teaching (mem. editorial bd. 1980-82, bd. dirs. 1985-88, Outstanding Paper award, 1979, 81), Am. Ednl. Research Orgn. Home: 147 Overhill Rd Orinda CA 94563-3110

BOXER, ALAN LEE, accountant; b. Denver, Sept. 9, 1935; s. Ben B. and Minnette (Goldman) B.; m. Gayle, Dec. 21, 1958; children: Michael E., Jodi S., Richard S. BSBA in Acctg., U. Denver, 1956. CPA, Colo. Audit mgr. Touche, Ross & Co. CPAs, Denver, 1956-60, Ballin, Milstein & Feinstein CPAs, Denver, 1960-61; prin. Alan L. Boxer, CPA, Denver, 1961-69; v.p and treas. Pawley Co., Denver, 1969-78; pres. Sci-Pro Inc., Denver, 1978-82; regional mgr. A.T.V. Systems, Inc., Denver, 1982-83; prin. The Enterprise Group, Denver, 1983-86; shareholder, pres. Allerdice, Baroch, Boxer & Co., CPAs, Denver, 1986-87; prin. Alan L. Boxer, CPA, Denver, 1987—. Bd. dirs. Anti-Defamation League, Denver, 1986-90, BMH Congregation, Denver, 1986—, treas. 1990-93, v.p. 1993—. Mem. Am. Inst. CPAs, Colo. Soc. CPAs, Bnai Brith #171 (pres. 1982, trustee 1983-89). Democrat. Jewish.

BOXER, BARBARA, U.S. senator; b. Bklyn., Nov. 11, 1940; d. Ira and Sophie (Silvershein) Levy; m. Stewart Boxer, 1962; children: Doug, Nicole. BA economics, Bklyn. Coll., 1962. Stockbroker, econ. rschr. N.Y. Securities Firm, N.Y.C., 1962-65; journalist, assoc. editor Pacific Sun, 1972-74; congl. aide to rep. 5th Congl. Dist. San Francisco, 1974-76; mem. Marin County Bd. Suprs., San Rafael, Calif., 1976-82; mem. 98th-102d Congresses from 6th Calif. dist., mem. armed services com., select com. children, youth and families; majority whip at large, co-chair Mil. Reform Caucus, chair subcom. on govt. activities and transp. of house govt. ops. com., 1990—, U.S. Senator from Calif., 1993—. Pres. Marin County Bd. Suprs., 1980-81; mem. Bay Area Air Quality Mgmt. Bd., San Francisco, 1977-82, pres., 1979-81; bd. dirs. Golden Gate Bridge Hwy. and Transport Dist., San Francisco, 1978-82; founding mem. Marin Nat. Women's Polit. Caucus; pres. Dem. New Mems. Caucus, 1983. Recipient Open Govt. award Common Cause, 1980, Rep. of Yr. award Nat. Multiple Sclerosis Soc., 1990, Margaret Sanger award Planned Parenthood, 1990, Women of Achievement award Anti-defamation League, 1990. Jewish. Office: US Senate 112 Hart Senate Office Bldg. Washington DC 20510-0505

BOXER, JEROME HARVEY, computer and management consultant; b. Chgo., Nov. 27, 1930; s. Ben Avrum and Edith (Lyman) B.; AA magna cum laude, East L.A. Coll., 1952; m. Sandra Schaffner, June 17, 1980; children by previous marriage: Michael, Jodi. AB with honors, Calif. State U., L.A., 1954. Lab. instr. Calif. State U., L.A., 1953-54; staff acct. Dolman, Freeman & Buchalter, L.A., 1955-57; sr. acct. Neiman, Sanger, Miller & Beress, L.A., 1957-63; ptnr. firm Glynn and Boxer, CPAs, L.A., 1964-68; v.p., sec. Glynn, Boxer & Phillips Inc., CPA's, L.A.and Glendale, 1968-90, pvt. practice cons., 1990—; pres. Echo Data Svcs., Inc., 1978-90; instr. data processing L.A. City Adult Schs.; tchr. lectr., cons. wines and wine-tasting; instr. photography. Mem. ops. bd. Everywoman's Village; bd. dirs., v.p. So. Calif. Jewish Hist. Soc.; co-founder Open Space Theatre; former officer Ethel Josephine Scantland Found.; past post adviser Explorer Scouts, Boy Scouts Am., also Eagle Scout. Recipient Youth Service award Mid-Valley YMCA, 1972-73; CPA, Calif., cert. systems profl. Mem. Am. Inst. CPAs, Calif. Soc. CPAs, Assn. for Systems Mgmt., Data Processing Mgmt. Assn., Am. Fedn. Musicians, Am. Jewish Hist. Soc., Friends of Photography, L.A. Photog. Ctr., Acad. Model Aeros., Nat. Model Railroad Assn., Maltese Falcons Home Brewing Soc., San Fernando Valley Silent Flyers, San Fernando Valley Radio Control Flyers, Associated Students Calif. State U., Los Angeles (hon. life), Acad. Magical Arts, Internal Brotherhood of Magicians, Soc. Preservation of Variety Arts, Les Amis du Vin, Knights of the Vine, Soc. Wine Educators, Napa Valley Wine Libr. Alumni Assn., L.A.-Bordeaux Sister City Affiliation, Soc. Bacchus Am., Paso Robles Dem. Club (pres. 1993), Wines and Steins, Cellarmasters, Paso Robles Vintners and Growers Assn., German Shepherd Dog Club Am., German Shepherd Dog Club Los Angeles County, Blue Key, Alpha Phi Omega. Clubs: Verdugo, Exchange, Kiwanis (pres. Sunset-Echo Park 1968), Braemar Country, Pacific Mariners Yacht, S.Coast Corinthian Yacht (former dir., officer), B'nai B'rith. Cons., contbr. Wine World Mag., 1974-82. Home and Office: 1660 Circle B Rd Paso Robles CA 93446-9515

BOXER, LESTER, lawyer; b. N.Y.C., Oct. 19, 1935; s. Samuel and Anna Lena (Samovar) B.; m. Frances Barenfeld, Sept. 17, 1961; children: Kimberly Brett, Allison Joy. AA, UCLA, 1955, BS, 1957; JD, U. So. Calif., 1961. Bar: Calif. 1962; U.S. Dist. Ct. (cen. dist.) Calif. 1962. Assoc. Bautzer & Grant, Beverly Hills, Calif., 1961-63; pvt. practice Beverly Hills, 1963-65, 69—; ptnr. Boxer & Stoll, Beverly Hills, 1965-69; pvt. practice, 1969—. Mem. Calif. Bar Assn., L.A. County Bar Assn., Beverly Hills Bar Assn., Friars Club. Office: 1875 Century Park E Ste 2000 Los Angeles CA 90067

BOYAJIAN, CAROLE L., graphic designer, interior designer; b. Fresno, Calif., Jan. 6, 1948; d. Armon K. and Louise (Josephine) B.;. BFA cum laude, The Art Ctr. Coll. Design, Los Angeles, 1969. Typographical liaison Doyle Dane Bernbach Advt., N.Y.C., 1969-70; prin. The Enchanted Nook Co., Pasadena, Calif., 1972-78; cons., pvt. practice pub. relations developer Ajijic, Jalisco, Mex., 1978-80; sales assoc. Forbes Monselle Inc., Los Angeles, 1980-84; prin. Carol Boyajian & Assocs., Beverly Hills, Calif., 1980—; co-owner ZERO Gallery, L.A., 1968-69; owner's rep./interior designer Robert Evans Co.; interior designer Internat. Mgmt. and Pub. Rels. div. of The Gordy Co., medical offices of Dr. Zion Yu and George Harrison. Cons. Los Angeles Theater Ctr., 1985. Recipient Cert. Merit, Nat. Fedn. Music Tchrs., Fresno, Calif., 1965. Mem. AIA (profl. affiliate Los Angeles chpt.), Nat. Fedn. Music, Network Exec. Women in Hospitality. Republican. Home: 365 W Alameda Ave Apt 308 Burbank CA 91506-3340 Office: PO Box 663 Beverly Hills CA 90213-0663

BOYCE, MARK STEPHEN, zoology educator; b. Yankton, S.D., May 24, 1950; s. John Harold and Mirriam (Dahl) B.; m. Jaren Jeanette Evers, May 29, 1971 (dec. 1981); 1 child, Cody James; m. Evelyn Hunter Merrill, July 31, 1987; 1 child, Aaron LaVon. BS, Iowa State U., 1972; MS, U. Alaska, 1974; MPhil, Yale U., 1975, PhD, 1977. Instr. U. Wyo., Laramie, 1976-77, asst. prof. Zoology, 1977-81, assoc. prof. Zoology, 1981-87, vis. prof. Math., 1984-85, prof. Zoology and Physiology, 1987—, dir. Nat. Park Rsch. Ctr., 1989-92; postdoctoral fellow Oxford (Eng.) U., 1982-83. Author: The Jackson Elk Herd, 1989; editor: North American Elk, 1979, Evolution of Life Histories of Mammals, 1988, The Greater Yellowstone Ecosystem, 1991; assoc. editor IMA Jour. Math. Applied Biology and Medicine, 1986—, Ecologia Montana, 1991—; contbr. articles to profl. jours. Recipient Outstanding Achievement award U. Alaska, 1974; Frederick Vanderbilt fellow Yale U., 1976, Fulbright fellow, India, 1991; exch. scholar NAS, Poland, 1982. Mem. Am. Soc. Naturalists, Am. Soc. Mammalogists, British Ecolog. Soc., The Wildlife Soc., Sigma Xi, Gamma Sigma Delta. Home: PO Box 3622 Laramie WY 82071-3622 Office: Dept Zoology and Physiology PO Box 3166 Laramie WY 82071-3166

BOYCE, ROBERT ABBOTT, service executive; b. Gallup, N.Mex., Apr. 10, 1942; s. George A. and Elizabeth (Coleman) B.; m. Shirley Cole, June 26, 1966 (div. 1987); children: Robert A. Jr., Jeffry H. LLB, LaSalle U., Chgo., 1974. Hotel credit mgr. Flamingo Hotel, Las Vegas, 1970-72; credit exec. Desert Inn Hotel, Las Vegas, 1972-75, 78-80, Aladdin Hotel, Las Vegas, 1975-78; exec. casino host Landmark Hotel, Las Vegas, 1980-85, Maxim Hotel, Las Vegas, 1985-86, Sahara Hotel, Las Vegas, 1986-89, Peppermill Hotel, Reno, 1989-92, Reno Hilton, 1992-93; dir. casino credit Gold River Gambling Hall and Resort, Laughlin, 1993—. Contbr. articles to popular mags. Cub scout exec. com. Boulder dam area Boy Scouts Am., Las Vegas, 1976-86; bd. dirs. Clark County Optimist Boys Home, Las Vegas, 1976-88. With USAF, 1960-65. Recipient Award of Merit Boulder dam area Boy Scouts Am., 1985. Mem. Optimists Club (pres. Las Vegas chpt. 1976, 84, outstanding service award 1988), Masons. Republican. Office: Gold River Gambling Hall and Resort 2700 S Casino Dr Laughlin NV 89029

BOYCE, RONALD REED, social and behavioral sciences educator, academic administrator; b. Los Angeles, Jan. 7, 1931; s. Reed S. and Martha Fern (Pusey) B.; m. Norma Rae Loraas, May 6, 1955; children: Renee Noreen, Susan Annette. BS, U. Utah, 1956, MS, 1957; PhD, U. Wash., 1960; BS, Seattle Pacific U., 1982, Seattle Pacific U., 1986. Instr. Western Wash. U., Bellingham, 1959; research assoc. Washington U., St. Louis, 1960-62; asst. prof. planning U. Ill., Urbana, 1962-64; assoc. prof. bus. and geography U. Iowa, Iowa City, 1964-65; prof. geography U. Wash., Seattle, 1965-76; dean social, behavioral scis. Seattle Pacific U., 1976—. Author: Economic Geography, 1978, Geography Perspectives on Global Problems, 1982, The Nature of Cities, 1985, Regional Development and the Wabash Basin, 1964; co-author: The United States and Canada, 1970, Seattle, Tacoma and the Southern Sound, 1986 and others. Councilman City of Woodway, 1969-74; chmn., farmland pres. Seattle C. of C., 1979-80; co-pres. Seattle-Beersheva Sister City com., 1985—; mem. tech. II com. City of Redmond, Wash., 1984-85; pres. Allied Arts Orch., Seattle, 1975-78. With U.S. Army, 1952-54. Recipient Service award Beersheva, Israel, 1978, Quadrenniel award Congress of South African Geographers, 1981; Nat. scholar Nat. Council of Social Sci., 1969; Am. Council Edn. fellow, 1978-79. Mem. Assn. Am. Geographers (pres. Bible speciality group 1981-84), Assn. Wash. Geographers (pres. 1976-78), Regional Sci. Assn., Sigma Xi. Democrat. Presbyterian. Home: 23606 112th Pl W Edmonds WA 98020-5252 Office: Seattle Pacific U Sch Social & Behavioral Scis 3rd and W Nickerson Seattle WA 98119

BOYD, EDWARD HASCAL, retired military officer; b. Kevil, Ky., Sept. 4, 1934; s. Lloyd E. and D. Irene (Steinbeck) B.; m. D. Ann Creecy, Jan. 13, 1956 (dec. Mar. 1970); children: Lawrence H., Debra A.; m. Margaret Lorene Hogan, Nov. 7, 1970; 1 child, Laura Irene. AA, Phoenix Coll., 1954; BS, Ariz. State U., 1956, MBA, 1972. Cert. secondary tchr., Ariz. Commd. 2d lt. USMC, 1956, advanced through ranks to col., 1980, exec. officer Marine Detachment USS Helena, 1959-60; assigned Marine Corps Recruit Depot, San Diego, 1961-63; instr. ops. and intelligence Landing Force Tng. Command USMC, 1963-65, mem. 1st Bn. 4th Marines, 1966-67, instr. Amphibious Warfare Sch., 1967-70, Hdqrs. USMC, 1973-76; assigned to Devel. Ctr. Marine Corps Devel. and Edn. Command, 1977-80; comdr. Hdqrs. Bn., Camp Pendleton, Calif., 1981-84; ret. USMC, 1984; substitute tchr. Mesa (Ariz.) Unified Sch. Dist., 1984—. Mem. Marine Corps Assn., Ret. Officers Assn., Williams AFB Officers Club, Alta Mesa Country Club, Delta Pi Epsilon, Alpha Tau Omega. Home: 5851 E Elmwood St Mesa AZ 85205-5833

BOYD, GARY HARLOW, oil company executive; b. San Francisco, May 3, 1936; s. Clarence Harlow and Angie Rachael (Harmon) B.; m. Olga Rose Marcon, Mar. 9, 1959; children: Gary C., Stephen J., Peter D., Douglas E. Grad. high sch. Retail mktg. rep. Texaco Inc., San Francisco, 1963-65, retail tng. supr., 1965-66; retail mktg. supr. Texaco Inc., Oakland, Calif., 1966-71; real estate agt. Texaco Inc., San Francisco, 1971-75, ops. supr., 1975-77; real estate agt. Texaco Inc., Phoenix, 1977-82; real estate supr. Texaco Refining & Mktg., Inc., El Paso, Tex., 1982-89; sr. real estate agt. Texaco Refining & Mktg., Inc., Phoenix, 1989—. Editor Texaco newspaper New Horizon, 1991 (Texaco Pres.'s Carpe Diem award). With USCG, 1954-63. Mem. Am. Inst. Real Estate Appraisers (resdl. mem.). Republican. LDS. Home: 8533 E Via De Viva Scottsdale AZ 85258 Office: Texaco Refining & Mktg Inc 3333 E Camelback Rd #170 Phoenix AZ 85018

BOYD, JAMES BROWN, molecular genetics educator; b. Denver, June 25, 1937; s. James and Ruth Ragland (Brown) B.; m. Susie Fay Staats, Apr. 23, 1960; children: Randall Ragland, Pamela Ann. BA, Cornell U., 1959; PhD, Calif. Inst. Tech., 1965. Postdoctoral fellow Max-Planck Institut for Biologie, Tubingen, W.Ger., 1965-68; asst. prof. dept. genetics U. Calif., Davis, 1969-71, asso. prof., 1971-77, prof., 1977—; vis. scholar Stanford (Calif.) U., 1988-89; mem. genetics study sect. NIH, 1976-80. Served with M.S.C. U.S. Army, 1959-60. Helen Hay Whitney fellow, 1965-68; NATO sr. scientist fellow, 1974; Guggenheim fellow, 1975-76; Sr. Am. von Humboldt prize, 1981-82. Mem. Genetics Soc. Am., Sierra Club, Sigma Xi. Home: 1615 Redwood Ln Davis CA 95616-1017 Office: U Calif Dept Molecular/Cellular Bio Davis CA 95616

BOYD, JOHN GARTH, manufacturing production and operations consultant; b. Greeley, Colo., Sept. 17, 1942; s. Jack Gardner and Madelyn Ilene (Bucher) B.; m. Cherie Kay Graves, Mar. 16, 1962 (div. June 1982); children: Jeffrey G., Daryl I., Peggy N.; m. Ellen Lea Meyers, Aug. 8, 1987; 1 child, Ian T. BA, U. No. Colo., 1963; MA, Colo. State U., 1965; MS, U. Colo., 1972. Teaching asst. Colo. State U., Ft. Collins, 1964-65; instr. No. Ariz. U., Flagstaff, 1965-67; teaching asst. U. Colo., Boulder, 1967-72; systems rep. Burroughs Corp., Englewood, Colo., 1972-76; mgr. Touche Ross & Co., Denver, 1977-84; chief fin. officer, chief operating officer Catalina Controls Corp., Longmont, Colo., 1984-86; ptnr. High Plains Ptnrship., Boulder, 1987—; adminstr. Martin Marietta Astronautics Group, Denver, 1988-92, honorarium instr. U. Colo. at Denver, Grad. Sch. Bus. Adminstrn. 1991—; instr. U. Denver, U. Coll., 1992—. Scoutmaster Boy Scouts Am., Boulder, 1969-72, troop scoutmaster, Denver, 1972-75; loaned exec. Colo. Gov.'s Mgmt. and Efficiency Study, 1982. NASA fellow, 1968. Mem. Am. Soc. Quality Control, Am. Prodn. and Inventory Control Soc. (treas. Denver 1983-84, pres. 1984-85, Gold award 1985). Avocations: hiking, mountain climbing, fishing, cross-country skiing. Office: High Plains Ptnrship 245 Berthoud Way Golden CO 80401-4813

BOYD, LEONA POTTER, retired social worker; b. Creekside, Pa., Aug. 31, 1907; d. Joseph M. and Belle (McHenry) Johnston. Grad. Ind. (Pa.) State Normal Sch., 1927, student Las Vegas Normal U., N.Mex., 1933, Carnegie Inst. Tech. Sch. Social Work, 1945, U. Pitts. Sch. Social Work, 1956-57; m. Edgar D. Potter, July 16, 1932 (div.); m. Harold Lee Boyd, Oct. 1972. Tchr. Creekside (Pa.) Pub. Schs., 1927-30, Papago Indian Reservation, Sells, Ariz., 1931-33; caseworker, supr. Indiana County (Pa.) Bd. Assistance, 1934-54, exec. dir., 1954-68, ret. Bd. dirs. Indiana County Tourist Promotion, hon. life mem.; former bd. dirs. Indiana County United Fund, Salvation Army, Indiana County Guidance Ctr., Armstrong-Indiana Mental Health Bd.; cons. assoc. Community Rsch. Assocs., Inc.; mem. Counseling Ctr. Aux., Lake Havasu City, Ariz., 1978-80; former mem. Western Welcome Club, Lake Havasu City, Sierra Vista Hosp. Aux., Truth or Consequences, N.Mex. Recipient Jr. C. of C. Disting. Svc. award, Indiana, Pa., 1966, Bus. and Profl. Women's Club award, Indiana, 1965. Mem. Am. Assn. Ret. Persons, Daus. Am. Colonists, Sierra County Hist. Soc., Common Cause (Washington and N.Mex.). Lutheran. Home: Phoenix Mountain Villa 13240 N Tatum Blvd Apt 137 Phoenix AZ 85032

BOYD, MARC ADAM, real estate company executive; b. Seattle, July 29, 1960; s. William Goldstein and June Roslyn (Bender) B. BA in Econs., U. Wash., 1990. Salesman Bon Marche, Seattle, 1976-79; mktg. specialist Better Bus. Bur., Seattle, 1979-85; property mgr. Boyd Real Estate Investments, Mercer Island, Wash., 1985-90; sec., treas., owner Boyd Real Estate Investments, Inc., Mercer Island, Wash., 1990—. Arbitrator Better Bus. Bur., Seattle, 1986—. Office: Boyd Real Estate Investments Inc 3801 Wallingford Ave N Seattle WA 98103

BOYD, RICHARD VICTOR, electrical engineer; b. Tacoma, Wash., May 13, 1942; s. Donald Frank and Doris Louise (Leonard) B.; m. Erna Sommer, July 3, 1968; 1 child, Mark Richard. BS, U. Wash., 1964; MDiv cum laude, Trinity Evang. Divinity Sch., Deerfield, Ill., 1974; MS, U. Ariz., 1986, PhD, 1993. Aero. engr. Rocketdyne, Canoga Park, Calif., 1964-65, Boeing, Seattle, 1965-69; elec. engr. Naval Undersea Warfare Engr. Sta., Keyport, Wash., 1987-90, U.S. Army Info. Systems Command, Ft. Huachucha, Ariz., 1990—. Author papers in field. Mem. IEEE, Am. Assn. Artificial Intelligence, Assn. Computing Machinery, Internat. Neural Network Soc., Tau Beta Pi. Home: 11824 80th Ave E Puyallup WA 98373

BOYD, SCOTT T, software engineer. BS, Abilene Christian Coll., 1983; MS, Tex. A&M U., 1987. Co-founder, software engr. The MacHax Group, Bryan, Tex., 1986—; software engr. Blue Meanie, X-Man Apple Computer, Cupertino, Calif., 1988—. Witer, programmer MacTutor; creator Ann. Best Hack Contest, MacHack, the Macintosh Tech. Conf., 1987-92; contbr. articles to profl. jours. Mem. Sierra Club, Nature Conservancy, Greenpeace. Mem. Assn. for Computing Machinery. Office: Apple Computer 20525 Mariani Cupertino CA 95014

BOYD, STOWE, software company executive, consultant; b. Boston, Sept. 24, 1953; s. Thomas Fyans and Martha (Bayles) B.; m. Sarah Hoover, Sept. 22,1 984; children: Keenan, Conrad. BS, U. Mass., Amherst, 1979; M Computer Sci., Boston U., 1986. Mem. staff ADR/Compass, Wakefield, Mass., 1987-88; v.p. engring. Meridian Software Systems, Irvine, Calif., 1988-91, pres., CEO, 1991—. Vice-pres. Back Bay Village Homeowners Assn., 1990-92. Mem. IEEE (com. chair 1988-89), Assn. Computing Machinery (nat. lectr. 1990-92, svc. award 1990), Object Oriented Programming Spl. Interest Group (chair software coun.), Phi Beta Kappa. Office: Meridian Software Systems 10 Pasteur St Irvine CA 92718

BOYD, WILLIAM ARTHUR, II, communications manager, editor, public relations professional; b. Washington, May 29, 1953; s. Donald Edward and Dorothymae (Phillips) B.; m. Cathy Ann Braman, Sept. 30, 1977; children: David James, Robin Elaine. Student, Am. U., 1971-74, George Mason U., 1975-76, U. Wash., 1976. Reporter, anchor Radio Sta. WAVA, Washington, 1973-76; reporter Radio Sta. KIRO, Seattle, 1976-77; press sec. mayoral campaign Seattle, 1977, press sec. congl. campaign, 1978; assignment editor, reporter Sta. KSTW-TV, Tacoma, Wash., 1979-86; prin. William Boyd Pub. Rels., Federal Way, Wash., 1986—; communications mgr., editor Weyerhaeuser, Federal Way, 1988—. Contbr. articles to Christian Sci. Monitor. Recipient 4 1st Pl. awards Wash. Press Assn., 1992, 93. Mem. Internat. Assn. Bus. Communicators (Gold Quill Award of Excellence, 1990, 91, 92, 6 Silver Six Awards, 1990, 91, 92, Gold Quill Award of Merit, 1992, 93, Seattle chpt. Communicator of Yr. 1992). Christian Scientist. Home: 1134 S 299th Pl Federal Way WA 98003-3751 Office: Weyerhaeuser 33663 Weyerhaeuser Way S Federal Way WA 98003

BOYD, WILLIAM HARLAND, historian; b. Boise, Idaho, Jan. 7, 1912; s. Harland D. and Cordelia (Crumley) B.; AB, U. Calif.-Berkeley, 1935, MA, 1936, PhD, 1942; m. Mary Kathryn Drake, June 25, 1939; children: Barbara A. Boyd Voltmer, William Harland, Kathryn L. Boyd Nemeyer. Tchr. Fall River High Sch., McArthur, Calif., 1937-38, Watsonville (Calif.) High Sch., 1941-42, San Mateo (Calif.) High Sch., 1942-44; prof. history Bakersfield Coll., 1946-73, chmn. social sci. dept., 1967-73. Pres., Kern County Hist. Soc., 1950-52; adv. com. Kern County Mus., 1955-60; chmn. Fort Tejon Restoration Com. Bakersfield, 1952-55, sec., 1955-60; mem. Kern County Hist. Records Commn., 1977—, Bakersfield Hist. Preservation Commn., 1984-87. Recipient Merit award Kern County Bd. Trade, 1960; commendation Kern County Bd. Suprs., 1952, 76, 78. Mem. Calif. Tchrs. Assn., Am. Hist. Assn., Phi Alpha Theta. Republican. Baptist. Author: Land of Havilah, 1952, (with G.J. Rogers) San Joaquin Vignettes, 1955, (with others) Spanish Trailblazers in the South San Joaquin, 1957, A Centennial Bibliography on the History Kern County, California, 1966, A California Middle Border, 1972, A Climb Through History, 1973, Bakersfield's First Bapt. Church, 1975, Kern Country Wayfarers, 1977, Kern County Tall Tales, 1980, The Shasta Route, 1981, Stagecoach Heyday in the San Joaquin Valley, 1983, Bakersfield's First Baptist Church A Centennial History, 1989. Contbr. to Ency. Brit. Home: 339 Cypress St Bakersfield CA 93304-1742

BOYDSTON, JAMES CHRISTOPHER, composer; b. Denver, July 21, 1947; s. James Virgal and Mary June (Wiseman) B.; m. Ann Louise Bryant, Aug. 20, 1975. BA in Philosophy, U. Tex., 1971. Lutenist and guitarist Collegium Musicum, U. Tex., Austin, 1968-70; tchr. classical guitar Extension div. The New Eng. Conservatory of Music, Boston, 1972-73. Arranger music: S. Joplins, "The Entertainer," 1976; arranger/composer/performer cassette recording: Wedding Music for Classical Guitar, 1988; inventor classical guitar bridge-saddle, 1990; author original poetry included in: The World of Poetry Anthology, 1991. Democrat. Home: 4433 Driftwood Pl Boulder CO 80301-3104

BOYER, CARL, III, educator, city official; b. Phila., Pa., Sept. 22, 1937; s. Carl Boyer Jr. and Elizabeth Campbell Timm; m. Ada Christine Kruse, July 28, 1962. Student, U. Edinburgh, Scotland, 1956-57; BA, Trinity U., 1959; MEd in Secondary Edn., U. Cin., 1959; postgrad., Calif. State U., Northridge, 1964-72. Tchr. Edgewood High Sch., San Antonio, Tex., 1959-60; libr. U. Cin., Cincinnati, Ohio, 1960-61; tchr. Eighth Avenue Elem. Sch., Dayton, Ky., 1961-62, Amelia High Sch., Amelia, Ohio, 1962-63; instr. Kennedy San Fernando Comm. Adult Sch., San Fernando, Calif., 1964-74, Mission Coll., San Fernando, 1971; tchr. San Fernando High Sch., San Fernando, Calif., 1963—; faculty chmn. San Fernando High Sch., dept. chmn.; cons. Sofia (Bulgaria) City Coun., 1991. Author, compiler 10 books on genealogy and family history; contbr. articles to profl. jours. Councilman City of Santa Clarita, Calif., 1987—, mayor pro tem, 1989-90, mayor, 1990-91; mem. Nat. League Cities Internat. Mcpl. Consortium, 1992—; mem. revenue and taxation com. League Calif. Cities, 1992—; sec. Calif. Contract cities Assn., 1992-93; trustee Santa Clarita C.C. Dist., 1973-81, pres., 1979-81; bd. dirs. Castaic Lake Water Agy., 1982-84, Newhall-Saugus-Valencia Fedn. Homeowners Assn., 1969-70, 71-72; prs. Del Prado Condominium Assn., Inc., Newhall, Calif.; exec. v.p. Canyon County Formation Com.; chmn. Santa Clarita City Formation Com., 1987. Mem. United Tchrs. L.A., New Eng. Hist. Geneal. Soc. Republican. Methodist. Home: PO Box 220333 Santa Clarita CA 91322-0333 Office: Santa Clarita City Hall 23920 Valencia Blvd Ste 300 Santa Clarita CA 91355-2175

BOYER, FORD SYLVESTER, hypnotherapist; b. Cadet, Mo., Jan. 12, 1934; s. Wilford Robert and Mary Elizabeth (DeClue) B.; m. Juelle-Ann Rupkalvis, May 2, 1970. BA in Psychology, U.S. Air Force Inst., 1957; DD, Am. Bible Inst., Kansas City, Mo., 1977; postgrad., John F. Kennedy U.; apprenticed, Spurling Hypnosis Lab., L.A., 1958=61. Cert. alcohol specialist. Adminstr. Getz Bros., San Francisco, 1969-73; supr. word processing U.S. Leasing Corp., San Francisco, 1977-82, dir. tng. and applications-word processing, 1982-84; computer cons Petaluma, Calif., 1984-87; massage therapist Petaluma, 1985-87; pvt. practice hypnotherapy Alameda, Calif., 1987—; cons. for chem. dependency Alameda, 1987—. Contbr. articles to profl. publs.; writer, pub.: (newsletter) Starfire, 1988—. With USAF, 1953-57, Korea. Mem. Am Coun. Hypnotist Examiners, Nat. Assn. Alcohol and Drug Abuse Counselors, Calif. Assn. Alcohol and Drug Abuse Counselors, Calif. Assn. Alcohol Recovery Homes. Home and Office: 3327 Cook Ln Alameda CA 94501-6939

BOYER, GLENN GORDON, author, painter; b. Pittsville, Wis., Jan. 5, 1924; s. Edwin Russell and Emma (Bliefeild) B.; m. Betty Ann Colby, Aug. 8, 1945 (div. May 1989); 1 child, Don. G.; m. Jane Winthrop Candia, Aug. 10, 1992. Commd. 2d lt. USAF, 1944, advanced through grades to lt. col., 1965; with U.S. Civil Svc. U.S. DOD, various, 1966-73; freelance writer, 1966—; pres. Chamiso Imprints, Rodeo, N.Mex., 1990—. Author: Illustrated Life of Doc Holliday, 1966, Suppressed Murder of Wyatt Earp, 1967, Wyatt Earp's Tombstone Vendetta, 1993, also 6 novels, 1981-86; collector, editor: I Married Wyatt Earp, 1976 (TV movie 1981); pub.: Wyatt Earp's Autobiography, 1981.

BOYER, JAY MARCUS, English language educator; b. Chgo., Aug. 31, 1947; s. John M. and Freida Maxine (Shoaf) B.; m. Roanne Phyllis Goldfein, May 21, 1977. BA, St. Louis U., 1969; MA, SUNY, Buffalo, 1971, PhD, 1976. Prof. Ariz. State U., Tempe, 1976—; lectr., speaker Ariz. Humanities Coun., 1979—. Author: As Far Away As China, 1990, Richard Brautigan, 1987, Sidney Lumet, 1993, Ishmael Reed, 1993; contbr. articles to periodicals. Capt. USAF, 1971-74. Office: Ariz State U English Dept Tempe AZ 85287

BOYER, LAURA MERCEDES, librarian; b. Madison, Ind., Aug. 3, 1934; d. Clyde C. and Dorcas H. (Willyard) Boyer. A.B., George Washington U., 1956; A.M., U. Denver, 1959; M.L.S., George Peabody U., 1961. Pub. sch. tchr., Kankakee, Ill., 1957-58; asst. circulation librarian U. Kans., Lawrence, 1961-63; asst. reference librarian U. of Pacific Library, Stockton, Calif., 1963-65, head reference dept., 1965-84, coordinator reference services, 1984-86; reference librarian Calif. State U.-Stanislaus, Turlock, 1987-90, ref. coord., 1990—. Author: The Older Generation of Southeast Asian Refugees: An Annoteted Bibliography, 1991; compiler of Play Anthologies Union List, 1976; contbr. articles to profl. jours. Mem. Am. Soc. Info. Sci., ALA, Calif. Library Assn., AAUP, Nat. Assn. for Edn. and Advancement of Cambodian, Laotian and Vietnamese Ams., DAR, Daughters of Am. Colonists, Phi Beta Kappa, Kappa Delta Pi, Beta Phi Mu. Republican. Episcopalian. Home: 825 Muir Rd Modesto CA 95350-6052

BOYER, ROBERT JAY, civil engineer, surveyor, land use planner; b. Fargo, N.D., Apr. 23, 1951; s. Kenneth Ward and Lucille Agnes (Kruse) B.; m. Eithne Mary Moore-Stevens, July 25, 1992. BSCE, U. N.D., 1973. Profl. engr., Alaska, Oreg., Wash.; lic. land surveyor, Alaska, Oreg. Constrn. engr. Santa Fe Internat., Orange, Calif., 1981; structural engr., sales mgr. HP Marine, Gothenburg, Sweden, 1981; player, instr., coach of basketball Travelodge All Stars, Nat. Basketball League, Bucks, Eng., 1981-82; engr. Boyer Engring., Portland, Oreg., 1982-83, Advance Engring., Wasilla, 1983; constrn. engr. State of Alaska, Anchorage, 1983-84; sanitation engr. City of Galena (Alaska), 1984-85; bldg. mgmt. specialist II State of Alaska, Anchorage, 1985-86; project engr. Engineered Concepts, Inc., Portland, Oreg., 1986-88; profl. engr., land surveyor, prin. Global Engring., Land Surveying, Planning Co., Portland, 1988—. V.p. Young Adult Ministry, Portland, 1980. Named Most Valuable Basketball Player Sioux Booster Club, Grand Forks, 1972. Mem. ASCE (Outstanding Sophomore Engring. Student Ladies Aux. 1971), Profl. Land Surveyors of Oreg., Nat. Soc. Profl. Engrs., Consulting Engrs. Counsel Oreg. (chair "new principals" com. 1991, membership com. 1992), Portland Skyliners, Tall Club. Roman Catholic. Home: 7315 SE Clay St Portland OR 97215-3528 Office: Global Engring/Land Survey 7315 SE Clay St Portland OR 97215-3528

BOYER, WILLIAM EDWARD, manufacturing professional; b. Silverton, Oreg., Aug. 4, 1931; s. William E. and Dorothy Marie (Gandy) B.; m. Evelyn Delores Holbert, June 6, 1951 (div. June 1969); m. Lorene Holt, Dec. 30, 1970; children: Richard, John, James, Diane, Claudette, Brenda. Registered mfg. engr. Sr. indsl. engr. Willamette Iron & Steel, Portland, Oreg., 1955-66; v.p., chief engr. S. Patkay & Assocs., El Monte, Calif., 1966-81; mfg. mgr. Barry Controls, Burbank, Calif., 1981—; mgmt. cons. various orgns., 1966-81. Home: 29013 N Dune Ln #104 Canyon Country CA 91351 Office: Barry Controls 4320 Vanowen St Burbank CA 91505

BOYETTE, BARBARIE ELAINE, consultant; b. Crockett, Tex., Apr. 8, 1952; d. Ronald Earl and Thelma Faye (Jackson) Gilmore; m. Will Charles Boyette, Mar. 2, 1978 (div. 1983); children: Donald, Aaron, Brie; m. Fred E. Baker, Dec. 31, 1992. BA in Polit. Sci., Calif. State U., Hayward, 1984; postgrad., Calif. State U., Turlock, 1985-86. Campus supr. Hayward Sch. Dist., 1978-83; caseworker Big Bros./Big Sisters, Belmont, Calif., 1983-84; exec. dir. E.C.H.O.S. Housing, Modesto, Calif., 1988-92; cons. Better Consult, Ceres, Calif., 1992—; commr. Human Svc. Commn., Hayward, 1980-84, Human Rels. Commn., Modesto, 1986—, County Affirmative Action Com., Modesto, 1987-92; mem. Ceres Pub. Rels. Com., 1987—. Mem. Rep. Cen. Com., Modesto, 1990; dir. ctrl. Calif. region Calif. Assn. Human Rights Orgn., 1990—; bd. dirs. Calif. Assn. Human Rights Orgn. Named Minority Woman of Yr., Stanislaus County, 1989. Mem. Modesto Civitan. Roman Catholic. Office: Better Consult 1651 Molly Ln Ceres CA 95307

BOYKIN, JAMES LESTER, aerospace engineer, consultant; b. Clarendon, Tex., Jan. 6, 1928; s. Garland Lester and Lucy Edna (Matthews) B.; m. Dulcie Mildred Ligon, Sept. 2, 1958; children: Tracy Lynette, Leslie Dee, James Russell, Robin Elisa. BSME, N.Mex. State U., 1951, BSEE, 1959. Comml. pilot rating. With Hughes Aircraft Co., 1951-54; fighter pilot U. S. Air Force, 1954-58; flight test engr., test ops. supr. N.Am. Aviation div. Rockwell Internat., L.A., 1959-63, Las Cruces, N.Mex., 1963-69; test ops. supr. LTV (Ling Temco Vaught), Las Cruces, 1969-71, Dynalectron Corp., Las Cruces, 1971-74; with Rockwell Internat., Las Cruces, 1974-85, ops. supr., 1978-85, project engr., 1981, sr. project engr., 1981-85; cons.; charter flying, instr., 1985—. Capt. USAF, 1946-48, 54-58; with USAFR, 1969. (ret.). Mem. Nat. Rifle Assn. (life), Air Force Assn., Res. Officers Assn., Lions (pres. 1975-76). Republican. Methodist. Home: 2390 Rosedale Dr Las Cruces NM 88005-1448

BOYKIN, RAYMOND FRANCIS, management science educator, consultant; b. Santa Monica, Calif., Nov. 18, 1953; s. Francis Raymond and Doris Elaine (Davis) B.; m. Shelley Lynne Ladd, July 30, 1977; children: Jennifer Lynne, Whitney Michele. BA in Quantitative Method, Calif. State U., Fullerton, 1975; MS in Mgmt. Sci., San Diego State U., 1976; PhD in Mgmt. Sci., St. Louis U., 1986. Indsl. engr. Rockwell Internat., L.A., 1976-77; sr. scientist Rockwell Internat., Richland, Wash., 1977-80; sr. mgmt. scientist Monsanto Co., St. Louis, 1980-86; prof. mgmt. sci. Calif. State U., Chico, 1986—; assoc. sr. cons. PLG, Inc., Newport Beach, Calif., 1986—; mem. tech. adv. com. State of Calif., Sacramento, 1988-90. Author, editor: Risk Analysis in the Chemical Industry, 1985; contbr. over 30 articles to profl. jours. and meetings. Mem. Soc. for Risk Analysis (chartered, ann. meeting chair 1984, 89, treas. 1989—), Inst. Mgmt. Sci. (Achievement award 1984). Democrat. Home: 862 Westmont Dr Chico CA 95926-7761 Office: Calif State U Coll of Bus Chico CA 95929-0011

BOYLAN, JOHN PATRICK, military career officer, navigator; b. Staten Island, N.Y., May 2, 1959; s. Francis G. and Gladys M. (Peterson) B.; m. Ellen M. Fantry, Nov. 27, 1982; children: Megan, Gary, Andrew. BA, Fairfield (Conn.) U., 1981; cert., Squadron Officer Sch., 1987; MA, Calif. State U., Stanislaus, 1992. Commd. 2d lt. USAF, 1981, advanced through grades to maj., 1993; flight instr. 310th air refuelling squadron USAF, Plattsburgh, N.Y., 1985-86; with standarization/evaluation to chief navigator tng. flight USAF, 1986-87, wing exec. officer, 1987-88; instr. 93rd air refueling squadron Strategic Air Command KC-135 USAF, Atwater, Calif., 1988-89, wing tactics officer 93rd bombardment wing KC-135 wing, 1989-90, instr., br. chief, 1990-93; weapon systems mgr. HQ Def. Mapping Agy. Fairfax, Va., 1993—. Tchr. religious edn. St. Jude Parish, Plattsburgh, 1984-86, minister lay eucharistic, 1986-88. Mem. Air Force Assn. (life). Roman Catholic. Lodges: K.C., Fairfield Fellows.

BOYLAN, RICHARD JOHN, psychologist, educator; b. Hollywood, Calif., Oct. 15, 1939; s. John Alfred and Rowena Margaret (Devine) B.; m. Charnette Marie Blackburn, Oct. 26, 1968 (div. June 1984); children: Christopher J., Jennifer April, Stephanie August; m. Judith Lee Keast, Nov. 21, 1987; stepchildren: Darren Andrew, Matthew Grant. BA, St. John's Coll., 1961; MEd, Fordham U., 1966; MSW, U. Calif., Berkeley, 1971; PhD in Psychology, U. Calif., Davis, 1984. Lic. psychologist, Calif.; lic. clin. social worker, Calif.; lic. marriage, family and child counselor, Calif. Assoc. pastor Cath. Diocese of Fresno, 1965-68; asst. dir. Berkeley (Calif.) Free Ch., 1970-71; psychiat. social worker Marin Mental Health Dept., San Rafael, Calif., 1971-77; dir. Calaveras Mental Health Dept., San Andreas, Calif., 1977-85; prof., coord. Nat. U., Sacramento, 1985-86; instr. Calif. State U., Sacramento, 1985-90, U. Calif., Davis, 1984-88; dir. U.S. Behavioral Health, Sacramento, 1988-89; pvt. practice psychotherapy, Sacramento, 1974—. Cons. Calif. State Legis., Sacramento, 1979-80; chmn. Calaveras County Bd. Edn., Angels Camp, Calif., 1981-84. Recipient Geriatric Medicine Acad. award NIH, 1984, Experiment Station grant USDA, Calif., 1983. Mem. Am. Psychol. Assn., Sacramento Valley Psychol. Assn. (pres.), Sacramento Soc. Profl. Psychologists (past pres.), Nat. Resources Def. Coun. Democrat. Home: 6724 Trudy Way Sacramento CA 95831-1924 Office: 2826 O St Sacramento CA 95816

BOYLE, CAROLYN MOORE, public relations executive, marketing communications manager; b. Los Angeles, Jan. 29, 1937; d. Cory Orlando Moore and Violet (Brennan) Baldock; m. Robert J. Ruppelt, Oct. 8, 1954 (div. Aug. 1964); children: Cory Robert, Traci Lynn; m. Jerry Ray Boyle, June 1, 1970 (div. 1975). AA, Orange Coast Coll., 1966; BA, Calif. State U., Fullerton, 1970; student, U. Calif., Irvine, 1970-71. Program coordinator Newport Beach (Calif.) Cablevision, 1968-70; dir. pub. relations Fish Communications Co., Newport Beach, 1970-74; mktg. rep. Dow Pharm. div. Dow Chem. Co., Orange County, Calif., 1974-77, Las Vegas, Nev., 1980-81; mgr. product publicity Dow Agrl. Products div. Dow Chem. Co., Midland, Mich., 1977-80; mgr. mktg. communications Dowell Fluid Services Region div. Dow Chem. Co. Houston, 1981-84; adminstr. mktg. communications Swedlow, Inc., Garden Grove, Calif., 1984-85; cons. mktg. communications, 1985-86; mgr. mktg. communications Am. Convertors div. Am. Hosp. Supply, 1986-87; mgr. sales support Surgidev Corp., Santa Barbara, Calif., 1987-88; owner Barrel House, Victorville, Calif., 1988-91, Saratoga Fences, Las Vegas, 1991; project comm. specialist nuclear waste divsn. Clark County Comprehensive Planning, Las Vegas, 1992—; guest lectr. Calif. State U., Long Beach, 1970; seminar coordinator U. Calif., Irvine, 1972; mem. Western White House Press Corps, 1972; pub. relations cons. BASF Wyandotte, Phila., 1981-82. Author: Agricultural Public Relations/Publicity, 1981; editor Big Mean AG Machine (internal mag.), 1977; contbr. numerous articles to trade publs.; contbg. editor Dowell Mktg. Newsletter, 1983; creator, designer Novahistine DMX Trial Size nat. mktg. program, 1977. Com. mem. Dow Employees for Polit. Action, Midland, 1978-80; bd. dirs. Dowell Employees for Polit. Action Com., Houston, 1983-84. World Campus Afloat scholar, U. Seven Seas, 1966-67; recipient PROTOS award, 1985. Mem. Pub. Relations Soc. Am. (cert.), Soc. Petroleum Engrs., Internat. Assn. Bus. Communicators. Episcopalian. Recipient first rights to televise President Nixon in Western White House. Office: 7904 Fanciful Ave Las Vegas NV 89128-4009

BOYLE, CHARLES KEITH, artist, educator; b. Defiance, Ohio., Feb. 15, 1930. Student, Ringling Sch. Art; B.F.A., U. Iowa. Prof. painting and drawing Stanford U., Calif., 1962-88. Group shows include Stanford U. Mus., 1964, San Francisco Mus. Art, 1965, Ann Arbor, Mich., 1965, Joslyn Art Mus., Omaha, 1970, San Jose Mus. Art, Calif., 1978; represented in permanent collections: San Francisco Mus. Art, Stanford U. Mus., Mead paper Corp., Atlanta, Nat. Fine Arts Collection, Washington, Oakland Mus., Continental Bank, Chgo., Seton Med. Ctr., Daily City, Calif. Grantee NEA, 1981-82, Pew Meml. Trust, 1986-87. Address: 6285 Thompson Creek Rd Applegate OR 97530

BOYLE, M. COLLEEN, business consultant, facilitator, speaker; b. San Francisco, Aug. 26, 1949; d. Thomas Daniel and Mary Margaret (Kenny) B.; m. John R. Goehl, Sept. 23, 1977 (div. 1983). Student, U. of Utah, 1968-70, 71-72, Gonzaga U., 1967-68, Weber State Coll., 1970-71. Cert. real estate broker. Owner Vail (Colo.) Golf Club Restaurant, 1975-80; ptnr. Total Beauty Ctr., Vail, 1979-81; real estate assoc. Coldwell Banker Timberline Property, Vail, 1981-83, Gore Range Properties, Vail, 1983-84; dir. mktg. and leasing Design Collection, Denver, 1984-85; mng. ptnr. Realty Comml. Assocs., Boulder, Colo., 1985-87; broker Perferred Properties, Denver, 1987-89; prin. Lifeworks Consulting, Denver, 1989—; ptnr. The Action Ctr., Denver, 1991—; pres. WIN/WIN Bus. Forum, Denver, 1989-91, mem. speaker's com., 1988—; mem. adv. bd. Keeping the Promise Children's Campaign, Denver, 1990—. Bd. dirs. Children's Candle Light Vigil, Denver, 1990-91, Minority Bus. Devel. Week, Denver, 1991—. Mem. NAFE, Nat. Assn. Women Bus. Owners (com.), LEADS Denver Tech. Ctr., Women's C. of C., Greater Denver C. of C. Home: 1407 E 10th Ave # 7 Denver CO 80218-3531 Office: The Action Ctr 910 16th St Ste 830 Denver CO 80202

BOYLES, ROBERT JOSEPH, avionics engineer; b. North Tonawanda, N.Y., Dec. 18, 1955; s. Robert F. and Bethea J. (Crispin) B.; m. Dawn Marie Lerette, June 7, 1980; children: Brandon, Jason, Andrew. Student, No. Ariz. U., 1979-80; BSEE, Ariz. State U., 1984; postgrad., U. Phoenix, 1986-87. Telecommunication technician Trans-West Telephone Co., Phoenix, 1980-83; digital circuit designer Sperry Space Systems, Phoenix, 1983-85; flight test instrn. engr. Garrett Turbine Engine Co., Phoenix, 1985-87; sr. project engr. Global-Wulfsberg Systems, Prescott, Ariz., 1987—; pvt. practice flight test instrn. engr. Prescott, 1987—. Comdr. AWANA, Prescott, 1987—. With USN, 1975-79. Mem. NRA. Office: Global-Wulfsberg 6400 Wilkinson Dr Prescott AZ 86301-6164

BOYNTON, DONALD ARTHUR, title insurance company executive; b. Culver City, Calif., Sept. 6, 1940; s. A.A. and Margaret Lena (Slocum) B.; m. Jean Carolyn Ferrulli, Nov. 10, 1962; children: Donna Jean, Michael Arthur; m. Sharon C. Burns, Nov. 18, 1984; children: Cynthia, David, Sharie. Student, El Camino Jr. Coll., 1960-62, Antelope Valley Jr. Coll., 1963-64, Orange Coast Coll., 1969-72; BA, Bradford U., 1977. With Title Ins. & Trust Co., 1958-63; sales mgr. Title Ins. & Trust Co., Santa Ana, Calif., 1980-81; dep. sheriff County of Los Angeles, 1963-65; with Transamerica Title Ins. Co., L.A., 1965-69, state coord., 1981-82; sr. title officer Calif. Land Title Co., L.A., 1969-72; asst. sec., systems analyst Lawyers Title Ins. Corp., 39 states, 1972-77; county mgr. Am. Title Co., Santa Ana, Calif., 1977-79; v.p., mgr. Orange County ops. Chgo. Title Ins. Co., Tustin, Calif., 1979-80; pres. Stewart Title Co. of Fresno, 1985-86; supr. builder svcs. Orange Coast Title Co., Santa Ana, 1986-89; sr. title officer TSG dept. Orange Coast/Record Title, Whittier, Calif., 1990—; sr. title officer, ednl. coord. State of Calif. for Orange Coast Title, 1993—. Mem. Calif. Trustees Assn., Orange County Escrow Assn., Calif. C.T.A., Optimists (sec.-treas.), Elks (life, chaplain), Rotary. Home: 9061 Bermuda Dr Huntington Beach CA 92646-7812 Office: Orange Coast Title-Hdqs 640 N Tustin Ave Santa Ana CA 92705

BOYNTON, ROBERT GRANVILLE, computer systems analyst; b. North Bend, Oreg., Aug. 11, 1951; s. Granville Clarence Jr. and Leatrice Anne (Yoder) B.; m. Sandra Lynn Harrold, Aug. 17, 1991. Student, Central Oreg. Community Coll., 1969-70. cert. career data processing Heald Coll. Bus., 1972. Computer operator Coca-Cola Bottling Co. Calif., San Francisco, 1973-76, data processing mgr., 1977-78; computer operator Warn Industries, Milwaukie, Oreg., 1979-81, computer programmer, 1981-85, analyst, 1983-85, computer systems analyst, 1985-90, info. systems team leader, 1990—. Vol. Oreg. Spl. Olympics, 1985-86. Democrat. Home: 5712 SE 130th Pl Portland OR 97236 Office: Warn Industries 13270 SE Pheasant Ct Portland OR 97222-1297

BOYNTON, WILLIAM LEWIS, electronic manufacturing company official; b. Kalamazoo, May 31, 1928; s. James Woodbury and Cyretta (Gunther) B.; ed. pub. schs.; m. Kei Ouchi, Oct. 8, 1953. Asst. mgr. Speigel J & R, Kalamazoo, 1947-48; served with U.S. Army, 1948-74, ret., 1974; with Rockwell/Collins div., Newport Beach, Calif., 1974-78, supr. material, 1978-81, coord., 1981-88; supr. coord. Rockwell/CDC, Santa Ana, Calif., 1981—, coord. investment recovery, 1982-86, shipping and material coord., 1987-88, material coord., 1988, environ. coord. Rockwell/DCD, Newport Beach, 1988-89, ret.; mem. faculty Western Mich. U., 1955-58. Trustee Orange County Vector Control Dist., 1980—, bd. sec. 1991, bd. v.p. 1992—; pres., 1993; rep. So. Calif. region Calif. Mosquito and Vector Control Assn. 1992—, v.p. bd. trustees, 1993; mem. adv. panel for bus./econ. devel. Calif. State Legislature, 1979-86. Decorated Bronze Star. Mem. Assn. U.S. Army, Assn. U.S. Army, Non-Commd. Officers Assn., Nat. Geog. Soc. Republican. Roman Catholic. Home and Office: 5314 W Lucky Way Santa Ana CA 92704-1048

BOYSON, SALLY J., neurologist; b. Phila., Feb. 24, 1952; d. John Evans Boyson II and Ruth (Erb) Boyson Paine. SB, MIT, 1974; MD, U. Pa., 1979. Diplomate Am. Bd. Psychiatry and Neurology; lic. med. dr. Colo., Pa. Intern U. Pa., Phila., 1979-80, resident in neurology, 1980-83, post-doctoral fellow neuropharmacology, 1983-85, from asst. instr. to asst. prof. neurology, 1979-86; asst. prof. neurology and pharmacology Health Scis. Ctr. U. Colo., Denver, 1986—, dir. Am. Parkinson Disease Info. and Referral Ctr., 1987-92, dir. Movement Disorders Clinic, 1988—; cons. and lectr. in field. Ad hoc reviewer Annals of Neurology, New Eng. Jour. Medicine; contbr. chpts. to books and numerous articles to profl. jours. Recipient Pfizer Med. Rsch. Merit award, 1984, Clin. Investigator Devel. award NIH, 1985, 90; Huntington's Disease Found. Am. fellow, 1984-85; grantee NSF, 1973, Hereditary Disease Found., 1983-84, 90, Am. Parkinson Disease Assn., 1990—, Dystonia Med. Rsch. Found., 1990, USPHS, 1986—, NIH, 1990—. Mem. AMA, AAAS, Soc. Neurosci., Am. Acad. Neurology (S. Weir Mitchell essay com. 1987-92), Colo. Soc. Clin. Neurologists, Phi Lambda Upsilon. Office: U Colo Health Scis Ctr 4200 E 9th Ave # B-183 Denver CO 80262-0001

BOZANICH, RICHARD ANTHONY, journalist; b. Long Beach, Calif., July 27, 1957; s. Michael Nicholas and Margaret Ruth (Neuzil) B. BA, U. So. Calif., 1979; MA, Am. U., 1984. Editor Harvard Bus. Sch., Boston, 1979-81; writer, editor The L.A. Times, 1981-83; reporter (intern) The L.A. Times, Washington, 1983-84; editor Dallas Morning News, 1985-86; news editor The Hollywood Reporter, L.A., 1986-87; mng. editor Daily Variety, L.A., 1987-92. Vol. AIDS Project, L.A., Jerry Brown's 1982 Senate campaign, L.A., Alan Cranston's Senate campaign, 1986, Dukakis for Pres. campaign, L.A., 1988, No on Proposition 96 & 102 campaign, L.A., 1988. Fellow Media Evaluation Conf. on Comml. Activities, Denver, 1979, Poynter Inst. for Media Studies, St. Petersburg, Fla., 1984. Mem. Soc. Profl. Journalists. Home: 36-190 E Ave de Las Montana Cathedral City CA 92234

BRAASCH, WILLIAM MICHAEL, computer software company executive; b. Chicago, Aug. 10, 1947; s. Robert John and Mary Rita (Burke) B.; m. Vera Lou Louie, June 23, 1979; children: Kristen, Andrea Mei, Lanceolot Joseph, Michelle Kai. BA in Math., Lewis U., 1969. Programmer, analyst Chgo. and Northwestern Rwy., 1969-73; project mgr. Indsl. Indemnity, San Francisco, 1973-76, Pacific Fareast Lines, San Francisco, 1976-78; pres. Braasch and Assocs., Oakland, Calif., 1978-81, Network Data Base Systems, Mountain View, Calif., 1981-83, Data Base Architects, Alameda, Calif., 1983—; lectr. in field. Contbr. articles in field to profl. jours.; designer text mgmt. sys. With U.S. Army, 1969-75. Mem. Info. Tech. Assn. Am., Software Entrepreneurs Forum, Tau Kappa Epsilon. Roman Catholic. Office: Data Base Architects Inc 980 Atlantic Ave Alameda CA 94501-1018

BRABSON, SHIRLEY STEBBINS, shop owner; b. Fairmont, Okla., Oct. 17, 1935; d. Robert Riley and Ettie Stebbins; m. George Dana Brabson, Jr., May 2, 1959; children: Jennifer, Robert, Andrew. BS, Okla. State U., 1956; M in City and Regional Planning, U. Calif., Berkeley, 1964. Shop owner QuiltWorks Inc., Albuquerque, 1985—. Office: The Quilt Works 11117 Menaul NE Albuquerque NM 87112

BRACEWELL, RONALD NEWBOLD, electrical engineering and computer science educator; b. Sydney, Australia, July 22, 1921; s. Cecil Charles and Valerie Zilla (McGowan) B.; m. Helen Mary Lester Elliott; children: Catherine Wendy, Mark Cecil. BS in Math. and Physics, U. Sydney, 1941, B in Engring., 1943, M. in Engring. with 1st class honors, 1948; PhD, Cambridge (Eng.) U., 1951. Sr. rsch. officer Radiophysics Lab., Commonwealth Sci. and Indsl. Rsch. Orgn., Sydney, 1949-54; vis. asst. prof. radio astronomy U. Calif., Berkeley, 1954-55; mem. elec. engring. faculty Stanford U., 1955—, Lewis M. Terman prof. and fellow in elec. engring., 1974-79, now prof. emeritus elec. engring.; Pollock Meml. lectr. U. Sydney, 1978; Tektronix Disting. Visitor, summer 1981; Christensen fellow St. Catherine's Coll., Oxford, autumn 1987; sr. vis. fellow Inst. Astronomy, Cambridge, U., autumn 1988; mem. adv. panels NSF, Naval Rsch. Lab., Office Naval Rsch., NAS, Nat. Radio Astronomy Obs., Jet Propulsion Lab. Adv. Group on Radio Experiments in Space, Advanced Rsch. Projects Agy. Author: The Fourier Transform and Its Applications, 1965, rev. edit., 1986, The Galactic Club: Intelligent Life in Outer Space, 1974, The Hartley Transform, 1986; co-author: Radio Astronomy, 1955; translator: Radio Astronomy (J.L. Steinberg and J. Lequeux); editor: Paris Symposium on Radio Astronomy, 1959; mem. editorial adv. bd. Planetary and Space Sci.; former mem. editorial adv. bd. Proceedings of the Astron. Soc. Pacific, Cosmic Search, Jour. Computer Assisted Tomography; mem. bd. Revs. Astronomy and Astrophysics, 1961-68; contbr. articles and revs. to jours., chpts. to books; patentee in field. Recipient Duddell Premium, Instn. Elec. Engrs., London, 1952, Inaugural Alumni award Sydney U., 1992; Fulbright travel grantee, 1954, William Gurling Watson traveling fellow, 1978, 86. Fellow IEEE (life), AAAS, Royal Astron. Soc.; mem. Inst. Medicine of NAS (fgn. assoc), Astron. Soc. Pacific (life), Am. Astron. Soc. (past councilor), Astron. Soc. Australia, Internat. Astron. Union, Internat. Sci. Radio Union, Internat. Acad. Astronautics. Home: 836 Santa Fe Ave Palo Alto CA 94305-1023 Office: Stanford U 329A Durand Bldg Stanford CA 94305

BRACHER, GEORGE, radiologist; b. Portland, Oreg., Mar. 20, 1909; s. George Michael and Anna (Ris) B.; m. Helen Arndt, Oct. 6, 1936; children: Randall W., Ann Louise. BS, U. Oreg., 1932, MD, 1934. Diplomate Am. Bd. Radiology. Intern St. Vincent's Hosp., Portland, 1935; resident fellow U. Chgo., 1936-38; asst. prof. radiology U. Oreg. Med. Sch., Portland, 1938-39; radiologist King County Hosp. System, Seattle, 1939-41, Hilo (Hawaii) Hosp., 1960-85, Lucy Henriques Med. Ctr., Kamuela, Hawaii, 1985—; pvt. practice Seattle and Spokane (Wash.), 1941-60; cons. radiologist Honokaa (Hawaii) Hosp., 1960—, Kohala (Hawaii) Hosp., 1960—, Kau Hosp., Pahala, Hawaii, 1960—; attending physician U. Hawaii Peace Corps Project, 1962-70. Pres. Hawaii County unit Am. Cancer Soc., Hilo, 1970, Hawaii Pacific div. Honolulu, 1972, chmn. Pacific and related islands com., 1975; founder Hawaii County Med. Soc. Scholarship Fund, Cancer Care Trust, Hilo. Mem. AMA, Hawaii Med. Assn., Hawaii County Med. Soc. (pres. 1969), Am. Coll. Radiology, Hawaii Radiologic Soc., Wash. Athletic Club, Hilo Yacht Club. Home: 134 Puako Beach Dr Kamuela HI 96743-9709 Office: Lucy Henriques Med Ctr PO Box 1108 Kamuela HI 96743-1108

BRACHTENBACH, ROBERT F., state justice; b. Sidney, Nebr., Jan. 28, 1931; s. Henry W. and Elizabeth A. (Morfeld) B.; m. Marilyn Hammond; children: Rick, Jeff, Randal, Curtis, David. BS, U. Wash., 1953, LLB, 1954. Bar: Wash. 1954. Instr. sch. law U. Calif., Berkeley, 1954-55; practiced in Selah, Wash., 1955-72; justice Supreme Ct. Wash., 1972—; chief justice Wash. Supreme Ct., 1981-83. Contbr. articles to law revs. Mem. Selah Sch. Bd., 1960-72; mem. Wash. State Ho. of Reps., 1963-67; trustee Eastern Wash. State Coll. Office: Supreme Ct Wash Temple of Justice Olympia WA 98504

BRADBERRY, BRENT ALAN, mathematics educator, retired naval officer; b. L.A., Aug. 18, 1939; s. Winsel T. and Eleanor M. (Martin) B.; m. Donna L. Cook, July 29, 1961; children: Keri, Kristen, Kassandra. BA, Pepperdine Coll., L.A., 1961; MS, U. Idaho, Moscow, 1968; PhD, Wash. State U., Pullman, 1987. Commd. ensign USN, 1961, advanced through grades to comdr., 1976; served as jr. officer U.S. Pacific Fleet, 1961-64; mem. faculty Naval ROTC program U. Idaho, 1964-67; ops. officer USS Rogers, 1967-71; mem. faculty math. U.S. Naval Acad., 1971-74; officer U.S. 2d Fleet, 1974-76; commanding officer USS Power, 1977; ops. officer USS Tarawa, 1978-80; with support activity USN Tactical Interoperability, 1981-82; ret. USN, 1982; teaching asst. Wash. State U., 1982-86; mem. faculty math. Lewis-Clark State Coll., Lewiston, Idaho, 1986—; adminstr. Math. In-Svc. Tchr. Edn. Grant, No. Idaho, 1988—. Contbr. articles to profl. jours. Chmn. U.S. Naval Acad. Faculty Forum, 1973, Lewis-Clark State Coll. Faculty

Assn., 1990—. Mem. Math. Assn. Am., Nat. Coun. Tchrs. Math., Idaho Coun. Tchrs. Math., U.S. Naval Inst. Democrat. Home: 615 E C St Moscow ID 83843-2731 Office: Lewis-Clark State Coll Lewiston ID 83501

BRADBERRY, BRUCE MARTIN, educator; b. Los Angeles, May 4, 1948; s. Winsel Taylor and Eleanor Monedel (Martin) B.; m. Lois Jane Adrian, Aug. 28, 1968; children: Carl, Brenda. BA, Pepperdine Coll., 1969, MA, 1975; EdD, UCLA, 1981. Assoc. dean admissions Pepperdine U., Malibu, Calif., 1972-77; admissions and records officer Indian Valley Colls., Novato, Calif., 1977-80; dir. admissions Cen. Wash. U., Ellensburg, 1980-82; tchr. Cottonwood (Idaho) Sch. Dist., 1982-83, Omak (Wash.) Sch. Dist., 1983-84, Whitepine Sch. Dist., Deary, Idaho, 1984—; announcer N.W. Pub. Radio, Pullman, Wash.; conductor Moscow (Idaho) Community Theatre, 1987—; choir dir. United Ch. of Moscow, 1984-89; football referee Idaho Activities Assn., Moscow, 1984—. Pres. Moscow Community Theatre, 1986-87. 1st lt. USAF, 1969-72. Mem. NEA, Whitepine Edn. Assn. (chief negotiator 1986-88). Democrat. Disciples of Christ. Home: 1420 Ridge Rd Moscow ID 83843-2535

BRADBURY, EDWIN MORTON, biochemistry educator; b. Cardiff, South Glamorgan, Wales, May 25, 1933; came to U.S., 1979.; s. Thomas Morton and Gladys Mabel (Manfield) B.; m. Antonija Trpkovic, Nov. 6, 1957; children—Andrew, Antonija, Vlado, Erna. B.Sc. with honours, King's Coll., London, 1955, Ph.D., 1958. Research scientist Courtauld Research Lab., 1958-62; head dept. molecular biology Portsmouth Poly., Eng., 1962-79; prof., chmn. dept. biol. chemistry U. Calif., Davis, 1979-92; mem. neutron beam com. Argonne Nat. Lab., 1983—, adv. com. Los Alamos Nat. Lab., 1983-88; leader Life Sci. Div., Los Alamos Nat. Lab., 1988—. Author: DNA Chromatin and Chromosomes, 1981. Editor: Organization and Expression of Eukaryotic Genome, 1977. Contbr. articles to profl. jours. Mem. editorial bd. Jour. Biol. Chemistry, 1983-88, European Jour. Biochemistry, 1976-81, Biopolymers, 1982-87, Internat. Jour. Biol. Macromolecules, 1976—, Cell Biophysics, 1983—, Biochemistry, 1989—; NMR in the Life Scis., 1986. Recipient Anniversary prize, Fedn. European Biochem. Socs., Hamburg, 1976. Home: 1303 Secret Bay St Davis CA 95616-2634 Office: U Calif Dept Biol Chemistry Davis CA 95616

BRADBURY, JOHN WYMOND, sales executive; b. Grants, N.Mex., July 8, 1960; s. John Platt and Ellen Adel (Wilder) B. BA with distinction, U. Colo., 1983. Area mgr. Premiere Wine Mchts., San Francisco, 1984-85; mgr. of fine wines Premiere Wine Mchts., Costa Mesa, Calif., 1985-88; dir. of fine accts. Premiere Wine Mchts., Walnut Creek, Calif., 1988-90; western div. mgr. Parducci Wine Cellars, 1991-92; gen. sales mgr. Western Wine Merchants-Western Distbg. Co., Denver, 1992—.

BRADBURY REID, ELLEN ADELE, art historian, director; b. Louisville, Ky., Feb. 26, 1940; d. Edward and Dulcinea (Straeffer) W.; m. John Platt Bradbury, Sept. 5, 1960 (div. 1980); m. Edward Brown Reid, 1990; children: John Wymond, Katharine Dulcinea Bradbury Lormand. BA, U. N.Mex., Alburquerque, N.Mex., 1961, MA, 1963; postgrad., Yale U., 1967. Registrar Mpls. Inst. of Arts, Mpls., 1969-74, curator of primitive art, 1974-76; dir. Museum of Fine Arts, Museum of N.Mex., Santa Fe, N.Mex., 1983-84, Recursos de Santa Fe, Santa Fe, N.Mex., 1984—. Author: I Wear the Morning Star, 1976; editor: (with Christopher Merrill) From the Faraway Nearby: Biography of Georgia O'Keeffe. Mem. Santa Fe (N.Mex.) Desert Chorale, 1987-90, Maxwell Mus. of Anthropology, Albuquerque, 1988-90. Mem. Ladies Assn. Democrat. Episcopalian. Home: 510 Alto St Santa Fe NM 87501-2517 Office: Recursos de Santa Fe 826 Camino De Monte Rey Santa Fe NM 87501-3961

BRADEN, BRENDA LOU, lawyer; b. Hutchinson, Kans., Dec. 6, 1940; d. Gene M. and Margaret (Smith) Rayl; m. Melvin M. Hoyt, Mar. 1, 1959 (div. Oct., 1977); children: Aron K., Lisa Hoyt Marlar, Brian G., Sean M.; m. John Buckley Braden, May 19, 1985. Student, Washburn U., 1971-73, JD, 1980; BS in Polit. Sci., U. Colo., 1976. Bar: N.Mex. 1980, Kans. 1981, Wash. 1988. Assoc. Kirk & Williams P.A., Albuquerque, New Mex., 1980; asst. atty. gen. Office of Atty Gen., Topeka, Kans., 1981-84; dep. atty. gen. Office of Atty Gen., Topeka, 1984-88; asst. code reviser Statute Law Com., Olympia, Wash., 1988-91; city atty. City of Hoquiam, Wash., 1991—; liason Kansas County and Dist. Attys. Assn., Topeka, 1984-88. Campaigner Robert Stephan for Atty. Gen., Topeka, 1986; bd. dirs. Am. Diabetes Assn., Topeka, 1987; mem. long range planning com. St. Mark's Episcopal Cathedral, Seattle, 1989-90; advisor Gray's Harbor Hist. Seaport, Aberdeen, Wash., 1991—. Mem. Wash. State Assn. Mcpl. Attys., Wash. Bar Assn. Office: City of Hoquiam 609 8th St Hoquiam WA 98550

BRADEN, GEORGE WALTER (LORD OF BOVER), company executive; b. L.A., Sept. 1, 1936; s. Paul Sumner and Evelyn Widney (Traver) B.; m. Trina Rose Thomas, July 3, 1964; children: Barbara Diane, Beverly Eileen Braden Christensen. BS, Calif. State U., 1963; grad. cert., U. So. Calif., 1990, Harvard U., 1991; postgrad., UCLA, 1990—; MBA, Chadwick U. Mgr. western region vet. div. Bristol-Myers, Syracuse, N.Y., 1970-79; pres. Braden Sales Assocs. Internat., Apple Valley, Calif., 1980—. Mem. Friends of Hoover Inst., Stanford, Calif.; charter mem. Rep. Presdl. Task Force, Washington, 1989—; commr. Rep. Presdl. Adv. Com., Washington, 1991—; active Nat. Rep. Senatorial Com. Capt. U.S. Army., 1985-93, major 1993—. Recipient Presdl. order Of Merit, Heritage Found.; numerous awards Boy Scouts of Am. Mem. Am. Mktg. Assn., Tex. A&M U. Internat. Assn. of Agri-Bus., President's Club. Mem. LDS Ch.

BRADFIELD, STEPHANIE ALISON, hospital association executive; b. Pasadena, Calif., June 24, 1950; d. Theodore C. and Karen (Coene) B.; m. John R. Balzar, Mar. 18, 1978. BA in Mass Communications, Calif. State U., Chico, 1972. Pub. info. officer Calif. Gov.'s Office Emergency Services, Sacramento, 1972-76; chief pub. info. Calif. Energy Commn., Sacramento, 1976-78, asst. exec. dir., 1978-80; chief office legis. and pub. affairs Calif. State Water Resouces Control Bd., Sacramento, 1980-85; pub. info. mgr. Gen. Telephone Calif., Santa Monica, 1985-87; pub. info. dir. GTE Calif., Thousand Oaks, 1987-88, pub. affairs dir. tel. ops., 1988-90; pub. affairs dir. Wash. State Hosp. Assn., Seattle, 1990—. Former bd. dirs. Coro Found. So. Calif., L.A., 1987-90, KCRW Found., Santa Monica. Mem. Pub. Relations Soc. Am., Women in Communications. Office: Wash State Hosp Assn 190 Queen Anne Ave N Fl 3D Seattle WA 98109-4926

BRADFORD, DAVID PAUL, judicial assistant; b. Lynwood, Calif., Mar. 23, 1955; s. William H. and Barbara E. (O'Leary) Johnson. AA, Citrus Coll., Azusa, Calif., 1975; BA in Polit. Sci., UCLA, 1978; postgrad., Calif. State U., L.A., 1984-85, U. W. L.A., 1990-91. Prin. clerk UCLA Brain Rsch. Inst., 1977-81; adminstrv. asst., supr. UCLA Hosp. and Clinics, 1977-81; dep. to atty. in residence matters office of registrar UCLA, 1981-85; office of clerk L.A. County Bd. Suprs., L.A., 1987-88; judicial asst., ct. clerk L.A. Superior Ct., L.A., 1988—; founder Bradford & Assocs., L.A., 1987—; rsch. dir. Citizenship Protection Fund, Santa Monica, 1992—. Active Domestic Violence Coun., Family Ct. Svcs. Domestic Violence Task Force. Recipient Cert. of Appreciation, Domestic Violence Coun., 1990. Mem. AFSCME (pres. local 575), N.Y. Acad. Scis., L.A. County Superior Ct. Clerks Assn. (pres. 1993), Acad. Polit. Scis., UCLA Alumni Assn. (life). Office: LA County Superior Ct Rm 245 Dept 8 111 N Hill St Los Angeles CA 90012

BRADFORD, GARRETT EUGENE, real estate agent; b. Fullerton, Calif., Nov. 1, 1970; s. Randell E. and Joan E. (Hager) B. Diploma, Marysville-Pilchuck High Sch., 1989. Realtor U.S.A. Realty, Inc., Arlington, Wash., 1989—. Office: USA Realty Inc 2730 172D NE Arlington WA 98223

BRADFORD, HOWARD, graphic artist, painter; b. Toronto, Ont., Can., July 14, 1919; came to U.S., 1923, naturalized, 1948; s. Robert E. and Emily (Beadle) B.; m. Dorothy Louise Bowman (div. Aug. 1967); children: Brock, Cyndra Lisa, Tal Scot, Heather, Delia Contess; m. Jane Kunkel, Apr. 1970 (div. Dec. 1979); m. Catherine Gerber, Jan. 1980 (div. June 1983); m. Christina Milhalitsianos, May 11, 1991. Student, Chouinard Art Inst., 1947-49, Jepson Art Inst., 1950-52. Instr. graphic arts center Sunset Sch., Carmel, Calif. One-man shows Landau Gallery, Los Angeles, 1950, Anthes Gallery, Los Angeles, 1950, Coast Gallery, Big Sur, Calif., 1960, Carmel Art Assn., 1973, 77, 80, 89, 91, 93, Pacific Grove Art Ctr., Calif., 1992; exhibited in group shows nationally and internationally with Am. Fedn. Arts, USIS, 1950—, Carmel Art Assn., 1970-93; represented in permanent collections Dallas Mus. Fine Arts, Mus. Modern Art, N.Y.C., Seattle Mus., Met. Mus., Los Angeles County Mus., Calif. State Fair, Library of Congress, San Diego Mus., N.Y. Pub. Library, High Mus., Atlanta, Morton Gallery, Palm Beach, Fla., Crocker Art Gallery, Sacramento, New Britain (Conn.) Mus., Boston Mus. Fine Arts, U. Wis., U. Ill., Bradley U., Albert and Victoria Mus., London, Phila. Mus. Fine Arts. With AUS, 1942-45, ETO. Guggenheim fellow for creative printmaking, 1960; recipient purchase awards Los Angeles County Mus., 1950, purchase awards Bradley U., 1951, purchase awards Nat. Serigraph Soc., 1951, 52, purchase awards Am. Color Print Soc., 1951, 52, 58, 60, purchase awards Library of Congress, 1951, 56, 57, purchase awards U. Ill., 1957, purchase awards Boston Printmakers, 1958, purchase awards Western Serigraph Inst., 1948, purchase awards N.W. Printmakers Soc., 1958, purchase awards Dallas Print Soc., 1952, painting awards Monterey Peninsula Mus., 1965, 68. Mem. Carmel Art Assn. Address: 684 Alice St Monterey CA 93940

BRADFORD, ROBERT EDWARD, supermarket executive; b. Roanoke, Va., June 27, 1931; s. Miller Hughes and Helen (Gardner) B.; m. Margaret Strader, Dec. 27, 1956 (div. June 1970); children: Joseph Charles, Stephen Frederick; m. Nancy Rourke, Nov. 12, 1970; 1 child, Laura Ann. BA, Washington and Lee U., 1954. News dir. WMAL Radio and TV, Washington, 1957-58; adminstrv. asst. rep. Richard Poff (Rep.-Va.), Washington, 1958-68; exec. dir. Ill. Rep. Com., Springfield, 1968-71; adminstrv. asst. to Sen. William Brock, Tenn. U.S. Congress, Washington, 1971-73; dir. govt. affairs Firestone Tire and Rubber Co., Washington, 1973-77; exec. v.p. Food Mktg. Inst., Washington, 1977-80; pres., chief exec. officer Nat. Restaurant Assn., Washington, 1980-81; sr. v.p. Great A&P Tea Co., Washington, 1981-83, Safeway Inc., Oakland, Calif., 1983—. Bd. dirs. Pub. Affairs Coun., Washington, 1983-86, Keep Am. Beautiful, N.Y.C., 1984—, Friends of Arts, San Francisco, 1984—, 2d Harvest, Chgo., 1985—, Nat. Easter Seals Soc., Chgo., 1986—, nat. chmn., 1992—; chmn. Nat. Easter Seals Telethon, 1988. Capt. U.S. Army, 1954-57. Recipient 17 Radio Journalism awards AP, 1954-57; Harvard U. fellow (hon.), 1970-71. Mem. F St. Club, Lakeview Club, Capitol Hill Club, River Bend Club. Republican. Methodist.

BRADFORD, ROBERT WILLIAM, hospital administrator, researcher; b. U.S. Panama Canal Zone, Mar. 22, 1931; s. George Finley and Paulene Isabella (Arnold) B.; m. Zoal Schuab (div.); m. Carole Elizabeth Yent Walsh, Jan. 1, 1978; children: Richard, Evelyn, Darcy, Greg. Degree in engring. (hon.), Stanford U., 1965; DSc, Medicina Alternatavia, Sri Lanka, 1984; PhD (hon.), Medicina Alternativa, Sweden, 1984. Dir. exptl. facilities design, rsch. lab. GE, Palo Alto, Calif., 1955-65; dir. switch tube devel., Stanford Linear Accelerator Stanford U., Palo Alto, Calif., 1965-76; dir. rsch. Am. Biologics Hosp. and Med. Ctr., Chula Vista, Calif., 1980—; cons. engr. Litton Industries, Varian Assocs., GE and others; founder, pres. Com. for Freedom Choice in Medicine, 1972—, Bradford Rsch. Inst., Mex., Fed. Republc Germany, and U.S. Co-author: Stanford Two-Mile Linear Accelerator, 1973; author: Now That You Have Cancer, 1977, Metabolic Management of Cancer, 1980, International Protocols in Cancer Management, 1983, Oxidology - Reactive Oxygen Toxic Species, 1985, Biochemistry of Live Cell Therapy, 1986; also monographs; patentee in electronics, physics. Sgt. USAF, 1951-55. Recipient Laureate of Labor award, The Netherlands, 1984, Diploma of Merit, Sci. and Hygiene French Nat. Health Assn., 1983, Merit of Excellence award Academie Diplomatique de la Paix-Pax Mundi, 1987; named Knight Commdr. Order of U.S. and Mex. St. John of Jerusalem, 1983. Mem. Am. Naturopathic Assn., Am. Holistic Med. Assn. (organizational mem.), Nat. Nutritional Foods Assn., Nat. Coun. Improved Health (v.p. 1991), N.Y. Acad. Scis. Republican. Presbyterian. Office: Am Biologics Hosp & Med Ctr 1180 Walnut Ave Chula Vista CA 91911-2690

BRADLEY, CHARLES WILLIAM, podiatrist; b. Fife, Tex., July 23, 1923; s. Tom and Mary Ada (Cheatham) B.; m. Marilyn A. Brown, Apr. 3, 1948 (dec. Mar. 1973); children: Steven, Gregory, Jeffrey, Elizabeth, Gerald. Student, Tex. Tech., 1940-42; D. Podiatric Medicine, Calif. Coll. Podiatric Medicine U. San Francisco, 1949, MPA, 1987, D.Sc. (hon.). Pvt. practice podiatry Beaumont, Tex., 1950-51, Brownwood, Tex., 1951-52, San Francisco, San Bruno, Calif., 1952—; assoc. clin. prof. Calif. Coll. Podiatric Medicine, 1992—; chief of staff Calif. Podiatry Hosp., San Francisco; mem. surg. staff Sequoia Hosp., Redwood City, Calif.; mem. med. staff Peninsula Hosp., Burlingame, Calif.; chief podiatry staff St. Luke's Hosp., San Francisco; chmn. bd. Podiatry Ins. Co. Am.; cons. VA. Mem. San Francisco Symphony Found.; mem. adv. com. Health Policy Agenda for the Am. People, AMA; chmn. trustees Calif. Coll. Podiatric Medicine, Calif. Podiatry Coll., Calif. Podiatry Hosp.; mem. San Mateo Grand Jury, 1989. Served with USNR, 1942-45. Mem. Am. Podiatric Med. Assn. (trustee, pres. 1983-84), Calif. Podiatry Assn. (pres. No. div. 1964-66, state bd. dirs., pres. 1975-76, Podiatrist of Yr. award 1983), Nat. Coun. Edn. (vice-chmn.), Nat. Acads. Practice (chmn. podiatric med. sect.), Am. Legion, San Bruno C. of C. (bd. dirs. 1978-91, v.p. 1992, bd. dir. grand jury assoc. 1990), Olympic Club, Commonwealth Club Calif., Elks, Lions. Home: 2965 Trousdale Dr Burlingame CA 94010-5708 Office: 560 Jenevein Ave San Bruno CA 94066-4477

BRADLEY, FRANCINE AGNES-MARIE, poultry scientist; b. Oxnard, Calif., May 12, 1954; d. William Homer and Alice Anna (Agoure) B. BS in Avian Scis., U. Calif., Davis, 1976, MS in Avian Scis., 1978, PhD in Physiology, 1982. Area poultry farm advisor U. Calif. Coop. Extension, Davis, 1985—. Contbr. articles to scientific jours. Mem. Am. Poultry Hist. Soc. (resolutions com. 1992), Japanese Poultry Sci. Assn., Poultry Sci. Assn. (dir. 1991—), World's Poultry Sci. Assn., Capital Agri-Women (pres. 1988-89), Yolo County Hist. Soc., Native Dau. of Golden West (past officer), Sigma Xi (pres. 1986), Phi Kappa Phi (dir. 1985—). Office: U Calif Avian Scis Davis CA 95616-8532

BRADLEY, JAMES ALEXANDER, software engineer, researcher; b. Van Nuys, Calif., May 16, 1965. BA in Math., Computer Sci., U. Colo., 1988, postgrad., 1991—. Software developer Sci. Computer Systems, Inc., Boulder, Colo., 1982-84; teaching asst. Boulder Valley Pub. Schs., Boulder, Colo., 1984-87; software engr. Martin Marietta Aerospace, Littleton, Colo., 1988-. Recipient NASA New Tech. award, Martin Marietta Aerospace, 1990. mem. Am. Math. Soc., Math. Assn. Am., Golden Key Honor Soc. Office: Martin Marietta Aerospace PO Box 179 Mailstop 4372 Denver CO 80201-0179

BRADLEY, KENNETH DANIEL, insurance consultant; b. Ft. Clayton, Panama Canal Zone, Feb. 13, 1949; s. William Perry and Dorothy Marie (Gill) B.; m. Millajean Miller, Nov. 21, 1987; 1 child, Ian Perry. BSBA, Seton Hall U., 1971. CPCU. Rating analyst Nat. Council on Compensation Ins., Lyndhurst, N.J., 1971-73; underwriter Cen. Mut. Ins. Co., N.Y.C., 1973-75; v.p. dept. casualty Am. Home Assurance Co., N.Y.C., 1975-85; v.p. Western region, Los Angeles, 1985-87; exec. v.p. Alliance Ins. Group, Burbank, Calif., 1987-92; ind. ins. cons. Marina del Rey, Calif., 1992—. Scoutmaster Boy Scouts Am., Clifton, N.J., 1975-76; umpire Lyndhurst Little League, 1966-67; coach Clifton Little League, 1976; soccer coach St. John Kanty Sch., Clifton, 1980-81. Mem. N.A.P.S.L.O., Underwriters Assn. L.A. Home: 4758 D La Villa Marina Marina Del Rey CA 90292

BRADLEY, THOMAS (TOM BRADLEY), former mayor; b. Calvert, Tex., Dec. 29, 1917; s. Lee Thomas and Crenner (Hawkins) B.; m. Ethel Mae Arnold, May 4, 1941; children: Lorraine, Phyllis. Student, UCLA, 1937-40; LL.B., Southwestern U., 1956, LL.D., 1980; LL.D., Brandeis U., 1974, Oral Roberts U., 1974, Pepperdine U., 1974, Loyola Marymount U., 1974, Calif. Lutheran U., 1974, Wilberforce U., 1974, Whittier Coll., 1976, Yale U., 1979, U. So. Calif., 1979, Princeton U., 1979, Bus Nat. U., Korea, 1979, Antioch U., 1983, N.C. Central U., 1983; Ph.D. (hon.), Humanity Research Ctr. Beverly Hills, 1976. Bar: Calif. 1956. Police officer Los Angeles, 1940-62; practiced in Los Angeles, 1956-73; mem. Los Angeles City Council, 1963-73; mayor of Los Angeles, 1973-93; founder, dir. Bank of Fin., Nat. Urban Coalition; pres. Nat. League Cities, 1974, also mem. nat. bd. dirs.; pres. League of Calif. Cities, 1979, So. Calif. Assn. Govts., 1968-69, Nat. Assn. Regional Councils, 1969-71; mem. Nat. Energy Adv. Council, Nat. Commn. on Productivity and Work Quality; mem. advisory bd., vice chmn. transp. com. U.S. Conf. Mayors; former mem. Council Intergovt. Relations; chmn. State, County and Fed. Affairs Com.; former chmn. Pub. Works Priority Com., Com. for Proposed Legis. bd. dirs. Nat. Urban Fellows. Mem. Calif. Democratic Central Com.; del. Dem. Nat. Mid-Term Conf., 1974; co-chmn. Dem. Nat. Conv., 1976; former mem. bd. dirs. Joint Com. Mental Health for Children; former mem. adv. council Peace Corps. Named African Methodist Episcopal Man of Yr., 1974; recipient Dr. Martin L. King, Jr. award, 1974, Pub. Ofcl. of Yr. award Los Angeles Trial Lawyers Assn., 1974, award CORO Found., 1978, award of merit Nat. Council Negro Women, 1978, John F. Kennedy Fellowship award Govt. of N.Z., 1978, Internat. Humanitarian award M.E.D.I.C., 1978, City Employee of Yr. award All City Employees Benefits Service Assn., 1983, Magnin award, 1984. Mem. Los Angeles Urban League, NAACP (Spingarn medal 1985), So. Calif. Conf. on Community Relations, Los Angeles Conf. Negro Elected Ofcls., UN Assn. Los Angeles (bd. dirs.), Kappa Alpha Psi. Democrat. Mem. African Methodist Episcopal Ch. (trustee). •

BRADLEY, WADE HARLOW, acquisitions specialist; b. Mpls.; s. Robert Douglas and Florence (Wells) B.; m. Alessandra Maria Benitez, June 30, 1984; children: Isabella Andrea, Francesca Alessandra. BS, U. Minn., 1983; postgrad., LaJolla Acad. Advt., 1984. Bus. cons. A.B.A. Investment Corp., LaJolla, Calif., 1987-88; pres. The Harlow Co., San Diego, 1987—; acquisitions specialist Pacific Capital Ptnrs., San Diego, 1989-90; v.p. corp. devel. Sundance Resources Inc., San Diego, 1990—; design cons. Forty Five Metro, LaJolla, 1983-85. Republican. Roman Catholic. Office: Sundance Resources Inc 12526 High Bluff Dr Ste 300 San Diego CA 92130-2067

BRADLEY, WALTER D., real estate broker, owner; b. Clovis, N.M., Oct. 30, 1946; s. Ralph W. and M. Jo (Black) B.; m. Debbie Shelly; children: Tige, Lance, Nicole. Student Eastern N.M. U., 1964-1967. Supr. Tex. Instruments, Dallas; mgr., salesman Nat. Chemsearch, Irving, Tex., Colonial Real Estate, Clovis, 1976; mem. N.Mex. Senate, 1989-92. V.p., bd. dirs. Clovis Indsl. Commn., 1983-86, pres. econ. devel., 1987; bd. dirs. United Way, Clovis, 1984-86, Curry County Blood Adv. Bd., Clovis, 1980-85; chmn. Curry County Reps., Clovis, 1984-88; Cosmos Soccer, Clovis, 1984. Mem. Realtors Assn. N.Mex. (v.p., bd. dirs. 1982-85, v.p. 1987-88), Clovis Bd. Realtors (pres. 1982, 93), Clovis C. of C., Curry County Jaycees, N.M. Jaycees. Baptist. Lodge: Lions. Home: 2020 Fairway Ter Clovis NM 88101-3130 Office: Colonial Real Estate PO Box 1154 Clovis NM 88102-1154

BRADO, MICHAEL WAYNE, infosystems specialist; b. Aberdeen, Wash., Oct. 26, 1958; s. Clarence Wayne and Karen (Copeland) B.; m. M. Rosela Bernabe Venture, Aug. 23, 1987 (div. Feb. 1993). BS, Wash. State U., 1982. Systems operator I Computing Svc. Ctr. Wash. State U., Pullman, 1980-82; firmware/diagnostics software engr. Altos Computer Systems, Inc., San Jose, Calif., 1982-84; corp. acct. mgr. Advanced Micro Devices, Sunnyvale, Calif., 1984-87, sr. prodn. control planner, bus. systems analyst, 1987-88, info. ctr. cons., 1988-91; sr. info. ctr. cons. Advanced Micro Devices, 1991—. Mem. working com. ASPEN, Sunnyvale, 1987—; registrar Campbell (Calif.) Reps., 1987. Mem. Am. Electronics Assn. (cert. 3COM local area and UNIX network system installation and adminstrn.), San Jose Seahawks Rugby Football Club, Elks. Lutheran. Home: 3003 Mauricia Ave Santa Clara CA 95051-6843 Office: Advanced Micro Devices 901 Thompson Pl # 196 Sunnyvale CA 94086-4518

BRADPIECE, THEODORE GRANT, mutual fund supervisor, venture capitalist; b. L.A., Aug. 31, 1965; s. Sidney and Naomi (Silton) B. BS in Mgmt., Tulane U., 1987. Account exec. Baraban Securities, Inc., Culver City, Calif., 1987-88; owner, mgr. Bradpiece Advising, L.A., 1987—; supr. mut. fund Assocs. Fin. Group, Inc., L.A., 1988—; mutual fund adminstr. Pacific Fin. Rsch., 1993. Mem. alumni admissions com. Tulane U., L.A., 1987—; trustee Tau Epsilon Phi Found., Inc., 1990—; co-chmn. young adult network Alumni and Friends United Synagogue Youth, 1991—. Mem. Nat. Assn. Securities Dealers, Tau Epsilon Phi (alumni mem.-at-large grand coun. 1987—, v.p. Epsilon Kappa chpt. alumni holding corp. 1987—). Democrat. Jewish. Home: 6326 1/2 Orange St Los Angeles CA 90034 Office: Pacific Fin Rsch Inc 9601 Wilshire Blvd Ste 800 Beverly Hills CA 90210

BRADSHAW, CARL JOHN, lawyer, consultant; b. Oelwein, Iowa, Nov. 1, 1930; s. Carl John and Lorraine Lillian (Thiele) B.; m. Katsuko Anno, Nov. 5, 1954; children: Carla K., Arthur Herbert, Vincent Marcus. BS, U. Minn., 1952, JD, 1957; LLM, U. Mich., 1958; MJur, Keio U., Tokyo, 1962. Bar: Minn. 1960, U.S. Supreme Ct., 1981, Calif. 1985,. Assoc. Graham, James & Rolph, Tokyo, 1961-63; assoc. prof. law U. Wash., Seattle, 1963-64; sr. v.p. Oak Industries, Inc., Crystal Lake, Ill., 1964-84, dir. internat. ops., 1964-70, dir. corp. devel., 1970-72, pres. communications group, 1972-78, chief legal officer, 1979-84; counsel Seki & Jarvis, L.A., 1985-87, Bell, Boyd & Lloyd, L.A., 1987; prin. The Pacific Law Group, L.A., Tokyo and Palo Alto, Calif., 1987—, The Asian Mktg. Group, Torrance, Calif., 1992—; participant Japanese-Am. program for cooperation in legal studies, 1957-61. Contbr. articles to legal and bus. jours. Bd. dirs. Japan-Am. Soc., Chgo., 1966-72; bd. dirs., fin. dir. San Diego Symphony Orch. Assn., 1980-81. Served to lt. (j.g.) USN, 1952-55. Fulbright scholar, 1958-59, Ford Found. scholar, 1960-61. Fellow Radio Club Am.; mem. Minn. Bar Assn., Calif. Bar Assn., ABA, Am. Soc. Internat. Law, Internat. Fiscal Assn., San Diego Bar Assn., Westwood Bar Assn., Order of Coif. Club: Regency (Los Angeles). Home: 12958 Robleda Cv San Diego CA 92128-1126 Office: Pacific Law Group 12121 Wilshire Blvd 2d Fl Los Angeles CA 90025

BRADSHAW, IRA WEBB, accountant; b. Hurricane, Utah, Jan. 7, 1929; s. Ira H. and Emma (Webb) B.; m. Nancy C. Wolfley, June 6, 1987; children: Jeffrey, Ingrid, Alison. BS, Utah State U., 1951. CPA, Nev. Staff acct. Conway, Moe & Hibbs, CPAs, Las Vegas, Nev., 1953-56, ptnr., 1957-61; ptnr. Bradshaw, Snow & Mathis, CPAs, Las Vegas, 1962-69; ptnr., dir. taxation Laventhol & Horwath, CPAs, Las Vegas, 1970-76; propr. Ira W. Bradshaw, CPA, Las Vegas, 1976-77; founding ptnr. Bradshaw, Smith & Co., CPAs, Las Vegas, 1978—; mem. Nev. State Bd. of Accountancy, Las Vegas, 1982-88, sec.-treas., 1983-84, pres., 1985-88, founder newsletter, 1985, editor, 1989-91. Advisor Nev. Dance Theater, Las Vegas, 1980—; mem. support coun. Utah State U., Logan, 1988-92. 1st lt. USAF, 1951-53. Mem. AICPA, Nev. Soc. CPA's (v.p. 1970-71, pres. 1971-72, Valuable Svc. award 1987). Republican. Mem. LDS Ch. Office: 5851 W Charleston Blvd Las Vegas NV 89102-1961

BRADSHAW, JAMES R., business educator; b. Beaver, Utah, Oct. 26, 1938; s. Lafey LaVel and Ilynn (Christensen) B.; m. Jeanie Bok Dong Chung, Sept. 4, 1964; children: Scott, Lisa, Jonathan, Mibi. BSBA in Edn., CSU, Cedar City, 1968; MS in Bus. Adminstrn./Edn., Utah State U., Logan, 1969; EdD in Bus. Report Writing, Brigham Young U., 1974. Missionary, dist. supr. Latter-Day Ch. Korea, 1958-61; with Mountain Fuel Supply co., Salt Lake City, 1964-66, State Bank of So. Utah, Cedar City, 1966-68, Cache Tractor & Implement Co., 1968-69; vis. prof. MBA program Chaminade U., 1977-85; vis. lectr. Cen. Mich. U., 1983—; with Brigham Young U., Hawaii, 1969—. Contbr. articles to profl. jours. With U.S. Army, 1961-64. Recipient David L. Sargent Manhood of Yr. award, 1968; NEA Title V fellow Utah State U., 1969; decorated U.S. Army Commendation medal; recipient David O. McKay Lectr. award, Brigham Young U., Hawaii, 1987, Disting. Teaching award, Cen. Mich. U., 1987, Outstanding Faculty of Yr. award/Bus. Div., Brigham Young U., Hawaii, 1988, Outstanding Tchr. of Yr. award/Bus. Div., 1988, 90. Mem. Hawaii Bus. Edn. Assn , Western Bus. Edn. Assn., Nat. Bus. Edn. Assn., Am. Bus. Communications Assn., Delta Pi Epsilon. Mormon. Home: Brigham Young U Box 1808 Laie HI 96762 Office: Brigham Young U PO Box 1808 Laie HI 96762-0921

BRADSHAW, JEFFREY MARK, cognitive scientist; b. Salt Lake City, June 5, 1956; s. Mark John and Elma (Singleton) B.; m. Kathleen Marie Peterson, Apr. 27, 1979; children: Robert William, Mary Elizabeth, Thomas Mark, Samuel Harris. BA, U. Utah, 1979; postgrad., Brigham Young U., 1979-80; PhD, U. Wash., 1993. Client aide program mgr., community support treatment Harborview Community Mental Health Ctr., Seattle, 1983-84; staff therapist, child and adolescent resident program Children's Indsl. Home, Tacoma, 1984-85; rsch. scientist, knowledge acquisition Advanced Tech. Ctr., Boeing Computer Svcs., Seattle, 1985-87, prin. investigator, intelligent decision systems, 1987-88, rsch. scientist NASA Ames corp. memory project, 1989-90; prin. investigator, process mgmt. Coordination Tech. Rsch. and Tech., Boeing Computer Svcs., Seattle, 1989—; cons. Computing Environ. for Graphical Belief Models NASA, Seattle, 1992—; co-prin. investigator bone-marrow transplant support tech. Fred Hutchinson Cancer

Rsch. Ctr., Seattle, 1992—. Author: (with others) Current Trends in Knowledge Acquisition, 1990, Uncertainty in Artificial Intelligence 5, 1990, Progress in Knowledge Acquisition for Knowledge Based Systems, 1990, AI Tools and Techniques, 1989, Knowledge Acquisition Tools for Expert Systems, 1988, Language and the Paradigms of Social Psychology, 1985, Knowledge Acquisition as Modeling, 1992; editorial bd. Knowledge Acquisition: An Internat. Jour., 1989—; contbr. numerous articles to profl. jours. Fulbright scholar European Inst. Cognitivie Scis. and Engring., Toulouse, France, 1993—. Mormon. Home: 13515 173rd Pl NE Redmond WA 98052

BRADSHAW, MURRAY CHARLES, musicologist; b. Hinsdale, Ill., Sept. 25, 1930; s. Murray Andrew Bradshaw and Marie (Novak) Orth; m. Doris Louise; children: Jean Marie, Murray Edward, Thomas Andrew. MusM in Piano, Am. Conservatory Music, Chgo., 1955, MusM in Organ, 1958; PhD in Musicology, U. Chgo., 1969. Prof. UCLA, 1966—; organist and choirmaster various churches in Ill., Ind., Calif., 1948—; music critic Gary Post Tribune, Ind., 1962-64. Author: The Origin of the Toccata, 1972, The Falsobordone, 1978, Francesco Severi, 1981, Girolamo Diruta The Transylvanian, 1984, Giovanni Luca Conforti, 1985, Gabriele Fattorini, 1986, Emilio de' Cavalieri, 1990; contbr. articles to profl. jours. Served with U.S. Army, 1954-56. Am. Philos. Soc. grantee, 1987. Mem. Internat. Musicol. Soc., Am. Musicol. Soc. (pres. local chpt. 1979-81), Am. Guild Organists, Ctr. for Medieval and Renaissance Studies. Home: 17046 Burbank Blvd # 3 Encino CA 91316 Office: UCLA Dept Musicology 405 Hilgard Ave Los Angeles CA 90024-1301

BRADSHAW, RALPH ALDEN, biochemistry educator; b. Boston, Feb. 14, 1941; s. Donald Bertram and Eleanor (Dodd) B.; m. Roberta Perry Wheeler, Dec. 29, 1961; children: Christopher Evan, Amy Dodd. BA in Chemistry, Colby Coll., 1962; PhD, Duke U., 1966. Asst. prof. Washington U., St. Louis, 1969-72, assoc. prof., 1972-74, prof., 1974-82; prof., chair dept. U. Calif., Irvine, 1982—; study sect. chmn. NIH, 1979, mem., 1975-79, 80-85; mem. sci. advisory bd. Hereditary Disease Found., 1983-87, ICN Nucleic Acids Research Inst., 1986-87; research study com. physiol. chem. Am. Heart Assn., 1984-86, mem. Council on Thrombosis, 1976-90; fellowship screening com. Am. Cancer Soc. Calif., 1984-87; chmn. adv. com. Western Winter Workshops, 1984-88; dir., chmn., mem. organizing com. numerous symposia, confs. in field including Proteins in Biology and Medicine, Shanghai, Peoples Republic China, 1981, Symposium Am. Protein Chemists, San Diego, 1985, chmn. exec. com. Keystone Symp. Mol. Cell. Biol., 1991—, bd. trustees, 1991—, Internat. Union Biochem. Mol. Biol., 1991—, U.S. Nat. Commn. Biochem., 1987—, chmn., 1992—. Mem. editorial bd. Archives Biochemistry and Biophysics, 1972-88, Jour. Biological Chemistry, 1973-77, 78-79, 81-86, assoc. editor, 1989—, Jour. Supramolecular Structure/Cellular Biochemistry, 1980-91, Bioscience Reports, 1980-87, Peptide and Protein Reviews, 1980-86, Jour. Protein Chemistry, 1980-90, IN VITRO Rapid Communication in Cell Biology, 1984—; editor Trends in Biochemical Sciences, 1975-91, editor-in-chief, 1986-91, J. Neurochem, 1986-90, Proteins: Structure, Functions & Genetics, 1988-92, Growth Factors, 1989—; assoc. editor: Protein Science, 1990-92; contbr. numerous articles to scientific jours. Recipient Young Scientist award Passano Found., 1976. Fellow AAAS; mem. Am. Chem. Soc. (Sect. award 1979), Am. Soc. Biol. Chemists (coun. 1987-90, treas. 1991—), Am. Peptide Soc., N.Y. Acad. Scis., Protein Soc. (acting pres. 1986-87), Am. Soc. for Neurochemistry, Am. Soc. for Cell Biology, Soc. for Neuroscience, The Endocrine Soc., Sigma Xi. Home: 25135 Rivendell Dr Lake Forest CA 92630-4134 Office: U Calif Irvine Dept Biol Chemistry CCM D240 Irvine CA 92717

BRADY, COLLEEN ANNE, communications consulting company executive; b. Springfield, Ill., July 17, 1951; d. Robert and Eleanor Brady. BA, So. Ill. U., 1973; MS, Humboldt State U., 1978. Instr. various adaptive Outward Bound programs, 1975-78; mgr. tech. publs. Wood/Harbinger Engring. Inc., Kirkland, Wash., 1980-82; pres. Tech. Communication Cons., Inc., Seattle, 1978—. Editor: Softball Tune-Up Guide, 1988, Softball Practice Guide, 1988, How to Write an Engineering Report, 1990. Fellow Demonstrative Evidence Specialist Assn. (founding fellow); mem. Soc. Tech. Communications (Tech. Recognition award 1987, '88), Emerald City Softball Assn. (rep. 1988—), Rise n' Shine. Office: Tech Communication Cons Inc 3043 California Ave SW Seattle WA 98116-3301

BRADY, JANE MARIETTE, cleaning company and ceramics executive; b. Ft. Meade, Md., May 31, 1955; d. Allison Purvis and Monique Jeannine (Hutteau) B.; m. Jose Luis Millan Velazquez, Aug. 29, 1975 (div. Oct. 1982); 1 child, Jovan Jay Millan. AS, Cochise Coll., 1975. LIc. real estate sales person, Ariz. Aircraft mechanic Hawthorne Aviation Co., Ft. Huachuca, Ariz., 1975-77; owner, mgr. Sincerely Ceramics, Tucson, 1984—, Constantly Cleaning, Tucson, 1984—. Served with U.S. Army, 1979-84, Korea. Morris Udall grantee, 1974-75. Mem. Royal Order Roadrunners. Roman Catholic. Home and Office: 4402 E Sylvane St Tucson AZ 85711-6346

BRADY, JOHN PATRICK, JR., electronics educator, consultant; b. Newark, Mar. 20, 1929; s. John Patrick and Madeleine Mary (Atno) B.; m. Mary Coop, May 1, 1954; children: Peter, John P., Madeleine, Dennis, Mary G. BSEE, MIT, 1952, MSEE, 1953. Registered profl. engr., Mass. Sect. mgr. Hewlett-Packard Co., Waltham, Mass., 1956-67; v.p. engring. John Fluke Mfg. Co., Inc., Mountlake Terrace, Wash., 1967-73; v.p. engring. Dana Labs., Irvine, Calif., 1973-77; engring. mgr., tech. advisor to gen. mgr. Metron Corp., Upland, Calif., 1977-78; ptnr. Resource Assocs., Newport Beach, Calif., 1978-86; prof. electronics Orange Coast Coll., Costa Mesa, Calif., 1977—, dean technology, 1983-84; instr. computers and electrinc engring. Calif. State U., Long Beach, 1982-84. Mem. evaluation team Accrediting Commn. for Community and Jr. Colls., 1982-92; mem. blue ribbon adv. com. on oversees technology transfer U.S. Dept. of Commerce, 1974-76. With USN, 1946-48. Mem. Measurement Sci. Conf. (dir. 1982-83), MIT (L.A.). Contbr. articles in field to profl. jours. Office: Orange Coast Coll Costa Mesa CA 92626

BRADY, ROBERT EUGENE, aircraft company executive, management consultant; b. Flint, Mich., Dec. 3, 1933; s. Frederick Johnathan and Lolita (Blakeley) B.; m. Diane Potter, June 16, 1956 (div. May 1980); children: Robert, Kim, Mike; m. Renagene Bickel, Aug. 8, 1981. BS, U. Md., 1957; MBA with honors, City U., Bellevue, Wash., 1982. Plant indsl. engr. supr. Chrysler Corp., Detroit, 1957-60; indsl. engr. supr. Boeing Co., Seattle, 1960-61, fin. mgr., 1961-63, 68-72, supt. quality control, 1963-68, exec. cons. mgr., 1972-82, mgr. electronics mktg. strategy, 1982-88, proposal mgr., 1988-91, mgr. process mgmt. cons., 1991—; instr. bus. adminstrn. City U., 1982-83. Bd. dirs. Sensible Growth Alliance, Issaquah, Wash., 1988—, Citizens for Local Govt. Sammamish Inc., Issaquah, 1990—, Coalition Wash. Communities, 1990—; founder Assn. Uninc. Community Clubs and Couns., 1990—; Rep. candidate for Wash. Senate, 1992. Mem. Issaquah C. of C., Western Wash. DX Club. Home: 1304 251st Ave SE Issaquah WA 98027

BRADY, THOMAS DENIS, controller; b. Prescott, Ariz., June 2, 1955; s. Ormond Denis and Mary (Mei) B.; m. Kimberley Jo Huber, Apr. 21, 1978. BSBA, Ariz. State U., 1977, BS in Fin., 1983. Lic. real estate agt., Ariz., ins. agt. Ariz. Controller Twin Knolls Market, Inc., Mesa, Ariz., 1977-81; ins. agt. William Kirkendale & Assocs., Phoenix, Ariz., 1981; supr. accounts receivable dept. Associated Grocers Ariz., Phoenix, 1981-84; asst. controller SW Restaurant Systems, Inc., Tempe, Ariz., 1984-86; controller, treas. SW Restaurant Systems, Inc., Tempe, 1986—, asst. sec., 1990; bd. dirs., treas. Dobbins Enterprises, Durable Products Inc., United Comml. Realty, Inc.; controller, treas. Canyon Provisions, Inc., Tempe, 1986—, also bd. dirs.; bd. dirs. Pinnacle Peak Butcher Shoppe, Inc., Continental Airport Parking Inc., Ocotillo Builders, Inc., S.W. Rent A Car, Inc., County Plaza, Inc., Travel Express, Inc., Bitter Root Cattle Co., Inc., Watson Lake Devel. Co., Inc. Active Dennis DeConcini for U.S. Senate campaign, 1976. Mem. Nat. Restaurant Assn., Ariz. Restaurant Assn., Mesa-Tempe-Chandler Bd. Realtors, Scottsdale Bd. Realtors, Nogales Beach Club, Inc. (bd. dirs.), Cancun Bay Club, Inc. (bd. dirs.). Democrat. Roman Catholic. Home: 3440 E Edgewood Ave Mesa AZ 85204-4807 Office: SW Restaurant Systems 1979 E Broadway Rd Ste 3 Tempe AZ 85282-1732

BRADY, THOMAS MICHAEL, business executive; b. Oakland, Calif., Apr. 3, 1962; s. Thomas Michael and Katharine Marie (Abrott) B.; m. Julia Ann Wetzel, July 6, 1992. BA, U. Calif., Berkeley, 1984. Cons. First Data Resources, Orinda, Calif., 1987; v.p. MBA Systems, Pasadena, Calif., 1987-91; regional mgr. Fortel Group, Santa Clara, Calif., 1991—; cons. Doctor Micro Computer, Pasadena, 1991—, UNX Systems, Pasadena, 1991—. Chmn. sister friendship com. to Japan City of Pasadena, 1993. Named to Outstanding Young Men of Am., 1990. Mem. Tournament of Roses Assn. (life), Kasukabe, Japan Student Exch., Pasadena Jaycees (bd. dirs. 1989-90). Roman Catholic. Home: 2235 S Treelane Ave Monrovia CA 91016

BRAGDON, PAUL ERROL, foundation administrator; b. Portland, Maine, Apr. 19, 1927; s. Errol Freemont and Edith Lillian (Somerville) B.; m. Nancy Ellen Horton, Aug. 14, 1954; children: David Lincoln, Susan Horton, Peter Jefferson. BA magna cum laude, Amherst Coll., 1950, DHL (hon.), 1980; JD, Yale U., 1953; LLD (hon.), Whitman Coll., 1985; DLitt. (hon.), Pacific U., 1988; DHL (hon.), Reed Coll., 1989. Bar: N.Y. 1954. With firm Dewey, Ballantine, Bushby, Palmer & Wood, N.Y.C., 1953-58, Javits, Trubin, Sillcocks, Edelman & Purcell, N.Y.C., 1961-64; counsel Tchrs. Ins. and Annuity Assn. Coll. Retirement Equities Fund, N.Y.C., 1958-61; asst. to mayor City of N.Y., 1964-65, exec. sec. to mayor, 1965, exec. asst. to pres. City Council, 1966-67; v.p. NYU, 1967-71; pres. Reed Coll., Portland, Oreg., 1971-88; pres. emeritus, 1988—; asst. for edn. to gov. State of Oreg., 1988-91; dir. Office Edn. Policy and Planning Oreg. Office Edn. Policy and Planning, 1990-91; pres. Med. Rsch. Found. Oreg., Portland, 1991—; bd. dirs. Tektronix, Inc. Trustee Amherst Coll., 1972-78, Oreg. Grad. Ctr. for Sci. and Tech., 1988—; chmn. Oreg. Partnership for Internat. Edn., 1989—. Mem. Phi Beta Kappa, Phi Beta Kappa Assocs., Beta Theta Pi. Clubs: Century (N.Y.C.), Univ. (N.Y.C.); City (Portland, Oreg.), Univ. (Portland, Oreg.). Office: Med Rsch Found Oreg PO Box 458 Portland OR 97207-0458

BRAGG, DARRELL BRENT, nutritionist, consultant; b. Sutton, W.Va., May 24, 1933; s. William H. and Gertrude (Perrine) B.; m. Elizabeth Hosse, Dec. 28, 1957; children: Roger, Larry, Teresa. BSc, W.Va. U., 1959, MSc, 1960; PhD, U. Ark., 1966. Instr. dept. animal sci. U. Ark., Fayetteville, 1965-67; asst. prof. U. Man., Winnipeg, Can., 1967-68, assoc. prof., 1970-74; assoc. prof. dept. poultry sci. U. B.C., Vancouver, Can., 1970-74, prof., head dept., 1975-86; industry cons., Vancouver, 1986-89; nutritionist, dir. quality assurance Rangen Aquaculture Feeds, Buhl, Idaho, 1990-92; sr. rsch. scientist Rangen Aquaculture Rsch. Ctr., Hagerman, Idaho, 1991-92; indsl. biochem. cons. Deutrel Labs. Inc., Palmdale, Calif., 1991—. Contbr. numerous articles to sci. jours. With U.S. Army, 1954-56. Recipient numerous rsch. grants from industry, univs. and govts. Mem. Poultry Sci. Assn. (nat. bd. dirs., v.p., pres. 1978-84), World Poultry Sci. Assn. (bd. dirs., v.p. 1975-86), Sigma Xi, numerous others. Home: PO Box 902521 Palmdale CA 93590-2521

BRAIDEN, ROSE MARGARET, art educator, illustrator, calligrapher; b. Los Angeles, Nov. 25, 1922; d. Sylvester and Margaret Mary (Hines) B.; B.A., Mt. St. Mary's Coll., Los Angeles; M.F.A., Calif. Coll. Arts and Crafts. Chmn. art dept. Bishop Montgomery High Sch., Torrance, Calif., 1958-68; chmn. humanities Mt. St. Mary's Coll., Los Angeles, 1968-70; prof. art Santa Barbara City Coll., 1970—; chmn. photo dept. Cate Sch., Carpinteria, Calif., 1982-89; founder Los Padres Water Color Soc., 1990. Illustrator: Choices, 1983, Leah, 1986, The Mystical Ferryboat, 1986, A Mother's Journal, 1990. Democrat. Roman Catholic. Address: 2929 Paseo Tranquillo Santa Barbara CA 93105

BRAINERD, JOHN CALHOUN, publisher, editor, Anglican Catholic priest; b. Chgo., Aug. 22, 1934; s. Henry Hall and Marion (Calhoun) B.; m. Medora Jane Watkins, July 11, 1959; children: John Watkins, Mary Gwyn, Anne Catherine. BA, U. No. Colo., 1956; MA, U. Denver, 1964; PhD in History, U. Colo., 1994. Ordained priest Anglican Cath. Ch., 1979. From instr. to prof. N.W. Jr. Coll., Rangely, Colo., 1968-75; tchr. Golden (Colo.) High Sch., 1975-87; priest, missionary Anglican Cath. Ch., Denver and Western States, 1979-85; publisher, editor Dayspring Press, Golden, Colo., 1983—. Author: The Faerie Way, 1988; editor 6 monthly periodicals (Dayspring Press). Republican. Home and Office: Dayspring Press 18600 W 58th Ave Golden CO 80403-1070

BRAITHWAITE, CHARLES HENRY, chemist, chemical engineering comsultant; b. Chgo., Dec. 16, 1920; s. Charles Henry and Wilhelmina (Hoth) B.; m. Bernice May Hyde, Apr. 29, 1949; children: Charles Henry III, Betty Susan Braithwaite Artman. AB, UCLA, 1941; BS in Chem. Engring., U. Mich., 1943; MS, Carnegie Inst. Tech., 1948, DSc, 1949. Registered profl. engr., Calif. Materials engr. Westinghouse Electric, East Pittsburgh, Pa., 1943-46; rsch. chemist Shell Oil Co., Wood River, Ill., 1949-51; dir. rsch. FMC Corp.-Chlor-Alkali div., South Charleston, W.Va., 1951-57; dir. R & D Productol Co., Santa Fe Springs, Calif., 1957-59; pres. Cal-Colonial Chemsolve, La Habra, Calif., 1960-87; forensic cons. Braithwaite Cons., Whittier, Calif., 1987—; forensic cons., 1987—. Patentee in field; contbr. articles on elec. insulation to tech. publs. Mem. Am. Chem. Soc., Am. Inst. Chem. Engrs., Soc. Plastics Engrs., Western Plastics Pioneers. Office: 11232 Tigrina Ave Whittier CA 90603-3241

BRAITHWAITE, WALT WALDIMAN, aircraft manufacturing company executive; b. Kingston, Jamaica, Jan. 19, 1945; s. Ivanhoe Alexander and Ivy Mary (Green) B.; m. Edwina Gerell Patrick, Apr. 7, 1967 (div. March 1976); 1 child, Charlene Maria; m. Rita Cecelia Wood, May 4, 1974; children: Catherine Cecelia, Rachel Christine. BS in Electromech. Engring., Am. Inst. Engring. & Tech., Chgo., 1965; MS in Computer Sci., U. Wash., Seattle, 1975; SM in Mgmt., MIT, Cambridge, 1981. Cert. computer tech. Systems engr. engring. div. The Boeing Co., Renton, Wash., 1979-80; Sloan fellow MIT The Boeing Co., 1980-81; program mgr. bus. planning and commitments 7/7/7 div. The Boeing Co., Renton, Wash., 1981-82, mgr. CAD/CAM integration engring. div., 1982-83; dir. program tech. mgmt. Nat. Airspace Systems Co. div. Boeing/Lockheed, Kent, Wash., 1983-84; chief engr. CAD/CAM integration engring. div. The Boeing Co., Renton, Wash., 1984; chief engr. engring. ops. 747/767 div. The Boeing Co., Everett, Wash., 1984-85, dir. computing systems 747/767 div., 1985-86; dir. program mgmt. 707/737/757 div. The Boeing Co., Renton, 1986-91, v.p. info. systems Boeing Comml. Airplane Group, 1991—; initial graphics exchange specification Nat. Bur. Standards, Calif., 1980. Author: Design and Implementation of Interpreters, 1978. Bd. dirs. City Art Works, Seattle, 1981-85. Recipeint Joseph Marie Jacquare Meml. award Am. Inst. Mfg. Tech., Mass., 1987, leadership award Computer and Automated Systems Assn., Seattle, 1987, Nat. Black Achievers award YMCA, Seattle, 1990. Mem. Soc. Mfg. Engrs., Greater Renton C. of C. (pres. 1990-91). Episcopalian. Office: The Boeing Co PO Box 3707 Seattle WA 98124-2207

BRAKENSIEK, JAY CLEMENCE, county safety officer; b. Troy, Mo., Apr. 23, 1954; s. Clemence Ernst and Juanita Geraldine (Gaylord) B.; m. Kathleen Lorraine Edmonds, Aug. 25, 1981 (div. 1991); children: Gregory Jay, Matthew James. BS in Biology, N.E. Mo. State U., 1977, MA in Biosci. Edn., 1981; MS in Indsl. Hygiene, U. So. Calif., 1991, hazardous waste mgmt. cert., 1991. Cert. tchr., Calif.; registered environ. assessor, Calif. cert. asbestos inspector, mgmt. planner, project designer. Geology lab. asst. U. Mo., Columbia, 1975-76; chemistry lab. asst. N.E. Mo. State U., Kirksville, 1977-78; lab. asst./phlebotomist Kirksville Osteo. Hosp., 1978-79, Huntington Meml. Hosp., Pasadena, Calif., 1979-90; instr. biology dept. Citrus Coll., Glendora, Calif., 1984-87; instr. life scis. Pasadena City Coll., 1985-88; cardiopulmonary technologist, respiratory care practitioner Huntingtom Meml. Hosp., Pasadena, Calif., 1983-90; safety officer L.A. County Dept. Pub. Works, Alhambra, Calif., 1990—, indsl. hygiene/asbestos coord., 1990. Mem. sch. bd. First Luth. Ch. and Sch., 1988—, asbestos cons., 1990; mem. Endowment Com., 1993. Nat. Inst. Occupational Health and Safety fellow U. So. Calif. Inst. Safety and Systems Mgmt., 1988, 89, 90, 91; recipient L.A. County Productivity and Quality awards cert. for Devel. and Implementation of Computerized Search Programs for Health and Safety Regulations, 1993. Mem. Am. Indsl. Hygiene Assn., Am. Conf. Govtl. Indsl. Hygienists, Nat. Safety Coun., County Safety Officers Orgn. Calif., U. So. Calif. Inst. Safety and Systems Triumvirate, N.E. Mo. State U. Alumni Assn., U. So. Calif. Gen. Alumni Assn. Democrat. Home: 1618 E South Mayflower Ave Monrovia CA 91016 Office: LA County Dept Pub Works Risk Mgmt 900 S Freemont Ave Alhambra CA 91803-1331

BRAKHAGE, JAMES STANLEY, filmmaker, educator; b. Kansas City, Mo., Jan. 14, 1933; s. Ludwig and Clara (Dubberstein) B.; m. Mary Jane Collom, Dec. 28, 1957 (div. 1987); children: Myrrena, Crystal, Neowyn, Bearthm, Rarc; m. Marilyn Jull, Mar. 30, 1989; children: Anton, Vaughn. Ph.D., San Francisco Art Inst., 1981. Lectr. Sch. Art Inst. Chgo., 1969-81; prof. U. Colo., Boulder, 1981; mem. Filmmakers Coop., N.Y.C., Canyon Cinema Coop., San Francisco, London Filmmakers Coop., Can. Filmmakers' Distbn. Ctr., Toronto; Faculty lectr. U. Colo., 1990-91. Films include Interim, 1952, Anticipation of the Night, 1958, The Dead, 1960, Blue Moses, 1962, Dog Star Man, 1964, Songs in 8mm, 1964-69, Scenes from Under Childhood, 1967-70, The Weir Falcon Saga, 1970, The Act of Seeing with One's Own Eyes, 1971, The Riddle of Lumen, 1972, Sincerity and Duplicity, 1973-80, The Text of Light, 1974, Desert, 1976, The Governor, 1977, Burial Path, 1978, Nightmare Series, 1978, Creation, 1979, Made Manifest, 1980, Salome, 1980, Murder Psalm, 1980, Roman Numeral Series, 1979-81, the Arabic series, 1980-82, Unconscious London Strata, 1982, Tortured Dust, 1984, The Egyptian Series, 1984, The Loom, 1986, Nightmusic, 1986, The Dante Quartet, 1987, Faust, parts I-IV, 1987-89, Marilyn's Window, 1988, Visions in Meditation, 1989-90, City Streaming, 1990, Glaze of Cathexis, 1990, Babylonian Series, 1989-90, Passage Through: A Ritual, 1990, A Child's Garden and the Serious Sea, 1991, Delicacies of Molten Horror Synapse, 1991, Christ Mass Sex Dance, 1991, Crack Glass Eulogy, 1992, Boulder Blues and Pearls and For Marilyn, Interpolations 1-5, 1992, Blossom Gift Favor, The Harrowing, Tryst Haunt, Study in Color and Black and White, Stellar, Atumnal, 1993; author: Metaphors on Vision, 1963, A Moving Picture Giving and Taking Book, 1971, The Brakhage Lectures, 1972, Seen, 1975, Film Biographies, 1977, Brakhage Scrapbook, 1982, Film at Wits End, 1989, I...Sleeping, 1989. Recipient Brussels Worlds Fair Protest award, 1958, Brandeis citation, 1973, Colo. Gov.'s Award for Arts and humanities, 1974, Jimmy Ryan Morris Meml. Found. award, 1979, Telluride Film Festival medallion, 1981 Maya Deren award Am. Film Inst., 1986, medal U. Colo., 1988, Outstanding Achievement award Denver Internat. Film Festival, 1988, MacDowell medal, 1989, Libr. Cong. Nat. Film Registry, 1992, Anthology Film Archives honor, 1993, The Colo. 100 certificate of Recognition, 1993; grantee Avon Found. 1965-69, NEA, 1974-75, 77, 80, 83, 88, U. Colo. Coun. Rsch. and Creative Work, 1983, Rocky Mountain Film Ctr., 1985; Rockefeller fellow, 1967-69, Guggenheim fellow, 1978. Democrat. Home: Apt 203 2142 Canyon Blvd Boulder CO 80302 Office: U Colo Film Studies Hunter 102 Campus Box 316 Boulder CO 80309

BRALVER, PETER JEFFREY, interdisciplinary ecologist; b. Detroit, Sept. 27, 1943; s. Richard Samuel and Eleanor Norma (Kirschbaum) B. Student, Pasadena Mus. of Art Sch., 1961, Chovinard Art Inst., 1962, L.A. Valley Coll., 1981-83. Book clk. and antiquarian, 1959-65, fine artist, 1955—, Zen monk, interdisciplinary ecologist, mathematician, artist, comml. art dir., 1966-67; cons. ecology and gen. sci., 1986—; cons. interdisciplinary ecology Wide Network Environ. Think Tank, 1987—, policy studies, 1993; ind. nuclear and earth scis. rsch., 1993. Contbr. articles to profl. jours.; editor, corr. Earth First! Jour., 1988—. Organizer, activist L.A. Earth First!, 1986—; ecol. analyst Earth First! Biodiversity Project, 1988—. Mem. N.Y. Acad. Scis., Earth Island Inst., Soc. for Conservation Biology, Am. Math. Soc., The Wilderness Soc., Sea Shepherd Conservation Soc. (ship's crew rsch. scientist deckhand 1988, shore crew 1992-93). Greens. Vedanta. Office: Earth First! WNETT Rsch PO Box 4381 North Hollywood CA 91617-0381

BRAMBLE, JOHN MYLES, city manager; b. Vancouver, Wash., May 3, 1946; s. Paul Eugene and Beulah Elizabeth (Henderson) B.; m. JoAnn Tolle, May 2, 1980; children: Scott Byron, Steven Tolle. BS, Oreg. State U., 1969; MPA, U. Nev., Las Vegas, 1978. Adminstrv. asst. City of Salem (Oreg.), 1969-73; research analyst Abt Assocs., Inc., Cambridge, Mass., 1973-74; dir. budget and mgmt. City of Las Vegas (Nev.), 1975-79; asst. city mgr., fin. dir. City of Belmont (Calif.), 1979-81; city mgr. City of Commerce City (Colo.), 1981-84, City of Pueblo (Colo.), 1984-87; city adminstr., City of Bell, Calif., 1988—. Fin. dir. Friends of Bell Found.; mem. exec. bd. Colo. Mcpl. League, 1982-83. Mem. Internat. City Mgmt. Assn., Denver Met. Mgrs. Assn. (chmn. 1983), Colo. City Mgmt. Assn. (pres-elect 1986-87), Kiwanis. Home: 9047 Chaney Ave Downey CA 90240-2413 Office: 6330 Pine Ave Bell CA 90201-1291

BRAME, MARILLYN A., hypnotherapist; b. Indpls., Sept. 17, 1928; d. David Schwalb and Hilda (Riley) Curtin; 1 child, Gary Mansour. Student, Meinzinger Art Sch., Detroit, 1946-47, U. N.Mex., 1963, Orlando (Fla.) Jr. Coll., 1964-65, El Camino Coll., Torrance, Calif., 1974-75; PhD in Hypnotherapy, Am. Inst. Hypnotherapy, 1989. Cert. and registered hypnotherapist. Color cons. Pitts. Plate Glass Co., Albuquerque, 1951-52; owner Signs by Marillyn, Albuquerque, 1952-53; design draftsman Sandia Corp., Albuquerque, 1953-56; designer The Martin Co., Orlando, 1957-65; pres. The Arts, Winter Park, Fla., 1964-66; supr. tech. publs. Gen. Instrument Corp., Hawthorne, Calif., 1967-76; pres. Camart Design, Westminster, Calif., 1977-86, Visual Arts, El Toro, Calif., 1978—; mgr. tech. publs. Archive Corp., Costa Mesa, Calif., 1986-90; adj. instr. Orange Coast Coll., Costa Mesa, 1985—; hynotherapist, Lake Forest, 1986—; bd. dirs. Am. Bd. Hypnotheraphy Orange County Chpt. Author: (textbook) Folkdancing is for Everybody; prodn. editor; (newsletter) Techniscribe, 1986, 1987; inventor, designer dance notation system MS Method; News Letter Editor: Am. Bd. Hypnotheraphy. Mem. Bd. govs. Lake Forest II Showboaters Theater Group, 1985-88, 90—. Mem. Soc. Tech. Communication (v.p. programs, 1987, newsletter editor 1986-87, newsletter prodn. editor 1985-86). Office: 22651 Lambert St Ste 101B Lake Forest CA 92630

BRAMWELL, MARVEL LYNNETTE, nurse; b. Durango, Colo., Aug. 13, 1947; d. Floyd Lewis and Virginia Jenny (Amyx) B. Diploma in lic. practical nursing, Durango Sch. Practical Nursing, 1968; AD in Nursing, Mt. Hood Community Coll., 1972; BS in Nursing, BS in Gen. Studies cum laude, So. Oreg. State Coll., 1980; cert. edn. grad. sch. social work, U. Utah, 1987, cert. counselor alcohol, drug abuse, 1988, MSW, 1992; M in Social Work, 1992. RN, Utah. Staff nurse Monument Valley (Utah) Seventh Day Adventist Mission Hosp., 1973-74, La Plata Community Hosp., 1974-75; health coordinator Tri County Head Start Program, 1974-75; nurse therapist, team leader Portland Adventist Med. Ctr., 1975-78; staff nurse Indian Health Service Hosp., 1980-81; coordinator village health services North Slope Borough Health and Social Service Agy., 1981-83; nurse, supr. aides Bonneville Health Care Agy., 1984-85; staff nurse Latter Day Saints Adolescent Psychiat. Unit, 1985-86; coordinator adolescent nursing CPC Olympus View Hosp., 1986-87, 91; charge and staff nurse adult psychiatry U. Utah, 1987-88; nursing supr. St. Joseph Villa, Salt Lake City, 1989-90; assisted with design and constrn. 6 high tech. health clinics in Ala. Arctic, 1982-83; psychiat. nurse specialist Community Nursing Svc. Contbr. articles to profl. jours. Active Mothers Against Drunk Driving; mem. acad. rev. com. Community Health Assn. Program U. Alaska Rural Edn., 1981-83. Recipient Cert. Appreciation Barrow (Alaska) Lion's Club, 1983, U.S. Census Bur., Colo., 1970. Mem. NOW, Nat. Assn. Social Workers, Assn. Women Sci., Am. Soc. Circumpolar Health. Home: 3406 Monte Verde Dr Salt Lake City UT 84109-3229

BRANCHAUD, JAMES HOWARD, electronics engineer; b. Alameda, Calif., Apr. 1, 1946; s. Howard James and A. Jean (Davis) B.; m. Michele Joyce Cooney, Aug. 20, 1983. Student, Coll. of San Mateo (Calif.), 1964-66, Honolulu Electronics Inst., 1973-77. Field svc. staff Bell & Howell Co., Honolulu, 1970—; owner The Wizard Werks, Kaneohe, 1978—. Pres. Kukui Plaza Owners Assn., Honolulu, 1975-87, Kaneohe Woods Assn. of Owners, 1987-92. With USN, 1966-70. Mem. Aloha Mustang Club, Hui'O'Kaaina, Elks. Home: 45-620 Koai'e Pl Kaneohe HI 96744 Office: Bell & Howell Co 46-132C Kahuhipa St Kaneohe HI 96744

BRAND, JAY LLOYD, psychology educator, researcher; b. Takoma Park, Md., June 14, 1959; s. Lewis Clayton and Naomi Jean (Reynolds) B.; m. Michelle DaVonn Esh, Dec. 12, 1989. Student, Union Coll., 1979; BA, So. Coll., 1982; MA, U. Louisville, 1985, PhD, 1990. Teaching asst. English dept. So. Coll., Collegedale, Tenn., 1977-79, 80-82; rsch. technician U. Louisville, 1982-85, lectr., 1985-89; asst. prof. La Sierra U., Riverside, Calif., 1989—; lectr. Jefferson Community Coll., Louisville, summer 1988; statis. and psychology cons. Loma Linda U., 1990—. Author: (chpt.) Risk & Effort, 1984. Instr. bible South Louisville SDA Ch., 1982-85; election vol. Dem. Party, Louisville, 1984. Mem. APA, So. Soc. for Philos. Psychology, Human Factors Soc., Sigma Xi (assoc.). Office: La Sierra U 4700 Pierce St Riverside CA 92515-8247

BRAND, LEONARD ROY, biology educator; b. Harvey, N.D., May 17, 1941; s. George Edward and Clara Leona (Kingsfield) B.; m. Kim Kwangho, Aug. 8, 1974; children—Dennis, Jenelle. B.A., La Sierra Coll., Riverside, Calif., 1964; M.A., Loma Linda U., 1966; Ph.D., Cornell U., 1970. Asst. prof. biology Loma Linda U., Loma Linda and Riverside, Calif., 1969-74, assoc. prof. biology, 1974-78, prof. biology, 1978-90, chmn. dept. biology, 1971-86, 88-90, chmn. dept. natural scis., 1990—, prof. biology and paleontology, 1990—. Contbr. articles to profl. jours. Recipient Zapara award for disting. teaching Loma Linda U., 1989; NSF grad. fellow, 1964-69. Mem. Animal Behavior Soc., Am. Soc. Mammalogists (A. Brazier Howell award 1967), Soc. Vertebrate Paleontologists, Geol. Soc. Am., Sigma Xi (Grant-in-Aid of Research 1968). Seventh-Day Adventist. Home: 6095 Alhambra Ave Riverside CA 92505-2262 Office: Loma Linda U Dept Natural Scis Loma Linda CA 92350

BRAND, MARY LOU, nurse; b. Colorado Springs, Colo., Apr. 19, 1934; d. Frederick William and Clara Irene (Morriss) B. BS, U. Denver, 1957; MA, U. Colo., 1963; postgrad., U. No. Colo., 1969-77. Cert. in spl. svcs., Colo. Staff nurse Presbyn. Med. Ctr., Denver, 1957-68; staff sch. nurse Denver Pub. Schs. Dist. I, 1958-90, counselor, 1963-90; cons. Sch. Health Counseling Edn. & Svcs., 1991—; co-dir. sch. nurse workshop U. Wyo. Summer Sch., Laramie, 1967, U. No. Colo., 1969, 70; RN, Nat. Coun. for Sch. Nurses, pres., 1968-69; mem. Colo. Sci. Fair Adv. Coun., 1986—, judge health & behavioral sci. category, 1985—. Contbr. articles to profl. jours. Profl. mem. Colo. div. ARC, 1958-90; mem. Rep. Nat. Com., 1982—. Recipient Florence Nightingale award U. Colo. Sch. Nursing, 1988, cert. appreciation for outstanding svc. Denver Pub. Schs., 1988, Edn. Svc. award, 1990. Fellow Am. Sch. Health Assn.; mem. AAHPERD (conf. dir. 1968, Schering/AAHPERD Nat. Sch. Nurse award 1972), ANA, NEA, Colo. Nurses Assn. (chmn. sch. nurses sect. 1963-68), Colo. Sch. Health Coun. (sec. 1981-82, v.p. 1983-84, pres. 1984-87, bd. dirs. 1984-87, 89-92, newsletter editor, recognition award 1986), Colo. Edn. Assn., Denver Classroom Tchrs. Assn. (area rep. 1987-89, award for svc. to children 1971), Internat. Platform Assn., Presbyn. Med. Ctr. Sch. Nursing Alumni Assn., Statue of Liberty-Ellis Island Found. Home: PO Box 2650 Littleton CO 80161-2650

BRAND, MYLES, academic administrator; b. N.Y.C., May 17, 1942; s. Irving Philip and Shirley (Berger) B.; m. Wendy Hoffman (div. 1976); 1 child: Joshua; m. Margaret Zeglin, 1978. BS, Rensselaer Poly. Inst., 1964, D (hon.), 1991; PhD, U. Rochester, 1967; hon. doctorate, Rensselaer Poly. Inst., 1991. Asst. prof. philosophy U. Pitts., 1967-72; from assoc. prof. to prof., dept. chmn. U. Ill., Chgo., 1972-81; prof., dept. head U. Ariz., Tucson, 1981-83; dir. cognitive sci. program U. Ariz., 1982-85; dean, social & behavioral scis. U. Ariz., Tucson, 1983-86; provost, v.p. acad. affairs Ohio State U., Columbus, 1986-89; pres. U. Oreg., Eugene, 1989—. Author: Intending and Acting, 1984; editor: The Nature of Human Action, 1970, The Nature of Causation, 1976, Action Theory, 1976. Bd. dirs. Ariz. Humanities Coun., 1984-85, Am. Coun. on Edn., Washington, 1992—. Recipient research award NEH, 1974, 79. Mem. Am. Philos. Assn., Phi Kappa Phi. Office: U Oreg Office of Pres Eugene OR 97403-1226

BRANDEMUEHL, JENNY ANGELA, organization development manager; b. Queens, N.Y., June 25, 1963; d. Augustus S. F. Fung and Angela H. (Yuan) Fung-Denzler; m. Mark Wesley Brandemuehl, July 2, 1988. BA, Wellesley (Mass.) Coll., 1985. Rsch. asst. dept. psychology Harvard U., Cambridge, Mass., 1983-84; asst. to dir. City & County of San Francisco Mission Mental Health Dist., 1984; with Standard Microsystems Corp., Hauppauge, N.Y., 1985-86; employee rels. and tng. mgr. Standard Microsystems Corp., Hauppage, N.Y., 1986-88; sr. employee rels. rep. Nat. Semiconductor Corp., Santa Clara, Calif., 1988-89; human resources cons., 1989-91; mgr. tng. and devel. Hewlett Packard Co., Santa Clara, 1991-92, orgn. devel. mgr., 1992—. Mem. No. Calif. Human Resources Coun., West Bay (Calif.) Wellesley Coll. Alumnae Assn. (bd. dirs., admissions officer 1990—), Women's Housing Connection Silicon Valley (human resources adv. com. 1992—). Office: Hewlett Packard Co 5301 Stevens Creek Blvd Santa Clara CA 95051-7201

BRANDENBURG, GLEN RAY, marine education administrator; b. Long Beach, Calif., July 28, 1950; s. Richard Stanley and Julia Amelia Brandenburg. B in Indsl. Arts, San Diego State U., 1974. Dir. Mission Bay Aquatic Ctr., San Diego, 1970—; cons. in field. Producer primary instrnl. video in field. Chmn. San Diego City Lakes Master Plan, 1975; asst. regatta dir. Olympic Rowing Venue, L.A., 1984; bd. dirs Boating Safety Ctr. Calif. Dept Boating and Waterwasys, 1976—. Mem. Calif. Boating Ctr. Dirs., U.S. Sailing, Nat. Boating Fedn., San Diego Assn. Yacht Clubs, Mission Bay Rowing Assn. (bd. dirs. 1975—), Boat/U.S. Democrat. Office: Mission Bay Aquatic Ctr 1001 Santa Clara Pl San Diego CA 92109-7299

BRANDENBURGH, DONALD CARTER, literary agent; b. Stuart, Iowa, July 4, 1931; s. Wilbur Hager and Esther Hadley (Carter) B.; m. Mary Isabelle Moore, June 5, 1953; children: Gregory, Curtis, Brenda. BA, William Penn Coll., 1953; MA, Whittier Coll., 1960; MDiv, Talbot Sch. Theology, La Mirada, Calif., 1970. Ordained minister Soc. of Friends, 1956; Pastor Paton (Iowa) Friends Ch., 1955-57; clk. So. Calif. Gas Co., L.A., 1958-59; minister Christian edn. Alamitos Friends Ch., Garden Grove, Calif., 1959-68; bus. adminstr. Calif. Yearly Meeting Friends Ch., Whittier, Calif., 1968-73; exec. dir. Nat. Sunday Sch. Assn., Whittier, 1973-74, Evang. Christian Publs. Assn., La Habra, Calif., 1974-80; assoc. pub., owner Home & Land mag., La Habra, 1981-85; lit. agt., owner, mgr. Brandenburgh & Assocs., Murrieta, Calif., 1986—. Bd. dirs. Friends Ctr., Azusa, Calif., 1986-87. Mem. La Habra Area C. of C. (chmn. trade fair com. 1987-88, 2d v.p. 1987-88, chmn. ambassador com. 1988-89), Greater L.A. Sunday Sch. Assn. (bd. dirs. 1962-82). Republican. Home and Office: 24555 Corte Jaramillo Murrieta CA 92562

BRANDES, STANLEY HOWARD, anthropology educator, writer; b. N.Y.C., Dec. 26, 1942; s. Emanuel Robert and Annette (Zalisch) B.; divorced; children: Nina Rachel, Naomi Carla. BA, U. Chgo., 1964; MA, U. Calif., Berkeley, 1969, PhD, 1971. Asst. prof. anthropology Mich. State U., East Lansing, 1971-75; asst. prof. anthropology U. Calif., Berkeley, 1975-78, assoc. prof., 1978-82, prof. anthropology, 1982—, chmmn. dept., 1990—; dir. Barcelona Study Ctr., U. Calif. and Ill., Spain, 1981-82. Author: Migration, Kinship and Community, 1975, Metaphors of Masculinity, 1980, Forty: The Age and the Symbol, 1985, Power and Persuasion, 1988; co-editor: Symbol as Sense, 1980. NIH fellow, 1967-71; NICHD research fellow, 1975-77; Am. Council Learned Socs. grantee, 1977. Fellow Am. Anthrop. Assn.; mem. Am. Ethnological Soc., Soc. for Psychol. Anthropology. Office: U Calif Dept Anthropology Berkeley CA 94720

BRANDIN, ALF ELVIN, retired mining and shipping company executive; b. Newton, Kans., July 1, 1912; s. Oscar E. and Agnes (Larsen) B.; m. Marie Eck, June 15, 1936 (dec. 1980); children: Alf R., Jon, Erik, Mark.; m. Pamela J. Brandin, Jan. 28, 1983. A.B., Stanford U., 1936. With Standard Accident of Detroit, 1936-42; bus. mgr. Stanford U., Calif., 1946-52; bus. mgr., exec. officer for land devel. Stanford U., 1952-59, v.p. for bus. affairs, 1959-70; sr. v.p., dir., mem. exec. com. Utah Internat. Inc., San Francisco, from 1970; pres. Richardson-Brandin, 1964-86, also bd. dirs.; bd. dirs. Hershey Oil Co.; vice chmn. bd. dirs. Doric Devel. Inc. Bd. govs. San Francisco Bay Area Council; trustee Reclamation Dist. 2087, Alameda, Calif.; bd. overseers Hoover Instn. on War, Revolution and Peace, Stanford; mem. VIII Olympic Winter Games Organizing com., 1960. Served as comdr. USNR, 1942-46. Mem. Zeta Psi. Clubs: Elk, Stanford Golf, Bohemian, Pauma Valley Country, Silverado Country; Royal Lahaina. Home: 668 Salvatierra St Palo Alto CA 94305-8538 Office: 550 California St San Francisco CA 94104-1006

BRANDMEYER, DONALD WAYNE, maritime consultant, retired foreign service officer; b. New London, Iowa, Aug. 22, 1919; s. Frederick Theodore, Jr. and Viola Jane (Wright) B.; m. Esther Delle Noss, Mar. 22, 1941 (div. Nov. 1953); children—Donna Delle, David Wayne, Dennis Ray, Debra Sue; m. Elizabeth Louise Hansen, Nov. 25, 1953. Student Burlington Coll. Commerce, 1936-37; B.A. in World Bus. and Econs. cum laude, San Francisco State U., 1951; postgrad. U. Calif.-Berkeley, 1952. Calif. State U.-Long Beach, 1958-61, U. Pitts., 1969. Registered marine surveyor; pvt. pilot; unltd. master mariner. Transp. officer Ft. MacArthur, Calif., 1940-42, transp. officer, exec. asst. to comdg. officer spl. services U.S. War Dept., 1942-44; from mate to master large vessels in fgn. service, 1944-46; marine supt. San Francisco Port of Embark, 1946-51, Naval Supply Ctr., Oakland, Calif., 1951-52; head terminal ops. br. U.S. Navy, Washington, 1952-54; sr. civilian advisor Army Transp. Bd., 1954-57; pres. Brandmeyer Internat., Rancho Palos Verdes, Calif., 1957—; sr. maritime advisor AID, Vietnam and UN, 1967-71; Cons. Internat. Maritime Orgn., 1978-79; U.S. rep. UN Conf. on Internat. Intermodal Transport of Container Cargo, Bangkok, 1972. Contbr. articles to periodicals. Pres. Mira Costa Terr. Homeowners Assn., 1979-80. Served with USN, 1937-40. Recipient commendation AID, Vietnam, 1969, Outstanding Service award and medal, Govt. of Vietnam, 1971, Highest Diplomatic Rank of Gen. Mem. Masters, Mates and Pilots Internat., Internat. Assn. Marine Surveyors (charter), World Affairs Council, Master Mariners Council. Republican. Club: Toastmasters.

BRANDNER, MARGARET ANNE SHAW, polygraph examiner; b. Denver, Sept. 4, 1937; d. Bertram James and Bessie (Syme) Shaw. BA in Elem. Edn., Loretto Heights Coll., 1959; polygraph examiner Rocky Mountain Security Inst., 1978; grad. Famous Writers' Sch., 1964, Inst. Forensic and Investigative Hypnosis, 1980; AAS. in Polygraph Tech., Pikes Peak Community Coll., 1982. Acct., Denver Children's Home, 1970; polygraph examiner, sec.-treas. The Brandner Corp., Green River, Wyo., 1978—; agt. Allstate Ins. Cos., 1989-91; acct., polygraph examiner Crime Prevention, Inc., 1991—. Mem. Green River Planning Commn., 1971-79; bd. dirs. Green River Co-op Pre-Sch., Inc., 1977-79; trustee Sweetwater County Sch. Dist. #2, 1986—, Sweetwater BOCES, 1992—, treas. region IV, 1987-91; vol. chmn. Arthritis Found., Sweetwater County, 1986-87, Sweetwater County United Way, 1984—. Roman Catholic. Office: 2800 Sunset Dr # 8 Rock Springs WY 82901-6038

BRANDOM, CHARLYNN, insurance and securities company official; b. St. Joseph, Mo., Dec. 13, 1953; d. C. Dudley and Marilyn V. (Wiegner) B. AA, Stephens Coll., Columbia, Mo., 1974; BFA, Stephens Coll., 1976; MS, Ariz. State U., 1980; life teaching cert., Maricopa County C.C., Phoenix. Cert. ins. agt., Ariz.; cert. for series 6, 22, 63 Nat. Assn. Securities Dealers. Patternmaker, seamstress Thimbleweeds, Scottsdale, Ariz., 1976; saleswoman Casual Corner, Scottsdale, 1976-77; asst. mgr., then mgr. Saks Fifth Avenue, Phoenix, 1977-78; mem. part-time faculty Glendale (Ariz.) C.C., 1978-80, Phoenix Coll., 1978-87; lectr. Ariz. State U., Tempe, 1980-84; owner, designer Char Designs, Ltd., Phoenix, 1982-87; agt., registered rep. N.Y. Life and NYLIFE Securities, Phoenix, 1987—; program speaker to various civic and bus. groups, including Svc. Corps Ret. Execs., Phoenix, 1990. Instr. Young Olympians, Inc., Scottsdale, 1987—. Mem. Nat. Assn. for Profl. Saleswomen (co-founder, charter, membership dir. 1991-92, program chmn. 1992-93, treas. 1993—), Nat. Assn. Women Bus. Owners (historian 1990-92), Phoenix Assn. Life Underwriters, Women Life Underwriters, Profl. Referral Source (charter, pres. 1991-92, v.p. 1992), Resources for Women, Stephens Coll. Alumnae Club (sec. Phoenix 1990-92, program speaker). Republican. Methodist. Office: NY Life 100 W Clarendon Ste 1500 Phoenix AZ 85013

BRANDON, ALLEN DEWAIN, neuropsychologist; b. Celina, Ohio, Oct. 10, 1957; s. Eldon DeWain and Janis Ann (Hines) B.; m. Helen Kathleen Bacon, June 20, 1981. BS, Colo. State U., 1980, MS, 1983, PhD, 1986. Lic. clin. psychologist, Colo. Mem. clin. staff Med. Sch. UCLA, 1986-87; dir. Rocky Mountain Neuropsychological Scis., Ft. Collins, 1987—; dir. psychology Charter Hosp. Ft. Collins, 1989—; clin. fellow Med. Sch. Harvard U., Boston, 1985-86; postdoctoral fellow Med. Sch. UCLA, 1986-87; adj. faculty Colo. State U., Ft. Collins, 1987—; cons. psychologist Poudre Valley Hosp., Ft. Collins, 1987—, McKee Med. Ctr., Loveland, Colo., 1987—. Co-author: (test manual) Electronic Finger Tapping Test, 1983, contbr. articles to profl. jours. Mem. United Meth. Men, Ft. Collins, 1987—. Grantee NIMH, 1981. Mem. Nat. Acad. Neuropsychologists, Internat. Neuropsychology Soc., Colo. Psychol. Assn., Colo. Head Injury Found. Office: Rocky Mountain 375 E Horsetooth Rd Fort Collins CO 80525-3155

BRANDON, KATHRYN ELIZABETH BECK, pediatrician; b. Salt Lake City, Sept. 10, 1916; d. Clarence M. and Hazel A. (Cutler) Beck; MD, U. Chgo., 1941; BA, U. Utah, 1937; MPH, U. Calif., Berkeley, 1957; children: John William, Kathleen Brandon McEnulty, Karen. Intern, Grace Hosp., Detroit, 1941-42; resident Children's Hosp. Med. Center No. Calif., Oakland, 1953-55, Children's Hosp., L.A., 1951-53; pvt. practice, La Crescentia, Calif., 1946-51, Salt Lake City, 1960-65, 86—; med. dir. Salt Lake City public schs., 1957-60; dir. Ogden City-Weber County (Utah) Health Dept., 1965-67; pediatrician Fitzsimmons Army Hosp., 1967-68; coll. health physician U. Colo., Boulder, 1968-71; student health physician U. Utah, Salt Lake City, 1971-81; occupational health physician Hill AFB, Utah, 1981-85; ; child health physician Salt Lake City-County Health Dept., 1971-82; cons. in field; clin. asst. U. Utah Coll. Medicine, Salt Lake City, 1958-64; clin. asst. pediatrics U. Colo. Coll. Medicine, Denver, 1958-72; active staff Primary Children's Hosp., LDS Hosp., and Cottonwood Hosp., 1960-67. Diplomate Am. Bd. Pediatrics. Fellow Am. Pediatric Acad., Am. Pub. Health Assn., Am. Sch. Health Assn.; mem. Utah Coll. Health Assn. (pres. 1978-80), Pacific Coast Coll. Health Assn., AMA, Utah Med. Assn., Salt Lake County Med. Soc., Utah Public Health Assn. (sec.-treas. 1960-66), Intermountain Pediatric Soc. Home: PO Box 58482 Salt Lake City UT 84158-0482 Office: 3236 E 3300 S Salt Lake City UT 84109-2247

BRANDON, MICHAEL PATRICK, sales executive; b. L.A., July 13, 1961; s. Jerome Doyle and Marguerite (Mullenaux) B. AB, U. Calif., Berkeley, 1983. Sales rep. C.D.M. Companies, Denver, 1984-85; retail leasing specialist Norris, Beggs & Simpson, San Francisco, 1985-88; rel estate cons. A.R. Jarvis & Assocs., San Francisco, 1988-90; ptnr., v.p. sales SF Video, San Francisco, 1990—; mem. Nat. Geographic Trans Americas Expedition, 1988. Bd. dirs. Bah Humbug Charity Ball, San Francisco, 1986—. Republican. Episcopalian. Home: 3824 Scott St San Francisco CA 94123 Office: San Francisco Video 3328 Steiner St Ste 2 San Francisco CA 94123

BRANDT, ELIZABETH ANNE, sociocultural and linguistic anthropology educator; b. Sanford, Fla., Oct. 20, 1945; d. Frederick Jacob and Anna Marie (Fellows) B.; m. Conrad Schott IV, June 8, 1974 (div. 1978); m. Silverio Casillas, Dec. 12, 1987. BA, Fla. State U., 1967; MA, So. Meth. U., 1969, PhD, 1970; postgrad., Phillips U., Marburg, Fed. Republic Germany, 1965-66. Asst. prof. U. Ill., Chgo., 1970-74; asst. prof. Ariz. State U., Tempe, 1974-75, assoc. prof., 1976—, chair program in linguistic anthropology, 1980—, chair interdisciplinary program in linguistics, 1979-80, 83-85, 1987-88; co-dir. Am. Indian Lang., Lit., Culture and History Inst., Tempe, 1989-90, dir., 1991-93; co-dir. Am. Indian Summer Seminars; contractor Nat. Park Svc., 1992-93. Co-author: Navajo Students at Risk, 1986; co-editor: Bilingualism and Language Contact, 1982; contbr. articles to profl. jours. Chair program com., exec. com. Ariz. Humanities Coun., Phoenix, 1989-91; exec. bd. Apache Cultural Survival Coalition, Tucson, 1990, Spirit of the Senses, Scottsdale, 1987-88. Grantee NEH, Alamo Navajo Community, 1987, NSF, Zuni Pueblo, 1986-87, N.Mex. Endowment for Humanities, Sandia Pueblo, 1989-90. Fellow Soc. for Applied Anthropology, Am. Anthrop. Soc.; mem. Linguistic Soc. Am., Soc. for Study of Indigenous Langs. of the Americas, Coun. on Anthropology & Edn., Am. Soc. Ethnohistory, Sigma Xi. Office: Ariz State U Dept Anthropology Tempe AZ 85287

BRANDT, JERRY, consultant; b. N.Y.C., Mar. 16, 1929; s. Sol and Fannie (BUrstein) Boorstein; m. Shirley Goodchild (div. 1975); children: Craig, Kim. BS in Mech. Engring., U. Ala., 1952; MS in Indsl. Mgmt., Stevens Inst. Tech., 1956. Test engr. Patt & Whitney Aricraft, Hartford, Conn., 1954-56, Combustion Engrs., N.Y.C., 1956-58, Burnes & Roe, Cape Kennedy, Fla., 1958-60; bus. mgr., prin. Gruye Brandt & Assocs., Palo Alto, Calif., 1960-65; bus. cons., prin. Interface Systems, Portola Valley, Calif., 1965—; COO Logical Machine, 1977; cons. Electrofusion Corp., 1977-91, McCutchen Mktg. Svc., 1991-92; pres. ULtra PUre System, 1981-85. Capt. USAF, 1952-54, ETO. Mem. Pi Tau Sigma. Home and Office: 35 Prado Ct Portola Valley CA 94028

BRANDVOLD, LYNN AIRHEART, chemist; b. Fargo, Apr. 9, 1940; d. Paul Evans and Corrine Louise (Lawrence) Airheart; m. Donald Keith Brandvold, Dec. 29, 1961; children: Evan Paul, Beth Louise. BS, N.D. State U., 1962, MS, 1964. Staff chemist N.Mex. Bur. Mines and Mineral Resources, Socorro, 1965-80, sr. chemist, 1980—; mem. Water Quality Control Commn., N.Mex., 1972—, Interstate Oil Compact Commn., 1982—; mem. adv. bd. N.Mex. Water Conf., 1975—. Contbr. articles on water chemistry, ore analysis and environ. issues to various publs. Asst. leader Socorro coun. Girl Scouts Am., 1982-83; team parent Am. Youth Soccor Orgn., Socorro, 1982-87; sec. Socorro Aquatics Club, 1987. Mem. Am. Chem. Soc., Soc. Mineral Analysts, Am. Water Resources Assn., Soc. Applied Spectroscopy (pres. 1980-81), N.Mex. Acad. Sci., N.Mex. Geol. Soc., Sigma Xi (chpt. pres. 1982-83). Republican. Methodist. Home: Star Rte 2 Box 93 Socorro NM 87801 Office: NMex Bur Mines and Mineral Resources Campus Sta Socorro NM 87801

BRANDWAJN, ALEXANDRE, software company executive; b. Hohne, Fed. Republic of Germany, Apr. 13, 1948; came to U.S., 1978; s. Rachmiel and Liba (Goldziuk) B.; m. Marlene Francette Chabbat, May 22, 1974; children: Elise Sophie, Xavier Marc. Telecommunications Engring. Diploma, ENST, Paris, 1971; D of Engring., U. Paris, 1972, BA in Lit., 1973, Docteur d'Etat, 1975. Researcher Inst. Rsch. Automatique and Informatique, Rocquencourt, France, 1971-75; prof. computer sci. Ecole Nat. Superieure des Telecommunications, Paris, 1975-79; sr. computer architect Amdahl Corp., Sunnyvale, Calif., 1979-82, mgr. performance analysis, 1982-85; pres. Pallas Internat. Corp., San Jose, Calif., 1983—; prof. computer engring. U. Calif., Santa Cruz, 1985—; cons. UCCEL Corp., Dallas, 1986-87, MCC, Austin, Tex., 1986-87, Amdahl Corp., Sunnyvale, 1985—. Contbr. articles to profl. jours. Mem. Assn. for Computing Machinery, Computer Measurement Group. Office: Pallas Internat Corp 1763 Valhalla Ct San Jose CA 95132-1653

BRANEN, ALFRED LARRY, food science educator; b. Caldwell, Idaho, Jan. 5, 1945; s. Alfred Lorenzo and Meara (Graves) B.; children: Arick, Greg; m. Laurel Jean Bruss, Nov. 19, 1972; 1 child, Joshua Rennie. BS, U. Idaho, 1967; PhD, Purdue U., 1970. Asst. prof. food sci. dept. U. Wis., Madison, 1970-74; asst. prof., assoc. prof. Wash. State U., Pullman, 1974-81, chmn. dept., 1979-81; prof. head dept. U. Nebr., Lincoln, 1981-83; assoc. dean for resident instrn. Coll. Agr., Coll. Agr., U. Idaho, Moscow, 1983-86, prof. food sci. & tech., 1986-93; dean Coll. Agr., U. Idaho, 1986-93; assoc. v.p. U. Idaho, Moscow, 1990-91; chmn. Western Regional Coun., Washington, 1986-90; mem. exec. bd. Consortium for Internat. Devel., Tucson, 1990-91. Co-editor: Antimicrobials in Foods, 1985, Handbook of Food Additives, 1989. Mem. Inst. Food Technologists. Office: U Idaho Coll Agr Moscow ID 83843

BRANIN, JOAN JULIA, financial planner; b. Newark, July 20, 1944; d. Alvin Edwin and Julia (White) B. B.A., Newark State Coll., 1966; M.A., Calif. State U., Long Beach, 1970; M.B.A., UCLA, 1979. CFP. Tchr. Los Alamitos (Calif.) Sch. Dist., 1966-70; sales mgr. Calif. Copy Products, 1970-73; with pharm. sales dept. Lederle Labs., L.A., 1973-75; med. mktg. analyst Am. Hosp. Supply, Glendale, Calif., 1975-78; corp. loan officer Security Pacific, Los Angeles, 1978-80; v.p. First Interstate Bank, 1980-84; v.p., mgr. Standard Chartered Bank, Chgo., 1984-88, v.p., mgr. Union Bank, L.A., 1988-89; v.p., mgr. Chase Manhattan Bank Pvt. Banking Group, L.A., 1989-91; fin. planner retirement and estate planning, Mass. Mut. Ins. Co., 1991—. Contbr. articles to profl. jours. Bd. dirs. L.A. Area Dance Alliance, Calif. Conf. Arts, Young Musicians Found., UCLA Internat. Student Ctr., 1983—, Leadership Coun. United Way Met. div., 1989—, Am. Diabetes Assn., 1989—, Am. Heart Assn., 1990—, Music Ctr. Unified Fund Cabinet and Spl. Gifts Com., CSULB Pres. Assocs. exec. bd., 1991—, Girl Scouts U.S. Chgo. chpt., 1987-88, OxBox Summer Sch. Arts Inst., 1987-88. Recipient Disting. Alumni award Calif. State U. Long Beach. Mem. Internat. Assn. for Fin. Planning, Homemakers Soc. Pasadena (bd. dirs.), Phi Kappa Phi, Pi Lambda Theta, Phi Delta Gamma, Kappa Delta Pi. Democrat. Home: 2043 Allen Ave Altadena CA 91001-3423

BRANKOVICH, MARK J., restaurateur; b. Rijeka, Yugoslavia, Mar. 4, 1922; came to U.S., 1951; s. Joseph M. and Rose (Haydin) B.; m. Marilyn J. Severin, Jan. 4, 1957; children: Mark, Laura. BA in Philosophy, U. Zurich, 1944; student, U. Geneva, 1945, U. Padua, Italy, 1947. Owner The Golden Deer, Chgo., 1953-55; mgr. Gaslight Club, N.Y.C., 1955-57; gen. mgr., exec. v.p., dir. Gaslight Club, Chgo., 1959-63; owner, mgr. Franchise Gaslight Club, L.A., 1963-66; owner Monte Carlo Italian Deli, Burbank, Calif., 1969—, Pinocchio Restaurant, Burbank, 1970—, Pinocchio West, Santa Monica, 1972—, Pinocchio Westwood (Calif.), 1978, Italia Foods Wholesale, Burbank, 1972. Mem. Presdl. Task Force, Washington, 1980—, Rep. Senatorial Inner Circle, 1986. Mem. Internat. Platform Assn. Serbian Orthodox. Home: 1250 Hilldale Ave West Hollywood CA 90069-1826 Office: Monte Carlo Italia Foods Inc 3103 W Magnolia Blvd Burbank CA 91505-3046

BRANN, ALTON JOSEPH, aerospace executive; b. Portland, Maine, Dec. 23, 1941; s. Donald Edward and Marjorie Margaret (Curran) B.; m. Dorothy Marie Mazeika, Sept. 7, 1963 (div. 1977); children—Katherine, Gregory, Alton; m. Anna Jeanine Beaudoin, June 10, 1977. B.A., U. Mass., 1969. Mgr. advanced programs Dynamics Research Corp., Wilmington, Mass., 1969-73; dir. engring. Litton Guidance & Control Systems, L.A., 1973-79, dir. program mgmt., 1979-81, v.p. engring., 1981-83, pres., 1983-86; group exec. Navigation Guidance and Control Systems Group, Beverly Hills, Calif., 1986-88; sr. v.p. Components and Indsl. Products Group Litton Industries, Beverly Hills, 1988-90, pres., chief operating officer, 1990—. Mem., UCLA Fifth Decade Com., 1984. Mem. IEEE (sr. mem.), Inst. Navigation, Air Force Assn., Optical Soc. Am., Los Angles World Affairs Council. Office: Litton Industries 360 N Crescent Dr Beverly Hills CA 90210-4867

BRANNAN, DAVID LEE, musician; b. Pendleton, Oreg., May 31, 1972; s. Jerry Lee and Donna Jean (Miller) B. Student, Blue Mountain Commun. Coll. Environ. aide U.S. Forest Svc., Ukaiah, Oreg., 1990-91. Percussionist, Oreg. East Symphony, Pendleton, 1989; bass, vocalist Blue Jazz, Pendleton, 1991—; mem. vocal quartet Five More or Less, Pendleton, 1992; percussionist coll. prodn. Little Shop of Horrors, Pendleton, 1991. Percussionist Valley Christian Ctr., Milton-Freewater, Oreg., 1991-93; performer Kiwanis Kapers, Pendleton. Recipient various music awards. Republican. Mem. Assembly of God Ch. Home: 812 College St Milton Freewater OR 97862

BRANNON, BRIAN RAY, consultant, writer, lawyer; b. New Hampton, Iowa, Mar. 5, 1944; s. Raymond Phillip and Andrea Yvonne (Robinson) B.; m. Jody Kent, June 21, 1973; children: Shannon Christine, Douglas Brian. BA, U. Iowa, 1966, JD, 1973. Bar: Iowa 1973, Colo. 1986. V.p., trust officer Iowa State Bank & Trust, Iowa City, 1973-76; sr. v.p., mgr. trust dept. 1st Nat. Bank Dubuque, Iowa, 1976-78, U.S. Bank, Grand Junction, Colo., 1978-81; cons., advisor, writer, Grand Junction, 1981—; bd. dirs. Kent News Co., Scottsbluff, Nebr., Adams Co., House Assit Corp. Capt. U.S. Army, 1966-70, Vietnam; Comdr. USAR, 1971-75. Decorated Bronze Star; Cross of Gallantry (Vietnam). Mem. Rotary (bd. dirs. Grand Junction 1991-92), Brookcliff Country Club. Republican. Roman Catholic. Home and Office: 2660 G 3/8ths Rd Grand Junction CO 81506

BRANSON, ALBERT HAROLD (HARRY BRANSON), magistrate judge, educator; b. Chgo., May 20, 1935; s. Fred Brooks and Marie (Vowell) B.; m. Siri-Anne Gudrun Lindberg, Nov. 2, 1963; children: Gunnar John, Gulliver Dean, Hanna Marie, Siri Elizabeth. BA, Northwestern U., 1957; JD, U. Chgo., 1963. Bar: Pa. 1965, Alaska 1972. Atty. Richard McVeigh law offices, Anchorage, 1972-73; ptnr. Jacobs, Branson & Guetschow, Anchorage, 1973-76, Branson & Guetschow, Anchorage, 1976-82; pvt. practice Law Offices of Harry Branson, Anchorage, 1982-84, 85-89; atty. Branson, Bazeley & Chisolm, Anchorage, 1984-85; U.S. magistrate judge U.S. Dist. Ct., Anchorage, 1989—; instr., adj. prof. U. Alaska Justice Ctr., 1980-93; U.S. magistrate, Anchorage, 1975-76. With U.S. Army, 1957-59. Mem. Alaska Bar Assn. (bd. dirs., v.p. bd. govs. 1977-80, pres. bd. govs. 1978-86, Disting. Svc. award 1992, Spl. Svc. award 1988, editor-in-chief Alaska Bar Rag 1978-86), Anchorage Bar Assn. (bd. dirs., bd. govs. 1982-86). Democrat. Office: US Dist Ct # 33 222 W 7th Ave Anchorage AK 99513-7525

BRANTHAVER, JAN FRANKLIN, research chemist; b. Davenport, Iowa, Mar. 12, 1936; s. Franklin Inglis and Ruth Matilda (Doering) B. BA, Millikin U., 1958; PhD, N.D. State U., 1976. Rsch. aide N.D. State U., Fargo, 1964-76; rsch. chemist Laramie (Wyo.) Energy Tech. Ctr., 1976-83; sr. staff rsch. scientist Western Rsch. Inst., Laramie, 1983—. Editor Metal Complexes in Fossil Fuels, 1987; contbr. numerous articles to profl. publs. With U.S. Army, 1959. Mem. Am. Chem. Soc. (sec. Wyo. sect. 1986-87, treas.

1990-93), Sigma Xi. Lutheran. Home: 1000 E Garfield St Apt 17 Laramie WY 82070-4065 Office: Western Rsch Inst 9th and Lewis St Laramie WY 82071

BRANTINGHAM, CHARLES ROSS, podiatrist, ergonomics consultant; b. Long Beach, Calif., Feb. 14, 1917; m. Lila Carolyn Price; children: Paul Jeffery, John Price, Charles Ross, James William. Student, Long Beach City Coll., 1935; D in Podiatric Medicine, Calif. Coll. Podiatric Medicine, 1939, postdoctoral student surgery, 1947. Diplomate Am. Bd. Podiatric Pub. Health. Resident in podiatry Podiatry Clinics, San Francisco, 1939-40; pvt. practice podiatry Long Beach, 1946-56; podiatrist, dir. Podiatric Group, Long Beach, 1956-71, Los Alamitos (Calif.) Podiatric Group, 1971-90; chief podiatry sect., dept. orthopedics Los Alamitos Med. Ctr., 1983-90; ergonomics educator and cons. Nipomo, Calif., 1990—; adj. prof. Calif. State U., Long Beach, 1972-89; vol. faculty Sch. Medicine U. So. Calif., L.A., 1965-92; cons. Specified Products Co., El Monte, Calif., 1969-91, Armstrong World Industries, Lancaster, Pa., 1983-91, Cert. Carpet Svcs., Lancaster, 1991—. Contbr. chpts. to books, articles to profl. jours. Patentee in field. Bd. dirs. Diabetes Assn. So. Calif., L.A., 1964-67; cons., bd. dirs. Comprehensive Health Planning Assn., L.A., 1969-72; pub. improvement and adv. cons. Long Beach City Coun. and Office of Mayor, 1957-67. With USN, 1942-46, to lt. comdr. (ret.) USNR. Fellow Am. Assn. Hosp. Podiatrists (pres. 1958-60), Am. Pub. Health Assn. (sect. coun. pres. 1986, Steven Toth award 1982), Am. Soc. Podiatric Medicine, Internat. Acad. Standing and Walking Fitness (pres. 1963—); mem. Am. Podiatric Med. Assn. (exec. coun. 1957-59, Hall of Sci. award 1973), Calif. Podiatric Med. Assn. (life, pres. 1950), Assn. Mil. Surgeons U.S. (life.), Res. Officers Assn. U.S., Exch. Club (local pres. 1948-49), Ind. Bus. Club (pres. 1958), Nat. Acad. Practice (award 1983). Republican. Mem. LDS Ch. Home and Office: 1541 Los Padres Dr Nipomo CA 93444-9625

BRANTINGHAM, PATRICIA LOUISE, criminology educator; b. St. Louis, June 28, 1943; d. Frederic Lawrence and Mary Louise (Kelley) Matthews; m. Paul J. Brantingham, Aug. 26, 1967; 1 child, Paul Jeffrey Jr. AB in Math., Barnard Coll., 1965; MA in Math., Fordham U., 1966; MSP in Planning, Fla. State U., 1974, PhD in Planning, 1977. System analyst Johnson & Johnson, New Brunswick, N.J., 1966-67, Technicon Corp., Terrytown, N.Y., 1967-68, Hunt-Wesson Foods, Fullerton, Calif., 1968-69, Census Processing Ctr., Tallahassee, Fla., 1971-74; asst. prof. Simon Fraser U., Burnaby, B.C., Can., 1977-80, assoc. prof., 1980-89, prof., 1989—; dir. program evaluation Dept. Justice Can., Ottawa, Ont., 1985-89; cons. crime prevention Tumbler Ridge New Town, B.C., 1980-82; cons. Dept. Justice, Can., 1978-81. Editor: Courts and Diversion, 1981, Enviromental Criminology, 1981, 2d edit. 1991; author: Patterns in Crime, 1984. Mem. Am. Planning Assn., Am. Soc. Criminology (program com. 1978, 85), Can. Criminal Justice Assn. Office: Simon Fraser U, Sch Criminology, Burnaby, BC Canada V5A1S6

BRANTINGHAM, PAUL JEFFREY, criminology educator; b. Long Beach, Calif., June 29, 1943; s. Charles Ross and Lila Carolyn (Price) B.; m. Patricia Louise Matthews, Aug. 26, 1967; 1 child, Paul Jeffrey Jr. BA, Columbia U., 1965, JD, 1968; Diploma in Criminology, Cambridge U., 1970. Bar: Calif. 1969. Asst. prof. Fla. State U., Tallahassee, 1971-76, assoc. prof., 1976-77; assoc. prof. Simon Fraser U., Burnaby, B.C., Can., 1977-85, assoc. dean faculty interdisciplinary studies, 1980-82, prof., 1985—; dir. spl. revs. Pub. Svc. Commn. Can., Ottawa, Ont., 1985-87. Editor: Juvenile Justice Philosophy, 1974, 2d edit. 1978, Environmental Criminology, 1981, 2d edit. 1991; author: Patterns in Crime. Recipient Eisenhower Watch award Columbia U., 1966; Ford Found. fellow, 1969-70. Mem. ABA, Calif. Bar Assn., Am. Soc. Criminology (chmn. nat. program 1978), Canadian Criminal Justice Assn. Home: 4680 Eastridge Rd, North Vancouver, BC Canada V7G 1K4 Office: Simon Fraser U, Sch Criminology, Burnaby, BC Canada V5A 1S6

BRANUM, PAUL MONROE, JR., marketing executive; b. Greenville, Tex., Aug. 27, 1960; s. Paul Monroe and Nicolet Cecil (Brown) B. BA in Polit. Sci. and History, Claremont Men's Coll., 1983; MBA in Internat. Bus., Calif. State U., Fullerton, 1989. Fgn. exch. specialist Thomas Cook Fgn. Currency, Costa Mesa, Calif., 1986-89; mktg. rsch. asst. The Copley Newspapers, La Jolla, Calif., 1989-90; rsch. analyst San Diego Conv. Ctr., 1991; mktg. rsch. analyst The Pennysaver, Vista, Calif., 1991—; cons. in field. Editor econ. ann.: 1990 Annual Review of San Diego Business; author: Ancestry of Paul M. Branum, 1993. Vol. Reagan's 1980 Presdl. Campaign. 1st lt. U.S. Army, 1983-85. Mem. Ams. for Med. Progress Edni. Found., James Madison Soc. of Claremont Men's Coll. (pres. 1982-83). Republican. Christian. Home: 3162 San Helena Oceanside CA 92056 Office: The Pennysaver 1300 Specialty Dr Vista CA 92083

BRASCH, KLAUS RAINER, biology educator; b. Berlin, Fed. Republic of Germany, Dec. 19, 1940; came to U.S., 1983; s. Heinz and Christel (Fauth) B.; m. Margaret Schoning, May 21, 1966; 1 child, Madeleine. BS, Concordia U., Montreal, Can., 1965; MS, Carleton U., Ottawa, Can., 1968, PhD, 1971. Prof. of biology Queen's U., Kingston, Ont., Can., 1973—; prof. biol. sci. U. Tulsa, Okla., 1983—; chmn. biology dept. Calif. State U., San Bernardino, 1990—; cons. Okla. Dept. Agr., Oklahoma City, 1988-90; mem. sci. policy adv. com. for Congressman George E. Brown Jr., chair Com. on Sci., Space and Tech., 1991. Mem. editorial bd. Cellular and Molecular Biology jour., 1989-92; contbr. chpts. to book, articles to profl. jours. Recipient Okla. Health Rsch. award Okla. Ctr. Avancement of Sci., U. Tulsa, 1988-90, Rsch. awards Nat. Rsch. Coun. of Can., 1973-83, U. Tulsa, 1986-89, NSF, 1991, 92, NSF-Tchr. Enhancement award Calif. State U., San Bernardino, 1992-94, also NIH Rsch. award, 1992-94. Mem. AAAS, Am. Soc. for Cell Biology, Can. Soc. for Cell Biology (bd. dirs. 1976), Assn. Lunar and Planetary Observers. Home: 29162 Rock Crest Ct Highland CA 92346-3929 Office: Calif State University Dept of Biology 5500 University Pky San Bernardino CA 92407-2318

BRASDA, BERNARD WILLIAM, trust company owner; b. La Crosse, Wis., May 3, 1938; s. George John and Olga Mary Olive (Hanson) B.; m. Carol June Welch, June, 1962 (div. 1979); children: George Allen, Norma Jean. BA, LaSalle Extension U., 1958; PhD (hon.), Juan Hauz U., 1979. Abstractor's asst. Las Cruces (N.M.) Abstract & Title Co., 1963-66; owner Grant County Abstract Co., Silver City, N.M., 1966-69; chief title officer Transam. Title Ins. co., Casa Grande, Ariz., 1969-72; title officer Title Ins. Co., Minn. and Phoenix, 1972-75; owner Brasda Title Service, Phoenix, 1975-76, 1979—; unit mgr. First Am. Title Ins. Co., Phoenix, 1976-79; instr. searching techniques, pvt. practice, 1975—. With U.S. Army, 1959-63. Republican. Office: Brasda Title Svc PO Box 2357 Phoenix AZ 85002-2357

BRASSELL, ROSELYN STRAUSS, lawyer; b. Shreveport, La., Feb. 19, 1930; d. Herman Carl and Etelka (McMullan) Strauss. BA, La. State U., 1949; JD, UCLA, 1962. Bar: Calif. 1963. Atty. CBS, Los Angeles, 1962-68, sr. atty., 1968-76, asst. gen. atty., 1976-83, broadcast counsel, 1983-91; pvt. practice law L.A., 1991—; instr. TV Prodn. Bus. and Legal Aspects, UCLA Extension, 1992. Co-writer: Life After Death for the California Celebrity, 1985; bd. editors U. Calif. Law Rev., 1960-62. Named Angel of Distinction Los Angeles Cen. City Assn., 1975. Mem. Calif. Bar Assn., Los Angeles County Bar Assn. (exec. com. 1970—, sect. chmn. 1980-81), Beverly Hills Bar Assn., Los Angeles Copyright Soc. (treas. 1977-78, sec. 1978-79, pres. 1981-82), Am. Women in Radio and TV (nat. dir.-at-large 1971-73, nat. pub. affairs chmn. 1977-78, Merit award So. Calif. chpt. 1989), NATAS, Women in Film, Los Angeles World Affairs Coun., U. Calif. Law Alumni Assn. (dir. 1971-74), Order of Coif, Alpha Xi Delta, Phi Alpha Delta. Republican. Home: 33331 Gildlion Cir Monarch Beach CA 92629 Office: 645 N Wilcox Ave Ste 1-D Los Angeles CA 90004

BRATSCH, STEVEN GARY, chemistry educator; b. Torrance, Calif., Nov. 26, 1951; s. Paul James and Marjorie Ruth (Hagen) B. BS, U. Tex., 1977, PhD, 1985. Lab. coord. U. Tex., Austin, 1985-86, instr., 1986-87; asst. prof. U. Conn., Storrs, 1987-88, S.W. Tex. State U., San Marcos, Tex., 1988-90; instr. Honolulu C.C., 1991—; cons. John E. Fetzer Inst., Kalamazoo, Mich., 1990—. Reviewer Jour. of Chem. Edn., 1984—; contbr. articles to profl. jours. Asst. dir. Inner Light Ministries, Honolulu, 1990—. Sgt. USAF, 1972-76. Mem. Internat. Union of Pure and Applied Chemistry (affiliate), Am. Chem. Soc., Sigma Xi. Home: 120 Kuine Pl Honolulu HI 96816

BRATTON, HOWARD CALVIN, judge; b. Clovis, N.Mex., Feb. 4, 1922; s. Sam Gilbert and Vivian (Rogers) B. B.A., U. N.Mex., 1941, LL.D., 1971; LL.B., Yale U., 1947. Bar: N.Mex. 1948. Law clk. U.S. Cir. Ct. Appeals, 1948; ptnr. Grantham & Bratton, Albuquerque, 1949-52; spl. asst. U.S. atty. charge litigation OPS, 1951-52; assoc., then ptnr. Hervy, Dow & Hinkle, Roswell, N.Mex., 1952-64; judge U.S. Dist. Ct. N.Mex., Las Cruces, 1964—, chief judge, 1978-87, sr. judge, 1987—; chmn. N.Mex. Jr. Bar Assn., 1952; pres. Chaves County (N.Mex.) Bar Assn., 1962; chmn. pub. lands com. N.Mex. Oil and Gas Assn., 1961-64, Interstate Oil Compact Commn., 1963-64; mem. N.Mex. Commn. Higher Edn., 1962-64, Jud. Conf. of U.S. Com. on operation of jury system, 1966-72, 79—, Jud. Conf. U.S. Com. on Ethics, 1987—. Bd. regents U. N.Mex., 1958-68, pres., 1963-64; bd. dirs. Fed. Jud. Ctr., 1983-87. Served to capt. AUS, 1942-45. Mem. Trial Judges Assn. 10th Circuit (pres. 1976-78), Nat. Conf. Fed. Trial Judges (exec. com. 1977-79), Sigma Chi. Home: 6760 Via Emma Dr Las Cruces NM 88005-4977 Office: US Dist Ct 200 E Griggs Ave Las Cruces NM 88001-3523

BRAUKER, WILLIAM CHARLES, public information officer; b. Coldwater, Mich., Aug. 2, 1948; s. Robert Glen and Margaret Mae (Elliget) B.; m. Christine Marie Kipp, Oct. 30, 1971 (div. July 1982); 1 child, Robert Eugene; m. Anne Elizabeth Jarvis, Oct. 15, 1983; children: Margaux Anne, Chelsea Elizabeth. BS in Journalism/Polit. Sci., Cen. Mich. U., 1973. Editor, pub. Harrison (Mich.) Star, 1976-78; press sec. U.S. Congressman Don Albosta, Washington, 1978-80; editor Dearborn Heights (Mich.) Leader, 1981-82; dir. pub. info. Madonna U., Livonia, Mich., 1982-83; sr. media rels. officer McAuley Health System, Ann Arbor, Mich., 1983-92; pub. info. officer City & County of Honolulu, 1992—. Chmn. Clare County Dem. Party, Harrison, 1976-78, Clare/Gladwin Intermediate Sch. Dist. Parents Adv. Com., Harrison, 1979-80. Office: 650 S King St Honolulu HI 96813

BRAULT, G(AYLE) LORAIN, healthcare executive; b. Chgo., Jan. 3, 1944; d. Theodore Frank and Victoria Jean (Pribyl) Hahn; m. Donald R. Brault, Apr. 29, 1971; 1 child, Kevin David. AA, Long Beach City Coll., 1963; BS, Calif. State U.-Long Beach, 1973, MS, 1977. RN, Calif. Dir. nursing Canyon Gen. Hosp., Anaheim, Calif., 1973-76; dir. faculty critical care masters degree program Calif. State U., Long Beach, 1976-79; regional dir. nursing and support svcs. Western region Am. Med. Internat., Anaheim, Calif., 1979-83; v.p. Hosp. Home Care Corp. Am., Santa Ana, Calif., 1983-85; pres. Hosp. Home Health Care Agy. Calif., Torrance, 1986-91; sr. v.p. NSI Inc., Torrance, Calif., 1991—; invited lectr. China Nurses Assn., 1983; cons. AMI, Inc., Saudi Arabia, 1983; advisor dept. grad. nursing Calif. State U., L.A., 1988, advisor Nursing Inst., 1990-91; guest lectr. dept. pub. health UCLA, 1986-87; assoc. clin. prof. U. So. Calif., 1988-92. Contbr. articles to profl. jours., chpts. to books. Commr. HHS, Washington, 1988. HEW advanced nurse tng. grantee, 1978. Mem. Women in Health Adminstrn. (sec. 1989, v.p. 1990), Nat. Assn. Home Care, Am. Orgn. Nursing Execs., Calif. Assn. Health Svcs. at Home (task force chmn. 1988, bd. dirs. 1989—, chmn. bd. dirs. 1990-93), Calif. League Nursing (bd. sec. 1983, program chmn. 1981-82), Am. Coll. Health Care Execs., Phi Kappa Phi, Sigma Theta Tau. Republican. Methodist. Home: 1032 E Andrews Dr Long Beach CA 90807-2406

BRAUN, ALAN F., hospitality sales executive; b. Chgo., Jan. 22, 1957; s. Frank Elmer and Janice Fonda (Posey) B. BS in Comm., Ill. State U., Normal, 1979. Conv. svc. mgr. Hyatt Regency O'Hare, Rosemont, Ill., 1979-80; dir. conv. svcs. Hyatt Regency Phoenix, 1980-83; sales mgr. Wild Bills Limousine Svc., Scottsdale, Ariz., 1984-86; dir. sales & mktg. Destination West, Inc., Scottsdale, 1986-90; pres. Western Meetings & Events, Inc., Scottsdale, 1990-92; dir. of sales Destination San Diego, 1992—. Mem. Meeting Planners Internat., Hotel Sales and Mktg. Assn., Soc. Incentive Travel Execs., San Diego Conv. & Visitors Bur. Office: Destination San Diego 8395 Camino Santa Fe San Diego CA 92121

BRAUN, GERRY COLE, oil company executive; b. Washington, Aug. 12, 1948; s. John Walter and Lary Hall (Dalton) B.; m. Christy Lynn Andersen, July 7, 1979; children: Scott, Paul, Brittany. BS, U. Tenn.; MBA, U. S.C. Cost acct. Star-Kist, Terminal Island, 1973-75; mgr. mfg. acctg. Federated Dept. Stores, L.A., 1975-77; chief acct. Santa Fe Internat., Orange, Calif., 1977-80; dir. planning and control Anaconda Advanced Tech. div. Arco, Dublin, Ohio, 1980-87; sr. systems cons. Arco Marine, Long Beach, Calif., 1987-89, mgr. materials and adminstrv. svcs., 1989-91; controller Arco Four Corners Pipe Line, Long Beach, 1992—. Mem. Jr. Achievement. Sgt. U.S. Army, 1971-73. Mem. L.A. Nat. Acctg. Assn., Strategic Planning Forum, Civic Club (treas. Va. chpt. 1966), Kappa Sigma. Democrat. Presbyterian. Home: 2110 Ironbark Cir Brea CA 92621-4417 Office: Arco Marine 300 Oceangate Long Beach CA 90802-6801

BRAUN, JEROME IRWIN, lawyer; b. St. Joseph, Mo., Dec. 16, 1929; s. Martin H. and Bess (Donsker) B.; children: Aaron Hugh, Susan Lori, Daniel Victor; m. Dolores Ferriter, Aug. 16, 1987. AB with distinction, Stanford U., 1951, LLB, 1953. Bar: Mo. 1953, Calif. 1953, U.S. Dist. Ct. (no. dist.) Calif., U.S. Tax Ct., U.S. Ct. Mil. Appeals, U.S. Supreme Ct., U.S. Ct. Appeals (9th cir.). Assoc. Long & Levit, San Francisco, 1957-58, Law Offices of Jefferson Peyser, San Francisco, 1958-62; founding ptnr. Farella, Braun & Martel (formerly Elke, Farella & Braun), San Francisco, 1962—; instr. San Francisco Law Sch., 1958-69; past chmn. and mem. lawyer reps. to 9th Cir. Jud. Conf., chair sr. adv. bd., 1990—; mem. U.S. Dist. Ct. Civil Justice Reform Act Adv. Com., 1991—; speaker various state bar convs. in Calif. Revising editor: Stanford U. Law Rev.; contbr. articles to profl. jours. Mem. Jewish Community Fedn. San Francisco, The Peninsula, Marin and Sonoma Counties, pres., 1979-80; past pres. United Jewish Community Ctrs. 1st lt. JAGC, U.S. Army, 1954-57. Recipient Lloyd W. Dinkelspiel Outstanding Young Leader award Jewish Welfare Fedn., 1967. Mem. ABA, Calif. Bar Assn. (chmn. adminstrn. justice com. 1977), Bar Assn. San Francisco (spl. com. on lawyers malpractice and malpractice ins.), State Bar Mo., Calif., San Francisco Bar Found. (past trustee), Calif. Acad. Appellate Lawyers (past pres.); Am. Judicature Soc. (past dir.), Stanford Law Sch. Bd. of Visitors, Am. Coll. Trial Lawyers (teaching trial and appellate advocacy com.), U.S. Dist. Ct. of No. Dist. Calif. Hist. Soc., 9th Cir. Ct. of Appeals Hist. Soc. (pres. 1990—), Mex.-Am. Legal Def. Fund (honoree), Order of Coif.

BRAUN, STEPHEN HUGHES, psychologist; b. St. Louis, Nov. 20, 1942; s. William Lafon and Jane Louise B.; BA, Washington U., St. Louis, 1964, MA, 1965; PhD (USPHS fellow in Clin. Psychology), U. Mo., Columbia, 1970; m. Penny Lee Prada, Aug. 28, 1965; 1 son, Damian Hughes. Asst. prof. psychology Calif. State U., Chico, 1970-71; dir. social learning div. Ariz. State Hosp., Phoenix, 1971-74; chief bur. planning and evaluation Ariz. Dept. Health Svcs., Phoenix, 1974-79; pres. Braun and Assocs., human svc. program cons.'s, Scottsdale, Ariz., 1979—; v.p. Ariz. Healthcare, 1991—; asst. prof. psychology Ariz. State U., 1971-79, vis. asst. prof. Ctr. of Criminal Justice, 1974-79, Ctr. for Pub. Affairs, 1979-81; cons. Law Enforcement Assistance Adminstrn., NIMH, Alcohol, Drug Abuse, and Mental Health Adminstrn., Ariz. Dept. Health Svcs., Ariz. Dept. Corrections, Ariz. Dept. Econ. Security, local and regional human svc. agys. NIMH rsch. grantee, 1971-74; State of Calif. rsch. grantee, 1971; cert. clin. psychologist, Ariz. Mem. Am. Psychol. Assn., Sigma Xi. Editorial cons.; contbr. articles to profl. pubs. Office: 6122 E Calle Tuberia Scottsdale AZ 85251

BRAUNEGG, GEORGE GWYER, management consultant, accountant; b. Charleroi, Pa., Nov. 29, 1957; s. George Francis and JoAnn Lynn (Gwyer) B.; m. Janet A. Louie, May 2, 1987. BS in Acctg., Indiana U. Pa., 1979; MBA, U. So. Calif., 1981. CPA, Calif. Cons., sr. cons., then mgr. KPMG Peat marwick, L.A., 1981-86; prin. Cast Mgmt. Cons., L.A., 1986—. Contbr. articles to fin. publs. Mem. AICPA (edn. subcom. mgmt. adv. svcs. divsn. 1989-91), Calif. Soc. CPAs. Office: Cast Mgmt Cons Ste 2040N 1620 26th St Santa Monica CA 90404

BRAVERMAN, DONNA CARYN, fiber artist; b. Chgo., Apr. 4, 1947; d. Samuel and Pearl (Leen) B.; m. William Stanley Knopf, Jan. 21, 1990. Student, U. Mo., 1965-68; BFA in Interior Design, Chgo. Acad. Fine Arts, 1970. Interior designer Ascher Dental Supply-Healthco., Chgo., 1970-72, Clarence Krusinski & Assocs. Ltd., Chgo., 1972-74, Perkins & Will Architects, Chgo., 1974-77; fiber artist Fiber Co-op Fibrecations, Chgo., 1977, Scottsdale, Ariz., 1977—. Exhibited in group shows at Mus. Contemporary Crafts, N.Y.C., 1977, James Prendergast Library Art Gallery, Jamestown, N.Y., 1981, Grover M. Herman Fine Arts Ctr., Marietta, Ohio, 1982, Okla. Art Ctr., 1982, Middle Tenn. State U., Murfreesboro, 1982, Redding (Calif.) Mus., 1983, Tucson Mus. Art, 1984, 86, The Arts Ctr., Iowa City, 1985, The Wichita Nat., 1986; in traveling exhibitions Ariz. Archtl. Crafts, 1983, Clouds, Mountains, Fibers, 1983; represented in permanent collections Phillips Petroleum, Houston, Metro. Life, Tulsa, Directory Hotel, Tulsa, Keys Estate Ariz. Biltmore Estates, Phoenix, Sohio Petroleum, Dallas, Reichold Chem., White Plains, N.Y., Rolm Telecommunications, Colorado Springs, Mesirow & Co., Chgo., Exec. House Hotel, Chgo., Cambell Estate, Ariz., Dictaphone Worldhead Quarters, Stratford, Conn., Davenport Bldg., Boston; contbr. articles to profl. jours. Home and Office: 1041 E Glenrosa Ave Phoenix AZ 85014-4435

BRAVERMAN, ROBERT ALLEN, lawyer; b. Oakland, Calif., July 9, 1940; s. Joseph Braverman and Elton Pearl Briggs Rayhill; m. Frances Ternus, Aug. 19, 1967 (div. 1974). BS in Bus. Adminstrn., U. Calif., Berkeley, 1963; JD, U. Calif., San Francisco, 1966. Bar: Calif. Legis. counsel Calif. Legislature, Sacramento, 1966-68; asst. pub. defender Pub Defender of Alameda County, Oakland, 1968-71; atty. in pvt. practice Oakland, 1972—; dir. Ct. Apptd. Atty. Program, Oakland, 1975; hearing officer Alameda County. Pres. Alameda County Dem. Lawyers, Oakland, 1988. With U.S. Army, 1959-63. Mem. Alameda County Bar Assn. (bd. dirs.), Sierra Club, Commonwealth Club, World Affairs Coun., Calif Attys. for Criminal Justice, Lawyers Club of Alameda County, Nat. Wildlife Fedn., Nature Conservancy, Nat. Travel Club. Presbyterian. Office: Law Offices 1611 Telegraph Ave # 1100 Oakland CA 94612

BRAVIN, DON ALAN, ophthalmologist; b. Richmond, Calif., Sept. 10, 1943; s. Aldo Peter and Laura Gertrude (Aversente) B.; m. Elvira Maria Mendez, Dec. 26, 1970; children: Michael, Rosanne, Melissa. MS, U. Calif., San Francisco, 1966; MD, U. Calif., 1968. Diplomate Am. Bd. Ophthalmology. Intern Los Angeles County/U. So. Calif. Med. Ctr., L.A., 1968-69; resident Gorgas Hosp., 1969-72; pvt. practice, Tulare, Calif., 1974—; mem. cons. staff St. Agnes Hosp., Fresno, Calif., 1975—, Kaweah Delta Dist. Hosp., Visalia, Calif., 1987—; mem. courtesy staff Community Hosp., Fresno, 1983—, Visalia Community Hosp., 1987—. Mem. active staff Tulare (Calif.) Dist. Hosp. Lt. M.C., USNR, 1972-74. Fellow Am. Acad. Ophthalmology; mem. AMA, Calif. Med. Assn., Am. Soc. Cataract and Refractive Surgery. Democrat. Roman Catholic. Office: 979 Gem St Tulare CA 93274 also: 5435 Hillsdale Dr Visalia CA 93291

BRAY, ALLEN ANTHONY, manufacturing executive; b. Milw., Apr. 30, 1949. BS, U. Wis.-Stout, 1971. Indsl. engr. Waukesha Mtr. Co., Wis., 1971-73; sr. process engr. Allis-Chalmers Corp., Milw., 1973-77; mgr. mfg. engring. Warner-Electric, Marengo, Ill., 1977-81; prodn. mgr. Energy Adaptive Grinding, Rockford, Ill., 1981-83; mgr. mfg. engring. Schlage Lock Co., Colorado Spgs., Colo., 1983--. Office: Schlage Lock Co 3899 Hancock Expy Colorado Springs CO 80911-1298

BRAY, ELIZABETH ANN, plant physiologist, molecular biologist; b. Ithaca, N.Y., Aug. 18, 1954; d. David William and Estella (Groom) B.; m. Mich Bradley Hein. BA, Mt. Holyoke Coll., 1976; MS, U. Minn., St. Paul, 1978, PhD, 1982. Rsch. asst. U. Minn., St. Paul, 1976-81; rsch. assoc. Mich. State U., East Lansing, 1982-83, Washington U., St. Louis, 1983-85; asst. prof. U. Calif., Riverside, 1985-92, assoc. prof., 1992—. Contbr. articles to profl. jours. Mem. Am. Soc. Plant Physiologists, Internat. Soc. for Plant Molecular Biology. Office: U Calif Dept Bot Plant Sci Riverside CA 92521

BRAY, JEFFREY HOWARD, credit analyst; b. Yreka, Calif., Dec. 24, 1951; s. Eugene Willis and Patricia Clare (Riffel) B.; m. Toni Jean Burket, July 12, 1975; children: Cole, Jess, Laura. BS, Calif. Poly. State U., San Luis Obispo, 1974. Agronomist Dunham and Livesay, Inc., Grenada, Calif., 1974-86; credit officer Farm Credit Svcs., Klamath Falls, Oreg., 1986-87; appraiser Farm Credit Svcs., Central Point, Oreg., 1987-88; credit analyst Farm Credit Svcs., Alturas, Calif., 1988—; mem. Calif. AG Prodn. Consultants Assoc., 1977—, pres., 1982-84, state dir., 1983-85. Dir. Siskiyou Co. Farm Bur., Yreka, Calif., 1983-85; mem. Am. Legion Post 122 Drum & Bugle Corps, Yreka, 1970—; adult leader Cub Scout Pack 51 & Pack 36, Montague, Calif., Yreka, 1987-92; asst. scoutmaster Boy Scout Troop 57, Yreka, 1992, scoutmaster, 1992—. Named one of Outstanding Young Man of Am., 1986. Mem. Am. Soc. Agronomy, Calif. AG Prodn. Consultants Assoc., Alpha Zeta Hon. AG Frat. Republican. Roman Catholic. Home: 2431 Ager Rd Montague CA 96064

BRAY, JO ANN ELIZABETH, travel agent; b. Santa Barbara, Calif., Aug. 4, 1943; d. Robert Ray Payne and Paulyne Elizabeth (Austin) Mason; m. Patrick Lee Jamieson, Aug. 12, 1962 (div. 1973); children: Juliann, Cherie, Robyne. AA, Lassen Coll., 1987. Adminstrv. sec. Kern County, Bakersfield, Calif., 1962-71, supr. welfare dept., 1974-77; exec. sec. J. G. Boswell Ranching, Taft, Calif., 1971-74; supr. welfare dept. Lassen County, Susanville, Calif., 1977-81; mem. emergency rm. staff Lassen Community Hosp., Susanville, 1981-83; correctional officer Calif. State Dept. Corrections, Susanville, 1983-89; mgr., agt. Lassen Comm. Travel, Susanville, 1990-91; owner, mgr. Ready "2" Travel, Susanville, 1991—. Talk show hostess KSUE Radio, Susanville, 1992; sec.-treas. Lassen County Arts Coun., 1984-86; mem. Lassen Vol. Hospice; mem. Critical Incident Stress Debriefing Team. Mem. LWC, Lassen County C. of C. Democrat. Roman Catholic. Home: PO Box 945 Susanville CA 96130

BRAY, JOHN DONALD, magazine publishing executive; b. Valparaiso, Ind., Jan. 7, 1938; s. John Donald Sr. and Marjorie Fair (Gold) B.; m. Mary Ellen Monti, Nov. 9, 1957; children: John L., James B. BA in Mgmt., St. Mary's Coll., Moraga, Calif., 1982. Various positions Pacific Telephone, Calif., 1966-83; v.p. mktg. Am. Telecorp, Redwood City, Calif., 1983-86; pres., pub. Procomm Enterprises mag., San Rafael, Calif., 1986—; advisor Nat. Centrex Users Group, Novi, Mich., 1986; mem. adv. bd. Golden Gate U., San Francisco, 1988—. Contbr. articles to profl. jours. With U.S. Army, 1961-63, Korea. Mem. Bus. Pubs. Assn. Office: Procomm Enterprises Inc 6 School St # 160 Fairfax CA 94930

BRAY, RICHARD DANIEL, literary program director; b. Albany, N.Y., June 19, 1945; s. Harry and Sylvia Jeanette (Weiss) B.; m. Suzannah Greentree, Aug. 17, 1980. AA, Pasadena City Coll., 1966; B.A., San Francisco State U., 1969. Pres. Guild Books, Inc., Chgo., 1979-88; instr. english Columbia Coll. Judge, Carl Sandburg award Friends of Chgo. Pub. Library, 1985-86; literature panelist for L.A. Dept. Cultural Affairs, 1989-90, Calif. Arts Coun., 1989-92, NEA, 1992—. Mem. lit. adv. bd. Ill. Arts Coun., 1985-87, multi-arts adv. com. Chgo. City Arts Program, 1985-87; bd. dirs. Friends of Chgo. Pub. Library, 1985-87, bd. dirs. Coun. Literary Mags. and Presses, 1987-92. Mem. Am. Booksellers Assn. (edn. com. 1987-89), Nat. Writers Union, Am. Writers Congress (exec. 1981-82), Am. Libr. Assn., Calif. Libr. Assn., Midwest PEN (mem. exec. bd. 1985-87). Avocation: magic. Office: PEN Ctr USA West 672 S Lafeyette Park Pl Los Angeles CA 90057

BRAY, R(OBERT) BRUCE, music educator; b. LaGrande, Oreg., July 24, 1924; s. Ernest C. and Leta M. (Haight) B.; m. Donna Marie Siegman, July 2, 1949 (div. 1980); children: Stephen Louis, Ruth Elizabeth, Katherine Ernestine, Anne-Marie. BA, U. Oreg., 1949, MMus, 1955; cert., U. Strasbourg, France, 1951; postgrad., U. Wash., 1960-61. Music tchr. Helen McCune Jr. High Sch., Pendleton, Oreg., 1951-54; dir. choral music Albany (Oreg.) Union High Sch., 1954-56; elem. music supr. Ashland (Oreg.) Public Schs., 1956-57; asst. prof. music Cen. Wash. U., Ellensburg, 1957-60; asst. prof. U. Idaho, Moscow, 1961-67, assoc. prof., 1967-74, prof., 1974-89, prof. emeritus, 1989—, sec. faculty, 1968-88. Editor: Oreg. Music Educator, 1954-57, Wash. Music Educator, 1957-60, U. Idaho Music, 1961-68, Idaho Music Notes, 1963-68, U. Idaho Register, 1974-88 ; editorial bd. Music Educators Jour., 1964-68. With USNR, 1942-46. Mem. AAUP, Music Educators Nat. Conf. (bd. dirs., pres. N.W. div. 1963-65, nat. exec. com. 1964-66), Phi Mu Alpha Sinfonia. Democrat. Episcopalian. Home: W 2411 Second Ave # 2 Spokane WA 99204-1124 Office: U Idaho Brink Hall Rm M6 Moscow ID 83844-1106

BRAZIER, JOHN RICHARD, lawyer, physician; b. Olean, N.Y., Mar. 11, 1940; s. John R. and Edith (Martin) B.; children: Mark, Jennifer. AAS, SUNY, Alfred, 1960; BS in Engring. Physics, U. Colo., 1963, MD, 1969; JD, Santa Clara U., 1989. Bar: Calif., 1989. Intern in surgery Downstate Med. Ctr., Bklyn., 1969-70; resident in surgery U. Colo., Denver, 1970-75; fellowship thoracic and cardiovascular surgery NYU, 1975-77; asst. prof. surgery UCLA, 1977-78; pvt. practice Northridge, 1978-84, Newport News, Calif., 1984-86, Sacramento, 1989—. Fellowship NIH, UCLA, 1972-74. Mem. ABA, AMA, ACS, Am. Coll. Chest Physicians, Calif. Bar, Sacramento County Bar Assn. Home: 1401 36th St Sacramento CA 95816-6606 Office: 915 21st St Sacramento CA 95814-3117

BRAZIER, LESLIE ANN, building services company executive; b. Coronado, Calif., Oct. 1, 1957; d. Lee Joseph and Arlette (Marie) Gaffrey; m. Robert John Brazier, June 18, 1983; 1 child, Julie Marie. AA in Acctg., Southwestern Coll., 1980. Accounts payable supr. Tracor Applied Scis., San Diego, 1980-82; staff acct. Pacific Recorders & Engring., San Diego, 1982-83; acctg. cons. San Diego, 1983-85; staff acct. Hyder & Co., Solana Beach, Calif., 1985-86; acctg. adminstr. Income Growth Mgmt., Solana Beach, 1986-88; v.p., owner Pacific Bldg. Svcs., Vista, Calif., 1988—. Contbr. articles to profl. jours. Assoc. mem. San Diego Rep. Party, 1992; contbg. mem. Calif. Pro-Life Coun., San Diego, 1991—, Nat. Right To Life, Washington, 1991—; active current issues Tri-City Christian Ch. Women's Ministries. Mem. Concerned Women for Am. (Capital hill ptnr. 1990—), Am. Inst. of Profl. Bookeepers, Kappa Alpha Theta (Gamma Sigma chpt.). Office: Pacific Bldg Svcs 770 Sycamore Ave #J116 Vista CA 92083

BRAZIER, ROBERT G., transportation executive. Student, Stanford U. With Airbone Aircraft Service Inc., 1953-63; v.p. ops. Pacific Air Freight Inc., 1963-68; sr. v.p. ops. Airbone Freight Corp., Seattle, 1968-73, exec. v.p., chief operating officer, 1973-78, pres., chief operating officer, dir., 1978—. Office: Airborne Freight Corp PO Box 662 Seattle WA 98111-0662*

BREAKER, RICHARD CARROLL, construction company executive; b. Cambridge, Nebr., Nov. 19, 1926; s. William C. and Clara (Ogorzolka) B.; m. Virginia C. Driscoll, Jan. 30, 1954; children: Kathryn, John, William, Michael. BS in Civil Engring., U. Colo., 1951. Registered profl. engr., Colo. Draftsman U.S. Geological Survey, Denver, 1946-47; engr. Colo. State Hwy. Dept., Denver, 1948-52; engr., estimator Peter Kiewit Sons Co., Denver, 1952-55; project mgr. Webb & Knapp Construction Corp., Denver, 1955-61; estimator Gerald H. Phipps, Inc., Denver, 1961-64, chief estimator, 1964-67, v.p., 1967-84, pres., CEO, 1984-92, also bd. dirs., vice chmn. bd. dirs., 1992—; dir. Gerald H. Phipps, Inc., Denver, 1967—. With USAF, 1944-46. Mem. Am. Arbitration Assn., Associated Gen. Contractors of Colo. (sec. 1986-87, treas. 1987-88), Rolling Hills Country Club, Denver Athletic Club, Denver Country Club. Roman Catholic.

BREASHER, PHILIP M., telecommunications executive; b. Patterson, Calif., July 14, 1941; s. James Franklin and Roselyn (Anderson) B.; m. Tillie Avila, Dec. 26, 1964; children: Galen, Gregory, Gail. AA, Modesto (Calif.) Jr. Coll., 1975. With Evans Telephone Co., Patterson, 1964-77, bus supr., 1978-81; sales mgr. Evans Telecommunications, Modesto, 1982-84; gen. mgr. Evans Telecommunications, Turlock, Calif., 1985-89; v.p. Evans-Executone, Inc., 1989-90; pres. Evans-Executone, Inc., Turlock, Calif., 1990—. Bd. deacons, trustee, Chmn. Evang. Covenant Ch., Patterson Recreational Commn., Patterson Planning Commn.; vice-mayor Patterson City Coun.; gen. chmn. Apricot Festival; bd. dirs. Turlock Econ. Devel. Com. With USN, 1959-63. Mem. Modesto-Stan Trade Club (bd. dirs. 1986-91), Modesto C. of C. (legis. commn.), No. Calif. Ofcl. Assn. (exec. bd. referee football team 1965-90), Sacramento Assn. Coll. Ofcls. (judge 1985-88), Lions (3d v.p. 1987, 2d v.p. 1988, 1st v.p. 1989, pres. 1990-91). Republican. Home: 300 N 5th St Patterson CA 95363-2236 Office: Evans-Executone Inc 4918 Taylor Ct Turlock CA 95380-9579

BRECHBILL, SUSAN REYNOLDS, lawyer, educator; b. Washington, Aug. 22, 1943; d. Irving and Isabell Doyle (Reynolds) Levine; B.A., Coll. William and Mary, 1965; J.D., Marshall-Wythe Sch. Law, 1968; children—Jennifer Rae, Heather Lea. Admitted to Va. bar, 1969, Fed. bar, 1970; atty. AEC, Berkeley, Calif., 1968-73, indsl. relations specialist AEC, Las Vegas, 1974-75; atty. ERDA, Oakland, Calif., 1976-77; atty. Dept. Energy, Oakland, 1977-78, dir. procurement div. San Francisco Ops. Office, 1978-85, asst. chief counsel for gen. law, 1985-93, acting asst. mgr. environ. mgmt. and support, 1992; mem. faculty U. Calif. Extension; speaker Nat. Contract Mgmt. Assn. Ann. Symposiums, 1980, 81, 83, 84, 88; speaker on doing bus. with govt. Leader Girl Scouts U.S.A., San Francisco area. Named Outstanding Young Woman Nev., 1974; recipient Meritorious Svc. award Dept. Energy, 1992. Mem. Va. State Bar Assn., Fed. Bar Assn., Nat. Contract Mgmt. Assn. (pres. Golden Gate chpt. 1983-84, N.W. regional v.p. 1984-86), Nat. Assn. Female Execs. Republican. Contbr. articles to profl. jours. Home: 67 Scenic Dr Orinda CA 94563-3426

BRECHIN, GARRY DAVID, leasing company executive, real estate company executive; b. Wellington, U.K., Dec. 29, 1944; came to U.S., 1969; s. William Charles (stepfather) and Lillian May (Shenton) Harbottle; m. Letitia S.L. Mau, July 21, 1977 (div. Dec. 1982); m. Lynn Suemi, Mar. 17, 1986. Grad. with honors in criminal law, Hendon Police Acad., London, 1961-64. Lic. real estate agt., Hawaii. Asst. comptr. Harrison Hotel (Seagrams), Harrison, B.C., Can., 1967-69; area dir. Tauck Tours, Inc., N.Y.C., 1969-77; adminstrv. v.p. Aloha Motors Ltd., Honolulu, 1977-81; exec. v.p. Shelton Motors Ltd., Honolulu, 1981-83; v.p. Continental Cars Ltd., Honolulu, 1983-85; pres. Plaza Suites, Inc., Honolulu, 1987-91, Global Leasing, Inc., Honolulu, 1985—; exec. v.p. Gen. Pacific Realty, Honolulu, 1987—. Mem. English Speaking Union (v.p. 1989-91), Waikiki Yacht Club (membership chmn.1992-93). Republican. Office: Global Leasing Inc 444 Hobron Ln #211 Honolulu HI 96815-1229

BRECKNER, WILLIAM JOHN, JR., retired air force officer, corporate executive, consultant; b. Alliance, Ohio, May 25, 1933; s. William John and Frances P. (Bertschey) B.; m. Cheryl V. Carmell, Aug. 30, 1963; children—William R., Kristen C. B.A., SUNY, 1976; postgrad., Harvard U., 1980. Vice commandant cadets U.S. Air Force Acad., Colo., 1976-79; comdr. 82d Flying Tng. Wing Williams AFB, Ariz., 1979-80; dep. chief staff logistics Hdqrs. Air Tng. Commd., Tex., 1980-83; chief staff Hdqrs. U.S. Air Force Europe, 1983-84; commdr. 17th Air Force, Sembach AFB, Fed. Republic Germany, 1984-86; maj. gen. U.S. Air Force, 1983-86, retired, 1986; advt. and mktg. cons., bd. dirs. Classic Fuels, Inc. Decorated D.S.M., 1986, Silver Star, 1972, Legion of Merit, 1973, Bronze Star medal, 1973, Air medal, 1968, 72, Purple Heart, 1972, 73, Republic of Vietnam Cross of Gallantry with palm, 1973. Mem. Nat. War Coll. Alumni Assn., Order Daedalians, Air Force Assn., Nam Prisoners of War Inc., Red River Valley Fighter Pilots Assn. Lutheran. Home: 2918 Chelton Dr Colorado Springs CO 80909

BREDDAN, JOE, systems engineering consultant; b. N.Y.C., Sept. 18, 1950; s. Hyman and Sylvia (Hauser) B. BA in Math. and Psychology, SUNY, Binghamton, 1972; MS in Ops. Research, U. Calif., Berkeley, 1975; PhD in Systems Engring., U. Ariz., 1978. Teaching and research assoc. Dept. Systems and Indsl. Engring. U. Ariz., Tucson, 1975-79; project engr. B.D.M. Services Co., Tucson, 1979-80; mem. tech. staff Bell Labs., Am. Bell, AT&T Info. Systems, Denver, 1980-86; staff mgr. AT&T, Denver, 1986-91; pvt. practice cons. Boulder, Colo., 1991—. Patentee in field. Regents scholar N.Y. State Bd. Regents, 1968. Home and Office: 8812 Elgin Dr Lafayette CO 80026

BREDE, ANDREW DOUGLAS, research director, plant breeder; b. Pitts., Feb. 4, 1953; s. James Faris and Adele Katherine (Konefal) B.; m. Linda Davis Rudd, Jan. 11, 1992; children from previous marriage: Loralee Elizabeth, Michael Douglas. BS, Pa. State U., 1975, MS, 1978, PhD, 1982. Asst. golf course supt. Valley Brook Country Club, McMurray, Pa., 1975-76; grad. rsch. asst. Pa. State U., University Park, 1976-82; assoc. prof. Okla. State U., Stillwater, 1982-86; dir. rsch. Jacklin Seed Co., Post Falls, Idaho, 1986—; v.p. Turfgrass Breeders Assn., Tangent, Oreg., 1989-91; chmn. variety review Lawn Inst., Pleasant Hill, Tenn., 1990-91. Contbr. articles to profl. jours. (21 to Agronomy Jour.), 120 to mags.; producer 15 ednl. videos. Rsch. grantee, 1983-86. Mem. Am. Soc. Agronomy, Am. Radio Relay League, Gamma Sigma Delta, Phi Epsilon Phi, Phi Kappa Phi, Phi Sigma. Republican. Office: Jacklin Seed Co 5300 W Riverbend Rd Post Falls ID 83854-9499

BREEDLOVE, S. MARC, psychology educator; b. Springfield, Mo., June 20, 1954; s. John T. and Lula (Collins) B.; children: Benjamin, Nicholas, Tessa. BA, Yale U., 1976; MA, UCLA, 1978, PhD, 1982. Prof. psychology U. Calif., Berkeley, 1982—. Cons. editor Hormones and Behavior; assoc. editor Jour. Neurosci.; co-editor: Behavioral endocrinology, 1991; contbr. articles to profl. jours. Recipient Angier prize, Yale U., 1976, Franz award, UCLA, 1979, Lindsley prize, Soc. for Neursci., 1982, Early Career award, Am. Psychol. Assn., 1987; named. Presdl. Young Investigator, NSF, 1985. Mem. Am. Psychol. Soc., Am. Psychol. Assn., Soc. for Neurosci., Soc. for Sci. Study of Sex. Office: University of California Dept Psychology Berkeley CA 94720

BREELAND, KEVIN MARK, mortgage loan officer; b. Hunstanton, Norfolk, Eng., Feb. 9, 1957; came to U.S., 1958; s. Allen H. Breeland Jr. and Frances Naomi O'Dell; m. Stacey Lynn Smith, Dec. 10, 1983 (div. Feb. 1986); 1 child, Brandon Allan O'Brien Breeland; m. Paula Christine Patterson, Mar. 25, 1989; children: Tara Brooke Breeland, Ryan Charles Breeland. Student, McNeese State U., Lake Charles, La., 1976. Sr. asst. mgr. Assocs. Fin. Svcs., various locations, La., Tex., 1979-82; loan officer Longview (Tex.) Savs., 1982-83; mortgage loan officer Lumberman's, Waco, Tex., 1984, Am. Nat. Bank, Waco, 1084-85; pres., loan office Mannda Equities Co., Dallas, 1985; collection officer No. Collection, Anchorage, 1985-87; mortgage loan officer Columbia Mortgage Co., Anchorage, 1987-88, GMAC Mortgage, Anchorage, 1988, Seattle Mortgage Co., Anchorage, 1988—. Author editorials; sports editor. Devel. chmn. Food Bank of Alaska, Anchorage, 1990-92, v.p., 1991-92. Mem. Alaskan Bay Owners Assn. (sec. 1990, pres. 1991—). Republican. Baptist. Home: 10871 Kauishak Bay Cir Anchorage AK 99515 Office: Seattle Mortgage Co 560 E 34th Ste 100 Anchorage AK 99503

BREEN, THOMAS ALBERT, financial services executive; b. Ft. Benning, Ga., Apr. 18, 1956; s. Thomas Alden and Anne Marie (Brun) B.; m. Linda Whitney, June 16, 1979; children: Matthew, Andrew. BSBA in Acctg., Colo. State U., 1979. CPA, Colo. With audit staff Coopers & Lybrand, Denver, 1979-81; audit supr. Hein & Assocs., Denver, 1981-84; v.p. fin. Orion Broadcast Group, Inc., Denver, 1984-89, Englewood, Colo., 1989—; bd. dirs. FN Realty Svcs., Inc., Pasedena, Calif., Vehicle Resource Corp., FNRS Fin. Corp. Mem. AICPA, Colo. Soc. CPA's. Office: Orion Broadcast Group Inc 6061 S Willow Dr Ste 117 Englewood CO 80111-5149

BREEZLEY, ROGER LEE, banker; b. Williston, N.D., Apr. 1, 1938. B.B.A., U. N.D. C.P.A., Oreg. Acct. Haskins & Sells, 1960-68; pres. Moduline Internat. Inc., 1968-77; with U.S. Bancorp, Portland, Oreg., 1977—, with corp. devel. and fin. analysis depts., 1977-79, sr. v.p. fin. analysis planning, 1979-80, exec. v.p., 1980-82, treas., 1980-87, vice chmn., 1982-87, chief oper. officer, 1983-87, dir., chmn., chief exec. officer, 1987—. Office: US Bancorp PO Box 4412 111 SW 5th Ave # 8837 Portland OR 97204-3604

BREGMAN, JENN SWENSON, lawyer; b. Williston, N.D., June 22, 1960; d. Richard Carl and Elisabeth (Jirgensons) Swenson; m. Jerry Lyle Bregman, Jan. 2, 1989. MusB magna cum laude, U. Denver, 1984; JD, UCLA, 1989. Bar: Calif. 1989, U.S. Ct. Appeals (9th cir.) 1989. Atty. Baker & McKenzie, L.A., 1989-90, Farmer & Ridley, L.A., 1990—. Contbr. article to profl. mag. Mem. L.A. County Bar Assn., Women's Lawyers Assn. L.A., Gamma Phi Beta. Democrat. Lutheran. Home: 11771 Texas Ave # 4 Los Angeles CA 90025-1621 Office: Farmer & Ridley 444 S Flower St Ste 2300 Los Angeles CA 90071-2956

BREIDENTHAL, ROBERT EDWARD, fluid mechanics educator, consultant; b. Washington, Oct. 9, 1951; s. Robert Edward Sr. and Ila May (Heller) B.; m. Cathy Jo Shisler, June 9, 1973 (div. Jan. 1991); children: Matthew John, Ian Thomas. BS in Aero. Engring., Wichita (Kans.) State U., 1973; MS, Calif. Inst. Tech., 1974, PhD, 1979. Post-doctoral rsch. fellow Calif. Inst. Tech., Pasadena, 1979-80; rsch. asst. prof. U. Wash., Seattle, 1980-83, asst. prof., 1983-87, assoc. prof., 1987—; cons. Boeing Aerospace Co., Kent, Wash., 1980-89, Rocketdyne div. Rockwell Internat., Canoga Park, Calif., 1987-90, Asea Brown Boveri Ltd., Baden, Switzerland, 1989—. Contbr. numerous articles to profl. jours.; inventor mineral wool prodn., shock wave kidney stone treatment, combuster design. Area chair Calif. Inst. Tech. Alumni Fund, Seattle U. dist., 1990. Recipient Earl R. Hutton scholarship, 1969-73, NSF fellowship, 1973-76, Donald W. Douglas fellowship, 1973-78. Mem. Am. Inst. Aerodyns. and Astronautics (fluid mechanics tech. com.), Am. Phys. Soc., Am. Geophys. Union, Soaring Soc. Am., Evergreen Soaring, Omicron Delta Kappa, Tau Beta Pi, Sigma Gamma Tau. Home: 10306 Sand Point Way NE Seattle WA 98125-8156 Office: U Wash FS-10 Seattle WA 98195

BREINER, RICHARD HARRY, judge; b. Milw., Feb. 28, 1935; s. James and Fannie (Appel) B.; m. Dorothy Landau, Oct. 30, 1960; children: Daniel James, Deborah Lynn. Student, Washington U., St. Louis, 1953-55; AB, U. Mo., Columbia, 1957; JD, U. Mo., 1961. Bar: Calif. 1962, Mo. 1961, U.S. Supreme Ct. 1973, U.S. Dist. Ct. (no. dist.) Calif. 1962, U.S. Ct. Appeals (9th cir.) 1976. Atty. U.S. Dept. Labor, San Francisco, 1961-62; assoc. Gladstein et al, San Francisco, 1962-65, Conn, Breiner, et al, San Rafael, Calif., 1965-77; dep. pub. def. County of Marin, San Rafael, 1965-70; dep. city atty. City of Tiburon (Calif.), 1965-77; city atty. City of Belvedere (Calif.), 1976-77; judge Marin County Superior Ct., San Rafael, Calif., 1977—, presiding judge, 1980-81, 85, 87-88, 93; assoc. judge pro tempore Ct. Appeal, 1983; assoc. justice pro tempore Calif. Supreme Ct., 1985; presiding judge appellate dept. Marin County Superior Ct., San Rafael, Calif., 1982, 84, justice, 1978, 82-84, 86, 88, 90, 91, 92, 93. Contbr. articles to profl. jours. Bd. dirs. The Branson Sch., Ross, Calif., 1988-91; trustee Big Bros. of Marin, San Rafael, 1973-84. 1st lt. U.S. Army, 1957-59. Mem. Calif. Judges Assn. (bd. dirs. 1984-87, v.p. 1986-87, chair jud. ethics com. 1989-90, Pres. award 1992), San Francisco Am. Inn. of Ct. (benchmaster 1988—, pres. 1992-93), Phi Beta Kappa. Democrat. Jewish. Office: Marin County Superior Ct Hall of Justice C92 San Rafael CA 94903

BREINER, ROSEMARY, contractor; b. Las Vegas, N. Mex., Oct. 25, 1937; d. Gregorio and Lucia (Madrid) Montoya; m. James Kilroy Breiner, Sept. 5, 1959; children: Alicia Kathleen, James Kilroy II, Terrance Kevin, Margaret Eileen. Student, U. Denver, 1956-58, 88-89. Pres. Breiner Constrn. Co., Inc., Denver, 1969—; mem. exec. bd. Associated Gen. Contractors (legis. com. 1988—, liaison to hispanic contractors 1990—), Denver, 1987—; S.W. Regional Dir. Women Constrn. Owners &Execs., Wash. State, 1988—. Mem. Nat. Resource Com. Sisters of St. Joseph (vice chair 1992), St. Louis, 1988—. Office: Breiner Constrn Co 1400 Oneida St Denver CO 80220

BREITBART, BARBARA RENEE, psychologist, administrator; b. N.Y.C.; d. Bernard John and Sally Etta (Horwitz) Garson; m. Sheldon Lewis Breitbart; children: Stacey Jana, Kevin Harrison. A.B., Syracuse U., 1973; M.A., Adelphi U., 1975, Ph.D., 1978. Lic. psychologist, N.Y. Pvt. practice Great Neck, N.Y., 1979-89; editor-in-chief Who's Who in The Biobehavioral Scis., 1983—; pres. Rsch. Inst. Psychophysiology, Sedona, Ariz., 1980—; pres., chief exec. officer Enchantment Resort, Sedona, 1990-92; cons. on wellness; editor Who's Who in the Biobehavioral Scis., N.Y.C., 1984—; columnist, lectr. on behavioral medicine and psychophysiology, 1978—; guest on radio talk shows. Bd. dirs. Sedona Cultural Pk., Ariz. Indian Living Treasures, La Chaine des Rotisseurs. Mem. Am. Psychol. Assn., Sedona-Oak Creek Canyon C. of C. (bd. dirs.).

BREITENBACH, MARY LOUISE MCGRAW, psychologist, drug rehabilitation counselor; b. Pitts., Sept. 26, 1936; d. David Evans McGraw and Louise (Schoch) Neel; m. John Edgar Breitenbach, Apr. 15, 1960 (dec. 1963); m. Joseph George Piccoli III, Aug. 15, 1987; 1 dau. Kirstin Amethyst. Postgrad., Oreg. State Coll., 1960-61; BA, Russell Sage Coll., Troy, N.Y., 1958; MEd, Harvard U., 1983. Lic. profl. counselor, Wyo.; lic. chem. dependency specialist, Wyo.; cert. addiction specialist, level III; nat. cert. addiction counselor II. Paraprofessional psychologist St. John's Episc. Ch., Jackson, Wyo., 1963-82; pvt. practice Wilson, Wyo., 1983—; counselor Curran/Seeley Found. Addiction Svcs., Jackson, 1989-91, Van Vleck House/ Tri-County Group Home, Jackson, 1986-89, others. Trustee Teton Sci. Sch., Kelly, Wyo, 1960-76; pres. bd. govs. Teton County Mus. Bd., Jackson; vestry mem. St. John's Ch., Jackson. Mem. Am. Psychol. Assn., Wyo. Psychol. Assn., Wyo. Assn. Counseling and Devel., Wyo. Assn. Addiction Specialists. Democrat. Episcopalian. Home and Office: Star Rte Wilson WY 83014

BREITWEISER, JAMES RUSSELL, insurance company executive; b. Ogden, Utah, Oct. 19, 1936; s. Elmer Ellsworth and Helen (Russell) B.; m. Rose Mary Holley; children: J. Curtis, Tricia R., Cherise H., Marci A. ASBA, Weber State U., 1958; BSBA, Utah State U., 1960; MSBA, Calif. State U., Sacramento, 1965; CLU, Am. Coll. Life Underwriters, 1975. Sales rep. Procter & Gamble, Stockton, Calif., 1960-62, J.B. Roerig (Div. of Pfizer Labs), Stockton, Calif., 1962-66; dist. sales mgr. Allstate Ins. Co., Bakersfield, Calif., 1966-68; ins. agt. N.Y. Life, New Eng. Life, Ogden, 1968-71; v.p. First Security Ins., Inc., Salt Lake City, 1971-77; pres. Integrated Fin. Mktg., Inc., Ogden, 1987—; owner, ins. agt. Breitweiser Ins. Svcs., Ogden, 1977-92; adj. instr. Weber State U., 1977-87; ins. cons. Ogden First Fed. Savs. and Loan, 1977—. Bd. dirs. Hospice No. Utah, 1993—. Served with USN, 1955-57. Mem. Ogden Exch. Club (pres. 1984-85), Ogden Assn. CLU (pres. 1984-85), Ogden Assn. Ind. Ins. Agts. (pres. 1980-81), Ind. Ins. Agts. of Utah Assn. (pres. 1990-91), Greater Ogden C. of C., Pi Kappa Alpha (hon.). Republican. Mem. LDS Ch. Home: 5278 S 1300 E Ogden UT 84403-4557 Office: Breitweiser Ins Svcs 4155 Harrison Blvd Ste 202 Ogden UT 84403-2463

BRELAND, ALBERT EDWARD, JR., psychiatrist; b. Hattiesburg, Miss., Dec. 29, 1939; s. Albert Edward and Gladys (Lee) B.; m. Annis Julia Pepper, Mar. 20, 1960 (div. 1970); children: Albert Edward III (dec.), Robert Lee; m. Nancy Viola Horner, Dec. 26, 1971; children: Adrienne Elizabeth, Kenneth Clifford. MD, U. Miss., 1963. Diplomate Am. Bd. Psychiatry and Neurology. Rotating intern U. Med. Ctr., Jackson, Miss., 1963-64, neurology resident, 1964-67; neurologist Swiss Ave. Med. Clinic, Dallas, 1967-68, VA Hosp., Jackson, Miss., 1970-74, Neurologic Physicians of Ariz., Inc., Mesa, 1974-84; med. officer CIA, S.E. Asia and Washington, 1984-92; resident in psychiatry U. Calif., San Diego, 1988-91; psychiatrist/neurologist VA Hosp., Sheridan, Wyo., 1992—; pres. med. staff Desert Samaritan Hosp., Mesa, 1980-81; dir. Muscular Dystrophy Clinic, Muscular Dystrophy Assocs., Phoenix/Mesa, 1975-83. Contbr. articles to profl. jours. Maj. U.S. Army, 1968-70. Am. Heart Assn. Stroke Coun. fellow, 1978. Mem. AMA, Maricopa County Med. Soc., Alpha Omega Alpha. Methodist. Office: VAMC Dept Psychiatry 1898 Fort Rd Sheridan WY 82801

BREM, ROBERT JOHN, psychotherapist, political theorist; b. Niagara Falls, N.Y., May 5, 1958; s. Joseph C. and Jane A. (Tiefel) B. Grad., Army & Navy Acad., 1976; AA, Scottsdale C.C., 1982; BS in Polit. Sci., Ariz. State U., 1985, MA in Polit. Sci., M in Counseling, 1989. Cert. counselor, NCC. Cons. ACORN, Phoenix, 1985; rsch. assoc. Ariz. State U., Tempe, 1985-89; crisis counselor Empact, Tempe, 1989-90; therapist Ctr. Against Sexual Abuse, Phoenix, 1989-90; clin. coord. Touchstone Community, Inc., Phoenix, 1990—; pvt. practice cons., therapist Tempe, 1991—; adj. prof. Rio Salado C.C., Phoenix, 1992; bd. dirs. Earth Trust, Phila., Ariz. Coun. for Sustainable Devel., Phoenix. Asspc. editor Jour. Dry Heat. Environ. activist Greenpeace, Green politics, Franciscan Renewal Ctr., Ariz., 1985—; mem. So. Poverty Law Ctr. Paul Harris fellow Rotary Internat., 1989. Mem. Internat. Platform Assn., Ariz. Counselor Assn. (del. 1991—), Greenpeace USA, Amnesty Internat. Democrat.

BREMER, DONALD DUANE, school administrator; b. Sioux City, Iowa, June 19, 1934; s. Donald Forbes and Irma Marjorie (Schaller) B.; m. Carol Louise Rankin, May 3, 1955; children—Douglas Duane, Robert Alan, Kevin Ray. B.A., Nebr. State U., 1958; M.A. sch. adminstr., Los Angeles State U., 1962; postgrad., U. Iowa, 1966, U. Calif., Riverside, 1967. Cert. tchr., Calif. Math. tchr. Chino Unified Sch. Dist., Calif., 1958-66; tchr. Chaffey Jr. Coll., Alta Loma, Calif., 1961-63; prin. summer sch., Chino Schs., 1966-67; vice prin. Ramona Jr. High Sch., Chino, 1967-77; prin. Boys Republic High Sch., Chino, 1978—, chmn. accreditation com., 1981-82. Com. chmn., asst. cubmaster Mt. Baldy coun. Boy Scouts Am., 1966-68; mem. Rep. Senatorial Com. Grantee NSF, 1964. With U.S. Army, 1954-56. Mem. NEA, Calif. Tchrs. Assn., Assn. Calif. Sch. Adminstrs., Chino Adminstrs. Assn. (treas. 1971-73, pres. 1973-74), Am. Legion, Chino C. of C., Toastmasters, Rotary (pres. 1990-91), Masons, Elks. Home: 12183 Dunlap Pl Chino CA 91710-2331 Office: Boys Republic High Sch Chino CA 91709

BREMS, DAVID PAUL, architect; b. Lehi, Utah, Aug. 10, 1950; s. D. Orlo and Gearldine (Hitchcock) B.; m. Johna Devey Brems; 1 child, Stefan Tomas Brems. B.S., U. Utah, 1973, M.Arch., 1975. Registered architect, Utah, Calif., Colo., Ariz., Wyo., N.Mex., Idaho, Mont., Wash. Draftsman, Environ. Assoc., Salt Lake City, 1971-73; draftsman/architect intern Environ. Design Group, Salt Lake City, 1973-76; architect/intern Frank Fuller AIA, Salt Lake City, 1976-77; prin. Edwards & Daniels, Salt Lake City, 1978-83; pres. David Brems & Assocs., Salt Lake City, 1983-86; prin. Gillies, Stransky, Brems, Smith P.C., Salt Lake City, 1986—; adj. prof. U. Utah Grad. Sch. Architecture, 1990—; mem. urban design com. Assist, Inc., Salt Lake City, 1982—, Salt Lake County Planning Commn., 1991—, chmn., 1992—; invited lectr. Wyo Soc. Architects, sch. engring. U. Utah, 1993. Prin. works include solar twinhomes Utah Holiday, (Best Solar Design award), Sun Builder, Daily Jour., Brian Head Day Lodge, Easton Aluminum, Four Seasons Hotel, Gore Coll. Bus., CMF Tooele, Utah Regional Corrections Facility, St. Vincents De Paul Ctr., Steiner Aquatic Ctr., U. Utah Football Support Facility, Sports Medicine West, West Jordan Community Water Park, Utah Nat. Guard Apache Helicopter Hangar & Armory, Kashmitter Residence, St. Thomas More Cat. Ch.; mem. Leadership Utah. Recipient awards AM. Concrete Inst., 1993. Mem. AIA (pres. Salt Lake chpt. 1983-84, pres. Utah Soc. 1987, chmn. Western Mountain Region conf., 1986, com. on design 1990—, chmn. com. on environment Utah chpt. 1993, sustainable architecture community Utah chpt. 1993, Honor awards 1983, 88, Merit awards 1983,85, 88, 93, chmn. Western Mountain Region honor awards 1988. PCI award 1988. IFRAA award 1988, Jr. Colo. West awards 1992), Am. Solar Energy Soc., Hobie Fleet 67 (commodore 1985-86)), Illuminating Engring. Soc. (assoc.), Bronze medalist 1991 Utah Summer Games, Silver Medalist 1992 Utah Summer Games. Home: 161 Young Oak Rd Salt Lake City UT 84108-1645

BREMSER, GEORGE, JR., electronics company executive; b. Newark, May 26, 1928; s. George and Virginia (Christian) B.; m. Marie Sundman, June 21, 1952 (div. July 1979); children: Christian Fredrick II, Priscilla Suzanne, Martha Anne, Sarah Elizabeth; m. Nancy Kay Woods, Oct. 27, 1983 (div. Feb. 1989). BA, Yale U., 1949; postgrad., U. Miami, 1959; MBA, NYU, 1962. With McCann-Erickson Inc., N.Y.C., 1952-61; asst. gen. mgr. McCann-Erickson Inc., Bogota, Columbia, 1955, gen. mgr., 1955-57; account supr. McCann-Erickson Inc., N.Y.C., 1958; v.p., mgr. McCann-Erickson Inc., Miami, Fla., 1959-61; with Gen. Foods Corp., White Plains, N.Y., 1961-71; v.p., gen. mgr. internat. div. Gen. Foods Europe, White Plains, N.Y., 1967; pres. Gen. Foods Internat., White Plains, 1967-71; group v.p. Gen. Foods Corp., White Plains, 1970-71; chmn., pres., chief exec. officer Texstar Corp., Grand Prairie, Tex., 1971-81; exec. v.p. Shaklee Corp., San Francisco, 1981-82; chmn., pres., chief exec. officer Etak Inc., Menlo Park, Calif., 1983-88, chmn., 1989—; bd. dirs. PBI Industries Inc. Trustee Union Ch., Bogota, 1956-57; Dem. county committeeman, Ridgewood, N.J., 1962-63; mem. New Canaan (Conn.) Town Council, 1969-73; founder, past pres. Citizens Com. for Conservation, New Canaan; mem. coun. Save the Redwoods League, 1987—. Served to 2d lt. USMC 1950-52, capt. Res. Mem. Phi Beta Kappa, Beta Gamma Sigma, Beta Theta Pi. Congregationalist. Clubs: New Canaan Country; Brook, Metropolitan, Yale (N.Y.C.); Block Island; Casino (Nantucket, Mass.); Explorers. Home: 535 Everett Ave Palo Alto CA 94301-1547 also: Mansion Beach Rd Block Island RI 02807 Office: care Etak Inc 1430 Obrien Dr Menlo Park CA 94025-1486

BRENGLE, THOMAS ALAN, computer scientist; b. San Diego, Sept. 22, 1952; s. Alan Seymour and Nadeene Marie (Clark) B.; m. Anita Anne Jones, June 22, 1974; children: Adam Thomas, Evan John. BS in Physics, Harvey Mudd Coll., 1974; MS in Physics, So. Ill. U., 1976. Research asst. So. Ill. U., Edwardsville, 1975-76; physicist Lawrence Livermore (Calif.) Nat. Lab., 1976-77, computer scientist, 1977-79, group leader, 1979-86, mgr. user service ctr., 1983-86, assoc. div. leader, 1986-91, staff tech. asst., 1991—.

Contbr. numerous articles to profl. jours. Bd. trustees Lammersville Sch. Dist., 1989—, clk., 1989-90, pres., 1990-91. Mem. ARRAY (sec./treas. nat. chpt. 1982-83, v.p. 1983-84, pres. 1984-85). Home: 16312 Diablo Ct Tracy CA 95376-9758 Office: Lawrence Livermore Nat Lab PO Box 808 L-548 Livermore CA 94551-0808

BRENNAN, BARBARA JANE, manufacturing company executive; b. Oklahoma City, Mar. 22, 1936; d. Chanc T. and Mary E. (Parker) Roos; m. Donald H. Brennan, Sept. 13, 1958 (dec. Feb. 1989); children: Bridget, Brian, Joe (dec.), Kerry, Patrick. Student, U. Okla., 1954-58. Dir. pub. relations The Rehab. Ctr., Albuquerque, 1972-76, coord. community svcs., 1976-81; gen. mgr. RC Ink, Albuquerque, 1981-88; pres./chief executive officer Stride, Inc., Albuquerque, 1988—; pres. Presentation, Inc., Albuquerque; bd. dirs. Very Spl. Arts N.Mex., 1992—. Ward chmn. Springfield (Va.) Dem. party, 1964; pres. Albuquerque High Sch. PTA, 1976-77; chmn. St. Patrick's Day Benefit Dinner, Albuquerque, 1981-83; pres. Little Bros. Good Shepherd Aux., Albuquerque, 1981-83. Named Woman on the Move Albuquerque YWCA, 1992. Mem. Rotary Club (Rotarian of Month Dec. 1991). Democrat. Roman Catholic. Office: Stride Inc 607 4th St NW Albuquerque NM 87102-2103

BRENNAN, CIARAN BRENDAN, accountant, independent oil producer, real estate developer; b. Dublin, Ireland, Jan. 28, 1944; s. Sean and Mary (Stone) B. BA with honors, Univ. Coll., Dublin, 1966; MBA, Harvard U., 1973; MS in Acctg., U. Houston, 1976. Lic. real estate broker, Calif.; CPA, Tex. Auditor Coopers & Lybrand, London, 1967-70; sr. auditor Price Waterhouse & Co., Toronto, Ont., Can., 1970-71; project acctg. specialist Kerr-McGee Corp., Oklahoma City, 1976-80; contr. Cummings Oil Co., Oklahoma City, 1980-82; chief fin. officer Red Stone Energies, Ltd., 1982, Hibernia Oil Inc., 1980—; treas., chief fin. officer Leonoco, Inc., 1982-87, JKJ Supply Co., 1983-87, Saturn Investments Inc., 1983-87, JFL Co., 1984-87, Little Chief Drilling & Energy Inc., 1984-85; pres. Ciaran Brennan Corp., 1990, Rathgar Securities, Inc., 1989-90; CFO Nationwide Industries, 1991—; bd. dirs., cons. sml. oil cos.; adj. faculty Okla. City U., 1977-86; vis. faculty Cen. State U., 1977-86. Contbr. articles to profl. jours. Mem. Inst. Chartered Accts. England and Wales, Inst. Chartered Accts. Can., Inst. Chartered Accts. in Ireland, AICPA, Tex. Soc. CPAs, Okla. Soc. CPAs, Calif. Soc. CPAs, L.A. Bd. Realtors. Republican. Roman Catholic.

BRENNAN, JERRY MICHAEL, economics educator, statistician, reseacher, clinical psychologist; b. Grosse Pointe, Mich., July 17, 1944; s. Walter X. and Aretta May (Gempler) B. Student Kalamazoo (Mich.) Coll., 1962-64, Pasadena (Calif.) City Coll., 1966-67; B.A., UCLA, 1969; M.A., U. Hawaii, 1973, Ph.D., 1978. Researcher, UCLA, 1968-69; researcher U. Hawaii, 1972, 74-78, cons., 1975, 77, 78, data analyst and statis. cons., 1979-80, lectr., 1976-80, asst. prof. econs., 1980—; pres. Sugar Mill Software, 1986—; cons. WHO; v.p. Forest Inst. Profl. Psychology. Light scholar, 1964-66. Mem. Am. Psychol. Assn., Soc. Multivariate Exptl. Psychology, Psychometric Soc., Western Psychol. Assn., AAUP, Hawaii Ednl. Research Assn. Contbr. psychol. articles to profl. jours. Address: 651 Kaumakani Honolulu HI 96825

BRENNAN, JOAN STEVENSON, judge; b. Detroit, Feb. 21, 1933; d. James and Betty (Holland) Stevenson; m. Lane P. Brennan, June 26, 1954 (div. 1970); children: Suzanne, Steven, Clayton, Elizabeth, Catherine. BA, Skidmore Coll., 1954; JD, Santa Clara U., 1973. Bar: Calif. Dep. dist. atty. Dist. Attys. Office, Santa Clara, Calif., 1974-78; legal counsel U.S. Leasing Internat., San Francisco, 1978-79; asst. U.S. atty. U.S. Dist. Ct. (no. dist.) Calif., San Francisco, 1980-82, U.S. Magistrate judge, 1982—. Mem. Nat. Assn. Women Judges, Nat. Assn. Magistrate Judges. Democrat. Office: US Dist Ct PO Box 36054 450 Golden Gate Ave San Francisco CA 94102

BRENNEMAN, RICHARD JAMES, writer, television producer; b. Abilene, Kans., July 23, 1946; s. Louis James and Sarah Marie (Larsen) B.; m. Carolyn Maraldo (div.); 1 child, Derald Jeremiah; m. Laura Shelton, May 1, 1982; children: Jacqueline Elizabeth, Samantha Marie. Student, Adams State Coll., 1963-65. Journalist Rev. Jour., Las Vegas, 1966-67; city editor Blade Tribune, Oceanside, Calif., 1967-71; assoc. editor Psychology Today, Del Mar, Calif., 1971-72; freelance writer Oakland, Calif., 1972-75; journalist Santa Monica (Calif.) Evening Outlook, 1976-80; freelance writer L.A., 1980-82; journalist Sacramento (Calif.) Bee, 1983-85; writer Napa, Calif., 1985—; ptnr. Back St. Prodns., L.A., 1993—; writer-in-residence Tantra Rsch. Inst., Oakland, 1972-74; cons. Robert D. Kahn & Assocs., Sacramento, 1986-90. Author: Deadly Blessings, 1990, Fuller's Earth, 1985; editor: Leela, 1975; contbr. articles to mags. and newspapers. Recognized for Best In-Depth Reporting Calif. Newspaper Pubs. Assn., 1988; recipient Berton J. Ballard award of merit State Bar Calif., 1977, 79, Silver Gavel award of merit ABA, 1979, Best Community Svc. award Greater L.A. Press Club, 1977, Nev. Press Assn., 1967. Mem. Authors Guild, Soc. for Rational Inquiry (bd. dirs. 1985-91), CHILD Inc. Home and Office: 3210 Buckeye Ct Napa CA 94558

BRENNEN, STEVEN RUSSELL, government executive; b. Fremont, Ohio, May 25, 1953; s. Russell E. and Ann (Murray) B. BA, Ohio State U., 1974, MPA, 1976. Adminstrv. asst. Mayor's Office, City of Columbus, Ohio, 1974-77; analyst Fin. Dept., City of Columbus, 1977-79; spl. asst. Congressman Wylie's Office, Washington, 1979-81; staff asst. govt. Ops. Com., Ho. of Reps., Washington, 1981-83; dir. Congl. rels. EDA, U.S. Dept. Commerce, Washington, 1983-86, dep. asst. sec., 1986-89; staff aide Exec. Office of Pres., Washington, 1990; asst. to adminstr. U.S. SBA, Washington, 1990-91; regional dir. Econ. Devel. Adminstrn., U.S. Dept. Commerce, Denver, 1991—. Roman Catholic. Office: US Dept Commerce-EDA 1244 Speer Blvd Denver CO 80204

BRENNER, DANIEL L., law educator; b. 1951. AB, MA, Stanford U., 1973, JD, 1976. Bar: Calif. 1976, D.C. 1977. Law clk. to Hon. Wm. Matthew Byrne Jr. L.A., 1976-77; atty. Wilmer, Cutler & Pickering, D.C., 1977-79; sr. adviser to chair FCC, D.C., 1979-86; adj. prof. UCLA, 1986—; lectr. Am. U., 1981, Yeshiva U., 1983. Author: (with Rivers) Conflicting Traditions in Media Law, 1982, (with Price & Meyerson) Cable Television and Other Nonbroadcast Video: Law and Policy, 1989. Trustee Stanford U., 1983-87; bd. dirs. Corp. Pub. Broadcasting, 1986-90. Mem. Assn. Def. Lawyers Am. (nat. law com. 1984—). Office: UCLA Sch Law 405 Hilgard Ave Los Angeles CA 90024-1301

BRENNER, WILLIAM IRWIN, cardiac surgeon; b. Bklyn., Dec. 30, 1943; s. Sidney Lionel and Shirley Lillian (Kirstein) B.; m. June Frances Avner, June 20, 1965; children: Eric Nathaniel, Evan Benjamin. BA, Columbia Coll., 1965; MD, NYU, 1969. Diplomate Am. Bd. Surgery, Am. Bd. Thoracic Surgery. Intern N.Y. U. Bellevue Med. Ctr., N.Y.C., 1969-70, resident, 1970-76; cardiac surgeon Kaiser-Permanente, L.A., 1976-91; staff cardiac surgeon Harbor-UCLA Med. Ctr., Torrance, Calif., 1991-92; chief cardiac surgery Santa Clara Valley Med. Ctr., San Jose, Calif., 1992—; asst. clin. prof. thoracic surgery UCLA, 1979—. Contbr. articles to profl. jours. Capt. USAR, 1969-78. Fellow ACS; mem. Soc. Thoracic Surgeons, Western Thoracic Surg. Soc., Assn. for Acad. Surgery, Am. Heart Assn. Office: Santa Clara Valley Med Ctr 751 S Bascom Ave San Jose CA 95128

BRENT, IRA MARTIN, psychiatrist; b. N.Y.C., Nov. 1, 1944; m. Terry Suffet. BS, L.I. U., 1966; MD, Chgo. Med. Sch., 1970. Diplomate Am. Bd. Psychiatry and Neurology; qualified med. examiner, Calif. Intern U. Calif. at Irvine Orange County Med. Ctr., Orange, 1970-71; resident in psychiatry Cedars Sinai Med. Ctr., 1973-76; pvt. practice psychiatry, 1976—; dir. dept. psychiatry and bariatrics St. Mary's Hosp., Decatur, Ill., 1984-89; dir. adult program Charter Hosp. of Sacramento, Calif., 1989-90; dir. partial hospitalization program CPC Heritage Oaks Hosp., Sacramento, 1990—; asst. clin. prof. psychiatry U. Calif., Davis. Served to capt. USAF, 1971-73. Fellow Am. Assn. Psychoanalytic Physicians; mem. Am. Coll. Nutrition, Am. Soc. Psychiat. Physicians, Calif. Med. Assn., Eldorado Med. Soc., Sacramento Med. Soc. Office: 87 Scripps Dr # 214 Sacramento CA 95825

BRENT, RICHARD SAMUEL, manufacturing company executive; b. Pitts., July 30, 1949; s. Irving J. and Sarah Evelyn (Weiss) B.; m. Sharon I. Levine, Aug. 17, 1969; children: Andrew, Sarah, Kirah. BA, Sonoma State Coll., 1972, teaching cert., 1973. Gen. mgr. Solar Warehouse, El Cajon, Calif., 1980-82; plant mgr., program mgr. Jet Air, Inc., El Cajon, 1982-85; program mgr. Solar Turbines, Inc., San Diego, 1985—. Editor: (booklet) Who Says You Can't Do Anything?, 1970. V.p. United Cerebral Palsy of San Diego, 1984; vice chmn. Nat. Kidney Found. of So. Calif., San Diego, 1989-90, chmn., 1990-91; loaned exec. United Way Am. of San Diego, 1986; mem. exec. adv. com. U. Phoenix. Named Outstanding Vol. of Yr., Combined Health Agys., 1989. Mem. Am. Def. Preparedness Assn., Solar Profl. Mgmt. Assn. (pres. bd. dirs. 1989), Nat. Security Indsl. Assn., Navy League U.S., Keeper's Club-Zool. Soc. San Diego. Home: 5402 Redland Pl San Diego CA 92115-2217

BRENTS, BARBARA GAYLE, sociology educator; b. Austin, Tex., Mar. 19, 1957; d. Walker Allen and Lorna Margaretta (McNamee) Brents; m. Michael Joseph Pawlak. BJ, U. Mo., 1979, M.Sociology, 1983, PhD in Sociology, 1987. Asst. editor pubs. Jewish Hosp. of St. Louis, 1978-80; teaching asst. U. Mo., Columbia, 1980-87; asst. prof. sociology U. Nev., Las Vegas, 1987-93, co-chmn. women's studies prog., 1989-91, assoc. prof., 1993—. Contbr. articles to profl. jours. Active Campaign for Choice, Las Vegas, Nevadans for Peace, 1990—; bd. dirs. ACLU, 1992—, Citizen Alert, 1993—. Midwest Coun. for Social Rsch. on Aging fellow, 1982-86; recipient Good Gal award So. Nev. Women's Polit. Caucus, 1992. Mem. Am. Sociol. Assn., Midwest Sociol. Soc. (student dir. 1982-83), Assn. for Humanist Sociology. Democrat. Home: 1015 Franklin Ave Las Vegas NV 89104 Office: University of Nevada Dept Sociology Las Vegas NV 89154

BRES, PHILIP WAYNE, automotive executive; b. Beaumont, Tex., Mar. 6, 1950; s. Roland Defrance Bres and Edna Gene (Griffith) Seale; m. Janet Vivian Meyer, May 16, 1987; children: Rachel Elizabeth, Rebecca Claire. BA, Lamar U., Beaumont, Tex., 1972; MBA, Stephen F. Austin State U., 1973. Distbn. mgr., bus. mgmt. mgr. Mazda Motors of Am., Houston, 1973-75; analyst, cons. C.H. McCormack and Assocs., Houston, 1975-76; assoc. Frank Gillman Pontiac/GMC/Honda, Houston, 1976-79, David Taylor Cadillac Co., Houston, 1979-80; pres. Braintrust Inc., Houston, 1980-83; sales mgr. Mossy Oldsmobile, Inc., Houston, 1983-84; gen. mgr. Mossy Nissan/Ford, Bellevue, Wash., 1984-86; dir. ops. Mossy Co., Encinitas, Calif., 1986-91; gen. mgr. Performance Nissan, Duarte, Calif., 1991—; seminar lectr. Rice U., Houston, 1980-83. Author: The Entrepreneurs Guide for Starting a Successful Business., 1982; contbr. (book) Business Planning for the Entrepreneur, 1983. Mem. Houston C. of C. (small bus. coun.), Opt Astron. Soc., Univ. Club, Phi Eta Sigma, Phi Kappa Phi. Republican. Home: 2423 E Woodlyn Rd Pasadena CA 91104-3447 Office: Performance Nissan PO Box 1500 Duarte CA 91009

BRESHEARS, GERRY EVERETT, theology educator; b. Albuquerque, Jan. 28, 1947; s. Galen Kurtz and Ruth Roselle (Stouffer) B.; m. Sherry Ann Veazey, Mar. 22, 1968; children: Donn Glen, David Randall. BS, U. N.Mex., 1968; MDiv, Conservative Bapt. Theol. Sem., 1975; PhD, Fuller Theol. Sem., 1984. Tchr. math. Jefferson County (Colo.) Pub. Schs., 1968-69, Faith Acad., Manila, 1969-72; machinist, bookkeeper C & C Mfg., Denver, 1972-75; machinist, foreman Lanmar Co., Pasadena, Calif., 1975-78; machinist Meister Engring., Pasadena, 1978-80; mem. part-time faculty Biola Coll., La Mirada, Calif., 1979-80; prof. system theology Western Sem., Portland, Oreg., 1980—; lectr. Western Evang. Sem., Portland, 1982, 84, Cannon Beach (Oreg.) Conf. Ctr., 1984, 86-91, Multnomah Sch. of the Bible, Portland, 1984, 90; vis. prof. Denver Sem., 1986, 88. Author: (with others) Christian Freedom: Essays, 1986, Celebrating the Word, 1987, Crystal, 1992; contbg. editor Jour. of Psychology and Theology, 1986—. Elder, tchr. Lents Bapt. Ch., Portland, 1981—; mem. adv. bd. North Portland Bible Coll., 1987—. Mem. Evang. Theol. Soc. (regional exec. com. 1985—, nat. pres.-elect 1992—), Dispensational Study Group (sec.-treas. 1986-90). Home: 2036 SE 54th Portland OR 97215 Office: Western Sem 5511 SE Hawthorne Blvd Portland OR 97215

BRESLAUER, GEORGE WILLIAM, political science educator; b. N.Y.C., Mar. 4, 1946; s. Henry Edward and Marianne (Schaeffer) B.; m. Yvette Assia, June 5, 1976; children: Michelle, David. BA, U. Mich., 1966, MA, 1968, PhD, 1973. Asst. prof. polit. sci. U. Calif., Berkeley, 1971-79, assoc. prof., 1979-90, prof., 1990—, chmn. dept., 1993—, chmn. Ctr. for Slavic and East European Studies, 1982-93; vice chmn. bd. trustees Nat. Coun. for Soviet and East European Rsch., Washington, 1988-91. Author: Khrushchev and Brezhnev as Leaders, 1982, Soviet Strategy in the Middle East, 1989; editor: Can Gorbachev's Reforms Succeed?, 1990, Learning in U.S. and Soviet Foreign Policy, 1991. Grantee Ford Found., 1982-84, Carnegie Corp., 1985-91, MacArthur Found., 1988—. Mem. Am. Assn. for Advancement Slavic Studies (bd. dirs., exec. com. 1990—). Office: 210 Barrows Hall U Calif Dept Polit Sci Berkeley CA 94720

BRESLOW, NORMAN EDWARD, biostatistics educator, researcher; b. Mpls., Feb. 21, 1941; s. Lester and Alice Jane (Philp) B.; m. Gayle Marguerite Bramwell, Sept. 7, 1963; children: Lauren Louise, Sara Jo. BA, Reed Coll., 1962; PhD, Stanford U., 1967. Trainee Stanford U., 1965-67; vis. research worker London Sch. Hygiene, 1967-68; instr. U. Wash., Seattle, 1968-69, asst. prof., 1969-72, assoc. prof., 1972-76, prof., 1976—, chmn. dept. biostats., 1983-93; statistician Internat. Agy. Research Cancer, Lyon, France, 1972-74; mem. Hutchinson Cancer Ctr., Seattle, 1982—; statistician Nat. Wilms' Tumor Study, 1969—; cons. Internat. Agy. Research Cancer, Lyon, 1978-79, Stats. and Epidemiology Research Corp., Seattle, 1980—. Recipient Spiegelman Gold medal Am. Pub. Health Assn., 1978, Preventive Oncology Acad. award, NIH, 1978-83; research grantee NIH, 1984—; sr. U.S. Scientist, Alexander Humboldt Found., Fed. Republic Germany, 1982; sr. Internat. fellowship Fogarty Ctr., 1990. Fellow AAAS, Am. Statis. Assn.; Internat. Statis. Inst., Inst. Medicine-Nat. Acad. Scis., Biometric Soc. (regional com. 1975-78). Office: Univ of Wash Dept of Biostatistics SC-32 Seattle WA 98195

BRESNAHAN, JAMES PATRICK, writer; b. Detroit, May 29, 1954; s. John Cleland and Georgine Anne (Kotal) B.; m. Janice Arleen Young, Oct. 28, 1972 (div. 1975); m. Jacqueline Leslie Housego, Jan. 30, 1988; 1 child, Kevin C. AA, Henry Ford Community Coll., Dearborn, Mich., 1980. Author: Four-Wheeled Missile, 1981; author screenplay: Jitterbug, 1987, Voices, 1989. Roman Catholic. Home: 7975 Locust Ave Fontana CA 92336-2838

BREST, PAUL A., law educator; b. Jacksonville, Fla., Aug. 9, 1940; s. Alexander and Mia (Deutsch) B.; m. Iris Lang, June 17, 1962; children: Hilary, Jeremy. AB, Swarthmore Coll., 1962; JD, Harvard U., 1965; LLD (hon.), Northeastern U., 1980, Swarthmore Coll., 1991. Bar: N.Y. 1966. Law clk. to judge U.S. Ct. Appeals (1st cir.), Boston, 1965-66; atty. NAACP Legal Def. Fund, Jackson, Miss., 1966-68; law clk. Justice John Harlan, U.S. Supreme Ct., 1968-69; prof. law Stanford U., 1969—, Kenneth and Harle Montgomery Prof. pub. interest law, Richard E. Lang prof. and dean, 1987—. Author: Processes of Constitutional Decisionmaking, 1992. Mem. Am. Acad. Arts and Scis. Home: 814 Tolman Dr Palo Alto CA 94305-1026 Office: Stanford U Sch Law Nathan Abbott Way at Alvarado Row Stanford CA 94305

BRETERNITZ, CORY DALE, archaeological company executive, consultant; b. Tucson, Apr. 9, 1955; s. David Alan and Barbara Blair (Myers) B.; m. Adrian Sue White, May 21, 1981; children: Jessie Lynn, Dylan Blair. BA, U. Ariz., 1978; MA, Wash. State U., 1982. Archaeologist Mus. No. Ariz., Flagstaff, 1973; lab. technician Lab. of Tree-Ring Rsch., Tucson, 1973-78; archaeologist Ariz. State Mus., Tucson, 1978, Nat. Pk. Svc., Albuquerque, 1976-79, Dolores (Colo.) Archaeol. Program, 1980-81; project dir. Navajo Nation Archaeology Program, Window Rock, Ariz., 1981-82, Profl. Svc. Industries, Inc., Phoenix, 1982-84; pres. Ctr. for Indigenous Studies in Ams., Phoenix, 1991—; pres., owner Soil Systems, Inc., Phoenix, 1984—. Mem. Ariz. Archaeol. Coun. (exec. com. 1976, editor 1989—), N.Mex. Archaeol. Coun., Colo. Coun. Profl. Archaeologists, Utah Profl. Archaeol. Coun., Am. Quaternary Assn., Soc. for Am. Archaeology, Am. Anthrop. Assn. Office: Soil Systems Inc 1121 N 2d St Phoenix AZ 85004

BRETOI, REMUS NICOLAE, aerospace engineer; b. St. Paul, Apr. 9, 1925; s. Nicolae and Elena (Puscas) B.; m. Yvonne Zumbusch, Dec. 28, 1953; children: Christopher Lee, Stephen Nicolae, Kim Ferdinand, Anita Elena. B Aero. Engring., U. Minn., 1945, MS in Aero. Engring., 1946; MBA, Golden Gate U., 1979. Registered profl. engr., Minn., Calif. Rsch. analyst N.Am. Aviation, Inc., El Segundo, Calif., 1946-48; flight control rsch. engr., then supr. Honeywell, Inc., Mpls., 1948-58, mil. products group planning staff, 1958-61; mgr. R & D Honeywell GmbH, Doernigheim, Fed. Republic Germany, 1961-63; sect. head guidance and control Honeywell Inc., Mpls., 1963-67; chief spl. projects office, control lab. NASA Elec. Rsch. Ctr., Cambridge, Mass., 1967-70; chief STOL experiments office, chief avionics rsch. br., staff asst. programs, rsch. engr./scientist NASA-Ames Rsch. Ctr., Moffett Field, Calif., 1970—, now, asst. chief extravehicular systems br., 1990—. Patentee aircraft control devices. Bd. dirs. Internat. Inst. Minn., St. Paul, 1959-67; pres. Casa Romana & Capela, Oakland, 1989-91; pres. parish coun. Holy Resurrection Romanian Orthodox parish, Oakland, 1984-88. Named Boss of Yr., Peninsula chpt. Am. Bus. Women's Assn., Palo Alto, Calif., 1972; named to Otto Bremer South St. Paul (Minn.) Hall of Excellence, 1987. Mem. AIAA, NSPE, Theta Tau, Sigma Gamma Tau. Home: 1095 Mcgregor Way Palo Alto CA 94306-2634 Office: NASA Ames Rsch Ctr MS 239-15 Moffett Field CA 94035

BREUER, MELVIN ALLEN, electrical engineering educator; b. L.A., Feb. 1, 1938; s. Arthur and Bertha Helen (Friedman) B.; m. Sandra Joyce Scalir, Apr. 7, 1967; children: Teri Lynn, Jeffrey Steven. BS in Engring., UCLA, 1959, MS in Engring., 1961; PhD in Elec. Engring., U. Calif., Berkeley, 1965. Asst. prof. U. So. Calif., Los Angeles, 1965-71, assoc. prof., 1971-80, prof., 1980—, chmn. elect. engring. systems dept., 1991—. Co-author: Diagnosis and Reliable Design, 1976, Digital Systems Testing and Testable Design, 1990; editor, co-author: Design Automation, 1972; editor: Digital Systems Design Automation, 1975, Jour. Design Automation, 1980-82; co-editor: Knowledge Based Systems for Test and Diagnosis, 1990; contbr. articles to profl. jours. Recipient Assocs. award U. So. Calif., 1991; Fulbright-Hays scholar, 1972. Fellow IEEE; mem. Sigma Xi, Tau Beta Pi, Eta Kappa Nu. Democrat. Home: 16857 Bosque Dr Encino CA 91436-3530 Office: U So Calif University Park Los Angeles CA 90089

BREUER, STEPHEN ERNEST, temple executive; b. Vienna, Austria, July 14, 1936; s. John Howard and Olga Marion (Haar) B.; came to U.S., 1938, naturalized, 1945; BA cum laude, UCLA, 1959, gen. secondary credential, 1960; m. Gail Fern Breitbart, Sept. 4, 1960 (div. 1986); children: Jared Noah, Rachel Elise; m. Nadine Bendit, Sept. 25, 1988. Tchr. L.A. City Schs., 1960-62; dir. Wilshire Blvd. Temple Camps, Los Angeles, 1962-88; exec. dir. Wilshire Blvd. Temple, 1980—; dir. Edgar F. Magnin Religious Sch., Los Angeles, 1970-80. Instr. Hebrew Union Coll., Los Angeles, 1965-76, U. Judaism, 1991; field instr. San Francisco State U., 1970-80, Calif. State U., San Diego, Hebrew Union Coll., 1977-81, U. of Judaism UCLA extension. Vice pres. Los Angeles Youth Programs Inc., 1967-77; youth adviser Los Angeles County Commn. Human Relations, 1969-72. Bd. dirs. Community Relations Conf. So. Calif., 1965-85; regional bd. mem. Union Am. Hebrew Congregations, 1986-88; bd. dirs. Alzheimer's Disease and Related Disorders Assn., 1984—, v.p. L.A. County chpt., 1984-86, pres., 1986-88, nat. exec. com., 1987—, nat. devel. chair, 1992—, Calif. state coun. pres. 1987-92, chmn. of Calif. gov.'s adv. com. on Alzheimer's disease, 1988—; mem. goals program City of Beverly Hills, Calif., 1985-91; bd. dirs. Echo Found., 1986-88, Wilshire Stakeholders, exec. com., 1987—, treas. Wilshire Community Prayer Alliance, 1986-88; active United Way. Recipient Service awards Los Angeles YWCA, 1974, Los Angeles County Bd. Suprs., 1982, 87, Ventura County Bd. Suprs., 1982, 87, Weinberg Chai Lifetime Achievement award Jewish Fed. Council Los Angeles, 1986, Steve Breuer Conference Ctr. in Malibu named in his honor Wilshire Blvd. Temple Camps. Mem. So. Calif. Camping Assn. (dir. 1964-82), Nat. Assn. Temple Adminstrs. (nat. bd. dirs. 1987—, v.p. 1991-93, pres. 1993—, Svc. to Judaism award 1989, Svc. to the Community award 1990), Nat. Assn. Temple Educators, Los Angeles Assn. Jewish Edn. (dir.), Profl. Assn. Temple Adminstrs. (pres. 1985-88), Assn. Supervision and Curriculum Devel., Am. Mgmt. Assn., So. Calif. Conf. Jewish Communal Workers, Jewish Profl. Network, Amnesty Internat., Jewish Resident Camping Assn. (pres. 1976-82), UCLA Alumni Assn., Wilderness Soc., Center for Environ. Edn., Wildlife Fedn., Living Desert, Maple Mental Health Ctr. of Beverly Hills, Los Angeles County Mus. Contemporary Art, People for the Am. Way, Assn. Reform Zionists Am., Union of Am. Hebrew Congregations (bd. dirs. Pacific SW region 1985-88). Office: Wilshire Blvd Temple 3663 Wilshire Blvd Los Angeles CA 90010-2798

BREUNIG, ROBERT HENRY, business executive; b. Phila., May 12, 1926; s. Robert Henry and Gertrude Florence (Burke) B.; m. Ruth Carolyn Cole, Aug. 30, 1947; children: Lynn Carol, Mark Robert, Christopher John, Eric Martin. BA, Ind. U., 1950; MA, Goddard Coll., 1979; PhD, Union Inst., 1981. Dir. advt. Am. Petroleum Inst., Washington, 1971-73; dir. pub. affairs Calif. State U., Long Beach, 1974-85; co-founder, exec. dir. Found. for the 21st Century, San Diego, 1985-87; sec. Found. for Pvt. Sector, San Diego, 1987—; dep. chmn. Sammis Co., San Diego, 1987-90; pres. Internat. Info. Transfer Co., Los Alamitos, Calif., 1990—; U.S. bd. dirs. Nichibai Trading Co., Osaka, Japan, Hohyo Kosan Co., Ltd., Tokyo. Active Pacific Intercultural Exch. Japan. With U.S. Army, 1943-46. Decorated Bronze star, Belgian Fourragere, Presdl. Citation. Episcopalian. Home: 3372 Cortese Dr Los Alamitos CA 90720-4306

BREW, DAVID ALAN, geologist; b. Clifton Springs, N.Y., Nov. 22, 1930; s. Clifford Ellsworth and Grace Louise (Crocker) B.; m. Alice Perrin Dickerman, Aug. 22, 1958; children: Elizabeth C., A. Perrin, Catherine L., Emily O. AB, Dartmouth Coll., 1948-52; student, U. Colo., 1955-56, U. Vienna, Austria, 1959-60; PhD, Stanford U., 1957-59, 64. Registered Geologist, Calif. Geologist U.S. Geol. Survey, Grand Junction, Colo., 1952-57, Menlo Park, Calif., 1957-59, 60-69; deputy asst. chief geologist mineral resources U.S. Geol. Survey, Washington, 1970-72; geologist U.S. Geol. Survey, Menlo Park, 1973-91, asst. chief branch Alaskan geology, 1991-92, geologist branch Alaskan geology, 1992—; chmn. Apl. Interagy. Task force for Preparation of Final Environ. Impact Statement on Trans-Alaska Pipeline, Washington, 1970-72; geol. names com. U.S. Geol. Survey, Reston, Va., 1985—; co-chmn. Glacier Bay Sci. Bd., Gustavus, Alaska, 1982-88. Author in field. Chmn. human resources com. PTA, L.A., 1969-70, Citizens Caucus, L.A., 1973-74; co-chmn. Stanford-U.S. Geol. Survey Fellowship Fund, 1986—; bd. dirs. Far West Ski Assn., San Francisco, 1966-70. Recipient Meritorious Svc. award U.S. Dept. Interior, Washington, 1972, Commendation for Outstanding Svc., 1972, Career Svc. award Nat. Civic Svc. League, Washington, 1973. Fellow Geol. Soc. of Am.; mem. Am. Geophysical Union, Am. Assn. Petroleum Geologists, Arctic Inst. of N.Am., Sociedad Geol. Peninsular, Sigma Xi. Home: 164 Doud Dr Los Angeles CA 94022 Office: U S Geol Survey MS904 345 Middlefield Rd Menlo Park CA 94025-3591

BREWBAKER, JAMES LYNN, horticulture and genetics educator; b. St. Paul, Oct. 11, 1926; s. Harvey Edgar and Jean (Turner) B.; divorced; children: Paul Harvey, Philip Lloyd, Perry Lynn, Pamela Barbara Jean; m. Kathryn Bradley, 1992. Student, So. Meth. U., 1945, U. Tex., 1945-46; BS in Gen. Sci. cum laude, U. Colo., 1948; PhD in Plant Breeding, Cornell U., 1952. NSF postdoctoral fellow U. Lund, Sweden, 1952-53; asst. prof. agronomy U. Philippines, Los Banos, 1953-55; assoc. geneticist biology dept. Brookhaven Nat. Lab., AEC, Upton, N.Y., 1956-61; assoc. prof. horticulture and genetics U. Hawaii, Honolulu, 1961-64, prof., 1964—; field staff geneticist Rockefeller Found., Bangkok, 1967-68; cons. IAEA, The Philippines, 1970; vis. prof. dept. plant breeding Cornell U., Ithaca, N.Y., 1974; vis. scientist Internat. Ctr. Tropical Agr., Cali, Colombia, 1978, Nigeria, 1989, Taiwan Agrl. and Forestry Rsch. Insts., 1981, Australia Nat. U., U. Queensland, 1985, 93; cons. in tropical agr. and agroforestry numerous countries, 1970—. Author: Agricultural Genetics, 1962 (trans. into 7 langs.), Experimental Design on a Spreadsheet, 1993; editor: Leucaena Rsch. Reports, 1980-90, Nitrogen Fixing Tree Rsch. Reports, 1983-88; mem. editorial bd. several jours.; contbr. over 200 articles to sci. jours. With USNR, 1944-46. Recipient Outstanding svc. award Korean Office Rural Devel., 1978, Excellence in Rsch. award U. Hawaii, 1980, G.J. Watumull Disting. Achievement award Internat. Agr., 1982, recognition Hawaii Senate, 1986, Internat. Inventor's award Swedish Inventors Assn., 1986, Scientist of Yr. award Achievement Rewards for Coll. Students, 1988, Superior Svc. award USDA, 1990, Rsch. award Nat. Coun. Comml. Plant Breeders, 1992. Fellow Am. Soc. Agronomy (Crop Sci. Rsch. award 1984), Crop Sci. Soc. Am.; mem. Am. Soc. Hort. Sci., Am. Soc. Forestry, Internat. Soc. Tropical Foresters, Nat. Sweet Corn Breeders Assn. (pres. 1987), Nitrogen Fixing Tree Assn. (founder, pres. 1981-90), Hawaiian Acad. Sci. (pres. 1978), Hawaiian Bot. Soc. (pres. 1967), Hawaii Crop Improvement Assn. (exec. sec. 1969-85), Sigma Xi (pres. Hawaii chpt. 1990), Phi Kappa Phi, Pi Mu Epsilon, Phi Eta Sigma, Phi Sigma, Gamma Sigma Delta (Disting Svc. award

1982). Republican. Presbyterian. Office: U Hawaii Dept Horticulture 3190 Maile Way Honolulu HI 96822-2279

BREWER, JANICE KAY, state legislator, property and investment firm executive; b. Hollywood, Calif., Sept. 26, 1944; d. Perry Wilford and Edna Clarice (Bakken) Drinkwine; m. John Leon Brewer, Jan. 1, 1963; children—Ronald Richard, John Samuel, Michael Wilford. Med. asst. cert. Valley Coll., Burbank, Calif., 1963, practical radiol. technician cert., 1963; D. Humanities, (hon.), Los Angeles Chiropractic Coll., 1970. Pres., Brewer Property & Investments, Glendale, Ariz., 1970—; mem. Ariz. Ho. of Reps., Phoenix, 1983-86, Ariz. Senate, 1987—. Committeeman, Republican Party, Phoenix, 1970, 1983; legis. liaison Ponderosa Rep. Women, Phoenix, 1980; bd. dirs. Westside Mental Healty Agy., Phoenix, 1983—. Named Woman of Yr., Chiropractic Assn. Ariz., 1983. Mem. Nat. Fedn. Rep. Women, Am. Legis. Exchange Council. Lutheran. Home: 6835 W Union Hills Dr Glendale AZ 85308-8058 Office: Office of State Senate 6835 W Union Hills Dr Glendale AZ 85308

BREWER, JOHN THOMAS, foreign language educator; b. Palo Alto, Calif., Mar. 1, 1938; s. Gardner Hunter and Lesley (Rogers) B. BA, Pomona Coll., 1959; PhD, U. Tex., 1962. Asst. prof. German U. Calif., Riverside, 1962-67; assoc. prof. German Wash. State U., Pullman, 1967—; chmn. dept. fgn. languages and lit., Pullman, 1982-87. Fulbright fellow, 1987-88. Mem. MLA, Am. Assn. Tchrs. of German, Rotary (pres. elect 1992-93). Republican. Presbyterian. Office: Wash State Univ Dept Fgn Languages and Lit Pullman WA 99164

BREWER, ROBERT FRANKLIN, retired horticulturist; b. Woodbury, N.J., May 25, 1927; s. George Beckett and Helen Rebecca (Schellenger) B.; m. Gladys Edna Meerwald, Nov. 28, 1947; children: Cynthia Roberta Sano, Robin Augusta Caldwell. BSc, Rutgers U., 1950, PhD, 1953. Rsch. fellow Rutgers U., New Brunswick, N.J., 1950-53; jr. chemist U. Calif., Riverside, 1953-55, asst. chemist, 1955-60, assoc. chemist, 1960-70, assoc. horticulturist, 1970-89; ret., 1990; cons. Aerojet Gen., Sacramento, 1963-65, Harvey Aluminum, The Dalles, Oreg., 1965-67, USPHS, Washington, 1980-81, 87, Multinat. Agribus. Systems, Washington, 1982, Pfizer Chem. Co., N.Y.C., 1984-89, Chem. Waste Mgmt., 1989-92. Mem. Riverside Civic League, 1966-70. With USN, 1945-60. Internat. Minerals Rsch. fellow, 1950-53. Mem. Am. Soc. for Horticultural Sci., Air Pollution Control Assn., Kiwanis (sec. Riverside chpt. 1962-63, Reedley, Calif. chpt. 1979-82, pres. Riverside chpt. 1965, Reedley chpt. 88-89, Outstanding Pres. 1989). Republican. Congregationalist. Home: 6879 S Reed Ave Reedley CA 93654-9714 Office: U Calif 9240 S Riverbend Ave Parlier CA 93648-9774

BREWER, ROY EDWARD, lawyer; b. Atlanta, Dec. 22, 1949; s. Roy Mullins and Martha Joann (Still) B.; m. Cahterine Elizabeth Schindler, May 5, 1979; 1 child, Garrett Edward. BA in Polit. Sci., U. Fla., 1971, MA in Polit. Sci., 1973; JD, U. Pacific, 1982. Bar: Calif., 1984, U.S. Dist. Ct. (ea. dist.) Calif. 1984. Regional planner North Cen. Fla. Regional Planning Council, Gainesville, Fla., 1975-78; dir. met. affairs Sacramento Met. C. of C., 1978-79; dir. land planning Raymond Vail and Assocs., Sacramento, 1979-84; pvt. practice Sacramento, 1984-89; ptnr. Hunter McCray Richey & Brewer, 1989—. Bd. dirs. Sacramento Symphony Assn., 1987—, Am. Lung Assn., 1988—; bd. dirs. Am. River Natural History Assn., 1986—, pres., 1988-89; bd. dirs. No. Calif. Rugby Football Union, 1985—, pres. 1985-88; chmn. Sacramento Ad-Hoc Charter Commn., 1988—; bd. dirs. Healthcare, 1987—, chmn., 1988-89; trustee ARC, 1989—; chmn. Local Govt. Reorgn. Com., 1988; co-founder, sec./treas. Fla. Rugby Football Union, 1974-78. Recipient Sacramento Regional Pride award for community devel., 1991, exceptional performers award Air Force Assn., 1991, Sacrementan of Yr. award 1991; named among Best and Brightest, Sacramento mag., 1985. Mem. Am. Inst. Cert. Planners, Sacramento Met. C. of C. (bd. dirs. 1985-87, v.p. 1988, pres.-elect 1989, pres. 1990), Am. Planning Assn. Office: Hunter McCray Richey Brewer 801 K St Fl 23D Sacramento CA 95814-3500

BREWER, SHERYL DENISE, nutritional consultant; b. Albuquerque, Mar. 29, 1958; d. Ernest E. and Virgie N. (Gentry) B.; m. William J. Brown, Sept. 30, 1990. BS, U. N.Mex., 1984, MPA, 1991. Lic. nutritionist. Pub. health nutritionist I Women, Infant, Childrens Program State of N.Mex., Albuquerque, 1985-87, pub. health nutritionist II Child & Adult Care Food Program, 1987-88; nutritional cons. A Better Life, Albuquerque, 1991—; vol. counselor Student Crisis Ctr., U. N.Mex., 1978-79; elected chartered bd. mem. Pre-Med. Professions Club, U. N.Mex., 1978-80; adv. bd. mem. Student Health Ctr., U. N.Mex., 1981; newsletter, ad hoc hunger, hospitality chairperson N.Mex. Community Nutrition Coun., Albuquerque, 1986-88. Pres. Pub. Adminstrn. Grad. Student Assn., Univ. N.Mex., 1988-89. Recipient Leadership award Pub. Adminstrn. Grad. Student Assn., U. N.Mex., 1989, Thesis Rsch. award Student Rsch. Allocation Com., U. N.Mex., 1989, 90; named Outstanding Young Women of Am., 1991. Mem. Nat. Assn. for the Edn. Young Children, Phi Kappa Phi, Pi Alpha Alpha. Home: 808 Valencia NE Albuquerque NM 87108

BREWER, THOMAS BOWMAN, university administrator; b. Fort Worth, July 22, 1932; s. Earl Johnson and Maurine (Bowman) B.; m. Betty Jean Walling, Aug. 4, 1951; children: Diane, Thomas Bowman. B.A., U. Tex., 1954, M.A., 1957; Ph.D., U. Pa., 1962. Instr. St. Stephens Episcopal Sch., Austin, Tex., 1955-56, S.W. Tex. State Coll., San Marcos, 1956-57; from instr. to asso. prof. N. Tex. State U., Denton, 1959-66; asst. prof. U. Ky., 1966-67; asso. prof. Iowa State U., 1967-68; prof. history, chmn. dept. U. Toledo, 1968-71; dean Tex. Christian U., Fort Worth, 1971-72, vice chancellor, dean univ., 1972-78; chancellor E. Carolina U., Greenville, N.C., 1978-82; v.p. acad. affairs Ga. State U., Atlanta, 1982-88; pres. Met. State Coll. of Denver, 1988-93. Editor: Views of American Economic Growth, 2 vols, 1966, The Robber Barons, 1969; gen. editor: Railroads of America Series. Mem. Econ. History Assn., Bus. History Assn., Am. Assn. Higher Edn. Home: 104 Javelin Austin TX 78734 Office: Office of Pres 104 Jauclin Dr Austin TX 78734

BREWSTER, RUDI MILTON, judge; b. Sioux Falls, S.D., May 18, 1932; s. Charles Edwin and Wilhemina Therese (Rud) B.; m. Gloria Jane Nanson, June 27, 1954; children: Scot Alan, Lauri Diane (Alan Lee), Julie Lynn Yahnke. AB in Pub. Affairs, Princeton U., 1954; JD, Stanford U., 1960. Bar: Calif. 1960. From assoc. to ptnr. Gray, Cary, Ames & Frye, San Diego, 1960-84; judge U.S. Dist. Ct. (so. dist.) Calif., San Diego, 1984—. Served to capt. USNR, 1954-82 Ret. Fellow Am. Coll. Trial Lawyers; mem. Am. Bd. Trial Advs., Internat. Assn. Ins. Counsel, Am. Inns of Ct. Republican. Lutheran. Office: US Dist Ct 940 Front St San Diego CA 92101-8902

BREZZO, STEVEN LOUIS, museum director; b. Woodbury, N.J., June 18, 1949; s. Louis and Ella Marie (Savage) B.; m. Dagmar Grimm, Aug. 10, 1975. B.A., Clarion State Coll., 1969; M.F.A., U. Conn., 1973. Chief curator La Jolla Mus. Contemporary Art, Calif., 1974-76; asst. dir. San Diego Mus. Art, 1976-78, dir., 1978—. Mem. Am. Assn. Mus. (del. to China 1981, to Italian mus. study trip 1982), Calif. Assn. Mus. (pres. 1992—), La Jolla Library Assn. (pres. 1980). Club: University (San Diego). Lodge: Rotary. Office: San Diego Museum of Art PO Box 2107 San Diego CA 92112-2107

BRICE, TOM LUTHER, state legislator; b. Fairbanks, Alaska, Feb. 6, 1965; s. Tom Liston and Jane Ann (Lawton) B. BA in Polit. Sci., U. Alaska, 1990. Mem. Alaska Ho. of Reps., 1993—; Legis. aide Alaska State Legislature, Juneau, 1991-92; camp coord. Fahrenkamp Camp, Fairbanks, 1990. Mem. Alumni Assn. U. Alaska, Kiwanis. Democrat. Episcopalian. Office: Alaska State Legislature 119 W Cushman St Ste 205 Fairbanks AK 99701

BRICKEN, MEREDITH STEPHANIE, information scientist; b. Baton Rouge, May 15, 1946; d. Wirt Alfred and Ann Noreen (Meredith) Williams; m. William Marion Bricken, Aug. 16, 1967; children: Ian Wirt, Colin William. BA in Social Scis., U. Calif. Santa Barbara, Goleta, 1968. Cert. tchr., Calif. Prof. sociology Royal Melbourne Inst. Tech., Australia, 1972-74; educator, curriculum designer Project Head Start, Columbus, Ohio, 1968-70, Coonara Sch., Melbourne, 1972-75, Laupahoehoe (Hawaii) Schs., 1979-81, Ellen Thatcher Children's Ctr., Palo Alto, Calif., 1982-83; info. designer Autodesk, Inc., Sausalito, Calif., 1988-89; rsch. scientist Human Interface Tech. Lab., U. Wash., Seattle, 1989-92; founder, mgr. interface tech. Oz...Internat., Ltd., Seattle, 1992—; cons. Human Interface Tech. Lab., Seattle, 1992—. Contbg. author: Cyberspace, 1993, Softwhere, 1992; editorial bd.: Presence Jour., 1991—; contbr. articles to computer graphics publs. Founder Coonara Alternative Sch., Melbourne, 1971. Mem. Assn. Computing Machinery, Special Interest Group in Computer Graphics, Special Interest Group in Computer-Human Interface (founding mem. Puget Sound chpt.), Electronic Frontier Found. Office: Oz Internat Ltd Seattle WA 98101

BRICKEN, WILLIAM MARION, scientist; b. Melbourne, Victoria, Australia, Apr. 27, 1945; s. William M. Sr. and Lois D. (Hickman) B.; m. Meredith S. VanNess Williams, Aug. 16, 1967; children: Ian, Colin. MS in Stats., Stanford U., 1983, PhD in Edn., 1987. Cert. tchr. Prin. Coonara Sch., Melbourne, 1972-75; asst. prof. State Coll. of Victoria, Melbourne, 1973-75; prin. scientist Advanced Decision Systems, Mountain View, Calif., 1984-88; dir. Autodesk Rsch. Lab, Sausalito, Calif., 1988-89; prin. scientist Human Interface Tech. Lab./Univ. Wash., Seattle, 1990—; co-founder Oz... Internat., Seattle, 1991—. Creator: Boundary Mathematics, 1983; designer: (computer program) VEOS, 1990; assoc. editor: Presence, Boston, 1991—. Mem. IEEE, AAAI, Assn. Computing Machinery, Spl. Interest Group on Computer Graphics. Office: HITL Univ Washington FJ-15 Seattle WA 98195

BRICKER, RUTH, national foundation administrator, real estate developer; b. Oak Park, Ill., Mar. 23, 1930; m. Neal S. Bricker; children: Daniel Baker, Cary, Dusty, Suzanne. MA in Urban Planning, postgrad. in pub. adminstrn. 1987-90; cert. mediator, 1992. Antioch U. Staff writer Artforum Mag., Los Angeles, 1966-69; western dir. Expts. in Art and Tech., Los Angeles, 1969-75; owner Empire Real Estate and Devel., Los Angeles, 1975-86; mng. gen. ptnr. LOMA, Loma Linda, Calif., 1988—; designer Trade-Off, a computer simulation for use in urban planning; developed programs in art and technology for Calif. State Coll.-Long Beach, U. So. Calif., UCLA; designer laser light wall Calif. Inst. Tech.; lectr. and cons. in field. Mem. Mayor's Housing Task Force, Los Angeles; councilor Loma Linda U. & Med. Sch. Internat. Inst. Kidney Diseases; mem. exec. com. Savings and Preserving Archtl. and Cultural Environ.; mem. Am. Found. for Pompidou Mus., Paris. Author: Getting Rich in Real Estate Partnerships, 1983; editor, contbg. author: Experiments in Art and Technology/Los Angeles jour., 1974-79.

BRICKER, SEYMOUR MURRAY, lawyer; b. N.Y.C., May 19, 1924; s. Harry and May (Glick) B.; m. Darlene M. Mohilef, July 29, 1951 (dec. Mar. 1987); children: Andrea Helene, Phillip Alan, Julie Ellen. Student, U. Okla., 1943-44; AB, U. Calif., Los Angeles, 1947; LLB, U. So. Calif., 1950. Bar: Calif. 1951. Atty. Calif. Jud. Coun., 1951-52; with legal dept. Universal Pictures, 1952-56; ptnr. Cohen & Bricker, 1956-68, Kaplan, Livingston, Goodwin, Berkowitz & Selvin, 1968-81, Mitchell, Silberberg & Knupp, 1982—; exec. v.p. Ed Friendly Prodns. Inc.; pres. Friendly/Bricker Prodns. Served with inf. AUS, 1943-46. Fellow Am. Bar Assn. Found.; mem. ABA (mem. council patent, trademark and copyright sect., past chmn. copyright div., past chmn. forum com. on entertainment and sports industries, mem. com. on Bicentennial program), Los Angeles Copyright Soc. (past pres.), Copyright Soc. U.S. (trustee), Calif. Copyright Conf. (past pres.), Acad. TV Arts and Scis. Home: 10445 Wilshire Blvd Los Angeles CA 90024-4606 Office: Mitchell Silberberg & Knupp 11377 W Olympic Blvd Los Angeles CA 90064

BRICKNER, RALPH GREGG, physicist; b. Cin., Nov. 28, 1951; s. Ralph Harold and Heloise Janet (Fagedes) B. BS in Physics, U. Cin., 1974; MS in Physics, U. Conn., 1975, PhD in Physics, 1981. Mem. staff Los Alamos (N.Mex.) Nat. Lab., 1981—. Contbr. articles to profl. jours., mags. Sec., rescue dir., v.p., then pres. Los Alamos Mountaineers, Inc., 1981—; mem. Los Alamos Ski Patrol, 1985-86. Mem. Am. Phys. Soc., Sigma Pi Sigma. Home: 377 Calle Loma Norte Santa Fe NM 87501 Office: Los Alamos Nat Lab C-3 MS-B265 Los Alamos NM 87545

BRIDE, ROBERT FAIRBANKS, lawyer; b. Washington, July 18, 1953; s. Noel Crawford and Jeanne Marie (Rafferty) B.; m. Carole Ann Hunter, 1975 (div. 1977); m. Tracy Viles Johnson, 1992. BA, Northwestern U., 1974; JD, U. Mich., 1978. Bar: Calif. Assoc. Sullivan, Jones and Archer, San Diego, 1978-80, Kosmo, Cho and Brown, Ventura, Calif., 1980-85; assoc. McGahan and Engle, Ventura, 1985-87, ptnr., 1987-88; founding ptnr. Engle and Bride, Ventura, 1988—; judge pro tempore Ventura County Superior Ct. and Mcpl. Ct., 1989—; arbitrator Ventura County Superior Ct., 1983—; prof. Pacific Legal Arts Coll., Camarillo, Calif., 1981-84; lectr. Assn. of Southern Calif. Defense Counsel, 1992. Sponsor Save the Children, 1988—, Santa Barbara Civic Light Opera, 1988—, Cato Inst., 1991—. Mem. ABA, Assn. So. Calif. Def. Counsel, Am. Soc. Law and Medicine, Ventura County Bar Assn., Bar Assn. U.S. Supreme Ct., Phi Beta Kappa, Pierpont Racquet Club. Republican. Roman Catholic. Home: 7262 Wolverine St Ventura CA 93003-7037 Office: Engle and Bride 353 San Jon Rd Ventura CA 93001

BRIDGES, EDWIN MAXWELL, education educator; b. Hannibal, Mo., Jan. 1, 1934; s. Edwin Otto and Radha (Maxwell) B.; m. Marjorie Anne Pollock, July 31, 1954; children: Richard, Rebecca, Brian, Bruce. BS, U. Mo., 1954; MA, U. Chgo., 1956, PhD, 1964. English tchr. Bremen Community High Sch., Midlothian, Ill., 1954-56; asst. prin. Griffith (Ind.) High Sch., 1956-60, prin., 1960-62; staff assoc. U. Chgo., 1962-64, assoc. prof., 1967-72; assoc. dir. Univ. Coun. for Edn. Adminstrn., Columbus, Ohio, 1964-65; asst. prof. Washington U., St. Louis, 1965-67; prof. U. Calif., Santa Barbara, 1972-74; prof. edn. Stanford (Calif.) U., 1974—; mem. nat. adv. panel Ctr. for Rsch. on Ednl. Accountability and Tchr. Evaluation, 1990—; external examiner U. Hong Kong, 1990-92; cons. World Bank, China, 1986, 89. Author: Managing the Incompetent Teacher, 1984, The Incompetent Teacher, 1986, Problem Based Learning for Adminstrators, 1992; contbr. articles to profl. jours. Named Outstanding Young Man of Ind., C. of C., 1960; named hon. prof. and cert. of honor So. China Normal U., 1989. Mem. Am. Ednl. Rsch. Assn. (v.p. 1974-75). Office: Stanford U Sch Edn Stanford CA 94305

BRIDGES, ROBERT MCSTEEN, mechanical engineer; b. Oakland, Calif., Apr. 17, 1914; s. Robert and Josephine (Hite) B.; BS cum laude in Mech. Engring., U. So. Calif., 1940; postgrad. UCLA; m. Edith Brownwood, Oct. 26, 1945; children: Ann, Lawrence, Robert. Engr. Nat. Supply Co., Torrance, Calif., 1940-41; design engr. landing gear and hydraulics Lockheed Aircraft Corp., Burbank, Calif., 1941-46; missile hydraulic controls design engr. Convair, San Diego, 1946-48; sr. staff engr. oceanic systems mech. design Bendix Corp., Sylmar, Calif., 1948—; adv. ocean engring. U.S. Congress. Com. chmn. Boy Scouts Am., 1961. Recipient award of Service Am. Inst. Aero. Engrs., 1965. Mem. Marine Tech. Soc. (charter; com. cables, connectors 1969), Tau Beta Pi. Republican. Patentee in field of undersea devices (54 internat., 14 U.S.), including deep ocean rubber band moor; inventor U.S. Navy sonobuoy rotochute; contbr. articles to profl. jours. and confs. Home: 10314 Vanalden Ave Northridge CA 91326-3326 Office: Allied Bendix Aerospace Corp Oceanics Div 15825 Roxford St San Fernando CA 91342-3537

BRIDGES, ROY DUBARD, JR., career officer; b. Atlanta, July 19, 1943; s. Roy D. and Elizabeth A. (Roberson) B.; m. Benita L. Allbaugh, Mar. 26, 1967; children: Tanya M., Brian N. BS in Engring. Sci., USAF Acad., 1965; MS in Astronautical Engring., Purdue U., 1966. Commd. 2d lt. USAF, 1965, advanced through grades to maj. gen., 1992; test pilot Air Force Flight Test Ctr., Edwards AFB, Calif., 1970-75; student Air Command and Staff Coll., Maxwell AFB, Ala., 1975-76; staff officer Hdqrs. USAF, Pentagon, Washington, 1976-79; dep. dir. plans Detachment 3, Air Force Flight Test Ctr., Henderson, Nev., 1979-80; astronaut (pilot) Johnson Space Ctr., NASA, Houston, 1980-86; comdr. 6510th Test Wing, Edwards AFB, Calif., 1986-89; comdr., Ea. Space and Missile Ctr., Patrick AFB, Fla., 1989-90; dep. chief of staff for test and resources Air Force Systems Command, Andrews AFB, Md., 1990-91; comdr. Air Force Flight Test Ctr., Edwards AFB, Calif., 1991—; pilot space shuttle Challenger, NASA,1985. Recipient Space Flight award Am. Astronautical Soc., 1986, Astronaut Engring. Alumnus award Purdue U., 1990. Mem. Soc. Exptl. Test Pilots, Air Force Assn. Methodist. Office: Air Force Flight Test Ctr AFFTC/CC Edwards AFB CA 95324

BRIDGES, WILLIAM BRUCE, electrical engineer, researcher, educator; b. Inglewood, Calif., Nov. 29, 1934; s. Newman K. and Doris L. (Brown) B.; m. Carol Ann French, Aug. 24, 1957 (div. 1986); children: Ann Marjorie, Bruce Kendall, Michael Alan; m. Linda Josephine McManus, Nov. 15, 1986. B.E.E., U. Calif. at Berkeley, 1956, M.E.E. (Gen. Electric Rice fellow), 1957, Ph.D. in Elec. Engring. (NSF fellow), 1962. Assoc. elec. engring. U. Calif., Berkeley, 1957-59, grad. research engr., 1959-61; mem. tech. staff Hughes Research Labs. div. Hughes Aircraft Co., Malibu, Calif., 1960-77, sr. scientist, 1968-77, mgr. laser dept., 1969-70; prof. elec. engring. and applied physics Calif. Inst. Tech., Pasadena, 1977—, Carl F Braun prof. engring., 1983—, exec. officer elec. engring., 1978-81; lectr. elec. engring. U. So. Calif., Los Angeles, 1962-64; Sherman Fairchild Disting. scholar Calif. Inst. Tech., 1974-75; chmn. Conf. on Laser Engring. and Applications, Washington, 1971; bd. dirs. Uniphase Corp. Author: (with C.K. Birdsall) Electron Dynamics of Diode Regions, 1966; contbr. articles on gas lasers, optical systems and microwave tubes to profl. jours.; assoc. editor: IEEE Jour. Quantum Electronics, 1977-82, Jour. Optical Soc. Am., 1978-83; inventor noble gas ion laser; patentee in field. Active Boy Scouts Am., 1968-82; bd. dirs. Ventura County Campfire Girls, 1973-76; mem. Air Force Sci. Adv. Bd., 1985-89. Recipient L.A. Hyland Patent award, 1969, Arthur L. Schawlow award Laser Inst. Am., 1986. Fellow IEEE (chmn. Los Angeles chpt. Quantum Electronics and Applications Soc. 1979-81, Quantum Electronics award 1988), Optical Soc. Am. (chmn. lasers and electro-optics tech. group 1974-75, objectives and policies com. 1981-86, 89-91, bd. dirs. 1982-84, v.p. 1986, pres.-elect 1987, pres. 1988, past pres. 1989), Laser Inst. Am.; mem. Nat. Acad. Engring., Nat. Acad. Scis., Am. Radio Relay League, Phi Beta Kappa, Sigma Xi, Tau Beta Pi, Eta Kappa Nu (One of Outstanding Young Elec. Engrs. for 1966). Lutheran. Office: Calif Inst Tech Watson Bldg 128-95 Pasadena CA 91125

BRIDGFORTH, ROBERT MOORE, JR., aerospace engineer; b. Lexington, Miss., Oct. 21, 1918; s. Robert Moore and Theresa (Holder) B.; student Miss. State Coll., 1935-37; BS, Iowa State Coll., 1940; MS, MIT, 1948; postgrad. Harvard U., 1949; m. Florence Jarnberg, November 7, 1943; children: Robert Moore, Alice Theresa. Asst. engr. Standard Oil Co., of Ohio, 1940; teaching fellow M.I.T., 1940-41, instr. chemistry, 1941-43, research asst., 1943-44, mem. staff div. indsl. cooperation, 1944-47; asso. prof. physics and chemistry Emory and Henry Coll., 1949-51; rsch. engr. Boeing Airplane Co., Seattle, 1951-54, rsch. specialist 1954-55, sr. group engr., 1955-58, chief propulsion systems sect. Systems Mgmt. Office, 1958-59, chief propulsion rsch. unit, 1959-60; chmn. bd. Rocket Rsch. Corp. (name now Rockcor, Inc.), 1960-69, Explosives Corp. Am., 1966-69. Fellow AIAA (assoc.), Brit. Interplanetary Soc., Am. Inst. Chemists; mem. AAAS, Am. Astronautical Soc. (dir.), Am. Chem. Soc., Am. Rocket Soc. (pres. Pacific NW 1955), Am. Ordnance Assn., Am. Inst. Physics, Am. Assn. Physics Tchrs., Tissue Culture Assn., Soc. for Leukocyte Biology, N.Y. Acad. Scis., Combustion Inst., Sigma Xi. Home: 4325 87th Ave SE Mercer Island WA 98040-4127

BRIDGMAN, JAMES CAMPBELL, lawyer; b. Boston, July 5, 1950; s. Howard Allen and Esther Campbell (Floyd) B. BA in French, Beloit Coll., 1973; M Marine Affairs, U. R.I., 1977; JD, U. Miami, Fla., 1981. Bar: Fla. 1981, Mass. 1982, U.S. Dist. Ct. Mass. 1982, U.S. Ct. Appeals (1st cir.) 1982, Calif. 1985, U.S. Dist. Ct. (no. dist.) Calif. 1985, U.S. Ct. Appeals (9th cir.) 1985, U.S. Supreme Ct. 1985, U.S. Dist. Ct. (ea. dist.) Calif. 1986, U.S. Dist. Ct. Hawaii 1986, Paraguay, 1993. Assoc. Law Office of Irving H. Sheff, Boston, 1983-85, Law Office of James C. Gahan, Boston, 1985; sole practice San Francisco, 1985-88; ptnr. Aspelin & Bridgman, San Francisco, 1988—; cons. internat. trade, U.S. law, internat. law Asuncion, Paraguay, 1990—; non-govtl. rep. 3d United Nations Conf. on Law of the Sea, 1973-81. Contbr. articles to profl. jours. Mem. ABA, Mass. Bar Assn., San Francisco Bar Assn., Assn. Trial Lawyers Am. Office: 220 Montgomery St Ste 813 San Francisco CA 94104-3410

BRIDWELL, NAIDYNE BROWN, classical languages educator; b. Owensboro, Ky., Jan. 6, 1924; d. Edward Mitchell and Nina (Nelson) Brown; m. Wilburn Fowler Bridwell, June 21, 1958; children: Marion Mitchell, Laura Naidyne. BA summa cum laude, Georgetown (Ky.) Coll., 1945; MA, U. Mich., 1950; postgrad. Am. Sch. Classical Studies, Athens, Greece, 1970, Northwestern U., 1972-75. Cert. all grade supr., Ill. Tchr. Latin, Washburn High Sch., Mpls., 1956-62, Forest View High Sch., Arlington Heights, Ill., 1965-68, John Hersey High Sch., Arlington Heights, 1968-84; prof. classical langs. Regis U., Denver, 1985—. Coord. host program for internat. students Colo. Sch. Mines, Golden. Mem. Vergilian Soc. (trustee 1979-82), Classical Assn. Mid. West and South (v.p. 1980-84, merit com. 1990—, Semple fellow 1970, V.P.'s award 1984), Am. Classical League, Colo. Classics Assn. (sec. 1991—), Nat. Com. for Promotion Latin and Greek (state liaison chmn. 1988-92), Archaeol. Inst. Am.

BRIDWELL, WILBURN FOWLER, food company executive; b. Atlanta, July 16, 1933; s. Floyd McRae and Marion (Fowler) B.; m. Naidyne Brown, June 21, 1958; children: Marion Mitchell, Laura Naidyne. BA, Vanderbilt U., 1955. Chemist Coca-Cola Co., Atlanta, 1955-59, Land O' Lakes Co., Mpls., 1956-61; food technologist Kroger Co., Cin., 1961-64; group leader Kraft Foods, Glenview, Ill., 1964-83; v.p. Hudson Industries, Troy, Ala., 1983-84; tech. dir. Rustco Products, Denver, 1984-86; prin. Bridwell Group, Denver, 1986—. Mem. Inst. Food Technologists, Am. Assn. Cereal Chemists (chmn. chem. levening 1984-87). Baptist.

BRIEGER, STEPHEN GUSTAVE, management consultant; b. Marburg, Ger., Sept. 7, 1935; came to U.S., naturalized, 1945; s. Heinrich and Kate L. (Steitz) B.; B.Sc., Springfield (Mass.) Coll., 1955; M.S., Fla. State U., 1970, Ph.D., 1972; m. Karen L. Jentes, Nov. 27, 1968; children—Jennifer B., Benjamin A. Tchr., Calif. schs., 1954-69; indsl. cons. mgmt. tng., 1960-70; mgmt. cons. Nebr. Criminal Justice System, 1972; research criminologist Stanford Research Inst., 1972-74; evaluation cons. Office Gov. Calif., 1974-76; mgmt. devel. assoc. Am. Electronics Assn., 1976-80; mgr. employee and mgmt. devel. ISS Sperry Univac, Santa Clara, Calif., 1980-83; mgr. tng. recruiting and devel. Lawrence Livermore Nat. Lab., U. Calif., 1983—; mem. faculty U.S. Internat. U., St. Mary's Coll., U. San Francisco. Mem. Am. Soc. Tng. and Devel., Am. Mgmt. Assn., Am. Electronics Assn. Author studies, reports in field. Home: 1665 Fairorchard Ave San Jose CA 95125-4935 Office: PO Box 5508 Livermore CA 94551-5508

BRIEN, LOIS ANN, psychologist, educator; b. Cleve., Sept. 24, 1928; d. Alexander and Anne Lois (Katz) B.; m. Melvin Lintz, June 1961 (div. June 1964). BFA, Ohio U., 1950; MA, U. Ala., 1953; PhD, U. Iowa, 1959. Instr. Auburn (Ala.) U., 1953-55; clin. instr. Baylor Coll. Medicine, Houston, 1959-64; diagnostician Houston Speech and Hearing Ctr., 1959-64; faculty, speech com. Case Western Reserve U., Cleve., 1965-69; faculty, psychology San Francisco State U., 1970-72; pvt. practice San Francisco, 1969-79; faculty Calif. Sch. Profl. Psychology, Berkeley, 1971-79; pvt. practice Palm Springs, 1981-82; faculty, women's studies San Diego State U., 1983-86; pvt. practice Encinitas, Calif., 1982—; prof. psychology Nat. U., San Diego, 1984-87, dean Sch. Psychology, 1987-91, dean emeritus, assoc. faculty, 1991—. Contbr. articles to profl. jours. and textbooks. Commr. Marin County Commn. on the Status of Women, 1974-77. U.S. Office Edn. grantee, 1970-71. Mem. NOW, Am. Psychol. Assn., Calif. Assn. Marriage, Family Therapy, Am. Assn. Marriage, Family Therapy, Am. Acad. Psychotherapists. Democrat. Jewish. Office: 1012 2nd St Ste 200 Encinitas CA 92024-5053 also: Nat U Sch of Psychology Dept Psychology University Park San Diego CA 92108-4194

BRIERLEY, JAMES ALAN, research administrator; b. Denver, Dec. 22, 1938; s. Everette and Carrie (Berg) B.; m. Corale Louise Beer, Dec. 21, 1965. BS in Bacteriology, Colo. State U., 1961; MS in Microbiology, Mont. State U., 1963, PhD, 1966. Research scientist Martin Marietta Corp., Denver, 1968-69; asst. prof. biology N.Mex. Inst. Mining and Tech., Socorro, 1966-68, from asst. prof. to prof. biology, chmn. dept. biology, 1969-83; research dir. Advanced Mineral Techs., Golden, Colo., 1983-88; chief biologist Newmont Metall. Svcs., Salt Lake City, 1988—; vis. fellow U. Warwick, Coventry, Eng., 1976, vis. prof. Catholic U., Santiago, Chile, 1983; cons. Mountain States Mineral Enterprises, Tucson, 1980, Sandia Nat. Lab., Albuquerque, 1976, Bechtel Civil and Minerals, Scottsdale, Ariz., 1984. Contbr. numerous articles to profl. jours.; patentee in field. Served to staff sgt. Air N.G., 1956-61. Recipient 32 research grants. Fellow AAAS; mem.

Am. Soc. Microbiology, Soc. Gen. Microbiology, Sigma Xi. Home: 2872 E Elk Horn Ln Sandy UT 84093-6595 Office: Newmont Metall Svcs 417 Wakara Way Ste 210 Salt Lake City UT 84108-1255

BRIERLEY, RICHARD GREER, business consultant; b. Kearney, N.J., July 1, 1915; s. Josiah Richards and Castella Sophia (Parker) B.; m. Margaret Jean LaLone, Aug. 24, 1940; children: Linda, Sandra, Martha, Ann. AB, Dartmouth Coll., 1936; MBA, Tuck Sch., 1937; AMP, Harvard U., 1952. Salesman Armstrong Cork Co., Lancaster, Pa., 1937-40; with Archer-Daniels-Midland Co., Mpls., 1940-64; exec. v.p. Arcaer-Daniels-Midland Co., Mpls., 1979-61, Drackett Co., Cin., 1961-66; pres., chief exec. officer Bristol Myers Can., Toronto, Ont., 1966-68; v.p. corp. planning Bristol Myers Co., N.Y.C., 1968-70; pres., chief exec. officer Stearns & Foster, Cin., 1970-75, chmn. bd. dirs., 1975-76; pres., chmn. bd. dirs. Brierley Assocs., Carefree, Ariz., 1976—; bd. dirs. Transcapital Fin. Corp., Cleve., Galleon Beach Club, Antiqua, W.I. Office: Brierley Assocs 34 Easy St PO Box 2659 Carefree AZ 85377

BRIERLY, KEPPEL, investment executive; b. Denver, Mar. 9, 1909; s. Justin Keppel and Pearl A. (Walters) B.; Engr. Mines, Colo. Sch. Mines, 1934; student, Denver U., 1936-37, U. Colo., 1939-41; m. Ruth E. Davis, Nov. 4, 1934; 1 child, Barbara Brierly Brann. Engr., Pub. Service Co. of Colo., Denver, 1930-38; coordinator, tchr. Denver pub. schs., 1938-41; pres. J & K Constrn. Co., Denver, 1946-68; pres. Denver Lions Found., 1967-68; bd. dirs. Colo. Leukemia Soc. Served to lt. col. AUS, 1941-45; lt. col. Res. ret. Decorated Bronze Star Medal; also VI Haakon (Norway); award (France). Registered profl. engr., Colo.; lic. real estate broker, Colo. Mem. Denver Assn. Home Builders (pres. 1949, hon. life mem.), Assoc. Bldg. Contractors Colo. (pres. 1956-57, Assoc. Gen. Contractors Am. (dir. 1956-65), hon. life mem.), Am. Arbitration Assn., Theta Tau, Kappa Sigma, Blue Key. Presbyterian. Clubs: Denver Press (life), Denver Athletic (life), Pinehurst Country (life), Lions (pres. 1963-64), Masons, Shriners, Royal Order Jesters (life). Home: 5151 Juniper St Littleton CO 80123-1533 Office: 601 Broadway Ste 206 Denver CO 80203-3424

BRIESMEISTER, RICHARD ARTHUR, chemist; b. Mansfield, Ohio, Apr. 21, 1942; s. Arthur Conrad and Eileen Patricia (Moore) B.; m. Margaret Knudson (div.); 1 child, Anne Marie Briesmeister Rowlison. BS in Chemistry, U. Wyo., 1965. Technician Los Alamos (N.Mex.) Nat. Lab., 1965-79, staff mem., 1980-85, project leader, 1985-88, dep. group leader, 1988-92, program officer, maintenance mgmt. office, 1992—. Mem. Am. Glovebox Soc. Office: Los Alamos Nat Lab MS D473 PO Box 1663 Los Alamos NM 87545-0001

BRIGGS, DEAN WINFIELD, engineering consulting company executive; b. Boise, Idaho, Sept. 27, 1953; s. William Winfield and Shirley Anne (Churchill) B.; m. Debbie K. Sakahara, Nov. 4, 1989. BSCE, U. Idaho, 1975, MSCE, 1978. Registered profl. engr., Alaska, Ariz., Calif., Colo., Fla., Hawaii, Idaho, Nev., Oreg., Tex., Wash., Wyo. Design engr. J-U-B Engrs. Inc., Boise, 1975-79, structural projects engr., 1980-83, mgr. structural dept., 1984-91; pres. Briggs Engring. Inc., Boise, 1986—. Mem. Boise City Bldg. Code Com., 1988—. Mem. Nat. Soc. Engrs., Constrn. Specifications Inst. (edn. chmn. 1988—), Prestressed Concrete Inst., Am. Concrete Inst., Structural Engrs. Assn. Idaho (bd. dirs. 1988—), Tau Beta Pi, Pi Delta Theta. Home: 3215 N Welford Ave Boise ID 83704-4399 Office: 1111 N Orchard St Ste 600 Boise ID 83705-1966

BRIGGS, DINUS MARSHALL, agriculturist; b. Stillwater, Okla., Mar. 5, 1940; s. Hilton Marshall and Lillian (Dinusson) B.; m. June Elaine Wolf, Sept. 2, 1962; children: Denise, Deborah. BS, S.D. State U., 1962; MS, Iowa State U., 1969, PhD, 1971. Asst. pastor Stroudsburg (Pa.) Meth. Ch., 1962-64; grad. asst. Iowa State U., Ames, 1964-66, research assoc., 1966-70; asst. prof. N.C. State U., Raleigh, 1970-75; asst. dir. Ark. Agrl. Expt. Sta., Fayetteville, 1976-82; assoc. dir. N.Mex. Agrl. Expt. Sta., Las Cruces, 1982—. Co-author: Modern Breeds of Livestock, 1980. Mem. Poultry Sci. Assn. (resolutions com. 1972-73), Am. Assn. Animal Sci., World's Poultry Sci., Sigma Xi. Lodge: Rotary. Home: 1927 Francine Ct Las Cruces NM 88005-5509 Office: NMex Agrl Experiment Sta PO Box 30003 Dept 3BF Las Cruces NM 88003-0003

BRIGGS, EDWARD SAMUEL, naval officer; b. St. Paul, Oct. 4, 1926; s. Charles William and Lois Ione (Johnson) B.; m. Nanette Parks, June 7, 1949; 1 child, Jeffrey Charles. BS, U.S. Naval Acad., 1949. Commd. ensign U.S. Navy, 1949, advanced through grades to vice adm., 1980; commanding officer USS Turner Joy, USS Jouett; asst. chief staff plans, chief of staff U.S. 7th Fleet, 1972-73; fleet ops. officer, asst. chief staff ops. U.S. Pacific Fleet, Makalapa, Hawaii, 1973-75; comdr. Crusier-Destroyer Group 3, San Diego, 1975-77, Navy Recruiting Command, Arlington, Va., 1977-79, Naval Logistics Command, U.S. Pacific Fleet, Naval Base, Pearl Harbor, Hawaii, 1979-80; dep. comdr.-in-chief U.S. Pacific Fleet, Pearl Harbor, 1980-82; comdr. Naval Surface Force U.S. Atlantic Fleet, 1982-84; ret., 1984. Decorated Bronze Star with combat device and one star, Air medals (2), Navy Commendation medal with combat device and two stars, Legion of Merit with combat device and four stars, D.S.M.; Vietnamese Navy Gallantry medal. Mem. Surface Navy Assn., U.S. Naval Acad. Alumni Assn., Naval Inst., Navy League. Home: 3648 Lago Sereno Escondido CA 92029-7902

BRIGGS, JAMES HENRY, II, engineering administrator; b. San Francisco, Dec. 25, 1953; s. James Henry and Barbara (Cordes) B.; m. Niwana Page, Sept. 1, 1979; children: Melanie Shannon, James Henry III. AA in Bus. Adminstrn., Albany (Ga.) Jr. Coll., 1976; BS in Computer Sci., U. N.C., Wilmington, 1979; BSEE, So. Tech., Marietta, Ga., 1985. Lic. 1st class radio telephone; registered profl. engr., Calif. Asst. chief engr. WECT-TV, Wilmington, 1978-82; maintenance supr. Cable News Network, Atlanta, 1982-85; mgr. engring. ops. KCOP-TV, L.A., 1985-87; sr. product support engr. Abekas Video Systems, Redwood City, Calif., 1987-92; dir. engring. D.T.S., Union City, Calif., 1991—. Editor: Video Prodn. in the 90's. Mem. Soc. Motion Picture and TV Engrs., Soc. Broadcast Engrs., Greenpeace, Toastmasters Club, Lions. Office: DTS 2500 Medallion Ste 198 Union City CA 94587

BRIGGS, ROBERT NATHAN, electrical engineer; b. Miami Beach, Fla., Dec. 22, 1946; s. Donald Hickes and Harriett Martha (Mercer) B.; m. Polly Elizabeth Partridge, Dec. 22, 1970; children: Nathan Michael, Carey Robert, Christopher Alan. BSEE, Northrop Inst. Tech., 1974; postgrad. in Physics, U. Nev., Las Vegas, 1978-81. Electronics engr. U.S. Dept. Energy Telcom Inc., Las Vegas, 1974-75; sr. fiber optics engr. U.S. Dept. Energy Holmes & Narver, Las Vegas, 1975-81; dir. quality assurance Am. Fiber Optics, Signal Hill, Calif., 1981-83; sr. staff engr. command and data handling lab. TRW, Inc., Redondo Beach, Calif., 1983-84, sr. sect. head telecommunications lab., 1984-85, sr. staff engr. electro-optic rsch. ctr., 1985-86, Tracking and Data Relay Satellite System Telemetry, Tracking and Command systems engr. spacecraft electronics system lab., 1986—. Mem. Am. Inst. Aeronautics and Astronautics, Inc., Optical Soc. Am. Home: 6532 Verde Ridge Rd Palos Verdes Peninsula CA 90274-4632 Office: TRW Inc Space and Tech Group One Space Park Redondo Beach CA 90278

BRIGGS, WINSLOW RUSSELL, plant biologist, educator; b. St. Paul, Apr. 29, 1928; s. John DeQuedville and Marjorie (Winslow) B.; m. Ann Morrill, June 30, 1955; children: Caroline, Lucia, Marion. B.A., Harvard U., 1951, M.A., 1952, Ph.D., 1956. Instr. biol. scis. Stanford (Calif.) U., 1955-57, asst. prof., 1957-62, asso. prof., 1962-66, prof., 1966-67; prof. biology Harvard U., 1967-73; dir. dept. plant biology Carnegie Instn. of Washington, Stanford, 1973-93. Author: (with others) Life on Earth, 1973; Asso. editor: (with others) Annual Review of Plant Physiology, 1961-72; editor (with others), 1972—; Contbr. (with others) articles on plant growth and devel. and photobiology to profl. jours. Recipient Alexander von Humboldt U.S. sr. scientist award, 1984-85; John Simon Guggenheim fellow, 1973-74, Deutsche Akademie der Naturforscher Leopoldina, 1986. Fellow AAAS; mem. Am. Soc. Plant Physiologists (pres. 1975-76), Calif. Bot. Soc. (pres. 1976-77), Nat. Acad. Scis., Am. Acad. Arts and Scis., Am. Inst. Biol. Scis. (pres. 1980-81), Am. Soc. Photbiology, Bot. Soc. Am., Nature Conservancy, Sigma Xi. Home: 480 Hale St Palo Alto CA 94301-2207 Office: Carnegie Inst Washington Dept Plant Biology 290 Panama St Palo Alto CA 94305-4170

BRIGHAM, JOHN ALLEN, JR., financial executive, environmentalist; b. San Francisco, June 17, 1942; s. John Allen, Sr. and Susan (Endberg) B.; m. Patricia Katherine Carney, Feb. 4, 1968; 1 child, Jennifer. BS in Acctg., San Jose State U., 1967. Acct. Shell Oil Co. Data Ctr., Palo Alto, Calif., 1963-66; asst. plant controller Brown Co., Santa Clara, Calif., 1966-68; budget mgr. Varian Assocs., Palo Alto, 1968-80; cost acctg. mgr. Adac Labs., San Jose, Calif., 1980-86; controller Crystal Tech., Palo Alto, 1986-90; environ. stock analyst, environ. industry stock newsletter, 1990—. Del. League Calif. Cities, 1974-78; mem. Saratoga (Calif.) City Council, 1974-78; vice-chmn. Santa Clara County Polity Planning Use Commn., 1975-78; chmn. Santa Clara Com. on Mass Transit, 1976-78; chmn. Open Space Bond Issue, 1976; treas. Calif. State Solar Bond Issue, 1976; mem. Castle Rock State Pk. Com., 1972-74; vice-chmn. Saratoga Hillside Com. 1978-79. Recipient 10 Yr. Sierra Club Activist award, 1989, Chpt. Svc. award, 1990, Spl. Achievement award, 1990; Local Outstanding Young Man of Am. award, 1974, Siemens USA Personality of the Month award, Jan. 1990. Mem. Am. Entomol. Soc., Archeol. Inst. Am., Nat. Acctg. Assn., Sierra Club (vice chmn., treas. Loma chpt. 1985—, internat. chmn. 1989—, Centennial chmn. 1990—, liaison to USSR and Mex., co-chair Earth Day 1990, taskforce 1989, chmn. fin. commn. 1985—), Am. Diabetes Soc. (treas., bd. dirs. Santa Clara County chpt.), Nat. Wildlife Fedn., Cousteau Soc., Planetary Soc., Nat. Audubon Soc. Republican. Roman Catholic.

BRIGHAM, RALPH ALLEN, university administrator; b. Aberdeen, S.D., July 25, 1949; s. Robert Over and Margaret Eugene (Krueger) B.; m. Susan Deborah Ransom, June 14, 1975 (div. July 1992); children: Robert Ransom, Matthew Paul. BS, No. Mont. Coll., Havre, 1972, MEd, 1978; DEd, Mont. State U., Bozeman, 1987. Guidance counselor Brady (Mont.) Pub. Schs., 1975-77; student activities coord. No. Mont. Coll., Havre, 1977-79, registrar, dir. admissions, 1979-82; asst. registrar Mont. State U., Bozeman, 1982-85, dir. career svcs., 1985—; cons. Coun. Advancement Experiential Learning Pathways, Denver, 1988—. Dir. Gallatin Devel. Corp., Bozeman, 1992; active Mont. Spl. Olympics, Bozeman, 1989-90. With U.S. Army, 1972-74. Mem. Rocky Mountain Coll. Placement Assn. (evaluation 1988), Western Coll. Placement Assn. (evaluator 1990), Coll. Placement Coun., Mont. Career Planning and Placement Assn. (pres. 1987-88), Bozeman Area C. of C. (pres. 1992, dir. 1989—), Phi Delta Kappa (pres. 1985-86), Kappa delta Pi. Home: 105 E Granite Apt D Bozeman MT 59715 Office: Mont State U Career Svcs 125 SUB Bozeman MT 59717

BRIGHT, DONALD BOLTON, environmental consultant; b. Ventura, Calif., Nov. 28, 1930; s. Claude Wilson and Ruby Thelma (Bolton) B.; m. Patricia Jean McLaughlin, Nov. 25, 1955; children: Debra Ann, Steven Allan. BA in Zoology, U. So. Calif., 1952, MS in Biology, 1957, PhD in Biology, 1967; postdoctoral studies, Ariz. State U., 1974. Cert. safety mgr., exec., hazardous materials supr., Calif.; registered environ. auditor, Calif. Instr. Fullerton (Calif.) Coll., 1960-67; prof., chmn. dept. biol. scis. Calif. State U., Fullerton, 1967-77; dir. commerce Port of Long Beach, Calif., 1977-78, dir. environ. affairs, 1975-78; exec. v.p. EFS, Inc., Los Angeles, 1978-79; pres. Bright & Assocs., Anaheim, Calif., 1979-88; chief exec. officer Environ. Audit Inc., Placentia, Calif., 1987—; Mem. Marine Sci. Coast Guard Adv. Com., Washington, 1977-80. Editor: Proc. National Magazine Science Edmc., 1970, Proc. Southern California Coastal Zone Supervisor, 1972; sci. advisor Am. Scientist mag., 1975-77; contbr. articles to profl. jours. Chmn. Calif. Regulatory Coastal Commn., Long Beach, 1973-75. Served to 1st lt. U.S. Army, 1952-55. Grantee NSF, 1969-75. Mem. Am. Inst. Planners, So. Calif. Acad. Sci. (v.p. 1975-78, fellow 1975), Western Soc. Naturalists, Sierra Club, Sigma Xi, Phi Sigma. Democrat. Presbyterian. Home: 921 Finnell Way Placentia CA 92670-4446 Office: Environ Audit Inc 1000A Ortega Way Placentia CA 92670-7125

BRILEY, DAVID WESLEY, landscape architect, environmental planner; b. San Diego, Dec. 25, 1952; s. Wesley Carol and Eunice (Sjogren) B. BA in Math., UCLA, 1974, MS in Kinesiology, 1976; M of Landscape Architecture and Environ. Planning, Calif. State Poly. U., 1992. Lic. landscape architect, Calif., Nev.; cert. natural resource expert. Project mgr. Crescent Bay Co., Santa Monica, Calif., 1983-87; owner Briley Assocs., Santa Monica, 1987—. Mem. Am. Soc. Landscape Architects (merit award 1991, honor award 1992), Assn. Environ. Profls., Internat. Assn. Landscape Ecology, Internat. Soc. Ecological Econs., Calif. Native Plant Soc., UCLA Alumni Assn., Santa Monica Rugby Club. Home: 909 Euclid St # 12 Santa Monica CA 90403 Office: Briley Assocs 1625 Olympic Blvd Santa Monica CA 90404-3822

BRILL, JAMES LATHROP, finance executive; b. Pasadena, Calif., Apr. 11, 1951; s. Richard H. and Elizabeth (Schmidt) B.; m. Deborah May, Dec. 16, 1978; 1 child, Samantha. BS, US Naval Acad., 1973; MBA, UCLA, 1980. Various positions Union Bank, L.A., 1980-88; sr. v.p. fin., chief fin. officer Merisel, Inc., El Segundo, Calif., 1988—, also bd. dirs. Lt. USN, 1973-78. Mem. US Naval Acad. Alumni Assn., UCLA Alumni Assn., Beta Gamma Sigma. Office: Merisel Inc 200 Continental Blvd El Segundo CA 90245-4510

BRILL, JOEL VICTOR, gastroenterologist; b. Phila., Jan. 28, 1956; s. Earl Burton and Lois Elaine (Werner) B.; m. Laurie Ann Lissner, May 17, 1980; children: Jacob, Zachary. BA, UCLA, 1976; MD, Chgo. Med. Sch., 1976. Diplomate Am. Bd. Internal Medicine, Gastroenterology. Intern Sepulveda (Calif.) VA Hosp., 1980-81, resident internal medicine, 1981-83; fellow gastroenterology U. So. Calif. Med. Ctr., Los Angeles, 1983-85; pvt. practice gastroenterology Covington, Menz, Brill, Ventura, Calif., 1985—; instr. in field. Fellow Am. Coll. Gastroenterology; mem. ACP, Am. Gastroent. Assn., Am. Soc. Gastrointestinal Endoscopy, Am. Soc. for Parentral and Enteral Nutrition. Democrat. Jewish. Office: Covington Menz & Brill Ste 404 168 N Brent St Ventura CA 93003

BRIMMER, CLARENCE ADDISON, federal judge; b. Rawlins, Wyo., July 11, 1922; s. Clarence Addison and Geraldine (Zingsheim) B.; m. Emily O. Docken, Aug. 2, 1953; children: Geraldine Ann, Philip Andrew, Andrew Howard, Elizabeth Ann. B.A., U. Mich., 1944, J.D., 1947. Bar: Wyo. 1948. Pvt. practice law Rawlins, 1948-71, mcpl. judge, 1948-54; U.S. commr., magistrate, 1963-71; atty. gen. Wyo. Cheyenne, 1971-74; U.S. atty., 1975; chief U.S. dist. judge Wyo. Dist. Cheyenne, 1975-92; mem. panel multi-dist. litigation, 1992—. Sec. Rawlins Bd. Pub. Utilities, 1954-66, Gov.'s Com. on Wyo. Water, 1963-65; sec. Wyo. Rep. Com., 1966, chmn., 1967-71, Rep. gubernatorial candidate, 1974; trustee Rocky Mountain Mineral Law Found., 1963-75. Served with USAAF, 1945-46. Mem. ABA, Wyo. Bar Assn., Am. Judicature Soc., Laramie County Bar Assn., Carbon County Bar Assn. Episcopalian. Clubs: Masons, Shriners. Office: US Dist Ct PO Box 985 Cheyenne WY 82003-0985

BRINDAMOUR, JEAN-LOUIS EDMOND, II, book publisher; b. San Francisco, Oct. 5, 1933; s. Jean-Louis Edmond and Margaret Catherine (Kelly) B. BA, San Francisco State U., 1956; MS, Columbia U., 1965, PhD, 1966. Asst. to asst. dir. Columbia U. Press, N.Y.C., 1960-66; mgr. pub. rels. Xerox Edn. Group, N.Y.C., 1966-67; asst. to pres., dir. new publs. Consol. Book Pubs., Chgo., 1968-71, dir. Eng. Lang. Inst. of Am., 1968-71; dir. spl. publs. Pyramid Publs., N.Y.C., 1971-74; v.p., gen. mgr. Celestial Arts, Millbrae, Calif., 1974-75; v.p. editorial & mktg. Beta Books, San Diego, 1976-77; mng. dir. Dawne-Leigh Publs., San Rafael, Calif., 1978-80; pres. Strawberry Hill Press, Portland, Oreg., 1976—; prof. speech therapy U. Ill., Chgo. Circle Campus, 1968-72; pub. cons. Brindamour & Assocs., San Francisco, 1976—; instr. cert. in pub. program U. Calif. Berkeley, 1976-90; lectr. in field. Author: (book) Some Heads Have Stomachs, 1964, (booklet) A Survey of Western Publishing, 1975, An Annotated Bibliography of Publishing, 1992; contbr. to book: Editors on Editing, 1993. Cons. Willamette Writers, Portland, Oreg., 1990—. Recipient Gold medal Cannes Film Festival, 1965, Spl. award Peace Corps, 1964, Spl. award MLA, 1971, Tunbridge award Lone Mtn. Coll., 1975. Mem. Willamette Writers, Women's Nat. Book Assn., Calif. Writers' Club, Bay Area Editors' Forum. Office: Strawberry Hill Press 3848 SE Division St Portland OR 97202-1641

BRINEGAR, CLAUDE STOUT, oil company executive; b. Rockport, Calif., Dec. 16, 1926; s. Claude Leroy Stout and Lyle (Rawles) B.; m. Elva Jackson, July 1, 1950 (div.); children: Claudia, Meredith, Thomas; m. Mary Katharine Potter Garrity, May 14, 1983. BA, Stanford U., 1950, MS, 1951, PhD, 1954. V.p. econs. and planning Union Oil (now Unocal), L.A., 1965; pres. pure oil div. Union Oil (now Unocal), Palatine, Ill., 1965-69; sr. v.p., pres. refining and mktg. Union Oil (now Unocal), L.A., 1969-73; U.S. sec. of transp. Washington, 1973-75; sr. v.p. adminstr. Unocal Corp., L.A., 1975-85, mem. exec. com., 1975-92, exec. v.p., chief fin. officer, 1985-91, also bd. dirs., vice chmn. bd., also bd. dirs.; founding dir. Consol. Rail Corp., Washington, 1974-75, 90—; bd. dirs. Maxicare Health Plans, Inc.; vis. scholar Stanford U., 1992—. Author: monograph on econs. and price behavior, 1970; contbr. articles to profl. jours. on statistics and econs. Chmn. Calif. Citizens Compensation Commn., 1990—; mem. regional selection panel White House Fellows Program, 1976-83, chmn., 1983. Mem. Am. Petroleum Inst. (bd. dirs. 1976-85, 88-91, hon. life dir. 1992), Calif. Club, Georgetown Club, Internat. Club, Boothbay Harbor Yacht Club, Southport Yahct Club, Phi Beta Kappa, Sigma Xi. Republican. Office: Unocal Corp Unocal Ctr 1201 W 5th St Los Angeles CA 90017-1461

BRINEGAR, DON EUGENE, real estate sales professional; b. Winston Salem, N.C., Mar. 17, 1929; s. Carl Adam and Polly Ann (Cumbie) B.; m. Sara S. Houser, July 9, 1955; children: Debra, Diane, Lori, Kay. BA, Rollins Coll., 1951; MBA, U. Mo., 1969. Commd. 2d lt. USAF, 1951, advanced through grades to major, pilot, 1951-55, 62-79, retired, 1979; pilot Pan Am. World Airlines, 1955-62; real estate broker John D. Noble, Phoenix, 1979-91; owner Brinegar Comml. Properties, Phoenix, 1991—. V.p. Jaycees, North Miami, Fla., 1962. Decorated D.F.C., Air medal with 7 oak leaf clusters. Mem. Phoenix Bd. Realtors, Ariz. Assn. for Indsl. Devel., Nat. Assn. Realtors (comml.-investment real estate coun.; cert. comml. investment mem.), Valley Forward. Republican. Home: 4513 W Port Au Prince Ln Glendale AZ 85306-3629 Office: Brinegar Comml Properties 5800 N 19th Ave Ste 209 Phoenix AZ 85015-2436

BRINEGAR, ELIZABETH ANNE, management assistant; b. Las Cruces, N.Mex., Nov. 4, 1953; d. Robert Winston and Helen Earlene (Ward) B.; m. Michael Carl Knox, Dec. 17, 1971 (div. June 1979); children: Michael Carl II, Rebecca Anne. BA in Bus. Adminstrn. magna cum laude, Coll. of Santa Fe, 1992. Rental property mgr. Enid, Okla., 1981-84; from clk.-stenographer to sec.-stenographer USAF, various locations, 1977-84; mgmt. asst. Contract Mgmt. div. USAF, Albuquerque, 1985-90, Phillips Lab., USAF, Albuquerque, 1990-93; USAF Hosp., Albuquerque, 1993—. Mentor, Edn. for Ministry, U. of the South, Sewanee, Tenn; mem. Daus. of the King, St. Mary's Episcopal Ch., Albuquerque. Named to Outstanding Young Women of Am., 1987. Republican.

BRINER, PAMELA JOAN, banker; b. Vancouver, B.C., Can., Apr. 21, 1950; came to U.S., 1953; d. James Henry and Margaret Elaine (Withrow) Pitman; m. Michael Charles Wasmann, Nov. 21, 1970 (div. Jan. 1975); m. John Gaylord Briner, May 17, 1975. Grad. high sch., San Mateo, Calif. Sales clk. Melart's, San Mateo, 1966-69; note clk. Wells Fargo Bank, San Mateo, 1969-70, 72-73; flight attendant Hughes Air West, San Francisco, 1970; receptionist Harris & Stroh, Hayward, Calif., 1970-72; office mgr. Sky Climber, Inc., Brisbane, Calif., 1973; new accounts to cashier Placer Nat. Bank/Bank of Alex Brown, Auburn, Calif., 1974-82; exec. officer The Bank of Commerce, N.A., Auburn, 1983—; bd. dirs. Auburn Palm Terr. Episcopalian. Office: The Bank of Commerce NA 540 Wall St # 5770 Auburn CA 95604-3907

BRING, KARL ELMER, lawyer; b. Mayville, N.D., May 26, 1959; s. Harold Almer and Esther Camille (Olson) B.; m. Susan Elaine VanCamp, Oct. 21, 1990. BSEE, N.D. State U., 1982; JD, U. Denver, 1985. Bar: Colo. 1985. Patent agt. Hewlett-Packard Co., Colorado Springs, Colo., 1984, atty., 1985-90; atty. Hewlett-Packard Co., Ft. Collins, Colo., 1990-92, sr. atty., 1992—. Bd. dirs. Colorado Springs Choral Soc., 1987-90; dem. candidate N.D. State Ho. of Reps., Dist. 20, 1980. Mem. IEEE, ABA, Colo. Bar Assn., Am. Intellectual Propery Law Assn., Am. Corp. Counsel Assn. Lutheran. Office: Hewlett-Packard Co 3404 E Harmony Rd M/S 79 Fort Collins CO 80525

BRINKER, CONNIE JUGE, graphoanalyst, document examiner; b. New Orleans, July 15, 1928; d. Edward Joseph and Faustine Madeline (Aleman) Juge; m. Robert William Brinker, Jan. 4, 1948; children: Richard, Susan, John, Craig, Randy. Student, Fullerton Coll., Calif., 1974-76. Master cert. graphoanalyst; cert. forensic document examiner. Cosmetologist various salons, Fullerton, Calif., 1967-79; owner/operator cosmetology salon Fullerton, 1979—; graphoanalyst and document examiner Brinker & Assocs., Fullerton, 1980—; instr. handwriting analysis, questioned documents; lectr. in field. Author: Reflections, 1984; contbr. articles to profl. jours. Active Boy Scouts Am., Girl Scouts U.S.A.; consolation minister St. Philip Beniz Cath. Community. Recipient Sharon Topper Humanitarian award, Fullerton Coll., 1976. Mem. Internat. Graphoanalysis Soc. (chpt. pres. 1978-79, Cooperator of Yr. 1977, Graphoanalyst of Yr. 1977), Nat. Assn. Document Examiners, Ind. Assn. Questioned Document Examiners, Am. Bd. Forensic Handwriting Analysts, Inc., Amvets Aux., World Assn. Document Examiners. Democrat. Roman Catholic. Office: Brinker and Assocs 107 N Woods Ave Fullerton CA 92632-1636

BRINSTER, KENNETH JOSEPH, construction manager; b. Dickinson, N.D., Jan. 12, 1953; s. Robert George and Dolores Bernadette (Frank) B. A of Engring., Mech. Engring. Tech., Oreg. Inst. Technology, 1973, B of Engring., Mech. Engring. Tech., 1976; MBA, Oreg. State U., 1985. Warehouse supr. Bechtel Group Inc., Sulawesi, Indonesia, 1976-78; nuclear quality control engr. Bechtel Group Inc., Midland, Mich., 1978-79; contract engr. Bechtel Group Inc., Jubail, Saudi Arabia, 1980-81; lead piping engr. Bechtel Group Inc., Kalimantan, Indonesia, 1982-83; maintenance supr. Container Corp. of Am., Renton, Wash., 1985-87; v.p. engring. Pyro Pacific Inc., Klamath Falls, Oreg., 1987-88; constrn. mgr. Harris Group Inc., Portland, Oreg., 1989—. Mem. ASME, U.S. Parachute Assn. Republican.

BRINTON, RICHARD KIRK, marketing executive; b. Hanover, Pa., Apr. 21, 1946; s. James Henry and Mabel (Adelung) B.; m. Joan Marita Ayo, Mar. 21, 1970; children: Katherine, Mark, Michael. BA in Liberal Arts, BS in Indsl. Engring., Pa. State U., 1968. Registered profl. engr., Ohio. From systems engr. to dir. mktg. AccuRay/ABB, Columbus, Ohio, 1968-82; group mktg. dir. AccuRay/ABB, London, 1982-84; internat. sales mgr. Flow Systems, Seattle, 1984, v.p. mktg., 1985-87; dir. mktg. and bus. devel. UTILX Corp., Seattle, 1987-90, v.p. mktg. and bus. devel., 1990-93, v.p. internat. ops., 1993—; chmn. Nippon FlowMole, Tokyo, 1991-93. Mem. World Trade Club Seattle (bd. dirs. 1993—). Home: 18137 149th Ave SE Renton WA 98058-9654 Office: UTILX Corp 22404 66th Ave S Kent WA 98032

BRISBIN, ROBERT EDWARD, insurance agency executive; b. Bklyn., Feb. 13, 1946; m. Sally Ann Tobler-Norton. BSBA, San Francisco State U., 1968. Cert. safety exec. Field rep. Index Research, San Mateo, Calif., 1969-82; mgr. loss control Homeland Ins. Co., San Jose, Calif., 1982-87; ins. exec. Morris and Dee Ins. Agy., San Luis Obispo, Calif., 1987—; prin., cons. Robert E. Brisbin & Assocs., Pismo Beach, Calif., 1972—; mgt. cons.; pres. Profl. Formulas Amino Acid Food Supplements, 1987-90. Author: Amino Acids, Vitamins and Fitness, 1986, Loss Control for the Small- to Medium-Sized Business, 1989, (with Carol Bayly Grant) Workplace Wellness, 1992; composer: Country Songs and Broken Dreams, 1978, America the Land of Liberty, 1980. Mem. Am. Soc. Safety Engrs., World Safety Orgn. (cert. safety exec.), UN Roster Safety Cons. Republican. Office: PO Box 341 Pismo Beach CA 93448-0341

BRISCOE, JOHN, lawyer; b. Stockton, Calif., July 1, 1948; s. John Lloyd and Doris (Olsen) B.; m. Valerie A. Breton, Aug. 21, 1976; children: John Paul, Katherine. JD, U. San Francisco, 1972. Bar: Calif. 1972, U.S. Dist. Ct. (no. and ea. dists.) Calif. 1972, U.S. Supreme Ct. 1976. Dep. atty. gen. State of Calif., San Francisco, 1972-80; ptnr. Washburn and Kemp, San Francisco, 1980-88; ptnr. Washburn, Briscoe and McCarthy, San Francisco, 1988—, chmn., 1990—; bd. dirs. San Francisco Bay Planning Coalition, 1990—; vis. scholar U. Calif. at Berkeley, 1990-93. Author: Surveying the Courtroom, 1984; editor: Reports of Special Masters, 1991; contbr. articles to profl. and lit. jours. Mem. ABA, San Francisco Bar Assn., Law of the Sea Inst. Roman Catholic. Office: Washburn Briscoe & McCarthy 55 Francisco St San Francisco CA 94133-2122

BRISCOE, JOHN FREDERICK, JR., food products executive; b. Altadena, Calif., Nov. 4, 1952; s. John Frederick and Guntrud Mardel

(Hilmers) B.; m. Debra Fae Burns, July 12, 1975. BA in Psychology, BA in Speech Communication, Calif. State U., Long Beach, 1975, MPA, 1979; MBA, Claremont Grad. Sch., 1990. Lic. broker, Calif. Sales mgr. Gen. Foods Inc., White Plains, N.Y., 1975-82; nat. trade devel. sales mgr. Kal Kan Inc., Vernon, Calif., 1982—; bd. dirs. Machine Tool Inc.; owner Crestwave, Property Mgmt. Co., Long Beach, Valif., 1991—. Dist. advancement chmn. Boy Scouts Am.; organizing com. Concerned Taxpayers of Kenilworth; mem. Apt. Owners Assn., San Marino Community Chest; registrar Voters L.A. County. Mem. Am. Logistics Assn., Phi Kappa Phi., Psi Chi Honor Frat., Calif. Indian Hobbyist Assn., Explorer Scouts., Theta Chi Internat. Coun. Lutheran. Office: Kal Kan Inc 3250 E 44th St Los Angeles CA 90058-2426 also: Crestwave 350 Redondo Ave Long Beach CA 90814-2655

BRISCOE, MARIANNE GRIER, development professional, educator; b. Orange, Calif., Nov. 25, 1945; d. Nelson Borland and Anne Kathryn (Houlihan) Grier; m. Alden Frank Briscoe, Aug. 10, 1968; 1 child, Stacy Anne. AB cum laude, Goucher Coll., 1967; cert. in medieval studies, Cath. U. Am., 1972; PhD, Cath. U., 1975. Cert. fund raising exec. Lectr. English lit. U. Mich., Flint, 1973; pub. info. officer Flint Charter Revision Commn., 1974-75; devel. officer The Newberry Library, Chgo., 1975-78, dir. devel., 1978-81; prin. The Briscoe Co., Chgo., 1981-84; assoc. dir. devel. U. Chgo., 1984-85, dir. corp. rels., 1985-89; centennial campaign dir. Sierra Club, San Francisco, 1989-91; sr. cons. Staley/Robeson/Ryan/St Lawrence, 1989-91; v.p. advancement St. Mary's Coll. Calif., Moraga, 1992—. Author, co-editor: Contexts of Early English Drama, 1989, Artes Praedicandi, 1992; contbr. articles to profl. jours. Founder Washington Sq. Consortium, Chgo., 1978-81; grant reviewer NEH, Washington, 1979-82. Brit. Acad. fellow, 1978-80, Newberry Library fellow, 1981, Med. Acad. fellow, 1974; Am. Philos. Soc. grantee, 1981. Mem. MLA, Nat. Soc. Fund Raising Execs. (nat. bd. dirs. 1984—, vice chmn. found. 1989-91), City Club San Francisco. Office: St Mary's Coll Calif PO Box 4300 Moraga CA 94575

BRISSENDEN-BENNETT, JO ANN, computer software consultant; b. L.A., Apr. 13, 1943; d. Owen Delton and Alvina Irene (Wynne) Spaur; m. Philip Hugh Brissenden, Sept. 8, 1961 (div. 1965); 1 child, Gina Lee Brissenden; m. Charles Alan Bennett, Nov. 24, 1988. Grad., El Camino Coll., L.A., 1965; postgrad., U. Calif., Berkeley, 1982. Acct., svc. rep. Pacific Telephone, L.A., 1961-72; bus rep., order dept. mgr. Pacific Telephone, Ventura, Calif., 1972-79; staff mgr. Pacific Telephone, San Francisco, 1979-82; bus. owner Committee Software, Sherman Oaks, Calif., 1982-90; software cons. Bennett & Assocs., Ojai, Calif., 1990—. Author: Training Manual, 1982. Troop leader Girl Scouts U.S., Ojai, 1991-92. Mem. NAFE, Ventura C. of C., Ojai C. of C. Republican. Roman Catholic. Office: Bennett and Assocs 415 E Villanova Rd Ojai CA 93023

BRITTAIN, JEFFREY CHARLES, insurance company executive; b. L.A., Dec. 4, 1949; s. Rupert Coakley and Florence Louise (Viano) B.; m. Mona Lisa Gonzales, Feb. 16, 1974; children: Christopher Matthew, Sean Marshall. Grad., U. Calif., San Diego, 1971. Supervisory underwriter Transam. Occidental Life Ins. Co., L.A., 1973-81; mgr. underwriting Western Growers Assurance, Irvine, Calif., 1981-88, Blue Cross of Calif., Westlake Village, 1988-90; v.p. underwriting Acordia of So. Calif., Anaheim, 1991—. Contbr. articles to Western Growers Yearbook and Small Group Newsletter. Bd. dirs. Covina (Calif.) Am. Little League, 1988; coach, umpire Conejo Valley Little League, 1989-93. Mem. Orange County Employee Benefits Assn. Home: 3301 Silver Spur Ct Thousand Oaks CA 91360-1041 Office: Acordia Benefit Svcs 2401 E Katella Ave Ste 400 Anaheim CA 92806-5951

BRITTEN, CRAIG ERIC, transportation sales executive; b. Moristown, N.J., May 10, 1946; s. Guido Fredolin and Dorothea Van Duyn Verbeck; m. Sherry Lynn Johnson, May 27,1967 (div. Aug., 1977); children: Sherryl Lynn Verbeck Rodgers, Edward Van Duyn Verbeck. Student, Tex. A&I U., 1969-70, U. Conn., 1970-72. Caretaker Alaska-Yukon Guides, White River, Alaska, 1979-80; camp cook L.D. Frome Outfitter, Afton, Wyo., 1980-82; mgr. Simon & Seaforts Grill, Anchorage, 1983-84; facilities mgr. Sodexho Alaska SA, Anchorage, 1984-86, ops. mgr., 1988-90; sales rep. S.E. Rykoff & Co., San Diego, 1987; gen. mgr. Alaska Produce Co., Anchorage, 1990-91; account executive Sea Land Svc. Co., Anchorage, 1991, sales mgr., 1992. Vol. Alaska Informational Radio Reading Ednl. Svc. 1991-92, Anchorage YMCA, 1991, Boys and Girls Club of Anchorage, 1992. With U.S. Navy, 1966-72. Office: Sea-Land Svc, Inc 2550 Denal St Ste 1604 Anchorage AK 99503

BRITTON, BOYD REINERT, radio executive; b. Boston, Aug. 17, 1947; s. J. Boyd and Ruth Gertrude (Reinert) B.; m. Marcy J. Katz, Nov. 19, 1981 (div. 1982). Student, Princeton U., 1964-65, 66-67, Emerson Coll., 1965-66, U.S. Def. Info. Sch., 1967, U.S. Def. Lang. Inst., 1967-68. News dir. Sta. WLYN Radio, Lynn, Mass., 1965, KUUU Radio, Seattle, 1970-71, KIIS-FM Radio, L.A., 1974-77, KTNQ/Ten-Q Radio, L.A., 1977-80, KHTZ-FM Radio, L.A., 1980-83; prodn. dir. KJOY/KJAX, Stockton, Calif., 1972; news anchor Malrite Broadcasting, Milwaukee, Denver, 1984-86; dir. news and pub. affairs KROQ-FM, L.A., 1987—. Compiler, performer rec. Hero in Hell, 1991. Mem. Arroyo Seco Coun., Pasadena, Calif., 1991. Sgt. U.S. Army, 1967-70, Vietnam. Recipient Golden Mike award So. Calif. Radio TV News Assn., 1981, Cert. for Best Newswriting, Calif. AP TV-Radio Assn., 1982. Office: KROQ-Infinity Broadcasting PO Box 10670 Burbank CA 91510

BRITTON, MARY KAY, data management executive; b. Great Falls, Mont., Sept. 27, 1939; d. Gerald Glen and Martha (Spitler) Emerson; m. Kent E. Gunnison, Sept. 7, 1963; (div. Jan., 1974); children: Mark E., Katie E.; m. James A. Britton, Dec. 10, 1977. BS, Lewis & Clark Coll., 1962. Elec. drafter Columbia Engrs. Svcs., Inc., Richland, Wash., 1975-76; drafter Westinghouse Hanford Co., Richland, 1976-77, supr. drawing and procedure control, 1977-79, supr. proj. Dalis (data base svc.), 1979-84, staff mgr. control & computer systems, 1984-87, mgr. data systems, 1987, mgr. data standards & adminstrn., 1987—. Guardian Ad Litem Ct. Jurisdiction, Benton-Franklin Counties, Wash., 1986-92; mem. bus. adv. com. Tri-City Area Vocat. Ctr., Richland, Wash., 1984-86. Mem. Assn. for Systems Mgmt., Nat. Mgmt. Assn. Office: Westinghouse Hanford Co PO Box 1970 Richland WA 99352-0539

BRITTON, SANDRA LOUCILLE MARY, artist, gallery owner; b. Morelia, Michoachan, Mexico, Apr. 22, 1948; d. Jose Trinidad Absalon Martinez y Ramirez and Rikki Marie Elizabeth (Anderson) Britton. BA, San Diego State U., 1983. came to U.S., 1948;. Karate instr. Karate-Do Centre, Del Mar, Calif., 1986-93; graphic artist, project mgr. Ecol. Rsch. Assoc., Del Mar, Calif., 1983-88; artist, gallery owner Sandra Britton Studio/Gallery, Pagosa Springs, Colo., 1988-93; judge Carlsbad (Calif.) Art League, 1991; artist, illustrator Jundokan Internat., Spokane, 1987—. Represented in five galleries throughout Southwest and Japan; prin. works include ltd. edition print Intergalactic Passage, 1991. Mem. Southwestern Assn. on Indian Affairs. Democrat. Home and Office: Sandra Britton Studio PO Box 2350 Pagosa Springs CO 81147

BRITTON, THOMAS WARREN, JR., management consultant; b. Pawhuska, Okla., June 16, 1944; s. Thomas Warren and Helen Viola (Haynes) B.; BS in Mech. Engring., Okla. State U., 1966, MS in Indsl. Engring. and Mgmt., 1968; m. Deborah Ann Mansour, Oct. 20, 1973; children: Natalie Dawn, Kimberly Ann. Cons., Arthur Young & Co., Los Angeles, 1968-72, mgr., 1972-76, prin., 1976-79, ptnr., 1979—, office dir. mgmt. svcs. dept., Orange County, Calif., 1980-87; ptnr. West Region Mfg., 1987-88, Price Waterhouse; ptnr.-in-charge west coast mfg. cons. practice, Nat. Aerospace and Def. Industry, 1988—; lectr. in field. Mem. City of San Dimas Creative Growth Bd., 1976-77, chmn. planning commn., 1977-83; trustee World Affairs Council of Orange County, 1980; benefactor, founders com., v.p. ann. fund, pres., chair long range planning, trustee South Coast Repertory Theater; trustee Providence Speech and Hearing Ctr.; mem. devel. com. U. Calif.-Irvine Med. Sch.; chmn. Costa Mesa Arts Council. Served to capt. USAR, 1971-86. Cert. mgmt. cons. Mem. Los Angeles Inst. CPAs, Mgmt. Adv. Svcs. Com., Am. Prodn. and Inventory Control Soc., Am. Inst. Indsl. Engrs., Greater Irvine Indsl. League, Okla. State Alumni Assn., Kappa Sigma Alumni Assn. Clubs: Jonathan, Ridgeline Country, Santa Ana Country. Home: 18982 Wildwood Cir Orange CA 92667-3137

BRIXEY, LORETTA SANCHEZ, strategic management consultant; b. Lynwood, Calif., Jan. 7, 1960; d. Ignacio Sandoval and Maria Socorro (Macias) S.; m. Stephen Simmons, May 5, 1990. BS in Econs., Chapman U., 1982; MBA, Am. U., 1984. Spl. projects mgr. Orange County Transp. Authority, Santa Ana, Calif., 1984-87; asst. v.p. Fieldman, Rolapp & Assocs., Irvine, Calif., 1987-90; assoc. Booz, Allen & Hamilton, L.A., 1990—; cons. Migrant Workers Edn., Santa Ana, 1991—. Orange County Rotary Found. scholar, 1984. Mem. Nat. Soc. Hispanic MBAs (pres. L.A. chpt.), Dem. of Orange County, Calif. Elected Women's Assn. for Edn. and Rsch., Assn. Mexican-Am. Educators. Roman Catholic. Office: Booz Allen & Hamilton Inc 523 W 6th St # 616 Los Angeles CA 90014

BROAD, ELI, financial services and home construction company executive; b. N.Y.C., June 6, 1933; s. Leon and Rebecca (Jacobson) B.; m. Edythe Lois Lawson, Dec. 19, 1954; children: Jeffrey Alan, Gary Steven. BA cum laude in Bus. Adminstrn., Mich. State U., 1954. CPA. Pres. SunAmerica Inc. (formerly Kaufman & Broad, Inc.), L.A., 1990—; CPA, 1954-56; asst. prof. Detroit Inst. Tech., 1956-57; co-founder SunAmerica Inc. (formerly Kaufman & Broad, Inc.), L.A., 1957, pres., CEO, 1957—; chmn., chief exec. officer Sun Life Ins. Co. Am. and Anchor Nat. Life Ins. Co., Balt., 1976—; chmn. Kaufman and Broad Home Corp., 1986—; bd. dir. Fed. Nat. Mortgage Assn., past dir. The Advest Group, Verex Corp.; mem. real estate adv. bd. Citibank, N.Y.C., chmn. Stanford Ranch Co., co-owner Sacramento Kings & Arco Arena, 1992—, mem. Calif. Bus. Roundtable, 1986—. Dir. devel. bd. Mich. State U., 1969-72; mem. Nat. Indsl. Pollution Control Council, 1970-73; co-founder Council Housing Producers; chmn. Los Angeles Mayor's Housing Policy Com., 1974-75; del. Dem. Nat. Conv., 1968; pres. Calif. Non-Partisan Voter Registration Found., 1971; bd. dirs. Nat. Energy Found., 1979-86, NCCJ, YMCA, L.A. United Way, Haifa U.; bd. dirs., trustee Windward Sch.; mem. acquisition com. Los Angeles County Mus. Art, 1979-81; exec. com. Internat. Forum for Los Angeles World Affairs Council; exec. com., bd. fellows Claremont Colls.; adv. bd. Inst. Internat. Edn.; founding chmn. Mus. Contemporary Art, L.A., 1980-83, trustee, 1980-93; dir. Los Angeles World Affairs Counsel, 1988—, chmn. designate 1992—, dir. D.A.R.E. Am. 1889—, trustee The Am. Fedn. of the Arts, 1988-91, vis. com. Grad. Sch. Mgmt., UCLA, 1972-90; trustee City of Hope, Calif. State Univs. and Colls.; trustee Pitzer Coll., 1979—, chmn. bd. trustees, 1972-79, trustee Dem. Nat. Com. Victory Fund, 1988, 1992. Recipient Man of Year award City of Hope, 1965; Golden Plate award Am. Acad. Achievement, 1971; Humanitarian award NCCJ, 1977; Housing Man of Yr. Nat. Housing Conf., 1979; Am. Heritage award Anti-Defamation League, 1984, Pub. Affairs award Coro Found., 1987, Honors award visual arts L.A. Arts Coun., 1989. Mem. Beta Alpha Psi. Clubs: Regency, Hillcrest Country (Los Angeles). Home: 1 Oakmont Dr Los Angeles CA 90049 Office: Sun Life Insurance Co 11601 Wilshire Blvd Los Angeles CA 90025

BROADBENT, HYRUM SMITH, chemistry educator, retired; b. Snowflake, Ariz., July 21, 1920; s. Hyrum Broadbent and Lorana Smith; m. Katherine Mary Miller, Sept. 9, 1942; children: Karen, David S., Justin M., Camille, Nathan E., Thomas A., Marla, Daniel H. BS, Brigham Young U., 1942; PhD, Iowa State U., 1946. Postdoctoral fellow Harvard U., Cambridge, Mass., 1946-47; asst. prof. chemistry Brigham Young U., Provo, Utah, 1947-49, assoc. prof., 1949-52, prof., 1952-85, prof. emeritus, 1985—; group leader med. chemistry div. Schering Corp., Bloomfield, N.J., 1958-59; vis. scientist Kettering Labs., Yellow Springs, Ohio, 1962-63, Eastman Kodak, Rochester, N.Y., 1970-71, Kuwait U., 1980, Konstanz U., Fed. Republic Germany, 1980; cons. various orgns. Contbr. articles to profl. jours.; patentee in field. Recipient Karl G. Maeser Teaching Excellence award Brigham Young U., Karl G. Maeser Research award Brigham Young U. Mem. Am. Chem. Soc. (pres. Salt Lake City chpt.), Royal Soc. Chemists, Internat. Soc. Heterocyclic Chemistry, Sigma Xi (pres. Brigham Young U. chpt.). Republican. Mormon. Home: 1147 Aspen Ave Provo UT 84604 Office: Brigham Young U 120 Eyring Sci Ctr Provo UT 84602

BROADHEAD, RONALD FRIGON, petroleum geologist, geology educator; b. Racine, Wis., July 22, 1955; s. Ronald Leslie and Thereise (Frigon) B. BS, N.Mex. Tech. U., 1977; MS, U. Cin., 1979. Geologist, Cities Svc. Oil Co., Oklahoma City and Tulsa, 1979-81; sr. petroleum geologist, head petroleum sect. N.Mex. Bur. Mines data section, Socorro, 1981—. mem. adj. faculty N.Mex. Tech. Coll., 1983—. Union Oil Co. summer fellow Duke U. Marine Lab., 1977. Mem. Am. Assn. Petroleum Geologists (Ho. of Dels., membership com.), Soc. Econ. Paleontologists and Mineralogists, N.Mex. Geol. Soc. (pres.), Roswell Geol. Soc., Four Corners Geol. Soc., West Tex. Geol. Soc., Sigma Xi. Office: NMex Bur Mines Campus Sta Socorro NM 87801

BROADHURST, NORMAN NEIL, foods company executive; b. Chico, Calif., Dec. 17, 1946; s. Frank Spencer and Dorothy Mae (Conrad) B.; BS, Calif. State U., 1969; MBA, Golden Gate U., 1975; m. Victoria Rose Thomson, Aug. 7, 1976; 1 child, Scott Andrew. With Del Monte Corp., San Francisco, 1969-76, product mgr., 1973-76; product mgr. Riviana Foods, Inc., div. Colgate Palmolive, Houston, 1976-78; new products brand devel. mgr. foods div. Coca Cola Co., Houston, 1978-79, brand mgr., 1979-82, mktg. dir., 1982-89; v.p. mktg. Beatrice Foods Co., Chgo., 1983-86; pres., chief operating officer Famous Amos Chocolate Chip Cookie Co., Torrance, Calif., 1986-88; corp. sr. v.p., gen. mgr. Kerr Group Inc., L.A., 1988-92, corp. sr. v.p., pres. Kerr Group Consumer Products. Chmn. youth soccer program Cystic Fibrosis; pres., chmn. South Coast Symphony, 1985-88; vice chmn. Lit. Vol. Am., Inc., 1992—. Recipient Cystic Fibrosis Community Svcs. award, 1982; vice-chmn. bd. dirs. Literacy Vols. Am., Inc., 1987—. Mem. Am. Mgmt. Assn., Am. Mktg. Assn., Toastmasters Internat. (past chpt. pres.). Home: 5009 Queen Victoria Rd Woodland Hills CA 91364-4757 Office: Kerr Group Inc 1840 Century Park E Los Angeles CA 90067-2101

BROCA, LAURENT ANTOINE, aerospace scientist; b. Arthez-de-Bearn, France, Nov. 30, 1928; came to U.S., 1957, naturalized, 1963; s. Paul L. and Paule Jeanne (Ferrand) B.; B.S. in Math., U. Bordeaux, France, 1949; Lic. es Scis. in Math. and Physics, U. Toulouse (France), 1957; grad. Inst. Technique Professionnel, France, 1960; Ph.D. in Elec. Engring., Calif. Western U., 1979; postgrad. Boston U., 1958, MIT, 1961, Harvard U., 1961; m. Leticia Garcia Guerra, Dec. 18, 1962; 1 dau., Marie-There Yvonne. Teaching fellow physics dept. Boston U., 1957-58; spl. instr. dept. physics N.J. Inst. Tech., Newark, 1959-60; sr. staff engr. advanced research group ITT, Nutley, N.J., 1959-60; examiner math. and phys. scis. univs. Paris (France) and Caen, Exam. Center, N.Y.C., 1959-69; sr. engr. surface radar div. Raytheon Co., Waltham, Mass., 1960-62, Hughes Aircraft Co., Culver City, Calif., 1962-64; asst. prof. math. Calif. State U., Northridge, 1963-64; prin. engr. astrionics lab. NASA, Huntsville, Ala., 1964-65; fellow engr. Def. and Space Center, Westinghouse Electric Corp., Balt., 1965-69; cons. and sci. adv. electronics, phys. scis. and math. to indsl. firms and broadcasting stations, 1969-80; head engring. dept. Videocraft Mfg. Co., Laredo, Tex., 1974-75; asst. prof. math. Laredo State U., summer, 1975; engring. specialist dept. systems performance analysis ITT Fed. Electric Corp., Vandenberg AFB, Calif., 1980-82; engring. mgr. Ford Aerospace and Communications Corp., Nellis AFB, Nev., 1982-84; engring. mgr. Arcata Assocs., Inc., North Las Vegas, Nev., 1984-85; sr. scientific specialist engring. and devel. EG&G Spl. Projects, Inc., Las Vegas, 1985—. Served with French Army, 1951-52. Recipient Published Paper award Hughes Aircraft Co., 1966; Fulbright scholar, 1957. Mem. IEEE, Am. Nuclear Soc. (vice chmn. Nev. sect. 1982-83, chmn. 1983-84), Am. Def. Preparedness Assn., Armed Forces Communications and Electronics Assn., Air Force Assn. Home: 5040 Lancaster Dr Las Vegas NV 89120-1445 Office: EG&G Spl Projects Inc PO Box 93747 Las Vegas NV 89193-3747

BROCK, CHARLES MICHAEL, water company executive; b. La Mesa, Calif., Nov. 22, 1952; s. Marvin Arthur and Louise Flora (Schliekelman) B.; m. Wilma Jo Stigaullde, Dec. 15, 1972 (div. Oct. 1982); children: Michael Donovan, Brieanna Rene, Matthew James; m. Joyceanna Lee Baxter, Feb. 14, 1988; 1 child, Mercedes Karee. Grad. high sch., Blythe, Calif. Mech. Jerry Pritchard Chevrolet, Roswell, N.Mex., 1972-78; founder, owner A&E Repair Svcs., Ehrenberg, Ariz., 1978-91; gen. mgr. Ehrenberg Water Co., 1991—. Bd. dirs. Ehrenberg Improvement Assn., 1978-80, pres., 1990-91; founder, pres. So. Colo. River Valley Mens Assn., Ehrenberg, 1989; bd. pres. Ehrenberg Fire Dist., 1989-92, 92—. Recipient Honor & Appreciation award Ehrenberg Improvement Assn., 1980. Republican. Roman Catholic. Home: PO Box 291 Lot 2 Lake Dr Ehrenberg AZ 85334 Office: Ehrenberg Water Co PO Bo 284 Ehrenberg AZ 85334

BROCK, JAMES WILSON, drama educator, playwright, researcher; b. Greensfork, Ind., May 23, 1919; s. Virgil Prentiss and Blanche (Kerr) B.; m. Martha Faught, June 1942 (div. Mar. 1956); m. Patricia Anne Clemons, Mar. 1956 (div. Nov. 1966); children: Lisa Anne, Tamsen Lee, Julie Michele; m. Marjorie Mellor, Feb. 1, 1969. AB, Manchester Coll., 1941; MA, Northwestern U., 1942, PhD, 1950. Assoc. prof. Albion (Mich.) Coll., 1946-56; asst. prof. Mich. State U., East Lansing, 1956-57, U. Mich., Ann Arbor, 1957-58; assoc. prof. Fla. State U., Tallahassee, 1958-59; prof. Calif. State U., Northridge, 1959-89; mng. dir. Plymouth (Mass.) Drama Festival, 1956-58. Author: (plays) Modern Chancel Dramas, 1964, (musical dance drama) The Summons, 1964; contbr. articles to profl. jours. Sgt. USAAF, 1942-45, Middle East, ETO. Decorated Bronze Star; fellow Ch. Soc. for Coll. Work, Eng., 1964; rsch. grantee Calif. State U. Found., 1964, 66, 67. Mem. Am. Soc. for Theatre Rsch., Nat. Theatre Conf., Theta Alpha Phi (sec.-treas. 1952-57), Delta Sigma Rho. Democrat. Episcopalian. Home: 55 E 700 S # 51 Saint George UT 84770

BROCK, LONNIE REX, manufacturing executive; b. Mattoon, Ill., Nov. 13, 1950; s. Lyman Dale and Margaret Mary (Barnett) B.; m. Mary Kathryn Greider, May 25, 1975; 1 child, Lonnie Rex II. BSBA in Acctg., Ea. Ill. U., 1977. CPA, Wis., Colo. Mem. audit staff Price Waterhouse, Milw., 1978-80; audit sr. Price Waterhouse, Denver, 1980-82, audit mgr., 1982-85; contr. Western Gas Resources, Inc., Denver, 1985-89, v.p., contr., 1988-89, v.p. fin., 1989-90, v.p., chief fin. officer, 1990—. With USAF, 1971-74. Mem. AICPA, Am. Mgmt. Assn., Colo. Soc. CPA, Ranch Golf Club, Troon North Golf Club. Republican. Home: 11150 E Blue Sky Dr Scottsdale AZ 85255 Office: Western Gas Resources Inc 12200 Pecos St Denver CO 80234-3439

BROCKENBROUGH, EDWIN CHAMBERLAYNE, surgeon; b. Balt., July 24, 1930; s. Edwin Chamberlayne Sr. and Martha Davis (Coale) B.; m. Jean McClure, May 4, 1968; children: John, Martha, Andrew, Ann, Susan. BA, Coll. William & Mary, 1952; MD, Johns Hopkins U., 1956. Intern Johns Hopkins Hosp., Balt., 1956-57, resident, 1957-59; sr. asst. surgeon Nat. Heart Inst., Bethesda, Md., 1959-61; chief resident surgery U. Wash., Seattle, 1961-64, faculty mem. dept. surgery, 1964-75; pvt. practice Seattle, 1975—; clin. prof. surgery U. Wash., 1984—; pres. King County Med. Soc., Seattle, 1992; trustee Health Resources N.W., Seattle. Contbr. chpt. to book and articles to profl. jours. Sr. asst. surgeon USPHS, 1959-61. Fellow Am. Coll. Surgeons (pres. Wash. State chpt. 1985), Seattle Surg. Soc. (sec. 1972); mem. North Pacific Surg. Assn. (councilor 1992), Pacific Coast Surg. Assn., Am. Rhododendron Soc. (pres. 1977-79, silver medal 1985). Republican. Episcopalian. Home: 3630 Hunts Point Rd Bellevue WA 98004 Office: 1560 N 115th St Seattle WA 98133

BROCKISH, ROBERT FRANCIS, software systems consultant; b. Denver, July 14, 1931; s. Maurice Alexander and Clara Elizabeth (Gwartney) B.; m. Carol Marie Scott, Feb. 23, 1952; children: Timothy, Theodore, Mary, Thomas, Margaret, Madeline, Milissa, Amy. BS in Math., Regis Coll., 1956; postgrad., Denver U., 1957-59. Computer programmer The Martin Co., Denver, 1956-59; data processing mgr. Thiokol Chem. Co., Brigham City, Utah, 1959-66; sr. programmer IBM Corp., Boulder, Colo., 1966-90; mem. exec. bd. Share, Chgo., 1963-64. lt. col. USMCR, 1949-52, Korea, ret. Res. 1974. Mem. Marine Corps Res. Officers Assn., The Ret. Officers Assn., Boulder Assn. Computing Machines, Marine Hist. Found., Marine Corps Assn., Korean War Vets. Assn., Colo. Hist. Soc., KC, Elks. Roman Catholic. Home: 4095 Darley Ave Boulder CO 80303-6520

BROCKMAN, RITA JO, school social worker; b. Omaha, Sept. 1, 1955; d. Ralph Quinton and Elvah Dare (Harmier) B.; m. Darryl Lynn Boam, June 19, 1982; children: Travis Keith, Rachel Lynn. BA in Social Work/Criminal Justice, Colo. State U., 1978. Social worker State of Wyo., Gillette, 1980-85, Campbell County Meml. Hosp., Gillette, 1985-87, Wyo. Children's Soc., Gillette, 1985-88, Campbell County Sch. Dist., Gillette, 1988—; mem. adv. bd. Wyo. Social Svcs. Dept., Rawlins, 1982-84, mem. child protection team, 1980-85. Chmn. Am. Cancer Soc., Gillette, 1985-87; leader Girl Scouts U.S.A., Gillette, 1988—; officer parent coun. Meadowlark Elem. Sch., Gillette, 1991—. Named No. 1 Parent Vol., Campbell County Sch. Bd., 1992. Home: 4 Cherokee Circle Gillette WY 82716 Office: Campbell County Sch Dist 2500 Dogwood Gillette WY 82716

BROCKMAN, WAYNE EDWARD, corporate executive; b. West Covina, Calif., Jan. 31, 1968; s. Leonard and Elinor (Rose) B. BSCS, Regents Coll., Albany, N.Y., 1992. Systems programmer McDonald Douglas Corp., Agoura, Calif., 1984-86; developer interactive entertainment group CinemaWare Corp., Westlake Village, Calif., 1987-88; pres. rsch. and devel. ThoughtWORX, Agoura, 1990—; cons. in field. Author: IUI Development System, TM-x System, 1989. Mem. IEEE, Assn. Computing Machinery, Am. Assn. Artificial Intelligence. Office: Thoughtworx R&D 29757 Strawberry Hill Dr Agoura Hills CA 91301

BRODERICK, DONALD LELAND, electronics engineer; b. Chico, Calif., Jan. 5, 1928; s. Leland Louis and Vera Marguerite (Carey) B.; m. Constance Margaret Lattin, Sept. 29, 1957; children: Craig, Eileen, Lynn. BSEE, U. Calif., Berkeley, 1950; postgrad., Stanford U., 1953-54. Jr. engr. Boeing Co., Seattle, 1950-52; design engr. Hewlett-Packard Co., Palo Alto, Calif., 1952-59; sr. staff engr. Ampex Computer Products, Culver City, Calif., 1959-60; dir. engring. Kauke & Co., Santa Monica, Calif., 1960-61; program mgr. Space Gen. Corp., El Monte, Calif., 1961-68, Aerojet Electronics Div., Azusa, Calif., 1968-89; prin. D.L. Broderick, Arcadia, Calif., 1989—. Contbr. articles to profl. jours. Mem. Jr. C. of C., Woodland Hills, Cailf., 1963-64. With USN, 1945-46. Fellow Inst. for Advancement of Engring; mem. IEEE (chmn. profl. group on audio 1955-59, mem. exec. com. San Francisco sect. 1957-59, chmn. San Gabriel Valley sect. 1964-71, chmn. sections. com. L.A. coun., 1971-72, chmn. L.A. coun. 1972-76, chmn. bd. WESCON conv. 1976-80, bd. dirs. IEEE Electronics Conv. Inc. 1981-84, Centennial medal 1984), AIAA (sec. L.A. sect., 1986-88, sec. nat. tech. com. on command control comm. and intelligence, Washington, 1985-89, chmn. devel. com. L.A. coun. 1986—). Home: 519 E La Sierra Dr Arcadia CA 91006-4321

BRODERICK, EDWARD MICHAEL, III, lawyer; b. Stamford, Conn., Nov. 4, 1947; s. Edward Michael Broderick and Lois Caroline (Brown) Contaras; m. Jeanine Lynn Bennett; children: Courtney Elizabeth, Ashley Noelle. BA, St. Anselm's Coll., Manchester, N.H., 1969; JD, St. John's U., N.Y.C., 1973. Bar: N.Y. 1974, Conn. 1974. Adminstrv. asst. of legis. affairs Royal Globe Ins. Cos., N.Y.C., 1970-74, atty., 1974-75; asst. gen. counsel and sec. Puritan Ins. Group, Stamford, 1975-79; sr. counsel Gen. Electric Credit Corp., Stamford, 1975-79; asst. gen. counsel ITT Fin. Corp., St. Louis, 1983-86; gen. counsel and sec. ITT Lyndon Ins. Group, St. Louis, 1979-86; v.p., gen. counsel Calfarm Ins. Group, Sacramento, 1986—. Mem. various Rep. campaigns, N.Y.C., Stamford and St. Louis, St. Louis Squires,, 1984-86. Mem. ABA, Conn. Bar Assn., N.Y. State Bar Assn. Republican. Roman Catholic. Office: Calfarm Ins Group 1601 Exposition Blvd Sacramento CA 95815-5103

BRODERICK, GLEN REID, engineer, consultant; b. Delta, Utah, Aug. 14, 1943; s. Cloy Lenord and Anna (Mortensen) B.; m. Mary (div. Oct. 1970); m. Liwliwa Bradago Manuel, Nov. 2, 1970; 1 child, Reid M. BS in Bus. Adminstrn., U. Redlands, 1983; MS in Telecommunications Mgmt., Golden Gate U., 1986. Test engr. GTE, Northlake, Ill., 1969-76; staff engr. GTE, Thousand Oaks, Calif., 1976-82; sr. planning analyst GTE, Thousand Oaks, 1982-86, mktg. product mgr., 1986-90; cons. engr. Infonet, El Segundo, Calif., 1990—. Coach Conejo Valley Little League, Thousand Oaks, 1985-90. Sgt. USAF, 1965-68. Latter Day Saints.

BRODERICK, HAROLD CHRISTIAN, interior designer; b. Oakland, Calif., Apr. 8, 1925; s. Harold Christian and Laura Jane (Lloyd) B. BA, U. Tex., 1947. A founder Arthur Elrod Assos., Inc., Palm Springs, Calif., 1954, now pres.; bd. dirs. The Living Desert. Mem. Planning Commn., City of Palm Springs, 1972-74; trust Palm Springs Desert Mus.; mem. devel. com. Barbara Sinatra Children's Ctr. Mem. Am. Soc. Interior Designers. Republican. Office: Arthur Elrod Assocs Inc 850 N Palm Canyon Dr Palm Springs CA 92262-4424

BRODIE, ALAN DAVID, physicist; b. Elmira, N.Y., Sept. 22, 1960; s. Ivor and Audrey (Leila) B.; m. Ellyn Dianne Segal, May 24, 1987. BSc cum laude, U. Santa Clara, Calif., 1981; MSc, Coll. William and Mary, Williamsburg, Va., 1983; PhD, Cambridge U., Eng., 1990. Physicist, engr. KLA Instruments, Santa Clara, 1987—. Contbr. articles to profl. jours. Mem. IEEE, Sigma Xi, Sigma Pi Sigma. Home: 998 Van Auken Cir Palo Alto CA 94303-3841 Office: KLA Instruments 3520 Bassett St Santa Clara CA 95054-2756

BRODIE, HOWARD, artist; b. Oakland, Calif., Nov. 28, 1915; s. Edward and Anna (Zeller) B. Student, Art Inst. San Francisco, Art Student's League, N.Y.C., U. Ghana, Accra; LHD (hon.), Acad. Art Coll., San Francisco, 1984. Mem. staff Life mag., Yank: the Army Weekly, Collier's, AP, CBS News, 1969-89; freelance artist, journalist, 1990—. Author: (book) Howard Brodie War Drawings, 1963; art journalist: (major wars) World War II, Korea, French Indo-China, Vietnam, (trials) Jack Ruby, Ray, Sirhan, My Lai, Charles Manson, Chicago Seven, Watergate, John Hinckley, Klaus Barbie of France, (famous people) John Wayne, Pres. Kennedy, James Jones; art at White House, 1946, 48; work represented in permanent collections Calif. Palace of the Legion Hon., San Francisco, Soc. Illustrators, N.Y., Libr. Congress, Washington, Air Force Acad., Colo.; prints, books: U.S. Army Infantry Mus., Ft. Benning, Ga., U.S. Army Mus., Presidio, Monterery, Oreg. Nat. Milt. Mus., The Hoover Instn. on War, Revolution and Peace, The Mus. of Books, Lenin Libr., Moscow, Gorky Sci. Libr., Moscow State U., Admiral Nimitz State Hist. Pk., Tex., Henry E. Huntington Libr. (award), San Marina, New Britain Mus. Am. Art, Conn.; guest on Merv Griffin Show, Charles Kuralt Sunday Morning program, Ted Koppel program, Night Line. Sgt., U.S. Army. Decorated Bronze Star; recipient honor medals Freedom Found., 1957, 58, 60, 61.

BRODY, ARTHUR, industrial executive; b. Newark, June 30, 1920; s. Samuel A. and Ruth (Marder) B.; m. Sophie Mark, Mar. 5, 1944; children: Janice, Donald. Student, Columbia U., 1939-42. Organizer, operator Library Service, 1940-42; exec. buyer L. Bamberger & Co., Newark, 1942-43; chmn. Brodart Co., Williamsport, Pa., 1946—, BDI Investment Corp., San Diego, Tura Inc., Lake Success, N.Y.; past mem. adv. panel study on librs. and industry Nat. Adv. Com. on Librs.; past pres. Friends of N.J. Librs. Past trustee Newark Symphony Hall., Ctr. for Book, Libr. of Congress, L.A. County Libr. Found., Friends of Libr. USA, San Diego Community Found.; past commr. San Diego Pub. Libr. With AUS, 1943-46. Mem. ALA, NEA, Green Brook Country Club, San Diego Yacht Club, Rancho Sante Fe Golf Club, Masons, Shriners. Office: Brodart Co 10983 Via Frontera San Diego CA 92127-1703

BRODY, DAVID, history educator; b. Elizabeth, N.J., June 5, 1930; s. Barnet and Ida (Gulker) B.; m. Susan Schapiro, Oct. 30, 1955; children: Sara Beth, Pamela, Jonathan. AB, Harvard U., 1952, MA, 1953, PhD, 1958. Asst. prof. Columbia U., N.Y.C., 1961-65; assoc. prof. Ohio State U., Columbus, 1965-67; prof. U. Calif., Davis, 1967—; visiting prof. U. Warwick, Coventry, Eng., 1972-73, Moscow State U., USSR, 1975, U. Sydney, Australia, 1984, Wayne State U., 1988-89. Author: Steelworkers in America, 1960, Labor in Crisis, 1965, Workers in Indsl. Am., 1980; co-author: America's History, 1987. Pres. Pacific Coast br. Am. Hist. Assn., 1991-92. Recipient Social Sci. Rsch. Coun. fellowship, 1966, NEH sr. fellowship, 1978, Guggenheim Found. fellowship, 1983, Fulbright sr. professorship, 1975. Fellow Soc. Am. Historians; mem. Am. Hist. Assn., Orgn. Am. Historians (exec. bd. 1976-79). Home: 62 Richardson Rd Kensington CA 94707 Office: Dept History U Calif Davis CA 95616

BRODY, JEFFREY M., newspaper editor, journalist; b. Chgo., Oct. 27, 1953; s. Leonard and Isabel (Dienstein) B.; m. Joyce Elaine Brown, Nov. 7, 1981; 1 child, Daniel Oren Brown Brody. BS in Journalism, U. Ill., 1975; MA in Econs., Sangamon State U., Springfield, Ill., 1987. Reporter The Plain Dealer, Wabash, Ind., 1975, The State Jour.-Register, Springfield, 1975-88; editor city desk The Sun, Bremerton, Wash., 1988—; vis. prof. ethics program Washington and Lee U., 1979; participant Poynter Inst. for Media Studies, 1989; contbg. editor Crain's Chgo. Bus., 1982-88. Author: (anthology) Economic Development in Illinois, 1986; editor: Hood Canal: Splendor at Risk, 1991; contbr. Ill. Issues mag., 1984-88. Bd. dirs. Ill. First Amendment Congress, Springfield, 1981, 83, Ill. Freedom of Info. Coun., Springfield, 1982-88. Recipient Excellence in Journalism award Soc. Profl. Journalists, 1990, 91, 92. Mem. Investigative Reporters and Editors. Home: 10902 Durham Pl NW Silverdale WA 98383 Office: The Sun 545 5th St Bremerton WA 98310

BRODY-WATTS, STELLA, nurse; b. Athens, Greece, Oct. 15, 1939; came to U.S., 1965; d. Isaac Leon and Alice (Levy) Leontsini; m. William Brody, June 11, 1963 (div. 1977); children: Suzanne, David, Alexia; m. Dan Pike Watts III, Nov. 19, 1977. AA in Nursing, El Camino Coll., Torrance, Calif., 1974. RN, Calif. Operating room nurse Bay Harbor Hosp., Lomita, Calif., 1974-76, Kaiser Hosp., Harbor City, Calif., 1976-78, Dr. Sheldon Thorrens, Torrance, 1978-79, Long Beach (Calif.) Meml. Hosp., 1979-85; recreational nurse Am. Travel Cons., Redondo Beach, Calif., 1985-89; pres. Lela Tours, Inc., Redondo Beach, 1990—; part time nurse South Bay Hosp., Redondo Beach, 1989—. Editor newsletter South Bay Women in Travel, 1988—. Mem. Assn. Oper. Rm. Nurses (editor newsletter South Bay chpt., pres. 1982-83), Opera Guild So. Calif. (bd. dirs. 1989—). Democrat. Jewish. Home: 513 Via La Selva Redondo Beach CA 90277-6506 Office: Lela Tours Inc 112 S Catalina Ave Redondo Beach CA 90277-3327

BROER, ROGER L., artist; b. Omaha, Nov. 9, 1945; s. Ludwig and Frieda B.; m. Merlene Julie Good, May 31, 1970; children: Juli Jyll, Zame Stockton. BA, Ea. Mont. Coll., 1974; postgrad., Cen. Wash. U., 1974-76. Artist in residence Alaska Arts Artist in the Schs., various towns, 1978-81, Wash. State Arts, 6 schs. in Wash., 1985-89; artist in the prisons, Wash. State Arts, 4 prisons in Wash., 1987-91; lectr. in field. One man and group shows throughout the U.S., Can. and Europe. Mem. Oglala Sioux tribe. With USAF, 1964-68. Over 25 nat. and internat. awards. Mem. Dream Catchers Artist Guild. Office: PO Box 6412 Kent WA 98064-6412

BROG, TERRENCE KENYON, ceramic engineer, corporate technology director; b. Hastings, Mich., Sept. 9, 1957; s. Kenneth Clair and Elizabeth Ann (Kenyon) B.; m. Jill Ann Hannum, May 22, 1982; children: Shaun Kenneth, Ryan Edward. BS, Kenyon Coll., 1979; MS in Nuclear Engring., U. Mich., 1982, MS in Metallurgical Engring., 1982, PhD, 1986. Rsch. engr. Champion Spark Plug Co., Detroit, 1985-87; rsch. engr. Coors Ceramics Co., Golden, Colo., 1987-90, dir. corporate tech., 1991. Author: (with others) Am. Soc. Metals Handbook, Vol. 2, 1990; patents pending in field. Mem. Am. Soc. Metals, Am. Ceramic Soc. (pres. Mich. chpt. 1986-87), Sigma Xi. Office: Coors Ceramics Co 4545 Mcintyre St Golden CO 80403-7201

BROGDEN, STEPHEN RICHARD, library administrator; b. Des Moines, Sept. 26, 1948; s. Paul M. and Marjorie (Kueck) B.; m. Melinda L. Raine, Jan. 1, 1983; 1 child, Nathan. BA, U. Iowa, 1970, MA, 1972. Caretaker Eya Fechin Branham Ranch, Taos, N.Mex., 1970-72; dir. Harwood Found. U. N.Mex., Taos, 1972-75; vis. lectr. U. Ariz., Tucson, 1975-76; rd. mgr. Bill and Bonnie Hearne, Austin, Tex., 1976-79; head fine arts Pub. Libr. Des Moines, 1980-90; dep. dir. Thousand Oaks (Calif.) Libr., 1990—. Author book revs., Annals of Iowa, 1980; columnist Taos News, 1973. Mem. Am. Libr. Assn., Calif. Libr. Assn., Films for Iowa Librs. (pres. 1983-86), Metro Des Moines Libr. Assn. (pres. 1980). Office: Thousand Oaks Library 1401 E Janss Rd Thousand Oaks CA 91360

BROGLIATTI, BARBARA SPENCER, television and motion picture executive; b. L.A., Jan. 8, 1946; d. Robert and Lottie (Goldstein) Spencer; m. Raymond Haley Brogliatti, Sept. 19, 1970. BA in Social Scis. and English, UCLA, 1968. Asst. press. info. dept. CBS TV, L.A., 1968-69, sr. publicist, 1969-74; dir. publicity Tandem Prodns. and T.A.T. Comm. (Embassy Comm.), L.A., 1974-77, corp. v.p., 1977-82, sr. v.p. worldwide publicity, promotion and advt. Embassy Comm., L.A., 1982-85; sr. v.p. worldwide corp. comm. Lorimar Telepictures Corp., Culver City, Calif., 1985-89; pres., chmn. Brogliatti Co., Burbank, Calif., 1989-90; sr. v.p. publicity, promotion and advt. Lorimar TV, 1991-92; sr. v.p. TV publicity, promotion and pub. rels. Warner Bros. Inc., Burbank, 1992—. Mem. bd. govs. TV Acad., L.A., 1984-86; bd. dirs. KIDSNET, Washington, 1987—, Nat. Acad. Cable Programming, 1992—; vice chmn. awards com. TV Acad.; mem. Hollywood Women's Polit. Com., 1992. Recipient Gold medallion Broadcast Promotion and Mktg. Execs., 1984. Mem. Am. Diabetes Assn. (bd. dirs. Los Angeles chpt. 1992), Dirs. Guild Am., Publicists Guild, Acad. TV Arts and Scis. (vice chmn. awards com.). Office: Warner Bros Studios Bldg 137 Ste 1057 4000 Warner Blvd Burbank CA 91552

BROIN, THAYNE LEO, geologist; b. Kenyon, Minn., Sept. 18, 1922; s. Oscar Arthur and Ella (Hoff) B.; m. Beverly Ruth Johnson, Dec. 21, 1949; children: Martin, Dana, Valerie. BS, St. Cloud U., 1943; MA, U. Colo., 1952, PhD, 1957. Instr. Colo. State U., Fort Collins, Colo., 1950-54, asst. prof., 1956-57; rsch. geologist Cities Svc. R & D Co., Tulsa, 1957-58, tech. group leader, 1958-60, head geol. rsch., 1960-65; rsch. coord. Cities Svc. Oil Co., Bartlesville, Okla., 1965-72; chief computer geologist Cities Svc. Oil Co., Tulsa, 1972-75, computer technology mgr., 1975-83; cons. Broin and Assocs., Colorado Springs, Tulsa, 1983—. Capt. USAF, 1943-48, South Pacific. Recipient Regents fellowship U. Colo., 1954, 55. Mem. Geol. Soc. Am., Tulsa Geol. Soc. (pres. 1971, 72), Sons of Norway (pres. 1991, 92). Home and Office: 5280 Champagne Dr Colorado Springs CO 80919

BROKAW, BETH FLETCHER, social worker, psychological assistant; b. Staunton, Va., Mar. 9, 1955; d. Forest and Helen (Tilson) Fletcher; m. David Wilson Brokaw, Oct. 15, 1988. BA, Muhlenberg Coll., 1977; MSW, Columbia U., 1978; MA, Rosemead Sch. Psychology, 1988, PhD, 1991. Lic. clin. social worker, Va., Calif. Clin. social worker Philhaven Hosp., Lebanon, Pa., 1978-80, Hollygrove Treatment Ctr. for Children, Hollywood, Calif., 1980-82, U. Va. Med. Ctr., Charlottesville, Va., 1982-85; dir. of counseling svcs. Trinity Presbyn. Ch., Charlottesville, 1983-85; clin. dir. Growing Edge Counseling Ctr., Arcadia, Calif., 1985-86; pvt. practice lic. clin. social worker Pasadena, Calif., 1985-91; psychol. asst. Pacific Psychol. Resources, Pasadena, 1991—; asst. prof. Rosemead Sch. Psychology, 1992—; student body pres. Rosemead Sch. of Psychology, Biola, U., La Mirada, Calif., 1989-90. Bd. dirs., 3d v.p. Rainbow Lake Club, Azusa, Calif., 1990. Mem. APA, NASW, Christian Assn. for Psychol. Studies. Office: Pacific Psychol Resources 200 E Del Mar Blvd Ste 120 Pasadena CA 91105

BROKAW, NORMAN ROBERT, artists' management company executive; b. N.Y.C., Apr. 21, 1927; s. Isadore David and Marie (Hyde) B.; children—David M., Sanford Jay, Joel S., Barbara M., Wendy E., Lauren Quincy. Student pvt. schs., Los Angeles. With William Morris Agy., Inc., Beverly Hills, Calif., 1943—, sr. agt. and co. exec., 1951-74, v.p. world-wide ops., 1974-80, exec. v.p., dir., 1980—, co-chmn. bd., 1986-91, pres., chief exec. officer, 1989-91, chmn. bd., chief exec. officer, 1991—. Pres. Betty Ford Cancer Center, Cedars-Sinai Med. Center, Los Angeles, 1978—; bd. dirs. Cedars-Sinai Med. Center; industry chmn. United Jewish Welfare Fund, 1975. Served with U.S. Army, World War II. Mem. Acad. Motion Picture Arts and Scis. Clubs: Hillcrest Country (Los Angeles). Home: 530 Vick Pl Beverly Hills CA 90210-1930 Office: William Morris Agy 151 S El Camino Dr Beverly Hills CA 90212-2775 also: William Morris Agy Inc 1350 Ave of the Americas New York NY 10019

BROM, ROBERT H., bishop; b. Arcadia, Wis., Sept. 18, 1938. Ed., St. Mary's Coll., Winona, Minn., Gregorian U., Rome. Ordained priest Roman Catholic Ch., 1963, consecrated bishop, 1983. Bishop of Duluth Minn., 1983-89; coadjutor bishop Diocese of San Diego, 1989-90, bishop, 1990—. Office: Diocese of San Diego Pastoral Ctr PO Box 85728 San Diego CA 92186-5728*

BROMBERGER, FREDERICK SIGMUND, English language educator; b. El Paso, Tex., Mar. 5, 1918; s. Frederick Sigmund and Agnes Ardena (Landstrom) B.; m. Corrine Aldridge, Oct. 21, 1944; children: Eric, Troy, Corinth, Matthew, Thrace. AB, Knox Coll., 1940; BA, U. Cin., 1941; PhD., U. So. Calif., 1964; postgrad., Harvard U., 1947, Stanford U., 1977. Tchr. Kemper Mil. Sch., Boonville, Mo., 1941-42; instr. English, U. Mo., Columbia, 1946-47; prof. U. Redlands, Calif., 1948-84, part-time prof., 1984—, instr. lit. and music Elderhostel programs, 1981—; spl. instr. U. Calif., Riverside, 1965. Author: (manual) Leadership in the U.S. Air Force, 1954; contbr. numerous articles to profl. jours. Chmn. citizen's adv. com. Redlands Unified Sch. Dist., 1964-66; mem. Redlands Cultural Arts Commn., 1987—; founding mem. Redlands Symphony Orch. Maj. USAAF, 1942-46, CBI. Recipient Directive Tchr. award Danforth Found., 1959; Top Tchr. award Alumni Assn. U. Redlands, 1983, Alumni Svc. award, 1992; grantee Lilly Found., 1977. Mem. Riverside-San Bernardino Orchid Soc. (pres. 1982-83), Redlands Hort. Soc. (pres. 1981-82), Redlands Fortnightly Club (pres. 1990). Republican. Congregationalist. Home: 136 E Hilton Ave Redlands CA 92373

BROMM, ROBERT DALE, senior nuclear engineer; b. San Pedro, Calif., Nov. 13, 1950; s. Robert and Olive Genevive (Hart) B.; m. Linda Suzanne Owens, June 30, 1973 (div. June 1986); children: Christina Ann, Ryan David; m. Margaret Rose Meusborn, Jan., 14, 1989; 1 adopted child, Mindy Christine. BSME, Calif. State Poly. U., 1973; MBA, Idaho State U., 1985. Registered profl. engr., Calif. Engr. Bechtel Power Corp., Norwalk, Calif., 1973-76; engring. specialist EG&G Idaho Inc., Idaho Falls, 1977-85; sr. remote systems and robotics engr. Fluor Daniel, Irvine, Calif., 1985—. Mem. Am. Nuclear Soc. (chmn. L.A. 1989), Mensa (loc. sec. SE Idaho chpt. 1985), Toastmasters (pres. Irvine 1988). Office: Flour Daniel 3333 Michelson Dr Irvine CA 92730-0001

BROMMER, GERALD FREDERICK, artist, writer; b. Berkeley, Calif., Jan. 8, 1927; s. Edgar C. and Helen (Wall) B.; m. Georgia Elizabeth Pratt, Dec. 19, 1948. B.S. Ed., Concordia Coll., Nebr., 1948; M.A., U. Nebr., 1955; postgrad. UCLA, U. So. Calif., Otis Art Inst., Chouinard Art Inst.; D.Litt., Christ Coll., 1985. Instr., St. Paul's Sch., North Hollywood, Calif., 1948-55, Lutheran High Sch., Los Angeles, 1955-76; one-person shows throughout country; exhibited in numerous group shows including Am. Watercolor Soc., NAD, Royal Watercolor Soc., London; represented in permanent collections Claremont Colls. (Calif.), Pacific Telesis, Laguna Beach Mus. Art, TRW, Cola Cola Co., Ky., Concordia Coll., Nebr., Ill., Mo., Utah State U., Provo; books include: Discovering Art History, 1981, revised edition, 1988, The Art of Collage, 1978, Drawing, 1978, Understanding Transparent Watercolor, 1993, Landscapes, 1977, Art in your World, 1977, Watercolor and Collage Workshop, 1986, Exploring Painting, 1989, Exploring Drawing, 1990, Art: Your Visual Environment, 1977, Movement and Rhythm, 1975, Space, 1974, Transparent Watercolor, 1973, Relief Printmaking, 1970, Wire Sculpture, 1968, Careers in Art, 1984, and others; editor: The Design Concept Series, 10 vols., 1974-75, Insights to Art series, 1977—; various texts; assoc. Hewitt Painting Workshops, Artist Workshop Tour Agy., Trillium workshops, Can. Grand Strand Watercolor workshops. Recipient prizes Am. Watercolor Soc., 1965, 68, 71, Watercolor U.S.A., 1970, 73, Los Angeles City Art Festival, 1970, 75, Calif. State Fair, 1975. Mem. Nat. Watercolor Soc. (treas., v.p., pres., awards 1972, 74, 78, 80), West Coast Watercolor Soc., Nat. Arts Club, Rocky Mountain Nat. Watermedia Soc., Watercolor USA Honor Soc., Nat. Art Edn. Assn. Republican. Lutheran. Club: Nat. Arts (N.Y.C.). Address: 11252 Valley Spring Ln North Hollywood CA 91602

BRON, WALTER ERNEST, physics educator; b. Berlin, Jan. 17, 1930; came to U.S., 1939, naturalized, 1946; s. Arthur and Edith (Seidel) B.; m. Ann Elisabeth Berend, June 1, 1952; children: Karen Susanne, Michelle Elise. B.M.E., N.Y. U., 1952; M.S., Columbia, 1953, Ph.D., 1958. Research assoc. IBM Watson Lab., Yorktown Heights, N.Y., 1957-58; research physicist IBM Watson Lab., 1958-66; assoc. prof. physics Ind. U., Bloomington, 1966-69; prof. Ind. U., 1969-86; prof. dept. physics U. Calif., Irvine, 1986—, chmn., 1989-92; lectr. George Washington U., 1955-56, Columbia, 1957, adj. lectr., 1964; vis. prof. Physikalisches Institut der Technischen Hochschule, Stuttgart, Germany, 1966-67; vis. scientist Max Planck Inst. for Solid State Research, Stuttgart, Germany, 1973-74, 81-82, 83. Contbr. articles sci. jours. Mem. Bloomington Environ. Quality and Conservation Commn., 1972-81, chmn., 1974-76. Served with AUS, 1954-56. Gen. Electric fellow, 1952-53; W. Campbell fellow, 1953-54, 56-57; Guggenheim fellow, 1966-67; sr. Scientist award Alexander von Humboldt Found., 1973. Fellow Am. Phys. Soc.; mem. European Phys. Soc., Sassafras Audubon Soc. (pres. 1976-78), Sigma Xi, Tau Beta Pi, Pi Tau Sigma. Home: 20 Mendel Ct Irvine CA 92715-4039 Office: U Calif Irvine Dept Physics Irvine CA 92717

BRONG, GERALD RUSSELL, business development specialist; b. Tacoma, July 20, 1939; s. Gordon Allen and Helen L. (Blatt) B.; m. Marlene Ann Lindauer, Sept. 18, 1960; children: Christopher Scott, Richard Karl. BA in Edn., Cen. Wash. U., 1961, MEd, 1965; EdD, Wash. State U., 1973. Registered PAC. Tchr. 6th grade Tacoma Sch. Dist., 1961-65; dir. faculty devel. instructional media svcs. program Wash. State U., Pullman, 1965-73, 74-82; dir., founder ednl. svcs. div. Community Computer Ctrs., Pullman, 1982-90; founder, pres., chief exec. officer Bus. Info. Inc., Ellensburg, Wash., 1990—; dir. futures planning task force Wash. State Libr., 1990-92; founding pgnr. GMB Partnership, Ellensburg, Wash., 1992—; founding cons., publ. editor Student Pub. Svcs., Inc., 1989-91; designer, coord. Power On symposium U. Idaho, 1989-90; del. White House Conf. on Small Bus., 1986; active delegations steering and planning coms. Wash. State Gov.'s Conf. on Small Bus., 1989; govtl. liaison officer rep. regional univ. to state and fed. govt.; cons., platform speaker, seminar leader numerous profl. and ednl. orgns. Editor Brong's Business Success News, 1990-92; contbr. articles on edn. orgns.; columnist Small Bus. News, Reuton, Wash., Yakima (Wash.) Herald-Republic, others; contbr. Technol. Horizons in Edn. Mem.-at-large Pullman City Coun., 1982-88; pres., chmn. Cen. Wash. U. Found., 1987-89; mem. Clearwater Econ. Devel. Assn., bd. dirs., 1983-85; bd. dirs. Palouse Econ. Devel. Coun., 1985-88; Ea. Wash. chmn. Wash. State Com. for Employer Support of Guard and Res. Mem. Internat. Communications Industry Assn. (founding bd. dirs. Better Govt. Fund, vice chmn. 1988-92), Assn. Ednl. Communications and Tech. (bd. dirs., mem. exec. com., pres. Wash. chpt., pres. membership div., Meml. scholar 1972), Cen. Wash. U. Alumni Assn. (pres. 1982-84), Rotary (pres. Pullman club 1979-80, team leader group study exch. project 1988). Republican. Home: RR 1 Box 1130 Ellensburg WA 98926-9733

BRONSTEIN, ARTHUR J., former linguistics educator; b. Balt., Mar. 15, 1914; s. Gershon and Bessie B.; m. Elsa Meltzer, May 15, 1941; children: Nancy Ellen, Abbot Alan. B.A., CCNY, 1934; M.A., Columbia U., 1936; Ph.D., NYU, 1949. Vis. scholar and rsch. assoc. in linguistics U. Calif., Berkeley, 1987—; prof. Queens Coll., N.Y.C., 1938-67; Fulbright prof. U. Tel Aviv, (Israel), 1967-68, U. Trondheim, (Norway), 1979; prof. linguistics Lehman Coll. and Grad. Sch., CUNY, 1968-83, prof. emeritus, 1983—; exec. officer PhD program in speech and hearing scis. CUNY, 1969-72; exec. officer Ph.D. program in linguistics Lehman Coll. and Grad. Sch., CUNY, 1981-83; cons. in field; with dept. linguistics U. Calif., Berkeley. Author: Pronunciation of American English, 1960, Essays in Honor of C.M. Wise, 1970, Biographical Dictionary of the Phonetic Sciences, 1977; project dir.: Dictionary of American English Pronunciation. Served with Signal Corps and AGD USAA, 1942-46. Fellow Am. Speech and Hearing Assn., Internat. Soc. Phonetic Sics., N.Y. Acad. Sci.; mem. MLA, Linguistics Soc. Am., Am. Dialect Soc., Am. Assn. Phonetic Scis., Dictionary Soc. N.Am., Phi Beta Kappa. Office: U Calif Dept Linguistics Berkeley CA 94720

BROOK, WINSTON ROLLINS, audio-video design consultant; b. Cameron, Tex., Aug. 20, 1931; s. Winston Marshall and Maude Katherine (Woody) B. BA, U. Denver, 1955. Lic. radiotelephone operator, FCC. Engr. Sta. WKNO-TV, Memphis, 1965-67; instr. Memphis State U., 1967-69; audio-visual dir. So. Coll. Optometry, Memphis, 1968-73; sr. cons. Bolt Beranek and Newman, Chgo. and Los Angeles, 1973-87; prin. Brook & Chavez Assocs., Los Angeles, 1987—; instr. various seminars and workshops; assoc. editor Theater Design & Tech. mag., N.Y.C., 1981-87; tech. cons. Sound & Video Contractor mag., Overland, Kans., 1987—. Co-author: Handbook for Sound Engineers, 1987; contbr. articles to profl. jours., 1978—. Mem. Audio Engring. Soc., Acoustical Soc. Am., U.S. Inst. for Theatre Tech. Democrat. Mormon. Home and Office: 5715 Calvin Ave Tarzana CA 91356-1108

BROOKBANK, JOHN W(ARREN), retired microbiology educator; b. Seattle, Apr. 3, 1927; s. Earl Bruce and Louise Sophia (Stoecker) B.; m. Marcia Ireland, Sept. 16, 1950 (div. 1978); children: Ursula Ireland, John W. Jr., Phoebe Bruce; m. Sally Satterberg Cahill, Aug. 6, 1983. BA, U. Wash., 1950, MS, 1953; PhD, Calif. Inst. Tech., 1955. Asst. prof. U. Fla., Gainesville, 1955-58, assoc. prof., 1958-68, prof. microbiology and cell sci., 1968-85, prof. emeritus, 1985—; vis. assoc. prof. U. Fla. Coll. Medicine, Gainesville, 1961-63, U. Wash., Seattle, 1965; cons. in field, Friday Harbor, Wash. 1986—. Author: Developmental Biology, 1978, (with W. Cunningham) Gerontology, 1988; editor: Improving Quality of Health Care of the Elderly, 1977, Biology of Aging, 1990; contbr. articles to profl. jours. Pres. Griffin Bay Preservation Com., Friday Harbor, 1985—, Bridge Council on Narcotics Addiction, Gainesville, 1974, Marine Environ. Consortium, 1986—; founding pres. Gainesville Regional Council on Alcoholism, 1976. Research grantee NIH, 1957-80, NSF, 1972-73. Mem. AAAS, Gerontol. Soc. Am., Seattle Tennis Club. Republican. Episcopalian. Home: PO Box 2688 Friday Harbor WA 98250-2688

BROOKE, CHARLES PATRICK, surgeon; b. Three Forks, Mont., Sept. 8, 1914; s. Enoch Marvin and Rachel Geneivive (Murray) B.; m. Helen Streeter, Oct. 16, 1942; children: Michael C., Patrick M. (dec.), James M., Virginia M., Mary A., Terrance J. BA in Biology, Carroll Coll., 1937; MD, St. Louis U., 1941; JD, U. Mont., 1964. Intern, resident Sacred Heart Hosp., Spokane, 1941-42; resident in orthopedics Camp White Army Hosp., Medford, Oreg., 1942; chief of staff Holy Family Hosp., St. Ignatius, Mont., 1947-53; pres. hosp. staff St. Patrick Hosp., Missoula, Mont., 1978-79; mem. staff Community Hosp.; solo practice law Missoula Gen. Hosp.; chief med. legal cons. ins. cos., 1966-85; mem. Mont. State Bd. Med. Examiners, 1965-75, also past pres.; prof. forensic medicine U. Mont. Law Sch., 1972-86; chief reconditioning svc. Surg. Svc. Camp Swift Regional Hosp., Tex.; chief surg. svc. Prisoner War Hosp. Camp Swift, Tex., 1977. Contbr. articles to profl. pubs. Pres. Missoula C. of C., 1975-76; pres. bd. dirs. MIssoula Civic Symphony, 1956-74. Maj. U.S. Army Med. Corps, 1941-46. Recipient Alumni Merit award St. Louis U., 1977; named to Carroll Coll. Alumni Hall of Fame, 1989. Mem. AMA, Western Mont. Bar Assn., Mont. Bar, Mont. Med. Assn., Am. Coll. Legal Medicine, Am. Legion (vice comdr.), Lions (v.p. Missoula chpt.), K.C. Republican. Roman Catholic. Home: 307 University Ave Missoula MT 59801-4349

BROOKE, EDNA MAE, business educator; b. Las Vegas, Nev., Feb. 10, 1923; d. Alma Lyman and Leah Mae (Ketcham) Shurtliff; m. Bill T. Brooke, Dec. 22, 1949; 1 child, John C. BS in Acctg., Ariz. State U., 1965, MA in Edn., 1967, EdD, 1975. Grad. teaching asst. Ariz. State U., Tempe, 1968-69; prof. bus. Maricopa Tech. Coll., Phoenix, 1967-72, assoc. dean instl. services, 1972-74; prof. bus. and acctg. Scottsdale (Ariz.) Community Coll., 1974—; cons. in field. Author: The Effectiveness of Three Techniques Used in Teaching First Semester Accounting Principles to Tech. Jr. College Students, 1974. Mem. Nat. Bus. Edn. Assn., Western Bus. Edn. Assn., Ariz. Bus. Edn. Assn., Am. Acctg. Assn., Delta Pi Epsilon. Home: 1330 E Calle De Caballos Tempe AZ 85284-2404 Office: Scottsdale Community Coll 9000 E Chaparral Rd Scottsdale AZ 85250-2699

BROOKE, TAL (ROBERT TALIAFERRO), company executive, author; b. Washington, Jan. 21, 1945; s. Edgar Duffield and Frances (Lea) B. BA, U. Va., 1969; M in Theology/Philosophy, Princeton (N.J.) U., 1986. V.p. pub. rels. nat. office Telecom Inc., 1982-83; pres., chmn. Spiritual Counterfeits Project, Inc., Berkeley, 1989—; guest lectr. Cambridge U., Eng., 1977, 86, Oxford and Cambridge U., 1979, 84; speaker in field. Author: Lord of the Air, 1990, When the World Will Be As One, 1989 (bestseller 1989-90), Riders of the Cosmic Circuit, 1986, Avatar of Night, 1987 (bestseller in India 1981-84), The Other Side of Death, Lord of the Air: The International Edition, 1976. Mem. Soc. of the Cin. Office: SCP Inc 2606 Dwight Way Berkeley CA 94704

BROOKES, VALENTINE, lawyer; b. Red Bluff, Calif., May 30, 1913; s. Langley and Ethel (Valentine) B.; m. Virginia Stovall Cunningham, Feb. 11, 1939; children: Langley Brookes Brandt, Lawrence Valentine, Alan Cunningham. A.B., U. Calif., Berkeley, 1934, J.D., 1937. Bar: Calif. 1937, U.S. Supreme Ct. 1942. Asst. franchise tax counsel State of Calif., 1937-40; dep. atty. gen. Calif., 1940-42; spl. asst. to U.S. atty. gen., asst. to solicitor gen. U.S., 1942-44; partner firm Kent & Brookes, San Francisco, 1944-70, Alvord & Alvord, Washington, 1944-50, Lee, Toomey & Kent, Washington, 1950-79; partner firm Brookes and Brookes, San Francisco, 1971-88, of counsel, 1988-90; legal cons. Orinda, Calif., 1990—; lectr. Hastings Coll. Law, U. Calif., 1941-48, U. Calif. Law Sch., Berkeley, 1948-70; cons. fed. taxation. Author: The Continuity of Interest Test in Reorganizations, 1946, The Partnership Under the Income Tax Laws, 1949, The Tax Consequences of

Widows Elections in Community Property States, 1951, Corporate Trasactions Involving Its Own Stock, 1954, Litigation Expenses and the Income Tax, 1957. Bd. dirs. Children's Hosp. Med. Center of N. Calif., 1963-74, v.p., 1968-70; trustee Oakes Found., 1957-70; regent St. Mary's Coll., Calif., 1968-88, pres. bd., 1970-72, emeritus mem., 1988—. Fellow Am. Bar Found. (life); mem. Am. Law Inst., ABA (chmn. com. on statute of limitations 1954-57, mem. council, tax sect. 1960-63), Calif. Bar Assn. (chmn. com. on taxation 1950-52, 60-61), Soc. Calif. Pioneers (v.p. 1964, 1975-86), Am. Coll. Tax Counsel, Phi Kappa Sigma, Phi Delta Phi. Republican. Clubs: Pacific Union, Orinda Country, World Trade. Home and Office: 7 Sycamore Rd Orinda CA 94563-1418

BROOKMAN, ANTHONY RAYMOND, lawyer; b. Chgo., Mar. 23, 1922; s. Raymond Charles and Marie Clara (Alberg) B.; m. Marilyn Joyce Brookman, June 5, 1982; children: Meribeth Brookman Farmer, Anthony Raymond, Lindsay Logan Christensen. Student, Ripon Coll., 1940-41; BS, Northwestern U., 1947; JD, U. Calif., San Francisco, 1953. Bar: Calif. 1954. Law clk. to presiding justice Calif. Supreme Ct., 1953-54; ptnr. Nichols, Williams, Morgan, Digardi & Brookman, 1954-68; sr. ptnr. Brookman and Talbot (formerly Brookman and Hoffman, Inc.), Walnut Creek, Calif., 1969-92, Brookman & Talbot Inc., Sacramento, 1992—; Pub. Contra Costa New Register. Pres. Young Reps. Calif., San Mateo County, 1953-54. 1st lt. USAF. Mem. ABA, Alameda County Bar Assn., State Bar Calif., Lawyers Club Alameda County, Alameda-Contra Costa County Trial Lawyers Assn., Assn. Trial Lawyers Am., Calif. Trial Lawyers Assn., Athenian Nile Club, Crow Canyon Country Club, Masons, Shriners. Republican. Office: 901 H St Ste 200 Sacramento CA 95814-1879 also: 1990 N California Blvd Walnut Creek CA 94596 also: 2119 W March Ln Ste A Stockton CA 95207

BROOKS, ALISON ANNE, lawyer; b. Toledo, Ohio, Nov. 21, 1954; d. Charles Thomas and Margaret Anne (Houser) Kopp; m. Charles N. Brooks, Oct. 6, 1979 (div. Dec. 1987); 1 child, Matthew Hunter; m. W. Gerald Flannery, Mar. 18, 1989. BA magna cum laude, Denison U., 1976; JD, U. Toledo, 1979. Bar: Mich. 1980, Calif. 1988, U.S. Dist. Ct. (ctrl., no., so. and ea. dists.) Calif. 1989. Rsch. atty. Charfoos & Charfoos, Detroit, 1979-80; staff atty. Ford Motor Co., Dearborn, Mich., 1981-87; sr. counsel Mitsubishi Motor Sales Am., Cypress, Calif., 1988-89; sr. assoc. Snell & Wilmer, Irvine, Calif., 1989—; Mem. exec. com., sustaining mem. Nat. Product Liability Adv. Coun., 1988-89. Editor jour. U. Toledo Law Rev., 1978-79. Mem. Red Ribbon Com., Orange County, Calif., 1990-92. Mem. ABA, Calif. Bar Assn., Assn. Trial Lawyers Am., Def. Rsch. Inst., Mortar Board, Phi Beta Kappa. Republican. Office: Snell & Wilmer 1920 Main St Ste 1200 Irvine CA 92714

BROOKS, ALISON LESLEY, neonatal intensive care nursery nurse; b. Portsmouth, Eng., June 14, 1958; came to U.S., 1981; d. Bazil Peter Kay and Kathleen Eileen (Stewart-Blacker) B.; m. Andrew Altounyan, Feb. 25, 1993. ASN, U. of State of N.Y., Albany, 1986; BSN, Holy Names Coll., 1993; postgrad., U. Calif., San Francisco, 1993—. RN. Staff nurse II intensive care nursery level II Community Hosp., Santa Rosa, Calif., 1984-87; staff nurse III intensive care nursery level III Children's Hosp. Oakland (Calif.), 1987—; staff nurse Planned Parenthood, Oakland, 1992—; chair Staff Nurse III Com., Oakland, 1992—; chair, mem. grief and bereavement fllow-up program Children's Hosp. Oakland, 1990—. Pres.'s scholar Holy Names Coll., 1990. Fellow Royal Geog. Soc.; mem. NAACOG, Calif. Nurses Assn. (scholar 1991), Neonatal Nurses Of No. Calif. Nat. Assn. Neonatal Nurses, East Bay Nursing Honor Soc., Omicron Alpha Kappa.

BROOKS, BRADFORD OLDHAM, immunotoxicologist, consultant; b. Dallas, May 5, 1951; s. Charles Raymond and Bettye June (Oldham) B.; m. Anita Marian Chandler, June 11, 1974; children: Nathaniel Bradford, Collin Chandler. BS in Biology, Harding U., 1973; MS in Microbiology, Mont. State U., 1976, PhD in Immunobiology, 1979. NIH/NAID fellow in preventive medicine Cornell U., Ithaca, N.Y., 1979-81, sr. rsch. assoc., asst. prof. preventive medicine, 1981-82; staff scientist health effects rsch. IBM Corp., Boulder, Colo., 1982-85, adv. scientist health effects rsch., 1985-89, sr. level scientist, health effects rsch. dept., 1989-92; mgr. Health Effects Rsch. Inst., 1992—; pres., chief exec. officer Immunocompetence Cons. Co., Longmont, Colo., 1983—. Co-author: Understanding Indoor Air, 1991, Immunotoxicology, 1991; contbr. articles to profl. jours. Bd. dirs. Mountain States Children's Home, Longmont, 1986-90. Mem. ASHRAE (assoc.), Am. Soc. for Microbiology, Am. Acad. Clin. Toxicology, Am. Assn. Immunologists, Am. Assn. for Testing and Materials, Internat. Soc. for Immunopharmacology. Office: IBM Corp PO Box 190 Boulder CO 80328-0001

BROOKS, DORIS JEAN, temporary employment firm executive; b. Highland Park, Mich., June 13, 1955; d. Virgil Eugene and Dora Ann (Corum) Davis; m. Roy Lee Thompson, June 15, 1973 (div. Jan. 16, 1978); m. Russell Joseph Brooks, Mar. 18, 1979; children: Shawn Christopher, Beth Ann Brooks. AA, North Seattle (Wash.) C.C., 1991. Ins. clk. Tenn. Farmers Mut. Ins. Co., Columbia, Tenn., 1973-75; office clk. Uncle Charlie's Sausage Co., Columbia, 1975-77; sec. Salvation Army, Seattle, 1977-78; ins. clk. Albany Ins. Co., Seattle, 1978-79; asst. customer svc. rep. Fred S. James & Co., Seattle, 1979-86; pres. Ins. Temps., Inc., Seattle, 1986—. Democrat. Methodist.

BROOKS, EDWARD HOWARD, college administrator; b. Salt Lake City, Mar. 2, 1921; s. Charles Campbell and Margery (Howard) B.; m. Courtaney June Perren, May 18, 1946; children: Merrillee Brooks Runyan, Robin Anne (Mrs. R. Bruce Pollock). B.A., Stanford U., 1942, M.A., 1947, Ph.D., 1950. Mem. faculty, adminstrn. Stanford U., 1949-71; provost Claremont (Calif.) Colls., 1971-81; v.p. Claremont U. Center, 1979-81; sr. v.p. Claremont McKenna Coll., 1981-84; provost Scripps Coll., 1987-89, pres., 1989-90; ret., 1990. Trustee EDUCOM, 1978-80, Webb Sch. of Calif., 1979-90, Menlo Sch. and Coll., 1985-88; bd. overseers Hoover Instn., 1972-78; bd. dirs. Student Loan Mktg. Assn., 1973-77; mem. Calif. Student Aid Commn., 1984-88, chmn., 1986-88. Served with AUS, 1942-45. Clubs: University (Los Angeles); Bohemian (San Francisco). Home: 337 8th St Manhattan Beach CA 90266-5629

BROOKS, GLENN ALLEN, telecommunications engineer; b. Pasadena, Calif., Mar. 23, 1960; s. Robert Allen and Sarah Eloise (Merritt) B.; m. Tracy Jo Williams, June 11, 1983; children: Joshua Allen Ray, Ashleigh Nicole, Jonathan Lincoln. AA, Golden West Coll., Huntington Beach, Calif., 1983; BS, San Diego State U., 1985; postgrad., U. Phoenix, 1992. Lic. foster child care, Calif.; notary pub. Orange County, Calif. Owner Moriah Recording Svcs., San Diego, 1983-84; intern, asst. account exec. Cox Cable, San Diego, 1985; intern, 2d engr. Studio West, San Diego, 1983-84; audio engr. KPBS-TV, San Diego, 1984-85, Group W., Santa Monica, Calif., 1985-86; owner Small World Prodns., Huntington Beach, Calif., 1986-90; editor Video General, Long Beach, Calif., 1988-89; audio engr. KSCI-TV, Los Angeles, 1986-88; syncronist, audio engr. Chace Prodns., Hollywood, Calif., 1988; materials coord. purchasing, TQM team facilitator, system controller 2 Rank Video, Garden Grove, Calif., 1989-93; pres. Brooks Concepts, Inc., Huntington Beach, 1990-92; sole proprietor BroCon Devels., 1993—; cons. in field. Mem. Internat. Alliance TV Sound Engrs. Republican. Home and Office: 5522 Harold Pl Huntington Beach CA 92647-2013

BROOKS, JAMES SPRAGUE, retired national guard officer; b. Los Angeles, Feb. 16, 1925; s. Julian Chesney and Louise Heegaard (Sprague) B.; m. Loa Mae Woolf, June 17, 1947; children—Georgia Lee (stepdau.), Kerri Louise (dec.), James Patrick. B.C.E., Oreg. State Coll., 1951. Commd. lt. Idaho N.G., 1947, advanced through grades to maj. gen., 1975; engring. staff officer Idaho Mil. Dept. Idaho N.G., Boise, 1951-64, engr. Budget and Property Office, 1953-64, chief staff, 1965-74, adj. gen., chief Bur. Disaster Svcs., state dir. Selective Svc., 1975-85; chmn. army res. forces policy com. Dept. Army, 1979. Contbr. articles to Aviation Digest. Nat. Guard Mag. Mem. Boise Mcpl. Airport Commn., 1963-90, Idaho Law Enforcement Planning Commn., 1975, Boise Met. Plan Steering Com., 1976, Boise County Comprehensive Planning Task Force, 1989—; chmn. Boise Mayor's Transit Adv. Com., 1991—. Served with USAAF 1943-46. Decorated Legion of Merit, D.S.M.; recipient Idaho Safe Pilot award, 1974; named Disting. Citizen, Idaho Statesman, 1977. Mem. N.G. Assn., U.S. Army, AF Assn., Retired Officers Assn., Tau Beta Pi, Sigma Tau.

BROOKS, KRISTINA MARIE, software and system development administrator; b. Ft. Leavenworth, Kans., Aug. 29, 1949; d. Allison Cochran and Geraldine (Nordell) B.; m. Patrick Dennis Joyce, Jan. 17, 1987; children: Michael Baxter Joyce, Elizabeth Benedict Joyce. BA, U. Wash., 1970; MAT, N.Mex. State U., 1972; MLS, U. Oreg., 1975; PhD, Oreg. State U., 1986. Tchr. La Mesa (N.Mex.) Schs., 1970-72, Browning (Mont.) Schs., 1972-73; libr. asst. CERL facility U.S. EPA, Corvallis, Oreg., 1975; online coord. Oreg. State U. Libr., Corvallis, 1975-82; mgr. applications programming System Devel. Corp., Santa Monica, Calif., 1982-87; tech. dir. Saztec Internat., Rolling Hills Estates, Calif., 1987-88; dir. applications devel. Maxwell Data Mgmt., Costa Mesa, Calif., 1988—. Contbr. chpt. to book, articles to profl. jours. Mem. Am. Soc. for Info. Sci. (chair SIGMGT 1985-86), Assn. for Computing Machinery. Office: Maxwell Data Mgmt 275 E Baker Ste A Costa Mesa CA 90815

BROOKS, SHEILA JEANNE, librarian; b. San Francisco, May 13, 1944; d. John W. Brooks and Flora A. (Adams) Farnbach. BA, U. Calif., Davis, 1966. Cert. secondary teaching, adminstr., librarian. Tchr. Ukiah (Calif.) Unified Schs., 1967-75, librarian, 1975—; instr. Santa Rosa Jr. Coll. Extension, Ukiah, 1969-71; mem. Instructional Media Ctr. Adv. Bd., Ukiah, 1987—; adv. Calif. Scholarship Fedn., Ukiah, 1974-87. Mem. Mendocino County Public Library Adv. Bd., Ukiah, 1972-88. C-Span Equipment grantee, 1992; recipient Century Award Remarkable Educator award Century Cable, 1993. Mem. Calif. Media and Library Educators Assn., Calif. Tchrs. Assn., Am. Fedn. Tchrs., Ukiah High Sch. Faculty Assn. (sec. 1986-87, treas. 1987-88), AAUW Women (v.p. membership Ukiah br. 1985-87). Democrat. Club: Oak Hill Pool (Ukiah) (pres. 1982, treas. 1983). Office: Ukiah High Sch 1000 Low Gap Rd Ukiah CA 95482-3798

BROOKS, TEMPE BOYCE-SMITH, manufacturing company executive; b. Summit, N.J., May 26, 1941; d. John III and Lee Ellis (Wootten) Boyce-Smith; m. John Emmert Brooks, June 14, 1963; children: Christine Brooks Macdonald, Cynthia, John Emmert Jr. BA in Zoology, Pomona Coll., 1963. Sec.-treas. Adams & Brooks, Inc., L.A., 1985—. Pres. bd. dirs. Jr. League of Pasadena, Calif., 1977-78, Pasadena Pub. Libr. Found., 1986-90, Project D.A.Y. Found., 1992—; pres. bd. trustees Westridge Sch. for Girls, Pasadena, 1985-88; vice chmn. United Way Planning Coun. Region II, San Gabriel Valley, 1978-88; bd. dirs. Calif. Coun. on Alcoholism, 1980-83; del. White House Conf. on Aging, 1981. Recipient 20th Century award Pasadena YWCA, 1982, Gold Key award L.A. United Way, 1985; named to Outstanding Young Women in Am., 1970. Mem. Pasadena Garden Club (treas. 1986-88), Cal Tech Assocs. Republican. Presbyterian. Home: 1118 Wellington Ave Pasadena CA 91103 Office: Adams & Brooks Inc 1915 S Hoover St Los Angeles CA 90007

BROOKSHAW, KEITH HENRY, college administrator; b. Southampton, Hampshire, Eng., June 25, 1949; s. Jack Arthur and Yvonne (de la Croix) B. m. Elva Antonia Luna, July 17, 1976; children: Elisia Angela, David Keith. AA, Foothill Coll., 1971; BA, U. Calif., Davis, 1973; MS, Calif. State U., Hayward, 1975; postgrad., U. So. Calif., 1993—. Counselor, instr. Foothill Coll., Los Altos Hills, Calif., 1975-79; psychology instr. Chabot Coll., Hayward, Calif., 1975-86; ESL instr. Calif. State U., Hayward, 1975-86; project dir. Santa Rosa (Calif.) Jr. Coll., summer 1979; counselor, instr. Indian Valley Coll., Novato, Calif., 1977-80, San Francisco City Coll., 1980-81; asst. dir. Sonoma State Univ., Rohnert Park, Calif., 1981-88; program dir. Shasta Coll., Redding, Calif., 1988—. Mem. pub. relations com. No. Counties Hispanic Coun., Red Bluff, Calif., 1990—, adv. bd. Migrant Edn.-Region II, Chico, Calif., 1991—; bd. dirs. Old Adobe Devel. Ctr., Petaluma, Calif., 1983-88. Mem. Phi Delta Kappa, Theta Chi. Democrat. Roman Catholic. Home: 11472 Thursday Ln Redding CA 96003 Office: Shasta Coll 11555 Old Oregon Trail Redding CA 96049

BROOM, ARTHUR DAVIS, chemistry educator; b. Panama Canal Zone, July 26, 1937; s. Thomas Selwyn and Georgia Mae (Stallings) B.; m. Mary Jo Duffin, June 13, 1960; children: Thomas, Laura, Carol. BS, U. Tex., 1959; PhD, Ariz. State U., 1965. Rsch. assoc. Johns Hopkin's U., Balt., 1965-66; rsch. assoc. U. Utah, Salt Lake City, 1966-67, asst. rsch. prof., 1967-69, asst. prof., 1969-71, assoc. prof., 1971-75, prof., 1975—, chair dept. med. chemistry, 1978—; mem. grant proposal rev. com. NIH Study Sect., Washington, 1981—, chair, 1992—; mem. grant proposal rev. com. Am. Cancer Soc., 1986-90. Contbr. numerous articles to profl. jours. Lectr. Am. Cancer Soc., Salt Lake City, U. Utah Speakers Bur., Salt Lake City. John R. Park fellow Poland, 1979, Fulbright fellow Fed. Republic of Germany, 1983. Mem. AAAS, Am. Assn. for Cancer Rsch., Am. Assn. Colls. of Pharmacy, Am. Chem. Soc., Rho Chi. Methodist. Office: U Utah Dept Medicinal Chemistry 308 Skaggs Hall Salt Lake City UT 84112

BROOMFIELD, ROBERT CAMERON, federal judge; b. Detroit, June 18, 1933; s. David Campbell and Mabel Margaret (Van Deventer) B.; m. Cuma Lorena Cecil, Aug. 3, 1958; children: Robert Cameron Jr., Alyson Paige, Scott McKinley. BS, Pa. State U., 1955; LLB, U. Ariz., 1961. Bar: Ariz. 1961, U.S. Dist. Ct. Ariz. 1961. Assoc. Carson, Messinger, Elliot, Laughlin & Ragan, Phoenix, 1962-65, ptnr., 1966-71; judge Ariz. Superior Ct., Phoenix, 1971-85, U.S. Dist. Ct. Ariz., Phoenix, 1985—; faculty Nat. Jud. Coll., Reno, 1975-82. Contbr. articles to profl. jours. Adv. bd. Boy Scouts Am., Phoenix, 1968-75; tng. com. Ariz. Acad., Phoenix, 1980—; pres. Paradise Valley Sch. Bd., Phoenix, 1969-70; bd. dirs. Phoenix Together, 1982—, Crisis Nursery, Phoenix, 1976-81; chmn. 9th Cir. Task Force on Ct. Reporting, 1988—; mem. Space and Facilities Com. of U.S. Jud. Conf., 1987—, chmn., 1990. Capt. USAF, 1955-58. Recipient Faculty award Nat. Jud. Coll., 1979, Disting. Jurist award Miss. State U., 1986. Mem. ABA (chmn. Nat. Conf. State Trial Judges 1983-84, pres. Nat. Conf. Met. Cts. 1978-79, chmn. bd. dirs. 1980-82, Justice Tom Clark award 1980, bd. dirs. Nat. Ctr. for State Cts. 1980-85, Disting. Svc. award 1986), Ariz. Bar Assn., Maricopa County Bar Assn. (Disting. Pub. Svc. award 1980), Ariz. Judges Assn. (pres. 1981-82), Am. Judicature Soc. (spl. citation 1985), Maricopa County Med. Soc. (Disting. Svc. medal 1979). Lodge: Rotary. Office: US Dist Ct US Courthouse & Fed Bldg 230 N 1st Ave Ste 3077 Phoenix AZ 85025-0069

BROPHY, DENNIS RICHARD, psychology and philosophy educator, administrator, clergyman; b. Milw., Aug. 6, 1945; s. Floyd Herbert and Phyllis Marie (Ingram) B.; B.A., Washington U., St. Louis, 1967, M.A., 1968; M.Div., Pacific Sch. Religion, 1971; ABD in Indstrl. and Orgnl. Psychology, Texas A & M U. Cert. coll. tchr., Calif. Edn. researcher IBM Corp., White Plains, N.Y., 1968-71; edn. minister Community Congl. Ch., Port Huron, Mich., 1971-72, Bethlehem United Ch. of Christ, Ann Arbor, Mich., 1972-73, Community Congl. Ch., Chula Vista, Calif., 1974; philosophy instr. Southwestern Coll., Chula Vista, 1975; assoc. prof. psychology and philosophy Northwest Coll., Powell, Wyo., 1975—, chmn. social sci. divsn., 1992—; religious edn. cons. Mont.-No. Wyo. Conf. United Ch. of Christ. Mem. Wyo. Council for Humanities, 1979-82. Mem. Wyo. Assn. Advancement of Humanities, Am. Psychol. Assn., Yellowstone Assn. of United Ch. of Christ, Phi Kappa Phi, Phi Beta Kappa, Sigma Xi, Omicron Delta Kappa, Theta Xi, Golden Key Nat. Honor Soc. Home: 533 Avenue C Powell WY 82435-2401 Office: Northwest Coll 231 W 6th St Powell WY 82435

BROPHY, TODD RANDALL, property management executive, rancher; b. Wray, Colo., Sept. 21, 1954; s. Desmond Daniel amd Delpha Jean (Bowman) B.; m. Caroline Brooks Lerew. BS in Agrl. Econs., Colo. State U., 1977; postgrad., U. Colo., Denver, 1980. Pres. A.S.L. Denver Inc., 1978-91; ptnr. Brophy Bros. Ranch, Wray, Colo., 1983—; v.p. Mktg. Mgmt. Plus, Inc, Aurora, Colo., 1991-92; owner Tao Mgmt., Aurora, 1992—; bd. dirs., sec., treas. Cherry Creek Marina, Inc., Denver, 1986-90, pres./mgr., 1990—; bd. dirs., sec., treas. Marine Devel., Inc., Denver, 1987—; bd. dirs., pres. Marina Assocs., Inc., Denver, 1987—; bd. dirs., sec. Masa Azul Ltd., Gunnison, Colo., 1988. Pub. Newsletter Agenda in field. Bd. dirs., pres. The Tiny Town Found. Inc., 1989-90. Mem. Inst. Real Estate Mgmt. (v.p. communication 1987-88, v.p. Tiny Town 1988-89, treas. 1990, sec. 1991, pres.-elect 1992), Leadership Centennial, Chief Exec. Officers Mgmt. Cos. Com., Home Builders Assn. (affiliate), Community Assns. Inst. Republican. Office: Tao Mgmt PO Box 441077 Aurora CO 80044

BRORBY, WADE, federal judge; b. 1934. BS, U. Wyo., 1956, JD with honor, 1958. Bar: Wyo. County and prosecuting atty. Campbell County, Wyo., 1963-70; ptnr. Morgan Brorby Price and Arp, Gillette, Wyo., 1961-88; judge U.S. Ct. Appeals (10th cir.), Cheyenne, Wyo., 1988—. With USAF, 1958-61. Mem. ABA, Campbell County Bar Assn., Am. Judicature Soc., Def. Lawyers Wyo., Wyo Bar Assn. (commr. 1968-70). Office: US Ct Appeals 10th Cir O'Mahoney Fed Bldg Rm 2016 PO Box 1028 Cheyenne WY 82002-0001

BROSELOW, STANLEY DAVID, electrical engineer; b. Phila., Aug. 3, 1925; s. Herman George and Dorothy Edyth B.; m. Bernyce Helene Shulman, Mar. 27, 1949; children: Stephen Mark, Hope Gail. BSEE, Drexel U., 1946. Construction mgmt. engr. U.S. Army Engr. Dist., Balt., 1946-61; chief, contract adminstrn. Corps of Engrs. Ballistic Missile Construction Office, Norton AFB, Calif., 1961-66; chmn. Western Regional Renegotiation Bd., L.A., 1966-79; procurement mgr. Hughes Aircraft Co., El Segundo, Calif., 1979-89. Mem. IEEE, Soc. Am. Mil. Engrs., ASCE, Nat. Contract Mgmt. Assn., Sigma Alpha Mu. Democrat. Jewish. Home: 7357 Paradiso Ct Las Vegas NV 89129-6481

BROSNAN, PETER LAWRENCE, documentary filmmaker; b. Bklyn., July 6, 1952; s. John Joseph and Audrey Barbara (Holran) B.; m. Lisa Anne Muller, June 30, 1990. BFA, NYU, N.Y.C., 1974; MA, U. So. Calif., 1979, Pepperdine U., 1993. Documentary filmmaker, writer L.A., 1980—; dir. DeMille Project, Hollywood Heritage, L.A., 1988—. Author: (screenplay) Heart of Darkness, 1992; co-author: (book) PML Report, 1989; writer: (documentary film) Ghosts of Cape Horn, 1980 (World Ship Trust award); producer, dir.: (TV documentary) The Lost City, 1992; writer, segment prodn.: (PBS Series) Faces of Culture, 1983-84 (Emmy 1984), Writer Marketing, 1984 (Emmy 1985). Democrat. Home: 3031 Angus St Los Angeles CA 90039

BROTHERTON, MAUREEN SALTZER, newspaper executive; b. Winchester, Mass., Mar. 21, 1959; d. William Charles Saltzer and Janet Ann (Quigley) Child; m. O. Lee Brotherton, June 27, 1981 (div. 1984). BS in Journalism summa cum laude, Boston U., 1981; postgrad., Northeastern U., Boston, 1984. Freelance corr. Concord (N.H.) Monitor, 1981-82; advt. sales rep. N.H. Times, Concord, 1981-82, circulation mgr., 1982-83; circulation and promotion mgr. Century Publs. Inc., Winchester, Mass., 1983-84, asst. gen. mgr., 1984-85; ad dir., ops. mgr. Provincetown (Mass.) Adv., 1985-86; gen. mgr. Healdsburg (Calif.) Tribune, Lesher Communications, 1986-87, Valley Times, Lesher Communications, Pleasanton, Calif., 1987-90; corp. oper. bd. dirs. Lesher Communications Inc., Walnut Creek, Calif.; pub., v.p. Victor Valley Daily Press div. Freedom Newspapers, Victorville, Calif., 1990—. Bd. dirs. Desert Communities United Way, campaign chmn., 1992, v.p., 1993; bd. dirs. Victor Valley Community Svcs. Coun., pres. 1993; hotline listener First Call for Help; treas. High Desert Regional Econ. Devel. Authority. Recipient Woman of Achievement award Bus. and Profl. Women, San Orco, 1991, Hall of Fame-Bus. award for State of Calif., 1992; Humanitarian award Desert Communs. United Way, 1991. Mem. Am. Newspaper Pubs. Assn., Calif. Newspaper Pubs. Assn. (2d Pl. Excellence award 1989, 1st v.p. so. unit 1993), Internat. Newspaper Mktg. Assn., Internat. Newspaper Advt. and Mktg. Execs. Assn. (Best TV Comml. 1992), Nat. Newspaper Assn., Admark-East Bay, Calif. Newspaper Advt. Execs. Assn., Pleasanton C. of C. (leadership com. 1988-90), Apple Valley C. of C., Victorville C. of C. (leadership com., fundraising com.), Rotary. Democrat. Home: 20672 Sholic Rd Apple Valley CA 92308-6367 Office: Victor Valley Daily Press PO Box 1389 Victorville CA 92393-1389

BROTMAN, CAROL EILEEN, adult education educator, advocate; b. L.A., Feb. 17, 1955; d. Hyman and Beverly Joanne (Krause) B. AA, L.A. Pierce Coll., 1977; BA, U. So. Calif., L.A., 1984; postgrad., UCLA, 1990, cert. legal asst., 1991. Cert. adult edn. tchr., Calif. Tchr. L.A. Unified Sch. Dist., 1986-88; tchr. adult edn. and ESL North Hollywood (Calif.) Adult Sch., 1988—. Founder Families for Quality Care, San Fernando Valley, Calif., 1983-86; mem. com. L.A. Pub. Libr. Cen. Libr., internat. langs. dept. Langs. Expertese and Resources Network, 1991; vol. paralegal Harriet Buhai Ctr. for Family Law, 1992—. Recipient Mayor's Commendation, 1984, Older Women's League, 1985. Mem. United Tchrs. of L.A., AAUW, Pomegranate Guild of Judaic Needlework. Home: 10921 Reseda Blvd Northridge CA 91326-2803 Office: North Hollywood Adult Sch 5231 Colfax Ave North Hollywood CA 91601-3097

BROTMAN, JEFFREY H., variety stores executive; b. 1942. JD, U. Wash., 1967. Ptnr. Lasher-Brotman & Sweet, 1967-74; with ENI Exploration Co., 1975-83; co-founder Costco Wholesale Corp., 1983, chmn. bd., chief exec. officer, 1983-88, chmn. bd., 1988—. Office: Costco Wholesale Corp 10809 120th Ave NE Kirkland WA 98033-5030

BROTMAN, RICHARD DENNIS, counselor; Detroit, Nov. 2, 1952; s. Alfred David and Dorothy G. (Mansfield) B.; m. Debra Louise Hobold, Sept. 9, 1979. AA, E. L.A. Jr. Coll., 1972; AB, U. So. Calif., 1974, MS, 1976. Instructional media coord. Audio-Visual Div., Pub. Library, City of Alhambra, Calif., 1971-78; clin. supr. Hollywood-Sunset Community Clinic, L.A., 1976—; client program coord. N. L.A. County Regional Ctr. for Developmentally Disabled, 1978-81; sr. counselor Eastern L.A. Regional Ctr. for Developmentally Disabled, 1981-85; dir. community svcs. Almansor Edn. Ctr., 1985-87; tng. and resource devel. Children's Home Soc. Calif., 1987-90; program supr. Pacific Clinics-East, 1990—; intern student affairs div., U. So. Calif., 1976. Corp. dir. San Gabriel Mission Players, 1973-75. Lic. marriage, family and child counselor, Calif.; cert. counselor Calif. Community Coll. Bd. Mem. Am. Assn. For Marriage and Family Therapy (approved supr.), Calif. Personnel and Guidance Assn. (conv. participant, 1976, 77, 79), Calif. Rehab. Counselors Assn. (officer), San Fernando Valley Consortium of Agys. Serving Developmentally Disabled Citizens (chmn. recreation subcom.), L.A. Aquarium Soc. Democrat. Home: 3515 Brandon St Pasadena CA 91107-4542 Office: Pacific Clinics 1217 Buena Vista Ave Duarte CA 91010-2408

BROTZMAN, PAUL DAVID, city manager; b. Sayre, Pa., Feb. 23, 1946; s. Elwood H. and Mabel E. (Stonell) B. m. Sharon Lynn Douglas, 1975 (div. 1981); m. Amy Jean Chong, Jan. 1, 1984. BS in Polit. Sci., Wilkes U., 1968. Asst. township mgr. S. Whitehall Township, South Whitehall, Pa., 1968-73; asst. city mgr. City Claremont, Calif., 1973-78; city mgr. City of Martinez, Calif., 1978-85, City of West Hollywood, Calif., 1985—. Bd. dirs. West Hollywood Homeless Orgn., 1989-92, West Side Urban Forum, L.A., 1990-92, Pub. Tech., Inc., Washington, 1990-92. Mem. Internat. City Mgmt. Assn. (Clarence Ridley award, 1988). Democrat. Home: 2573 Laurel Pass Los Angeles CA 90046-1403 Office: City of West Hollywood 8611 Santa Monica Blvd West Hollywood CA 90069-4182

BROUGH, BRUCE ALVIN, public relations and communications executive; b. Wayland, N.Y., Nov. 22, 1937; s. Alvin Elroy and Marjorie Huberta (McDowell) B.; m. Jane Virginia Koethen, Aug. 9, 1958; children: John David, Pamela Marjorie, Robert Bruce. BS in Pub. Rels., U. Md., 1960; MS in Mass Communications, Am. U., Washington, 1967. Comm. mgr. IBM Corp., various locations, 1965-74; owner, pres. Bruce Brough Assocs., Inc., Boca Raton, Fla., 1974-75; worldwide press rels. rep. Tex. Instruments Inc., 1975-76; v.p. pub. rels. Regis McKenna Inc., 1976-77; pres., prin. Pease/Brough Assocs., Inc., Palo Alto, Calif., 1978-80, Franson/Brough Assocs., Inc., San Jose, Calif., 1980-81; sr. v.p., dir. Advanced Tech. Network Hill and Knowlton, Inc., San Jose, 1981-86; sr. v.p., gen. mgr. Hill and Knowlton, Inc., Santa Clara, Calif., 1989; mgr. corp. pub. rels. Signetics Corp., 1986-87; mktg. comm. mgr. Corp. Ctr. Philips Components divsn. Philips Internat., B.V., Eindhoven, The Netherlands, 1987-89; dir. corp. communications Centigram Communications Corp., San Jose, Calif., 1989-90; pvt. practice cons. San Jose area, 1991—; lectr. San Jose State U., 1977-83, 91—; cons. communications and pub. rels., 1986—. Author: Publicity and Public Relations Guide for Business, 1984, revised edit., 1986, The Same Yesterday, Today and Forever, 1986; contbg. editor Family Bible Ency., 1973. Recipient Sustained Superior Performance award NASA, 1964, award Freedom's Found., 1963. Mem. Pub. Rels. Soc. Am. (accredited), Soc. Tech. Communications, Nat. Press Club, Sigma Delta Chi. Republican. Episcopalian. Home: 155 Rabbits Run Rd Santa Cruz CA 95060-1540 Office: Mktg/Comm Ptnrs 155 Rabbits Run Rd Santa Cruz CA 95060

BROUGH, FARRELL LYNN, computer software engineer. AA in Computer Sci., Ctrl. Wyo. Coll., 1972; BS in Computer Sci., Brigham Young U.,

1974, MS in Computer Sci., 1992. Programmer, analyst Control Data Corp., Mpls., 1974-75; owner, co-mgr. Brough Livestock Co., Inc., Riverton, Wyo., 1975-77; programmer analyst in systems programming Data Systems Corp., Riverton, 1977-82, mgr. in systems programming, 1982-85; sr. systems analyst Hercules Aerospace, Salt Lake City, 1985-91; software developer WordPerfect Corp., Orem, Utah, 1991—. Pres. Sertoma Club of Riverton, 1979-80. Mem. IEEE, Assn. Computing Machinery, Phi Kappa Phi.

BROUGHAM, GLEN SCOTT (ROCKY BROUGHAM), marketing consultant, entertainer; b. Kankakee, Ill., Nov. 22, 1950; s. Glen Everal and Mary Alice (Youmans) B. BA in Communications, So. Ill. U., 1974. Owner, mgr. Jeremiah's Trading Post/Taum Sauk Wilderness, Springfield, Mo., 1974-79; mktg. cons., mfrs. rep. Brougham Prodns., Denver, 1980-83; advt. sales mgr., account exec. TCI/United Cable of Colo., 1984-87; mktg. cons., mfrs. rep. Brown and Bigelow, St. Paul, 1988—; entertainer "Rocky the Colo. Leprechaun", 1983—. Author: (books) Hikes of the Ozark Plateau, 1979, Colorado Pub Crawl, 1987; monthly newspaper column. Recipient Commendation for Saving a Life, USAF, 1970, Fundraiser Cert. Merit ARC, 1992; named One of 50 People to Watch, Denver Mag., 1986, Best Advt. Item, Colo. Mac Starwards, 1989, Outstanding Young Men of Am., 1980, 83, 86, 90. Mem. Denver Advt. Fedn., Am. Press Assn., Colo. Press Assn., Nat. Speleological Soc. (past officer), BPOE (past officer). Home: PO Box 608 Evergreen CO 80439-0608

BROUGHER, CRAIG WILLIAM, owner, founder; b. Spokane, Wash., May 23, 1962; s. Gayle Kermit and Carol Ann (Hodge). BS, Wash. State U., 1987. V.p. Brougher Ranch Inc., Wilbur, Wash., 1985—; rsch. asst. Wash. State U., Pullman, 1986-88; cons. Brougher Earth Resources, Pullman, 1988-89; rsch. assoc. Internat. Ambassador Program, Spokane, Wash., 1989-90; pres. Pangaea Internat., Wilbur, 1990—; ind. researcher Wash. State U., Pullman, 1986-89; prin. investigator of sci. rsch., 1990. Candidate Wilbur City Coun., 1991. Mem. Am. Geophys. Union, Geologic Soc. of Am., Am. Soc. for Photogrammetric Engring. and Remote Sensing, Wilbur C. of C. Lutheran. Office: Pangaea Internat SW 106 Pope St Wilbur WA 99185-0168

BROUGHTON, CHARLES OMER, military officer, history and geography educator; b. Peoria, Ill., Jan. 21, 1934; s. Omer Donald and Estella Pauline (Miller) B.; m. Sally Josephine Wabel, Sept. 3, 1960; children: Charles Christopher, Thomas Allen, Matthew Joseph. BS, U. Ill., 1961; MA, Mont. State U., 1991. Cert. tchr., Mont. Enlisted U.S. Marine Corps, 1952, advanced through grades to col., 1980; host nation support negotiator Hdqrs. U.S. European Command, Stuttgart, Germany, 1983-87; part-time faculty NATO Logistics Coll., Hamburg, Germany, 1983-87; support officer War Fighting Ctr., Quantico, Va., 1987-89; ret. U.S. Marine Corps, 1989; adj. faculty Mont. State U., Bozeman, 1990—. Ruling elder Presbyn. Ch., Woodbridge, Va., 1969-71, Coronado, Calif., 1980-83, Bozeman, 1991-92. Most decorated Marine at time of retirement from USMC. Mem. Acacia Frat. (pres. 1958), Masons. Democrat. Home: 10663 Bridger Canyon Rd Bozeman MT 59715 Office: Mont State U Bozeman MT 59717

BROUGHTON, JAMES WALTER, real estate development executive, consultant; b. Atlantic City, Dec. 16, 1946; s. Walter Lennie and Janet Caroline (Mossman) B.; m. Sharon Carter, Mar. 10, 1980; children—Jennifer Christine, Matthew James. Student U. Colo.-Colorado Springs, 1967-68, U. Md., 1968-70, U. Colo.-Denver, 1972-73. Asst. regional sales dir. Del E. Webb Corp., Denver, 1972-76; dir. mktg. Interval Internat. Miami, Fla., 1981-82, exec. dir. Time Sharing Inst., Miami, 1981-82; pres. J. Broughton, Inc., Miami, 1976-83, Spectrum Mktg. Group, Denver, 1983-84, Ocean Resorts Devel. Co., Ventura, Calif., 1984—; sr. v.p. Fairfield Communities, Inc., Atlanta, 1985; chmn., pres. CEO Lexes Leisure Group, Las Vegas, 1985—; bd. dirs. Resort Computer Corp., Denver, 1983—, Spectrum Group, Denver, 1983—, Internat. Found. Time Sharing, Washington, 1983—, Internat. Resort Group, Inc., Las Vegas, 1992—; pub. Time Sharing Ency., 1981, Time Sharing Ind. Rev., 1981. Contbr. articles to profl. jours. Served with USAF, 1964-71. Mem. Am. Resort Devel. Assn. (recruitment award 1983, bd. dirs. 1985—, exec. com. 1988—, meetings coun. chmn. 1991—), Nat. Time Sharing Council (chmn. 1984—, bd. govs. 1984—, recruitment award 1984), Interval Internat. (adv. bd. 1982—), Urban Land Inst. (recreational devel. coun. 1993—). Republican. Office: Lexex Leisure Group 1500 E Tropicana Ave Ste 110 Las Vegas NV 89119-6516

BROUGHTON, RAY MONROE, economic consultant; b. Seattle, Mar. 2, 1922; s. Arthur Charles and Elizabeth C. (Young) B.; BA, U. Wash., 1947, MBA, 1960; m. Margret Ellen Ryno, July 10, 1944 (dec.); children: Linda Rae Broughton Hellenthal, Mary Catherine Broughton Boutin; m. Carole Jean Packer, 1980. Mgr. communications and managerial devel. Gen. Electric Co., Hanford Atomic Products Ops., Richland, Wash., 1948-59; mktg. mgr., asst. to pres. Smyth Enterprises, Seattle, 1960-62; dir. rsch. Seattle Area Indsl. Council, 1962-65; v.p., economist (mgr. econ. rsch. dept.) First Interstate Bank of Oreg., N.A., Portland, 1965-87; ind. economic cons., 1987—; mem. econ. adv. com. to Am. Bankers Assn., 1980-83; mem. Gov.'s Econ. Adv. Council, 1981-88; dir. Oregonians for Cost Effective Govt., 1989-90; instr. bus. communications U. Wash., Richland, 1956-57. Treas., dir. Oreg. affiliate Am. Heart Assn., 1972-78, chmn., 1980-81, dir., 1980-84. Served to 1st lt. U.S. Army, 1943-46; ETO. Mem. Western Econ. Assn., Pacific N.W. Regional Econ. Conf. (dir. 1967—), Nat. Assn. Bus. Economists (co-founder chpt. 1971), Am. Mktg. Assn. (pres. chpt. 1971-72), Alpha Delta Sigma. Episcopalian. Author: Trends and Forces of Change in the Payments System and the Impact on Commercial Banking, 1972; contbg. editor Pacific Banker and Bus. mag., 1974-80.

BROWER, DAVID ROSS, conservationist; b. Berkeley, Calif., July 1, 1912; s. Ross J. and Mary Grace (Barlow) B.; m. Anne Hus, May 1, 1943; children: Kenneth David, Robert Irish, Barbara Anne, John Stewart. Student, U. Calif., 1929-31; DSc (hon.), Hobart and William Smith Colls., 1967; DHL (hon.), Claremont Colls. Grad. Sch., 1971, Starr King Sch. for Ministry, 1971, U. Md., 1973; PhD in Ecology (hon.), U. San Francisco, 1973, Colo. Coll., 1977; other hon. degrees, New Sch. for Social Rsch., 1984, Sierra Nev. Coll., 1985, Unity Coll., Maine, 1989. Editor U. Calif. Press, 1941-52; exec. dir. Sierra Club, 1952-69, bd. dirs., 1941-43, 46-53, 83-88, mem. editorial bd., 1935-69, hon. v.p., 1972—; dir. John Muir Inst. Environ. Studies, 1969-71, v.p., 1968-72; pres. Friends of the Earth, 1969-79; founder, chmn. Friends of the Earth Found., 1972-84, bd. dirs.; founder Environ. Liaison Ctr., Nairobi, 1974; founder, chmn. Earth Island Inst., San Francisco, 1982—; founder, pres. Earth Island Action Group, 1989; founder Earth Island Law Ctr. and Earth Island Voters, 1991; founder biennial Fate and Hope of the Earth Confs., N.Y.C., 1982, Washington, 1984, Ottawa, 1986, Managua, 1989; activist in conservation campaigns, Kings Canyon Nat. Pk., 1938-40, Dinosaur Nat. Monument, 1952-56, North Cascades Nat. Pk., 1955-68, Cape Cod, Fire Island, Point Reyes nat. seashores, 1960-68, Redwood Nat. Pk., 1963-68, Grand Canyon 1952-68, population and growth control and nuclear proliferation issues, Nat. Wilderness Preservation System, 1951-64, conservation lectr., U.S., 1939—, Finland, 1971, Sweden, 1972, Kenya, 1972, 74, Italy, 1972, 74, 79, 82, 91, N.Z., 1974, Japan, 1976, 78, 90, 92, USSR, 1985, 88, 90, 91, 92, France, 1970, 90-91, Fed. Republic Germany, 1989, Berlin, 1990, Nicaragua, 1988, 89; founder Trustees for Conservation, 1954, sec., 1960-61, 64-65; founder Sierra Club Found., 1960; bd. dirs. Citizens Com. Natural Resources, 1955-78; chmn. Natural Resources Coun. Am., 1955-57; bd. dirs. North Cascades Conservation Coun., from 1957, Rachel Carson Trust for Living Environment, 1966-72, cons. expert, from 1973; founder, steering com. League Conservation Voters, 1969-80; founder Les Amis de la Terre, Paris, 1970; founder, guarantor Friends of the Earth U.K., 1970-88; chmn. Earth Island Ltd., London, 1971-74; active Restoring-the-Earth movement, from 1986, founder Green Circle vol. corps., 1990, leader del. to Lake Baikal, Siberia, 1988, 90, 91, 92, mem. various adv. bds. including Found. on Econ. Trends, Nat. Strategy, Coun. Econ. Priorities, Zero Population Growth, Earth Day 1990; mem. Com. on Nat. Security. Initiator, designer, gen. editor: Sierra Club Exhibit Format Series, 20 vols., 1960-68, Friends of the Earth series The Earth's Wild Places, 10 vols., 1970-77, Celebrating the Earth series, 3 vols., 1972-73; numerous other films and books, biographee in Encounters with the Archdruid (John McPhee), 1970; (autobiography) Vol. 1, For Earth's Sake: The Life and Times of David Brower, 1990, Vol. 2, Work in Progress, 1991; contbr. articles to nat. mags., profl. publs., others; subject video documentary produced for Sta. KCTS, Seattle, shown nationally on PBS; contbr. to U.S. Army mountain manuals, instruction, 1943-45. Participant in planning for 1992 UN Conf. on Environment, Rio de Janiero, 1987-92. Served as 1st lt. with 10th Mountain div. Inf. AUS, 1943-45; maj. Inf.-Res. ret. Decorated Bronze Star; recipient awards Calif. Conservation Coun., 1953, Nat. Parks Assn., 1956, Bklyn. Coll. Libr. Assn., 1970, also Carey-Thomas award, 1964, Paul Bartsch award Audubon Naturalist Soc. of Cen. Atlantic States, 1967, Golden Ark award the Prince of The Netherlands, 1979, Golden Gadfly award Media Alliance, San Francisco, 1984, Rose award World Environment Festival, Ottawa, Can., 1986, Strong Oak award New Renaissance Ctr., 1987, Lewis Mumford award Architects Designers Planners for Social Responsibility, 1991; hon. fellow John Muir Coll., U. Calif., San Diego, 1986. Noated Nobel Peace Prize, 1978, 79. Mem. Nat. Parks and Conservation Assn. (hon.), The Mountaineers (hon.), Appalachian Mountain Club (hon.), Sierra Club (1933—, John Muir award 1977), Am. Alpine Club (hon.). Office: Earth Island 300 Broadway San Francisco CA 94133

BROWER, MYRON RIGGS, architect, interior designer, educator; b. Muscatine, Iowa, Dec. 8, 1949; s. Myron Orson and Marcene P. (Shafnett) B. BArch, Ariz. State U., 1973, BA in Edn., 1977; MA in Arch. History, U. Va., 1992. Registered architect, Ariz. Architect in tng. Fenlason Assocs., Architects, Tempe, Ariz., 1975-77; pvt. practice architecture Scottsdale, Ariz., 1977—; prof. Scottsdale Community Coll., 1982—. Mem. Soc. Archtl. Historians, Mensa.

BROWN, AARON DONALD, environmental scientist; b. Binghamton, N.Y., Sept. 29, 1954; s. Donald F. and Patricia Brown. BA, Oberlin Coll., 1976; MSc, U. Mich., 1977; PhD, Utah State U., 1985. Cert. profl. soil scientist. Researcher, instr. Chiang Mai (Thailand) U., 1977-79; rsch. and teaching asst. Utah State U., Logan, 1980-84; rsch. soil scientist U. Calif., Riverside, 1984-91; asst. rsch. environ. chemist U. Calif., Santa Barbara, 1991—. Contbr. articles to profl. jours. Mem. AAAS (Klauber award 1983), Am. Geophys. Union, Internat. Soc. Soil Sci., Soil Sci. Soc. Am., Phi Kappa Phi. Office: U Calif Marine Sci Inst Santa Barbara CA 93106

BROWN, ALANNA KATHLEEN, English language educator; b. Austin, Tex., Mar. 7, 1944; d. Harry Wesley and Tex-Rozelle (Rounds) B. BA, U. Calif., Santa Barbara, 1966, MA, 1968, PhD, 1974. Asst. prof. Mont. State U., Bozeman, 1973-78, asst. dean, 1978-83, univ. honors dir., 1982-85, assoc. prof. English, 1978—; speaker, cons. Mont. Com. for Humanities, Missoula, 1974—. Contbr. articles to profl. jours. NEH humanities fellow, Columbia U., 1975-76; Danforth Found. assoc., 1975-85; NEH Summer Seminars recipient Columbia U., 1981, U. Ariz., 1987; recipient Burlington No. Teaching award Burlington Found. Mont. State U., 1989. Mem. Phi Kappa Phi (chpt. sec. 1989-92, chpt. pres. 1992—). Democrat. Office: Mont State U English Dept Bozeman MT 59717

BROWN, ALEXANDER CROSBY, JR., electrical engineer; b. Newport News, Va., July 3, 1936; s. Alexander Crosby Brown and Louise (Applewhite) Watson; m. Ulla Hildagard Schmitz, May 8, 1965; children: Julia, Michael. BEE, Rensselaer Polytech., 1959; MS, George Washington U., 1972, DSc, 1987. Engr. Bellcomm Inc., Washington, 1966-69, RCA Svc., Lanham, Md., 1969-72; sr. engr. Atlantic Rsch. Corp., Alexandria, Va., 1972-76; pvt. practice cons. Springfield, Va., 1976-77; sr. engr. Tracor, Lexington, Md., 1977; engring. specialist Loral DSD, Litchfield Park, Ariz., 1977-90; inventor Phoenix, 1990—. Recipient Cert. of Recognition NASA, 1984. Mem. IEEE (sr. mem., sec. Phoenix sect. 1984, vice chmn. 1985, chmn. 1986; combined electron devices soc, microware theory and techniques soc., atennas and progation soc., chapt. publ 1980, chmn. 1981), Electron Devices Soc., Microwave Theory and Techniques Soc. (Antennas and Propagation Soc. chpt. publ. 1980, chmn. 1981), Phoenix Conf. Computers and Comm. (program chmn. 1988), Sigma Xi. Republican. Home and Office: 202 W Interlacken Dr Phoenix AZ 85023-5259

BROWN, ALFRED, social worker; b. Boston, June 1, 1931; s. Abraham and Ida (Winer) B.; m. Diane Carl, Sept. 6, 1959; children: Kara Suzanne, David Eli. BS in BA, Boston U., 1955, MS in Social Sci., 1959. Youth dir. Elizabeth Peabody House, Somerville, Mass., 1959-60; youth dir. Jewish Community Ctr., Tucson, 1960-62, San Francisco, 1962-63; div. dir. Dept. Social Svcs., San Francisco, 1963-74; program mgr. U.S. Dept. Health & Human Svcs., Region IX, San Francisco, 1974—; field supr. B'nai B'rith Youth Orgn., San Mateo, Calif., 1968-72; cons. New Careers Fed. Project, San Francisco, 1967-68; assoc. dir. Child Abuse Rsch. Project, San Francisco, 1965-66; conductor workshops in employment. Pres. United Homeowners Assn. of San Mateo, 1986-87; bd. dirs. Conflict Resolution Orgn., San Mateo, 1985-88; chmn. Human Resources Commn., San Mateo, 1977-78. Mem. Am. Orthopsychiatric Assn., Masons. Office: US Dept Health & Human Svcs 50 United Nations Plz San Francisco CA 94102-4912

BROWN, ANTHONY B., finance executive; b. Mpls., Apr. 5, 1922; s. Wayland Hoyt and Adele (Birdsall) B.; m. Mary Alice Ann Anderson, July 28, 1956. BS, Rutgers U., 1949; postgrad. U. So. Calif., 1968-69; PhD, U. Beverly Hills, 1986. Cert. data processing systems profl. Sr. system analyst Thrifty Corp., L.A., 1957-69; system engr. Informatics Gen., Inc., L.A., 1969-73; contract instr. computer software York U., 1970, McGill U., U. Victoria, 1971, USMC, Boston U., W.Va. U., U. Guelph, 1972; sr. system engr. Jet Propulsion Lab., La Canada, Calif., 1974-76; sr. system engr. Informatics Gen., Inc., Anchorage, L.A., Washington, 1976-78; supr. project control Hughes Aircraft Co., L.A., 1978-81; contr. western ops. Contel Corp., Redondo Beach, Calif., 1981-88. Author: A Century of Blunders--America's China Policy 1844-1949. Rep. precinct capt., presdl. election, 1964; vol. Reason Found.; chmn. bd. govs. La Brea Vista Townhouses, 1967-68; active numerous animal welfare orgns. Served with Finance Corps, U.S. Army, 1951-57. Decorated Bronze Star. Fellow Brit. Interplanetary Soc.; mem. AAAS, The Planetary Soc., Nature Conservancy, Town Hall of Calif., Assn. Computer Machinery (chpt. sec. 1973-74), Assn. Systems Mgmt., Mensa, Intertel, Armed Forces Communications and Electronics Assn., Assn. Inst. Cert. Computer Profls., Am. Assn. Fin. Profls., Am. Def. Preparedness Assn., Washington Legal Found., Am. Security Council (mem. nat. adv. bd.), Calif. Soc., SAR, Mil. Order World Wars, Aircraft Owners and Pilots Assn., Internat. Platform Assn., Theodore Roosevelt Assn., Res. Officers Assn., Delta Phi Epsilon. Republican. Club: Los Angeles Athletic. Lodges: Masons, Shriners, Nat. Sojourners. Home: 4333 Redwood Ave Marina Del Rey CA 90292-6424

BROWN, ARTHUR, mining executive; b. Germiston, Union South Africa, Oct. 27, 1940; s. Harry and Elsie (vandenBerg) B.; m. Tiia Haab, Oct. 7, 1961; children: Lisa Anne, Hayley Elaine, Laura Kathleen. Mining Engr., Witwatersrand Tech. Coll., South Africa, 1960. Supr. foreman Va. Gold Mining Co., South Africa, 1958-60; supt., project mgr. Cementation Co., South Africa and Can., 1960-67; engr. Hecla Mining Co., Wallace, Idaho, 1967-72, mgr. mines, 1972-80, v.p. ops., 1980-83, sr. v.p. ops., 1983-85, exec. v.p., 1985-86, pres., 1986-87, chief exec. officer, chmn., 1987—, dir., 1983—; chmn. bd. dirs. Acadia Mineral Ventures Ltd.; bd. dirs. Granduc Mines Ltd., Am. Colloid Co. Contbr. articles on mining. Mayor, City of Pinehurst (Idaho), 1983-86. Mem. AIME, Can. Inst. Metall. and Mining Engrs., Idaho Mining Assn. (pres. 1989-91), Idaho Assn. Commerce and Industry (bd. dirs.), Am. Mining Congress (bd. dirs.), The Silver Inst. (pres. 1989-92), World Gold Coun. (bd. dirs.), The Gold Inst. (bd. dirs.), Western Regional Coun., Wallace Gyro Club (pres. 1983-85). Republican. Home: PO Box 4566 Coeur D Alene ID 83814-1960 Office: Hecla Mining Co PO Box C-80000 6500 Mineral Dr Coeur D Alene ID 83814

BROWN, ARTHUR CARL, JR., retired minister; b. Stockton, Calif., Dec. 16, 1915; s. Arthur Carl and Maud (Twitchings) B.; m. Inez Lundquist, May 10, 1940 (dec. Aug. 1982); 1 child, Arthur Carl III. BA, Coll. of the Pacific, 1937; MA, San Francisco Theol. Sem., 1939, BD with honors, 1940; postgrad., Stanford U., 1949-50. Ordained to ministry Presbyn. Ch., 1940. Pastor Presbyn. Ch., Sedro Woolley, Wash., 1940-44, Community Ch., Santa Clara, Calif., 1944-46; assoc. pastor First Presbyn. Ch., San Jose, Calif., 1946-49; minister edn. First Presbyn. Ch., Palo Alto, Calif., 1949-51; organizing pastor Covenant Presbyn. Ch., Palo Alto, 1951-74; pastor Trinity Presbyn. Ch., Santa Cruz, Calif., 1974-78; outreach assoc. Los Gatos (Calif.) Presbyn. Ch., 1978-81; commr. to gen. assembly United Presbyn. Ch., 1947, 52, 59; moderator San Jose Presbytery, 1950, chmn. various coms., 1950-78; mem. Synod Golden Gate and Synod of Pacific coms. Synod of Calif., 1947-82; pastor emeritus Covenant Presbyn. Ch.; moderator Bellingham Prebytery-Synod of Wash., 1943. Treas., chmn. fin. com., bd. dirs. Internat. House, Davis, Calif., 1984-90, chmn. internat. house nominating com., 1990-93, mem. internat. devel. com., pers. com., 1991—. Republican. Home: 4414 San Ramon Dr Davis CA 95616-5018

BROWN, BART A., JR., consumer products company executive; b. Louisville, 1933. LLB, U. Louisville, 1955; LLM, Georgetown U., 1957, JD. With Irs, 1970-76, with Keating, Muething, Klekamp, Brown & Gardner, 1976-90; chmn. bd. Circle K Corp., Phoenix, Ariz., 1990—; chief exec. officer Circle K. Corp., Phoenix, 1971—, also bd. dirs. Office: Circle K Corp Box 52084 1601 N 7th St Phoenix AZ 85006

BROWN, BEN MAURICE, diagnostic radiologist, psychiatrist; b. Mar. 7, 1943; came to U.S., 1953; s. Maurice and Kate (Muehlendorf) B.; m. Claudia Brower, 1975; 1 child, Keith. AB in Philosophy and Psychology, U. Calif., Berkeley, 1965; MD, Stanford U., 1969. Diplomate Am. Bd. Psychiatry and Neurology, Am. Bd. Radiology. NIMH postdoctoral fellow U. Calif., Berkeley, 1969-70; intern St. Mary's Hosp., San Francisco, 1970-71; resident in psychiatry Stanford, Calif., 1971-74; resident in radiology U. Calif., San Francisco, 1980-82; fellow in radiology Stanford, 1982-83; pvt. practice psychiatry San Francisco, 1974-75; staff psychiatrist, lectr. dept. psychiatry U. Ariz. Health Scis. Ctr., Tucson, 1975-79; asst. clin. prof. radiology and neurosurgery Oreg. Health Scis. U., Portland, 1984—; radiologist, chief Magnetic Resonance Ctr. Kaiser-Sunnyside Med. Ctr., Clackamas, Oreg., 1983—; bd. dirs. Kaiser-N.W. Permanente, Portland, 1992—. Contbr. articles to profl. jours.; presenter in field. NIMH predoctoral fellow, 1965-68. Mem. Am. Coll. Radiology, Radiol. Soc. N.Am., Oreg. Radiol. Soc. (exec. com. 1987-88), Pacific N.W. Radiol. Soc. (edn. chmn. 1987-88). Home: 2221 Sw 1st Ave Ste 2424 Portland OR 97015 Office: Kaiser Sunnyside Med Ctr Dept Radiology 10180 SE Sunnyside Rd Clackamas OR 97015

BROWN, BYRON WILLIAM, JR., biostatistician, educator; b. Chgo., Apr. 21, 1930; s. Byron William and Ruth (Munson) B.; m. Janet Louise Hyde, July 30, 1949; children: Byron William III, Eric Paul, Alan Thomas, Nancy Ellen, Mark Andrew, Lisa Anne. BA in Math., U. Minn., 1952, MS in Stats., 1955, PhD in Biostats., 1959. Asst. prof. biostats. La. State U. Med. Sch., New Orleans, 1956-57; from lectr. to assoc. prof. Sch. Pub. Health, U. Minn., 1957-65, prof., head biostats., 1965-68; prof. biostats., head div. Stanford U., Calif., 1968—, chmn. dept. health research and policy, 1988—; cons. govt. and industry. Co-author: Statistics: A Biomedical Introduction; Contbr. articles to profl. jours., books, encys. Served with USAF, 1949. Fellow AAAS, Am. Statis. Assn. (sect. pres., assoc. editor Jour.), Am. Heart Assn.; mem. Inst. Medicine of NAS (elected), Biometrics Soc. (pres. Western N.Am. region 1978), Inst. Math. Stats., Soc. for Clin. Trials (pres. 1988), Internat. Stats. Inst. (elected), Phi Beta Kappa, Sigma Xi. Home: 981 Cottrell Way Stanford CA 94305-1057

BROWN, CARL WILLIAMSON, business executive, consultant; b. Pomona, Calif., Feb. 5, 1944; s. William Newton and Louise (Cofield) B.; m. Linda Ann Siebers, Oct. 23, 1971; children: Erin Candace, Colin Travis. Student, Cath. U., Coll. of Marin, U. Calif., Berkeley, Merritt Coll., Northeastern U., Santa Clara, Calif., St. Mary's Coll., Moraga, Calif. System programmer Pacific Intermoutain Express, Oakland, Calif., 1969-71, mgr. system programming, 1971-76; ind. cons., 1976-78; strategic planner Levi Strauss & Co., 1978-80, mgr. teleprocessing systems, 1980-84; pres. X.Net, Inc., 1984—. Bd. dir. Orinda (Calif.) Assn., 1978-81. Mem. Ind. Computer Cons. Assn. (bd. dirs. Norcal San Francisco chpt. 1988, chmn. profl. standards com., pres. at-large chpt. 1992), Software Svcs. Assn, Unicorn Consortium.

BROWN, CAROL ELIZABETH, educator; b. Boise, Idaho, Jan. 26, 1950; d. Mason Oliver Brown and Hazel (Metcalf) Henderson; m. Richard Bruce Wodtli, Aug. 16, 1989. BS in Art, U. Wis., 1972; MS in Acctg., U. Oreg., 1977; PhD in Computer Sci., Oreg. State U., 1989. CPA. Bookkeeper Stone Fence Inc., Madison, Wis., 1972-74; staff acct. Baillies, Denson, Erickson & Smith, Madison, 1974-75, Minihan, Kernutt, Stokes & Co., Eugene, 1977-78; instr. Oreg. State U., Corvallis, 1978-89, asst. prof., 1989-92, assoc. prof., 1992—. Contbr. articles to profl. jours. Bd. dirs. United Way of Benton County, Corvallis, 1989—, vol. acct., 1982-86. Recipient Outstanding Vol. Svc. award United Way of Benton County, 1986; rsch. grant Oreg. State U., 1988, 90, Scholarship award, 1993; rsch. grant TIAA-CREF, 1990, 91. Mem. Am. Acctg. Assn. (program adv. com. 1990-91, artifical intelligence/expert systems sect., chairperson elect 1992—, vice-chairperson 1991-92), Inst. Mgmt. Accts. (dir. manuscripts Salem Oreg. area 1990—, bd. dirs. 1990—, Cert. Merit 1990-91, rsch. grant 1993), Oreg. Soc. of CPA (computer svcs. com. vice-chmn. 1990-91, com. mem. 1989—, Cert. Recognition for Leadership Excellence 1989-90, Outstanding Svc. award 1990-91), Am. Assn. for Artificial Intelligence, Assn. for Computing Machinery, IEEE Computer Soc., others. Home: 1145 NW 20th Corvallis OR 97330 Office: Oreg State U Coll of Bus Bexell Hall 200 Corvallis OR 97331-2603

BROWN, CAROLYN SMITH, communications educator, consultant; b. Salt Lake City, Aug. 12, 1946; d. Andrew Delbert and Olive (Crane) Smith; m. David Scott Brown, Sept. 10, 1982. BA magna cum laude, U. Utah, 1968, MA, 1972, PhD, 1974. Instr. Salt Lake Ctr., Brigham Young U., Salt Lake City, 1976-78; vis. asst. prof. Brigham Young U., Provo, 1978; asst. prof. Am. Inst. Banking, Salt Lake City, 1977—; prof., chmn. English, communication and gen. edn. depts. Latter Day Saints Bus. Coll., Salt Lake City, 1973—, acad. dean, 1986—; founder, pres. Career Devel. Tng., Salt Lake City, 1979—; field mktg. dir. Systems Internat./Prformax Inc., Mpls., 1978—, Carlson Learning Co., Mpls., 1978—; cons. in-house seminars 1st Security Realty Svcs., USDA Soil Conservation Svc., Utah Power & Light, Utah Soc. Svcs., Adminstrv. Office of Cts., HUD, Intermountain Health Care, Continental Bank. Author: Writing Letters & Reports That Communicate, 6 ed., 1985; contbr. articles to profl. jours. Demi-soloist Utah Civic Ballet (now Ballet West), Salt Lake City, 1964-68; active Mormon Ch. Named Tchr. of Month, Salt Lake City Kiwanis, 1981; NDEA fellow, U. Utah, 1972. Mem. Am. Bus. Communications Assn. (lectr. West/N.W. regional chpt. 1987), Delta Kappa Gamma (2d v.p. 1977-79), Lambda Delta Sigma (Outstanding Woman of Yr. 1983), Kappa Kappa Gamma (Outstanding Alumnus in Lit. 1974). Republican. Clubs: Alice Louise Reynolds Literary (Salt Lake City) (v.p. 1978-79, sec. 1985-86). Office: LDS Bus Coll 411 E South Temple Salt Lake City UT 84111-1392

BROWN, CATHEY ANN, newspaper publisher; b. Gainesboro, Tenn., Feb. 25, 1954; d. Ray O. and Margaret Rosland (Haile) Hix; m. Gerald Spencer Brown, Mar. 5, 1983; 1 child, Jessica Lauren. BS in English Journalism, Tenn. Tech. U., 1977. Sec., bookkeeper U.S. Armed Forces, Stuttgart, Germany, 1971-72; avt. specialist Petroleum Info., Denver, Houston, 1977-79; editor Stapleton Innerline, Denver, 1979-82; publisher, owner Stapleton Innterline, Innerline Pub., Denver, 1982-89; pub., owner The Beacon Review, Century Pub., Denver, 1989—. mem. Rocky Mountain Ski Writers Assn. (1st v.p. 1987-89). Republican. Methodist. Office: Century Pubs 1805 S Bellaire #235 Denver CO 80222

BROWN, CHARLES IRVING, corporate executive; b. Bombay, India, Jan. 14, 1932; s. Charles Irving and Frances Belcher (Woods) B. (parents Am. citizens); m. Kathleen Mae Shrum, July 2, 1960; children: Dana Scott, Tracy Ann, Kelly Mae. BA in Geology, Williams Coll., 1954; MBA with distinction, Harvard U., 1959. Asst. mgr. credit dept. First Nat. City Bank of N.Y., Rio de Janeiro, Brazil, 1954-57; v.p. fin. Western Nuclear Inc., Denver, 1959-73, also dir.; v.p. fin. and mktg. Energy Fuels Corp., Denver, 1974-82, also dir.; fin. cons., 1982-92; sr. v.p., chief fin. officer, dir. Integrated Med. Systems Inc., Golden, Colo., 1990-92; bd. dirs. Original Sixteen-to-One Mine, Allegheny, Calif., 1ZZO Systems, Inc., Denver, Colo.; trustee Colo. Outward Bound, Colo. State U. Research Found. Mem. Denver Athletic Club, Am. Alpine Club. Home: 2691 S Pinehurst Dr Evergreen CO 80439-8909 Office: Ste 400 15000 W 514th Ave Golden CO 80401

BROWN, CLARK TAIT, English language educator; b. N.Y.C., Dec. 27, 1935; s. Clark Tait and Winnifred (Wilson) B.; m. Noël Doyle, Dec. 19, 1965; children: Scott, Thomas, Elizabeth, Holly. AB, U. Calif., Berkeley, 1958, MA, 1959, postgrad., 1960-61; postgrad., U. Paris, 1959-60. Instr. Calif. State U., Chico, 1968-70, prof., 1970—; instr. U. Calif., Berkeley, 1968, Stanford (Calif.) U., 1968-70; cons. Ednl. Testing Svc., Emeryville, Calif.,

1973—. Author: The Disciple, 1968; author short stories. Fellow Nat. Endowment Humanities, 1976. Office: Calif State Univ Dept English Chico CA 95929

BROWN, CORRICK, musician, conductor. Mus. dir., condr. Santa Rosa (Calif.) Symphony Orch. Office: Santa Rosa Symphony Orch Luther Burbank Ctr Arts 50 Mark West Springs Rd Santa Rosa CA 95403-1476

BROWN, CYNTHIA JANE, language educator; b. Phila., June 10, 1948; d. Wendell Stimpson and Jane Christian (Bowden) B.; m. Samuel Spender Sweet, May 24, 1980 (div. 1982); m. Arthur Charles Ludwig, June 20, 1993. BA, U. N.H., 1970; MA, U. Calif., Berkeley, 1973, PhD, 1978. Teaching asst. dept. French U. Calif., Berkeley, 1971-76, 77; lectr. Ecole Normale Superieure, France, 1976-77; lectr. French, Italian U. N.H., Durham, 1978-79; asst. prof. French, Italian U. Calif., Santa Barbara, 1979-85, assoc. prof., 1985—, chair dept. French, Italian, 1991—. Author: The Shaping of History & Poetry in Late Medieval France, 1985, critical edition of André de la Vigne's Ressource de la Chrestienté (1494), 1989; contbr. articles to scholarly publs. Grantee NEH, 1980, 84, Am. Coun. Learned Socs., 1987-88. Mem. Medieval Acad. Am., Am. Assn. Tchrs. of French, Modern Lang. Assn., Internat. Courtly Love Soc. Office: Univ Calif Dept French/Italian Santa Barbara CA 93106

BROWN, DALE ROBERT, sales and marketing executive; b. San Leandro, Calif., Apr. 23, 1967; s. Delmar Edwin and Maureen Diane (McGhee) B. Mem. ops. staff Nat. Car Rental, Stockton, Calif., 1982-84; gen. store mgr. Circle K Corp., Lathrop, Calif., 1984-87; sales trainer Venture Out Inc., Hayward, Calif., 1987-89; nat. sales mgr. Ventuno, Inc., Fremont, Calif., 1989-93; v.p. sales Champion Duplicators, Inc., Fremont, Calif., 1993—; human resources cons. Courtlandt Group, Modesto, Calif., 1988—; ptnr. Sutherland & Brown Investments, Turlock, Calif., 1990—. Author: Setting Your Life Course, 1989. Office: Champion Duplicators Inc 43301 Osgood Rd Fremont CA 94539-5656

BROWN, DANIEL WARREN, public relations executive; b. Portchester, N.Y., Oct. 26, 1930; s. Malcolm Doughty and Helen Ann (Warren) B.; m. Helen June Sproule, Mar. 15, 1953 (div. 1958); 1 child, Peter; m. Jean Frances High, Aug. 2, 1958; 1 child, Daniel Warren; stepchildren: Carole Hoppe, Fredric Hoppe, Catherine Hoppe. BA, Columbia U., 1952; MA in Journalism, U. Wis., 1971. Reporter Sun-Tattler, Hollywood, Fla., 1956-57, Miami Herald, Fla., 1957-61; dir. Combined Fed. Campaign, San Diego, 1980-82; dir. pub. affairs Aerojet, Sacramento, 1982-91; owner Hartman Brown & Assocs., Sacramento, 1991—. Lt. Col. USMC, 1952-55, 61-80. Decorated Legion of Merit, Joint Svcs. Commendation medal, Navy Commendation medal. Mem. Pub. Relations Soc. Am. (chpt. pres. 1988), Sutter Club. Republican. Office: Hartman Brown & Assocs PO Box 601581 Sacramento CA 95860-1581

BROWN, DAVID EUGENE, school superintendent; b. June 25, 1941; m. Ilse Brown; children: Doug, Peter, Kristen, Megan, Cameron. BA, Occidental Coll., 1966; MA, U. So. Calif., 1968, PhD, 1977. Cert. std. jr. coll., std. high sch. 7-12, std. supervision 7-12, instrn., adminstrv. svcs. K-12. Tchr. German U. So. Calif., 1966-67, Calif. State U., Long Beach, 1968-70, Calif. Inst. Arts, 1969-70; tchr. world history, U.S. history, English, govt. Morningside High Sch., 1970-74, dir. activities, 1973-75; asst. prin. San Marino High Sch., 1975-78; prin. La Canada High Sch., 1978-80; supt. San Marino Unified Sch. Dist., 1980-87, Irvine (Calif.) Unified Sch. Dist., 1987—; mem. adv. com. State Supt. Bill Honig, 1990—. Contbr. articles to profl. jours. Pres. North San Gabriel Valley Data Processing Consortium, 1982-84, Santa Anita Industry Edn. Coun., 1982-85; chair San Marino Com., 1982-87, Calif. State Citizens Com., 1990-91, Irvine Children's Fund Found., 1990—. Acad. grantee Occidental Coll.; NDEA fellow U. So. Calif., 1967-70. Mem. Assn. Calif. Sch. Adminstrs. (chair student affairs com. region XV 1977-80, sec. 1979-80, v.p. 1980-82, pres. 1982-83, state bd. dirs. 1985-88, state v.p., pres.-elect, pres., past pres. 1988-92), Western Assn. Schs. and Colls. (accreditation team mem., team chmn.), Foothill Track Starters Assn. (pres. 1981-82). Office: Irvine USD Barranca Pky Irvine CA 92714*

BROWN, DEAN NAOMI, state official, geologist; b. Fairbanks, Alaska, Mar. 9, 1944; d. James Heuston and Betty (Jefford) Alexander; m. Jim McCaslin Brown, Sept. 1, 1963 (div. 1987); children: Robin Wendy, Shelly Reneé. BS in Geology, U. Wis., 1967. Lectr. geology U. Ind., Kokomo, 1971-72; geologist, landman Amax Coal Co., Indpls., 1974; asst. and field constrn. engr. Trans-Alaska pipeline Fluor Alaska, Inc., 1975-76; environ. geologist Civil Engrs./Alaska, Wasilla, 1977; various positions to acting dir. agr. Alaska Dept. Natural Resources, 1978-87; office mgr. Northwind Aviation, Anchorage, 1987-88; geologist Placer Dome U.S., Inc., Nome, Alaska, 1988; journeyman carpenter Ensearch Corp., Bradley Lake, Alaska, 1989; no. regional mgr. div. land and water mgmt. Alaska Dept. Natural Resources, Fairbanks, 1990; dep. dir. forestry Alaska Dept. Natural Resources, Anchorage, 1990-93, acting state forester, 1993—; adj. prof. natural resource econs. Alaska Pacific U., 1991, 93. Vol. Iditarod Trail Com. Recipient cert. of appreciation City of Valdez, Alaska, 1976, Anchorage Sch. Dist., 1983, 4-H Leaders, Palmer, Alaska, 1987, cert. of achievement Susitna coun. Girl Scouts U.S.A., 1982, Outstanding Achievement award Alaska Dept. Natural Resources, 1986. Mem. Alaska Geologic Soc., Aircraft Owners and Pilots Assn., Alaska Airman's Assn., Alaska Horse Breeders Assn. (bd. dirs. 1984-90), Ninety-Nines. Home: PO Box 870366 Wasilla AK 99687-0366 Office: Alaska Dept Natural Resources 3601 C St Ste 1058 Anchorage AK 99503-5937

BROWN, DEE ALEXANDER, author; b. La., 1908; s. Daniel Alexander and Lulu (Cranford) B.; m. Sara B. Stroud, Aug. 1, 1934; children—James Mitchell, Linda. B.S., George Washington U., 1937; M.S., U. Ill., 1951. Librarian Dept. Agr., Washington, 1934-42, Aberdeen Proving Ground, Md., 1945-48; agrl. librarian U. Ill. at Urbana, 1948-72, prof., 1962-75. Author: Wave High the Banner, 1942, Grierson's Raid, 1954, Yellowhorse, 1956, Cavalry Scout, 1957, The Gentle Tamers: Women of the Old Wild West, 1958, The Bold Cavaliers, 1959, They Went Thataway, 1960, (with M.F. Schmitt) Fighting Indians of the West, 1948, Trail Driving Days, 1952, The Settler's West, 1955, Fort Phil Kearny, 1962, The Galvanized Yankees, 1963, Showdown at Little Big Horn, 1964, The Girl from Fort Wicked, 1964, The Year of the Century, 1966, Bury My Heart at Wounded Knee, 1971, The Westerners, 1974, Hear That Lonesome Whistle Blow, 1977, Tepee Tales, 1979, Creek Mary's Blood, 1980, The American Spa, 1982, Killdeer Mountain, 1983, Conspiracy of Knaves, 1987, Wondrous Times on the Frontier, 1991; contbr.: Growing Up Western, 1990; editor: Agricultural History, 1956-58, Pawnee, Blackfoot and Cheyenne, 1961. Served with AUS, 1942-45. Recipient A.L.A. Clarence Day award, 1971, Christopher award, 1971, Illinoisian of Yr., Ill. News Broadcasters Assn., 1972, W.W.A. Golden Saddleman award, 1984. Mem. Authors Guild, Soc. Am. Historians, Western Writers Am., Beta Phi Mu. Home: 7 Overlook Dr Little Rock AR 72207-1619

BROWN, DONALD JEROULD, geologist, consultant; b. Salt Lake City, Nov. 4, 1926; s. Clyde Dudley and Clara Edith (Nielson) B.; m. Joe Ann Carrol Johnson, Dec. 15, 1955; children: Tai Elizabeth, Seth Folsom, Ero Johnson. BS, Univ. Utah, 1955, postgrad., 1959-60. Registered geologist, geol. engr. Engring. geologist Gen. Electric Co., Richland, Wash., 1955-67; environ. engr. Atlantic Richfield Hanford Co., Richland, 1967-76; prin. engr. Rockwell Hanford Ops., Richland, 1976-78; sr. project mgr. Rockwell Hanford Ops., 1978-79, dept. mgr., 1979-81, sr. sci. advisor, 1981-85; adv. engr. Westinghouse Hanford Co., Richland, 1985—. V.p. United Cerebral Palsy Assn., Benton and Franklin Counties, 1963; mem. exec. bd. Blue Mountain coun. Boy Scouts Am., Richland, 1969. With USN, 1946-48. Recipient Silver Beaver award Boy Scouts Am., 1964. Fellow Geol. Soc. Am.; mem. Am. Assn. Petroleum Geologists. Republican. Mormon. Home: 1306 Farrell Ln Richland WA 99352-3202 Office: Westinghouse Hanford Co PO Box 1970 MSIN B4-63 Richland WA 99352

BROWN, EDMUND GERALD, JR. (JERRY BROWN), former governor of California; b. San Francisco, Apr. 7, 1938; s. Edmund Gerald and Bernice (Layne) B. B.A., U. Calif.-Berkeley, 1961; J.D., Yale U., 1964. Bar: Calif. 1965. Research atty. Calif. Supreme Ct., 1964-65; atty. Tuttle & Taylor, Los Angeles, 1966-69; sec. state Calif., 1970-74; Gov. of State of Calif., 1975-83; chmn. Calif. Dem. Party, 1989-90; Dem. candidate for Pres. of United States, 1992. Trustee Los Angeles Community Colls., 1969. Address: 3022 Washington St San Francisco CA 94115

BROWN, FREDERICK CALVIN, physicist, educator; b. Seattle, July 6, 1924; s. Fred Charles and Rose (Mueller) B.; m. Joan Schauble, Aug. 9, 1952; children—Susan, Gail, Derek. B.S., Harvard U., 1945, M.S., 1947, Ph.D., 1950. Physicist Systems Research Lab., Harvard (NDRC), 1945-46; staff physicist Naval Research Lab., Washington, 1950; physicist Applied Physics Lab., U. Wash., 1950-51; asst. prof. Reed Coll., Portland, Oreg., 1951-55, U. Ill., Urbana, 1955-58; assoc. prof. U. Ill., 1958-61, prof., 1961-87, prof. emeritus, 1987—; assoc. Center for Advanced Study, 1969-70; prin. scientist, area mgr. Xerox Palo Alto Research Center, 1973-74; prof. U. Wash., Seattle, 1987; cons. prof., applied physics dept. Stanford, 1973-74. Author: The Physics of Solids-Ionic Crystals, Lattice Vibrations and Imperfections, 1967; Contbr. articles profl. jours. Recipient Alexander von Humboldt sr. scientist award U. Kiel, 1978; NSF sr. postdoctoral fellow Clarendon Lab., Oxford, 1964-65. Fellow Am. Phys. Soc. Home: 2414 E Discovery Pl Langley WA 98260-8305 Office: U Wash Dept Physics FM-15 Seattle WA 98195

BROWN, GARY ROSS, lawyer, magistrate; b. Denver, Nov. 11, 1947; s. F. Ross and Leona R. (Temple) B.; m. Kelly Ann Simms, May 31, 1969; children: Julie Marie, Phillip Ross. BA, Lewis and Clark Coll., 1969; JD, U. Denver, 1973. Bar: Colo. 1973, U.S. Dist. Ct. Colo. 1973. Assoc. Clarence L. Bartholic, Denver, 1973-75; sole practice, Denver and Estes Park, Colo., 1975—; U.S. magistrate U.S. Dist. Ct. Colo. with specific jurisdiction over Rocky Mountain Nat. Park, 1980—; judge adv. gen. Colo. Dept. Military Affairs. Served with Colo. Army N.G., 1969—. Named Soldier of Yr., Colo. Army N.G., 1975. Mem. Masons (presiding officer Rocky Mountain Consistory), Rotary (pres. Estes club). Presbyterian.

BROWN, GAY WEST, school psychologist; b. L.A., Nov. 20, 1953; d. James Dale and Ola Maye (Daniels) West; m. Lorenzo Hubbard, Nov. 26, 1977 (dec. Feb. 1990); 1 child, Loren Rochelle; m. Fred Lyndle Brown, Jr., Dec. 28, 1992. BA, Calif. State U., Dominguez Hills, 1975; MS, U. So. Calif., 1976; PhD, UCLA, 1991. Lic. ednl. psychologist; cert. sch. psychologist. Student counselor Dignity Ctr. for Drug Abuse, L.A., 1974-76; community health worker Am. Indian Free Clinic, Compton, Calif., 1974-76; student psychologist Martin Luther King Hosp., L.A., 1976-77; counselor aide Washington High Sch., L.A., 1974-77; vocat. counselor Skill Ctr., L.A., 1977-78; sch. psychologist L.A. Unified Sch. Dist., 1978—, tchr., advisor, 1988-90; psychol. asst. Verdugo Hills (Calif.) Mental Health, 1984-85; counselor, coord. Crenshaw High Sch., L.A., 1985-87; asst. behavior sci. cons. Coalition Mental Profls., L.A., 1992—; psychol. asst., Martin Luther King Hosp., L.A., 1992—. Mem. APA, Nat. Assn. Sch. Psychologists, Calif. Assn. Sch. Psychologists, L.A. Assn. Sch. Psychologists, Assn. Black Psychologists (sec. 1992—), Pan African Scholars Assn., Delta Sigma Theta. Democrat. United Methodist. Office: Virgil Middle Sch 152 N Vermont Ave Los Angeles CA 90004

BROWN, GEORGE EDWARD, JR., congressman; b. Holtville, Calif., Mar. 6, 1920; s. George Edward and Bird Alma (Kilgore) B.; 4 children. B.A., UCLA, 1946; grad. fellow, Fund Adult Edn., 1954. Mgmt. cons. Calif., 1957-61; v.p. Monarch Savs. & Loan Assn., Los Angeles, 1960-68; mem. Calif. Assembly from 45th Dist., 1959-62, 88th-91st congresses from 29th Dist. Calif., 93d Congress from 38th Dist. Calif., 94th-103rd Congresses from 36th (now 42nd) Dist. Calif.; mem. standing com. on agr., chmn. sci. space and tech. com. 94th-101st Congresses from 36th Dist. Calif., 1987; mem. agriculture com., mem. sci., space and tech. com.; chmn. Office of Tech. Assessment; coll. lectr., radio commentator, 1971. Mem. Calif. Gov.'s Adv. Com. on Housing Problems, 1961-62; mem. Mayor Los Angeles Labor-Mgmt. Com., 1961-62, Councilman, Monterey Park, Calif., 1954-58, mayor, 1955-56; candidate for U.S. Senate, 1970. Served to 2d lt., inf. AUS, World War II. Mem. Am. Legion, Colton C. of C., Urban League, Internat. Brotherhood Elec. Workers, AFL-CIO, Friends Com. Legislation, Ams. for Dem. Action. Democrat. Methodist. Lodge: Kiwanis. Office: US House of Representatives 2300 Rayburn House Office Bldg Washington DC 20515-0542*

BROWN, GEORGE HARDIN, English language and classics educator; b. Denver, Feb. 14, 1931; s. LeRoy Joseph and Mary Catherine (George) B.; m. Phyllis Rugg, Nov. 24, 1979; children: Austin, Malcolm. BA in Humanities and Letters with honors, St. Louis U., 1955, Ph.L. in Philosophy, 1956, MA in English, 1959; PhD in English, Harvard U., 1971. Mem. Soc. of Jesus (Jesuits), 1949-71; ordained priest in Roman Cath. Ch., 1962, laicized, 1971. Asst. prof. English St. Louis U., 1969-71; asst. prof. English Stanford (Calif.) U., 1971-77, assoc. prof. English, 1977-87; prof. English and French Stanford U., Cliveden, Eng. and Tours, France, 1982, 89; prof. English and classics Stanford (Calif.) U., 1987—; prof. religious studies Santa Clara U., Durham, Eng., 1989, 93. Author: Bede the Venerable, 1987; editor: Hero and Exile: Essays by S.B. Greenfield, 1989; contbr. articles to profl. jours. and encys. Contbr. to various orgns.; super donor Stanford U. Blood Bank; coord. Gregorian Mass Liturgy, St. Ann's Chapel, Palo Alto, Calif., 1971—. Dexter Travel fellow Harvard U., 1968, Am. Coun. Learned Socs. fellow, 1975, Nat. Endowment for the Humanities fellow, 1978; Mellon Rsch. grantee Mellon Found., Stanford U., 1974. Mem. MLA (exec. com. Old English 1971-73), Medieval Assn. Pacific (pres. 1992-94, exec. coun. 1976-79), Medieval Acad. Am. (exec. coun. 1991—, chmn. com. regional assns. and ctrs. 1978-81), Philol. Assn. Pacific Coast (exec. coun. 1983-86), Internat. Soc. Anglo-Saxonists (1st v.p. 1991, pres. 1993—). Democrat. Home: 451 Adobe Pl Palo Alto CA 94306-4501 Office: Stanford U Dept English Bldg 40 Stanford CA 94305-2087

BROWN, GEORGE STEPHEN, physicist; b. Santa Monica, Calif., June 28, 1945; s. Paul Gordon and Frances Ruth (Moore) B.; m. Nohema Fernandez, Aug. 8, 1981; 1 child, Sonya. BS, Calif. Inst. Tech., 1967; MS, Cornell U., 1968, PhD, 1973. Mem. tech. staff Bell Labs., Murray Hill, N.J., 1973-77; sr. research assoc. Stanford (Calif.) U., 1977-82, rsch. prof. applied physics, 1982-91; prof. physics U. Calif., Santa Cruz, 1991—; assoc. dir. Stanford Synchrotron Radiation Lab., Stanford, 1980-91. Mem. editorial bd. Rev. Sci. Instruments, 1983-86; contbr. articles to profl. jours. Fellow Am. Phys. Soc. Home: 740 Alameda Redwood City CA 94061 Office: U Calif Dept Physics Santa Cruz CA 95064

BROWN, H. DOUGLAS, English educator; b. Ntondo, Zaire, July 26, 1941; came to U.S., 1959; s. Henry D. and Ethel D. (White) B.; m. Mary Bjornson, June 3, 1963; children: Stefanie Diana, Jeffrey Douglas. BA, Linfield Coll., 1963; MDiv, Am. Bapt. Sem., 1966; MA, UCLA, 1968, PhD, 1970. Asst. prof. U. Mich., Ann Arbor, 1970-75, assoc. prof., 1975-78; assoc. prof. U. Ill., Urbana, 1978-81, prof., 1981-83; prof. San Francisco State U., 1983—; dir. Am. Lang. Inst., San Francisco, 1983—. Author: Principles of Language Learning and Teaching, 1980, 3d edit., 1994, A Practical Guide to Language Learning, 1989, Breaking the Language Barrier, 1991, (series) Vistas, 1991, Teaching by Principles, 1994. Mem. Am. Bapt. Community Ch., Walnut Creek, Calif., 1983—. Mem. Tchrs. of English to Speakers of Other Langs. (pres. 1979-81, Disting. Svc. award 1986), Calif. Tchrs. of English to Speakers of Other Langs., Am. Coun. on Teaching Fgn. Langs., Am. Assn. Applied Linguistics. Office: San Francisco State U Dept English 1600 Holloway Ave San Francisco CA 94132-1722

BROWN, H. WILLIAM, urban economist, private banker; b. L.A., Sept. 6, 1933; s. Homer William Brown and Carol Lee (Thompson) Weaver; m. Shirley Rom, Jan. 18, 1953 (div. 1962); 1 child, Shirlee Dawn. BA in Pub. Adminstrn., Calif. State U., 1956; MA in Bus. Adminstrn., Western States U., 1983, Phd in Urban Econs., 1984. Pres. Real Estate Econs., Sacramento, 1956-60; dir. spl. projects Resource Agy. Calif., Sacramento, 1960-65; program planning officer U.S. Dept. Housing and Urban Devel., Washington, 1965-66; asst. dir. regional planning U.S. Dept. Commerce, Washington, 1967-69; dir. internat. office Marshall and Stevens, Inc., L.A., 1970-72; vice chmn., CEO Investment Property Econ. Cons., 1972—; chmn., CEO The Northpoint Investment Group, San Francisco, 1986—; chmn. Trade and Devel. Ctr. For UN, N.Y. 1983-88, pres. Ctr. for Habitat and Human Settlements, Washington 1977-90. Author: The Changing World of the Real Estate Market Analyst-Appraiser, 1988. Mem. Internat. Real Estate Inst. (fgn. lectr. 1983—), Le Groupe d'Elegance (charge d'affaires, pvt. bankers club). Office: Northpoint Investment Group 2310 Powell St Ste 205 San Francisco CA 94133-1425

BROWN, HANK, senator; b. Denver, Feb. 12, 1940; s. Harry W. and Anna M. (Hanks) B.; m. Nana Morrison, Aug. 27, 1967; children: Harry, Christy, Lori. BS, U. Colo., 1961, JD, 1969; LLM, George Washington U., 1986, M in Tax Law, 1986. Bar: Colo. 1969; CPA, Colo. Tax acct. Arthur Andersen, 1967-68; asst. pres. Monfort of Colo., Inc., Greeley, 1969-70; corp. counsel Monfort of Colo., Inc., 1970-71; v.p. Monfort Food Distbg., 1971-72, v.p. corp. devel., 1973-75, v.p. internat. ops., 1975-78, v.p. lamb div., 1978-80; mem. 97th-101st Congresses from Colo. 4th dist., 1981-90; mem. Colo. State Senate, 1972-76, asst. majority leader, 1974-76; U.S senator from Colo. Washington, 1991—. With USN, 1962-66. Decorated Air medal. Mem. Colo. Bar Assn. Republican. Congregationalist. Office: US Senate 716 Hart Senate Bldg Washington DC 20510

BROWN, HARRY LESTER, materials scientist, metallurgical engineer; b. Brimfield, Mass., June 29, 1924; m. 1946; 3 children. MetE, Colo. Sch. Mines, 1950, MSc, 1951. Engr. Phillips Petroleum Co., Kans., 1951-54; mem. staff Los Alamos (N.Mex.) Sci. Lab., 1954-67; sr. scientist water reactor safety program Phillips Petroleum Co. atomic energy div. and successors, Idaho, 1967-73; project engr. materials tech. br. Aerojet Nuclear, 1973-75; staff specialist documentation fuels and materials div. EG&G Idaho, Idaho, 1977-80, sr. engr., tech. reviewer/editor materials sci. div., 1980-86; cons. EG&G, Idaho, 1986—. With USAAF, 1942-45, ETO. Address: 1867 Michael St Idaho Falls ID 83402

BROWN, HERMIONE KOPP, lawyer; b. Syracuse, N.Y., Sept. 29, 1915; d. Harold H. and Frances (Burger) Kopp; m. Louis M. Brown, May 30, 1937; children—Lawrence D., Marshall J., Harold A. BA, Wellesley Coll., 1934; LLB, U. So. Calif., 1947. Bar: Calif. 1947. Story analyst 20th Century-Fox Film Corp., 1935-42; assoc. Gang, Kopp & Tyre, Los Angeles, 1947-52; ptnr. to sr. ptnr. Gang, Tyre, Ramer & Brown, Inc., Los Angeles, 1952—; lectr. copyright and entertainment law U. So. Calif. Law Sch., 1974-77. Contbr. to profl. publs. Fellow Am. Coll. Trust and Estate Coun.; mem. Calif. Bar Assn. (chair probate law cons. group nd. legal specialization 1977-82, trust and probate law sect., exec. com. 1983-86, advisor 1986-89), L.A. Copyright Soc. (pres. 1979-80), Order of Coif, Phi Beta Kappa. Office: Gang Tyre Ramer & Brown Inc 6400 W Sunset Blvd Los Angeles CA 90028-7392

BROWN, IDALYN STOLL, neuropsychologist; b. Columbia, S.C.; d. Philip Cunningham and Charles Loreen (Mc Leod) Stoll; m. Carol Eugene Brown, June 1, 1956; children: Susan Stoll Brown Tate, Michael Ashley. BA in Music, Coker Coll., 1956; BS in Psychology, Salem Coll., 1978; MS in Psychology, Francis Marion U., 1980; PhD in Psychology, U. Ga., 1983. Dir. diagnostic svcs. S.C. Dept. Mental Retardation, Florence, 1984; fellow in neuropsychology Bowman Gray Sch. Medicine, Winston-Salem, N.C., 1985-86, rsch. asst. prof., 1986-91; head neuropsychology program Valley Children's Hosp., Fresno, Calif., 1991—; asst. prof. (part time) St. Andrews Presbyn. Coll., Laurinburg, N.C., 1984, Wake Forest U., Winston-Salem, 1986-91, Salem Coll., Winston-Salem, 1986-91; lectr. in field. Contbr. articles to profl. jours. Mem. Internat. Neuropsychol. Soc., Soc. for Neurosci., So. Soc. for Philosophy & Psychology, Phi Beta Kappa, Phi Kappa Phi. Office: Valley Children's Hosp Rehab Ctr 3151 N Millbrook Fresno CA 93703

BROWN, IONA, violinist, orchestra director; b. Salisbury, Wiltshire, England, Jan. 7, 1941. Studied with Hugh Maguire, London, Remy Principe, Rome, Henryk Szeryng, France. Violinist Nat. Youth Orch. of Gt. Britain, 1955-60, Philharmonia Orch. of London, 1963-66; violinist Acad of St. Martin in the Fields, 1964—, concertmaster, dir., 1974—; artistic dir. Norwegian Chamber Orch., Oslo; prin. guest dir. L.A. Chamber Orch., 1987-91, City of Birmingham Symphony Orch., England, 1992—. Office: LA Chamber Orch 315 W 9th St Bldg 801 Los Angeles CA 90015-4208

BROWN, JACK D(ELBERT), chemist, researcher; b. Boise, Idaho, June 21, 1954; s. Robert and Shirley Fay (Piper) B.; m. Leslie Anne Terry, June 12, 1981; children: Lauren Anne, Justin Andrew. Student, Boise State U., 1973-76; BS, Utah State U., 1983, PhD, 1987. Post-doctoral researcher Colo. State U., Ft. Collins, 1986-88; sr. rsch. chemist Syntex Chemicals Inc., Boulder, Colo., 1988-90; prin. rsch. chemist, Tech. Ctr. Syntex Chemicals Inc., Boulder, 1990—. Co-author: (book chpt.) Metabolism of Food Disaccarides, 1983; co-inventor; contbr. articles to profl. jours. Explorer Scout advisor Boy Scouts Am., Boulder, 1991. Mem. AAAS, Am. Chem. Soc., Sigma Xi. Home: 11329 Chase Way Westminster CO 80020-6811 Office: Syntex Chemicals Inc 2075 N 55th St Boulder CO 80301

BROWN, JACK H., supermarket company executive; b. San Bernardino, Calif., June 14, 1939. Student, San Jose State U., UCLA. V.p. Sages Complete Markets, San Bernardino, 1960-71, Marsh Supermarkets, Yorktown, Ind., 1971-77; pres. Pantry Supermarkets, Pasadena, Calif., 1977-79; pres. mid-west div. Cullum Cos., Dallas, 1979-81; pres., chief exec. officer Stater Bros. Markets, Colton, Calif., 1981—; chmn. bd. dirs. Stater Bros. Inc., 1986—; dir. Life Savs. & Loan Assn., San Bernardino. Trustee, U. Redlands, Calif.; bd. dirs. Goodwill Industries of Inland Empire, San Bernardino; bd. councillors Calif. State U., San Bernardino. With USNR, 1956-62. Named Sagamore of the Wabash, Gov. Ind., 1978. Recipient Horatio Alger award of Disting. Ams., 1992, Bus. Exec. of Yr. award U. So. Calif., 1993; Calif. State U., San Bernadino Sch. Bus. named in his honor, 1992. Mem. Western Assn. Food Chains (v.p., bd. dirs., pres. 1987-88), Calif. Retailers Assn. (bd. dirs.), Food Mktg. Inst. (vice chmn.), So. Calif. Grocers Assn., Food Employers Council (bd. govs.), Elks. Republican. Presbyterian. Office: Stater Bros Markets 21700 Barton Rd Colton CA 92324-4408

BROWN, JAMES CARRINGTON, III (BING BROWN), public relations and communications executive; b. Wilmington, Del., May 17, 1939; s. James Carrington Jr. and Virginia Helen (Miller); m. Carol Osman, Nov. 3, 1961. Grad. security mgmt. group, Indsl. Coll. of the Armed Forces; BBA, Ariz. State U., 1984. Newsman, disc jockey, program dir. various radio stas., Ariz., 1955-60; morning news editor Sta. KOY, Phoenix, 1960-61; staff writer, photographer Prescott (Ariz.) Evening Courier, 1961; bus. editor, staff writer, photographer Phoenix Gazette, 1961-65; various communications positions Salt River Project, Phoenix, 1965-89; pres. Carrington Communications, Phoenix, 1989—; cons. comm., freelance writing, photography The Browns, Phoenix, 1965—; pub. info. officer Water Svcs. Dept., City of Phoenix, 1991—; instr. Rio Salado C.C., Phoenix, 1989—; guest lectr. various colls. and univs., 1975—; prof. Walter Cronkite Sch. Journalism and Telecomm., Ariz. State U., 1990—. Bd. dirs Theodore Roosevelt coun. Boy Scouts Am., 1985-89, mem. adv. coun., 1990—; mem. environment com. Phoenix Futures Forum, 1991-93; deacon Meml. Presbyn. Ch., 1980-82, elder, 1985-87; spl. gifts com. United Way, Phoenix, 1986-89. Recipient Golden Eagle award Boy Scouts Am., 1992. Mem. Western Systems Coordinating Coun. (chmn. pub. info. com. 1969-89), Ariz. Newspapers Assn. (Billy Goat award, Allied Mem. of Yr. 1985), Ariz. Broadcasters Assn., Western Energy Supply and Transmission Assocs. (mem. pub. info. com. 1967-89), Phoenix Press Club (pres. 1982-83), Pub. Rels. Soc. Am., Nat. Acad. TV Arts and Scis., Ariz. Zool. Soc., Heard Mus. Anthropology and Primitive Art. Republican. Home and Office: Carrington Communications 3734 E Campbell Ave Phoenix AZ 85018-3507 also: Phoenix Water Svcs Dept 455 N 5th St Phoenix AZ 85004

BROWN, JAMES CHANDLER, college administrator; b. Garden City, N.Y., Aug. 5, 1947; s. Harry Chandler and Lillian Marie (Cutter) B. BA, Susquehanna U., Selinsgrove, Pa., 1970; License es Lettres, Geneva U., 1978; postgrad., Stanford U., 1984. Rsch. asst. Geneva (Switzerland) U., 1972-79; asst. Galerie Jan Krugier, Geneva, 1978-81; coord. pubs. So. Oreg. State Coll., Ashland, 1982-84; dir. pubs. So. Oreg. State Coll., 1984—; cons. in field. Author: How to Sharpen Your Publications (brochure, Case award) 1985, College Viewbook (booklet), 1985. Sec. bd. dirs. Schneider Mus. Art, Ashland, 1985—. Canton of Geneva grantee, 1974-79; awardee, Coun. for Advancement and Support of Edn., 1987, 88. Mem. Coun. for Advancement and Support of Edn. Methodist. Home: 385 Guthrie St Ashland OR 97520-9999 Office: Southern Oreg State College 1250 Siskiyou Blvd Ashland OR 97520-2268

BROWN, JAMES COOKE, inventor, non-profit organization administrator, writer; b. Tagilarin, Bohol, The Philippines, July 21, 1921; came to U.S., 1929; s. Bryan Burtis and Violet Mary (Cooke) B.; m. Evelyn Ruth Hamburger, July 21, 1985; children: Jefferson O'Reilly, Jill O'Reilly, Jennifer Fuller. BA in Philosophy and Math., U. Minn., 1946, PhD in Philosophy, Sociology and Math. Stats., 1952. Instr. sociology Wayne State U., Detroit, 1949-50; asst. prof. Ind. U., Bloomington, 1950-52; dir. statis. controls Inst. for Motivation Rsch., Croton-on-Husdon, N.Y., 1954-55; asst. prof. sociology and humanities, assoc. prof. sociology, philosophy U. Fla., Gainesville, 1955-63, 70; dir., then chmn. Loglan Inst., Inc., Gainesville and San Diego, 1964—. Author: Loglan 1: A Logical Language, 1966, 4th edit., 1989, (novel) The Troika Incident, 1970; inventor game Careers, Loglan lang. Home and Office: 3009 Peters Way San Diego CA 92117-4313

BROWN, JAMES HAROLD, software engineer, consultant; b. Dallas, May 1, 1961; s. Harold James and Sally (Cross) B.; m. Lorraine Ann Rice, May 22, 1982; children: Travis James, Alex Forest, Katie Beth. Student, Brigham Young U., 1980-82. Salesman/programmer Commodity Computer Corp., Provo, Utah, 1982-84; hardware designer Golden West Computers, Provo, 1982-84; software engr. Novell Inc., Provo, 1984—; teacher's asst. Brigham Young U., Provo, 1981-82. Tech. editor: Netware 386 User's Guide, 1989. First responder Emergency Med. Svcs. Mem. Assn. Computing Machinery, Nat. Eagle Scout Assn. Mem. LDS Ch. Office: Novell Inc Mail Stop C-22-1 122 East 1700 South Provo UT 84606

BROWN, J'AMY MARONEY, journalist, media relations consultant; b. L.A., Oct. 30, 1945; d. Roland Francis and Jeanne (Wilbur) Maroney; m. James Raphael Brown, Jr., Nov. 5, 1967 (dec. July 1982); children:James Roland Francis, Jeanne Raphael. B.A., U. So. Calif., 1967. Reporter L.A. Herald Examiner, 1966-67, Lewisville Leader, Dallas, 1980-81; editor First Person Mag., Dallas, 1981-82; journalism dir. Pacific Palisades Sch., L.A., 1983-84; free-lance writer, media cons., 1984-88; press liaison U.S. papal visit, L.A., 1987; media dir., chief media strategist Tellem Inc., communication cons., 1990-93. Auction chmn. Assn. Pub. Broadcasting, Houston, 1974, 75; vice chmn. Dallas Arts Council, 1976-80; vice chmn. Met. March of Dimes, Dallas, 1980-82; del. Dallas Council PTAs, 1976-80. Recipient UPI Editors award for investigative reporting, 1981. Mem. Women Meeting Women, Women in Communications, Am. Bus. Women's Assn. Republican. Roman Catholic. Home: 13101 Nimrod Pl Los Angeles CA 90049-3632

BROWN, JANICE, university official; b. Reno, July 22, 1935; d. Charles Emmett Brown and Sarah Margaret (Harrison) Selin. BS, U. Nev., 1957. Sec. to pres. Bonanza Air Lines, Las Vegas, Nev., 1957-58; sec. to comdg. officer U.S. Naval Supply Depot, Guam, Marianas Islands, 1958-61; sales promotion agt. Air France, Los Angeles, 1961-62, asst. cargo sales mgr., 1962-67; sec. Pangborn, Douglass & Morgan, Reno, 1968-74; sec. to assoc. dean of students U. Nev., Reno, 1974-80, mgt. analyst, 1980-84, rsch. analyst, 1984-88, sr. rsch. analyst, asst. dir. for instnl. analysis, 1988—. Mem. Rocky Mountain Assn. for Instnl. Rsch. (Nev. corr. 1987—), Assn. Instnl. Rsch., Univ. Club, Delta Delta Delta. Republican. Home: 3080 Achilles Dr Reno NV 89512-1332 Office: U Nev Office Planning Budget Analysis Reno NV 89557

BROWN, JERRY See BROWN, EDMUND GERALD, JR.

BROWN, JOHN OLLIS LANGFORD, JR., surgeon, educator; b. Nashville, May 16, 1946; s. John O. Sr. and Marie Louise (Faulkner) B.; m. Kimberly Ann Brown, Dec. 8, 1990; children: John O. III, William L. BA, Harvard U., 1967; MD, Yale U., 1973. Diplomate Am. Bd. Surgery. Clin. instr. U. Calif., Sacramento, 1979; surgeon Kaiser Hosp., Portland, Oreg., 1979—; dir. Clark County Sch. Bd., Vancouver, Wash., 1991—. Candidate Clark County Sch. Bd., Vancouver, Wash., 1991—. Mem. Nat. Med. Assn., Portland Surg. Soc. Republican. Episcopalian. Home: 14205 SE 15th Cir Vancouver WA 98684-7536

BROWN, KATHLEEN, lawyer, state treasurer; d. Edmund G. and Bernice Brown; m. George Rice (div. 1979); children: Hilary, Alexandra, Zebediah; m. Van Gordon Sauter, 1980; 2 stepsons. BA in History, Stanford U., 1969; grad., Fordham U. Sch. Law. Mem. L.A. Bd. Edn., 1975-80; with O'Melveny & Myers, N.Y.C., then L.A.; commr. L.A. Bd. Pub. Works, 1987-89; elected Treas. of Calif., 1990. Democrat. Address: Office of State Treas PO Box 942809 Sacramento CA 94209-0001*

BROWN, KEITH LAPHAM, retired ambassador; b. Sterling, Ill., June 18, 1925; s. Lloyd Heman and Marguerite (Briggs) B.; m. Carol Louise Liebmann, Oct. 1, 1949; children: Susan, Briggs (dec.), Linda, Benjamin. Student, U. Ill., 1943-44, Northwestern U., 1946-47; LLB, U. Tex., 1949. Bar: Tex., Okla., Colo. Assoc. Lang, Byrd, Cross & Ladon, San Antonio, 1949-55; v.p., gen. counsel Caulkins Oil Co., Oklahoma City, 1955-70, Denver, 1955-70; pres. Brown Investment Corp., Denver, 1970-87; U.S. ambassador to Kingdom of Lesotho, 1982-84, Denmark, 1985-92; founder, developer Vail Assocs., Colo., 1962; developer Colo. State Bank Bldg., Denver, 1971; U.S. amb. to Denmark, Copenhagen, 1988-92; retired, 1992. Chmn. Republican Nat. Fin. Com., 1985-88; hon. trustee, past pres. bd. Colo. Acad. With USN, 1943-46. Mem. Denver Country Club, Univ. Club. Presbyterian. Address: 365 Mill Creek Cir Vail CO 81657

BROWN, LES, insurance counselor, business planner; b. Bklyn., Apr. 25, 1926; s. Robert and Rose (Solomon) B.; m. Doris Goldstein, Nov. 15, 1929; children: Sandy E., Joanie S., Gil W. Student, U. N.C., 1946-47, Columbia Sch. Broadcasting, 1947. Radio announcer various stas., 1948-49; sales mgr. Armour and Co., Bklyn., 1949-51; pres. Brown Bros., Rockville Ctr., N.Y., 1951-63; sales rep. Conn. Gen. Life, Queens, N.Y., 1963-76; sales rep. Lincoln Nat. Life, Albuquerque, 1976-79, Phoenix, 1979-89; ret., 1989; cons. Exec. Svc. Corp. Ariz. Bd. dirs. Anytown Am., Phoenix, 1985—, Consumer Credit Cons., Phoenix, 1981-85; founder, past pres. Fairview Jewish Meml. Cemetery, Albuquerque, 1978; mem. many animal conservation orgns. With Mcht. Marine, 1943-45, 82d Airborne, AUS, 1945-46. Mem. KP (past chancellor). Office: Lincoln Nat Life 410 N 44th St Ste 200 Phoenix AZ 85008-1501

BROWN, LEWIS FRANK, lawyer; b. Cleveland, Miss., Aug. 4, 1929; s. Frank C. and Lula Y. (Armstrong) B.; m. Dorothy Jean Fitzgerald, Mar. 29, 1956; children: Lewis G., Orville Frank. AA, Vallejo (Calif.) Coll., 1955; BA, Calif. State U., San Francisco, 1957; JD, Lincoln U., 1965. Bar: Calif. 1970. Tchr. Vallejo Unified Sch. Dist., 1957-64; cons. Greenleigh Assocs., N.Y.C., 1964-66, Contra Costa County Office Econ. Opportunity, Martinez, Calif., 1966-70; assoc. Solano Legal Assistance, Vallejo, 1970-71; ptnr. Beeman, Bradley, Brown & Beeman, Vallejo, 1977—; cons. Exec. Office of Pres. Lyndon B. Johnson. Committeeman Solano County Dems., 1959-67; mem. planning commn. City of Vallejo, 1963-65, city councilman, 1965-69, vice mayor, 1967-69. Recipient Commendation award Solano County Dist. Atty., 1982, Jones County, Miss. Bd. Suprs., 1988, Laurel, Miss. May and City Coun., 1988, Resolution awds. Sen. Barry Keene and Thomas H. Hannigan, 1982, City of Vallejo Civic Leader award, 1982, Nat. Laurel, Miss. Oak Park High Sch. Alumni Assn. Alumni of Yr., 1988, NAACP Citizen of the Yr. award, Vallejo br., 1982; park named in his honor, Vallejo, 1969. Mem. NAACP (Golden Heritage award, Citizen of the Yr. 1985), NAACP Million Dollar Club, Oak Park High Sch. Alumni Assn., Calif. Bar Assn., Solano County Bar Assn. (sec.-treas. 1971), Charles Houston Bar Assn., Nat. Bar Assn. (life). Rescue Mission Ch. of God in Christ. Home: 400 Lakeside Dr Vallejo CA 94589-2106 Office: Brown & Bradley 538 Georgia St Vallejo CA 94590-6096

BROWN, LILLIAN ERIKSEN, retired nursing administrator, consultant; b. Seattle, Feb. 7, 1921; d. Peter Louis and Lena (Lien) Eriksen; m. Jan. 21, 1942 (div. Nov. 1963); children: Patricia Lee, Michael Gregory, Kevin William. Student, U. Calif., Berkeley, 1939-40; diploma, St. Luke's Hosp. Sch. Nursing, San Francisco, 1943; AB, Calif. State U., San Francisco, 1952; MPA, U. So. Calif., 1975. RN, Calif. Pub. health nurse San Francisco Dept. Health, 1946-50; asst. dir. nursing San Francisco Gen. Hosp., 1950-56; dir. nursing Weimar (Calif.) Med. Ctr., 1956-62, Orange County Med. Ctr., Orange, Calif., 1962-76; assoc. dir. hosp. and clins., dir. nursing, lectr. U. Calif. Med. Ctr., Irvine, 1976-82; assoc. hosp. administr. King Khalid Eye Specialist Hosp., Riyadh, Saudi Arabia, 1982-86; cons. AMI-Saudi Arabia Ltd., Jeddah, 1986-90; chmn. Western Teaching Hosp. Coun. Dirs. Nursing, 1972-75, 80-81; mem. planning project com. Calif. Dept. Rehab., 1967-69, mem. adv. com., 1970-73; mem. ad hoc president's com. on hosp. governance U. Calif., 1981-82; pres. dirs. nursing coun. Hosp. Coun. So. Calif., 1972-74, mem. pers. practices com., 1976-78, 80-83, area rep., 1975-82; mem. dept. nursing adv. com. to establish baccalaureate program U. So. Calif., 1980-82; mem. adv. bd. various coll. nursing programs. Contbr. articles to profl. jours. Sec. Olive (Calif.) Little League, 1967-72; mem. com. on emergency med. svcs. Orange County Health Planning Coun., 1977-78, mem. health promotion task force, 1978-79. 2d lt. Nurse Corps, U.S. Army, 1944-45. Recipient Lauds and Laurels award U. Calif., Irvine, 1981. Fellow Am. Acad. Nurses; mem. ANA (cert. nurse adminstr. advanced), Nat. League for Nursing, APHA, Am. Orgn. Nurse Execs., Nat. Critical Care Inst. Edn., Calif. Nurses Assn. (Lillian E. Brown award named in her honor 1989), Calif. Orgn. for Nurse Execs. (hon.), Calif. Soc. for Nursing Svc. Adminstr., NOW. Republican. Home: 1806 N Nordic Pl Orange CA 92665-4637

BROWN, MARK STEVEN, medical physicist; b. Denver, July 12, 1955; s. Clarence William and Gail Margaret (Farthing) B.; m. Mary Linda Avery, Oct. 9, 1988. Student, Northwestern U., 1973-74; BS, Colo. State U., 1977; PhD in Phys. Chemistry, U. Utah, 1984. GE postdoctoral fellow Yale U. Sch. Medicine, New Haven, 1984-86, assoc. rsch. scientist, 1986-87; rsch. asst. prof. U. N.Mex. Sch. Medicine, Albuquerque, 1987-89; med. physicist Swedish Med. Ctr. Porter Meml. Hosp., Englewood, Colo., 1989-92; instr. C.C. Denver, Denver, 1990, 91; asst. clin. prof. radiology U. Colo. Sch. Medicine, Denver, 1991-92, asst. prof. radiology, 1992—. Author: (with others) NMR Relaxation in Tissues, 1986; contbr. articles to profl. jours. Mem. Floyd Hill Homeowners Assn., Evergreen, Colo., 1990. Mem. Am. Chem. Soc., Soc. for Magnetic Resonance in Medicine, Soc. for Magnetic Resonanace Imaging. Home: 560 Hyland Dr Evergreen CO 80439-4809 Office: Univ Colo Health Scis Ctr Dept Radiology Box A034 4200 E 9th Ave Denver CO 80262

BROWN, MARK TERRILL, hotel executive, electronics executive; b. Dodge City, Kans., June 21, 1953; s. Maynard Virgil and Evelyn Christina (Lietzan) B.; m. Donna Rae Seibel, June 11, 1977; children: Amanda Marie, Jennifer Lee. Student, St. Mary of the Plains Coll., 1971-72; BS in Bus., Colo. U., 1991. Owner War Eagle Jewelers, Liberal, Kans. and Estes Park, Colo., 1967—; gen. mgr. Moreno Tewahay Inc., Estes Park, 1979-88, treas., 1988-91, pres., 1991—; pres. Hobit Industries, Estes Park, 1985—; v.p. The Estes Park Trolley Corp., 1987—; gov. Best Western Internat., 1985—; bd. dirs. Colo. Connections. Inventor auotomatic telephone quotation system, Hobit 2000, 1985. Planning commr. Town of Estes Park, 1988—, trustee 1984-88; bd. dirs. Estes Park C. of C., 1983-84; commr. econ. devel. Larimer County, 1988—; bd. dirs. Internat. Aspenfest, pres. 1981-83. Mem. Am. Hotel & Motel Assn., Colo. Wyo. Hotel & Motel Assn., Estes Park Accomodations Assn. (pres. 1983-84). Republican. Roman Catholic. Lodge: Elks. Office: Moreno Tewanay Inc PO Box 1466 Estes Park CO 80517-0282

BROWN, MARK THOMAS, accountant; b. Vancouver, Wash., July 27, 1956; s. Arlie Don and Shirley Ann (Plummer) B.; m. Patricia Sue Martin, Apr. 24, 1982; children: Sheena Marie, Melissa Sue. BS, Portland (Oreg.) State U., 1978. CPA, Oreg. Cost analyst Portland Wire and Iron, 1978; tax auditor Oreg. Dept. of Revenue, Salem, 1979-81; acctg. ptnr. Kent and Snow, CPAs, Oregon City, Oreg., 1981—. Mem. AICPAs, Oreg. Soc. CPAs, Kiwanis (pres. Milw. chpt. 1990—). Office: Kent and Snow CPAs Ste 100 8305 SE Monterey Ave Portland OR 97266-7728

BROWN, MARY HELEN, state official; b. Shelby, Mont., Feb. 20, 1958; d. Ray V. and Elsie Jean (Neilsen) Robbins; m. Dale R. Brown, June 30, 1984; 1 child, Ryan D. Adminstrn. Clk., Family Tng. Ctr., Glasgow, Mont. Office mgr. Larson Clothing, Shelby, Mont., 1980-84; assessor property tax Toole County Assessor, Dept. of Revenue, Shelby, 1984-91; property tax clk. II Toole County Appraisal, Dept. of Revenue, Shelby, 1991—. Dir. Parents of Creative and Performing Arts, Shelby, 1990—; vol. Toole County Sr. Citizen Ctr.; active Shelby Booster Club, 1990—, Cut Bank Snowgoers, 1992—. Mem. Internat. Assn. Assessing Officers, Jaycees Mont. (dir. region 2 1992, v.p. 1992, program mgr. 1991, Top 3 pres. 1990), Toole County Community Concert, Harley Owners Group, Am. Bikers Aiming for Edn. Republican. Methodist. Home: 504 1st St S Shelby MT 59474 Office: Toole County Appraisal Office Courthouse Shelby MT 59474

BROWN, MERWIN L., utility executive; b. Wichita, Kans., Mar. 31, 1944; s. Charles M. and June L. Brown; m. Cheryl Ann Clark, July 25, 1964; 1 child, Merwin M. BS in Nuclear Engring., Kans. State U., 1966, PhD in Nuclear Engring., 1973. Rsch. analyst Ariz. Pub. Svc. Co., Phoenix, 1971-76, mgr. rsch., 1976-83; dir. program devel. Gas-Cooled Reactor Assocs., San Diego, 1983-85; dir. R & D, Pacific Gas & Electric Co., San Ramon, Calif., 1985-87; dir. electric supply bus. planning Pacific Gas & Electric Co., San Francisco, 1987-89; dir. R & D, Pacific Gas & Electric Co., San Ramon, 1989—; design advisor Engring. R & D Ctr., Ariz. State U., Tempe, 1981-82. Rsch. advisor Ariz. Dept. Transp., Phoenix, 1980-83; mem. Ariz. Solar Energy Commn., Phoenix, 1982-83. Fellow AEC, 1966-70. Office: Pacific Gas & Electric Co 3400 Crow Canyon Rd (R&D) San Ramon CA 94583

BROWN, MICHAEL DAVID, environmental engineer; b. Berkeley, Calif., July 19, 1948; s. Philip Kier and Edith (Bernhard) B.; m. Barbara Ann Johnston; children: Chandra, Benjamin. BS in Environ. Engring., Calif. Poly. State U., 1975; MBA, Golden Gate U., 1981. Registered profl. engr., Calif., Pa. Engr. Calif. Regional Water Quality Control Bd., San Luis Obispo, 1974-75; chief environ. engr. Garretson-Elmendorf-Zinov-Reibin, San Francisco, 1975-79; pres. Brown Vence & Assocs., San Francisco, 1979—, also bd. dirs.; bd. dirs. Gensmith Inc., San Francisco, 1984-86, Energy Systems Design, Menlo Park, Calif., 1982-84. Author: Solid Waste Transfer Techniques, 1975, Resource Recovery Case Studies, 1982; contbr. chpt. to book. Pres. Point Richmond (Calif.) Neighborhood Coun., 1984-85, Crestmont Sch., Richmond, Calif., 1984, treas., 1983. Mem. Govtl. Refuse Collection and Disposal Assn. Democrat. Jewish. Office: Brown Vence & Assocs 120 Montgomery St Ste 680 San Francisco CA 94104-4309

BROWN, MICHAEL DEWAYNE, lawyer; b. Guymon, Okla., Nov. 11, 1954; s. Wayne E. and R. Eloise (Ferguson) B.; m. Tamara Ann Oxley, July 19, 1973; children: Jared Michael, Amy Aryann. Student, Southeastern State Coll., 1973-75; BA in Polit. Sci. and English, Cen. State U., Edmond, Okla., 1978; JD, Oklahoma City U., 1981. Bar: Okla. 1982, U.S. Dist. Ct. (no. and we. dists.) Okla. 1982, U.S. Ct. Appeals (10th cir.) 1982, U.S. Ct. Appeals (D.C. cir.) 1987. Assoc. Long, Ford, Lester & Brown, Enid, Okla., 1982-87; sole practice Enid, 1987—; adj. prof. state and local govt. law legis. Oklahoma City U.; cons. No. Okla. Devel. Assn., Enid, 1983-91; gen. counsel Alpha Oil Co., Duncan, Okla., 1985—, Physicians Mgmt. Svc. Corps., 1985-90, Physicians of Okla., Inc., Physicians Med. Plan Okla., Inc., City Nat. Bank & Trust Co., 1987-88, Stanfield Printing Co., 1987—, Hammell Newspapers, Inc., 1987-90, Dillingham Ins., 1989-91, Suits Rig Corp., Suits Drilling Co., 1989-91; chmn. bd. dirs. Okla. Mcpl. Power Authority, Edmond, 1982-88, judges & stewards commr. Internat. Arabian Horse Assn., 1991—. Councilman City of Edmond, 1981; cons. Okla. Reps., Oklahoma City, 1983; bd. dirs. Okla. Christian Home, Edmond, 1985; Rep. nominee 6th Dist. U.S. Congress, 1988; co-chmn. Nat. Challengers Polit. Coalition, 1989-91. Michael D. Brown Hydroelectric Power Plant and Dam named in his honor, Kaw Reservoir, Okla., 1987. Mem. Okla. Bar Assn. (assoc. bar examiner 1984—), MD Physicians Okla., Ariz. and La., MD Physicians of Tulsa. Mem. Christian Ch. (Disciples of Christ). Home and Office: 8373 Larkspur Rd Boulder CO 80302-9322

BROWN, NANCY DIANE, public relations executive; b. Oakland, Calif., Jan. 12, 1961; d. H. Douglas and Janet (Roberts) Mooers; m. Cory Noel Brown, Sept. 13, 1986. BA, U. Oreg., 1983. Accredited pub. rels. Intern PACIFICOMM Pub. Rels., Eugene, 1983; asst. account exec. Arnold & Co. Pub. Rels., Boston, 1983-84; account exec. Ralph Silver Assocs., San Francisco, 1984-86; sr. account exec. Pam Hunter & Assocs., St. Helena, Calif., 1986-87; prin. Brown Miller Communications, Martinez, Calif., 1987—. Wine columnist Costco Connection, 1988; food columnist Diablo Mag., 1989. Mem. Am. Inst. of Wine and Food (bd. dirs. 1990-92), Pub. Rels. Soc. Am., Napa Valley Wine Libr., Kappa Alpha Theta (editor, historian Alpha Xi chpt. 1982). Democrat. Office: Brown Miller Communications 1330 Arnold Dr Ste 242 Martinez CA 94553-6538

BROWN, PATRICIA ANNE, counselor; b. Sewickley, Pa., Dec. 12, 1947; d. Camillo J. and Virginia (Forcone) Iacobucci; m. W. Gerald Brown (div. Feb. 1981); children: David, Kathryn. BA cum laude, James Madison U., 1969; MEd, U. Ariz., 1978, postgrad. Tchr. midsch. Robinson Twp. (Pa.) Sch. Dist., 1969-70, Cherry Hill (N.J.) Sch. Dist., 1970-76; crisis couselor Suicide Crisis Prevention Ctr., Tucson, 1976-77; crisis and bereavement counselor St. Joseph Hosp., Albuquerque, 1980-83; counselor Albuquerque Pub. Schs., 1982-87; dir. mktg., v.p. sales Western Data Systems, Inc., Albuquerque, 1986-90, sec., bd. dirs., 1987-90; mktg. cons. Presentation Express & Sunflower Resources, Albuquerque, 1990-91, Rivera Tech. Enterprises, Albuquerque, 1991; counselor A.P.S., Albuquerque, 1991—. Mem. publs. and publicity Bernalillo Med. Aux. Wives, Albuquerque, 1978-81; coord. fashion show, 1981; mem. bldg. and fundraising com. Ronald McDonld House, Albuquerque, 1982-83. Winner Best Presentation U. N.Mex. and Wellness Symposium, 1988; named Danforth Scholar, 1993. Mem. Albuquerque Sch. Counselors Assn. (East area rep. 1991-92), Nat. Sch. Counselors Assn., Kappa Delta Pi, Sigma Phi Lambda. Home: 927 Tramway Ln NE Albuquerque NM 87122

BROWN, PATRICIA LYNN, information consultant, librarian; b. Torrance, Calif., Apr. 23, 1954; d. William Charles and Louise Patricia (Zultowsky) B. BA, U. Calif., Irvine, 1976; MLS, UCLA, 1978. Info. splist. NASA Indsl. Application Ctr., L.A., 1978-80; interim libr. L.A. Pub. Libr., 1981; sr. reference libr. L.A. Times, 1981-88; divsn. dir. Savage Info. Svcs., Torrance, Calif., 1988-93; sr. system cons. Dialog Info. Svcs., Marina Del Ray, Calif., 1993—. Editor: (book series) Custom Online Guide (COG), 1990—; contbr articles to profl. jours. Treas. Friends of the Robert Louis Stevenson br. of L.A. Pub. Libr., 1985—. Mem. ALA, So. Calif. Online Users Group (mem. steering com.), Spl. Librs. Assn. (So. Calif. chpt., career guidance com. chair 1990-92, Information Tech. online section chair 1992—, community rels. officer 1992-93). Home: 2268 India St Los Angeles CA 90039 Office: Dialog Info Svcs 4640 Admiralty Way Ste 201 Marina Del Rey CA 90292

BROWN, PAUL FREMONT, aerospace engineer, educator; b. Osage, Iowa, Mar. 10, 1921; s. Charles Fremont and Florence Alma (Olson) B.; m. Alice Marie Culver, Dec. 5, 1943; children—Diane, Darrell, Judith, Jana. BA in Edn. and Natural Sci., Dickinson State Coll., 1942; BS in Mech. Engring., U. Wash., 1948; MS in Cybernetic Systems, San Jose State U., 1971. Profl. quality engr., Calif., 1978; cert. reliability engr., Am. Soc. Quality Control, 1976. Test engr., supr. Boeing Aircraft Corp., Seattle, 1948-56; design specialist, propulsion systems, Lockheed Missiles and Space Co., Sunnyvale, Calif., 1956-59; supr. system effectiveness, 1959-66, staff engr., 1966-76, mgr. product assurance, 1976-83; v.p. research, devel. Gen. Agriponics Inc. of Hawaii, 1971-76; owner Diversatek Engring. and Product Assurance Conss., 1983—; coll. instr., lectr., San Jose State U. Active in United Presbyn. Ch., 1965—; scoutmaster, Boy Scouts Am., 1963-65. Served to 1st lt., USAF, 1943-46. Recipient awards for tech. papers, Lockheed Missiles and Space Co., 1973-75. Mem. Am. Soc. Quality Control, AIAA. Clubs: Toastmasters (Sunnyvale, Calif.). Author: From Here to Retirement, 1988; contbr. articles to profl. jours. Home and Office: 19608 Braemar Dr Saratoga CA 95070-5046

BROWN, PETER HARRISON, architect, construction consultant, development manager; b. N.Y.C., Apr. 25, 1943; s. William Seltzer and Sara (Ervin) B.; m. Barbara Elaine Allbut, Feb. 14, 1986. BArch, Cornell U., 1967; MArch, Columbia U., 1968. Registered architect N.Y. Architect/planner Gruzen Ptnrship., N.Y.C., 1968-70, 75-78, Norval White Assocs., Brooklyn Heights, N.Y., 1970-74; assoc. ptnr., project mgr. Skidmore, Owings & Merrill, N.Y.C., 1978-85; assoc. ptnr., mgr. project Skidmore, Owings & Merrill, L.A., 1985-86; ptnr. Teubner and Brown, L.A., Costa Mesa and Santa Barbara, Calif., 1988—. Mem. AIA. Club: U. (N.Y.C.). Home: 1601 Mira Vista Ave Santa Barbara CA 93103-1881 Also: 255 S Grand Ave Los Angeles CA 90012 Office: Teubner and Brown 601 W 5th St Ste 220 Los Angeles CA 90071-2004

BROWN, POLLY SARAH, psychologist; b. Cambridge, Mass., Dec. 30, 1952; d. David Randolph and Sally (England) B. BA in Psychology, Computer Sci., Mills Coll., Oakland, Calif., 1976; MA in Cognitive Psychology, U. Denver, 1982, PhD in Cognitive Psychology, 1985. Computer programmer Argonne (Ill.) Nat. Lab., 1976-77; tech. writer ESL, Sunnyvale, Calif., 1977-78; instr. psychology, rsch. asst., computer programmer U. Denver, 1978-85; postdoctoral rsch. human factors IBM Rsch., Yorktown Heights, N.Y., 1985-87; human factors scientist IBM, San Jose, Calif., 1987-91; cons. human-computer interaction Xerox XSoft, Palo Alto, Calif., 1992; human-computer interaction specialist Palo Alto, 1992—. Patentee highlighting tool, 1988; contbr. articles to profl. jours. Tchr. First Congl. Ch., Palo Alto, 1990-92; mem. NOW. Mem. Human Factors Soc., Assn. for Computing Machinery (spl. interest group in computer-human interaction 1985—), Sierra Club, Phi Beta Kappa. Democrat. Home: 410 Sheridan Ave Apt 444 Palo Alto CA 94306-2020

BROWN, RANDALL EMORY, geologist; b. Eugene, Oreg., May 28, 1917; s. Percy Walker and Zula (Correll) B.; m. Helene Kerr, Jan. 21, 1950; children: Derek Jeffrey, Kevin Randall. AB, Stanford U., 1938; MA, Yale U., 1941. Registered geologist. Chief sampler, resident geologist M.A. Hanna Co., Darrington, Wash., 1941; geologist Oreg. Dept. Geology and Mineral Industries, Portland, 1941-42, U.S. Geol. Survey, 1942-45, U.S. Army, Corps Engrs., Portland, 1945-47, Gen. Electric Co. Hanford Works, Richland, Wash., 1947-65; sr. rsch. scientist Battelle Meml. Inst., Richland, 1965-71; asst. prof. Cen. Wash. U., Ellensburg, Wash., 1971-72; instr. Columbia Basin Coll., Pasco, Wash., 1972-73; cons. Pasco, 1973—; panelist radio and TV sci. program Hanford Sci. Forum, 1954, 56. Contbr. articles to profl. jours. Asst. supr. Franklin County Conservation Dist., Pasco, 1972—. Fellow AAAS, Geol. Soc. Am.; mem. Assn. Ground Water Scientists and Engrs., Nat. Water Well Assn., N.W. Sci. Assn. (pres. 1969-70), Sigma Xi. Republican. Episcopalian (lay reader). Home: 504 N Road 49 Pasco WA 99301-3042

BROWN, RANDY LEE, systems engineer; b. Yakima, Wash., Oct. 9, 1963; s. Jack Leroy Brown and Carol Ann (Litchtenburg) Myers. Student, Yakima Valley Vocat. Skills Ctr., 1980-82, Phoenix Inst. Tech., 1982-83. Electronic technician Easy Enterprises Amusements, Yakima, 1983-84; svc. mgr. Cliff Miller's Computers Inc., Yakima, 1984—. Named State Champion radio TV repair Vocat. Industries Clubs Am., 1982. Home: 608 S Yakima Ave Wapato WA 98951-1261 Office: Cliff Millers Computers Inc 22 N 2d St Yakima WA 98901

BROWN, RICHARD ALLEN, IV, air force officer, software administrator; b. Balt., Sept. 12, 1959; s. Richard Allen and Alfredia (Williams) B.; 1 child, La Rishia Coreece Brown. BS in Physics, Benedict Coll., Columbia, S.C., 1981; MA in Computer Resource Mgmt., Webster U., St. Louis, 1988. Commd. 2d lt. USAF, 1981, advanced through grades to capt., 1985; space systems dir. USAF, Diyabakir, Turkey, 1985-86; orbital analyst USAF, Colorado Springs, Colo., 1986-88, team supr., 1988-89, software test mgr., 1989-91, software test dir., 1991—. Author: (poetry) Love is Simply Beautiful, 1987, 89, 90. Named to Outstanding Young Men of Am., 1989. Mem. NAACP, Alpha Phi Alpha (Alpha Man of Yr. 1990, assoc. editor 1989-91). Mem. African Methodist Episcopal Ch. Home: 6565 Lindal Dr Colorado Springs CO 80915 Office: HQ AFSPACECOM/DONC Stop 4 Cheyenne Mountain AFB Colorado Springs CO 80914

BROWN, RICHARD M., professional baseball team executive; b. Chgo., Nov. 16, 1942; m. Sandra Spellman; children: Scott, Todd. BA, UCLA, 1964, JD, 1967. With legal staff FTC, Xerox Corp.; div. counsel Bechtel Power Corp., 1974-79; v.p., gen. counsel Avery Internat.; v.p., gen. counsel, sec. Golden West Broadcasters, 1981-83; legal counsel Calif. Angels, from 1981, mem. bd. dirs., 1986—, pres., chief exec. officer, 1990—; ptnr. Jeffer, Mangels, Butler & Marmano, Century City, Calif., 1989-90. Capt. U.S. Army JAGC, 1968-71. Mem. ABA, State Bar Calif., Sports Lawyers Assn., Acad. TV Arts and Scis. Office: Calif Angels Anaheim Stadium Anaheim CA 92806*

BROWN, ROBERT FREEMAN, mathematics educator; b. Cambridge, Mass., Dec. 13, 1935; s. Irving and Charlotte (Frankel) B.; m. Brenda Webster, June 16, 1957; children: Geoffrey, Matthew. AB, Harvard Coll., 1957;

postgrad., Am. U., 1959; PhD, U. Wis., 1963. Asst. prof. UCLA, 1963-68, assoc. prof., 1968-73, prof., 1973—. Author: Lefschetz Fixed Point Theorem, 1970, Applied Finite Math, 1977, Essentials of Finite Math, 1990, Finite Mathematics, 1992. Mem. Am. Math. Soc., Math. Assn. Am. (gov. 1986-89, Lester Ford award 1983). Democrat. Episcopalian. Office: Univ Calif Dept Math Los Angeles CA 90024

BROWN, ROBERT HAROLD, emeritus geography educator; b. Rochester, N.Y., Sept. 16, 1921; s. Harold Cecil and Marion (Johnson) B.; m. Helene Adeline Zukey, Sept. 1, 1945; children: Suzanne Odette, Kurtis Johnson. BS, U. Minn., 1948, MA, 1949; PhD, U. Chgo., 1957. Mem. faculty St. Cloud (Minn.) State Coll., 1949-64; prof. geography dept. U. Wyo., 1964-85. Author: Political Areal Functional Organization, 1957, (with Phillip Tideman) Atlas of Minnesota Occupancy, 3d edit., 1969, Wyoming Occupance Atlas, 1970, Wyoming: A Geography, 1980, The Global-Economy Urban Heirarchy, 1991, The Pervasive Spirit: Concepts for a Personal Religious Philosophy, 1992, Sedona: Arizona's Red Rock Community, 1993. Served to 1st lt. AUS, 1939-45; with USAF, 1951-52. Mem. Assn. Am. Geographers. Home: 10910 W Welk Dr Sun City AZ 85373-1845

BROWN, ROBERT HENRY, physics educator; b. Sioux Falls, S.D., Aug. 27, 1915; s. Harry Joseph and Isabel E. (Ross)B.; m. Ruth Frances Miler, May 26, 1942; children: Rebecca Sue, Judith Ann. BA, Union Coll., Lincoln, Nebr., 1940; MS, U. Nebr., 1942; PhD, U. Wash., 1950. Asst. instr. physics U. Nebr., 1940-42; rsch. engr. Sylvania Electronic Products Co., 1942-45; head sci. dept. Can. Union Coll., Lacombe, Alta., 1945-47; instr. physics U. Wash., 1948-49; mem. faculty Walla Walla Coll., 1947-70, prof. physics, 1954-70, v.p., 1961-70; pres., prof. Union Coll., Lincoln, 1970-73; dir. Geosci. Rsch. Inst., Berrien Springs, Mich., 1973-80; prof. geophysics Andrews U., Berrien Springs, 1973-80; prof. physics Loma Linda (Calif.) U., 1980-88. Mem. Am. Phys. Soc., Am. Geophys. Union, Geochem. Soc., Sigma Xi. Republican. Seventh-day Adventist. Home: 12420 Birch St Yucaipa CA 92399-4218

BROWN, RODNEY JAY, dean, consultant; b. Coalville, Utah, Oct. 6, 1948; s. John Parley and Vera (Bisel) B.; m. Sandra Claire Wood, May 28, 1971; children: Shauna Marie, Carla Rae, David Michael. BS, Brigham Young U., 1972; MS, Utah State U., Logan, 1973; PhD, N.C. State U., Raleigh, 1977. Rsch. assoc. Weizmann Inst. of Sci., Rehovot, Israel, 1977-79; asst. prof. dept. nutrition and food scis. Utah State U., 1979-83, assoc. prof. dept. nutrition and food scis., 1983-84, assoc. prof., head dept. nutrition and food scis., 1985-87, prof., head dept. nutrition and food scis., 1987-91; dean Coll. Agr. Utah State U., Logan, 1991—. Contbr. numerous articles to profl. jours. Mem. AAAS, Am. Chem. Soc., Am. Dairy Sci. Assn. (mem. editorial bd. Jour. Dairy Sci. 1981-91, chair dairy foods div. 1993-94), Inst. Food Technologists (chair dairy tech. div. 1991-92), Rotary, Phi Kappa Phi. LDS. Home: 615 Circle Pl Providence UT 84332-9435 Office: Utah State U Coll Agriculture Logan UT 84322-4800

BROWN, ROGER A., lawyer; b. Hawthorne, Calif., July 30, 1946; s. Finus Austin and Dorothy (Grove) B.; m. Sheila Anne Monaghan, Aug. 28, 1970; children: Allison, Julia. AB, Calif. State U., Fullterton, 1968; JD, U. Calif., Hastings, 1972. Bar: Calif. 1973. Dep. dist. atty. Yolo County Dist. Atty., Woodland, Calif., 1973-78; enforcement chief Calif. Fair Polit. Practices Commn., Sacramento, 1978-88; ptnr. Weintraub Genshlea Hardy Erich & Brown, Sacramento, 1988-90; pvt. practice Sonora, Calif., 1990—. Mem. adv. bd. Yolo County Sexual Assault Ctr., Davis, Calif., 1977; mem. Cen. Sierra Arts Coun. Sonora, 1991-92; counsel Alioto for Mayor, San Francisco, 1991, Dianne Feinstern for Gov., 1992. Mem. Calif. Polit. Attys. Assn., Yolo County Attys. Assn. (pres.), Bay Area Prosecutors Assn., Art in Pub. Pls., Rotary Internat., Phi Sigma Kappa, Pi Sigma Alpha. Office: 38 N Washington St Sonora CA 95370

BROWN, RONALD MALCOLM, engineering corporation executive; b. Hot Springs, S.D., Feb. 21, 1938; s. George Malcolm and Cleo Lavonne (Plumb) B.; m. Sharon Ida Brown, Nov. 14, 1964 (div. Apr. 1974); children: Michael, Troy, George, Curtis, Lisa, Brittney. AA, Southwestern Coll., 1970; BA, Chapman Coll., 1978. Commd. USN, 1956, advanced through grades to master chief, 1973, ret., 1978; engring. mgr. Beckman Inst., Fullerton, Calif., 1978-82; mech. engring. br. mgr. Northrop Corp., Hawthorne, Calif., 1982-83; dir. of ops. Transco, Marina Del Rey, Calif., 1983-85; v.p. ops. Decor Concepts, Arcadia, Calif., 1985—; design dir. Lockheed Aircraft Corp., Ontario, Calif. Mem. Soc. Mfg. Engrs., Inst. Indsl. Engrs., Nat. Trust for Hist. Preservation, Fleet Res. Assn., Am. Film Inst., Nat. Mgmt. Assn.

BROWN, RUDOLPH VALENTINO, JR., architect; b. Fort Myers, Fla., Nov. 17, 1953; s. Rudolph Valentino Brown and Mary Louise (Pierce) Jones; m. Terri Lynn Richardson, Jan. 24, 1987; children: Rudolph Valentino III, Randall Vincent. BArch, Tuskegee (Ala.) Coll., 1978, MArch, 1980. Registered architect. Draftsman, carpenter Jones Constrn. Co., Fort Myers, 1972-73; designer, draftman Mount Herman Bapt. Ch., Fort Myers, 1978; laborer Tuskegee Hist. Site, Nat. Park Svc., 1978; architect Nat. Park Svc. Site Tuskegee Inst. Nat. Hist., 1978, Nat. Park Svc., Lakewood, Colo., 1979, Nat. Park Svc., DSC-TWE, Denver, 1980-88; project mgr., designer J.A. Walker Co., Inc., Denver, 1988-89; designer, constn. mgr. RTR, Inc., Denver, 1980-90; architect USDA Forest Svc., Lakewood, 1990—; designer, cons. Mount Herman Bapt. Ch., Fort Myers, 1978, Lighthouse Community Ch., Denver, 1982-83. Architect Cleetwood Toliet Facilities, 1984 (Honor award 1984); mem. design team U.S.G.S. Observatory, 1987 (Cert. Excellence 1987). Bd. dirs. East Denver YMCA, 1987-88; mem. US Forest Svc. Nat. Task Force, Washington, 1992. Recipient Svc. to Youth plaque East Denver YMCA, 1988, Parkhill NAACP Community Thank You plaque ParkHill Community, 1988., Cert. of Appreciation White River Nat. Forest, 1993. Mem. Associated Photographer Internat., Constrn. Stecification Inst., Internat. Conf. of Bldg. Officials, Alpha Phi Omega (1st v.p. 1977-78, Svc. award 1978, cert. 1982). Democrat. Baptist. Home: 9920 E Ohio Ave Denver CO 80231 Office: US Forest Svc 11177 W 8th Ave Lakewood CO 80225

BROWN, SHIRLEY ANNE, nurse; b. San Diego, Jan. 8, 1955; d. Martin Laurel and Beverly Jean (Eacock) B.; m. Dennis J. Van Beek, Aug. 4, 1990; 1 child, Daniel Martin. BS in Nursing magna cum laude, Seattle Pacific U., 1979; M in Nursing, U. Wash., 1984. RN, Wash. Staff nurse Swedish Hosp. Med. Ctr., Seattle, 1979-80, Ballard (Wash.) Community Hosp., 1980-83; nurse clinician Community Home Health Care, Seattle, 1983-89; clinician ambulatory care and specialist occupational health CHEC Med. Ctr., Seattle, 1989-91; clinician ambulatory care Sunrise Med. Ctr., Everett, 1991; clinic adminstr. Paine Field Occupational Medicine Clinic, Everett, 1991—; cons. in field; historian USAFR, Washington, 1988—, jr. v.p., 1989—. Vol. ARC, 1988. Capt. USAFR, 1985—. Mem. Am. Assn. Occupational Health Nurses (edn. chmn. 1984-85), USAF Assn., Reserve Officers Assn. (historian dept. Wash. 1988—, jr. v.p. 1989—, Seattle chpt. USAF committeeman 1987-90, v.p. Air Force 1991—), Assn. Mil. Surgeons U.S., Order of Eastern Star, Sigma Theta Tau. Methodist. Home: 6512 208th St SW Apt 9F Lynnwood WA 98036-7404 Office: Paine Field Occupational Medicine Clinic Everett WA 98203

BROWN, SPENCER L., surgeon; b. Boston, July 30, 1954; s. Samuel and Phyllis Lillian (Perlman); m. Lauren Carole Pinter, May 25, 1980; children: Joshua Samuel, Benjamin Harrison. BA, Brandeis U., 1972; MD, Boston U., 1986. Mem. staff UCLA Med. Ctr., 1980-87; surgeon L.A. Thorasic and Cardiovascular Assocs., 1987—. Mem. AMA, Am. Coll. Surgeons. Office: 2080 Century Park E # 1807 Los Angeles CA 90067

BROWN, STEPHANIE DIANE, psychologist, consultant, researcher; b. Mpls., July 19, 1944; d. Samuel Benjamin and Stephanie (Sanko) B.; m. Robert Francis Harris, Sept. 9, 1978; 1 child, Makenzie. BS, U. Calif., Berkeley, 1966; MS, Calif. State U., San Jose, 1974; PhD, Calif. Sch. Profl. Psychology, 1977. Advt. rep. Koratron Co., San Francisco, 1966-68; rsch. asst. Stanford Rsch. Inst., Menlo Park, Calif., 1968-69; rsch. analyst Baumeister & Dole, Palo Alto, Calif., 1969-70; rsch. assoc. dept. psychiatry Stanford (Calif.) U. Med. Sch., 1972-75; founder, dir. Stanford Alcohol Clinic, 1977-85; cons. psychologist, Menlo Park, 1986—; rsch. assoc. Mental Rsch. Inst., Palo Alto, 1989—; dir. The Addictions Inst., Menlo Park, 1989—; cons. Monte Villa Hosp., Gilroy, Calif., 1977-80, O'Connor Hosp., Campbell, Calif., 1984-87, Kids Are Spl., San Jose, Calif., 1986-88, Merritt Peralta Inst., Oakland, Calif., 1988-89. Author: Treating the Alcoholic, 1985, Treating Adult Children of Alcoholics, 1988, Adult Children of Alcoholics in Treatment, 1989, Safe Passage, 1991. Recipient Outstanding Instr. award Stanford U., 1980, Community Svc. award Calif. Soc., 1986; Bronze Key award Nat. Coun. on Alcoholism, 1983, Humanitarian award, 1984; Academic Specialist grantee, 1991. Mem. APA, Am. Group Psychotherapy Assn., Assn. for Med. Edn. and Rsch. in Substance Abuse, No. Calif. Group Psychotherapy Assn., Nat. Assn. for Children Alcoholics (adv. bd.). Democrat. Office: The Addictions Inst 445 Burgess Dr Menlo Park CA 94025-3442

BROWN, STEVEN BRIEN, radiologist; b. Ft. Collins, Colo., Jan. 18, 1952; s. Allen Jenkins and Shirley Irene (O'Brien) B.; m. Susan Jane DiTomaso, Sept. 10, 1983; children: Allison Grace, Laura Anne. BS, Colo. State U., 1974; MD, U. Calif., San Diego, 1978. Diplomate Am. Bd. Radiology, Radiol. Soc. N. Am. Intern U. Wash., Seattle, 1978-79; resident in radiology Stanford (Calif.) U., 1979-82; fellow in interventional and neuro-radiology Wilford Hall, USAF Med Ctr., San Antonio, 1982-83; staff radiologist Wilford Hall, USAF Med Ctr., 1983-86, Luth. Med. Ctr., Wheat Ridge, Colo., 1986—; chief angiography and interventional radiology Luth. Med. Ctr., 1987—, asst. chief dept. med. imaging, 1992—; pres. Luth. Med. Ctr. Joint Venture, 1992-93. Contbr. articles to profl. jours. Mem. Rep. Nat. Com., Washington, 1984—, Nat. Rep. Senatorial Com., 1985—, Rep. Presdl. Task Force, 1986—. Maj. USAF, 1982-86. Fellow Radiol. Soc. N.Am.; mem. Rocky Mt. Radiol. Soc., Am. Coll. Radiology, Soc. Cardiovascular and Interventional Radiology, Western Neuroradiol. Soc., Am. Soc. Neuroradiology, Colo. Preferred Physicians Orgn. (bd. dirs. 1987-89), World Wildlife Orgn., Colo. Angio Club. Republican. Presbyterian. Office: Luth Med Center 8300 W 38th Ave Wheat Ridge CO 80033-6099

BROWN, THOMAS ARCHER, artist; b. N.Y.C., Dec. 13, 1917; s. Lowell Huntington and Constance (McKelvey) B.; m. Katherine Jones, Dec. 16, 1940; children: Sara Stuart, Connie Pretti. Student, U. Laussane, Switzerland, N.Y. Sch. Fine and Applied Art, Colorado Springs Fine Arts Ctr, Colo. Represented at The Crespi Gallery, N.Y.C., Little Studio Ltd., N.Y.C., Liona Duncan Gallery, N.Y.C., Sante Fe Art Festival, The Paint Pot, Santa Fe, Contemporayy Art Gallery, N.Y.C., Paull Five Gallery, L.A., The Barn Gallery, Sante Fe, Greenville (S.C.) Mus. Art, Telfair Acad., Savanna, Ga., Ga. Mus. Art, Athens, The Morse Gallery Art, Winter Park, Fal., Fla. Union, Gainesville, Collectors of Am. Art, N.Y.C., William R. Mayer, Riverdale, N.Y.C., others. With U.S. Army, 1945-46. Home: PO Box 5392 Santa Fe NM 87502

BROWN, THOMAS HAROLD, French language educator; b. Copperton, Utah, July 23, 1930; s. Harold King and Emma (Featherstone) B.; m. Sheila Ann Dorius, June 30, 1955; children: Emma Rebecca, John B., Alison, Thomas C., Elizabeth, Michael. BA, Brigham Young U., 1955; MA, U. Ill., 1957, PhD, 1960. Prof. French Brigham Young U., Provo, Utah, 1959—; vis. prof. U. Ariz., Tucson, 1962, U. Colo., Boulder, 1968; Fulbright lectr. U.S. Govt., Canary Islands, Spain, 1965-66. Author: French, 1965, Langue et Littérature, 1967, Tranches de Vie, 1986, Pas à pas, 1991. Mem. MLA, Assn. Can. Studies in U.S. Democrat. Mormon. Home: 1635 N 1550 E Provo UT 84604-5734 Office: Brigham Young U 4004 Jesse Knight Hum Bldg Provo UT 84602

BROWN, THOMAS RAYMOND, marketing company executive; b. Hammond, Ind., Nov. 6, 1947; s. Harvey Raymond and Cristina (Frunzio) B.; m. Constance Gladys, June 17, 1972; children: Katherine, Elizabeth Anne. BA in Letters and Sci., U. Calif., Berkeley, 1972. Pvt. practice comml. photographer Tom Brown Photography, Oakland, Calif., 1972-78; various oper. dept. positions Western Pacific RR, San Francisco, 1978-80, gen. mgr., 1980-82; sr. v.p. intermodal Western Pacific RR, Oakland, Calif., 1982-83; pres. Riss Intermodal, Alameda, Calif., 1983—. Office: Riss Intermodal # 101 1100 Marina Village Pkwy Alameda CA 94501

BROWN, TIMOTHY DONELL, professional football player; b. Dallas, July 22, 1966. BA, U. Notre Dame, 1988. Wide receiver L.A. Raiders, 1988—. Recipient Heisman trophy, 1987. Office: L.A. Raiders 332 Center St El Segundo CA 90245

BROWN, TOD DAVID, bishop; b. San Francisco, Nov. 15, 1936; s. George Wilson and Edna Anne (Dunn) B. BA, St. John's Coll., 1958; STB, Gregorian U., Rome, 1960; MA in Theology, U. San Francisco, 1970, MAT in Edn., 1976. Dir. edn. Diocese of Monterey, Calif., 1970-80, vicar gen., clergy, 1980-82, chancellor, 1982-89, vicar gen., chancellor, 1983-89; pastor St. Francis Xavier, Seaside, Calif., 1977-82; bishop Roman Catholic Diocese of Boise, Idaho, 1989—. Named Papal Chaplain Pope Paul VI, 1975. Mem. Cath. Theol. Soc. Am., Cath. Biblical Assn., Canon Law Soc. Am., Equestrian Order of the Holy Sepulchre in Jerusalem. Office: Diocese of Boise 303 Federal Way Boise ID 83705

BROWN, WADE H., aerospace manufacturing executive; b. Glen Ridge, N.J., Sept. 22, 1940; s. John Henry and Kathryn A. (Nofsinger) Frankenbach B.; m. Katherine Manchester, May 17, 1991. BA in Chemistry, U. Ky., 1964. Rsch. chemist Geigy Rsch. Labs, Ardsley, N.Y., 1965-69; project mgr. Geigy Indsl. Chemicals, Ardsley, 1969-71; sr. salesman Ciba-Geigy Corp., Ardsley, 1971-74, product mgr., 1974-76, advt. dir., 1976-80; strategic planner Ciba-Geigy Corp., Basel, Switzerland, 1981-83; bus. mgr. Ciba-Geigy Corp., Fountain Valley, Calif., 1983-86; pres. ABB Composites Inc., Irvine, Calif., 1986-88, Rand Am. Corp., Irvine, 1988-90; dir. Kaiser Aerotech Corp., San Leandro, Calif., 1990—; dir. Polysil Inc., Chatsworth, Calif., 1985—. Patentee in field. County committeeman Conservative Party, N.Y.C., 1968-69. Sgt. U.S. Army, 1964-65. Fellow Am. Inst. Chemists; mem. Soc. for the Advancement Materials & Processes, Am. Soc. Metals, Am. Inst. Aero. & Astronautics, Sierra, U.S. Recreational Ski Assn. Republican. Episcopalian. Home: 20 Hall Dr Orinda CA 94563-3613 Office: Kaiser Aerotech Corp 880 Doolittle Dr San Leandro CA 94577-1020

BROWN, WALTER CREIGHTON, biologist; b. Butte, Mont., Aug. 18, 1913; s. D. Frank and Isabella (Creighton) B.; m. Jeanette Snyder, Aug. 20, 1950; children: Pamela Hawley, James Creighton, Julia Elizabeth. AB, Coll. Puget Sound, 1935, MA, 1938; PhD, Stanford U., 1950. Chmn. dept. Clover Park High Sch., Tacoma, Wash., 1938-42; acting. instr. Stanford U., Calif., 1949-50; instr. Northwestern U., Evanston, Ill., 1950-53; dean sci. Menlo Coll., Menlo Park, Calif., 1955-66, dean instrn., 1966-75; rsch. assoc., fellow Calif. Acad. Sci., San Francisco, 1978—; lectr. Sillman U., Philippines, 1954-55, dir. rsch. Program on Ecology and Systematics of Philippine Amphibians and Reptiles, 1958-74; ; vis. prof. biology Stanford U., 1962, 64, 66, 68, Harvard U., Cambridge, Mass., 1969, 72. Author: Philippine Lizards of the Family Gekkonidae, 1978, Philippine Lizards of the Family Scincidae, 1980, Lizards of the genus Emoia (Scincidae) with Observations of Their Evolution and Biogeography, 1991; contbr. 73 articles to profl. jours. Served with U.S. Army, 1942-46. Fellow AAAS; mem. Am. Soc. Ichthyologists and Herpetologists, Sigma Xi. Office: Calif Acad Scis Dept Herpetology Golden Gate Park San Francisco CA 94118-4501

BROWN, WALTER FRANKLIN, information systems executive; b. Phila., Apr. 3, 1952; s. Benjamin Franklin and Fidele Adeste (Van Beverhoudt) B.; m. Marie Magdalena Guerra, Aug. 8, 1971; 1 child, Angelique. AA in Acctg. and Data Processing, Chaffey Coll., Alta Loma, Calif., 1980; Diploma in Bibl. Studies, Pinecrest Bible Tng. Ctr., Salisbury Center, N.Y., 1984; BSBA, Calif. State Poly. U., 1984. From mfg. cons. to nat. mgr. tech. services Xerox Computer Services, Los Angeles, 1978-85, mgr., major account support, 1985-89, mgr. nat. account mktg., 1990-92; mgr. strategic planning Xerox Computer Svcs., L.A., 1992—. Deacon Ctrl. Assembly of God Ch., Ontario, Calif., 1985-88, First Assembly of God Ch., Chino, Calif., 1991—. Mem. Am. Mgmt. Assn., Data Processing Mgmt. Assn., Am. Prodn. and Inventory Control Soc. Democrat. Home: 11887 Roswell Ave Chino CA 91710-1547 Office: Xerox Computer Svcs 5310 Beethoven St Los Angeles CA 90066-7056

BROWN, WALTER FREDERICK, lawyer; b. L.A., July 28, 1926; s. Walter Andrew and Emily Anna (Weber) B.; m. Barbara Mae Porter Stahmann, Aug. 6, 1950; children: Jeffrey David, Kendall Paul, David Walter. BA, U. So. Calif., 1949, JD, 1952; MA, Boston U., 1961; MLS, U. Oreg., 1975. Bar: Calif. 1952, U.S Tax Ct. 1954, U.S. Supreme Ct. 1955, Oreg. 1981; cert. Am. Assn. Law Librarians. Assoc. prof. and law librarian Northwestern Sch. Law Lewis and Clark Coll., Portland, Oreg., 1970-80; mem. Oreg. Senate, Salem, 1975-87; gen. counsel Oreg. Consumer League, Portland, 1987-89; county counsel, dep. dist. atty. Malheur County, Vale, Oreg., 1989-91; dep. dist. atty. Gilliam County, Condon, Oreg., 1991—; gen. counsel Oreg. Consumer League, Portland, 1991—; chmn. Senate Agrl. and Forestry Com., 1985, Senate Task Force Vet.'s Home Loans, 1985-87; chmn., mem. capitol constrn. subcom. joint ways and means com., 1983, Senate Bus. and Consumer Affairs Com., 1981; senate co-chmn. Joint Legis. Counsel Com., 1979-87; mem. Legis. Emergency Bd., 1983-84; Senate co-vice chmn. Joint Trade and Econ. Devel. Com., 1985-87; commr. Gov.'s Commn. Sr. Services, 1985-87; vice chmn. Senate Judiciary Com., 1975, 79, 81, 83, 85, Labor Com., 1983, Elections Com., 1981. Contbr. articles to law jours. Pres. Clackamas County Citizens Assn., Oreg., 1974-74; asst. moderator Atkinson Meml. Ch., Unitarian Universalist; mem. state bd. Oreg. Common Cause; bd. dirs. Oreg. Consumer League; treas. United Consumers Oreg.; active Oreg. Hist. Soc. Comdr. JAGC, USN, 1944-70. Recipient Oreg. Civil Liberties Union award, 1983, Oreg. Environ. Council award, 1975, 79, 81, 83, 85, Trout Unltd. award Oregon City, 1975, Liberty award Oreg. Conf. Seventh-day Adventists, 1985. Mem. Am. Assn. Retired Persons, Oreg. State Coun. of Sr. Citizens, State Bar of Calif., Oreg. State Bar, Nat. Coalition Against the Misuse of Pesticides, Oreg. Natural Resources Coun., Consumers Union, Oreg. Fair Share, Pub. Concern Found., N.W. Coalition for Alternatives to Pesticides, Citizens Utility Bd. Oreg., Pub. Citizen, Natural Resources Def. Coun., Nat. Eagle Scout Assn., Oreg. Meml. Assn., Rachel Carson Coun., Am. Legion (award 1981, 82), VFW, Nat. Officers Assn., Ctr. for Sci. in the Pub. Interest, Oreg. Small Woodlands Assn., Sierra Club, Oreg. State Grange, Mazamas, Coalition for Free and Open Elections, United We Stand Am., Northwest Farmers Union, Masons, Delta Theta Phi, Phi Beta Kappa, Phi Kappa Phi, Kappa Sigma. Democrat. Unitarian Universalist. Home and Office: 16 SW Monticello Dr Lake Oswego OR 97035-1416

BROWN, WARREN SHELBURNE, JR., psychology educator; b. Loma Linda, Calif., Sept. 8, 1944; s. Warren Shelburne and Lois Marie (Jarzyna) B.; m. Janet Ann Lawson, Aug. 19, 1966; children: Warren Shelburne III, Charise Leanne. BA, Point Loma Coll., 1966; MA, U. So. Calif., 1969, PhD, 1971. Postdoctoral trainee UCLA Brain Rsch. Inst., 1971-73; instr. Point Loma Coll., San Diego, 1970-75; asst. rsch. psychologist dept. psychiatry UCLA, 1973-75, prof. dept. psychiatry, 1975-82; prof. psychology Fuller Grad. Sch. Psychology, Pasadena, Calif., 1982—; mem. UCLA Brain Rsch. Inst., 1973—; guest prof. neurology Univ. Hosp., Zurich, Switzerland, 1976-77; vis. scholar dept. comm. and neurosci. U. Keele, U.K., 1986; dir. Travis Inst. for Biopsychosocial Rsch., Pasadena. Contbr. chpt. to The Dual Brain, 1985; over 40 rsch. articles. Recipient Career Devel. award NIMH, Bethesda, Md., 1975-80; participant Program for Exch. Scientists, NSF, Washington, 1986. Mem. AAAS, APA, Soc. Psychophysiol. Rsch., Internat. Neuropsychol. Soc., N.Y. Acad. Sci. Democrat. Nazarene. Office: Fuller Grad Sch Psychology 180 N Oakland Ave Pasadena CA 91101

BROWN, WILLIAM EDWIN, construction executive, educator; b. Belknap, Ill., Jan. 11, 1934; s. Samuel Edwin and Sarah Elizabeth (Kean) B. BS, So. Ill. U., 1956, MS, 1957; PhD, Ohio State U., 1964. Asst. instr. So. Ill. U., Carbondale, 1955-56; instr. U. Tenn., Knoxville, 1956-57; asst. prof. Ohio Sate U., Columbus, 1957-64, asst. to dean, 1964-67; prof. Trenton State Coll., N.J., 1967-76; regional dir. State of Calif., Sacramento, 1976-80; owner Dial One Bear Tavern Construction, Inc., Sacramento, 1979—; seminar dir. Dial One of No. Calif., 1985—; part-time prof. Calif State U., Sacramento, 1986—. Adv. Phi Alpha Delta, Trenton State Coll. Served with USAR, 1955-62. Mem. Am. Soc. Engring. Educators, Optimist (v.p. 1965-67), Phi Delta Kappa, Epsilon Phi Tau. Republican. Methodist. Home: 1110 Sierra Dr Sacramento CA 95864-4924

BROWN, WILLIAM ERNEST, retail executive; b. Sydney, N.S., Can., Aug. 21, 1929. Grad., Sydney Acad., 1948; student, Dalhousie U., Halifax, N.S. V.p. Brown's Jewellers Ltd., Sydney, 1950-70; pres. William Ernest Brown Ltd., Beverly Hills, Calif., 1970—; chmn. William Ernest Brown of Beverly Hills, Inc., 1989—. Author: Cosmetic Surgery, 1970, 2d edit., 1980. Mem. Copeley Soc. Boston. Office: William Ernest Brown Inc 442 N Canon Dr Beverly Hills CA 90210

BROWN, WILLIAM OSCAR, retired railroad executive; b. El Paso, Tex., May 16, 1915; s. Benjamin McCulloch and Alice Lillian (Drisdale) B.; m. Phyllis Ann Disano, July 6, 1940; children: William Drisdale, Marcia Jean. BSME, Rice U., 1937; postgrad., Stanford U., 1958, MIT, 1964. Registered profl. engr. With So. Pacific Transp. Co., 1937—; asst. supt. motive power So. Pacific Transp. Co., Sacramento, 1955-58, supt. mech. dept., 1959-67; asst. chief mech. officer So. Pacific Transp. Co., San Francisco, 1968-69, chief mech. officer, 1970-78, ret., 1978; mech. adv. mem. Trailer Train Corp., Chgo., 1970-78, Assn. Am. R.R. mech. divsn., Washington, 1970-78. Mem. ASME, So. Pacific Ret. Execs. Club (pres. 1987-88), Green Hills Country Club, Engrs. Club San Francisco. Republican. Baptist. Address: 1130 Murchison Dr Millbrae CA 94030

BROWN, YVONNE MARGARET ROSE, nursing educator, dean; b. Strasbourg, Sask., Can., Nov. 19, 1940; d. Ernest Brör and Isabella Margareta (Johanson) Forsman; m. F. Barry Brown, June 22, 1963; children: Tanya Lee Cestnick, Tyson Barry. BS in Nursing, U. Sask., Saskatoon, 1963, BA, 1969, M in Continuing Edn., 1983. RN. Gen. duty nurse Univ. Hosp., Saskatoon, 1963-64, 69-74; lectr. anatomy and physiology Centralized Teaching Program, Saskatoon, 1964-66; clin. instr. obstetrical nursing U. Sask., Saskatoon, 1966-67, lectr. nursing, 1975-83, asst. prof., 1983-88, assoc. prof., 1988-93, dean coll. nursing, 1990—, prof., 1993—; mem. steering com. nursing to Minister of Health, Regina, Sask., 1990—; mem. adv. com. nursing edn. to Minister of Health, Regina, 1988-89. Author: (with others) Perinatal Crisis of the Rural Saskatchewan Family, 1990; contbr. articles to profl. jours.; producer: (videotapes) Leopold's Maneuvers and Auscultation of Fetal Heart Sounds, 1983 (Amtec Award Excellence 1984), Postpartum Assessment, 1985 (Amtec Chmns. Choice award 1986), Thinking About Nursing?, 1988. Coord. Perinatal Loss Support Group, Saskatoon, 1983-90; founder, coord. Baby Loss Support Group, Saskatoon, 1988-89. Undergrad. scholar U. Saskatchewan, 1953, 59, 62, grad. studies scholar U. Saskatchewan, 1980; rsch. grantee U. Saskatchewan, 1988, Royal Univ. Hosp., 1990. Mem. Can. Nurses Assn., Can. Assn. Univ. Schs. Nursing, Saskatchewan RN Assn., Nursing Edn. Spl. Interest Group. Office: U Saskatchewan, Coll Nursing, Saskatoon, SK Canada S7N 0W0

BROWNE, JOSEPH PETER, librarian; b. Detroit, June 12, 1929; s. George and Mary Bridget (Fahy) B.; A.B., U. Notre Dame, 1951; S.T.L., Pontificium Athenaeum Angelicum, Rome, 1957, S.T.D., 1960; MS in L.S., Cath. U. Am., 1965. Joined Congregation of Holy Cross, Roman Cath. Ch., 1947, ordained priest, 1955; asst. pastor Holy Cross Ch., South Bend, Ind., 1955-56; libr., prof. moral theology Holy Cross Coll., Washington, 1959-64; mem. faculty U. Portland (Oreg.), 1964-73, 75—, dir. libr., 1966-70, 76—, dean Coll. Arts and Scis., 1970-73, asso. prof. libr. sci. 1967—, regent, 1969-70, 77-81, chmn. acad. senate, 1968-70, 1987-88; prof., head dept. libr. sci. Our Lady of Lake Coll., San Antonio, 1973-75; chmn. Interstate Libr. Planning Coun., 1977-79. Mem. Columbia River chpt. Huntington's Disease Soc. Am., 1975-90, pres., 1979-82; pastor St. Birgitta Ch., Portland, 1993—. Recipient Culligan award U. Portland, 1979. Mem. Cath. Libr. Assn. (life, pres. 1971-73), ALA, Cath. Theol. Soc. Am., Pacific N.W. Libr. Assn. (pres. 1985-86), Oreg. Libr. Assn. (pres. 1967-68), Nat. Assn. Parliamentarians, Oreg. Assn. Parliamentarians (pres. 1985-87), Archdiocesan Hist. Commn. (pres. 1985-90), Mensa Internat., All-Ireland Cultural Soc. Oreg. (pres. 1984-85). Democrat. Club: KC. Home: 11820 NW Saint Helens Rd Portland OR 97231 Office: U Portland 5000 N Willamette Blvd Portland OR 97203-5750

BROWNE, MARY STEPHANIE, counselor, therapist; b. Milw., Nov. 1, 1963; d. Richardson E. and Jeannie (Jones) B. BA in Criminal Justice, U. N.Mex., 1986; M in Counseling magna cum laude, Webster U., 1992. Lic. social worker. Dir. child care programs YMCA, Albuquerque, 1984-87; probation officer Laguna (N.Mex.) Indian Pueblo, 1987-88; dir., therapist Hogares, Inc., Albuquerque, 1988-92; teen and family counselor, dir. Mountainside YMCA, Albuquerque, 1992—; speaker in field. Active Big

Bros./Big Sisters, 1984—, Greater Albuquerque Vol. Assn., 1992—; juvenile probation vol., 1984-86; charity ball project dir. Hogares Silverhouse, 1987-88; bd. dirs. YMCA, 1988-92, sec., 1988-92; bd. dirs. YMCA Leadership Club, 1984—; judge academic decathalon Albuquerque Pub. Schs., 1989—; mem. steering com. Albuquerque Gang Task Force, 1993—; bd. dirs. Child Abuse Prevention Assn. Albuquerque, 1992—, v.p., 1993—; dir. Hoover Middle Sch. Initiative for High Risk Students "Fade to Reality" Video Program, 1992—; mentor for pregnant teens YWCA, 1992—. Recipient Woman on the Move award YWCA, Albuquerque, 1988. Episcopalian. Home: 3003 Adams Albuquerque NM 87110 Office: Mountainside YMCA 12500 Comanche NE Albuquerque NM 87111

BROWNE, STEVEN EMERY, video editor; b. New Haven, Dec. 23, 1950; s. Robert Walter and Sara Elizabeth Brown; m. Michele Catherine Osterhout, June 16, 1979; children: Nikole, Kristopher, Kate. BS in TV/Radio, Ithaca Coll., 1973; postgrad., U. So. Calif., 1973-74. Page NBC, Burbank, Calif., 1975; apprentice editor Sta. KNBC-TV, Burbank, 1975; prodn. asst. Komack Co., Los Angeles, 1975-77; asst. editor Bob Best's Producers TV Services, Los Angeles, 1977; freelance editor Los Angeles, 1977-79; staff editor Video Transitions, Hollywood, Calif., 1979-86, sr. staff editor, 1986-87; staff editor Encore Video, Inc., Hollywood, 1987-88, Modern Videofilm, Hollywood, 1988-89; sr. editor Video Rsch. Corp., 1990-92; supervising editor New Wave Prodns., Hollywood, Calif., 1992—; cons. EECO Video Systems, 1984-86. Author: Video Tape Post Production Primer, 1982, 2d edit., 1993, Getting That Job In Hollywood, 1983, Video Editing, 1988, 2d edit., 1993, Film/Video Terms and Concepts, 1992. Mem. Internat. Alliance of Theatrical Stage Employees, Film and Video Tape Editors Guild. Office: 910 N Citrus Ave Los Angeles CA 90038-2402

BROWNE, WALTER SHAWN, journalist, chess player; b. Sydney, Australia, Jan. 10, 1949; s. Walter Francis and Hilda Louis (Leahy) B.; m. Raquel Emilse Facal, Mar. 9, 1973; 1 stepson, Marcello Facal. Grad. high sch. Chess player, 1957—, U.S. jr. champion, 1966, Australian champion, 1968-69, U.S. Open champion, 1971-73, Nat. Open champion, 1971-73, 75, 84, 86-87, 91, U.S. champion, 1974-78, 80-83, Pan-Am. champion, 1974, Internat. German champion, 1975, mem. U.S. Olympic Team, 1974, 78, 82, 84, Nat. and U.S. Open Blitz chess champion, 1989, Pan-Pacific Blitz chess champion, 1991; columnist Chess Life & Rev., Berkeley, Calif., 1973—; lectr. in field. Publisher: Strongest International Chess Tourneys, 1978-85; editor in chief quar. mag. Blitz Chess. Named Internat. Master Fedn. Internat. des Eshecs, 1969, Internat. Grandmaster, 1969; 1st pl. Venice, 1971; 1st pl. Rejkavik, Iceland, 1978; 1st pl. Wijk Am. Zee, Holland, 1974, 80; 1st pl. Indonesia, 1982; 2d-3d World Open, Phila., 1988; only 8 time winner Nat. Open, Can. Open champion, 1991, U.S. class champion, 1991' 6 time American Open champion. Mem. World Blitz Chess Assn. (pres., founder, pub., editor Blitz Chess 1988—). Address: 8 Parnassus Rd Berkeley CA 94708

BROWNELL, JEFF ALLEN, artist; b. Sacramento, July 10, 1953; s. Warren Ellsworth and Barbara (Hussey) B.; m. Debra Richards (div. Jan. 1980); children: Sarah Ann, Jessica Jane; m. Erika Stefka Wyniarcuk, Jan. 10, 1981; 1 child, Andreya Alvina. Student, Sierra Coll., Rocklin, Calif., 1972-74. coord. Evening for the Arts, South Lake Tahoe, Calif., 1989-90; founder Artist in Motion, South Lake Tahoe, 1991-92, Artist Underground, South Lake Tahoe, 1991-92; coord., founder Native Am. Ann. Pow-Wow Art Show, South Lake Tahoe, 1991-92. Artist: People of the Washo, 1991-92, Petroglyphs/Sacred Places, 1991-92, Don't Look Down Series, Mountain Tops/Lake Tahoe, 1989-92. Mem. Artvision (v.p. 1991-92), Tahoe Tallac Assn. (coord. arts 1988-92), Artist Underground (pres. 1990-92) Tahoe Art League (promoter art shows 1992). Home: PO Box 9984 South Lake Tahoe CA 96158

BROWNHILL, BUD H., canine behavior therapist; b. Fort Erie, Ont., Can., May 22, 1941; came to U.S., 1958; s. Charles B. and June M. (Ott) B. Student, Fullerton (Calif.) Coll., 1960-62, Fanshaw Coll., London, Ont. Can., 1971-73, Brock U., Ont., Can., 1977. Cert. canine behavior therapist in aggression solving, trainer, Calif. Owner Brownhill Basics Dog Tng., N.Y., Ariz., Calif., Can., Dogs-Calif. Tng., Anaheim, 1988—; presenter seminars to dog tng. assns. in U.S. and Can.; speaker on dog-bite prevention to various orgns. lectr. seminars on dog tng. anti-aggression to tng. assns. and pvt. industry, U.S. A. and Can. Recipient High in Trials awards Am. Kennel Club, Can. Kennel Club, Bermuda Kennel Club, Mex. Kennel Club; winner U.S. Chesapeake Nat., 1989, Shuffle Bd. Champion, 1980; 1st pl. Gaines Western U.S. Obedience Championship, 1985, 3d pl. tie World Series Obedience Competition, 1985; recipient Calif. State award, Golden State award. Mem. NRA, Calif. Handlers Advanced Obedience Handling Soc., Internat. Platform Assn., Am. Amateur Trap-Shooting Assn. (class winner 1978, 79), Long Beach German Shepherd Club (obedience chmn. 1985-90), Dog Owners Internat. Travel (internat. chmn. 1987-90), Doberman Club (Santa Ana, obedience cons. 1984-86), Orange Coast Obedience Club (program dir. 1984), Can. Nat. Assn. (provincial rep. 1980). Office: Dogs-Calif Tng 2230 W Colchester Dr # 14 Anaheim CA 92804-4286

BROWNING, JAMES ROBERT, federal judge; b. Great Falls, Mont., Oct. 1, 1918; s. Nicholas Henry and Minnie Sally (Foley) B.; m. Marie Rose Chapell. BA, Mont. State U., Missoula, 1938; LLB with honors, U. Mont., 1941, LLD (hon.), 1961; LLD (hon.), Santa Clara U., 1989. Bar: Mont. 1941, D.C. 1950, U.S. Supreme Ct. 1952. Spl. atty. antitrust div. Dept. Justice, 1941-43, spl. atty. gen. litigation sect. antitrust div., 1946-48, chief antitrust dept. N.W. regional office, 1948-49; asst. chief gen. litigation sect. antitrust div. Dept. Justice (N.W. regional office), 1949-51, 1st asst. civil div., 1951-52; exec. asst. to atty. gen. U.S., 1952-53; chief U.S. (Exec. Office for U.S. Attys.), 1953; pvt. practice Washington, 1953-58; lectr. N.Y.U. Sch. Law, 1953, Georgetown U. Law Center, 1957-58; clk. Supreme Ct. U.S., 1958-61; judge U.S. Ct. Appeals 9th Circuit, 1961—, chief judge, 1976-88; mem. Jud. Conf. of U.S., 1976-88, exec. com. of conf., 1978-87, com. on internat. conf. of appellate judges, 1987-90, com. on ct. adminstrn., 1969-71, chmn. subcom. on jud. stats., 1969-71, com. on the budget, 1971-77, adminstrn. office, subom. on budget, 1974-76, com. to study U.S. jud. conf., 1986-88, com. to study the illustrative rules of jud. misconduct, 1985-87, com. on formulation of standard of conduct of fed. judges, 1969, Reed justice com. on cont. edn., tng. and adminstrn., 1967-68; David T. Lewis Disting. Judge-in-residence, U. Utah, 1987; Blankenbaker lectr. U. Mont., 1987, Sibley lectr. U. Ga., 1987, lectr. Human Rights Inst. Santa Clara U. Sch. Law, Strasbourg. Editor-in-chief, Mont. Law Rev. Dir. Western Justice Found.; chmn. 9th Cir. Hist. Soc. 1st lt. U.S. Army, 1943-46. Decorated Bronze Star; named to Order of the Grizzly, U. Mont., 1973; scholar in residence Santa Clara U., 1989, U. Mont., 1991; recipient Devitt Disting. Svc. to Justice award, 1990. Fellow ABA (judge adv. com. to standing com. on Ethics and Profl. Responsibility 1973-75); mem. D.C. Bar Assn., Mont. Bar Assn., Am. Law Inst., Fed. Bar Assn. (bd. dirs 1945-61, Nat. council 1958-62), Inst. Jud. Adminstrn., Am. Judicature Soc. (chmn. com. on fed. judiciary 1973-74, bd. dirs. 1972-75), Herbert Harley award 1984), Am. Soc. Legal History (adv. bd. jour.), Nat Lawyers Club (bd. govs. 1959-63). Office: US Ct Appeals 9th Cir PO Box 193939 San Francisco CA 94119-3939

BROWNING, JESSE HARRISON, entrepreneur; b. Kingsville, Mo., July 27, 1935; s. Jesse Harrison and Anna Love (Swank) B.; m. Vicki Carol Thompson, Dec. 21, 1957; children: Caroline Kaye, Marcia Lynn, Nanci Ann, Susan Louise. Student, U. Wash., 1955-61; MPA, U. So. Calif., 1988. Cert. mfg. engr. Field engr. The Boeing Co., Los Angeles, 1961-64; gen. mgr. SPI, Los Angeles, 1964-70; chmn. Browning Inc., Los Angeles, 1970—, Indsl. Systems, Los Angeles, 1979-87, Vapor Engring., Los Angeles, 1979-87. Patentee in field. Mem. Palos Verdes Breakfast Club, Los Angeles C. of C., Am. Helicopter Soc., Am. Electroplaters Soc., Soc. Mfg. Engrs. Lutheran. Home and Office: 16301 Inglewood Rd NE Bothell WA 98011-3908

BROWNING, WILLIAM DOCKER, federal judge; b. Tucson, Az., May 19, 1931; s. Horace Benjamin and Mary Louise (Docker) B.; m. Courteny Browning (div.); children: Christopher, Logan, Courtenay; m. Zerilda Sinclair, Dec. 17, 1974; 1 child, Benjamin. BBA, U. Ariz., 1954, LLB, 1960. Bar: Ariz. 1960, U.S. Dist. Ct. Ariz. 1960, U.S. Ct. Appeals (9th cir.) 1965, U.S. Supreme Ct. 1967. Pvt. practice Tucson, 1960-84; judge U.S. Dist. Ct., Tucson, 1984—; mem. jud. nominating com. appellate ct. appointments, 1975-79. Del. 9th Cir. Jud. Conf., 1968-77, 79-82; trustee Inst. for Ct. Mgmt., 1978-84; mem. Ctr. for Pub. Resources Legal Program. 1st lt. USAF, 1954-57, capt. USNG, 1958-61. Fellow Am. Coll. Trial Lawyers, Am. Bar Found.; mem. ABA (spl. com. housing and urban devel. law 1973-76, com. urban problems and human affairs 1978-80), Ariz. Bar Assn. (chmn. merit selection of judges com. 1973-76, bd. gove. 1968-74, pres. 1972-73, Outstanding Mem. 1980), Pima County Bar Assn. (exec. com. 1964-68, med. legal screening panel 1965-75, pres. 1967-68), Am. Bd. Trial Advocates, Am. Judicature Soc. (bd. dirs. 1975-77), Fed. Judges Assn. (bd. dirs.). Office: US Dist Ct US Courthouse Rm 301 55 E Broadway Blvd Tucson AZ 85701-1719

BROWNLEE, WILSON ELLIOT, JR., history educator; b. Lacrosse, Wis., May 10, 1941; s. Wilson Elliot Sr. and Pearl (Woodings) B.; m. Mary Margaret Cochran, June 25, 1966; children: Charlotte Louise, Martin Elliot. BA, Harvard U., 1963; MA, U. Wis., 1965, PhD, 1969. Asst. prof. U. Calif., Santa Barbara, 1967-74, assoc. prof., 1974-80, prof. history, 1980—; vis. prof. Princeton (N.J.) U., 1980-81; chmn. dept. history U. Calif., Santa Barbara, 1984-87, acad. senate, 1983-84, 88-90, systemwide acad. senate, 1992-93; acting dir. U. Calif.-Santa Barbara Ctr., Washington, 1990-91; chmn. exec. com. dels. Am. Coun. Learned Socs., N.Y.C., 1988-90, bd. dirs.; bd. dirs. Nat. Coun. on Pub. History, Boston; bicentennial lectr. U.S. Dept. Treasury, 1989; faculty rep. U. Calif. Bd. Regents, 1991-93.. Author: Dynamics of Ascent, 1974, 79, Progressivism and Economic Growth, 1974; co-author: Women in the American Economy, 1976, Essentials of American History, 1976, 80, 86, America's History, 1987, 93. Chair schs. com. Harvard Club, Santa Barbara, 1971-80, 85, 86; pres. Assn. for Retarded Citizens, Santa Barbara, 1982-84; 1st v.p. Assn. for Retarded Citizens Calif., Sacramento, 1983-84; pres. Santa Barbara Trust for Hist. Preservation, Santa Barbara, 1986-87. Charles Warren fellow Harvard U., 1978-79, fellow Woodrow Wilson Ctr., Washington, 1987-88; recipient Spl. Commendation, Calif. Dept. Parks and Recreation, 1988. Mem. Am. Hist. Assn., Orgn. Am. Historians, Econ. History Assn., Am. Tax Policy Inst. Office: U Calif Dept History Santa Barbara CA 93106

BROWNSTEIN, RONALD JAY, correspondent; b. N.Y.C., Apr. 6, 1958; s. David Leo and Shirley Hannah (Burkhoff) B.; m. Nina J. Easton, May 27, 1983; 1 child, Taylor David. BA in English Lit., SUNY, Binghamton, 1979. Chief staff writer Ralph Nader, Washington, 1979-83; polit. corr. Nat. Jour., Washington, 1983-86, West Coast corr., 1986-89; nat. polit. corr. L.A. Times, 1990—. Author: The Power and The Glitter, The Hollywood-Washington Connection, 1991; co-author: Reagan's Ruling Class, 1982, Who's Poisoning America, 1981. Recipient Exceptional Merit in Media award Nat. Women's Polit. Caucus, 1989; U.S. Japan Soc. Leadership fellow, 1993. Office: Los Angeles Times Times Mirror Sq Los Angeles CA 90012-3816

BROWN-STIGGER, ALBERTA MAE, respiratory clinician; b. Columbus, Ohio, Nov. 11, 1932; d. Sylvester Clarence and Malinda (Mason) Angel; grad. Antelope Valley Coll., 1961; AA, L.A. Valley Coll., 1975; BS, Calif. State U., Dominguez Hills, 1981; m. Norman Brown, Dec. 29, 1967 (dec. Jan. 1989); children: Charon, Charles, Stevan, Carole; m. A.C. Stigger, June 14, 1992. Nurses aid, vocat. nurse, respiratory therapist St. Bernardines Hosp., 1965-69, Good Samaritan Hosp., L.A., 1969-70, Midway Hosp., L.A., 1973-81; allergy nurse, instr. respiratory therapy VA Hosp., L.A., 1970—, also acting dept. head; nurse, respiratory splty. unit Jerry L. Pettis Meml. Hosp., Loma Linda, Calif., 1984—; instr. L.A. Valley Med. Technoogists Sch., Compton Coll. seminar instr., 1979. Active Arrowhead Allied Arts Coun. of San Bernardino; CPR instr. Am. Heart Assn. Lic. vocat. nurse; R.N. Mem. Am. Assn. Respiratory Therapy, Nat. Honor Soc., Eta Phi Beta. Democrat. Baptist. Clubs: Social-Lites, Inc. of San Bernardino, (pres.) Order Eastern Star. Patentee disposable/replaceable tubing for stethoscope. Home: Orangewood Estates 1545 N Hancock St San Bernardino CA 92411 Office: Jerry L Pettis JA Hosp Loma Linda CA 92357

BRUBAKER, CRAWFORD FRANCIS, JR., government official, aerospace consultant; b. Fruitland, Idaho, Apr. 23, 1924; s. Crawford Francis and Cora Susan (Flora) B.; m. Lucile May Christensen, May 5, 1945; children: Eric Stephen, Alan Kenneth, Craig Martin, Paul David. BA, Pomona Coll., 1946; MBA, U. Pa., 1948. Office mgr. Lockheed Calif. Co., Burbank, 1948-54, sales adminstr., 1954-57, with fighter contracts div., field office rep., 1959-65, asst. dir. fighter sales, 1965-69, dep. mgr. bid and proposals, 1969-74, mgr. govt. sales, 1974-76; dir. internat. mktg. devel. and policy Lockheed Corp., Burbank, 1976-83; dep. asst. sec. for aerospace U.S. Dept. Commerce, Washington, 1983-87; internat. aerospace cons., 1987—; vice chmn. Industry Sector Adv. Com., Washington, 1979-83; mem. Aero. Policy Rev. Com., Washington, 1983-87. Vice chmn. So. Calif. Dist. Export Coun., L.A., 1980-83, 88-91, chmn., 1992—. Lt. (j.g.) USN, 1943-45, PTO. Mem. AIAA, Am. Defense Preparedness Assn., Sigma Alpha Epsilon. Republican. Presbyterian.

BRUBAKER, JOHN E., bank executive; b. 1941. CEO 1st Bank Ill., Chgo., 1967-89; chmn. bd., pres., CEO, dir. Ctrl. Bank Walnut Creek, Calif., 1989-92; COO, sr. exec. v.p., now pres., CEO Bay View Fed. Bank, San Mateo, Calif., 1992—. Office: Bay View Federal Bank 2121 S El Camino Real San Mateo CA 94403

BRUCE, CAROL, museum professional; b. Bedford, Ind., Sept. 22, 1954; d. Robert Dean and Dorothy Rae (Faulk) Bruce; 1 child, Martin Richard Linville II. BA in Communications, U. Colo., 1980, BA in U.S. History, 1980. Pub. info. coord Pikes Peak Libr. Dist., Colorado Springs, Colo., 1980-85; prog. coord. Colorado Springs Pioneers Mus., Colorado Springs, 1985—; cons. in pub. rels. Editor tchrs. manual: A Teacher's Guide, 1990. Chmn. Springspree Festival, Colorado Springs, 1988—; mem. Festival of Lights steering com., Colorado Springs, 1988—; steering com. Kennedy Ctr. Imagination Cel., 1988—. NEH grantee, 1987; Kellogg Found. fellow, 1986, 87. Mem. Am. Assn. Mus. United Ch. of Christ.

BRUCE, DICKSON DAVIES, JR., history educator; b. Dallas, Apr. 11, 1946; s. Dickson Davies and Helen (Woodcock) B.; m. Mary Macreeda Watson, Sept. 28, 1967; 1 child, Emily Sarah. BA, U. Tex., 1967; MA, U. Pa., Phila., 1968, PhD, 1971. Prof. history U. Calif., Irvine, 1971—. Author: And They All Sang Hallelujah, 1974, Violence and Culture in the Antebellum South, 1979, The Rhetoric of Conservatism, 1982, Black Writing From the Nadir, 1989, Archibald Grimké, 1993. Recipient James Mooney award So. Anthropol. Soc., 1973, Huntington Libr. Fellowship, San Marino, Calif., 1975, Fulbright Lectureship USIA, Szeged, Hungary, 1987-88. Mem. Orgn. Am. Historians, Soc. Historians of Early Am. Republic, So. Hist. Assn. Democrat. Office: U Calif Irvine CA 92717

BRUCE, JOHN ALLEN, foundation executive, educator; b. Kansas City, Mo., Sept. 17, 1934; BA, Wesleyan U., Middletown, Conn., 1956; MDiv, Gen. Theol. Sem., N.Y.C., 1959; PhD, U. Minn., 1972. Ordained to ministry Episcopal Ch., 1959. Clergyman, 1959-68; prof. U. Ala., Tuscaloosa, 1972-74; exec. dir. E.C. Brown Found., Portland, Oreg., 1974—; cons. to philanthropies and corp. programs; clin. prof. community medicine Sch. Medicine, Oreg. Health Scis. U., Portland, 1976—. Author, editor various scholarly publs. Exec. producer various ednl. films on family life, health and values. Bd. dirs. various community orgns. Served to lt. USN, 1964-67. Recipient various awards and grants from med. orgns. and related groups. Mem. Nat. Coun. on Family Rels. (Disting. Service to Families award 1979), Oreg. Coun. on Family Rels. (pres. 1981), Cosmos Club. Republican. Office: EC Brown Found 101 SW Main St Ste 500 Portland OR 97204

BRUCE, ROBERT KIRK, college administrator; b. Evanston, Ill., Nov. 7, 1942; s. Robert Kirk and Irma Bertha (Roese) B.; m. Judith Lee Chjlopecki, July 13, 1968; children: Michael, James, Suzanne, Gary, Meredith. BS in Edn., No. Ill. U., DeKalb, 1967; MA, Ctrl. Mich. U., Mt. Pleasant, 1972, EdS, 1974. Edn. writer Rockford (Ill.) Morning Star, 1969-70; coord. News Bur. Ctrl. Mich. U., Mt. Pleasant, 1970-75; dir. News Bur. U. Oreg., Eugene, 1975-78; dir. univ. rels. Kans. State U., Manhattan, 1978-82; dir. univ. info. U. Nebr., Lincoln, 1982-89; asst. v.p. Oreg. State U., Corvallis, 1989—; cons. U. Ariz., Tucson, 1984, Barton County C.C., Great Bend, Kans., 1984, Glassboro (N.J.) State Coll., 1988. Mem. Mayor's Task Force on Pub. Artwork, Manhattan, Kans., 1981; bd. dirs. Lincolnfest Celebration, Lincoln, Nebr., 1983-87, Oreg. Spl. Olympics, 1976-78. With USNR, 1965-73. Recipient Pub. Rels. awards ACPRA, AAC, Washington, 1971-74. Mem. Coun. for Advancement and Support of Edn. (medal awards 1980—), Am. Legion, Lincoln C. of C. (chmn. com. 1983-89), Century Club (bd. dirs. 1990—). Democrat. Roman Catholic. Home: 1075 Charlemagne Pl NW Corvallis OR 97330 Office: Oreg State U AdS 524 Corvallis OR 97331

BRUCE, THOMAS EDWARD, thanatologist, psychology educator; b. Vinton, Iowa, Dec. 3, 1937; s. George Robert and Lucille Etta (Aurner) B.; m. Mary A. Bohner, Jan. 29, 1969 (div. 1990); children: Scott Thomas and Suzanne Laura (twins). BA, U. No. Iowa, 1961, MA, 1964; postgrad., U. Colo., 1968-71; MA, U. San Francisco, 1985. Lic. psychology educator, counselor, Calif. Tchr. various Iowa high schs., 1961-65; sociologist, counselor Office Econ. Opportunity, Denver, 1965-66; social sci. educator Arapahoe Coll., Littleton, Colo., 1966-69; lectr. U. Colo., Boulder, 1968-71; psychology educator Sacramento City Coll., Calif., 1972—; thanatology cons. for hospices, survivor support groups, No. Calif., 1984—. Author: Grief Management: The Pain and the Promise, 1986, Thanatology: Through the Veil, 1992; contbr. articles to profl. publs. Co-founder, bd. dirs. Bereavement Resources Network, Sacramento, 1983-87; profl. dir. Children's Respite Ctr., Sacramento, 1985-88; pres.-elect., bd. dirs. Hospice Care of Sacramento, 1979-85. With U.S. Army, 1955-58. Recipient Pres.'s award Nat. Hospice Orgn., 1985. Mem. Sacramento Mental Health Assn. (Vol. Svc. award 1985, 87), Assn. for Death Edn. and Counseling, Thanatology Found., Am. Fedn. Tchrs., Faculty Assn. Calif. C.C.'s, Pi Gamma Mu, Phi Delta Kappa. Presbyterian. Office: Sacramento City Coll 3537 Freeport Blvd Sacramento CA 95822

BRUCH, JOHN CLARENCE, JR., engineer, educator; b. Kenosha, Wis., Oct. 11, 1940; m. Susan Jane Tippett, Aug. 19, 1967. BCE, U. Notre Dame, 1962; MCE, Stanford U., 1963, PhD in Civil Engring., 1966. Acting instr. engring. Stanford (Calif.) U., 1966; asst. prof. engring. U. Calif., Santa Barbara, 1966-74, assoc. prof. engring., 1974-78, prof. engring., 1978—. Grantee NSF, 1987-92, faculty grantee U. Calif., 1968. Mem. Am. Soc. Civil Engrs., Sigma Xi, Tau Beta Pi. Office: U Calif Mech Engring Dept Santa Barbara CA 93106

BRUCK, GLENN R., geologist; b. Mpls., Nov. 17, 1956; s. Wilbur L. and Wendy Bruck. BSc, U. Wis., 1979; MSc, Ariz. State U., 1983. Cert. profl. geologist, Ind. Geologist Péwé Assocs., Tempe, Ariz., 1981, Ariz. Dept. Water Resources, Phoenix, 1982-83; geologist region V U.S. EPA, Chgo., 1983-84; geologist region X U.S. EPA, Seattle, 1984—; mem. faculty South Seattle Community Coll., 1990—, Green Rive Community Coll., Auburn, Wash., 1992—. Author: (portolio and maps) Engineering Geology in Arizona, 1982. Counselor Boy Scouts Am., Hudson, Wis., 1977-79, counselor, Seattle, 1990—. Rsch. grantee Ariz. State U., 1981. Mem. Geol. Soc. Am. (agy. rep. 1988—), Am. Geophys. Union, Assn. Ground Water Scientists and Engrs., N.W. Geol. Soc., Gamma Theta Upsilon Internat. Office: US EPA 1200 6th Ave Seattle WA 98101

BRUCK, NATALIE RENEE, elementary school educator; b. Long Beach, Calif., June 21, 1967; d. Ernie and Mia (Gray) B. Student, Saddleback Jr. Coll., Mission Viejo, Calif., 1985-86; degree in Communications, U. Calif., Santa Barbara, 1990; postgrad., U. Calif., Irvine, 1992-93. Hostess Fieldstone Co., Newport, Calif., 1987-90; tchr. math. Culverdale Elem. Sch., Irvine, 1990-91, tchr. phys. edn., 1991-92; elem. tchr. Irvine Unified Sch. Dist., 1992, Culverdale Elem. Sch., 1992—; counselor Camp Frasier, Irvine, 1987-90, dir., 1990-91; tchr. phys. edn. YMCA, Newport Beach, Costa Mesa, Calif., 1990—. Mem. Kappa Alpha Theta.

BRÜDERLIN, BEAT DOMINIK, computer science educator; b. Basel, Switzerland, July 28, 1955; came to U.S., 1988; s. Kurt Wilhelm and Mia (Hossdorf) B. MS in Physics, U. Basel, 1981; PhD in Computer Sci., Swiss Fed. Inst. Tech., Zurich, 1987. Head geometric algorithms CAD Systems AG, Basel, 1981-84; asst. prof. computer sci. U. Utah, Salt Lake City, 1987—; cons. HEPE AG, Däniken, Switzerland, 1986-88. Author: Rule-Based Geometric Modelling. Grantee NSF, 1989, 91, U. Utah, 1989, NSF Sci. & Tech. Ctr. for Computer Graphics & Visualization, 1991. Mem. IEEE, Assn. for Computing Machinery, Soc. for Indsl. & Applied Math. Office: U Utah Computer Sci Dept 3190 MEB Salt Lake City UT 84112

BRUDNO, BARBARA, lawyer, educator; b. Chgo., Oct. 2, 1941; d. A. Edward and Bunnie (Shine) B. B.A., U. Calif., Berkeley, 1963, M.A. in Philosophy, 1964, J.D., 1967. Bar: Calif. 1967, N.Y. 1980. Law clk. to presiding justice Calif. Supreme Ct., 1967-68; asst. prof. law UCLA, 1968-70, assoc. prof., 1970-72, prof., 1972-82; prof. Bklyn. Law Sch., 1981-85; assoc. Baer Marks & Upham, N.Y.C., 1980-81; pvt. practice, N.Y.C., 1985-88, L.A., 1988-89, of counsel Ashen, Martin, Seldon, Lippman & Scilleri, L.A., 1989—; vis. prof. law Boalt Hall Sch. Law U. Calif., Berkeley, spring 1975, Inst. on Internat. and Comparative Law, Paris, summer 1984; bar rev. lectr. in constl. law, 1979. Mem. ABA, Copyright Soc. U.S.A., Los Angeles County Bar Assn., L.A. Copyright Soc., Beverly Hills Bar Assn., Assn. of Bar of City of N.Y. Author: Poverty, Inequality and the Law, 1976; Income Redistribution Theories and Programs, 1977. Office: 2049 Century Park E Bldg 1900 Los Angeles CA 90067-3121

BRUENN, RONALD SHERMAN, financial company executive; b. Yakima, Wash., June 21, 1940; s. William H. and Reta (Eggars) B.; m. Virginia Mae Pollard, June 10, 1961 (div. 1981); m. Vicky A. Lindstrom, Apr. 16, 1983 (div. 1988); children: Bradly Dean, Vikki Lee. BA, Wash. State U., 1962. Exec. sales Pillsbury Inc., 1963-68; field sales mgr. Revlon Inc., N.Y.C., 1968-86; v.p. sales/mktg. Stericon Inc., L.A., 1986-88; pres., CEO Sr. Fin. Mkt. Svc., Inc., Yakima, Wash., 1988—; lectr. in field. Active Rep. Party, Yakima, 1990. Mem. YMCA, Elks. Home: 5406 Meadow Ln Yakima WA 98908 Office: Sr Fin Mktg Svc Inc 120 N 50th Ave Yakima WA 98908

BRUGGEMAN, LEWIS LEROY, radiologist; b. N.Y.C., Sept. 9, 1941; s. Louis LeRoy and Edwina Jane (Mickel) B.; m. Ann Margaret Kayajan, May 28, 1966; children: Gretchen Ann, Kurt LeRoy. AB, Dartmouth Coll., 1963, B in Med. Sci., 1965; MD, Harvard U., 1968. Intern Los Angeles County Harbor Gen. Hosp., Torrence, Calif., 1968-69; resident in diagnostic radiology Columbia Presbyn. Med. Ctr., N.Y.C., 1969-72; chief dept. radiology Bremerton (Wash.) Naval Regional Med. Ctr., 1972-74; pvt. practice diagnostic radiology South Coast Med. Ctr., South Laguna, Calif., 1974—, dir. dept. radiology, 1983—, hosp. bd. trustees, 1985-87; pvt. practice diagnostic radiology Saddleback Community Hosp., Laguna Hills, Calif., 1974—; pres., chmn. bd. dirs. South Coast Med. Group Inc., South Laguna, Calif., 1983—; pres. So. Coast Radiol. Med. Group Inc., South Laguna, 1986—; bd. trustees South Coast Med. Ctr. Found., 1993—. Lt. comdr. Med. Corps USN, 1972-74. Mem. AMA, Radiol. Soc. N.Am., Am. Coll. Radiology, Calif. Med. Assn., Calif. Radiol. Soc., Dartmouth Club Orange County. Office: S Coast Radiol Med Group 28 Monarch Bay Pla Ste J South Laguna CA 92677

BRUGGER, PAUL RAYMOND, gaming professional; b. Glendale, Calif., July 31, 1942; s. Paul Joseph and Rita Marie (Wirth) B.; m. Carol Ann Tarleton, May 12, 1965; children: John-Paul, Eric, Joel, Beth, Dann, Elyn, KayCee. Student, Glendale Coll., 1960-64, L.A. City Coll., 1961, Western Nev. Community Coll., 1978-79, U. Nev., Las Vegas, 1981. Engring. asst. Nev. Controls, Inc., Minden, 1968; prodn. test technician Raven Electronics, Reno, 1968-69; electronics specialist Nev. Gaming Control Bd., Carson City, 1969-81; mgr. field support Summit Systems, Inc., Las Vegas, 1981-82; dist. mgr. Cal-Omega, Inc., Las Vegas, 1982-83; project engr. Sierra Control Systems, Carson City, 1983-85; electronics engr., mktg. mgr. Bally Systems, Reno, 1985-89; account exec. Computerland, Carson City, 1990-91; svc. mgr. Aristocrat, Inc., Reno, 1991—; owner, gaming cons. Paul R. Brugger Cons. Svcs., Carson City, 1979—. Adult leader Nev. Area coun. Boy Scouts Am., 1971-. With USN, 1964-68. Mem. IEEE (sr., sect. chmn. 1988-90). Republican. Mormon. Office: Aristocrat Inc 750A South Rock Blvd Reno NV 89502

BRULAND, RAYMOND VELAUSE, avionics engineer; b. Blaine, Wash., Feb. 19, 1917; s. Reimers Olai and Laura Marie (Hall) B.; m. Mary Emelda Kiss, Nov. 23, 1940; children: Melinda Rey, Richard Ray, Steven Ray. Student, U. Wash., 1934-35, Capitol Radio Engring. Inst., Washington, 1936-39. Various positions as radio engr. Calif., 1937-45; chief radio engr. to comm. supt. Pan Am.-Grace Airways, Lima, Peru, 1945-50; supt. comm. engr. Braniff Internat. Airways, Dallas, 1950-55; tech. rep. Collins Radio Co., Madrid and Geneva, 1955-57; mgr.-cen. Europe Collins Radio

Co., Geneva, 1957-60; aviation product mgr. to dir. product lines Collins Radio Co., Cedar Rapids, Iowa, 1960-62; v.p., gen. mgr. Europe Collins Radio Internat., Geneva and London, 1962-66; dir. so. region Collins Radio Co., Dallas, 1966; dir. mktg. Litton Aero Products Div. Inter-Am. Ops., Inc., Woodland Hills, Calif., 1967-82; pres.mktg. Inter-Am. Ops., Inc., Woodland Hills and Sedona, Ariz., 1982-89. Contbr. articles to profl. jours. Home: 420 Windsong Dr Sedona AZ 86336-3751

BRULL, EUGENE EDWIN, JR., investment company executive; b. Oak Park, Ill., Aug. 17, 1940; s. Eugene Edwin Brull Sr. and Mildren Josephine (Havlatko) Christian; m. Margaret Anne Forgette, May 4, 1963; children: Robin Rene, Aimee Janine, Tanja Gretchen. AB in Chemistry, Washington U., 1962; MS in Physics, Trinity Coll., 1971; MS in Mgmt., Renssallaer Polytech. Inst., 1987. Rsch. engr. Rocketdyne div. N.Am. Aviation, Canoga Park, Calif., 1962-67; sr. rsch. chemist United Technologies Rsch. Ctr., East Hartford, Conn., 1967-85; commodity mgr. Northrop Corp., Hawthorne, Calif., 1985-93; pres., CEO Brull Haz Ltd., Las Vegas, 1991—; real estate broker. Author (book) Stamps, 1987; inventor Delta Thermatron, 1982, Compu Marketer, 1991. Lobbyist North Redondo Traffic Com., Redondo Beach, 1988-90. Fellow Gemological Inst. Am.; mem. Kappa Sigma. Office: Brull Haz Ltd 516 S 4th St Las Vegas NV 89101

BRUMBAUGH, ROLAND JOHN, bankruptcy judge; b. Pueblo, Colo., Jan. 21, 1940; s. Leo Allen and Ethel Marie (Brummett) B.; m. Pamela Marie Hultman, Sept. 8, 1967; children—Kenneth Allen, Kimberly Marie. B.S. in Bus. with honors, U. Colo., 1968, J.D., 1971. Bar: Colo. 1971, U.S. Dist. Ct. Colo. 1972, U.S. Ct. Appeals (10th cir.) 1973, U.S. Supreme Ct. 1980. Legal intern HUD, Denver, 1971-72; sole practice, Denver, 1972-75; chief dep. city atty. City of Lakewood, Colo., 1975; dep. dir. Colo. Dept. of Revenue, Denver, 1975-78; asst. U.S. atty. Dist. of Colo., Denver, 1978-82; judge U.S. Bankruptcy Ct. Dist. of Colo., Denver, 1982—; lectr. in field. Author: Colorado Liquor and Beer Licensing-Law and Practice, 1970; Handbook for Municipal Clerks, 1972. Contbr. articles to profl. jours. Served with USAF, 1962-65. Recipient numerous awards for excellence in law. Mem. Colo. Bar Assn., Alpha Kappa Psi, Beta Gamma Sigma, Rho Epsilon, Sigma Iota. Home: 1845 Sherman St #400 Denver CO 80203 Office: US Dist Ct 400 Columbine Bldg 1845 Sherman St Denver CO 80203-1132

BRUMMETT, ROBERT EDDIE, pharmacology educator; b. Concordia, Kans., Feb. 11, 1934; s. Gordon Legonia and Gladys Leona (Anderson) B.; m. Naomi Deen Weaver, Dec. 19, 1955; children: Randall, Wendy, Robin, Philip. BS, Oreg. State U., 1959, MS, 1960; PhD, U. Oreg., 1964. Registered pharmacist, Oreg. Asst. prof. pharmacology Oreg. State U., Corvallis, 1961-62; asst. prof. otolaryngology Oreg. Health Scis. U., Portland, 1964-70, assoc. prof. otolaryngology and pharmacology, 1970-80, prof. otolaryngology and Pharmacology, 1981—; mem. Oreg. Coun. on Alcohol and Drug Problems, Salem, 1979-85; instr. Am. Acad. Otolaryngology, Washington, 1964—; mem. adv. panel otorhinolaryngology U.S. Pharmacoeia, 1985—, mem. drug info. adv. panel, 1988—, mem. coun. on naturopathic physicians formuling, 1990—. Patentee in field; contbr. 100 articles to profl. jours. Comdr. U.S. Power Squadron, Portland, 1982-86, adminstr. officer, 1986—, dist. ednl. officer, 1991—. Grantee NIH, 1969—, Deafness Research Found., 1970, Med. Research Found., 1979, 83. Mem. AAAS, Am. Acad. Otolaryngology (instr. 1964—), Head and Neck Surgery, Associated Researchers in Otolaryngology, Sigma Xi. Republican. Club: Hayden Island Yacht (Portland) Lodge: Elks. Home: 545 N Hayden Bay Dr Portland OR 97217 Office: Oreg Health Scis U 3181 SW Sam Jackson Park Rd Portland OR 97201-3011

BRUN, JUDY KAY, university administrator, consultant; b. Petoskey, Mich.; d. Lester Jasper and Beatrice Winona (Hoar) Kalbfleisch; m. Torben Otto Brun, June 29, 1968; 1 child, Christian Tor Brun. BS, Mich. State U., 1964; MS, Iowa State U., 1967, PhD, 1970. Cert. home economist; lic. nutritionist. Tchr. Clarkston (Mich.) High Sch., Clarkston, 1964-66, James Madison Mem. High Sch., Madison, Wis., 1967-68; asst. prof. Chgo. State Univ., 1971-74, U. Ill., Champaign, 1974-78; dir. rsch. and evaluation Nat. Dairy Coun., Ill., 1978-86; v.p. div. Nutrition Edn. Nat. Dairy Coun., Rosemont, Ill., 1986-89; pres. Brun and Assocs., Sante Fe, 1989—; prof., chair Iowa State U., Ames, 1990—; pres., bd. dirs. Soc. for Nutrition Edn., Oakland, 1987-90, pres. Soc. for Nutrition Edn. Found., editorial bd. Jour. of Nutritional Edn., 1981-87. Contbr. rsch. articles to mags. Recipient Prof. Achievement award, Iowa State U., 1986. Mem. Soc. for Nutrition Edn. (pres. 1989-90), Am. Home Econs. Assn. Office: 973 Nambe Loop Los Alamos NM 87544 also: Iowa State U 219 MacKay Hall Ames IA 50011

BRUN, KIM ERIC, photographer; b. San Diego, Jan. 31, 1947; s. Henry Milton and Laurel Elizabeth (Von Heeringen) B.; m. Susan Eileen Headley, Nov. 5, 1990; children: Brittany Nicole, Blaine Eric. BA, Humboldt State U., 1973; MBA, San Diego State U., 1976. Asst. rsch. physyologist Naval Personal Rsch. and Devel. Ctr., San Diego, 1973-76; sales rep. Sparkletts Water Co., San Diego, 1977-78; photographer Kim Brun Photography, San Diego, 1978-84, Kim Brun Studios, Inc., San Diego, 1984—. Co-author: Computer-Based Management Info Systems and Organization Behavior, 1980; photographer 23 nat. mag. covers, 7 interior design books. Bd. dirs. San Diego Oceans Found., 1993—. Sgt. U.S. Army, 1968-70, Vietnam. Decorated Bronze star for valor with two oak leaf clusters. Mem. Am. Soc. Mag. Photographers (treas. 1985-87, bd. dirs. 1987-88), San Diego Fly Fishers, Sierra Club.

BRUN, MARGARET ANN CHARLENE, buyer, planner; b. Toledo, June 19, 1945; d. John Joseph and Maude Elizabeth (Harrell) Bartos; m. Paul Joseph Brun, June 17, 1967. Student, Phoenix Coll., 1964-67, Glendale C.C., 1991—. Cert. purchasing mgr. Controller material inventory Digital Equipment Corp., Phoenix, 1975-76, controller prodn. inventory, 1976-77, prodn. control planner, 1977-79, inventory control planner, 1979, buyer, 1979-91; buyer, planner ASM Am., Inc., 1991—. Named Buyer of Yr., Purchasing World mag., 1987. Mem. Purchasing Mgmt. Assn. Ariz. affiliate of Nat. Assn. Purchasing Mgmt. Democrat. Methodist.

BRUNACINI, ALAN VINCENT, fire chief; b. Jamestown, N.Y., Apr. 18, 1937; s. John N. and Mary T. Brunacini; B.S., Ariz. State U., 1970, M.P.A., 1975; m. Rita McDaugh, Feb. 14, 1959; children—Robert Nicholas, John Nicholas, Mary Candice. Mem. Phoenix Fire Dept., 1959—, bn. chief, then asst. fire chief, 1971-78, fire chief, 1978—; condr. nat. seminar on fire dept. mgmt., 1970—. Redford scholar, 1968. Mem. Am. Soc. Public Adminstrn. (Superior Service award 1980), Nat. Fire Protection Assn. (chmn. fire service sect. 1974-78, dir. 1978), Internat. Assn. Fire Chiefs, Soc. Fire Service Instrs. Author: Fireground Command; also articles in field. Office: Office of Fire Chief 520 W Van Buren St Phoenix AZ 85003-1632*

BRUNDIN, BRIAN JON, lawyer; b. St. Paul, Oct. 11, 1939; s. Milton E. Brundin and LuVerne (Johnson) Roddan; m. Carolyn Bagley, June 30, 1961; children: Iana L. Sayer, Ian S., Dane E. BBA in Acctg. cum laude, U. Alaska, 1961; JD, Harvard U., 1964. Bar: Alaska 1966, U.S. Ct. Appeals (9th cir.) 1966, U.S. Supreme Ct. 1986; CPA, Alaska. Assoc. Hughes, Thorsness, Gantz, Powell & Brundin, Anchorage, 1966-70, ptnr., 1970—, prin. ptnr., 1975—, chair comml. div. and corp. sect., 1970—, vice chmn., 1972-76, chmn., 1976-82; instr. acctg. and law U. Alaska, 1965-69; bd. dirs., pres. Brundin, Inc., 1979—, Kyak Oil, Inc., 1985-90; bd. dirs., sec. Far North Fishermen, Inc., 1981-85; trustee Humana Hosp. Alaska, 1982-83; adv. bd. World Trade Ctr. Alaska, 1992—. Chmn. subcom. on sales taxes Operation Breakthrough, Anchorage, 1968; mem. U. Alaska Bd. Regents, 1969-77, chmn. fin. com., 1970-75, v.p. 1973-75, pres., 1975-77; mem. Alaska Postsecondary Commn., 1973-75; founder, trustee U. Alaska Found., 1974—, pres., 1974-77, mem. exec. com., 1987—, chmn. Bullock prize for excellence com., 1989—; Alaska chmn. Harvard U. Law Sch. Fund, 1975-78; mem. adv. bd. alaska Ctr. for Internat. Bus., 1986-88. Capt. U.S. Army, 1964-66. Mem. ABA, AICPA, Anchorage Bar Assn. (legis. com.), Alaksa Bar Assn. (ethics and client security, corp. banking, bus. law and taxation WICHE, higher edn.), Am. Soc. Hosp. Attys., Am. Soc. Atty./CPAs, Alaska Soc. CPAs, U. Alaska Alumni Assn. (pres. Anchorage chpt. 1968-69), Sons of Norway, Pioneers of Alaska Igloo 15, Am. Legion, Amvets, Lions, Rotary.

BRUNEAU, BILL, architect; b. Phila., May 29, 1948; s. William Francis and Mabel Frances (Quiroli) B.; children: Nicole Domenique, Mercedes Angelina, William Robert, Michelangelo Joseph. BArch., Pa. State U., 1970; MArch., U. Colo., 1971; M. of Urban Design, Harvard U., 1974; Cert. in City Planning, U. Florence, Italy, 1969; Cert. in Urban Econs., MIT, 1970. Registered architect Colo., Calif., Mo., Mass., Wyo., Minn. Urban designer planning dept. City of Aurora, Colo., 1977-80; project interior architect Cannell & Chaffin, Denver, 1980-82; dir. architecture URS Co., Denver, 1982-84; mgr. facilities Frontier Airlines, Denver, 1984-86, United Airlines, Chgo., 1986-87; sr. aviation planner Burns & McDonnell, Denver, 1987-91; dir. facilities Continental Airlines, 1991; pres. Fountain of Youth Mktg. Internat., 1991; instr. U. Colo., Denver, 1972, Community Coll. Denver, Red Rocks, Colo., 1975-80, Boston Archtl. Ctr., 1972-74; prin. Bruneau Urban Design and Architecture Assocs., Denver, 1980-87; pres. Rocky Mountain Constrn. Mgmt., Inc., Aurora, 1982. Contbr. articles to profl. jours. Vol. YMCA, Colo., Denver Art Mus., Denver Nat. History Mus., Zoological Soc., Math Counts; lectr. career days Colo.; Sunday sch. tchr., counselor and planning commr. Harvard U. fellow, 1973; recipient award of Merit City and County of Denver, 1972; named Outstanding Young Man of Am., 1976. Mem. AIA, AAAE, AOCI, Am. Soc. Interior Designers, Am. Inst. Certified Planners, Illuminating Engring. Soc. Presbyterian. Home: 5440 Vale Dr Denver CO 80222-2337 Office: Stapleton Plaza Office Ctr Ste 3500 Denver CO 80207

BRUNELLO, ROSANNE, sales executive; b. Cleve., Aug. 26, 1960; d. Carl Carmello and Vivan Lucille (Caranna) B.; divorced, 1991. Student, U. Cin., 1978-81, Cleve. State U., 1981-82. Indsl. sales engr. Alta Machine Tool, Denver, 1982; mem. sales./purchases Ford Tool & Machine, Denver, 1982-84; sales/ptnr. Mountain Rep. Enterprises, Denver, 1984-86; pres., owner Mountain Rep. Ariz., Phoenix, 1986—; pres. Mountain Rep. Oreg., Portland, 1990—, Mountain Rep. Wash., 1991—, Mountain Rep. of Midwest, Chgo., 1992—; sec. Computer & Automated Systems Assoc., 1987, vice chmn., 1988, chmn., 1989. Active mem. Rep. Party, 1985—; mem. Phoenix Art Mus. Mem. NAFE, Soc. Mfg. Engrs. (pres. award 1988), Computer Automated Assn. (sec. 1987, vice chmn. 1988 chmn. 1989), Italian Cultural Soc., Tempe C. of C., Vocat. Ednl. Club Am. (mem. exec. bd., pres. 1987—). Roman Catholic. Office: Mountain Rep Ariz 255 S Kyrene Rd Unit 207 Chandler AZ 85226-4460

BRUNER, CINDY HULL, judge; b. Waterbury, Conn., Apr. 26, 1949; d. Harry Garfield Jr. and Ella Betsey (Houghton) Hull; m. Jack Dennis Bruner, Sept. 24, 1988; children. BS, U. Vt., 1979; JD, U. Colo., 1984. Bar: Colo. 1984, U.S. Dist. Ct. Colo., 1985. Law clk. U.S. Dist. Ct., Denver, 1984-85; dep. dist. atty. Adams County, Brighton, Colo., 1985-91; count. ct. judge 17th Jud. Dist., Brighton, 1991—. Mem. Colo. Bar Assn., Adams County Bar Assn. Office: Hall of Justice 17th Jud Dist 1931 E Bridge St Brighton CO 80601

BRUNETTI, MELVIN T., federal judge; b. 1933; m. Gail Dian Buchanan; children: Nancy, Bradley, Melvin Jr. Grad., U. Nev., 1960; JD, U. Calif., San Francisco, 1964. Mem. firm Vargas, Bartlett & Dixon, 1964-69, Laxalt, Bell, Allison & Lebaron, 1970-78, Allison, Brunetti, MacKenzie, Hartman, Soumbeniotis & Russell, 1978-85; judge U.S. Ct. Appeals (9th cir.), Reno, 1985—. Mem. Council of Legal Advisors, Rep. Nat. Com., 1982-85. Served with U.S. Army N.G., 1954-56. Mem. ABA, State Bar of Nev. (pres. 1984-85, bd. govs. 1975-84), Washoe County Bar Assn., Carson City Bar Assn. Office: US Ct Appeals 300 Booth St Rm 5003 Reno NV 89509-1946 also: US Courthouse 9th Circuit 300 Booth St Rm 5003 Reno NV 89509

BRUNI, JOHN RICHARD, broadcasting executive; b. Bklyn., Apr. 24, 1951; s. Albert P. and Doris L. (Burke) B.; m. Cynthia C., Aug. 20, 1988; 1 child, Summer Lee. Studio engr. Top NY DJ's, N.Y.C., 1973-76; soundman, cameraman Today Show and Nightly News NBC Network News, N.Y.C., 1976-78; soundman, electronic journalist for San Francisco Bur., Today Show and Nightly News with Tom Brokaw NBC Network News, San Francisco, 1978-91. Author: Risks, 1993. Recipient Emmy award NATAS, 1983, 84. Presbyterian.

BRUNING, JANET ANN, accountant; b. Milw., Feb. 17, 1942; d. Frederick H. and Delores J. Waldmann; m. Carl A. Bruning, July 17, 1978 (div.); children: Debra L., Brian C. BS in Bus. Mgmt., Park Coll., 1991. Acct. Yuma (Ariz.) Proving Ground, 1985-88, Williams AFB, Mesa, Ariz., 1988-91, Bur. Indian Affairs, Coolidge, Ariz., 1991—. Mem. NAFE, Am. Soc. Mil. Comptr. (treas.-sec.-v.p. 1977-91), Toastmasters (treas.-sec.-v.p., pres. 1988-91), Mensa. Home: 2131 E Juanita Mesa AZ 85204

BRUNK, GUNTER WILLIAM, health science association administrator; b. Berlin, Germany, Mar. 4, 1934; came to U.S., 1955; s. Erwin and Anna (Hoepner) B.; m. Sharon Elizabeth Genske, Aug. 16, 1969; children: Steve Erwin, Christopher Allan, Michelle Anna, Samantha Elizabeth. BS with distinction, U. Ariz., 1976, MPA, 1977, cert. in gerontology, 1977. Lic. long-term care adminstr. Enlisted USAF, 1955, advanced through grades, 1955-75, ret., 1975; adminstr. The Evan. Luth. Good Samaritan Soc., St. Croix Falls, Wis., 1977-80, Eugene, Oreg., 1980-87; exec. dir. The Evan. Luth. Good Samaritan Soc., Honolulu, 1987—; mem. joint tech. com. Dept. Health Svcs. State of Hawaii, Honolulu, 1988—. Active Hawaii Literacy Program, Oahu, 1988—. Mem. Am. Coll. Healthcare Adminstrs. (past pres.), Rotary (bd. dirs. Kaneohe, Hawaii chpt. 1988—, past pres. 1990—, Paul Harris fellow), Bayview Golf Club (adv. bd. 1990—), Kaneohe Yacht Club. Roman Catholic. Home: 44-010 Aina Moi Pl Kaneohe HI 96744 Office: The Evang Lutheran Good Samaritan Soc 45-090 Namoku St Kaneohe HI 96744

BRUNN, DAVID KEVIN, computer consultant; b. Dayton, Ohio, Oct. 22, 1956; s. Russell Owen and Peggy (Harten) B. BA in Graphic Design, U. Oreg., 1980, MFA in Graphic Design, 1986. Instr. Oreg. Art Inst., Portland, 1988, U. Oreg. Continuation Ctr., Portland, 1987-90; computer cons. Brunn Cons., Lake Oswego, Oreg., 1990—; adj. instr. U. Oreg., 1987, others; presenter various workshops in field; exhibitor group shows. Contbr. articles to profl. jours. Roman Catholic. Office: Brunn Consultants 12375 Mt Jefferson Ter Apt 4K Lake Oswego OR 97035-1465

BRUNNER, EARL CHESTER, JR., school administrator; b. L.A., Dec. 13, 1924; s. Earl Chester and Louise Esther (Jones) B.; m. Laurine Adams, July 28, 1948; children—Earl Claude, David Arnold, Michael Bruce, Karl Martin, Kurt Lafi, Laurine Louise. B.S., Brigham Young U., 1950, M.Ed., 1957. Tchr., Las Vegas Sch. Dist., Nev., 1950-52, biology Las Vegas High Sch., 1953-57, sci. and math. Ch. Coll. W. Samoa, Apia, Western Samoa, 1958-60; tchr. Las Vegas pub. schs., 1960-63, elementary prin., 1963-82; chief librarian Branch Genealogical Library, Las Vegas, Nev., 1980—, dir. Las Vegas Family History Ctr., 1988—. Committeeman, Republican Central Com., Las Vegas, 1974-82; scoutmaster, dist. commr. Boy Scouts Am., Las Vegas, 1960-82. Recipient Scout award Boy Scouts Am. 1975. Republican. Mormon. Home: 330 N 9th St Las Vegas NV 89101-3033 Office: Las Vegas Family History Ctr 509 S 9th St Las Vegas NV 89101-7010

BRUNNER, NORMAN JAMES, airport administrator; b. Owosso, Mich., Nov. 6, 1942; s. Norman Henry and Ella Louise (Dimke) B.; m. Belle Aimee, July 15, 1972. BA in Govt. cum laude, Chapman U., Orange, Calif., 1973; student, L.A. C.C., Okinawa, Japan, 1978, Santa Ana (Calif.) Coll., 1982-85; MA in Mgmt., Webster U., 1986. Lic. adult edn. instr., coll. instr., karate instr. Karate instr. Japanese Karate Assn., Japan, U.S. Vietnam, 1958—; calibrator Arctic Rsch. Inc., Clare, Mich., 1959-61; commd. USMC, 1968, advanced through grades to capt., 1985; athletic dir. Highridge Apts., Palos Verdes, Calif., 1972-74; instr. L.A. C.C., Okinawa, 1977-78; med. claims approver Equitable Life Assurance, Brea, Calif., 1981-82; election supr. Orange County Registrar of Voters, Santa Ana, 1982-85; bn. comdr. 303d Inf. Bn., Long Beach, Calif., 1985—; asst. dir. Fullerton (Calif.) Airport, 1985—; accident prevention counselor FAA Flight Stds., Long Beach, 1991—; pvt. pilot FAA, Oklahoma City, 1989—. Vol. tax counselor IRS, Camp Pendleton, Calif., 1976-78. Mem. Ret. Officers Assn., Assn. Airport Execs., Calif. Assn. Airport Execs. (exec. mem. 1990—), Aircraft Owners-Pilots Assn., Fullerton Airport Pilot's Assn. Republican. Lutheran. Office: Fullerton Mcpl. Airport 4011 W Commonwealth Ave Fullerton CA 92633

BRUNNI, CONNI M., healthcare administrator; b. Conneaut, Ohio, May 7, 1961; d. Gordon Leland and Florence May (Brown) Dodge; m. Scott C. Brunni, Oct. 16, 1982; children: Clarissa Joanne, Nicholas Robert. BS with honors, Calif. State U., Bakersfield, 1982. Preferred banking officer Bank of Am., Bakersfield, 1982-87; asst. v.p. San Joaquin Bank, Bakersfield, 1987-90; exec. dir. Bakersfield Meml. Physicians' IPA, 1990—. Bd. dirs. Kern County chpt. Am. Lung Assn., 1988—, Family to Family Project, H. Weill Meml. Child Guidance Clinic, Bakersfield, 1987-89; vice chmn. Project Clean Air, Bakersfield, 1989—; mem. Bakersfield Rep. Assembly, 1989-90; chmn. Kern County Young Reps., 1982; chmn. Charter Hosp. Adv. Bd., 1991; mem. Bakersfield Water Bd. Mem. Am. Bus. Womens Assn. (sec. 1984-85), Bakersfield C. of C., Kern County Dairymaids (treas. 1985-86). Office: Bakersfield Meml Physicians 400 34th St Bakersfield CA 93301-2237

BRUNO, JUDYTH ANN, chiropractor; b. Eureka, Calif., Feb. 16, 1944; d. Harold Oscar and Shirley Alma (Farnsworth) Nelson; m. Thomas Glenn Bruno, June 1, 1968; 1 child, Christina Elizabeth. AS, Sierra Coll., 1982; D of Chiropractic, Palmer Coll. of Chiropractic West, Sunnyvale, Calif., 1986. Diplomate Nat. Bd. Chiropractic Examiners. Sec. Bank Am., San Jose, Calif., 1965-67; marketer Memorex, Santa Clara, Calif., 1967-74; order entry clk. John Deere, Milan, Ill., 1977; system analyst Four Phase, Cupertino, Calif., 1977-78; chiropractic asst. Dr. Thomas Bruno, Nevada City, Calif., 1978-81; chiropractor Chiropractic Health Care Ctr., Nevada City, 1987-91; pvt. practice Cedar Ridge, Calif., 1991—. Area dir. Cultural Awareness Coun., Grass Valley, Calif., 1977—; vol. Nevada County Library, Nevada City, 1987-88, Decide Team III, Nevada County, 1987—, Active Parenting of Teen Facilitator Nev. Union High Sch.; mem., vol. task force health care Nev. County C. of C., 1993. Mem. Am. Chiropractic Assn., Toastmasters (sec. 1988, pres. 1989, edn. v.p. 1990). Republican. Office: Chiropractor Health Care 12720 Colfax Hwy PO Box 1718 Cedar Ridge CA 95924

BRUNSEN, WILLIAM HENRY, finance educator, consultant, researcher; b. Friend, Nebr., Aug. 18, 1940; s. William H. and Lorene Lavern (Schrock) B.; m. Judith Elaine Williamson, Feb. 22, 1964; children: William Eric, Lori Elaine. BS in Econs., Eastern N.Mex. U., 1968; MA in Econs., U. Nebr., 1972, PhD in Fin., 1976. Cert. mgmt. acct. Legis. asst. Nebr. Legislature, Lincoln, 1971-80; fin. officer Peterson Constrn., Lincoln, 1980-83; asst. prof. fin. Western Carolina U., Cullowhee, N.C., 1983-85, No. Ariz. U., Flagstaff, 1985-87; assoc. prof. fin. Eastern N.Mex. U., Portales, 1987—. Co-author: Commercial Banking, 1985; contbr. articles to profl. jours. With USAF, 1961-65. Fulbright scholar, West Berlin, Fed. Republic Germany, 1968-69. Mem. Fin. Mgmt. Assn., S.W. Fin. Assn., Nat. Assn. Accts., Inst. Cert. Mgmt. Accts. Home: PO Box 2024 Portales NM 88130-2024 Office: Eastern NMex U PO Box 2024 Portales NM 88130-2024

BRUNSON, ADRIEL, video producer, writer; b. Lubbock, Tex., Aug. 9, 1949; s. Paul Lawrence and Vida Grace (Harrison) B.; m. Zoe Ann Hilliard, (div. Feb. 16, 1984); children: Dustin, Seth, Faith; m. Kathleen Lucille Luker, May 16, 1992. Grad., Abilene (Tex.) Christian U., 1970. Composer, performer Cedar Creek Band, 1970-77; mng. engr. Cedar Creek Studio, 1974-77; owner Radiant Star Studio, 1977-81, Brunson Prodns., Ft. Collins, Colo., 1981—. Writer over 250 scripts for mktg. films, tng. films and documentaries. Recipient numerous Gold and Silver Keys, Best of Class, Best of Show awards Bus./Profl. Advt. Assn., Bronze award N.Y. Music Video Competition, 1980. Home and Office: Brunson Prodns 701 Westshore Ct Fort Collins CO 80525

BRUNVAND, DANA KARI, editor, English educator; b. Moscow, Idaho, June 11, 1964; d. Jan Harold and Judith Darlene (Ast) B. BA, U. Utah, 1985, MA, 1988. Asst. editor Western Am. Lit., Logan, 1988—. Asst. editor Western American Literature. Mem. Western Lit. Assn. (treas. 1989—).

BRUSKI-MAUS, BETTY JEAN, state legislator; b. Ekalaka, Mont., Sept. 15, 1927; d. Dave and Grace Berry Lunder; m. Jerome B. Bruski, 1946 (dec.); children: Bruce, Beverly, Cherie (Mrs. Roshau), Vicki (Mrs.Tullius), Jacqueline (Mrs. Levenseller), William, Thomas, Gregory, Grace , Michelle; m. Ernest M. Maus, Jan. 3, 1992; 10 stepchildren. Ptnr., pres. Red Top Ranch Corp., Wibaux, Mont., 1946-91; owner, operator Sew-Art Shop, Wibaux, Mont., 1966-68; mem. Mont. State Senate, 1991—; vice chairwoman Hwys. Com. Mont. State Senate. Recipient sr. artists award N.D. Arts and Badlands Arts Assn., 1979. Mem. VFW Auxiliary (dist. v.p.), Coun. Cath. Women (diocesan pres.), Mont. Tourism Orgn. (dir.), Good Sams, Sons of Norway, Custer Country. Address: Box 234 Wibaux MT 59353

BRUSSARD, PETER FRANS, biologist, educator; b. Reno, June 20, 1938; s. William and Evelyn (Anderson) B.; Janet E. McDonald, Oct. 1962 (div. Dec. 1969); 1 child, William R.; m. Trudy Elizabeth Byers, Dec. 20, 1969; 1 child, Peter H. AB, Stanford U., 1960, PhD, 1969; MS, U. Nevada, 1965. Asst. prof. Cornell U., 1969-75, assoc. prof., 1975-85; prof., head biology dept. Montana State U., Bozeman, 1985-89; prof., chmn. biology dept. U. Nev., Reno, 1989—; dir. Rocky Mountain Biol. Lab, Crested Butte, Colo., 1979-88. Editor: Ecological Genetics, 1978; contbr. articles and book revs. to profl. publ. Served to lt. USNR. NSF Rsch. grantee, 1971-75, 77-78, 81-85; NIH Rsch. grantee, 1971-74; rsch. grantee Nat. Geog. Soc., 1988-91. Fellow Am. Assn. Advanced Sci.; mem. Soc. Study Evolution (coun. 1978-80), Am. Soc. Naturalists (treas. 1980-83), Soc. Conservation Biology (sec., treas. 1985-90, pres.-elect 1991-93, pres. 1993—), Soc. Sci. Exploration (coun. 1983-85). Democrat. Episcopalian. Home: 1400 Granite Dr Reno NV 89509-3924 Office: U Nev 142 FA Reno NV 89557

BRUSSEAU, MARK LEWIS, environmental educator, researcher; b. Pontiac, Mich., June 17, 1958. PhD, U. Fla., 1989. Asst. prof. U. Ariz., Tucson, 1989-93, assoc. prof., 1993—; vis. scientist on groundwater rsch. dept. environ. engring, Tech. U. of Denmark, 1989; mem. groundwater contamination com. USDA, 1990—; mem. exploratory rsch. proposal rev. panel EPA, 1990—; mem. subsurface sci. program rsch. proposal rev. panel U.S. Dept. of Energy, 1990—; cons. EPA, Office of Sci. Rsch., USAF, Ariz. Dept. Environ. Quality. Assoc. editor Jour. Contaminant Hydrology, 1990—; contbr. over 30 articles to profl. jours. Rsch. fellow Air Force Office Sci., 1990, U.S. Dept. Energy, 1992; recipient Emil Truog award for Outstanding PhD, Soil Sci. Soc. Am., 1990, Young Scientist postdoctoral rsch. Am. Chem. Soc., 1990, Young Faculty award U.S. Dept. Energy, 1992, Young Investigator award NAS, 1993. Mem. Assn. Groundwater Scientists and Engrs., Am. Geophys. Union, Am. Chem. Soc., Internat. Assn. Hydrogeologists, Soil Sci. Soc. Am., Phi Kappa Phi, Sigma Xi. Office: U Ariz Soil and Water Sci Dept 429 Shantz Tucson AZ 85721

BRUST, DAVID, physicist; b. Chgo., Aug. 24, 1935; s. Clifford and Ruth (Klapman) B.; BS, Calif. Inst. Tech., 1957; MS, U. Chgo., 1958, PhD, 1964. Rsch. assoc. Purdue U., Lafayette, Ind., 1963-64; rsch. assoc. Northwestern U., Evanston, Ill., 1964-65, asst. prof. physics, 1965-68; theoretical rsch. physicist U. Calif., Lawrence Radiation Lab., Livermore, Calif., 1968-73; cons. Bell Telephone Lab., Murray Hill, N.J., 1966. Campaign co-ordinator No. Calif. Scientists and Engrs. for McGovern, 1972. NSF travel grantee, 1964; NSF rsch. grantee, 1966-68. Mem. Am. Phys. Soc., Am. Assn. Coll. Profs., Internat. Solar Energy Soc., Pacific Assn. of AAU, Nature Conservancy, Sierra Club, Sigma Xi. Office: PO Box 13130 Oakland CA 94661-0130

BRUTOSKY, SISTER MARY VERONICA, art and English language educator, artist, writer, poet; b. Connellsville, Pa., Apr. 27, 1932; d. Stephen Joseph and Mary Elizabeth (Takacs) B. BA in English, History, Mt. St. Mary's Coll., 1959; BFA, Otis Art Inst., 1975; MA in Painting, Calif. State U., Fresno, 1984. Joined Sisters of St. Joseph of Carondelet, Roman Cath. Ch., 1950. Tchr. elementary, high schs. Cath. Schs. System, Calif., 1953-82; part-time instr. Calif. State U., Fresno, 1981-84, Fresno City Coll., 1984—; founder, dir. Internat. Registry for Religious-Wo/men-Artists, Fresno, 1978—; art cons. Duplicast Corp., Fresno, 1978-82; curator, installation dir. group show U. San Francisco, 1982, ECLIPSE, 1978, others. Exhbns. include Phebe Conley Gallery, Calif. State U., Fresno, 1984, Cedar Clinton Libr., 1982-83, Plums Contemporary Art Gallery, Fresno, 1989-90, Heritage Gallery, Fresno, 1990, Franklin Gallery Art, Citrus Heights, Calif., 1991, New Eng. Fine Art Inst., 1993, Nat. Invitational Exhbn. Am. Contemporary Art, 1993; designer windows Our Lady of Guadalupe Ch., L.A., 1976, ceramic side altars Our Lady of Guadalupe Ch., Hermosa Beach, 1972; producer video: Easter Light: New Life, 1992; poetry collections include A Quality of Love, 1990, World Treasury of Golden Poems, Sisters Today,

1991. Home: 1315 N Van Ness Ave Fresno CA 93728-1937 Office: Fresno City Coll 1101 E University Ave Fresno CA 93741-0001

BRUTTING, THOMAS CHARLES, architect; b. N.Y.C., July 8, 1954; s. Charles Christian and Dorothy Martha (Kasil) B.; m. Laura Jean Kinzie, June 24, 1978 (div. Apr. 12, 1986); 1 child, Michael; m. M.W. Henderson, Sept. 30, 1986; step-children: Matthew, Sarah. BArch, Tulane U., 1977. Registered profl. architect. Architect Russo & Sonder, N.Y.C., 1977-78, Leibowitz & Bodouva, N.Y.C., 1978-80, HSR Architects, Madison, Wis., 1980-82, Strang Ptnrs., Madison, Wis., 1983-86, Engelbrecht & Griffin, Des Moines, 1986-89, Hardison, Komatsu, Ivelich & Tucker, San Francisco, 1989—. Pres. Old Market Pl. Neighborhood Assn., Madison, 1981-84; bd. dirs. Bethel Outreach, Madison, 1984-86. Recipient John Lawrence fellowship AIA, 1976. Mem. AIA. Episcopalian. Home: 795 Buena Vista W San Francisco CA 94117 Office: Hardison Komatsu et al 400 Second St Ste 200 San Francisco CA 94107

BRUYERE, HAROLD JOSEPH, JR., pharmacy educator; b. Wausau, Wis., Aug. 5, 1947; s. Harold Joseph and Katherine Mary (Iversen) B.; m. Alice May Hendrickson, Dec. 20, 1975; children: Kimberly, Travis. BS, U. Wis., Madison, 1969, PhD, 1982. Project specialist U. Wis., Madison, 1971-81, teaching asst., 1981-82, asst. scientist, 1982-86, clin. asst. prof., 1986-87; asst. prof. Sch. Pharmacy U. Wyo., Laramie, 1987-92, assoc. prof. Sch. Pharmacy, 1992—; ad hoc reviewer biomed. rsch. grants U. Wyo., 1988—; referee publs. in developmental toxicology, 1974—; presenter at nat. sci. meetings. Contbr. chpts. to books, articles and abstracts to profl. publs. Bd. dirs. Am. Heart Assn. of Wyo.-Albany County, 1991—. With U.S. Army, 1969-71. Grantee Wis. Heart Assn., 1985-86, 86-87, Wyo. Heart Assn., 1988-89, Am. Heart Assn., 1989-92. Mem. AAAS, Am. Heart Assn. Wyo. (cert. of appreciation 1990), Am. Assn. Colls. Pharmacy, Teratology Soc., Midwest Teratology Soc., Am. Legion, Sigma Xi. Democrat. Roman Catholic. Home: 1408 E Park Ave Laramie WY 82070-4148 Office: Sch Pharmacy Univ Wyo PO Box 3375 Laramie WY 82071-3375

BRYAN, A(LONZO) J(AY), service club official; b. Washington, N.J., Sept. 17, 1917; s. Alonzo J. and Anna Belle (Babcock) B.; student pub. schs.; m. Elizabeth Elfreida Koehler, June 25, 1941 (div. 1961); children: Donna Elizabeth, Alonzo Jay, Nadine; m. Janet Dorothy Onstad, Mar. 15, 1962 (div. 1977); children: Brenda Joyce, Marlowe Francis, Marilyn Janet. Engaged as retail florist, Washington, N.J., 1941-64. Fund drive chmn. ARC, 1952; bd. dirs. Washington YMCA, 1945-55, N.J. Taxpayers Assn., 1947-52; mem. Washington Bd. Edn., 1948-55. Mem. Washington Grange, Sons and Daus. of Liberty, Soc. Am. Florists, Nat. Fedn. Ind. Businessmen, Florists Telegraph Delivery Assn., C. of C. Methodist. Clubs: Masons, Tall Cedars of Lebanon, Jr. Order United Am. Mechanics, Kiwanis (pres. Washington (N.J.) 1952, lt. gov. internat. 1953-54, gov. N.J. dist. 1955, sec. N.J. dist. 1957-64, sec. S.E. area Chgo. 1965-74; editor The Jersey Kiwanian 1958-64, internat. staff 1964-85); Breakfast (pres. 1981-82) (Chgo.); sec., treas. Rocky Mtn. Kiwanis Dist., 1989; pres. South Denver, 1990-91; editor Rocky Mountain Kiwanian, 1990—. Home: 8115 S Poplar Way Englewood CO 80112-3135 Office: 11005 Ralston Rd # 204G Arvada CO 80004-4551

BRYAN, CAROLINE ELIZABETH, quality assurance professional; b. Washington, Dec. 4, 1951; d. Carter Royston and Anna Marie (Schneider) B. BA, Vassar Coll., 1973. Programmer Santa Barbara Rsch. Ctr., Goleta, Calif., 1975-77; tester, software developer and sr. test technician Johnson Controls, Inc., Milw., 1977-85; cons. Cap Gemini Am., Cranford, N.J., 1986-90; quality assurance engr. PRC, Inc., McLean, Va., 1990-91; software quality assurance engr. Unify Corp., Sacramento, 1991—; cons. AT&T, Lincroft and Middletown, N.J., 1986-90. Editor (newsletter) Captain America, 1989. Fellow Murphy Ctr. for Codification of Human and Organizational Law; mem. IEEE (assoc.), Assn. for Computing Machinery, Am. Philatelic Soc., Am. Topical Assn. Democrat. Roman Catholic. Home: 1730 Tehama Dr Woodland CA 95695 Office: Unify Corp 3901 Lennane Dr Sacramento CA 95834-1946

BRYAN, GORDON REDMAN, JR., nuclear power engineering consultant; b. Cleve., Dec. 1, 1928; s. Gordon Redman and Iola (Schecter) B.; m. Janet Louise McIntyre, Aug. 1, 1951 (div. Oct. 1986); children: Gordon L., Steven G.; m. Judith Hager, July 5, 1987. BA, Brown U., 1951; MS, George Washington U., 1970. Commd. ensign USN, 1951, advanced through grades to capt., 1971; comdg. officer 4 navy ships and 5 shore commands, 1965-78, submarine squadron, 1972-74; ret., 1978; marine design cons. various aerospace and engring. cos., Seattle, 1979-81; engring. cons. U.S. Nuclear Regulatory Commn. and U.S. Dept. Energy, Seattle, 1982—. Decorated Legion of Merit. Mem. Am. Nuclear Soc., Am. Radio Relay League, N.Y. Acad. Scis., Rotary. Republican. Home and Office: PO Box 2153 20271 Pugh Rd NE Poulsbo WA 98370

BRYAN, JOHN RODNEY, management consultant; b. Berkeley, Calif., Dec. 29, 1953; s. Robert Richard and Eloise (Anderson) Putz; m. Karen Nelson, Jan. 20, 1990. BA in Chemistry, U. Calif., San Diego, 1975; MBA, Rutgers U., 1985. Agt. Prudential, San Diego, 1975-79; sales mgr. Herman Schlorman Showrooms, L.A., 1980-83; pvt. practice mgmt. cons. Basking Ridge, N.J., 1983-85; mgmt. cons. Brooks Internat. Corp., Palm Beach Gardens, Fla., 1985-88; pvt. practice San Diego, 1988—; with Western Productivity Group, 1990—. Elder La Jolla Presbyn. Ch., 1991—. Mem. ASPA, Inst. Indsl. Engring., Rutgers Club So. Calif., Beta Gamma Sigma. Office: Applied Control Mgmt Effectiveness Systems 5796 Scripps St San Diego CA 92122-3210

BRYAN, RICHARD H., senator; b. Washington, July 16, 1937; married; 3 children. B.A., U. Nev., 1959; LL.B., U. Calif.-San Francisco, 1963. Bar: Nev. 1963. Dep. dist. atty. Clark County, Nev., 1964-66; public defender Clark County, 1966-68; counsel Clark County Juvenile Ct., 1968-69; mem. Nev. Assembly, 1969-73, Nev. Senate, 1973-79; atty. gen. State of Nev., 1979-83, gov. Nev., 1983-89, U.S. Senator from Nevada, 1989—; mem. U.S. Senate coms. on commerce, sci. and transp., banking, joint econ.; mem. Dem. Policy Com.; chmn. western region Dem. Senate Campaign Com.; chmn. Senate Consumer Subcom. Bd. dirs. March of Dimes; former v.p. Nev. Easter Seal Soc.; former pres. Clark County Legal Aid Soc. Served with U.S. Army, 1959-60. Recipient Disting. Svc. award Vegas Valley Jaycees. Mem. ABA, Clark County Bar Assn., Am. Judicature Soc., Nat. Gov.'s Assn. (com. econ. devel. and technol. innovation, com. internat. trade and fgn. relations, task force on adult literacy, task force on jobs growth and competitiveness, chmn. subcom. tourism), Council of State Govts. (past pres.), Phi Alpha Delta, Phi Alpha Theta. Democrat. Clubs: Masons, Lions, Elks. Office: US Senate 364 Russell Senate Bldg Washington DC 20510-2804*

BRYAN, ROBERT J., federal judge; b. Bremerton, Wash., Oct. 29, 1934; s. James W. and Vena Gladys (Jensen) B.; m. Cathy Ann Welander, June 14, 1958; children: Robert James, Ted Lorin, Ronald Terence. BA, U. Wash., 1956, JD, 1958. Bar: Wash. 1959, U.S. Dist. Ct. (we. dist.) Wash. 1959, U.S. Tax Ct. 1965, U.S. Ct. Appeals (9th cir.) 1985. Assoc., then ptnr. Bryan & Bryan, Bremerton, 1959-67; judge Superior Ct., Port Orchard, Wash., 1967-84; ptnr. Riddell, Williams, Bullitt & Walkinshaw, Seattle, 1984-86; judge U.S. Dist. Ct. (we. dist.) Wash., Tacoma, 1986—; mem. State Jail Comm., Olympia, Wash., 1974-76, Criminal Justice Tng. Com., Olympia, 1978-81, State Bd. on Continuing Legal Edn., Seattle, 1984-86; mem., sec. Jud. Qualifications Commn., Olympia, 1982-83. Author: (with others) Washington Pattern Jury Instructions (civil and criminal vols. and supplements), 1970-85. Chmn. 9th Ct. Jury Com., 1991-92. Served to maj. USAR. Office: US Dist Ct 1717 Pacific Ave Rm 4427 Tacoma WA 98402-3224

BRYAN, SHARON ANN, lawyer; b. Kansas City, Mo., Dec. 18, 1941; d. George William and Dorothy Joan (Henn) Goll; children: Lisa Ann, Holly Renee. BJ, U. Mo., 1963; diploma Stanford Radio and TV Inst., 1961; postgrad. NYU Sch. Arts and Sci., 1963-64; Personal Fin. Planning profl. designation UCLA, 1986; JD, U. So. Calif., 1989. Proofreader, copy editor Cadwalader, Wickersham, and Taft, N.Y.C., 1963-64; manuscript editor, writer nonsci. sects. N.Y. State Jour. Medicine, Med. Soc. State of N.Y., N.Y.C., also mng. editor Staffoscope, 1965-66; manuscript editor Transactions, also editor Perceiver, Am. Acad. Ophthalmology and Otolaryngology, Rochester, Minn., 1969-72, hist. writer, 1972-82; atty. Burkley, Moore, Greenberg & Lyman, Torrance, Calif., 1989-91; Christopher M. Moore & Assocs., 1991—; writer publicity articles Ft. Lee (Va.) Community Theatre. Mem. vol. honor roll Soc. of Meml. Sloan-Kettering Cancer Center; active N.Y. Hosp. Women's League, 1965-67 ; docent Los Angeles County Mus. Natural History; vol. Harriet Buhai Ctr. Mem. ABA, Am. Med. Writers Assn. (editor conv. bull. 1966), AAAS, Internat. Platform Assn., N.Y. Acad. Scis., NOW, Women's Lawyers Assn. of L.A. (bd. govs. 1991—, chmn. family law sect.), L.A. County Bar Assn. (del. to State Bar Calif.), Assn. Trial Lawyers Am., South Bay Women Lawyers Assn. (recording sec.), Kappa Tau Alpha, Kappa Alpha Theta (chmn. membership com. N.Y. chpt. 1966). Author: Pioneering Specialists: History of the American Academy of Ophthalmology and Otolaryngology. Home: 533 Via Del Monte Palos Verdes Peninsula CA 90274-1205

BRYANS, CHRISTOPHER LOREN, non-commissioned officer; b. Enid, Okla., Oct. 22, 1955; s. Elwood Robert and Carol Jean (Deel) B.; m. April Ann Kramme, Apr. 10, 1982. AAS in Comm. Ops. Tech., C.C. of USAF, 1988, AAS in Tech. and Mil. Sci., 1991; BA in History, Calif. State U., San Bernardino, 1992. Enlisted USAF, 1973, advanced through grades to sr. master sgt.; aero. station radio operator 1961 comm. group USAF, Clark AB, Philippines, 1974-75; ground radio operator 1st aeromed. evacuation squadron USAF, Pope AFB, N.C., 1975-77; aero. station shift supr. 27th comm. squadron USAF, Anderson AFB, Guam, 1977-79; noncom. officer in charge 2d combat comm. group radio ops. USAF, Patrick AFB, Fla., 1979-82; noncom. officer deployment planning 1st combat com. group USAF, Lindsey Air Station, Germany, 1982-85; noncom. officer 33d comm. group USAF, March AFB, Calif., 1985-87, instr. communicative skills divsn. chief strategic air comd. Noncommd. Officer Profl. Military Edn. Ctr., 1987-92; supt. ops. 353d spl. ops. comm. squadron USAF, Kadena AFB, Japan, 1992—; instr. USAF suprs. course, 1987-91, jr. ROTC leadership course, 1987-91. Bd. dirs. Creative Arts Festival, Lindsey AFB, 1985; internat. friendship dinner host Internat. Svcs. Ctr. U. Calif., Riverside, 1988-90; chmn., bd. elders Riverside Bible Ch., 1988. Named Vol. of Yr., Vol. Ctr. of Riverside, 1987. Mem. Phi Alpha Theta, Phi Kappa Phi. Home: PSC 79 Box 20858 APO AP 96364 Office: USAF 353d Spl Ops Comm APO AP 96368

BRYANT, ALAN WILLARD, human resources executive; b. Glen Ridge, N.J., Aug. 17, 1940; s. Alan Willard and Clara Sherman (Clark) B.; m. Karen Koenig; children: Hilary Ann, Christopher Bowman. AB, Dartmouth Coll., 1962, MBA, 1963; postgrad., St. Mary's U. Law, San Antonio, 1964-65. Specialist profl. placement spacecraft dept. GE, King of Prussia, Pa., 1965-66; foreman, methods analyst TV dept. GE, Syracuse, N.Y., 1966-67; specialist salaried employment armament dept. GE, Springfield, Mass., 1967-68; specialist profl. and salaried compensation info. systems equipment div. GE, Phoenix, 1968-70; mgr. personnel relations nuclear energy dept. GE, Wilmington, N.C., 1970-72; mgr. relations practices TV receiver products dept. GE, Portsmouth, Va., 1972-76; mgr. employee and community relations meter bus. dept. GE, Somersworth, N.H., 1976-85; mgr. human resources operation GE, San Jose, Calif., 1985—; mem. sr. staff positive mgmt. leadership course GE, Fairfield, Conn., 1981—, mem. staff exec. assessment and devel., 1987—; speaker nat. conf. Am. Mgmt. Assn., 1986, U.S.-Japan Inst., 1991. Author in field. Pres., campaign chair United Way of Strafford County, Dover, N.H., 1980-81; founding pres. Strafford Hospice Care, Somersworth, 1982-85; trustee Wentworth Douglass Hosp., Dover, 1982-85. Served to capt. U.S. Army, 1963-65. Recipient Pub. Svc. award Gov. Ariz., 1970, Pub. Svc. award Gov. N.H., 1982, 84. Mem. Soc. for Human Resource Mgmt., Bay Area Human Resource Execs. Coun. (pres. 1992-93), No. Calif. Human Resources Coun., Santa Clara County Mfg. Group Working Coun., Dover C. of C. (pres. 1984-85) Rotary (Disting. Svc. award 1985). Republican. Home: 119 El Porton Los Gatos CA 95030-1125 Office: GE Nuclear Energy 175 Curtner Ave MC 920 San Jose CA 95125-1014

BRYANT, CAROL LEE, public health educator, psychotherapist, consultant; b. L.A., Aug. 17, 1946; d. John Thomas and Janice Hathaway (Haislip) B.; m. Norman Alexander, June 4, 1966 (div. 1975); children: Ian Alexander, Colin Alexander; m. Reinhard Alexander Fritsch, June 14, 1983. AA, Diablo Valley Jr. Coll., Pleasant Hill, Calif., 1975; BA, San Francisco State U., 1978; MA in Transpersonal Counseling, John F. Kennedy U., Orinda, Calif., 1982, MA in Clin. Psychology, 1982; PhD in Clin. Psychology, Sierra U., 1986. Lic. marriage, family, and child counselor, Calif. Instr., tchr. Community Recreation YWCA, Walnut Creek, Calif., 1970-80, John F. Kennedy U., Orinda, Calif., 1980-81; adminstrv. dir. Touchstone Counseling Svc., Walnut Creek, 1981-83; tchr. Diablo Valley Jr. Coll., 1984; exec. dir. Battered Women's Alternatives, Concord, Calif., 1984-85, Child Abuse Prevention Coun., Walnut Creek, 1985-90; psychotherapist InVision Assocs., Lafayette, Calif., 1984—; pub. health educator Mariposa (Calif.) Health Dept., 1990—; cons. Computer Using Educators, Menlo Park, Calif., 1988-90; lectr. in field; mem., v.p. Mariposa Mental Health Adv. Bd., Mariposa Drug and Alcohol Adv. Bd., maternal-child health adv. bd. John C. Fremont Hosp. Found. Contbr. articles to profl. jours. and books. Chmn. No. Calif. Legis. Children and Family Coalition, Berkeley, 1987-90; adv. bd., chmn. Women's Recovery Ctr., Bass Lake, Calif., 1990-92; coord./mem. No. Calif. Child Death Review Coalition, San Francisco, 1988-90, Children and Family Trust Fund Com., Concord, 1989-90. Mem. Assn. Marriage Family Therapists. Home: 4821 Crystal Aire Dr Mariposa CA 95338-9663 Office: Mariposa Pub Health Dept PO Box 5 Mariposa CA 95338-0005

BRYANT, DON ESTES, economist, scientist; b. Truman, Ark., May 18, 1917; s. James Monroe and Olivia (Mayfield) B.; m. Jess Ann Chailer, Jan. 27, 1956; children: Stephen Williamson (dec.), Patrice Ann. Student, Cass Tech. Trade Coll., 1938-41. Pres., founder Consol. Aircraft Products, El Segundo, Calif., 1949-57, Trilan Corp., El Segundo, 1957-62, The Am. Inventor, Palos Verdes Estates, Calif., 1962-68; chmn., founder Message Control Crop., Palos Verdes Estates, 1968-70; scientist Econ. Rsch., Palos Verdes Estates and Lake Arrowhead, Calif., 1970—; cons. Svc. Corps. Ret. Execs. Assn.-SBA, L.A., 1965-67; founder Bryant Inst. and Club U.S.A. (United to Save Am.), 1991, J. Ayn Bryant and Assocs., 1991. Inventor missle and satellite count-down systems for USAF, 1958; formulator sci. of human econs.; host TV talk show World Peace Through Free Enterprise, 1985; author: 10-book children's series The 1, 2, 3's of Freedom and Economics, 1988. Served with USN, 1935-37. Republican. Roman Catholic. Home: 282 S Sunset Lake Arrowhead CA 92352-9999 Office: Econ Rsch PO Box 1023 Lake Arrowhead CA 92352-1023

BRYANT, GARRY EUGENE, photojournalist, educator; b. Boulder, Colo., Aug. 23, 1954; s. Ralph Eugene Bryant and Frances Lorene (Alcorn) Gilpin; m. Dalene Day, Sept. 6, 1985; children: Sterling Quinn, Ian William, Ailene. BA, Brigham Young U., 1986. Missionary LDS Ch., Pitts., 1978-80; photographer The Sun Advocate, Price, Utah, 1981; photographer, photo editor The Daily Universe-Brigham Young U., Provo, Utah, 1981-83; photographer The Herald Jour., Logan, Utah, 1983-84, Ogden (Utah) Standard-Examiner, 1984-85; photojournalist Deseret News, Salt Lake City, 1985—; adj. prof. Brigham Young U., Provo, 1988—. Author: Journal Mass Media Ethics, 1987, Special Report on Photojournalism Ethics, 1990, The Augustan Soc. Omnibus, 1993; assoc. editor: (mag.) The Rangefinder, 1983-90; editor: (newsletter) Saltire, 1992—. Sgt. USAF, 1972-76. Named Utah Photographer of Yr., Soc. Profl. Journalists, 1984, Best News and Sports photo Associated Press, Utah-Idaho Office, Salt Lake City, 1991. Mem. Nat. Press Photographers Assn. (region 9 student chmn. 1984-90, Coll. Photographer of Yr. 1982), Am. Coll. Heraldry, The Augustan Soc., St. Andrews Soc. Utah (historian 1991—), Clan Kennedy Soc. Am. (Rocky Mountain rep. 1989—), Scottish-Am. Mil. Soc. Post 1847 (sec., historian 1992—), Noble Co. Rose (knight), Internat. Chivalric Inst., Hibernian Soc. Utah, Heraldry Soc. Ireland. Democrat. Church of Jesus Christ of Latter Day Saints. Home: 319 E Mansfield Ave South Salt Lake UT 84115-4033 Office: Deseret News 30 East 100 South Salt Lake City UT 84110

BRYANT, GARY LEE, federal agency executive; b. Stockton, Calif., Dec. 10, 1943; s. Arnold and Dorothy J. (Miller) B.; m. Leah Song Wha Kim, Dec. 30, 1967; 1 child, Andrea. BS in Zoology, Pacific Union Coll., 1966; MA in Biology, Calif. State U., Long Beach, 1974. Engring. tech. U.S. Borax Chem. Co., Boron, Calif., 1970-71; fishery biologist U.S. Bur. Reclamation, Tracy, Calif., 1972-74; environ. specialist U.S. Bur. Reclamation, Salt Lake City, 1974-76; regional fishery biologist U.S. Bur. Reclamation, Boulder City, Nev., 1976-78, supr. environ. specialist, 1978-84; fellowship Dept. Interior, Washington, 1985-86; regional loan program mgr. U.S. Bur. Reclamation, Boulder City, 1986-88, regional planning and loans officer, 1988—. Contbr. articles to profl. jours. 1st lt. U.S. Army, 1967-70. Mem. Water Reuse Assn. Calif., Desert Pupfish Soc., Colo. River Water Users. Republican. Office: US Bur Reclamation PO Box 61470 Boulder City NV 89006-1470

BRYANT, HILDA MARIE, journalism educator; b. Big Rapids, Mich., Feb. 4, 1928; d. George Ray and Mary Jane (White) Mallett; m. Robert Lee Bryant, Sept. 2, 1949; adopted children : Michael Kimm (dec.), Victoria Lee Bryant Avery. BA in Journalism, U. Wash., 1965, MA, 1969. Instr. English Seattle Pacific U., 1965-67; social/racial issues reporter Seattle Post-Intelligencer, 1967-82; investigative reporter/producer KIRO-TV, Seattle, 1982-88; asst. prof. dept. comm. Seattle U., 1988—; war corres. newspaper Vietnam, 1974; TV war corres. Afghanistan, 1979, 80, 84, 91; fgn. corres. TV, Bangladesh, 1988; specialist on Afghanistan for radio and TV; cons. The Sun, Seattle U. Mag., 1990-92, Wash. Journalism Edn. Assn., 1990-92; media cons. Habitat for Humanity, Wash. chpt., 1991-92; cons. feminist textbook: A Place inthe News, Columbia U. Press, 1990. Author: Are You Listening, Neighbor, 1971; author collected essays: The Red Man in America, 1970. Recipient Nat. Journalism Edn. Rsch. Warren Price award, 1969, Nat. Gold Medal, Mass Media Brotherhood award for in-depth racial newspaper coverage Nat. Coun. Christians and Jews, N.Y.C., 1968, Regional Emmy awards Nat. Assn. TV Artists, 1985, 86, 87, Global Media award Metro. TV, Internat. Population Inst., 1990, many others; Poynter Inst. broadcast teaching fellow, 1990, Gannett Found. media ethics fellow, 1991, Internat. Radio and TV Soc. broadcast faculty fellow, 1992, Seattle U. grant, 1990. Mem. Soc. Profl. Journalists (sec. Western Wash. chpt. 1991-92), Wash. Press Assn. (life), Nat. Fedn. Presswomen (life), Wash. Journalism Edn. Assn., Seattle U. Profl. Ethics Ctr., Olympic Health and Racquet Club, Intiman Theater Dinner and Conversation Group. Democrat. Methodist. Home: 1605 5th St N #501 Seattle WA 98109 Office: Seattle Univ Broadway and Madison Seattle WA 98122

BRYANT, HURLEY DOUGLAS, JR., marketing professional; b. Kansas City, Mo., July 4, 1944; s. Hurley Douglas Bryant Sr. and Lulrene (Whiles) Brown; m. Margie Lou Fugina, Nov. 19, 1971; children: Erin McCell, Shaunna Lynn, Blake Douglas. BBA, Benedictine Coll., Atchison, Kans., 1971; MPA, U. Okla., 1975; postgrad., U. Kans., 1977, UCLA, 1991. Cert. mktg./mdsing. Commd. 2d lt. U.S. Army, 1963, advanced through grades to lt. col., ret., 1983; cons. Sci. Applications Internat., Kansas City, Kans., 1984; program mgr. Perceptronics, Inc., Atlanta, 1984-87, comml. products mgr., 1987-88; dep. dir. Perceptronics, Inc., Woodland Hills, Calif., 1988-90; dir. bus. devel. Perceptronics, Inc., Woodland Hills, 1990—; product mgr. Profl. Truck Driving Simulators joint venture Perceptronics, Inc. and 1st Ann Arbor (Mich.) Corp., Woodland Hills, 1991; dist. mgr. Burns Internat. Security Svcs., L.A., 1991—. Leader Atchison area Boy Scouts Am., 1976-83, YMCA Trailblazers, 1992; dir. Trinity Luth. Ch., Atchison, 1977-83. Mem. Kiwanis. Home: 15793 Milne Cir Moorpark CA 93021-3233 Office: Burns Internat Security Svc 292 S La Cienega Blvd Beverly Hills CA 90211-3330

BRYANT, JACK KENDALL, civil engineer; b. Enid, Okla., Nov. 1, 1925; s. Theodore Claude and Esther Annabell (Moon) B.; m. Ann Yerkes, June, 1946 (div. 1974); children: John Kendall, Mary Ann; m. Peggy Ann Hamblin, June 9, 1974. BS in Engring., U. Ark., 1950; MS, U. So. Calif., 1960, MPA, 1965. Registered civil engr., Calif. Civil engr. L.A. County Engrs. Dept., 1963-71; prin. Jack K. Bryant and Assoc., Inc., L.A., 1971—. Bd. dirs. Goodwill Industries So. Calif., L.A., 1966—, chmn., 1972-73. Fellow ASCE (life); mem. Am. Pub. Works Assn. (assoc.), Masons (past master 1971-72). Republican. Methodist. Office: 2601 Airport Dr Ste 310 Torrance CA 90505

BRYCHEL, RUDOLPH MYRON, engineer; b. Milw., Dec. 4, 1934; s. Stanley Charles and Jean Ann (Weiland) B.; m. Rose Mary Simmons, Sept. 3, 1955; children: Denise, Rita, Rudolph Myron Jr., Patrick, Bradford, Matthew. Student, U. Wis., Stevens Point, 1953, U.S. Naval Acad., 1954-55, U. Del., 1957, Colo. State U., 1969, North Park Coll., Chgo., 1973, Regis U., Denver, 1990-91. Lab. and quality tech. Thiokol Chem. Co., Elkton, Md., 1956; final test insp. Martin Aircraft Co., Middle River, Md., 1956-57; system final insp. Delco Electronics Co., Oak Creek, Wis., 1957-58; test equipment design engr. Martin Marietta Co., Littleton, Colo., 1958-64; prodn. supr. Gates Rubber Co., Denver, Colo., 1964-65; freelance mfr., quality and project engr. Denver and Boulder, Colo., Raton, N.Mex., 1965-67; quality engr. IBM, Gaithersburg (Md.), Boulder (Colo.), 1967-73; sr. quality engr. Abbott Labs., North Chicago, Ill., 1973-74; instrumentation and control engr. Stearns Roger Co., Glendale, Colo., 1974-81; staff quality engr. Storage Tech., Louisville, Colo., 1981-83; sr. quality engr. Johnson & Johnson Co., Englewood, Colo., 1983-84; quality engr., cons. Staodynamics Co., Longmont, Colo., 1984-85; sr. engr. for configuration and data mgmt. Martin Marietta Astronautics Group, Denver, 1985-91; freelance cons. Littleton, Colo., 1991—. With USN, 1953-56. Mem. Am. Soc. Quality Control (cert. quality engr.), Regulatory Affairs Profl. Soc., Soc. for Tech. Communications (regional chpt. chmn. 1970), KC. Democrat. Roman Catholic. Home and Office: 203 W Rafferty Gardens Ave Littleton CO 80120-1710

BRYDON, HAROLD WESLEY, entomologist, writer; b. Hayward, Calif., Dec. 6, 1923; s. Thomas Wesley and Hermione (McHenry) B.; m. Ruth Bacon Vickery, Mar. 28, 1951 (div.); children: Carol Ruth, Marilyn Jeanette, Kenneth Wesley. AB, San Jose State Coll., 1948; MA, Stanford U., 1950. Insecticide sales Calif. Spray Chem. Corp., San Jose, 1951-52; entomologist, fieldman, buyer Beech-Nut Packing Co., 1952-53; mgr., entomologist Lake County Mosquito Abatement Dist., Lakeport, Calif., 1954-58; entomologist, adviser Malaria Eradication Programs AID, Kathmandu, Nepal, 1958-61, Washington, 1961-62, Port-au-Prince, Haiti, 1962-63; dir. fly control research Orange County Health Dept. Santa Ana, Calif., 1963-66; free-lance writer in field, 1966—; research entomologist U. N.D. Sch. Medicine, 1968; developer, owner Casierra Resort, Lake Almanor, Calif., 1975-79; owner Westwood (Calif.) Sport Shop, 1979-84; instr. Lassen Community Coll., Susanville, Calif., 1975—; bio control cons., 1980—. Mem. entomology and plant pathology del. People to People Citizen Ambassador Program, China, 1986; citizen ambassador 30th Anniversary Caravan to Soviet Union, 1991, Vietnam Initiative Del., 1992. Contbr. profl. jours. and conducted research in field. Served with USNR, 1943-46. Recipient Meritorious Honor award for work in Nepal, AID, U.S. Dept. State, 1972. Mem. Entomol. Soc. Am., Am. Mosquito Control Assn., Pacific Coast Entomol. Soc., Am. Legion. Republican. Methodist. Club: Commonwealth of California. Lodges: Masons, Rotary. Home: PO Box 312 Westwood CA 96137-0312

BRYDON, RUTH VICKERY, educator; b. San Jose, Calif., June 2, 1930; d. Robert Kingston and Ruth (Bacon) Vickery; m. Harold Wesley Brydon, Mar. 28, 1951 (div.); children—Carol Ruth Brydon Koford, Marilyn Jeanette, Kenneth Wesley. B.A., Stanford U., 1952; student San Jose State Coll., 1964-65, MA Calif. State Coll.-Chico, 1987. Cert. tchr., Calif., cert. sch. adminstr. Tchr., Lincoln Sch., Kathmandu, Nepal, 1959-60; tchr. Am. Sch., Port-au-Prince, Haiti, 1962-63; tchr. social studies Norte Vista High Sch., Riverside, Calif., 1965-67, chmn. social studies dept., 1966-67; tchr. home econs., social studies Westwood (Calif.) High Sch., 1967-90, mentor tchr., 1984-85; media specialist Lake Havasu High Sch., 1990-91; history instr. Mohave Community Coll. Lake Havasu Campus, 1990—; coord. extended day classes Lassen Coll., 1977-84. Co-chairperson Almanor Art Show, 1980-84. NDEA grantee, 1967. Mem. Commonwealth Club Calif. Episcopalian. Home: 2681 N Cisco Dr Lake Havasu City AZ 86403-5020

BRYNGELSON, JIM, educational administrator; b. Billings, Mont., Mar. 8, 1941; s. Ivan Carl and Clarie (Ellingwood) B.; m. Judy Bryngelson, June 29, 1969; children: Joy, Nick. BS, U. Mont., 1959; MS, Purdue U., 1967; EdS, U. No. Colo., 1974, EdD, 1976. Tchr. sci. Littleton Pub. Schs., Colo., 1964-66, sch. counselor, 1967-73, sch. psychologist, 1974-75; spl. edn. cons., Steamboat Springs, Colo., 1975-78; dir. edn. Yellowstone Edn. Ctr., Billings, Mont., 1978-90, supr. treatment team, 1990—; pres. Self Esteem Assocs., Billings, 1980—. Bd. dirs. Tumbleweed Foster Homes, Billings, 1980-84, Rocky Mountain Little League, Billings, 1982, Mental Health Assn., Billings, v.p., 1986-87, pres. 1987-88. Recipient Disting. Educator award Charles Kettering Found., 1983; named U.S. Cultural Exchange Delegate to

Republic of China, 1986. Fellow Assn. Supervision and Curriculum Devel., Sch. Adminstrs. Mont., Council Exceptional Children, Council for Children with Behavior Disorders, Mont. Assn. Supervision and Curriculum Devel. (bd. dirs. 19887-89), Council for Adminstrs. Spl. Edn., Albert Schweitzer Soc., John Dewey Soc., Phi Delta Kappa (v.p. 1984-85, pres 1985-86); mem. Mont. Educators Emotionally Disturbed (charter). Democrat. Lutheran. Home: 1144 Henry Rd Billings MT 59102-0811 Office: Youth Dynamics 2601 Uir Ln Billings MT 59102

BRYSON, BRUCE ALAN (RANDY), corporate executive, nurse; b. Eugene, Oreg., July 28, 1946; s. Milton L. and Margaret J. (Ryker) B.; m. Cassandra A. Coleman, Mar. 16, 1984; children: Stacey, Leslie. Student, U. Oreg., 1964-66; AS, Lane Community Coll., Eugene, 1971; student, Linfield Coll., 1987—. RN, Oreg. Nurse VA, Roseburg, Oreg., 1971, Kapiolani Ob.-Gyn. Hosp., Honolulu, 1971-72; dir. North Pacific Raceway, Eugene, 1972; nurse Sacred Heart Gen. Hosp., Eugene, 1972-74, Queens Med. Ctr., Honolulu, 1974-77; owner Warmuth Co., Santa Cruz, Calif., 1977-83; admissions specialist Rep. Health Corp., Gresham, Oreg., 1983-86; nurse mgr. Sacred Heart Gen. Hosp., Eugene, 1986-88; exec. dir. Nat. Consortium Chem. Dependency Nurses, 1987—; pres. Momentum Mgmt., Eugene, 1990—; cons. State of Oreg. and Idaho, 1987-90; rep. div. nursing Dept. Pub. Health, Washington, 1988-90; dir. family svcs. Nelson Inst., Boise, Idaho. Contbr. articles to profl. jours. Mem. Nat. Consortium Chem. Dependency Nurses (charter), Izaak Walton League. Home: 2210 Burlington Dr Eugene OR 97405-1104 Office: Momentum Mgmt Ste 510 1720 Willow Creek Cir Eugene OR 97402

BRYSON, DOROTHY PRINTUP, retired educator; b. Britton, S.D., Dec. 2, 1894; d. David Lawrence and Marion Harland (Gamsby) Printup; m. Archer Butler Hulbert, June 16, 1923 (dec. Dec. 1933); children: Joanne Woodward, Nancy Printup; m. Franklin Fearing Wing, Oct. 15, 1938 (dec. Mar. 1942); m. Arthur Earl Bryson, Feb. 15, 1964 (dec. Apr. 1979). AB, Oberlin Coll., 1915; AM, Radcliffe Coll., 1916; LHD (hon.), Colo. Coll., 1989. Instr. Latin, Tenn. Coll., Murfreesboro, 1916-18; tchr. Latin, prin. high sch., Britton, 1918-20; instr. classics Colo. Coll., Colorado Springs, 1921-22, 23-25, sec., instr., head resident, 1951-60; tchr. latin San Luis Prep. Sch., Colorado Springs, 1934-36, 41-42, Sandia Sch., Albuquerque, 1937-39, Westlake Sch., L.A., 1946-49; exec. dir. YWCA, Colorado Springs, 1942-46, 49-51; editor western history Stewart Commn., Colorado Springs, 1934-41; ret., 1960. Editor: Overland to the Pacific, 5 vols., 1934-41. Bd. dirs. Day Nursery, Colorado Springs 1933-37. Fellow Aelioian Lit. Soc., 1920-21; scholar U. Chgo., 1920-21. Mem. LWV (v.p., bd. dirs. Colorado Springs 1943-45), Women's Ednl. Soc. Colo. Coll. (pres., bd. dirs. 1955—), Tuesday Discussion Club, Pikes Peak Posse of Westeners, Phi Beta Kappa, Gamma Phi Beta. Republican. Episcopalian. Home: 107 W Cheyenne Rd Apt 610 Colorado Springs CO 80906-2509

BRYSON, GARY SPATH, cable television and telephone company executive; b. Longview, Wash., Nov. 8, 1943; s. Roy Griffin and Marguerite Elizabeth (Spath) B.; children: Kelly Suzanne, Lisa Christine. A.B., Dartmouth Coll., 1966; M.B.A., Tuck Sch., 1967. With Bell & Howell Co., Chgo., 1967-79; pres. consumer and audio-visual group Bell & Howell Co., 1977-79; chmn. bd., chief exec. officer Bell & Howell Mamiya Co., Chgo., 1979-81; exec. v.p. Am. TV & Communications Corp., subs. Time, Inc., Englewood, Colo., 1981-88; v.p. diversified group US West, Englewood, 1988-89, pres. cable communications div., 1989-92; pres., CEO TeleWest Internat., 1992—. Mem. Phi Beta Kappa, Sigma Alpha Epsilon. Republican. Lutheran. Home: Rm 1180 4643 S Ulster St Denver CO 80237 Office: US West 4643 S Ulster St Ste 1180 Denver CO 80237

BRYSON, JOHN E., utilities company executive; b. N.Y.C., July 24, 1943; m. Louise Henry. B.A. with great distinction, Stanford U., 1965; student, Freie U. Berlin, Federal Republic Germany, 1965-66; J.D., Yale U., 1969. Bar: Calif., Oreg., D.C. Asst. in instrn. Law Sch., Yale U., New Haven, Conn., 1968-69; law clk. U.S. Dist. Ct., San Francisco, 1969-70; co-founder, atty. Natural Resources Def. Council, 1970-74; vice chmn. Oreg. Energy Facility Siting Council, 1975-76; assoc. Davies, Biggs, Strayer, Stoel & Boley, Portland, Oreg., 1975-76; chmn. Calif. State Water Resources Control Bd., 1976-79; vis. faculty Stanford U. Law Sch., Calif., 1977-79; pres. Calif. Pub. Utilities Commn., 1979-82; ptnr. Morrison & Foerster, San Francisco, 1983-84; sr. v.p. law and fin. So. Calif. Edison Co., Rosemead, 1984; exec. v.p., chief fin. officer SCEcorp. and So. Calif. Edison Co., 1985-90; chmn. of bd., CEO SCE Corp. and So. Calif. Edison Co., Rosemead, 1990—; lectr. on pub. utility, energy, communications law.; former mem. exec. com. Nat. Assn. Regulatory Utility Commrs., Calif. Water Rights Law Rev. Commn., Calif. Pollution Control Financing Authority; former mem. adv. bd. Solar Energy Research Inst., Electric Power Research Inst., Stanford Law Sch.; bd. dirs. Pacific Am. Income Shares Inc. Mem. bd. editors, assoc. editor: Yale U. Law Jour. Bd. dirs. World Resources Inst., Washington, Calif. Environ. Trust, Claremont U. Ctr., Grad. Sch., Stanford U. Alumni Assn.; trustee Stanford U., 1991. Woodrow Wilson fellow. Mem. Calif. Bar Assn., Oreg. Bar Assn., D.C. Bar Assn., Nat. Assn. Regulatory Utility Commrs. (exec. com. 1980-82), Stanford U. Alumni Assn. (bd. dirs. 1983-86), Phi Beta Kappa. Office: So Calif Edison Co PO Box 800 2244 Walnut Grove Ave Rosemead CA 91770-3714

BUBB, BRIAN DAVID, lawyer; b. Balt., June 22, 1962; s. Donald Lewis Sr. and Louise Mary (Masimore)B. BBA in Fin., Albright Coll., 1985; JD, Pepperdine U., 1988. Assoc. Howarth & Smith, L.A., 1988—. Mem. ABA, Am. Trial Lawyers Assn., Calif. Bar Assn., L.A. County Bar Assn. Republican. Baptist. Home: 234 S Figueroa St Ste 1432 Los Angeles CA 90012

BUBB, HARRY GEIPLE, insurance company executive; b. Trinidad, Colo., Dec. 16, 1924; s. Harry H. and Grace Alleine (Geiple) B.; m. Berdel Edrie Letcher, June 9, 1951; children—Melinda, Howard, Susan, John, Mary. BA in Econs, Stanford U., 1946, MBA, 1949; grad., Advanced Mgmt. Program, Harvard U., 1973. With Pacific Mut. Life Ins. Co., 1949—, asst. v.p., 1966-68, then v.p., 1968-72, sr. v.p. group ins., 1972-75, pres., 1975—, chief exec. officer, 1986-90, chmn. bd., 1987-90, chmn. bd. emeritus, 1990—; bd. dirs., mem. exec. com. Pacific Mut. Life. Bd. dirs. Calif. Health Decisions, Orange County Bus. Com. for Arts; mem. adv. coun. Calif. State Parks Found.; trustee Newport Harbor Art Mus. Served as pilot USNR, World War II. Mem. Calif. C. of C. (bd. dirs.), Lincoln Club of Orange County, Balboa Yacht Club, California Club, Center Club. Home: 27 Beacon Bay Newport Beach CA 92660-7218 Office: Pacific Mut Life Ins Co 700 Newport Center Dr Newport Beach CA 92660-6397

BUBULKA, GRACE MARIE, trauma administrator, nursing education director; b. Phila., June 26, 1951; d. Joseph John and Ida (Gryniewicz) B.; children: Karen, Billy, Joan. BS in Nursing, Villanova U., 1973; MS in Nursing, Widener U., 1984. Course coordinator U. Pa., Phila., 1978-79; supr., head nurse Lankenau Hosp., Phila., 1973-84; clin. specialist AEMC, Phila., 1984-85; affiliate faculty Widener U., Chester, Pa., 1985-89; trauma cons. Norristown, Phila., 1986-89, Valley Children's Hosp., Fresno, Calif., 1989—; lectr. in field. Author: Ants In My Toothbrush (Camp Nursing), Beyond Reality (Near Death Experience); contbr. articles to profl. jours. Recipient Mayor's Recognition award Borough Coun., 1986. Mem. Emergency Nurses Assn. (founder Valley Forge chpt.), Am. Trauma Soc., Sigma Theta Tau. Home: 3757 W Wathen Fresno CA 93711 Office: Valley Children's Hosp 3151 N Millbrook Ave Fresno CA 93703-1497

BUCCELLATI, GIORGIO, archeology educator; b. Milan, Italy, Feb. 8, 1937; came to the U.S., 1959; s. Mario and Maria (Rodolfi) B.; m. Marilyn Kelly, Apr. 11, 1966; 1 child Federico Alessandro. PhD in Ancient History, Catholic U., Milan, 1954-58; cert. in German, U. of Bonn, Germany, summer 1956; student of Philosophy, U. of Innsbruck, Austria, 1958-59; MA in Philosophy, Fordham U., 1959-60; PhD in Oriental Langs., U. Chgo., 1960-65. Instr., dept. of History Loyola Univ., Chgo., 1963-65; asst. prof. UCLA, 1965-68, assoc. prof., 1968-74; vis. prof. Pontifical Biblical Inst., 1971; prof. Ancient Near East, History UCLA, 1974—; vis. prof. Univ. of Aleppo, 1979; trustee, mem. exec. com., chmn. Damascus Com., NEH Fellowship com., Am. Schs. of Oriental Rsch., 1986-89; guest curator Elba to Damascus Exhibit, Mus. of Natural History, L.A., 1986; mem. screening com. Coun. for Internat. Exchange of Scholars, 1983; co-dir. Archaeological Exhibit on Mesopotamian Archeology Govt. of India, 1982; dir. Inst. of Archaeology, UCLA, 1973-83, Internat. Inst. for Mesopotamian Studies, 1976—; prin. investigator Linguistic Analysis of Old Babylonian Texts, NEH, 1972-77; chmn. Grad. Archaeology Program, UCLA, 1971-73; rsch. asst. Univ. Chgo., 1962-63. Author (with others): The Amorities of the Ur III Period, 1966, Cities and Nations of Ancient Syria, 1967, Cuneiform Texts from Nippur: The Eighth and Ninth Season, 1969, IIMAS Field Encoding Manual, 1978, Terqa Preliminary Report, 10: The Fourth Season-Introduction and the Stratigraphic Record, 1979, Mozan 1. The Soundings of the First Two Seasons, 1988; editor: Studi Sull'Oriente e al Bibbia offerti al P. Giovanni Rinaldi, 1967, Approaches to the Study of the Ancient Near East: Gelb Volume, 1973, (with others) The Shape of the Past: Studies in Honor of Franklin D. Murphy, 1981; contbr. articles to profl. jours., numerous editorial positions held. Fellow Am. Schs. of Oriental Rsch., Univ. Calif. Humanities Inst.; mem. Internat. Com. for the Publ. of the Texts of Ebla. Office: UCLA Near Eastern Langs 405 Hilgard Ave Los Angeles CA 90024

BUCCIGROSSI, DAVID ERIC, physician; b. Riverside, Calif., Sept. 12, 1956; s. Sam Anthony and Geraldine (Ligman) B.; m. Debbie Lee Winkelbauer, Sept. 7, 1985. BA, U. Calif., San Diego, 1979; MD, U. Calif., 1984. Diplomate Am. Bd. Internal Medicine. Guitar instr. San Diego, 1973-78; chemistry instr. U. Calif., San Diego, 1978-81; chemistry reasearcher Scripps Inst. Oceanography U. Calif., 1978-80; intern, then resident U. Wash., Seattle, 1984-87; ptnr. specializing in internal medicine So. Calif. Permanente Med. Group, San Diego, 1990—. Family Practice Preceptorship grantee U. Calif., San Diego, 1981. Mem. Am. Coll. Physicians, A. Baird Hasting Soc. Democrat. Roman Catholic. Office: So Calif Permanente Med Group 6860 Avenida Encinas Carlsbad CA 92008

BUCCO, MARTIN, writer, educator; b. Newark, Dec. 3, 1929; s. Mario and Anna (DiSalvo) B.; m. Edith Ann Erickson, Aug. 26, 1956; 1 child, Tamara. BA, Highlands U., 1952; MA, Columbia U., 1957; PhD, U. Mo., 1963. Instr. N.D. State Coll., Valley City, 1958-59, U. Mo., Columbia, 1959-63; prof. Colo. State U., Ft. Collins, 1963—; vis. prof. U. of the Pacific, Stockton, Calif., 1980-81; cons. in field. Author: The Voluntary Tongue, 1957, Frank Waters, 1969, Wilbur Daniel Steele, 1972, An American Tragedy Notes, 1974, E.W. Howe, 1977, Rene Wellek, 1981, Western American Literary Criticism, 1984, Critical Essays on Sinclair Lewis, 1986, Main Street: The Revolt of Carol Kennicott, 1993; mem. editorial bd. Rocky Mountain Rev., 1984—. Wurlitzer Found. grantee, 1956-57, NEH grantee, 1977; vis. scholar U. Wales, Swansea, Eng., 1989. Mem. Western Am. Lit. (exec. sec. 1982-87). Home: 140 Circle Dr Fort Collins CO 80524-4108 Office: Colo State U Dept English Fort Collins CO 80523

BUCHANAN, BRYCE JOHN, accountant, consultant; b. Dec. 6, 1965; s. Hayle and Melva Lois (Taylor) B.; m. Kimberli Anne Kellett, Aug. 12, 1988; 1 child, Tyler. BS cum laude, Brigham Young U., 1990, MS with honors, 1990. Systems/acctg. cons. Provo, Utah, 1987-90; acct. Price Waterhouse, Phoenix, 1991—. Varsity Scout coach Boy Scouts Am., Mesa, Ariz., 1991. Home: 540 N May St Apt 1121 Mesa AZ 85201-4464 Office: Price Waterhouse 1850 N Cnetral Ave Phoenix AZ 85004-4563

BUCHANAN, TERI BAILEY, public relations executive, marketing agency owner; b. Long Beach, Calif., Feb. 24, 1946; d. Alton Hervey and Ruth Estelle (Thompson) Bailey; m. Robert Wayne Buchanan, Aug. 14, 1964 (div. May 1979). BA in English with highest honors, Ark. Poly. Coll., 1968. With employee communications AT&T, Kansas City, Mo., 1968-71; freelance writer Ottawa, Kans., 1971-73; publs. dir. Ottawa U., 1973-74; regional info. officer U.S. Dept. Labor, Kansas City, 1974; owner, operator PBT Communications, Kansas City, 1975-79; sr. pub. affairs rep., sr. editor, exhibit supr., communications specialist Standard Oil/Chevron, San Francisco, 1979-84; owner The Resource Group/Mktg. Pub. Relations, San Francisco, 1984—; mem. faculty pub. rels. master's program Golden Gate U., San Francisco, 1987. Pub. rels. trainer Bus. Vols. for Arts, San Francisco, 1985—; mem. San Francisco Conv. and Visitors Bur., Napa Conf. and Visitors Bureau. Recipient Internat. Assn. Bus. Communicators Bay Area Gold and Silver awards, 1984. Mem. Publicity Club, Napa C. of C. Democrat. Episcopalian. Office: The Resource Group Studio B 340 Bryant St San Francisco CA 94107 also: 1325 Imola Ave West Ste 515 Napa CA 94559

BUCHEGER, RONALD R., corporate executive; b. Park Falls, Wis., Mar. 1, 1948; s. Robert L. and Luana (Pichler) B.; m. Ruth M. Thielke, June 17, 1972. AAS in Computers, Milw. Sch. Engring., 1974, BEE, 1974; Master of Mgmt., Northwestern U., 1986. Registered profl. engr., Wis. Applications engr. Giddings & Lewis Machine Tool Co., Fond du Lac, Wis., 1974-76; various positions Baxter Healthcare Corp., Deerfield, Ill., 1976-90, mgr. rsch. and devel., dir. rsch. and devel., dir. tech. ops., dir. bus. devel., gen. mgr.; mgr., product devel. mktg. Acuson Corp., Mountain View, Calif., 1990-92; sr. dir. product devel. Applied Immune Scis., Santa Clara, Calif., 1992—; bd. dirs. Linus Techs., Inc., Reston, Va. Patentee in field. With U.S. Army, 1968-71. Mem. IEEE, Am. Assn. Med. Instrumentation. Republican. Roman Catholic. Home: 905 Montevino Dr Pleasanton CA 94566-6315 Office: Applied Immune Scis 5301 Patrick Henry Dr Santa Clara CA 95054-1114

BUCHHOLZ, JOHN NICHOLAS, pharmacology educator; b. Cahose, N.Y., Nov. 2, 1956; s. Walter Lawrence and Teresa Marie (Touzin) B.; m. Melisa Audrey Erick, June 22, 1981 (div. Apr. 1987); 1 child, Nickolaus Erick. BS, Loma Linda U., 1980, MS, 1983, PhD, 1988. Asst. prof., asst. rsch. Loma Linda U., U. Calif., Irvine, 1991—; cons. Allergan Pharms., Irvine, 1990—. Contbr. articles to profl. jours. Fellowship Am. Heart Assn., 1989, NIH, 1991; rsch. grant Am. Fedn. Aging Rsch. 1992. Mem. Soc. for Neurosci., Sigma Xi. Republican. Home: 12168 Mt Vernon Ave #36 Grand Terrace CA 92324 Office: U Calif Dept Pharmacology Irvine CA 92717

BUCHMAN, MATTHEW LIEBER, legal administrator; b. Phila., Mar. 14, 1958; s. A Sander and Joan Sue (Katzen) B. BA in Geology, Bates Coll., 1976-80. Sole proprietor Unicorn Boat Works, Seattle, 1982-85; network adminstr. Ulin, Dann & Lambe, Profl. Svc. Corp., Seattle, 1985-89; automation systems mgr. Betts, Patterson & Mines, Profl. Svc., Seattle, 1989-92; dir. legal div. CMIS, Inc., Redmond, Wash., 1992—. Vol. Civic Light Opera. Regents scholar, 1976. Mem. Assn. Systems Mgrs. (membership chair 1990-91, v.p. 1991-92), 1ONET Users Group (officer 1988-90). Democrat. Jewish. Home: 347 N 76th St Seattle WA 98103-4613 Office: CMIS Inc 16307 NE 83d Redmond WA 98052

BUCHSBAUM, HARVEY WILLIAM, neurologist, educator; b. Newark, Sept. 7, 1935; s. Max A. and Henrietta (Mentzel) B.; m. Ruby Francis Weihrauch, Aug. 22, 1959; children: Steven, Karen, Cynthia. BA, Hamilton Coll., 1957; MD, Albany State U., 1961, postgrad., 1963; postgrad., Neurologic Inst., 1966. Diplomate Am. Bd. Neurology. Asst. prof. U. Ariz., Tucson, 1968, clin. prof., 1977—; med. dir. Aetna, Tucson, 1991—; chief of staff Tucson Med. Ctr., 1978-80. Pres. Crippled Children, Tucson, 1972; bd. dirs. Rehab. Inst., Tucson, 1990—. Capt. U.S. Army, 1966-68. Home: 7720 N Christie Dr Tucson AZ 85718

BUCHTA, EDMUND, engineering executive; b. Wostitz, Nikolsburg, Czechoslovakia, May 11, 1928; came to U.S., 1979; Kaufmann, Deutsche Wirtschaftoberschule, Bruenn, Czechoslovakia, 1942-45. Shop foreman Messerklinger, Ernsting, Austria, 1949-51; constrn. foreman Hinteregger, U.S. Mil. Project, Salzburg, Siezenheim, Austria, 1951-52, Auserehl Constrn. Corp., N.Y.C., 1963; pres. Grout Concrete Constrn. Ltd., Edmonton, Alta., Can., 1966-73; pioneer & explorer Canol Project Parcel B and Land Ownership N.W. Can., 1968—; pres. Barbarosa Enterprises Ltd., Yellowknife, Can., 1971—; owner Canol Project Parcel B, 1968. With German Mil., 1943-45. Named Emperor of the North, McLean Mag., Can., 1976. Mem. TRW, Automobile Club Calif. Home: PO Box 7000-713 Redondo Beach CA 90277

BUCK, ALAN CHARLES, forensic investigator; b. Chgo., Oct. 26, 1931; s. Axel Harris and Mabel Anna (Kleutgen) B.; m. Kay Collins, Mar. 27, 1992. BS, U. Ill., 1954, MS, 1959; PhD, U. Hawaii, 1967; postgrad., Stanford U., 1961-63. Sr. lectr. Kampala (Uganda), Makerere U., 1967-69; sr,. researcher NASA, Houston, 1969-75; mgr. environ. affairs Gulf Interstate Eng. Co., Houston, 1975-78; pres. Practical Scis., Inc., Cypress, Calif., 1978-87, Chem. Applications Techs., Cypress, Calif., 1987—; sr. scientist Environ. Forensics, Cypress, Calif., 1990—; pres. Detroit Testing Labs., 1980-81; sr. scientist Am. Stas. Testing Bur., N.Y.C., 1984-86; sr. cons. Ecoserve, Pitts., 1990-91; spl. cons. Nat. Tech. Svcs., Fullerton, Calif., 1992—. Patentee in field. With U.S. Army, 1950-52. USPH PhD Tng. grantee, 1961-63; U. Ill. Alumni scholar, 1950-52. Mem. Am. Chem. Soc. (pub. rels. com. dir. 1987), Aerospace Medicine (edit. review 1970-74), Undersea Med. Soc. (Edit. review 1971-75). Home: 6073 Nauru St Cypress CA 90630

BUCK, CARL NELSON, electronics executive; b. Plainfield, N.J., June 29, 1952; s. Robert R. and Lucille M. (Nelson) B. BSEE, Princeton U., 1974; MS, U. Md., 1976; MBA, Stanford U., 1978. Product mgr. Intel, Santa Clara, Calif., 1978-79, 81-83; product mktg. mgr. Intel, Hillsboro, Oreg., 1979-81; mktg. mgr. Aehr Test Systems, Menlo Park, Calif., 1983-86, major account mgr., 1986-88, bus. unit mgr., 1988-90, v.p. engring., 1990—. Contbr. articles to profl. jours. Founder Sta. WLOP, Beaverton, Oreg., 1980—; musician Good Times Soc. Band, Palo Alto, Calif., 1985—, West Valley Light Opera, Saratoga, Calif. 1983, 92. Mem. IEEE. Office: Aehr Test Systems 1667 Plymouth St Mountain View CA 94043

BUCK, CHRISTIAN BREVOORT ZABRISKIE, independent oil operator; b. San Francisco, Oct. 18, 1914; s. Frank Henry and Zayda Justine (Zabriskie) B.; student U. Calif., Berkeley, 1931-33; m. Natalie Leontine Smith, Sept. 12, 1948; children—Warren Zabriskie, Barbara Anne. Mem. engring. dept. U.S. Potash Co., Carlsbad, N.Mex., 1933-39; ind. oil operator, producer, Calif., 1939-79, N.Mex., 1939—; owner, operator farm, ranch, Eddy County, N.Mex., 1951-79; dir. Belridge Oil Co. until 1979; dir. Buck Ranch Co. (Calif.). Served with RAF, 1942-45. Democrat. Episcopalian. Club: Riverside Country (Carlsbad). Home: PO Box 5368 599 Lariat Circle # 2 Incline Village NV 89450 Office: PO Box 2183 Santa Fe NM 87504-2183

BUCK, LAWRENCE RICHARD, fund raising executive; b. Albuquerque, Jan. 31, 1953; s. Richard Arthur and Mary Farris (Van Allen) B. BS in Phys. Sci., Colo. State U., 1976; MBA in Mktg., Calif. State U., San Bernardino, 1983. Ordained minister Evang. Ch. Alliance, 1991. Asst. to the dean Internat. Sch. of Theology, San Bernardino, 1977-78, asst. to the pres., 1978-80, deve. adminstr., 1980-82, donor rels. coord., 1982-83, asst. planning officer, 1983-84, dir. mktg., 1984-86; devel. adminstr. The JESUS Film Project, Campus Crusade for Christ Internat., San Bernardino, 1986-87, assoc. devel. officer, 1987—; cons., com. mem. ann. fund com. Calif. State U., San Bernardino, 1987-88; bd. dirs. Genesis Counseling Svc., 1992—. Mem. bd. councillors Calif. State U. Sch. Bus. and Pub. Adminstrn., San Bernardino, 1984—. Named one of Outstanding Young Men in Am., U.S. Jaycees, 1984. Mem. Am. Mktg. Assn. (charter mem. Calif. Inland Counties chpt.), Nat. Soc. Fund Raising Execs. (cert. fund raising exec., Inland Communities chpt.), Calif. State U. San Bernardino Alumni Assn. (bd. dirs. 1984—, bus. chpt. pres. 1984—). Republican. Mem. Evang. Free Ch. Office: The JESUS Film Project Arrowhead Springs 90-15 San Bernardino CA 92414

BUCK, LINDA DEE, recruiting company executive; b. San Francisco, Nov. 8, 1946; d. Sol and Shirley D. (Setterberg) Press; student Coll. San Mateo (Calif.), 1969-70; divorced. Head hearing and appeals br. Dept. Navy Employee Rels. Svc., Philippines, 1974-75; dir. human resources Homestead Savs. & Loan Assn., Burlingame, Calif., 1976-77; mgr. VIP Agy., Inc., Palo Alto, Calif., 1977-78; exec. v.p., dir. Sequent Personnel Svcs., Inc., Mountain View, Calif., 1978-83; founder, pres. Buck & Co., San Mateo, 1983-91. Publicity mgr. for No. Calif., Osteogenesis Imperfecta Found. Inc., 1970-72; cons. Am. Brittle Bone Soc., 1979-88. Jewish.

BUCKINGHAM, MICHAEL JOHN, oceanography educator; b. Oxford, Eng., Oct. 9, 1943; s. Sidney George and Mary Agnes (Walsh) B.; m. Margaret Penelope Rose Barrowcliff, July 15, 1967. BSc with hons., U. Reading (Eng.), 1967, PhD, 1971. Postdoctoral rsch. fellow U. Reading, 1971-74; sr. sci. officer Royal Aircraft Establishment, Farnborough, Eng., 1974-76; prin. sci. officer Royal Aircraft Establishment, 1976-82; exchange scientist Naval Rsch. Lab., Washington, 1982-84; vis. prof. MIT, Cambridge, 1986-87; sr. prin. sci. officer Royal Aircraft Establishment, 1983-86, 1987-90; prof. oceanography Scripps Instn. of Oceanography, La Jolla, Calif., 1990—; vis. prof. Inst. Sound and Vibration rsch., Southampton, Eng., 1990—; cons. Commn. of European Communities, Brussels, Belgium, 1989—; dir. Arctic rsch. Royal Aerospace Establishment, Farnborough, 1990—. Editor-in-chief Jour. Computational Acoustics; author: Noise in Electronic Devices and Systems, 1983; patentee in field; contbr. articles to profl. jours. Recipient Clerk Maxwell Premium, Inst. Electronic and Radio Engrs. London, 1972, A.B. Wood Medal, Inst. Acoustics, Bath, Eng., 1982, Alan Burman Pub. award, Naval Rsch. Lab., 1988, Commendation for Disting. Contbns. to ocean acoustics Naval Rsch. Lab., 1986. Fellow Inst. Acoustics (U.K.), Inst. Elec. Engrs. (U.K.); mem. Acous. Soc. Am. (chmn. acoustical oceanography tech. com. 1991—)., Sigma Xi. Home: 7921 Caminito Del Cid La Jolla CA 92037-3404 Office: Scripps Inst Oceanography Marine Phys Lab La Jolla CA 92093

BUCKINGHAM, RICHARD JOHN, accountant; b. Flint, Mich., Oct. 11, 1945; s. George Edward and Irma Clair (French) B.; m. Janet Gail Jefferies, Aug. 26, 1973 (div. Apr. 1992); children: Robert John, Richmond James; m. Doña M. Voights, Nov. 22, 1992. BS in Acctg., U. Colo., 1973; M in Taxation, U. Denver, 1984. CPA, Colo. Staff acct. Brock, Cordle & Assoc., Longmont, Colo., 1973-75; tax mgr. Smith, Brock & Gwinn, Denver, 1975-88; pvt. practice Arvada, Colo., 1988-92, Northglenn, Col., 1992—. With U.S. Army, 1969-70. Office: 10460 Wyandot Northglenn CO 80234

BUCKLEY, DAVID WHITAKER, consulting engineering geologist; b. Oakland, Calif., July 15, 1951; s. James Meredith and Muriel Donna (Hammel) B.; m. Amy Lee Cheng, Oct. 7, 1962; 1 child, Susanna. BA, U. Calif., Santa Barbara, 1975; MS, Purdue U., 1977. Engring. geologist Lowney and Assocs., Palo Alto, Calif., 1978-83, Earth Systems Cons., Palo Alto, 1983-85, PSC Assocs., Mountain View, Calif., 1985-88, Terrasearch, Inc., San Jose, Calif., 1988-92; pvt. practice cons. San Jose, 1992—. Mem. Assn. Engring. Geologists, Nat. Water Well Assn., Earthquake Engring. Rsch. Inst. Home and Office: 3452 Lisbon Dr San Jose CA 95132-1316

BUCKLEY, WILLIAM RANDOLPH, computer scientist; b. Artesia, Calif., Nov. 29, 1957; s. William Edgar and Bonnie Jean Pless (Hansen) B. BS in Phys. Sci., Calif. Poly, San Luis Obispo, 1986; tech. cert. computer ops. & programming, Control Data Inst., Anaheim, Calif., 1976. Pres. Amran, Huntington Beach, Calif., 1984-92, dir. emeritus, 1992—. Pub. The Core War Newsletter, 1986-91; contbr. articles to profl. jours.; columnist Hobnobbing with the Hyper Hacker for ASCII Mab., 1988—. Mem. Internat. Core Wars Soc. (dir. 1987—), Internat. Soc. on Systems Scis. (chmn. spl. interest group on artificial life 1990—). Home: 5712 Kern Dr Huntington Beach CA 92649-4535 Office: Amran 5712 Kern Dr Huntington Beach CA 92649-4535

BUCKLIN, LOUIS PIERRE, business educator, consultant; b. N.Y.C., Sept. 20, 1928; s. Louis Lapham and Elja (Barricklow) B.; m. Weylene Edwards, June 11, 1956; children: Randolph E., Rhonda W. Student, Dartmouth Coll., 1950; MBA, Harvard U., 1954; PhD, Northwestern U., 1960. Asst. prof. bus. U. Colo., Boulder, 1954-56; instr. in bus. Northwestern U., Evanston, 1958-59, assoc. dean Grad. Sch. Bus. Adminstrn., 1981-83; prof. bus. adminstrn. U. Calif., Berkeley, 1960-93, prof. emeritus, 1993—; vis. prof. Stockholm Sch. Econs., 1983, INSEAD, Fontainebleau, France, 1984, Erasmus U., Rotterdam, The Netherlands, 1993—; prin. Bucklin Assocs., Lafayette, Calif., 1975—; mem. adv. bd. Gemini Cons., San Francisco, 1987—. Author: A Theory of Distribution Channel Structure, 1966, Competition Evolution in The Distributive Trades, 1972, Productivity in Marketing, 1979; editor: Channels and Channel Institutions, 1986. Mem. City of Lafayette Planning Commn., 1990-93. Capt. USMC, 1951-53, Korea. Mem. Am. Mktg. Assn. (Paul D. Converse award 1986), Inst. Mgmt. Sci., Lafayette-Langeac Soc. (bd. dirs. 1988-92). Republican. Office: U Calif Haas Sch Bus Berkeley CA 94720

BUCKMAN, JAMES F., internist, gastroenterologist. MD, U. Wash., Seattle, 1966. Pvt. practice specializing in gastroenterology Albuquerque, 1974-89; med. dir. Qual-Med HMO, Albuquerque, 1989-90, Bellevue, Wash., 1991—; state surgeon N.Mex. Army N.G., Santa Fe, 1985-90. Fellow Am. Coll. Gastroenterology; mem. N.G. Assn. U.S. Office: Qual-Med 2331 130th Ave NE Bldg C Bellevue WA 98005-1753

BUCKNER, PHILIP FRANKLIN, newspaper publisher; b. Worcester, Mass., Aug. 25, 1930; s. Orello Simmons and Emily Virginia (Siler) B.; m. Ann Haswell Smith, Dec. 21, 1956; children: John C., Frederick S., Catherine A. AB, Harvard U., 1952; MA, Columbia U., 1954. Reporter Lowell (Mass.) Sun, 1959-60; pub. East Providence (R.I.) Post, 1960-62; asst. to treas. Scripps League Newspapers, Seattle, 1964-66, div. mgr., 1966-71; pres. Buckner News Alliance, 5 newspapers, Seattle, 1971—. Office: Buckner News Alliance Ste 2300 2101 4th Ave Seattle WA 98121-2317

BUCKWOLD, VICTOR EPHRAIM, microbiologist; b. Winnipeg, Man., Can., Dec. 30, 1964; came to U.S., 1991; s. Morley M. and Gudney (Nordal) B. BSc in Gen. Biology, U. Winnipeg, 1987, BSc in Biology, 1989; MSc in Microbiology, U. Manitoba, 1992. Asst. demonstrator chemistry lab. U. Winnipeg, 1986, undergrad. rsch. asst. dept. chemistry, 1988-89; rsch. asst. dept. chemistry biotech. lab. Manitoba Rsch. Coun.-Indsl. Tech. Ctr., Winnipeg, 1986; tech. writer, editor VisAid Devices Wuerz Pub., Winnipeg, 1987-89; technician forestry br. plant pathology lab. U. Manitoba, Winnipeg, 1989, grad. rsch. asst., jr. scientist ABI Biotech. Inc., 1989-91, grad. rsch. asst. Rh Pharms. and dept. microbiology, 1991; grad. rsch. asst. Children's Hosp. and dept. microbiology U. So. Calif. Sch. Medicine, L.A., 1991, grad. rsch. asst. Howard Hughes Med. Inst., 1991-92, grad. rsch. asst. dept. microbiology, 1992—; indsl. rsch. asst. NRC, Can., 1990. Mem. AAAS, Am. Soc. Microbiology, Can. Soc. Biochem. Molecular Biology, N.Y. Acad. Scis., Oxygen Soc. Jewish. Home: 1-500 N Maryland Ave Glendale CA 91206 Office: U So Calif Sch Medicine Dept Microbiology 2011 Zonal Ave Los Angeles CA 90033

BUCY, RICHARD SNOWDEN, aerospace engineering and mathematics educator, consultant; b. Washington, July 20, 1935; s. Edmond Howard and Marie (Glinke) B.; m. Ofelia Teresa Rivva, Aug. 25, 1961; children: Phillip Gustav, Richard Erwin. B.S. in Math., MIT, 1957; Ph.D. in Math. Stats., U. Calif.-Berkeley, 1963. Researcher in math. Rsch. Inst. Advanced Studies, Towson, Md., 1960-61, 63-64; rsch. asst. U. Calif., Berkeley, 1961-63; asst. prof. math. U. Md., College Park, 1964-65; assoc. prof. aerospace engring. U. Colo., Boulder, 1965-66; prof. aerospace engring. and math. U. So. Calif., Los Angeles, 1966—; professeur associe French Govt., Toulouse, 1973-74, Nice, 1983-84, 90-91; vis. prof. Technische Universität Berlin, 1975-76; co-dir. NATO Advanced Study Inst. on Non-linear Scholastic Problems, Algarve, Portugal; cons. to industry. Author: Filtering for Stochastic Processes, 1968, 2d edit., 1987, Nonlinear Stochastic Problems, 1984; editor Jour. Info. Scis., Jour. Modelling and Sci. Computing; founding editor (jour.) Stochastics, 1971-77; contbr. numerous articles to profl. publs. Recipient Humboldt prize Govt. W. Germany, Berlin, 1975-76; Air Force Office Sci. Sch. grantee, 1965-81, NATO Rsch. grantee, 1979—. Fellow IEEE (del. to Soviet Acad. of Scis. Info. Theory Workshop); mem. Am. Math. Soc. Republican. Home: 240 S Juanita Ave Redondo Beach CA 90277-3438 Office: U So Calif Dept Aerospace Engring Los Angeles CA 90089-1191

BUDD, ROBERT WESLEY, trade association executive; b. Laramie, Wyo., Apr. 22, 1956; s. William H. and Carolyn (Mockler) B.; m. Lynn Maree Bourn, Aug. 3, 1985; children: Joseph Byron, Jacob Varner, Margaret Carolyn. BS in Animal Sci. and Agrl. Bus., U. Wyo., 1979. Ranch hand Budd Ranches, Inc., Big Piney, Wyo., 1972-79; exec. sec. Wyo. Stock Growers Assn., Cheyenne, 1979-85, exec. v.p., 1985—; mgr. Wyo. Beef Coun., Cheyenne, 1979-85; pub. guide Diamond Tail Outfitters, Greybull, Wyo., 1981—. Author: Send Fresh Horses, 1987, A Wide Spot in the Road, 1990. Mem. Wyo. Hist. Trails Adv. Bd., 1984-89, Wyo. Coun. for Humanities, 1985-89; mem. pub. relations com. Cheyenne Frontier Days, 1988—; coord. com. chmn. Wyo. Rangeland, 1989—; active Nat. Security Forum Air War Coll., 1989. Named Outstanding Young Men in Am., 1987, 88, Outstanding Agrl. Businessman Cheyenne C. of C., 1989. Mem. Nat. Cattlemen's Assn., Soc. for Range Mgmt., Wyo. Assn. Trade Execs., Cheyenne C. of C. (pres. 1988), Young Men's Literary Club of Cheyenne. Republican. Episcopalian. Home: 6551 Moreland Ave Cheyenne WY 82009-3207 Office: Wyo Stock Growers Assn 113 E 20th St Cheyenne WY 82001-3701

BUDDENBOHM, HAROLD WILLIAM, aerospace project engineer; b. Wellington, Kans., Aug. 8, 1959; s. Harold William Buddenbohm (dec.) and Dorothy Ruth (Webber) B. BSMechE, U Ill, 1981; MBA, Pepperdine U., 1984, MS in Tech. Mgmt., 1991. With Rockwell Internat., Canoga Park, Calif., 1981-84, design engr., 1984-85, project engr., 1985-91, turbomachinery market devel. engr., 1991-92, strategic planning mgr., 1992—. Patentee turbine tip sealing. Recipient Achievement, Leadership, and Tech. Utilization awards. Republican. Presbyterian. Home: 4720 Escobedo Dr Woodland Hills CA 91364-4511 Office: Rockwell Internat PO Box 7922 6633 Canoga Ave Canoga Park CA 91309-7922

BUDZINSKI, JAMES EDWARD, interior designer; b. Gary, Ind., Jan. 4, 1953; s. Edward Michael and Virginia (Caliman) B. Student U. Cin., 1971-76. Mem. design staff Perkins & Wills Architects, Inc., Chgo., 1973-75, Med. Architectonics, Inc., Chgo., 1975-76; v.p. interior design Interior Environs., Inc., Chgo., 1976-78; pres. Jim Budzinski Design, Inc., Chgo., 1978-80; dir. interior design Robinson, Mills & Williams, San Francisco, 1980-87, dir. design, interior architecture Whisler Patri, San Francisco, 1987-90; dir. design and mktg. Deepa Textiles, 1990—; instr. design Harrington Inst. Design, Chgo.; cons. Chgo. Art Inst., Storwal Internat., Inc.; speaker at profl. confs. Designs include 1st Chgo. Corp. Pvt. Banking Ctr., 1st Nat. Bank Chgo. Monroe and Wabash Banking Ctr., 1978, IBM Corp., San Jose, Deutsch Bank, Frankfort, Crowley Maritime Corp., San Francisco, offices for Brobeck, Phleger and Harrison, offices for chmn. bd. Fireman's Fund Ins. Cos., Nob Hill Club, Fairmont Hotel, San Francisco, offices for Cooley, Godword, Castro, Huddleson, and Tatum, Palo Alto, Calif, offices for Pacific Bell Acctg. div., San Francisco, showroom for Knoll Internat., San Francisco, lobby, lounge TransAm. Corp. Hdqrts, San Fransisco, offices for EDAW, San Francisco, showroom for Steelcase Inc., Bally of Switzerland, N.Am. Flagship store, San Francisco; corp. Hqrs. Next Inc., Redwood City, Calif., Schafer Furniture Design, Lobby Renovation 601 California, San Francisco, Bennedetti Furniture Inc. Furniture Design. Pres. No. Calif. chpt. Design Industries Found. for AIDS. Office: Deepa Textiles 333 Bryant St San Francisco CA 94107-1421

BUECHLER, MELANIE KAY, computer programmer and analyst; b. Racine, Wis., Oct. 4, 1966; d. Robert Carl and Lois Diane (Hanson) B. BS, N.E. Mo. State U., 1988; MS, U. Utah, 1990. Tutor, grader math. dept. N.E. Mo. State U., Kirksville, 1985-88, computer/office asst. Pickler Meml. Libr., 1987-88, preceptor Joseph Baldwin Acad., 1987-88; computer programmer/analyst Info. Systems Ctr. VA, Salt Lake City, 1990—; grad. teaching asst. math. dept. U. Utah, 1988-90. Mem. Am. Math. Soc., Soc. for Indsl. and Applied Math., Kappa Mu Epsilon (v.p. 1987-88, conv. presenter 1987). Lutheran. Office: VA Info Systems Ctr 295 Chipeta Way Salt Lake City UT 84108-1228

BUECHNER, JOHN C., academic administrator. Dir. govtl. rels., then dir. pub. affairs U. Colo. System Office, Denver, until 1989; chancellor U. Colo., Denver, 1988—. Office: U Colo-Denver Office of Chancellor 1200 Larimer St Denver CO 80204-5300

BUEHLER, MARILYN KAY HASZ, secondary education educator; b. Garden City, Kans., July 19, 1946; d. Benjamin Bethel and Della Marie (Appel) Hasz; m. Brice Edward Buehler, July 23, 1966. BA in English, Washburn U., 1970; MA in Reading Edn., Ariz. State U., 1976; DHL (hon.), No. Ariz. U., 1989. Cert. tchr. English and secondary edn. Vol. probation officer, co-facilitator Maricopa County Probation Office, Phoenix, 1972; adult edn. tchr. Phoenix Union High Sch., 1972-73; tchr. English Trevor G. Browne High Sch., Phoenix, 1973; tchr. Title I Carl Hayden High Sch., Phoenix, 1974; tchr. English Camelback High Sch., Phoenix, 1975, Central High Sch., Phoenix, 1976-85, North High Sch., Phoenix, 1985—; chmn. awareness facilitator Phoenix Union High Sch. System, 1986—; speaker Partnrships in Edn., Phoenix, 1991—. Bd. dirs. Ariz. Edn. Found., Phoenix, 1990—, North High-Ariz. Pub. Svc. Partnership Com., 1991—. Named Ariz. State Tchr. of Yr., State of Ariz./AEF, 1989; recipient award of honor for outstanding contbns. to edn. Nat. Sch. Pub. Rels. Assn., 1989, others. Mem. NEA, Nat. Coun. Tchrs. English, Classroom Tchrs. Assn., Nat. Writers Club, Nat. State Tchrs. of Yr. Democrat. Office: North High Sch 1101 E Thomas Rd Phoenix AZ 85014

BUEHRING, GERTRUDE CASE, tumor biology educator; b. Chgo., May 28, 1940; d. Theodore Johnston and Rosemary (Lawrence) Case; m. William Richard Buehring, Aug. 24, 1962; children: Anna, Jessica. BA in Biology, Stanford U., 1962; PhD in Genetics, U. Calif., Berkeley, 1972. Postdoctoral fellow U. Calif., Berkeley, 1972-73, asst. prof., 1973-80, assoc. prof. medical microbiology and tumor biology, 1980—; vis. prof. U. Innsbruck, Austria, 1981-82, U. Wis., 1990. Research grantee Nat. Cancer Inst., 1974-77, U. Calif. Cancer Research Coordinating Com., 1983-84, Pardee Found., 1985-86. Mem. AAAS, Am. Assn. Cancer Research, Tissue Culture Assn., Internat. Assn. Breast Cancer Rsch., Sigma Xi. Office: U Calif Sch Pub Health Berkeley CA 94720

BUEL, JAMES WES, food service executive; b. Long Beach, Calif., May 21, 1937; s. James Buel and June (von Opperman) B.; m. Renee J. Ellis; children: Frank, Roddy, Tammy, Ty, Wesley, Elise. BS, Calif. Poly. State U., 1963. Food service mgr. Dole Philippines, 1964-69; dir. food and beverage Hyatt Hotels Asia, Philippines, 1969-79; food service dir. Western Innkeepers, Los Angeles, 1979-83, Service America, Long Beach, Calif., 1983-88; food service mgr. Lucky Food Stores, Redlands, Calif., 1988-90; with Newport Diversified, Santa Fe Springs, Calif., 1990—; cons. in field. Author: Food Service in the Philippines, 1977, Food Service in Asia, 1978, Food Service Software, 1991. Coun. bd. dirs. Boy Scouts Am., 1987—; v.p. Am. Assn., Manila, 1977; mem. Buena Park Vision 2010 Commn. Recipient Cert. Leadership Cornell U., 1979; named Fullbright exchange student, 1958. Mem. James Beard Found., Calif. Poly. Alumni Assn., Global Holelies Club (life). Republican.

BUFFINGTON, GARY LEE ROY, safety standards engineer, construction executive; b. Custer, S.D., Dec. 6, 1946; s. Donald L. B. and Madge Irene (Selby) Lampert; m. Kathleen R. Treloar, Aug. 3, 1965; children: Katherine, Lowell, Gary Jr. BS in Bus. Edn., Black Hill State Coll., 1971; AA in Criminal Justice, U. S.D., 1972, MS, 1974. Cert. safety profl., EMT, law enforcement officer, mine safety and health adminstrn. instr., OSHA instr.; Canadian registered safety profl.; lic. pvt. investigator. Contract miner Homestake Mining Co., Lead, S.D., 1966-72; dep. sheriff, criminal investigator Pennington County Sheriff's Dept., Rapid City, S.D., 1972-77; fed. mine inspector U.S. Dept. of Labor, Mine Safety and Health Adminstrn., Birmingham, Ala., 1977-79; supr., spl. investigator U.S. Dept. of Labor, Mine Safety and Health Adminstrn., Birmingham, 1979-81; supr., mine inspector U.S. Dept. of Labor, Mine Safety and Health Adminstrn., Grand Junction, Colo., 1981-83; safety and security mgr. Black & Veatch Engrs. Stanton Energy Ctr., Orlando, Fla., 1983-87; loss control mgr. Black & Veatch Engrs. AES Thames Cogeneration Plant, Uncasville, Conn., 1987-90; loss control mgr. Trans-Mo. River Tunnel project Black & Veatch, Engrs.-Architects, Kansas City, Mo., 1990-92; mgr. safety and security. metro rail constrn. mgr. Parsons-Dillingham, L.A., 1992—; mem. ANSI A-10 Accredited Standards Com., Washington, 1984—, Mine Safety and Health Adminstrn. Standards Com., Arlington, Va., 1981-83. Named Police Officer of the Year, Sundown Optimist Club, Rapid City, 1975; recipient Meritorious Achievement award, U.S. Dept. of Labor, Arlington, 1979, Monetary Spl. Achievement award, U.S. Dept. Labor, Arlington, 1980. Mem. Am. Soc. Safety Engrs., World Safety Orgn., Am. Indsl. Hygiene Assn., Am. Soc. for Indsl. Security, Nat. Safety Council, Moose Lodge. Republican. Lutheran. Home: 505 N Kenwood St #1 Glendale CA 91206 Office: Parsons-Dillingham 523 W 6th St Ste 400 Los Angeles CA 90014

BUFFINGTON, LINDA BRICE, interior designer; b. Long Beach, Calif., June 21, 1936; d. Harry Bryce and Marguerite Leonora (Tucciarone) Van Bellehem; student El Camino Jr. Coll., 1955-58, U. Calif., Irvine, 1973—; children: Lisa Ann, Phillip Lynn. Cert. gen. contractor, interior designer, Calif.; lic. gen. contractor, Calif. with Pub. Fin., Torrance, Calif., 1954-55, Beneficial Fin., Torrance and Hollywood, Calif., 1955-61; interior designer Vee Nisley Interiors, Newport Beach, Calif., 1964-65, Leon's Interiors, Newport Beach, 1965-69; ptnr. Marlind Interiors, Tustin, Calif., 1969-70; owner, designer Linda Buffington Interiors, Villa Park, Calif., 1970—; cons. builders, housing developments. Mem. Bldg. Industry Assn., Internat. Soc. Interior Designers (past sec. Orange County chpt., 1988-89, pres./ internat. bd. rep. 1990-91), Nat. Assn. Home Builders. Republican. Office: 17853 Santiago Blvd Ste # 107 Villa Park CA 92667

BUFFINGTON, NANCY CATHERINE, policy strategist, consultant; b. Logan, Utah, Mar. 24, 1939; d. Fred Roberts and Lucy (Harris) Coburn; children: William, Timothy, Sheryl, Sharlene. BA in Liberal Arts/Polit. Sci., Antioch U., Seattle, 1989; PhD in Govt. and Health Policy, Union Inst., 1992. Aquatic and women's health dir. Jewish Community Ctr., 1968-72; program dir., coord. Cardio-Pulmonary Rsch. Inst., 1970-74; mem. Wash. State Senate, 1975-79; pub. affairs clients Wash. Natural Gas Co., 1976-78, numerous other organizations; founder, pres. Medina Med., Inc., 1978-90; founder, CEO Buffington Assocs., Inc., Seattle, 1992—; mem. exec. adv. com. Sch. Bus. and Econs., Seattle Pacific U., 1984—. Contbr. articles to profl. jours. Bd. dirs. King County Med. Aux., 1987-88, Bellevue Downtown Assn., 1983-85, United for Wash., 1981-87, Goodwill Industries, 1976-87, Seattle Children's Home, 1979-81, Am. Heart Assn., 1976-80, West Seattle YMCA, 1967-71; bd. dirs., sec.-treas. Commun. Health Assn., 1977-86; bd. dirs., pres. Pvt. Sector Initiatives, 1979-81; bd. dirs. internat. dist. Community Health Ctr., 1993-; mem. fin. com. Bellevue Downtown Park, 1985-86; mem. Puget Sound Work Edn. Coun., 1975-81, acad. svc. sch. bus. and econs. Seattle Pacific U., others; active Seattle Mcpl. League, Virginia Mason Soc. Recipient numerous awards. Mem. AAUW, Am. Assn. for Pub. Opinion, Am. Polit. Sci. Assn., LWV (Child Haven vol. 1990), Rotary (internat. dist. 1992-), Rural Devel. Inst. (bd. dirs 1993-), Union Inst. Alumni Assn.

BUFFMIRE, JUDY ANN, rehabilitation services administrator, psychologist; b. Salt Lake City, June 5, 1929; d. William Henry Broyles and Audrey Francis (Cook) Broyles Ballinger; m. LaMar Lee Buffmire, Nov. 28, 1948; children—Kathryn Ann, Shanna Lee. B.S. cum laude, U. Utah, 1966, M.S., 1967, Ph.D., 1969. Asst. prof. dept. spl. edn. U. Utah, 1967-76; state program specialist Utah State Office Edn., Salt Lake City, 1976-77; dep. dir. Utah Social Services, Salt Lake City, 1978-80; dir. State Div. Family Services, Salt Lake City, 1981-82, dir. State Div. Registration, Salt Lake City, 1982-83, dir. State Div. Rehab., Salt Lake City, 1983—; rep. Utah House of Reps., 1992—. Contbr. articles to profl. publs. Mem. Presdl. Adv. Council on Ednl. and Profl. Devel., 1974-77; chmn. Utah Adv. Com. on Handicapped, 1975-77, chmn. State Mental Health Adv. Com., Salt Lake City, 1977-78, Regional VIII Adoption Resource Ctr., Salt Lake City, 1980; mem. State Bd. Fin. Instns., Salt Lake City, 1981-83; vol. therapist Parents United, Inc., Salt Lake City, 1982-84. Utah State Bd. Edn. scholar 1967; NDEA scholar, 1968-69; recipient Disting. Grad. award Wasatch Acad., 1976; named Bureaucrat of Yr., Utah Issues, 1982; Pub. Service Adminstr. of Yr., Nat. Assn. Social Workers, 1983. Mem. Utah Psychol. Assn., Delta Kappa Gamma (pres. 1983-84). Democrat. Presbyterian. Avocations: cooking; camping; fishing; running rivers; traveling. Home: 765 E 4255 S Salt Lake City UT 84107-3042 Office: UT State Office of Rehabilitation 250 E 500 S Salt Lake City UT 84111-3204

BUFFORD, SAMUEL LAWRENCE, federal judge; b. Phoenix, Ariz., Nov. 19, 1943; s. John Samuel and Evelyn Amelia (Rude) B.; m. Julia Marie Metzger, May 13, 1978. BA in Philosophy, Wheaton Coll., 1964; PhD, U. Tex., 1969; JD magna cum laude, U. Mich., 1973. Bar: Calif., N.Y., Ohio. Instr. philosophy La. State U., Baton Rouge, 1967-68; asst. prof. Ea. Mich. U., Ypsilanti, 1968-74; asst. prof. law Ohio State U., Columbus, 1975-77; assoc. Gendel, Raskoff, Shapiro & Quittner, L.A., 1982-85; atty. Paul, Weiss, Rifkind, Wharton & Garrison, N.Y.C., 1974-75, Sullivan Jones & Archer, San Francisco, 1977-79, Musick, Peeler & Garrett, L.A., 1979-81, Rifkind & Sterling, Beverly Hills, Calif., 1981-82, Gendel, Raskoff, Shapiro & Quittner, L.A., 1982-85; U.S. bankruptcy judge Ctrl. Dist. Calif., 1985—; adj. prof. law U. So. Calif., 1988—; bd. dirs. Fin. Lawyers Conf., L.A., 1987-90, Bankruptcy Forum, L.A., 1986-88; lect. U.S.-Romanian Jud. Delegation, 1991;cons. Calif. State Bar Bd. Bar Examiners, 1989-90. Editor-in-chief Am. Bankruptcy Law Jour., 1990—; contbr. articles to profl. jours.; columnist Norton Bankruptcy Advisor, 1988—. Younger Humanist fellowship NEH. Mem. ABA, L.A. County Bar Assn. (past chmn. ethics com.), Order of Coif. Office: US Bankruptcy Ct 255 E Temple St Ste 1582 Los Angeles CA 90012-3308

BUGBEE-JACKSON, JOAN, sculptor; b. Oakland, Calif., Dec. 17, 1941; d. Henry Greenwood and Jeanie Ogden (Abbot) B.; m. John Michael Jackson, June 21, 1973; 1 child, Brook Bond. BA in Art, U. Calif., San Jose, 1964, MA in Art/Ceramics, 1966; student Nat. Acad. Sch. Fine Arts, N.Y.C., 1968-72, Art Students League, N.Y.C., 1968-70. Apprentice to Joseph Kiselewski, 1970-72; instr. art Foothill (Calif.) Jr. Coll., 1966-67; instr. design De Anza Jr. Coll., Cupertino, Calif., 1967-68; instr. pottery Greenwich House Pottery, N.Y.C., 1969-71, Craft Inst. Am., N.Y.C., 1970-72, Cordova (Alaska) Extension Center, U. Alaska, 1972-79, Prince William Sound Community Coll., 1979—; one-woman exhbns. in Maine, N.Y.C., Alaska and Calif.; group exhbns. include Allied Artists Am., 1970-72, Nat. Acad. Design, 1971, 74, Nat. Sculpture Soc. Ann., 1971, 72, 73, Alaska Woman Art Show, 1987, 88, Cordova Visual Artists, 1991, 92; pres. Cordova Arts and Pageants Ltd., 1975-76; commns. include Merle K. Smith Commemorative plaque, 1973, Bob Korn Pool Commemorative Plaque, 1975, Eyak Native Monument, 1978, Anchorage Pioneer's Home Ceramic Mural, 1979, Alaska Wildlife Series Bronze Medal, 1980, sculpture murals and portraits Alaska State Capitol, 1981, Pierre De Ville Portrait commn., 1983, Robert B. & Evangeline Atwood, 1985, Armin F. Koernig Hatchery Plaque, 1985, Cordova Fishermen's Meml. Sculpture, 1985, Alaska's Five Govs., bronze relief, Anchorage, 1986, Reluctant Fisherman's Mermaid, bronze, 1987, Charles E. Bunnell, bronze portrait statue, Fairbanks, 1988, Alexander Baranof monument, Sitka, Alaska, 1989, Wally Noerenberg Hatchery Plaque, Prince William Sound, Alaska, 1989, Russian-Alaskan Friendship Plaque (edit. of 4), Kayak Island, Cordova, Alaska and Vladivostok & Petropavlovsk-Kamchatskiy, Russia, 1991, Sophie-Last Among Eyak Native People, 1992; also other portraits. Bd. dirs. Alaska State Coun. on the Arts, 1991—. Scholarship student Nat. Acad. Sch. Fine Arts, 1969-72; recipient J.A. Suydam Bronze medal, 1969; Dr. Ralph Weiler prize, 1971; Helen Foster Barnet award, 1971; Daniel Chester French award, 1972; Frishmuth award, 1971; Allied Artists Am. award, 1972; C. Percival Dietsch prize, 1973; citation Alaska Legislature, 1981, 82. Fellow Nat. Sculpture Soc. Address: PO Box 374 Cordova AK 99574

BUGEL, JOE, professional football team coach; b. Pitts., Mar. 10, 1940; m. Brenda Bugel; children: Angie, Holly, Jennifer. B in Physical Edn., Western Ky. U., Bowling Green, 1963; M in Guidance and Counseling, Western Ky. U., 1964. Asst. coach Western Ky. U., 1964-68, U.S. Naval Acad., 1969-72, Iowa State U., 1973, Ohio State U., 1974, Detroit Lions, NFL, 1975-76; asst. coach, offensive line coach Houston Oilers, 1977-80; asst. coach Washington Redskins, 1981-89, offensive coord., 1981-82, asst. head coach-offense, 1983-89; head coach Phoenix Cardinals, 1990—. Office: Phoenix Cardinals 8701 S Hardy Tempe AZ 85284*

BUHLER, JILL LORIE, editor, writer; b. Seattle, Dec. 7, 1945; d. Oscar John and Marcella Jane (Hearing) Younce; 1 child, Lori Jill Scopinich; m. John Buhler, 1990; stepchildren: Christie, Cathie Vsetecka, Mike. AA in Gen. Edn., Am. River Coll., 1969; BA in Journalism with honors, Sacramento State U., 1973. Reporter Carmichael (Calif.) Courier, 1968-70; mng. editor Quarter Horse of the Pacific Coast, Sacramento, 1970-75, editor, 1975-84; editor Golden State Program Jour., 1978, Nat. Reined Cow Horse Assn. News, Sacramento, 1983-88, Pacific Coast Jour., Sacramento, 1984-88, Nat. Snaffle Bit Assn. News, Sacramento, 1988; pres., chief exec. officer Communications Plus, Port Townsend, Wash., 1988—; mag. cons., 1975—. Interviewer Pres. Ronald Regan, Washington, 1983; mng. editor Wash. Thoroughbred, 1989-90. Mem. 1st profl. communicators mission to USSR, 1988; bd. dirs. Carmichael Winding Way, Pasadena Homeowners Assn., 1985-87; mem. scholarship com. Thoroughbred Horse Racing's United Scholarship Trust. Recipient 1st pl. feature award, 1970, 1st pl. editorial award Jour. Assn. Jr. Colls., 1971, 1st pl. design award WCHB Yuba-Sutter Counties, Marysville, Calif., 1985. Mem. Am. River Jaycees (Speaking award 1982), Am. Horse Publs. (1st Pl. Ediatorial award 1983, 86), Port Townsend C. of C. (trustee, v.p. 1993), Mensa (bd. dirs., asst. local sec., activities dir. 1987-88, membership chair 1988-90), Intertel Thoroughbred Horse Racing's United Scholarship Trust (Scholarship com.), Kiwanis Internat. (chair MEP com., treas. 1992-94), 5th Wheel Touring Soc. (Sacramento) (v.p. 1970). Republican. Roman Catholic. Home: 440 Adelma Beach Rd Port Townsend WA 98368-9612

BUHLER, LUIS PALTENGHÉ, financial executive; b. N.Y.C., Mar. 26, 1953; s. Louis Lee Buhler and Julie Hubbell (Paltenghé) Dougherty. BA in Econ., Stanford U., 1975, MBA, 1982; MA in Urban Studies, Occidental Coll., 1978. Dir. fin. adminstrn., grants mgr. Levi Strauss Found. and Community Affairs Dept., San Francisco, 1977-80; mgr. internat. planning and reporting Cummins Engine co., Columbus, Ind., 1982-84; asst. contr. Cummins Brasil S.A., Sao Paulo, Brazil, 1985-86; v.p. Delta-Valentine, Inc., San Francisco, 1987-88; treas., dir. finance Trans Ocean Ltd., San Bruno, Calif., 1988—; bd. dirs. E.J. Electric Installation Co., N.Y.C. mem. Exec. com. Lincoln Club No. Calif., 1991-92; bd. dirs. Calif. Rep. League, 1974-82, 87—; chmn. CRL Com. of 100, 1988—; pres. Vanished Children's Alliance, 1989-90. Office: Trans Ocean Ltd San Bruno CA 94066

BUHLER, RICHARD GERHARD, minister; b. Cottonwood, Ariz., July 18, 1946; s. Henry Richard and A. Genevieve (Woodward) B.; m. Linda M. Bates, Dec. 9, 1966; children: Karin, Kristin, Karise, Kenneth, Kevin, Kim, Keith. BA, Biola U., 1968, LLD, 1990; cert., Omega Ctr., Santa Ana, Calif., 1978. Announcer Sta. KBBI-FM, L.A., 1964-68; writer, editor Sta. KFWB-AM, L.A., 1968-71, Sta. KNX-AM Radio, Racho, L.A., 1971-73; asst. pastor Atwater (Calif.) Bapt. Ch., 1973-79, Omega Fellowship, Santa Ana, 1975-78; pastor El Dorado Ch., Long Beach, Calif., 1978-84; radio host Branches Communications, Costa Mesa, Calif., 1981—; host Tabletalk daily radio program, Costa Mesa, 1990—, Talk From the Heart radio show, 1981-90. Author: Love...No Strings Attached, 1986, Pain and Pretending, 1988, New Choices, New Boundaries, 1991, The First Book of Self Tests, 1993. Recipient Angel award Religion in Media, L.A., 1986. Mem. Writer's Guild Am. Republican. Mem. Internat. Ch. of Foursquare Gospel. Office: Branches Communications PO Box 6688 Orange CA 92613-6688

BUHLMANN, MICHAEL RICHARD, progammer, analyst; b. Aitkin, Minn., Nov. 3, 1960; s. Richard Hans Buhlmann and Jo Ann (Kuhn) Peters. Student, Nat. Univ., Irvine, Calif., 1987, Santiago Coll., 1984—. Programmer Alexandria (Minn.) Credit Union, 1981-82; programmer, cons. Great Western Computers, Rancho Cucmonga, Calif., 1982-83, Synergistic Mgmt. Systems, Riverside, Calif., 1983-84; programmer Shearson, Lehman Mortgage, San Bernardino, Calif., 1984-85; programmer analyst Challenge Cook Bros., Industry, Calif., 1985-88, So. Calif. Rapid Transit Dist., L.A., 1988-90; sr. programmer analyst Walt Disney, Burbank, Calif., 1990—. French Horn player U.S. Army Res., Bell, Calif., 1983—, Symphonic Band of Orange, Calif., 1984—. Republican. Home: PO Box 6747 Orange CA 92613

BUI, PHILIP PHU-VAN, mathematics and science educator; b. Saigon, Vietnam, Oct. 13, 1955; came to U.S., 1975; s. Gia Van Bui and Quy Thi Tran; m. Thanh Huong Thi Le, May 30, 1992. Cert., U. Saigon, 1975; BA, U. Calif., Berkeley, 1983. Cert. phys. sci., math., lang. devel. tchr., Calif. Tchr. trainer Expt. in Internat. Living, Brattleboro, Vt., 1986; ednl. cons. UN High Commr. for Refugees, Hong Kong, 1987; instr. math. Coll. Alameda, Calif., 1988—; tchr. sci. Oakland (Calif.) Pub. Schs., 1988—. Editor Noi Vong Tay Mag., 1979-82, Indochina Jour., 1989—; contbr. numerous articles to mags. Tchr. sci. Peace Corp, Togo, West Africa, 1983-85, tech. coord., 1985. Mem. Vietnamese Fishermen Assn. Am. (gen. sec., bd. dirs. 1988—), Calif. Tchr. Assn., Calif. Sci. Tchr. Assn., Vietnamese Pastoral Coun. (dir. communication Oakland diocese 1989—). Roman Catholic. Office: Roosevelt Jr High Sch 1926 19th Ave Oakland CA 94606

BUIDANG, GEORGE, educator, administrator, consultant, writer; b. Danang, Vietnam, Dec. 30, 1924; came to U.S., 1981; s. Bui Dang Do and Ha Thi Yen; m. Pham Thi Hong, Feb. 25, 1951; children: Bui Tu Long, Bui Nguyen Khanh, Bui Minh Hoang, Bui Thi Tuong Vi. Head translator

USMC, 1956-61; dep. employment officer Hdqrs. Support Activity Saigon USN, 1962-65; asst. dir. Cen. Tng. Inst. U.S. Army, Vietnam, 1966; pers. dir. Foremost Dairies Vietnam of Foremost-McKesson Internat., 1966-75; instr. of French Un Bateau Pour L'Asie Du Sud-Est, Brussels, Belgium, 1980; asst. dir. edn. Career Resources Devel. Ctr., Inc., San Francisco, 1981-93; ind. cons. San Francisco, 1993—. Author: Using WordPerfect 5.0, 1989, Using Lotus 1-2-3 Release 2.2, 1991, Using WordPerfect 5.1, 1991, Using Microsoft Windows 3.1, 1993. Recipient Outstanding Performance award Bd. of Dirs., 1987. Republican. Roman Catholic. Home: Apt 411 565 Geary St San Francisco CA 94102-1660 Office: 655 Geary St San Francisco CA 94102

BUIE, JAMES RANDALL, auditor; b. Pontiac, Mich., July 18, 1953; s. James Brent and Christine (DeHart) B. BS, U. Tenn., 1977. CPA, Ill. Auditor Heller Fin., Chgo., 1979-85; auditor, staff officer 1st Nat. Bank Chgo., 1985-87; internal auditor Citicorp, Dallas, 1987-88, Las Vegas (Nev.) Valley Water Dist., 1988—. Mem. Inst. Internal Auditors. Democrat. Baptist. Home: 8141 Leger Dr Las Vegas NV 89128-4773

BUKLAREWICZ, PAUL JOSEPH, educator; b. Bayonne, N.J., Dec. 7, 1949; s. Joseph Anthony and Regina (Skowronski) B.; m. Arlene Louise Kiesnowski, Nov. 22, 1970. BBA, Pace U., 1972; MS in Bus. Edn., Utah State U., 1977. Tchr. Bayonne High Sch., 1974-75; asst. prof. Agrl. and Tech. Coll., SUNY, Farmingdale, 1976-82; instr. II Kapiolani C.C., U. Hawaii, Honolulu, 1982-88; instr. Aeon Intercultural Corp., Kurashiki, Japan, 1988-90; internat. pub.-writer, photographer, 1980—; v.p. Urawatandai Hawaii Coll., Hilo, 1991—; office automation cons., N.Y., Honolulu, 1980-88. Contbr. articles to profl. jours. Pres., bd. dirs. Big Island Art Guild, Hilo, 1992; docent Volcano (Hawaii) Art Ctr., 1991-92. With U.S. Army, 1972-74. Grantee N.Y. State Edn. Dept., 1980. Mem. Am. Soc. Media Photographers, Japanese C. of C. and Industry. Home: PO Box 854 Volcano HI 96785-0854 Office: Urawatandai Hawaii Coll 139 Kapiolani St Hilo HI 96720

BUKOVNIK, GARY A., artist; b. Cleve., Apr. 10, 1947; s. Raymond Peter and Betty (Kisthardt) B. Graphic designer Turner Communications, Atlanta, 1970-75; represented in permanent collections at Art Gallery of Hamilton, Ont., Art Inst. Chgo., Atlanta Bot. Garden, BankAmerica Corp., San Francisco, Bklyn. Mus., Citibank, N.Y., Fine Arts Mus. San Francisco, Hunt Inst. Bot. Documentation, Pitts., Ill. Bell Telephone Co., Chgo., IBM, Atlanta, N.Y., Libr. Congress, Met. Mus. Art, N.Y., Mus. Fine Arts, Boston, Oakland Mus., others; author: Flowers: Gary Bukovnik, Watercolors and Monotypes, 1990; illustrator: A Taste of San Francisco, 1990, From a Breton Garden, 1990. One person shows at Ansorena, Madrid, 1991, Kurts Bingham Gallery, Memphis, 1990, 91, 93, Galerie Kutter, Luxembourg, 1988, 91, Atlanta Bot. Garden, 1987, Cleve. Playhouse, 1986, 89, Staempfli Gallery, N.Y., 1983, 84, 86, 87, 89, 91, Bklyn. Mus., 1984, Carnegie Inst., Pitts., 1981, Concept Art Gallery, Pitts., 1984, 86, 88, 90, 92, Garden Ctr. of Greater Cleve., 1992, de Saisset Mus. Santa Clara Univ., 1991; group shows include Fine Arts Mus. San Francisco, 1990, 91, So. Alleghenies Mus. Art, Pa., 1987, Shasta Coll. Gallery, Calif., 1987, Bergen Mus., 1986, Wave Hill Gallery, N.Y., 1984, City of Aubusson, France, 1992, others. Poster donor, San Francisco Symphony, 1981—, Cleve. Inst. Music, 1990, 92, The Met. Opera, 1991. Recipient George Bunker award, Print Club of Phila., 1981, Award of Merit, Am. Soc. Mub. pub., Washington, 1982, Arts Commn. of San Francisco, 1988. Home: 1179 Howard St San Francisco CA 94103-3925

BUKOWINSKI, MARK STEFAN TADEUSZ, geophysics educator; b. Trani, Italy, Oct. 17, 1946; came to U.S., 1962; s. Stanley K. and Jadwiga Teresa (Jezierski) B.; m. Halina V. Mudy, June 20, 1970; children: Katherine, Anne, John, Christopher. BS in Physics, UCLA, 1969, PhD in Physics, 1975. Asst. rsch. geophysicist Inst. Geophysics and Planetary Physics, UCLA, 1975-78; asst. prof. U. Calif., Berkeley, 1978-82, assoc. prof., 1982-89, prof., 1989—. Assoc. editor: Jour. Geophys. Rsch., 1988-91; mem. bd. editors: Phys. Earth Planetary Internat., 1992—; contbr. over 50 articles to sci. jours. NSF grantee, 1976—, Inst. Geophysics and Planetary Physics. Mem. AAAS, Am. Geophys. Union (mem. mineral physics com. 1988-90), Mineralog. Soc. Am. (mem. publs. com. 1988-91, chair 1991-92). Home: 5738 Laurelwood Pl Concord CA 94521-4807 Office: U Calif Berkeley Dept Geology and Geophysics Berkeley CA 94720

BUKOWSKI, JAMES BERNARD, insurance broker, consultant; b. Chgo., Dec. 31, 1944; s. Bernard Vincent and Virginia Marie (Wierzbowski) B.; m. Susan Frankida Dussing, May 28, 1972; children: Katherine Susan, Janis Sofia. Student, St. John's Sem. Coll., 1961-65; BA, U. Calif., Santa Barbara, 1967; PhD, Ind. U., 1972; MIM, Am. Grad. Sch. Internat. Mgmt., 1978. CPCU. Asst. prof. Augustana Coll., Rock Island, Ill., 1972-77; asst. v.p. Johnson & Higgins of Calif., L.A., 1979-93; v.p. constrn. svcs. Minet Ins. Svcs., Inc., L.A., 1993—; instr. Ins. Edn. Assn., Newport Beach, Calif., 1988—. Dir. Internat. Vis. Coun., L.A., 1986—, Triunfo YMCA, Agoura Hills, Calif., 1990—. Exch. fellow Internat. Rsch. and Exch. Bd., Zagreb, Yugoslavia, 1970. Mem. Soc. CPCUs (L.A. chpt. dir. 1992-94), Toastmasters Internat. Democrat. Roman Catholic. Home: 5662 Walnut Ridge Dr Agoura Hills CA 91301 Office: Minet Ins Svcs Inc 333 S Grand Ave Los Angeles CA 90071

BUKOWSKI, JEFFREY DAVID, career officer; b. Reading, Pa., Dec. 28, 1965; s. Ronald Stanley and Sandra Lynn (Distasio) B. BA in History and Polit.Sci., U. Pa., 1987. Commd. ensign U.S. Navy, 1987, advanced through grades to lt.; communications officer USS Elliot, San Diego, 1988-89, main propulsion asst., 1989-90, navigator, 1990; flag lt. and aide Comdr., Cruiser-Destroyer Group FIVE, San Diego, 1990—. Mem. World Affairs Coun. San Diego, 1991—. Recipient Navy Achievement medal, 1990, 91, 92, Navy Commendation medal, 1990. Mem. Zool. Soc. San Diego. Roman Catholic. Office: Comdr Cruiser Destroyer Group FIVE FPO AP San Diego CA 96001-4703

BUKRY, JOHN DAVID, geologist; b. Balt., May 17, 1941; s. Howard Leroy and Irene Evelyn (Davis) Snyder. Student, Colo. Sch. Mines, 1959-60; BA, Johns Hopkins U., 1963; MA, Princeton U., 1965, PhD, 1967; post-grad., U. Ill., 1965-66. Geologist U.S. Army Corp Engrs., Balt., 1963; research asst. Mobil Oil Co., Dallas, 1965; geologist U.S. Geol. Survey, La Jolla, Calif., 1967-84, U.S. Minerals Mgmt. Service, La Jolla, 1984-86, U.S. Geol. Survey, Menlo Park, Calif., 1986—; research assoc. dept. geol. research div. U. Calif.-San Diego, 1970—; cons. Deep Sea Drilling Project, La Jolla, 1967-87; lectr. Vetlesen Symposium, Columbia U., N.Y.C., 1968, 3d Internat. Planktonic Conf., Kiel, Fed. Republic Germany, 1974; shipboard micropaleontologist on D/V Glomar Challenger, 5 Deep Sea Drilling Project cruises, 1968-78; mem. stratigraphic correlations bd. NSF/Joint Oceanographic Instns. for Deep Earth Sampling, 1976-79. Author: Leg I of the Cruises of the Drilling Vessel Glomar Challenger, 1969, Coccoliths from Texas and Europe, 1969, Leg LXIII of the Cruises of the Drilling Vessel Glomar Challenger, 1981; editor: Marine Micropaleontology, 1976-83, mem. editorial bd. Micropaleontology, 1985-90. Mobil Oil, Princeton U. fellow, 1965-67; Am. Chem. Soc., Princeton U. fellow, 1966-67. Fellow AAAS, Geol. Soc. Am., Explorers Club; mem. Hawaiian Malacological Soc., Paleontol. Rsch. Inst., Am. Assn. Petroleum Geologists, Soc. Econ. Paleontologists and Mineralogists, Internat. Nannoplankton Assn., European Union Geoscis., The Oceanography Soc., Nat. Sci. Tchrs. Assn., U. Calif. at San Diego Ida and Cecil Green Faculty Club, San Diego Shell Club, Princeton Club No. Calif., Sigma Xi. Office: US Geol Survey MS-915 345 Middlefield Rd Menlo Park CA 94025-3591

BULITT, PATRICIA ANN, choreographer, performer, ethnologist; b. Trenton, N.J., Dec. 16, 1949; d. Harold Richard and Miriam C. (Gross) B. BA, U. Ariz., 1972. Dance and movement specialist; project dir. Eskimo Dance Music Documentary Project; project dir. Our Neighbors Dance Their Dances, Berkeley, Calif.; choreographer, performer outdoor dance projects. Vol. Berkeley Women's Health Collective, 1978-82; grad. sch. bd. mem. Calif. Dance Educator's Assn., 1973-85; mem. East Bay Citizens for Creek Restoration. Nat. Endowment for Arts choreography fellow, 1984, UCLA fellow, 1984, Dorland Mountain Colony Artist fellow, 1986; L.J. Skaggs and Mary C. Skaggs grantee, 1983-87, Chevron USA grantee, 1978, 79, 81, 85, Calif. Arts Coun. grantee, 1986, 87, East Bay Community Found. grantee, 1992; Kyoto, Japan for Theatre scholar, 1984. Address: 2138 Mckinley Berkeley CA 94703

BULL, VIVIAN ANN, economics educator; b. Ironwood, Mich., Dec. 11, 1934; d. Edwin Russell and Lydia (West) Johnson; m. Robert J. Bull, Jan. 31, 1959; children: R. Camper, W. Carlson. BA, Albion (Mich.) Coll., 1956; postgrad., London Sch. Econs., 1957; PhD, NYU, 1974. Economist Nat. Bank Detroit, 1955-59; with Bell Telephone Labs., Murray Hill, N.J., 1960-62; prof. econs. Drew U., Madison, N.J., 1960-92, assoc. dean, 1978-86; bd. dirs. Chem. Bank N.J., Morristown; trustee Africa U., Zimbabwe; treas. Joint Expedition to Caesareu Maritime Archaeology, 1971—. Author: Economic Study The West Bank: Is It Viable?, 1975. Trustee, assoc. Am. Schs. Oriental Rsch., 1982-90; trustee, Colonial Symphony Soc., 1984-92, The Albright Inst. of Archaeol. Record; commr. Downtown Devel. Commn., Madison, 1986-92; mem. univ. senate United Meth. Ch., 1989—, gen. bd. higher edn., 1988-92; mem. planning bd. Coll. Bus. Adminstrn., Africa U., Zimbabwe, 1990-91; exec. com. Nat. Assn. Commns. on Salaries, United Meth. Ch., 1986-92. Fulbright scholar, 1956, Paul Harris fellow Rotary Internat., 1988; named Disting. Alumna Albion Coll., 1979; recipient SAlute to Policy Makers award Exec. Women N.J., 1986. Mem. Nat. Assn. Bank Women, Phi Beta Kappa. Home: Presidents House Linfield Coll 900 S Baker St McMinnville OR 97128-6894 Office: Linfield Coll 900 S Baker St McMinnville OR 97128

BULLARD, RICHARD FORREST, mathematics educator; b. Seattle, July 3, 1937; s. Harold C. and Hazel (Andersen) B.; m. Mary E. Day, June 29, 1963; children: Elizabeth, Lisa, Christopher. BS, U. Wash., 1959, MS, 1961; postgrad., Calif. State U., Sacramento, 1967. Instr. math. San Joaquin Delta Coll., Stockton, Calif., 1964-67; rsch. asst. San Joaquin Delta Coll., 1967-69, dir. fin. aid, 1969-80, instr. math., 1980—. Pres. bd. dirs. First Unitarian Ch., Stockton, 1980-82; exec. sec. Weberstown Homes Assn., Stockton, 1982—. Mem. San Joaquin Delta Coll. Found. (exec. sec. 1975-80), Calif. Assn. of Student Aid Adminstrs. (treas. 1976-77), Calif. Community Coll. Student Aid Adminstrs. (pres. 1977-78), San Joaquin Delta Coll. Tchrs. Assn. (pres. 1986-87), Masons, Order DeMolay (Legion of Honor 1962). Republican. Unitarian. Office: San Joaquin Delta College 5151 Pacific Ave Stockton CA 95207-6370

BULLARD, THAIS JEANNE, real estate executive; b. Austin, Tex.; d. Fred Mason and Bess (Mills) B. AB, Vassar Coll., Poughkeepsie, N.Y., 1950; AM, U. Tex., Austin, 1951, postgrad., 1962-67, 76-79; postgrad., U. Hawaii, 1989-91. Geologist in charge, micropaleontology lab. Exxon Corp., Corpus Christi, Tex., 1951-56; exploration geologist North Tex. div. Ensearch Corp., Dallas, 1956-61; rsch. assoc. Inst. Latin Am. Studies U. Tex., Austin, 1964-66; head team sociometric rsch. Tracor, Inc., Austin, 1966-67; owner Valverde Park Residences, Taos, N.Mex., 1970—. Author: Mexico's Natural Gas: The Beginning of an Industry, 1968. E.D. Farmer fellow U. Tex., Mexico, 1962-64, Ford Found. fellow U. Tex., Guatemala, 1965, Mexico, 1966. Mem. Am. Assn. Petroleum Geologists (assoc.). Home and Office: PO Box 512 Austin TX 78767-0512 also: 469 Ena Rd #3411 Honolulu HI 96815

BULLARD, WILLIS GALE, military career officer, anesthesia consultant; b. Inavale, Nebr., Nov. 18, 1940; s. Dale J. and Edna K. (Elliott) B.; m. Judith Anderson, Feb. 2, 1963; children: Deborah Ann, Leigh-Ann, Shari Lynne. RN, Mary Lanning Meml. Sch. Nursing, 1962; CRNA, Creighton Meml. Sch. Anesthesia, 1964; BS in Anesthesiology, Mt. Marty Coll., 1975; MA, U. No. Colo., 1978. Commd. 2d lt. USAF, 1966, advanced through grades to col., 1988; staff nurse anesthetist USAF Hosp., Grand Forks AFB, N.D., 1966-68, Carswell AFB Ft. Worth, 1969-72, Sault Ste. Marie, Mich., 1972-74, Holloman AFB Allamogordo, N.Mex., 1975-78; instr. in nurse anesthesiology USAF Med. Ctr. Wilford Hall, San Antonio, 1978-82; chief nurse anesthesist 804th Med. Group, Incirlik AB, Turkey, 1982-83; assoc. dir. nurse anesthesia residency Wilford Hall Med. Ctr., 1983-87, dir. nurse anesthesia residency program, 1987-90; sr. nurse anesthetist USAF Hosp. USAF Acad., Colorado Springs, Colo., 1990—; sr. mil. mem. Uniformed Svcs. Task Force, Am. Assn. Nurse Anesthesists, 1987—; chief cons. Air Force Surgeon Gen. Office, Bolling AFB, Wash., 1988—. Contbr. articles to profl. jours. Decorated Air Force Commendation medal. Mem. Am. Assn. Nurse Anesthesists, Air Force Assn. Nurse Anesthesists (treas. 1981-82), Tex. Assn. Nurse Anesthesists, Air Force Assn., Nurse Anesthetists. Republican. Roman Catholic. Home: Sr Officers Qtrs # 4114 U S A F Academy CO 80840 Office: USAF Hosp USAF Academy CO 80840

BULLER, DENNIS WILSON, engineering and testing company executive; b. Santa Monica, Calif., May 19, 1944; s. Russell Paris and Winifred Ellen (Danley) B.; m. Frances Alda Edsall, Apr. 10, 1971 (div. Dec. 1980); 1 child, Sean Michael; m. Maura Anne O'Connor, Jan. 2, 1988 (stepchildren: Jeremy James Stevenson, Shawn Cameron Stevenson. Student, Calif. Poly. Inst., San Luis Obispo, 1962-64, 64-65, U. N.Mex., 1970-72. Enlisted man USN, 1966, advanced through grades to chief petty officer, 1975; resigned, 1979; mech. technician Air Products & Chem., Inc., Allentown, Pa., 1979-80; asst. plant mgr. LHZ Plant, Air Products & Chem., Inc., Long Beach, Calif., 1980-81; chief design engr. med. gases group Liquid Air Corp., San Francisco, 1981-83; dist. mgr. Crest/Good Mfg. Co., Inc., Syosset, N.Y., 1984—; owner, mgr. Taurus Engring. & Testing, Stockton, Calif., 1992—; cons., Stockton, 1984—. Chmn. pack com. Cub Scouts Am., Stockton, 1988; coach Stockton Youth Soccer Assn., 1990; v.p. Bear Creek High Sch. Parent-Tchr.-Student Assn., Stockton, 1991-92. Sr. chief petty officer USNR ret. Mem. Am. Legion. Office: Taurus Engring & Testing Ste 391 9120 Thornton Rd Stockton CA 95209

BULLIN, CHRISTINE NEVA, arts administrator; b. New Plymouth, N.Z., Apr. 13, 1948; d. Kenneth and Hazel Iris B. B.A., Wellesley Coll., 1969; M.L.A., Simmons Coll., 1973. Dir., Opera New England, Boston, 1974-78; with San Francisco Opera, 1978-81; mgr. San Francisco Opera Ctr., 1981—. Office: Western Opera Theater War Memorial Opera House San Francisco CA 94102

BULLOCK, BRUCE LEWIS, technology company executive; b. Bartlesville, Okla., July 28, 1947; s. Oakle Porter and Jane (Livingston) B.; m. Cheryl Kea Williams; children: Aimee, Chad. BS in Physics, U. Calif., Riverside, 1970, BS in Math., 1970; MS in Computer Sci., U. Calif., Irvine, 1988. Group head, intelligent systems Hughes Rsch. Lab., Malibu, Calif., 1971-82; v.p. Teknowledge, Inc., Palo Alto, Calif., 1982-83; chmn., CEO Teknowledge Fed. Systems, Inc., Thousand Oaks, Calif., 1983-87, ISX Corp., Westlake Village, Calif., 1988—; bd. dirs. IS Robotics Corp., Cambridge, Mass.; sci. advisor NASA, Washington, 1992—; mem. Navy Rsch. Adv. Com., Washington, 1983; vis. staff mem. Stanford U. Artificial Intelligence Lab., 1975. Contbr. articles to profl. jours. Howard Hughes staff doctoral fellow Hughes Aircraft Co., 1973-75. Office: ISX Corp 4353 Park Terr Westlake Village CA 91361

BULLOCK, DONALD WAYNE, educator, educational computing consultant; b. Tacoma Park, Md., Mar. 24, 1947; s. B.W. and Margaret (Harris) B.; m. Pamela Louise Hatch, Aug. 7, 1971. AA in Music, L.A. Pierce Coll., Woodland Hills, Calif., 1969; BA in Geography, San Fernando Valley State Coll., 1971; Cert. Computer Edn., Calif. Luth. U., 1985, MA in Curriculum-Instrn., 1987. Tchr. music Calvary Luth. Sch., Pacoima, Calif., 1970-71; elem. tchr. 1st Luth. Sch., Northridge, Calif., 1971-73; elem. tchr. Simi Valley (Calif.) Unified Sch. Dist., 1973—, computer insvc. instr., 1982-85, computer mentor tchr., 1985-87, mentor tchr. edn. tech., 1992-93; lectr. Calif. Luth. U., Thousand Oaks, 1985-92; ednl. computer cons. DISC Ednl. Svcs., Simi Valley, 1985—; speaker profl. confs. Contbr. articles to profl. publs. Pres. Amen Choir, Van Nuys, Calif., 1981-83. Recipient Computer Learning Month grand prize Tom Snyder Prodns., 1988, Computer Learning Found., 1990, Spl. Commendation of Achievement, Learning mag. profl. best tchr. excellence awards, 1990; grantee Tandy-Radio Shack, Inc., 1985, Calif. Dept. Edn., 1985. Mem. NEA, Assn. for Supervision and Curriculum Devel., Internat. Soc. Tech. in Edn., Computer Using Educators Calif., Gold Coast Computer Using Educators (bd. dirs. 1988-89), Basset Hound Club Am., Basset Hound Club So. Calif. Home: 2805 Wanda Ave Simi Valley CA 93065-1528 Office: Knolls Elem Sch 6334 Katherine Rd Simi Valley CA 93063-4439

BULLOCK, J(AMES) ROBERT, judge; b. Provo, Utah, Dec. 16, 1916; s. James A. and Norma (Poulton) B.; m. Ethel Hogge, Aug. 29, 1949; children: James Robert Jr., C. Scott, David A., Steven H. BS, Utah State U., 1938; JD with honors, George Washington U., 1942. Bar: U.S. Ct. Appeals (D.C. cir.) 1942, Utah 1946, Colo. 1946, U.S. Supreme Ct. 1969. Ptnr. Aldrich, Bullock & Nelson, Provo, 1950-73; judge 4th Dist. Ct. Utah, 1973-85; sr. judge Dist. Cts. Utah, 1985—, chmn. bd. sr. judges, 1988-92; mem. Utah Jud. Coun., 1973-83, chief judge, 1981-83. Utah State Rep., 1963-67; mem. Utah Constn. Revision Commn., 1969-76, vice chmn. 1974-76. Comdr. U.S. Navy, 1941-46, ETO, PTO. Mem. ABA, Utah Bar Assn. (pres. 1972-73, Judge of the Yr. 1983), Am. Inns of Ct. (charter), Riverside Country Club, Rotary (pres. 1958-59), Order of Coif, Phi Delta Phi. Home and Office: 1584 Willow Ln Provo UT 84604-2802

BULTHUIS, DOUGLAS ALLEN, marine research scientist; b. Bellingham, Wash., Feb. 15, 1948; s. Peter and Winifred (Elenbaas) B.; m. Pamela Marie Spillman, June 26, 1970; children: Brian Michael, Karen Anne, Jonathan Mark. AB in Edn., Calvin Coll., Grand Rapids, Mich., 1970; MS in Limnology, Mich. State U., 1973; PhD in Botany, Latrobe U., Melbourne, Australia, 1982. Marine scientist Marine Pollution Studies Group, Melbourne, 1973-80; sr. marine scientist Marine Sci. Labs., Queenscliff, Australia, 1980-85, rsch. mgr., 1985-88; rsch. coord. Padilla Bay Nat. Estuarine Rsch. Res., Mt. Vernon, Wash., 1988—. Contbr. articles to profl. jours. Grantee Marine Sci. and Tech.-Australia, 1985, NOAA, 1991, 1989-92. Mem. Estuarine Rsch. Fedn., Pacific Estuarine Rsch. Soc. (sec.-treas. 1990-92), Am. Soc. Limnology and Oceanography, Am. Sci. Affiliation. Office: Padilla Bay Nat Estuarine Rsch Res 1043 Bay View-Edison Rd Mount Vernon WA 98273

BULTMANN, WILLIAM ARNOLD, historian; b. Monrovia, Calif., Apr. 10, 1922; s. Paul Gerhardt and Elsa (Johnson) B.; AB, UCLA, 1943, PhD, 1950; m. Phyllis Jane Wetherell, Dec. 28, 1949; 1 child, Janice Jane. Assoc. prof. history Central Ark. U., Conway, 1949-52, prof., 1954-57; assoc. prof. Ohio Wesleyan U., Delaware, 1957-61, prof., 1961-65; prof. Western Wash. U., Bellingham, 1965-87, chmn. dept., 1968-70, dean arts and scis., 1970-72, provost, 1971-73; vis. assoc. prof. U. Tex., Austin, 1952-53; vis. prof. U. N.H., summers 1965, 66; acad. cons. Wash. Commn. for Humanities, 1973-87, Nat. Endowment for Humanities, 1976-87; reader Ednl. Testing Service Princeton, 1973-85. Bd. dirs. Bellingham Maritime Heritage Found., 1980-85; mem. The Nature Conservancy, 1992—, Washington Arboretum Found., 1992—; adminstrv. officer Bellingham Power Squadron, 1981-82, comdr., 1982-84. Fulbight sr. lectr. Dacca (Bangladesh) U., 1960-61; Ohio Wesleyan U. rsch. fellow, 1964; Fund for Advancement Edn. fellow for fgn. study, 1953-54; recipient rsch. award Social Sci. Rsch. Coun., 1957. Mem. AAUP. Am. Hist. Assn., Nat. Tropical Botanical Garden Soc., Nat. Boating Fedn., Wash. Arboretum Found., Ch. Hist. Soc., Conf. Brit. Studies, Pacific, Pacific N.W. confs. Brit. studies, Mystery Writers of Am., Interclub Boating Assn. Washington, Seattle Power Squadron, Phi Beta Kappa, Phi Delta Kappa, Pi Gamma Mu. Episcopalian. Clubs: Park Athletic Recreation, Bellingham Yacht (chmn. pub. rels. com. 1981-86), Squalicum Yacht (trustee 1979-82), Birch Bay Yacht; Wash. Athletic. Co-author: Border Boating, 1978; co-founder, mem. editorial bd. Albion, 1968-84; mng. editor Brit. Studies Intelligencer, 1973-80; co-editor Current Research in British Studies, 1975; editor Jib Sheet, 1981-86; feature writer, columnist Sea mag., 1974—; feature writer Venture mag., 1981-85, Poole Publs., 1988—. Home: 1600 43d Ave E Ste 101 Seattle WA 98112

BUMGARDNER, LARRY G., academic administrator; b. Chattanooga, June 10, 1957; s. Walter G. and Kathryn (Hamrick) B. BA, David Lipscomb Coll., 1977; JD, Vanderbilt U., 1981. Bar: Tenn. 1981, U.S. Dist. Ct. (cen. dist.) Tenn. 1982, Calif. 1984, U.S. Dist. Ct. (cen. dist.) Calif. 1985. From reporter to copy editor Nashville (Tenn.) Banner, 1975-79; editor Tenn. Attorneys Memo, Tenn. Jour., Nashville, 1979-83; dir. founds. Pepperdine U., Malibu, Calif., 1983-85, asst. v.p. communications and grants, 1985-92, assoc. vice chancellor for founds. and rsch., asst. prof. comms., 1992—. Contbr. numerous articles to various pubs. Mem. ABA, Calif. Bar Assn. Home: 24321 Baxter Dr Malibu CA 90265 Office: Pepperdine U 24255 Pacific Coast Hwy Malibu CA 90263-4785

BUNCHMAN, HERBERT HARRY, II, plastic surgeon; b. Washington, Feb. 23, 1942; s. Herbert H. and Mary (Halleran) B.; m. Marguerite Fransioli, Mar. 21, 1963 (div. Jan. 1987); children: Herbert H. III., Angela K., Christopher. BA, Vanderbilt U., 1964; MD, U. Tenn., 1967. Diplomate Am. Bd. Surgery, Am. bd. Plastic Surgery. Resident in surgery U. Tex., Galveston, 1967-72, resident in plastic surgery, 1972-75; practice medicine specializing in plastic surgery Mesa, Ariz., 1975—; chief surgery Desert Samaritan Hosp., 1978-80. Contbr. articles to profl. jours. Eaton Clin. fellow, 1975. Mem. AMA, Am. Soc. Plastic and Reconstructive Surgery, Am. Soc. Aesthetic Plastic Surgery, Singleton Surgical Soc., Tex. Med. Assn., So. Med. Assn. (grantee 1974), Ariz. Med. Assn. Office: Plastic Surgery Cons PC 1520 S Dobson Rd Ste 314 Mesa AZ 85202-4783

BUNDE, CON, communication educator, state legislator; b. Mankato, Minn., Aug. 4, 1938; s. Ralph Louis and Leona Dorothy (Lehman) B.; m. Angelene Hammer, Aug. 22, 1964; children: Joy, Kurt. BA, Ctrl. Wash. U., 1966, MS, 1970; AA, Anchorage C.C., 1970. Cert. speech pathologist. Speech therapist Gig Harbor (Wash.) Schs., 1967-68, Anchorage Sch. Dist., 1968-70; asst. prof. speech comm. Anchorage C.C., 1970-88; prof. U. Alaska, Anchorage, 1988-93; mem. Alaska Ho. of Reps., Juneau, Anchorage, 1993—; pilot Ketchum Air Svc., Anchorage, 1975—; seminar leader in field. Mem. citizens adv. coun. Dept. Fish and Game, Anchorage, 1991-92, instr. bowhunter edn. program; active Anchorage Community Theater; mem. citizen's adv. bd. U. Alaska Anchorage Aviation Airframe and Power Plant degree program. With U.S. Army, 1956-59. Mem. Alaska Sled Dog Racing Assn. (pres. 1970-78), Alaska Airmen's Assn., Alaska Bowhunter Assn. (bd. dirs. 1991-92), Alaska Sportfishing Assn., Alaska Outdoor Coun. Republican. Office: Alaska State Legislature Ho of Reps 716 W 4th Ave Anchorage AK 99501

BUNDESEN, FAYE STIMERS, educator, investment and management company owner; b. Cedarville, Calif., Sept. 16, 1932; d. Floyd Walker and Ermina Elizabeth (Roberts) Stimers; m. Allen Eugene Bundesen, Dec. 27, 1972; children—William, David, Edward Silvius; Ted, Eric Bundesen. B.A., Calif. State U.-Sacramento, 1955; M.A., Calif. State U.-San Jose, 1972. Licensed real estate broker, Calif. Elem. sch. tchr. San Francisco Pub. Schs., 1955-60; elem. and jr. high sch. tchr., lang. arts specialist Sunnyvale (Calif.) Schs., 1978-83; cons. Santa Clara County Office of Edn. and Sunnyvale Sch. Dist., 1983-86; v.p. Bundesen Enterprises, Elk Grove, Calif., 1975-81, pres., 1981—. Bd. dirs. Sunnyvale Sch. Employees' Credit Union, 1983-86, v.p., 1984-86; mem. City of San Jose Tenant/Landlord Hearing Com., 1983-86, v.p., 1984-85. Mem. Assn. Supervision and Curriculum Devel., Calif. Scholarship Fedn. (life), AAUW, Tri-County Apartment Assn., Calif. Apartment Assn., Nat. Apartment Assn., Santa Clara County Real Estate Bd., Calif. Assn. Realtors, Nat. Assn. Realtors, Sacramento Assn. Realtors. Presbyterian. Office: PO Box 2006 Elk Grove CA 95759-2006

BUNN, CHARLES NIXON, strategic business planning consultant; b. Springfield, Ill., Feb. 8, 1926; s. Joseph Forman and Helen Anna Frieda (Link) B.; student U. Ill., 1943-44; BS in Engring., U.S. Mil. Acad., 1949; MBA, Xavier U., Cin., 1958; m. Cecine Cole, Dec. 26, 1951 (div. 1987); children: Sisene, Charles; m. Marjorie Fitzmaurice, Apr. 5, 1988. Flight test engr. Gen. Electric Co., Cin., also Edwards AFB, Calif., 1953-59; sr. missile test engr., space systems div. Lockheed Aircraft Corp., USAF Satellite Test Center, Sunnyvale, Calif., 1959-60, 63-70, economist, advanced planning dept., 1961-63; economic and long-range planning cons., Los Altos, Calif., 1970-73; head systems planning, economist, strategic bus. planning, Western Regional hdqrs. U.S. Postal Service, San Bruno, Calif., 1973-78; strategic bus. planning cons., investment analysis cons., 1978-79; strategic bus. planning Advanced Reactor Systems dept. Gen. Electric Co., Sunnyvale, Calif., 1979-84; strategic planning cons., 1984—. Served with inf. paratroops U.S. Army, 1944-45, with inf. and rangers, 1949-53, Korea. Decorated Battle Star (5). Mem. Nat. Assn. Bus. Economists, World Future Soc., Sigma Nu. Episcopalian. Home and Office: 222 Incline Way San Jose CA 95139-1525

BUNN, DOROTHY IRONS, court reporter; b. Trinidad, Colo., Apr. 30, 1948; d. Russell and Pauline Anna (Langowski) Irons; m. Peter Lynn Bunn; children: Kristy Lynn, Wade Allen, Russell Ahearn. Student No. Va. Community Coll., 1970-71, U. Va., Fairfax, 1971-72. Registered profl. reporter; cert. shorthand reporter. Pres., chief exec. officer Ahearn Ltd., Springfield, Va., 1970-81, Bunn & Assocs., Glenrock, Wyo., 1981—; cons.

Bixby Hereford Co., Glenrock, 1981-89, co-mgr., 1989—. Del., White House Conf. on Small Bus., Washington, 1986. Mem. NAFE, Am. Indian Soc., Nat. Ct. Reporters Assn., Wyo. Shorthand Reporters Assn. (chmn. com. 1984-85), Nat. Fedn. Ind. Businesses (guardian 1991—), Nat. Fedn. Bus. and Profl. Women (2nd v.p. 1993—, pub. rels. chair). Avocations: art, music. Home: PO Box 1602 Bixby Hereford Co Glenrock WY 82637 Office: Bunn & Assocs 81 Bixby Rd Glenrock WY 82637

BUNN, JAMES LEE, state senator; b. McMinnville, Oreg., Dec. 12, 1956; s. Benjamin Adam and Viola Mae (Fulgham) B.; m. Cindy Lou Mishler, Sept. 9, 1978; children: James Jr., Matthew, Phillip, Malachi. AA, Chemeketa Community Coll., Salem, Oreg., 1977; BA in Biology, N.W. Nazarene Coll., Nampa, Idaho, 1979. Farmer Oreg.; senator from dist. 15 Oreg. State Senate, 1987—; exec. dir. Oreg. Rep. Party. With Oreg. N.G. Res. Mem. Nazarene Ch. Home: 8157 SW River Bend Rd Mcminnville OR 97128-8627 Office: Office of State Senate State Capitol Salem OR 97310

BUNNELL, DAVID J., JR., pediatrician; b. Crawfordsville, Ind., Apr. 17, 1929; s. David J. and Alice (Thompson) B.; m. Cynthia Sue Briner; children: Beth Anne, Sharon Leigh, David Cedric, Thomas J., William Lewis. AB, Kenyon Coll., 1951; MD, Johns Hopkins U., 1955. Diplomate Am. Bd. Pediatrics. Intern Johns Hopkins Hosp. Harriet Lane Home, Balt., 1956; resident Johns Hopkins Hosp. Harriet Lowe Home, Balt., 1957-58; fellow, lectr. Johns Hopkins Sch. Medicine, Balt., 1957-58; pvt. practice pediatrics Newport Beach, Calif., 1963—; asst. prof. pediatrics U. Calif., Irvine, 1963-79, assoc. prof. pediatrics, 1980—; mem. Orange County Health Planning Coun., 1974-80, Med. Quality Rev. Com. of Med. Bd. Calif., 1987—. Mem. Lincoln Club of Orange County, 1978—, Rep. State Cen. Com., 1982—. With USAF, 1957-62. Fellow Am. Acad. Pediatrics; mem. AMA, Calif. Med. Assn. (ho. of dels.), Orange County Med. Assn., Orange County Pediatric Soc., L.A. Pediatric Soc., S.W. Pediatric Soc. Presbyterian. Home: 1301 Santiago Dr Newport Beach CA 92550-4945 Office: Harbor Pediatric Med Group 1901 Westcliff Dr Newport Beach CA 92660-4945

BUNTING, DAVID CUYP, economics educator, consultant; b. Chgo., Sept. 22, 1940; s. Van Asmus and Jane (Whitemore) B.; m. Susan Jean Wilkins, Oct. 28, 1978; children: Maxwell C., N. Henri. BS, Ohio State U., 1962, MA, 1964; MS, U. Wis., 1966; PhD, U. Oreg., 1972. Asst. prof. Ea. Wash. U., Cheney, 1971-76, assoc. prof., 1976-80, prof., 1980—; cons. Bonneville Power Adminstrn., Spokane, Wash., 1985—. Author: Rise of Large American Corporations, 1987; contbr. articles to profl. jours. Soccer coach Spokane Youth Sports Assn., 1985—. Mem. Am. Econ. Assn., Social Sci. History Assn., Western Social Sci. Assn., Bus. History Conf., Econ. History Assn. Democrat. Home: 2311 E 17th Ave Spokane WA 99223-5121 Office: Ea Wash U Dept Economics Cheney WA 99004

BUNTON, CLIFFORD ALLEN, chemist, educator; b. Chesterfield, Eng., Jan. 4, 1920; came to U.S., 1963, naturalized, 1978; s. Arthur and Edith (Kirk) B.; m. Ethel Clayton, July 28, 1945; children—Julia Margaret, Claire Jennifer. B.Sc., Univ. Coll., London, 1941, Ph.D., 1945; hon. degree, U. Perugia, Italy, 1986. Successively asst. lectr., lectr., reader Univ. Coll., 1944-63; prof. chemistry U. Calif., Santa Barbara, 1963-90, prof. emeritus, 1990—, chmn. dept., 1967-72; Commonwealth Fund fellow U. Columbia, 1948-49; Brit. Council vis. lectr., Chile and Argentina, 1960; vis. prof. UCLA, 1961, U. Toronto, 1962, U. Sao Paolo, Brazil, 1973, U. Lausanne, Switzerland, 1976, 79; adj. prof. U. Chile, Santiago, 1990—; mem. policy com. U. Chile-U. Calif. Coop. Program, chmn. sci. and engring. sub-com., 1969—. Contbr. articles to profl. jours. Recipient Tolman medal, So. Calif. sect. Am. Chem. Soc., 1987. Fellow AAAS; mem. N.Y. Acad. Sci., Am. Chem. Soc. (Calif. sect.), Chem. Soc. (London); corr. mem. Chilean Acad. Scis. (1974). Home: 935 Cocopah Dr Santa Barbara CA 93110-1204

BUNZEL, JOHN HARVEY, political science educator, researcher; b. N.Y.C., Apr. 15, 1924; s. Ernest Everett and Harriett (Harvey) B.; m. Barbara Bovyer, May 11, 1963; children—Cameron, Reed. A.B., Princeton U., 1948; M.A., Columbia U., 1949; Ph.D., U. Calif.-Berkeley, 1954; LL.D., U. Santa Clara, 1976. Mem. faculty San Francisco State U., 1953-56, 63-70, vis. scholar Ctr. Advanced Study in Behavioral Scis., 1969-70; mem. faculty Mich. State U., East Lansing, 1956-57, Stanford U., Calif., 1957-63; pres. San Jose State U., Calif., 1970-78; sr. research fellow Hoover Inst. Stanford U., Calif., 1978—; mem. U.S. Commn. on Civil Rights, 1983-86. Author: The American Small Businessman, 1962; Anti-Politics in America, 1967; Issues of American Public Policy, 1968; New Force on the Left, 1983, Challenge to American Schools: The Case For Standards and Values, 1985, Political Passages: Journeys of Change Through Two Decades 1968-1988, 1988, Race Relations on Campus: Stanford Students Speak, 1992; contbr. articles to profl. jours., popular mags., newspapers. Weekly columnist San Jose Mercury-News. Bd. dirs. No. Calif. Citizenship Clearing House, 1959-61; mem. Calif. Atty. Gen.'s Adv. Com., 1960-61; del. Calif. Democratic Conv., 1968; del. Dem. Nat. Conv., 1968. Recipient Presdl. award No. Calif. Polit. Sci. Assn., 1969, cert. of Honor San Francisco Bd. Suprs., 1974, Hubert Humprey Pub. Policy award Policy Studies Orgn., 1990; grantee Ford Found., Rockefeller Found., Rabinowitz Found. Mem. Am. Polit. Sci. Assn. Home: 1519 Escondido Way Belmont CA 94002-3634 Office: Stanford U Hoover Inst Stanford CA 94305

BURAS, NATHAN, hydrology and water resources educator; b. Barlad, Romania, Aug. 23, 1921; came to U.S., 1947; s. Boris and Ethel (Weiser) B.; m. Netty Stivel, Apr. 13, 1951; 1 child, Nir H. BS with highest honors, U. Calif., Berkeley, 1949; MS, Technion, Haifa, Israel, 1957; PhD, UCLA, 1962. Registered profl. engr., Israel. Prof. hydrology and water resources Technion, 1962-80, dean, 1966-68; vis. prof. Stanford (Calif.) U., 1976-81; prof., head of dept. hydrology and water resources U. Ariz., Tucson, 1981-89, prof. hydrology and water resources, 1989—; cons. Tahal, Ltd., Tel Aviv, 1963-73, World Bank, Washington, 1972-76, 79-81, Regional Municipality of Waterloo, Ont., Can., 1991—, U.S. AID, Washington, 1992—, Great No. Paper Co., 1992—. Author: Scientific Allocation of Water Resources, 1972; editor: Control of Water Resources Systems, 1976. Mem. Israel-Mex. Mixed Commn. on Sci. Cooperation, 1976, So. Ariz. Water Resource Assn., 1982—; active Pugwash Workshops, 1991, 92. Named Laureat du Congres, Internat. Assn. Agrl. Engring., 1964; recipient Cert. of Appreciation, USDA., 1970. Fellow Ariz.-Nev. Acad. Sci., ASCE (life), Am. Geophys. Union, Am. Water Resources Assn. (charter). Jewish. Home: 5541 E Circulo Terra Tucson AZ 85715-1003 Office: U Ariz Dept Hydrologand Water Resources Tucson AZ 85721

BURAWA, CHRISTOPHER MARK, editor; b. Reykjavik, Iceland, Dec. 17, 1959; came to U.S., 1971; s. George and Aslaug (Hermanniusdottir) B. AA, Prince Georges C.C., Largo, Md., 1979; BA, Ariz. State U., 1987. Rsch. asst. Ariz. Ctr. for Medieval and Renaissance Studies, Ariz. State U., Tempe, 1987-89, assoc. editor acad. and adminstrv. documents, 1989—. Editor: The Computer and the Brain: Perspectives on Human and Artificial Intelligence, 1989. Scholar Tenn. Wesleyan Coll., 1977. Mem. Am. Soc. Indexers, Sigma Tau Delta. Lutheran. Office: Ariz State U Tempe AZ 85287-1103

BURCH, CLAIRE, writer; b. N.Y.C., Feb. 19, 1925; d. Albert I. and Dorothy (Denhoff) Cohen; m. Bradley A. Burch, Apr. 24, 1944 (dec. 1967); children: Laurie, Emily, Elizabeth. BA, Washington Square Coll., N.Y.C., 1947. Editor, writer N.Y.C., 1947-50; freelance writer, 1950-68; adj. prof. Union of Experimenting Colls., Antioch, N.Y., 1968-74; editor, freelance writer various nat. mags., N.Y.C., 1974-78; contbg. editor No. Calif. Psychiat. Network News, Berkeley, 1978-83; mng. editor No. Calif. Network News, Berkeley, 1983—; exec. dir. Art and Edn. Media Inc., Berkeley; conducted numerous workshops in field. Author: Stranger in the Family, 1972, You Be the Mother Follies, 1985, Goodbye My Coney Island Baby, 1988, Solid Gold Illusion, 1988, Shredded Millions, 1988, Homeless in the Nineties, 1990; filmmaker (documentaries) James Baldwin, Entering Oakland (People's Choice award), Alfonia (People's Choice award), The Clown Uptown, Thumbed a Ride to Heaven, Baby Don't Cry, Oracle Rising, Remembering the Summer of Love and other Songs by Claire Burch, James Baldwin Part II. Recipient Andrew Carnegie award, 1981; grantee Ctr. for Ind. Living, 1989, City of Berkeley, 1989, 90, 91, Calif. Arts Coun., 1991, 92, 93. Home: 2747 Regent St Berkeley CA 94705-2525 Office: Art and Edn Media Inc 2747 Regent St Berkeley CA 94705-1212

BURCH, EARL ALLEN, JR., psychiatrist, psychopharmacologist; b. Charleston, S.C., Mar. 30, 1947; s. Earl A. Sr. and Minnie Janelle (Maloney) B.; m. Betty Kay Thompson, Sept. 6, 1969; 1 child, Jeffery Hall Brandenburg. BS in Biology, Augusta Coll., 1969; student, U. Tenn.-Oak Ridge, 1969-70; MD, Med. Coll. Ga., 1975. Diplomate Am. Bd. Psychiatry and Neurology. Resident in psychiatry William S. Hall Psychiat. Inst., Columbia, S.C., 1975-78; asst. prof. sch. medicine U. S.C., Columbia, 1978-82, assoc. prof., 1982-83; assoc. prof. sch. medicine Tulane U., New Orleans, 1983-88, prof., 1988-91; staff psychiatrist Salt Lake City VA Med. Ctr., 1991—. Co-author various book chpts., video/audio tapes; contbr. articles to profl. jours. Office: VA Med Ctr 500 Foot Hill Dr Salt Lake City UT 84148

BURCH, HAMLIN DOUGHTY, III, retired sheet metal man; b. Oakland, Calif., June 14, 1939; s. Hamlin D. Burch II and Bernice I. (Ingerski) Bortscheller; m. Zettie A. Honeycutt, Nov. 16, 1957 (div. 1974); children: Paula Christine Grothaus, Victoria Jaylee Alberti, Hamlin D. IV. Grad., Modesto (Calif.) High Sch. Sheet metal worker Fred L. Hill., Modesto, 1960-62, Olson's Plumbing, Turlock, 1962-64, Hansen's Inc., Modesto, 1964-74; Lang's Engerprises, Modesto, 1974-87; sheet metal worker Mendenhall, Sacramento, 1985-87, South Valley Mech., San Juan Baptiste, 1987-88, Brott Mech., Tulare, 1988; ret. Brott Mech. Republican. Mem. LDS Ch.

BURCH, MARY LOU, housing advocate, executive; b. Billings, Mont., Apr. 4, 1930; d. Forrest Scott Sr. and Mary Edna (Hinshaw) Chilcott; m. J. Sheldon Robinson, June 18, 1949 (div. 1956); m. G. Howard Burch, Nov. 27, 1957 (div. 1984); children: Julie Lynne Scully, Donna Eileen, Carol Marie Kimball, Alan Robert, Christine Philips Spruill Enomoto. AA, Grant Tech. Coll., Sacramento, 1949; AB, Sacramento State Coll., 1955; student, U. Alaska, 1976-78, Santa Rosa (Calif.) Jr. Coll., 1987. Diagnostic tchr. Calif. Youth Authority, Perkins, 1955-57; com. chmn. on pub. info. Sequoia Union High Sch. Dist., So. San Mateo County, Calif., 1970-72; exec. dir. Presbyn. Hospitality House, Fairbanks, Alaska, 1979-80; realtor Century 21 Smith/Ring, Renton, Wash., 1980-81; cons. Fairbanks, Alaska, 1981-84; exec. dir. Habitat for Humanity of Sonoma County, Santa Rosa, Calif., 1986-89, Affordable Housing Assoc., Santa Rosa, Calif., 1989-90; pvt. cons. in housing and orgn. Scottsdale, Ariz., 1991—; bd. dirs. Hosp. Chaplainey Svcs, Santa Rosa, Villa Los Alamos Homeowners Assn.; cons. Access Alaska, Anchorage, 1983; contractor Alaka Siding, Fairbanks, 1982-83. Named vol. of the year, Hosp. Chaplaincy Svcs., 1987. Democrat. United Ch. of Christ. Home and Office: 1678 W Pine Cone Prescott AZ 86303

BURCHARD, THOMAS KIRK, psychiatrist; b. Boston, Feb. 16, 1948; s. Charles Henry and Helen (Schwob) B.; m. Geri Diane Margolese. BS, Antioch Coll., 1970; MD, U. Va., 1973. Intern Cin. Children's Hosp., 1974-75; adult psychiatry resident Sepulveda VA Hosp., L.A., 1975-77; child psychiatry fellow UCLA, 1977-79; dir. Mental Health Ctr. child and family programs Community Hosp. of the Monterey Peninsula, Monterey, Calif., 1979-91, dir. child and adolescent outpatient programs, 1991—; instr. Antioch-West, Pacific Grove, Calif., 1982. Fellow Am. Orthopsychiatric Assn.; mem. AMA, Am. Acad. Child and Adolescent Psychiatry, Am. Psychiat. Assn., Calif. Med. Assn., No. Calif. Psychiat. Assn. Office: Community Hosp of Peninsula Holman Hwy Monterey CA 93940

BURCHETTE, MARISSA JEANETTE, SR., executive secretary; b. Bainbridge, Md., Nov. 21, 1967; d. Danny Layell and Veronica Joyce (Berry) B. Sec. Dyncorp, Lakehurst, N.J., 1986-88; exec. sec. POPI, Winston-Salem, 1988-89; computer cons. Glendale Coll., Duarte, Calif., 1989; exec. sec. James Montgomery Cons. Engr., Pasadena, Calif., 1989—. Mem. NAFE. Roman Catholic. Office: Montgomery Watson 250 N Madison Ave Pasadena CA 91109

BURCIAGA, JUAN GUERRERO, federal judge; b. Roswell, N.Mex., Aug. 17, 1929; s. Melesio Antonio and Juana (Guerrero) B.; m. Carolyn Jacoby, Oct. 28, 1958 (dec.); children: Lisa Anne, Lora Anne, Amy Virginia, Carlos Antonio, Pamela. BS, U.S. Mil. Acad., 1952; JD, U. N.Mex., 1963. Bar: N.Mex. 1964. Assoc., then ptnr. firms in Albuquerque, 1964-79; judge U.S. Dist. Ct. N.Mex., 1979—; lectr. U. N.Mex. Sch. Law, 1970-71. Bd. dirs. Albuquerque YMCA, 1964-74, NCCJ, Albuquerque, 1969-73; urban renewal commnr. City of Albuquerque, 1972-76. Served as officer USAF, 1952-60. Mem. Am. Bar Assn., Am. Judicature Soc. (dir.), Def. Research Inst., Am. Bd. Arbitration, Am. Trial Lawyers Assn., Am. Bd. Trial Advocates, Albuquerque Bar Assn. Democrat. Roman Catholic. Office: US Dist Ct PO Box 67 Albuquerque NM 87103-0067

BURCZYK, MARY ELIZABETH, corporate communications executive; b. Racine, Wis., Aug. 19, 1953; d. Raymond and Dolores Cecelia (Swencki) B. BS, U. Wis., 1975; MBA, Northwestern U., 1985. Dir. pub. rels. Indsl. Fabrics Assn. Internat., St. Paul, 1976-80; mgr. pub. info. and audience devel. St. Paul Chamber Orch., 1980-81; dir. pub. rels. Mental Health Assn. Minn., Mpls., 1981-83; sr. v.p. On-Line Communications Corp., Chgo., 1986-90; v.p. corp. communications Catellus Devel. Corp., San Francisco, 1990—. Office: Catellus Devel Corp 201 Mission St San Francisco CA 94105-1831

BURDETTE, ROBERT SOELBERG, accountant; b. Salt Lake City, Apr. 28, 1955; s. Grant Edward and Jewel Irene (Soelberg) B.; m. Marne Marie Erekson, June 21, 1977 (div. May 1985); children: Aaron Edward, Melissa Marie, Barton Allen; m. Conna Lee Jolley, Feb. 1, 1990; children: Seth Robert, Mark Jacob. BA, U. Utah, 1979; M in Taxation, Wash. Inst. Grad. Studies, 1993. CPA, Utah. Staff acct. Huber & Assocs., Salt Lake City, 1979-80; acctg. mgr. Huntsman-Christensen Corp., Salt Lake City, 1980-81; supervising tax specialist Leverich & Co., Salt Lake City, 1982-83; tax ptnr. Burdette & Hymas CPAs, Salt Lake City, 1983—; compt. Art Beats, Inc., Salt Lake City, 1988-90; prof. law in taxation Washington Sch. Law, 1991. Conv. del. Salt Lake County Rep. Party, 1980, Utah State Rep. Party, 1992; missionary Ch. Jesus Christ of Latter-Day Saints, 1974-76; basketball coach Salt Lake Boys & Girls Club, 1989; scout master Boy Scouts Am., Sandy, Utah, 1986-87. Mem. AICPA, Utah Assn. CPAs (taxation com. 1983), Nat. Assn. Tax Practioneers, Intermountain Soc. Practicing CPAs, CPA Law Forum (bd. adv.), Nat. Soc. Tax Profls. Home: 1756 Wilson Ave Salt Lake City UT 84108-2917 Office: Burdette & Hymas CPAs 4444 S 700 E Salt Lake City UT 84107

BURDICK, DOROTHY JEANNETTE, advertising, publishing executive, consultant; b. Baltimore, Jan. 10, 1935; d. Harvey Nathan and Bessie Bell (Day) Jones; m. Martin Myrl Burdick, June 16, 1956; children: Robert Myrl, Linda Lee. BS, U. Md., 1957. Tchr., 1957—; owner Welcoming You Greeting Svcs., Littleton, Colo., 1985—; founder, bd. dirs. Christians United Publ., Littleton, Colo., 1990—. Author adult Christian edn. curriculum. Del. Rep. County Assembly, Golden, Colo., 1992; commr. Presbyn. USA Gen. Assembly, Baltimore, 1991, Denver Presbytery, 1993; mem. City Hostess Internat., v.p. 1991-92. Mem. Women Bus. Owners (founder), Welcome Svcs. Internat. (pres. 1992-93), South Metro C. of C., Aurora C. of C., Alpha Gamma Delta. Republican. Home and Office: PO Box 621544 Littleton CO 80162

BURDSALL, DEAN LEROY, accountant; b. Indpls., June 4, 1935; s. Ralph Kirk and Florence Geraldine (Duncan) B.; m. Georgia Lee Vent, June 1, 1957; children: Kevin, Craig, Scott, Jeffrey. BA, Pasadena Coll., 1957. CPA, Calif. Staff acct. Peat, Marwick, Mitchell & Co., San Jose, Calif., 1960-68; corp. controller GRT Corp., Sunnyvale, Calif., 1968-71; prin. Brooks, Stednitz & Rhodes Accountacy Corp., San Jose, 1971—. Treas. Santa Clara Valley Youth for Christ, San Jose. With U.S. Army, 1958-60. Mem. AICPA (mem. peer rev. com. 1991-93, mem. PCP exec. com. 1993—), Calif. Soc. CPAs (mem. quality rev. com. 1989-93, mem. acctg. prins. and auditing standards com. 1987—), Calif. Group Acctg. Firms Assn. (chmn. 1988-89). Home: 6531 Gillis Dr San Jose CA 95120

BURE, PAVEL, professional hockey player; b. Moscow, Mar. 31, 1971. Wing Vancouver (Can.) Canucks. Recipient Calder Meml. trophy, 1991-92. Office: Vancouver Canucks, 100 N Renfrew St, Vancouver, BC Canada U5K 3N7

BURG, ANTON BEHME, chemist, retired educator; b. Dallas City, Ill., Oct. 18, 1904; s. Frank Winchester and Sadie Quinton (Hornby) B. BS, U. Chgo., 1927, MS, 1928, PhD, 1931. Researcher Kimberley-Clark Co., Neenah, Wis., 1928-29; rsch. asst. U. Chgo., 1929-31, instr., 1931-39; from asst. prof. to prof. U. So. Calif., L.A., 1939-74, dept. head, 1940-50, prof. emeritus, 1974—; cons. in field. Contbr. numerous articles to profl. jours. Fellow AAAS; mem. Am. Chem. Soc. (Mallinckrodt award Tolman medal 1969), AAUP, Sigma Xi, Phi Beta Kappa. Home: 459 W 38th St Los Angeles CA 90037 Office: U So Calif Los Angeles CA 90089-0744

BURG, BARRY RICHARD, history educator, writer; b. Denver, Aug. 2, 1938; s. H.D. and Florence Burg; m. Kathleen Semrau, June 12, 1965 (div. 1980); children: Jenny Anne, John Eliot; m. Judith Marie Harbour, July 17, 1982. BA, U. Colo., 1960; MA, Western State Coll., Gunnison, Colo., 1963; PhD, U. Colo., 1967. Lectr. U. Colo., Denver, 1965-67; with Ariz. State U., Tempe, 1967—, dir. honors program, 1978-82, prof. history, 1977—. Author: Richard Mather of Dorchester, 1976, Sodomy & the Pirate Tradition, 1982, An American Seafarer in the Age of Sail: The Intimate Diaries of Philip C. Van Bushkirk, 1851-1870, 1993. Lt. U.S. Army, 1961-62. Fulbright scholar Pakistan, 1982-83, Indonesia, 1989-90; Ford Found. fellow Mass. Hist. Soc., 1969-70. Office: Ariz State U History Dept Tempe AZ 85287

BURG, GARY G., vocational expert; b. L.A., Aug. 24, 1956; s. George J. and Kathleen A. (Doheny) B.; m. Diane Teresa Giliotti, Aug. 5, 1978; children: Sean Douglas, Anthony Christian. BA in Psychology, Calif. State U., Los Angeles, 1978, MS in Rehab. Counseling, 1982. Diplomate Am. Bd. Vocat. Experts; cert. vocat. evaluation specialist, cert. ins. rehab. specialsit. Counselor East Valley Community Health Ctr., West Covina, Calif.; evaluation and tng. counselor Goodwill Industries So. Calif., L.A.; vocat. counselor, evaluator PAR Services, Santa Fe Spring, Calif.; exec. dir. West Mountain Community Services, Crestline, Calif.; vocat. evaluator, mgr. Anfuso Work Evaluation Ctr. Inc., Pasadena, Calif.; owner, dir. Testing, Evaluation And Mgmt., El Monte, Riverside and Temecula, Calif.; forensic vocat. expert Testing Evaluation And Mgmt., Riverside; assoc. prof. Calif. State U., L.A.; lectr. in field. Past bd. dirs. Crestline Area Presch., Contact the Helpline, San Bernardino, Calif., East Valley Community Health Ctr., South Hills Little League, West Covina, Assn. Retarded Citizens, San Gabriel Valley, Calif., West End Industry Edn. Coordination Counsel, San Bernardino County. Mem. Am. Bd. Vocat. Experts (membership chair 1991-93, bd. dirs. 1992-94), Calif. Assn. Rehab. Profl., Inland Empire Rehab. Group, Nat. Rehab. Assn., Nat. Assn. Rehab. Profl. Pvt. Sector, Calif. Vocat. Evaluators and Work Adjustment Assn. (bd. dirs. 1987—, pres. 1989—). Office: Testing Evaluation And Mgmt 3737 Main St Ste 520 Riverside CA 92501

BURG, GERALD WILLIAM, religious organization administrator; b. Pitts., Oct. 16, 1923; s. Julius Samuel and Anna (Shapiro) B.; student Walsh Inst., 1940-43; m. Flavia Kafton, Aug. 12, 1945; children—Cindy, Melinda, Andrew. Engring. rep. U.S. Rubber Co., 1943-45; adminstr. Beverly Hills (Calif.) B'nai B'rith, 1945-52, Univ. Synagogue, Brentwood, 1952-55; exec. dir. Wilshire Blvd. Temple, Los Angeles, 1956-80; mgmt. and fin. cons., 1980-85; adminstr. Sinai Temple, 1985—. Mem. Jewish relations com. Los Angeles council Boy Scouts Am., 1959-85; mem. Mayor's Adv. Com. on Community Activities, Los Angeles, 1963-73; chmn. Crime Prevention Fifth Councilmanic Dist., Los Angeles, 1968-73. Bd. dirs. McCobb Home for Boys, Los Angeles Psychiat. Service, Maple Ctr. for Crises Intervention, Save a Heart Found., Didi Hirsch Community Mental Health Services, pres., 1975-77; bd. dirs., chmn. finances, chmn. adminstrv. com. Community Care and Devel. Services, 1975-92. Mem. Nat. (bd. dirs., pres. 1975-77), Western (pres. 1969-71, bd. dirs.), So. Calif. (pres. 1958-60) assns. temple adminstrs., NCCJ (bd. dirs. brotherhood antytown 1966-82), Los Angeles Jewish Communal Execs. (dir.). Mem. B'nai B'rith (youth dir. 1945-82, Akiba award 1950, Beverly Hills pres. 1953-54). Club: Sertoma (v.p. 1973-82). Home: 5115 Kester Ave Apt 202 Sherman Oaks CA 91403-1365 Office: Sinai Temple 10400 Wilshire Blvd Los Angeles CA 90024-4600

BURG, JEROME STUART, financial planning consultant; b. N.Y.C., Aug. 2, 1935; s. Norman and Ruth (Schkurman) B.; m. Janis Elaine Lyon, May 26, 1974; children: Jeffrey Howard, David Matthew, Audree, Harriet, Robert, Stephanie. Student, Temple U., 1953-56; CLU, Am. Coll., 1973, chartered fin. cons., 1984; cert. fin. planner, Coll. Fin. Planning, 1983. Pres., CEO Jerome Burg Assoc., Inc., Cherry Hill, N.J., 1963-79, Contemporary Fin. Planning, Scottsdale, Ariz., 1979-89; sr. acct. mgr. Acacia Group, Phoenix, 1989—; instr. Glendale and Scottdale C.C., 1983—, Nat. Inst. Fin., N.J., 1984-90. Pres. N.J. Assn. Life Underwriters, Trenton, 1963-65; instr. Jr. Achievement, Scottsdale, 1985-89; 1st v.p. Pres. Cabinet-Acacia Group, Washington, 1991, 93, co-pres., 1992. With U.S. Army, 1956-58. Mem. Internat. Assn. Fin. Planning (bd. dirs. Greater Phoenix chpt. 1982—), Inst. Cert. Fin. Planners. Office: Acacia Group 3200 E Camelback Rd Phoenix AZ 85018

BURGAMY, MICHAEL BARNET, distributing and manufacturing company executive; b. Lubbock, Tex., July 6, 1945; s. Estes D. and Nona Marie (Pevehouse) B.; m. Susan Jane White, Sept. 9, 1972; children: Aaron Michael, Sarah Estes. BS in Engring. Mgmt., U.S. Air Force Acad., 1968. Real estate broker Berry& Stark, Denver, 1972-74; CFO Star Aviation Corp., Denver, 1974-76; pres. CGS Distbg. Inc., Denver, 1976—; CEO Perky-Pet Products, Denver, 1991—. Participant, Fifty for Colo., Denver, 1988, Pub. Edn. Coalition, Denver, 1988—; bd. dirs. Stanley Brit. Primary Sch., Denver, 1984, Graland Country Day Sch., Denver, 1986-92. Capt. USAF, 1968-72. Mem. Nat. Lawn and Garden Distbrs. Assn. (bd. dirs. 1986-88). Office: CGS Distributing Inc 4747 Ivy St Denver CO 80216-6413 also: Perky-Pet Products Co 2201 S Wabash Denver CO 80231

BURGARINO, ANTHONY EMANUEL, environmental engineer, consultant; b. Milw., July 20, 1948; s. Joseph Francis Burgarino and Mardelle (Hoeffler) T.; m. Gail Fay DiMatteo, Mar. 13, 1982; children: Paul Anthony, Joanna Lynn. BS, U. Wis., 1970; MS, Ill. Inst. Tech., 1974, PhD, 1980. Registered profl. engr., Ariz. Sales engr. Leeds & Northrup, Phila., 1970-72; rsch. asst. Ill. Inst. Tech., Chgo., 1972-75; chemist City of Chgo., 1975-79; instr. Joliet (Ill.) Jr. Coll., 1978-79; project engr. John Carollo Engrs., Walnut Creek, Calif., 1980—; cons. City of Clovis, Calif., 1981-83, City of Fresno, Calif., 1983—, City of Phoenix, 1981-90, City of Yuma, Ariz., 1989—, City of Santa Maria, Calif., 1991—. Contbr. articles to profl. jours. EPA grantee, 1970-72; NSF fellow, 1973, Ill. Inst. Tech. Rsch. Found. fellow, 1974. Mem. Am. Water Works Assn. Roman Catholic. Home: 4355 Oakdale Pl Pittsburg CA 94565-6258 Office: John Carollo Engrs 450 N Wiget Ln Walnut Creek CA 94598

BURGE, WILLARD, JR., software company executive; b. Johnson City, N.Y., Oct. 2, 1938; s. Willard Sr. and Catherine Bernice (Matthews) B.; m. Carol Crockenberg, June 16, 1961; children: Willard III, Pennie Lynn. Registered profl. engr., Ohio. Indsl. engr. Harnischfeger Corp., Escanaba, Mich., 1966-67; sr. indsl. engr. Gen. Electric, Ladson, S.C., 1968-74; advanced mfg. engr. Gen. Electric, Mentor, Ohio, 1971-74; corp. staff engr. Eaton Corp., Willoughby Hills, Ohio, 1974-79, supr. N/C programming, 1979-80, supr. mfg. engring., 1980-82, mgr. mfg. systems engring., 1982-87; bus. unit mgr. MSC Products, Eaton Corp., Costa Mesa, Calif., 1987-91; pres., CEO CAM Software, Inc., Provo, Utah, 1991—; bd. dirs. CAM Software, Inc. Presenter in field. With U.S. Army, 1957. Mem. Soc. Mfg. Engrs. Republican. Home: 95 N Paradise Dr Orem UT 84057 Office: CAM Software 750 North 200 West Ste 208 Provo UT 84601

BURGER, JOHN BARCLAY, systems architect, computer scientist; b. Blackwell, Okla., Jan. 8, 1936; s. William B. and Avis (Winkler) B.; m. Janet Olivia Polf, Dec. 27, 1988; children: John Barclay, Carolyn Avis. BS in Computer Sci., U. Okla., 1961; MBA in Engring. Tech., Fla. Inst. Tech., 1976; MBA, Harvard U., 1980. Computer sci. instr. U. Okla., Norman, 1958-61; sr. avionics programmer Gen. Dynamics-Ft. Worth, 1961-62; dir. systems engring. GE, Daytona Beach, Fla., 1962-72; systems mgr. City of Melbourne, Fla., 1972-79; pub. utilities industry adminstr. Gen. Systems Div., IBM, Atlanta, 1979-82; dir. MIS Seminole Electric Coop., Inc., Tampa, Fla., 1982-85, Fla. Employers Svc. Co., Sarasota, Fla., 1985-88; program mgr. Ball Systems Engring. Div., San Diego, 1988-89; sr. tech. specialist Northrop B-2 Div., Pico Rivera, Calif., 1989—; chief info. officer, bd. dirs.

Waters Ins. Svc. Corp., Sarasota; chief info. officer, cons. Fla. Chamber Fund, Sarasota, 1986-92. Copyright numerous computer software programs. Mem. Elfin Soc. GE, Daytona Beach, 1970; bd. dirs. Suncoast Mental Health Ctr., Sarasota, 1985. Col. USAFR, 1955-86. Named Man of Yr., Huntsville, Ala. C. of C., 1964, Best Speaker, Lions Club, 1972. Mem. IEEE (spl. interest group chmn. 1990-91), AIAA (pres. 1988-89), Soc. Logistics Engrs. (program chmn. 1989-91), Greater L.A. Zoo Assn. (docent, vol., contbr.), L.A. County Mus. of Art (contbr.). Democrat. Mem. 1st Christian Ch. Home: 1344 W 5th St # 36 Glendale CA 91201

BURGESS, CLARA WOODWARD, executive; b. Hobson, Mont., Oct. 24, 1918; d. Herbert Starr and Ethel (Warren) Woodward; m. William H. Burgess; children: Sarah Louise, Margaret Warren. Student, U. Minn., 1937-41, U. So. Calif., 1948. Dir. law clks. Covington, Burling, Rubles, Acheson & Shorb, Washington, 1943-45; with juvenile crime prevention bur. Pasadena (Calif.) Police Dept., 1946-49; dir. women's aux. Aux. Goodwill Industries, 1949-55; dir. Sta. KCET Channel 28 Ednl. TV, 1966, treas., 1968—. Chmn. youth activities Women's Civic League, 1948-51; bd. dirs., Pasadena auxiliary Boy's Rep., 1950-55; bd. dirs. Huntington Meml. Tumor Clinic Auxiliary, 1951-54, Pasadena Family Svc., 1964-66, Pasadena Art Mus., Pasadena Symphony Assn., Women's Auxiliary Goodwill Industries, 1949-55, Inst. Internat. Edn., 1970-72; founder Pasadena Chpt. of Hope, 1963; pres. Pasadena Philarm. Com., 1962-64; trustee Pasadena Cultural Found., 1966-72; active So. Calif. Opera Guild, L.A. World Affairs Coun., 1954—, The Diadames of the Child Care League, Rep. Club of the Desert, YWCA, Tiempo de Los Ninos of Desert Hosp., Encore of L.A. Philharm. Assn.; pres. Palm Springs Friends of L.A. Philharm.; pres. Show Case Assocs.; pres'. cir., dir. western art coun. Palm Springs Desert Mus.; pres'. cir. McCallum Theatre of Performing Arts, Coll. of the Desert; founding mem. Pasadena Art Alliance, 1955—. Mem. So. Calif. Symphony Assn., Nat. Inst. Social Scis., L.A. Music Ctr., Calif. Assocs., L.A. Ballet Soc., Ballet Guild of Deserts, Les Dames de Champagne de Los Angeles, Blu Ribbon 400, Muses, Town Club, Valley Hunt Club, Pathfinders, River Club, Odonnell Golf Glub, Desert Riders (pres.), Vintage Club, So. Calif. Alpha Phi Alumni Assn. (pres. 1949-50). Home: 550 Palisades Dr Palm Springs CA 92262-5644

BURGESS, HENRY ERNEST, academic administrator, English language educator; b. Anaconda, Mont., Nov. 27, 1929; s. James Arthur and Loretta Margaret (Gillespie) B.; m. Dorothy Eileen Mehrens, June 28, 1958; children: Jean, Theresa, Kathleen, Mary, Judy, Margaret, Thomas, Sarah. BA in Philosophy, Carroll Coll., 1951; MA in English Lit., U. Mont., 1957. Instr. in English Carroll Coll., Helena, Mont., 1958-63, asst. prof. English, 1963-73, assoc. prof. English, 1978-83, prof. English, 1983—, head dept. English, 1978—; mem. bd. pardons Deer Lodge, Mont., 1971-75, chmn., 1975-91; chair com. on ind. higher edn. State of Mont., Helena, 1973-74, chair task force on corrections Mt. Coun. on Criminal Justice Standards and Goals, Helena, 1972-73; mem. Mont. Crime Control Commn., Helena, 1975-77; mem. Gov.'s Commn. on Criminal Justice, Helena, 1987—; head boxing coach Carroll Coll., 1958-78. With USNR, 1952-53, Korea. Mem. Ancient Order Hibernians (pres. 1984-86). Democrat. Roman Catholic. Home: 1506 Leslie Ave Helena MT 59601-2019 Office: Carroll Coll Helena MT 59625

BURGESS, J. WESLEY, psychiatrist; b. Mar. 5, 1952; m. Diane Froh. BS, Purdue U., 1974; PhD, N.C. State U., 1979; MD, U. Miami, 1987. Diplomate Am. Bd. Med. Examiners,. Rsch. asst. N.C. Mental Health Dept., 1975-79; with Caribbean Primate Rsch., La Pargaera, P.R.; instr. psychology U. Calif., Davis, 1979-81; assoc. rsch. psychiatrist NPI UCLA, 1981-84; instr. Western Grad. Sch. Psychology, 1989-90; intern Stanford U., 1987-88, resident in psychiatry, 1988-91, staff psychiatrist geropsychiat. clinic, 1989-90, chief resident, 1990-91; teaching faculty Pacific Grad. Sch. Psychology, 1990-92; dir. adolescent div. Ctr. Mood Disorders, L.A., 1991—; prof. Calif. Sch. Profl. Psychology, 1991-92; expert panel Superior Ct. Calif., L.A.; speaker Pharmacology Bd. Ciba Geigy. Contbr. articles to profl. jours. Neuropsychiatric Inst. fellow UCLA, 1981-83, Stanford/NIH fellow, 1990-91; recipient Mead Johnson award Psychiatry, 1991. Mem. AMA (Physician's Recognition award), No. Calif. Psychiat. Soc. (Resident award 1991), Coll. Physicians and Surgeons (lic.), Coll. Qualified Med. Examiners, L.A. County Med. Assn., So. Calif. Pediatric Assn., Am. Psychiat. Assn., Calif. Psychiat. Assn., So. Calif. Psychiat. Soc., Am. Assn. Advancement Psychotherapy, Internat. Soc. Adolescent Psychiatry, Am. Soc. Adolescent Psychiatry, Am. Assn. Geriatric Psychiatry, Calif. Med. Assn. Office: 1990 S Bundy Dr Ste 790 Los Angeles CA 90025-5203

BURGESS, JOSEPH JAMES, JR., artist, educator; b. Albany, N.Y., July 13, 1924; s. Joseph James and Marie (Southwell) B.; m. Anna Kang, Aug. 25, 1959; children: Ian Tai Kyung, Dana Tai Soon. BA, Hamilton Coll., Clinton, N.Y., 1947; MA, Yale U., 1948; postgrad., Pratt Inst., Bklyn., 1950-52; MFA, Cranbrook Acad. Art, Bloomfield Hills, Mich., 1954. Asst. prof. fin arts, dept. head St. Lawrence U., Canton, N.Y., 1954-55; instr. art, chmn. art dept. Flint (Mich.) Community Jr. Coll., 1956-65, dir. DeWaters Art Ctr., 1956-65; asst. prof. design Ariz. State U., Tempe, 1965-66; instr. dept. continuing edn. Coll. of Santa Fe (N.Mex.), 1977-82; lectr. audio visual dept. Santa Fe Pub. Libr., 1981-82; asst. prof. art Highlands U., Las Vegas, N.Mex., 1982-83; instr. art Santa Fe Community Coll., 1987-90; instr. art workshops Valdes Corp., Santa Fe, 1988—; owner design studio and retail outlet Origins, Carmel, Calif., 1966-75, K/B Designs, 1960—; dir. Blair Galleries, Santa Fe, 1976-80. One man shows: Albany Inst. History and Art, 1958; group shows: Ball State Tchrs. Coll., 1958, Palace of Legion of Honor, San Francisco, 1959, DeWaters Art Ctr., 1964, Pasadena Art Mus., 1968, Santa Fe Festival of Arts, 1979, 80; group shows include Detroit Inst. Arts, 1956, Mus. Modern Art, N.Y.C., 1956, Flint Inst. Arts, 1956-65, Albany Inst. of History and Art, 1957; author: Three Chinese Poems, 1962, Four Chinese Poems, 1961, A Random Poem, 1973, others; contbr. articles to profl. jours. With USNR, 1943-46. Mem. Phi Beta Kappa. Home: PO Box 2151 Santa Fe NM 87504-2151 Office: K/B Designs PO Box 2151 Santa Fe NM 87504-2151

BURGESS, LARRY LEE, corporate executive; b. Phoenix, May 13, 1942; s. Byron Howard and Betty Eileen (Schook) B.; m. Sylvia Wynnell, Sept. 30, 1964 (div. Dec. 1984); children: Byron, Damian; m. Mary Jane Ruble, Mar. 10, 1985. BSEE, MSEE, Naval Postgrad. Sch. Officer USN, Washington, 1964-85; corp. exec. Martin Marietta, Denver, 1985—; pres. L & M Investments, Denver, 1987—. Coach Youth Activities, Corpus Christi, Tex., 1976-78; speaker in local schs., Littleton, Colo., 1987-90. Inducted into the Kans. Basketball Hall of Fame, 1993. Mem. AIAA (dir.), SASA, Armed Forces Comm. and Electronic Agy. Republican. Home: 3 Red Fox Ln Littleton CO 80127 Office: Martin Marietta PO Box 179 DC 4001 Denver CO 80201

BURGESS, MARY ALICE (MARY ALICE WICKIZER), publisher; b. San Bernardino, Calif., June 21, 1938; d. Russell Alger and Wilma Evelyn (Swisher) Wickizer; m. Michael Roy Burgess, Oct. 15, 1976; children from previous marriage: Richard Albert Rogers, Mary Louise Rogers Reynnells. AA, Valley Coll., San Bernardino, 1967; BA, Calif. State U., San Bernardino, 1975, postgrad., 1976-79; postgrad., U. Calif., Riverside, 1976-79. Lic. real estate salesman, Calif.; real estate broker, Calif. Sec.-treas. Lynwyck Realty & Investment, San Bernardino, 1963-75; libr. asst. Calif. State U., San Bernardino, 1974-76, purchasing agt., 1976-81; co-pub. The Borgo Press, San Bernardino, 1975—. Co-pub: (with Robert Reginald) Science Fiction and Fantasy Book Review, 1979-80; co-author (with M.R. Burgess) The Wickizer Annals: The Descendents of Conrad Wickizer of Luzerne County, Pennsylvania, 1983, (with Douglas Menville and Robert Reginald) Futurevisions: The New Golden Age of the Science Fiction Film, 1985, (with Jeffrey M. Elliot and Robert Reginald) The Arms Control, Disarmament and Military Science Dictionary, 1989; author: The Campbell Chronicles: A Genealogical History of the Descendants of Samuel Campbell of Chester County, Pennsylvania, 1989, (with Boden Clarke) The Work of Katherine Kurtz, 1992-93, (with Michael Burgess and Daryl F. Mallett) State and Province Vital Records Guide; editor: Cranberry Tea Room Cookbook, Still The Frame Holds, Defying the Holocaust, Risen from the Ashes: A Story of the Jewish Displaced Persons in the Aftermath of World War II, Being a Sequel to Survivors (Jacob Biber), 1989, Ray Bradbury: Dramatist (Ben P. Indick), 1989, Across the Wide Missouri: The Diary of a Journey from Virginia to Missouri in 1819 and Back Again in 1821, with a Description of the City of Cincinnati, (James Brown Campbell), Italian Theatre in San Francisco, Into the Flames: The Life Story of a Righteous Gentile, Jerzy Kosinski: The Literature of Violation, The Little Kitchen Cookbook, Victorian Criticism of American Writers, 1990; co-editor and pub. (with Robert Reginald) of all Borgo Press publs.; also reviewer, indexer, researcher and editor of scholarly manuscripts. Chmn. new citizens Rep. Women, San Bernardino, 1967; libr. San Bernardino Geneal. Soc., 1965-67; vol. Boy Scout Am., Girl Scouts U.S., Camp Fire Girls, 1960s. Recipient Real Estate Proficiency award Calif. Dept. Real Estate, San Bernardino, 1966. Mem. City of San Bernardino Hist. and Pioneer Soc., Calif. State U. Alumni Assn., Cecil County (Md.) Hist. Soc., Gallia County (Ohio) Hist. and Geneal. Soc., DAR (membership and geneal. records chmn. 1964-66, registrar and vice regent San Bernardino chpt. 1965-67). Office: The Borgo Press PO Box 2845 San Bernardino CA 92406-2845

BURGESS, MICHAEL, library science educator, publisher; b. Fukuoka, Kyushu, Japan, Feb. 11, 1948; came to U.S., 1949; s. Roy Walter and Betty Jane (Kapel) B.; m. Mary Alice Wickizer, Oct. 15, 1976; stepchildren: Richard Albert Rogers, Mary Louise Reynnells. AB with honors, Gonzaga U., 1969; MLS, U. So. Calif., 1970. Periodicals librarian Calif. State U., San Bernardino, 1970-81, chief cataloger, 1981—, prof., 1984—; editor Newcastle Pub. Co., North Hollywood, Calif., 1971-92; pub. Borgo Press, San Bernardino, 1975—, St. Willibrord's Press, San Bernardino, 1991—, Brownstone Books, San Bernardino, 1991—, Sidewinder Press, San Bernardino, 1991—, Unicorn & Con, San Bernardino, 1991—, Burgess & Wickizer, San Bernardino, 1991—; Emeritus Enterprises, 1993—; assoc. editor SFRA Review, 1993—. Author 70 books, including A Guide to Science Fiction & Fantasy in the Library of Congress Classification Scheme, 1984, 2d edit. 1988, Mystery & Detective Fiction in the Library of Congress Classification Scheme, 1987, (as M. R. Burgess) The House of the Burgesses, 1983, (under pseudonym R. Reginald) Contemporary Science Fiction Authors, 1975, Science Fiction & Fantasy Literature (2 vols.), 1979 (Outstanding Book of Yr. Choice Mag. 1980), Science Fiction & Fantasy Awards, 1981, 2d edit., 1991, 3d edit., 1993, Stella Nova, 1970, The Work of Robert Reginald, 2d edit., 1992, Reference Guide to Science Fiction, Fantasy and Horror, 1992 (Outstanding Academic Book of Yr. Choice Mag. 1993, Outstanding Reference Book Am. Libraries, Booklist & Reference Books Bulletin), (under pseudonym Lucas Webb) The Attempted Assassination of John F. Kennedy, (under pseudonym C. Everett Cooper) Up Your Asteroid!, 1977, (under pseudonym Boden Clarke) The Work of Jeffrey M. Elliot, 1984, Lords Temporal & Lords Spiritual, 1985; (with others) The Work of R. Reginald, 1985, 2d edit., 1993, Western Fiction in the Library of Congress Classification Scheme, 1988; (under pseudonym R. Reginald, with others) Things To Come, 1977, If J.F.K. Had Lived, 1982, The Paperback Price Guide No. 2, 1982, Tempest in a Teapot, 1983, The Work of Julian May, 1985, Futurevisions, 1985, The Work of George Zebrowski, 1986, 2d edit., 1990, The Arms Control, Disarmament, and Military Security Dictionary, 1989, (with Sheikh Ali and Jeffrey M. Elliot) The Trilemma of World Oil Politics, 1991, (with Hal W. Hall) The Work of Louis L'Amour, 1991, Science Fiction and Fantasy Literature 1975-91, 1992, Reginald's Science Fiction Fantasy Awards, (with Daryl F. Mattett) 2nd edit., 1991, 3d edit., 1993, (with Mary A. Burgess) The Work of Katherine Kurtz, 1993, (with Jerry Hewett and Daryl F. Mallett) The Work of Jack Vance, 1993, (with Margaret Aldiss) The Work of Brian W. Aldiss, 1992; (as M. R. Burgess, with Mary Burgess) The Wickizer Annals, 1983; (under pseudonym Boden Clarke, with James Hopkins) The Work of William F. Nolan, 1988; editor: Ancestral Voices, 1975, Alistair MacLean, 1976, Ancient Hauntings, 1976, Phantasmagoria, 1976, R.I.P., 1976, The Spectre Bridegroom & Other Horrors, 1976, John D. MacDonald, 1977, Dreamers of Dreams, 1978, King Solomon's Children, 1978, They, 1978, Worlds of Never, 1978, Science Fiction & Fantasy Book Review, 1980, The Holy Grail Revealed, 1982, Candle for Poland, 1982, The Work of Bruce McAllister, 1985, rev. edit. 1986, The Work of Charles Beaumont, 1986, 2d edit., 1990, The Work of Colin Wilson, 1989, The Work of Chad Oliver, 1989, The Work of Ross Rocklynne, 1989, The Work of Ian Watson, 1989, The Work of Reginald Bretnor, 1989, The Work of Pamela Sargent, 1990, The Work of Dean Ing, 1990, The Work of Jack Dann, 1990, Hancer's Price Guide to Paperback Books, 3d edit., 1990, To Kill or Not to Kill, 1990, (with Mary Burgess) California Ranchos, 1988; editor: 15 scholarly series, including Milford Series: Popular Writers of Today (60 vols.), Science Fiction (63 vols.), Supernatural and Occult Fiction (64 vols.), Lost Race and Adult Fantasy Fiction (69 vols.), Forgotten Fantas(24 vols.), Stokvis Studies in Historical Chronology and Thought (15 vols.), editor 6 reprint series, 2 jours.; author over 135 articles; outside reader Anatomy of Wonder, 1981, Fantasy Literature, 1990, Horror Literature, 1990. Recipient MPPP award, 1987, Lifetime Collectors award for Contbn. to Bibliography, 1993, Pilgrim award, 1993; named title II fellow U. So. Calif., 1969-70. Mem. ALA, NEA, AAUP, Blue Earth County Hist. Soc., Calif. Tchrs. Assn., Kent Hist. Soc., Sci. Fiction Writers Am., Calif. Faculty Assn. (statewide librs. task force 1986-89, editor newsletter 1987-89), Calif. Libr. Assn., San Bernardino Hist. and Pioneer Soc., Grant County Hist. Soc., Internat. Assn. for Fantastic in Arts, Internat. Geneal. Soc., Internat. PEN, U.S.A. Ctr. West, Ky. Hist. Soc., Nat. Geneal Soc., Sci. Fiction Rsch. Assn., Horror Writers Am., Upper Cumberland Valley Geneal Assn., ACLU, World SF. Office: Borgo Press PO Box 2845 San Bernardino CA 92406-2845 also: Calif State U Libr 5500 University Pky San Bernardino CA 92407

BURGESS, ROBERT JOHN, marketing consultant, writer, educator; b. Metarie, La., Aug. 4, 1961; s. John Jacob and Doris Claire (Keating) B. BSBA summa cum laude, U. Denver, 1983; MBA, Loyola U., Chgo., 1984. Sr. rsch. analyst United Bank Denver, 1984-85; sr. rsch. analyst Adolph Coors Co., Golden, Colo., 1985-88; sr. mgr. market rsch. U.S. West, Englewood, Colo., 1988-90; pres. Mktg. Advs., Inc., Englewood, 1990—. Author: Blitzed, 1992; columnist monthly mktg. jour. Quick Consult, 1992; inventor Keystone Beer, 1988. Mem. Colo. Rep. Party, Denver, 1983—. Mem. Am. Mktg. Assn. (pres. Colo. chpt. 1990-92, Outstanding Mktg. Rschr.-Peak awards 1992, grantee 1992), Market Rsch. Assn., South Metro Denver C. of C. (counselor 1992—), Colo. State U. Mktg. Club (hon.), Beta Gamma Sigma, Mu Kappa Tau (lifetime). Roman Catholic. Office: Mktg Advs Inc 6702 S Ivy Way Ste # B1 Englewood CO 80112

BURGESS, WILLIAM HENRY, entrepreneur; b. Mpls., June 30, 1917; s. Gerald Henry and Louise (Bailey) B.; m. Clara Ethel Woodward, June 21, 1941; children: Sarah Louise Burgess Cadenhead, Mali. BBA, U. Minn., 1939; MBA, Harvard U., 1941. Indsl. engr. R.R. Donnelly & Sons Co., Chgo., 1941-42; mgmt. engr. Hollister & Evans, Los Angeles, 1946; founder, pres. Electronic Splty. Co., Los Angeles, 1949-66, chmn. bd., 1949-69; founder, chmn. bd., pres. Shavex Corp., Los Angeles, 1949-62; chmn. bd. Continental Controls Corp., 1972-78, Internat. Controls Corp., Boca Raton, Fla., 1978-86; founder, chmn. bd. dirs. C.M.S. Digital, 1984—; entrepreneur, 1969—; pres., chmn. bd. William H. Burgess Found.; founder, dir. Titech, Inc., 1966-90; bd. dirs. Early Calif. Industries; mem. L.A. panel arbitrators N.Y. Stock Exch., 1971—; mem. nat. adv. bd. Ctr. Privatization, 1985—; mem. Nat. Forum Found., 1984—, Am. Space Frontier Com., 1985—, Coun. Nat. Policy, 1985—. Mem. council regents Forest Lawn, 1959-65; vice chmn. commerce and industry United Crusade, 1968-70; mem. adv. bd. Pasadena YWCA, 1955-57; bd. dirs. Jr. Achievement So. Calif., 1965-70, adv. council, 1971-75; founding mem. Los Angeles Music Center, 1964; dir. The Founders, 1971-78; v.p., bd. dirs. Calif. Inst. Tech. Assocs., 1964-65, 70-78; bd. overseers, vis. com. Harvard U., 1964-70; bd. dirs. Huntington Meml. Tumor Clinic, 1958-60; life mem., trustee Pasadena Mus. Modern Art, 1956-74; mem. pres.'s council Calif. Inst. Tech., 1968-71; mem. Pasadena Tournament of Roses Assn., 1971-74; bd. govs. Otis Art Inst., 1967-74; bd. dirs. So. Calif. council Inst. Internat. Edn., 1970-72; founding fellow, bd. dirs. L.S.B. Leakey Found., 1969-79; trustee San Gabriel Valley Found. Boy Scouts Am., 1968-69; mem. Nat. Assn. Eagle Scouts, 1974—; world ambassador Internat. Student Center, UCLA, 1970-73; mem. pres.'s adv. council U. Redlands, 1971-74; mem. Econ. Round Table, 1970-75; mem. curriculum adv. com. U. So. Calif. Bus. Sch., 1972-78; mem. orthopedic council Los Angeles Orthopedic Hosp., 1972-75; mem. vol. adv. com. Calif. Atty. Gen., 1971-78; hon. adv. bd. Internat. Profl. Tennis Assn., 1967-71; life mem. Nat. Ednl. Tennis Found.; nat. adv. bd. Am. Security Council, 1971—; bd. dirs. Palm Springs Friends Philharm., 1974-78, Coachella Valley YMCA, 1977-78; trustee Space Age Hall Sci., 1973-76, Palm Springs Desert Mus., 1974-77; mem. Rep. Nat. Com. Served to lt. USNR, 1941-45. Recipient Rep. Minnesotan award U. Minn., 1939, Bus. Achievement award Harvard Bus. Sch. Club So. Calif., 1963; citation for Distinguished Service DAV, 1963; Outstanding Achievement award U. Minn., 1964. Mem. Nat. Inst. Social Scis. (life), Chief Execs. Forum (dir. 1969-73), Young Pres. Orgn. (nat. dir. 1958-67, internat. pres. 1966), Palm Springs World Affairs Council (dir. 1974—, v.p. 1980), Harvard Bus. Sch. Club So. Calif. (pres., dir. 1955-56, dir. 1970-74), Internat. Mktg. Inst. (adv. council 1959-63), L.A. World Affairs Council (v.p. and dir. 1962-80, treas. 1964), Soc. for Improvement of Human Functioning, Metric Soc., Tarrytown One Hundred (founding mem.), Tailhook Assn., U. Minn. Alumni Assn., U.S. Lawn Tennis Assn. (life), Tennis Patrons Assn. So. Calif. (bd. govs. 1966), Pasadena Foothill Tennis Patrons Assn. (hon. bd. mem. 1964-74), Chief Exec. Forum, Valley Hunt Club, Harvard Club, California Club, Lincoln Club, Tennis Club, Desert Riders Club, Desert Rats Club, O'Donnell Golf Club, Phi Delta Theta Alumni Assn., Phi Delta Theta. Presbyterian. Office: 550 Palisades Dr Palm Springs CA 92262-5644

BURGESS, WILLIAM VANDER, education educator; b. Brownfield, Ill., June 5, 1934; s. Felix Siegfried and Verna Gertrude (Stockdale) B.; m. Mary Etta Layman, Aug. 20, 1961; children: Eric, Sara, Brian. BS, U. Ill., 1955; MS, So. Ill. U., 1962; PhD, U. Calif., Berkeley, 1970. Cert. nurseryman, Calif. Tchr. agr. Rosiclare (Ill.) High Sch., 1955-56, St. Francisville (Ill.) High Sch., 1960-63, Mt. Auburn (Ill.) High Sch., 1963-64; supt. schs. Mt. Auburn Unit Dist., 1964-65; prof. edn. U. San Francisco, 1968-92, dir. secondary tchr. internship, 1971-73, dean summer session and spl. programs, 1973-75, chmn. dept. orgn. and leadership, 1984-86, chmn. faculty council Sch. Edn., 1978-80, 84-86, assoc. dean Sch. Edn., 1990-92; ret., 1992; pres. William V. Burgess & Assocs., San Ramon, Calif., 1983—. Editor: Current Issues in Organizational Leadership, 1983; co-editor: Handbook of High Speed Machining Technology, 1985. Arbitrator Better Bus. Bur., San Francisco, 1983—; docent Strybing Arboretum, San Francisco, 1982—. Served with U.S. Army, 1956-59. Grantee NSF, Washington, 1978, Calif. Community Colls., Sacramento, 1979. Mem. Phi Delta Kappa (pres. 1985-86, Svc. award 1986, coord. Area 2J 1990—). Democrat. Home: 9593 Davona Dr San Ramon CA 94583-3743

BURGET, FRANZ ANTHONY, III, import-export executive; b. Terre Haute, Ind., Sept. 23, 1939; s. Frank Anthony and Elizabeth (Arnhold) B.; m. Utako Sugai, Sept. 1, 1958 (dec. 1964); children: F.A. Yukio IV, Alden O. BA, U. Miami, 1961; MA, Kokkusai Kristokyo, Tokyo, 1962, Columbia U., 1964; EdD, Columbia U., 1966. Instr. Tokyo Inst. Fgn. Lang., 1962-63; dir. NDEA inst. Columbia U., N.Y.C., 1965-68; asst. prof. U. Hawaii, Honolulu, 1968-70; assoc. prof. Sophia U., Tokyo, 1970-72; mng. dir. foodstuffs Dodwell, Ltd., Tokyo, 1972-74; pres. El Senor K.K., Tokyo, 1974-80; mng. dir. Asia New England Fish Co., Seattle, 1980-83; mng. dir. foodstuffs U.S. World Trade, Seattle, 1983-86; pres. Security Pack Trading Corp., Seattle, 1986—; bd. dirs. Wash. Dist. Export Coun., Seattle, Wash. State Internat. Trade Fairs, Seattle, 1984-89. Treas. Northwest AIDS Found., Seattle, 1987-88; active V. Mason Med. Found., Seattle, 1989—; lectr. Internat. Trade Ad., Seattle, 1987—; adminstr. USITA. Mem. Evergreen Partnership, Columbia Tower Club. Democrat. Roman Catholic. Office: Security Pack Trading Corp 1101 Boylston Ave Seattle WA 98101-2818

BURGON, M. KENT, securities trader, dealer; b. Murray, Utah, Dec. 7, 1936; s. Marvin H. Burgon and Bernice Kemp; m. Joan Willmore, Dec. 1, 1961; children: Josh G., M. Justin, Jeremy K., Nicole, Gretchen, Matthew J. Student, U. Utah, 1955-59. Branch mgr. Dun & Bradstreet, Tacoma, Wash., 1959-67; stockbroker Blyth & Co., Salt Lake City, 1967-74; v.p. Dain Bosworth, Salt Lake City, 1974-79; 1st v.p. Shearson Lehman Bros., Salt Lake City, 1979—; Dir. Utah State Svcs. Bd., Salt Lake City, 1986—. with USANG, 1953-61. Republican. Mem LDS Ch. Home: 8360 Sublette Cir Sandy UT 84093-1164 Office: Shearson Lehman Bros 60 E South Temple Salt Lake City UT 84111-1004

BURGSTAHLER, SHERYL ELAINE, information systems specialist; b. Seattle, June 19, 1948; d. Jerome Gustin and Elaine Minerva (Christen) Larsson; m. David Curtis Burgstahler, Aug. 28, 1988; 1 child, Travis Jerome. BS in Math. Edn., U. Wash., 1970, MS in Math., 1975, PhD, 1992. Adminstr. Dept. Def. PREP Sch., Osan Air Base, South Korea, 1975-76; chmn. dept. math. and computer sci. St. Martin's Coll., Lacey, Wash., 1980-84, project dir. computers and individuals with disabilities, 1982-84, assoc. dir. microcomputer resource ctr., 1981-84, dir. computer insvc., 1982-84; mgr. micro support group U. Wash., Seattle, 1984-88, mgr. desktop computing svc., 1988-91, asst. dir. info. systems computing and comm., 1991—; tchr. U. Wash., 1974-75, U. Md./L.A. City Coll., South Korea, 1976, Ft. Steilacoom C.C., Tacoma, 1977-79, U. Puget Sound, Tacoma, 1978-79, Seattle Pacific U., 1981, St. Martin's Coll., 1978-84, U. Wash., 1984—; presenter in field. Contbr. articles to profl. publs. Vol. U. Wash., Vets. Hosp., Children's Hosp. and Med. Ctr., Seattle, Shriners' Hosp., Honolulu, Osan orphanage. Mem. Math. Assn. Am., Nat. Coun. Tchrs. Math., Western Wash. Math. Cons., Wash. State Math. Coun. (regional dir. 1981-83, co-chair secondary workshops 1983), Assn. Computer Edn. Specialists, Nat. Consortium for Computers in Edn., Computer CurbCuts, Assn. Higher Edn. and Disablility, Consortium Sch. Networking, Assn. Computing Machinery (spl. interest group in univ. and coll. computing svcs., chair internat. computer conf. 1991, dir. disabilities, opportunities, internetworking and tech. 1992—). Home: 3608 43d NE Seattle WA 98105 Office: Computing & Communication JE 25 Seattle WA 98195

BURHANS, FRANK MALCOLM, mechanical engineer; b. Hagerstown, Md., Dec. 11, 1920; s. William Humphrey Sr. and Ethel Adella (Forthman) B.; m. Jean Maria Dermott, Oct. 10, 1943; children—Stephen William, Douglas Allan, Jeffrey Malcolm. B.E. in Mech. Engring., Johns Hopkins U., 1942; postgrad. U. Conn., 1942-43. Registered profl. engr., Wash. Design engr. Pratt & Whitney, East Hartford, Conn., 1942-55, Ford Motor Co., Dearborn, Mich., 1955-58; sr. design engr. Fairchild Engine Div., Deer Park, N.Y., 1958-59; sr. specialist engr. Turbine Div. Boeing Co., Seattle, 1959-66, prin. engr. Boeing Aircraft Engine Installations, 1967-86. Active Boy Scouts Am. Served with AC, U.S. Army, 1945-47. Recipient Silver Beaver award Boy Scouts Am. Mem. AIAA, ASME. Presbyterian (elder). Club: Masons (past master) (Bellevue). Pioneering designer gas turbines and gas turbine installations.

BURHENNE, HANS JOACHIM, physician, radiology educator; b. Hannover, Germany, Dec. 27, 1925; emigrated to U.S., 1955, naturalized, 1959; s. Adolph and Clara (Ditges) B.; m. Linda Jean Warren, Oct. 20, 1978; children by previous marriage: Mark, Antonia, Yvonne. Matura, Gymnasium, Salzburg, Austria, 1944; M.D. magna cum laude, Maximilian Med. Sch., Munich, 1951. Intern Monmouth Med. Center, Long Branch, N.J.; resident in radiology Peter Bent Brigham Hosp., Boston, 1955-59; instr. Harvard U., 1958-59; chmn. dept. radiology Children's Hosp., San Francisco, 1960-78; clin. prof. radiology U. Calif., San Francisco, 1960-78; prof. radiology U. B.C., 1978—, head dept. radiology, 1978-91. Author: (with A.R. Margulis) Alimentary Tract Roentgenology, 4th edit., 1989, Practical Alimentary Tract Radiology, 1993, Sierra Spring Ski Touring, 1971, Biliary Lithotripsy, 1990; editor: Mammography, 1969; editorial bd.: Radiologica Clinica, 1964-90, Oncology, 1973-77, Gastrointestinal Radiology, 1976—, Western Jour. Medicine, 1975-79, Radiology, 1983-91, Lithotripsy and Stone Disease, 1988—. Chmn. bd. dirs. Cathedral Sch., San Francisco, 1976-77; bd. dirs. Sterling-Winthrop Imaging Rsch. Inst., 1989-92. NIH fellow, 1959; recipient Walter B. Cannon medal, 1982, Forsell Lecture and medal Swedish Acad. Medicine, Stockholm, 1990. Fellow Am. Coll. Radiology (counselor 1973-77), Royal Coll. Physicians Can., Royal Coll. Surgeons Ireland (hon. faculty radiology); mem. Calif. Radiol. Soc. (pres. 1977-78), Internat. Soc. Radiology (exec. com. 1985—, chmn. diagnostic radiology 1990), Soc. Gastrointestinal Radiologists (pres. 1977), Internat. Soc. Biliary Radiology (pres. 1989-91). Home: 1063 W 7th Ave #1, Vancouver, BC Canada V6H 1B2 Office: 10th Ave and Heather St, Vancouver, BC Canada V5Z 1M9

BURICK, JOHN EARLE, account executive; b. Santa Cruz, Calif., July 13, 1962; s. Robert James Burick and Susan Merle (Wilkinson) Miller; m. Brandin Leigh Meek; 1 child, Bogart Christopher. BA in Comm., Calif. State U., Fullerton, 1986. Press aide to Senator John Garamendi, Calif. Senate, Sacramento, 1982-83; field rep. Gregorio for State Senate Campaign, Palo Alto, Calif., 1984; legis. dir. CSUF Assoc. Students, Inc., Fullerton, Calif., 1985-86; polit. reporter Toronto Sun Corp., Washington, 1988-91; dir. comm. LIMIT Initiative 553/557 Campaigns, Tacoma, Wash., 1991-92; account exec. N.W. Strategies, Seattle, 1993—. 1st lt. Wash. Army N.G., 1987—. Mem. Pub. Rels. Soc. Am. Republican. Roman Catholic. Home:

240-118th Ave SE Apt 21 Bellevue WA 98005 Office: NW Strategies 111 Queen Anne N Ste 500 Seattle WA 98109

BURK, GARY MAURICE, health care facility planner; b. Dallas, Nov. 8, 1943; s. Houston Maurice and Evelyn (Howell) B. BArch, Tex. Tech U., 1968; MArch, U. Ill., 1970. Registered architect; NCARB cert. Asst. prof. Tex. Tech U., Lubbock, 1970-79; project designer Hellmuth, Obata & Kassabaum, Dallas, 1979-80; assoc. Richard Ferrara, Architect, Dallas, 1980-83; cons. designer Myrick, Newman, Dahlberg, Dallas, 1982-83; assoc. prof. Calif. State U., Pomona, Calif., 1983-85; sr. facility planner Am. Med. Internat., L.A., 1985-86; dir. facilities planning URS Cons., Cleve., 1986-88, URS Consultants, N.Y. and N.J., 1988-91; sr. med. planner Ellerbe Becket, Inc., L.A., 1991—; cons. City Hosp./St. Thomas Med. Ctr., Merger Task Force, Akron, 1988-89, L.A. County Pub. Health Programs and Svcs., 1992—, Palo Alto (Calif.) Med. Found., 1992—; dir. Hosp. of the Future research studio, 1985. Mem. Dallas Civic Chorus, 1980-83, St. Alban's Parish Choir, Cleveland Heights, Ohio, 1987-88, All Saints Parish Choir, Hoboken, N.J., 1988-90, Cleve. Opera Assocs., 1987-88; mem. steering com. Judith Resnik Women's Health Ctr., Summa Health System, Akron, 1989-91, Friends of N.Y. Philharm, 1990-91. Research grantee Tex. Tech U., 1976. Mem. AIA (ednl. fellow 1968, Calif. coun.), Am. Soc. for Testing Materials, Com. on Architecture for Health. Democrat. Episcopalian. Home: 2160 Century Park E Apt 410 Los Angeles CA 90067 Office: Ellerbe Becket Inc 2501 Colorado Ave Ste 300 Santa Monica CA 90404

BURKART, JORDAN V., financial consultant; b. Marshall, Tex., Dec. 7, 1935; s. William Jordan and Lois (Vincent) B.; m. Marcia Marcotte, Aug. 24, 1969; children: Ashley, Frazer. BS, So. Meth. U., 1958; MBA, Harvard U., 1963. Assoc. Glore Forgan, William R. Staats, Inc., L.A., 1964-67; 1st v.p. Blyth Eastman Dillon & Co., L.A., 1967-74; v.p. Crocker Nat. Bank, L.A., 1974-79, sr. v.p., 1979-85; sr. v.p., treas. Crocker Nat. Corp., L.A., 1982-85; corp. fin. cons. L.A., 1986—. Served to lt. (j.g.) USNR, 1958-61. Club: Jonathan (Los Angeles).

BURKE, ARTHUR THOMAS, engineering consultant; b. Pueblo, Colo., Nov. 26, 1919; s. Daniel Michael and Naomi Edith (Brashear) B.; BS, U.S. Naval Acad., 1941; postgrad. UCLA; m. Regina Ahlgren Malone, June 15, 1972; children: Arthur Thomas, Craig Timothy, Laura Ahlgren, Scott Ahlgren. With USN Electronics Lab. Center, San Diego, 1947-72, sr. satellite communications cons., 1964-72, satellite communications engring. cons., 1974—. Judge, San Diego Sci. Fair, 1960—. With USN, 1938-46; comdr. Res., ret. Recipient Superior Performance award USN Electronics Lab. Center, 1967. Mem. IEEE (mem. San Diego membership com. 1958-68), AAAS, San Diego Astronomy Assn., San Diego Computer Assn., Am. Radio Relay League. Patentee electronic bathythermograph. Home and Office: 4011 College Ave San Diego CA 92115-6704

BURKE, DENNIS ANDREW, lawyer; b. Phila., Sept. 27, 1956; s. Charles Judson and Margret Rita (Fillapone) B.; m. Aree Lian Gerberg, Aug. 28, 1982; children: Andrew Lawrence, Nicholas Charles. BS in Fin., Siena Coll., Loudonville, N.Y., 1978; JD, Calif. Western Sch. Law, 1982. Bar: Calif., 1982. Assoc. Rose, Klein & Marias, San Diego, 1983-85; mng. atty. workers compensation dept. Ludecke & Denton, San Diego, 1985-92; mng. atty. Jones, Nelson, Ford & Screeton, San Diego, 1992—; speaker on workers' compensation Calif. Trial Lawyers Assn., Continuing Edn. Bar. Mem. San Diego County Bar Assn., San Diego Trial Lawyers Assn., Calif. Applicants Attys. Assn. (pres. San Diego 1988-92, state bd. govs. 1988-92, speaker). Office: Jones Nelson Ford Screeton 2555 5th Ave Ste 617 San Diego CA 92103

BURKE, EDMOND WAYNE, judge; b. Ukiah, Calif., Sept. 7, 1935; s. Wayne P. and Opal K. B.; children from previous marriage: Kathleen R., Jennifer E.; m. Anna M. Hubbard, Dec. 29, 1990. A.B., Humboldt State Coll., 1957, M.A., 1958; J.D., U. Calif., 1964. Bar: Calif., Alaska. Individual practice law Calif. and Alaska, 1965-67; asst. atty. gen. State of Alaska, 1967; asst. dist. atty. Anchorage, Alaska, 1968-69; judge Superior Ct., Alaska, 1970-75; justice Supreme Ct. State of Alaska, Anchorage, 1975—, chief justice, 1981-84. Republican. Presbyterian.

BURKE, JOHN CHARLES, social worker; b. N.Y.C., May 11, 1946; s. Charles John and Mary Rosalma (DeMott) B.; m. Kathleen Killough, Aug. 4, 1972; children: Eric John, Colleen Lee. BA in Sociology, Siena Coll., 1970; MS in Counseling, Laverne U., 1989; MBA, Chapman U., 1990. Owner, mgr. Burke's Apts., Saugerties, N.Y., 1973-76; owner, operator, tchr. Burke's Studio and Sch. Photography, Saugerties, 1973-76; outdoor recreation expert PM Mag., Channel 8 WFAA TV, Dallas, 1978; child placement worker Tex. Dept. Human Resources, Dallas, 1976-79; social worker State of Alaska Div. Family and Youth Svcs., Anchorage, 1979—; pres., CEO Internat. Bus. Devel. Corp., Anchorage, 1992; instr. Am. Inst. Banking, Am. Bankers Assn.; speaker in field. Contbr. articles to profl. publs. With U.S. Army, 1970-71. Roman Catholic. Home: 7500 Chalet Ct Anchorage AK 99516-1155

BURKE, MICHAEL FRANCIS, chemistry educator; b. Gallup, N.Mex., Jan. 29, 1939; s. Frank J. and Mary (Noonen) B.; m. Virginia Ann Giles, Jan. 30, 1960; children: Patricia, Colleen, Michael K., Timothy. BS in Chemistry, Regis Coll., 1960; postgrad., Kansas State U., 1961-63; PhD in Chemistry, Va. Poly. Inst. and State U., 1965. Sci. tchr. De La Salle High Sch., New Orleans, 1960-61; rsch. assoc. Purdue U., Lafayette, Ind., 1965-67; asst. prof. U. Ariz., Tucson, 1967-73, assoc. prof., 1973—; program dir. NSF, Washington, 1978-79; bd. dirs. Bioaffinity Systems, Inc., Torrance, Calif., Sorbent Tech., Ltd., Cardiff, U.K.; cons. in field; presenter over 100 seminars in 15 countries. Contbr. over 40 articles to sci. publs. Recipient Sustained Superior Performance award NSF, 1979. Mem. Am. Chem. Soc. Democrat. Roman Catholic. Home: 7602 E Waverly St Tucson AZ 85715-4230 Office: U Ariz Dept Chemistry Tucson AZ 85721

BURKE, YVONNE WATSON BRATHWAITE (MRS. WILLIAM A. BURKE), lawyer; b. L.A., Oct. 5, 1932; d. James A. and Lola (Moore) Watson; m. William A. Burke, June 14, 1972; 1 dau., Autumn Roxanne. A.A., U. Calif., 1951; B.A., UCLA, 1953; J.D., U. So. Calif., 1956. Bar: Calif. 1956. Mem. Calif. Assembly, 1966-72, chmn. urban devel. and housing com., 1971, 72; mem. 93d Congress from 37th Dist. Calif., 94th-95th Congresses from 28th Dist. Calif., House Appropriations Com.; chmn. Congl. Black Caucus, 1976; ptnr. Jones, Day, Reavis & Pogue, L.A.; dep. corp. commr., hearing officer Police Commn., 1964-66; atty., staff McCone Commn. (investigation Watts riot), 1965; bd. dirs. Ednl. Testing Svc.; past chair L.A. fr. Red. Res. Bank; U.S. adv. bd. Nestle. Vice chmn. 1984 U.S. Olympics Organizing Com.; bd. dirs. or bd. advisers numerous orgns.; regent U. Calif., Bd. Ednl. Testing Service; Amateur Athletic Found.; bd. dirs. Ford Found., Brookings Inst.; bd. supr's. 2d Dist., L.A. County Bd. of Supr's., 1992. Recipient Profl. Achievement award UCLA, 1974, 84; named one of 200 Future Leaders Time mag., 1974; recipient Achievement awards C.M.E. Chs.; numerous other awards, citations.; fellow Inst. Politics John F. Kennedy Sch. Govt. Harvard, 1971-72; Chubb fellow Yale, 1972. Office: Hall of Adminstrn Supr 2d Dist, Kenneth Hahn 500 West Temple St Los Angeles CA 90012

BURKEE, IRVIN, artist; b. Kenosha, Wis., Feb. 6, 1918; s. Omar Lars and Emily (Quardokas) B.; diploma Sch. of Art Inst. Chgo., 1945; m. Bonnie May Ness, Apr. 12, 1945; children: Brynn, Jill, Peter (dec.), Ian. Owner, silversmith, goldsmith Burkee Jewelry, Blackhawk, Colo., 1950-57; painter, sculptor, Aspen, Colo., 1957-78, Pearce, Ariz., Pietrasanta, Italy, 1978—; instr. art U. Colo., 1946, 50-53, Stephens Coll., Columbia, Mo., 1947-49. John Quincy Adams travel fellow, Mex., 1945. Executed copper mural of human history of Colo. for First Nat. Bank, Englewood, Colo., 1970, copper mural of wild birds of Kans. for Ranchmart State Bank, Overland Park, Kans., 1974; exhibited Art Inst. Chgo., Smithsonian Instn. (award 1957), Milw. Art Inst., Krannert Mus., William Rockhill Nelson Gallery, St. Louis Art Mus., Denver Art Mus.; represented in permanent collections several southwestern galleries, also pvt. collections throughout U.S.; work illustrated in books Design and Creation of Jewelry, Design through Discovery, Walls. Mem. Nat. Sculpture Soc., Sedona Chamber Music Soc. Address: HC1 Box 398 Pearce AZ 85625

BURKETT, EUGENE HERBERT, insurance sales manager; b. Johnson AFB, Japan, Aug. 15, 1948; came to U.S., 1949.; s. Eugene Roy and Jane W. (Lavene) B.; m. Anna Lee, June 14, 1973; children: David, Justin, Erik, Catherine. BA in Speech, U. So. Fla., 1970, MA in Speech, 1972. Theater dir. Berkeley (Calif.) St. Theater, 1973-77; instr. Berkeley Adult Sch., 1977; agent, instr. John Hancock Mutual Life, Oakland, Calif., 1977-82, Acacia Mutual Life, Oakland, Calif., 1982-86; gen. agent Transamerica Occidental Life, Felton, Calif., 1986-91; sales mgr. ASG Life & Health Ins. Svcs. Inc., Santa Cruz, Calif., 1991—; instr. Life Underwriters Tng. Coun., Santa Cruz, 1992—. Bd. dirs. San Lorenzo Valley on site coun. Unified Sch. Dist., Felton, Calif., 1988, Santa Cruz County (Calif.) Child Abuse Prevention Coun., 1987-88; asst. choir dir., choir mem. St. Peter and St. Paul's Orthodox Ch., Benlomond, Calif. Recipient Million Dollar Round Table award, 1983, 84. Mem. Nat. Assn. Life Underwriters (Health Ins. Quality award 1989, Nat. Sales Achievement award 1983-89, Nat. Quality award 1983-89), Exchange Club of Felton-Ben Lomand (pres. 1987-88, Disting. Pres. award 1988), Santa Cruz County Life Underwriters Assn. (nat. committeeman 1989—, pres. 1988-89, past pres. award 1989, bd. dirs. 1987—). Office: ASG Life & Health Ins Svcs Inc 1044 41st Ave Santa Cruz CA 95062

BURKETT, JOHN DAVID, professional baseball player; b. New Brighton, Mass., Nov. 28, 1964. With San Francisco Giants, 1987, 90—; mem. Nat. League All-Star Team, 1993. Office: San Francisco Giants Candlestick Park San Francisco CA 94124

BURKETT, WILLIAM RAY, JR., state official; b. Augusta, Ga., Aug. 31, 1943; s. William Ray and Frances (DeLong) B.; m. Wanda Yvonne Kleppe, Apr. 1, 1968; children: William Ray III, Heather Gabrielle. Grad. high sch., Jacksonville Beach, Fla. Reporter Jacksonville (Fla.) Jour., 1961-64; contbg. editor Bahams Handbook & Bus. Ann., Nassau, 1969-70; reporter Harrisburg (Pa.) Evening News, 1970-72; pub. affairs rep. Am. Fedn. of State, County and Mcpl. Employees, Washington, 1972-73; copy editor Seattle Times, 1973; editorial staffer Outdoor Empire Pub. Co., Seattle, 1973-76; pub info. officer II Ariz. Game & Fish Dept., Phoenix, 1976-78; pub. info. officer III, bd. sec. Wash. Liquor Control Bd., Olympia, 1978-84; pub. info. officer IV Wash. State Patrol, Olympia, 1984—. Author: Sleeping Planet, 1964; author/exec. producer TV and radio spots, 1985—; feature writer Sunday mag. Flatimes-Union Jour., 1964-67; Sunday editor Augusta Chronicle, 1967-68; editor: The Cecil Field Afterburner, 1968-69; contbr. articles to profl. jours. Pres. Faith Home, Episcopal Svcs. for Youth, Tacoma, 1989-91; vice chmn. police media rels. subcom. Goodwill Games, 1989; chair AAMVA Reg. IV Media Rels. com., Olympia, 1992—, mem. standing com. for consumer edn. and pub. affairs, Washington, 1987—; bd. dirs. Wash. Safety Restraint Coalition. With U.S. Army, 1965-67. Recipient Telly award, 1990, Mobius Broadcast awards, 1989, Clio award, 1992, others. Mem. Pub. Rels. Soc. Am., Ducks Unltd. Office: Washington State Patrol Gen Adminstrn Bldg AX12 Olympia WA 98504

BURKHART, BRUCE WELLS, college educator; b. Raleigh, N.C., July 21, 1939; m. Catherine Ray; children: Lee, Katy, Dottie. BS, U. Ariz., 1962, MEd, 1964, MS in Botany, 1964, M in Biology, 1966. Prof. biology Rio Hondo Coll., Whittier, Calif., 1962—. Home: 2530 S Cardillo Ave Hacienda Heights CA 91745-4441

BURKHART, CATHERINE RAY, secondary school educator; b. Tucson, Mar. 2, 1939; m. Bruce Burkhart; children: Lee, Katy, Dottie. BA, U. Ariz., 1961, MEd, 1966. Tchr. Whittier (Calif.) High Sch. Dist., 1966—; Editor SCTE newsletter; mentor teacher. Home: 2530 S Cardillo Ave Hacienda Heights CA 91745-4441

BURKHART, LONA JANE TANKERSLEY, rancher; b. L.A., Oct. 15, 1930; d. Drew E. and Jane Irwin (Nicholas) Tankersley; widowed 1990; 1 child, Raymond Houston. Grad. high sch., Barstow, Calif., 1948. Rancher Ariz., 1949-50, Calif., 1950-72, Nev., 1972-80, Oreg., 1980—; owner, operator Sequoia-Kings Pack Trains, Independence, Calif., 1956-70, Rodeo String-High Sierra Rodeo Stock, Independence, Calif., 1965-70; lectr. Nat. Cowboy Symposium and Celebration, Lubbock, Tex., 1989-92. Author poetry. Activist in promoting ranchers role in conservation of the land and wildlife, 1985-92; chmn. BLM Grazing Bd., Independence, 1964-65. Named nominee Cowgirl Hall of Fame, Herford, Tex., 1991. Republican. Home: Box 825 Madras OR 97741

BURKHAUSER, TERESA ELAINE, company planning executive; b. Enid, Okla., Oct. 18, 1955; d. Cleo Veryl and Gladys Elaine (West) Winter; m. Ralph Ottokar Burkhauser, Sept. 30, 1978; 1 child, Cody Steven. Diploma, Altus High Sch., 1973. Tour and travel mgr. Caesars Tahoe Hotel and Casino, Stateline, Nev., 1980-82, sales mgr., 1982-85, nat. sales mgr., 1985-89, convention svcs. mgr., 1989-90; owner, meeting and conv. planner Mountain View Planners, Garnerville, Nev., 1990—. Mem. Sac. Soc. Assn. Execs., No. Calif. Soc. Assn. Execs., Am. Soc. Assn. Execs., So. Calif. Soc. Assn. Execs., Tahoe Douglas C. of C. Office: Mountain View Planners PO Box 2273 Gardnerville NV 89410-2273

BURKHOLDER, JOYCE LYNN, clinical social worker; b. Phila., Oct. 28, 1951; d. J. Edward and Mae Elizabeth (Wood) B.; m. Dirk Denier Vandergon, May 31, 1983; children: Austin Edward, Alexandra Mae. BSW, Temple U., 1975; MSW, Calif. State U., Sacramento, 1985. Lic. clin. social worker, Nev. Caseworker Silver Springs Martin Luther Sch., Plymouth Meeting, Pa., 1974-76; counselor Turning Point Youth Svc., Ambler, Pa., 1976-77; dir., counselor Aquarian Effort Alternative House, Sacramento, Calif., 1978-81; dir. social svcs., case mgr. Truckee Meadows Hosp., Reno, 1983-84; clin. social worker U. Calif. Davis Med. Ctr., Sacramento, 1985-86; cons. Greater Nev. Home Health Care, Revo, 1988-90; sec., bd. dirs. Pathways, Reno, 1990—; pvt. practice, 1993—; instr. U. Nev., Reno, 1991. Bd. dirs. Aux. to Washoe County Med. Soc., Reno, 1989-90; vol. Planned Parenthood of No. Nev., Reno, 1990. Mem. Nat. Assn. Social Workers. Home: 4288 Bitterroot Rd Reno NV 89509-0617

BURLAND, BRIAN BERKELEY, novelist, poet, painter; b. Paget, Bermuda, Apr. 23, 1931; s. Gordon Hamilton and Honor Alice Croydon (Gosling) B.; m. Charlotte Ann Taylor, 1952 (div. 1958); children: Susan, Anne, William; m. Edwina Ann Trentham, 1962 (div. 1979); 1 child, Benjamin; m. Isabella Scott Lee Petrie, 1990. Grad., Aldenham Sch., Elstree, Eng., 1948; student, U. Western Ont., Can., 1948-51. Mng. dir. Burland Estates, Ltd., Gosling Estates, Ltd.; 1st v.p. G.H. Burland & Co., Ltd., 1951-56; assoc. editor Bermudian Mag., 1957; lectr. Am. Sch., London, 1974, Washington and Lee U., Va., 1973; writer in residence So. Sem., Va., 1973, Bermuda Writers Conf., 1978, U. Hartford, Conn., 1981-82; guest fellow Yale U., 1982-83; vis. prof. Conn. Coll., 1986-87; judge P.E.N. Syndicated Fiction Project, 1985; narrator stories and poems BBC, 1968—. Author: A Fall from Aloft, 1968, A Few Flowers for St. George, 1969, Undertow, 1970, The Sailor and The Fox, 1973, Surprise, 1975, Stephan Decator, 1976, The Flight of the Cavalier, 1980, Love is a Durable Fire, 1985(childrens book) St. Nicholas and the Tub, 1964; (poetry) To Celebrate a Happiness that is America, 1971. Fellow Royal Soc. Lit.; mem. Poetry Soc. Am., Author's Am., PEN, Am. Ctr. Soc., Royal, Yacht (Bermuda), Chelsea Arts (London). Office: c/o Mary Cunnane W W Norton & Co 550 Fifth Ave New York NY 10110

BURLEIGH, RITA JEAN, educator; b. Santa Monica, Calif., Mar. 19, 1943; d. Charles Patrick and Jeanne (DeWitt) Loftus; m. Thomas William Scott, June 12, 1965 (div. 1975); children: Graham Robert, Shelly Amber; m. Edward William Burleigh, Oct. 23, 1980; children: Edward William, Rebecca Dawn. BA, U. Redlands, 1965, MA, 1967; MLS, Immaculate Heart Coll., L.A. 1969; PhD Claremont (Calif.) U., 1990. Librarian, Pomona Pub. Library, Calif., 1967-69, U. La Verne, Calif., 1970-72, Rio Hondo Coll., Whittier, Calif., 1973-79; learning resources dir. Citrus Coll., Glendora, Calif., 1979-86, assoc. dean instrn., 1986-90, dean adminstrv. svcs., 1990-92; v.p. instruction, 1992—; pres. San Gabriel Community Colls. Library Coop., 1982-86. Corr. sec. Pomona Valley Art Assn., 1979; mem. exec. coun. Coun. Calif. Community Coll. Staff Developers; draft bd. mem. U.S. Selective Service, 1981-92; sr. warden St. Paul's Episcopal Ch., Pomona, 1984. Fellow Claremont Grad. Sch., 1984-87. Mem. Assn. Calif. Community Coll. Adminstrs., Calif. C.C. Librarians (sec.-treas. 1985), Mortarboard. Rotary. Republican. Office: Citrus Community Coll Dist 1000 W Foothill Blvd Glendora CA 91740-1885

BURLESKI, JOSEPH ANTHONY, JR., information services professional; b. Poughkeepsie, N.Y., June 30, 1960; s. Joseph Anthony Burleski Sr. and Fredeline Cyr; m. Judith Ann Lezon, June 10, 1989. BSBA, Marist Coll., 1982; MBA Mktg., U. Phoenix, 1992; grad. in human rels. and effective speaking, Dale Carnegie, 1990. Computer operator IBM Corp., Poughkeepsie, 1982-83, lead/sr. computer operator, 1983-84, systems programmer, 1984-85, assoc. systems programmer, 1985-86, mgr. offshift computer ops., 1986-87; mgr. info. processing IBM Corp., Boulder, Colo., 1987-88, mgr. MVS systems programming, 1988-91; mgr. location and field svcs. devel. Integrated Systems Solutions Corp. (subs. IBM), Boulder, 1991-93, mgr. location and field svc. devel. ind. test, 1992-93; mgr. VM/VSE svcs. Integrated Systems Solutions Corp. (subs. IBM Corp.), Boulder, 1993—; mem. IBM Data Processing Ops. Coun., Poughkeepsie, 1983—; grad. asst. Dale Carnegie Inst., Boulder, 1990—. Coach Spl. Olympics, 1987—; mem. Order of the Arrow Hon. Soc., sec., editor, 1976-77, pres. 1977-78, treas. 1980-81; patrol leader, store dir., asst. camp dir. Boy Scouts Am., Cub Scouts Summer Camp, 1985-87. Mem. Marist Coll. Alumni Assn. (contbr.), Vigil Nat. Honor Soc., IBM Runners' Club. Roman Catholic. Home: 1826 Lashley St Longmont CO 80501-2061 Office: ISCC Corp 7R6A/024W 5600 N 63rd St Boulder CO 80314

BURLESON, GEORGE ROBERT, physics educator; b. Baton Rouge, Oct. 12, 1933; s. George Larkin and Maurine (Vaughn) B.; m. Carol Elaine Yowell, June 8, 1960; children: Geoffrey Larkin, Christopher Arnold. BS, La. State U., 1955; MS, Stanford U., 1957, PhD, 1960. Rsch. asst. High Energy Physics Lab., Stanford (Calif.) U., 1956-60; rsch. assoc. Argonne (Ill.) Nat. Lab., 1960-64; asst. prof. Northwestern U., Evanston, 1964-72; assoc. prof. physics N.Mex. State U., Las Cruces, 1972-77, prof., 1977—; guest scientist Los Alamos (N.Mex.) Nat. Lab., 1972-74. Contbr. over 90 articles to profl. jours. Rsch. grantee U.S. Dept. Energy, 1976—. Mem. Am. Phys. Soc., N.Mex. Acad. Sci., LAMPF Users Group (bd. dirs. 1984-86), Sigma Xi, Phi Kappa Phi. Office: NMex State U Physics Dept Box 3D Las Cruces NM 88003

BURLINGAME, ALMA LYMAN, chemist, educator; b. Cranston, R.I., Apr. 29, 1937; s. Herman Follett and Rose Irene (Kohler) B.; children: Mark, Walter. BS, U. R.I., 1959; PhD, MIT, 1962. Asst. prof. U. Calif., Berkeley, 1963-68, assoc. chemist, 1968-72, rsch. chemist, 1972-78; prof. U. Calif., San Francisco, 1978—. Editor: Topics in Organic Mass Spectrometry, 1970, Mass Spectrometry in Health and Life Science, 1985, Biological Mass Spectrometry, 1990; contbr. articles to profl. jours. With USAR, 1954-62. Guggenheim Found. fellow, 1970. Fellow AAAS. Office: U Calif Dept of Pharmaceutical Chemistry San Francisco CA 94143-0446

BURLINGAME, JONATHAN DONALD, journalist, musicologist; b. Gloversville, N.Y., Apr. 2, 1953; s. Roy G. and Rita M. (Wood) B. Student, Fla. Inst. Tech., 1971-73. Reporter, critic Leader-Herald, Johnstown, N.Y., 1973-82; reporter Schenectady Gazette, 1983-84; writer, editor TV Data, Glen Falls, N.Y., 1984-86, mgr. nat. programming, 1986; West Coast writer TV Data, Burbank, Calif., 1986-89; TV columnist United Feature Syndicate, Burbank, 1988—, sr. editor, 1991—. Contbg. author music Emmy mag., 1986—; author liner notes albums by Michel Legrand, Henry Mancini, David Shire, others, 1990—; contbr. numerous articles to newspapers and mags. Office: United Media 200 Park Ave New York NY 10166

BURLINGAME, JUDY LOUISE, educator, coach; b. Denver, Dec. 3, 1960; d. David Graham Burlingame and Susan Louise (Johnson) Pucci. Student, Colo. Coll., 1980-81; BS, U. Colo., 1984. Cert. tchr., Colo. Tchr. biology Douglas County Schs., Castle Rock, Colo., 1985-88; tchr. health, phys. edn. Denver Pub. Schs., 1989-91, substitute tchr., 1991—; varsity lacrosse and field hockey coach Colo. Schoolgirls' Lacrosse Assn., 1986-93, v.p., 1989-91. Vol. Peregrine Found., Denver, 1990, Colo. Hist. Soc., Denver, 1990-92, Craig Hosp. Coach State champion team Colo. Schoolgirls' Lacrosse Assn., 1990, 93. Mem. NEA, U.S. Women's Lacrosse Assn., Colo. Hist. Soc., Nat. Wildlife Assn. Home: PO Box 1502 Evergreen CO 80439

BURNASH, ROBERT JOHN CHARLES, hydrologist; b. Bklyn., Aug. 17, 1931; s. James Francis and Marion Josephine (Olifiers) B.; BS, Bucknell U., 1953; postgrad. Naval Postgrad. Sch., 1954; m. Jeanne Carolyn Mack, July 11, 1953; children: Charles, Kathleen, Mary, Elizabeth, David, Daniel. Hydrologist, Nat. Weather Svc. River Forecast Ctr., Cin., 1957-62, prin. asst., Sacramento River Forecast Ctr., 1963-71, hydrologist in charge Calif.-Nev. River Forecast Ctr., 1972-87, retired 1987—; guest lectr. hydrologic systems Australian Water Resources Council, Melbourne, Perth, Brisbane, Sydney, 1984; World Meteorological Orgn. lectr. U. Calif., Davis, 1983-86, 89, 91; prin. organizer Internat. Tech. Conf. on Mitigation of Natural Hazards through Real-Time Data Collection and Hydrological Forecasting, World Meteorol. Orgn., Sacramento, 1983; cons. Hydrologic Svcs., 1987—. With USNR, 1953-56. Recipient Bronze medal Dept. Commerce, 1970, Silver medal, 1975, Gold medal, 1980; Outstanding Pub. Svc. award NOAA, 1978. Fellow Am. Meteorol. Soc. (Outstanding Forecaster award 1979, Robert E. Horton meml. lectr. 1983); mem. Am. Geophys. Union, AAAS, N.Y. Acad. Scis., Calif.-Nev. Alert Users Group (hon. life), Western Snow Conf., Assn. State Flood Plain Mgrs., Delta Mu Delta, Phi Lambda Theta. Author: (with others) The Sacramento Model. Contbr. articles to profl. jours. Originator real time event reporting telemetering systems and ALERT flood warning system. Home: 3539 Ridgeview Dr El Dorado Hills CA 95762

BURNETT, ERIC STEPHEN, environmental consultant; b. Manchester, Eng., Apr. 5, 1924; s. William Louis and Edith Winifred (Gates) B.; came to U.S., 1963; naturalized, 1974; BSc in Physics (with honors), London U., 1954; MS in Environ. Studies, Calif. State, Dominguez Hills, 1976; PhD in Environ. Engring., Calif. Coast U., 1982; Reg. Environ. Auditor. children: Diana, Ian, Brenda, Keith. Program mgr. Brit. Aircraft Corp., Stevenage, Eng., 1953-63; sr. systems engr. RCA, Princeton, N.J., 1963-66; project mgr. Gen. Electric Co., Valley Forge, Pa., 1966-67; dept. head TRW systems Group, Redondo Beach, Calif., 1967-72; dir. energy and pollution control ARATEX Svcs., Inc., Calif., 1974-81, dir. tech. devel., 1981-83, staff cons., 1983-91; cons., lectr. in spacecraft sensor tech., energy conservation, environ. and contamination controls. With Royal Air Force, 1942-47. Assoc. fellow AIAA; mem. Inst. Environ. Scis. (sr.). Contbr. articles in field to profl. jours. Home and Office: 22901 Leadwell St West Hills CA 91307-2120

BURNETT, JOHN LAURENCE, geologist; b. Wichita, Kans., Aug. 28, 1932; s. Virgil Milton and Bertha Maurine (Van Order) L.; m. Annetta J. Saywell, July, 2, 1954 (div. 1975); children: John Forrester, Laurence Gregory. AB in Geology, U. Calif., Berkeley, 1957, MS in Mining, 1960. Cert. engring. geologist; registered geologist. Geologist Calif. Div. Mines and Geology, Sacramento, Calif., 1958—; courts expert superior ct. of L.A., 1967-71; instr. geology U. Calif. Extension, Berkeley, 1967-75, Cosumnes River Coll., 1981-88. Pvt. U.S. Army, 1955. Fellow Geol. Soc. of Am.; mem. Assn. of Engring. Geologists, Soc. of Mining Metallurgy and Exploration. Unitarian. Office: Calif Div Mines and Geology 620 Bercut Dr Sacramento CA 95814-0131

BURNETT, LYNN BARKLEY, health science educator; b. Reedley, Calif., Oct. 20, 1948; s. Charles Erbin and Ruth Clarice (Erickson) B. BS, Columbia Pacific U., MSc; diploma in nat. security mgmt. Nat. Def. U. of U.S.; PhD in Physiology and Psychology, Columbia Pacific U.; EdD in Higher Edn. Nova U.; Faculty of Laws, U. London. Cert. community coll. tchr., Calif., instr. in advanced first aid, emergency care, basic CPR, ACLS, Pediatric ALS. Med. advisor Fresno County Sheriff's Depart., 1972—, assoc. dir. Cen. Valley Emergency Med. Svcs. System, Fresno, Calif., 1974-75; faculty Fresno City Coll., 1978—, prof. health sci., 1981-87, dir. continuing edn. in health, Calf. State U. Fresno, 1981—, adj. faculty West Coast Christian Coll., 1989-92, med. and health commentator Sta. KVPR-FM Valley Pub. Radio, 1990— lectr., cons. in field; co-dir. conjoint rsch. program of Stanford U. Sch. Medicine and Dept. Health Sci. Calif. State U., Fresno, 1986; established pilot paramedic programs Fresno County, 1974-75; dir. Cent. Valley's Inaugural Paramedic Tng. Program, 1975; established CPR tng. Programs Fresno Fire Dept., 1968, Fresno Police Dept., 1972, Fresno County Sheriff's Dept., 1973. Chmn. Fresno County steering com. The Chem. People, 1983-86, Generation at Risk, 1987; mem. Emergency Med. Care Com. Fresno County, 1979-85, vice chmn., 1984-85; mem. Calif. State

Commn. Emergency Med. Services, 1974-75; mem. Fresno County Adv. Bd. on Drug Abuse, 1984—, chmn. drug adv. bd., 1985-88; chmn. pub. edn. Fresno County unit Am. Cancer Soc., 1984-87, 90-92, bd. dirs. 1984—, v.p., 1985-87, pres. elect 1987-88, pres. 1988-90, past. pres., 1990-92, chmn. nominations and leadership devel. Fresno County unit, 1990-92, task force cancer and underserved populations Fresno County unit, 1992—, youth and cancer, Calif. Divsn. Am. Cancer Soc., 1992; com. mem. Early Detection and Treatment, Prevention amd Risk Reduction, Fresno County Unit Am. Cancer Soc., 1993;; chmn. Alcohol, Drug adv bd. Fresno County, 1992—; pres. Fresno County Safety Coun., 1985—; mem. steering com. Fresno Health Promotion Coalition, chmn. com. on crime, violence and safety, 1987-89; chmn. bd. Fresno County Drug and Alcohol Prevention Coalition, Inc., 1991-92; mem. med. staff, steering com. All-Star Football Game. 1965—; emergency med. cons. Dept. Intercollegiate Atheltics Calif. State U., Fresno, 1982—; mem. Community Collaborative of Fresno Tomorrow, Inc., com. Juvenile Crime Benchmarks, 1990—; mem. core com. Student Assistance Program for Substance Abuse and Related Problems Fresno City Coll., 1989—; mem. coms. on bus. and industry and govt. Fresno County Master Plan Adv. Body for Comprehensive Coordination of Substance Abuse Svcs.; faculty advanced trauma life support and trauma nurse tactics Valley Med. Ctr., 1982—; bd. dirs. Calif. div. Am. Cancer Soc.; chmn. com. pub. policy Fresno County Drug, Alcohol Prevention Coalition, Inc., 1992—; mem. cancer svcs. adv. bd., Calif. Cancer Ctr., 1992—; mem. com. biomedical ethics Fresno Community Hosp. and Med. Ctr., 1992—; subcom. mem. Resuscitation Status, Advance Directives, and Organ Donation, Protocol for Consultations and Med. Records, Intramural and Extramural Bioethics Edn., 1993; mem. com. emergency cardiac care, Central Valley Divsn. of Am. Heart Assn., 1992—; mem.steering com., subcom. neighborhood revitalization and svc. coord., Oper. "Weed and Seed", office of U.S. attorney gen. eastern dist. Calif., 1992—; chmn. master plan adv. body to reduce alcohol and other drug abuse in Fresno County. Recipient State Service medal Calif. Mil. Dept., 1980; Bronze medal Am. Heart Assn., 1974, Appreciation award Am. Cancer Soc., 1985. Mem. AAAS, Am. Coll. Preventive Medicine, Am. Acad. Forensic Scis. (alt. del. People's Republic of China, citizen ambassador program People to People Internat. 1986), Am. Assn. Suicidology, N.Y. Acad. Scis., Internat. Platform Assn., Fresno County Bar Assn. Republican. Baptist. Avocations: reading, musical conductinggs. Coauthor: manuscript for motion picture Quarantine. Home: PO Box 4512 Fresno CA 93744-4512

BURNETTE, ROBERT VANCE, marketing and engineering professional; b. Kearney, Nebr., Dec. 24, 1955; s. Willie Napoleon and Noma (Manker) B.; m. Debra Ann Heath, June 11, 1977 (div. Sept. 1983); children: Robert Vance Jr., John Michael, Brian Jospeh; m. Katharine Elizabeth Anthes, Dec. 17, 1982 (div. Aug. 1991); children: Scott James, Danielle Katherine; m. Cheryl Arline Poe, May 22, 1992. BSEE, U.S. Naval Acad., 1977; MBA, U. New Haven, 1983. Cert. profl. engr. Commd. lt. USN, 1977, advanced through grades to lt. comdr., 1981; master tng. specialist USN, New London, Conn., 1984-86; resigned USN, 1986; mktg. rep. Harris Corp., Melbourne, Fla., 1986-89, Gen. Dynamics (Convair), San Diego, 1989-91, Flam & Russell, Inc., San Diego, 1991—; cons. Nat. Coun. for Examiners for Engrng. and Surveying, Clemson, S.C., 1990—. Mem. IEEE, Am. Soc. Naval Engrs., Antenna Measurement Techniques Assn., Naval Acad. Alumni Assn., Navy League. Republican. Home and Office: 2415 B Village Way Oceanside CA 92054-4576

BURNEY, VICTORIA KALGAARD, business consultant, civic worker; b. Los Angeles, Apr. 12, 1943; d. Oscar Albert and Dorothy Elizabeth (Peterson) Kalgaard; children: Kim Elizabeth, J. Hewett. BA with honors, U. Mont., 1965; MA, U. No. Colo., 1980; postgrad. Webster U., St. Louis, 1983-84. Exec. dir. Hill County Community Action, Havre, Mont., 1966-67; community orgn. specialist ACCESS, Escondido, Calif., 1967-68; program devel. and community orgn. specialist Community Action Programs, Inc., Pensacola, Fla., 1968-69; cons. Escambia County Sch. Bd., Fla., 1969-71; pres. Kal Kreations, Kailua, Hawaii, 1974-77; instr., dir. office human resources devel. Palomar Coll., San Marcos, Calif., 1978-81; chief exec. officer IDET Corp., San Marcos, 1981-87; cons. County of Riverside, Calif., 1983. Mem. San Diego County Com. on Handicapped, San Diego, 1979; cons. tribal resource devel., Escondido, Calif., 1979; mem. exec. com. Social Services Coordinating Council, San Diego, 1982-83; mem. pvt. sector com. and planning and rev. com. Calif. Employment and Tng. Adv. Council, Sacramento, 1982-83; bd. mgrs. Santa Margarita Family YMCA, Vista, Calif., 1984-86; bd. dirs. North County Community Action Program, Escondido, 1978, Casa de Amparo, San Luis Rey, Calif., 1980-83; mem. San Diego County Pub. Welfare Adv. Bd., 1979-83, chairperson, 1981; assoc. mem. Calif. Rep. Cen. Com., Sacramento, 1984-85, 89—; ofcl. San Diego County Rep. Cen. Com., 1985—, exec. com., 1987-92, 2nd vice-chmn. 1991-92; chmn. 74th Assembly Dist. Rep. Caucus, 1989-90; chmn. Working Ptnrs., 1987-90; trustee Rancho Santa Fe Community Ctr., 1991-92. Mem. Nat. Assn. County Employment and Tng. Adminstrs. (chairperson econ. resources com. 1982-85), Calif. Assn. Local Econ. Devel., San Diego Econ. Devel. Corp., Oceanside Econ. devel. Council (bd. dirs. 1983-87), Oceanside C. of C., San Marcos C. of C. (bd. dirs. 1982-85), Carlsbad C. of C. (indsl. council 1982-85), Escondido C. of C. (comml. and indsl. devel. council 1982-87), Vista C. of C. (vice chairperson econ. devel. com. 1982-83), Vista Econ. Devel. Assn., Nat. Job Tng. Partnership, San Diego County Golden Eagle Club, Rancho Santa Fe Rep. Women's Club Federated.

BURNIECE, THOMAS FRANCIS, III, engineering executive; b. Mpls., May 28, 1941; s. Thomas Francis Jr. and Virginia June (Nelson) B.; m. Carol Grace Brandberg, Nov. 10, 1960 (div. Dec. 1988); children: Bruce Thomas, Deborah Carol, William Brian, Kari Lynn; m. Valerie E. Norwood, May 31, 1992. B.E.E., U. Minn., 1964; M.S. in Engrng., Ariz. State U., 1969; postgrad. MIT, 1987. Engr. to sr. engr. Motorola, Scottsdale, Ariz., 1964-69; sr engr., prin. engr. Control Data Corp., Mpls., 1969-74, unit mgr. sect. mgr., 1974-80, dir. engrng., 1980-81; engrng. group mgr. Digital Equipment Corp., Colorado Springs, Colo., 1981-91; sr. v.p. engrng. Maxtor Corp., San Jose, Calif., 1991—; chmn. engrng. dean's adv. council U. Colo., Colorado Springs, 1982-85; mem. Higher Edn. Council, Colo. Assn. Commerce and Industry, Denver, 1982-83. Patentee magnetic read head, 1976, track density increasing apparatus, 1975. Mem. Gov.'s Task Force on Excellence in Edn., Denver, 1983-84; football coach Scottsdale, Ariz., Edina, Minn., 1964-77; hockey coach Edina and Wayzata, Minn., Colorado Springs, 1969-83. Recipient Tech. excellence award Control Data Corp., 1977. Republican. Lutheran. Home: 17150 Los Robles Way Los Gatos CA 95030

BURNISON, BOYD EDWARD, lawyer; b. Arnolds Park, Iowa, Dec. 12, 1934; s. Boyd William and Lucile (Harnden) B.; m. Mari Amaral; children: Erica Lafore, Alison Katherine. BS, Iowa State U., 1957; JD, U. Calif., Berkeley, 1961. Bar: Calif. 1962, U.S. Supreme Ct. 1971, U.S. Dist. Ct. (no. dist.) Calif. 1962, U.S. Ct. Appeals (9th cir.) 1962, U.S. Dist. Ct. (ea. dist.) Calif. 1970, U.S. Dist. Ct. (ctrl. dist.) Calif., 1992. Dep. counsel Yolo County, Calif., 1962-65; of counsel Davis and Woodland (Calif.) Unified Sch. Dists., 1962-65; assoc. Steel & Arostegui, Marysville, Calif., 1965-66, St. Sure, Moore & Hoyt, Oakland, 1966-70; ptnr. St. Sure, Moore, Hoyt & Sizoo, Oakland and San Francisco, 1970-75; v.p. Crosby, Heafey, Roach & May, P.C., Oakland, 1975—, also bd. dirs. Adviser Berkeley YMCA, 1971—; adviser Yolo County YMCA, 1962-65, bd. dirs. 1965; bd. dirs. Easter Seal Soc. Crippled Children and Adults of Alameda County, Calif., 1972-75, Moot Ct. Bd., U. Calif., 1960-61; trustee, sec., legal counsel Easter Seal Found., Alameda County, 1974-79, hon. trustee, 1979—. Fellow ABA Found. (life); mem. ABA (labor rels. and employment law sect., equal employment law com. 1972—), Nat. Conf. Bar Pres.'s, State Bar Calif. (spl. labor counsel 1981-84, labor and employment law sect. 1982—), Alameda County Bar Assn. (chmn. memberships and directory com. 1973-74, 80, chmn. law office econs. com. 1975-77, assn. dir. 1981-85, pres., 1984, vice chmn. bench bar liaison com. 1983, chmn. 1984, Disting. Svc. award 1987, bd. dirs. 1993—), Alameda County Bar Found. (bd. dirs. 1993—), Yolo County Bar Assn. (sec. 1965), Yuba Sutter Bar Assn., Bar Assn. San Francisco (labor law sect.), Indsl. Rels. Rsch. Assn., Sproul Assoc. Boalt Hall Law Sch. U. Calif. Berkeley, Iowa State Alumni Assn., Order Knoll, Round Hill Country Club, Rotary (Paul Harris fellow), Pi Kappa Alpha, Phi Delta Phi. Democrat. Home: PO Box 743 2500 Caballo Ranchero Dr Diablo CA 94528 Office: Crosby Heafey Roach & May 1999 Harrison St Oakland CA 94612-3515

BURNLEY, KENNETH S., school system administrator; m. Eileen Burnley; children: Traci, Trevor. BS, U. Mich., MA, PhD. Tchr. various schs. Mich.; asst. track coach U. Mich.; tchr., coord., asst. prin., prin., dir. Ypsilanti Bd. Edn.; instr. Ea. Mich. U.; asst. supt. instrn. Waverly Bd. Edn.; supt./CEO Fairbanks (Alaska) North Star Borough Sch. Dist.; supt. schs. Colorado Springs (Colo.) Sch. Dist. 11, 1987—; speaker in field. Bd. dirs. Colo. Nat. Bank Exch. Named Supt. of Year, Am. Assn. Sch. Adminstrs., 1993. Mem. Colo. Springs C. of C. (bd. dirs.). Office: Colorado Springs School Dist 11 115 N El Paso St Colorado Springs CO 80903-2599*

BURNS, ALEXANDRA DARROW (SANDRA BURNS), health program administrator; b. West Point, Ky., Mar. 28, 1946; d. Eugene Alexander and Phyllis Anna (Kedroski) Darrow; m. Maurice Edward Burns Jr., Sept. 8, 1966 (div. May 1985); 1 child, Megan Alexandra. BS in Journalism, U. Colo., 1967, MA in Guidance and Counseling, 1974. Cert. ins. rehab. specialist, rehab. counselor. Probation and parole officer Office of Probation and Parole, Olympia, Wash., 1969-70; employment counselor Div. Employment, Denver, 1971-73; rehab. counselor Colo. Div. Rehab.-Blind Svcs., Denver, 1973-77; rehab. supr. Colo. Div. Rehab., Denver, 1978-81, program supr. rehab. ins. svcs. for employment, 1981-91; program adminstr. Americans With Disabilities Act, Denver, 1991—. Vice chmn. Juvenile Parole Bd., Denver, 1982-91, acting chmn., 1987, chmn., 1988-91; del. Dem. County Caucus, Aurora, Colo., 1986; coun. del. Girl Scouts U.S.A., 1988-90, coleader Brownie troop, 1988-9-, mem. area svc. team, 1989-90; mem. adv. bd. Indsl. Commn., 1983-86; mem. Jr. Symphony Guild, 1986-87; sec., bd. dirs. Mission Viejo Homeowners Assn., 1989-90. Mem. Nat. Rehab. Assn., Nat. Rehab. Adminstrn. Assn., Colo. Rehab. Adminstrn. Assn. (bd. dirs. 1988—, pres.-elect pvt. sector div. 1989, pres. 1990-91), Zonta (corr. sec. 1984-86). Episcopalian. Home: 15770 E Mercer Pl Aurora CO 80013-2559 Office: Colo Div Rehab Ste 3400 4th Fl 1575 Sherman St Denver CO 80203-1714

BURNS, BRENT EMIL, electrical engineer; b. Wynnewood, Okla., Dec. 3, 1952; s. Frank Brent and Dorothy Esther (Westberg) B. BSEE, U. Okla., 1978, MSEE, 1979; PhD of Elec. Engrng., Stanford U., 1987. Rschr. Northrop Rsch. Ctr., Palos Verdes, Calif., 1985—. With U.S. Army, 1972-74. Scholarship NSF 1979-82. Mem. IEEE, Electrochem. Soc., Tau Beta Pi, Eta Kappa Nu. Home: 6638 El Rodeo Rd Rancho Palos Verdes CA 90274 Office: Northrop ESD PO Box 5032 Hawthorne CA 90251

BURNS, CONRAD RAY, senator; b. Gallatin, Mo., Jan. 25, 1935; s. Russell and Mary Frances (Knight) B.; m. Phyllis Jean Kuhlmann; children: Keely Lynn, Garrett Russell. Student, U. Mo., 1952-54. Field rep. Polled Hereford World Mag., Kansas City, Mo., 1963-69; pub. rels. Billings (Mont.) Livestock Com., 1969-73; farm dir. KULR TV, Billings, 1974; pres., founder No. Ag-Network, Billings, 1975-86; commissioner Yellowstone County, Billings, 1987-89; U.S. Senator from Montana, 1989—. With USMC, 1955-57. Mem. Nat. Assn. Farm Broadcasters, Am. Legion, Rotary, Masons, Shriners. Republican. Lutheran. Office: US Senate 183 Dirksen Bldg Washington DC 20510-2603*

BURNS, DAN W., manufacturing company executive; b. Auburn, Calif., Sept. 10, 1925; s. William and Edith Lynn (Johnston) B.; 1 child, Dan Jr. Dir. materials Menasco Mfg. Co., 1951-56; v.p., gen. mgr. Hufford Corp., 1956-58; pres. Hufford div. Siegler Corp., 1958-61; v.p. Siegler Corp., 1961-62, Lear Siegler, Inc., 1962-64; pres., dir. Electrada Corp., Culver City, Calif., 1964; pres., chief exec. officer Sargent Industries, Inc., L.A., 1964-85, chmn. bd. dirs., 1985-88; now chmn. bd. dirs., chief exec. officer Arlington Industries, Inc.; bd. dirs. Gen. Automotive Corp., Dover Tech. Internat., Inc. Bd. dirs. San Diego Aerospace Mus., Smithsonian Inst., Nat. Acad. Sci., The Pres.'s Cir. Capt. U.S. Army, 1941-47; prisoner of war Japan; asst. mil. attache 1946, China; a.d.c. to Gen. George C. Marshall 1946-47. Mem. Orgn. Am. States Sports Com. (dir.), L.A. Country Club, St. Francis Yacht Club, Calif. Club, Conquistador del Cielo. Home: 10851 Chalon Rd Los Angeles CA 90077

BURNS, DANIEL HOBART, management consultant; b. Atlanta, Jan. 26, 1928; s. Hobart H. and Florence (Kuhn) B.; B.A., U. Ala., 1949; grad. Armed Forces Staff Coll., 1966, Air Command and Staff Coll., 1969, Air War Coll., 1972; postgrad. U. S.C., 1975, Regent Coll., U. B.C., 1978-79, Trinity Episcopal Sch. for Ministry, 1979-80; m. Barbara Ann Grimsley, Jan. 15, 1949 (div. July 1974); children—Eric Grimsley, Daniel Hobart, Barbara Bennett, Arlene Chester; m. Ann Lyn Horrell, Sept. 28, 1979; children: Jessica Florence, Stephen John. Account exec. Sta. WCOS, Columbia, S.C., 1949-51; sales mgr. sta. WIS, Columbia, 1951-57; ins. agt. Aetna Life Ins. Co., Columbia, 1957-60; propr. Daniel H. Burns Co., mgmt. cons., broker, Columbia, 1960—; pres., dir. Nat. Search, Inc., 1966—, Indsl. Surveys, Inc., 1968—; Alliance Bldg. Industries, 1971-84; cons., Ednl. TV Network, govts. of Israel, Greece, W. Ger., Fed. Grants Projects, S.C. Ednl. TV Network; guest lectr. U. S.C.; cons. sales mgmt. and market analysis, analytical and conceptual problem solving; owner Western Rare Books-Fine Art, 1983—, Internat. Galleries, Empire Gallery, Empire Pub. Co. Pres., Schneider Sch. PTA, 1963-66; supr. registration City of Columbia, 1962-69; asst. project dir., statewide law enforcement edn. through TV, 1966-69; cons. Pitts. Leadership Found., 1980-81; dist. commr. Boy Scouts Am.; pres., committeeperson Boulder County Rep. Party; pres., bd. dirs. Internat. Communications Resources Found.; bd. dirs. Travelers Aid Assn. Am., Nat. Council USO; Columbia Sch. Theology for Laity; bd. dirs., exec. com. Consol. Agys. of United Funds; Richland County chpt. Nat. Found. Served with USAAF, 1943-46; lt. col. USAF ret. Mem. S.C. Football Ofcls. Assn., Columbia Real Estate Bd., Air Force Assn., Am. Y-Flyer Yacht Racing Assn., AAUP, Am. Mgmt. Assn., Nat. Assn. Ednl. Broadcasters, Soc. for Advancement Mgmt., Am. Soc. Real Estate Appraisers, Interprofl. Cons. Council, Nat. Assn. Security Dealers, Soc. Am. Archivists, Nat. Hist. Soc., Internat. Platform Assn., Hist. Columbia Found., S.C. Press Assn., Columbia C. of C., Am. Soc. Personal Adminstrn., Sierra Club, Columbia Lyric Opera, Internat. Christian Leaders, Fellowship Christian Athletes, English Speaking Union, N. Am. Yacht Racing Union, Sigma Phi Epsilon. Episcopalian/Anglican. Clubs: Charleston (S.C.) Yacht; Yachting of Am., Workshop Theatre, First Nighters, Columbia Squash Racquets, Town Theatre, Masons (Shriner), Lions. Author publs. in field. Home: 7425 Empire Dr Boulder CO 80303-5007 Office: PO Box 1725 Boulder CO 80306-1725

BURNS, DANIEL MICHAEL, manufacturing company financial executive; b. Phila., Sept. 18, 1927; s. Michael John and Louise Ruth (Haun) B.; m. Margery Fay Mueller, Apr. 23, 1966; children: Jeremy Michael, Elizabeth Louise. Cert. in fin., U. Pa., 1957. Mgr. cost acctg. Electric Storage Battery Co., Phila., 1953-58; asst. treas., contr. Eversharp, Inc., Culver City, Calif., 1958-70; dir. corp. fin. analysis Warner-Lambert Co., Morris Plains, N.J., 1970-73; treas., contr. Schick Electric, Inc., Lancaster, Pa., 1973-76; v.p. fin. Chloride Power Electronics, Laguna Hills, Calif., 1976-91; chief fin. officer Altus Corp., Laguna Hills, 1991-93, also bd. dirs.; bd. dirs. UP Systems, Inc., Caledonia, N.Y., CHC Holding Corp., Burgaw, N.C., Chloride Power Electronics, Inc., Burgaw. Sgt. 1st class U.S. Army, 1950-52. Mem. Fin. Execs. Inst., Inst. Mgmt. Accts., Saddlebrook Resorts Country Club. Home: 27441 Via Caudaloso Mission Viejo CA 92692 Office: Burns Travel Ind 27660 Margueritr Mission Viejo CA 92692

BURNS, DENISE RUTH, artist; b. Bellville, N.J., Oct. 17, 1943; d. A. Richard and Ruth Jean (Landers) Culkin; m. Robert P. Burns Jr., Apr. 8, 1960; children: Michael R, David R. Studied, Sergei Bonjart Sch. Art, 1971-73; studied with Dan McCaw, Scottsdale Sch. Art, 1980, 89, studied with J. Asaro, 1988. One-woman shows include Off White Gallery, 1984, 85, 86, 93; two-woman show May Gallery, 1993; group shows include May Galleries, Scottsdale, Ariz., 1987-92, Roy Miles Gallery, London, 1993; featured in Swart Mag., 1992. Instr. Chambersburg (Pa.) Art Alliance, 1985-86, 87-89, Omaha Artist Group, 1988, Pocono Pines (Pa.), 1989, Catalina Art Assn., Avalon, Calif., 1990-91; dir.Plein Art Painters Show, Catalina Island, 1986-92; judge Big Bear Art Festival, 1986, Children's Show, L.A. County Libr., Avalon, 1990. Recipient 2nd Pl. award Scottsdale Art Sch., 1991; named Emerging Artist by Am. Artist Mag., 1984, Best of Show by Catalina Art Festival, 1984, 86, 87, 89-91. Mem. Plein Air Painters Am. (dir., founder), Catalina Art Assn. (pres. 1985, 86), Oil Painters of Am. Home: PO Box 611 Avalon CA 90704

BURNS, DONALD SNOW, registered investment advisor, financial and business consultant; b. Cambridge, Mass., July 31, 1925; s. Jules Ian and Ruth (Snow) B.; m. Lucy Lee Keating, July 15, 1947 (div.); children: Julie Ann Wrigley, Patti B. Boyd, Laurie Bidegain, Wendi Collins, Loni Monahan, Robin. Student, Williams Coll., 1943-44; M in Baking, Am. Inst. of Baking, 1947. Baker O'Rourke Baking Co., Buffalo, 1946-49; gen. mgr. Glaco Co. of So. Calif., L.A., 1949-51; regional mgr. Glaco Div. of Ekco Prodn. Co., Chgo., 1951-53, gen. mgr., 1953-56; pres. McClintock Mfg. Div. Ekco Prodn. Co., Chgo., 1956-61; v.p. Ekco Products Co., Chgo., 1961-67; pres., chmn. Prestige Automotive Group, Garden Grove, Calif., 1967-78; chmn. Prestige Holdings Ltd., Newport Beach, Calif., 1978—; chmn. bd. Newport Nat. Bank, Newport Beach, 1961-67; bd. dir. Securitas Trust, Monte Carlo, Monaco, Am. Safety Equipment Co., Glendale, Calif., Internat. Tech. Corp., Torrance, Calif., Escorp, San Luis Obispo, Calif.; dir. Internat. Rectifier, El Segundo. Author: (short story) The Goose that Neighed, 1967, (books) Two and a Half Nickels, 1970, Light My Fire, 1979. Mem. Calif. State U. Adv. Bd., Fullerton, 1973-76; bd. dirs. Santiago Coll. Found., Santa Ana, Calif., 1989-90, Orange County Sheriff's Adv. Coun., Calif., 1978—, pres., 1987-88; chmn. bd. trustees Orme Sch. Mayer Ariz., 1976-78. With USNR, 1943-46. Mem. Jonathan Club. Office: Prestige Holdings Ltd 22912 Mill Creek Rd Laguna Hills CA 92653

BURNS, JAMES ALVIN, pharmacist; b. East Chicago, Ind., Sept. 24, 1935; s. Mallin Christie and Mary Jeannette (Sholes) B.; m. Suzanne Kay Sherk, Aug. 19, 1967 (div. Dec. 1978); children: Anthony J., Ellen K. BS, Purdue U., 1957. Lic. pharmacist Calif., Ind., Va. Pharmacist Haney's Prescription Ctrs., Hammond, Ind., 1957-58, 60-61, Moore's Arville Pharmacy, Arlington, Va., 1958-60, various pharmacies, So. Calif., 1981-83, L.M. Caldwell Pharmacist, Santa Barbara, Calif., 1983—; sales rep. Eli Lilly & Co., Calif., 1961-80; sales mgr. Rossin Corp., Goleta, Calif., 1980-81. With U.S. Army, 1958-60. Mem. Calif. Pharmacists Assn., Santa Barbara Pharmacists Assn., Masons (past master 1976). Republican. Methodist. Home: 5096D Rhoads Ave Santa Barbara CA 93111-2664

BURNS, JAMES M., federal judge; b. Nov. 24, 1924. BA in Bus. Adminstrn., U. Portland, 1947; JD cum laude, Loyola U., Chgo., 1950. Sole pracitce Portland, 1950-52; dist. atty. Harney County, Oreg., 1952-56; ptnr. Black, Kendall, Tremaine, Booth & Higgins, Portland, 1956-66; judge Oreg. Cir. Ct., Multnomah County, 1966-72; mem. faculty Nat. Jud. Coll., 1972—; judge U.S. Dist. Ct. Oreg., Portland, 1972—, chief judge, 1979-84; Mem. Oreg. Criminal Law Revision Commn., 1967-72; chmn. continuing legal edn. com. Oreg. State Bar, 1965-66; faculty advisor Nat. Jud. Coll., 1971. Mem. Oreg. Cir. Judges Assn. (pre. 1969-70), U.S. Jud. Conf. (com. on adminstrn. of probation system 1978-87). Office: US Dist Ct 602 US Courthouse 620 SW Main St Portland OR 97205-3023

BURNS, MARVIN GERALD, lawyer; b. Los Angeles, July 3, 1930; s. Milton and Belle (Cytron) B.; m. Barbara Irene Fisher, Aug. 23, 1953; children: Scott Douglas, Jody Lynn, Bradley Frederick. BA, U. Ariz., 1951; JD, Harvard U., 1954. Bar: Calif. 1955. Mem. De Castro, West, Chodorow & Burns, Inc., L.A., 1984—. Bd. dirs., v.p. Inner City Arts for Inner City Children. With AUS, 1955-56. Clubs: Beverly Hills Tennis, Sycamore Park Tennis. Home: 10350 Wilshire Blvd PH4 Los Angeles CA 90024 Office: Ste 1800 10960 Wilshire Blvd Los Angeles CA 90024-3881

BURNS, MARY FERRIS, accountant; b. Corpus Christi, Tex., Aug. 24, 1952; d. Wilbur Glenn and Lena (Faught) Ferris; m. Douglas Keith Burns, Dec. 26, 1975. BA, Baylor U., 1974; MLS, U. Tex., Austin, 1975; BS, U. Tex., Dallas, 1982; MA, U. Fla., 1978. CPA, Tex., Wash. Reference libr., Latin Am. collection U. Fla., Gainesville, 1975-78; reference libr., Fondren Libr. So. Meth. U., Dallas, 1978-79; libr. Tex. A&M U., College Station, 1979-81; auditor, provider reimbursement div. Blue Cross & Blue Shield of Tex., Dallas, 1983-84; internal auditor U. Tex. Health Sci. Ctr. at Dallas, 1984-85, adminstrv. svcs. officer Biomed. Comm. Resource Ctr., 1985-87; adminstrv. svcs. mgr. Div. of Lab. Animal Medicine Stanford U., 1988-89, adminstrv. svcs. mgr. Dept. of Microbiology and Immunology, 1989; dir. adminstrn. RIDES for Bay Area Commuters, Inc., San Francisco, 1989-93; cons. Centro Intenacional de Desarrollo Humano en America Latina, Cuernavaca, Mex., 1975. Contbg. editor: Hispanic American Periodicals Index, 1975, 76. Mem. AICPA, Calif. Soc. of CPA's, Wash. Soc. of CPA's., Soc. for Human Resource Mgmt.

BURNS, PATRICIA HENRIETTA, religious association founder and administrator; b. L.I., N.Y., Dec. 9, 1934; d. Henri Jacob and Rolanda Katherine (Berger) Verwayen; m. John Christopher Burns, sept. 10, 1933 (dec. Jan. 1977); children: Stephanie, David, John. Student, Warren Harding, 1952, Maricopa Tech. Coll., 1978-86, Rio Salado Community Coll., 1980-88, Lamson Bus., 1981. Advt. mgr. W. T. Grant Phoenix Area Stores, 1970-74; with securities sales dept. Waddell & Reed Securities, Phoenix, 1975-76; commr.'s aide Maricopa County Superior Ct., Phoenix, 1976-82; sec. to dept. mgrs. Motorola, Inc., Chandler, Ariz., 1984-92; pres. Non-Denominational Bible Prophecy Study Assn., Tempe, 1983—. Author: The Book of Revelation Explained, 1982.

BURNS, ROBERT CHARLES, multimedia software developer, computer programmer; b. Phila., Dec. 17, 1961; s. Washington and Paula Christine (Schmidt) B. BS in Computer Sci., U. Puget Sound, 1987. Computer programming cons. Weyerhaeuser Paper Co., Tacoma, 1984-88; computer systems analyst Boeing Computer Svcs., Seattle, 1988—. Mem. Assn. Computing Machinery (spl. interest group computer human interface), Assn. Software Design., Puget Chi, Bay Chi. Roman Catholic.

BURNS, ROBERT OBED, retired physicist; b. Emporia, Kans., Jan. 16, 1910; s. Elmer Emmett and Catherine (Crocker) B.; widowed. BS in Physics, Knox Coll., 1931; MS in Physics, U. Ill., 1933, PhD in Physics, 1937. Grad. asst. U. Ill., Urbana, 1931-37; physicist, then asst. dir. rsch. engrng. Celotex Corp., various locations, 1937-43; physicist, transition aide, engrng. div. war rsch. U. Calif., San Diego, 1943-46; head devel. dept. Navy Electronics Lab., San Diego, 1946-49; chief scientist U.S. Army Electronics Warfare Ctr., Ft. Monmouth, N.J., 1952-54, U.S. Army Electronics Proving Ground, Ft. Huachuca, Ariz., 1954-56; devel. coord. Office Naval Rsch., Washington, 1956-59; dir. long range planning, dir. tech. analysis & adv. group Dep. Chief Naval Ops., Office of Chief of Naval Ops., Washington, 1959-75; retired, 1975. Author: Innovation--the Management Connection, 1975. Mem. Tucson Com. on Fgn. Rels.; supr. Great Decisions program Fgn. Policy Assn. Mem. UN Assn. USA (bd. dirs.). Republican. Home: Apt 4138 8700 N La Cholla Blvd Tucson AZ 85741

BURNS, THOMAS DONALD, electrical engineer; b. Albuquerque, Apr. 10, 1956; s. Donald John and Virginia Marie (Gutierrez) B.; m. Karen Lynn Houser, Aug. 6, 1983; children: Kiri Ann, James Christopher Helmer. BSEE, U. N.Mex., 1978. Engrng. technician USAF Weapons Lab., Albuquerque, 1976-78; elec. engr. Storage Tech. Corp., Louisville, Colo., 1979-82; sr. regulatory engr. Auto-Trol Tech., Thornton, Colo., 1982—. Author: Information About FCC Class A and Class B Testing, 1989, 91, 93, FCC Rule Change Updates, 1991, Preparing for FCC Testing, 1993. Mem. Nat. Assn. Radio and Telecomm. Engrs. (cert. EMC engr.), The Country Club (organizing com. for Colo. Country Classic nat. country western dance competition). Republican. Roman Catholic. Home: 1700 Sussex St Lafayette CO 80026-1931 Office: Auto-Trol Tech 1700 Sussex St Lafayette CO 80026

BURNS, THOMAS GORDON, petroleum company executive; b. Chgo., Aug. 5, 1940; s. Gordon Taylor and Mildred (Birmingham) G.; m. Louise Evelyn Toppe, May 2, 1964; children: Erik Thomas, Michael Edward Louis. BS, MIT, 1962, MS, 1963. Group assoc. Caltex Corp., N.Y.C., 1963-66; petroleum chem. sales coord. Caltex Deutschland, Frankfurt, Fed. Republic Germany, 1966-68, asst. to mng. dir., 1968-71, ops. supt., 1971-73; project devel. specialist Chevron Chem. Co., San Francisco, 1974-78; supr. supply Chevron Corp., San Francisco, 1978-81, asst. mgr. econs., 1981-86, mgr. econs., 1986—. Author proc. World Petroleum Congress, 1988, 92; contbr. articles to profl. jours. Mem. Western States Petroleum Assn. (chair com. economists 1986—), Natural Gas Supply Assn. (chair info. resources com. 1988-90). Office: Chevron Corp 225 Bush ST 1622 San Francisco CA 94104

BURNSIDE, ROGER EDWARD, forest entomologist, natural resource manager; b. Detroit Lakes, Minn., July 12, 1952; s. Clarence E. and Marianne M. (Hoffman) B.; m. Eileen Kay Geiger, Aug. 30, 1975; children: April, Sara. BS in Biology, Chemistry, Bemidji State U., 1975; MS in Entomology, plant Pathology, N.D. State U., 1979. Plant health specialist Minn. Dept. Natural Resources, Bemidji, 1975, 76, forest inventory specialist, 1975-76; tutor reading, math Kenai Peninsula Borough Sch. Dist., Tyonek, Alaska, 1980-81; natural resource officer Alaska Dept. Natural Resources, Anchorage, 1981-90, natural resource mgr. insects and disease div. forestry, 1990—. Mem. Soc. Am. Foresters, Nat. Audubon Soc. Office: Alaska Dept Natural Resources/Divsn Forestry 3601 C St PO Box 107005 Anchorage AK 99510-7005

BURNWEIT, RICHARD CHRIS, political science educator, college official; b. Bridgeport, Conn., June 14, 1950; s. Edwin Chris and Lois Jane (Parmelee) B. BA in History, Claremont McKenna Coll., 1972; MA in Polit. Sci., U. Calif., Santa Barbara, 1983, postgrad., 1986. Asst. dir. learning resources Westmont Coll., Santa Barbara, 1973—, adj. prof. polit. sci., 1981—. Compiler: Californians on Capitol Hill: Bibliography of California's Congressional Delegation 1955 to Present, 1992; contbr. biog. articles to Political Parties and Elections in the U.S.: An Ency., 1991, Ency. U.S. Congress, 1993. Mem. Santa Barbara Pers. Bd., 1976-79. Mem. Am. Polit. Sci. Assn., Western Polit. Sci. Assn., Orgn. Am. Historians, Calif. Preservation Found., Soc. Calif. Archivists. Presbyterian. Home: 308 S Santa Cruz St Ventura CA 93001 Office: Westmont Coll 955 La Paz Rd Santa Barbara CA 93108-1099

BURR, KAREN LYNNE, sales executive; b. Upland, Calif., Sept. 22, 1964; d. H. C. and Rosemary Evelyn (Holland) J. BA, Calif. State U., Fullerton, 1987. TV co-producer City of Walnut, Calif., 1985-88; in sales Homes and Land mag., Upland, 1989-92; sales exec. Mobilecomm/BellSouth Paging, Ontario, Calif., 1992—. Apostolic Pentecostal Ch. Home: 7422 Via Salsipuedes Rancho Cucamonga CA 91730

BURRELL, GARLAND E., JR., federal judge; b. L.A., July 4, 1947. BA in Sociology, Calif. State U., 1972; MSW, Washington U., Mo., 1973; JD, Calif. We. Sch. Law, 1976. Bar: Calif. 1976, U.S. Dist. Ct. (ea. dist.) Calif. 1976, U.S. Ct. Appeals (9th cir.) 1981. Dep. dist. atty. Sacramento County, Calif., 1976-78; dep city atty. Sacramento, 1978-79; asst. U.S. atty., dep. chief civil divsn. Office of U.S. Atty. for Ea. Dist. Calif., 1979-85, asst. U.S. atty., chief civil divsn., 1990-92; litigation atty. Stockman Law Corp., Sacramento, Calif., 1985-86; sr. dep. city atty. Office of City Atty., Sacramento, 1986-90; judge U.S. Dist. Ct. (ea. dist.) Calif., Sacramento, 1992—. With USMC, 1966-68. Office: Dist Ct 650 Capital Mall Sacramento CA 95814*

BURRI, BETTY JANE, research chemist; b. San Francisco, Jan. 23, 1955; d. Paul Gene and Carleen Georgette (Meyers) B.; m. Kurt Randall Annweiler, Dec. 1, 1984. BA, San Francisco State U., 1976; MS, Calif. State U., Long Beach, 1978; PhD, U. Calif. San Diego, La Jolla, 1982. Research asst. Scripps Clinic, La Jolla, 1982-83, research assoc., 1983-85; research chemist Western Human Nutrition Rsch. Ctr., USDA, San Francisco, 1985—. Contbr. articles to profl. jours. Affiliate fellow Am. Heart Assn., 1983, 84; grantee NIH, 1982, 85, USDA, 1986-92. Mem. Assn. Women in Sci. (founding dir. San Diego chpt.), N.Y. Acad. Sci., Union Concerned Scientists, Am. Inst. Nutrition, Am. Soc. Clin. Nutrition. Office: Western Human Nutrition Rsch Ctr PO Box 29997 San Francisco CA 94129-0997

BURRIS, BILL BUCHANAN, JR., automotive manufacturing executive; b. San Diego, Jan. 7, 1957; s. Bill Buchanan Sr. and Marjorie Ellen (Halliburton) B. BA in Biology, Westmont Coll., 1981. Svc. technician Mesa Porsche Audi Ferrari, La Mesa, Calif., 1981, Alan Johnson Porsche Audi, Inc., San Diego, 1981-82; svc. trainer Volkswagen Am., Inc., Culver City, Calif., 1982-84; sr. svc. trainer, dist. svc. mgr. Porsche Cars N.Am., Inc., Reno, 1984-88; mgr. nat. svc. tng. Jaguar Cars, Inc., Mahwah, N.J., 1988-90; body svc. group mgr. Toyota Motor Sales, U.S.A., Inc., Torrance, Calif., 1991—. Author: Training Value and Statistical Analysis, 1991. Exec. advisor Jr. Achievement Inc., 1993. Mem.. ASTD, Nat. Inst. Automotive Svc. Excellence (cert. master automobile technician), Soc. Automotive Engrs. (subcom. 1988—), Am. Mgmt. Assn., Inter-Industry Conf. on Auto Collision Repair. Office: Toyota Motor Sales USA Inc 19001 S Western Ave M/D S-102 Torrance CA 90509-2991

BURRIS, DUANE, software developer; b. St. Louis, Nov. 27, 1956; s. Hubert Wayne and Marjorie (Graham) B.; m. Brenda Joyce Keegan, Apr. 21, 1978; children: Ashley Keegan Burris, Andrew James Zebadiah Burris. AA in Liberal Arts, Glendale (Ariz.) C.C., 1976; AA in Constrn., Rio Salado Coll., 1981; BS in Computer Sci., Grand Canyon U., 1988. Cert. network engr.; cert. folio cons. Gen. foreman Mardian Constrn., Phoenix, 1978-83, scheduling mgr., 1983-84, info. systems mgr., 1984-90; pres. Witan Industries, Glendale, 1990—; adj. prof. Grand Canyon U., Phoenix, 1988; cons. Teknow!, Phoenix, 1989. Author (software) XQLLIB, 1989; inventor BNC tool. Foresight N.W. Christian Ch., Phoenix, 1989-92, Sunday sch. tchr., 1980-92; cons. Jr. Achievement, Phoenix, 1989. Recipient Cert. Appreciation Ariz. Alliance of Bus., 1988, 89, Grand Canyon U., 1988; named Outstanding Capenter Ariz. Gov. Bruce Babbit, 1981. Mem. IEEE, Assn. for Computing Machinery, Peoria Econ. Devel. Group, Novell Profl. Developers. Republican. Office: Witan Industries 12237 N 47th Dr Glendale AZ 85304

BURROUGHS, KATE, entomologist; b. Hayward, Calif., Oct. 31, 1953; d. Erwin Solon and Mary Adele (Henderson) B.; m. David Lincoln Henry Jr., July 12, 1975; 1 child, Michael David Burroughs Henry. BS in Entomology, U. Calif., Berkeley, 1975. Cert. Am. Registry of Profl. Entomologists. Entomologist Calif. Dept. of Food & Agr., Sonoma, 1975-78; entomologist, pvt. cons. Sebastopol, Calif., 1978-80; entomologist Harmony Farm Supply, Sebastopol, 1980—; mem. USDA Nat. Sustainable Agriculture Adv. Coun., 1993. Author: Future is Abundant, 1980; editor: Environmentally Friendly Gardening Techniques, 1990; contbr. articles to profl. jours. Mem. com. Calif. Cert. Organic Farmers, Santa Cruz, 1976—. Mem. Assn. Applied Insect Ecologists (profl. mem., pres. 1989-90), Am. Soc. Enology & Viticulture. Democrat. Office: Harmony Farm Supply 3244 Gravenstein Hwy N Sebastopol CA 95472-2354

BURROWS, RONNA MAY, secondary education educator, business owner; b. Denver, Apr. 14, 1956; d. Gerald Ray and Evangeline Veronica (Wickham) Holtzinger; m. Lawrence McDevitt Burrows, Aug. 4, 1984; children: Bradley, Sarah, Katherine, Laura Evangeline. BE, Colo. State U., 1979. Cert. secondary sch. educator, type A bus./office educator, mktg. and distributive educator. Tchr., coord. Platte County Sch. Dist., Wheatland, Wyo., 1979-81, Cripple Creek (Colo.)-Victor Schs., 1983-84; substitute tchr. Jefferson County Pub. Schs., Lakewood, Colo., 1984-92; tchr., coord. Evergreen (Colo.) High Sch., 1992-93; owner Color Changers, Denver, 1991—. Mem. Com. on Ministry, Denver Presbytary, 1990-93; elder, chair of edn. North Presbyn. Ch., Denver, 1987-90, chair pastor nominating com., 1990. Named to DECA Hall of Fame, 1980. Republican. Presbyterian. Home: 2970 Sheridan Blvd Denver CO 80214

BURRY, KENNETH ARNOLD, physician, educator; b. Monterrey Park, Calif., Oct. 2, 1942; s. Frederick H. and Betty Jean (Bray) B.; m. Mary Lou Tweedy, June 4, 1964 (div. 1981); 1 child, Michael Curtis; m. Katherine A. Johnson, Apr. 3, 1982; 1 child, Lisa Bray. B.A., Whittier Coll., 1964; M.D., U. Calif.-Irvine, 1968. Diplomate Am. Bd. Ob-Gyn, Am. Bd. Reproendocrine. Intern, Orange County Med. Ctr., Calif.; resident U. Oreg. Med. Sch.; sr. research fellow U. Wash., Seattle, 1974-76; asst. prof. Oreg. Health Sci. U., Portland, 1976-80, assoc. prof., 1980-89, prof., 1989—; dir. Oreg. Reproductive Research and Fertility Program, Portland, 1982—; dir. Fellowship Program, Portland, 1984—, asst. chmn. Dept. Ob-Gyn, 1986—, dir. divsn Reproendocrine, 1992—; sci. presentations to profl. assns. Author: In Vitro Fertilization and Embryo Transfer, Oregon Health Sciences University Patient Handbook, 1984 (with others). Contbr. abstracts, articles to profl. publs. Served to capt. U.S. Army, 1969-71. Decorated Bronze Star, Air medal, Army Commendation medal oak leaf cluster; recipient Combat Med. badge. Fellow Am. Coll. Ob-Gyn; mem. Endocrine Soc., Am. Fertility Soc., Am. Fedn. Clin. Research, Soc. Reproductive Endocrinologists, Soc. Reproductive Surgeons, Pacific Coast Obstet. and Gynecol. Soc. Republican. Lutheran. Home: 8630 SW Pacer Dr Beaverton OR 97005-6980 Office: Oreg Health Scis U 3181 SW Sam Jackson Park Rd Portland OR 97201-3011

BURSTEIN, DAVID, astronomy educator; b. Englewood, N.J., May 19, 1947; s. Bernard and Mildred (Mindlin) B.; m. Gail Kelly, June 19, 1971; children: Jonathan, Elizabeth. BS in Physics with honors, Wesleyan U., Middletown, Conn., 1969; PhD in Astronomy, U. Calif., Santa Cruz, 1978. Research fellow dept. terrestrial magnetism Carnegie Instn., Washington, 1977-79; research assoc. Nat. Radio Astronomy Obs., Charlottesville, Va., 1979-82; asst. prof. dept. physics Ariz. State U., Tempe, 1982-88, assoc. prof., 1988—. Contbr. over 130 articles to astronomy and astrophysicas jours. Named Outstanding Tchr. Ariz. State Golden Key, 1989, Ariz. State Faculty of Yr., Disabled Student Resources, 1990. Mem. Am. Astron. Soc., Internat. Astron. Union, Sigma Xi. Office: Ariz State U Dept Physics Tempe AZ 85283

BURTON, AL, producer, director, writer; b. Chgo.; s. D. Chester and Isabelle (Olenick) G.; m. Sally Lou Lewis, Jan. 8, 1956; 1 dau., Jennifer. BS cum laude, Northwestern U. Exec. v.p. creative affairs Norman Lear-Embassy Communications, Inc., 1973-83; exec. producer-cons. Universal TV, 1983-92; exec. prodr., v.p. syndication Castle Rock Entertainment, 1992—; bd. dirs. Pilgrim Group Funds; mem. Second Decade council Am. Film Inst., adv. bd. Samantha Smith Found. Producer Johnny Mercer's Mus. Chairs, 1952-55, Oscar Levant Show, 1955-61; creative producer Teen-Age Fair, 1962-72; exec. producer Charles in Charge, CBS-TV, 1984-85, Tribune Entertainment, 1986-91, Together We Stand, CBS-TV, 1986-87, Nothing Is Easy, 1987-88, The New Lassie, 1989-92; creative supr. Mary Hartman, Mary Hartman, Fernwood 2Night, America 2Night; prodn. supr. One Day At a Time, Facts of Life, Silver Spoons, The Jeffersons, Square Pegs, Different Strokes; composer-lyricist theme songs for Facts of Life, Different Strokes, Charles in Charge, The New Lassie (Genesis award, 1992), Together We Stand, Nothing Is Easy; cons. Domestic Life CBS-TV, 1983-84, Alan King Show, 1986. Shared Emmy award for outstanding comedy series All in the Family, 1978-89, Producers award Nat. Coun. for Families and TV, 1984, Jackie Coogan award for Oustanding Contbn. to Youth through Entertainment, 1991; honored for Different Strokes, NCCH, 1979-80; honored by Calif. Gov.'s Com. for employment of the handicapped for Facts of Life, 1981-82, for Charles in Charge, 1988; recipient Youth in Film award Charles in Charge, 1990, Genesis award for portrayal animal issues The New Lassie, 1992; spl. commendation Entertainment Industries Coun. for The New Lassie and Charles in Charge, 1990. Mem. AFTRA, Chmn.'s Coun. of Caucus for Producers, Writers and Dirs., Dirs. Guild Am., Writers Guild Am., Acad. TV Arts and Scis., Acad. Magical Arts. Office: Castle Rock Entertainment Inc 335 N Maple Dr Ste 135 Beverly Hills CA 90210

BURTON, BERTHA EDWINA, advocate, consultant; b. Columbia, S.C., Apr. 19, 1949; d. B. T. and Georgie (Lott) B. BA cum laude, Johnson C. Smith U., 1971; MSW, U. S.C., 1974. Recreational therapy coord. Mecklenburg County Mental Health, Charlotte, N.C., 1969-71; tchr. Columbia (S.C.) Pub. Schs., 1971-72; dir. social work Gaston Meml. Hosp., Gastonia, N.C., 1972; instr. Benedict Coll., Columbia, 1974-76, King Meml. Coll., Columbia, 1976-77; addiction cons. Mid-Carolina Coun. on Alcoholism, Columbia, 1976-78; trainer, cons. Urban Mgmt. Cons., San Francisco, 1980-82; sch. out-reach cons. Community Human Scvs. Project, Monterey, Calif., 1982-85; prison rep. Friends Outside Correctional Tng. Facility, Soledad, Calif., 1987—; DUI cons. Community Human Svcs. Project, Monterey, 1981-85; career cons. Urban Mgmt. Cons., San Francisco, 1980-82; cen. regional cons. Friends Outside, San Jose, Calif., 1989—. NIMH grantee, 1972. Mem. Family and Corrections Network, NASW, Kiwanis (charter), Delta Sigma Theta. Office: Correctional Tng Facility PO Box 686 Soledad CA 93960-0686

BURTON, EDWARD LEWIS, industrial procedures and training consultant; b. Colfax, Iowa, Dec. 8, 1935; s. Lewis Harrison and Mary Burton; m. Janet Jean Allan, July 29, 1956; children: Mary, Cynthia, Katherine, Daniel. BA in Indsl. Edn., U. No. Iowa, 1958; MS in Indsl. Edn., U. Wis.-Stout, 1969; postgrad., Ariz. State U., 1971-76. Tchr. apprentice program S.E. Iowa Community Coll., Burlington, 1965-68; tchr. indsl. edn. Keokuc (Iowa) Sr. High Sch., 1965-68, Oak Park (Ill.)-River Forest High Sch., 1968-70; tchr. Rio Salado Community Coll., Phoenix, 1972-82; tchr. indsl. edn. Buckeye (Ariz.) Union High Sch., 1970-72; cons. curriculum Westside Area Career Opportunities Program - Ariz. Dept. Edn.; instr. vocat. automotive Dysart High Sch., Peoria, Ariz., 1979-81; tng. adminstr. Ariz. Pub. Service Co., Phoenix, 1981-90; tng. devel. cons. NUS Corp., 1991—; mem. dispatcher tng. com. Western Systems Coord. Coun., Salt Lake City, 1986-90; owner Aptitude Analysis Co., 1987—; mem. IEEE Dispatcher Tng. Work Group, 1988-91. Editor: Bright Ideas for Career Education, 1974, More Bright Ideas for Career Education, 1975. Mem. Citizens Planning Com., Buckeye, 1987-90, Town Governing Coun., Buckeye, 1990-91. NDEA grantee, 1967. Mem. NEA (life), Ariz. Indsl. Edn. Assn. (life), Personnel Testing Council of Ariz., NRA (life, endowment), Cactus Combat League, Mensa (test proctor 1987—), Masons. Republican. Methodist. Home: 19845 W Van Buren St Buckeye AZ 85326-9134

BURTON, FREDERICK GLENN, laboratory director; b. Greensburg, Pa., Nov. 30, 1939; s. Frederick Glenn and Vivian Baird (Chambers) B.; m. Jeanne Marie Nesper, May 29, 1968. BA, Coll. Wooster, 1962; MA, Wesleyan U., 1966; PhD, U. Rochester, 1971. Instr. Ohio Agrl. Experiment Sta., Wooster, 1962-64; postdoctoral fellow Salk Inst., San Diego, 1971-73; from rsch. scientist to sr. rsch. scientist Battelle N.W., Richland, Wash., 1974-85; project mgr. Battelle Meml. Inst., Columbus, Ohio, 1985-89; lab dir. Battelle Tooele (Utah) Ops., 1990—; cons. Immunodiagnostics Inc., Oceanside, Calif., 1973-74. Mayor City of West Richland, 1976-81. With USAR, 1964-70. Recipient honor Fed. Lab. Consortium, 1986. Mem. Am. Chem. Soc., Controlled Release Soc. Home: 90 Lakeview Tooele UT 84074-9668 Office: Battelle Tooele Ops 11650 Stark Rd Tooele UT 84074-9712

BURTON, JOHN PAUL, lawyer; b. New Orleans, Feb. 26, 1943; s. John Paul and Nancy (Key) B.; m. Anne Ward; children: Jennifer, Susanna, Derek, Catherine. BBA magna cum laude, La. Tech. U., 1965; LLB, Harvard U., 1968. Bar: N.Mex. 1968, U.S. Dist. Ct. N.Mex. 1968, U.S. Ct. Appeals (10th cir.) 1973, U.S. Supreme Ct. 1979. Assoc., Rodey, Dickason, Sloan, Akin & Robb, Albuquerque, 1968-74, dir., 1974—, chmn. comml. dept., 1980-81, mng. dir. Santa Fe, N.Mex., 1986-90; lectr. workshops, seminars. Author: (book) Boundary Disputes in New Mexico, 1992; contbr. articles to legal publs. Mem. Nat. Coun. Commrs. on Uniform State Laws, 1989—, drafting com. UCC Article 5, 1990—, legis. coun., 1991—; vice chmn. St. Simeon's Found., 1988-89; com. chmn. N.Mex. Harvard Law Sch. Fund; pres. Brunn Sch., 1987-89. Fellow Am. Coll. Real Estate Lawyers, Lex Mundi Coll. of Mediators, State Bar Found.; mem. ABA (pvt. litigation com. of antitrust sect., comml. code com. bus. law sect.), N.Mex. State Bar Assn. (chmn. litigation and antitrust sect. 1985-86; mem. com. to revise antitrust laws 1985-87), Am. Law Inst. (rep. to UCC Article 5 drafting com. 1992—, mem. consultative panel on complex litigation 1988-93, uniform comml. code Articles 2, 5 & 9, 1990—, mortgages 1990—, easements 1990—, servitudes 1991—, suretyship 1991—, torts 1992—, product liability 1992—), Am. Coll. Mortgage Attys., Am. Arbitration Assn. (panel arbitrators), Am. Bankruptcy Inst., Conf. Consumer Fin. Law. Office: Rodey Dickason Sloan Akin & Robb PA PO Box 1357 Santa Fe NM 87504-1357

BURTON, KENNETH RAYMOND, insurance executive; b. Ogden, Utah, July 27, 1944; s. Kenneth Taylor and Elizabeth (Tonks) B.; m. Susan Wideman, June 2, 1967; children: Amy, Kenneth W., Rebecca, Michelle, Jacqueline. BS in Banking and Fin., Weber State U., 1969, A in Ins. Sales, 1980. CLU. Pilot USAF, Wash., Okla. Thailand and, Okinawa, 1969-74; agt. N.Y. Life, Wash., Utah, 1974-80; ind. agt. SUF, Utah, 1980-82; mgr. sales Lincoln Nat. Life, Utah, 1982-84, State Mut. Assurance, Utah, 1984-86; owner Burton & Assocs., Utah, 1986—. Bd. dirs. Utah Transit Authority, Salt Lake City, 1986-92, sect. to bd. dirs., 1990-92. Lt. col. Utah Air N.G., Saudi Arabia. Home and Office: 2563 S 1825 E Ogden UT 84401-3051

BURTON, LOREN G., school system administrator; b. Ogden, Utah, June 16, 1939; s. Dale Shirtliff and Belva Ginger (Marriott) B.; m. Annette Jean Laughlin, June 22, 1962; children: Stephen, Greg, Lori, Brad, Jeanine, Becky, John, Mike. AS, Weber State Coll., 1959; BS, U. Utah, 1964, MS, 1967, EdD, 1975. Supt. Granite Sch. Dist., Salt Lake City, 1987—, tchr., coach, counselor, 1964-68, asst. prin., 1968-74, 75-77, intern adminstrv. asst., 1977-78, prin. Kennedy Jr. High Sch., 1978-81, dir. west area, 1981-82, asst. supt. west area, 1982-87, asst. supt. adminstrv. svcs., 1987; chmn. Concortium of Supts., Salt Lake City, 1990—; mem. State Adv. Com. on Tchr. Edn., Salt Lake City, 1988-89. Del. polit. conventions, Utah, 1966, 69, 71; leader Boy Scouts Am., Utah, 1967—; leader community athletic programs, 1968—; leader Ch. of Jesus Christ of Latter-Day Saints, Utah, 1959—; mem. exec. bd. Jr. Achievement, Salt Lake City, 1988-90; mem. Utah Partnership, Salt Lake City, 1990—. Recipient Fellow's award U. Utah, 1985. Mem. Granite Assn. Sch. Adminstrs., Am. Assn. Sch. Adminstrs., Utah Sch. Supts. Assn., Nat. Fedn. Urban Suburban Sch. Dists., Utah State PTA (v.p. 1988—), Utah High Sch. Activities Assn., Phi Delta Kappa. Republican. Home: 4985 S 1645 E Salt Lake City UT 84117-5972 Office: Granite Sch Dist 340 E 3545 S Salt Lake City UT 84115

BURTON, PAUL FLOYD, social worker; b. Seattle, May 24, 1939; s. Floyd James and Mary Teresa (Chovanak) B.; BA, U. Wash., 1961, MSW, 1967; m. Roxanne Maude Johnson, July 21, 1961; children: Russell Floyd, Joan Teresa. Juvenile parole counselor Div. Juvenile Rehab. State of Wash., 1961-66; social worker VA, Seattle, 1967-72, social worker, cons. Work Release program King County, Wash., 1967-72; supr., chief psychiatry sect. Social Work Svc. VA, Topeka, Kans., 1972-73; pvt. practice, Topeka and L.A., 1972—; chief social work svc. VA, Sepulveda, Calif., 1974—, EEO coord. Med. ctr., 1974-77. Mem. Nat. Assn. Social Workers (newsletter editor Puget Sound chpt. 1970-71), Acad. Cert. Social Workers, Ctr. for Studies in Social Functioning, Am. Sociol. Assn., Am. Public Health Assn., Am. Hosp. Assn., Soc. Hosp. Social Work Dirs., Assn. VA Social Work Chiefs (founder 1979, charter mem. and pres. 1980-81, newsletter editor 1982-83, 89-91). Home: 14063 Remington St Arleta CA 91331-5359 Office: 16111 Plummer St Sepulveda CA 91343

BURTON, RANDALL JAMES, lawyer; b. Sacramento, Feb. 4, 1950; s. Edward Jay and Bernice Mae (Overton) B.; m. Joan Ellen Mather, June 16, 1979 (div. Aug. 1987); children: Kelly Jacquelyn, Andrew Jameson; m. Kimberly D. Rogers, Apr. 29, 1989. B.A., Rutgers U., 1972; J.D., Southwestern U., 1975. Bar: Calif. 1976, U.S. Dist. Ct. (ea. dist.) Calif. 1976, U.S. Dist. Ct. (no. dist.) Calif., 1990, U.S. Supreme Ct. 1991. Assoc., Brekke & Mathews, Citrus Heights, Calif., 1976; pvt. practice, Sacramento, 1976—. Bd. dirs. North Highlands Recreation and Park Dist.; chmn. Local Bd. 22, Selective Service, 1982-86; pres. Active 20-30 Club of Sacramento, 1987. Recipient Disting. Citizen award, Golden Empire Council, Boy Scouts Am. Mem. Sacramento Bar Assn., Sacramento Young Lawyers Assn., North Highlands C. of C. (past pres., dir.). Presbyterian. Lodge: Rotary (pres. Foothill-Highlands club 1980-81). Office: Ste 224 1540 River Park Dr Sacramento CA 95815-4609

BURTON, RICHARD ROGHAAR, architect; b. Ogden, Utah, Dec. 17, 1941; s. Laurence S. and Marguerite (Roghaar) B.; m. Linda M., Dec. 28, 1960; children: Deborah Lynn, Kathleen Ann, Colleen Elizabeth. BArch, U. Utah, 1968. Lic. architect, UT, 1972, Ariz., 1972, N.Mex., 1979. Designer John L. Piers, Architect, Ogden, UT, 1968-72; project architect Mascarella Merry & Assocs. Architects, Tucson, 1972-77; architect, pres. Burton & Assocs. Architects, Tucson, 1977—. Chmn. Bd. Adjustment, Tucson, 1974-92, v.p. Catalina coun. Boy Scouts Am., Tucson, 1980-89, Boys Clubs, Tucson, 1978-80; stake pres. LDS Ch.; gov. Ariz. Optimist Clubs, 1981-82. Mem. Nat. Coun. Archtl. Registration Bds., Optimists Club Am. (pres. Uptown Tucson club 1976-78), Tucson C. of C. (chmn. bd.). Republican.

BURTON, RONALD ALLAN, lawyer; b. San Francisco, Oct. 16, 1939; s. Raymond Aubrey and Helen Beatrice (Parkison) B. BA, San Francisco State U., 1964; JD, Georgetown U., 1967. Bar: D.C. 1969, Calif. 1969, U.S. Supreme Ct. 1972. Pvt. practice San Francisco, 1969—; real estate broker Offices of Ronald A. Burton, San Francisco, 1979—. With U.S. Army, 1958-65. Mem. Islam Shrine, San Francisco Masons, Elks. Republican. Home: PO Box 470542 San Francisco CA 94123 Office: Ste 2000 One Sansome St San Francisco CA 94104

BURWASH, PETER FRANCIS, tennis management company executive; b. Brockville, Ont., Can., Feb. 10, 1945; s. Stanley Ernest and Barbara Hilda (Wright) B.; m. Lynn harvey, June 1, 1984; 1 child, Kimberly. BPE, U. Toronto, 1967. Profl. tennis player, 1967-74; pres. Peter Burwash Internat., Honolulu, 1974—. Host radio series on tennis CBS; Author: Tennis for Life, Total Tennis, Vegetarian Primer, Aerobic Workout Book for Men, Who Cares? A Wakeup Call for Svc. and Leadership. Mem. Young Pres.'s Orgn., U.S. Profl. Tennis Assn., U.S. Tennis Assn., Honolulu Club. Office: Peter Burwash Internat PO Box 10627 Honolulu HI 96816

BURWELL, BILL LOREN, production coordinator; b. Litchfield, Ill., Nov. 10, 1952; s. Herbert Loren and Duella Louise (Johnson) B.; m. Susan Marie Chelgren. Student, So. Ill. U., 1970-78; cert. EMT, Belleville Community Coll., 1978. Audio engr. Miss. River Festival, Edwardsville, Ill., 1970-78; stage tech. So. Ill. U., Edwardsville, 1970-78, various co., West U.S., 1978-89; audio engr. Phoenix Symphony Hall, 1978-89; owner, pres. Stage & Studio Svcs., Phoenix, 1978—, F-Stop Prodns., Scottsdale, Ariz., 1989—; cons. Mill Ave. Theater, Tempe, Ariz., 1989. Presbyterian. Home: 7921 E San Miguel Ave # 5 Scottsdale AZ 85250-6558 Office: F-Stop Prodns PO Box 9486 Scottsdale AZ 85252-9486

BUSBY, RON D., janitorial service executive; b. Houston, Nov. 26, 1958; s. Willie T. and Carlos L. (Ray) B. BS, Fla. A&M U., 1981; MBA, Atlanta U., 1982. Sales rep. Xerox, Houston, 1984-85; product mgr. IBM, Houston, 1985-88; nat. acct. exec. Coca-Cola, U.S.A., Dallas, 1988-89; pres. Super Clean Janitorial Svc., Oakland, Calif., 1989—. Mem. Black Porsche Club, Kappa Alpha Psi (v.p.). Home: 5798 Balmoral Dr Oakland CA 94619 Office: Super Clean Janitorial Svc 5798 Balmoral Dr Oakland CA 94619

BUSCH, COREY, professional baseball team executive. Exec. v.p. San Francisco Giants, Nat. League. Office: care San Francisco Giants Candlestick Park San Francisco CA 94124-3998

BUSCH, JOYCE IDA, small business owner; b. Madera, Calif., Jan. 24, 1934; d. Bruno Harry and Ella Fae (Absher) Toschi; m. Fred O. Busch, Dec. 14, 1956; children: Karen, Kathryn, Kurt. BA in Indsl. Arts & Interior Design, Calif. State U., Fresno, 1991. Cert. interior designer Calif. Stewardess United Air Lines, San Francisco, 1955-57; prin. Art Coordinates, Fresno, 1982—, Busch Interior Design, Fresno, 1982—; art cons. Fresno Community Hosp., 1981-83; docent Fresno Met. Mus., 1981-84. Treas. Valley Children's Hosp. Guidance Clinic, 1975-79, Lone Star PTA, 1965-84,; mem. Mothers Guild Jan Joaquin Mem. Hosp., 1984-88. Mem. Am. Soc. Interior Designers, Illuminating Engring. Soc. N.Am. Republican. Roman Catholic. Club: Sunnyside Garden (pres. 1987-88).

BUSCH, MARC ALLEN, computer engineer; b. L.A., Oct. 23, 1953; s. Joseph Harry and Molly May (Landau) B.; m. Pamela Lynn Hayden-Moses, Aug. 16, 1981 (div. 1985); m. Virginia Rae Klein, Apr. 17, 1988; 1 child, Nicholas William. AS, L.A. Pierce Community Coll., 1977; BS in Engring., Calif. State U., Long Beach, 1984. Cert. net wave engr. Liaison engr. Western Digital Corp., Newport Beach, Calif., 1979-81; tech. support engr. Western Digital Corp., Irvine, Calif., 1987; computer product specialist Hamilton/Avnet Electronics, Costa Mesa, 1981-84; mfg. engr. Ford Aerospace & Communications Corp., Newport Beach, Calif., 1985-86; mfg. engring. supr. Excellon Photonics, Costa Mesa, Calif., 1986; sys. support specialist Wyle Labs., Garden Grove, Calif., 1987; western reg. tech. svcs. mgr. CPU Corp., Fountain Valley, Calif., 1987-88; applications engr. Zoran Corp., Santa Clara, Calif., 1988-89; pres. VBMB Computers, Laguna Niguel, Calif., 1989—; sr. applications engr. Archive Corp., Costa Mesa, Calif., 1982; sr. network engr. Contel Customer Support, San Diego, 1989-90; sr. tech. staff FileNet Corp., Costa Mesa, Calif., 1990; sr. test engr. Toshiba Am. Corp., Irvine, 1990-91; network specialsit Unocal Corp., 1991, Alternative Resources Corp., Anaheim, Calif., 1991, Creative Bus. Concepts, Laguna Hills, Calif., 1992—. Mem. Nat. Wildlife Fedn., DAV. Democrat.

BUSCH, THOMAS ANTHONY, broadcast executive; b. Phila., Nov. 1, 1947; s. Benjamin Francis and Catherine Elizabeth (Langell) B.; m. Florence Margaret Francis, Sept. 3, 1977; children: Stephen, Kathleen. BA in

Psychology, Boston Coll., 1969. Announcer Sta. WLDB, Atlantic City, 1966-70; chief engr. Sta. KIAK, Fairbanks, Alaska, 1973-75; chief engr., asst. mgr. Sta. KNOM, Nome, Alaska, 1970-73, gen. mgr., 1975—; dir. Iditarod Trail Com., Inc., Wasilla, Alaska, 1984-90. Pres. Kegoayah Kozga Assn., Nome, 1977-85, Nome Preschool Assn., Inc., 1983-88. Mem. Soc. Broadcast Engrs. (cert. broadcast technologist), Nat. Assn. Radio and Telecommunications Engrs. (cert. 1st class engr.), Alaska Broadcasters Assn. (bd. dirs. 1979—, pres. 1982-83, sec.-treas. 1984-92, v.p., 1992-93, Alaska Broadcaster of Yr. 1986), Rotary (bd. dirs. Nome chpt. 1989—, pres 1992-93, sec. 1993—). Roman Catholic. Home: PO Box 1017 Nome AK 99762-1017 Office: Sta KNOM PO Box 988 Nome AK 99762-0988

BUSENBERG, STAVROS NICHOLAS, mathematics educator; b. Jerusalem, Israel, Oct. 16, 1941; came to U.S. 1957; s. George Eurybiades and Panayota (Kotopoulea) B.; m. Bernadette Eleanor Egan, June 21, 1969; children: George, John. BME, Cooper Union, N.Y.C., 1962; MS, Ill. Inst. Tech., Chgo., 1964; PhD, Ill. Inst. Tech., 1967. Instr. math. Loyola U., Chgo., 1966-67; rsch. fellow Sci. Ctr. of Rockwell Internat., Thousand Oaks, Calif., 1967-68; asst. prof. Harvey Mudd Coll., Claremont, Calif., 1968-73; assoc. prof. Harvey Mudd Coll., 1973-79, prof. math., 1979—; mem. grad. faculty Claremont Grad. Sch., 1971—; dir. Math. Clinic, Harvey Mudd Coll., 1981-82, 1990—; cons. Oak Ridge Nat. Lab., 1979-82. Author: Models and Analysis of Vertically Transmitted Diseases, 1992; editor: Differential Equations and Applications, 1981, Delay Differential Equations and Dynamical Systems, 1991; contbr. articles to profl. jours.; assoc. editor Jour. Math. Analysis and Applications; editorial bd. Jour. Math. Biology. NSF grantee, 1971—; Fulbright Rsch. prof., 1988. Mem. Am. Math. Soc., Math. Assn. Am. (sci. policy com. 1987—), Soc. for Indsl. and Applied Math. Office: Harvey Mudd College 301 East 12th St Claremont CA 91711

BUSH, GARY GRAHAM, research scientist; b. Atlanta, Dec. 29, 1950; s. Hubert Henry and Mary Meredith (Raper) B.; m. Freeda Charline Leach, Nov. 20, 1982; children: Joseph David, Deborah Gail. BS in Physics, Ga. Inst. Tech., 1972, MS in Nuclear Engring., 1974, MSEE and MS in Physics, 1976, PhD in Elec. Engring., 1983. Sr. engr. Intel Magnetics, Santa Clara, Calif., 1984-85; sr. staff scientist Lockheed Missile & Space Co., Inc., Palo Alto, Calif., 1985—; prin. scientist Micromagnetics Lab., R & D div. Lockheed Missiles & Space Co., Palo Alto, Calif., 1989—; owner DosTek, San Jose, Calif., 1987—; cons. Becket & Co., Inc., San Jose, 1989—, Applied Math Models Co., Atlanta, 1990—, NASA/Langley, Hampton, Va., 1992. Mem. IEEE (sr.), Eta Kappa Nu, Sigma Xi (assoc.). Home: 5505 Castle Manor Dr San Jose CA 95129-4169

BUSH, JAMES MICHAEL, systems engineer; b. Anchorage, Sept. 17, 1955; s. James Rolland and Ann (Prestor) B.; m. Donna Louise Getzfried, June 4, 1977; children: Julia Katheryn, James Anthony. BS, San Jose State U., 1977; MS, Wright State U., 1981. Engr. Lockheed Missiles & Space, Sunnyvale, Calif., 1982—; tchr. Young Astronauts, Santa Clara, Calif., 1989—. Contbr.: Surface Cleaning, 1985. Capt. USAF, 1977-81. Republican. Office: Lockheed Missiles & Space 1111 Lockheed Way Sunnyvale CA 94086

BUSH, JUNE LEE, real estate executive; b. Philippi, W.Va., Sept. 20, 1942; d. Leland C. and Dolly Mary (Costello) Robinson; m. Jerry Lee Coffman, June 15, 1963 (div. 1970); 1 child, Jason Lance; m. Richard Alfred Bush, May 20, 1972. Grad., Fairmont State Coll., 1962, Dale Carnegie, Anaheim, Calif., 1988. Exec. sec. McDonnell Douglas, Huntington Beach, Calif., 1965-72; adminstrv. asst. Mgmt. Resources, Inc., Fullerton, Calif., 1978-80; bldg. mgr. Alfred Gobar Assocs., Brea, Calif., 1980—; treas. Craig Park East, Fullerton, 1982, bd. dirs., 1982-84. Author instrn. manual Quality Assurance Secretarial Manual, 1971. Sec. PTA, La Palma, 1974. Mem. Gamma Chi Chi. Home: 6600 E Canyon Hills Rd Anaheim Hills CA 92807 Office: Alfred Gobar Assocs Inc 721 W Kimberly Ave Placentia CA 92670

BUSH, RONALD L., literature educator; b. Phila., June 16, 1946; s. Raymond J. and Esther (Schneyer) B.; m. Marilyn Wolin, Dec. 14, 1969; 1 child, Charles. BA, U. Pa., 1968, Cambridge (Eng.) U., 1970; PhD, Princeton U., 1974. Asst. prof. lit. Harvard U., Cambridge, Mass., 1974-79, assoc. prof., 1979-82; assoc. prof. Calif. Inst. Tech., Pasadena, 1982-85, prof., 1985—. Author: The Genesis of Ezra Pound's Cantos, 1976, T.S. Eliot: A Study in Character and Style, 1984; editor T.S. Eliot: The Modernist in History, 1991. NEH fellow, 1977-78, 92-93. Mem. MLA (exec. com., div. 20th-century English lit.). Office: Calif Inst Tech Div Humanities Pasadena CA 91125

BUSH, SARAH LILLIAN, historian; b. Kansas City, Mo., Sept. 17, 1920; d. William Adam and Lettie Evelyn (Burrill) Lewis; m. Walter Nelson Bush, June 7, 1946; children: William Read, Robert Nelson. AB, U. Kans., 1941; BS, U. Ill., 1943. Clk. circulation dept. Kansas City Pub. Library, 1941-42, asst. librarian Paseo br., 1943-44; librarian Kansas City Jr. Coll., 1944-46; substitute librarian San Mateo County Library, Woodside and Portola Valley, Calif., 1975-77; various temporary positions, 1979-87; owner Metriguide, Palo Alto, Calif., 1975-78. Author: Atherton Lands, 1979, rev. edition 1987. Editor: Atherton Recollections, 1973. Pres., v.p. Jr. Librarians, Kansas City, 1944-46; courtesy, yearbook & historian AAUW, Menlo-Atherton branch (Calif.) Br.; asst. Sunday sch. tchr., vol. Holy Trinity Ch., Menlo Park, 1955-78; v.p., membership com., libr. chairperson English reading program, parent edn. chairperson Menlo Atherton High Sch. PTA, 1964-73; founder, bd. dirs. Friends of Atherton Community Library, 1967—, oral historian, 1968—, chair Bicentennial event, 1976; bd. dirs. Menlo Park Hist. Assn., 1979-82, oral historian, 1973—; bd. dirs. Civic Interest League, Atherton, 1978-81; mem. hist. county commn. Town of Atherton, 1980-87; vol. Allied Arts Palo Alto Aux. to Children's Hosp. at Stanford, 1967—, oral historian, 1978—, historian, 1980—; vol. United Crusade, Garfield Sch., Redwood City, 1957-61, 74-88, Encinal Sch., 1961-73, program dir., chmn. summer recreation, historian, sec.; vol. Stanford Mothers Club, 1977-81, others; historian, awards chairperson Cub Scouts Boy Scouts Am.; vol. dir. Atherton Heritage Assn. 1989—; bd. dirs. Atherton Heritage Rm., 1989—; mem. Guild Gourmet, 1971—. Recipient Good Neighbor award Civic Interest League, 1992. Mem. PTA (life). Episcopalian.

BUSH, STANLEY GILTNER, secondary education educator; b. Kans. City, Mo., Nov. 4, 1928; s. Dean Thomas and Sallie Giltner (Hoagland) B.; m. Barbara Snow Adams, May 23, 1975; stepchildren: Deborah Gayle Duclon, Douglas Bruce Adams. BA, U. Colo., 1949, MA, 1959, postgrad., 1971; postgrad., U. Denver, 1980, 85, 90. Tchr. Gering (Nebr.) Pub. Schs., 1949-51, 54-57, Littleton (Colo.) Pub. Schs., 1957-91; emergency plan dir. City of Littleton, 1961—; safety officer Littleton Pub. Schs., 1968—; founder, chief Arapahoe Rescue Patrol, Inc., Littleton, 1957-92; pres. Arapahoe Rescue Patrol, Inc., 1957—, Expedition, Inc., Littleton, 1973—. Contbr. chpts. to Boy Scout Field Book, 1984; co-author: Managing Search Function, 1987; contbr. articles to profl. jours. Safety advisor South Suburban Parks Dist., Littleton, 1985—; advisor ARC, Littleton, 1987—, Emergency Planning Com., Arapahoe County, Colo., 1987—; coord. search and rescue Office of Gov., Colo., 1978-82. Sgt. U.S. Army, 1951-54. Shell Oil Co. fellow, 1964; recipient Silver Beaver award Boy Scouts Am., 1966, Vigil-Order of Arrow, 1966, Award of Excellence Masons, 1990. Mem. Nat. Assn. for Search and Rescue (life, Hall Foss award 1978), Colo. Search and Rescue Bd., NEA (life). Methodist. Home: 2415 E Maplewood Ave Littleton CO 80121-2817 Office: Littleton Ctr 2255 W Berry Ave Littleton CO 80165

BUSH, WILLIAM READ, computer scientist; b. San Francisco, Feb. 8, 1950; s. Walter Nelson and Sarah Lillian (Lewis) B. AB, Harvard Coll., 1972; JD, Boston U., 1977; MS, U. Calif., Berkeley, 1985, PhD, 1992. Mem. tech. staff Computer Corp. of Am., Cambridge, 1973-77; sr. programmer Harvard U., Cambridge, 1977-82; teaching asst. U. Calif., Berkeley, 1982-83, rsch. asst., 1983-84, postgrad. rschr., 1986-90, computer scientist, 1991—; cons. computer scientist AKM Assocs., San Mateo, Calif., 1986-89, prin. investigator, 1989-91, 93. Contbr. articles to profl. jours. Mem. IEEE, Assn. for Computing Machinery.

BUSHEHRI, ALI, business management company executive; b. Santa Cruz, Calif., May 28, 1957; s. S. Reza and S. Catherine (Ghahremani) B.; m. Nassrin Barabi, Feb. 9, 1985. BS in Mech. Engring., U. Mo., Rolla, 1981. Engring. planning Bechtel Nat. Inc., San Francisco, 1981-86, sr. planner, 1986-87, asst. to mgr. of engring., 1987-89; pres. CMA Internat., Ltd., Walnut Creek, Calif., 1989—; bd. dirs. Oz Techs. Inc., Hayward, Calif., Procon Technologies, Inc., Santa Clara, Calif.; cons. Xerxes Group Inc., Oakland, Calif., 1986-88. Bd. dir. Iranian-Am. Rep. Coun., San Francisco, 1988, pres. Contra Costa County, 1989. Mem. Am. Mgmt. Assn., Entrepreneur Inst. Home: 142 Del Monte Dr Walnut Creek CA 94595-1713

BUSHMAN, EDWIN FRANCIS ARTHUR, engineer, plastics consultant, rancher; b. Aurora, Ill., Mar. 16, 1919; s. George J. and Emma (Gengler) B.; B.S., U. Ill., 1941, postgrad., 1941-42, Calif. Inst. Tech., 1941; m. Louise Kathryn Peterson, Jan. 3, 1946; children: Bruce Edwin, Gary Robert, Joan Louise, Karen Rose, Mary Elisabeth, Paul George. Jr. engr, Gulf Refining Co. Gulf Oil Corp., Mattoon, Ill., 1940-41; engr. radio and sound lab. war rsch. div. U. Calif. at Navy Electronics Lab., Pt. Loma, San Diego, 1942-45; project engr. Bell and Howell Co., Lincolnwood, Ill., 1945-46; research cons., Scholl Mfg. Co., Inc., Chgo., 1946-48; project engr. deepfreeze div. Motor Products Corp., North Chicago, Ill., 1948-50; research and product design engr. Bushman Co., Aurora, Ill. also Mundelein, Ill., 1946-55; with Plastics div. Gen. Am. Transp. Corp., Chgo., 1950-68, tech. dir., 1950-55, mgr. sales and sales engring. Western states, Compton, Calif., 1955-68, sales and sales engring. research and devel. div., 1962-64; with USS Chems., 1968-70; plastics cons. E.F. Bushman Co., 1970—, Tech. Conf. Assocs., 1974-80. Program mgr. Agriplastics Symposium Nat. Agrl. Plastics Conf., 1966; program mgr. Plastics in Hydrospace, 1967; originator Huisman Plastics awards, 1970, Un-Carbon Polymer prize and Polymer Pool Preserve Plan, 1975, Polymer Independence award, 1977, 78. Bd. dirs. Coastal Area Protective League, 1958-66, Lagunita Community Assn., 1959-66 (pres. 1964-65), Calif. Marine Parks and Harbors Assn., 1959-69. Sr. editor Plastic Trends mag., 1985-90. Recipient Western Plastics Man of Yr. award, 1972. Mem. Soc. Plastics Industry Inc. (chpt. pres. 1971-72), Soc. Plastic Engrs. (Lundberg award 1981), Western Plastics Pioneers, Western Plastics Mus. and Pioneers, Plastics Pioneers Assn., Sunkist Growers, Cal. Citrus Nurserymen's Soc., Calif. Farm Bur. Fedn. U. Ill. Alumni Assn., Soc. for Advancement Materials and Process Engring., Geopolymers Inst. Roman Catholic. Moose. Author various profl. and strategic resource papers. Patentee in field of plastics, carbon and colored glass fibers, process, and applications. Home: 19 Lagunita Ln Laguna Beach CA 92651-4237 Office: PO Box 581 Laguna Beach CA 92652-0581

BUSHNELL, ASA SMITH, law enforcement community relations manager, writer; b. Springfield, Ohio, Sept. 15, 1925; s. Asa Smith and Thelma Lucille (Clark) B.; m. Dorothy B. Longstreth, Apr. 24, 1946 (div. July 1951); m. Betty Ann Hunsaker, Nov. 3, 1951 (div. July 1986); children: Carolyn, Larry, Mark; m. Cheryl Stone Cross, Aug. 23, 1986; stepchildren: Michelle, Peggi, Rochelle. BA in History, Princeton U., 1947. Reporter, sports editor Tucson Citizen, 1948-51, city editor, 1952-55, staff writer, 1962-64, asst. mng. editor, editorial page editor, 1971-83; spl. agt. FBI, Detroit, 1951-52; mng. editor Town Topics, Princeton, 1955-59; pub. rels. dir. Atty. Gen.'s Office of N.J., Trenton, 1959-62; editor Montesano (Wash.) Vidette, 1964-69, Palisadian Post, Pacific Palisades, Calif., 1969-71; community rels. mgr. Pima County Sheriff's Dept., Tucson, 1983—. Contbr. articles to newspapers and mags. Bd. dirs. 88-Crime, Tucson, 1980—, pres., 1990-92; bd. dirs., v.p. Crime Prevention League, Tucson, 1982—; dir., vice chmn. Citizens Traffic Safety Task Force, Tucson, 1988—; bd. dirs. Gateway LARC, Tucson, 1979—, Tucson Coun. on Alcoholism and Drug Dependence, 1976—, Nat. Coun. on Alcoholism, N.Y.C., 1983-90. With USMC, 1943-45. Recipient Meritorious award Nat. Assn. Secs. of States, 1983, Outstanding Community Svc. award Tucson Metro C. of C., 1984, Outstanding Leadership award Tucson Tomorrow, 1985, NCA Bronze Key Tucson Coun. on Alcoholism, 1988, Disting. Svc. award Nat. Coun. on Alcoholism, 1990. Mem. Soc. Former FBI Agts. (western v.p. 1976-77), Soc. Ex-FBI Agts. Tucson (pres. 1975-76), Tucson Press Club (life, pres. 1954-55), Alano Club (life, pres. 1982-83), Rotary Club Tucson (sr. active, pres. 1986-87), Princeton U. Class (sec. 1982—). Baptist. Home: 4985 E Silver St Tucson AZ 85712-5726

BUSHNELL, BILL, theatrical director, producer; b. Detroit, Apr. 30, 1937; s. William Harrison and Margaret (Gable) B.; m. Scotty Bushnell (div. 1976). BA in Theater Arts, Denison U., 1959; postgrad., U. Kans., 1959-60; MA in Theater History and Mgmt., Ohio State U., 1962. Press. and promotion dir. Cleve. Playhouse, 1962-63; exec. dir. Center Stage, Balt., 1964-66; mng. dir. Am. Conservatory Theatre, San Francisco, 1966-69; pres. Williams Prodns., San Francisco and L.A., 1969-75; mng. artist L.A. Actors' Theatre, 1975-78, artistic producing dir., trustee, mem. exec. com., 1978-85; also trustee, mem. exec. com., 1978—; artistic dir. L.A. Theatre Ctr., 1985-91; dir., producer Calif. Repertory Co., 1991—; lectr. Calif. State U., Long Beach; co-host TV talk show Burman & Bushnell: On the Arts. Dir. numerous theatrical prodns. including Tamer of Horses, 1986, Foolin' Around With Infinity, 1987, Sarcophagus, 1987, Cat's-Paw, 1988, Stars in the Morning Sky, 1988, A Burning Beach, 1989, Death of a Salesman, 1989, Piano, 1990, The Crucible, 1990, The Night of the Iguana (Nat. Theatre Norway), 1991, Life is a Dream, 1991, The Doctor and the Devils, 1992, As You Like It, 1992; dir. films Prisoners, 1973, The Four Deuces, 1974; producer and dir. TV programs. Mem. city bldg. adv. coun., v.p. cultural affairs St. Spring St. Assn., 1983-91. Recipient Margaret Harford award L.A. Drama Critics Circle, 1977, Spl. award, 1986, 92, The Illusion Producer award, 1990; Drama-Logue Outstanding Achievement in Theatre award 1980, Drama-Logue Disting. Achievement award, 1982, 87, Best 1st Film award Berlin Film Festival, 1974, Margo Jones award, 1984, Theatre award NAACP, 1987, Olof Palme Nuclear Age Issues award Educators for Social Responsibility, 1987. Mem. L.A. Arts Advocates (acting pres. 1979-81), Calif. Theatre Coun. (v.p. 1978-82, pres. 1982-84, bd. dirs., mem. exec. com. 1978-87), L.A. Theater Alliance (v.p. 1979-82), Am. Arts Alliance (theatre rep. 1982-91), Am.-Russian Theatre Initiative (bd. govs. 1988—).

BUSHNELL, RODERICK PAUL, lawyer; b. Buffalo, Mar. 6, 1944; s. Paul Hazen and Martha Atlee B.; m. Suzann Yvonne Kaiser, Aug. 27, 1966; 1 child, Arlo Phillip. BA, Rutgers U., 1966; JD, Georgetown U., 1969. Bar: Calif. 1970, U.S. Supreme Ct. 1980. Atty. dept. water resources Sacramento, 1969-71; ptnr. Bushnell, Caplan & Fielding, San Francisco, 1971—; adv. bd. dirs. Bread & Roses, Inc., Mill Valley, Calif. Bd. dirs. Calif. Lawyers for the Arts, Ft. Mason, San Francisco, 1985—. Mem. Assn. Trial Lawyers Am., San Francisco Bar Assn. (arbitrator), San Francisco Superior Ct. (arbitrator), Calif. Bar Assn., Lawyers Club of San Francisco, Calif. Trial Lawyers Assn., San Francisco Trial Lawyers Assn., No. Calif. Criminal Trial Lawyers Assn., San Francisco Bay Club, Commonwealth Club. Democrat. Office: Bushnell Caplan & Fielding 901 Market St Ste 230 San Francisco CA 94103-1789

BUSHRE, PETER ALVIN, financial executive; b. Ketchikan, Alaska, Dec. 14, 1943; s. Robert Almon and Violet Orene (Neal) B. BS, U. Ariz., 1967, MA in Acctg., 1971. Staff auditor Peat Marwick Mitchell & Co., Honolulu, 1971-72; sr. auditor Touche Ross & Co., Anchorage, 1972-73; sr. legis. auditor State of Alaska, Juneau, 1973-76, comptroller, 1976-78, treas., 1978-83; comptroller Alaska Permanent Fund Corp., Juneau, 1983-93, CFO, 1993—; pres. Bushre Trading and Investment Co., Douglas, Alaska, 1980—. Republican. Baptist. Home: PO Box 28 Douglas AK 99824-0001

BUSICK, CHARLES PHILIP, ski shop owner, retired military officer; b. Covington, Ky., Sept. 4, 1928; s. Brazel Pinckney and Elise (Gardner) B.; m. Elizabeth MacKinnon, Oct. 6, 1959 (div. Apr. 1979); m. Anna Bell, July 3, 1985; children: Robert Paul, Charles Norman, Lisa Anne. B of Gen. Edn., U. Omaha, 1963; M of Aerospace Mgmt., U. So. Calif., 1969; M in History, N.Mex. State U., 1983; grad., Naval War Coll., 1969-70. Supply clk. Ea. Airlines, Miami, Fla., 1947-48; commd. 2d lt. USAF, 1950, advanced through grades to col., 1969, ret., 1977; owner Busick Ski Haus, Cloudcroft, N.Mex.; project officer AWACS devel., 1973; base civil engr. 49th Tactical Fighter Wing, Holloman AFB, N.Mex., 1974-76; base comdr. George AFB, Victorville, Calif., 1976. Mem. Cloudcroft Neighborhood Watch, 1987-91. Decorated Silver Star, DFC (2), Air medal (13), Legion of Merit, Meritorious Svc. medal (2), others. Republican. Baptist. Home: 1001 Corona Ave PO Box 501 Cloudcroft NM 88317 Office: Busick Ski Haus Hwy 130 S Cloudcroft NM 88317

BUSIG, RICK HAROLD, mining executive; b. Vancouver, Wash., June 21, 1952; s. Harold Wayne and Ramona (Riley) B. AA, Clark Coll., Vancouver, 1972; BA in Econs., U. Wash., 1974. CPA, Wash. Acct., Universal Svcs., Seattle, 1975-78; acct., acctg. mgr., controller Landura Corp., Woodburn, Oreg., 1978-80; asst. controller Pulte Home Corp., Laramie, Wyo., 1980-81; treas., controller Orcal Cable, Inc., Sparks, Nev., 1981-82; controller Saga Exploration Co., Reno, Nev., 1982—; acct. Sterling Mine Joint Venture, Beatty, Nev., 1982—. Del. Nev. State Dem. Conv., Reno, 1984, Las Vegas, 1988. Recipient Spaatz award CAP. Mem. AICPA, Wash. Soc. CPA's, Oreg. Soc. CPA's. Home: 2735 Lakeside Dr #A Reno NV 89509 Office: Saga Exploration Co 2660 Tyner Way Reno NV 89503-4926

BUSKUHL, CARL THOMAS, economic financial consultant; b. Brisbane, Australia, July 27, 1952; s. Paul E. and Joyce Marie (Clarke) B.; m. Gayle Hoxie, May 24, 1980; children: Travis Lloyd, Curtis Paul. BA in Fin., U. Puget Sound, 1977. Fin cons., account exec. Merrill Lynch, La Jolla, Calif., 1977-82; v.p. Detwiler, Ryan and Co., San Diego, Calif., 1982-84; investment assoc. Jensen Securities, Portland, Ore., 1984-85; fin. analyst U.S. Dept. Energy BPA, Portland, 1985-88, Sacramento (Calif.) Mcpl. Utility Dist., 1988-90; sr. cons. Resource Mgmt. Internat., Rancho Cordova, Calif., 1990-91; fin. specialist Bonneville Power Adminstrn. U.S. Dept. Energy, Portland, Oreg., 1991—. With USMC, 1970-72. Mem. Assn. Gov. Accts., Masons, Sigma Nu. Republican. Methodist. Office: US Dept Energy BPA Bonneville Power Adminstrn PO Box 3621 Portland OR 97208-3621

BUSS, DIETRICH G., history educator; b. Tokyo, Sept. 20, 1939; s. Bernhard August and Katharine (Wenzel) B.; m. Miriam Eleanore Epp, July 30, 1966; children: Eric, Julie, Natalie. BA, Biola Coll., La Mirada, Calif., 1963; MA, Calif. State U., L.A., 1965; PhD, Claremont Grad. Sch., Calif., 1976. Faculty mem. Culter Acad., L.A., 1965-66; prof. history Biola U., La Mirada, 1966—; chmn. dept. history Biola U., 1977—. Author: Henry Villard, 1978; contbr. Dictionary of Christianity in America, 1990, Blackwell Dictionary of Evangelical Biography, 1992, Encyclopedia U.S.A., 1992. Mem. La Mirada Hist. Heritage Commn., 1976—. Recipient Charles J. Kennedy award, Econ. and Bus. Hist. Soc., 1978. Mem. Orgn. Am. Historians, Conf. Faith and History, Econ. and Bus. Hist. Soc. Evangelical Free Ch. Am. Home: 14779 Mansa Dr La Mirada CA 90638-3033 Office: Biola University 13800 Biola Ave La Mirada CA 90639-0001

BUSS, JERRY HATTEN, real estate executive, sports team owner; Children: John, Jim, Jeanie, Jane. BS in Chemistry, U. Wyo.; MS, PhD in Chemistry, U. So. Calif., 1957. Chemist Bur. Mines; past mem. faculty dept. chemistry U. So. Calif.; mem. missile div. McDonnell Douglas, Los Angeles; partner Mariani-Buss Assos.; former owner Los Angeles Strings; chmn. bd., owner Los Angeles Lakers (Nat. Basketball Assn.); until 1988 owner Los Angeles Kings (Nat. Hockey League). Office: care LA Lakers PO Box 10 3900 W Manchester Blvd Inglewood CA 90306

BUSS, SAMUEL RUDOLPH, mathematics educator, researcher; b. New Haven, Conn., Aug. 6, 1957; s. Martin John and Nancy Jane (Macpherson) B.; m. Teresa Paula Thacker, June 7, 1980; children: Stephanie, Ian. BS in Math. and Physics, Emory U., 1979; MA in Math., Princeton U., 1982, PhD in Math., 1985. VLSI engr. Proximity Designs Corp. (now Franklin Electronic Pub.), 1980-82; researcher Math. Scis. Rsch. Inst., Berkeley, Calif., 1985-86; instr. U. Calif., Berkeley, 1986-88; asst. prof. math. U. Calif., San Diego, 1988-90, assoc. prof., 1990—; co-organizer workshop on feasible math., Ithaca, 1989; organizer workshops on proof theory, complexity and logic, San Diego, 1990, Prague, 1991. Author: Bounded Arithmetic, 1986; co-editor: Feasible Mathematics, 1990; patentee in field; contbr. articles to profl. jours. NSF fellow, 1979-80, 82-84, 85-88, Sloan Found. fellow, 1984-85; NSF grantee, 1988—. Mem. IEEE (organizing com. mem. for logic in computer sci. conf.). Office: U Calif San Diego Math Dept La Jolla CA 92093

BUSS, TERESA THACKER, software engineer; b. Canton, Ga., Jan. 4, 1957; d. Paul Reed and Geneva (McWhorter) Thacker; m. Samuel Rudolph Buss, June 7, 1980; children: Stephanie Samantha, Ian Paul. BS, Oglethorpe U., 1976. Programmer analyst Emory U. Computing Ctr., Atlanta, 1976-80; contract programmer Sellers Software Co., Atlanta, 1979-80; sr. programmer analyst Proximity Tech. Inc., Ft. Lauderdale, 1980-82; software engr. Exxon Office Systems, Princeton, N.J., 1982-85; sr. systems analyst U. Calif., Berkeley, 1985-88, Sci. Applications Internat. Corp., San Diego, 1988—. Pres. Wyman Club Princeton U., 1983-85; mem. PTA, San Diego, 1990—. Shell Cos. Found. scholar Oglethorpe U., 1975-76; recipient Sally Hull Welter award, 1976. Mem. San Diego Zool. Soc. Democrat. Baptist. Office: SAIC Comsystems 10770 Wateridge Cir San Diego CA 92121

BUSSE, LEONARD WAYNE, banker, financial consultant; b. Chgo., June 29, 1938; s. Edward William and Elsie Helen (Weidner) B.; m. Gretchen Gnuam Beal, Sept. 7, 1963; children: Whitney Lee, Carter Douglas. BS, Purdue U., 1960; postgrad., Northwestern U., 1964-67. CPA, Ill. With Continental Ill. Corp., Chgo., 1963-88, v.p., 1973-81, sr. v.p., 1981-85; dir. Vectra Banking Corp., Denver, 1993—; head internat. banking dept. Continental Ill. Corp., Chgo., 1985; exec. v.p. Continental Bank, Chgo., 1985-88; cons. Busse Group, Vail, Colo., 1989-93; pres., COO, and dir. The Pacific Bank, San Francisco, 1993—; bd. dirs. Vectra Banking Corp., Denver, 1993—. Bd. dirs. McGraw Wildlife Found., Elgin, Ill., 1982-92, Vectra Banking Corp., Denver, 1993. Mem. AICPA. Republican. Lutheran.

BUSSE, MICHAEL CLIFFORD, newspaper advertising executive; b. Milw., Dec. 28, 1942; s. Clifford August and Lucille Minnie (Retzlaff) B.; Gloria Jean Olsen, June 8, 1968; children: Bradford Michael, Kurtis Mountaine. Student, Chapman U., 1960-61, Fullerton (Calif.) Coll., 1961-62, El Camino Coll., 1971-72, Cerrtius Coll., 1972-73. Yellow pages sales rep. Gen. Telephone and Electronics, Long Beach, Calif., 1968-70; account exec. L.A. Times, 1970-73, L.A. Times/N.Y. Advt. Bur., N.Y.C., 1973-78; co-op advt. L.A. Times, 1978-83; display advt. mgr. west side edit. L.A. Times, Santa Monica, Calif., 1983-85; display advt. mgr. Orange County L.A. Times, Costa Mesa, Calif., 1985-89; new bus. devel. group mgr. L.A. Times, 1989—. Author: (video) Newspaper Co-Op Network, 1990 (Achievement award 1990), Newspaper Advertising Co-Op Network, 1990 (Achievement award 1991), The Non-Traditional Sell, 1991; contbr. articles to profl. jours. With U.S. Army, 1965-67, Vietnam. Recipient Outstanding Leadership/Promotions and Advt. Chmn. Orange County Centennial Commn., 1989, Ann. Leadership award Newspaper Advt. Bur., 1990; named Regional Dir. fo Yr. Newspaper Co-Op Network, 1991. Mem. Am. Legion, Newspaper Advt. Co-Op Network (bd. dirs. 1990-92, regional dir. 1989—, pres. 1983-84, John Maione award 1986), Purple Heart Assn., Newspaper Assn. of Am. (mktg. ops. com. 1992-93, chmn. co-op coun. 1992-93, bd. govs. 1992-93),. Republican. Lutheran. Home: 3805 E Sycamore Orange CA 92669 Office: LA Times Mirror Square Los Angeles CA 90053

BUSSEY, GEORGE DAVIS, psychiatrist; b. Salta, Argentina, Apr. 14, 1949; s. William Harold and Helen (Wygant) B.; m. Moira Savage, July 26, 1975; children: Andrew Davis, Megan Elizabeth. BS, U. Denver, 1969; MD, Ea. Va. Med. Sch., 1977; JD, U. Hawaii, 1993. Intern Eastern Va. Grad. Sch. Medicine, 1977-78; resident Ea. Va. Grad. Sch. Medicine, 1978-79, Vanderbilt U. Hosp., Nashville, 1979-81; staff psychiatrist Hawaii State Hosp., Kaneohe, 1981-82; asst. prof. dept. psychiatry U. Hawaii, Honolulu, 1982-84; dir. adult svcs. Kahi Mohala Hosp., Ewa Beach, Hawaii, 1983-89; clin. dir. Queens Healthcare Plan, Honolulu, 1988—; clin. assoc. prof. Dept. Psychiatry U. Hawaii, Honolulu, 1990—. Mem. U. Hawaii Law Rev., 1991-93; contbr. articles to profl. jours. Fellow Am. Psychiat. Assn., Hawaii Psychiat. Soc. (treas. 1982-83, pres. 1985-87).

BUSSEY, PATRICIA JEAN, interior designer, real estate company executive; b. Long Beach, Calif., Nov. 10, 1923; d. Charles Davenport and Nora Augustine (Bills) Hamilton; m. Henry Dillon, July 15, 1945 (dec. 1957); children: Patrick H., Michael C.; m. Frederick Ernest Bussey, Sept. 16, 1961. Student, U. Calif., San Francisco, 1963; real estate cert., Anthony's Sch., 1982. Sec. N. Am. Aviation, Inglewood, Calif., 1942-44, Juvenile and Adult Probation, Oakland, Calif., 1946-50; model May Co., Los Angeles, 1944-45; stenographer Los Angeles Hall Records, 1944-45; adminstrv. asst. ABMA Werner Von Braun, Oakland, 1950-52, Piper and Aero Commander Sales, Oakland, 1953-57; owner, pres. Paticia Bussey Interior Design, Oakland Castro Valley, Calif., 1957—; sales agt. Peter Mattie Co., San Francisco, 1982—; owner, mgr., apt. bldgs., restaurants. Bd. dirs. 4,000,000 Coop, Castro Valley, 1975-76. Republican. Clubs: Blackhawk (Danville, Calif.), Lakes (Palm Desert, Calif.).

BUSSIERES, YVAN, supermarket chain executive; b. 1945. Pres. Provigo Inc., Montreal, Que., Can.; chmn. bd., CEO Provigo Corp., San Rafael, Calif. Office: Provigo Distbn Inc, 800 Rene-Levesque Blvd W, Montreal, PQ Canada H3B 4S7 also: Univa, 1250 Rene-Levesque Blvd W 41st F, Edmonton, AB Canada T5J 2G9

BUSSINGER, ROBERT E., service executive; b. Dayton, Ohio, Jan. 26, 1932; s. Albert G. and Louise B. (Hoffman) B.; m. Doreen L. Fine, Jan. 25, 1957 (div. 1978); children: Leslie E., Daniel M., David M. Student, U. Dayton, 1955-56, U. Redlands, 1957-59. Broker Bussinger Ins., Carmel, Calif., 1962-69; broker, dealer Esper Corp., Carmel, 1969-72; owner Esperanto Coffee House, Carmel, 1971-75; gen. mgr. Gen. Store Restaurant, Carmel, 1976-77; food svc. dir. Lodge at Pebble Beach (Calif.), 1977-79; resort v.p., gen. mgr. TransAm. Corp., Big Sur, Calif., 1979—, Ventana Inn Resort, Big Sur, 1979—. Bd. dirs. Grovemont Theater, Monterey, 1990—, chmn., 1991, 92; bd. dirs. Monterey Peninsula Mus. Art, 1990—. With USN, 1951-55. Mem. Nat. Restaurant Assn., Calif. Hotel Assn., Monterey County Hospitality Assn. (bd. dirs.), Carmel Bus. Assn., Calif. Hotel Sales Mktg. Assn., Monterey County Restaurant Assn. (bd. dirs.), Bug Sur C. of C. (bd. dirs. 1984—, pres. 1984-89), Am. Inst. Wine and Food (bd. dirs. 1990—), Monterey Advt. Club (v.p. 1985-87). Home and Office: Ventana Big Sur CA 93920

BUSTER, EDMOND BATE, metal products company executive; b. Whitt, Tex., Oct. 20, 1918; s. Edmond Bate and Emma Lee (Johnston) B.; m. Beatrice Keller, Oct. 24, 1939; children: John Edmond, Robert William, Susan Lynn, Steven K., James L., Brian R. A.A., Menlo Jr. Coll., 1937; B.S. in Mining Engring, U. Calif. at Berkeley, 1940. With Tex. Co., Santa Paula, Calif., 1937-40, Tidewater Asso. Oil Co., Ventura, 1940-42; supr. mfg. and engring. Douglas Aircraft Co., Long Beach, 1942-45; pres. Pacific Rivet and Machine Co., Alhambra, 1945-52, Pacific Fasteners, inc., Alhambra, 1951-54; v.p. Milford Rivet and Machine Co., Alhambra, 1952-54; sales mgr. S & C Electric Co., Chgo., 1954-56; v.p. West Coast ops. Townsend Co., Santa Ana, 1956-67; exec. v.p. West Coast ops. Townsend Co., 1967-82; pres. Cherry Textron, 1982-85, chmn., 1985-86; pres. Camalisa, Panama, 1965—; dir. Morehouse Engring. Corp., 1968-74, Orange County regional bd. U.S. Nat. Bank, 1969-73, First Fed. Savs. & Loan Assn., 1974-82; mem. regional bd. Calif. Fed. Bank, 1982-92; cons., bd. dirs. Airdrome Parts Co., Long Beach, Calif., 1987—. Mem. adv. bd. Calif. State U., Fullerton, 1961-81, chmn., 1971-81; chmn. Disneyland awards com., 1971-72; trustee St. Joseph Found., 1970-76, 78-82, chmn., 1982; trustee Chapman Coll., Orange, 1972—, exec. vice chmn., 1976—; trustee Calif. Coll. Medicine of U. Calif. at Irvine, 1973—, vice chmn., 1976-79, chmn., 1979-91; chmn. Community Airport Coun., 1974-86. Recipient Outstanding Humanitarian award NCCJ, 1980. Mem. IEEE, Nat. Aeros. Assn., Mchts. and Mfrs. Assn. (v.p., bd. dirs., chmn. 1985, chmn. exec. com. 1986), Airplane Owners and Pilots Assn., Nat. Pilots Assn., Am. Mgmt. Assn., Theta Tau. Clubs: Santa Ana Country, Balboa Bay, Pacific. Home: 1841 Beverly Glen Dr Santa Ana CA 92705-3383 Office: 1224 E Warner Ave Santa Ana CA 92705-5484

BUTCHER, JACK ROBERT, manufacturing executive; b. Akron, Ohio, Dec. 10, 1941; s. William Hobart and Marguerite Bell (Dalton) B.; m. Gloria Jean Hartman, June 1, 1963; children: Jack R. II, Charlotte Jean. BA in Math., Jacksonville U., 1964. Pres. Portableacher Corp., Hesperia, Calif., 1977—; v.p. Nice Day Products, Hesperia, 1980-85; pres. The Mark of Profl. Mgmt. and Design Co., Hesperia, 1983—, Nice Day Products, Hesperia, 1985—; co-owner JB Scale Co., Hesperia, Calif., 1991—. Author: (poem) Something Good, 1978; patentee in field. Mem. Internat. Platform Assn., Masons, Shriners, Royal Order of Jesters. Address: PO Box 402540 Hesperia CA 92340

BUTCHER, RICHARD KENT, sales representative; b. Scottsbluff, Nebr., June 20, 1949; s. Richard Walter and Donna Beth (Winchell) B.; m. Cheryl Ann Morton, June 8, 1969; children: James William, Shelly Rene, Sherry Rene. BS in Agronomy, Agrl. Econs., U. Nebr., 1971. Agriculturalist Gt. Western Sugar Co., Lovell, Wyo., 1972-75; farmer Butcher Farms, Morrill, Nebr., 1975-78; sr. sales rep. Monsanto Agrl. Co., Sterling, 1978-83; sales specialist Monsanto Agrl. Co., Ft. Collins, Colo., 1983-89, sr. sales specialist, 1989—; trainer co. internal Monsanto Agrl. Co., Sterling, Ft. Collins, 1979—, regional mgr. adv. team, Ft. Collins, 1987—, gen. mgr. adv. bd., Sterling, Ft. Collins, 1983-87. Author: (pamphlet) Colorado Conservation Tillage Guide, 1980 (Achievement award 1980); co-producer (video) Low Rate Application Guidelines, 1989. Coach Sterling Soccer Assn., 1980-83, Sterling Baseball Assn., 1982-83, Ft. Collins Soccer Assn., 1984-86, Ft. Collins Baseball League, 1984-87. 2d lt. U.S. Army, 1971-72. Mem. Colo. Conservation Tillage Assn. (founding/bd. mem. 1988—), Rocky Mountain Plant Food and Agrl. Chem. Assn. (v.p. 1986, bd. dirs. 1980-86), Residue Mgmt. Work Group USDA-Soil Conservation Svc. (adv. bd. 1991—), Colo. Aerial Applicators Assn., Colo. Assn. Wheat Growers, Colo. Corn Growers Assn. Home: 2212 Ouray Ct Fort Collins CO 80525 Office: Monsanto Agrl Co 2212 Ouray Ct Fort Collins CO 80525

BUTLER, ALDIS PERRIN, advertising agency executive; b. New Haven, Dec. 7, 1913; s. Sidney Perlin and Margaret Taylor (Simpson) B.; m. Louise B. Smith, Sept. 9, 1936; children: Louise Butler Johnson, Aldis Perrin Butler, Jr., Margaret Butler McKenna. BA, Dartmouth Coll., 1936. V.p. Young and Rubicam, Inc., N.Y.C., 1953-54; v.p., gen. mgr. Young and Rubicam, Inc., Detroit, 1954-59; v.p. J. Walter Thompson Co., N.Y.C., 1959-62; sr. v.p., dir. Benton & Bowles, Inc., N.Y.C., 1962-66; chmn. bd. Butler-Turner Advt., Vero Beach, Fla., 1966-82; v.p. mktg. Metapath, Inc., Foster City, Calif., 1984; chmn. bd. Livingston/Sirutis Advt., Belmont, Calif., 1984-85; pvt. practice cons. Sonoma, Calif., 1986—. Chmn. Am. Heart Assn., Vero Beach, Fla., 1973-75; chmn. ARC, Vero Beach, 1973-75; chmn. Civic Arts Com., Vero Beach, 1969-76. Served to lt. USNR, 1943-46, PTO. Recipient Silver Medal award Am. Advt. Fedn., 1979. Mem. Sonoma Valley C. of C. Democrat. Episcopalian. Club: Adcraft (life mem.) (Detroit). Home and Office: 202 Avenida Barbera Sonoma CA 95476-8053

BUTLER, ARTHUR MAURICE, university administrator; b. Osaka, Japan, Mar. 18, 1947; came to U.S., 1949; s. John Elzie Jr. and Connie Mae (Hartzel) B.; m. Celine Marie Bell, Sept. 19, 1970. BA in Polit. Sci., Calif. State Coll., San Bernadino, 1977. Asst. dir. pub. safety Calif. State Coll., 1975-81, dir. pub. safety, 1981-87, dir. adminstrv. svcs., 1987—; exec. dir. Found. for Calif. State U., San Bernardino, 1987—; bd. dirs. Western Assn. Coll. Aux. Svcs., Calif., Inland Bus. Coun. on Emergency Preparedness, San Bernadino. Vice chair City Personnel Bd., Riverside, Calif., 1981-88; chair Selective Svc. Bd., Riverside, 1980—; chair, chpt. pres. Arrowhead United Way, San Bernadino, 1987—; active Calif. Rep. Cen. Com. Sacramento, 1982-84. mem. Nat. Assn. Coll. Aux. Svcs. (dir. region 1 1988-89), Newcomen Soc., Serra Club (trustee, sec. Riverside chpt. 1985-90), Victoria Club, Pi Sigma Alpha. Roman Catholic. Office: Calif State U San Bernardino 5500 University Pky San Bernardino CA 92407-2318

BUTLER, BYRON CLINTON, physician, cosmologist, gemologist, scientist; b. Carroll, Iowa, Aug. 10, 1918; s. Clinton John and Blance (Prall) B.; m. Jo Ann Nicolls; children: Marilyn, John Byron, Barbara, Denise; 1 stepdau., Marrianne. MD, Columbia Coll. Physicians and Surgeons, 1943; ScD, Columbia U., 1952; grad., Gemol. Inst. Am., 1986. Intern Columbia Presbyn. Med. Ctr.; resident Sloane Hosp. for Women; instr. Columbia Coll. Physicians and Surgeons, 1950-53; dir. Butler Rsch. Found., Phoenix, 1953-86, pres., 1970—; pres. World Gems/G.S.G., Scottsdale, Ariz., 1979—, World Gems Software, 1988, World Gems Jewelry, 1990—; cosmologist, jewelry designer Extra-Terrestrial-Alien Jewelry & Powerful Personal Talismans, 1992—. Featured in life; patentee in field; discovery of cause of acute fibrinolysis in humans; research on use hypnosis for relief of pain in cancer patients, use of tPA (tissue plaminogen activator) in acute coronary occlusion treatment. Bd. dirs. Heard Mus., Phoenix, 1965-74; founder Dr. Byron C. Butler, G.G., Fund for Inclusion Research, Gemol. Inst. Am., Santa Monica, Calif., 1987. Served to capt. M.C. AUS, 1944-46. Grantee Am. Cancer Soc., 1946-50, NIH, 1946-50. Fellow AAAS; mem. Am. Genstones Trade Assn. Home: 6302 N 38th St Town Paradise Valley AZ 85253-3825

BUTLER, JAMES HALL, oceanographer, atmospheric chemist; b. San Antonio, June 25, 1948; s. Franklin Hall and Audrey (Chaffin) B.; m. Sherie Jean Kittrell, Dec. 30, 1972 (dec. 1982); m. Kathleen Ann Hawes, Aug. 4, 1984; children: Stephanie, Michael. BA in Biology, U. Calif., Santa Barbara, 1970; MS in Natural Resources, Humboldt State U., 1975; PhD in Chem. Oceanography, Oreg. State U., 1986. Regional mgr., lab. dir. Environ. Rsch. Cons., Arcata, Calif., 1975-79; instr. dept. oceanography Humboldt State U., Arcata, 1979-82; rsch. assoc. U. Colo., Boulder, 1986-89; rsch. chemist NOAA, Boulder, 1989—; cons. on coastal planning, wastewater use cities of Arcata, Trinidad and Watsonville, County of Humboldt, Calif., 1977-81. Contbr. articles to Nature, Marine Chemistry, other profl. pubis. Sec. Homeowners' Assn., Boulder, 1990—; mem. Supt. Schs. Adv. Com., Longmont, Colo., 1991—. Mem. AAAS, Am. Geophys. Union, Oceanography Soc. (charter), Sigma Xi. Democrat. Office: NOAA 325 Broadway Boulder CO 80303

BUTLER, JAMES PATRICK, minister; b. Phoenix, Mar. 17, 1957; s. Howard Manuel and Mabel (Jennings) B.; m. Cynthia Lynn Carpenter, May 31, 1980; children: Stephen James, William Scott. BA, Grand Canyon U., 1980; MDiv, Southwestern Bapt. Theol. Sem., 1984, DMin, 1990. Ordained minister Laveen (Ariz.) Bapt. Ch., 1984. Chaplain extern Baylor Univ. Med. Ctr., Dallas, 1982; pastor Laveen (Ariz.) Bapt. Ch., 1984-89; chaplain New Life Treatment Ctr., Phoenix, 1989-90; pastor Community Meth. Ch., Buckeye, Ariz., 1991—; co-spiritual dir. Walk to Emmaus Retreat, 1988, spiritual dir., 1989. Mem. Estrella Baptist Assn. (ch. tng. dir. 1985-86, exec. bd. mem. 1988-89, moderator 1989). Home: 808 E Eason Ave Buckeye AZ 85326-2504

BUTLER, JOHN MICHAEL, II, international business consultant; b. Arlington, Tex., Apr. 1, 1969; s. Ronald Ray Butler and Lou Ann (Owen) Malone. BA in Polit. Sci. and Russian Studies, U. Denver, 1991; student, Leningrad State Polytechnic U., 1992, U. St. Petersburg, Russia, 1993. cons. Baltic Commodities Co., St. Petersburg, Russia, 1992, Western Govs. Assn., Denver, 1992. Law clk. Bourke Jacobs Luber, Denver, 1989-90; Presdl. advanceman The White House, Washington, 1989-91; cons. Western Govs. Assn., Denver, Colo., 1993. Precinct committeeman Denver County Rep. Com., 1990; mem. exec. bd. Colo. Rep. Party, 1990; state chmn. Coll. Reps. Colo., 1990-91. Coors scholar, Milliken scholar, Woodward scholar U. Denver, 1989; named Outstanding Young Men of Am., 1989. Mem. Sigma Iota Rho, Pi Sigma Alpha, Beta Theta Pi. Baptist.

BUTLER, KENT ALAN, electrical engineer; b. Payson, Utah, Aug. 31, 1958; s. Kenneth David and Cherril (Benson) B.; m. Shauna Alexander, Apr. 10, 1987. BSEE, Brigham Young U., 1983. Engr. Ford Aerospace and Communications, Inc., Palo Alto, Calif., 1983-85; sr. engr. Boeing Mil. Airplane Co., Seattle, 1985-86, Novell, Inc., Provo, Utah, 1986—. Served in Korea-Seoul Mission for Mormon Church, 1977-79. Mem. IEEE, Tau Beta Pi, Eta Kappa Nu. Republican. Mormon. Office: Novell Inc MS E-12-1 Provo UT 84606

BUTLER, LESLIE ANN, advertising agency owner, artist; b. Salem, Oreg., Nov. 19, 1945; d. Marlow Dole and Lala Ann (Erlandson) Butler. Student Lewis and Clark Coll., 1963-64; BS, U. Oreg, 1969; postgrad. Portland State U. 1972-73, Lewis & Clark Coll., 1991. Creative trainee Ketchum Advt., San Francisco, 1970-71; asst. advt. dir. Mktg. Systems, Inc., Portland, Oreg., 1971-74; prodn. mgr., art dir., copywriter Finzer-Smith, Portland, 1974-76; copywriter Gerber Advt., Portland, 1976-78; freelance copywriter, Portland, 1983-84, 83-85; copywriter McCann-Erickson, Portland, 1980-81; copy chief Brookstone Co., Peterborough, N.H., 1981-83; creative dir. Whitman Advt., Portland, 1984-87; prin. L.A. Advt., 1987—. Co-founder, v.p., newsletter editor Animal Rescue and Care Fund, 1972-81. Recipient Internat. Film and TV Festival N.Y. Finalist award, 1985, 86, 87, 88, Internat. Radio Festival of N.Y. award, 1984, 85, 88, Hollywood Radio and TV Soc. Internat. Broadcasting award, 1981, TV Comml. Festival Silver Telly award, 1985, TV Comml. Festival Bronze Telly, 1986, AVC Silver Cindy, 1986, Los Angeles Advt. Women LULU, 1986, 87, 88, 89 Ad Week What's New Portfolio, 1986, N.W. Addy award Seattle Advt. Fedn., 1984, Best of N.W. award, 1985, Nat. winner Silver Microphone award, 1987, 88, 89. Mem. Portland Advt. Fedn. (Rosey Finalist award 1986), Portland Art Assn., Assn. Research and Enlightenment, Nat. Wildlife Fedn., ASPCA, Friends and Advocates of Urban Natural Areas, People for Ethical Treatment of Animals. Home and Office: 7556 SE 29th Portland OR 97202

BUTLER, LILLIAN CATHERINE, biochemistry educator; b. Chgo., Dec. 1, 1919; d. William Joseph and Lillian Eleanor (Kennedy) B. BS, U. Ill., 1941; MS in Biochemistry, U. Tex., 1945; PhD in Nutrition, U. Calif.-Berkeley, 1953. Assoc. prof. U. Ill., Champaign/Urbana, 1956-58; vis. scientist NIH, Endocrinology Sect., Bethesda, Md., 1958-60; rsch. biochemist and supr. VA Hosp., Diabetes Rsch. Unit, Birmingham, Ala., 1960-63; assoc. prof. rsch. Coll. Medicine, U. Ala., Birmingham, 1963-66; assoc. prof. nutrition U Md., College Park, 1967-78; ret. Author/editor: Nutrition from Infancy Through the Geriatric, 1976; contbr. articles to profl. jours. Nat. Inst. Cancer postdoctoral fellow, 1953-55, Nat. Inst. Arthritis and Metabolic Diseases fellow, 1949-53. Mem. Am. Chem. Soc., Am. Inst. Nutrition, Ariz. Watercolor Guild, Sigma Xi, Iota Sigma Pi, Sigma Delta Epsilon.

BUTLER, MELVIN LYNN, hospital administrator, gastroenterologist; b. Melber, Ky., Apr. 8, 1938; s. Markie Lane and Audrey (Springer) B.; m. Cornelia Pinckney, Aug. 15, 1959 (div. 1977); m. Shirley Bergstrom, Aug. 19, 1978; children: Markie II, Clinton, Mark, Ciaren. BS, U. Ala., Tuscaloosa, 1960; MD, U. Ala., Birmingham, 1964; MHA, Webster U., 1986, MBA, 1990. Diplomate Am. Bd. Internal Medicine and Gastroenterology. Intern U. Hosp., Birmingham, 1964; resident, internal medicine and gastroenterology Brooke Army Med. Ctr., San Antonio, 1968-72; commd. 2d lt. U.S. Army, 1965, advanced through grades to col., 1978; chief dept. medicine Brooke Army Med. Ctr. U.S. Army, San Antonio, 1982-84; project mgr. Saudi Arabian N.G. Hosp. U.S. Army, Ryadh, Saudi Arabia, 1984-85; dep. chief of staff Health Svcs. Command U.S. Army, San Antonio, 1988-90; comdr. Frankfurt (Germany) Army Med. Ctr. U.S. Army, 1986-88; comdr. Letterman Army Hosp. U.S. Army, San Francisco, 1990—; presenter at profl. confs. Contbr. sci. articles to profl. jours. Decorated Legion of Merit. Fellow ACP, Am. Coll. Physician Execs.; mem. Am. Gastroenterol. Assn., Am. Coll. Legal Medicine, Am. Soc. Law and Medicine. Episcopalian. Home: 514 B Simonds Loop San Francisco CA 94129 Office: Letterman Army Hosp San Francisco CA

BUTLER, PATRICK DAVID, helicopter mechanic; b. Rochester, N.H., July 24, 1952; s. Patrick and Mary Elizabeth (McDonald) B. BS in Engring. Tech., Northrop U., 1987. Helicopter mechanic European Helicopter Establishment, Taif, Saudi Arabia, 1978, Carribean Marine Svc., San Diego, Calif., 1978, Nat. Helicopter Svc., Van Nuys, Calif., 1979-80, 84—, Airspur Helicopter Airlines, L.A., 1985; A&P mechanic Continental Airlines, L.A., 1985; detail parts insp. Pacific Airmotive Corp., Burbank, Calif., 1986-87; helicopter mechanic Hevi-Lift Helicopters, Mt. Hagen, Papua, New Guinea, 1990. With USAF, 1972-76. Mem. AIAA.

BUTLER, ROBERT ALLEN, engineering manager; b. Weslaco, Tex., Sept. 28, 1944; s. Robert Oren and Luna Belle (Beachum) B.; m. LInda Mildred Kriegbaum, Dec. 31, 1969 (div. June, 1978); children: Kerry Amber, Robert James. BS in Physics summa cum laude, Calif. State U., Fresno, 1966; MS in Physics, U. Hawaii, 1967. Faculty Fullerton (Calif.) Jr. Coll., 1968-70; engr. autonetics div. Rockwell Internat., Anaheim, Calif., 1967-72; sr. engr. Boeing Co., Seattle, 1972-77, Intel Corp., Sunnyvale, Calif., 1977-78; prin. engr. Boeing Co., Seattle, 1978-89, mgr., 1989—. Author: Family Records of Revolutionary War Pension Applicants, 1983; composer (with others) 109 Brand New Old Time Fiddle Tunes, 1990; other folk music and classical compositions including Sinfonia Concertante in G Major, Op. 10. Recipient NSF Tng. grant, U. Hawaii, 1966-67. Mem. Boeing Mgmt. Assn., Seattle Geneal. Soc. (life), S. King County Geneal. Soc. (life, v.p. 1985-86), Skandia Folkdance Soc., N.W. Folkdancers, Inc., Allspice Internat. Folkdance Band. Republican. Congregationalist. Home: Box 5635 Kent WA 98064

BUTOW, ROBERT JOSEPH CHARLES, history educator; b. San Mateo, Calif., Mar. 19, 1924; s. Frederick W.C. and Louise Marie B.; m. Irene Elkeles; 1 child, Stephanie Cecile. BA magna cum laude, Stanford U., 1947, MA, 1948, PhD, 1953. Instr. history Princeton U., 1954-59, asst. prof., 1959-60, rsch. assoc. Ctr. of Internat. Studies, 1954-60; assoc. prof. East Asian history and internat. studies U. Wash., Seattle, 1960-66, prof., 1966-90, prof. emeritus, 1990—. Author: Japan's Decision to Surrender, 1954, 67, Tojo and the Coming of the War, 1961, 69, The John Doe Associates: Backdoor Diplomacy for Peace, 1941, 1974. 2d lt. U.S. Army, 1943-46. Social Sci. Rsch. Coun. grantee, 1956-57, Rockefeller Found. grantee, 1956-57; mem. Inst. for Adv. Study, 1962-63; Guggenheim fellow, 1965-66, 78-79, Woodrow Wilson Ctr. fellow, 1987-88, Japan Found. fellow, 1987-88. Mem. Assn. Mems. of Inst. Advanced Study, Soc. Historians of Am. Fgn. Rels., World War Two Studies Assn. Office: U Wash Thomson Hall Jackson Sch Internat Studies DR-05 Seattle WA 98195

BUTOWICK, GEORGE VINCENT, portfolio manager; b. Chgo., Aug. 29, 1945; s. Alfons Paul and Gertrude Louise (Provost) B.; m. Patricia Ann Varga, Dec. 30, 1967; 1 child, Steven George. BS in Acctg., U. Ill., Chgo., 1967; MBA, U. Mich., 1974. CFA. Various positions Ford Motor Credit Co., Dearborn, Mich., 1970-81, investment officer, 1981-88; v.p. U.S. Municipal and Corp. Financing, San Francisco, 1989—. Vol. Am. Red Cross, Detroit, 1976-86; sr. patroller Nat. Ski Patrol, Milford, Mich., 1976-87. Lt. j.g. USN, 1967-69. Mem. Inst. CFA, Fin. Analysts Fedn., Assn. for Investment Mgmt. and Rsch.

BUTRIMOVITZ, GERALD PAUL, financial planner, securities analyst, investment advisor; b. Detroit; B.A., Wayne State U., 1969; M.Sc., Ohio State U., 1973; Ph.D., U. Md., 1977; postgrad. U. Wash., 1978, Inst. for Legis. Assts., Nat. Def. U., 1978, Golden Gate U., 1985—. AAAS congl. sci. fellow, cons. to U.S. Congress, Washington, 1978-80, writer bills on fiscal budgets and health, 1979; asst. prof., affiliate in health policy U. Calif.-San Francisco, 1980-82, biotechnology analyst, cons. 1982-84, Mt. Zion Hosp., San Francisco, 1984; pres. Gerald Butrimovitz and Assocs. Adv. Svcs. Author: Hospital Cost Containment, 1979; lobbied for NIH Nutrition Ctr. Program, 1977-80; dir. polit mobilization Am.-Israel Pub. Affairs Com. Leadership Coun., San Francisco; fin., investment and endowment coms. Jewish Children and Family Svcs.; bd. dirs. Jewish Community Ctr., Jewish Community Relations Coun. Fellow Nat. Acad. Clin. Biochemists; mem. Internat. Assn. Fin. Planners and Practitioners, Internat. Fedn. Tech. Analysts, Am. Assn. Individual Investors (bd. dirs., founder fin. planning 1983-88), Tech. Securities Analysts Assn. (pres. 1990, co-dir. mentor program 1991-92, dir. long range planning com. 1992-93, chmn.-elect 1993), Nat. Assn. Securities Dealers (registered prin.), Coll. for Fin. Planning, Inst. Cert. Fin. Planners, Internat. Bd. Standards Practices for Certified Fin. Planners, Internat. Fedn. Tech. Analysts, Sigma Xi.

BUTTCHEN, TERRY GERARD, real estate company executive, consultant; b. Madison, Wis., July 15, 1958; s. Elmer John and Margaret Katherine (Falkenstein) B. BS, U. Wis.-Platteville, 1980, MS, 1981. Sr. key account mgr. Searle Pharms., St. Louis, 1981-84; reg. mgr. Am. Hosp. Supply, St. Louis, 1984-87; pres. Titan Cons., Inc., San Francisco, 1987—; pres. Ameri-Swiss Internat., San Francisco, 1988—; instr. Dale Carnegie Seminars, St. Louis, 1984—. Congl. aide Rep. Party, Wis., 1981; bd. dirs. U. Wis.-Platteville, 1989—; chmn. bd. dirs. March of Dimes, No. Calif. chpt. Recipient Humanitarian award, U. Calif., 1987. Mem. Nat. Inter-Fraternity Conf., Delta Sigma Phi (nat. v.p. 1987—, nat. new mem. commr. 1988—), Order of Omega. Republican. Office: 1275 Washington Ave Apt 353 San Leandro CA 94577

BUTTERFIELD, ANTHONY SWINDT, photographic oscillograph paper distributing company executive; b. Jackson, Mich., Apr. 20, 1931; s. William Swindt and Sally (Jackson) B.; m. Sarah Pennell, May 16, 1964; children: Sally Butterfield Klotz, Annie Pennell, Anthony Swindt Jr. BA, Williams Coll., 1954. Sales engr. Macklin Co., Jackson, Mich., 1956-58; dispatcher Indsl. Asphalt Co., Los Angeles, 1958-60; salesman U.S. Motors, San Francisco, 1960-62; account exec. Xerox Corp., San Francisco, 1962-82; owner, mgr. Pacific Coast Photo Co., Santa Cruz, Calif., 1985—. Republican. Home and Office: Pacific Coast Photo Co 280 Cress Rd Santa Cruz CA 95060-1036

BUTTERWORTH, EDWARD LIVINGSTON, retail company executive; b. Los Angeles, May 24, 1914; s. Esther (Livingston) B.; m. Shirley Townsend, Oct. 12, 1946; children: Edward, Lynne, Kenneth, David, Lorell. BA, Stanford U., 1936, LLB, 1939. Ptnr. Butterworth & Waller, Los Angeles, 1946-77; pres., chief exec. officer, dir. Fedco Inc., Santa Fe Springs, Calif., 1977—. Mayor City of Arcadia, Calif., 1968-72; pres. San Gabriel Valley council Boy Scouts Am., 1980; mem. Arcadia Arboretum Commn.; U.S. del. Internat. Conf. of Local Authorities, Am. Mcpl. Assn., 1963. Felix Frankfurter scholar Harvard U., 1936-37. Mem. Order of Coif, Phi Beta Kappa. Methodist. Office: Fedco Inc 9300 Santa Fe Springs Rd Santa Fe Springs CA 90670-2610

BUTTERWORTH, ROBERT ROMAN, psychologist, researcher, media therapist; b. Pittsfield, Mass., June 24, 1946; s. John Leon and Martha Helen (Roman) B. BA, SUNY, 1972; MA, Marist Coll., 1975; PhD in Clin. Psychology, Calif. Grad. Inst., 1983. Asst. clin. psychologist N.Y. State Dept. Mental Hygiene, Wassaic, 1972-75; pres. Contemporary Psychology Assocs., Inc., L.A. and Downey, Calif., 1976—; cons. L.A. County Dept. Health Svcs.; staff clinician San Barnardino County Dept. Mental Health, 1983-85; staff psychologist State of Calif. Dept. Mental Health, 1985—; media interviews include PA, L.A. Times, N.Y. Times, USA Today, Wall St. Jour., Washington Post, Redbook Mag., London Daily Mail and many others; TV and radio interviews include CBS, NBC and ABC networks, Oprah Winfrey Show, CNN Newsnight, Can. Radio Network, Mut. Radio Network and many others. Served with USAF, 1965-69. Mem. Am. Psychol. Assn. for Media Psychology, Calif. Psychol. Assn., Nat. Accreditation Assn. Psychoanalysis. Office: Contemporary Psychology Assocs Inc PO Box 76477 Los Angeles CA 90076-0477

BUTTON, LARRY IRVIN, food service executive; b. Portland, Oreg., Dec. 4, 1946; s. Lloyd Irvin and Enid K. (Lewis) B.; m. Gretchen Mary Illk, July 11, 1970; children: Aaron Lewis, Joshua Corbett. BS, Portland State U., 1968. Exec. chef Tiffany Food Svc., Portland, 1985-88; dir. catering Benson Hotel, Portland, Oreg., 1988—; cons. for food and beverage, Portland, 1982—. Bd. chair Boy Scouts Am., Portland, 1989-92; com. chair fund raising Oreg. Mus. of Sci. and Industry, Portland, 1988-91. Mem. Oreg. Catering Execs. (pres.-founder 1990—). Office: The Benson Hotel 309 SW Broadway Portland OR 97205

BUXBAUM, JAMES MONROE, business administration educator; b. Jamaica, N.Y., Mar. 8, 1928; s. Edward J. and Theresa (Gross) B. BA cum laude, Harvard U., 1949; JD, Columbia U., 1955; PhD, Claremont Grad. Sch., 1979. Bar: Calif. 1959. Story editor, assoc. producer Seahunt and Aquanauts TV series, 1957-60; producer Flipper TV series, 1964-66; exec. v.p. Ivan Tors Films, Hollywood, Calif., 1967-68; gen. mgr. Am. Film Inst. Ctr. for Advanced Film Studies, Beverly Hills, Calif., 1968-69; prof. Calif. Poly. State U., San Luis Obispo, 1978—. Author: The Corporate Politeia, 1981. Mem. Pilgrims of U.S., Hasty Pudding, Inst. of 1770, Phi Delta Phi, Delta Psi. Office: Calif Poly State U Dept Bus Adminstrn San Luis Obispo CA 93407

BUXBAUM, RICHARD M., legal educator, lawyer; b. 1930. A.B., Cornell U., 1950, LL.B., 1952; LL.M., U. Calif.-Berkeley, 1953; Dr. (hon.) U. Osnabrück, 1992, Eôtrôs Lorand U., Budapest, 1993. Bar: Calif. 1953, N.Y. 1953. Practice law, pvt. firm, Rochester, N.Y., 1957-61; prof. U. Calif.-Berkeley, 1961—. dir. U. Calif. Ctr. German and European Studies. Editor-in-chief Am. Jour. Comparative Law. Recipient Humboldt prize, 1991, German Order of Merit, 1992. Mem. German Soc. Comparative Law (corr.) Office: Am Jour Comparative Law U Calif Sch Law 225 Boalt Hall Berkeley CA 94720-2499

BUXTON, GLENN, marketing professional, public relations executive; b. San Diego, Jan. 12, 1953. Student, U. Nev., Las Vegas, 1988—. Owner West Coast Pub. Rels. Concerts/Mgmt., 1978-83; dir. mktg. and entertainment Paddlewheel Hotel and Casino, Las Vegas, 1988-89; dir. advt. and publicity MGM Marina Hotel and Casino, Las Vegas, 1989-90; dir. casino promotions Showboat Hotel/Casino/Bowling Ctr., Las Vegas, 1990-91; dir. mktg. Rio Suite Hotel & Casino, Las Vegas, 1991-92, Pioneer Hotel & Gambling Hall, Laughlin, Nev., 1992—; course instr. U. Nev., Las Vegas, 1990—; cons. resort rels. to Nev. U.S. Sen., 1988. Sgt. U.S. Army, 1984-88. Mem. Pub. Rels. Assn. of Las Vegas, Am. Mktg. Assn., Advt. Fedn., Pub. Rels. Soc. Am., Internat. Gaming Bus. Exposition (seminar leader 1989—, seminar program com. 1990—). Republican. Unitarian. Home: PO Box 32703 Laughlin NV 89028-2703 Office: Pioneer PO Box 29664 Laughlin NV 89029

BUXTON, KENNETH ARTHUR, educator, academic dean; b. Balt., Aug. 1, 1944; s. William Wallace and Ruth (Martin) B.; children: Karen, James. BA, U. Redlands, 1966; M in Internat. Studies, Claremont (Calif.) Grad. Sch., 1976. Tchr., theater dir. Dunn Sch., Los Olivos, Calif., 1984—, chair math dept., 1989-91, acad. dean, 1991—. Recipient Klingenstein award Columbia U., 1988. Home and Office: Dunn Sch PO Box 98 Los Olivos CA 93441-0098

BUXTON, RICHARD MILLARD, financial executive; b. Denver, July 8, 1948; s. Charles Roberts and Janet (Millard) B.; m. Consuelo Gonzalez, June 15, 1974; 1 child, Richard Fernando. B.A. with distinction, Stanford U., 1970; M.B.A., Harvard U., 1975. Mgr. ops. planning Western Fed. Savs., Denver, 1975-78; sr. fin. analyst Rocky Mountain Energy Co., Denver, 1978-83; dir. fin. analysis, treas. Frontier Devel. Group, Inc., Denver, 1983-85; treas. Frontier Holdings, Inc., Denver, 1985-86; dir. fin. svcs. K N Energy, Inc., Denver, 1986-91, v.p. strategic planning and fin. svcs., 1991—. Mem. Nat. Investor Rels. Inst., Fin. Execs. Inst., Colo. Harvard Bus. Sch. Club, Rocky Mountain Stanford Club (bd. dirs. 1982-84), Columbine Country Club. Presbyterian. Home: 17 Wedge Way Littleton CO 80123-6629 Office: KN Energy Inc PO Box 281304 Lakewood CO 80228-8304

BUYDOS, GEARY STEPHAN, television producer; b. Johnstown, Pa., Feb. 15, 1950; s. George Peter and Pauline Patricia (DeLasko) B. BA in Electronic Engring., Ohio State U., 1972; AA in Telecommunications, San Diego City Coll., 1978. Projectionist WOSU-TV, Columbus, Ohio, 1969-72; projectionist, cameraman WIMA-TV, Lima, Ohio, 1972-75; audio technician KFMB-TV News, San Diego, 1978-79, photographer, 1979-80; photographer, producer PM Mag., KFMB-TV, San Diego, 1980-85, sr. photographer, producer, 1985-88; exec. producer PM Mag. KFMB-TV, San Diego, 1988-90, producer Assignment San Diego, 1990—; lectr. San Diego City High Schs., 1988—; instr. San Diego City Coll., 1990—. Mem. NATAS (6 Emmy awards 1980, 82, 86, 88, 89, 90, 92, 93), NRA, Greenpeace, Defenders of Wildlife, Harley Owners Group. Office: KFMB-TV 7677 Engineer Rd San Diego CA 92111-1582

BUZARD, KURT ANDRE, ophthalmologist; b. Lakewood, Colo., Apr. 9, 1953; s. Donald Keith and Sonja Marie (Vik) B.; m. Carol Ann Moss, Aug. 4, 1989. BA in Math. and Physics, Northwestern U., 1975; MA in Applied Physics, Stanford, U., 1976; MD, Northwestern U., 1980. Diplomate Am. Bd. Ophthalmology, Nat. Bd. Med. Examiners. Intern medicine L.A. County-U. So. Calif. Med. Ctr., 1980-81; resident Jules Stein Eye Inst. UCLA, 1982-85; fellow cornea/refractive surgery Richard C. Troutman, MD, 1985-86; ophthalmologist, corneal specialist Las Vegas, Nev., 1986—; staff physician Rancho Los Amigos Hosp., 1981-82; clin. asst. prof. div. ophthalmology dept. surgery U. Nev. Sch. Medicine, 1988—; clin. asst. prof. dept. ophthalmol. medicine Tulane U. Med. Ctr., New Orleans, 1991; med. dir. S.W. Eye Procurement Ctr., Las Vegas, 1989—; affiliate Humana Hosp.-Sunrise, 1989—, Las Vegas Surg. Ctr., 1989—, Las Vegas Surg. Ctr., Med. Ctr. So. Nev., 1989—; assoc. staff Valley Hosp., Las Vegas, 1986—; mem. med. adv. bd. Donor Orgn. Referral Svc. Author: (with Richard Troutman) Corneal Astigmatism: Etiology, Prevention and Management, 1992; contbr. articles to profl. jours. Mem. Las Vegas C. of C., 1989. Recipient Rsch. award Jules Stein Inst., L.A., 1985. Fellow Am. Acad. Ophthalmology, Am. Coll. Surgeons; mem. Am. Soc. Cataract and Refractive Surgery, AMA, Assn. for Rsch. in Vision and Ophthalmology, Castroviejo Soc., Colombian Soc. Ophthalmology (corr.), Eye Bank Assn. of Am.-Paton Soc., Internat. Soc. for Eye Rsch., Internat. Soc. Refractive Keratoplasty (long-range planning com., alternative rep. to Am. Acad. Ophthalmology, bd. dirs. 1992-94), Pan Am. Assn. Ophthalmology, Pan Am. Implant Assn., Phi Eta Sigma, Phi Beta Kappa. Office: 2575 Lindell Rd Las Vegas NV 89102-5409

BUZUNIS, CONSTANTINE DINO, lawyer; b. Winnipeg, Man., Can., Feb. 3, 1958; came to U.S., 1982; s. Peter and Anastasia (Ginakes) B. BA, U. Man., 1980; JD, Thomas M. Cooley Law Sch., 1985. Bar: Mich. 1986, U.S. Dist. Ct. (ea. and we. dists.) Mich. 1986, Calif. 1986, U.S. Dist. Ct. (so. dist.) Calif. 1987, U.S. Supreme Ct. 1993. Assoc. Church, Kritselis, Wyble & Robinson, Lansing, Mich., 1986, Neil, Dymott, Perkins, Brown & Frank, San Diego, 1987—. Sec., treas. Sixty Plus Law Ctr., Lansing, 1985; active Vols. in Parole, San Diego, 1988—; bd. dirs. Hellenic Cultural Soc., 1993—. Mem. ABA, Fedn. Bar Assn., Assn. Trial Lawyers Am., Mich. Bar Assn., Calif. Bar Assn., San Diego County Bar Assn., San Diego Trial Lawyers Assn., So. Calif. Def. Counsel, State Bar Calif. (gov. 9th dist./young lawyers div. 1991—, 3d v.p. young lawyers div. 1992-93), San Diego Barristers Soc. (bd. dirs. 1991-92), Pan Arcadian Fedn., Order of Ahepa, Phi Alpha Delta. Home: 3419 Overpark Rd San Diego CA 92130-1865 Office: Neil Dymott Perkins et al 1010 2d Ave Ste 2500 San Diego CA 92101-4959

BYDALEK, DAVID ALLEN, educator; b. Kankakee, Ill., June 14, 1943; s. Paul Daniel and Earleen Doris (Shrontz) B.; m. Karen Mildred Gebauer, Jan. 24, 1968; children: Karin, Peggy, Gabriel. BS in Edn., Ea. Ill. U., 1965; MS in Edn., No. Ill. U., 1967; EdD, Ariz. State U., Tempe, 1979. Instr. Ind. U., Ft. Wayne, 1967-69; instr., dept. chair Gateway Community Coll., Phoenix, 1969-90; instr. Mesa (Ariz.) Community Coll., 1990—, chair dept., 1992—. Author: A Means for Individualized Progression in Bookkeeping, 1972, A Supplement to Teach Accounting Principles, 1977. Mem. Maricopa County Colls. Faculty Assn. (pres. 1979), Delta Pi Epsilon (pres. 1978). Office: Mesa Community Coll 1833 W Southern Ave Mesa AZ 85202-4866

BYER, ADAM MIKAEL, statistician, game inventor; b. Antioch, Calif., Jan. 10, 1963; s. Morse Justin and Margot O.; m. Lizette Byer, Sept. 24, 1988. BA in Math., U. Calif., Berkeley, 1985. Actuary Coopers & Lybrand, San Francisco, 1986-89; sr. statistician Calif. Judicial Coun., San Francisco, 1989—; owner Cherry St. Games, Berkeley, 1991—. Inventor board game Kinesis, 1991. Democrat. Jewish. Home: 3900 Enos Ave Oakland CA 94619

BYERS, PAMELA MCLUCAS, book publishing executive; b. Boston, July 25, 1947; d. John Luther and Patricia Newmaker (Knapp) McLucas; m. Jeffrey Olan Byers, March 21, 1970; 1 child, Katherine McLucas. BA, Wellesley Coll., 1969; PhD, Rutgers U., 1975. Publicity assoc., asst. pub. rels. mgr. John Wiley & Sons, N.Y.C., 1976-79, product mgr., 1979-83; mgr. mktg. planning Doubleday & Co., N.Y.C., 1984, mgr. non-trade sales, 1985, dir. advt. and publicity, 1986-87; dir. mktg. reference divsn. Simon & Schuster, N.Y.C., 1987, assoc. pub. reference divsn., 1988-89; assoc. pub., v.p. mktg. Harper, San Francisco, 1990-91; v.p. ops. Harper Collins, San Francisco, 1992. Campaign mgr. Dem. orgn. various state legis. races, Queens County, N.Y., 1976-84; pres., exec. mem. West Queens Ind. Dem. Club, N.Y.C., 1976-89; dist. leader Dems. Queens County, N.Y.C., 1984-86; elder Sunnyside (N.Y.) Reformed Ch., 1986-89, Old First Presbyn. Ch., San Francisco, 1991—. Named Woodrow Wilson fellow, 1969-75. Mem. Phi Beta Kappa. Home: 180 Lippard Ave San Francisco CA 94131 Office: Harper Collins San Francisco 1160 Battery St San Francisco CA 94111

BYERS-JONES, CHARMIAN, association executive; b. Elizabeth, N.J., June 26, 1913; d. George Bartram and Helen Wilder (Haines) Woodruff; children: Valerie W. Gage, Nicholas Gilman, Charmian G. Abel. BA, Smith Coll., 1934. Staff mem. Paper Mill Playhouse, Millburn, N.J., 1938-39; pres. The 99's women pilots assn., Oklahoma City, 1960—; pres. B-J's Garden Nursery, Eugene, Oreg., 1962-75. Honoree Internat. Forest of Friendship, Atcheson, Kans., 1990. Mem. Actors Equity, Jr. League, Phi Beta Alumnae. Republican. Presbyterian.

BYLUND, DAVID JOHN, pathologist; b. Jamestown, N.Y., Mar. 16, 1954; s. John Eric and Doris Josephine (Samuelson) B.; m. Audrey Jean Kline, July 7, 1979; children: D. Quentin, Lukas, Travis, Audra. AB, Hamilton Coll., 1976; MD, Vanderbilt U., 1980. Diplomate Am. Bd. Pathology. From intern to resident USN Hosp., San Diego, 1980-84; staff pathologist Scripps Clinic, La Jolla, Calif., 1988—. Comdr. USNR, 1980-88. Fellow Coll. Am. Pathologists, Am. Soc. Clin. Pathologists; mem. U.S.-Can. Acad. Pathology (diplomate). Office: Scripps Clinic Dept Pathology 211C 10666 N Torrey Pines Rd La Jolla CA 92037

BYNOE, PETER CHARLES BERNARD, real estate developer, legal consultant; b. Boston, Mar. 20, 1951; s. Victor Cameron Sr. and Ethel May (Stewart) B.; m. Linda Jean Walker, Nov. 20, 1987. BA, Harvard U., 1972, JD, 1976, MBA, 1976. Bar: Ill. 1982; cert. real estate broker, Ill. Exec. v.p. James H. Lowry & Assocs., Chgo., 1977-82; chmn., chief exec. officer Telemat Ltd., Chgo., 1982—; mng. dir. Howard Ecker & Co. Real Estate, Chgo., 1986-87; of counsel Davis, Barnhill & Galland, Chgo., 1987-88; exec. dir. Ill. Sports Facilities Authority, Chgo., 1988-92; mng. gen. ptnr. Denver Nuggets, 1989-92. Chmn. Chgo. Landmarks Commn., 1985; bd. dirs. Goodman Theatre, Chgo., 1986, Boys and Girls Clubs of Chgo., 1987. Mem. Chgo. Architecture Found., Chgo. Bar Assn., Chgo. Bd. Realtors, Ill. Bar Assn., Ill. Preservation Council, Urban Land Inst., Harvard Bus. Sch. Alumni Council (bd. dirs. 1987). Democrat. Clubs: International (Chgo.), East Bank. Office: Telemat Ltd 919 N Michigan Ave Ste 2300 Chicago IL 60611

BYRD, GILL ARNETTE, professional football player; b. San Francisco, Feb. 20, 1961. Degree in Bus. Adminstrn. and Fin., San Jose State, 1982. Cornerback San Diego Chargers, 1983—. Office: San Diego Chargers PO Box 609609 San Diego CA 92120

BYRD, MARC ROBERT, florist; b. Flint, Mich., May 14, 1954; s. Robert Lee and Cynthia Ann (Poland) B.; m. Bonnie Jill Berlin, Nov. 25, 1975 (div. June 1977). Student, Ea. Mich. U., 1972-75; grad., Am. Floral Sch., Chgo., 1978. Gen. mgr., dir. flowers shop; designer Olive Tree Florist, Palm Desert, Calif., 1978-79, Kayo's Flower Fashions, Palm Springs, 1979-80; owner, designer Village Florist, Inc., Palm Springs, 1980-85; pres. Mon Ami Florist, Inc., Beverly Hills, 1986-87; gen. mgr. Silverio's, Santa Monica, 1987; gen. mgr., hotel florist, creative dir. Four Seasons Hotel, Beverly Hills, 1988-90; owner, ptnr. Marc Fredericks, A Flower Design Firm, Beverly Hills, 1990—. Author: Celebrity Flowers, 1989. Del., Dem. County Conv., 1972, Dem. County Conv., 1972, Dem. State Conv., 1972, Dem. Nat. Conv., 1972. Mem. Soc. Am. Florists, So. Calif. Floral Assn., Desert Mus., Robinson's Gardens. Republican. Mem. Dutch Reformed Ch. Home: 4255 Duquesne Ave Culver City CA 90232-2807 Office: Marc Fredericks 8441 Warner Dr Culver City CA 90232-2428

BYRD, RONALD DALLAS, civil engineer; b. Reno, Nov. 30, 1934; s. Eugene Richard and Helen Madelyn (Hursh) B.; m. Irene Josephine Phenix, Sept. 19, 1953; children: Kevin Gregory, Helen Christine, Stephanie Irene. BSCE, U. Nev., 1960. Registered profl. engr., Nev., Calif., Oreg., Wash., Idaho., Wyo. Staff engr. Sprout Engrs., Sparks, Nev., 1960-64, design engr., 1964-67; office mgr. Sprout Engrs., Seattle, 1967-70; exec. v.p. SE&A Engrs., Seattle, 1970-72, Sparks, 1972—; also bd. dirs. SE&A Engrs.; bd. dirs. ABS Land Co.; cons. Engrs. Coun. of Nev. Pres.-elect Engrs. Council of Nev., 1992-93. Fellow ASCE (sec. 1966-67); mem. NSPE (bd. dirs. 1983-86), Am. Pub. Works Assn., U. Nev. Reno Engring. Alumni Assn. (sec. 1985-86), U. Nev. Reno Alumni Assn. (pres. 1989-90), Kiwanis (pres. Sparks club 1971-72), Rotary (pres. Federal Way, Wash. club 1971-72, bd. dirs. Reno Sunrise 1992—), Elks, Masons. Republican. Methodist. Home: 50 Rancho Manor Dr Reno NV 89509-3956 Office: SE&A Inc 950 Industrial Way Sparks NV 89431-6092

BYRNE, GEORGE MELVIN, physician; b. San Francisco, Aug. 1, 1933; s. Carlton and Esther (Smith) B.; BA, Occidental Coll., 1958; MD, U. So. Calif., 1962; m. Joan Stecher, July 14, 1956; children: Kathryne, Michael, David; m. Margaret C. Smith, Dec. 18, 1982. Diplomate Am. Bd. Family Practice, 1971-84. Intern, Huntington Meml. Hosp., Pasadena, Calif., 1962-63, resident, 1963-64; family practice So. Calif. Permanente Med. Group, 1964-81, physician-in-charge Pasadena Clinic, 1966-81; asst. dir. Family Practice residency Kaiser Found. Hosp., L.A., 1971-73; clin. instr. emergency medicine Sch. Medicine, U. So. Calif., 1973-80; v.p. East Ridge Co., 1983-84, sec., 1984; dir. Alan Johnson Porsche Audi, Inc., 1974-82, sec., 1974-77, v.p., 1978-82. Bd. dirs. Kaiser-Permante Mgmt. Assn., 1976-77; mem. regional mgmt. com. So. Calif. Lung Assn., 1976-77; mem. pres.'s circle Occidental Coll., L.A. Drs. Symphony Orch, 1975-80; mem. profl. sect. Am. Diabetes Assn. Fellow Am. Acad. Family Physicians (charter); mem. Am., Calif., L.A. County Med. Assns., Calif. Acad. Family Physicians, Internat. Horn Soc., Am. Radio Relay League (Pub. Service award), Sierra (life). Home and Office: 528 Meadowview Dr La Canada Flintridge CA 91011-2816

BYRNE, JAMES M., state official; b. Washington, Aug. 15, 1940; s. Milton Lee and Cornelia (Garnett) B.; m. Dorothy Roberts, Aug. 23, 1965; children: Burke Lee, Betsy Caroline. BS in Physics, Va. Poly. Inst. and State U., 1962; MS in Nuclear Engring., U. Utah, 1969. Registered profl. engr., Calif. Sr. reactor engr. mech. engring. dept. U. Utah, Salt Lake City, 1969-78; nuclear engr. Utah Energy Office, Salt Lake City, 1978-80, asst., then dep. dir., 1980-81, dir., 1981-82; mem. Utah Pub. Svc. Commn., Salt Lake City, 1982—; dir. Western Solar Utilization Network, Portland, Oreg., 1980-86, chmn., 1984-86. Contbr. articles on fast reactor physics, pulsed neutron generator measurements and reactor operation to profl. jours. Bd. dirs. Neighborhood Coun., Salt Lake City, 1978-83, chmn., 1983-90. Office: Utah Pub Svc Commn PO Box 45585 160 East 300 South Salt Lake City UT 84145

BYRNE, JAMES PETER, sales and marketing executive; b. Santiago, Chile, July 10, 1956; came to U.S., 1972; s. James Eamon and Catherine Jane (Riley) B.; m. Gail Diane McDaniel, Apr. 13, 1988. BA in English, Pomona Coll., 1978. Purchasing mgr. Casablanca Fan Co., Industry, Calif., 1981-84, regional sales mgr., 1984-88, nat. mktg. mgr., 1988-90; sales and mktg. mgr. Homestead Products, Compton, Calif., 1990-92, v.p. sales and mktg., 1992—.

BYRNE, JOHN VINCENT, academic administrator; b. Hempstead, N.Y., May 9, 1928; s. Frank E. and Kathleen (Barry) B.; m. Shirley O'Connor, Nov. 26, 1954; children: Donna, Lisa, Karen, Steven. AB, Hamilton Coll., 1951; MA, Columbia U., 1953; PhD, U. So. Calif., 1957. Research geologist Humble Oil & Refinery Co., Houston, 1957-60; assoc. prof. Oreg. State U., Corvallis, 1960-66, prof. oceanography, 1966—, chmn. dept., 1968-72, dean Sch. Oceanography, 1972-76, acting dean research, 1976-77, dean research, 1977-80, v.p. for research and grad. studies, 1980-81, pres., 1984—; adminstr. NOAA, Washington, 1981-84; Program dir. oceanography NSF, 1966-67. Recipient Carter teaching award Oreg. State U., 1964. Fellow AAAS, Geol. Soc. Am., Am. Meteorol. Soc.; mem. Am. Assn. Petroleum Geologists, Am. Geophys. Union, Sigma Xi, Chi Psi. Club: Arlington (Portland, Oreg.). Home: 3520 NW Hayes Ave Corvallis OR 97330-1746 Office: Oreg State U Office of Pres Corvallis OR 97331

BYRNE, NOEL THOMAS, sociologist, educator; b. San Francisco, May 11, 1943; s. Joseph Joshua and Naomi Pearl (Denison) B.; m. Dale W. Byrne, Aug. 6, 1989. BA in Sociology, Sonoma State Coll., 1971; MA in Sociology, Rutgers U., 1975, PhD in Sociology, 1987. Instr. sociology Douglass Coll., Rutgers U., New Brunswick, N.J., 1974-76, Hartnell Coll., Salinas, Calif., 1977-78; from lectr. to assoc. prof. depts. sociology and mgmt. Sonoma State U., 1978—; rsch. dir. mgmt. grads. survey project Sonoma State U., Rohnert Park, Calif., 1983-86, 89, chmn. Dept. of Mgmt., 1990-91; cons. prof. Emile Durkheim Inst. for Advanced Study, Grand Cayman, Brit. West Indies, 1990—; family bus. rsch. project, 1987-88. Contbr. articles and revs. to profl. lit. Recipient Dell Pub. award Rutgers U. Grad. Sociology Program, 1976, Louis Bevier fellow, 1977-78. Mem. AAAS, Am. Sociol. Assn., Pacific Sociol. Assn., Acad. of Mgmt., Assn. of Mgmt., N.Y. Acad. Sci., Soc. for Study Symbolic Interaction (rev. editor Jour. 1980-83), Soc. for Study Social Problems, Commonwealth Club. Democrat. Home: 4773 Ross Rd Sebastopol CA 95472-2114 Office: Sonoma State U Sch Bus and Econs Rohnert Park CA 94928

BYRNE, ROBERT LEO, writer; b. Dubuque, Iowa, May 22, 1930; s. Thomas Edward and Clara Louise (Loes) B.; m. Josefa Anna Heifetz, 1957 (div. 1977); 1 child, Russell; m. Cynthia Louise Laffoon, May 6, 1991. BSCE, U. Colo., 1954. Jr. engr. City of San Francisco, 1954-55; asst. editor Western Construction Mag., San Francisco, 1955-60, editor, 1960-76; freelance writer Marin and Sonoma counties, 1977—. Author: (books) Writing Rackets, 1969, McGoorty: The Story of a Billiard Bum, 1972, 84, Memories of a Non-Jewish Childhood, 1970, The Tunnel, 1977, Byrne's Standard Book of Pool and Billiards, 1978, 87, The Dam, 1981, Byrne's Treasury of Trick Shots, 1982, Always A Catholic, 1981, Cat Scan, 1983, Skyscraper, 1984, Mannequin, 1988; (collections of quotations) The 637 Best Things Anybody Ever Said, 1982, The Other 637 Best Things Anybody Ever Said, 1982, The Third and Possibly The Best 637 Best Things Anybody Ever Said, 1986, The 1911 Best Things Anybody Ever Said, 1988, The Fourth 637 Best Things Anybody Ever Said, 1990, Byrne's Advanced Technique in Pool and Billiards, 1990, Every Day is Father's Day, 1989; (videos) Byrne's Standard Video of Pool, Vol. I and II; editor Mrs. Byrne's Dictionary, 1976. Office: Buffalo Billiards 8492 Gravenstein Hwy Cotati CA 94931

BYRNE, WILLIAM MATTHEW, JR., federal judge; b. Los Angeles, Sept. 3, 1930; s. William Matthew Sr. and Julia Ann (Lamb) B. BS, U. So. Calif., 1953, LLB, 1956; LLD, Loyola U., 1971. Bar: Calif. Ptnr. Dryden, Harrington & Schwartz, 1960-67; asst. atty U.S. Dist. Ct. (so. dist.) Calif., 1958-60; atty. U.S. Dist. Ct. (cen. dist.) Calif., Los Angeles, 1967-70, judge, 1971—; exec. dir. Pres. Nixon's Commn. Campus Unrest, 1970; instr. Loyola Law Sch., Harvard U., Whittier Coll. Served with USAF, 1956-58. Mem. ABA, Fed. Bar Assn., Calif. Bar Assn., Los Angeles County Bar Assn. (vice chmn. human rights sect.), Am. Judicature Soc. Office: US Dist Ct 312 N Spring St Los Angeles CA 90012-4701

BYZEWSKI, MARK T., sales representative; b. Columbus, Ohio, Oct. 10, 1960; s. Earnest and Ellen Irene (Wolfgram) B. BFA, U. N.D., 1983; MFA, U. Miss., 1986. Resident asst. U. Housing, U. Miss., Oxford, 1985-86; grad. teaching asst. U. Miss., 1984-86; cook Bonanza Family Restaurant, Grand Forks, N.D., 1986-87; math/art tchr. Raymondsville (Tex.) Ind. Sch. Dist., 1987-88, Rio Hondo (Tex.) Ind. Sch. Dis.t, 1988-89; tchr. math. Harlingen (Tex.) Ind. Sch. Dist., 1989; 2nd lead Barella & Sons, Inc., Colorado Springs, Colo., 1989-90; sales clk. Art Hardware, Colorado Springs, 1990—. Artist lithographic prints The Arts Place, Grand Forks, 1990. Mem. Coll. Art Assn. Roman Catholic. Home: 2313 Lexington Village Ln Colorado Springs CO 80916-4605

CABANYA, MARY LOUISE, software development executive, rancher; b. Denver, Nov. 3, 1947; d. Dareo and Hellen Etta (Charley) Mattivi; m. Robert L. Cabanya, Jan. 6, 1978. BS in Math., U. So. Colo., 1969; postgrad., Regis U., 1985. Flight test engr. Boeing Co., Seattle, 1969-75; computer scientist Telephone Computing Service, Seattle, 1975-77; support engr. Digital Equipment Corp., Denver, 1977-79; cons. computer systems Colorado Springs, Colo., 1979-92; program mgr. Digital Equipment Corp., Colorado Springs, 1980-92; owner, operator ostrich ranch Little Pines Ranch, Colorado Springs. Mem. Rocky Mountain Ratite Assn., Am. Ostrich Assn., Aircraft Owners Pilots Assn. Republican. Roman Catholic.

CABLE, RICHARD ALBERT, manufacturing executive; b. Port Townsend, Wash., Apr. 22, 1950; s. Anton and Josephine Elizabeth (Kiesel) C.; m. Glenda Gaye Swain, Aug. 12, 1972; children: Emily Serena, Grant Michael. B in Mgmt. Sci. and Mktg., U. Wash., 1972; MBA, U. Nev., 1974. CPA, cert. mgmt. acct. Sr. acct. Crown Zellerbach Co., Camas, Wash., 1974-77, mgr. acctg., 1977-79; asst. controller Crown Zellerbach Co., West Linn, Oreg., 1979-82; controller Crown Zellerbach Co., Los Angeles, 1982-83; corp. controller Grant and Roth Plastics, Hillsboro, Oreg., 1983-84, corp. gen. mgr., 1984-87, also sec. bd. dirs.; proprietor Ragg, Inc., West Linn, Oreg., 1986—; chief fin. officer, sec.-treas. Dee Forest Products, Hood River, Oreg., 1987-91, v.p., 1989-91; market rschr. Swain's Gen. Store, Port Angeles, Wash., 1972, co-dir., 1980—, co-owner, buyer, 1991—. Cub master Boy Scouts Am., Camas, 1977-79, West Linn, 1986, asst. scoutmaster Oregon City, Oreg., 1982. Mem. AICPA, Assn. MBA Execs., Nat. Assn. Accts. (bd. dirs. Portland chpt.), Wash. Soc. CPAs, Am. Soc. Quality Control, Olympic Peninsula Explorers Volksspot Club (pres. 1992—), Beta Gamma Sigma. Republican. Mormon. Clubs: Clark County Kennel (Vancouver, Wash.) (bd. dirs. 1977-79), Portland Borzoi (treas. 1977-80). Lodge: Elks. Office: Swains Gen Store 602 E 1st St Port Angeles WA 98362-3304

CABOT, HUGH, III, painter, sculptor; b. Boston, Mar. 22, 1930; s. Hugh and Louise (Melanson) C.; m. Olivia P. Taylor, Sept. 8, 1967; student Boston Museum, 1948, Ashmolean Mus., Oxford, Eng., 1960, Coll. Ams., Mexico City, 1956, San Carlos Acad., Mexico City. Portrait, landscape painter; sculptor in bronze; one-man shows: U.S. Navy Hist. and Recreation Dept., U.S. Navy Art Gallery, The Pentagon, Nat. War Mus., Washington, La Muse de la Marine, Paris; group shows include: Tex. Tri-state, 1969 (1st, 2d, 3d prizes). Served as ofcl. artist USN, Korean War. Named Artist of Yr., Scottsdale, Ariz., 1978, 30th ann. Clubs: Salmagundi (N.Y.C.). Author, illustrator: Korea I (Globe).

CABRAL, DARIEN, economic development director; b. L.A., May 26, 1949; s. Flavio Emmanuel and Louise Michelle (Cohen) C.; m. Graciela Martinez (div. 1982); 1 child, Adrian Rael; m. Lynne Davidson, Dec. 31, 1984. BBA, Coll. Santa Fe, 1981; M in Internat. Mgmt., Am. Grad. Sch. Internat. Mgmt., 1984. Rsch. coord. Ariz. Farmworkers Union, El Mirage, 1986; field coord. Save the Children Southwest Hispanic Program, Espanola, N.Mex., 1987; dir. econ. devel. Small Bus. Asst. Ctr., Espanola, 1988—; founder, bd. pres., N.Mex. Community Devel. Loan Fund., Albuquerque, organizer, bd. pres., Artes Hispanos Del Norte. Flamenco guitarist, L.A., Spain, Mexico, 1970-78; contbr. articles to profl. jours. Organizer arts, N.Mex. State Legis., Santa Fe, 1989, mktg. legis., 1991. Levinson Found. Bus. Devel. grantee, 1990; Coll. Santa Fe Spain Meml. scholar, 1981. Home: RR 14 Box 241D Santa Fe NM 87505-9810

CACHO, PATRICK THOMAS, relocation management company executive; b. N.Y.C., Oct. 23, 1950; s. Enrique Fredrico and Johanna (O'Connor) C.; m. Marilyn Jane Ribera, Sept. 7, 1985; children: James Patrick, Daniel John. BA in Psychology, CUNY, 1976. Cert. relocation profl. Dir. ops. PHH Homequity, San Mateo, Calif., 1980-87; pres., CEO Western Relocation Mgmt. subs. Century 21 and Met. Life Ins., Walnut Creek, Calif., 1987—, also bd. dirs.; mem. Nat. Brokers Commn. Congress, Century 21 Internat., Irvine, Calif., 1991—. Mem. Employee Relocation Coun. Republican. Roman Catholic. Office: Western Relocation Mgmt 1350 Treat Blvd Ste 400 Walnut Creek CA 94596

CACIOPPO, PETER THOMAS, government bank liquidator; b. N.Y.C., Jan. 31, 1947; s. Joseph Eugene and Sistina Elizabeth (Attardo) C.; m. Rhonda Jean Thomas, Nov. 12, 1983. BSBA, U. Mo., 1969. Cert. fin. planner. Examiner FDIC, St. Louis, 1972-82, Nat. Assn. of Securities Dealers, Kansas City, Mo., 1983-84; fin. cons. Merrill Lynch, Overland Park, Kans., 1984-87; pres. Centrex Fin., Kansas City, 1987-88; v.p. S.W. Bank, Vista, Calif., 1988-89; bank liquidation specialist, account officer FDIC, Irvine, Calif., 1990—. Mem. Phi Kappa Psi (treas. 1973-79). Home: 12642 Hinton Way Santa Ana CA 92705

CADD, GARY GENORIS, molecular biologist; b. Richland, Wash., Sept. 2, 1953; s. Robert Milton and Pauline Helen (Bybee) C.; m. Debra Jean Mastrude, Aug. 27, 1982. BS with honors, Western Wash. U., Bellingham, 1982; MS, U. Calif., Davis, 1984; PhD, U. Wash., 1990. Sr. fellow Hughes Med. Rsch. Inst., Seattle, 1990-92; mem. staff dept. physiology and biophysics U. Wash., Seattle, 1992—. Contbr. articles to profl. jours. Bd. dirs. Amnesty Internat., Puget Sound, Wash., 1990—, pres., 1993—, UN Assn., Seattle, 1988, pres., 1990—, mem. nat. coun., N.Y.C., 1990—. With USN, 1972-75, Viet Nam. Fellow Andrew Mellon Found., 1992—. Mem. AAAS, Viet Nam Vets. Leadership Program. Home: 1212 NE Ballinger Pl Seattle WA 98155-1138

CADES, JULIUS RUSSELL, lawyer; b. Phila., Oct. 30, 1904; s. Isaac and Ida Frieda (Russell) C.; m. Charlotte Leah McLean, Nov. 28, 1938; 1 son, Russell McLean. A.B., U. Pa., 1925, LL.B. cum laude, 1928, LL.M. (Gowan research fellow corp. law), 1930. Bar: Pa. 1928, Hawaii 1930, U.S. Supreme Ct. 1936. Practice in Honolulu, 1929—; partner firm Cades Schutte Fleming & Wright (and predecessor), 1934—; chmn. com. to promote uniformity of legislation of U.S. for Hawaii, 1949-60, mem., 1962-66; mem. Jud. Council State Hawaii, 1966-71; bd. dirs. Universal Corp. Writer on taxation, gen. semantics, jurisprudence; contbr. articles to law jours. Chmn. bd. commrs. Hawaii Bd. Pub. Instrn., 1945; bd. govs., violin and viola player Honolulu Symphony Orch., 1930-65; Chmn. bd. regents U. Hawaii, 1941-43; trustee, bd. dirs. Honolulu Acad. Arts, 1950-51, Watumull Found., 1955—; treas., bd. dirs. Honolulu Art Soc., 1936-50; bd. dirs. Contemporary Mus.,

1967—, chmn., 1980-83; mem. Honolulu Social Sci. Assn., 1948—. Decorated Order Brit. Empire; Order of Distinction for Cultural Leadership Hawaii. Fellow Am. Bar Found. (life); mem. ABA (del. Hawaii 1950-53), Bar Assn. Hawaii (pres. 1946-48), Am. Law Inst. (life), Am. Judicature Soc. (dir. 1969-73), Social Sci. Assn., Honolulu Com. on Fgn. Rels., Pacific Club, Order of Coif. Home: 2186 Round Top Dr Honolulu HI 96822-2059 Office: PO Box 939 Honolulu HI 96808-0939

CADOGAN, EDWARD JOHN PATRICK, manufacturing company executive, marketing professional; b. London, Dec. 22, 1939; came to U.S., 1959, naturalized, 1964; BS in Mktg., L.I. U., 1971; MBA, U. Dayton, 1977; m. Wanda Maxine Evans, Dec. 30, 1975. Sr. field engr. Fairchild Camera & Instrument Corp., Syosset, N.Y., in Vietnam and Okinawa, 1964-69; mgr. Honeywell Mut. Alarm Corp., N.Y.C., 1971-72; sales engr. CAI/div. Recon-Optical, Barrington, Ill., 1972-75; mktg. engr. Cin. Electronics Corp., 1977-78; mktg. mgr. electro-optics Electronic Warfare Centre, Systems Rsch. Labs., Dayton, Ohio, 1978-82; regional mgr. Fairchild Weston Systems, Inc., Dayton, 1982-89; sales mgr. IR products Litton Electron Devices, 1990-92, govt. mktg. mgr., 1992—. Mem. Republican Nat. Com. With USAF, 1959-63. Mem. Assn. MBA Execs., Assn. Old Crows, Tech. Mktg. Soc. Am., Am. Def. Preparedness Assn., Air Force Assn., Assn. Unmanned Vehicle Systems, Nat. Contract Mgmt. Assn. Home: 416 W Curry St Chandler AZ 85224-1540 Office: 1215 S 52nd St Tempe AZ 85281-6921

CADWALLADER, FAY MARGARET, social worker; b. New Orleans, Jan. 2, 1964; d. Joseph Dale and Maria Natalie (Lovoi) C. Lic. in cosmetology, Glen Dow Acad. Hair Design, 1985; BA in Social Work, Southeastern La. U., 1988; M in Social Work, Walla Walla Coll., 1993. Recreation asst. Tamarack Ctr., Spokane, 1989-90, residential counselor, 1990-91, profl. staff orgn. pres., 1990-91, designated shift supr., 1990-91, admissions, discharge, aftercare coord., 1991—. Mem. NAFE, NASW, Profl. Svc. Orgn. Mem. Assemblies of God Ch. Home: E 1221 Excaliber Spokane WA 99218 Office: Tamarack Ctr W 2901 Ft George Wright Spokane WA 99204

CADY, JOSEPH HOWARD, management consultant; b. Dallas, Feb. 2, 1959. BS in Bus. Adminstrn., San Diego State U., 1981, MBA, 1988. Cert. profl. cons. to mgmt. Project coord. Mitsubishi Bank of Calif., Escondido and L.A., 1979-82; ind. mgmt. cons. San Diego, 1985-87; sr. cons. Deloitte & Touche, San Diego, 1989-90; mng. ptnr. CS Cons. Group, San Diego, 1990—; guest lectr. U. San Diego, 1987-93, Southwestern Coll., Chula Vista, Calif., 1990; speaker in field. Contbr. articles to profl. jours. Mem. Cons. Roundtable of San Diego. Office: CS Cons Group 3150 Sandrock Rd San Diego CA 92123

CAESAR, CAROL ANN, psychologist, consultant; b. Jacksonville, Fla., June 10, 1945; d. David Union and Helen Claudia (Casper) Richards; m. Vance Ray Caesar, Apr. 22, 1967; 1 child, Eric Roy. BS in Edn. and Biology, U. Fla., 1968; M in Edn. Guidance and Counseling, Fla. Atlantic U., 1975; PhD, Calif. Sch. of Profl. Psychology, 1987. Lic. psychologist, Calif. Instr. in sci. Palm Springs Jr. High Sch., Hialeah, Fla., 1968-71; therapist Long Beach (Calif.) Counseling Ctr., 1986; chief behavioral scientist Long Beach Meml. Hosp. Family Practice, 1987-90; owner Carol Ann R. Caesar Psychologist, Seal Beach, Calif., 1989—; psychoanalyst St. Mary Med. Ctr., Long Beach, 1987-90; bd. dirs. Long Beach chpt. Am. Heart Assn. Bd. dirs. House for Abuse Children/Women, Long Beach, 1987-88, Am. Cancer Soc., Long Beach, 1989-90; officer, bd. dirs. Family Svcs., Long Beach, 1988-89. Mem. APA, Calif. Psychol. Assn., Fla. Oceanographic Soc., Indian River Plantation Soc., South Fla. Humane soc., Stuart Animal Shelter, Long Beach Psychol. Assn., Long Beach Yacht Club, Olo Ranch Country Club. LDS. Home: 110 Ocean Ave Seal Beach CA 90740-6027 Office: Ste 200 550 Pacific Coast Hwy Seal Beach CA 90740-6336

CAFFERKY, MICHAEL EDWIN, health services marketing professional; b. Clarkston, Wash., Feb. 28, 1950; s. Allan Brian Cafferky and Josephine Lois Vickery Wilcott; m. Marlene Bertha Anderson, Dec. 29, 1974; children: Bryan, Nolan. BA, Atlantic Union Coll., South Lancaster, Mass., 1973; MDiv, Andrews U., 1978; MPH, Loma Linda U., 1979; PhD, Southwest U., New Orleans, 1991. Pastor, health educator Ohio Conf. of SDA, Mt. Vernon, Ohio, 1979-82; asst. dir. community health Kettering (Ohio) Med. Ctr., 1983-85, mktg. info. mgr., 1986; pres., founder Advance Mktg. Group, Upland, Calif., 1987-88; dir. mktg. Doctors' Hosp. of Montclair, Calif., 1988-89; dir. bus. devel. Pacific Hosp. of Long Beach, Calif., 1989—; cons. in field; adj. faculty U. Laverne, Calif., 1987-88. Author: Patients Build Your Practice: Word of Mouth Marketing for Healthcare Practitioner, 1993. Vol. Radio Amateur Civil Emergency Svc., Fontana, Calif., 1991—; adv. bd. Interfaith Action for Aging, Long Beach, 1992—; treas. Wrigley Village Bus. Assn., Long Beach, 1992; co-chair mktg. Long Beach Bus. Beautiful, 1992. Recipient Medallion award Nat. Philanthropy Day L.A., 1992. Mem. Am. Coll. Healthcare Execs., Am. Hosp. Assn., Am. Mktg. Assn., Healthcare Execs. of So. Calif., Long Beach C. of C. Home: 14031 Champlain Ct Fontana CA 92336-3502 Office: Pacific Hosp of Long Beach 2776 Pacific Ave Long Beach CA 90806

CAFFREY, AUGUSTINE JOSEPH, physicist; b. Lawrence, Mass., June 29, 1948; s. Andrew Augustine and Evelyn Frances (White) C.; m. Adele Pauline Boison, Aug. 3, 1974; children: David J., Anna M. AB, Holy Cross Coll., Worcester, Mass., 1973; MA, Johns Hopkins U., 1977, PhD, 1987. Sr. scientist EG&G Idaho, Inc., Idaho Falls, 1980—. Contbr. articles to profl. jours. Sgt. U.S. Army, 1969-71. Recipient R&D-100 award R&D mag., 1992. Mem. IEEE, Am. Physical Soc., Am. Assn. Physics Tchrs., N.Y. Acad. Scis. Office: EG & G Idaho Inc PO Box 1625 Idaho Falls ID 83415-2114

CAFLISCH, RUSSEL EDWARD, mathematics educator; b. Charleston, W.Va., Apr. 29, 1954; s. Edward George and Dorothy Gail (Barrett) C.; m. Margo Thole, June 2, 1984. BS, Mich. State U., 1975; MS, NYU, 1977, PhD, 1978. Vis. mem. faculty NYU, 1978-79, asst. prof., 1983-84, assoc. prof., 1984-88, prof., 1988-89; asst. prof. Stanford (Calif.) U., 1979-82; prof. UCLA, 1989—; cons. Naval Studies Bd., Washington, 1990, Inst. for Def. Analyses, Alexandria, Va., 1985-90; prin. investigator URI Ctr. for Analysis of Heterogeneous and Nonlinear Media, N.Y.C., 1986-89. Alfred P. Sloan rsch. fellow, 1984-89, Hertz grad. fellow, 1975-78. Home: 1146 Embury St Pacific Palisades CA 90272 Office: UCLA Math Dept Los Angeles CA 90024

CAGLIERO, GIORGIO, computer company executive; b. Torino, Italy, May 22, 1952; came to U.S., 1991; s. Giovanni and Teresa (Carminati) C.; m. Laura Allori, Oct. 28, 1978; 1 child, Federica. BS in Physics, Liceo Segre, Torino, 1970; M in Electronics, Politecni, Politecnico, Torino, 1975; postgrad. in bus. administrn., Unione Industriale, Torino, 1987. Registered profl. electronic engr. System engr. S.I.A. Panavia, Torino, 1975-76; pvt. practice systems cons., 1976-77; founder, pres. Spin Engring., Torino, 1977-80; founder, CEO Infos SpA, Torino, Dusseldorf, Paris, Barcelona, 1978-90; founder, pres. I.T. Ptnrs., Inc., Carlsbad, Calif., 1991—; pres. GLF Corp., Carlsbad, 1991—, Albatross Inc., Henderson, Nev., 1991—. Home: 4353 Citrus Dr Fallbrook CA 92028

CAHILL, RICHARD FREDERICK, lawyer; b. Columbus, Nebr., June 18, 1953; s. Donald Francis and Hazel Fredeline (Garbers) C.; m. Helen Marie Girard, Dec. 4, 1982; children: Jacqueline Michelle, Catherine Elizabeth, Marc Alexander. Student, Worcester Coll., Oxford, 1973; BA with highest honors, UCLA, 1975; JD, U. Notre Dame, 1978. Bar: Calif. 1978, U.S. Dist. Ct. (ea. dist.) Calif. 1978, U.S. Dist. Ct. (cen. dist.) Calif. 1983, U.S. Dist. Ct. (so. dist.) Calif. 1992, U.S. Ct. Appeals (9th cir.) 1992. Dep. dist. atty. Tulare County Dist. Atty., Visalia, Calif., 1978-81; staff atty. Supreme Ct. of Nev., Carson City, 1981-83; assoc. Acret & Perochet, Brentwood, Calif., 1983-84, Thelen, Marrin, Johnson & Bridges, L.A., 1984-89; ptnr. Linton, Cushman & Hammond, Pasadena, Calif., 1989—. Mem. Pasadena Bar Assn., L.A. County Bar Assn., Assn. So. Calif. Defense Counsel, Notre Dame Legal Aid and Defender Assn. (assoc. dir.), Assn. Southern Calif. Defense Counsel, Phi Beta Kappa, Phi Alpha Delta (charter, v.p. 1977-78), Pi Gamma Mu, Phi Alpha Theta (charter pres. 1973-74), Phi Eta Sigma, Sigma Chi. Republican. Roman Catholic. Home: 2015 Fox Ridge Dr Pasadena CA 91107-1009 Office: Linton Cushman & Hammond 180 S Lake Ave Ste 540 Pasadena CA 91101-2683

CAHN, MATTHEW ALAN, political scientist, educator; b. L.A., 1961; s. Donald and Rosalyn Cahn. BA, U. Calif., Berkeley, 1987; MA, U. So. Calif., L.A., 1988, PhD, 1991. Lectr. San Francisco State U., 1989-90, San Jose (Calif.) State U., 1989-91, U. San Francisco, 1990-91; prof. Calif. State U., Northridge, 1991—. Author: Environmental Deceptions, 1993; co-author: Western Governments and Environmental Policy, 1991. Mem. Amnesty Internat.; bd. dirs. AIDS Care Inc. Haynes fellow Haynes Found., 1989-90. Mem. ACLU, Western Polit. Sci. Assn., Am. Polit. Sci. Assn., Sierra Club.

CAHN, ROBERT NATHAN, physicist; b. N.Y.C., Dec. 20, 1944; s. Alan L. and Beatrice (Geballe) C.; m. Frances C. Miller, Aug. 22, 1965; children: Deborah, Sarah. BA, Harvard U., 1966; PhD, U. Calif., Berkeley, 1972. Rsch. assoc. Stanford (Calif.) Linear Accelerator Ctr., 1972-73; rsch. asst. prof. U. Wash., Seattle, 1973-76; asst. prof. U. Mich., Ann Arbor, 1976-78; assoc. rsch. prof. U. Calif., Davis, 1978-79; sr. staff physicist Lawrence Berkeley Lab., 1979-91, div. dir., 1991—. Author: Semi Simple Lie Algebras and Their Representations, 1984; co-author: Experimental Foundations of Particle Physics, 1989. Fellow Am. Phys. Soc. (sec., treas. div. of particles and fields 1992—).

CAILLIET, MARCEL EMILE, artist, educator; b. Dijon, France, Sept. 8, 1914; came to U.S., 1926; s. Lucien and Valentine Marguerite (Thome) C.; m. Helene Amoy, May 20, 1940 (dec. Feb. 1986); m. Dorothy Kirk Frederick, Nov. 30, 1986; children: Jon, Michelle, Lorella. BS, Villanova U., 1938; BA, U. So. Calif., 1940, MFA, 1941. Cert. tchr. fine arts. V.p. Far East ops. Grolier, Inc., N.Y.C., 1948-62; tchr./lectr. pvt. studio/sch., Honolulu, 1962-70; sales mgr., v.p. United Realty, Inc., Honolulu, 1970-80; painter, lectr. pvt. studio, Honolulu, 1980—. Executed 8 murals in Ct. of the Flowers, San Francisco Exposition, 1930; exhibited in one-man shows and travelling exhbns.; numerous paintings in pvt. collections worldwide. Lt. USN, 1941-46, PTO. Mem. Windward Artists Guild (Hawaii), Cercle Francais (Hawaii). Roman Catholic. Home and Office: 411 Dune Cir Kailua HI 96734

CAIN, PATRICIA JEAN, accountant; b. Decatur, Ill., Sept. 28, 1931; d. Paul George and Jean Margaret (Horne) Jacka; m. Dan Louis Cain, July 12, 1952; children: Mary Ann, Timothy George, Paul Louis. Student, U. Mich., 1949-52, Pasadena (Calif.) City Coll., 1975-76; BS in Acctg., Calif. State U., L.A., 1977, MBA, 1978; M in Taxation, Golden Gate U., Los Angeles, 1988; Diploma in Pastry, Hotel Ritz, Paris, 1991. CPA, Calif.; cert. personal fin. planner; cert. advanced fin. planner. Tax supr. Stonefield & Josephson, L.A., 1979-87; chief fin. officer Loubella Extendables, Inc., L.A., 1987—; participant program in bus. ethics U. So. Calif., L.A., 1986; trainer for A-Plus in house tax Arthur Andersen & Co., 1989-90; instr. Becker CPA Rev. Course, 1989—. Bd. dirs. Sierra Madre coun. Girl Scouts U.S.A., 1968-73, treas., 1973-75, nat. del., 1975; mem. Town Hall, L.A., 1987—, L.A. Bus. Forum, 1991—. Listed as one of top six tax experts in L.A. by Money mag., 1987. Mem. AICPA (chair nat. tax teleconf. 1988), Am. Women's Soc. CPAs (bd. dirs. 1986-87, v.p. 1987-90), Calif. Soc. CPAs (chair free tax assistance program 1983-85, high road com. 1985-86, chair pub. rels. com. 1985-89, microcomputer users discussion group taxation com., fin. com./speaker computer show and conf. 1987—, planning com. and speaker San Francisco Tax and Microcomputer show 1988, state com. on taxation 1991—, speaker Tax Update 1992, dir. L.A. chpt.), Internat. Arabian Horse Assn., Wrightwood Country Club, Beta Alpha Psi. Democrat. Episcopalian. Home: 3715 Fairmeade Rd Pasadena CA 91107-3048 Office: Loubella Extendables Inc 5540 Harbor St Commerce CA 90040

CAIN, VIRGINIA HARTIGAN, retired judicial educator, consultant; b. Bklyn., May 1, 1922; d. James Gerard and H. Virginia (Williams) Hartigan; m. Edmund Joseph Cain, Dec. 3, 1944; children: Edmund Joseph III, Mary Ellen McMullen, James Michael. AB, NYU, 1943; MEd, U. Del., 1963; postgrad., U. Nev., 1972. Personnel counselor R & D Labs., Ft. Monmouth, N.J., 1943-47; elem. and secondary tchr. and counselor Reno, 1968-73; dir. children in placement project Nat. Coun. Juvenile and Family Ct. Judges, Reno, 1974-76; asst. tng. dir. Nat. Coll. Juvenile Justice, Reno, 1976-80, curriculum dir., 1980-83, child support enforcement project dir., 1983-86; cons. juvenile and family law Reno, 1987—; adj. asst. prof. U. Nev., Reno; mem. adv. bd. Com. To Aid Abused Women, Nat. Assn. Family Counselors in Juvenile Ct., 1981-82; del.-at-large White House Conf. on Families, 1980; mem. Gov.'s Adv. Com. on Youth, 1985—; mem. Washoe County Adv. Bd. Human Services, 1987—. Author numerous poems. Co-chair Nev. Friends of Gov.'s Mansion, 1989; mem. Nev. Gov.'s Commn. on Status of Women, 1966-70, 72-81; del. Nat. Dem. Convs., 1970, 72, 80, 92; Dem. chmn. Nev. chpt. ERA, 1980-82; mem. Dem. Nat. Com., 1980-82, 1990—, Assn. State Dem. Chairs, exec. bd., Dem. Task Force Orgn.; mem. platform accountability commn., 1982; 1st vice chmn. Nev. Dem. Com., 1980-82, ; mem. exec. bd. Cen. Com., 1988—; coord. Nev. Women for Clinton/Gore, 1992, No. Nev. for Clinton/Gore; mem. No. Nev. Chairwoman for Clinton/Gore; Dem. 1st vice chair State of Nev., 1980-84, 90-95; mem. adv. bd. Mental Health Assn. Nev., 1966-72; mem. Nev. Gov.'s Commn. on Girl's Tng. Sch., 1972-76; mem. exec. com. Washoe County Dem. Central Com., 1966-80; Nev. mem. Compliance Rev. Commn., 1972-76; mem. Nev. Charter Com., 1972-74; No. Nev. Coord. for Senator Edward Kennedy, 1979-80, Gov. of Nev., 1972; active campaign worker for Adlai Stevenson, John F. Kennedy, Jimmy Carter; bd. dirs. United Way No. Nev., Planned Parenthood Nev.; mem. Nat. Com. for Support Pub. Schs.; mem. Sr. Citizens Adv. Bd. Washoe County; former chmn. early childhood edn. and legis. com. Del. PTA Bd.; former mem. adv. bd. Washoe Assn. For Mentally Retarded; co-program chmn. 21st Ann. South Pacific Regional Conf., Child Welfare League Am.- Nat. Coun. Juvenile Ct. Judges, 1976; numerous other civic polit. activities; elected 1st vice chair Nev. Dem. State Com.; mem. Dem. Nat. Com.; apptd. Washoe County Adv. Bd. Human Rels. and Svcs. Recipient Woman of Achievement award Nevada Women's Fund, 1993, various service and profl. awards. Mem. AAUW, LWV, NEA, Internat. Soc. Family Law, Children's Def. Fund, Women's Polit. Caucus, Nat. Women's Polit. Caucus, Nat. Assn. Counsel for Children, Nat. Assn. State Dem. Chairs (presdl. elector 1992, treas. 1993), Reno Bus. and Profl. Women (legis. chmn.), Nev. Art Gallery, Croesus Corp. Investment Club (pres.), Nat. Jud. Educators Assn., Univ. Club. Nev. Faculty Wives, Caughlin Club. Roman Catholic. Home: 3710 Clover Way Reno NV 89509-5246

CAINE, CAROL WHITACRE, business owner; b. Vandergrift, Pa., Mar. 14, 1925; d. Guy Alvin and Genevra Madeline (Lash) Whitacre; m. Charles Clyde Caine, Dec. 27, 1948; children: Christopher, Charles Lash. BS, Ohio State U., 1951. Part-time med. and x-ray technician Internal Medicine Lab., 1950-70; co-owner Transceiver Ctrs. of Columbus, Ohio, 1968-79, PIP Printing, Cheyenne, Wyo., 1981—. Mem. AAUW (bd. dirs. Cheyenne chpt. 1984-86), Wyo. Media Profls., Am. Soc. Radiol. Technologists, Am. Soc. Med. Tech., Nat. Fedn. Press Women, Zonta (bd. dirs. Cheyenne chpt. 1988-92), Order of Eastern Star, Alpha Phi (life). Home: 3304 Sunrise Hills Dr Cheyenne WY 82009-4528 Office: PIP Printing 1718 Capitol Ave Cheyenne WY 82001-4528

CAINE, STEPHEN HOWARD, data processing executive; b. Washington, Feb. 11, 1941; s. Walter E. and Jeanette (Wenborne) C. Student Calif. Inst. Tech., 1958-62. Sr. programmer Calif. Inst. Tech., Pasadena, 1962-65, mgr. systems programming, 1965-69, mgr. programming, 1969-70; pres. Caine, Farber & Gordon, Inc., Pasadena, 1970—; lectr. applied sci. Calif. Inst. Tech., Pasadena, 1965-71, vis. assoc. elec. engring., 1976, vis. assoc. computer sci., 1976-84. Dir. San Gabriel Valley Learning Ctrs., 1992—. Mem. Pasadena Tournament of Roses Assn., 1976—. Mem. AAAS, Nat. Assn. Corrosion Engrs., Am. Ordnance Assn., Assn. Computing Machinery, Athanaeum Club (Pasadena), Houston Club. Home: 77 Patrician Way Pasadena CA 91105-1039

CAINES, KENNETH L.D., management consulting executive; b. N.Y.C.; s. Clarence and Monica C.; BS in Psychology and Sociology, NYU; postgrad. Calif. State Coll., UCLA, ; m. Josephine A. Robinson. pres. People Oriented Systems, Santa Ana, Calif., 1969—; v.p. Band Aide, 1984-87; dir. Joken Human Factors Assocs 1967-76. lectr. civil and social systems U. Calif.-Irvine, 1970-71. V.p. tech. adv. com. on testing Calif. Fair Employment Practices Commn., 1967-71; mem. U. Calif. at Irvine-Project 21 Com. on Population Growth, 1971-72; pres. Orange YMCA, 1973; mem. exec. bd. Orange County coun. Boy Scouts Am., 1970-73; mem. Orange County Grand Jury, 1980-81. Mem. Orange Planning Commn., 1973-76. Bd. dirs. Orange County United Way, 1971-73, Orange County Community Housing Corp., 1986—. Served with USAAF. Named Citizen of Year Orange YMCA, 1972. Mem. IEEE, Am. Mgmt. Assn., Serenity Foster Care Homes (treas.), Assn. Profl. Cons. Office: People Oriented Systems 2060 N Tustin Ave Santa Ana CA 92701-2143

CAIRNS, DIANE PATRICIA, motion picture literary agent; b. Fairbanks, Alaska, Mar. 2, 1957; d. Dion Melvin and Marsha Lala (Andrews) C. BBA, U. So. Calif., 1980. Literary agt. Sy Fischer Agy., L.A., 1980-85, Internat. Creative Mgmt., L.A., 1985—.

CAIRNS, SHIRLEY ANN, financial planner; b. Hundred, W.Va., Sept. 26, 1937; d. John Martin and Thelma Irene Stiles; children: John Michael, Lyle Dennis, Glynis Ann. BS, W.Va. U., 1959, MA, 1964; MPA, Harvard U., 1989. Cert. fin. planner; enrolled agt. IRS. Tchr., head bus. edn. dept. Sutherlin (Oreg.) High Sch., 1964-80; registered rep., 1980-83; prin. Shirley A. Cairns & Assocs., 1983—. Active Oreg. State Dem. 4th dist. Cen. Com., 1982—, sec. exec. com., 1991—; active Oreg. Dem. Rules Com., 1991—, Oreg. Dem. Exec. Com., 1985-88; active Oreg. Dem. Cen. Com., 1982—, Oreg. Orgn. Com., 1989-91; active Douglas County Tourist Adv. Com., 1985-89, Douglas County Dem. Cen. Com., 1980—; pres. Douglas County Dem. Women's Fedn., 1992—; bd. dirs. Oreg. Dem. Women's Fedn.; state chair Oreg. Assn. C.C. Trustees, 1992; del. Dem. Nat. Conv., 1984, mem. rules com., 1988; mem. Roseburg dist. adv. com. Bur. Land Mgmt., 1987-90; mem. Oreg. Port Adv. Com., 1988-91; bd. dirs. Calapooia Water Dist.; active Leadership Am. Alumni, 1989—; trustee Umpqua Community Coll., 1989—. Mem. AAUW, Nat. Women's Polit. Caucus, Oreg. Women's Polit. Caucus, Internat. Assn. Fin. Planners, Oreg. Soc. Enrolled Agts. (bd. dirs. 1990-92), Inst. Cert. Fin. Planners, Roseburg C. of C., Douglas County C. of C. (pres. 1990). Home: PO Box 76 Oakland OR 97462-0076 Office: 2713 NW Harvard Ste 110 Roseburg OR 97470-0399

CAKEBREAD, STEVEN ROBERT, minister; b. Pittsburg, Calif., June 19, 1946; s. Robert Harold Cakebread and Mildred Irene (McQeen) Cowing; m. Margaret Anne Spandall, July 16, 1967; children: Robert, Scott, Andrew. ABS, Nazarene Bible Coll., Colorado Springs, Colo., 1977; BA, Mid. Am. Nazarene Coll., 1979; MDiv, Am. Bapt. Sem. of the West, Berkeley, Calif., 1983. Ordained to ministry Ch. of the Nazarene, 1980, Am. Bapt. Ch., 1984. Pastor Ch. of the Nazarene, Brookfield, Md., 1978-80; hosp. chaplain VA Hosp., San Francisco, 1988—, Oakland (Calif.) Naval Hosp./ Operation Desert Storm, 1990-91, Naval Reserves/Naval Base, San Francisco, 1985—; pastor 21st Ave Bapt. Ch., San Francisco, 1984-92, Yountville Community Ch., Yountville, Calif., 1992—; Coun. mem. Coun. of Chs., San Francisco, 1988. E-5 USN, 1966-70, Vietnam. Decorated Humanitarian Svc. medal USN, Navy Achievement medal (Desert Storm). Mem. Naval Res. Assn., ABA/USA Chaplains Coun., Am. Legion. Office: Am Baptist Personnel Svc 35 E 19th St Antioch CA 94509-5107

CALA, JOHN JOSEPH, management consultant; b. San Mateo, Calif., Dec. 11, 1960; s. Joseph Charles and Patricia Jean (Murphy) C.; m. Susan Jeanett Hailey; children: Melonie, Brianna, Dominic. AB, Occidental Coll., 1983; MBA, Stanford U., 1988. Acct. exec. Data Resources, L.A., 1983-86; mng. cons. Towers Perrin, San Francisco, 1988—. Contbr. articles to profl. jours. Office: Towers Perrin 333 Bush St Ste 1600 San Francisco CA 94104-2836

CALARCO, ANTONINO PIETRO ROMEO, health education administrator; b. Oakland, Calif., May 9, 1929; s. Francesco and Domenica (Musorofiti) C.; m. Alice Catherine Erlinger, Jan. 24, 1959; children: Catherine, Teresa, Steven, Andrea Flower, Peter, Veronica. BS, U. Calif., Berkeley, 1950, MA, San Francisco State U., 1954; MPH, U. Calif., Berkeley, 1955. Cert. health edn. specialist. Health educator Butte County Dept. Pub. Health, Oroville, Calif., 1955-56, health edn. and safety coord., 1956-64, health edn. and project coord., 1964-68, dir. health edn., project dir. for drug control resource ctr, 1968-74, health edn. svcs. coord., 1974-78, dir. health edn., 1978-92; instr. Butte C.C., Oroville, 1992—; lectr. Calif. State U., Chico, 1976. Pres. Calif. Conf. Local Dirs. of Health Edn., Sacramento, 1967, 84; former chairperson Calif. Health Manpower Coun., Thirteen Northeastern Counties High Blood Pressure Control Project, others; advisor to pub. health, sch., med. mental health and human svc. orgns., local and area programs in maternal and child health, perinatal programs, and others; chair St. Johns Cath. Pastoral Coun., 1992—. With U.S. Army, 1951-53. Recipient Award for Disting. Svc., Calif. Med. Assn., 1989, bronze and silver medallions Calif. affiliate Am. Heart Assn., 1977, 92; named Young Man of Yr., Jr. C. of C., Chico, 1959. Fellow APHA, Soc. for Pub. Health Edn. Roman Catholic. Home: 1297 E Lindo Ave Chico CA 95926

CALBOM, CHERIE MARIE, nutritionist; b. Seattle, Dec. 20, 1947; d. Martis C. and Esther L. (Batdorf) Scalf; m. John Edward Calbom Jr., Oct. 27, 1984. MS in Nutrition, Bastyr Coll., 1990. Cert. nutritionist. Clin. nutritionist St. Luke Med. Ctr., Bellevue, Wash., 1989-90, Trillium Health Products, Seattle, 1990-92; nutritional cons., speaker Trillium Health Products, 1990—. Author: Juicing for Life, 1992, 1993, (monthly column) Choices mag., 1990-93. Grantee Project Cure, Washington, 1988. Mem. Am. Coll. Nutrition, Soc. Nutrition Edn. Republican. Episcopalian. Home: W 1907 Dean Ave Spokane WA 99201

CALCOTT, PETER HOWARD, quality assurance director, researcher; b. London, July 2, 1948; came to U.S., 1976; s. Derrick Ellis and Winifred Elsie (Washington) C.; m. Katherine Nathaniel, Dec. 21, 1975; children: Nicholas Aaron, Julian Spencer. BS in Biochemistry, U. East Anglia, Eng., 1969; PhD in Molecular Biology, U. Sussex, Eng., 1972. Post-doctoral position McGill U., Montreal, Quebec, Can., 1972-74, asst. prof., 1974-76; asst. prof. Wright State U., 1976-80, assoc. prof., 1980-81; project mgr. Dow Chem., Midland, Mich., 1981-83; sr. group leader Monsanto Co., St. Louis, 1983-86, rsch. mgr., 1986-88, mgr. product chemistry/quality control, 1988-90, dir. public rels., 1990-92; dir. quality assurance Miles Inc., Berkeley, Calif., 1992—; cons. Lallemand Yeast, Montreal, 1972-86, VA Hosp., Dayton, 1976-81, Dept. Defense, D.C. 1979—, West Vaco, D.C., 1976-80. Author: Freezing and Thawing Microbes, 1976; editor: Continuous Cultures of Cells, 1983; contbr. articles to profl. jours. Bd. dirs. U. East Anglia Expdn., Norwich, Eng., 1968, Childgrove Sch., St. Louis, 1990. Grantee NSF, Dayton, 1975, Dept. of Def., Dayton, 1976-81. Fellow Am. Soc. Microbiology; mem. Can. Soc. Microbiology, Sigma Xi. Office: Miles Inc 4th and Parker Berkeley CA 94701

CALDEN, GERTRUDE BECKWITH, civic worker; b. Santa Paula, Calif., Apr. 18, 1909; d. Ralph Leslie and Bernice (Hart) Beckwith; grad. Woodbury Coll., 1928; postgrad. U. Calif., Berkely, 1935-50, U. Calif., Santa Barbara, 1935-50, Santa Barbara City Coll.; m. Raymond A. MacMillan, Nov. 7, 1929 (div. 1948); 1 son, Thad C.; m. 2d Guy C. Calden, Jr., Dec. 16, 1961 (dec. 1967). Assoc. dir. Students Internat. Travel Assn., N.Y.C., 1949-51; lectr. on self-improvement to schs., colls., women's clubs So. Calif., 1951-54; cons., tchr., counselor Marymount Sch., Santa Barbara, 1953-54; adminstrv. asst. to pres. Resin Industries, Santa Barbara, Calif., 1954-58; adminstrv. asst. to corp. cons. Grant C. Ehrlich, Santa Barbara, 1958-61; treas. Wire Co. Am., Goleta, Calif., 1959-60; dir. Investors Research Fund. Inc., 1980—, exec. com. 1991—. Pres. Roosevelt Sch. PTA, 1944-46; sec. Jefferson Sch. PTA, 1941-42; chmn. tchr. recognition divsn. Santa Barbara County Selective Tchrs. Recruitment Coun., 1960-61; mem. adv. com. to bd. govs. Calif. C.Cs., 1970; bd. dirs. community council Santa Barbara City Coll., 1956-62, pres., 1961-62; bd. dirs. U. Calif., Santa Barbara Affiliates, 1975, pres., 1978-80, life mem., 1980—; trustee Found. for Santa Barbara City Coll., 1975-83, pres., 1977-79; emeritus bd. dirs., 1979—; trustee Found. for U. Calif., Santa Barbara, 1978-80; appropriations com. Santa Barbara Found., 1981-86; pres. Santa Barbara Citizens Adult Edn. Adv. Council; women's bd. Santa Barbara Mental Health Assn.; bd. dirs. Work Tng. Programs, Inc., 1968-90 , Central Counties USO, 1969-71, Channel City Women's Forum, 1987—; mem. Citizens Commn. Civil Disorders U. Calif., Isla Vista, 1970-71; mem. Pres.'s Nat. Adv. Council on Adult Edn., 1974-80; mem. Am. Friends of Wilton Park, 1974—; bd. dirs. Rec. for Blind, Santa Barbara Unit, 1974-78, Alexander House, 1976-81; pres. Friends of Hospice, Santa Barbara, 1980-82; pres. Montecito Republican Women's Club, 1963-65; bd. dirs. Santa Barbara Rep. Assembly, 1963-66, v.p., 1964; bd. dirs. Santa Barbara County Fedn. Rep. Women's Clubs, 1963-82, pres., 1966-69;

bd. dirs. So. div. Calif. Fedn. Rep. Women, 1966-69; mem. 13th Congl. Dist. Rep. Com., 1965—; asso. mem. Calif. Rep. Central Com., 1967-68, mem., 1969-84; mem. Santa Barbara County central com., 1970-74, sec., 1971-74; mem. Rep. Presdl. Task Force, 1982-93. Named Women of Yr., Rep. Hall of Fame, Greater Santa Barbara Area, 1974; fellow Wilton Park Internat. Conf., Sussex, Eng., 1972. Mem. Santa Barbara Personnel Assn. (sec. 1957-58), Santa Barbara C. of C. (edn. com. 1955, 57-61), Am. Assn. for UN, Family Service Agy., Am. Field Service, Mental Health Assn., Santa Barbara Hist. Soc., Citizens Planning Assn. of Santa Barbara County, St. Francis Hosp. Guild, LWV, Santa Barbara Council Women's Clubs, Calif. Hist. Soc., Univ. Affiliates U. Calif. Santa Barbara. Club: Zonta (pres. Santa Barbara 1956-57, 59-60, chmn. IX dist. Amelia Earhart Scholarship com. 1957-58). Contbr. poems to anthology Gossamer Wings. Address: 819 E Pedregosa St Santa Barbara CA 93103

CALDER, CLARENCE ANDREW, educator, researcher, mechanical engineer; b. Baker, Oreg., Oct. 30, 1937; s. Clarence Leroy and Viola Mary (Lucas) C.; m. Judy Lee Wood, Dec. 15, 1961; children: Brian Andrew, Gregory Clarence, Kaylene Ellen, Chad Warner, Jared Lucas. BSME, Oreg. State U., Corvallis, 1960; MS, Brigham Young U., 1962; PhD, U. Calif., Berkeley, 1969. Registered profl. engr., Oreg., Calif. Project engr. Sandia Corp., Albuquerquqe, 1962-64; asst. prof. mech. engr. Wash. State U., Pullman, 1969-74; sr. rsch. engr. Lawrence Livermore (Calif.) Nat. Lab., 1974-78; assoc. prof. Oreg. State U., Corvallis, 1978—; vis. sr. lectr. U. Auckland, N.Z., 1986; tech. cons. Lawrence Livermore Nat. Lab., 1978-88. Contbr. articles to profl. jours. Mem. ASME, Am. Soc. Engring. Edn., Soc. for Exptl. Mechs. (treas. 1982-85, pres. 1987-88). Republican. LDS. Office: Oreg State U Dept Mech Engring Corvallis OR 97331

CALDER, ROBERT MAC, aerospace engineer; b. Vernal, Utah, Oct. 16, 1932; s. Edwin Harold and Sydney (Goodrich) C.; m. Yoshiko Iemura, Feb. 14, 1959; children: Suzanne, Alexis, Irene, John. BSChemE, U. Utah, 1956, M.S. in Math. and Geology (NSF grantee), 1967; postgrad., U. Wash., 1964, Utah State U., 1965, U. Iowa, 1966. Cert. secondary tchr., Utah. Tchr. Utah Pub. Schs., 1958-79. V.p. Sydney Corp., Bountiful, Utah, 1958-82; sr. engr. aero. div. Hercules Inc., Magna, Utah, 1979—; owner RMC Enterprises, Nations Imports; cons. in field, 1960—; cultural exchange participant to Israel, Egypt, 1983, 87. Active Boy Scouts Am., 1945-75, instr., Philmont Scout Ranch, 1972, asst. scoutmaster Nat. Jamboree Troop, 1973; instr. hunter safety and survival, Utah Dept. Fish and Game, 1964-74; state advisor U.S. Congl. Adv. Bd., 1982—; mem. Rep. Nat. Com. Capt. USAF, 1956-70. Mem. AIAA, NRA (life), Am. Quarter Horse Assn., Internat. Platform Assn., Oratorio Soc. Utah, The Planetary Soc., Hercules Toastmasters Club (treas. 1980, v.p. edn. 1981, pres. 1982). Mormon. Home: PO Box 268 Bountiful UT 84011-0268 Office: PO Box 98 Magna UT 84044-0098

CALDERA, LOUIS EDWARD, state legislator, lawyer; b. El Paso, Tex., Apr. 1, 1956; s. Benjamin Luis and Soledad (Siqueiros) C. BS, U.S. Mil. Acad., 1978; JD, MBA, Harvard U., 1987. Bar: Calif. 1987. Commd. 2nd lt. U.S. Army, 1978, advanced through ranks to capt., 1982, resigned commn., 1983; assoc. O'Melveny & Myers, L.A., 1987-89, Buchalter, Nemer, Fields & Younger, L.A., 1990-91; deputy county counsel County of L.A., 1991-92; mem. Calif. State Assembly, 46th Dist., L.A., 1992—. Democrat. Roman Catholic. Home: 234 S Figueroa St No 1239 Los Angeles CA 90012 Office: State Capitol Rm 2176 Sacramento CA 95814

CALDERON, LINDA MARY, safety manager; b. Springfield, Mass., Feb. 1, 1950; d. Victor Frank and Lorraine Ruth (Perusse) Antienowicz; 1 child, Will. BS in Microbiology, Ariz. State U., 1977. Bd. cert. safey profl. Microbiology technician Armour-Dial, Phoenix, 1976; histology technician Phoenix Meml. Hosp., 1977-78; soils technician U.S. Forest Service, Flagstaff, Ariz., 1979; secondary sch. tchr. Logan (N.Mex.) Schs., 1980-81, Ft. Sumner (N.Mex.) Schs., 1981-83; industrial hygienist Westinghouse Electric Co., Carlsbad, N.Mex., 1984-89, mgr. safety and plant prodn., 1989—. With USMC, 1968-70. Mem. Am. Soc. Safety Engrs., Am. Indsl. Hygiene Assn., Bd. of Cert. Safety Profls. Republican. Roman Catholic. Home: 2835 Western Way Carlsbad NM 88220 Office: Westinghouse Electric PO Box 2078 Carlsbad NM 88221

CALDERON-VAN STANE, ZULMA CECILIA, business executive; b. San Jose, Costa Rica, Sept. 5, 1943; came to U.S., 1963; d. Eduin and Elisa (Barrantes) Calderon; m. John Van Stane, Dec. 21, 1963. BS, U. Dominguez Hills, Carson, Calif., 1974. Chief teller United Calif. Bank, L.A., 1965-74; officer City of L.A., 1974-84; CEO Z&P Inc., Inglewood, Calif., 1984—. Ombusman Spanish Srs., others; community activist. Office: Z&P Inc 10231 Hawthorne Blvd Inglewood CA 90304

CALDERWOOD, NEIL MOODY, telephone traffic engineer, consultant, retired; b. Vinalhaven, Maine, June 19, 1910; s. Austin Shirley and Eliza Louise (Carver) C.; m. Katherine Foster Mariani, Oct. 13, 1940; children: John Carver, James Foster, Bruce Glidden. BSCE, U. Maine, Orono, 1932, MS in Math., 1935. Sr. engr. Resettlement Adminstrn., Camden, Maine, 1935-37; sr. engr. Pacific Telephone, San Francisco, 1937-42, staff engr., dist. traffic engr., gen. traffic engr., staff dir. network ops., 1946-75; telecom. expert Internat. Telecom. Union, UN, Geneva, 1975-76; cons. telephone numbering plans Libyan Govt., Benghazi, Tripoli, 1976; traffic engring. cons. Las Vegas Telephone Co., 1952, Hawaiian Telephone Co., 1963; expert witness Public Utilities Commn. of Calif. hearings on all number calling cases, San Francisco and L.A., 1962-64. Lt. comdr. USNR, 1942-46. Mem. Am. Rose Soc., Pierce-Arrow Soc., Telephone Pioneers, Mus. Soc. San Francisco. Republican. Home: 49 Dolores Way Orinda CA 94563

CALDERWOOD, WILLIAM ARTHUR, physician; b. Wichita, Kans., Feb. 3, 1941; s. Ralph Bailey and Janet Denise (Christ) C.; m. Nancy Jo Crawford, Mar. 31, 1979; children: Lisa Beth, William Arthur II. MD, U. Kans., 1968. Diplomate Am. Bd. Family Practice. Intern Wesley Med. Ctr., Wichita, 1968-69; gen. practice family medicine Salina, Kans., 1972-80, Peoria, Ariz., 1980—; pres. staff St. John's Hosp., Salina, 1976; 28th jud. dist. coroner State of Kans., Salina, 1973-80; clin. instr. U. Kans., Wichita, 1978-80; cons. in addiction medicine VA Hosp., 1989—. Inventor, patentee lighter-than-air-furniture. Lt., M.C., USN, 1969-70. Fellow Am. Acad. Family Physicians; mem. AMA, Ariz. Med. Soc. (physicians med. health com., exec. com. 1988-92), Maricopa County Med. Soc., Ariz. Acad. Family Practice (med. dir. N.W. Orgn. Vol. alternatives 1988-91), Am. Med. Soc. on Alcoholism and Other Drug Dependencies (cert.), Shriners. Home: 7015 W Calavar Peoria AZ 85381 Office: 14300 W Granite Valley Dr Sun City West AZ 85375-5783

CALDWELL, ALLAN BLAIR, health services company executive; b. Independence, Iowa, June 13, 1929; s. Thomas James and Lola (Ensminger) C.; B.A., Maryville Coll., 1952; B.S., N.Y.U., 1955; M.S., Columbia U., 1957; M.D., Stanford U., 1964; m. Elizabeth Jane Steinmetz, June 13, 1955; 1 child, Kim Allistair; m. Susan A. Koss, Feb. 12, 1984. Med. intern Henry Ford Hosp., Detroit, 1964-65; resident Jackson Meml. Hosp., Miami, Fla., 1956-57; admstr. Albert Schweitzer Hosp., Haiti, 1957-58; asst. admstr. Palo Alto-Stanford Hosp. Center, 1958-59; asso. dir. program in hosp. adminstrn. U. Calif. at Los Angeles, 1965-67; dir. bur. profl. service Am. Hosp. Assn., Chgo., 1967-69; v.p. Beverly Enterprises, Pasadena, Calif., 1969-71; exec. v.p., med. dir. Nat. Med. Enterprises, Beverly Hills, Calif., 1971-73; pres., chmn. bd. Emergency Physicians Internat., 1973—, Allan B. Caldwell, M.D., Inc., 1973—; dir. indsl. medicine Greater El Monte Community Hosp., South El Monte, Calif., 1973-83; pres. Am. Indsl. Med. Services, 1978—; chmn. bd. dirs. Technicraft Internat., Inc., San Mateo, Calif., 1970-76; pres., med. dir. Shelton-Livingston Med. Group, 1984—; dir. Career Aids, Inc., Glendale, Calif., 1969-75; cons. TRW Corp., Redondo Beach, Calif., 1966-71; lectr. UCLA, 1965—, Calif. Inst. Tech., 1971—, Calif. State U., Northridge, 1980-85; examiner Civil Service Commn., Los Angeles, 1966; adviser Western Center for Continuing Edn. in Hosps. and Related Health Facilities, 1965—; cons. Los Angeles Hosp. and Nursing and Pub. Health Dept., 1965—; adv. council Calif. Hosp. Commn., 1972-78; commr. Emergency Med. Services Commn. Bd. dirs. Comprehensive Health Planning Assn. Los Angeles County, 1972-76; vice chmn. Emergency Med. Care Commn., Los Angeles County, 1977-78, chmn., 1978-79. Recipient Geri award Los Angeles Nursing Home Assn., 1966, Outstanding Achievement award Health Care Educators, 1978; USPHS scholar, 1961-63. Diplomate Am. Bd. Med. Examiners. Mem. Am., United (pres. 1971-72) hosp. assns., Am. Coll. Hosp. Adminstrs., Am., Calif. med. assns., Los Angeles County Med. Assn., Am. Coll. Emergency Physicians (v.p. 1975-77 dir. continuing med. edn. for Western U.S., Hawaii, Australia, N.Z., 1976-84), Hosp. Fin. Mgmt. Assn., Am. Indsl. Hygiene Assn., Rolls Royce Owners' Club (dir. 1982—, vice chmn. 1982, chmn. 1983), Classic Car Club of Am. (life 1983). Home: 4405 Medley Pl Encino CA 91316-4344 Office: 1414 S Grand Ave Ste 123 Los Angeles CA 90015

CALDWELL, BRIAN YANCY, marketing executive; b. Los Alamos, N.Mex., Nov. 27, 1961; s. Gary Lee and Cyrella Lou (Rue) C.; m. Debra Lee Sadler, Dec. 26, 1981. BS, Syracuse U., 1983. Sales mgr. Storer Cable Communications, East Windsor, N.J., 1983-86; mktg. mgr. Storer Cable Communications, Woodbury, N.J., 1986-89; dir. mktg. Heritage Cablevision, Wilmington, Del., 1989-90, Continental Cablevision, Stockton, Calif., 1990—. Recipient Grand prize Cable Advt. Bur., 1987, cert. of merit Broadcast Promotion and Mktg. Exec., 1990. Mem. Cable TV Adminstrs. and Mktg. (cert. excellence 1992), Nat. Acad. Cable Programming, Exchange Club. Home: 3233 Estate Dr Stockton CA 95209 Office: Continental Cablevision 6505 Tam O Shanter Stockton CA 95210

CALDWELL, COURTNEY LYNN, lawyer, real estate consultant; b. Washington, Mar. 5, 1948; d. James Morton and Moselle (Smith) C. Student, Duke U., 1966-68, U. Calif., Berkeley, 1967, 1968-69; BA, U. Calif., Santa Barbara, 1970, MA, 1975; JD with highest honors, George Washington U., 1982. Bar: D.C. 1984, Wash. 1986, Calif. 1989. Jud. clk. U.S. Ct. Appeals for 9th Cir., Seattle, 1982-83; assoc. Arnold & Porter, Washington, 1983-85, Perkins Coie, Seattle, 1985-88; dir. western ops., assoc. gen. counsel MPC Assocs., Inc., Irvine, Calif., 1988-91, sr. v.p., 1991—. Named Nat. Law Ctr. Law Rev. Scholar, 1981-82. Mem. Calif. Bar Assn., Wash. State Bar Assn., D.C. Bar Assn., Urban Land Inst. Office: MPC Assocs Inc 4199 Campus Dr Ste 210 Irvine CA 92715-2698

CALDWELL, DAN EDWARD, political science educator; b. Oklahoma City, May 12, 1948; s. John Edward and Hester Evelyn (Kiehn) C.; m. Lora Jean Ferguson, Mar. 21, 1970; children: Beth Christine, Ellen Claire, John Ferguson. BA in History, Stanford U., 1970, MA in Polit. Sci., PhD in Polit. Sci., 1978; MA in Internat. Rels., Tufts U., 1971. Staff mem. Office Emergency Preparedness, Exec. Office of Pres., Washington, 1972; rsch. and teaching fellow Stanford (Calif.) U., 1975-78; assoc. dir. Ctr. for Fgn. Policy Devel., Brown U., Providence, 1982-84; prof. polit. sci. Pepperdine U., Malibu, Calif., 1978-82, 84—, pres. faculty orgn., 1980-81, 89-90; dir. Forum for U.S.-Soviet Dialogue, Washington, 1984—, pres., 1989-91. Author: American-Soviet Relations, 1981, The Dynamics of Domestic Politics and Arms Control, 1991; editor: Henry Kissinger, 1985. Elder Pacific Palisades (Calif.) Presbyn. Ch.; co-chmn. Ground Zero, L.A., 1982. With USN, 1971-74. Named Prof. of Yr., Pepperdine U. Student Alumni Assn., 1992.; rsch. fellow U.S. Inst. Peace, 1987, Pew faculty fellow Harvard U. Kennedy Sch. Govt., 1990. Mem. Internat. Inst. Strategic Studies (London), Am. Polit. Sci. Assn., Internat. Studies Assn. (sect. exec. com. 1982-87, dir. sect. on Am.-Soviet rels. 1984-86, fellow 1977), Coun. on Fgn. Rels. Home: 654 Radcliffe Ave Pacific Palisades CA 90272 Office: Pepperdine U Social Sci Div 24255 Pacific Coast Hwy Malibu CA 90263

CALDWELL, DAVID ORVILLE, physics educator; b. Los Angeles, Jan. 5, 1925; s. Orville Robert and Audrey Norton (Anderson) C.; m. Miriam Ann Planck, Nov. 4, 1950 (div. Apr. 1978); children: Bruce David, Diana Miriam; m. Edith Helen Anderson, Dec. 29, 1984. BS in Physics, Calif. Inst. Tech., 1947; postgrad., Stanford U., 1947-48; MA in Physics, UCLA, 1949, PhD in Physics, 1953. From instr. to assoc. prof. physics MIT, Cambridge, 1954-63; vis. assoc. prof. physics Princeton U., N.J., 1963-64; lectr. physics dept. U. Calif., Berkeley, 1964-65; prof. physics U. Calif., Santa Barbara, 1965—; cons. U. Calif. Radiation Lab., Berkeley, 1957-58, 64-67, Am. Sci. and Engring., Boston, 1959-60, Inst. Def. Analysis, Washington, 1060-67, U.S. Dept. Def., Washington, 1966-70; dir. U. Calif. Inst. for Research at Particle Accelerators, 1984—. Contbr. numerous articles to profl. jours. Served to 2d lt. USAAF, 1943-46. Recipient von Humboldt Sr. Disting. Sci. award, 1987; research grantee Dept. Energy, 1966—; Ford Found. fellow, 1961-62, NSF fellow, 1953-54, 1960-61, Guggenheim fellow, 1971-72. Fellow Am. Phys. Soc.; mem. Phys. Soc. (exec. com. 1976-78). Democrat. Office: U Calif Santa Dept Physics Santa Barbara CA 93106

CALDWELL, DENNIS DANA, manufacturing executive; b. Seattle, Sept. 25, 1942; s. James Warren Reed and Helen Mae (Thompson) Caldwell; m. Terry Lou Meeker, Nov. 22, 1961 (div. 1979); children: Tiffany, Dennis Jr.; m. Leslie Joyce Todd, July 2, 1983; 1 child, Patrick. BA, Nat. U., 1982. Cert. prodn. and inventory mgmt. Gen. foreman Deutsch Co., Oceanside, Calif., 1961-72; prodn. mgr. Rexair Inc., Cadillac, Mich., 1972-73; planning mgr. Capacitor Specialists Inc., Escondido, Calif., 1973-76; prodn. control mgr. Emcon Div. Ill. Tool Works, San Diego, 1976-80; prodn. mgr. Kyocera Corp., San Diego, 1980-86, Palomar-Msi Inc., Escondido, 1986—. Chmn. Escondido Edn. Compact, 1991. Mem. ASME, Am. Prodn. and Inventory Control Soc. (v.p. 1982-84), Escondido C. of C. Republican. Office: Palomar Msi Inc 2310 Aldergrove Ave Escondido CA 92029

CALDWELL, DOUGLAS RAY, oceanographer, educator; b. Lansing, Mich., Feb. 16, 1936; s. Ray Thornton and Pearl Elizabeth (Brown) C.; m. Joan Hannauer, Sept. 9, 1961; children: Michael G., Elizabeth C., Katherine L. AB, U. Chgo., 1955, BS, 1957, MS, 1958, PhD, 1964. Research assoc. U. Chgo., 1963; post doctoral study Cambridge U., Eng., 1963-64; research asst. Inst. Geophysics, La Jolla, Calif., 1964-68; asst. prof. Oreg. State U., Corvallis, 1968-73, assoc. prof., 1973-78, prof., 1978—, assoc. dean, 1983-84, dean, 1984—. Office: Oreg State U Coll of Oceanography Oceanography Admin Bldg 104 Corvallis OR 97331

CALDWELL, HOWARD BRYANT, English language educator; b. London, Ky., Jan. 28, 1944; s. Stratton and Linda Emily (Bryant) C. BA, Berea (Ky.) Coll., 1966; MA, U. Calif., Berkeley, 1977. Cert. adult edn. tchr. Tchr. L.A. Unified Sch. Dist., 1977—. Mem. L.A. County Mus. Art, N.Y. Met. Mus. Art, L.A. World Affairs Coun. With USAF, 1966-70, The Philippines. Mem. United Tchrs. L.A., London Victory Club. Republican. Baptist.

CALDWELL, JONI, small business owner; b. Chgo., Aug. 8, 1948; d. Bruce Wilber and Eloise Ethel (Ijams) C. BS in Home Econs. Edn., Mich. State U., 1970; MA in Psychology, U. San Francisco, 1978. Cret. high sch. and coll. tchr., Mich. Instr. Northwestern Mich. Coll., Traverse City, 1972-78, Mott Community Coll., Flint, Mich., 1974-78; tchr. Grand Blanc (Mich.) High Sch., 1970-73, Clio (Mich.) High Sch., 1974-78; parent educator, vol. coord. Family Resource Ctr., Monterey, Calif., 1981-82; owner, gen. mgr. Futons & Such, Monterey, 1982—. Bd. dirs., v.p., pres. Ch. Religious Sci., Monterey, 1984-87; mem. bd. stewards Pacific Coast Ch., Monterey, 1988-92, v.p.; bd. dirs. YWCA, Monterey, 1986-88. Mem. New Monterey Bus. Assn. (bd. dirs. 1984—, v.p., past pres.), Monterey C. of C. (cons. workshop com. 1985-87, Small Bus. Excellence award 1990). Home: 29 Portola Ave Monterey CA 93942-1171 Office: Futons & Such 484 Lighthouse Ave Monterey CA 93940-1457

CALDWELL, MARK R., industrial sales executive; b. Denver, June 3, 1953; s. Ben Robert and Mary Anne (Anderies) C.; m. Constance Anton, May 5, 1979; children: Gregory Robert, Christine Alexandra. BA, Metro State Coll., 1978. With sales M. L. Foss, Denver, 1980-82; sales rep. Hendrie & Bolthoff, Denver, 1982-86, Centurion, Denver, 1986-89; sales and territory mgr. KSC, Denver, 1989—. Pres. Edn. and Spiritual Queen of Peace, Aurora, Colo., 1991—; tchr. Rainbow Program for Children Facing Crisis in Death, Aurora, 1992—. Mem. KC (3d degree). Republican. Roman Catholic. Home: 5947 S Odessa Cir Aurora CO 80015 Office: KSC 7000 Broadway # 1-105 Denver CO 80221

CALDWELL, PAUL WILLIS, JR., aerospace executive; b. Asheville, N.C., Apr. 5, 1930; s. Paul Willis and Martha Gill (Jarnagin) C.; m. Marion Louise Thielges, Feb. 11, 1961; children: Pamela Ann, Lisa Diane. BSBA, U. N.C., Chapel Hill, 1952. Jr. auditor Graham S. DeVane CPA, Morganton, N.C., 1956-58; acct., Systems Devel. Labs. Hughes Aircraft Co., Culver City, Calif., 1958-61, supr. fin. planning rsch. and devel. fin., 1961-69; head fin. analysis and controls Hughes Aircraft Co., Culver City, 1969-75, asst. to contr. Electro-Opt. and Data Systems Group, 1975-77; mgr. fin. contr. analyst Hughes Aircraft Co., El Segundo, Calif., 1977-84, mgr. fin. bus. mgmt. and audit, 1984-90, ret., 1989. Bd. dirs., treas. Casa de Los Amigos HUD sr. housing devel., 1991—; mem. Young Reps., Torrence, Calif., 1963-64. Capt. USAFR, 1952-64. Mem. Jr. C. of C., U. N.C. Alumni Assn. (pres. L.A. chpt. 1982-84). Republican. Methodist. Home: 4820 Maricopa St Torrance CA 90503-2818

CALDWELL, PETER DEREK, pediatrician, pediatric cardiologist; b. Schenectady, N.Y., Apr. 16, 1940; s. Philip Graham and Mary Elizabeth (Glockler) C.; m. Olga Hoang Hai Miller, May 31, 1969. BA, Pomona Coll., 1961; MD, UCLA, 1965. Intern King County Hosp., Seattle, 1965-66; resident in pediatrics U. Wash., 1969-71, fellow in pediatric cardiology, 1971-73; pvt. practice Hawaii Permanente Med. Group, Honolulu, 1973—. Author: Bac-Si: A Doctor Remembers Vietnam, 1990, Adventurer's Hawaii, 1992; contbr. articles to profl. jours. Lt. comdr. USNR, 1966-69. Fellow Am. Acad. Pediatrics; mem. Am. Coll. Sports Medicine, Wilderness Med. Soc., Internat. Soc. Mountain Medicine. Office: Kaiser Punawai Clinic 94-235 Leoku St Waipahu HI 96797

CALDWELL, ROBERT JOHN, newspaper editor; b. LaGrande, Oreg., Feb. 28, 1949; s. Donald John and Barbara Cecelia (Joyce) C.; m. Vicki J. Meierjurgen, June 12,1971 (div. 1980); 1 child, Elizabeth Anne; m. Lora Beth Cuykendall, Mar. 10, 1981; children: Katherine, Eleanor. BS in Journalism, U. Oreg., 1971. Mng. editor Albany (Oreg.) Dem.-Herald, 1976-78, Valley Newspapers, Kent, Wash., 1978; editor Springfield (Oreg.) News, 1978-82; pub. Gresham (Oreg.) Outlook, 1982-83; copy editor The Oregonian, Portland, 1983-84, regional editor, 1984-85, met. editor, 1985—. Mem. Soc. Profl. Journalists (pres. Willamette Valley chpt. 1978), Investigative Reporters and Editors. Home: 3122 SW Willow Pky Gresham OR 97080-9496

CALDWELL, STRATTON FRANKLIN, kinesiologist; b. Mpls., Aug. 25, 1926; s. Kenneth Simms and Margaret Mathilda (Peterson) C.; m. Mary Lynn Shaffer, Aug. 28, 1955 (div. May 1977); children: Scott Raymond, Karole Elizabeth; m. Sharee' Deanna Ockerman, Aug. 6, 1981; 1 stepchild, Shannon Sharee' Calder. Student, San Diego State Coll., 1946-48; BS in Edn. cum laude, U. So. Calif., 1951, PhD in Phys. Edn., 1966; MS in Phys. Edn., U. Oreg., 1953. 0, 1971-92; teaching asst. dept. phys. edn. UCLA, 1953-54, assoc. in phys. edn., 1957-65, vis. asst. prof. phys. edn., 1967; dir. phys. edn. Regina (Sask., Can.) Young Men's Christian Assn., 1954-56; tchr. sec. grades, dir. athletic Queen Elizabeth Jr.-Sr. High Sch., Calgary, Alta., Can., 1956-57; asst. prof. phys. edn. San Fernando Valley State Coll., Northridge, Calif., 1965-68, assoc. prof., 1968-71; prof. phys. edn. dept. kinesiology Calif. State U., Northridge, 1971-91, prof. kinesiology, 1991-92, prof. Kinesiology emeritus, 1992; vis. assoc. prof. phys. edn. U. Wash., Seattle, 1968, U. Calif., Santa Barbara, 1969. Author (with Cecil and Joan Martin Hollingsworth) Golf, 1959, (with Rosalind Cassidy) Humanizing Physical Education: Methods for the Secondary School Movement Program, 5th edit., 1975; also poetry, book chpts., articles in profl. jours., book revs. With USN, 1944-46. Recipient Meritorious Performance and Profl. Promise award Calif. state U., 1986, 87, 89, Disting. Teaching award, 1992; AAPHERD fellow, 1962, Am. Coll. Sports Medicine fellow, 1965, Can. Assn. for Health, Phys. Edn., and Recreation fellow, 1971. Fellow Am. Alliance for Health, Phys. Edn., Recreation and Dance (Centennial Commn. 1978-85, cert. appreciation 1985), Am. Coll. Sports Medicine; mem. Calif. Assn. for Health, Phys. Edn., Recreation and Dance (pres. L.A. coll. and univ. unit 1969-70, v.p. phys. edn. com. 1970-71, mem. editorial bd. CAHPER Jour. 1970-71, mem. forum 1970-71, Disting. Svc. award 1974, Honor award 1988, Verne Landreth award 1992), Nat. Assn. for Phys. Edn. in Higher Edn. (charter), Sport Art Acad., Nat. Assn. for Sport and Phys. Edn., N.Y. Acad. Scis., N.Am. Soc. for Sports History, Sport Lit. Assn., Acad. Am. Poets, Phi Epsilon Kappa (Svc. award 1980), Alpha Tau Omega (charter,Silver Circle award 1976), Phi Delta Kappa, Phi Kappa Phi, others. Republican. Mem. Christian Ch. Home: 80 N Kanan Rd Oak Park CA 91301-1105 Office: Calif State U Dept Kinesiology 18111 Nordhoff St Northridge CA 91330-0001

CALDWELL, THOMAS MICHAEL, facilities director; b. Beardstown, Ill., June 29, 1946; s. Carl and E. Lou (Bullard) C.; children: Tamera Lynn, Thomas Adam, Elizabeth R., Benjamin T. BS, U. N.Mex., 1975. Ptnr. Solar Retrofit Inc., Albuquerque, N.Mex., 1978-81; maint. data collections W.B.C. Consultants, Tucson, 1981-82; facilities dir. EG&G, Albuquerque, 1983-90; owner T's Weldry, Los Lunas, N.Mex., 1988—; ptnr. D&T Solar Lazers, Albuquerque, 1983; exec. v.p. Solar Detox. Corp., Albuquerque, 1990—. Co-designer human powered vehicle, Boing 888. With USN, 1965-69. Mem. Rio Grande Human Powered Vehicle Assn. (pres.). Democrat. Roman Catholic. Home: 418 Vista Dr Los Lunas NM 87031-8536

CALDWELL, WALTER EDWARD, editor, small business owner; b. L.A., Dec. 29, 1941; s. Harold Elmer and Esther Ann (Fuller) C.; m. Donna Edith Davis, June 27, 1964; 1 child, Arnie-Jo. AA, Riverside City Coll., 1968. Sales and stock professional Sears Roebuck & Co., Riverside, Calif., 1963-65; dispatcher Rohr Corp., Riverside, Calif., 1965-67; trainee Aetna Fin., Riverside, 1967-68; mgr. Aetna Fin., San Bruno, Cal., 1968-70, Amfac Thrift & Loan, Oakland, Calif., 1970-74; free lance writer San Jose, Calif., 1974-76; news dir. Sta. KAVA Radio, Burney, Cal., 1977-79; editor-pub. Mountain Echo, Fall River Mills, Calif., 1979—. Contbg. author Yearbook of Modern Poetry, 1976. Del. Farmers and Ranchers' Congress, St. Louis, 1985; participant Am. Leadership Conf., San Diego, 1989; pres. United Way, Burney, Calif., 1979, co-chmn., 1977, chmn., 1979; disaster relief worker ARC, Redding, Calif., 1988-91, disaster action team leader, 1991—; bd. dirs. Shasta County Women's Refuge, Redding, 1988-91; bd. dirs. Shasta County Econ. Devel. Task Force, Redding, 1985-86, exec. bd. dirs., 1988; bd. dirs. Shasta County Econ. Devel. Corp., 1986-90; pres. Intermountain Devel. Corp., 1989; leader Girl Scouts U.S., San Jose, 1973-76; announcer various local parades; trustee Mosquito Abatement Dist., Burney, 1978-87, 89—, chmn., 1990—; commr. Burney Fire Protection Dist., 1987-91, v.p., 1990, pres. 1991; bd. dirs. Crossroads, 1985; past chmn. Burney Basin Days Com., 1984—; candidate Shasta County Bd. Suprs., 1992. Cpl. USMC, 1959-63. Mem. Burney Basin C. of C. (advt. chmn. 1982, Community Action award 1990, 93), Fall River Valley C. of C. (bd. dirs. 1991), Internat. Platform Assn., Am. Legion (Citation of Recognition 1987, Community Action award 1989), Rotary (pres. 1977-78, chmn. bike race 1981-85), Lions (student speaker chmn. Fall River club 1983—, 1st v.p. 1991, pres. 1992, co-chmn. disaster com., newsletter chmn. dist. 4-C1 1989-91), Moose, Masons, Shriners (sec.-treas. Intermountain club). Republican. Home: 20304 Elm St Burney CA 96013 Office: Mountain Echo Main St Fall River Mills CA 96028

CALDWELL, WILLIAM MACKAY, III, business executive; b. Los Angeles Apr. 6, 1922; s. William Mackay II and Edith Ann (Richards) C.; BS, U. So. Calif., 1943; MBA, Harvard U., 1948; m. Mary Louise Edwards, Jan. 16, 1946 (dec. 1980); children: William Mackay IV, Craig Edwards, Candace Louise; m. Jean Bledsoe, Apr. 27, 1985. Sec.-treas., dir. Drewry Photocolor Corp., 1957-60, Adcolor Photo Corp., 1957-60; treas., dir. Drewry Bennetts Corp., 1959-60; sr. v.p., chief fin. officer Am. Cement Corp., 1960-67; sr. v.p. corp., 1966-70, pres. cement and concrete group, 1967-70; pres., chmn. bd., chief exec. officer Van Vorst Industries, 1969; pres. Van Vorst Corp., Washington, 1969-77; chmn. bd., pres. So. Cross Industries, U.S. Bedding Co., 1979-84, St. Croix Mfg. Co., 1979-81, Hawaiian Cement Corp.; pres. Englander Co., 1979-84; v.p., dir. Am. Cement Internat. Corp., Am. Cement Properties; chmn. Kyco Industries Inc., 1982—; pres. BHI Inc., 1984—; cons. prof. U. So. Calif. Mem. men's com. Los Angeles Med. Center; bd. dirs. Commerce Assocs., Calif. Mus. Sci. and Industry, U. So. Calif. Assocs., bd. dirs. Pres.'s Circle; bd. dirs. Am. Cement Found. Served to lt. USNR, 1943-46. Mem. Newcomen Soc., Friends Huntington Library, L.A. Country Club, Town Hall Club, Calif. Club (L.A.), Trojan Club, Annandale Golf Club, Eldorado Country Club, Chaparell Golf Club, Harvard Bus. Sch. of So. Calif. (dir. 1960-63), Kappa Alpha, Alpha Delta Sigma, Alpha Pi Omega. Presbyterian. Office: PO Box 726 Pasadena CA 91102-0726

CALDWELL-LEE, LAURIE NEILSON, lawyer; b. Portland, Oreg., Jan. 22, 1947; d. Duncan Reese and Lilian (Schwichtenberg) Neilson; m. Douglas Caldwell, Sept. 13, 1968 (div. Aug. 1987); children: Jessica, Ashley; m. Alan

M. Lee, Jan. 1, 1988; stepchildren: Erin Lee, Sam Lee. BA, U. Oreg., 1969; JD, Lewis & Clark Coll., 1980. Bar: Oreg. 1980, U.S. Dist. Ct. Oreg. 1980. Assoc. Urbigkeit, Hinson & Abele, Oregon City, Oreg., 1980-85, Gleason, Scarborough, McNeese, O'Brien & Barnes, P.C., Portland, Oreg., 1985-88; ptnr. Bullivant, Houser, Bailey, Pendergrass & Hoffman, Portland, 1989—; speaker legal seminars Oreg. State Bar, 1984-86, 88, 90, 92, 93, Oreg. Law Inst., 1989, Oreg. Soc. CPAs, 1986-90, 92, Nat. Bus. Inst., 1990, Portland Tax Forum, 1991. Contbr. articles to profl. jours. Mem. activities coun. Portland Art Mus., 1989—, Nature Conservancy, Portland, 1990; bd. dirs. The Dougy Ctr., Portland, 1989-91; mem. N.W. Planned Giving Roundtable, 1992—; past chair, past sec., com. mem. exec. com. estate planning and adminstrn. sect. Oreg. State Bar, Lake Oswego, 1982-88. Fellow Am. Coll. Trust and Estate Coun.; mem. ABA, Oreg. Women Lawyers (charter), Estate Planning Coun. Portland Inc. (bd. dirs., chair planning com. 22d Ann. Estate Planning Seminar 1992), Oreg. State Bar, Multnomah County Bar Assn., Clackamas County Bar Assn. Office: Bullivant Houser Bailey 300 Pioneer Tower 888 SW 5th Ave Portland OR 97204-2089

CALFEE, DAVID WALKER, municipal court judge, lawyer; b. Richmond, Calif., Sept. 23, 1921; s. Tsar N. and Leona (Jones) C.; m. Mary Helen Bergman, May 15, 1943; children: David, Kent, Shirley Heinrich, Laura Marlow. A.B. in Polit. Sci., Stanford U., 1942; J.D., U. Calif.-San Francisco, 1949. Bar: Calif. 1950, U.S. Dist. Ct. Calif. 1950, U.S. Ct. Appeals (9th cir.) 1950. Ptnr. Calfee, Gregg, Moses & Calfee, Richmond, Calif., 1950-58; judge Bay Mcpl. Ct., Richmond, 1959-81; of coun. Whiting, Rubenstein, Swager & Levy, Richmond, 1981-86. Served to maj. USMC, 1943-46; PTO. Decorated D.F.C.; named Man of Yr. Richmond Jr. C. of C., 1965; recipient Silver Beaver award Boy Scouts Am. Mt. Diablo Coun., 1963, Order of the Coif Man of The Yr., 1965, Human Rights award Richmond Soromists, 1985. Mem. Richmond Bar Assn. (pres. 1956). Republican. Methodist. Lodge: Rotary (pres. 1983-84) (Richmond). Home: 17201 Creekside Dr Meadow Vista CA 95722-9579 Office: PO Box 709 Meadow Vista CA 95722-0709

CALHOON, JOHN CHARLES, media company executive; b. Gallup, N.Mex., Mar. 28, 1957; s. John Clifton and Florence Josephine (Allman) C. Student, U. Oreg., 1975-76; BS in Electronics Engring. Tech., DeVry Inst., Phoenix, 1979. Chief technician Western Geophys. Co., Houston, 1979-81, field svc. engr., 1982-84, instrument supr., 1985-89; technician GECO U.S., Houston, 1981-82; owner, mgr. A to Z Co., Anchorage, 1985, Mobile Tech., Redmond, Wash., 1990—, Advanced Tng. Concepts, Bellevue, Wash., 1991-92; v.p. Advanced Media Group, Inc., Redmond, 1991—. Office: Advanced Media Group Inc 16770 NE 79th St Ste 202 Redmond WA 98052

CALHOUN, GORDON JAMES, lawyer; b. Pitts., Sept. 3, 1953; s. Bertram Allen and Dorothy Mae (Brown) C.; m. Jane Ann Walchli, May 7, 1982; children: Andrew Michael, Megan Jane. BA, John Hopkins U., 1975; JD, Stanford U., 1978. Bar: Calif. 1978, U.S. Dist. Ct. (no., cen., ea. and so. dists.) Calif. 1979, U.S. Ct. Appeals (9th cir.) 1980. Assoc. Long & Levit, 1978-83, Parkinson & Wolf, 1983-84; ptnr. Wolf & Leo, 1984-91, Lewis, D'Amato, Brisbois & Bisgaard, 1991—. Mem. ABA (real property, probate and trust law sect., litigation sect., tort and ins. practice sect.), Am. Trial Lawyers Assn. Office: Lewis D'Amato Brisbois et al 221 N Figueroa St Los Angeles CA 90012-2601

CALHOUN, JAMES CLAY, electrical and mechanical engineer; b. Tucson, Ariz., Dec. 31, 1962; s. Ronald Brian Sr. and Sherion Kay (Hester) C.; m. Mary Lue Horvet, Mar. 7, 1987. BSME, U. Ariz. Registered profl. engr., Calif., Ariz. Sr. elec. designer Taylor Engrs., Inc., Scottsdale, Ariz., 1978-87, WR Acorn Engring., Tucson, 1987-89; asst. dir. mech. and elec. engring., chief elec. engr. AC Martin & Assocs., L.A., 1989—. Republican. Home: 28028 Aumond Ave Canyon Country CA 91351 Office: Albert C Martin & Assocs 811 W 7th St Los Angeles CA 90017-3408

CALKINS, JERRY MILAN, anesthesiologist, educator, administrator, biomedical engineer; b. Benkelman, Nebr., Sept. 10, 1942; s. Robert Thomas and Mildred Rachel (Stamm) C.; m. Connie Mae Satterfield, Oct. 17, 1964; children: Julie Lynn, Jenifer Ellan. BSChemE, U. Wyo., 1964, MSChemE, 1966; PhD in Chem. Engring., U. Md., 1971; MD, U. Ariz., 1976. Diplomate Am. Bd. Anesthesiology. Lectr. engring. U. Md., College Park, 1970-71; asst. prof. engring. Ariz. State U., Tempe, 1971-73; asst. prof. anesthesiology U. Ariz., Tucson, 1979-84, assoc. prof., 1984; assoc. prof., vice chmn. dept. U. N.C., Chapel Hill, 1984-86; clin. assoc. U. N.Mex., Albuquerque, 1986-88, chmn. dept. anesthesiology Lovelace Med. Ctr., 1986-88; chmn. dept. anesthesiology Maricopa Med. Ctr., Phoenix, 1988—; clin. prof. anesthesiology U. Ariz., 1988—; adj. assoc. prof. indsl. engring. N.C. State U., 1984-86; dir. med. engring. lab. Harry Diamond Labs., Washington, 1968-71; cons. Bur. Med. Devel., FDA, Washington, 1977-86; asst. prof. engring., bd. dir. advanced biotech. Lab. Ariz. Health Sci. Ctr., Tucson, 1979-84. Coauthor: Future Anesthesia Delivery Systems, 1984, High Frequency Ventilation, 1986; editor Annals Biomed. Engring., 1979, Clin. Monitoring, 1984—; contbr. numerous articles to profl. jours., chpts. to books. Recipient Outstanding Tchr. award Upjohn Co., 1979; spl. fellow NIH, 1970. Mem. AMA, AICE, Am. Soc. Anesthesiologists, Am. Soc. Artificial Internal Organs, Closed and Lowflow Anesthesia Systems Soc. (pres. 1986-88), Soc. Tech. Anesthesia (pres. 1993—), Ariz. Med. Assn., Ariz. Soc. Anesthesiology, Maricopa County Med. Assn., Masons, Sigma Xi. Republican. Office: Maricopa Med Ctr Phoenix AZ 85010

CALKINS, ROBERT BRUCE, aerospace engineer; b. Pasadena, Calif., Apr. 10, 1942; s. Bruce and Florence May (Bennit) C.; m. Dana B. Ericson. BS in Aerospace Engring., Calif. State Polytech., 1965; BA in Applied Math., San Diego State U., 1970; MS in Computer Sci., Wright State U., 1984. Project engr. U.S. Air Force Flight Test Ctr., El Centro, Calif., 1965-75; sr. engr. U.S. Air Force Aero. Systems Div., Dayton, Ohio, 1975-85; prin. engr. Douglas Aircraft Co., Long Beach, Calif., 1985-90; project engr. McDonnell Douglas Missile Systems Co., Long Beach, 1990—. Recipient U.S. Presidential citation, Fed. Govt., 1967. Fellow AIAA (Disting. Svc. award 1992, assoc., chmn. tech. standards com.); mem. SAFE Assn. (sec. chpt. 1 1991, pres. chpt. 1 1992). Home: 7901 Southwind Cir Huntington Beach CA 92648-5458 Office: McDonnell Douglas 3855 N Lakewood Blvd Long Beach CA 90846-0001

CALL, JOSEPH RUDD, accountant; b. Pensacola, Fla., Oct. 18, 1950; s. Melvin Eliason and Doris Mae (Rudd) C.; m. Nola Jean Pack, Dec. 20, 1973; children: Benjamin, Jeremy, Joshua, Rebecca, Jacob. BS, Brigham Young U., 1974. CPA, Calif., Idaho; cert. fin. planner, 1986. Small bus. specialist Deloitte, Haskins & Sells, L.A., 1974-78; audit mgr. Rudd, DaBell & Hill, Rexburg, Idaho, 1978-80, audit ptnr. Rudd & Co., 1980-82, ptnr. in charge Idaho Falls office, 1982—. Mem. task force Small Bus. High Tech. Devel. State of Idaho, 1983; pres. Bonneville-Idaho Falls Crimestoppers, Inc., 1984-85; bd. dirs. Idaho Falls symphony Soc., 1988-91. Mem. Am. Inst. CPAs (hon. mention on CPA exam 1975, exec. coms. pvt. cos. 1989—), Calif. Soc. CPAs., Idaho Soc. CPAs (pres. S.E. Idaho chpt. 1983-84, state bd. dirs. 1984-88, pres.-elect 1987, pres. 1988-89), Idaho Falls C. of C. (bd. dirs. 1984-88, chmn. bd. dirs. 1986-87), Rexburg C. of C. (dir. 1981-82), Eastern Idaho Sailing Assn. (rear commodore 1983-89). Mormon. Office: Rudd & Co/Chartered 725 S Woodruff Ave Idaho Falls ID 83401-5286

CALL, MERLIN WENDELL, lawyer; b. Long Beach, Calif., Nov. 25, 1931; s. True and Bernice (Johnson) C.; m. Kathryn J. Gage, Dec. 22, 1956 (div.); children: Christopher, Lori. AB, Stanford U., 1951, JD, 1953. Bar: Calif. Assoc. Tuttle & Taylor, L.A., 1955-60, ptnr., 1960—; mem. bd. visitors Stanford Sch. Law, 1987-90. Chmn. bd. trustees Westmont Coll., Santa Barbara, Calif., 1988—, Fuller Found., Pasadena, Calif., 1987—, Mission Aviation Fellowship, Redlands, Calif., 1974-78, Gospel Broadcasting Assn., 1967-78; mem. Town Hall of Calif., L.A., 1958—; trustee Fuller Theol. Sem. Pasadena, 1963-78, 83—, AirServ Internat., Redlands, 1984-91. 1st lt. U.S. Army, 1953-55. Mem. Calif. Club, Phi Beta Kappa, Order of Coif. Home: 1660 La Loma Rd Pasadena CA 91105-2158 Office: Tuttle & Taylor 355 S Grand Ave Fl 40 Los Angeles CA 90071-3101

CALL, OSBORNE JAY, retail executive; b. Afton, Wyo., June 4, 1941; s. Osborne and Janice C.; m. Tamra Compton, Dec. 16, 1977; children—Thad, Crystal. Student, Ricks Coll., Rexburg, Idaho, Brigham Young U., Provo, Utah. Engaged in petroleum mktg., 1960-68; v.p. Caribou Four Corners, Afton, 1964-68; pres. Flying J Inc. (retail and wholesale gasoline and real estate devel. co.), Brigham City, Utah, 1968—; dir. No. div. First Security Bank, Brigham City. Office: Flying J Inc 770 W 2250 S Brigham City UT 84302-4181 also: Flying J Inc 50 W 990 S Brigham City UT 84302

CALL, RICHARD WILLIAM, health facility administrator; b. L.A., Oct. 17, 1924; s. Asa Vickry and Margaret (Fleming) C.; m. Nancy Banning, Nov. 29, 1952; children: Leslie, Kate, Nancy. AB, Stanford U., 1945, MD, 1947; postgrad., Harvard U., 1953. Diplomate Am. Bd. Internal Medicine. Intern L.A. County Hosp., 1947-48; resident Hosp. of the Good Samaritan and L.A. County Hosp., 1948-50; pvt. practice, L.A., 1953-57; corp. med. dir. Union Oil Co. Calif., L.A., 1957-83; pres. Seaver Inst., L.A., 1983—; bd. dirs. investment funds and convertible funds Trust Co. West, L.A. Past pres. bd. govs., trustee Natural History Mus., L.A., 1970—; bd. dirs. Santa Anita Found., L.A., 1978—; trustee, chmn. bd. emeritus Children's Hosp., L.A., 1971—; bd. dirs. Exec. Svc. Corps. Fellow ACP. Republican. Episcopalian. Office: Seaver Inst 800 W 6th St Ste 1410 Los Angeles CA 90017-2717

CALLAHAN, JAMES CALVIN, state offical; b. Leadville, Colo., Dec. 3, 1942; s. Cecil James and Frances Morine (Parr) C.; m. Antoinette Jo, Apr. 15, 1964; children: Ian James, Lara Jan. Student, U. Colo., 1961-64. Sr. engr. Div. Wildlife, State of Colo., Denver, 1964-77, sr. land agt., 1977—. Mem. Royal Order of Scotland, Masons (venerable master Denver). Methodist. Home: 562 Melody Dr Northglenn CO 80221 Office: Div Wildlife 6060 Broadway Denver CO 80216

CALLAHAN, MARILYN JOY, social worker; b. Portland, Oreg., Oct. 11, 1934; d. Douglas Q. and Anona Helen (Bergemann) Maynard; m. Lynn J. Callahan, Feb. 27, 1960 (dec.); children: Barbara Callahan Baer, Susan Callahan Sewell, Jeffrey Lynn. BA, Mills Coll., 1955; MSW, Portland State U., 1971, secondary teaching cert., 1963. Bd. cert. diplomate in clin. social work; lic. clin. social worker, Oreg. Developer, adminstr. ednl. program Oreg. Women's Correctional Ctr., Oreg. State Prison, Salem, 1966-67; mental health counselor Benton County Mental Health, Corvallis, Oreg., 1970-71; inst. tchr. Hillcrest Sch., Salem, Oreg., 1975-81; social worker protective svcs. Mid Willamette Valley Sr. Svcs. Agy., Salem, 1981-88; psychiat. social worker dept. forensics Oreg. State Hosp., 1988—; part-time pvt. practice care mgmt. of elderly/disabled; therapist for ct. referred adult sex offenders; panel mem. Surgeon Gen.'s NW Regional Conf. on Interpersonal Violence, 1987; speaker in field; planner, organizer Seminar on Age Discrimination, 1985. Mem. NASW (bd. dirs. Oreg. chpt.), Oreg. Gerontol. Assn., Catalina 22 Nat. Sailing Assn. Home: 2880 Mountain View Dr S Salem OR 97302-5471 Office: Oreg State Hosp Forensics Dept 2600 Center St NE Salem OR 97310-0530

CALLAHAN, MICHAEL CHARLES, military officer; b. Washington, July 29, 1949; s. John Arthur Callahan and Celia Louise (Pierce) Karl; m. V. LuAnn Gustaveson, Oct. 18, 1976; children: Lawrence Arthur, Erin Louise, Patrick Charles. BSBA, Fla. State U., 1974; MA in Computer Resource Mmgt., Webster U., 1987. Commd. 2d lt. USAF, 1974, lt. col., 1991; F-4D weapons system officer 421 TAC Fighter Squadron, Hill AFB, Utah, 1976-78; instr. pilot Det 4 40 ARRS, Hill AFB, 1978-79; ops. officer Det 7 37 ARRS, Minot, N.D., 1979-82; chief H-1 acads. 1550 Combat Crew Tng. Wing, Kirtland AFB, N.Mex., 1982-84, chief ops. analysis, 1983-84; USAF SAR coodr. HQ ARRS, Scott AFB, Ill., 9184-86, chief U.S. Mission Control Ctr., 1986-88; USSOUCOM search and rescue liaison officer OL-I ARS, Quarry Heights, Panama, 1988-91; chief Alaskan Rescue Coordination Ctr. OLE-Det 5 ARS, Elmendorf AFB, 1991—; U.S. del. SICOFAA SAR Com., S.Am., 1989-92, SAR Planning Com., Vladsvostok, CIS, 1992. Mem. Ctrl. Jr. High Adv. Com., Anchorage, 1992; pres. Elders Quorum, Anchorage, 1992. Decorated DFC, Bronze Star, Air medal with V, Air medal with 3 oak leaf clusters, Air Force Commendation medal, Meritorious Svc. medal with 3 oak leaf clusters. Mem. Air Rescue Assn. (Outstanding Achievement 1990-91), Dadaelions. Republican. LDS. Home: Apt A 5550 H St Elmendorf AFB AK 99506 Office: OL-E Det 5 ARS Ste 5 6900 9th St Elmendorf AFB AK 99506

CALLAN, JOSI IRENE, museum director; b. Yorkshire, Eng., Jan. 30, 1946; came to U.S., 1953; d. Roger Bradshaw and Irene (Newbury) Winstanley; children: James, Heather, Brett Jack; m. Patrick Marc Callan, June 26, 1984. BA in Art History summa cum laude, Calif. State U., Domingues Hills, 1978, MA in Behavioral Scis., 1981. Dir. community rels./alumni affairs Calif. State U., Dominguez Hills; adminstrv. fellow office chancellor Calif. State U., Long Beach, assoc. dir. univ. svcs. office chancellor, 1979-85; dir. capital campaign, assoc. dir. devel. Sta. KVIE-TV, Sacramento, 1985-86; dir. project devel. Pacific Mountain Network, Denver, 1986-87; dir. mktg. and devel. Denver Symphony Orch., 1988-89; assoc. dir. San Jose (Calif.) Mus. Art, 1989-91, dir., 1991—; asst. prof. sch. social and behavioral scis. Calif. State U., Dominguez Hills, 1981—; mem. adv. com. Issues Facing Mus. in 1990s JKF U., 1990-91. Mem. com. arts policy Santa Clara Arts Coun., 1990-92; chair San Jose Arts Roundtable, 1992—; active ArtTable, 1992—, Community Leadership San Jose, 1992-93; mem. adv. bd. Bay Area Rsch. Project, 1992—; mem. Calif. Arts Coun. Visual Arts Panel, 1993, Santa Clara Arts Coun. Visual Arts Panel, 1993; bd. dirs. YWCA, 1993—. Fellow Calif. State U., 1982-83. Mem. AAUW, Am. Mus. Assn., Nat. Soc. Fund Raising Execs. (bd. dirs. 1991), Colo. Assn. Fund Raisers, Art Mus. Devel. Assn., We. Mus. Assn., Calif. State U. Alumni Coun. (pres. 1981-83), Rotary Internat. Office: San Jose Museum of Art 110 S Market St San Jose CA 95113

CALLAWAY, HOWARD HOLLIS, business executive; b. La Grange, Ga., Apr. 2, 1927; s. Cason Jewell and Virginia (Hand) C.; m. Elizabeth Walton, June 11, 1949; children: Elizabeth Callaway Considine, Howard Hollis Jr., Edeard Cason, Virginia Callaway Martin, Ralph Walton. Student, Ga. Inst. Tech., 1944-45; BS, U.S. Mil. Acad., 1949. Commd. 2d lt. AUS, 1949, advanced through grades to 1st. lt., 1952; resigned, 1952; mem. 89th Congress from 3d Ga. dist.; U.S. sec. Army Washington, 1973-75; campaign mgr. Pres. Ford Com., 1975-76; CEO Crested Butte (Colo.) Mountain Resort, 1975—; bd. dirs. SCI systems, Inc., Hunstville, Ala., CML, Acton, Mass. Mem. Nat. 4-H Svc. Com., 1957-73; chmn. trustees Ida Cason Callaway Found., Pine Mountain, Ga., Freedoms Found. at Valley Forge; former mem. bd. regents Univ. System Ga.; Rep. candidate for gov. Ga., 1966; candidate in Rep. Primary for U.S. Senate from Colo., 1980; chmn. Colo. Rep. Party, 1981-87, chmn. GOPAC, 1987-93; mem. Def. Base Realignment and Closure Commn., 1992. 1st lt. inf. AUS, 1949-52. Mem. World Pres.' Orgn. (past pres.), Young Pres.' Orgn. (past pres.), Chief Execs. Orgn., Capital City Club (Atlanta), Piedmont Driving Club (Atlanta), Bohemian Club (San Francisco), Phi Delta Theta. Episcopalian. Home: Mt Crested Butte CO 81225 Office: 1900 Grant St Ste 850 Denver CO 80203

CALLEN, LON EDWARD, county official; b. Kingman, Kans., Mar. 31, 1929; s. Cleo Paul and Josephine Nell (Mease) C.; BA in Math. and Physics, U. Wichita (Kans.), 1951; m. Barbara Jean Sallee, Oct. 12, 1954; children: Lon Edward, Lynnette J. Commd. 2d lt. USAF, 1951, advanced through grades to lt. col., 1968; comdr. Tuslog Detachment 93, Erhac, Turkey, 1966-67; sr. scientist Def. Atomic Support Agy., Washington, 1967-71; ret., 1971; dir. emergency preparedness City-County of Boulder, Colo., 1976—; bd. dirs. Boulder County Emergency Med. Svcs. Coun., 1977, Boulder County Amateur Radio Emergency Svcs., 1978—. Mem. hon. awards com. Nat. Capital Area council Boy Scouts Am., 1971; chmn. Boulder County United Fund, 1976-82; mem. asst. staff Indian Princesses and Trailblazer programs Boulder YMCA, 1974-78. Decorated Joint Svc. Commendation medal; recipient cert. achievement Def. Atomic Support Agy., 1970. Mem. AAAS, Am. Ordnance Soc., Am. Soc. Cybernetics, Planetary Soc., Math. Assn. Am., N.Y. Acad. Scis., Fedn. Am. Scientists, Nat. Assn. Atomic Vets., Union Concerned Scientists, Boulder County Fire Fighters Assn., Colo. Emergency Mgmt. Assn., Ret. Officers Assn., Colo. Front Range Protective Assn., Mensa, Sigma Xi, Pi Alpha Pi. Clubs: Boulder Knife and Fork, Boulder Gunbarrel Optimists, Denver Matrix, U. Colo. Ski, U. Wichita. Author articles in field. Home: 4739 Berkshire Ct Boulder CO 80301-4055 Office: Box 471 County Courthouse Boulder CO 80306

CALLENDER, WILLIAM LACEY, savings and loan executive, lawyer; b. Oakland, Calif., Feb. 1, 1933; s. William Clarence and Doris (Lacey) C.; m. Joan Ingram, Dec. 14, 1968; 1 child, William Ingram; 1 child from previous marriage, Suzanne. AA, Hartnell Jr. Coll., Salinas, Calif., 1952-53; student, U. Calif., Berkeley, 1953-54; BA in Econs., Fresno State Coll., 1955; JD, U. So. Calif., 1960. Bar: Calif. 1960, U.S. Dist. Ct. (so. dist.) Calif. 1960. V.p., sr. atty. Calif. Fed. Savs. & Loan Assn., Los Angeles, 1975-81, v.p., asst. gen. counsel, 1981-82, sr. v.p., gen. counsel, sec., 1982-83, exec. v.p. adminstrn., sec., 1985-87; pres., chief exec. officer Calif. Fed. Bank (formerly Calif. Fed. Savs. and Loan Assn.), L.A., 1987—; bd. dirs. Calif. Fed. Bank, CalFed Inc., L.A. Mem. Calif. League Savs. Instns. (legis. and regulation com. 1987—), Order of Coif. Republican. Episcopalian. Office: Calif Fed Bank 5700 Wilshire Blvd Los Angeles CA 90036-3659

CALLIHAN, C. MICHAEL, lieutenant governor, former state senator; b. Spokane, Wash., Aug. 7, 1947; s. Collis and Dorothy C.; m. Debra McDonald, 1990. BA, Western State Coll., 1973. Gunnison county assessor, 1975-79; mem. Colo. Ho. of Reps., 1979-80, Colo. Senate, 1982-86; lt. gov. State of Colo., 1986—; chmn. Colo. Commn. Indian Affairs, 1987—; pres. Western Equity Assn., Inc. With USN, Vietnam. Recipient Outstanding Advocate award SBA, 1989; named Colo. Elected Official of Yr. United Vet. Com. of Colo., 1991. Mem. Am. Legion, VFW, Colo. Civil Air Patrol (maj.), Lions. Democrat. Office: Office of Lt Gov 130 State Capitol Denver CO 80203*

CALLIS, DANIEL LEON, artist, paralegal; b. Shirley, Mass., May 7, 1958; s. Robert Edward and Carol Louise (Tetman) C.; m. Stephanie Sue Linam, May 25, 1985 (div. 1991); 1 child, Owen. BA, U. Tex., El Paso, 1985. Legal asst. Butt, Thornton and Baehr, P.C., Albuquerque, 1991-93, paralegal, 1993—. Author: (novel) Lovely Days of Jeff, 1992; one-man show: Camera Graphics, Albuquerque, 1992; group shows: Albuquerque, 1987, Montserrat Gallery, N.Y.C., 1992, Agora Gallery, N.Y.C., 1992. Vol. Necessities of Life Bank, Albuquerque, 1991; writer, player variety show Sta. KUNM, Albuquerque, 1992-93. Democrat. Home: 211 Graceland Dr SE Albuquerque NM 87108

CALLISON, NANCY FOWLER, nurse; b. Milw., July 16, 1931; d. George Fenwick and Irma Esther (Wenzel) Fowler; m. B.G. Callison, Sept. 25, 1954 (dec. Feb. 1964); children: Robert, Leslie, Linda. Diploma, Evanston Hosp. Sch. Nursing, 1952; BS, Northwestern U., 1954. RN, Calif. Staff nurse, psychiat. dept. Downey VA Hosp., 1954-55; staff nurse Camp Lejeune Naval Hosp., 1955, 59-61; obstet. supr. Tri-City Hosp., Oceanside, Calif., 1961-62; pub. health nurse San Diego County, 1962-66; sch. nurse Rich-Mar Union Sch. Dist., San Marcos, Calif., 1966-68; head nurse San Diego County Community Mental Health, 1968-73; dir. patient care services Southwood Mental Health Ctr., Chula Vista, Calif., 1973-75; program cons. Comprehensive Care Corp., Newport Beach, Calif., 1975-79; dir. Manpower Health Care, Culver City, Calif., 1979-80; dir. nursing services Peninsula Rehab. Ctr., Lomita, Calif., 1980-81; clinic supr., coordinator utilization and authorizations, acting dir. provider relations Hawthorne (Calif.) Community Med. Group, 1981-86; mgr. Health Care Delivery Physicians of Greater Long Beach, Calif., 1986-87; cons. Quality Rev. Assocs., West L.A., 1988-93; case mgr. Mercy Physicians Med. Group, 1992—; clin. coord., translator Flying Samaritans, 1965—, mem. internat. bd. dirs., 1975-77, 79-86, 89—, dir. San Quentin project, 1991—, pres. South Bay chpt., 1975-81, v.p., 1982-85, bd. dirs. San Diego chpt., 1987—, pres. San Diego chpt. 1991—, adminstr. Clinica Esperanza de Infantil Rosarito Beach 1990-93. Mem. Nat. Assn. Female Execs., Aircraft Owners and Pilots Assn., U.S.-Mex. Border Health Assn., Calif. Assn. of Quality Assurance Profls., Cruz Roja Mexicana (Delegacion Rosarito 1986-92).

CALLISS, FRANK WILLIAM, computer science educator; b. London, Jan. 1, 1962; came to U.S., 1990.; BSc with honours, New U. Ulster, Coleraine, No. Ireland, 1986; PhD, U. Durham, Eng., 1989. Asst. prof. computer sci. Ariz. State U., Tempe, 1990—. Editor Proc. Maintenance Workshop, 1987, 88; contbr. articles to profl. jours. Mem. IEEE, Assn. for Computing Machinery, Brit. Computer Soc. Office: Ariz State U Dept Computer Sci Tempe AZ 85287-5406

CALLISTER, LOUIS HENRY, JR., lawyer; b. Salt Lake City, Aug. 11, 1935; s. Louis Henry and Isabel (Barton) C.; B.S., U. Utah, 1958, J.D., 1961; m. Ellen Gunnell, Nov. 27, 1957; children—Mark, Isabel, Jane, Edward, David, John Andrew, Ann. Bar: Utah 1961. Asst. atty. gen. Utah, 1961; sr. ptnr. Callister, Duncan & Nebeker, Salt Lake City, 1961—; bd. dirs. Am. Stores Co., Quailbluff Devel. Co. Vice-chmn. Salt Lake City Zoning Bd. Adjustment, 1979-84; bd. govs. Salt Lake Valley Hosps., 1983-91; treas. exec. com. Utah Rep. Com., 1965-69; chmn. Utah chpt. Rockefeller for Pres. Com., 1964-68; sec., trustee Salt Lake City Police Hon. Cols., 1982—; trustee Utah Econ. Devel. Corp., 1992—, U. Utah, 1987—, vice-chmn., 1989—. Mormon. Home: 1454 Tomahawk Dr Salt Lake City UT 84103-4225 Office: Callister Duncan Nebeker 800 Kennecott Bldg Salt Lake City UT 84133

CALLISTER, MARION JONES, federal judge; b. Moreland, Idaho, June 6, 1921; m. Nina Lynn Hayes, June 7, 1946; children—Nona Lynn Callister Haddock, Lana Sue Callister Meredith, Jenny Ann Callister Thomas, Tamara Callister Banks, Idonna Ruth Callister Andersen, Betty Patricia Callister Jacobs, Deborah Jean Hansen, Mary Clarice Fowler, David Marion, Nancy Irene Callister Garvin, Michelle, Kimberly Jane. Student, Utah State U., 1940-41; B.S.L., U. Utah, 1950, J.D., 1951. Bar: Idaho 1951. Dep. pros. atty. Bingham County, Idaho, 1951-52; asst. U.S. atty. Dist. of Idaho, 1953-57, U.S. atty., 1975-76; pvt. practice, 1958-69; judge Idaho Dist. Ct. 4th Jud. Dist., 1970-75; judge U.S. Dist. Ct. Idaho, Boise, 1976—, chief judge, 1981-88. Served with U.S. Army, 1944-46. Decorated Purple Heart. Republican. Mormon. Office: US Dist Ct PO Box 040 550 W Fort St Boise ID 83724

CALLOS, PHYLLIS MARIE, association executive; b. Oakland, Calif., Nov. 6, 1923; d. William Earl Canova and Jessie Marian Andrea (Jensen) Cowan; m. Reno Gelso Bresso, Jan. 24, 1943 (div. 1948); children: William Andrew Bresso Callos; m. Albert Callos, Feb. 26, 1949; 1 stepchild, Cheryl Callos Brooke. Adminstrv. asst. Calif. Rsch. Assocs., Albany, 1956-58; coowner Legal/Tech. Secretarial Svc., Oakland, 1959-61; office mgr., legal sec. Smith, Parrish, Paduck & Clancy, Oakland, 1961-79; asst. to pres. Citizens for Law and Order, Oakland, 1980-86, nat. pres., 1986—; bd. dirs. Crime Victims United, Sacramento, 1992—, Jud. Reform Found., Oakland, 1991—, Coalition of Victims Equal Rights, Sacramento, 1991—. Editor, writer CLO News, 1983—. Chmn. City of Oakland Residential Rent Arbitration Bd., 1984-87; pres. Piedmont Area Rep. Women, 1981-83. Recipient Proclamation Mayor and City Coun., Oakland, 1987, Clock Victims of Crime, Alameda, Calif., 1990, Plaques State of Calif., Sacramento, 1991, Justice for Murder Victims, San Francisco, 1992. Mem. DAR (vice-regent Piedmont chpt. 1981-82), Soc. Mayflower Descs., Daus. Calif. Pioneers, Nat. Soc. Magna Charta Dames, Descs. of Robert the Bruce, Descs. of Knights of the Garter, The Roush Family in Am., Sons Union Veterans of Civil War (aux.). Repubican. Episcopalian. Office: Citizens for Law and Order Box 13308 Oakland CA 94661

CALLOW, KEITH MCLEAN, judge; b. Seattle, Jan. 11, 1925; s. Russell Stanley and Dollie (McLean) C.; m. Evelyn Case, July 9, 1949; children: Andrea, Douglas, Kerry. Student, Alfred U., 1943, CCNY, 1944, Biarritz Am. U., 1945; BA, U. Wash., 1949, JD, 1952. Bar: Wash. 1952, D.C. 1974. Asst. atty. gen. Wash., 1952; law clk. to justice Supreme Ct. Wash., 1953; dep. pros. atty. King County, 1954-56; ptnr. Little, LeSourd, Palmer, Scott & Slemmons, Seattle, 1957-62, Barker, Day, Callow & Taylor, 1964-68; judge King County Superior Ct., 1969-71, Ct. of Appeals Wash., Seattle, 1972-84; presiding chief judge Ct. of Appeals Wash., 1985-90; justice State Supreme Ct. Wash., Olympia, 1985-90, chief justice, 1989-90; 2d v.p. Conf. of Chief Justices; lectr. bus. law U. Wash., 1956-62, Shefelman Disting. lectr., 1991; faculty Nat. Jud. Coll., 1980, Seattle U. Environ. Law, 1992; coorganizer, sec. Coun. of Chief Judges, 1980; mem. Fed. Cts. Study Com., 1989-90; legal adviser Nat. Ct. & Ministry of Justice, Republic of Estonia, 1993. Editor works in field. Chief Seattle coun. Boy Scouts Am.; adviser Gov. Health Care Commn. State of Washington, 1991-92; pres. Young Men's Rep. Club, 1957. With AUS, 1943-46. Decorated Purple Heart; recipient Brandeis award Wash. State Trial Lawyers Assn., 1981, Douglas award, 1990. Fellow Am. Bar Found.; mem. ABA (chmn. com. on judiciary 1984-90), Wash. State Bar Assn. (mem. exec. com., appellate Judges Conf.),

D.C. Bar Assn., Seattle-King County Bar Assn., Estate Planning Coun., Navy League, Rainier Club (sec. 1978, trustee 1989-92), Coll. Club, Harbor Club, Forty Nine Club (pres. 1972), Masons, Rotary, Psi Upsilon, Phi Delta Phi. Office: US Embassy, Kentmonni 20, Tallinn EE0001, Estonia

CALVERT, KEN, congressman; b. Corona, Calif., June 8, 1953. AA, Chaffey Coll., 1973; BA Econs., San Diego State U., 1975. Corona/ Norco youth chmn. for Nixon, 1968, 82; county youth chmn. rep. Vesey's Dist., 1970, 43d dist., 1972; congl. aide to rep. Vesey, Calif., 1975-79; gen. mgr. Jolly Fox Restaurant, Corona, Calif., 1975-79, Marcus W. Meairs Co., Corona, Calif., 1979-81; pres., gen. mgr. Ken Calvert Real Properties, Corona, Calif., 1981—; Reagan-Bush campaign worker, 1980; co chmn. Wilson for Senate Campaign, 1982, George Deukmejian election, 1978, 82, 86, George Bush election, 1988, Pete Wilson senate elections, 1982, 88, Pete Wilson for Gov. election, 1990; mem. 104th Congress from Calif. dist., 1993—; mem. natural resources com., sci., space and tech. com., 1993—; former v.p. Corona/ Norco Rep. Assembly; chmn. Riverside Rep. Party, 1984-88, County Riverside Asset Leasing; bd. realtors Corono/ Norco. Exec. bd. Corona Community Hosp. Corp. 200 Club; mem. Corona Airport adv. commn.; adv. com. Temescal/ El Cerrito Community Plan. Mem. Riverside County Rep. Winners Circle (charter), Lincoln Club (co-chmn., charter, 1986-90), Corona Rotary Club (pres. 1991), Elks, Navy League Corona Norco, Corona C. of C. (pres. 1990), Noroco C. of C., Monday Morning Group, Corona Group (past chmn.), Econ. Devel. Ptnrship., Silver Eagles (March AFB support group, charter). Office: US Representative 1523 Longworth Washington DC 20515-0543*

CALVIN, DOROTHY VER STRATE, computer company executive; b. Grand Rapids, Mich., Dec. 22, 1929; d. Herman and Christina (Plakmyer) Ver Strate; m. Allen D. Calvin, Oct. 5, 1953; children: Jamie, Kris, Bufo, Scott. BS magna cum laude, Mich. State U., 1951; MA, U. San Francisco, 1988; EdD, U. San Francisco, 1991. Mgr. data processing. Behavioral Rsch. Labs., Menlo Park, Calif., 1972-75; dir. Mgmt. Info. Systems Inst. for Prof. Devel., San Jose, Calif. 1975-76; systems analyst, programmer Pacific Bell Info. Systems, San Francisco, 1976-81; staff mgr., 1981-84; mgr. applications devel. Data Architects Inc., San Francisco, 1984-86; pres. Ver Strate Press, San Francisco, 1986—. Instr., Downtown C.C., San Francisco, 1980-84, Cañada C.C., 1986—, Skyline Coll., 1988—; mem. computer curriculum adv. coun. San Francisco City Coll., 1982-84. V.p. LWV, Roanoke, Va., 1956-58; pres. Bulliss Purissima Parents Group, Los Altos, Calif., 1962-64; bd. dirs. Vols. for Israel, 1986-87. Mem. NAFE, Assn. Systems Mgmt., Assn. Women in Computing, Phi Delta Kappa. Democrat. Avocations: computing, gardening, jogging, reading. Office: Ver Strate Press 1645 15th Ave San Francisco CA 94122-3523

CALVIN, MELVIN, chemist, educator; b. St. Paul, Minn., Apr. 8, 1911; s. Elias and Rose I. (Hervitz) C.; m. Genevieve Jemtegaard, 1942; children: Elin, Karole, Noel. BS, Mich. Coll. Mining and Tech., 1931, DSc, 1955; PhD, U. Minn., 1935, DSc, 1969; hon. rsch. fellow, U. Manchester, Eng., 1935-37; Guggenheim fellow, 1967; DSc, Nottingham U., 1958, Oxford (Eng.) U., 1959, Northwestern U., 1961, Wayne State U., 1962, Gustavus Adolphus Coll., 1963, Poly. Inst. Bklyn., 1962, U. Notre Dame, 1965, U. Gent, Belgium, 1970, Whittier Coll., 1971, Clarkson Coll., 1976, U. Paris Val-de-Marne, 1977, Columbia U., 1979, Grand Valley U., 1986. With U. Calif., Berkeley, 1937—; successively instr. chemistry, asst. prof., prof., Univ. prof., dir. Lab. Chem. Biodynamics U. Calif., 1963-80, assoc. dir. Lawrence Berkeley Lab., 1967-80; Peter Reilly lectr. U. Notre Dame, 1949; Harvey lectr. N.Y. Acad. Medicine, 1951; Harrison Howe lectr. Rochester sect. Am. Chem. Soc., 1954; Falk-Plaut lectr. Columbia U., 1954; Edgar Fahs Smith Meml. lectr. U. Pa. and Phila. sect. Am. Chem. Soc., 1955; Donegani Found. lectr. Italian Nat. Acad. Sci., 1955; Max Tishler lectr. Harvard U., 1956; Karl Folkers lectr. U. Wis., 1956; Baker lectr. Cornell U., 1958; London lectr., 1961, Willard lectr., 1982; Vanuxem lectr. Princeton U., 1969; Disting. lectr. Mich. State U., 1977; Prather lectr. Harvard U., 1980; Dreyfus lectr. Grinnell Coll., 1981, Berea Coll., 1982; Barnes lectr. Colo. Coll., 1982; Nobel lectr. U. Md., 1982; Abbott lectr. U. N.D., 1983; Gunning lectr. U. Alta., 1983; O'Leary disting. lectr. Gonzaga U., 1984; Danforth lectr. Dartmouth Coll., 1984, Grinnell Coll., 1984; R.P. Scherer lectr. U. S. Fla., 1984; Imperial Oil lectr. U. Western Ont., Can., 1985; disting. lectr. dept. chemistry U. Calgary, Can., 1986; Melvin Calvin lectr. Mich. Tech. U., 1986; Eastman prof. Oxford (Eng.) U., 1967-68. Author: (with G. E. K. Branch) The Theory of Organic Chemistry, 1940, Isotopic Carbon, (with others), 1949, Chemistry of Metal Chelate Compounds, (with Martell), 1952, Path of Carbon in Photosynthesis, (with Bassham), 1957, (with Bassham) Photosynthesis of Carbon Compounds, 1962, Chemical Evolution, 1969; contbr. articles to chem. and sci. jours. Recipient prize Sugar Research Found., 1950, Flintoff medal prize Brit. Chem. Soc., 1953, Stephen Hales award Am. Soc. Plant Physiologists, 1956, Nobel prize in chemistry, 1961, Davy medal Royal Soc., 1964; Virtanen medal, 1975, Priestley medal, 1978, Am. Inst. Chemists medal, 1979, Feodor Lynen medal, 1983, Sterling B. Hendricks medal, 1983, Melvin Calvin Medal of Distinction Mich. Tech. U., 1985, Nat. Medal of Sci., 1989, John Ericsson award/medal U.S. Dept. Energy, 1991. Mem. Britain's Royal Soc. London (fgn. mem.), Am. Chem. Soc. (Richards medal N.E. chpt. 1956, Nichols medal N.Y. chpt. 1958, award for nuclear applications in chemistry, pres. 1971, Gibbs medal Chgo. chpt. 1977, Priestley medal 1978, Desper award Cin. chpt. 1981), Am. Acad. Arts and Scis., Nat. Acad. Scis., Royal Dutch Acad. Scis., Japan Acad., Am. Philos. Soc., Sigma Xi, Tau Beta Pi, Phi Lambda Upsilon. Office: U Calif Dept Chemistry Berkeley CA 94720

CALVO, KEVIN EDWARD, orthotist, prosthetist, consultant; b. New Orleans, Jan. 11, 1957; s. Ellen (McConnell) C.; m. Lisa Northey; children: Brandon James, Nicholas Edward, Robert Raymond. Student, Delgado Coll., New Orleans, 1978, Tulane U., 1978, UCLA, 1979-80, NYU, 1980. Cert. orthotic/prosthetic practitioner. Orthotic and prosthetic technician Lambert Limb & Brace, New Orleans, 1977-78; prosthetic/orthotic asst. Harbor Orthopedics, San Diego, 1978-80; chief of orthotic/prosthetic lab. VA Hosp., La Jolla, Calif., 1980-82, rsch. prosthetist, 1980-88; owner, practitioner Bionics, Orthotics & Prosthetics, San Diego, 1981—; educator in orthopedic residency program U. Calif. San Diego, La Jolla, 1981—; vol. orthotic prosthetic svcs. Calexico (Calif.) Valley Orthopedic Clinic, 1979-86. Author: Orthopedic Rehabilitation, 1992; patentee knee brace. VA grantee, 1980-88. Mem. Internat. Soc. Orthotists and Prosthetists, Am. Acad. Orthotics and Prothestics, Calif. Orthotics and Prosthetics Assn., Am. Orthotic and Prosthetic Assn. Office: Bionics Orthotics and Prosthetics 3737 Moraga Ave # 220 San Diego CA 92101

CAMARILLO, RICHARD JON, professional football player; b. Whittier, Calif., Nov. 29, 1959. Student, Cerritos Jr. Coll., Washington U. With New England Patriots, 1981-87, L.A. Rams, 1988; punter Phoenix Cardinals, 1989—. Office: Phoenix Cardinals 8701 S Hardy Tempe AZ 85284

CAMENZIND, MARK J., research chemist; b. Palo Alto, Calif., Nov. 17, 1956; s. Paul V. and Mildred Martha Camenzind; m. Dorothy L. Hassler. SB in Chemistry, MIT, 1978; PhD in Inorganic Chemistry, U. Calif., Berkeley, 1983. Postdoctoral fellow U. B.C., Vancouver, 1983-86; rsch. chemist Salutar, Inc., Sunnyvale, Calif., 1987, Balazs Analytical Lab., Sunnyvale, 1987—. Contbr. rsch. papers to profl. jours. Mem. ASTM, Semicondr. Equipment and Materials Internat., Am. Chem. Soc. Office: Balazs Analytical Lab 1380 Borregas Ave Sunnyvale CA 94089

CAMERON, CHARLES HENRY, petroleum engineer; b. Greeley, Colo., Oct. 21, 1947; s. Leo Leslie and Naomi Tryphena (Phillips) C.; m. Cheryl Christine Debelock, Aug. 30, 1969; 1 child, Ericka Dawn. AS, Mesa State Coll., 1968; BS in Geology, Mesa Coll., 1978; AS in Hazardous Materials Tech., Front Range C.C., Wesminister, Colo., 1990. Retardation technician Colo. State Home and Tng. Sch., Grand Junction, 1967-69; journeyman carpenter Brotherhood of Carpenters and Joiners, Grand Junction, 1969-76; hydrocompaction mgr. Colo. Dept. Hwys., Grand Junction, 1975-77; rsch. geologist Occidental Oil Shale, Inc., Grand Junction, 1977-78; geol. engr. Cleveland Cliffs Iron Co., Morgantown, W.Va., 1978-81; tech. advisor Ute Indian Tribe, Ft. Duchesne, Utah, 1981-86; ops. mgr. Charging Ute Corp., Golden, Colo., 1986-87; cons. Golden, 1987-90; petroleum engr., hazardous materials mgr. U.S. Dept. Interior/Bur. of Indian Affairs, Ft. Duchesne, 1990—. Contbr. articles to profl. jours. Mem. Colo. Oil Field Investigators Assn. Home: 255 E 200 N Vernal UT 84078 Office: BIA Uintah & Ouray Agy Fort Duchesne UT 84026

CAMERON, DUNCAN FERGUSON, museum consultant; b. Toronto, Ont., Can., Feb. 1, 1930; s. Charles Gordon and Winnifred Petrie (Peppderdene) C.; m. Nancy Tousley, Apr. 24, 1975. Adminstr. Royal Ont. Museum, Toronto, 1956-62; pres. Janus Ltd., Toronto, 1962-70; nat. dir. Can. Conf. Arts, Toronto, 1968-71; dir. Bklyn. Mus., 1971-73; prin. P.S. Ross & Partners, Toronto, 1975-77; dir. Glenbow-Alta. Inst., Calgary, 1977-88, dir. emeritus, 1988—. Author articles in field; frequent guest lectr. Fellow Mus. Assn., Can. Mus. Assn.; mem. Internat. Coun. Mus., Am. Assn. Mus., Can. Art Mus. Dirs. Orgn. (past pres.), Commonwealth Assn. Mus. (past pres.), Order St. Lazarus of Jerusalem, Masons. Anglican. Home: 3438 6th St SW, Calgary, AB Canada T2S 2M4

CAMERON, ELSA SUE, curator, consultant; b. San Francisco, Nov. 19, 1939; d. L. Don and Betty (Jelinsky) C.; m. Michael Lerner, Dec. 24, 1979. BA, San Francisco State U., 1961, MA, 1965; teaching credential, 1962. Curator Randall Jr. Mus., San Francisco, 1963-65, Fine Arts Mus. Downtown Ctr., San Francisco, 1976-80, San Francisco Airport Galleries, 1980—; exec. dir. Community Arts, Inc., San Francisco, 1973—; reporter Council on Mus., N.Y.C., 1973-80; asst. prof. art edn. U. So. Calif., Los Angeles, 1982-83; cons. U. Art Mus., Berkeley, 1980-82, instr. 1981, 101 California Venture, San Francisco, 1986—; exhibitions curator OM & M/ Olympia & York, L.A., 1988—; cons. Art in Pub. Pls., Miami, Fla., 1988; cons. John Wayne Airport, Orange County, 1990-91, Hankyu Dept. Store, Osaka, Japan, 1992—. Reporter: (book) The Art Museum as Educator, 1977, (exhibit catalogue) Airport Cafe, 1986. Fellow NEA, 1973, 77. Mem. Western Regional Conf. (v.p. 1974-75), Am. Assn. Museums. Office: San Francisco Internat Airport Exhbn PO Box 8097 San Francisco CA 94128-8097

CAMERON, JAMES DUKE, state justice; b. Richmond, Calif., Mar. 25, 1925; s. Charles Lee and Ruth M. (Mabry) C.; m. Suzanne Jane Pratt, Aug. 16, 1952 (div. 1982); children: Alison Valerie, Craig Charles, Jennifer Elaine; m. Paula Manardo, July 25, 1992. A.B., U. Calif. at Berkeley, 1950; J.D., U. Ariz., 1954; LL.M., U. Va., 1982; LLD (hon.), U. Nev., 1991. Bar: Ariz. 1954. Practice in Yuma, 1954-60, 61-65; judge Superior Ct. Yuma County, 1960, US. Ct. Appeals Ariz., 1965-70; justice U.S. Supreme Ct., Ariz., 1970—, vice chief justice, 1971-75, chief justice, 1975-80; mem. faculty appellate judges seminar Inst. Jud. Adminstrn., 1968-80; bd. dirs. State Justice Inst., 1986—. Author: Arizona Appellate Forms and Procedures, 1968, also article. Mem. Ariz. Bd. Pub. Welfare, 1961-64, chmn., 1963-64; Mem. Eagle Scout bd. rev. Theodore Roosevelt council Boy Scouts Am., 1968—; Alternate del. Republican Nat. Conv., 1952; treas. Ariz. Rep. Party, 1958-60; Trustee Yuma City-County Library, 1958-67. Served with AUS, World War II. Mem. ABA (chmn. appellate judges conf. jud. adminstrn. div. 1977-78, jud. mem.-at-large 1986-88, bd. govs.), Ariz. Bar Assn., Yuma County Bar Assn. (past pres.), Ariz. Acad. Inst. Jud. Adminstrn., Nat. Inst. Justice (adv. com. 1984-86), Conf. Chief Justices U.S. (chmn. 1978-79), Am. Judicature Soc., Am. Law Inst., Masons, Shriners, Ariz. Club, Lambda Chi Alpha, Phi Alpha Delta, Delta Theta Phi. Office: Bonnett Fairbourn et al Ste 1100 4041 N Central Ave Phoenix AZ 85012

CAMERON, JUDITH ELAINE MOELLERING, jewelry designer and manufacturer; b. Eagle Grove, Iowa, May 26, 1943; d. Albert Edwin and Marion (Trask) Moellering; m. William Ewen Cameron, Aug. 13, 1966 (div. 1970). BA, Drake U., 1965; Cert. Inst. Essential Integration, 1991, Jin Shinjyutsu Therapy Tng., 1992; lic. massage therapist, N.Mex., 1992. Polit. intern, Washington, 1965; model, asst. buyer, copywriter, Yonkers, Des Moines, 1962-66; asst. to columnist Harlan Miller, 1962-65; dir. pers. 4th Northwestern Nat. Bank, Mpls., 1966; head copywriter SPF Advt., Mpls., 1966-68; dir. spl. projects program U. Minn., Mpls., 1968-70; cons. pub. rels. Fed. Republic of Germany, Italy, Spain, 1970-71; mgr. Jetset Sportswear, Footville, Wis., 1971-72; artist Almunecar, Spain, 1972-74; dir. pub. rels. Topspin, Totalplan Sports Internat., A.G., Madrid, 1974-76, mng. dir., Madrid and London, 1976-80; European mgr. Siam Internat. Amalgamated Mfrs. Ltd., London, 1977-80; European rep. Siam Cement Trading Co., London, 1979-80; European mgr. Third Wave Electronics Co., Inc., London, 1980-82; exec. v.p., dir. Electronic Specialty Products, Inc., N.Y.C., 1983-84; pres. Q.E.D., Ltd., Hong Kong, 1981-85, Comml. Brain, Inc., N.Y.C. and N.Mex., 1984—, Judith Cameron of Santa Fe, 1988-93, mgr. End of the Trail/Sante Fe and CD's T Shirt Co., 1992; gen. mgr. H & B Enterprises, Santa Fe, 1992-93. Bd. dirs. N.Mex. Repertory Theater; mem. N.Mex. Task Force, Arts Advocacy, Fashion Coun., Rep. Nat. Com. 8 one-woman exhibitions of paintings, Spain; 4 group exhbns., Europe. Mem. NAFE, Reps. Abroad, Women Bus. Owners of N.Y., Iowa Soc. N.Y. (founding mem., pres.), Coun. Internat. Rels., Spotlighters, Am. Crafts Coun., Alpha Phi.

CAMERON, JUDITH LYNNE, educator, hypnotherapist; b. Oakland, Calif., Apr. 29, 1945; d. Alfred Joseph and June Estelle (Faul) Moe; m. Richard Irwin Cameron, Dec. 17, 1967; 1 child, Kevin Dale. AA in Psychol., Sacramento City Coll., 1965; BA in Psychol., German, Calif. State U., 1967; MA in Reading Specialization, San Francisco State U., 1972; postgrad., Chapman Coll.; PhD, Am. Inst. Hypnotherapy, 1987. Cert. tchr., Calif. Tchr. St. Vincent's Catholic Sch., San Jose, Calif., 1969-70, Fremont (Calif.) Elem. Sch., 1970-72, LeRoy Boys Home, LaVerne, Calif., 1972-73; tchr. Grace Miller Elem. Sch., LaVerne, Calif., 1973-80, resource specialist 1980-84; owner, mgr. Pioneer Take-out Franchises, Alhambra and San Gabriel, Calif., 1979-85; resource specialist, dept. chmn. Bonita High Sch., LaVerne, Calif., 1984—; mentor tchr. in space sci. Bonita Unified Sch. Dist., 1988—, rep. LVTV; owner, therapist So. Calif. Clin. Hypnotherapy, Claremont, Calif., 1988—; bd. dirs., recommending tchr., asst. dir. Project Turnabout, Claremont, Calif.; Teacher-in-Space cons. Bonita Unified Sch. Dist., LaVerne, 1987—; advisor Peer Counseling Program, Bonita High Sch., 1987—; advisor Air Explorers/Edwards Test Pilot Sch., LaVerne, 1987—; mem. Civil Air Patrol, Squadron 68, Aerospace Office, 1988—; selected amb. U.S. Space Acad.-U.S. Space Camp Acad., Huntsville, Ala., 1990; named to nat. teaching faculty challenger Ctr. for Space Edn., Alexandria, Va., 1990; regional coord. East San Gabiel Valley Future Scientists and Engrs. of Am. Vol. advisor Children's Home Soc., Santa Ana, 1980-81; dist. rep. LVTV Channel 29, 1991; regional coord. East San Gabriel Valley chpt. Future Scientists and Engrs. of Am., 1992; mem. internat. invesigation Commn. UFOs, 1991. Named Tchr. of Yr. Bonita High Sch., 1988-89, Continuing Svc. award, 1992, La Verne, Calif. Space Ambassador U.S. Space Camp, 1990. Mem. Internat. Investigations Com. on UFOs, Coun. Exceptional Children, Calif. Assn. Resource Specialists, Calif. Elem. Edn. Assn., NEA, Calif. Tchrs. Assn., Calif. Assn. Marriage and Family Therapists, Planetary Soc., Mutual UFO Network, Com. Scientific Investigation L5 Soc., Challenger Ctr. for Space Edn., Calif. Challenger Ctr. Crew for Space Edn., Ornage County Astronomers. Republican. Clubs: Chinese Shar-Pei Am., Concord, Rare Breed Dog, Los Angeles. Home: 3257 N La Travesia Dr Fullerton CA 92635-1455 Office: Bonita High Sch 115 W Allen Ave San Dimas CA 91773-1437

CAMERON, KENNETH ALLAN, geologist, educator; b. Oregon City, Oreg., July 18, 1953; s. Richard Dale and Janis May (Hieb) C.; m. Ellen Jean Sandberg, Mar. 16, 1979; children: Eric Collin, Laura Elaine. BSc, Portland State U., 1976, MSc, 1980. Registered geologist, Oreg. Teaching asst. Portland (Oreg.) State U., 1977-79, instr., 1986—; geologist U.S. Bur. Mines, Spokane, Wash., 1976-77, U.S. Geol. Survey, Vancouver, Wash., 1981-90, Oreg. Dept. Environ. Quality, Portland, 1990—; dir. Haggard Astron. Obs., Oregon City, 1989—; geol. cons. Northwest Archaeol. Investigations, Portland, 1990—. Contbr. articles to sci. jours. Recipient award of merit John Inskeep Environ. Learning Ctr., Oregon City, 1988. Mem. Am. Geophys. Union, Northwest Sci. Assn., U.S. Geological Soc. (Meritorious Svc. award, 1987), Sigma Xi. Home: 14708A SE Rupert Dr Portland OR 97267-1207 Office: Oreg Dept Environ Quality 811 SW 6th St Portland OR 97204

CAMERON, RICHARD IRWIN, property manager; b. Twin Falls, Idaho, Feb. 12, 1941; s. Wilbur Richard and Rose (Steinberg) C.; m. Judith Lynne Moe, Dec. 17, 1967; 1 child, Kevin Dale. Student, U. Idaho; BA, Idaho State U., 1963. Lic. real estate broker. Owner, mgr. Four C Ranches, Twin Falls, 1962-65, Cameron's Marina and Garage, Twin Falls, 1965-67; mgr. Doggie Diner Restaurants, Oakland, Calif., 1967-68; mgr. Bartels & Blaine A&W Restaurant, San Mateo, Calif., 1968-70, supr., gen. mgr., 1970-73; area supr. McDonalds Corp., L.A., 1973-78; pres. CamWal Enterprises, Inc., Alhambra, Calif., 1978-84, Four C Svcs., Inc., San Gabriel, Calif., 1979-85, Four C Properties, Fullerton, Calif., 1979—; cons. Enterprise Pub. Co., La Mirada, Calif., 1989—; v.p. pub. rels. Infinity Hypnosis Group, Orange County Calif., 1992—. Vol. counselor Children's Home Soc., Santa Ana, Calif., 1980-84; mem. Friends of the Observatory, Air/Space Mus., San Diego, Calif. With U.S. Air Guards, 1963-64. Recipient Nat. Franchisee of Yr. award Pioneer Take-Out Corp., L.A., 1984. Mem. Nat. Franchisees Assn. (bd. dirs. 1980-85), Nat. Restaurant Assn., Rotary, Elks. Republican. Home and Office: Four C Properties 3257 N La Travesia Dr Fullerton CA 92635-1455

CAMMALLERI, JOSEPH ANTHONY, corporate director, retired air force officer; b. Bronx, N.Y., Feb. 2, 1935; s. Leo Anthony and Angela Marie (Mirandi) C.; BS, Manhattan Coll., 1956; M.S., Okla. State U., 1966; postgrad. Golden Gate U., 1974—; children: Anthony R., Aaron L., Thomas K., Jeffrey A. Cert. life ins. instr., Calif. Commd. 2d lt. USAF, 1956, advanced through grades to lt. col., 1973; trainee flight crew, 1956-58; crew mem. B-52, 1958-64; behavioral scientist Aerospace Med. Rsch. Labs., Wright-Patterson AFB, Ohio, 1966-68; EB-66 crew mem. Tahkli AFB, Thailand, 1968-69; faculty mem. dept. life and behavioral scis. USAF Acad. (Colo.), 1969-74, assoc. prof., dir. operational psychology div., 1972-74, B-1 human factors engring. mgr. Air Force Flight Test Center, Edwards AFB, Calif., 1974-76, chief handbook devel., 1976-77; ret., 1977; account exec. Merrill Lynch, Pierce, Fenner & Smith, Sherman Oaks, Calif., 1977-80; acad. program rep. U. Redlands (Calif.), 1980-84, regional dir. admissions assessment, 1984—, mem. faculty Whitehead Ctr., 1979—, assoc. dean admissions, 1986-89; fac lty Golden Gate U., 1975-80; account exec. Humanomics Ins., 1989-90; corp. dir. tng. and edn. Fin. West Group, 1990-92, prin. CEO Spectrum Securities, Inc., Westlake Village, Calif., 1992—; adj. faculty Calif. Luth. U., 1990—, Antioch U., 1992—; sec., 7th Ann. Narrow Gauge Conv. Com., Pasadena, Calif., 1986. Contbr. articles to profl. jours. Sec. com. centennial celebration Rio Grande So. Ry., Dolores, Colo., 1991; North L.A. County Liaison Offcr. USAF Acad., 1992—; USAF Acad. Liason Officer, North Los Angeles County, 1992—. Decorated D.F.C., Air medal (5), Meritorious Service medal. Mem. Nat. Ry. Hist. Soc., Ry. and Locomotive Hist. Soc., Rocky Mountain R.R. Club, L.A. Live Steamers, Nat. Model R.R. Assn., Colo. R.R. Hist. Found. (life), Santa Fe Ry. Hist. Soc., USAF Acad. Athletic Assn. (life), DAV, Psi Chi. Home: 3093 Charlotte St Newbury Park CA 91320-4450 Office: Spectrum Securities Inc Westlake Village CA 91361-4222

CAMMANS, STEPHEN CHARLES, finance executive; b. Nephi, Utah, Sept. 9, 1954; s. Francis Carolus and Helen (Lunt) C.; m. Victoria Payne, Nov. 17, 1979; children: Miriam, Joseph Lemar. B, Calif. State Polytechnic U., 1978. CPA. Acct. Schultz, Meggelin, et al, Covina, Calif., 1977-87, jr. partner, 1987-89; controller Ameritec Corp., Covina, 1989-92, v.p., 1992—; dir. Hollfelder Found., Covina, 1988—. Asst. scoutmaster Boy Scouts of Am., Covina, 1977-78, scoutmaster, Pomona, Calif., 1982; scout coord. Cub Scouts of Am., Chino, 1989-92. Republican. Home: 11923 Roswell Chino CA 91710 Office: Ameritec Corp 760 Arrow Grand Cir Covina CA 91722

CAMP, ALIDA DIANE, lawyer, law educator; b. N.Y.C., Feb. 14, 1955; d. Seymour and Pearl (Aisen) C.; m. Roger Morris Arar, June 3, 1984. BA, SUNY-Binghamton, 1976; JD, Columbia U., 1980. Bar: N.Y. 1981, U.S. Dist. Ct. (so. and ea. dists.) N.Y. 1982, Calif. 1986, U.S. Dist. Ct. (cen. dist.) Calif. 1987. Student intern U.S. Atty.'s Office, N.Y.C., 1979-80; assoc. Kaye, Scholer, Fierman, Hays & Handler, N.Y.C., 1980-83; asst. prof. bus. law grad. sch. bus. adminstrn. U. Mich., Ann Arbor, 1983-86, sr. faculty adviser Mortarboard, 1983; cons. Treat Mgmt, L.A., 1986; v.p. bus. and legal affairs Concorde-New Horizons Corp, L.A., 1987—; vol. atty. mediator-negotiator Calif. Lawyer for the Arts.; vol. Lawyers for Arts, N.Y.C., 1982-83; alumni adviser shc. law Columbia U., 1985—. Editor Columbia Jour. Law and Soc. Problems, 1979-80; contbr. articles to profl. jours. Mem. Am. Mus. Natural History, N.Y.C., 1983—; mem. Nature Conservancy, 1988—. Harlan Fiske Stone scholar Columbia U., 1978, 80. Mem. ABA, Columbia U. Law Sch. Alumni Assn., Beverly Hills Bar Assn., Phi Beta Kappa. Jewish. Home: 155 S Elm Dr Beverly Hills CA 90212-3321 Office: Concorde-New Horizons Corp 11600 San Vicente Blvd Los Angeles CA 90049-5102

CAMP, WILLIAM CURTIS, engineering research company executive; m. Linda Bobier, Nov. 27, 1985. BSME, U. N.Mex., 1970, MBA, 1974. Engr., mgr. Kirtland Air Force Base, 1970-77; fin. analyst U.S. Dept. Energy, 1977-79; advanced planner Pub. Svc. Co. N.Mex., 1979-82, dir. fin. mgmt., 1982-85; treas., chief fin. officer Sci. and Engring. Assocs., Inc., 1985—; pres. Soup'r Salad Restaurant, 1979-83. State rep. N.Mex., 1985-88; chmn. budget com. LWV, 1991, treas. 1991—; mem. Albuquerque Energy Consv. Bd., 1977-78; coach Young Am. Football League, 1975-77. Maj. USAR, 1968—. Recipient numerous cake baking awards including Best of Show, N.Mex. State Fair, 1981, Best Chiffon, 1981, 83, 90. Mem. Albuquerque C. of C. (bd. dirs. 1989—, vice chmn. 1990-91, chmn. govt. divsn., chmn. bus. opportunities task force 1989-90), U. N.Mex. Alumni Assn. (bd. dirs. 1977-80, legis. com. 1983-84), Kiwanis Club (bd. dirs. 1972-74, chmn. youth com. 1974-75). Home: 7708 Spring Ave NE Albuquerque NM 87110-7332

CAMPANA, MICHAEL EMERSON, hydrogeology educator, researcher; b. N.Y.C., May 13, 1948; s. John Pilgrim and Ruth Ellen (Emerson) C. BS in Geology, Coll. of William and Mary, 1970; MS in Hydrology, U. Ariz., 1973, PhD in Hydrology, 1975. Cert. profl. geologist, Ind.; cert. profl. hydrogeologist, Am. Inst. Hydrology. From asst. to assoc. rsch. prof. Desert Rsch. Inst., Reno, 1976-83, 84-89; from asst. to assoc. prof. geology U. Nev., Reno, 1976-83, 84-89; assoc. prof. geology Ga. State U., Atlanta, 1983-84; vis. assoc. prof. earth scis. U. Calif., Santa Cruz, 1988-89; assoc. prof. hydrogeology U. N.Mex., Albuquerque, 1989—; mem. Nat. Rsch. Coun. Com., Washington, 1988-90, EPA workshop ground water ecology, 1992-93. Mem. editorial bd. Journal of Ground Water, 1984-89; contbr. articles to profl. jours. Active Amnesty Internat., 1987—. Numerous rsch. grants including U.S. Dept. Interior, State of Nev., NSF, U.S. Dept. Energy, 1976—. Mem. Internat. Assn. Hydrogeologists, N.Am. Benthological Soc., Geol. Soc. Am., Am. Geophys. Union, Am. Inst. Hydrology, Assn. Ground Water Scis. and Engrs., Am. Water Resources Assn. (pres. N.Mex. sect. 1993—), N.Mex. Geol. Soc. (chair Rocky Mountain ground water conf. 1993), Soc. Ind. and Applied Maths. Home: 4808 Ridgecrest Cir SE Albuquerque NM 87108-4435 Office: Univ NMex Dept Earth & Planetary Scis Albuquerque NM 87131-1116

CAMPANY, ANDREW DANIEL, mechanical engineer; b. Watertown, N.Y., Nov. 20, 1956; s. Lyle Fredrick and Viola Cecilia (Wilcox) C.; m. Suzanne Rocco, Aug. 14, 1982; 1 child, Alycia Danielle. AS in Engring. Sci., Jefferson Community Coll., 1976; BSME, Rochester Inst. Tech., 1979; postgrad., U. Colo., 1986-89. Registered profl. engr., Colo. Dynamics engr. Rocketdyne div. Rockwell Internat. Corp., Canoga Park, Calif., 1979-81; sr. product engr. Lord Corp., Erie, Pa., 1981-84; group leader Gates Rubber Co., Denver, 1984-88; project engr. OEA, Inc., Aurora, Colo., 1988-92; supr. project engring. Special Devices, Inc., Newhall, Calif., 1993—; cons. 1992—. Patentee in field. Mem. Pi Tau Sigma. Home: 27114 Baxard Pl Valencia CA 91354 Office: Special Devices Inc 16830 W Placerita Canyon Rd Newhall CA 91321

CAMPBELL, ALICE DEL CAMPILLO, biochemist, researcher; b. Santurce, Puerto Rico, May 30, 1928; d. José Adrian and Julia Pilar (Rivera) del Campillo; m. Allan McCulloch Campbell, Sept. 5, 1958; children: Wendy Alice, Joseph Lindsay. AB, Columbia U., 1947; MS, NYU, 1953; PhD, U. Mich., 1960. Research asst. Pub. Health Research Inst., N.Y.C., 1947-48, NYU, 1948-54; instr. biochemistry Sch. Medicine, San Juan, Puerto Rico, 1954-56; research assoc. U. Rochester, N.Y., 1960-68; sr. research assoc. Stanford U., Calif., 1968—. Contbr. articles to sci. jours. Fellow Am. Inst. Chemists; mem. Am. Chem. Soc., Sigma Xi (sec., treas. 1985-86, v.p. Stanford chpt. 1986-87), Phi Sigma (Beta chpt.). Home: 947 Mears Ct Stanford CA 94305 Office: Stanford U Dept Biological Scis Stanford CA 94305

CAMPBELL, ANDREW GARRETT, scientist; b. N.Y.C., June 19, 1960; s. ATtar Rowley and Doreen Estelle (Job) C. BS, CUNY, 1981; CPhil, UCLA, 1984, PhD, 1987. Scientist U. Calif., Los Angeles; supplemental investigator, sr. postdoctoral fellow NIH-UCLA, 1991—; cons. Migliara/

Kaplan Assocs., Towson, Md., 1990, Key Communications Mktg. Rsch., Long Beach, Calif., 1986-87, Bremshield Corp., L.A., 1985—. Contbr. articles to profl. jours. UCLA fellow, 1982-84.

CAMPBELL, ANDREW ROBERT, geology educator; b. Boston, Apr. 6, 1954; s. Robert Wellington and Laura (Mason) C.; m. Kathryn Elaine Glesener, Aug. 11, 1984; children: Alison Elaine, Robert Marshall. BS in Geology with honors, Ind. U., 1977; MA in Geology, Harvard U., 1979, PhD in Geology, 1983. Asst. prof. N.Mex. Tech, Socorro, 1983-88, assoc. prof., 1988—. Assoc. editor: Economic Geology, 1991—; contbr. articles to profl. jours. Recipient 5 NSF grants for geology rsch., numerous other grant awards. Mem. Am. Mineralogical Soc., Soc. Econ. Geologists, N.Mex. Geol. Soc. Office: N Mex Tech DeptGeoscience Socorro NM 87801

CAMPBELL, ARTHUR WALDRON, lawyer, educator; b. Bklyn., Mar. 29, 1944; s. Wilburn Camrock and Janet Louise (Jobson) C.; m. Drusilla Newlon Green, June 7, 1969; children: Wilburn Camrock, Matthew Patrick. BA, Harvard U., 1966; JD, W.Va. U., 1971; M in Criminal Justice, Georgetown U., 1975. Bar: W.Va. 1971, D.C. 1971, Calif. 1974. Asst. U.S. atty. U.S. Justice Dept., Washington, 1971-73; clin. instr. D.C. Consortium Univs., 1973-76; law prof. Calif. Western Sch. Law, San Diego, 1976—; cons. W.Va. State Legis. Com. to Rewrite Criminal Code, 1972-73; chmn. Va. sect. Nat. Assn. Criminal Def. Lawyers Strike Force on Grand Jury Abuse, 1975-76; mem. ABA Com. on Privacy, Washington, 1974, D.C. Bar Landlord and Tenant Com., 1975, Neighborhood Legal Svcs., San Diego, 1982; pvt. prac. 1976—; chief exec. officer Trudar Prodns. Inc., San Diego, 1981—; devel. real estate Trudar Prodns. Inc., 1982—. Author: (legal treatise) Law of Sentencing, 1978, 2d edit., 1991, (coursebook) Entertainment Law, 1993, (books) Discoveries of a Workaholic, 1988, Meditations for Recovering Workaholics, 1990. Pres. Peace Store, San Diego, 1986. Recipient Harvard Nat. scholarship, 1962-63, Am. Jurisprudence awrd Lawyers Coop. Pub. Co., 1970-71, Prettyman Fellowship, Georgetown U., 1971-73; middle weight boxing champion Harvard U., 1964-65. Mem. Fed. Defenders, Appellate Defenders, Peace Through Law Inst., World Svc. Orgn. for Workaholics Anonymous (sec. 1990-91), San Diego Workaholics Anonymous (founder). Home: 4891 Sparks Ave San Diego CA 92110-1358 Office: Calif Western Sch Law 350 Cedar St San Diego CA 92101-3113

CAMPBELL, BEN NIGHTHORSE, U.S. senator; b. Auburn, Calif., Apr. 13, 1933; m. Linda Price; children: Colin, Shanan. BA, Calif. U., San Jose, 1957. Educator Sacramento Law Enforcement Agy.; mem. Colo. Gen. Assembly, 1983-86, U.S. Ho. Reps., 1987-93; U. S. Senator from Colorado, 1993—; rancher, jewelry designer, Ignacio, Colo. Chief No. Cheyenne Tribe. Named Outstanding Legislator Colo. Bankers Assn., 1984, Man of Yr. LaPlata Farm Bur., Durango, Colo., 1984; named one of Ten Best Legislators Denver Post/Channel 4, 1986. Mem. Am. Quarter Horse Assn., Am. Brangus Assn., Am. Indian Edn. Assn., Aircraft Owners and Pilots Assn. Democrat. Office: US Senate 380 Russell Sen Office Bldg Washington DC 20510*

CAMPBELL, COLIN HERALD, mayor; b. Winnipeg, Man., Can., Jan. 18, 1911; s. Colin Charles and Aimee Florence (Herald) C.; BA, Reed Coll., 1933; m. Virginia Paris, July 20, 1935; children: Susanna Herald, Corinna Buford, Virginia Wallace. Exec. sec. City Club of Portland, 1934-39; alumni sec., dir. endowment adminstrn. Reed Coll., 1939-42, exec. sec. N.W. Inst. Internat. Rels. 1940-42, instr. photography, 1941-42; contract engr. Kaiser Co., Inc., 1942-45; asst. pers. dir. Portland Gas & Coke Co., 1945-48; dir. indsl. rels. Pacific Power & Light Co., Portland, 1948-76. Mem. Oreg. Adv. Com. on Fair Employment Practices Act, 1949-55; trustee, chmn., pres. Portland Symphonic Choir, 1950-54; trustee Portland Civic Theater, 1951-54; bd. dirs. Portland Symphony Soc., 1957-60, Community Child Guidance Clinic, 1966-68; active United Way, 1945-75; bd. dirs. Contemporary Crafts Assn., 1972-76, treas., 1975-76; bd. dirs. Lake Oswego Corp., 1961-65, 71-73, 74-76, corp. sec., 1964, pres., 1973-74, treas., 1975-76; mem. Com. on Citizen Involvement, City of Lake Oswego, 1975-77; chmn. Bicentennial Com., Lake Oswego; sec.-treas. Met. Area Communications Commn., 1980-85; treas. Clackamas County Community Action Agy., 1980-82, chmn., 1982-85; mem. fin. adv. com. W. Clackamas County LWV, 1974-76, 78-80; councilman City of Lake Oswego, 1977-78, mayor, 1979-85, chmn. libr. growth task force, 1987-89, chmn. hist. rev. bd., 1990-92; chmn. energy adv. com. League Oreg. Cities, 1982-84; mem. adv. bd., chmn. fin. com. Lake Oswego Adult Community Ctr. 1985-88; pres. Oswego Heritage Coun., 1992—; active county Blue Ribbon Com. on Law Enforcement, 1987-89. Mem. Edison Electric Inst. (exec. com.), N.W. Electric Light and Power Assn., Lake Oswego C. of C. (v.p. 1986-87, chmn. Land Use com. 1990-91), Nat. Trust for Hist. Preservation, Oreg. Art Mus., Pacific N.W. Pers. Mgmt. Assn. (past regional v.p.), St. Andrews Soc., Oreg. Hist. Soc., Rotary (treas. Lake Oswego chpt. 1990—). Republican. Presbyterian. Home: 1219 Maple St Lake Oswego OR 97034-4729

CAMPBELL, DAVID ALAN, retail store manager; b. Berkeley, Calif., Oct. 20, 1954; s. Percy Ralph and Margaret Ann (Lawrence) C.; m. Diana Kay Pritchard, Aug. 31, 1977; children: Esther Jean, David Lawrence. BS, Calif. State U., Hayward, Calif., 1976. Store mgr. K Mart Corp., Great Falls, Mont., 1974—. Office: K Mart 7454 4400 10th Ave S Great Falls MT 59401

CAMPBELL, DAVID RANDALL, equipment manufacturing company executive; b. Rupert, Idaho, Aug. 26, 1928; s. Charles Newton and Rhoda (Randall) C.; m. Mary Elizabeth May, Jan. 3, 1951; children: Colin, Heather, Anne, Catherine, Bonnie, Allison, Rebecca. Student, Utah State U., 1946-48, U. Utah, 1951-53, 57-59. Salesman Home Furniture Co., Rupert, 1951-57; ptnr. Kenyon Farms, Oakley, Idaho, 1952-57; pres. Campbell Mfg. Inc., Salt Lake City, 1958-59; mgr. Cambelt div. Eimco Corp. Campbell Mfg. Inc., 1969-74; pres., owner Cambelt Internat. Corp., 1974-89, chmn. bd., CEO, 1989—. Numerous patents in field. Pres. Internat. Visitors-Utah Coun., Salt Lake City, 1974-75, 88, bd. dirs., 1990—; commr. Clan Campbell, Utah, 1990-92, trustee Clan Campbell USA, 1989-93, v.p. Clan Campbell N.Am., 1993—; former high councilman and bishop LDS Ch.; former dist. chmn., dist. rep. to county, dist. chmn. to state Nat. Rep. Com.; singer Utah Chorale. Recipient award of merit Internat. Visitors-Utah Coun., 1990. Mem. Utah Scottish Assn. (pres. 1987-88). Home: 8800-B Kings Hill Dr Salt Lake City UT 84121 Office: Cambelt Internat Corp 2420 West 1100 South Salt Lake City UT 84104

CAMPBELL, DAVID SCOTT, lawyer; b. Ft. Ord, Calif., Jan. 20, 1954; s. Robert E. and Helen L. (Moses) C.; m. Shellene G., Mar. 15, 1986; children: HEather, Damon. BS, Georgetown U., 1976; MPA, U. N.Mex., 1981, JD, 1986. Bar: N.Mex. Vol. U.S. Peace Corps, Foumban, Cameroon, Africa, 1976-78; cons., trainer U.S. Peace Corps, Cameroon, Tonga, Africa, 1978-81; asst. to mayor City of Albuquerque, 1981-83; law clk. Eaves Law Firm, Albuquerque, 1983-86; atty. Cole & Myers, Albuquerque, 1987-89; city atty. City of Albuquerque, 1989—; dir. N.Mex. State Bd. of Bar Commrs., Albuquerque, 1988-89. Chmn. Good Govs. Group, Albuquerque, 1988-89; key person, chmn. United Way, Albuquerque, 1982; mem. Leadership Albuquerque, 1988. Named N.Mex. Jaycees Outstanding Young New Mexican of Yr. 1992, Eagle Scout, 1969; recipient Young Lawyer award N.Mex. Bar Found., 1989. Mem. N.Mex. Common Cause (dir. 1983—, v.p. 1985-86), N.Mex. State Bar Assn. (prof. devel. com., pres. young lawyers div. 1988-89), N.Mex. Mcpl. Attys. Assn. (pres. 1990-91), Greater Albuquerque Vols. Assn. (founder 1981-82), Georgetown U. Alumni Assn. Democrat. Home: 1701 Caqua NE Albuquerque NM 87110 Office: City of Albuquerque PO box 1293 Albuquerque NM 87103

CAMPBELL, DEMAREST LINDSAY, writer, artist, designer; b. N.Y.C.; d. Peter Stephen III and Mary Elizabeth (Edwards) C.; m. Dale Gordon Haugo. BFA in Art History, MFA in S.E. Asian Art History, MFA in Theatre Design. Art dir., designer murals and residential interiors Campbell & Haugo, 1975—. Designed, painted and sculpted over 150 prodns. for Broadway, internat. opera, motion pictures. Mem. NOW, Asian Art Mus. Soc., San Francisco. Mem. United Scenic Artists, Scenic & Title Artists and Theatrical Stage Designers., Sherlock Holmes Soc. London, Amnesty Internat., Nat. Trust for Hist. Preservation (Gt. Brit. and U.S.A. chpt.), Shavian Malthus Soc. (charter Gt. Brit. chpt.).

CAMPBELL, DOUGLAS MICHAEL, computer science educator; b. San Pedro, Calif., May 4, 1943; s. Quinn Anslow and Joan Campbell; m. Jill Yvonne Thomas, Feb. 4, 1966; children: Heather, Micah, Matthew, Susannah. BA, Harvard U., 1967; PhD, U. N.C., 1971. Prof. math. dept. Brigham Young U., Provo, Utah, 1971-81, prof. computer sci., 1982—; pres. Timp Software, Orem, Utah, 1986—. Author: Whole Craft of Number, 1976, People, Problems, Results, 1981 (Sci. Book of Month), Tales of the Comet, 1986. Fulbright fellow India, 1983; recipient Maeser Rsch. award Brigham Young U., 1980. Mem. Phi Beta Kappa. Democrat. Mormon. Home: 758 E 100N Orem UT 84057 Office: Brigham Young U Computer Sci Dept Provo UT 84602

CAMPBELL, DOUGLAS NORMAN, air force officer, pilot; b. Verdun, France, June 30, 1955; came to U.S., 1957; s. Norman Joseph and Eva Nell (Fowler) C.; m. Theresa Cecilia Collins, May 29, 1982; 1 chld, Patricia Lorraine. BA in Polit. Sci., North Ga. Coll., 1976; MA in History, U. Nev., Las Vegas, 1990. Commd. ensign U.S. Navy, 1977; intersvc. transfer to U.S. Air Force, 1984, advanced through grades to maj., 1992. Mem. Nature Conservancy, Nat. Parks and Conservation Assn. Office: Holloman AFB Det 4 4444 OPS GP Alamogordo NM 88310

CAMPBELL, FREDERICK HOLLISTER, lawyer, historian; b. Somerville, Mass., June 14, 1923; s. George Murray and Irene Ivers (Smith) C.; A.B., Dartmouth, 1944; J.D., Northwestern U., 1949; postgrad. Indsl. Coll. Armed Forces, 1961-62; M.A. in History, U. Colo., 1984, PhD in History, 1993; m. Amy Holding Strohm, Apr. 14, 1951; 1 dau., Susan Hollister. Served with USMCR, 1944-46; joined USMC, 1950, advanced through grades to lt. col., 1962; admitted to Ill. bar, 1950, U.S. Supreme Ct. bar, 1967, Colo. bar, 1968; judge adv. USMC, Camp Lejeune, N.C., Korea, Parris Island, S.C., El Toro, Calif., Vietnam, Washington, 1950-67; asso. editor Callaghan and Co., Chgo., 1949-50; practiced law, Colorado Springs, Colo., 1968-88; ptnr. firm Gibson, Gerdes and Campbell, 1969-79; pvt. practice law, 1980-88; gen. counsel 1st Fin. Mortgage Corp., 1988—, vice chmn., corp. sec., 1993—; hon. instr. history U. Colo., Colorado Springs, 1986—; vis. instr., Colo. Coll., 1993. Mem. Estate Planning Coun., Colorado Springs, 1971-81, v.p., 1977-78. Rep. precinct committeeman, 1971-86; del. Colo. Rep. State Conv., 1972, 74, 76, 80, alt., 1978; trustee Frontier Village Found., 1971-77; bd. dirs. Rocky Mountain Nature Assn., 1975—, pres., 1979-92, Rocky Mountain Nat. Park Assocs. 1986—, v.p. 1986-92, sec. 1992—. Mem. Colo. Bar Assn., El Paso County Bar Assn., Am. Arbitration Assn., Marines Meml. Club, Phi Alpha Theta. Congregationalist. Author: John's American Notary and Commissioner of Deeds Manual, 1950. Contbr. articles to profl. jours. Home and Office: 2707 Holiday Ln Colorado Springs CO 80909-1217

CAMPBELL, GAYLON SANFORD, soil physicist; b. Blackfoot, Idaho, Aug. 20, 1940; s. Hazelton Sanford and Rosalie (Barrus) C.; m. Judith Harris, Aug. 5, 1964; children: Tamsin, Julia Bee, Karine, Colin, Cecily, Scott, Nigel, Stuart, Gillian. BS in Physics, Utah State U., 1965, MS in Soil Physics, 1966; PhD in Soils, Wash. State U., 1968. Asst. prof. soils Wash. State U., Pullman, 1971-75; assoc. prof. soils Wash. State U., 1975-80, prof. soils, 1980—; vis. prof. U. Nottingham, England, 1984-85. Author: Introduction to Environmental Biophysics, 1977, Soil Physics with BASIC, 1985; contbr. articles to profl. jours; patentee Krypton hygrometer. NSF fellow 1966-68, Sr. Vis. fellow British Sci. Rsch. Coun., Nottingham, England, 1977-78. Fellow Am. Soc. Agronomy, Soil Sci. Soc. Am. Mem. LDS Ch. Office: Wash State U Dept Crop and Soil Scis Pullman WA 99164-6420

CAMPBELL, GORDON MUIR, mayor; b. Vancouver, B.C., Can., Jan. 12, 1948; s. Charles Gordon and Margaret Janet (Muir) C.; m. Nancy J. Chipperfield, July 4, 1970; children: Geoffrey Gordon, Nicholas James. AB, Dartmouth Coll., 1970; MBA, Simon Fraser U., 1978. Tchr. Can. Univ. Service Overseas, Yola, Nigeria, 1970-72; exec. asst. to mayor City of Vancouver, 1972-76, alderman, 1984-86, mayor, 1986—; project mgr. Marathon Realty Devel. Co., Vancouver, 1976-81; pres. Citycore Devel. Corp., Vancouver, 1981-86. Recipient Outstanding Alumni award Simon Fraser U., 1987. Office: City of Vancouver, 453 W 12th Ave, Vancouver, BC Canada V5Y 1V4

CAMPBELL, GREGORY RAY, anthropology educator, researcher; b. Cin., Aug. 1, 1955; s. Ray Floyd and Wanda June (Castor) C. AA in Behavioral and Social Sci., Chaffey Community Coll., Alta Loma, Calif.; BA in History, UCLA, BA in Anthropology; MA in Anthropology, U. Okla., PhD in Anthropology. Acting asst. prof. dept. Afro-ethnic studies Calif. State U., Fullerton, 1988; acting asst. prof. dept. Am.-Indian studies and anthropology UCLA, 1988; asst. prof. U. Mont., Missoula, 1988-92, assoc. prof., 1992—; vis. adj. instr. U. Okla., Norman, 1985-93, clin. anthropologist dept. family medicine, 1986-87; cons. No. Cheyenne Tribe of Mont., Lame Deer, 1980—; rsch. affiliate Ctr. for Population Study, U. Mont., 1988—, curator of ethnology, 1988—. Inst. Am. Cultures fellow, 1987-88; NEA grantee, 1984-85, Okla. Found. for the Humanities grantee, 1985. Mem. Am. Soc. for Ethnohistory, Soc. for Med. Anthropology, Infectious Disease Study Group, Cultural Survival, Plains Anthropol. Assn. Office: Univ Mont Dept Anthropology Missoula MT 59812

CAMPBELL, HARRY WOODSON, geologist, mining engineer; b. Carthage, Mo., Jan. 14, 1946; s. William Hampton and Elizabeth Verle (LeGrand) C. BSEE, Kans. State U., 1969; MBA, U. Oreg., 1973, BS in Geology, 1975; MS in Geology, Brown U., 1978. Registered profl. engr., Wash.; cert. profl. geologist, Va. Geologist, mining engr. and phys. scientist U.S. Bur. Mines, Spokane, 1980—. Served with U.S. Army, 1969-71. Recipient Spl. Achievement award U.S. Bur. Mines, 1983, 86, 88. Mem. Geol. Soc. Am., Soc. Mining Engrs. Office: US Bur Mines E 360 3d Ave Spokane WA 99202

CAMPBELL, HOWARD ERNEST, mathematician, educator; b. Detroit, Sept. 20, 1925; s. Howard E. and Marie Easter (Brown) C.; m. Ramona Ann Anderson, July 30, 1972; children: Tanaquil Ruth, Howard Blaine, Thane George, Lowell Lete, Scott Baker. Student, Stevens Inst. Tech., 1943-44; BSEE, U. Wis., 1946, MS in Math., 1947, PhD in Math., 1949. Teaching asst. U. Wis., Madison, 1946-49; instr. U. Pa., Phila., 1949-51; asst. prof. Emory U., Atlanta, 1951-56; from asst. to assoc. prof. Mich. State U., East Lansing, 1956-63; prof., chmn. U. Idaho, Moscow, 1963-79, prof. math., 1979-80, prof. emeritus, 1981—; lectr. math Calif. Poly. State U., San Luis Obispo, 1984-90; from mem. to chmn. com. of examiners Coll. Entrance Exam. Bd. and Edn. Testing Svc., 1968-72; mem. accreditation team Commn. Higher Schs. N.W. Assn., 1968; cons. Future Resources and Devel. Corp. (Famous Artists Schs.), 1970. Author: The Structure of Arithmetic, 1970, Concepts of Trigonometry, 1981, Concepts of College Algebra, 1982, Concepts of Algebra and Trigonometry, 1982, (with Paul Dieker) Calculus, 1975, Calculus with Analytic Geometry, 2d edit., 1978, 3d edit., 1982; contbr. articles to profl. jours. Rsch. grantee USAR Office Sci. Rsch., 1952, 57-58, NSF, 1958-60. Mem. Sigma Xi, Pi Mu Epsilon. Home: 2679 Bamboo Dr Lake Havasu City AZ 86403

CAMPBELL, IAN DAVID, opera company director; b. Brisbane, Australia, Dec. 21, 1945; came to U.S., 1982; m. Ann Spira; children: Benjamin, David. BA, U. Sydney, Australia, 1966. Prin. tenor singer The Australian Opera, Sydney, 1967-74; sr. music officer The Australia Council, Sydney, 1974-76; gen. mgr. The State Opera of South Australia, Adelaide, 1976-82; asst. artistic adminstr. Met. Opera, N.Y.C., 1982-83; gen. dir. San Diego Opera, 1983—; guest lectr. U. Adelaide, 1978; guest prof. San Diego State U., 1986—; cons. Lyric Opera Queensland, Australia, 1980-81; bd. dirs. Opera Am., Washington, 1986—; chmn. judges Met. Opera Auditions, Sydney, 1989. Recipient Peri award Opera Guild So. Calif., 1984; named Headliner of Yr., San Diego Press Club, 1991. Assoc. fellow Australian Inst. Mgmt.; mem. Kona Kai Club, Rotary, San Diego Press Club (Headliner award 1991). Office: San Diego Opera PO Box 988 San Diego CA 92112-0988

CAMPBELL, JAMES EDWARD, physicist, consultant; b. Kingsport, Tenn., Jan. 13, 1943; s. Edward Montroe and Iola (Church) C.; m. Judy Priscilla Cameron, June 12, 1966; children: Jennifer Marie, James Kyle. BA in Math., Physics, Catawba Coll., 1965; PhD in Physics, Va. Tech. Inst., 1969. Nuclear radiation expert Naval Weapons Evaluation Facility, Albuquerque, 1970-76; mem. tech. staff Sandia Nat. Labs., Albuquerque, 1976-80; v.p. Intera Techs., Inc., Denver, 1980-88; disting. mem. tech. staff Sandia Nat. Labs., Albuquerque, 1988—; bd. dirs. TechLaw, Inc., Denver, 1983-88. Contbr. articles to profl. jours. Recipient IEEE Outstanding Paper award, 1991, NDEA fellowship, 1965-68, Acad. Honors scholarship, Catawba Coll., 1961-65. Mem. AAAS, Am. Phys. Soc. Republican. Lutheran. Office: Sandia Nat Labs Divsn 6613 Albuquerque NM 87185

CAMPBELL, JOHN FRANK, engineering and construction executive, financial manager; b. Inglewood, Calif., Nov. 11, 1947; s. John Bennington and Eugenia Ann (Binczik) C.; m. Vicky Lynn Bell, Mar. 6, 1976; children: John James, Jeremy Alan, Jason Alexander. BS in areospace engring., Va. Poly. Inst., 1970; MBA in internat. and multinat. bus., Golden Gate U., 1979. Test program mgr. David Taylor Model Basin, Carderock, Md., 1966-74; project adminstr. Bechtel, Inc., Gaithersburg, Md., 1974-75; project engr. Bechtel, Inc., Houston, 1976; asst. projects mgr. Bechtel Civil, San Francisco, 1977-80; mgr. mgmt. info. and planning Bechtel Group, Inc., San Francisco, 1981-88; info. svcs. mgr. Bechtel Corp., San Francisco, 1988-89, planning and reporting mgr., 1989-90, comml./svcs. mgr., 1990—; mem. conf. bd. charter Coun. Mgmt. Info. Execs., 1987-89. Mem. PTA, San Ramon, Calif., 1986-91. Mem. Sigma Gamma Tau. Republican. Roman Catholic. Home: 9485 Thunderbird Pl San Ramon CA 94583-3625 Office: Bechtel Corp 45 Fremont St San Francisco CA 94105-2204

CAMPBELL, KATHERINE ANN, editor, writer, communications executive; b. San Rafael, Calif., Nov. 16, 1949; d. Walter Franklin Campbell and Dorothy Ellen (Wilson) Coupe; m. John Edward Van Veenendaal, Nov. 16, 1975; children: Mark Campbell, Michael Campbell. AA, Santa Rosa Community Coll., Calif., 1970; BA in Journalism, San Francisco State U., 1979. Editor, reporter Davis (Calif.) Enterprise, 1980-82; sr. communications officer Bank Am., San Francisco, 1982-84; sr. editor Pacific Gas and Electric Co., San Francisco, 1984-90; prin. Campbell Communications, Berkeley, Calif., 1990—. Com. mem. Equal Rights Advocates, San Francisco, 1990, Literacy Vols. Am., Berkeley, 1990. Recipient Compass Award for Excellence Pub. Rels. Soc. Am., 1989; named Bay Area Best for Writing Internat. Assn. of Bus. Communicators, 1986, Gold Quill, 1988. Mem. Nat. Assn. Real Estate Editors, Women in Communications, Inc. Office: Campbell Communications 1609 Edith St Berkeley CA 94703-1306

CAMPBELL, LAUGHLIN ANDREW, mathematician, educator; b. Detroit, May 9, 1942; s. Laughlin Austin and Mary Kennerly (Holmes) C.; m. Janet Rhonda Gore, May 28, 1971 (div. July 1978); life ptnr. Roberta Grubb. ScB, MIT, 1963; Lic. ès Sc., U. Paris, 1964; MA, Princeton U., 1967, PhD, 1970. Asst. prof. math. U. Calif., San Diego, 1969-76; mem. tech. staff, engring. specialist, rsch. scientist The Aerospace Corp., L. A., 1978—. Reviewer Math. Revs., 1978—. Mem. IEEE, Am. Math. Soc., Assn. Computing Machinery. Achievements include first publication of solution of the Galois case of the Jacobian conjecture. Office: Aerospace Corp M1-102 PO Box 92957 Los Angeles CA 90009-2957

CAMPBELL, MARTIN JAMES, chemist; b. Eugene, Oreg., Nov. 3, 1965; s. Paul Hayden and Myrna Josephine (Pruner) C.; m. Janee Hayworth, Sept. 8, 1991. BS in Chemistry, Oreg. State U., 1988. Phys. sci. tech. U.S. Bur. Mines, Albany, Oreg., 1988-90, chemist, 1990—. Mem. Am. Chem. Soc., Toastmasters Internat. Office: US Bur Mines 1450 Queen Ave SW Albany OR 97321-2198

CAMPBELL, MICHAEL LEE, computer science researcher; b. L.A., Nov. 25, 1958; s. Earl J. and Lee (Fitch) C.; m. Asya Glozman, Jan. 23, 1961; children: Sasha Madeline, Alice Edie. BS in Math., U. Calif., Riverside, 1980; MS in Computer Sci., UCLA, 1982, PhD in Computer Sci., 1986. Mem. tech. staff electro-optical and data systems group Hughes Aircraft, El Segundo, Calif., 1982-88; sr. staff computer scientist Hughes Rsch. Labs., Malibu, Calif., 1988-92; engring. specialist computer systems divsn. Aerospace Corp., El Segundo, 1992—; lectr. dept. computer sci. UCLA, 1987-88. Contbr. articles to profl. jours. Mem. Computer Soc. of IEEE, Assn. for Computing Machinery, Sigma Xi (chpt. pres.). Office: Aerospace Corp PO Box 92957 Los Angeles CA 90009-2957

CAMPBELL, PHILIP LAROCHE, computer scientist; b. Bangor, Maine, Dec. 14, 1950; s. Ashley Sawyer and Mary Letitia (Fishier) C.; m. Mary Susan Ingram, Dec. 14, 1979; children: Katharine Skye, Benjamin Ingram, Rosalie Windham, Peter Greenleaf. BS in Psychology, Brigham Young U., 1975, MS in Computer Sci., 1983. Mem. tech. staff Sandia Nat. Labs., Albuquerque, 1983—. Mem. Assn. for Computing Machinery. Mem. LDS Church. Office: Sandia Nat Labs Box 5700 Albuquerque NM 87185-5700

CAMPBELL, REGINALD LAWRENCE, industrial hygienist, educator; b. Hartford, Conn., Apr. 8, 1943; s. Reginald L. and Etta M. (Ashton) C. Student Amherst Coll., 1961, Yale U. Sch. Medicine, 1965-67; AS, Hahnemann Med. Coll., 1975; BA, Fairmont State Coll., 1977; MS, Marshall U., 1980. Propr., dir. Campbell Clin. Lab., Amherst, Mass., 1963-65; staff therapist St. Joseph's Hosp., Stamford, Conn., 1966-67; staff therapist Yale-New Haven Hosp., 1967-70; asst. rsch. cardiothoracic surgery Yale U. Sch. Medicine, 1967-70; guest lectr. Royal Melbourne (Australia) Hosp., Monash U., 1968, Royal North Shore Hosp., U. Sydney (Australia), 1968; chief anesthetic technologist Montreal (Que.) Gen. Hosp., McGill U. Sch. Medicine, 1970; tech. dir. sect. respiratory disease svcs. Danbury (Conn.) Hosp., 1970-72; dir. respiratory program adj. faculty Western Conn. State Coll., Danbury, 1970-72; sr. instr. medicine Sch. Respiratory Therapy, Hahnemann Med. Coll., Phila., 1972-75, asst. prof. dept. medicine Coll. Allied Health Professions, 1974-75; adminstr. So. W.Va. Lung Ctr., Inc., Beckley, 1975-77; cons. respiratory therapy program Fairmont (W.Va.) State Coll., 1975-76, Bluefield (W.Va.) State Coll., 1975-76; tech. cons. W.Va. Gov.'s Coal Worker's Respiratory Disease Control Program, 1975-78; indsl. hygienist Nat. Mine Health and Safety Acad., U.S. Dept. Interior, Beckley, W.Va., 1978-79; instr. occupational lung diseases and occupational health Nat. Mine Health and Safety Acad., U.S. Dept. Labor, Beckley, 1979-87; chief indsl. hygienist dept. def. Preventive Medicine Meddac, Ft. Huachuca, Ariz., 1987—; chief exec. officer Campbell Assocs., Inc., Sierra Vista, 1988—; guest lectr. mil. history and firearms various mil. instns., 1965-69. Contbr. articles to profl. jours. Squadron comdr. CAP, Beckley, 1978-80, Lewisburg, 1980-83, wing staff, 1983-87, CAP, Sierra Vista, Ariz., 1988-91; chmn. Cochise County Local Emergency Planning Com., 1988—; mem. Pa. Gov.'s Task Force on Black Lung, 1974-75. Mem. Am. Public Health Assn., Am. Assn. Indsl. Hygiene, Am. Assn. Safety Engrs., Am. Assn. for Respiratory Therapy, Can. Soc. Respiratory Technologists, Am. Thoracic Soc. (asso. mem.), Mil. Hist. Soc. S. Africa, Mil. Hist. Soc. Australia, Wheelchair Pilots Assn., Kappa Delta Pi, Yale Sch. Respiratory Therapy Alumni Assn. (pres. 1966-71), Lions, Masons, Ruritan. Republican. Presbyterian. Home: 6641 S Ranch Rd Hereford AZ 85615 Office: Preventive Medicine MEDDAC Fort Huachuca AZ 85613-7040

CAMPBELL, RICHARD ALDEN, business consultant; b. Bend, Oreg., July 31, 1926; s. Corlis Eugene and Lydia Amney (Peck) C.; m. Edna Mary Seaman, June 12, 1948; children: Stephen Alden, Douglas Niall (dec.), Carolyn Joyce. B.S. in Elec. Engring., U. Ill., 1949, M.S. in Elec. Engring., 1950. With TRW Inc., Redondo Beach, Calif., 1954-87, exec. v.p., 1979-87; bd. dirs. Novadyne Computer Systems, Inc. Patentee in radio communications. Bd. dirs. U. Ill. Found., Hugh O'Brian Youth Found. With USN, 1944-46. Recipient Alumni Honor award U. Ill. Coll. Engring. Mem. Am. Electronics Assn. (pres. 1969, dir. 1970), IEEE (sr.), Sigma Xi, Phi Kappa Phi, Tau Beta Pi, Eta Kappa Nu, Sigma Tau, Pi Mu Epsilon, Phi Eta Sigma. Republican. Clubs: Kiwanis (Palos Verdes, Calif.); Rolling Hills Country, Rancheros Visitadores, Los Caballeros.

CAMPBELL, ROBERT HEDGCOCK, investment banker; b. Ann Arbor, Mich., Jan. 16, 1948; s. Robert Miller and Ruth Adele (Hedgcock) C.; m. Katherine Kettering, June 17, 1972; children: Mollie DuPlan, Katherine Elizabeth, Anne Kettering. BA, U. Wash., 1970, JD, 1973. Bar. Wash. 1973, Wash. State Supreme Ct. 1973, Fed. 1973, U.S. Dist. Ct. (we. dist.) Wash. 1973, Ct. Appeals (9th cir.) 1981. Assoc. Roberts & Shefelman, Seattle, 1973-78, ptnr., 1978-85; sr. v.p. Shearson Lehman Bros., Inc., Seattle, 1985-87, mng. dir., 1987—; dir., treas. Nat. Assn. Bd. Lawyers, Hinsdale, Ill., 1982-85; pres., trustee Wash. State Soc. Hosp. Attys., Seattle, 1982-85. Contbr. articles to profl. jours. Trustee Bellevue (Wash.) Schs. Found., 1988-91, pres., 1989-90; nation chief Bellevue Eastside YMCA Indian Princess Program, 1983-88; trustee Wash. Phikeia Found., 1983-91;

mem. Wash. Gov.'s Food Processing Coun., 1990-91. Republican. Home: 8604 NE 10th St Bellevue WA 98004-3915 Office: Lehman Bros 999 3d Ave Ste 4000 Seattle WA 98104

CAMPBELL, SARA MOORES, minister; b. Hollywood, Calif., Nov. 23, 1943; d. Richard Arnold and Gretchen Cora (Stahl) M.; m. Charles Curtis Campbell, Mar. 21, 1970. BA, Wake Forest U., 1965; MAT, Duke U., 1969; MDiv, Harvard Div. Sch., 1982. Ministerial fellowship Unitarian Universalist Assn. Min. First Universalist Ch. of Southold, N.Y., 1982-86, Unitarian Ch. of Rockville, Md., 1986-91; sr. min. Unitarian Soc. of Santa Barbara, Calif., 1991—; mem. Unitarian Universalist Assn. Commn. on Governance, 1990-93. Author: Into the Wilderness, 1990; contbr. articles to profl. jours. Bd. mem. Interfaith Coalition for Affordable Housing, Md., 1989-90, Transition House, Santa Barbara, 1992; sec., bd. mem. Community Action of Southold (N.Y.) Town. Mem. Unitarian Universalist Mins. Assn. (v.p. 1985-87). Office: Unitarian Soc Santa Barbara 1535 Santa Barbara St Santa Barbara CA 93101

CAMPBELL, SCOTT ROBERT, lawyer, former food company executive; b. Burbank, Calif., June 7, 1946; s. Robert Clyde and Jenevieve Anne (Olsen) C.; m. Teresa Melanie Mack, Oct. 23, 1965; 1 son, Donald Steven. B.A., Claremont Men's Coll., 1970; J.D., Cornell U., 1973. Bar: Ohio 1973, Minn. 1976, Calif. 1989; U.S. Ct. Appeals (9th cir.) 1989, U.S. Ct. Appeals (5th cir.) 1991; U.S. Dist. Ct. (no. dist.) Calif., 1989, U.S. Dist. Ct. (cen. and so. dists.) Calif., 1990, U.S. Dist. Ct. (so. dist.) Ohio, 1974; U.S. Tax Ct., 1991. Assoc. atty. Taft, Stettinius & Hollister, Cin., 1973-76; atty. Mpls. Star & Tribune, 1976-77; sr. v.p., gen. counsel, sec. Kellogg Co., Battle Creek, Mich., 1977-89; ptnr. Furth Fahrner Mason, San Francisco, 1989—; U.S. del. ILO Food and Beverage Conf., Geneva, 1984; participant, presenter first U.S.-USSR Legal Seminar, Moscow, 1988; speaker other legal seminars. Mem. ABA, Ohio Bar Assn., Minn. Bar Assn., Calif. Bar. Assn., Am. Soc. Corp. Secs. Office: Furth Fahrner & Mason 1000 Furth Bldg 201 Sansome St San Francisco CA 94104-2303

CAMPBELL, SID ELLIS, production company executive; b. Montgomery, Ala., Sept. 29, 1944; s. John Selwyn and Audress Magnolia (Langston) C.; m. Leonor Cantu (div. 1972); 1 child, Kimberlee Dawn Marie. Student, U. Md., Okinawa, Alameda Coll., Contra Costa Coll., Ryukyu U., Japan. 7th Deg. Black Belt. Chief instr. Sid Campbell's Shorin-Ryu Karate Studios, Oakland, Calif., 1966—; pres. Gong Prodns. Internat., Oakland, Calif., 1972—, Movie Media Corp., Oakland, Calif., 1972-84, Tonfa Police Baton Acad., Oakland, Calif., 1980—; dir. Pathways to the Orient Sports Acad., 1991-92, Tao of the Fist Fraternity, 1990—; dir., founder Coliseum Martial Arts Expo, 1980—; choreographer action sequences for TV and motion pictures including: Yellow Faced Tiger, Death Machines, Weapons of Death, Shadow Fight. Author: Ninja Shuriken Throwing, over 50 books and over 200 short stories on martial arts; actor Ninja Busters, Weapons of Death, Death Machines, Master Demon, others; video instr. Boots, Buckles & Blades, Fist Load Weaponry, Super Nunchaku, Police Baton; screenwriter (motion pictures) Falcon Claw, China Bomb, Ninja Busters, Bushwhackers, Wingless, others. With USN, 1962-66. Inducted into the Profl. World Assns. Hall of Fame. Mem. U.S. Police Def. Tactics Assn. (nat. advisor 1984—), U.S. Shorin-Ryu Karate Assn. (v.p. 1976-85).

CAMPBELL, THOMAS GORDY, private investor, retired naval officer; b. Atlanta, Dec. 9, 1932; s. Bennie Thomas and Margaret (Gordy) C.; m. Ann Morgan, May 5, 1957. BS in Bus., U. Fla., 1956; cert. in aero. engring., U. So. Calif., 1960; mil. staff cert., Armed Forces Staff Coll., Norfolk, Va., 1970; MBA, U. Chgo., 1979. Commd. ensign USN, 1950, advanced through grades to capt., 1977; ret., 1979; security dir. Northrop Corp., Rolling Meadows, Ill., 1980-88; prin. Campbell Group, Langley, Wash., 1988—; dir. Ill. Port Dist., Chgo., 1979-85; mem. workshop faculty Am. Soc. for Indsl. Security, Arlington, Va., 1987-88. Pres. Jackson Boulevard Hist. Dist., Chgo., 1979-81; chmn. conservation Whidbey Island Audubon Soc., Oak Harbor, Wash. Mem. Assn. Naval Aviation, Exptl. Aircraft Assn., War Birds Am., Assn. Old Crows (pres. Windy City chpt. 1983-86, Leadership award 1988), Wash. State U.-Whidbey Island Beach Watchers, Master Gardeners. Home and Office: PO Box 695 Langley WA 98260

CAMPBELL, THOMAS J., congressman; b. Chgo., Aug. 14, 1952; s. William J. and Marie Campbell; m. Susanne Martin. BA, MA in Econs. with highest honors, U. Chgo., 1973, PhD in Econs. with highest dept. fellowship, 1980; JD magna cum laude, Harvard U., 1976. Law clk. to presiding justice U.S. Ct. Appeals (D.C. cir.), 1976-77; law clk. to Justice Byron R. White U.S. Supreme Ct., Washington, 1977-78; assoc. Winston & Strawn, Chgo., 1978-80; White Ho. fellow Office Chief of Staff and White Ho. of Counsel, Washington, 1980-81; exec. asst. to dep. atty. gen. Dept. Justice, Washington, 1981; dir. Bur. Trade Competition FTC, Washington, 1981-83, head del. to OECD, Paris, com. experts on restrictive bus. practices, 1982, 83; mem. 101st-102nd Congresses from 12th Calif. dist., 1989—; mem. com. on sci., space and tech., com. on judiciary, banking, fin. and urban affairs 101st Congress from 12th Calif. dist., 1989—; prof. Stanford Law Sch., 1983-89. Referee Jour. Polit. Economy, Internat. Rev. Law and Econs. Mem. San Francisco Com. on Fgn. Relations. Mem. ABA (antitrust sect., coun. 1985-88, program chmn. 1983-84). Office: US Ho of Reps 313 Cannon House Office Bldg Washington DC 20515 also: 599 N Mathilda Ave Ste 105 Sunnyvale CA 94086 also: 7415 Eigleberry St Ste D Gilroy CA 95020

CAMPBELL, TOM, chiropractor; b. Bklyn., Oct. 27, 1954; s. Charles Marvin and Edna Marie (Sacer) C.; m. C. Lynn Hearn, July 2, 1983. AA in Social Scis., Fla. Tech. U., 1974; BA in Police Sci. and Adminstrn., Seattle U., 1977; DC, Life Chiropractic Coll., 1983; student, L.A. Chiropractic Coll., 1984—. Cert. chiropractor Nat. Bd. Chiropractic Examiners, -Physiotherapy, Wash., Fla., Fla. Physiotherapy. Examining doctor Jerry S. Torrence, D.C., Miami, Fla., 1983-84; pvt. practice Chiropractic Physician-Clinical Doctor, 1984—. State rep. Wash. State House of Reps., 1993-94. Capt. USAR. Fellow Internat. Coll. of Chiropractors; mem. Am. Chiropractic Assn. (alt. del. House of Dels.), Wash. State Chiropractic Assn. (chmn. mem. com. 1984-85, dist. 4A 1985-86, dir. exec. bd. 1985-88, v. chmn. disciplinary bd. 1990—, pres. award outstanding achievement in the mem. com. 1985, legislative affairs com. 1986, Dist. of the Yr. award 1985-86, named Chiropractor of the Yr. 1987, 89, 90, 91), Fla. Chiropractic Assn., Pierce County Chiropractic Assn., Chiropractic Rehabilitation Assn. (bd. dirs.). Democrat. Home: Box 443 Spanaway WA 98387

CAMPBELL, WESLEY GLENN, economist, educator; b. Komoka, Ont., Can., Apr. 29, 1924; s. Alfred E. and Delia (O'Brien) C.; m. Rita Ricardo, Sept. 15, 1946; children: Barbara Campbell Gray, Diane Campbell Porter, Nancy. B.A., U. Western Ont., 1944; M.A., Harvard, 1946, Ph.D., 1948; LLD (hon.), Pepperdine U., 1990, Okla. Christian Coll., 1977. Instr. econs. Harvard, 1948-51; research economist U.S. C. of C., 1951-54; dir. research Am. Enterprise Assn., 1954-60; dir. Hoover Instn. War, Revolution and Peace, Stanford, Calif., 1960-89, counselor, 1989—; Co-dir. project on Am. competitive enterprise, fgn. econ. devel. and aid program, spl. com. to study fgn. aid program U.S. Senate, 1956-57; mem. Pres.'s Commn. on White House Fellows, 1969-74, President's Com. on Sci. and Tech., 1976; mem. personnel adv. com. to Pres., 1980-81; mem. adv. bd. Ctr. for Strategic and Internat. Studies, 1980-85; dir. Hutchins Ctr. for Study Dem. Instns., 1981-87; bd. dirs. NSF, 1972-78, NSB, 1990—; mem. Com. on Present Danger, 1976—; chmn. Pres.'s Intelligence Oversight Bd., 1981-90; spl. advisor U.S. Delegation to 43d Session Gen. Assembly of UN; mem. Pres.'s Fgn. Intelligence Adv. Bd., 1981-90; chmn. Am. panel Joint Com. Japan-U.S. Cultural and Ednl. Coop., 1983-89; chmn. Japan-U.S. Friendship Commn., 1983-89; trustee Ronald Reagan Presdl. Found., 1985-90, chmn., 1985-87. Co-author: The American Competitive Enterprise Economy, 1952; Editor, prin. author: The Economics of Mobilization and War, 1952; contbr. articles to profl. jours. Trustee Herbert Hoover Presdl. Libr. Assn.; mem. bd. regents U. Calif., 1968—, chmn., 1982-83. Recipient Gold and Silver Star Order of Sacred Treasure, Govt. of Japan, 1989. Fellow Royal Econ. Soc.; mem. Am. Econ. Assn., Phila. Soc. (pres. 1965-67), Mont Pelerin Soc. (dir. 1980-86). Clubs: Bohemian (Cal.), Cosmos (Cal.), Commonwealth (Cal.). Home: 26915 Alejandro Dr Los Altos CA 94022-1932 Office: Stanford Univ Hoover Instn Stanford CA 94305

CAMPBELL, WILLIAM JACKSON, biochemist; b. Wichita Falls, Tex., Oct. 23, 1929; s. Henry Morrison and Lela Pearl (Graves) C.; m. Vivian Delores Orr, Dec. 24, 1951 (div. Sept. 1959); children: Raymond D., Boyd W., Cindy Lou; m. Irma Grace Dunton, June 23, 1964. BA, North Tex. State Coll., 1949; BS in Pharmacy, U. Tex., 1952, MS in Pharmacy, 1953; PhD, Ohio State U., 1960. Program adminstr. Nat. Inst. Gen. Med. Sci., Bethesda, Md., 1964-74; exec. dir. Am. Assn. Clin. Chemistry, Washington, 1974-82; pres. Stanbio Lab., San Antonio, 1982-90; quality assurance scientist Nat. Health Labs., LaJolla, Calif., 1990—. With U.S. Army, 1953-64; capt. USPHS, 1964-74. Mem. Am. Assn. Clin. Chemistry (exec. dir. 1974-82), Am. Chem. Soc. Office: Nat Health Labs 7590 Fay Ave La Jolla CA 92037

CAMPBELL, WILLIAM STEEN, writer, magazine publisher; b. New Cumberland, W.Va., June 27, 1919; s. Robert N. and Ethel (Steen) C.; m. Rosemary J. Bingham, Apr. 21, 1945 (dec. Dec. 1992); children: Diana J., Sarah A., Paul C., John W. Grad., Steubenville (Ohio) Bus. Coll., 1938. Cost accountant Hancock Mfg. Co., New Cumberland, 1938-39; cashier, statistician Weirton Steel Co., W.Va., 1939-42; travel exec. Am. Express Co., N.Y.C., 1946-47; adminstr., account exec. Good Housekeeping mag., 1947-55; pub. Cosmopolitan mag., 1955-57; asst. dir. circulation Hearst Mags., N.Y.C., 1957-61; gen. mgr. Motor Boating mag., 1961-62; v.p., dir. circulation Hearst Mags., 1962-85; pres. Internat. Circulation Distbrs., 1978-81, Mags., Meetings, Messages, Ltd., 1986—; with Periodical Pubs. Svc. Bur. subs. Hearst Corp., Sandusky, Ohio, 1964-85, v.p., chief exec., 1964-69, pres., chief exec., 1970-85; dir. Audit Bur. Circulations, 1974-86, Periodical Pubs. Svc. Bur., 1964-85, Nat. Mag. Co., Ltd., London, Randolph Jamaica Ltd., Omega Pub. Corp. Fla., Hearst Can. Ltd., 1964-85; former chmn. Cen. Registry, Mag. Pubs. Assn.; chmn. bd. trustees Hearst Employees Retirement Plan, 1971-85; mem. pres.' coun. Brandeis U., 1974—; chmn. nat. corp. and found. com. U. Miami, 1979-85; dir. Broadway Assn., 1985-90, v.p. 1988-90. Served to lt. col. USAF, 1942-46, ETO. Recipient Lee C. Williams award Mag. Fulfillment Mgrs. Assn.; Torch of Liberty award Anti-Defamation League, 1979. Mem. Campbell Clan Soc., Mil. Order of World Wars, Masons. Home and Office: 1150 Coast Village Rd Santa Barbara CA 93108-2722

CAMPBELL, WILLIS PRESTON, photographer; b. Portsmouth, Va., May 16, 1945; s. Willis Preston Campbell and Dorothy Lee (Eshman) Collier; m. Sherelyn Douglas, Dec. 13, 1975; children: Jonathan, Paul. BA, Westmont Coll., Santa Barbara, Calif., 1967; MA, U. Calif., Santa Barbara, 1971. Cert. profl. photographer. Owner Willis Preston Campbell Photography, Santa Cruz, Calif., 1977—. Republican. Baptist. Home: 107 Moore Creek Rd Santa Cruz CA 95060-2321 Office: 1015 Cedar St Santa Cruz CA 95060-3803

CAMPER, JOHN SAXTON, public relations and marketing executive; b. Trenton, N.J., Apr. 24, 1929; s. Thomas Emory and Mildred Ruth (Burke) C.; m. Ferne Arlene Clanton; children: Susan Jennifer, John Saxton III. BS in History and Econs., U. Nebr., 1968. Enlisted U.S. Army, 1948, commd. to 1st lt., advanced through ranks to maj., 1972, ret., 1972; regional mktg. officer First Bank System, Mont., 1978-83; lectr., instr. mktg. and advt. pub. rels.; pres. Camper Comm., Helena, 1983—; dir. Profl. Devel. Ctr., Mont., 1984-91. Decorated Legion of Merit. Mem. Helena Advt. Fedn. (1st pres., founder), Rotary Internat. Republican. Methodist.

CAMPHAUSEN, FRED HOWARD, physicist; b. L.A., Aug. 23, 1933; s. Fred Henry and Eloise (Ingebretsen) C.; BA in Physics, U. Calif., 1961; m. Martina Simon, Apr. 2, 1956 (div.); children: Raymond Thomas, Karin Maria; m. 2d, Marianna P. Dembinski, Aug. 2, 1980. With Naval Weapons Cen., China Lake, Calif., 1961-88, physicist, project mgr. electronic warfare test and evaluation, 1980-88; owner, mgr., Mountain High West, 1980—. With U.S. Army, 1953-56. Mem. Naval Aviation Execs. Inst., Assn. of Old Crows, Am. Alpine Club, Sierra Club. Republican. Roman Catholic. Club: Vägmarken, Eastern Sierra Mountaineers. Contbr. articles to profl. jours. Home and Office: 2765 Sierra Vista Way Bishop CA 93514-3046

CAMPOS, JOAQUIN PAUL, III, chemical physicist, technical specialist; b. L.A., Feb. 16, 1962; s. Joaquin Reyna and Maria Luz (Chavez) C.; m. Barbara Ann Esquivel, Oct. 31, 1987; children: Courtney Luz, Nathaniel Alexander. Student, U. Calif., Santa Cruz, 1980-85, UCLA, 1985-86. Tutor U. Calif., Santa Cruz, 1980-82, admissions liaison, 1982-84; chem. teaching assoc. L.A. Unified Sch. Dist., 1985-87; pvt. tutor Santa Clara, L.A., 1987-89; tech. specialist Alpha Therapeutics Corp., L.A., 1989—; cons. L.A. Unified Sch. Dist., 1985-87. Docent in tng. L.A. Mus. of Sci. and Industry, 1989—. Scholar, grantee So. Calif. Gas Co., L.A., 1980-84, Sloan Rsch. fellow, 1981-82. Mem. Am. Chem. Soc., N.Y. Acad. Sci., Am. Inst. Chemists, Am. Assn. Physics Tchrs., AAAS, Fedn. Am. Scientists, Internat. Union of Pure and Applied Chemistry, So. Calif. Paradox User Group, Math. Assn. Am. Office: Alpha Therapeutics Corp 5555 Valley Blvd Los Angeles CA 90032-3548

CAMPOS, LEONARD PETER, psychologist; b. Arecibo, P.R., Dec. 24, 1932; s. Joseph Gervasio Campos and Emma (Roman) Crespi; m. Mary Lois Cole, Oct. 1, 1961 (div. 1976); children: David, Elizabeth, Barbara; m. Lee Barrett, June 13, 1986 (div. 1992). BA cum laude, CCNY, 1955; PhD, Mich. State U., 1963. Diplomate Am. Bd. Profl. Psychology, Am. Bd. Forensic Psychology. Asst. prof. U. of Pacific, Stockton, Calif., 1963-66; staff psychologist Calif. Youth Authority, Stockton, 1966-70; cons. psychologist Sacramento, 1970—. Author: You Can Redecide Your Life, 1989, Introduce Yourself to Transactional Analysis,1992. With U.S. Army, 1955-57. Mem. Am. Psychol. Assn., Calif. Psychol. Assn., Sacramento Valley Pscyhol. Assn. (pres. Div. I 1988-89, pres. Divsn. II 1992), Nat. Hispanic Psychol. Assn. Office: 1820 Professional Dr # 5 Sacramento CA 95825-2120

CAMPOS, SANTIAGO E., federal judge; b. Santa Rosa, N.Mex., Dec. 25, 1926; s. Ramon and Miquela Campos; m. Patsy Campos, Jan. 27, 1947; children: Theresa, Rebecca, Christina, Miquela Feliz. J.D., U. N.Mex., 1953. Bar: N.Mex. 1953. Asst., 1st asst. atty gen. State of N.Mex., 1955-57; judge 1st Jud. Dist. N.Mex., 1971-78; judge U.S. Dist. Ct. N.Mex., Santa Fe, 1978—, sr. judge, 1992—. Served as seaman USN, 1944-46. Mem. State Bar of N.Mex., First Jud. Dist. Bar Assn. (hon.), Order of Coif. Office: US Dist Ct PO Box 2244 Santa Fe NM 87504-2244

CAMPRA, FRANCES L., retail executive; b. Iron Mountain, Mich., July 2, 1940; d. John Secundo and Catherine (Carollo) Campra; m. Robert Brantley, Sept. 13, 1976; children: Scott, Katrina. BA, U. Mich., 1962. Mgmt. trainee Emporium, San Francisco, 1962-63; asst. buyer Macy's, San Francisco, 1963-64, 65-67; buyer children's Macy's, 1968-69, buyer jrs., 1969-71, merchandise adminstr., 1971-74, v.p., 1974-87, grp. v.p., 1987-91; sr. v.p., 1992—. Home: 718 Steiner St San Francisco CA 94117-1617 Office: Macy's Stockton/O'Farrell St San Francisco CA 94117

CANAKA, TOGO W(ILLIAM), real estate and financial executive; b. Portland, Oreg., Jan. 7, 1916; s. Masaharu and Katsu (Iwatate) T.; m. Jean Miho Wada, Nov. 14, 1940; children: Jeannine, Christine, Wesley. AB cum laude, UCLA, 1936. Editor Calif. Daily News, 1935-36, L.A. Japanese Daily News, 1936-42; documentary historian War Relocation Authority, Manzanar, Calif., 1942; staff mem. Am. Friends Service Com., Chgo., 1943-45; editor to head publs. div. Am. Tech. Soc., 1945-52; pub. Chgo. Pub. Corp., 1952-56; pub. School-Indsl. Press, Inc., L.A., 1956-60; chmn. Gramercy Enterprises, L.A.; dir. T.W. Tanaka Co., Inc.; city commr. Community Redevel. Agy., L.A., 1973-74; dir. L.A. Wholesale Produce Market Devel. Corp., 1979-89, Fed. Res. Bank, San Francisco, 1979-89; mem. adv. bd. Calif. First Bank, L.A., 1976-78, bd. dirs. Meth. Hosp., So. Calif., 1978-93. Author: (with Frank K. Levin) English Composition and Rhetoric, 1948; (with Dr. Jean Bordeaux) How to Talk More Effectively, 1948; (with Alma Meland) Easy Pathways in English, 1949. Mem. citizens mgmt. rev. com. L.A. Unified Sch. Dist., 1976-77; adv. coun. to assessor L.A. County, 1981-84; bd. dirs. Goodwill Industries of So. Calif.; trustee Wilshire United Meth. Ch., 1976-78, Calif. Acad. Decathlon, 1978-81; adv. bd. Nat. Safety Coun., L.A., Visitors and Conv. Bur., 1984-88, Am. Heart Assn., 1984-88, New Bus. Achievement, Inc., YMCA Met. L.A., Boy Scouts Am. Coun., 1980-86; mem. adv. council Calif. World Trade Comm., 1986-87; active Nat. Strategy Info. Ctr. N.Y., Internat. City of Care Found., Nat. Wellness Community, Western Justice Ctr. Found.; trustee Whittier Coll. Recipient merit award Soc. Advancement Mgmt., 1950, mag. award Inst. Graphic Arts, 1953, 1st award Internat. Council Indsl. Editors, 1955, UNESCO Literacy award, 1974, L.A. Archbishop's Ecumenical award, 1986. Mem. L.A. Area C. of C. (dir. 1974-76), Japan-Am. Soc. So. Calif. (coun. 1960-78), Petroleum Club, Lincoln Club, Masons, Shriners, Rotary (dir., pres. L.A. club 1983-84), Phi Beta Kappa, Pi Sigma Alpha, Pi Gamma Mu. Home: 949 Malcolm Ave Los Angeles CA 90024-3113 Office: 626 Wilshire Blvd Los Angeles CA 90017-3209

CANALES, CHARLES JOHN, personnel director; b. L.A., June 24, 1944; s. Carlos A. and Jennie (De LaTorre) C.; children: Christopher, Caryn, Stephen, Aaron, Justin, Marie. Student, Glendale Coll. of Law, 1972-73, Calif State U., Domingues Hills, Carson, 1990-91. Head civil svc. advocate L.A. County Dept. Health Svcs., L.A., 1979-87; personnel dir. Olive View Med. Ctr., Sylmar, Calif., 1987—; curriculum advisor West Valley Adult Occupationa Tng. Ctr. Woodland Hills, Calif., 1989-92, L.A. Mission Coll., San Fernando, Calif., 1990—. Mem. steering com. N.E. Community Action Project United Way, San Fernando, Calif., 1967-90; regional mem. United Way Adult Literacy Com., 1990-91. With U.S. Marines, 1964-70. Mem. L.A. County Hispanic Mgrs. Assn., So. Calif. Personnel Mgrs. Assn., L.A. County Dept. Health Svcs. Personnel Coun. (exec. dir. 1991-93, Golden Hind award 1982). Republican. Office: Olive View Med Ctr Personnel Dept 14445 Olive View Dr Sylmar CA 91342-1495

CANAN, PENELOPE, sociology educator; b. Miami, Fla., Oct. 3, 1946; d. Christopher Michael and Mary Rita (Kershaw) C.; m. Thomas E. Austin, June 10, 1967 (div. June 1977); m. Reid T. Reynolds, July 19, 1986; 1 child, Lily Canan Reynolds. BA, U. N.C., 1969; MA, U. Denver, 1972, PhD, 1976. Asst. prof. sociology U. Va., Charlottesville, 1977-78; vis. prof. sociology U. Hawaii, Honolulu, 1978-80, asst. prof. urban and regional planning, 1980-83; asst. prof. sociology U. Denver, 1983-89, assoc. prof. sociology, 1989—, co-dir. polit. litigation project, 1984—; cons. Colo. State Govt., 1984-86, Hawaii State Govt., 1981-83, City and County of Hawaii; mem. environ. programme on ozone depletion UN, 1990-91, 93—. Contbr. articles to profl. jours. Co-founder Hawaii Women's Polit. Action League, Honolulu, 1980. Mem. Am. Sociol. Assn. (chair sect. environment and tech. 1993—), Law & Soc. Assn., Soc. for Applied Sociology (v.p. 1988-89), Sigma Xi. Democrat. Home: 65 S Jackson St Denver CO 80209 Office: Univ Denver Dept Sociology Denver CO 80208-0209

CANBY, WILLIAM CAMERON, JR., federal judge; b. St. Paul, May 22, 1931; s. William Cameron and Margaret Leah (Lewis) C.; m. Jane Adams, June 18, 1954; children—William Nathan, John Adams, Margaret Lewis. A.B., Yale U., 1953; LL.B., U. Minn., 1956. Bar: Minn. 1956, Ariz. 1972. Law clk. U.S. Supreme Ct. Justice Charles E. Whittaker, 1958-59; asso. firm Oppenheimer, Hodgson, Brown, Baer & Wolff, St. Paul, 1959-62; asso., then dep. dir. Peace Corps, Ethiopia, 1962-64; dir. Peace Corps, Uganda, 1964-66; asst. to U.S. Senator Walter Mondale, 1966; asst. to pres. SUNY, 1967; prof. law Ariz. State U., 1967-80; judge U.S. Ct. Appeals (9th cir.), Phoenix, 1980—; bd. dirs. Ariz. Center Law in Public Interest, 1974-80, Maricopa County Legal Aid Soc., 1972-78, D.N.A.-People's Legal Services, 1978-80; Fulbright prof. Makerere U. Faculty Law, Kampala, Uganda, 1970-71. Author: American Indian Law, 1988; also articles; note editor: Minn. Law Rev, 1955-56. Precinct and state committeeman Democratic Party Ariz., 1972-80; bd. dirs. Central Ariz. Coalition for Right to Choose, 1976-80. Served with USAF, 1956-58. Mem. State Bar Ariz., Minn. Bar Assn., Maricopa County Bar Assn., Phi Beta Kappa, Order of Coif. Office: US Ct Appeals 9th Circuit 6445 US Courthouse 230 N 1st Ave Phoenix AZ 85025-0230

CANDAU, EUGENIE, librarian; b. San Francisco, Jan. 26, 1938; d. Pierre and Marie Catherine (Lassallette) C. BA, San Francisco State U., 1974; MLS, U. Calif., Berkeley, 1978. Libr. Louise Sloss Ackerman Fine Arts Libr. San Francisco Mus. of Modern Art, 1968—; mem. exec. bd. ARLIS/NA, 1990-91. Commr. Berkeley Civic Arts Commn., 1984-91; com. mem. Berkeley Design Review Com., 1988-91; bd. dirs. Berkeley Art Ctr., 1991—. Mem. Coll. Art Assn., Art Librs. Soc. of N.Am. Office: San Francisco Mus Modern Art 401 Van Ness Ave San Francisco CA 94102-4522

CANDLIN, FRANCES ANN, psychotherapist, social worker, educator; b. Phila., July 18, 1945; d. Francis Townley and Wilma (David) C. BA magna cum laude, Loretto Heights Coll., Denver, 1967; MSW, St. Louis U., 1971. Diplomate Am. Bd. Clin. Social Work; cert. social worker; lic. clin. social worker, Colo. Recreational therapist trainee Jewish Hosp., St. Louis, 1970-71; social worker trainee Jefferson Barracks VA Hosp., St. Louis, 1970-71; social worker Adams County Juvenile Probation, Brighton, Colo., 1972-74, Boulder (Colo.) County Social Svcs., 1974-75; sch. social worker Adams County Sch. Dist. #50, Westminster, Colo., 1975-80; workshop presenter Human Enrichment Cons., Denver, 1980-90; pvt. practice Denver, 1980—; dir. Madison St. Counseling Ctr., Denver, 1991—; cons. Mountain Plains Regional Ctr., Denver, 1981-85, Dept. Edn., Topeka, 1981-87, Dept. Spl. Edn., Nebr., Colo., Mo., N.Mex., Utah, 1982-86. Bd. dirs. Denver Sch. for Gifted, 1982-86, Weaver Found., 1985-86, St. Mary's Acad., Englewood, Colo., 1985-88. Recipient stipend NIMH, 1969, VA Social Work Trainee, 1970. Mem. NASW, NOW, Acad. Cert. Social Workers, Assn. Humanistic Psychology, Assn. Transpersonal Psychology, Colo. Assn. Clin. Social Workers, County Assn. Clin. Social Workers, Vajra Soc. (bd. dirs. 1990—). Office: Madison St Counseling Ctr 123 Madison St Denver CO 80206-5417

CANFIELD, BRIAN A., communications company executive; b. New Westminister, B.C., Canada, July 9, 1938; s. Orra Wells and Effie Beatrice (Dunham) C.; m. Beverly Irene Gillies, Apr. 15, 1961; children: Brian Robert, Bruce Martin, Nancy Susan. Area gen. mgr. B.C. Telephone Co., Burnaby, 1983-85, v.p. tech. support, 1985-88, exec. v.p. tel. ops., 1988-89, pres., COO, 1989-91, pres., chief exec. officer, 1991—, chmn., CEO, 1993—; chmn. bd. Microtel Ltd., MPR Teltech Ltd., BC TEL Svcs. Inc.; bd. dirs. Can. Telephones and Supplies Ltd., BC TEL Mobility-Cellular Inc., BC TEL Mobility-Paging, BC TEL Mobile Ltd., Telecom Leasing Can. Ltd., Prism Systems Inc., Telestat Can.; mem. adv. coun. faculty commerce and bus. adminstrn. U. B.C., Stentor Coun. CEOs; bd. govs. Bus. Coun. B.C. Bd. dirs. Royal Columbian Hosp. Found., Royal Trust, Vancouver Bd. of Trade. Office: BC TEL Co, 3777 Kingsway, Burnaby, BC Canada V5H 3Z7

CANFIELD, GRANT WELLINGTON, JR., association administrator, management consultant; b. Los Angeles, Nov. 28, 1923; s. Grant Wellington and Phyllis Marie (Westland) C.; m. Virginia Louise Bellinger, June 17, 1945; 1 child, Julie Marie. BS, U. So. Calif., 1949, MBA, 1958. Personnel and indsl. relations exec., Los Angeles, 1949-55; employee relations cons., regional mgr. Mchts. and Mfrs. Assn. Los Angeles, 1955-60; v.p., orgnl. devel. cons. Hawaii Employers Council, Honolulu, 1960-75; pres., dir. Hawaiian Ednl. Council, 1969-92, chmn., CEO, 1989-92, chmn. emeritus, 1992; faculty assignments Calif. State U., L.A., 1957-59, U. So. Calif., 1958-59, U. Hawaii, 1963-72; exec. v.p. Hawaii Garment Mfrs. Assn., 1965-75, Assn. Hawaii Restaurant Employers, 1966-75; exec. dir. Hawaii League Savs. Assns., 1971-78; exec. dir. Pan-Pacific Surg. Assn., 1980-81, exec. v.p., 1982-83; exec. dir. Hawaii Bus. Roundtable, 1983-89; sec., treas. Econ. Devel. Corp. Honolulu, 1984-85; sec., treas. Hawaii Conv. Park Council, Inc., 1984-86, hon. dir., 1986-88. Co-author: Resource Manual for Public Collective Bargaining, 1973. Bd. dirs. Hawaii Restaurant Assn., 1974-76, bd. dirs. Hawaii chpt. Nat. Assn. Accts., 1963-67, nat. dir., 1965-66; bd. dirs. Vol. Service Bur. Honolulu, 1965-66, pres., 1966-68; bd. dirs. Vol. Info. and Referral Service Honolulu, 1972-75, Goodwill Vocat. Tng. Ctrs. of Hawaii, 1973-81, Girl Scout council Pacific, 1961-65, 71-72; bd. dirs. Hawaii Com. Alcoholism, 1962-71, co-chmn., 1964-68; pres., dir. Friends of Punahou Sch., 1972-75; mem. community adv. bd. Jr. League Honolulu, 1968-70; exec. bd. Aloha council Boy Scouts Am., 1962-65; bd. regents Chaminade U., 1983-85. Served to 1st lt. inf. AUS, 1943-46. Decorated Bronze Star, Purple Heart, Combat Inf. badge. Mem. Am. Soc. Assn. Execs. (cert. assn. exec.), Inst. Mgmt. Cons. (cert.), Am. Soc. Tng. and Devel., Soc. for Human Resource Mgmt., Pacific Club, Rotary, Masons. Home: 1950 W Dry Creek Rd Healdsburg CA 95448-9747 Office: PO Box 637 Healdsburg CA 95448

CANN, JOHN RUSWEILER, biophysics educator; b. Bethlehem, Pa., Dec. 11, 1920; s. John Henry and Anna (Rusweiler) C.; m. Minerva Elda Butz, Sept. 7, 1946; children: Susan Austin, Richard L., David C. BS in Chemistry, Moravian Coll., 1942; MS in Chemistry, Lehigh U., 1943; MA in Chemistry, Princeton U., 1945, PhD in Phys. Chemistry, 1946. Rsch. assoc.

Cornell U., Ithaca, N.Y., 1947; rsch. fellow Calif. Inst. Tech., Pasadena, 1947, sr. rsch. fellow, 1948-50; asst. prof. biophysics U. Colo. Med. Ctr., Denver, 1951-56, assoc. prof. biophysics, 1956-63; USPHS spl. rsch. fellow Carlsberg Found. Biol. Inst., Copenhagen, 1961-62; prof. biophysics U. Colo. Med. Ctr., Denver, 1963-91, emeritus prof., 1991—; adj. prof. biochemistry Kans. State U., Manhattan, 1987-91; mem. adv. panel molecular biology div. of biol. and med. sci. NSF, 1967-70. Mem. editorial bd. Jour. Biol. Chemistry, 1982, 88—, Archives of Biochemistry and Biophysics, 1980—, Internat. Jour. Peptide and Protein Rsch., 1978-88; co-author: (with D.W. Talmadge) The Chemistry of Immunity in Health and Disease, 1961; co-author Interacting Macromolecules: The Theory and Practice of Their Electrophoresis, Ultracentrifugation and Chromatography, 1970; contbr. articles to profl. jours.; reviewer manuscripts for sci. jours. Recipient John Amos Comenius award Moravian Coll., 1968, Med. Alumni award U. Colo., Denver, 1976; rsch. support grantee NIH, 1952-91. Fellow AAAS; mem. Am. Chem. Soc., Am. Assn. Biol. Chemists, Biophysics Soc., Sigma Xi (past pres. U. Colo. chpt.). Office: U Colo Health Sci Ctr B121 Dept Biochemistry/Biophysics/Genetics 4200 E 9th Ave Denver CO 80262

CANN, WILLIAM HOPSON, former mining company executive; b. Newark, June 17, 1916; s. Howard W. and and Ruth (Hopson) C.; m. Mildred E. Allen, Mar. 7, 1942 (dec. 1982); children: William Hopson, Sharon Lee, John Allen, Lawrence Edward; m. Nancy B. Barnhart, Nov. 17, 1984. A.B. magna cum laude, Harvard, 1937; LL.B., 1940. Bar: N.Y. 1941, Calif. 1947. Assoc. Chadbourne, Parke, Whiteside & Wolfe (and predecessors), N.Y.C., 1940-53; asst. to pres. Rockwell Internat. Corp., 1953-60, v.p., sec., 1960-75; coordinator for stockholder relations Cyprus Mines Corp., Los Angeles, 1975-76; corp. sec. Cyprus Mines Corp., 1977-85, ret., 1985. Former mem. adv. bd. Family Svc. of Los Angeles. Served to 1st lt. USAAF, 1942-45. Mem. Am. Soc. Corp. Secs. (past pres.), Phi Beta Kappa. Episcopalian. Club: Rocky Mountain Harvard (Denver). Home: 4505 S Yosemite St Denver CO 80237-2533

CANNADY, EDWARD WYATT, JR., retired physician; b. East St. Louis, Ill., June 20, 1906; s. Edward Wyatt and Ida Bertha (Rose) C.; m. Helen Freeborn, Oct. 20, 1984; children by previous marriage: Edward Wyatt III, Jane Marie Starr. AB, Washington U., St. Louis, 1927, MD, 1931. Intern in internal medicine Barnes Hosp., St. Louis, 1931-33, resident physician, 1934-35, asst. physician, 1935-74, emeritus, 1974—; asst. resident Peter Bent Brigham Hosp., Boston, 1933-34; fellow in gastroenterology Washington U. Sch. Medicine, 1935-36, instr. internal medicine 1935-74, emeritus, 1974—; cons. internal medicine Washington U. Clinics, 1942-74; physician St. Mary's Hosp., East St. Louis, 1935-77, pres. staff, 1947-49, chmn. med. dept., 1945-47; physician Christian Welfare Hosp., 1935-77, chmn. med. dept., 1939-53, dir. electrocardiography, 1936-77; dir. electrocardiography Centreville Twp. Hosp., East St. Louis; mem. staff Meml. Hosp., Belleville, Ill., St. Elizabeth Hosp., Belleville; pres. C.I.F. Dir. health service East St. Louis pub. schs., 1936-37; chmn. med. adv. bd. Selective Svc., 1941-45; pres. St. Clair County Coun. Aging, 1961-62; chmn. St. Clair County Home Care Program, 1961-68, St. Clair County Med. Soc. Com. Aging, 1960-70; del. White House Conf. Aging, 1961, 71, 81; mem. Adv. Coun. Improvement Econ. and Social Status Older People, 1959-66; bd. dirs., exec. com. Nat. Council Homemaker Svcs., 1966-73, chmn. profl. adv. com. 1971-73; bd. dirs. St. Louis Met. Hosp. Planning Commn., 1966-70; mem. Ill. Coun. Aging, 1966-74; mem. Gov.'s Council on Aging, 1974-76; mem. Ill. Regional Heart Disease, Cancer and Stroke Com.; mem. exec. com. Bi-State Regional Com. on Heart Disease, Cancer and Stroke; pres. Ill. Joint Council to Improve Health Care Aged, 1959-61; dir. Ill. Coun. Continuing Med. Edn., 1972-77, v.p., 1974-75. Trustee McKendree Coll., 1971-79; adv. bd. Belleville Jr. Coll. Sch. Nursing, 1970-78; bd. dirs. United Fund Greater East St. Louis, 1953-58. Recipient Disting. Service Award Am. Heart Assn., 1957, Disting. Achievement award, 1957; award Ill. Public Health Assn., 1971; Greater Met. St. Louis award in geriatrics, 1976. Diplomate Am. Bd. Internal Medicine. Fellow Am. Coll. Cardiology, Am. Geriatrics Soc., ACP (gov. 1964-70); mem. AMA (ho. dels. 1961-71, mem. aging com.; editorial adv. bd. Chronic Illness News Letter 1962-70, chmn. Ill. delegation 1964-66, mem. council vol. health agys.), Am. (dir. 1956-62, personnel and personnel tng. com. 1956-60), Ill. (pres. 1950-51) heart assns., St. Clair County (pres. 1952, bd. censors 1953-57), Ill. (sec. cardiovascular sect. 1957, chmn. sect., 1958-59; chmn. com. on aging, 1959-69, speaker Ho. Dels. 1964-68, pres. 1969-70) med. socs., Mason, St. Clair Country Club, Palmbrook Country Club (Sun City, Ariz.), Sun Cities Physicians Club, Palmbrook Country Club, Beta Theta Pi, Nu Sigma Nu, Alpha Omega Alpha. Presbyterian. Contbr. articles to med. jours. Address: 14406 Bolivar Sun City AZ 85351

CANNIFF, PAUL JOSEPH, JR., software development engineer. BS, Villanova U., 1984. Software engr. Avant-Garde Inc., Mt. Laurel, N.J., 1984-86; software engr. Microsoft Corp., Redmond, Wash., 1986-89, mgr. software devel., 1989&. Office: Microsoft Corp One Microsoft Way Redmond WA 98052

CANNON, CHRIS J., lawyer; b. Milw., Feb. 15, 1954; s. John Edward and Delphine Mary (Bruckwick) C.; m. Anne E. Libbin, July 20, 1985; children: Abigail, Rebecca. Student, Sophia U., Tokyo, 1973-74; BA in English, U. Notre Dame, 1976; JD, Southwestern U., 1979. Law clk. U.S. Dist. Judge William T. Swiegert, San Francisco, 1979-81; pub. defender Santa Clara, Calif., 1981-82; asst. fed. pub. defender San Francisco, 1982-89; ptnr. Sugarman & Cannon, San Francisco, 1989—. Contbr. articles to profl. jours. Mem. ACLU, Am. Coll. Trial Lawyers, Nat. Assn. Criminal Def. Lawyers, Fed. Bar Assn. (treas. 1987-90), Fed. Indigent Def. Panel, Calif. Attys. Criminal Justice. Democrat. Office: Sugarman & Cannon 600 Harrison St Ste 535 San Francisco CA 94107-1370

CANNON, JAMES DEAN, accountant, financial analyst, military officer; b. Redding, Calif., May 27, 1964; s. Ronald Dean Cannon and Laureen Day (Snyder) White; m. Narcia Denise McCurtain. BA, U. Ariz., 1987; MBA, Nat. U., San Diego, 1989. Contract contr. Lockheed Missiles and Space, Sunnyvale, Calif., 1987-90; contr. Metwest Inc., Phoenix, 1990-92, The Dial Corp., Phoenix, 1992—. Mem. Young Reps., Sunnyvale, 1987-90; officer Ariz. Nat. Guard, Phoenix, 1992—. 1st lt. USAR, 1985—. Mem. Inst. for Cert. Mgmt. Accts. (contr. coun.). Office: Metwest Contr 9201 N 7th Ave Phoenix AZ 85021-3560

CANNON, KEVIN FRANCIS, sculptor; b. N.Y.C., Nov. 27, 1948; s. Connell and Maud (Brogan) C. AA, CCNY, 1971. One-man shows include Willard Gallery, N.Y.C., 1982, James Corcoran Gallery, L.A., 1984, Charles Cowles Gallery, N.Y.C., 1985-86, Rena Bransten Gallery, San Francisco, 1987, New Gallery, Houston, 1987, and others; exhibited in group shows Ft. Worth Gallery, 1984, Am. Crafts Mus., N.Y.C., 1986, Charles Cowles Gallery, N.Y.C., 1987, Modern Objects Gallery, L.A., 1987 and others; represented in permanent collections Lannan Found., Cin. Mus., Bklyn. Mus., Am. Crafts Mus., JB Speed Art Mus., Albuquerque Mus. Nat. Endowment for the Arts grantee, 1986.

CANNON, LOUIS SIMEON, journalist, reporter; b. N.Y.C., June 3, 1933; s. Jack and Irene (Kohn) C.; m. Virginia Oprian, Feb. 2, 1953 (div. 1983); children: Carl, David, Judy, Jack; m. Mary L. Shinkwin, Sept. 7, 1985. Student, U. Nev., 1950-51, San Francisco State U., 1951-52. Reporter Lafayette Sun, Calif., 1957; editor Newark (Calif.) Sun, 1957-58, Merced Sun Star, Calif., 1958-60, Contra Costa Times, Calif., 1960-61; reporter, editor San Jose Mercury News, Calif., 1961-65; Washington corr. Ridder Pubs., Washington, 1959-72; reporter The Washington Post, Washington, 1972—; western bur. chief The Washington Post, L.A., 1990—. Author: President Reagan: the Role of a Lifetime, 1991, Reagan, 1982, Ronnie and Jesse, 1969, Reporting: An Inside View, 1977, The McCloskey Challenge, 1972. Recipient Gerald R. Ford prize Gerald Ford Libr., 1988, Merriman Smith award White House Corrs. Assn., 1986, Aldo Beckman award, 1984, Washington Journalism Rev. award, 1985, Disting. Reporting of Pub. Affairs award Am. Polit. Sci. Assn., 1968. Mem. Soc. of Profl. Journalists, Authors Guild. Home: PO Box 436 Summerland CA 93067 Office: Washington Post 10 100 Santa Monica Blvd # 745 Los Angeles CA 90067

CANNON, SHERRI DETTMER, management consultant; b. Ft. Wayne, Ind., Apr. 21, 1958; d. Siemon John and Gertrude (Schroeder) D.; m. David A. Cleveland, Aug. 13, 1978 (div. July 1984); m. Roger Kerm Cannon, July 21, 1989. BA, Ind. U., 1979. Sales rep. Procter & Gamble Co., Orange, Calif., 1979-81, dist. sales rep., 1981; unit sales mgr. Procter & Gamble Co., San Francisco, 1982-84; mgr. spl. assignment Procter & Gamble Co., Cin., 1984-85; dist. sales mgr. Procter & Gamble Co., L.A., 1985-88; prin. Cannon & Assocs., Rancho Palos Verdes, Calif., 1988—; seminar presenter Nat. Seminars Inc., Kansas City, Kans., 1989—; cons. Eveready Battery Co., Inc., St. Louis, 1988—. Named one of Outstanding Young Women in Am., 1985. Mem. NAFE, Am. Soc. for Tng. & Devel., Nat. Speakers Assn. Home: 1681 W 22d St San Pedro CA 90732 Office: Cannon & Assocs 28901 S Western Ave Ste 423 San Pedro CA 90732-2122

CANNONITO, FRANK BENJAMIN, mathematics educator; b. N.Y.C., Oct. 19, 1926; s. John Cannonito and Harriet Ruth (Sniffin) Nemeth; m. Jeanne Beth Bressler, Apr. 28, 1953 (div. 1972); children: Julie M., Carol M.; m. Janet Mary Ferguson Leslie, July 10, 1985. BS, Columbia U., 1959, MA, 1961; PhD, Adelphi U., 1964. Asst. prof. math. U. Calif., Irvine, 1965-70, assoc. prof., 1970-77, prof., 1977-91, prof. emeritus, 1991—; mem. Math. Scis. Rsch. Inst., Berkeley, Calif., 1988-89. Co-editor: Word Problems, 1973; contbr. articles to profl. jours. With USAAC, 1943-45. Columbia scholar, 1959-60, George Pfeiffer scholar Columbia U., 1959-60. Mem. London Math. Soc. Home: 4 Russell Ct Irvine CA 92715 Office: U Calif Dept Math Irvine CA 92717

CANOVA-DAVIS, ELEANOR, biochemist, researcher; b. San Francisco, Jan. 18, 1938; d. Gaudenzio Enzio and Catherine (Bordisso) Canova; m. Kenneth Roy Davis, Feb. 10, 1957; children: Kenneth Roy Jr., Jeffrey Stephen. BA, San Francisco State U., 1968, MS, 1971; PhD, U. Calif., San Francisco, 1977. Lab. asst. Frederick Burk Found. for Edn., San Francisco, 1969-71; research , teaching asst. U. Calif., San Francisco, 1972-77, asst. research biochemist, 1980-84; NIH postdoctoral fellow U. Calif., Berkeley, 1977-80; sr. scientist Liposome Tech., Menlo Park, Calif., 1984-85, Genentech, Inc., South San Francisco, 1985—. Contbr. articles to profl. jours. Recipient Nat. Rsch. Svc. award NIH, 1977-80; grantee Chancellor's Patent Fund, U. Calif., San Francisco, 1976, Earl C. Anthony Trust, 1975; grad. div. fellow U. Calif., San Francisco, 1972-73. Mem. Am. Chem. Soc., Calif. Scholarship Fedn., Sequoia Woods Country Club, Protein Soc., Am. Peptide Soc. Roman Catholic. Home: 2305 Bourbon Ct South San Francisco CA 94080-5367 Office: Genentech Inc 460 Point San Bruno Blvd South San Francisco CA 94080-4918

CANSECO, JOSE, professional baseball player; b. Havana, Cuba, July 2, 1964; s. Jose and Barbara (dec.) C.; m. Esther Haddad, October 25, 1988. Player various minor league teams, 1982-85; outfielder Oakland (Calif.) Athletics, 1985-92, Texas Rangers, 1992—; mem. Am. League All-Star Team, 1986, 88, 89, 90. Appeared in instructional video, Jose Canseco's Baseball Camp, 1989. Named Most Valuable Player So. League, 1985, Am. League, 1988, Am. League Rookieof Yr. The Sporting News, 1986, Baseball Writers' Assn. Am., 1986; first player to have 40 home runs and 40 stolen bases in same season, 1988; mem. ChampionshipTeam, 1989. Office: care Texas Rangers 1250 Copeland Road Arlington TX 76010

CANTOR, ROBERT FRANK, computer company executive; b. N.Y.C., Apr. 29, 1943; s. Myron David and Phyllis Jane (Singerman) C.: m. Nancy Marie Carpenter, May 3, 1970 (div.); 1 child, Michelle; m. Brenda Le Cousins, May 5, 1984; children: Anthony, Samuel, Matthew. BSBA, Pa. State U., 1965, MSBA, 1967. Indsl. engr. IBM, 1967, with software devel., 1968-72; adv. planner banking and security Kingston, N.Y., 1973-78; program mgr. strategy and bus. practices at div. hdqrs. Harrison, N.Y., 1978-80; mgr. tech. products planning Boulder, Colo., 1980-83; program mgr. OEM supplies, 1983-91; mem. faculty loan program Xavier U., New Orleans, 1972-73; program mgr. spl. delivery products Lexmark Internat., Inc., Boulder, 1991—; bd. dirs. and pres. Colo. Neurodiagnostic Inst., Boulder. Inventor in field. Mem. Beta Gamma Sigma. Republican. Mem. Bahai Faith. Office: LexMark Internat Inc 6555 Monarch Rd Boulder CO 80301

CANTWELL, MARIA E., congresswoman. Grad., Miami U. Former rep. Dist. 44 State of Wash.; mem. 103rd Congress from 1st Wash. dist., Washington, D.C., 1993—; owner pub. rels. firm. Office: US Ho Reps Office Ho Mems Washington DC 20515

CAO, DAC-BUU, software engineer; b. Ninh Hoa, Khanh Hoa, Vietnam, Feb. 21, 1949; came to U.S., 1980; s. Thuan and Tiep Thi (Le) C.; m. Amy My-Hao Luong, Nov. 11, 1967; children: Valerie Phuong-Bao, Jesse Chau, Mike Minh-Chau. B of Law, U. Saigon, Vietnam, 1972; BS in Computer Sci., U. Calif., Irvine, 1985; MS in Computer Sci., West Coast U., L.A., 1991. Spl. corr. Progress Daily News, Saigon, 1965-69, mng. editor, 1969-72; asst. editor Dem. Daily News, Saigon, 1973-74; programmer, analyst Eaton Corp., Costa Mesa, Calif., 1981-85; system design engr. EPC Internat., Newport Beach, Calif., 1985-89; sr. application specialist McDonnell Douglas System Integration, Cypress, Calif., 1989-91; sr. systems engr. Unigraphics div. EDS Corp., 1991—. Author: (Vietnamese) Tien Don Yeu Dau, 1969, Ngon Doi Tuyet Vong, 1970; inventor protector for motor vehicles. Recipient Vietnamese Journalism award Nat. Press Coun., U.S. Govt., 1966, Systems Integration MVP award McDonnell Douglas Corp., 1990. Mem. IEEE Computer Soc., Acad. of Am. and Internat. Law, Assn. for Computing Machinery, Am. Assn. for Artificial Intelligence. Republican. Buddhist. Office: Electronic Data Systems Corp 10824 Hope St Cypress CA 90630

CAO, DIANSHENG, science researcher; b. Keshan, Heilongjian, China, Feb. 17, 1962; came to U.S., 1986; s. Ying Xiuqien Cao and Xiuqien Wei; m. Xiaoqian Chang, Aug. 15, 1986; 1 child, Allen. BS, Jilin U., Chang Chun, People's Rep. of China, 1983, MS, 1986; ME, U. Utah, 1990, PhD, 1991. Rsch. ass't. Nat. Optoelectronic Labs., Chang Chun, 1983-86, U. Utah, Salt Lake City, 1986—; coord. dept. material sci. Clin. Rsch. Assocs., Provo, Utah, 1991—. Contbr. articles to profl. jours. Office: Clin Rsch Assocs Provo UT 84604

CAO, THAI-HAI, industrial engineer; b. Saigon, Republic of Vietnam, July 8, 1954; came to U.S., 1975; s. Pho Thai and Anh Ngoc (Nguyen) C.; m. Hue Thi Tran, June 29, 1979; children: Quoc-Viet Thai, Quoc-Nam Thai, Huyen-Tran Thai. BS in Indsl. Engring., U. Wash., 1980; grad., Gen. Electric Mfg. Mgmt. Prgm., 1982. Mfg. engr. GE, San Jose, Calif., 1980-82; mgr. mfg. engring. and quality assurance Broadcast Microwave div. Harris Corp., Mountain View, Calif., 1982-85; mgr. mfg. engring. John Fluke Mfg. Co., Everett, Wash., 1986-90; mgr. quality engring. Advanced Tech. Labs., Bothell, Wash., 1990—; cons. total quality mgmt. Vinatek. Mem. Am. Soc. Quality Control (chmn. membership com. 1987—), Soc. Vietnamese Profls. (pres. 1988), Soc. Mfg. Engrs., Inst. Indsl. Engrs., Am. Prodn. and Inventory Control. Home: 23502 22d Ave SE Bothell WA 98021

CAPELLE, MADELENE CAROLE, soprano, educator, music therapist; b. Las Vegas, Nev., July 29, 1950; d. Curtis and Madelene Glenna (Healy) C. BA, Mills Coll., 1971; MusM, U. Tex., 1976; postgrad., Ind. U., 1976-77; diploma cert., U. Vienna, Austria, 1978. Cert. K-12 music specialist, Nev. Prof. voice U. Nev. Clark County Coll., Las Vegas, 1986—; music therapist Charter Hosp., Las Vegas, 1987—; pvt. practice child music therapy, Las Vegas, 1989—; music specialist Clark County Sch. Dist., Las Vegas, 1989—; contract music therapist Nev. Assn. for Handicapped, Las Vegas, 1990; guest voice coach U. Basel, Switzerland, 1992; artist-in-residence, Nev., Wyo., S.D., N.D., Oreg., Idaho, 1988—; mem. cons. roster Wyo. Arts Coun., 1988—; cons., U.S. rep. Princess Margaret of Romania Found. Opera singer, Europe, Asia, S.Am., U.S., Can., Australia, 1978—; roles include Cio Cio San in Madama Buttrfly, Tosca, Turandot and Fidelio; featured guest All Things Considered PBS radio, 1985; co-writer (one-woman show) The Fat Lady Sings, 1991 (Women's Awareness award). Cons. Children's Opera Outreach, Las Vegas, 1985—; artist Musicians Emergency Found., N.Y.C., 1978-82; vol. Zoo Assn., Allied Arts, Ziegfeld Club (first Junior Ziegfeld Young Woman of Yr.), Las Vegas, 1979—; clown Very Spl. Arts, Nev., Oreg., S.D., 1989-90; goodwill and cultural amb. City of Las Vegas, 1983; panelist Kennedy Ctr., Washington, 1982; artist Benefit Concerts for Children with AIDS; mem. Nev. Arts Alliance. Mem. Nat. Assn. Tchrs. Singing, Performing Arts Soc. Nev., Brown Bag Concert Assn. (bd. dirs.), Make A Wish Found. Democrat. Home: 3266 Brentwood St Las Vegas NV 89121

CAPENER, REGNER ALVIN, minister, electronics engineer; b. Astoria, Oreg., Apr. 18, 1942; s. Alvin Earnest and Lillian Lorraine (Lehtosaari) C.; divorced; children: Deborah, Christian, Melodie, Ariella; m. Della Denise Melson, May 17, 1983; children: Shelley, Danielle, Rebekah, Joshua. Student, U. Nebr., 1957-58, 59-60, Southwestern Coll., Waxahachie, Tex., 1958-59, Bethany Bible Coll., 1963-64. Ordained minister Full Gospel Assembly Ch., 1971. Engr., talk show host Sta. KHOF-FM, Glendale, Calif., 1966-67; youth min. Bethel Union Ch., Duarte, Calif., 1966-67; pres. Intermountain Electronics, Salt Lake City, 1967-72; assoc. pastor Full Gospel Assembly, Salt Lake City, 1968-72, Long Beach (Calif.) Christian Ctr., 1972-76; v.p. Refuge Ministries, Inc., Long Beach, 1972-76; pres. Christian Broadcasting Network-Alaska, Inc., Fairbanks, 1977-83; gen.mgr. Action Sch. of Broadcasting, Anchorage, 1983-85; pres., pastor House of Praise, Anchorage, 1984—; chief engr. KTBY-TV, Inc., Anchorage, 1988—; pres. R & DC Engring., Anchorage, 1992—; area dir. Christian Broadcasting Network, Virginia Beach, 1977-83; cons., dir. Union Bond and Trust Co., Anchorage, 1985-86; author, editor univ. courses,1 984-85; dep. gov. Am. Biog. Inst. Rsch. Assn., 1990—; adviser Anchorage chpt. Women's Aglow Internat., 1990-91. Author: Spiritual Maturity, 1975, Spiritual Warfare, 1976, The Doctrine of Submission, 1988, A Vision for Praise, 1988, Ekklesia, 1993; author, composer numerous gospel songs; creator numerous broadcasting and electronic instrument inventions. Sec., Christian Businessmen's Com., Salt Lake City, 1968-72; area advisor Women's Aglow Internat., Fairbanks, 1981-83; local co-chmn. campaign Boucher for Gov. Com., Fairbanks, 1982; campaigner for Boucher, Anchorage, 1984, Clark Gruening for Senate Com., Barrow, Alaska, 1980; TV producer Stevens for U.S. Senate, Barrow, 1978; fundraiser City of Refuge, Mex., 1973-75; statewide rep. Sudden Infant Death Syndrome, Barrow, 1978-82; founder Operation Blessing/Alaska, 1981; mem. resch. bd. advisors Am. Biog. Inst., 1990—; advisor Anchorage chpt. Women's Aglow Internat., 1990-91. Mem. Soc. Broadcast Engrs., Internat. Soc. Classical Guitarists (sec. 1967-69), Alaska Broadcaster's Assn., Nat. Assn. Broadcasters, Anchorage C. of C. Republican. Office: TAD Tellecomunications Inc Ste 203A 555 W Northern Lights Blvd Anchorage AK 99503

CAPIZZI, MICHAEL ROBERT, lawyer; b. Detroit, Oct. 19, 1939; s. I.A. and Adelaide E. (Jennelle) C.; m. Sandra Jo Jones, June 22, 1963; children: Cori Anne, Pamela Jo. BS in Bus. Adminstrn., Eastern Mich. U., 1961; JD, U. Mich., 1964. Bar: Calif. 1965, U.S. Dist. Ct. (so. dist.) Calif. 1965, U.S. Ct. Appeals (9th cir.) 1970, U.S. Supreme Ct. 1971. Dep. dist. atty. Orange County, Calif., 1965-68, head writs, appeals and spl. assignments sect., 1968-71, asst. dist. atty., dir. spl. ops., 1971-86; legal counsel, mem. exec. bd. Interstate Organized Crime Index, 1971-79, Law Enforcement Intelligence Unit, 1971-86, chief asst. dist. atty., 1986-90, dist. atty., 1990—; instr. criminal justice Santa Ana Coll., 1967-76, Calif. State U., 1976-87. Commr. City Planning Commn., Fountain Valley, Calif., 1971-80, vice chmn., 1972-73, chmn., 1973-75, 79-80. Fellow Am. Coll. Trial Lawyers; mem. Nat. Dist. Attys. Assn., Calif. Dist. Attys. Assn. (outstanding prosecutor award 1980), Calif. Bar Assn., Orange County Bar Assn. (chmn. cts. com. 1977, chmn. coll. of trial advocacy com. 1978-81, bd. dirs. 1977-81, sec.-treas. 1982, pres. 1984). Office: Orange County Dist Atty 700 Civic Center Dr W Santa Ana CA 92701-4045

CAPLAN, EDWIN HARVEY, university dean, accounting educator; b. Boston, Aug. 24, 1926; s. Henry and Dorothy (Nathanson) C.; m. Ramona Hootner, June 20, 1948; children—Gary, Dennis, Jeffrey, Nancy. B.B.A., U. Mich., 1950, M.B.A., 1952; Ph.D., U. Calif., 1965. C.P.A., Calif., Mich. Ptnr. J.J. Gotlieb & Co., C.P.A.s, Detroit, 1953-56; prof. acctg. Humboldt State U., 1956-61, U. Oreg., 1964-67; prof. U. N.Mex., Albuquerque, 1967—, assoc. dean Sch. Mgmt., 1982-83, dean Sch. Mgmt., 1989-90; cons. in field. Contbr. articles to profl. jours. Served to 1st lt. U.S. Army, 1944-46. Mem. Am. Acctg. Assn., AICPA, Nat. Assn. Accts. Home: 8201 Harwood Ave NE Albuquerque NM 87110-1517 Office: Univ N Mex Anderson Sch Mgmt Albuquerque NM 87131

CAPLAN, FRANK, management consultant, educator; b. Detroit, Oct. 15, 1919; s. Frank and Marguerite (Hummel) C.; m. Shirley Ellen Rickard, May 28, 1942; children: Janice Joyce, James Arthur, Joel Anthony, Judith Jill. B in Mech. Engring., Cornell U., 1942. Plant engr. Camillus (N.Y.) Cutlery Co., 1945-52; quality engr. supr. GE, Syracuse, N.Y., Evendale, Ohio, 1952-57; quality mgr., corp. quality cons. Westinghouse Electric Co., Cheswick and others, Pa., 1957-64; dir. engring. and product assurance Atlas Chem. Industries, Valley Forge, Pa., 1964-69; sr. systems engr. Gen. Systems Co., Pittsfield, Mass., 1969-76; mgr., quality system planning Motorola, Inc., Schaumburg, Ill., 1976-82; v.p., corp. quality systems Gull Inc., Smithtown, N.Y., 1982-86; pres. Quality Svcs. Inc., Smithtown, 1983-89; pres. Quality Scis. Cons. Inc., Issaquah, Wash., 1989—, also bd. dirs.; mem. adj. faculty dept. engring. SUNY, Stony Brook, 1983-86. Author: The Quality System, 1980, 2d edit., 1990; editor-in-chief: (jour.) Quality Engring., 1988—. Chmn. civil def., Camillus, 1948; mem. Franklin Twp. (Pa.) Sch. Bd., 1962-64; pres. The Crossings Homeowners Assn., Buffalo Grove, Ill., 1980-81; founder, v.p., exec. sec., fellow Nat. Ednl. Quality Initiative, Smithtown and Issaquah, 1986—. 1st lt. U.S. Army, 1942-45, lt. col. Res. ret. Named Engr. of Yr., Engrs. Week Joint Com., L.I., 1990. Fellow Am. Soc. for Quality Control (chmn. electronics div. 1979-80, chmn. L.I. sect. 1986-88, McDermond award 1980, Saddoris award 1987, Ralph A. Evans award 1989, Eugene L. Grant award 1991); mem. Triangle (nat. pres., Svc. Key 1968, Outstanding Alumnus award 1961). Home and Office: Quality Scis Cons Inc 22531 SE 42D Ct Issaquah WA 98027-7241

CAPLAN, JOHN ALAN, executive search company executive; b. San Mateo, Calif., Aug. 24, 1945; s. Julian and Sylvia Yetta (Peterman) C.; m. Andrea Illyne Wiener, June 25, 1967; children: Jay Wesley, Cynthia Rochelle. BS, San Jose State U., 1967; MBA, U. Calif., Berkeley, 1968. With Shell Oil Co., 1970-73; mgr. Mattel, Inc., Hawthorne, Calif., 1972-73; v.p. Syntex Corp., Palo Alto, Calif., 1973-85, Valid Logic Systems, San Jose, 1985-86; sr. v.p. Howe-Lewis Internat., Palo Alto, 1986—. Bd. dirs. Jr. Achievement, Santa Clara, Calif., 1987; mem. MBA adv. bd. U. Santa Clara, 1986-89. With USAR, 1968-72. Democrat.

CAPLIN, TY, country club owner, professional golfer; b. Plymouth, Mich., Sept. 5, 1935; s. Carl James and Helynn (Tyler) C.; m. Nancy Lou Rickman, Mar. 26, 1960; children: Kimberly Joy, Catherine Ann, Kristen Lynn. BS in Liberal Arts, Mich. State U., 1960. Asst. golf profl. Tripoli Country Club, Milw., 1963, Aptos (Calif.) Golf Club, 1964; teaching golf profl. Olympic Club, San Francisco, 1964-65; head golf profl. Mira Vista Country Club, El Cerrito, Calif., 1966-69, Las Positas Golf Course, Livermore, Calif., 1970-71, Castlewood Country Club, Pleasonton, Calif., 1972-78; owner, dir. golf Elkhorn Country Club, Stockton, Calif., 1978—; cons. Sacramento City Recreation, 1986. Bd. dirs. Jr. Golf Assn. No. Calif., Santa Cruz, 1972-80. With U.S. Army, 1961-62. Recipient Jr. Advisor award Jr. Golf Assn. No. Calif., 1986. Mem. Nat. Profl. Golfer's Assn. (bd. dirs. 1992—), No. Calif. Profl. Golfers Assn. (bd. dirs., pres. 1984-86, various offices 1982—, Profl. of Yr. 1985, 86, Bill Strausbaugh award 1988, 89, 90, 91), Profl. Golfers Assn. Am. (Class A), Stockton C. of C. (mem. com. 1982-92, Small Bus. Person of Yr. 1991). Republican. Lutheran. Office: Elkhorn Country Club 1050 Elkhorn Dr Stockton CA 95209

CAPORASO, FREDRIC, food science educator; b. Jersey City, May 28, 1947; s. Pat and Florence L. C.; m. Karen Denise Kuhle, Dec. 5, 1981; children: Robert, Michael, Daniel, Allison. BS, Rutgers U., 1969, MS, 1972; PhD, Pa. State U., 1975. Asst. prof. food sci. U. Nebr., Lincoln, 1975-78; mgr. food sci. Am. McGaw Labs., Irvine, Calif., 1978-82; chmn. food sci. and nutrition Chapman U., Orange, Calif., 1982—; dir. Food Sci. Rsch. Ctr. Chapman U., 1988—. Editor: 9th International Herpetological Proceedings, 1985; contbr. articles to profl. jours. Mem. So. Calif. Inst. Food Technologists (chmn. 1987-88), Inst. Food Technologists (exec. bd. sensory evaluation div. 1983-87, sci. lecturer 1993—), Food Sci. Adminstrs. (coord. 1989-91). Office: Chapman U Food Sci and Nutrition Dept Orange CA 92666

CAPORASO, KAREN DENISE, financial planner; b. Alhambra, Calif., May 23, 1953; d. Robert S. and Vivian J. (Scharff) Kuhle; m. Fredric Caporaso, Dec. 5, 1981; 1 child, Allison Marie. BS in Fin., Chapman U., 1988, BS in Bus. Econs., 1988. CFP. Supr. payroll and acctg. Am. Med. Optics, Irvine, Calif., 1983-85; acct. Liberty Capital Markets, Newport Beach, Calif., 1985-89; stock broker Baraban Securities, Inc., Anaheim,

Calif., 1990-92; registered rep. First Fin. Planners/FFP Securities, Tustin, Calif., 1992—; registered rep. FFP Adv. Svcs., Inc. Mem. Internat. Assn. Fin. Planners, Orange County Soc. of Inst. CFPs. Office: First Fin Planners 17772 E 17th St # 107 Tustin CA 92680

CAPOZZI, KEVIN LEO, holding company executive; b. Kelowna, B.C., Can., July 19, 1957; came to U.S., 1991; s. Joseph Jasper Capozzi and Stella Clara (Bakony) Abbey; m. Lailey Elizabeth Wallace, Dec. 7, 1988. Student, U. So. Calif., 1975-78. Tech. sales rep. Black & McDonald, Toronto, Ont., Can., 1978-80; v.p. ops. Capri Ctr., Kelowna, 1980-87; pres. Bitec Devel. Corp., Vancouver, B.C., 1986-87; exec. v.p. Pan Abode Internat., Richmond, B.C., 1987-91; mng. ptnr. Terrell Plaza Ptnrs., San Antonio, 1991—; v.p. Eagle Fund Corp., San Antonio, 1991—; pres. South Bay Enterprises Ltd., Ketchum, Idaho, 1991—; bd. dirs. South Arm Devel., Vancouver. Mem. Young Entrepreneurs Orgn. (founding bd. dirs. Vancouver 1990—), Wine Club (founding pres. Vancouver 1990). Roman Catholic. Home: 106 Shaun Ln PO Box 5795 Ketchum ID 83340 Office: South Bay Enterprises Ltd Box 4216 141 Northwood Ketchum ID 83340

CAPPA, DONALD, business educator, management consultant; b. San Francisco, Aug. 29, 1930; s. Dominick Navarro and Ruth (Bergman) C.; m. Maryann Freer, Dec. 31, 1950 (div. June 1985); children: Janice Faye Rodondi, James Donald, Christopher Louis; m. Diana Estelle Barry, m. Aug. 21, 1986. Cert. in indsl. mgmt., Coll. San Mateo, 1960, AA, 1961; BA in Mgmt., Golden Gate U., 1973, MA, 1976. Engring. asst. Standard Oil of Calif., San Francisco, 1950-60; pres. Marina Ski Corp., San Francisco, 1960-73; instr. bus. Chabot Coll., Hayward, Calif., 1974—; co-host TV series Sta. KPIX-TV, San Francisco, 1967-71; cons. Hayward (Calif.) Park and Recreation Assn., 1985-86, Plumbers Union 44, San Leandro Calif., 1985—; regional dir. U.S. Naval Sea Cadets, San Francisco, 1985—; ski cons. Sta. KPIX-TV and Sta. KSFO, San Francisco, 1961-72. Co-advisor Arlington, Va. chpt. Distributive Edn. Clubs Am. Lodge: Lions (pres. 1981-82). Office: Chabot Coll 25555 Hesperian Blvd Hayward CA 94545-2447

CAPPEL, CONSTANCE, consulting company executive, author; b. Dayton, Ohio, June 22, 1936; d. Adam Denison and Mary Louise (Henry) C.; m. R.A. Montgomery Jr., June 16, 1962 (div. Apr. 1980); children: Raymond A. Montgomery III, Anson Cappel Montgomery. BA, Sarah Lawrence Coll., 1959; MA, Columbia U., N.Y.C., 1961; PhD, The Union Inst., Cin., 1991. Editor Newsweek, N.Y.C., 1961-63, Vogue, N.Y.C., 1964-66; grad. prof. Goddard Coll., Plainfield, Vt., 1975-79; founder, chief exec. officer, pub. Vt. Crossroad Press, Waitsfield, 1972-82; comml. realtor Investmark, Dayton, 1985-87; prin. Cappel Cons., San Francisco, 1986—. Author: Hemingway in Michigan, 1966 (paperback 1977), Vermont School Bus Ride, 1977. Founder Women's Rights Project/ACLU, Vt., 1973-74. McDowell Colony fellow, Peterborough, N.H., 1972, 74. Mem. Am. Mgmt. Assn. Commonwealth Club Calif., Hemingway Soc., Little Traverse Yacht Club. Episcopalian. Office: PO Box 553 Bodega Bay CA 94923

CAPPS, JAMES LEIGH, II, lawyer, military career officer; b. Brunswick, Ga., Dec. 17, 1956; s. Thomas Edwin Sr. and Betty Marie (Greenhill) C.; m. Nancy Ann Fisher, June 25, 1978; children: Bonnie Lynn, James Leigh III. AA, Seminole Community Coll., Sanford, Fla., 1976; BA in History, U. Cen. Fla., 1981; JD, U. Fla., 1987. Bar: Fla. 1987, U.S. Ct. Mil. Appeals 1988, Colo. 1990. Enlisted USAF, 1977, advanced through grades to capt., 1985; med. svc. specialist USAF, MacDill AFB, Fla., 1977-79; air weapons controller USAF, Fed. Republic of Germany, 1982-84; claims officer USAF, Homestead AFB, Fla., 1987-88, area def. counsel, 1988-90; dep. staff judge adv. USAF, Onizuka AFB, Calif., 1990—. Democrat. Home: 625B Perimeter Rd Mountain View CA 94043 Office: USAF Judge Advs Office Onizuka AFB CA 94088

CARANCI, JOHN ANTHONY, JR., funeral director; b. North Providence, R.I., Feb. 18, 1952; s. John Anthony and Anna Frances (Lombardo) C.; m. Beverly Ann Wright, Sept. 6, 1975; children: Carrie Ann, John III. Grad., Calif. Coll. Mortuary Sci., L.A., 1973. Cert. funeral dir., Calif.; lic. embalmer, Calif. Staff mem. Palm Springs Mortuary, Palm Springs, Calif., 1970-73; embalmer, counselor, funeral dir. Wiefels & Son Mortuary, Palm Springs, 1973-77, mgr., funeral dir., embalmer, 1979—; embalmer, funeral dir. Prata Funeral Home, Providence, R.I., 1977-79; lectr., tour host Wiefels & Son Mortuary, Palm Springs, 1980—. V.p. Loren Arny Meml. Scholarship Fund, 1980—; bd dirs. Palm Springs High Sch. Booster Club, 1985—; vol. athletic trainer Palm Springs High Sch. Named Boss of Yr., Palm Springs Jr. C. of C., 1991. Mem. Orange Belt Funeral Dirs. Assn. (sec., treas. 1988—), Elks. Roman Catholic. Home: 67-380 Rango Rd Cathedral City CA 92234 Office: Wiefels & Son Mortuary 666 Vella Palm Springs CA 92264

CARBONE, LESLIE ANNE, chief of staff, writer; b. Salem, Mass., Oct. 12, 1964; d. Robert Francis and Mary Anne (Homan) C. BS, Am. U., 1988. Sr. assoc. Bus.-Industry PAC, Washington, 1986-87; dep. dir. Congl. Majority Com., Arlington, Va., 1987-88; dir. Accuracy In Academia, Washington, 1988-89, exec. dir., 1989-92; chief of staff Office of Assemblyman Ferguson, Newport Beach, Calif., 1992—. Exec. editor Campus Report, 1989-92; author Conservative Rev. mag., 1991-92. Nat. dir. Young Ams. for Freedom, Washington, 1989-90, Exemplary Svc. award DuPage County, 1989; mem. Young Reps. Mem. Univ. Profs. for Acad. Order (commendation award 1992). Roman Catholic.

CARDEN, JOY CABBAGE, education executive; b. Livermore, Ky., Dec. 15, 1932; d. Henry L. and Lillie (Richardson) Cabbage; m. Donald G. Carden, Dec. 19, 1954; children: Lynn Kehlenbeck, Tom Carden, Bob Carden, Jan Blount, Jim Carden. BA, Ky. Wesleyan, 1955; MA, U. Ky., 1975. Instr. music Owensboro (Ky.) City Schs., 1955-57; founder, dir. Musical Arts Ctr., Lexington, Ky., 1980-88; edn. specialist Roland Corp., L.A., 1989, dir. edn., 1993—. Author: Music in Lexington Before 1840, 1980, Guide to Electronic Keyboards, 1988; composer ensembles for electronic keyboards. Mem. Music Tchrs Nat. Assn. (commd. composer 1987), Nat. Guild Piano Tchrs. (state chmn. 1980-88), Nat. Conf. Piano Pedagogy (com. chmn. 1990), Ky. Music Tchrs. Assn. (state chmn. 1980-88), Music Tchrs. Calif. Home: 118 Redondo Ave Long Beach CA 90803-2667 Office: Roland Corp 7200 Dominion Cir Los Angeles CA 90040-3696

CARDEN, THOM(AS) RAY, counseling psychologist; b. Indpls.; s. Howard Ray Carden and Mary Ola Eacret; m. Shirley A. Towles, 1953 (div. 1968); m. Anita Van Natter, May 26, 1973; children: Thom H., Kevin L., Shawn D., Dennis P., Suzanne M., Marlene, Cindy, Lorrie, Linda, Alayne. AA in Psychology, Cerritos Coll., 1973; BA in Psychology, Calif. State U., Northridge, 1975; MS in Psychology, U. So. Calif., 1976; PhD in Psychology, Walden U., 1980. Tchr. spl. edn. L.A. Unified Schs., 1976-81; spl. developmental disabilities resource cons. Torrance (Calif.) Unified Sch. Dist., 1977-78; founder, educator, counselor Western Inst. for Sexual Edn. and Rsch., Northridge, Calif., 1977-84; pvt. practice Northridge, 1977—; devel. workshops for Calif. Coun. on Adult Edn., L.A., Santa Barbara, 1977-78; mem. Calif. State Coun. for Devel. Disabled. Author: Birth Control for Disabled, 1977, V.D. is Very Dangerous, 1977, Sexuality Tutoring for Developmentally Disabled Persons, 1976, (computer program) Personality Index Spectral Analysis, 1987; contbr. articles to profl. jours. With USN, 1950-51. Republican. Mormon.

CARDENAS, HENRY STEVEN, chiropractor, industrial safety consultant; b. L.A., Sept. 27, 1964; s. Enrique Rivera and Sylvia Teresa (Chavez) C. BS in Biology, BA in Psychology, U. Calif., Irvine, 1987; DC, L.A. Coll. Chiropractic, 1990. Cert. ind. disability evaluator. Pvt. practice chiropractor Brea, Calif., 1991—; indsl. safety cons. Orange County, Calif., 1992. Mem. Internat. Chiropractic Assn., Am. Chiropractic Assn., Orange County Chiropractic Assn., Hispanic C. of C. of Orange County, Costa Mesa Mens Golf Club. Office: 375 W Central Ave Brea CA 92621

CARDER, JOHN ARTHUR, market technician; b. Albuquerque, June 3, 1955; s. John Morton Carder and Paula Millicent (Young) O'Neil; m. Susan Potter Burchell, Oct. 11, 1977. BS, U. Colo., 1978. Chartered market technician. Prin. Carder Trust Coordination, 1982—, Topline Investment Graphics, Boulder, Colo., 1988—. Mem. Market Technicians Assn. Office: Topline Investment Graphics PO Box 4283 Boulder CO 80306

CARDER, LARRY WILLIAM, display and exhibit executive; b. Cumberland, Md., July 2, 1958; s. Kenneth Milton and Patricia Ann (Terry) C.; m. Terrill Ann Brockway, Aug. 13, 1983; children: Mandy Lynn, Casey James. Student, The Citadel, 1977-81. Jr. engr. Gen. Dynamics, Charleston, S.C., 1981; designer Ralph M. Parsons, Pasadena, Calif., 1981-82; gen. mgr. KMC/Alco, Culver City, Calif., 1982-88; pres. Exhibit Systems Calif., Culver City, 1988-90; v.p. Subia, Hawthorne, Calif., 1990-91; nat. sales mgr. N/S Corp., Inglewood, Calif., 1991; div. mgr. Exhibit Group, L.A., 1992—; cons. R&K Industries, Inc., Inglewood, Calif., 1988. Bd. dirs., coach Culver City Babe Ruth, 1985-88. With USMC, 1979-80. Recipient Design award Nimlok, 1989. Mem. Mil. Order of The Stars and Bars, SCV, Sons of Union Civil War Vets. Republican. Home: 2742 Greenfield Ave Los Angeles CA 90064-4032 Office: Exhibit Group 7026 E Slauson Ave Los Angeles CA 90040

CARDIN, SUZETTE, nurse manager; b. Attleboro, Mass., Feb. 4, 1950; d. Wilfred W. and Vera E. (Broadbent) C.; m. Edward R. Barden, May 10, 1986; children: Luke Edward, Helen Elizabeth. Diploma, Children's Hosp. Sch. Nursing, Boston, 1970; BSN, Southeastern Mass. U., 1974; MS, U. Md., 1978; postgrad., UCLA, 1990—. RN, Calif. Nursing instr. Fall River (Mass.) Diploma Sch. Nursing, 1974-76; staff nurse SICU Johns Hopkins Hosp., Balt., 1977-78; dir. critical care nursing Med. Ctr. Hosp. Vt., Burlington, 1978-83; nurse mgr. UCLA Med. Ctr., 1984—; editorial cons. Dimensions of Critical Care Nursing, 1989-92, Clin. Issues in Critical Care Nursing, 1989-93. Co-editor: Personnel Management in Critical Care Nursing, 1989-92, AACN Clin. Issues in Critical Care Nursing, 1989-92, Critical Care Nursing, 1992. Recipient award Profl. Businesswomen, 1973, award Maxicare Ednl. & Rsch. Found. Mem. AACN (chair various coms., co-editor CCRN newsletter 1985-86, mem. cert. com. 1984-85, liaison AANN cert. bd. 1986-88, pres. Vt. chpt. 1979-81, mem. program com. 1987-88, NTI com. 1987-88, recipient scholarship, 1992), Am. Heart Assn., Children's Hosp. Alumnae Assn. (recipient One-C scholarship, 1992), Sigma Theta Tau (co-editor newsletter Gamma Tau chpt. 1987-89). Home: 2102 Farrell Ave Redondo Beach CA 90278-1819

CARDINE, GODFREY JOSEPH, state supreme court justice; b. Prairie Du Chien, Wis., July 6, 1924; s. Joseph Frederick and Mary (Kasparek) C.; m. Janice Irene Brown, Sept. 14, 1946; children: Susan, John, Lisa. BS in Engring., U. Ill., 1948; JD with honors, U. Wyo., 1954. Bar: Wyo. 1954, U.S. Dist. Ct. Wyo. 1954, U.S. Ct. Appeals (10th cir.) 1954. Assoc. Schwartz, Bon & McCrary, Casper, Wyo., 1954-66; dist. atty. Natrona County, Wyo., 1966-70; ptnr. Cardine, Vlastos & Reeves, Casper, 1966-77; prof. law U. Wyo., Laramie, 1977-83; justice Wyo. Supreme Ct., Cheyenne, 1983-88, 90—, chief justice, 1988-90; mem. Wyo. State Bd. Law Examiners, 1973-77; faculty mem., dir. Western Trial Advocacy Inst., Laramie, 1981—; adj. prof. trial advocacy Harvard U. Law Sch., 1991; bd. advisors Land and Water Law Rev., 1985-90; jud. assoc. editor Georgetown U. Cts., Health Sci. and the Law, 1989—; mem. ad hoc com. to rev. bar assn. rules and by-laws, 1987-88. Contbr. articles to profl. jours. Active Little League Baseball, Casper, 1960-62, Gov.'s Com. on Dangerous Drugs, 1968-71; Iniciator Alternative Dispute Resolution Program State of Wyo., 1989; chmn. Alternative Dispute Resolution Com., 1990—. Served to 1st lt. USAF, 1943-46, PTO. Fellow Internat. Soc. Barristers; mem. ABA (judicial adminstrn. div.), Assn. Trial Lawyers Am., Wyo. State Bar (pres. 1977-78, minor cts. com. 1966-69), Chi Epsilon, Phi Alpha Delta. Club: Potter Law (pres. 1953-54). Lodge: Rotary. Home: PO Box 223 Cheyenne WY 82003-0223 Office: Wyo Supreme Ct Supreme Ct Bldg Cheyenne WY 82002

CARDLE, MARIA JOAN PASTUSZEK, child psychologist, educator; b. Chester, Pa., Mar. 5, 1959; d. Michael Joseph and W. Joan (Burczynski) Pastuszek; m. James Angus Cardle, Sept. 14, 1985. BA in Psychology, U. Notre Dame, 1981; MA in Child Psychology, U. Minn., 1984, PhD in Child Psychology, 1986. Lic. psychologist, Nev. Psychologist Children's Behavioral Svcs., Las Vegas, Nev., 1986-88, Human Behavior Inst., Las Vegas, 1986-88; dir. Child Focus Psychol. Svcs., Las Vegas, 1988—; lectr. U. Nev., Las Vegas, 1988-89, Sch. Medicine, 1989—. Contbr. articles to mag. Lectr. Las Vegas Libr., 1987; psychol. participant Boulder City (Nev.) Presch. Screening, 1988, 89, 90, 91, 92, Children's Devel. Ctr., Las Vegas, 1990. Named Disting. Woman in Nev., Assn. Disting. Women, 1990. Mem. APA, Soc. for Rsch. in Child Devel., Nev. Psychol. Assn. (treas., sec. 1989-90), So. Nev. Assn. Lic. Psychologists (pres. 1990—). Office: Child Focus 2501 Green Valley Pky Ste 126 Henderson NV 89014-2158

CARDONA, STEVEN CARL, management consultant; b. San Jose, Calif., Aug. 10, 1956; s. Carl Caesar and Jacqueline Marie (Kabrich) C.; m. Sarah Megan Kelly, Oct. 24, 1992. Student, U. Calif. San Diego, 1974-76; BA in Econs., UCLA, 1979; postgrad., U. Notre Dame, 1979-80; MBA in Fin., U. So. Calif., 1982. Account mktg. rep. IBM Corp., L.A., 1982-87; we. regional sales mgr. GE Info. Svcs., GE Co., San Francisco, 1988-89; sr. cons. Dale Watson & Assocs., Inc., San Jose, 1989-90; mgr. Nolan, Norton & Co./KPMG Peat Marwick, L.A., 1990—. Contbr. articles to profl. jours. Mem. Calif. Young Reps., Manhattan Beach, Calif., 1985—; mem. Rep. Senatorial Inner Cir., 1988-90; legis. intern U.S. Ho. of Reps., Washington, 1981; lectr. Sacred Heart Parish, Saratoga, Calif., 1987-90; mem. L.A. Youth Motivational Task Force, 1982-87. Mem. KC, Churchill Club (Palo Alto), Commonwealth Club (steering com. 1990, Santa Clara Valley), Beta Theta Pi. Republican. Roman Catholic. Home: 12723 Trent Jones Ln Tustin CA 92680 Office: Nolan Norton & Co/ KPMG Peat Marwick 725 S Figueroa St 29th Fl Los Angeles CA 90017

CARDOZA, ANNE DE SOLA, screenwriter, illustrator, producer, sculptor, novelist; b. N.Y.C., Nov. 18, 1941; d. Sara Nunez de Sola and Michael Cardoza. BS in Creative Writing, English, NYU, 1964; MA in Creative Writing, English, San Diego State U., 1979; diploma Hollywood Scriptwriting Inst., 1984; diploma Alexandra Inst. Painting, San Diego, 1988. Pres. Anne Cardoza Prodns., Psyche - Toons, Jungian Art. Author of 33 books including In The Chips: 101 Ways to Make Money with your Personal Computer, 1985, High Paying Jobs in Six Months or Less, 1984, Understanding Robotics, 1985, Careers in Robotics, 1985, Careers in Aerospace, 1985, Homehealth Careers, 1993, Winning Resumes for Computer Personnel, 1993, (novels) Psyche Squad, The One Who Invented Writing, 1991, and various short stories; co-author: Winning Tactics for Women Over 40, 1988, (screenplay and novel) Midnight Shift, 1989, Playpen Hostages, 1989, (screenplay) Black Snow Melting, 1990, Why so Many Thousands of American Children Are MIssing Overseas, 1991, The Encyclopedia of Scriptwriting A to Z, 1992; author 17 screenplays; contbr. articles to various publs., film scripts, 2 novelettes and collections of short stories. Office: PO Box 4333 San Diego CA 92164-4333

CARDOZA, MARVIN EDMUND, lawyer, retired banker; b. Half Moon Bay, Calif., Aug. 25, 1913; s. Manuel Edmund and Valda Malvina (Oleson) C.; m. Mafalda Cecelia Angelini, Aug. 16, 1936; children: Michael, Jill M., Jack. AA, San Mateo (Calif.) Jr. Coll., 1933; cert., Am. Inst. Banking, 1941; LLB, U. San Francisco, 1946. Bar: Calif. 1947. From various corp. titles to v.p. Bank of Am., San Francisco, 1934-78; atty. Brit. Motor Car Distbrs., San Francisco, 1978—; mem. Calif. State Fair Bd., Sacramento, 1962-69, Calif. mem. exec. com., 1967-69; gov. USO, Washington, 1967-80; dir. J.A.C.S., Washington, 1980-89. Commr. Pub. Utilities Commn., San Francisco, 1970-72, pres. 1972, San Francisco Police Commn., 1972-76, pres. 1975; pres. U. San Francisco Alumni Assn., 1965-66; regent St. Mary's Cathedral, San Francisco, 1990, v.p. bd. regents; foreman San Francisco Civil Grand Jury, 1982-83. With USN, 1942-45. Named Humanitarian of the Yr., Met. YMCA, 1979; recipient Cert. of Appreciation, USO, 1986. Mem. Bankers Club of San Francisco (hon., asst. sec. 1970-78), World Trade Club of San Francisco, The Olympic Club (treas. 1980-81). Roman Catholic. Office: Brit Motor Car Distbrs 901 Van Ness Ave San Francisco CA 94109-6993

CARDWELL, MICHAEL DEXTER, law enforcement official; b. L.A., Nov. 5, 1950; s. Harvey Debs and Bettie Lee (Craig) C.; m. Kathleen Marie McMahon, Dec. 24, 1980; stepchildren: Edward Charles Anderson, William Charles Anderson. AS in Math. and Sci., Victor Valley Coll., 1988, AS in Adminstrn. of Justice, 1988; grad., FBI Nat. Acad., 1989. With San Bernardino (Calif.) County Sheriff's Dept., 1972—, undercover narcotics detective, 1976-77, homicide detective, 1977-79, SWAT unit comdr., 1983-91, detective div. comdr., 1987-91; de facto chief of police Town of Apple Valley, Calif., 1991—; security planner, tactical unit comdr. Olympic Integrated Threat Assessment Group, 1983-84; San Bernardino Sheriff's rep. to Olympic Anti-Terrorist Operation Ctr., L.A., 1984; security planning con. South Korean Nat. Police, San Bernardino, 1984; co-founder Law Enforcement Incident Command System, San Bernardino, 1985; designer spl. ops. tng. facility San Bernardino County Regional Tng. Ctr., 1985. Contbr. articles, photographs to mags. Recipient Cert. of Commendation, County Bd. Suprs., 1985, Calif. Atty. Gen., 1990, Achievement award Nat. Assn. Counties, 1987. Mem. Calif. Homicide Investigators Assn., Calif. Peace Officers Assn., FBI Nat. Acad. Assocs., Internat. Assn. Bomb Technicians and Investigators, Internat. Assn. Chiefs of Police, Nat. Tactical Officers Assn., Rotary. Home: PO Box 492 Victorville CA 92393-0492 Office: Apple Valley Sheriff's Sta PO Box 429 Apple Valley CA 92307-0008

CAREAGA, ROGELIO ANTONIO, economics educator, consultant; b. Asunción, Paraguay, Sept. 16, 1942; came to U.S., 1963; s. Enrique A. Sosa and Fredesvinda D. Careaga-Pena; m. Anne Appleton Makepeace, June 14, 1969 (div. 1982); m. Rebecca Ruth Westwood, Dec. 8, 1990; children: Julia Maria, John Manuel. BA in History with honors, Stanford U., 1967, MA in Econs., 1968, PhD in Polit. Economy, 1979. Internat. banking officer Wells Fargo Bank, San Francisco, 1979-82; pres. Stanford Bus. Internat., Palo Alto, Calif., 1982-84; prof. Colo. Coll., Colorado Springs, 1984, prof. econs., 1986-88; with corp. banking Hibernia Bank, San Francisco, 1984-85; prof. econs. San Jose (Calif.) State U., 1988—; cons. Conempa Consortium, Asunción, 1990-91, Govt. of Paraguay, Asunción, 1992; advisor to pres. candidate and pres. elect of Paraguay, 1993. Fulbright scholar, 1963. Mem. Am. Econ. Assn. Office: San Jose State Univ Economics Dept 1 Washington Square San Jose CA 95192

CAREY, KATHRYN ANN, advertising and public relations executive, editor, consultant; b. Los Angeles, Oct. 18, 1949; d. Frank Randall and Evelyn Mae (Walmsley) C.; m. Richard Kenneth Sundt, Dec. 28, 1980. BA in Am. Studies with honors, Calif. State U., L.A., 1971. Tutor Calif. Dept. Vocat. Rehab., L.A., 1970; teaching asst. U. So. Calif., 1974-75, UCLA, 1974-75; claims adjuster Auto Club So. Calif., San Gabriel, 1971-73; corp. pub. rels. cons. Carnation Co., L.A., 1973-78; cons., adminstr. Carnation Community Svc. Award Program, 1973-78; pub. rels. cons. Vivitar Corp., 1978; sr. advt. asst. Am. Honda Motor Co., Torrance, Calif., 1978-84; exec. dir. Am. Honda Found., 1984—; adminstr. Honda Matching Gift and Vol. Program, Honda Involvement Program; mgr. Honda Dealer Advt. Assns., 1978-84; cons. advt., pub. rels., promotions. Editor: Vivitar Voice, Santa Monica, Calif., 1978, Rod Machado's Instrument Pilots' Survival Manual, c. 1991; editor Honda Views, 1978-84, Found. Focus, 1984—; asst. editor Friskies Research Digest, 1973-78; contbg. editor Newsbriefs and Momentum, 1978—, Am. Honda Motor Co., Inc. employees publs. Calif. Life Scholarship Found. scholar, 1967. Mem. Advt. Club L.A., Pub. Rels. Soc. Am., So. Calif. Assn. Philanthropy, Coun. on Founds., Affinity Group on Japanese Philanthropy (pres.), Ninety-Nines, Am. Quarter Horse Assn., Aircraft Owners and Pilots Assn., Los Angeles Soc. for Prevention Cruelty to Animals, Greenpeace, Ocicats Internat., Am. Humane Assn., Humane Soc. U.S., Elsa Wild Animal Appeal. Office: Am Honda Found 700 Van Ness Ave Torrance CA 90501-1490

CAREY, OMER LIGON, academic administrator; b. Ellsworth, Ill., Jan. 24, 1929; s. George Franklin and Nola (Thompson) C.; m. Carol Lucille Grant, June 21, 1954; children: Gayle, Craig, Dale, Bryan, Grant. BA, Ill. Wesleyan U., 1954; MBA, Ind. U., 1960, D in Bus. Adminstrn., 1962. Chair mgmt. dept. Alaska Pacific U., Anchorage. Co-author: Financial Tools for Small Business, 1983, Opportunity Management: Strategic Planning for Smaller Business, 1985, Essential of Financial Management, 1990, (monograph) Personnel Policies of Small Business, 1964, Bristol Bay: Its Potential and Development, 1976; editor: The Military-Industrial Complex and United States Foreign Policy, 1969. Regional v.p. N.W. chpt. Nat. Assn. for Retarded Citizens, Irvine, Tex., pres. Wash. Assn. for Retarded Citizens, Olympia, 1969-71, Alaska Assn. for Retarded Citizens, Anchorage, 1974-75. Fulbright fellow C.I.E.S., 1987. Mem. Treasury Mgmt. Assn. (cert. cash mgr.), Fin. Execs. Inst. Alaska (treas. 1989-90, v.p. 1990-91, pres. 1991-92), Fin. Mgmt. Assn., Blue Key, Phi Kappa Phi, Beta Gamma Sigma. Republican. Methodist. Office: Alaska Pacific U 4101 University Dr Anchorage AK 99508-4672

CAREY, RICHARD EDWARD, company executive, pastor; b. Pocatello, Idaho, July 12, 1957; s. Max Edward and Flora Lee (Wright) C.; m. Patricia Ann Wilson, June 4, 1977; children: Jennifer Lynn (dec.), Joshua Richard, Jonathan David. Cert., Idaho State U., 1976, ICC Bible Coll., 1982. Ordained to ministry Idaho Christian Ctr., 1987, Nat. Fellowship of Chs., 1992. Stockman/checker Albertsons, Inc., Pocatello, 1973-76; machinist Bucyrus Erie Co., Pocatello, 1976-83; lead machinist Gen. Products Machine Shop, Pocatello, 1983-91; pres. Idaho Micro Systems Inc., Pocatello, 1987—. Author: (book) The Victorious Life, 1981, software programs, 1983—. asst. pastor Idaho Christian Ctr., Pocatello, 1987-91; sr. pastor Faith Christian Ctr., Blackfoot, Idaho, 1991—; pres. Pocatello Color Computer Club, 1984-86. Named Outstanding Young Man of Am., 1987. Republican. Home and Office: Idaho Micro Systems Inc 180 N Fisher Ave Blackfoot ID 83221

CAREY, STAN, sports administrator, football coach; b. Atlanta, June 17, 1955; s. Morris Stanton Sr. and Dorothy (Kirkman) C. Student, DeKalb C.C., Decatur, Ga., 1975-77, Atlanta Tech., 1976, Gallaudet Coll., 1979. Coaching aide Atlanta Falcons, 1971-78, Washington Redskins, 1979, Ga. Tech., Atlanta, 1981-82, L.A. Rams, 1983, UCLA, 1983, U. So. Calif., 1984; assoc. gen. mgr., asst. head coach Gainesville (Ga.) Rams, 1983-86; gen. mgr., spl. teams coach Seattle Raiders, 1989; pres., CEO Am. Pacific N.W. Sports, Seattle, 1989—; asst. gen. mgr., player Sno-King Blue Knights, Edmonds, Wash., 1990; v.p. Seattle Panthers, 1991; v.p. exec. ops., football dir., asst. head coach Seattle Skyhawks, 1992-93; head coach, exec. v.p., dir. football ops. N.W. Huskys; cons. United Cerebral Palsy, Seattle, 1990. Worker Jerry Lewis MDA Telethon, 1973—; charity golfer United Cerebral Palsy, 1974—, Ga. Spl. Olympics, 1974; campaign aide Reagan-Bush, Atlanta, 1980, 84, campaign worker Bush-Quayle, Atlanta, 1988, Seattle, 1992; active Rep. Cen. Com., 1992. Mem. NFL Players Assn., Kiwanis Internat. Episcopalian. Address: Am Pacific NW Sports PO Box 21481 Seattle WA 98111-3481

CARIGNAN, MARC ALFRED, software engineer; b. Manchester, N.H., Aug. 29, 1963; s. Maurice Alfred and Denise Georgette (Cote) C. BS in Computer Sci., U. N.H., 1985. Software engr. No. Telecom Inc., Concord, N.H., 1985-87; sr. software engr. Digital Equipment Corp., Nashua, N.H., 1987-89; devel. mgr. Oracle Systems Inc., Redwood Shores, Calif., 1989-91; sr. software engr. Verity, Inc., Mountain View, Calif., 1991—. Mem. IEEE, Assn. of Computing Machinery. Democrat. Home: 445 Noe St San Francisco CA 94114 Office: Verity Inc 1550 Plymouth St Mountain View CA 94043

CARLANDER, JOHN ROBERT, art educator; b. Moorhead, Minn., Mar. 22, 1943; s. Roy Arthur and Agnes Ingeborg (Erickson) C.; m. Marilyn Lee Strange, Dec. 29, 1965; children: Jay Robert, Lee Allan. BA, Concordia Coll., 1965; MFA, Bowling Green (Ohio) State U., 1968. Instr. Ashland (Ohio) Coll., 1967-69; asst. prof. Concordia Coll., Moorhead, 1969-72; assoc. prof. Augustana Coll., Sioux Falls, S.D., 1972-80; prof. Westmont Coll., Santa Barbara, Calif., 1980—. Dir. Red River ARt Ctr., Moorhead, 1970-72. Mem. Coll. Art Assn., Mus. Contemporary Art L.A., Phi Kappa Phi (pres. 1991—). Democrat. Lutheran. Home: 743 Palermo Dr Santa Barbara CA 93105-4449 Office: Westmont Coll 955 La Paz Rd Santa Barbara CA 93108-1099

CARLBERG, RALPH NORMAN, financial executive; b. Bremerton, Wash., Aug. 4, 1943; s. Norman Enggland Carlberg and Evelyn Grace (Ridley) Osterberg; m. Cathryn Emery, Apr. 23, 1966 (div. 1980); children: Whitney, Reid. BS in Bus., Econs., Western Wash. U., 1966. Plant contr. Corning (N.Y.) Glass Works, 1968-72; plant acctg. mgr. R.T. French Co., Shelley, Ind., 1972-78; div. contr. R.T. French Co., Idaho Falls, Idaho, 1978-83; dir. fin. and human resources R.T. French Co., Rochester, N.Y., 1983-88; v.p. fin. Crescent Foods, Seattle, 1988-91; prin. Sound Strategies, Seattle, 1991-92; v.p. fin. EZ Loader Boat Trailers, Spokane, Wash., 1992—. Bd. dirs. Civitans, Idaho Falls, 1976-81. With USN, 1966-68.

CARLE, HARRY LLOYD, social worker, career development specialist; b. Chgo., Oct. 26, 1927; s. Lloyd Benjamin and Clara Bell (Lee) C.; BSS, Seattle U., 1952; MSW, U. Wash., 1966; m. Elva Diana Ulrich, Dec. 29, 1951; adopted children: Joseph Francis, Catherine Marie; m. Karlen Elizabeth Howe, Oct. 14, 1967 (dec. Feb. 1991); children: Kristen Elizabeth and Sylvia Ann (twins), Eric Lloyd. Indsl. placement and employer rels. rep. State of Wash., Seattle, 1955-57, parole and probation officer, Seattle and Tacoma, 1957-61, parole employment specialist, 1961-63, vocat. rehab. officer, 1963-64; clin. social worker Western State Hosp., Ft. Steilacoom, Washington and U.S. Penitentiary, McNeil Island, Wash., 1964-66; exec. dir. Community Action Council/Social Planning Council, Everett, Wash., 1966-77; career devel. counselor, 1962—; employment and edn. counselor Pierce County Jail Social Services, Tacoma, 1979-81; dir. employment devel. clinic, coord. vocat. program North Rehab. Facility, King County Div. Alcoholism & Substance Abuse, Seattle, 1981-90; counselor Northgate Outpatient Ctr. Lakeside Recovery , Inc., Seattle, 1991; community orgn./agy. problems mgmt. cons., 1968—; mem. social service project staff Pacific Luth. U., Tacoma, 1979-81. Cons. to pres. Geneal. Inst., Salt Lake City, 1974-78. Served with USN, 1944-46. U.S. Office Vocat. Rehab. scholar, 1965-66. Mem. Seattle Geneal. Soc. (pres. 1974-76), Soc. Advancement Mgmt. (chpt. exec. v.p. 1970-71), Acad. Cert. Social Workers, Nat. Assn. Social Workers, Pa. German Soc., Henckel Family Nat. Assn., various hist. and geneal. socs. in Cumberland, Perry and Lancaster counties, Pa., Peoria and Fulton Counties, Ill., Seattle Japanese Garden Soc., Olympia-Yashiro Sister City Assn., Puget Sound Koi Soc., Dr. Sun Yat-sen Garden Soc. Vancouver (B.C., Can.), Kubota Garden Found. (Seattle), Bloedel Reserve (Banbridge Island, Wash.). Roman Catholic. Home: KarlensGarten 1425 10th Pl N Edmonds WA 98020-2629

CARLEONE, JOSEPH, mechanical engineer; b. Phila., Jan. 30, 1946; s. Frank Anthony and Amelia (Ciaccia) C.; m. Shirley Elizabeth Atwell, June 29, 1968; children: Gia Maria, Joan Marie. BS, Drexel U., 1968, MS, 1970, PhD, 1972. Civilian engrng. trainee, mech. engr. Phila. Naval Shipyard, 1963-68; grad. asst. in applied mechanics Drexel U., Phila., 1968-72, postdoctoral rsch. assoc., 1972-73, NDEA fellow, 1968-71, adj. prof. mechanics, 1974-75, 77-82; chief rsch. engr. Dyna East Corp., Phila., 1973-82; chief scientist warhead tech. Aerojet Ordnance Co., Tustin, Calif., 1982-88. v.p., gen. mgr. warhead systems div. GenCorp. Aerojet Precision Weapons, Tustin, 1988-89; v.p., dir. armament systems, Aerojet Electronics Systems Div., Azusa, Calif., 1989—. Mem. ASME, Sigma Xi, Tau Beta Pi, Pi Tau Sigma, Phi Kappa Phi. Contbr. articles to profl. jours.; researcher explosive and metal interaction, ballistics, projectile penetration, impact of plates. Home: 19741 Marsala Dr Yorba Linda CA 92686-2824 Office: Aerojet Electronic Systems Azusa CA 91702

CARLETON, JOHN LOWNDES, psychiatrist; b. Seattle, Dec. 26, 1925; s. John Phillip and Lilian (Lowndes) C.; m. Marie Pak, June 12, 1948 (div. 1968); children: John Phillip II, Pakie Ann, Daniel Lowndes; m. Ellen Andree Masthoff, Apr. 14, 1985; children: Kip, Talitha Ellen. BA, U. Louisville, 1946; MD, Northwestern U., 1950. Diplomate Am. Bd. Psychiatry and Neurology. Physician Howe Sound Mining Co., Holden, Wash., 1950-52; resident psychiatrist Johns Hopkins Hosp., Balt., 1955-57; asst. psychiatrist Moses Shephard and Enoch Pratt Hosp., Towson, Md., 1957-58; pvt. practice Santa Barbara, Calif., 1958—; trustee The Masserman Found. for International. Accords, Chgo., 1986—. Editor: Man for Man, 1973, Dimensions of Social Psychiatry, 1978; editor-in-chief Am. Jour. of Social Psychiatry, 1980-87; contbr. articles to profl. jours. Capt. USAR, 1952-54. Recipient Congress medal, State of Israel, 1974, City of Opatija, 1976, Portugal, 1978, Paris, France, Osaka, Japan, Rio de Janeiro, Brazil, 1983, 83, 86. Fellow ACP, Wold Assn. Social Psychiatry (pres., pres.-elect, sec. gen.), Am. Assn. Social Psychiatry (founding sec., pres., founder), Am. Psychiat. Assn. (life fellow), Am. Coll. Psychiatrists; mem. AMA, Calif. Med. Assn., Santa Barbara County Med. Assn. Home and Office: 310 Malaga Dr Santa Barbara CA 93108

CARLEY, JOHN BLYTHE, retail grocery executive; b. Spokane, Wash., Jan. 4, 1934; s. John Lewis and Freida June (Stiles) C.; m. Joan Marie Hohenleitner, Aug. 6, 1960; children: Christopher, Kathryn, Peter, Scott. AA, Boise Jr. Coll., 1955; student, U. Wash., 1956-57, Stanford U. Exec. Program, 1973. Store dir. Albertson's Inc., Boise, Idaho, 1961-65, grocery merchandiser, 1965-70, dist. mgr., 1970-73, v.p. gen. mdse., 1973, v.p. corp. merchandising, 1973-75, v.p. retail ops., 1975-76, sr. v.p. retail ops., 1976-77, exec. v.p. retail ops., 1977-84, pres., 1984-91; pres., COO Albertson's Inc., Boise, 1991—; also bd. dirs. Albertson's Inc., Boise, Idaho. Republican. Roman Catholic. Clubs: Arid, Hillcrest Country (Boise). Office: Albertson's Inc PO Box 20 250 E Parkcenter Blvd Boise ID 83706-3999*

CARLSON, BRADLEY DEE, research and development engineer; b. Logan, Utah, June 11, 1951; s. Donald Bud and Elaine (Pitcher) C.; m. Lana Louise King, June 13, 1972; children: Heather, Cameron Brad. BSME, Utah State U., 1973; MSEE, Ariz. State U., 1990. Mfg. engr. Sperry Flight Systems, Phoenix, 1972-75, planner, 1975-76, buyer, 1976-78, prodn. mgr., 1980-84; prin. R & D engr. Lucas Sensing Systems, Phoenix, 1985-92; v.p. engrng. Cline Labs., Phoenix, 1992—. Inventor protractor system, ortho ranger and dual axis clinometer. Mem. Phi Kappa Phi. LDS. Home: 4115 W Meadow Dr Glendale AZ 85308-4014 Office: Cline Labs Ste 5 2501 W Behrend Phoenix AZ 85027

CARLSON, CARL EDWARD, petroleum geologist; b. La Crosse, Kans., Jan. 30, 1922; s. Carl Edward and Laura (Pine) C.; m. Iris May Spielman, Aug. 18, 1947; 1 child, Dwight Jesse. BA in Geology, U. Wyo., 1948, MA in Geology, 1949. Cert. profl. geologist, Wyo.; cert. profl. geol. scientist Am. Inst. Petroleum Geologists. Geologist Mobil Oil Corp., Wyo., 1949-52; dist.. geologist Mobil Oil Corp., Mont., Wyo., 1957-63; dist. exploration supt. Mobil Oil Corp., Tex., 1963-66; area exploration mgr. for Can. and U.S., Mobil Oil Corp., 1966-76, geol. cons. in 30 states, 1976-82; ind. petroleum geologist, Wyo., 1982—. Lt. (j.g.) USNR, 1942-46, PTO. Scholar U. Wyo., 1940. Fellow Geol. Soc. Am.; mem. Am. Assn. Petroleum Geologists (cert. petroleum geologist), Sigma Xi, Phi Kappa Phi. Republican.

CARLSON, CARL G., arbitrator, mediator; b. Somerville, Mass., May 8, 1924; s. Gustav A. and Ruth E. (Nelson) C.; m. Estelle E. Panaccione, Jan. 27, 1950. BS, Cornell U., 1953; student, N.Y. Law Sch., N.Y.C., 1959-60. Cert. Am. Arbitration Assn. Indsl. rels. trainee Westinghouse Electric Corp., Pitts., 1953-57; supr. pers. Deloo Remy div. Gen. Motors, New Brunswick, N.J., 1957-65; dir. indsl. and labor rels. Johnson Bronze Co., New Castel, Pa., 1965-67; corp. dir. labor rels. Dow Chem. Co., Midland, Mich., 1967-71; asst. PM gen. U.S. Postal Svc., Washington, Chgo., 1971-79; postmaster, sec. mgr. U.S. Postal Svc., Colorado Springs, Colo., 1979-82; dir. employee and labor rels. U.S. Postal Svc., Flagstaff, Ariz., 1983-89; arbitrator, mediator Breckenridge, Colo., 1991—. Contbr. articles on labor/mgmt. rels. to publs. Former vice chmn. Republican Party, N.J.; chmn. Indsl. Commn., New Brunswick, 1956-58, N.J. State Indsl. Safety Com., Trenton, 1957-60.

CARLSON, CHARLES LONG, controller, accountant; b. Olean, N.Y., Jan. 10, 1917; s. Charles Julius and Edna (Long) C.; m. June Helena Kreamer, Apr. 10, 1948; children: Yvonne, Shaun, Linda, Maria. B.S. in Bus. Adminstrn., U. Buffalo, 1938. C.P.A., N.Y., Calif. Ptnr., Merle Moore & Co., C.P.A.'s, Tucson, 1954-55; sec.-treas., comptroller Infilco, Tucson, 1955-64; comptroller Traveler Boat Div., Stanray Corp., Chgo. and Danville, Ill., 1964-65; comptroller Dorsett Plastics Co., Santa Clara, Calif., 1966; v.p., sec.-treas. Daniel, Mann, Johnson & Mendenhall, Los Angeles, 1966-82, bus. cons., sec., 1982—; dir. numerous subsidiaries of Infilco & DMJM; sec., dir. Infilco (Australasia) Ltd., Infilco (Can.) Ltd., Infilco Mexicana; sec. Gale Separator Co., Catalina Constrn. Co. (both Tucson); sec.-treas. Beach Ocean Inc., 1985—, Honolulu condo Inc., 1985-86; bus. mgr. Westwil Ltd., 1986-92, Hampwil Ptnrs., 1986—; asst. treas. Fuller Co., Catasauqua, Pa.; dir. Gen. Steel Co., Ft. Worth, 1960-64; instr. St. Bonaventure U., Olean, 1948. Republican county committeeman, Olean, 1939. Mem. Tucson C. of C. tax study com., 1960; team orgn. chmn. Olean Gen. Hosp. drive, 1952; gen. chmn. Community Chest campaign, Olean, 1950. Served to 2d lt. USAAF, 1944-45. Mem. Am. Inst. C.P.A.'s. Mem. Ch. of Nazarene. Home and Office: 4515 Prairie Rd Paso Robles CA 93446

CARLSON, CURTIS EUGENE, orthodontist, peridontist; b. Mar. 30, 1942; m. Dona M. Seely; children: Jennifer Ann, Gina Christine, Erik Alan. BA in Divisional Scis., Augustana Coll., 1965; BDS, DDS, U. Ill., 1969; cert. in peridontics, U. Wash., 1974, cert. in orthodontists, 1976. Dental intern Oak Knoll Navy Hosp., Oakland, Calif., 1969-70; dental officer USN, 1970-72; part-tine dentist VA Hosp., Seattle, 1972-73; part-time peridontist Group Health Dental Coop., Seattle, 1973-76, part-time orthodontist, 1976-78; clin. instr. U. Wash., 1976; prin. Bellevue (Wash.) Orthodontic and Peridontic Clinic, 1976—; clin. instr., trainer Luxar Laser Corp., Bothell, Wash., 1992—; presenter in field. Master of ceremonies Auctioneer Friendship Fair, Augustana Coll., 1965, orientation group leader, 1965, mem. field svcs. com. for high sch. recruitment, 1965. Mem. ADA, Am. Acad. Peridontology, Am. Assn. Orthodontics, Western Soc. Peridontology (bd. dirs. 1984-85, 86, program chmn. 1986, v.p. 1988, pres. elect 1989, pres. 1990), Seattle King County Dental Soc. (grievance, ehtics and pub. info. coms.), Wash. State Dental Assn., Wash. State Soc. Peridontists (program chmn., pres. elect 1987, pres. 1988, 89), Wash. Assn. Dental Specialists (com. rep. 1987, 88, 89), Omicron Kappa Upsilon (dental hon. fraternity), Pi Upsilon Gamma (social chmn. 1964, pres. 1965). Home: 16730 Shore Dr NE Seattle WA 98155-5634 Office: Bellevue Orthodontic Peridontic Clinic 1248 112th Ave NE Bellevue WA 98004-3712 also: Luxar Corp 19204 N Creek Pkwy Ste 100 Bothell WA 98011-8009

CARLSON, DENNIS NOBEL, minister, religious organization executive; b. Lincoln, Nebr., Mar. 26, 1946; s. Nobel August and Hildur Eulila (Bengtson) C.; m. Annalee Whieldon, Aug. 10, 1968; children: Jonathan Dennis, Julie Ann. Ordained to ministry Seventh-day Adventist, 1974. Pastor Seventh-day Adventist Ch., East Dayton, Ohio, 1970-72, Willoughby and Brooklyn, Ohio, 1972-74, Mansfield, Ohio, 1974-80, Puyallup, Wash., 1980-84; dir. stewardship edn. and communication Wash. Conf. Seventh-day Adventists, Bothell, 1984-86, exec. sec., 1986—, mem. exec. com., 1981-83; mem. exec. com. Ohio Conf., Mt. Vernon, 1978-80, mem. K-16 Bd. Edn., 1978-80. Contbr. articles to profl. jours. Office: Wash Conf Seventh-day Adventists 20015 Bothell Everett Hwy Bothell WA 98012-7198

CARLSON, GARY LEE, public relations executive, director, producer; b. Yakima, Wash., Oct. 15, 1954; s. Glenn Elmer and Helen Mary (McLean) Carlson. AA, Yakima Community Coll., 1975; BA in Communications, U. Wash., 1977. Dir. pub. affairs Sta. KCMU, Seattle, 1976-77; dir. programming and promotions Sta. KAPP-TV, Yakima, 1978-80; dir. promotions Sta. WBZ-TV, Boston, 1980-84; producer Sta. KCBS-TV, Los Angeles, 1985; dir. creative services Metromedia Producers, Los Angeles, 1985-86; dir. promotion publicity 20th Century Fox, Los Angeles, 1986—. Producer, dir.: M*A*S*H* 15th Ann. Campaign, 1987 (Internat. Film and TV Festival N.Y. award), The Fox Tradition, 1988 (Internat. Film and TV Festival N.Y. award, Clio Finalist award, 1988, Telly award, 1988, B.P.M.E. award, 1988); producer, writer, dir. Consumer Reports, 1983 (Internat. Film and TV Festival N.Y. award, Houston Internat. Film and TV award). Mem. Broadcast Promotion and Mktg. Execs., Nat. Assn. TV Program Execs., Beta Theta Pi. Home: 1510 Rock Glen Ave Glendale CA 91205-2063 Office: 20th Century Fox Film Corp PO Box 900 Beverly Hills CA 90213-0900

CARLSON, MARGARET ELLEN, marketing executive; b. Boise, Idaho, Apr. 5, 1955; d. Lloyd Erwin Johnson and Janet Ellen (Austad) Parks; m. James Dahllund Carlson, July 28, 1979; children: Matthew James, Brett John. BA in Psychology, U. Idaho, 1976; MBA, Wash. State U., 1982. Supr. Boise Cascade Corp., 1977-79; mktg. asst. Foodways Nat., Inc., Boise, 1982-83, asst. product mgr., 1983-85, product mgr. weight watchers desserts, 1985-86, product mgr. weight watchers entrees, 1986-87, product mgr. new products, 1987-88; gen. mgr. ventures Ore-Ida Foods, Inc., Boise, 1988-90, v.p. human resources, 1990-92, v.p. bus. devel., 1992-93, v.p. spl. product mktg., 1993—. Mem. adv. bd. U. Idaho Coll. Bus. & Econs.; chmn. Am. Festival Ballet, Boise, 1991-92. Mem. Kappa Kappa Gamma (pres. Boise Alumni group 1986). Office: Ore-Ida Foods Inc 220 W Parkcenter Blvd Boise ID 83706-3998

CARLSON, MITCHELL LANS, international technical advisor; b. Boulder, Colo., Nov. 24, 1951; s. DeVon M. and Mary (Ackley) C. BA in History and Internat. Affairs, Lewis and Clark Coll., 1974; MA in Environ. Planning, UCLA, 1978; postgrad., U. Calif., Berkeley, 1978-80. Rsch. asst. Sch. Architecture and Urban Planning UCLA, 1977-78; project planner Calif. Energy Resource Conservation and Devel. Commn., Sacramento, 1977-78, Vastu-Shilpa Found., Ahmedabad, India, 1978-79; various positions with UN, 1974-92; chief tech. adviser UN (UNDP), Bangkok, Thailand, 1992—. Home: 502 Mapleton Ave Boulder CO 80304 Office: care UNDP/PNP, GPO Box 618, Bangkok Thailand 10501

CARLSON, NANCY LEE, English language educator; b. Spokane, Wash., June 1, 1950; d. Catherine Esther Paight. BS, Wash. State U., 1973; MEd, curriculum specialist, Ea. Wash. U., 1987. Tchr. Stevenson-Carson Sch. Dist., Wash., 1973-74, Spokane Sch. Dist., 1974—; vis. faculty Ea. Wash. U., 1989-91; active steering com. Spokane County Children's Alliance, 1992—. Spokane County co-chmn. Sen. Slade Gordon campaign, 1988; Rep. precinct committeeperson, 1988-90, 92—; bd. dirs. Spokane Civic Theater, 1986—, sec., 1992—; mem. Spokane Human Svcs. Adv. Bd., 1986—, chmn., 1990-92; mem. affordable housing com. Spokane County, 1990-91; mem. adv. bd. City Spokane Community Ctrs., 1990-92; treas. Inland Empire for Africa, Spokane, 1985-86; vice chmn. Ea. Wash. phone bank for Sen. Dan Evans, Spokane, 1984; mem. Mayor's Task Force on the Homeless, 1987-88; mem. Spokane County adv. bd. for. Sen. Slade Gordon, 1989—; mem. Spokane Human Svcs. Bd., 1986-92, chmn. 1990-92; mem. Community Ctrs. Bd., 1990-92; bd. dirs. West Ctrl. Community Ctr., 1993—. Mem. NEA, Nat. Coun. Tchrs. English, Wash. Coun. Tchrs. English, Assn. for Supervision and Curriculum Devel., Wash. Edn. Assn., Spokane Edn. Assn., Wash. State U. Alumni Assn. (area rep. 1987-90). Republican. Presbyterian. Office: Rogers High Sch Sch Dist # 81 E 1622 Wellesley Spokane WA 99207

CARLSON, NATALIE TRAYLOR, publisher; b. St. Paul, Feb. 15, 1938; d. Howard Ripley and Maxine (Johnson) Smith; m. James S. Carlson, Oct. 6, 1990; children: Drew Michael, Dacia Lyn, Dana Ann. BA, Jacksonville (Ala.) State U., 1975. Dir. Madison County Assn. of Mental Health, Anniston, Ala., 1966-67; campaign mgr. U.S. Senatorial Race, No. Ala., 1968; pub. rels. Anniston Acad., 1970-76; journalist The Anniston Star, 1970-74, The Birmingham News, Anniston, 1972-76; dir. Ala. affiliate, Am. Heart Assn., Birmingham, 1976-77; mgr. San Vincent New Home div., San Diego County Estates Realty, 1978-79; dir. sales Blake Pub. Co., San Diego, 1980-86; pres. Century Publ., San Diego, 1986—. Alternate del. at large Rep. Nat. Conv., San Francisco, 1964; fin. chmn. Madison County Rep. Exec. Com., Huntsville, Ala., 1966-69; pres. Madison County Rep. Women, Huntsville, 1967, 68; Diocesan Conv. del. Grace Episcopal Ch., Ala., 1975; active Nat. Rep. Party, 1962—; mem. St. James Episcopal Ch., Newport Beach, 1990—. Recipient 1st Pl. newswriting award AP, 1971, 72, 73; named Outstanding Woman of Yr., Huntsville Area Jaycees, 1967. Mem. Long Beach Area C. of C., Palm Springs C. of C., Greater Del Mar C. of C., Encino C. of C., Kappa Kappa Gamma.

CARLSON, PAUL EDWIN, real estate developer, writer; b. San Francisco, June 29, 1944; s. Carl John and Marguerite Eutha (Kovatch) C.; m. Sharon Raye Hammond, Nov. 14, 1964; children: Kimberley, Davin, Christina. AA, Yosemite Coll., 1964; BA, Calif. State U., Long Beach, 1971; cert. shopping ctr. mgr., Internat. Council of Shopping Ctrs. Mgmt. Sch., 1981. Vice and narcotics officer Modesto and Los Angeles Police Depts., Calif., 1964-69; owner Universal Prodns., N.Y.C. and Modesto, 1963-73; gen. mgr. City Investing Co., N.C.Y. and Beverly Hills, Calif., 1973-75; sr. v.p. The Koll Co., Newport Beach, Calif., 1975-79; v.p. Irvine Co., Newport Beach, 1979-80; owner Willows Shopping Ctr., Concord, Calif., 1980-83; sr. v.p. Lee Sammis Co., Irvine, 1983-85; pres. Am. Devel. Co., Costa Mesa, Calif., 1985-86; chmn. bd. The Carlson Co., Newport Beach, 1986—; guest lectr. U. So. Cal., U. Calif., Los Angeles, Orange Coast Coll.; real estate cons. Bank of Am., Union Bank, Chevron U.S.A., Aetna Life Ins. Co., James Lang Wooten, Eng., Peoples Republic of China. Author three screenplays for Police Story; comedy writer The Tonight Show, Sat. Night Live, Late Night with David Letterman; pub. Property Mgrs. Handbook. mem. Calif. State Juvenile Justice Commn., Rep. Senatorial Inner circle, Washington; past chmn. City of Newport Beach Traffic Commn.; pres. bd. trustees Mt. Diablo Hosp.; v.p., bd. dirs. City of Concord Pavillion; bd. dirs. Concord Visitors and Conv. Bur. Mem. Am. Cancer Soc. (bd. dirs. Contra Costa County), Internat. Coun. Shopping Ctrs. (state ops. chmn.). Republican. Home: 140 Jasmine Creek Dr Corona Del Mar CA 92625-1421 Office: The Carlson Co 3 Corporate Plaza Dr Ste 100 Newport Beach CA 92660-7905

CARLSON, RALPH JENNINGS, communications executive; b. Sept. 19, 1929, Salt Lake City; s. Arthur J. and Lizette (Russell) C.; m. Catheryn Jane Kallas, Aug. 1951; children: Ralph Steven, Brent Jennings, Lloyd Daryl, Rex Neil, Julie Ann, Jana Lynn. Student U. Utah, 2 yrs.; grad. in bus. adminstrn. Alexander Hamilton Inst., 1966. Pres. Carlson Communications Internat., Holiday Broadcasting Co., KRSP-AM-FM, Holiday Broadcasting of ELKO/KRJC-FM, Central Broadcasting Co. KSMK-FM, KUSW Worldwide Radio, Salt Lake City; ptnr. A & R Meats, Inc. Vice-chmn. Utah Multiple Sclerosis Soc., 1976-78; dist. chmn. Jordan dist. Great Salt Lake council Boy Scouts Am., 1966, activities chmn., 1967-70; stake high council East Jordan stake, 2d counselor union 28th ward Ch. of Jesus Christ of Latter-day Saints. Served with U.S. Army, 1951-53. Recipient Silver Beaver award Boy Scouts Am., 1968, Scouters Tng. award, 1969; U. Utah Journalism award, 1979. Mem. Utah Broadcasters Assn. (pres. 1978), Utah Advt. Fedn. (dir.), Rocky Mountain Broadcasters Assn. (pres. 1979), Nat. Radio Broadcasters Assn. (bd. dirs. 1984-86), Utah AP Broadcasters (pres. 1976), Nat. Exchange Club (v.p. 1981-87, pres. 1982—, pres. Sugarhouse/Cottonwood 1971, 83, sec. 1978, pres., 1979-80, nat. bd. dirs. 1981-85, v.p. western region, 1986—), Salt Lake City Track Club (pres. 1982). Address: Station KRSP PO Box 7760 Salt Lake City UT 84107

CARLSON, RALPH WILLIAM, JR., food products company executive; b. Oak Park, Ill., Dec. 28, 1936; s. Ralph W. and Evelyn Marie (Benson) C.; m. Donna Drevs, Feb. 9, 1963; children: Daniel, Karen, Susan, Robert, Kathleen. B.A., Mich. State U., 1958; M.B.A., U. Chgo., 1965; J.D., De Paul U., 1976. Bar: Ill. Group product mgr. The Kendall Co., Chgo., 1966-70; dir. mktg. Ovaltine Products Co. div. Sandoz, Inc., Chgo., 1970-76; mgr. new products Arco Polymers, Inc. subs. Atlantic Richfield Co., Chgo., 1976-78; mgr. internat. fleet ops. Arco Transp. Co., Long Beach, Calif., 1978-81; mgr. mktg. planning Arco Solar Industries, Woodland Hills, Calif., 1981-85; mgr. trademark licensing Sunkist Growers Assn., Inc., Ontario, Calif., 1986—; part-time instr. mktg. UCLA, 1989—. Mem. Oak Park (Ill.) Sch. Bd., 1976-78; bd. dirs. Phila. Maritime Exchange, 1978-79; trustee Cornelia Connelly Sch., 1990—. Served to lt. USNR, 1958-63. Mem. ABA, Am. Mktg. Assn., Calif. Solar Energy Soc. (dir. 1983-85), U.S. Naval Inst., Delta Chi. Republican. Roman Catholic. Club: Economic (Chgo.); Newfoundland of So. Calif. (bd. dirs. 1985—). Home: 9117 Wagner River Cir Fountain Vly CA 92708-6449 Office: Sunkist Growers Assn 720 E Sunkist St Ontario CA 91761-1861

CARLSON, RICHARD MERRILL, aeronautical engineer, research executive; b. Preston, Idaho, Feb. 4, 1925; s. Carl and Oretta C.; m. Venis Johnson, Nov. 26, 1946; children: Judith, Jennifer, Richard. BS in Aero. Engring., U. Wash., Seattle, MS; PhD in Engring. Mechanics, Stanford U. Registered profl. engr., Calif., chartered engr., U.K. Chief aeros., structures engr. Hiller Aircraft, Menlo Pk., Calif., 1949-64; engr. rotary wing div. Lockheed Calif. Co., Burbank, 1964-72; chief advanced systems rsch. Air Mobility R&D Lab. U.S. Army, Moffett Field, Calif., 1972-76, dir. Rsch. & Tech. Labs., Ames Rsch. Ctr., 1976—; lectr. Stanford U.; designated engring. rep. FAA. Contbr. articles to profl. jours. Lt. (j.g.) AC, USN, 1943-46. Recipient Meritorious Civilian Svc. awards U.S. Army, 1975, 77, 83, Presdl. Rank Meritorious Exec., 1987; Consol.-Vultee fellow, 1947. Fellow AIAA, Royal Aero. Soc., Am. Helicopter Soc. (hon.); mem. NAE, Swedish Soc. Aeros. and Astronauts, Sigma Xi, Elks. Mem. LDS Ch. Office: US Army Rsch & Tech Lab Activity Ames Rsch Ctr Moffett Field CA 94035

CARLSON, ROBERT CODNER, industrial engineering educator; b. Granite Falls, Minn., Jan. 17, 1939; s. Robert Ledin and Ada Louise (Codner) C.; children: Brian William, Andrew Robert, Christina Louise. BSME, Cornell U., 1962; MS, Johns Hopkins U., 1963, PhD, 1976. Mem. tech. staff Bell Tel. Labs., Holmdel, N.J., 1962-70; asst. prof. Stanford (Calif.) U., Stanford, 1970-77; assoc. prof. Stanford (Calif.) U., 1977-82, prof. indsl. engring., 1982—; program dir., lectr., cons. various spl. programs U.S., Japan, France, 1971—; cons. Japan Mgmt. Assn., Tokyo, 1990—, Raychem, Menlo Park, Calif., 1989—, GKN Automotive, London, 1989—, Rockwell Internat., L.A., 1988—; vis. prof. U. Calif., Berkeley, 1987-88, Dartmouth Coll., Hanover, N.J., 1978-79; vis. faculty Internat. Mgmt. Inst., Geneva, 1984, 88. Contbr. articles to profl. jours. Recipient Maxwell Upson award in Mech. Engring. Cornell U., 1962; Bell Labs. Systems Engring. fellow, 1962-63, Bell Labs. Doctoral Support fellow, 1966-67. Mem. Ops. Rsch. Soc. Am. (chmn. membership com. 1981-83), Inst. Mgmt. Scis., Inst. Indsl. Engrs., Am. Soc. Engring. Edn., Am. Prodn. and Inventory Control Soc. (bd. dirs. 1975-81), Internat. Material Mgmt. Soc., Tau Beta Pi, Phi Kappa Phi, Pi Tau Sigma, Soc. of Enophiles Club (Woodside, Calif.). Office: Stanford Univ Dept Indsl Engring/Engring Mgmt Stanford CA 94305

CARLSON, ROBERT ERNEST, freelance writer, architect, lecturer; b. Denver, Dec. 6, 1924; s. Milton and Augustine Barbara (Walter) C.; m. Jane Frances Waters, June 14, 1952 (div. June 1971); children: Cristina, Bob, Douglas, Glenn, James. BS in Archtl. Engring., U. Colo., 1951. Registered architect, Colo. Architect H.D. Wagener & Assocs., Boulder, Colo., 1953-75; pvt. practice architect Denver, 1975-82; health and promotion cons. Alive & Well Cons., Denver, 1982-85; freelance writer Denver, 1985—; mem. Colo. Gov.'s Coun. for Fitness, Denver, 1975—; state race walking chmn. U.S. Track & Field, Denver, 1983—; bd. dirs. Colo. Found. for Phys. Fitness, Denver, 1987—; lectr. in field. Author: Health Walk, 1988. Vol. Colo. Heart Assn., 1985—, Better Air Campaign, 1986-87, Cystic Fibrosis, 1989-91, Multiple Sclerosis Soc., 1988-91, Qualife, 1989—, March of Dimes, 1989, United Negro Coll. Fund, 1989, bd. trustees, 1990. With U.S. Army, 1943-46, ETO. Decorated Bronze Star; named One of Ten Most Prominent Walking Leaders in U.S.A., Rockport Walking Inst., 1989. Mem. Colo. Author's League, Phidippides Track Club (walking chmn. 1981-85), Rocky Mountain Rd. Runners (v.p. 1983-84), Front Range Walkers Club (founder, pres. Denver chpt. 1985—), Lions (bd. dirs. 1965-72). Episcopalian. Home and Office: 2261 Glencoe St Denver CO 80207-3834

CARLSON, ROGER DAVID, psychologist, clergyman, educator; b. Berkeley, Calif., Nov. 19, 1946; s. George Clarence and Elizabeth (Norris) C.; m. Ema T. Paviolo, June 11, 1977. AB, Calif. State U., Sacramento, 1968, MA, 1969; PhD, U. Oreg., 1972. Assoc. prof. psychology Lebanon Valley Coll., Annville, Pa., 1972-85; rsch. assoc. Eugene Pub. Schs., 1985-87; assoc. prof. edn. Williamette U., Salem, Oreg., 1987-88; assoc. prof. psychology Ea. Wash. U., 1991-92; adj. faculty Linfield Coll., 1993—; pastor Coburg United Meth. Ch., 1992—; vis. scholar dept. history and philosophy of sci. Cambridge (Eng.) U., 1979-80; temporary sr. mem. Wolfson Coll.; vis. assoc. prof. psychology Whitman Coll., Walla Walla, Wash., 1988-89, 90-91, cons., 1989—. Contbr. rsch. papers, jour. articles and book chpts. on numerous subjects in field. Mem. Friends Radio Sta. KPFA, v.p. 1969, pres. 1970. Recipient Presdl. Sports award. Fellow Am. Coll. Heraldry; mem. Am. Psychol. Assn., Western Psychol. Assn., Am. Psychol. Soc., Am. Coll. Psychol., Soc. for Philosophy and Psychology (exec. com. 1975-76), SAR, Airplane Owners and Pilots Assn., Sons Union Vets Civil War, Am. Radio Relay League, Psi Chi, Vasa order. Methodist. Home: 39413 Deerhorn Rd Springfield OR 97478-9521

CARLSON, RONALD FRANK, educator, fiction writer; b. Logan, Utah, Sept. 15, 1947; s. Ed and Verna (Mertz) C.; m. Georgia Elaine Craig, June 14, 1969; children: Nicholas George Carlson, Colin Edwin. BA, U. Utah, 1970, MA, 1972. English tchr. Hotchkiss Sch., Lakeville, Conn., 1971-81; artist in edn. Utah Arts Coun., Salt Lake City, 1982-87, Idaho Arts Com., Boise, 1983-89, Alaska Arts Com., Anchorage, 1984-87; instr. continuing edn. U. Utah, Salt Lake City, 1982-86; writer-in residence Ariz. State U., Tempe, 1986-87, asst. prof. English, 1987-88, assoc. prof. English, 1988—, dir. creative writing, 1989—. Author: (novels) Betrayed by F. Scott Fitzgerald, 1977, Truants, 1981, (collection of stories) The News of the World, 1987, Plan B for the Middle Class, 1992, (story) Milk (Best Am. Stories 1987). Bd. dirs., founder Class of '65 West High Schlarship Fund, Salt Lake City, 1985—. Mem. Writers Guild of Am. West. Office: Ariz State Univ Dept English Tempe AZ 85287

CARLSON, SHAWN ERIC, physicist; b. Long Beach, Calif., Mar. 11, 1960; s. Devere Milfred Carlson Sr. and Beverly Ann Graham Bennett. BS in Physics, Applied Math., U. Calif., Berkeley, 1981; MS in Physics, UCLA, 1983, PhD in Physics, 1989. Ind. magician San Francisco, 1977-89; v.p. R & D Flowgram Software Assocs., San Francisco, 1989-91; rsch. physicist Lawrence Berkeley Labs., 1990—; sci. and tech. cons. Com. for Sci. Investigation of Claims of Paranormal, 1985—; speaker in field; bd. dirs. Bay Area Skeptics, San Francisco. Author: Satanism in America, 1989; columnist, sci. writer Humanist Mag., Buffalo, 1991—. Investigator faith-healers, Satanism Com. for Sci. Examination of Religion, Buffalo, 1987, 89. Mem. AAAS. Home: 6331 Fairmount Ave Apt 302 El Cerrito CA 94530 Office: Lawrence Berkeley Labs MS 50-232 Berkeley CA 94720

CARLSTROM, R. WILLIAM, retired special education educator; b. Seattle, Oct. 22, 1944; s. Roy Albert Carlstrom and Dorothy (Anderson) Hart; m. Ann Scheffer, July 29, 1967; children: Trina Anderson Schmoll, Paul Scheffer. BA, Lewis & Clark Coll., 1967; MA, U. Wash., 1970. Tchr. Shoreline Pub. Schs., Seattle, 1968-71; program coordinator fo adult handicapped City of Seattle, 1971-72; spl. edn. tchr. South Shore Middle Sch., Seattle, 1972-75, Sharples Jr. High, Seattle, 1975-78, Ryther Child Ctr., Seattle, 1978-89; sec., treas., bd. dirs. Glaser Found., Inc., Edmonds, Wash., 1974-86, exec. dir., 1983-91, trustee, 1983—; adv. com. mem. U. Wash. Dentistry for Handicapped, Seattle, 1979; pres., cons. Funding Resources Group, Edmonds, 1984—; co-founder, trustee Snohomish County Youth Community Found., 1992—; pres. Current Health Techs., Inc., 1992—, N.P. Mktg.; trustee St. Regis Clinics, 1992—. Coun. mem. U. Wash. Grad. Sch. for Dentistry, 1979—; trustee Edmonds Unitarian Ch., 1980-81, Pub. Edn. Fund, Dist. 15, Edmonds, 1986—, Home Care Wash.; pres. Madrona Middle Sch. PTA, Edmonds, 1983-84. Grantee Seattle Masonic Temple, 1974-75, Fed. Govt., 1970-71. Mem. Seattle Tchrs. Assn., Pacific N.W. Grantmakers Forum, Nat. Council on Founds. Democrat. Club: Harbor Square Athletic. Office: NP Mktg 144 Railroad Ave Ste 107 Edmonds WA 98020

CARLTON, RICHARD ANTHONY, management consultant, educator, author; b. Henderson, N.C., Feb. 4, 1951. BA, U. Mo., 1972. Prin. Loadmaster Magnetics, Wichita, Kans., 1975-77; dir. music svcs. Bellestreet Prodns., Kansas City, Mo., 1977-78; prin. Carlton Unltd., Costa Mesa, Calif., 1978-82; pres. Desert Wind Communications, Inc., Costa Mesa, 1982-85; sr. assoc. R.A. Carlton Consultancy, Costa Mesa, 1985—. Feature writer periodical Kitchen Bath Design, 1986; author: Computers for Manufacturing Technology, 1991; contbg. editor periodicals Furniture Design and Manufacturing, 1987—, Cabinet Maker, 1988—, Sports Car mag., Calif. Sports Car. Sustaining mem. Rep. Nat. Com., Washington, 1987—, CAP, Costa Mesa, 1987—; mem. Whale Adoption Project, Woods Hole, Mass., 1988—; charter mem. Battle of Normandy Mus., Caen, France, 1988—. With USAF, 1971-75, SEA, ETO. Mem. AIAA, IEEE, Am. Mgmt. Assn., Am. Helicopter Soc., Vietnam Vets. Am., Helicopter Assn. Internat., ACM, Soc. Mfg. Engrs., Am. Legion, Challenger Mus. (charter mem.), Naval Inst., Am. Cons. League, Am. Air Mus. (charter mem.), Tailhook Assn., Air Force Assn., Air Force Sgts. Assn. Republican.

CARLTON-ADAMS, GEORGIA M., psychotherapist; b. Kansas City, Mo.; d. George Randolph Carlton and Harriett Marie (Smith) Carlton-Witt; m. John Adams. Student, Kansas City (Mo.) Jr. Coll., Rockhill Coll., Trinity Coll., Dublin, Ireland, 1973, City U. of London (Eng.), 1978. Owner Pure White Electric Light and Magic, Lakewood, Calif., 1985—; dir., owner Trauma Buddy's, Lakewood, 1988—; clin. hypotherapist Inner Group Mgmt., Cerritos, Calif., 1989—; cons. Rockwell, McDonnell Douglas, Long Beach, Calif., 1987-90; owner In Print mag., 1990—; staff counselor FHP. Author: Handbook for the Living, 1990. Adv. Greater Attention Victims Violent Crimes; active Animal Rights Pet Protection Soc., Calif. Preventive Child Abuse Orgn., Sierra Club. Mem. Calif. Astronomy Assn., Acoustic Brain Rsch., Inner Group Mgmt., NLP Integration Soc. (pres. 1988-89), British Psychol. Assn., C. of C. Home and Office: 744 Chestnut # 11 Long Beach CA 90813

CARMACK, DAVID EARL, songwriter, musician; b. St. Louis, June 24, 1946; s. Earl Raymond and Marie (Bonebrake) C. Agt. Nat. Security Agy., Balt. and Washington, 1968-71; songwriter, musician, performer U.S.A. and Can., 1972-86; cons. to mentally ill, to lawyers for mental health cases and procedures, to state and local legislatures and other mental health orgns. Composer, performer over 200 songs. Pres. bd. dirs. Survivors on Our Own, Phoenix, 1989-91. Sgt. U.S. Army, 1967-68. Named Best Single Performer and Songwriter in Mo., Country Music Assn., 1975, Best Single Performer and Songwriter in Ariz., Country Music Assn., 1983. Home and Office: 2002 E Tierra Buena Phoenix AZ 85022-3478

CARMAN, MICHAEL DENNIS, museum director; b. Monahans, Tex., Nov. 6, 1938; s. Herbert Charles and Marie Noelie (Watkins) C.; m. Malica Jean Brunet, Jan. 27, 1967 (div. June 1984); m. Sharon Ruth Morrisson, Nov. 29, 1985. BA in History, San Diego State U., 1970, MA in History, 1973. Commd. USN, 1956, advanced through grades to petty officer I, resigned, 1966; curator San Diego Hist. Soc., 1973-77, Pioneers Mus., Colorado Springs, Colo., 1978-82; chief curator Network Curatorial Services, Colorado Springs, 1982-84; dir. Ariz. State Capitol Mus., Phoenix, 1984—. Author: United States Customs and the Madero Revolution, 1975; contbr. articles to profl. jours. Mem. Am. Assn. Mus. (MAP evaluator 1980-86, curator com., sec. 1982-83), Am. Assn. State and Local History (rep. 1974-77, cons. 1975—), Mus. Assn. Ariz., Cen. Ariz. Mus. Assn. (v.p. 1987-89). Club: Phoenix City. Office: Ariz State Capitol Mus 1700 W Washington St Phoenix AZ 85007-2812

CARMICHAEL, GARY ALAN, secondary education educator; b. Saco, Mont., May 7, 1964; s. Glen Alan Carmichael and Jerri Ruth (Haines) Maclay. BA, U. Mont., 1989. Cert. tchr., Mont. Telecommunication specialist, social studies chmn., libr. media specialist Saco Pub. Schs., 1990—; mem. adv. com. NMCC, Mont., 1992; coach speech, debate, drama team, Saco, 1990—. Pres. Circle K Internat., U. Mont., 1988, gov., Mont. dist., 1986. Mem. ALA, Mont. Libr. Assn., Theta Chi (pres.), U. Mont. Alumni Assn. Office: Saco Pub Schs Hwy 341 Saco MT 59261

CARMONY, KEVIN BRACKETT, computer software manufacturing company executive; b. Ogden, Utah, Sept. 26, 1959; s. Clifford Conrad and Marion Janette (Fletcher) C.;. BA in Bus. and Econs., Weber State U., 1983. Dist. mgr. Consol. Theatres, Salt Lake City, 1980-82; founder, chief exec. officer Streamlined Info. Systems, Inc., Ogden, 1982-91; pres. New Quest Technologies, Inc., Salt Lake City, 1991-92; v.p. tech. Franklin Quest Co., Salt Lake City, 1992—; bd. dirs. Pro Image, Inc., Salt Lake City. Trustee Weber State U., 1992-93; exec. v.p., COO I.N.V.U., Inc., 1993—; elder's pres. LDS Ch., Ogden, 1987-89, Stake Mission pres., 1989-92. Named Outstanding Bus. Grad., Weber State U., 1983. Mem. Internat. Platform Assn. Republican. Home: 48 W 300 S # 2701N Salt Lake City UT 84101 Office: Franklin Quest Co 2550 S Decker Lake Blvd Salt Lake City UT 84119

CARNAHAN, KARLYN TASTO, insurance company executive; b. Hayward, Calif., Aug. 30, 1958; d. Harry Lloyd and Mary Jane (Muirhead) Tasto; m. Douglas Ralph Carnahan, June 30, 1979; children: Jeffrey Douglas, Rebecca Mary. BS Engring. Tech., Cogswell Coll., San Francisco, 1979; MBA, Stanford U., 1987. CPCU. Loss control cons. Fireman's Fund, Santa Rosa, Calif., 1979-82, underwriter, 1982-85; mktg. mgr. Fireman's Fund Ins. Co., Concord, Calif., 1987-89; asst. v.p. tng. Fireman's Fund Ins. Co., Novato, Calif., 1989-92, asst. v.p. mktg., 1992—. Mem. CPCU.

CARNAHAN, ORVILLE DARRELL, state legislator, retired college president; b. Elba, Idaho, Dec. 25, 1929; s. Marion Carlos and Leola Pearl (Putnam) C.; m. Colleen Arrott, Dec. 14, 1951; children: Karen, Jeanie, Orville Darrell, Carla. B.S., Utah State U., 1958; M.Ed., U. Idaho, 1962, Ed.D., 1964. Vocat. dir., v.p. Yakima Valley Coll., Yakima, Wash., 1964-69; chancellor Eastern Iowa Community Coll. Dist., Davenport, 1969-71; pres. Highline Coll., Midway Wash., 1971-76; assoc. Utah Commr. for Higher Edn., Salt Lake City, 1976-78; pres. So. Utah State Coll., Cedar City, 1978-81, Salt Lake Community Coll., Salt Lake City, 1981-90; pres. emeritus Salt Lake Community Coll. (formerly Utah Tech. Coll.), Salt Lake City, 1990—; mem. Utah Ho. of Reps.; cons. to various orgns. Active Boy Scouts Am. Served with U.S. Army, 1952-54, Korea. Mem. Am. Vocat. Assn., NEA, Idaho Hist. Soc., Utah Hist. Soc., Alpha Tau Alpha, Phi Delta Kappa, Rotary Internat. Mem. Ch. of Jesus Christ of Latter-Day Saints. Home: 2112 Quailbrook Dr Salt Lake City UT 84118-1120 Office: Salt Lake Community Coll 4600 S Redroad Rd Salt Lake City UT 84130

CARNATHAN, GILBERT WILLIAM, pharmaceutical company executive, research scientist; b. Quincy, Mass., Nov. 1, 1951; s. Gilbert Caldwell and Regina Marie (Layden) C.; m. Jane Ellen Gabel, July 9, 1972; children: Paul Max, Jesse Gilbert. BS, Northeastern U., Boston, 1974; MS, U. Mass., 1979, PhD, 1982. Rsch. scientist G.D. Searle & Co., Skokie, Ill., 1980-85; sect. mgr. Rorer Cen. Rsch., King of Prussia, Pa., 1985-90; dir. product devel. Cortech, Inc., Denver, 1990—. Contbr. 28 articles to profl. jours. Chairperson Rorer Blood Drive/ARC, King of Prussia, 1989-90; coach Hyland Hills (Colo.) Bantam B Hockey Team, 1991-93. Mem. AAAS, Inflammation Rsch. Assn., Project Mgmt. Inst., Drug Info. Assn. Office: Cortech Inc 6850 N Broadway Denver CO 80221-2852

CARNEY, DEBORAH LEAH TURNER, lawyer; b. Great Bend, Kans., Aug. 19, 1952; d. Harold Lee and Elizabeth Lura (Dillon) Turner; m. Thomas J.T. Carney, Mar. 20, 1976; children: Amber Blythe, Sonia Briana, Ross Dillon. BA in Human Biology, Stanford U., 1974; JD, U. Denver, 1976. Bar: Kans. 1977, U.S. Dist. Ct. Kans. 1977, U.S. Ct. Appeals (10th cir.) 1982, Colo. 1984, U.S. Dist. Ct. Colo. 1984, U.S. Supreme Ct. 1989, U.S. Claims Ct. 1990. With Turner & Boisseau, Great Bend, 1976-84, of counsel, 1984—; assoc. Lutz & Oliver, Arvada, Colo., 1984-85; prin. Deborah Turner Carney, P.C., Golden and Lakewood, Colo., 1985-92; shareholder Deborah & T.J. Carney, P.C., Golden/Lakewood, Colo., 1992—. Author (newsletter) Profl. Solutions, 1984; editor Apple Law newsletter, 1984-86; contbr. articles to profl. jours. Mem. ABA (computer divsn.), Kans. Bar Assn., Assn. Trial Lawyers Am., Colo. Trial Lawyers Assn., Kiwanis (bd. dirs. Denver club 1988-90, trustee 1990—, sec. 1992—). Republican.

CARNEY, HEATH JOSEPH, aquatic ecologist, educator; b. Lyon, France, Aug. 7, 1955; s. Stephen McLure and June (Kempf) C. BS, Coll. William and Mary, 1979; MS, U. Mich., 1981; PhD, U. Calif., Davis, 1987. Rsch. asst. U. Mich., Ann Arbor, 1979-82; aquatic ecology fellow U. Calif., Davis, 1982-87, rsch. ecologist, 1989—; asst. prof., rsch. fellow dept. biology Ind. U., Bloomington, 1987—; cons. U. Mich., 1980-81, Harvard U., 1988—, U. Calif. Berkeley, 1989—. Contbr. articles to profl. jours. Grantee EPA, NOAA, NSF, MAB/UNESCO. Mem. AAAS, Am. Soc. Limnology and Oceanography, Ecol. Soc. Am., Am. Phycol. Soc. Am., Soc. Internat. Limnologiae, Internat. Assn. Ecology, Union Concerned Scientists, Sierra Club, Sigma Xi, Phi Beta Kappa. Office: U Calif Inst Ecology Davis CA 95616

CARNEY, RICHARD EDGAR, foundation executive; b. Marshall, Tex., Dec. 11, 1923; s. Edgar Lester and Lillian (Sansom) C.; m. Adrienne McAndrews, 1973 (div. 1981). Student, Culver-Stockton Coll., 1942, 46, Washington U., St. Louis, 1946-48; Taliesin fellow, Spring Green, Wis. and Scottsdale, Ariz., 1948-55. Aide to Frank Lloyd Wright, 1952-59; asst. to sec.-treas. Frank Lloyd Wright Found., Scottsdale, 1959-62, exec. asst. to pres., 1962-85, treas., 1962—, mng. trustee, ceo, 1985—; dir. admissions, student adviser Frank Lloyd Wright Sch. Architecture, Scottsdale, 1962—; treas. Taliesin Architects, Scottsdale, 1962—; exhbn. com. Scottsdale Ctr. for Arts, 1985-91; mem. Gov.'s Commn. on Taliesin, State of Wis., 1988-89; organizer, bd. dirs. Taliesin Preservation Commn., Spring Green, 1990—. Set designer, performer theatrical prodns., Taliesin, Spring Green, 1960—. Trustee Unity Chapel, Inc., Spring Green, 1980—; mem. Task Force on Higher Edn., Scottsdale, 1991—. Sgt. U.S. Army, 1942-46, ETO. Recipient Alumni of Yr. award Culver-Stockton Coll., 1962. Home and Office: Frank Lloyd Wright Found Taliesin West Scottsdale AZ 85261

CARNICOM, GENE E., health services administrator; b. Miami, Fla., Nov. 13, 1944; s. Francis Eugene and Kathleen (Kitchens) C.; m. Sharon Boisseau Brown, 1966; m. Lillian Helen Baehr, Mar. 22, 1970; children: Patrick Dylan, Danielle Brooke; m. Clare Helminiak, Nov. 1, 1984; children: Whitney Alexis, Heath Britten, James Tiberius Kirk. BA in Social Welfare, San Diego State U., 1971, MSW, 1972; PhD, Southeastern U., 1981. Diplomate Am. Bd. Clin. Social Workers; cert., Acad. Cert. Social Workers. Lic. Social Worker, Mont. Coord., Beach Area Free Clinic, San Diego, 1970-72; program cons. Balt. City Dept. Social Services, 1973; chief of social work Balt. City Jail, 1974-76; hosp. social work dir. Pine Ridge (S.D.) Indian Health Service Hosp., 1980-81; dir. mental health and social service USPHS Indian Health Service Hosp., Mescalero, N.Mex., 1981-84; alternate health resources coordinator Alaska Native Med. Ctr., Anchorage, 1984-88; med. social worker IHS Ft. Peck Service Unit, Mont., 1988-89; dir. profl. services Parker (Ariz.) Indian Hosp., 1989—; mem. faculty U. Md., 1972-76, Community Coll. Balt., 1973-76, Morgan State U., 1974-76, Webster Coll., 1977-80, Oglala Sioux Community Coll., 1980-81, Park Coll., 1982-84, Golden Gate U., 1982-84, N.Mex. State U., 1982-84. Steering com. Community Congress San Diego, 1980-82; bd. dirs. Innercity N.W. Neighborhood Corp., 1970-72; exec. dir. Retred, Inc., 1971-72; site selection task force Community Corrections Program of Md. Dept. Corrections, 1973-74; grad. council Webster Coll., San Antonio, 1978-80; coordinator child protection team Pine Ridge Indian Reservation, 1980-81, coordinator Mescalero Apache Indian Reservation Child Protection Team, 1981-84, Alaska AIDS Network; sr. leader 4-H; comdr. Sierra Blanca CAP Cadet Squadron, 1982-84. Served with USNR, 1962-68, to capt. U.S. Army, 1974-80; capt. USPHS, 1980—. Decorated Army Commendation medal; recipient Isolated Hardship Duty award USPHS, 1981, Hazardous Duty award, 1981, USPH Pub. Health Svc. Commendation medal, 1989. Mem. Nat. Assn. Social Workers (Diplomate in Social Work), Am. Anthrop. Assn., Soc. Med. Anthropology, Assn. Mil. Surgeons U.S., Am. Pub. Health Assn., Profl. Assn. Commd. Corps of USPHS, Indian Health Service Computer Users Group, Mensa. Democrat. Contbr. articles profl. jours. Office: USPHS Indian Hosp RR 1 Box 12 Parker AZ 85344-9703

CARNINE, DOUGLAS WAYNE, education educator, author; b. Sullivan, Ill., Oct. 7, 1947; s. Wayne J. and Olive F. (Emel) C.; m. Linda M. McRoberts, June 10, 1970; children: Berkley, Leah. BS, U. Ill., 1969; MS, U. Oreg., 1970; PhD, U. Utah, 1974. Asst. prof. U. Oreg., Eugene, 1975-81, assoc. prof., 1981-87, prof., 1987—. Author: Theory of Instruction, 1982, Learning Pascal, 1989. Office: U Oreg 805 Lincoln St Eugene OR 97401-2810

CARO, MIKE, gaming authority; b. Joplin, Mo., May 16, 1944; s. Peter Klaus and Marguerite (Zuercher) C.; m. Bonita Marie Polniak, June 6, 1965 (div. June 1972); m. Phyllis Marsha Goldberg. Gen. mgr. Huntington Park (Calif.) Casino, 1985; chief strategist Bicycle Club, Bell Gardens, Calif., 1984-85; founder Mad Genius Brain Trust; actor, instr. video tape Play to Win Poker, 1988. Author: Caro on Gambling, 1984, Mike Caro's Book of Tells-The Body Language of Poker, 1985, Poker for Women - A Course in Destroying Male Opponents at Poker and Beyond, 1985, New Poker Games, Gambling Times Quiz Book, Bobby Baldwin's Winning Poker Secrets, Caro's Fundamental Secrets of Poker, 1991; editor-in-chief Poker Player; poker editor Gambling Times; mng. editor B&G Pub.; contbr. articles to gambling mags.; developer programming tools Mike Caro's Poker Engine, audio tapes Real Life Strategy, Positive Poker, Pro Poker Secrets, Pro Hold on Secrets, 1992, four-color deck, 1992. Mailing address: 4535 W Sahara Ste 105 Las Vegas NV 89102

CARPENTER, ADELBERT WALL, air force officer; b. Darby, Pa., July 31, 1943; s. Adelbert and Maxine (Wall) C.; m. Nancy Ann Jackson, June 24, 1967; children: Kristin L., Kimberly L., Kelli L. BS in Internat. Affairs, U.S. Air Force Acad., 1967; MS in Systems Mgmt., U. So. Calif., 1974. Commd. 2d lt. U.S. Air Force, 1967, advanced through grades to col., 1988; comdr. 70th Tactical Fighter Squadron, Moody AFB, Ga., 1985-87; dir. programs Hdqrs. USAF in Europe, Ramstein AB, Germany, 1987-90; comdr. 377th Combat Support Wing, Ramstein AB, 1990-91; vice comdr. 2d Air Force, Beale AFB, Calif., 1991—. Decorated Legion of Merit, Air medals (5). Mem. Air Force Assn. (life), Assn. USAF Acad. Grads. (life), Daedalians. Presbyterian. Office: 2d Air Force Beale AFB CA 95903

CARPENTER, BRUCE H., college president; b. Rapid City, S.D., Feb. 5, 1932; s. Ralph A. Carpenter and Anna F. (Davis) Langworthy; m. Olivia J. clark, Nov. 23, 1953 (div. 1974); children: Lynne A., Ralph D.; m. Kathryn A. West, June 7, 1975. BA, Calif. State U., Long Beach, 1957, MA, 1958; PhD, UCLA, 1962. Prof. Calif. State U.-, Long Beach, 1962-72, assoc. acad. v.p., 1972-75; provost, acad. v.p. Western Ill. U., Macomb, 1975-82; pres. Eastern Mont. Coll., Billings, 1982—; bd. dirs. Norwest Bank Billings. Contbr. articles to profl. jours. Chmn. Macomb United Way, 1982; mem. exec. bd. Billings United Way, 1983, pres. 1986; bd. dirs. Billings YMCA, 1985-91, Deaconess Hosp. Found., 1988—. Cpl. U.S. Army, 1952-54. NSF research grantee, 1963-70. Mem. AAAS, Am. Soc. Plant Physiologists, N.Y. Acad. Scis., Am. Assn. State Coll. and Univs. (bd. dirs. 1989—), Rotary (bd. dirs. Billings Club, pres. 1992). Office: Ea Mont Coll 1500 N 30th St Billings MT 59101-0298

CARPENTER, DAVID ROLAND, life insurance executive; b. Fort Wayne, Ind., Mar. 24, 1939; s. Geary W. and Rita (Ueber) C.; m. Karen Woodard, Oct. 20, 1963 (div. Apr. 1975); children: Kimberly, Clayton; m. Leila E.M. Sjogren, Sept. 20, 1980; 1 dau., Michelle. BBA, U. Mich., 1961, MS, 1962. Sr. v.p. Booz, Allen Cons., Newport Beach, Calif., 1976-77; v.p. Tillinghast, Nelson & Warren, Newport Beach, Calif., 1977-80; chief mktg. officer Transam. Occidental Life Ins. Co., L.A., 1980-81, exec. v.p., chief mktg. officer, 1981-82, pres., 1982—, chief operating officer, 1982-83, pres., dir., chief exec. officer, 1983-93, also chmn.; exec. v.p. Transamerica Corp., 1993—; group v.p. Transam. corp., 1990-93, exec. v.p., 1993—; dir. Transam. Life & Annuity Co., Transam. Assurance Co., Transam. Ins. Corp., First Transam. Life Ins. Co. Trustee, founding chmn. Alliance for Aging Rsch., 1986-92, bd. dirs.; chmn. bd. dirs. Cen. City Assn., 1985—, chmn., 1987-88, Ind. Colls. So. Calif., 1988—; bd. dirs. UniHealth Am., 1988—, chmn., 1985-88; gov. Ford's Theatre, 1985—; bd. visitors Anderson Grad. Sch. of Mgmt., UCLA; founding chmn. Calif. Med. Ctr. Found., 1985-92, bd. dirs. Fellow Soc. Actuaries (bd. dirs. 1978-81); mem. Am. Acad. Actuaries (v.p. 1981-83), Internat. Ins. Soc. (gov. 1987—), Assn. Calif. Life Ins. Cos. (chmn. 1991-92), L.A. C. of C. (bd. dirs. 1984—). Presbyterian. Office: Transam Occidental Life Ins Co 1150 S Olive St Los Angeles CA 90015-2211

CARPENTER, DONALD BLODGETT, real estate appraiser; b. New Haven, Aug. 20, 1916; s. Fred Donald and Gwendolen (Blodgett) C.; m. Barbara Marvin Adams, June 28, 1941 (dec. Aug. 1978); m. 2d, Lee Burker McGough, Dec. 28, 1980 (div. Apr. 1987); children—Edward G., John D., William V., Andrew J., Dorothy J. and James J. McGough. PhB, U. Vt., 1938; postgrad., Sonoma State U., 1968-69, Mendocino Community Coll., 1977, Coll. of Redwoods, 1984-85. Reporter Burlington (Vt.) Daily News, 1938-39; guide chair operator Am. Express Co., N.Y. World's Fair, 1939; underwriter G.E.I. Corp., Newark, 1939-40; sales corr. J. Dixon Crucible Co., Jersey City, 1940-41, asst. office mgr., priorities specialist, 1941-42; sales rep. J. Dixon Crucible Co., San Francisco, 1946-52; field supr. Travelers Ins. Co., San Francisco, 1952-58; gen. agt. Gen. Am. Life Ins. Co., San Francisco, 1958-59; western supr. Provident Life & Accident Ins. Co., San Francisco, 1959-60; brokerage supr. Aetna Life Ins. Co., San Francisco, 1960-61; maintenance cons. J.I. Holcomb Mfg. Co., Mill Valley, Calif., 1961-68; ednl. svc. rep. Marquis Who's Who, Inc., 1963-68; sales rep. Onox, Inc., Mendocino, Calif., 1965-68; tchr., coach Mendocino Jr.-Sr. High Sch., 1968; real property appraiser Mendocino County, 1968-81; instr. Coll. of Redwoods, 1985-87; real estate appraiser Carpenter Appraisal Svcs., 1982-88, ret. Active numerous civic orgns.; co-chmn. Citizens for Sewers, 1971-72; mem. Mendocino County Safety Coun., 1981; sponsor mem. Mendocino Art Ctr., 1965—. With USNR, 1942-46; lt. comdr., comdg. officer res. unit, 1967-68, ret., 1968. Sec. of Navy Commendation with ribbon, 1946, other awards, certificates; companion Mil. Order World Wars; named Community Sportsman of Yr., 1971. Mem. Res. Officers Assn. U.S. (life; chpt. pres. 1954, 56, state v.p. 1958-61), Ret. Officers Assn. (life, chpt. survivors assistance area counselor 1979—, chpt. scholarship com. 1986-91), Save-The-Redwoods League, Marines Meml. Assn., Mendocino County Employees Assn. (dir. 1981), Mendocino County Hist. Soc., Mendocino Hist. Rsch. Inc. (docent 1982-88), Nat. Assn. Uniformed Svcs. (life), Mendocino Coast Geneal. Soc. (pres. 1991-93), Nat. Ret. Tchrs. Assn., Calif. Ret. Tchrs. Assn., Naval Order of U.S. (life), Naval Res. Assn. (life), Navy League of U.S. (life), U.S. Naval Inst. (life), Am. Diabetes Assn., Alumni Assn. U. Vt. (founding pres. San Francisco Alumni Club 1964), Mendocino Coast Stamp Club (charter, dir. 1983—), Rotary Internat. (club pres. 1975-76, dist. gov. area rep. 1977-78, Dist. Gov. awards 1974, 76, dist. amb. scholarship, 1978-81, 89-90, dist. group study exchange com. 1981-88, 90-93, dist. found. alumni com. 1991-92, Paul Harris fellow 1979—, Rotarian of the Yrs. 1969-88, club historian 1989—), Am. Legion (post comdr. 1972-73, state citation for outstanding community svc. 1972, past comdrs. Calif., life), Mendocino Coast Land Devel. Corp. (dir 1991—), Mendocino Cardinal Booster Club (charter, life, pres. 1971), U. Vt. Catamount Fraternity Club (charter), Old Mill Club, Kappa Sigma (Scholarship-Leadership award 1937-38). Republican. Congregationalist. Home: PO Box 87 10801 Gurley Ln Mendocino CA 95460-0087

CARPENTER, FRANK CHARLES, JR., retired electronics engineer; b. L.A., June 1, 1917; s. Frank Charles and Isobel (Crump) C.; A.A., Pasadena City Coll., 1961; B.S. in Elec. Engring. cum laude, Calif. State U.-Long Beach, 1975, M.S. in Elec. Engring., 1981; m. Beatrice Josephine Jolly, Nov. 3, 1951; children—Robert Douglas, Gail Susan, Carol Ann. Self-employed design and mfgr. aircraft test equipment, Los Angeles, 1946-51; engr. Hoffman Electronics Corp., Los Angeles, 1951-56, sr. engr., 1956-59, project mgr., 1959-63; engr.-scientist McDonnell-Douglas Astronautics Corp., Huntington Beach, Calif., 1963-69, spacecraft telemetry, 1963-67, biomed. electronics, 1967-69, flight test instrumentation, 1969-76; lab. test engr. Northrop Corp., Hawthorne, Calif., 1976-82, spl. engr., 1982-83; mgr. transducer calibration lab. Northrop Corp., Pico-Rivera, Calif., 1983-86. Served with USNR, 1941-47. Mem. IEEE (sr.), Amateur Radio Relay League. Contbr. articles to profl. jours. Patentee transistor squelch circuit; helicaland whip antenna. Home: 2037 Balearic Dr Costa Mesa CA 92626-3514

CARPENTER, JACK DUANE, forester; b. Lawrence, Kans., Jan. 20, 1951; s. Duane Ora and Normagene (Barlow) C.; m. Gwendolyn Ann McGee, Aug. 13, 1977; children: Ernest Peter Jack, Stella Ann, Modesta Lynn. BS in Forestry, U. Mo., 1973. Cert. para-archeologist, silviculturist. Postal clk. U. Mo., Columbia, 1970-73; vol. Peace Corps, San Jose, Costa Rica, 1973-75; timber marker forestry tech. USDA Forest Svc., Kaibab Nat. Forest, Williams Ranger Dist., Williams, Ariz., 1976-77; timber sale adminstr. USDA Forest Svc., Carson Nat. Forest, Tres Piedras Dist., N.Mex., 1977-86; forester USDA Forest Svc., Carson Nat. Forest, Questa Ranger Dist., N.Mex., 1986-91; supr. forester USDA Forest Svc., Carson Nat. Forest, Tres Piedras Dist., N.Mex., 1991—; facilitator N.Mex. Forestry Camp, Cuba, N.Mex., 1990—, Habitat Typing, Taos, N.Mex., 1992—. Foster parent N.Mex. Dept. Human Svcs., Taos, 1986—, mem. steering com. Foster Parent Conf., 1993, work com. Family to Family Initiative, 1993; sectional commd. N.Mex. Dist. Royal Rangers, Albuquerque, 1990—. Named Foster Parent of Yr., Taos County Dept. Human Svcs., Taos, 1991. Mem. Am. Forests, Soc. of Am. Foresters, Gideon's Internat., Citizen's Rev. Bd. #19 (cert. of appreciation 1993). Republican. Mem. Assembly of God Ch. Home: Box 5810 Taos NM 87571 Office: USDA Forest Svc Carson Nat Forest PO Box 38 Tres Piedras NM 87577

CARPENTER, JOHN EVERETT, retired prinicipal; b. Tarrytown, N.Y., Nov. 27, 1923; s. Everett Birch and Mary (Avery) C.; student Union Coll., 1943; B.A., Iona Coll., 1946; M.A., Columbia, 1949, profl. diploma, 1961; m. Marie F. McCarthy, Nov. 14, 1944; 1 son, Dennis Everett. Tchr., Blessed Sacrament High Sch., New Rochelle, N.Y., 1946-50; tchr., adminstr. Armonk (N.Y.) pub. schs., 1950-62; dir. guidance Ridge Street Sch., Port Chester, N.Y., 1962-64; counselor Rye (N.Y.) High Sch., 1964-66, prin., 1966-78, ret.; guest lectr. Served to lt. USNR; now lt. comdr. ret. Res. Decorated Bronze Star medal. Mem. Middle States Assn. Colls. and Schs. (commn. on secondary schs.), Am. (life), Westchester-Putnam-Rockland (past pres.) personnel and guidance assns., NEA, Am. Legion (past comdr.), Phi Delta Kappa, Kappa Delta Pi. Rotarian (past pres., Paul Harris fellow). Clubs: Tarrytown Boat (past commodore), Green Valley Elks. Home: 321 N Paseo De Los Conquist Green Valley AZ 85614-3140

CARPENTER, PETER ROCKEFELLER, trust company executive; b. Sunbury, Pa., Apr. 18, 1939; s. Alvin Witmer and Katherine (Rockefeller) C.; m. Janet Ross Buck, Aug. 24, 1963; children: Karen Louise Althaus, Jean Ellen, Peter Alvin. BA, Pa. State U., 1962. Mgr. dept. J.C. Penney Co., Menlo Park, N.J., 1964-67; ops. mgr. Allstate Ins. Co., Summit, N.J., 1967-73; adminstrv. mgr. Prudential Property & Casualty, Scottsdale, Ariz., 1973-75; v.p. Fortune Properties, Scottsdale, 1975-76; life underwriter Conn.

Mutual Life, Phoenix, 1976-81; v.p. and dir. sales and mktg. No. Trust Bank, Phoenix, 1981-89; v.p. M&I Marshall & Ilsley Trust Co., 1989—. Sec. exec. bd. Samuel Gompers Rehab. Ctr., 1981-84, chmn. bd., 1984-91; div. chmn. Phoenix United Way, 1981, 82, 86, 90; Rep. committeeman, Phoenix, 1978-86; bd. dirs. Scottsdale Boys Club, Scottsdale Cultural Coun. Adv., Herberger Theatre Ctr. With USN, 1962-64. Mem. Nat. Assn. Life Underwriters, Pa. State U. Alumni Assn. (dir. 1979-86), Son of Am. Revolution, Ariz. Club, U.S. Navy League, Kiwanis (Disting. lt. gov.), Masons, Sigma Alpha Epsilon. Lutheran. Home: 8526 E San Bruno Dr Scottsdale AZ 85258-2532 Office: M&I Marshall & Ilsley Trust Co 1 E Camelback Rd Ste 340 Phoenix AZ 85012-1648

CARPENTER, PHILIP BRIAN, software engineer; b. Evansville, Ind., June 5, 1956; s. Max Burns and Alberta (Leaf) C. BA, U. Evansville, 1978. Geophysicist U.S. Naval Oceanographic Office, Bay Saint Louis, Miss., 1978-83; sci. programmer Xontech, Van Nuys, Calif., 1983-86; sales support UNIRAS, Chatsworth, Calif., 1986-87; software engr. SimGraphics Engring., Pasadena, Calif., 1988, Jet Propulsion Lab., Pasadena, 1988-89; mem. tech. CADAM, Burbank, Calif., 1989-90; software engr. Rockwell, Downey, Calif., 1990, Jet Propulsion Lab., Pasadena, 1991-92, R. Greenberg Assocs., 1993—; cons. Visual Concepts Engring., Sylmar, Calif., 1992, Consol. Films, Hollywood, Calif., 1992. Pub. (books) Vindicators, 1989, Vindicators Plus, 1991. Mem. IEEE (affiliate). Home: 66 S Grand Oaks # 4 Pasadena CA 91107

CARPENTER, RAY WARREN, materials scientist and engineer, educator; b. Berkeley, Calif., 1934; s. Fritz Josh and Ethel Thordis (Davisson) C.; m. Ann Louise Leavitt, July 10, 1955; children: Shannon R., Sheila A., Matthew L. BS in Engring., U. Calif., Berkeley, 1958, MS in Metallurgy, 1959, PhD in Metallurgy, 1966. Registered profl. engr., Calif. Sr. engr. Aerojet-Gen. Nucleonics, San Ramon, Calif., 1959-64; sr. metallurgist Stanford Rsch Inst., Menlo Park, Calif., 1966-67; mem. sr. rsch. staff Oak Ridge (Tenn.) Nat. Lab., 1967-80; prof. Solid State Sci. & Engring. Ariz. State U., Tempe, 1980—, dir. Facility for High Resolution Electron Microscopy, 1980-83, dir. Ctr. for Solid State Sci., 1985-91, also bd. dirs. Ctr. for Solid State Sci.; chmn. doctoral program on Sci. and Engring. of Materials Ariz. State U., 1987-90; vis. prof. U. Tenn., 1976-78; adj. prof. Vanderbilt U., Nashville, 1979-81. Contbg. author books; contbr. articles to profl. rsch. jours. and symposia. Recipient awards, Internat. Metellographic Soc. and Am. Soc. for Metals competition, 1976, 77, 79; Faculty Disting. Achievement award Ariz. State U. Alumni Assn., 1990. Mem. Electron Microscopy Soc. Am. (pres. 1989, dir. phys. sci. 1980-83), Metall. Soc. of AIME, Materials Rsch. Soc., Am. Phys. Soc., Am. Ceramic Soc., Sigma Xi. Office: Ariz State U Ctr Solid State Sci Tempe AZ 85287-1704

CARR, DAVID ROBERT, oil trading company executive; b. Albany, N.Y., Oct. 10, 1950; s. Edward James Carr and Janice Mary (O'Connell) Foster; m. Katharine Gage, Dec. 15, 1980 (div. July 1985); 1 child, Matthew Robert. BS in Marine Transp., U.S. Merchant Marine Acad., Kings Point, N.Y., 1972; MBA, Calif. State U., Long Beach, 1993. 3d officer Reynolds Metals Co., Corpus Christi, Tex., 1972-74; transp. cons. John J. McMullen Assocs., N.Y.C., 1974-76; supr., vessel coord. Continental Oil Co., Stamford, Conn., 1977-79; vessel operator Teekay Shipping Co., Inc., L.A. and Nassau, Bahamas, 1979-81; claims mgr. Interpetrol U.S.A., Inc., N.Y.C., 1981-83, Teekay Shipping Co., Inc., Long Beach, 1984-89, Westport Petroleum, Inc., Pasadena, Calif., 1990—. Mem. Am. Petroleum Inst., U.S. Merchant Marine Acad. Alumni Assn. (treas. L.A./Long Beach chpt. 1989-91). Democrat. Roman Catholic.

CARR, JACQUELYN CARNEY, speech pathologist, educator; b. Redding, Calif., Mar. 3, 1956; d. James Robert and Maria Cora (Barni) Carney; m. Phillip John Carr, June 27, 1981; 1 child, Thomas Kennedy. AA, Shasta Community Coll., 1977; BA, Humboldt State U., 1979, MA, 1981. Cert. clin. competence in speech pathology, Calif.; clin. rehab. credential, Calif. Tchr. spl. day class Junction Sch. Dist., Palo Cedro, Calif., 1981-82, 83-87, Redding (Calif.) Sch. Dist., 1987-89, Shasta County Office Edn., 1989—; pvt. practice speech pathology Redding, 1987—; cons. in field. Mem. Dem. Women Shasta County, Redding, 1989—; sec. Shasta County Grand Jury, Redding, 1990-91. Mem. AAUW, Am. Speech, Lang. and Hearing Assn., Calif. Speech, Lang. and Hearing Assn. Office: Shasta County Office Edn 1644 Magnolia Ave Redding CA 96001-1513

CARR, JEANETTE IRENE, human resources executive; b. Santa Monica, Calif., Aug. 13, 1955; d. John Joseph and Barbara Carr. BS in Bus., U. La Verne, 1985. Cert. compensation profl. Compensation coord. TRW-Def. and Space Systems, Redondo Beach, Calif., 1977-79; human resources mgr. Chase Bank Internat., L.A., 1979-80; CHQ compensation/benefits adminstr. Pertec Computer Corp., Culver City, Calif., 1980-82; human resources adminstr. to Colo. Hughes Aircraft Co., El Segundo, Calif., 1982-87; compensation mgr. Aerospace Corp., El Segundo, 1987-93; human resources mgr. St. Mary-Corwin Med. Ctr., Pueblo, Colo., 1993—. Pres. Hermosa Beach (Calif.) Hist. Soc., 1990-92, bd. dirs., 1987-90; v.p. Le Parc Assn., Walteria, Calif., 1988—; vol. assoc. buyer UN Assn.-Harbor Chpt., San Pedro, Calif., 1980—; dir. Am. Cetacean Soc., San Pedro, 1977-80. Named for Outstanding Pub. Svc., City of Hermosa Beach, 1987, 90. Mem. Am. Compensation Assn. (cert. compensation profl.), Electronic Salary and Wage Assn., N.Mex. Compensation Assn., Rocky Mountain Compensation Assn. (southern area rep.), Am. Electronics Assn., So. Colo. Assn. Human Resource Profls., L.A. Compensation and Benefits Assn., Dolphins Jr. Women's Club (San Pedro, v.p. 1989—). Office: St Mary-Corwin Med Ctr 1008 Minnequa Ave Pueblo CO 81004-3798

CARR, KATHERINE ANN CAMACHO, nurse midwife; b. Chgo., Oct. 14, 1949; d. Raymond James and Pearl Mae (Davis) Totleben; m. F. Dean Carr, Jan. 10, 1976; children: Christopher Edward, Jonathan James. BSN, Loyola U., 1971; MSN and cert. nurse midwife, U. Ill., 1974; PhD, U. Wash., 1989. Pub. health nurse Chgo. Dept. Health, Maternal and Infant Care Project, 1971-72; nurse-midwife Ill. Masonic Med. Ctr. and Chgo. Bd. Health, 1974-77; instr. U. Wash., 1977-78, 83-84; co-founder, staff nurse-midwife, clin. coord. Birthplace, Seattle, 1978-80; dir. midwifery svcs. Group Health Coop. of Puget Sound Eastside Hosp., Seattle, 1980-83; nurse-midwife Healthcare for Women, Providence Hosp., Seattle, 1985-88, Va. Mason Clinic, Seattle, 1989-91; clin. assoc. prof. Sch Nursing Pacific Luth. U., Seattle, 1989-91; locum tenens nurse-midwife Va. Mason Hosp., Community Clinic Svc., Seattle, 1991; staff nurse-midwife Highline Community Nurse-Midwifery Svc., Seattle, 1991—; mem. faculty community based nurse-midwifery ednl. program Frontier Sch. MIdwifery and Family Nursing, Hyden, Ky., 1991—; rsch. asst. U. Wash., 1984-85; clin. faculty mem. Sch. Nursing, U. Wash., 1979—; mem. faculty Seattle Midwifery Sch., 1978-88; mem. cons. bd. Preparation for Expectant Parents, 1978-82; mem. ad hoc com. birthctr. regulation devel., State of Wash., 1979-81; mem. access to maternity care com., 1990-92; cons. in field. Contbr. articles to profl. publs. Hester McClaws scholar, 1988; WHO fellow 1976, NIH predoctoral fellow, 1987; Kaiser Family Found. grantee 1983. Mem. Am. Coll. Nurse-Midwives (bd. dirs. 1983-85, mem. numerous coms., 1983—, Midwife of Yr. in Wash. State 1986, Regional award for excellence 1992), Midwives Assn. of Wash. State (bd. dirs. 1983-86, 87-91, legis. com. 1989-90, other coms., Midwife of Yr. 1987), NAACOG (continuing edn. faculty 1974-84), Wash. State Nurses Assn., Internat. Childbirth Edn. Assn. Unitarian. Home and Office: 902 17th Ave E Seattle WA 98112

CARR, NOLY CRUZ, real estate broker, notary public; b. Mabalacat, Pampanga, Philippines, Jan. 31, 1940; came to U.S., 1970; s. Efipanio and Isabel (DelaCruz) Carreon; m. Libby C. Carr, June 21, 1967; children: Beth C., Cathy C. BS in Elem. Edn., Philippine Normal Coll., Manila, 1964. Tchr. Mabalacat Elem. Sch., Pampanga, 1964-65; prin. elem. dept. and dean St. Peter's Coll., Iligan City, Philippines, 1965-67; stock clk. J.W. Robinson, Pasadena, Calif., 1970-71; supr. mailroom Clinton E. Frank Advt., Los Angeles, 1971-73; supr. shipping Eldon Office Products, Carson, Calif., 1974-80; traffic mgr. Internat. Rectifier, El Segundo, Calif., 1980-81; assoc. realtor Century 21-Crown Equitites, Long Beach, Calif., 1981-88; real estate broker and owner Realty Square, Long Beach, 1988—. Pres. Mabalacat Residents of So. Calif., Gardena, 1986. Mem. Long Beach Dist. Bd. Realtors. Home: 19352 New Haven Ln Huntington Beach CA 92646 Office: Realty Square 1736 W Willow St Long Beach CA 90810-3034

CARR, VICTORIA, publishing executive; b. Wildwood, N.J., Jan. 9, 1956; d. Phillip William and Ruth Emelia (Borkowski) Calamaro; m. William Carr, Dec. 31, 1986. BS in Dietetics, Fla. State U., 1979. Salesperson World Class Resorts, Houston, 1980-86; owner, pub. The Fortune Group, Incline Village, Nev., 1986—; cons. Resorts Internat., Australia, 1985. Author: America's Most Beautiful Drive: Lake Tahoe's Shoreline Tour, 1987. Vol. Planned Parenthood, Reno, 1992. Mem. Vegetarians for Health (founder, pres. 1989—). Office: Fortune Group PO Box 1758 Crystal Bay NV 89402

CARRANZA, FERMIN ALBERT, periodontology educator; b. Buenos Aires, Argentina, Feb. 28, 1926; came to U.S., 1974; s. Fermin Alberto and Olga Ernestina (Falco) C.; m. Rita Maria Ostivar, Dec. 12, 1953; children: Fermin A., Patricia I., Laura V. DDS, U. Buenos Aires, 1948; cert. periodontics, Tufts U., 1952. Asst. prof. periodontology Tufts U., Boston, 1955-56; adj. prof. pathology U. Buenos Aires, 1961-65, prof., chmn. periodontics, 1966-74; dir. postdoctoral periodontics program UCLA Sch. Dentistry, 1976-80, prof., chmn. periodontology, 1974—; attending dentist UCLA Hosp, 1974—; dir. UCLA Clin Research Ctr. for Periodontal Disease, 1974—. Author: Glickman's Clinical Periodontology, 5th edit., 1979, 6th edit., 1984, 7th edit., 1990; contbr. articles to profl. jours. Recipient Sci. award Internat. Assn. Dental Research, W.G. Gies Found. award. for Latin-Am. Scientists, 1977. Fellow AAAS; mem. ADA, Am. Acad. Periodontology, Western Soc. Periodontology, Calif. Soc. Periodontists (award 1988), Internat. Assn. Dental Research, Pan Am. Assn. Peridontology, Calif. Dental Assn., Assn. Odontologica Argentina (hon.), Soc. Argentina de Periodontologia, Acad. de Estomatologia del Peru (hon.), Soc. Espanola de Parodoncia (hon), Soc. Colombiana de Periodoncia (hon.), Soc. Chilena de Parodontologia (hon.), Sigma Xi, Omicron Kappa Upsilon. Home: 10577 Eastborne Ave Los Angeles CA 90024-6045 Office: UCLA 405 Hilgard Ave Los Angeles CA 90024-1301

CARRARO, JOSEPH JOHN, senator, small business owner, consultant; b. N.Y.C., Nov. 12, 1944; s. Joseph George and Katherine (Dankert) C.; m. Linda JOyce Foster; children: Kitty, Mia, Joey, Lisa, Lindy. BA, U. N.Mex., 1968, M.Mgmt., 1981; Fin., N.Y. Inst. Fin., 1969; postgrad., Anderson Sch. Bus., 1983. Analyst Merrill, Lynch, Pierce, Fenner & Smith, N.Y.C., 1967-69; stock broker Quinn & Co., Albuquerque, 1969-71; communications cons. N.Y. Tel. Co., N.Y.C., 1971-73; owner Carraro's Pizza & Italian Restaurants, Albuquerque, 1973—; senator State of N.Mex., Santa Fe, 1984—; lobbyist N.Mex. Restaurants, Santa Fe, 1979-80. Charter mem. Citizens Adv. Group, Albuquerque, 1975; participant Emergency Care Alliance, Albuquerque, 1980; founder Project Share-Homeless Feeding, Albuquerque, 1981—. Named Outstanding Legislator of Yr. Nat. Rep. Legis. Assn., 1987. Mem. Exec. Mgmt. Assn. N.Mex. (pres. 1981-84), Albuquerque C. of C. (Small Bus. of Yr. 1984), N.Mex. Restaurant Assn. Home: 10216 Carraro Pl NW Albuquerque NM 87114-4505

CARREY, NEIL, lawyer, educator; b. Bronx, N.Y., Nov. 19, 1942; s. David L. and Betty (Kurtzburg) C.; m. Karen Krysher, Apr. 9, 1980; children: Jana, Christopher; children by previous marriage: Scott, Douglas, Dana. BS in Econs., U. Pa., 1964; JD, Stanford U., 1967. Bar: Calif. 1968. Mem. firm, v.p. corp. DeCastro, West, Chodorow & Burns, Inc., L.A., 1967—; instr. program for legal paraprofls. U. So. Calif., 1977-89; lectr. U. So. Calif. Dental Sch., 1987—. Author: Nonqualified Deferred Compensation Plans-The Wave of the Future, 1985. Officer, Vista Del Mar Child Care Center, Los Angeles, 1968-84; treas. Nat. Little League of Santa Monica, 1984-85, pres., 1985-86, coach, 1990—, coach Bobby Sox Team, Santa Monica, 1986-88, bd. dirs. 1988, umpire in chief, 1988; referee, coach Am. Soccer Youth Orgn., 1989—; curriculum com. Santa Monica-Malibu Sch. Dist., 1983-84, community health adv. com., 1988—, chmn., 1989—, athletic adv. com., chmn., 1988-90, dist. com. for sch. based health ctr., 1991—, gender equity com., chmn., 1992-93. Mem. U. Pa. Alumni Soc. So. Calif. (pres. 1971-79, dir. 1979-87), Alpha Kappa Psi (disting. life). Republican. Jewish. Club: Mountaingate Tennis (Los Angeles). Home: 616 23d St Santa Monica CA 90402 Office: 10960 Wilshire Blvd 18th flr Los Angeles CA 90024-3881

CARRICK, DAVID STANLEY, electrical engineer; b. Staines, Middlesex, Eng., Jan. 2, 1914; came to U.S., 1929, naturalized, 1938; s. David John and Ethel May (Bignel) Carrick; m. Marjorie Huey, Jan. 6, 1945; children: Paul David, Robert Peter. BSEE, U. Colo., 1949; MSEE, U. N.Mex., 1956. Engr. U.S. Bur. of REclamation, Billings, Mont., 1949-52; elec. engr. in nuclear weapons Prodn. and Quality Assurance Sandia Nat. Lab., Albuquerque, 1952-70; design engr. Western Elec., Omaha, 1970-74; dept. and night mgr. GTE, Albuquerque, 1974-80. Election judge Bernalillo County, Albuquerque, 1974-79; meals on wheels vol. Lovilace Hosp., Albuquerque, 1986—; vol. docent N.Mex. Mus. Nat. History, Albuquerque, 1987—; bd. dirs. Storehouse, Albuquerque, 1989—. With USN, 1942-45. Democrat. Congregationalist. Home: 808 Dakota SE Albuquerque NM 87108

CARRICO, DONALD JEFFERSON, public transit system manager; b. Dallas, June 15, 1944; s. Ivan and Helen Mae (Jefferson) C.; m. Prudence Louise Cornish, Aug. 17, 1968; children: Bryan Jefferson, Alan Jefferson. BSBA, Ohio State U., 1967; MA in Bus. Mgmt., Cen. Mich. U., 1977. Commd. 2d lt. USAF, 1967, advanced through grades to maj., 1979; various supervisory positions USAF Air Freight Terminals, 1967-72; mgr. passenger travel and cargo br. USAF Transp. Div., Rickenbacker AFB, Ohio, 1972-74; transp. and air terminal insp. USAF Insp. Gen. Team, Hawaii, 1974-76; liaison officer US Naval Supply Ctr., Pearl Harbor, Hawaii, 1976-78; transp. staff officer USAF Hdqrs. Tactical Air Command, Langley AFB, Va., 1978-83; chief transp. USAF Transp. Div., Incirlik AB, Turkey, 1983-85, Williams AFB, Ariz., 1986-88; vehicle fleet mgr. V&B Svcs., Phoenix, 1989-91; asst. mgr. dispatch svcs. Phoenix Transit System, 1991-92. Logistics chief Gilbert Food Bank Community Food Dr., Gilbert, Ariz., 1987, chmn. 1988; asst cubmaster Pack 282 Boy Scouts Am., Gilbert, 1987; mem. Town of Gilbert Gen. Plan Rev. Task Force, 1992—, total quality mgmt. rsch. panel Transp. Rsch. Bd., Washington, 1992—. Decorated Bronze Star. Home: 683 E Washington Ave Gilbert AZ 85234-6401

CARRIGAN, JIM RICHARD, federal judge; b. Mobridge, S.D., Aug. 24, 1929; s. Leo Michael and Mildred Ione (Jaycox) C.; m. Beverly Jean Halpin, June 2, 1956. Ph.B., J.D., U. N.D., 1953; LL.M. in Taxation, NYU, 1956; LLD (hon.), U. Colo., 1989, Suffolk U., 1991. Bar: N.D. 1953, Colo. 1956. Asst. prof. law U. Denver, 1956-59; vis. assoc. prof. NYU Law Sch., 1958, U. Wash. Law Sch., 1959-60; jud. adminstr. State of Colo., 1960-61; individual practice law Denver, 1961-62; prof. law U. Colo., 1961-67; partner firm Carrigan & Bragg (and predecessors), 1967-76; justice Colo. Supreme Ct., 1976-79; judge U.S. Dist. Ct. Colo., 1979—; mem. Colo. Bd. Bar Examiners, 1969-71; lectr. Nat. Coll. State Judiciary, 1964-77; bd. dirs. Nat Bd. Trial Advocacy, 1978-91; adj. prof. law U. Colo., 1984, 1991—; chmn. bd. dirs. Nat. Inst. Trial Advocacy, 1986-88, also mem. faculty, mem. exec. bd., trustee. Editor-in-chief: N.D. Law Rev., 1952-53, Internat. Soc. Barristers Quar., 1972-79; editor: DICTA, 1957-59; contbr. articles to profl. jours. Bd. regents U. Colo., 1975-76; bd. visitors U. N.D. Coll. Law, 1983-85. Recipient Disting. Svc. award Nat. Coll. State Judiciary, 1969, Outstanding Alumnus award U. N.D., 1973, Regent Emeritus award U. Colo., 1977, B'nai Brith Civil Rights award, 1986, Thomas More Outstanding Lawyer award Cath. Lawyers Guild, 1988, Svc. award Nat. Inst. Trial Advocacy, 1992, Disting. Svc. award Nat. Assn. Blacks in Criminal Justice (Colo. chpt.), 1992. Fellow Colo. Bar Found., Boulder County Bar Found.; mem. ABA (action com. on tort system improvement 1985-87, TIPS sect. long range planning com. 1986-90, coun. 1987-91, task force on initiatives and referenda 1990—, size of civil juries task force 1988-90), Am. Law Inst., Colo. Boulder Denver County Bar Assns., Cath. Lawyers Guild, Boulder Law Club, Internat. Soc. Barristers, Internat. Acad. Trial Lawyers, Fed. Judges Assn. (bd. dirs. 1985-89), Am. Judicature Soc. (bd. dirs. 1985-89), Tenth Cir. Dist. Judges Assn. (sec. 1991-92, v.p. 1992—), Denver Athletic Club, Order of Coif, Phi Beta Kappa. Roman Catholic. Office: US Dist Ct US Courthouse 1929 Stout St Denver CO 80294-2900

CARRIKER, ROBERT CHARLES, history educator; b. St. Louis, Aug. 18, 1940; s. Thomas B. and Vivian Ida (Spaunhorst) C.; m. Eleanor R. Gualdoni, Aug. 24, 1963; children: Thomas A., Robert M., Andrew J. BS, St. Louis U., 1962, AM, 1963; PhD, U. Okla., 1967. Asst. prof. Gonzaga U., Spokane, Wash., 1967-71, assoc. prof., 1972-76, prof. history, 1976—. Author: The Kalispell People, 1973, Fort Supply, Indian Territory, 1970, 90; editor: (with Eleanor R. Carriker) Army Wife on the Frontier, 1975; book rev. editor Columbia mag. 1987—. Mem. Wash. Lewis and Clark Trail Com., 1978—; commr. Wash. Maritime Bicentennial, Olympia, 1989-92; bd. dirs. Wash. Commn. for Humanities, Seattle, 1988—; trustee Wash. State Hist. Soc., Tacoma, 1981-90. Burlington No. Found. scholar, 1985; recipient Disting. Svc. award Lewis and Clark Trail Heritage Found., 1989. Mem. Western Hist. Assn., Phi Alpha Theta (councilor 1985-87). Roman Catholic. Office: Gonzaga U 502 E Boone Ave Spokane WA 99258-0001

CARRILLO, GILBERTO, engineer; b. San Diego, Sept. 22, 1926; s. Manuel C. and Francisca (Ruiz) C.; m. Maria de Lourdes Paez, Jan. 21, 1957; children: Gilbert A., Elizabeth, Evelyn, Fernando, Mary Lou. BS with honors, San Diego State U., 1951. Materials and process engr. Convair Div. Gen. Dynamics, San Diego, 1950-56, Douglas Aircraft Co., El Segundo, Calif., 1956-60; tech. dir. Torco Products, Inc., Mexico City, 1960-68; mgr., environ. engr. Rohr Industries, Riverside, Calif., 1969—; gen. chmn. First Soc. Advancement Materials and Process Engring. Internat. Environ. Symposium and Tech. Conf., 1991. Contbr. articles to profl. jours.; patentee in field. Served as sgt. USAAF, 1945-46, Japan. Mem. Soc. for Advancement Materials and Process Engring. (nat. chpt.: gen. chmn., internat. symposium and tech. conf. 1988; Inland Empire chpt.: chmn. arrangements com. 1972-76, chmn. scholarships 1976-82, gen. chmn. 1982-83, Best Paper award, 1983), VFW. Republican. Roman Catholic. Home: 5535 Montero Dr Riverside CA 92509-5608 Office: Rohr Industries Materials Engring 8200 Arlington Ave Riverside CA 92503-1499

CARROLL, DANA, academic researcher, administrator, educator; b. Palm Springs, Calif., Sept. 2, 1943; s. William Robert and Harriet Merrill (Dana) C.; divorced; children: Adam Slade, Jessica Ann. BS, Swarthmore (Pa.) Coll., 1965; PhD, U. Calif., Berkeley, 1970. Postdoctoral fellow Beatson Inst. for Cancer Rsch., Glasgow, Scotland, 1970-72, Carnegie Instn. of Washington, Balt., 1972-75; asst. prof. Sch. of Medicine U. Utah, Salt Lake City, 1975-81, assoc. prof., 1981-85, prof., co-chmn., 1985—; mem. grant rev. panel devel. biology NSF, Washington, 1988-91. Contbr. numerous articles to profl. jours. Coach Utah Youth Soccer Assn., Salt Lake City, 1982-86. Jane Coffin Childs Meml. Fund Med. Rsch. fellow, 1970-72; USPHS fellow, 1973-75; Cancer Rsch. scholar Am. Cancer Soc., 1983. Mem. Am. Soc. for Microbiology, AAAS, Am. Soc. Biochemistry and Molecular Biology, Am. Chem. Soc. Home: 237 Elizabeth St Salt Lake City UT 84102-2544 Office: U Utah Sch Medicine Dept Biochemistry Salt Lake City UT 84132

CARROLL, DAVID TODD, computer engineer; b. West Palm Beach, Fla., Apr. 8, 1959; s. David Irwin and Lois Ellen (Spriggs) C. Student, U. Houston, 1978-81. Lab. technician Inst. for Lipid Rsch., Baylor Coll. Medicine, Houston, 1978-81; software specialist Digital Equipment Corp., Colorado Springs, Colo., 1982-86, systems engr., 1986-91, systems support cons., 1991—. Mem. AAAS, Digital Equipment Corp. Users Soc. Home: 7332 Aspen Glen Ln Colorado Springs CO 80919-3024 Office: Digital Equipment Corp 305 S Rockrimmon Blvd Colorado Springs CO 80919-2303

CARROLL, EARL HAMBLIN, federal judge; b. Tucson, Mar. 26, 1925; s. John Vernon and Ruby (Wood) C.; m. Louise Rowlands, Nov. 1, 1952; children—Katherine Carroll Pearson, Margaret Anne. BSBA, U. Ariz., 1948, LLB, 1951. Bar: Ariz., U.S. Ct. Appeals (9th and 10th cirs.), U.S. Ct. of Claims, U.S. Supreme Ct. Law clk. Ariz. Supreme Ct., Phoenix, 1951-52; assoc. Evans, Kitchel & Jenckes, Phoenix, 1952-56, ptnr., 1956-80; judge U.S. Dist. Ct. Ariz., Phoenix, 1980—; spl. counsel City of Tombstone, Ariz., 1962-65, Maricopa County, Phoenix, 1968-75, City of Tucson, 1974, City of Phoenix, 1979; designated mem. U.S. Fgn. Intelligence Surveillance Court by Chief Justice U.S. Supreme Ct., 1993—. Mem. City of Phoenix Bd. of Adjustment, 1955-58; trustee Phoenix Elem. Sch. Bd., 1961-72; mem. Gov.'s Council on Intergovtl. Relations, Phoenix, 1970-73; mem. Ariz. Bd. Regents, 1978-80. Served with USNR, 1943-46; PTO. Recipient Nat. Service awards Campfire, 1973, 75, Alumni Service award U. Ariz., 1980, Disting. Citizen award No. Ariz. U., Flagstaff, 1983, Bicentenial award Georgetown U., 1988, Disting. Citizen award U. Ariz., 1990. Fellow Am. Coll. Trial Lawyers, Am. Bar Found.; mem. ABA, Ariz. Bar Assn., U. Ariz. Law Coll. Assn. (pres. 1975), Phoenix Country Club, Sigma Chi (Significant Sig award 1991), Phi Delta Phi. Democrat. Office: US Dist Ct US Courthouse & Fed Bldg 230 N 1st Ave Ste 6000 Phoenix AZ 85025-0005

CARROLL, FRANK RICHARD, chef; b. Norfolk, Va., July 28, 1947; s. Frank Belcher and Delma Iona (Ramsey) C.; m. Cheryl Ann King, June 3, 1969; children: Frank R., Jr., Marla Lynn. Diploma in Bus., U. Miami, 1970; Diploma in Culinary Arts with hons., Western Culinary Inst., Portland, Oreg., 1990. V.p. Carroll Oil Co., Ft. Meyers, Fla., 1970-75, pres., 1975-80; owner/builder Cherimar Devel. Co., Evergreen, Colo., 1981-86; working chef Evergreen Conf. Ctr., Evergreen, 1986-89; exec. chef Adventure Treks, Denver, 1990-91, Tiger Run R.V. Resort, Breckenridge, Colo., 1992—; chef cons. Bed & Breadfast Rocky Mountains, Denver, 1991—, Colo. Whitewater Expdns., Salida, 1989-90. With U.S. Army Nat. Guard, 1970-76. Mem. Colo. Chef's DeCuisine, Nat. Off-Road Bicycle Assn., Rotary (sec. Ft. Myers Club 1979), Kiwanis (v.p. Evergreen chpt. 1985), Nat. Model Railroad Assn. (bd. dirs. Rocky Mountain region 1984). Episcopalian. Home: 251 S Clarkson St Denver CO 80209-2123 Office: Bed & Breakfast-Rocky Mountains 906 S Pearl St Denver CO 80209-4224

CARROLL, JAMES ROBERT, construction engineer, engineering executive; b. Cin., Dec. 22, 1940; s. Robert J. and Ruth Ann (Krumpelbeck) C.; m. Gloria J. Mutcher, Feb. 27, 1971; children: Monique, Heather. BSCE, U. Detroit, 1963; MBA, Boise State U., 1980. Profl. engr., Idaho. Project engr. Morrison Knudsen Corp., Republic of Vietnam, 1965-67; estimator Morrison Knudsen Corp., Boise, Idaho, 1967-70; engring. mgr. Morrison Knudsen Corp., Langdon, N.D., 1970-75; dir. tng. Morrison Knudsen Corp., Boise, 1975-77; dir. engring. Morrison Knudsen Corp., Saudi Arabia, 1977-80; constrn. mgr. Morrison Knudsen Corp., Colombia, 1980-84; div. engr. Morrison Knudsen Corp., Boise, 1984-88, dir. planning and devel., 1988-90, v.p. mktg., 1990—; instr. Boise State U., 1985-87; mem. CII Project Orgn. Task Force, Austin, Tex., 1985-91. Author manuals in field. With USMC, 1963-64. Fellow ASCE; mem. Am. Soc. Macro Engring., Constr. Industry Inst. Libertarian. Roman Catholic. Office: Morrison Knudsen Corp MK Plz Boise ID 83729

CARROLL, JOEL, retired mathematician; b. Hallettsville, Tex., Apr. 8, 1924; s. Norman and Otealia (Hargrove) C.; m. Anne M. Merriweather, Aug. 20, 1960; children: Joel Anson, Bernard Eugene, Harlan Patrick. BA, Roosevelt U., 1950; MS, DePaul U., Chgo., 1952. Analytical statistician U.S. Railroad Retirement Bd., Chgo., 1952-54; asst. mathematician Argonne nat. Lab., Lemont, Ill., 1954-55; computing engr. North Am. Aviation Inc., L.A., 1955-58; mathematician Land-Air, Inc., Point Mugu, Calif., 1958-61, Gen. Precision, Inc., Glendale, Calif., 1961-63; sr. engr. Northrop Corp., Hawthorne, Calif., 1963-65; computer specialist Douglas Aircraft Co., Santa Monica, Calif., 1965-66; mathematician Naval Ocean System Ctr., San Diego, 1966-80, scientist, 1980-88. Moderator San Diego Assn. United Ch. of Christ, 1980-81; mem. Town Hall of Calif.; past moderator, past treas., past deacon Congl. Ch. With USNR, 1943-45. Recipient Superior Accomplishment award Dept. of Navy, 1968, Spl. Achievement award Naval Ocean System Ctr., San Diego, 1974. Fellow Harry S. Truman Libr. Inst. (hon.); mem. AAAS, ACLU, Am. Math. Soc., N.Y. Acad. Scis., Kiwanis (past sec.), Pi Mu Epsilon. Home: 13307 Olive Grove Dr Poway CA 92064-3945

CARROLL, LARRY LESTER, estate planner; b. Freer, Tex., Sept. 1, 1935; s. Lester Edward and Anna Lee (Whitley) C.; m. Catherine Joy DeAngelis, May 11, 1990. BA in Elem. Edn., L.A. State Coll., 1962; MA in Elem. Edn., Mont. State U., 1968, PhD, 1972; D of Common Law, Universal Life U., 1993. Lic. real estate broker, ins. broker, securities dealer. Tchr. elem. sch. Kalispell, Mont., 1956-57, Red Lodge, 1957-59; pub. sch. adminstr. Bozeman, Mont., 1963-68; prof. edn. Mont. State U., Bozeman, 1968-75; sales rep. U.S. Surg. Equipment, Hartford, Conn., 1975-80, Howmedica-Cope, Dallas, 1980-90; estate planner Investors Tax Svc., Stockton, Calif., 1990—; pres. U.S. Bar, 1993—, Nev. Common Law U., 1993—; instr. Real Estate Sch., Helena, Mont., 1966-68, Tyler, Tex., 1988-90, Securities Licensing Sch., Tyler, 1988-90, Estate and Tax Planning Sch., Tyler, 1988-90; author license preparation course materials for real estate, ins. and securities courses. Named Outstanding Young Man Bozeman Jr. C. of C., 1968; winner Humerous Speech state contest Toastmasters, Bozeman, 1970. Mem. Ch. of Christ. Office: Investors Tax Svc 1052 Rivara Rd Stockton CA 95207

CARROLL, PAT, actress; b. Shreveport, La., May 5, 1927; d. Maurice Clifton and Kathryn Angela (Meagher) C.; children: Sean, Kerry, Tara. Student, Immaculate Heart Coll., 1944-47, Catholic U., 1950; Litt.D. (hon.), Barry Coll., Miami, Fla., 1969. pres. Sea-Ker, Inc., Beverly Hills, Calif., 1979—; pres. CARPA Prodns., Inc., N.Y.C. Profl. debut in stock prodn. A Goose for the Gander, 1947; supper club debut at Le Ruban Bleu, N.Y.C., 1950; appeared on numerous television shows, 1950—, including: Red Buttons Show, 1951, Caesar's Hour, 1956-57 (Emmy award), Danny Thomas Show, 1961-63, The Ted Knight Show, 1985, She's the Sheriff, 1987-1988; Broadway debut in Catch a Star, 1955 (Tony nomination); appeared in motion picture With Six You Get Eggroll, 1968; producer, actress: Gertrude Stein Gertrude Stein Gertrude Stein for colls. and univs. (Grammy award 1980, Drama Desk award, Outer Critics Circle award); Shakespeare debut as nurse in Romeo and Juliet and Falstaff in The Merry Wives of Windsor, Shakespeare Theater at the Folger, 1986 (Helen Hayes award 1987); voice of Ursula, the wicked squidwitch, in The Little Mermaid, 1989; appeared in The Show-Off, 1992—, Roundabout Theater Company. Pres. Center of Films for Children, 1971-73; bd. regents Immaculate Heart Coll., Hollywood, Calif., 1970. Mem. Actors Studio, Actors Fund (life), Actors Equity Assn., Screen Actors Guild, AFTRA, Acad. Television Arts and Scis. (trustee 1958-59), Am. Youth Hostel (life), Del. and Hudson Canal Hist. Soc., George Heller Meml. Fund. Office: care Craig Agy 8635 Wonderland Ave Los Angeles CA 90046-1452

CARROLL, PAULA MARIE, security company executive; b. Fresno, Calif., July 17, 1933; d. Paul Edward Mikkelsen and Helen Marie (Anderson) Mack; m. Herman S. Carroll Jr., April 25, 1954. V.p., co-owner Cen. Valley Alarm Co., Inc., Merced, Calif., 1963—; pres., co-owner Cen. Valley Alarm Co., Inc., Merced, 1988—. Author: Life Wish, 1986, Moment to Moment, 1992. Mem. Hospice of Merced and Mariposa Counties, Calif., 1979; pres., founder Consumers for Med. Quality Inc., Merced, 1981; chair Ombudsman, Merced, 1982-85; coord. 15th congl. dist. AARP/Vote, Calif., trainer Health Care Am. AARP. Recipient Celebrating Women award Merced County, 1987, Pres.'s award Calif. Trial Lawyers Assn., 1987; named Woman Distinction Soroptimist Internat., 1986; Consumers for Med. Quality grantee Calif. Trial Lawyers Assn., 1987. Mem. AARP, Western Burglar and Fire Alarm Assn., Soc. Law and Medicine, Hastings Ctr. Inst. of Society, NAFE, Internat. Platform Assn., Josephson Inst. for Advancement Ethics, Health Care Am., Inst. Rsch. Assn. (assoc.), Am. Assn. Ret. Persons, Commonwealth Club Calif., Beta Sigma Phi. Home: 3271 Alder Ave Merced CA 95340-1702 Office: Cen Valley Alarm Co Inc 620 W 14th St Merced CA 95340-5911

CARROLL, ROBERT ALAN, manufacturing executive; b. Boston, Sept. 25, 1935; s. Stephen John and Helene Ann (Roache) C.; m. Dixie Lee; children: Linda, Scott, Sean. BA in Sci., Harvard U., 1972. Mfg. mgr. Am. Sci. and Engring., Cambridge, Mass., 1968-79; mgr. prodn. ops. sect. Motorola, Scottsdale, Ariz., 1979—. Mem. AAAS, N.Y. Acad. Scis., Ariz. Artist Guild, Copley Soc. Home: 5983 N 83d St Scottsdale AZ 85253

CARROTT, JOHN ARDEN, manufacturing executive; b. Columbus, Ohio, Dec. 18, 1947; s. Donald Forwein and Marion Randall (Miller) C.; m. Nancy Elizabeth Loftus, Oct. 2, 1970 (div. Sept. 1986); children: Andrew Alan, Christopher Thomas; m. Jerri Lynn Stetler, May 22, 1987. ASEE, Capital Radio Engring. Inst., Washington, 1973; B of Tech. in Computer Tech., N.Y. Inst. Tech., Old Westbury, 1976; AS in Computer Sci., R.I. Jr. Coll., Warwick, 1981; postgrad., Kennedy-Western U. Research specialist U. R.I. Sch. Oceanography, Narragansett, 1974-78; sr. engr. Data Gen., Providence, 1978-81; pres. Sequoia Computers, Cranston, R.I., 1981-83; dir. research & devel. SCI, Inc., Huntsville, Ala., 1983-84; pres. Diversified Digital Systems, Huntsville, 1984, Universal Systems of Ala., Albertville, 1985; dir. engring. Mets, Inc., Pompano Beach, Fla., 1985-87; v.p. Fairview, Inc., Orlando, Fla., 1987; chief exec. officer Ocean Electronic Systems, Sunnyvale, Calif., 1988—; cons. John A. Carrott & Assocs., 1989—. Patentee security monitoring and tracking systems. Served with USN, 1967-73. Mem. World Trade Ctr., VFW, Smithsonian Assn. Roman Catholic.

CARRUTHERS, PETER AMBLER, physicist, educator; b. Lafayette, Ind., Oct. 7, 1935; s. Maurice Earl and Nila (Ambler) C.; m. Jean Ann Breitenbecher, Feb. 26, 1955; children: Peter, Debra, Kathryn; m. Lucy J. Marston, July 10, 1969; m. Cornelia B. Dobrovolsky, June 20, 1981; m. Lucy Marston Carruthers, Mar. 3, 1990. B.S., Carnegie Inst. Tech., 1957, M.S., 1957; Ph.D., Cornell U., 1960. Asst. prof. Cornell U., N.Y., 1961-63, assoc. prof., 1963-67, prof. physics, atomic and solid state physics, nuclear studies, 1967-73; div. leader, theoretical div. Los Alamos (N.Mex.) Sci. Lab., 1973-80, group leader of elem. particles and field theory, 1980-85, sr. fellow, 1980-86; prof., dept. head physics U. Ariz., Tucson, 1986-93, dir. Ctr. for Study Complex Systems, 1987—; vis. asso. prof. Calif. Inst. Tech., 1965, vis. prof., 1969-70, 77-78; mem. physics adv. panel NSF, 1975-80, chmn., 1978-80; trustee Aspen Center for Physics, 1976-82, chmn. exec. com., 1977-79, chmn. bd. trustees, 1979-82, advisor, 1982-89, hon. trustee, 1989—; mem. High Energy Physics Adv. Panel, 1978-82, com. on U.S.-USSR cooperation in physics NAS, 1978-82; cons. SRI Internat., 1976-81, MacArthur Found., 1981-82, 84-88, Inst. for Def. Analysis, 1985-89; chmn. Ariz. Superconducting Super Collider Tech. Com., 1986-89; editor Multiparticle Prodn. Dynamics, 1988. Author: (with R. Brout) Lectures on the Many-Electron Problem, 1963, Introduction to Unitary Symnetry, 1966, Spin and Isospin in Particle Physics, 1971; editor: (with D. Strottman) Hadronic Matter in Collision, 1986, Hadronic Multiparticle Dynamics, 1988, (with J. Rafelski) Hadronic Matter in Collision, 1988; cons. editor Harwood Soviet Physics Series. Trustee Santa Fe Inst., 1984-86, v.p., 1985-86, mem. sci. bd. 1986-93. Recipient Merit award Carnegie Mellon U., 1980; Alfred P. Sloan research fellow, 1963-65; NSF sr. postdoctoral fellow U. Rome, 1967-68; Alexander von Humboldt sr. fellow, 1987—. Fellow AAAS, Am. Phys. Soc. (panel on pub. affairs 1984-86), Univs. Rsch. Assn. (Superconducting Super Collider bd. overseers 1990-93. Home: 2220 E Camino Miraval Tucson AZ 85718-4939 Office: Univ Ariz Dept Physics PAS Bldg 81 Tucson AZ 85721

CARSON, EDWARD MANSFIELD, banker; b. Tucson, Nov. 6, 1929; s. Ernest Lee and Earline M. (Mansfield) C.; m. Nadine Anne Severns, Dec. 13, 1952; children: Dawn, Tod. BSBA, Ariz. State U., 1951; grad. in banking, Rutgers U., 1963. With First Interstate Bank of Ariz., Phoenix, 1951-85, exec. v.p., 1969-72, chief adminstrv. officer, 1972-75, vice chmn. bd., 1975-77, pres., chief exec. officer, 1977-85, also bd. dirs.; pres. First Interstate Bancorp, L.A., from 1985, now chmn. bd., chief exec. officer, also bd. dirs.; bd. dirs. Inspiration Resources Corp., Ramada Inns, Inc., First Interstate Bank of Oreg. Bd. fellows Am. Grad. Sch. Internat. Mgmt. Recipient Service award Ariz. State U. Alumni Assn., 1968; named to Ariz. State U. Alumni Assn. Hall of Fame, 1977. Mem. Assn. Res. City Bankers, Assn. Bank Holding Cos. (bd. dirs.). Clubs: Paradise Valley Country, Thunderbirds, Los Angeles Country, Calif.; Phoenix Country. Office: 1st Interstate Bancorp Po Box 54068 633W 5th St Los Angeles CA 90071*

CARSON, ELIZABETH LORRAINE NEAL, logistics management specialist, small business owner; b. Glendale, Calif., Oct. 2, 1958; d. Harold Dean and Viola Gertrude (Neal) Donaldson; m. Robert Lawrence Chally, Aug. 7, 1981 (div. Sept. 1985); m. Richard W. Carson, Oct. 5, 1992. BS, Spring Arbor Coll., 1979; MS, Air Force Inst. Tech., 1988. Loan sec. Sacramento (Calif.) Savs. and Loan, 1979, acctg. clk., 1979-81; equipment specialist trainee Civil Svc. USAF, McClellan AFB, 1981-84, equipment specialist, 1984-86; logistics specialist Civil Svc. USAF, L.A. AFB, 1986-88; dep. systems program mgr. Civil Svc. USAF, Sacramento, 1988-89, chief, resource and plans, 1989-90, program mgr., 1990-93, integrated weapon system mgr., program mgmt. process action team rep., 1991-92; adj. prof. Colo. Tech. Coll., Colorado Springs, 1989-91; advisor Logistics Adv. Bd., Colorado Springs, 1988-92; integrated weapon system mgmt. program mgr., process action team mem. Air Force Material Command Creation, 1991—; co-owner Colors of Nature Gallery, Chapel Hills Mall, Colorado Springs. Organist/pianist Orangevale Free Meth. Ch., 1971-76, fin. com. 1981-82, music com., 1971-76, 80-85, chmn. music com., 1984. Mem. Soc. Reliability Engrs., Soc. Logistics Engrs., Sigma Iota Epsilon. Republican. Office: Colors of Nature Gallery 1710 Briargate Blvd # 477 Colorado Springs CO 80920

CARSON, JAMES MATTHEW, technology transfer engineer; b. Mantua, N.J., Feb. 14, 1944; s. George Donald and Bernice Evelyn (Stow) C.; m. Susan Elizabeth Dobratz, Dec. 17, 1966; children: Katherine Susan, Sara Alexis. BS, USAF Acad., 1966; MS, Drexel U., 1972, PhD, 1978; grad., Air War Coll., 1987. Registered profl. engr., Colo. Commd. 2d lt. USAF, 1966, advanced through grades to capt., 1969; materials engr. Air Force Materials Lab., Dayton, Ohio, 1966-70; asst. prof. USAF Acad., Colo., 1972-76; resigned, 1976; rsch. engr. E.I. DuPont de Nemours & Co., Inc., Seaford, Del., 1978-80; sr. rsch. engr. Engring. Rsch. Inst., U. N.Mex., Albuquerque, 1980-88; engring. cons., Albuquerque, 1988-92; mem. tech. transfer staff Sandia Nat. Labs., Albuquerque, 1992—; mobilization asst. to comdr. Phillips Lab., Albuquerque, 1990—. Contbr. articles to profl. jours. Col. USAFR. Mem. ASME, Sigma Xi, Tau Beta Pi, Pi Tau Sigma. Home: 902 Ganado Ct SE Albuquerque NM 87123-4111 Office: Sandia Nat Labs Divsn 4212 Albuquerque NM 87185-5800

CARSON, LILLIAN GERSHENSON, psychotherapist; b. N.Y.C., Mar. 22, 1933; d. Joseph and Helen E. (Tucker) Gershenson; m. Ralph Carson, July 19, 1978 (dec. June 1983); children from previous marriage: Susan Gevirtz, Steven Gevirtz, Carrie Gevirtz Wicks; m. Sam T. Hurst, Dec. 11, 1984. BA, UCLA, 1968, MSW, 1970, DSW, 1979. Lic. clin. social worker, Calif. Psychotherapist parent-infant consultation program, dept. child psychiatry Cedars Sinai Hosp., L.A., 1970; dir. counseling Zahm Sch. Individual Edn., L.A., 1970-72; dir. clinic L.A. Psychoanalytic Soc., 1972-82; pvt. practice psychotherapy, L.A., 1970—; case supr. So. Calif. Counseling Ctr.; instr. Calif. State Mental Health Tng. Ctr.; exec. com. dean's coun. UCLA Sch. Social Welfare, tchr., field work supr., 1985-87, field instr., 1986-87; cons. Santa Monica Child Devel. Ctrs.; mem. exec. com., sec.-treas. Psychiat. Med. Group So. Calif., 1973-74; mem. profl. bd. L.A. County Mental Health Assn., 1974; bd. dirs. Friends of UCLA Child Care Svcs., 1981, adv. coun., editorial bd., 1989; mem. adv. coun. L.A. Child Devel. Ctr., 1981; staff mem. Westwood Psychiat. Hosp.; invited guest 20th birthday celebration meetings Hempstead Clinic, London, 1972, participant seminar by Anna Freud, 1978; founding mem. Inst. for The Study of Men and Women U. So. Calif.; mem. Betty Friedan Think Tank, editorial bd. UCLA Working Parents Newsletter; facilatator salon series Inst. for Study of Women and Men. Nat., 1989. Author: The Joy of Grandparenting, 1993. Bd. dirs. Girls Inc., 1989—, chmn. golden circle, exec. com. sec., 1992; facilitator Santa Barbara County Advs. on Behalf of Children, Partnership for Children, Santa Barbara; commr. Santa Barbara County Children's Commn., 1989. Fellow Calif. Soc. Clin. Social Work (nominating com. 1974-77), Am. Orthopsychiat. Assn.; mem. Ctr. Improvement of Child Caring, Nat. Assn. Social Workers, Acad. Cert. Social Workers, Nat. Assn. Edn. of Young Children.

CARSON, MARVIN WAYNE, municipal employee; b. Henryetta, Okla., Apr. 20, 1955; s. William Walter and Pauline Janet (Gasaway) Wells. Student, U. Alaska, 1986. Data tech. Veco Inc., Prudhoe Bay, Alaska, 1979-81; engring. aide Arco Alaska, Inc., Anchorage, 1981, info. systems coord., 1981-82; systems analyst Municipality of Anchorage, 1982-85, 89-92, data and systems security officer, 1985-88; supr. systems support Mcpl. Light and Power, Anchorage, 1992—; distbr. Amway Corp., 1987—. Pres. Jr. Achievement, Bellingham, Wash., 1973. With USAF, 1973-79. Decorated USAF Commendation medal. Mem. Assn. Records Mgrs. (bd. dirs. 1982-83), Data Processing Mgmt. Assn., Masons. Home: 1370 Valencia St # 1 San Francisco CA 94110 Office: Mcpl Light and Power Systems Divsn 1200 E 1st Ave Anchorage AK 99501

CARSON, STANLEY, ophthalmologist; b. Lansford, Pa., Dec. 26, 1937; s. Jacob Martin and Josephine Mary (Tocek) Ogozalek; m. Alexandra Gale Mayberry, Dec. 17, 1988. BA, U. So. Calif., 1963, MD, 1966. Diplomate Am. Bd. Ophthalmology. Physician pvt. practice Long Beach, Calif., 1971—; chief of staff Long Beach Meml. Hosp., 1990, 91. With USAF, 1955-59. Republican. Office: 2888 N Long Beach Blvd Ste 150 Long Beach CA 90806-1586

CARSON, VIRGINIA GOTTSCHALL, academic administrator, biology educator; b. Pitts.; d. Walter Carl and Rosalie (Paulin) Gottschall; m. John Richard Carson; children: Margaret Rosalie, Kenneth Robert. BA in Math., Calif. State U., L.A., 1960, MA in Psychology, 1965; PhD in Physiology, UCLA, 1970. Asst. prof. dept. biology Chapman U., Orange, Calif., 1971-77, pre-med. advisor, 1974—, assoc. prof. dept. biology, 1977-83, chmn. div. natural sci., 1983-91, prof. dept. biology, 1983—, chmn. dept. biology, 1993—; asst. rsch. pharmacologist U. Calif., Irvine, 1972-81, assoc. rsch. pharmacologist, 1981-83, 91—; assoc. prof. So. Calif. Coll. Optometry, Fullerton, 1979-83. Contbr. numerous articles to profl. jours. Elder First Presbyn. Ch. Orange, 1990-93; chmn. home econs. adv. com. Orange Unified Sch. Dist., 1989—; chmn. faculty Chapman U., 1987-88. NIH fellow UCLA, 1972-74. Mem. Orange County Sci. Edn. Assn. (bd. dirs. 1989—, chmn. 1993—), Grad. Women in Sci. (chpt. sec. 1989-93, pres. 1993—). Republican. Home: 717 S Yorba St Orange CA 92669-5043 Office: Chapman Univ 333 N Glassell St Orange CA 92666-1099

CARSON, WALLACE PRESTON, JR., state supreme court chief justice; b. Salem, Oreg., June 10, 1934; s. Wallace Preston and Edith (Bragg) C.; m. Gloria Stolk, June 24, 1956; children: Scott, Carol, Steven (dec. 1981). BA in Politics, Stanford U., 1956; JD, Willamette U., 1962. Bar: Oreg. 1962, U.S. Dist. Ct. Oreg. 1963, U.S. Ct. Appeals (9th cir.) 1968, U.S. Supreme Ct. 1971, U.S. Ct. Mil. Appeals 1977; lic. comml. pilot FAA. Pvt. practice law Salem, Oreg., 1962-77; judge Marion County Cir. Ct., Salem, 1977-82; assoc. justice Oreg. Supreme Ct., Salem, 1982-92, state chief justice, 1992—. Mem. Oreg. Ho. of Reps., 1967-71, maj. leader, 1969-71; mem. Oreg. State Senate, 1971-77, minority floor leader, 1971-77; dir. Salem Area Community Council, 1967-70, pres., 1969-70; mem. Salem Planning Commn., 1966-72, pres., 1970-71; co-chmn. Marion County Mental Health Planning Com., 1965-69; mem. Salem Community Goals Com., 1965; Republican precinct commiteeman, 1963-66; mem. Marion County Rep. Central Exec. Com., 1963-66; com. predinct edn. Oreg. Rep. Central Com., 1965; vestryman, acolyte, Sunday Sch. tchr., youth coach St. Paul's Episcopal Ch., 1935—; task force on cts. Oreg. Council Crime and Delinquency, 1968-69; trustee Willamette U., 1970—; adv. bd. Cath. Ctr. Community Services, 1976-77; mem. comporehensive planning com. Mid-Willamette Valley Council of Govts., 1970-71; adv. com. Oreg. Coll. Edn. Tchr. Edn., 1971-75; pres. Willamette regional Oreg. Lung Assn., 1974-75, state dir., exec. com., 1975-77; pub. relations com. Williamette council Campfire Girls, 1976-77; criminal justice adv. bd. Chemeketa Community Coll., 1977-79; mem. Oreg. Mental Health Com., 1979-80; mem. subcom. Gov's Task Force Mental Health, 1980; you and govt. adv. com. Oreg. YMCA, 1981—. Served to col. USAFR, 1956-59. Recipient Salem Disting. Svc. award, 1968; recipient Good Fellow award Marion County Fire Svc., 1974, Minuteman award Oreg. N.G. Assn., 1980; fellow Eagleton Inst. Politics, Rutgers U., 1971. Mem. Marion County Bar Assn. (sec.-treas. 1965-67, dir. 1968-70), Oreg. Bar Assn., ABA, Willamette U. Coll. Law Alumni Assn. (v.p. 1968-70), Salem Art Assn., Oreg. Hist. Soc., Marion County Hist. Soc., Stanford U. Club (pres. Salem chpt. 1963-64), Delta Theta Phi. Home: 1309 Hillendale Dr SE Salem OR 97302-3347 Office: Oreg Supreme Ct Supreme Ct Bldg Salem OR 97310*

CARSON, WAYNE GILBERT, general contracting company executive; b. Chariton, Iowa, Nov. 23, 1931; s. Earl Roscoe and Nora Viola (Sheldon) C.; m. Joan Farquer, Nov. 26, 1960 (div. Oct. 1969); children: Scott B., Sondra Dee; m. Kathleen Jean Sanders, Apr. 27, 1975. BS, Iowa State U., 1954; postgrad., Loyola U., Chgo., 1963-65. Foreman casting dept. Revere Copper & Brass, Chgo., 1954-55, asst. prodn. mgr., 1957-60; fin. salesman Investors Diversified Svcs., Chgo., 1960-62; tchr. Chgo. Bd. Edn., 1962-64; sales engr. Essex Internat., Chgo., 1964-75; owner, mgr. Sunlite Constrn. Co., Chgo., 1975-77, Sunlite Devel. Co., Glenwood Springs, Colo., 1977-85, Sunlite Builders, San Diego, 1985—. With USN, 1955-57. Mem. Nat. Home Builders Assn. (pres. 1982-84).

CARSRUD, ALAN LEE, business educator; b. Denver, July 23, 1946; s. George E. Carsrud and Clara Lee (Jones) Harrell; 1 child, Nichel David Victor. BA, Tex. Christian U., 1968; MA, U. N.H., 1972, PhD, 1974; postdoctoral, U. Tex., 1979-81. Instr. psychology U. N.H. and Nasson Coll., 1971-73; asst. prof. psychology SUNY, Brockport, 1973-75, Tex. A&M U., College Station, 1975-77; coord. psychological svcs. and rsch. Travis State Sch. Tex. Dept. Mental Health, 1977-79; adj. asst. prof. psychology Southwestern U., Georgetown, Tex., 1978-81, St. Edward's U., Austin, Tex., 1978-81; mng. dir. Univ. Cons. Internat., 1978—; rsch assoc., cons. psychologist R. Helmreich, Inc., 1980-83; rsch. scientist dept. psychology U. Tex., Austin, 1981-83, co-dir., lectr. dept. mgmt., 1982-86; assoc. prof. entrepreneur program grad sch. bus. U. So. Calif., 1986-90; mng. dir., chief exec. officer Pacific Scientific Techs., 1989—; vis. prof. Sch. Bus. and Mgmt. Pepperdine U., 1989—; vis. assoc. prof., researcher Entrepreneurial Studies Ctr. and Ctr. for Internat. Bus. Edn. and Rsch. UCLA, 1990—. Cons. editor: Asian Entrepreneur, 1989—; assoc. editor Entrepreneurship and Regional Devel., 1988—; contbr. articles to profl. jours. Recipient Outstanding Rsch. award 29th World Conf. on Small Bus., 1984; UK Advanced Mgmt. Programme Internat. Trust Durham U. Bus. Sch. Rsch. fellow, 1989; Salzburg Seminar fellow, 1987; Am. Participant Program U.S. Info. Agy. grantee, 1988. Methodist. Office: 120 Palos Verdes Blvd # A Redondo Beach CA 90277-5807

CARTÉ, GEORGE WAYNE, geophysicist, mayor; b. Buhl, Idaho, Sept. 8, 1940; s. Harold D. Carte and Reba E. (Lammert) Magoon; m. Katherine I. Williams, Sept. 8, 1962; children: Charles M., Theresa L., Jeannette M., Suzanne E. AAS, Columbia Basin Coll., Wash., 1962; BS in Geol. Engring., U. Idaho, 1964; postgrad. U. Hawaii, 1978-79. Hydraulic engr. U.S. Geol. Survey, Anchorage, 1964-66; seismologist AK Tsunami Warning Ctr., Palmer, Alaska, 1966—; instr. Mat-Su Community Coll., Palmer, 1971-72, 81. Mayor City of Palmer, 1981—; chmn. Palmer Planning and Zoning Commn., 1968-78; mem. Mat-Su Borough Planning Commn., 1975-78. Mem. Alaska Conf. of Mayors, 1982—, Mat-Su Borough Econ. Devel. Commn., 1989—; chmn. Palmer-Saroma Japan Sister City. Recipient cert. of achievement Anchorage Fed. Exec. Assocs., 1981, 87. Mem. Alaska Mcpl. League (bd. dirs. 1983—, pres. 1986-87, trustee joint ins. arrangement 1989—), Earthquake Engring. Rsch. Inst., Am. Geophys. Union, Tsunami Soc., Alaska Geol. Soc. Mem. Pentecostal Ch. Home: 367 N Valley Way Palmer AK 99645-6137 Office: 910 S Felton St Palmer AK 99645-6599

CARTER, DAVID J., Canadian provincial government official; b. Moose Jaw, Sask., Can., Apr. 6, 1934. BA, U. Manitoba, 1958; Licentiate in Theology, St. John's Coll., Winnipeg, 1961; D.Div., St. John's Coll., 1968; B. in Sacred Theology, U. B.C., 1968. Chaplain U. Calgary, 1965-69, So. Alta. Inst. Tech., 1965-69, Mount Royal Coll., 1965-69; dean Anglican Diocese of Calgary, 1969-79; with NOVA, Alta., 1982-86; rep. for Calgary Millican Alta. Legislature, 1979-82, rep. for Calgary Egmont, 1982-93, speaker, 1986-93; archivist Anglican Diocese of Calgary, 1966-88; senator U. Calgary, 1971-77. Rector Cathedral Ch. of the Redeemer, Calgary; hon. chmn. Lupus Erythematosus Soc. Alta.; dir. Trinity Place Found. Alta., Calgary Canucks Jr. Hockey Team, Calgary Exhbn. & Stampede 1986-90; founding chmn. Alta. Social Care Facilities Rev. Com., 1979-82; mem. numerous govt. and legis. coms.; spl. advisor Minister of Edn. Mem. Calgary C. of C., Commonwealth Parliamentary Assn. (pres. Alta. br., mem. exec. com. Can. region). Office: PO Box 39, Elkwater, AB Canada T0J 1C0

CARTER, DAVID LAVERE, soil scientist, researcher, consultant; b. Tremonton, Utah, June 10, 1933; s. Gordon Ray and Mary Eldora (Hirschi) C.; m. Virginia Beutler, June 1, 1953; children: Allen David, Roger Gordon, Brent Ryan. BS, Utah State U., 1955, MS, 1957; PhD, Oreg. State U., 1961. Soil scientist USDA Agrl. Research Service, Corvallis, Oreg., 1956-60; research soil scientist, line project leader USDA Agrl. Research Service, Weslaco, Tex., 1960-65; rsch. soil scientist USDA Agrl. Rsch. Svc., Kimberly, Idaho, 1965-68, supervisory soil scientist, rsch. leader, 1968-86, supervisory soil scientist, rsch. leader, dir., 1986—; cons., adviser to many projects and orgns. Contbr. articles to profl. jours.; author, co-author books. Recipient Emmett J. Culligan award World Water Soc. Fellow Am. Soc. Agronomy (cert.), Soil Sci. Soc. Am. (cert.); mem. Soil Conservation Soc. Am. (Soil Conservation award 1985), AAAS, Internat. Soc. Soil Sci., Western Soc. Soil Sci., CAST, Internat. Soc. Soil Sci., OPEDA. Mormon. Office: Siol & Water Mgmt Rsch USDA-ARS 3793 N 3600 E Kimberly ID 83341-9801

CARTER, DAVID S., psychology educator; b. Pasadena, Calif., Aug. 27, 1946; s. William S. and Barbara G. (Gerschler) C.; m. Gloria Alvarado; children: Benjamin Alvarado, Chelsea Alvarado. MA in Psychology, Calif. State U., Fullerton, 1975; PhD in Psychology, U. Calif., Riverside, 1980. Social sci. analyst U.S. Forest Svc., Riverside, 1979-80; prof. psychology Mont. Tech., Butte, 1980—; statis. cons. in psychol. testing. Contbr. articles to profl. jours. 1st lt. U.S. Army, 1966-69. Mem. Sigma Xi. Office: Mont Coll Mineral Sci/Tech HSS Dept Butte MT 59701

CARTER, EDWARD WILLIAM, retail executive; b. Cumberland, Md., June 29, 1911; s. S. and Rose P. C.; m. Christine Dailey; children: William Dailey, Ann Carter Huneke; m. Hannah Locke Caldwell, 1963. AB, UCLA, 1932; MBA cum laude, Harvard, 1937; LLD (hon.), Occidental Coll., 1962. Account mgr. Scudder, Stevens & Clark, L.A.; mdse. mgr. May Co., L.A.; chmn. emeritus bd. dirs. Carter Hawley Hale Stores, Inc., L.A.; bd. dirs. Stamford Rsch. Inst., Palo Alto, Calif., Businessmen's Council, N.Y.C., chmn. bd. regents U. Calif., Berkeley. Trustee Occidental Coll., Brookings Instn., L.A. County Mus. Art, Nat. Humanities Ctr. Com. Econ. Devel.; bd. dirs. Assocs. Harvard Grad. Bus. Sch., Stanford Rsch. Inst., Santa Anita Found., L.A. Philhar. Assn.; mem. vis. com. UCLA Grad. Sch. Mgmt.; mem. Woodrow Wilson Internat. Ctr. Coun., Havard Bd. Overseers Com. Depts. Econs., Art Mus. and Univ. Resources, Coun. on Fgn. Rels. Mem. Bus. Coun., Harvard U. Bus. Sch. Alumni Assn. (bd. dirs.). Clubs: Calif. (Los Angeles), Los Angeles Country; Pacific Union, Bohemian, Burlingame Country (San Francisco); Cypress Point (Pebble Beach). Office: Carter Hawley Hale Stores 12233 W Olympic Blvd Bldg 320 Los Angeles CA 90064-1060

CARTER, GARY LEE, artist; b. Hutchinson, Kans., Mar. 12, 1939; s. Phillip M. and Louise E. (Sloan) C.; m. MarLys Taylor, Feb. 6, 1976; children: Jeffrey T., Suzanne. AA, Southwestern Coll., 1968; BFA with honors, Art Ctr. Coll. of Design, 1971. Staff artist Art Works Design Studio, Tucson and La Jolla, Calif., 1971-72; Western artist Tucson, 1972-75; prin., owner Gary Carter Wester Art Lithography, West Yellowstone, Mont., 1975—. Featured in numerous mags. Adopted into Crow Tribe, 1991. Mem. Cowboy Artists of Am. (pres. 1986-87). LDS. Office: 12075 Marina Loop West Yellowstone MT 59758-9717

CARTER, JANE FOSTER, agriculture industry executive; b. Stockton, Calif., Jan. 14, 1927; d. Chester William and Bertha Emily Foster; m. Robert Buffington Carter, Feb. 25, 1952; children: Ann Claire Carter Palmer, Benjamin Foster. BA, Stanford U., 1948; MS, NYU, 1949. Pres. Colusa (Calif.) Properties, Inc., 1953—; owner Carter Land and Livestock, Colusa, 1965—; sec.-treas. Carter Farms, Inc., Colusa, 1975—. Author: If the Walls Could Talk, Colusa's Architectural Heritage, 1988; author, editor: Colusa County Survey and Plan for the Arts, 1981, 82, 83, Implementing the Colusa County Arts Plan, 1984, 85, 86. Mem. Calif. Gov.'s Commn. on Agr., Sacramento, 1979-82, Calif. Rep. Cen. Com., 1976—; del. Rep. Nat. Conv., Kansas City, Mo., 1976, Detroit, 1980, Dallas, 1984; trustee Calif. Hist. Soc., 1979-89, regional v.p., 1984-89; sec. Calif. Reclamation Bd., 1983—; mem. Heritage Preservation Com. City of Colusa, 1976—, chmn., 1977-83, vice chmn., 1983-91; bd. dirs. Colusa Community Theatre Found., 1980—, English Speaking Union, San Francisco, 1992— ; trustee Calif. Preservation Found., 1989—; trustee, bd. dirs. Leland Stanford Mansion Found., Sacramento, 1992—. Recipient award of Merit for Historic Preservation Calif. Hist. Soc., 1989, Design award Calif. Preservation Found., 1990. Mem. Sacramento River Water Contractors Assn. (exec. com. 1974—), Francisca Club, Kappa Alpha Theta. Episcopalian. Home and Office: 909 Oak St Colusa CA 95932-2229

CARTER, JANICE JOENE, telecommunications executive; b. Portland, Oreg., Apr. 17, 1948; d. William George and Charline Betty (Gilbert) P.; m. Ronald Thomas Carter, June 13, 1968; children: Christopher Scott, Jill Suzanne. Student, U. Calif., Berkeley, 1964, U. Portland, 1966-67, U. Colo., Boulder, 1967-68; BA in Math, U. Guam, 1970. Computer programmer Ga.-Pacific Co., Portland, 1972-74; systems analyst ProData, Seattle, 1974-79; systems analyst, mgr. Pacific Northwest Bell, Seattle, 1979-80; data ctr. mgr. Austin Co., Renton, Wash., 1980-83; developer shared tenent svcs. Wright-Runstad, Seattle, 1983-84; system adminstr. Hewlett-Packard, Bellevue, Wash., 1984; telecom. dir. Nordstrom, Inc., Seattle, 1984—; mem. large customer panel AT&T, Seattle, 1987—. Ski instr. Alpental, Snoqualmie Pass, Wash., 1984-87; bd. dirs. Educationally Gifted Children, Mercer Island, Wash., 1978-80; mem. curriculum com. Mercer Island Sch. Bd., 1992—; mem. Sweet Adelines. Mem. Telecom. Assn., Internat. Comm. Assn., System 85/ETN User Group. Office: Nordstrom Inc 1321 2d Ave Seattle WA 98101

CARTER, JOY EATON, electrical engineer, consultant; b. Comanche, Tex., Feb. 8, 1923; d. Robert Lee and Carrie (Knudson) Eaton; m. Clarence J. Carter, Aug. 22, 1959; 1 child, Kathy Jean. Student, John Tarleton Agrl. Coll., 1939-40; B Music cum laude, N. Tex. State Tchrs. Coll., 1943, postgrad., 1944-45; postgrad., U. Tex., 1945; MSEE, Ohio State U., 1949, PhDEE and Radio Astronomy, 1957. Engr. aide Civil Service Wright Field, Dayton, Ohio, 1945-46; instr. math. Ohio State U., Columbus, 1946-48, asst., then assoc. Rsch. Found., 1947-49, from instr. to asst. prof. elec. engring., 1949-58; rsch. engr. N.Am. Aviation, Columbus, 1955-56; mem. tech. staff Space Tech. Labs. (later TRW Inc.), Redondo Beach, Calif., 1958-68; sect. head, staff engr. electronics rsch. labs. The Aerospace Corp., El Segundo, 1968-72, staff engr. and mgr. system and terminals, USAF Satellite Communications System Program Office, 1972-77, mgr. communications subsystem Def. Satellite Communications System III Program Office, 1978-79; cons. Mayhill, N.Mex., 1979—. Active Mayhill Vol. Fire Dept.; bd. dirs. Mayhill Community Assn., 1988—, sec. bd. dirs. 1988—; co-chair music com. Mayhill Bapt. Ch., 1988—, trustee, 1989—; bd. dirs. Otero County Farm Bur., 1987—. Named Cow Belle of Yr. Otero Cow Belles, 1988. Mem. IEEE (sr., life), Am. Astron. Soc., Am. Nat. Cattle Women (sec. Otero CowBelles chpt. 1986-87, 1st v.p. 1988, historian 1989), Calif. Rare Fruit Growers, Native Plant Soc. N.Mex., Sacramento Mountains Hist. Soc. (bd. dirs. 1986—), Sun Country Walking Horse Assn., Sigma Xi (life), Eta Kappa Nu (life), Sigma Alpha Iota (life), Alpha Chi, Kappa Delta Pi, Pi Mu Epsilon, Sigma Delta Epsilon. Home and Office: PO Box 23 Mayhill NM 88339-0023

CARTER, L. PHILIP, neurosurgeon, consultant; b. St. Louis, Mo., Feb. 26, 1939; s. Russell G. and Dorothy Ruth (Zerwick) C.; m. Marcia L. Carlson, Aug. 26, 1960 (div. Apr., 1989); children: Kristin, Melinda, Chad Philip; m. Colleen L. Harrington, Oct. 20, 1990. MD, Wash. U., 1964. Active staff Barrow Neurol. Inst., Phoenix, 1976-88, dir. microsurg. lab., 1978-88, chief cerebral vascular surgery, 1983-88; prof. neurosurgery, chief neurosurg. svcs. Coll. Medicine U. Ariz., Tucson, 1988—; med. cons. Flowtronics, Inc., Phoenix, 1980—; vis. prof. Japan Neurosurg. Soc., Kyoto, 1983. Co-editor: Cerebral Revascularzation for Stroke, 1985; contbr. articles to profl. jours. Cons. Ariz. Head Injury Found., 1988—, Ariz. Epilepsy Found., 1973-75. Capt. USAF, 1965-67. Recipient Internat. Coll. Surgeons fellowship, 1973, Ariz. Disease Control for the Study of Treatment of Stroke grant, 1986. Fellow Am. Heart Assn., Am. Coll. Surgeons; mem. Ariz. Neurol. Soc. (sec., treas. 1985-91), Western Neurosurg. Soc. (program chmn. 1990), Am. Assn. Neurol. Surgeons, Rocky Mtn. Neurosurg. Soc. Republican. Home: 2701 E Camino Pablo Tucson AZ 85718-6625 Office: Univ Ariz Med Ctr 1501 N Campbell Ave Tucson AZ 85724-0001

CARTER, LARRY ALEXANDER, brokerage firm executive; b. Joplin, Mo., Nov. 9, 1940; s. Samuel E. and Laura L. (House) C.; m. Jan. 24, 1962 (div.); children: Larry Vince, Donna Diane, Mitchell Alexander; m. Gail Carter, Apr. 28, 1989; children: Jacques Gabriella. Student, Cerritos Coll., Long Beach State Coll., UCLA, Calif. Orange Coast Coll. Police officer South Gate (Calif.) Police Dept., 1963-65; narcotics expert Long Beach (Calif.) Police Dept., 1965-75; pvt. practice constrn., 1975-76; v.p., office mgr. Diversified Securities, Inc., El Toro, Calif., 1976-89; v.p. Diversified Securities, Inc., Crestline, 1989—; speaker in field. Recipient Calif. Commn. on Police Officer Standards and Tng. Advanced cert., 1974; named DSI Top Ten Mem., 1977—. Mem. Saddleback C. of C., Lake Arrowhead C. of C., Crestline C. of C., Narcotics Officers Assn., Crest Forest Community Assn. (dir.), Rotary. Republican. Baptist. Address: PO Box 3271 Crestline CA 92325 Office: 396-A Hartman Cir Cedar Pines Park CA 92322

CARTER, MARGARET L., legislator; b. La., Dec. 29, 1935; d. Emma Carter; 9 children. BA, Portland State U., 1972; MEd, Oreg. State U., 1973; postgrad., Washington State U. Community organizer, asst. dir. Community Action Agy., Shreveport, La.; tchr. Albina Youth Opportunity Sch., Portland; counselor Portland Community Coll.; mem. Oreg. Ho. of Reps., Salem, 1984—; mem. Joint Trade and Econ. Devel. com., 1985—, co-chair 1989—, Human Resources com., 1985, vice chair, 87, Edn. com., 1985, 87, 89, Conf. com. on Dr. Martin Luther King State Holiday, co-chair, 1985, Joint Health Care com. 1986. Founder, mus. dir. Joyful Sound Singers Piedmont Ch. Christ; vol. counselor various juvenile detention ctrs. and women's prisons, voter registration drives in Portland's black neighborhoods, Project Pride; organizer Oreg. chpt. of Sickle Cell Anemia Found.; founder Oreg. Black Leadership Conf.; mem. Oreg. State Commn. on Post Secondary Edn. and the Oreg. Alliance for Black Sch. Educators, Spl. Commn. for the Parole Bd. on the Matrix System; mem. Gov.'s Task Force on Pregnancy and Substance Abuse, 1989—, Coun. on Alcohol and Drugs, 1989—. Recipient Jeanette Rankin award Oreg. Women's Polit. Caucus, 1985. Mem. Nat. Organ. Black Legis. Elected Women (v.p. 1985), Nat. Black Caucus (exec. com.), Blacks in Gov. (regional pres.), Alpha Kappa Alpha. Democrat. Home: 2948 NE 10th Ave Portland OR 97212-3240 Office: Oreg State Legis H-478 State Capitol Salem OR 97310

CARTER, MARY ELIZABETH ARKLEY, author; d. Robert Pickering and Elizabeth May (Holzlin) Arkley; m. William P. Lyon III; children: William P. Lyon Carter, Robert A. Lyon Carter, Victoria Elizabeth Carter. Student, U. Oreg., Pitzer Coll., Claremont, Calif. Lectr. fiction Writers Workshop, U. Iowa, Iowa City, 1986-71, Grad. Program in Writing, Boston U., 1971-72, 78-81; fiction faculty MFA Writing Program Goddard Coll., Vt., Fall 1979; writer-in-residence Coll. of William and Mary, Williamsburg, Va., 1979-80; prof. creative writing U. Ariz., Tucson, 1981-90, dir. creative writing program, 1981-87; prof. internat. studies U. Ariz., London, 1986-90; faculty grad. summer program U. Puget Sound, Tacoma, 1971; freelance editor, book reviewer; literary cons. Author: A Fortune in Dimes, 1963, The Minutes of the Night, 1965, La Maestra, 1973, A Member of the Family, 1974, Tell Me My Name, 1975; author numerous short stories, book revs.; contbr. articles to profl. jours. Nat Endowment for Arts grantee, 1986; fellow MacDowell Colony, Peterborough, N.H., 1973, 74, 75, 77, 78, 80, Fondation Karolyi, Vence, France, 1973-74, 77, Va. for the Creative Arts, Wavertree, 1972-73, Ossabaw Found., Ga., 1973. Democrat. Anglican Ch.

CARTER, MELVIN WHITSETT (MEL CARTER), artist, educator; b. Ill., Nov. 19, 1941; s. Mallory and Claudia (Whitsett) C. BFA, U. Ill., 1963; MFA, U. Gunajuato, Mex., 1968. Tchr. art Denver Pub. Schs., 1963-68; instr. Fine Arts Community Coll., Denver, 1968-71; coord. Fine Arts Community Auraria, Denver, 1971-89; artist, instr. Art Students League Denver, 1987—; artist cons., bd. dirs. Cherry Creek Arts Festival, Denver, 1991-92. Exhibited numerous group shows and one-man shows, 1964-90; illustrator: Occupational Communications, 1969; artist with others (book) Figure Drawing Workshop, 1985. Commr. art Mayors Commr. Art, Culture, Film, 1992; artist advisor, bd. dirs. Cherry Creek Arts Festival, Denver, 1991. Sgt. USAF, 1959-61. Named Prof. Art, Colo. Community Colls. Abroad, Rome, Paris, London, 1970, Outstanding Educator Am., Bd. Dirs., Washington, 1974, State of Colo., 1987; recipient medal Excellence in Higher Edn., U. Tex., Austin, 1989; Fulbright scholar USIA, Netherland Am. Agy., 1987. Home: 1330 Gilpin St Denver CO 80218-2511 Office: Art Students League Denver 200 Grant St Denver CO 80203

CARTER, MICHAEL RAY, freelance artist, singer, composer; b. L.A., Dec. 2, 1953; s. Richard Eugene and Sarah Ann (Carter) C.; m. Janet Lynette Siefman, Sept. 15, 1978 (div. Apr. 1987). Student, Cypress (Calif.) Coll., 1976-77. Ind. collector, appraiser memorabilia and Am. oak antiques San Diego, 1965—, freelance artist,, 1976—; pres., founder M.R. Carter's Am. Character Co., San Diego, 1988—; co-chair programming and mktg. New Year's Love '91, Sea World, San Diego, 1990. Author poetry; songwriter, storyteller. Charter, founding mem. Gene Autry Western Herritage Mus., L.A., 1988; mem. Buffalo Bill Hist. Ctr., Cody, Wyo.; asst. nat. foreman Buck Jones Western Corral 1, Lompoc, Calif., 1989-90. Recipient 2d place award Ft. Verde Days Assn., Inc., 1985, art placement award Roy Rogers-Dale Evans Mus., 1986, best of show award UNISYS Corp., 1987, 90. Mem. Western Music Assn. (founding, voting mem. 1988), N.Am. Hunting Club (life, charter, founding), State of Liberty-Ellis Island Found. (charter). Internat. Platform Assn., Am. Lyceum Assn. Republican. Office: PO Box 27464 San Diego CA 92198-1464

CARTER, RICHARD BERT, church and retired government official; b. Spokane, Wash., Dec. 2, 1916; s. Richard B. and Lula Selena (Jones) C.; BA in Polit. Sci., Wash. State U., 1939; postgrad. Georgetown U. Law Sch., 1941, Brown U., 1944, Brigham Young U. Extension, 1975-76; m. Mildred Brown, Sept. 6, 1952; children: Paul, Mark, Janis, David. Advt. credit mgr. Elec. Products Consol., Omaha, 1939-40; pub. communications ofcl., investigator FBI, Washington, 1940-41, Huntington, W.Va., 1941, Houston, 1942, Boston, 1943, S. Am., 1943, Providence, 1944-45, N.Y.C., 1945, Salt Lake City, 1945, P.R., 1946-48, Phoenix, 1948-50, Washington, 1950-51, Cleve., 1952-55, Seattle, 1955-75, ret., 1975; assoc. dir. stake and mission pub. communications dept. Ch. Hdqrs., Ch. of Jesus Christ of Latter-day Saints, Salt Lake City, 1975-77. Dist. chmn. Chief Seattle coun. Boy Scouts Am., 1967-68, coun. v.p., 1971-72, coun. commr., 1973-74, nat. coun. rep., 1962-64, 72-74, area II, Eagle Scout Assn., 1984—. Mem. Freedoms Found. Valley Forge, Utah chpt., 1988—; bd. dirs. Salvation Army, 1963, United Way, 1962-63, mem. allocations com., 1962, 1987-88. Served to 1st lt., Intelligence Corps, U.S. Army, 1954. Recipient Silver Beaver award Boy Scouts Am., 1964, Vigil Honor, 1971; named Nat. Media Man-of-Month Morality in Media, Inc., N.Y.C., 1976. Mem. Profl. Photographers Am., Internat. Assn. Bus. Communicators, Am. Security Council (nat. adv. bd.), Internat. Platform Assn., Sons Utah Pioneers (pres. 1982, Disting. Svc. award 1985), SAR (pres. Salt Lake City chpt. 1987-88, Law Enforcement Commendation medal 1987, Meritorious Svc. medal 1989, Pres.-Gen.'s Program Excellence award, Oliver R. Smith medal 1990, Grahame T. Smallwood award 1990, Liberty medal 1991, Patriot medal 1992), Utah State Soc. (pres. 1989-90), Amicus Club (chmn. membership com. Deseret Found. 1988—, world sr. games adv. com. 1987—), William Carter Family Orgn. (nat. pres.), Nat. Assn. Chiefs of Police (Am. Police Hall of Fame, John Edgar Hoover Distin. Pub. Svc. medal 1991), Scabbard and Blade, Am. Media Network (nat. adv. bd.), Assn. Former Intelligence Officers, Alpha Phi Omega, Pi Sigma Alpha, Sigma Delta Chi, Phi Delta Theta. Mem. LDS Ch. (coord. pub. communications council Seattle area 1973-75, br. pres. 1944-45, dist. pres. 1954-55, high priest 1958—, stake pres. counselor 1959-64, stake Sunday Sch. pres. 1980-81, temple staff 1987—). Clubs: Bonneville Knife and Fork (bd. dirs. 1982-85), Rotary (dir., editor The Rotary Bee, 1982-83, Paul Harris fellow 1982, Richard L. Evans fellow 1987, Best Club History in Utah award 1988, Best Dist. Newsletter award 1983, Rotarian of Month 1988). Author: The Sunbeam Years-An Autobiography, 1986; assoc. editor FBI Investigator, 1965-75; contbg. author, editor: Biographies of Sons of Utah Pioneers, 1982; contbr. articles to mags. Home: 2180 Elaine Dr Bountiful UT 84010-3120

CARTER, ROBERT SPENCER, private investor; b. Oakmont, Pa., Aug. 18, 1915; s. Robert Spencer and Adele Rebecca (Crowell) C.; m. Cynthia Root, Dec. 31, 1937; children—Lief Hastings, Delight Carter Willing. B.A., Harvard U., 1937. Underwriter, Atlantic Mutual Ins. Co., N.Y.C., 1939-51; marine mgr. Gen. Ins. Co. of Am., Seattle, 1951-59; pvt. investor, Medina, Wash., 1959—. Author: Sail Far Away, 1978. Contbr. articles to profl. jours. Trustee, Archaeol. Inst. Am. Boston, 1980-87. Clubs: Cruising of Am., Seattle Yacht, Corinthian, Explorers.

CARTER, ROBERTA ECCLESTON, educator, therapist; b. Pitts.; d. Robert E. and Emily B. (Bucar) Carter; divorced; children: David Michael Kiewlich, Daniel Michael Kiewlich. Student Edinboro State U., 1962-63; BS, California State U. of Pa., 1966; MEd, U. Pitts., 1969; MA, Rosebridge Grad. Sch., Walnut Creek, Calif., 1987. Tchr., Bethel Park Sch. Dist., Pa., 1966-69; writer, media asst. Field Ednl. Pub., San Francisco, 1969-70; educator, counselor, specialist Alameda Unified Sch. Dist., Calif., 1970—; master trainer Calif. State Dept. Edn., Sacramento, 1984—; personal growth cons., Alameda, 1983—. Author: People, Places and Products, 1970, Teaching/Learning Units, 1969; co-author: Teacher's Manual Let's Read, 1968. Mem. AAUW, NEA, Calif. Fedn. Bus. and Profl. Women (legis. chair Alameda br. 1984-85, membership chair 1985), Calif. Edn. Assn., Alameda Edn. Assn., Charter Planetary Soc., Oakland Mus., Exploratorium, Big Bros. of East Bay, Alameda C. of C. (svc. award 1985). Avocations: aerobics, gardening, travel, tennis. Home: 1516 E Shore Dr Alameda CA 94501-5758

CARTER, THOMAS SMITH, JR., retired railroad executive; b. Dallas, June 6, 1921; s. Thomas S. and Mattie (Dowell) C.; m. Janet R. Hostetter, July 3, 1946; children: Diane Carter Petersen, Susan Jean, Charles T., Carol Ruth. B.S. in Civil Engring., So. Meth. U., 1944; MS in Engring. Mgmt., Kans. U., 1991. Registered profl. engr., Mo., Kans., Okla., Tex., La., Ark. Various positions Mo. Kans. Tex. R.R., 1941-44, 46-54, chief engr., 1954-61, v.p. ops., 1961-66; v.p. Kansas City So. Ry. Co., La. and Ark. Ry. Co., 1966—; pres. Kansas City So. Ry. Co., 1973-86, also bd. dirs., chmn. bd., 1981-91; pres. La. and Ark. Ry. Co., 1974-86, also bd. dirs., chmn. bd., 1981-91, chief exec. officer, 1981-91; bd. dirs. Kansas City So. Industries, Assn. Am. R.R.; adj. prof. Rockhurst Coll., 1992-93; instr. Johnson County Community Coll., 1992-93. Served with C.E. AUS, 1944-46. Fellow ASCE; mem. Am. Ry. Engring. Assn. (life), NSPE, Kansas City Club, Hide-A-Way Lake Club. Home: 1892 Woodhaven Dr Henderson NV 89014-0927

CARTER, WILLIAM GEORGE, III, army officer; b. Buffalo, June 18, 1944; s. William George Jr. and Elaine Ruth (Weber) C.; m. Linda Fay Yener, Oct. 2, 1965; children: Kris Ann, William George. BS, U. Tampa, 1972; MA, U. Shippensberg, 1982; MPE, U. Pitts., 1984. Commd. 2d. lt. U.S. Army, 1965, advanced through grades to maj. gen., 1992; various command and staff positions, 1964-77; exec. officer 3d Brigade, 1st Armored Div., Bamberg, Fed. Republic Germany, 1977-79; comdr. 1st Bn., 52d Inf., Bamberg, 1979-81, G3 1st Armored Div., VII U.S. Corps, Ansbach, Fed. Republic Germany, 1981-83; chief Plans and Integration Office, Hdqrs. U.S. Army, Washington, 1983-86; comdr. 1st Brigade, 4th Inf. Div., Ft. Carson, Colo., 1986-88; exec. asst. Office Chief of Staff Army, Washington, 1988-89; asst. div. comdr. 1st Inf. Div., Ft. Riley, Kans., 1989-91; comdr. Nat. Tng. Ctr., Ft. Irwin, Calif., 1991—. Decorated Legion of Merit with silver oak leaf cluster, Bronze Star with V device and two oak leaf clusters, Purple Heart with two oak leaf clusters. Mem. Soc. of the Big Red One, Alpha Chi. Office: HHC Nat Tng Ctr Fort Irwin CA 92310

CARTIER, CAROL JEAN MCMASTER, social worker; b. Spokane, Wash., Sept. 11, 1954; d. Gilbert Clayton and Thelma L. (Wentworth) McMaster; m. Robert Alan Cartier, Sept. 20, 1986. AA, Green River Community Coll., Auburn, Wash., 1976; BSW, Ea. Wash. U., 1981, MSW, 1983. Cert. social worker, Wash. Counselor Family Counseling Svcs., Spokane, 1983-84; med. social worker Harbors Home Health Svcs., Aberdeen, Wash., 1984—; case mgr. AIDS prevention program and maternity support svc. Grays Harbor County Health Dept., Aberdeen, 1989—; social worker III Wash. State Dept. Health Svc., Aberdeen, 1989-90; cons. Grays Harbor County Health Dept., 1989-90. Vol. sta. supr. Sr. Companion Program, Aberdeen, 1986—, mem. adv. bd., 1985—; facilitator People Living with AIDS Support Group, Aberdeen, 1989—. Fellow Ea. Wash. U. Alumni Assn.; mem. NASW, Ocean Shores C. of C., Ocean Shores Community Club. Home: PO Box 1352 Ocean Shores WA 98569-1352 Office: Grays Harbor County Health Dept 2109 Sumner Ave Aberdeen WA 98520-3600

CARUSO, MARK JOHN, lawyer; b. L.A., Apr. 27, 1957; s. John Mondella and Joyce Dorothy (Baldi) C.; m. Judy F. Velarde, Aug. 15, 1987. BA, Pepperdine U., 1979, JD, 1982. Bar: Calif. 1982, U.S. Dist. Ct. (cen. dist.) Calif. 1982, U.S. Ct. Appeals (9th cir.) 1983, N.Mex. 1987, U.S. Dist. Ct. N.Mex. 1987, U.S. Ct. Appeals (10th cir.) 1987. Pvt. practice, Burbank, Calif., 1982—, Albuquerque, 1987—; mem. House labor com., House consumer and pub. affairs com., workers compensation oversight interim com., ct., correction and justice interim com. Col., aide-de-camp to gov. State of N.Mex., 1987; chmn. N.Mex. Mcpl. Boundary Commn., 1988—; del. Rep. Nat. Conv., 1988, 92; mem. jud. com. house labor com., workers compensation oversight com. N.Mex. Ho. of Reps., 1990, 92, 93. Recipient platinum award N.Mex. Free Enterprise Adv., 1986. Mem. Albuquerque Hispano C. of C., Greater Albuquerque C. of C. Office: 4302 Carlisle Blvd NE Albuquerque NM 87107-4811

CARVER, FRANK GOULD, theology educator; b. Crookston, Nebr., May 27, 1928; s. Frank Alonzo and Greeta G. (Gould) C.; m. Betty Joan Ireland, Mar. 31, 1949; children: Mark Erwin, Carol Denise. BA, Taylor U., 1950; BD, Nazarene Theol. Sem., 1954; MTh, Princeton Theol. Sem., 1958; PhD, New Coll., U. Edinburgh, Scotland, 1964. Pastor Ch. of Nazarene, Kimball, Nebr., 1954-56, Edison, N.J., 1956-58, Edinburgh, Scotland, 1959; from asst. to full prof. Pasadena/Point Loma (Calif.) Nazarene Coll., 1961—, chmn. dept. philosophy and religion, 1967-82, 1991—, dir. grad. programs in religion, 1981—, dir. summer ministries, faculty officer, 1986-89; Mem. numerous coms. including curricular exceptions, academic policy, coun. on ednl. policy and program, graduate studies, profl. devel., rank and tenure and many others Point Loma Nazarene Coll., San Diego, Calif.; guest prof. Olivet Nazarene Coll., fall 1972, Nazarene Theol. Sem., 1976, 79, 81, 85, Nazarene Theol. Coll., S. Africa, 1979, Inst. Biblico Nazareno Ensenada, Mex., 1987; mem. Ch. Growth Symposium, 1978-79; mem. curriculum com. Enduring Word Series, 1976-80; many lecturing positions. Author: Peter the Rock Man, 1973, Matthew Part One: To Be a Disciple, 1984, Matthew Part Two: Come. . .and Learn From Me, 1986, The Cross and the Spirit: Peter and the Way of the Holy, 1987; editor: Thank God and Take Courage, 1992; contbr. articles to profl. jours.; editorial bd. Lockman Found., 1961—. Tchr. adult Sunday Sch. Pasadena First Ch. Nazarene, San Diego First Ch. Nazarene, 1961-89. Mem. Inst. Biblical Rsch. (West Coast chmn. 2 terms, nat. exec. com. 2 terms), Soc. Biblical Lit., Wesleyan Theol. Soc. (1st v.p. 1985-86, pres. 1986-87), Evangel. Theol. Soc. Home: 403795 Porte De Palmas San Diego CA 92122-5135 Office: Point Loma Nazarene Coll 3900 Lomaland Dr San Diego CA 92106-2810

CARVER, JOHN GUILL, physicist; b. Mt. Juliet, Tenn., Feb. 10, 1924; s. Henry Gilliam and Inez (Cook) C.; m. Elva Emily Kattelman, Apr. 21, 1956; children: John Jr., Linda Lee, Karen Emily, Susan Aline. BS in Physics, Ga. Inst. Tech., 1950; MS, Yale U., 1951, PhD, 1955. Registered profl. elec. engr., Ohio, registered profl. nuclear engr., Calif. Field svc. engr. Philco Corp., Phila., 1946-48; nuclear engr. dept. atomic power equipment Gen. Electric, Cin., 1955-60; nuclear engr., mgr. irradiations physics Gen. Electric, San Jose, Calif., 1960-67; mgr. advanced rsch. Rockwell Internat., Downey, Calif., 1967-72; supr. electro-optics Rockwell Internat., Seal Beach, Calif., 1972-78; prin. engr. Rockwell Internat., Downey, 1978-84; prin. cons. Rockwell Internat., Seal Beach, 1984-89; cons. in electro-optical physics Karsulin Enterprises, Orange, Calif., 1989—. Contbr. articles to profl. jours. Elder Forest Dale Ch. of Christ, Cin., 1957-60, Valley Ch. of Christ, Livermore, Calif., 1964-67, East Anaheim (Calif.) Christian Ch., 1969—. 1st lt. USAAF, 1943-46. Rockefeller Found. fellow, 1955-56. Fellow AAAS, AIAA (assoc.); mem. Am. Phys. Soc., Soc. Photo-Optical Instrumentation Engrs., N.Y. Acad. Scis., Am. Nuclear Soc. Office: Karsulin Enterprises PO Box 3774 Orange CA 92665

CARVER, JUANITA, plastic company executive; b. Indpls., Apr. 8, 1929; d. Willard H. and Golda M. Ashe; children: Daniel Charles, Robin Lewis, Scott Alan. Cons. MOBIUS, 1983— ; pres. Carver Corp., Phoenix, 1977—. Bd. dirs. Scottsdale Meml. Hosp. Aux., 1964-65, now assoc. Republican. Methodist. Patentee latch hook rug yarn organizer. Home: 9866 Reagan Rd # 126 San Diego CA 92126

CASALS, ROSEMARY, professional tennis player; b. San Francisco, Sept. 16, 1948. Profl. tennis player, 1968—; nat. championships and major tournaments include U.S. Open singles (finalist), 1970, 71, U.S. Open doubles, 1967, 71, 74, 82, U.S. Open mixed doubles, 1975, Wimbledon doubles, 1967, 68, 70, 71, 73; nat. championships and major tournaments include Wimbledon mixed doubles, 1971, 73, finalist with Dick Stockton, 1976; finalist with Dick Stockton Italian doubles, 1967, 70; finalist with Dick Stockton Family Circle Cup (winner), 1973, Wightman Cup, 1967, 76-81; Wightman Cup Bridgeston doubles championships (finalist), 1975, Spalding mixed doubles, 1976, 77, U.S. Tennis Assn. Atlanta doubles, 1976, Fedn. Cup, 1967, 76-81; winner 1st Virginia Slims tournament, 1970; 3d place Virginia Slims Championships, 1976, 4th place, 1977, 78; winner Murjani-WTA championship, 1980; Fla. Fed. Open doubles, 1980; pres. sports promotion co. Sportswoman, Inc., Sausalito, Calif., 1981—; Mem. Los Angeles Strings team, World Team Tennis, 1975-77. Virginia Slims Event tennis winner, 1986, doubles winner (with Martina Navratilova), 1988, 89. Mem. Women's Internat. Tennis Assn. (bd. dirs.). Office: Sportswoman Inc PO Box 537 Sausalito CA 94966-0537

CASANI, JOHN RICHARD, electrical engineer; b. Phila., Sept. 17, 1932; s. John Charles and Julia Jean (Bateman) C.; divorced; 1 son, John Charles; m. J. Lynn Seitz, Dec. 13, 1969; children: Jason, Josh, Drew. BSEE, U. Pa., 1955, DSc, 1992. Spacecraft mgr. Jet Propulsion Lab., Pasadena, Calif., 1966-70, project mgr. Mariner Mars 69, 1970-71, spacecraft mgr. Mariner Venus Mercury, 1971-73, div. mgr. guidance and control, 1973-75, Voyager project mgr., 1975-77, Galileo project mgr., 1977-88, asst. lab. dir., 1988—. Recipient Exceptional Svc. medal, NASA, 1965, Outstanding Leadership medal, 1974, 81. Fellow AIAA (Space Systems award 1979, Astronautics Engr. award 1981); mem. NAE, Internat. Acad. Astronautics. Republican. Roman Catholic. Home: 281 S Orange Grove Blvd Pasadena CA 91105-1748 Office: Jet Propulsion Lab 4800 Oak Grove Dr Pasadena CA 91109-8099

CASARREAL, KENIA MARIA, management and organization consulting executive; b. Manzanillo, Oriente, Cuba, Jan. 3, 1946; came to U.S., 1946; d. Diego Casarreal and Amelia Suarez; m. Leo Clouser, Dec. 26, 1965 (div. 1975); m. Jacob Adajian, Nov. 11, 1987; children: Leo and Kimberly (twins). BA in Indsl. Sociology summa cum laude, Marion Coll.; M in Counseling Psychology and Spl. Edn., Calif. State U., L.A.; M in Statis. Measurements, Calif. State U.; PhD in Orgnl. Psychology, Claremont Grad. Sch.; postdoctoral studies, UCLA. Head Health Care Devel. div. TransAm. Life Cos., 1986-88; sr. v.p. Primary Prevention Program The Louis Pasteur Inst., 1988; founder, pres. K. C. Assocs., 1988—; pvt. cons. in field. Apptd. to Nat. Insts. Sci.-Nat. Ctr. for Health Svc. Rsch., 1985; bd. dir. AIDS Project, L.A., 1989—; mem. Friends of L.A. Commn. Status for Women, 1989—; mem. Health Ptnrs. Weingut Ctr., 1992. Fellow Claremont Grad. Sch., 1980. Mem. APA, Am. Planning Assn., Am. Assn. Healthcare Execs., Assn. Mgmt. Design, Am. Mgmt. Assn. Office: K C Assocs 2209 Live Oak Dr W Los Angeles CA 90068

CASCIO, WAYNE FRANCIS, human resource and management educator, consultant, researcher; b. Jamaica, N.Y., Mar. 2, 1946; s. Frank Bernard and Rose Joan (Ingrao) C.; m. Dorothy Meyers, Aug. 23, 1975; 1 child: Joseph Francis. BA, Holy Cross Coll., 1968; MA, Emory U., 1969; PhD, U. Rochester, 1973. Diplomate Am. Bd. Profl. Psychology, 1980. Asst. prof. to assoc. prof. Fla. Internat. U., 1973-80; vis. assoc. prof. psychology and mgmt. U. Calif.-Berkeley, 1980-81; prof. mgmt. U. Colo. Denver, 1981—; vis. scholar U. Pa., 1987-88; vis. prof. U. Geneva, 1991-92. Author: Applied Psychology in Personnel Management, 4th edit. 1991; Human Resources Management: An Information Systems Approach, 1981; Costing Human Resources: The Financial Impact of Behavior in Organizations, 3d edit., 1991; Managing Human Resources: Productivity, Quality of Worklife, Profits, 3d edit., 1992. Mem. editorial bd. Asia Pacific HRM, 1990—, Human Performance, 1987—, Organizational Dynamics, 1989—. Served to 1st lt. USNG, 1969-75. Recipient award for excellence in research and creative endeavor U. Colo., 1983, 90. Fellow Am. Psychol. Assn.; mem. Acad. Mgmt. (Disting. Faculty award 1988), Soc. Indsl. and Orgnl. Psychology (pres. 1992-93). Republican. Roman Catholic. Home: 24353 Paragon Pl Golden CO 80401-9221 Office: 1250 14th St Denver CO 80204-5300

CASCIOLA, STEVEN GEORGE, personal care and beauty industry executive; b. Detroit, Mar. 25, 1948; s. Guy and Josephine (Tarantino) C.; m. Anne Ryan, June 17, 1989. Ariz. State. Profl. singer, 1964-73; pres. Fashion Media, Inc., Seattle, 1975-81; sales/ed. mgr. Vidal Sassoon, Inc., L.A., 1982-83; dir. creative svcs. Image Labs, L.A., 1983-86; industry cons. S.C. Communications, L.A., 1986-91; nat. sales dir. Alexia Alexander, Inc., L.A., 1991—; cons. various mags. and industry orgns. Contbr. articles to profl. jours. Mem. So. Calif. Rsch. Lodge, Grand Lodge State Calif. (committeeman, past master assn), Burbank Masonic Lodge ((worshipful master 1992), Internat. Platform Assn., Pasadena Scottish Rite (officer 1988-93), Philos. Rsch. Soc. (vol. 1982-88), Veritat Orgn. Inc. (cons. 1986-88).

Republican. Roman Catholic. Home: 616 S Burnside Ave Apt 202 Los Angeles CA 90036-3978

CASE, DOUGLAS NELSON, student services specialist; b. Chgo., Dec. 20, 1954; s. Ronald Nelson and Anna Jean (Brown) C. BSBA with honors, San Jose State U., 1976; postgrad., San Diego State U., 1977-78. Coord. frat. and sorority life San Diego State U., 1978—. Bd. dirs. Project Concern Internat., 1974-82; active ACLU, 1978—; pres. Coll. Area Community Coun., 1989-90, mem. coun., 1980-90; parliamentarian San Diego County Dem. Ctrl. Com., 1987—; pres. San Diego Dem. Club, 1991-92; del. Dem. Nat. Convention, 1992; bd. dirs. Lobby for Individual Freedom and Equality, 1987—, Gay and Lesbian Alliance Against Defamation, San Diego, 1993—; mem. Mayor's Adv. Bd. on Gay and Lesbian Issues, San Deigo, 1992; mem. Calif. Dem. State Ctrl. Com., 1991—. Named Citizen of the Yr.-Coll. Area, Mid-City C. of C., 1990; recipient Community Svc. aard Coll. Area Com. Coun., 1988, Doug Scott Polit. Action award, 1990, City Coun. Spl. Commmendation San Diego City Coun., 1990. Mem. ACLU (San Diego Decade Club award, 1992), Am. Coll. Pers. Assn., Nat. Assn. Student Pers. Adminstrs., Assn. Frat. Advisors, Inc. (treas. 1987-90, nat. pres. 1990-91), Uptown Dem. Club (pres. 1993), Kappa Sigma (nat. scholarship commn. 1987—). Home: 5444 Reservoir Dr Apt 20 San Diego CA 92120-5144 Office: San Diego State U Housing & Residential Life Office San Diego CA 92182

CASE, JAMES BOYCE, physical scientist; b. Lincoln, Ill., Oct. 26, 1928; s. Richard Warren and Blanch Irene (Boyce) C.; m. Clare Karlin Criger, Sept. 20, 1958 (dec. Mar. 1983); 1 child, James Christian. Student, Oreg. State Coll., 1946-47; BS, Stanford U., 1950; MS, Ohio State U., 1957, PhD, 1959. Cartographer Inter-Am. Geodetic Survey, Costa Rica, Brazil, 1950-55; photogrammetrist Broadview Rsch. Corp., Washington, 1960-61; prin. scientist Autometric Corp., Alexandria, Va., 1961-71; physical scientist Def. Mapping Agy., Washington, 1971-89; editor in chief Am. Soc. for Photogrammetry and Remote Sensing, Bethesda, Md., 1975—. Co-author (books) Manual of Photogrammetry, 1966, Manual of Photogrammetry, 1980, Handbuch der Vermessunskunde, 1972. Chair Iron County Dem. Com., Cedar City, Utah, 1991—. Am. Geographical Soc. rsch. fellow, 1957-58; NSF rsch. grantee, 1959. Fellow The Royal Geographical Soc.; mem. AAAS, AARP (pres. Cedar City chpt. 1992-93), Kiwanis, The Photogrammetric Soc. (hon.); mem. emeritus The Soc. of the Sigma Xi, Am. Soc. for Photogrammetry and Remote Sensing. Home: PO Box 1669 Cedar City UT 84721-1669

CASE, LEE OWEN, JR., college official; b. Ann Arbor, Mich., Nov. 5, 1925; s. Lee Owen and Ava (Comin) C.; m. Dolores Anne DeLoof, July 1950 (div. Feb. 1958); children: Lee Douglas, John Bradford; m. Maria Theresia Breninger, Feb. 27, 1960; 1 adopted dau., Ingrid Case Dunlap. AB, U. Mich., 1949. Editor Washtenaw Post-Trib, Ann Arbor, 1949; dir. pub. rels. Edison Inst., Dearborn, Mich., 1951-54; field rep. Kersting, Brown, N.Y.C., 1954-58; campaign dir. Cumerford Corp., Kansas City, Mo., 1958-59; v.p. devel., pub. rels. U. Santa Clara, 1959-69; v.p. planning, devel., Occidental Coll., L.A., 1969-90; ret.; bd. visitors South Western U. Law Sch., L.A., 1981—; mem. Sr. Cons. Network. Chmn. Santa Clara City Proposition A, 1966; mem. Santa Clara County Planning Com. on Taxation and Legis., Santa Clara, 1968. Served to 1st lt. USAAF, 1943-46. Mem. Am. Coll. Pub. Relations Assn. (bd. dirs. 1968-74), Council for Advancement and Support Edn. (founding bd. dirs. 1974-75), 1st Tribute for Distinction in Advancement, Dist. VII, 1985), Santa Clara C. of C. (pres. 1967), Santa Clara County C. of C. (founding bd. dirs. 1968), Town Hall. Republican. Club: University (Los Angeles). Lodge: Rotary. Home and Office: 2633 Risa Dr Glendale CA 91208-2355

CASELLA, LYNN FRANCISCO, communications executive, educator; b. Salinas, Calif., Aug. 22, 1940; d. Cyrus Peter Francisco and Barbara (Kent) Lievsay; m. Joseph Anthony Casella, June 28, 1969; children: Christina Lynn, Kelly Jo. AA, Pasadena (Calif.) City Coll., 1963; BA, UCLA, 1966; MA, U. La Verne, 1987. Cert. secondary English/history tchr., Calif. Tchr., English and history Pasadena City Schs., 1967-68; tchr., English, photo publs. L.A. City Schs., 1968-84; tchr., English Upland (Calif.) High Sch., 1984-86; market communications mgr. San Antonio Community Hosp., Upland, 1986-89; lectr. Calif. State U., Pomona, 1988-89; free-lance writer various, 1985-86, 89—; dir. fund devel. communications Hoag Hosp. Found., Newport Beach, Calif., 1990-92; pub. Lynn F. Casella Communications, Upland, 1988—; advt. exec. Uber Advt. and Design, Upland, 1992—; tchr. English, photog. publs. Rialto (Calif.) Unified Schs., 1992—; nat. judge Columbia U., Scholastic Press, N.Y.C., 1984-85; market comm. mgr. San Antonio Community Hosp., 1986, 89; secondary tchr. Chaffey Joint Union High Sch. Dist., Ontario, Calif., 1984-86; lectr. Calif. Poly Tech., Pomona, 1988-89, others. Editor: The Man and the Mountain: Sydney Laurence's Mt. McKinley, 1990; bus. editor Elan mag., 1988; editor/writer various newsletter, 1990; contbr. hist. articles to jours. Candidate Upland Unified Sch. Dist. Bd. Edn., 1989; publicity specialist Inland Empire Ad Club, Claremont, Calif., 1988-89. Recipient first place publ. Med. Mktg. Assn., Upland, 1989. Mem. Nat. Assn. Hosp. Devel., Nat. Soc. Fund Raising Execs. Home: 2081 N Palm Ave Upland CA 91784-1476 Office: Eisenhower High Sch 301 Newport Blvd 1321 N Lilac Rialto CA 92376

CASERIA, CAROL SHULER, elemenatry school educator; b. Marion, Kans., Dec. 25, 1919; d. Harry Elston and Edith May (Mosher) Shuler; m. Armando Caseria, Feb. 20, 1943; children: Priscilla, Philip, Jeffrey. BA, Wichita State U., 1941; MA, U. of Redlands, 1966. Cert. elem. edn., standard supervision. Tchr. English, history Nortonville (Kans.) High Sch., 1941; file clk. Dept. of Agr., Lincoln, Nebr., 1942; clk. typist Air Transport Command, Gravelly Point, Va., 1942-43; prin., tchr. Nursery-Kindergarten, Ft. Myer, Va., 1947-51; kindergarten tchr. Weisbaden (Fed. Republic Germany) Am. Nursery Kindergarten, 1953-55; prin. tchr. St. Michael's Kindergarten, Arlington, Va., 1956-60; tchr. kindergarten Edison Elem. Sch., Redondo Beach, Calif., 1960-63; tchr. kindergarten, 1st-2nd grades Grand Terrace (Calif.) Elem., 1963-65; intern supr. Liason Calif. State U., Colton, 1965, 66, 68; tchr. Colton Joint Unified Sch. Dist., 1965—. Aide-participant White House Golden Ann. Conf. on Children and Youth, Washington, 1960. Mem. NEA, Calif. Tchrs. Assn., Am. Colton Educators (rep.), AAUW, Panhellenic, Beta Sigma Phi, Alpha Phi. Home: 26037 Holly Vista Blvd San Bernardino CA 92404-3516 Office: Lincoln Elem Sch 444 E Olive St Colton CA 92324-2799

CASERIO, MARJORIE CONSTANCE, academic administrator; b. London, Feb. 26, 1929; came to U.S., 1953; d. Herbert C. and Doris May (House) Beckett; m. Frederick F. Jr. Caserio, Mar. 9, 1957; children: Brian, Alan. BSc in Chemistry, U. London, 1950; MA in Organic Chemistry, Bryn Mawr Coll., 1951, PhD in Organic Chemistry, 1956. Rsch. chemist Fulmer Rsch. Inst., Buckinghamsnire, Eng., 1952-53; post-doctoral fellow Calif. Inst. Tech., Pasadena, 1956-59, sr. rsch. fellow, 1959-65; from. asst. prof. to prof. chemistry U. Calif., Irvine, 1965-90, chair dept. chemistry, 1987-90; vice-chancellor academic affairs U. Calif., San Diego, 1990—. Contbr. articles to profl. jours. Recipient Cert. of Achievement, Leadership of Women Orange County, 1983; Sir John Dill scholar, 1950; Fulbright travel award, 1950; Guggenheim fellow, 1975-76. Fellow AAAS; mem. Am. Chem. Soc. (Garvan medal 1975) Grad. Women in Sci. (hon.), Sigma Xi. Office: U Calif San Diego Acad Affairs 0001 La Jolla CA 92093

CASEY, BARBARA A. PEREA, state representative, educator; b. Las Vegas, N.Mex., Dec. 21, 1951; d. Joe D. and Julia A. (Armijo) Perea; m. Frank J. Casey, Aug. 5, 1978. BA, N.Mex. U., 1972; MA, Highland U., Las Vegas, N.Mex., 1973. Instr. N.Mex. Highlands U., Las Vegas, 1972-74; tchr. Roswell Ind. Schs., Roswell, N.Mex., 1974—; mem. N.Mex. Ho. of Reps., 1984—; instr. N.Mex. Mil. Inst., Roswell, 1977-82, Roswell Police Acad., 1984. Mem. NEA (Adv. of of Yr.), AAUW, Am. Bus. Women's Assn., N.Mex. Endowment for Humanities. Democrat. Roman Catholic. Home: 1214 E 1st St Roswell NM 88201-7960

CASEY, DENETTE C., health club owner; b. Cleve., Oct. 5, 1954; d. James Charles Sr. and Elizabeth Louise (Clark) C.; children: Shakir Aswad Johnson, Asha Chelise Johnson. Student, Ohio State U., 1974; AA, Mohegan C.C., 1976; BA, Golden State U., 1986. Co-owner Transcontinental Photographic Enterprises, Balt. and San Diego, 1979-87; pers. asst. civilian Pers., Hickam AFB, Hawaii, 1983-85; adminstrs. asst. Naval Ocean Systems Ctr., San Diego, 1985-88; adminstr. San Diego State U., 1988—; owner, operator Sasha's Internat., San Diego, 1989—, Sasha's Internat. Health and Fitness Club, San Diego, 1992—. Freelance writer small bus. series Voice and Viewpoint, 1990-91. CEO Oak Park Little League, San Diego, 1987-89; program coord. Bus. League of Balt., 1981-82; founder, coord. bus. directory Bayview Bapt. Ch., San Diego, 1990-91; mem. adv. bd. African Am. Women's Conf., 1992—. Baptist. Home: 8751 Vista Del Oro Way San Diego CA 92104

CASEY, JOHN THAYER, artist, retired educator; b. New London, Conn., June 27, 1931; s. John Joseph and Marguerite Virginia (Whitney) C.; m. Patricia Carolyn Park, Aug. 4, 1956 (div. Dec. 1980); children: Kathleen Gail, Brian Wayne; m. Florine Anne Ferguson Dixon, Oct. 13, 1990. BA, U. Oreg., 1958; MFA, Calif. Coll. Arts and Crafts, 1962; postgrad., San Jose State Coll., 1962-63. Teaching scholar Calif. Coll. Arts and Crafts, Oakland, 1961-62; assoc. prof. art Western Oreg. State Coll., Monmouth, 1965-88, assoc. prof. emeritus, 1988—; vis. instr. Oreg. State U., Corvallis, summer 1966. Exhibited in group shows Denver Art Mus., 1962, Oakland Art Mus., 1963, Seattle Art Mus., 1967, 71, Portland Art Mus., 1969-72; one-man shows include Oreg. State U., Corvallis, 1966, Salishan Lodge Gallery, Gleneden Beach, Oreg., 1972, Western Oreg. State Coll., Monmouth, 1987; represented in permanent collections Coos Art Mus., Coos Bay, Oreg., U. Oreg., Sch. Architecture and Allied Arts, Eugene, Oreg., State of Oreg., Salem, Pendleton, Monmouth. Bd. dirs. Mid-Valley Arts Coun., Salem, Oreg., 1986-89. Staff sgt. USAF, 1950-54. Democrat. Unitarian. Home: 2125 Oak Grove Rd NW Salem OR 97304-9511

CASEY, JOSEPH T., corporate executive; b. 1931; married. B.S., Fordham U. With Arrow Surgical Supply Co., 1947-51, Am. Lumbermen's Mutual Casualty Co. of Ill., 1951-52, Thoroughbred Racing Protective Bur. Inc., 1952-55; mgr. audits Touche, Ross, Bailey & Smart, 1955-63; controller Litton Industries Inc., Beverly Hills, Calif., 1963-67, v.p. fin., 1967-69, sr. v.p. fin., 1969-76, exec. com., exec. v.p. fin., 1976-91, vice chmn., chief fin. officer, 1991—. Office: Litton Industries Inc 360 N Crescent Dr Beverly Hills CA 90210-4867

CASEY, MARK EVAN, environmental services executive; b. St. Louis, July 1, 1954; s. John Louis C. and Myra Alice (Lovan) Tourville; m. Jennifer S. Tseng, Aug. 31, 1986; children: Caroline, Evan. BS, U. Mo., 1976; MBA, U. Va., 1983. Project mgr. Trammell Crow Co., Charlotte, N.C., 1983-85; pres. NC Properties, Inc., Ft. Collins, Colo., 1986-89, Risk Removal, Inc., Ft. Collins, 1989—; bd. dirs. NC Properties, Inc.; adj. faculty Colo. State U., Ft. Collins, 1988-89. Active City Water Bd., Ft. Collins, 1988—; grad. Leadership Ft. Collins, 1987-88. Capt. USMC, 1976-81. Democrat. Mem. Christian Ch. Home: 900 W Oak St Fort Collins CO 80521 Office: Risk Removal Inc PO Box 2106 Fort Collins CO 80522-2106

CASEY, PATRICIA CAROLYN, social worker; b. Roseburg, Oreg., Aug. 27, 1936; d. Clarence Wayne and Mary Elizabeth (Frederick) Park; m. John Joseph Casey, Aug. 4, 1956 (div. 1980); children: Kathleen, Brian; m. Mark Preston Siegel, Mar. 14, 1987. BA in Social Work, San Francico State U., 1962; MSW, Portland State U., 1989. Caseworker Santa Clara County Welfare, San Jose, Calif., 1962-63; community svc. worker Mid Willamette Valley Community Action Agy., Salem, Oreg., 1974-78; asst. dir. Marion Polk Yamhill Coun. on Aging, Salem, 1978-83; teen mother program dir. YWCA, Salem, 1984-87; counselor Clackamas Family Ct. Svc., Oregon City, Oreg., 1987-88; social work intern VA Hosp., Portland, Oreg., 1988, Oreg. Health Scis. U., Portland, 1988-89; med. social worker Salem Hosp., 1989—; commr. Polk County Welfare Dept., Dallas, Oreg., 1964-67; planning coun. MWV Manpower Consortium, Salem, 1975-83. Producer: (TV program) Sr. Citizens Today, 1980-81; prodn. coord.: (documentary films) Special Special, 1981, Conspiracy of Silence, 1981. Commr. Marion-Polk Boundary Commn., Salem, 1977-81; mem. Oreg. Women's Polit. Caucus, Salem, 1987—. Named Outstanding Young Woman of Am., 1970. Mem. Nat. Assn. Social Workers, City Club. Democrat. Unitarian. Home: 482 Ewald Ave SE Salem OR 97302-4700 Office: Salem Hosp PO Box 14001 Salem OR 97309-5014

CASEY, PATRICK ANTHONY, lawyer; b. Santa Fe, Apr. 20, 1944; s. Ivanhoe and Eutimia (Casados) C.; m. Gail Marie Johns, Aug. 1, 1970; children: Christopher Gaelen, Matthew Colin. BA, N.Mex. State U., 1970; JD, U. Ariz., 1973. Bar: N.Mex. 1973, U.S. Dist. Ct. N.Mex. 1973, Ariz. 1973, U.S. Ct. Appeals (10th cir.) 1979, U.S. Supreme Ct. 1980. Assoc. firm Bachicha & Corlett, Santa Fe, 1973-75; assoc. firm Bachicha & Casey, Santa Fe, 1975-77; pvt. practice law, Santa Fe, 1977—. Bd. dirs. Santa Fe Sch. Arts and Crafts, 1974, Santa Fe Animal Shelter, 1975-81, Cath. Charities of Santa Fe, 1979-82, Old Santa Fe Assn., 1979-88; bd. dirs. United Way, 1986-89, N.Mex. State U. Found., 1985—. With USN, 1961-65; Vietnam. Mem. Assn. Trial Lawyers Am. (state del. 1988-89, bd. govs. 1990-91, 93—), ABA, Western Trial Lawyers Assn. (bd. dirs. 1988—, parlimentarian 1990-91, gov. 1987-90, treas. 1991-93), N.Mex. Trial Lawyers Assn. (dir. 1977-79, 85—, treas. 1979-83, pres. 1983-84), Bar Assn. 1st Jud. Dist. (pres. 1980), Am. Legion, VFW, Vietnam Vets. of Am., Elks, Rotary. Office: 1421 Luisa St Ste Q Santa Fe NM 87501-4073

CASEY, THOMAS CLARK, trust company executive; b. Akron, Ohio, Dec. 17, 1929; s. Thomas W. and Portia (Clark) C.; m. Tanya Seely, July 2, 1958; children: Tate, Doug, John, Gary, Brad, Nina, Mimi, Tom W. BA, Bowdoin Coll.; MBA, Stanford U.; cert. fin. svcs. counselor, Northwestern U. Sales rep. Acushnet Co., New Bedford, Mass., 1953-55, Reeves Rubber Co., San Clemente, Calif., 1957-59; gen. mgr. Polymer Corp., Santa Ana, Calif., 1956-61; from trust officer to pres. 1st Am. Trust Co., Santa Ana, 1965—. Bd. overseers Bowdoin Coll., 1989—, bd. dirs. Hoag Meml. Hosp., 1982—; chmn. Orange County com. So. Calif. Bldg. Fund, 1986—; co-chmn. capital expenditure rev. com. United Way, 1982—; sec., bd. dirs. Hoag Hosp. Found., 1988—; bd. dirs. Newport Ctr. Assn., 1976—, pres., 1979; past pres. bd. trustees Mesa Unified Sch. Dist., 1974-75. Mem. L.A. Soc. Fin. Analysts, Calif. Bankers Assn., Orange County Soc. Investment Mgrs., Newport-Irvine Estate Planning Coun., Orange County Fin. Soc. (founding bd. dirs.). Office: 1st Am Trust Co 2161 San Joaquin Hills Rd Newport Beach CA 92260

CASH, R. D., natural gas and oil executive; b. Shamrock, Tex., 1942. BSIE, Tex. Tech U., 1966. With Amoco Prodn. Co., 1966-76; v.p. Mountain Fuel Supply Co. subs. Questar Corp., 1976-79, pres., CEO, 1980-84, now also chmn. bd.; pres. Wexpro Co., 1979-80; pres., CEO Questar Corp., 1984—, also chmn. bd., 1985—. Office: Questar Corp 180 E First S St Salt Lake City UT 84111-1502*

CASHATT, CHARLES ALVIN, retired hydro-electric power generation company executive; b. Jamestown, N.C., Nov. 14, 1929; s. Charles Austin and Ethel Buren (Brady) C.; m. Wilma Jean O'Hagan, July 10, 1954; children: Jerry Dale, Nancy Jean. Grad. high sch., Jamestown. Bldg. contractor, Jamestown, 1949-50; 1954-58; powerhouse foreman Tri-Dam Project, Strawberry, Calif., 1958-66; power project mgr. Merced Irrigation Dist., Calif., 1966-92; ret. 1992; mem. U.S. com. large dams, 1988-92. Contbr. articles to ASCE pub. and books. Pres. Merced County Credit Union, 1981-82. Served with USAF, 1950-54. Mem. Am. Legion. Republican. Lodge: Elks, Odd Fellows.

CASHMAN, MICHAEL RICHARD, small business owner; b. Owatonna, Minn., Sept. 26, 1926; s. Michael Richard and Mary (Quinn) C.; m. Antje Katrin Paulus, Jan. 22, 1972 (div. 1983); children: Janice Katrin, Joshua Paulus, Nina Carolin. BS, U.S. Mcht. Marine Acad., 1947; BA, U. Minn., 1951; MBA, Harvard U., 1953. Regional mgr. Air Products & Chems., Inc., Allentown, Pa., 1959-64; then pres. so. div. Air Products & Chems., Inc., Washington, 1964-68; mng. dir. Air Products & Chems., Inc. Europe, Brussels, 1968-72; internat. v.p. Airco Indsl. Gasses, Brussels, 1972-79; pres. Continental Elevator Co., Denver, 1979-81; assoc. Moore & Co., Denver, 1981-84; prin. Cashman & Co., Denver, 1984—. Creator continental walking baton, 1987. Committeeman Denver Rep. Com., 1986—, congl. candidate, 1988; chmn. "Two Forks or Dust" Ad Hoc Citizens Com.. Lt. (j.g.) USN, 1953-55. Mem. Bdlg. Owners and Mgrs. Assn., Colo. Harvard Bus. Sch. Club, Royal Golf de Belgique, Belgian Shooting Club, Rotary, Phi Beta Kappa. Home: Apt 802 2512 S University Blvd Denver CO 80210-6152

CASILLAS, MARK, lawyer; b. Santa Monica, Calif., July 8, 1953; s. Rudolph and Elvia C.; m. Natalia Settembrini, June 2, 1984. BA in History, Loyola U., L.A., 1976; JD, Harvard U., 1979. Bar: N.Y. 1982, Calif. 1983. Clk. to chief judge U.S. Ct. Appeals (10th cir.), Santa Fe, 1979-80; assoc. Breed, Abbott & Morgan, N.Y.C., 1980-82; counsel Bank of Am. Nat. Trust and Savs. Assn., San Francisco, 1982-84; assoc. Lillick & Charles, San Francisco, 1984-87, ptnr., 1988—; counsel Internat. Bankers Assn. in Calif., L.A., 1984-89. Mng. editor Harvard Civil Rights-Civil Liberties Law Rev., 1978-79. Mem. ABA (apptd. mem. airfin. subcom. 1991—), N.Y. Bar Assn., Calif. Bar Assn. (vice-chmn. fin. instn. com. 1987-88), Internat. Bar Assn., The Japan Soc., Bankers Club. Office: Lillick & Charles 2 Embarcadero Ctr San Francisco CA 94111-3807

CASKIE, WILLIAM WIRT, accountant, securities broker; b. N.Y.C., May 9, 1945; s. John Minor and Rosa Maria (Marchese) C.; BS in Physics, Georgetown U., 1967; MBA in Ops. Research, NYU, 1970; BS magna cum laude in Acctg., Golden Gate U., 1976. Tchr. math. N.Y.C. pub. schs., 1968-71; statistician Fed. Res. Bank of San Francisco, 1972-74; pvt. practice acctg., Marina Del Rey, Calif., 1977—; registered rep. Fin. Network Investment Corp., 1986-92, H.D. Vest Fin. Svcs., 1993—. Mem. Assn. Bus. and Tax Cons., Nat. Assn. Enrolled Agts., Calif. Soc. Enrolled Agts., Mensa, Fin. Network Investment Corp. (registered rep.). Home and Office: 557-1/2 Washington Blvd Marina Del Rey CA 90292-5438

CASPE, NAOMI, children's entertainer, educator; b. Colorado Springs, Colo., Apr. 21, 1954; d. Leonard and Neva Jean (Hayutin) C.; m. Douglas Kim Kipping, Aug. 26, 1990. BA, Mills Coll., 1987. Cert. storyteller. Owner Jester Enterprises and The Magic Makers, Oakland, Calif., 1982—; tchr. Oakland Mus., 1992—. Artist: (book) Facepainting, 1991 (Parents Choice award 1991), video mime Bodybonding, 1990. Nat. Women's Book grantee, San Francisco, 1987. Mem. Nat. Assn. for Perpetuation of Storytelling, World Clown Assn. Office: Magic Makers 564 Melrose Ave San Francisco CA 94127

CASPER, GERHARD, university president, law educator; b. Hamburg, Germany, Dec. 25, 1937; s. Heinrich and Hertha C.; m. Regina Koschel, Dec. 26, 1964; 1 child, Hanna. Legal state exam., U. Freiburg, U. Hamburg, 1961; LL.M., Yale U., 1962; Dr.iur., U. Freiburg, Germany, 1964. Asst. prof. polit. sci. U. Calif., Berkeley, 1964-66; assoc. prof. law and polit. sci. U. Chgo., 1966-69, prof., 1969-76, Max Pam prof. law, 1976-80, William B. Graham prof. law, 1980-87, William B. Graham Disting. Svc. prof. law, 1987-92, dean law sch., 1979-87, provost, 1989-92; prof. law Stanford (Calif.) U., 1992—, pres., 1992—; vis. prof. law Cath. U., Louvain, Belgium, 1970, U. Munich, 1988, 91; bd. dirs. Ency. Britannica. Author: Realism and Political Theory in American Legal Thought, 1967, (with Richard A. Posner) The Workload of the Supreme Court, 1976; co-editor: The Supreme Ct. Rev., 1977-91. Fellow Am. Acad. Arts and Scis.; mem. Internat. Acad. Comparative Law, Am. Bar Found. (bd. dirs. 1979-87), Coun. Fgn. Rels., Am. Law Inst. (coun. 1980—), Oliver Wendell Holmes Devise (permanent com. 1985—).

CASPY, BARBARA JANE, social worker; b. N.Y., Jan. 11, 1945; d. Harold Brooks Mandel and Lillian (Metzger) Rost; m. Avram Caspy, Apr. 24, 1966; children: Nick Walker, Karen Caspy Nielsen. BA, Bklyn. Coll., 1966; MSW, Rutgers U., 1984. Lic. clin. social worker, Nev. Family counselor Family Svc. Agy. Princeton, N.J., 1984; pvt. practice clin. social work Princeton, 1985-87; social worker Trenton (N.J.) Psychiat. Hosp., 1987-89; clin. social worker So. Nev. Adult Mental Health Svcs., Las Vegas, Nev., 1989-92, Irwin Lehrhoff and Assocs., Las Vegas, 1992—; social work cons. Family Infant Resource Ctr., Princeton, 1985-88; group facilitator Rutgers Med. Sch. Sexuality Seminar, Piscataway, N.J., 1984-87. Mem. Nat. Assn. Social Workers (diplomate clin. social work), Nat. Rifle Assn. (life).

CASSENS, NICHOLAS, JR., ceramics engineer; b. Sigourney, Iowa, Sept. 8, 1948; s. Nicholas and Wanda Fern (Lancaster) C.; B.S. in Ceramic Engring., Iowa State U., 1971, B.S. in Chem. Engring., 1971; M.S. in Material Sci. and Engring., U. Calif., Berkeley, 1979; m. Linda Joyce Morrow, Aug. 30, 1969; 1 son, Randall Scott, Jr. research engr. Nat. Refractories and Minerals Corp., Livermore, Calif., 1971-72, research engr., 1972-74, sr. research engr., 1974-77, staff research engr., 1977-84, sr. staff research engr., 1984—. Mem. Am. Ceramic Soc. Democrat. Patentee in field, U.S., Australia, S.Am., Japan, Europe. Home: 4082 Suffolk Way Pleasanton CA 94588-4117 Office: 1852 Rutan Dr Livermore CA 94550-7635

CASSIDY, CHARLES PHILIP, construction contractor; b. Needham, Mass., Aug. 31, 1937; s. Philip Irving and Viola Dorathea (Lindoff) C.; m. Pat Chaingtong, July 16, 1976 (div. July, 1981); 1 child, William; m. Billie Sue Llewellyn, Sept. 12, 1981; children: Crystal, Christopher. Grad., Air War Coll., 1976; BA, Chapman Coll., 1977; M in Aero. Sci., Embry-Riddle Aero. U., 1986. Commd. 2d lt. USAF, 1958, advanced through grades to lt. col., 1975, served as pilot, world wide, Vietnam Vet., ret., 1987; owner Sheetrock Svcs., Eagle River, Ark., 1990—; acad. advisor continuing edn. Embry-Riddle Aero. U., 1987—. Author tng. manual for B-52 maintenance officers, 1980. Decorated Air medal with one oak leaf cluster, 1969. Republican. Episcopalian. Home: 10917 Gakona Cir Eagle River AK 99577-8238

CASSIDY, DEVALLO FRANCIS, film manager, writer, consultant; b. Chgo., June 7, 1937; s. DeVallo Francis and Catherine Mary (Crowe) C. Grad., St. Mary's Coll., Winona, Minn., 1959. Advt. writer, planner Cada Inc., Chgo., 1964-65; head divsn. writer McMaster Carr Supply Co., Chgo., 1966-79; prodn. coord. 7-West, Hollywood, Calif., 1979, Osmond Prodns., Hollywood, Calif., 1980-82; prodn. mgr. Colman Group Inc., Hollywood, Calif., 1982-88, Rapport Films Inc., Hollywood, Calif., 1988-90, Stiles-Bishop Prodns. Inc., Hollywood, Calif., 1982—; dir. various community and regional theatres, Chgo., suburbs, Ill., 1964-79; cons. plays, various waiver theaters, L.A., 1982-88; cons. film, TV, various independent Prodn. Cos., L.A., 1982—. Author, editor Skunk Hollow Ski Mag., 1972-73; author Combat Survival soft books, 1962-63 (Best in AF 1963), articles in Popular Science, 1972, Popular Mechanics, Poetry Review, 1972,74. With USAF, 1960-64. Mem. Am. Film Inst., Nat. Geographic Soc., Smithsonian Inst. (Nat. Assocs.). Roman Catholic. Office: Stiles Bishop Prodns Inc 3255 Bennett Dr Los Angeles CA 90068

CASSIDY, DONALD LAWRENCE, former aerospace company executive; b. Stamford, Conn., May 26, 1933; s. John Dingee and Ursula Agnes (Lynch) C. BS, MIT, 1954; grad. mgmt. policy inst., U. Southern Calif., L.A., 1973. Jr. exec. Johns-Manville Corp., N.Y.C., 1954-55; contracting officer U.S. Army Signal Corps Electric Lab., Ft. Monmouth, N.J., 1955-57; with contract dept. field svc. and support div. Hughes Aircraft Co., L.A., 1957-69, mgr. contracts support systems, 1969-78; dir. contracts Hughes Aircraft Co., Long Beach, Calif., 1978-87, group v.p. bus. ops., 1987, v.p., chief contracts officer, 1987-92. 1st lt. U.S. Army, 1955-57. Mem. Am. Def. Preparedness Assn. (L.A. chpt. bd. dirs.), Nat. Contract Mgmt. Assn., Nat. Security Indsl. Assn., Aerospace Industries Assn. (procurement finance coun. exec. group). Republican. Office: Hughes Aircraft Co 7200 Hughes Terr Westchester CA 90045

CASSIDY, RICHARD ARTHUR, environmental engineer, governmental water resources specialist; b. Manchester, N.H., Nov. 15, 1944; s. Arthur Joseph and Alice Ethuliette (Gregoire) C.; m. Judith Diane Maine, Aug. 14, 1971; children: Matthew, Amanda, Michael. BA, St. Anselm Coll., 1966; MS, U. N.H., 1969, Tufts U., 1972. Field biologist Pub. Service Co. of N.H., Manchester, 1968; jr. san. engr. Mass. Div. Water Pollution Control, Boston, 1968-69; aquatic biologist Normandeau Assocs., Bedford, N.H., 1969-70; hydraulic engr. New Eng. div. U.S. Army C.E., Waltham, Mass., 1971-77, environ. engr., Portland Dist., Oreg., 1977-81, supr., environ. engr., 1981—. Contbr. articles to books and profl. jours. Den leader Pack 164 and 598 Columbia Pacific council Cub Scouts Am., Beaverton, Oreg., 1982-83, Webelos leader, 1984-85, 90-91, troop 764 committeeman, 1985-87, asst. scoutmaster, 1992, scoutmaster, 1993-, Columbia Pacific council Boy Scouts Am., 1985-87; mem. Planning Commn. Hudson, N.H., 1976-77. Recipient commendation for exemplary performance Mo.-Miss. flood, 1973, commendation for litigation defense, 1986, commendation for mgmt. activities, 1987, 91. Mem. Am. Inst. Hydrology (cert., profl. ethics com. 1986, v.p. Oreg. sect. 1987-89, pres. Oreg. sect. 1990-92), Internat. Tng in Communication (pres. West Way Club 1989-90), N.Am. Lake Mgmt. Soc. Democrat. Roman Catholic. Home: 7655 SW Belmont Dr Beaverton OR 97005-6335 Office: Portland Dist CE Chief Reservoir Reg and Water Quality Sect-PO Box 2946 Portland OR 97208

CASSIDY, SAMUEL H., lawyer, state legislator; children: Rachael Kathryn, Sarah Woyneve, Samuel H. IV. BA, U. Okla., 1972; JD, U. Tulsa, 1975; postgrad., Harvard U., 1991. Bar: Okla., 1975, U.S. Supreme Ct. 1977, U.S. Ct. Appeals (10th cir.), 1977, Colo. 1982. Ptnr. Cassidy, Corely & Ganem, Tulsa, 1975-77, Seigel, Cassidy & Oakley, Tulsa, 1977-79, Beustring, Cassidy, Faulkner & Assocs., Tulsa, 1979-82; pvt. practice Pagosa Springs, Colo., 1982—; mem. Colo. State Senate, 1991—; bd. dirs. Capital Reporter; instr. U. Tulsa, 1978-81, Tulsa Jr. Coll., 1979; owner High Country Title Co.; developer Townhome Property, Mountain Vista; ptnr. Wee Share Internat., 1987-89, Hondo's Inc.; pres., Sam Cassidy, Inc.; mem. agriculture and natural resources com. 1991-92, state, military and vet. affairs com., 1991-92, local govt. com. 1991, legal svcs. com. 1991-92, hwy. legislative review com. 1991-93, nat. hazards mitigation coun., 1992-93, appropriations com., 1993, judiciary com., 1993 ; adv. bd. Colo. Econ. Devel., 1993; exec. com. legis. coun., 1993, senate svcs. com. 1993; elected Senate Minority Leader, exec. com. Colo. Gen. Assembly. Mem. State Dem. Ctr. Com., 1987—; mem. steering com. Clinton/Gore campaign. Named Outstanding Legislator for 1991 Colo. Bankers Assn.,; recipient Outsatnding Legis. Efforts award Colo. Counties, Guardian of Small Bus. award, NFIB; fellow Gates Found., 1991. Mem. Colo. Bar Assn., S.W, Colo. Bar Assn., Nat. Conf. State Legis. (Colo. rep., task force on state-tribe rels.), Rotary (hon. mem., sustaining Paul Harris fellow), Club 20 (chmn. bd. dirs.), San Juan Forum. Office: State Senate PO Box 129 Pagosa Springs CO 81147

CASTAGNETTO, PERRY MICHAEL, retail sales executive; b. San Francisco, Jan. 22, 1959; s. William Joseph and Patricia Mary (Williams) C. BA, San Jose State U., 1985. Lic. real estate agt., Calif. Asst. mgr. Emerald Hills Golfland, San Jose, 1978-85; dept. mgr. Orchard Supply Hardware, San Jose, 1987—; owner, pres. Castagnetto Enterprises, San Jose, 1991—. Mem. Kappa Sigma (Outstanding alumni 1985, 87). Home: 450 Avenida Arboles San Jose CA 95123-1428

CASTAIN, RALPH HENRI, physicist; b. L.A., Nov. 23, 1954; s. Henry Ulrich and Anni (Springmann) C.; m. Cynthia Ellen Nicholson, Dec. 28, 1976; children: Kelson, Alaric. BS in Physics, Harvey Mudd Coll., 1976; MS in Physics, Purdue U., 1978, MSEE in Robotics, PhD in Nuclear Physics, 1983. Sr. engr. Harris Semiconductor, Palm Bay, Fla., 1978-79; mem. staff Jet Propulsion Lab., Pasadena, Calif., 1983-84; mem. staff Los Alamos (N.Mex.) Nat. Lab., 1984-92, chief scientist nonproliferation and arms control, 1992—; cons. Jet Propulsion Lab., Pasadena, 1984-91. Editor, contbr. to Dept. Energy Office Arms Control publs. Recipient Maths. award Bank of Am., 1972, Gold Seal, State of Calif., 1972; Calif. State scholar, 1972-76. Mem. IEEE, Am. Phys. Soc., Internat. Neural Network Soc., VLSI Spl. Interest Group (chmn. electronics com.). Home: 431 Bryce Ave Los Alamos NM 87546-3605 Office: Las Alamos Nat Lab NAC MS-F650 Los Alamos NM 87545

CASTANEDA, OMAR SIGFRIDO, creative writing educator; b. Guatemala, Guatemala, Sept. 6, 1954; came to U.S. 1957; s. Hector-Neri and Miriam (Mendez) C.; m. Mary L. Slater, July 13, 1972 (div. Dec. 1978); children: Omar C., Bleu C.; m. Jill C. Jepson, Aug. 11, 1984 (div. Jan. 1991). BA, Ind. U., 1980, MFA, 1983. Assoc. instr. Ind. U., Bloomington, Ind., 1980-83; fgn. expert Beijing Tchrs. Coll., Beijing, Republic China, 1983-84; vis. asst. prof. Rollins Coll., Winter Park, Fla., 1985-88; vis. asst. prof. Western Wash. U., Bellingham, 1989-90, asst. prof., 1990-92; assoc. prof., 1992—. Author: Cunuman, 1987, Among the Volcanoes, 1991, Abuela's Weave, 1993, Remembering to Say Mouth or Face, 1993; contbr. articles to profl. jours. Sgt. USAF, 1972-76. NEA Orgnl. grantee, 1992-93; recipient Fulbright, 1989-90, Critchfield, Rollins Coll., Winter Pk., Fla., 1988, Fla. Arts grant, Fla. State Div. Cultural Affairs, 1988-89, Ernest Hemingway fellowship, Ind. U., Bloomington, Ind., 1980-81. Mem. MLA, Associated Writing Programs, Soc. Children's Book Writers. Home: 910 20th St Apt 304 Bellingham WA 98225-6773 Office: Western Wash U Eng Dept Bellingham WA 98225

CASTBERG, EILEEN SUE, construction company owner; b. Santa Monica, Calif., Mar. 12, 1946; d. George Leonard and Irma (Loretta) Conroy; m. David Christopher Castberg, Oct. 27, 1967; children: Eric, Christopher. Grad. high sch., U. High Sch., L.A., 1964; certificate, Anthony Schs., 1990. Lic. real estate agt., Calif. Exec., co-founder Advanced Connector Telesis, Inc., Santa Ana, Calif., 1986-87; exec. Western Energy Engrs., Inc., Costa Mesa, Calif., 1987-89; owner Dave Castberg and Assoc., Inc., Ramona, Calif., 1989 --; cons. Watt Asset Mgmt., Santa Monica, 1990-91. Mem. choir Ramona Luth. Ch.; 3d v.p. Holy Cross Luth. Ch. Women's League, Cypress, Calif., 1983. Mem. San Diego Bd. Realtors, Ramona Real Estate Assn., Intermountain Rep. Women's Fedn. (pres.), Ramona Christian Women's Club. Republican.

CASTEEL, CHERYL THEODORA, security officer; b. Dallas, Oct. 11, 1955; d. Richard Lee Taylor and Robbie Roy (Collins) Bowling; m. James A. Grade, June 18, 1977 (div. 1980); 1 child, James Robert Grade; m. James L. Casteel, Dec. 13, 1980 (dec. 1991); children: Janice, Marjeen, Sabrina, Thresea, Terris (dec.); 1 adopted child, Dawn; 1 stepdaughter, Shawna. AA, Cochise Coll., Sierra Vista, Ariz., 1981. Sec. Batchelder Ins., Sierra Vista, 1973-77; truck driver J&C Trucking, Sierra Vista, 1977-79; sec. Dental Clinic, Fort Huachuca, Ariz., 1979-81; bus. mgr. Mr. Photo, Sierra Vista, 1980; paraprofl. Buena High Sch., Sierra Vista, 1981-89, day security officer, 1989—. Actress Tombstone Vigilantes and Tombstone Vigilets, 1986—. Coach Spl. Olympics, Sierra Vista, 1982-88; sec., treas. Anonymous Program, 1984-86; foster parent for Cochise County, 1983-86; advisor Vocat. Industries of Am., Sierra Vista, 1980-91; chmn. Jim Casteel Scholarship Fund, Sierra Vista, 1991—. Named Outstanding Vocat. Industries Clubs Am. advisor for Ariz., 1983, Nat. Outstanding VICA advisor for Ariz., 1985. Mem. NEA, Ariz. Ednl. Assn. (Outstanding Young Woman of Am. 1987). Democrat. Baptist. Home: PO Box 937 Sierra Vista AZ 85636

CASTELLANI, VICTOR, foreign language and literature educator, wine consultant; b. Bklyn., Feb. 14, 1947; s. Anthony Joseph and Frances Agnes (Pajer) C.; m. Cheryl Ann Beauford; children: Stephen Beauford, Julia Beauford. BA in Greek and Latin, Fordham Coll., 1968; PhD in Classics, Princeton U., 1971. Adj. instr. Fordham U., Bronx, N.Y., 1970-71; instr. U. Denver, 1971-72, asst. prof., 1972-80, assoc. prof., 1980—, dir. classical studies, 1973—, chmn. dept. fgn. langs. and lits., 1981-85, 89—. Coll./univ. educators adv. coun., Denver Ctr. Theatre Co., 1993—. Contbg. editor Rocky Mountain Wine Guide, Littleton, Colo., 1983-85; contbr. articles, revs. and papers to profl. jours., books and confs.; leader Denver Wine Symposia, 1980—. Democratic precinct committeeman, Denver, 1980-82. Recipient Book award Columbia Tchrs. Coll., N.Y.C., 1968; NDEA Title IV and Princeton U. nat. fellow, 1968-71; Colo. Humanities Program project planning grantee, Denver, 1984, ACLS Travel grantee, 1990, NEH grantee, 1992. Mem. Am. Philological Assn., Am. Classical League, Am. Assn. for Italian Studies, MLA, Philological Assn. Pacific Coast, Classical Assn. Middle West and South, Rocky Mountain MLA (pres. 1984), ProRiesling Verein (Trier, Germany). Democrat. Roman Catholic. Home: 1901 S High St Denver CO 80210-3313 Office: Univ Denver Dept Fgn Langs and Lits Denver CO 80208

CASTELLANO, JOSEPH ANTHONY, chemist, management consulting firm executive; b. N.Y.C., Oct. 28, 1937; s. Joseph John and Marie Antoinette (Gallo) C.; m. Rosalie Ann Fantaci, Aug. 28, 1960; children: Joseph, Thomas, Laura. BS in Chemistry, CCNY, 1959; MS in Chemistry, Poly. Inst. N.Y., 1964, PhD in Chemistry, 1969. Cert. profl. chemist; cert. community coll. instr. Research chemist Witco Chem. Co., Paterson, N.J., 1959-62; sr. research chemist Thiokol Chem. Corp., Denville, N.J., 1962-65; mem. tech. staff, project mgr. RCA Labs., Princeton, N.J., 1965-73; chmn., CEO Princeton Materials Sci., 1973-75; ops. mgr. Fairchild Camera and Inst. Corp., Palo Alto, Calif., 1975-77; mgr. ops. Kylex, Mt. View, Calif., 1977-78; pres. Stanford Resources, San Jose, Calif., 1978—; cons. scientist Princeton U., 1970-72; lectr. Rutgers U., Kent State U., SUNY-Binghamton, NASA Research Ctr., USAF Materials Lab., Office Naval Research, IBM Research Ctrs., RCA Labs., Motorola and various profl. and trade assns. Author: Handbook of Displa Technology, 1992; editor Electronic Display World, The Electronic Display Industry Service; contbr. articles to profl. jours.; patentee in field. Recipient RCA Doctoral Study award, RCA Labs. Outstanding Achievement award Indsl. Rsch. mag.'s IR-100 award, David Sarnoff Team award in Sci. Fellow Am. Inst. Chemists; mem. AAAS, Am. Chem. Soc., Am. Assn. Advancement Sci., N.Y. Acad. Sci., Royal Chem. Soc., Soc. Info. Display, Profl. and Tech. Cons. Assn., Soc. Tech. Comm., N.Y. Acad. Sci., Sigma Xi. Roman Catholic. Home: 7017 Elmsdale Dr San Jose CA 95120-3225 Office: Stanford Resources Inc PO Box 20324 San Jose CA 95160-0324

CASTELLANO, MICHAEL ANGELO, research forester; b. Bklyn., June 26, 1956; s. Biagio and Mildred Anne (Cucco) C.; m. Elizabeth Marie Phillips, July 14, 1979; children: Nicholas Aaron, Daniel Robert Feller, Kelly Marie, Katlyn Morgan. AAS, Paul Smiths Coll., 1978; BS, Oreg. State U., 1982, MS, 1984, PhD, 1988. Forest technician Weyerhauser Co., Columbus, Miss., 1979; forester trainee USDA Forest Svc., Pacific N.W., Corvallis, Oreg., 1980-84, forester, 1984-87, rsch. forester, 1987—; cons. CSIRO, Div. of Forestry, Australia, 1988-92, Spanish-Am. Binational Prog., Barcelona, 1987, 91. Author: Key to Hypogeous Fungi, 1989, (agr. handbook) Mycorrhizae, 1989; contbr. articles to profl. jours. Bishop LSD Ch. Named one of Outstanding Young Men, Am. JayCees, 1984. Mem. Soc. Am. Foresters, N.Am. Truffling Soc. (advisor), Soil Ecology Soc., Mycol. Soc. of Am. (nomenclature 1986), Sigma Xi. Home: 1835 NW Garfield Ave Corvallis OR 97330-2535 Office: USDA Forest Svc 3200 SW Jefferson Way Corvallis OR 97331-4401

CASTER, SEAN CAUTHERS, industrial engineer, consultant; b. Goleta, Calif., June 28, 1970; s. John Corbett and Angela Louise (Parker) C. BA in Anthropology, Stanford U., 1992, BS in Indsl. Engring., 1992. Data analyst Earthcalc, Inc., Modesto, Calif., 1988; mktg. and planning intern Inland Fisher Guide-GM, Warren, Mich., 1991; indsl. engr. McMaster-Carr Supply Co., Santa Fe Springs, Calif., 1992—; project cons. Silicon Graphics, Mountain View, Calif., 1991-92. Recipient Champion-Acad. Decathlon award County of Stanislaus-Edn., 1988. Mem. Inst. Indsl. Engrs., Sigma Nu (rush chmn. 1990-92). Democrat. Home: 524 S Catalina # B Redondo Beach CA 90277 Office: McMaster-Carr Supply Co 9630 Norwalk Blvd Santa Fe Springs CA 90670-2392

CASTLE, ALFRED, administrator; b. Washington, Dec. 22, 1948; m. Mary Ann Slagle (div. 1979). BA, Colo. State U., 1971, MA, 1972; postgrad., U. N.Mex., Columbia U., 1980, U. N.Mex. Chmn., div. humanities Sunset Hill Sch., Kansas City, 1973-75; teaching asst. U. N.Mex., Alburquerque, 1975; prof., history N.Mex. Mil. Inst., Roswell, 1976-83; exec. dir. NMMI Fedn. N.Mex. Mil. Inst., 1983-87; v.p. devel. Hawaii Pacific U., Honolulu, 1987—; trustee Samuel N. and Mary Castle Found., Honolulu, 1987—, pres.-elect, 1992—; trustee Acad. Pacific, Honolulu, 1987—, Hawaiian Hist. Soc., Honolulu, 1988—. Author: Century of Philanthropy, 1992; contbr. articles to profl. jours., chpts. to books. Trustee, Hawaii Food Bank, Honolulu, 1987—, Hawaii Sch. Girls, Honolulu, 1987—, Henry Dorothy Castle Fund, Robert Black Mem. Trust. NEH fellow, 1978, 79-80, 81, 86, 91, Hoover fellow, 1983, 86, 90, 93, Coolidge fellow, 1988. Mem. Assn. Grantmakers Hawaii, Govrs. Coun. Children Youth, Coun. Founds. Episcopalian. Home: 725 Kapiolani Honolulu HI 96813 Office: Hawaii Pacific U 1188 Fort Street Mall Honolulu HI 96813-2713

CASTLE, CHRISTIAN LANCELOT, lawyer; b. Houston; s. James Christian and Mary Margeret (Barord) C.; m. Katherine Isobel Charleson, June 30, 1987. BA magna cum laude, UCLA, 1983, MBA, JD, 1987. Bar: Calif. 1988. Assoc. Loeb and Loeb, L.A., 1987-89, Cooper,Epstein and Hurewitz, Beverly Hills, Calif., 1989-91; dir. bus. and legal affairs A & M Records, Inc., Hollywood, Calif., 1991—; musician, 1967-84. Mem. UCLA Law Rev., 1984-86; editor: First Amendment Handbook, 1990; contbr. articles to profl. jours. Mem. ABA, NARAS, Gordonstoun Assn., Am. Sailing Assn. Office: A&M Records 1416 N La Brea Ave Los Angeles CA 90028-7563

CASTLE, EMERY NEAL, agricultural and resource economist, educator; b. Eureka, Kans., Apr. 13, 1923; s. Sidney James and Josie May (Tucker) C.; m. Merab Eunice Weber, Jan. 20, 1946; 1 dau., Cheryl Diana Delozier. B.S., Kans. State U., 1948, M.S., 1950; Ph.D., Iowa State U., 1952. Agrl. economist Fed. Res. Bank of Kansas City, 1952-54; from asst. prof. to prof. dept. agrl. econs. Oreg. State U., Corvallis, 1954-65; dean faculty Oreg. State U., 1965-66, prof., head dept. agrl. econs., 1966-72, dean Grad. Sch., 1972-76, Alumni disting. prof., 1970, prof. univ. grad. faculty econs., 1986—; v.p., sr. fellow Resources for the Future, Washington, 1976-79; pres. Resources for the Future, 1979-86; Kellogg lectr. Nat. Assn. State Univs. and Land Grant Colls., 1980; bd. dirs. Agrl. Devel. Coun., 1980-85, Winrock Internat. Inst. for Agrl. Devel., 1984-87; chmn. Water Policy Rev. Bd. Oreg., 1975; mem. State Water Resources Bd., 1964-72, 74-75; mem. President's Commn. on Univ. Goals, Oreg. State U., 1969-70; vice chmn. Environ. Quality Commn. Oreg., 1988—. Author: U.S.-Japanese Agricultural Trade Relations, 1982, Global Natural Resources: Energy, Minerals and Food, 1984; mem. editorial bd. Land Econs., 1969—; contbr. articles to profl. jours. Recipient Alumni Disting. Service award Kans. State U., 1976; Disting. Service award Oreg. State U., 1984. Fellow AAAS, Am. Assn. Agrl. Economists (pres. 1972-73), Am. Acad. Arts and Scis. Home: 1112 NW Solar Pl Corvallis OR 97330-3640 Office: Oreg State U 307 Ballard Hall Corvallis OR 97331

CASTLEBERRY, ARLINE ALRICK, architect; b. Mpls., Sept. 19, 1919; d. Bannona Gerhardt and Meta Emily (Veit) Alrick; m. Donald Montgomery Castleberry, Dec. 25, 1941; children: Karen, Marvin. B in Interior Architecture, U. Minn., 1941; postgrad., U. Tex., 1947-48. Designer, draftsman Elizabeth & Winston Close, Architects, Mpls., 1940-41, Northwest Airlines, Mpls., 1942-43, Cerny & Assocs., Mpls., 1944-46; archtl. draftsman Dominick and Van Benscotten, Washington, 1946-47; ptnr. Castleberry & Davis Bldg. Designers, Burlingame, Calif., 1960-65; prin. Burlingame, 1965-90. Recipient Smith Coll. scholarship. Mem. AIA, Am. Inst. Bldg. Designers (chpt. pres. 1971-72), Commaisini, Alpha Alpha Gamma, Chi Omega. Democrat. Lutheran. Home and Office: 3004 Canyon Rd Burlingame CA 94010-6019

CASTOR, JON STUART, management consultant; b. Lynchburg, Va., Dec. 15, 1951; s. William Stuart and Marilyn (Hughes) C.; m. Stephanie Lum, Jan. 7, 1989; 1 child, David Jon. BA, Northwestern U., 1973; MBA, Stanford U., 1975. Mgmt. cons. Menlo Park, Calif., 1981—. Dir. Midwest Consumer Adv. Bd. to FTC, 1971-73; v.p., dir. San Mateo coun. Boy Scouts Am., 1991—; trustee Coyote Point Mus. Environ. Edn., San Mateo, 1992—. Office: 830 Menlo Ave Menlo Park CA 94025

CASTOR, WILBUR WRIGHT, futurist, author, consultant; b. Harrison Twp., Pa., Feb. 3, 1932; s. Wilbur Wright and Margaret (Grubbs) C.; m. Donna Ruth Schwartz, Feb. 9, 1963; children: Amy, Julia, Marnie. BA, St. Vincent Studies, 1959; PhD, Calif. U. Advanced Studies, 1990. Sales rep. IBM, Pitts. and Cleve., 1959-62; v.p. data processing ops. Honeywell, Waltham, Mass., 1962-80; pres., chief exec. officer Aviation Simulation Tech., Lexington, Mass., 1980-82; sr. v.p. Xerox Corp., El Segundo, Calif., 1982-89; freelance cons., 1989—. Author: (play) Un Certaine Soirée, 1958, (mus. comedy) Breaking Up, 1960, (book) The Information Age and the New Productivity, 1990; contbr. articles to profl. jours. Mem. Presdl. Rep. Task Force; pres., bd. dirs. Internat. Acad., Santa Barbara; active Town Hall Calif. Served to capt. USN, 1953-58, with USAFR, 1958-76. Recipient Disting. Alumnus of Yr. award St. Vincent Coll., 1990. Mem. World Bus. Acad., The Strategy Bd., U. Denver "Netthink", World Future Soc., Aircraft Owners and Pilots Assn., Caballeros Country Club, Rolling Hills (Calif.) Club, Tennis Club, U.S. Senator's Club. Home: 19 Georgeff Rd Rolling Hills CA 90274-5272

CASTRO, DAVID ALEXANDER, construction executive; b. L.A., Dec. 30, 1950; s. Victor A. and Guadalupe (Valdez) C.; m. Katherine Winfield Taylor, Sept. 30, 1990; 1 child, Sarah Taylor. A Liberal Arts, U. Md., 1976, BS in Bus. and Mgmt., 1978; A Engring. Asst., C.C. USAF, 1986; MS in Systems Mgmt., Golden Gate U., 1991. Enlisted USAF, 1970, advanced through grades to Chief Master Sgt., 1989; quality control mgr. 6950 security wing USAF, Royal AFB Chicksands, U.K., 1976-79; supr. engring. support 2851 civil engring. squadron USAF, McClellan AFB, Calif., 1979-82, inspector major projects 2851 civil engring. squadron, 1982-85, supt. engring. svcs. 2851 civil engring. squadron, 1985-87; dep. dir. pub. works tech. assistance team USAF, Beni Seuf, Egypt, 1987-88; contract mgr., then program mgr. 60 civil engring squadron USAF, Travis AFB, Calif., 1988-91; ret. USAF, 1991; acct. rep. Met. Life Ins. Co., Fairfield, Calif., 1991-92; construction mgr. Pacifica Svcs. Inc., Travis AFB, Calif., 1992—; mem. USAF Enlisted Coun., Washington, 1984-86. Group leader Neighborhood Watch, North Highlands, Calif., 1983-86; vol. Loaves and Fishes, Sacramento, 1984-86, Christman Promise, Sacramento, 1983-85; coach Little League Baseball, U.K. and Sacramento, 1976-81. Mem. Air Force Assn. (named Outstanding Airman 1985), Air Force Sgts. Assn., Travis Chiefs Group (treas. 1990-92), Am. Legion. Republican. Roman Catholic. Home: 1354 James St Fairfield CA 94533-6451

CASTRO, JOSEPH ARMAND (JOE CASTRO), music director, pianist, composer, orchestrator; b. Miami, Ariz., Aug. 15, 1927; s. John Loya and Lucy (Sanchez) C.; m. Loretta Faith Haddad, Oct. 21, 1966; children: John Joseph, James Ernest. Student, San Jose State Coll., 1944-47. Mus. dir. Herb Jeffries, Hollywood, Calif., 1952, June Christy, Hollywood, 1959-63, Anita O'Day, Hollywood, 1963-65, Tony Martin, Hollywood, 1962-64, Tropicana Hotel, Las Vegas, Nev., 1980—, Desert Inn, Las Vegas, 1992-93; orch. leader Mocambo Night Club, Hollywood, 1952-54; soloist Joe Castro Trio, L.A., N.Y.C., Honolulu, 1952-65, Sands Hotel, Desert Inn, Las Vegas, 1975-80; mus. dir. Folies Bergere, 1980-89. Recs. include Cool School with June Christy, 1960, Anita O'Day Sings Rodgers and Hart, 1961, Lush Life, 1966, Groove-Funk-Soul, Mood Jazz, Atlantic Records, also albums with Teddy Edwards, Stan Kenton, Jimmy Borges with Joe Castro Trio, 1990, Loretta Castro with Joe Castro Trio, 1990, Honolulu Symphony concerts; command performance, Queen Elizabeth II, London Palladium, 1989, Concerts with Jimmy Borges and Honolulu Symphony Pops Concerts, 1991; jazz concert (with Nigel Kennedy) Honolulu Symphony, 1990; jazz-fest, Kailua-Kona, Hawaii, 1990; arrangements Tropicana Hotel, 1989-92. With U.S. Army, 1946-47. Roman Catholic. Home: 2812 Colanthe Ave Las Vegas NV 89102-2026 Office: Tropicana Hotel 3801 Las Vegas Blvd S Las Vegas NV 89109-4317

CASTRO, LEONARD EDWARD, lawyer; b. L.A., Mar. 18, 1934; s. Emil Galvez and Lily (Meyers) C.; 1 son, Stephen Paul. A.B., UCLA, 1959, J.D., 1962. Bar: Calif. 1963, U.S. Supreme Ct. 1970. Assoc. Musick, Peeler & Garrett, Los Angeles, 1962-68, ptnr., 1968—. Mem. ABA, Internat. Bar Assn., Los Angeles County Bar Assn. Office: Musick Peeler & Garrett 1 Wilshire Blvd Ste 2000 Los Angeles CA 90017-3806

CASTRUITA, RUDY, school superintendent. BA in Social Sci., Utah State U., 1966, MS in Sch. Adminstrn., 1967; EdD, U. So. Calif., 1983. Cert. adminstrv. svcs., std. secondary, pupil svcs. Dir. econ. opportunity program City of El Monte, Calif., 1966-67; secondary tchr., counselor, program coord. El Monte Union High Sch. Dist., 1967-75, asst. prin. Mountain View High Sch., 1975-80; prin. Los Alamitos (Calif.) High Sch. Los Alamitos Unified Sch. Dist., 1980-85; asst. supt. secondary divsn. Santa Ana (Calif.) Unified Sch. Dist., 1985-87, assoc. supt. secondary divsn., 1987-88, supt., 1988—; adj. prof. Calif. State U., Long Beach, 1981-88, mem. adv. com. dept. ednl. adminstrn., 1983-86; adj. prof. U. San Francisco, 1984-88; mem. State Tchr. of Yr. Selection Com., 1988, Student Tchr. Edn. Project Coun., SB 620 Healthy Start Com., SB 1274 Restructuring Com., Joint Task Force Articulation, State High Sch. Task Force; mem. Latino eligibility study U. Calif., mem. ednl. leadership inst.; mem. state adv. coun. Supt. Pub. Instrn.; Delta Epsilon lectr. U. So. Calif.; rep. Edn. Summit; mem. selection com. Calif. Ednl. Initiatives Fund; co-chair subcom. at risk youth Calif. Edn. Com., 1989; mentor supt. Harvard Urban Supt.'s Program, 1993—. Chair Orange County Hist. Adv. Coun., South El Monte Coordinating Coun.; mem. exec. coun. Santa Ana 2000; mem. articulation coun. Rancho Santiago C.C. Dist.; active Hacienda Heights Recreation and Pks. Commn., Santa Ana City Coun. Stadium Blue Ribbon Com.; exec. dir. Orange County coun. Boy Scouts Am.; mem. adv. com. Bowers Mus.; mem. exec. bd. El Monte Boys Club; hon. lifetime mem. Calif. PTA; bd. dirs. Santa Ana Boys and Girls Club, Orange County Philharm. Soc., Santa Ana Pvt. Industry Coun., El Monte-South El Monte Consortium, Drug Use is Life Abuse, EDUCARE sch. edn. U. So. Calif. Named Supt. of Yr. League United Latin Am. Citizens, 1989; state finalist Nat. Supt. Yr. award, 1992. Mem. ASCD, Assn. Calif. Sch. Adminstrs. (rep. region XVII secondary prins. com. 1981-85, presenter region XVII 1984, Calif. Supt. of Year award 1991, Marcus Foster award 1991), Calif. Sch. Bds. Assn. (mem. policy and analysis com.), Assn. Calif. Urban Sch. Dists. (pres. 1992—), Orange County Supts. (pres.), Santa Ana C. of C. (bd. dirs.), Delta Epsilon (pres. 1990-91), Phi Delta Kappa. Office: Santa Anna USD 1405 French St Santa Ana CA 92701*

CATALA, HENRY LEON, electrical engineer; b. San Rafael, Calif., Feb. 16, 1951; s. Henry Frank and Carolyn Louise (Bottarini) C. BSEE and Computer Sci., Santa Clara U., 1973, MSEE, 1976. Engr. GTE Govt. Systems, Mountain View, Calif., 1973-76; design engr. Nat. Semicondr., Santa Clara, Calif., 1975-79; sr. engr. Memorex Corp., Santa Clara, 1979, Diasonics Inc., Sunnyvale, Calif., 1979-80; engring. mgr. GTE Govt. Systems, Mountain View, Calif., 1980—. Tchr. religious edn. Transfiguration Ch., San Jose, calif., 1980-90, Holy Spirit Ch., San Jose, 1990—. Mem. IEEE, Tau Beta Pi, Eta Kappa Nu. Republican. Office: GTE Govt Systems PO Box 7188 100 Ferguson Dr Mountain View CA 94039

CATALANO, DENNIS MICHAEL, organic laboratory project and marketing manager; b. Reading, Pa., Mar. 10, 1956; s. Dima James and Margarite Rebecca (Mirabella) C.; m. Patricia Clare Korff, May 6, 1978; children: Emily, Patrick, Ian, Julia. BS in Chemistry, Biology, U. Dayton, 1977. Chemist Gulf South Rsch. Inst., New Orleans, 1978-80; mgr. gas chromatography mass spectrometry Mead CompuChem, Research Triangle Park, N.C., 1980-82; dioxin lab. mgr. IT Corp., Knoxville, Tenn., 1982-86; organic lab. mgr. Ecova Co., Redmond, Wash., 1986-87, Weyerhaeuser, Federal Way, Wash., 1987—. Contbr. articles to sci. publs. Grantee NSF, 1975-76. Democrat. Roman Catholic. Home: 3715 204th Ct NE Redmond WA 98053-9365 Office: Weyerhaeuser WTC 2F25 32901 Weyerhaeuser Way S Federal Way WA 98003

CATALANO, JOHN GEORGE, management consultant; b. Rockford, Ill., Jan. 28, 1950; s. Francis Richard and Angela C.; m. Kathryn Swaney, Sept. 20, 1980; 1 child, F. Richard. BSBA, U. Ill., 1972. Sales rep. Metal Fabricators, Inc., Rockford, Ill., 1972-76; v.p. sales/mktg. Metal Fabricators, Inc., 1976-82, pres., chief exec. officer, 1982-86; pres. Catalano & Co., Rockford, 1986-88, Greenbrae, Calif., 1988-91; CEO, pres. Casa Blanca Works, Greenbrae, 1991—. Pub. (monthly newsletter) BusinessMac, (directory) Chicago Computer Training Directory, 1987; contbr. articles to profl. jours. Recipient Silver Beaver award, Boy Scouts Am., 1988, Silver Wreath, 1986. Mem. Am. Mgmt. Assn., Apple Profl. Exch. (gen. mgr. 1989-90), Apple Cons. Rels. Bd., Marin County C. of C. Republican. Office: 148 Bon Air Ctr Greenbrae CA 94904-1702

CATALANO, MICHAEL ALFRED, rheumatologist, clinical scientist; b. N.Y.C., Jan. 25, 1947. BS, Boston Coll., Chestnut Hill, Mass., 1968; MD, Yale U., 1972. Rheumatologist Arthritis Ctr. Hawaii, Honolulu, 1980-84; dir. Ciba-Geigy, Summit, N.J., 1984-86, exec. dir., 1986-90; v.p. clin. rsch. Synergen, Inc., Boulder, Colo., 1990-93; tech. cons., 1993—. Mem. Am. Soc. Clin. Pharmacology and Therapeutics (vice chairperson), Am. Coll. Rheumatology (co-chairperson), Am. Fedn. Clin. Rsch., Am. Coll. Sports Medicine.

CATALINO, KENNETH JAMES, political cartoonist; b. San Diego, June 13, 1950; s. Joseph and Lena (Barranco) C.; m. Janine Huff. BA, San Diego State U., 1973. Asst. cost ctr. supr. Ralph M. Parsons Co., Pasadena, Calif., 1976-81; dir. pers. adminstrn. Ensench Alaska Svcs., Anchorage, 1981-88; editorial cartoonist Anchorage Times, 1990—. Recipient 1st Pl. award Soc. Profl. Journalists, 1990, 1st and 2d Pl. awards Soc. Profl. Journalists, 1991. Mem. Am. Assn. Editorial Cartoonists, Ala. Press Club (1st pl. awards 1990, 91, 92). Home: 1544 W 14th Ave Anchorage AK 99501 Office: Anchorage Times PO Box 10040 Anchorage AK 99510-0040

CATANZARO, MARCI-LEE, nursing educator; b. Cin., July 27, 1941; d. Peter Charles and Martha (Radel) C. BSN, Spalding Coll., Louisville, 1970; MSN, U. Wash., 1971; PhD, Union Inst., Cin., 1980. Instr. Seattle Cen.

Community Coll., 1971-74, curriculum specialist, 1974-76; svcs. coord. Nat. Multiple Sclerosis Soc., Seattle, 1976-82; assoc. prof. nursing U. Wash., Seattle, 1982—; dir. Am. Assn. Marriage and Family Therapists, Seattle, 1988—. Editor/author: Nursing Research: Theory and Practice, 1988 (ANA Book of the Yr. 1988). Sci. explainer Pacific Sci. Ctr., Seattle, 1980—;/ trustee Nat. Multiple Sclerosis Soc., 1987—. Recipient Outstanding Pub. Svc. award, U. Wash., 1988, Hope award, Nat. Multiple Sclerosis Soc., 1988; Am. Nurses Found. scholar, 1986. Fellow Western Acad. Nursing; mem. Rehab. Nursing Found. (rsch. com.), Western Inst. Nursing, Nat. Multiple Sclerosis Soc. (treas. 1988-90), Sigma Theta Tau. Democrat. Roman Catholic. Office: Univ of Wash Physiological Nursing SM-28 Seattle WA 98195

CATE, FLOYD MILLS, electronic components executive; b. Norfolk, Va., Aug. 2, 1917; s. Floyd Mills and Ellen (Lewis) C.; m. Ann Willis, Jan. 31, 1943; 1 child Carol Cate Webster. B.A. U. Tenn., 1940; student exec. program UCLA, 1958; B.A. (hon.) Calif. Inst. Tech., 1947. With special sales dept. Cannon Electric Co., Los Angeles, 1940-46, western sales mgr., 1946-50, with internat. sales dept., 1950-57, v.p. sales, mktg., 1957-62, pres. internat. sales, 1958-62, v.p. sales and mktg. electronics, 1962-69; v.p. sales, mktg. divsn. Japan Aviation Electronics Zemco, Irvine, Calif., 1977-80, cons., 1977-80; pres., owner F.E.S. Cons., San Clemente, Calif., 1968—; 2R engring. cons. dir., San Marcos, Calif., 1987— . Co-chmn. Ron Packard for Congress, San Clemente, 1984; chmn. adhoc com. Sea Sade Village, 1986—; pres. Assn. Shorecliffs Residence, San Clemente, 1986—; dir. La Christianitos pagents Samaritan Hosp. Guild. Mem. IEEE, Internat. Electric Electronic Engrs., Shorecliff Golf Club (bd. dirs. San Clemente), San Clemente C. of C., San Clemente Hist. Soc., Shorecliff Golf Club (bd. dirs. San Clemente). Democrat. Roman Catholic. Club: Shorecliff Golf (bd. dirs. San Clemente). Office: 205 Via Montego San Clemente CA 92672-3625

CATHCART, GEORGE LEBLANC, journalist, educational administrator; b. N.Y.C., Sept. 2, 1947; s. James Armstrong and Anna Adelaide (LeBlanc) C.; m. Violet Cheshire Duane, Dec. 21, 1974 (dec. 1980); m. Mary Katherine Robbins, Dec. 18, 1982; children: Anna Elizabeth, Charles Carew Robbins. BA in Journalism, George Washington U., 1981; student, U. Denver, 1965-66. Pub. rels. asst. Sea Pines Co., Hilton Head, S.C., 1972-73; mng. editor Island Packet, Hilton Head, 1973-77; freelance writer Hilton Head, 1977-83; news editor Island Packet, Hilton Head, 1983; writer Ariz. State U., Tempe, 1984-85, asst. dir. news bur., 1985-87, dir. news bur., 1987—. Co-author: Moonshadows, 1977; contbr. articles to mags.; author, producer multi-media show Ascend Steeply, 1982. 1st lt. U.S. Army, 1966-69, Vietnam. Recipient Interpretive Reporting award S.C. Hosp. Assn., Merit award Internat. Assn. Bus. Communicators, 1990, 91, Excellence award, 1992; winner News Story award S.C. Press Assn., 1973, Sports Story award, 1975, Community Svc. award, 1975. Mem. Trout Unlimited (bd. dirs. Zane Grey chpt., sec. 1990-92), Ariz. Flycasters, Hon. Soc. Phi Kappa Phi. Home: 15843 S 33d Pl Phoenix AZ 85044 Office: Ariz State Univ Tempe AZ 85287-1803

CATHCART, JAMES B., geologist; b. Berkeley, Calif., Nov. 22, 1917; s. James B. and Lydia Pauline (Anderson) C.; m. Doris Lee Mapes, Nov. 12, 1944; children: Janet, James D. AB, U. Calif., Berkeley, 1939. Geologist US Geol. Survey, Denver, 1942-88, geologist emeritus, 1988—. Contbr. articles to profl. jours. Vol. Boy Scouts Am., Denver, 1950-60. With USN, 1945-46. Recipient Superior Svc. award U.S. Dept. Interior, 1984, Meritorious Svc. award, 1986. Fellow Geol. Soc. Am.; mem. Am. Assn. Petroleum Geology (emeritus), Soc. Econ. Geologists (sr.). Home: 17225 W 16th Pl Golden CO 80401-2754 Office: US Geol Survey Denver Fed Ctr Denver CO 80225

CATHERWOOD, HUGH ROBERT, public administration consultant; b. Chgo., July 6, 1911; s. Robert and Lucy Cotton (Morris) C.; m. Frances Maughs, May 31, 1941 (dec. 1963); children: Jane, Nancy; m. Jean Williams, Sept. 5, 1967. BA, Yale U., 1933. Project dir. Griffenhagan Assocs., 1935-42; dir. budget and pers. City of Denver, 1947-53; pres. Western Wood Preserving, Denver, 1954-60, Shannon (Ireland) Repair Svcs., 1960-64; ptnr., pub. adminstrn. cons. Kansas-Denver Assocs., Denver, 1967—; clients include cities of Houston, Amarillo, El Paso, Texarkana, Tex., Boulder, Colorado Springs, Denver, Colo., states of Mont., La., Mich., Va., numerous counties and individual corps.; chief of party J.L. Jacobs Co., Govt. of Saudi Arabia, Riyadh, 1966-67; arbitrator Fed. Mediation and Conciliation Svc. Contbr. articles and opinion pieces to various publs. Lt. comdr. USNR, 1947-92. Mem. Univ. Club N.Y., Univ. Club Chgo., Univ. Club Denver, Denver Country Club, Denver City Club, Colo. Physicians for Social Responsibility (bd. dirs.) SCORE (officer). Democrat. Episcopalian. Home and Office: 130 Lafayette St Denver CO 80218

CATHEY, DEAN EDWARD, fire chief officer; b. Long Beach, Calif., July 19, 1946; s. Robert Edward and Marie Gertrude (Gillette) C.; m. Barbara Anne Boring, Sept. 11, 1971 (div. Jan. 1988); m. Yanira Estrada Buchholz. BA in Mgmt., U. Redlands, 1981; postgrad., Nat. Fire Acad., Emmitsburg, Md., 1985. Firefighter L.A. City Fire Dept., 1970—. Producer (videotape) Coalinga Earthquake, 1983. Staff sgt. USAF, 1966-70. Mem. Calif. Fire Chief Assn. (L.A. chpt.), L.A. Fire Dept. Chief Officers Assn., L.A. Firefighters/Paramedics Sertoma Club, Nat. Fire Protection Assn. Democrat.

CATHEY, SHARON SUE RINN, educational administrator; b. Reed City, Mich., June 11, 1940; d. Sherwood and Ellen (Hutson) Rinn.; m. Jerry A. Cathey, June 25, 1960; children: Joel A., Julie A. BA in Edn., San Francisco State U., 1962; postgrad., U. Mich., 1972-74, U. Calif., 1975-77; MA in Edn., U. Nev., 1988, EdDin doctorate curriculum and instrn., 1991. Tchr. Laguna Salada Union Sch. Dist., Pacifica, Calif., 1962-64, Redwood City (Calif.) Sch. Dist., 1964-66, Lapeer (Mich.) Sch. Dist., 1970-74; tchr., choral dir. Pine Middle Sch., Reno, 1978-84; tchr. Washoe County Sch. Dist., Reno, 1985—; adminstrv. elem. edn. cons. Washoe County Sch. Dist., 1991-92; adminstrv. cons. Nev. State Dept. Elem. Edn., Carson City, 1990—; prin. Anderson Elem. Sch., Reno, 1992—; diagnostician Thompsn Learning Ctr., Reno, 1987-89; asst. U. Nev., 1988-90; cons. Nev. State Bd. Elem. Edn., 1990, Computer Users Educators of No. Nev. Nev. ESSA grantee, 1977. Mem. AAUW (pres. 1976-78), Washoe County Tchrs. Assn., Internat. Reading Assn. (state pres.-elect 1991, pres. 1992, IRA presentations, 1990-93, local pres. 1993-94), Nat. Reading Assn. (presentations 1989, 91), Nat. Coun. Tchrs. English (presenter 1990, 92), Phi Kappa Phi, Delta Kappa Gamma (state pres. 1989-91, state v.p. 1990). Republican. Episcopalian. Home: 814 Glen Meadow Dr Sparks NV 89434-1539

CATON, CHARLES ALLEN, physician; b. Clovis, N.Mex., Oct. 13, 1937; s. Lewis O. and Mildred L. (Shepherd) C.; m. Marilyne Lois Hancock, June 21, 1959; children: Karen, Katherine, Kenneth. BS in Biology with honors, U. N.Mex., Albuquerque, 1960; MD, Baylor U., 1964. Diplomate Am. Bd. Emergency Medicine. Rotating intern Baylor U., Houston, 1965; emergency physician McKay Dee Hosp., Ogden, Utah, 1969-81, St. Benedict's Hosp., Ogden, 1981—; pres. Care Plus, P.C., Roy, Utah, 1984—; emergency physician Humana Hosp. Davis North, Layton, Utah, 1989—; clin. instr. dept. family medicine U. Utah, Salt Lake City, 1974-93; med. cons. Weber State U., Ogden, 1975-81, So. Pacific Transp. Co., Ogden, 1984-90; surveyor Accreditation Assn. Ambulatory Health Care, Skokie, Ill., 1983-93; pres. Care Plus, Inc., Ogden and Roy, 1984-93. Capt. USAF, 1964-68, Vietnam. Decorated D.F.C., Bronze Star, Air Medal with oak leaf cluster. Fellow Am. Coll. Emergency Physicians (chpt. pres. 1975); AMA, Utah Med. Assn. (del. 1980), Weber County Med. Soc. (pres. 1982). Republican. Office: Care Plus PC 5924 S 1900 W Roy UT 84067-2310

CATRAMBONE, EUGENE DOMINIC, public relations consultant; b. Chgo., June 5, 1926; s. Nicola and Maria Theresa (Catrambone) C.; m. Mary Gloria Gaimari, Mar. 26, 1951; children: Mary, Eugene Jr., Jane, David, Jill. BA, St. Benedict Coll., 1950; postgrad., Kans. State U., 1952-54; MA, DePaul U., 1960; postgrad., UCLA, 1962-63. Cert. secondary tchr., coll. instr., Calif. Tchr. high schs. Chgo., 1950-62, L.A., 1963-88; cons. pub. rels. Westlake Village, Calif., 1986—; tech. writer U. Chgo., 1956-59, Douglas Missile div. USN, L.A. and Ventura, Calif., 1962-75; reporter, editor Las Virgenes Enterprise, Calabasas, Calif., 1968-75; evening instr. L.A. City Coll., 1965-68. Author: Requiem for a Nobody, 1993, The Golden Touch: Frankie Carle, 1981; poem "Exit dust", 1982; contbr. articles on edn. to profl. publs., 1959-60, feature stories to local newspapers, 1968-75. Sgt. U.S. Army, 1944-46. Recipient Fostering Excellence award L.A. Unified Sch. Dist., 1986-87, nominee Apple award, 1986. Mem. NEA (life), Calif. Tchrs. Assn., Book Publicists So. Calif., United Tchrs. L.A., Am. Legion, Westlake Village Men's Golf Club (pub. rels. editor 1986—, bd. dirs., pres. 1989—). Democrat. Roman Catholic. Home: 31802 Tynebourne Ct Westlake Vlg CA 91361-4132 Office: Golden Touch Assocs PO Box 1064 Agoura Hills CA 91376-1064

CATRETT, JOHN THOMAS, III, minister; b. Pascegoula, Miss., June 20, 1947; s. John T. Catrett II and Dorothy M. (Demouey) Morgan. BA in Ministry, Midwest Christian Coll., 1971, BA in Christian Edn., 1972; postgrad., Ky. Christian Coll., 1987—. Student minister Cere Christian Ch., Red Rock, Okla., 1969-71; student youth minister Forest Hills Christian Ch., Oklahoma City, 1971-72; youth minister Davis Park Christian Ch., Enid, Okla., 1972-74, Sandusky Area Christian Ch., Tulsa, 1974-85; minister Cen. Christian Ch., Carlsbad, N.Mex., 1986—; chmn. trustees Midwest Christian Coll., Oklahoma City, 1984-85; regional bd. dirs. Dallas Christian Coll. Donor ARC, 1974—; asst. coach T-Ball Team, 1980-82; coach Basketball Jr. High Teams, 1979-81; mem. N.Mex. for Life, 1987—, Camp Fire Bd., 1987—, Little League Umpires, 1987—; pres. N.Mex. Christian Conv., 1990, treas., 1991—. Home: 1114 W Ash St Carlsbad NM 88220-4421

CATTANACH, RICHARD L., contractor; b. Stanley, Wis., Feb. 28, 1942; s. Bert Cornwall and Katherine Mary (Lamont) C.; m. Mary M. Cattanach, May 7, 1976; children: Thomas Burke, Shaun Eric, Eric Lamont. BBA, U. Wis., Whitewater, 1964; MSBA, U. Denver, 1966; PhD, Ariz. State U., 1971. CPA, Alaska, Ariz. Asst. prof. U. Miss., Oxford, 1971-73, U. Denver, 1973-74; contr. Alaska Bank of Commerce, 1974-77; asst. to v.p. Nat. Tech. Inst. for the Deaf, Rochester, N.Y., 1977-80; v.p. Unit Co., Anchorage, 1980—; Dir. Workers Compensation Com. of Alaska, 1980-91; chmn. Mgmt./Labor Ad Hoc Workers Compensation Com., 1983-92. Mem. Associated Gen. Contractors (sec.-treas. 1991, v.p. 1992, pres. 1993), Fin. Exec. Inst. (sec. to pres. 1985-88). Episcopalian. Office: Unit Co 8101 Old Seward Hwy Anchorage AK 99518

CATTANEO, JACQUELYN ANNETTE KAMMERER, artist, educator; b. Gallup, N.Mex., June 1, 1944; d. Ralph John and Gladys Agnes (O'Sullivan) Kammerer; m. John Leo Cattaneo, Apr. 25, 1964; children: John Auro, Paul Anthony. Student Tex. Woman's U., 1962-64. Portrait artist, tchr. Gallup, N. Mex., 1972; coord. Works Progress Adminstrn. art project renovation McKinley County, Gallup, Octavia Fellin Performing Arts wing dedication, Gallup Pub. Library; formation com. mem. Multi-modal/Multi-Cultural Ctr. for Gallup, N.Mex.; exch. with Soviet Women's Com., USSR Women Artists del., Moscow, Kiev, Leningrad, 1990; Women Artists del. and exch. Jerusalem, Tel Aviv, Cairo, Israel; mem. Artists Del. to Prague, Vienna and Budapest.; mem. Women Artists Del. to Egypt and Israel, 1992. One-woman shows include Gallup Pub. Libr., 1963, 66, 77, 78, 81, 87, Gallup Lovelace Med. Clinic, Santa Fe Station Open House, 1981, Gallery 20, Farmington, N.Mex., 1985—, Red Mesa Art Gallery, 1989, Soviet Restrospect Carol's Art & Antiques Gallery, Liverpool, N.Y., 1992, N.Mex. State Capitol Bldg., Santa Fe, 1992, Lt. Govt. Casey Luna-Office Complex, Women Artists N.Mex. Mus. Fine Arts, Carlsbad, 1992; group shows include: Navajo Nation Library Invitational, 1978, Santa Fe Festival of the Arts Invitational, 1979, N.Mex. State Fair, 1978, 79, 80, Catharine Lorillard Wolfe, N.Y.C., 1980, 81, 84, 85, 86, 87, 88, 89, 91, 92, 4th ann. exhbn. Salmagundi Club, 1984, 90, 3d ann. Palm Beach Internat., New Orleans, 1984, Fine Arts Ctr. Taos, 1984, The Best and the Brightest O'Brien's Art Emporium, Scottsdale, Ariz., 1986, Gov.'s Gallery, 1989, N.Mex. State Capitol, Santa Fe, 1987, Pastel Soc. West Coast Ann. Exhbn. Sacramento Ctr. for Arts, Calif., 1986-90, gov.'s invitational Magnifico Fest. of the Arts, Albuquerque, 1991, Assn. Pour La Promotion Du Patrimone Artistique Français, Paris, Nat. Mus. of the Arts for Women, Washington, 1991, Artists of N.Mex., Internat. Nexus '92 Fine Art Exhbn., Trammell Corw Pavilion, Dallas, Carlsbad (N.Mex.) Mus. Fine Art; represented in permanent collections: Zuni Arts and Crafts Ednl. Bldg., U. N.Mex., C.J. Wiemar Collection, McKinley Manor, Gov.'s Office, State Capitol Bldg., Santa Fe, Historic El Rancho Hotel, Gallup, N.Mex., Sunwest Bank. Fine Arts Ctr., En Taos, N.Mex., Armand Hammer Pvt. Collection, Russell Gallery & Studio, Albuquerque, Dallas & Assocs., Ruidoso, N.Mex., Dallas Summers, Galaria Impi, Netherlands, Woods Art and Antiques, Liverpool, N.Y. Mem. Dora Cox del. to Soviet Union-U.S. Exchange, 1990. Recipient Cert. of Recognition for Contbn. and Participation Assn. Pour La Patrinome Du Artistique Français, 1991, N.Mex. State Senate 14th Legislature Session Meml. # 101 for Artistic Achievements award, 1992. Mem. Internat. Fine Arts Guild, Am. Portrait Soc. (cert.), Pastel Soc. of W. Coast (cert.), Mus. N.Mex. Found., Mus. Women in the Arts, Fechin Inst., Artists' Co-op. (co-chair), Gallup C. of C., Gallup Area Arts and Crafts Council, Am. Portrait Soc. Am., Pastel Soc. N.Mex., Catharine Lorillard Wolfe Art Club of N.Y.C. (oil and pastel juried membership), Chautaugua Art Club, Soroptimists (Internat. Woman of Distinction 1990).0). Address: 210 E Green St Gallup NM 87301

CATTANEO, JOHN LEO, contractor, consultant, business owner; b. Gallup, N.Mex., Sept. 21, 1944; s. Auro and Nellie (Motta) C.; m. Jacquelyn A. Kammerer, Apr. 25, 1964; children: John Auro, Paul Anthony. Student, U. Tex., El Paso, 1962, St. Joseph's U., Albuquerque, 1963. With Cattaneo Constrn., Gallup, 1962-64, 68—, from foreman to co-owner, 1964-68; pres. Cattaneo Enterprises Inc., Gallup, 1984—; contractor Restoration Hist. Zuni Mission Our Lady of Guadalupe 1629, 1965-68, Restoration Gallups His. Chief Theatre, 1986. Mem. Downtown Devel. Signage Com., Gallup, 1986-88. Recipient Papel Blessing from Pope Paul VI for restoration of Our Lady of Quadalupe Mission. Mem. Principe Luigi Club, Elks. Roman Catholic. Office: Cattaneo Constrn PO Box 568 Gallup NM 87319-0451 also: Constrn Shop 191 Wyatt Gallup NM 87301

CATTELL, RODERIC GEOFFREY GALTON, computer scientist; b. Urbana, Ill., May 4, 1953; s. Raymond Bernard and Alberta Karen (Schuettler) C.; m. Nancy Worner, Aug. 11, 1973 (div. 1981); 1 child, Eric; m. Susan Gail Fraenkel, Feb. 14, 1987; children: Aaron, Elliott. BS in Computer Sci. and Psychology, U. Ill., 1974; PhD in Computer Sci., Carnegie-Mellon U., 1978. Rsch. scientist Carnegie-Mellon U., Pitts., 1978, Xerox PARC, Palo Alto, Calif., 1978-84; 2d level mgr. Sun Microsystems, Mountain View, Calif., 1984-88, disting. engr., 1988—; mem. tech. adv. bd. several object-oriented software cos., 1988—; chmn. Object Data Mgmt. Group, 1991—. Author: Formalization and Automatic Derivation of Code Generators, 1978, Object Data Management, 1991, The Object Databse Standard ODMG-93, 1993; also articles. Mem. IEEE, Assn. for Computing Machinery. Office: Sun Microsystems 2550 Garcia Ave Mountain View CA 94043

CATTERTON, MARIANNE ROSE, occupational therapist; b. St. Paul, Feb. 3, 1922; d. Melvin Joseph and Katherine Marion (Bole) Maas; m. Elmer John Wood, Jan. 16, 1943 (dec.); m. Robert Lee Catterton, Nov. 20, 1951 (div. 1981); children: Jenifer Ann Dawson, Cynthia Lea Uthus. Student, Carleton Coll., 1939-41, U. Md., 1941-42; BA in English, U. Wis., 1944; MA in Counseling Psychology, Bowie State Coll., 1980; postgrad., No. Ariz. U., 1987—. Registered occupational therapist. Occupational therapist VA, N.Y.C., 1946-50; cons. occupational therapist Fondo del Seguro del Estado, Puerto Rico, 1950-51; dir. rehab. therapies Spring Grove State Hosp., Catonsville, Md., 1953-56; occupational therapist Anne Arundel County Health Dept., Annapolis, Md., 1967-78; dir. occupational therapy Eastern Shore Hosp. Ctr., Cambridge, Md., 1979-85; cons. occupational therapist Kachina Point Health Ctr., Sedona, Ariz., 1986; regional chmn. Conf. on revising Psychiat. Occupational Therapy Edn., 1958-59; instr. report writing Anne Arundel Community Coll., Annapolis, 1974-78. Editor Am. Jour. Occupational Therapy, 1962-67. Active Md. Heart Assn., 1959-60; mem. task force on occupational therapy Md. Dept. of Health, 1971-72; chmn. Anne Arundel Gov. Com. on Employment of Handicapped, 1959-63; mem. gov.'s com. to study vocat. rehab., Md., 1960; com. mem. Annapolis Youth Ctr., 1976-78; mem. ministerial search com. Unitarian Ch. Anne Arundel County, 1962; curator Dorchester County Heritage Mus., Cambridge, 1982-83; v.p., officer Unitarian-Universalist Fellowship Flagstaff, 1988—. Mem. P.R. Occupational Therapy Assn. (co-founder 1950), Am. Occupational Therapy Assn. (chmn. history com. 1958-61), Md. Occupational Therapy Assn. (del. 1953-59), Ariz. Occupational Therapy Assn., Pathfinder Internat., Dorchester County Mental Health Assn. (pres. 1981-84), Internat. Platform Assn., Ret. Officers Assn., Air Force Assn. (Barry Goldwater chpt., sec. 1991-92), Severn Town Club (treas. 1965), Internat. Club (Annapolis, publicity chmn. 1966), Toastmasters, Newcomers (Sedona, pres. 1986), Zero Population Growth, Delta Delta Delta. Republican. Home: 415 Windsong Dr Sedona AZ 86336-3745

CATZ, BORIS, physician; b. Troyanov, Russia, Feb. 15, 1923; s. Jacobo and Esther (Galbmilion) C.; came to U.S., 1950, naturalized, 1955; B.S., Nat. U. Mexico, 1941, M.D., 1947; M.S. in Medicine, U. So. Calif., 1951; m. Rebecca Schechter; children—Judith, Dinah, Sarah Lea, Robert. Intern, Gen. Hosp., Mexico City, 1945-46; prof. adj., sch. medicine U. Mexico, 1947-48; research fellow medicine U. So. Calif., 1949-51, instr. medicine, 1952-54, asst. clin. prof., 1954-59, assoc. clin. prof., 1959-83, clin. prof., 1983—; pvt. practice, Los Angeles, 1951-55, Beverly Hills, Calif., 1957—; chief Thyroid Clinic Los Angeles County Gen. Hosp., 1955-70; sr. cons. thyroid clin. U. So. Calif.-Los Angeles Med. Center, 1970—; clin. chief endocrinology Cedars-Sinai Med. Ctr., 1983-87. Served to capt. U.S. Army, 1955-57. Boris Catz lectureship named in his honor Thyroid Research Endowment Fund, Cedars Sinai Med. Ctr., 1985. Fellow ACP, Am. Coll. Nuclear Medicine (pres. elect 1982), Royal Soc. Medicine; mem. AMA, AAAS, Cedars Sinai Med. Ctr. Soc. for History of Medicine (chmn.), L.A. County Med. Assn., Calif. Med. Assn., Endocrine Soc., Am. Thyroid Assn., Soc. Exptl. Biology and Medicine, Western Soc. Clin. Research, Am. Fedn. Clin. Research, Soc. Nuclear Medicine, So. Calif. Soc. Nuclear Medicine, N.Y. Acad. Scis., Los Angeles Soc. Internal Medicine, Am. Soc. Internal Medicine, Calif. Soc. Internal Medicine, Collegium Salerni, Cedar Sinai Soc. of History of Medicine, Beverly Hills C. of C., Phi Lambda Kappa. Jewish. Mem. B'nai B'rith. Club: The Profl. Man's (past pres.). Author: Thyroid Case Studies, 1975, 2d edit., 1981. Contbr. numerous articles on thyroidology to med. jours. Home: 300 S El Camino Dr Beverly Hills CA 90212-4212 Office: 435 N Roxbury Dr Beverly Hills CA 90210-5027

CAUDILL, JAMES MASON, public relations executive; b. Detroit, Sept. 16, 1950; s. Estill and Naomi (Oakley) C.; m. Elaine O'Donnell, Oct. 30, 1971 (div. 1983); children: Heather, Stacy, Megan; m. Charlotte Lee Banach, Sept. 14, 1991. BA, Wayne State U., 1974; MA, Western Mich. U., 1979. Editor Leader Publs., Dearborn Heights, Mich., 1970-72; dir. pub. rels. various Mich. sch. dists., Dearborn, 1972-79; v.p. Carl Byoir & Assocs., Detroit, San Francisco, 1979-84; v.p. pub. rels. Amfac Hotels & Resorts, San Francisco, 1984-85; sr. v.p., assoc. dir. Ketchum Pub. Rels., San Francisco, 1985-92; prin. Caudill and Co., Sausalito, Calif., 1992—; instr. pub. rels., Golden Gate U., San Francisco, 1986—. Mem. Pub. Rels. Soc. Am. (past pres. San Francisco chpt.; Silver Anvil award, 1980, 84, chair 1993), Pub. Rels. Roundtable (bd. dirs.). Democrat. Methodist. Home: 114 Lincoln Dr Sausalito CA 94965-1653 Office: Caudill and Co 114 Lincoln Dr Sausalito CA 94965-1653

CAUDILL, TERRY LEE, accountant; b. Nampa, Idaho, Aug. 10, 1947; s. Loyd A. and Melda M. (Youree) C. BA in Math., N.W. Nazarene Coll., 1969; BS in Acctg., U. Nev., Reno, 1977. CPA, Nev. Audit mgr. Fox & Co. CPA's, Reno, 1977-83; chief internal auditor Circus Circus Enterprises, Inc., Las Vegas, 1983-84, v.p., chief acctg. officer, treas., 1984—. Mem. Internat. Assn. Hospitality Accts., Am. Inst. CPA's. Office: Circus Circus Enterprises Inc 2880 Las Vegas Blvd S Las Vegas NV 89109-1120

CAUDRON, JOHN ARMAND, safety engineer, technical forensic investigator; b. Compton, Calif., Sept. 26, 1944; s. Armand Robert and Evelyn Emma (Hoyt) C.; m. Marilyn Edith Fairfield, Mar. 16, 1968; children: Melita, Rochelle. AA, Ventura Coll., 1965; BA, Calif. State U., Fullerton, 1967; postgrad., U. Nev., 1975-78; MS, U. So. Calif., 1980. Dist. rep. GM, Reno, 1969-75; mgr. Snyder Rsch. Lab., Reno, 1976-78, v.p., El Monte, Calif., 1978-82, pres., 1982-85; prin. Fire and Accident Reconstruction, Rowland Heights, Calif., 1985—. Pub. accident reconstrn. newsletter. With U.S. Army, 1967-69. Mem. ASCE, Am. Soc. Safety Engrs., Nat. Fire Protection Assn., Geol. Soc. Am., Firearms Rsch. and Identification Assn. (pres. 1978—), Am. Soc. Metals, Nat. Safety Coun., Nat. Soc. Profl. Engrs., Nat. Assn. Profl. Accident Redonstruction Specialists, Ft. Tejon Hist. Assn. (info. adviser 1983—). Republican. Baptist. Avocations: hiking, traveling, photography. Office: Fire & Accident Reconstrn 17524 E Colima Rd Ste 360 La Puente CA 91748-1750

CAUGHEY, GEORGE HERBERT, pulmonary physician; b. Balt., Feb. 13, 1953; s. Winslow Spaulding and Helen McDowell (Hill) C.; m. Michelle Beer, June 8, 1975; children: Devin, Robert, Bennett, Willa. BS in Chemistry, Ariz. State U., 1975; MD, Stanford U., 1979. Med. intern and resident Pa. Hosp., Phila., 1979-82; postdoctoral fellow U. Calif., San Francisco, 1983-86, instr. medicine, 1986-88, asst. prof. medicine, 1988-92, assoc. prof. medicine, 1992—; assoc. staff mem. Cardiovascular Rsch. Inst., San Francisco, 1988—. Contbr. articles to profl. jours., chpts. to books. Recipient Merck award in Chemistry, Ariz. State U., 1975, others; RJR Nabisco rsch. scholar, 1989; NIH Clin. Investigator grantee, U. Calif.-San Francisco, 1986. Mem. Am. Thoracic Soc., Am. Physiol. Soc., Am. Soc. for Clin. Investigation. Office: Univ Calif PO Box 911 San Francisco CA 94143-0911

CAUGHLAN, GEORGEANNE ROBERTSON, retired physics educator; b. Montesano, Wash., Oct. 25, 1916; d. George Duncan and Anna (McLeod) Robertson; m. Charles Norris Caughlan, June 21, 1936 (div. 1975); children—Cheryl Karen, Kevin Michael, Kerry Jan, Deirdre Norrine. B.S. in Physics, U. Wash., 1937, Ph.D. in Physics, 1964. Faculty Mont. State U., Bozeman, 1957—; instr. physics Mont. State U., 1957-61, asst. prof., 1961-65, asso. prof., 1965-74, prof. physics, 1974-84, prof. emeritus, 1984—, acting dean grad. studies, 1977-78, acting v.p. acad. affairs, 1978; condr. research, cons. in field. NSF grantee, 1965-77. Fellow Am. Phys. Soc.; mem. Am. Astron. Soc., Internat. Astron. Union, Phi Beta Kappa, Sigma Xi. Episcopalian. Home: 1002 E Kagy Blvd Bozeman MT 59715-5834 Office: Mont State Univ Dept Physics Bozeman MT 59717

CAUGHLIN, STEPHENIE JANE, organic farmer; b. McAllen, Tex., July 23, 1948; d. James Daniel and Betty Jane (Warnock) C. BA in Family Econs., San Diego State U., 1972, MEd, 1973; M. in Psychology, U.S. Internat. U., San Diego, 1979. Cert. secondary life tchr., Calif. Owner, mgr. Minute Maid Svc., San Diego, 1970-75; prin. Rainbow Fin. Svcs., San Diego, 1975-78; tchr. San Diego Unified Sch. Dist., 1973-80; mortgage broker Santa Fe Mortgage Co., San Diego, 1980-81; commodity broker Premex Commodities, San Diego, 1981-84; pres., owner Nationwide Futures Corp., San Diego, 1984-88; owner, sec. Nationwide Metals Corp.; owner, gen. mgr. Seabreeze Organic Farm, 1984—. Sec. Arroyo Sorrento Assn., Del Mar, Calif., 1978—. Mem. Greenpeace Nature Conservancy, DAR, Sierra Club, Jobs Daus. Republican. Avocations: horseback riding, swimming, skiing, gardening. Home and Office: 3909 Arroyo Sorrento Rd San Diego CA 92130-2610

CAULFIELD, BARBARA ANN, federal judge; b. Oak Park, Ill., Dec. 2, 1947; d. Edward F. and Lucille M. (Kloth) C.; m. Stephen A. Mayo, July 12, 1985; children: Katherine, John, Jefferson, Alexander, Elizabeth. BS, Northwestern U., 1969, JD, 1972. Bar: Ill. 1972, Calif. 1982, Alaska 1983. Dir. research Chgo. Law Enforcement Group, 1972-73; instr. law Northwestern U., Chgo., 1973-74; assoc. prof. U. Oreg., Eugene, 1974-78; prof. U. Calif. Hastings, San Francisco, 1978-83, dean acad. affairs, 1980-81; ptnr. Brobeck, Phleger & Harrison, San Francisco, 1983-90; sr. counsel Pacific Bell, 1991; judge U.S. Dist. Ct. (no. dist.) Calif., San Francisco, 1991—; assoc. dir. Nat. Inst. for Trial Advocacy, San Francisco, 1979-82; lawyer rep. U.S. Ct. Appeals (9th cir.), San Francisco, 1984-87; Brendan Brown lectr. Cath. U. Am., Washington, 1984. Author: Questions Raised by Privacy, 1977, Child Abuse and Neglect, 1979, California Criminal Evidence, 1980, Civil RICO, 1987. Founder Child Advs. Assn., Chgo., 1972; bd. dirs. Nat. Com. to Prevent Child Abuse, Chgo., 1974-83, Lawyer's Com. for Urban Affairs, Chgo., 1986—. Named Citizen of Yr., Chgo. C. of C., 1974; recipient spl. commendation U. Calif. San Francisco, 1982. Mem. ABA (coun. criminal justice sect. 1980-84, chmn. litigation sect. com. 1983-86), Calif. Bar Assn., Alaska Bar Assn., Am. Law Inst., Queen's Bench, Assn. Trial Lawyers Am. Office: US Dist Ct PO Box 36060 450 Golden Gate Ave San Francisco CA 94102 also: US Dist Ct Rm 18425 Po Box 36060 San Francisco CA 94102

CAUSEY, GILL TERRY, recreation company executive; b. L.A., May 22, 1950; s. Gill B. and June Celeste (Hillman) C. BA, Whittier Coll., 1972. With Causey & Rhodes Devel. Co., Newport Beach, Calif., 1972-75, Causey Investment Co., Laguna Beach, Calif., 1973-80, B&C Wines Importers, Kamuela, Hawaii, 1980-86; pres. Charter Locker, Inc., Kailua-Kona, Hawaii, 1986—, Big Island Yacht Sales, Inc., Kailua-Kona, Hawaii, 1986-93, Paradise Rafting Adventures, Inc., Agana, Guam, 1991—; v.p. Atoll Express, Inc., Kailua-Kona, 1988—; dir. Pelorus Maritime Ltd., Rarotonga, Cook Islands, Causey Trust Investments, newport Beach. Vice pres. Nancy Griffith, Inc., Kailua-Kona, 1987—. Mem. Pacific Ocean Rsch. Found., nat. Assn. Charterboat Operators, Kona Sailing Club, Hawaii Yacht Club. Presbyterian. Office: Charter Locker Inc 74-425 Kaelakehe Pkwy Kailua Kona HI 96740

CAVAGNARO, EDMUND WALTER, radio station executive; b. San Francisco, Feb. 25, 1952; s. Walter John and Loretta (Monahan) C.; m. Barbara Ann Goode, June 10, 1978; 1 child, Elizabeth. BA, U. Calif., Berkeley, 1974; MJ, Northwestern U., 1975. Adminstrv. asst. San Francisco Bd. Suprs., 1976-77; editor KCBS Radio, San Francisco, 1978-81, asst. mng. editor, 1981-83, mng. editor, 1984-85, asst. dir. news and programming, 1985-88, dir. news and programming, 1988—. Chmn. Bay Region Emergency Broadcast System Com., San Francisco, 1991—; mem. fire task force City of Oakland, Calif., 1991-92; vol. basketball and baseball coach YMCA, San Francisco, 1991-92. Recipient Peabody award U. Ga., 1990, duPont-Columbia award Columbia U., 1990. Mem. Radio-TV News Dirs. Assn. (Edward R. Murrow award 1990). Office: KCBS-AM 1 Embarcadero Ctr San Francisco CA 94111

CAVALLERO, HAZEL HELEN, properties corporation executive; b. Burntmill, Colo., Mar. 18, 1913; d. Walter Merwin and Elizabeth Belle (Donley) Heller; m. John Walter Miller, June 4, 1937 (dec. Dec. 1943); m. Robert Angelo Cavallero, May 10, 1950; 1 child, Robert Clive. BA, U. Ill., 1941; MA, Stanford U., 1950. Pres. CSI, Inc., San Mateo, Calif., 1979—. Bd. dirs. Peninsula Vols., Menlo Park, Calif., 1962-74. Lt. (j.g.) USN, 1943-45. Republican. Episcopalian. Home: One Baldwin Ave # 323 San Mateo CA 94401 Office: 181 2nd Ave Ste 314 San Mateo CA 94401-3815

CAVANAGH, JOHN CHARLES, advertising agency executive; b. San Francisco, Dec. 19, 1932; s. John Timothy and Alicia Louise (McDowell) C.; m. Mary Ann Anding, Apr. 10, 1959; children: Karen, Brad. Student, U. Hawaii, 1950; B.S., U. San Francisco, 1954. Pub. rels. rep. Kaiser Industries Corp., Oakland, Calif., 1956-58; pub. rels. mgr. Kaiser Cement & Gypsum Corp., Oakland, 1958-63; pub. relations dir. Fawcett-McDermott Assos. Inc., Honolulu, Hawaii, 1964-66; ops. v.p. Fawcett-McDermott Assos. Inc., 1966-69, exec. v.p., 1969-73, pres., dir., 1973-75; pres., dir. Fawcett McDermott Cavanagh Inc., Honolulu, 1975-87, Fawcett McDermott Cavanagh Calif., Inc., San Francisco, 1975-87; pres. The Cavanagh Group/Advt. Inc., Honolulu, 1987—. Served to 1st. lt. 740th Guided Missile Bn. AUS, 1954-56. Named Advt. Man of Yr. Honolulu Advt. Fedn., 1985. Mem. Pub. Rels. Soc. Am. (accredited, v.p. 1970, pres. Hawaii chpt. 1971), Advt. Agy. Assn. Hawaii (pres. 1973), Am. Assn. Advt. Agys. (chmn. Hawaii coun. 1980-81), Affiliated Advt. Agys. Internat. (chmn. 1984-85), Sonoma County Ad Club, Fountaingrove Country Club, Outrigger Canoe Club, Commonwealth Club of Calif. Home and Office: 1142 Auahi St Ste 3007 Honolulu HI 96814 also: 3750 St Andrews Dr Santa Rosa CA 95403

CAVENAGH, DESMOND WARING, JR. (TIM CAVENAGH), quality assurance professional; b. Watertown, N.Y., Dec. 24, 1937; s. Desmond Waring and Margaret Agatha (Moscoe) C.; m. Jackie Marie Baumer, Dec. 14, 1963 (div. Oct. 1972); m. Martha Schaller Heavner, Feb. 11, 1977; stepchildren: Emily Suzanne, Ronald Stewart. AAS, SUNY, Farmingdale, 1958; police acad. cert., Allan Hancock Coll., 1970; BS, Sussex Coll., London, 1981. Electronic technician GE, Syracuse, N.Y., 1958-60; field technician GE, Clear, Alaska, 1960-61, Sacramento, 1961-62; field technician GE, Vandenberg AFB, Calif., 1962-77, radar system specialist, 1977-89; leader quality assurance Martin Marietta, Vandenberg AFB, Calif., 1989—. Capt. Sheriff's Dept. Res. Forces, Santa Maria, Calif., 1966—. Mem. Am. Soc. Quality Control (vice chmn. Calif. Ctrl. Coast div. 1992), Peace Officers Rsch. Assn., Elks. Republican. Home: 4357 Countrywood Dr Santa Maria CA 93455 Office: Martin Marietta Box 5158 Bldg 488 Vandenberg AFB CA 93437

CAVEZZA, CARMEN JAMES, career officer; b. Scranton, Pa., Nov. 15, 1937; s. James Vincent and Rose (Verdetto) C.; m. Joyce Mae Mathews, Apr. 30, 1960; 1 child, Peggy Joi Cavezza Anders. BA in Polit. Sci., The Citadel, 1961; MA in Govt., U. Miami, 1961; MS in Internat. Affairs, George Washington U., 1977, MPhil, 1992; grad. inf. officers' basic course, Fort Benning, 1961, grad. inf. officers' advanced course, 1967; grad., USM Corps. Commd. and Staff Coll., 1972, U.S. Nat. War Coll., 1977. Commd. 2d lt. U.S. Army, 1961, advanced through grades to lt. gen.; bn. comdr. 2d Inf. Div. U.S. Army, Republic of Korea, 1975-76; div. chief mil. pers. U.S. Army, Alexandria, Va., 1977-81; comdr. 197th Inf. Brigade (mech.) U.S. Army, Fort Benning, Ga., 1981-84; asst. div. comdr. 82d Airborne Div. U.S. Army, Fort Bragg, N.C., 1986-87; comdg. gen. 7th Inf. Div. (light) and Fort Ord, Calif. U.S. Army, 1987-89; comdg. gen. Inf. Ctr. U.S. Army, Fort Benning, 1989-91; comdg. gen. I Corps and Fort Lewis, Wash. U.S. Army, 1991—. Decorated D.S.M., Silver Star with oak leaf cluster, D.F.C. with oak leaf cluster, Bronze Star with four oak leaf clusters, Purple Heart, Legion of Merit with two oak leaf clusters, Meritorious Svc. medal with two oak leaf clusters, Army Commendation medal with three oak leaf clusters. Mem. Assn. of U.S. Army, The Citadel Alumni Assn., Rotary (Columbus, Ga.). Home: Quarters # 1 Fort Lewis WA 98433 Office: I Corps Fort Lewis GA 98433

CAVNAR, SAMUEL MELMON, author, publisher, activist; b. Denver, Nov. 10, 1925; s. Samuel Edward and Helen Anita (Johnston) C.; m. Peggy Nightengale, Aug. 14, 1977; children by previous marriage: Dona Cavnar Hambly, Judy Cavnar Bentrim; children: Heather Anne Hicks, Heide Lynn. Student pub. schs., Denver. Dist. mgr. U.S. C. of C., various locations, 1953-58; owner Cavnar & Assocs., mgmt. cons., Washington, Las Vegas, Nev., Denver and Reseda, Calif., 1958—; v.p. Lenz Assoc. Advt., Inc., Van Nuys, Calif., 1960—; dist. mgr. Western States Nu-Orm Plans, Inc., Los Angeles, 1947-52; cons. to architect and contractor 1st U.S. Missile Site, Wyo., 1957-58; prin. organizer Westway Corp. and subsidiaries, So. Calif. Devel. Co., 1958—; chmn. bd. Boy Sponsors, Inc., Denver, 1957-59; pres. Continental Am. Video Network Assn. Registry, Inc., Hollywood, Calif., 1967—; pres. United Sales Am., Las Vegas and Denver, 1969—; sr. mgmt. cons. Broadcast Mgmt. Cons. Service, Hollywood, Las Vegas, Denver, Washington, 1970—; pres., dir., exec. com. Am. Ctr. for Edn., 1968—; pub. Nat. Ind., Washington, 1970—, Nat. Rep. Statesman, Washington, 1969—, Nat. Labor Reform Leader, 1970—, Nat. Conservative Statesman, 1975—; owner Ran Vac Pub., Las Vegas and Los Angeles, 1976—; ptnr. P.S. Computer Services, Las Vegas, 1978—, C & A Mgmt., Las Vegas, 1978—, Westway Internat., 1983—; lectr. in field; spl. cons. various U.S. senators, congressmen, 1952—. Author: Run, Big Sam, Run, 1976, The Girls on Top, 1978, Big Brother Bureaucracy, The Cause and Cure, 1977, Kiddieland West, 1980, Games Politicians Play: How to Clean Up Their Act, 1981, A Very C.H.I.C. President, 1981, How to Clean Up Our Act, 1982, Assassination By Suicide, 1984, How to Get Limited Government, Limited Taxes, 1985, Tax Reform or Bust, 1985, At Last: Real Tax Reform, 1986, On the Road to a Real Balanced Budget, 1989, It's Time for Term Limitation, 1990, Clinton's "Investments": Just More Taxes, 1993, Hillary-Billary's New Road to Socialism, 1993. Nat. gen. chmn. Operation Houseclean, 1966-81; nat. candidate chmn. Citizens Com. To Elect Rep. Legislators, 1966, 68, 70, 72-74, 85—; mem. Calif. and Los Angeles County Rep. Cen. Coms., 1964-70; nat. gen. chmn. Project Prayer, 1962—; exec. dir. Project Alert, 1961—; nat. chmn. Nat. Labor Reform Com., 1969—; sustaining mem. Rep. Nat. Com., 1964—; Western states chmn. and nat. cochmn. Am. Taxpayers Army, 1959—; area II chmn. Calif. Gov.'s Welfare Reform Com., 1970; chmn. Com. Law and Order in Am., 1975; mem. Nev. State Rep. Com., 1972—; mem. Clark County Rep. Com., 1972—; bd. dirs. Conservative Caucus, Las Vegas, 1974, 76, 82, 92; Rep. candidat for U.S. Senate from Nev., 1976, 82, 92; Rep. nominee for U.S. Congress from 30th dist. Calif., 1968, 70; nat. chmn. Return Pueblo Crew, 1968, Citizens League for Labor Reform, 1984—; nat. co-chmn. U.S. Taxpayers Forces, 1985—; pres., trustee Community Youth Activities Found., 1977—; nat. chmn. Operation Bus Stop, 1970—, P.R.I.D.E. Com., 1981—, Positivics Program, 1982—; co-chmn. Question 8 Com., 1980-82, S.H.A.F.T.E.D. Tax Repeal Com., 1982 C.H.I.C. Polit. Edn. Com., 1977—, People Against Tax Hikes Com., 1983—; bd. dirs., Nev. co-chmn. Pres. Reagan's Citizen's Com. for Tax Reform, 1985-86; nat. chmn. Term Limitation Com., 1988—. Served with USN, 1942-45, USAF, 1950-53, Korea; comdr. USCG Aux., 1959-60. Recipient Silver medal SAR. Mem. Am. Legion (comdr. 1947-48, mem. nat. conv. disting. guest com. 1947-52), DAV, VFW, Am. Security Council (nat. adviser 1966—), U.S. C. of C. (sr. mem. rep. 1986—). Home: 301A Misty Isle Ln Las Vegas NV 89107-1135 Office: 1615 H St NW Washington DC 20062

CAWDREY, NANCY TOWNSEND, educator; b. Ft. Benning, Ga., Dec. 19, 1948; d. Donald Dean and Jane (Wilson) D.; m. Steven Wiley Cawdrey, July 23, 1971; 1 child, Morgan Dunlop. Student, Am. U. in Paris, 1968; BA, George Washington U., 1970. Co-dir. Kilworthy House, Tavistock, Devon, Eng., 1971-77; co-founder Spring Creek Community, Thompson Falls, Mont., 1979—, dir. edn., 1983-85, dir. admissions, 1985-87, alumni rels./fundraising, 1987-90, acting dir., 1990, co-dir., 1990-91; sch. rep. Round Square Conf. Represented in permanent collection Nordstrom Corp.; galleries: Kootenai Galleries, Bigfork, Mont., The Company Store Gallery, Sandpoint, Idaho, Le Petite Gallerie, Bozeman, Mont. Home and Office: Spring Creek Community 1342 Blue Slide Rd Thompson Falls MT 59873

CAWLEY, RHYA NOEL, theater and film writer; b. Bklyn., Apr. 9, 1947; d. Sidney Saraby and Beverly Leonora (Fields) Dash; divorced. Fine arts cert., Dash Sch. Art, 1972; BA in Fine Arts and Edn., St. Thomas Aquinas Coll., 1974; MA in Comms., N.Y. Inst. Tech., 1982; MA in Film and Telecommunications, San Diego State U., 1992. Graphic artist Warner Bros. Publs., N.Y.C., 1975-80; research mgr. Frank Barth Pub. Relations, N.Y.C., 1982-84; freelance writer N.Y., N.J., 1984—; agent AFH/ROBB Group, L.A., 1992-93. Author: (screenplay) Slow Dancing, 1992, (book) The Coral Canyon Circus, 1987, (TV series) The San Diego Kids, 1992; author, lyricist, librettist (musical) Mia Moonchild, 1987; poetry in Am. Anthology of Poetry, 1986. Democrat. Jewish. Home: 16345 Bassett Ct Ramona CA 92065

CAYETANO, BENJAMIN JEROME, lieutenant governor, former state senator and representative; b. Honolulu, Nov. 14, 1939; s. Bonifacio Marcos and Eleanor (Infante) C.; m. Lorraine Gueco, Sept. 20, 1958; children: Brandon, Janeen, Samantha. B.A., UCLA, 1968; J.D., Loyola U., 1971. Bar: Hawaii 1971. Practiced in Honolulu, 1971-86; mem. Hawaii Ho. of Reps., 1975-78, Hawaii Senate, 1979-86; lt. gov. State of Hawaii, 1986—; bar examiner Hawaii Supreme Ct., 1976-78, disciplinary bd., 1982-86; arbitration panel 1st Cir. Ct. State of Hawaii, 1986; adv. U. Hawaii Law Rev., 1982-84. Mem. bd. regents Chaminade U., 1980-83; mem. adv. council U. Hawaii Coll. Bus. Adminstrn., 1982-83. Recipient Excellence in Leadership Medallion Asia-Pacific Acad. Consortium for Pub. Health, 1991, UCLA Alumni award for excellence in pub. svc., 1993. Democrat. Office: Office of Lt Gov 14th fl 235 S Beretania St Honolulu HI 96813

CAYWOOD, THOMAS ELIAS, educator, consultant; b. Lake Park, Iowa, May 9, 1919; s. Harry E. and Alice A. (Bollenbach) C.; m. Mary E. Miller, June 6, 1941; children: Ann, Beth, Kay Dee. AB, Cornell Coll., Mt. Vernon, Iowa, 1939; MA, Northwestern U., 1940; PhD, Harvard U., 1947. Sr. mathematician Inst. Air Weapons Rsch. U. Chgo., 1947-50, coord. rsch., 1950-52; supr. ops. rsch. Armour Rsch. Found., Chgo., 1952-53; mng. ptnr. Caywood-Schiller Assocs., Chgo., 1953-70; v.p. Caywood-Schiller div. A.T. Kearney and Co., Chgo., 1970-78; lectr. grad. sch. bus. U. Chgo., 1953-58, 78-86, sch. bus. econs. Calif. State U., Hayward, 1981—; pres. Investigacion de Operaciones S.A. (Mex.), 1959-60; mem. R & D bd. Dept. Def., 1952-53, chmn. panel on ordinance transport and supply, 1959-64, def. sci. bd., 1960-64. Bd. dirs. Cornell Coll. Alumni Assn., 1962-65, trustee, 1964—, pres. bd. trustees 1970-73. Mem. Am. Math Assn., Am. Inst. Indsl. Engrs., Am. Math Soc., Inst. Mgmt. Sci., Ops. Rsch. Soc. Am. (editor 1961-68, pres. 1969-70), Cosmos Club. Home: 704 Argyle Ave Flossmoor IL 60422-1204 Office: Calif State U Sch Bus & Econs Hayward CA 94542

CAZIER, BARRY JAMES, electrical engineer, software developer; b. Phoenix, May 10, 1943; s. James Henry and Dorothy Marie (Lynton) C.; m. Susan Arline Shewey, June 13, 1964 (dec. July 1979); children: Suzanne, Bryan. Student, Colo. Sch. Mines, 1961-62; BSEE, U. Colo., 1965; student advanced bus. adminstrn., Ariz. State U., 1974-77. Mfg. mgmt. Gen. Electric, Richland, Wash., 1965-66, Warren, Ohio, 1966-67; system engr. Gen. Electric, Schenectady, N.Y., 1967-69; project mgr. Honeywell, Phoenix, 1970-80, dir. field ops., 1980—; prin. Cazier Software Designs, Scottsdale, Ariz., 1985—. adv. Jr. Achievement, Phoenix, 1972. Club: IBM PC Users (Phoenix). Home: 6616 E Desert Cv Scottsdale AZ 85254 Office: Honeywell 16404 N Black Canyon Hwy Phoenix AZ 85023-3095

CECH, JOHN EDWARD, continuing education administrator; b. Livingston, Mont., June 17, 1962; s. James B. and Theresa (Polilo) C.; m. Victoria S. Brown, Sept. 8, 1989. BA in Computer Sci., Ea. Mont. Coll., Billings, 1985. Computer instr. Ea. Mont. Coll., 1984-86; computer cons. U.S. Bur. Reclamation and U.S. Bur. Land Mgmt., Mont., Wyo., Colo., Nebr., 1986-87; dir. computer applications program Rocky Mountain Coll., Billings, 1987-89, dir. continuing edn. and summer session, 1989—; computer cons. United Way of Billings, 1989. Author: Using VAX/VMS, 1986. Bd. dirs. Greater Rose Park After Sch. Programs, Billings, 1991—; mem. Billings Sports Com., 1991—; mem. tech. com. Sch. Dist. 2, Billings, 1991—; site chairperson United Way of Billings, 1990. Named to Outstanding Young Men of Am., 1990. Mem. Billings Com. on Fgn. Rels., Billings Rotary, Billings Town and Gown Soc. Democrat. Roman Catholic. Office: Rocky Mountain Coll 1511 Poly Dr Billings MT 59105

CECH, THOMAS ROBERT, chemistry and biochemistry educator; b. Chicago, Ill., Dec. 8, 1947; m. Carol Lynn Martinson; children: Allison E., Jennifer N. BA in Chemistry, Grinnell Coll., 1970, DSc (hon.), 1987; PhD in Chem., U. Calif., Berkeley, 1975; DSc (hon.), U. Chgo., 1991. Postdoctoral fellow dept. biology MIT, Cambridge, Mass., 1975-77; from asst. prof. to assoc. prof. chemistry U. Colo., Boulder, 1978-83, prof. chemistry and biochemistry also molecular cellular and devel. biology, 1983—, disting. prof., 1990—; research prof. Am. Cancer Soc., 1987—; investigator Howard Hughes Med. Inst., 1988—; co-chmn. Nucleic Acids Gordon Conf., 1984; Phillips disting. visitor Haverford Coll., 1984; Vivian Ernst meml. lectr. Brandeis U., 1984, Cynthia Chan meml. lectr. U. Calif., Berkeley; mem. Welch Found. Symposium, 1985; Danforth lectr. Grinnell Coll, 1986; Pfizer lectr. Harvard U., 1986; Verna and Marrs McLean lectr. Baylor Coll. Medicine, 1987; Harvey lectr., 1987; Mayer lectr. MIT, 1987; Martin D. Kamen disting. lectureship, U. Calif., San Diego, 1988; Alfred Burger lectr. U. Va., 1988; Berzelius lectr. Karolinska Inst., 1988; Osamu Hayaishi lectr. Internat. Union Biochemistry, Prague, 1988; Beckman lectr. U. Utah, 1989, HHMI lectr. MIT, 1989; Max Tishler lectr. Merck, 1989; Abbott vis. scholar U. Chgo., 1989; Herriott lectr. Johns Hopkins U., 1990; J.T. Baker lectr., 1990; G.N. Lewis lectr. U. Calif., Berkeley, 1990; Sonneborn lectr. Ind. U., 1991; Sternbach lectr. Yale U., 1991; W. Pauli lectr., Zürich, 1992; Carter-Wallace lectr. Princeton U., 1992; Hastings lectr. Harvard U., 1992; Stetten lectr. NIH, 1992; Dauben lectr. U. Wash., 1992; Marker lectr. U. Md., 1993; Hirschmann lectr. Oberlin Coll., 1993; Beach lectr. Purdue U., 1993. Assoc. editor Cell, 1986-87; mem. editorial bd. Genes and Development; dep. editor Science mag. NSF fellow, 1970-75, Pub. Health Service research fellow Nat. Cancer Inst. 1975-77, Guggenheim fellow, 1985-86; recipient medal Am. Inst. Chemists, 1970, Research Career Devel. award Nat. Cancer Inst., 1980-85, Young Sci. award Passano Found., 1984, Harrison Howe award, 1984, Pfizer award, 1985, U.S. Steel award, 1987, V.D. Mattia award, 1987, Louisa Gross Horowitz prize, 1988, Newcombe-Cleveland award AAAS, 1988, Heineken prize Royal Netherlands Acad. Arts and Scis., 1988, Gairdner Found. Internat. award, 1988, Lasker Basic Med. Rsch. award, 1988, Rosenstiel award, 1989, Warren Triennial prize, 1989, Nobel prize in Chemistry, 1989, Hopkins medal Brit. Biochemical Soc., 1992; named to Esquire Mag. Register, 1985, Westerner of Yr. Denver Post, 1986. Mem. AAAS, Am. Soc. Biochem. Molecular Biology, NAS, Am. Acad. Arts and Scis., European Molecular Biology Orgn. Office: U Colo Dept Chemistry & Biochemistry Boulder CO 80309

CECI, JESSE ARTHUR, violinist; b. Phila., Feb. 2, 1924; s. Luigi Concezio and Catherine Marie (Marotta) C.; m. Catherine Annette Stevens, Aug. 5, 1979. BS, Juilliard Sch. Music, 1951; license de concert, L'Ecole Normale de Musique, Paris, 1954; MusM, Manhattan Sch. Music, 1971. Assoc. concertmaster New Orleans Philharm. Orch., 1953-54; violinist Boston Symphony Orch., 1954-59, N.Y. Philharm. Orch., N.Y., 1959-62, Esterhazy Orch., N.Y.C., 1962-68; concertmaster Denver Symphony Orch., 1974-89, Colo. Symphony Orch., 1989—; over 50 solo performances of 22 major works; mem. Zimbler Sinfonietta, Boston, 1957-59; participant Marlboro Festival Chamber Orch. Vt., summmers 1960-62, 65, Marlboro Festival Chamber Orch. European-Israeli tour, 1965, Grand Teton Festival, Wyo., 1972, N.Mex. Festival, Taos, 1980, Carmel (Calif.) Bach Festival, 1987—, Whistler (B.C., Can.) Mozart Festival, 1989-90; mem. faculty N.Y. Coll. Music, 1961-71, NYU, 1971-74, U. Colo., 1975-79; guest faculty Univ. Denver, 1986; mem., assoc. concertmaster Casals Festival Orch., San Juan, P.R., 1963-77; violinist Cleve. Orch. fgn. tours, 1967, 73, 78, Cin. Symphony Orch. world tour, 1966; 1st violinist N.Y. String Quartet in-residence at U. Maine, Orono, summer 1969; concertmaster Minn. Orch., summers 1970-71; guest concertmaster Pitts. Symphony Orch., Pitts., L.A., 1988, mem. N.Y. Philharmonia Chamber Ensemble in-residence at Hopkins Ctr., Dartmouth U., summer 1973; recitalist, Paris, 1963, Amsterdam, 1963, recitalist Carnegie Recital Hall, N.Y.C., 1963, Town Hall, N.Y.C., 1968, 70, Alice Tully Hall, N.Y.C., 1972; fgn. tour Pitts. Symphony Orch., 1989. Concertmaster Denver Chamber Orch., 1985-90; faculty Congress of Strings, Dallas, 1985. Served to cpl. U.S. Army, 1943-46, PTO. Fulbright fellow Paris, 1951-52. Democrat. Roman Catholic. Office: Colo Symphony Orch 1031 13th St Denver CO 80204-2156

CEDOLINE, ANTHONY JOHN, psychologist; b. Rochester, N.Y., Sept. 19, 1942; s. Peter Ross and Mary J. (Anthony) C.; m. Clare Marie De Rose, Aug. 16, 1964; children: Maria A., Antonia C., Peter E. Student, U. San Francisco, 1960-62; BA, San Jose State U., 1965, MS, 1968; PhD in Ednl. Pscyhology, Columbia Pacific U., 1983. Lic. ednl. psychologist, sch. adminstr., marriage, family, child counselor, sch psychologist, sch. counselor, social worker, Calif.; Lic. real estate broker, Calif. Mng. ptnr. Cienega Valley Vineyards and Winery (formerly Almaden Vineyards) and Comml. Shopping Ctrs., 1968—; coord. psychol. svcs. Oak Grove Sch. Dist., San Jose, Calif., 1968-81, asst. dir. pupil svcs., 1977-81; dir. pupil svcs. Oak Grove Sch. Dist., San Jose, 1981-83; pvt. practice, ednl. psychologist Ednl. Assocs., San Jose, 1983—; co-dir. Biofeedback Inst. of Santa Clara County, San Jose, 1976-83; ptnr. in Cypress Ctr.-Ednl. Psychologists and Consultancy, 1978—; cons., program auditor for Calif. State Dept. Edn.; instr. U. Calif., Santa Cruz and LaVerne Coll. Ext. courses; guest spkr. San Jose State U.; lectr., workshop presenter in field. Author: Occupational Stress and Job Burnout, 1982, A Parents Guide to School Readiness, 1971, The Effect of Affect, 1975; contbr. articles to profl. jours. and newspapers. Founder, bd. dirs. Lyceum of Santa Clara County, 1971—. Mem. NEA, Calif. Tchrs. Assn., Calif. Assn. Sch. Psychologists, Nat. Assn. Sch. Psychologists, Council for Exceptional Children, Calif. Assn. for Gifted, Assn. Calif. Sch. Adminstrs., Calif. Personnel & Guidance Assn., Biofeedback Soc. Am., Nat. Assn. Realtors, Calif. Assn. Realtors, San Jose Realty Bd., Tau Delta Phi. Home and Office: 1183 Nikulina Ct San Jose CA 95120-5441

CEGUERRA, LOURDES OBIETA, marketing professional; b. Quezon City, Luzon, Philippines, July 30, 1963; came to U.S., 1980; d. Bernard and Lina (Obieta) C.; m. Donald Roberts, Mar. 21, 1987 (div. Sept. 1991). BA in Econs., BA in Computer Sci., U. Calif., Berkeley, 1985; postgrad., Pa. State U., 1992. Software engr. Software Rsch. Assn., San Francisco, 1985-86; tech. account mgr. Ask/Ingres Corp., Burlington, Mass., 1986-90; mktg. mgr. Digital Equipment Corp., San Francisco, 1990—. Mem. U. Calif. Honors Students Soc., Omicron Delta Epsilon.

CELENTANO, FRANCIS MICHAEL, artist, art educator; b. N.Y.C., May 25, 1928; s. Michael Anthony and Rafaela (Valentino) C. B.A., NYU, 1951, M.A. in Art History, 1957. Lectr. C.W. Post Coll., L.I., N.Y., 1961-63, N.Y. Inst. Tech., Old Westbury, N.Y., 1965-66; from assoc. prof. to prof. Sch. Art, U. Wash., Seattle, 1966—. One-man exhbns. include: Howard Wise Gallery, N.Y.C., 1963, Foster/White Gallery, Seattle, 1971, 73, 75, 78, Diane Gilson Gallery, Seattle, 1981, 82, Fountain Gallery, Portland, Oreg., 1983, Greg Kucera Gallery, Seattle, 1986, 89, 91, Safeco Plaza, Seattle, 1990. Laura Russo Gallery, Portland, 1990, Woodside/Braseth Gallery, 1993; retrospective exhbn. Portland Ctr. for the Visual Arts, 1986, Whatcom County Mus., Bellingham, Washington, 1992; represented in permanent collections: Mus. of Modern Art, N.Y.C., Albright-Knox Mus., Buffalo, Seattle Art Mus., Fed. Res. Bank of San Francisco, Wash. State Arts Commn., King County Arts Commn., Univ. Hosp., Seattle. Fulbright scholar Rome, 1958; fed. regional fellow in painting Western States Arts Fedn. Nat. Endowment for the Arts, 1990. Office: Univ of Wash Sch of Art DM-10 Seattle WA 98195

CELIS, MANUEL, international manufacturing company executive; b. El Paso, Tex., Oct. 20, 1944; m. Carolyn Louis McGowan, June 8, 1965; children: Manuel Jr., Stephen. BSBA, Rollins Coll., 1978. Sales rep. R&R Electronics, El Paso, Tex., 1966-70; mgr. Magnavox, El Paso, 1970-72; systems test foreman Stromberg-Carlson Corp., Lake Mary, Fla., 1972-80; mfg. mgr. Oster Corp., Mex., 1980-84; plant mgr. Zenith Corp., Mex., 1984-86; ops. mgr. Zenith Corp., 1986-88; exec. dir., v.p. Mex. ops. Sanyo Mfg. Corp., San Diego, 1989—. With USAF, 1961-65. Mem. Am. Mgmt. Assn. Republican. Home: 1734 Sherbrooke St San Diego CA 92139-3970 Office: Sanyo Mfg Corp 2001 Sanyo Ave San Ysidro CA 92173-2229

CELLA, JOHN ANTHONY, chemist; b. Chgo., Apr. 28, 1926; s. John Anthony and Rose Catherine (Ginocchio) C.; m. Marie Frances Ullrich, Feb. 26, 1949; children: John Anthony, Mary Lee, Leslie Ann Johnson, William. BS, DePaul U., Chgo., 1947; PhD, U. Notre Dame, 1950. Rsch. chemist Armour & Co., Chgo., 1950-52; rsch. chemist/grp. leader G.D. Searle & Co., Skokie, Ill., 1952-61; asst. to pres. Julian Labs., Franklin Park, Ill., 1961-63; v.p. Alberto Culver, Melrose Park, Ill., 1963-72; v.p., bd. dirs., exec. com. Elizabeth Arden, N.Y.C., Indpls., 1972-86; chem. cons. San Diego, 1986—. Contbr. articles to profl. jours.; patentee in field. Bd. dirs. Am. Cancer Soc., Indpls., 1980-81. Recipient Disting. Alumni award, DePaul U., Chgo., 1973; named Chicagoan of the Yr. in Sci., Chgo. Assn. Commerce and Industry, 1960. Fellow Soc. Cosmetic Chemists; mem. Am. Chem. Soc., Sigma Xi. Home: 16435 Calle Pulido San Diego CA 92128-3250

CELLI, KENNETH DANA, lawyer; b. San Francico, June 9, 1956; s. Ronald Louis Celle and Florene Paula (Resnick) Fields; m. Barbara Lynn Paul, May 31, 1986. Student, U. Hartford, 1974-75; BA, UCLA, 1980; JD, Whittier Coll., 1987. Bar: Calif. 1988. Dep. dist. atty. Los Angeles County Dist. Atty.'s Office, L.A., 1988-90; pvt. practice, San Rafael, Calif., 1990—; prof. Whittier Coll. Sch. Law, L.A., 1989-90. Co-chmn. L.A. Beautiful, Inc., 1988-89. Mem. Calif. State Bar, Marin County Bar Assn., Calif. Attys. for Criminal Justice, Calif. Pub. Defenders Assn., Assn. Dep. Dist. Attys., Italian Am. Lawyers Assn., Phi Alpha Delta. Office: 1299 4th St Ste 405 San Rafael CA 94901-3030

CENARRUSA, PETE T., secretary of state; b. Carey, Idaho, Dec. 16, 1917; s. Joseph and Ramona (Gardoqui) C.; m. Freda B. Coates, Oct. 25, 1947; 1 son, Joe Earl. B.S. in Agr., U. Idaho, 1940. Tchr. high sch. Cambridge, Idaho, 1940-41, Carey and Glenns Ferry, Idaho, 1946; tchr. vocat. agr. VA, Blaine County, Idaho, 1946-51; farmer, woolgrower, nr. Carey, 1946—; mem. Idaho Ho. of Reps., 1951-67, speaker, 1963-67; sec. state Idaho, 1967-90, 91-94; mem. Idaho Bd. Land Commrs., Idaho Bd. Examiners; pres. Idaho Flying Legislators, 1953-63; chmn. Idaho Legis. Council, 1964—, Idaho Govt. Reorgn. Com.; Idaho del. Council State Govts., 1963—. Elected ofcl., mem. BLM Adv. Coun., Boise Dist.; Rep. adminstr. Hall of Fame, 1978. Maj. USMCR, 1942-46, 52-58. Named Hon. Farmer Future Farmers Am., 1955; named to Agrl. Hall of Fame, 1973; Idaho Athletic Hall of Fame, 1976, Basque Hall of Fame, 1983. Mem. Blaine County Livestock Mktg. Assn., Blaine County Woolgrowers Assn. (chmn. 1954), Carey C. of C. (pres. 1952), U. Idaho Alumni Assn., Gamma Sigma Delta, Tau Kappa Epsilon. Republican. Office: Office of Sec State State Capitol Rm 203 Boise ID 83720*

CENOTTO, LAWRENCE ARTHUR, historian, publisher, writer; b. St. Louis, Oct. 20, 1931; s. Lawrence and Mary (Smith) C.; m. Barbara Mary Grogan, June 10, 1952 (div. 1976); children: Lawrence A., Lisa D., Lee A., Locke A., Laird A.; m. Darlene Bernice Wassink, Oct. 23, 1976. AA, Compton (Calif.) Coll., 1951. Class A broadcasting lic. Clk. So. Calif. Edison, Compton, Alhambra, Calif., 1955-57; radio, TV broadcaster various stations, Wyo., Mont., Calif., 1957-63; news dir. KBEE Radio, Modesto, Calif., 1963-64; reporter-photgrapher Sacramento (Calif.) Bee, 1964-67; legis. asst. Gene Chappie, Calif. Assemblyman, Sacramento, 1967-74; founder, pub. Scenic 88 Fun Times, Jackson, Calif., 1975-85; archivist County Amador, Jackson, 1983—; announcer Cable TV Slivick Prodns., Pine Grove, Calif, 1990—; researcher various hist. cons., Jackson, Calif., 1975—. Author, editor, pub. Historical Jackson Guidebook, 1981, Italian Centennial Booklet, 1981, Logan's Alley Vol. I, 1985, Vol. II, 1987. Founder Amador County Young Republicans, 1968; mem., past chmn. Amador Cunty Rep. Ctrl. Com., Jackson, 1970s. Mem. Jackson Rotary Club. Home: 557 Clinton Rd Jackson CA 95642 Office: Amador County Archives 38 Summit St Jackson CA 95642

CEO, RAYMOND ANTHONY, college official; b. Bklyn., Apr. 16, 1956; s. Angelo John and Elizabeth (Bruno) C.; m. Regina Mae McAleer, Feb. 11, 1979; children: Heather Elizabeth, Raymond Anthony Jr. BSBA, Embry-Riddle Aero. U., Prescot, Ariz., 1991. Mail clk. AFSA Data Corp., Long Beach, Calif., 1978-79, account analyst, 1979-80, group leader, 1980-83; fin. aid counselor Embry-Riddle Aero. U., 1983-86, loan and scholarship coord., 1986-89; dir. fin. aid Prescott Coll., 1989—. Mem. Nat. Assn. Vets. Programs Adminstrs., Nat. Assn. Student Fin. Aid Adminstrs., Western Assn. Student Fin. Aid Adminstrs., Ariz. Assn. Fin. Aid Adminstrs. (rep.-at-large 1991-92, v.p. 1992—), Ariz. Assn. Collegiate Registrars and Admissions Officers, Ariz. Vet. Programs Adminstrs. Democrat. Roman Catholic. Home: 5428 E Sapphire Dr Prescott AZ 86301 Office: Prescott Coll 220 Grove Ave Prescott AZ 86301

CEPPOS, JEROME MERLE, newspaper editor; b. Washington, Oct. 14, 1946; s. Harry and Florence (Epstein) C.; m. Karen E. Feingold, Mar. 7, 1982; children: Matthew, Robin. B.S. in Journalism, U. Md., 1969; post-grad., Knight-Ridder Exec. Leadership Program, 1989-90. Reporter, asst. city editor, night city editor Rochester Democrat & Chronicle, N.Y., 1969-72; from asst. city editor, to nat. editor, to asst. mng. editor The Miami Herald, Fla., 1972-81; assoc. editor San Jose Mercury News, Calif., 1981, mng. editor, 1983—; mem. nat. adv. bd. Knight Ctr. Specialized Reporting, U. Md.; mem. Accrediting Coun. on Edn. in Journalism and Mass Comm. Mem. AP Mng. Editors (bd. dirs.), Am. Soc. Newspaper Editors, Calif. Soc. Newspaper Editors (bd. dirs., pres.), Soc. Profl. Journalists, Silicon Valley Capital Club. Home: 14550 Pike Rd Saratoga CA 95070-5359 Office: San Jose Mercury News 750 Ridder Park Dr San Jose CA 95190-0001

CERASO, CHUCK MARTIN, artist, educator; b. Manchester, Conn., June 30, 1951; s. Mario Rocco and Mary (Culotta) C. Student, U. Notre Dame, 1969-72, New Orleans Acad. Fine Art, 1978-80, Cape Sch. Art, 1987. Freelance artist, tchr. New Orleans, Louisville, Colo., 1974—; instr. art Arvada (Colo.) Ctr. for Arts and Humanities, 1988—, Boulder (Colo.) County Sch. Dist., 1988—. Exhibited paintings in numerous shows, 1980-91. Mem. ECKANKAR (regional ECK spiritual aide 1991—), Colo. Satsang Soc. Home and Office: 565 East St Louisville CO 80027

CERATO, KAREN LEE, clinical dietitian; b. Sacramento, Apr. 19, 1963; d. Richard R. and Donna (Miller) Auwaerter; m. John V. Cerato, Oct. 26, 1991. BS in Dietetics, U. Calif., Davis, 1987. Registered dietitian. Dietetic intern U. Wis., Madison, 1988; clin. dietitian Mercy San Juan Hosp., Carmichael, Calif., 1988-89, chief clin. dietitian, 1989-92; chief clin. dietitian Mercy San Juan Hosp., Mercy Am. River Hosp., 1992—; preceptor food svc. mgmt. Am. River Coll., Carmichael, 1989—; preceptor dietetics U. Calif., Davis, 1990—. Contbr. columns to The Bridge newletter, 1987-90. Mem. Am. Dietetic Assn., Clin. Nutrition Mgmt. Office: Mercy San Juan Hosp 6501 Coyle Ave Carmichael CA 95608

CERBONE, ROBERT, sales executive; b. Bklyn., Jan. 29, 1960; s. Frank James Sr. and Margaret (Castore) C.; m. Deborah Sue Boyle, Sept. 23, 1989. BA in Physics, Adelphi U., 1982; MBA in Mktg., L.I. U., 1985. Sales engr. Logitek, Farmingdale, N.Y., 1981-82; systems support specialist Porta Systems Corp., Syosset, N.Y., 1982-83; sales engr. Rhode & Schwarz, New Hyde Park, N.Y., 1983-84; regional sales rep. Chyron Corp., Melville, N.Y., 1984-86; sales engr. Ampex Systems Corp., Redwood City, Calif., 1986-87, dist. mgr., 1987-89, dir. southcentral region, 1989-91, mgr. hdqs. sales programs, 1991, dir. eastern region, 1991—. Mem. Soc. Broadcast Engrs. Roman Catholic.

CEREGHINO, WARREN WOOD, television news executive; b. San Mateo, Calif., May 6, 1937; s. Raimondo Ernesto and Mary Melissa (Wood) C.; m. Donna Jeanne Olson, June 22, 1963 (div. 1984); children: Todd Warren, Josh Mathew; m. Marilyn Ardis Haese, Feb. 23, 1985; children: Andrew Arthur, Erik Raymond. BA, Ariz. State U., 1961. News editor KPHO-TV Channel 5, Phoenix, 1960-63; news dir. KOVR-TV Channel 13, Sacramento, 1963-66; media dir. Coun. Calif. Growers, San Francisco, 1966-68; news dir. KTVU-TV Channel 2, San Francisco, 1968-71; news editor KNBC-TV Channel 4, L.A., 1971-89; news dir. KTLA-TV Channel 5, L.A., 1989—; cons. Gannett Found., Rochester, N.Y., 1985-89; lectr. UCLA Ext., 1979-89, U. So. Calif., L.A., 1980-90. With USAF, 1961-62. Recipient Geo. Foster Peabody award U. Ga., 1991, Golden Mike award Radio-TV News Assn. So. Calif., 1990. Episcopalian. Office: KTLA-TV 5800 Sunset Blvd Los Angeles CA 90028

CERNAK, KEITH PATRICK, health care and financial consultant; b. Northampton, Mass., Mar. 17, 1954; s. Samuel and Geraldine (Dykstra) C.; m. Kristin Freedman, Sept. 10, 1983; 1 child, Emily Samantha. BA magna cum laude, U. Mass., 1976; MPH, U. Hawaii, 1980; MBA, UCLA, 1984. Healthcare researcher U. Hawaii, Honolulu, 1978; health planning cons. Guam Health Planning Agy., Agana, 1979; rsch. dir. Hawaii Dept. Health, Honolulu, 1980-81; grad. instr. UCLA Sch. Pub. Health, 1981; mgmt. cons. Am. Med. Internat., Beverly Hills, Calif., 1982; asst. v.p. Crocker Bank, L.A., 1984-86; v.p. Weyerhaeuser, San Francisco, 1986-90; health rsch. dir. Evergreen Med. Ctr., Seattle, 1992—; pub. hosp. dist. and health care cons.; presenter in field. Author papers in field. Cabinet mem. Shepherd of the Hills Ch., Berkeley, Calif., 1988-90. Health Svc. scholar U. Hawaii, 1978. Mem. UCLA Sch. Mgmt., Beta Gamma Sigma. Home: 1904 212th Ave SE Issaquah WA 98027-9518

CERNY, JOSEPH, III, chemistry educator, scientific laboratory administrator, university dean and official; b. Montgomery, Ala., Apr. 24, 1936; s. Joseph and Olaette Genette (Jury) C.; m. Barbara Ann Nedelka, June 13, 1959 (div. Nov. 1982); children: Keith Joseph, Mark Evan; m. 2d Susan Dinkelspiel Stern, Nov. 12, 1983. BS in Chem. Engring., U. Miss.-Oxford, 1957; postgrad. Fulbright scholar, U. Manchester, Eng., 1957-58; PhD in Nuclear Chemistry, U. Calif.-Berkeley, 1961; PhD in Physics (hon.), U. Jyväskylä, Finland, 1990. Asst. prof. chemistry U. Calif., Berkeley, 1961-67, assoc. prof., 1967-71, prof., 1971—, chmn. dept. chemistry, 1975-79, head nuclear sci. div., 1979-84, assoc. dir. Lawrence Berkeley Lab., 1979-84; dean grad. div. U. Calif., 1985—, provost for research, 1986—; mem. Nat. Acad. Scis. Physics Commn., chair nuclear physics panel, 1983-86; mem. NASA Adv. Coun., Univ. Rels. Task Force, 1991-93, NRC Study of Rsch. Doctorates, 1992-94. Editor: Nuclear Reactions and Spectroscopy, 4 vols., 1974; contbr. numerous articles to field to profl. jours. Served with U.S. Army, 1962-63. Recipient E.O. Lawrence award U.S. AEC, 1974; Guggenheim fellow, 1969-70; recipient Nuclear Chemistry award Am. Chem. Soc., 1984, A. von Humboldt Sr. Scientist award, 1985. Fellow AAAS, Am. Phys. Soc.; mem. Am. Chem. Soc., Assn. Grad. Schs. (v.p., pres.-elect 1992-94). Democrat. Home: 860 Keeler Ave Berkeley CA 94708-1324 Office: U Calif 309 Sproul Hall Berkeley CA 94720

CERRI, ALBERTO, management consultant executive; b. Mar del Pata, Buenos Aires, Argentina, Oct. 13, 1948; came to U.S., 1964; s. Alberto Roman and Milagro (Climent) C.; m. Christina M. Gastaldi, Jan. 17, 1978; children: Alberto A., Patrick L. AA in Bus. Adminstrn., Santa Ana Coll., 1970; Contracts in Architecture/Engring., U. Buenos Aires, 1978; postgrad. studies in small bus. mgmt., Cath. U. La Plata, Argentina, 1985; BS in bus. mgmt., U. Laverne, 1993. Lic. income tax preparer. Acctg. dept. supr. Security Indsl. Supply, South Gate, Calif., 1970-71; fin. mgr. Ullom, Kahn & Assoc., Santa Ana, Calif., 1971-74; mng. ptnr. Estudio Enterprise, La Plata, 1974-86; exec. dir. Cerrico Enterprises, Santa Ana, 1986—. Contbr. articles to profl. jours. Pres. Buenos Aires regional chpt. Argentine Coun. Small Bus., 1983-86; treas. C. of C., Argentina, 1985-86; mem. Entrepreneurs' Guild, 1989; com. chair Orange County coun. Boy Scouts Am., 1990-91. Mem. Nat. Soc. Pub. Accts., Calif. Assn. Ind. Accts. Roman Catholic.

CERRITO, ORATIO ALFONSO, real estate investor, financial advisor; b. Cleve., Mar. 10, 1911; s. Carl and Lillian (DiVita) C.; m. Rita McCue, Oct. 9, 1931 (div. 1946); children: Lillian, Rita-Diane; m. Maria Capri, Dec. 18, 1947; children: Miriam, Linda, Claudia. Student, John Carroll U., 1935; LLB, Cleve. Law Sch., 1940. Bar: Ohio, 1941, U.S. Dist. Ct. (no. dist.) Ohio, 1950. Foreman Chase Brass and Copper Co., Euclid, Ohio, 1931-41; assoc. Sindell & Sindell, Attys. at Law, Cleve., 1941-42; law violations investigator Wage-Hour div. U.S. Dept. Labor, Cleve., 1942-44; price officer Allied Control Commn. of Allied Mil. Govt., Rome, 1944-45; hdqs. distbn. officer UNRRA, Athens, 1945-46; pres., gen. mgr. U.S. Store Fixture Co., Cleve., 1946-52; account exec. Research Inst. Am., Cleve., 1952-54, So. Calif., 1954-60; regional mgr. indsl. div. Marlin, So. Calif., 1960-81; fin. advisor, mgr. O.A. Cerrito Family Trust, Fountain Valley, Calif., 1981—. Home and Office: 18173 Santa Cecilia Cir Fountain Valley CA 92708-5613

CHABOT-FENCE, DENE, industrial engineer; b. Long Beach, Calif., Dec. 20, 1932; s. Marvin Carl and Jessica May Castleberry (Albrecht) Fence. AA, Am. River Coll., Sacramento, 1965; BS, Calif. Inst. Tech., 1966, U. San Francisco, 1983; MS, U. San Francisco, 1985. Research technician Calif. Inst. Tech., Pasadena, 1960-66; engr. various firms, Calif., 1966-80; design engr. J.R. Simplot, Helm, Calif., 1980-85; project engr. J. Oakley & Assocs., Fresno, Calif., 1985-86; prin. engr. Handypersons, Fresno, 1986-87; design engr. Heublein Wines, Madera, Calif., 1987-88, Bruce Industries, Dayton, Nev., 1988-91; bus. entrepreneur Vitamin Villa, The Natural Gourmet Cafe, Carson City, Nev. Patentee in field. Mission pilot Airlifeline, Sacramento. Served with USAF, 1950-54, Korea. Mem. Am. Assn. Indsl. Hygiene (cert.), 99's (chmn. local chpt. 1985-86). Democrat. Home: 5959 Sedge Rd Carson City NV 87901

CHACKEL, CHARLES VICTOR, communications executive; b. San Francisco, Nov. 20, 1947; s. Reno D. and Betty J. Chackel; m. Kathryn A. Fitzhugh, Aug. 30, 1969; children: Geoffrey C., Ryan R. BSBA, U. Oreg., 1970. Dist. mgr. Kraft Foods, Inc., Eugene, Oreg., 1970-72; design cons. Obie Communications Corp., Eugene, 1972-74; account exec. Sta. KUGN-AM, Eugene, 1974-76, sales mgr., 1976-81; gen. mgr. Sta. KUGN-FM, Eugene, 1981-83; v.p., gen. mgr. Sta. KUGN-AM-FM, Eugene, 1983—; bd. dirs. CBS Radio Affiliates, N.Y.C., 1986—, Arbitron Radio, Beltsville, Md., 1988—. Bd. dirs. Youth for Christ, Eugene, 1985—, Community Substance Abuse, 1987—, Children's Relief Nursery, 1981-83, Oreg. Bach Festival, 1981-83. Mem. Oreg. Assn. Broadcasters (bd. dirs. 1987—), Mid-Oreg. Advt. Club, Eugene Arts Found., Rotary, Eugene Country Club. Republican. Office: Sta KUGN 4222 Commerce St Eugene OR 97402-5496

CHACON, MICHAEL ERNEST, computer networking specialist; b. L.A., Feb. 14, 1954; s. Ernest Richard and Teresa Marie (Venegas) C.; children: Mylan Grahm, Aubrie Sarah, Christina Nabseth, Caitlyn Nasbeth, Julia Anna. Student, Pierce Coll., 1972-74, Boise State U., 1980-82. Systems cons. MEC & Assocs., Riverside, Calif., 1986-91; regional mgr. Inacom Corp., Garden Grove, Calif., 1991—; cons. in field; lectr. Microsoft Corp., Bellvue, Wash., 1990-92. Author: Understanding Networks, 1991; contbr. articles to profl. jours. Named to Dean's List, Pierce Coll., 1973, 74. Mem. Lake Elsinore Sportsman Assn., L.A. World Affairs Coun., 3Com Adv. Coun. (bd. dirs. pres. 1986-92). Office: Inacom Corp 11842 Monarch St Garden Grove CA 92641

CHADA, SHARON LYNNE WACHTEL, psychologist; b. Coronado, Calif., Aug. 9, 1960; d. Arthur and Barbara Savaine (Propp) Wachtel; m. Sunil Chada, Apr. 16, 1985. BA in Psychology, UCLA, 1984; MA, Calif. Sch. Profl. Psychology, 1990. Mental health counselor New Eng. Fellowship for Rehab. Alternatives, Worcester, Mass., 1986-87; program dir. Alternatives Unltd., Plainville, Mass., 1987-88; psychology doctoral intern Eye Crisis & Counseling Svcs., Escondido, Calif., 1989-90, Psychiatric & Counseling Svcs. No. County, Vista, Calif., 1990-91, San Diego State U., 1992-93. Mem. Am. Psychol. Assn., Calif. Psychol. Assn. Democrat. Jewish.

CHADWICK, ROGER PARKS, wholesale and retail manufacturing executive; b. Winchester, Va., Mar. 14, 1963; s. Ralph W. and Dorothy Ann (Coleman) C. BSBA, Christopher Newport Coll., 1985. With Hawaiian Tropic, Inc., Lahaina, Hawaii, 1985-86; sales rep. Island Optics, Inc., Honolulu, Hawaii, 1986-87; sales rep. Chadwick Hawaii, Inc., Lahaina, 1987-89, dir. of sales, 1989-90, chief operating officer, 1990—; dir. of sales Hawaiian Sunlight, Inc., Indianatlatic, Fla., 1990—, West Maui Polo Club Sportswear, Inc., 1990—; dir. retail ops. Watch-N-See, Inc. Office: Chadwick Hawaii Inc 721 Wainee St # 211 Lahaina HI 96761-1510

CHADWICK, SHARON STEVENS, librarian; b. Syracuse, N.Y., June 1, 1951; d. Robert Harold and Melba Frances (Hurlburt) Stevens; m. Gary Robert Chadwick, May 27, 1972. BS in Chemistry, Clarkson Coll. Tech., 1973; MSLS, Syracuse U., 1975; MS in Chemistry, SUNY, Oswego, 1980. Asst. librarian SUNY, Oswego, 1977-78; chemistry, physics bibliographer Syracuse U., 1978-79; sci. librarian Humboldt State U., Arcata, Calif., 1980—. Mem. ALA, Am. Chem. Soc., Med. Libr. Assn., N.Y. Acad. Scis., Self-Help for Hard of Hearing, Nat. Captioning Inst., Humane Soc. U.S. Home: 190 Willow Ln Arcata CA 95521-9210 Office: Humboldt State U The Libr Arcata CA 95521

CHAFFEE, JAMES ALBERT, protective services official; b. Balt., Aug. 14, 1952; s. John Dempster and Elizabeth May (Holden) C.; m. Virginia Rose Braun, Oct. 4, 1980; children: Andrew James, Thomas John, Elizabeth Mary. AA, Alan Hancock Coll., 1973; BA, Chapman Coll., 1980; MBA, St. Thomas Coll., 1986. Lic. EMT, L.A. County; lic. police officer, Minn. Police officer Minnetonka (Minn.) Police Dept., 1976-87, police supr., 1982-87; pub. safety dir. City of Chanhassen, Minn., 1987-90; dir. security Walt Disney Studios, Burbank, Calif., 1990—; dir. S.W. Metro Drug Task Force, Chanhassen, 1988-90; adv. com. 1991 U.S. Open, Chaska, Minn., 1989-90. Founding mem. Chanhassen Rotary Club, 1987, v.p., 1990; pres. Emblem Sch. Site Coun., Saugus, Calif., 1992. With USAF, 1972-76. Mem. Chief Spl. Agts. Assn. (dir. 1991—), Am. Soc. for Indsl. Security, Community Police and Security Team. Republican. Roman Catholic. Office: Walt Disney Studios 500 S Buena Vista St Burbank CA 91521-5130

CHAFFEE, MAURICE AHLBORN, geologist; b. Wilkes-Barre, Pa., Jan. 10, 1937; s. William Galbraith and Sarah Hollenback (Ahlborn) C.; m. Annette Fern Eckdahl, Aug. 8, 1959; children: Bradley Alan, Kim Annette Chaffee Laurie. Degree in geol. engring., Colo. Sch. Mines, 1959; MS, U. Ariz., 1964, PhD, 1967. Geologist N.J. Zinc Co., Austinville, Va., 1960-62; grad. student U. Ariz., Tucson, 1962-67; geologist U.S. Geol. Survey, Denver, 1967—. Editorial bd. Jour. Geochem. Exploration, 1975—; contbr. over 100 articles to profl. pubs. Capt. U.S. Army, 1959-64. Fellow Soc. Econ. Geologists (membership sec. 1982-87), Assn. Exploration Geochemists (v.p. 1986-88, pres. 1988-89). Presbyterian. Office: US Geol Survey Federal Ctr MS 973 Denver CO 80225

CHAFFEE, WALTER KENNETH, winery plant manager; b. Riverside, Calif., Jan. 27, 1950; s. Willard Leslie and Betty Lou (Zane) C.; m. Diana Lynn Dow, Dec. 19, 1970; children: Scott, Andy. Student, Fresno State U., 1968-71, Stanislaus State Coll., 1983-85. Rec. clerk Ernest & Julio Gallo Winery, Fresno, Calif., 1971-72, prodn. supr., 1972-74, prodn. supt., 1974-78; prodn. mgr. Ernest & Julio Gallo Winery, Livingston, Calif., 1978-85, plant mgr., 1985—. Co-editor: Tactical Bidding, 1991, The Tools of Bidding, 1992. Nat. charity vol. Am. Contract Bridge League, Memphis, 1992, pres., 1989-92; mem. sch. bd. Sacred Heart Sch., Turlock, Calif., 1985-86; fgn. exch. parent Youth for Understanding, Washington, 1989-92. Am. Soc. Encology and Viticulture, Arrowhead Club (booster 1987-92). Republican. Home: PO Box 144 Hilmar CA 95324 Office: E&J Gallo Winery 18000 W River Rd Livingston CA 95334

CHAGALL, DAVID, journalist, author; b. Phila., Nov. 22, 1930; s. Harry and Ida (Coopersmith) C.; m. Juneau Joan Alsin, Nov. 15, 1957. Student, Swarthmore Center Coll., 1948-49; B.A., Pa. State U., 1952; postgrad., Sorbonne, U. Paris, 1953-54. Social caseworker State of Pa., Phila., 1955-57; sci. editor Jour. I.E.E., 1959-61; pub. relations staff A.E.I.-Hotpoint Ltd., London, 1961-62; mktg. research assoc. Chilton Co., Phila., 1962-63; mktg. research project dir. Haug Assos., Inc. (Roper Orgn.), Los Angeles, 1964-74; research cons. Haug Assos., 1976-79; investigative reporter for nat. mags., 1975—. Author: Diary of a Deaf Mute, 1960, The Century God Slept, 1963, The Spieler For The Holy Spirit, 1972, The New Kingmakers, 1981, The Sunshine Road, 1988; pub.: Inside Campaigning, 1983; contbr. syndicated column, articles, revs., stories and poetry to mags., jours., newspapers; contbg. editor: TV Guide, Los Angeles Mag. Apptd. to Selective Svc. Bd., 1991; bd. dirs. Chosen Prophetic Ministries, 1991. Recipient U. Wis. Poetry prize, 1971; nominee Nat. Book award in fiction, 1972, Pulitzer prize in letters, 1973, Disting. Health Journalism award, 1978; Presdl. Achievement award, 1982; Carnegie Trust grantee, 1964. Home: PO Box 85 Agoura Hills CA 91376-0085

CHAI, WINBERG, political science educator, foundation chair; b. Shanghai, China, Oct. 16, 1932; came to U.S., 1951, naturalized, 1973; s. Ch'u and Mei-en (Tsao) C.; m. Carolyn Everett, Mar. 17, 1966; children: Maria Maylee, Jeffrey Tien-yu. Student, Hartwick Coll., 1951-53; BA, Wittenberg U., 1955; MA, New Sch. Social Rsch., 1958; PhD, NYU, 1968. Lectr. New Sch. Social Rsch., 1957-61; vis. asst. prof. Drew U., 1961-62; asst. prof. Fairleigh Dickinson U., 1962-65; asst. prof. U. Redlands, 1965-68, assoc. prof., 1969-73, chmn. dept., 1970-73; prof., chmn. Asian studies CCNY, 1973-79; disting. prof. polit. sci., v.p. acad. affairs, spl. asst. to pres. U. S.D., Vermillion, 1979-82; prof. polit. sci., dir. internat. programs U. Wyo., Laramie, 1988—; chmn. Third World Conf. Found., Inc., Chgo., 1982—; pres. Wang Yu-fa Found., Taiwan, 1989—. Author: (with Ch'u Chai) The Story of Chinese Philosophy, 1961, The Changing Society of China, 1962, rev. edit., 1969, The New Politics of Communist China, 1972, The Search for a New China, 1975; editor: Essential Works of Chinese Communism, 1969, (with James C. Hsiung) Asia in the U.S. Foreign Policy, 1981, (with James C. Hsiung) U.S. Asian Relations: The National Security Paradox, 1983; (with Carolyn Chai) Beyond China's Crisis, 1989, In Search of Peace in the Middle East, 1991, Chinese Human Rights, 1993; (with Cal Clark) Political Stability and Economic Growth, 1991; co-translator: (with Ch'u Chai) A Treasury of Chinese Literature, 1965. Haynes Found. fellow, 1967, 68; Ford Found. humanities grantee, 1968, 69, Pacific Cultural Found. grantee, 1978, 86, NSF grantee, 1970, Hubert Eaton Meml. Fund grantee, 1972-73, Field Found. grantee, 1973, 75, Henry Luce Found. grantee, 1978, 80, S.D. Humanities Com. grantee, 1980, Pacific Culture Fund grantee, 1987, 90-91. Mem. Am. Assn. Chinese Studies (pres. 1978-80), AAAS, AAUP, Am. Polit. Sci. Assn., N.Y. Acad. Scis., Internat. Studies Assn., NAACP. Democrat. Home: 1071 Granito Dr Laramie WY 82070-5045 Office: PO Box 4098 Laramie WY 82071-4098

CHAIM, ROBERT ALEX, academic administrator, educator; b. Stockton, Calif., Oct. 25, 1947; s. Alex Jr. and Carmen Lorraine (Rodriques-Lopez) C.; m. Diane Leonora Gregonis, May 30, 1971 (dec. 1973); m. Linda Jean Riley, Dec. 22, 1976. AA, San Joaquin Delta Coll., 1967; BA, Sacramento State Coll., 1970; cert. in secondary teaching, U. Pacific, 1972, ArtsD, 1980. Instr. English lang. U. Pacific, Stockton, 1973-77; lectr. lang. of law U. Pacific, Sacramento, 1977—; asst. to dean McGeorge Sch. Law, Sacramento, 1977-81, asst. dean students, 1981—; cons. grammar, usage and linguistics numerous law orgns. and pvt. law firms, Calif., 1978—; mem. curriculum com. law sch. U. San Fernando, Calif., 1979; mem. ABA/Assn. Am. Law Schs./Law Sch. Admission Coun. Joint Task Force on Fin. Aid, 1991—. Editor-in-chief Stauffer Legal Rsch. Series, 1978—; contbr. articles to scholarly books and profl. jours. Mem. Elk Grove (Calif.) Community Planning Adv. Couns., 1986-88, vice-chmn., 1987; mem. scholarship com. Centro Legal de Calif., Sacramento, 1987—, curriculum adv. com. Elk Grove Unified Sch. Dist., 1988, scholarship com. Sacramento Country Day Sch., 1988; bd. advisors St. Hope Acad. Youth Orgn., 1991—. Recipient Meritorious Svc. award Asian-Am. Law Students Assn., Sacramento, 1986, 87, Outstanding Svc. award La Raza Law Students Assn., 1988. Mem. ABA (assoc., legal edn. and bar admissions sect.), Nat. Assn. Fgn. Student Affairs, Assn. Am. Law Schs. (mem. legal rsch. and writing sect, student svcs. sect., student svc. com. 1990-91, law admission coun. joint task force on fin. aid 1991—), Lions Club (judge 53rd annual multiple dist. four, final speaker contest, 1990). Office: U of Pacific McGeorge Sch Law 3200 5th Ave Sacramento CA 95817-2705

CHAIT, ARTHUR LYLE, management consultant; b. Phila., Mar. 20, 1947; s. Solomen J. and Ethel G. (Katz) C.; m. Susan Smith, Oct. 16, 1982; children: Stephen, Audrey. BS, Rutgers U., 1969; MBA, U. Pitts., 1974. Rsch. engr., customer svcs. mgr., lab. mgr., rsch. dir. Harbison-Walker div. Dresser Industries, Pitts., 1969-80; dir. Booz Allen & Hamilton, N.Y.C., 1980-82; v.p., div. pres. PA Consulting Group, Princeton, N.J., 1982-88; sr. v.p., gen. mgr. SRI Internat., Menlo Park, Calif., 1988—. Contbr. tech. and mgmt. articles to profl. jours.; inventor in field. Mem. Tech. Transfer Soc. (pres. No. Calif. chpt. 1990—), Am. Ceramic Soc., Planning Forum, KERAMOS Nat. Ceramic Engring. Honor Soc. Office: SRI International 333 Ravenswood Ave Menlo Park CA 94025

CHALK, EARL MILTON, retired art director; b. Deerlodge, Mont., Sept. 14, 1927; s. Forrest A. and Jeanette Curtis (Robinson) C.; m. Carole Estelle, Feb. 9, 1963 (div. 1974); children: Teri, Kevin, Quinn. BFA, U. Wash., 1953. Artist Facilities Boeing, Seattle, 1954-57; writer, artist Facilities Boeing, Renton, Wash., 1957-60; supr. mfg. Facilities Boeing, Seattle, 1960-65; sr. supr. planning Facilities Boeing, Auburn, Wash., 1965-71, art dir. mfg. engring., 1971-87; ret., 1987—; artist and writer fabrication divsn. Auburn, 1954-87; artist Puget Sound Group of North West Painters, Seattle, 1968-78; co-mgr., owner Art Galary, 1967-74. 1st class petty officer USN, 1945-49. Recipient Rotary scholarship U. Wash., 1953. Home and Office: 1803 7th Ave SE Puyallup WA 98372

CHALLEM, JACK JOSEPH, public relations, advertising and magazine writer; b. Montreal, Quebec, Can., May 29, 1950; came to U.S., 1954; s. Alex and Sara Bella (Novak) C.; m. Renate Lewin, Sept. 30, 1977; 1 child, Evan G. BA, Northeastern Ill. U., 1972. Advt. mgr. J.R. Carlson Labs., Arlington Heights, Ill., 1973-78; editor-in-chief Physician's Life Mag., Evanston, Ill., 1978; contbg. editor Health Quarterly, New Canaan, Conn., 1979-83, Your Good Health Rev., New Canaan, 1979-83; graphics mgr. Eberline Instrument Corp., Santa Fe, 1979-81; sci. writer, media rels. specialist Los Alamos (N.Mex.) Nat. Lab., 1981-88; contbg. editor Let's Live Mag., L.A., 1978—; writer KVO Advt. & Pub. Rels., Beaverton, Oreg., 1988—. Author: What Herbs Are All About, 1979, Vitamin C Updated, 1983, Making the Most of Your Vitamins and Minerals, 1993; contbr. Natural Health Mag., 1992—; editor: The Nutrition Reporter Newsletter, 1992—. contbr. articles to profl. jours. Mem. NRA, Nat. Health Fedn., Pub. Rels. Soc. Am. Home: 6782 SW 167th Pl Beaverton OR 97007-6310

CHALLONER, ANTHONY DORIAN, aerospace engineer; b. Runcorn, Cheshire, Eng., June 7, 1947; came to U.S., 1979; s. Frederick and Nicky (Notara) C.; m. Kathryn Ruth Campbell, June 20, 1969; children: Christine, Byron, David. B in Applied Sci., U. Toronto, Ont., Can., 1969, M in Applied Sci., 1971. Cons. Communications Rsch. Ctr. Can. Govt., Ottawa, Can., 1971-76; project engr. Spar Aerospace Products Ltd., Toronto, 1976-79; scientist/engr. Hughes Aircraft Co., El Segundo, Calif., 1979—. Patentee in field. Mem. AIAA, IEEE. Republican. Episcopalian. Office: Hughes Aircraft Co EI/DIIO PO Box 902 El Segundo CA 90245

CHAMBERLAIN, ADRIAN RAMOND, state official; b. Detroit, Nov. 11, 1929; s. Adrian and Leila (Swisher) C.; m. Melanie F. Stevens, May 19, 1979; children: Curtis (dec.), Tracy, Thomas (dec.). BS, Mich. State U., 1951, D Engring., 1971; MS, Wash. State U., 1952; PhD, Colo. State U., 1955; LittD, Denver U., 1974. Registered profl. engr., Colo. lic. real estate broker, Colo., 1981-91. Rsch. engr. Phillips Petroleum Co., 1955; rsch. coord., civil engr. Colo. State U., 1956-57, chief civil engr. sect., 1957-61, acting dean engring., 1959-61, v.p., 1960-66, exec. v.p., treas., governing bd., 1966-69, pres., 1969-80; chmn. bd. dirs. Univ. Nat. Bank, 1964-69, dir., 1964-74; pres., dir. Mitchell & Co., Inc., 1981-85; exec. v.p. Simons, Li & Assocs., Inc., 1985-87; pres., chief exec. officer Chemagnetics, Inc., Ft. Collins, Colo., 1987-89; exec.

dir. Colo. Dept. Hwys., Denver, 1987-91, Colo. Dept. Transp., Denver, 1991—; chmn. NSF Commn. Weather Modification, 1964-66; mem. Nat. Air Quality Criteria Adv. Com., 1967-70; vice-chmn. rsch. and tech. coord. com. FHWA of Transp. Rsch. Bd. NRC, 1991—; exec. dir. Colo. Dept. Hwys., 1987-91, Colo. Dept. Transp., 1991—. Colo. commr. Western Interstate Commn. on Higher Edn., 1974-78; pres. State Bd. Agr. System, 1978-80; trustee Cystic Fibrosis Found., 1971-84; trustee Univ. Corp. for Atmospheric Rsch., 1967-72, 74-81, chmn. bd. trustees, 1977-79; pres. Black Mountain Ranch, Inc., 1969-85; bd. dirs. Nat. Ctr. for Higher Edn. Mgmt. Systems, 1975-80, chmn. bd. dirs., 1977-78; bd. visitors Air U., USAF, 1973-76, chmn., 1975-76; exec. com. Nat. Assn. State Univs. and Land Grant Colls., 1976-80, pres.-elect, 1978-79, chmn., 1979-80; mem. adv. coun. to dir. NSF, 1978-81; chmn. Ft. Collins-Loveland Airport Authority, 1983-86; bd. dirs. Synergetics Internat. Inc., 1987-90; mem. exec. com. strategic hwy. rsch. commn. Transp. Rsch. Bd. NRC, 1989-93, chmn. strategic transp. rsch. study hwy. safety, 1989-90, exec. com., 1991—, vice-chmn. 1992, chmn. 1993; mem. Gov.'s Cabinet, State of Colo., 1987—; mem. Info. Mgmt. Commn., 1988—. Fulbright student U. Grenoble, 1955-56. Mem. ASCE, Am. Assn. State Hwy. and Transp. Ofcls. (policy com. 1987-92, v.p. 1990-91, pres. 1991-92, bd. dirs. 1992—, chmn. standing com. on adminstrn. 1993—), Order of Aztec Eaglex Mex., Sigma Xi, Tau Beta Pi, Phi Kappa Phi, Chi Epsilon. Home: 4200 Westshore Way Fort Collins CO 80525-3214 Office: Dept Transp 4201 E Arkansas Ave Rm 262 Denver CO 80222-3400

CHAMBERLAIN, BARBARA KAYE, state legislator, publishing company executive; b. Lewiston, Idaho, Nov. 6, 1962; d. William Arthur and Gladys Marie (Humphrey) Greene; m. Dean Andrew Chamberlain, Sept. 13, 1986; 1 child, Kathleen Marie. BA in English cum laude, BA in Linguistics cum laude, Wash. State U., 1984. Temp. sec. various svcs., Spokane, Wash., 1984-86; office mgr. Futurefast: The History Co., Melior Publs., Spokane, 1986-87, dir. mktg. and prodn., 1987-88, v.p., 1988-89; founder, owner PageWorks Publ. Svcs., Post Falls, Idaho, 1989—; mem. dist. 2 Idaho State Ho. of Reps., 1990-92; Idaho State Senate, 1992—. Author North Idaho's Centennial, 1990; editor Washington Songs and Lore, 1988. Bd. dirs. Mus. North Idaho, Coeur d'Alene, Idaho, 1990-91, Northwest Water Watch, Coeur d'Alene, 1992—. Mem. AAUW, NOW, LWV, Women in Comm., Inc., Nat. Women's Polit. Caucus, Women Legislators Lobby, Idaho Women's Network, No. Idaho Pro-Choice Network, Idaho Citizen's Network, Idaho Conservation League, Mensa, Post Falls C. of C. Democrat. Office: PO Box 1893 Post Falls ID 83854

CHAMBERLAIN, OWEN, nuclear physicist; b. San Francisco, July 10, 1920; divorced 1978; 4 children; m. June Steingart, 1980 (dec.). AB (Cramer fellow), Dartmouth Coll., 1941; PhD, U. Chgo., 1949. Instr. physics U. Calif., Berkeley, 1948-50, asst. prof., 1950-54, assoc. prof., 1954-58, prof., 1958-89, prof. emeritus, 1989—; civilian physicist Manhattan Dist., Berkeley, Los Alamos, 1942-46. Recipient Nobel prize (with Emilio Segré) for physics, for discovery anti-proton, 1959, The Berkeley citation U. Calif., 1989; Guggenheim fellow, 1957-58; Loeb lectr. at Harvard U., 1959. Fellow Am. Phys. Soc., Am. Acad. Arts and Scis.; mem. Nat. Acad. Scis., Berkeley Fellows. Office: U Calif Physics Dept Berkeley CA 94720*

CHAMBERLAIN, STEVEN MICHAEL, software engineer; b. Meriden, Conn., Jan. 16, 1938; s. Lynn P. and Leilabelle (Stevens) C.; m. Judith Maxine Johnson, Apr. 14, 1962; children: Charlotte, Michael, Randy. BA, U. Conn., 1961. Engr. computing North Am. Aviation, Anaheim, Calif., 1961-64; mem. tech. staff Sci. Data Systems, Santa Monica, Calif., 1964-66; sr. systems analyst Programming Scis. Corp., Century City, Calif., 1966-71, Actron Industries, Monrovia, Calif., 1971-72; sr. tech. staff Magnavox, Torrance, Calif., 1972—. Author numerous tech. papers. Mem. IEEE Computer Soc., Assn. for Computing Machinery, Nat. Mgmt. Assn., Inst. of Navigation. Office: 2829 Maricopa St Torrance CA 90503

CHAMBERLAIN, WILLIAM EDWIN, JR., management consultant; b. St. Louis, June 8, 1951; s. William Edwin Sr. and Grace (Salisbury) C. AA in Bus. Mgmt., Mesa (Ariz.) Community Coll., 1983; BBA, U. Phoenix, 1988. Tng. and human resources devel. specialist Motorola, Inc., Phoenix, 1979-87; pres., seminar speaker Chamberlain Cons. Svcs., Chino Valley, Ariz., 1987—. Curator, dir. ops. U.S. Wolf Refuge and Adoption Ctr. Mem. ASTD, Network for Profl. Devel.

CHAMBERLAIN, WILTON NORMAN, former professional basketball player; b. Phila., Aug. 21, 1936. Student, U. Kans., 1954-58. Player Harlem Globetrotters, 1958-59, Phila. (later San Francisco) Warriors, 1959-65, Phila. 76ers, 1965-68, Los Angeles Lakers, 1968-73; coach San Diego Conquistadors, Am. Basketball Assn., 1973-74. Actor, Conan The Destroyer, 1982; author: A View from Above, 1991. Player, Nat. Basketball Assn. All-Star Game, 1960-69, 71-73; rookie of yr. Nat. Basketball Assn., 1960; Most Valuable Player, Nat. Basketball Assn., 1960, 66-68, Nat. Basketball Assn. Playoffs, 1972; inducted Naismith Meml. Basketball Hall of Fame, 1978; named to Nat. Basketball Assn. 35th Anniversary All-Time Team, 1980; mem. Nat. Basketball Assn. Championship Team, 1967, 72; holder Nat. Basketball Assn. record for most points scored in one game with 100. Office: care Seymour Goldberg 16633 Ventura Blvd Ste 1400 Encino CA 91436-1829

CHAMBERLIN, EUGENE KEITH, historian, educator; b. Gustine, Calif., Feb. 15, 1916; s. Charles Eugene and Anina Marguerite (Williams) C.; B.A. in History, U. Calif. at Berkeley, 1939, M.A., 1940, Ph.D., 1949; m. Margaret Rae Jackson, Sept. 1, 1940; children—Linda, Thomas, Rebecca, Adrienne (dec.), Eric. Tchr. Spanish, Latin, Lassen Union High Sch. and Jr. Coll., Susanville, Calif., 1941-43; tchr. history Elk Grove (Calif.) Joint Union High Sch., 1943-45; teaching asst. history U. Calif., Berkeley, 1946-48; instr. history Mont. State U., Missoula, 1948-51, asst. prof., 1951-54; asst. prof. to prof. San Diego City Coll., 1954-78; cab driver San Diego Yellow Cab Co., 1955-74, 79, 86; vis. prof. history Mont. State Coll., Bozeman, summer 1953, U. Calif. Extension, 1965-68, San Diego State Coll., 1965-68, others; instr., coordinator history lectures San Diego Community Colls.-TV, 1969-77; prof. San Diego Miramar Coll., 1978-83; prof. history San Diego Mesa Coll., 1983-86; mem. adv. com. Quechan Crossing Master Plan Project, 1989-90. Huntington Library-Rockefeller Found. grantee, 1952; Fulbright-Hays grantee, Peru, 1982; recipient merit award Congress of History San Diego County, 1978; Outstanding Educator award, San Diego City Coll., 1970; recipeint award for dedicated svc. to local history San Diego Hist. Soc., 1991. Mem. AAUP (various coms., nat. council 1967-70, pres. Calif. conf. 1968-70, acting exec. sec. 1970-72), San Diego County Congress of History (pres. 1976-77, newsletter editor 1977-78), Am. Hist. Assn. (life, Beveridge-Dunning com. 1982-84, chmn. 1984), Pacific Coast Council on Latin-Am. Studies, Cultural Assn. of the Californias, The Westerners (Calif., S.D. chpts.), E Clampus Vitus (historian 1970—, chpt. pres. 1972-73, dir. 1983-89, grand council mem. 1972—, dir. T.R.A.S.H 1979—, pres. 1983-84), Phi Alpha Theta (sec. U. Calif. Berkeley chpt. 1947-48, organizer and faculty adv., Mont. State U. chpt. 1948-54). Democrat. Mem. Ch. of the Brethren (del. 200th Annual Conf. 1986). Author numerous booklets on SW Am. history and numerous articles on Mexican NW to profl. jours. Home: 3033 Dale St San Diego CA 92104-4929

CHAMBERLIN, ROBERT JOSEPH, marketing executive; b. Weatherford, Tex., July 4, 1929; s. Tracy W. and Dorothy (O'Hare) C.; children: Russell R., Robin T. BA in Mktg., Duke U., 1951, BS in Psychology, 1951. Salesman, broker, reg. rep. NASD, 1951-62; v.p./dir. sales Hawaii Clay Products, Inc., 1963-68; with various auto sales and leasing mgmt. dealerships L.A., 1969-80; owner Modern Methods of Merchandising Inc., Canoga Park, Calif., 1981-92, Am. Nat. Energy Progs., Inc., Canoga Park, 1981-92, All Am. Dist., Inc., Canoga Park, 1981-92, Am. Atlas Sales & Leasing, Inc., Canoga Park, 1981-92, All Am. Fin. Svcs., Inc., Canoga Park, 1981-92; founder, pres., ceo, chmn. bd. Clasped Hands Inc. and subs, Valencia, Calif., 1988-92; owner Natural Pure Artesian Water, Valencia, Calif., 1991-92; past owner/operator supper clubs in Hawaii; producer nightclub, radio and tv shows featuring jazz artists incl. Herb Jeffries, Anita O'Day, Ray McKinley and Glen Miller Orch., Buddy Rich, Joe Williams, Billy Daniels. With USMC, 1944-48, 51-52; PTO. Decorated Silver Star, Bronze Star, Purple Heart; recipient Golden State award for outstanding profl. achievement and superior leadership, Calif., 1990, award of honor, 1990, others. Mem. Am. Vets. Alliance, AMVETS, Am. Legion, Am. Mgmt. Assn., Better Bus. Bur., Optimists Internat., Am. Entrepreneur's Assn., L.A. World Affairs Coun., Passport Club, Internat. Bottled Water Assn., Smithsonian Instn., Am. Film Inst., Mus. Natural History, Internat. Platform Assn., Gene Autry Western Heritage Mus. (founder), Smithsonian Inst. (assoc.), Mus. Nat. History, Granada Hills C. of C., Shoe 'n Slipper Club (pres. 1949-51), Jaycees, Lambda Chi Alpha. Democrat. Baptist. Home and Office: 27778 Hopkins Ave Valencia CA 91355

CHAMBERS, CAROLYN SILVA, communications company executive; b. Portland, Oreg., Sept. 15, 1931; d. Julio and Elizabeth (McDonnell) Silva; widowed; children: William, Scott, Elizabeth, Silva, Clark. BBA, U. Oreg. V.p., treas. Liberty Comm., Inc., Eugene, Oreg., 1960-83; pres. Chambers Comm. Corp., Eugene, 1983—; chmn., bd. dirs. Chambers Constrn. Co., 1986—; bd. dirs., dep. chair of bd. Fed. Res. Bank of San Francisco, 1982-92. Mem. Sacred Heart Med. Found., 1980—; mem. Sacred Heart Gov. Bd., 1987-92; mem. U. Oreg. Found., 1980—, pres., 1992-93; chair U. Oreg. Found. The Campaign for Oreg., 1988-89; pres., bd. dirs. Eugene Arts Found.; bd. dirs., treas., dir. search com. Eugene Symphony; mem. adv. bd. Eugene Hearing and Speech Ctr., Alton Baker Park Commn., Pleasant Hill Sch. Bd.; chmn., pres., treas. Civic Theatre, Very Little Theatre; negotiator, treas., bd. dirs., mem. thrift shop Jr. League of Eugene. Recipient Webfoot award U. Oreg., 1986, Pioneer award, 1983, Woman Who Made a Difference award, 1989, Pres.'s medal U. Oreg., 1991, Disting. Svc. award U. Oreg., 1992. Mem. Nat. Cable TV Assn. (mem. fin. com., chmn. election and by-laws com., chmn. awards com., bd. dirs. 1987—, Vanguard award for Leadership 1982), Pacific Northwest Cable Comm. Assn. (conv. chmn., pres.), Oreg. Cable TV Assn. (v.p., pres., chmn. edn. com., conv. chmn., Pres.'s award 1986), Calif. Cable TV Assn. (bd. dirs., conv. chmn., conv. panelist), Women in Cable (charter mem., treas., v.p., pres., recipient star of cable recognition), Wash. State Cable Comm. Assn., Idaho Cable TV Assn., Community Antenna TV Assn., Cable TV Pioneers, Eugene C. of C. (first citizen award, 1985). Home: PO Box 640 Pleasant Hill OR 97455-0640 Office: Chambers Comm Corp PO Box 7009 Eugene OR 97401-0009

CHAMBERS, CLYTIA MONTLLOR, public relations consultant; b. Rochester, N.Y., Oct. 23, 1922; d. Anthony and Marie (Bambace) Capraro; m. Joseph John Montllor, July 2, 1941 (div. 1958); children: Michele, Thomas, Clytia; m. Robert Chambers, May 28, 1965. BA, Barnard Coll., N.Y.C., 1942; Licence en droit, Faculte de Droit, U. Lyon, France, 1948; MA, Howard U., Washington, 1958. Assoc. dir. dept. rsch. Coun. for Fin. Aid to Edn., N.Y.C., 1958-60; asst. to v.p. indsl. rels. Sinclair Oil Corp., N.Y.C., 1961-65; writer pub. rels. dept. Am. Oil Co., Chgo., 1965-67; dir. editorial svcs., v.p. Hill & Knowlton Inc., N.Y.C., 1967-77; sr. v.p., dir. spl. svcs. Hill & Knowlton Inc., L.A., 1977-90; sr. cons. Hill & Knowlton Inc., 1990—; cons. and trustee Childen's Inst. Internat., L.A., 1988-93. Co-author: The News Twisters, 1971; editor: Critical Issues in Public Relations, 1975. Mem. Calif. Rare Fruit Growers (editor Fruit Gardener 1979—). Home: 11439 Laurelcrest Dr Studio City CA 91604-3872

CHAMBERS, DOROTHY ROSE, educator; b. Yakima, Wash., May 8, 1941; d. George Milford and Blance Mary (McCarthy) Hollenbeck; B.S. in Speech and Lang. Therapy, Marquette U., 1964; M.A. in Spl. Edn., San Francisco State U., 1969; m. Thomas M. Chambers, Aug. 14, 1971; adopted children—David, Monique, Christopher, George, Elizabeth. Speech pathologist Mpls. Pub. Schs., 1964-65, Milbrae (Calif.) Sch. Dist., 1965-68; reading specialist Dept. Def., Landstuhl, Germany, 1970-71; tchr. children with extreme learning problems Portland (Oreg.) Public Schs., 1971-80, dept. chmn. spl. edn., 1980-84, program specialist program devel., 1984-86; diagnostic specialist assessment program spl. edn., 1986—; cert. instr. develop. therapy U. Ga., 1982; instr. Portland State U., D.C.E., 1982, 83. HEW Dept. Rehab. fellow, 1969. Mem. Am. Speech and Hearing Assn. (cert. in clin. competence), Common Cause, Cousteau Soc., NEA, Oreg. Edn. Assn., Nat. Council Exceptional Children (presenter nat. conv. 1984). Democrat. Roman Catholic. Author: PEACHES (Pre-Sch. Ednl. Adaptation for Children Who Are Handicapped), 1978. Home: 12414 SE Oatfield Rd Portland OR 97222-6956 Office: Portland Pub Schs 501 N Dixon St Portland OR 97227-1804

CHAMBERS, GARY LEE, lawyer; b. Inglewood, Calif., June 6, 1953; s. George Edmund and Beverly Jean (Shuler) C.; m. Dalyn Valerie Myhra, Dec. 7, 1985; children: Garrett Ryan, Brendan Kyle. BA, U. Redlands (Calif.), 1975; JD, Western State U., Fullerton, Calif., 1978. Bar: Calif. 1979, U.S. Dist. Ct. (cen. dist.) Calif. 1979, U.S. Supreme Ct. 1982. Assoc. Law Offices of Murray Palitz, Westminster, Calif., 1979; pvt. practice law Orange, Calif., 1979-80; assoc. Law Offices Giles, Callahan et al, Tustin, Calif., 1980-81, Law Offices of Mark E. Edwards, Tustin, 1981-82; ptnr. Edwards, Chambers & Hoffman, Tustin, 1983-88, Chambers, Hoffman & Noronha, Santa Ana, Calif., 1989-92, Chambers, Noronha & Lowry, Santa Ana, Calif., 1992—; mem. tech. adv. staff Impact Gen., 1990—. Editorial adv. bd. James Pub. Co., 1988—. Mem. Orange County Trial Lawyers Assn. (bd. govs. 1984-92, pres. 1990), Calif. Trial Lawyers Assn. (bd. govs. 1986-93, sec. 1991-93, Chpt. Pres. of Yr. 1990, Presdl. award of merit 1987, 92, rated AV by Martindale-Hubbel). Democrat. Christian Ch. Office: Chambers Hoffman & Noronha # 1450 1851 E 1st St Santa Ana CA 92704-4208

CHAMBERS, JONATHAN GOETZ, film producer; b. Wilmington, Del., Sept. 24, 1955; s. David Everett and Marie Louise (Goetz) C. BS in Film, Syracuse U., 1977. Prin. Chambers Co., L.A., 1980-90; pres. Chambers Co. Enterprises, Inc., Altadena, Calif., 1990—. Assoc. producer (films) Taste of Hemlock, 1988, One Cup of Coffee, 1991. Recipient Silver award Film & Tape Festival, 1979. Lutheran. Office: Chambers Co Enterprises Inc 1171 E Mendocino St Altadena CA 91001-2524

CHAMBERS, KENNETH CARTER, astronomer; b. Los Alamos, N.Mex., Sept. 27, 1956; s. William Hyland and Marjorie (Bell) C.; m. Jeanne Marie Hamilton, June 28, 1986; children: Signe Hamilton, William Hamilton. BA in Physics, U. Colo., 1979, MS in Physics, 1982; MA in Physics and Astronomy, Johns Hopkins U., 1985, PhD in Physics and Astronomy, 1990. Rsch. asst. dept. physics U. Colo., Boulder, 1982-83; rsch. asst. dept. physics and astronomy Johns Hopkins U., Balt., 1983-86; mem. instrument team Hopkins Ultraviolet Telescope, Balt., 1983-86; rsch. asst. Space Telescope Sci. Inst., Balt., 1986-90; postdoctoral fellow Leiden (The Netherlands) Obs. Leiden U., 1990-91; asst. prof. Inst. Astronomy U. Hawaii, Honolulu, 1991—; Contbr. articles to Astrophys. Jour., Nature mag., Phys. Rev.; contbr. conf. procs. in field. Mem. Am. Astron. Soc. (Chretein award 1989), Am. Phys. Soc. Office: Inst for Astronomy U Hawaii 2680 Woodlawn Dr Honolulu HI 96822

CHAMBERS, LOIS IRENE, insurance agency executive; b. Omaha, Nov. 24, 1935; d. Edward J. and Evelyn B. (Davidson) Morrison; m. Peter A. Mscichowski, Aug. 16, 1952 (div. 1980); 1 child, Peter Edward; m. Frederick G. Chambers, Apr. 17, 1981. Clk. Gross-Wilson Ins. Agy., Portland, Oreg., 1955-57; sec., bookkeeper Reed-Paulsen Ins. Agy., Portland, 1957-58; office mgr., asst. sec., agt. Don Biggs & Assocs., Vancouver, Wash., 1958-88, v.p. ops., 1988-89, automation mgr., 1989-91, mktg. mgr., 1991—; automation cons. Chambers & Assocs., Tualatin, Oreg., 1985—; chmn. adv. com. Clark Community Coll., Vancouver, 1985-93, adv. com., 1993—. Mem. citizens com. task force City of Vancouver, 1976-78, mem. Block Grant rev. task force, 1978—. Mem. Ins. Women of S.W. Wash. (pres. 1978, Ins. Woman of Yr. 1979), Nat. Assn. Ins. Women, Nat. Users Agena Systems (charter; pres. 1987-89), Soroptimist Internat. (Vancouver)(pres. 1978-79, Soroptimist of the Year 1979-80). Democrat. Roman Catholic. Office: Don Biggs & Assocs 916 Main St PO Box 189 Vancouver WA 98666-0189

CHAMBERS, MARJORIE BELL, historian; b. N.Y.C., Mar. 11, 1923; d. Kenneth Carter and Katherine (Totman) Bell; m. William Hyland Chambers, Aug. 8, 1945; children: Lee Chambers-Schiller, William Bell, Leslie Chambers Trujillo, Kenneth Carter. AB cum laude, Mt. Holyoke Coll., South Hadley, Mass., 1943; MA, Cornell U., 1948; PhD, U. N.Mex., 1974; LLD honoris causa, Ctrl. Mich. U., 1977; LHD (hon.), Wilson Coll., 1980, Northern Michigan U., 1982. Staff asst. Am. Assn. UN, League of Nations Assn., N.Y.C., 1944-45; program specialist dept. rural sociology Cornell U., Ithaca, N.Y., 1945-46, rsch. asst. dept. speech and drama, 1946-48; substitute tchr. Los Alamos (N.Mex.) Pub. Schs., 1962-65; project historian U.S. AEC, Los Alamos, 1965-69; adj. prof. U. N.Mex., Los Alamos, 1970-76, 84-85; pres. Colo. Women's Coll., Denver, 1976-78; dean Grad. Sch. Union Inst., Cin., 1979-82, mem. core faculty Grad. Sch., 1979—; interim pres. Colby-Sawyer Coll., New London, N.H., 1985-86; vis. prof. Cameron U., Lawton, Okla., 1974; commr., vice-chair N.Mex. Commn. on Higher Edn., Santa Fe, 1987-91; chair citizen adv. bd. U.S. Army Command and Gen. Staff Coll., Ft. Leavenworth, Kans., 1990—; mem. bd. dirs. Coun. Ind. Colls. and Univs., Santa Fe, 1991—; rep. Los Alamos County Labor Mgmt. Bd. Contbr. articles to profl. jours. Chair Los Alamos County Coun., 1976, councilor, 1975-76, 79; candidate N.Mex. 3d Congl. Dist., 1982, lt. gov. N.Mex., 1986; chair Sec. of Navy's Advisor Bd. on Edn. and Tng., Washington and Pensacola, Fla., 1987-89; acting chair, vice-chair adminstrn. Pres. Carter's Com. for Women, Washington, 1977-80; chair Los Alamos County Pers. Bd., 1983-90; mem. nat. adv. coun. U.S. SBA, 1990—; mem., editor Los Alamos and N.Mex. Rep. Ctrl. com., 1982—; trustee Colby-Sawyer Coll., New London, N.H., 1980-89. Recipient Teresa d'Avila award Coll. St. Teresa, Winona, Minn., 1978, Disting. Woman award U. N.Mex. Alumni Assn., Albuquerque, 1990, N.Mex. Disting. Pub. Svc. award Gov. and Awards Coun., Albuquerque, 1991; named Outstanding N.Mex. Woman Gov. and Com. on Status of Women, Albuquerque, 1988, 89. Mem. AAUW (life, nat. pres. 1975-79, pres. Edn. Found.), DAR, Bus. and Profl. Women (Los Alamos parliamentarian and dist. parliamentarian 1991-93), Women's Polit. Caucus (gov. bd., conv. keynoter, vice-chair Rep. caucus 1971—), Internat. Women's Forum, N.Mex. Hist. Soc., Los Alamos Hist. Soc. (pres.). Presbyterian.

CHAMBERS, MILTON WARREN, architect; b. L.A., Aug. 5, 1928; s. Joe S. and Barbara N. (Harris) C.; m. Elizabeth M. Smith, Nov. 27, 1949; children: Mark, Michael, Daniel, Matthew. Student, Coll. of Sequoias, 1948-49, Harvard U., 1990. Lic. architect, Calif., Nev., Colo., Hawaii, Mont.; cert. Nat. Coun. Archtl. Registration Bds. Apprentice architect Kastner & Kastner Architects, Visalia, Calif., 1950-57; project architect Wurster, Bernardi & Emmons, Architects, San Francisco, 1958-63, Claude Oakland, Architect, San Francisco, 1964-65; chief architect Bank of Am., San Francisco, 1965-68; pres., owner Milton W. Chambers, Architect, San Rafael, Calif., 1969-82, The Chambers Group, Architects, Rancho Mirage, Calif., 1983—. Architect, designer St. Margaret's Episcopal Church, 1988. Foreman Marin County Grand Jury, San Rafael, 1976; mem. Archtl. Design Rev. Bd., Rancho Mirage, 1986—; trustee Marywood Sch., Rancho Mirage, 1990—. Cpl. U.S. Army, 1946-48, PTO, 50-51. Mem. AIA (pres. Calif. Desert chpt. 1986-87, dir. Calif. Coun. 1989-90), Rotary Internat., Terra Linda Rotary Club (pres. 1975-76, dist. gov. 1993-94), Rancho Mirage Rotary Club (pres. 1986-87). Republican. Episcopalian. Office: The Chambers Group 70390 Highway 111 Ste 101 Rancho Mirage CA 92270

CHAMBERS, PETER R., psychologist; b. L.A., Aug. 23, 1953; s. Ralph James and Eileen Lucy (Allsworth) C. Student U. Calif., Riverside, 1975-77; BA, Chapman Coll., 1978; MA, U.S. Internat. U., 1980, PhD, 1982. Researcher, Rancho Los Amigos Hosp., Downey, Calif., 1972-76; counselor educator Free Clinic of Orange County, Anaheim, Calif., 1976-78; psychotherapist Care Manor Hosp., Orange, Calif., 1978-80; asst. adminstr. Cabrillo Med. Ctr., San Diego, 1980-81, psychologist Cabrillo Mental Health Group, 1982, prof. Nat. U.; evaluation and guidance unit Orange County Mental Health, Orange, 1982-91; pvt. practice, 1992—; instr. Calif. Community Coll.; asst. clin. prof. U. Calif. Irvine Sch. Medicine, Irvine, 1987. Mem. expert witness panel State of Calif., County of Orange. Mem. Am. Psychol. Assn, Am. Acad. Forensic Scis., Calif. Psychol. Assn., Soc. Adolescent Medicine.

CHAMBERS, RICHARD H., retired federal judge; b. Danville, Ill., Nov. 7, 1906; s. William R. and Lida J. (Spencer) C.; m. Mary Martin, Nov. 24, 1945 (dec. Oct. 1987); children: Martha Chambers Froese, Janet Chambers Crews (dec.); m. Eileen A. Engett, Sept. 16, 1989. A.B., U. Ariz., 1929, LL.D., 1976; LL.B., Stanford, 1932; LL.D., U. Pacific, 1972. Bar: Ariz. bar 1932. Practice law in Tucson, 1932-41, 45-54; judge Ct. of Appeals, 9th Circuit, Tucson, 1954-77; sr. judge Ct. of Appeals, 9th Circuit, from 1977. Served from capt. to maj. USAAF, 1942-45. Recipient Law medal Gonzaga U., 1974. Mem. Am. Law Inst., Am. Bar Assn., Phi Gamma Delta. Republican. Club: Old Pueblo (Tucson).

CHAMBERS, STEPHEN L.E., university administrator; b. Flagstaff, Ariz., July 24, 1956; s. LeRoy O. and Geraldine (Fisher) C.; m. Mary Elizabeth Elliott, May 4, 1991. BS in Polit. Sci., No. Ariz. U., 1977, MA in Sociology, 1979, PhD in History and Polit. Sci., 1985; student, Calif. West Sch. Law, 1977. Rsch. analyst No. Ariz. U., Flagstaff, 1978-80, rsch. asst., 1980-82, program dir., 1982-83, mgmt. rsch. analyst, 1983-87, interim dir. inst. rsch., 1987-88, asst. dir. inst. rsch., 1988-89, assoc. dir. univ. planning, analysis, 1989—; mem. Ariz. Hist. Sites Rev. Com., 1986—. Contbr. articles to profl. jours. Elections marshall Coconino County, Flagstaff, 1978-82; active Big Sisters No. Ariz., Flagstaff, 1987—; vice chmn. adv. com. Ariz. Hist. Preservation, 1991—; chmn. tech. support com. Ariz. Bd. Regents, 1991-92, mem. commn. on status of women, 1989-91, mem. enrollment mgmt. task force, 1992—, mem. ethnic minority student goal setting tech. assistance com., 1993—; mem. Flagstaff Main St. Found. Recipient cert. award DAR, 1986; named Outstanding Young Men Am. U.S. Jaycees, 1989; rsch. grantee Navajo and Hopi Rels. Com./U.S. Govt., 1982; program grantee U.S. Dept. Edn., 1979—; acad. scholar R.O. Raymond Found., Phoenix, 1974-76. Mem. Mus. No. Ariz., Flagstaff Symphony Assn., Assn. for Study of Higher Edn., Am. Assn. for Higher Edn., Ariz. Assn. Instl. Rsch. (founder 1987-88), Ctr. for Study of Presidency, Nat. Trust Historic Preservation, Ariz. Hist. Soc., Assn. for Instl. Rsch., Soc. Coll. and Univ. Planning, Phi Alpha Theta. Democrat. Roman Catholic. Office: No Ariz U PO Box 4132 Flagstaff AZ 86011

CHAMBERS, STEVEN RALPH, geochemist, environmental consultant; b. Columbus, Ohio, Feb. 22, 1961; s. Guy W. and Rita A. (Burns) C. BS in Geology magna cum laude, UCLA, 1984; PhD in Geochemistry, Stanford U., 1991. Supr. lab. Inst. Geophysics and Planetary Physics UCLA, 1982-85; teaching asst. dept. geology Stanford (Calif.) U., 1985-88, geochemist ocean drilling program, 1987-88, rsch. asst. dept. geology, 1988-91; postgrad. rsch. chemist div. geol. rsch. Scripps Inst. Oceanography, La Jolla, Calif., 1991-92; cons. chemist Erler and Kalinowski, Inc., San Mateo, Calif., 1992—; chair project for environ. rsch. Stanford U., 1989-91. Editor: Stanford University Project for Environmental Research: Student Research 1989, 1990; contbr. articles to profl. jours. Mem. Am. Soc. Limnology and Oceanography, Geol. Soc. Am., Geochem. Soc., Oceanography Soc., Phi Beta Kappa. Home: 935 Holly Rd Belmont CA 94002 Office: Erler and Kalinowski Inc Ste 320 1730 S Amphlett Blvd San Mateo CA 94402

CHAMBERS, THOMAS DOANE, professional basketball player; b. Ogden, Utah, June 21, 1959; m. Erin C.; children: Ericka, Skylar. Attended, U. Utah. Player San Diego Clippers, 1981-83, Seattle SuperSonics, 1983-88, Phoenix Suns, 1988-93, Utah Jazz, 1993—. Mem. Nat. Basketball Assn. All-Star Team, 1987-91; Most Valuable Player, Nat. Basketball Assn. All-Star Game, 1987; All-NBA second team, 1989, 90. Office: care Utah Jazz Delta Ctr 301 West S Temple Salt Lake City UT 84101

CHAMBERS, VIRGINIA ELLEN, community volunteer, retired photographer; b. St. Paul, Apr. 17, 1927; d. Carlton Gardner and Lillian (Cox) Annable; m. Newell LeMoine Bradley, Oct. 26, 1946 (dec. Aug. 1968); children: Rosalind (dec.), Newell Jr., Lawrence, Stephan; m. Stanley Lancaster Chambers, July 22, 1979. Student, Morningside Coll., Sioux City, Iowa, 1945, Nebr. U., 1961-62. Telephone operator Northwestern Bell, Sioux City, 1946-48, Norfolk, Nebr., 1949-52, Des Moines, 1962-67; owner cocktail lounge Tucson, 1968-72; photographer Jones & Presnell, Charlotte, N.C., 1975-79. Founder, active Gen. Fedn. Women's Clubs-Ariz., pres. S.W. dist., 1986-88, treas., 1990-92, recording sec., 1992—; founder London Bridge Woman's Club, Lake Havasu, pres. 1981-83; v.p. Homemaker's Extension Club, Lake Havasu, 1988; vol. Festival Arts Assn., Lake Havasu, Cancer Soc., Easter Seal Soc., Heart Fund, Jazz Festival; mem. state legis. com. Am. Assn. Ret. Persons, Friends of Libr.; sec. Mohave County (Ariz.) Dem. Cen. Com., 1988-91; mem. Dem. Assn. of Havasu. Mem. Apple User's Club, Old English Costume Club., Lake Havasu Hist. Soc. Home: 1847 Willow Ave Lake Havasu City AZ 86403

CHAMBON, CHARLES WILLIAM, electrical engineer; b. Colorado Springs, Colo., Apr. 15, 1954; s. George William and Myrtle Ines (Elliott) C. BSEE, U. Colo., 1982, MSEE, 1985, postgrad., 1985—. Asst. prof. engrng. graphic design, instr. physics U. Colo., Colorado Springs, 1981-82; rschr. with Robert Burton and Ronald M. Sego Defense Advanced Rsch.

Project, 1979-85. Active Pikes Peak Jaycees, Colorado Springs Jaycees, Colorado Springs Police Dept. Named Community Fund Raiser of Yr., Colo. Jaycees, 1984, Jaycee of Yr., Pikes Peak Jaycees, 1982, 84, Outstanding Young Coloradan, Colo. Jaycees and JCI Senate, 1984, Outstanding Young Man Am., U.S. Jaycees, 1983; recipient Award of Appreciation, Rocky Mountain Multiple Sclerosis Ctr. Denver, 1983, Cert. of Merit, Colo. Engring. Coun., 1982. Mem. IEEE, Acoustics, Speech and Signal Processing Soc. of IEEE, Automatic Control Soc. of IEEE, Aerospace and Electronic Systems Soc. of IEEE, AAAS (disabled resource group 1981—), Am. Radio Relay League, Denver Radio League, Lookout Mountain Repeater Group, Squaw Mountain Ham Club, Pueblo Ham Club, Telstar Ham Club, Amateur Radio Emergency Svc., Pikes Peak FM Assn., Wilderness on Wheels Found., Cheyenne Mountain Repeater Group (pres., founder 1981—), Rocky Mountain Pedals and Chords Organ Club, Eta Kappa Nu (Theta Chi chpt., pres. 1982-83, Award of Appreciation 1984). Home: 2823 W Vintah St Colorado Springs CO 80904-2429

CHAMP, STANLEY GORDON, scientific company executive; b. Hoquiam, Wash., Feb. 15, 1919; s. Clifford Harvey and Edna Winnifred (Johnson) C.; m. Anita Knapp Wegener, Sept. 6, 1941; children: Suzanne Winnifred Whalen, Colleen Louise Szurszewski. BS, U. Puget Sound, 1941; MS, U. Wash., 1950; postgrad., MIT, 1955, 57, UCLA, 1959. Cert. tchr., adminstr., Wash. Tchr. Lake Washington Sch. Dist., Kirkland, Wash., 1942-48; prof. math. U. Puget Sound, Tacoma, 1948-51; supr. mathematician Puget Sound Naval Shipyard, Bremerton, Wash., 1951-55; rsch. specialist Boeing Co., Seattle, 1955-68; v.p. R.M. Towne & Assocs., Seattle, 1968-75; founder, pres. Dynac Scis., Tacoma, 1975—; cons. R.M. Towne Assocs., Seattle, Yantis Assocs., Bellevue, Wash. Contbr. articles to profl. jours.; patent method and apparatus determination soil dynamics insitu. Mem. N.Y. Acad. Sci., Phi Delta Kappa. Presbyterian. Home: 1540 S Fairview Dr Tacoma WA 98465-1314

CHAMPION, MARGE (MARJORIE CELESTE CHAMPION), actress, dancer, choreographer; b. L.A., Sept. 2, 1923; d. Ernest and Gladys (Basquette) Belcher; m. Art Babbitt (div.); m. Gower Champion, Oct. 5, 1947 (div. 1973); children: Blake (dec.), Gregg; m. Boris Sagal, Jan. 1, 1977 (dec. 1981). Student pub. schs., Los Angeles. stage debut L.A. Civic Opera, 1936; movie debut (under name Marjorie Bell) in The Castles, 1938; live action model for cartoon heroines in: Walt Disney prodns. Blue Fairy in Pinocchio, 1938, Snow White, 1937, Hippo and Storks in Fantasia; appeared on Broadway musicals Dark of the Moon, 1945, Beggar's Holiday, 1946; first profl. appearance with Gower Champion as Gower and Bell Normandie Roof, Montreal, Que., Can., 1947; N.Y. debut as Marge and Gower Champion at Hotel Plaza, 1947; weekly show Admiral Broadway Review, Dumont and NBC TV Network, 1949, Marge and Gower Champion Show, 1957; with husband staged dances for revues: Lend an Ear, 1949, Make A Wish, Small Wonder; movies include: Showboat, 1951, Lovely to Look At, 1952, Everything I Have is Yours, 1952, Give A Girl a Break, 1953, Three for the Show, 1955, Jupiter's Darling, 1955, The Swimmer, 1968, The Party, 1968, The Cockeyed Cowboy of Calico County, 1970, That's Entertainment, Part 2, 1976; various TV appearances, including TV show Toast of the Town, 1953; Three for Tonight, 1955, Shower of Stars, 1956, GE Theatre, 1957, Dinah Shore Show, 1958, Telephone Hour, 1960; acting debut Hemingway and All Those People, Indpls., 1958; title role: Sabrina Fair, 1960; choreographer: Queen of the Stardust Ballroom, 1975 (Emmy award), 1992, Day of the Locust, 1975; author: (with Marilee Zdenek) Catch the New Wind, 1972, God is a Verb, 1974; dialogue coach and choreographer: The Awakening Land, NBC-TV, 1978, Masada, ABC-TV, 1979, Diary of Ann Frank, NBC-TV, 1980, When the Circus Comes to Town, CBS-TV, 1980; appeared: TV series Fame, 1982; dir., choreography: TV prodn. I Do, I Do, 1983, Stepping Out, Berkshire Theatre Festival, 1988, 89, Lute Song, 1989, She Loves Me, 1990; dancer: 5-6-7-8, Dance!, Radio City Music Hall, 1983, No No Nanette, St. Louis Muny Opera, 1990. Recipient Legend of Dance award, 1991. Office: care Paperny Sher 15060 Ventura Blvd Ste 100 Sherman Oaks CA 91403-2426

CHAN, ALLEN FONG, protective services official; b. Union City, Calif., Mar. 9, 1957; s. Herbert Quai and Christine (Lee) C. Student, Ohlone Coll., Fremont, Calif., 1975-79; BS in Recreation Adminstrn., Calif. State U., Hayward, 1979. Recreation specialist City of Newark (Calif.) Recreation Dept., 1973-79, police aide, 1981-83, police officer, 1983—; instr. Ohlone Coll., Fremont; supervising recreation coordinator City of Fremont (Calif.) Community Services, Recreation, 1978-79, park ranger, 1979-83; communication operator City of Hayward (Calif.) Police Dept., 1980-81. Advisor Newark Police Explorers, Boy Scouts Am., 1983—; coordinating officer, Sch. Safety Patrol, Newark, 1987—; basketball ofcl. Mission Valley Athletic League, Fremont, Calif., 1975-79; site ofcl. Cath. Youth Orgn., Fremont, 1975-79; active Alameda County (Calif.) Spl. Olympics, 1981; chmn. local chpt. Internat. Spl. Olympic Winter Games, 1989; chmn. law enforcement torch run Calif. Spl. Olympics, 1989; bd. dirs. Fremont Softball League, 1979-80. Named Outstanding Young Men. Am., 1982. Mem. Police Officers Rsch. Assn. Calif., Calif. Orgn. Police and Sheriffs, Calif. Parks and Recreation Soc., Newark Police Assn. (sec. 1985-88, pres. 1988-90), Calif. Law Enforcement Adminstrn. (bd. dirs. 1988—). Democrat. Office: City of Newark Police Dept 37101 Newark Blvd Newark CA 94560-3796

CHAN, JERRY KUM NAM, corporate controller; b. Singapore, Singapore, Apr. 11, 1960; came to U.S., 1982; s. Shu Wing Chan and Yeok Han Yeong. BS with honors, U. Mass., 1985; MBA, Santa Clara U., 1987. Info. officer Ministry of Def., Singapore, 1978-82; fin. analyst Plain Heaven Ltd., Singapore, 1980-82; corp. contr. Supertex Inc., Sunnyvale, Calif., 1987—. Vol. Habitat for Humanity, Calif. Mem. Inst. Mgmt. Assn., Nat. Assn. accts. Baptist.

CHAN, LOREN BRIGGS, technical writing specialist; b. Palo Alto, Calif., Sept. 10, 1943; s. Shau Wing and Anna Mae (Chin) C.; m. Frances Anastasia Chow, Apr. 19, 1975 (div. Jan. 1988); children: Karen Monique, Pierre Bénédict, Marc Henri. AB, Stanford U., 1965, AM, 1966; MS, Golden Gate U., 1988; PhD, UCLA, 1971. Teaching asst. UCLA, 1968-69, teaching assoc., 1969-70; lectr. in history Calif. State U., Northridge, 1970-71; lectr. in history San Jose (Calif.) State U., 1971-72, asst. prof. history, 1972-76, assoc. prof. history, 1976-80; lectr. history Calif. State U., Hayward, 1980-81; prodn. test technician Nicolet Paratronics Corp., Fremont, Calif., 1982; computer svc. technician Bell-Northern Rsch., Mountain View, Calif., 1982-83; rsch. analyst Bell-No. Rsch., Mountain View, 1984-85, tech. writer, 1985-87; sr. tech. writer StrataCom, Inc., Campbell, Calif., 1987-88; tech. writer Sun Microsystems, Mountain View, 1988-90, sr. tech. writer, 1990—. Author: Sagebrush Statesman, 1973, SPARCstation 1 Installation Guide, 1989, Collected Technical Support Notes, 1988, SPARCstation 2 Installation Guide, 1990, Desktop Storage Pack Installation Guide, 1989-90, SPARCstation 10 Installation Guide, 1992; editor: Chinese-American History Reader, 1976; contbr. articles to profl. jours. Radio sta. trustee ARC, Menlo Park, Calif., 1975-80. Recipient Presdl. Sports award Pres.'s Coun. on Phys. Fitness and Sports, 1973. Mem. Nat. Geog. Soc., Chinese Inst. Engrs., Am. Radio Relay League, Confederate Stamp Alliance, Buick Club of Am., San Jose Aquatics Masters Swim Club. Democrat. Christian Scientist. Home: 5719 Makati Cir Apt D San Jose CA 95123-6211

CHAN, MICHAEL CHIU-HON, chiropractor; b. Hong Kong, Aug. 31, 1961; came to U.S., 1979; s. Fuk Yum and Chun Wai (Ma) C. D of Chiropractic, Western States Chiropractic Coll., 1985; fellow, Internat. Acad. Clin. Acupuncture, 1986. Assoc. doctor Widoff Chiropractic Clinic, Phoenix, 1986, Horizon Chiropractic Clinic, Glendale, Ariz., 1986-88; dir. North Ranch Chiropractic Assoc., Scottsdale, Ariz., 1988-91; pvt. practice Phoenix, 1991—; dir. Neighborhood Chiropractic, Phoenix, 1988-89. Contbr. articles to profl. jours. Mem. Am. Chiropractic Assoc., Coun. on Diagnostic Imaging, Paradise Valley Toastmaster Club. Office: 6544 W Thomas Rd Ste 37 Phoenix AZ 85033

CHAN, PETER WING KWONG, pharmacist; b. L.A., Feb. 3, 1949; s. Sherwin T.S. and Shirley W. (Lee) C.; m. Patricia Jean Uyeno, June 8, 1974; children: Kristina Dionne, Kelly Alison, David Shoichi. BS, U. So. Calif., 1970, D in Pharmacy, 1974. Lic. pharmacist, Calif. Clin. instr. U. So. Calif., 1974-76; staff clin. pharmacist Cedars-Sinai Med. Ctr., L.A., 1974-76; 1st clin. pharmacist in ophthalmology Alcon Labs., Inc., Ft. Worth, 1977—, formerly in Phila. monitoring patient drug therapy, teaching residents, nurses, pharmacy students, then assigned to Tumu Tumu Hosp., Karatina, Kenya, also lectr. clin. ocular pharmacology tng. course, Nairobi, Cairo, Athens, formerly dist. sales mgr. Alcon/BP, ophthal. products div. Alcon Labs., Inc., Denver; v.p., gen. mgr. Optikem Internat., Sereine Products Div., Optacryl, Inc., Denver; formerly product mgr. hosp. pharmacy products Am. McGaw div. Am. Hosp. Supply Corp.; past internat. market mgr. IOLAB subs. Johnson & Johnson, past dir. new bus. devel. Iolab Pharms., dir. Internat. Mktg., dir. new products mktg.; bus. and mktg. strategies cons. to pharm. and med. device cos.; ptnr., chmn. Pre Free Techs., Inc.; ptnr. Vitamin Specialties Corp.; bd dirs. SUDCO Internat., L.A. Del. Am. Pharm. Assn. House of Dels., 1976-78; bd. dirs. Calif. Youth Theatre at Paramount Studios, Hollywood 1986-87, 91-93. Recipient Hollywood-Wilshire Pharm. Assn. spl. award for outstanding svc., 1974. Mem. Chinese Am. Pharm. Assn., Am. Pharm. Assn., Calif. Pharm. Assn., Hollywood-Wilshire Pharm. Assn. (bd. dirs. 1972-76), Am. Soc. Hosp. Pharmacists, Am. Pharm. Assn. Acad. of Pharmacy Practice, U. So. Calif. Gen. Alumni Assn., Granada Hills High Sch. Highlanders Booster Club (bd. dirs. 1991, 92, 93, chmn.-Project 2000), OSAD Centurions, Phi Delta Chi. Democrat. Home: 10251 Vanalden Ave Northridge CA 91324-1240 Office: Chan & Assocs PO Box 7398 Northridge CA 91327-7398

CHAN, RAY CHI-MOON, accountant; b. Hong Kong, Dec. 26, 1957; came to U.S., 1980; s. Kwok-Fai and Shun-Ying (Choi) C.; m. Judy Owyoung, June 14, 1986. BS (hon.), U. Hong Kong, 1980; MS in Acctg., Calif. State U., 1986. Mech. engr. State Calif., Sacramento, 1981-86; acct. Grant Thornton, Sacramento, 1987-89; ptnr. Chan & NG CPAs, Sacramento, 1989—. Vol. Asian Legal Svcs. Outreach, Sacramento, 1982-86; chief fin. officer Chinese Am. Coun. Sacramento, 1986-89; treas. Camellia Symphony, Sacramento, 1986-90; bd. mem. Asian Community Svc. Ctr., Jinan-Sacramento Sister Cities Corp., 1992. Mem. South Sacramento Rotary Club, AICPA, Calif. Soc. CPAs. Office: Chan & NG CPAs 1414 K St Ste 305 Sacramento CA 95814

CHAN, RIX SIU-WONG, electrical engineer; b. Hong Kong, Dec. 13, 1962; came to U.S., 1982; s. Kum Chen and Nin Hing (Yang) C. BSEE cum laude, U. Wis., Milw., 1985; MSEE, Purdue U., 1986. Elec. engr. Cyperchron Corp., Cold Spring, N.Y., 1986-90; sr. elec. engr. Codar Tech., Inc., Longmont, Colo., 1991—; adj. prof. CUNY-Queens Coll., Flushing, N.Y., 1988-90. Mem. IEEE, Assn. for Computing Machinery, Tau Beta Pi. Home: 2400 17th Ave # 305 D Longmont CO 80503

CHAN, STEVEN S., electronics company executive; b. Kowloon, Hong Kong, Oct. 6, 1949; came to U.S., 1967; s. Yit-Ming and Cheong-Yuen (Lee) C.; m. Rosa T. Cho; children: James, Janey. BSEE, Worcester Poly. Inst., 1971; postgrad., Cornell U., 1972; MSEE, Worcester Poly. Inst., 1980. Dir. elec. engring. labs. Alden Rsch. Labs., Holden, Mass., 1971-72; v.p. engring. Adams-Smith Inc., Boxboro, Mass., 1972-79; staff engr. AMPEX Corp., Redwood City, Calif., 1980-82; mgr., dir. LSI Logic Corp., Milpitas, Calif., 1982-85, v.p. application specific integrated circuits, 1986-87; v.p. systems engring. Headland Tech., Fremont, Calif., 1988-89; v.p. and gen. mgr. media group Chips and Techs., San Jose, Calif., 1990-92; founder, pres. AuraVision Corp., Fremont, Calif., 1992—; speaker at various industry confs., 1978—. Patentee in field; contbr. articles to profl. jours. Mem. IEEE, Eta Kappa Nu, Pi Mu Epsilon, Tau Beta Pi. Home: 2518 Euclid Pl Fremont CA 94539 Office: AuraVision Corp 47865 Fremont Blvd Fremont CA 94538

CHAN, TAK-BIU (BUDDY T. B. CHAN), investment company executive; b. Hong Kong, Oct. 1, 1961; s. Peter P.F. and Vivian P.K. (Chan) Chan; m. Yuko Takeshita, Apr. 27, 1988; children: Christina Akie, Catherine Yoshie. Diploma, Oxford Coll. Applied Sci., Eng., 1984; BSc, DSc, Pacific Western U., 1986. Founder, dir. Buddy Electronics & Systems Ltd., Hong Kong, 1979—; exec. dir. Peter Chan (Secs.) Ltd., Hong Kong, 1983—; gen. mgr. Pacific Essential Ltd., Hong Kong, 1987-92, dir., 1987—; editor Hong Kong Economist Newspaper Ltd., 1987-92; mng. dir. Concord Securities Ltd., Hong Kong, 1987—; mgr. Essential Projects Corp., U.S., 1988—, Essential Tech. Ltd., Can., 1988—; bd. dirs. Pacific Essential Ltd., Buddy Electronics & Systems Ltd., Concord Securities Ltd., Essential Projects Corp., Essential Tech. Ltd., Hong Kong Economist Newspaper Ltd. Author: Application of Robotic Technology in Rehabilitation Medicine, A Restaurant Served by Robots--A Feasibility Study, The Illustrated Encyclopedia of Robotic Technology, The Share Registration Program--An Advance Approach. Recipient cert. Dir. of the Assn. for Mgmt. Excellence, U.S., 1989, Internat. Bus. Inst., U.S., 1989, Hong Kong Productivity Coun., 1988, Japan Found. and Japan Assn. Internat. Edn., 1987, Stock Exch. of Hong Kong Ltd., 1987, Hallmark Medallion, World Decoration of Excellence, 1989, Leader in Sci. award Am. Biog. Inst., 1989, Award of Honor, Internat. Civil Aviation Orgn., 1979; fellow Oxford Coll. Applied Sci., 1984. Fellow Internat. Biog. Assn. UK; mem. Robotic Internat. (sr.), Soc. Mfg. Engrs. USA (sr.), Nat. Svc. Robot Assn. USA (charter), Hong Kong Inst. Fishery (exec. com.), N.Y. Acad. Scis. (sustaining), Am. Biog. Inst. Rsch. Assn. (dep. gov. 1989-90), ASME, German Assn. Engrs., French Soc. Mech. Engrs., Can. Soc. Mech. Engring., Engring. Inst. Can., Robotic Soc. Am., Japan Indsl. Robot Assn., Robotics Soc. Japan, Engring. Mgmt. Soc., IEEE, Inst. Sci. Tech. UK, Laser Soc. Japan, ABI Rsch. Bd. Advisers. Office: 2873 Japonica Pl, Coquitlam, BC Canada V3E 2V6

CHAN, VIVIEN WAI-FAN, biochemist; b. Hong Kong, May 3, 1967; came to U.S., 1985; d. Peter Kai-Lai and Rosamund Yee-Hing Chan. BA in Chemistry, Coll. Wooster, 1989; postgrad., U. Calif., 1989—. Grad. rschr. U. Calif., San Francisco, 1989—; tutor Coll. of Wooster, Ohio, 1986-89, lab. asst., 1986. Contbr. articles to profl. jours. Vol. interpretor U. Calif., San Francisco, 1992; dir. fin. Grad. Students Assn., San Francisco, 1990-92. Predoctoral fellowship Howard Hughes Med. Inst., 1989—, Nuclear Chemistry fellowship Am. Chem. Soc., 1987. Mem. Am. Chem. Soc., Phi Beta Kappa, Iota Sigma Pi, Sigma Xi. Office: U Calif Box 0552 Hooper Found San Francisco CA 94143

CHAN, YIM HUNG, psychiatrist; b. Hong Kong, Jan. 24, 1959; s. Pak Woon and Bo Ying (Lam) C. BA, Cornell U., 1981; MD, Albany Med. Coll., 1986. Diplomate Am. Bd. Psychiatry and Neurology. Intern, resident St. Mary's Hosp. and Med. Ctr., San Francisco, 1986-90; clin. instr. U. Calif., San Francisco, 1990-92, asst. clin. prof. psychiatry, 1992—; attending physician St. Mary's Hosp. and Med. Ctr., San Francisco, 1991—, Villa Fairmont Hosp., San Leandro, Calif., 1991-93; staff psychiatrist Sunset Day Treatment, San Francisco, 1991—; team leader physician San Francisco Gen. Hosp., 1990-91; attending physician St. Luke's Hosp. and Med. Ctr., San Francisco, 1990—, Calif. Pacific Med. Ctr., San Francisco, 1993—. Mem. Asian AIDS Task Force, San Francisco, 1986, Asian Pacific AIDS Coalition, San Francisco, 1987—; bd. dirs. Family Svc. Agy., San Francisco, 1993—. Mem. Am. Psychiat. Assn., No. Calif. Psychiat. Soc., Calif. Psychiat. Soc. Office: Asian Am Psychiat Practice 490 6th Ave # 302 San Francisco CA 94118

CHANCE, KATHY LYNN, wholesale distribution executive, owner; b. Seattle, June 12, 1957; d. Wright Andrew and Mary Ruth (Marzolla) Carleton; m. Bill Craig Chance, July 19, 1986; children: Jessica Lynn, Justin Carleton. AA in Bus., Butte Community Coll., 1981; BS in Bus., Calif. State U., Chico, Calif., 1986. Office mgr. Kauffmans Mens Store, Chico, Calif., 1978-81; bookkeeper Pacific Stihl, Chico, Calif., 1981-86; acct. Aerojet, Sacramento, Calif., 1986-87; mgr., owner Pacific Stihl, Chico, 1987—. Mem. coms. Chico C. of C., 1986—; mem. Omega Nu, Chico, 1987—; newsletter editor Calif. Women for Agriculture, Chico, 1986—; mem. Calif. Farm Bus., 1985—. Mem. Chico Ad Club, Employer Adv. Group. Republican. Office: Pacific Stihl Inc 11096 Midway Chico CA 95928

CHANCE, KENNETH DONALD, engineer; b. Denver, July 27, 1948; s. John Jefferson and Evelyn Pauline (Jacobs) C. AA, Red Rocks Coll., Golden, Colo., 1982. Stationery operating engr. EG&G Rocky Flats, Golden, 1980—. Office: EG&G Rocky Flats Rocky Flats Util Bldg 707 Golden CO 80402

CHANCEY, VELTON RAY (SONNY), plant manager; b. Tahoka, Tex., Dec. 9, 1943; s. Tull Ray and Mary Alice (Hines) C.; m. Betty Jo Williams, June 19, 1966; children: Cheryl Lynn Kruse, Jennifer Lee. AA, Ea. N.Mex. U., Roswell, 1969; BBA, Ea. N.Mex. U., Portales, 1971. Engr. trainee/pumper Gen. Am. Oil Co. Tex., Loco Hills, N.Mex., 1964-68; dir. phys. plant Ea. N.Mex. U., Roswell, 1971-78, N.Mex. Mil. Inst., Roswell, 1978—. Mem. Assn. Phys. Plant Adminstrs., Am. Inst. Plant Engrs., Assn. Energy Engrs., N.Mex. Horse Breeders, N.Mex. Horseman's Assn., Delta Sigma Pi. Republican. Mem. Ch. of Christ. Home: RR 3 1601 Springfield Rd Roswell NM 88201 Office: NMex Mil Inst 101 W College Blvd Roswell NM 88201

CHANDLER, BRUCE FREDERICK, internist; b. Bohemia, Pa., Mar. 26, 1926; s. Frederick Arthur and Minnie Flora (Burkhardt) C.; m. Janice Evelyn Piper, Aug. 14, 1954; children: Barbara, Betty, Karen, Paul, June. Student, Pa. State U., 1942-44; MD, Temple U., 1948. Diplomate Am. Bd. Internal Medicine. Commd. med. officer U.S. Army, 1948, advanced through grades to col., 1967; intern Temple U. Hosp., Phila., 1948-49; chief psychiatry 7th Field Hosp., Trieste, Italy, 1950; resident Walter Reed Gen. Hosp., Washington, 1949-53; battalion surgeon 2d Div. Artillery, Korea, 1953-54; chief renal dialysis unit 45th Evacuation Hosp. and Tokyo Army Hosp., Korea, Japan, 1954-55; various assignments Walter Reed Gen. Hosp., Fitzsimons Gen. Hosp., Letterman Gen. Hosp., 1955-70; comdg. officer 45th Field Hosp., Vicenza, Italy, 1958-62; pvt. practice internist Ridgecrest (Calif.) Med. Clinic, 1970-76; chief med. svc. and out-patients VA Hosps., Walla Walla, Spokane, Wash., 1976-82; med. cons. Social Security Adminstrn., Spokane, Wash., 1983-87; ret. Panel mem. TV shows, 1964-70; lectr.; contbr. numerous articles to med. profl. jours. Decorated Legion of Merit. Fellow ACP, Am. Coll. Chest Physicians; mem. AMA, Am. Thoracic Soc., N.Y. Acad. Scis., So. European Task Force U.S. Army Med. Dental Soc. (pres., founder 1958-62). Republican. Methodist. Home: 6496 N Callisch Ave Fresno CA 93710-3902

CHANDLER, DAVID BENJAMIN, toxicologist; b. Fresno, Calif., Feb. 5, 1953; s. Hubert Eugene and Louise Elizabeth (Burke) C.; m. Margaret Lourdes Garcia, Jan. 8, 1983; 1 child, Tyler Benjamin. BS, BA, U. Calif., Santa Barbara, 1976; PhD, U. Calif., Davis, 1982. Diplomate Am. Bd. Toxicology, Am. Bd. Applied Toxicology. Rsch. asst. dept. Psychol. Scis. U. Calif., Davis, 1981-82; postdoctoral fellow dept. Neurology U. Miss., Jackson, 1982-83; assoc. dir. pulmonary rsch. dept. Medicine U. Ala. VA Hosp., Birmingham, 1983-88, chief pulmonary macrophage rsch, 1985-88; rsch. asst. prof. Medicine U. Ala., Birmingham, 1986-88, Sch. Medicine, Birmingham, 1986-88; assoc. dir. Oreg. Poison Ctr. Oreg. Health Sci. U., Portland, 1988—, assoc. prof. Emergency Medicine, 1992—; with Pesticide Analytical Responce Ctr., 1988—; chmn. credentialling com. Am. Bd. of Toxicology, 1992—, Triennial Water Quality Standards Rev. State of Oreg., 1992—. Contbr. articles to profl. jours. Mem. Am. Coll. of Toxicology, Soc. for Risk Analysis, Am. Acad. of Clin. Toxicology, Soc. of Toxicology, Am. Soc. for Pharmacology and Exptl. Therapeutics, Am. Thoracic Soc., Sigma Xi. Democrat. Office: Oreg Health Sci Univ 3181 SW Sam Jackson Pk Rd Portland OR 97201-3098

CHANDLER, DOUGLAS EDWIN, zoology educator; b. Oak Park, Ill., Oct. 1, 1945; s. Herbert Edwin and Jeannette (Willard) C. BS in Chemistry, U. Rochester, 1967; MA in Biochemistry, Johns Hopkins U., Balt., 1969; PhD in Physiology, U. Calif., San Francisco, 1977. Postdoctoral fellow U. Calif., San Francisco, 1977-79, U. Coll. Sch. Medicine, London, 1979-80; asst. prof. Ariz. State U., Tempe, 1980-85; assoc. prof. Ariz. State U., 1985-90, prof. zoology, 1990—. Contbr. articles to profl. jours.; guest editor Microscopy Rsch. & Technique, 1988—, mem. editorial bd., 1990—. With USN, 1969-73. NIH rsch. career devel. awardee, 1985-90; NSF grantee, 1981—. Mem. Am. Soc. Cell Biology, Soc. for Developmental Biology. Office: Arizona State Univ Dept Zoology Tempe AZ 85287-1501

CHANDLER, FLOYD COPELAND, fine arts educator; b. San Diego, Dec. 5, 1920; s. Floyd Fedrick and Benadah (Sullivan) C. Cert., S.D. Acad. Fine Arts, 1937, Otis Art Inst., L.A., 1941, Art Students League N.Y., N.Y.C., 1950; BA, San Diego State U., 1964; MA, Claremont Grad. Sch., 1969. Designer Farr Screen Prossing Corp., N.Y.C., 1950; advt., art dept. Preferred Utilities Mfg. Corp., N.Y.C., 1951-54; free-lance mural work and porature N.Y.C., 1947-53; head art dept. Desert Sun High Sch., Idyllwild, Calif., 1954; fine arts instr. adult sch. San Diego Unified Sch. Dist., 1955-71; dept. head continuing edn. div. San Diego C.C., 1971-79, fine arts instr., 1980—; curator San Diego Art Inst., 1960-70; chmn. city-wide art shows Adult Educator of San Diego, 1969-75; curator Balboa Park, San Diego, 1960-70. Exhibited in group shows at Chapellier Studio Gallery, N.Y.C., 1950, Mus. Natural History, San Diego, 1969, Thackeray Fine Arts Gallery, San Diego, 1969-80, The Jerome Ariz. Hist. Mine Mus., 1970-92, Southwestern Arts Ltd. Art Gallery, Carmel, Calif., 1975-77, Pratt Gallery, San Diego, 1992—, Antiques West Mall, 1993, Fine Arts Gallery, San Diego, 1993; contbr. paintings to mags. With USCG, 1942-46. Recipient Grumbacher Golden Palette award. Mem. Art Students League N.Y. (life), Calif. Coun. Adult Edn., San Diego Adult Educators Assn., Fine Arts Assn. San Diego, Del Gardens Art Assn. Republican. Christian Scientist. Home: 4121 Texas St San Diego CA 92104-1615

CHANDLER, GREGORY, lawyer; b. Ft. Knox, Ky., Nov. 23, 1957; s. Samuel and Agnes Lillie (Wideman) C.; m. Sunae Chong, Feb. 8, 1990. BA, Harvard U., 1983; JD, U. Tex., 1987. Bar: Calif. 1992, U.S. Dist. Ct. (no. dist.) Calif. 1992, U.S. Ct. Appeals (9th cir.) 1992, U.S. Ct. Vets. Appeals 1992. Atty. Swords to Plowshares, San Francisco, 1992—. Mem. Inner City Outings, San Francisco, 1991; vol. atty. Homeless Advocacy Project, San Francisco, 1992; judge adv. gen.'s corps. U.S. Army. Capt. U.S. Army, 1988-91. Mem. Bar Assn. of San Francisco, Alameda County Bar Assn., Contra Costa Bar Assn., Harvard Club of San Francisco, Sierra Club. Home: 10944 San Pablo Ave # 522 El Cerrito CA 94530 Office: Swords to Plowshares 400 Valencia St San Francisco CA 94103

CHANDLER, JOHN C., nuclear engineer; b. Gulfport, Miss., Oct. 31, 1946; s. Thomas Alfred and Jo Beth (Majure) C., Jr.; m. Lynne Blair Bratcher, Aug. 1, 1967 (div. 1976); 1 dau., Gwendolyn Amy. B.S., Miss. State U., 1968; M.S. in Nuclear Engring, U. Wash., 1980. Nuclear engr. Ingalls Nuclear Ships Co., Pascagoula, Miss., 1968; advanced engr. Westinghouse Hanford Co., Richland, Wash., 1973-79; nuclear engr. Middle South Services, New Orleans, 1979-80; sr. engr. Exxon Nuclear Co., Inc., Richland, Wash., 1980-86; program dir. reload & reactor physics svcs. EI Internat., Inc., Idaho Falls, Idaho, 1986-87; chief engr. John Elston Assocs., Richland, Wash., 1987—. Contbr. articles to profl. jours. Advisor CAP, Richland, 1973-76. Served to capt. USAF, 1968-73. Mem. Am. Nuclear Soc.

CHANDLER, KRIS, computer consultant, educator; b. Cleveland Heights, Ohio, June 26, 1948; d. Gerhard A. and Hanna R. (Rittmeyer) Hoffmann; children: Karen, Heidi. BSBA with honors and spl. distinction U. So. Colo., 1984, postgrad., 1984-85; MBA, U. Ark., 1987; PhD in C.C. Adminstrn. Colo. State U. Owner, mgr. V&W Fgn. Car Svc., Canon City, Colo., 1970-80; prin. The Chandlers, Computer Cons., Pueblo, Colo., 1982—; ptnr. Jak Rabbit Software, 1989—; faculty Pikes Peak Community Coll., U. So. Colo., also mgr. Sch. Bus. microcomputer lab. Bd. dirs. Canon City Community Svc. Ctr., 1978-80, Canon City chpt. ARC, 1978-81. Mem. Assn. for Computing Machinery, Data Processing Mgmt. Assn. (advisor student chpt. Pikes Peak Community Coll. 1989—), U. So. Colo. Honors Soc. (pres.), U. So. Colo. Grad. Assn. (founder), Alpha Chi, Sigma Iota Epsilon. Home and Office: 401 S Neilson Ave Pueblo CO 81001-4238

CHANDLER, MARK JOSEPH, city and county official; b. Albuquerque, June 30, 1956; s. Everett Marston and Arlene Byrdell (Bahr) C. AB in Econs. with honors, U. Calif., Davis, 1978; MBA in Internat. Bus., U. Calif., Berkeley, 1983; postgrad., Tokyo Acad. Japanese, 1983-84. Mgr. market devel. P.I.E. Nationwide, Walnut Creek, Calif., 1980-83; mgr. market analysis U.S. Sprint, Kansas City, Mo., 1984-87; coord. internat. bus. City and County of San Francisco, 1987—. Mem. adv. coun. for CCSF Ctr. Internat. Trade; bd. dirs. San Francisco Trade Office, Inc. Mem. Pacific Rim Comm. Forum (founding), San Francisco Planning and Urban Rsch. Assn., Golden Gate Nat. Park Assn., San Francisco C. of C. (consular corps com.), Nature Conservancy, Marine Mammal Ctr., World Affairs Coun., Commonwealth Club. Democrat. Home: 1557 Noe St San Francisco CA 94131-2331

CHANDLER, MICHAEL STEPHEN, communications consultant; b. Brunswick, Ga., Dec. 16, 1959; s. Harold Aubrey and Emily Juanita (Sleeth) C.; m. Pamela Jeanette Morrow, Sept. 12, 1985; 1 child, Felic Jamison. AA, Pensacola Jr. Coll., 1979; BS, U. West Fla., 1982. Analyst NASA HQ, Washington, 1980-81; account mgr. Motorola, Inc., San Diego, 1988—; cons.

Western Maquiladora Assoc., 1991—, Otay C. of C., 1990—. Chmn. pac com. Boy Scouts of Am., 1990. Lt. USN, 1983-88. Republican. Methodist. Office: 9980 Carroll Canyon Rd San Diego CA 92131

CHANDLER, TERTIUS, historian; b. Dedham, Mass., Feb. 6, 1915; m. Margot Muller Tegelstrom. Grad. cum laude, Harvard U., 1937; PhD, Clayton U., 1988. Author: Godly Kings and Early Ethics, 1976, Progress, 1976, The Tax We Need, 1982, Chandler's Half-Encyclopedia, 1983, 4000 Years of Urban Growth, 1987; editor: Digsig, 1977-82, Solutions, 1978-82; contbr. chpt. to Readings for the 21st Century, 1991. Candidate for U.S. Ho. of Reps., 1980, 82. Home: 2500 Buena Vista Way Berkeley CA 94708-1928

CHANDLER, THOMAS FRANKLIN, food products executive; b. Cobourg, Ontario, Canada, Jan. 11, 1947; s. Thomas Francis and Esther Elizabeth (Fabry) C.; m. Janet Elaine Roy, June 28, 1969. BE in Sci., U. Western Ontario, 1969; MA in Sci., U. Waterloo, Ontario, 1984. Registered profl. engr., Ontario. Project engr. Canada Packers, Toronto, Ontario, 1969-71, Campbell Soup, Toronto, 1971-77; engring. mgr. Redpath Sugar, Toronto, 1977-80, v.p. mfg., 1980-90; pres. Western Sugar, Denver, 1990—. Mem. Assn. Profl. Engrs., Sugar Industry Techs. (v.p. 1989—). Home: 32990 Woodland Dr Evergreen CO 80439-9720 Office: Western Sugar 1700 Broadway Denver CO 80290-0101

CHANDONNET, ANN FOX, journalist, poet; b. Lowell, Mass., Feb. 7, 1943; d. Leighton Dinsmore Fox and Barbara Amelia (Cloutman) Curran; m. Fernand Leonce Chandonnet, June 11, 1966; children: Yves, Alexandre. BS in Edn. magna cum laude, Lowell (Mass.) State Coll., 1964; MS in Eng. Lit., U. Wis., 1965. Cert. in secondary edn., Mass., Calif. Tchr. Kodiak (Alaska) High Sch., 1965-66; instr. Lowell (Mass.) State Coll., 1966-69; sec. First Enterprise Bank, Oakland, Calif., 1972-73; freelance writer Calif. and Alaska, 1972—; instr. Eagle River Community Coll., Eagle River, Alaska, 1976-82; feature writer Anchorage Times newspaper, 1982—. Author: (poems) Ptarmigan Valley, 1980, Auras, Tendrils, 1984, Canoeing in the Rain, 1990, (history) On the Trail of Eklutna, 1985, (children's book) Chief Stephen's Parky, 1989. Recipient Wis. Union award, 1965, Utah Wilderness Soc. Poetry award, 1990. Mem. Niagara-Erie Writers, Phi Delta Kappa (Excellence in Edn. Writing 1989), Literary Artist Guild of Alaska (founder 1980-82). Home: 6552 Lakeway Dr Anchorage AK 99502-1949 Office: Anchorage Times PO Box 100040 Anchorage AK 99510-0040

CHANDOR, STEBBINS BRYANT, pathologist; b. Boston, Dec. 18, 1933; s. Kendall Stebbins Bryant and Dorothy (Burrage) C.; m. Mary Carolyn White, May 30, 1959; children: Stebbins Bryant Jr., Charlotte White. B.A., Princeton U., 1955; M.D., Cornell U., 1960. Diplomate Am. Bd. Pathology. Intern Bellevue Hosp., N.Y.C., 1960-61, resident, 1965-66; resident Stanford U. Med. Ctr., Palo Alto, Calif., 1962-65; instr. Cornell U., Ithaca, N.Y., 1966; asst. prof. U. So. Calif. Med. Ctr., Los Angeles, 1969-73, assoc. prof., 1974-76; assoc. prof. SUNY, Stony Brook, 1976-80; prof., chmn. dept. pathology Marshall U. Sch. Medicine, Huntington, W.Va., 1981-91; assoc. dean for clin. affairs Marshall U. Sch. Medicine, 1990-91; prof., vice chmn. Sch. Medicine U. So. Calif., L.A., 1991—; pathologist Tripler Army Med Ctr, Honolulu, 1966-69; dir. immunopathology U. So. Calif., Los Angeles County Med. Ctr., 1969-76; dir. clin. lab. Univ. Hosp., Stony Brook, N.Y., 1978-80; dir. JMMS Labs., Huntington, W.Va., 1981-91; dir.labs. U. So. Calif. U. Hosp., L.A., 1991—. Contbr. articles to profl. jours. Pres. San Marino Tennis Found., 1975. Served to maj. USAR, 1966-69. Decorated Army Commendation medal; recipient Physicians Recognition award AMA, 1983, 86, 89. Fellow Am. Soc. Clin. Pathologists (project dir. commr. continuing edn., bd. dirs. 1990—), Coll. Am. Pathologists (state commr. I&A program 1987-91, dist. commr. 1991—); mem. Calif. Soc. Pathologists (sec.-treas. 1974-75, pres. elect. 1975-76), Assn. Am. Pathologists, W.Va. Assn. Pathologists (pres. 1985-86), Assoc. Pathol. Chmn. Acad. Clin. Lab. Physical Sci. (rep. CAS 1991—), Princeton Club, Valley Club (v.p. 1975), City Club (v.p. 1988-89, pres. 1989-90), San Gabriel Country Club. Republican. Episcopalian. Home: 855 S Oak Knoll Ave Pasadena CA 91106-4419 Office: U So Calif Sch Medicine 2011 Zonal Ave Los Angeles CA 90033-1054

CHANDRA, ABHIJIT, engineering educator; b. Calcutta, India, Jan. 4, 1957; came to U.S., 1980; s. Ramesh Kumar and Sandhya (Dey) C.; m. Dolly Day, June 4, 1984; children: Koushik, Shoma. B of Tech. with honors, Indian Inst. Tech., Kharagpur, India, 1978; MS, U. N.B., Fredericton, Can., 1980; PhD, Cornell U., 1983. Sr. rsch. engr. GM Rsch. Labs., Warren, Mich., 1983-85; asst. prof. U. Ariz., Tucson, 1985-89, assoc. prof. engring., 1989—; cons. Goodyear Tire and Rubber Co., Akron, Ohio, 1988-89, Advanced Ceramic Rsch., Tucson, 1990—, ALCOA, Pitts., 1990—. Editor: Developments in Boundary Element Method, 1991; contbr. articles to tech. publs. Alexander von Humboldt fellow, 1991; recipient Presdl. Young Investigator award NSF, 1987, Arc Welding Achievement award J. F. Lincoln Arc Welding Found., 1989. Mem. ASME (sec. So. Ariz. sect. 1988-89), Sigma Xi. Office: U Ariz Aerospace and Mech Engring Bldg 16 Tucson AZ 85721

CHANDRAMOULI, RAMAMURTI, electrical engineer; b. Sholinghur, Madras, India, Oct. 2, 1947; s. Ramamurti and Rajalakshmi (Ramamurti) Krishnamurti; m. Ranjani, Dec. 4, 1980; children: Suhasini, Akila. BSc, Mysore U., 1965, BE, 1970, MEE, Pratt Inst., 1972; PhD, Oreg. State U., 1978. Instr., Oreg. State U., Corvallis, 1978; sr. engr. R & D group, mem. tech. staff spacecraft datasystems sect. Jet Propulsion Lab., Pasadena, Calif., 1978-81; staff engr., design automation group Am. Microsystems Inc., Santa Clara, Calif., 1982-83; staff software engr. corp. computer-aided design Intel, Santa Clara, 1983-86; project leader computer-aided design Sun Microsystems, Mountain View, Calif., 1986-93; tech. mktg. engr. Mentor Graphics, San Jose, Calif., 1993—; adj. lectr. Calif. State U.-Fullerton, 1987—. Sec., South India Cultural Assn., L.A., 1980-81; bd. dirs. Am. Assn. East Indians. Mem. IEEE, IEEE Computer Soc., Sigma Xi, Eta Kappa Nu. Home: 678 Tiffany Ct Sunnyvale CA 94087-2439 Office: Mentor Graphics 1001 Ridder Park Dr San Jose CA 95131-2314

CHANG, ANTHONY KAI UNG, state legislator; b. Sept. 5, 1944. Mem. exec. com. Nat. Conf. State Legislatures, 1988-91. Mem. Hawaii Senate from 13th Dist. Democrat. Office: State Senate 217 Propsect St # B11 Honolulu HI 96813

CHANG, CHIH-WEI DAVID, computer company executive; b. Chang-Hwa, Taiwan, Republic of China, Sept. 28, 1955; came to U.S., 1982; s. Chun-Wen and Kuichen (Wu) C.; m. Heng-Chun Shen, Sept. 12, 1981; 1 child, Louisa Yun-Ru. BSEE, Chung-Yuan U., Chung-Li, Taiwan, 1977; MSEE, Tatung Inst. of Tech., Taipei, 1979; MS in Computer Engring., U. So. Calif., 1984, PhDEE, 1988. Project mgr. Sinotek Co., Taipei, Taiwan, 1981-82; project engr. Quotron Systems, L.A., 1985-88; sr. staff engr. Pyramid Tech., Mt. View, Calif., 1988-91; project leader Hal Computer Systems, Campbell, Calif., 1991—; adj. prof. San Jose (Calif.) State U., 1989-91. Contbr. articles to profl. jours. With Republic of China Navy, 1979-81. Mem. IEEE, Assn. of Computing Machinery. Home: 6062 Allante Dr San Jose CA 95129 Office: HAL Computer 1315 Dell Ave Campbell CA 95008

CHANG, DEBORAH, lawyer, educator; b. Man, W.Va., Feb. 15, 1960; d. C.H. Joseph and Chung Sook (Chun) C. BA, Kans. U., 1983; JD with honors, Drake U., 1986. Bar: Conn. 1986, Ariz. 1991, U.S. Dist. Ct. Conn., 1987, U.S. Dist. Ct. Ariz. 1991, U.S. Dist. Tex. 1992. Law clk. to judge Conn. Appellate Ct., Hartford, 1986-87; assoc. Day, Berry & Howard, Hartford, 1987-91, Snell & Wilmer, Phoenix, 1991—, 1991—; instr. Law Sch. U. Conn., Hartford, 1988-91. Contbr. articles to profl. jours. Counsel Ariz. Kids Project, McKinney Scholarship Fund, Fairfield, 1989-91; speaker, adv. AIDS Project Hartford & Discrimination Forums, 1988—, vol., 1989. Named one of 20 Young Lawyers Whose Work Makes a Difference ABA Young Lawyers' div., 1990; recipient Women of Distinction award Soroptimist Internat. of the Ams., 1990. Mem. ABA (young lawyer's divsn. award 1990), State Bar of Ariz., Conn. Bar Assn. (young lawyers sect., mem. legal aid com., mem. human rights com.), Maricopa County Bar Assn. (AIDS assistance com. young lawyers divsn.). Office: Snell & Wilmer One Arizona Ctr Phoenix AZ 85004-0001

CHANG, DONALD S. M., fire dept. chief; b. Honolulu, Mar. 16, 1934; s. Thomas and Rose (Lee) C.; m. Frances M. Spencer, Dec. 28, 1957; children: Kathy, Kimberley, Randall. Diploma fire adminstrn., U. Hawaii, 1952-54, 57-58. Fire fighter Honolulu Fire Dept., 1957-62, fire equipment operator I, 1963, fire equipment operator II, 1963-69, fire lieutenant, 1969-71, fire capt., 1971-76, fire battalion chief, 1976-88, fire asst. chief, 1988-90, fire dep. chief, 1990-92, fire chief, 1993—; field rep. Hawaii Fire Fighters Assn.; mem bd. dirs. Hon. Fire Dept. Fed. Credit Union, 1968-79; pres. Hon. Fire Dept. Fireman's Fund, 1966-76. Mem. Western Fire Chief's Assn., Hawaii Fire Chiefs Assn., Hawaii State Fire Coun. (pres.), Internat. Assn. Fire Chiefs. Home: 98-324 Ponohale St Aiea HI 96701 Office: Honolulu Fire Dept 3375 Koapaka St Ste H425 Honolulu HI 96819*

CHANG, FRANKLIN, entomologist, educator; b. Princeton, N.J., Feb. 12, 1942; s. Jonathan H. and Anita C.; m. Cheryl S. Creech, June 24, 1967 (div. June 1983); children: Michael Jonathan, Dustin Steven; m. Chiou-Ling Hsu, May 22, 1985; 1 child, Anthony Brian. BS with honors, U. Md., 1963; postgrad., Purdue U., 1963-64; PhD, U. Ill., 1969. Registered profl. entomologist. Biol. technician USDA-ARS, Beltsville, Md., 1960-63, biol. aide insect physiology pioneering lab., 1963-64; rsch. asst. dept. entomology Purdue U., West Lafayette, Ind., 1964-65; asst. prof., biologist Alma (Mich.) Coll., 1969-70; prof., entomologist U. Hawaii at Manoa, Honolulu, 1970—, chair dept. entomology, 1991—. Contbr. articles to profl. jours. Dir. Hawaiian Sci. and Engring. Fair, Honolulu, 1975. USDA rsch. grantee, 1986-88, 88-90, CDFA, 1991-93. Mem. AAAS, NEA, Entomol. Soc. Am. (editorial bd. 1988—, chair editorial bd. 1992, chair arrangements com. Pacific br. 1985), Hawaiian Entomol. Soc. (pres. 1979), Am. Registry Profl. Entomologists (cert. bd. 1991), Sigma Xi, Beta Beta Beta, Gamma Sigma Delta, Alpha Zeta. Home: 5090 Likini St PH 103 Honolulu HI 96818 Office: U Hawaii at Manoa Dept Entomology 3050 Maile Way Honolulu HI 96822-2271

CHANG, KANG-TSUNG, geography educator; b. Taitung, Taiwan, Republic of China, Jan. 30, 1943; came to U.S., 1966; s. Ching-Tu and Yeh (Yang) C.; m. Lillian R. Hsu, Aug. 30, 1971; children: Gary, Mark. BS, Nat. Taiwan U., 1965; MA, Clark U., 1969, PhD, 1971. Asst. prof. Calif. State U., Northridge, 1971-74, Clark U., Worcester, Mass., 1974-76; assoc. prof. U. N.D., Grand Forks, 1976-82, prof.f geography, 1982-86; prof.f geography U. Idaho, Moscow, 1986—; vis. assoc. prof. U. Minn., Mpls., 1980; vis. rsch. prof. Nat. Taiwan U., Taipei, 1985. Contbr. articles to profl. publs. Mem. Assn. Am. Geographers, Am. Congress Surveying and Mapping, Sigma Xi. Home: 1016 Virginia Ave Moscow ID 83843-9442 Office: U Idaho Dept Geography Moscow ID 83843

CHANG, KUO-TSUN, aerospace scientist, mathematician; b. Hanchow, China, Jan. 26, 1922; came to U.S., 1947; s. Tien-Tsu and Yueh-Hsiang (Lou) C.; m. Rose M.Y. Fei; children: Timothy T., Juliann L., Gray T. BSCE, St. Johns U., Shanghai, 1943; MCVE, Rensselaer Poly. Inst., 1948; M Aero. Engring., U. Wash., 1950; PhD in Engring. Mechanics, Stanford U., 1952. Mem. staff China Nat. Aviation Corp., Dinjan, India, 1943-45, Shanghai, 1945-47; project engr., scientist Airesearch Mfg. Co., L.A., 1952-72; internat. sales rep. Garrett Corp., Kyoto, Japan, 1972-80, UOP (Chgo.), Beijing, 1980-84; ind. computer cons. Saratoga, Calif., 1984—. Patentee spacecraft control moment gyro; contbr. to profl. publs. Republican. Presbyterian.

CHANG, LEE-HONG, chemistry educator; b. Taipei, Taiwan, Aug. 25, 1954; s. Ru-Chuan and Tswei-Chin (Lin) C. BS, Fu-Jen Cath. U., Taipei, 1976; MS, Nat. Taiwan U., Taipei, 1978; PhD, Ohio State U., 1985. Postdoctoral fellow U. Calif., San Francisco, 1985-86, asst. rschr., 1986-89; mgr. Biomed. Magnetic Resonance Lab., U. Calif., San Francisco, 1987—; asst. adj. prof. U. Calif., San Francisco, 1989—. Scholar Dr. Huang's Meml. Found., 1977, 78; recipient Rsch. award The Whitaker Found., 1992—. Mem. AAAS, Soc. Magnetic Resonance in Medicine, N.Y. Acad. Scis., Phi Tau Phi. Office: U Calif Rm S-926 Box 0446 San Francisco CA 94143-0446

CHANG, LEH, research and medical technologist; b. Taipei, Taiwan, Aug. 21, 1960; came to U.S., 1984; d. Song-Nein and Hwei-Jao (Sun) C. AA, Taiwan Adventist Coll., Taipei, 1983; BS, Loma Linda U., 1988, MS, 1990. Lab. technician Taiwan Adventist Hosp., Taipei, 1982-84; venipuncturist Loma Linda (Calif.) U. Med. Ctr., 1986-88, med. technologist, 1988—, rsch. technologist, 1990—. Co-contbr. chpt. to booKK. Recipient Young Investigator's award 6th Ann. Meeting Clin. Applications Cytometry, 1991; pediatric rsch. grantee Loma Linda U., 1992. Mem. AAAS, Am. Soc. for Med. Tech., Calif. Soc. for Med. Tech., N.Y. Acad. Scis. Adventist. Office: Loma Linda U Med Ctr 11234 Anderson St Rm 2563 Loma Linda CA 92354

CHANG, MICHAEL MOONKI, psychiatrist, educator; b. Seoul, Feb. 17, 1944; came to U.S., 1957; s. Chi Whan and Pung Yoon (Min) C.; m. Yun Suk Lee, May 30, 1974; children: Kenneth K., Samantha S. Student, Internat. Christian U., Mitaka, Japan, 1965; AB, U. Calif., Berkeley, 1966; PhD in Biochemistry, Brandeis U., 1970; MD, Yale U., 1979. Diplomate Am. Bd. Psychiatry and Neurology. Postdoctoral fellow Roche Inst. Molecular Biology, Nutley, N.J., 1970-72; chief biochemistry Korean Inst. Sci. and Tech., Seoul, 1972-76; resident in psychiatry UCLA Med. Sch., 1979-82, ass.t prof., 1983-84; chief resident Sepulveda (Calif.) VA Hosp., 1982-83; ward chief Brentwood (Calif.) VA Hosp., 1983-84; asst. prof. Loma Linda (Calif.) U. Med. Sch., 1984-88; chief alcohol and drug treatment Loma Linda VA Hosp., 1984-88; dir. substance abuse treatment program Honolulu VA Med. Ctr., 1988—; assoc. prof. U. Hawaii Med. Sch., Honolulu, 1988—; mem. Mental Health Spl. Users Group, Loma Linda, 1982-87; dir. Substance Abuse Program, Honolulu, 1988—. Contbr. articles to profl. jours.; inventor synthesis of substance P, enzymatic determination of blood urea nitrogen. Fellow Calif. Heart Assn., 1961, Rosenthiel fellow Brandeis U., 1966-70; rsch. grantee Loma Linda U., Computerized Med. Records for Substance Abuse Programs, VA., 1985-88. Buddhist. Office: Honolulu VA Med Ctr PO Box 50188 Honolulu HI 96850

CHANG, PING-TUNG, mathematics educator; b. Nan-King, China, Oct. 16, 1935; came to U.S., 1963; s. Sun and Y. K. (Wang) C.; 1 child, Susanna San-San. BE, Nat. Taiwan Normal U., Taipei, 1960; MS in Math., Ind. State U., 1966; PhD, Ga. State U., 1977. Asst. prof., chair div. natural sci. Mt. St. Paul Coll., Waukesha, Wis., 1966-68; tchr. math. Brooker T. Washington High Sch., Atlanta, 1970-73; asst. prof. math. Gordon Jr. Coll., Barnesville, Ga., 1973-78; assoc. prof. math. Augusta (Ga.) Coll., 1978-83; assoc. prof. Laredo (Tex.) State U., 1983-88; coord. math., prof. math. U. Alaska, Anchorage, 1988—; vis. prof. math. Taiwan Normal U. Grad Sch. Math., Taipei, summer 1979. Author: A Comparative Study of Math Education Between ROC & USA, 1985, Teach Mathematics in Junior High School, 1985, Remedial Math Education for Disadvantaged, 1985; (coll. textbook) Teaching Mathematics in the Elementary School, 1989; contbr. several articles to profl. jours. Grantee Pacific Cultural Found., 1982-83, Laredo State U., 1984, U. Alaska Dept. Edn., 1990—, Dwight D. Eisenhower Math and Sci. grant Mat-Su Math Coop. Project, 1990—. Mem. Am. Math. Soc., Math. Assn. Am., Nat. Coun. Tchrs. Math., N.Y. Acad. Scis., Math. Assn. Two-Yr. Colls. (nat. devel. program in math. com. 1974-80), Assn. for Supervision and Curriculum Devel., Pi Mu Epsilon, Matanuska-Susitna Lion Club. Office: U Alaska Matanuska-Susitna Coll PO Box 2889 Palmer AK 99645

CHANG, POHUA PAUL, computer engineer; b. Taipei, Taiwan, Aug. 16, 1966; came to U.S., 1980; BS in Computer Sci., U. Calif., Berkeley, 1987; MS in Elec. and Computer Engring., U. Ill., 1989, PhD in Elec. and Computer Engring., 1991. Staff rsch. mem. Intel Corp., Santa Clara, Calif., 1991—; local arrangement chair Internat. Symposium Microarchitecture, Portland, Oreg., 1992, mem. program com., 1992; coord. Internat. Microarchitecture Conf. Contbr. articles to profl. jours. Mem. Intel. Polit. Rep., Washington, 1992. Mem. Assn. Computing Machinery, IEEE Computer Soc.

CHANG, ROBERT SHIHMAN, virology educator; b. Quangdong, China, July 26, 1922; came to U.S., 1947; m. Yinette Yangsen Yu, June 12, 1951; children: Jeffrey, Holly, Charlene, Garrick. BS, St. John's U., Shanghai, China, 1943, MD, 1946; DSc, Harvard U., 1952. Rsch. assoc. Harvard U. Sch. of Pub. Health, Boston, 1952-54, asst. prof., 1954-60, assoc. prof., 1960-68; prof. U. Calif., Davis, 1968—. Recipient Presdl. award 4th Internat. Polio Congress, 1957, Excellence in Teaching award Kaiser Found. Hosps., 1975, 93. Fellow Am. Acad. Microbiology, Am. Coll. Preventive Medicine. Home: 1620 Holly Ln Davis CA 95616-1010 Office: U Calif Med Microbiology Dept Davis CA 95616

CHANG, RODNEY EIU JOON, artist, dentist; b. Honolulu, Nov. 26, 1945; s. Alfred Koon Bo and Mary Yet Moi (Char) C.; m. Erlinda C. Feliciano, Dec. 4, 1987; children: Bronson York, Houston Travis, Rochelle Jessica. BA in Zoology, U. Hawaii, 1968; AA in Art, Triton Coll., 1972; DDS, Loyola U., 1972; MS in Edn., U. So. Calif., 1974; MA in Painting and Drawing, U. No. Ill., 1975; MA in Community Leadership, Cen. Mich. U., 1976; BA in Psychology, Hawaii Pacific U., 1977; MA in Psychology of Counseling, U. No. Colo., 1980; PhD in Art Psychology, The Union Inst., 1980; MA in Computer Art, Columbia Pacific U., 1989. Pvt. practice dentist Honolulu, 1975—; dir. SOHO too Gallery and Loft, Honolulu, 1985-89; freelance artist Honolulu, 1982—; founder Pygoya Internat. Art Group, 1990—; founder Art Cap Group, Slap Caps Co., Honolulu, 1993; columnist Milk Cap News; dir. ann. Honolulu City Hall Hawaiian Computer Art Exhbn., 1990-92; speaker on art psychology and computer art, also numerous TV and radio interviews. Author: Mental Evolution and Art, 1980, Rodney Chang: Computer Artist, 1988, Commentaries on the Psychology of Art, 1980; host (radio show) Disco Doc Hour, Sta. KISA; one-man shows include Honolulu Acad. Arts, 1986, Shanghai State Art Mus., People's Republic of China, 1988, Retrospective Exhbn. 1967-87, Ramsay Gallery, Honolulu, 1987, Visual Encounters Gallery, Denver, 1987, The Bronx Mus. of the Arts, N.Y.C., 1987, Nishi Noho Gallery, N.Y.C., 1987, Eastern Wash. U. Gallery of Art, 1988, Salon de la Jeune Peinture, Paris, 1989, Holter Art Mus., Mont., 1989, Las Vegas Art Mus., 1990, Forum Art Sch. Gütershoh, Fed. Republic of Germany, 1990, Siggraph-Dallas, 1990, Tartu State Art Mus., Estonia/USSR, 1990, U. Oregon Continuation Ctr., Portland, 1991—, Kauai Art Mus., Hawaii, 1993; conceived, produced 1st milk cap art exhbn., Arts of Paradise Gallery, Waikiki Beach, 1993. Judge Jr. Miss Contest, Honolulu, 1981. Served to capt., U.S. Army, 1973-74. Mem. ADA, Hawaii Dental Assn., Assn. of Honolulu Artists (pres. 1989), Nat. Computer Graphics, Acad. Gen. Dentistry, Hawaii Space Soc., Bernice Bishop Mus. Honolulu. Roman Catholic. Office: 2119 N King St Ste 206 Honolulu HI 96819-4550

CHANG, STEVEN DANIEL, investment company executive; b. Honolulu, June 25, 1968; s. Hing Dat Sum and Lorene Mary (Anastasi) C. BS in Biology, BA in Econs., Stanford U., 1989, MD, 1993. Pres. BMI, Inc., Honolulu, 1986—, Steven D. Chang Group, Inc., Honolulu, 1991—. Mem. AMA, Nat. Assn. Security Dealers, Honolulu Bd. Realtors. Republican. Roman Catholic. Home: 2305 Round Top Dr Honolulu HI 96822

CHANG, TAIPING, marketing executive, magazine publisher; b. Tainan, Taiwan, Republic of China, Apr. 20, 1949; came to U.S., 1975; d. Lanfeng Chang and Shuchun Liu; m. David R. Knechtges, June 7, 1976; 1 child, Jeanne Y. BA, Tunghai U., 1971, MA, 1974; PhD, U. Wash., 1981. Lectr. Tunghai U., Taichung, Taiwan, 1974-75; asst. prof. Pacific Luth. U., Tacoma, 1986-88; publisher Asia Pacific Bus. Jour., Seattle, 1988—; pres. Asia Media Group, Inc., Seattle, 1989—; bd. dirs. Chong-Wa Benevolent Assn., Seattle, No. Seattle (Wash.) C.C.; chmn. World Trade Club-Taiwan Forum, Seattle, 1991—. Editor: Editor-in-Chief, 1988. Named Woman of Yr., Asia Am. Soc., Seattle, 1990. Mem. Rotary Club. Office: Ste 2328 2001 6th Ave Seattle WA 98121

CHANICK, RICHARD ALAN, executive, president; b. Pueblo, Colo., May 18, 1953; s. Richard and Marion Arlene (Bodycomb) C.; m. Mary Margaret Bareis, June 7, 1975. BS, USAF Acad., 1975. Cert. personnel cons. Pilot tng., capt. USAF, Phoenix, 1975-76; instr. pilot tng. USAF, San Antonio, 1976; instr. pilot USAF, Phoenix, 1977-82; pres. VSP Search, Phoenix, 1982—, 1990—; dir. The Bus. Jour., Phoenix, 1989-91; employment cons., CBS News. Author weekly column on pers. issues The Bus. Jour. Project dir. Boys & Girls Club of Phoenix, 1983, exec. coun. mem., 1987-90. Named Inc. 500 Pres., 1987. Office: VSP Search/VSP Internat 1430 E Missouri Ave Ste 275 Phoenix AZ 85014-2454

CHAO, CHIH HSU, research mechanical engineer; b. Shantung, China, Aug. 2, 1939; s. Ching Fung and Ching Chih (Lin) C.; BS, Nat. Taiwan U., 1962; MS, U. Calif.-Berkeley, 1965, PhD, 1972; m. Grace Yng Chu, Apr. 15, 1967; children: Henry Shaw, Lily Yuin. Rsch. asst., applied mechanics U. Calif.-Berkeley, 1965-72; rsch. engr. Boeing Co., Seattle, 1966-67; rsch. scientist, mgr. engring. analysis, chief engr. dir. Physics Internat. Co., San Leandro, Calif., 1969—; cons. engr. Registered profl. engr., Calif. Bd. dirs. Chinese Am. Polit. Assn., San Francisco Bay Area Sci. Fair. Mem. ASME (sect. chmn.), Nat. Soc. Profl. Engrs., Calif. Soc. Profl. Engrs. (chpt. v.p.), Nat. Apt. and Property Owners Assn. Democrat. Roman Catholic. Contbr. research papers in field to profl. jours. Home: 1018 Contra Costa Dr El Cerrito CA 94530-2710

CHAO, DANIEL KUNG-HUA, financial executive; b. Alexandria, Va., Mar. 26, 1951; s. Edward Ching-te and Vera (Lin) C.; m. Lily Wai-fong Wong, Nov. 4, 1989; children: Tamara, Jonathan. BA, Stanford U., 1973; MA, Fletcher Sch. Law & Diplomacy, 1976, PhD, 1978; advanced profl. cert., NYU, 1981. V.p. Chem. Bank, N.Y.C., 1978-85, Citicorp Investment Bank, San Francisco, 1985-86; v.p. and mgr. Bechtel Fin. Svcs., Inc., San Francisco, 1986—; mem. exporters coun. Pvt. Export Funding Corp.; bd. dirs. S.E. Asia Bus. Coun. Contbr. chpt. to book and articles to profl. jours. Mem. Fgn. Affairs Counsel. Office: Bechtel Fin Svcs Inc 50 Beale St San Francisco CA 94119-3965

CHAO, JAMES MIN-TZU, architect; b. Dairen, China, Feb. 27, 1940; s. T. C. and Lin Fan (Wong) C.; came to U.S., 1949, naturalized, 1962; m. Kirsti Helena Lehtonen, May 15, 1968. BArch, U. Calif., Berkeley, 1965. Registered architect, Calif.; cert. instr. real estate, Calif. Intermediate draftsman Spencer, Lee & Busse, Architects, San Francisco, 1966-67; asst. to pres. Import Plus Inc., Santa Clara, Calif., 1967-69; job capt. Hammaberg and Herman, Architects, Oakland, Calif., 1969-71; project mgr. B A Premises Corp., San Francisco, 1971-79; constrn. mgr. The Straw Hat Restaurant Corp., 1979-81, mem. sr. mgmt., dir. real estate and constrn., 1981-87; mem. mktg. com. Straw Hat Coop. Corp., 1988-91; pvt. practice architect, Berkeley, Calif., 1987—; pres. Food Svc. Cons. Inc., 1987-89; pres., chief exec. officer Stratsac, Inc., 1987-92; prin. architect Alpha Cons. Group Inc., 1991—; v.p. Intersyn Industries Calif., 1993—; lectr. comml. real estate site analysis and selection for profl. real estate seminars; coord. minority vending program, solar application program Bank of Am.; guest faculty mem. N.W. Ctr. for Profl. Edn.; bd. dirs Ambrosia Best Corp., 1992—. Patentee tidal electric generating system; author first comprehensive consumer orientated performance specification for remote banking transaction. Recipient honorable mention Future Scientists Am., 1955. Mem. AIA, Encinal Yacht Club (bd. dir. 1977-78). Republican.

CHAPGIER, PIERRE ANDRE, financing company executive; b. Perigueux, Dordogne, France, Jan. 18, 1941; came to U.S., 1979; s. Andre and Jeanne (Duclos) C.; m. Florence Baumgartner, Apr. 18, 1980; children: Julie, Kevin, Dylan. Degree engring., French Naval Acad., 1960-62, Ecole Centrale Paris, 1962-65; MBA, Institut Europeen D'Administration Des Enterprises, Fontainebleau, France, 1969. Dept. head Societe Centrale Pour L'Equipement Du Territoire, Paris, 1965-68; assoc. McKinsey and Co., Paris, 1969-72; ptnr. Interfinexa, Paris, 1972-74; exec. v.p. Meridien Hotels, Paris, 1974-79; pres. Meridien Hotels Investment Group, Inc., N.Y.C., 1980-85; founder, pres. Jukedy, Inc., L.A., 1986—. Translator: Managing By Results, 1969. Roman Catholic. Home: 1891 Kimberly Ln Los Angeles CA 90049 Office: Jukedy Inc 2001 S Barrington # 102 Los Angeles CA 90025

CHAPIAN, GRIEG HOVSEP, artist; b. Varna, Bulgaria, May 27, 1913; s. Joseph and Perouzé (Cholakian) C.; m. Constance Nunes, Sept. 25, 1938; children: Grieg Andrew, Peter John; m. Martha Jane Coleman, July 6, 1963. Student, Cooper Union, N.Y.C., 1930-31, Beaux Arts Inst. Design, N.Y.C., 1931-36, Nat. Acad. of Design, N.Y.C., 1931-36. Dir. Murray Art Schs., Wilkes-Barre and Scranton, Pa., 1948-50, Cooper Sch. Art, Cleve., 1950-55; dean Pan Am. Art Sch., N.Y.C., 1960-66; instr. Am. Art Sch., N.Y.C., 1963-66, Fine Arts Gallery, Albuquerque, 1969-75; founder, dir. Albuquerque Inst. Art, 1974—; exhbns. chmn. Albuquerque Festival, 1970-73; lectr., conservator, demonstrator, judge, juror in numerous shows in U.S.; judge Nat. Art Show. First wartime exhibit sponsored by Internat.

Union Marine and Shipbldg. Workers Am., Camden, N.J., 1944 (Grand prize, 1st prize); one-man shows Ada Artizt Gallery, N.Y.C., 1960; State Fair Fine Arts Gallery, Albuquerque, 1969, Coronado Town Hall, Albuquerque, 1970, Mesilla Gallery, Las Cruces, N.Mex., 1972, Geronimo Springs Mus., Truth of Consequences, N.Mex., 1972, N.Mex. Art League, Albuquerque, 1972, U. Eastern N.Mex., Portales, 1973, The Gallery, Conroe, Tex., 1975; exhibited in group shows including Allied Artists Am., N.Y.C., Pa. Acad. Fine Arts, Phila., Soc. Ind. Artists, N.Y.C., Mus. City of N.Y., Vandome Galleries, N.Y.C., Nassau County Art League, Long Beach (N.Y.) Art Assn., Art League L.I., Douglastown, N.Y., Santa Fe Art Guild, N.Mex. Art League, 1959—, N.Mex. State Fair, 1969—, Artists Equity, Albuquerque, 1969—, Southwestern Watercolor Soc., Albuquerque, Am. Artists Profl. League, N.Y.C., 1971-72, Western Watercolor Assn., Lubbock, Tex., 1972, Albuquerque Inst. Art, 1975; murals executed Auto Racing Syndicate South Africa, Johannesburg, 1939; represented in permanent collections U. Eastern N.Mex., N.Mex. State FAir, also numerous pvt. Collections. Pres. N.Mex. Art League, 1991. Recipient numerous prizes and awards for figure, landscape, still life, genre paintings and mural designs including 1st prize for oils N.Mex. State Fair, 1973; purchase prize, 1974; 2d ann. purchase prize Grant County Art Guild, 1987, Silver City, N.Mex., 1990; Nat. Acad. Design scholar, 1931-36. Mem. N.Mex. Art League (1st prize for oils and best of show in graphics 1969, 70, 71, Best of Show award 1990), Artists Equity Assn. (pres. Albuquerque chpt. 1973-74), Am. Artists Profl. League, Long Beach Art Assn., Nassau County Art Leagues, Rotary Club (Amarillo chpt.). Address: 1850 Gretta St NE Albuquerque NM 87112 also: care Galeria on the Pla PO Box 1017 Mesilla NM 88046

CHAPLIN, GEORGE, newspaper editor; b. Columbia, S.C., Apr. 28, 1914; s. Morris and Netty (Brown) C.; m. Esta Lillian Solomon, Jan. 26, 1937; children: Stephen Michael, Jerry Gay. BS, Clemson Coll., 1935; Nieman fellow, Harvard U., 1940-41; HHD (hon.), Clemson U., 1989; LHD (hon.), Hawaii Loa Coll., 1990. Reporter, later city editor Greenville (S.C.) Piedmont, 1935-42; mng. editor Camden (N.J.) Courier-Post, 1946-47, San Diego Jour., 1948-49; mng. editor, then editor New Orleans Item, 1949-58; asso. editor Honolulu Advertiser, 1958-59, editor in chief, 1959-86, editor at large, 1986—; Pulitzer prize juror, 1969, 83; mem. selection com. Jefferson fellowships East-West Ctr.; chmn. Gov.'s Conf. on Year 2000, 1970; chmn. Hawaii Commn. on Year 2000, 1971-74; co-chmn. Conf. on Alt. Econ. Futures for Hawaii, 1973-75; charter mem. Goals for Hawaii, 1979—; alt. U.S. rep. South Pacific Commn., 1978-81; chmn. search com. for pres. U. Hawaii, 1983; chmn. Hawaii Gov.'s Adv. Council on Fgn. Lang. and Internat. Studies, 1983—; rep. of World Press Freedom Com. on missions to Sri Lanka, Hong Kong, Singapore, 1987. Editor, officer-in-charge: Mid-Pacific edit. Stars and Stripes World War II; Editor: (with Glenn Paige) Hawaii 2000, 1973. Bd. dirs. U. Hawaii Rsch. Corp., 1970-72, Inst. for Religion and Social Change, Hawaii Jewish Welfare Fund; mem. bd. govs. East-West Ctr., Honolulu, 1980-89, chmn., 1983-89; mem. bd. govs. Pacific Health Rsch. Inst., 1984-90, 93—, Straub Pacific Med. Found., 1989—, Hawaii Pub. Schs. Found., 1986-87; trustee Clarence T.C. Ching Found., 1986—; Am. media chmn. U.S.-Japan Conf. on Cultural and Ednl. Interchange, 1978-86; co-founder, v.p. Coalition for Drug-Free Hawaii, 1987-90; panelist ABA Conv., 1989; mem. Civilian Adv. Group, U.S. Army, Hawaii, 1985—. Capt. AUS, 1942-46. Decorated Star Solidarity (Italy), Order Rising Sun (Japan), Prime Minister's medal (Israel). Recipient citations Overseas Press Club, 1961, 72, Headliners award, 1962, John Hancock award, 1972, 74, Distinguished Alumni award Clemson U., 1974, E.W. Scripps award Scripps-Howard Found., 1976, Champion Media award for Econ. Understanding, 1981, Judah Magnes Gold medal Hebrew U. Jerusalem, 1987, Herbert Harley award Am. Judicature Soc., 1991; inductee Honolulu Press Club Hall of Fame, 1987. Mem. Soc. Nieman Fellows, Honolulu Symphony Soc., Pacific and Asian Affairs Council (dir.), Internat. Press Inst., World Future Soc., Japan-Am. Soc. Honolulu, Am. Soc. Newspaper Editors (dir., treas. 1973, sec. 1974, v.p. 1975, pres. 1976), Friends of East-West Ctr. Clubs: Pacific, Waialae Country. Home: 4437 Kolohala St Honolulu HI 96816-4938 Office: care Honolulu Advertiser PO Box 3110 Honolulu HI 96802-3110

CHAPMAN, BRUCE KERRY, institute executive; b. Evanston, Dec. 1, 1940; s. Landon Lincoln Chapman and Darroll Jesamine (Carlson Swanson) Shinn; m. Sarah Gilmore Williams, Aug. 22, 1976; children: Adam Winthrop, Andrew Howard. BA cum laude, Harvard U., 1962; Doctorate (hon.), Monmouth (Ill.) Coll., 1983. Pub. Advance Mag., Washington, Cambridge, Mass., 1960-64; editorial writer N.Y. Herald Tribune, N.Y.C., 1965-66; cons., speech writer Wash. State Commn. on Civil Disorders, Seattle, 1966-71; mem. city coun. City of Seattle, 1971-75; sec. of state State of Wash., Olympia, 1975-81; dir. U.S. Census Bur., Washington, 1981-83; dep. asst. to Pres. The White House, Washington, 1983-85; U.S. amb. State Dept. (UN Offices), Vienna, 1985-88; sr. fellow Hudson Inst., Indpls., 1988-91; pres. Discovery Inst., Seattle, 1991—. Author: The Wrong Man in Uniform, 1967, (with G. Gilder) The Party that Lost Its Head, 1966; author (documentary film) A Memory for the Future, 1975-76; author, dir. (documentary film) The Market, 1976. V.p. Harvard Young Reps., Cambridge, 1962; candidate for gov. State of Wash., 1980. Episcopalian. Office: Discovery Inst 1201 3d AVe 40th Fl Seattle WA 98101-3099

CHAPMAN, CHRISTOPHER ERIC, computer engineering technologist, researcher; b. Des Moines, Oct. 24, 1970; s. Roger Ross and Joan Marie (Curtis) C. Student, Santa Clara U., 1990—. Intern 3 Com, Santa Clara, Calif., LSI Logic, Santa Clara; systems engr., computer asst. Hitachi MicroSystems, San Jose, Calif., 1991-92; rsch. asst. Rohm Systems/Siemens, Santa Clara, Calif., 1992; owner The Phoenix Advisers, Cupertino, Calif., 1992—; cons. The Phoenix Advisers, 1987-92; physics rsch. asst., Santa Clara, 1992—. Vol. Amnesty Internat., 1991-92, Keep Our Cities Clean, Cupertino, Calif., 1992. Santa Clara U. scholar, 1990-93. Home and Office: 10349 Leola Ct # 1 Cupertino CA 95014-3419

CHAPMAN, ELAINE GRACE, engineer; b. St. Johnsbury, Vt., Dec. 30, 1956; d. Frederick Elmer and Marie Louise (Warner) Chapman; m. Richard Dale Smith, Jan. 5, 1985; 1 child, Jeffrey. BS, Rensselaer Poly. Inst., Troy, N.Y., 1978; M.Eng., Rensselaer Poly. Inst., 1980. Student intern engr. Stauffer Chem. Co., Dobbs Ferry, N.Y., 1977; engr. Battelle Pacific N.W. Labs., Richland, Wash., 1980-81; rsch. engr. Battelle Pacific N.W. Labs., 1981-83, sr. rsch. engr., 1983—. Contbr. articles to profl. jours. Mem. Lower Columbia Basin Audubon Soc. (pres. 1981-82, 86-87). Office: Battelle Pacific NW Labs PO Box 999 Richland WA 99352-0999

CHAPMAN, JOHN SHERWOOD, lawyer; b. Twin Falls, Idaho, July 6, 1936; s. Marshall Byron and Dorothy (Parsons) C.; m. Judith June Day, May 28, 1966 (div. July 1982); children: Christina Jean, Heidi Suzanne, Elizabeth June. BA, U. Idaho, 1958; JD, Stanford U., 1961. Bar: Idaho 1962, U.S. Dist. Ct. Idaho 1962, U.S. Supreme Ct. 1975, U.S. Ct. Appeals (9th cir.) 1982. Assoc. Hawley, Troxell, Boise, Idaho, 1961-64; ptnr. Martin, Chapman, Schild & Lassaw, Boise, 1965—; Chmn. adv. coun. Martin Peace Inst., U. Idaho. Precinct committeeman Ada County Cen. Com.; mem. Idaho State Cen. Com., treas., 1974-75; former chmn. State Dem. Pledge Fund; mem. state exec. com. Idaho Dem. Party, 1974-84; treas. Gov. John V. Evans' re-election campaign; del. Nat. Dem. Conv., N.Y., 1976, 80; state fin. chmn. Carter/Mondale Campaign, 1980; active United Way of Ada County; bd. dirs., former state chmn. Idaho Ptnrs. of the Alliance; bd. dirs., mem. exec. com. Boise chpt. ARC, chmn., 1985-86; trustee Boise State U. Found.; former bd. dirs. Boise YMCA; chmn. Idaho Commn. on Arts, 1986; mem., past pres. Boise Estate Planning Council; state legal counsel Clinton/Gore Campaign, 1992; mem. U. Idaho Found., 1992—. Named Boise's Young Man of Yr., Boise Jaycees, 1965, One of Outstanding Young Men of Am., U.S. Jaycees, 1966, Disting. Citizen of Idaho, Idaho Statesman, 1976. Fellow Am. Coll. Trust and Probate Counsel; mem. Internat. Assn. Fin. Planners (pres. 1989-90), Boise Rotary Club. Democrat. Episcopalian. Home: PO Box 2898 Boise ID 83701 Office: Martin Chapman Schild & Lassaw PO Box 2898 Boise ID 83701-2898

CHAPMAN, JUDI, Indian tribes and organizations consultant, lobbyist; b. Pierre, S.D., July 23, 1941; d. Francis Andrew and Leona Phyllis (Cook) Larson. Student, St. Olaf Coll., 1963, U. Mont., 1975. Dir. Edn.-Social Svcs. Mt. Plains, Glasgow, Mont., 1970-72; legis. asst. Congressman Pat Williams, Washington, 1979-91; cons., 1991—; cons. Nat. Commn. on Librs., Info. Sci., Washington, 1991—; reviewer Head Start, Washington, 1992—; contract work with Blackfoot Tribe, Affiliated Tribes NW Indians, Solish-Koofenai Coll., Ft. Bellenap Coll., Dull Knife Coll., Nat. Comsn. Native Am., Alaska Natives, Native Hawaiian Housing, Kauffman & Assocs. Reader Adminstrn. for Native Ams., 1992—; state Dem. Committeewoman, Missoula County; coord. Discover the Indian Vote, 1992; county coord. Williams for Congress, Missoula, 1978; mem. Missoula Women for Peace, 1991—; mem. precinct com. Dem. Party, Missoula, 1991—, mem. issues com., 1991—, Clinton del. Dem. Nat. Conv., 1992; bd. dirs. City-County Health Bd., Missoula, 1992—, City-County Water Quality Dist., City-County Air Pollution Control Bd., Missoula Indian Alcohol and Drug Svcs., 1992—. Mem. Mont. Indian Edn. Assn., Nat. Congress-Am. Indians. Home and Office: 2300 Hilda Missoula MT 59801

CHAPMAN, LORING, psychologist, neuroscientist; b. L.A., Oct. 4, 1929; s. Lee E. and Elinore E. (Gundry) Scott; children: Robert, Antony, Pandora. B.S., U. Nev., 1950; Ph.D., U. Chgo., 1955. Lic. psychologist, Oreg., N.Y., Calif. Rsch. fellow U. Chgo., 1952-54; rsch. assoc., asst. prof. Cornell U. Med. Coll., N.Y.C., 1955-61; rsch. dir. Music Rsch. Found., N.Y.C., 1958-61; assoc. prof. in residence Neuropsychiat. Inst., UCLA, 1961-65; rsch. prof. U. Oreg., Portland, 1965; br. chief NIH, Bethesda, Md., 1966-67; prof., chmn. dept. behavioral biology Sch. Medicine U. Calif., Davis, 1967-81; prof. psychiatry Sch. Medicine U. Calif., 1977—, prof. neurology, 1977-81, prof. human physiology, 1977-81; vice chmn. div. of sci. basic to medicine, 1976-79; condr. research in field of behavioral and sensory physiology, brain function, neuropharmacology; vis. prof. U. Sao Paulo, Brazil, 1959, 77, Univ. Coll., London, 1969-70, U. Florence, Italy, 1979-80; clin. prof. Georgetown U., 1966-67; mem. Calif. Primate Research Center, 1967—; dir. research Fairview Hosp., 1965-66; cons. Nat. Inst. Neurol. Disease and Stroke, 1961—, Nat. Cancer Inst., 1977—, Nat. Inst. Child Health & Human Devel., 1967—, mem. research and tng. com., 1968-72. Author: Pain and Suffering, 3 vols, 1967, Head and Brain 3 vols, 1971, (with E.A. Dunlap) The Eye, 1981; assoc. editor courtroom medicine series updates, 1965—; contbr. sci. articles to publs. Recipient Thornton Wilson prize, 1958, Career award USPHS, 1964, Commonwealth Fund award, 1970; grantee NASA, 1969—; grantee NIH, 1956—; grantee Nat. Inst. Drug Abuse, 1971—; Fogarty Sr. Internat. fellow, 1980. Mem. Am. Acad. Neurology, Am. Physiol. Soc., Am. Psychol. Assn., Royal Soc. Medicine (London), Am. Neurol. Assn., Am. Assn. Mental Deficiency, Aerospace Med. Assn., Soc. for Neurosci. Home: 205 Country Pl Apt 188 Sacramento CA 95831-2076 Office: U Calif Med Ctr Dept Psychiatry 2315 Stockton Blvd Sacramento CA 95817-2201

CHAPMAN, ORVILLE LAMAR, chemist, educator; b. New London, Conn., June 26, 1932; s. Orville Carmen and Mabel Elnora (Tyree) C.; m. Faye Newton Morrow, Aug. 20, 1955 (div. 1980); children: Kenneth, Kevin; m. Susan Elizabeth Parker, June 15, 1981. B.S., Va. Poly. Inst., 1954; Ph.D., Cornell U., 1957. Prof. chemistry Iowa State U., 1957-74; prof. chemistry UCLA, 1974—; Cons. Mobil Chem. Co. Recipient John Wilkinson Teaching award Iowa State U., 1968, award Nat. Acad. Scis., 1974; Founders prize Tex. Instruments; George and Freda Halpern award in photochemistry N.Y. Acad. Scis., 1978. Mem. Am. Chem. Soc. (award in pure chemistry 1968, Arthur C. Cope award 1978, Midwest award 1978, Havinga medal 1982, McCoy award UCLA, 1985). Home: 1213 Roscomare Rd Los Angeles CA 90077-2202 Office: UCLA Dept Chemistry 405 Hilgard Ave Los Angeles CA 90024

CHAPMAN, PAUL JAMES, grocery retail chain controller; b. Seattle, Aug. 28, 1949; s. Jean Thomas and Margret L. (Buck) C.; m. Lynn Eileen Hreha, June 15, 1974; children: Lesha Victoria, Crisotpher Ryan, Matthew Paul. BA, U. Wash., 1975. Retail clk., 3d man in charge Tradewell Stores, Seattle, 1966-69, 72-77; contr. Cemco Howard S. Wright Constrn., Seattle, 1977-84; contr. Cemco Products Inc., Everett, Wash., 1984-86, Thrifty Foods of Burlington (Wash.), Inc., 1986—. Bd. dirs. Skagit Valley YMCA, Mt. Vernon, Wash., 1988—, treas., 1990, pres. bd., 1991-92. Sgt. U.S. Army, 1969-72, Vietnam. Decorated Bronze Star; named Vol. of Yr. Skagit Valley YMCA, 1991. Roman Catholic.

CHAPMAN, RICHARD LEROY, public policy researcher; b. Yankton, S.D., Feb. 4, 1932; s. Raymond Young and Vera Everette (Trimble) C.; m. Marilyn Jean Nicholson, Aug. 14, 1955; children: Catherine Ruth, Robert Matthew, Michael David, Stephen Raymond, Amy Jean. BS, S.D. State U., 1954; postgrad., Cambridge (Eng.) U., 1954-55; MPA, Syracuse U., 1958, PhD, 1967. With Office of Sec. of Def., 1958-59, 61-63; dep. dir. rsch. S.D. Legis. Rsch. Coun., 1959-60; mem. staff Bur. of the Budget, Exec. Office of Pres., Washington, 1960-61; profl. staff mem. com. govt. ops. U.S. Ho. of Reps., Washington, 1966; program dir. NIH, Bethesda, Md., 1967-68; sr. rsch. assoc. Nat. Acad. Pub. Adminstrn., Washington, 1968-72, dep. exec. dir., 1973-76, v.p., dir. rsch., 1976-82; sr. rsch. scientist Denver Rsch. Inst., 1982-86; mem. adv. com. Denver Rsch. Inst. U. Denver, 1984-86; ptnr. Milliken Chapman Rsch. Group Inc., Denver, 1986-88; v.p. Chapman Rsch. Group, Inc., Littleton, 1988—; cons. U.S. Office Pers. Mgmt., Washington, 1977-81, Denver, 1986—; cons. CIA, Washington, 1979, 80, 81, Arthur S. Fleming Awards, Washington, 1977-81; exec. staff dir., cons. U.S. Congressman Frank Denholm; lectr. on sci., tech., govt. and pub. mgmt. Contbr. over 50 articles, revs., Congl. staff reports to profl. publs. Mem. aerospace com. Colo. Commn. Higher Edn., Denver, 1982-83; chmn. rules com. U. Denver Senate, 1984-85; bd. dirs. S.E. Englewood Water Dist., Littleton, 1984-88, pres., 1986-88; mem. strategic planning com. Mission Hills Bapt. Ch., 1986; bd. dirs. Lay Action Ministry Program, 1988—, chmn., 1992—; established Vera and Raymond Chapman Scholarship Fund, S.D. State U.; active S.D. State U. Found. Bd., 1992—; mem. Fairfax County Rep. Ctrl. Com., Va., 1969-71, Fairfax County Com. of 100, 1979-82. With U.S. Army, 1955-57, Korea, capt. Res. Syracuse U. Maxwell Sch. fellow, 1957-58, 63-64, Brookings Inst. fellow, 1964-65. Mem. AAAS, IEEE, Tech. Transfer Soc. (bd. dirs. 1987—, Pres.'s award 1991), Engring. Mgmt. Soc., Fed. Lab. Consortium (nat. adv. com. 1989—), S.D. State U. Found. (bd. dirs. 1992—), Futures Soc., Masons, Commandery, Order of DeMolay (Cross of Honor 1982), Rotary Internat. Found. (fellow 1954-55, Paul Harris fellow 1989), Southglenn Country Club, Met. Club. Republican. Office: Chapman Rsch Group 5601 S Broadway Ste 306 Littleton CO 80121-8030

CHAPMAN, ROBERT GALBRAITH, retired hematologist, administrator; b. Colorado Springs, Colo., Sept. 29, 1926; s. Edward Northrop and Janet Galbraith (Johnson) C.; m. Virginia Irene Potts, July 6, 1956; children: Lucia Tully Chapman Chatzky, Sarah Northrop, Robert Bostwick. Student, Westminster Coll., 1944-45; BA, Yale U., 1947; MD, Harvard U., 1951; MS, U. Colo., 1958. Diplomate Am. Bd. Internal Medicine and Pathology. Intern Hartford (Conn.) Hosp., 1951-52; resident in medicine U. Colo. Med. Ctr., Denver, 1955-58; fellow in hematology U. Wash., Seattle, 1958-60; chief resident in medicine U. Colo., Denver, 1957-58, instr. medicine, 1960-62, asst. prof. medicine, 1962-68, assoc. prof., 1968-91; chief staff VA Hosp., Denver, 1968-70; dir. Belle Bonfils Meml. Blood Ctr., Denver, 1977-91; mem. regionalization com. Am. Blood Commn., Washington, 1985-87, Colo.sickle cell com., Denver, 1978-91, gov.'s AIDS Coun., 1987-88; trustee Coun. Community Blood Ctrs., v.p., 1979-81, pres., 1989-91, mem. rsch. inst. bd. Palo Alto Med. Found., 1991—. Contbr. articles to profl. jours. Served as capt. USAF, 1953-55. USPHS fellow, 1958-60. Fellow ACP; mem. Am. Assn. Blood Banks, Mayflower Soc., Denver Med. Soc., Colo. Med. Soc., Western Soc. Clin. Rsch., Am. Soc. Hematology, Denver Country Club, Am. Radio Relay League. Mem. United Ch. Christ. Home: 47 La Rancheria Carmel Valley CA 93924-9424

CHAPPELL, DAVID JAY, language educator, state legislator; b. Centralia, Wash., Feb. 27, 1960; s. Fred Joseph and Lois (Carico) C.; m. Joan Ellen Koehler, Dec. 28, 1984; children: Christopher Mykal, Camille Amaliyah. BE, We. Wash. U., 1983; M in Ednl. Leadership and Supervision, U. Portland, 1991. Cert. tchr., Wash. Tchr. Spanish W.F. West High Sch., Chehalis, Wash., 1983—; mem. Wash. State Ho. of Reps., Olympia; police interpreter Lewis County (Wash.) Law Enforcement Agys., 1983—. Vol. leader Lewis County Young Life, Centralia, 1983-86; dir., vol. Wash. State Jr. Sportsmans Boys Conservation Camp, Oveas Island, Wash., 1987—; coach WF West Rifle Team, 1988-92; res. police officer Centralia Police Dept., 1988—; mem. Centralia Planning Commn., 1990—, Gov.'s Substance Abuse Coun., Olympia, 1993—; foster parent Dept. Social & Health Svcs., Centralia, 1990—; respite care provider Dept. Devel. Disabilities, Centralia, 1990—; pro-act team mem. Unified Narcotic Enforcement Team, Lewis County, 1991—; appointee Gov.'s Juvenile Justice Adv. Commn., Olympia, Wash., 1991—. Mem. NRA. Democrat. Presbyterian. Home: 520 N Rock St Centralia WA 98531 Office: Wash State Ho of Reps John L O'Brien Bldg 303 Olympia WA 98504

CHAPPELL, DAVID WELLINGTON, religion educator; b. Saint John, N.B., Can., Feb. 3, 1940; came to U.S., 1966; s. Hayward Lynsin and Mary Elvira (Mosher) C.; m. Bertha Vera Bidulock, Aug. 23, 1960 (div. Jan. 1976); children: Cynthia Joan, Mark Lynsin David; m. Stella Quemada, July 11, 1981. BA, Mt. Allison U., Sackville, N.B., 1961; BD, McGill U., Montreal, Can., 1965; PhD, Yale U., 1976. Min. United Ch. Can., Elma, Ont., Can., 1964-66; prof. U. Hawaii, Honolulu, 1971—; asst. prof. U. Toronto, Can., 1977-78; vis. prof. U. Pitts., 1982; vis. lectr. Taisho U., Tokyo, 1986-88; dir. East West Religions Project, Honolulu, 1980—, Buddhist Studies Program, U. Hawaii, 1987-92. Editor: T'ien-t'ai Buddhism, 1983, Buddhist and Taoist Practice, 1987; editor Buddhist-Christian Studies jour., 1980—. Mem. Am. Acad. Religion, Assn. Asian Studies, Internat. Assn. Buddhist Studies, Soc. Buddhist-Christian Studies (v.p.). Democrat. Home: 47 696 Hui Kelu St # 1 Kaneohe HI 96744

CHARBONNEAU, RALPH GRAY, air cargo leasing company executive; b. Osborne, Kans., Jan. 4, 1929; s. Alvarez Emery and Jessie Lucinda (Haskins) C.; m. Martha Habegger, May 19, 1957; children: Eric Gray, Christine Rebecca. BA, Doane Coll., Crete, Nebr., 1950; postgrad., Army Lang. Sch., Monterey, Calif., 1952, Pacific Coast Banking Sch., Seattle, 1968-69. Trainee Mercantile Bank & Trust Co., Kansas City, Mo., 1955-56; loan officer City Nat. Bank & Trust Co., Kansas City, 1956-63; mgr. ICD Seattle-First Nat. Bank, 1963-69; mng. dir. Seattle-First Nat. Bank Switzerland, Zurich, 1969-74; v.p. internat. Seattle First Nat. Bank, 1974-78, v.p., mgr. Europe, Can. and Australasia, 1980-88; gen. mgr. Seattle-First Nat. Bank Switzerland, 1978-80; v.p., mgr. Transiplex, Seattle, 1988—; prof. internat. banking Am. Inst. Banking, Seattle, 1984—. Advisor book, Internat. Banking, 1987, 90. Precinct officer Rep. Party, Seattle, 1989. With USAF, 1951-55. Mem. Canadian Soc. (bd. dirs. 1989), Australian-N.Z. Am. Soc. (bd. dirs. 1989), Swiss Soc. Congregationalist. Home: 1531 Sunset Ave SW Seattle WA 98116-1648 Office: Transiplex Inc 2580 S 156th St PO Box 68515 Seattle WA 98168

CHARBONNEAU, ROBERT BRUCE, university official, natural resourcess consultant; b. Worcester, Mass., Oct. 4, 1960; s. Philip Paul and Statia Marie (Polturak) C. BS in Environ. Scis. cum laude, U. Mass., 1983; M City Planning, U. Calif., Berkeley, 1988. Registered environ. assessor, Calif. 2firefighter, EMT, Northboro Fire Dept., Northborough, Mass., 1978-86; sr. san. engr.'s aide div. water pollution control Mass. Dept. Environ. Quality Engring., Westboro, 1981; biologist, water qualaity specialist IEP Inc., Northborough, 1984-86; environ. resstoration project coord., environ. planner U. Calif. Office Environ. Health and Safety, Berkeley, 1987-89, cons. on Strawberry Creek restoration project, 1989-92; environ. assessment coord. Office of Pres., U. Calif. Office Environ. Health and Safety, Oakland, 1992—; due diligence coord. Office of Pres., U. Calif. Systemwide, 1989—; speaker in field. Author: (booklet) Walking Tour of Campus Natural History, U. Calif., Berkeley, 1990. Coord. disaster svcs. ARC, Northborough, 1976-78; charter mem. Berkeley Citizens for Creek Restoration, 1989. Grantee U. Calif., Berkeley, 1987. Mem. Assn. Environ. Profls., Soc. for Ecol. Restoration and Mgmt., Watershed Mgmt. Assn., Bay Area Resource Mgrs. Assn., Sierra Club, Berkeley Hiking Club (bd. dirs. 1987-91). Office: U Calif Environ Protection Svcs Office of Pres 300 Lakeside Dr 12th Fl Oakland CA 94612-3550

CHARLES, MARY LOUISE, newspaper columnist, photographer, editor; b. L.A., Jan. 24, 1922; d. Louis Edward and Mabel Inez (Lyon) Kusel; m. Henry Loewy Charles, June 19, 1946; children: Susan, Henry, Robert, Carol. AA, L.A. City Coll., 1941; BA, San Jose (Calif.) State U., 1964. Salesperson Roos Bros., Berkeley, Calif., 1945-46; ptnr. Charles-Martin Motors, Marysville, Calif., 1950-54; farm editor Indep. Herald, Yuba City, Calif., 1954-55; social worker Sutter County, Yuba City, 1955-57; social worker Santa Clara County, San Jose, 1957-61, manual coordinator, 1961-73, community planning specialist, 1973-81; columnist Sr. Grapevine various weekly newspapers, Santa Clara, 1981-86; editor Bay area Sr. Spectrum Newspapers, Santa Clara, 1986-90; columnist, 1990—; founder, pres. Triple-A Coun. Calif., 1978-80. Vice chmn. Santa Clara County Sr. Care Commn., 1987-89, chmn., 1989-91, social svcs. com. 1993—; mem. Calif. Legis. Roundtable, 1975—. With WAVE, USNR, 1942-45. Recipient Social Welfare award Daniel E. Koshland Found., 1973, Friends of Santa Clara County Human Rels. Commn. award, 1992; named 24th State Assembly Dist. Woman of Yr., 1990. Mem. NASW, LWV, Nat. Coun. Sr. Citizens (bd. dirs. 1988—), Svc. Employees Internat. Union (mem. local 535, state exec. bd. dirs. 1973—, pres. sr. mems. and retiree chpt. 1982—), Congress of Calif. Srs. (bd. dirs. 1987—, region IV pres. 1992—, trustee 1993—), Older Women's League of Calif. (edn./resource coord. 1987-89, pres. 1990-91), Am. Soc. on Aging (co-chair women's concerns com. 1985-86, awards com. 1990—), Nat. Coun. on Aging., Calif. Specialists on Aging (treas. 1985-93), Calif. Srs. Coalition (chmn. 1986, treas. 1993—), Calif. Writers Club. Home and Office: 2527 Forbes Ave Santa Clara CA 95050-5547

CHARLESTON, STEVE, bishop. Bishop Diocese of Alaska, Fairbanks, 1991—. Office: Diocese of Alaska 1205 Derali Way Fairbanks AK 99701-4137*

CHARLEY, PHILIP JAMES, testing laboratory executive; b. Melbourne, Australia, Aug. 18, 1921; came to U.S., 1940, naturalized; 1948; s. Walter George and Constance Mary (Macdonald) C.; BS, U. Wis., 1943; MS in Mech. Engring., U. So. Calif., 1947, PhD in Biochemistry, 1960; m. Katherine Truesdail, Jan. 31, 1948; children: James Alan, Linda Kay, William John. Test engr. Gen. Electric Co., Schenectady, 1943-44; lectr. in engring. U. So. Calif., L.A., 1947-49; project engr. Standard Oil of Calif., El Segundo, 1948-55; v.p. Truesdail Labs., L.A., 1955-70, pres., 1970—. Served to lt. Royal Can. Elec. and Mech. Engrs., 1943-45. Recipient Dueul award U. So. Calif., 1960, rsch. assoc., 1960-65; registered profl. engr., Calif.. Ariz., Nev. Mem. AAAS, ASTM, ASME, Am. Soc. Metals, Am. Soc. Safety Engrs., Am. Chem. Soc., Sigma Xi, Tau Beta Pi, Beta Theta Pi. Republican. Club: Rotary. Home: 1906 Calle De Los Alamos San Clemente CA 92672-4309 Office: Truesdail Labs Inc 14201 Franklin Ave Tustin CA 92680-7094

CHARLTON, JOHN KIPP, pediatrician; b. Omaha, Jan. 26, 1937; s. George Paul and Mildred (Kipp) C. A.B., Amherst Coll., 1958; M.D., Cornell U., 1962; m. Susan S. Young, Aug. 15, 1959; children: Paul, Cynthia, Daphne, Gregory. Intern, Ohio State U. Hosp., Columbus, 1962-63; resident in pediatrics Children's Hosp., Dallas, 1966-68, chief pediatric resident, 1968-69; nephrology fellow U. Tex. Southwestern Med. Sch., Dallas, 1969-70; pvt. practice medicine specializing in pediatrics, Phoenix, 1970; chmn. dept. pediatrics Maricopa Med. Ctr., Phoenix, 1971-78, 84-93, assoc. chmn. dept. pediatrics, 1979-84, med. staff pres., 1991; med. dir., bd. dirs. Crisis Nursery, Inc., 1977—; sr. clin. lectr. dept. pediatrics U. Ariz. Pres. Maricopa County Child Abuse Coun., 1977-81; bd. dirs. Florence Critenton Svcs., 1980-83, Ariz. Children's Fund, 1987-91; mem. Gov.'s Coun. on Children, Youth and Families, 1984-86. Officer M.C., USAF, 1963-65. Recipient Hon Kachina award for volunteerism, 1980, Jefferson award for volunteerism, 1980, Horace Steel Child Advocacy award, 1993. Mem. Am. Acad. Pediatrics, Ariz. Pediatric Soc., Maricopa County Pediatric Soc. (past pres.). Author articles, book rev. in field. Home: 6230 E Exeter Blvd Scottsdale AZ 85251-3060 Office: Maricopa Med Ctr 2601 E Roosevelt St Phoenix AZ 85008-4973

CHARLTON, SHANNON BRUCE, golf course architect; b. Manchester, Iowa, Apr. 27, 1957; s. William Stuart and Lois (McCord) C.; m. Maridee Huston, Jan. 2, 1988. B of Landscape Architecture, U. Ariz., 1990. Landscape architect Shoneberger & Assocs., Phoenix, 1980-81; v.p. golf course architect Robert Trent Jones II, Palo Alto, Calif., 1981—. Runner-up Best New Pub. Golf Course (Univ. Ridge, Madison, Wis.), Golf Digest Mag., Edinburgh USA-Brooklyn Park, Minn., 1980. Mem. Am. Soc. Golf Course Architects (environ. com. 1990—), Am. Soc. Landscape Architects (No. Calif. chpt.), U. Ariz. Alumni Fund. Office: Robert Trent Jones II 705 Forest Ave Palo Alto CA 94301

CHARNAY, JOHN BRUCE, marketing and fundraising professional; b. N.Y.C., Apr. 4, 1949; s. David Buckley and Shirley Renee Kraft (Miller) C.;

m. Carolyn Agnes Hemighaus; children: Matthew Brandon, Katharine Bridget. BA in Polit. Sci., U. Pa., 1971; MS in Journalism, Columbia U., 1973; JD, Southwestern U., L.A., 1977. Pub. rels. dir. 4 Star Prodns., Beverly Hills, Calif., 1973-76; news editor Hollywood (Calif.) Reporter, 1976-78; sr. account supr. ICPR Pub. Rels., L.A., 1978-80; v.p. corp. communications Glendale (Calif.) Fed. Savs., 1980-85; pub. rels. dir. L.A. (Calif.) County Mus. Natural History, 1985-88; devel. dir., capital campaigns dir., mktg. dir. L.A. County Mus. Natural History, 1988—. With U.S. ANG, 1970-77. Mem. Am. Mktg. Assn. (seminar leader), Pub. Rels. Soc. Am. (fin. instns. sect.), Pub. Rels. Com. (chmn.), Internat. Assn. Bus. Communicators (v.p. profl. devel.), Pub. Club L.A. (internship and program com. chmn.), Mktg. Club L.A. (founder), Greater L.A. Press Club, L.A. Advt. Club, ABA, Calif. Bar Assn., L.A. County Bar Assn., Savs. Instn. Mktg. Soc. Am., Nat. Investor Rels. Inst., Am. Bus. Communicators Assn., Sales & Mktg. Execs. Internat., L.A. Soc. Pub. Rels. Counselors, Sigma Delta Chi. Republican.

CHARNEY, MICHAEL JEFFREY, corporate communications specialist; b. Atlanta, Apr. 17, 1959; s. Alan Charney and Shirley Ann Mark. BA in Journalism with highest honors, U. S.C., 1981; MA in Communications with highest honors, Ohio State U., 1982. Mgr. pub. rels. Raytheon Co., Lexington, Mass., 1982-87; mgr. media rels., employee communications Rockwell Internat. World Hdqrs., El Segundo, Calif., 1987-91; dir. communications Rockwell Internat. Rocketdyne Div., Canoga Park, Calif., 1991—. Recipient Bell Ringer award Publicity Club Boston, 1986, Award of Excellence L.A. Press Club, 1992, 93, Gold Quill award Internat. Assn. Bus. Communicators, 1990, 91, 92, Design Recognition award Libr. of Congress, 1990, Nat. Award of Excellence Aerospace Writers' Assn., 1991, 92. Mem. Pub. Rels. Soc. Am. (Prism award 1989, 90, 91), Publicity Club L.A. (v.p. bd. dirs. 1991-92, "Pro" award 1988, 89, 90, 91, 92, Excellence in Corp. Communications award 1992, 93), San Fernando Valley Pub. Rels. Exec. Coun., Nat. Mgmt. Assn. (bd. dirs. 1991-92, Top Mgr. of Yr. 1993-94). Home: 2116 Oak St Santa Monica CA 90405 Office: Rockwell Internat Rocketdyne Divsn 6633 Canoga Ave Canoga Park CA 91303

CHAROBEE, DANNY DAVID, publishing executive, photographer; b. Charleroi, Pa., Apr. 22, 1950; s. Louis Edward and Frances (Kokoska) C.; m. Sheryl Ann Alducka, May 22, 1976; 1 child, David Louis. BS, Pa. State U., 1972; postgrad., U. Pitts., 1978-79. Probation officer Allegheny County Juvenile Ct., Pitts., 1973-79; comml. photographer Charobee Photography, Irvine, Calif., 1979-82; sales mgr. Off Duty Mag., Costa Mesa, Calif., 1982-84, U.S. advt. mgr., 1984-89; bus. mgr. Off Duty Ent., Costa Mesa, Calif., 1989-90; pres. Pacific Coast Media, Irvine, 1990—; cons. Lefebvre Advt., Anaheim, 1988-89. Pub. mag. Internat. Fire Chiefs; photographer unique home features, Showcase mag., 1980, Home Buyers Guide, 1979-82. Recipient Sales Achievement award, Off Duty Mag., 1982, Merit award, U. Pitts., 1978. Mem. Am. Logistics Assn. (sec. 1990-91, dir. 1982-91). Office: Off Duty Ent 3303 Harbor Blvd Costa Mesa CA 92626-1530

CHARTCHAIGANAN, SUWIT, food and beverage concession executive; b. Bangkok, Thailand, Feb. 8, 1954; came to U.S., 1974; s. Liang Ua Chua and Apiwan Chartchaiganan; m. Oranuj Durongbhandhu, June 14, 1980; children: Christopher Chart, Brittany Nan. Student, Glendale (Calif.) City Coll., 1976-78, Calif. State U., L.A., 1979-81. Cert. computer system operation and programming. Stations mgr. Al-Sal Oil Co., L.A., 1974-78; gen. mgr. Pinterex, L.A., 1978-80; bar mgr. Pastel, Bevery Hills, Calif., 1980-88; gen. mgr. B.C. Club, Hollywood, Calif., 1988-89; food and beverage mgr. Marriott, L.A., 1989—; gen. mgr. L.A. United Airport Group, Minority Bus. Enterprise, L.A., 1991—. Contbr. articles to profl. jours. Home: 9281 Longacres Ave Pico Rivera CA 90660-5949 Office: L A United Airport Group 201 World Way Los Angeles CA 90045-5807

CHARTERS, CYNTHIA GRACE, artist, educator; b. Fort Bragg, Calif., Sept. 14, 1949; d. Morris James and Virignia Lola (Davis) C.; m. William Terrance Foley, Aug. 30, 1970 (div. 1983); m. Peter Vladimir Tkacheff, Jan. 31, 1987; 1 child, Alexandra Petrovna. BA in Art, U. Calif., Davis, 1972, BS in Design, 1972, MA, 1981. Curator, registrar R.L. Nelson Gallery, U. Calif., Davis, 1982-85; lectr. art Calif. State U.-Stanislaus, Turlock, 1985-87, art lectr., dir. univ. art gallery, 1988-91; guest lectr., panelist, cons. for numerous civic and pvt. orgns. including Sacramento Met. Arts Commn., Sacramento City Coll., Inst. Design and Exptl. Art, Sacramento; juror art exhbns.; artist in residence Yosemite (Calif.) Nat. Park, 1988. Represented numerous pvt. collections. Arts commr. City of Turlock, 1989-90. Mem. Am. Assn. Museums, Assn. Coll. and Univ. Museums and Galleries, Coll. Art Assn.

CHARTIER, VERNON LEE, electrical engineer; b. Ft. Morgan, Colo., Feb. 14, 1939; s. Raymond Earl and Margaret Clara (Winegar) C.; m. Lois Marie Schwartz, May 20, 1967; 1 child, Neal Raymond. BSEE, BS in Bus., U. Colo., 1963. Registered profl. engr., Pa.; cert. electromagnetic compatibility engr. Rsch. engr., cons. Westinghouse Electric Co., East Pittsburgh, Pa., 1963-75; principal engr. high voltage phenomena Bonneville Power Adminstrn., Vancouver, Wash., 1975—. Contbr. articles to profl. jours. Fellow IEEE (mem. fellow com.); mem. IEEE Power Engring. Soc. (past chmn. fellows com.), Internat. Conf. Large High Voltage Electric Systems (U.S. rep. to study com. 36 on interference), Acoustical Soc. Am., Bioelectromagnetics Soc., Internat. Electrotech. Commn. (U.S. rep. to subcom. on High Voltage Lines & Traction Systems), Chartier Family Assn. Baptist. Home: 5190 SW Dover Ln Portland OR 97225-1021 Office: Bonneville Power Adminstrn PO Box 491 Vancouver WA 98666-0491

CHASE, JUDITH HELFER, librarian, educator, musician; b. Elizabethton, Tenn., Feb. 19, 1939; d. Edward Conley and Faith (Clemons) Helfer; m. William Clark Chase, Aug. 8, 1970. BS in Music Edn., East Tenn. State U., 1962; postgrad., Bradley U., 1963-64, U. Tenn., Knoxville, 1968; student, German Ctr. for Internat. Music Edn., 1969-70; postgrad., Oreg. Inst. Tech., 1975-77; M in Music, U. Oreg., 1984; ML, U. Wash., 1986. Music specialist Morristown (Tenn.) City Schs., 1962-63, Peoria (Ill.) County Schs., 1963-64, Anne Arundel County Bd. Edn., Annapolis, 1964-69, 70-73; ch. organist, pvt. practice piano tchr. Elizabethton, Tenn. and Klamath Falls, Oreg., 1973-77; with med. records dept. Merle West Med. Ctr., Klamath Falls, 1977-79; media svcs. cataloger, libr. aide, music specialist Klamath County Sch. Dist., 1977-85; med. libr. aide of aux., 1987-89; asst. prof., reference and documents librarian Oreg. Inst. Tech., Klamath Falls, 1986-89; asst. catalog libr. Francis Marion Coll., Florence, S.C., 1989-90, Klamath County Pub. Libr., Klamath Falls, 1992; catalog libr. Weyerhaeuser Corp. Libr., Tacoma, Wash., 1992-93; bassoonist, counselor Brevard (N.C.) Music Ctr., summer 1961; unit leader Nat. Music Camp, Interlochen, Mich., summer 1964. Dir. youth choir St. Paul's Episcopal Ch., Klamath Falls., 1975-84; mem. aux. Klamath Arts Coun., 1976-84; mem. online coord. com. Interinstitnl. Libr. Coun. Oreg. State Systems Higher Edn., 1989; soprano Klamath Symphonic Choir, 1977-84; libr. Plum Ridge Symphony, Klamath Falls, 1979-84, v.p. guild, 1980-82; bd. dirs., libr. Klamath Youth Symphony, 1983-89; mem. FMC Artist Series Com., 1989-90; alto Masterworks Choir, Florence, S.C., 1990. Bassoon scholar, 1957, 58-62, 63, 63-64. Mem. ALA (govt. documents roundtable 1987—, resources and tech. svcs. div. 1988—), AAUW, Med. Libr. Assn. (ednl. media and tech. svcs. sect. 1988-92), Music Libr. Assn., Pacific N.W. Libr. Assn., Online Audiovisual Catalogers, MacDowell Evening Music Club, Nat. Fedn. Music Clubs, Delta Omicron (pres. alumni chpt. 1967-68, Mae Chenoweth Grannis grantee 1984), Kappa Delta Pi. Episcopalian. Office: Weyerhaeuser Corp Libr 33663 Weyerhaeuser Way S Tacoma WA 98477

CHASE, LARRY J., communications executive; b. Akron, Ohio, May 5, 1945; m. George Ramsey and Phyllis (Bugh) Chase; m. Patricia A. Alexander, Aug. 26, 1967 (div. 1980); children: Benjamin, Jeremy; m. Sara A., July 2, 1982; 1 child, Kerri. Student, Kent State U., 1963-65; BA in Communications, Boise State U., 1972. Radio announcer, TV weatherman KBOI Radio and TV, Boise, Idaho, 1969-84; promotion mgr. KBCI TV, Boise, Idaho, 1974-76, account exec., 1976-78; local sales mgr. KPVI-TV, Pocatello, Idaho, 1978-79; sta. mgr. KPCI-TV, Pocatello, Idaho, 1979-81; ops. mgr. KIVI-TV, Boise and Nampa, Idaho, 1981-82; gen. mgr. KIVI-TV, Boise and Nampa, 1982—. Pres. bd. dirs. YMCA, Boise, 1987-89; bd. dirs. Idaho Children's Trust Fund, Boise, 1985-89; elected to ABC Affiliate Bd. of Govs., 1991. With USAF, 1965-69. Named Distin. Citizen Idaho Statesman newspaper, Boise, 1985, Exec. of the Yr., Exec. Women Internat., 1985. Mem. Idaho Advt. Fedn. (vice-chmn. 1986-88, chmn. 1988-92), Idaho State Broadcasters (legis. chmn. 1987—, bd. dirs. 1990—), Am. Advt. Fedn. (lt. gov. 1984-86, Silver medal 1990), Boise Area C. of C. (chmn. 1987), Rotary Club. Home: 3278 Snowflake Way Boise ID 83706-5260 Office: Sta KIVI-TV 1866 E Chisholm Dr Nampa ID 83687-6899

CHASE, LORIENE ECK, psychologist; b. Sacramento; d. Walter and Genevieve (Bennetts) Eck; m. Leo Goodman-Malauth, 1946 (div. 1951); 1 child, Leo; m. Allen Chase, Mar. 4, 1960 (div.); m. Clifton W. King, 1974. AB, U. So. Calif., 1948, MA, 1949, PhD, 1953. Psychologist Spastic Children's Found., L.A., 1952-55, Inst. Group Psychotherapy, Beverly Hills, Calif., 1957-59; pvt. practice, 1953—; v.p. VSP Exec. Relocation Consultants. Condr., Dr. Loriene Chase Show, ABC-TV, Hollywood, Calif. 1966—; cons. Camarillo State Hosp.; bd. dirs., pres.'s circle U. So. Calif.; founding mem. Achievement Rewards for Coll. Scientists; bd. dirs. Chase-King Personal Devel. Ctr., L.A.; v.p. Chase-King Prodns. Inc., L.A., Shell Beach, Calif.; exec. bd. Cancer Rsch. Ctr., L.A. Author: The Human Mircle; writer syndicated newspaper column Casebook of Dr. Chase; columnist Westways mag. With Waves World War II. Recipient Woman of Yr. in Psychology award Am. Mothers Com. Mem. AFTRA, Diadames, Assn. Media Psychologists, Les Dames de Champagne, Dame de Rotisseur, Nat. Art Assn., Screen Actors Guild, Internat. Platform Assn., Internat. Studies for the Study of Subtle Energies and Energy Medicine, Assn. for the Study of Dreams, Assn. for Past Life Rsch. and Therapy, Regency Club, Lakeside Country Club, Santa Maria Country Club. Home: 1465 Valley Ranch Circle Prescott AZ 86303

CHASE, RICHARD BARTH, operations management educator; b. L.A., May 4, 1939; s. Louis R. and Sally (Barth) C.; m. Harriet Levine, Jan. 27, 1962; children: Laurie, Andrew, Glenn. BS, UCLA, 1962, MBA, 1963, PhD, 1966. Asst. prof. UCLA, 1966-68; assoc. prof. Pa. State U., University Park, 1968-69; assoc. prof. U. Ariz., Tucson, 1970-75, prof., 1975-85; prof. ops. mgmt. U. So. Calif. Sch. Bus., L.A., 1985—; vis. prof. Inst. for Mgmt. Devel., Lausanne, France, 1976-77, Harvard U., Boston, 1988-89; dir. Ctr. for Ops. Mgmt., L.A., 1985—; examiner Malcolmb Baldridge Nat. Quality Award, 1989; bd. govs. Acad. Mgmt., 1985-87. Co-author: Management: A Life Cycle Approach, 1981, Production and Operations Management, 1989, Service Management Effect, 1990. Fellow Decision Scis. Inst., Acad. Mgmt.; mem. Ops. Mgmt. Assn. (bd. dirs. 1985-87), Beta Gamma Sigma, Omega Rho. Office: U So Calif Sch Bus Ctr Ops Mgmt Los Angeles CA 90089-1421

CHASE, RICHARD LIONEL ST. LUCIAN, geology and oceanography educator; b. Perth, Australia, Dec. 25, 1933; s. Conrad Lucien Doughty and Vera Mabel (Saw) C.; m. Mary Malcolm Nafe, Aug. 28, 1965; children: Sarah, Samuel, Elijah. B.Sc. with honors, U. Western Australia, 1956; Ph.D., Princeton U., 1963. Geologist Geosurveys of Australia, Adelaide, 1956-57; sr. asst. geologist Ministere des Mines, Que., Can., 1959; geologist Ministerio de Minas, Venezuela, 1960-61; postdoctoral fellow Woods Hole (Mass.) Oceanographic Instn., 1963-64; asst. scientist, 1964-68; asst. prof. U. B.C., Vancouver, 1968-73; assoc. prof. U. B.C., 1973-78, prof. dept. geol. scis., 1978-80, prof. depts. geol. scis. and oceanography, 1980—, acting head dept. geol. scis., 1990-91. Contbr. articles to profl. jours. Mem. Am. Geophys. Union, Geol. Assn. Can., Geol. Soc. Am. Club: Faculty U. B.C. Home: 4178 W 12th Ave, Vancouver, BC Canada V6R 2P6 Office: U BC, 6339 Stores Rd, Vancouver, BC Canada V6T 1Z4

CHASIN, JUDITH TRIPP, psychotherapist; b. Phoenix, Nov. 24, 1948; d. Arnold Carl and Miriam Roseman (Gregg) Johnson; m. Michael Jay Tripp (div. 1981); 1 child, Gwyneth Dawn; m. Gilbert Edwin Chasin, Sept. 9, 1985. BA, U. Calif., Santa Cruz, 1970; MA, John F. Kennedy U., Orinda, Calif., 1982; teaching cert., Sonoma State U., 1972; cert., Acupressure Inst., Berkeley, Calif., 1992. Cert. tchr., Calif.; lic. marriage and family counselor, Calif. Tchr. handicapped and emotionally handicapped students Mt. Diablo Unified Sch. Dist., Concord, Calif., 1972-84; tchr., supr. John F. Kennedy U., Orinda, 1984-86; psychotherapist Affiliated Psychol. Svcs., San Francisco, 1983-87; workshop leader, wilderness workshop leader Awakening to the Heart of the Feminine, Berkeley, Calif., 1985-92; cons. Grace Cathedral, San Francisco, 1988-92; psychotherapist Live Oak Counseling Ctr., San Francisco, 1987—; mem. conf. com. Assn. for Transpersonal Psychology, 1984-88; mem. Women's Dream Quest, Grace Cathedral, San Francisco, 1987-91; coord. no. Calif. com. Toward the True Meaning of Peace, Costa Rica, 1988-89. Vol. Berkeley High Sch. Health Ctr., 1992, Clinton/Gore campaign, Berkeley, 1992. Mem. Calif. Assn. Marriage and Family Counselors, Assn. Humanistic Psychology. Democrat. Home: 816 Contra Costa Ave Berkeley CA 94707 Office: Live Oak Counseling Ctr 1637 Irving St San Francisco CA 94122

CHATFIELD, CHERYL ANN, investment bank executive, writer, educator; b. King's Park, N.Y., Jan. 24, 1946; d. William David and Mildred Ruth (King) C.; m. Gene Allen Chasser, Feb. 17, 1968 (div. 1979); m. James Bernard Arkebauer, Apr. 16, 1983 (div. 1987). BS, Cen. Conn. Coll., 1968, MS, 1972; PhD, U. Conn., 1976. Cert. gen. prin. securities. Tchr. Bristol East High Sch., Conn., 1968-77; adminstr. New Britain Schs., Conn., 1977-79; prof. Ariz. State U., Phoenix, 1979; stockbroker J. Daniel Bell, Denver, 1980-83, Hyder and Co., Denver, 1983-84; stockbroker; chief exec. officer Chatfield Dean & Co., Denver, 1984-90, Women Securities Internat., 1990-92; tchr. investment seminars Front Range Community Coll., Denver, 1984-86; speaker women's groups, Denver, 1983-86. Author: Low-Priced Riches, 1985, Selling Low-Priced Riches, 1986, (newspaper columns) For Women Investors, 1982-84, Commentary, 1985-86; editor, founder (newsletter) Women in Securities . Project bus. cons. Jr. Achievement, Denver, 1986. Mem. NAFE, AAUW, Aircraft Owners and Pilots Assn., Internat. Women's Forum, Kappa Delta Pi. Republican. Roman Catholic. Avocation: flying. Office: 2801 Rodeo Rd Ste B-217 Santa Fe NM 87505

CHATFIELD, JOAN, church administrator; b. Elizabeth, N.J., Oct. 7, 1932; d. Henry Summers and Angela Dorothea (McCahill) Chatfield. BA, Manhattanville Coll., 1956; MA, U. San Francisco, 1968; PhD, Grad. Theol. Union, Berkeley, Calif., 1983. Secondary sch. tchr. Cath. Sch. Dept., Hawaii, 1956-72; dir. Maryknoll (N.Y.) Mission Inst., 1974-78; exec. dir. Inst. for Religion and Social Change, Honolulu, 1980—; ecumenical officer Roman Cath. Diocese of Honolulu, 1983-90, chair ecumenical commn., 1983—; dean Sch. Humanities and Fine Arts Chaminade U. Honolulu, 1990—; pres. Hawaii Inst. for Theol. Studies, Honolulu, 1988—; v.p. Western Fellowship for the Profs. of Mission, Calif., 1989—; bd. dirs. Interfaith Ministries of Hawaii, Honolulu, 1985—. Contbr. articles to profl. jours. Vice chair City & County Status of Women, Honolulu, 1981-86; pres. Project Realize Effective Support Programs for the Elderly through Chs. and Temples, Honolulu, 1983—; bd. dirs. Honolulu Theater for Youth, 1983-88, 91—. Named Tchr. of Yr., Finance Factors, Honolulu, 1964, one of Women of Note, Honolulu Status of Women Commn., 1982; recipient Pres.'s award Internat. Assn. Mission Studies, 1988. Mem. AAUW (chair ednl. found. program, pres. 1986-88), Am. Soc. Missiology (pres. 1984-86), Rotary. Democrat. Home: 2880 Oahu Ave Honolulu HI 96822-1726 Office: Inst Religion and Social Change 3146 Waialae Ave Honolulu HI 96816-1510

CHATHAM, SHERRI IRENE, practical nurse; b. Sheridan, Wyo., Sept. 3, 1958; d. Richard Lee and Mary Louise (George) C.; children: Cameron, Aimée. Student, Mont. State U., 1977-78; diploma nursing, Great Falls Vocat.-Tech., 1980. Staff nurse Columbus Hosp., Great Falls, Mont., 1980—, Columbus Convenience Care, Great Falls, 1986-88; office nurse Internal Medicine Specialists, Great Falls, 1988—; mem. Mont. State Bd. Nursing, 1987—; lab. technician Meadow Gold Dairy/Borden Foods, Great Falls, 1990—; dress designer Heirloom Originals, Great Falls, 1979-90. Vol. ARC, Great Falls, 1980—, Rescue Mission for Homeless, Great Falls; asst. Boy Scouts Am., Great Falls; active Mont. Rep., Helena; saxophonists Winds of Mont., Great Falls. Mem. Salvation Army Christian Nurses, Am. Legion Aux. Office: Internal Medicine Specialists 400 15th Ave S Ste 208 Great Falls MT 59405

CHATLOSH, DIANE LYNN, psychology educator; b. Menominee, Mich., Sept. 19, 1955; d. Joseph A. and Viola Josephine (Wery) C. BS, Northern Mich. U., 1977; MS, U. Wisc., 1982; PhD, U. Iowa, 1988. Asst. prof. psychology Ball State U., Muncie, Ind., 1987-89, Calif. State U., Chico, 1989—. Author book chpts. and jour. articles in field. Recipient Soc. award Delta Kappa Gamma, Oshkosh, Wisc., 1981. Rsch. Svc. award NIMH, 1982, Don Lewis Dissertation of Yr. award U. Iowa, 1987. Mem. Am. Psychol. Assn., Midwestern Psyhol. Assn., Sigma Xi (Grant-in-Aid of Rsch. award 1986), Psi Chi. Office: Calif State U Dept Psychology Chico CA 95929-0234

CHATROO, ARTHUR JAY, lawyer; b. N.Y.C., July 1, 1946; s. George and Lillian (Leibowitz) C. BChemE, CCNY, 1968; JD cum laude, New York Law Sch., 1979; MBA with distinction, NYU, 1982. Bar: N.Y. 1980, Ohio 1992. Process engr. Standard Oil Co. of Ohio, various locations, 1968-73; process specialist BP Oil, Inc., Marcus Hook, Pa., 1974-75; sr. process engr. Sci. Design Co., Inc., N.Y.C., 1975-78; mgr. spl. projects The Halcon SD Group, N.Y.C., 1978-82; corp. counsel, tax and fin. The Lubrizol Corp., Wickliffe, Ohio, 1982-85; sr. counsel spl. investment projects The Lubrizol Corp., Wickliffe, 1989-90; gen. counsel Lubrizol Enterprises, Inc., Wickliffe, 1985-89; chmn. Correlation Genetics Corp., San Jose, Calif., 1990-91; gen. counsel Agrigenetics Co., Eastlake, Ohio, 1990-92; dir. comml. contracting Agrigenetics, L.P., San Diego, 1992—. Mem. Met. Parks Adv. com., Allen County, Ohio, 1973. Mem. ABA, Am. Chem. Soc., Am. Inst. Chem. Engrs., N.Y. State Bar Assn., Cleve. Bar Assn., Am. Corp. Counsel Assn., Jaycees (personnel dir. Lima, Ohio chpt. 1972-73), Omega Chi Epsilon, Beta Gamma Sigma. Club: Toastmasters. Home: Apt 4204 7655 Palmilla Dr 7655 Palmilla Dr San Diego CA 92122 Office: Agrigenetics LP 4980 Carroll Canyon Rd San Diego CA 92121

CHATTERJEE, ANIL KUMAR, mechanical engineer, consultant; b. Calcutta, India, May 27, 1923; came to U.S., 1951; s. Narayan Chandra and Indu (Banerjee) C.; m. Maya Mukherjee, Dec. 14, 1958; children: Bikash K., Pallab R. BME, U. Jadavpur, Calcutta, 1948; MS, Va. Poly. Inst., 1952; postgrad, U. Minn., 1952-56. Registered profl. engr., Calif., N.Y. Sr. staff engr. Ellerbe & Co., 1956-58; asst. prof. U. Akron, Ohio, 1958-61; engring. specialist Valve div. TRW, Cleve., 1961-66; sr. staff engr. Union Carbide, Tonawanda, N.Y., 1966-67, Torrax div. Carborundum Co., Niagara Falls, N.Y., 1967-74; engring. specialist, sr. staff engr. Acres Am. Inc., Buffalo, 1974-77; sr. rsch. engr. SRI Internat., Menlo Park, Calif., 1978-80; pres. Chatterjee & Assocs. Inc., Newark, Calif., 1980—; engring. cons. World Bank, UNIDO, U.S. AID, Caribbean Community SECRTT, Asian Devel. Bank. Co-author: Biomass Conversion Processes for Energy and Fuels, 1981; contbr. articles to profl. jours.; patentee in field. Fulbright scholar New Delhi, 1951; recipient 1st prize for paper Am. Soc. Engring. Edn., 1960. Mem. ASME (bd. dirs. 1961-66), AIChE. Democrat. Hindu. Home: 4883 Windermere Dr Newark CA 94560 Office: Chatterjee & Assocs Inc Newark CA 94560

CHATTERJEE, BIJOY GOPAL, defense contractor executive, computer scientist; b. Bhagalpur, Bihar, India, Oct. 8, 1937; came to U.S., 1962; s. Amala Pada and Annapurna (Mukherjee) C.; m. Joya Banerjea, May 22, 1965; children: Arjun Bijoy, Indra Neel. BSEE, Bihar Inst. Tech., 1959; MSEE, U. Calif., Berkeley, 1964. Subdivisional officer Bihar State Electric, Samastipur, Bihar, 1959-61; asst. prof. Bihar Inst. Tech., Sindri, Bihar, 1961-62; computer programmer Univ. Calif., Berkeley, 1962-66; engring. mgr. RCA Computer Systems, Cherry Hill, N.J., 1966-71; asst. dir. Travellers Ins. Co., Hartford, Conn., 1971-74; engring. mgr. Inst. for Advanced Computation, Moffett Field, Calif., 1975-79; engring. dir. ESL Inc., Sunnyvale, Calif., 1980—. Democrat. Hindu. Home: 127 Mary Way Los Gatos CA 95032-4817 Office: ESL Inc 495 E Java Dr Sunnyvale CA 94089-1150

CHATTERJEE, SIDDHARTHA, computer scientist; b. Chandernagore, India, May 1, 1963; s. Benoy Lal and Jharna C.; m. Sarmita Mukherjee, Feb. 6, 1990. B of Technology with honors, Indian Inst. Tech., Kharagpur, India, 1985; MS, Carnegie Mellon U., 1988, PhD, 1991. Vis. scientist Rsch. Inst. for Advanced Computer Sci., Moffett Field, Calif., 1991—. Recipient Pres.'s Gold medal Indian Inst. Tech., 1985. Mem. IEEE Computer Soc., Assn. for Computing Machinery, Sigma Xi.

CHAUNCEY, TOM, retired radio and television executive.; b. Houston, Jan. 20, 1913; s. Brinkley and Lucille Dunn (Weber) C.; 6 children; student pub. schs.; LHD (hon.) Ariz. State U., 1983. Owner, Tom Chauncey Jeweler, 1940-61; v.p., gen. mgr. Sta KPHO, 1941-48; pres. Sta. KOPO, Tucson, 1947-76; v.p., mng. dir. KOOL Radio-TV, Inc., 1948-55, exec. v.p., gen. mgr., 1955-57, pres., gen. mgr., 1957-61, pres., 1961-81, chmn. bd., pres., chief exec. officer, 1981-82, owner, chief exec. officer Sta. KOOL-AM-FM, 1982-86; owner, 26 Bar Ranch, Ceear Creek Cattle Co., Tom Chauncey Arabians, Tom Chauncey Properties; pres., mng. dir. Old Pueblo Broadcasting Co., (KOLD-TV), Tucson, 1957-69; daily columnist TV Views, Ariz. Republic, Phoenix Gazette, (weekly) Broadcasting mag., 1960-61; former chmn. bd. CBS TV Network Affiliates 1961-62; dir. Valley Nat. Bank; mem. nat. com. Support Free Broadcasting; rep. of pres. U.S., ambassador, Nigeria, 1960. Grand marshal J.C. World Championship Rodeo and Parade, 1963; former nat. trustee City of Hope; former mem. Ariz. Nat. Livestock Show; past Ariz. chmn. Radio Free Europe; former mem. bd. Phoenix Symphony Assn., Phoenix Art Mus., Muscular Dystrophy Assn. Am.; gen. campaign. chmn. Greater Phoenix-Scottsdale United Fund Campaign; former mem. bd., v.p., pres. Phoenix Better Bus. Bur.; mem. Citizen's Action Com.; voting mem. Ariz. State U. Found.; former mem. Phoenix Baseball Stadium Com., U. Ariz. Found., chmn. Ariz. com. A.R.C.; past dir. at large for Ariz. Am. Cancer Soc.; past dir. and pres. Community Council; exec. v.p., mem. bd., Incorporator, co-founder Barrow Neurol. Inst.; mem. Com. for Phoenix Civic Plaza Dedication Ceremonies, 1972, Ariz. Commn. on Nat. and Internat. Commerce; past nat. chmn. Broadcaster's adv. com. U.S. Savs. Bonds; past dir. United Cerebral Palsey Assn. Central Ariz.; past mem. Phoenix All-Am. City Com.; chmn. Ariz. Motion Picture Adv. Bd.; past chmn. adv. bd. on radio and TV, Ariz. State U.; bd. dirs. Central Ariz. Water Conservation Dist.; Nat. Cowboy Hall of Fame bd. dir. 1979—; pres., bd. dirs. Ariz. Children's Found. Named Man of Yr., City of Hope, 1962, NCCJ, 1967, B'nai B'rith Anti-Defamation League, 1975; Citizen of Yr., Phoenix Real Estate Bd., 1965; recipient Nat. Sch. Bell award, 1961; award U.S. Treasury Dept., 1961; Tom Chauncey award United Fund, 1962; Jesse Owens award; George Foster Peabody award, Disting. Achievement award Coll. Pub. Programs Ariz. State U., 1984. Mem. Ariz. (past pres., past dir., past mem. legis. com.), Met. Phoenix (past pres., dir.) broadcasters assns., Nat. Assn. Broadcasters, Nat. Acad. TV Arts and Scis. (Bd. Govs. award Phoenix chpt. 1962, past Ariz. bd. gov.), Mus. Broadcasting (hon.), Nat. Retail Jewelers Assn. (past dir.), Phoenix C. of C., Ariz. Quarterhorse Breeders Assn., Ariz. State Horseman's Assn., Ariz. Heart Inst. 1974—, Arabian Horse Assn. Ariz. (dir. 1972), Ariz. Hereford Assn., Ariz. Retail Jewelers Assn., Am. Gem Soc., TV Pioneers, Phoenix Press Box Assn. (life), Phoenix Thunderbirds, Navy League, Newcomen Soc. N. Am., Sigma Delta Chi. Elk. Clubs: Phoenix Country, Phoenix Execs.; Paradise Valley Country; Rancheros Vistacores; Cowman's. Author: Educational Contributions of Commercial Television, 1960. Tom and Dorothy Chauncey Student Loan Fund established at Ariz. State U. Home: 18000 N Scottsdale Rd Scottsdale AZ 85255-9617

CHAUNCEY, TOM WEBSTER, II, lawyer; b. Phoenix, May 30, 1947; s. Tom Webster and Kathryn (Geare) C.; m. Mary Kathleen LaCroix, Dec. 28, 1972. BA in Sociology with honors, Northwestern U., 1970; JD, Ariz. State U., 1973. Bar: Ariz. 1973, U.S. Dist. Ct. Ariz. 1973. Ptnr., mgt. com. Gust Rosenfeld, Phoenix; exec. v.p., counsel KOOL Radio-TV, Inc., Phoenix, 1972-82; gen. counsel, sta. mgr. KOOL-AM-FM, Phoenix, 1982-86; chmn. Cameras in the Courtroom Com., 1979-86; mem. bd. CBS Radio Network Affiliates, 1984-86. V.p. 1st Amendment Coalition, 1981-83, pres., 1984-85; bd. dirs. Park Found. of Phoenix, 1980-84, NCCJ, 1978—, rep. nat. exec. bd. 1986—; bd. dirs. Ariz. Bus.-Industry-Edn. Coun., Inc., 1979-83, Friendly House, 1983-84, Ariz. Community Found., 1981-85; mem. fin. com. YMCA Phoenix and Valley of Sun, 1974-80, mem. camp com., 1978-80; bd. dirs., mem. Project Pool It, Valley Forward Assn., 1977-83; mem. media adv. bd. Traffic Accident Reduction Task Force, 1980; bd. dirs. Meml. Hosp. Found., 1978-83, planning com., 1980-83, community rels. com., 1982-83; bd. dirs. Barrow Neurol. Found., 1979-89, mem. exec. com., 1980-89, v.p., 1983-85, pres., 1985-89, mem. investment com. 1985-89; bd. dirs. Ariz. Hist. Soc., 1982-84, mem. bldg. com., 1983, bylaws com., 1983; bd. dirs. Cen. Ariz. Mus. chpt., 1979-84, St. Joseph's Meml. Hosp., 1989-91; mem. fin. com., 1989-91, mem. strategic planning com., 1990-91, Found. for Blind Children, 1990-91, fin. com., 1990-91,, mem. pers. com., 1990-91; mem. Crisis Nursery, 1988-90; mem. Walter Cronkite Found. for Journalism and Telecommunications, Ariz. State U., 1982—, mem. fundraising com., 1986—, nominating com., 1986—; mem. task force on productivity Ariz. Supreme Ct. Commn. on Cts., 1988-89; mem. Maricopa County voter awareness com. 1986-88. Fellow Ariz. State Bar Found.; mem. ABA, Ariz. Bar Assn. (pub. rels. com. 1975-86, fee arbitration com. 1976-86), FCC Bar Assn., Lawyer-Pilots Bar Assn. (lawyer), Maricopa County Bar Assn. (past dir. Young Lawyers sect.), Ariz. Trial Lawyers Assn., Phoenix Assn. Def. Counsel, Orme Sch. Alumni Assn., Northwestern U. Alumni Assn. Phoenix (pres. 1975-76), Ariz. State U. Alumni Assn., Ariz. State U. Law Alumni Assn., Phoenix Press Club, Nat. Assn. Broadcasters, Ariz. Broadcasters Assn. (bd. dirs. 1985-86), Met. Phoenix Broadcasters (bd. dirs. 1976-86, v.p. 1984-85, pres. 1985-86), Phi Delta Phi, Sigma Delta Chi, Phi Gamma Delta. Office: Gust Rosenfeld 201 N Central Ave Ste 3300 Phoenix AZ 85073-3300

CHAVE, KEITH ERNEST, oceanographer, educator; b. Chgo., Jan. 18, 1928; s. Ernest John and Winnifred (Carruthers) C.; m. Edith Hunter, May 19, 1969; children: Alan D., Warren T. PhB, U. Chgo., 1948, SM, 1951, PhD, 1952. Research geochemist Chevron Research, La Habra, Calif., 1952-59; prof. geology Lehigh U., Bethlehem, Pa., 1959-67; prof. oceanography U. Hawaii, Honolulu, 1967—; pres. Palau Marine Research Inst., Koror, Palau, 1979—. Contbr. articles to profl. jours. Grantee NSF, 1960-80, ONR, 1960-80, NOAA Sea, 1970-86, ACS-PRF, 1960-88. Fellow AAAS; mem. Alex. Von Humboldt Stiftung (sr. U.S. Scientist), Geochem. Soc., Am. Geophys. Union, Am. Soc. Limnology and Oceanography, Sigma Xi. Home: 4935 Mana Pl Honolulu HI 96816-4009 Office: U Hawaii 1000 Pope Rd Honolulu HI 96822-2336

CHAVEZ, ALBERT BLAS, financial consultant; b. L.A., Jan. 1, 1952; s. Albert Blas and Yolanda (Garcia) C. BA, U. Tex., El Paso, 1979; MBA, Stanford U., 1985. CPA, Calif. Mem. profl. staff Deloitte Haskins and Sells, L.A., 1980-83; planning analyst corp. fin. planning Boise (Idaho) Cascade Co., 1984; treasury analyst corp. treasury RCA Corp., N.Y.C., 1985; asst. contr. RCA/Ariola Records, Mexico City, 1986; fin. analyst corp. exec. office GE Co., Fairfield, Conn., 1987-90; fin. cons. Entertainment Industry and Litigation Support Svcs., L.A., 1990-91; sr. v.p., chief fin. officer El Dorado Comm., Inc., L.A., 1991—. Bd. dirs., treas. L.A. Conservation Corps, 1990—. Mem. AICPA, Calif. Soc. CPAs, L.A. Trial Lawyers Assn. (affiliate mem.). Democrat. Home: 11701 Texas Ave # 312 Los Angeles CA 90025 Office: El Dorado Comm Inc Ste 307 2130 S Sawtelle Blvd Los Angeles CA 90025

CHAVEZ, DAVID MARIO, lawyer; b. Farmington, N.Mex., Jan. 15, 1955; s. David Flavio and Maria Delfinita (Gomez) C.; m. Grace Angela Coca, Sept. 26, 1981; children: Dominic, Alisha. BS, U. N.Mex., 1977; JD, U. Pa., 1980. Bar: N.Mex. 1980. Asst. dist. atty. Office Dist. Atty., Farmington, 1980-82; pvt. practice, Farmington, 1982—; spl. asst. atty. gen. child support enforcement div. Human Svcs. Dept., Farmington, 1989—; instr. bus. law San Juan Coll., Farmington, 1986. Mem. Sacred Heart Sch. Bd., Farmington, 1991—, Legal Svcs. Community Bd., Farmington, 1992—; col. a.d.c. Office Gov. N.Mex., Farmington, 1992. Recipient Disting. Svc. award Office Dist. Atty., 1982; scholar U. N.Mex., 1973-74, U. Pa., 1977. Mem. N.Mex. Bar Assn. (community edn. com. 1988—, bar disciplinary com. 1988—), San Juan County Bar Assn., N.Mex. Trial Lawyers Assn. Office: 333 E Main St Farmington NM 87401

CHAVEZ, EDWARD L., councilman; b. L.A., Dec. 9, 1963; s. Abenicio Pacheco and Magdalena (Peralta) C. BA, UCLA, 1989; AA, Rio Hondo Coll., Whittier, Calif., 1985; postgrad., Claremont (Calif.) Grad. Sch. Tchr. Whittier Union High Sch. Dist., 1990-91; adminstrv. asst. to state assemblywoman Sally Tanner Calif. Legislature, 1991-92. Councilman City of La Puente, Calif., 1990—; pres. bd. edn. Bassett Unified Sch. Dist., La Puente, 1987-91. Democrat. Roman Catholic. Office: City of La Puente 15900 E Main St La Puente CA 91744-4788

CHAVEZ, GILBERT ESPINOZA, bishop; b. Ontario, Calif., Mar. 19, 1932; ed. St. Francis Sem., El Cajon, Calif., Immaculate Heart Sem., San Diego, U. Calif., San Diego. Ordained priest Roman Cath. Ch., 1960; titular bishop of Magarmel and aux. bishop Diocese of San Diego, 1974—. Office: 1535 3rd Ave San Diego CA 92101-3192*

CHAVEZ, MARTIN JOSEPH, state senator, attorney; b. Albuquerque, Mar. 2, 1952; s. Lorenzo Armijo and Sara (Baca) C.; m. Margaret Chavez de Aragon, July 28, 1988; children: Martinique, Ezequiel Lorenzo. BS, U. N.Mex., 1975; JD, Georgetown, 1978. Mem. Med. Rev. Commn., 1990—; bd. dirs. Senior Arts Project, 1987—, Tree New Mex., 1991-92. State sen. State of N.Mex., Santa Fe, 1988—; mem. Citizens Rev. Bd., 1988—. Mem. N.Mex. Bar Assn. Home: 612 Palisades NW Albuquerque NM 87105

CHAYASIRISOBHON, SIRICHAI, physician, neurologist; b. Bangkok, Thailand, Oct. 15, 1944; came to U.S., 1979; s. Sui Po Tseng and Chantana Chayasirisobhon; m. Wanpen Chayasirisobhon; 1 child, Victor. BSc, Mahidol U., Bangkok, 1969, MD, 1971. Diplomate Am. Bd. Psychiatry and Neurology, Am. Bd. Electroencephalography. Intern Ministry of Pub. Health, Bangkok, 1971-72; resident dept. medicine & neurology Ramathipbodi Hosp.-Mahidol U., Bangkok, 1972-73; resident dept. neurology & neurosurgery Somdej Chaopraya Hosp., Bangkok, 1973-74; intern Royal Victoria Hosp.-McGill U., Montreal, Que., 1974-75, resident dept. medicine, 1975-76; resident dept. neurology Montreal Neurol. Inst. and Hosp.-McGill U., 1976-77; 6-month resident various other hosps., Montreal, 1977-79; fellow in epilepsy, electroencephalography & neurophysiology Lafayette Clinic-Wayne State U., Detroit, 1979-81; staff neurologist Lafayette Clinic, Detroit, 1980-82; asst. prof. dept. neurology Wayne State U., Detroit, 1981-83; staff neurologist dept. neurology Kaiser PermanenteMed. Ctr., Bellflower, Calif., 1983-88; co-dir. regional epilepsy program Kaiser PermanenteMed. Group Southern Calif., Anaheim, 1988—, dir. electroencephalography and neurogiagnostic lab., 1988—; assoc. prof. dept surg. neurology and epilepsy ctr. Charles R. Drews U., L.A., 1984—; acting dir. & adminstrv. dir. dept. neurology, clin. dir. sleep clinic Lafayette Clinic, 1981-82; asst. clin. prof. dept. neurology U. Calif.-Irvine, 1986-91, assoc. clin. prof., 1992—; vis. prof. Siriraj Med. Sch. Mahidol U., Bangkok, 1992; guest speaker various meetings. Author over 40 publs. in field. Recipient numerous rsch. grants. Mem. Am. Acad. Neurology, Am. Epilepsy Soc., Am. Med. Electroencephalographic Assn., Am. Electroencephalographic Soc., Western Electroencephalographic Soc. (chmn. membership com. 1988-91, bd. dirs. 1988-91), Thai Physician Assn. Am. (chmn. edn. & publ. Western chpt. 1986-91, mem. adv. bd. Western chpt. 1992—). Office: Kaiser Permanente Med Ctr 411 N Lake View Anaheim CA 92807

CHAYKIN, ROBERT LEROY, manufacturing and marketing executive; b. Miami, Fla., May 2, 1944; s. Allan Leroy and Ruth (Levine) C.; m. Patty Jean Patton, Feb. 1971 (div. May 1975); m. Evelyn Marcy Slodzina, Sept. 3, 1989; children: Michelle Alee, Catrina Celia, Ally Sue. BA in Polit. Sci., U. Miami, Fla., 1965, LLB, 1969. Owner, operator Serrating Svcs. Miami, 1969-71, Serrating Svcs. Las Vegas, Nev., 1971-84; pres. Ser-Sharp Mfg., Inc., Las Vegas, 1984—; nat. mktg. dir. Coserco Corp., Las Vegas, 1987—. Patentee in mfg. field. With U.S. Army, 1962. Recipient 2d degree black belt Tae Kwon Do, Profl. Karate Assn., 1954-61.

CHAZEN, MELVIN LEONARD, chemical engineer; b. St. Louis, Sept. 26, 1933; s. Saul and Tillie (Kramer) C.; m. Dorothea Glazer, June 29, 1958; children: Jamie Lynn, Avery Glazer. BS in Chem. Engring., Washington U., St. Louis, 1955. Registered profl. engr., Mo. Thermodynamics engr. Bell Aerospace Textron, Buffalo, 1958-59; devel. engr. Bell Aerospace Textron, 1959-62, project engr., 1962-65, chief sec. rocket engines, 1965-72, prog. mgr., tech. dir., 1972-74, project engr., 1974-84, chief engr. rocket devel., 1984-87; sr. staff engr. TRW-Applied Tech. div., Redondo Beach, Calif., 1987—; bd. dirs. Unimed Corp., Rochester. Contbr. articles to profl. jours. Mem. Alpha Chi Sigma. Home: 12522 Inglenook Ln Cerritos CA 90701-7837 Office: TRW Applied Tech Divsn One Space Park Redondo Beach CA 90278

CHECKETTS, KEITH THOMAS, psychology educator; b. Ogden, Utah, June 4, 1935; s. Thomas Leroy and Mable Marie (Wright) C.; m. Carol Donaldson, Aug 09, 1961; children: Mary Elizabeth, Melinda, Ruth, Michelle, Thomas Keith, Stanford Donaldson. BS, Utah State U., 1959; PhD, U. Minn., 1965. Cert. sch. counseling, sch. psychology. Tchr. Odgen (Utah) City Schs., 1959-61; instr. counselor U. Minn., Mpls., 1961-65; asst. prof. Utah State U., Logan, 1965-68; assoc. prof. Utah State U., 1968-74; visiting prof U. Penn., Phila., 1974-75; prof. Utah State U., 1975—; bd. trustees Am. Coll. Testing, Iowa City; cons. The Coll. Bd., N.Y., Ednl. Testing Svc., Princeton, N.J. Mem. Nat. Assn. State Bd. Edn. (bd. dirs.), Nat. Coun. Accreditation Tchr. Edn. (bd. examiners), Utah State Bd. Edn. (chmn. 1986-89, 92—). Mem. LDS Ch. Home: 1495 E 1140 N Logan UT 84321-2815

CHEDDAR, DONVILLE GLEN, chemist, educator; b. St. Mary, Jamaica, June 8, 1946; came to U.S., 1968; s. Joshua A. and Delmaria Adassa (Wilson) C.; children: Michael Glen, Angela Rose. BS in Chemistry, U. Oreg., 1973; PhD in Chemistry, U. Ariz., 1980. Lectr. U. West Indies, Kingston, Jamaica, 1981-83; rsch. biochemist U. Ariz., Tucson, 1984—. Contbr.: (textbook) Flash Photolysis and Pulse Radiolysis, 1983; contbr. articles to jours. Photochemistry and Photobiology, Biochemistry, Archives of Biochemistry and Biophysics. Group leader Youth Summer Program, Tucson, 1978. Office: Univ Ariz Bioscience W Tucson AZ 85721-0001

CHEDID, JOHN G., bishop; b. Eddid, Lebanon, July 4, 1923. Educated, Sems. in Lebanon and Pontifical Urban Coll., Rome. Ordained priest Roman Cath. Ch., 1951. Titular bishop of Callinico and aux bishop St. Maron of Bklyn., 1981. Office: Aux Bishop of St Maron 333 S San Vicente Blvd West Hollywood CA 90048-3313*

CHEE, PERCIVAL HON YIN, ophthalmologist; b. Honolulu, Aug. 29, 1936; s. Young Sing and Den Kyau (Ching) C.; m. Carolyn Tong, Jan. 27, 1966; children: Lara Wai Lung, Shera Wai Sum. BA, U. Hawaii, 1958; MD, U. Rochester, 1962. Intern Travis AFB Hosp., Fairfield, Calif., 1962-63; resident Bascom Palmer Eye Inst., Miami, Fla., 1965-68, Jackson Meml. Hosp., Miami, 1965-68; partner Straub Clinic, Inc., Honolulu, 1968-71; practice medicine specializing in ophthalmology, Honolulu, 1972—; mem. staffs Queen's Med. Center, St. Francis Hosp., Kapiolani Children's Med. Center, Honolulu; clin. assoc. prof. surgery U. Hawaii Sch. Medicine, 1971—; cons. Tripler Army Med. Center. Mem. adv. bd. Services to Blind; bd. dirs. Lions Eye Bank and Makana Found. (organ bank), Multiple Sclerosis Soc. Served to capt. USAF, 1962-65. Fellow Am. Acad. Ophthalmology, ACS; mem. AMA, Pan Am. Med. Assn., Pan Pacific Surg. Assn., Am. Assn. Ophthalmology, Soc. Eye Surgeons, Hawaii Ophthal. Soc. Pacific Coast Ophthal. Soc., Am. Assn. for Study Headache, Pan Am. Ophthal. Found. Contbr. articles to profl. pubs. Home: 3755 Poka Pl Honolulu HI 96816-4409 Office: Kukui Pla 50 S Beretania St Ste C116 Honolulu HI 96813-2298

CHEESEMAN, DOUGLAS TAYLOR, JR., wildlife tour executive, photographer, educator; b. Honolulu, July 16, 1937; s. Douglas Taylor Cheeseman and Myra (Bettencourt) Ehrlich; m. Gail Macomber, Apr. 7, 1963; children: Rosie M., Ted F. BA, San Jose (Calif.) State U., 1959, MA, 1964. Cert. secondary tchr., Calif. Naturalist Crater Lake (Oreg.) Nat. Park, summers 1959-60; tchr. biology Woodside High Sch., Redwood City, Calif., 1961-65; teaching asst. U. Colo., Boulder, 1966-67; prof. biology De Anza Coll., Cupertino, Calif., 1967—, dir. environ. study area, 1970—, dir. Student Ecology Rsch. Lab., 1990—; pres. Cheeseman's Ecology Safaris, Saratoga, Calif., 1981—; instr. wildlife and natural history photography, Saratoga, 1984—; rsch. cooperator Fish and Wildlife Svc., 1972—, guest lectr. numerous conservation groups, No. Calif., 1978—; speaker on rainforest destruction, zone depletion, global warming; participant, speaker to save planet; speaker Calif. Acad. Antarctic Ecology; expidition leader Sengey Vavilov, Antarctic, 1994; active in saving flora and fauna in third world. Photographs represented in books and on calendars. Recipient Outstanding Svc. and Tchr. award, Pres.'s award De Anza Coll., 1988, Nat. Leadership award U. Tex., Austin, 1989; NSF fellow, 1969, 71; NEDA Title III grantee, 1970. Mem. Ecol. Soc. Am., Am. Ornithologists Union, Am. Soc. Mammalogists, Brit. Trust Ornitology, Brit. Ornithologists Union, AfricanWildlife Soc., Marine Mammal Soc. (founding), Calif. Native Plants Soc., Bay Area Bird Photographers (co-founder), Santa Clara Valley Audubon Soc. (bd. dirs., v.p., program chmn. 1983—), Cooper Soc. Home: 20800 Kittridge Rd Saratoga CA 95070-6322 Office: De Anza Coll Dept Biology Cupertino CA 95014

CHEEVER, DAN J., bank executive; b. Watertown, S.D., Aug. 23, 1955; s. Gene G. and JoAnn (Coughlin) C.; m. Janet Olsen, Sept. 5, 1981; children: Nicole M., Alison L. BS in Bus./Acctg., U. S.D., 1977; postgrad. advanced exec. program, Northwestern U., Evanston, Ill., 1991. CPA, Colo. Sr. auditor Ernst & Whinney, Denver, 1977-80; asst. contr. Empire Savs., Denver, 1980-81; sr. v.p., treas. Silverado Banking, Denver, 1981-88; sr. v.p., treas. PriMerit Bank, Las Vegas, 1989-90, exec. v.p., chief fin. officer, 1990-91, pres., COO, 1991-92, pres., CEO, 1992—, also bd. dirs.; bd. dirs. PriMerit Investor Svcs. Mem. adv. bd. dirs. Las Vegas Natural History Mus., 1990, St. Jude's Ranch for Children. Mem. Fin. Mgrs. Soc. Republican. Roman Catholic. Office: PriMerit Bank 3300 W Sahara Ave Las Vegas NV 89102-6066

CHEIFETZ, LORNA GALE, psychologist; b. Phoenix, Mar. 22, 1953; d. Walter and Ruth Cheifetz. BS, Chapman Coll., Orange, Calif., 1975; D of Psychology, Ill. Sch. Profl. Psychology, 1981. Psychology intern Cook County Hosp., Chgo., 1979-80; clin. psychologist City of Chgo., 1980-84, Phoenix Inst. for Psychotherapy, 1984-87; pvt. practice Phoenix, 1987—; cons. to judges, attys., cts., 1984—; adj. faculty Met. U., Phoenix, 1984-88, Ill. Sch. Profl. Psychology, 1982-86. Contbr. chpt. to book Listening and Interpreting, 1984; contbg. editor Internat. Jour. Communicative Psychoanalysis and Psychotherapy, 1991—. Cons., vol. Ariz. Bar Assn. Vol. Lawyer Program, 1985—; co-coord. Psychology Info. Referral Svc., Maricopa County, Ariz., 1984—. Named Psychologist of Yr. Ariz. Bar Assn., 1987. Mem. Am. Psychol. Assn. (activist 1989—), Ariz. Psychol. Assn. (activist 1989—), Maricopa Psychol. Soc., Nat. Register Health Svc. Providers in Psychology, Soc. for Psychoanalytic Psychotherapy, Assn. Family and Concilliation Cts., Phoenix Psychoanalytic Study Group. Office: 2211 E Highland Ave Ste 135 Phoenix AZ 85016-4833

CHEN, BASILIO, engineering executive; b. Panama, Republic of Panama, Mar. 10, 1953. BEE, Calif. State Poly. U., 1974; MAS, U. Brit. Columbia, Vancouver, 1976. Engr. Nat. Inst. Tech., Panama, 1970, Wescom, Inc., Santa Clara, Calif., 1978-79; engring. mgr. Rolm, Corp., Santa Clara, 1979-81; cons. Engring. Mgmt. cons., Daly City, Calif., 1981-84; pres. Evotech, Inc., Burlingame, Calif., 1984—. Life mem. Gway Sen Assn., San Francisco, 1990. Mem. IEEE, Profl. Assn. Tech. Cons., Internat. Computer Cons. Assn., Asian Am. Mfrs. Assn., Eta Kappa Nu, Tau Beta Pi. Office: Evotech Inc 875 Cowan Rd Ste 203B Burlingame CA 94010-1204

CHEN, FRANCIS F., physics and engineering educator; b. Canton, Kwangtung, Republic of China, Nov. 18, 1929; s. M. Conrad and Evelyn (Chu) C.; m. Edna Lau Chen, Mar. 31, 1956; children: Sheryl F., Patricia A., Robert F. AB, Harvard U., 1950, MA, 1951, PhD, 1954. Research staff mem. Princeton (N.J.) Plasma Physics Lab., 1954-69; prof. elec. engring. UCLA, 1969—; chmn. plasma physics div. Am. Phys. Soc., N.Y.C., 1983. Author: Introduction to Plasma Physics and Controlled Fusion, 1974, 2d edit., 1984; contbr. over 100 articles to sci. jours. Fellow IEEE, Am. Phys. Soc.; mem. N.Y. Acad. Scis., Fusion Power Assocs., Phi Beta Kappa. Office: U Calif L A 56-125B Engr IV Mail code 159410 Los Angeles CA 90024

CHEN, HAN-PING, computer scientist; b. Quemoy, Fukien, China, Aug. 6, 1949; came to U.S., 1972; s. Chao-Kwi and Chin-Hua C. BS, Chiao Tung U., Hsinchu, Taiwan, 1970; PhD, UCLA, 1981. Sr. engr. Delphi Communications, L.A., 1977-79; prin. engr. Litton Data Systems, Van Nuys, Calif., 1979; project mgr. Xerox Corp., El Segundo, Calif., 1979-82; mgr. Mattel Electronics, Hawthorne, Calif., 1982-84, Hughes Aircraft Co., El Segundo, 1985-89; pres. Teledata, L.A., 1989—. Mem. IEEE, Chinese Am. Profl. Soc. (pres. 1989—), Eta Kappa Nu, Tau Beta Pi, PhiKappa Phi, Upsilon Pi Epsilon. Home: 341 S Maple Dr Los Angeles CA 90212

CHEN, JEI-PO, physician; b. Chia-Yi, Taiwan, Republic of China, July 27, 1936; came to U.S., 1967; s. Chin-Shu and Fu-Yon (Kuo) C.; m. Suphie Lin, May 23, 1967; 1 child, Charles. MD, Nat. Taiwan U., 1965. Rotating intern Sisters of Charity Hosp., Buffalo, 1967-68, resident in internal medicine, 1968-71; fellow in hematology L.I. Jewish Med. Ctr., New Hyde Park, N.Y., 1972-73; mem. governing bd. Doctors Hosp. of Montclair and Ontario (Calif.) Hosp., Calif., 1991—; v.p. Chemco Internat. Co. Mem. Med. Soc. Calif., Med. Soc. San Bernardino County. Address: 534 N Campus Ave Ontario CA 91764-3302

CHEN, JOHN CALVIN, child psychiatrist; b. Augusta, Ga., Apr. 30, 1949; s. Calvin Henry Chen and Lora (Lee) Liu. BA, Pacific Union Coll., 1971; MD, Loma Linda U., 1974; PhD in Philosophy, Claremont Grad. Sch., 1984; JD, UCLA, 1987. Bar: Calif. 1987; diplomate Am. Bd. Psychiatry and Neurology, 1982. Gen. resident in psychiatry Loma Linda U. Med. Ctr., 1975-77; fellow in child and family psychiatry Cedars-Sinai Med. Ctr., L.A., 1977-78; psychiat. cons. San Bernadino (Calif.) County Mental Health Dept., 1979-83; pvt. practice psychiatry Claremont, Calif., 1980-84; fellow in child and family psychiatry U. So. Calif., L.A., 1983-84; law clk. to Hon. William P. Gray U.S. Dist. Ct., L.A., 1987-88; mental health psychiatrist L.A. County Mental Health Dept., L.A., 1988—; adj. instr. philosophy Fullerton (Calif.) Coll., 1989-90. Univ. fellow Claremont Grad. Sch., 1980-81. Office: Mental Health Clinic Cen Juvenile Hall 1605 Eastlake Ave Los Angeles CA 90033

CHEN, NAI-FU, finance educator; b. Hong Kong, Nov. 24, 1950; came to U.S., 1968; s. Lee (Wong) Chen;m. Victoria Ma, Feb. 1, 1975; children: Nicole, Ellen. AB in Math., U. Calif., Berkeley, 1972, PhD in Math., 1975; PhD in Finance, UCLA, 1981. Asst. prof. math. U. So. Calif., L.A., 1976-78; asst. prof. econs. U. Calif., Santa Barbara, 1980-81; asst. prof. finance U. Chgo., 1981-85, assoc. prof. finance, 1985-89; prof. finance U. Calif., Irvine, 1989—; prof., head fin. Hong Kong U. Sci. and Tech., 1990—; docent fin. Swedish Sch. Econs. and Bus. Adminstrn., Helsinki, 1991—; exec. cons. Roll & Ross Asset Mgmt., Culver City, Calif., 1989—. Contbr. articles to profl. jours. Mem. Am. Finance Assn.

CHEN, PETER WEI-TEH, mental health services administrator; b. Fuchow, Fukien, Republic of China, July 20, 1942; came to U.S., 1966; s. Mao-Chuang and Sheu-Lin (Wang) C.; m. Lai-Wah Mui, Nov. 8, 1969; children: Ophelia Mei-Chuang, Audrey Mei-Hui. BA, Nat. Chung Hsing U., Taipei, Taiwan, Republic of China, 1964; MSW, Calif. State U., Fresno, 1968; D of Social Work, U. So. Calif., 1976. Case worker Cath. Welfare Bur., L.A., 1968-69; psychiat. social worker L.A. County Mental Health Svcs., 1969-78, mental health svcs. coordinator, 1978; sr. rsch. analyst Jud. and Legis. Bur. L.A. County Dept. Mental Health, 1978-79; Forensic In-Patient Program dir. L.A. County Dept. Mental Health, 1979-86, chief Jail Mental Health Svcs., 1986-89, asst. dep. dir. Adult Svc. Bur., 1989, dir. specialized commnunity programs, 1989—; pres. Orient Social and Health Soc., Los Angeles, 1973-75; bd. dirs. Am. Correctional Health Assn., 1986-87. Author: Chinese-Americans View Their Mental Health, 1976. Bd. dirs. San Marino (Calif.) Community Chest, 1986-87; trustee San Marino Schs. Found., 1987-90; advisor San Marino United Way, 1989—. 2d lt. Chinese Marine Corps, Taiwan, Republic of China, 1964-65. Recipient several community service awards. Mem. Nat. Assn. Social Workers (bd. dirs. Calif. chpt. 1979-80), Nat. Correctional Health Assn., Forensic Mental Health Assn. Calif. Clubs: Chinese of San Marino (pres. 1987-88), San Marino City. Home: 2161 E California Blvd San Marino CA 91108-1348 Office: LA County Dept Mental Health 505 S Virgil Ave Los Angeles CA 90020-1403

CHEN, STEPHEN SHAU-TSI, psychiatrist, physiologist; b. Tou-Nan, Yun-Lin, Taiwan, Aug. 18, 1934; s. R-Yue and Pi-Yu (Huang) C.; m. Clara Chin-Chin Liu, Sept. 7, 1936; children: David, Timothy, Hubert. MD, Nat. Taiwan U., Taipei, 1959; PhD, U. Wis., 1968. Diplomate Am. Bd. Psychiatry and Neurology, also sub. bd. Geriatric Psychiatry. Intern Nat. Taiwan U. Hosp., 1959; instr. dept. physiology U. Wis., Madison, 1968-71, asst. prof., 1971-75; resident in psychiatry SUNY, Stony Brook, 1975-78; asst. prof. psychiatry dept. psychiatry U. Pitts., 1978-80; asst. prof. psychiatry dept. psychiatry and behavioral sci. U. Wash., Seattle, 1981-86, clin. asst. prof. psychiatry, 1986—; chief mental health clinic VA Med. Ctr., Tacoma, 1981-85. Contbr. articles to Am. Jour. Physiol., Jour. Physiology, Can. Jour. Physiology and Pharmacology, Acta Physiol. Fellow Wis. Heart Assn., 1966-68. Mem. APA, North Pacific Soc. Neurology and Psychiatry, Formosan Assn. for Pub. Affairs (pres. Seattle chpt. 1986-88, bd. dir. Washington chpt. 1988-89). Presbyterian. Office: VA Med Ctr Psychiatry Svc Tacoma WA 98394

CHEN, THEODORE TIEN YIU, academic, financial administrator; b. Shanghai, Kiangsu, People's Republic of China, Sept. 1, 1946; arrived in Can., 1965; s. Hung Chuan and Ming Yih Chen; m. Yuli Tang, May 5, 1973; children: Emily Helen, Timothy Evan. B of Commerce, McGill U., 1969; MBA, U. B.C., 1971. Cert. mgmt. acct. Credit officer Fed. Bus. Devel. Bank, Vancouver, B.C., 1972; spl. projects analyst Gulf Oil Can. Ltd., Vancouver, 1973; corp. fin. analyst B.C. Forest Products Ltd., Vancouver, 1973-74; faculty fin. mgmt. B.C. Inst. Tech., Burnaby, 1974-77; mgr. fin. planning & analysis Freightliner of Can. Ltd., Burnaby, 1977-79; mgr. budgets & fin. analysis B.C. Liquor Distbn. Br., Vancouver, 1979-87; assoc. dir. Enterprise Ctr. Simon Fraser U., Burnaby, 1988-89; asst. dean adminstrv. svcs. Vancouver Community Coll., 1989-90, dir. fin. svcs., 1990-92; cert. mgmt. accountant Theodore T.Y. Chen, Vancouver, 1992—; sessional instr. Simon Fraser U., Burnaby, 1988—. Co-author: Advanced Management Accounting, 1978. Vice chmn., sec. Newbern Meml. Chinese Alliance Ch., Vancouver, 1986-88, 91—; treas. Alzheimer Soc. of B.C., Vancouver, 1987-88. Mem. Soc. Mgmt. Accts. of B.C. (bd. dirs. 1986-88, ednl. svcs. com. 1984-86).

CHEN, YUNG-LIN, research chemist, consultant; b. Keelung, Taiwan, Republic of China, Oct. 26, 1952; came to U.S., 1977; s. Chian-Hsing Chen and Jao-Jeng Yang; m. Yu-Ying Maria Chen, Feb. 2, 1978; children: Kai-Shi, Kenny, Kai-Jay, Keith. BS, Nat. Chung-Hsing, Taichung, Taiwan, 1974; MS, Iowa State U., 1983, PhD, 1986. Rsch. assoc. Carnegie Mellon Univ., Pitts., 1986-88; sr. rsch. chemist J & W Sci., Folsom, Calif., 1988—; cons. United West Coast Trading Inc., Richmond, Calif., 1986—. Mem. AAAS, Am. Chem. Soc., Chinese Am. Chem. Soc. Office: J & W Sci 91 Blue Ravine Rd Folsom CA 95630-4714

CHENEY, DICK (RICHARD BRUCE CHENEY), former secretary of defense, former congressman; b. Lincoln, Nebr., Jan. 30, 1941; s. Richard Hebert and Marjorie Lauraine (Dickey) C.; m. Lynne Anne Vincent, Aug. 29, 1964; children: Elizabeth, Mary Claire. B.A., U. Wyo., 1965, M.A., 1966; postgrad., U. Wis., 1966-68. Staff aide to Gov. Warren Knowles, Wis., 1966; mem. staff Congressman William A. Steiger, 1969; spl. asst. to dir. OEO, Washington, 1969-70; dep. to counsellor to Pres. The White House, Washington, 1970-71; asst. dir. Cost of Living Council, 1971-73; dep. asst. to Pres. The White House, Washington, 1974-75, asst. to Pres., 1975-77; ptnr. Bradley, Woods and Co., 1973-74; mem. 96th-100th Congresses from Wyo., 1979-89, Rep. Whip, 1987-88; sec. U.S Dept. of Defense, Washington, 1989-92; sr. fellow Am. Enterprise Inst., Washington, 1993—; chmn. Rep. Conf., 1981-87; chmn. Rep. Policy Com. Named One of 10 outstanding young men in Am., U.S. Jaycees, 1976; Congl. fellow Am. Polit. Sci. Assn., 1968-69. Republican. Office: Am Enterprise Inst 1150 17th St NW Washington DC 20036

CHENEY, ELIZABETH JOAN, secretarial service company executive; b. Oshkosh, Wis., Oct. 17, 1924; d. Edward John and Esther Johanna (Deysenroth) Haase; m. William George Cheney, May 18, 1946 (div. May 1959); children: Stephen Charles, Susan Elizabeth, Lee Edward. Profl. sec. cert., Oshkosh Bus. Coll., 1946; student, Victor Valley Coll., 1970-86. Sec., med. asst. John W. Stevens, M.D., Apple Valley, Calif., 1957-58; sec. to mgr. Apple Valley Inn, 1958-61, Hesperia (Calif.) Inn., 1961-62; dep. city clk., sec. City of Victorville, Calif., 1962-66; exec. sec. Tatum Constrn. Corp., Victorville, 1967-69, Victor Valley Coll., 1970-86; owner, mgr. Letter Perfect Secretarial Service, Apple Valley, 1987—; cons., sec. AAUW, VVC, Victorville, 1985—. Vol. sec. Apple Valley Sci. and Tech. Ctr., 1989—, Apple Valley Airport Commn., San Bernardino County Horseman's Assn., Victorville; mem. water and sewer adv. com. Town Apple Valley. Mem. Macintosh/Apple Computer User Group for Victor Valley Area (sec., 1990—, bd. dirs.). Lutheran. Office: Letter Perfect Secreterial Svc PO Box 652 Apple Valley CA 92307-0011

CHENG, HENG-DA, computer scientist; b. Shenyang, Liaoning, China, May 1, 1944; came to U.S., 1980; s. Ji Cheng and Yu-Zhi Pan; m. Xiaohong Hao (Haybina Hao); children: Yang-Yang, Yue-Yue, Lydia. BS, Harbin (China) Inst. Tech., 1967; MS, Wayne State U., 1981; PhD, Purdue U., 1985. Instr. Harbin Shipbuilding Inst., 1971-76; rschr., technician Harbin Railway Sci. and Tech. Rsch. Inst., Harbin, 1976-78; vis. asst. prof. U. Calif., Davis, 1985-86; asst. prof. Concordia U., Montreal, Que., Can., 1987-88; assoc. prof. Tech. U. Nova Scotia, Halifax, Can., 1988-91, Utah State U., Logan, 1991—; co-chair Vision Interface '90, The Fourth Can. Conf., Halifax, 1990; com. mem. Vision Interface '92, 1992. Co-editor: Pattern Recognition: Architectures, Algorithms and Applications, 1991; contbr. articles to profl. jours. and confs.; reviewer sci. jours. and confs. Grantee Natural Scis. and Engring. Rsch. Coun. Can., NSF, 1987—. Mem. IEEE Soc. (sr.), IEEE Computer Soc., IEEE Circuits and System Soc., IEEE Geosci. and Remote Sensing Soc., IEEE Robotics and Automation Soc., IEEE System, Man and Cybernetics Soc., IEEE Signal Processing Soc., IEEE Engring. in Medicine and Biology Soc., Assn. for Computing Machinery. Office: Utah State Univ Dept Computer Sci Logan UT 84322-4205

CHENG, WAN-LEE, industrial technology educator, mechanical engineer; b. Yi-Hsin, Chaing-Su, Republic of China, Dec. 28, 1945; came to U.S., 1971; s. Teh-Chih and Mei-Nung (Shih) C.; m. Viki Shu-Whei Lu, Dec. 16, 1972; children: Julie Wheichung, Paul Yichung, Lisa Yenchung. BS, Chung Yuan U., Taiwan, 1969; MEd, Sul Ross State U., 1972; PhD, Iowa State U., 1976. Mech. engr. Taiwan Power Co., Taipei, 1970-71; instr. Iowa State U., Ames, 1974-76; asst. prof., then prof. U. N.D., Grand Forks, 1976-85; prof., chmn. dept. design and industry San Francisco State U., 1985—; cons. High-Tech Mobile Lab., N.D. Vocat. Edn. Dept., Bismarck, 1984-85; vis. prof. Nat. Sci. Coun. and Chung Yuan U., Taiwan, Republic of China, 1990-91. Author computer software; contbr. articles to profl. jours.; mem. rev. bd. Jour. Indsl. Tech., 1986—. Session elder 1st Presbyn. Ch., Grand Forks, 1984-85; session elder Lakeside Presbyn. Ch., 1989-91. Recipient Indsl. Arts Profl. Devel. award N.D. Indsl. Arts Assn., Bismarck, 1985, Outstanding Teaching and Faculty Devel. award Burlington No. Found., Grand Forks, 1985, Outstanging Prof. Indsl. Tech. award Nat. Assn. Indsl. Tech., 1992; 10 grants U. N.D., 1979-85. Mem. Soc. Mfg. Engrs. (sr.), Chinese Inst. Engrs. (v.p. 1993), Chung Yuan Alumni Assn. No. Calif. (pres. San Francisco 1987-88), Joint Alumni Assn. Chinese Univs. and Colls. No. Calif. (pres. San Francisco, 1988-89), Phi Kappa Phi, Epsilon Pi Tau (trustee Gamma Gamma chpt. Grand Forks 1984-85, Laureate award Beta Beta chpt. San Francisco 1991). Office: San Francisco State Univ Dept of Design and Industry 1600 Holloway Ave San Francisco CA 94132-1722

CHENOWETH, WALTER A, real estate developer; b. L.A., Feb. 4, 1930; s. Walter A. and Jean (Stone) C.; m. Charlanne Swanson, Feb. 7, 1953; children: Walter A. III, Elizabeth. BA, UCLA, 1953; MBA, Harvard U., 1959. Various positions IBM, 1959-70; pres. Computer Intelligence Corp., San Diego, 1970-74; sr. v.p. Coldwell Banker Comml. Real Estate, Carlsbad, Calif., 1974-86; pres. Sterling Pacific Devel., Rancho Santa Fe, Calif., 1986—; dir. Computer Intelligence Corp., San Diego, 1970-80, Home Thrift & Loan, San Diego, 1988—. Home: PO Box 1808 Rancho Santa Fe CA 92067 Office: Sterling Pacific Devel PO Box 2287 Rancho Santa Fe CA 92067

CHENOWETH, WILLIAM LYMAN, consulting geologist; b. Wichita, Kans., Sept. 16, 1928; s. Bertrum and Bessie (Lyman) C.; m. Miriam Bernadine Pawlicki, Jan. 6, 1955; children: Mary, Martin, Peter, Paul. AB, Wichita State U., 1951; postgrad., N.Mex. Sch. of Mines, 1949; MS, U. N.Mex., 1951. Geologist AEC, Navajo Indian Reservation, Ariz., 1953-55, project geologist, 1955-57, area geologist, 1957-62; project geologist AEC, Grand Junction, Colo., 1962-74, staff geologist, 1975-77; staff geologist U.S. Dept. of Energy, Grand Junction, 1977-81, chief geologist, 1981-83; pvt. practice cons. geologist Grand Junction, 1984—; rsch. assoc. N.Mex. Bur. Mines, Socorro, 1984—. Editor: Colorado Uranium, 1981. Staff sgt. USNG, 1955-59. Fellow Geol. Soc. Am.; mem. Am. Assn. Petroleum Geologists (chmn. nuclear minerals com. 1982—), Rocky Mountain Assn. Geologists (Cert. of Recognition 1980), N.Mex. Geol. Soc. Democrat. Roman Catholic. Home: 707 Brassie Dr Grand Junction CO 81506-3911

CHERIS, ELAINE GAYLE INGRAM, business owner; b. Ashford, Ala., Jan. 8, 1946; m. Samuel David Cheris, June 8, 1980; 1 child, Zachariah Adam Abraham. BS, Troy State U., 1971. Aquatics dir. Yale U., New Haven, 1976-79; owner, mgr. Cheyenne Fencing Soc., Denver, 1980—; chmn. organizing com. World Fencing Championships, 1989; chmn. World Jr./Cadet Fencing Championships, 1993. Author: Handbook for Parents - Fencing, 1988, 2d edit., 1992; editor Yofen Mag., 1988-90, 1992—. Mem. Gov.'s Coun. on Sports and Fitness, Colo., 1990—; commr. Colo. State Games-Fencing, 1989—. Mem. U.S. Olympic Team, 1980, 88 (6th place fencing), 92; named Sportswoman of Yr. Fencing, YWCA, 1980, 81, 82, to Sportswomen Hall of Fame, 1982; mem. U.S. World Championship Fencing Team, 1982, 85, 87, 90, 91, 92, 93, U.S. Maccabiah Fencing Team, 1981 (1 gold, 1 silver medal); recipient Gold Medal of Honor from Fedn. Internat. d'Escrime. Mem. AAPHERD, U.S. Fencing Assn. (youth chmn. 1988-90, editor Youth Mag., 1988-90, 92—, chmn. Colo. divsn., 1992—), Féderation International d'Escrime (co-chmn. Atlanta fencing project '96). Jewish. Office: Cheyenne Fencing Soc 5818 E Colfax Ave Denver CO 80220

CHERKIN, ADINA, interpreter, translator; b. Geneva, Nov. 22, 1921; came to U.S., 1940; d. Herz N. and Genia (Kodriansky) Mantchik; m. Arthur Cherkin, Mar. 14, 1943 (div. Sept. 1980); children: Della Peretti, Daniel Craig. BA, UCLA, 1942, MA in Russian Linguistics, 1977. Pvt. practice med. interpreter L.A., 1942-80; translator UCLA Med. Sch., 1970-79; pres. acad. forum Jewish studies Herz Mantchik Amity Cir., L.A., 1973—. Author numerous poems. Active L.A. Internat. Vis. Coun., 1991—; pub. rels. Judge Stanley Mosk's Campaign, L.A., 1960; vol. Gov. Cranston's Campaign, 1960. Recipient Community Svc. award L.A. City Coun., 1992. Mem. Am. Soc. for Technion Israel Inst. Tech. (nat. bd. regents 1991—). Home and Office: 2369 N Vermont Ave Los Angeles CA 90027

CHERN, SHIING-SHEN, mathematics educator; b. Kashing, Chekiang, China, Oct. 26, 1911; s. Lien Ching and Mei (Han) C.; m. Shih-ning Chern, July 28, 1939; children—Paul, May. B.S., Nankai U., Tientsin, China, 1930; M.S., Tsing Hua U., Peiping, 1934; D.Sc., U. Hamburg, Germany, 1936, D.Sc. (hon.), 1972; D.Sc. (hon.), U. Chgo., 1969, SUNY-Stony Brook, 1985; LL.D. honoris causa, Chinese U., Hong Kong, 1969; Dr. Math (hon.), Eidgenossische Technische Hochschule, Zurich, Switzerland, 1982. Prof. math. Nat. Tsing Hua U., China, 1937-43; mem. Inst. Advanced Study, Princeton, N.J., 1943-45; acting dir. Inst. Mathematics, Academia Sinica, China, 1946-48; prof. math. U. Chgo., 1949-60, U. Calif., Berkeley, 1960-79; prof. emeritus U. Calif., 1979—; dir. Math. Scis. Rsch. Inst., 1981-84, dir. emeritus, 1984—; dir. Inst. Mathematics, Tianjin, P.R., China. hon. prof. various fgn. univs.; Recipient Chauvenet prize Math. Assn. Am., 1970, Nat. Medal of Sci., 1975, Wolf prize Israel, 1983-84. Fellow Third World Acad. Sci. (founding mem. 1985); mem. NAS, Am. Math. Soc. (Steele prize 1983), Am. Acad. Arts and Scis., N.Y. Acad. Scis. (hon. life), Am. Philos. Soc., Indian Math. Soc. (hon.), Brazilian Acad. Scis. (corr.), Academia Sinica, Royal Soc. London (fgn.), Academia Peloritana (corr. mem. 1986), London Math. Soc. (hon.)., Acad. des sciences Paris (fgn. mem.), Acad. der Lincei Rome (stranieri). Home: 8336 Kent Ct El Cerrito CA 94530-2548 Office: Univ Calif Berkeley Dept of Mathematics Berkeley CA 94720

CHERNIN, PETER, motion picture company executive. Pres. entertainment group Fox Broadcasting Co., L.A.; chmn. Twentieth Century Fox Film Corp., Beverly Hills, Calif., 1992—. Office: 20th Century Fox Film Corp PO Box 900 Beverly Hills CA 90213

CHERNOFF-PATE, DIANA, interior designer, small business owner; b. San Mateo, Calif., Apr. 7, 1942; d. Fred Eugene and Nadine (Chernoff) Pate; 1 child, Kim Renee. BA in Design, U. Calif., Berkeley. Lic. cosmetologist, Calif. Owner, mgr. Diana Interiors, Napa, Calif.; co-owner, v.p., mgr. ops. Stickney Enterprises, Redwood, Calif., Stickney Restaurants and Bakeries, Redwood; pub. rels. specialist, coord. passenger svc. tng. TWA, San Francisco; adminstr. Internat. Fed. Employees Benefits, 1973, Pension Funds, 1982. Author: Cooking for Profit. Co-sponsor Stanford Athletic Fund, Stanford U.; mem. Frank Lloyd Wright Found. Mem. LWV (Carmel br.), NAFE, Embroiderers Guild of Am. (founder San Mateo and Santa Clara chpts.), World Affairs Coun., Designers Lighting Forum, Inst. Noetic Scis., Am. Assn. Retired Persons, Am. Soc. Phys. Rsch., San Francisco De Young Mus., San Francisco Asian Mus., San Francisco Ballet, Commonwealth Club Calif. Home: 1220 Cayetano Dr Napa CA 94558

CHERRY, LEE OTIS, scientific institute director; b. Oakland, Calif., Nov. 20, 1944; s. Knorvel and Lucy (Grayson) C.; m. Lauren Michelle Waters, Aug. 30, 1980; children: Aminah L., Jamilah L. AA, Merritt Community Coll., Oakland, Calif., 1965; BSEE, San Jose State U., 1968. Systems analyst IBM, San Francisco, 1968-69; elec. engr. Pacific Gas & Elec., Oakland, Calif., 1969-79; project mgr. Navy Facility, Dept. Def., Washington, 1979-84, San Bruno, Calif., 1984—; co-founder, exec. dir. African Sci. Inst., Oakland, 1967—; sr. cons. Devel. Cons. & Assocs., Oakland, 1972—; proprietor L & L & Assocs., Oakland, 1980—. Pubr. mo. mag. "Technology Transfer", 1979-83, quar. newspaper "SciTech", 1988—; developer calendar: Blacks in Science, 1986—. Mem. Ghanaian-Am. C. of C. (co-founder, bd. dirs. 1990—). Office: African Scientific Inst PO Box 12161 Oakland CA 94604-2161

CHESHIRE, WILLIAM POLK, newspaper columnist; b. Durham, N.C., Feb. 2, 1931; s. James Webb and Anne Ludlow (McGehee) C.; m. Lucile Geoghegan, Aug. 1, 1959; children—William Polk, Helen Wood Cheshire Elder, James Webb. A.B., U. N.C., Chapel Hill, 1958. Reporter Richmond News Leader, Va., 1958-61; assoc. editor Canton (N.C.) Enterprise, 1961-62, Charleston Evening Post, S.C., 1963-68, The State, Columbia, S.C., 1968-72; editorial dir. Capital Broadcasting Co., Raleigh, N.C., 1972-75; editorial page editor Greensboro Record, N.C., 1975-78; editor-in-chief Charleston Daily Mail, W.Va., 1978-84; editor, editorial pages Washington Times, 1984-87; editor, editorial pages The Ariz. Republic, Phoenix, 1987-93, sr. editorial columnist, 1993—; prof. journalism U. Charleston, 1979-83; commentator Voice of Am., 1986-87. Dir. comm. N.C. Senate Campaign, 1972; bd. dirs. Sunrise Mus., Charleston United Way, 1978-84. With USCG, 1952-56. Recipient Council for the Def. Freedom award, 1980, George Washington Honor medal Freedoms Found., 1975; named Disting. Fellow in Journalism, Heritage Found., 1987; Media fellow Hoover Instn., 1991. Mem. N.C. Soc. Cin. (pres. 1988-91), Phila. Soc., Nat. Press Club, Phoenix Country Club, Ariz. Club, Sigma Delta Chi (pres. Piedmont chpt. 1978). Anglican. Office: The Ariz Republic 120 E Van Buren St Phoenix AZ 85004-2200

CHESNUT, CAROL FITTING, economist; b. Pecos, Tex., June 17, 1937; d. Ralph Ulf and Carol (Lowe) Fitting; m. Dwayne A. Chesnut, Dec. 27, 1955; children: Carol Marie, Michelle, Mark Steven. BA magna cum laude, U. Colo., 1971; student Hastings Coll. Law, 1991—. Research asst. U. Colo., 1972; head quality controller Mathematica, Inc., Denver, 1973-74; cons. Mincome Man., Winnipeg, Can., 1974; cons. economist Energy Cons. Associates, Inc., Denver, 1974-79; exec. v.p. tng. ECA Intercomp, 1980-81; gen. ptnr. Chestnut Consortium, S.F., 1981—; sec., bd. dirs. Critical Resources, Inc., 1981-83. Rep. Lakehurst Civic Assn., 1968; staff aide Senator Gary Hart, 1978; Dem. precinct capt., 1982-88. Mem. ABA, Am. Mgmt. Assn., Soc. Petroleum Engrs., Am. Nuclear Soc. (chmn. conv. space activities for 1989, chair of spouse activities 1989), Am. Geophys. Union, Assn. Women Geoscientists (treas. Denver 1983-85), ACLU, NOW, AAUW (1st v.p. 1989-90), Associated Students of Hastings (rep.), Amador Valley Quilters, Century Club, Phi Beta Kappa, Phi Chi Theta. Unitarian. Office: 100 McAllister St Apt 2101 San Francisco CA 94102-4944

CHESTER, MARVIN, physics educator; b. N.Y.C., Dec. 29, 1930; s. Herman and Sadye Chester; m. Sandra (div. 1963); children: Lisa, Karen; m. Elfi Bollert, July 30, 1977; children: Chiam Peter, Sadye Vera. BS, CCNY, 1952; PhD, Calif. Inst. Tech., 1961. Prof. physics U. Calif., L.A., 1961-92, prof. emeritus, 1992—; sr. rsch. fellow U. Sussex, Eng., 1973. Author: Primer of Quantum Mechanics, 1987; contbr. articles to profl. jours. Recipient Alexander von Humboldt award, Von Humboldt Stifftung, 1974-75. Mem. Am. Phys. Soc., N.Y. Acad. Sci. Office: UCLA Dept Physics Los Angeles CA 90024

CHESTER, SHARON ROSE, photographer, natural history educator; b. Chgo., July 12, 1942; d. Joseph Thomas and Lucia Barbara (Urban) C. BA, U. Wis., 1964; grad., Coll. San Mateo, 1972-74; postgrad., U. Calif., Berkeley, 1977; grad., San Francisco State U., 1989. Flight attendant Pan Am. World Airways Inc., San Francisco, 1965; free lance photographer San Mateo, Calif., 1983—; stock photographer Comstock, N.Y.C., 1987—; lectr. Soc. Expdns., Seattle, 1985-91, Abercrombie & Kent, Chgo., 1992—. Author: (checklist) Birds of the Antarctic and Sub-Antarctic, 1986; translator: Field Guide to the Birds of Chile, 1989; co-author: The Birds of Chile, 1993; photos featured in Sierra Club Book: Mother Earth Through the Eyes of Women Photographers and Writers, 1992; photographer mag. cover King Penguin and Chick for Internat. Wildlife Mag., 1985, Sierra Club Calendar, 1986; exhibited photos at Royal Geog. Soc., London, 1985. Mem. Calif. Acad. Sci. Home: 724 Laurel Ave Apt 211 San Mateo CA 94401-4131

CHESTERFIELD, RHYDONIA RUTH EPPERSON, financial company executive; b. Dallas, Tex., Apr. 23, 1919; d. Leonard Lee and Sally E. (Stevenson) Griswold; m. Chad Chesterfield, Apr. 21, 1979. BS Southwestern U., 1952; BS, North Tex. U., 1954, ME, 1956; PhD, Bernardean U., 1974, Calif. Christian U., 1974, LLD (hon.), 1974. Evangelist with Griswold Trio, 1940-58; tchr., counselor Dallas public schs., 1952-58, L.A. pub. schs., 1958-74; pres. Griswold-Epperson Fin. Enterprise, L.A., 1974—; pres. GEC Enterprises, 1979—; guest speaker various schs., chs. and civic orgns. in U.S. and Can. Author: Little Citizens series, Cathedral Films; contbr. articles on bus. to profl. publs. Fellow Internat. Naturopathic Assn.; mem. L.A. Inst. Fine Arts, Assn. of Women in Edn. (hon.), Internat. Bus. and Profl. Women, Calif. C. of C., L.A. C. of C., Pi Lambda Theta (hon.), Kappa Delta Pi (hon.). Office: 10790 Wilshire Blvd Apt 202 Los Angeles CA 90024-4426

CHETWYND, LIONEL, screenwriter, producer, director; b. London, Jan. 29; s. Peter and Betty (Dion) C.; m. Gloria Carlin, June 2; children: Michael Anthony, Joshua Stephen. BA with honors, Sir George Williams U., Montreal, Que., 1963; B in Civil Law, McGill U., Montreal, Que., 1967; postgrad., Trinity Coll. of Oxford (Eng.) U., 1968. Bar: PQ 1967. With acquisition/distbn. dept. Columbia Pictures, London, 1968-72; screenwriter, 1971—; mem. faculty Grad. Film Sch., NYU; lectr. screenwriting Frederick Douglass Ctr., Harlem. Writer: (stage prodns.) Maybe That's Your Problem, 1971, Bleeding Great Orchids, 1971, (feature films) The Apprenticeship of Duddy Kravitz, 1974 (also adaptor, Acad. award nomination 1974), Morning Comes, 1975 (also dir.), Two Solitudes, 1978 (also producer, dir., Grand award Salonika 1979), Quintet, 1978, Hot Touch, 1981 (Genie nomination), The Hanoi Hilton, 1987 (also dir.), (TV films) Johnny, We Hardly Knew Ye, 1976 (also producer, George Washington Honor medal Freedom Found. 1976), It Happened One Christmas, 1977 (citation Am. Women in Film and TV 1979), Goldenrod, 1977 (also producer), A Whale for the Killing, 1980, Miracle on Ice, 1981 (Christopher award 1981), Escape From Iran: The Canadian Caper, 1981, Sadat, 1983 (NAACP Image award 1983), Children in the Crossfire, 1984 (Prix D'Association Mondiale des Amis de L'Enfants 1985, award Monte Carlo Internat. TV Festival 1985), To Heal a Nation, 1988 (also producer, Vietnam Vets. Meml. Fund Patriots award, George Washington Honor medal Freedom Found. 1989), The American 1776 (official U.S. bicentennial film); co-writer, co-producer (stage prodn.) We The People...200, 1987; exec. producer (TV film) Evil in Clear River, 1988 (Spl. award Am. Jewish Com., Christopher award); writer, dir., exec. producer So Proudly We Hail (Bnai Zion Creative Achievement award 1990), Heroes of the Desert Storm, 1991; exec. prodr., writer, creator (PBS documentary series) Reverse Angle, 1993. Co-chair Arts and Entertainment Commn. for Reagan/Bush, Los Angeles, 1978-80; exec. bd. dirs. Can. Ctr. for Advanced Cinema Studies, Toronto, 1986—; mem. exec. bd. LA chpt. Am. Jew. Com. Served as sgt. Black Watch of Can., 1956-58. Mem. Acad. Motion Picture Arts and Scis., Acad. TV Arts and Scis., Writers Guild Am. (exec. bd. 1972-76, nat. exec. 1975, Writers Guild award 1974), Writers Guild Britain, Can. Bar Assn., Dirs. Guild Am., Broadcast Music, Inc., Assn. Can. TV and Radio Artists. Jewish. Office: care Gang Tyre Raymer & Brown 6400 W Sunset Blvd Los Angeles CA 90028-7392

CHEUNG, WESLEY HOI PANG, corporate treasurer, insurance executive; b. Kowloon, Hong Kong, Dec. 2, 1956; came to U.S., 1965; s. Wai Mui (Kong) C.; m. Arlene D.G. Gabalis, Sept. 22, 1991. Student, U. Hawaii, 1980. Acctg. clk. Nat. Mortgage and Fin., Honolulu, 1980-85, asst. supr., 1985-86; acctg. supr. Goodstill Anderson Quinn & Stifel, Honolulu, 1986-88; acctg. mgr. Triad Ins. Agy. Inc., Honolulu, 1988-90, treas., 1990—. Home: Triad Ins Agy Inc 855 Makahiki Way # 304 Honolulu HI 46826

CHEVERTON, WILLIAM KEARNS, science corporation executive; b. Corpus Christi, Tex., Dec. 20, 1944; s. Milton Robbins and Pauline (Kearns) C. Student, San Diego State Coll., 1962-65, Chapman Coll., 1965-68; PhD, LaJolla U., San Diego, 1980. Lic. ins. broker, Calif. Pres. WYBSQUIZ Scientific, LaJolla, 1980—. Contbr. articles to profl. publs. Cons./vol. YMCA, C. of C., Ednl. Insts., Rep. Party, Boy Scouts Am., scoutmaster, 1968-78. Named Kiwanian of Yr., Kiwanis Club, 1986. Mem. Camelopard High Intelligence Group, Mensa High Intelligence Group, DRONK Radio Network. Republican.

CHEW, KA-WING, dentist; b. Hong Kong, Mar. 16, 1957; s. Pui-Wan and Shun-Chuk (Chan) C.; m. Connie Kan. AS, City Coll. of San Francisco, 1978; BS, San Francisco State U., 1981; DDS, Northwestern U., 1985. Assoc. dentist Stanley Lee, DDS, San Jose, Calif., 1986-87; staff dentist N.E. Med. Svc., San Francisco, 1987-92; prvt. practice San Francisco, 1992—. Mem. San Francisco Dental Soc. Ethics Com. Mem. ADA, Calif. Dental Assn., San Francisco Dental Soc., Acad. Gen. Dentistry, full Gospel Businessmen's Fellowship Internat., Assemblies of God Chinese Christian Ctr. Home: 2375 24th Ave # 2 San Francisco CA 94116-2332

CHEW, LINDA LEE, fundraising management consultant; b. Riverside, Calif., Mar. 3, 1941; d. LeRoy S. and Grace (Ham) Olson; m. Dennis W. Chew, July 23, 1965; children—Stephanie, Erica. B.Mus., U. Redlands, 1962. Cert. fund raising exec. Dir. pub. events U. Redlands (Calif.), 1962-69; dir. fin. and communications San Gorgonio council Girl Scouts U.S.A., Colton, Calif., 1969-71; exec. dir. United Cerebral Palsy Assn. Sacramento-Yolo Counties, 1972-73; fin. devel. dir. San Francisco Bay coun. Girl Scouts U.S.A., 1973-76; chief devel. and pub. info. East Bay Regional Park Dist., Oakland, Calif., 1976-86; cons. Chew & Assocs., Alamo, Calif., 1986—; pres. Providence Hosp. Found., Oakland, 1991-92. Bd. dirs. Planned Parenthood Contra Costa County, 1980-82, San Ramon Valley Edn. Found., 1984-88; Calif. Conservation Corps Bay Area Ctr. Adv. Bd., 1988-89; Mem. AAUW (pres. Redlands br. 1968-69), Nat. Soc. Fund Raising Execs. (nat. bd. dirs. 1981-90, nat. vice chmn. 1982-84, pres. Golden Gate chpt. 1979-80, bd. dirs. 1987-90, Abel Hanson Meml. award 1977, Outstanding Fund Raising Exec. 1988), Assn. Healthcare Philanthropy (Region 11 cabinet mem. 1991—), Nat. Pk. and Recreation Assn., Am. Guild Organists (dean Riverside-San Bernardino chpt. 1969-71), Pub. Rels. Soc., Calif. Pk. and Recreation Soc. Office: 170F Alamo Pla Ste 400 Alamo CA 94507

CHHABILDAS, LALIT CHANDRA, research scientist; b. Bombay, May 10, 1945; came to U.S., 1966; s. Chhabildas Chhaganlal and Jadiben Chhabildas (Chhaganlal) Mandalaywala; m. Annette Helen Winslow, Aug. 23, 1971; children: Nomita Ann, Natrisha Helen. ISc, U. Rangoon, Burma, 1964; BSc, U. Bombay, 1966; PhD, Rensselaer Poly. Inst., 1971. Teaching asst., then rsch. asst. Rensselaer Poly. Inst., Troy, N.Y., 1966-71, postdoctoral assoc., 1971-73; rsch. assoc. Cornell U., Ithaca, N.Y., 1973-76; mem. tech. staff Sandia Nat. Labs., Albuquerque, 1976-88, sr. mem. tech. staff, 1989—, project mgr., 1990—; meeting coord. Aeroballistic Range Assn., Albuquerque, 1987-88; project leader Hypervelocity Activities, Sandia, 1988-90. Editor conf. procs. 1988 Aeroballistic Range Assn., 1988; contbr. articles to tech. publs. New hiring coord. Sandia Asian mems., 1989. Mem. AIAA, Am. Phys. Soc., Sigma Xi. Home: 3716 Tewa Dr NE Albuquerque NM 87111-4318 Office: Exptl Impact Physics 1543 PO Box 5800 Albuquerque NM 87185-5800

CHI, CHANG HWI, computer scientist; b. Hamheung, Korea, Dec. 23, 1934; came to U.S. 1954; s. Yongha and Soaei (Shin) C.; m. Keum Young, Mar. 16, 1963; children: David, Danny, Thomas, Susan. BS, MIT, 1958, MS, 1960; PhD, Poly. Inst. Bklyn., 1969. Sr. engr./project mgr. Perkin Elmer Corp., Norwalk, Conn., 1969-75; chief scientist/prog. mgr. Hughes Aircraft Co., El Segundo, Calif., 1975-90; engring. mgr. Dataline Engring., Thousand Oaks, Calif., 1990—. Editor: Periodic Structure, 1980; patentee in field. Mem. IEEE, Optical Soc. Am. Office: Dataline Engineering 1634 Aspenwall Rd Westlake Village CA 91361-1704

CHI, DONNA SHERMAN, controller; b. Albany, Ga., May 18, 1954; d. Dan Melton and Emalene (Camp) Sherman; m. Robert K. Newcomb, June 26, 1973 (div. Jan. 1983); m. David Chi, Oct. 15, 1986. AA in Bus. Adminstrn., Darton Coll., 1975; BS in Bus. Adminstrn., Ga. Southwestern Coll., 1976; MBA, Pepperdine U., 1992. Acct. Pate & Co. CPA's, Atlanta, 1976-78; contr. Ramada Inn, Athens, Ga., 1978-81; fin. analyst Westinghouse Electric, Athens, 1981-85; asst. contr. Corning Glass Works, Wilmington, N.C., 1985-87; bus. unit contr. Hiram Walker Internat. Liqueurs, L.A., 1987—. Mem. AMA, NAFE. Home: 11119 Camarillo St North Hollywood CA 91602-1248 Office: 10 Universal City Plz Ste 1700 Universal City CA 91608-1002

CHIA, FU-SHIANG, university dean, zoology educator; b. Shantung, China, Jan. 15, 1931; emigrated to Can., 1969, naturalized, 1975; s. Chien-Ming Chia and Hsu-Tsie Chang; m. Sharon Simonds, Apr. 27, 1963; children: Alisa, Maria. B.Sc., Taiwan Normal U., 1955; M.Sc., U. Wash., 1962, Ph.D., 1964. Asst. prof. biology Sacramento State U., 1964-66; sr. research officer U. Newcastle upon Tyne and Dove Marine Lab., Eng., 1966-69; asst. prof. zoology U. Alta. (Can.), Edmonton, 1969-71; asso. prof. U. Alta. (Can.), 1971-75, prof., 1975—, also chmn. dept. zoology., dean Faculty of Grad. Studies and Research, 1983—. Editor: (with M.E. Rice) Settlement and Metamorphosis of Marine Invertebrate Larvae, 1978. Fellow AAAS; mem. Am. Soc. Zoologists, Can. Soc. Zoologists, Sigma Xi. Office: U Alta, Dept Zoology, Edmonton, AB Canada T6G 2E9

CHIANG, ALBERT CHIN-LIANG, electrical engineer; b. Putai, Taiwan, Jan. 25, 1937; s. San Chi and Chiu (Hsu) C.; BS in Elec. Engring., Nat. Taiwan U., 1959; MS in Elec. Engring., Chiaotung U., Taiwan, 1963; PhD, U. So. Calif., 1968; m. Steffie F.L. Huang, Dec. 24, 1966; children: Margaret, Stacy, Kathy, George. Came to U.S., 1963, naturalized, 1973. Research asst. U. So. Calif., Los Angeles, 1963-68; engr. specialist Litton Industries, Woodland Hills, Calif., 1968-70; dir. internat. sales Macrodata Co., Woodland Hills, Calif., 1970-77; pres. Tritek Internat. Co., Woodland Hills, Calif., 1977—. Mem. IEEE, Sigma Xi, Eta Kappa Nu. Home: 24132 Lupin Hill Rd Hidden Hills CA 91302-2430 Office: Tritek Internat Co 20121 Ventura Blvd Woodland Hills CA 91364-2546

CHIANG, YAOJEN PETER, marketing professional; b. Taipei, Taiwan, Dec. 7, 1964. BS in Biology, U. Calif., Irvine, 1985, MBA, 1988. Dir. mktg. Berkeley Antibody Co., Inc., Richmond, Calif., 1988—. Office: Babco 4131 B Lakeside Dr Richmond CA 94806

CHIASSON, ROBERT BRETON, veterinary science educator emeritus; b. Griggsville, Ill., Oct. 9, 1925; s. Placid Nelson and Anna Marie Chiasson; m. Frances Marguirete Kientzle, Oct. 24, 1944; children: Phyllis, Robert, Sarah, John, William, Mary, Annette, Laura. AB, Ill. Coll., 1949; MS, U. Ill., 1950; PhD, Stanford U., 1956. Spl. supr. Ill. State Mus., Springfield, 1949-50; instr. in zoology U. Ariz., Tucson, 1951-55, asst. prof. in zoology, 1956-60, assoc. prof. in zoology, 1960-65, prof. in zoology and biology, 1965-75, prof. in vet. sci., 1975-93, prof. emeritus, 1993—; vis. scientist U. Edinburgh, Scotland, 1976-77, U. Lueven, Belgium, 1985; cons. editor Wm. C. Brown Co. Pubs., Dubuque, Iowa, 1968—. Author (lab. texts): Laboratory Anatomy of the White Rat, 5th edit., 1988, Laborty Anatomy of the Cat, 8th edit., 1989, Laboratory Anatomy of the Shark, 5th edit., 1988, various others; contbr. articles to profl. jours. Air quality advisor County of Pima, Tucson, 1978-87; bd. dirs. Ariz. Consumers Coun., 1974-85; sr. arbitrator Better Bus. Bur., Tucson, 1980—. With U.S. Army, 1944-46, ETO. Named Fulbright Prof., 1969-70. Mem. Am. Assn. Vet. Anatomists, Am. Physiol. Soc., Am. Soc. Zoologists, World Assn. Vet. Anatomists, N.Y. Acad. Sci., Sigma Xi, Gamma Sigma Delta (award of merit 1984). Home: 6941 E Calle Jupiter Tucson AZ 85710-5437 Office: U Ariz Dept Vet Sci Tucson AZ 85721

CHICKS, CHARLES HAMPTON, mathematician; b. Sandpoint, Idaho, Nov. 10, 1930; s. Ralph Raymon and Emma Marie (Robbins) C.; m.

Barbara Jean Thomson, June 19, 1956; children: Kathryn A. Foust, Steven H., R. David, Vicki L. BA, Linfield Coll., 1953; postgrad., Stanford U., 1956-57; MA, U. Oreg., 1956, PhD, 1960. Engring. specialist GTE-Sylvania, Mountain View, Calif., 1957-69; staff engr. ESL Inc., Sunnyvale, Calif., 1969-91; lectr. Santa Clara (Calif.) U., 1964-86. Trustee Linfield Coll., McMinnville, Oreg., 1972—, Am. Bapt. Sem. of the West, Berkeley, Calif., 1982—; v.p. Am. Bapt. Chs. of the West, 1992-93. Mem. Am. Math Soc. Republican. Baptist. Home: 925 Kamsack Ct Sunnyvale CA 94087-5211

CHICOREL, MARIETTA EVA, publisher; b. Vienna, Austria; came to U.S., 1939, naturalized, 1945; d. Paul and Margaret (Gross) Selby. AB, Wayne State U., 1951; MALS, U. Mich., 1961. Asst. chief library acquisitions div. U. Wash., Seattle, 1962-66; project dir. Macmillan Info. Scis., Inc., N.Y.C., 1968-69; pres. Chicorel Library Pub. Corp., N.Y.C., 1969-79, Am. Library Pub. Co., Inc., 1979—; pub. cons. Creative Solutions Co., 1986—; asst. prof. dept. libr. sci. CUNY (Queens Coll.), 1986—; mem. edn. com. Gov.'s Commn. on Status of Women, Wash., 1963-65; instr. libr. scis. No. Ariz. U., Flagstaff, 1990; bd. dirs. Skills Devel. Tng. counseling; pub. cons. creative solutios. Chief editor: Ulrich's International Periodicals Directory, 1966-68; editor, pub.: Chicorel Indexes, 1969—; founding editor: Jour. Reading, Writing and Learning Disabilities International, 1985-90; contbr. chpt. on univs. to Library Statistics: A Handbook of Concepts, Definitions and Terminology, 1966. Mem. ALA (exec. bd. tech. svcs. divsn. 1965-68, chmn. libr. materials price index com. 1968-69, councillor 1969-73), Am. Assn. Profl. Cons., Am. Book Prodrs. Assn., Book League N.Y. (bd. govs. 1975-79), Am. Soc. for Info. Sci., Can. Libr. Assn., Pacific N.W. Libr. Assn., N.Y. Libr. Club, N.Y. Tech. Svcs. Librarians. Home and Office: PO Box 4272 Sedona AZ 86340-4272

CHIDESTER, GENE ROGER, computer company executive, educator; b. Murray, Utah, Nov. 17, 1948; s. Max B. and Clista Z. (Byington) C.; m. Robyn LaVonne Johnson, Aug. 19, 1972; children: Melissa, Brandon, Nicole, Ryan, Matthew. BS in Acctg., Brigham Young U., 1976. Fin. analyst Corvallis (Oreg.) div. Hewlett-Packard, 1976-77, gen. acctg. supr., 1978-79; mfg. planning mgr. personal Computer div. Hewlett-Packard, Corvallis, 1980-83; materials mgr. N.W. Integrated Circuit div. Hewlett-Packard, Corvallis, 1984-88; materials mgr., dir. mfg. Evans and Sutherland Computer Corp., Salt Lake City, 1989—; instr. acctg. and tax Linn Benton Community Coll., Albany, Oreg., 1978-79; instr. acctg. and ops. mgr. Oreg. State U., Corvallis, 1980-88; adj. prof. Westminster Coll., Salt Lake City, 1992—. Mem. task force Salt Lake City Baseball Stadium Task Force, 1992; vice chmn. Davis County (Utah) Dist. Republicans, 1992. Mem. Am. Prodn. and Inventory Control Soc., Brigham Young U. Mgmt. Soc., Brigham Young U. Cougar Club. Mormon. Home: 207 Valley View Dr North Salt Lake UT 84054 Office: Evans & Sutherland Computer 540 Arapeen Dr Salt Lake City UT 84108

CHIEFFALO, MARIO VICTOR (VIC CHIEFFALO), magazine executive; b. Italy, Aug. 24, 1934; came to U.S. from Uruguay, 1948, naturalized 1954; s. Rosario and Teresa C.; m. Mary Ruth Rector, June 3, 1958; 1 child, Belinda. BS, La. State U., 1961; B in Fgn. Trade, Am. Inst. Fgn. Trade, 1962. Mgr. export sales Cotton Producers Assn., Atlanta, 1963-66; mem. advt. sales staff This Week mag., N.Y.C., 1966-69, Am. Home r ag., N.Y.C., 1969-71, Reader's Digest, N.Y.C., 1971-74; mgr. advt. Iberian edit., Spain, 1974; mgr. west coast advt. sales So. Living mag., San Francisco, 1975-92, cons., 1992—. Served to petty officer U.S. Navy, 1955-58. Mem. San Francisco Mag. Reps., Moraga Country Club.

CHIEFFO, ALEXANDER BERNARD, aerospace engineer, consultant; b. N.Y.C., Sept. 17, 1920; s. Nicholas and Rosina (Cetta) C.; m. Charlotte Sieglestein, Sept. 17, 1955 (dec. 1963); m. Evelyn Osgood, Dec. 30, 1965. BS, City Univ. of N.Y., Brooklyn, 1945. Registered profl. engr., N.Y. Mgr. C&G Electronics Co., Jamaica, N.Y., 1945-47; electronic designer Worldwide Electronics Co., N.Y.C., 1947-49; sr. instr. Radio TV Instn., N.Y.C., 1949-51; sr. tech. writer Hazeltine Electronics, L.I., N.Y., 1951-55; mgr. tech. publs. Thompson Ramo Wooldridge, Redondo Beach, Calif., 1955-63; sr. tech. mgr. ITT Fed. Labs., San Fernando, Calif., 1963-65; sr. program mgr. Advanced Communications Inc., Chatsworth, Calif., 1965-67; sr. tech. mgr. 3 Tech. R&D Co.'s, L.A., 1967-78; sr. systems engr. TRW Electronics & Def. sector, Redondo Beach, 1978-86; engring. mgmt. cons., Redondo Beach, 1986—. Patentee in nuclear safety field. Appointed lifetime mem. gov.'s com. for employment of the handicapped. Republican. Home: 13443 Reindeer St Moreno Valley CA 92553

CHIEN, KUEI-RU, chemical physicist; b. Nantung, Kiangsu, China, Dec. 14, 1945; came to U.S. 1969; s. Hun-Wen and Jang-Jen (Tsao) C.; m. Ming-Hsia Lee, July 25, 1983. BS, Nat. Taiwan Normal U., 1968; PhD, MIT, 1973. Research assoc. MIT, Cambridge, Mass., 1973-74, Cornell U., Ithaca, N.Y., 1974-76; with TRW, Redondo Beach, Calif., 1976-83; sr. staff engr. Hughes Aircraft, El Segundo, Calif., 1983-85; sect. head Hughes Aircraft, 1985-87, sr. scientist, 1987-88, dept. mgr., 1988—. Contbr. articles to profl. jours.; inventor in laser field. Recipient Outstanding Publ. of Yr. award Hughes Electro-optical Data System Group. Mem. Optical Soc. Am., Sigma Xi. Home: 17310 Evening Star Ave Cerritos CA 90701-4421 Office: Hughes Aircraft 2000 El Segundo Blvd E1-B118 El Segundo CA 90245

CHIKALLA, THOMAS DAVID, science facility administrator; b. Milw., Sept. 9, 1935; s. Paul Joseph and Margaret Ann (Dittrich) C.; m. Ruth Janet Laun, June 20, 1960; children: Paul, Mark, Karyn. BS in Metallurgy, U. Wis., 1957, PhD in Metallurgy, 1966; MS in Metallurgy, U. Idaho, 1960. Research scientist Gen. Electric Co., Richland, Wash., 1957-62; sr. research scientist Battelle Pacific N.W. Labs., Richland, 1964-72, sect. mgr., 1972-80, programs mgr., 1980-83, dept. mgr., 1983-86, assoc. dir., 1986—; tchr. U. Wis., Madison, 1962-64. Contbr. articles to profl. jours. Fellow AEC. Fellow Am. Ceramic Soc. (counselor 1974-80); mem. AAAS, Am. Nuclear Soc., Sigma Xi. Republican. Roman Catholic. Clubs: Desert Ski (pres. 1958-59), Alpine. Home: 2108 Harris Ave Richland WA 99352-2021 Office: Battelle Pacific NW Labs Battelle Blvd Richland WA 99352

CHILBERG, DENNIS ERVIN, county commissioner; b. Kendrick, Idaho, July 14, 1944; s. Robert E. and Dorothy H. (Candler) C.; m. Leora Lynn Stephens, Nov. 10, 1970 (div. May 1992); children: Mark, Kim, Frank, Robert; m. Janell Downard, Nov. 27, 1992. BS in Agr., U. Idaho, 1966. Budget dir. State of Idaho, Boise, 1971-73, dir. adminstrn., 1973-76; pres. Family Tng. Ctr., Glasgow, Mont., 1977-78; fin. dir. N.W. Regional Found., Spokane, Wash., 1979-82; treas. Spokane County, Spokane, 1983-92, commr., 1993—. Mem. Wash. State Housing Fin. Com., Seattle, 1987-93, appt. chmn., 1993—; chmn. bd. United Ch. of Christ, Wash.-No. Idaho Conf., 1990-91; active in polit. campaigns. With U.S. Army, 1967-69, Germany. Mem. Wash. Assn. County Treas. (pres. 1986-87), Nat. Assn. Treas. and Fin. Officers, Govt Fin. Officers Assn. Democrat. Mem. United Ch. of Christ.

CHILD, CARROLL CADELL, research nursing administrator; b. Vicksburg, Miss., Nov. 10, 1949; s. John Clifton and Marie Adelaide (Gerwig) C.; m. Nicole Louise Child, Feb. 11, 1984; children: Dylan Christopher, Brendan Thomas. BA in Philosophy, So. Ill. U., 1972; BSN with honors, U. Calif., San Francisco, 1980. RN, Calif. Nurse supr. USDA/U. Calif., Berkeley; clin. rsch. supr. drug studies unit U. Calif., San Francisco; rsch. nurse educator Stanford (Calif.) U.; clin. trials coord. Community Consortium U. Calif., San Francisco; participant, co-presenter V Internat. Conf. on AIDS, Montreal, Que., Can., 1989, VI Internat. Conf. on AIDS, San Francisco, 1990, VIII Internat. Conf. on AIDS, Amsterdam, 1992; co-presenter univ.-wide task force on AIDS conf. U. Calif., Berkeley, 1990. Contbr. to profl. jours. Mem. Internat. AIDS Soc., Assn. Nurses in AIDS Care, Assn. Rsch. Nurses.

CHILDERS, THOMAS DALLAS, software engineer; b. Bridgeport, Conn., July 12, 1958; s. Dallas Childers, Jr. and Eleanora Penny (Horvath) Salanave; m. Nancy Ann Malcolm, July 18, 1992. Student, MIT, 1976-79. Programmer MIT, Cambridge, Mass., 1978-79; systems specialist Fireman's Fund Ins. Co., San Rafael, Calif., 1979-83; software engr. Viasoft, Inc., Sunnyvale, Calif., 1984; cons. Fireman's Fund Ins. Co., San Rafael, 1985-86, Levi Strauss Co., San Francisco, 1987, IBM, San Jose, Calif., 1988; software engr. E-Net Corp., Larkspur, Calif., 1988-89, Oracle Corp., Redwood Shores, Calif., 1989—. Contbr. articles to profl. jours. Mem. IEEE, AAAS, Nat. Systems Programmers Assn., Computer Measurement Group. Unitarian. Home: 34 El Camino Corte Madera CA 94925 Office: Oracle Corp 500 Oracle Pky Redwood Shores CA 94065

CHILDS, JOHN DAVID, computer hardware and services company executive; b. Washington, Apr. 26, 1939; s. Edwin Carlton and Catherine Dorothea (Angerman) C.; m. Margaret Rae Olsen, Mar. 4, 1966 (div.); 1 child, John-David. Student Principia Coll., 1957-58, 59-60; BA, Am. U., 1963. Jr. adminstr. Page Communications, Washington, 1962-65; account rep. Friden Inc., Washington, 1965-67; Western sales dir. Data Inc., Arlington, Va., 1967-70; v.p. mktg. Rayda, Inc., Los Angeles, 1970-73, pres., 1973-76, chmn. bd., 1976-84; sr. v.p. sales Exec. Bus. Systems, Encino, Calif., 1981—; sr. assoc. World Trade Assocs., Inc., 1976—. Pres. Coll. Youth for Nixon-Lodge, 1959-60, dir. state fedn.; mem. OHSHA policy formulation com. Dept. Labor, 1967. Served with USAFR, 1960-66. Mem. Assn. Data Ctr. Owners and Mgrs. (chmn. privacy com. 1975, sec. 1972-74, v.p. 1974). Democrat. Christian Scientist. Office: 15613 Ventura Blvd Encino CA 91436-3145

CHILDS, MARIAN TOLBERT, nutritionist, educator; b. Twin Falls, Idaho, Nov. 18, 1925; d. Edward and Helen (Mills) Tolbert; m. Morris Elsmere Childs, Nov. 26, 1952; children: Robert E., Mary E., Ruth E., Amy E. BS, U. Calif., Berkeley, 1946; PhD, U. Calif., 1950. Asst. prof. U. Ill., 1950-54; asst. prof. nutrition U. Wash., Seattle, 1969-81; assoc. prof. medicine U. Wash., 1981-90, assoc. prof. emeritus, 1990—. Contbr. articles to profl. jours. NIH fellow, 1976-78; recipient Borden award, 1943. Mem. Am. Inst. Nutrition, Sigma Xi, Iota Sigma Xi. Home: 7857-56th Pl NE Seattle WA 98115 Office: Univ Wash DL10 Seattle WA 98195

CHILES, JOHN HUNTER, III, futurist; b. Sharon, Pa., Oct. 2, 1938; s. John Hunter Jr. and Edythe Mae (Lawes) C.; m. Dianna Margaret Chiles, Dec. 7, 1991; children: John, Jeannie, Drew Ann, Edward, Dana, Dacia. BSEE, Va. Poly. Inst., 1960; MBA, Pitts. U., 1968. Registered profl. engr., Pa. Dir. strategic mktg. ops. Westinghouse Electric Corp., Pitts., 1960-81; dir. office policy U.S. Dept. Energy, Washington, 1981-83; mgr. mktg. and strategic planning Bechtel Power Corp., San Francisco, 1983-88; mng. cons. Mgmt. Analysis Co., San Diego, 1988-91; chief ops. officer Cash Planning Resources, Inc., San Diego, 1991-92; pres. Chiles Cons. Co., San Diego, 1992—; vice chmn. Dine Power Authority of the Navajo Nation, Window Rock, Ariz., 1991—; chmn. Nema Power Equipment Survey, N.Y.C., 1975-81. Editorial bd. Electric Light and Power Mag., 1972-81; contbr. articles to profl. jours. Polit. appointee, dir. Office of Policy, Planning and Analysis, U.S. Dept. Energy, Washington, 1981-83. 1st lt. U.S. Army, 1962-65. Mem. Whispering Palms Country Club. Republican. Home and Office: PO Box 3445 Rancho Santa Fe CA 92067

CHILTON, DAVID SHADRACH, structural engineer; b. St. Louis, Aug. 15, 1955; s. Wendel Morris and Lucy (Queal) C.; m. Michelle Sari Suffian, July 25, 1982; children: Arielle Jennifer, Dustin Scott. BSCE, U. Mo., Columbia, 1979; MSCE, U. Alaska, 1989. Registered profl. engr., Alaska, Mo. Structural engr. HNTB, Kansas City, Mo., 1980-83, USKH, Anchorage, Alaska, 1983-84, Century Engring., Anchorage, 1984-86, Ch2m Hill NW, Inc., Anchorage, 1986—. Author papers in field. Mem. ASCE, Earthquake Engring. Rsch. Inst. (sec.-treas. Alaska chpt. 1991). Home: 221 Langnes Ct Anchorage AK 99515-3367 Office: Ch2m Hill NW Inc 2550 Denali Ste 800 Anchorage AK 99503

CHIMENTO, THOMAS CARMINE, JR., neuroscientist; b. Queens, N.Y., Nov. 27, 1957; s. Thomas Carmine and Rose (DeLuca) C.; m. Catherine Anne Egli, Oct. 12, 1986; children: Matthew Anthony, Jonathan Hayes. BA, L.I. U., 1979; PhD, U. Calif., San Francisco, 1989. Lab. supr. L.I. U., Southampton, N.Y., 1977-79; staff rsch. assoc. U. Calif., San Francisco, 1981-85; rsch. assoc. Nation Rsch. Coun./NASA, Moffett Field, Calif., 1990—. Author conf. abstracts in field of neuroscience; contbr. articles to profl. jours. Mem. San Francisco Coun. Parent Participation Nursery Schs., 1991, 92. Recipient Nat. Rsch. Coun. fellowship NAS, 1990, 91, Calif. Regents fellowship Regents of Calif., 1983, N.Y. State Regents scholarship, 1975. Mem. Soc. for Neuroscience, Internat. Neural Network Soc., Assn. for Rsch. in Otolaryngology. Home: 213 Gold Mine Dr San Francisco CA 94131-2523 Office: NASA Ames Rsch Ctr MS239-11 Moffett Field CA 94035-1000

CHIN, DENNIS LEW, safety officer; b. San Francisco, July 27, 1935; s. Eugene and Hilda (Young) C.; children: Pamela, Roxanne. AB, U. Calif., Berkeley; PhD, U. Minn. Rsch. scientist Wadsworth Ctr. Labs. and Rsch., Albany, N.Y., 1970-91; safety officer Desert Rsch. Inst., Reno, 1991—. Mem. Am. Soc. Testing Materials, Am. Soc. Microbiology, N.Y. Acad. Scis., Sigma Xi. Republican. Presbyterian. Office: Desert Rsch Inst 7010 Dandini Blvd Reno NV 89512

CHIN, LLEWELLYN PHILIP, lawyer; b. Saigon-Cholon, Vietnam, June 4, 1957; s. Thomas and Quoc Kim (Sam) C. AA, Glendale (Calif.) Coll., 1980; BS, U. So. Calif., L.A., 1982; JD, Columbia U., 1986. Bar: Calif. 1988, U.S. Dist. Ct. (cen. dist.) Calif. 1988, U.S. Ct. Appeals (9th cir.) 1988. Sr. counsel Calif. Assn. of Realtors, L.A., 1989—; polit. cons. Robert Kwan for Alhambra Sch. Bd., Monterey Park, Calif., 1988; bus. cons. Larry L. Berg, Inc., L.A., 1986-88; speaker in field. Columnist L.A. County Bar Real Property Newsletter; contbr. articles to profl. jours. Bd. dirs. Chinese Am. Polit. Action Com., Alhambra, 1986—, Oriental Am. Svc. Ctr., L.A., 1990, Chinese-Am. PTA, 1993, Orgn. Chinese Ams., 1993, Golden Tours, Alhambra, 1993; mem. L.A. County Ctrl. Com., Dem. Party, 1988-90; exec. com. Alhambra Dem. Club, 1988-90; precinct capt. Dukakis for Pres., 1988; coord. SW Voter Registration Project, 1988; vol. Clinton for Pres., 1993; candidate Alhambra City Coun., 1993. Beren Found. scholar, 1983-86, Harlan Fisk Stone scholar, 1986. Mem. ABA (vice chair, purchase and sale of residential real estate subcom.), L.A. County Bar Assn. (disaster relief com., corp. counsel, elderline, continuing edn. com., gen. property subsection steering com.), So. Calif. Fgn. Trade Assn., Calif. Trial Lawyers Assn., So. Calif. Chinese Lawyers Assn., Calif. State Bar (exec. mem., real property sect., continuing edn. of the bar com.), Alhambra C. of C. (legis. com.). Democrat. Office: Calif Assn Realtors 525 S Virgil Ave Los Angeles CA 90020-1431

CHIN, MARJORIE SCARLETT, controller, business executive; b. Reno, Mar. 24, 1941; d. Wing Yee and Jessie (Wong) Echavia; m. Manford Jeffrey Chin, Dec. 26, 1969. AA, Contra Costa Coll., 1969; BS, John F. Kennedy U., 1988. Treas., contr. Maya Corp., South San Francisco, 1977-78; fin. and pers. coord. Garretson-Elmendorf-Zinov, San Francisco, 1978-82; bus. mgr. Cyclotomics, Berkeley, Calif., 1982-85; contr. JTS Leasing Corp., South San Francisco, 1985-88; contr., office mgr. Barbary Coast Steel Corp., Emeryville, Calif., 1988-90; cons. WAM, 1990-91, U. Calif., Berkeley, 1992-93; sr. acct. Computers Resources Group, San Francisco, 1993—; bd. dirs. Experience Unlimited, Pleasant Hill, Calif. Vol. driver ARC, Richmond, Calif., 1978; vol. UNICEF, San Francisco, 1980. Mem. NAFE, AAUW, Nat. Assn. Accts. (bd. dir.), Calif. Fedn., Bus. & Profl. Women Club (sec. 1980—). Home: 1069C Mohr Ln Concord CA 94518-4001

CHIN, SUE SOONEMARIAN (SUCHIN CHIN), conceptual artist, portraitist, photographer, community affairs activist; b. San Francisco; d. William W. and Soo-Up (Swebe) C. Grad. Calif. Coll. Art, Mpls. Art Inst., (scholar) Schaeffer Design Ctr.; student, Yasuo Kuniyoshi, Louis Hamon, Rico LeBrun. Photojournalist, All Together Now show, 1973, East-West News, Third World Newscasting, 1975-78, Sta. KNBC Sunday Show, L.A., 1975, 76, Live on 4, 1981, Bay Area Scene, 1981; graphics printer, exhbns. include Kaiser Ctr., Zellerbach Pla., Chinese Culture Ctr. Galleries, Capricorn Asunder Art Commn. Gallery (all San Francisco), Newspace Galleries, New Coll. of Calif., L.A. County Mus. Art, Peace Pla. Japan Ctr., Congress Arts Communication, Washington, 1989; SFWA Galleries, Inner Focus Show, 1989—, Calif. Mus. Sci. and Industry, Lucien Labaudt Gallery, Salon de Medici, Madrid, Salon Renacimento, Madrid, Life Is a Circus, SFWA Gallery, 1991, Sacramento State Fair, AFL-CIO Labor Studies Ctr., Washington, Asian Women Artists (1st prize for conceptual painting, 1st prize photography), 1978; represented in permanent collections L.A. County Fedn. Labor, Calif. Mus. Sci. and Industry, AFL-CIO Labor Studies Ctr., Australian Trades Coun., Hazeland and Co., also pvt. collections. Del. nat., state convs. Nat. Women's Polit. Caucus, 1977-83, San Francisco chpt. affirmative action chairperson, 1978-82, nat. conv. del., 1978-81, Calif. del., 1976-81. Recipient Honorarium AFL-CIO Labor Studies Ctr., Washington, 1975-76; award Centro Studi Ricerche delle Nazioni, Italy, 1985; bd. advisors Psycho Neurology Found. Bicentennial award L.A. County Mus. Art, 1976, 77, 78. Mem. Asian Women Artists (founding v.p., award 1978-79, 1st award in photography of Orient 1978-79), Calif. Chinese Artists (sec.-treas. 1978-81), Japanese Am. Art Coun. (chairperson 1978-84, dir.), San Francisco Women Artists, San Francisco Graphics Guild, Pacific/Asian Women Coalition Bay Area, Chinatown Coun. Performing and Visual Arts. Chmn., Full Moon Products; pres., bd. dir. Aumni Oracle Inc. Address: PO Box 421415 San Francisco CA 94142-1415

CHIN, SUSAN WONG, educator; b. Stockton, Calif., Mar. 14, 1946; d. Wee Poy and Yik Gee (Fong) Wong; m. Harvey Victor Chin, Sept. 8, 1968; children: Christina, Cherilyn. BA, U. Calif., Berkeley, 1968; secondary credential, U. San Francisco, 1970; cert. data processing, Merritt Coll., 1984; MBA with distinction, Nat. U., 1988. Office mgr. J.L. Burke, CPA, Oakland, Calif., 1983; instr. Coll. Alameda (Calif), 1984—; faculty senator Coll. Alameda Faculty Senate, 1987-90. Sch. vol. Joaquin Miller Sch., Oakland, 1971-87. Recipient Cert. of Leadership, Nat. U., Oakland, 1987. Mem. Assn. Computing Machinery, Peralta Fedn. Tchrs., Peralta Asian Pacific Am. Assn. (v.p.), Asian Pacific Ams. in Higher Edn., Future Bus. Leaders Am. (profl.), Phi Beta Lambda. Democrat. Methodist. Office: Coll Alameda 555 Atlantic Ave Alameda CA 94501-2109

CHIN, WANDA WON, graphics designer; b. L.A., July 10, 1952; d. John Ah and Lui Shui (Leung) Chin; m. Terry Paul Dickey, Feb. 3, 1982; children: Emile, Pierre. BA, UCLA, 1974. Graphic designer KCOP-13 TV, L.A., 1977-78, KTTV-11 TV, L.A., 1978; exhibits designer U. Alaska Mus., Fairbanks, 1979-84, coord. exhibits, 1984—. Artist fiber sculptures: Trading Ways, 1983, Magnetic Forces, 1985, Vuelo, 1986, Thrust Away, 1990; artist metal sculpture: Transformations, 1991. Panelist Dept. Natural Resources, Art in Pub. Places, Fairbanks, 1988-89; mem. State of Alaska Coun. on Arts, 1991—; bd. dirs. Dance Omnium, 1982; mem. gov.'s tourism coord. com. State of Alaska, 1992; organizer, designer Arctic Winter Games, 1986. Fellow Kellogg Found., 1982, 87, NEA/Rockefeller Found., 1976. Mem. Fairbanks Arts Assn., Am. Assn. of Mus., Mus. Alaska, Inst. Alaska Native Arts, North Star Borough Chinese Assn., Asian Am. Women in Am. Project. Office: Univ of Alaska Mus 907 Yukon Dr Fairbanks AK 99775-1200

CHINCHINIAN, HARRY, pathologist, educator; b. Troy, N.Y., Mar. 7, 1926; s. Ohaness and Armen (Der Arakelian) C.; m. Mary Corcoran, Aug. 22, 1952; children: Armen, Marjorie, Matthew. BA, U. Colo., 1952; MS, Marquette U., 1956, MD, 1959. Co-dir. Pathologists Regional Labs., Lewiston, Idaho, 1964—; chief of staff Tri-State Hosp., Clarkston, Wash., 1967, St. Joseph's Hosp., Lewiston, 1971; assoc. prof. pathology Wash. State U., Pullman, 1972—. Author: Antigens To Melanoma, 1957, Parasitism and Natural Resistance, 1958; co-author: Malakoplakia, 1957, Pneumocystis, 1965. Pres. Am. Cancer Soc., Asotin County, Wash., 1968, Lewiston Roundup, 1972-73, N.W. Soc. Blood Banks, 1973-74. Sgt. U.S. Army, 1944-46. Fellow Am. Coll. Pathologists (cert., lab. inspector 1970—). Home: 531 Silcott Rd Clarkston WA 99403 Office: Pathologists Regional Labs Box 956 Lewiston ID 83501

CHING, ERIC SAN HING, health care and insurance administrator; b. Honolulu, Aug. 13, 1951; s. Anthony D.K. and Amy K.C. (Chong) C. BS, Stanford U., 1973, MS, MBA, 1977. Fin. analyst Mid Peninsula Health Service, Palo Alto, Calif., 1977; acting dep. exec. dir. Santa Clara County Health Systems Agy., San Jose, Calif., 1977-78; program officer Henry J. Kaiser Family Found., Menlo Park, Calif., 1978-84; dir. strategic planning Lifeguard Health Maintenance Orgn., Milpitas, Calif., 1984-90; v.p. strategic planning and dir. ops. Found. Life Ins. Co., Milpitas, 1986-90; sr. planning analyst Kaiser Found Health Plan, Oakland, Calif., 1990—; adj. faculty Am. Pistol Inst., 1991—. Mem. vol. staff Los Angeles Olympic Organizing Com., 1984; mem. panel United Way of Santa Clara County, 1985, panel chmn., 1986-87, mem. com. priorities and community problem solving, 1987-90, Project Blueprint, 1988-90. Mem. NRA, ACLU, Am. Soc. Law Enforcement Trainers, Internat. Assn. Law Enforcement Firearms Instrs., Soc. Competitive Intelligence Profls., Stanford Alumni Assn., Stanford Bus. Sch. Alumni Assn., Stanford Swordmasters (pres. 1980-89). Office: Kaiser Found Health Plan Inc One Kaiser Pla 25th Fl Oakland CA 94612

CHING, FRED YET-FAN, aerospace engineer; b. Toishan, Kwangung, People's Republic of China, Mar. 27, 1957; s. Lloyd Lap-Chi and Lena Yuen-Wah (Moy) C.; m. Fenny Siauw; BS with honors in Mech. and Aerospace Engring., Ill. Inst. Tech., 1979; MS in Aerospace Engring., Ga. Inst. Tech., 1980. Engr. scientist McDonnell Douglas Corp., Long Beach, Calif., 1981-84; sr. project engr. HR Textron, Valencia, Calif., 1984—. Contbr. Articles to profl. jours. Mem. ASME, ASTM, AIAA, Soc. Advancement Material and Process Engring. Office: HR Textron Inc 25200 Rye Canyon Rd Santa Clarita CA 91355-1204

CHING, LORI SAU-KIN, internal auditor; b. Fukuoka, Japan, Jan. 18, 1960; came to U.S., 1961; d. Clarence B.W. and Melicent (Chong) C. BA, U. Pa., 1982; MBA, U. Mich., 1984. CPA, Hawaii. Staff auditor Ernst & Whinney, Honolulu, 1984-86, sr. auditor, 1986-88, audit mgr., 1988-89; audit mgr. Ernst & Young, Honolulu, 1989-90; asst. v.p., internal auditor Liberty Bank, Honolulu, 1990—; bd. dirs. Make-A-Wish Hawaii, Inc., Honolulu, 1988—, treas. 1988-93, pres. 1993—. Treas. Associated Chinese Univ. Women, Honolulu, 1990, fin. chair, 1991, v.p. 1993; sec. U. Pa. Club of Hawaii, Honolulu, 1991—; mem. Chinese C. of C. of Hawaii, Honolulu, 1992—; v.p. Honolulu Chinese Jaycees, 1992—, treas., 1991-92, dir., 1989-91. Named Outstanding Officer of Yr., Honolulu Chinese Jaycees, 1991-92, one of Outstanding Young Woman of Am., 1991; recipient Presdl. award of Honor, Hawaii Jaycees, 1991, named Outstanding Officer of Yr., Outstanding Community Devel. V.P., 1992-93. Mem. Hawaii Soc. CPAs, Am. Inst. CPAs, Inst. Internal Auditors, Internat. Frat. Delta Sigma Pi (v.p. 1984). Office: Liberty Bank 99 N King St Honolulu HI 96817

CHING, STEFANIE W., realtor; b. Honolulu, Oct. 29, 1966; d. Norman K.H. and Jocelyn C. H. (Lee) C. BBA in Fin., U. Hawaii at Manoa, 1988; postgrad., U. Hawaii, Manoa, 1992—. Realtor-assoc. Grad. Realtor Inst. Fin. analyst Am. Savs. Bank, F.S.B., Honolulu, 1988-89; realtor-assoc. Herbert K. Horita Realty, Inc., Honolulu, 1989—; part-time auditor Kahala Hilton, Honolulu, 1990-92; mem. project sales team Herbert K. Horita Realty, Inc., Honolulu, 1993—. Mem. NAFE, NAR, HAR, Honolulu Bd. Realtors, Internat. Platform Assn., Million Dollar Club, Phi Kappa Phi, Beta Gamma Sigma, Phi Eta Sigma. Home: 5339 Manauwea St Honolulu HI 96821-1917 Office: Herbert K Horita Realty Inc Ste 110 2024 N King St Honolulu HI 96819

CHINN, LELAND JEW, science educator; b. Sacramento, Calif., Oct. 19, 1924; s. Ned J. and Fung Peng (Leong) C.; married, July 25, 1959; 1 child, Karen Celeste. AA, Sacramento Coll., 1946; BS, U. Calif., Berkeley, 1948; PhD, U. Wis., 1951. Rsch. investigator G.D. Searle & Co., Skokie, Ill., 1952-62, sr. rsch. investigator, 1962-70, group leader atherosclerosis, steroid & prostaglandin rsch., 1970-75, chmn. sexual disorders and reproduction rsch. com., 1975-78; rsch. fellow G.D. Searle & Co. and NutraSweet Co., Skokie, 1976-86; adj. prof. Biola U., La Mirada, Calif., 1986—; rsch. asst. Wis. Alumni Rsch. Found., U. Wis., 1948-51; vis. scientist U. So. Calif., L.A., 1968; mem. Am. Steroid Chemistry and Biochemistry del. to People's Rep. of China, U.S. Nat. Acad. Scis., 1976. Author: Selection of Oxidants in Synthesis. Oxidation at the Carbon Atom, 1971; co-author: The Chemistry and Biochemistry of Steroids, 1969. Fellow AAAS; mem. Am. Chem. Soc., N.Y. Acad. Scis., Phi Beta Kappa, Sigma Xi, Phi Lambda Epsilon. Home: 10333 Lundene Dr Whittier CA 90601-2032 Office: Biola Univ 13800 Biola Ave La Mirada CA 90639-0001

CHINN, PHYLLIS ZWEIG, mathematics educator; b. Rochester, N.Y., Sept. 26, 1941; d. Julian and Gladys Elizabeth (Weinstein) Z.; m. Daryl Ngee Chinn, Dec. 31, 1968; children: Allison Hai-Ting, Wesley Chee. BA, Brandeis U., 1962; MAT, Harvard U., 1963; MS, U. Calif., San Diego, 1966, PhD, Santa Barbara, 1969. Asst. prof. Towson State Coll. Balt., 1969-75; assoc. prof. Humboldt State U., Arcata, Calif., 1975-83, prof., 1984—; exch. prof. U. Cen. Fla., Orlando, 1983-84. Dir. Redwood Area Math Project,

1988—. Author: (bibliography) Women in Science and Math, 1979, 3rd edit., 1988; also monograph. Contbr. articles to profl. jours. Conf. coord. Nat. Women's Studies Assn., Arcata, 1982, Expanding Your Horizons in Sci. and Math, Arcata and Orlando, 1980-89. Calif. State U. grantee, 1977, NSF, 1992—. Mem. Assn. for Women in Math., Women and Math., Assn. for Women in Sci., Nat. Council of Tchrs. of Math., Math. Assn. Am., Calif. State U. Task Force on Status of Women in Sci., Engring. and Math., Phi Beta Kappa, Phi Kappa Phi. Office: Humboldt State U Math Dept Arcata CA 95521

CHINN, ROBERTA NAOMI, research psychologist, educator; b. Sacramento, Apr. 5, 1955; d. Guy Gordon and Clara Helen (Chan) C. BS, U. Calif., Davis, 1977; MA, U. Pacific, 1980; PhD, La State U., 1984. Teaching and research asst. U. Pacific, Stockton, Calif., 1977-79; teaching and research asst. La. State U., Baton Rouge, 1979-82, instr., 1982-83, research asst., 1983-84; tech. writer USAF, N.Y.C., 1984-85; lectr. U. Mo., Rolla, 1985-86; vis. asst. prof. U. Nev., Reno, 1986-87; asst. prof. U. No. Colo., Greeley, 1987-90; test validation and devel. specialist Dept. Consumer Affairs State of Calif., Sacramento, 1990—. Contbr. numerous articles to profl. jours. Mem. Calif. Scholarship Fed. (life). Calif. State scholar, 1973; travel grantee We. Psychol. Assn., 1979. Mem. AAAS, Am. Psychol. Assn., Am. Ednl. Research Assn., Psi Chi. Democrat. Office: Calif State Dept Consumer Affairs Cen Testing Unit Sacramento CA 95814

CHINN, STEVEN DOUGLAS, podiatrist, medical educator; b. Culver City, Calif., Oct. 10, 1958; s. John Lee and Norma Katherine (Wong) C.; m. Joni Leung, July 23, 1988. BS, Calif. Coll. Podiatric Medicine, 1982, DPM, 1984, MS, 1985. Asst. prof. Calif. Coll. Podiatric Medicine, San Francisco, 1986—; pvt. practice Ocean Ave. Podiatry Group, San Francisco, 1987—; asst. clin. prof. U. Calif., San Francisco, 1987—, San Francisco Gen. Hosp., 1987—. Author (with others): Complications of Laser Surgery, 1990, 92. Fellow Am. Coll. Foot Orthopedists; mem. Am. Coll. Foot Surgeons (assoc.), Calif. Podiatric Med. Assn., San Francisco-San Mateo Podiatric Med. Assn. (v.p. 1989-92). Office: Ocean Ave Podiatry Group 2411 Ocean Ave Ste 101 San Francisco CA 94127

CHINN, THOMAS WAYNE, typographic company executive; b. Marshfield, Oreg., July 28, 1909; s. Wing Chin and Shee Lee; student U. Calif.; m. Daisy Lorraine Wong, June 8, 1930; 1 son, Walter Wayne Chinn. Propr., Chinn Linotype Co., San Francisco, 1937-42; owner Calif. Typesetting Co., 1949-56; typographer, 1956-71; pres. Gollan Typography, Inc., San Francisco, 1971-80. Mem. San Francisco Mayor's Citizens Com., 1958—; mem. San Francisco Twin Bicentennial History Com., 1974-76; mem. Nat. Am. Revolution Bicentennial Advisory Com. on Racial, Ethnic and Native Am. Participation, 1974-76; governing mem. San Francisco YMCA, 1972-82; founding pres., Chinese Hist. Soc. Am., San Francisco, 1963, pres., 1964-66, 75-76; foreman Civil Grand Jury, City and County of San Francisco, 1983-84. Author: Bridging the Pacific: San Francisco Chinatown and Its People, 1989, A Historian's Reflections of Chinese American Life in San Francisco 1919-91, 1993. Recipient awards of merit Conf. Calif. Socs., 1976, 81, Am. Assn. State and Local History, 1976, San Francisco Laura Bride Powers Meml. award, 1987. Mem. Calif. Hist. Soc. (award of merit 1970, trustee 1981-83), E Clampus Vitus, The Westerners. Clubs: Masons (32 deg.) (past master lodge), Shriners. Editor: A History of the Chinese in California-A Syllabus, 1969; editor, co-pub. Chinese Digest, 1st newspaper in English for Chinese-Ams., 1935-37; contbr. articles to hist. jours.

CHIOLIS, MARK JOSEPH, television producer, video consultant; b. Walnut Creek, Calif., Dec. 29, 1959; s. Richard Spiro and Muriel Marie (Kottinger) C. Student aeronautics, Sacramento Community Coll., 1980-82; student, American River Coll., 1982. With on-air ops. Sta. KRBK-TV, Sacramento, 1979-81; on-air ops. trainer, crew chief Sta. KVIE-TV, Sacramento, 1981-85; trainer on air ops., ops. crew chief Sta. KRBK-TV, Sacramento, 1981-84; producer, dir., ops. crew chief Sta. KVIE-TV, Sacramento, 1985-87, Sta. KRBK-TV, Sacramento, 1984-87; prodn. mgr., producer, dir. Sta. KVIE-TV, Sacramento, 1987—; production mgr., producer, dir. spl. programs, comml. productions Sta. KRBK-TV, Sacramento, 1987—; with on-air ops. Sta. KVIE-TV, Sacramento, 1980-82; regional sales mgr. BTS-Broadcast T.V. Systems, Inc., 1992—; promotion chmn. Capital Concour d'Elegance, Sacramento, 1984—, gen. chmn., 1987-89. Producer (music videos) Running Wild, Running Free, 1984, Rocket Hot-/The Image, 1984 (Joey award 1985); producer, dir. (music video) Haunting Melodies, 1991; dir. (documentary) Behind Closed Doors, 1984; producer, dir. FLIGHTLOG, The Jerry Reynolds Show, CountryMile country music show, 1991; dir. (video camera) Reno Nat. Championship Air Races, 1992, Money Insights. Video producer Calif. N.G., 1980-82; video trainer Am. Cancer Soc., Sacramento, 1983-85; cons. Sacramento Sheriff's Dept., Sacramento, 1984—, United Way-WEAVE, Sacramento, 1984-85; bd. dirs. Woodside Homeowners Assn., 1989—. Recipient Gold Addy award, 1986, 87, Addy award, 1989. Mem. Am. Advt. Fedn., Sacramento Advt. Club (awards video producer 1984—, chmn. judging 1988-89, bd. dirs. 1989—, co-chair awards banquet 1989-90), Aircraft Owners and Pilots Assn., Computer Users Group. Republican. Office: Broadcast TV Systems Inc 4827 N Sepulveda Blvd Ste # 150 Sherman Oaks CA 91403

CHIONG, ANGELICA CECILIA, city planner, consultant; b. Lima, Peru, Nov. 22, 1953; came to U.S., 1966; d. Enrique and Regina (Andrade) C. BS in Bus. Adminstrn., U. Calif., Berkeley, 1976, M of City Planning, 1978. Planner/analyst City of Berkeley, 1975-77; analyst Spanish Speaking Unity Coun., Oakland, Calif., 1978-81; planner City and County of San Francisco, 1981-90, dist. planner, 1990—. Author profl. reports and issues paper. Bd. dirs. Brava! For Women in the Arts, San Francisco, 1989-92, Community Edn. Svcs., San Francisco, 1981-82; community liaison Mayor's Task Force on NEMissionIZ, San Francisco, 1991-92; mem. Task Force on Gas Sta. Conversions, San Francisco, 1989-90; mem. MALDEF Leadership Devel. and Advocacy, San Francisco, 1982-92; coord. Mission Neighborhood Family Ctr., San Francisco, 1973. Grad. Minority Program fellow U. Calif. Berkeley, 1976-78. Mem. Gay and Lesbian Planners, Internat. Fedn. Profl. and Tech. Engrs., Mcpl. Planners Assn., Cheuk Fung Y Chuang Martial Arts Sch. Office: City/County San Francisco 450 McAllister St 4th Fl San Francisco CA 94102

CHIPMAN, PATRICK GEORGE, mechanical engineer; b. Flint, Mich., Aug. 17, 1961; s. James Andrew and Olga Marie Chipman. BSME, U. Mich., 1983. Owner Earthwise Prodns., San Diego, 1989—; assoc. global Energy Network, Internat., San Diego, 1990—; Inventor computer chip pin straightener, Earth-Sun-Moon orrery; designer T-shirts; animator Folding/Morphing Dymaxion World Map. Mem. Buckminster Fuller Inst., Tau Beta Pi. Office: Earthwise Prodns 1580 Corsica St San Diego CA 92111

CHISHOLM, DONALD WILLIAM, political science educator; b. Coronado, Calif., July 16, 1953; s. William Kaiser and Mary Katherine (Carmichael) C. AB, U. Calif., Berkeley, 1975, MA, 1977, PhD, 1984. Instr. Mich. State U., East Lansing, 1983-84; vis. lectr. U. Calif. San Diego, La Jolla, 1984-86; asst. prof. Ohio State U., Columbus, 1986-89; asst. prof. polit. sci. UCLA, 1989—; vis. asst. prof. U. Calif., Berkeley, 1986-87. Author: Coordination Without Hierarchy: Informal Structures in MultiOrganizational Systems, 1989; contbr. articles to profl jours. Recipient Leonard D. White award Am. Polit. Sci. Assn., 1985. Mem. Am. Polit. Sci. Assn., Western Polit. Sci. Assn., Midwest Polit. Sci. Assn., San Onofre Surfing Club, Velo Allegro Cycling Club, Surfrider Found., Phi Beta Kappa. Home: 4000 E Colorado St Long Beach CA 90814-2819 Office: UCLA Dept Polit Sci Los Angeles CA 90024

CHISHOLM, TOM SHEPHERD, environmental engineer; b. Morristown, N.J., Nov. 28, 1941; s. Charles Fillmore and Eileen Mary (Fenderson) C.; m. Mary Virginia Carrillo, Nov. 7, 1964; children: Mark Fillmore, Elaine Chisholm. Student, Northeastern U., Boston, 1959-61; BS in Agrl. Engring., N.Mex. State U., 1964; MS in Agrl. Engring., S.D. State U., 1967; PhD in Agrl. Engring., Okla. State U., 1970. Registered profl. engr., Ariz., La.; cert. Class A indsl. wastewater operator. Agrl. engr. U.S. Bur. Land Mgmt., St. George, Utah, 1964-65; asst. prof. U. P.R., Mayaguez, 1970-74, La. State U., 1974-77; assoc. prof. S.D. State U., 1977-81; environ. engr. Atlantic Richfield Subsidiary, Sahuarita, Ariz., 1981-86, Ariz. Dept. Environ. Quality, Phoenix, 1986-88; environ. mgr. Galactic Resources, Del Norte, Colo., 1988-91; v.p. M&E Cons., Inc., Phoenix, 1991—; cons. various mfrs., Calif., Tex., Ill., Mex., 1980-91. Contbr. articles to profl. jours. NSF fellow, 1965-66, 68-69. Mem. Am. Soc. Agrl. Engrs. (faculty advisor student chpt. 1978-79), Phi Kappa Phi, Sigma Xi, Alpha Epsilon, Beta Gamma Epsilon. Home: 2323 E Paradise Dr Phoenix AZ 85028-1018 Office: M&E Cons Inc 2338 W Royal Palm Rd Ste E Phoenix AZ 85021-9339

CHITTICK, ARDEN BOONE, steamship agency executive; b. Sunnyside, Wash., Aug. 5, 1936; s. Herbert Boone and Maude Ellen (George) C.; m. Nina Sorensen, Apr. 16, 1960; children: Kyle, Kirsten. BS, Wash. State U., 1964. Ops. mgr. Kerr Steamship Co. Inc., Seattle, 1979-81, marine mgr. PNW, 1981-84; dist. ops. mgr. Merit Steamship Agy. Inc., Seattle, 1984-86, Pacific N.W. ops. mgr., 1986-87; ops. mgr. Internat. Shipping Co. Inc., Seattle, 1987-89, v.p. ops., 1989-91, regional v.p. ops., 1991—; v.p. Internat. Shipping Co. Inc., Portland, Oreg., 1991—; v.p. Marine Exch. of Puget Sound, Seattle, 1982-88; pres. Puget Sound Steamship Operators Assn., Seattle, 1987, v.p., 1983, 86. Troop com. mem. Boy Scouts Am., Bainbridge Island, Wash., 1984. Capt. USMCR, 1957-64; comdr. USCG, 1964-79. Mem. Puget Sound Coast Guard Officers Assn. (pres. 1978), Propeller Club of U.S. (gov. Seattle chpt. 1984-87, 89—). Republican. Methodist. Home: 8380 NE Blakely Heights Dr Bainbridge Is WA 98110-3200 Office: Internat Shipping Co Inc 1111 3rd Ave Bldg Ste 1825 Seattle WA 98101

CHIU, CHU-TSEN, surgeon; b. Tainan, Taiwan, Republic of China, Dec. 19, 1947; came to U.S. 1975; s. Ping-Hong and Li-Chu Chiu; m. Susan Wu, Jan. 10, 1974; 1 child, Alice. MD, Taipei Med. Coll., 1973. Diplomate Am. Bd. Surgery, Am. Bd. Colon and Rectal Surgery. Resident Meth. Hosp., Bklyn., 1976-80; fellow U. Tex. Med. Sch., Houston, 1980-81; pvt. practice surgery Monterey Park, Calif., 1981—; dir. Gen. Bank, L.A., 1985—. Fellow ACS, Am. Soc. Colon and Rectal Surgeons. Office: 500 N Garfield # 311 Monterey Park CA 91754

CHIU, MARTIN THOMAS, financial planner; b. L.A., Nov. 7, 1964; s. Loy Mai and Ellen (Chan) C. BS, Calif. State U., Long Beach, 1988. Cert. fin. planner. Fin. planner Titan Value Equities Group, Inc., Tustin, Calif.; owner Mapco. Mem. U.S. Profl. Tennis Assn., Internat. Assn. Fin. Planners, Chinese Assn. Orange County (bd. dirs.). Office: Titan Value Equities Group Inc 3155 Arlotte Ave Long Beach CA 90808-4411

CHIU, PETER YEE-CHEW, physician; b. China, May 12, 1948; came to U.S., 1965; naturalized, 1973; s. Man Chee and Yiu Ying (Cheng) C. BS, U. Calif., Berkeley, 1969, MPH, 1970, DrPH, 1975; MD, Stanford U., 1983. Diplomate Am. Bd. Family Practice; registered profl. engr., Calif.; registered environ. health specialist, Calif. Asst. civil engr. City of Oakland, Calif., 1970-72; assoc. water quality engr. Bay Area Sewage Services Agy., Berkeley, 1974-76; prin. environ. engr. Assn. Bay Area Govts., Berkeley, 1976-79; intern San Jose (Calif.) Hosp., 1983-84, resident physician, 1984-86; ptnr. Chiu and Crawford, San Jose, 1986-89, Good Samaritan Med. Group, San Jose, 1989-90, The Permanente Med. Group, 1991—; adj. prof. U. San Francisco, 1979-83; clin. asst. prof. Stanford U. Med. Sch., 1987—. Contbr. articles to profl. publs.; co-authored one of the first comprehensive regional environ. mgmt. plans in U.S.; composer, pub. various popular songs Southeast Asia, U.S. Mem. Chinese for Affirmative Action, San Francisco, 1975—; bd. dirs. Calif. Regional Water Quality Control Bd., Oakland, 1979-84, Bay Area Comprehensive Health Planning Council, San Francisco, 1972-76; mem. Santa Clara County Cen. Dem. Com., 1987—; mem. exec. bd. Calif. State Dem. Cen. Com. Recipient Resident Tchr. award Soc. Tchrs. Family Medicine, 1986, Resolution of Appreciation award Calif. Regional Water Quality Control Bd., 1985. Fellow Am. Acad. Family Physicians; mem. Am. Pub. Health Assn., Chi Epsilon, Tau Beta Pi. Democrat. Office: The Permanente Med Group 770 E Calaveras Blvd Milpitas CA 95035-5462

CHMIEL, KENNETH WALTER, rail systems executive; b. Terre Haute, Ind., Feb. 12, 1944; s. Walter and Celia Grace (Brown) C.; m. Margareta Kuplis, Oct. 17, 1970; children: Nikolas, Alexander. BS in Aeronautical Engring., U. Mich., 1966; MBA, Harvard U., 1973. Engr. Boeing Aircraft Co., Seattle, 1967-70; asst. to pres. Bendix Aerospace Group, Southfield, Mich., 1973-74, Bendix Dashoaveyor Co., Ann Arbor, Mich., 1974-75; mgr. pricing and contracts Bendix Avionics Div., Fort Lauderdale, Fla., 1975-76, mgr. inventory control, 1976-78; mgr. materials Bendix Test Systems Div., Teterboro, N.J., 1977-80, dir. mfg., 1980-81; plant mgr. Flight Systems div. Allied Signal Aerospace, Montrose, Pa., 1981-86; asst. gen mgr. flight systems div. Allied Signal Aerospace, Teterboro, 1986-87; pres. Electrodynamics div. Allied Signal Aerospace, North Hollywood, Calif., 1987-89; corp. v.p. mfg. ops. Morrison Knudsen Corp., Boise, Idaho, 1989-90, exec. v.p. Rail Systems Group, 1990—. Mem. Arid Club. Republican. Roman Catholic.

CHO, LEE-JAY, social scientist, demographer; b. Kyoto, Japan, July 5, 1936; came to U.S., 1959; s. Sam-Soo and Kyung-Doo (Park) C.; m. Eun-Ja Chun, May 20, 1973; children—Yun-Kyong, Sang-Mun, Jeremy. BA, Kookmin Coll., Seoul, Korea, 1959; MA in Govt., George Washington U., 1962; MA in Sociology (Population Council fellow), U. Chgo., 1964, PhD in Sociology, 1965; D in Econs. (hon.), Dong-A U., 1982; DSc in Demography, Tokyo U., 1983; D in Econs., Keio U., Tokyo, 1989. Statistician Korean Census Council, 1958-61; research assoc., asst. prof. sociology Population Research and Tng. Center, U. Chgo., 1965-66; asso. dir. Community and Family Study Center, 1969-70; sr. demographic adv. to Malaysian Govt., 1967-69; assoc. prof. U. Hawaii, 1969-73, prof., 1973-78; asst. dir. East-West Population Inst., East-West Center, Honolulu, 1971-74; dir. East-West Population Inst., East-West Center, 1974-92; pres. pro tem East-West Center, 1980-81, v.p., 1987—; cons. in field; mem. Nat. Acad. Scis. Com. on Population and Demography; mem. U.S. 1980 Census Adv. Com., Dept. Commerce. Author: (with others) Differential Current Fertility in the United States, 1970,editor: (with others) Introduction to Censuses of Asia and the Pacific: 1970-74, 1976, (with Kazumasa Kobayashi) Fertility Transition in East Asian Populations, 1979, (with Suharto, McNicoll and Mamas) Population Growth of Indonesia, 1980, The OWN Children of Fertility Estimation, 1986, (with Y.H. Kim) Economic Development of Republic of Korea: A Policy Perspective, 1989; contbr. (with Suharto, McNicoll and Mamas) numerous articles on population to profl. jours. Bd. dirs. Planned Parenthood Assn., Hawaii, 1976-77. Ford Found. grantee, 1977-79; Population Council grantee, 1973-75; Dept. Commerce grantee, 1974-78; recipient Award of Mugunghwa-Jang, govt. Republic of Korea, 1992. Mem. Internat. Statis. Inst. (tech. adv. com. World Fertility Survey), Internat. Union Sci. Study Population, Population Assn. Am., Am. Statis. Assn., Am. Sociol. Assn., N.E. Asia Econ. Forum (founding chmn.). Home: 1718 Halekoa Dr Honolulu HI 96821-1027 Office: 1777 East-West Rd Honolulu HI 96848

CHO, ZANG HEE, physics educator; b. Seoul, Korea, July 15, 1936; came to U.S., 1972; p. Byung-Soon Cho and Kang Ae Yu. BSc, Seoul Nat. U., 1960, MSc, 1962; PhD, Uppsala (Sweden) U., 1966. Assoc. prof. Stockholm U., 1971-76, UCLA, 1972-78; prof. Columbia U., N.Y.C., 1979-85, U. Calif., Irvine, 1985—; assoc. dir. Imaging Rsch. Ctr., Columbia U., 1979-84; dir. Nuclear Magnetic Resonance rsch. U. Calif., Irvine, 1985—. Editor: IEEE Nuclear Science, 1974, Computers Medical Biology, 1976, Image Science, Springer & Verlag, 1984, Imaging Science & Technology, 1989. Named Disting. Scientist, Asilomar, 1982; recipient Grand Sci. prize, Seoul, 1984, Sylvia Sorkin Greenfield award, Am. Assn. Med. Physicists, 1989. Fellow IEEE (editor Trans. Nuclear Sci. 1974), Third World Acad. Sci. (assoc.). Home: 29 Harbor Point Corona Del Mar CA 92625 Office: Univ Calif Dept Radiological Sci Irvine CA 92717

CHOA, WALTER KONG, chemical company official; b. Rangoon, Burma, Aug. 10, 1948; came to U.S., 1974; s. Keng Hong and Kim (Tan) C.; m. Teresa Yeap Myint, Sept. 29, 1979; 1 child, Patricia. BS in Chemistry, Rangoon U., 1967. R & D chemist Diversey Chems., Des Plaines, Ill., 1975-80; mgr. tech. svc. Diversey Wyandotte, Mich., 1980-85, Diversey Wyandotte Metals, 1985-88; western mgr. tech. svc. Novamax Techs. (U.S.), Inc., City of Industry, Calif., 1988—. Mem. Am. Electroplaters and Surface Finishers Assn. (appreciation award L.A. br. 1983). Home: 3561 Cotter Rim Ln Diamond Bar CA 91765 Office: Novamax Techs (US) Inc 15010 E Don Julian Rd City of Industry CA 91746

CHOCK, CLIFFORD YET-CHONG, family practice physician; b. Chgo., Oct. 15, 1951; s. Wah Tim and Leatrice (Wong) C. BS in Biology, Purdue U., 1973; MD, U. Hawaii, 1978. Intern in internal medicine Loma Linda (Calif.) Med. Ctr., 1978-79, resident in internal medicine, 1979; resident in internal medicine U. So. Calif.-L.A. County Med. Ctr., L.A., 1980; physician Pettis VA Clinic, Loma Linda, Calif., 1980; pvt. practice Honolulu, 1981—; physician reviewer St. Francis Med. Ctr., Honolulu, 1985—, chmn. family practice care, 1990—, chmn. utilization rev., 1990-91, acting chmn. credentials com., 1992, chmn. care evaluation com., 1990—; physician reviewer Peer Rev. Orgn. Hawaii, Honolulu, 1987—. Mem. Am. Acad. Family Physicians. Office: 321 N Kuakini St Ste 513 Honolulu HI 96817-2361

CHODERA, JERRY, mechanical engineer; b. Medina, Ohio, May 19, 1947; s. Joseph John and Marcella Ellaine (Damon) C.; m. Marie Grace Buonocore, June 29, 1972; children: John Damon, Kristin Ann. BS in Mech. Engring., Case Inst. Tech., 1969; postgrad., U. fla., 1969-70. Registered profl. engr., Calif., Ohio. Apollo launch crew engr. Boeing Atlantic Test Ctr., Cape Canaveral, Fla., 1969-70; sr. plant engr. B. F. Goodrich Co., Akron, Ohio, L.A., 1970-75; sr. project engr. AMF-Tire Equipment Div., Santa Ana, Calif., 1975-78; v.p. Wescal Industries, Rancho Dominguez, Calif., 1978—. Committeman Boy Scouts of Am., 1988—. Recipient Bausch and Lomb Sci. award, 1965. Mem. ASME, Case Inst. Tech. Alumni Assn., Mensa. Presbyterian. Office: 18033 S Santa Fe Ave East Rancho Dominguez CA 90221-5579

CHOE, JOSEPH JONG KOOK, mortgage banker; b. Seoul, Republic of Korea, Mar. 15, 1961; s. Eung S. and Koja (Lee) C. Student, Santa Monica (Calif.) Coll., 1981, UCLA, 1982. Loan officer Southwest Savs. & Loan, Los Angeles, 1984-85; v.p. I.G.F.S. Inc., Los Angeles, 1986-87; pres. Investree, Inc., Los Angeles, 1985-87; sr. loan cons. Merchant Bank of Calif., Beverly Hills, 1987-88; pres. Fin. Am., Los Angeles, 1988-92; v.p. Coast Bank, Long Beach, Calif., 1992—. Mem. Korean Jr. League Am. (L.A. chpt., treas., counselor 1982-83), Wooriro Club (L.A. chpt., treas. 1987—). Office: Coast Bank 5354 E 2d St Long Beach CA 90803

CHOI, KWANG-CHUL, construction company executive; b. Je-Cheon, Korea, June 24, 1955; came to Guam, 1977.; s. Kee-Joon Choi and Bok-Dong Park; m. Sun-Haeng Rhee, Sept. 18, 1977; 1 child, Minna. BS, Seoul (Korea) Nat. U., 1977; MS, U. Calif., Berkeley, 1981, PhD, 1992. Registered profl. engr., Calif. Field constrn. engr. Dillingham Corp., Guam, 1978-80; project controls engr. Bechtel Corp., San Francisco, 1981-86, sr. systems analyst, 1989-92, IS mgr., 1992—; constrn. mgmt. cons. Berkeley, 1986-87; rsch. asst. U. Calif., Berkeley, 1987-89. Mem. ASCE, Am. Assn. Cost Engrs., Assn. Computing Machinery. Home: 730 Farmhill Ct Walnut Creek CA 94598 Office: Bechtel Corp 50 Beale St PO Box 193965 San Francisco CA 94119

CHOI, YONG, store owner; b. Seoul, Korea, Jan. 1, 1937; came to U.S., 1960; s. Sung Doo and Soon Kyung Choi; m. Kwang Ja, Dec. 18, 1965; children: Chul, Mihee, Mili. BBA, Yun Se U., Seoul, 1959. Mgr. N.Y. World's Fair Korean Pavilion, N.Y.C., 1964-65; pres. Richard Cosmetic Inc., N.Y.C., 1965-68; v.p. K.B.S. Trading Co., Honolulu, 1969-75; owner franchise 7-Eleven Food Store, Palo Alto, Calif., 1975—. Fund raiser Sight First Program Lions Club, Palo Alto, Calif. 1993 (made Guiness Book of Records for fastest around the world no layovers trip completed on a commercial airplane, 35hrs 14min., 19,731 miles for charity). Mem. South Palo Alto Lions Club (pres. 1979-80, 92). Republican. Baptist. Office: 7-Eleven Food Store 708 Colorado Ave Palo Alto CA 94303

CHOJNACKY, CYNTHIA COFFER, communications coordinator; b. Ponca City, Okla., Feb. 14, 1955; d. Henry Ford and Helene Martha (Lewis) C.; m. David Carl Chojnacky, May 28, 1977; 1 child, Michal Jean. BA in Journalism, U. Ariz., 1977; MA in Polit. Sci., Colo. State U., 1984. Forestry reporter Albany (Oreg.) Democrat-Herald News, 1977-79; higher edn. reporter Standard-Examiner, Ogden, Utah, 1979; government reporter Standard Examiner, Ogden, 1985-86; univ. rels. rep. Colo. State U., Fort Collins, 1981-83; writer, editor Forest Svc., Ogden, Utah, 1986-87; communications coord. Forest Svc., Ogden, 1987—, pub. affairs team leader, steelhead and salmon strategy, 1992-93; mem. UOFU Pub. Adminstrs. Practitioners Adv. Group, Salt Lake City, 1989-91; cons., mem. Forest Svc. Customer Expectations Team, 1991-93; mem., reporter Forest Svc. Orgn. Improvement Team, (regional), 1992—. Developer (workshops) Real Time Customer Svc., 1991; contbr. articles to newspapers. Mem. Pub. Rels. Soc. Am., Nature Conservancy, Sierra Club, Assn. Forest Svc. Employees for Environ. Ethics, Wilderness Soc., Pi Sigma Alpha. Mem. Christian Ch. Home: 1387 36th St Ogden UT 84403 Office: Forest Svc Intermt Region 324 25th St Ogden UT 84401

CHOLE, RICHARD ARTHUR, otolaryngologist, educator; b. Madison, Wis., Oct. 12, 1944; s. Arthur Steven and Wendy Elveyn (Danielczyk) C.; m. Cynthia Beiseker, Dec. 27, 1969; children: Joseph Michael, Timothy Thomas, Katharine, Melinda. Student, U. Calif., Berkeley, 1962-65; MD, U. So. Calif., 1969; PhD in Otolaryngology, U. Minn., 1977. Diplomate Am. Bd. Otolaryngology (alt. bd. examiner). Rotating intern U. So. Calif. Med. Ctr., 1969-70; med. fellow dept. surgery Sch. Medicine, U. Minn., 1972-73, med. fellow dept. otolaryngology, 1973-77; asst. prof. dept. otolaryngology-head and neck surgery Davis Sch. Medicine, U. Calif., 1977-81, assoc. prof., 1981-84, prof., 1984—, acting chmn. dept., 1985, chmn., 1985—; mem. sci. rev. com. Deafness Rsch. Found., 1986—; mem. communicative disorders rev. com. Nat. Inst. Deafness and Communication Disorders, 1989—; staff cons. Dept. Air Force, David Grant USAF Med. Ctr., Travis AFB, Calif., 1981—; keynote speaker 92d Japan Oto-Rhino-Laryngol. Soc. Meeting, Fukuoka City, 1990; faculty mem. 4th Internat. Cholesteatoma Conf., Niigata City, Japan, 1992; lectr. in field. Mem. editorial bd. Laryngoscope, 1985-87; mem. exec. editorial bd. Otolaryngology-Head and Neck Surgery, 1990—; contbr. numerous articles to profl. jours., book chpts., revs.; patentee in field. Mem. profl. edn. com. Am. Cancer Soc., 1977-78, Sacramento Noise Control Hearing Bd., 1977—, Greater Sacramento Profl. Standards Rev. Orgn., 1978-79; deacon 1st Bapt. Ch., Davis, 1979-82, elder, 1983-88. Recipient 1st pl. award Am. Acad. Ophthalmology and Otolaryngology, 1977, care recognition awards U. Calif., Davis, 1988-91; rsch. grantee NIH, Nat. Inst. Aging, Nat. Inst. Neurol. and Communicative Disorders and Stroke, Nat. Inst. on Deafness and Other Communication Disorders, Deafness Rsch. Found., Am. Otol. Soc., U. Calif., 1978-91. Mem. Collegeum ORLAS (U.S. group), Am. Acad. Otolaryngology-Head and Neck Surgery (Honors award 1984, com. on rsch. 1987—, rsch. coordinating coun. 1987—, continuing edn. com. 1991—), Am. Otol. Soc. (trustee rsch. fund 1986—, sec.-treas. 1989—), Assn. for Rsch. in Otolaryngology (award of merit com. 1988—), Am. Laryngol., Rhinol. and Otol. Soc., Am. Soc. for Bone and Mineral Rsch., Assn. Acad. Depts. Otolaryngology-Head and Neck Surgery (coun. 1986—), Calif. Med. Assn. (sci. adv. panel, sect. on otolaryngology-head and neck surgery 1986—), Sacramento Soc. Otolaryngology and Maxillofacial Surgery, Soc. Univ. Otolaryngologists-Head and Neck Surgeons. Office: U Calif-Davis Sch Medicine Dept Otorhinolaryngology 2500 Stockton Blvd Sacramento CA 95817-2208

CHOMKO, STEPHEN ALEXANDER, archaeologist; b. Bklyn., Nov. 18, 1948; s. Paul and Lucy Isabella (Bisaccio) C.; m. Leslie M. Howard, Aug. 1972 (div. 1980). BA in Anthropology cum laude, Beloit Coll., 1970; MA in Anthropology, U. Mo., 1976, PhD in Anthropology, 1992. Mem. rsch. staff Nassau County Mus. Natural History, Glen Cove, N.Y., 1969-71; grad. rsch. asst. U. Mo., Columbia, 1972-74, 75-78; rsch. asst. Ill. State Mus., Springfield, 1974-75; dist. archaeologist Bur. Land Mgmt., Rawlins, Wyo., 1978-80; archaeologist Office of Fed. Inspector, Denver, 1980-82; dir. Paleo Environ. Cons., Wheat Ridge, Colo., 1980-86; archaeologist Interagy. Archaeol. Svcs., Denver, 1982-92; chief rsch. and resource mgmt. Mesa Verde (Colo.) Nat. Park, 1992—. Writer, dir. (video program) Our Past Our Future, 1992; contbr. articles to profl. jours. Grantee Cave Rsch. Found., Yellow Springs, Ohio, 1976; recipient Anthropology Scholarship U. Mo., Columbia, 1978, Quality Performance award Nat. Park Svc., Denver, 1992. Mem. Soc. Am. Archaeology, Am. Anthropol. Assn., Am. Quaternary Assn., Wyo. Assn. Profl. Archaeologists (exec. com. 1979-82), Mont. Archaeol. Soc., Plains Anthropol. Soc. (v.p. 1988-89, bd. dirs. 1986-89). Home: 6880 W 36th Pl Wheat Ridge CO 80033 Office: Nat Park Svc 12795 W Alameda Ave Denver CO 80225

CHONG, LOO TIMOTHY, newspaper editor; b. Yuma, Ariz., Dec. 8, 1965; s. Loo Shee and Evelyn Leona (Shumpert) C. Student, U. Ariz., 1983-84; AA in Gen. Studies, Ariz. Western Coll., 1986; BS in Journalism, No. Ariz. U., 1989. Asst. entertainment editor The Lumberjack, Flagstaff, Ariz.,

1986, entertainment editor, 1987; copy editor The Idaho Statesman, Boise, Idaho, 1989; copy editor, TV editor The Yuma Daily Sun, 1989—. Author: (news/commentary column) Open Season, 1987-89 (1st pl. award gen. news column 1989), Journalists Notebook, 1993—; (humor column) Switching Channels, 1990-93. Office: The Yuma Daily Sun 2055 Arizona Ave Yuma AZ 85364

CHONG, RICHARD DAVID, architect; b. Los Angeles, June 1, 1946; s. George and Mabel Dorothy (Chan) C.; m. Roze Gutierrez, July 5, 1969; children: David Gregory, Michelle Elizabeth. BArch, U. So. Calif., 1969; MArch, UCLA, 1974. Registered architect, Utah, Calif., Wyo., Wash. Assoc. Pulliam, Matthews & Assocs., Los Angeles, 1969-76; dir. Asst. Community Design Ctr., Salt Lake City, 1976-77; prin. Richard D. Chong & Assocs., Salt Lake City and L.A., 1977—; planning cons. Los Angeles Harbor Dept., 1974-76; asst. instr. So. Calif. Inst. Architecture, Santa Monica, 1973-74; vis. design critic Calif. State Poly. U., Pamona, 1975, U. Utah, Salt Lake City, 1976-78; design instr. Calif. State Poly. U., 1975-76; adj. asst. prof. urban design, U. Utah, 1980-84; bd. dirs. Utah Housing Coalition, Salt Lake City; Salt Lake City Housing Adv. and Appeals Bd., 1976-80. Author: Design of Flexible Housing, 1974; prin. works include Airmen's Dining Hall, 1985 (1st Pl. Mil. Facility Air Force Logistics Command, 1986), Oddfellows Hall, 1984 (Heritage Found. award, 1986). Mem. Task Force for the Aged Housing Com. Salt Lake County, Salt Lake City, 1976-77; Salt Lake City Mortgage Loan Instns. Rev. Com., 1978; bd. dirs. Neighborhood Housing Svcs. of Fed. Home Loan Bank Bd., Salt Lake City, 1979-81, devel. com.; vice-chmn. Water Quality Adv. Coun., Salt Lake City, 1981-83; vice-chmn. Salt Lake City Pub. Utilities Bd., 1985-87; mem. adv. bd. Pub. Utilities Commn., Salt Lake City, 1985—; bd. dirs. Kier Mgmt. Corp.; bd. mem. Camp Kostopulos. Mem. AIA (jury mem. Am. Soc. Interior Designers Annual awards 1981-82, treas. Salt Lake chpt. 1988-89, treas. Utah Soc. 1991, sec. Utah Soc. 1992), Am. Inst. Planning (juror Annual Planning award 1984-85), Am. Planning Assn., Am. Arbitration Assn., Nat. Panel Arbitrators, Salt Lake City C. of C. (mem. housing com. 1977). Democrat. Club: Ft. Douglas Country (Salt Lake City). Office: Richard D Chong & Assocs 248 Edison St Salt Lake City UT 84111-2307 also: 261 S Figueroa Ste 370 Los Angeles CA 90012

CHOO, VINCENT KI SENG, mechanical engineering educator; b. Pahang, Malaysia, Aug. 27, 1952; came to U.S., 1983; s. Sang and Ling Yeng (Chong) C.; m. Charlene Cox, May 18, 1984; children: Nathaniel I., Christopher T., Joshua K. BS with honors, Nottingham (Eng.) U., 1977; PhD, Liverpool (Eng.) U., 1982. Postdoctoral rsch. asst. Imperial Coll., London, 1982; vis. asst. prof. U. Wash., Seattle, 1983-84; assoc. prof. N.Mex. State U., Las Cruces, 1985—; cons. Flow Industries, Kent, Wash., 1983, Boeing Aircraft Co., Seattle, 1984, Sund Defibrator, A.B., Stockholm, 1985. Author: Multiaxial Testing of Composite Materials, 1986, Fundamentals of Composite Materials, 1990. GE Found. grantee, 1989, Am. Chem. Soc. grantee, 1987. Mem. Am. Soc. for Composites, Soc. for the Advancement of Material and Process Engrng. Home: 2040 Boise Dr Las Cruces NM 88001-5135 Office: NMex State U Mech Engrng Dept Las Cruces NM 88003-0001

CHOOK, EDWARD KONGYEN, disaster medicine educator; b. Shanghai, China, Apr. 15, 1937; s. Shiu-heng and Shuiking (Shek) C.; m. Ping Ping Chew, Oct. 30, 1973; children by previous marriage: Miranda, Bradman. MD, Nat. Def. Med. Ctr., Taiwan, 1959; MPH, U. Calif., Berkeley, 1964, PhD, 1969; ScD, Phila. Coll. Pharmacy & Sci., 1971. Assoc. prof. U. Calif., Berkeley, 1966-68; dir. higher edn. Bay Area Bilingual Edn. League, Berkeley, 1970-75; prof., chancellor United U. Am., Oakland and Berkeley, Calif., 1975-84; regional adminstr. U. So. Calif., L.A., 1984-90; vis. prof. Nat. Def. Med. Ctr., Taiwan Armed Forces U., 1982—, Tongju U., Shanghai, 1992—, Foshan U., People's Republic of China, 1992—; founder, pres. United Svc. Coun., Inc., 1971—; pres. Pan Internat. Acad., Changchun, China, San Francisco, 1992—; pres. U.S.-China Gen. Devel. Corp., 1992—; pub. Power News, San Francisco, 1979—; mem. Nat. Acad. Scis./NRC, Washington, 1968-71. Trustee Rep. Presdl. Task Force, Washington, 1978—; mem. World Affairs Coun., San Francisco, 1989—; deacon Am. Bapt. Ch.; sr. advisor U.S. Congl. Adv. Bd.; mem. Presdl. Adv. Commn., 1991—. Mem. Rotary (chmn. cm. 1971—). Office: 555 Pierce St # 1338-9 Albany CA 94706

CHOU, CHUNG-KWANG, bio-engineer; b. Chung-King, China, May 11, 1947; came to U.S. 1969, naturalized 1979; s. Chin-Chi and Yu-Lien (Hsiao) C.; m. Grace Wong, June 9, 1973; children: Jeffrey, Angela. BSEE, Nat. Taiwan U., 1968; MSEE, Washington U., St. Louis, 1971; Ph.D., U. Wash., Seattle, 1975. Postdoctoral fellow U. Wash., Seattle, 1976-77, asst. prof., 1977-81, rsch. assoc. prof., 1981-85; rsch. scientist, head biomed. engring. sect., dir. dept. radiation rsch., div. radiation oncology, City of Hope Nat. Med. Ctr., Duarte Calif., 1985—; cons. Nat. Coun. Radiation Protection and Measurement, 1978—. Assoc. editor Jour. of Bioelectromagnetics, 1988—; contbr. articles to profl. jours. Served to 2d lt. Army of Taiwan, 1968-69. Fellow IEEE (com. on man and radiation 1990—, standard coordinating com., subcoms.); mem. Internat. Microwave Power Inst. (1st spl. award of decade 1981, Outstanding Paper award 1985), N.Am. Hyperthermia Soc., Bioelectromagnetics Soc. (bd. dirs. 1981-84), Radiation Rsch. Soc., Electromagnetic Acad., Sigma Xi, Tau Beta Pi. Mem. Christian Ch. Office: City of Hope Nat Med Ctr Divsn Radiation Oncology Duarte CA 91010

CHOU, YUE HONG, education educator, researcher; b. Taipei, Taiwan, Oct. 14, 1952; came to U.S., 1978; s. Chang Shong and Chin-Lien (Cheng) C.; m. Grace Minn-Chue Liau, Aug. 11, 1978; children: Jason Hsun, Jonathan Wayne. BS, Nat. Taiwan U., Taipei, 1975; MA, Ohio State U., 1979, PhD, 1983. Asst. prof. Northwestern U., Evanston, Ill., 1984-87; assoc. prof. U. Calif., Riverside, 1987—; prin. investigator U.S. Forest Svc., Riverside, 1989—, U.S. Dept. Navy, Riverside, 1990—, So. Calif. Assn. of Govts., L.A., 1990—; co-investigator County of Riverside, 1990—. Contbr. articles to profl. jours. Moderator Internat. Symposium on the Role of Taiwan, L.A., 1988, Enviorn. Systems Rsch. Inst., Palm Springs, Calif., 1990—; invited speaker U.S. Forest Svc., Riverside, 1990—. U.S. Forest Svc. grantee, 1990—, USMC grantee, 1991—. Mem. Am. Assn. Geographers, Am. Congress on Surveying and Mapping, Am. Soc. for Photogrammetry and Remote Sensing, Am. Cartographic Assn., Urban and Regional Info. Systems Assn., Math. Assn. Am. Presbyterian. Office: U Calif Earth Scis Dept Riverside CA 92521

CHOW, FRANKLIN SZU-CHIEN, obstetrician-gynecologist; b. Hong Kong, Apr. 15, 1956; came to U.S., 1967; s. Walter Wen-Tsao and Jane Ju-Hsien (Tang) C. BS, CCNY, 1977; MD, U. Rochester, 1979. Diplomate Am. Bd. Ob-Gyn. Intern Wilmington (Del.) Med. Ctr., 1979-80, resident in ob-gyn, 1980-83; practice medicine specializing in ob-gyn Vail (Colo.) Valley Med. Ctr., 1983—, chmn. obstetrics com., 1984-85, 86-87, chmn. surg. com., 1987-88, vice chief of staff, 1989-91, chief of staff, 1991-92. Named to Athletic Hall of Fame, CCNY, 1983. Fellow Am. Coll. Ob-Gyn's; mem. AMA, Colo. Med. Soc., Intermountain Med. Soc. (pres. 1985-86), Internat. Fedn. Gynecol. Endoscopists, Am. Assn. Gynecol. Laparoscopists, Gynecologic Laser Soc., Am. Soc. Colposcopy and Cervical Pathology. Home: 171 Chaparral PO Box 5657 Vail CO 81658-5657 Office: Vail Valley Med Ctr 181 W Meadow Dr Ste 600 Vail CO 81657

CHOW, JOHN (KUNG-YAO), systems manager; b. Shanghai, China, Mar. 14, 1947; came to U.S., 1979; s. John (Wan-Kong) and Shu-Ching (Kwok) C.; m. Rosalind Liang, Feb. 4, 1981; children: Alfred, Serena. BS, U. San Francisco, 1989. Systems analyst Computerized Automotive Mgmt. Systems, San Francisco, 1982-86; sr. systems analyst Reynolds & Reynolds Info. Systems, Dayton, Ohio, 1986-88; pres. Bus. Records Mgmt. Systems, Inc., Wilmington, Del., 1986—; systems mgr. U. Calif., San Francisco, 1988—. Recipient award of excellence Photographers Forum mag., 1990. Christian. Office: U Calif 612 Forbes Blvd South San Francisco CA 94080

CHOW, JUDY, educator; b. Taipei, Taiwan, China, Feb. 13, 1954; came to U.S., 1964; d. Charles and Lucy (Chu) C.; m. Steve Lee, July 3, 1982; children: Andrew Chow Lee, Mike Chow Lee. BA, UCLA, 1975, MLS, 1977. Libr. LA County Pub. Libr., 1979-84, LA Pub. Libr., 1984-90; faculty mem. LA Community Coll., 1990—. Mem. Calif. Libr. Assn., Faculty Assn. of Calif. Community Colls. Buddhist. Office: LA Community Coll 4800 Freshman Dr Culver City CA 90230

CHOW, MOO-PING, environmental engineer, consultant; b. Youngchow, Jiangsu, China, Dec. 17, 1927; came to U.S., 1954; s. Shin-Ting and Wei-Jian Chow; m. Lin-Lin Chow, Nov. 17, 1955; children: George, Ellen, Betty. BSCE, Chao-Tung U., Shanghai, China, 1947; MS in San. Engring., U. N.C., 1960. Asst. prof. Sun Yat Sen U., Canton, China, 1948-49; engr. san. div. Taiwan Bur. Pub. Works, Taipei, 1950-59; san. engr. various cons. engring. cos., San Francisco and Lansing, Mich., 1960-67; engr. san. div., sr. process analyst City and County San Francisco, 1968—; cons. to Taiwan, 1972, 76, 88, China, 1980, 83, 86, 88—, UN, 1989. Mem. Am. Acad. Environ. Engrs. (diplomate), Water Pollution Control Fedn., Am. Water Works Assn. Home: 3091 Medina Dr San Bruno CA 94066 Office: Bur Water Pollution Control 750 Phelps St San Francisco CA 94124

CHOW, PAUL CHUAN-JUIN, physics educator; b. Beijing, China, Aug. 1, 1926; came to U.S., 1955; s. C. K. and Baode (Shen) C.; m. Vera Chow, June 25, 1965; children: Maria, Theresa, Teh-Han. BA, U. Calif., Berkeley, 1960; PhD, Northwestern U., 1965. Fishing boat capt. Fisheries Taiwan/UNRRA, China Coast, 1946-55; rsch. scientist U. So. Calif., L.A., 1965-67, U. Tex., Austin, TEx., 1967-68, 1970; from asst. prof. to assoc. prof. Calif. State U., Northridge, 1968-80, prof., 1980—; adj. prof. Beijing (China) Inst. Tech.; advisor S. China Normal U., Expert bur., State Coun., Beijing, China; cons. World Bank, Control Data Corp., UNDP, Chinese State Edn. Commn. Bd. dirs. L.A.-Guangzhou Sister City, L.A., chmn. Sci & Tech. Ctr., L.A. Mem. Am. Phys. Soc.

CHOW, PHILIP YEONG-WAI, engineering company executive, consultant; b. Medan, Sumatra, Indonesia, Aug. 8, 1923; s. Chee-Yee and Khoo Oi-Toh; m. Toh-Cheen Tan, May 2, 1952; children: Yan-Chiew, Chee-Chiew, Sharon Chen-ru Chow Chia, Chen-Yin Chow Noah. BSCE, U. Ariz., 1950; MS, U. Ill., 1952; diploma, Imperial Coll. Sci. and Tech., London, 1953. Lic. profl. engr., U.K., Singapore (Malaysia), Calif. Ptnr. Steen Sehested and Ptnrs., Singapore, 1953-65; project engr. Santa Fe Internat., San Francisco, 1966-71; mng. dir. T.Y. Lin S.E. Asia, Singapore, 1971-76; from exec. v.p. to chmn. T.Y. Lin Internat., San Francisco, 1976—; task group chmn. Fedn. Internat. Precontraint, London, 1978-86. Co-author: (chpt.) Handbook of Structural Concrete, 1983; patentee in field of structural engineering and high-pressure prestressed concrete pressure vessels; contbr. articles to profl. jours. Fellow ASCE (aerospace task force, Best Paper on Aerospace 1990), Am. Concrete Inst. (com. chmn. 1978-86), Inst. Civil Engrs. U.K., Ins. Structural Engrs. U.K.; mem. Soc. Naval Architects and Marine Engrs. Democrat. Methodist. Home: 3 Harran Cir Orinda CA 94563

CHOW, TEH-HAN P., marketing consultant; b. Austin, Tex., Aug. 16, 1968; s. Paul C. and Vera (Chow) C. BS in Mktg., Calif. State U., 1992. Exec. mgr. Golden Life Med. Group, Tarzana, Calif., 1988-92; mng. ptnr. Pacific Cons., Northridge, Calif., 1992-; pub. rels. mgr. Holiday Inn Lido Beijing Hotel, Beijing, People's Republic of China, 1992—; bd. dirs. Sci. and Tech. Ctr., 1990—. Mem. adv. bd. Am. Express Connections Mag., N.Y.C., 1991-92. Founder Com. for Preservation of Giant Panda, 1984-87. Mem. Am. Assn. Promotion Sci. in China (bd. dirs.), Am. Mktg. Assn.

CHOW, WINSTON, engineering research executive; b. San Francisco, Dec. 21, 1946; s. Raymond and Pearl C.; m. Lilly Fah, Aug. 15, 1971; children: Stephen, Kathryn. BSChemE, U. Calif. Berkeley, 1968; MSChemE, Calif. State U., San Jose, 1972; MBA cum laude, Calif. State U., San Francisco, 1985. Registered profl. chem. and mech. engr.; instr.'s credential Calif. Community Coll. Chem. engr. Sondell Sci. Instruments, Inc., Mountain View, Calif., 1971; mem. research and devel. staff Raychem Corp., Menlo Park, Calif., 1971-72; supervising engr. Bechtel Power Corp., San Francisco, 1972-79; sr. project mgr. water quality and toxic substances control program Electric Power Rsch. Inst., Palo Alto, Calif., 1979-89, program mgr., 1990—. Contbr. author Water Chlorination, vols. 4, 6; contbr. articles to profl. publs. Pres., CEO Directions, Inc., San Francisco, 1985-86, bd. dirs., 1984-87, chmn. strategic planning com., 1984-85; mem. industry com. Am. Power Conf., 1988—; mem. Dist. Cen. Com., 1990—, chmn., 1992—; mem. strategic long-range planning and restructuring com. Sequoia Union High Sch. Dist., 1990—. Recipient Grad. Disting. Achievement award, 1985; Calif. Gov.'s Exec. fellow, 1982-83. Mem. ASME, Am. Inst. Chem. Engrs. (profl. devel. recognition award), NSPE, Calif. Soc. Profl. Engrs. (pres. Golden Gate chpt. 1983-84, v.p. 1982-83, state dir.), Calif. Water Pollution Control Assn., Air and Waste Mgmt. Assn., Calif. State U. Alumni Assn. (bd. dirs., treas. 1989-91), Calif. Alumni Assn., Beta Gamma Sigma. Democrat. Presbyterian. Office: Electric Power Rsch Inst 3412 Hillview Ave Palo Alto CA 94304-1395

CHOY, HERBERT YOUNG CHO, federal judge; b. Makaweli, Kauai, Hawaii, Jan. 6, 1916; s. Doo Wook and Helen (Nahm) C.; m. Dorothy Helen Shular, June 16; 1945. B.A., U. Hawaii, 1938; J.D., Harvard U., 1941. Bar: Hawaii 1941. Law clk. City and County of Honolulu, 1941; assoc. Fong & Miho, 1946; ptnr. Fong Miho & Choy, Honolulu, 1947-57; atty. gen. Ter. of Hawaii, 1957-58; ptnr. Fong, Miho, Choy & Robinson, 1958-71; judge U.S. Ct. Appeals, 9th circuit, Honolulu, 1971—. Trustee Hawaii Loa Coll., 1963-79. Served with Hawaii Territorial Guard, 1941-42, AUS, 1942-46, lt. col. USAR, ret. Decorated Order Civil Merit (Korea), 1973. Fellow Am. Bar Found.; mem. Am., Hawaii bar assns. Office: US Ct Appeals PO Box 50127 Honolulu HI 96850-0001

CHRESSANTHIS, JAMES ANDREW, cinematographer, documentary director; b. Phila., May 9, 1953; s. Andrew George and Angeline (Nichols) C.; m. Robin Lynne Becker, July 7, 1979. Student, Rensselaer Poly. Inst., 1970-72; BFA, Ariz. State U., 1975; MFA, So. Ill. U., 1977, Am. Film Inst., L.A., 1988. Assoc. prof. Western Mich. U., Kalamazoo, 1977-85; cinematographer music videos MTV and various record cos., 1987—; cons. Sony Corp. Am., L.A., 1986—. Dir. photography: Leather Jackets (Columbia-Tri-Star), 1990, Death Dreams (Lifetime/ABC), 1991, Public Enemy #2 (Showtime), 1991, Father and Son (NBC), 1993, Majority Rule (Lifetime/ABC), 1992, Hexed (Columbia Studios), 1993; documentary dir. Voices That Care (Fox Network), 1991, Bridge for the Children, 1991. Grantee Ford Found., 1981; recipient Ace award for cinematography Nat. Acad. Cable Programming, 1991, Red Ribbon award for documentary Am. Film and Video Festival, 1991. Democrat. Greek Orthodox. Office: Lyons/Sheldon Agy 8344 Melrose Ave Ste 20 Los Angeles CA 90069

CHRIST, RONALD LEE, surgeon; b. Akron, Ohio, Sept. 19, 1935; s. Henry and Kathryn (Ellis) C.; m. Deborah Ann Styer, Apr. 28, 1990; children: Kathryn, Theresa, Leslie, Kurt, Sara. BS, U. Akron, 1957; MD, Ohio State U., 1961. Diplomate Am. Bd. Surgery. Intern Akron City Hosp., 1961-62; resident surgery Montefiore Med. Ctr., Bronx, N.Y., 1967-71; pvt. practice surgery Yuma, Ariz., 1971—; chief staff Yuma Regional Med. Ctr., 1979; dir. So. Ariz. Bank, Yuma. Mem., pres. dist. bd. Crane Elem. Sch., Yuma, 1982-88. Comdr. USN, 1962-67. Fellow ACS; mem. AMA, Ariz. Med. Assn. (dir. 1980-92), Yuma County Med. Soc. Republican. Office: 1763 W 24th St Yuma AZ 85364

CHRISTENSEN, ALBERT SHERMAN, federal judge; b. Manti, Utah, June 9, 1905; s. Albert H. and Jennie (Snow) C.; m. Lois Bowen, Apr. 4, 1927; children: A. Kent, Karen D., Krege B. Student, Brigham Young U., intermittently 1923-27; J.D., Nat. U., 1931. Bar: D.C. 1932, Utah 1933. Asst. bus. specialist U.S. Dept. Commerce, 1930-32; practiced in Provo, Utah, 1933-42, 45-54; U.S. dist. judge Dist. of Utah, Salt Lake City, 1954—; sr. fed. judge, 1972—; mem. com. on revision laws Jud. Conf. U.S., 1960-68, com. on ct. adminstrn., 1968-75, adv. com. rules of civil procedure, 1972-82, rev. com., 1977-78, jud. ethics com., 1978-82, Temporary Emergency Ct. Appeals, 1972-93; bd. Utah Bar Examiners, 1939-42; chmn. Ad Hoc Com. Am. Inns of Ct. 1983-85. Republican congressional candidate, 1939. Served from lt. to lt. comdr. USNR, 1942-45. Recipient Chmn.'s award Am. Inns of Ct. Found., 1988,; Fulbright award Nat. Ctr., George Washington U., 1990. Mem. ABA (awarded medal 1990), Utah Bar Assn. (pres. 1951-52, Judge of Yr. award 1977), Utah Jr. Bar Assn. (pres. 1937-38), Utah County Bar Assn. (pres. 1936-37, 47-48). Mem. Ch. Jesus Christ of Latter-day Saints.

CHRISTENSEN, ALLEN CLARE, agriculturalist, educator; b. Lehi, Utah, Apr. 14, 1935; s. Clare Bernard and Relia Sarah (Allen) C.; m. Kathleen Ruth Atwater, Dec. 19, 1958; children: Ann Marie, Allen Clare Jr., James Lynn, Niel Daniel, Eric Wayne. BS with Honors, Brigham Young U., 1957; MS, U. Calif.-Davis, 1960; PhD, Utah State U., 1979. Cert. Am. Registry Profl. Animal Scientists. Vocat. agr. tchr. White Pine County Schs., Lund, Nev., 1961-64; from asst. to assoc. prof. agr. Calif. State Poly. U., Pomona, 1964-73, prof., 1973—, dean coll. agr., 1980-85, 87—; acting provost and acad. v.p., 1985-87; cons. Agrl. Edn. Found., Templeton, Calif., 1971-85, AID, Washington, 1983—, W.K. Kellogg Found., Battle Creek, Mich., 1984, Lesotho Agrl. Coll., Maseru, 1989; trustee Consortium for Internat. Devel., Tucson, Ariz., 1980—, vice chair of bd., 1988-89, chmn. 1992—; mem. deans' coun. Calif. Agr. Leadership Program, Templeton, 1980-85, 87—, chair 1989-91; mem. joint com. on agr. rsch. and devel., AID, 1982-87, chmn. strengthening grant panel bd. internat. food and agrl. devel., 1983-87; chair BIFAD panel Human Capital Devel., 1985-87; apptd. by Gov. Wilson to Calif. State Bd. for Food and Agr., 1991—, NASULGC Board on Agr., 1992—. Author: (with others) Working in Animal Science, 1978. Contbr. articles to profl. jours. Pres. Chino, Calif Latter-day Saint Stake, 1979-88, mem. exec. bd. Old Baldy coun. Boy Scouts Am., 1988-89; bd. dirs. So. Calif. Agrl. Land Found., 1988—. Recipient Hon. State Farmer Degree, Calif. Assn. Future Farmers Am., 1983, Disting. Svc. award Calif. Assn. Future Farmers Am. , 1992. Mem. Am. Soc. Animal Scis., Poultry Sci. Assn., Golden Key Nat. Honor Soc. (hon.), Phi Beta Delta, Phi Kappa Phi, Gamma Sigma Delta (Outstanding Faculty award of Merit, 1976, pres. 1969-70), Alpha Zeta. Republican. Mormon. Office: Calif State Poly U Coll Agriculture 3801 W Temple Ave Pomona CA 91768-4041

CHRISTENSEN, CAROLINE, vocational educator; b. Lehi, Utah, Oct. 5, 1936; d. Byam Heber and Ruth (Gardner) Curtis; m. Marvin Christensen, June 16, 1961; children: Ronald, Roger, Robert, Corlyn, Richard, Chad. BS, Brigham Young U., 1958, MS, 1964. Sec. Brigham Young U., Provo, Utah, 1954-58; instr. bus. Richfield (Utah) High Sch., 1958-61, Sevier Valley Applied Tech. Ctr., Richfield, 1970-92. Historian, Sevier Sch. Dist. PTA, 1968, 69; chmn. Heart Fund Dist., 1983, Voting Dist., 1988-90. Mem. Utah Edn. Assn., Am. Vocat. Assn., Utah Vocat. Assn., Nat. Bus. Edn. Utah Bus. Edn. Assn. (sec. 1986-87), NEA, Western Bus. Edn. Assn., Sevier Valley Tech. Tchrs. Assn. (sec. 1971-92, pres. 1986-87), Delta Pi Epsilon (historian), Delta Kappa Gamma (treas. 1975-90, pres. 1990-92, state nominating com.), Phi Beta Lambda (advisor 1988-92).

CHRISTENSEN, DANA LANE, controller; b. Great Falls, Mont., June 21, 1961; s. Wayne Marinus and Helen Katherine (Hickman) C.; m. Evelyn Carol Heintzelman, Mar. 1, 1985; children: Bob, Steve, Kelli, Adam, Tyler. B in Adminstrn., Eastern Mont. Coll., 1990. CPA, Mont. Contr. Conrad & Bischoff Oil Co., Idaho Falls, Idaho, 1990, Woodside Homes Corp., Ogden, Utah, 1990-93, Atherton Constrn., Salt Lake City, 1991—. Republican. Mem. Church of Jesus Christ of Latter Day Saints. Home: 528 N 550 E Orem UT 84057 Office: Atherton Construction Inc 127 S 500 E Ste 600 Salt Lake City UT 84102

CHRISTENSEN, DONN WAYNE, insurance executive; b. Atlantic City, Apr. 9, 1941; s. Donald Frazier and Dorothy (Ewing) C.; BS, U. Santa Clara, 1964; m. Marshella Abraham, Jan. 26, 1963 (div.); children: Donn Wayne, Lisa Shawn; m. Mei Ling Fill, June 18, 1976 (div.); m. Susan Kim, Feb. 14, 1987; stepchildren: Don Kim, Stella Kim. West Coast div. mgr. Ford Motor Co., 1964-65; agt. Conn. Mut. Life Ins. Co., 1965-68; pres. Christensen & Jones, Inc., L.A., 1968—; v.p. Rsch. Devel. Systems Inc.; investment advisor SEC, 1985—. Pres. Duarte Community Drug Abuse Coun., 1972-75; pres. Woodlyn Property Owners Assn., 1972-73; mem. L'Ermitage Found., 1985—, Instl. Rev. Bd. White Meml. Hosp., L.A., 1975—. Recipient Man of Yr. award L.A. Gen. Agts. and Mgrs. Assn., numerous. Mem. Nat. Life Underwriters Assn., Calif. State Life Underwriters Assn., Investment Co. Inst. (assoc.), Soc. Pension Actuaries, Foothill Community Concert Assn. (pres. 1970-73). Registered investment advisor, SEC, 1984. Office: 709 E Colorado Blvd Ste 270 Pasadena CA 91101-2196

CHRISTENSEN, GORDON JOHNSON, prosthodontist, lecturer, researcher; b. Logan, Utah, Nov. 10, 1936; s. Wilford Emanuel and Janet (Johnson) C.; m. Rella Parisi, Nov. 21, 1959; children: William G., Michael G., Carlene. DDS, U. So. Calif., 1960; MS in Dentistry, U. Wash., 1963; PhD, Denver U., 1972. Diplomate Am. Bd. Prosthodontics. Asst. prof. U. Wash., Seattle, 1962-65; assoc. prof. U. Ky., Lexington, 1965-68; prof., assoc. dean U. Colo., Denver, 1968-76; co-dir. Clin. Rsch. Assocs., Provo, Utah, 1976-87, sr. cons., 1987—; prosthodontist Gordon J. Christenson P.C., Provo, Utah, 1976—; dir. Gordon J. Christensen Practical Clin. Courses, Provo, Utah, 1981—; bd. dirs. Found. of Acad. of Gen. Dentistry; cons. U.S. Army Dental Corps Comdrs., 1987—, U. Utah Engring. Sch., 1970-80, U. Iowa, Expanded Function Aux. Program, 1973-75, Ft. Ord, Calif., 1973-78, Wm. Beaumont Gen. Hosp., El Paso, Tex., 1973-78, Fitzsimons Army Med. Ctr., Denver, 1970-78, VA Hosp., Denver, 1969-76, NIMH Clin. Rsch. Ctr., Lexington, Ky., 1965-68, Wright Patterson AFB Hosp., Dayton, Ohio, 1965-68; appointments to Utah Valley Regional Med. Ctr., Provo, 1976—, Colo. Gen. Hosp., Denver, 1968-76, Univ. Hosp., Lexington, 1965-68, Univ. Hosp., Seattle, 1963-65; lectr. in U.S. and internationally. Co-editor Clin. Rsch. Assocs. Newsletter, 1977—; assoc. editor Jour. Pedodontics, 1975-80; mem. editorial bd. Current Opinion in Dentistry, 1989—, Jour. of Esthetic Dentistry, 1989—, Am. Jour. of Dentistry, 1989—, Internat. Jour. of Periodontics and Restorative Dentistry, 1988—, Jour. of Operative Dentistry, 1978—. Jour. of Am. Acad. of Gold Foil Operators, 1968-76; editorial cons. Jour. of Am. Dental Assn., 1988—; section editor Jour. of Prosthetic Dentistry, 1980-85; contbg. editor Am. Acad. Esthetic Dentistry, 1980-82, Dental Students, 1980-82. Active LDS Ch., Boy Scouts Am., 1963-93; profl. coord. United Way, 1988. Capt. U.S. Army, 1960-63. Recipient Achievement award Alumni Assn. SCADA, 1968, Man of Yr. award Am. Coll. Dentists, 1986, Disting. Svc. award Brigham Young U. Acad. Dentists, 1987, Award of Distinction Acad. Dentistry Internat., 1988, Pieere Fauchard Acad. award, 1989, Disting. Alumnus award U. Wash. Dental Alumni Assn., 1989, Award for svc. to dental profession Delta Sigma Delta, 1990, Utah Dental award, 1991, Internat. Achievement award Alpha Omega, 1991, Fauchard Gold Medal award, 1992; voted # 1 Dental Lectr. in U.S. Dentist Mag., 1987, 88, 89; Gordon Christensen Recognition Lecture award established in his honor Chgo. Dental Soc., 1990. Fellow Royal Coll. Surgeons, Acad. Gen. Dentistry (hon.), Acad. Dentistry Internat., Am. Coll. Dentists, Internat. Coll. Dentists, Am. Coll. Prosthodontists; mem. Am. Coll. Oral Implantology, Current Opinion in Dentistry (editorial bd. 1991—), Internat. Congress Oral Implantologists, Fedn. Prosthodontic Orgns. (clin. review com. 1991—), Fedn. Dentiare Internat., Christian Dental Soc., Internat. Coll. Prosthodontists, Omicron Kappa Upsilon, Phi Kappa Phi, Alpha Tau Epsilon. Home: 4100 North Devonshire Dr Provo UT 84604 Office: Clin Rsch Assocs 3707 N Canyon Rd Ste 7A Provo UT 84604

CHRISTENSEN, GWEN JOYNER, media director, diaconal minister; b. Mpls., Feb. 21, 1930; d. Albert and Victoria (Krienke) J.; children: Grant, Vicki, Emily, Bert. BA, Hamline U., 1951; MA, Sch. Theology, Claremont, Calif., 1989. Cert. tchr., United Meth. Christian Educator, United Meth. Communicator; ordained to ministry United Meth. Ch. as diaconal min., 1980. Tchr. English local jr. high sch. Mpls., 1951-52; dir. jr. high sch. sect. United Meth. Ch., Mpls., 1952-54; dir. media ctr. United Meth. Ch., L.A., 1975—; diaconal min. United Meth. Ch., Pasadena, Calif., 1980—; cons. media for ch. workshops and seminars; vice-chair Bd. Diaconal Ministry, 1988-89; reviewer Am. Film Festival. Contbg., writer Ch. Tchrs. mag., 1986—. Supt. Sunday sch. local ch. United Meth. Ch., Tujunga, Calif., 1960-63, tchr. Sunday sch. local ch., Glendale, Calif., 1977—, chair ministries coun., Glendale, 1985-86. Recipient Bishop's award Calif.-Pacific conf. United Meth. Ch., 1991. Mem. United Meth. Communicators, United Meth. Women, Religious Pub. Rels. Coun., Christian Edn. Fellowship.

CHRISTENSEN, ROBERT WAYNE, JR., financial and leasing company executive; b. Chester, Calif., Nov. 11, 1948; s. Robert Wayne and Ann (Forsyth) C.; m. Debra Schumann, Dec. 6, 1988; 1 child, Heather. BA with honors, Coll. Gt. Falls, 1976; MBA, U. Puget Sound, 1978. Cert. flight instr. Corp. pilot Buttrey Food Stores, Gt. Falls, Mont., 1972-74; asst. to pres. Pacific Hide & Fur, Gt. Falls, 1974-76; fin. analyst Olympia Brewing Co., Olympia, Wash., 1977; pres., chief exec. officer Republic Leasing, Olympia, 1978—; pres. PacWest Fin. Corp., Olympia, 1984—; bd. dirs. Republic Leasing, Olympia, Wash. Independent Bancshares, Olympia, 1982—, PacWest Fin. Corp., Olympia. Served to sgt. USAF, 1969-72. Mem. Nat. Vehicle Leasing Assn. (bd. dirs. 1978—, 2d. v.p. 1984, pres. 1986), Western Assn. Equipment Lessors, Western Leasing Conf., Mensa,

Rotary (bd. dirs. 1982—, v.p. 1986-88, pres. 1988—). Office: Republic Leasing The Republic Bldg PO Box 919 Olympia WA 98507-0919

CHRISTENSEN, STEVEN BRENT, data processing executive; b. Salt Lake City, Feb. 26, 1959; s. Raymond David and Marlene Kay (Manheim) C. BA in Human Resource Devel. cum laude, Brigham Young U., 1983, MLS, 1990. Tng. specialist Am. Express Co., N.Y.C., 1983; mgr. C&J Clark Inc., Orem, Utah, 1984-86; mgr. computer svc. Valcom Computers, Provo, Utah, 1987; cons. Castle Computer Systems, Orem, 1988-91; systems mgr. tech. libr. Dugway (Utah) Proving Ground, 1991—. Vol. asst. Found. Ancient Rsch., Provo, 1987-88. Named one of Outstanding Young Men Am., 1983. Mem. ALA, Spl. Librs. Assn., Am. Soc. Tng. and Devel., Internat. Platform Assn. Republican. Home: 1579 E 8730 S Sandy UT 84093-1550 Office: US Army Dugway Proving Ground Tech Libr AHN JOD-I Dugway UT 84022-5000

CHRISTENSON, ANDREW LEWIS, archaeologist; b. Seattle, Feb. 15, 1950; s. Carl James and Geraldine (Beleu) C. BA in Anthropology, UCLA, 1973, MA in Anthropology, 1976, PhD in Anthropology, 1981. Curator, archaeology Mus. of Cultural History, UCLA, L.A., 1980-83; assoc. scientist So. Ill. Univ., Carbondale, Ill., 1983-87; adj. faculty Prescott (Ariz.) Coll., 1988—; archaeologist CSWTA, Inc., Tuba City, Ariz., 1990—; archaeology cons. U.S. Army, Washington, 1980, Zuni (N.Mex.) Archaeology Program, 1989-90, Nat. Park Svcs., 1990—; assoc. editor Western U.S., Bull. of History of Archaeology, 1990—. Co-editor: (book) Modeling Change in Prehistoric Subsistence Economies, 1980; Co-author: (book) Prehistoric Stone Technology on Northern Black Mesa Arizona, 1987; editor: (book) Tracing Archaeology's Past, 1989. Grantee Am. Philosophical Soc., 1985, NEH, 1985, S.W. Pks. and Monuments Assn., 1987. Mem. Soc. for Am. Archaeology (com. on the history of archaeology). Home and Office: 229 Creekside Cir # D Prescott AZ 86303-5611

CHRISTENSON, CHARLES ELROY, art educator; b. Gary, Ind., Jan. 2, 1942; s. Christian Monroe and Violet May (Kirkland) C.; m. Coral Yvette Demar, Feb. 26, 1966 (div. May 1990); children: Michael Eric, Tessa Diahann, Leah Renee. Student, U. Tex., 1960-63; BFA, San Francisco Art Inst., 1966; MFA, U. Wash., Seattle, 1970. Staff artist Taylor Press, Dallas, 1962-63; freelance artist San Francisco, 1963-64, 65-66; comml. artist The Emporium, San Francisco, 1964-65; art educator U. Wash., 1970-71, Shoreline Community Coll., Seattle, 1971-75; art educator North Seattle Community Coll., Seattle, 1971—, acting chmn. humanities div., 1978-79, gallery dir., 1977—; advisor art group North Seattle C.C., 1978—; juror Equinox Arts Festival, Everett, Wash., 1981; curator exhbns. Wash. C.C. Humanities Conv., Bellevue, 1986, 87; bd. advisors Noon Star Prodns., Seattle, 1992—; co-owner, tour leader Sketching and Touring Through France, Seattle, 1992—. Writer, illustrator: Simple Crafts for the Village, 1968; author poems. Vol. Am. Peace Corps, Andra Pradesh, India, 1966-68; beef leader Riverview Champs-4-H Club, Everett, 1980-81; coach Snohomish (Wash.) Youth Soccer, 1982-88; mem. Seattle Art Mus. Recipient Beyond War Found. award, 1987, Gov.'s Faculty Recognition award, 1987; Seattle Community Coll. Dist. grantee, 1988, Fulbright grantee India, 1990—; named to Humanities Exemplary Status, Wash. Community Coll. Humanities Assn., 1987. Mem. Wash. C.C. Humanities Assn., Smithsonian Inst., Artist's Trust, Seattle C.C. Fedn. Tchrs. (human div. rep. 1977-78), Nat. Coun. for Social Studies, Nat. Campaign for Freedom Expression, Amnesty Internat. Office: North Seattle Community Coll 9600 College Way N Seattle WA 98103-3599

CHRISTENSON, VICKI, nursing educator; b. Lafayette, Ind., Mar. 22, 1947; d. Charles LeRoy and Mary Anne (Hazelgrove) Wallace; m. Donald Martin Christenson, Oct. 30, 1964; children: Candi, David Martin. ADN, Spokane C.C., 1984; BSN (magna cum laude), Gonzaga U., 1988; M in Nursing, Wash. State U., 1991. Cert. BLS, PALS, ACLS, maternal child/adolescent nursing. Teaching asst., Rogers High Sch., No. Ctrl. High Sch. Sch. Dist. 81, Spokane, Wash., 1979-81; staff nurse, Adult Orthopedics Holy Family Hosp., Spokane, Wash., 1984-85; pediatric critical care, staff nurse, clin. nurse specialist Sacred Heart Med. Ctr., Spokane, Wash., 1985—; nursing instr. Spokane C.C., 1988-93; cardiovascular clin. nurse specialist Empire Health Svcs., Spokane, 1990-91; cons. Plummer Community Clinic, 1991, St. John Clinic, 1991, Coulee City Hosp., 1991, Spokane C.C., 1991, Valley Med. Ctr., 1991, YMCA Infant Ctr., 1992—. Editor: Heart Gram, Empire Health Svcs. and Community Hosps., 1990-91. Mem. AACN (spl. interest cons. region 18), Am. Heart Assn., Wash. State Nurses Assn., Wash. Jr. Golf Assn., Wash. State Univ. Alumni, Northwest Pediatric Critical Care Symposium, Inland Empire Nurses Assn. (nominating com. 1985-89, conv. com. 1992—, 2d v.p. & program chair, bd. dirs. 1989-91, newsletter author 1989-91), Gonzaga Univ. Alumni (advisor), Sigma Theta Tau (publicity com., co-editor newsletter 1991—). Home: W 2107 Dalton Spokane WA 99205 Office: Intercollegiate Ctr for Nursing Edn W 2917 Ft George Wright Dr Spokane WA 99204

CHRISTIAENS, CHRIS (BERNARD F. CHRISTIAENS), financial analyst, senator; b. Conrad, Mont., Mar. 7, 1940; s. Marcel Jules and Virgie Jeanette (Van Spyk) C. BA in Chemistry, Coll. Gt. Falls, 1962, postgrad., 1984—. Fin. and industry mgr. Rice Motors, Gt. Falls, Mont., 1978-84; senator State of Mont., 1983-87, 1991—, majority whip 49th legis., 1985-86; fin. planner Jack Stevens CPA, Gt. Falls, 1984-85; adminstr., fin. analyst Gt. Falls Pre-Release, 1986—; owner Old Oak Inn-Bed and Breakfast, 1989—. Chmn. Balance of State Pvt. Industry Council, Mont. 1984—; mem. Mont. Human Rights Commn., 1981-84; bd. dirs. St. Thomas Child and Family Ctr., Gt. Falls, 1983—, Coll. Gt. Falls, 1984—; bd. dirs., treas. Gt. Falls Community Food Bank, 1984-86; Dem. committeeman, Cascade County, Mont., 1976-82; Mont. del. to Nat. Rules Conv., 1980; pub. chmn. Cascade County chpt. ARC, 1986; mem. adv. bd. Cambridge Court Sr. Citizen Apt. Complex, 1986; bd. dirs. Cascade County Mental Health Assn., 1986—; treas. Cascade County Mental Health Ctr.; vice-chmn. Gov.'s Task Force on Overcrowding; mem. regional jail com.; mem. Re-Leaf Great Falls com., 1989—, mem. steering com. Named one of Outstanding Young Men of Am., Jaycees, 1976; recipient Outstanding Young Alumni award Coll. Gt. Falls, 1979. Roman Catholic. Clubs: Gt. Falls Ski, Toastmasters. Lodge: Optimists. Home: 709 4th Ave N Great Falls MT 59401-1509 Office: Great Falls Pre-Release Svcs Inc 1019 15th St N Great Falls MT 59401-1238

CHRISTIAN, ANN SEGER, state government lawyer; b. Waterloo, Iowa, Oct. 11, 1954; d. David Edmund and Dorothy Ann (Reinhart) Seger; m. Thomas Embree Christian, July 21, 1978. BA in Social Work, U. Iowa, 1976, JD magna cum laude, 1980. Bar: Oreg. 1981. Worker income maintenance Iowa Dept. of Welfare, Cedar Rapids, 1976-77; assoc. Multnomah Defenders, Inc., Portland, Oreg., 1982-86, asst. dir., 1986-88; dir. Indigent Def. Svcs. divsn. Office of State Ct. Adminstrn., Salem, Oreg., 1988—. Bd. dirs. Vancouver (Wash.) Humane Soc., 1988-89. Mem. Oreg. Bar Assn., Phi Beta Kappa.

CHRISTIAN, DONALD JACOBS, computer engineer; b. Bryan, Tex., Mar. 8, 1951; s. John Donald and Marlan Francis (Jacobs) C.; m. Sally Elizabeth Christian, Dec. 21, 1974; children: Mary, John, James, William. BS, Ohio State U., 1974; MS, So. Meth. U., 1981. Computer engr. Tex. Instruments, Dallas, 1974-85; product mgr. Allen-Bradley Co., Milw., 1985-88; dept. mgr. FMC Corp. Tech. Ctr., Santa Clara, Calif., 1988—. Patentee in robotics, machine vision, automation, electronic music; contbr. to profl. publs. Mem. IEEE (sr. mem.), Soc. Mfg. Engrs. (sr. mem., cert.), Machine Vision Assn. (bd. dirs. 1990—). Office: FMC Corp Tech Ctr 1205 Coleman Ave Santa Clara CA 95050-4337

CHRISTIAN, PAULETTE THERESE, cosmetics executive, educator; b. Orleans, Vt., Jan. 9, 1947; d. Raymond Josephat and Gertrude (Poirier) Benoit; m. Robert Anthony Christian, June 10, 1981. AA, Scottsdale (Ariz.) Community Coll., 1976, Glendale Community Coll., 1991; postgrad., Westmore Acad. of Cosmetic Arts, 1987; diploma in beauty therapy, Aesthetics Unltd., Phoenix, 1988; BS, No. Ariz. U., 1992. Cosmetic sales exec. Colorful You, Phoenix, 1981—; curriculum developer, educator Glendale (Ariz.) Community Coll., 1985—; speaker various ednl. orgns., 1985—. Author various works in field. Mem. NAFE, Ariz. Soc. Profl. Image Cons., Nat. Cosmetology Assn., Am. Inst. Esthetics, Robert Schuller's Eagle Club (Orange, Calif.), 500 Club (Phoenix). Republican. Roman Catholic. Office: Colorful You 7873 N 49th Ave Glendale AZ 85301-8012

CHRISTIAN, ROLAND CARL (BUD CHRISTIAN), retired English and speech communications educator; b. LaSalle, Colo., June 7, 1938; s. Roland Clyde and Ethel Mae (Lattimer) C.; m. Joyce Ann Kincel, Feb. 15, 1959; children: Kathleen Marie, Kristine May Sweet. BA in English and Speech, U. No. Colo., 1962, MA, 1966. Cert. tchr., N.Y., Colo. Tchr. Southside Jr. High Sch., Rockeville Ctr., N.Y., 1962-63, Plateau Valley High Sch., Collbran, Colo., 1963-67; prof. English Northeastern Jr. Coll., Sterling, Colo., 1967-93, prof. emeritus, 1993—; presenter seminars, workshops, Sterling, 1967—; emcee/host Town Meeting of Am., Sterling, 1976. Author: Be Bright! Be Brief! Be Gone! A Speaker's Guide, 1983, Potpourrivia, A Digest of Curious Words, Phrases and Trivial Information, 1986, Nicknames in Sports: A Quiz book, 1986; lit. adv. New Voices mag., 1983—; contbr. Ways We Write, 1964, The Family Treasury of Great Poems, 1982, Our Twentieth Century's Greatest Poems, 1982, Anti-War Poems; vol. II, 1985, Impressions, 1986, World Poetry Anthology, 1986, American Poetry Anthology, 1986, Chasing Rainbows, 1988, The Poetry of Life, 1988, Hearts on Fire, 1988, Wide Open Magazine, 1986, 87, 88; columnist South Platte Sentinel, 1988—. Served with U.S. Army, 1956-59. Recipient Colo. Recognition of Merit scholarship, 1956, Merit cert. Poets Anonymous, 1983, Award of Merit (9), 1985, 86, Golden Poet of Yr. award World of Poetry Press, 1985, 86, 87, 88, Joel Mack Tchr. of Yr. award Northeastern Jr. Coll., 1986; Jr. Coll. Found. grantee, 1986, 87. Mem. NEA, AAUP, Jr. Coll. Faculty Assn. (sec./treas. 1970-72), Colo. Edn. Assn., Nat. Council Tchrs. of English, Poets of Foothills. Roman Catholic. Home: 1027 Park St Sterling CO 80751-3753 Office: Northeastern Jr Coll Humanities and Human Svcs Sterling CO 80751

CHRISTIAN, SUZANNE HALL, financial planner; b. Hollywood, Calif., Apr. 28, 1935; d. Peirson M. and Gertrude (Engel) Hall; children: Colleen, Carolyn, Claudia, Cynthia. BA, UCLA, 1956; Master's, Redlands U., 1979; cert. in fin. planning, U. So. Calif., 1986. Cert. fin. planner. Instr. L.A. City Schs., 1958-59; instr. Claremont (Calif.) Unified Schs., 1972-84, dept. chair, 1981-84; fin. planner Waddell & Reed, Upland, Calif., 1982—, sr. account exec., 1986; corp. mem. Pilgrim Place Found., Claremont; lectr. on fin., estate and tax planning for civic and profl. groups; host TV show Money Talks. Author: Strands in Composition, 1979. Mem. legal and estate planning com. Am. Cancer Soc., 1988—; bd. dirs. YWCA-Inland Empire, 1987; treas. Fine Arts Scripps Coll. Recipient Silver Crest award Torchmark, 1985-87, 92. Mem. Inst. Cert. Fin. Planners, Internat. Assn. Fin. Planners, Planned Giving Roundtable, Estate Planning Coun. Pomona Valley, Claremont C. of C. (pres. elect, bd. dirs.), Curtain Raisers Club of Gairison (pres. 1972-75), Circle of Champions, Rotary Internat. (bd. dirs.), Kappa Kappa Gamma (pres. 1970-74). Home: PO Box 1237 Claremont CA 91711-1237 Office: Waddell & Reed 1317 W Foothill Blvd Ste 222 Upland CA 91786-3673

CHRISTIAN, WILLIAM RICHARDSON, lawyer; b. Columbia, S.C., Mar. 18, 1950; s. Frank Lester Christian and Mary (Richardson) Flaherty; m. Bonnie L. Christian, June 21, 1982; children: Amy, William, Jonathan, Austin, Lindsey. BA in Acctg., Calif. State Coll., Fullterton, 1970; JD, U. Calif., 1973. CPA. Ptnr. Willis, Butler, Scheifly, Leydorf & Grant, L.A., 1973-81; tax ptnr. Pepper, Hamilton & Scheetz (merged with Willis et al), L.A., 1981-83; ptnr. Hufstedler, Miller, Kaus & Beardsley, L.A., 1983-90; Rodi, Pollock, Pettker, Galbraith & Phillips, L.A., 1990—; lectr. U. So. Calif, U. Calif., L.A., Calif. State U., Northridge, Fullerton; adj. prof. Golden Gate U.; trustee Wynn Found., L.A., 1984-90. Author: Subchapters Taxation, 1990; assoc. editor Hastings Law Jour., 1972-73. Mem. ABA (tax, corp. and estate planning sects.), L.A. County Bar Assn. (mem. tax sect., com. chmn. death and gift inheritance tax, bus. law, real property, probate and anti-trust sects.), Calif. State Bar Assn. (Conf. del. 1976-89), Order of Coif. Office: Rodi Pollock Pettker et al 801 S Grand Ste 400 Los Angeles CA 90017

CHRISTIANSEN, ERIC ALAN, software development executive; b. Salt Lake City, May 14, 1958; s. Don Parley and Lilian Patricia (Clegg) C.; m. April Gay Willes, Jan. 9, 1988; 1 child, Amber. BS in Computer Sci., West Coast U., L.A., 1981. Software engr. Lear Siegler Astronics, Santa Monica, Calif., 1980-82; sr. software specialist Digital Equipment Corp., Culver City, Calif., 1982-83; software cons. L.A., 1983-84; v.p. Mindcode Devel. Corp., Salt Lake City, 1984-85; software cons. Van Nuys, Calif., 1985-89; sr. software engr. ITT Gilfillan, Van Nuys, 1989-90; asst. v.p. Wells Fargo Nikko Investment Advisors, San Francisco, 1990—; strategic advisor Tri-Pacific Cons. Corp., Alameda, Calif., 1991—; guest lectr. George Mason U. and Joint Tactical Command, Control, and Comm. Agy., 1991. Developer (comml. software program) Structurer preprocessor enhancing command interface and language for VAX/VMS, 1989; contbr. articles to profl. jours. Sunday sch. tchr. Ch. of LDS, Concord, Calif., 1992. Mem. IEEE, Assn. for Computing Machinery, Digital Equipment Computer Users Soc. (local user group bd. 1988-90). Republican. Office: Wells Fargo Nikko Investment Advisors 45 Fremont St San Francisco CA 94105

CHRISTIANSEN, MARJORIE MINER, nutrition educator; b. Canton, Ill., Feb. 28, 1922; d. John Ernest and Margaret Ellen (Wilson) Miner; m. Theodore Leo Christiansen, Aug. 10, 1951; 1 dau., Karen Lee. Student Joliet Jr. Coll., 1939-41, Iowa State U., 1941-42; B.S., U. N.Mex., 1949, M.A., 1955; Ph.D., Utah State U., 1967. Instr. sci. and nutrition Regina Sch. Nursing, Albuquerque, 1950-64, project dir., 1966-69; project dir., adj. prof. U. Albuquerque, 1969; prof. home econs. James Madison U., Harrisonburg, Va., 1969-84, prof. emeritus, 1984—; nutrition cons. Mental Devel. Ctr., Albuquerque, 1968-69; project dir. Dietary Mgmt. Seminars, VA Regional Med. Program, 1973-76. Mem. adv. Com. on spl. edn. Harrisonburg (Va.) pub. schs., 1972-84. Utah State U. fellow, 1963-67; grantee Corn Products Co., 1965, Nurse Tng. Act Pub. Health Service, 1966-69. Mem. Am. Dietetic Assn., N.Mex. Dietetic Assn. Methodist. Contbr. articles to profl. jours. Home: 10008 Wellington NE Albuquerque NM 87111

CHRISTIANSEN, ROBERT LORENZ, geologist; b. Kingsburg, Calif., June 13, 1935; s. Lorenz Walter and Sara (Hugo) C.; m. Susan Eloise Putnam, June 23, 1962; children: Peter Putnam, John Robert, Catherine Sara. BS, Stanford U., 1956, MS, 1957, PhD, 1961. Geologist Utah Constr. Co., San Francisco, 1957-58, Stanford Rsch. Inst., Menlo Park, Calif., 1960-61; geologist U.S. Geol. Survey, Denver, 1961-71, Hawaii Nat. Park, 1971-73; geologist U.S. Geol. Survey, Menlo Park, 1973—, chief igneous and geothermal processes br., 1987-91; coord. monitoring and rsch. U.S. Geol. Survey, Mt. St. Helens, Wash., 1980; rev. panelist Costa Rican Elec. Inst., San Jose, 1984-86; cons. UN, Nairobi, Kenya, 1987. Contbr. articles on volcanology, igneous petrology and tectonics to profl. jours. With U.S. Army, 1958. Fellow Geol. Soc. Am.; mem. AAAS, Am. Geophys. Union, Mineral. Soc. Am. Office: US Geol Survey 345 Middlefield Rd # 910ms Menlo Park CA 94025-3591

CHRISTIANSEN, SUSAN PUTNAM, artist, educator, consultant; b. Fresno, Calif., Sept. 4, 1938; d. Murray and Iolene Lazelle (Lund) Putnam; m. Robert Lorenz Christiansen, June 23, 1962; children: Peter Putnam and John Robert (twins), Catherine Sara. BA in Biology, Art, Stanford U., 1960, MA in Edn., 1961. Cert. secondary tchr., Calif. Tchr. sci. and art Blach Sch., Los Altos, Calif., 1961-62; tchr. art appreciation Jefferson County Schs., Denver, 1963-68; docent Denver Art Mus., 1963-70; docent trainer, classroom aide Palo Alto (Calif.) Sch. Dist. and Cultural Ctr., 1973-84; art cons. Children's Hosp., Stanford, Calif., 1985-90; researcher Creative Svcs., Stanford Alumni Assn., 1989-92; docent Stanford Mus. Art, 1982—; freelance artist, illustrator, cons., 1973—; children's art tchr., painter Hilo Art Ctr., Big Island, Hawaii, 1971-73; chmn. African art lecture group Stanford Mus. Art, 1990—. Illustrator signs in Hawaii Volcanoes Nat. Pk., 1971-73, U.S. Geol. Survey, 1977, Photographic Atlas of Mid-Atlantic Rift Valley, 1977; muralist Children's Hosp., 1979-84; painter, illustrator Stanford Centennial exhibit, 1991. Mem. organizing com. edn. Palo Alto Centennial, 1992-93. Mem. Stanford Alumni Assn. (nomination com. 1970), Nat. Trust for Historic Preservation, Coun. for Arts (v.p. spl. projects com. 1989—), Stanford Hist. Soc., Palo Alto Hist. Assn., Inst. for Rsch. on Women and Gender, Pacific Art League of Palo Alto. Democrat. Home: 1118 Harker Ave Palo Alto CA 94301

CHRISTIANSON, DANA PAUL, art director; b. La Mesa, Calif., Oct. 8, 1957; s. Carl Alfred and Johanna (Cassol) C.; m. Deborah Jill Christianson, Jan. 26, 1986; children: Jon Carl, Joseph Andrias and Caitlin Elizabeth (triplets). BA, San Diego State U., 1987. Asst. art dir. Cinematronics, El Cajon, Calif., 1983-88; art dir. Blue Sky Software Inc., San Diego, 1989—. Roman Catholic. Home: 11020 Crystal Springs Rd Santee CA 92071

CHRISTIANSON, ROGER GORDON, biology educator; b. Santa Monica, Calif., Oct. 31, 1947; s. Kyle C. and Ruby (Parker) C.; m. Angela Diane Rey, Mar. 3, 1967; children: Lisa Marie, David Scott, Stephen Peter. BA in Cell and Organismal Biology, U. Calif., Santa Barbara, 1969, MA in Biology, 1971, PhD in Biology, 1976. Faculty assoc. U. Calif., Santa Barbara, 1973-79, staff rsch. assoc., 1979-80; asst. prof. So. Oreg. State Coll., Ashland, 1980-85, assoc. prof., 1985-93, prof., 1993—; coord. gen. biology program So. Oreg. State Coll., 1980—; instr. U. Calif., Santa Barbara, summers 1976, 78, 80. Contbr. articles to profl. jours. Active Oreg. Shakespeare Festival Assn., Ashland, 1983-87; mem. bikeway com. Ashland City Coun., 1986-88; coord. youth program First Bapt. Ch. Ashland, 1981-85, mem. ch. life commn., 1982-88, organizer Bike Oreg., 1982—, Frontline staff, 1985—, Mex. Orphanage short-term mission work, 1986—, bd. deacons, 1993—; ofcl. photographer Ashland High Sch. Booster Club, 1987-92; youth leader jr. and sr. high sch. students Grace Ch., Santa Barbara, Calif., 1973-80. Mem. AAAS (chair Pacific div. edn. sect. 1985—, coun. mem. Pacific div. 1985—), Am. Mus. Natural History, Oreg. Sci. Tchrs. Assn., Assn. Biologists for Lab. Edn., Assn. Biology Lab. Educators, Beta Beta Beta. Republican. Home: 430 Reiten Dr Ashland OR 97520-9724 Office: So Oreg State Coll Dept Biology 1250 Siskiyou Blvd Ashland OR 97520

CHRISTIE, HANS FREDERICK, retired utility company subsidiaries executive, consultant; b. Alhambra, Calif., July 10, 1933; s. Andreas B. and Sigrid (Falk-Jorgensen) C.; m. Susan Earley, June 14, 1957; children: Brenda Lynn, Laura Jean. BS in Fin., U. So. Calif., 1957, MBA, 1964. Treas. So. Calif. Edison Co., Rosemead, 1970-75, v.p., 1975-76, sr. v.p., 1976-80, exec. v.p., 1980-84, pres., dir., 1984-87; pres., chief exec. officer The Mission Group (non-utility subs. SCE Corp.), Seal Beach, Calif., 1987-89, ret., 1989, cons., 1989—; bd. dirs. Gt. Western Fin. Corp., L.A., Ducommun Inc., L.A., Untramar Corp., N.Y., Am. Mut. Fund, Inc., I.H.O.P. Corp., AECom Tech., L.A., Nichols Inst., Internat. House of Pancakes, Inc., Smallcap World Fund, L.A., Bond Fund Am., Inc., L.A., Tax-Exempt Bond Fund Am., L.A., Capital Income Builder, L.A., Capital World Bond Fund, L.A., Capital World Growth Fund, Capital World Groth and Income Fund, Intermediate Bond Fund Am., L.A., Capital World Growth 2d Income Fund, L.A.; trustee Cash Mgmt. Trust Am., New Economy Fund, L.A., Am. Funds Income Series, L.A., The Am. Funds Tax-Exempt Series II, Am. High Income Trust, L.A., U.S. Treasury Fund Am., L.A. Trustee Occidental Coll., L.A.; pres. Nat. History Mus. L.A. County; bd. councillor sch. pub. adminstrn. U. So. Calif. With U.S. Army, 1953-55. Named Outstanding mem. Arthritis Found., L.A., 1975, Outstanding Trustee, Multiple Sclerosis Soc. So. Calif., 1979. Mem. Pacific Coast Elec. Assn. (bd. dirs. 1981-87, treas. 1975-87), L.A. C. of C. (bd. dirs. 1983-87), Calif. Club. Republican. Home: 548 Paseo Del Mar Palos Verdes Estates CA 90274-1260 Office: PO Box 144 Palos Verdes Estates CA 90274-0144

CHRISTMAN, HELEN DOROTHY NELSON, resort executive; b. Denver, Nov. 25, 1922; d. Hector C. and Dorothy C. (Hansen) Russell; m. James Ray Christman, Aug. 7, 1942 (dec. June 1986); children: J. Randol, Linda Rae. Student, Colo. U., 1940-42. Producer Sta. KRMA-TV, Denver, 1960-62; resident mgr. Mana Kai Maui, Maui, Hawaii, 1974-76, exec. coord., 1976-78; pres. Resort Apts., Inc., 1986—; bd. dirs. Kihei Community Assn. Pres. Stephen Knight PTA, Denver, 1957; radio and TV chmn. Colo. PTA, 1958-59; producer ednl. TV programs for PTA, Denver County, 1960-61; bd. dirs. Maui United Way, 1983—, Am. Lung Assn. Hawaii, Maui; precinct pres. Maui Reps.; chmn. Maui County Rep. Com., 1989-91; mem. adv. bd. State of Hawaii Reapportionment Com., Maui, 1991—. Mem. Delta Delta Delta, Women's Golf Club (chmn. Silverswood chpt.), Maui Country Club (chmn. women's golf assn. 1987), Waiehu Women's Golf Assn. (pres. 1992-93), Maui Liquor Commn. Address: 3448 Hookipa Kihei HI 96753

CHRISTOPHER, LEE NEIL, investment company executive, author; b. Hartwell, Ga., June 14, 1940; d. Neil and Ressie Mae (Locke) C.; m. Allen Hermann, May 19, 1979; children: Miriam, Mary, Neil, Scott. BA, Loretto (Colo.) Heights Coll., 1962; MEd, Tulane U., 1980. V.p. So. Small Bus. Investment Co., Inc., New Orleans, 1962—, Fidelity Band & Mktg. Co. Inc., New Orleans, 1962—; tchr. Barnes Bus. Coll., Denver, 1984-85, 89-91. Author: Sonnets for a Sunday Afternoon, 1992, A Workshop With Anne, 1992, Experiments, 1992, Apollinaire Inspirations, 1992, Translations, Apollinaire a Beginning, 1992; co-editor: Bombay Gin, 1993; contbr. articles to profl. jours. Mem. Assn. Retarded Citizens, Nat. Writers Assn.

CHRISTOPHER, SUSAN ROXANNE, pre-school teacher; b. Everett, Wash., May 14, 1952; d. Kenneth Duane and Clara Aletha (Green) Atwell; children: Peter, Candi, Tim. BA in Social Psychology, Warner Pacific Coll., Portland, Oreg., 1975. Presch. tchr. Holladayland, Portland, 1973-75; day care dir. Miss Muffet's, Klamath Falls, Oreg., 1975-76; kindergarten thcr. Oak Park Day Care, Salem, Oreg., 1976-78; presch. tchr. Children's Nest, Marysville, Wash., 1984-86; day care dir. Calvary Kiddie Korner, Marysville, 1986-89; presch. tchr. Marysville Day Care, 1989—; children's dir. of ministry Edmonds (Wash.) Ch. of God, 1981—. Mem. Ch. of God.

CHRISTY, THOMAS PATRICK, human resources executive, educator; b. Urbana, Ill., May 18, 1943; s. Edward Michael and Iona Theresa (Rogers) C.; m. Marjorie Anne McIntyre, June 1966 (div. May 1973); children: Thomas Patrick Jr., Derek Edward; m. Sandra Allen Stern, May 19, 1984; children: Patrick Edward, Margaret Allen. BA in Psychology, Adams State Coll., 1965. Tchr. Colorado Springs Pub. Sch., 1965-69; regional personnel dir. Forest Service USDA, Washington, 1969-81; sr. account exec. Mgmt. Recruiters Inc., Costa Mesa, Calif., 1981-84; v.p. Coleman & Assoc. Inc., Santa Monica, Calif., 1984; asst. v.p. Union Bank, Los Angeles, 1984-88; v.p., human resources dir. TOPA Savs. Bank, Los Angeles, 1988-89, Cenfed Bank, Pasadena, Calif., 1989-91; v.p., regional human resources mgr., nat. dir. tng. Tokio Marine Mgmt., Inc., Pasadena, 1991—; assoc. prof. Coll. Bus. Mgmt., Northrop U., L.A., 1985-91; adj. prof. Coll. Bus. Mgmt., UCLA, 1991—; bd. dirs. Human Resources Mgmt. Inst., L.A.; mem. editorial rev. bd. Calif. Labor Letter, L.A. Arbitrator Bus. and Consumer Arbitrator program Better Bus. Bur., Los Angeles and Orange County; mem. Calif. Rep. Assembly. Mem. AAUP, Pers. and Indsl. Rels. Assn. (pres.), Soc. Human Resources Mgmt. (Calif. state legis. affairs dir.), Employment Mgmt. Assn., Soc. Profls. in Dispute Resolution, Merchants and Mfrs. Assn. (bd. dirs.), Am. Compensation Assn., Japanese Am. Soc. So. Calif., Merchant and Mfrs. Assn. L.A. (bd. dirs.), Adams State Coll. Alumni Assn. (Calif. state pres.), Town Hall Calif., Valley Hunt Club, L.A. Athletic Club, Beach Club, Sigma Pi Alumni Assn. Episcopalian. Home: 1730 Banning Way San Marino CA 91108-1714 Office: Tokio Marine Mgmt Inc 800 E Colorado Blvd Ste 830 Pasadena CA 91101-2132

CHRITTON, GEORGE A., film producer; b. Chgo., Feb. 25, 1933; s. George A. and Dorothea (Goergens) C.; m. Martha Gilman, Aug. 26, 1956 (div. May 26, 1978); children: Stewart, Andrew, Douglas, Laura, Neil, Lyle. BA, Occidental Coll., 1955; postgrad., Princeton U., 1955-57. With various U.S. govt. agys., 1960-89; gen. ptnr. Margeo Investment Co., L.A., 1963-76; pres. Wildacre Prodns., Inc., L.A., 1990—; pres., chief exec. officer Fin. Svcs. Bancorp., Reno, 1990—. Actor appearing in Steven Ray Allen, 1990. Mem. Am. Fgn. Svc. Assn., Washington, 1960—; chmn. bd. Neighborhood Learning Ctr., Capitol Hill, Washington, 1985-87; vol. Options House, Hollywood, Calif.; vol. coord. Rebuild L.A. Maj. USAF, 1957-60. Named Princeton Nat. Fellow, 1955-56, Vis. Fellow & Lectr. U. Calif., 1987-88. Mem. AFTRA, Nat. Assn. Ind. Film & T.V. Prodrs., Phi Beta Kappa, Phi Gamma Delta, Alpha Mu Gamma, Alpha Phi Gamma. Office: Wildacre Prodns Inc PO Box 719 Beverly Hills CA 90213-0719

CHU, ALLEN YUM-CHING, automation company executive, systems consultant; b. Hong Kong, June 19, 1951; arrived in Can., 1972; s. Luke King-Sang and Kim Kam (Lee) C.; m. Janny Chu-Jen Tu, Feb. 27, 1993. BSc in Computer Sci., U. B.C., Vancouver, Can., 1977; BA in Econs., U. Alta., Edmonton, Can., 1986. Rsch. asst. dept. neuropsychology and rsch. Alta. Hosp., Edmonton, 1977-78; systems analyst dept. agr. Govt. of Alta., Edmonton, 1978-81; systems analyst for computing resources City of Edmonton, 1981-86; pres. ANO Automation Inc., Vancouver, 1986—.

Mem. IEEE Computer Soc., N.Y. Acad. Sci. Office: ANO Automation Inc, 380 W 2d Ave 2d Flr, Vancouver, BC Canada V5Y 1C8

CHU, CHRISTOPHER KAR FAI, graphic designer; b. Hong Kong, July 20, 1955; came to U.S., 1957; s. Joseph K. Woo and Marion Sui Sin Pau; m. Faye Allison Mark, July 30, 1988; children: Bethany Joy, Hannah Lynne. AA, City Coll. San Francisco, 1981; BS, San Jose State U., 1984. Journeyman clk. Safeway Stores, Inc., San Francisco, 1974-85; sr. designer, art dir. Neumeier Design Team, Atherton, Calif., 1985—. Recipient Silver award, Murphy awards, 1987, certificate of Distinction, N.Y. Creativity Show, 1988, 89, 90, 91, award of Excellence, Print Regional Design Ann., 1988, Print Computer Art & Design Ann., 1991, Distinctive Merit award, N.Y. Art Dirs. Club, cert. of Design Excellence, Print Mag., award of Merit Brit. Designers & Art Dirs., and others. Home: 182 Exbourne Ave San Carlos CA 94070 Office: Neumeier Design Team 915 Waverley St Palo Alto CA 94301

CHU, DEEING, architect, small business owner; b. Shanghai, Jan. 21, 1943; came to U.S., 1980; d. Shen Zhi and Yong Zhen (Yuan) C.; m. Daniel Chang, Aug. 23, 1968; 1 child, Erik Y. BARch, Qing Hua U., Beijing, 1965; MArch, So. Calif. Inst. Architecture, Santa Monica, Calif., 1980. Designer Archtl. Rsch. Acad. of China, Beijing, 1965-79, CRS, Houston, 1981; designer Rosswou Internat., Santa Monica, 1982-83, prin., 1982-89; ptnr. Rosswou, Inc., Santa Monica, 1990—. Mem. AIA, Asian Am. Architects/Engrs. Assn. Office: Rosswou Inc 2450 Broadway Ave # 650 Santa Monica CA 90404

CHU, GEORGE HAO, biomaterial scientist, biochemist; b. Beijing, Jan. 12, 1939; came to U.S., 1966; s. Tsu-You and Betty H.C. (Chiang) C.; m. Celia Chien-Chiang Wang, Oct. 10, 1970; children: Raymond, Wellington. BS with honors, U. Calif., Davis, 1967, MS, 1969. Biochemist Inst. chemistry, Acad. Simica, Taipei, Republic of China, 1962-66; rsch. asst. dept. food sci. U. Calif., Davis, 1966-69; biochemist Vivonex & Co., Mountain View, Calif., 1969-71; rsch. asst. dept. medicine Stanford (Calif.) U., 1971-77; prodn. mgr. Collagen Corp., Palo Alto, Calif., 1977-79, dir. tech. ops., 1980-85, sr. rsch. scientist, 1985-89, prin. scientist, 1989—; cons. Collagen Corp., 1975-77. Patentee in field; contbr. articles to sci. jours. Mem. AAAS, Am. Chem. Soc., Parenteral Drug Assn., Soc. Biomaterials. Office: Collagen Corp 2500 Faber Pl Palo Alto CA 94303-3308

CHU, JUDY MAY, psychology educator, city official; b. L.A., July 7, 1953; d. Judson and May C.; m. Michael Eng, Aug. 8, 1978. BA in Math., UCLA, 1974; MA in Clin. Psychology, Calif. Sch. Profl. Psychology, 1977, PhD, 1979. Lectr. UCLA, 1980-86; assoc. prof. L.A. City Coll., 1981-88; prof. East L.A. Coll., Monterey Park, 1988—. Author, editor: Linking Our Lives: Chinese American Women in Los Angeles, 1984; contbr. articles profl. jours. Mayor City of Monterey Park, 1990-91; city councilmember, 1988—; mem. Garvey Sch. Dist. bd. edn., 1985-88; chair Commn. for Sex Equity, L.A. Unified Sch. Dist., 1984-85; bd. dirs. Rebuild L.A. Named Dem. of the Yr., 59th Assembly Dist. Dem. Com., 1989, UCLA Alumni of the Yr., 1991; recipient Asian Pacific Family Ctr. Achievement award, 1990, Asian Pacific Legal Ctr. award for pub. svc., 1989; named one of 88 Leaders for 1988 L.A. Times, 1988. Mem. Red Cross (bd. dirs., v.p. 1987—, recipient leadership award West San Gabriel Valley chpt.), San Gabriel Valley United Way (bd. dirs., named Vol. of Yr. 1989), San Gabriel Valley Med. Ctr. (bd. dirs.), Asian Youth Ctr. (pres. bd.), West San Gabriel Valley Juvenile Diversion Project (bd. dirs.), Soroptimists. Office: City Hall 320 W Newmark Ave Monterey Park CA 91754-2818

CHUA, LEON O., electrical engineering and computer science educator; b. June 28, 1936; m. Diana Chua; children: Amy Lynn, Michelle Ann, Katrin Faye, Cynthia Mae. SM, MIT, 1961; PhD, U. Ill., 1964; D honoris causa, Ecole Poly. Lausanne, Switzerland, 1983; honorary doctorate, U. Tokushima, Japan, 1984. Asst. prof. Purdue U., Lafayette, Ind., 1964-67, assoc. prof., 1967-70; prof. U. Calif., Berkeley, 1972—; cons. various electronic industries; Miller Rsch. prof. Miller Inst., 1976. Author: Introduction to Nonlinear Network Theory, 1969; co-author: Computer-Aided Analysis of Electronic Circuits: Algorithms and Computational Techniques, 1975, Linear and Nonlinear Circuits, 1987; dep. editor Internat. Jour. Circuit Theory and Applications; contbr. numerous articles to profl. jours. Patentee in field. Recipient Frederick Emmons Terman award, 1974, Alexander von Humboldt Sr. U.S. Scientist award Tech. U. Munich, 1982-83, Vis. U.S. Scientist award Japan Soc. for Promotion Sci., 1983-84, Myril B. Reed Best Paper prize, 1985, Prof. Invite Internat. award French Ministry Edn., 1986; Cambridge (Eng.) U. sr. vis. fellow, 1982. Fellow IEEE (Browder J. Thompson Meml. Prize award 1967, W.R.G. Baker Prize award 1973, Centennial medal 1985, Guillemin-Cauer prize 1985); mem. Soc. Circuits and Systems IEEE (editor Trans. on Cirs. and Systems 1973-75, pres. 1976). Office: Univ Calif Dept Elec Engring & Computer Sci Berkeley CA 94720

CHUAN, RAYMOND LU-PO, scientific researcher, consultant; b. Shanghai, China, Mar. 4, 1924; came to U.S., 1941; s. Peter Shao-Wu and Katherine (Tao) C.; m. Norma Nicoloff, Dec. 21, 1951 (dec. 1973); m. Eugenia Nishimine Sevilla, Apr. 23, 1982; children: Jason, Alexander. BA, Pomona Coll., 1944; MS, Calif. Tech. U., 1945, PhD, 1953. Rsch. assoc., then dir. Engring. Ctr. U. So. Calif., L.A., 1953-63, adj. prof. Sch. Engring., 1957-63; pres. Celestial Rsch. Corp., South Pasadena, Calif., 1963-68; staff scientist Atlantic Rsch., Costa Mesa, Calif., 1968-72, Celesco, Costa Mesa, 1972-76, Brunswick Corp., Costa Mesa, 1976-88; v.p. Femtometrics, Costa Mesa, 1985—; cons. NASA, Hampton, Va., 1972-82. Patentee in field; contbr. papers to sci. jours. Co-founder, chmn. bd. dirs. Sequoyah Sch., Pasadena, Calif., 1958-72. Mem. AAAS, Am. Geophys. Union. Home: PO Box 1183 Hanalei HI 96714 Office: Femtometrics Unit R 1001 W 17th St Costa Mesa CA 92627

CHUCK, STEVEN LEE, physician; b. Encino, Calif., Nov. 28, 1958; s. Gilbert and Aileen Chuck; m. Loretta Yin, May 27, 1984; 1 child, Bryan Yin Chuck. BA, U. Calif., Davis, 1980; MD, U. Calif., San Francisco, 1984. Cert. nat. bds., infectious diseases Am. Bd. Internal Medicine. Intern U. Calif., San Francisco, 1984-85, resident, 1985-87, chief resident, 1987-88, fellow, 1988—. Author (with others): Handbook of Medical Treatment, 1988, Internal Medicine, 1990; contbr. articles to profl. jours.; inventor pause transfer and protein engring. Recipient Physician Scientist award NIH, 1990. Mem. Alpha Omega Alpha, Phi Beta Kappa, Phi Kappa Phi. Presbyterian. Office: U Calif San Francisco CA 94143-0654

CHUCK, WALTER G(OONSUN), lawyer; b. Wailuku, Maui, Hawaii, Sept. 10, 1920; s. Hong Yee and Aoe (Ting) C.; m. Marian Chun, Sept. 11, 1943; children: Jamie Allison, Walter Gregory, Meredith Jayne. Ed.B., U. Hawaii, 1941; J.D., Harvard U., 1948. Bar: Hawaii 1948. Navy auditor Pearl Harbor, 1941; field agt. Social Security Bd., 1942; labor law insp. Terr. Dept. Labor, 1943; law clk. firm Ropes, Gray, Best, Coolidge & Rugg, 1948; asst. pub. prosecutor City and County of Honolulu, 1949; with Fong, Miho & Choy, 1950-53; ptnr. Fong, Miho, Choy & Chuck, 1953-58; pvt. practice law Honolulu, 1958-65, 78-80; ptnr. Chuck & Fujiyama, Honolulu, 1965-74; ptnr. firm Chuck, Wong & Tonaki, Honolulu, 1974-76, Chuck & Pai, Honolulu, 1976-78; pres. Walter G. Chuck Law Corp., Honolulu, 1980—; dist. magistrate Dist. Ct. Honolulu, 1956-63; gen. ptnr. M & W Assocs., Kapalama Investment Co.; bd. dirs. Aloha Airlines, Inc., Honolulu Painting Co., Ltd. Chmn. Hawaii Employment Rels. Bd., 1955-59; bd. dirs. Nat. Assn. State Labor Rels. Bds., 1957-58, Honolulu Theatre for Youth, 1977-80; chief clk. Hawaii Ho. of Reps., 1951, 53, Hawaii Senate, 1959-61; govt. appeal agt. SSS, 1953-72; former mem. jud. coun. State of Hawaii; mem. exec. com. Hawaiian Open; dir. Friends of Judiciary History Ctr. Inc., 1983—; former mem. bd. dirs. YMCA. Capt. inf. Hawaii Territorial Guard. Fellow Internat. Acad. Trial Lawyers (founding, bd. dirs.), Am. Coll. Trial Lawyers; mem. ABA (chmn. Hawaii sr. lawyers div., former mem. ho. of dels.), Hawaii Bar Assn. (pres. 1963), Am. Trial Lawyers Assn. (former editor), U. Hawaii Alumni Assn. (Disting. Svc. award 1967, dir., bd. govs.), Law Sci. Inst., Assoc. Students U. Hawaii (pres.), Am. Judicature Soc., Internat. Soc. Barristers, Am. Inst. Banking, Chinese C. of C. Republican. Clubs: Harvard of Hawaii, Waialae Country (pres. 1975), Pacific, Oahu Country. Home: 2691 Aaliamanu Pl Honolulu HI 96813-1216 Office: 201 Merchant St Ste 2210 Honolulu HI 96813-2957

CHUM, HELENA L., research institute official, chemist, researcher; b. Sao Paulo, Brazil, Dec. 26, 1946; came to U.S., 1976.; BSc in Chemistry and Chem. Edn., U. Sao Paulo, 1968, PhD in Phys. Chemistry, 1972. Asst. prof. U. Sao Paulo, 1971-78; cons. Colo. State U., Ft. Collins, 1978-79; sr. scientist Solar Energy Rsch. Inst., Golden, Colo., 1979-83, prin. scientist, 1983-86, br. mgr., 1986—. Author: Electrochemical Biomass, 1985; patentee fractionation biomass, supercritical processing, membrane separation. Tech. advisor to Congressman David Skaggs, 1988-89. Recipient Francis Van Morris award Midwest Rsch. Inst., 1988, R&D 100 award R & D mag., 1990, excellence in tech. transfer award Fed. Lab. Consortium, 1990. Mem. Am. Chem. Soc. (membership chmn. cellulose, paper and textile div. 1986-88, program chmn. 1988-90, chmn.-elect 1990-91, coord. chemistry and pub. policy 1990, coord. energy 1993). Office: Solar Energy Rsch Inst 1617 Cole Blvd Golden CO 80401

CHUMMERS, PAUL, performing company executive. Dir. Utah Symphony Orch., Salt Lake City. Office: Utah Symphony Orch 123 W South Temple Salt Lake City UT 84101-1496*

CHUN, ALVIN, management consultant, engineer, risk communicator, training manager; b. San Francisco, Jan. 15, 1950. BSEE, U. Calif., Berkeley, 1972; MS in Mech. Engring., Stanford (Calif.) U., 1975. Environ. engr. U.S. EPA Region 9, San Francisco, 1975-79, chief air sect., 1979-81, chief tech. evaluation sect., 1981-83, spl. projects mgr., 1983-85, sr. mgmt. analyst, 1985-88, sr. environ. health policy advisor, 1988—; trainer Zenger Miller Program, San Francisco. Career counselor Stanford U., 1985—; exec. Combined Fed. Campaign, Treasure Island, Calif., 1990—. Capt./engr. dir. USPHS, 1972—. Mem. Bay Area Orgnl. Devel. Network, USPHS Commd. Officers Assn. (pres. San Francisco chpt. 1980-82). Office: USPHS-US EPA Region 9 75 Hawthorne St San Francisco CA 94105-3901

CHUN, LOWELL KOON WA, architect; b. Honolulu, Sept. 2, 1944; s. Kwai Wood and Sara Lau C. BA in Eng., U. Hawaii, 1967; BArch, Cornell U., 1971. Registered profl. architect, Hawaii. Archtl. designer Wilson, Okamoto & Assocs., Honolulu, 1972-74; architect, planner Aotani & Assocs., Inc., Honolulu, 1974-82; design planner Daniel, Mann, Johnson & Mendenhall, Manila and Honolulu, 1982-84; architect, planner Alfred A. Yee div. Leo A. Daly Co., Honolulu, 1984-87; prin. Lowell Chun Planning & Design, Honolulu, 1987-89; dir. planning Daniel, Mann, Johnson & Mendenhall, Honolulu, 1989; assoc. AM Ptnrs., Inc., Honolulu, 1989-92; planning svcs. officer Hawaii Community Devel. Authority, Honolulu, 1992—; rsch. bd. advisors Am. Biog. Inst., Raleigh, S.C., 1990—; dep. dir. gen. The America's, 1990—; mem. IBC adv. coun. Internat. Biog. Centre, Cambridge, Eng., 1990—. Prin. author: Kauai Parks and Recreation Master Plan, 1978, Hawaii State Recreation Plan (Maximum Fed. Eligibility award 1980), Maui Community Plans, 1981, Pauahi Redevel. Project, Honolulu, 1974, State Tourism Plan, Physical Resources Element, 1977, City & County of Honolulu Urban & Regional Design Plans, 1979, Hilo Civic Center Master Development Plan, 1989, New Communities, U. Petroleum and Minerals, Dhahran, Saudi Arabia, 1982, Lake Pluitt Resdl./Comml. District, Jakarta, Indonesia, 1982, Destination Resorts: Key Biscayne, Fla., Sint Maarten, Netherlands Antilles, St. Croix, U.S. Virgin Islands, Palm Springs, Calif., 1988, The Imperial Plaza Residential Commercial Complex, 1989, Kailua Elderly Housing Community Master Plan, 1990, Waimano Ridge Master Development Plan, 1991, and others. Advisor, locations officer Maitreya Inst., Honolulu, 1983-84; v.p., treas. Kagyu Theg Chen Ling Tibetan Ctr., Honolulu, 1982, 84; rep. Environ. Coalition to Hawaii State Legislature, 1974; mem. Waikiki Improvement Assn., Phys. Improvement Task Force, 1990, Hawaii Soc. Corp. Planners, 1991. Recipient Master Plan award Nat. Assn. Counties, 1975. Mem. AIA, Am. Planning Assn. (local exec. com. mem.-at-large 1987-88), Sierra Club (local vice-chmn. 1974-76), Cornell Club of Hawaii (Honolulu). Buddhist. Home: 456 N Judd St Honolulu HI 96817-1754 Office: Hawaii Community Devel Authority Ste 1001 677 Ala Moana Blvd Honolulu HI 96813

CHUN, WENDY SAU WAN, investment company executive; b. China, Oct. 17, 1951; came to U.S., 1975, naturalized, 1988; d. Siu Kee and Lai Ching (Wong) C.; m. Tan Ng Wong, Jan. 1992; stepchildren: Sze Ho, Sze Man. BS, Hong Kong Bapt. Coll., 1973; postgrad. U. Hawaii-Manoa, 1975-77. Real estate saleswoman Tropic Shores Realty Co., Honolulu, 1977-80; pres., prin., broker Advance Realty Investment Co., Honolulu, 1980—; owner Video Fun Centre, Honolulu, 1981-83; pres. Asia-Am. Bus Cons., Inc., Can., 1983—; bd. dirs., exec. dir. B.P.D. Internat., Ltd., Hong Kong; exec. dir. Asia-Am. Bus. Cons., Inc., Hong Kong br., 1985—; pres. Asia-Am. Internat., Ltd., Honolulu, 1989; pres. Maurey Internat., Ltd., Hong Kong, 1990. Mem. Nat. Assn. Realtors. Avocations: singing, dancing, swimming, dramatic performances. Home: 2333 Kapiolani Blvd Apt 3302 Honolulu HI 96826-4473

CHUNDURI, NARENDRA R., engineer, computer consultant; b. Kakinada, South Andhra, India; came to U.S., 1978; s. Lakshminarayana and Anjamma C.; m. Pongprapa Kasemsnat, June 8, 1985. BS, Andhra (India) State U., Eluru, 1972; MS, Andhra (India) State U., Waltair, 1975; MBA, Calif. State U., Long Beach, 1981, postgrad. Inventory controller Savin Corp., Cerritos, Calif., 1979-81; programmer-analyst Starkist, Long Beach, 1981-84; mem. computing staff Hughes Aircraft Co., El Segundo, Calif., 1984-87; mem. tech. support Aerospace Corp., El Segundo, 1987-89, mem. tech. staff, 1989-91, project mgr., 1992—; cons. Dr. C. V. Chelapati & Assocs., Huntington Beach, Calif., 1981—. Mem. Soc. Cost Evaluation and Analysis, Assn. MBA Execs. Office: Aerospace Corp 2350 E El Segundo Blvd El Segundo CA 90245

CHUNG, BYUNG HWA, marketing executive; b. Seoul, South Korea, Nov. 19, 1966; came to U.S. 1982; s. Joon Sang and Kyu Ye (Yang) C. BS, U. Calif., Berkeley, 1990. Internat. mktg. mgr. EXP Computers, Sunnyvale, Calif., 1990-91; pres. Informatrix, Inc. (formerly Infomatrix), Sunnyvale, Calif., 1991—. Presbyterian. Home: 611 San Conrada Terr # 4 Sunnyvale CA 94086 Office: Informatrix Inc 780 Montague Expy Ste 306 San Jose CA 95131

CHUNG, KEA SUNG, television broadcasting executive; b. Pusan, Korea, Jan. 2, 1935; came to U.S., 1973; s. Tae In and Dou Kum (Lee) C.; m. Ok Soon Yang, June 20, 1958; children: Hee Sung, Yun Hee, Jaeh Hoon, Juneho. BS in Bus. Adminstrn., Cen. Mo. State U., 1957; D Bus. Mgmt. (hon.), Calif. Internat. U., 1982. Pres. Polynesian Fair, Inc., Honolulu; pres., CEO KBFD, TV, Honolulu; pres. The Asia Network, Honolulu, Voice of Korea, Honolulu; dir. Hawaii Korea Nat. Tourism Corp., Honolulu. Past pres. Korean Community Coun. Hawaii, Honolulu; chmn. Temple Constrn. of Dae Won Sa Buddhist Temple, Honolulu; hon. mem. adv. coun. Dem. and Peaceful Unification of Korea. Recipient Merit Sus award Ministry of Culture and Info., Republic of Korea, 1978, Nat. Merit award Pres. Republic of Korea, 1990. Mem. Korean Press Club Hawaii (past pres.), Am. Soc. Travel Assn. (past dir.), Korean Athletic Assn. (past dir.), Hawaii TV Broadcasters Assn. (dir.), Hawaii Korean C. of C. (past pres.), Hibiscus Lions Club (hon., charter pres. 1987). Office: KBFD TV 1188 Bishop St PH-1 Honolulu HI 96813

CHUNG, STEWART, architect; b. Hong Kong, Sept. 2, 1956; came to U.S., 1973; s. Shek-Chuen and Alice (Wong) C. BArch, U. So. Calif., 1979; MArch, Harvard U., 1982. Prin. SCA Architects, South Pasadena, Calif., 1984—; mem. adv. com. Cerritos Coll., Norwalk, Calif., 1985—; commr. South Pasadena Design Rev. Bd., 1992—. Lt. comdr. USNR, 1985—. Mem. AIA. Republican.

CHUNG, SUE FAWN, educator, researcher; b. L.A., Mar. 11, 1944; d. Walter K. and Jane Beverly (Chan) C.; m. Alan Moss Solomon, Apr. 17, 1980; children: Walter Moss, Alexander Moss. BA, UCLA, 1965; AM, Harvard U., 1967; PhD, U. Calif., Berkeley, 1975. Lectr. San Francisco State U., 1971-73; asst. prof. U. Nev., Las Vegas, 1975-79, assoc. prof., 1979—, dir. internat. programs, 1985-87; mem. media panel NEH, 1992; dir. Asia and Nevada project Nev. Humanities Com., 1992—. Editor: Nev. Pub. Affairs Jour., 1987. Mem. com. Nev. Dance Theater, Las Vegas, 1988. ACLS fellow, 1977, U. Calif. fellow, 1968-70; U. Nev. grantee, 1976, 81. Mem. Am. Hist. Assn., Assn. for Asian Studies, Soc. for Qing Studies, U.S.-China Friendship Assn. (co-founder Las Vegas chpt. 1975), Chinese Hist. Assn., Harvard U. Alumni Assn., UCLA Alumni Assn., Phi Kappa Phi (v.p. Las Vegas chpt. 1986-88). Democrat. Home: 1105 Vegas Valley Dr Las Vegas NV 89109-1536 Office: Univ Nev 4505 S Maryland Pky Las Vegas NV 89154-5020

CHURCH, ALONZO, mathematics and philosophy educator; b. Washington, June 14, 1903; s. Samuel Robbins and Mildred Hannah Letterman (Parker) C.; m. Mary Julia Kuczinski, Aug. 25, 1925 (dec. Feb. 1976); children—Alonzo, Mary Ann, Mildred Warner. A.B., Princeton U., 1924, Ph.D., 1927, D.Sc. (hon.), 1985; D.Sc. (hon.), Case Western Res. U., 1969, SUNY, Buffalo, 1990. Faculty Princeton U., 1929-67, prof. math., 1947-61, prof. math. and philosophy, 1961-67; prof. philosophy and math. UCLA, 1967-90, ret. Author: Introduction to Mathematical Logic, vol. I, 1956; editor: Jour. Symbolic Logic, 1936-79; contbr. articles to math. and philos. jours. Mem. Am. Acad. Arts and Scis., Assn. Symbolic Logic, Am. Math. Soc., AAAS, Nat. Acad. Scis., Brit. Acad. (corr.), Am. Philos. Assn. (pres. Pacific div. 1973-74).

CHURCH, LORENE KEMMERER, government official; b. Jordan, Mont., Oct. 18, 1929; d. Harry F. and Laura (Stoller) Kemmerer; m. Scott Johnston, Sept. 8, 1948 (div. 1953); children: Linda M., Theodore O.; m. Fred C. Church, May 9, 1956; children: Ned B., Nia J. Student, Portland Community Coll., 1973-76, Portland State U., 1978-79. Sec. intelligence div. IRS, Portland, Oreg., 1973-75; trade asst. Internat. Trade Adminstrn., U.S. Dept. Commerce, Portland, 1975-84, internat. trade specialist, 1984—. Recipient high performance award U.S. Dept. Commerce, 1986, spl. act and svc. award, 1987, quality step award, 1990, 92. Mem. NAFE, World Affairs Coun., N.W. China Coun., Portland C. of C. (Europe 1992 com. 1988-89, internat. trade adv. bd. 1988-89). Democrat. Roman Catholic. Home: 19725 SW Pike St Beaverton OR 97007 Office: US Dept Commerce US&FCS 121 SW Salmon St Portland OR 97204-2901

CHURCHILL, BONNIE JEANE, columnist, writer; b. Chicago, Ill., Dec. 5, 1937; d. Wesley Roy and Mildred (Gibson) C. AA, UCLA, 1966. Youth columnist L.A. Times; syndicated columnist Nat. News Syndicate, Chgo.; internat. syndicated columnist Nat. News Syndicate; radio commentator Comm. Interat., L.A., 1970—; pres. Churchill Inc., L.A., 1985—. Author: Expand Your Learning Power, 1980, Guide to Beauty. Founder Project Advance, L.A., 1976. Named Woman of Excellence Boy Scouts Am., 1992, Woman of Yr. Theta Sigma Phi; recipient Press award Nat. Press Honor. Mem. Press Club, Hollywood Women's Press Club. Home: 1423 N Orange Grove Hollywood CA 90046

CHURCHILL, WILLIAM DELEE, retired educator, psychologist; b. Buffalo, Nov. 4, 1919; s. Glenn Luman and Ethel (Smith) C.; AB, Colgate U., 1941; MEd, Alfred U., 1951; EdD, U. Rochester, 1969; m. Beulah Coleman, Apr. 5, 1943; children: Cherylee, Christie. Tchr. secondary sci., Canaseraga, N.Y., 1947-56; dir. guidance Alfred-Almond Sch., Almond, N.Y., 1956-63; grad. asst. U. Rochester, 1963-65; asst. prof. psychology Alfred (N.Y.) U., 1965-66; assoc. prof. edn. Ariz. State U., Tempe, 1966-86. Lt. col. USAAF, 1942-79, PTO. Mem. Ariz. Psychol. Assn. Author: Career Survey of Graduates, 1973. Home: 11454 N 85th St Scottsdale AZ 85260-5727

CHURCHMAN, DAVID ALAN, history educator; b. N.Y.C., July 20, 1938; s. Stanley and Elizabeth (Lawson) C. BA, U. Mich., 1960, MA, 1964; PhD, UCLA, 1972. Social worker Dept. Pub. Social Svcs., Bakersfield, Calif., 1964-65; tchr. Am. Internat. Sch., Tangier, Morocco, 1965-66, Newtown (Pa.) High Sch., 1966-68; rsch. assoc. UCLA, 1972-76; prof. negotiations and conflict management Calif. State U., Dominguez Hills, 1976—; bd. dirs. Wildlife on Wheels, L.A., 1985—, Orangutan Found., L.A., 1986-92, New South African Trade Orgn., 1993—; Calif. coord. Nat. Coun. U.S.-Arab Rels., 1993—; cons. Nat. Inst. Drug Abuse, State of Hawaii, Minn., N.Mex., Tribal Am. Corp., UCLA Harbor Gen. Hosp., others; adv. bd. Bur. Land Mgmt., Calif., 1984-87. Author: Negotiation Tactics, 1988, 1993, (with others) Evaluation Workshop, 1971, American Indian Life Environments, 1975; contbr. numerous articles to profl. jours. 1st lt. U.S. Army, 1960-62. Grantee NSF, Calif. Dept. Fish and Game, Calif. Community Found., Chevron, Arco, Carnation and others; Malone fellow Nat. Coun. on U.S.-Arab Rels., 1993. Mem. Am. Assn. Zool. Parks and Aquariums, Internat. Assn. Zoo Educators. Republican. Office: Calif State U BSGP Dominguez Hills CA 90747

CHUTE, PHILLIP BRUCE, management consultant; b. Saugus, Mass., Aug. 19, 1938; s. Ernest Yorke and Dorothy (Bruce) C.; m. Elizabeth Boyd; children: Brian, Elaine. Student, Northeastern U., Boston, 1961-62; AA, Pasadena City Coll., 1965; BS, Calif. State U., L.A., 1977. Fin. reporter Dun & Bradstreet, L.A., 1961-62; mgr. Crocker Citizens Bank, L.A., 1962-64; acct. Cons. Rock Prod., L.A., 1965-74; pres. Phillip B. Chute, Corp., Riverside, Calif., 1974—; prin. Keogler Morgan & Co., Riverside, 1991; pres. Pacific Fin. Advisors Corp., 1992—. Author: American Independent Business, 1984, AIB Handbook, 1988. Pres. Riverside County Tax Commn. Assn., 1978; active Calif. Bapt. Coll., Riverside, 1990-93. With U.S. Army, 1957-60, Germany. Recipient Clyde Hurley writing award Kiwanis Internat., 1988, 89, Writing award, 1990. Republican. Home: 6710 Mountain Laurel Ct Highland CA 92346 Office: Phillip B Chute Corp 4100 Central Ave Riverside CA 92506

CHYBA, CHRISTOPHER F., planetary scientist; b. Balt., Oct. 28, 1959; s. Herman Joseph and Mary (Santora) C. BA, Swarthmore Coll., 1982; MPhil, Cambridge (Eng.) U., 1985; PhD, Cornell U., 1991. Nat. rsch. coun. assoc. NASA Ames Rsch. Ctr., Moffett Field, Calif., 1991—; mem. USSR-U.S. Exobiology Expedition to Northeastern Siberia, 1991. Contbr. articles to profl. publs. Del. U.S.-USSR Emerging Leaders Summit, Phila., 1988; mem. delegation to Chernobyl (USSR) Am. Ctr. for Internat. Leadership, 1989. Marshall scholar, Brit. govt., 1982-85; Sage fellow, 1985-87. Mem. Am. Astron. Soc., Am. Geophys. Union, Internat. Soc. for Study of Origin of Life, Phi Beta Kappa, Sigma Xi. Office: NASA Ames Rsch Ctr Space Divsn MS245-3 Moffett Field CA 94035

CICCIARELLI, JAMES CARL, immunology educator; b. Toluca, Ill., May 26, 1947; s. Maurice Cicciarelli and Helen Ippolito; divorced; 1 child, Nicola. BS, Tulane U., 1969; PhD, So. Ill. U., 1977. Lic. clin. lab. dir., Calif. Postdoctoral fellow dept. surgery UCLA, 1977-79, asst. prof. immunology, 1980-87, assoc. prof., 1987-91; prof. urology and microbiology U. So. Calif., L.A., 1992—; lab. dir. Metic Transplant Lab., Inc., L.A., 1984—; bd. dirs. So. Calif. Organ Procurement Agy., 1987—; clin. lab. dir. Am. Bd. Bioanalysis, 1991—; mem. histocompatibility com. United Network Organ Sharing, 1991—. Contbr. articles to sci. jours., chpts. to books. NIH rsch. grantee, 1985-88. Mem. Am. Soc. Histocompatibility and Immunogenetics, Internat. Transplant Soc., Am. Soc. Transplant Physicians. Republican. Roman Catholic. Home: 1527 Manhattan Ave Hermosa Beach CA 90254-3637 Office: USC Dept Urology Metic Transplant Lab 2100 W 3rd St Ste 280 Los Angeles CA 90057

CICHOKE, ANTHONY JOSEPH, JR., writer, health consultant, chiropractor; b. Peoria, Ill., Nov. 23, 1931; s. Anthony Joseph Sr. and Margaret Mary (Conwell) C.; m. Margaret A. Kovner, Feb. 24, 1962; children: Anthony Joseph III, Michael David, William F., Margaret Kathleen. BS in Social Sci., John Carroll U., 1954; student, Army Lang. Sch., Monterey, Calif., 1955; MA in Speech and Theater, St. Louis U., 1964; MA in Speech Sci. Pathology and Audiology, U. Minn., 1967; postgrad., Case Western Res. U., 1969; D. Chiropractic, Nat. Coll. Chiropractic, Lombard, Ill., 1973; postgrad., Western States Chiropractic Coll., 1975. Diplomate Am. Chiropractic Bd. Nutrition. Actor, promoter Schubert Orgn., N.Y.C., 1960-61; entertainment dir., producer U.S. Army and 2d Army, Ft. Eustis, Va., 1961-62; actor, tchr. radio announcer U. Minn., Mpls., 1964-67; tchr., researcher Eastman Dental Ctr., Rochester, N.Y., 1967-68; team physician Portland State U. Amateur Athletic Union, 1975-84; instr. and lectr. on sports medicine, nutrition, and chiropractic medicine at seminars, convs. and various colls. and univs; researcher. Contbr. over 100 articles to profl. journals; editor Nutritional Prospectives mag, 1979; producer Blockheads, London, 1984-85, This was Burlesque, L.A., 1985. Chmn. sports medicine com. Amateur Athletic Union, 1975—; mem. postgrad. faculty numerous chiropractic colls. 1st lt. U.S. Army, 1955-59. Grantee U.S. Office Edn., 1965-67, Case We. Res. U., 1968-69, U. Minn., 1965-67, NIH, 1968-69. Fellow Internat. Assn. Study of Pain (diplomate), Internat. Coll. Chiropractic; mem. Am. Chiropractic Assn. (coun.

orthopedics, 3 man posture com., coun. sports injuries, past pres. and v.p. coun. nutrition), N.Y. Acad. Scis., Orthomolecular Med. Soc., Acad. Orthomolecular Psychiatry, Acad. Sports Medicine, U.S. Sports Acad., Found. Chiropractic Edn. and Rsch., Metabolic Rsch. Found. Republican. Roman Catholic. Office: PO Box 16189 Portland OR 97216-0189

CIERNIA, JAMES RICHARD, financial advisor; b. St. Paul, Sept. 22, 1933; s. Albert Joseph and Lillian Caroline (Kemski) C.; m. Mary Elizabeth Friese, Aug. 4, 1956; children: Karen M., Mark J., Jennifer M., Scott W. BA, Calif. State U., Long Beach, 1954; PhD, Clayton U., 1983. CLU. Group ins. mgr. Conn. Gen. Life Ins. Co., Long Beach, 1957-60; account exec. Johnson and Higgins, L.A., 1960-65; v.p. Behrendt-Levy, L.A., 1965-67; pres., owner Ciernia Co., Denver, 1967-73; sr. v.p. Frank B. Hall Inc., Denver, 1973-75;; with RNC Capital Mgmt., L.A., 1978-85; owner, mgr., cons. Ciernia Co., San Luis Obispo, Calif., 1985--. Bd. dirs. Colo. Comprehensive Planning Coun., 1970, Cen. City Opera House Assn., 1973. Lt. (j.g.) USN, 1951-53. Mem. Nat. Assn. Securities Dealers, Mensa, San Luis Obispo Country Club (bd. dirs. 1979-80). Home and Office: 153 Country Club Dr San Luis Obispo CA 93401-8918

CIMOCHOWICZ, DIANE MARIE, naval petty officer; b. Jacksonville, Fla., Aug. 13, 1955; d. Richard Clarence and Edith Darlene (Johnson) C. AS in Mgmt., Hawaii Pacific Coll., 1986, BSBA, 1986; cert. total quality mgmt. (TQM), Hawaii Pacific U., 1992. Cert. total quality mgmt. cons. Enlisted USN, 1974, advanced through grades to petty officer first class; ops. specialist USN, Naples, Italy, 1975-77; ops. specialist, instr. USN, Dam Neck, Va., 1977-78; resigned USN, 1978, reenlisted, 1980; photographer USN, San Diego, 1980-82, Honolulu, 1982-92, San Diego, 1992—; owner ICON, Columbia, Md., 1978-79; owner, operator In Other Words, Honolulu, 1988. Mem. NAFE, Nat. Audubon Soc., Federally Employed Women, Fleet Res. Assn., Associated Photographers Internat., Nat. Honor Frat. Bus. Adminstrn., Delta Mu Delta. Democrat. Office: Fleet Imaging Ctr Pacific Naval Air Sta Miramar CA 92145

CIOFFI-REVILLA, CLAUDIO, political science educator; b. May 7, 1951. BS, Instituto Patria, Mexico City, 1969; D suma cum laude in Polit. Sci., U. Florence, Italy, 1977; PhD, SUNY, Buffalo, 1979. Asst. prof. U. N.C., 1978-81; asst. to assoc. prof. U. Ill., Urbana-Champaign, 1981-88; assoc. prof. dept. polit. sci. U. Colo., Boulder, 1988—; bd. dirs. Long-Range Analysis of War Project, U. Colo. Author: The Scientific Measurement of International Conflict, 1990, Mathematical Models in International Relations, 1979; contbr. articles to Math. and Computer Modeling, Synthese, IFAC Procs., Am. Polit. Sci. Rev., Am. Jour. Polit. Sci., Internat. Studies Quarterly, others. Recipient Outstanding Pub. Svc. award United Nations Assn., 1989, various rsch. grants NSF, Young Leadership Program award Atlantic Coun. of U.S., 1981-82; elected Academician, Internat. Medici Acad., 1985. Mem. AAAS, Internat. Polit. Sci. Assn., Am. Polit. Sci. Assn., N.Y. Acad. Scis., Consortium for Math. Applications. Office: Univ Colo Campus Box 333 Boulder CO 80309-0333

CIPRIANO, PATRICIA ANN, teacher, consultant; b. San Francisco, Apr. 24, 1946; d. Ernest Peter and Claire Patricia (Croak) C. BA in English, Holy Names Coll., Oakland, Calif., 1967; MA in Edn. of Gifted, Calif. State U.-L.A., 1980. Cert. tchr., tchr. gifted, adminstrv. svc., Calif. Tchr. English, math. Bancroft Jr. High Sch., San Leandro, Calif., 1968-79, 83-85, coord. gifted edn., 1971-79; tchr. English, math., computers San Leandro High Sch., 1979-83, 85—, mentor tchr., 1991—, chmn. English dept., 1992—, coord. gifted and talented edn., 1981-83; cons. Calif. State Dept. Edn., various Calif. sch. dists. Recipient Hon. Svc. award Tchr. of Yr., Bancroft Jr. High Sch. PTA, 1973; bd. dirs. Calif. Curriculum Correlating Coun. Mem. NEA, Calif. Assn. for Gifted, World Coun. Gifted and Talented, Cen. Calif. Coun. Tchrs. English (past pres.), Calif. Assn. Tchrs. English (bd. dirs., past pres.), Nat. Coun. Tchr. English (bd. dirs.), San Leandro Tchrs. Assn., Calif. Tchrs. Assn., Computer Using Educators, Assn. for Supervision and Curriculum Devel., Calif. Math. Coun., Nat. Coun. Tchrs. Math., Cirriculum Study Commn., Delta Kappa Gamma (past pres.). Roman Catholic. Avocations: reading, piano, calligraphy, tennis, photography. Contbr. articles to profl. jours. Office: San Leandro High Sch 2200 Bancroft Ave San Leandro CA 94577-6198

CIRE, RICHARD CAMILE, distribution executive; b. Alexandria, La., Mar. 16, 1933; s. Leonce Benoit and Mathilde Meeker (Marshall) C.; m. Shirley Ann Bell, Nov. 25, 1954; children: Chaille Camile, Frank Leonce, Dana Michelle. BS in Mech. Engring., Tex. A&M U., 1954. Design engr. Gen. Dynamics, Fort Worth, 1954-57; sr. mfg. engr. Tex. Instruments, Dallas, 1957-68; div. sales mgr. Varo Microcircuit Products, Garland, Tex., 1969-73; v.p. sales Micropac Industries, Garland, 1969-73, Western area sales mgr., 1976-77; product mgr. Bourns, Inc., Riverside, Calif., 1973-75, Pulse Engring., San Diego, 1975-76; ptnr. Rical Assocs., Huntington Beach, Calif., 1977-82; v.p. ops. Ital Electronic Sales, Inc., Industry, Calif., 1982—. 1st lt. U.S. Army, 1955-57. Republican. Home: 23712 Bower Cascade Pl Diamond Bar CA 91765 Office: ITAL Electronic Sales Inc 15405 Proctor Ave Industry CA 91745

CITRIN, WILLIE, physician; b. Amberg, Germany, Mar. 18, 1947; s. Abe and Dora (Bril) C. BA, Rutgers U., 1968; MD, N.J. Coll. Medicine, 1972. Chief medicine Parkview Community Hosp., Riverside, Calif., 1984-87; chief of staff Parkview Community Hosp., 1987-8. Mem. Am. Coll. Physicians, Am. Soc. Internal Medicine, AMA, Calif. Med. Assn., Calif. Soc. Internal Medicine. Office: 3975 Jackson St Ste 203 Riverside CA 92503-3938

CITRON, M. SLOANE, publisher; b. Amarillo, Tex., Feb. 20, 1956; s. Ralph and Joesphine C.; m. Judith Ann Feuerstein, Aug. 29, 1982; children: Joshua, Arielle, Avital. BA, Claremont McKenna Coll., 1978; cert. of pub., Harvard U., 1978; MBA, Stanford U., 1980. Gen. mgr. Meyer Publs., Miami, Fla., 1981-85; pub. Internat. Voyager, Miami, 1985-86; pres. Westar Media, Inc., Redwood City, Calif., 1986—. Bd. dirs. North Calif. Jewish Bull., San Francisco, 1990, Flame, San Francisco, 1990. Recipient Presdl. Citation Am. Soc. Interior Designers, 1989, Circle of Hope Am. Cancer Soc., 1990. Republican. Jewish. Office: Westar Media Inc 656 Bair Island Rd Redwood City CA 94063-2744

CIVITELLO, ROBERT CHARLES, interior painting company owner; b. Phila., Mar. 8, 1947; s. Nicolas Charles and Ester Mary (Nardelli) C.; m. Patricia Ann Olbrat, May 6, 1967; children: Robert, Craig. Student, El Camino Coll., 1980-82. Ticket agt. Nat. Agt., Phila., 1968-77; supr. Pan Am. World Airways, L.A., 1980-91; owner Quality Interior Painting, Redondo Beach, Calif., 1991—; cons. to various airlines on baggage theft and baggage claims, L.A., 1980-91. With U.S. Navy (Seabees), 1966-68, Vietnam. Mem. Vietnam Vets. Am. (pres. Redondo Beach 1990—). Home and Office: # E 2102 Manhattan Beach Blvd Redondo Beach CA 90278-1202

CLABAUGH, ELMER EUGENE, JR., lawyer; b. Anaheim, Calif., Sept. 18, 1927; s. Elmer Eugene and Eleanor Margaret (Heitshusen) C.; m. Donna Marie Organ, Dec. 19, 1960 (div.); children: Christopher C., Matthew M. BBA cum laude, Woodbury U.; BA summa cum laude, Claremont McKenna Coll., 1958; JD, Stanford U., 1961. Bar: Calif. 1961, U.S. Dist. Ct. (cen. dist.) Calif., U.S. Ct. Apls. (9th cir.) 1961, U.S. Sup. Ct. 1971. With fgn. svc. U.S. Dept. State, Jerusalem and Tel Aviv, 1951-53; Pub. Adminstrn. Svc., El Salvador, Ethiopia, U.S., 1953-57; dep. dist. atty. Ventura County, Calif., 1961-62; pvt. practice, Ventura, Calif., 1962—; mem. Hathaway, Clabaugh, Perrett and Webster and predecessors, 1962-79, Clabaugh & Perloff, Ventura, 1979—; state inheritance tax referee, 1968-78. Bd. dirs. San Antonio Water Conservation Dist., Ventura Community Meml. Hosp., 1964-80; trustee Ojai Unified Sch. Dist., 1974-79; bd. dirs. Ventura County Found. for Parks and Harbors, 1982—, Ventura County Maritime Mus., 1982—. With USCGR, 1944-46, USMCR, 1946-48. Mem. Calif. Bar Assn., Am. Arbitration Assn., NRA, Safari Club Internat., Mason, Shriners, Phi Alpha Delta. Republican. Home: 241 Highland Dr Channel Island River CA 93035 Office: 1190 S Victoria Ave Ventura CA 93003-6507

CLABOTS, JOSEPH PAUL, cardiothoracic surgeon; b. Milw., May 2, 1951; s. Thomas F. and Mary Jane (Graves) C.; m. M. Teresa Garcia Otero, May 29, 1976. BA, St. Louis U., 1973; MD, Washington U., St. Louis, 1977. Diplomate Am. Bd. Thoracic Surgery. Mem. staff St. Joseph Hosp., Tacoma, Wash., 1986—. Fellow ACS; mem. Soc. Thoracic Surgeons. Office: 314 S K St Ste 306 Tacoma WA 98498

CLAES, DANIEL JOHN, physician; b. Glendale, Calif., Dec. 3, 1931; s. John Vernon and Claribel (Fleming) C.; AB magna cum laude, Harvard U., 1953, MD cum laude, 1957; m. Gayla Christine Blasdel, Jan. 19, 1974. Intern, UCLA, 1957-58; Bowyer Found. fellow for rsch. in medicine, L.A., 1958-61; pvt. practice specializing in diabetes, L.A., 1962—; v.p. Am. Eye Bank Found., 1978-83, pres., 1983—, dir. rsch., 1980—; pres. Heuristic Corp., 1981—. Mem. L.A. Mus. Art, 1960—. Mem. AMA, Calif. Med. Assn., L.A. County Med. Assn., Am. Diabetes Assn., Internat. Diabetes Fedn. Clubs: Harvard and Harvard Med. Sch. of So. Calif.; Royal Commonwealth (London). Contbr. papers on diabetes mellitus, computers in medicine to profl. lit. Office: Am Eyebank Found 15327 W Sunset Blvd Ste 236 Pacific Palisades CA 90272-3674

CLAEYS, RICHARD G., electric power industry communications executive; b. Albany, Calif.; s. Reder and Gladys (Knudsen) C.; m. Luisa Tosi, June 14, 1964; children: Eric, Carla, Justin. BA in English, St. Mary's Coll., 1963; MS in Journalism, Boston U., 1964. Dir. pub. rels. Conn. Gen. Ins. Co., 1964-79; v.p. corp. Comm. Met. Life Ins., N.Y., 1979-85; dir. corp. comm. Electric Power Rsch. Inst., Palo Alto, Calif., 1985-93, v.p., 1993—. Contbr. articles to profl. jours. Mem. program com. U.S. Coun. Energy Awareness, N.Y.C.; mem. Pub. Rels. Seminar, Washington. Fellow Pub. Rels. Soc. Am. (chmn. energy and natural resources sect.), Arthur W. Page Soc. Office: Electric Power Rsch Inst 3412 Hillview Ave Palo Alto CA 94304

CLAFLIN, DOUGLAS MORGAN, software engineer; b. West Covina, Calif., Oct. 4, 1963; s. Glenn Millard and Avon Eloise (Rhoads) C. BS, U. Calif., Riverside, 1986; MS, Claremont Grad. Sch., 1992. Software engr. Lockheed Aircraft Svc. Co., Ontario, Calif., 1986—; cons. Canyon Mortgage Co., Upland, Calif., 1989—, Etiwanda (Calif.) Sch. Dist., 1990—. Mem. IEEE, Assn. Computing Machinery, Math. Assn. Am. Home: 13233 Highland Ave Etiwanda CA 91739

CLAGUE, WILLIAM DONALD, university administrator; b. Mobile, Ala., Nov. 29, 1920; m. Betty Louise Scrogum, 1944; children—William Donald, Gayle Annette Clague Graef. B.A., Bridgewater Coll., 1941; M.Ed., U. Va., 1954, Ed.D., 1960. Cert. tchr., administr. Tchr., Baker High Sch., Mobile; instr. Bridgewater Coll., Columbia U., N.Y.C., 1941-48; dean students Bridgewater Coll., 1948-66; dean grad. and profl. studies, U. of La Verne, Calif., 1966-82, v.p. acad. affairs, 1975-83, exec. v.p., 1983-87, prof. ednl. mgmt., 1987—; cons. to Calif. pub. schs., Los Angeles, 1970—. Contbr. articles to profl. jours. Pres., David and Margaret Home for Girls, La Verne, 1983-87; mem. La Verne Sch. Bd., 1970—; chair Pomona Valley 5 city Red Cross Bd., 1991-92. Named Disting. Prof. Bridgewater Coll., 1950-66, Community Builder of the Yr., 1984, Citizen of the Yr., La Verne, 1985. Mem. La Verne C. of C. (v.p. 1984—, pres. 1986), Phi Delta Kappa. Lodge: Rotary (pres. 1969-70) (La Verne). Office: U La Verne 1950 3d St La Verne CA 91750

CLAIR, THEODORE NAT, psychologist; b. Stockton, Calif., Apr. 19, 1929; s. Peter David and Sara Renee (Silverman) C.; A.A., U. Calif. at Berkeley, 1949, A.B., 1950; M.S., U. So. Calif., 1953, M.Ed., 1963, Ed.D., 1969; m. Laura Gold, June 19, 1961; children—Shari, Judith. Tchr., counselor Los Angeles City Schs., 1957-63; psychologist Alamitos Sch. Dist., Garden Grove, Calif., 1963-64, Arcadia (Calif.) Unified Sch. Dist., 1964-65; head psychologist Wiseburn Sch. Dist., Hawthorne, Calif., 1966-69; asst. prof. spl. edn., coordinator sch. psychology program U. Iowa, Iowa City, 1969-72; dir. pupil personnel services Orcutt (Calif.) Union Sch. Dist., 1972-73; adminstr. Mt. Diablo Unified Sch. Dist., 1973-77; program dir., psychologist San Mateo County Office of Edn., Redwood City, 1977—; assoc. prof. John F. Kennedy U. Sch. Mgmt., 1975-77; pvt. practice as ednl. psychologist and marriage and family counselor, Menlo Park, Calif., 1978—, Menlo Park, Calif., 1977—; dir. Peninsula Vocat. Rehab. Inst., 1978—; adj. faculty Nat. U., 1992—; psychologist Coll. Counseling Svc., Menlo Pk., 1992—, Calif. Pacific Hosp., San Francisco, 1993-. Served with USNR, 1952-54. Mem. Am. Assn. Counseling and Devel., Calif. Assn. Marriage and Family Counselors, Am. Psychol. Assn., Nat. Rehab. Assn., Phi Delta Kappa. Club: Palo Alto B'nai B'rith (pres.). Author: Phenylketonuria and Some Other Inborn Errors of Amino Acid Metabolism, 1971; mem. editorial adv. bd. Psychology in Schs., 1972—; editor Jour. Calif. Ednl. Psychologists, 1992—; contbr. articles to profl. jours. Home and Office: 56 Willow Rd Menlo Park CA 94025-3654

CLAIRE, ANNE MARIE ARANCIBIA, strategic research coordinator; b. Tehachapi, Calif., Dec. 23, 1948; d. Franklyn Richard and Cleo Patricia (Arancibia) Stenberg; m. Richard George Barager, June 14, 1970 (div. July 1979); 1 child, Jennifer Claire. BA in English Lit., George Fox Coll., Newberg, Oreg., 1971; MLS, U. Oreg., 1973. Teaching asst. George Fox Coll., 1970-71; bus. libr. Multnomah County Pub. Libr., Portland, Oreg., 1975-76; evening reference libr. Clackamas Community Coll., Oregon City, Oreg., 1977-79; govtl. documents libr. U.S. Bonneville Power Adminstrn., Portland, Oreg., 1979; reference libr. U.S. Western Solar Utilization Network, Portland, Oreg., 1980-82; corp. libr. NERCO Inc., Portland, Oreg., 1982-84; reference libr. Pacific Power Libr., Portland, Oreg., 1984-85; strategic rsch. coord. Pacific Power Strategic Planning, Portland, Oreg., 1985—; part-time reference libr. Lewis & Clark Coll., Portland, Oreg., 1973-79. Author: Clackamas Community Coll. Libr. Handbook, 1978. Mem. libr. task force Multnomah County Commn., Portland, 1985. Mem. Portland Area Spl. Librs. (sec. 1983-84), Portland City Club. Democrat. Episcolalian. Office: Pacific Power 920 SW 6th Ave Ste 675 PFFC Portland OR 97204-1236

CLAIRE, FRED, professional baseball team executive. A.A., Mt. San Antonio Coll.; B.A. in Journalism, San Jose State Coll., 1957. Formerly sports writer and columnist Long Beach Ind. Press Telegram and Whittier News; sports editor Pomo Progress-Bull, Calif., until 1969; dir. publicity Los Angeles Dodgers, Nat. League, 1969-75, v.p. pub. relations and promotions, 1975-82, exec. v.p., from 1982, now exec. v.p. player personnel, 1987—; bd. dirs. Major League Baseball Promotion Corp. Bd. dirs. Greater Los Angeles Vistors and Conv. Bur. Named The Sporting News Major League Exec. of Yr., 1988. Mem. Echo Park C. of C. Los Angeles Rotary. Office: Los Angeles Dodgers 1000 Elysian Park Ave Los Angeles CA 90012-1112*

CLARAMUNT, JAVIER FERNANDO, manufacturing company executive; b. Montevideo, Uruguay, Apr. 30, 1960; came to U.S., 1986; s. Mariano and Alicia (Fernandez) C.; m. Elena Robiano; children: Diego, Joshua, Mark. B in Exact Scis., Poitiers Acad (France), Buenos Aires, 1978; MS in Mech. Engring., U. Buenos Aires, 1986. Registered profl. engr., Calif. Tech. mgr. Acilay S.A., Buenos Aires, 1980-83; applications engr. Edal S.A. Mori Seiki Rep., Buenos Aires, 1984-86; engring. mgr. Republic Lagun CNC Corp., Harbor City, Calif., 1986-88, v.p., gen. mgr., 1988—; gen. mgr. Conquest Industries, Paramount, Calif., 1988; v.p., gen. mgr Lagun CNC Corp., Harbor City, Calif., 1988—. Republican. Roman Catholic. Home: 15544 Wiemer Ave Paramount CA 90723 Office: Republic Lagun CNC Corp 800 Spruce Lake Dr Harbor City CA 90710

CLARINGBULL, K(ATHARINE) RUTH, business executive; b. Essex, Eng., July 12, 1949; came to U.S., 1977; m. Philip Claringbull, Aug. 21, 1971; children: Daniel, Nicholas, Thomas, John. BA with honors, U. Reading, Berkshire, Eng., 1970. Mgr. regional mktg. bus. intelligence ctr. SRI Internat. (formerly Stanford Rsch. Inst.), Menlo Park, Calif., 1977-88; regional dir. SRI Internat. (formerly Stanford Rsch. Inst.), Menlo Park, 1988—.

CLARK, ALAN BARTHWELL, city administrator; b. Bklyn., Dec. 29, 1936; s. James and Elizabeth Clark; m. Mary Ann Rawlins, June 27, 1964; 1 son, David Edward. BA, Bklyn. Coll., 1958; MLS, Pratt Inst., 1960. Libr. Bklyn. Pub. Libr., 1958-66; asst. dir. Greenwich (Conn.) Pub. Libr., 1966-69; asst. dir. Albuquerque Pub. Libr., 1969-71, dir., 1971-79; dir. cultural svcs. City of Albuquerque, 1979—; instr. edn. U. N.Mex., 1975-78. With U.S. Army, 1960-62. Mem. ALA (life), South Western Libr. Assn., N.Mex. Libr. Assn. Episcopalian. Home: 1005 Stuart Rd NW Albuquerque NM 87114-1927 Office: Albuquerque Bernalillo County Libr System 501 Copper Ave NW Albuquerque NM 87102-3129*

CLARK, ALLEN LEROY, geologist; b. Delaware, Iowa, Sept. 29, 1938; s. Charles Leo and Velda Marie (Meader) C.; m. Jennifer Lea Cook, Oct. 10, 1981; children: Brett Harlan, Holly Lin. BS, Iowa State U., 1961; MS, U. Idaho, 1963, PhD, 1967; postgrad., Stanford U., 1969-72. Exploration geologist Kennecott Copper Corp., Spokane, Wash., 1965-67; geologist U.S. Geol. Survey, Menlo Park, Calif., 1967-72; office chief U.S. Geol. Survey, Reston, Va., 1972-78; sr. staff geologist U.S. Geol. Survey, Reston, 1978-80; exec. dir. Internat. Inst. for Resource Devel., Vienna, Austria, 1980-83; program dir. East-West Ctr., Honolulu, 1983—; adj. prof. U. Hawaii, 1983—; cons. United Nations, 1983-92, Asian Devel. Bank, Manila, 1985-87, Econ. and Social Commn. of Asia and Pacific, Bangkok, Thailand, 1985-92. Author 7 books: contbr. almost 200 articles to profl. jours. and mags. Scoutmaster Boy Scouts Am., Sunnyvale, Calif., 1968-72; mem. Save Our Bays and Beaches, Honolulu, 1971—. Fellow Geol. Soc. Am., Soc. Econ. Geologists, Am. Assn. Petroleum Geologists; mem. Assn. Geologists for Internat. Devel., Internat. Assn. Math. Geologists, Sima Xi, Sigma Gamma Epsilon. Home: 1135 Koohoo Pl Kailua HI 96734 Office: East West Ctr 1777 East West Rd Honolulu HI 96848

CLARK, ANNE MARGARET EBERHARDT, management consultant; b. San Diego, May 25, 1961; d. Duane Orrin and Melva Lee (Gibson) Eberhardt; m. Jeffrey Raphiel Clark, Mar. 15, 1985; children: Jeffrey Raphiel Jr., Mary Anne Elizabeth. BS in Fin., Brigham Young U., 1983, MBA, 1988. Property acct. Kirby Exploration Co. of Tex., Houston, 1984-85; asst. controller Tex. Meridian Resources, Houston, 1986; mgmt. cons. Grant Thornton, Salt Lake City, 1988-92. Editor Dialogue, 1988-92. Fin. com. mem. Utah Girl Scouts, Salt Lake City, 1990-91; recording sec. Profl. Rep. Women, Salt Lake City, 1992. Home: 1428 Michigan Ave Salt Lake City UT 84105

CLARK, ARTHUR JOSEPH, JR., mechanical and electrical engineer; b. West Orange, N.J., June 10, 1921; s. Arthur Joseph and Marjorie May (Courter) C.; BS in Mech. Engring., Cornell U., 1943; MS, Poly. Inst. Bklyn., 1948; MS in Elec. Engring., U. N.Mex., 1955; m. Caroline Katherine Badgley, June 12, 1943; children: Arthur Joseph, III, Durward S., David P. Design engr. Ranger Aircraft Engines Co., Farmingdale, N.Y., 1943-46; sr. structures engr. propeller div. Curtis Wright Co., Caldwell, N.J., 1946-51; mgr. space isotope power dept., also aerospace nuclear safety dept. Sandia Labs., Albuquerque, 1951-71, mgr. environ. systems test lab., 1971-79, mgr. mil. liaison dept., 1979-86; pres. Engring. Svcs. Cons. Firm, 1987; mem. faculty U. N.Mex., 1971-75; invited lectr. Am. Mgmt. Assn. Pres. Sandia Base Sch. PTA, 1960-61; chmn. finance com. Albuquerqe chpt. Am. Field Svc., 1964-66; chmn. Sandia Labs. div. U.S. Savs. Bond drive, 1972-74, chmn. employee contbn. drive, 1973-75; active local Boy Scouts Am., 1958-66. Recipient Order Arrow, Boy Scouts Am., 1961, Order St. Andrew, 1962, Scouters Key award, 1964; cert. outstanding service Sandia Base, 1964. Fellow ASME (nat. v.p. 1975-79, past chmn. N.Mex. sect.); mem. IEEE (sr.), Cornell Engring. Soc., Theta Xi. Clubs: Kirtland Officers, Four Hills Country. Home: 905 Warm Sands Albuquerque NM 87123-4332

CLARK, BRIAN THOMAS, mathematical statistician, operations research analyst; b. Rockford, Ill., Apr. 7, 1951; s. Paul Herbert and Martha Lou (Schlensker) C.; m. Suzanne Drake, Nov. 21, 1992. B.S. cum laude, No. Ariz. U., 1973; postgrad. Ariz. State U., 1980-82. Math. aide Center for Disease Control, Phoenix, 1973-74, math. statistician, 1979-83; math. Statistician Ctrs. for Disease Control, Atlanta, 1983-84 ops. research analyst U.S. Army Info. Systems Command, Ft. Huachuca, Ariz., 1984—; math. statistician U.S. Navy Metrology Engring. Center, Pomona, Calif., 1974-79. Mem. Am. Statis. Assn., Am. Soc. Mil. Comptrs. Republican. Mormon. Office: US Army Info Systems Command Dep Chief Staff Resource Mgmt Chargeback Test Divsn Fort Huachuca AZ 85613

CLARK, BURNILL FRED, television executive; b. Horton, Kans., Nov. 8, 1941; s. Fred Charles and Mildred Anna (Magner) C.; m. Diane Rae Oswald, Aug. 25, 1963; children: Michelle Rae, Marcie Diane, Melissa Esther. BA, U. Denver, 1963, MA, 1964; postgrad., Mich. State U., 1964, Harvard U., 1981. Producer, dir., prodn. mgr. Nebr. Ednl. TV Network, Lincoln, 1965-73, asst. network program mgr., 1973-75; asst. gen. mgr., dir. programming Sta. KCTS-TV, Seattle, 1975-82, gen. mgr., 1982-87; exec. dir. KCTS Assn., Seattle, 1983-87, pres., chief exec. officer, 1987—; chmn. U.S. Pub. TV Internat. Consortium, Washington, 1987—, Pacific Rim Co-Prodn. Assn., 1987—, PBS Border Consortium, Vancouver, B.C., Can., 1984—; bd. govs. Pacific Mountain Network, Denver, 1983-90, chmn., 1984-86; bd. dirs. Pub. TV Outreach Alliance, 1985—, Washington, 1987—; mem. PBS program mgr. adv. com., 1978-82, PBS program adv. com. 1982-85, Frontline mgmt. bd. and editorial adv. bd., 1983—, mem. exec. com. PBS Bd., 1987-91, chmn. nominating com. PBS bd., 1990-91; mem. adv. planning com. Am.'s Pub. TV Stas., 1987—; trustee Am's. Pub. TV Stas. Bd., Washington, 1991—; headed study of advanced TV systems, 1992. Mem. TV and Radio Commn. of Meth. Ch., Lincoln, 1966-69; bd. dirs. N.W. Ctr. for the Retarded, Seattle, 1983-85; chmn. media adv. com. Washington Give Five Leadership Coun., 1988-90. Fellow U.S. Japan Soc. Leadership Program; mem. N.W. Devel. Officers Assn. (bd. dirs. 1988-90), Rotary (chmn. program com. 1988-90, bd. dirs. 1993—, trustee svc. found. 1990-93), Phi Beta Kappa, Alpha Epsilon Rho. Methodist. Office: Sta KCTS-TV 401 Mercer St Seattle WA 98109-4699

CLARK, CALEB MORGAN, political scientist, educator; b. Washington, June 6, 1945; s. Tanner Morgan and Grace Amanda (Kautzmann) C.; B.A., Beloit Coll., 1966; Ph.D., U. Ill., 1973; m. Janet Morrissey Sentz, Sept. 28, 1968; children—Emily Claire, Grace Ellen, Evelyn Adair. Lectr., N.Mex. State U., Las Cruces, 1972-75, asst. prof., 1975-78, assoc. prof. govt., 1978-81; assoc. prof. polit. sci. U. Wyo., Laramie, 1981-84, prof., 1984-92, U. Auburn, 1992—, prof., head polit. sci. NDEA fellow, 1966-69; Woodrow Wilson dissertation fellow, 1969-70; grantee N.Mex. Humanities Coun., 1975, Wyo. Coun. for Humanities, 1982, U.S. Dept. Edn., 1983-85, Pacific Cultural Found., 1984-86. Am. Coun. Learned Socs., 1976, Met. Life Edn., 1978-80, NEH, 1978, NSF, 1981. Mem. Am. Polit. Sci. Assn., Western Polit. Sci. Assn., Assn. Asian Studies, Southern Polit. Sci. Assn. , Internat. Studies Assn. (exec. dir. West 1981-84), Phi Beta Kappa (treas. 1983-91), Pi Eta Sigma, Phi Kappa Phi. Author: (with Robert L. Farlow) Comparative Patterns of Foreign Policy and Trade, 1976; (with Karl F. Johnson) Development's Influence on Yugoslav Political Values, 1976; Taiwan's Development, 1989; (with Bih-er Chou and Janet Clark) Women in Taiwan Politics, 1990; (with Steve Chan) Foresight, Flexibility and Fortuna in Taiwan's Devel., 1991; mng. editor IS Notes, 1984-92; co-editor: North/South Relations, 1983, State and Development, 1988, Polit. Stability and Economic Development, 1991, The Evolving Pacific Basin, 1992; cons., assoc. editor Soviet Union, 1974-77, World Affairs, 1975-84, Social Sci. Jour., 1978-80; contbr. articles to profl. jours.

CLARK, CHARLES SUTTER, interior designer; b. Venice, Calif., Dec. 21, 1927; s. William Sutter and Lodema Ersell (Fleeman) C. Student Chouinard Art Inst., Los Angeles, 1950-51. Interior designer LM.H. Co., Gt. Falls, Mont., 1956-62, Andreason's Interiors, Oakland, Calif., 1962-66, Western Contact Furnishers Internat., Oakland, 1966-70, Design Five Assocs., Lafayette, Calif., 1972-73; owner, interior designer Charles Sutter Clark Interiors, Greenbrae, Calif., 1973-91, San Rafael, Calif., 1991—. Served with USAF, 1951-55. Recipient prizes Mont. State Fair, 1955-55. Mem. Am. Soc. Interior Designers. Home: 429 El Faisan Dr San Rafael CA 94903-4517

CLARK, CLAUDE, art educator; b. Rockingham, Ga., Nov. 11, 1915; s. John Henry and Estella (Graham) C.; m. Effie Mary Lockhart, June 13, 1943; children: Claude Lockhart, Alcie Shasta. Profl. diploma, Phila. Mus. Sch. of Art, 1939; BA in Art Edn., Sacramento State U., 1958; MA in Painting, U. Calif., Berkeley, 1962. Artist grade I WPA/Fed. Art Project, Phila., 1939-42; tchr. Phila. Pub. Schs., 1945-48; assoc. prof. Talladega (Ala.) Spl. Schs., 1948-55; instr. Alameda (Calif.) County Spl. Schs., 1959-68; instr. Merritt Coll., Oakland, Calif., 1968-81, ret., 1981. Author: (manual) Black Art Perspective, 1970; exhibited in group and one-man shows, including

NCA Exhbns., 1988, Salvador Bakis Brazil Introspectives Contemporary Art by Ams. and Brazilians of African Descent, 1989, traveling 50 Yr. Retrospective Exhbn., 1990. Carnegie Mellon Found. grantee, 1949, 50, 51. Mem. Assn. Study Classical, African and Civili, Nat. Congress of Artists, AAUP (emeritus), NAACP. Home: 788 Santa Ray Ave Oakland CA 94610-1737

CLARK, DAVID GILLIS, educator, author; b. Lubbock, Tex., May 14, 1933; s. James Cuthbert and Lena Drusilla (Gillis) C.; m. Alice Ann Cappon, Dec. 21, 1974; 1 child from previous marriage, Andrew; children: Sarah, Matthew. BA, Tex. Tech U., 1955; MA, U. Iowa, 1956; PhD, U. Wis., 1965. Radio-TV news editor Sta. KCBD-TV, Lubbock, 1952-54; reporter, photographer Lubbock Avalanche Jour., 1956, Lincoln (Nebr.) Star, 1958-59; instr. U. Nebr., Lincoln, 1958-59, U. Cin., 1959-64; tennis coach U. Wis., Madison, 1962-63, instr., 1964-65, from asst. prof. to assoc. prof., 1967-73; asst. prof. Stanford U., Palo Alto, Calif., 1965-67; chair, prof. dept. tech. journalism Colo. State U., Ft. Collins, 1973-91, acting dean Coll. of Arts, Humanities and Social Scis., 1991—; asst. to provost, 1992—. Co-author: You and Media, 1973, Random House Guide to Technical and Scientific Communication, 1987; co-editor: Mass Media and the Law, 1970, The American Newspaper by Will Irvin, 1989. Mem. AAUP, Assn. for Edn. in Journalism and Mass Communication, Soc. Profl. Journalism. Home: PO Box 87 Bellvue CO 80512-0087 Office: Colo State U Office of Provost V P Acad Affairs Fort Collins CO 80523

CLARK, DAVID NEIL, chemist; b. Buffalo, June 24, 1953; s. Ronald Squire and Caroline (Willard) C.; m. Jane Harriet Cline, Jan. 8, 1977; children: Daniel Squire, Sarah Elizabeth. BS, Clarkson Coll. Tech., Potsdam, N.Y., 1975; PhD, MIT, 1979. Rsch. chemist IIT Rsch. Inst., Chgo., 1983-87; assoc. mgr. hazardous material lab. Battelle Meml. Inst., Columbus, Ohio, 1987-88; projects mgr. Battelle Meml. Inst., 1988-89; chem. surety mgr. Battelle Meml. Inst., Tooele, Utah, 1989—; state chem. officer Utah N.G., 1990. Contbr. articles to profl. jurs. Capt. U.S. Army, 1975-83. Decorated Army Commendation medal. Mem. Am. Chem. Soc., Am. Def. Preparedness Assn., N.G. Assn., Chem. Corps Regiment, Sigma Xi. Home: 129 Lakeview Tooele UT 84074-9669 Office: Battelle 11650 Stark Rd Tooele UT 84074-9712

CLARK, DONALD ROWLEE, public relations consultant; b. Seattle, July 3, 1925; s. Donald Hathaway and Mildred (Taylor) C.; m. Joyce Douglass, Dec. 21, 1947; children: Kimberly, Jennifer, Lorinda. BA in Journalism, U. Wash., 1949, postgrad., 1960-61. Bus. mgr. Northgate Jour., Seattle, 1955-59; pres. Clark & Gropp Advt. Inc., Seattle, 1959-67; v.p., account supr. Lennen & Newell, Inc., Seattle, 1967-72; prin. Don Clark Communications Planner, Seattle, 1972—. Author: Wild Blue Yonder, 1972, The Brother XII, 1990; pub. editor Sr. Svcs. of Seattle, 1987—. Pres. Chaos-In-Depth, Seattle, 1966-74; editorial cons. ARC, Seattle, 1988—; vol. Arthritis Found., Campfire Girls; trustee Pacific N.W. Writers Conf. With USN, 1943-46. Mem. Cannon Hunters Assn. of Seattle (head hunter-chaos), Rotary. Home and Office: 13547 Linden Ave N Seattle WA 98133-7532

CLARK, DOUGLAS KENNETH, city manager; b. Long Beach, Calif., Mar. 6, 1947; s. Kenneth Elmer and Clintine Edelweiss (Crain) C.; m. Marle-Elisabeth Lecouté, May 27, 1972; 1 child, Philip Douglas. BA cum laude, Whittier Coll., 1969, MAT, 1970; postgrad., Ctr. for Urban & Regional Studies, Birmingham (England) U., 1970-71. Asst. planner City of Costa Mesa, Calif., 1972-73, assoc. planner, 1973-76, chief advance planning, 1976-78, asst. devel. svcs. dir., 1978-81, devel. svcs. dir., 1981-86; city mgr. City of Larkspur, Calif., 1986-89, City of Escondido, Calif., 1989—. Mem. bd. United Way, North San Diego County, 1989—, vice chair, 1991, chair-elect, 1992, campaign com., 1992, campaign com. Marin County, 1988; cubmaster Boy Scouts Am., Marin County, 1986-88; mem. Marin County Emergency Med. Care Com., 1988-89. Rotary Found. fellow Birmingham (England) U., 1970-71. Mem. Internat. City Mgmt. Assn. (Clarence E. Ridley award 1992), Urban Land Inst., Rotary (sec. Marin County 1988-89).

CLARK, DREW, secondary education educator, state legislator; b. Jacksonville, Ill., Dec. 7, 1946; s. Robert Donald and Roberta Ruth (Wheelan) C.; m. Lainie (Joyce Elaine) Peters, Aug. 6, 1970. BS in Math., Ill. Coll., 1968. Cert. math., physics tchr., Colo. Tchr. Elmwood (Ill.) High Sch., 1968-69, Adams County Sch. Dist. 12, Northglenn, Colo., 1973—; mem. Colo. Ho. of Reps., 1993—, mem. edn., transp. coms. Elder Rocky Mountain Christian Ch., Niwot, Colo., 1991—; host fgn. exch. students. With U.S. Army, 1969-71, Vietnam. Republican. Home: 876 Dearborn Pl Boulder CO 80303 Office: Ho of Reps Rm 271 State Capitol Denver CO 80203

CLARK, EARNEST HUBERT, JR., tool company executive; b. Birmingham, Ala., Sept. 8, 1926; s. Earnest Hubert and Grace May (Smith) C.; m. Patricia Margaret Hamilton, June 22, 1947; children: Stephen D., Kenneth A., Timothy R., Daniel S., Scott H., Rebecca G. BS in Mech. Engring, Calif. Inst. Tech., 1946, MS, 1947. Chmn., chief exec. officer Friendship Group, Baker Hughes, Inc. (formerly Baker Oil Tools, Inc.), L.A., 1947-89, v.p., asst. gen. mgr., 1958-62, pres., chief exec. officer, 1962-69, 75-79, chmn. bd., 1969-75, 79-87, 87-89, ret., 1989; ret. The Friendship Group, Newport Beach, Calif., 1989; bd. dirs. CBI Industries, Inc., Honeywell Inc., Kerr-MGee Corp., Beckman Instruments Inc., Am. Mutual Fund. Chmn., bd. dirs. YMCA of U.S.A.; past chmn. bd. YMCA for Met. L.A.; mem. nat. coun. YMCA; trustee Harvey Mudd Coll. With USNR, 1944-46, 51-52. Mem. AIME, Am. Petroleum Inst., Petroleum Equipment Suppliers Assn. (bd. dirs.), Tau Beta Pi. Office: Friendship Group W Tower # 3000 5000 Birch St Newport Beach CA 92660

CLARK, EDGAR SANDERFORD, insurance broker, consultant; b. N.Y.C., Nov. 17, 1933; s. Edgar Edmund, Jr., and Katharine Lee (Jarman) C.; student U. Pa., 1952-54; BS, Georgetown U., 1956, JD, 1958; postgrad. INSEAD, Fontainbleau, France, 1969, Golden Gate Coll., 1973, U. Calif., Berkeley, 1974; m. Nancy E. Hill, Sept. 13, 1975; 1 dau., Schuyler; children by previous marriages: Colin, Alexandra, Pamela. Staff asst. U.S. Senate select com. to investigate improper activities in labor and mgmt. field, Washington, 1958-59; underwriter Ocean Marine Dept., Fireman's Fund Ins. Co., San Francisco, 1959-62; mgr. Am. Fgn. Ins. Assn., San Francisco, 1962-66; with Marsh & McLennan, 1966-72, mgr. for Europe, resident dir. Brussels, Belgium, 1966-70, asst. v.p., mgr. captive and internat. div., San Francisco, 1970-72; v.p., dir. Risk Planning Group, Inc., San Francisco, 1972-75; v.p., dir. global constrn. group Alexander & Alexander Inc., San Francisco, 1975—; lectr. profl. orgns.; guest lectr. U. Calif., Berkeley, 1973, Am. Grad. Sch. Internat. Mgmt., 1981, 82, Golden Gate U., annually 1985-91. Served with USAF, 1956-58. Mem. Am. Mgmt. Assn., Am. Risk and Ins. Assn., Internat. Insurance Soc., Chartered Ins. Inst., Am. Soc. Internat. Law, Soc. Calif. Pioneers San Francisco, Meadow Club, Fairfax, Calif., World Trade San Francisco. Republican. Episcopalian. Mem. editorial adv. bd. Risk Mgmt. Reports, 1973-76. Home: 72 Millay Pl Mill Valley CA 94941-1501 Office: Alexander & Alexander Inc 2 Embarcadero Ctr Ste 1400 San Francisco CA 94111-3821

CLARK, EDWARD ALAN, immunologist, microbiologist, educator; b. Long Beach, Calif., Sept. 3, 1947; s. Elliott Goss and Iris E. (Price) C.; children: Tomas, Sashya. BS in Psychology/Zoology, UCLA, 1969, PhD in Microbiology/Immunology, 1977. Researcher UCLA, 1968-77; rsch. asst. Univ. Coll., London, 1977-79; from asst. prof. to assoc. prof. microbiology U. Wash., Seattle, 1979-90, prof., 1990—, dir. program lymphocyte activation, 1989—, adj. prof. immunology, 1991—, core stafff scientist Regional Primate Rsch. Ctr., 1979—; mem. study sect. exptl. immunology NIH, 1990—; mem. adv. bd. Tissue Antigens, 1990—. Assoc. editor Jour. Clin. Immunology, 1988—; sect. editor Jour. Immunology 1992—; contbr. articles to profl. jours. Mem. AAAS, Am. Assn. Immunologists. Office: Dept Microbiology SC-42 U Wash Med Ctr Seattle WA 98195

CLARK, EDYTHE AUDREY, home economist, educator; b. Jeffersonville, Ind., Dec. 26, 1929; d. John Foster and Martha Willey (Long) Eberts; m. Paul Stoner Clark, Sept. 9, 1950; children: Robert, Randall, Barbara, Steven. BS, Northwestern U., 1951; MS, Calif. State U., Northridge, 1971; PhD, U. So. Calif., 1978. Instr. Calif. State U., Northridge, 1971-73, asst. prof., 1973-80, assoc. prof., 1980-84, prof., 1984—, dept. chmn., 1983—; child devel. cons. 1985—. Author: (with others) Readings in Developmental Psychology, 1988; contbr. articles to profl. jours. V.p. L.A. County Am. Lung Assn., 1990-91. Recipient USDA grant, 1979-81, Drown Found. grant, 1988. Mem. Am. Home Econs. Assn., Nat. Coun. Adminstrs. Home Econs. (pres. 1990), Nat. Coun. Family Rels., Kappa Omicron Nu. Presbyterian. Office: Calif State U 18111 Nordhoff St Northridge CA 91330-0001

CLARK, EZEKAIL LOUIS, chemical engineering consultant; b. Gomel, Russia, June 29, 1912, came to U.S., 1914, naturalized, 1919; s. Louis Elia and Pauline (Rapoport) C.; m. Freida Cohen, June 29, 1933; children: Alvin M., Charlotte S. Clark Landay. BSChemE, Northeastern U., 1937. Process engr. Cities Svc. Co., 1943-45; supr. coal hydrogenation research U.S. Bur. Mines, 1945-54; supr. pilot plant labs. Israel Mining Industries, 1954-56; self-employed cons., 1956-64; pres., founder Pressure Chem. Co., 1964-74; chief coal gasification br. Dept. of Energy, 1974-78; chem. engring. cons., Scottsdale, Ariz., 1978—; bd. dirs. Pressure Chem. Co., 1990; assoc. prof. chem. engring. Haifa Technion, 1955, U. Pitts., 1951-52; lectr. Cath. U., 1954. Recipient McAfee award Pitts. Sect. Am. Inst. Chem. Engrs., 1988. Fellow Am. Inst. Chem. Engrs. (chmn. Pitts. sect. 1973-74); mem. Am. Chem. Soc. Contbr. articles on coal conversion to gaseous and liquid fuels, oil shale utilization, petroleum tech. to profl. jours. Home and Office: 4200 N Miller Rd Scottsdale AZ 85251-3624

CLARK, GARY C., football player; b. Radford, Va., May 1, 1962. Student, James Madison U. With Jacksonville Bulls, 1984-85, Washington Redskins, 1985-92, Phoenix Cardinals, 1993—. Named to Pro Bowl team, 1986, 87, 90, 91. Office: care Phoenix Cardinals 8701 South Hardy Tempe AZ 85284

CLARK, GARY KENNETH, religious ministries executive; b. New Castle, Pa., June 17, 1936; s. Stanley Kenneth and Melba Sunshine (Brickner) C.; m. Dorothy Agnes MacGregor, Aug. 23, 1958; children: Bethany Jane, Nathan Douglas, David Stanley, Kathryn Joy. BA, Barrington (R.I.) Coll., 1958; MDiv, Gordon Sem., Wenham, Mass., 1965, M of Christian Edn., 1969; DDiv (hon.), Trinity Coll., Nigeria, 1990. Asst. pastor Woodlawn Bapt Ch., Pawtucket, R.I., 1958-61; pastor Calvary Covenant Ch., Cranston, R.I., 1961-63, 1st Bapt. Ch., Salem, N.H., 1963-85; pres. Holy Spirit Renewal Ministries, Pasadena, Calif., 1984—; internat. field coord. Assn. of Internat. Mission Svcs., Pasadena, 1989—; assoc. dir. of program Lausanne Congress of World Evangelism, Manila, Philippines, 1988-89; pastor Christian Ctr. Renewal Ch., Arcadia, Calif., 1991—; pres. Gordon-Cornwell Sem. Alumni, Wenham, 1978-84. Editor: (newsletter) Lausanne Internat., 1988-89, Refreshing Times, 1985—, AD2000, 1987-89. Mem. ABC Ministers Coun., Rotary Internat. Republican. Baptist. Home: 1386 N Sierra Bonita Ave Pasadena CA 91104-2647

CLARK, GLEN EDWARD, chief judge; b. Cedar Rapids, Iowa, Nov. 23, 1943; s. Robert M. and Georgia L. (Welch) C.; m. Deanna D. Thomas, July 16, 1966; children: Andrew Curtis, Carissa Jane. BA, U. Iowa, 1966; JD, U. Utah, 1971. Bar: Utah 1971, U.S. Dist. Ct. Utah 1971, U.S. Ct. Appeals (10th cir.) 1972. Assoc. Fabian & Clendenin, 1971-74, ptnr., 1975-81, dir., chmn. banking and comml. law sect., 1981-82; judge U.S. Bankruptcy Ct. Dist. Utah, Salt Lake City, 1982—; bd. govs. nat. Conf. Bankruptcy Judges, 1988-91; mem. com. on bankruptcy edn. Fed. Jud. Ctr., 1989-92; vis. prof. U. Utah, Salt Lake City, 1977-79, 83; pres. Nat. Conf. Bankruptcy Judges, 1992-93; chair bd. trustees Nat. Conf. Bankruptcy Judges Endowment for Edn., 1990-92. With U.S. Army, 1966-68. Finkbine fellow U. Iowa. Fellow Am. Coll. Bankruptcy; mem. Utah Bar Assn., Order of Coif. Presbyterian. Office: US Bankruptcy Ct US Courthouse Rm 361 350 S Main St Salt Lake City UT 84101-2106

CLARK, HENRY BENJAMIN, JR., retired food company executive, community service volunteer; b. Chevy Chase, Md., Oct. 8, 1915; s. Henry Benjamin and Lena (Sefton) C.; m. Geraldine D. Putman, July 25, 1942; children: Putman D., Sefton R. B.C.S., Northwestern U., 1937; M.B.A., Harvard U., 1940. Analyst Castle & Cooke, Inc., Honolulu, 1946-50, asst. sec., 1950-58, asst. treas., 1956-58, treas., 1958-70, v.p., 1962-70, exec. v.p., dir., 1970-80, vice chmn. bd., 1980-81, chmn. bd., pres., 1982-83, chmn., 1981-85, ret., 1985. Chmn. Honolulu Acad. Arts; bd. dirs. Honolulu YMCA, Acad. of Pacific, Hanahauoli Sch., McInerny Found., Goodwill Industries, Palolo Chinese Home, Rehab. Hosp. Pacific. Served to lt. comdr. USNR, 1940-45. Mem. Hawaii Bus. Roundtable, C. of C., Phi Kappa Psi. Clubs: Pacific, Outrigger, Pacific-Union. Office: Honolulu Acad Arts 900 S Beretania St Honolulu HI 96814-1495

CLARK, JAMES H., electronics executive; b. Ft. Worth, Tex., 1944. BS, U. New Orleans, 1971; MS, U. Utah, 1974, PhD. Founder, chmn. bd. Silicon Graphics, Inc., 1981—; bd. dirs. Paracomp. Home: 2040 Broadway Ave San Francisco CA 94115 Office: Silicon Graphics Inc PO Box 7311 2011 N Shoreline Blvd Mountain View CA 94039-1389*

CLARK, JAMES HENRY, publishing company executive; b. Chgo., Aug. 30, 1931; s. James Henry and Mildred Beth (Rutledge) C.; children: Garrette Elizabeth, James Henry. A.B., U. Calif.-Berkeley, 1959. With personnel dept. Fireman's Fund, San Francisco, 1959-60; coll. textbook salesman Prentice-Hall Inc., Berkeley, 1960-63; regional editor Prentice-Hall Inc., 1963-64; editor Prentice-Hall Inc., Englewood Cliffs, N.J., 1964-67; dir. Western editorial office, Belmont, Calif., 1967-68; asso. pub. Aldine Pub. Co., Chgo., 1969; editor-in-chief coll. div. Harper & Row Pubs., Inc., N.Y.C., 1969-70; pub., v.p. Harper & Row Pubs., Inc., 1970-77; dir. Univ. Press, U. Calif.-, Berkeley, 1977—. Served with USAF, 1949-53. Mem. Am. Assn. Univ. Presses (pres. 1986.). Office: U Calif Univ Press 2120 Berkeley Way Berkeley CA 94720-0001

CLARK, JAMES ORIE, II, food technologist; b. South Bend, Ind., Nov. 3, 1950; s. James Orie Sr. and Anna Katherine (Yelich) C.; m. Janet Lee Jenkins, Mar. 31, 1973. AS in Gen. Sci., Mohegan Community Coll., Norwich, Conn., 1976; BS in Food Sci. & Tech., Oreg. State U., 1983; AS in Electronics Engring., Oreg. Polytech. Inst., Portland, 1986. Quality control technician Frito Lay, Inc., Beaverton, Oreg., 1983-84; mgr. R & D Allen Fruit Co., Inc., Newberg, Oreg., 1984-88; tech. dir. Allen Fruit Co., Inc., Newberg, 1989-90, ops. mgr., 1990—; quality assurance mgr. Tree Top, Inc., Selah, Wash., 1988-89. Scoutmaster Boy Scouts Am., Japan & Spain, 1976-79; asst. dist. commr. Boy Scouts Am. (Wood Badge, 1979), Rota, Spain, 1978-79; with USN, 1971-79. Mem. Inst. Food Technologists, Nat. Food Processors Assn. (co. rep.), Am. Soc. for Quality Control, Am. Chem. Soc., Am. Inst. Chemists, Northwest Cherry Briners Assn., Northwest Food Processors Assn. Home: 1468 Woodland Ave Woodburn OR 97071 Office: Allen Fruit Co Inc 500 E Illinois St Newberg OR 97132-2307

CLARK, JANET EILEEN, political scientist, educator; b. Kansas City, Kans., June 5, 1940; d. Edward Francis and Mildred Lois (Mack) Morrissey; AA, Kansas City Jr. Coll., 1960; AB, George Washington U., Washington, 1962, MA, 1964; PhD, U. Ill., 1973; m. Caleb M. Clark, Sept. 28, 1968; children: Emily Claire, Grace Ellen, Evelyn Adair. Staff, U.S. Dept. Labor, Washington, 1962-64; instr. social sci. Kansas City (Kans.) Jr. Coll., 1964-67; instr. polit. sci. Parkland Coll., 1970-71; asst. prof. govt., N.Mex. State U., Las Cruces, 1971-77, assoc. prof., 1977-80; assoc. prof. polit. sci. U. Wyo., 1981-84, prof., 1984—. Co-author: Women, Elections and Representation, 1987, The Equality State, 1988, Women in Taiwan Politics: Overcoming Barriers to Women's Participation in a Modernizing Society, 1990; editor Women & Politics, 1991—. Wolcott fellow, 1963-64, NDEA Title IV fellow, 1967-69. Mem. Internat. Soc. Polit. Psychology Gov. Coun., 1987-89. Mem. NEA (pres. chpt. 1978-79), Am. Polit. Sci. Assn., Western Polit. Sci. Assn. (exec. coun. 1984-87), Western Social Sci. Assn. (exec. coun. 1978-81, v.p. 1982, pres. 1985), Women's Caucus for Polit. Sci. (treas. 1982, pres. 1987), LWV (exec. bd. 1980-83, treas. 1986-90, pres. 1991—), Women's Polit. Caucus, Beta Sigma Phi (v.p. chpt. 1978-79, sec. 1987-88, treas. 1988-89, v.p. 1989-90, pres. 1990-91), Phi Beta Kappa, Chi Omega (prize 1962), Phi Kappa Phi. Democrat. Lutheran. Book rev. editor Social Sci. Jour., 1982-87. Contbr. articles to profl. jours. Home: 519 S 12th St Laramie WY 82070-4021

CLARK, JEFFREY RAPHIEL, research and development company executive; b. Provo, Utah, Sept. 29, 1953; s. Bruce Budge and Ouida (Raphiel) C.; m. Anne Margaret Eberhardt, Mar. 15, 1985; children: Jeffrey Raphiel, Mary Anne Elizabeth. BS, Brigham Young U., 1977, MBA, 1979. CPA, Tex. Fin. analyst Exxon Coal USA, Inc., Houston, 1979-83; constrn. mgr. Gen. Homes, Inc., Houston, 1983-84; controller Liberty Data Products, Houston, 1984-86; v.p. Tech. Rsch. Assocs., Inc., Salt Lake City, 1987—; also dir. Tech. Rsch. Assocs., Inc. Scoutmaster Boy Scouts Am., Salt Lake City, 1989-91. Mem. AICPA, Salt Lake C. of C. (legis. action com.), Rotary (treas. 1988-90). Republican. Mormon. Home: 1428 Michigan Ave Salt Lake City UT 84105-1609 Office: Technical Rsch Assocs 2257 S 1100 E Salt Lake City UT 84106

CLARK, JEFFRY RUSSELL, counseling psychologist, consultant, researcher; b. Wareham, Mass., Oct. 12, 1950; s. John Russell and Barbara Jean (Roberts) C.; children: Stephen Russell, Jeffry John Taylor. BS, Trinity Coll., 1975; MEd, Am. U., 1979; PhD, Stanford U., 1990. Social worker Monmouth Family Ctr., Middletown, N.J., 1975-76; counselor Annandale (N.J.) Correctional Ctr., 1977, Temple Hills (Md.) Counseling Ctr., 1977-79; adminstrv. dir. Stanford (Calif.) Counseling Inst., 1979-82; counselor Emergency Treatment Ctr., Palo Alto, Calif., 1981-87, dir. tng., 1985-86; dir. adolescent and family svcs. Mid Peninsula Family Svc., Palo Alto, 1986—, dir. parenting in divorcing families program, 1990—; pvt. practice family counseling, Palo Alto, 1986—; cons. Peninsula Children's Ctr. Served with USMC, 1969-71. Mem. APA, AACD, Assn. Advancement Behavior Therapy, Western Psychol. Assn., Annandale Jaycees (pres. 1978-79). Democrat. Research on children of divorce, stress, insomnia, parenting in divorcing families. Home: 2081 Hanover St Palo Alto CA 94306-1243

CLARK, JOANN, nurse; b. Tulsa, Dec. 27, 1953; d. Cecil James and Virginia (McGowan) C. ADN, Tulsa Jr. Coll., 1976. RN, Wash. Staff nurse St. John's Med. Ctr., Tulsa, 1976-79, Providence Hosp., Everett, Wash., 1980—. Mem. AACN (sec.-elect Evergreen chpt. 1992), Am. Soc. Post Anesthesia Nurses, Northwest Post Anesthesia Nurses Assn. Republican. Roman Catholic. Office: Providence Hosp 916 Pacific Ave Everett WA 98201

CLARK, LARRY KENNETH, marketing professional; b. Huntington, W.Va., Sept. 14, 1945; s. Dewey and Ruth (Sydenstricker) Sexton; m. Terrie Lee Bodie, July 30, 1981 (div. 1987); m. Sheryl C. Carlson, May 28, 1988; children: Ava Renee, Michael Christopher. Student, U. Md., 1967, Embry-Riddle U., 1985, N.Am. U., 1989. Line pilot Petroleum Helicopters Inc., Lafayette, La., 1968-72; dir. flight ops. Offshore Logistics Inc., Lafayette, 1972-81; mktg. mgr. Honeywell Inc., Phoenix, 1981—; owner The Little Airplane Co., Phoenix, 1985—; designated engring. rep. test pilot FAA, 1979-91, airline transport pilot, 1974—. Named Hon. Citizen of Tex. Larry Clark Day, Tex. Senate, 1988. Mem. Deer Valley Airport Pilot Assn. (bd. dirs. 1989-93), Vietnam Helicopter Pilots Assn. (exec. dir. 1983-86), Internat. Aerobatic Club (2d Pl. 1992). Home: 16645 N 29th Dr Phoenix AZ 85023 Office: Honeywell 5353 W Bell Rd Phoenix AZ 85308

CLARK, LISA R., manufacturing management professional; b. Kansas City, Kans., Dec. 31, 1967; d. Howard Eugene and Norma Jean (Jacks) C. Student, U. N.Mex., 1986-91. Mem. AIX tech. support IBM, Austin, Tex., 1990, 91; mfg. mgmt. asst. Gen. Mills, Inc., Albuquerque, 1992—. Excel scholar U. N.Mex., 1986-90; named one of Outstanding Young Women of Am., 1991. Mem. IEEE, Soc. Women Engrs., Eta Kappa Nu. Roman Catholic. Home: 7300 Valley Forge NE Albuquerque NM 87109 Office: Gen Mills Inc 3501 Paseo del Norte NE Albuquerque NM 87113

CLARK, LLOYD, historian, educator; b. Belton, Tex., Aug. 4, 1923; s. Lloyd C. and Hattie May (Taylor) C.; m. Jean Reeves, June 17, 1950; children: Roger, Cynthia, Candyce. BSJ, So. Meth. U., 1948; B in Fgn. Trade, Am. Grad. Sch. Internat. Mgmt., 1949; MPA, Ariz. State U., 1972. String corr. A.P., Dallas, 1941-42; editor, pub. Ex-Press, Arlington, Tex., 1945-48; publicity mgr. Advt. Counselors Ariz., Phoenix, 1949; reporter Phoenix Gazette, 1949-65; asst. pub. Ariz. Weekly Gazette, 1965-66; founder Council on Abandoned Mil. Posts-U.S.A., 1966; project cons. City of Prescott, Ariz., 1971-72; dep. dir. adminstrv. svcs. No. Ariz. Coun. Govts., Flagstaff, 1972-73; regional adminstr. South Eastern Ariz. Govts. Orgn., Bisbee, 1973-75; local govt. assistance coordinator Ariz. Dept. Transp., Phoenix, 1975-80, program adminstr., 1980-83; history instr. Rio Salado Community Coll., Phoenix, 1983-89; editor and pub. Clark Biog. Reference, 1956-62. Bd. dirs. Friends of Channel 8, 1984-86; mem. transit planning com. Regional Pub. Transit Authority, 1988, Phoenix Citizen's Bond Com., 1987; bd. dirs. Friends of Ariz. Highways Mag., 1989—. Served to lt. AUS, 1942-46; maj., 1966-70; col. Res. Recipient Ariz. exemplary gen. news coverage award, 1960, outstanding news reporting, 1961; Lloyd Clark Journalism scholarship named in honor U. Tex. at Austin Alumni Assn., 1992. Mem. Am. Grad. Sch. Internat. Mgmt. Alumni Assn. (pres. Phoenix chpt. 1965), Ariz. Hist. Soc. (bd. dirs. cen. Ariz. chpt. 1992-93), Sharlot Hall Hist. Soc. (life mem.), Res. Officers Assn., Ex-Students Assn. U. Tex. at Arlington (life mem., pres. 1946-48), The Westerners (sheriff Phoenix Corral 1986-88), Sigma Delta Chi (pres. Valley of Sun chpt. 1964). Club: University (Phoenix). Author: Lloyd Clark's Scrapbook, Vol. 1, 1958, Vol. 2, 1960. Address: PO Box 1489 Surprise AZ 85374

CLARK, LOYAL FRANCES, public affairs specialist; b. Salt Lake City, July 16, 1958; d. Lloyd Grant and Zina (Okelberry) C. Student, Utah State U., 1976-78. Human resource coord. U.S. Forest Svc., Provo, Utah, 1984—, fire info. officer, 1987—, pub. affairs officer, interpretive svcs. coord., edn. coord., 1988—; mem. Take Pride in Utah Task Force, Salt Lake City, 1989—; chairperson Utah Wildlife Ethics Com., Provo, 1989—. Instr. Emergency Svcs., Orem, Utah, 1990—. Recipient Presdl. Award for Outstanding Leadership in Youth Conservation Programs Pres. Ronald Reagan, 1985, Superior Svc. award USDA, 1987, Exemplary Svc. award U.S. Forest Svc., 1992. Mem. Nat. Wildlife Fedn., Nat. Assn. Interpretation, Utah Soc. Environ. Educators, Utah Wildlife Fedn. (bd. dirs. 1981-85, v.p. 1985-87, Achievement award 1983, 85, 87), Utah Wilderness Assn., Am. Forestry Assn., Nature Conservancy. Office: Uinta Nat Forest 88 W 100 N Provo UT 84601-4452

CLARK, MICHAEL, artist, educator; b. Richmond, Calif., Aug. 20, 1948; s. Samuel Marvin and Johnnie Mae (Gibson) C.; m. Pamela Joyce Hansen, Aug. 20, 1975; 1 child, April. AA, San Jose City Coll., 1972; BA, Boise State U., 1975, MA, 1983. Tchr. Buhl (Idaho) Sch. Dist. One, 1975-82; grad. asst. Boise (Idaho) State U., 1982-83; profl. artist Kemmerer, Wyo., 1983-90; dir. outreach Western Wyo. Coll., Kemmerer, 1990—; mem. accreditation team Idaho State Dept. Edn., 1980. Exhibited in group shows (Best of Show award 1987, 92, 1st Pl. Profl. award 1992). Precinct capt. Dem. Party, Kemmerer, 1987; vice chair Sch. Bd., Kemmerer, 1988-90; chmn. Lincoln County Sch. Bd., 1992; bd. dirs. Wyo. Adult Continuing Community Edn., 1993—. With U.S. Army, 1968-70, Vietnam. Decorated Combat Inf. badge; named Outstanding Young Educator, Rotary, 1979. Mem. Wyo. Adult and Continuing Community Edn. Assn. (bd. dirs. 1993—), C. of C. Office: Western Wyo Coll Outreach 1004B Elk St Kemmerer WY 83101

CLARK, MICHAEL P., English educator; b. Marlin, Tex., May 27, 1950; s. Burton Francis and Nelda (Blount) C.; m. Kathleen Mack, 1971 (div. 1973); m. Katherine Weber, May 26, 1977. BA magna cum laude, Rice U., 1972; MA, U. Calif., Irvine, 1973, PhD, 1977. Asst. prof. U. Mich., Ann Arbor, 1977-83; prof. in English and comparative lit. U. Calif., Irvine, 1983—. Author: Michael Foucault, 1983, Jacques Lacan, 1989; contbr. articles to profl. publs. Mem. MLA, Rocky Mountain MLA. Office: U Calif Dept English & Comp Lit Lit Irvine CA 92717

CLARK, MICHAL CHARLES, social services director; b. Bakersfield, Calif., Apr. 30, 1945; s. Henry Benjamin and Betty Jean (Bray) C.; m. Norleen Smith, June 8, 1973; children: Matthew, Amanda, Marlana. BA, UCLA, 1966; PhD, Stanford U., 1969. Asst. prof. U. Tex., Austin, 1969-70, Ariz. State U., Tempe, 1970-72; assoc. prof. Calif. State U., Bakersfield, 1972-74, adj. lectr., 1978—; assoc. prof. St. John's U., Collegville, Minn., 1974-76; coord. gen. edn. Coll. of St. Benedict, St. Joseph, Minn., 1975-77; ops. officer Owen Clark Plumbing, Bakersfield, Calif., 1977; self-employed speculative builder Bakersfield, 1977-87; exec. dir. Kern Regional Ctr., Bakersfield, 1986—; pres. Nat. Down Syndrome Congress, Chgo., 1990-92; pres. Assn. Regional Ctr. Agys., Sacramento, 1991-93; chair So. Calif. Conf. Regional Ctr. Dirs., L.A., 1989-91. Editor: Understanding Student Behavior, 1969; presenter in field; contbr. articles to profl. jours. Campaign mgr. City Coun. Election, Bakersfield, 1982; mem. Spl. Edn. Adv. Com., Bakersfield, 1988-91; pres. Found. for Advocacy, Conservatorship and Trusts, L.A., 1989-91. Mem. Am. Assn. Mental Retardation, Assn. Severe Handicaps, Assn. Retarded Citizens, Kern Down Syndrome Parent Group (pres. 1984-88, founder 1984). Republican. Roman Catholic. Office: Kern Regional Ctr 3200 N Sillect Ave Bakersfield CA 93308

CLARK, MICHEAL DALE, management consultant; b. Grants Pass, Oreg., Apr. 12, 1954; s. Dale Albert and Wanda Lee (Story) C.; m. Terralyn Denison, Aug. 24, 1974; 1 child, Brittany Lauren. BS, U. Oreg., 1978. Property tax mgr. Denny's Inc., LaMirada, Calif., 1981-84; dir. property taxes Motel 6, Inc., Santa Barbara, Calif., 1984-87; v.p., ptnr. Ad Valorem Tax, Inc., Mt. Prospect, Ill., 1987—, P.R. Datasystems, Inc., Covina, Calif., 1990—. Author: (software) Professional Property Tax Management System, 1988. Mem. Inst. Property Taxation (com. chair). Republican. Office: Ad Valorem Tax Inc 750 S Terrado Plz # 231 Covina CA 91723-3419

CLARK, PATRICIA ANN, federal judge; b. Buffalo, July 26, 1936; d. Andrew A. and Mary (Gardner) Zacher; m. James A. Clark, Mar. 25, 1960; B.A., Goucher Coll., Towson, Md., 1958; postgrad. Duke U., 1958-60; LL.B., U. Colo., 1961. Bar: Colo. 1961, U.S. Dist. Ct. D.C. 1961. With Transamerica Title Ins. Co., 1962-65; assoc. Holme, Roberts and Owen, 1965-70, ptnr., 1970-74; judge U.S. Bankruptcy Ct., Denver, 1974—. Commr., Colo. Civil Rights Commn., 1969-72; trustee Waterman Fund, 1978—; mem. transition adv. com. U.S. Cts., 1980-84, com. jud. resources, 1987—. Recipient Disting. Alumni award U. Colo. Sch. Law, 1984. Mem. Colo. Bar Assn., Denver Bar Assn. Office: US Dist Ct 400 Columbine Bldg 1845 Sherman St Denver CO 80203-1190

CLARK, PATTI LYNN, secondary education educator; b. Elgin, Ill., Aug. 29, 1950; d. Donald F. and Gloria F. (Tedei) C. BA in Spl. Edn., No. Ill. U., 1972; MA in Learning Disabilities, U. No. Colo., 1980; Adminstrv. Cert., San Diego State U., 1987. Elem. tchr. Schaumburg (Ill.) Sch. Dist., 1972-76; program specialist N.W. Colo. Bd. Coop. Svcs., Steamboat, 1976-81; retail office products Steamboat Bus. Ctr., 1981-83; resource specialist Grossmont Sch. Dist., LaMesa, Calif., 1983-85, Sweetwater Union High Sch., Chula Vista, Calif., 1985—; cons. Learning Solutions Network, Sacramento, 1989-90. Mem. ASCD, Calif. Sch. Leadership Acad., Sweetwater Union High Sch. Dist. Curriculum, Calif. Consortium Ind. Study, Nat. Dropout Prevention Network. Office: Sweetwater High Sch 2900 Highland Ave National City CA 91950

CLARK, R. BRADBURY, lawyer; b. Des Moines, May 11, 1924; s. Rufus Bradbury and Gertrude Martha (Burns) C.; m. Polly Ann King, Sept. 6, 1949; children: Cynthia Clark Maxwell, Rufus Bradbury, John Atherton. BA, Harvard U., 1948, JD, 1951; diploma in law, Oxford U., Eng., 1952; D.H.L., Ch. Div. Sch. Pacific, San Francisco, 1983. Bar: Calif. 1952. Assoc. O'Melveny & Myers, L.A., 1952-62, sr. ptnr., 1961—, mem. mgmt. com., 1983-90; bd. dirs. So. Calif. Water Co., Econ. Resources Corp., Brown Internat. Corp., Automatic Machinery & Electronics Corp., John Tracy Clinic, also pres. 1982-88. Editor: California Corporation Laws, 6 vols, 1976—. Chancellor Prot. Episcopal Ch. in the Diocese of L.A., 1967—, hon. canon, 1983—. Capt. U.S. Army, 1943-46. Decorated Bronze Star with oak leaf cluster, Purple Heart with oak leaf cluster; Fulbright grantee, 1952. Mem. ABA (subcom. on audit letter responses, com. on law and acctg., task force on legal opinions), State Bar Calif. (chmn. drafting com. on gen. corp. law, 1973-81, drafting com. on nonprofit corp. law 1980-84, mem. exec. com. bus. law sect. 1977-78, 84-87, sec. 1986-87, mem. com. nonprofit corp. law 1991—), L.A. County Bar Assn., Calif. Club, Harvard Club, Chancery Club, Alamitos Bay Yacht Club (Long Beach, Calif.). Republican. Office: O'Melveny & Myers 400 S Hope St Los Angeles CA 90071-2801

CLARK, RAYMOND OAKES, banker; b. Ft. Bragg, N.C., Nov. 9, 1944; s. Raymond Shelton and Nancy Lee (McCormick) C.; m. Patricia Taylor Slaughter; children: Matthew Patrick, Geoffry Charles. BBA, U. Ariz., 1966; postgrad. U. Wash., 1984-86. Mgmt. trainee First Interstate Bank, Phoenix, 1966, credit analyst, 1968-69, asst. br. mgr., Scottsdale, Ariz., 1969-72, asst. v.p., br. mgr., Tempe, Ariz., 1972-90, v.p. br. mgr. Scottsdale, 1990-92, v.p. br. mgr. Phoenix, 1992—. Pres., bd. dirs. Sun Devil Club, Tempe, 1975—; pres. Tempe Diplomats, 1979-89; pres. Tempe Diablos, 1975—; major chmn. Fiesta Bowl, Tempe, 1975-79; bd. dirs. Maricopa County Bd. Mgrs., Phoenix, 1973, YMCA, Tempe, 1974, Tempe Design Rev. Bd., 1983-87. Named one of Outstanding Young Men of Am., Tempe Jaycees, 1977, Ariz. Jaycees, 1978, U.S. Jaycees, 1979. Bd. dirs., treas. East Valley div. Am. Heart Assn., 1989-92. Served with U.S. Army, 1966-68. Mem. Tempe C. of C. (pres. 1979-80). Republican. Episcopalian. Lodge: Kiwanis (dist. lt. gov. 1980).

CLARK, RICHARD WALTER, educator, consultant; b. Mt. Pleasant, Iowa, Apr. 14, 1936; s. Samuel Richard and Floreine Eunice (Walz) C.; m. Rosemary Helma Savage, June 10, 1958; children: Melissa O'Neal, Cameron Clark. BA, U. Wash., 1957, MA, 1963, PhD, 1970. Cert. tchr., prin., supt., Wash. Lectr., grad. asst. U. Wash., Seattle, 1960-61; tchr. Bellevue (Wash.) Pub. Schs., 1961-65, adminstr., 1965-91, dep. supt., to 1991; sr. assoc. Ctr. for Ednl. Renewal, U. Wash., Seattle, 1987—; cons. Pew Charitable Trusts, Phila., 1988—, MacArthur Found., Chgo., 1991-92, Coalition of Essential Schs., Brown U., Providence, 1990—, Ednl Commn. of the States, Denver, 1990-91, Calgary (Alta., Can.) Bd. Edn., 1990-91, others. Author: Effective Speech, 1982, 85, (with others) Glencoe English 10, 11, 12, 1981, 85; contbr. chpts. to books, articles to profl. jours. Pres. Youth Eastside Svcs., Bellevue, 1972; mem. Seattle King County Mcpl. League. Capt. USMC, 1957-63. Recipient Outstanding Performance Pub. Svc. award Seattle King County Mcpl. League, 1987; named Educator of Yr., Lions Club, 1991. Mem. ASCD, Am. Edn. Rsch. Assn., Am. Assn. Sch. Adminstrs., Wash. Assn. Sch. Adminstrs., Speech Communication Assn., Nat. Soc. Study of Edn., Phi Delta Kappa. Methodist. Home and Office: 14426 NE 11th Pl Bellevue WA 98007

CLARK, RICHARD WARD, food industry executive, consultant; b. N.Y.C., Oct. 23, 1938; s. Richard Leal and Dorothy Jane (Whittaker) C. BA with honors, U. Rochester, N.Y., 1960; MBA in Fin., U. Pa., 1962. Corp. planning analyst Campbell Soup Co., Camden, N.J., 1965-67; asst. product mgr. Gen. Mills, Inc., Mpls., 1967-70; sr. fin. analyst McKesson Corp., San Francisco, 1970-71, asst. div. controller, 1971-72, div. controller, 1972-78, gen. mgr. grocery products devel., 1978-79; v.p., controller McKesson Foods Group/McKesson Corp., 1979-85, dir. strategic planning, 1985-87; v.p. fin., chief fin. officer Provigo Corp. (Market Wholesale Grocery Co.), San Rafael, Calif., 1987-89; cons. and hotel devel. Napa Valley Assocs., S.A., San Francisco, 1990—; bd. dirs. Taylor Cuisine, Inc., San Francisco. Author: Some Factors Affecting Dividend Payout Ratios, 1962; musician (album) Dick Clark at the Keyboard, I Love a Piano, 1990. Adv. bd. Salvation Army, San Francisco, 1984—, chmn., 1993—; bd. dirs. Svcs. for Srs., San Francisco, 1990-92. Lt. (j.g.) USNR, 1962-64, PTO. Sherman fellow U. Rochester, 1960. Mem. Fin. Execs. Inst., Bohemian Club, Beta Gamma Sigma. Republican. Presbyterian. Home: 2201 Sacramento St Apt 401 San Francisco CA 94115-2314

CLARK, SALLY NEWBERT, middle level education educator; b. Waldoboro, Maine, Dec. 16, 1934; d. Bernard A. and Arolyn A. (Feyler) Newbert; m. Donald C. Clark, Jan. 26, 1957; children: Susan Lynn, Janet Kathleen May. BA with honors, Calif. State U., L.A., 1960; MA, Pasadena (Calif.) Coll., 1965; EdD, U. Ariz., 1977. Tchr. bus. Pacoima Jr. High Sch., L.A., 1960, Pasadena City Coll., 1961-66; asst. prof. bus. edn. Calif. State U., L.A., 1966-71; tchr. bus. Pima Community Coll., Tucson, 1974-76; asst. prof. bus., sr. lectr. U. Ariz., Tucson, 1977—; co-dir. mid. level support group Tucson Sch./Univ. Partnership; cons. in field. Co-author: (chpt.) National Business Education Association Yearbook, 1979; editor Jour. Adolescent Rsch., 1986—; co-author Ariz. Mid. Schs.: A Survey Report, 1990; co-editor Schs. in the Mid.: A Decade of Growth and Change, 1992, Restructuring Ariz.'s Mid. Schs.: The Report of the Supt.'s Task Force on Mid. Level, 1991; rev. bd. Rsch. in Mid. Level Edn.; contbr. articles to profl. jours. Ariz. Dept. Edn. Rsch. grantee, 1978. Mem. Am. Ednl. Rsch. Assn., Nat. Bus. Edn. Assn., Nat. Mid. Sch. Assn., Ariz. Bus. Edn. Assn., Western Regional Mid. Level Assn. (bd. dirs., co-dir. rsch. com. 1989—), Western Bus. Edn. Assn., Phi Delta Kappa, Delta Pi Epsilon chpt. Beta Pi (charter). Office: U Ariz Coll Edn PO Box 404 Tucson AZ 85721-0001

CLARK, THOMAS JOSEPH, optometrist, former mayor; b. San Diego, July 13, 1926; s. Thomas Joseph and Marjorie Sarah (Harper) C.; B.S., U. Calif.-Berkeley, 1950, M.S., 1951, D.Optometry, 1951; m. Lois Olney, Feb. 22, 1952; children—Paul, James, Carol. Pvt. practice optometry, Long Beach, 1951—; mem. park commn. City Long Beach, 1963-66, mem. city council, 1966—, mayor, 1975-80, 82-84; pres. Los Angeles County div. League of Cities, 1978-79; bd. dirs. League of Calif. Cities, 1976—, pres. 1981-82. Chmn., Los Altos YMCA, Long Beach, 1959-61. Served with AUS, 1944-46. Mem. Am., Calif. optometric assns., Long Beach Optometric Soc. (pres. 1955-56), Ind. Cities Los Angeles County (pres. 1968-69), Calif. Pub. Employees Retirement System (bd. dirs. 1990—). Republican. Methodist. Clubs: Masons, Elks, Rotary. Home: 2267 Albury Ave Long Beach CA 90815-2105 Office: 5479 Abbeyfield St Long Beach CA 90815

CLARK, THOMAS RYAN, retired federal agency executive, business and technical consultant; b. Aberdeen, Wash., Sept. 16, 1925; s. George O. and Gladys (Ryan) C.; m. Barbara Ann Thiele, June 14, 1948; children: Thomas R. III, Kathleen Clark Sandberg, Christopher J.T. Student, U. Kans., 1943-44; BS, U.S. Mil. Acad., 1948; MSEE, Purdue U., 1955; cert., U.S. Army Command and Gen. Staff Coll., 1960, Harvard U., 1979. Commd. C.E., U.S. Army, 1948, advanced through grades to col., 1968; ret. U.S. Army, 1968; program mgr. U.S. AEC, Washington, 1968-75; dep. mgr. Dept. of Energy, Albuquerque, 1976-83; mgr. Nev. ops. Dept. of Energy, Las Vegas, 1983-87, ret., 1987; cons. in field Las Vegas and Albuquerque, 1987—; mem. adv. bd. Dept. Chem. and Nuclear Engring., U. N.Mex., 1984—; mem. statewide adv. bd. Desert Research Inst., U. Nev., 1985-88. Editor, co-author: Nuclear Fuel Cycle, 1975. Trustee Nev. Devel. Authority, Las Vegas, 1984-88, Nat. Atomic Mus. Found., 1993. Decorated Legion of Merit, Bronze Star; named Disting. Exec., Pres. of U.S., 1982. Mem. Las Vegas C. of C. (bd. dirs. 1983-87), Sigma Xi, Tau Beta Pi, Eta Kappa Nu, Rotary Club of Albuquerque (pres. 1993-94). Episcopalian. Lodge: Rotary.

CLARK, THOMAS SULLIVAN, lawyer; b. Bakersfield, Calif., Dec. 12, 1947; s. Walter J. and Ruth Virginia (Sullivan) C.; m. Barbara H. Langston, June 14, 1969. BA in History, U. So. Calif., 1969, JD, 1973. Gen. counsel Income Equities Corp., Los Angeles, 1972-74; campaign cons. Huntington Beach, Calif., 1974-75; prosecutor Office of Kern County Dist. Atty., Bakersfield, 1975-78; ptnr. Arrache, Clark & Potter (formerly Rudnick, Arrache & Clark), Bakersfield, 1978—; cons. Vol. Attys. Program, Bakersfield, 1985—. Bd. dirs. Kern Bridges Youth Found., pres. 1987-89; bd. dirs. Bakersfield City Sch. Dist. Ednl. Found., Bakersfield Med. Found. Mem. Calif. Bar Assn., Kern County Bar Assn. (client cons. 1984—), Community Assns. Inst., Kern County Hist. Soc., Kern County U. So. Calif. Alumni Assn. (bd. dirs., v.p. 1985-88, pres. 1988—). Republican. Roman Catholic. Club: Petroleum. Lodge: Rotary (bd. dirs. Bakersfield club 1982). Office: Arrache Clark & Potter 5401 California Ave Ste 301 Bakersfield CA 93309-0702

CLARK, WALLACE THOMAS, III, instrumental scientist; b. Bakersfield, Calif., Sept. 9, 1953; s. Wallace Thomas II and Betty Joe (Seibert) C.; m. Kathleen Gay Bunch, Nov. 14, 1981; children: Alethea Rae, Wallace Thomas IV. BS in Physics, N.Mex. Inst. Mining and Tech., 1975; MS in Physics, Idaho State U., 1978; PhD in Instrumental Scis., U. Ark., 1982. Devel. assoc. III Union Carbide/Martin Marietta, Oak Ridge, Tenn., 1982-85; mem. tech. staff AT&T Bell Labs., Holmdel, N.J., 1985-86; sr. staff mem. BDM Corp., Albuquerque, 1986-89; chief scientist BDM Mgmt. Svcs. Co., Kirtland AFB, N.Mex., 1991; imaging scientist, data analyst BDM Internat., Albuquerque, 1991—. Contbr. articles to Jour. Radiation Effects, Rsch. and Engring. Participant Albuquerque Ground Water Project, 1991. Mem. Instrument Soc. Am., Optical Soc. Am., Inst. Hazardous Materials Mgmt. Home: 7208 Mesa de Arena NW Albuquerque NM 87120-1518 Office: BDM Internat 1801 Randolph Rd SE Albuquerque NM 87106-4295

CLARK, WILL (WILLIAM NUSCHLER CLARK, JR.), professional baseball player; b. New Orleans, Mar. 13, 1964. Student, Miss. State U. Baseball player Class A Calif. League Team, Fresno, 1985, San Francisco Giants, 1986—; mem. U.S. Olympic baseball team, 1984. Recipient Gold Glove award, 1991, Silver Slugger, 1989, 91; named to All-Star team, 1988-92, Coll. All-Am. Team Sporting News, 1984-85; Nat. RBI leader, 1988. Office: San Francisco Giants Candlestick Park San Francisco CA 94124-3998

CLARKE, ALLEN RICHARD, lawyer; b. Lima, Ohio, Oct. 21, 1957; s. George W. and Jane (Lindsay) C.; m. Kathleen A. Neel, May 16, 1987. BA, Marietta Coll., 1979; JD, U. Va., 1984. Bar: Ariz. 1984, U.S. Dist. Ct. Ariz. 1984, U.S. Ct. Appeals (9th cir.) 1986, U.S. Ct. Appeals (5th cir.) 1987, U.S. Supreme Ct. 1990. With Lewis and Roca, Phoenix, 1984–. Mem. bd. mgmt. YMCA, Phoenix, 1986-91. Mem. Phi Beta Kappa. Home: 6123 E Edgemont Ave Scottsdale AZ 85257-1050 Office: Lewis and Roca 40 N Central Ave Phoenix AZ 85004-4424

CLARKE, DAVID MARSHALL, college president, Jesuit priest; b. Chewalah, Wash., Nov. 28, 1927; s. Melvin L. and Louise M. (Van Bibber) C. B.S., Gonzaga U., 1949, M.S. in Organic Chemistry, 1949, Licentiate in Philosophy, 1958; Ph.D. in Phys. Chemistry, Northwestern U., 1953; Licentiate in Sacred Theology, Weston Coll., 1965. Instr., asst. prof. chemistry and math. Gonzaga U., Spokane, Wash., 1949-50, 56-61, asst. prof. chemistry, 1966-68, assoc. prof., 1968-70, acad. v.p., 1968-69, exec. v.p., 1969-70; research scientist Weston Obs., Boston Coll., 1961-65; provost, acad. v.p. St. Francis Coll., Joliet, Ill., 1970-72; pres. Regis Coll., Denver, 1972—; mem. Commn. on Edn. Credits and Credentials, Washington, 1981-85, Commn. on Higher Edn. and Adult Learner, 1986—; bd. dirs. Midwest Research Inst., 1982—; mem. exec. com. Ind. Coll. Funds Am., 1985—; apptd. mem. Denver Edn. Council on Higher Edn., 1987—. Mem. Denver Commn. Community Relations, 1975-83; trustee, mem. exec. com. N.W. Assn. Pvt. Colls. and Univs., 1968-70; trustee Gonzaga U., 1968-70, Coll. Holy Cross, 1969-78, Regis Coll., 1972—, Denver Inst. Healt, Loyola U., New Orleans, 1982-85; trustee, chmn. acad. com. Loyola U., Chgo., 1971-80; bd. dirs. Assn. Jesuit Colls. and Univs., 1973—; mem. adv. bd. Colo. Youth Leadership Seminar, Sisters of St. Francis, 1987; appointed to Denver Edn. Council on Higher Edn., 1987. Named to 10 most disting., Denver Bus. Magt., 1985; recipient Disting. Alumni Merit award Gonzaga U., 1987, Serra Trust award, 1990. Mem. Am. Chem. Soc., Pres.'s Assn., Sigma Xi, Delta Epsilon Sigma, Phi Lambda Upsilon, Alpha Sigma Nu. Address: 3333 Regis Blvd Denver CO 80221-1099

CLARKE, JACK FREDERICK, psychologist; b. Portland, Oreg., Feb. 3, 1936; s. Jack C. and Florence H. (Seaquist) C.; m. Janice A. Cessna, Mar. 30, 1958; children: Scott A., Kristin A., Kerry S. BA, U. Redlands, 1958; MS, U. Oreg., 1965; PhD, Ariz. State U., 1971. Lic. psychologist, marriage & family therapist. Dist. scout exec. Boy Scouts Am., Portland, 1959-62, Eugene, Oreg., 1962-65; counselor, tchr. Eugene Sch. Dist., 1965-68; counseling psychologist U. Nev., Reno, 1970—; appointed mem. Nev. Bd. Marriage & Family Therapist Examiners, 1977-79. Mem. AACD, APA, Assn. for Counselor Edn. & Supervision (treas. 1980-84), Western Assn. for Counselor Edn. & Supervision (pres. 1978-79). Methodist. Home: 901 Sierra Manor Dr Reno NV 89511-9406 Office: U Nev Counseling Ctr (080) Reno NV 89557

CLARKE, PETER, communications educator; b. Evanston, Ill., Sept. 19, 1936; s. Clarence Leon and Dorothy (Whitcomb) C.; m. Karen Storey, June 4, 1962 (div. 1984); 1 child, Christopher Michael. B.A., U. Wash., 1959; M.A., U. Minn., 1961, Ph.D., 1963. Dir., asst. prof. Comm. Rsch. Ctr. U. Wash., Seattle, 1965-68, assoc. prof. sch. comm., 1967-72, dir. sch. comm., 1971-72; prof. dept. journalism U. Mich., Ann Arbor, 1973-74, chmn., prof. dept. journalism, 1975-78, chmn., prof. dept. comm., 1979-80; dean, prof. Annenberg Sch. Comm., U. So. Calif., L.A., 1981-92, prof., 1993—; cons. for various fed. and state govt. commns. on mass media and social problems. Co-author: (with Susan H. Evans) Covering Campaigns: Journalism in Congressional Elections, 1983; editor: New Models for Communication Research, 1973; co-editor: (with Susan H. Evans) The Computer Culture, 1985; contbr. articles to profl. jours. Grantee U.S. Office of Edn., 1967-69, NSF, 1973-78, ABC-TV, 1984, IBM, 1987, other granting agys. Mem. Am. Assn. for Pub. Opinion Rsch., Am. Sociol. Assn., Internat. Comm. Assn., Am. Polit. Sci. Assn., Internat. Assn. Mass Comm. Rsch., Am. Psychol. Assn., Am. Statis. Assn., Assn. Edn. in Journalism and Mass Comm. (chmn. rsch. com., mem. exec. com.), Am. Assn. Schs. and Dept. Journalism (exec. com.). Office: U So Calif Annenberg Sch Comm 3502 S Hoover St Los Angeles CA 90089-0281

CLARKE, PETER ANTHONY, real estate company executive; b. Columbus, Ohio, Dec. 29, 1933; s. George Caleb and Cecilia Ruth (Noonan) C.; m. Mimi Cahill, Nov. 22, 1978; 1 child, Caleb Anthony. BA, U. Cin., 1957. Lic. real estate broker, Calif., Hawaii. Acctg. machine sales Nat. Cash Register, Cin., 1958-61; computer sales Honeywell, San Francisco, 1961-62; comml. real estate sales rep. Damon Raike & Co., San Francisco, 1963-70; exec. dir. Ctr. Properties, Honolulu, 1970-72; pres. Clarke & Cramer, Inc., San Francisco, 1973—. Mem. Soc. of Indsl. and Office Realtors (chpt. pres. 1992, bd. dirs. 1991-94, Largest Dollar Volume Intra City award 1992), Rotary Club, Hibernian Newman Club (pres. 1988), Outrigger Canoe Club (Hawaii). Roman Catholic. Home: 20 Geldert Dr Tiburon CA 94920 Office: Clarke & Cramer Inc 300 Montgomery St San Francisco CA 94104

CLARKE, PHILIP JOSEPH, radio announcer; b. Pomona, Calif., Nov. 30, 1956; s. Edward James and Mary Ann (Kipp) C. Grad. high sch., Lancaster, Calif.; student, Navy Submarine Sch., 1975; announcing cert., Columbia Sch. of Broadcasting, San Diego, 1983-84. Enlisted USN, 1975; sonar operator USS Snook, San Diego, 1976-78, USS Billfish, New London, Conn., 1980-82; repair parts petty officer USN Fleet Anti-submarine Tng. Ctr., San Diego, 1982-84; morning drive announcer KXTL-AM Radio, Butte, Mont., 1984—. Author: (book poetry) Reflections, 1983. Literacy trainer, LVA Butte Literacy Program, 1992. Recipient Certs. of Appreciation D.A.R.E. Program, Butte, 1989, Big Brothers and Sisters, Butte, 1991, ARC, 1992, Wiseriver Vol. Fire Co., 1992. Mem. KC (3rd degree knight), Butte Jaycees. Republican. Roman Catholic. Home: 108 3rd St W SP # 4 Box 314 Whitehall MT 59759

CLARKE, RANDALL LEE, real estate broker; b. Portland, Oreg., Oct. 25, 1958; s. Elmo Lee and Margie Madeline (Zill) C.; m. Sharon Ann Susanka, May 24; children: William C. Porter, Jacob C. Porter, Sky M. Clarke, Rose M. Clarke. Grad., Realtors Inst., Portland, Oreg., 1985-90. Real estate agt. Republic Real Estate Co., Portland, Oreg., 1984-85, The Realty Group, Portland, Oreg., 1985-90; real estate assoc. broker Hasson Co., Portland, Oreg., 1990—. Mem. Hist. Preservation League of Oreg., 1992. Named Top Producer, Hasson Co., 1991, Top 5 Producers, Handel, Hasson & Jones Co., 1990. Mem. Nat. Assn. Realtors, Oreg. Assn. Realtors, Portland Bd. Realtors, Mil. Vehicle Collectors Club of Oreg., Oreg. Vintage Motorcycle Club, Pacific Coast Land Rover Club, Land Rover Owners Club. Home: 3392 SE Brooklyn Portland OR 97202

CLARKE, RICHARD ALAN, electric and gas utility company executive, lawyer; b. San Francisco, May 18, 1930; s. Chauncey Frederick and Carolyn (Shannon) C.; m. Mary Dell Fisher, Feb. 5, 1955; children: Suzanne, Nancy C. Stephen, Douglas Alan. AB Polit. Sci. cum laude, U. Calif., Berkeley, 1952, JD, 1955. Bar: Calif. 1955. Atty. Pacific Gas and Electric Co., San Francisco, 1955-60, sr. counsel, 1970-74, asst. gen. counsel, 1974-79, v.p., asst. to chmn., 1979-82, exec. v.p., gen. mgr. utility ops., 1982-85, pres., 1985-86, chmn. bd., chief exec. officer, 1986—; ptnr. Rockwell, Fulkerson and Clarke, San Rafael, Calif., 1960-69; bd. dirs. Potlach Corp., Bank Am. Corp.; mem. exec. com. Edison Electric Inst.; mem. The Bus. Coun., Assn. Edison Illuminating Cos., Pres.'s Coun. on Sustainabel Devel. Chmn. Bay Area Coun.; mem. Bay Area Econ. Forum, The Bus. Roundtable, The Calif. Bus. Roundtable; trustee Com. for Econ. Devel.; trustee Boalt Hall Trust, Sch. Law U. Calif.-Berkeley; bd. govs. San Francisco Symphony; mem. adv. bd. Walter A. Haas Sch. Bus. U. Calif., Berkeley. Mem. Pacific Coast Elec. Assn., Pacific Coast Gas Assn., Calif. C. of C. (past dir.), San Francisco C. of C. (past dir., v.p. econ. devel.), Marin Tennis Club. Office: Pacific Gas & Electric Co 77 Beale St San Francisco CA 94177

CLARKE, URANA, musician, writer, educator; b. Wickliffe-on-the-Lake, Ohio, Sept. 8, 1902; d. Graham Warren and Grace Urana (Olsaver) C.; artists and tchrs. diploma Mannes Music Sch., N.Y.C., 1925; cert. Dalcroze Sch. Music, N.Y.C., 1950; student Pembroke Coll., Brown U.; BS, Mont. State U., 1967, M of Applied Sci., 1970. Mem. faculty Mannes Music Sch., 1922-49, Dalcroze Sch. Music, 1949-54; adv. editor in music The Book of Knowledge, 1949-65; v.p., dir. Saugatuck Circle Housing Devel.; guest lectr. Hayden Planetarium, 1945; guest lectr., bd. dirs. Roger Williams Park Planetarium, Providence; radio show New Eng. Skies, Providence, 1961-64, Skies Over the Big Sky Country, Livingston, Mont., 1964-79, Birds of the Big Sky Country, 1972-79, Great Music of Religion, 1974-79; mem. adv. com. Nat. Rivers and Harbors Congress, 1947-58; instr. continuing edn. Mont. State U. Chmn. Park County chpt. ARC, 1967-92, chmn. emeritus 1992—, co-chmn. county blood program, first aid instr. trainer, 1941-93; instr. ARC cardio-pulmonary resuscitation, 1976-84; mem. Mont. Commn. Nursing and Nursing Edn., 1974-76; mem. Park County Local Govt. Study Commn., 1974-76, chmn., 1984-86; mem. Greater Yellowstone Coalition. Mem. Am. Acad. Polit. Sci., Am. Musicol. Soc., Royal Astron. Soc. Can., Inst. Nav., Maria Mitchell Soc. Nantucket, N.Am. Yacht Racing Union, AAAS, Meteoritical Soc., Internat. Soc. Mus. Research, Skyscrapers (sec.-treas. 1960-63), Am. Guild Organists, Park County Wilderness Assn. (treas.), Trout Unlimited, Nature Conservancy, Big Sky Astron. Soc. (dir. 1965—), Sierra Club. Lutheran. Club: Cedar Point Yacht. Author: The Heavens are Telling (astronomy), 1951; Skies Over the Big Sky Country, 1965; also astron. news-letter, View It Yourself, weekly column Big Skies, 1981—; contbr. to mags, on music, nav. and astronomy. Pub. Five Chorale Preludes for Organ, 1975; also elem. two-piano pieces. Inventor, builder of Clarke Adjustable Piano Stool. Address: Log-A-Rhythm 9th St Island Livingston MT 59047

CLARKSON, LAWRENCE WILLIAM, airplane company executive; b. Grove City, Pa., Apr. 29, 1938; s. Harold William and Jean Henrietta (Jaxtheimer) C.; m. Barbara Louise Stevenson, Aug. 20, 1960; children: Michael, Elizabeth, Jennifer. BA, DePauw U., 1960; JD, U. Fla., 1962. Counsel Pratt & Whitney, West Palm Beach, Fla., 1967-72, program dep. dir., 1972-75, program mgr., 1974-75; v.p., mng. dir. Pratt & Whitney, Brussels, Belgium, 1975-78; v.p. mktg. Pratt & Whitney, West Palm Beach, 1978-80; v.p. contracts Pratt & Whitney, Hartford, Conn., 1980-82, pres. comml. products div., 1982-87; sr. v.p. Boeing Comml. Airplanes Group, Seattle, 1988-91; corp. v.p. planning and internat. devel. Boeing Co., Seattle, 1992—; dir. Partnership for Improved Air Travel, Washington, 1988—. Trustee DePauw U., Greencastle, Ind., 1987—; corp. coun. Interlochen (Mich.) Ctr. for the Arts, 1987, trustee, 1988—; trustee Seattle Opera, 1990—, chmn. , 1991—, pres. Japan-Am. Soc., Wash., pres. Wash. State China Rels. com., chmn. Nat. Bur. of Asia Rsch., Coun. Fgn. Rels. Capt. USAF, 1963-66. Mem. N.Y. Yacht Club, Seattle Yacht Club, Met. Opera Club, Wings Club (bd. govs. 1987—). Episcopalian. Home: 13912 NE 31st Pl Bellevue WA 98005-1881 Office: The Boeing Co PO Box 3707 Seattle WA 98124-2207

CLARNO, BEVERLY ANN, state legislator, farmer; b. Langlois, Oreg., Mar. 29, 1936; d. Howard William and Evelyn June (Young) Boice; m. Roy Clarno, July 15, 1991; children: Dan, Don, Randy, Cindi. Student, Marleherst Coll., 1985, Lewis & Clark Law Sch., 1985-87. Real estate broker Lake Realty and Hatfield & Skopil, Lake Osewego, Oreg., 1984-85; pres. T & H Hog Farms, Wasco, Oreg., 1973-76; securities examiner State of Oreg., Salem, 1981-83; circuit ct. clerk Deschutes County, Bend, Oreg., 1987-88; state legislator State of Oreg., 1988—. Recipient Cost Cutting award, Citizens for Cost Effective Govt., Portland, 1991. Mem. Boys & Girls Aid Soc., Kiwanis Club, Lions Club, High Desert Mus., Eastern Star. Republican. Methodist. Home: 25249 Dodds Rd Bend OR 97701-9320

CLARREN, STERLING KEITH, pediatrician; b. Mpls., Mar. 12, 1947; s. David Bernard and Lila (Reifel) C.; m. Sandra Gayle Bernstein, June 8, 1970; children: Rebecca Pia, Jonathan Seth. BA, Yale U., 1969; MD, U. Minn., 1973. Pediatric intern U. Wash. Sch. Medicine, Seattle, 1973-74, resident in pediatrics, 1974-77, asst. prof. dept. pediatrics, 1979-83, assoc. prof., 1983-88, prof., 1988, Robert A. Aldrich chair in pediatrics, 1989—; head divsn. congenital defects U. Wash. Sch. Medicine, 1987—; dir. dept. congenital defects Children's Hosp. and Med. Ctr., Seattle, 1987—. Contbr. articles to profl. jours.; patentee for orthosis to alter cranial shape. Cons.

pediatrician Maxillofacial Rev. Bd., State of Wash., Seattle, 1984—, chmn. Health-Birth Defects Adv. Com., Olympia, 1980—; mem. fetal alcohol adv. com. Children's Trust Found., Seattle, 1988—; mem. adv. bd. Nat. Orgn. on Fetal Alcohol Syndrome. Rsch. grantee Nat. Inst. Alcohol Abuse & Alcoholism, 1982—. Mem. AAAS, Am. Acad. Pediatrics, Soc. for Pediatric Rsch., Teratology Soc., Rsch. Soc. on Alcoholism (pres. fetal alcohol study group 1993), Am. Cleft Palate Assn., N.Y. Acad. Scis. Home: 8515 Paisley Dr NE Seattle WA 98115-3944 Office: Children's Hosp and Med Ctr Divsn Congenital Defects PO Box C-5371 Seattle WA 98105

CLARY, WARREN POWELL, natural resource researcher; b. Lewellen, Nebr., Sept. 8, 1936; s. Oren Vernen and Naomi F. (Riggs) C.; m. Jeanne Carlholm, Aug. 18, 1957; children: David Warren, Douglas Oren, Diane Jeanne. BS, U. Nebr., 1958; MS, Colo. State U., 1961, PhD, 1972. Range conservationist Rocky Mountain Forest and Range Exptl. Sta., Flagstaff, Ariz., 1960-65; plant ecologist Rocky Mountain Forest and Range Exptl. Sta., Flagstaff, 1965-76; project leader So. Forest Exptl. Sta., Pineville, La., 1976-77; project leader Intermountain Rsch. Sta., Provo, Utah, 1977-84, Boise, Idaho, 1984—. Contbr. articles to profl. jours. Methodist. Office: Intermountain Rsch Sta 316 E Myrtle St Boise ID 83702-7693

CLAUSEN, ALF HEIBERG, composer; b. Mpls., Mar. 28, 1941; s. Alf and Magdalene (Heiberg) C.; m. Judy Kaye Landstrom, June 5, 1965; children: Karen Leigh, Scott Owen, Kyle Evan; m. Sally Maureen Taron, Jan. 9, 1993. BA, N.D. State U., 1963; postgrad., U. Wis., 1963; diploma in music composition and arranging, Berklee Coll. Music, 1966; studies with John Bavicchi, William Maloof, Herb Pomeroy, Earle Hagen. Composer, orchestrator; pres. Karleigh Music Co.; instr. music The Dick Grove Music Workshops; instr. music arranging and composition UCLA; adjudicator Playboy All-Star Intercollegiate Jazz Festival Competition, Western Div. Intercollegiate Jazz Festival Competition; composer Los Angeles Neophonic Orch. Concert Series, 1968. Composer, orchestrator (films) Mr. Mom, Force Five, An Eye for an Eye, Fast Walking, Forced Vengeance, Airplane II: The Sequel, Natty Gann, Splash, Micki & Maude, Weird Science, Dragnet, Number One With a Bullet, (TV shows) Father Murphy, Christine Cromwell, The Simpsons (Emmy nomination), Little House on the Prairie, Shell Game, The Mississippi, Fame, Wizards & Warriors, Partners in Crime, Dads, Lime Street, Harry, Alf, Moonlighting (6 Emmy nominations), Bronk, Jigsaw, The FBI, Ripley's Believe It Or Not, Scene of the Crime, Trauma Center (TV films) Happy Endings, Rememberance of Love, Miss All-American Beauty, This is Kate Bennett, For Ladies Only, The Other Lover, Letting Go, The Long Way Home, Double Agent, Murder in Three Acts, My First Love, Police Story, She Knows Too Much, Stranded; orchestrator (films) Buddy, Buddy, Jinxed, The Beastmaster, Table for Five, Up the Creek, Miracles, My Science Project, Wise Guys, Into the Night, Lots of Luck, The Last Starfighter, Ferris Bueller's Day Off; (TV movies) Sparkling Cyanide, Princess Daisy, Quarterback Princess, Caribbean Mystery, I Want to Live, Legs, Six Months With an Older Woman, Two of a Kind (Emmy award), Listen to Your Heart, Mirrors; composer, arranger, producer (albums) Into the Night, Moonlighting, The Beastmaster, The Last Starfighter, North Tex. State Lab Band (Grammy nomination), numerous others. Recipient Clio nomination, N.Y.C., 1979, One O'Clock award North Tex. State U., Denton, 1978, 79, 80, Alumnus Recognition award Berklee Coll. Music, 1984, Alumni Achievement award N.D. State U., 1986; U. Wis. scholar; Nat. Endowment Arts, Berklee Coll. Music fellow. Mem. ASCAP, Nat. Assn. Jazz Educators, Songwriters Guild, Soc. Composers and Lyricists, Nat. Acad. Rec. Arts and Scis. (mem. jazz crafts com.), Acad. TV Arts and Scis. (8 Emmy nominations), Am. Fedn. Musicians, Screen Actors Guild, Blue Key, Phi Kappa Phi, Kappa Kappa Psi. Democrat. Lutheran.

CLAUSEN, BRET MARK, industrial hygienist, safety professional; b. Hayward, Calif., Aug. 1, 1958; s. Norman E. and Barbara Ann (Wagner) C.; m. Cheryl Elaine Carlson, May 24, 1980; children: Kathrine, Eric, Emily. BS, Colo. State U., 1980, MS, 1983. Diplomate Am. Acad. Indsl. Hygiene; cert. indsl. hygienist, safety profl., hazard control mgr., hazardous materials mgr. Assoc. risk mgmt., indsl. hygienist, safety rep. Samsonite Corp., Denver, 1980-83, mgr. loss prevention, 1984-88; health, safety and environment rep. Storage Tech., Longmont, Colo., 1984; sr. project cons. Occusafe Inc., Denver, 1988; prin. program administr. indsl. hygiene Rockwell Internat., Golden, Colo., 1988-89; sr. prin. HS & E area engr. EG&G Rocky Flats, Inc., Colden, 1990, mgr. indsl. hygiene programs, 1990-91, mgr. indsl. hygiene, 1991—. Mem. Am. Indsl. Hygiene Assn. (pres. Rocky Mtn. sect. 1988-89, past pres. 1990), Am. Soc. Safety Engrs. (profl.), Am. Bd. Indsl. Hygiene (cert. in comprehensive practice), Bd. Cert. Safety Profls. (cert. in comprehensive practice and mgmt. aspects), Bd. Hazard Control Mgmt. (cert master level), Inst. Hazardous Materials Mgmt. (cert. sr. level), Ins. Inst. Am. (assoc. risk mgmt.). Republican. Lutheran. Home: 16794 Weld County Rd 44 La Salle CO 80645 Office: EG&G Rocky Flats Inc PO Box 464 Mail Stop T452D Golden CO 80402-0464

CLAUSEN, EDWIN GEORGE, history educator; b. San Francisco, Aug. 1, 1946; s. Edwin George and Shirley Ann (Stephens) C.; 1 child, Ahren Edwin. BA, U. Calif., Riverside, 1970; MA, U. Calif., Santa Barbara, 1972, PhD, 1979. Lectr. Chinese U. Hong Kong, 1975-76; faculty rsch. fellow U. Calif., Santa Barbara, 1978-79; asst. prof. Lafayette Coll., Easton, Pa., 1979-82; asst. prof. Pacific Luth. U., Tacoma, Wash., 1983-87, assoc. prof. history, 1987—, chair history dept., 1991—; dir. Global Studies Program, 1990—; dir. CUST exch., 1989-92, dir. Chinese Studies Program, 1992-93; vis. lectr./rsch. specialist Chungdu U., China, 1988-89; project dir. PLU Team, Edn. for Third World Devel., U. Mich., Ann Arbor, 1985-88; cons. Pacific World Telecourse, Unit 3, U. Calif., San Diego, 1988, Project on Blacks and Chinese in the Pacific Northwest, 1983-84; project evaluator Assn. for the Humanities in Idaho, 1983-84. Editorial bd. Assn. of Asian Studies on the Pacific Coast, 1988—, Occasional Papers Series; co-author, producer: To Facilitate Inclusion and Nobility: The Chinese and Asian Immigrant Connections, 1978; co-author: (books) Revolution and Foreign Policy: Sino-African Relations, 1949-1976, 1981, Chinese and African Professional in CA, 1982; co-editor: Pluralism, Racism and Public Policy, 1981, Roads Of Freedom The Struggle Against Dependence in the Developing World, 1989; contbr. articles to profl. jours. Fulbright Hays Curriculum Devel. award, Thailand, 1988, Burlington No. Found. award, 1986-87; Calif. Coun. for the Humanities in Pub. Policy fellow, 1978-79, Am. Luth. Ch. fellow for rsch., 1984, 88-89; ACLS travel grantee, 1984, South Seas Soc. travel award, Singapore, 1984, Nancy Kittle Trust rsch. award, 1979, U. Calif. Patent Fund Rsch. grantee, 1977; Regents of U. Calif. fellow, 1978-79, U. Calif./U.S. State Dept. fellow, 1975-76. Mem. Assn. Third World Studies, Assn. Asian Studies, Amnesty Internat. Office: Pacific Luth U History Dept Tacoma WA 98447

CLAUSNER, MARLIN DAVID, JR., forest products company executive; b. San Juan, Puerto Rico, Dec. 26, 1941; s. Marlin David and Aida Margaret (Jordan) C.; m. Linda Marie Nuxoll, Feb. 4, 1984; children: Karin, Ronald. BS, U.S. Naval Acad., 1965; MBA, Dartmouth Coll., 1972. Commd. ensign USN, 1965, advance through grades to lt., 1970, surface warfare officer, 1965-70; mfg. mgr. Potlatch Corp., Lewiston, Idaho, 1974-82; resource mgr. Potlatch Corp., Lewiston, 1982-88, v.p. western wood products div., 1988—. Active Idaho Community Found., Boise, 1988—. Mem. Western Wood Products Assn. (bd. dirs. 1988—), Nat. Forest Products Assn. (dir. 1988—), Intermountain Forest Industries Assn. (v.p. 1991—). Office: Potlatch Corp Box 1016 Lewiston ID 83501

CLAUSSEN, BONNIE ADDISON, II, aerospace company executive; b. Pueblo, Colo., Jan. 11, 1942; s. Bonnie A. I and Gertrude A. (Poe) C.; m. Charlotte J. Dipert, July 11, 1961; children: Christopher Addison, Raymond Dale. BS in Math., U. So. Colo., 1967; postgrad., Pa. State U., King of Prussia, 1968-69. Programmer Gen. Electric Corp., King of Prussia, 1967-69, sr. programmer, 1969-71; project mgr. Martin Marietta Aerospace Co., Denver, 1971-79; co-founder, exec. v.p. CTA, Inc., Englewood, Colo., 1979—, also bd. dirs. Designer: (software) Real-Time Flight, 1967-78, Viking Mars Lander Flight, 1975; contbr: Real-Time Simulation Publs., 1975-78. Served with USAF, 1962-65. Recipient Pub. Service medal Nat. Aeronautics and Space Adminstrn., 1976. Republican. Office: CTA Inc 5670 Greenwood Plaza Blvd Englewood CO 80111-2448

CLAUSSEN, KELLI, artist; b. Virginia, Minn., Oct. 30, 1943; d. Luke O'Farrell and Sarah (Haryn) Suihkonen; m. Paul Kelly, Nov. 1964 (div. 1969); children: Christopher, Stephanie, Mechelle; m. Howard Boyd Claussen, Nov. 17, 1989. BS in Visual Arts, Ind. State U., 1990. Artist Arlington, Wash., 1990—. Exhibited in group shows at Salmon Days Art Show, 1990, 3 juried shows at Ind. U., 1987-90. Mem. Woman Artist Mus., Washington, 1990-91, Seattle Art Mus., 1991-92. Roman Catholic. Home and Office: 19632 Meadowlake Rd Snohomish WA 98290

CLAUSSEN, RONALD VERNON, federal transportation agency administrator; b. Davenport, Iowa, Feb. 6, 1938; s. Elmer Arthur and Mary Elizabeth (Negus) C.; m. Martha Elizabeth Walls, Jan. 26, 1961 (div. 1988); children: Terry, Traci. AA in Bus. Adminstrn., Palmer Jr. Coll., 1970; BA in Pub. Adminstrn., Upper Iowa U., 1974; MBA, Cen. Mich. U., 1977. Police officer City of Davenport, Iowa, 1961-67; transp. specialist Rock Island (Ill.) Arsenal Activity U.S. Dept. Def., 1967-69, traffic mgr. Savanna (Ill.) Army Depot, 1969-70; storage specialist personal property U.S. Dept. Def., Chgo. and Atlanta, 1970-73; traffic mgmt. specialist Rock Island Arsenal U.S. Dept. Def., 1973-74; sr. storage specialist personal property U.S. Dept. Def., Falls Church, Va., 1974-82; chief of transp. Army Aviation Ctr. U.S. Dept. Def., Ft. Rucker, Ala., 1982-85; dep. dir. personal property U.S. Dept. Def., Oakland, Calif., 1985-88; dep. dir. inland traffic U.S. Dept. Def., Oakland, 1988-93; dep. asst. chef od staff ops., 1993—; instr. bus. Fairfax County (Va.) Adult Edn., 1977-83; instr. seminar George Mason U., Fairfax, 1977-83; adj. faculty U. Va., Falls Church, 1977-83, Embry-Riddle Aero. U., Daytona Beach, Fla., 1983—; sole propr. Claussen Assocs. Bus. Mgmt. and Mktg.; bd. dirs DNA Internat., 1992—. Co-author: Warehouse Emergency Operations, 1982; contbr. to profl. orgns. Mem. supervisory com. San Francisco Bay Area unit Internat. Longshoremen and Warehousemen Fed. Credit Union. Sgt. USAF, 1956-60. Recipient Commander's award/medal Oakland (Calif.) Army Base. Mem. Meeting Planners Internat., Nat. Def. Transp. Assn. (bd. dirs. 1987-93, chpt. pres.), Soc. Govt. Meeting Planners (nat. pres. 1987-89, chpt. pres. 1986-87, Sam Gilmer Award Excellence 1990, Members' Choice award 1992), No. Calif. Meeting Planners Internat., Am. Legion, Shriners, Mason, Scottish Rite, Delta Nu Alpha (chpt. pres., region v.p., Pres.'s citation 1991). Republican. Lutheran. Home: 1009 Cedar Ter San Pablo CA 94806-3798 Office: Mil Traffic Mgmt Command Western Area Oakland Army Base Oakland CA 94626-5000

CLAY, JAMES RAY, mathematics educator; b. Burley, Idaho, Nov. 5, 1938; s. Charles Milton Clay and Dahlia LaRae Carlson; m. Carol Cline Burge, June 12, 1959; children: Thea Patricia, Christine Marie, Terri Susan. BS in Math., U. Utah, 1960; MS in Math., U. Wash., 1962, PhD in Math., 1966. Asst. prof. U. Ariz., Tucson, 1966-69, assoc. prof., 1969-74, prof., 1974—, assoc. head math. dept., 1969-72; guest prof. U. Tuebingen, Germany, 1972-73, Kings' Coll. U. London, 1973, Technische U. Muenchen, Munich, Germany, 1979-80, 87, U. Edinburgh, Scotland, 1980, U. Stellenbosch, South Africa, 1989, U. der Bundeswehr, Hamburg, Germany, 1990, Nat. Cheng Kung U., Tainan, Taiwan, 1991; postdoctorate dir. Hubert Kiechle, Technische U. Muenchen, 1991-93; lectr. in field. Author: Trigonometry—A Motivated Approach, 1977, Nearrings: Geneses and Applications, 1992; contbr. 41 articles to profl. jours. With USN, 1956-59. Recipient Dist. Sr. U.S. Scientist award Humboldt Found., 1972-73, Am. Men of Sci. Mem. Am. Math. Soc. Mem. LDS Ch. Home: 2201 N Frannea Dr Tucson AZ 85712 Office: U Arizona Dept Mathematics Bldg 89 Tucson AZ 85721

CLAYTON, CHARLES ANDREW, chemist; b. St. Louis, Sept. 21, 1957; s. Charles Ivy and Peggy Lee (Van Pelt) C.; m. Susan Kay Ellis, Dec. 11, 1976; children: Stephanie Nichol, Charles Daniel, Eric Milburn. Student, Point Loma Coll., 1975-76; BS, Calif. State U., Bakersfield, 1979. Chemist Witco Chem., Bakersfield, 1979-86; tech. mgr. S.E. Koch Materials, Charleston, S.C., 1986-90; tech. mgr. western Koch Materials, Salt Lake City, 1990—. Mem. Am. Chem. Soc., Assn. Asphalt Paveing Technologist, Asphalt Emulsion Mfrs. Assn. Republican. Methodist. Office: Koch Materials PO Box 196 North Salt Lake City UT 84054

CLAYTON, DONALD W., utilities, energy executive; b. Bakersfield, Calif., 1936. BS, La. State U., 1959. Sr. v.p. ops. Meridian Oil, Inc., Houston, 1985-87, pres., CEO, 1987-92; pres., dir. Burlington Resources, Inc., Seattle, 1992—. Office: Burlington Resources Inc 999 3rd Ave Ste 4500 Seattle WA 98104*

CLAYTON, JEFFREY ALAN, geologist; b. Des Moines, Aug. 24, 1955; s. George Adrian Clayton and Lola Lee (Crane) Jackman; m. Julie Blair Lawrence, Sept. 29, 1992; 1 child, Grayland Robert Clayton. AA, Sacramento City Coll., 1983; BS, U. Calif., Davis, 1986, MS, 1989. Carpenter Uhlenbrock Constrn. Co., 1980-83; resident apt. mgr. Casa del Rey, Davis, Calif., 1984-90; with Wallace-Kuhl and Assocs., 1989; project geologist Roger Foott Assocs., West Sacramento, Calif., 1990—. Umpire Davis Little League, 1992. Mem. Am. Quaternary Assn., Geol. Soc. of Am. Libertarian. Baptist. Office: Roger Foott Assocs Inc 1450 Harbor Blvd # G West Sacramento CA 95691

CLAYTON, LAWRENCE DEAN, mechanical engineer, researcher; b. Salt Lake City, July 3, 1957; s. Vaughn Allen and Marjorie Patricia (Johnson) C.; m. Linda Lujan, Sept. 20, 1985 (div. Feb. 1987); 1 child, Benjamin Lawrence; m. Lori Lee Ann Martinez, Mar. 25, 1989; 1 child, Alec Martin. BS, U. Utah, 1979, MS, 1985. Engr. Ford Aerospace, Newport Beach, Calif., 1979-81; teaching asst. U. Utah, Salt Lake City, 1981-83; project engr. Quartex, Inc., Salt Lake City, 1983-84; R & D engr. Quartztronics, Inc., Salt Lake City, 1984—; cons. Quartex, Inc., 1983; founding co-owner Micro-Analytical Pubs., Salt Lake City, 1987—. Author: Finite Element Analysis on Micro-Computers, 1988; contbr. articles to profl. jours. U. Utah shcolar, 1976. Mem. Phi Kappa Phi, Pi Kappa Alpha, Tau Beta Pi. Democrat. LDS. Home: 1729 Colchester Ct Sandy UT 84092-5400 Office: Quartztronics Inc 1020 Atherton Dr # C Salt Lake City UT 84123-3402

CLAYTON, MAYME AGNEW, librarian, cultural organization administrator; b. Van Buren, Ark., Aug. 4, 1923; d. Jerry Monique and Mary Dorothy (Knight) Agnew; m. Andrew Lee Clayton, Jan. 22; children: Avery Virgle, Renai Vonzelle, Lloyd Leoinard. BA, U. Berkeley, 1974; MLS, Goddard Coll., 1975; PhD, Sierra U., 1983. Libr. Dohney and Engring. Libr. U. So. Calif., L.A., 1954-56; libra. Law Libr./Afro Am. Libr. UCLA, 1956-71; co-owner Universal Books, Hollywood, Calif., 1971-72; owner Third World Ethnic Books, L.A., 1972—; owner, founder, dir. Western States Black Rsch. Ctr., L.A., 1972—; exec. dir., founder Black Am. Cinema Soc., L.A., 1974—; rschr. Western States Black Rsch. Ctr., L.A., 1972—; cons. Black Am. Cinema Soc. Awards Ind. Filmmakers, L.A., 1978—, Cable TV, L.A., 1990—. Exec. prodr. Black Talkies Film Festival, 1975—; artist. Cons. Dr. Mayme Clayton Golf Tournament, L.A., 1979—. Recipient Rosa Parks award So. Christian Leadership Conf., 1990, L.A. Mayor's award, 1992, Living Legend award L.A. County Suprs. and Librs., 1993; named Woman of Yr., L.A. Sentinel, 1991. Mem. NAACP, Urban League, Coin Club, Western Ave. Golf Club (trophy), Cougars Golf Club (trophy), Iota Phi Lambda (hon.). Office: Western States Black Rsch Ctr 3617 Montclair St Los Angeles CA 90018

CLAYTON, WILLIAM ALEXANDER, JR., restaurant executive, consultant, councilman; b. Denver, July 2, 1946; s. William Alexander Sr. and Barbara Jean (Kimber) C.; m. Joan Smyth, June 13, 1970; children: Daniel Alexander, Jennifer Ann. BA in Econs. and Math., U. Denver, 1969. Various positions Walt Disney Prodns., Denver and Orlando, Fla., 1965-76; controller Tommy Wong's Island, Denver, 1976-78; mgr. Denny's Inc., Denver, 1978-79; pres. High Country Restaurants, Denver, 1979-84, Snaxco, Inc., Denver, 1982—. Mayor pro tem City of Englewood, Colo., 1988-89, councilman, 1988-91; bd. dirs. Ct. House Inc., 1990—; advisor Boy Scouts Am., 1980—. Mem. Nat. League Cities (nat. policy com. 1989-91), Colo. Mpcl. League (policy com. Denver chpt. 1989-91), Englewood C. of C. (bd. dirs. 1990-92, mem. bd. adjustment and appeals, 1992—). Republican. Home: 958 E Cornell Ave Englewood CO 80110-1717

CLAYTON-HILL, KELLI, public relations executive; b. Ft. Belvoir, Va., Feb. 25, 1965; d. Frank William Clayton and Billie (Kelley) Clayton; m. Jeff Hill, July 7, 1990. BA, Loyola Marymount U., 1987. Acct. exec. Dateline Communications, L.A., 1987-89, McNeil Communications, Honolulu, 1989-90; dir. mktg. and communications Lambrecht & Assocs., Auburn, Calif., 1990-91; owner Clayton-Hill Communications, Auburn, 1991—. Contbr. articles to profl. jours. Named Voice scholar Loyola Marymount U., 1984-87. Mem. Auburn Caring About Kids Coun., Am. Advt. Soc., Pub. Rels. Soc. Am. Democrat. Methodist. Home and Office: 11250 Sunrise Ridge Cir Auburn CA 95603-6009

CLEAR, ROBERT DOUGLAS, lighting and vision researcher; b. Berkeley, Calif., June 28, 1947; s. Charles Gerald and André (Sapiro) C.; m. Sue Ann Arrigo, Nov. 24, 1973 (div. Dec. 1977); m. Barbara Lynne Judd, May 1, 1985; children: Charles Judson, Emily Cleardaughter. AB, U. Calif., Berkeley, 1969; PhD, U. Calif., San Diego, 1975. Lectr. chemistry Calif. Poly. U., Pomona, 1974-75; term scientist Lawrence Berkeley Lab., 1975-84, staff scientist II, 1984—. Contbr. articles to profl. jours. Mem. Illuminating Engring. Soc. (coms. 1985—). Democrat. Office: Lawrence Berkeley Lab MS 46-125 1 Cyclotron Rd Berkeley CA 94720

CLEARY, GARY WYNN, health products company executive; b. Visalia, Calif., May 1, 1942; s. Charles M. and Virginia C. (Lawson) C.; children: Sean, Colin. PharmD, U. Calif., San Francisco, 1966; PhD, Rutgers U., 1973; MBA, U. Miami, 1982. Investigator, drug sect. U.S. FDA, N.Y.C., 1966-68; rsch. scientist Cutter Labs., Berkeley, Calif., 1972-74; project leader Alza Corp., Palo Alto, Calif., 1974-79; dir. pharmaceutics R&D Key Pharms., Miami, Fla., 1979-83; mgr. pharmaceutics Genentech, Inc., South San Francisco, Calif., 1983-85; chmn., chief tech. officer Cygnus Therapeutic Systems, Redwood City, Calif., 1985—; chmn. Nichiban Cygnus, Tokyo, 1990—, Nor Cal Pharma Disc Group, San Francisco, 1985-88. Contbr. articles to profl. jours. Capt. USPHS, 1966-68. Johnson & Johnson rsch. fellow, 1970-72; named Entrepreneur of Yr. in Life Sci., Inst. Am. Entrepreneurs, 1991. Mem. Am. Assn. Pharmacol. Scs., Controlled Release Soc. (bd. govs. 1992-94), N.Y. Acad. Sci., Internat. Soc. for Bioengring. and the Skin. Office: Cygnus Therapeutic Systems 400 Penobscot Dr Redwood City CA 94063

CLEARY, SHIRLEY JEAN, artist, illustrator; b. St. Louis, Nov. 14, 1942; d. Frank and Crystal (Maret) C.; m. (Leo) Frank Cooper, June 18, 1982; stepchildren: Clay Cooper, Alicia Cooper, Curt Cooper. BFA, Wash. U., St. Louis, 1964; MFA, Tyler Sch. of Art of Temple U., Phila.. Rome, Italy, 1968; student, The Corcoran, Washington, 1967-71. Prin. works include illustrations in mags. Flyfishing Quar., Fly Fishers Magazine, Flyfishing News, Mont. Outdoors, Flyfisherman, Flyfishing Heritage; contbr. articles to profl. jours., 1986, 88; exhibited in Am. in Paint and Bronze, Mo. Hist. Soc., St. Louis, 1987, Women in Wildlife, Wild Wings, Mpls., 1985-87, Am. Miniatures, Settlers West Galleries, Tucson, 1984; artist 1990 Oreg. Trout Stamp (artist of yr. award 1992, Assn. N.W. Steelheaders print winner 1992). Bd, mem. Mont. State Arts Coun., Mont., 1973-81, Helena Civic Ctr., Mont., 1983-89, mem. leadership Helena, 1985. Grantee Apprenticeship Grant, Western Starts Art Found., Artist in Residence, River Meadow, Jackson, Wyo., 1989-93, Herning Hojskole, Herning, Denmark, 1981, Wyo. Artist in the Schools, Sheridan, Wyo., 1977; named Arts for Parks Top 100 Artist, 1989, Jackson (Wyo.) One Fly Artist of Yr., 1990-92. Mem. Helena Arts Coun., Mont. Dem. Party, Miniature Art Soc. of N.J., Mont. Miniature Soc., MOnt. Assn. Female Execs., Pat Barnes Mo. River Chpt. of Trout Unlimited, Coll. Art Assn., Women Artists of the West. Democrat. Home: 1804 Beltview Dr Helena MT 59601-5801

CLEARY, WILLIAM JOSEPH, JR., lawyer; b. Wilmington, N.C., Aug. 14, 1942; s. William Joseph and Eileen Ada (Gannon) C.; AB in History, St. Joseph's U., 1964; JD, Villanova U., 1967. Bar: N.J. 1967, U.S. Ct. Appeals (3d cir.) 1969, Calif. 1982, U.S. Ct. Appeals (9th cir.) 1983, U.S. Supreme Ct., 1992. Law sec. to judge N.J. Superior Ct. Jersey City, 1967-68; assoc. Lamb, Blake, H&D, Jersey City, 1968-72; dep. pub. defender State of N.J., Newark, 1972-73; 1st asst. city corp. counsel, Jersey City, 1973-76; assoc. Robert Wasserwald, Inc., Hollywood, Calif., 1984-86, 88-89, Gould & Burke, L.A., 1986-87; pvt. practice, 1989—. Mem. ABA, N.J. State Bar, Calif. Bar Assn., L.A. County Bar, Alpha Sigma Nu, Nat. Jesuit Honor Soc. Democrat. Roman Catholic. also: 1853 1/2 N Canyon Dr Los Angeles CA 90028

CLEAVER, JAMES EDWARD, radiologist, educator; b. Portsmouth, England, May 17, 1938; came to the U.S., 1964; s. Edward Alfred and Kathleen Florence (Cleveley) C.; m. Christine J. Cleaver, Aug. 8, 1964; children: Jonathon, Alison. BA, St. Catharine's Coll., 1961; PhD, U. Cambridge, 1964. Rsch. fellow Mass. Gen. Hosp., Boston, 1964-66; asst. rsch. biophysicist lab. radiobiology environ. health U. Calif., San Francisco, 1966-68, asst. prof. radiology, 1968-70, assoc. prof. radiology, 1970-74, prof. radiology, 1974—; assoc. prof. radiology Imperial Cancer Rsch. Fund, London, 1973-74. Contbr. articles to profl. jours. Recipient Lila Gruber award Am. Acad. Dermatology, 1976. Mem. Nat. Coun. on Radiation Protection, Radiation Rsch. Soc. (councillor 1982-84, rsch. award 1973, Luigi Provasoli award 1992). Office: U Calif PO Box 750 San Francisco CA 94143-0001

CLECAK, DVERA VIVIAN BOZMAN, psychotherapist; b. Denver, Jan. 15, 1944; d. Joseph Shalom and Annette Rose (Dveirin) Bozman; m. Pete Emmett Clecak, Feb. 26, 1966; children: Aimée, Lisa. BA, Stanford U., 1965; postgrad., U. Chgo., 1965; MSW, UCLA, 1969. Lic. clin. social worker, Calif.; lic. marriage, family and child counselor, Calif. Social work supr. Harbor City (Calif.) Parent Child Ctr., 1969-71; therapist Orange County Mental Health Dept., Laguna Beach, Calif., 1971-75, area coordinator, 1975-79; pvt. practice psychotherapy Mission Viejo, Calif., 1979—; founder, exec. dir. Human Options, Laguna Beach, 1981—; mem, co-chmn. domestic violence com. Orange County Commn. on Status of Women, 1979-81; mem. mental health adv. com. extension U. Calif., Irvine, 1983, counseling psychologist, 1980, lectr., 1984-85; lectr. Saddleback Community Coll., Mission Viejo, 1981-82, Chapman Coll., Orange, 1979; field instr. UCLA, 1970-71, 77-78. Recipient Women Helping Women award Saddleback Community Coll., 1987, Cert. for child abuse prevention Commendation State of Calif. Dept. Social Svcs., 1988, Community Svc. award Irvine Valley Coll. Found., 1989. Mem. NASW, Calif. Marriage Family and Child Counselors' Assn., Phi Beta Kappa. Office: 28261 Marguerite Pky Ste 255 San Juan Capistrano CA 92692-3722

CLEGG, JOHN CARDWELL, electrical engineering educator; b. Heber, Utah, Sept. 19, 1927; s. Henry Cardwell and Marion Garland (Davis) C.; m. Helen Truman, Dec. 10, 1953; children: J. Scott, Paul T., Suzanne, D. Bruce, James C., Sarah Jane, Jared T., M. Ruth. BSEE, U. Utah, 1949, MSEE, 1954, PhD in Elec. Engring., 1957. Registered profl. engr., Utah. Farmer Heber, 1945; engr. GE, Schenectady, N.Y., 1949-53, TRW, L.A., 1957-61; prof. elec. engring. Brigham Young U., Provo, Utah, 1961—; cons. TRW Systems, L.A., 1961-68, Becton Dickinson, Salt Lake City, 1975-78, Office Energy Related Inventions, U.S. Dept. Commerce, 1988—. 5 patents in field. County del. Rep. Party, Provo, 1978, 88. Recipient Spl. Recognition award U.S. Sec. of Energy, 1988, Gov.'s award State of Utah, 1988. Mem. IEEE (sr., edn. coord. 1963-65), Illuminating Engrs. Soc. (nat. com., Educator of the Yr. 1988). Home: 1785 N 1500 E Provo UT 84604-5714 Office: Brigham Young U Provo UT 84602

CLEM, LANE WILLIAM, bank officer; b. Sioux City, Iowa, Feb. 25, 1944; s. Clifford Lester and Sadie Doris (Ellis) C.; m. Ruth Marie Gaetke, June 18, 1965; children: Timothy Lane, Jonathan Dean, Pamela Jean. Student, Azusa Pacific U., 1962-65, N.W. Intermediate Banking Sch., 1988, Indiana U., 1990-92; ABA, Nat. Compiance Sch., 1992. Teller Crocker Bank, Maywood, Calif., 1970-71; asst. ops. officer Bank of Am., L.A., 1971-74; ops. officer 1st Interstate Bank of Oreg., Portland, 1974-79, dept. mgr., 1979-92; regional compicnae officer retail banking Interstate Bank of Oreg., Porltand, 1992—. Named Disting. Lt. Gov. by Kiwanis, Pacific N.W., 1983. Mem. Nazarene Ch. Office: 1st Interstate Bank Oreg NA 1300 SW 5th Ave Portland OR 97201-5606

CLEMENS, WILLIAM ALVIN, vertebrate paleontology educator; b. Berkeley, Calif., May 15, 1932; s. Vincent Alvin and Estella (Osborn) C.; m. Dorothy Elise Thelen, Jan. 22, 1955; children: Catherine, Elisabeth, Diane, William. B.A., U. Calif.-Berkeley, 1954, Ph.D., 1960. Instr. to assoc. prof. dept. zoology U. Kans., Lawrence, 1961-67, curator Mus. Natural History, 1961-67; assoc. prof. dept. paleontology U. Calif.-Berkeley, from 1967, now prof., curator Mus. Paleontology, 1967—, chmn. dept. paleontology, dir. mus., 1987-89; Miller research prof. Miller Inst., 1982-83. Contbr. articles to profl. jours. Served with U.S. Army, 1954-56. NSF fellow U. Coll. London,

1960-61; sr. postdoctoral fellow Royal Holloway Coll., 1968-69; Guggenheim fellow, 1974-75; Humboldt-Pries, A. von Humboldt Stiftung U. Munich, 1978-79. Fellow Zool. Soc. London, Linnean Soc. London, Geol. Soc. Am., Calif. Acad. Sci. Home: 920 Spruce St Berkeley CA 94707-2425 Office: Univ Calif Dept Paleontology 3 Earth Sci Bldg Berkeley CA 94720

CLEMENT, BETTY WAIDLICH, literacy educator, consultant; b. Honolulu, Aug. 1, 1937; d. William G. Waidlich and Audrey Antoinette (Roberson) Malone; m. Tom Morris, Jan. 16, 1982; 1 child, Karen A. Bratesani. BA in Elem. Edn., Sacramento State U., 1960; MA in Elem. Reading, U. No. Colo., 1973, MA in Adminstrn., EdD in Edn. & Reading, 1980. Elem. sch. tchr. pub schs., Colo., Calif., 1960-66; reading specialist, ESEA title I various locations, 1966-75; grad. practicum supr. U. No. Colo. Reading Clinic, Greeley, 1976-77; grant cons. Colo. Dept. Edn., Denver, 1978-81; adj. prof. U. Colo., Denver, 1981-82; adult edn. tutor, cons. various orgns., Boulder, Colo., 1983-87; student tchr. supr. U. San Diego, 1989-90; adult literacy trainer for vols. San Diego Coun. on Literacy, 1988—. adj. prof. reading Southwestern Coll., Chula Vista, Calif., 1990—; presenter various confs. Co-author, editor: Adult Literacy Tutor Training Handbook, 1990. Grantee Fed. Right-to-Read Office Colo. Dept. Edn., 1979, Southwestern Coll., 1992. Fellow San Diego Coun. on Literacy (chair coop. tutor tng. com.); mem. Whole Lang. Coun. San Diego, Calif. Reading Assn. Office: Southwestern Coll Communication Arts 900 Otay Lakes Rd Chula Vista CA 91910

CLEMENT, RONALD E., communications executive; b. Colorado Springs, Colo., Dec. 31, 1948; s. Carl E. and Ardith (Perkins) C.; m. Tharon Clement, Feb. 20, 1968 (div. July 1969); 1 child, Stacy; m. Cindy M. Moore, Aug. 30, 1975; children: Justin, Desiree. Student, Anchorage Community Coll., Ark., 1975-76. Gen. mgr. Sourdough Broadcasters, Anchorage, 1976—. Mem. Advt. Fedn. (treas. 1980-81). Office: KHAR-KKLU 11259 Tower Rd Anchorage AK 99515-2938

CLEMENT, STEPHEN LE ROY, agricultural researcher; b. Ventura, Calif., Aug. 25, 1944; s. Edward Le Roy and Eleanor Eileen (Summers) C.; m. Mary Anne Lindeman, Dec. 21, 1981; 1 child, Kevin Matthew. BS in Entomology, U. Calif., Davis, 1967, PhD in Entomology, 1976. Postdoctoral researcher U. Calif., Davis, 1977; asst. prof. entomology Ohio State U., Ohio Agrl. Rsch. Devel. Ctr., Wooster, 1977-81; rsch. entomologist USDA, Agrl. Rsch. Svc., Rome, Italy, 1982-86; mem. agrl. mission U.S. Embassy, Rome, 1982-86; rsch. entomologist USDA, Agrl. Rsch. Svc., Pullman, Wash., 1986—; seasonal ranger-naturalist U.S. Park Svc., Yellowstone Nat. Park, 1970-72; mem. peer rev. panel agrl. rsch. grants USDA Coop. States Rsch. Svc., Washington, 1987; mem. adv. team Food Agrl. Orgn. UN, Rome, 1982. Contbr. articles to profl. jours. 1st lt. U.S. Army, 1967-70, Vietnam. Decorated Bronze Star for Valor (Vietnam); Sigma Xi grantee, 1976, U.S. EPA grantee, 1977-81. Office: Wash State U USDA Agrl Rsch Svc 59 Johnson Hall Pullman WA 99164-6402

CLEMENT, WALTER HOUGH, retired railroad executive; b. Council Bluffs, Iowa, Dec. 21, 1931; s. Daniel Shell and Helen Grace (Hough) C.; AA, San Jose (Calif.) City Coll., 1958; PhD, World U., 1983; m. Shirley Ann Brown, May 1, 1953; children: Steven, Robert, Richard. Designer, J.K. Konerle & Assocs., Salt Lake City, 1959-62; with U.P. R.R. Co., 1962—, class B draftsman, Salt Lake City, 1971-75, sr. right of way engr. real estate dept., 1975-80, asst. dist. real estate mgr., 1980-83, asst. engr. surveyor, 1983-87; owner, pres. Clement Sales and Svc. Co., Bountiful, Utah, 1987—. Mem. Republican Nat. Com., Rep. Congl. Com. With USN, 1950-54, Korea. Lic. realtor, Utah. Mem. Am. Ry. Engring. Assn., Execs. Info. Guild (assoc.), Bur. Bus. Practice. Methodist. Home: 290 W 1200 N Bountiful UT 84010-6826

CLEMENTE, PATROCINIO ABLOLA, psychology educator; b. Manila, Philippines, Apr. 23, 1941; s. Elpidio San Jose and Amparo (Ablola) C.; came to U.S., 1965; B.S.E., U. Philippines, 1960; postgrad. Nat. U., Manila, 1961-64; M.A., Ball State U., 1966, Ed.D., 1969; postgrad. U. Calif., Riverside, 1970, Calif. State Coll., Fullerton, 1971-72. High sch. tchr. gen. sci. and biology, div. city schs., Quezon City, Philippines, 1960-65; doctoral fellow dept. psychology Ball State U., Muncie, Ind., 1966-67, dept. spl. edn., 1967-68, grad. asst. dept. gen. and exptl. psychology, 1968-69; tchr. educable mentally retarded high sch. level Fontana (Calif.) Unified Sch. Dist., 1969-70, intermediate level, 1970-73, dist. sch. psychologist, 1973-79, bilingual edn. counselor, 1979-81; resource specialist Morongo (Calif.) Unified Sch. Dist., 1981-83, spl. day class tchr., 1983-90, tchr. math, sci., Spanish, English, 1990—; adj. assoc. prof. Chapman Coll., Orange, Calif., 1982-91. Adult leader Girl Scouts of Philippines, 1963-65; mem. sch. bd. Blessed Sacrament Sch., Twentynine Palms, Calif. State bd. scholar Ball State U., 1965-66. Fellow Am. Biographical Inst. (hon. mem. research bd. advisors, life); mem. Council for Exceptional Children, Am. Assn. on Mental Deficiency, Nat. Assn. of Sch. Psychologists, Found. Exceptional Children, Assn. for Children with Learning Disabilities, N.Y. Acad. Scis., AAAS, Assn. for Supervision and Curriculum Devel., Roman Catholic. Home: PO Box 637 Twentynine Palms CA 92277-0637

CLEMENTI, MARK ANTHONY, sport psychologist; b. Milw., Oct. 11, 1955; s. Anthony Clementi and Liz (Coffman) Schmidt; m. Christina Masterson-Clementi, Oct. 26, 1988. BA, Humboldt State U., 1977; MA, Sonoma State U., 1988; PhD, Fla. State U., 1991. Sport psychologist pvt. practice, Kentfield, Calif., 1991-92; psychology editor, columnist GOLFWEEK Mag., Winter Haven, Fla., 1991-92, Inside Golf, Port Orchard, Wash., 1992; author One Publ. Co., San Jose, 1991-92; owner Inside Game (Golf Sch.), Rohnert Park, Calif., 1992; psychol. cons. Fla. State U. Track Team, Tallahassee, 1989-91; cons. Sauer Golf Sch., 1991, S.W. Athletic Clin., 1990, Seminole Jr. Golf Camp, 1990. Author: (Audio tapes) INSIDE GAME-Golf, INSIDE GAME-Tennis, 1991; contbr. articles to profl. jours. Featured speaker Rotary Internat., Terra Linda, Calif., 1992, Marin Breakfast Club, San Rafael, Calif., 1992, Lion's Internat., San Rafael, Calif., 1992; community columnist Ind. Jour., Novato, Calif., 1992, Golf Expo '92, Seattle, 1992; featured guest on KNBR radio's Sports Phone 68, San Francisco, 1992. Recipient Cert. Appreciation award Lion's Internat., San Rafael, Calif., 1992. Mem. Ctr. for Performance Enhancement, Assn. Advancement of Applied Sport Psychology, Internat. Assn. Sport Psychology, Seminole Golf Course. Home: 1406 Parkway Dr Rohnert Park CA 94928 Office: 919-B Sir Franc Drake Blvd Kentfield CA 94904

CLEMENTS, GEORGE FRANCIS, mathematics educator; b. Colfax, Wash., Apr. 17, 1931; s. Harry Frank and Louise May (Schmidt) C.; m. Anna Bell, June 18, 1952; children: Ellen, Mark, Eric, Owen. BSME, U. Wis., 1953; MA, Syracuse U., 1957, PhD, 1962. Asst. prof. math. U. Colo., Boulder, 1962-68, assoc. prof. math., 1968-76, prof. math., 1976—. Contbr. articles to profl. jours. With U.S. Army, 1953-55. Mem. Am. Math. Soc. Unitarian. Home: 2954 3d St Boulder CO 80304 Office: Univ Colo Dept Math Box 426 Boulder CO 80309

CLEMENTS, JOHN ROBERT, real estate professional; b. Richmond, Ind., Nov. 2, 1950; s. George Howard and Mary Amanda (McKown) C. Grad. high sch., Phoenix. Sales assoc. Clements Realty, Inc., Phoenix, 1973-75; office mgr. Clements Realty, Inc., Mesa, Ariz., 1975-78; v.p., co-owner Clements Realty, Inc., Phoenix, 1978-80; broker, assoc. Ben Brooks & Assocs., Phoenix, 1980-88; pres. John R. Clements, P.C., 1984—; broker, assoc. Rainbow Real Estate Group, Inc. (formerly Prince Realty, Inc.), Phoenix and Mesa, Ariz., 1988—. Real Estate dir. Circle K Corp., Western Region, 1989-92; bd. dirs., v.p. Big Sisters Ariz., Phoenix, 1974-80; trustee Ariz. Realtors Polit. Action Com., 1975-85, Realtors Polit. Action Com., Ill., 1985-88; appointee Govtl. Mall Co., Ariz., 1986—, commr. chair, 1991—. Mem. Ariz. Assn. Realtors (bd. dirs., pres. 1981) Mesa-Chandler-Tempe Bd. Realtors (past bd. dirs., pres., 1978), Nat. Assn. Realtors (past bd. dirs.), Residential Sales Coun. Realtors (bd. govs. 1986—, v.p. 1990, pres. 1991), Nat Mktg. Inst., Ariz Country Club. Republican. Presbyterian. Home: 3618 N 60th St Phoenix AZ 85018-6708 Office: Rainbow Realty Group Inc 4647 N 32nd St Ste 100 Phoenix AZ 85018-3346

CLEMMER, EDITH, artist; b. Phila., Dec. 6, 1920; d. George Henry and Regina (Donnelly) Hoopes; m. Elwood Gregg Clemmer, Jan. 22, 1943; children: Peter Laird, Leonore, Philip, Mary Regina, Edith Ellen. Student, Dobbins Comml. Art Sch., Phila., 1938-39. Freelance artist, Oreg., 1978—. Exhibited in group shows at Oreg. Watercolor Co. Ann. Show, 1990, 92; represented in permanent collection Clemmer's Furniture Store, 1990—. Recipient Best of Show and Best of Category awards Gladstone (Oreg.) Art Guild, 1992, Best of Category and outstanding award Clackamas County, Canby, Oreg., 1992. Mem. Watercolor Soc. Oreg., Brush and Palette Art Assn. Home and Studio: 10070 SE Orient Dr Boring OR 97009

CLEMONS, LYNN ALLAN, land use planner, public affairs officer; b. New Orleans, Oct. 23, 1946; s. Gaylord Wilson and Jessica Monica (McDonald) C. BS, Colo. State U., 1973. Planner outdoor recreation Bur. Outdoor Recreation, Denver, 1974-75; planner outdoor recreation Bur. Land Mgmt., Golden, Co., 1975-77, Winnemucca, Nev., 1977—; pub. affairs officer Bur. Land Mgmt., Winnemucca, 1989—. Co-author environ. impact statements. With USN, 1968-69, Vietnam. Recipient Spl. Achievement award Dept. of Interior, 1988, 91. Mem. Am. Radio Relay League, U.S. Chess Fedn., No. Nev. Amateur Radio Club (sec.-treas. 1992), Winnemucca Amateur Trap Assn. (sec.-treas. 1981), Assn. for Preservation Tech., Wilderness Soc., One Moccasin Toastmasters Club (officer, Competent Toastmaster award 1988). Roman Catholic. Office: Bur Land Mgmt 705 E 4th St Winnemucca NV 89445

CLEMONS, STEVEN CRAIG, non-profit organization director; b. Salina, Kans., Aug. 27, 1962; s. Craig Ridenour and Elisabeth Claire (Caldwell) C. BA in Polit. Sci., UCLA, 1985, MA in Polit. Sci., 1987. Coord., liaison Soviet Ctr. Rand Corp., Santa Monica, Calif., 1983-86; exec. dir. Japan Am. Soc. So. Calif., L.A., 1987—; speech writer Consulate Gen. of Japan, L.A., 1985-87; lectr., writer, cons., L.A., 1987—. Tech. cons.: (movie) Rising Sun; contbr. articles to profl. jours. Bd. dirs. L.A. Chamber Music Festival, 1989—, Japan Studies Inst., San Diego, 1989—, Japan Program at La Jolla (Calif.) Day Sch., 1989—, U. Calif. San Diego Career Adv. Group, La Jolla, 1990—; advisor L.A. Festival, 1991—; exec. dir. Japan Week L.A., 1989—; adv. bd. mem Bollens/Ries Meml. Lecture, UCLA, 1992—. Episcopalian. Office: Japan Am Soc So Calif 505 S Flower St Los Angeles CA 90071

CLENDENEN, BRIAN, sales and marketing executive; b. New London, Conn., Mar. 4, 1946; s. William H. and Ethel Lorraine (Clifford) C.; m. Karen Van Vleet, Nov. 21, 1980 (div.). BS in Bus., U. Conn., New Brittain, 1968. Lic. radio broadcaster. Regional sales rep. ARTEC Distbn., Burlington, Vt., 1979-81; owner Video Realm Computer, Computer Realm, Realm of the Coin, Saratoga Springs, N.Y., 1981-83; regional sales mgr. Thorn EMI, N.Y.C., 1982-86; sr. v.p. Ingram Video, Nashville, 1986-88; v.p. sales and mktg. Imperial Entertainment Corp., Hollywood, Calif., 1988—; bd. dirs. Ingram Distbn., Nashville. Author: (movie) Demon Cop, 1988. Active Santa Fund for Kids Downtown Merchants Assn., Saratoga Springs, 1981, 82; fund raiser United Way, Nashville, 1986-88. Mem. Nat. Assn. Video Distburs., Video Software Dealers Assn., Antique Auto Club Am., Theta Alpha Phi. Home: 13912 Old Harbor Ln Apt 204 Marina Dl Rey CA 90292-7322 Office: Imperial Entertainment Corp 4640 Lankershim Blvd # 4 Toluca Lake CA 91602-1841

CLEVE, GEORGE, conductor; b. Vienna, Austria, 1936; student Mannes Coll. Music, N.Y.C.; studies with Pierre Monteux, George Szell, Franco Ferrara; D.F.A. (hon.), U. Santa Clara. Music dir., co-founder Midsummer Mozart Festival; music dir. Winnipeg Symphony; music dir., condr. San Jose Symphony, 1972—; guest condr. San Francisco Symphony, Royal Philharm., London, Minn. Orch., Kansas City Philharm., St. Louis Symphony, Boston Symphony, St. Paul Chamber Orch., N.Y. Philharm., Cleve. Symphony, Pitts. Symphony, Denver Symphony, Honolulu Symphony, Balt. Symphony, Mostly Mozart Festival, N.Y.C. Recipient 1st Community Arts program award City of San Jose. Office: San Jose Symphony Orch 99 Almaden Blvd Ste 400 San Jose CA 95113-1600

CLEVELAND, CARL S(ERVICE), JR., academic administrator, educator, physician; b. Webster City, Iowa, Mar. 29, 1918; s. Carl S. Sr. and Ruth R. (Ashworth) C.; m. Mildred G. Allison, Mar. 28, 1939 (dec. 1979). D in Chiropractic, Cleveland Chiropractic Coll., Kansas City, 1945; BS in Physiology, U. Nebr., 1947. Cert. tchr., Kans., Calif. Instr. Cleveland Chiropractic Coll., Kansas City, Mo., 1939—, dean, 1945-55, pres., 1976-82, prof. physiology, 1975—; exec. v.p. Cleveland Chiropractic Coll., L.A., 1976-82, pres., 1982-92, chancellor, 1992—; pres. bd. trustees Unity Temple, Kansas City, 1969-78; pres. bd. trustees Unity Sch. Practical Christianity, Kansas City, 1969-78; speaker nat., internat. lecture tours The Sci. Award Medallion, Rsch. Award World Chiro Congress, Montreaux, Switzerland, 1970. Mem. Internat. Chiropractors Assn. (bd. control), Mo. Chiropractic Assn. (pres. 1962-63), North Ctrl. Assn. Colls. and Schs., Delta Sigma Chi, Beta Chi Rho, Sigma Chi, Sigma Chi Psi. Republican. Office: Cleveland Chiropractic Coll 590 N Vermont Ave Los Angeles CA 90004-2196

CLEVELAND, GERALD LLOYD, university dean; b. Conde, S.D., Apr. 18, 1931; s. Lloyd Edward and M. Frances (Miesen) C.; m. Ramona June Morgan, Sept. 11, 1952; children: Debra, Linda, Sara. BBA in Acctg. summa cum laude, U. S.D., 1953; MBA, U. Minn., 1957; PhD, U. Wash., 1965. Instr./assoc. prof. U. S.D., Vermillion, 1956-59; lectr./asst. prof. U. Wash., Seattle, 1959-67; assoc. prof. Seattle U., 1967-69, prof. acctg., dean Sch. Bus., 1969-76; prof. acctg., dean Coll. Bus. and Econs. U. Idaho, Moscow, 1976-77; prof. U. Idaho, 1977-87; chmn. dept. acctg. Seattle U., 1978-84; dean. Sch. Bus. and Econs., prof. acctg. Cen. Wash. U., Ellensburg, 1987—; adv. com. Acctg. Career Awareness, Seattle, 1981-88; Wash. adv. com. for Acctg. Transfer Edn., 1973-75; mem. exec. com. Western Assn. Collegiate Schs. Bus., 1975-77; vis. lectr. acctg. and fin. Bristol (Eng.) Poly. Inst., 1984-85; vis. prof. Massey U., New Zealand, 1985; cons., expert witness for FTC, 1978-79, pvt. cons., 1963— ; frequent speaker in field. Contbr. chpts. to books, articles to profl. jours. Mem. Lake Forest Park Civil Service Commn., Seattle, 1982-84, regional selection panel White House Fellows program, 1974; mem. acctg. adv. com. Shoreline Community Coll., Seattle, 1969-75. Served to 1st lt. U.S. Army, 1954-56, capt. USAR. Mem. Am. Acctg. Assn., Fin. Execs. Inst. (bd. dirs. Seattle chpt. 1974-76, 78-80, edn. com. 1971-74), Phi Eta Sigma, Beta Gamma Sigma, Beta Alpha Psi. Office: Cen Wash U Sch Bus and Econs Ellensburg WA 98926

CLEVENGER, JEFFREY GRISWOLD, mining company executive; b. Boston, Sept. 1, 1949; s. Galen William and Cynthia (Jones) C. BS in Minig Engring., N.Mex. Inst. Mining & Tech., Socorro, 1973. Engr. Phelps Dodge, Tyrone, N.Mex., 1973-78, gen. mine foreman, 1979-81, mine supt., 1981-86; mine supt. Phelps Dodge, Morenci, Ariz., 1986, gen. supt., 1987; asst. gen. mgr. Chino Mines Co., Hurley, N.Mex., 1987-88; asst. gen. mgr. Phelps Dodge, Morenci, 1988-89, gen. mgr., 1989-92; sr. v.p. Cyprus Copper Co., Tempe, Ariz., 1992-93, sr. v.p., pres., 1993—; pres. Phelps Dodge Morenci, Inc., 1989-92, Morenci Water & Electric Co., 1989-92, Cyprus Minerals, 1993. Contbr. articles to profl. jours. Recipient Disting. Achievement award N.Mex. Inst. Mining & Tech., 1988. Mem. Am. Inst. Mining Engrs. (chmn. southwest N.Mex. chpt. 1982), Soc. Mining Engrs. (Robert Peele award 1984), Rotary, Elks. Home: 4575 N Launfal Phoenix AZ 85018 Office: Cypris Copper Co PO Box 22015 1501 Fountainhead Pky Tempe AZ 85285-2015

CLEVENGER-BURDELL, KATHERINE ROSE, health educator, county official; b. Gallup, N.Mex., Dec. 29, 1943; d. James Byron and Lena (Frank) Huffman; m. Galen Malcolm Clevenger, July 1, 1967 (dec. 1975); m. Jonathan Henry Burdell, May 15, 1977. BA, Ariz. State U., 1965, MA, 1976. Cert. health edn. specialist, Ariz. Rsch. asst. Nat. Ctr. for Health Edn., San Francisco, 1978-79; family therapist Huron Valley Inst., Dexter, Mich., 1979-82, Out WWayne County Youth Svcs., Westland, Mich., 1979-82; cons., trainer and evaulator Community Devel. Inst., Chgo., 1981-83; cons. on policy devel. dept. dietetics U. Mich. Hosps., Ann Arbor, 1983-84; supr. crisis clinic Phoenix South Mental Health, 1985-86; pub. rels. cons. A-Z Womens Ctr., Inc., Phoenix, 1986-89; AIDS health educator Maricopa County Pub. Health Dept., Phoenix, 1989-91; health educator Maricopa County Health Plan, Phoenix, 1991—; tng. dir. Maricopa County Head Start, Phoenix, 1972-77. Designer sterling silver jewelry. Bd. dirs. Phoenix YWCA, 1975-77; vol., lobbyist Planned Parenthood Affiliates Mich., 1981-82, Ariz. Assn. for Gifted and talented, 1985; vol. press room Babbitt for Pres. Com., Phoenix, 1988. Mem. Ariz. Pub. Health Assn. (legis. com. 1989-91), Beta Kappa (chpt. pres.), Pi Lambda Theta.

CLEWE, JANE ELIZABETH, computer programmer; b. San Francisco, July 26, 1954; d. Thomas Hailey and Elizabeth Jane (Robb) C.; m. Joan Ellen Klein, Dec. 20, 1977 (div. May 1980); m. Deborah Doenges White, Sept. 23, 1981. BSE cum laude, Princeton U., 1977. Programmer, analyst System Devel. Corp., Santa Monica, Calif., 1977-80; sr. systems programmer, v.p. City Nat. Bank, L.A., 1981-90; sr. systems programmer Systematics, Inc., L.A., 1991—. Coord. Wilderness Women, Long Beach, Calif., 1980-90; vol. Mus. Neon Art, L.A., 1989—. Mem. Assn. Women in Computing (pres. L.A. chpt. 1992—), So. Calif. Women for Understanding, L.A. Gay and Lesbian Scientists, Computer Profls. for Social Responsibility. Office: Systematics Inc 1801 W Olympic Blvd Los Angeles CA 90006-3779

CLIFFORD, NATHAN JOSEPH, cardiologist; b. Denver, Apr. 19, 1929; s. Donald Francis and Anna (Karchmer) C.; m. Maryellen Baptist, June 12, 1954; 1 child, William Barnett. BS in Pharmacy, U. Colo., Boulder, 1951; MD, U. Colo., Denver, 1956. Diplomate Am. Bd. Internal Medicine. Physician USPHS Indian Hosp., Whiteriver, Ariz., 1957-58; med. officer in charge USPHS Indian Hosp., Owyhee, Nev., 1958-59; med. resident Kings County Hosp., Bklyn., 1959-61; cardiology fellow Mercy Hosp., San Diego, 1961-63; physician Buenaventura Clinic, Ventura, Calif., 1963-67, Internal Medicine and Cardiology P.C., Greeley, Colo., 1967-90; med. officer Phoenix Indian Med. Ctr., 1990—, chief of staff, 1992; clin. prof. medicine U. Colo., Denver, 1967—. Named Tchr. of Yr. No. Colo. Med. Ctr., 1974. Fellow ACP (Disting. Internist award Colo. chpt. 1988); mem. Am. Heart Assn. Roman Catholic. Home: 6302 N 73d St Scottsdale AZ 85250 Office: Phoenix Indian Med Ctr 4212 N 16th St Phoenix AZ 85016

CLIFFORD, STEVEN FRANCIS, science research director; b. Boston, Jan. 4, 1943; s. Joseph Nelson and Margaret Dorothy (Savage) C.; children from previous marriage: Cheryl Ann, Michelle Lynn, David Arthur. BSEE, Northeastern U., Boston, 1965; PhD, Dartmouth Coll., 1969. Postdoctoral fellow NRC, Boulder, Colo., 1969-70; physicist Wave Propagation Lab., NOAA, Boulder, 1970-82, program chief, 1982-87, dir. lab., 1987—; mem. electromagnetic propagation panel, NATO, 1989-91; vis. scientist closed acad. city Tomsk, Siberia, USSR. Author: (with others) Remote Sensing of the Troposphere, 1978; contbr. 120 articles to profl. jours.; patentee in acoustic scintillation liquid flow measurement, single-ended optical spatial filter. Recipient 4 Outstanding publs. awards Dept. Commerce, 1972, 75, 89. Fellow Optical Soc. Am. (editor atmospheric optics 1978-84, advisor atmospheric optics 1982-84), Acoustical Soc. Am., Ainstical Soc.; mem. IEEE (sr.), Internat. Radio Sci. Union, Am. Geophys. Union. Office: NOAA Wave Propagation Lab 325 Broadway St Boulder CO 80303-3328

CLIFFORD, WALTER HOWARD, television producer; b. Wausau, Wis., July 14, 1912; s. Walter and Katherine (Clarke) C.; m. Margaret Ellis, Nov. 1935 (div. 1945); 1 child, Sally Mae (Mrs. William Weber); m. Phyllis Jean Rice, Nov. 18, 1946 (div. 1961); 1 child, Karen Lynn (Mrs. Randy Doran); m. Joan Grant, Apr., 1961 (dec.); m. Henrietta Thompson, Oct. 6, 1967. BBA, U. Puget Sound, 1934. Asst. sports editor Tacoma Ledger, 1935-36; chief photographer, aviation editor Tacoma News Tribune, 1936-56; dir. advt. pub. rels. Pacific No. Airlines, Seattle, 1956-67; regional pub. rels. mgr. Western Air Lines, Seattle, 1967-77; v.p. pub. affairs Aeroamerica, Seattle, 1978; pres. Sourdough Enterprises, Seattle, 1978—; mgr. corp. communications Tour Alaska, Seattle, 1987-88; dir. corp. communications Princess Tours, Seattle, 1988-89, dir. pub. rels., 1989-92; assoc. producer MEC Prodns., Delray Beach, Fla., 1993—. Author: Guidebook Alaska Game Fishing, 1958, Much About Totems, 1962, Skagway Story, 1975, Rails North, 1980, Doing The White Pass, 1985; editor: ATPA Travel Times, 1964-69, Alaska News Rev., 1961-84, Alaska Blue Book Tour Guide, 1960-86; travel editor: Alaska Mag., 1970-72; developer first water ski safe release binding. Dir. Seattle Pub. Rels. Roundtable, 1963-64, 73-75. With USMC, 1944-46. Mem. Pub. Rels. Soc. Am. (accredited), Puget Sound Sportswriters and Sportscasters (pres. 1986-88), N.W. Outdoors Writers Assn., Wash. Press Assn., Seattle-Tacoma Newspaper Guild (pres. 1955), Pacific N.W. INdsl. Editors Assn. (pres. 1970), Soc. Am. Travel Writers (chmn. Western chpt. 1980-82), Internat. Airline Ski Fedn. (pres. 1976-84). Home: 16401 3d SW Normandy Park WA 98166

CLIFT, WILLIAM BROOKS, III, photographer; b. Boston, Jan. 5, 1944; s. William Brooks C. and Anne (Pearmain) Thomson; m. Vida Regina Chesnulis, Aug. 8, 1970; children: Charis, Carola, William. Free lance comml. photographer in partnership with Steve Gersh under name Helios, 1963-71; pres. William Clift Ltd., Santa Fe, 1980-85; cons. Polaroid Corp., 1965-67. Photographer one-man shows, Carl Siembab Gallery, Boston, 1969, Mus. Art, U. Oreg., Eugene, 1969, New Boston City Hall Gallery, 1970, U. Mass., Berkshire Mus., Pittsfield, Mass., William Coll., Addison Gallery of Am. Art, Wheaton Coll., Mass., Worcester Art Mus., 1971, Creative Photography Gallery, MIT, 1972, St. John's Coll. Art Gallery, Santa Fe, 1973, Wiggin Gallery, Boston Pub. Library, 1974, Australian Ctr. for Photography, Sydney, 1978, Susan Spiritus Gallery, Newport Beach, Calif., 1979, MIT Creative Photography Gallery, 1980, William Lyons Gallery, Coconut Grove, Fla., 1980, Eclipse Gallery, Boulder, Colo., 1980, Atlanta Gallery of Photography, 1980, Phoenix Art Mus., 1981, Jeb Gallery, Providence, 1981, Portfolio Gallery, 1981, Images Gallery, Cin., 1982, Boston Atheneum, 1983, Bank of Santa Fe, 1984, Susan Harder Gallery, N.Y.C., 1984, Cleve. Art Mus., 1985, Art Inst. Chgo., 1987, Amon Carter Mus., Ft. Worth, 1987, Clarence Kennedy Gallery, Cambridge, Mass., 1988, Equitable Gallery, N.Y.C., 1993; exhibited in group shows Gallery 216, N.Y., N.Y. Grover Cronin Gallery, Waltham, Mass., 1964, Carl Seimbab Gallery, Boston, 1966, Lassall Jr. Coll., 1967, Hill's Gallery, Santa Fe, Tyler Mus. Art, Austin, Tex., Dupree Gallery, Dallas, 1974, Quindacqua Gallery, Washington, 1978, Zabriskie Gallery, Paris, 1978, Am. Cultural Ctr., Paris, 1978; photographer AT & T Project-Am. Images, 1978, Seagram's Bicentennial Project, Courthouse, 1975-77, Readers Digest Assn. Project, 1984, Hudson River Project, 1985-92; author: Photography Portfolios, Old Boston City Hall, 1971, Photography Portfolios, Courthouse, 1979, Photography Portfolios, New Mexico, 1975, Certain Places, Photographs, 1987, A Hudson Landscape, Photographs, 1993. Nat. Endowment for Arts photography fellow, 1972, 79; Guggenheim fellow, 1974, 80, N.Mex. Gov.'s Excellence in The Arts award, 1987. Home and Office: PO Box 6035 Santa Fe NM 87502-6035

CLIFTON, CHAS STANHOPE, outdoor and environmental writer, educator; b. Del Norte, Colo., June 13, 1951; s. Otis Stanhope and Betty Ruth (Treece) C.; m. Mary T. Currier, July 3, 1977. BA in English, Reed Coll., 1973; MA in Religious Studies, U. Colo., 1988. Reporter Colorado Springs (Colo.) Sun, 1979-82; staff writer Colo. Coll., Colorado Springs, 1983-84; dir. mktg. Johnson Books, Boulder, Colo., 1984-86; mng. editor Colo. Outdoor Jour., Canon City, Colo., 1986-87; natural resources reporter Canon City Daily Record, 1987-90; freelance writer, 1982—; instr. Pueblo (Colo.) C.C., 1988-92, U. So. Colo., 1992—. Author: Encyclopedia of Heresies & Heretics, 1992; editor: Witchcraft Today series including The Modern Craft Movement, 1992, Modern Rites of Passage, 1993, Witchcraft & Shamanism, 1994; contbg. editor GNOSIS: Jour. Western Inner Traditions, 1988—; columnist Colo. Wildlife; contbr. articles to popular mags. Recipient 1st place disting. achievement award for local govt. news Inland Daily Press Assn., 1988. Mem. Colo. Wildlife Fedn. (Media of Yr. award 1989), Nat. Wild Turkey Fedn., Arkansas Valley Trout Unltd. (pres. 1988-89). Home: PO Box 227 Florence CO 81226

CLIFTON, MICHAEL EDWARD, English language educator; b. Reedley, Calif., Jan. 6, 1949; s. Edward Eugene and Helen May (Peters) C.; m. Anita May Bernardi, June 22, 1973. BA, Calif. State U., Fresno, 1971, MA with distinction, 1977; PhD, Ind. U., 1984. Tchr. English Hoover High Sch., Fresno, 1971-74; assoc. instr. Ind. U., Bloomington, 1978-80; lectr. Calif. State U., Fresno, 1982—; reader, presenter Internat. Assn. Fantastic in Arts, Ft. Lauderdale, Fla., 1988-93, Houston, Tex., 1987, Am. Imagery Assn., San Francisco, 1986, Eaton Conf., U. Calif. Riverside, 1985. Contbr. articles to popular mags. and profl. jours. Chair Landmarks Preservation Coun., Tower Dist. Design Rev. Com.; bd. dirs. Fresno City and County Hist. Soc., Tower Dist. Preservation Assn., Inc. Mem. MLA, AAUP. Democrat. Home: 921 N San Pablo Ave Fresno CA 93728-3627 Office: Calif State U Dept English Peters Bldg Fresno CA 93740

CLIFTON, ROBERT BLAINE, educator, aviation maintenance training consultant; b. Sabina, Ohio, Dec. 1, 1937; s. Ulysis Blaine and Olive Imogene

(Storer) C.; m. Regina Esposito, Aug. 26, 1961; children: Christopher Blaine, Jennifer Regina. Cert. teaching, UCLA, 1970; B in Vocat. Edn., Calif. State U., Long Beach, 1971, MA, 1973. Mechanic Los Angeles Airways, 1959-62, 63-66, ERA Helicopters, Anchorage, 1962; FAA designee, engring. flight test technician Hughes Tool Co., Culver City, Calif., 1966-69; asst. prof. aviation tech. Orange Coast Coll., Costa Mesa, Calif., 1969-74, assoc. prof., 1974-79, prof., 1979—, asst. div. chmn. tech., 1979-84; aviation tech. program coord., 1986—; designated mech. examiner FAA, Long Beach, 1971—; mem. exec. com. Aviation Tech. Edn. Coun., 1986—, pres. western region, 1991—. Creator (films) Aviation Tech. Tng., 1974. coach Huntington Beach (Calif.) Youth Soccer Club, 1985-86, Am.Youth Soccer Orgn., 1978-85, 1992—, Westminster (Calif.) Lil' Miss Softball, 1979-83, Little League Baseball, Huntington Beach, 1972-79. Served with U.S. Army, 1956-59. Mem. Am. Vocat. Assn., Calif. Assn. Vocat. Edn., Am. Helicopter Soc., Calif. Internat. Tech. Edn. Commn., 101st Airborne Div. Assn., Orange Coast Coll. Airframe and Powerplant Club (chmn. 1976-86), Kappa Delta Pi. Republican. Roman Catholic. Office: Orange Coast Coll 2701 Fairview Rd Costa Mesa CA 92626-5561

CLINCH, HARRY ANSELM, former bishop; b. San Anselmo, Calif., Oct. 27, 1908. Educ., St. Joseph College, Mountain View, Calif, St. Patrick's Seminary, Menlo Park, Calif. ord. priest June 6, 1936; ord. titular bishop of Badiae and auxiliary bishop of Monterey-Fresno Feb. 27, 1957. Appointed first bishop of Monterey in Calif., installed Dec. 14, 1967,served to 1982. Address: Retired Bishop Of Monterey 3400 Paul Sweet Rd-C 232 Santa Cruz CA 95065

CLINCH, NICHOLAS BAYARD, III, business executive; b. Evanston, Ill., Nov. 9, 1930; s. Nicholas Bayard Jr. and Virginia Lee (Campbell) C.; m. Elizabeth Wallace Campbell, July 11, 1964; children: Virginia Lee, Alison Campbell. Student, N.Mex. Mil. Inst., Roswell, 1948-49; AB, Stanford U., 1952, LLB, 1955. Bar: Calif. 1959. Expedition leader First Ascent, Gasherbrum I (26,470 ft.), Pakistan, 1958, First Ascent, Masherbrum (25, 660 ft.), Pakistan, 1959-60; assoc. Voegelin, Barton, Harris & Callister, L.A., 1961-68; pvt. practice Washington, 1968-70; v.p., counsel Lincoln Savs. & Loan Assn., L.A., 1970-74; exec. dir. Sierra Club Found., San Francisco, 1975-81; environ. cons. Fluor Corp., Grass Valley, Calif., 1981-84; v.p., sec. Communicom Corp. Am., Denver, 1984—; dir. Growth Stock Outlook Inc., Potomac, Md. Author: A Walk in the Sky, 1982. Leader Am. Antarctic Mountaineering Expdn., Sentinel Range, 1966-67; co-leader Chinese Am. Ulugh Muztagh Expdn., Kun Lun Range, Xinjiang, 1985; co-founder, trustee Calif. League Conservation Voters, San Francisco, 1972—. 1st lt. USAF, 1956-57. Recipient John Oliver La Gorce medal Nat. Geog. Soc., Washington, 1967. Fellow Royal Geog. Soc., Explorers Club; mem. ABA, Am. Alpine Club (hon., pres. 1967-70), Appalachian Mountain Club (hon.), State Bar Calif., Alpine Club (London), Chinese Assn. Sci. Expdns. (hon.). Republican. Episcopalian. Home: 2001 Bryant St Palo Alto CA 94301 Office: Communicom Corp Am 4100 E Mississippi Ave Ste 1750 Denver CO 80222

CLINE, ATHOL LOUIS, analytical chemist; b. Caldwell, Idaho, May 15, 1936; s. Floyd O. and Eva R. (Deel) C.; m. Martha Oros, 1959 (div. 1971); children: Kathleen Diane Cline-Garrison, Gretchen Elizabeth Cline-Riley; m. Maria Otero, Aug. 27, 1971; 1 child, Rebecca Helena. BA, Whitman Coll., 1958; MA, U. Oreg., 1960; PhD, U. Ky., 1964. Registered environ. assessor, Calif. Postdoct. USPHS, Madison, Wis., 1964-66; USPHS postdoctoral fellow U. Ill. Med. Sch., Madison, Wis., 1966-68; asst. prof. U. Ariz. Med. Sch., Tucson, 1968-71; dir. rsch. and devel. Cen. Feed Mills Assn., Bitan Aharon, Israel, 1971-77; math instr. Walla Walla (Wash.) Community Coll., 1978-80; dir. rsch. and devel. Mezquital Del Oro, Hermosillo, Mex., 1980-82; gen. mgr. Am. Analytical Labs., Inc., Tucson, 1982-85, owner, chief exec. officer, 1985—; ptnr. Am. Analytical Labs. de Mexico S.A. de C.V., Hermosilio, Sonora, Mex., 1991—; chmn. environ. lab. adv. com. to the asst. dir. Ariz. Dept. Health Svc., 1989-90. Bd. dirs. Congregation Anshei Israel, 1991—; active Congregation Anshei Israel. Fellow Am. Inst. Chemists; mem. AAAS, Am. Chem. Soc., Am. Water Works Assn., Sigma Xi. Democrat. Jewish. Home: 5755 E 6th St Tucson AZ 85711-2419 Office: 3441 E Milber St Tucson AZ 85711-2031

CLINE, BRYAN M., industrial engineer; b. Springfield, Oreg., Mar. 18, 1959; s. Charles Frederick and Ilse Maria (Rausch) C. AAS with honors, Shoreline Community Coll., 1981; student, U. Mont., 1982; BA, U. Wash., 1984; MBA, Seattle U., 1991. Lifeguard City of Seattle, 1978-85; indsl. engring. mgr. The Boeing Co., Seattle, 1985—. Seattle Milk Fund scholar, 1977. Mem. U.S. Postal Commemorative Soc. Democrat. Lutheran.

CLINE, CAROLYN JOAN, plastic and reconstructive surgeon; b. Boston; d. Paul S. and Elizabeth (Flom) Cline. BA, Wellesley Coll., 1962; MA, U. Cin., 1966; PhD, Washington U., 1970; diploma Washington Sch. Psychiatry, 1972; MD, U. Miami (Fla.) 1975. Diplomate Am. Bd. Plastic and Reconstructive Surgery. Rsch. asst. Harvard Dental Sch., Boston, 1962-64; rsch. asst. physiology Laser Lab., Children's Hosp. Research Found., Cin., 1964, psychology dept. U. Cin., 1964-65; intern in clin. psychology St. Elizabeth's Hosp., Washington, 1966-67; psychologist Alexandria (Va.) Community Mental Health Ctr., 1967-68; research fellow NIH, Washington, 1968-69; chief psychologist Kingsbury Ctr. for Children, Washington, 1969-73; sole practice clin. psychology, Washington, 1970-73; intern internal medicine U. Wis. Hosps., Ctr. for Health Sci., Madison, 1975-76; resident in surgery Stanford U. Med. Ctr., 1976-78; fellow microvascular surgery dept. surgery U. Calif.-San Francisco, 1978-79; resident in plastic surgery St. Francis Hosp., San Francisco, 1979-82; practice medicine, specializing in plastic and reconstructive surgery, San Francisco, 1982—. Contbr. chpt. to plastic surgery textbook, articles to profl. jours. Mem. Am. Bd. Plastic and Reconstructive Surgeons (cert. 1986), Royal Soc. Medicine, Calif. Medicine Assn., Calif. Soc. Plastic and Reconstructive Surgeons, San Francisco Med. Soc. Address: 490 Post St Ste 735 San Francisco CA 94102

CLINE, DAVID BRUCE, physicist; b. Kansas City, Kansas, July 12, 1933; s. Andrew B. Cline and Ella M. Jacks; married; children: Heather, Bruce, Richard, Yasmin. BS, MS, Kansas State Univ., 1960; PhD, Univ. Wis., 1965. Asst. prof. physics Univ. Wis., Madison, 1965-66, assoc. prof. physics, 1966-68, prof. physics, 1969; prof. physics and astronomy UCLA, 1969—; vis. appts. U. Hawaii, Lawrence Berkeley (Calif.) Lab., Fermilab, CERN; mem. various high energy physics adv. panels and program coms., theory and lab. astrophysics panel, panel on particles NRC Astronomy & Astrophysics Survey Com.; past co-dir. Instit. for Accelerator Physics at U. Wis.; founder Ctr. for Advanced Accelerators, UCLA, 1987. Editor numerous books. With U.S. Army, 1956-58. Recipient Sloan fellow A.P. Sloan Found., 1967. Fellow N.Y. Acad. Scis; mem. Phi Beta Kappa. Democrat. Office: UCLA Dept Physics 405 Hilgard Ave Los Angeles CA 90024

CLINE, FRED ALBERT, JR., librarian, conservationist; b. Santa Barbara, Calif., Oct. 23, 1929; s. Fred Albert and Anna Cecelia (Haberl) C. AB in Asian Studies, U. Calif., Berkeley, 1952, MLS, 1962. Resident Internat. House, Berkeley, 1950-51; trainee, officer Bank of Am., San Francisco, Düsseldorf, Fed. Republic Germany, Kuala Lumpur, 1954-60; adminstrv. reference libr. Calif. State Libr., Sacramento, 1962-67; head libr. Asian Art Mus. San Francisco, 1967—. Contbg. author: Chinese, Korean and Japanese Sculpture in the Avery Brundage Collection, 1974; author, editor: Ruth Hill Cooke, 1985. Bd. dirs. Tamalpais Conservation Club, 1990—; mem. Greenpeace, Bay Area Trails Preservation Coun., Calif. Oak Found., The Desert Protective Coun. Sgt. M.C., U.S. Army, 1952-54. Mem. Soc. for Asian Art, Metaphys. Alliance (sec., bd. dirs. San Francisco chpt. 1988-91), Nature Conservancy, Sierra Club. Democrat. Home: 825 Lincoln Way San Francisco CA 94122-2323 Office: Asian Art Mus San Francisco Golden Gate Park San Francisco CA 94118-4598

CLINE, PLATT HERRICK, author; b. Mancos, Colo., Feb. 7, 1911; s. Gilbert T. and Jessie (Baker) C.; m. Barbara Decker, Sept. 11, 1934. Grad., N.Mex. Mil. Inst., 1930; student, Colo. U., 1930-31; LittD, No. Ariz. U., 1966, BS, 1982. Advt. solicitor Denver Post, 1931; with Civilian Conservation Corps., 1934-36; Nat. Monument ranger, 1936; pub. Norwood (Colo.) Post, 1937-38; advt. mgr. Coconino Sun, Flagstaff, Ariz., 1938-41; mng. editor Holbrook Tribune-News, 1941-45; editor Coconino Sun, 1945-46; mng. editor Ariz. Daily Sun, 1946-53, pub., 1953-69, pres., 1969-76, v.p., 1976—; rsch. assoc. Mus. No. Ariz., 1976—, adj. prof. history, 1983—. Author: They Came to the Mountain, 1976, Mountain Campus, 1983, The View From Mountain Campus, 1990; Mountain Town, Flagstaff in the 20th Century, 1993. Mem. Ariz. Commn. Indian Affairs, 1952-55, Norwood (Colo) Town Coun., 1937-38; chmn. Flagstaff Citizen of Yr. Com., 1976—; bd. dirs., past pres. Raymond Edn. Found., No. Ariz. U. Found.; bd. dirs. Transition Found; trustee Flagstaff Community Hosp., 1954-58. Recipient Ariz. Master Editor-Pub. award, 1969, El Merito award Ariz. Hist. Soc., 1976; named Flagstaff Citizen of Yr., 1976, Disting. Citizen No. Ariz. U. Alumni, 1983, Dedicatee No. Ariz U. Libr., 1988. Mem. Ariz. Newspapers Assn. (past pres., Golden Svc. award 1989), No. Ariz. Pioneers Hist. Soc. (trustee 1972-75), Sigma Delta Chi, Phi Alpha Theta, Masons. Home: PO Box 578 Flagstaff AZ 86002-0578 Office: 417 W Santa Fe Ave Flagstaff AZ 86001-5395

CLINE, ROBERT STANLEY, air freight company executive; b. Urbana, Ill., July 17, 1937; s. Lyle Stanley and Mary Elizabeth (Prettyman) C.; m. Judith Lee Stucker, July 7, 1979; children: Lisa Andre, Nicole Lesley, Christina Elaine, Leslie Jane. BA, Dartmouth Coll., 1959. Asst. treas. Chase Manhattan Bank, N.Y.C., 1960-65; v.p. fin. Pacific Air Freight Co., Seattle, 1965-68; exec. v.p. fin. Airborne Express (formerly Airborne Freight Corp.), Seattle, 1968-78, vice chmn., CFO, dir., 1978-84, chmn., CEO, dir., 1984—; bd. dirs. N.C. Machinery Co., Seafirt Corp., Safeco Corp. Trustee Seattle Repertory Theatre, 1974-90, chmn. bd., 1979-83; trustee Children's Orthopedic Hosp. Found., 1983-91, Corp. Coun. of Arts, 1983—; bd. dirs. Washington Roundtable, 1985—; chmn. bd. dirs. Children's Hosp. Found., 1987-89; trustee United Way of King County, 1991-93. With U.S. Army, 1959-60. Home: 1209 39th Ave E Seattle WA 98112-4403 Office: Airborne Express PO Box 662 Seattle WA 98111

CLINE, RUSSELL BRIAN, aerospace engineer; b. Lancaster, Ohio, Dec. 13, 1959; s. Russell Max and Sarah Elaine (Shoup) C.; 1 child, Sarah Chanelle. BS in Aero. and Astron. Engring., Ohio State U., 1982; MS in Aerospace Engring., U. Ariz., 1987; student, USAF Acad., 1978-81. Mem. tech. staff Hughes Aircraft Co.-Missile Systems Group, Tucson, 1982-84, masters fellow, 1984-87, mem. tech. staff II, 1988-89, staff engr., 1989-91, sr. staff engr., 1991—. Co-inventor rolling diaphragm actuation system. Bd. dirs. Coronado Ridge Homeowners Assn., Inc., Tucson, 1990. Named one of Outstanding Young Men of Am., U.S. Jaycees, 1985. Mem. Tucson Men's Sr. Baseball League. Republican. Home: 10121 E Lost Trails St Tucson AZ 85748-1819 Office: Hughes Aircraft Co PO Box 11337 Bldg 805 M/S M-1 Tucson AZ 85734

CLINE, WILSON ETTASON, retired administrative law judge; b. Newkirk, Okla., Aug. 26, 1914; s. William Sherman and Etta Blanche (Roach) C.; m. G. Barbara Verne Pentecost, Nov. 1, 1939 (div. Nov. 1960); children: William, Catherine Cline MacDonald, Thomas; m. Gina Lana Ludwig, Oct. 5, 1969; children: David Ludwig, Kenneth Ludwig. Student, U. Ill., 1932-33; A.B., U. Okla., 1935, B.S. in Bus. Adminstrn., 1936; J.D., U. Calif., Berkeley, 1939; LL.M., Harvard U., 1941. Bar: Calif. 1940. Atty. Kaiser Richmond Shipyards, 1941-44; pvt. practice Oakland, 1945-49; prof., asst. dean, dean Eastbay Div. Lincoln U. Law Sch., Oakland, 1946-50; atty., hearing officer, asst. chief adminstrv. law judge, acting chief adminstrv. law judge Calif. Pub. Utilities Commn., San Francisco, 1949-80, ret., 1981, dir. gen. welfare Calif. State Employees Assn., 1966-67, chmn. retirement com., 1965-66, mem. member benefit com., 1980-81, mem. ret. employees div. council dist. C, 1981-82; executor estate of Warren A. Cline. Past trustee Cline Ranch Trust, various family trusts. Mem. ABA, State Bar Calif., Conf. Calif. Pub. Utility Counsel (steering com. 1967-71), Am. Judicature Soc., Boalt Hall Alumni Assn., Harvard Club of San Francisco, Commonwealth Club San Francisco, Sleepy Hollow Swim and Tennis Club (Orinda, Calif.), Masons (Orinda lodge # 494 sec. 1951-55, past Master 1949), Sirs (Peralta chpt. 12), Phi Beta Kappa (pres. No. Calif. assn. 1969-70), Beta Gamma Sigma, Delta Sigma Pi (Key award 1936), Phi Kappa Psi, Phi Delta Phi, Pi Sigma Alpha. Democrat. Mem. United Ch. Christ. Home: 110 St Albans Rd Kensington CA 94708-1035 Office: PO Box 11120 3750 Harrison St Unit 304 Oakland CA 94611-0120

CLIPSHAM, ROBERT CHARLES, veterinarian; b. Kansas City, Kans., June 27, 1955; s. Robert Berkley and Diana Ruth (Jordan) C.; m. Priscilla Sue Harlan, June 27, 1990. BS in Vet. Sci., Kans. State U., 1978, DVM, 1980; Cert. of Internship, U. Calif., Davis, 1981. Intern avian medicine U. Calif. Teaching Hosp., Davis, 1980-81; clinician McClaves Vet. Hosp., Reseda, Calif., 1981-82, Animal Med. Ctr., Hawthorne, Calif., 1982-83, Capri Pla. Pet Clinic, Tarzana, Calif., 1983-85, Valley Vet. Clinic, SimiValley, Calif., 1985-87; owner In-Flight Avicultural Svc., SimiValley, 1987-88, Calif. Exotics Clinic, SimiValley, 1988—; guest instr. Moorpark (Calif.) Jr. Coll., 1987-92; aviculture advisor World Wildlife Fund, Washington, 1989—; bd. dirs. Wildlife on Wheels, L.A., 1987-91. Author: Veterinary Clinics of North America, 1991; contbg. author: Diseases of Caged and Aviary Birds, 3d edit., 1992; contbr. articles to profl. jours. Mem. Am. Vet Med. Assn., Am. Fedn. Aviculture, Assn. Avian Vets., Calif. Vet. Med. Assn., Am. Assn. Avian Pathologists, Model Avicultural Plan (bd. dirs. 1989—), So. Calif. Vet. Med. Assn., Am. Assn. Zool. Parks & Aquariums, Am. Assn. Lab. Animal Practitioners, Am. Assn. Lab. Animal Sci., Am. Assn. Zool. Practitioners. Republican. Address: 560 N Moorpark Rd # 168 Thousand Oaks CA 91360 Office: Calif Exotics Clinic 1464 Madera Rd Unit N-122 Simi Valley CA 93065

CLITHERO, DONLEY JAMES, broadcast executive; b. Emmett, Idaho, Oct. 15, 1941; s. Charles Hubert and Clara Marriam (Storms) C.; children: Christina, Diana, Monika. Student, DeVry Tech. Inst., Chgo., 1968. Core layer Hult Plywood, Junction City, Oreg., 1964-67; studio engr. KVIQ-TV, Eureka, Calif., 1968-70; chief engr. KPIC-TV, Roseburg, Oreg., 1970-77, station mgr., 1978—. Active United Way (Roseburg, Oreg. chpt. pres., 1980-81, campaign chmn., 1982, 1990), vol. Easter Seals, bd. dirs. Umpqua Valley Arts Assn. With USAF, 1961-64, Germany. Recipient George Gratke award Greater Douglas United Way, Roseburg, Oreg., 1991. Mem. A.D.A.P.T., Wildlife Safari, Roseburg Kiwanis Club, Roseburg Exec. Club, Roseburg Country Club. Republican.

CLODIUS, ALBERT HOWARD, history educator; b. Spokane, Wash., Mar. 26, 1911; s. William Sr. and Mary Hebner (Brown) C.; m. Wilma Charlene Candler, June 3, 1961; children: Helen Lou Namikas, John Charles Parker. BA in Edn., Ea. Wash. State U., 1937; postgrad., Stanford U.; MA in History, Claremont (Calif.) Coll., 1948, PhD in History, 1953. Cert. secondary edn. tchr., Calif. Editorial asst. Pacific N.W. Quarterly, U. Wash., Seattle, 1938-40; reader Stanford U., Palo Alto, Calif., 1940-42; instr. Claremont-McKenna Coll., 1946-50; asst. prof. Pepperdine U., L.A., 1952-53; instr. Ventura (Calif.) Community Coll., 1953-76; adj. prof. Northrop U., L.A., 1977-85; prof. Nat. U., San Diego, 1987-88; ret., 1988. English conversation tchr., vol. internat. student ctr. U. Calif., L.A., 1979—. John R. and Dora F. Haynes Found. fellow, 1950-52; Clarence D. Martin scholar Ea. Wash. State U., 1936-37. Mem. Plato Soc. U. Calif. Democrat. Unitarian. Home: 4838 Salem Village Pl Culver City CA 90230-4324

CLOONAN, CLIFFORD B., electrical engineer, educator; b. Chugwater, Wyo., Aug. 28, 1928; s. Clifford Brokaw and Jessie Fern (Dowler) C.; m. Ann Jean Worstell, Mar. 23, 1951; children: Clifford Cameron, Alison Ann, Kevin Allen. Student, S.D. State Coll., 1945-46; B.S., U. Colo., 1955; M.S., Mont. State Coll., 1961; postgrad., Utah State U., 1964, Colo. U., 1967-69; Ph.D., Colo. U., 1975. Systems engr. Collins Radio Co., Cedar Rapids, Iowa, 1955-57; asst. prof. Calif. Poly. State U., San Luis Obispo, 1957-62, assoc. prof., 1962-67, prof. elec. engring., 1967-90, prof. emeritus, 1990—; rsch. assoc. Mont. State Coll., 1960-61; electronic scientist Environ. Sci. Services Adminstrn., Boulder, Colo., 1966-68; cons. McDonnell Aircraft Co., St. Louis, TRW, Redondo Beach, Calif., Hewlett-Packard, Santa Rosa, Calif. Served with inf. AUS, 1946-47; Served with Signal Corps, 1951-53. NSF fellow, 1968-69. Mem. IEEE, Am. Radio Relay League, Sigma Xi, Phi Kappa Phi. Republican. Baptist. Home: 650 Lilac Dr Los Osos CA 93402-3822

CLOPINE, GORDON ALAN, consulting geologist, educator; b. Los Angeles, Nov. 28, 1936; s. Walter Gordon and Sara Elizabeth (Donahue) C.; m. Sara Rose Lapinski, Mar. 2, 1979; children: William, Susan, Russell, Cynthia. BS, U. Redlands, Calif., 1958; MS, U. Houston, 1960. Registered geologist, Calif., Ariz.; cert. profl. geol. scientist, Calif., registered environ. assessor, Calif. Pres. Clopine Geol. Svcs., Inc., cons. geologists, Redlands, 1961—; prof. San Bernardino Valley Coll., San Bernardino, Calif., 1961-84, dean instrn., 1978-81; lectr. U. Redlands, 1961—; mem. extension faculty U. Calif.-Riverside, 1965—, field leader geol. field studies and natural environ. series. Author numerous reports and studies on geol. hazards in So. Calif. and San Andreas Fault Zone. Pres. San Bernardino County Mus. Assn., 1972. Fellow Geol. Soc. Am.; mem. Am. Inst. Profl. Geologists (cert. profl. geol. scientist). Republican. Research on geologic field studies; lecturer and researcher on San Andreas fault zone in So. Calif.; geologic hazards investigation. Home and Office: Clopine Geol Services 13093 Burns Ln Redlands CA 92373-7415

CLOSE, JAY CHARLES, oil and gas geologist; b. St. Louis, June 4, 1961; s. John Charles and Jean Reynolds (Gowran) C. AB, Wittenberg U., 1983; MS, Miami U., Ohio, 1985; PhD, So. Ill. U., 1988. Supr. Geology Resource Enterprises, Inc., Salt Lake City, 1988—. Assoc. editor: Internat. Jour. Coal Geology, Amsterdam, The Netherlands, 1990—; contbr. numerous articles to profl. jours. Vol. various amateur radio assns., Salt Lake City, 1992—. Mem. Am. Assn. Petroleum Geologists, Am. Inst. Profl. Geologists (assoc., cert.), Geol. Soc. of Am., Rocky Mountain Assn. Geologists, Soc. Economic Paleontologists and Mineralogists, Soc. Petroleum Engrs., Soc. for Organic Petrology, Sigma Xi. Republican. Presbyterian. Office: Resource Enterprises Inc 360 Wakara Way Salt Lake City UT 84108

CLOUD, JAMES MERLE, university and hospital administrator; b. Winston-Salem, N.C., Feb. 16, 1947; s. Merle Vail and Jane Crawford (Moore) C.; B.A., U. N.C., 1970; Ph.D., Columbia Pacific U., 1979. Co-founder Wholistic Health and Nutrition Inst., Mill Valley, Calif., 1974, dir. edn., 1974-76, dir. health resource consultation, 1976-78; dir., v.p. No. Calif. Internat. Coop. Coun., 1975-77; admissions dir. Columbia Pacific U., 1978-84, sec.-treas., dir., 1978-84; v.p. Calif. U. for Advanced Studies, Novato, 1984-85; dir. Wholistic Health and Nutrition Inst., 1974-85; adminstr. Autumn Care Convalescent Hosp., 1989-90; founder Memorobics Seminars of Memory Skills for Fgn. Lang. Study, 1992, Speed Learning Systems, 1992; sec., dir. Citizens of Marin Against Crime, 1983. Columnist Ukiah Penny Pincher, 1990. Mem. Assn. Holistic Health (v.p. 1976, dir.), Airplane Owners and Pilots Assn., Am. Assn. Active Srs. (v.p. 1988-89), Internat. Friends of the Iron Horse (founder, pres. 1990—), Internat. Assn. of Body Mechanics (pres. 1991—), Mendocino County Railway Soc. (dir. 1991), Nat. Assn. of Railway Passengers, Train Riders Assn. of Calif., Pacific Internat. Trapshooters Assn. Author: The Healthscription, 1979, Directory of Active Senior Organizations and Communications Resources, 1989; anthologies of poems: Aeolus, 1971, No One Loves With Solitude, 1970; columnist The New Penny Pincher, Ukiah, 1991. Home: 4286 Redwood Hwy San Rafael CA 94903-2645

CLOUGHERTY, DENNIS PAUL, physicist; b. Boston; s. Martin John and Leslie Pearl (Babbin) C. SB in Physics, MIT, 1982, SBEE, 1982, SMEE, 1982, PhD, 1989. Sr. engr. Steinbrecher Corp., Woburn, Mass., 1982-84; pres. Ambit Technologies, Santa Barbara, Calif., 1984—; cons. Commonwealth of Mass., Boston, 1986-89, Los Alamos (N.Mex.) Nat. Lab., 1986-90, Mass. Gen. Hosp., Boston, 1986-89, Akzo Chem., 1991—; instr. MIT, 1988-89; rsch. fellow Univ. Calif., Santa Barbara, 1989-92; mem. Materials Processing Ctr., MIT, 1990-92; asst. prof. U. Vt., 1992—, lectr. U. Calif., San Diego, 1992. Author numerous articles in profl. pubs. Mem. Am. Physical Soc., Inst. of Elec. and Electronic Engrs., Boston Computer Soc., MIT Enterprise Forum, Materials Rsch. Soc., Sigma Xi, Eta Kappa Nu.

CLOUSER, MICHAEL ALLEN, lawyer; b. Harrisburg, Pa., Feb. 15, 1963; s. Earl Edgar and Wenda Lee (Corbin) C. BS in Acctg. with highest honors, Coll. of William and Mary, 1986; JD cum laude, U. Miami, 1989. Bar: Calif. 1989. Bus. mgmt. intern Nordenfjord World U., Thisted, Denmark, summer 1985; assoc. Latham and Watkins, L.A., 1989-91, Gansinger, Hinshaw and Buckley, L.A., 1991—; rsch. asst. in field. Mng. editor: U. Miami Law Rev.; editor: U. Miami Entertainment and Sports Law Rev. Recipient full acad. scholarship, Paul, Landy, Beiley & Harper, P.A., acad. scholarship Pa. Women's Club. Mem. ABA, L.A. Bar Assn., Calif. Bar Assn., Beverly Hills Bar Assn., Marina Tae-Kwon-Do Club, Marina Athletic Club. Home: 411 W Manchester Ave Playa Del Rey CA 90293-7733 Office: Gansinger Hinshaw & Buckley Ste 2900 355 S Grande Ave Los Angeles CA 90071

CLOW, WILLIAM HAMMOND, secondary school educator; b. Portland, Oreg., Nov. 24, 1939; s. William H. Sr. and Dorothy G. (Greenwood) C.; m. Arlayne H. Larson, Aug. 28, 1982; children: Erik Benjaminson, Kristiann Benjaminson. BA, U. Portland, 1963; MA in Latin, U. Wash., 1968, PhD, 1985; MA in French, Middlebury (Vt.) Coll., 1972. High sch. Latin tchr. Vancouver (Wash.) Pub. Schs., 1963-64; high sch. Latin-French tchr. Bellevue (Wash.) Pub. Schs., 1964-71, jr. high French tchr., 1972-77, high sch. French tech., 1979-87, middle sch. Math-Sci. tchr., 1988—; exch. tchr. Wash. State/Victoria, Australia Exch., Melbourne, 1978. Mem. NEA. Democrat. Roman Catholic. Home: 11015 NE 140th St Kirkland WA 98034 Office: Bellevue Pub Schs PO Box 90010 Bellevue WA 98009-9010

CLOWERS, MYLES LEONARD, history educator; b. Pine Bluff, Ark., Feb. 19, 1944; s. Myles Leonard and Bernice Lorene (Teague) C.; m. Catherine Jean Bouslog, Sept. 23, 1964 (div. 1974); 1 child, Lee William; m. Linda Diane Davis, Jan. 2, 1979. Student, Fullerton (Calif.) Jr. Coll., 1962-64; BA, Calif. State U., Fullerton, 1966; MA, Calif. State U., 1970, U. Calif., Riverside, 1968-69; MS in Edn. and Computers, National Univ., 1985. Prof. history San Diego City Coll., 1971—; cons. in field; participan Midwest/Far West Reg. Conf. on Ednl. Computing, 1985; policy bd. mem. Calif. History-Social Sci. Project, 1990—. Co-author: Understanding American History Through Fiction, 2 fols. (with Warren Beck), 1974, Understanding American Politics Through Fiction (with Lorin Letendre), 1973, 2d edit. 1977, Understanding Sociology Through Fiction (with Steve Mori), 1976; contbr. articles to profl. jours.; editor medial rev. sect. Community Coll. Social Sci. Quar., 1975-77; assoc. editor Community Coll. Social Sci. Quar., 1975-77; editorial adv. bd. in Western Civilizations, Collegiate Press, 1988. Mem. San Diego Italian Cultural Assn. Recipient Golden Apple awards, Alpha Gamma Sigma, 1983, 84, 85; Fulbright grantee, 1981-82, 87, 90; Julian virtue Fellow in Econ. and Entrepreneur History, Pepperdine U., 1980. Mem. Am. Historical Assn., Am. Political Sci. Assn., Nat. Conference on Higher Edn., Community Coll. Humanities Assn., Conf. on Italian Politics and Soc., Brit. Politics Grp., Fulbright Alumni Assn., Am. Cultural Assn., Phi Alpha Theta. Democrat. Home: 10279 Caminito Agadir San Diego CA 92131-1719 Office: San Diego City College 1313 12th Ave San Diego CA 92101-4787

CLOWES, ALEXANDER WHITEHILL, surgeon, educator; b. Boston, Oct. 9, 1946; s. George H.A. Jr. and Margaret Gracey (Jackson) C.; m. Monika Meyer. AB, Harvard U., 1968, MD, 1972. Resident in surgery Case Western Reserve, Cleve., 1972-74, 76-79; rsch. fellow in pathology Harvard Med. Sch., Boston, 1974-76; fellow in vascular surgery Brigham and Womens Hosp. Harvard Med. Sch., 1979-80; asst. prof. U. Wash., Seattle, 1980-85, assoc. prof., 1985-90, assoc. chmn. dept. surgery, 1989-91, acting chmn. dept. surgery, 1992—; prof. U. Wash., 1990—; adj. prof. pathology U. Wash., Seattle, 1992. Contbr. chpts. to books; author numerous sci. papers. Trustee Marine Biol. Labs., Woods Hole, Mass., 1989; bd. dirs. Seattle Chamber Music Festival, 1990. Recipient NIH Rsch. Career Devel. award, 1982-87; NIH Tng. fellow, 1974-77; Loyal Davis Traveling Surg. scholar ACS, 1987. Mem. Am. Assn. Pathologists, Am. Heart Assn. Coun. on Arteriosclerosis, Am. Soc. Cell Biology, Internat. Soc. Applied Cardiovascular Biology, North Pacific Surg. Assn., Seattle Surg. Soc., Soc. Vascular Surgery, Cruising Club Am., Quisset Yacht Club, Sigma Xi. Episcopalian. Home: 702 Fullerton Ave Seattle WA 98122-6432 Office: U Wash Dept Surgery RF-25 Seattle WA 98195

CLOWES, GARTH ANTHONY, electronics executive, consultant; b. Didsbury, Eng., Aug. 30, 1926; came to U.S., 1957; s. Eric and Doris Gladys (Worthington) C.; m. Katharine Allman Crewdson, July 29, 1950; children: John Howard Brett, Peter Miles, Vicki Anne. BSc HNC, Stockport Coll., Cheshire, Eng., 1953; postgrad., UCLA, 1965-66, Birmingham (Eng.) Coll. Tech., 1955-56. Gen. mgr., v.p., dir. Eldon Industries, Inc., El Segundo, Calif., 1962-69; chief exec. officer, founder Entex Industries, Inc., Compton,

Calif., 1969-83; pres., founder Entex Electronics, Inc., Valley Ford, Calif., 1983—; pres., founder TTC, Inc., Carson, Calif., 1984-86; pres. Universal Telesis Electronics, Inc., Carson, 1986-87; gen. mgr. Matchbox Toys (U.S.A.) Ltd., Moonachie, N.J., 1987-88; dir. gen. Matchbox Spain, S.A., Valencia, 1988-89; cons. Matchbox Internat. Ltd., worldwide, 1986-89. Inventor electronic voice recognition devices, numerous others. Mem. pres.'s com. UNICEF, N.Y., 1972-74, Senate Adv. Bd., Washington, 1982-83; cons. Interracial Coun., L.A., 1967-69. Mem. Knights of Malta. Home: 13950 Coast Hwy 1 Valley Ford CA 94972

COATE, LESTER EDWIN, educational institution administrator; b. Albany, Oreg., Jan. 21, 1936; s. Lester Francis and Mildred Roxana (Clarck) C.; m. Marilyn Nan Robinson (dec.); chidlren: Steven, David, Carol; m. Cheryl Diane Mizer, Dec. 20, 1973. BS, Oreg. State U., 1959; MS, San Diego State U., 1969; PhD, U.S. Internat. U., 1973; vis. scholar, U. Wash., 1985-86. Engr. Los Angeles County, L.A., 1959-61; mng. ptnr. Robinson & Coate, Valley Center, Calif., 1961-64; asst. to pres. White House, Washington, 1970-71; environ. dir. San Diego County, San Diego, 1971-73; dep. regional adminstr. U.S. EPA, Seattle, 1973-86; v.p. fin. and adminstrn. Oreg. State U., Corvallis, 1986-92; vice chancellor bus. and adminstrv. svcs. U. Calif., Santa Cruz, 1992—; cons. Parsons Engring., Pasadena, Calif.; bd. dirs. U. Calif. Santa Cruz Found.; rsch. com. Goals/QPC. Author: Regional Environmental Management, 1974; contbr. articles to profl. jours. Fellow Am. Acad. Environ. Engrs., White House Fellows, Salzburg Fellows; mem. Nat. Assn. Coll. and Univ. Bus. Officers (chmn. fin. com.), C. of C. (past v.p.), Rotary (past pres.), Phi Kappa Phi. Home: 217 Venetian Rd Aptos CA 95003 Office: Univ Calif Santa Cruz CA 95064

COATES, ROSS ALEXANDER, art educator; b. Hamilton, Ont., Can., Nov. 1, 1932; s. Ralph Mansfield and Dorothea (Alexander) C.; m. Agnes Dunn, 1955 (div. 1979); children: Meagan Scott, Arwyn Alexandra; m. Marilyn Kathleen Lysohir, Sept. 27, 1980. BFA, Sch. of the Art Inst. of Chgo., 1956; MA, NYU, 1960, PhD, 1972. Asst. prof. Montclair (N.J.) State Coll., 1965-68; art tutor Canon Lawrence Coll., Lira, Uganda, 1968-70; chair fine arts dept. Russell Sage Coll., Troy, N.Y., 1971-76; prof. Wash. State U., Pullman, 1976—, chair art dept., 1976-84; vis. instr. in art Kansas City (Mo.) Art Inst., 1963-64. Editor: Gods Among Us, 1990; numerous one man shows and group exhibitions. Idaho Arts Commn. fellow, 1990. Mem. Coll. Art Assn. Office: Wash State U Fine Art Dept Pullman WA 99164

COATES, WAYNE EVAN, agricultural engineer; b. Edmonton, Alberta, Can., Nov. 28, 1947; came to U.S., 1981; s. Orval Bruce Wright and Leora (Raesler) C.; m. Patricia Louise Williams, Aug. 28, 1970. BS in Agr., U. Alberta, 1969, MS in Agrl. Engring., 1970; PhD in Agrl. Engring., Okla. State U., 1973. Registered profl. engr., Ariz., Sask. Forage systems engr. Agr. Can., Melfort, Sask., 1973-75; project engr., tech. advisor, asst. sta. mgr. Prairie Agrl. Machinery Inst., Humboldt, Sask., 1975-81; cattle, grain farmer pvt. practice, Humboldt, 1975-81; assoc. prof. U. Ariz., Tucson, 1981—; adj. prof. U. Catamarca, Argentina, 1992—; cons. Paraguayan Govt. UN Devel. Program, 1987-90, Argentine Govt., univs. and pvt. industry, 1991—, also govt., univ., and agrl. orgns.; cons. on Middle East agrl. projects; speaker at internat. confs., Australia, Paraguay, Argentina, U.S. Designer farm equipment primarily for alternative crops and tillage; contbr. articles to profl. jours. Pres. Sunrise Ter. Village Townhomes Homeowners Assn., Tucson, 1990-92. Grantee USDA, Washington, 1981—, Ariz. Dept. Environ. Quality, Phoenix, 1989—, U.S. Dept. of Energy, Washington, 1991—, agrl. industries western U.S., 1982—. Mem. Am. Soc. Agrl. Engrs. (chmn. Ariz. sect. 1984-85, vice-chmn. Pacific region 1988-89, dir. dist. 4 1991-93, rep. to AAAS Consortium of Affiliates for Internat. Programs 1992, internat. dir.-elect 1993—), Am. Soc. Engring. Edn., Soc. Automotive Engrs., Air and Waste Mgmt. Assn., Can. Soc. Agrl. Engring., Australian Soc. for Agrl. Engring., Asian Assn. for Agrl. Engring., Sigma Xi. Office: Univ Ariz Dept Agrl Biosystems Engr Tucson AZ 85721

COBB, JEWEL PLUMMER, retired college president; b. Chgo., Jan. 17, 1924; divorced; 1 child. A.B., Talladega Coll., 1944; M.S., N.Y. U., 1947, Ph.D. in Biology, 1950. Fellow Nat. Cancer Inst., 1950-52; instr. anatomy U. Ill. Coll. Medicine, 1952-54; mem. rsch. surgery staff Postgrad. Med. Coll., N.Y. U., 1955, asst. prof., 1955-60; Cancer Rsch. Found. prof. biology Sarah Lawrence Coll., 1960-69; prof. zoology, dean Conn. Coll., 1969-76; prof. biology, dean Douglass Coll., Rutgers U., 1976-81; pres. Calif. State U., Fullerton, 1981-90, pres. emerita, prof. emerita, 1990—; Calif. State Trustee prof. Calif. State U., L.A.; former mem. commn. acad. affairs Am. Coun. on Edn.; mem. Nat. Inst. Medicine; bd. dirs. 21st Century Found., CPC Internat., Inc., Allied Signal Corp., Travelers Ins. Co., First Interstate Bancorp, Ga.-Pacific. Trustee Drew U. Medicine and Sci., Calif. Inst. Tech. Recipient Alumnae Woman of Yr. award N.Y. U., 1979. Fellow N.Y. Acad. Scis., Tissue Culture Assn.; mem. AAUW, Sigma Xi. Office: Calif State U Los Angeles CA 90032-8500

COBB, JOHN BOSWELL, JR., clergyman, educator; b. Kobe, Japan, Feb. 9, 1925; s. John Boswell and Theodora Cook (Atkinson) C.; m. Jean Olmstead Loftin, June 18, 1947; children: Theodore, Cliford, Andrew, Richard. M.A., U. Chgo. Div. Sch., 1949, Ph. D., 1952. Ordained to ministry United Meth. Ch., 1950. Pastor Towns County Circuit, N.Ga. Conf., 1950-51; faculty Young Harris Coll., Ga., 1950-53, Candler Sch. Theology and Emory U., 1953-58, Sch. Theology, Claremont, Calif., 1958-90; Avery prof. Claremont Grad. Sch., 1973-90; ret., 1990; mem. commn. on doctrine and doctrinal standard United Meth. Ch., 1968-72; mem. commn. on mission, 1984-88. Author: A Christian Natural Theology, 1965, The Structure of Christian Existence, 1967, Christ in a Pluralistic Age, 1975, (with Herman Daly) For the Common Good, 1989. Dir. Center for Process Studies. Fulbright prof. U. Mainz, 1965-66; fellow Woodrow Wilson Internat. Ctr. for Scholars, 1976. Mem. Am. Acad. Religion, Am. Metaphys. Soc.

COBB, ROWENA NOELANI BLAKE, real estate broker; b. Kauai, Hawaii, May 1, 1939; d. Bernard K. Blake and Hattie Kanui Yuen; m. James Jackson Cobb, Dec. 22, 1962; children: Shelly Ranelle Noelani, Bret Kimo Jackson. BS in Edn., Bob Jones U., 196l; broker's lic., Vitousek Sch. Real Estate, Honolulu, 198l. Lic. real estate broker, Honolulu; cert. residential broker. Bus. mgr. Micronesian Occupational Ctr., Koror Palau, 1968-70; prin. broker Cobb Realty, Lihue, Hawaii, 1983—; sec. Neighbor Island MLS Svc., Honolulu, 1985-87, vice chmn., 1987-88; chmn. MLS Hawaii, Inc., Honolulu, 1988-90. Assoc. editor Jour Entymology, 1965-66. Sec. Koloa Community Assn., 1981-89, pres., 1989; mem. Kauai Humane Soc., YWCA, Kauai Mus.; bd. dirs. Wong Care Home. Mem. Nat. Assn. Realtors (grad. Realtors Inst., cert. residential specialist), Hawaii Assn. Realtors (cert. tchr., state bd. dirs. 1984, v.p. 1985), Kauai Bd. Realtors (v.p. 1984, pres. 1985, Realtor Assoc. of Yr. award 1983, Realtor of Yr. award 1986), Kauai Mus., Soroptimists (bd. dirs. Lihue 1986-89, treas. 1989). Office: 3016 Umi St Ste 206 Lihue HI 96766-1346

COBB, ROY LAMPKIN, JR., computer sciences corporation executive; b. Oklahoma City, Sept. 23, 1934; s. Roy Lampkin and Alice Maxine (Ellis) C.; B.A., U. Okla., 1972; postgrad. U. Calif., Northridge, 1976-77; m. Shirley Ann Dodson, June 21, 1958; children—Kendra Leigh, Cary William, Paul Alan. Naval aviation cadet U.S. Navy, 1955, advanced through grades to comdr., 1970; ret., 1978; mktg./project staff engr. Gen. Dynamics, Pomona, Calif., 1978-80; mgr. dept. support svcs. Computer Scis. Corp., Point Mugu, Calif., 1980—. Decorated Navy Commendation medal, Air medal. Mem. Assn. Naval Aviators, Soc. Logistic Engrs. (editor Launchings 1990—). Republican. Methodist. Club: Las Posas Country. Home: 2481 Brookhill Dr Camarillo CA 93010-2112 Office: Computer Scis Corp PO Box 42273 Port Hueneme CA 93044-4573

COBB, SHIRLEY ANN, public relations specialist, journalist; b. Oklahoma City, Jan. 1, 1936; d. William Ray and Irene (Fewell) Dodson; m. Roy Lampkin Cobb, Jr., June 21, 1958; children: Kendra Leigh, Cary William, Paul Alan. BA in Journalism with distinction, U. Okla., 1958, postgrad., 1972; postgrad., Jacksonville U., 1962. Info. specialist Pacific Missle Test Ctr., Point Mugu, Calif., 1975-76; corr. Religious News Svc., N.Y.C., 1979-81; splty. editor fashion and religion Thousand Oaks (Calif.) News Chronicle, 1977-81; pub. rels. cons., Camarillo, Calif., 1977—; media mgr. pub. info City of Thousand Oaks, 1983—. Contbr. articles to profl. jours. Trustee Ocean View Sch. Bd., 1976-79; pres. Point Mugu Officers' Wives Club, 1975-76, 90—, Calif. Assn. Pub. Info. Ofcls. (pres. 1989-90, Paul Clark Lifetime Achievement award 1993); bd. dirs. Camarillo Hospice, 1983-85; sec. Conejo Valley Hist. Soc., 1993. Recipient Spot News award San Fernando Valley Press Club, 1979. Mem. Pub. Rels. Soc. Am. (L.A. chpt. liaison 1991), Sigma Delta Chi, Phi Beta Kappa, Chi Omega. Republican. Clubs: Las Posas Country, Town Hall of Calif. Home: 2481 Brookhill Dr Camarillo CA 93010-2112 Office: 2400 Willow Ln Thousand Oaks CA 91360

COBB, TIMOTHY LEE, physician assistant, military officer; b. Indpls., Nov. 20, 1948; s. John and Norma Alice (Lacey) C.; m. Sandra Lynn Sleeper, May 10, 1975; children: Elizabeth Anne Cobb, Sarah Ann Cobb. AA, St. Petersburg Jr. Coll., Fla., 1972; B of Health Scis., Duke U., 1977. Cert. physican asst.; cert. orthopedic physician asst. Physician asst. emergency medicine Carteret Gen. Hosp., Morehead City, N.C., 1977-80; commd. 2d lt. USAF, 1980, advanced through grades to major, 1989; physician asst. emergency medicine USAF Hosp., Robins AFB, 1980-83; physician asst. dept. medicine David Grant USAF Med. Ctr., Travis AFB, Calif., 1983-86, resident in othropedic surgery, 1986-87; instr. in surgery Uniformed Svcs. U. of Health Scis., Bethesda, Md., 1988—; orthopedic physician asst. Malcolm Grow USAF Med. Ctr., Andrews AFB, Md., 1987-89, 11th Air Force Regional Hosp., Elmendorf AFB, Anchorage, 1989—; officer-in-charge dept orthopedic surgery Malcolm Grow USAF Med. Ctr., Andrews AFB, 1987-89. Contbr. articles to profl. jours. Decorated Purple Heart, Vietnamese Cross of Gallantry. Fellow Am. Acad. Physician Assts., Am. Soc. of Orthopedic Physicians Assts., Soc. of Air Force Physician Assts.; mem. Am. Acad. Pain Mgmt. (clin.), Assn. of Mil. Surgeons of the U.S. Home: 19505 N Montague Loop Eagle River AK 99577-8718 Office: 3rd Air Force Med Ctr Dept Orthopedic Surgery Elmendorf AFB AK 99505

COBBAN, WILLIAM AUBREY, paleontologist; b. Anaconda, Mont., Dec. 31, 1916; s. Ray Aubrey and Anastacia (McNulty) C.; m. Ruth Georgina Loucks, Apr. 15, 1942; children—Georgina, William, Robert. B.A., U. Mont., 1940; Ph.D., Johns Hopkins U., 1949. Geologist Carter Oil Co., Tulsa, 1940-46; paleontologist U.S. Geol. Survey, Washington, 1948-92, emeritus scientist, 1992—. Contbr. numerous articles to profl. jours. Recipient Meritorious Service award Dept. of Interior, Washington, 1974, Paleontol. medal Paleontol. Soc. Am., 1985, Disting. Svc. award. U.S. Dept. Interior, 1986. Fellow Geol. Soc. Am., AAAS; mem. Rocky Mountain Assn. Geologists (hon., Disting. Pioneer Geologist award 1985), Mont. Geol. Soc. (hon.), Wyo. Geol. Assn. (hon.); mem. Paleontol. Soc., Soc. Econ. Paleontologists and Mineralogists (Raymond C. Moore Paleontolgoy medal 1990), Am. Assn. Petroleum Geologists, Phi Beta Kappa, Sigma Xi. Republican. Mem. United Ch. of Christ. Office: U S Geol Survey Federal Ctr Box 25046 MS 919 Denver CO 80225

COBBS, HARTZELL JAMES, healthcare consultant; b. Eugene, Oreg., Oct. 17, 1942; s. Hartzell Miller and LaVancy May (Hoffman) C.; m. Joy Ann Harter, Aug. 27, 1965; children: Justin, Stephen. BTh, N.W. Christian Coll., 1966; D of Religion, Claremont Sch. of Theology, 1970. Assoc. minister First Christian Ch., Sacramento, 1970-71; sr. minister South Bay Christian Ch., Redondo Beach, Calif., 1971-76; exec. v.p. Idaho Health Care Assn., Boise, Idaho, 1976-81; exec. dir. Oreg. Health Care Assn., Portland, 1981-87; sr. v.p. C&M Assocs., Portland, 1988; pres. Cobbs & Co., Portland, 1989—; internat. lectr. Intercare, 1984—; mem. Govs. Commn. on Fin. Long-Term Care, Salem Oreg., 1988-89; v.p. Mountain State Health Corp, Boise, 1984—. Pres. Redondo Beach Coordinating Coun., Redondo Beach, Calif., 1975; drug counselor The Center, Honolulu, 1970; bd. dirs. Emergency Housing Ctr., Sacramento, 1970-71. Mem. Am. Soc. Health Care Assn. Execs. (pres. 1986-87), Am. Health Care Assn. (bd. dirs. 1986-87). Democrat. Disciples of Christ. Home and office: 7160 SW Raleighwood Ln Portland OR 97225-1931

COBIANCHI, THOMAS THEODORE, engineering and marketing executive, educator; b. Paterson, N.J., July 7, 1941; s. Thomas and Violet Emily (Bazzar) C.; m. Phyllis Linda Asch, Feb. 6, 1964; 1 child, Michael. Student, Clemson U., 1963; BS, Monmouth Coll., 1968, MBA, 1972; postgrad., U.S. Internat. U., 1992—, Wharton Sch., U. Pa., 1987. Sales mgr. Westinghouse Electric Corp., Balt., 1968-74; sr. internat. sales engr. Westinghouse Electric Corp., Lima, Ohio, 1975-77; program mgr. Westinghouse Electric Corp., Pitts., 1977-78, mgr. bus. devel., 1978-82; dir. mktg. Westinghouse Electric Corp., Arlington, Va., 1982-86; acting dir., engring. mgr. General Dynamics Corp., San Diego, 1986-89; dir. bus. devel. RPV Programs Teledyne Ryan Aero., San Diego, 1989-90; pres. Cobianchi & Assocs., San Diego, 1990; v.p. strategic planning and program devel. S-Cubed div. Maxwell Labs., Inc., San Diego, 1991—; instr., lectr. various ednl. instns. Active various polit. and ednl. orgns.; mem. bus. adv. coun. U.S. Internat. U.; bd. dirs. Cath. Charities San Diego; vol. exec., sect. chmn. United Way San Diego. Mem. Armed Forces Communications and Electronics Assn. (acting chmn. 1988), Princeton Club of Washington, Nat. Aviation Club, General Dynamics Health Club, Delta Sigma Pi. Home: 16468 Calle Pulido San Diego CA 92128-3249

COBLE, HARVEY LAWRENCE, manufacturing company executive; b. Niles, Mich., Oct. 12, 1944; s. David John and Lucille (Lloyd) C.; m. Elizabeth Pauline Peckham, May 19, 1970. BA in Polit. Sci. with honors, Mich. State U., 1967; JD, Stetson U., 1970. Mgr. toy div. Phillips Enterprises, Phoenix, 1972-73; pres. Golden Dawn Enterprises, San Diego, 1974—. Vol., San Diego Dem. Party, 1976, 80, 84, 88, 92. Home: 3806 Box St San Diego CA 92103 Office: Golden Dawn Enterprises 4616 5th Ave San Diego CA 92101

COBLE, HUGH KENNETH, engineering and construction company executive; b. rochester, pa., Sept. 26; s. John L. and Victoria (Neilson) C.; m. Constance Stratton, June 2, 1956; children: Keith Allen, Kimberly Ann, Jon Arthur, Scott Arnold, Neal Stewart. BSChemE, Carnegie Mellon U., 1956; postgrad., UCLA, 1966, U. Houston, 1963-65, Stanford U., 1981. Engr. Standard Oil Calif., El Segundo, 1956-61; sales mgr. Turco Products, Houston, 1961-63; sales dir. W.R. Grace, Houston, 1963-65; pres., bd. dirs. Fluor Corp., Irvine, Calif., 1966—. Bd. dirs. John Henry Found., Orange, Calif., 1992—; trustee Scripps U., Claremont, Calif., 1991—; mem. adv. bd. Thunderbird U., Phoenix, 1992—. Mem. Am. Petroleum Inst., Am. Inst. Chem. Engrs. (bd. dirs. 1983-88). Presbyterian.

COBURN, JACK WESLEY, physician, researcher, educator; b. Fresno, Calif., Aug. 6, 1932; s. Glenn Walton and Eula May (Rishel) C.; m. Kathryn Helen Rorem, Feb. 1, 1958; children: Elizabeth Louise Callander, Laurel Helen Wright, Rachel Kathryn Vandenberg. BS cum laude, U. Redlands, 1953; MD, UCLA, 1957. Diplomate Am. Bd. Internal Medicine. Intern UCLA Hosp., 1957-58, resident, 1960-61; resident physician U. Wash. Hosps., Seattle, 1958-60; asst. prof. medicine UCLA Sch. Medicine, 1965-70, assoc. prof. medicine, 1970-73, prof. medicine, 1973-84; coord. NIH tng. program VA Med. Ctr. UCLA, 1967-75; chief nephology sect. VA Wadsworth Med. Ctr., L.A., 1970-81; dir. nephology tng. UCLA Combined Hosps., L.A., 1980-84; staff physician VA Med. Ctr., L.A., 1985—; pvt. practice Beverly Hills, Calif., 1985—; attending physician Cedars-Sinai Med. Ctr., L.A., 1985—; adj. prof. medicine UCLA Sch. Medicine, 1985—; cons. Hoffman LaRoche Labs., Nutly, N.J., 1973-82; vice chmn. Dept. Medicine UCLA, 1979-80; editorial bd. mem. Kidney Internat., N.Y.C., 1982—, Am. J Kidney Diseases, N.Y.C., 1987—, Seminars in Nephrology, Phila., 1984—. Author: Disorders of Mineral Metabolism, 1980, Aluminum and Kidney, 1989; also articles. Medical Adv. Com. Nat. Kidney Found., Southern Calif, 1970-82. Recipient Human Nutrition award Am. Inst. Nutrition, 1981, Medical Investigator award VA, 1982, Frederick Bartter award Am. Soc. Bone & Mineral Rsch., 1986, spl. award Nat. Kidney Found., 1990. Democrat. Home: 627 Lachman Ln Pacific Palisades CA 90272-2802 Office: 9400 Brighton Way Beverly Hills CA 90210-4714

COBURN, MARJORIE FOSTER, psychologist, educator; b. Salt Lake City, Feb. 28, 1939; d. Harlan A. and Alma (Ballinger) Polk; m. Robert Byron Coburn, July 2, 1977; children: Polly Klea Foster, Matthew Ryan Foster, Robert Scott Coburn, Kelly Anne Coburn. B.A. in Sociology, UCLA, 1960; Montessori Internat. Diploma honor grad. Washington Montessori Inst., 1968; M.A. in Psychology, U. No. Colo., 1979; Ph.D. in Counseling Psychology, U. Denver, 1983. Licensed clin. psychologist. Probation officer Alameda County (Calif.), Oakland, 1960-62, Contra Costa County (Calif.), El Cerrito, 1966, Fairfax County (Va.), Fairfax, 1967; dir. Friendship Club, Orlando, Fla., 1963-65; tchr. Va. Montessori Sch., Fairfax, 1968-70; spl. edn. tchr. Leary Sch., Falls Church, Va., 1970-72, sch. administr., 1973-76; tchr. Aseltine Sch., San Diego, 1976-77, Coburn Montessori Sch., Colorado Springs, Colo., 1977-79; pvt. practice psychotherapy, Colorado Springs, 1979-82, San Diego, 1982—; cons. spl. edn., agoraphobia, women in transition. Mem. Am. Psychol. Assn., Am. Orthopsychiat. Assn., Phobia Soc., Council Exceptional Children, Calif. Psychol. Assn., Acad. San Diego Psychologists, AAUW, NOW, Mensa. Episcopalian. Lodge: Rotary. Contbr. articles to profl. jours.; author: (with R.C. Orem) Montessori: Prescription for Children with Learning Disabilities, 1977. Office: 826 Prospect St Ste 101 La Jolla CA 92037-4206

COCHRAN, ANDREW VERITY, army officer; b. Alexandria, Va., May 25, 1963; s. Douglas and Ruth (Gelbach) McCord; m. Christine Marie Eckman (div. June 1991); m. Pamela Joan Bryan, Dec. 21, 1991. BA, U. S.C., 1985. Commd. 2d lt. U.S. Army, 1986, advanced through grades to capt., 1990; platoon leader Battery D, 1st Bn. 59th Air Def. Artillery, Wachernhiem, Germany, 1986-89; bn. adjutant Hdqrs. and Hdqrs. Battery, 1st Bn., 44th Air Def. Artillery, Ft. Lewis, Wash., 1990-91; asst. ops. officer Hdqrs. and Hdqrs. Battery, 3d Bn., 2d Air Def. Artillery, Dahran, Saudi Arabia, 1991; battery comdr. Battery C, 3d Bn., 2d Air Def. Artillery, Ft. Lewis, 1991—. Asst. scout master Boy Scouts Am., Steilacoom, Wash., 1990-91; com. mem. Steilacoom (Wash.) Steilacoom, Wash., 1990-91; mem. Crime Watch, University Place, Wash., 1992. Decorated Bronze star. Home: 5409 78th Ave Ct W Tacoma WA 98467 Office: C 3-2 ADA Fort Lewis WA 98433

COCHRAN, ANNE WESTFALL, public relations executive; b. Cairo, Ill., Sept. 16, 1954; d. Howard Thurston and Flora Isabelle (Stone) Westfall; m. Charles Eugene Cochran, June 14, 1975; 2 children. BA in Advt., So. Ill. U., 1974; MA in Communications, U. Wis., Milw., 1975. Dir. advt. Sight and Sound Systems Inc., Milw., 1975-76; nat. publicity/promotions mgr. 20th Century Fox Classics, Los Angeles, 1981-85; nat. publicity dir. Cannon Films Inc., Los Angeles, 1985-86; publicist, staff writer Warner Bros. Inc., Burbank, Calif., 1986-87; v.p. mktg. Cinetel Films, Inc., Los Angeles, 1987; v.p. publicity and promotion U.S. Cineplex Odcon Films, Inc., Los Angeles, 1987-89; ptnr. Jones Cochran Assocs., Beverly Hills, Calif., 1989-92; sr. v.p. corp. and motion picture divsns. Bender, Goldman & Helper, L.A., 1992—; mktg. cons., L.A., 1976-81. Bd. dirs. Case de Rosas Sunshine Mission, L.A., 1990. Mem. Publicists Guild. Democrat. Mem. Ch. Religious Sci. Home: 3641 Shannon Rd Los Angeles CA 90027 Office: Bender Goldman & Helper 11500 W Olympic Blvd Ste 655 Los Angeles CA 90027

COCHRAN, FRED WILLIAM, JR., sales management executive, consultant; b. Oakland, Calif., July 9, 1938; s. Fred William and Dolores Pearl (Rogers) C.; m. Marie Blanche Brereton, Sept. 18, 1968 (div. June 1982); children: Jeff, Lori, Gregory; m. Karen Lou Wiget, Oct. 11, 1986; 1 child, Fred William III. BS in Bus., San Francisco State U., 1960. Sales rep. Chesebrough-Ponds, Inc., N.Y.C., 1960-68; no. dist. mgr. Schick Safety Razor, Culver City, Calif., 1968-74; western regional mgr. Consol. Foods, Centralia, Ill., 1974-77; gen. mgr. Phototron Photo Finisher, Rialto, Calif., 1977-82; v.p. sales Stony Ridge Winery, Pleasanton, Calif., 1982-86; dir. sales Internat. Tobacco, Martinez, Calif., 1986-92; pvt. practice real estate appraisal Martinez, Calif., 1992—; nat. sales mgr. Stony Ridge Winery; sales cons. Schick Safety Razor Co. Author tng. manual Internat. Tobacco Co. Named Top Exec. of Yr., Internat. Tobacco, 1990. Republican. Home: 217 Augustine Dr Martinez CA 94553

COCHRAN, JACQUELINE LOUISE, general management executive; b. Franklin, Ind., Mar. 12, 1953; d. Charles Morris and Marjorie Elizabeth (Rohrbaugh) C. BA, DePauw U., 1975; MBA, U. Chgo., 1977. Fin. analyst Pan Am World Airways, N.Y.C., 1977-79, Gen. Bus. Group W. R. Grace & Co., N.Y.C., 1979-80; sr. fin. analyst Gen. Bus. Group div. W. R. Grace & Co., N.Y.C., 1980-81, mgr. fin. analysis, 1981-82; dir. fin. planning and analysis Gen. Bus. Group div. W. R. Grace & Co., N.Y.C., 1982-85; v.p. fin. Am. Breeders Svc. div. W. R. Grace & Co., DeForest, Wis., 1985-87, v.p. feed ops. Grace Animal Svc. div., 1987-89; gen. mgr., chief ops. officer SoftKat div. W. R. Grace & Co., Chatsworth, Calif., 1990; pres. SoftKat div. W.R. Grace & Co., Chatsworth, Calif., 1990-92; vice-chmn., chief adminstrv. officer Baker & Taylor, Inc., 1992, pres. SoftKat div., 1992. Bd. visitors DePauw U., 1993—. Recipient Women of Distinction award Madison (Wis.) YWCA, 1987; named to Acad. Women Achievers YWCA N.Y., 1984. Mem. ABCD, The Microcomputer Industry Assn. (adv. coun. 1992), Phi Beta Kappa, Alpha Lambda Delta, Delta Delta Delta (advisor scholarship com. Madison chpt. 1985-89, treas. 1986-89, house corp. bd. dirs. 1986-89, fin. advisor 1989-90). Republican. Methodist.

COCHRAN, JEFFERY KEITH, engineering educator; b. Ramey AFB, P.R., Oct. 11, 1952; s. Billy Gene and Joy Lynn (Powers) C. BS in Enring., Purdue U., 1973, MS in Nuclear Engring., 1976, MS in Indsl. Engring., 1982, PhD in Indsl. Engring., 1984. Registered profl. engr., Ariz. Assoc. engr. Aerojet Nuclear Co., Idaho Falls, Idaho, 1973; engr. Stone and Webster Engring. Corp., Boston, 1974; rsch. asst. NASA, West Lafayette, Ind., 1975-76; staff mem. Los Alamos (N.Mex.) Nat. Lab., 1976-80; sr. rsch. scientist Battelle N.W. Lab., Richland, Wash., 1984; asst. prof. Ariz. State U., Tempe, 1984-88, assoc. prof., 1988—; prin. investigator NSF, Washington, 1987-92, Inst. for Mfg. and Automation Rsch., L.A., 1988-93, Motorola, Inc., Schaumburg, Ill., 1986-87, Honeywell, Inc., West Covina, Calif., 1985-86. Contbr. articles to profl. jours. Fellowship Lilly Found., 1982-84, Los Alamos Nat. Lab., 1978-79. Mem. Inst. of Indsl. Engrs. (sr.), Soc. of Mfg. Engrs. (sr.), Soc. for Computer Simulation, Ops. Rsch. Soc. of Am., Am. Soc. of Engring. Edn., Assn. for Computing Machinery, IEEE Computer Soc. Office: Ariz State U Dept Indsl/Mgmt Systems Engring Tempe AZ 85287

COCHRAN, JOHN ARTHUR, economics educator; b. Des Moines, Sept. 25, 1921; s. Arthur John and Lena (McCowin) C.; m. Mary Leffler, July 10, 1943; children: Jacquelyn Sue, Cynthia Elizabeth, Catherine Edna. A.B., Drake U., 1943; cert., U. Exeter, Eng., 1945; M.A., Harvard U., 1948, Ph.D., 1949. Teaching asst. MIT, Cambridge, 1947-48; teaching fellow Harvard U. (Cambridge), 1948-49; asst. prof. econs. U. Ill., Urbana, 1949-56; monetary economist Fed. Res. Bank N.Y., 1956-57; assoc. prof. econs. So. Ill. U., Carbondale, 1957-62; prof. econs. Ariz. State U., Tempe, 1962—, chmn. dept. econs., 1962-67; vis. prof. U. Colo., 1965, NYU, 1980; chmn. fund mgrs., Pub. Safety Retirement Fund of Ariz., 1984—. Author: Money, Banking and the Economy, 1967, (5th edit.), 1983; contbr. articles to profl. jours. Mem. Ariz. Acad. Sponsors Ariz. Town Halls for Ariz. Leaders, 1962—, Presbyn. Mission del Sol Ch. (pres. Presbyn. Men 1991-93); trustee Presbyn. Ch., 1964-67, elder United Presbyn. Ch. Session, 1986-89. 1st lt. AUS, 1943-46, 51-52. Mem. Midwest Econ. Assn. (sec.-treas. 1960-62), Phi Beta Kappa (pres. chpt. 1976-77), Phi Kappa Phi (pres. chpt. 1985-86), Beta Gamma Sigma (pres. chpt. 1985-86). Home: 116 E Greentree Dr Tempe AZ 85284-3147 Office: Arizona State U Tempe AZ 85287

COCHRAN, PAUL TERRY, cardiologist, educator; b. Sullivan, Ind., Jan. 27, 1938; s. Charles Harold and Mary Josephine (Ring) C.; m. Linda Diane Stogsdill, Mar. 11, 1972; children: Kelli Marie, Mary Kathleen. BA, DePauw U., 1960; MD, Western Res. U., 1964. Diplomate Am. Bd. Internal Medicine, Am. Bd. Cardiovascular Disease. Resident in internal medicine N.C. Meml. Hosp., Chapel Hill, 1964-67; fellow in cardiology Georgetown U. Med. Ctr., Washington, 1967-69; cardiologist Gallatin Med. Group, Downey, Calif., 1971-72; asst. prof. medicine U. N.Mex., Albuquerque, 1972-76, assoc. prof., 1976-77, clin. prof., 1984—; pvt. practice, Albuquerque, 1977—; staff cardiologist Presbyn. Health Care Svcs., Albuquerque, 1977—, trustee, 1986—, pres. med. staff, 1988-90; bd. dirs. Physicians Mut. Liability Ins. Co., Albuquerque. Contbg. auuthor: Essentials of the Cardiac Physical Diagnosis, 1987. Maj. M.C., USAF, 1969-71. Fellow ACP (councilor N.Mex. 1982-84), Am. Coll. Cardiology (bd. govs. N.Mex. 1978-81); mem. Am. Heart Assn. (fellow coun. on clin. cardiology, exec. com. 1984-88), N.Mex. Med. Soc. (councilor 1986-91), Greater Albuquerque Med. Assn. (pres. 1984-85), Phi Beta Kappa. Methodist. Home: 6401 Zapateco NW Albuquerque NM 87107 Office: SW Cardiol Assocs 1101 Medical Arts Ave NE Albuquerque NM 87102

COCHRAN, WENDELL, science editor; b. Carthage, Mo., Nov. 29, 1929; s. Wendell Albert and Lillian Gladys (Largent) C.; m. Agnes Elizabeth

Groves, Nov. 9, 1963; remarried Corinne Des Jardins, Aug. 25, 1980. A.B., U. Mo., Columbia, 1953, A.M. in Geology, 1956, B.J., 1960. Geologist ground-water br. U.S. Geol. Survey, 1956-58; reporter, copyeditor Kansas City (Mo.) Star, 1960-63; editor Geotimes and Earth Sci. mags., Geospectrum newsletter, Alexandria, Va., 1963-84; v.p. Geol. Survey Inc., Bethesda, Md., 1984-86. Co-author: Into Print: A Practical Guide to Writing, Illustrating, and Publishing, 1977; sr. editor: Geowriting: A Guide to Writing, Editing and Printing in Earth Science, 1973; contbr. articles to profl. jours. and encys. Mem. geol. socs. Washington, London, Assn. Earth Sci. Editors (award Outstanding Contbns. 1982), Dog in the Night-time. Home: 4351 SW Willow St Seattle WA 98136-1769

COCHRAN, WILLIAM MICHAEL, librarian; b. Nevada, Iowa, May 6, 1952; s. Joseph Charles and Inez (Larson) C.; m. Diane Marie, July 24, 1971. BA, U. Iowa, 1979, MA with distinction in Libr. Sci., 1983; MA in Pub. Adminstrn., Drake U., 1989. Dir. Red Oak (Iowa) Pub. Libr., 1984; patron svcs. libr. Pub. Libr. of Des Moines, 1984-87; program coord. LSCA State Libr. of Iowa, Des Moines, 1987-88, dir. libr. devel., 1988-89, asst. state libr., 1989-90; coord. South Ctrl. Fedn. Librs., Billings, Mont., 1990—; dir. Parmly Billings Libr., 1990—. Author: A Centry of Iowa Libraries in Association: A History of the Iowa Library Association 1890-1990, 1990; contbr. articles to profl. jours. Bd. dirs. Literacy Vols. Am., 1991—; consult the pub. com. mem. Billings Mont. Sch. Dist. # 2, 1992—. Recipient Gov's. Vol. award, 1990; Extending Libr. Svcs. to the Disabled grantee U.S. Dept. of Edn. through Mont. State Libr., 1993, U.S. Dept. of Housing and Urban Devel. through City of Billings, 1993, Literacy Resource Ctr. grantee Community Devel. Block Grant, 1992, Family Literacy Programs grantee State Libr. of Iowa from U.S. Dept. Edn., 1988. Mem. ALA (intellectual freedom round table 1991—, libr. hist. round table 1989—, assn. specialized and coop. libr. agys. 1988-90, ALA/ILA fed. rels. coord. 1985-86), Nat. Agrl. Libr. Rural Info. Ctr. (state libr. coord. for Iowa 1988-90), Mountain Plains Libr. Assn. (cont. edn. com. chair 1991-92, blue ribbon task force on grad. libr. edn. 1992, pub. libr./trustees sect. 1991—, state agy. coops. & systems sect. 1991—), Pacific Northwest Libr. Assn. (collection devel. interest group 1992—, libr. instr. interest group 1992—, mgmt. interest group 1992—, intellectual freedom interest group 1993—, libr. devel. interest group 1993—), Mont. Libr. Assn. (bd. dirs. 1991—, pub. libr. divsn. 1991—, chair 1991-92, legislative com. chair 1992—, task force on lobbying chair 1992—, ad hoc com. on Mont. Libr. edn. 1991-92), Mont. Libr. Svcs. Adv. Coun. (planning com. 1991), Mont. Ctr. for the Book (exec. com. 1990—, fundraising com. chair 1991-92), Mont. State Libr. Commn. Collection Mgmt. Com., Mont. Gov's. Conf. on Libr. and Info. Svcs., Mont. Libr. Fedn. Coords. (spokesperson 1991), Mont. Telecommunications Adv. Coun., Iowa Libr. Assn. (exec. bd. 1989-90, govtl. affairs com. 1985-87, chair 1986-87, exec. asst. rels. com. 1989-90, assn. coll. rsch. libr. pub. libr. forum 1989-90, local hist. round table chair 1985), Iowa Blue Ribbon Task Force on Librs., State Libr. of Iowa Regional Libr. Study Com., Iowa Libr. Friends (bd. dirs. 1985-87, legis. liaison com. chair 1985-87), Southwest Iowa Regional Libr. System Adv. Bd., White House Conf. on Libr. and Info. Svcs. (del.-at-large, personal topic discussion group, elected mem. of conf. recommendations com.), Libr. Admnstrn. and Mgmt. Assn. (govtl. affairs com. 1992—, pub. rels. sect., govtl. advocacy skills com. 1992—, program chair for 1994 Miami conf. 1992—, fundraising and fin. devel. sect. 1992—, libr. orgn. and mgmt. sect. 1992—, personnel admnstrn. sect. 1992—), Pub. Libr. Assn. (mktg. pub. libr. svcs. sect. 1992—), Writer's Voice of the YMCA (Billings chpt. steering com. 1991—), Rotary Internat. (rotarian com. 1992—). Office: Parmly Billings Library 510 N Broadway Billings MT 59101

COCKELL, WILLIAM ARTHUR, JR., naval officer; b. Oswego, N.Y., Aug. 12, 1929; s. William Arthur and Alice Amelia (Barlow) C. B.A., Ohio State U., 1950; M.A., cert. (Russian Inst. grantee), Columbia U., 1952; J.D. with distinction, (Henry M. Bates scholar; Jerome S. Freud scholar), U. Mich., 1959. Bar: Mich. 1961. Commd. ensign U.S. Navy, 1953, advanced through grades to rear adm., 1980; exec. asst. to comdr. Allied Forces, So. Europe, 1969-70; comdg. officer U.S.S. Farragut, 1970-71; head, strategic concepts section Office Chief of Naval Ops., Washington, 1972-73, exec. dir. Exec. Panel, spl. asst. to Chief of Naval Ops., 1974-75; comdr. Destroyer Squadron 13, 1975-77; asst. chief of staff (plans) CINCPACFLT, 1977-78; exec. asst. to chief Naval Ops., Washington, 1978-81; comdr. Cruiser-Destroyer Group Five, 1981-83; comdr. surface combatant force Seventh Fleet, 1982, 83; comdr. Task Force 71 (KAL-007 search and salvage force) Seventh Fleet, 1983; comdr. tng. command U.S. Pacific Fleet and dep. chief of staff for tng. CINCPACFLT, 1983-85; ret., 1986; dep. under sec. of def. for research and engring. Dept. Def., 1986; dep. asst. then spl. asst. to pres. for nat. security affairs, 1986-87, 87-88; sr. dir. def. policy NSC, 1987-88; corp. vice pres. Sci. Applications Internat. Corp., 1989—; bd. dirs. Ethics and Pub. Policy Ctr., Washington; mem. U.S. Def. Sci. Bd., Naval Intelligence Cons. Seminar; cons. to chmn. U.S. Joint Chiefs of Staff. Decorated D.S.M., Legion of Merit. Mem. U.S. Naval Inst., Soc. Nautical Research, Navy Records Soc., U.S. Strategic Inst., Am. Mil. Inst., Am. Assn. Advancement Slavic Studies, Naval Hist. Found., Ulysses S. Grant Assn., Order of Coif, Phi Beta Kappa, Pi Sigma Alpha. Episcopalian. Home: 3222 Browning St San Diego CA 92106 Office: 10260 Campus Point Dr San Diego CA 92121-1522

COCKRELL, FRANK BOYD, II, film production company executive; b. Redding, Calif., May 3, 1948; s. Alfred Marion Sr. and Blanche Delma (Webb) C.; m. Grace Marie Louise Whest, Sept. 20, 1986; children: Catherine, Francis V, Ross, Sabrina, Brooke, Amanda, Richard. AA, Shasta Jr. Coll., 1968; BS, Sacramento (Calif.) State U., 1970; postgrad., U. Pacific, 1970-72. Pres., chmn. Als Towing & Storage Co., Sacramento, 1976-78, Compacts Only Rental Cars, Sacramento, 1976-78; film producer, actor, comedian Sacramento, L.A. and Las Vegas, Nev., 1976—; pres., chmn. Cockrell Prodns., Inc., L.A., 1984—, Palm Spring Employment Agy., Inc., Palm Desert, Calif., 1986; chmn. Contractor's Surety and Fidelity Co., Ltd., CNR Constrn. Co., Inc., U.S. Mining Corp.; CEO First Am. Contractors Bonding Assn., Inc. Author: Vietnam History, 1970. Candidate Assembly 6th Dist. Rep. Party, Sacramento, 1974; mem. Sacramento Rep. Cen. Com., 1975-76, Calif. State Cen. Rep. Com., 1974-76. Bank of Am. scholar, 1966, Shasta Coll. scholar, 1967. Lodge: Optimists (pres. Sacramento chpt. 1975-76, lt. gov. 1976-77). Office: Cockrell Prodns Inc PO Box 1731 Studio City CA 91614-0731

COCKRUM, DAN JAMES, small business owner; b. Modesto, Calif., Jan. 4, 1945; s. Frank James and Phyllis (Clifton) C.; m. Suzanne Marie Nelson, Sept. 10, 1966; children: Sean James, Jason Daniel. BS in Mech. Engring., Calif. Poly. U., 1966; MBA, Stanislaus U., 1978. Mech. engr. Gen. Dynamics Corp., San Diego, 1966-67; distbn. engr. Pacific Gas & Electric Co., Sacramento, 1969-73; dist. supt. Pacific Gas & Electric Co., Modesto, Calif., 1973-80; div. engr. Pacific Gas & Electric Co., Stockton, Calif., 1980-85; area mgr. Pacific Gas & Electric Co., Antiock, Calif., 1985-86; ops. mgr. Pacific Gas & Electric Co., Modesto, 1986-87; pres. Calif. Water Labs., Modesto, 1987-89; gen. mgr. Western Regional Lab., Modesto, 1989-90; owner, founder Pro-10 Minute Oil Change, Modesto, 1979—; vice chmn. Stanislaus County Hazardous Waste Adv. Bd., Modesto, 1988—; dir., treas. Convenient Automotive Svc. Inst., Bethesda, Md., 1989-92. Contbr. articles to profl. jours. Patroller Nat. Ski Patrol, Dodge Ridge, Calif., 1991—; div. chmn. San Joaquin United Way, Stockton, Calif., 1980. 1st lt. U.S. Army, 1967-69, Vietnam. Named Div. Speaker of Yr., 1984; recipient Army Accommodation medal U.S. Army, 1969. Mem. Convenient Automotive Svc. Inst. (dir. 1989-92, pres. 1987-88), Modesto Engr. Club. Office: Pro 10 Minute Oil Change 3037 Sisk Rd Modesto CA 95350

COCKRUM, WILLIAM MONROE, III, investment banker, consultant, educator; b. Indpls., July 18, 1937; s. William Monroe C. II and Katherine J. (Jaqua) Moore; m. Andrea Lee Deering, Mar. 8, 1975; children: Catherine Anne, William Monroe IV. AB with distinction, DePauw U., 1959; MBA with distinction, Harvard U., 1961. With A.G. Becker Paribas Inc., L.A., 1961-84, mgr. nat. corp. fin. div., 1968-71, mgr. pvt. investments, 1971-74, fin. and adminstrv. officer, 1974-80, sr. v.p., 1975-78, vice chmn., 1978-84, also bd. dirs.; prin. William M. Cockrum & Assocs., L.A., 1984—; mem. faculty Northwestern U., 1961-63; vis. lectr. grad. sch. mgmt. UCLA, 1984-88, adj. prof., 1988—; bd. dirs. Knapp Communications Corp. Mem. Monterey Club (Palm Desert, Calif.), Deke Club (N.Y.C.), UCLA Faculty Club, Alisal Golf Club (Solvang, Calif.), Bel-Air Country Club (L.A.), Delta Kappa Epsilon.

CODDING, GEORGE ARTHUR, JR., political science educator; b. Salem, Oreg., June 23, 1923; s. George Arthur and Maude Fern (Corlies) C.; m. Yolanda Celeste Legnini, June 17, 1961; children: Christine Diane, George Arthur III, William Henry, Jennifer Celeste. Student, Willamette U., 1940-42; B.A., U. Wash., 1943, M.A., 1948; D. Polit. Sci, U. Geneva, 1952. Lectr. dept. polit. sci. U. Pa., 1953-55, asst. prof., 1955-61; assoc. prof. polit. sci. U. Colo., Boulder, 1961-65, prof. polit. sci., 1965—, chmn. dept., 1971-73, dir. B.A. in Internat. Affairs Program, 1977—; vis. prof. Grad. Inst. Internat. Studies U. Geneva, 1973-74; tech. sec. Internat. Telecommunications Union, 1949; cons. sec.-gen., 1964-65; cons. UNESCO, 1957-58, 73, Nat. Commn. Causes & Prevention of Violence, 1968-69, Australian Fedn. Comml. Broadcasters, 1973, Office Telecommunications, Dept. Commerce, 1975, Telecommunications Policy, Exec. Office of Pres., 1976-77, FCC, 1979, Internat. Inst. Communications, 1982, 84, 85, 88, 89, 92, 93; mem. adv. bd. Gen. Elec. Space Broadcast, 1967-70. Author: The International Telecommunication Union, 1952, Broadcasting Without Barriers, 1959, The Federal Government of Switzerland, 1961, The Universal Postal Union, 1964, Governing the Commune of Veyrier: Politics in Swiss Local Government, 1967, (with William Safran) Ideology and Politics: The Socialist Party of France, 1979, (with Anthony M. Rutkowski) The International Telecommunication Union in a Changing World, 1982, The Future of Satellite Communications, 1990; editorial bd.: Monograph Series in World Affairs, 1964-78, Telecommunications Policy, 1987—; mem. adv. bd.: Denver Jour. Internat. Law and Policy, 1971—. Exec. bd. Southeastern Pa. chpt. Ams. for Democratic Action. Served with USNR, 1943-46. Guggenheim fellow, 1958-59; Faculty fellow U. Colo., 1965-66, 73-74; SSRC Behavioral Scis. Evaluation Panel; NSF grad. fellow, 1969-73; NSF grantee, 1979-80. Mem. Am., Internat. polit. sci. assns., Internat. Studies Assn. (mem. governing council 1972-73, pres. West 1972-73), Am. Soc. Internat. Law, Pi Sigma Alpha. Club: Trout Unlimited (pres. 1976). Home: 6086 Simmons Dr Boulder CO 80303-3032

CODDINGTON, IQBAL JWAIDEH, anthropology educator; b. Baghdad, Iraq, Nov. 25, 1935; d. Abdul Massih Elias and Jamila Jwaideh; m. Joseph Mark Coddington, June 20, 1970 (div. 1990). BA in English Lit., Baghdad U., 1955; two diplomas in Edn., London U., 1961, 62; MSc in Edn., Ind. U., 1964, MA in Antrhopology, 1970, PhD in Anthropology, 1980. Cert. tchr. Calif. community colls. Adj. asst. prof. Okla. U., Norman, 1981-85; administr., reseacher Arab Gulf State Folklore Ctr., Qatar, Persian Gulf, 1985-87; asst. prof. DeAnga Coll., Cupertino, Calif., 1988-89; post doctoral scholar, researcher U. Calif., Berkeley, 1988—; prof. Cogswell Coll., Cupertino, Calif., 1990—; vis. scholar U. Calif., Berkeley, 1988—; pub. lectr., participant pub. seminars and confs. Co-chmn. internat. visitors com. Neighbors Abroad, Palo Alto, Calif., 1988—. Mem. AAUW (chmn. relation com. 1988-89, chmn. women's health issues com. 1990, bd. dirs., chmn. cultural diversity com. 1991—), Am. Anthrop. Assn., Mid. East Studies Assn., Assn. Mid. East Women's Studies. Democrat. Roman Catholic. Home: PO Box 60417 Palo Alto CA 94306-0417

CODIKOW, STACY E., film producer; b. L.A., Feb. 12, 1964. BA, U. So. Calif., 1984. Producer, coord. Cagney & Lacey, LA, 1984-86; tchr. U. So. Calif. Seminars, L.A., 1990. Producer: (feature films) Hollywood Heartbreak, 1987, Fatal Instinct, To Kill for, 1991, (video) Video Roommate, 1988. Mem. Women in Film, Ind. Features Project, Univ. So. Calif. Cinema Alumni Assn. Office: Nucleus Entertainment 1093 Broxton Ave Ste 602 Los Angeles CA 90024

CODY, MICHAEL ALBERT, university administrator; b. Elmhurst, Ill., Jan. 3, 1934; s. William James and Ruth Muriel (Helton) C.; m. Waltraud Maria Ebert, Dec. 23, 1958 (div. Sept. 1973); children: Doris Jean, Michele Marlene, Angela Maria; m. Gretchen Anne Rogers, July 13, 1974; children: Michaelli Daun, Kimberly Leigh. BA, Bradley U., 1955, MA, 1956; MAS, U. Ala., Huntsville, 1974; postgrad., Command and Staff Coll., 1971, Def. Systems Mgmt. Coll., 1976, U.S. Army War Coll., 1981. Enlisted U.S. Army, advanced through grades to col.; ret. brig. gen. N.Mex. State Guard; with Command and Staff Coll., 1971; dir. U.S. Army War Res. Hdqrs. Dept. Army, Washington, 1974-77; with Defense Systems Mgmt. Coll., 1976; comdr. maintenance depot 8th Maintenance Bn., Hanau, Germany, 1977-79; dep. dir. logistics Fifth U.S. Corps, Frankfort, Germany, 1979-80; with U.S. Army War Coll., 1981; dir. material mgmt. U.S. Army Missile Command, Redstone Arsenal, Ala., 1981-84; dir. logistics Def. Nuclear Agy., Albuquerque, 1984-87; exec. dir. United Way of Santa Fe (N.Mex.), 1988-89; dir. mil. and govt. affairs, instr. U. Phoenix, Albuquerque, 1988-91; asst. dir., adj. prof. Grad. Ctr. Webster U., Albuquerque, 1991—; mgmt. and communications cons., 1990—. Contbr. articles to profl. jours. State chmn. Congl. Medal of Honor Soc. Heroes Program, N.Mex., 1990—; mem. N.Mex. State Com., Employer Support Guard and Res., 1989—. Recipient Profiles of Courage award Vietnam Vets. Am., N.Mex., 1990, Patriotism award Congl. Medal of Honor Soc., 1989. Mem. Assn. U.S. Army (pres. exec. bd. 1985-93, partiotism award 1988), Mil. Order World Wars (adjutant 1988-89, patriotism award 1989), Vietnam Vets. N.Mex., Ret. Officers Assn., Greater Albuquerque C. of C. (chmn. mi. rels. com. 1990, 91, 92, Superior Svc. award 1991, 93, Achievement award 1992). Home: 1716 Singletary Dr NE Albuquerque NM 87112-4842 Office: Webster U Ste B-395 8500 Menaul NE Albuquerque NM 87112

COE, GAIL ALLISON, restaurant executive; b. Denver, Oct. 15, 1960; d. Fred Capron and Bernice Charlotte (Behrens) C.; m. M. Nickolai Mathison, July 21, 1985. BS in Econs., UCLA, 1986. Fin. mgr. Bycel, Grey & Plebuch, Santa Barbara, Calif., 1983-84; contr. Nipper's div. Internat. Source Mgmt., Beverly Hills, Calif., 1984-87; pres. Lahaina Coolers Restaurant & Bar div. Coe Mgmt. Inc., Lahaina, Hawaii, 1989—, Kona Coolers Restaurant & Bar div. Coe Mgmt. Inc., Waikoloa, Hawaii, 1992—. Bd. dirs. Lahaina Town Action Com., 1990-91; originator Historic Lahaina Fun Run, 1990, 91;; me. Aloha Festivals Com., Maui, 1991. Mem. West Maui Taxpayers Assn., NOW, C. of C. Republican. Office: Lahaina Coolers Restaurant 180 Dickenson St Lahaina HI 96761

COE, MARGARET LOUISE SHAW, community service volunteer; b. Cody, Wyo., Dec. 25, 1917; d. Ernest Francis and Effie Victoria (Abrahamson) Shaw; m. Henry Huttleston Rogers Coe, Oct. 8, 1943 (dec. Aug. 1966); children: Anne Rogers Hayes, Henry H.R., Jr., Robert Douglas II. AA, Stephens Coll., 1937; BA, U. Wyo., 1939. Asst. to editor The Cody Enterprise, 1939-42, editor, 1968-71. Chmn. bd. trustees Buffalo Bill Hist. Ctr., Cody, 1966—, Cody Med. Found., 1964—; commr. Wyo. Centenniel Commn., Cheyenne, 1986-91. Recipient The Westerner award Old West Trails Found., 1980, Gold Medallion award Nat. Assn. Sec. of State, 1982, Disting. Alumni award U. Wyo, 1984, Govs. award for Arts, 1988; inducted Hall of Fame Nat. Cowgirl Hall of Fame, 1983. Mem. P.E.O., Delta Delta Delta. Republican. Episcopalian. Home: 1400 11th St Cody WY 82414-4206

COE, WILLIAM CHARLES, psychology educator; b. Hanford, Calif., Oct. 22, 1930; s. Bernard and Bertha (Vaughan) C.; m. Charlene L. Brown; children: Karen Ann, William Vaughan. B.S., U. Calif., Davis, 1958; postgrad., Fresno State Coll., 1960-61; Ph.D. (NSF fellow), U. Calif., Berkeley, 1964. Rsch. helper Fresno State Coll., 1960-61; rsch. asst. U. Calif., Berkeley, 1961-62, 63-64; NSF rsch. fellow U. Calif., 1963-64; clin. psychology trainee VA Hosp., San Francisco, 1962-63; staff psychologist Langley Porter Neuropsychiat. Inst., San Francisco, 1964-66; pvt. practice psychology Fresno, Calif., 1965-88; asst. clin. prof. med. psychology U. Calif. Sch. Medicine, San Francisco, 1965-66; instr. corr. div. U. Calif., Berkeley, 1967-76; asst. prof. psychology Fresno State Coll., 1966-68; assoc. prof. psychology Calif. State U., Fresno, 1968-72; prof. Calif. State U., 1972—, chmn. dept. psychology, 1979-84; instr. Calif. Sch. Profl. Psychology, Fresno, 1973, Northeastern U., Boston, 1974; research assoc. U. Calif., Santa Cruz, 1975; cons. Tulare and Kings County Mental Health Clinics, Kingsview Corp., 1966-68, Visalia Unified Sch. Dist., 1967-68; Head Start Program, Fresno, 1970-71, Fig Garden Hosp., Fresno, 1972-73, Concentrated Employment Program, Fresno, 1973-74, VA Hosp., Fresno, 1974; vis. prof.U. Queensland, Australia, 1982. Author: (with T.R. Sarbin) The Student Psychologists Handbook: A Guide to Source, 1969, Hypnosis: A Social Psychological Analysis of Influence Communication, 1972, Challenges of Personal Adjustment, 1972, (with L. Gagnon and D. Swiercinsky) instructors Manual for Challenges of Personal Adjustment, 1972, Psychology X118: Psychological Adjustment, 1973, (with T.R. Sarbin) Mastering Psychology, 1984; Contbr.: chpts. to Behavior Modification in Rehabiliation Settings, 1975, Helping People Change, 1975, 80, Encyclopedia of Clinical Assessment, 1980, Hypnosis: The Cognitive-Behavioral Perspective, 1989, Hypnosis: Current Theory, Research and Practice, 1990, Theories of Hypnosis: Current Models and Perspectives, 1991, Contemporary Hypnosis Research, 1992; contbr. articles to profl. jours. Served with USAF, 1951-55. Decorated D.F.C., Air medal with oak leaf cluster.; NSF grantee, 1967, 71. Fellow Am. Psychol. Assn. (pres. div. 30 psychol. hypnosis 1986-87), Soc. for Clin. and Exptl. Hypnosis; mem. Western Psychol Assn., Calif. Psychol Assn., San Francisco Psychol Assn. (editor San Francisco Psychologist 1966), Central Calif. Psychol. Assn. (pres. 1969, dir. 1972-73), Assn. for Advancement Behavior Therapy, Phi Beta Kappa, Sigma Xi, Phi Kappa Phi, Psi Chi. Office: Calif State U Dept Psychology Dept Psychology Fresno CA 93740-0011

COELHO, TONY, former congressman; b. Los Banos, Calif., June 15, 1942; s. Otto and Alice (Branco) C.; m. Phyllis Butler, June 10, 1967; children: Nicole, Kristin. B.A., Loyola U., Los Angeles, 1964. Agr. asst. to Rep. B.F. Sisk, 1965-70, adminstrv. asst., 1970-78; mem. 96th-101st Congresses from 15th Calif. Dist., 1979-89; chmn. Dem. Congl. Campaign Com., 1981-87; majority whip 100th, 101st Congress, 1987-89; resigned, 1989; mng. dir. Wertheim Schroder & Co., Inc.; pres., CEO Wertheim Schroder Investment Svcs., Inc.; bd. dirs. Circus Circus Enterprises, Inc., Condyne Tech. Inc., ICF Internat., Inc., Inst. for Lab. Medicine Inc., Svc. Corps. Internat., Tanknology Environ. Inc., United Medicorp Inc. V.p., bd. dirs. Epilepsy Found. Am. Roman Catholic. Office: 787 7th Ave Fl 5 New York NY 10019-6018

COFER, BERDETTE HENRY, public management consulting company executive; b. Las Flores, Calif.; s. William Walter and Violet Ellen (Elam) C.; m. Ann McGarva, June 27, 1954 (dec. Feb. 20, 1990); children: Sandra Lea Cofer-Oberle, Ronald William; m. Sally Ann Shepherd, June 12, 1993. AB, Calif. State U., Chico, 1950; MA, U. Calif., Berkeley, 1960. Tchr. Westwood (Calif.) Jr.-Sr. High Sch., 1953-54, Alhambra High Sch., Martinez, Calif., 1954-59; prin. adult and summer sch. Hanford (Calif.) High Sch., 1959-60, asst. supt. bus., 1960-67; dean bus. svcs. West Hills Coll., Coalinga, 1967-76; vice chancellor Yosemite Community Coll. Dist., Modesto, 1976-88; pres. BHC Assocs., Inc., Modesto, 1988—; chmn. Valley Ins. Program Joint Powers Agy., Modesto, 1986-88. Contbr. articles to profl. publs. Pres. Coalinga Indsl. Devel. Corp., 1972-74, Assn. for Retarded Citizens, Modesto, 1985; mayor City of Coalinga, 1974-76; foreman Stanislaus County Grand Jury, Modesto, 1987-88. 1st lt. USAF, 1951-53. Recipient Outstanding Citizen award Coalinga C. of C., 1976, Walter Starr Robie Outstanding Bus. Officer award Assn. Chief Bus. Officers Calif. Community Colls., 1988. Mem. Assn. Calif. C. C. Adminstrs. (life), Commonwealth Club Calif. (San Francisco), Elks, Lions (dist. gov. 1965-66), Phi Delta Kappa (pres. Kings-Tulare chpt. 1962-63). Democrat. Home and Office: 291 Leveland Ln # 2 Modesto CA 95350-2255

COFER, SUZANNE MARIE, educator; b. Wenatchee, Wash., Oct. 29, 1948; d. Earl Raymond Anthony and Wanda Elaine (Haworth) Desilet; m. Donald Frank Cofer, Aug. 30, 1975. BA in English Edn., Wash. State U., 1971; MPA, U. Wash., 1986. Cert. elem. and secondary educator. Tchr. Horsham (Australia) High Sch., 1972-74, Blaine (Wash.) High Sch., 1974-77, Fife (Wash.) High Sch., 1977-78; part-time faculty, program mgr. Pierce Coll., Tacoma, 1978-80; adminstrv. asst. Wash. State Ho. of Reps., Olympia, 1981-84; rsch. analyst Wash State Ho. of Reps., Olympia, 1987-89; coun. mem. City of Tumwater, Wash., 1990—; tchr. New Century High Sch., Lacey, Wash., 1992—. Del. Dem. Nat. Conv., San Francisco, 1984; chair Pub. Safety Com. City of Tumwater, 1991—. Mem. Wash. State Hist. Soc., Nat. Trust for Hist. Preservation, Tumwater C. of C. Democrat. Office: City of Tumwater 555 Israel Road SW Tumwater WA 98512 also: New Century High Sch 8929 Martin Way E Olympia WA 98516-5932

COFFEY, KATHRYN R(OBINSON) (KAY COFFEY), civic worker; m. Clarence W. Coffey; children: Clarence William, Kathryn Ann. BS in Govt., West Tex. State U., 1937; HHD (hon.), Northwestern State U., Natchitoches, La., 1987. Active Lakeview Presbyn. Ch., New Orleans, 1944—, deacon, 1968-71, bd. dirs. kindergarten and nursery sch., 1965-68; mem. com. on home and family nurture Presbytery South La., 1967-69; mem. exec. com., chmn. dept. relation to pub. schs. Greater New Orleans Fedn. Chs., 1970-76; mem. Presbyn. campus life com. Presbytery New Orleans, 1978-82; mem. various coms. Orleans Parish (La.) Sch. Bd., 1953-77; active PTA, including bd. dirs. New Orleans Council, 1956-75, pres., 1965-67, v.p., chmn. legis. services and pres. Dist One La., 1967-72, mem. legis. com. Nat. Congress, 1969-72; mem. New Orleans Pub. Library Bd., 1956-62; v.p., chmn. membership com. Civic Council New Orleans, 1952-75; organizer, exec. sec. New Orleans Citizens for Support of Pub. Schs., 1968-76; bd. dirs., mem. coms. La. Assn. Mental Health, 1968-71; mem. juvenile delinquency com. La. Commn. Law Enforcement and Adminstrn. Criminal Justice, 1968-70; pres. La. Orgns. for State Legis., 1972-76; com. mem., bd. dirs. regional adv. group La. Regional Med. Program Inc., 1970-76; numerous activites for gifted edn. and spl. edn., including: founder, v.p., legis. chmn. Greater New Orleans Spl. Edn. PTA, 1971-77; mem. exec. com. La. Adv. Council for Learning Disabilities, 1972-76; co-chmn. Speak Out for Spl. Children, New Orleans, 1972-77; mem. Task Force for Implementation of Act 368 of 1972, La., 1972-76; spl. hearing officer Fed. Dist. Ct., New Orleans, 1973-77; chmn. La. Adv. Com. for Gifted and Talented, 1973-76; pres., organizer Assn. Gifted and Talented Students Inc., 1973-86; editor newsletter, 1973-81, contbg. editor, 1981-87; com. mem., chmn. nomination com. La. Gov.'s 4-C Policy Bd., 1974-77; project reader Office Gifted and Talented, Office Edn., 1975-76; mem. La. Coalition on Handicapped, 1975-88; mem. U. New Orleans Task Force on Gifted and Talented, 1976-82; regional rep. La. Gov.'s White House Conf. on Handicapped, 1977; bd. dirs. Nat. Assn. Gifted Children, 1977-86; mem. La. Gov.'s Adv. Com. on Edn. of Handicapped, 1978-81; mem. adv. bd. Gifted Advocacy Info. Network, 1979-83; mem. adv. bd. Inst. Gifted and Talented Edn., N.J. Dept. Edn., 1978-81; rev. editor Jour. Edn. of Gifted, Assn. for Gifted, 1980-82; vice-chmn. bd. dirs. La. Sch. for Math., Sci. and the Arts, Natchitoches, 1981-85, chmn. bd., 1985-87; mem. adv. bd. Gifted Children's Newsletter, 1981—; mem. Gov.'s Adv. Com. Ednl. Block Grants. Mem. Gov.'s Commn. on Law Enforcement and Adminstrn., Criminal Justice, Juvenile Delinquency Com., 1970. Recipient Life Membership in La. PTA, Edward Hynes PTA, 1954; cert. of merit Mayor New Orleans, 1969; life Membership of Nat. Congress Parents and Tchrs., New Orleans Council PTA's, 1970; award for outstanding service Gov.'s Commn. on Law Enforcement and Adminstrn. Criminal Juvenile Deliquency Com., 1970; Outstanding Scouter award Greater New Orleans Fedn. Chs., 1972, Outstanding Citizen award Council Exceptional Children, 1974; award for outstanding service Dir. Office Gifted and Talented, Office Edn., 1976; award of appreciation Assn. Gifted and Talented Students, 1980, award for outstanding service Isnt. Gifted and Talented Edn., N.J. Dept. Edn., 1980; named Hon. Senator, Lt. Gov. and Pres. of La. Senate, 1975; award for outstanding service Inst. Arts and Humanities Inc., Kansas City, Mo., 1982; Conv. Parent of Yr., Nat. Assn. Gifted Children, 1982; award for service to bd. dirs. Nat. Assn. Gifted Children, 1987; Spl. Edn. Pioneer award for outstanding contbn. to edn. for children La. Dept. Edn., 1987; Kathryn Robinson Day declared by Mayor of Natchitoches, Nov. 19, 1987; awarded "hon. student" status, 1987; awarded 9th degree award Northwestern State U. La., Natchitoches, 1987; U. New Orleans Library designated Kay Coffey Archives, 1987; Kay Coffey Libr. of Benjamin Franklin Hi Sch., New Orleans, named in her honor, 1987. Home: 6400 Sealpoint Ct Rancho Palos Verdes CA 90274-5870

COFFEY, SHELBY, III, newspaper editor. Editor, exec. v.p. L.A. Times. Office: Los Angeles Times Times Mirror Sq Los Angeles CA 90053

COFFILL, MARJORIE LOUISE, civic leader; b. Sonora, Calif., June 11, 1917; d. Eric J. and Pearl (Needham) Segerstrom; A.B. with distinction in Social Sci., Stanford U., 1938, M.A. in Edn., 1941; m. William Charles Coffill, Jan. 25, 1948, (dec.); children: William James, Eric John. Asst. mgr. Sonora Abstract & Title Co. (Calif.), 1938-39; mem. dean of women's staff Stanford, 1939-41; social dir. women's campus Pomona Coll., 1941-43, instr. psychology, 1941-43; asst. to field dir. ARC, Lee Moore AFB, Calif., 1944-46; partner Riverbank Water Co., Riverbank and Hughson, Calif., 1950-68. Mem. Tuolumne County Mental Health Adv. Com., 1963-70; mem. central advisory coun. Supplementary Edn. Ctr., Stockton, Calif., 1966-70; mem.

advisory com. Columbia Jr. Coll., 1972-89, pres., 1980—; pres. Columbia Found., 1972-74, bd. dirs., 1974-77; mem. Tuolumne County Bicentennial Com., 1974—; active PTA, ARC. Pres., Tuolumne County Rep. Women, 1952—, assoc. mem. Calif. Rep. Central Com., 1950. Trustee Sonora Union High Sch., 1969-73, Salvation Army Tuolumne County, 1973—; bd. dirs. Lung Assn. Valley Lode Counties, 1974—, life 1986—. Recipient Pi Lambda Theta award, 1940; Outstanding Citizen award C. of C., 1974, Citizen of Yr. award, 1987; named to Columbia Coll. Hall of Fame, 1990. Mem. AAUW (charter mem. Tuolumne County br., pres. Sonora br. 1965-66). Episcopalian (mem. vestry 1968, 75). Home: 376 Summit Ave Sonora CA 95370-5728

COFFIN, DAVID R., networking executive; b. Indpls., Nov. 21, 1954; s. Forrest Hill and Ann (Pardee) C.; m. Kala J. Marietta, May 31, 1980. BSEE with honors, Lehigh U., 1976; MS in Systems Engrng. with honors, Ariz. State U., 1979; MBA, Harvard Bus. Sch., 1982. Computer engr. Honeywell Info. Systems, Phoenix, 1976-80; product line mgr. Gould/Modicon, Andover, Mass., 1980-81; mktg. mgr. Intel/System Group, Phoenix, 1982-86; dir., gen. mgr. Bull/Networked MicroSystems, Phoenix, 1986-91; pres., CEO irys Networking Corp., Phoenix, 1991—; chmn. Sonoran Vista, Phoenix, 1987-; speaker various seminars. Author: Availability Analysis of Distributed Information Networks, 1979; contbr. articles to profl. jours. Active various charities, Phoenix, 1988—. Recipient electrical engr. honors Eta Kappa Nu, 1976, system engr. honors Alpha Pi Mu, 1979.

COFFIN, HAROLD WALTER, lawyer; b. Benson, Minn., Aug. 8, 1908; s. Alecander and Ella Beatrice (Devereux) C.; m. Virginia Lee Maguire, Aug. 10, 1938; children: Sara Lee Coffin Fernandez, Melissa Ray Coffin Willis. Student, Kenyon Coll., 1926-27; BA, U. Idaho, 1930, LLB, 1933. Atty., sec. Vermont Loan & Trust Co., 1938-40; ptnr., of counsel Paine, Hamblen, Coffin, Brooke & Miller, Spokane, Wash., 1940—. Trustee Comstock Found., 1972—, Ea. Wash. State Hist. Soc.; pres., bd. dirs. Ea. Wash. Mus. Found., Spokane, 1984—; chancellor Episc. Diocese of Spokane, 1975—. Fellow ABA (ho. of dels. 1949-51); mem. Am. Coll. Probate Counsel, Wash. State Bar Assn. (pres. 1950-51, bd. govs. 1947-49), Spokane County Bar Assn. (pres. 1945). Republican.

COFFIN, THOMAS M., judge; b. St. Louis, May 30, 1945; s. Kenneth C. and Agnes M. (Ryan) C.; m. Penelope Teaff, Aug. 25, 1973; children: Kimberly, Laura, Colleen, Corey, Mary, Brendan, T.J. BA, St. Benedict's Coll., 1967; JD, Harvard, 1970. Bar: Mo. 1970, Calif. 1972, Oreg. 1982, U.S. Dist. Ct. (so. dist.) Calif. 1971, U.S. Dist. Ct. Oreg. 1980, U.S. Ct. Appeals (9th cir.) 1971. Asst. U.S. atty., chief criminal divsn. U.S. Attys. Office, San Diego, 1971-80; asst. U.S. atty., supr. asst. U.S. atty. U.S. Attys. Office, Eugene, Oreg., 1980-92; U.S. Magistrate judge U.S. Dist. Ct., Eugene, Oreg., 1992—; sr. litigation counsel U.S. Dept. Justice, 1984. Mem. Oreg. Bar Assn. Office: US Dist Ct 211 E 7th Ave Eugene OR 97401

COFFINGER, MARALIN KATHARYNE, retired air force officer, consultant; b. Ogden, Iowa, July 5, 1935; d. Cleo Russell and Katharyne Frances (McGovern) Morse. BA, Ariz. State U., 1957, MA, 1961; diploma, Armed Forces Staff Coll., 1972, Nat. War Coll., 1977; postgrad., Inst. for Higher Def. Studies, 1985. Commd. 2nd lt. USAF, 1963, advanced through grades to brig. gen., 1985; base comdr., dep. base comdr. Elmendorf AFB, Anchorage, Alaska, 1977-79; base comdr. Norton AFB, San Bernardino, Calif., 1979-82; chmn. spl. and incentive pays Office of Sec. Def., Pentagon, Washington, 1982-83; dep. dir. pers. programs USAF Hdqrs., Pentagon, Washington, 1983-85; command dir. NORAD, Combat Ops., Cheyenne Mountain Complex, Colo., 1985-86; dir. pers. plans USAF Hdqrs., Pentagon, Washington, 1986-89; ret. USAF, 1989. Bd. dirs. Ariz. Epilepsy Soc., Phoenix, 1989-90; mem., dedication ceremonies keynote speaker Vietnam Meml. Com., Phoenix, 1990. Decorated Air Force D.S.M., Def. Superior Svc. medal, Legion of Merit, Bronze Star.; recipient Nat. Medal of Merit. Mem. NAFE, Air Force Assn. (pres. Sky Harbor chpt. 1990), Nat. Officers Assn., Ret. Officers Assn., Internat. Platform Assn., Ariz. State U. Alumni Assn. (Profl. Excellence award 1981). Roman Catholic. Home: 8531 E San Bruno Dr Scottsdale AZ 85258-2577

COFIELD, PHILIP THOMAS, educational association administrator; b. Monmouth, Ill., July 3, 1951; s. Earl Crescant and Vera (Shunick) C.; m. Louise Ann Trapkus, June 13, 1981; children: Calla, Megan. BA in English, St. Ambrose U., 1973. Dir. Jr. Achievment of Quad Cities, Davenport, Moline, Iowa, Ill., 1980-83; account exec. Jr. Achievment Inc., 1983-85; pres., chief exec. officer Jr. Achievment of Utah, Salt Lake City, 1985—. Established Utah Bus. Hall of Fame, 1991. Mem. Utah Coun. on Economic Edn. (bd. dirs.), Salt Lake area C. of C., Rotary Club, (com. co-chmn. Salt Lake City). Office: Jr Achievment of Utah 182 S 600 E Salt Lake City UT 84102-1909

COGGIN, CHARLOTTE JOAN, cardiologist, educator; b. Takoma Park, Md., Aug. 6, 1928; d. Charles Benjamin and Nanette (McDonald) Coggin; BA, Columbia Union Coll., 1948; MD, Loma Linda U., 1952, MPH, 1987; Intern, Los Angeles County Gen. Hosp., Los Angeles, 1952-53, resident in medicine, 1953-55; fellow in cardiology Children's Hosp., Los Angeles, 1955-56, White Meml. Hosp., Los Angeles., 1955-56; research assoc. in cardiology, house physician Hammersmith Hosp., London, 1956-57; resident in pediatrics and pediatric cardiology Hosp. for Sick Children, Toronto, Ont., Can., 1965-67; cardiologist, co-dir. heart surgery team Loma Linda (Calif.) U., asst. prof. medicine, 1961-73, assoc. prof., 1973-91, prof. medicine, 1991—, asst. dean Sch. Medicine Internat. Programs, 1973-75, assoc. dean, 1975—, spl. asst. to univ. pres. for internat. affairs, 1991, co-dir., cardiologist heart surgery team missions to Pakistan and Asia, 1963, Greece, 67, 69, Saigon, Vietnam, 1974, 75, to Saudi Arabia, 1976-87, People's Republic China, 1984, 89-91, Hong Kong, 1985, Zimbabwe, 1988, Kenya, 1988, Nepal, 1992, China, 1992, Zimbabwe, 1993; mem. Pres's. Advisory Panel on Heart Disease, 1972—; hon. prof. U. Manchuria, Harbin, People's Republic China, 1989, hon. dir. 1st People's Hosp. of Mundanjiang, Heilongjiang Province, 1989. Apptd. mem. Med. Quality Rev. Com.-Dist. 12, 1976-80. Recipient award for service to people of Pakistan City of Karachi, 1963, Medallion award Evangelismos Hosp., Athens, Greece, 1967, Gold medal of health South Vietnam Ministry of Health, 1974, Charles Elliott Weinger award for excellence, 1976, Wall Street Jour. Achievement award, 1987, Disting. Univ. Svc. award Loma Linda U., 1990; named Honored Alumnus Loma Linda U. Sch. Medicine, 1973, Outstanding Women in Gen. Conf. Seventh-day Adventists, 1975, Alumnus of Yr., Columbia Union Coll., 1984. Diplomate Am. Bd. Pediatrics. Mem. Am. Coll. Cardiology, AMA (physicians adv. com. 1969—) Calif. Med. Assn. (com. on med. schs., com. on member services), San Bernardino County Med. Soc. (chmn. communications com. 1975-77, mem. communications com. 1987-88, editor bull. 1975-76), Am. Heart Assn., AAUP, Med. Research Assn. Calif., Calif. Heart Assn., AAUW, Am. Acad. Pediatrics, World Affairs Council, Internat. Platform Assn., Calif. Museum Sci. and Industry MUSES (Outstanding Woman of Year in Sci. 1969), Am. Med. Women's Assn., Loma Linda Sch. Medicine Alumni Assn. (pres. 1978), Alpha Omega Alpha, Delta Omega. Author: Atrial Septal Defects, motion picture (Golden Eagle Cine award and 1st prize Venice Film Festival 1964); contbr. articles to med. jours. Democrat. Home: 11495 Benton St Loma Linda CA 92354-3682 Office: Loma Linda U Med Ctr Loma Linda CA 92354

COGGINS, DOUGLAS EDWARD, lawyer; b. Plainfield, N.J., June 7, 1955; s. John Thomas Jr. and Margaret Helen (Rapp) C. AB, U. Calif., Berkeley, Calif., 1977; JD, U. San Diego, 1981. Dep. pub. defender Orange County Pub. Defender, Santa Ana, Calif., 1982-88; lawyer, sole practice Irvine, Calif., 1989—. Named Regents scholar U. Calif. Berkeley, 1972. Mem. Calif. State Bar Assn., Orange County Bar Assn. Democrat. Roman Catholic. Home: 323 14th St #3 Huntington Beach CA 92648

COGGINS, FRANK EDWARD, lawyer, military institute administrator; b. Paris, Tex., Nov. 8, 1946; s. Homer Dale and Dorothy Ann (Murrell) C.; m. Theresa Marie Borgman, Aug. 14, 1981 (div. 1983); m. Judy Hardage, Aug. 24, 1989 (div. 1990). AA, N.Mex. Mil. Inst., 1967; BBA, U. Ky., 1969, JD, 1975. Bar: Ky. Asst. treas. Liberty Nat. Bank (formerly United Ky. Bank), Louisville, 1975-78; atty., ptnr. Coggins, Watson & Llewellan, Louisville, 1978-80; sec., gen. counsel Andalex Resources, Inc., Louisville, 1980-85; mgr. Berco Ltd., Hamilton, Bermuda, 1986-88; asst. v.p. devel. N.Mex. Mil. Inst., Roswell, 1988-92, adj., legal advisor, 1992—. Chmn. planned giving Ea. N.Mex. Med. Ctr. Found., Roswell, 1990—. With USN, 1969-72, Japan/Far East. Mem. Ky. Bar Assn., Chaves County (N.Mex.) Bar Assn., Roswell Country Club, Royal Bermuda Yacht Club, Pecos Valley Rotary (pres.-elect 1992-93). Republican. Baptist. Office: NMex Mil Inst 101 W College Blvd Roswell NM 88201

COGHILL, JOHN BRUCE, state official; b. Fairbanks, Alaska, Sept. 24, 1925; s. William Alexander and Winefred (Fortune) C.; m. Frances Mae Gilbert, 1948; children: Patricia, John Jr., James, Jerald, Paula, Jeffry. Grad. high sch., Nenana, Alaska. Ptnr. Coghill's Inc., Nenana, Alaska, 1948—; owner Tortella Lodge & Apts., 1951, J.B. Coghill Oil Co., 1958-87, Nenana Fuel Co., 1960-87; mem. from senate dist. J Alaska State Legislature, Juneau, 1959-64, 85-90; chmn. resources com., chmn. majority caucus, vice chmn. transp., mem. oil and gas com., spl. joint com. on tax policy, nre revenue work group and fin. budget subcommittees on DNR, DEC and fish & game; lt. gov. State of Alaska, 1990—; mayor City of Nenana, 1962-84; ptnr. Coghill's, Inc.; sec. Nenana Industries, Nenana Fuel Co. Mem. sch. bd., 1948-59; mem. Alaskan territorial Ho. of Reps., 1953, 57, Alaska Constl. Conv., 1955; spl. asst. to gov. State of Alaska, 1967; sec. North Commn., 1968-72; chmn. Alaska Statehood Commn., 1980-83. Sgt. Alaska Command U.S. Army, 1944-46. Mem. VFW, Am. Legion, Eagle Hist. Soc., Pioneers of Alaska, Lions Club, Masons, Eagles, Moose. Office: Office of Lt Gov PO Box 110015 Juneau AK 99811-0015

COGHLAN, JAMES THOMAS, insurance executive; b. Rockville Centre, N.Y., Mar. 25, 1955; s. Gerald Joseph and Jean Theresa (Strype) C.; m. Wendy Suzanne Wines, Nov. 8, 1980; children: Colleen, Kevin, Megan. BS in Fin., Siena Coll., 1977. Comml. underwriter Sentry Ins., Scottsdale, Ariz., 1977-81, comml. large account underwriter, 1981-84, comml. sales/mktg. specialist, 1982-84, mass merchandising specialist, 1984-86, sales mgr., 1986—. Home: 104 Boomfield Way Folsom CA 95630

COGNATA, JOSEPH ANTHONY, football commissioner; b. Ashtabula, Ohio, Feb. 11, 1946; s. Joseph and Ella Jane (Dispense) C.; m. Betty Jean Jacobs, Dec. 17, 1978; children: Lisa Ann, Joseph Anthony Jr. Student, Kent State U., 1964-66. Sales rep. Endicott Buick, Pompano Beach, Fla., 1977-80; sales mgr. Fla. Chrysler Plymouth, West Palm Beach, Fla., 1980-82; owner, CEO So. States Football Club, Tequesta, Fla., 1982-85; backfield/spl. teams coach San Jose (Calif.) Bandits Minor League Football System, 1987-90; asst. head coach Calif. Outlaws Minor League Football System, Hayward, Calif., 1990-91; scout Profl. Spring Football League, Meadowlands, N.J., 1991-92; commr., co-founder golden West Football League, Sacramento, 1991—; commr. West Coast Amateur Football League, Mountain View, Calif., 1992—; pres., CEO, commr. Pacific Western Football Alliance, Sacramento, 1992—. Author: Complete Football Playbook, 1989. Lutheran. Home and Office: 107 S Mary Ave # 33 Sunnyvale CA 94086

COHAN, ANTHONY ROBERT, writer, publisher; b. N.Y.C., Dec. 28, 1939; s. Philip and Mary Helen (Foster) C.; m. Ruthane Capers, Apr. 15, 1965 (div. June 1971); m. Masako Takahashi, June 1, 1971; 1 child, Maya. BA, U. Calif., Santa Barbara, 1961. Author L.A., 1965—; pub. Acrobat Books, L.A., 1975—. Author: (fiction) Opium, 1984, Canary, 1981, Dreamtown, 1993, (essays) The Flame, 1981; lyricist for 8 albums, 1981—. Mem. ASCAP, NARAS, PEN (dir. Writers-in-Prison com. 1991-92), Authors Guild.

COHEN, ADAM LLOYD, inventor, composer; b. N.Y.C., Oct. 7, 1958; s. Leonard Wallis and Bernice Shiela (Cohen) Cohen. BS, MIT, 1985. Engr. Dataproducts Corp., Woodland Hills, Calif., 1986-87; project mgr. 3D Sysems, Inc., Valencia, Calif., 1987-91; publisher, editor, cons. F Cubed, L.A., 1991-92; v.p. R&D Soligen, Inc, Northridge, Calif., 1991—. Coauthor: (book) Rapid Prototyping and Manufacturing, 1992; editor, writer, founder (newsletter) Rapid Prototyping Report, 1991-92; editor, founder Rapid Prototyping Directory, 1991; inventor: resin film recoating for stereo lithography, 1992. Recipient fellowship MIT 1985, grant MIT 1985, grant MIT Coun for the Arts, 1985, Fulbright scholarship, London, 1985. Mem. Soc. of Mfg. Engrs. Office: Soligen Inc 19921 Bryant St Northridge CA 91324

COHEN, ALAN JAY, psychiatrist; b. Phila., Aug. 30, 1956; s. Harry Wallace and Shirley Vita (Berman) C.; m. Shannon Ruth Bowman, June 25, 1989; children: Brendan Harris, Hallie Patricia. BA, Oberlin Coll., 1978; MD, Jefferson Med. Coll., Phila., 1982. Diplomate Am. Bd. Psychiatry and Neurology. Resident U. Calif., San Francisco, 1982-86; fellow Inst. Pa. Hosp., Phila., 1987; pvt. practice Comprehensive Psychiat. Svcs., Walnut Creek, Calif., 1989—; asst. prof. psychiatry U. Calif., San Francisco, 1982-86; fellow Inst. Pa. Hosp., Phila., 1987; attending physician AIDS focus unit San Francisco Gen. Hosp., 1987-90, East Bay Hosp., Doctors Hosp., Brookside Hosp.; lectr. Franklin Inst. and Sci. Mus., Phila., 1975-76; med. rschr. Johns Hopkins U., 1976; dir. clin. rsch. East Bay Hosp., Richmond, Calif., 1991—; prin. rsch. investigator Burroughs-Wellcome. Contbr. articles to profl. jours. Lectr., cons. Family Night Workshops, San Francisco, 1988-90; musician Friends of the River, San Rafael, Calif., 1990. NSF fellow, 1978, NIH fellow, 1979; recipient Baldwin Keyes Psychiatry prize Jefferson Med. Coll., 1982. Mem. AMA, Am. Psychiat. Assn., North Calif. Psychiat. Soc., Am. Thyroid Found., Sigma Xi (assoc.). Office: Comprehensive Psychiat Svcs 37 Quail Ct Ste 200 Walnut Creek CA 94596-5595 also: 2340 Ward St # 201 Berkeley CA 94705

COHEN, ANNE CONSTANT, biologist; b. Durham, N.C., Mar. 1, 1935; d. Frank Woodbridge Constant and Carolyn Anne (Cook) Colwell; m. Daniel Morris Cohen, Nov. 4, 1955; children: Carolyn Annette Leech, Cynthia Sarah Cohen. BA, Stanford U., 1956; MS, U. Md., 1972; PhD, George Washington U., 1987. Waitress Stanford U., Palo Alto, Calif., 1953-56, rsch. asst., 1956; mus. technician Smithsonian Instn., Washington, 1963-66; teaching asst. U. Md., College Pk., 1969-70; mus. technician Smithsonian Instn., Washington, 1973-76, mus. specialist, 1976-82; project dir. Natural History Mus. L.A., 1987; postdoctoral fellow UCLA, 1987-91, biol. researcher, 1991—. Contbr. more than 21 rsch. articles to sci. jours. Grantee NSF, 1987-92, Mead Found., 1983-85, Learner-Gray Fund, 1981; recipient award for Exceptional Svcs., Smithsonian Instn., 1979, Antarctic Svc. medal NSF, 1967. Mem. Soc. Women Geographers, Western Soc. Naturalists, Crustacean Soc., Biol. Soc. of Washington (councillor 1980-81), Ctr. for Study of Evolution, Sigma Xi. Office: Natural History Mus of LA Div Life Science 900 Exposition Blvd Los Angeles CA 90007

COHEN, ARNOLD NORMAN, gastroenterologist; b. N.Y.C., Nov. 5, 1949; s. Norman and Edna Clara (Arnold) C.; m. Colleen Ruth Carey; children: Eric Arnold, Leslie Carey. BA summa cum laude, Hobart Coll., 1971; MD, Harvard U., 1975. Diplomate Am. Bd. Internal Medicine, Am. Bd. Gastroenterology. Resident internal medicine U. Pa., Phila., 1975-78, asst. instr. medicine, 1977-78; fellow gastroenterology, instr. medicine Northwestern U., Chgo., 1978-80; asst. clin. prof. medicine U. Wash. Med. Sch., Seattle, 1980—; mem. faculty Spokane (Wash.) Family Medicine Residency, 1980—; pvt. practice gastroenterology Spokane, 1980—; mem. various coms. St. Lukes-Deaconess Hosp., Spokane, 1980—; pres. med. staff St. Lukes Hosp., 1985-86. Contbr. articles to profl. jours. Fellow ACP, Am. Coll. Gastroenterology; mem. Am. Soc. Gastrointestinal Endoscopy, Am. Gastroent. Soc., Wash. Med. Soc., Spokane Internal Med. Soc., Phi Beta Kappa, Alpha Omega Alpha. Home: 3514 S Jefferson St Spokane WA 99203-1441 Office: Spokane Gastroenterology PS 801 W 5th Ave Spokane WA 99204-2823

COHEN, CLARENCE BUDD, aerospace engineer; b. Monticello, N.Y., Feb. 7, 1925; s. Isidor and Dora Cohen; m. Beatrice Sholofsky, Jan. 1, 1947; children: William David, Deborah Ann. BAE, Rensselaer Poly. Inst., 1945, MAE, 1947; MA, Princeton U., 1952, PhD, 1954. Aerospace research scientist NASA, Cleve., 1947-56; assoc. chief. spl. projects br. TRW Electronics and Def., Redondo Beach, Calif., 1957-87, head hypersonics research section, 1957-61; mgr. aerodynamics dept. TRW Electronics and Defense, Redondo Beach, Calif., 1961-63, mgr. aero scis. lab., 1966-69, dir. tech. application, 1970-80, dir. technology, 1980-87; cons. in field. Contbr. articles to profl. jours; patentee manned spacecraft with staged reentry. Trustee, vice chmn. Northrup U., 1991—; With USNR, 1943-46. Recipient Class of 1902 Rsch. Prize, Rensselaer Poly. Inst., 1945; Guggenheim fellow Princeton U., 1950-52. Fellow AIAA; mem. Licensing Execs. Soc., Research Soc. Am. (past pres.), Indsl. Research Inst. (emeritus), Sigma Xi. Club: King Harbor Yacht. Home: 332 Via El Chico Redondo Beach CA 90277-6756

COHEN, HARRY BRUCE, psychologist, educator; b. Bklyn., Mar. 1, 1938; s. Saul and Bessie (Levinson) C.; m. Adrienne Mann, Mar. 21, 1961; children: Jonathan Raphael, Alexander Benjamin. BA, Brandeis U., 1959; MA, McGill U., 1961, PhD, 1964. Lic. clin. psychologist, Calif. Post-doctoral fellow Stanford (Calif.) U. Coll. Medicine, 1964-66, rsch. assoc., 1966-68, asst. prof. Psychiatry, 1968-72; asst. prof. Psychiatry U. Calif., Irvine, 1972-80, adj. asst. prof. Psychiatry, 1980—; psychologist II Orange County Health Care Agy., Santa Ana, Calif., 1980—. Contbr. over 40 papers to sci. jours. Mem. APA (Rsch. award 1971), Sigma Xi, Brandeis U. Alumnae Orgn. (exec. com. So. Cal. chpt.). Office: 255 Thalia St Laguna Beach CA 92651

COHEN, JAMES ROBERT, oncologist, hematologist. BA in English Lit., Cornell U., 1967, MD, 1971. Diplomate Am. Bd. Internal Medicine, Am. Bd. Oncology. Intern N.Y. Hosp./Meml. Sloan Kettering Cancer Ctr., N.Y.C., 1971-72, resident in medicine, 1972-73; sr. resident in medicine U. Calif., San Francisco, 1973-74; postdoctoral fellow in hematology, oncology Stanford (Calif.) U. Sch. Medicine, 1976-78, clin. instr., 1978-85, clin. assoc. prof., 1986-93; pvt. practice San Jose, Calif., 1978—; clin. assoc. in medicine U. Nebr. Sch. Medicine, 1975-76; chmn. div. oncology Good Samaritan Hosp., 1981-83, dir. med. oncology, 1983—; bd. dirs. Hospice of the Valley, 1979-85, v.p. profl. svcs., 1981-83, pres. bd. dirs., 1983-85; clin. investigator No. Calif. Oncology Group, 1977-88; mem. regional steering com. Calif. Cancer Registry, 1987—, chmn., 1990-92. Contbr. articles to profl. jours. Maj. USAF, 1974-76. Fellow ACP; mem. ACS (liaison assoc. in cancer), AAAS, Santa Clara County Med. Soc., Calif. Med. Assn., Calif. Soc. Internal Medicine, Am. Soc. Internal Medicine, Am. Soc. Clin. Oncology, N.Y. Acad. Sci., Am. Acad. Med. Adminstrs., Am. Coll. Oncology Adminstrs., Alpha Omega Alpha. Home: 20585 Sprawling Oak Ct San Jose CA 95720 Office: 2410 Samaritan Dr San Jose CA 95124

COHEN, JEREMY PATRICK, lawyer; b. Grant, Nebr., Oct. 26, 1960; s. Gerald Morris and Carolyn (Ruth) C.; m. Mary Ellen Cohen, Dec. 19, 1987; 1 child, Maeve. BA, Creighton U., 1982; JD, U. Denver, 1986, LLM in Taxation, 1992. Bar: Colo. 1986, Nebr. 1992, U.S. Dist. Ct. Colo. 1987, U.S. Ct. Appeals (10th cir.) 1987. Assoc. Robinson, Waters, O'Dorisio & Rapson, Denver, 1986-89, Grant, McHendrie, Haines & Crouse, Denver, 1989-91, Kelley, Scritsmlr & Byrne, P.C., North Platte, Nebr., 1991-93; prin. Jeremy P. Cohen, P.C., Lakewood, Colo., 1993—. Mem. ABA, Colo. Bar Assn., Denver Bar Assn., 1st Jud. Dist. Bar Assn. Democrat. Roman Catholic. Office: Ste 900 143 Union Blvd Lakewood CO 80228

COHEN, LEONARD, hospital management company executive; b. 1925; married. BS, UCLA, 1948; LLB, Loyola U., 1951. Ptnr. Ervin, Cohen & Jessup, 1952-68; with Nat. Med. Enterprises, Los Angeles, 1968—, pres., chief operating officer, 1983—, now also vice-chmn., dir.; vice chmn., dir. The Hillhaven Corp., Tacoma, Wash., 1992—; bd. dirs. L.A. Met. YMCA. With U.S. Army, 1942-46. Office: Nat Med Enterprises Inc 2700 Colorado Ave Santa Monica CA 90404-3570

COHEN, MARC M., architect; b. N.Y.C., Dec. 25, 1952; s. Louis Harold and Harriet Cohen; m. Jane Jacobson; children: Benjamin, Gabriel. AB in Architecture, Princeton U., 1974; MArch, Columbia U., 1977. Lic. architect, Calif. With Architect's Workshop VISTA, Phila., 1974-75; project engr. United Way of Penobscot Valley, Bangor, Maine, 1977-78; architect E.W. Tarbell & Assocs., Bangor, 1978-79; facility architect NASA Ames Rsch. Ctr., Moffett Field, Calif., 1979-83, rsch. architect, 1983-88, configuration control mgr., 1992—; rsch. teaching asst. U. Mich., Ann Arbor, 1989-90. Designer, inventor Space Sta. Wardroom Table; patentee in field; contbr. articles to profl. jours. NASA grad. study fellow, U. Mich., 1988-89; recipient NASA Space Act award for patent on space sta. architecture. Mem. AIAA. Home: 700 College Ave Menlo Park CA 94025-5204 Office: NASA Ames Rsch Ctr Mail Stop 240-10 Moffett Field CA 94035-1000

COHEN, MARLENE ZICHI, clinical nursing researcher; b. Bklyn., June 1, 1951; m. David Marshall Cohen, Mar. 5, 1978. BS in Nursing, U. Mich., 1974, MS, 1981, PhD in Nursing, 1984. RN Univ. Hosp., Ann Arbor, Mich., 1974-75, asst. head nurse, 1975-76, head nurse, 1976-78; mental health profl. Aftercare Program, Ann Arbor, 1979-80; teaching and research asst. U. Mich., Ann Arbor, 1979-84; asst. prof. Eastern Mich. U., Ypsilanti, Mich., 1984-85, U. Iowa, Iowa City, 1985-90; asst. rsch. scientist City of Hope Nat. Med. Ctr., Duarte, Calif., 1990-92; dir., Office of Nursing Rsch. Dept. of Nursing and Kenneth Norris Jr., Comprehensive Cancer Ctr. Univ. of Southern Calif., L.A., 1992—; manuscript reviewer Western Jour. Nursing Rsch., 1985—, Image, 1989—, Qualitative Health Rsch., 1989—, Rsch. in Nursing and Health, 1990—, Clin. Nursing Rsch., 1991—. Contbr. articles to profl. jours. and publs. Research grantee NIH, 1986-90, N.Am. Nursing Diagnosis Assn., 1987. Mem. ANA, Coun. on Psychiat. and Mental Health Nursing, Coun. Nurse Researchers, Hadassah Nurses Coun. (internat. adv. bd.), Western Soc. for Rsch. in Nursing, Oncology Nursing Soc., Sigma Theta Tau (pres. Gamma chpt. 1986-90, reviewer internat. rsch. grants program). Home: 1866 Euclid Ave San Marino CA 91108-1609 Office: Univ of Southern Calif Dept of Nursing, 106 Leavey Hall 320 West 15th St Los Angeles CA 90015

COHEN, MAX MARK, surgeon; b. Glasgow, Scotland, Feb. 11, 1939; came to U.S., 1987; s. Harry and Rachel (Goldstein) C.; children: Simon, Talya; m. Marilyn Silverstein. MB ChB, U. Glasgow, 1963. Intern U. Glasgow Hosps., 1963-64, resident surgery, 1964-69; surgical rsch. fellow U. B.C., 1969-70, Harvard U., Cambridge, Mass., 1970-71; chief resident surgery Vancouver Gen. Hosp., 1971-72; asst. prof. surgery, then assoc. prof. surgery U. B.C., Vancouver, Can., 1972-80; assoc. prof. surgery, then prof. surgery U. Toronto, Ont., Can., 1980-87; prof. surgery U. Pa., Phila., 1987—, U. Colo., Denver, 1989—; chmn. surgery Grad. Hosp., Phila., 1987-89; chmn. surgery Rose Med. Ctr., Denver, 1989—; dir. Rose Videoscopic Surgery Ctr., Denver, 1991—. Editor: Biological Protection with Prostaglandins (2d vols.), 1985; editorial bd. Can. Jour. Surgery, 1983-87, Jour. Laparoendoscopic Surgery, 1992—; assoc. editor Clin. and Investigative Medicine, 1985-89; contbr. articles to profl. jours. Grantee Med. Rsch. Coun. Can., 1974-86. Fellow ACS, Royal Coll. Surgeons Edinburgh, Royal Coll. Surgeons Can.; mem. Soc. Am. Gastrointestinal Endoscopic Surgeons, Soc. Univ. Surgeons, Undersea Med. Soc., Am. Gastroenterology Assn., Am. Coll. Physician Execs., Can. Assn. Gen. Surgeons (chmn. rsch. com. 1984-87), Anti Def. League (bd. dirs. 1992). Office: Rose Med Ctr 4567 E 9th Ave Denver CO 80220-3941

COHEN, NATALIE SHULMAN, biochemical researcher; b. N.Y.C., Jan. 16, 1938; d. Isaac and Emma (Medve) Shulman; m. Donald S. Cohen, Sept. 7, 1958; children: Julie Elisabeth, Susan Louise. BA, Cornell U., 1959; MS, NYU, 1961, PhD, 1965. Rsch. fellow Calif. Inst. Tech., Pasadena, 1966-70; rsch. assoc. sch. medicine U. So. Calif., L.A., 1970-73, 74-77; sr. rsch. assoc. U. So. Calif., 1977-89, asst. prof., 1989—; rsch. assoc. sch. medicine U. Ariz., Tucson, 1973-74; panelist Howard Hughes doctoral fellowship program NRC, Washington, 1991-93; ad hoc reviewer NSF, 1985—. Contbr. articles to profl. jours. NSF fellow, 1959-64, Woodrow Wilson hon. fellow, 1959; Rsch. grantee Am. Diabetes Assn., 1977-78, NSF, 1988-89, Greater L.A. affiliate Am. Heart Assn., 1991-93. Mem. AAAS, Am. Soc. Biochemistry and Molecular Biology, U. So. Calif. Med. Faculty Women's Assn., Sigma Xi, Phi Beta Kappa. Democrat. Jewish. Office: U So Calif Sch Medicine 2011 Zonal Ave Los Angeles CA 90033-1034

COHEN, PAUL FREDERICK, software engineer; b. L.A., Dec. 29, 1944; s. Samuel Jehudah and Lucille Katherine (Stern) C. AB, UCLA, 1966; AM, U. Ill., 1967, PhD, 1975. Rsch. assoc. U. Ill. Coll. Medicine, Urbana, 1975-77; assoc. prof. Cen. State U., Wilberforce, Ohio, 1977-79; staff engr. Lockheed Missiles & Space Co., Inc., Sunnyvale, Calif., 1980—; vis. asst. prof. Santa Clara (Calif.) U., 1979-80. Recipient Grad. Traineeship NSF, 1966; Regents scholar UCLA, 1964. Mem. IEEE Computer Soc., Assn. for Computing Machinery (spl. interest group on Ada, chmn. Bay Area spl. interest group on Ada 1985-87), Phi Beta Kappa. Office: Lockheed Missiles & Space Orgn 76-11 Bldg 563 PO Box 3504 Sunnyvale CA 94088-3504

COHEN, RICHARD SCHLEY, physician; b. Eugene, Oreg., Sept. 22, 1945; s. Morris H. and Gladys (Schley) C.; m. Susan Gail Bostrom, Sept. 16, 1972; children: Jill, Thomas. BA, Northwestern U., 1967; MA, U. Ill., Chgo., 1969, MD, 1973. Diplomate Am. Bd. Otolaryngology, Head and Neck Surgery. Intern Univ. Hosp., San Diego, 1973-74; resident U. Chgo., 1974-77; private practice Grants Pass, Oreg., 1977-92; mem. clinical faculty U. Oreg., Portland, 1982-92, med. staff Josephine Meml. Hosp., pres. 1990, med. staff So. Oreg. Med. Ctr., pres. 1980. Designer Cohen Wing ventilating tube. Fellow Am. Coll. Surgeons; mem. Oreg. Med. Assn. (del. 1988-92); Josephine County Med. Soc. (pres. 1985). Office: Head and Neck Assocs 1600 NW 6th St South Ste Grants Pass OR 97526

COHEN, ROBERT F., lawyer, journalist; b. N.Y.C., Feb. 19, 1951; s. Abraham and Ruth Hope (Sunshine) C.; life ptnr. Patrick A. Kahill, Aug. 14, 1984. BA, SUNY, Stony Brook, 1975; BS in Law, Glendale U., 1990, JD, 1992. Bar: Calif. 1992, U.S. Dist. Ct. (cen. dist.) Calif. 1992, U.S. Dist. Ct. (no. dist.) Calif. 1993. Radio news anchor, news dir. various radio stas., 1972-79; radio news reporter Sta. WCBS, N.Y.C., 1979-80; broadcast bus. journalist Wall St. Jour., Bus. Week, UPI, N.Y.C., 1980-86; systems supr. Dern, Mason & Floum, L.A., 1988-89; paralegal Perkins Coie, L.A., 1989-92; pvt. practice Culver City, Calif., 1992—. Editor-in-chief Glendale Law Rev., 1991-92. Vol. fund-raiser AIDS Project L.A., 1989—, vol. attorney, 1993—; col. 1992 Voter Registration Drive, L.A., 1992. Mem. AFTRA, ACLU, State Bar Calif., L.A. County Bar Assn., Lawyers for Human Rights. Democrat. Office: 7121 Raintree Circle Culver City CA 90230-4416

COHEN, ROBERT STEPHEN, drama educator; b. Washington, July 14, 1938; s. Lester Ellis and Lydia Rita (Goldblatt) C.; m. Lorna Lee Buck, Nov. 13, 1972; children: Michael Geoffrey, Whitney. Student, Dartmouth Coll., 1956-58; BA, U. Calif., Berkeley, 1961; DFA, Yale U., 1965. Prof. drama U. Calif., Irvine, 1965—, chmn. drama dept., 1970-91; artistic dir. Theatre 40, Beverly Hills, Calif., 1991-92; stage dir. Colo. Shakespeare Festival, Boulder, 1982-88, Utah Shakespearean Theatre, Cedar City, 1985-93, FRP in Medieval Drama, Irvine, 1985-91. Author: Giraudoux, 1968, Acting Professionally, 1972, Creative Play Direction, 1974, Acting Power, 1978, Theater, 1981, Acting One, 1984, Acting in Shakespeare, 1990. NEH grantee, 1989. Mem. Actors Equity Assn., Am. Theatre Critics Assn., Phi Beta Kappa. Office: U Calif Irvine Dept Drama Irvine CA 92717

COHEN, SEYMOUR I., lawyer; b. N.Y.C., Apr. 15, 1931; s. Fred and Nettie (Sederer) C.; m. Rhoda Goldner, July 22, 1956; children: Cheryl Lynn, Marcy Ann, Lori Beth. BBA cum laude, CCNY, 1951; LLB, Bklyn. Law Sch., 1954, JD, 1967; MBA, NYU, 1960. Bar: N.Y. 1954, U.S. Tax. Ct. 1954, Calif. 1973, U.S. Dist. Ct. (cen. dist.) Calif. 1973, U.S. Ct. Appeals (9th cir.) 1973, U.S. Supreme Ct. 1976; CPA, Ohio, Calif. Staff acct. S.D. Leidesdorf, N.Y.C., 1958-61; mgr., acct. Rockwell, Columbus, Ohio, and L.A., 1961-69; mgr. contracts Logicon, L.A., 1970-71; mgr. internal audit Daylin, 1971-72; contr. NYSE Co., 1972-73; pvt. practice, Torrance, Calif., 1973—. Mem. AICPA, L.A. County Bar Assn. (appellate ct. com. 1979—, svcs. com. 1981-82), S. Bay Bar Assn. (pres. 1986-87, chmn. referral svc. 1977-81), State Bar Calif. (client trust fund commr. 1983, 84), Ohio Inst. CPAs, N.Y. Inst. CPAs, Calif. Inst. CPAs, Inst. Mgmt. Accts., L.A. Trial Lawyers Assn., N.Y. State Bar Assn., Calif. State Bar Assn. Jewish. Republican. Home: 30691 Via La Cresta Palos Verdes Peninsula CA 90274-5353 Office: 18411 Crenshaw Blvd Ste 411 Torrance CA 90504-5081

COHEN, SHAYNE DEL, consultant; b. San Rafael, Calif., Aug. 17, 1946; d. Irving Wolf and Sylvia (Danzig) C. Student, U. Calif., Davis, 1964-66; BA in Community Devel., Friends World Coll., 1970; MA in Internat. Adminstrn., Sch. for Internat. Tng., Brattleboro, Vt., 1974; PhD in Internat. Law, Columbia Pacific U., 1988. Vol. leader Office of Econ. Opportunity, San Francisco, 1967-68; resource devel. Inter Tribal Coun. Nev., Reno, 1970-77; planner Reno Spark Indian Colony, 1978-88; ind. cons. Reno, 1988—; bd. dirs. Radke & Assocs., Las Vegas, Nev., Game Plan, Inc., Salt Lake City. Author: Nevada Indian History and Government, 1980; editor: Coyote Tales, 1991, (manual) Tribal Government Records Management Manual, 1986; newspaper columnist, 1974-77. Bd. dirs. Nev. State Welfare Policy Bd., Carson City, 1988—; state coord. Sister Cities Internat., Alexandria, Va.; dir. Friends of VISTA. Named to Esquire Register Esquire Mag., 1985. Mem. Nat. Fedn. Press Women (state pres. 1985—), Nev. Women's Fund (bd. dirs. 1985-90). Office: 2450 Lymbery St # 205 Reno NV 89507

COHEN, STANLEY NORMAN, geneticist, educator; b. Perth Amboy, N.J., Feb. 17, 1935; s. Bernard and Ida (Stolz) C.; m. Joanna Lucy Wolter, June 27, 1961; children: Anne, Geoffrey. B.A., Rutgers U., 1956; M.D., U. Pa., 1960. Intern Mt. Sinai Hosp., N.Y.C., 1960-61; resident Univ. Hosp., Ann Arbor, Mich., 1961-62; clin. assoc. arthritis and rheumatism br. Nat. Inst. Arthritis and Metabolic Diseases, Bethesda, Md., 1962-64; sr. resident in medicine Duke U. Hosp., Durham, N.C., 1964-65; Am. Cancer Soc. postdoctoral rsch. fellow Albert Einstein Coll. Medicine, Bronx, 1965-67, asst. prof. devel. biology and cancer, 1967-68; mem. faculty Stanford (Calif.) U., 1968—, prof. medicine, 1975—, prof. genetics, 1977, chmn. dept. genetics, 1978-86, K.-T Li Prof., 1993—; mem. com. recombinant DNA molecules NAS-NRC, 1974; mem. com. on genetic experimentation Internat. Council Sci. Unions, 1977—. Mem. editorial bd.: Jour. Bacteriology, 1973-79; assoc. editor: Plasmid, 1977-86. Trustee, mem. bd. overseers U. Pa. Med. Ctr. With USPHS, 1962-64. Recipient Burroughs Wellcome Scholar award, 1970, Mattia award Roche Inst. Molecular Biology, 1977, Albert Lasker basic med. rsch. award, 1980, Wolf prize, 1981, Marvin J. Johnson award, 1981, Disting. Grad. award U. Pa. Sch. Medicine, 1986, Disting. Svc. award Miami Winter Symposium, 1986, Nat. Biotech. award, 1989, LVMH Inst. de la Vie prize, 1988, Nat. Medal Sci., 1988, City of Medicine award, 1988, Nat. Medal of Tech., 1989, Am. Chem. Soc. Spl. award 1992; Guggenheim fellow, 1975; Josiah Macy Jr. Found. faculty scholar, 1975-76. Mem. AAAS, NAS (chmn. genetics sect. 1988-91), Am. Acad. Microbiology, Am. Soc. Biol. Chemists, Genetics Soc. Am., Am. Soc. Microbiology (Cetus award 1988), Am. Soc. Pharmacology and Exptl. Therapeutics, Am. Soc. Clin. Investigation, Assn. Am. Physicians, Inst. Medicine, Phi Beta Kappa, Sigma Xi, Alpha Omega Alpha. Office: Stanford U Sch Med Dept Genetics M-320 Stanford CA 94305

COHEN, S(TEPHEN) MARSHALL, university dean, philosophy educator; b. N.Y.C., Sept. 27, 1929; s. Harry and Fanny (Marshall) C.; m. Margaret Dennes, Feb. 15, 1964; children: Matthew, Megan. B.A., Dartmouth Coll., Hanover, N.H., 1951; postgrad., Harvard U., 1953; M.A., Oxford U., Eng., 1977. Jr. fellow, Soc. of Fellows Harvard U., 1955-58, asst. prof. philosophy and gen. edn., 1958-62; asst. prof. U. Chgo., 1962-64, assoc. prof., 1964-67; assoc. prof. Rockefeller U., N.Y.C., 1967-70; prof. philosophy CUNY, 1970-83, exec. officer program in philosophy Grad. Sch., 1975-83; prof. philosophy and law U. So. Calif., L.A., 1983—, dean div. humanities, 1983—, interim dean Coll. Letters, Arts and Scis., 1993-94; lectr. Lowell Inst., Boston, 1957-58; vis. fellow All Souls Coll., Oxford, Eng., 1976-77; mem. Inst. for Advanced Study, Princeton, N.J., 1981-82. Editor: The Philosophy of John Stuart Mill, 1961, (with Gerald Mast) Film Theory and Criticism, 1974, (with Thomas Nagel and Thomas Scanlon) War and Moral Responsibility, 1974, (with Roger Copeland) What is Dance?, 1983; editor Philosophy and Public Affairs, 1970—, Philosophy and Society series, 1977-83, Ethical, Legal and Political philosophy Series, 1983—. Rockefeller Found. humanities fellow, 1977, Guggenheim fellow, 1976-77. Mem. Am. Philos. Assn., Soc. Ethical and Legal Philosophy, Am. Coun. Learned Socs. (bd. dirs. 1987-91, 93—), Coun. on Internat. Ednl. Exch. (bd. dirs. 1991—). Democrat. Jewish. Office: U So Calif Divsn Humanities Los Angeles CA 90089-4012

COHEN, SUSAN GLORIA, organizational researcher; b. N.Y.C., Apr. 22, 1952. BA, SUNY, Buffalo, 1972; MA, Whitworth Coll., 1977; MPhil, MA, Yale U., 1984, 86, PhD, 1988. Social worker Children's Home Soc., Spokane, Wash., 1972-74; dir. YWCA, Spokane, 1974-79; consumer analyst Group Health coop., Seattle, 1979-80; cons. Exec. Devel. Assoc., Westport, Conn., 1986-87; rsch. scientist U. So. Calif., L.A., 1988—; facilitator Consumer Panel Telephone Co., 1987-90; cons. in field. Contbr. articles to profl. jours. Mem. N.O.W., 1975—, N.A.R.A.L., 1988—. Mem. Brandeis Barbein, Acad. Mgmt. Office: U So Calif Ctr for Effective Orgns G S B A Los Angeles CA 90089-1421

COHEN, WILLIAM B., vascular surgeon; m. Joy L. Cohen; 1 child, Lauren L. Student, Colgate U., 1959; grad., NYU, 1963. Diplomate Am. Bd. Surgery; spl. cert. in vascular surgery. Attending surgeon Cedars/Sinai Med. Ctr., L.A., St. Vincents Hosp. Med. Ctr., L.A. Maj. U.S. Amry, 1969-71. Mem. So. Calif. Vascular Surgery Soc., Internat. Soc. for Cardio Vascular Surgery, Peripheral Vascular Surgery Soc., Clin. Soc. for Vascular Surgery. Office: 8631 W 3d St Ste 925E West Hollywood CA 90048-5955

COHN, DANIEL HOWARD, laboratory director; b. Santa Monica, Calif., Aug. 24, 1955; s. Sidney Lorber and Mynda Ellen (Zimmerman) C.; m. Ludmila Bojman, May 16, 1982; children: Zachary, Marissa, Rachel. BA, U. Calif., Santa Barbara, 1977; PhD, Scripps Inst. Oceanography, 1983. Rsch. scientist, asst. prof. Cedars-Sinai Med. Ctr./UCLA, 1988—; postdoctoral fellow U. Wash., Seattle, 1983-88; mem. genetics tng. program UCLA, 1988—; reviewer various jours. and granting agys. Editorial bd. various jours.; contbr. articles to profl. jours. and books. Grant reviewer, bd. dirs. Concern Found. for Cancer Rsch., L.A., 1988—. Recipient Martin Kamen award U. Calif., San Diego, 1983, Eckhart prize Scripps Inst. Oceanography, 1983; postdoctoral award NIH, 1985-88, grantee, 1988—. Mem. AAAS, Phi Beta Kappa. Democrat. Jewish. Office: Cedars-Sinai Med Ctr 8700 Beverly Blvd Los Angeles CA 90048

COHN, JOSEPH THEODORE, radio music and program director; b. New Orleans, Nov. 13, 1958; s. Lee Stern Cohn and Grace Dee (Cohen) Block. Summer TV workshop, UCLA (jazz history), 1978; BA, U. Ariz., 1980. Jazz host KUAT Radio, Tucson, 1978-80; on air talent KWFM Radio, Tucson, 1980-83; program dir. The Music Channel, Phoenix, 1984-85; on air talent KSTM Radio, Phoenix, 1983-87, KJZZ Radio, Phoenix, 1983-87; music dir. KPLU Radio, Seattle-Tacoma, 1987—. Mem. adv. bd. Imperials Music and Youth, Seattle, 1993-93. Nominee: Jazz Station of Yr. The Gavin Report, 1988, 89, Jazz Person of Yr. 1988-91; named Jazz Station of Yr. 1990, 91, Jazz Radio Person of Yr. Gavin Report, 1992; recipient FLO Best Sound award Nat. Pub. Radio, KPLU, Seattle, 1989, 92. Office: KPLU S 121st and Park Tacoma WA 98447

COHN, LAWRENCE STEVEN, physician, educator; b. Chgo., Dec. 21, 1945; s. Jerome M. and Francis C.; BS, U. Ill., 1967, MD, 1971; m. Harriett G. Rubin, Sept. 1, 1968; children: Allyson and Jennifer (twins). Intern, Mt. Zion Hosp., San Francisco, 1971-72, resident, 1972-73; resident U. Chgo., 1973-74; practice medicine specializing in internal medicine, Paramount, Calif.; pres. med. staff Charter Suburban Hosp., 1981-83; mem. staff Long Beach Meml. Hosp., Harbor Gen. Hosp; assoc. clin. prof. medicine UCLA. Maj. USAF, 1974-76. Recipient Disting. Teaching award Harbor-UCLA Med. Ctr., 1980, 90; diplomate Am. Bd. Internal Medicine. Mem. A.C.P., AMA, Calif. Med. Assn., L.A. County Med. Assn., Am. Heart Assn., Soc. Air Force Physicians, Phi Beta Kappa, Phi Kappa Phi, Phi Lambda Upsilon, Phi Eta Sigma, Alpha Omega Alpha. Home: 6608 Via La Paloma Palos Verdes Peninsula CA 90274-6449 Office: 16415 S Colorado Ste 202 Paramount CA 90723

COHN, NATHAN, lawyer; b. Charleston, S.C., Jan. 20, 1918; s. Samuel and Rose (Baron) C.; 1 son, Norman; m. Carolyn Venturini, May 18, 1970. J.D., San Francisco Law Sch., 1947. Bar: Calif. 1947, U.S. Supreme Ct. 1957. Pvt. practice law, San Francisco, 1947—; judge pro tem Mcpl. Ct., Superior Ct. Mem. Calif. State Recreation Commn., 1965-68; former mem. Democratic State Central Com. Served to 1st lt. USAF, 1950-55. Fellow Am. Bd. Criminal Lawyers (past pres.), Am. Acad. Matrimonial Lawyers, Am. Bd. Trial Advs. (diplomate, chpt. pres. 1984), Internat. Acad. of Law and Sci., Assn. Trial Lawyers Am., Calif. Trial Lawyers Assn., San Francisco Trial Lawyers Assn. (past pres.), Criminal Trial Lawyers Assn. No. Calif., Irish-Israeli-Italian Soc. (co-pres., co-founder), Internat. Footprinters Assn. (chpt. 1 San Francisco), Regular Vets. Assn., Roundtable, Calamari Club, Godfather Club, Press Club (life), Lawyers Club of San Francisco, Masons (32 degree), Shriners, B'nai B'rith, South of Market Boys, Ancient Order Hibernians Am. (hon. life). Jewish. Columnist San Francisco Progress, 1982-86; condr. and author seminars in field. Office: 693 Sutter St San Francisco CA 94102-1023

COHN, ROBERT GREER, literary arts educator; b. Richmond, Va., Sept. 5, 1921; s. Charles Alfred and Susan (Spilberg) C.; m. Dorrit Zucker-Hale, June 20, 1947 (div. 1963); children: Stephen A., Richard L.; m. Valentina Catenacci, Oct. 26, 1965. BA in Romance Langs., U. Va., 1943; PhD in French, Yale U., 1949. Instr. Yale U., New Haven, 1949-50; asst. prof. Swarthmore (Pa.) Coll., 1952-54, Vassar Coll., Poughkeepsie, N.Y., 1954-59; from asst. to full prof. French lit. Stanford (Calif.) U., 1959-91, prof. emeritus, 1992—. Author: L'OEuvre De Mallarmé, 1951, Toward the Poems of Mallarmé, The Poetry of Rimbaud, 1973, The Writer's Way in France, 1960; founding editor Yale French Studies, 1948. Guggenheim Found. fellow, 1956, 1985, Nat. Found. for the Humanities fellow, 1969. Home: 6 Maywood Ln Menlo Park CA 94025-5357 Office: Stanford U Bldg C Rm 12 Stanford CA 94305

COIT, R. KEN, financial planner; b. L.A., Aug. 26, 1943; s. Roger L. and Thelma D. C.; BS, U. Ariz., 1967; MBA, Pepperdine U., 1981; m. Donna M. Schemanske, Oct. 8, 1977; children—Kristin M., Shannon, Darren, Lauryn. Prin. Coit Fin. Group, 1981; mem. adj. faculty Coll. Fin. Planning, Denver, 1978-79; pres. Walnut Creek adv. bd. Summit Bank, 1987—. Mem. dean's adv. bd. Pepperdine U., 1988-91; nat. bd. advisor Coll. Pharmacy U. Ariz.; bd. dirs., chmn. investment com. East Community Found. Recipient Outstanding Alumnus award Pepperdine U. Sch. Bus. and Mgmt., 1986. Mem. Internat. Assn. Fin. Planners (chpt. pres. 1978-79), Inst. Cert. Fin. Planners, Am. Investors Co., East Bay Gourmet Club, Blackhawk Country Club. Office: 1655 N Main St Ste 270 Walnut Creek CA 94596-5395

COKE, FRANK VAN DEREN, museum director, photographer; b. Lexington, Ky., July 4, 1921; s. Sterling Dent and Elisabeth (Van Deren) C.; m. Eleanor Barton, 1943 (div. 1980); children: Sterling Van Deren, Eleanor Browning; m. Joan Gillberry Morgan, 1983. BA, U. Ky., 1956; MFA, Ind. U., 1958; postgrad., Harvard U.; LHD (hon.), San Francisco Acad. of Art, 1986. With Van Deren Hardware Co., Lexington, 1946-56; pres. Van Deren Hardware Co., 1953-56; asst. prof. art U. Fla., 1958-61; assoc. prof. art Ariz. State U., 1961-62; prof., dir. art mus. U. N.Mex., 1962-66, chmn. dept., 1963-70, dir. art mus., 1973-79; dep. dir., then dir. Internat. Mus. Photography, Rochester, N.Y., 1970-72; dir. dept. photography San Francisco Mus. Modern Art, 1979-87; bd. dirs. Internat. Folk Art Found.; chmn. Albuquerque Fine Arts Adv. Com.; cons. in field; Disting. vis. prof. art Ariz. State U., 1988-91. Author: books and catalogues, including Taos and Santa Fe: The Artist's Environment, 1882-1942, 1963, The Painter and the Photograph, 1972, One Hundred Years of Photographic History, 1975, Avant-Garde Photography in Germany, 1919-1939, 1981, Faces Photographed, 1984, Joel-Peter Witkin, 1985, Photography: A Facet of Modernism, 1986, Secular and Sacred: Photographs of Mexico by Van Deren Coke, 1992. Served as officer USNR, 1942-45. Recipient Photography Internat. award, 1955, 56 (2), Modern Photography Internat. award, 1956, U.S. Camera Internat. award, 1957, 58, 60, New Talent USA Art in Am. award, 1960, Gov.'s award State of N.Mex., 1986, Educator of Yr. Leica Medal of Excellence, 1987, Josef Sudek medal Ministry of Culture of the Czech Socialist Republic, 1989, Disting. Internat. Career in Photography award, 1992, Internat. Photomeeting, Rep. San Marino, Peer award The Friends of Photography, San Francisco, 1992; Guggenheim fellow, 1975; Fulbright teaching fellow U. Auckland, N.Z., 1989. Mem. Coll. Art Assn. (bd. dirs. 1973-77, 88-92), Soc. Photog. Edn. (bd. dirs. 1965-70).

COKER, PAMELA LEE, software company executive; b. L.A., Nov. 2, 1948; d. Frank Bethell Coker and Wilma (Sheets) Bradley; 1 child, Loren Underwood. BA, U. Calif., San Diego, 1970; PhD, U. Calif., Irvine, 1975. Asst. prof. Claremont (Calif.) Grad. Sch., 1974-81; founder Computer Cognition Corp., San Diego, 1981-88; founder, CEO Acucobol, Inc., San Diego, 1988—; cons. IBM Adv. Coun., 1991—, NCR Adv. Coun., 1992—. Honoree Nat. Assn. Corp. Dirs., 1990; recipient Exporter of Yr. award, San Diego Small Bus. Assn., 1992. Mem. Am. Electronics Assn., Info. Tech. Assn. Am., UCSD Connect-Tech. & Entrepreneurship, San Diego C. of C. (small bus. of month award 1992), UCSD Alumni Assn. (bd. dirs. 1989—). Office: Acucobol Inc 7950 Silverton Ave Ste 201 San Diego CA 92126

COLANDREA, THOMAS RICHARD, quality assurance professional; b. N.Y.C., May 7, 1938; s. Tom and Julia (Kronenthal) C.; m. Virginia June, May 7, 1960; children: Angela, Tom. BS in Metall. Engrng., U. Mo., 1959; MS in Engrng. Sci., Rensselaer Polytechnic Inst., 1965; MBA, Western New Eng. Coll., 1972. Registered profl. engr., Calif.; cert. quality engr., reliability engr., lead auditor. Mgr. quality systems to dir., Quality Assurance Div. Gen. Atomics, Inc., San Diego, 1974-89; pres. Colandrea & Assocs., Inc., San Diego, Calif., 1989—; expert witness, quality assurance advisor mgmt., tng. instr. in quality. Fellow Am. Soc. Quality Control (recipient Basile award 1987, voted Quality Assurance Person of Yr. energy div. 1981); mem. ASME. (nuclear QA commn.). Office: Colandrea & Assocs Inc PO Box 27121 San Diego CA 92198-1121

COLANGELO, JERRY JOHN, professional sports executive; b. Chicago Heights, Ill., Nov. 20, 1939; s. Larry and Sue (Drancek) C.; m. Joan E. Helmich, Jan. 20, 1961; children: Kathy, Kristen, Bryan. B.A., U. Ill., 1962. Partner House of Charles, Inc., 1962-63; assoc. D.O. Klein & Assocs., 1964-65; dir. merchandising Chgo. Bulls basketball club, 1966-68; gen. mgr. Phoenix Suns basketball club, 1968-87, now also exec. v.p., until 1987, pres., chief exec. officer, 1987—. Mem. Basketball Congress Am. (exec. v.p., dir.), Phi Kappa Psi. Republican. Baptist. Clubs: University, Phoenix Execs. Office: Phoenix Suns 2910 N Central Ave PO Box 1369 Phoenix AZ 85012*

COLBERT, EDWARD BRUCE, software engineering company executive; b. Detroit, July 24, 1957; s. Raymond and Arlene Sue (Barnett) C.; m. Judy Ann Pearlman, May 19, 1990. BS with honors, U. Mich., 1979, MS, 1981. Mem. tech. staff TRW, L.A., 1981-86; pres. Absolute Software Co., Inc., L.A., 1986—. Contbr. articles to profl. jours.; inventor object-oriented software devel. method. Mem. ACM, ACM Spl. Interest Group on Ada (vice chair 1989—), L.A. ACM (chair software engrng. 1986-87), IEEE, Planetary Soc., Sierra Club. Office: Absolute Software Co Inc 4593 Orchid Dr Los Angeles CA 90043-3320

COLBERT, OLGA, historian; b. Madrid, June 20, 1959; came to U.S., 1984; d. Mariano Lopez Calderon and Angeles Valero Lopez; m. Randall Scott Colbert, Sept. 2, 1983. BA, U. Madrid, 1981; MA, U. N.D., 1989. Tchr. Virgen del Bosque High Sch., Madrid, 1982-83, Climax (Minn.) High Sch., 1985-88, U. N.D., Grand Forks, 1988-89, U. Md., 1989—. Mem. NEA.

COLBURN, GENE LEWIS, insurance and industrial consultant; b. Bismarck, N.D., July 12, 1932; s. Lewis William and Olga Alma (Feland) C.; PhD, City U. L.A., 1983. Pres., gen. mgr. Multiple Lines Ins. Agy., Auburn, Wash., 1953-79; ins. and risk mgmt. cons., Auburn, Wash., 1980—; pres. Feland Safe Deposit Corp.; bd. dirs. Century Svc. Corp. subs. Capital Savs. Bank, Olympia, Wash.; mem. exec. com. Great Repub. Life Ins. Co., Portland, Oreg., 1971-75; mem. Wash. State Ins. Commrs. Test Devel. Com., 1986-87. cons. indsl. risk mgmt. Councilperson Auburn City, 1982-85; mayor-pro tem, City of Auburn, 1984; co-incorporator, chmn. bd. SE Community Alcohol Ctr., 1971-75; mem. Wash. State Disaster Assistance Coun., 1981-82, founding mem.; pres. Valley Cities Mental Health Ctr., 1980; mem. instn. rev. com. Auburn Gen. Hosp., 1978—; prin. trustee Dr. R. B. Bramble Med. Rsch. Found., 1980-90; bd. dirs. Wash. Assn. Chs. (Luth. Ch. in Am.), Asian Refugee Resettlement Mgmt. div., 1981-83, Columbia Luth. Home, Seattle, 1985-87, Wash. Law Enforcement Officers and Fire Fighter's Pension Disability Bd., Auburn, 1980-84. Cert. ins. counselor, 1978. Recipient Disting. Alumni award Green River Community Coll., 1982. Fellow Acad. Producer Ins. Studies (charter); mem. Internat. Platform Assn. Lodge: Auburn Lions (past pres.). Office: 720 L St SE Auburn WA 98002-6219

COLBURN, PAUL LEROY, healthcare administrator; b. San Pedro, Calif., Mar. 23, 1948; s. Francis Hervey and Lois Katherine (Egner) C.; m. Lorraine Nares, June 1, 1974 (div. Mar. 1982); 1 child, Jessica Lynne; m. Krista Sue Kline, Oct. 9, 1982; children: Sean Michael Kline, Christian Eric Kline. AS, Long Beach City Coll., 1977; BS, U. Phoenix, Costa Mesa, Calif., 1986. Cert. diagnostic radiology, Nat., Calif. Supr. computed tomography Torrance Meml. Med. Ctr., Calif., 1978-86; dir. dept. radiology Coastal Communities Hosp., Santa Ana, Calif., 1986-89; tech. dir. Moran, Rowen and Dorsey, Inc., Orange, Calif., 1989-90; dir. radiology Western Med. Ctr., Santa Ana, Calif., 1990—; instr. Long Beach City Coll., Calif., 1987, Orange Coast Coll., 1989—; editorial cons. R.T. Image mag., 1990—. Contbr. tech. manual for stereotactic neurosurgery, 1984. With USAF, 1966-68. Mem. Am. Soc. Radiologic Technologists (del. 1989-91), Calif. Soc. Radiologic Technologists (mem. Nominations Com. 1986-87, sec. and treas. 1987-88, pres. elect 1988-89, pres. 1989-90, chmn. bd. 1990-91, 1st place award Technologist Essay Competition 1984). Republican. Lutheran. Home: 15232 Vichy Cir Irvine CA 92714-3154 Office: Western Med Ctr Santa Ana CA 92705

COLBURN, RALPH JONATHAN, minister; b. Wheatland, N.D., Oct. 22, 1916; s. Franklin and Alvina (Ritter) C.; m. Julia Elizabeth Rowland, Apr. 10, 1954; children: Mark Jonathan, Timothy Joel. AA, Long Beach (Calif.) City Coll., 1936; BTh, Bible Inst. of L.A., 1940; BA, Westmont Coll., Santa Barbara, Calif., 1941. Ordained minister, 1941. Founding pastor Grace Community Ch., Seal Beach, Calif., 1939-42; pastor First Brethren Ch., Compton, Calif., 1942-48; nat. youth dir. Fellowship of Brethren Chs., Winona Lake, Ind., 1948-54; founding pastor Grace Brethren Ch., Ft. Lauderdale, Fla., 1955-68; pastor Community Grace Brethren Ch., Long Beach, Calif., 1968-78; assoc. pastor Grace Ch., Cypress, Calif., 1978—; exec. sec. Nat. Fellowship of Grace Brethren Ministers, Winona Lake, 1975—; officer Brethren Missionary Herald Bd., Winona Lake, 1961—. Mem. Biola Alumni Assn., Westmont Coll. Alumni Assn. Republican. Home: 3490 E La Jara St Long Beach CA 90805-3847 Office: Grace Ch 5100 Cerritos Ave Cypress CA 90630

COLBURN, WAYNE ALAN, pharmaceutical company executive; b. Allegan, Mich., Sept. 10, 1947; s. Albert Burton and Vena Maie (Wilson) C.; m. Nancy Druckenbrodt, Aug. 2, 1969 (div. June 1982); m. Gail Laura Englert, Mar. 9, 1985; children: Kurt Alan, Adrian Marie, Trent Andrew. BA, Albion Coll., 1969; PhD, SUNY, Buffalo, 1977. Rsch. biochemist Upjohn Co., Kalamazoo, Mich., 1970-75; rsch. fellow Nat. Inst. Environ. Health Scis., Park, N.C., 1977-78; mgr. rsch. Hoffmann-La Roche Inc., Nutley, N.J., 1978-85; dir. rsch. Parke-Davis/Warner-Lambert, Ann Arbor, Mich., 1985-90; v.p. Harris Labs., Phoenix, 1990—; cons. Cornell Med. Coll., N.Y.C., 1981—; adj. prof. Med. Coll. Va., Richmond, 1987—, U. Pitts., 1984—. Author, editor: Peptide, Peptoid and Protein Pharmacokinetics/Pharmacodynamics, 1991; author: Classical and Population Pharmacokinetics, 1988. Fellow Am. Assn. Pharm. Scientists (chmn. 1990), Am. Coll. Clin. Pharmacology (regent 1991-96); mem. Am. Soc. for Clin. Pharmacology and Therapeutics, Drug Info. Assn., Assocs. of Clin. Pharmacology, Internat. Soc. of the Study of Xenobiotics. Office: Harris Labs Inc 4639 S 36th St Phoenix AZ 85040

COLBY, BARBARA DIANE, interior designer, consultant; b. Chgo., Dec. 6, 1932; d. Raymond R. and Mertyl Shirley (Jackson) C.; 1 son, Lawrence James. Student Wright Jr. Coll., 1950, Art Inst. Chgo., UCLA. Owner, F.L.S., Los Angeles, 1971-77; ptnr. Ambiance Inc., Los Angeles, 1976-77; owner Barbara Colby, Ltd., Los Angeles, 1977-81; bus. adminstr. Internat. Soc. Interior Designers, Los Angeles, 1982—; owner Chromanetics, Glendale, Calif., 1981—; instr. Otis/Parsons Sch. Design, Los Angeles Fashion Inst. Design and Merchandising; dir. color Calif. Coll. Interior Design, Costa Mesa, Calif., 1987; also lectr. in field. Author: Color and Light Influences and Impact, 1990; contbg. editor Giftware News. Instr. L.A. County Regional Occupation Program, 1990—. Recipient award for Best Children's Room, Chgo. Furniture Show, 1969, award Calif. Design Show '76, 1976. Mem. Am. Soc. Interior Designers (cert.), Color Mktg. Group of U.S. (chairholder). Author: Color and Light: Influences and Impact, 1990; contbr. articles to profl. jours. Office: 245 W Loraine St Ste 309 Glendale CA 91202

COLBY, ROBERT LESTER, psychologist; b. N.Y.C., Jan. 21, 1941; came to Can., 1966; s. Allen Michael and Beatrice Dorethea (Kalkut) C.; m. Catherine Colby. BA, NYU, 1963; MS, L.I. U., 1965. Rsch. fellow Ctr. for Ednl. Disabilities, Guelph, Ont., Can., 1967-69; lectr. U. Guelph, 1967-69; dir., chief psychologist Psychol. Svcs. of County Sch. Bd., Brantford, Ont., Can., 1969-83; pvt. practice psychology Vancouver, B.C., Can., 1980—; clin. field placement supr. Simon Fraser U., Vancouver, 1984-86, lectr. Justice Inst. B.C., 1984-86; clin. dir. Personnel Inst. Can., Vancouver, 1984-89; pres. Grad. Tests Tng., Inc., Vancouver, 1984—, Colby Gallagler & Assocs., Inc.,

Vancouver, 1984—; cons. to govt. agys. and depts., Can., 1984—. Chmn. Interagy. Coordinating Com., Brantford, 1975-77; bd. dirs. Ont. Antipoverty Coordinating Com., Brantford, 1975-77. Mem. APA, Can. Psychol. Assn., B.C. Psychol. Assn. (bd. dirs. 1985—, chmn. ethics com. 1985-89, sec.-treas. 1988, pres. 1990-92, past pres. 1992-93), N.S. Psychol. Assn., Hong Kong Psychol. Assn., Can. Mental Health Assn., Soc. for Psychol. Study of Social Issues.

COLBY, TAMARA, editor; b. Hightstown, N.J., July 9, 1960; d. Patrick Joseph and Rosemary Frances (Burns) C.; m. John Francis Murray Boozang, Nov. 2, 1987; children: Karen Marie, Sharon Lynn, Kevin Patrick; stepchildren: Lauren, Erin, R.J. BA in English, Villanova U., 1982; MEd, Columbia U., 1986; postgrad., U. Seattle, 1993—. Copy editor Matthew Bender & Co. Inc., N.Y.C., 1982-85; sr. editor children's lit. divsn. Wildcat Press, Seattle, 1985-89; pub. mgr. Chandler-Ball & Werik Pubs., Seattle, 1990—. Author: (with Karen Ball) 101 Home Decorating Tips; (with Nancy Hedinger) On The Road Again; (with Dena Mastrodomenico) Life After Retail. Chmn. homeless com. Christ the King Ch., New Vernon, 1982-83; coach field hockey Morristown (N.J.) High Sch., 1984-85; vol. Hands Together, Inc., 1990—, Project Literacy, 1991—; Sunday sch. tchr. Holy Family, Seattle, 1992—. Mem. LWV (bd. dirs. 1991—), Villanova U. Alumni Assn. Roman Catholic. Office: Werik Gardens 7030 15th Ave NW Seattle WA 98117

COLE, CHARLES EDWARD, state attorney general; b. Yakima, Wash., Oct. 10, 1927; married; 3 children. BA, Stanford U., 1950, LLB, 1953. Law clk. Vets. Affairs Commn. Territory of Alaska, Juneau, 1954, Territorial Atty. Gen.'s Office, Fairbanks, Alaska, 1955-56, U.S. Dist. Ct. Alaska, Fairbanks, 1955-56; city magistrate City of Fairbanks, 1957-58; pvt. practice law, 1957-90; atty. gen. State of Alaska, 1990—; profl. baseball player, Stockton, Calif. and Twin Falls, Idaho, summers of 1950, 51, 53. With U.S. Army, 1946-47. Mem. Calif. State Bar, Washington State Bar Assn., Alaska Bar Assn. Office: Law Dept State of Alaska Office of Atty Gen PO Box 110300 Juneau AK 99811-0300

COLE, DAVID RODNEY, mining executive; b. White Plains, N.Y., July 13, 1931; s. Thomas Harris and Helene Louise (Fischer) C.; m. Marjofie Ann Davis, Nov. 7, 1959; 1 child, John W. Owen (adopted). BS in Mining Engring., Colo. Sch. Mines, 1952, MS in Mining Engring., 1956. Registered profl. engr., Colo. Jr. mining engr. Colo. Standard Lead-Zinc Mines, Inc., Lake City, Colo., 1952; mining engr. Tech-Ser Mining Co., Silverton, Colo., 1956-57; project engr. Idorado Mining Co., Ouray, Colo., 1957-61; sr. metal mine inspector Colo. Bur. Mines, Grand Junction, 1961-67; ops. mgr. Strategic Minerals Exploration Co., Grand Junction, 1967-69; pres. Colo. Mining Assn., Denver, 1969—; mem. Nat. Def. Exec. Res., Emergency Minerals Adminstrn., U.S. Dept. Interior, 1970—. Patentee in field. Sec.-treas., bd. dirs. CMA Found., 1977—. Cpl. U.S. Army, 1953-54. Mem. ASME, Colo. Hwy. Users Conf. (sec. 1988—), Am. Mining Congress (bd. western govs. 1969—), Am. Soc. Assn. Execs., Nat. Soc. Profl. Engrs., Colo. Sch. Mines Alumni Assn. (pres. 1975-76). Republican. Home: 3050 Quail St Lakewood CO 80215-7142 Office: Colo Mining Assn 1600 Broadway Ste 1340 Denver CO 80202-4913

COLE, DAVID WINSLOW, personal care industry executive; b. Toledo, Sept. 20, 1947; s. Robert Winslow and Marjorie Lucile (Rottman) C.; m. Nancy Carol Gerathy, July 3, 1971; 1 child, Kevin. BS, Miami U., Oxford, Ohio, 1969. From field sales rep. to unit mgr. Procter and Gamble Co., Chgo. and St. Louis, 1970-76; dist. mgr. frozen foods Quaker Oats Co., Detroit, 1976-78; ea. regional mgr. frozen foods Quaker Oats Co., Severna Park, Md., 1978-82; nat. sales mgr. confectionery products Quaker Oats Co., Chgo., 1982-85; mgmt. cons. Northeastern Orgn., Inc., Trumbull, Conn., 1985-86; dir. field sales Cadbury U.S.A. subs. Cadbury Schweppes PLC, Stamford, Conn., 1986-88; dir. sales Peter Paul Cadbury Products subs. Hershey (Pa.) Chocolate Co., 1988-89; v.p. sales Personal Care Products div. Weyerhauser Co., Federal Way, Wash., 1989, exec. v.p. sales, 1989, v.p., gen. mgr., 1990-93; exec. v.p., COO Paragon Trade Brands, Federal Way, Wash., 1993—. Bd. dirs. Bay View Homeowners Assn., Federal Way, 1989-90. Mem. Nat. Food Brokers Assn. (mem. prin. adv. group 1987-88, contbr. articles to assn. publs., author tng. program), Twin Lakes Golf and Country Club (mem. bd. trustees 1990-91). Office: Paragon Trade Brands 505 S 336th St Federal Way WA 98003-6328

COLE, DOUGLAS LEON, pharmaceutical company executive; b. Great Bend, Kans., Mar. 5, 1947; s. Jack Kellam and Maxine Virginia (Hickman) C.; m. Lucille Judith Kotalik, Aug. 21, 1976; children: Brian David, Laura Elaine, Adam Kellam. BS, Ft. Hays State U., Hays, Kans., 1969; PhD, U. Ill., 1975. Sr. rsch. chemist Merck Sharp & Dohme, Rahway, N.J., 1974-78, assoc. dir., 1983-85; group leader Lederle Labs., Pearl River, N.Y., 1978-83; dir. Marion Labs., Kansas City, Mo., 1985-89, Marion Merrell Dow Inc., Kansas City, 1989-91, ISIS Pharms., Carlsbad, Calif., 1991—. Author and presenter in field. With U.S. Army, 1969-75. Mem. Am. Chem. Soc., Assn. Ofcl. Analyst-Chemists, Drug Info. Assn. Home: 6863 Caminito Montanoso Apt 13 San Diego CA 92119-2348 Office: ISIS Pharms Inc 2280 Faraday Ave Carlsbad CA 92008-7208

COLE, GERALD AINSWORTH, retired zoology educator; b. Hartford, Conn., Dec. 25, 1917; s. Elbert Charles and Ida Nell (Ainsworth) C.; m. Jean Palmer Hascall, Mar. 11, 1944; children: Wendy A., Sally J., Thomas H., Stephen W., Jeffrey V. AB, Middlebury Coll., 1939; MS, St. Lawrence U., 1941; PhD, U. Minn., 1949. Teaching asst. U. Minn., Mpls., 1946-49; asst. prof., assoc. prof. U. Louisville, 1949-58; assoc. prof., prof. Ariz. State U., Tempe, 1958-80; instr., researcher Minn. Biology Station, Lake Itasca, 1964-70; prof. emeritus, zoology Ariz. State U., 1980; invited prof. U. Louisville, 1982. Co-author: Limnology in North America, 1963, Desert Biology, 1968; author: Textbook of Limnology, 1975; contbr. articles to profl. jours. Capt. U.S. Army, 1942-46. Fellow Ariz. Acad. Sci., 1964 (pres. 1971-72). Mem. Sigma Xi (sec. 1978). Democrat. Home: 1759 W Mariposa Ct Chandler AZ 85224

COLE, JOE CLINTON, hospitality industry executive; b. Phoenix, Aug. 13, 1938; s. Irion DuPree and Irene (Arendell) C.; m. Marianne Elizabeth Gilbert, Dec. 29, 1962; children: Gregory Manning, Cheryl Janice. BA, U. Ariz., 1961; postgrad., U. Wis., 1968-69. Reporter, editor The Ariz. Rep., Phoenix, 1961-88; v.p. corp. communications Aztar Corp., Phoenix, 1988—. With U.S. Army, 1961-65. Home: 605 E Myrtle Ave Phoenix AZ 85020-4929 Office: Aztar Corp 2390 E Camelback Rd Phoenix AZ 85016-3448

COLE, JULIAN WAYNE (PERRY COLE), computer educator, consultant, programmer, analyst; b. LaFayette, Ala., Dec. 16, 1937; s. William Walter and Hattie Lucille (Berry) C.; m. Judith Elaine Riley, June 27, 1959; children—Jeffrey Paul, Jarrett David. B.S. in Bus. Adminstrn., Ariz., State U., 1967; M. in Computer Sci., Texas A&M U., 1969. Joined U.S. Air Force, 1956, advanced through grades to capt., 1970, ret., 1978; programmer/analyst Hewlett Packard Corp., Colorado Springs, Colo., 1978-79, Digital Equipment Corp., Colorado Springs, 1979-85; lectr. U. Colo., Colorado Springs, 1978-92; tng. dir. System Devel. Corp., Colorado Springs, 1979-85; tng. dir. Unisys Corp., Colorado Springs, 1986-91; computer cons., Colorado Springs, 1980—; sr. systems analyst, tech. trainer MCI, Inc., Colorado Springs, 1992—; pres. Advanced Info. Methodology and Systems, Colorado Springs, 1982—. Author: ANSI Fortran IV, 1978; ANSI Fortran IV with Fortran 77 Extensions, 1983, ANSI Fortran 77: Structured Problem Solving Approach, 1987. Mem. Assn. Computing Machinery (chmn. 1981-82), Data Processing Mgmt. Assn., Beta Gamma Sigma, Phi Kappa Phi, Upsilon Pi Epsilon. Republican. Baptist. Club: Business. Home: 735 Big Valley Dr Colorado Springs CO 80919-1004 Office: MCI 2424 Garden of the Gods Colorado Springs CO 80919

COLE, LARRY DON, former mayor; b. Barron, Wis., May 17, 1937; s. John Herschel Cole and Leona Ruby (Bastian) Day; m. Rita Arlene Wanner, Oct. 11, 1957; children: Jeffrey Allen, Monica Lee. Installer Western Electric Co., Oreg., 1956-59; serviceman Nat. Cash Register, Salem, Coos Bay, Oreg., 1959-66; account exec. Moore Bus. Forms, Eugene, Portland, Oreg., 1966-83; mayor, CEO, City of Beaverton, Oreg., 1985-92; mem. Nat. Adv. Coun. on Environ. Policy and Tech., Washington, 1990—. Planning commr. City of Beaverton, 1973-76, chmn. bd. design rev., 1975-76, councilman, pres. coun., 1977-84. Mem. Nat. League Cities (bd. dirs. 1990-92), League Oreg. Cities (bd. dirs. 1989-90). Home: 11650 SW Clifford St Beaverton OR 97005-5879

COLE, MALVIN, neurologist, educator; b. N.Y.C., Mar. 21, 1933; s. Harry and Sylvia (Firman) C.; A.B. cum laude, Amherst Coll., 1953; M.D. cum laude, Georgetown U. Med. Sch., 1957; m. Susan Kugel, June 20, 1954; children: Andrew James, Douglas Gowers. Intern, Seton Hall Coll. Medicine, Jersey City Med. Ctr., 1957-58; resident Boston City Hosps., 1958-60; practice medicine specializing in neurology, Montclair and Glen Ridge, N.J., Montville, N.J., 1963-72, Casper, Wyo., 1972—; teaching fellow Harvard Med. Sch., 1958-60; Research fellow Nat. Hosp. for Nervous Diseases, St. Thomas Hosp., London, Eng., 1960-61; instr. Georgetown U. Med. Sch., 1961-63; clin. assoc. prof. neurology N.J. Coll. Medicine, Newark, 1963-72, acting dir. neurology, 1965-72; assoc. prof. clin. neurology U. Colo. Med. Sch., 1973-88, prof., 1988—; mem. staff Wyo. Med. Ctr., Casper, U. Hosp., Denver. Served to capt. M.C., AUS, 1961-63. Licensed physician, Mass., N.Y., Calif., N.J., Colo., Wyo.; diplomate Am. Bd. Psychiatry and Neurology, Nat. Bd. Med. Examiners. Fellow ACP, Am. Acad. Neurology, Royal Soc. Medicine; mem. Assn. Research Nervous and Mental Disease, Acad. Aphasia, Am. Soc. Neuroimaging, Internat. Soc. Neuropsychology, Harveian Soc. London, Epilepsy Found. Am., Am. Epilepsy Soc., Am. EEG Soc., N.Y. Acad. Sci., Osler Soc. London, Alpha Omega Alpha. Contbr. articles to profl. jours. Office: 246 S Washington St Casper WY 82601-2921

COLE, RICHARD GEORGE, public administrator; b. Irvington, N.J., Mar. 11, 1948; s. Warner W. and Laurel M. (Wilson) C. AS in Computer Sci., Control Data Inst., Anaheim, Calif., 1972; BA in Sociology with high honor, Calif. State U., Los Angeles, 1974; MA in Social Ecology, U. Calif., Irvine, 1976; postgrad., So. Oreg. State Coll., 1979. Computer operator Zee Internat., Gardena, Calif., 1971; teaching asst. U. Calif., Irvine, 1974-75; planner Herman Kimmel & Assocs., Newport Beach, Calif., 1976-78; program analyst The Job Council, Medford, Oreg., 1980-81, compliance officer, 1981-82; mgr. adminstrv. svcs. The Job Coun., Medford, Oreg., 1982—; instr. Calif. Community Coll.; chmn. bd. trustees Job Council Pension Trust, Medford, 1982—; mem. curriculum adv. com. Rogue Community Coll., Grants Pass, Oreg., 1986; mgr. computer project State of Oreg., Salem, 1983-84; mem. Oreg. Occupational Info. Coordinating Com., Salem, 1982-84. Pres. bd. trustees Vector Control Dist., Jackson County, Oreg., 1985, treas., 1986, bd. dirs., 1984-87, mem. budget com., 1988—, sec., 1988-89; cand. bd. dirs. Area Edn. Dist., Jackson County, 1981; treas. Job Svc. Employer Com., Jackson County, 1987— (Spl. Svc. award 1991); dir. fin. joint pub. venture System Devel. Project, Salem, Oreg., 1986-89; mem. adv. bd. New Jobs Planning, Medford, Oreg., 1987-88, Fin. Audit and Risk Mgmt. Task Force, 1987—, chm., 1989-90. Fellow LaVerne Noyes, U. Calif., Irvine, 1974; Dr. Paul Doehring Found. scholar, Glendale, Calif., 1973; Computer Demonstration grantee State of Oreg., Salem, 1983; recipient Award of Fin. Reporting Achievement Govt. Fin. Officers Assn. of U.S. and Can., 1989-90, Fin. Ops. recognition Vector Control Dist., Jackson County, Oreg., 1990, Nat. 2d Pl. Chpt. award Jackson County Job Svc. Employer Com., 1989, Oreg. Job Svc. Employer Com. Stat award, 1991, Oreg. Individual Citation award Internat. Assn. Profls. in Employment Security, 1993. Mem. Soc. for Human Resources Mgmt., Assn. So. Oreg. Pub. Adminstrs., Oreg. Employment and Tng. Assn., Pacific N.W. Personnel Mgmt. Assn. (chpt. treas. 1985-87, orgnl. liaison dir. 1988-89, Appreciation award 1985), Govt. Fin. Officers Assn., Oreg. Mcpl. Fin. Officers assn., The Nature Conservancy. Home: 575 Morey Rd Talent OR 97540-9725 Office: The Job Coun 3069 Crater Lake Ave Medford OR 97504-4799

COLE, TERRI LYNN, organization administrator; b. Tucson, Dec. 28, 1951; m. James R. Cole II. Student, U. N.Mex., 1975-80; cert., Inst. Orgn. Mgmt., 1985. Cert. chamber exec. With SunWest Bank, Albuquerque, 1971-74, employment adminstr., 1974-76, communications dir., 1976-78; pub. info. dir. Albuquerque C. of C., 1978-81, gen. mgr., 1981-83, pres., 1983—; pres. N.Mex. C. of C. Execs. Assn., 1986-87, bd. dirs., 1980—; bd. regents Inst. for Orgn. Mgmt., Stanford U., 1988—, vice chmn., 1990-91, chmn., 1991; bd. dirs. Hosp. Home Health, Inc. Recipient Bus. Devel. award Expn. Mgmt. Inc., 1985, Women on Move award YWCA, 1986; named one of Outstanding Women of Am., 1984. Mem. Am. C. of C. Execs. Assn. (chmn. elect bd. 1992—). Republican. Office: Greater Albuquerque C of C PO Box 25100 Albuquerque NM 87125-0100

COLELLI, MARC VINCENT, educational administrator, priest; b. Lake Charles, La., Sept. 30, 1959; s. Vincent Robert and Barbara Ethel (Miller) C. BA, U. St. Thomas, Houston, 1981; MDiv, U. Toronto, Ont., Can., 1986; M of Sci. in Adminstrn., U. Notre Dame, 1987; postgrad., St. Mary's Coll. Ordained priest Roman Cath. Ch., 1986. Priest Holy Rosary Ch., Toronto, 1986-87; pastor Christ the King Parish, Pleasant Hill, Calif., 1987—; dir. devel. Bishop O'Dowd High Sch., Oakland, Calif., 1987—; mem. priest senate Diocese of Oakland. Mem. Oakland Airport Ctr. Inc. Mem. Congregation of St. Basil, Nat. Cath. Devel. Conf., Nat. Soc. Fund Raising Execs. Republican. Home and Office: Bishop O'Dowd High Sch 9500 Stearns Ave Oakland CA 94605

COLEMAN, ALAN BROUSE, financial management educator; b. San Francisco, Jan. 11, 1929; s. Alan Brouse and Hazel Virginia (Deane) C.; m. Janet M. Saville, July 4, 1953; children: Kathleen, Frances Jennifer. BA, U. San Francisco, 1952; MBA, Stanford U., 1956, PhD, 1960. Mem. faculty Grad. Sch. Bus. Harvard U., 1958-62, Stanford U., 1962-70; dean ESAN, Lima, Peru, 1963-66; v.p., treas. U.S. Natural Resources, Inc., 1970-71; pres., chief exec. officer Yosemite Park and Curry Co., Calif., 1971-73; pres., chief adminstrv. officer Sun Valley Co., Idaho, 1973-74; Caruth Prof. fin. mgmt. So. Meth. U., Dallas, 1974-88, pres., chief exec. officer S.W. Sch. Banking Found., 1980-88, dean Edwin L. Cox Sch. Bus., 1975-81; pres. Alan B. Coleman, Inc., Cons., 1981—; bd. dirs. Centex Corp., Dallas, Sterling Bancshares, Houston. Treas., trustee Family Svc. Assn. Mis-Peninsula; bd. dirs. Stanford Credit Union; adv. dir. Army and Air Force Exch. Svc. World Hdqrs., Dallas. 1st lt. U.S. Army, 1952-54. Recipient Palmas Magisteriales, Orden de Commendador (Peru); Ford Found. fellow, 1956-57; Am. Numis. Soc. fellow, 1980—. Mem. Beta Gamma Sigma. Author: (with Hempel and Simonson) Bank Management: Text and Cases, 1983, 86, 90 (with Robichek) Management of Financial Institutions, 1967, 77, (with Vandell) Case Problems in Finance, 1962, (with Marks) Cases in Commerical Bank Management, 1962. Office: PO Box 35 The Sea Ranch CA 95497-0035

COLEMAN, ARLENE FLORENCE, nurse practitioner; b. Braham, Minn., Apr. 8, 1926; d. William and Christine (Judin) C.; m. John Dunkerken, May 30, 1987. Diploma in nursing, U. Minn., 1947, BS, 1953; MPH, Loma Linda (Calif.) U., 1974. RN, Calif. Operating room scrub nurse Calif. Luth. Hosp., L.A., 1947-48; indsl. staff nurse Good Samaritan Hosp., L.A., 1948-49; staff nurse Passavant Hosp., Chgo., 1950-51; student health nurse Moody Bible Inst., Chgo., 1950-51; staff nurse St. Andrews Hosp., Mpls., 1951-53; pub. health nurse Bapt. Gen. Conf. Bd. of World Missions, Ethiopia, Africa, 1954-66; staff pub. health nurse County of San Bernadino, Calif., 1966-68, sr. pub. health nurse, 1968-73, pediatric nurse practitioner, 1973—. Contbr. articles to profl. jours. Bd. dist. missions Bapt. Gen. Conf., Calif. 1978-84; adv. coun. Kaiser Hosp., Fontana, Calif., 1969-85; bd. dirs. Casa Verdugo Retirement Home, Hemet, Calif., 1985—; adv. coun. Bethel Seminary West, San Diego, 1987—; active Calvary Bapt. Ch., Redlands, Calif. 1974—. With USPHS, 1944-47. Calif. State Dept. Health grantee, 1973. Fellow Nat. Assn. Pediatric Nurse Assocs. and Practitioners; mem. Calif. Nurses Assn. (state nursing coun. 1974-76). Democrat.

COLEMAN, BARBARA LEE, city official; b. L.A., Apr. 2, 1948; d. Merrill Franklin and Vivian Berniece (Koller) Hale; m. Carl Weinstein, July 9, 1976 (div. Dec. 1988); 1 child, Dena Lynn; m. Basil Bruce Coleman, May 1, 1989 (dec. Oct. 1990). AA in Sociology, East L.A. Coll., 1969; BS in Recreation Edn., Calif. State U., L.A., 1972. Tchr. arts and crafts East L.A. YWCA, 1967-68; resident and day camp counselor West San Gabriel Valley YMCA, Alhambra, Calif., 1967-68; counselor Happy Day Nursery and Day Camp, Monterey Park, Calif., 1968-72; playground leader City of Las Vegas (Nev.), 1973-76, summer dist. coord., 1977, recreation leader, 1978-79, community sch. coord., 1979-93, recreation specialist, 1993—; bus driver Clark County Sch. Dist., Las Vegas, 1973-78. Editor Checkered Flag newsletter, 1984-86. Advisor Tri-Hi-Y, West San Gabriel YMCA, 1966-68; asst. leader Sierra Madre coun. Girl Scouts U.S.A., 1967-68, leader Frontier coun., 1976-77, 85-86. Mem. Nat. Recreation and Park Assn. (sec. Pacific S.W. regional coun. 1989-90), Nev. Recreation and Park Soc. (hist. chmn. 1981-84, sec. 1981-83, mem.-at-large 1983-84, 87-88, chmn. bylaws 1983-89, 91—, v.p. South 1985-86, pres. 1989-90, past pres. 1990-91, citation 1985, program excellence award 1988, 92), Nev. Assn. for Community Edn. (sec.-treas. 1984—), Sports Car Club Am. (asst. regional execs. Las Vegas region 1984-86, membership com. 1985-88, chief timing and scoring 1980—), Calif. Sports Car Club. Office: City of Las Vegas Dept Parks & Leisure Activities 749 Veterans Memorial Dr Las Vegas NV 89101

COLEMAN, DALE LYNN, electronics engineer, aviator, educator; b. Topeka, June 17, 1958; s. Dale R. Coleman and Linda C. (Parks) Meiergerd; m. Patricia Bermódez, Nov. 20, 1982; 1 child, Athena C. AS in Electronic Engring. Tech. with honors, Cleve. Inst. Electronics, 1987, postgrad. Electronics technician Litton G & CS, L.A., 1979-82; sr. electronics technician Cedars-Sinai Med. Ctr., L.A., 1982-85; svc. engr. Litton AMS, San Diego, 1985-86; assoc. electrical engr. IMED Corp. R & D, San Diego, 1987—; communications officer USCG Aux., San Diego, 1987—; participant Space Life Scis. (SLS) mission Space Sta. Freedom, NASA. Co-author: The Art of Hsin Hsing Yee Ti Kenpo Kung Fu, 1991; contbr. articles to various publs. Mem. UN Assn., 1979—, sr. officer USCG Aux., 1980—; USCG liaison U.S. Naval Sea Cadet Corps, NAS Miramar, 1985—; liaison NASA, 1992—. With USN, 1976-79. Named Outstanding Citizen, Exch. Club, San Diego, 1989, Outstanding Grad., Cleveland Inst. Electronics, 1990. Mem. IEEE, Planetary Soc., Nat. Space Soc., Star Trek Assn. for Revival (chpt. pres. 1973-79, legion of honor 1975). Office: IMED Corp R & D 9775 Businesspark Ave San Diego CA 92131-1699

COLEMAN, DONALD LEE, physician; b. Granite City, Ill., Sept. 8, 1936; s. Leo Mickel Coleman and Charlotte Aileen (Booth) Grondona; children: Michelle, Suzanne, Gregory. BS, St. Louis U., 1958; MD, U. Ill., Chgo., 1962; MPH, UCLA, 1968. Cert. in aerospace medicine. With USAF, 1964-75; intern St. Mary's Hosp., San Francisco, 1962-63; resident USAF, 1967-70; med. dir. Granite City (Ill.) Steel Co., 1975-79; dir. occupational medicine and epidemiology Monsanto Co., St. Louis, 1979-85; pres., founder Summit Med. Assocs., Breckenridge and Erie, Colo., 1985—; pres., founder BioVentures, Inc., Worcester, Mass., 1988-89. Brig. gen. U.S. Air NG, 1976-91, ret. Office: Summit Med Assocs 0303 Overlook Dr PO Box # 1537 Breckenridge CO 80424-1537

COLEMAN, LEWIS WALDO, bank executive; b. San Francisco, Jan. 2, 1942; s. Lewis V. and Virginia Coleman; m. Susan G.; children: Michelle, Gregory, Nancy, Peter. B.A., Stanford U., 1965. With Bank Calif., San Francisco, 1963-73; with Wells Fargo Bank, San Francisco, 1973-86, exec. v.p., chmn. credit policy com., until 1986; vice chmn. Bank Am., San Francisco, 1986—.

COLEMAN, MICHAEL B., artist; b. Provo, Utah, June 25, 1946; s. Blaine and Kathryn (Anderson) C.; m. Jacqueline Morgan, June 1, 1968; children: Michael, Jennifer, Nicholas, Nathaniel. Student, Brigham Young U. One man shows include Kennedy Galleries, Inc., N.Y.C., Wunderlich & Co., Inc., N.Y.C., J.N. Bartfield Galleries, N.Y.C., Buffalo Bill Hist. Ctr., Cody, Wyo., C.M. Russell Mus., Great Falls, Mont., Gerald Peters Gallery, Santa Fe; 1st Nat. Parks stamp and print, 1988, Boone and Crockett Club stamp and print, Alaskan Profl. Hunters Assn. stamp and print, 1985-87. Recipient Silver medal Nat. Acad. Western Art, 1992, Gold medal, 1993; named one of Top Twelve Wildlife Artists Sports Afield Mag. Mem. Nat. Assn. Wildlife Artists (Silver medal 1992). Home: 2822 Rolling Knolls Dr Provo UT 84604-4382

COLEMAN, ROBERT TRENT, social worker, rehabilitation consultant; b. Gary, Ind., Feb. 4, 1936; s. Robert Clinton and Lucille Verna C.; m. Dorothy Agnes, Aug. 1957; children: Sean, Bryce, Daniel; m. 2d, Patricia Lou, June 13, 1976; m. 3d Polly Anderson, Sept. 15, 1984. BA in Speech Therapy, U. Wash., Seattle, 1962; postgrad. in speech U. Redlands, 1963-64; MS in Rehab. Counseling, U. Oreg., 1971. Cert. rehab. counselor, cert. ins. rehab. specialist. Social worker, San Bernardino City Welfare Dept., 1963-64; correctional counselor Calif. Rehab. Center, Norco, 1964-67; sr. counselor Job Corps, Clearfield, Utah, 1967; assoc. dir. Ednl. Systems Corp., Washington, 1968-69; ptnr. Black Fir Jade Mines, Big Sur, Calif., 1971-76; vocat. specialist Internat. Rehab. Assn., San Diego, 1976-77; vocat. rehab. counselor Sharp Hosp., San Diego, 1977-80; clin. coord. San Diego Pain Inst., 1981; cons. in rehab. counseling, career guidance, human rels., Carlsbad, Calif., 1981-83; propr. R.T.C. Cons. Svcs., Escondido and San Diego, 1983—; vocat. rehab. expert Civil Ct., 1983—. Commr., Handicapped Appeals Commn., San Marcos, Calif., 1981-83. Served with U.S. Army, 1955-58. Mem. Am. Assn. for Counseling and Devel. (pres.), San Diego Career Guidance Assn. (pres. 1984), Assn. Indsl. Rehab. Reps. (pres. 1983), Am. Rehab. Counseling Assn., Nat. Assn. Rehab. Profls. in Pvt. Sector (standards and ethics com. 1986—, chmn. 1988-90). Republican. Home: 538 Glenheather Dr San Marcos CA 92069-2005 Office: 365 W 2nd Ave # 215 Escondido CA 92025-4230

COLEMAN, ROGER DIXON, bacteriologist; b. Rockwell, Iowa, Jan. 18, 1915; s. Major C. and Hazel Ruth Coleman; A.B., UCLA, 1937; postgrad. Balliol Coll., Oxford (Eng.) U., 1944; MS, U. So. Calif., 1952, PhD, 1957; m. Lee Aden Skov, Jan. 1, 1978. Sr. laboratorian Napa (Calif.) State Hosp., 1937-42; dir. Long Beach (Calif.) Clin. Lab., 1946-86, pres., 1980—; mem. Calif. State Clin. Lab. Commn., 1953-57. Served as officer AUS, 1942-46. Diplomate Am. Bd. Bioanalysts. Mem. Am. Assn. Bioanalysts, Am. Assn. Clin. Chemists, Am. Soc. Microbiologists, Am. Chem. Soc., Am. Venereal Disease Assn., AAAS (life), Calif. Assn. Bioanalysts (past officer), Med. Research Assn. Calif., Bacteriology Club So. Calif., Sigma Xi, Phi Sigma (past chpt. pres.). Author papers in field. Home: 7 Laguna Woods Dr Laguna Beach CA 92677-2829 Office: PO Box 7073 Laguna Beach CA 92607-7073

COLEMAN, ROGER WILLIAM, institutional food distribution company executive; b. Newark, Mar. 30, 1929; s. Bernard Simpson and Evelyn (Bornstein) C.; m. Ruth Rykoff (div. Apr. 1982); children—William, Wendy, Paul (dec.), Eric; m. Francesca Marie Wessilius, Sept. 1983. B.S., UCLA, 1950. Gen. mgmt. positions Rogay Food Supply div. S. E. Rykoff & Co., Los Angeles, 1951-58; purchasing and gen. mgmt. positions S.E. Rykoff & Co., Los Angeles, 1958-63, gen. mgr., 1963-67, pres., chief exec. officer, 1967-86; pres., chief exec. officer John Sexton Inc., 1983-86; pres., chief exec. officer Rykoff-Sexton, Inc., 1986-92, ret., 1992, cons., advisor, also bd. dirs. Bd. dirs. L.A. Conv. Ctr., Reiss-Dis Child Study Ctr., La. chpt. ARC, NCCJ. Mem. Nat. Inst. Food Svc. (bd. dirs.), Calif. C. of C. (bd.dirs.), L.A. C. of C. (bd. of dirs.). Clubs: Los Angeles Athletic, Hillcrest Country, Regency, Met., Carlton, World Trade and Stock Exchange, Pebble Beach, Beach and Tennis of Pebble Beach, La Costa Country. Home: 515 Homewood Rd Los Angeles CA 90049-1905 Office: Rykoff-Sexton Inc PO Box 21917 761 Terminal St Los Angeles CA 90021-1182*

COLEMAN, RONNY JACK, fire chief; b. Tulsa, May 17, 1940; s. Clifford Harold and Elizabeth Ann (Teter) C.; m. Susan René Calvert, July 18, 1963 (div. Jan. 1971); children: Lisa René, Christopher Alan; m. Marie Katherine McCarthy, Nov. 18, 1972. AS in Fire Sci., Rancho Santiago Coll., 1971; BS in Polit. Sci., Calif. State U., Fullerton, 1974; postgrad. in vocat. edn., Calif. State U., Long Beach. Tanker, foreman U.S. Forest Svc., Trabuco, Calif., 1960-62; ops. chief Costa Mesa (Calif.) Fire Dept., 1962-73; fire chief San Clemente (Calif.) Fire Dept., 1973-85, Fullerton (Calif.) Fire Dept., 1985—; pres. Phenix Tech., Inc., San Clementa, 1971—. Author: Management of Fire Service Operations, 1975, Fire Truck Toys for Men and Boys, Vols. I and II, 1978, Alpha to Omega: History of Fire Sprinklers, 1983; patentee firefighter helmets. Chmn. Pete Wilson's Fire Brigade, San Clemente, 1990, United Fund Dr., Costa Mesa, 1968. Cpl. USMC, 1957-60. Rayford-Worsted scholar, 1968, Moore scholar, 1961; named Polyurethane Man of Yr. Polyurethane Assn., 1988, Richard Parmalee award Am. Fire Sprinkler Assn., 1989. Mem. Internat. Assn. Fire Chiefs (pres. 1988-89), Nat. Fire Protection Assn., League of Calif. Cities (pres. fire chiefs dept. 1988-89), Orange County Fire Chief's Assn. (pres. 1983-84), Orange County Burn Assn. (bd. dirs. 1990). Republican. Home: 211 Calle Salida San Clemente CA 92672-2128 Office: Fullerton Fire Dept 312 E Commonwealth Ave Fullerton CA 92632-2099

COLEMAN, TED, health educator, consulting executive; b. Anderson, S.C., Oct. 31, 1953; m. Carol A. Barber; children: Ryan, Randy, Preston, Brady, Landon. AA, Anderson Coll., 1973; BA, Brigham Young U., 1979, MHEd, 1980; PhD, Purdue U., 1983. Registered health educator. Grad. instr. Purdue U., West Lafayette, Ind., 1980-83; asst. prof. Calif. State U., San Bernardino, 1983-85, Utah State U., Logan, 1985-91; sr. trainer Quest Internat., Granville, Ohio, 1988—. Contbr. articles to profl. jours. Chmn. Cache Valley AIDS Task Force, 1987-88, Cache Valley chpt. Am. Cancer Soc. 1987-88, bd. dirs. Named Advisor of Yr., Utah State U., 1988. Mem. AAHPERD (v.p. health S.W. dist. 1990-91, Health Profl. of Yr. award 1990), Utah Assn. Health Phys. Edn. Recreation and Dance (v.p. health 1988-89, Honor award 1990), Mortar Bd. (Top Prof. 1990, 91), Eta Sigma Gamma (Prof. of Yr. 1988, Outstanding Leadership and Svc. award 1989, Disting. Svc. award 1991, edit. assoc. The Eta Sigma Gamman/The Health Educator, 1992—).

COLEMAN, WILLIAM GILBERT, electric power industry executive; b. Little Rock, Aug. 1, 1951; s. Wendel Holmes, Jr., and Fredericka (Shafer) C.; m. Robin Rae Crank. BA, U. N.Mex., 1974. Environ. analyst Ark. Power & Light Co., Little Rock, 1974-78, environ. coord., 1978-80, mgr. environ. affairs, 1980-83; loaned exec. environ. and govt. affairs Edison Electric Inst., Washington, 1984-85; regional mgr. Electric Power Rsch. Inst., Washington, 1985-89; sr. technology transfer adminstr. Electric Power Rsch. Inst., Palo Alto, Calif., 1989-91, mgr. tech. transfer, 1992—. Appointee Gov.'s State Policy Adv. Com., Ark., 1977-80, Ark. Council for Environ. Edn., Ark., 1975-79; trustee Ark. Museum of Sci. & History, 1982-83. Named Forest Conservationist of Yr. Ark. Wildlife Fedn., 1983, Shared Conservation Orgn. of Yr., 1979, 84, Ark. Wildlife Fedn. Shared Conservation Orgn. of Yr., 1984, Gulf Oil Co. Mem. AMORC. Democrat. Home: 32 Hillbrook Dr Menlo Park CA 94028-7934 Office: Electric Power Rsch Co PO Box 10412 Palo Alto CA 94303-0813

COLEMAN, WILLIAM ROBERT, optometrist; b. Newport, R.I., Aug. 29, 1916; s. Frank and Mae Markel; m. Monique Coleman; children: Philippe Charles, Kevin Charles, Tina-Lise. BS, So. Calif. Coll. Optometry, L.A., 1948, OD, 1949. Pvt. practice San Bernardino, Calif., 1951—. Mem. San Bernardino County Mus. Commn., 1962-67; chmn. San Bernardino Bicentennial Commn., 1974-76; bd. dirs. nat. historic site Friends of Touro Synagogue, 1955—; v.p. Touch Am. History, 1985—. 1st lt. U.S. Army, World War II. Mem. Manuscript Soc. (treas. 1981-86, pres. 1986-88), Am. Antiquarian Soc., Grolier Club, Orange Belt Optometric Assn. (pres. 1976-77), So. Calif. chpt. Manuscript Soc. (pres. 1972-74, 83-84).

COLES, DWIGHT ROSS, software engineer; b. Albion, Ill., Nov. 30, 1952; s. Glenn Joseph and Helen Mae (Cowling) C.; m. Elizabeth Coles; 1 child, Tyler Ross. BSME, N.Mex. Inst. Mining & Tech., 1974, MS in Extractive Metallurgy, 1975. Metall. engr. Inspiration (Ariz.) Consolidated Copper Co., 1975-79; process engr./mgr. Cal West Metals, Socorro, N.Mex., 1979-80; software engr. Fluor Mining & Metals, Redwood City, Calif., 1980-84; sr. software engr. Signetics, Albuquerque, 1984-85; sr. software engr./mgr. BDM Corp., Albuquerque, 1985-89; sr. software engr., project mgr. Re/Spec Inc., Albuquerque, 1989—; cons. Sandia Nat. Labs., 1989—. Editor: History of First Christ Church of Albion, Ill., 1990; contbr. articles to profl. jours. Instr. N.Mex. Hunter Safety Prog., Albuquerque, 1985—. Mem. N.Mex Tech. Alumni (treas. 1990—), N.Am. Ingres Users Assn. (pres. 1992-93), N.Mex. Ingres Users Assn. (founding mem., pres.). Disciples of Christ. Office: Re/Spec Inc 4775 Indian School Rd NE # 300 Albuquerque NM 87110-3927

COLGREN, RICHARD DEAN, flight controls engineer; b. Seattle, June 13, 1961. BS in Aeronautics and Astronautics, U. Wash., 1982; MS in Elec. Engring., U. So. Calif., 1987, PhD in Elec. Engring., 1993. Engr. Northrop Corp., Pico Rivera, Calif., 1982-84; sr. engr. Lockheed Corp., Burbank, Calif., 1984—. Co-author: Progress in Simulation, 1993; contbr. articles to profl. jours.; assoc. editor Jour. Theoretical and Computer Graphics; patentee in field. Mem. IEEE (sr.), AIAA (sect. chmn. 1989-90, 91, ACC rev. chmn. 1992), Nat. Tech. Com. (sec., Sr. Mem. award 1989, Assoc. Fellow award 1991). Office: Lockheed B-311 P/B-6 D/25-33 PO Box 250 Sunland CA 91041-2533

COLLA, VIRGINIA COVERT, director choral activities, educator; b. Oklahoma City, July 8, 1937; d. Harry Thomas and Sadie Virginia (Campbell) Tucker; m. Terry Howard Covert, May 31, 1963 (div. Dec. 1970); m. Richard Joseph Colla, Oct. 3, 1981. AA, Mt. San Antonio Coll., 1957; MusB, U. of the Pacific, 1960; MA, Occidental Coll., 1970; D in Mus. Arts, U. Ill., 1986. Tchr. vocal music Havencourt Jr. High Sch., Oakland, Calif., 1960-61, Modesto (Calif.) High Sch., 1961-70; dir. choral activities San Diego Mesa Coll., 1970-84; asst. prof., dir. choral activities U. Nebr., Lincoln, 1984-86; assoc. prof., dir. choral and vocal activities Calif. State U., Turlock, 1986—; minister of music St. Paul's Episcopal Ch., Modesto, 1962-68, First Presbyn. Ch., Modesto, 1969-70; artistic dir. The Clarion Singers, San Diego, 1981-84. Mem. Am. Choral Dirs. Assn. (life, pres. Western div. 1975-77), Music Edn. Nat. Conf., Calif. Music Educators Assn. (Eunice Skinner award 1989). Republican. Presbyterian. Office: Calif State U Stanislaus Dept of Music Turlock CA 95380

COLLARD, LORRAINE FULLMER, violin instructor; b. Salt Lake City, Mar. 25, 1957; d. Merlin Don and Mary Suz Anne (Christensen) F.; m. Steven Robert Collard, June 26, 1981; children: Grant, Christopher, Michael. MusB, Brigham Young U., 1980; MA in Music, San Diego State U., 1986. Cert. music tchr., Calif., Utah. Instr. violin Calif., Utah, 1970—; tchr. string orch. Nebo Sch. Dist., Payson, Utah, 1980-81; substitute tchr. Poway, City Schs., Escondido Dists., San Diego, 1982-84; instr. group lessons in violin, San Diego, 1991—. Violinist San Jose State U. Chamber Orch., 1975-77, San Jose State U. Orch., 1975-77, San Diego State U. Quartet, 1976-77, Brigham Young U. Philharmonic, 1977-79, Brigham Young U. Chamber Orch., 1978-79, San Diego State U., 1982-85; concertmaster U. San Diego, 1981-82; active mem. LDS Ch.; den mother cub scouts Boy Scouts Am., San Diego, 1984-85; asst. concertmaster Palomar Orch., San Marcos, Calif., 1989-91; coord. Handel's Messiah Orch., San Diego, 1988-92. Rudolph Giskin Meml. scholar San Jose State U., 1975, Gov. scholar State of Calif., 1975, San Jose Tchr.'s Assn. scholar, 1975, music scholar Brigham Young U., 1977-79, grad. scholar San Diego State U., 1982-83; recipient music award Bank of Am., 1975, 3d runner-up award Miss Am. County Pageant, 1975, Swimsuit Competition award, 1975. Mem. Suzuki Assn. Am., Suzuki Music Assn. Calif.

COLLEN, MORRIS FRANK, physician; b. St. Paul, Nov. 12, 1913; s. Frank Morris and Rose (Finkelstein) C.; m. Frances B. Diner, Sept. 24, 1937; children: Arnold Roy, Barry Joel, Roberta Joy, Randal Harry. BEE, U. Minn., 1934, MB with distinction, 1938, MD, 1939. Diplomate Am. Bd. Internal Medicine. Intern Michael Reese Hosp., Chgo., 1939-40; resident Los Angeles County Hosp., 1940-42; chief med. service Kaiser Found. Hosp., Oakland, Calif., 1942-43; chief of staff Kaiser Found. Hosp., San Francisco, 1953-61; med. dir. Permanente Med. Group, West Bay Div., 1953-79, dir. med. methods research, 1962-79, dir. tech. assessment, 1979-83, cons. div. research, 1983—; chmn. exec. com. Permanente Med. Group, Oakland, 1953-73; dir. Permanente Services, Inc., Oakland, 1958-73; lectr. Sch. Pub. Health, U. Calif., Berkeley, 1966-78; lectr. info. sci. U. Calif., San Francisco, 1970-85; lectr. U. London, 1972, Stanford U. Med. Ctr., 1973, 75, 84-86, Harvard U., 1974, Johns Hopkins U., 1976, also others; cons. Bur. Health Services, USPHS, 1965-68, chmn. health care systems study sect., 1968-72, mem. adv. com. demonstration grants, 1967; advisor VA, 1968; cons. European region WHO, 1968-72; cons. med. fitness program U.S. Air Force, 1968; cons. Pres.'s Biomed. Research Panel, 1975; mem. adv. com. automated Multiphasic Health Testing, 1971; discussant Nat. Conf. Preventive Medicine, Bethesda, Md., 1975; mem. com. on tech. in health care NAS, 1976; mem. adv. group Nat. Commn. on Digestive Diseases, U.S. Congress, 1978; mem. adv. panel to U.S. Congress Office of Tech. Assessment, 1980-85; mem. peer rev. adv. group TRIMIS program Dept. Def., 1978-90; program chmn. 3d Internat. Conf. Med. Informatics, Tokyo, 1980; chmn. bd. sci. counselors Nat. Library Medicine, 1985-87. Author: Treatment of Pneumococcic Pneumonia, 1948, Hospital Computer Systems, 1974, Multiphasic Health Testing Systems, 1977, Informatics: A Historical Review, 1991; editor: Permanente Med. Bull., 1943-53; mem. editorial bd. Preventive Medicine, 1970-80, Jour. Med. Systems, Methods Information Medicine, 1980-93, Diagnostic Medicine, 1980-84, Computers in Biomed. Rsch., 1987-93; contbr. articles to med. jours., chpts. to med. books. Johns Hopkins Centennial scholar, 1976; fellow Ctr. Adv. Studies in Behavioral Scis., Stanford, 1985-86; scholar-in-residence Nat. Libr. Medicine, 1987-93; recipient Pioneer award Computers in Health Care Jour., 1992. Fellow ACP, Am. Coll. Cardiology, Am. Coll. Chest Physicians, Am. Inst. Med. & Biol. Engring.; mem. AMA, Inst. Medicine of NAS (chmn. tech. subcom. for improving patient records 1990, chmn. workshop on informatics in clin. preventive medicine 1991), Am. Fedn. Clin. Rsch., Salutis Unitas (v.p. 1972), Soc. Adv. Med. Systems (pres. 1973), Nat. Acad. Practice in Medicine (chmn. 1983-88, co-chmn. 1989-91), Am. Coll. Med. Informatics (pres. 1987-88), Am. Med. Informatics Assn. (bd. dirs. 1989-91), Internat. Med. Informatics Assn. (hon.), Internat. Health Evaluation Assn. (bd. dirs. 1985-93, Lifetime Achievement award 1992, Computers in Healthcare Pioneer award 1992), Alpha Omega Alpha, Tau Beta Pi. Home: 4155 Walnut Blvd Walnut Creek CA 94596-5834 Office: 3451 Piedmont Ave Piedmont CA 94611-5463

COLLETT, MERRILL JUDSON, management consultant; b. Winona Lake, Ind., Feb. 20, 1914; s. Charles Alfred and Dora (Jenkins) C.; m. Jeannette Luger, Dec. 10, 1938 (div.); m. Aagot Lunde, Oct. 12, 1955 (dec. Oct. 1985); m. Carol LaVerne, Feb. 1, 1987. BA, Stanford (Calif.) U., 1934; MPA, Syracuse (N.Y.) U., 1938. Pers. dir. Bonneville Power Adminstrn., Portland, Oreg., 1946-50; dir. pers. and mgmt. prodn., mktg. adminstrn. USDA, Washington, 1950-52; exec sec. requirements com. Def. Prodn. Adminstrn., Washington, 1952-54; dir. wartime organizational planning Office Def. Mobilization, Washington, 1954-58; co-owner Collett and Clapp, P.R., 1958-65; founder, pres. Exec. Mgmt. Svc., Arlington, Va., 1967-82; program assoc. Coalition to Improve Mgmt. in State and Local Govt., Pitts., 1983—; editor-at-large The Bureaucrat, Washingt, 1981—; cons. for mgmt. Tucson Met. Ministry, 1985-88. Contbr. articles to profl. jours. Moderator Calvary Bapt. Ch., Washington, 1981-83; bd. dirs. Efforts from Ex-Convicts, Washington, 1967-83, Bacone Coll., Muskogee, Okla., 1980-86, 91—, Tucson Met. Ministry, 1989-91. Lt. USNR, 1943-46. Mem. Internat. Pers. Mgmt. Assn. (hon. life, Stockberger award), Ariz. Pers. Mgmt. Assn. (hon. life).

COLLEY, BARBARA MARIE, financial executive; b. Pomona, Calif., May 5, 1958; d. Robert Weldon and Ethel Pancoast (Hosking) Toms; m. Ronald Winslow, Mar. 24, 1979 (div. 1981); m. Glenn Turner Colley, Nov. 21, 1987; children: Sean, Jennifer, Caleb. BS, Calif. Poly. Inst., 1988. Acct. Avery Label, Azusa, Calif., 1978-82; pvt. practice in acctg., 1986-90; acct. County of Orange, Santa Ana, Calif., 1988-89; CFO Hillcrest, LaVerne, Calif., 1989—. Mem. Calif. Poly. Acctg. Alumni (bd. dirs. 1992, 93, Scholarship 1987). Republican. Mem. Ch. LDS. Office: Hillcrest 2705 Mountain View Dr La Verne CA 91750

COLLEY, PETER MICHAEL, playwright, screenwriter; b. Scarborough, Yorkshire, Eng., Jan. 3, 1949; came to U.S., 1985; s. Thomas and Irene (Firth) C.; m. Ellen Ross Jenkins, Nov. 22, 1984. BA with honors, U. Sheffield, Eng., 1971; postgrad., U. Western Ont. Resident playwright Actors Alley Repertory Theatre, L.A., 1989; v.p. Castle Moon Prodns., 1989; resident playwright Grand Theatre, London, Ont., Can., 1973-76; pres. Buckingham Internat. Prodns., 1991—; instr. in playwrighting Theatre Ont. Author: (plays) The Saga of Regin, 1971, The Donnellys, 1974, You'll Get Used to It, 1975, The Huron Tiger, 1978, I'll Be Back Before Midnight, 1979, Heads, You Lose, 1981, The Mark of Cain, 1984, Beyond Suspicion, 1991, (films) The Mark of Cain, 1986, Illusions, 1992; co-author: (plays) The Vaudevillians Mus., 1979, When the Reaper Calls, 1990. Mem. ACTRA Writers Guild, Playwrights Union of Can., Writers Guild Am., Dramatists Guild. Office: Buckingham Internat Prodns Ste 123 20929-47 Ventura Blvd Woodland Hills CA 91364

COLLIER, MARSHA ANN, publishing executive; b. N.Y.C., Dec. 4, 1950; d. Samuel Schleimer and Claire (Schmelzer) Tracy; 1 child, Susan Marie. Student, Miami Dade Jr. Coll., 1968-70, U. Miami, 1970-72. Advt. account exec. Miami (Fla.) Herald, 1977; spl. projects mgr. Daily News, L.A., 1977-84; pres. Collier Advt. & Promotion Inc., Northridge, Calif., 1984—; bridal show dir. Daily News, L.A., 1978-83; gen. mgr. Dodger Blue, L.A., 1082-83; pub. So. Calif. Autoracing Newspaper, 1985-88, Score News (ofcl. publ. of Score Internat.), 1986-90, Northridge Bus. News. Mem. Am. Autoracing Writers and Broadcasters Assn., Advt. Club L.A., So. Calif. Mktg. Dirs. Assn., Internat. Coun. Shopping Ctrs., Northridge C. of C. (bd. dirs., Businessperson of Yr.), Chatsworth C. of C., Granada Hills C. of C., Calabasas C. of C., Rotary. Republican. Office: 18620 Plummer St Northridge CA 91324-2245

COLLIER, RICHARD BANGS, philosopher, foundation executive; b. Hastings, Nebr., Aug. 12, 1918; s. Nelson Martin and Stella (Butler) C. BA, U. Wash., 1951. Fgn. aid officer GS14, civil aviation Am. embassy, Bangkok, Thailand, 1958-63; founder, dir. Pleneurethics Society, Tacoma, 1963—; founder Inst. Ethics & Sci., Tacoma, 1988—. Carnegie fellow Inst. Pub. Affairs, Grad. Sch., U. Wash., 1950-51. Nat. adv. bd. Am. Security Council. Capt. USAF, 1965-66. Recipient Rep. Presdl. Legion of merit. Mem. Assn. Supervision & Curriculum Devel., Soc. Health & Human Values, Royal Inst. Philosophy (Eng.), Nat. Rep. Senatorial Inner Circle (Presdl. commn.). Author: Pleneurethic, 20 vols., 1964-93, Pleneurethics: A Philosophical System Uniting Body, Brain and Mind, 2d edit. 1990. Home: PO Box 1256 Tacoma WA 98401-1256

COLLINGS, CELESTE LOUISE (SHORTY VASSALLI), marketing executive, professional artist; b. Highland Park, Ill., Dec. 9, 1948; d. Robert Zane Jr. and Laura (Vasaly) C.; m. John Austin Darden III, July 17, 1971 (div. July 1975); 1 child, Desiree Anne; m. John Cochran Barber, Dec. 13, 1984. BA, U. Ariz., 1970; postgrad., N.Mex. State U., 1975; completed mktg. mgr. seminar, U. Calif., Irvine, 1978; cert. of achievement, Wilson Learning Course, 1983. Art tchr. Devargas Jr. High Sch., Santa Fe, 1971; artist, pvt. tchr. Las Cruces, N.Mex., 1971-75; sales rep. Helpmates Temp. Services, Santa Ana, Calif., 1975-76; sales account mgr. Bristol-Myers Products, N.Y.C., 1976-82; sales mgr. Profl. Med. Products, Greenwood, S.C., 1982-85; mktg. mgr. med. products Paper-Pak Products, La Verne, Calif., 1985-88; owner Multi-Media West, Newport Beach, Calif., 1988—; mgmt. trainee Bristol-Myers, Kansas City, Mo., 1978; sales trainee Profl. Med. Products, Greenwood, 1983, product strategy, 1984, chmn. nat. adv. com., 1983-84; owner and pres. Accent Shoji Screens, Newport Beach, Calif., 1981—. Exhibited in one-woman art shows at Nancy Dunn Studio and Gallery, San Clemente, Calif., 1980, The Collectables, San Francisco, 1980, Gallery 141, Orange Calif., 1992, Laguna Beach (Calif.) Festival of the Arts Art-A-Fair, 1981, Ariz. Inter-Scholastic Hon. Exhibit, 1st place award, 1962-66, Glendale Fed. Savs. Art Exhitibition, 1982; numerous others. Mem. Orange County Performing Arts Ctr., Colona Del Mar, Calif., 1981, Orange County Visual Artists, 1990, Orange County Ctr. for Contemporary Art, 1993; asst. dir. Orange County Satelittle, Womens Caucus for Art, organizer, 1993. Recipient 10 sales awards Bristol-Meyers, 1976-82, Western Zone Sales Rep. award Profl. Med. Products, 1984, Gainers Club award, 1984; named Nat. Sales Rep. of Yr. Profl. Med. Products, 1984. Mem. Humanities Assocs., U. Ariz. Alumni Assn., Kappa Alpha Theta Alumni.

COLLINGS, CHARLES LEROY, supermarket executive; b. Wewoka, Okla., July 11, 1925; s. Roy B. and Dessie L. C.; m. Frances Jane Flake, June 28, 1947; children—Sandra Jean, Dianna Lynn. Student, So. Methodist U., 1943-44, U. Tex., 1945. Sec., contr., dir. Noble Meat Co., Madera, Calif., 1947-54; chief acct. Montgomery Ward & Co., Oakland, Calif., 1954-56; with Raleys, Sacramento, 1956—; sec. Raleys, 1958—, pres., 1970—, CEO, 1993—, also dir. Bd. dirs. Pro Athlete Outreach, Youth for Christ. With USNR, 1943-46. Mem. Calif. Grocers Assn. (dir., officer, past chmn.), Calif Retailers Assn. (bd. dir.). Republican. Baptist. Home: 6790 Arabella Way Sacramento CA 95831-2325 Office: Raley's PO Box 15618 Sacramento CA 95852-1618

COLLINS, ALLAN WAYNE, state official, civil engineer; b. L.A., Aug. 10, 1934; s. Ross Meredith and Erma Druscilla (Fogg) C.; m. Joanne Virginia Pluess, June 16, 1956; children: Karen Holmes, Kenneth, David, Michael. BSCE, U. Calif., Berkeley, 1956; MS in Mgmt., U.S. Naval Postgrad. Sch., 1964. Registered profl. engr., Ariz., D.C. Commd. ensign USN, 1956, advanced through grades to capt., 1976, ret., 1982; dep. county engr. County of Miricopa, Phoenix, 1982-88, asst. county mgr. pub. works dir., engr., 1988-91; asst. state engr. maintenance Ariz. Dept. of Transp., Phoenix, 1991—; fed. region IX county rd. advisor Fed. Hwy. Adminstrn., Ariz., Calif., Nev. and Hawaii, 1989-91. Mem. solid mgmt. waste adv. bd. State of Ariz., Phoenix, 1987—. Mem. ASCE (pres. Ariz. chpt. 1988), Am. Pub. Works Assn. (v.p. Ariz. chpt. 1992, pres. Ariz. chpt. 1993), Am. Planning Assn., Nat. Assn. County Engrs. (v.p. western region 1988-90, sec., treas. 1990—, pres.-elect 1990-91), Soc. Am. Mil. Egnrs. (post bd. dirs. Phoenix chpt. 1985), Ariz. Assn. County Engrs. Presbyterian. Home: 7012 N 23d St Phoenix AZ 85020 Office: Ariz Dept of Transp 206 S 17th Ave Rm 176A Phoenix AZ 85007

COLLINS, CURTIS ALLAN, oceanographer; b. Des Moines, Sept. 16, 1940; s. Ralph Charlie and Noma Lovella (Buckley) C.; m. Judith Ann Petersen, Dec. 22, 1962; children: Nathaniel Christopher and Hillary Victoria. BS, U.S. Mcht. Marine Acad., 1962; MS, Oreg. State U., 1964, PhD, 1967. Instr. Chapman Coll. (Calif.) in Barcelona, Spain, 1964; 3d mate on ship Reynolds Metals, Corpus Christi, Tex., 1967-68; research scientist Govt. of Can., Nanaimo, B.C., 1968-70; ocean engr. Cities Service Oil, Tulsa, 1970-72; program dir. NSF, Washington, 1972-87, prof., chmn. dept. oceanography, Naval Postgrad. Sch., Monterey, 1987—; guest investigator Woods Hole Oceanographic Instn. (Mass.), 1983; commr. Moss Landing Harbor Dist., 1993—. Served to capt. USNR. Decorated Nat. Def. medal; recipient Admiral E.S. Land award Dept. Commerce, 1962, Meritorious Service award NSF, 1987; grad. fellow NSF, 1963. Mem. Am. Geophys. Union (Oceans Scis. award 1985, pres. ocean scis. sect.), Ocean Soc. Japan, Am. Meteorol. Soc. Home: 24010 Ranchito Del Rio Ct Salinas CA 93908-9652 Office: Naval Postgrad Sch Code OCCO Monterey CA 93943-5000

COLLINS, DANE H., artist, new product developer; b. Champaign, Ill., Feb. 2, 1961; s. Ronald Milton Collins and Beverly Carolyn (Brown) Patnaude; m. Leigh Ann Paulsen, Oct. 4, 1989. Student, Iowa State U., 1979-82. Acct. exec. Phoenix Pub., Inc., 1982-83, advt. mgt., 1983-85; comml. artist Jackie Awerman Assocs., Phoenix, 1983-88; acct. svcs. supr. The Lutzker Group, Phoenix, 1985-86; advt. dir. Intersouth Communications, Scottscale, Ariz., 1986-87; mktg. dir. Ariz. Bus. & Devel., Phoenix, 1988-89; v.p. S.W. Communications, Phoenix, 1988-90, Balloon Buddies, Inc., Mesa, Ariz., 1988-90; mktg. dir. Orange-Sol, Inc., Gilbert, Ariz., 1989-93, art/mktg. dir., 1993—; cons. Continental Am. Corp., Wichita, Kans., 1990-92, Ariz. Bus. & Devel., Phoenix, 1990-91. Illustrator: (books) Power, Influence, Sabotage: The Corporate Survivor's Coloring Book & Primer, 1986, Good Morning Mr. President, 1988; patentee decorative message display. Vol. DeNovo, Phoenix, 1984, Cystic Fibrosis Found., Scottsdale, 1985, Aid to Women's Ctr., Phoenix, 1987, Dayspring U.M.C. Missions for Homeless, Tempe, Ariz., 1990. Mem. Phoenix Soc. Communicating Arts. Republican. Methodist. Home and Office: 2650 E South Fork Dr Phoenix AZ 85044-8976

COLLINS, FERN SHARON, secretary/administrative reports clerk; b. Denver, Jan. 20, 1945; d. Royce Donald and Viola Fern (Sundgren) Grimes; m. James Marsh Rasmussen, Dec. 21, 1966 (div. Aug. 1981); children: Alan James, Michael Royce, Carol Ann; m. Steven Edward Collins, Sept. 18, 1982. Grad., Golden (Colo.) High Sch., 1962. Clk. Mountain Bell, Denver, 1962-67; homemaker Denver, 1967-81; sec./adminstrv. reports clk. US West, Denver, 1981—. Logistic asst. Denver Grand Prix, 1990, 91, St. Patricks Day Parade, Denver, 1992; asst. Cinco DeMayo, Denver, 1992.

COLLINS, GEORGE TIMOTHY, computer software consultant; b. Connersville, Ind., Aug. 21, 1943; s. Robert Emerson and Oma (Richie) C.; m. Martha Elizabeth Holt, Apr. 30, 1966; children: Kirsten Stephanie, Eowyn Erika. BA in Math., Ind. U., 1966; MS in Computer Sci., Rensselaer Poly. Inst., 1971. Engr. program analyst Sikorsky Aircraft, Stratford, Conn., 1966-70; research mathematician Peter Eckrich, Ft. Wayne, Ind., 1970-75; sr. systems analyst Pyrotek Data Service, Ft. Walton Beach, Fla., 1975-77; sr. aerosystems engr. Gen. Dynamics, Ft. Worth, 1977-79; sr. specialist Electronic Data Systems, Las Vegas, Nev., 1979-81; sr. assoc. CACI Fed., San Diego, 1981-82; prin., gen. mgr. Structured Software Systems, Escondido, Calif., 1982-88; sr. software engr. Sci. Applications Internat. Corp., San Diego, 1988—; cons. Hi-Shear Corp., Los Angeles, 1973-75. Developer (computer model and data base) Aircraft Stores Interface, 1975; (computer model) TAC Disrupter, 1981; co-developer (computer model) Tactical Air Def., Battle Model, 1978, Tactical Air and Land Ops., 1980; prime contbr. (computer data collection and analysis system) Mobile Sea Range, 1988-90; contbr. (computer communications system) Lightweight Deployable Communications, 1990, Joint Advanced Spl. Ops. Radio System, 1992. Bd. dirs. Family and Children's Service, Ft. Wayne, 1974. Mem. Assn. Computing Machinery (assoc.). Unitarian. Club: North County Chess (Escondido). Home: 121 W 8th Ave Escondido CA 92025-5001

COLLINS, JAMES FRANCIS, toxicologist; b. Balt., Jan. 26, 1942; s. James Murphy and Mary M. (Dolan) C.; m. Barbara Joan Betka, June 21, 1969; children: Chris, Cavan. BS, Loyola Coll., Balt., 1963; PhD, U.N.C., 1968. Diplomate Am. Bd. Toxicology. Fellow NIH, Bethesda, Md., 1968-75; faculty mem., rsch. chemist U. Tex. Health Sci. Ctr. and VA Med. Ctr., San Antonio, 1975-86; staff toxicologist Calif. EPA and Dept. Health Svcs., Berkeley, Calif., 1986—; instr. U. Calif. Berkeley/Extension, 1987—. Contbr. numerous articles to profl. jours., publs. Mem. Am. Soc. Biochemistry and Molecular Biology. Democrat. Roman Catholic. Home: 822 Rogers Way Pinole CA 94564-2409 Office: Calif EPA 2151 Berkeley Way Annex 11 Berkeley CA 94704-1011

COLLINS, JOHN JOSEPH, lawyer; b. Los Angeles, Calif., Dec. 13, 1936; s. James Edward Collins and Helen Agnes Howard; m. Patricia Lynn Stephens; children: James H., Cynthia A. Collins Lilly, Robert J., Pamela M. Birmingham, John J. Jr., Lauren P., William S., Andrea E. AB, U. Santa Clara, Santa Clara, 1958; LLB, Loyola U., L.A., 1961. Dep. county counsel Office of County Counsel, L.A., 1961-64; assoc. ptnr. mg. ptnr. Collins and Collins, L.A., 1964-81, Pasadena, Calif., 1981—; mg. ptnr. Collins Collins Muir Traver, Pasadena, 1984—. Bd. dirs. Soc. Friendly Sons of St. Patrick, L.A., 1964—, pres., 1980. Fellow Am. Coll. Trial Lawyers; mem. ABA, Pasadena Bar Assn., L.A. County Bar Assn. (trustee 1991-93), Calif. State Bar Assn., Calif. Def. Counsel (treas., bd. dirs. 1985—, pres. 1993), Pasadena Bar Assn. (pres. 1990), Am. Bd. Trial Advocates (pres. L.A. chpt. 1989, nat. bd. dirs. 1985—, diplomate), Assn. So. Calif. Def. Counsel (bd. dirs. 1975-80, pres. 1982-84). Home: 7 Emerald Bay Laguna Beach CA 92651 Office: Collins Collins Muir & Traver 265 N Euclid Ave # 300 Pasadena CA 91101-1571

COLLINS, LOU, management consultant; b. Meremac, Okla., Feb. 29, 1936; s. Hoyal and Doris (Dilley) C.; m. Cheryl Pottorff, May 31, 1975; children: Colleen, Heidi, Jaime, Andrew. Degree in Theol. Counseling, Freelandia Inst., 1980. Field ops. mgr., supt. foreman various contracting firms, Calif., Okla., Oreg., N.Mex., 1957-76; owner, chief exec. officer C&L Developers, Central Point, Oreg., 1976-81; ops. mgr. LoLo (Mont.) Springs Resort, 1981-84; property mgr. Hyder & Co., Solana Beach, Calif., 1984-87; ops. mgr. housing Calif. State Poly. U., Pomona, 1987—. Served as sgt. 1st class U.S. Army, 1953-57. Mem. Cachuho, Acuho, Nat. Geographic Soc., Nat. Audubon Soc., Smithsonian Inst., Am. Mgmt. Assn., NRA, Am. Legion. Democrat. Office: Calif State Poly U 3801 W Temple Ave Pomona CA 91768-2557

COLLINS, MICHAEL PAUL, earth science educator, consultant; b. Chula Vista, Calif., Jan. 2, 1959; s. William Henry and Linda Lee (Capron) C.; m. Elizabeth Anne Funk, May 31, 1981 (div. Jan. 1989); m. Dawn Ann Good, Oct. 27, 1990; children: Christopher M., Matthew R. A in Gen. Studies, Clatsop Community Coll., Astoria, Oreg., 1983; BS in Sci. Edn., Oreg. State U., 1987, BS in Geology, 1987; MS in Environ. Sci., U. Alaska, Anchorage. Cert. tchr., Wash., Alaska. Emergency med. technician II, fireman Sitka (Alaska) Fire Dept., 1978-80; paramedic Medix Ambulance, Astoria, 1980-83; cartographer technician U.S. Geol. Survey, Grants Pass, Oreg., 1985; earth sci. tchr. Lake Oswego (Oreg.) Sch. Dist., 1987-88, Gladstone (Oreg.) Sch. Dist., 1988-90; radon technician Radon Detection Systems, Portland, Oreg., 1988-90; mktg. dir. Evergreen Helicopters of Alaska, Inc., Anchorage, 1990-91; chemistry/math tchr. Anchorage Sch. Dist., 1991—; instr. Alaska Jr. Coll., Anchorage, 1992—; cons. earth sci. edn. Harvard U., Cambridge, Mass., 1992—. Co-author: Merrill Earth Science Lab Activities, 1989. Active Alaska Resource Devel. Coun., Anchorage, 1990—. With USCG, 1977-81. Mem. NEA, Am. Assn. Petroleum Geologists, Geol. Soc. Am., Nat. Sci.

Tchr. Assn., Alaska Geol. Soc. Inc., Nat. Assn. Geology Tchrs. Home: 5740 Rocky Mountain Ct Apt A Anchorage AK 99504-4832 Office: Chugiak High Sch PO Box 770218 Eagle River AK 99577

COLLINS, MICHAEL SEAN, obstetrician-gynecologist; b. Yankton, S.D., Sept. 8, 1951; s. Edward Daniel and Joyce (Slatky) C.; m. Judy Furman, Sept. 20, 1975; children: Lauren, Sean, Carolyn. BS, Davidson Coll., 1973; MD, Med. U. S.C., 1977. Diplomate Am. Bd. Ob-Gyn. Chief resident in ob-gyn Med. U. S.C., Charleston, 1980-81; instr. in ob-gyn U. Oreg. Health Scis. Ctr., Portland, 1981—; chmn. dept. ob-gyn Good Samaritan Hosp., Portland, 1983-85; cons. Prepared Childbirth Assn., Portland, 1981—, Triplet Connection, L.A., 1985—. Fellow Am. Coll. Ob-Gyn; mem. AMA, Oreg. Med. Assn., Oreg. Ob-Gyn Soc., Pacific Coast Ob-Gyn Soc., Pacific Northwest Ob-Gyn Soc., Am. Fertility Soc., Porsche Club Am., Oreg. Ob-Gyn Soc. (vice chmn. 1991—). Republican. Roman Catholic. Home: 716 NW Rapidan Ter Portland OR 97210-3129 Office: Cascade Ob-Gyn Ste 120 1130 NW 22d Ave Portland OR 97210-2934

COLLINS, RICK (VERNON ELDEN), oil company executive; b. Lewiston, Maine, June 9, 1948; s. Elden Ross and Elaine Beverly (Robinson) C.; married (div. 1984); 1 child, Jordan Vernon. BS in Engring. Mgmt., Norwich U., 1970; MS in Arctic Engring., U. Alaska, 1986, MS in Civil Engring., 1988. Constrn. mgr., supr. S.A. Collins & Son, Inc., Rangeley, Maine, 1964-69; plant engr. New Eng. Telephone, 1970-71; commanding officer 89th Ord Det U.S. Army, Ft. Benning, Ga., 1971-74; logistics chief and commanding officer 696th Ord Co and HHC 6th Ord Bn., 1974-75; ops. officer 543rd Ord Det, U.S. Army, Ft. Leonard Wood, Mo., 1976-78; chief spl. ops. J-3 8th U.S. Army, Seoul, Korea, 1979; commanding officer 176th Ord Det U.S. Army, Fort Richardson, Alaska, 1979-81; sr. project mgr. Alyeska Pipeline Svc. Co., Anchorage, 1981-88, area mgr. pump stations 1 and 2, 1988-90; marine terminal mgr. Alyeska Pipeline Svc. Co., Valdez, Alaska, 1990—; leadership and engring. cons. in field. Author: (adventure stories) Hunting in Alaska, 1981; contbr. articles to profl. jours. Pres. Valdez C. of C., 1991-93; bd. dirs. State C. of C., Juneau, Alaska, 1991-93; coll. coun. Valdez C.C., 1992; bd. dirs. Valdez Devel. Inst., 1992. Col. USAR. Recipient Meritorious Svc. medal U.S. Army, 1975, 79, 81, Army Commendation medal U.S. Army, 1974, 84. Mem. ARC, Project Mgmt. Inst., Equality Lodge #497 Masonic (lectr. 1975—). Democrat. Home: PO Box 596 1500 Dewey Ct Valdez AK 99686

COLLINS, THOMAS STEPHEN, off highway vehicle/expedition consultant; b. San Francisco, Feb. 2, 1950; s. Thomas Joseph and Helen Bernice (McAuliffe) C.; m. Jane Louise Anderson, Nov. 9, 1990; 1 child, Shannon Alexis. BS in Conservation, Calif. State U., San Jose, Calif., 1973. Seasonal ranger Calif. State Pks., Big Basin, 1968-70; water quality inspector Santa Clara County, San Jose, Calif., 1970-72; waiter Captain's Anchorage Restaurant, Aspen, Colo., 1973-82; carpenter freelance, Aspen, Colo., 1974—; cons. self-employed Basalt, Colo., 1988—; team mem. First North-South Motorized Traverse, Madagascar, 1987; first Motorized Traverse of Siberia's Elictare River Valley, 1990; expedition leader First Continuous North-South Motorized Traverse of Colo. Continental Divide, 1989; co-organizer, head instr. Range Rover Driving Acad., Aspen, Colo., 1990. Recipient 2d place Camel Trophy, Madagascar, 1987, 3d Highest Speed in U.S. award Internat. Speed Skiing Sprint Series, 1985, 10th place S.W. Motorcycle Enduro, Am. Motorcycle Assn., 1983, 4th place Class 4 Baja 1000, 1992; selected and trained Camel Trophy Champions, 1993. Mem. NRA, Blue Ribbon Coalition, Colo. Off Hwy. Vehicle Coalition, Rocky Mtn. Elk Found., Mtn. Trail Riders Assn. Office: US Camel Trophy PO Box 587 Snowmass CO 81654

COLLINS, VERNON O., real estate sales executive; b. Bunevista, Colo., June 25, 1947; s. Vernon Ollen and Anna Maude (Wilson) C.; 1 child, Rebecca. BS in Bus./Mktg., U. Colo., 1971, MBA, 1973; mgmt. assoc. degree, Red Rocks Coll., 1990. Pres. Collins & Assocs., Lakewood, Colo., 1971-90; ptnr. Collins & Pierce Real Estate, Aurora, Colo., 1988-90. Author: Improving Customer Service, 1989; speaker in field. With USNR, 1968-90. Mem. Art Reach (coord.). Republican. Roman Catholic. Office: Collins & Assocs PO Box 441103 Aurora CO 80044-1103

COLLINS, WILLIAM LEROY, telecommunications engineer; b. Laurel, Miss., June 17, 1942; s. Henry L. and Christene E. (Finnegan) C. Student, La Salle U., 1969; BS in Computer Sci., U. Beverly Hills, 1984. Sr. computer operator Dept. Pub. Safety, Phoenix, 1975-78, data communications specialist, 1978-79, supr. computer ops., 1981-82; mgr. network control Valley Nat. Bank, Phoenix, 1979-81; mgr. data communications Ariz. Lottery, Phoenix, 1982-85; mgr. telecommunications Calif. Lottery, Sacramento, 1985—; Mem. Telecomm. Study Mission to Russia, Oct. 1991. Served as sgt. USAF, 1964-68. Mem. IEEE, Nat. Systems Programmers Assn., Centrex Users Group, Accunet Digital Svcs. User Group, Telecommunications Assn. (v.p. edn. Sacramento Valley chpt. 1990-93), Assn. Data Communications Users, Soc. Mfg. Engrs., Data Processing Mgmt. Assn., Am. Mgmt. Assn., Assn. Computing Machinery, K.C. Roman Catholic. Home: 116 Valley Oak Dr Roseville CA 95678-4378 Office: Calif State Lottery 600 N 10th St Sacramento CA 95814-0393

COLLIS, KAY LYNN, economist, business consultant; b. Dallas, July 15, 1958; d. Martin Edward and Norma June C. AA, Tyler Jr. Coll., 1978; BBA, Sam Houston State U., 1982. Mgr. World Fin. Corp., Bryan, Tex., 1977-81; ops. analyst Republic Bank Dallas, 1983-85; asst. v.p. MBank, Dallas, 1985-87; v.p., Murray Fed. Savs., 1987-90; owner KC Enterprises, 1990—; advisor Collis Cons. Co., Sulphur Springs, Tex., 1983—. Vol. Speaker Bur., Arthritis Found., 1983—; mem. Better Bus. Bur. Mem. NAFE, Fin. Women Internat. (group pres. 1989-90, Tex. mktg./pub. rels. 1990-91), Las Vegas C. of C., Nat. Fedn. Ind. Bus. Owners. Republican. Episcopalian. Home: 7058 Montcliff Las Vegas NV 89117 Office: 3355 Spring Mountain # 60 Las Vegas NV 89102

COLLMER, RUSSELL CRAVENER, data processing executive, educator; b. Guatemala, Jan. 2, 1924; s. G. Russell and Constance (Cravener) C.; B.S., U. N.M., 1951; postgrad. Calif. Inst. Tech., 1943-44; M.S., State U. Iowa, 1955; m. Ruth Hannah Adams, Mar. 4, 1950; 1 son, Reed Alan. Staff mem. Mass. Inst. Tech., Lincoln Lab., Lexington, 1955-57; mgr. systems modeling, computer dept. Gen. Electric, Phoenix, 1957-59; mgr. ARCAS Thompson Ramo Wooldridge, Inc., Canoga Park, Cal., 1959-62; assoc. mgr. tech. dir. CCIS-70 Bunker-Ramo Corp., 1962-64; sr. assoc. Planning Rsch. Corp., Los Angeles, 1964-65; pres. R. Collmer Assocs., Benson, Ariz., 1965—; pres. Benson Econ. Enterprises Corp., 1968-69. Lectr. computer scis. Pima Community Coll., Tucson, 1970—. Served with USAAC, 1942-46, to capt. USAF, 1951-53. Mem. IEEE, Am. Meteorol. Soc., Assn. for Computing Machinery, Phi Delta Theta, Kappa Mu Epsilon. Republican. Baptist. Office: R Collmer Assocs PO Box 864 Benson AZ 85602-0864

COLLOPY, BERNARD JAMES, family practice physician; b. Ft. Collins, Colo., Oct. 26, 1927; s. Joseph Patrick Collopy and Lydia Margaret Troutman; m. Dinah Marie Umsted, Oct. 6, 1956; children: Leslie, Christopher, Margaret, Erin, Thomas, John. BS, U. Wyo, 1951; MD, Creighton U., 1958. Diplomate Am. Bd. Family Practice. Staff physician M&I Hosp. & Clinics, Miami, Ariz., 1959-66, asst. med. dir., 1966-71, med. dir., 1971-78; dir. emergency rm. El Dorado Hosp., Tucson, 1978-81; pvt. practice Miami, 1981—. Fellow Am. Coll. Family Practice. Democrat. Roman Catholic. Home: 30 Chaparral Miami AZ 85539 Office: 2M Miami Gardens Dr Miami AZ 85539-9737

COLMAN, RONALD WILLIAM, computer science educator; b. L.A., Sept. 13, 1930; s. William Maynard Colman and Edna Eliza (Halford) Smith. BA in Math., UCLA, 1957; PhD in Computer Sci., U. Calif., Irvine, 1976. Electronics tech. Lockheed Aircraft Corp., Burbank, Calif., 1952-53; staff specialist Western Electric Co., N.Y.C., 1957-58; assoc. math. Burroughs Corp., Pasadena, Calif., 1958-60; sr. computer analyst Beckman Instruments, Inc., Fullerton, Calif., 1960-62; mgr. L.A. dist. Digital Equipment Corp., L.A., 1962-64; chmn. computer sci. Calif. State U., Fullerton, 1964-80; prof. computer sci. Calif. State U., Northridge, 1980-89; ptnr. Windward Ventures, Venice, Calif.; chmn. session on heuristic search Internat. Joint Conf. on Artificial Intelligence, Stanford, 1973; chmn. nat. symposium on computer sci. edn. Assn. Computing Machinery, Anaheim, Calif., 1976; chmn. registration Nat. Computer Conf., Anaheim, 1978, 80. With USN, 1948-52. Home: 770-C 26th St San Pedro CA 90731

COLN, WILLIAM ALEXANDER, III, pilot; b. Los Angeles, Mar. 20, 1942; s. William Alexander and Aileen Henrietta (Shimfessel) C.; m. Lora Louise Getchel, Nov. 15, 1969 (div. July 1979); 1 child, Caryn Louise. BA in Geography, UCLA, 1966. Cert. airline transport pilot, flight engr. Commd. USN, Pensacola, Fla., 1966; pilot, officer USN, Fighter Squadron 102, 1969-71, Port Mugu, Calif., 1975-77; pilot, officer USNR, Port Mugu, Calif., 1971-75, advanced through grades to lt. comdr., 1978; ret. USNR, 1984; airline pilot Delta Airlines, Inc. (formerly Western Airlines Inc.), Los Angeles, 1972—. Recipient Nat. Def. medal USN, 1966. Mem. Nat. Aero. Assn., Airline Pilots Assn., Aircraft Owners and Pilots Assn., UCLA Alumni Assn., Am. Bonanza Soc., Internat. Platform Assn. Democrat. Club: Santa Barbara (Calif.) Athletic. Home: 519 W Quinto St Santa Barbara CA 93105-4829 Office: Delta Air Lines Inc Los Angeles Internat Airport Los Angeles CA 90009

COLSON, KENNETH MERRITT, anthropologist, educator; b. San Francisco, Jan. 22, 1939. BA, U. Calif., Berkeley, 1961; MA, San Francisco State Coll., 1969. With probation dept. San Mateo County, Belmont, Calif., 1962-69; instr. San Francisco State Coll., 1966-68, Can. Coll., Redwood City, Calif., 1967-69, West Valley Coll., Saratoga, Calif., 1967—. Lt. Saratoga Fire Dist., 1981—. NEH fellow, 1972, 92, Fulbright-Hays fellow, 1977, 90. Fellow Am. Anthrop. Assn.; mem. Soc. C.C. Anthropologists, Soc. Linguistic Anthropology. Office: West Valley Coll 1400 Fruitvale Ave Saratoga CA 95070

COLT, HENRI GASTON, physician; b. Rochester, N.Y., Feb. 28, 1956; s. George Simon and Franceska (Ziegelhofer) C.; m. Edwige Pionnier, Oct. 18, 1985. BS, Jacques Audiberti Coll., Antibes, France, 1974; MD, U. Nice, 1982. First asst. cardiothoracic surgery Inst. Arnault Tzanck, St. Laurent Duvar, France, 1979-81; gen. surgeon Svc. Internat. Tech. Assistance, Reunion Island, France, 1982-83; pvt. practice Reunion Island, 1984-85; resident in internal medicine Shadyside Hosp., Pitts., 1985-88; fellow in pulmonary medicine Oreg. Health Scis. U., Portland, 1988-90; asst. prof. laser ctr. St. Marguerite Hosp., Marseille, France, 1990-92; asst. prof. pulmonary div. U. Calif. Med. Ctr., San Diego, 1992—; assoc. dir. pulmonary spl. procedures and laser unit U. Calif., San Diego, 1992—, chief ambulatory chest clinic, 1992—. Contbr. articles to profl. jours.; author teaching videotapes. Named Eagle Scout with Palms Boy Scouts Am.; grantee Oreg. Lung Assn., 1990, French Assn. for Fight Against Cystic Fibrosis, 1991. Fellow Am. Coll. Chest Physicians, Am. Soc. Laser Medicine and Surgery; mem. Am. Thoracic Soc., European Laser Soc., Internat. Bronchoesophagological Soc., Conseil de L'Ordre National des Medecins France. Office: U Calif Med Ctr 225 Dickinson St San Diego CA 92103

COLTON, ARLAN MILLER, urban planner; b. Bronx, N.Y., Aug. 6, 1955; s. Stanley S. and Evelyn Louise (Miller) C. BS in Pub. Adminstrn., U. Ariz., 1977, MS in Urban Planning, 1979. Planner Pima County Planning Dept., Tucson, 1979-81, sr. planner, 1981-84, prin. planner, zoning adminstr., 1984-88; mgr. Ariz. State Land Dept., Tucson, 1988—; chair adv. com. Pima Assn. Govts. Environ. Planning, Tucson, 1983-84. Pres. bd. govs. Villa Paraiso Condominium, Tucson, 1983-88; mem. Temple Emanu-el. Named one of Outstanding Young Men of Am., Jaycees, 1983. Mem. Am. Planning Assn. (dir. region V 1990—), Am. Inst. Cert. Planners, Ariz. Planning Assn. (officer 1981-88, pres. 1987-88), Common Cause, Sierra Club (pres. Ariz. chpt. 1979-81). Democrat. Jewish. Home: 2601 E La Cienega Dr Tucson AZ 85716-1545 Office: Ariz State Land Dept 233 N Main Ave Tucson AZ 85701-7200

COLTON, ROY CHARLES, management consultant; b. Phila., Feb. 26, 1941; s. Nathan Hale and Ruth Janis (Baylinson) C.; B.A., Knox Coll., 1962; M.Ed., Temple U., 1963. With Sch. Dist. of Phila., 1963-64; systems analyst Wilmington Trust Co., 1967-69; exec. recruiter Atwood Consultants Inc., Phila., 1969-71; pres. Colton Bernard Inc., San Francisco, 1971—; occasional lectr. Fashion Inst. Tech., Phila. Coll. Textiles and Scis. Served with AUS, 1964-66. Mem. San Francisco Fashion Industries, San Francisco C. of C., Calif. Exec. Recruiter Assn., Nat. Assn. Exec. Recruiters, Am. Apparel Mfrs. Assn., Am. Arbitration Assn. (panel arbitrators), Am. Mgmt. Assn. Office: Colton Bernard Inc 870 Market St Ste 822 San Francisco CA 94102

COLVER, C. PHILLIP, engineering consultant; b. Coffeyville, Kans., Oct. 21, 1935; m. Carol Jean Cope (div.); children: Jeanne, John, Suzanne; m. A. Dominique Baudaux. AA, Coffeyville Coll., 1955; BSChemE, U. Kans., 1958, MSChemE, 1960; PhD in Chem. Engring., U. Mich., 1963. Registered profl. engr., Colo., Okla. Asst. prof. U. Okla., Norman, 1963-67, acting dir., 1966, assoc. prof., 1967-71, dir., 1970-74, prof., 1971-76, assoc. dean of engring., 1974-75; cons. Colver Tech. Cons., Aspen, Colo., 1976—; vis. prof. U. Colo., Boulder, 1977-78; dir. sponsored rsch. NSF/NASA, 1964-75; cons. Phillips Petroleum Co., Bartlesville, Okla., 1967-73; pres. Computer Design Data Cons. Svcs., Norman, 1970-73; chmn. Cryogenic Area Nat. Program Com. of Aiche, 1970; papers chmn. Heat Transfer and Energy Conversion div. Papos Aiche, 1972; best paper com. Nat. Heat Transfer Conf., 1972. Editor: Heat Transfer Chem. Engring. Progress Symposium, 1973. Recipient Best Paper award Cryogenic Engring. Conf., 1965; Esso fellow U. Mich., 1960-61. Mem. Am. Nat. Standards Inst., Nat. Fire Protection Assn., Internat. Assn. Arson Investigators, Sigma Xi, Phi Lambda Upsilon, Sigma Tau, Tau Beta Pi. Office: Colver Tech Cons 855 Mountain Laurel Dr Aspen CO 81611-2345

COLVIN, DONALD ANDREW, marketing consultant; b. Toronto, Ont., Can., Apr. 15, 1915; s. Norman Buchanan and Margaret Jean (Bone) C.; m. Ruth McMurtrie, June 17, 1950. BA in Econs., Princeton U., 1936. Dir. advt. Ametek Corp., N.Y.C., 1936-55; account exec. Ketchum Communications, Pitts., 1956-60; sr. v.p., gen. mgr. Ketchum Communications, Houston, 1960-78; pres. Don Colvin & Assocs., Houston, 1978-81, Sun City West, Ariz., 1981—. Bd. dirs. Houston Grand Opera Assn., 1969-71, Sun Cities Art Mus., 1991—; trustee Sun Cities Symphony Assn., 1986—. Vol. ambulance driver Am. Field Svc., 1943-45, NATOUSA, ETO. Mem. Briarwood Country Club. Home and Office: 12635 W Paintbrush Dr Sun City West AZ 85375-2525

COLVIN, GARY ROBERT, irrigation engineer; b. Safford, Ariz., May 18, 1956; s. Robert J. and Verna Rae (Cluff) C.; Pamela Jean Colvin, Apr. 23, 1982; children: Bobbi J., Jaci J., Dana R. AA in Agr.-Bus., Eastern Ariz. Coll., 1982; BS in Agr.-Mechanics & Irrigation, U. Ariz., 1985. Cert. water, wastewater treatment plant operator class 3. Farm mgr. Colvin Farms, Eden, Ariz., 1975-83; irrigation cons. Desert Agr. and Tech. Systems, Buckeye, Ariz., 1985-87; gen. mgr. Buckeye Irrigation Co., 1987—; bd. dirs. Agr.-Bus. Coun., Phoenix. Mem. Am. Soc. Agrl. Engr., Am. Water Works Assn., Irrigation Assn., Ariz. Farm Bur. Assn., Buckeye Citizen's Planning Group, Buckeye Valley C. of C. (v.p. 1990-91), Elks. Republican. Mem. LDS Ch. Home: 8234 S Johnson Rd Buckeye AZ 85326-9146 Office: Buckeye Irrigation Co PO Box 726 Buckeye AZ 85326-0160

COLVIN, LANCE ELLIOTT, credit manager; b. Houston, Oct. 13, 1944; s. Emmett and Mary Lee (Dietterich) C.; m. Lila Joan Ramsey, Aug. 21, 1971; children: Justin, Danae. BA in Edn., Spanish, North Tex. State U., 1968; Advanced Teaching Cert., U. Wash., 1972. cert. credit exec. Tchr. Skykomish (Wash.) Sch. Dist., 1968-72, Mountlake Sch., Mountlake Terrace, Wash., 1972-73; asst. credit mgr. to br. credit mgr. GE Credit Corp., Bellevue, Wash., 1973-77; corp. credit. mgr. Jay Jacobs, Inc., Seattle, 1977-79; asst. credit mgr. Pacific Water Works Supply, Seattle, 1979-84, corp. credit mgr., 1984—; speaker in field. Mem. Nat. Assn. Credit Mgmt. (founder, chair credit trade group, chmn. 1987-90). Home: 11217 NE 147th St Kirkland WA 98034-1010 Office: Pacific Water Works Supply Inc 602 Valley Ave NE Puyallup WA 98372-2518

COLVIN, LLOYD DAYTON, electrical engineer; b. Spokane, Wash., Apr. 24, 1915; s. George R. and Edna M. Colvin; m. Iris Venita Atterbury, Aug. 11, 1939; 1 child, Joy Victoria. BS, U. Calif., 1938; grad., AUS Command Gen. Staff Coll., Ft. Leavenworth, Kans., 1947, U. Heidelberg, Fed. Republic of Germany, 1955. Registered elec., mech., constrn. and asbestos engr. Elec. engr. Pacific Gas and Electric Co., San Francisco, 1938-40; commd. 2d lt. U.S. Army, 1938, advanced through grades to col., ret., 1961; pres. Drake Builders, Richmond, Calif., 1962—. Co-author: (with Iris Colvin) How We Started Out Building Our Own Home in Our Spare Time and Went On to Make a Million Dollars in the Construction Business, 1967. Mem. Yasme Found. (pres.), various amateur radio clubs. Home and Office: Drake Builders 5200 Panama Ave Richmond CA 94804-5498

COLVIS, JOHN PARIS, aerospace engineer, mathematician, scientist; b. St. Louis, June 30, 1946; s. Louis Jack and Jacqueline Betty (Beers) C.; m. Nancy Ellen Fritz, Mar. 15, 1969 (div. Sept. 1974); 1 child, Michael Scott; m. Barbara Carol Davis, Sept. 3, 1976; 1 child, Rebecca Jo; stepchildren: Bruce William John Zimmerly, Belinda Jo Zimmerly Little. Student, Meramec Community Coll., St. Louis, 1964-65, U. Mo., 1966, 72-75, Palomar Coll., San Marcos, Calif., 1968, U. Mo., Rolla, 1968-69; BS in Math., Washington U., 1977. Assoc. system safety engr. McDonnell Douglas Astronautics Co., St. Louis, 1978-81; sr. system safety engr. Martin Marietta Astronautics Group-Strategic Systems Co., Denver, 1981-87; sr. engr. Martin Marietta Astronautics Group-Space Launch Systems Co., Denver, 1987—; researcher in field. Precinct del., precinct committeeman, congl. dist. del., state del. Rep. Party; mem. state adv. bd. Colo. Christian Coalition. Lance cpl. USMC, 1966-68, Vietnam. Mem. AAAS, Math. Assn. Am., Colo. Home Educators' Assn. (pres. 1989), Colo. Christian Coalition (state bd. dirs.). Evangelical. Home: 4978 S Hoyt St Littleton CO 80123-1988 Office: Martin Marietta Astronautics Group-SLS PO Box 179 Denver CO 80201-0179

COLWELL, JAMES LEE, humanities educator; b. Brush, Colo., Aug. 31, 1926; s. Francis Joseph and Alice (Bleasdale) C.; BA, U. Denver, 1949; MA, U. No. Colo., 1951; cert. Sorbonne, Paris, 1956; diploma U. Heidelberg (Ger.), 1957; A.M. (Univ. fellow), Yale U., 1959, PhD (Hale-Kilborn fellow), 1961; m. Claudia Alsleben, Dec. 27, 1957; children—John Francis, Alice Anne. Tchr. high sch., Snyder and Sterling, Colo., 1948-52; civilian edn. adviser U.S. Air Force, Japan, 1952-56; assoc. dir. Yale Fgn. Student Inst., summers 1959-60; asst. dir. European div. U. Md., Heidelberg, 1961-65; dir. Office Internat. Edn., assoc. prof. Am. lit. U. Colo., Boulder, 1965-72; prof. Am. studies, chmn. lit. U. Tex. Permian Basin, Odessa, 1977-82, dean Coll. Arts and Edn., 1972-77, 82-84, K.C. Dunagan prof. humanities, 1984-87, prof. emeritus, 1988—. Mem. nat. adv. council Inst. Internat. Edn., 1969-75. Vice pres. Ector County chpt. ARC, 1974-76; mem. Ector County Hist. Commn., 1973-75. Served with USAAF, 1945; brig. gen. USAF Res. Ret. Mem. AAUP, Am. Studies Assn., Western Social Sci. Assn. (life; pres. 1974-75), MLA, NEA (life), Orgn. Am. Historians (life), South Central MLA, Permian Basin Hist. Soc. (life; pres. 1980-81), Air Force Assn. (life), Air Force Hist. Found. (life), Res. Officers Assn. (life), Ret. Officers Assn. (life), Phi Beta Kappa. Unitarian-Universalist. Contbr. articles to learned jours. Home: 4675 Gordon Dr Boulder CO 80303-6747

COMBIE, JOAN DIANE, biotechnology researcher; b. New London, N.H., June 30, 1946. BS, Colby-Sawyer Coll., 1968; MS, U. Ky., 1978, PhD, 1982. Toxicologist, med. toxicologist, 1982-87; dir. rsch., v.p., co-owner J.K. Rsch., Bozeman, Mont., 1987—. Contbr. 42 articles to profl. jours.; patentee in field. Mem. Am. Soc. Microbiology, Soc. Indsl. Microbiology. Office: JK Rsch 210 S Wallace Ave Bozeman MT 59715-4857

COMBIE, ROBERT GRAHAM, hotel executive; b. New London, N.H., Mar. 30, 1956; s. Graham Robert and Helen Louise (Rhodes) C. Student, Bunker Hill C.C., Charlestown, Mass., 1976, U. Mass., 1976-77. Mgr. rooms div. Seattle Hilton/Park Hilton, 1980-82, Holiday Inn-Crown Plaza, Seattle, 1982-85; cons. on operational analysis HMR Inc., Seattle, 1986-87; mgr. resort ops. Beachwood Resort, Blaine, Wash., 1987-88; gen. mgr. Hampton Inn-Seattle Airport, 1988—; mem. adv. bd. Wash. State Div. Devel. Disabilities, Olympia, 1991-92. Mem. Hotel and Motel Assn. (cert. hotel adminstr.), Seattle Hotel Mgrs. Assn. Office: Hampton Inn-Seattle Airport 19445 International Blvd Seattle WA 98188

COMBS, J. ANDREW, software systems specialist; b. Amityville, N.Y., Sept. 19, 1950; s. Andrew Grafton and Wilhelmina (Jackson) C.; m. Carol Keene, May 29, 1973 (div. Feb. 1977); m. Terry Lou Savage, July 1, 1982; children: Andrew, Joshua, Jonathan, Katherine, Alicia. BS in Physics, Duke U., 1972; MS in Meteorology, Fla. State U., 1974; PhD in Nuclear Engring., MIT, 1981. Rsch. assoc. MIT, Cambridge, Mass., 1978-81; postdoctoral scholar U. Calif., Davis, 1982-84; pres. World Rsch. Inst. for Sci. and Tech., N.Y.C., 1984—; v.p. Inter Linear Tech., Alameda, Calif., 1990—. Co-architect modular system software, 1989-92; contbr. articles to profl. publs.; patentee tiled vector plotting method. Mem. AAAS, Am. Phys. Soc., N.Y. Acad. Scis., Sigma Xi. Home: 24775 Townsend Ave Hayward CA 94544 Office: Inter Linear Tech Ste 120 1320 Harbor Bay Pkwy Alameda CA 94501

COMBS, KATHRYN LOUISE, economics educator; b. Ft. Wayne, Ind., May 30, 1957; d. Ernest Franklin and Cecilia Joy (Prevost) C.; m. Russell John Pylkki, Aug. 1, 1981. BA in Econs., Wash. State U., 1978; MA in Econs., U. Minn., 1985, PhD in Econs., 1988. Forecaster Pacific N.W. Bell, Seattle, 1979-81; asst. prof. Calif. State U., L.A., 1986—; vis. asst. prof. U. So. Calif., L.A., 1989-90. Author: (with others) Advances in Applied Microeconomics, vol. 5, 1990. Mem. Com. on Status of Women in Econs. Profession. Sloan Found scholarship, 1985; faculty grantee Calif. State U., 1987, 88, 89, 90, 92. Mem. Am. Econ. Assn., Western Econ. Assn. Internat. Office: Calif State U 5151 State University Dr Los Angeles CA 90032

COMBS, W(ILLIAM) HENRY, III, lawyer; b. Casper, Wyo., Mar. 18, 1949; s. William Henry and Ruth M. (Wooster) C.; m. Patricia M. Bostwick, Aug. 30, 1970; 1 child, J Bradley. Student, Northwestern U., 1967-69; BS, U. Wyo., 1972, JD, 1975. Bar: Wyo. 1975, U.S. Dist. Ct. Wyo. 1975, U.S. Ct. Appeals (10th cir.) 1990, U.S. Supreme Ct. 1990. Assoc. Murane & Bostwick, Casper, 1975-77, ptnr., 1978—. Mem. com. on resolution of fee disputes. Mem. ABA (tort and ins. practice, law office mgmt. sects.), Natrona County Bar Assn., Def. Rsch. Inst., Am. Judicature Soc., Def. Lawyers Assn. Wyo., Assn. Ski Def. Attys., U.S. Handball Assn., Am. Water Ski Assn., U.S. Ski Assn., Casper Boat Club, Casper Petroleum Club, Wyo. Athletic Club, Porsche Club Am., BMW Club Am., Sports Car Club Am. Republican. Episcopalian. Office: Murane & Bostwick 201 N Wolcott St Casper WY 82601-1930

COMES, ROBERT GEORGE, research scientist; b. Bangor, Pa., July 7, 1931; s. Victor Francis and Mabel Elizabeth (Mack) C.; student U. Detroit, 1957-58, Oreg. State Coll., 1959-60, U. Nev., 1960, Regis Coll., 1961-62; m. Carol Lee Turinetti, Nov. 28, 1952; children: Pamela Jo, Robert G. II, Shawni Lee, Sheryl Lynn, Michelle Ann. Tech. liaison engr. Burroughs Corp., Detroit, 1955-60, mgr. reliability and maintainability engring., Paoli, Pa., 1962-63, Colorado Springs, Colo., 1963-67; sr. engr. Martin Marietta Corp., Denver, 1960-62; program mgr., rsch. scientist Kaman Scis. Corp., Colorado Springs, 1967-75; dir. engring. Sci. Applications, Inc., Colorado Springs, 1975-80; mgr. space def. programs Burroughs Corp., Colorado Springs, 1980-82; tech. staff Mitre Corp., Colorado Springs, 1982-85; dir. Colorado Springs opn. Beers Assoc., Inc., 1985; dir. space programs Electro Magnetic Applications, Inc., Colorado Springs, 1985-87; dir. Space Systems, Profl. Mgmt. Assocs., Inc., 1987-88; mgr. Computer Svcs., Inc., Colorado Springs, 1989—; dir. mktg. Proactive Techs., Inc., Colorado Springs, 1990—; chmn. Reliability and Maintainability Data Bank Improvement Program, Govt.-Industry Data Exch. Program, 1978-80—; cons. in field. Youth dir. Indian Guides program YMCA, 1963-64; scoutmaster Boy Scouts Am., 1972-73; chmn. bd. dirs. Pikes Peak Regional Sci. Fair, 1972-84. Served with USAF, 1951-55. Mem. AAAS, IEEE, Inst. Environ. Scis., Soc. Logistics Engrs., Am. Soc. Quality Control. Lutheran. Club: Colorado Springs Racquet. Author: Maintainability Engineering Principles and Standards, 1962. Inventor Phase Shifting aircraft power supply, 1957. Home: 4309 Tipton Ct Colorado Springs CO 80915-1034 Office: Proactive Tech Inc 4309 Tipton Ct Colorado Springs CO 80915-1034

COMFORT, PATRICK CONNELL, lawyer; b. Tacoma, Sept. 21, 1930; s. Arthur Blaine and Claire Gertrude (Connell) C.; children: Christopher, Erin, Sean, Kathleen, Maureen. AB, Gonzaga U., 1952; LLB, NYU, 1955. Bar: Wash. 1955, U.S. Dist. Ct. (western dist.) 1958, U.S. Ct. Appeals (9th cir.) 1966, U.S. Supreme Ct. 1973. Ptnr. Comfort & Comfort, Tacoma, 1958-60, Comfort Dolack Hansler Billett Hulscher Rosenow & Burrows, Tacoma,

1960-76; sole practice, Fircrest, Wash., 1976-88, ptnr. Comfort & Smith, Tacoma, 1988—; real estate developer. Chmn. Heart Fund Dr. Pierce County; chmn. cabinet Bellarmine Devel. Fund Dr.; co-chmn. St. Joseph's Psychiat. Unit Fund Dr.; rep. 26th dist. Ho. State of Wash., 1960-64; town atty. Town of Fircrest, Wash., 1977—; bd. visitors U. Puget Sound Sch. Law; mem. Found Bd. Tacoma Community Coll., 1990—. With U.S. Army, 1955-57. Named Outstanding Young Man Am., U.S. Jaycees, 1964. Mem. ABA (del. 1987-93), Wash. State Bar Assn. (gov. 6th dist. 1981-84, pres. 1985-86, chmn. lawyers assistance program 1988—, spl. award honor 1984), Tacoma-Pierce County Bar Assn. (trustee 1971-74, pres. 1980). Republican. Roman Catholic. Club: Fircrest Golf (pres. 1974). Avocations: golf, bowling. Home: 1902 Bridgeport Way W Apt 405 Tacoma WA 98466-4843 Office: 2121 70th Ave W Ste C Tacoma WA 98466-7664

COMISSIONA, SERGIU, conductor; b. Bucharest, Romania, June 16, 1928; came to U.S., 1969; naturalized, 1976; s. Isaac and Jean L. (Haufrecht) C.; m. Robinne Florin, July 16, 1949. Studied with Constantin Silvestri and Eduoard Lindenberg, 1928; ed. music conservatoire, Bucharest; Mus.D. (hon.), Peabody Conservatory Music, 1972; LHD (hon.), Loyola Coll., Balt., 1973, Towson State U., 1980; D.F.A. (hon.), Washington Coll., Chestertown, Md., 1980, Western Md. Coll., 1977, U. Md., 1981, Johns Hopkins U., 1982. Operatic conducting debut in Faust at Sibiu, 1945, conducting debut Bucharest Opera Orch., 1946; violinist Bucharest Radio Quartet, 1946, Rumanian State Ensemble Orch., 1947, asst. condr., 1948, music dir., 1950-55; prin. condr. Rumanian State Opera, 1955-59; founder, condr. Ramat Gan (Israel) Chamber Orch., 1960-67; music dir. Haifa (Israel) Symphony, 1960-66, Israel Chamber Orch., 1960-67, Goteburg (Sweden) Symphony Orch., 1966-67, Balt. Symphony Orch., 1969-84, condr. laureate, 1984—; music dir. Houston Symphony Orch., 1983-88, N.Y.C. Opera, 1987-89, Helsinki Philharm. Orch. (also chief condr.), 1990-93, Vancouver Symphony, 1990—, Orquesta Sinfonica de RTVE, Madrid, 1990—; Am. debut with Phil. Orch., 1965; mus. adviser, condr. No. Ireland Orch., 1967-68; artistic dir. Temple U. Music Festival, 1976-80, music advisor, prin. condr., 1977-80; music dir., prin. condr. Chautauqua Symphony Orch. Summer Festival, 1976-80; music adviser Am. Symphony Orch., 1978-82; artistic advisor Houston Symphony Orch., 1980-83; permanent guest condr. Radio Philharm. Orch. of Netherlands, 1982-83, chief condr., 1983-89; with London Symphony, Stockholm Philharm., Swedish Radio Orch.; founder Joseph Meyerhoff Hall, Balt.. Decorated Order Merit 2d Class Rumania; winner internat. competition for young condrs. Besancon, France, 1954; recipient Gold medal award City of Goteborg, 1973, Ditson Condr.'s award Columbia U., 1979. Mem. Royal Swedish Acad. Music (hon.). Address: ICM Artists 40 W 57th St New York NY 10019 also: Audrey Michaels 122 E 76th St New York NY 10021

COMPERT, CINDY ELLEN, product specialist; b. N.Y.C., May 24, 1961; d. Murray Jules Compert and Rhoda (Kleinman) Kamisher. BA magna cum laude, NYU, 1983, MBA, 1986. Rsch. asst. econ. and securities rsch. Merrill Lynch & Co., Inc., N.Y.C., 1984, data base adminstr. econ. and securities rsch., 1984-85; tech. cons. Info. Builders, Inc., N.Y.C., 1985-86, project leader, 1986-87, mgr. mainframe support, 1987-89, mgr. midrange support, 1989-90; br. tech. mgr. Info. Builders, Inc., L.A., 1990-91, regional mktg. specialist, 1991—. Mem. Marina Sailing, Inc., Phi Beta Kappa. Home: PO Box 3772 Manhattan Beach CA 90266 Office: Info Builders Inc Ste 290 300 Continental Blvd El Segundo CA 90245

COMPTON, ALLEN T., state supreme court justice; b. Kansas City, Mo., Feb. 25, 1938; m. Sue Ellen Tatter; 3 children. B.A., U. Kans.; LL.B., U. Colo. Staff atty. legal services office in Colo., later entered pvt. practice; supervising atty. Alaska Legal Services, Juneau, 1970-73; sole practice Juneau, 1973-76; judge Superior Ct., Alaska, 1976-80; justice Alaska Supreme Ct., Anchorage, 1980—. Mem. 4 bar assns. including Juneau Bar Assn. (past pres.). Office: Alaska Supreme Ct 303 K St Anchorage AK 99501-2013*

COMPTON, LINN, technical writer; b. Klamath Falls, Oreg., Apr. 27; d. Arthur McConnell Compton and Florence (Crews) Nelson. BA, Evergreen State Coll., Olympia, Wash., 1972; BS, U. Wash., 1991. Tech. writer ESCA Corp., Redmond, Wash., 1984-87; sr. tech. writer Aldus Corp., Seattle, 1987-92, Microsoft Corp., Redmond, Wash., 1992—. Mem. adv. bd. extension cert. program U. Wash., Seattle, 1989—. Mem. Soc. Tech. Communications (sr., Disting. Publ. 1989, Excellence Publ. 1990), ACM SIGCHI. Home: 511 N 79th St Seattle WA 98103

COMPTON, MERLIN DAVID, Spanish language educator; b. Ogden, Utah, July 22, 1924; s. George Albert and Margaret Estella (Mattson) C.; m. Avon Allen Compton, June 17, 1950; children: Terry Ann Compton Harward, Todd Merlin, Tamara Jane Compton Hauge, Timothy George, Tina Louise. BA, Brigham Young U., 1952, MA, 1954; PhD, UCLA, 1959. Asst. prof. Adams State Coll., Alamosa, Colo., 1959-63; assoc. prof. Weber State Coll., Ogden, Utah, 1963-64; prof. Spanish Brigham Young U., Provo, Utah, 1964-89. Author: Ricardo Palma, 1982, Trayectoria de las Tradiciones de Ricardo Palma, 1989. Staff sgt. USAF, 1943-46. Mem. Phi Kappa Phi. Mem. LDS Ch. Home: 1015 S River Rd # 27 Saint George UT 84770

COMPTON, RUSSELL FREDERICK, orthopaedic surgeon; b. Chgo., Mar. 26, 1921; s. Russell Frederick and Kathryn Amelia (Fitzpatrick) C.; m. Ruth Evelyn O'Dea, Aug. 8, 1953; children: Dianne Marie, Russell Frederick, Joan Catherine, Robert Arthur. BS, U. Ill., 1951, MD, 1951; PhB, Mt. Carmel Coll., 1942. Diplomate Am. Bd. Orthopedic Surgery. Intern Harbor UCLA Med. Ctr., Torrance, Calif., 1951-52; resident in gen. surgery U. Colo Denver Gen. Hosp., 1952-53; pvt. practice orthopedic surgery Pasadena, Calif., 1957-86; orthopedic surgeon U. So. Calif., L.A., 1957—. Sgt. Signal Corps, U.S. Army, 1942-46, PTO. Orthopaedic Surgery fellow Mayo Clinic, 1953-56. Fellow Am. Acad. Orthopaedic Surgeons; mem. Pasadena Med. Soc. (pres. 1968-69), L.A. County Med. Assn. (councilor 1977-83), Stardusters (pres. 1984-85), La Canada Flintridge Country Club. Republican. Roman Catholic. Home and Office: 784 Starlight Heights Dr La Canada Flintridge CA 91011-1834

COMRIE, BERNARD STERLING, linguistics educator; b. Sunderland, England, May 23, 1947; came to U.S., 1979; s. Clifford Reginald Herbert and Ellen (Coulton) C.; m. Akiko Kumahira, Feb. 10, 1985; children: Amanda Mariko Kumahira Comrie, Michael Masaru Kumahira Comrie. BA, U. Cambridge, 1968, PhD, 1972. Rsch. fellow King's Coll., Cambridge, 1970-74; sr. asst. in rsch. U. Cambridge, 1972-74, univ. lectr. in linguistics, 1974-78; assoc. prof. linguistics U. So. Calif., L.A., 1978-81, prof. linguistics, 1981—. Author: Aspect, 1976, Language Universals and Linguistic Typology, 1981, Tense, 1985; editor: The World's Major Languages, 1987 (Outstanding Acad. Book 1987-88), Studies in Language, Amsterdam, Netherlands, 1991—. Recipient Rsch. grant Social Sci. Rsch. Coun., London, 1975-78, NSF, 1985-86, 90—. Mem. Linguistic Soc. Am., Linguistics Assn. Great Britain, Philological Soc. Office: Dept Linguistics Univ So Calif Los Angeles CA 90089-1693

COMSTOCK, DALE ROBERT, mathematics educator; b. Frederic, Wis., Jan. 18, 1934; s. Walter and Frances (Lindroth) C.; m. Mary Jo Lien, Aug. 18, 1956; children—Mitchell Scott, Bryan Paul. B.A., Central Wash. State Coll., 1955; M.S., Oreg. State U., 1962, Ph.D., 1966. Tchr. math. Kennewick (Wash.) High Sch., 1955-57, 59-60; instr. Columbia Basin Coll., Pasco, Wash., 1956-57, 59-60; programmer analyst Gen. Electric Co., Hanford Atomic Works, Richland, Wash., 1963; prof. math. Cen. Wash. U., Ellensburg, 1964—, dean Grad. Sch. and Research,, 1970-90; on leave as sr. program mgr. U.S. ERDA, also Presdl. interchange exec., 1976-77; mem. Pres.'s Commn. on Exec. Devel., 1976-77; on leave as dean in residence Council Grad. Schs. in U.S., 1984-85; cons. NSF India program, 1968, 69, USIA, India, 1985, NSF, Saudi Arabia, 1986; mem. grant proposal rev. panels NSF, 1970, 71, 76, 77, 89, 90; pres. Western Assn. Grad. Schs., 1979-80, Sec., treas., 1984-90; pres. N.W. Assn. Colls. and Univs. for Sci., 1988-89. Served with AUS, 1957-59. NSF fellow, 1960-61; grantee, summer 1964. Mem. Am. Math Soc., Math. Assn. Am., Assn. Computing Machinery (exec. com.), Soc. Indsl. and Applied Math., Northwest Coll. and Univ. Assn. for Sci. (pres. 1980-83). Methodist. Home: 1311 Brick Rd Ellensburg WA 98926-9562 Office: Cen Wash U Dept Math Ellensburg WA 98926

COMTOIS, MARY ELIZABETH, drama educator, dramaturg; b. Pitts.; d. Walter R. and Helen (Jones) Hart; m. Richard J. Comtois, Nov. 1961; children: Katherine Ann., Elizabeth. BA, Wellesley Coll., 1948; postgrad., Royal Acad. Dramatic Art, London, 1950; MA, San Francisco State U., 1961; PhD, U. Colo., 1970. Co-founder, mng. dir. Group 20 Players, Theater on the Green, Boston, 1952-55; play and story editor Kermit Bloomgarden Prodns., N.Y.C., 1955-60; faculty, chmn. dept. theater arts Rutgers U., New Brunswick, N.J., 1970-84; exec. dir. U. Wash., Seattle, 1985-89, head playwriting, 1985—; mem. adv. bd. Seattle Children's Theater, 1987-89. Author: Contemporary American Theater Critics, 1977. Mem. N.W. Playwrights Guild (founder, bd. dirs. 1986), Nat. Assn. Schs. Theatre (commr. 1986-91), Univ. Resident Theatre Assn. (pres. 1990-92). Democrat. Home: 6527 51st Ave NE Seattle WA 98115-7740 Office: U Wash Sch Drama DX-20 Seattle WA 98195

CONANT, DAVID ARTHUR, architectural acoustician, educator, consultant; b. Biloxi, Miss., Dec. 22, 1945; s. Roger and Lillian Rose May (Lovell) C.; m. Nancy Hayes, June 17, 1972; children: Christopher, Tyler. BS in Physics, Union Coll., 1968; MA in Geology, Columbia U., 1972; BArch, Rensselaer Poly. Inst., 1975, MArch, 1975. Faculty fellow Lamont-Doherty Geol. Obs., Palisades, N.Y., 1970-72; teaching asst. Rensselaer Poly. Inst., Troy, N.Y., 1973-76; asst. prof. dept. architecture Calif. State Poly. U., Pomona, 1976-78; sr. cons. Bolt Beranek Newman Inc., Canoga Park, Calif., 1977-87; prin. McKay Conant Brook, Inc., Westlake Village, Calif., 1987—; cons. IBM Bldg. Energy Rsch. Group, Marina Del Rey, Calif., 1976-77, Expo '93, Taejon, Korea; prin. acoustical cons. Euro Disneyland, Paris; lectr. acoustics UCLA. Co-author: (textbook) Fundamentals and Abatement of Highway Traffic Noise, 1980; author computer software. Instr., vol. Upward Bound, Schenectady, N.Y., 1967-68; overseas vol. Am. Friends Svc. Com., Yugoslavia and Denmark, 1967. With U.S. Army, 1968-70. Recipient Honor award Am. Inst. Architects, 1991. Mem. ASHRAE, Acoustical Soc. Am., Nat. Coun. Acoustical Cons., Constrn. Specifications Inst., Sigma Xi (univ. chpts. lectr. physics). Republican. Presbyterian. Home: 1504 Grissom St Thousand Oaks CA 91362 Office: McKay Conant Brook Inc 5655 Lindero Canyon Rd Ste 325 Thousand Oaks CA 91362

CONCANNON, KEVIN WILLIAM, state agency administrator; b. Portland, Maine, Dec. 17, 1940; s. Stephen Patrick and Katherine Anne (Feeney) C.; m. Mary Eileen Mackasey, Aug. 21, 1965; children: Timothy, Michael, Stephen, John. BA, St Francis Xavier Univ., Antigonish, N.S., 1964; MSW, Maritime Sch. Social Work, 1966; postgrad. U. Conn., 1973, Harvard U., 1987. Cert. social worker, rehab. specialist. Psychiat. social worker N.B. Govt., Saint John, 1966-68; assoc. dir. Diocesan Human Relations Svc., Portland, Maine, 1968-75; dir. of C & YSPP Exec. Dept. Augusta, Maine, 1975-77; dir. mental retardation Maine Dept. Mental Health, Augusta, 1977-80, commr. corrections, 1980-82; commr. Maine Dept. Mental Health and Mental Retardation, 1980-87; adminstr. Oreg. Mental Health Div., 1987; dir. Oreg. Dept. Human Resources, Salem, 1987—; adj. prof. social work Portland State U., 1987—; treas. Nat. Assn. Commn. of Mental Health, Washington, 1983—; dir., 1982—; treas. Nat. Assn. State Mental Health Program Dirs., 1983-86, pres.-elect, 1986-87, pres. 1987-88; cons. State of Ala., Montgomery, 1983, Atty. Gen. N.H., 1980-81. Chmn. Citizens for Mcpl. Reform, Portland, 1975; chmn. U. Conn. adv. com., Concord, N.H., 1983-86; chmn. Legis. Commn. of Children, Augusta, 1983-84; bd. dirs. United Way Oreg., 1988-89, Greater Portland United Way, 1985-87; mem. nat. adv. bd. Boston U. Psychiat. Rsch. and Tng. Ctr., 1984-87, Children's Mental Health of Robert Woods Johnson Found., 1988—; trustee Maine Council on Devel. Disabilities, 1977-87; bd. dirs. Project Mainstay, Inc., 1984-87; mem., trustee Mid-Maine Med. Ctr., Waterville, 1973—; mem. bd. dirs Oreg. Spl. Olympics, 1989—; trustee Oreg. Chpt. Am. Cancer Soc., 1989—; mem. Am. Public Welfare Assn. (chair refugee & immigration com. 1989-92), Oreg. Commn. on Agrl. Workers, 1988-92, Gov.'s Commn. on Workforce, Oreg., 1991-93, Nat. Coun. State Legis. Imm. Policy Com., 1992-94, Nat. Acad. Health Policy Vulnerable Populations Com., 1992-94, Portland Leaders Roundtable, 1991-94, Multnomah Founders Adv. Coun., 1991—, Oreg. Occupational Info. Coord. Coun., 1991-94. Recipient Trustee Svc. award Seton Hosp., 1975, Community Mental Health award Area V Mental Health, 1982, Outstanding Svc. award Maine Devel. Disability Council, 1983, Leadership award Maine State Prison Staff, 1981, Pub. Leadership award Maine State Legislature, 1987, Award Maine State Alliance for the Mentally Ill, 1987, First Pub. Policy Leadership award Opportunity Housing of Bangor, 1987, Engstrom award for U.S. Leadership Nat. Assn. Private Residential Facilities for MR/DD, 1987, Leadership award Oreg. Alliance for Mentally Ill, 1988, Non-speedy award Paralyzed Vets. Am., Oreg. chpt., 1989, Disting. Svc. award Oreg. State U. Ctr. For At Risk Children, 1991. Mem. Am. Coll. Mental Health Adminstrn., Am. Assn. Mental Deficiency, Nat. Assn. State Mental Health Program Dirs. (Leadership award 1988), Am. Pub. Welfare Assn. (pres., commn. self-sufficiency 1993), Maine Rehab. Assn., St. Francis Xavier Alumni. Democrat. Roman Catholic. Office: Oreg Dept Human Resources 500 Summer St NE Salem OR 97310-1012

CONCEPCIÕN, DAVID ALDEN, arbitrator, educator; b. Carmel, Calif., Aug. 6, 1935; s. Don Dominador Cuales Concepciõn and Elma Elizabeth Davis; m. Ann Martin Worster, Dec. 3, 1960; children: Leslie Martin Concepciõn Mayns, David Worster. BA, U. Calif., Santa Barbara, 1959. Adminstrv. exec. Lawrence Berkeley Lab. U. Calif., Berkeley, 1962-70, dir. mgmt. analysis, 1970-75; assoc. dean adminstrn. Hastings Coll. Law U. Calif., San Francisco, 1975-80; pvt. practice Berkeley, 1980—; mem. adv. bd. Calif. Pub. Employee Rels. at U. Calif., Berkeley, 1978—. Contbr. articles to profl. jours. Capt. USMC, 1959-62. Mem. Nat. Acad. Arbitrators, Am. Arbitration Assn. (mem. No. Calif. Adv. Coun. 1980—, mem. nat. bd. dirs. 1980-86, Disting. Svc. award 1990), Soc. Profls. in Dispute Resolution, Indsl. Rels. Rsch. Assn., Soc. Fed. Labor Rel. Profls. Democrat. Mem. United Ch. Christ. Office: 65 Stevenson Ave Berkeley CA 94708

CONCUS, PAUL, mathematician; b. L.A., June 18, 1933; s. Wulf and Flora (Malin) C.; m. Celia Gordon, Mar. 22, 1959; children: Marian, Adriane. BS, Calif. Inst. Tech., 1954; AM, Harvard U., 1955, PhD, 1959. Sr. scientist Lawrence Berkeley (Calif.) Lab., 1960—; adj. prof. U. Calif., Berkeley, 1978—; trustee Math. Sci. Rsch. Inst., Berkeley, 1984—; cons. in field. Author, editor books in field; contbr. articles to profl. jours. Sr. vis. fellowship Sci. Rsch. Coun., Eng., 1971; grantee various U.S. govt. agys. Mem. Soc. Indsl. and Applied Math. (chmn. section com. 1986—), Tau Beta Pi. Office: U Calif Lawrence Berkeley Lab 50A-2129 Berkeley CA 94720

CONDIE, CAROL JOY, anthropologist, research facility administrator; b. Provo, Utah, Dec. 28, 1931; d. LeRoy and Thelma (Graff) C.; m. M. Kent Stout, June 18, 1954; children: Carla Ann, Erik Roy, Paula Jane. BA in Anthropology, U. Utah, 1953; MEd in Elem. Edn., Cornell U., 1954; PhD in Anthropology, U. N.Mex., 1973. Edn. coordinator Maxwell Mus. Anthropology, U. N.Mex., Albuquerque, 1973, interpretation dir., 1974-77; asst. prof. anthropology U. N.Mex., 1975-77; cons. anthropologist, 1977-78; pres. Quivira Research Ctr., Albuquerque, 1978—; cons. anthropologist U.S. Congl. Office Tech. Assessment, chair Archeol. Resources Planning Adv. Com., Albuquerque, 1985-86; leader field seminars Crow Canyon Archeol. Ctr., 1986—; appointee Albuquerque dist. adv. coun., bur. land mgmt. U.S. Dept. Interior, 1989; study leader Smithsonian Instn. Tours, 1991; mem. Albuquerque Heritage Conservation Adv. Com., 1992. Author: The Nighthawk Site: A Pithouse Site on Sandia Pueblo Land, Bernalillo County, New Mexico, 1982, Five Sites on the Pecos River Road, 1985, Data Recovery at Eight Archeological Sites on the Rio Nutritas, 1992, Data Recovery at Eight Archeological Sites on Cabresto Road near Questa, 1992; co-editor: Anthropology of The Desert West, 1985; contbr. articles to profl. jours. Mem. Downtown Core Area Schs. Com., Albuquerque, 1982. Ford Found. fellow, 1953-54; recipient Am. Planning Assn. award, 1985-86, Gov.'s award, 1986. Fellow Am. Anthrop. Assn.; mem. Soc. Am. Archeology (chmn. native Am. rels. com. 1983-85), N.Mex. Archeol. Coun. (pres. 1982-83, hist. preservation com. 1988), Albuquerque Archeol. Soc. (pres. 1992), Maxwell Mus. Assn. (bd. dirs.), Las Arañas Spinners and Weavers Guild (pres. 1972). Democrat. Home and Office: Quivira Research Ctr 1809 Notre Dame Dr NE Albuquerque NM 87106-1011

CONDIE, MICHAEL WILFRED, dermatologist; b. Mayville, N.D., Apr. 26, 1939; s. Wilfred Alexander and Violet Elizabeth (Corey) C.; m. Joanne Colleen Balestra, Aug. 23, 1986. BA, Pomona Coll., 1962; MD, U. Ky., 1966. Diplomate Am. Bd. Dermatology. Intern U. Utah Med. Ctr., Salt Lake City, 1966-67; resident in dermatology Stanford U. Med. Ctr., Palo Alto, Calif., 1967-68, 70-72; pvt. practice Huntington Beach, Calif., 1972-74, Mission Viejo, Calif., 1974-75; dermatologist Sunnyvale (Calif.) Med. Clinic, 1975—; asst. clin. prof. dermatology Stanford U. Med. ctr., 1975—. Active Prince of Peace Luth. Ch., Saratoga, Calif., 1984—. Lt. comdr. USN, 1968-70, Vietnam. Fellow Am. Acad. Dermatology; mem. San Francisco Dermatology Soc., Stanford Club Los Gatos/Saratoga (pres. 1987-89, bd. dirs. 1984—), Pomona Coll. Alumni Assn. (bd. dirs. Peninsula chpt. 1989—), Alpha Omega Alpha. Home: 51 Bay Tree Ln Los Altos CA 94022 Office: Sunnyvale Med Clinic 201 Old San Francisco Rd Sunnyvale CA 94086

CONDIT, GARY A., congressman; b. Apr. 21, 1948. AA, Modesto Jr. Coll.; BA, Calif. State Coll. Councilman City of Ceres, Calif., 1972-74, mayor, 1974-76; supr. Stanislaus County, Calif., 1976-82; assemblyman State of Calif., 1982-89; mem. 101st-103rd Congresses from 15th (now 18th) Calif. Dist., 1989—; mem. agriculture com., mem. govt. ops. com. Democrat. Office: US House of Representatives 1123 Longworth Washington DC 20515-0518*

CONDIT, PHILIP MURRAY, business executive, engineer; b. Berkeley, Calif., Aug. 2, 1941; s. Daniel Harrison and Bernice (Kemp) C.; m. Madeleine K. Bryant, Jan. 25, 1963 (div. June 1982); children: Nicole Lynn, Megan Anne; m. Janice Condit, Apr. 6, 1991. BS MechE, U. Calif., Berkeley, 1963; MS in Aero. Engring., Princeton U., 1965; MS in Mgmt., MIT, 1975. Engr. The Boeing Co., Seattle, 1965-72, mgr. engring., 1973-83, v.p., gen. mgr., 1983-84, v.p. sales and mktg., 1984-86, exec. v.p., 1986-89, exec. v.p., gen. mgr. 777 div., 1989, now pres; mem. adv. council Dept. Mech. and Aerospace Engring., Princeton (N.J.) U., 1984—; chmn. aero. adv. com. NASA Adv. Coun., 1988-92; bd. dirs. John Fluke Mfg. Co., 1987—. Co-inventor Design of a Flexible Wing, 1965. Mem. Mercer Island (Wash.) Utilities Bd., 1975-78; bd. dirs. Camp Fire, Inc.; mem. exec bd. chief Seattle council #609, Boy Scouts Am., 1988-90; trustee Mus. of Flight, Seattle, 1990—. Co-recipient Laurels award Aviation Week & Space Tech. magazine, 1990; Sloan fellow MIT, Boston, 1974. Fellow AIAA (aircraft design award 1984, Edward C. Wells tech. mgmt. award 1982), Royal Aero. Soc.; mem. NAE, Soc. Sloan Fellows (bd. govs. 1985-89), Soc. Automotive Engrs. Clubs: Rainier, Columbia Tower (Seattle). Office: Boeing Comml Airplane Group PO Box 3707 7755 E Marginal Way S Seattle WA 98124-2207

CONDIT, RALPH HOWELL, chemist; b. Hollywood, Calif., May 12, 1929; s. Daniel Dale and Anne Elisabeth (Howell) C.; m. Mitzi Helena Grauer, Mar. 20, 1966; children: Carl Daniel, Cedric Alan. BA in Physics, Princeton U., 1951, PhD in Chemistry, 1960. Rsch. adminstr. Air Force Office Sci. Rsch., Washington, 1958-60; chemist Lawrence Livermore Lab., Livermore, Calif., 1960-90; cons. on plutonium technology Livermore, 1990—; cons. Air Force Office Sci. Rsch., 1965-74; chmn. bd. Geos Corp., Livermore, 1967-72. Contbr. articles to profl. jours. Chmn. Livermore Bicentennial Edn. Com., 1975-76. Mem. Am. Chem. Soc., Am. Physical Soc., Am. Nuclear Soc., AAAS. Home: 4669 Almond Cir Livermore CA 94550-5039 Office: Lawrence Lab L 362 Livermore CA 94550

CONDON, STANLEY CHARLES, gastroenterologist; b. Glendale, Calif., Feb. 1, 1931; s. Charles Max and Alma Mae (Chinn) C.; m. Vaneta Marilyn Mabley, May 19, 1963; children: Lori, Brian, David. BA, La Sierra Coll., 1952; MD, Loma Linda U., 1956. Diplomate Nat. Bd. Med. Examiners; cert. Am. Bd. Internal Medicine. Intern L.A. County Gen. Hosp., 1956-57, resident gen. pathology, 1959-61; resident internal medicine White Meml. Med. Ctr., L.A., 1961-63, attending staff out-patient clinic, 1963-64; active jr. attending staff L.A. County Gen. Hosp., 1964-65; dir. intern-resident tng. program Manila Sanitarium and Hosp., 1966-71; chief resident internal medicine out-patient clinic Loma Linda U. Med. Ctr., 1972-74, attending staff, asst. prof. medicine, 1976-91, assoc. prof. medicine, 1991—, med. dir. nutritional support team, 1984—. Contbr. articles to profl. jours. Capt. U.S. Army, 1957-59. Fellow ACP; mem. AMA, San Bernardino County Med. Soc., Calif. Med. Assn., Am. Soc. for Parenteral and Enteral Nutrition, Am. Gastroenterological Assn., So. Calif. Soc. Gastroenterology, Inland Soc. Internal Medicine, So. Calif. Soc. Gastrointestinal Endoscopy. Republican. Seventh-day Adventist. Home: 11524 Ray Ct Loma Linda CA 92354 Office: Loma Linda U Med Ctr 115234 Anderson St Loma Linda CA 92350

CONE, EDWIN EARL, lumber company executive; b. Portland, Oreg., Aug. 10, 1916; s. Edwin Earle and Emma Louise (Ziegler) C.; m. June Elizabeth Woldt, Jan. 31, 1943; children: Barbara Jean, Richard Bruce, Susan Elizabeth (dec.), Douglas Earl, Gregory Paul. BA, Willamette U., 1941. Ptnr., gen. mgr. Cone Lumber Co., Goshen, Oreg., 1941-88, cons., 1988—. Mayor City of Eugene, Oreg., 1958-69, councilman, 1953-54; state rep. from Lane County Oreg. State Legis., 1955, 57. Athletic field house, chapel named in honor of him and his wife Willamette U., Salem, Oreg.; orch. pit named in honor of him and his wife Hult Ctr. Performings Arts; endowed chair sch. bus. adminstrn. U. Oreg.; named Eugene's First Citizen, 1974, Boss Yr. Springfield Jaycees, 1979; recipient Bus. Adminstrn. Dean's Award U. Oreg., 1974, Pioneer Award, 1980. Mem. Masons, Al Kader Shrine, Travelers' Century Club, Knights Round Table, Eugene Country Club. Republican. Methodist. Home: 2130 Olive St Eugene OR 97405-2838 Office: Cone Lumber Co PO Box 7128 Eugene OR 97401-0028

CONE, JUNE ELIZABETH, civic worker; b. Portland, Oreg., Sept. 29, 1918; d. Otto Warner and Signa Elizabeth (Johannson) Woldt; m. Edwin Earl Cone, Jan. 31, 1943; children: Barbara Jean, Richard Bruce, Susan Elizabeth (dec.), Douglas Earl, Gregory Paul. BA, Willamette U., 1942. Charter mem. Com. for Performing Arts, Eugene, Oreg., Assistance League Eugene; endowed chair sch. bus. adminstrn. U. Oreg., mem. libr. bd., chmn. steering com. Fgn. Student Friendship Found.; mem. bd. overseers Lewis and Clark Coll., Portland. Athletic field house, chapel named in honor of her and her husband Willamette U., Salem, Oreg.; orch. pit named in honor of her and her husband Hult Ctr. Performing Arts, Eugene; named One of Eugene Outstanding Women Yr., 1968; recipient Woman of Achievement for Yr. award Quota Club, 1969, Lestle J. Sparks Medallion Disting. Svc., Willamette U., 1992. Mem. Travelers Century Club, PEO Sisterhood, Eugene Fortnightly Club, Monday Book Club. Republican. Methodist. Home: 2130 Olive St Eugene OR 97405-2838

CONE, LAWRENCE ARTHUR, research medicine educator; b. N.Y.C., Mar. 23, 1928; s. Max N. and Ruth (Weber) C.; m. Julia Haldy, June 6, 1947 (dec. 1956); m. Mary Elisabeth Osborne, Aug. 20, 1960; children: Lionel Alfred. AB, NYU, 1948; MD, U. Berne, Switzerland, 1954. Diplomate Am. Bd. Internal Medicine, Am. Bd. Infectious Diseases, Am. Bd. Allergy and Immunology, Am. Bd. Med. Oncology. Intern Dallas Meth. Hosp., 1954-55, resident internal medicine, 1955; resident Flower 5th Hosp., N.Y.C., 1957-59, Met. Hosp., N.Y.C., 1959-60; rsch. fellow infectious diseases and immunology NYU Med. Sch., N.Y.C., 1960-62; from asst. prof. to assoc. prof. N.Y. Med. Coll., N.Y.C., 1962-72, chief sect immunology and infectious diseases, 1962-72; assoc. clin. prof. medicine Harbor UCLA Med. Sch., 1984—; career scientist Health Rsch. Coun. N.Y.C., 1962-68; chief sect. immunology and infectious diseases Eisenhower Med. Ctr., Rancho Mirage, Calif., 1973—, chmn. dept. medicine, 1976-78, past pres. med. staff, 1984-90; cons. infectious disease Desert Hosp., Palm Springs, Calif., 1980-85. Contbr. articles to profl. jours. Bd. dirs. Desert Bighorn Research Inst., Palm Desert, Calif., 1986—. Served to capt. Med. Service Corps, U.S. Army, 1955-57. Fellow ACP, Internat. AIDS Soc., Royal Soc. Medicine, Am. Coll. Allergy, Am. Acad. Allergy and Immunology, Am. Soc. Infectious Diseases, Am. Geriatric Soc. (founding fellow western div.); mem. Am. Soc. Microbiology, Am. Fedn. for Clin. Rsch., Faculty Soc. UCLA, Woodstock Artists Assn., Tamamisk Country Club, Coachella Valley Gun and Wildlife Club Faculty Soc. UCLA Harbor Med. Ctr., Lotus Club (N.Y.C.). Republican. Office: Probst Profl Bldg 3900 Bob Hope Dr Rancho Mirage CA 92270-1731

CONGDON, ROGER DOUGLASS, theology educator, minister; b. Ft. Collins, Colo., Apr. 6, 1918; s. John Solon and Ellen Avery (Kellogg) C.; m. Rhoda Gwendolyn Britt, Jan. 2, 1948; children: Rachel Congdon Lidbeck, James R., R. Steven, Jon B., Philip F., Robert N., Bradford B., Ruth A. Mahner, Rebecca Congdon Skones, Rhoda J. Miller, Marianne C., Mark Alexander. BA, Wheaton Coll., 1940; postgrad, Eastern Bapt. Sem., 1940-41; ThM, Dallas Theol. Sem., 1945; ThD, Dallas Theology Sem., 1949.

Ordained to ministry Bapt. Ch., 1945. Exec. sec., dean Altanta Bible Inst., 1945-49; prof. theology Carver Bible Inst., Atlanta, 1945-49; prof. Multnomah Sch. of the Bible, Portland, Oreg., 1950-87; pastor Emmanuel Bapt. Ch., Vancouver, Wash., 1985—; served as past dean of faculty, dean of edn., v.p., chmn. library com., chmn. achievement-award com., chmn. lectureship com., advisor grad. div. and mem. pres.'s cabinet all at Multnomah Sch. of the Bible; chmn. Chil Evang. Fellowship of Greater Portland, 1978—; founder, pres. Preaching Print Inc., Portland, 1953—. Founder, speaker semi-weekly radio broadcast Bible Truth Forum, KPDQ, Portland, Oreg., 1989—; author: The Doctrine of Conscience, 1945. Chmn. Citizen's Com. Info. on Communism, Portland, 1968-75. Recipient Outstanding Educators of Am. award, 1972, Loraine Chafer award in Systematic Theology, Dallas Theol. Sem. Mem. Am. Assn. Bible Colls. (chmn. testing com. 1953-78), N.Am. Assn. Bible Colls. (N.W. rep. 1960-63), Near East Archaeol. Soc., Evang. Theol. Soc. Republican. Home: 16539 NE Halsey St Portland OR 97230-5607 Office: Emmanuel Bapt Ch 14810 NE 28th St Vancouver WA 98682-8357

CONGER, HARRY CALVIN, hazardous waste service company executive; b. Iowa City, Iowa, June 10, 1931; s. Ernest and Christine (Foster) C.; m. Marilyn Ann Bergman, Dec. 22, 1950 (div. Jan. 1984); children: Kristine, Carolyn, Melissa; m. Lisa Diane Homan, Sept. 1990. BS in Chemistry, U. Iowa, 1953; grad. Advanced Mgmt. Program, Harvard U., 1980. Start-up engr. Universal Oil Products, Chgo., 1956-58; v.p., gen. mgr. Calgon Water Mgmt. Div., Pitts., 1959-82; pres. Olin Water Svcs., Kansas City, Kans., 1982-84; pres., chief exec. officer Waste-Tech Svcs., Inc., Golden, Colo., 1984-92; chmn., CEO Vanguard Environ. Solutions Inc., Wheat Ridge, Colo., 1993—; bd. dirs. Indsl. Specialty Chem., Washington, Waste-Tech Svcs., Chgo. Author: Treatment of Oil Field Waste, 1965; author papers in field. Bd. dirs. Foothills Art Ctr., Golden, 1989, Sch. for Emotionally Disturbed Children, Evergreen, Colo., 1988. 1st lt. USAF, 1954-56, Korea. Mem. Indsl. Specialty Chem. Assn. (pres. 1983-89), Soc. Petroleum Engrs. (Outstanding Contbn. Cert. 1967), Am. Water Works Assn. (Cert. of Recognition 1969). Office: Vanguard Environ Solutions 12325 W 52d Ave Wheat Ridge CO 80033-1916

CONGER, HARRY MILTON, mining company executive; b. Seattle, July 22, 1930; s. Harry Milton Jr. and Caroline (Gunnell) C.; m. Phyllis Nadine Shepherd, Aug. 14, 1949 (dec.); children: Harry Milton IV, Preston George; m. Rosemary L. Scholz, Feb. 22, 1991. D in Bus. Adminstrn. (hon.), S.D. Sch. Mines and Tech., 1983; D. in Engring. (hon.), Colo. Sch. Mines, 1988, hon. degrees. Registered profl. engr., Ariz., Colo. Shift foreman Asarco, Inc., Silver Bell, Ariz., 1955-64; mgr. Kaiser Steel Corp. Eagle Mountain Mine, 1964-70; v.p., gen. mgr. Kaiser Resources, Ltd., Fernie, B.C., Can., 1970-73, Consolidation Coal Co. (Midwestern div.), Carbondale, Ill., 1973-75; v.p. Homestake Mining Co., San Francisco, 1975-77; pres. Homestake Mining Co., 1977-78, pres., chief exec. officer, 1978-82, chmn., pres., chief exec. officer, 1982-86, chmn., chief exec. officer, 1986—; also bd dirs.; bd. dir. CalMat, Inc., ASA Ltd., Pacific Gas & Electric Co., Baker Hughes Inc.; chmn. Am. Mining Congress., 1986-89. Trustee Calif. Inst. Tech. With C.E., U.S. Army, 1956. Recipient Disting. Achievement medal Colo. Sch. Mines, 1978, Am. Mining Hall of Fame, 1990. Mem. NAE, Am. Inst. Mining Engrs. (disting., Charles F. Rand gold medal 1990), Mining and Metallurgy Soc. Am., Mining Club, Bohemian Club, Commonwealth Club, Pacific Union Club, World Trade Club, Diablo Country Club. Republican. Episcopalian. Office: Homestake Mining Co 650 California St San Francisco CA 94108-2788

CONGREVE, MARIO RICARDO, producer, television editor, educator; b. Concepcion, Chile, Nov. 27, 1957; came to U.S., 1979; s. Mario Congreve Wilson and Iris (Stratta) Trabucco. BA in Cinema and Photography, So. Ill. U., 1982; MA in Humanities, Calif. State U.-Dominguez Hills, 1988. Prodn. asst. Polycom Teleprodns., Mission Viejo, Calif., 1985; TV editor Christian Family Movement, L.A., 1985; prodn. coordinator Stanton Films, Redondo Beach, Calif., 1985-87; videographer Cole, Green and Assocs., Lomita, Calif., 1985—; chyron operator Shop TV Network, Hollywood, Calif., 1987—; media specialist Calif. State U., Carson, Calif., 1985—; chyron operator Metroplex, 1989; cameraman Ford Motors, 1989; owner Pacific View Prodns., 1988. Dir. award winning TV commls., Concepcion, 1986, 87. Fulbright scholar, 1979; grad. equity fellow Calif. State U., 1988. Mem. Soc. Motion Picture and TV Engrs., Am. Film. Inst., Rotary (Dist. 651 scholarship 1981). Home: PO Box 1092 Redondo Beach CA 90278-0092 Office: Calif State U Dominguez Hills 1000 E Victoria St Carson CA 90747-0005

CONKLIN, HAL (HAROLD CONKLIN), arts association executive; b. Oakland, Calif., Dec. 11, 1945; s. Ralph Harold and Stella (Garabedian) C.; m. Barbara Elaine Lang, Mar. 25, 1972; children: Nathaniel, Joseph Lucas, Zachary. Student, Calif. State U., Hayward, 1967-71. Editor New Focus Mag., Santa Barbara, Calif., 1969-72; co-dir. Community Environ. Coun., Santa Barbara, 1972-82; pres. Santa Barbara Renaissance Fund, 1983—. Councilman City of Santa Barbara, 1977—; bd. dirs. Santa Barbara Redevel. Agy., 1978—, Calif. Local Govt. Commn., Sacramento, 1979—, Nat. League of Cities, 1987-89. Mem. League of Calif. Cities (bd. dirs. 1986—, pres. 1991-92), Calif. Resource Recovery Assn. (pres. 1978-82). Methodist. Home: 214 El Monte Dr Santa Barbara CA 93109-2006 Office: City of Santa Barbara 735 Anacapa St Santa Barbara CA 93101-2298

CONLEY, ELIZABETH SIMONA, lawyer; b. Pnoenix, Sept. 22, 1942; d. Vincent de Paul and Edna Harriet (Broderick) C.; m. William Charles Siska, July 25, 1975; children: Sean Paul, William, Margaret, Güs. BA, Mundelein Coll., Chgo., 1965; MA, U. Iowa, 1974; JD, U. Utah, 1986. Bar: Utah 1986, U.S. Dist. Ct. Utah 1986. Tchr. St. Mary Ctr. for Learning, Chgo., 1986-76; lectr. Mundelein Coll., Chgo., 1976-77; dir. tng. Triax Co., Alpine, Utah, 1981; adj. asst. prof. U. Utah, Salt Lake City, 1978—; assoc. Giauque and Williams, Salt Lake City, 1986-87; jud. clk. Hon. Bruce S. Jenkins, Salt Lake City, 1987-88; assoc. Davis, Graham & Stubbs, Salt Lake City, 1989, Parsons, Behle & Latimer, Salt Lake City, 1989—. Author: Mass Media, 1972 (mag. Maxi award, 1975). Mem. ABA, Utah State Bar Assn. (exec. bd.), Utah Women Lawyers, Salt Lake County Bar Assn., Utah Trial Lawyers Assn. (bd. govs.). Roman Catholic. Office: Parsons Behle Latimer 201 S Main St Ste 1800 Salt Lake City UT 84111-2215

CONLEY, PHILIP JAMES, JR., retired air force officer; b. Providence, May 22, 1927; s. Philip James and Lillian Loretta (Burns) C.; m. Shirley Jean Andrews, Jan. 26, 1956; children: Sharon, Kathleen, Anne, James. BS, U.S. Naval Acad., 1950; MS, U. Mich., 1956, Rensselaer Poly. Inst., 1963. Commd. 2d lt. USAF, 1950, advanced through grades to maj. gen., 1979; dep. chief staff, ops. Air Force Systems Command, Andrews AFB, Washington, 1974-75; chief staff Air Force Systems Command, 1975-78; comdr. Air Force Flight Test Center, Edwards AFB, Calif., 1978-82, Hanscom AFB, Mass., 1983; ret., 1983. Decorated Legion Merit with oakleaf cluster, Air medal (2), D.F.C., D.S.M. (2). Mem. Air Force Assn., Order of Daedalians, U.S. Naval Acad. Alumni Assn., Am. Legion, Vikings Club (L.A.). Roman Catholic. Home: 930 Camino Viejo Santa Barbara CA 93108-1920

CONLEY, ZEB BRISTOL, JR., art gallery director; b. Andrews, N.C., Feb. 12, 1936; s. Zeb Bristol and A. Elizabeth (Faircloth) C.; student N.C. State Coll., 1954-55, Mars Hill Coll., 1955-57, Coll. William and Mary, 1957-61; m. Betty Ann Wiswall, May 25, 1974; stepchildren—Peter Wiswall Betts, Stephen Wood Betts, Frederick Beale Betts, III. Designer, Seymour Robins, Inc., N.Y.C., 1961; with First Nat. Bank, Las Vegas (N.Mex.), 1964-65; gen. mgr. Swanson's Inc., Las Vegas, 1965-73, v.p., 1969—; dir. Jamison Galleries, Santa Fe, 1973—, guest curator Alfred Morang: A Retrospective at Mus. of S.W. Midland, Tex., 1985; sec. Marbasconi, Inc., d.b.a. Jamison Galleries, 1974-80, pres., 1980—. Republican. Office: c/o The Jamison Galleries 560 Montezuma # 103 Santa Fe NM 87501

CONLIN, WILLIAM RICHARD, II, columnist; b. Sacramento, Apr. 14, 1913; s. William Sr. and Clara Mabel (Schaadt) C.; (widowed); 1 child, William Richard III. AA, Yuba Coll., 1932; AB, Stanford U., 1934. City editor Sacramento Union, 1942-43, sports editor, 1946-59, editor, 1959-62, asst. to pub., 1962-66, sports editor, 1966-76; sports editor Sacramento Bee, 1982-86, ret., 1986. Lt. USN, 1943-45, PTO. Mem. Nat. Football Found., Mil. Order of World Wars, Elks, Alpha Sigma Phi, Sigma Delta Chi. Republican. Roman Catholic. Home: 1362 8th Ave Sacramento CA 95818 Office: Sacramento Bee 2100-Q Sacramento CA 95852

CONLON, FAITH E(LEANOR), publishing company executive, editor; b. Glen Rock, N.J., Oct. 15, 1955; d. Andrew Joseph and Edythe Victoreen (VanRees) C.; m. John Llwelynn McKittrick, Mar. 21, 1992; 1 child, Connor Andrew. BA in Am. Studies, Middlebury (Vt.) Coll., 1978. Asst. editor Anchor Books, Doubleday & Co., N.Y.C., 1979-80; assoc. editor Madrona Pubs., Seattle, 1981-82; pub., co-owner Seal Press, Seattle, 1982—; faculty, guest lectr. Denver (Wash.) Pub. Inst., 1990—; faculty U. Wash. Extension Pub. Workshop, Seattle, 1990. Chairperson Citizens Party, Seattle, 1984; bd. mem. Fair Budget Action Campaign, Seattle, 1989-90; precinct com. person King County Dms., Seattle, 1991—. Recipient Carey-Thomas award Pubs. Weekly, N.Y.C., 1988, Small Bus. award Seattle Mayor's Small Bus. Task Force, 1992, Excellence in Pub. award Pacific Northwest Booksellers Assn. Mem. Pacific Northwest Book Pubs. Assn. Democrat. Office: Seal Press 3131 Western Ave Ste 410 Seattle WA 98121

CONNELL, BRIAN LINDSAY, family medicine educator; b. Glasgow, Scotland, June 4, 1947; came to U.S., 1986; s. Robert Lindsay and Jean Elizabeth (Turnbull) C.; m. Marie Lang dePutron, Aug. 14, 1976; children: Shannon, Lindsay, Darryl. BSc, U. Toronto, Ont., Can., 1969; MD, U. Toronto, 1973; diploma in Christian studies, U. B.C., Vancouver, 1977; JD, Simon Greenleaf U., 1991. Cert. in family medicine and emergency medicine Coll. Family Physicians Can.; diplomate Am. Bd. Family Practice. Intern North York Gen. Hosp., Toronto, Ont., Can., 1973-74; assoc. physician Lorne Park Med. Group, Mississaga, Ont., 1974-76; pvt. practice Orillia, Ont., 1977-87; resident U. Calif., Irvine, 1987-88; asst. prof. family medicine Loma Linda (Calif.) U. Sch. Medicine, 1988-90, assoc. prof., 1990—; coroner Province of Ont., 1978-86; pres. med. staff Orillia Soldiers Meml. Hosp., 1985-86; med. dir. family medicine ctrs. Loma Linda U., 1988—, med. dir. family medicine residency, 1989—; med. dir. Heritage Garden Health Care Ctr., Loma Linda, 1988—; examiner Med. Bd. Calif., 1991—. Author: Contract in Blood, 1988. Vol. tchr. Simon Greenleaf Sch. Law, Anaheim, Calif., 1992—; advisor, cons. Western Ctr. for Law and Religious Freedom, Anaheim, 1990—. Fellow Am. Acad. Family Physicians; mem. AMA, Coll. Family Physicians of Can., Christian Legal Soc., Christian Concilation Svcs. of Orange County, Calif. Med. Assn., Calif. Acad. Family Physicians, San Bernardino Med. Assn. Republican. Mem. Evangelical Free Ch. Home: 6290 E Via Ribazo Anaheim Hills CA 92807-2334 Office: Loma Linda U Family Med Ctr 25455 Barton Rd B104 Loma Linda CA 92354

CONNELL, EVAN SHELBY, JR., author; b. Kansas City, Mo., Aug. 17, 1924; s. Evan Shelby and Elton (Williamson) C. Student, Dartmouth, 1941-43; AB, U. Kans., 1946-47; grad. study, Stanford U., 1947-48, Columbia U., 1948-49. Editor Contact mag., Sausalito, Calif., 1960-65. Author: The Anatomy Lesson and Other Stories, 1957, Mrs. Bridge, 1959, The Patriot, 1960, Notes From a Bottle Found on the Beach at Carmel, 1963, At the Crossroads: Stories, 1965, The Diary of a Rapist, 1966, Mr. Bridge, 1969, Points for a Compass Rose, 1973, The Connoisseur, 1974 (Calif. Literature Silver medal 1974), Double Honeymoon, 1976, A Long Desire, 1979, The White Lantern, 1980, St. Augustine's Pigeon, 1980, Son of the Morning Star: Custer and the Little Bighorn, 1984 (Nat. Book Critics Circle award nominee 1984, L.A. Times Book award 1985), The Alchymist's Journal, 1991; editor: Jerry Stoll's I Am A Lover, 1961, Women by Three, 1969. Served as naval aviator 1943-45. Eugene Saxton fellow, 1953, Guggenheim fellow, 1963; Rockefeller Found. grantee, 1967; recipient Am. Acad. Inst. Arts and Letters award, 1987. Office: Fort Marcy 13 320 Artist Rd Santa Fe NM 87501 also: care Elizabeth McKee 22 E 40th St New York NY 10016

CONNELL, JAMES JOSEPH, JR., international trading company executive; b. Balt., Aug. 6, 1928; s. Joseph James and Katherine Evelyn (Dietrich) C.; m. Elaine Therese Elvig, Oct. 14, 1950; children: Katherine, James, Elizabeth. BA, U. Kans., 1950; MS, San Francisco State U., 1967. Credit analyst Anglo Calif. Nat. Bank, San Francisco, 1953-54; export trader Mark Ross & Co. Internat., San Francisco, 1954-66, export mgr., 1966-72, v.p., 1987—; v.p. Global Mdsing. Corp., San Francisco, 1966—. Pres. Soc. for Asian Art, San Francisco, 1984-86; v.p. San Francisco Craft and Folk Art Mus., 1982-89; bd. dirs. Rudolph Schaeffer Sch. of Design, San Francisco, 1981-90. Served to lt. (j.g.) USN, 1950-53, comdr. Res. ret. Mem. Internat. Mgr.'s Assn. (pres. 1972). Office: Mark Ross & Co Internat 5 Dorman Ave San Francisco CA 94124-1898

CONNELL, ROBERT IVEY, mathematics educator, researcher; b. Fort Campbell, Ky., Dec. 29, 1955; s. Julius Clyburn and Lois Isabelle (Thompson) C.; m. Donna Marie Satler White, June 8, 1979 (div.); children Judd Ivey, Rachelle Marie, Juli Elizabeth; m. Jean Marie Law, May 30, 1986 (div.); 1 child, Luke Aaron. BS in Physics, Brigham Young U., 1980; MS in Physics, U. N.Mex., 1984, PhD in Physics, 1988. Commd. 2d lt. USAF, 1980, advanced through grades to maj., 1993; chief atmospheric phenomenology Air Force Weapons Lab., Albuquerque, 1980-85; rsch. asst. Plasma Tech. Br., Naval Rsch. Lab., Washington, 1986-87; chief laser kinetics br. Frank J. Seiler Lab., USAF Acad., Colo., 1987-91; dir. sophomore math. USAF Acad., Colo., 1991—. Contbr. articles to profl. jours. Recipient John E. Anderson Acad. scholarship, 1978, Air Force ROTC scholarship, 1978, Air Force Inst. Tech. scholarship, 1985. Mem. AAAS, Am. Phys. Soc. Home: 17955 Red Rocks Dr Monument CO 80132

CONNELL, WILLIAM D., lawyer; b. Palo Alto, Calif., Apr. 1, 1955; s. Robert Charles and Audrey Elizabeth (Steele) C.; m. Kathyn Lynn Mleko, Aug. 13, 1977; 1 child, Hilary Anne. BA in Polit Sci. with honors, Stanford U., 1976; JD cum laude, Harvard U., 1979. Bar: Calif. 1979, U.S. Dist. Ct. (cen., no. and ea. dists.) Calif. 1979, U.S. Ct. Appeals (9th cir.) 1979. Assoc. Gibson, Dunn & Crutcher, L.A., 1979-80; assoc. Gibson, Dunn & Crutcher, San Jose, Calif., 1980-87, ptnr., 1988—. Mem. Christian Legal Soc. Mem. Stanford Alumni Assn. (life), Commonwealth Club Calif., The Churchill Club, Silicon Valley Capital Club (founder), Sports Car Club Am., Phi Beta Kappa. Republican. Office: Gibson Dunn & Crutcher Telesis Tower 26th Flr 1 Montgomery St San Francisco CA 94104-4505

CONNELLEE-CLAY, BARBARA, quality assurance auditor, labratory administrator; b. Hereford, Tex., Dec. 4, 1929; d. Herman and Audrey Stella (Carroll) Galbraith; m. Rodger Sadosa Connellee, 1950 (dec.); m. Edward Lee Clay, 1983; children: Alison Elaine Stephens, Rebecca Diane Connellee Crabtree, Calvin Clay, Larry Clay, Becky Clay. BS, U. N.Mex., 1976, MBA, 1981; Cert. advanced facilitator, Quality Circle Inst.; insp. Occupational Safety and Health Adminstrn. Mem. adminstrv. staff U. Calif. Los Alamos Nat. Lab., 1976—. Editor nuclear materials tech. div. Safety and News bulletin. Pres., Wesleyan Service Guild, 1958. Recipient Women at Work award region 8 Dept. Labor Council on Working Women, 1983, N.Mex. Women at Work Spl. award Coun. Working Women Inst. Women and Minority Affairs, 1985. Mem. NAFE, Women in Sci., Assn. for Quality and Participation (cert. facilitator). United Methodist (past dir. edn.). Address: PO Box 1663 MS E583 Los Alamos NM 87544

CONNELLY, THEODORE SAMPLE, communications executive; b. Middletown, Conn., Oct. 15, 1925; s. Herbert Lee and Mabel Gertrude (Wells) C.; B.A., Wesleyan U., 1948, postgrad., 1951; postgrad. U. Paris, 1950. Sec., Nat. Com. on Edn., Am. Trucking Assn., Inc., Washington, 1952-54; dir. public affairs Nat. Automobile Club, San Francisco, 1955-62; pres., chmn. Connelly Corp., San Francisco, 1963—; treas. Ednl. Access Cable TV Corp.; dir. Mission Neighborhood Centers, Inc., Neighborhood Devel. Corp.; mem. adv. com. on Calif. motor vehicle legis., 1955-62, Calif. State C. of C. com. on hwys., 1958-62. Trustee, sec., v.p. Lincoln U.; sec. Lincoln U. Found., 1968-82; bd. dirs. San Francisco Program for Aging; founder, dir. Communications Library, 1963—, Communications Inst., 1978—; founding mem. Calif. Council for UN Univ., 1976; organizer Internat. Child Art Collection; co-founder African Research Commn., 1970; established Connelly Fund, 1981; mem. founding regents Am. Pan-Pacific U., 1991; co-established awds. for excellence in writing about communications, 1981—. Served with USNR, 1943-54. Recipient cert. of merit San Francisco Jaycees, 1959; award of merit USPHS, 1980, citation U.S. Dept. H&HS, 1981; commendations U.S. Coun. for World Communications, 1983. Mem. AAAS, AAUP, Public Relations Round Table San Francisco, Atlanta Hist. Soc., Asian Mass Communication and Info. Centre (Singapore), NAACP, SAR, UN Assn. U.S.A. Club: Dolphin Swimming and Boating (San Francisco), Golden Gate Swimmer. Author/compiler: BCTV Bibliography on Cabletelevision, 1975—; Electromagnetic Radiation, 1976; CINCOM: Courses in Communications, 1978—; editor: An Analysis of Joint Ventures in China, 1982; contbr. articles to profl. jours.; producer, writer, dir. numerous TV programs. Office: Lock Box 472139 Marina Sta San Francisco CA 94147-2139

CONNER, FINIS F., electronics company executive; b. Gadsden, Ala., July 28, 1943; s. William Otis and Vera Belle (Beasley) C.; m. Julie Machura, July 15, 1972. BS in Indsl. Mgmt., San Jose State U., 1969. Pres. Mastec Corp., Cupertino, Calif., 1969-71; original equipment mfr. market mgr. Memorex, Santa Clara, Calif., 1971-73; founder, western regional mgr. Shugart Assocs., Sunnyvale, Calif., 1973-79; founder, exec. v.p. sales and mktg., bd. dirs. Seagate Tech., Scotts Valley, Calif., 1979-85; founder, chairman, chief exec. officer Conner Peripherals Inc., San Jose, Calif., 1985—. With USN Air Res. Mem. Eldorado Country Club, Monterey Peninsula Country Club, Preston Trails Country Club, The Vintage Club, Big Horn Country Club, Castle Pines Country Club (Denver). Democrat. Office: Conner Peripherals 3081 Zanker Rd San Jose CA 95134-2128

CONNER, LAURIE CATHERINE, marketing and sales executive; b. Kew Gardens, N.Y., Sept. 1, 1954; d. Ernest Grant and Evelyn Edna (Nervi) C. BSCE, Duke U., 1976; MSCE, Stanford (Calif.) U., 1978; MBA, Harvard U., 1980. Process engr. Exxon Corp., Benicia, Calif., 1977-78; sr. fin. analyst Internat. Paper Co., N.Y.C., 1980-82; area sales mgr. Raychem Corp., Menlo Park, Calif., 1982-84; nat. sales mgr. TraceTek Raychem Corp., 1984-87; nat. sales mgr. Crystallume, Menlo Park, 1987-88, dir. mktg. and sales, 1988-89, v.p. mktg. and sales, 1989—. Mem. Harvard Club (No. Calif., N.Y.C.), Duke U. Alumni Assn., Internat. Electronic Packaging Soc., Am. Soc. of Materials. Home: 1950 Gough St #301 San Francisco CA 94109 Office: Crystallume 125 Constitution Dr Menlo Park CA 94025

CONNER, LINDSAY ANDREW, lawyer; b. N.Y.C., Feb. 19, 1956; s. Michael and Miriam (Mintzer) C. BA summa cum laude, UCLA, 1976; MA, Occidental Coll., 1977; JD magna cum laude, Harvard U., 1980. Bar: Calif. 1980, U.S. Dist. Ct. (cen. dist.) Calif. 1983. Assoc. Kaplan, Livingston, Goodwin, Berkowitz & Selvin, Beverly Hills, Calif., 1980-81, Fulop & Hardee, Beverly Hills, 1982-83, Wyman, Bautzer, Kuchel & Silbert, L.A., 1983-86; ptnr., entertainment dept. head Hill Wynne Troop & Meisinger, L.A., 1986—. Author: (with others) The Courts and Education, 1977; editor: Harvard Law Rev., 1978-80. Trustee L.A. Community Coll., 1981—, bd. pres., 1989-90; pres. Calif. Community Coll. Trustees, 1992-93. Mem. ABA, L.A. County Bar Assn., UCLA Alumni Assn. (life), Harvard-Radcliffe Club, Phi Beta Kappa. Office: Hill Wynne Troop & Meisinger 10940 Wilshire Blvd Los Angeles CA 90024-3915

CONNER, PATRICK JOHN, material financial analyst; b. Glendale, Calif., Oct. 6, 1965; s. Charles Allison and Audrey A. (Adams) C. BS, San Diego State U., 1988; MBA, U. So. Calif., 1991. Mktg. assoc. Selecta Switch, Inc., Covina, Calif., 1982-86; buyer Sundstrand Corp., San Diego, 1987-89; trading contr. Trust Co. of the West, L.A., 1989-90; material fin. analyst Northrop Corp., Pico Rivera, Calif., 1990—. Mem. South Hills Country Club, Sigma Alpha Epsilon. Republican. Home: 1858 E Palm Dr Covina CA 91724

CONNOLLY, JOHN EARLE, surgeon, educator; b. Omaha, May 21, 1923; s. Earl A. and Gertrude (Eckerman) C.; m. Virginia Hartman, Aug. 12, 1967; children: Peter Hart. John Earle, Sarah. A.B., Harvard U., 1945, M.D., 1948. Diplomate: Am. Bd. Surgery (bd. dirs. 1976-82), Am. Bd. Thoracic and Cardiovascular Surgery, Am. Bd. Vascular Surgery. Intern. in surgery Stanford U. Hosps., San Francisco, 1948-49, surg. research fellow, 1949-50, asst. resident surgeon, 1950-52, chief resident surgeon, 1953-54, surg. pathology fellow, 1954, instr. surgery, 1957-60, John and Mary Markle Scholar in med. scis., 1957-62; surg. registrar professional unit St. Bartholomew's Hosp., London, 1952-53; resident in thoracic surgery Bellevue Hosp., N.Y.C., 1955; resident in thoracic and cardiovascular surgery Columbia-Presbyn. Med. Ctr., N.Y.C., 1956; from instr. to assoc. prof. surgery Stanford U., 1957-65; prof. U. Calif., Irvine, 1965—, chmn. dept. surgery, 1965-78; attending surgeon Stanford Med. Ctr., Palo Alto, Calif., 1959-65; chmn. cardiovascular and thoracic surgery Irvine Med. Ctr. U. Calif., 1968—; attending surgeon Children's Hosp., Orange, Calif., 1968—, Anaheim (Calif.) Meml. Hosp., 1970—; vis. prof. Beijing Heart, Lung, Blood Vessel Inst., 1990, A.H. Duncan vis. prof. U. Edinburgh, 1984; Hunterian prof. Royal Coll. Surgeons Eng., 1985-86; Kinmonth lectr. Royal Coll. Surgeons, Eng., 1987; mem. adv. coun. Nat. Heart, Lung, and Blood Inst.-NIH, 1981-85; cons. Long Beach VA Hosp., Calif., 1965—. Contbr. articles to profl. jours.; editorial bd.: Jour. Cardiovascular Surgery, 1974—, chief editor, 1985—; editorial bd. Western Jour. Medicine, 1975—, Jour. Stroke, 1979—, Jour. Vascular Surgery, 1983—. Bd. dirs. Audio-Digest Found., 1974—; bd. dirs. Franklin Martin Found., 1975-80; regent Uniformed Svcs. U. of Health Scis., Bethesda, 1992—. Served with AUS, 1943-44. Recipient Cert. of Merit, Japanese Surg. Soc., 1979, 90. Fellow ACS (gov. 1964-70, regent 1973-82, vice chmn. bd. regents 1980-82, v.p. 1984-85), Royal Coll. Surgeons Eng. (hon.), Royal Coll. Surgeons Ireland (hon.), Royal Coll. Surgeons Edinburgh (hon.); mem. Am. Surg. Assn., Soc. Univ. Surgeons, Am. Assn. Thoracic Surgery (coun. 1974-78), Pacific Coast Surg. Assn. (pres. 1985-86), San Francisco Surg. Soc., L.A. Surg. Soc., Soc. Vascular Surgery, Western Surg. Assn., Internat. Cardiovascular Soc. (pres. 1977), Soc. Internat. Chirurgie, Soc. Thoracic Surgeons, Western Thoracic Surg. Soc. (pres. 1978), Orange County Surg. Soc. (pres. 1984-85), James IV Assn. Surgeons (councillor 1983—). Clubs: California (Los Angeles); San Francisco Golf, Pacific Union, Bohemian (San Francisco); Cypress Point (Pebble Beach, Calif.); Harvard (N.Y.C.); Big Canyon (Newport Beach). Home: 7 Deerwood Ln Newport Beach CA 92660-5108 Office: U Calif Dept Surgery Irvine CA 92717

CONNOLLY, THOMAS JOSEPH, bishop; b. Tonopah, Nev., July 18, 1922; s. John and Katherine (Hammel) C. Student, St. Joseph Coll. and St. Patrick Sem., Menlo Park, Calif., 1936-47, Catholic U. Am., 1949-51; JCD, Lateran Pontifical U., Rome, 1952; DHL (hon.), U. Portland, 1972. Ordained priest Roman Cath. Ch., 1947. Asst. St. Thomas Cathedral, Reno, 1947, asst., rector, 1953-55; asst. Little Flower Parish, Reno, 1947-48; sec. to bishop, 1949; asst. St. Albert the Gt., Reno, 1952-53; pastor St. Albert the Gt., 1960-68, St. Joseph Ch., Elko, 1955-60, St. Theresa's Ch., Carson City, Nev., 1968-71; bishop Baker, Oreg., 1971—; Tchr. Manogue High Sch., Reno, 1948-49; chaplain Serra Club, 1948-49; officialis Diocese of Reno; chmn. bldg. com., dir. Cursillo Movement; moderator Italian Cath. Fedn.; dean, mem. personnel bd. Senate of Priests; mem. Nat. Bishops Liturgy Com., 1973-76; region XII rep. to adminstrv. bd. Nat. Conf. Cath. Bishops, 1973-76, 86-89, mem. adv. com., 1974-76; bd. dirs. Cath. Communications Northwest, 1977-82. Club: K.C. (state chaplain Nev. 1970-71). Home: 63255 Overtree Rd Bend OR 97701-9759 Office: Bishop of Baker PO Box 5999 Bend OR 97708*

CONNOLLY-O'NEILL, BARRIE JANE, interior designer; b. San Francisco, Dec. 22, 1943; d. Harry Jr. and Jane Isabelle (Barr) Wallach; m. Peter Smith O'Neill, Nov. 27, 1983. Cert. of design, N.Y. Sch. Interior Design, 1975; BAF in Environ. Design, Calif. Coll. Arts and Crafts, 1978. Profl. model Brebner Agy., San Francisco, 1963-72; TV personality KGO TV, San Francisco, 1969-72; interior designer Barrie Connolly & Assocs., Boise, Idaho, 1978—; bd. dirs. Zoo Boise. Bd. dirs. Zoo Boise. Recipient Best Interior Design award Mktg. and Merchandising Excellence, 1981, 84, 91, Best Interior Design award Sales and Mktg. Coun., 1985, 86, Best Residential Design award Boise Design Revue Com., 1983, Grand award Best in Am. Living, Nat. Assn. Home Builders, 1986, 89, 2 Gold Nuggett Merit awards, 1990, Street of Dreams, People's Choice award, 1991, Award for Best Interior Merchandising MAME, Portland, 1991, Nat. award, 1992,. Mem. Nat. Assn. Home Builders (Nat. Silver award for best interior design 1991), Am. Soc. Interior Designers (affiliate), Inst. Residential Mktg. (Silver awrd 1991).

CONNOR, DAVID JOHN, health care executive, accountant; b. Indpls., Oct. 26, 1953; s. David J. Jr. and Amy (Thomas) C.; m. Beatrice U. Maier, Apr. 24, 1982; children: David C., Brian A. BBA, U. Notre Dame, 1975; MBA, Capital U., 1988. CPA, Ohio. Various positions Coopers & Lybrand, Cin., 1975-84; sr. v.p., chief fin. officer Mount Carmel Health, Columbus, Ohio, 1984-91, St. Anges Med. Ctr., Fresno, Calif., 1991—; chmn. bd. dirs. Health Response, Columbus, 1990-91; bd. dirs., treas. Cen. Valley Health Plan, 1991—; bd. dirs. Health Matrix Corp., Columbus, Hosp. Choice

Health Plan; bd. dirs., mem. fin. com. Holy Cross Health Systems, South Bend, Ind., 1987-91. Bd. dirs. Gladden Community House, Columbus, 1987-88; corp. fund raiser United Appeal, Cin., 1981; active Up Down Towners, Cin., 1980-82, Columbus Zoo Capital Campaign task force; mem. Leadership Fresno, 1992-93. Recipient Community Svc. award, Ohio Ho. of Reps., Columbus, 1988. Mem. Ohio Soc. CPAs, Calif. Soc. CPAs, Healthcare Fin. Mgrs. Assn., Ohio Hosp. Assn. (fin. com. 1989-91), Calif. Assn. Hosps. and Health Systems and Hosp. Coun. (fin. com. 1992—), Columbus C. of C., Notre Dame Club, Monogram Club. Office: St Anges Med Ctr 1303 E Herndon Fresno CA 93720

CONNOR, GARY EDWARD, manufacturing company marketing executive; b. S.I., N.Y., Nov. 13, 1948; s. Everett M. and Josephine (Amato) C.; B.S. in Elec. Engring., U. Md., 1973; M.B.A., U. Santa Clara (Calif.), 1979. Quality assurance engr. Frankford Arsenal, 1973; quality assurance engr., field service engr. Lockheed Electronics Co., 1973-74; group leader memory test engring. sect. head bipolar product engring. Nat. Semicondr. Corp., 1975-79; internat. mktg. mgr. Am. Microsystems Inc., 1979-80; mktg. mgr. GenRad-STI, Santa Clara, 1980-82; prodn. mktg. exec. AMD, Sunnyvale, Calif., 1982-86; dept. mgr. IDT, Santa Clara, Calif., 1986—. Mem. IEEE, Electronics Internat. Adv. Panel, Am. Security Council (nat. adv. bd.), Franklin Mint Collectors Soc. Republican. Home: 5121 Kozo Ct San Jose CA 95124-5527 Office: IDT 2670 Seely Ave San Jose CA 95134

CONNOR, JOHN WILLIAM, anthropology educator; b. Butler, Pa., May 24, 1930; s. John Francis and Mary Agnes (Bruner) C.; m. Joan Caryl Lovering, Mar. 31, 1988. AA, Sacramento City Coll., 1959; BA, Calif. State U., Sacramento, 1961, MA, 1966; PhD, U. Calif., Davis, 1972. Asst. hydrologist Dept. Water Resources, Sacramento, 1956-61; high sch. English and history tchr. Grant Sch. Dist., Sacramento, 1961-66; from instr. to prof. of anthropology Calif. State U., Sacramento, 1967—; rsch. assoc. Inst. for Personality Rsch., U. Calif., Berkeley; mem. Fulbright Com., 1992. Author: A Study of the Marital Stability of Japanese War Brides, 1976, Tradition and Change in Three Generations of Japanese Americans, 1977, Acculturation and the Retention of an Ethnic Identity in Three Generations of Japanese Americans, 1977; mem. editorial bd. Jour. Psychoanalytic Anthropology, 1986; also articles. With U.S. Army, 1948-56. Fellow NEH, 1977-90, Fulbright fellow, Japan, 1981-82, China, 1988-89. Fellow Am. Anthropol. Assn., Soc. for Psychol. Anthropology, S.W. Anthropol. Soc., Calif. Folklore Soc. Home: 5 Colby Ct Sacramento CA 95825-7005 Office: Calif State U Dept Anthrop 6000 Jay St Sacramento CA 95819-6106

CONNORS, KEVIN GERARD, venture capitalist; b. LaGrange, Ill., Nov. 1, 1961; s. John Murray and Helen Jean (Ruhaak) C.; m. Mary Katherine McEvoy, Aug. 20, 1988; children: Erin Kane, John Patrick. BSEE, U. Notre Dame, 1983; MSEE, U. Dayton, Ohio, 1985; MBA, Harvard U., 1987. Engr. Delco Products div. GM, Juarez, Mex. and Dayton, 1983-85; venture capitalist Genesis Seed Fund, Phila., 1987-88, DSV Ptnrs., Newport Beach, Calif., 1988—; bd. dirs. Vesitec Medical, Pilot Cardiovascular, Vital Signals. Mem. Notre Dame Club Orange County (bd. dirs.), Harvard Bus. Sch. of Orange County. Roman Catholic. Office: DSV Ptnrs 620 Newport Center Dr Ste 990 Newport Beach CA 92660-8009

CONOMIKES, GEORGE SPERO, management consultant executive, publisher; b. Canastota, N.Y., Oct. 8, 1925; s. Spero P. and Mary (Pappas) C.; m. Lynne Rowland; children: Melanie, Spero. AB with honors, Middlebury Coll., 1950; AM in Econs., U. Chgo., 1956. Research assoc., project dir. Indsl. Relations Ctr., U. Chgo., 1951-55; dir. Dept. of Commerce, U. Chgo., 1955-57; pres. Bus. Forum, Inc., Chgo., 1958-70; pres. Conomikes Assoc., Inc., Greenwich, Conn., 1970-74, L.A., 1974—; lectr. in econs. U. Chgo., 1955-58; guest lectr. Purdue U., NYU, Loyola U., Chgo., U. So. Calif., UCLA, U. Tex., Tufts U., U. Puerto Rico, U. Iowa, U. Tenn., U. Minn., Georgetown U., Marquette U., U. Md., Temple U., U. Oreg., Emory U. Contbg. editor: Stock Market Handbook, 1969; editor, pub. Conomikes Reports, 1982—, Conomikes Medicare Hotline, 1991—; author: Successful Practice Management Techniques, 1988. Served with USAAF, 1943-45. Republican. Clubs: Riviera Tennis (Pacific Palisades, Calif.). Office: Conomikes Assocs Inc 6033 W Century Blvd Ste 990 Los Angeles CA 90045-6418

CONOVER, CLARENCE MILLARD, retired mathematics educator; b. Santa Rosa, Mo., Oct. 17, 1939; s. Frank T. and Viola (Reed) C. BS in Edn., NE Mo. State U., 1962, MA in Math. Edn., 1964. Cert. tchr., Mo., secondary tchr., Ariz. With mail rm. U.S. Safety Svc., Kansas City, Mo., 1957-58; math. tchr. Westwood High, Mesa (Ariz.) Pub. Schs., 1962-92, Mesa Jr. Coll., 1968-92; math. dept. head Westwood High, Mesa, 1976-84; tchr. ESL math. in Spanish, 1991-92. V.p. Optimist Club, Mesa, 1967. With USAR, 1957-77. Recipient award NSF, 1975. Mem. NEA, Ariz. Edn. Assn., Mesa Edn. Assn. (head sch. rep. 1982-92). Democrat. Home: 1500 W 8th St # 3 Mesa AZ 85201

CONOVER, ROBERT WARREN, librarian; b. Manhattan, Kans., Oct. 6, 1937; s. Robert Warren and Grace Darline (Grinstead) C.; BA, Kans. State U., 1959; MA, U. Denver, 1961. Librarian, supervising librarian County of Fresno, Calif., 1961-66; county librarian County of Yolo, Woodland, Calif., 1967-68; dir. City of Fullerton (Calif.) Pub. Library, 1968-73, City of Pasadena (Calif.) Pub. Library, 1973-80, Palos Verdes Library Dist., Palos Verdes Peninsula, Calif., 1980-85, City of Commerce (Calif.) Pub. Library, 1985—. Recipient Pres.'s award Fresno Jaycees, 1963. Mem. ALA, Orange County Libr. Assn. (pres. 1971), Spl. Librs. Assn., Calif. Libr. Assn. (pres. Yosemite chpt. 1965, mem. coun. 1981), Santiago Libr. System Coun. (pres. 1972), Univ. Club, L.A. Athletic Club, Pi Kappa Alpha. Episcopalian. Office: City of Commerce Pub Libr 5655 Jillson St Commerce CA 90040-1485

CONQUEST, LOVEDAY LOYCE, biostatistics educator; b. Hilo, Hawaii, Jan. 22, 1948; d. Jay Walter and Daisy Eloise (Yamaguchi) C.; m. Fred Lee Kleinschmidt, May 28, 1983. AB, Pomona Coll., 1970; MS, Stanford U., 1972; PhD, U. Wash., 1975. Asst. prof. U. Hawaii, Honolulu, 1975; vis. asst. prof. biostats. U. Wash., Seattle, 1976-78, asst. prof., 1978-83, assoc. prof., 1983—, assoc. dean, 1991—. Assoc. editor Biometrics, 1989-93; contbr. articles to profl. jours. Speaker math. workshops Expanding Your Horizons, Seattle, 1985—. Recipient Outstanding Teaching award U. Wash., 1986, Disting. Teaching award, 1987; grantee NIH, 1970-75. Fellow Am. Statis. Assn. (pres. Puget Sound chpt. 1984-87); mem. Biometric Soc. (pres. West N.Am. region 1989), English-Speaking Union (nat. bd. dirs. 1989-95), Women's Univ. Club, Wash. Athletic Club, Phi Beta Kappa (bd. electors U. Wash. chpt. 1983—, pres. 1985-89), Sigma Xi (pres. U. Wash. chpt. 1983), Delta Kappa Gamma. Office: U Wash HR-20 3737 15th Ave NE Seattle WA 98195-0001

CONRAD, JOHN WILFRED, fine arts educator, ceramist; b. Cresson, Pa., Aug. 3, 1935; s. Wilfred L. and Elizabeth S. (Bouch) C.; m. Barbara J. Daugherty, 1963; children: William Thomas, Kristin Elizabeth. BS, Indiana U. of Pa., 1958; MFA, Carnegie Mellon U., 1963; PhD, U. Pitts., 1970. Tchr. art Penn-Hills Sr. High Sch., Pitts., 1959-64; part-time instr. Carnegie Mellon U., Pitts., 1960-64; prof. fine arts Mesa Coll., San Diego, 1966—, chmn. dept., 1980-82, 85-88; chief officer Falcon Co., San Diego, 1983—. Author: Ceramic Formulas: The Complete Compendium, 1973, Contemporary Ceramic Techniques, 1979, Contemporary Ceramic Formulas, 1980, Ceramic Windchimes, 1983, Advanced Ceramic Manual, 1988, Studio Potter's Dictionary, 1990. Recipient Outstanding Alumni award Ind. U. Pa., 1993. Mem. Ceramic Artists San Diego, Nat. Coun. on Edn. for the Ceramic Arts (co-chair 1993 San Diego conf.), Mex.-Am. Educators Exch., Chinese-Am. Ceramic Educators Exch., Allied Artists San Diego. Home and Office: 770 Cole Ranch Rd Encinitas CA 92024-9715

CONRAD, PAUL FRANCIS, editorial cartoonist; b. Cedar Rapids, Iowa, June 27, 1924; s. Robert H. and Florence G. (Lawler) C.; m. Barbara Kay King, Feb. 27, 1954; children: James, David, Carol, Elizabeth. B.A., U. Iowa, 1950. Editorial cartoonist Denver Post, 1950-64, L.A. Times, 1964-93; cartoonist L.A. Times Syndicate, 1973—; Richard M. Nixon chair Whittier Coll., 1977-78. Exhibited sculpture and cartoons, Los Angeles County Mus. Art, 1979; author: The King and Us, 1974, Pro and Conrad, 1979, Drawn and Quartered, 1985, CONArtist, 1993. Served with C.E. AUS, 1942-46, PTO. Recipient Editorial Cartoon award Sigma Delta Chi, 1963, 69, 71, 81-82, 87, Pulitzer prize editorial cartooning, 1964, 71, 84, Overseas Press Club award, 1970, 81, Journalism award U. So. Calif., 1972, Robert F. Kennedy Journalism award, 1st Prize, 1985, 90, 92, 93, Hugh M. Hefner 1st Amendment award, 1990. Fellow Soc. Profl. Journalists; mem. Phi Delta Theta. Democrat. Roman Catholic. Office: LA Times Syndicate 23133 Hawthorne Blvd Los Angeles CA 90505

CONRADY, JAMES LOUIS, audio visual technician; b. Santa Ana, Calif., May 22, 1933. AA in Electronics, Orange Coast Coll., 1953; BA in Social Sci., Chapman Coll., 1964. Audio visual technician Centralia Sch. Dist., Buena Park, Calif., 1960—. With USN, 1954-56. Mem. SAR, Assn. Audio Visual Technicians, The Soc. Photo-Technologists, Internat. Comm. Industries Assn., Gen. Soc. Mayflower Descendants. Presbyterian. Office: Centralia Sch Dist 6625 La Palma Ave Buena Park CA 90620-2899

CONRAN, JAMES MICHAEL, state government official; b. N.Y.C., Mar. 15, 1952; s. James Adrian and Mary Ellen (McGarry) C.; m. Phyllis Jean Thompson, Aug. 1, 1984; children: Michael O., Thomas O. BA, Calif. State U., Northridge, 1975; M in Urban Studies, Occidental Coll., 1978. Mgr. regulatory rels. Pacific Bell, San Francisco, 1985-88, mgr. pub. affairs & pub. issues, 1988-91; dir. State of Calif. Dept. Consumer Affairs, Sacramento, 1991—. Contbr. articles to profl. jours. Bd. dirs. Fight Back! Found., L.A., 1991—, Disabled Children's Computer Group, Orinda, Calif., Telecomm. Edn. Trust Fund-Calif. Pub. Utilities Commn., San Francisco, 1990-91; chair adminstrv. sect. United Calif. State Employees Campaign, Sacramento; mem. Stream Preservation Commn., Orinda, 1988-91, Calif. Rep. Party Cen. Com., Orinda, 1992; del. Rep. Nat. Conv., Houston, 1992; regional chair Bush-Quayle campaign, Orinda, 1992. Fellow Coro Found., 1977, Levere Meml. Found., 1976. Mem. Coro Assocs., Calif. Agenda for Consumer Edn., Sigma Alpha Epsilon. Roman Catholic. Home: 33 Southwood Dr Orinda CA 94563

CONROE, MARK GUSTAV, commercial real estate developer; b. Hartford, Conn., Jan. 21, 1958; s. Wallace Weller and Marie-Anne (Langenskiold) C. Student, U.S. Mil. Acad., 1976-78; BS in Civil Engring., Stanford U., 1980, MS in Civil Engring., 1981, MBA, 1985. Engr. Sohio Petroleum Co., San Francisco, 1982-83; cons. McKinsey & Co., Dallas, 1984; ptnr. Mozart Devel. Co., Palo Alto, Calif., 1985—. Bd. dirs. San Francisco Child Abuse Coun., 1983-85; bd. dirs., treas. Cancer Support & Edn. Ctr., Menlo Park, Calif., 1989-93; chmn. bd. dirs. Bayshore Workers, East Palo Alto, Calif., 1991—; chmn. honor code com. Stanford (Calif.) U., 1979-81. Shidler grantee The Shidler Group, Stanford U., 1985; Pepsico fellow Pepsico Found., Stanford U., 1984. Mem. Urban Land Inst. Office: Mozart Devel Co 435 Tasso St # 300 Palo Alto CA 94301-1545

CONRON, JOHN PHELAN, architect; b. Brookline, Mass., Dec. 4, 1921; s. Carl Edward and Katherine (Phelan) C. Student, U. So. Calif., 1940-41; B.Arch., Yale U., 1948. Draftsmn. Whelan & Westman, Boston, 1948-52; owner, prin. John P. Conron (Architect), Santa Fe, N.Mex., 1952-61; ptnr. Conron-Lent Architects, Santa Fe, 1961-86, Conron-Muths (restoration architects), Santa Fe and Jackson Hole, Wyo., 1975-88, Conron-Woods Architects, Santa Fe, 1986—; pres. The Centerline, Inc., Santa Fe, 1952-86. Prin. works include Centerline, Inc., Santa Fe, KB Ranch, nr. Santa Fe, Henry R. Singlton residence, Lamy, N.Mex., Amtech Tech. Corp., Santa Fe, restorations Stephen W. Dorsey Mansion State Monument, Colfax County, N.Mex., Palace of Govs., Santa Fe, Pipe Spring Nat. Monument, Ariz.; editor La Cronica de Nuevo Mexico, 1976—; co-editor N.Mex. Architecture mag., 1960-66, editor, 1966—. Vice Chmn. N.Mex. Cultural Properties Com., 1968-80; founder v.p. Las Trampas Found., 1967-80; trustee Internat. Inst. Iberian Colonial Art, Santa Fe, pres., 1978—; bd. dirs. Preservation Action., 1976-80; bd. dirs. Hist. Soc. N.Mex., 1976—, pres, 1982-86. Served with USAAF, 1941-45. Recipient Merit award AIA, 1962, Spl. Commendation award, 1970. Fellow AIA, Am. Soc. Interior Designers (pres. N.Mex. chpt. 1966-68, 74-75, regional v.p. 1970-73, Historic Preservation award for restoration Palace of Govs. 1980); mem. N.Mex. Soc. Architects (past pres.), Am. Soc. Man Environ. Relations (dir. 1973-86), Hist. Soc. N.Mex. chpt. Am. Soc. interior (1st v.p. 1979-83, pres. 1983-87, bd. dirs. 1987—). Office: Conron & Woods Architects 1807 2d St Ste 44 Santa Fe NM 87501

CONSTANT, CLINTON, chemical engineer, consultant; b. Nelson, B.C., Can., Mar. 20, 1912; came to U.S., 1936, naturalized, 1942; s. Vasile and Annie (Hunt) C.; m. Margie Robbel, Dec. 5, 1965. BSc with honors, U. Alta., 1935, postgrad., 1935-36; PhD, Western Res. U., 1939. Registered profl. engr. Devel. engr. Harshaw Chem. Co., Cleve., 1936-38, mfg. foreman, 1938-43, sr. engr. semi-works dept., 1948-50; supt. hydrofluoric acid dept. Nyotex Chems., Inc., Houston, 1943-47, chief devel. engr., 1947-48; mgr. engring. Ferro Chem. Co., Bedford, Ohio, 1950-52; tech. asst. mfg. dept. Armour Agrl. Chem. Co. (name formerly Armour Fertilizer Works), Bartow, Fla., 1952-61, mfg. research and devel. div., 1961-63; mgr. spl. projects Research div. (co. name changed to USS Agri-Chems 1968), Bartow, Fla., 1963-65, project mgr., 1965-70; chem. adviser Robert & Co. Assocs., Atlanta, 1970-79; chief engr. Almon & Assocs., Inc., Atlanta, 1979-80; project mgr. Engring. Service Assocs., Atlanta, 1980-81; v.p. engring. ACI Inc., Hesperia, Calif., 1981-83; sr. v.p., chief engr. MTI (acquisition of ACI), Hesperia, 1983-86; engring. cons. San Bernardino County APCD, Victorville, Calif., 1986-90; instr. environ. chemistry Victor Valley C.C., 1990; pvt. cons. Victorville, Calif., 1991—; cons. in engring., 1992—. Author tech. reports, sci. fiction; patentee in field. Fellow AAAS, Am. Inst. Chemists, Am. Inst. Chem. Engrs., N.Y. Acad. Scis., AIAA (assoc.); mem. Am. Chem. Soc., Am. Astron. Soc., Astron. Soc. Pacific, Royal Astron. Soc. Can., NSPE, Am. Water Works Assn., Calif. Water and Pollution Control Assn., Air Pollution Control Assn., Soc. Mfg. Engrs., Calif. Soc. Profl. Engrs.

CONSTANTIKES, PENELOPE LOUISE, political research consultant; b. Mount Vernon, Ohio, Aug. 17, 1956; d. Theodore John and Frances Louise (Grubb) C.; 1 child, Camille Marie Gulley. Student, U. Idaho, 1979-80, Boise State U., 1975-78, 90-92. Realtor Boise, 1981-88; dir. legis. info. ctr. Idaho Statehouse, 1992, 93; campaign mgr. Russ Newcomb for Senate, Twin Falls, Idaho, 1992—. Columnist Contractor-Bldg. Contractors of S.W. Idaho, 1987-88. Chmn. Boise Design Rev. Com., 1988—; mem. Boise City Sign Ordinance Task Force, 1990—; del. Idaho State Rep. Conv., Boise, 1990, Project Stride, Idaho Rep. Party, 1990; mem. Ada County Rep. Women. Home: 507 Village Ln Boise ID 83702

CONSTANTINEAU, CONSTANCE JULIETTE, banker; b. Lowell, Mass., Feb. 18, 1937; d. Henry Goulet and Germaine (Turner) Goulet-Lamarre; m. Edward Joseph Constantineau; children: Glen Edward, Alan Henry. Student, Bank Adminstrn. Inst. and Am. Inst. Banking, 1975-87. Mortgage sec. The Cen. Savs. Bank, Lowell, 1955-57; head teller First Fed. Savs. & Loan, Lowell, 1957-59, Lowell Bank & Trust Co., Lowell, 1973-74; br. mgr. Century Bank & Trust Co., Malden, Mass., 1975-78; v.p. purchasing, mgr. support svcs. First Nat. Bank Albuquerque, 1983—; mem. planning purchasing mgr.'s conf. Bank Adminstrn. Inst., San Antonio, Orlando, Fla., New Orleans; treas. polit. action com. First Nat. Bank, 1986. Bd. dirs., historian Indian Pueblo Cultural Ctr., Albuquerque, 1986-89. Mem. Fin. Women Internat., In-Plant Mgmt. Assn. (charter). Home: 13015 Deer Dancer Tr NE Albuquerque NM 87112 Office: First Nat Bank Albuquerque 40 First Plaza Ctr NW Albuquerque NM 87102-3338

CONSTINE, KAREN ROBIN, public affairs executive; b. L.A., Jan. 20, 1960; d. Herbert Edward and Roberta Irene (Feldstein) C. BA in Comm. Studies with honors, U. Account exec. The Blaine Group, L.A., 1983-84; dir. pub. affairs for L.A. area Kaiser Permanente Med. Care Program, Pasadena, Calif., 1984-88; dep. to Councilwoman Joan Milke Flores, L.A. City Coun., 1988-91; pub. affairs assoc. Pacific Enterprises, L.A., 1991-92, mgr. pub. affairs, 1992-93; pvt. practice as cons. West Hollywood, Calif., 1993—; chief of staff Councilmember Laura Chiel, 1993—; freelance writer short stories L.A. Times, 1987-88. Transp. commr. City of West Hollywood, Calif., 1988-91; pub. affairs and media advisor L.A. Festival, 1990—; mem. loan com. Arts Inc., L.A., 1991-93. Mem. Women in Pub. Affairs, L.A. Pub. Affairs Officers Assn., So. Calif. Assn. Philanthropists, Publicity Club L.A. (pres. 1991-92). Democrat.

CONTI, DANIEL JOSEPH, health science association administrator; b. Somerville, N.J., Feb. 22, 1949; s. Daniel A. and Helen (Glab) C.; m. Carolynn E. Frush, Aug. 10, 1982; children: Jonathan Daniel, Joshua Joseph. BS, St. Bonaventure U., 1970; MS, U. Ariz., 1979. Physiologist Los Angeles County Occupational Health Dept., 1979-80; program dir. Inst. Health Mgmt., San Francisco, 1980-82; owner, pres. Health Mgmt. Cons., San Francisco, 1982-86; v.p., chief ops. officer Nat. Inst. Cardiovascular Tech., Inc., Newport Beach, Calif., 1986-87; also bd. dirs. Nat. Inst. Cardiovascular Tech., Inc., Newport Beach; pres., chief exec. officer Nat. Inst. Cardiovascular Tech., Inc., Newport Beach, Calif., 1987-89; founder Health Resource Group, 1989—; chmn. heart at work com. Orange County chpt. Am. Heart Assn., 1988-90, state chmn. worksite subcom., 1989-91, bd. dirs., 1989-90. Pub. wellness newsletter The Pulse, 1989—; editor Health Mgmt. Newsletter, 1982-84. Coord. Orange County Men's Community Bible Study. Republican. Mem. Christian Ch. Office: Health Resource Group PO Box 196540166 Irvine CA 92713-9700

CONTI, ISABELLA, psychologist, consultant; b. Torino, Italy, Jan. 1, 1942; came to U.S., 1964; d. Giuseppe and Zaira (Melis) Ferro; m. Ugo Conti, Sept. 5, 1964; 1 child, Maurice. J.D., U. Rome, 1966; Ph.D. in Psychology, U. Calif.-Berkeley, 1975. Lic. psychologist. Sr. analyst Rsch. Inst. for Study of Man, Berkeley, Calif., 1967-68; postgrad. rsch. psychologist Personality Assessment and Rsch. Inst., U. Calif.-Berkeley, 1968-71; intern U. Calif.-Berkeley and VA Hosp., San Francisco, 1969-75; asst. prof. St. Mary's Coll., Moraga, Calif., 1978-84; cons. psychologist Conti Resources, Berkeley, Calif., 1977-85; v.p. Barnes & Conti Assocs., Inc., Berkeley, 1985—; pres. Lisardco, El Cerrito, Calif., 1989—; v.p. ElectroMagnetic Instruments, Inc., El Cerrito, Calif., 1985—. Author: (with Alfonso Montuori) From Power to Partnership, 1993; contbr. articles on creativity and mgmt. cons. to profl. jours. Regents fellow U. Calif.-Berkeley, 1972; NIMH predoctoral rsch. fellow, 1972-73. Mem. Am. Psychol. Assn. Office: Lisardco 1318 Brewster Dr El Cerrito CA 94530

CONTO, ARISTIDES, advertising agency executive; b. N.Y.C., Feb. 10, 1931; s. Gus Dimitrios and Osee (Kenney) C.; BA, Champlain Coll., 1953; MS in Journalism, UCLA, 1958, certificate in indsl. rels., 1965; m. Phyllis Helen Wiley, June 22, 1957; 1 son, Jason Wiley. Reporter, City News Svc., L.A., 1958; dir. pub. rels. Galaxy Advt. Co., Los Angeles, 1959-60; news media chief Los Angeles County Heart Assn., 1960-61; pub. rels. assoc. Prudential Ins. Co., L.A., 1961-64; advt. mgr. Aerospace Controls Co., L.A., 1964-65; comml. sales promotion coord. Lockheed-Calif. Co., Burbank, 1965-73; pres. Jason Wiley Advt. Agy., L.A., 1973—; dir. Tower Master, Inc., L.A. With U.S. Army, 1955-56. Recipient advt. awards. Mem. Nat. Soc. Published Poets, L.A. Press Club, Bus.-Profl. Advt. Assn. L.A.s, Pub. Rels. Soc. Author: The Spy Who Loved Me, 1962; The Diamond Twins, 1963, (screenplays) Lannigan, 1973, Haunted Host, 1976, Captain Noah, 1977, Government Surplus, 1983. Office: 3539 Ocean View Blvd Glendale CA 91208-1211

CONTOS, PAUL ANTHONY, engineer, investment advisor; b. Chgo., Mar. 18, 1926; s. Anthony Dimitrios and Panagiota (Kostopoulos) C.; m. Lilian Katie Kalkines, June 19, 1955 (dec. Apr. 1985); children: Leslie, Claudia, Paula, Anthony; m. Shirley Elsa Saxton, Mar. 7, 1987. Student, Am. TV Inst., Chgo., 1946-48, U. Ill., 1949-52, 53-56, Ill. Inst. Tech., 1952-53, U. So. Calif., 1956-57. Engr. J.C. Deagan Co., Inc., Chgo., 1951-53, Lockheed Missile and Space Co., Inc., Sunnyvale, Calif., 1956-62; engring. supr. Lockheed Missile and Space Co., Inc., Sunnyvale, 1962-65, staff engr., 1965-88; pres. PAC Investments, Saratoga, Calif., 1984-88; pres. PAC Investments, San Jose, Calif., 1988—, also advisor, 1984—. Served with U.S. Army, 1944-46, ETO. Decorated Purple Heart. Mem. DAV (life, commdr. Chgo. unit 1948-51), VFW (life), Pi Sigma Phi (pres. 1951-53). Republican. Greek Orthodox. Home and Office: 1009 Blossom River Way Apt 105 San Jose CA 95123-6304

CONVISER, RICHARD, health consultant; b. N.Y.C., Apr. 21, 1944; s. Harry and Pauline (Diner) C. BA, Reed Coll., Portland, Oreg., 1965; PhD, Johns Hopkins U., 1970. Asst. prof. U. Pitts., 1970-73, U. Ill., Urbana, 1973-76; freelance writer Woodford Creek, Glendale, Oreg., 1976-78; lectr. So. Oreg. State Coll., Ashland, 1978-80; asst. prof. Rensselaer Poly. Inst., Troy, N.Y., 1980-84; health policy specialist Empire Blue Cross/Blue Shield, N.Y.C., 1984-86; health policy analyst N.J. Dept. Health, Trenton, 1986-88; cons. Health Policy Rsch. and Analysis, West Linn, Oreg., 1988—; mem. Pres. Commn. on Student Life, chair alumni-student rels. com. Reed Coll. Vice chair Coalition for AIDS Edn., Portland, 1990-92; dir. Reed Coll. Alumni Bd., Portland, 1991-95; editor Cascade AIDS Project Speakers Bur., Portland, 1991-93. Recipient Fellowships NSF, 1965-70, 70, Nat. Endowment for Humanities, 1979. Mem. APHA, Reed Coll. Chamber Orch.

CONWAY, JOHN E., judge; b. 1934. BS, U.S. Naval Acad., 1956; LLB magna cum laude, Washburn U., 1963. Assoc. Matias A Zamora, Santa Fe, 1963-64; ptnr. Wilkinson, Durrett & Conway, Alamogordo, N.Mex., 1964-67, Durrett, Conway & Jordon, Alamogordo, 1967-80, Montgomery & Andrews, P.A., Albuquerque, 1980-86; city atty. Alamogordo, 1966-72; Mexico State Senate, 1970-80, minority leader, 1972-80; judge U.S. Dist. Ct. N.Mex., Albuquerque, 1986—. 1st lt. USAF, 1956-60. Mem. ABA, Nat. Commrs. on Uniform State Laws, N.Mex. Bar Assn., N.Mex. Judicial Coun. (vice chmn. 1972, chmn. 1973-75, disciplinary bd. of Supreme Ct. on N.Mex., vice chmn. 1980, chmn. 1981-85), The Albuquerque Lawyers Club, Albuquerque Bar Assn. Office: US Dist Ct PO Box 1160 Albuquerque NM 87103-1160*

CONWAY, MICHAEL J., airline company executive; b. 1945. BBA, CUNY, 1969. Acct. Price Waterhouse & Co., until 1980; v.p. controller Continental Airlines, 1980-81; with Am. West Airlines, 1981—, formerly sr. v.p., exec. v.p., 1983-84, pres., chief oper. officer, from 1984, now pres., chief exec. officer, also bd. dirs. With USMC, 1969-74. Office: Am W Airlines Inc 4000 E Sky Harbor Blvd Phoenix AZ 85034-3899*

CONWAY, RICHARD, English language educator; b. Pitts., Jan. 21, 1936; s. Henry S. and Dorothy Blanche (Faddis) C. ; m. Esther Fredholm, Sept. 5, 1960; children: Lauren, Bryan. BA, Pa. State U., 1958, MA, 1963; PhD, U. Denver, 1973. Instr. English, U. N.D., Grand Forks, 1961-63, Fairleigh Dickinson U., Teaneck, N.J., 1963-65, U. Wash., Seattle, 1865-67; asst. prof. St. Paul's Coll., Lawrenceville, Va., 1974-75; freelance writer, 1975-79; mem. faculty, chmn. dept. English, Lamar (Colo.) C.C., 1979—; coord. Colo. Film Network Series, Lamar, 1979-91; mem. State Faculty Adv. Coun., Denver, 1987—. Contbr. articles and fiction to various publs. Vice pres. S.W. Arts Coun., Lamar, 1980-82; bd. dirs. Sta. KANZ, PBS, Garden City, Kans., 1986—; mem. Lamar Pub. Sch. Bd., 1988. Named Instr. of Yr., Lamar C.C., 1989, 90, 92. Democrat. Transcendentalist. Home: 404 Willow Valley Lamar CO 81052 Office: Lamar CC 2401 S Main St Lamar CO 81052

CONWAY, ROBERT PATRICK, personal property development company executive; b. Iowa County, Wis., Oct. 26, 1914; s. Hugh and Minnie (Bell) C.; m. Helen Marie Smelich, 1939 (dec. June 1991); children: Patricia, Flo, Robert Patrick, Kathleen, Loretta, Harold (dec.), Helene; m. Nelle McElravy, Aug. 27, 1992. Diploma, Dodgeville (Wis.) Tchrs. Coll., 1933. CLU. Co. clk. CCC, Wis., 1933-34; dist. clk. CCC, Camp McCoy, Wis., 1934; rural tchr. Spring Valley Sch., Clyde, Wis., 1935-36; with Phelps Dodge Corp., Ajo, Ariz., 1936-42; part-time agt. State Farm Ins., Ajo, 1938-42; spl. agt. State Farm Ins., Albuquerque, 1942-55, dist. mgr., 1955-83; CEO Conway Enterprises, Albuquerque, 1984—; founder Am. Coll., Bryn Mawr, Pa. Chmn. fundraising Salk Inst., N.Mex., 1968; founder, 1st pres. Medic Alert Chpt., 1975-80; state chmn. March of Dimes, N.Mex., 1955-65; past pres. Coun. Ind. Colls., N.Mex., Santa Fe. Recipient various ins. awards. Mem. N.Mex. Bd. Optometry, N.Mex. State Assn. Life Underwriters (past pres), Serra Internat. (nat. com. 1988-92, pres. Albuquerque club), Elks (life), others. Republican. Roman Catholic.

COOK, ALBERT THOMAS THORNTON, JR., financial advisor; b. Cleve., Apr. 24, 1940; s. Albert Thomas Thornton and Tyra Esther (Morehouse) C.; m. Mary Jane Blackburn, June 1, 1963; children: Lara Keller, Thomas, Timothy. BA, Dartmouth Coll., 1962; MA, U. Chgo., 1966. Asst. sec. Dartmouth Coll., Hanover, N.H., 1972-77; exec. dir. Big Brothers, Inc., N.Y.C., 1977-78; underwriter Boettcher & Co., Denver, 1978-81; asst. v.p. Dain Bosworth Inc., Denver, 1981-82, Colo. Nat. Bank, Denver, 1982-84; pres. The Albert T.T. Cook Co., Denver, 1984—; arbitrator Nat. Assn. Securities Dealers, N.Y.C., 1985—, Mcpl. Securities Rulemaking Bd., Washington, 1987—. Pres. Etna-Hanover Ctr. Community Assn., Hanover, N.H., 1974-76; mem. Mayor's Task Force, Denver, 1984; bd. dirs. Rude Park Community Nursery, Denver, 1985-87, Willows Water

Dist., Colo., 1990—, sec.; trustee The Iliff Sch. Theol., Denver, 1986-92; mem. Dartmouth Coll. Com. on Trustees, 1990-93. Mem. Dartmouth Alumni Coun. (exec. com., chmn. nominating and trustee search coms. 1987-89), University Club, Cactus Club (Denver), Dartmouth Club of N.Y.C., Yale Club, Lions (bd. dirs. Denver chpt. 1983-85, treas. 1986-87, pres. Denver Found. 1987-88), Delta Upsilon. Congregationalist. Home: 7099 E Hinsdale Pl Englewood CO 80112-1610 Office: One Tabor Ctr 1200 17th St Ste 1303 Denver CO 80202

COOK, BRUCE MARTIN, urban planner; b. L.A., Aug. 14, 1954; s. Leon and Rose (Shink) C.; m. Jacqueline Arlette Goodsell, Aug. 22, 1976; children: Laurence Allen, Rebecca Michelle, Melinda Elisabeth. BS, UCLA, 1976. Asst. planner City of Pomona (Calif.), 1981-85; assoc. planner City of Rancho Cucamonga (Calif.), 1985-88; sr. planner City of Yorba Linda (Calif.), 1988—. Facilitator Planner's Day in Sch. Program for Orange County, Calif., 1992; asst. dir. for profl. devel. Orange County sect. Am. Planning Assn., 1989-91. Mem. Am. Inst. Cert. Planners. Office: City of Yorba Linda 4845 Casa Loma Ave Yorba Linda CA 92686

COOK, DAVID BRUCE, computer scientist; b. Des Moines, Nov. 13, 1957; s. George Hubert and Elizabeth Anne (Harvey) C. BS in physics and Computer Sci. with hon, Iowa State U., 1980. Sr. engr. M/A Com Linkabit, Inc., San Diego, 1981-86; staff scientist Western Rsch. Corp., San Diego, 1986-87; mgr., network resources Pacific Communications Scis., Inc., San Diego, 1987-90; dir. software Litel Instruments, Inc., San Diego, 1991-92; dir. engring., 1991—; cons., ind. software developer Network Group, San Diego, 1986—. Author: Vax DCL Programmers Reference, 1990; contbr. articles to profl. jours. Mem. IEEE Computer Soc., Nat. Assn. Rocketry (trustee 1980-83, selected U.S. Nat. team, 1980), Assn. Computing Machinery, San Diego Rocketry Club (DART) (pres. 1985-86, treas. 1989-90). Republican. Home: 7866 Hemphill Dr San Diego CA 92126-3522

COOK, DIERDRE RUTH GOORMAN, English language educator; b. Denver, Nov. 4, 1956; d. George Edward and Avis M. (Wilson) Goorman; m. Donald Robert Cook, Apr. 4, 1981; 1 child, Christen. BA in Theatre Arts, Colo. State U., 1980, postgrad. Cert. secondary tchr. Tchr. Centennial High Sch., Fort Collins, Colo., 1983-87; educator Poudre High Sch., Fort Collins, 1987—; curriculum devel. com. Poudre R-1 Sch. Dist., Fort Collins, 1984—, instrnl. improvement com., 1985—, trainer positive power leadership, 1986-87; communication con. Woodward Gov. Co., Fort Collins, 1991, 92; evaluation visitation team North Ctrl. Evaluation, Greeley, Colo., 1991. Campaign worker Rep. Party, Littleton, Colo., 1980, Ft. Collins, 1984, 88; mem. Colo. Juvenile Coun., Ft. Collins., 1986, 88, loaned exec., 1987; Leadership Ft. Collins; leader Girl Scouts Am., 1991—. NEH scholar, 1992; named Disting. Tchr. 1993 Colo. Awards Coun.; recipient Tchr. Excellence award Poudre High Sch., 1992. Mem. ASCD, NEA, Colo. Edn. Assn., Poudre Edn. Assn. (rep. 1989, 90, 91), Nat. Speech Communication Assn., Nat. Forensics League (degree for outstanding distinction 1992), Nat. PTO, Kappa Kappa Gamma (pres. 1985-90). Home: 1600 Burlington Ct Fort Collins CO 80525 Office: Poudre R-1 Sch Dist 201 Impala Dr Fort Collins CO 80521

COOK, DONALD E., pediatrician; b. Pitts., Mar. 24, 1928; s. Merriam E. and Bertha (Gwin) C.; BS, Colo. Coll., 1951; MD, U. Colo., 1955; m. Elsie Walden, Sept. 2, 1951; children: Catherine, Christopher, Brian, Jeffrey. Intern, Fresno County Gen. Hosp., Calif., 1955-56; resident in gen. practice Tulare (Calif.) County Gen. Hosp., 1956-57; resident in pediatrics U. Colo., 1957-59; practice medicine specializing in pediatrics, Aurora, Colo., 1959-64, Greeley (Colo.) Med. Clin., Greeley Sports Medicine Clin., 1964-93, mem. exec. com., 1990-92; med. adv. Centennial Develop. Svcs., Inc., clin. faculty U. Colo., clin. prof., 1977—; organizer, dir. Sports Medicine Px Exam Clinic for indigent Weld Co. athletes, 1990-93; mem. adv. bd. Nat. Center Health Edn., San Francisco, 1978-80; mem. adv. com. on maternal and child health programs Colo. State Health Dept., 1981-84, chmn., 1981-84; preceptor Sch. Nurse Practitioner Program U. Colo., 1978-88. Mem. Weld County Dist. 6 Sch. Bd., 1973-83, pres., 1973-74, 76-77, chmn. dist. 6 accountability com., 1972-73; mem. adv. com. dist. 6 teen pregnancy program, 1983-85; mem. Weld County Task Force on teen-aged pregnancy, 1986-89, Dream Team Weld County Task Force on sch. dropouts, 1986-92, Weld County Interagy. Screening Bd., Weld County Community Ctr. Found., 1984-89, Weld County Task Force Speakers Bur. on AIDS, 1987—; mem. Weld County Task Force Adolescent Health Clinic; mem. Task Force Child Abuse, C. of C.; bd. dirs. No. Colo. Med. Ctr., 1993; mem. Task Force on access to health care; group leader neonatal group Colo. Action for Healthy People Colo. Dept. Pub. Health, 1985-86; co-founder Colorodoans for seatbelts on sch. buses, 1985-90; co-founder, v.p. Coalition of primary care physicians, Colo., 1986; mem. adv. com. Greeley Cen. Drug and Alcohol Abuse, 1984-86, Rocky Mtn. Ctr. for Health Promotion and Edn., 1984—, bd. dirs., 1984—, v.p., 1992—; rep. coun. on med. specialty soc., AAP, 1988-89, mem. coun. pediatric rsch., 1988-89, oversight com. fin., oversight com. communications, rep. to nat. PTA, 1990—, mem. coun. on govt. affairs, 1989-90, rep. to coun. sects. mgmt. com., mem. search com. for new exec. dir.; med. cons. Sch. Dist. 6, 1989—; adv. com. bd. comm., adv. com. bd. membership comm., adv. com. bd. finance, adv. com. bd. dirs. AAP 1990-91, AAP com. govt. affairs, 1990; bd. dirs. N. Colo. Med. Ctr., 1993—, United Way Weld County, 1993—. With USN, 1946-48. Recipient Disting. Svc. award Jr. C. of C., 1962, Disting. Citizenship award Elks, 1975-76, Svc. to Mankind award Sertoma Club, 1972, Spark Plug award U. No. Colo., 1981; Mildred Doster award Colo. Sch. Health Coun. for sch. health contbns., 1992. Diplomate Am. Bd. Pediatrics. Mem. Colo. Soc. Sch. Health Com. (chmn. 1967-78), Am. Acad. Pediatrics (alt. dist. chmn. 1987-93, dist. chmn. dist. VIII 1993, chmn. alt. dist. chmn. com. 1991-93, chmn. sch. health com. 1975-80, chmn. Colo. chpt. 1982-87, mem. task force on new age of pediatrics 1982-85, Ross edn. and award com. 1985-86, media spokesperson Speak Up for Children 1983—, mem. coun. sects. mgmt. 1991-92, mem. search com., exec. dir.), AMA (chmn. sch. and coll. health com. 1980-82, James E. Strain Community Svc. award 1987, coun. pediatric practice), Adams Aurora Med. Soc. (pres. 1964-65), Weld County Med. Soc. (pres. 1968-69), Colo. Med. Soc. (com. on sports medicine, 1980-90, com. chmn. 1986-90, chmn. com. sch. health 1988-91, A.H. Robbins Community Svc. award 1974), Centennial Pediatric Soc. (pres. 1982-86), Rotary (bd. dirs. Greely chpt. 1988-91). Republican. Methodist. Home: 1710 21st Ave Greeley CO 80631-5143 Office: Greeley Sports Medicine Clinic 1900 16th St Greeley CO 80631-5189

COOK, DONALD LLOYD, physicist, researcher; b. Ypsilanti, Mich., Jan. 7, 1948; s. Orwin Seymour and Muriel Harriet (Veurink) C.; m. Margaret Ann Kramer, Feb. 12, 1972; children: Julia Allison, Cynthia Lauren. BSE, U. Mich., 1970; SM, MIT, 1974, PhD, 1976. Staff mem. Plasma Fusion Ctr., MIT, Cambridge, 1976-77; staff mem. Sandia Nat. Labs., Albuquerque, 1977-81, supr., 1981-84, mgr., 1984—; conf. chmn Dept. Energy Inertial Confinement Fusion Physics Conf., 1986, 91. Contbr. numerous articles to profl. jours. Sandia Nat. Labs. chmn. United Way, 1990. Mem. Am. Phys. Soc., Am. Nuclear Soc. (chair fusion energy div. 1989-90), Sigma Xi. Presbyterian. Office: Sandia Nat Labs Dept 1202 PO Box 5800 Albuquerque NM 87185

COOK, DOUGLAS NEILSON, theatre educator, producer, artistic director; b. Phoenix, Sept. 22, 1929; s. Neil Estes and Louise Y. (Wood) C.; m. Joan Stafford Buechner, Aug. 11, 1956; children: John Richard, Peter Neilson, Stephen Barton. Student, Phoenix Coll., 1948-49, U. Chgo., 1949-50, UCLA, 1950-51, Los Angeles Art Inst., 1948; B.F.A., U. Ariz., 1953; M.A., Stanford U., 1955; postgrad., Lester Polakov Studio Stage Design, 1966-67. Instr. San Mateo (Calif.) Coll., 1955-57, Nat. Music Camp, Interlochen, Mich., 1961; asst. prof. drama U. Calif., Riverside, 1957-66; assoc. prof., chair theatre dept. U. Calif., 1967-70; head dept. Pa. State U., University Park, 1970-88, sr. prof. theatre arts, 1988-92; prof. emeritus Pa. State U., 1992—. Actor Corral Theatre, Tucson, 1952-53, Orleans (Mass.) Arena Theatre, 1953; dir., designer Palo Alto (Calif.) Community Theatre, 1954, Peninsula Children's Theatre, 1956-57; assoc. producer Utah Shakespearean Festival, Cedar City, 1964-90, producing artistic dir., 1990—; producer Pa. State Festival Theatre, State College, 1970-85, The Nat. Wagon Train Show, 1975-76. Instl. rep. Juniata Valley council Boy Scouts Am., 1973-77; bd. dirs. Central Pa. Festival Arts, 1970-75, 84-87, v.p., 1984-86; bd. dirs. Nat. theatre Conf., 1980-90, v.p. 1983-85, pres. 1987-88. Recipient disting. alumni award U. Ariz., 1990. Mem. AAUP, Shakespeare Theatre Assn. Am. (v.p. 1990-92, pres. 1993—), Nat. Assn. Schs. Theatre, Am. Theatre Assn. (bd. dirs. 1977-86, exec. com. 1979-80, pres. 1984-85), U.S. Inst. Theatre Tech., Am. Soc. Theatre Rsch., Univ. Resident Theatre Assn. (bd. dirs. 1970-88, v.p. 1975-79, pres. 1979-83), Theatre Assn. Pa. (bd. dirs. 1972-76). Home: 5725 N 20th Pl Phoenix AZ 85016 Office: Utah Shakespearean Festival 351 W Center St Cedar City UT 84720-2498

COOK, FREDA MAXINE, retired councilwoman; b. Johnson County, Kans., July 13, 1928; d. Fred Charles and Eva Mathilda (Smith) Richardson; m. Thomas Warner Cook, June 24, 1951. Diploma, Cen. Bus. Coll., Kansas City, Mo., 1947. Legal sec. Carl G. Helm, Atty., La Grande, Oreg., 1949-65; adminstrv. sec. City of La Grande, 1965-84, councilmember, 1989-92. Bd. dirs. La Grande Downtown Assn., 1989, United Way of Union County, 1991-95; sec.-treas. Friends of La Grande Mainstreet, 1990; supporting mem. Ea. Oreg. Regional Arts Coun., 1985; mem. adv. bd. N.E. Oreg. Heritage Fund, 1989—. Named Woman of Yr. Soroptimist of La Grande, 1990, Woman of Yr. La Grande C. of C., 1992-93; recipient Pres.' Svc. award La Grande C. of C., 1989. Mem. La Grande C. of C., Soroptimist Internat. of La Grande (pres. 1982-83). Republican. Presbyterian.

COOK, GARY DENNIS, music educator; b. Jackson, Mich., Jan. 20, 1951; s. Jerome D. and Mary Jane (Read) C.; m. Kirsten M. Odmark, June 3, 1972; children: Tekla M., Tamara K. MusB, U. Mich., 1972, MusM, 1975. Instr. music La. Tech. U., Ruston, 1972-75; timpanist/prin. percussion Tucson Symphony Orch., 1976—; asst. dir. bands U. Ariz., Tucson, 1975-77, asst. prof. music, 1975-80, assoc. prof. music, 1981-90, prof. music, 1990—. Author: Teaching Percussion, 1988; co-author: The Encyclopedia for Percussion; contbr. articles to profl. jours. and ency. Charles and Irene Putnam award for excellence in teaching in the College of Fine Arts. Mem. Percussive Arts Soc., Coll. Music Soc., Music Tchrs. Nat. Assn., Am. Fedn. Musicians, Pi Kappa Lambda, Kappa Kappa Psi, Phi Mu Alpha. Office: U Ariz Sch Music Tucson AZ 85721

COOK, GREGORY D., mortgage banking company executive; b. Billings, Mont., Aug. 20, 1948; m. Margo L. Stahl, Apr. 6, 1974; children: Michael, Shanna, Jason. Student, Santa Barbara City Coll., 1970-71, Calif. Poly. State U., 1971-73. Zone mgr. Investors Diversified Svcs. Mktg. Corp., Mpls., 1974-78; fin. cons. Self-Mortgage Banking, Calif., 1978-90; pres. Am. Trust Deed Investment Corp., Billings, Mont., 1990—; mem. SEC, N.Y.C., 1974-78, Nat. Assn. Securities Dealers, N.Y.C., 1974-78, Mortgage Bankers Assn., Washington, 1980-82. Author: (book) Investing in Trust Deeds - Maximizing Wealth, 1992. With U. S. Army, 1968-71. Democrat. Home: 4321 Loma Vista Dr Billings MT 59106

COOK, LODWRICK MONROE, petroleum company executive; b. Castor, La., June 17, 1928; married. B.S., La. State U., 1950, B.S. in Petroleum Engring., 1955; M.B.A., So. Meth. U., 1965. Petroleum engr. Union Producing Co., 1955-56; with Atlantic Richfield Co., Los Angeles, 1956—; engring. trainee Atlantic Richfield Co., Inc., Los Angeles, 1956-61, adminstrv. asst., 1961-64, sr. personnel dept., then personnel mgr., 1964-67, labor reins. con., 1967-69, mgr. labor reins. dept., 1969-70, v.p., gen. mgr. product div. Western area, 1970-72, v.p. mktg. products div., 1972-73, v.p. corp. planning div., 1973-74, v.p. products div., 1974-75, v.p. transp. div., 1975-77, sr. v.p. transp. div., 1977-80, exec. v.p., dir., 1980-85, pres., chief exec. officer, 1985, chmn., chief exec. officer, 1986—. 1st lt. U.S. Army, 1950-53. Mem. Nat. Petroleum Council, Am. Petroleum Inst. (bd. dirs.). Office: Atlantic Richfield Co PO Box 2579 515 S Flower St Los Angeles CA 90071-2200

COOK, LOUISA FAY, retired electrical engineer; b. Yuma, Ariz., Sept. 28, 1925; d. Roy Edmond and Addalisa Katherine (Morton) Simons; m. George William Cook, Apr. 9, 1954; children: Robert Louis, Barbara Louise Cook Price, Rosemary Ann. BSEE, U. Ariz., 1947. Registered profl. engr., Ariz. Engring. aide U.S. Bur. Reclamation, Yuma, 1942-46; planning engr. power system Salt River Project, Phoenix, 1947-55, 62-64; engring. aide Sperry Flight Systems, Phoenix, 1966; elec. field engr. Bechtel Power Corp., Palo Verde, Ariz., 1977-86; ret., 1986. Fin. sec. Los Arcos United Meth. Ch., Scottsdale, Ariz., 1963—. Mem. IEEE (life), Soc. Women Engrs. (life).

COOK, LYLE EDWARDS, retired fund raising executive, consultant; b. Astoria, Oreg., Aug. 19, 1918; s. Courtney Carson and Fanchon (Edwards) C.; m. Olive Freeman, Dec. 28, 1940; children: James Michael, Ellen Anita Cook Otto, Mary Lucinda Cook Vaage, Jane Victoria. A.B. in History, Stanford U., 1940, postgrad., 1940-41. Instr. history Yuba Jr. Coll., Marysville, Calif., 1941-42; methods analyst Lockheed Aircraft Corp., 1942-45; investment broker Quincy Cass Assocs., Los Angeles, 1945-49; mem. staff Stanford U., 1949-66, asst. dean Sch. Medicine, 1958-65; sr. staff mem. Lester Gorsline Assos., Belvedere, Calif., 1966-72, v.p., 1967-70, exec. v.p., 1970-72; v.p. univ. relations U. San Francisco, 1973-75; fund-raising and planning cons., 1975; dir. fund devel. Children's Home Soc. Calif., 1976-78; exec. dir. That Man May See, Inc., San Francisco, 1978-87; co-founder, trustee, chmn. bd. The Fund Raising Sch., 1977-86; spl. cons. NIH, 1960-62. Mem. Marin County Grand Jury, 1987-88. Mem. Nat. Soc. Fund Raising Execs. (bd. dirs. 1976-88, chmn. certification bd. 1988-90, recipient first Nat. Chmn.'s award 1981, named Outstanding Fund Raising Exec. 1987), Stanford Assocs., Belvedere Tennis Club, Theta Delta Chi. Democrat. Episcopalian. Home: 25 Greenwood Bay Dr Belvedere Tiburon CA 94920

COOK, LYNETTE RENÉ, illustrator, educator; b. Herrin, Ill., Jan. 1, 1961; d. Kenneth Severin Cook and Charlotte Cecelia Cook-Fuller. BS, Miss. U. Women, 1981, BFA, 1982; MFA, Calif. Coll. Arts and Crafts, 1984. Freelance artist San Francisco, 1983—; art instr. U. Calif. Extension, Berkeley, 1989—, Calif. Acad. Scis., San Francisco, 1988—; artist, photographer Morrison Planetarium/Calif. Acad. Scis., San Francisco, 1984—; guest lectr. U. Calif., Santa Cruz, 1989—. Group exhbns. include: Oakland (Calif.) Mus., 1984, 87, 89, Wrubel Gallery, Berkeley, 1985, Assn. Med. Illustrators Conv., Cin., 1985, Strybing Arboretum, San Francisco, 1986, 90, AAAS, Washington, 1986, Ga. Mus. Art, 1987, Lawrence Hall Sci., Berkeley, 1987-88, Smithsonian Mus. Natural History, Washington, 1988-90, Santa Barbara (Calif.) Mus. Natural History, 1989, Hayden Planetarium, Am. Mus. Natural History, N.Y.C., 1991-92, Cleve. Mus. Natural History 1992-93, NASA Ames Rsch. Ctr., Mountain View, Calif., 1992, Calif. Acad. Scis., San Francisco, 1992; represented in permanent collection Guild Natural Sci. Illustrators travelling exhibit; illustrator notecubes, wrapping paper for The Nature Co., 1990. Coord. art project Environ. Protection Act. 1990, San Francisco, 1990. Recipient Bronze award Art of Calif. Mag., 1992. Mem. Guild Natural Sci. Illustrators (corr. sec. 1987—), Calif. Guild Natural Sci. Illustrators (sec. 1986-87), Internat. Assn. Astron. Arts, Phi Kappa Phi. Office: Morrison Planetarium Calif Acad Scis Golden Gate Park San Francisco CA 94118-4501

COOK, M(ELVIN) GARFIELD, chemical company executive; b. Woodbury, N.J., June 17, 1940; s. Melvin Alonzo and Wanda (Garfield) C.; m. Margo Dawn Taylor, Aug. 24, 1965; children: Dawn Ann, Melvin, Katherine, JoAnn, Carol, Mary, Taylor, Stephen, Michael. BS in Physics, U. Utah, 1966. Rsch. assoc. IRECO Chems., Salt Lake City, 1966-67; gen. mgr. Mesabi Blasting, Inc., Biwabik, Minn., 1967-69; v.p. ops. IRECO Chems., 1969-71, exec. v.p., 1971-72, pres., chief exec. officer, 1972-89; chmn. Non-Invasive Med. Tech. Corp., 1988—; dir. Def. Systems, Inc., Salt Lake City, Nobel Ins. Ltd.; advisor on explosives and propellants Dept. Def., Washington, 1979-81—; chmn. bd. govs. Inst. of Makers of Explosives, Washington, 1972-89. Author: Everlasting Burnings, 1981, Ency. Modern Explosives, 1972—, (with M.A. Cook) Science and Mormonism, 1967. V.p. N.E. Bench Region Coun., Salt Lake City, 1974; vice chmn. Utah Symphony, 1988-90; chmn. voting dist. Rep. Party, 1973. With USAR, 1958-66. Mem. Mayflower Soc., Rotary. Mem. LDS Ch. Office: IRECO Inc 11th Fl Crossroads Tower 50 S Main St Salt Lake City UT 84144-0103

COOK, MICHAEL DAVID, artist, educator; b. Ramey, Puerto Rico, July 16, 1953; s. Richard Monroe and Doris Elenor (Atkins) C.; children: Nigel R., Avery A.; m. Vera Sprunt. BFA, Fla. State U., 1975; MA, U. Dallas, 1976; MFA, U. Okla., 1978. Vis. artist U. Ill., Champaign, 1978-80; asst. prof. U. Ill., Chgo., 1980-82; asst. prof. art U. N.Mex., Albuquerque, 1987—; vis. lectr. U. Calif., Berkeley, 1983-85, Davis, 1985; spl. guest faculty San Francisco Art Inst., 1985. Exhibited works in numerous group and individual shows including Ctr. for Continuing Arts, Santa Fe, 1991, Mus. Fine Arts, Santa Fe, 1990, Janet Steinberg Gallery, San Francisco, 1986, Greyson Gallery, Chgo., 1983, New Mus. Contemporary Art, N.Y.C., 1983-84. NEA fellow, 1985, Ill. Arts Coun. fellow, 1982; Ford Found. grantee, 1979, 78, U. N.Mex. grantee, 1990; named Outstanding Tchr. of Yr. U. N.Mex., 1990. Office: U NMex Dept Art Art History Albuquerque NM 87131

COOK, PAUL M., chemical manufacturing company executive; b. Ridgewood, N.J.. BSChemE, MIT, 1947. With Stanford Rsch. Inst., Palo Alto, Calif., 1949-53, Sequoia Process Corp., 1953-56; with Raychem Corp., Menlo Park, Calif., 1957—, former pres., chief exec. officer, until 1990, now chmn., bd. dirs. Recipient Nat. Medal Tech., 1988. Mem. NAE. Office: Raychem Corp 300 Constitution Dr Menlo Park CA 94025-1111*

COOK, PHILIP WILLIAM, social services administrator, writer; b. Ft. Worth, Dec. 15, 1948; s. Frederick George and Evantha (Hipple) C.; m. Marion Prucha (div. 1980); m. Deborah Marie Brunton, Aug. 16, 1984; children: Colin Maxwell, Ethan William. BS in Journalism, U. Oreg., 1979. News dir. Sta. KEXL, San Antonio, 1972-76, Sta. KBOY, Medford, Oreg., 1976-77, Sta. KYTE, Portland, Oreg., 1979-82, Sta. KWJJ, Portland, Oreg., 1981-82, Sta. KVEW-TV, Kennewick, Wash., 1986-88; reporter Sta. KPNW, Eugene, Oreg., 1976-79; asst. news dir. Sta. KCRL-TV, Reno, 1983-86; exec. dir. PACE Inst. for Families in Transition, Lake Oswego, Oreg., 1989—; legis. liaison PACE Inst. for Families in Transition, Salem. Recipient Best Newscast award Sigma Delta Chi, 1976, Best Series-Radio award AP, 1982. Office: PACE Inst for Families Box 118 7981 SW Nyberg Rd Tualatin OR 97062

COOK, RONALD LEE, chemist; b. Riverside, Calif., Dec. 31, 1954; m. Diane L. Cook, Aug. 20, 1977. BA, U. No. Colo., 1977; PhD in Chemistry, Utah State U., 1983. Sr. electrochemist Eltron Rsch., Inc., Aurora, Ill., 1984-89, rsch. mgr., 1990-91; prin. scientist TDA Rsch., Inc., Wheat Ridge, Colo., 1992—. Contbr. articles to profl. jours.; patentee (9) in field. Mem. Am. Chem. Soc., Am. Ceramics Soc., Sigma Xi. Office: TDA Rsch Inc 12345 W 52nd Ave Wheat Ridge CO 80033

COOK, SHARON EVONNE, university official; b. Pocatello, Idaho, July 16, 1941; d. Willard Robert and Marian (Bartlett) Leisy; m. John Fred Cook, June 19, 1971 (div. Nov. 1980). BEd, No. Mont. Coll., 1970; M in Secondary Edn., U. Alaska, Juneau, 1980; EdD, U. San Francisco, 1987. Cert. secondary sch. tchr., Alaska. Loan officer 1st Nat. Bank, Havre, Mont., 1964-68; adminstrv. asst. Alaska State Legis., Juneau, 1970-71; tchr. Juneau Dist. High Sch., 1971-75; instr. Juneau Dist. Community Coll., 1975-79; assoc. prof. U. Alaska, Juneau, 1979-90, dean Sch. Bus. and Pub. Adminstrn., 1986-90; assoc. dean Coll. Tech., Boise (Idaho) State U., 1990—; editor in chief office tech. McGraw Hill Book Gregg Div., N.Y.C., 1983-84; mem. exec. bd. statewide assembly U. Region V Vocat. Assn., 1978-80, del. 1982. Treas. Alaska State Vocat. Assn., 1980-82, pres.-elect, 1986, pres., 1987; pres. U. Alaska Juneau Assembly, 1978-80, v.p., 1980-82. No. Mont. Coll. scholar, Havre, 1968-70; named Outstanding Tchr., U. Alaska, 1976. Republican. Home: 2551 S Swallowtail Ln Boise ID 83706-6130 Office: Boise State U Coll Tech Assoc Dean's Office 1910 University Dr Boise ID 83725-0001

COOK, STANLEY JOSEPH, English educator, academic programs administrator, poet; b. Spicer, Minn., June 9, 1935; s. William Joseph and Lillie Esther (Feeland) C.; m. Janet Lucille Terry, Oct. 9, 1964 (div. June 1988); children: John Hildon, Laurel Erin; m. Michaela Dianne Higuera, Dec. 18, 1989; 1 step-child, Richard Scott. BA, U. Minn., 1957; MA, U. Utah, 1966, PhD (NDEA fellow), 1969. Project specialist in English, U. Wis., Madison, 1967; instr. English, U. Utah, Salt Lake City, 1968-69; prof. English and modern langs. Calif. State Poly. U., Pomona, 1969—; cons. communications. Served with USMCR, 1958-64. NSF grantee, 1966; Calif. State U. and Colls. grantee, 1973-74. Mem. SUBUD, AAUP, NEA, Phi Beta Kappa. Democrat. Roman Catholic. Editor: Language and Human Behavior, 1973, Man Unwept: Visions from the Inner Eye, 1974; author: (with others) The Scope of Grammar: A Study of Modern English, 1980, Cal Poly through 2001: A Continuing Commitment to Excellence, 1987; fieldworker Dictionary of Am. Regional English, 1986—. Home: 1744 N Corona Ave Ontario CA 91764-1236 Office: Calif State Poly U 3801 W Temple Ave Pomona CA 91768-2557

COOK, STEPHEN CHAMPLIN, retired shipping company executive; b. Portland, Oreg., Sept. 20, 1915; s. Frederick Stephen and Mary Louise (Boardman) C.; m. Dorothy White, Oct. 27, 1945; children: Mary H. Cook Goodson, John B., Samuel D., Robert B. (dec.). Student, U. Oreg., 1935-36. Surveyor U.S. Engrs. Corp., Portland, Oreg., 1934-35; dispatcher Pacific Motor Trucking Co., Oakland, Calif., 1937-38; manifest clk. Pacific Truck Express, Portland, 1939; exec. asst. Coastwise Line, San Francisco, 1940-41, mgr. K-Line svc., 1945-56; chartering mgr. Ocean Svc. Inc. subs. Marcona Corp., San Francisco, 1956-75, ret., 1975; cons., San Francisco, 1976-78. Author 1 charter party, 1957. Mem. steering com. Dogwood Festival, Lewiston, Idaho, 1985-92; sec. Asotin County Reps., Clarkston, Wash., 1986-88; adv. bd. Pt. Clarkston Commrs., 1989-93. Lt. USN, 1941-45, PTO. Recipient Pres.'s award Marin (Calif.) coun. Boy Scouts Am., 1977, Order of Merit, 1971, 84, Skillern award Lewis Clark coun., 1982, Silver Beaver award 1987; Lewis-Clark Valley Vol. award, 1987, Youth Corps award Nat. Assn. Svc. and Conservation Corps., 1990. Mem. Clarkston C. of C. (Pre.'s Spl. award 1983), Asotin County Hist. Soc. (hon. life, pres. 1982-83, bd. dirs.), VFW. Republican. Mem. Stand for United Ch. of Christ.

COOK, WILLIAM ROBERT, theology educator; b. Portland, Oreg., Nov. 18, 1928; s. Floyd Newton and Alice (Schmidt) C.; m. Elaine Lucille Johnson, June 8, 1951; children: David, Kimberly. BA, Westmont Coll., 1951; ThM, Dallas Theol. Sem., 1955, ThD, 1960; postgrad., Hebrew U., Jerusalem, Israel, 1975. Pastor Galvin (Wash.) Bible Chapel, 1955-58; assoc. prof. Bible and Greek Northwestern Coll., Mpls., 1960-65; dean of students Western Conservative Bapt. Sem., Portland, 1966-69, acad. v.p., 1969-86, prof. bibl. theology, 1965—. Author: Theology of John, 1979; author chpt. in book: God What is He Like?, 1977; contbr. numerous articles to profl. jours. Mem. Evang. Theol. Soc. Office: Western Conservative Bapt Sem 5511 SE Hawthorne Blvd Portland OR 97215-3399

COOKE, M. MICHAEL, county official; b. Denver, Apr. 3, 1954; d. James Bernard and Marylou (Bastien) Kenney; m. John B. Madden, Oct. 20, 1973 (div. 1985); children: Amy Elizabeth, Declan John; m. Dennis Ray Cooke, Aug. 6, 1988. Student, Arapahoe C.C., Denver, 1972-73, 85, Colo. Real Estate Sch., 1976. Student loan adviser Bank of Denver, 1973-75; sales assoc. Heritage West Realty, Lakewood, Colo., 1976-85; v.p., treas. Spanish Peaks Constructors, Inc., Commerce City, Colo., 1981-85; payroll sec. Kenney Constrn. Co., Inc., Commerce City, 1980-87; ind. child care provider Highlands Ranch, Colo., 1984-93; vice chmn. Douglas County Bd. Commrs., Colo., 1993—. Coord. 9 Health Fair, Denver, 1984—; adv. panel Denver Mus. Natural History, Denver, 1986-88; mem. violations com. Highlands Ranch Community Assn., 1988-90, bd. dirs., 1990-92; pres. Highlands Ranch Jaycees, 1986-87. Mem. U.S. Jr. C. of C. (senatorship award 1988), Colo. Jaycees (bd. dirs. 1985-86, v.p. 1987-88), Arapahoe Jaycees (pres. 1989-90). Republican. Roman Catholic. Home: 8934 S Round Rock St Highlands Ranch CO 80126

COOKE, SUZETTE ALLEN, state representative; b. Bellingham, Wash., Aug. 27, 1949. BA, Western Wash. U., 1972. Recreation supr. City of Seattle, 1972-75; dir. Kent (Wash.) Parks and Recreation Dept. Sr. Activity Ctr., 1975-81; exec. dir. Kent C. of C., 1981-92; rep. 47th Dist. Washington State, 1993—; Mem. Ho. Human Svcs. Com., Appropriations Com., Health Care Com. Former ex-officio bd. mem. Wash. State Small Bus. Improvement Coun.; mem. Wash. Rsch. Coun., Valley Area Transp. Alliance, Fist Christian Ch. of Kent; former mem. King County Housing Rehab. Adv. Com., Valley Med. Ctr. Citizens Adv. Coun. Mem. Wash. C. of C. Execs. (past pres.), Assn. Wash. Bus. (former bd. and exec. com. mem.), Wash. State Sr. Ctr. Dirs. Assn. (founding organizer), Rotary Club Kent (com. chmn.). Home: 25307 144th Ave SE Kent WA 98042 Office: 320 John L O'Brien Bldg Olympia WA 98504

COOKSON, PATRICIA KAY, lawyer; b. Cleve., Mar. 3, 1953; d. Henry Theodore and Ann Josephine (Kenik) Rogalski; m. David Wesley Cookson,

June 19, 1983. BA, Kent (Ohio) State U., 1975; JD, John Marshall Law Sch., Cleve., 1978. Bar: Calif. 1979. Assoc. Law Offices of Gary Schweitzer, San Diego, 1979-81; dep. dist. atty. Office of the Dist. Atty., San Diego, 1981-88; assoc. Law Firm of Schall, Boudreau & Gore, Inc., San Diego, 1988—; apptd. asst. presiding judge El Cajon dist. San Diego County (Calif.) Mcpl. Ct., 1992; barrister Am. Inn of Ct., San Diego, 1985-87; instr. San Diego Police Acad., 1984-87, San Diego Police Dept., 1984-87, San Diego Shriff's acad., 1986, 88, Miramar Coll., San Diego, 1985-86. Vol. Am. Cancer Soc., San Diego, 1988—; speaker Women's Crisis Ctr., San Diego, 1987-88. Named Female Prosecutor of the Yr., Dist. Atty., 1987. Mem. San Diego County Bar Assn., San Diego Trial Lawyers Assn., Calif. Trial Lawyers Assn., Assn. Trial Lawyers Am., ABA, Barristers Club. Republican. Roman Catholic. Office: Schall Boudreau & Gore 501 W Broadway San Diego CA 92101-3536

COOLEY, EDWARD H., castings manufacturer; b. 1922; grad. in mech. engring., Swarthmore Coll.; postgrad. Harvard U., 1947; married. With Dana Corp., 1947-49, Ore Saw Chain Corp., 1950-55; pres., dir. Precision Castparts Corp., Portland, Oreg., 1955—, now chmn., chief exec. officer. Office: Precision Castparts Corp 4600 SE Harney Dr Portland OR 97206-0898*

COOLEY, ELIZABETH ANNEEN, research scientist, consultant; b. Berkeley, Calif., June 29, 1960; d. Oktay Sinanoglu and Yvonne Anneen (Esler) Hecht; m. Bruce Edwin Cooley, Sept. 6, 1980 (div. 1993). BS, U. Oreg., 1984, PhD, 1991. Project sec. Oreg. Rsch. Inst., Eugene, 1984-85, rsch. asst. I, 1985-86, rsch. asst. II, 1986-87, project coord., 1987-89, rsch. assoc., 1989-91, prin. investigator, rsch. scientist, 1991—, also bd. dirs.; chair orgnl. norms com. Oreg. Rsch. Inst., 1987, chair sci. support coun., 1987-89, mem. human resources and devel. com., 1992—; instr. continuing edn. U. Oreg., 1992; cons., trainer various sch. dists. and rehab. facilities, Oreg., 1991—. Contbr. articles to profl. jours.; writer, producer instrnl. videotapes; presenter in field. Adv. bd. Bethel Big Brother/Big Sister Program, 1986, Uhlhorn Apts., 1990-91; mem. devel. com. Lane County Direction Svc., 1986; mem. program evaluation com. Eugene Vol. Action Ctr., 1988; active Oreg. Dept. Edn. Deaf/Blind Working Group, 1987-88. Mem. Internal Stress Mgmt. Assn., Assn. Behavior Analysis, Nat. Head Injury Found., Assn. Retarded Citizens, Assn. for Persons with Severe Handicaps, Coun. for Exceptional Children, Oreg. Head Injury Found. Home: 3877 N Shasta Loop Eugene OR 97405 Office: Oreg Rsch Inst 1899 Willamette Eugene OR 97401

COOLEY, LELAND FREDERICK, writer, prose, news and commentary; b. Oakland, Calif., June 8, 1909; s. Arthur Montague and Anita Beatrice (Lewis) C.; m. Regina Francoise Verreth; children: Pamela Lee, Allison Smith Cooley; step-children: Michael Dunn, Elizabeth Dunn. With Mcht. Marine, South Pacific and worldwide, 1926-29; assoc. editor Sta. KNX News Dept., Hollywood, Calif., 1932-36; corr. Transradio Press, Europe, 1936; newscaster sports and spl. events KHJ Mut. Network, L.A., 1937; tech. dir. Paramount Pictures, Hollywood, Calif., 1937-38; writer and master of ceremonies Andre Kostelanetz Show, Sta. CBS Radio, N.Y.C., 1939-40; dir. daytime radio and experimental TV Ruthrauff & Ryan, Advt., N.Y.C., 1940-46; dir. TV McCann-Erickson Advt., 1946-50; producer-dir.-writer Perry Como Show, CBS TV Network, N.Y.C., 1950-56; exec. producer Paramount TV, Sta. KTLA, Hollywood, Calif., 1957-58. Author: (novels) The Run for Home, 1958, God's High Table, 1973, The Richest Poor Folks, 1963 (named to One Hundred Best Books List 1963), The Trouble With Heaven, 1966, Condition Pink, 1967, California, 1973 (awarded U. Calif. F.O.L. Hist. Fiction award, The Americana award 1973, Stein & Day Publ. 1984), The Art Colony, 1975, The Dancer, 1978, Imaginology, 1984, Judgment at Red Creek, 1992. With USCGR, 1942-46. Recipient Christopher award, N.Y.C., 1956. Mem. Radio & TV Dirs. Guild (founding mem.), Dutch Treat Club-West (founding mem.), Acad. of TV Arts and Scis., Writers Guild of Am. West, Authors League and Authors Guild, PEN (past pres.).

COOMBS, C'CEAL PHELPS (MRS. BRUCE AVERY COOMBS), air company executive, civic worker; b. nr. Portland, Oreg.; d. Perry Edwin and Flora (Gowey) Phelps m. Bruce Avery Coombs, Nov. 28, 1929; children: Keith Avery, Glinda C'Ceal (Mrs. Nick E. Mason). BS, U. Idaho, 1929; postgrad., Wash. State Coll., 1941. Tchr. pub schs., Idaho, 1929-30; adminstrv. asst. Coombs West-Air Co. and Coombs Flying C Ranches, Yakima, Wash., 1945—; lobbyist for civic activities Wash. Legislature, 1947—; genealogist, notary pub., Wash., 1960—. Del. White House Conf. on Children and Youth, 1960, Wash. State White House Conf. on Edn., 1955; mem. Wash. Citizens Coun., Nat. Coun. Crime & Delinquency, 1956—; bd. dirs., mem. exec. com. Wash. State Coun. Crime & Delinquency, 1956—, chmn., 1970-71, recipient Spl. State award, 1972, 76; mem. Allied Sch. Coun. Wash. 1951-53; mem. Western regional scholarship com. Ford Found., 1955-57; chmn. regional dist. Wash. Cities Legislation, 1960; chmn. Yakima County Sch. Bd., 1957-59; mem. Yakima County Health Dept., 1959-60; city councilwoman Yakima, 1959-61, asst. mayor, 1960; mem. Wash. Libr. Commn., 1960, 64-68, 72—, vice chmn., 1965-70, 75-76, recipient gov's. citation, 1976; del. UNESCO Conf. Crime & Delinquency, Kyoto, Japan, 1970, Caracus, Venezuela, 1980; del. to Internat. Libr. Assn., Toronto, 1968, Washington, 1975, del. to worldwide seminar, Seoul, 1976, London, Brussels, 1977; del. Internat. Fedn. Librs., Manila, 1980; trustee Wash. 4-H Found., 1960-79, chmn., 1969—, hon. trustee, 1979—; bd. mem. Wash. State Friends of Librs., 1976, pres., 1977; mem. bd. Yakima County Law and Justice; mem. Gov.'s Mansion Found., Washington; mem. Wash. State Com. for promoting writing & publ. of history of Wash. State Libr., 1990. Recipient Outstanding Citizen award Western Correctional Assn., 1974, Lobbyist Honor award Third House Orgn. of the Washington State Legislature, 1988, Ptnr. 4-H State Recognition, Wash. State 4-H Found., 1991; named one of 100 women in Centennial Wash. state publ. Mem. Am. Libr. Trustee Assn. (regional dir. 1962—, pres. 1967-68), C. of C., Oreg. Hist. Soc., Idaho Hist. Soc., Elmore County Hist. Soc., Washington County Hist. Soc., Calif. Hist. Soc., Windsor (Conn.) Hist. Assn. (life), Friends of Tewkesbury Abbey Eng. (life), Daus. Am. Colonists, Founders and Patriots, New Eng. Hist. Geneal. Soc., Conn. Hist. Soc., Dorchester (Mass.) Antiquarian and Hist. Soc., Conn. Soc. Genealogists, Ft. Simcoe Restoration Soc. (life), ALA (internat. trustee citation 1966, mem. bd. 1972—, coun. 1967-68, 71-72), Pacific N.W. Libr. Assn. (chmn. trustee sect. 1962-63), Wash. Libr. Assn. (chmn. 1960, trustee award 1967), Wash. State Libr. Found., Nat. Soc. Crown of Charlemagne, LWV, Allied Arts Coun., Broadway Theatre League, Nat. Aviation Assn., Am. Aviation Assn., P.E.O., Federated Women, Colonial Dames (state rec. sec., pres. local chpt., XVII Century award for outstanding contbn. 1988), Altrusa, Nat. Soc. Magna Charta Dames, Descs. of Conqueror and His Companions, Friends of N.Y.C. Libr., Order of the Crown of Charlemagne, Sovereign Colonial Soc. Ams. Royal Descent (life), Friends of the Washington Libr. (life).

COOMBS, JIM LE, secondary education educator, coach; b. Wheatridge, Colo., June 14, 1964; s. Leroy G. Coombs and Johnnie M. (Lyles) Maschoff. BS, Calif. Polytech. U., 1987. Cert. secondary edn. tchr., Calif. Asst. head football coach Cathedral City (Calif.) High Sch., 1985, head varsity baseball coach, 1985—; dir. student activities, student govt. San Dimas (Calif.) High Sch., 1992—; athletic camp asst. Stanford U., Palo Alto, 1990—. Educator Community Edn. on Child Growth & Devel., La Verne, Calif., 1990—. Mem. Nat. Tchrs. Assn., Calif. Tchrs. Assn., Calif. Baseball Coaches Assn., Calif. Football Coaches Assn., So. Calif. Basketball Ofcls., Fellowship of Christian Athletes. Republican. Baptist. Home: 222 E Foothill Sp 60 Pomona CA 91768 Office: San Dimas High Sch San Dimas CA 91773

COOMBS, MICHAEL JOHN, research center administrator; b. London, June 2, 1946; came to U.S., 1986; s. George Henry and Doris Elvina (Richardson) C.; m. Margaret Thomson, Nov. 24, 1983. BA, U. London, 1969; PhD in Psychology, U. Liverpool, 1978. Group leader Man Machine Rsch. group U. Liverpool, Eng., 1978-82; rsch. fellow in computer sci. U. Strathclyde, Glasgow, Scotland, 1982-83, lectr. in computer sci., 1983-85; prin. scientist Computing Rsch. Lab., N.Mex. State U., Las Cruces, 1986-87, assoc. dir., 1987—; dir. Rsch. Ctr., Phys. Sci. Lab., N.Mex. State U., Las Cruces, 1992—; cons. U.S. Army Info. Processing Adv. Bds., 1987—. Mem. editorial bd. Internat. Jour. Man Machine Studies, 1983—, Jour. Exptl. and Theoretical Army Info., 1990—; contbr. numerous articles to profl. jours. Recipient Freedom award City of London, 1985. Mem. Cognitive Sci. Soc., Am. Assn. Artificial Intelligence, Phi Kappa Phi. Home: PO Box 3315-UPB Las Cruces NM 88003 Office: Phys Sci Lab Box 30002 Las Cruces NM 88003-0002

COOMBS, ROBERT EUGENE, social worker; b. Cedaredge, Colo., Nov. 10, 1936; s. Oliver Clarence and Mary Ruth (Baker) C.; m. Virginia Marie Preyer, Sept. 19, 1968; children: Michael, Bonnie, Jeanne, Jodeen. BA in Biology, Pacific Union Coll., 1968, MA in Biology, 1971; MA in Counseling Psychology, Sierra U., 1986. Counselor Family Support Network, Napa, Calif., 1987; social worker child protective svc. emergency response Glenn County Social Svcs., Willows, Calif., 1987—; part time family counselor intern Glenn County Mental Health, Willows, 1988-89; intern counselor Family Svcs. Assn., Chico, Calif., 1992—. Mem. NASW, Internat. Soc. for Study Multiple Personality and Dissociation, Calif. Assn. Marriage and Family Therapists. Office: Glenn Cty Dept Social Svcs 135 N Enright Ave Willows CA 95988-2700

COOMBS, WILLIAM ELMER, accountant, lawyer; b. Keosauqua, Iowa, Jan. 17, 1911; s. Elmer Clyde and Myra Ann (Moon) C.; AB in Econs., U. Calif., L.A., 1933; JD, Loyola U., 1954; m. Katheryn Rose Logan, Oct. 20, 1934 (dec. May 1984); children: Katheryn M. Coombs (Mrs. Floyd Kirkendoll), Rose Ann (Mrs. Luciano Siracusa); m. Elta Louise Pfister, Feb. 17, 1985 (dec. Oct. 1990). CPA, Calif.; bar: Calif. 1955, U.S. Dist. Ct. (cen. dist.) Calif. 1955, U.S. Dist. Ct. (no. dist.) Calif. 1957, U.S. Supreme Ct. 1960, U.S. Ct. Appeals (9th cir.) 1963, U.S. Dist. Ct. (so. dist.) Calif. 1980. Acct., Shell Oil Co., L.A., 1933-36, So. Calif. Edison Co., L.A., 1936-37; auditor State of Calif., L.A., 1937-41; sr. acct. Arthur Andersen & Co., 1941-43; contr. Case Constrn. Co., San Pedro, Calif., 1943-46; C.P.A., Roberts & Coombs, 1946-49, Deloitte, Plender, Griffths & Co., 1949-52; contr. Ford J. Twaits Co., L.A., 1952-55; overseas auditor Morrison-Knudsen Internat., San Francisco, 1955-56; asst. prof. bus. Calif. State U., Chico 1956-58; sec.-treas., dir., house counsel Matich Corp., Colton, Calif. 1958-61; practiced law in Rialto, 1962-88, Laguna Beach, Calif., 1989-92, Newport Beach Calif. 1992—; mem. Calif. Senate, 1967-73, Calif. Regional Econ. Devel.Coun., 1984-87; city atty. Rialto, 1977-81, Big Bear Lake, Calif., 1980-82; bd. dirs. Calif. Taxpayers Assn., 1976-89; semi-ret., 1989—. Mem. Rialto City Planning Commn., 1960-62; councilman, Rialto, 1962-67; bd. dirs. Regional Econ. Devel. Council, 1964-67, pres., 1966-67. Mem. ABA, AICPA, Am. Arbitration Assn. (arbitrator constrn. disputes 1982—), Calif. State Bar Assn., Calif. Soc. CPAs (pres. citrus belt chpt. 1966-67), San Bernardino County Bar Assn. Author reference book: Construction Accounting and Financial Management, 1958. Home and Office: 1455 Superior Ave # 304 Newport Beach CA 92663-6123

COONEY, DANIEL ELLARD, aeronautical engineer; b. Deland, Fla., Oct. 25, 1949; s. William P. and Ruth E. C.; m. Marguerite R. Williams, Nov 17, 1990; children: Michael, Aaron. BS in Aerospace Engring., U. Fla., 1972; MA in Counseling, A.G. Theological Sem., 1987. Registered aeronautical engr., Kans.; cert. airline pilot. Project engr. Bede Aircraft Inc., Newton, Kans., 1972-78; CAD mgr. Lear Avia Corp., Reno, 1978-82; CAD cons. Aerospace CAD/CAM Svcs., Reno, 1982-89; chief engr. Scaled Composites Inc., Mojave, Calif., 1989—. Patents in field. Office: Scaled Composites 1624 Flight Line Airport Hanger 78 Mojave CA 93501-1663

COONEY, JOHN RICHARDSON, lawyer; b. Chgo., July 31, 1942; s. James B. and Kathleen A. (Kinane) C.; m. Jill L. Marron; children Matthew, James, Sean, Laura, Marron Anne. BA, JD, U. N.Mex., 1965. Bar: N.Mex. 1965. Assoc. Modrall, Sperling, Roehl, Harris and Sisk, Albuquerque, 1965-70, ptnr., 1970—, pres., 1993—; adj. faculty Sch. Law U. N.Mex., 1973-80. Fellow Am. Bar Found; mem. ABA, N.Mex. Bar Assn. (pres. 1980-81), N.Mex. Bar Found. (pres. 1982, sec.-treas. 1983-89). Office: Modrall Sperling Roehl Harris & Sisk 500 4th St NW Ste 1000 Albuquerque NM 87102

COONEY, KEVIN PATRICK, research computer engineer; b. Muscatine, Iowa, Dec. 14, 1955; s. Keith Eugene and Marjorie Ann (Schaer) C. BSCE, U. Colo., 1984, MSCE in Bldg. Energy Engring., 1988. Registered profl. engr., Wis. Mgr. Winterstash Foods, Telluride, Colo., 1976-78; lead carpenter Back of Nowhere Engring., Telluride, 1978-80; land survey party chief Bur. Land Mgmt., Denver, 1981-84; design engr. Sturm & Ballard, Lakewood, Colo., 1984-85; rsch. asst. U. Colo., Boulder, 1986-88; rsch. scientist Johnson Controls, Inc., Milw., 1988-91; sr. rsch. scientist Johnson Controls, Inc., Boulder, 1991—; R & D product cons. Hind, Inc., San Luis Obispo, Calif., 1990—. Contbr. articles to profl. jours. McCabe Meml. scholar, 1988. Mem. ASHRAE (tech. com. 1988—), Internat. Solar Energy Soc., Assn. Energy Engrs. Office: Johnson Controls Inc 250 Arapahoe Rm 303 Boulder CO 80302

COONEY, MIKE, state official; b. Washington, Sept. 3, 1954; s. Gage Rodman and Ruth (Brodie) C.; m. Dee Ann Marie Gribble; children: Ryan Patrick, Adan Cecelia, Colin Thomas. BA in Polit. Sci., U. Mont., 1979. State rep. Mont. Legislature, Helena, 1976-80; exec. asst. U.S. Sen. Max Baucus, Butte, Mont., 1979-82, Washington, 1982-85, Helena, Mont., 1985-89; sec. of state State of Mont., Helena, 1989—. Committeeman Lewis & Clark Dem. Cen. Com., Helena, Mont., 1986-88. Mem. Nat. Secs. of State. Roman Catholic. Home: PO Box 754 Helena MT 59624-0754 Office: Office Sec of State 225 State Capitol Helena MT 59620-9999*

COONEY, PATRICIA NOEL, lawyer; b. Oakland, Calif., Dec. 5, 1950; d. Robert Joseph and Mary Kathryn (Rhodes) C.; m. Kenneth Joseph Moore, Oct. 30, 1985; 1 child, Madeleine Cooney Moore. AB, U. Calif., Berkeley, 1981; JD, Golden Gate U., 1984. Bar: Calif. 1985, N.D. 1985. Pvt. practice Berkeley, 1990—. Office: 1108 Fresno Ave Berkeley CA 94707

COONS, ELDO JESS, JR., manufacturing company executive; b. Corsicana, Tex., July 5, 1924; s. Eldo Jess and Ruby (Allison) C.; m. Beverly K. Robbins, Feb. 6, 1985; children by previous marriage: Roberta Ann, Valerie, Cheryl. Student engring., U. Calif., 1949-50. Owner C & C Constrn. Co., Pomona, Calif., 1946-48; sgt. traffic div. Pomona Police Dept., 1948-54; nat. field dir. Nat. Hot Rod Assn., L.A., 1954-57; pres. Coons Custom Mfg., Inc., Oswego, Kans., 1957-68; chmn. bd. Borg-Warner Corp., 1968-71; pres. Coons Mfg., Inc., Oswego, 1971-84; pres. E.B.C Mgmt. Cons., Lake Havasu City, Ariz., 1984—. Mem. Kans. Gov.'s Adv. Com. for State Architects Assn. Served with C.E., AUS, 1943-46. Named to Exec. and Profl. Hall Fame, Recreational Vehicle/Mobile Homes Hall of Fame, Internat. Hot Rod Hall of Fame, 1961, Internat. Drag Racing Hall of Fame, 1991; recipient Paul Abel award Recreation Vehicle Industry Assn., 1978, 1st Ann. New Product award Kans. Gov.'s Office and Kans. Engring. Soc. 1982-83. Mem. Oswego C. of C. (dir.), Nat. Juvenile Officers Assn., Am. Legion, AIM (fellow pres.'s coun.), Mcpl. Officers Assn., Oswego C. of C., Young Pres.'s Orgn. Masons (K.T., Shriner), Rotary (pres. Oswego 1962-63). Originator 1st city sponsored police supervised dragstrip. Home and Office: EBC Mgmt Cons 2634 Diablo Dr Lake Havasu City AZ 86403-8450

COOPER, AUSTIN MORRIS, chemist, chemical engineer, consultant, researcher; b. Long Beach, Calif., Feb. 1, 1959; s. Merril Morris and Charlotte Madeline (Wittmer) C. BS in Chemistry with honors, Baylor U., 1981; BSChemE with honors, Tex. Tech U., 1983, MSChemE, 1985. Solar energy researcher U.S. Dept. Energy, Lubbock, Tex., 1983-85; advanced mfg. and process engring. mgr. McDonnell Douglas Space Systems Co., Huntington Beach, Calif., 1986-87, chem.-process line mgr., 1987-89, sr. material and process engr., 1989—. Contbr. articles to profl. jours. Mem. Am. Inst. Chem. Engrs., Am. Chem. Soc., Soc. Advancement of Materials and Process Engrs., Sigma Xi, Omega Chi Epsilon, Kappa Mu Epsilon, Beta Beta Beta.

COOPER, DOUGLAS E., consultant, executive; b. New Boston, Ohio, May 21, 1912; s. Frank G. and Norma Irene (Elhoff) C. BS, Eastern Ky. U., 1939; MS, U. Tenn., 1940; PhD, Purdue U., 1943. Cert. tchr., Calif. Chief chemist Bristol Labs., Syracuse, N.Y., 1943-59; rsch. assoc. Ethyl Corp. Rsch. Labs., Ferndale, Mich., 1959-69; rsch. assoc. Ethyl Corp. Comml. Devel., Baton Rouge, 1969-75, liaison med. mfg., 1975-77; pres. Cooper Assoc., Rocklin, Calif., 1979-88, Sacramento, Calif., 1988—; researcher in field. Contbr. articles to profl. sci. jours.; patentee in field. Mem. SIRS, Alpha Chi Sigma, Phi Lambda Upsilon, Sigma Xi. Republican. Presbyterian. Home: Arden Commons 1732 Avondale Ave Sacramento CA 95825

COOPER, GEORGE RYAN, lawyer; b. Denver, Nov. 29, 1954; s. Kemp Goodloe and Winifred Ann (Bucher) C. BA, U. Chgo., 1977; JD, U. Denver, 1982. Bar: Colo. 1983. Staff atty. Manville Corp., Denver, 1983; in-house counsel Knightwood & Brooks, Ltd., Mpls., 1983-84; assoc. atty. Nunn & Assocs., Denver, 1984-85, Thomas Leadabrand & Assocs., Lakewood, Colo., 1985-86, Thomas Scheffel & Assocs., Denver, 1988-89; in-house counsel Centennial Precious Metals, Denver, 1986-90; assoc. atty. Bath & Assocs., Denver, 1990-91; sole practitioner Denver, 1991—. Mem. Phi Beta Kappa. Office: 4155 E Jewell Ave # 222 Denver CO 80222

COOPER, GINNIE, library association executive; b. Worthington, Minn., 1945; d. Lawrence D. and Ione C.; 1 child, Daniel Jay. Student, Coll. St. Thomas, U. Wis., Parkside; BA, S.D. State U.; MA in Libr. Sci., U. Minn. Tchr. Flandreau (S.D.) Indian Sch., 1967-68, St. Paul Pub. Schs., 1968-69; br. libr. Wash. County Libr., Lake Elmo, Minn., 1970-71, asst. dir., 1971-75; assoc. adminstr., libr. U. Minn. Med. Sch., Mpls., 1975-77; dir. Kenosha (Wis.) Pub. Libr., 1977-81; county libr. Alameda County (Calif.) Libr., 1981-90; dir. librs. Multnomah County Libr., Portland, Oreg., 1990—. Chair County Mgr. Assn.; county adminstr. Mayor's Exec. Roundtable. Mem. ALA (mem. LAMA, PLA and RASD coms., elected to coun. 1987, 91, mem. legislation com. 1986-90, mem. orgn. com. 1990—), Calif. Libr. Assn. (pres. CIL, 1985, elected to coun. 1986, pres. Calif. County Librs. 1986), Oreg. Libr. Assn. Office: Multnomah County Libr 205 NE Russell St Portland OR 97212-3708

COOPER, JAMES RANDALL, electrical engineer; b. Monahans, Tex., Feb. 11, 1960; s. James Edward and Betty (Porter) C.; m. Marla Sandra Berlin, Aug. 11, 1990. BS in EE, Tex. Tech U., 1982, MSEE, 1983, PhDEE, 1986. Tech. group leader Maxwell Labs., San Diego, 1986-93; chief engr. SAIC, San Diego, 1993—. Patentee in field. Mem. IEEE (contbr. articles to jour.).

COOPER, JAMES RAY, JR., information services professional; b. Montgomery, Ala., May 26, 1949; s. James Ray and Bernice (Goldfelt) C.; m. Jane Mohr, Apr. 6, 1974. Student, Calif. Inst. of Tech., 1967-69, Pasadena (Calif.) City Coll., 1969-71; BA, Calif. State U., L.A., 1973; MA, U. Calif. at San Diego, La Jolla, 1975. Cert. data processor. Programming instr. Control Data Inst., L.A., 1975-78; programming mgr. Integral Bus. Computing, Torrance, Calif., 1978-80; cons. Western Data Corp., Seattle, 1980-82; data processing mgrs. Princess Tours, Seattle, 1982-85; software mgr. Continental Healthcare Tech., Seattle, 1985-88; cons. Sierra Systems Cons., Seattle, 1988-89, James Cooper Cons., Bainbridge Island, Wash., 1989-90; dir. cen. svcs. Benton County, Prosser, Wash., 1990—; computer sci. instr. Chapman Coll., Silverdale, Wash., 1984-89, Benton City Community Sch., 1992—. Contbr. articles to profl. jours. Income tax preparer V.I.T.A., Richland, Wash., 1991—. Mem. Data Processing Mgmt. Assn., Inst. for Cert. of Computer Profls., Assn. for City/County Info. Systems (sec., treas. 1992-94). Home: Rt 2 Box 2167D Benton City WA 99320 Office: Benton County Cen Svcs 620 Market St Prosser WA 99350

COOPER, JON HUGH, public television executive; b. Wynnewood, Okla., Aug. 6, 1940; s. John Hughes and Sarah Edna (Ray) C.; m. L. Ilene Batty, Dec. 16, 1961 (div. Jan. 1984); children: Jon Shelton, Geoffrey Harold; m. Patricia Carol Kyle, Jan. 28, 1989; children: Cynthia Lynne, Jennifer Jon Kyle. BA, Okla. State U., 1962; postgrad., U. Ariz., U. Denver, U. Colo., Denver. Mgmt. positions with Evening Star Broadcasting, Washington and Lynchburg, Va., 1962-67; producer, program mgr., dir. prodn. Sta. KUAT-AM-TV, Tucson, 1967-73; exec. dir. Rocky Mountain Network, Denver, 1973-77; exec. dir. Pacific Mountain Network, Denver, 1977-79, also bd. dirs.; gen. mgr. Sta. KNME-TV, Albuquerque, 1979—; lectr. speech and journalism U. Ariz., 1967-73; mem. interconnection com. PBS, 1983-92, bd. dirs. 1986-92, mem. exec. com., 1988-90, 91-92; bd. dirs. PBS Enterprises and Nat. Satacast, 1990—; bd. dirs. Natvie Am. Pub. Broadcasting Consortium, Pacific Mountain Network Japan Survey Team. Bd. dirs., co-chmn. cultural devel. Sisters Cities Albuquerque, 1987-90; host N.Mex. Internat. Student Program; bd. dirs., v.p., pres. Pueblo Los Cerros Homeowners Assn., 1987-88; bd. dirs. Samaritan Counseling Ctr., Albuquerque, 1987, Albuquerque Coun. for Internat. Visitors, N.Mex. Better Bus. Bur., 1991—; bd. advisors Pub. TV Outreach Alliance, 1992—; mem. N.Mex. Edn. Tech. Coun., 1992—; chmn. N.Mex. Commn. Pub. Broadcasting, 1992—. Named Govt. Bus. Adv. of Year U.S. Hispanic C. of C. Region II, 1990.

COOPER, LARRY S., cleaning network executive, textile consultant; b. Bklyn., June 14, 1957; s. Jack and Evelyn (Weinfeld) C.; m. Tryna Lee Giordano, Dec. 31, 1975;a children: Jonathan, Jennifer, Jillian. Student, U. Colo., 1975-78. Cert. master cleaner, sr. level carpet inspector. Owner Cooper's Carpet Cleaners, Boulder, Colo., 1975-79; pres. Profl. Cleaning Network, Denver, 1979—; owner Textiles Cons., Denver, 1986—. Chmn. Broomfield (Colo.) Connection, 1988-90; council mem. City of Broomfield, 1989—. Named Cleanfax Man of Yr., Clean Fax Mag., 1990. Mem. Profl. Carpet and Upholstery Cleaners Assn. (pres. 1980-81, 84-86), Internat. Inst. of Carpet and Upholstery Cert. (v.p. 1984-85, pres. 1985-87, chmn. bd. 1988, chmn. cert. bd. 1990—). Office: Profl Cleaning Network 6445 Downing St Denver CO 80229-7225

COOPER, LOUISA SINCLAIR, artist; b. Honolulu, July 24, 1931; d. William Taylor and Mary Lydia (Barrette) S.; m. George Dunton Witter, July 4, 1952 (div. May 1966); children: Martha S., George D. Jr., Elizabeth, James; m. Clifford Dennis Cooper, June 19, 1976. Student, U. Calif., Berkeley, 1949-51; BA in Studio Art, U. Calif., Irvine, 1976; postgrad., Laguna Beach Sch. Art, Ecole Migros, Geneva. One-woman shows include Pauahi Tower Gallery, Honolulu, 1989, 91, Contemporary Mus., Honolulu, 1992, Queen Emms Gallery, Honolulu, 1993; exhibited in group shows at Am. Artists Profl. League, 1986, 88, Salamagundi Artists Non-Members Show, N.Y., 1991, Women Artists of West, L.A., 1991, Nat. Art League 61st Ann. Exhbn., N.Y., 1991, Oil Painters Am., Chgo., 1993. Mem. Am. Artists Profl. League, Oil Painters Am., Nat. Mus. Women in Arts, Assn. Hawaii Artists, Honolulu Acad. Arts, Cath. Artists of 90s, Rockport Art Assn. Home: 1036 Mokulua Dr Kailua HI 96734 Office: 1000 S Bayfront Balboa Island CA 92662

COOPER, RICHARD KENT, physicist; b. Detroit, Apr. 13, 1937; s. John Joseph and Helen Irene (Wertz) C.; m. Lorna Hamilton Goss, Aug. 31, 1957 (div. 1986); children: Preston Allen, Erika Cooper Prueitt, Lindsay Anne; m. Lila Valerie Levi, May 14, 1986. BSEE, Calif. Inst. Tech., Pasadena, 1958; MSEE, Calif. Inst. Tech., 1959; MS in Physics, U. Ariz., 1962, PhD in Physics, 1964. Prof. physics Calif. State U.-Hayward, 1965-76; staff mem. Los Alamos (N.Mex.) Nat. Lab., 1976—; cons. Lawrence Livermore Nat. Lab., 1966-76. Patentee in field. Fulbright scholar, 1964-65. Mem. Am. Phys. Soc., Sigma Xi. Unitarian. Office: Los Alamos Nat Lab PO Box 1663 Los Alamos NM 87545-0001

COOPER, RON, resource planner; b. Doylestown, Pa., May 2, 1948; s. Frank E. and Jacquelin T. C.; children: Noah, Harper. BA in Econs., Ursinus Coll., 1970; M of Landscape Architecture, U. Mass., 1974. Sr. planner Adirondack Pk. Agy., Ray Brook, N.Y., 1974-77; asst. planning dir. City of Bozeman, Mont., 1977; exec. dir. Flathead Basin Environ. Impact Study, Kalispell, Mont., 1977-82; sr. natural resource aide Senator Max Baucus, Washington, 1983-86; profl. staff mem. Senate Environ. and Pub. Works Com., U.S. Senate, Washington, 1986-89; exec. dir. Yellowstone Ecosystem Study The Wilderness Soc., Bozeman, 1989-91; clean water coord. Nat. Wildlife Fedn., Bozeman, 1991-92, natural resource cons., 1992—. Author: (report) Keeping Clean Waters Clean, 1992, Yellowstone Ecosystem, 1991; contbr. numerous articles to profl. jours. Recipient Citation, Gov. Ted Schwinden, 1983. Home: 1201 S Bozeman Bozeman MT 59715 Office: PO Box 1562 Bozeman MT 59771

COOPER, STEVEN JON, health care management consultant, educator; b. Oct. 19, 1941; B.A., U. Calif., Los Angeles, 1966; M.Ed., Loyola U., 1973; postgrad. Union Sch., 1977—; m. Sharon M. Lepack; children: Robin E., Erik S. Ednl. coordinator dept. radiology Mt. Sinai Hosp. Med. Ctr., Chgo., 1969-72; chmn. dept. radiol. scis. U. Health Scis., Chgo. Med. Sch., VA Hosp., North Chicago, 1972-79; v.p. C&S Inc., Denver, 1980-81; pres. Healthcare Mktg. Corp., Denver, 1981-84; corp. officer Sharon Cooper Assocs. Ltd., Englewood, Colo., 1984—; cons. HEW; lectr. in field. Served with USAF, 1960-64, USAFR, 1964-66. Mem. W.K. Kellogg Found. grantee.

Mem. Am. (mem. edn., curriculum review coms., task force), Ill. (chmn. annual meeting 1976, program Midwest conf., 1977) socs. radiol. tech., Coll. Radiol. Scis., Am. Hosp. Radiology Adminstrs. (mem. edn. com., treas. Midwest region, nat. v.p.), AMA (com. on allied health edn. and accreditation), Kiwanis (charter), Sovereign Order of St. John of Jerusalem, Knights of Malta, Inverness Club (bd. dirs.), Sigma Xi. Author numerous publs. in field. Home: 8522 E Dry Creek Pl Englewood CO 80112-2701 Office: 9085 E Mineral Cir Ste 160 Englewood CO 80112-3418

COOPER, THOMAS MCNEIL, electronics technician; b. Wallace, Idaho, Jan. 14, 1951; s. John William and Jean Eldora (McNeil) C.; m. Lisa Karin Berg, Jan. 14, 1981. BS in Zoology, Coll. of Idaho, 1973; MS in Chemistry, Western Wash. U., 1979; postgrad., Oreg. State U., 1980-91. Chemist North Idaho Phosphate Co., Kellogg, Idaho, 1973-75, Rockwell Internat., Hanford, Wash., 1977; Lakewood mgr. Western Wash. U., Bellingham, 1977-79; sr. rsch. asst. Oreg. State U., Corvallis, 1980-91; sr. electronics technician Caltech Submillimeter Obs., Hilo, Hawaii, 1991—; adviser Helco IRP Adv. Group, Hilo, 1992. Bd. dirs. Naalehu (Hawaii) Main St., Inc., 1992—, Discovery Harbor Community Assn., Waiohinu, Hawaii, 1992—. Mem. Am. Solar Energy Soc., Internat. Solar Energy Soc., Solar Energy Assn. Oreg., Sigma Xi. Home: PO Box 652 Naalehu HI 96772 Office: Caltech Submillimeter Obs 1059 Kilauea Ave Hilo HI 96720

COOPER, WILLIAM CLARK, physician; b. Manila, P.I., June 22, 1912 (father Am. citizen); s. Wibb Earl and Pearl (Herron) C.; MD, U. Va., 1934; MPH magna cum laude, Harvard U., 1958; m. Ethel Katherine Sicha, May 1, 1937; children: Jane Willoughby, William Clark, David Jeremy, Robert Lawrence. Intern, asst. resident U. Hosps., Cleve., 1934-37; commd. asst. surgeon USPHS, 1940, advanced through grades to med. dir., 1952; chief occupational health Field Hqrs., Cin., 1952-57; mem. staff div. occupational health USPHS, Washington, 1957-62, chief div. occupational health, 1962-63; ret., 1963; rsch. physician, prof. occupational health in residence Sch. Pub. Health, U. Calif.-Berkeley, 1963-72; med. cons. AEC, 1964-73; sec.-treas. Tabershaw-Cooper Asso., Inc., 1972-73, v.p., sci. dir., 1973-74; v.p. Equitable Environ. Health Inc., 1974-77; cons. occupational medicine, 1977—. Served to 1st lt. M.C., U.S. Army, 1937-40. Diplomate Am. Bd. Internal Medicine, Am. Bd. Preventive Medicine, Am. Bd. Indsl. Hygiene. Fellow AAAS, Am. Pub. Health Assn., Am. Coll. Chest Physicians, Am. Coll. Occupational Medicine, Royal Soc. Medicine (London); mem. Internat. Commn. on Occupational Health, Western Occupational Med. Assn., Am. Indsl. Hygiene Assn., Cosmos Club. Contbr. articles to profl. jours. Home: 8315 Terrace Dr El Cerrito CA 94530

COOPER, WILLIAM SECORD, information science educator; b. Winnipeg, Man., Can., Nov. 7, 1935; m. Helen Clare Dunlap, July 22, 1964. BA, Principia Coll., 1956; M.Sc., MIT, 1959; Ph.D., U. Calif.-Berkeley, 1964. Alexander von Humboldt scholar U. Erlangen, Germany, 1964-65; asst. prof. info. sci. U. Chgo., 1966-70; assoc. prof. info. sci. U. Calif., Berkeley, 1971-76, prof., 1976—; acting dir. Inst. Library Research, 1970-71; Miller prof. Miller Inst., Berkeley, 1975-76. Hon. research fellow Univ. Coll., London, 1977-78. Mem. AAAS, Assn. Symbolic Logic, Am. Soc. Info. Sci., ACM. Office: U Calif Sch Libr and Info Studies Berkeley CA 94720

COOPERSMITH, FREDRIC S., financial planning executive; b. N.Y.C.; s. Phillip and Ruth L. (Brown) C.; divorced; children: Lisa, Jeffrey, Steven. BS, NYU, MBA. Cert. life underwriter; cert. fin. planner; chartered fin. cons. Cons. fin. planning Englewood, N.J., 1961—; adj. prof. fin. NYU, Rutgers U.; vis. lectr. in fin. planning Wharton Sch. U. Pa. Contbr. articles to profl. jours. Lt. U.S. Army. Named Man of Yr., Nat. C. of C.; recipient Man in Fin. award Finance Club (N.Y.C.). Mem. Internat. Assn. Fin. Planners, Nat. Council Fin. Planners, Nat. Assn. Estate and Fin. Planners, Duke U. Met. Alumni Club, Princeton Club. Club: NYU (N.Y.C.). Lodge: Masons.

COOR, LATTIE FINCH, university president; b. Phoenix, Sept. 26, 1936; s. Lattie F. and Elnora (Witten) C.; m. Ina Fitzhenry, Jan. 18, 1964 (div. 1988); children: William Kendall, Colin Fitzhenry, Farryl MacKenna Witten. AB with high honors (Phelps Dodge scholar), No. Ariz. U., 1958; MA with honors (Univ. scholar, Universal Match Found. fellow, Carnegie Corp. fellow), Washington U., St. Louis, 1960, PhD, 1964; LLD (hon.), Marlboro Coll., 1977, Am. Coll. Greece, 1982, U. Vt., 1991. Adminstrv. asst. to Gov. Mich., 1961-62; asst. to chancellor Washington U., St. Louis, 1963-67, asst. dean Grad. Sch. Arts and Scis., 1967-69, dir. internat. studies, 1967-69, asst. prof. polit. sci., 1967-76, vice chancellor, 1969-74, univ. vice chancellor, 1974-76; pres. U. Vt., Burlington, 1976-89; prof. public affairs and pres. Ariz. State U., Tempe, 1990—; cons. HEW; spl. cons. to commr. U.S. Commn. on Edn., 1971-74; chmn. Commn. on Govtl. Rels., Am. Coun. on Edn., 1976-80; dir. New Eng. Bd. Higher edn., 1976-89; co-chmn. joint com. on health policy Assn. Am. Univs. and Nat. Assn. State Univs. and Land Grant Colls., 1976-89; mem. pres. commn. NCAA, 1987-90, chmn. div. I, 1989. Trustee Am. Coll. Greece. Mem. Nat. Assn. State Univs. and Land Grant Colls. (chmn. bd. dirs. 1991-92), New Eng. Assn. Schs. and Colls. (pres. 1981-82), Am. Coun. on Edn. (bd. dirs. 1991-93). Office: Ariz State U Office of President Tempe AZ 85287

COORS, JEFFREY H., brewery company executive; b. Denver, Feb. 10, 1945; s. Joseph Coors. B.Chem. Engring., Cornell U., 1967, M.Chem. Engring., 1968. With Coors Porcelain Co., 1968-70; with Adolph Coors Co., Golden, Colo., 1970-92, pres., 1985-89; chmn., chief exec. officer Coors Techs. Cos., Golden, 1989-92; pres. ACX Techs., Golden, 1992—. Office: ACX Techs Golden CO 80403

COORS, JOSEPH, brewery director; b. 1917; m. Anne Coors; children: Jeff, Peter, Joseph Jr., Gover, John. Grad., Cornell U., 1939. With Adolph Coors Co., Golden, Colo., v.p., from 1947, vice chmn., 1975, pres., 1977-85, vice chmn., 1982—, chief oper. officer, 1982-87. Former regent U. Colo. Office: Adolph Coors Co BC350 Golden CO 80401

COORS, PETER HANSON, beverage company executive; b. Denver, Sept. 20, 1946; s. Joseph and Holly (Hanson) C.; m. Marilyn Gross, Aug. 23, 1969; children: Melissa, Christien, Carrie Ann, Ashley, Peter, David. B.S. in Idsl. Engring., Cornell U., 1969; M.B.A., U. Denver, 1970. Prodn. trainee, specialist Adolph Coors Co., Golden, Colo., 1970-71, dir. fin. planning, 1971-75, dir. market research, 1975-76, v.p. self distbn., 1976-77, v.p. sales and mktg., 1977-78, sr. v.p. sales and mktg., 1978-82, div. pres. sales, mktg. and adminstrn., 1982-85, pres. brewing div.; pres. Coors Brewing Co., Golden, Colo., 1989—, Coors Distbn. Co., 1976-82, 1976-81, chmn., from 1981, dir.; dir. Adolph Coors Co., 1973—, asst. sec.-treas., 1974-76; dir. CADCO, 1975-85; exec. v.p. Adolph Coors Co., Golden, Colo., 1991—; vice-chmn., CEO Coors Brewing Co., Golden, Colo., 1991—. Bd. dirs. Nat. Wildlife Fedn., 1978-81, Wildlife Legis. Fund, 1987—; hon. bd. dirs. Colo. Spl. Olympics Inc., 1978—; trustee Colo. Outward Bound Sch., 1978—, Adolph Coors Found., Pres.'s Leadership Com., U. Colo., 1978—; chmn. Nat. Commn. on the Future of Regis Coll., 1981-82, chmn. devel. com., 1983—, now trustee. Mem. Nat. Indls. Adv. Council, Opportunities Ctrs. of Am., Young Pres.' Orgn., Ducks Unlimited (nat. trustee 1979, sr. v.p., mem. mgmt. com., exec. com. 1982—, dir. Can. 1982—, pres. 1984-85, chmn. bd. 1986—). Club: Met. Denver Exec. (dir 1979, pres. 1981—). Office: Adolph Coors Co BC350 Golden CO 80401*

COORS, WILLIAM K., brewery executive; b. Golden, Colo., Aug. 11, 1916. BSChemE, Princeton U., 1938, MSChemE, 1939. Pres. Adolph Coors Co., Golden, Colo., from 1956, Chmn. bd., 1970—, also corp. pres. Office: Adolph Coors Co BC350 Golden CO 80401*

COPE, NANCY ELIZABETH, television news producer; b. Woodbury, N.J., Dec. 4, 1952; d. William Fox and Kathryn Florence (Pime) C. B.S., U. Tenn., 1974. News reporter, editor Houston News Svc., 1975-78; news assignment editor Sta. KHOU-TV, Houston, 1978-79; news producer Sta. KTRK-TV, Houston, 1979-86, exec. producer, 1986-89, Sta. KGO-TV, San Francisco, 1989—. Mem. Soc. Profl. Journalists, NOW, Internat. Platform Assn., Radio-TV News Dirs. Assn. Office: Sta KGO-TV 900 Front St San Francisco CA 94111-1427

COPEK, PETER JOSEPH, director humanities center, educator; b. Chgo., May 28, 1945; s. Peter Joseph and Catherine Mary (Balchunas) C. BS, Loyola U., Chgo., 1967; MA, Northwestern U., Evanston, Ill., 1969, PhD, 1973. Asst. prof. English Oreg. State U., Corvallis, 1972-77, assoc. prof. English, 1977—, dir. ctr. for the humanities, 1978—. Contbr. articles to profl. jours. Rockefeller Found. fellow, 1975; Nat. Endowment for the Humanities grantee, 1977-82, NEH grantee, 1984-89, John Ben Snow Trust grantee, 1987. Mem. Modern Lang. Assn., Soc. for Cinema Studies. Office: Oreg State U Humanities Ctr 811 SW Jefferson Ave Corvallis OR 97333-4506

COPELAND, PHILLIPS JEROME, former university administrator, former air force officer; b. Oxnard, Calif., Mar. 22, 1921; s. John Charles and Marion Moffatt) C.; student U. So. Calif., 1947-49; BA, U. Denver, 1956, MA, 1958; grad. Air Command and Staff Coll., 1959, Indsl. Coll. Armed Forces, 1964; m. Alice Janette Lusby, Apr. 26, 1942; children: Janette Ann Copeland Bosserman, Nancy Jo Copeland Briner. Commd. 2d lt. USAAF, 1943, advanced through grades to col. USAF, 1964, pilot 8th Air Force, Eng., 1944-45; various flying and staff assignments, 1945-51; chief joint tng. sect. Hdqrs. Airsouth (NATO), Italy, 1952-54; asst. dir. plans and programs USAF Acad., 1955-58; assigned to joint intelligence, Washington, 1959-61; plans officer Cincpac Joint Staff, Hawaii, 1961-63; staff officer, ops. directorate, then team chief Nat. Mil. Command Center, Joint Chiefs Staff, Washington, 1964-67; dir. plans and programs USAF Adv. Group, also adviser to Vietnamese Air Force, Vietnam, 1967-68; prof. aerospace studies U. So. Calif., L.A., 1968-72, exec. asst. to pres., 1972-73, assoc. dir. office internat. programs, 1973-75, dir. adminstrv. services Coll. Continuing Edn., 1975-82, dir. employee relations, 1982-84. Decorated D.F.C., Bronze Star, Air medal with 3 clusters; Medal of Honor (Vietnam). Mem. Air Force Assn., Order of Daedalians. Home: 81 Cypress Way Palos Verdes Peninsula CA 90274-3416

COPELLO, ANGELO GENE, health services administrator; b. Passaic, N.J., Jan. 27, 1959; s. Angelo F. and Jean Constance (DeLorenzo) C. BA, Eckerd Coll., 1980; MS, U. Tenn., 1984; MDiv, Vanderbilt U., 1984, DDiv, 1985. Clin. social worker, rsch. ethics and social scis. specialist. Dir., asst. prof. AIDS project Vanderbilt U. Med. Sch., Nashville, 1985-90; dir. San Mateo (Calif.) AIDS Prog., 1990—; mem. San Francisco AIDS Planning Coun., 1990—; dir. Fifth Internat. Conf. on AIDS Edn., Budapest, 1991—; mem. ethics com. San Mateo County Gen. Hosp.; conf. chmn. Third Internat. Conf. on AIDS Edn., 1989; mem. FDA Monitoring Bd., 1988. Contbg. author: AIDS: Confronting the Issues, 1989, AIDS Benchbook, 1991; mem. editorial bd. Jour. of AIDS Edn. and Prevention, N.Y.C., 1987—; contbr. articles to profl. jours. Mem. Mayor's Task Force on AIDS, Nashville, 1989, Tenn. AIDS Coun., Nashville, 1985-90, AIDS com./Tenn. Med. Assn., Nashville, 1989; pres. Nashville CARES, Inc., 1987-89; bd. dirs. Alive Hospice, Inc., Nashville, 1989. Recipient Presdl. scholarship Eckerd Coll., St. Petersburg, Fla., 1976, Miller Community Svc. award, 1980, Svc. citation Nashville Mayor's Office, 1990, Svc. award Nashvile CARES, Inc., 1990; nominated Social Worker of Yr. Tenn. chpt. Nat. Assn. Social Workers, 1988. Mem. Internat. Soc. AIDS Edn. (pres. 1988-89), Clin. Ethics Guild, Internat. AIDS Soc., Soc. Health and Human Values, Am. Pub. Health Assn., Calif. Conf. Local AIDS Dirs. (exec. com. 1991—, sec.-treas. 1991-92, pres.-elect 1992-93, pres. 1993—), Calif. Assn. AIDS Agys. (bd. dirs.), Life AIDS Lobby (chair, San Francisco Bay Area aids intergovernmental com., 1993—). Episcopalian. Office: San Mateo County AIDS Program 3700 Edison St San Mateo CA 94403-4496

COPENHAVER, JAMES, performing company executive. Dir. Colo. Symphony Orch., Denver. Office: Colorado Symphony Orchestra 1031 13th St Denver CO 80204*

COPI, IRVING MARMER, philosophy educator; b. Duluth, Minn., July 28, 1917; s. Samuel Bernard and Rose (Marmer) Copilowish; m. Amelia Glaser, Mar. 20, 1941; children: David Marmer, Thomas Russell, William Arthur, Margaret Ruth. B.A., U. Mich., 1938, M.S., 1940, M.A. (Univ. fellow 1946-47), 1947, Ph.D., 1948; postgrad., U. Chgo., 1938-39. Instr. philosophy U. Ill., 1947-48; faculty U. Mich., 1948-69, prof. philosophy, 1958-69, research assoc., 1951-52; research assoc. Engring. Research Inst., 1954-59; research logician Inst. Sci. and Tech., 1960-61; prof. philosophy U. Hawaii, Honolulu, 1969-91; research assoc. U. Calif., Berkeley, 1954; vis. lectr. Air Force U., 1958-66, Georgetown U. Logic Inst., 1960; vis. prof. Princeton, 1959-60, U. Hawaii, 1967; acad. visitor London Sch. Econs., 1975; Cons. Office Naval Research, 1952. Author: Introduction to Logic, 8th edit, 1990, Symbolic Logic, 5th edit, 1979, Introduccion a la Logica, 1962, Introduzione alla Logica, 1965, Theory of Logical Types, 1971, Li-tse Hsueh, 1972, Tarkasastra Ka Paricaya, 1973, Lo-chi-Kai-lun, 1973, Introducao a Logica, 1974, Mavo Lelogika, 1977, Lógica Simbólica, 1979, Einführung in die Logik, Kursenheit 1, 1983, Einführung in die Logik, Kursenheit 2, 1984, Informal Logic, 2d edit., 1992, Einführung in die Logik, Kurseinheit 3, 1987; also numerous essays. Editor: (Plato): Theaetetus, 1949, (with J.A. Gould) Readings in Logic, 1964, 2d edit., 1972, (with R.W. Beard) Essays on Wittgenstein's Tractatus, 1966, (with J.A. Gould) Contemporary Readings in Logical Theory, 1967, Contemporary Philosophical Logic, 1978. Faculty fellow Fund Advancement Edn., 1953-54; Guggenheim fellow, 1955-56; Fulbright sr. fellow, 1975. Mem. Am. Philos. Assn., Assn. Symbolic Logic, Mich. Acad. Letters, Arts and Scis., AAUP (chpt. pres. 1968-69), Phi Beta Kappa, Phi Kappa Phi. Democrat. Jewish (pres. congregation 1962-63). Home: 1618 Kamole St Honolulu HI 96821-1426

COPMAN, LOUIS, radiologist; b. Phila., Jan. 17, 1934; s. Jacob and Eve (Snyder) C.; m. Avera Schuster, June 8, 1958; children: Mark, Linda. BA, U. Pa., 1955, MD, 1959. Diplomate Am. Bd. Radiology; Nat. Bd. Med. Examiners. Commd. ensign Med. Corps USN, 1958; advanced through grades to capt. M.C. USN, 1975; ret.; asst. chief radiology dept. Naval Hosp., Pensacola, Fla., 1966-69; chief radiology dept. Doctors Hosp., Phila., 1969-73; radiologist Mercer Hosp. Ctr., Trenton, N.J., 1973-75; chmn. radiology dept. Naval Hosp., Phila., 1975-84; chief. radiology dept. Naval Med. Clinic, Pearl Harbor, Hawaii, 1984-89; pvt. practice radiologist Honolulu, 1989-92; cons. Radiology Services, Wilmington, Del., 1978-84, Yardley (Pa.) Radiology, 1979-84. Author: The Cuckold, 1974. Recipient Albert Einstein award in Medicine, U. Pa., 1959. Mem. AMA, Assn. Mil. Surgeons of the U.S., Royal Soc. Medicine, Radiol. Soc. N.Am., Am. Coll. Radiology, Photographic Soc. Am., Sherlock Holmes Soc., Phi Beta Kappa, Alpha Omega Alpha. Jewish. Home: PO Box 384767 Waikoloa HI 96738 Office: 68-1771 Makanahele Pl Waikoloa HI 96738-4767

COPPERMAN, WILLIAM H, value engineer, consultant; b. Cleve., Dec. 4, 1932; s. Jack Jason and Ruth (Rollnick) C.; m. Rena June Dorn, Dec. 26, 1954; children: Randy Lee, David Marc. BS, Duquesne U., 1954; MBA, U. So. Calif., L.A., 1962; JD, U. San Fernando, 1977. Cert. value specialist. Corp. mgr., value engr. Hughes Aircraft Co., L.A., 1957-89; pres. Copperman Assocs. in Value Engring., Inc., L.A., 1983—; bd. dirs. Miles Value Found., Washington; cert. bd. SAVE, Chgo., 1986-88. Author books, video tape series in value engring.; contbr. articles to profl. jours. Recipient Outstanding Achievement award U.S. Army, 1986, Value Engring. award Purchasing Mag., Washington, 1987, Achievement in Value Engring. U.S. Army, 1977, 78, 79, 80, 82. Mem. Soc. Am. Value Engrs. (exec. v.p. 1975—). Office: Copperman Assocs in Value Engring PO Box 5488 Playa Del Rey CA 90296

COPPERSMITH, SAM, congressman, lawyer; b. Johnstown, Pa., May 22, 1955; m. Beth Schermer, Aug. 23, 1983; children: Sarah, Benjamin, Louis. AB in Econs. magna cum laude, Harvard U., 1976; JD, Yale Law Sch., 1982. Fgn. svc. officer U.S. Dept. State, Port of Spain, Trinidad, 1977-79; law clk. to Judge William C. Canby Jr. U.S. Ct. Appeals (9th cir.), Phoenix, 1982-83; atty. Sacks, Tierney & Kasen, P.A., Phoenix, 1983-86; asst. to Mayor Terry Goddard City of Phoenix, 1984; atty. Jones, Jury, Short & Mast P.C., Phoenix, 1986-88, Bonnett, Fairbourn & Friedman P.C., Phoenix, 1988-92; mem. 103d Congress from 1st Ariz. Dist., 1993—. Former dir., pres. Planned Parenthood Ctrl. and No. Ariz.; former chair City of Phoenix Bd. of Adjustment; Phoenix Citizens Bond Com., 1988; RPTA Community Forum; City of Phoenix Surface Transp. Com.; former v.p. Greater East Phoenix Neighborhood Assn.; former dir. Ariz. Community Svc. Legal Assistance Found., 1986-89. Mem. Ariz. Bar Assn., Calif. Bar Assn., Maricopa County Bar Assn.,. Democrat. Office: US House of Representatives Washington DC 20515

COPPI, ROBIN ELLEN, nurse; b. Chgo., Dec. 20, 1957; d. Robert Edward and Jane Eloise (Penny) Graefen; m. Stephen Dominick Coppi, Apr. 7, 1984; children: Shelley Ann, Scott Stephen. BSN in Critical Care, Calif. State U., L.A., 1979; postgrad., Chapman U., 1980-81. RN, Calif.; cert. pub. health, Calif., critical care RN, cert. advanced cardiac life support, cert. basic life support. Unit sec. II Foothill Presbyn. Hosp., Glendora, Calif., 1976-78; med./surg. staff nurse Intercommunity Med. Ctr., Covina, Calif., 1978-79, spl. procedures nurse, 1979-81; surg. charge nurse Foothill Presbyn. Hosp., Glendora, Calif., 1981-83; community educator Foothill Community Edn. Ctr., Glendora, 1982-89; intensive care nurse III Foothill Presbyn. Hosp., Glendora, 1983-86, intensive/cardiac care charge nurse, 1986-90, nurse clinician intensive svcs., 1990—; instr. Foothill Community Edn., Glendora, 1982-89; speaker Am. Heart Assn., San Gabriel Valley, 1981—; com. mem. utilization rev., clin. ladder, policy and procedures, Foothill Presbyn. Hosp., 1983—. Editor: (newsletter) Phi-News, 1987-92. Vol. Stephen Ministries, Covina, Calif., 1982-84, Intercommunity Med. Ctr., Covina, 1970-75; advisor Tall Flag unit La Puenta (Calif.) High Sch., 1978-80; deacon Christ Luth. Ch., West Covina, Calif., 1980-82, coun. sec., 1982-84. Scholar Blue Cross of So. Calif., 1979, Inter-Community Aux., Covina, 1979, Alpha Tau Delta, 1979. Mem. AACN, Toastmasters Internat. (treas. 1980-81, sec. 1981-82, 1st place and runner up speaker awards West Covina chpt. 1981, 82, 83), Alpha Tau Delta (chpt. pres. 1984-87, nat. pres. 1991—), Alpha Tau Delta (nat. sec. 1987-91). Office: Foothill Presbyn Hosp Nursing Dept 250 S Grand Ave Glendora CA 91740-4218

COPPIN, ANN STACY, information specialist; b. Pasadena, Mar. 2, 1944; d. Alvin W. and Inez T. (Thomason) Stacy; m. Frederic A. Coppin, July 9, 1969; children—Stacy M., Thomas A. B.S. in Geology, U. Redlands, 1966; M.S. in Geology, N.Mex. Inst. Mining and Tech., 1970; M.L.S., U. Ariz., 1974. Librarian Ariz.-Sonora Desert Mus., Tucson, 1973; supr. tech. info. service Chevron Oil Field Research Co., La Habra, Calif., 1974-92; team leader tech. info. svc. Chevron Petroleum Tech. Co., La Habra, 1992—. Contbr. articles to profl. jours. NDEA fellow, 1968-69; Lunar Sci. Inst. vis. grad. fellow, 1974. Mem. Am. Soc. for Info. Sci., Spl. Libraries Assn., Assn. for Women Geoscientists (v.p. L.A. chpt. 1991), Western Assn. of Map Librs., So. Calif. Tech. Processors Group, Geosci. Info. Soc., Beta Phi Mu. Office: Chevron Petroleum Tech Co 1300 S Beach Blvd La Habra CA 90631-6300

COPPLE, RONALD LLOYD, insurance agent, financial advisor, estate planner; b. Kansas City, Mo., Aug. 4, 1945; s. James Edward and Grace Marie (Snyder) C.; m. Neva G. Craig, Feb. 12, 1966 (div. Apr. 1980); children: Ronald Lloyd Jr., Dawn M.; m. Pamela Ann King, June 2, 1990; children: Cari Casbere, Jessie Casbere. Student, City Coll., Seattle, 1973-77, U. Wash., 1977-79. Registered health underwriter. Electrician Boeing Co., Renton, Wash., 1966-67; claims investigator Retail Credit Co., Seattle, 1967-70; agt., advisor Mut. of Omaha, Mercer Island, Wash., 1970—. With USN, 1963-66, Vietnam. Decorated Bronze Star, Purple Heart with three clusters, Spl. Combat medal with one cluster; named Citizen of Yr. Federal Way (Wash.) Soccer Assn., 1981; recipient Pres.'s award Federal Way Referees' Assn., 1991, Nat. Quality award Life Underwriters Assn., Wash., 1976, 78, 80, 82, 85, 87, 88, Health Ins. Quality award, 1989, 90, 91. Fellow Life Underwriters Tng. Coun.; mem. Wash. State Life Underwriters (chmn. security 1989-90, health 1990—), Cascade Life Underwriters (membership com. 1989—), Tacoma, Pierce Co. Life Underwriters, Nat. Health Underwriters Assn. (Quality Achievement awards 1984, 87, 88), U.S. Youth Soccer Assn. (regional referee 1984-89, tournament coord. 1986-87, chmn. workshop 1986, nat. championships 1986-87), Washington State Youth Soccer Assn. (bldg. chmn. 1991—, state chmn. 1986—, jud. chmn. 1985—, Outstanding Chmn. award 1989, Pres. award 1991, chmn. workshop 1986—0, Totem Coccer Club (coach, v.p. 1975-82). Home: 29113 32d Pl S Auburn WA 98001

COPPLE, WILLIAM PERRY, judge; b. Holtville, Calif., Oct. 3, 1916; s. Perry and Euphie (Williams) C.; m. Nancy Matson, May 30, 1981; children by previous marriage—Virginia (Mrs. Richard Schilke), Leonard W., Steven D. A.B., U. Calif. at Berkeley, 1949, LL.B., 1951. Bar: Ariz. 1952. Various positions with U.S. Govt., also pvt. employers, 1936-48; practice in Yuma, Ariz., 1952-65; U.S. dist. atty. Dist. Ariz., Phoenix, 1965-66; judge U.S. Dist. Ct. Dist. Ariz., 1966—; Mem. Ariz. Hwy. Commn., 1955-58, Gov. Ariz. Com Fourteen for Colo. River, 1963-65; chmn. Yuma County Democratic Central Com., 1953-54, 59-60. Mem. Am. Bar Assn. Office: US Dist Ct US Courthouse & Fed Bldg 230 N 1st Ave Ste 7025 Phoenix AZ 85025-0077

COPPOCK, RICHARD MILES, nonprofit association administrator; b. Salem, Ohio, Mar. 17, 1938; s. Guy Lamar and Helen Angeline (Johnston) C.; m. Rita Mae McArtor, June 20, 1961 (div. 1973); 1 child, Carole; m. Trelma Anne Kubacak, Nov. 21, 1973; children: James, Lori. BS, USAF Acad., 1961; MSME, U. Colo., 1969. Commd. 2d lt. USAF, 1961, advanced through grades to lt. col., 1983, ret., 1983; exec. v.p., treas. Assn. Grads. USAF Acad., Inc., Colo., 1983—; bd. dirs. Air Acad. Nat. Bank, Colo.; v.p. Nat. Assns. in Colorado Springs. Decorated D.F.C., Air medal; named Outstanding Alumnus Salem High Sch., 1980. Mem. Colorado Springs C. of C. (mil. affairs coun. 1985-90), VFW (life), Am. Legion, Air Force Assn., Ret. Officers Assn., Elks. Republican. Methodist. Home: 2513 Mirror Lake Ct Colorado Springs CO 80919-3515 Office: USAF Acad Assn Grads Ste 100 3116 Academy Dr USAF Academy CO 80840-4475

COPPOLA, FRANCIS FORD, director, producer, film writer; b. Detroit, Apr. 7, 1939; s. Carmine C.; m. Eleanor Neil; children: Gian-Carlo (dec.), Roman, Sofia. B.A., Hofstra U., 1958; Master of Cinema, UCLA, 1968. Pub. mag. San Francisco, 1975-76. Artistic dir., Zoetrope Studios.; dir. motion pictures including Dementia 13, 1964, You're a Big Boy Now, 1967, Finian's Rainbow, 1968, The Rain People, 1969, One from the Heart, 1981; writer: motion pictures This Property Is Condemned, 1966, Reflections In a Golden Eye, 1967, The Rain People, 1969, Is Paris Burning, 1966, Patton, 1970, The Great Gatsby, 1974; writer, producer and dir. motion pictures The Godfather (Acad. awards for Best Screenplay and Best Picture, nominee for Best Dir., Film Dir.'s award Dirs. Guild Am. 1972), The Godfather, Part II, 1974 (Acad. awards for Best Screenplay, Best Dir. and Best Picture), The Conversation, 1974 (Golden Palm award Cannes Film Festival 1974), Apocalypse Now, 1979, Rumble Fish, 1983; producer TV movie The People; producer, dir. motion picture The Outsiders, 1983; producer: motion pictures THX 1138, 1971, The Escape Artist, 1982, The Black Stallion Returns, 1983; exec. producer motion picture Black Stallion, 1979; exec. producer motion picture Hammett; dir., co-screenwriter The Cotton Club, 1984; co-exec. producer Mishima, 1985; dir. Peggy Sue Got Married, 1986, Gardens of Stone, 1987, Tucker: The Man and His Dream, 1988, The Godfather, Part III (also writer), 1990, Bram Stoker's Dracula, 1992; dir. play Private Lives, opera The Visit; exec. producer motion picture Lionheart; dir., co-screenwriter Life Without Zoe segment in film New York Stories, 1990. Mem. Dirs. Guild Am. Inc. Office: Am Zoetrope 916 Kearny St San Francisco CA 94133-5138

CORAM, DAVID JAMES, protective services official; b. San Diego, Oct. 17, 1962; s. Thomas Harry and Joan Catherine (Rueter) C.; m. Irma Elizabeth Aquino, Jan. 14, 1989 (dec. July 1992); children: Catherine May, Corinna Briann. AS with honors, Miramar Coll., 1989; honor grad. police acad. basic tng., Southwestern Coll., 1986. Computer oper. Cubic Data Systems, San Diego, 1981-83, Electronic Data Systems, San Diego, 1983-84; ct. svc. officer San Diego County Marshal, 1985-86, deputy marshal, 1986—. Mediator San Diego Community Mediation Ctr., 1990—. Awarded Gold medal soccer Ariz. Police Olympics, 1990, 91, Silver medal, 1993, Marksmanship award San Diego Marshal, Outstanding Young Men of Am. award, 1989. Mem. Calif. State Marshal's Assn., San Diego County Marshal's Assn. (parliamentarian 1988, dir. 1989-91, 93), Soc. Profls. in Dispute Resolution (local and nat.), Nat. Physique Com., N.Am. Natural Bodybuilding Assn. Republican. Office: San Diego County Marshal 220 W Broadway San Diego CA 92101

CORAY, JEFFREY WARREN, assistant principal, instructor; b. Chgo., July 16, 1958; s. Warren George and Rose (Paul) C. Student, U. Calif., Berkeley, 1976-77; BA, Occidental Coll., 1980. Instr. Damien High Sch., La

Verne, Calif., 1982—, dir. student activities, 1983-87, chair social sci. dept., 1986-88, asst. prin. student activities, 1987-88, asst. prin. acad. affairs, instr. social sci., 1988—; cons. advanced placement program N.J. Coll. Bd., 1987—, exam reader, 1988—. Mem. Omicron Delta Epsilon. Republican. Roman Catholic. Home: PO Box 116 La Verne CA 91750-0116 Office: Damien High Sch 2280 N Damien Ave La Verne CA 91750-5116

CORBETT, KEVIN PATRICK, petroleum geologist; b. L.A., Apr. 24, 1956; s. Max Worrell and Charlotte Winifred (Gary) C.; m. Cynthia D. Miller, Apr. 21, 1984. BS in Geology, U. Alaska, 1979; MS in Geology, Tex. A&M U., 1982; PhD in Geology, UCLA, 1989. Registered geologist, Calif. Geologist Tex. Oil & Gas Corp., Sacramento, Calif., 1982-84; instr. Pasadena (Calif.) City Coll., 1985-87; asst. prof. Weber State U., Ogden, Utah, 1988-90; advanced rsch. geologist Marathon Oil Co., Littleton, Colo., 1990—. Contbr. articles to profl. jours. Fellow Am. Fedn. Mineralogical Soc., 1985-87; Penrose Rsch. grantee, 1986; Wayne Lowell Meml. Geology scholar Pasadena City Coll., 1976. Mem. Geol. Soc. Am., Am. Geophys. Union, Am. Assn. Petroleum Geologists. Democrat. Office: Marathon Oil Co Petroleum Tech Ctr PO Box 269 Littleton CO 80160-0269

CORBETT, LORI CHRISTINE, structural drafting company executive; b. Soda Springs, Idaho, Sept. 30, 1958; d. William Brent Corbett and Willadean (Woolsey) Noe. Student, Idaho State U., 1978. Draftsman EG&G Idaho, INEL Site, 1978-79; design draftsman Bithell Engring., Pocatello, Idaho, 1979-81; structural detailer Brower Detailing, Pocatello, 1981, Intermountain Detailers, Pocatello, 1981-87; owner, mgr. Corbett Structural, Inc., St. Anthony, Idaho, 1988—. Exhibited sculptures in group shows, Pacific Flyway Decoy Assn., Sacramento, Calif., 1991 (2d place award), Idaho Woodcarving Guild, Boise, 1992 (1st and best in show awards), First of Am. Ducks Unltd., Clare, Mich., carvings featured in PBS TV Series Outdoor Idaho, 1991. Office: 115 E Main St Ste 10 Saint Anthony ID 83445

CORBOY, JAMES MCNALLY, investment banker; b. Erie, Pa., Nov. 3, 1940; s. James Thomas and Dorothy Jane (Schluraff) C. ; m. Suzanne Shaver, July 23, 1965; children: Shannon, James McNally. BA, Allegheny Coll., 1962; MBA, U. Colo., 1986. Sales staff Boettcher & Co., Denver, 1964-70; sales staff Blyth Eastman Dillon, Denver and Chgo., 1970-74, William Blair & Co., Chgo., 1974-77; mgr. corp. bond dept. Boettcher & Co., Denver, 1977-79; ptnr. in charge William Blair & Co., Denver, 1979-86; first v.p. Stifel, Nicolaus & Co., Denver, 1986-88; pres., chief exec. officer J.M. Corboy, Inc., Denver, 1988—; gen. ptnr. Corboy & Co., L.P.; pres., chief exec. officer Telluride (Colo.) Aero Ctr., Inc. With USMC, 1962-67. Mem. Securities Industry Assn., Nat. Assn. Securities Dealers (bd. arbitrators), Am. Arbitration Assn. (bd. arbitrators), Country Club at Castle Pines, Met. Club. Republican. Presbyterian. Home: Castle Pines Village 4212 Morningstar Dr Castle Rock CO 80104 Office: 5251 DTC Pkwy Ste 1200 Englewood CO 80111

CORBRIDGE, JAMES NOEL, JR., chancellor, educator; b. Mineola, N.Y., May 27, 1934; s. James Noel Sr. and Edna (Springer) C.; children: Loren, Stuart. AB, Brown U., 1955; LLB, Yale U., 1963. Assoc. Lord, Day & Lord, N.Y.C., 1963-65; asst. prof. law U. Colo., Boulder, 1965-67, assoc. prof., 1967-73, prof., 1973—, v.p. student affairs, 1970-72, v.p. student and minority affairs, 1972-74, vice chancellor acad. affairs, 1974-77, interim vice chancellor acad. services, 1979-81, acting vice chancellor acad. affairs, 1986, chancellor, 1986—; vis. scholar Inst. for Advanced Legal Studies U. London, 1977, 85, Univ. Linkoping, Sweden, 1985. Contbr. articles to profl. jours. Served to lt. (j.g.) USNR, 1957-60. Mem. Colo. Bar Assn., Boulder County Bar Assn., Internat. Assn. Water Lawyers, Internat. Water Resources Assn. Episcopalian. Club: Boulder Country. Home: 7229 Four Rivers Rd Boulder CO 80301-3737 Office: U Colo Campus Box 17 Boulder CO 80309

CORCIA, VITO PETER, insurance company executive; b. Orange, N.J., Feb. 11, 1938; s. Peter Vito and Pauline (Uricoli) C.; 1 child, Peter Anthony; m. Joyce Elizabeth Stripko, Aug. 21, 1976. BS in Mgmt., Rutgers U., 1973; postgrad., Lincoln U., 1978-80. Supr. home office Fireman's Fund Ins. Co., San Francisco, 1970-82; claims cons. Sunset Claims Svc., San Francisco, 1982-90; instr. claims seminars Ins. Edn. Assn., San Francisco, 1982—; supr. liability claims Wausau Ins., San Francisco, 1990—; arbitration panelist Interco. Arbitration, San Francisco, 1982—; instr. computer seminar Wausau (Wis.) Ins., 1992. Author legal briefs, 1982—; author newsletter Gen. Topics, 1991; author mag. Work Simplification, 1992. Sgt. U.S. Army, 1962-68. Mem. KC (warden 1978—), Am. Numismatic Assn., Rutgers Alumni Assn., Delta Sigma Pi (life). Republican. Roman Catholic. Office: Wausau Ins Co 425 Market St San Francisco CA 94120-7847

CORDER, LOREN DAVID (ZEKE), quality assurance engineer; b. Nampa, Idaho, Sept. 9, 1949; s. H. Burton and E. Eldora (Crill) C.; m. Sheryl Ann Kinney, 1968 (div. 1971); m. Charlene Louise Brown, 1972; children: Jesse A., Nathaniel A., Quintan A., Dana A. (dec.). Cert., USAF Electronics, Chanute AFB, Ill., 1970, Ctr. For Employment Tng., Nampa, 1980. Fabrication process engr. Micron Semiconductor Inc., Boise, Idaho, 1981-83; assembly engr. Micron Tech., Inc., Boise, Idaho, 1983-85, quality assurance engr., 1986—; trustee Idaho Migrant Coun., Boise, 1980-82; mem. adv. bd. Ctr. For Employment Tng., Nampa, 1982-90. Contbr. articles to Surface Mt. Tech., Test and Measurement World and Semiconductor Internat. With USAF, 1969-72. Mem. AAAS, ASME (affiliate), EOS/ESD Assn., Am. Soc. Metals Internat., Inst. Environ. Scis. (sr.), Soc. Mfg. Engrs., Planetary Soc., Foresters, Treasure Valley Antique Power Assn., Early Day Gas Engine and Tractor Assn., Inc. Office: Micron Semiconductor Inc 2805 E Columbia Rd # 502 Boise ID 83706-9698

CORDER, RODNEY JOE, computer engineer; b. Baldwin Park, Calif., Oct. 10, 1962; s. Jimmie Dean and Ruby Jo (Morrison) C.; m. Kathi Mae Blakley, Apr. 11, 1987; children: Brittany Rose Corder, Brian James Corder. BSEE, Calif. State Poly. U., Pomona, 1984. Technician aide Jet Propulsion Lab., Pasadena, Calif., 1981-83; engr. Rockwell Internat. Semiconductor, Newport Beach, Calif., 1983-88; dir. engring. Togai Infralogic Inc., Irvine, Calif., 1988-90; v.p. of engring. New Media Corp., Irvine, 1991—; engring. cons. ITT Cannon, Santa Ana, Calif., 1990-91, TRW Electronic Products, Inc., San Luis Obispo, Calif., 1990-91; bd. dirs. New Media Corp., Irvine, 1990—, Ickety, Ackety, Oop, Inc., Rancho Cucamonga, Calif., 1991—. Patentee in field. Office: New Media Corp B-101 15375 Barranca Pkwy Irvine CA 92718

CORDES, FAUNO LANCASTER, retired nuclear medicine technologist; b. San Francisco, Nov. 3, 1927; d. Frederick Carl and Faun-Hope (Lancaster) C. AA, U. Calif. Berkeley, 1946, BA in Psychology, 1948; MA in Geography, San Francisco State U., 1991. Chief hematology rsch. technician NIH and U. Calif. Lab. of Exptl. Oncology, San Francisco, 1949-53, City of Hope Med. Ctr., Duarte, Calif., 1953-59; nuclear medicine technologist Mt. Zion Hosp., U. Calif., San Francisco, 1959-92; exec. com. Soc. Nuclear Medicine, No. Calif. Tech. Soc., San Francisco, 1968-81. Contbr. over 31 articles to profl. publs. Mem. AAAS, Soc. Nuclear Medicine, Soc. Woman Geographers, Calif. Acad. Scis., Antarctican Soc., Gleeson Libr. Assocs., Sigma Xi. Home: 355 Arballo Dr San Francisco CA 94132

CORDOVA, ALEXANDER M., city clerk; b. Phoenix, June 22, 1943; s. Alexander A. and Violet (Moreno) C.; m. Becky Cordova, June 28, 1969 (div. 1976); m. Joyce Hendricks, June 12, 1982. Student, Ariz. State U., 1962, Phoenix Coll., 1965. Cert. mcpl. clk. Aid City of Phoenix, 1965-67, agt. I, 1967-70, oper. analyst, 1970-72, election supr., 1974-80, elections and gen. svcs. adminstr., 1980-86, chief dep. city clk., 1986—. Mem. Internat. Right of Way Assn., 1975-85, Statewide Election Reform, 1987-88. With USN, 1962-64. Mem. Ariz. Mcpl. Clks., Internat. Inst. Mcpl. Clks., Am. Mgrs. Assn., Internat. Assn. County Recorders, Election Ofcls. and Treas., Am. Legion. Roman Catholic. Office: City of Phoenix 251 W Washington Phoenix AZ 85254

CORDOVA, DONALD E., lawyer; b. Trinidad, Colo., Jan. 26, 1938. AB, Regis Coll., 1961; JD, U. Colo., 1964. Bar: Colo. 1964. Asst. U.S. atty. Colo., 1964-68, mem. Denver County Ct. Judicial Selection Commn., 1968-71; ptnr. Cordova, DeMoulin, Harris & Mellon, P.C., Denver; judge U.S. Bankruptcy Ct., Denver. Mem. ABA (mem. litigation sect.), Denver Bar Assn. (v.p. 1981-82, pres. 1987-88) Colo. Bar Assn. (v.p. 1978-79, mem. bd. govs 1970-72, 80-82, 86-89, Supreme Ct. com. on pattern jury instructions 1987-90), Fedn. of Ins. and Corp. Counsel, Acad. of Hosp. Attys., Colo. Def. Lawyers Assn., Am. Soc. Law and Medicine, Hispanic Bar Assn. (pres. 1984), Denver Law Club (pres. 1977-78). Office: US Custom House 721 19th St Denver CO 80202-2504

CORDRAY, RICHARD LYNN, electronics engineering executive; b. Tulsa, Jan. 27, 1952; s. Austin Edwin and Barbara Lee (Kline) C.; m. Barbara Scott Lamb, May 9, 1975; children: Michael Scott, Carol Ann. BS in Elec. Engring., Rice U., 1974, MEE, 1975, PhD, 1978. Rsch. engr. Tektronix, Inc., Beaverton, Oreg., 1978-81, program mgr., 1981; v.p. N.W. Instrument Systems, Beaverton, 1981-84; program mgr. Intel, Hillsboro, Oreg., 1984-85, Spacelabs, Inc., Redmond, Wash., 1985-89; pres. Image Tech., Redmond, 1989—. Bd. dirs. English Hill Homeowners Assn., Redmond, 1987-89. Mem. IEEE, Soc. for Info. Display. Home: 17613 NE 142nd St Redmond WA 98052-1237 Office: Image Tech 2739 152d Ave NE Redmond WA 98052

CORIELL, BRUCE RICHARD, clergyman, chaplain; b. Millington, N.J., Aug. 15, 1956; s. Richard and Kathleen Veronica (Franolich) C.; m. Eleanor Ann Sents, Aug. 19, 1978; children: Richard Bruce, Alyssa Kathleen. BA, Wheaton (Ill.) Coll., 1978; MDiv, Princeton Theol. Sem., 1981; postgrad., Vanderbilt U., 1989. Ordained to ministry Am. Bapt. Ch., 1981. Assoc. chaplain DePauw U., Greencastle, Ind., 1981-85; asst. chaplain Vanderbilt U., Nashville, 1986-88; coll. chaplain Colo. Coll., Colorado Springs, 1988—. Chair Martin Luther King, Jr. Holiday Com., Colorado Springs, 1988—; bd. dirs. Gay and Lesbian Community Ctr., Colorado Springs, 1992, San Luis Valley Christian Community Svcs., 1990-91, United Way, others; mem. Pikes Peak Peace and Justice Commn., Colorado Springs, 1991—. Harold Vanderbilt scholar, 1985-88. Mem. Am. Acad. Religion, Nat. Assn. Coll. and Univ. Chaplains, Assn. Coll. and Univ. Religious Affairs (exec. bd.). Office: Colo Coll Shove Meml Chapel Colorado Springs CO 80903

CORK, RANDALL CHARLES, anesthesiology educator; b. St. Paul, Oct. 6, 1948; s. Willis Lawson and Ruth (Plotz) C.; m. Patricia Bee (dec. Sept. 1990); 1 child, Malcolm; m. Dixie Holmes. BS in Engring., Ariz. State U., 1970, MS in Engring., 1972, PhD, 1974; MD, U. Ariz., 1977. Systems engr. Honeywell Info. Systems, Phoenix, 1970-74; asst. prof. U. Ariz. Dept. Anesthesiology, Tucson, 1980-86, assoc. prof., 1986-93; prof. dept. anesthesiology La. State U., New Orleans, 1993—; lectr. dept. anesthesiology U. Zimbabwe, Harare, 1983-84; sect. head cardiac anesthesia Tucson VA Med. Ctr., 1991-93. Contbr. chtps. to books and articles to profl. jours. Cons. physician Tucson Spl. Olympics, 1991-93. Rsch. grantee Am. Cancer Soc., Janssen Pharm., 1984-85, Bristol Labs., 1984-85, Organin, 1984-85, Am. Heart Assn., 1985-86, Stuart Pharms., 1987-88, Hoffman-LaRoche, 1987-88, DuPont Pharms., 1989-90, Glaxo Inc., 1990-91, 91-92, Maruishi Pharms. Co., 1990-91, Anaquest, 1991-92, Astra Pharms., 1991-92. Fellow Am. Coll. Angiology; mem. AMA, Am. Soc. Anesthesiologists, Internat. Anesthesia Rsch. Soc., Ariz. State Soc. Anesthesiologists, N.Y. Acad. Scis., Soc. Cardiovascular Anesthesiologists, Soc. Critical Care Medicine, Soc. Ambulatory Anesthesia, U. Oxford Anesthesic Rsch. Soc.

CORLESS, DOROTHY ALICE, nurse educator; b. Reno, Nev., May 28, 1943; d. John Ludwig and Vera Leach (Wilson) Adams; children: James Lawrence Jr., Dorothy Adele. RN, St. Luke's Sch. Nursing, 1964. Flight nurse Lisle Air Svc., Fresno, 1968-71; author, adminstr. FEMA/NIMH Disaster Grants Fresno County Mental Health Dept., 1970—; pvt. practice mental health nurse Fresno, Calif., 1972—. Maj. USAFR, 1972—. Mem. NAFE, Forensic Mental Health Assn. Calif. Peace Officer's Assn. Home: 2890 Huntington Blvd Apt 161 Fresno CA 93721-2355 Office: Fresno County Health Dept PO Box 11867 Fresno CA 93775

CORMACK, RICHARD LOWELL, environmental specialist; b. Chanute, Kans., Mar. 9, 1948; s. Francis Lowell and Virginia Mae (Roseberry) C.; m. Fumi Matsumoto, June 5, 1985; 1 child, Bryan Toshio. BA in Chemistry, Ottawa (Kans.) U., 1966; MS in Environ. Quality Sci., U. Alaska, 1980. Water resources planner Tanan Chiefs Conf., Fairbanks, Alaska, 1979-80; environ. specialist Alaska Dept. Environ. Conservation, Juneau, 1980—. Home: PO Box 34736 Juneau AK 99803 Office: Alaska Dept Environ Conservation PO Box 0 Juneau AK 99801

CORMACK, WILLIAM MACINTOSH, grain exporting company executive; b. Bklyn., Aug. 16, 1941; s. David Charles Cormack and Catherine T. (Balmes) Finneran; m. Maryann Cyr, Oct. 6, 1962; children: Debra Ann, Colleen Michelle. Student, Hofstra U., 1959-60, Pace U., 1960-62. With Meadowbrook Nat. Bank, Garden City, N.Y., 1958-61; with Louis Dreyfus Corp., N.Y.C., 1961-64, Kansas City, Mo., 1964-68, Portland, Oreg., 1968-71; v.p. United Grain Corp., Portland, 1971-85, exec. v.p., 1985-87, pres., cheif exec. officer, 1987—; bd. dirs. Portland Merchants Exchange, Nat. Grain Trade Coun. Chmn. World Trade Club, 1990, Oreg. Trade Program, 1987-89; v.p. TEGMA, 1992-93; active Terminal Elev. Grain Merchants Assn., Edgefield Childrens Ctr. Democrat. Roman Catholic. Home: 13525 SW Hyland Park Ct Beaverton OR 97005-5635 Office: United Grain Corp 200 SW Market St Ste 1700 Portland OR 97201-5794

CORMIE, DONALD MERCER, investment company executive; b. Edmonton, Alta., Can., July 24, 1922; s. George Mills and Mildred (Mercer) C.; m. Eivor Elisabeth Ekstrom, June 8, 1946; children: John Mills, Donald Robert, Allison Barbara, James Mercer, Neil Brian, Buce George, Eivor, Robert. BA, U. Alta., 1944, LLB, 1945; LLM, Harvard U., 1946. Bar: Alta. 1947. Queens counsel, 1964; sessional instr. faculty law U. Alta., 1947-53; sr. ptnr. Cormie, Kennedy, Edmonton, Barristers, 1954-87; instr. real estate law Dept. of Extension, U. Alta., 1958-64; pres., bd. dirs. Collective Securities, Ltd., Cormie Ranch, Inc., Sea Investors Corp.; With Can. Mcht. Marine, 1943-44. Recipient Judge Green Silver medal in law. Mem. Law Soc. Alta., Dean's Coun. of 100 Ariz. State U., World Bus. Coun., Chief Execs. Forum (bd. dirs. 1976-79), Can. Bar Assn. (mem. coun. 1961-76, chmn. adminstrv. law com. 1963-66, chmn. taxation 1972-82, v.p. Alta. 1968-69). Home: 5101 N Casa Blanca # 314 Scottsdale AZ 85253 Office: 10405 Jasper Ave # 216-21, Edmonton, AB Canada T5J 3S2

CORMIER, MARK STEPHEN, poet, philosopher; b. Dover, Del., Nov. 25, 1960; s. Rene Victor and Margaret Mary (Moreau) C. AB, Dartmouth Coll., 1982. With Pacific Stock Exch., San Francisco, 1983—; activist Clamor Press, San Francisco, 1986—; drummer One Mike Stand; tchr. Princeton Rev. Author: (books) Homespun Threads, 1986, I Hear a Tear, 1987; editor : (books) Dr. Irony, 1986, 26 Flowers in the Alphabet, 1988; moderator Café Babar Open Poetry, 1986-88; writer San Francisco Examiner, 1989; participant Mad Dog in Fog roundtable, 1988—, House of Shield Bull Session, 1989—. Home: 428 Haight St San Francisco CA 94117-3506 Office: Pacific Stock Exch 220 Bush St San Francisco CA 94104-3502

CORNABY, KAY STERLING, lawyer, former state senator; b. Spanish Fork, Utah, Jan. 14, 1936; s. Sterling A. and Hilda G. C.; m. Linda Rasmussen, July 23, 1965; children: Alyse, Derek, Tara, Heather, Brandon. AB, Brigham Young U., 1960; postgrad. law Heidelberg (Ger.), 1961-63; JD, Harvard U., 1966. Bar: N.Y. 1967, Utah 1969, U.S. Patent and Trademark Office 1967. Assoc. Brumbaugh, Graves, Donahue & Raymond, N.Y.C., 1966-69; ptnr. Mallinckrodt & Cornaby, Salt Lake City, 1969-72; sole practice, Salt Lake City, 1972-85; mem. Utah State Senate, 1977-91, majority leader, 1983-84; shareholder Jones, Waldo, Holbrook & McDonough, Salt Lake City, 1985—; mem. adv. coun. Salt Lake Dist. SBA, 1984-91. Mem. Nat. Commn. on Uniform State Laws, 1988—; mem. adv. bd. U. Mich. Ctr. For Study Youth Policy, 1990—, Utah State Jud. Conduct Commn., 1983-91, chmn. 1984-85; bd. dirs. KUED-KUER Pub. TV and Radio, 1982—; bd. dirs. Salt Lake Conv. and Visitors Bur., 1985—. Mem. New York Bar, Utah Bar, Utah Harvard Alumni Assn. (pres. 1977-79), Harvard U. Law Sch. Alumni Assn. (v.p. 1979—); Alta Club. Office: Jones Waldo Holbrook & McDonough 1500 1st Interstate Pla 170 S Main St Salt Lake City UT 84101-1605

CORNELIUS, MARION EDNA, biologist, educator; b. Aurora, Mo., Mar. 10, 1930; d. Delmar Marion and Bessie Orine (Walters) Standridge; m. Robert Andrew Cornelius, Sept. 4, 1949; children: David Andrew, Deborah Ruth, Elizabeth Diana. BSSE, John Brown U., 1952; MS, Kans. State Tchrs. Coll., 1963; EdD, U. Ariz., 1980. Tchr. biol. sci. and home econ. John Brown Mil. Acad., Ark., 1952-55, Springdale (Ark.) High Sch., 1955-56, Stella (Mo.) High Sch., 1956-58, Goodman (Mo.) High Sch., 1958-60, Gorin (Mo.) High Sch., 1960-61; tchr. biol. sci. Southeast High Sch., Kansas City, Mo., 1961-70; prof. biol. sci. Cen. Ariz. Coll., Coolidge, 1970—; cons. Casa Grande (Ariz.) Counseling, 1970—; child birth educator Local Hosps., Casa Grande, 1972—. Author: Teachers Guide for Green Version BSCS Biology, 1969, 13 Teaching Modules for Physiology Anatomy, 1980, Oral Individual Testing: Content Comprehension, 1980, Audio-Video Tape - Gaming and Simulations, 1991. Named Outstanding 2 Yr. Coll. Biologist in Nation, Nat. Assn. Biology Tchrs., 1992, Master Tchr., Nisod, 1991. Mem. NSTA (awards com. 1988-89), State Curriculum Coordination Com., Ariz. Biology Conf. (pres. 1979-80), Sci. Tchrs. Mo. (pres. 1968-70), Kansas City Tchrs. Assn. (pres. 1964-68). Republican. Baptist. Home: 842 E Palm Parke Cir Casa Grande AZ 85222-2112 Office: Cen Ariz Coll 8470 N Overfield Rd Coolidge AZ 85228-9030

CORNWALL, JOHN MICHAEL, physics educator, consultant, researcher; b. Denver, Aug. 19, 1934; s. Paul Bakewell and Dorothy (Zitkowski) C.; m. Ingrid Linderos, Oct. 16, 1965. AB, Harvard U., 1956; MS, U. Denver, 1959; PhD, U. Calif., 1962. NSF postdoctoral fellow Calif. Inst. Tech., Pasadena, 1962-63; mem. Inst. Advanced Study, Princeton, N.J., 1963-65; prof. physics UCLA, 1965—; vis. prof. Niels Bohr Inst., Copenhagen, 1968-69, Inst. de Physique Nucléaire, Paris, 1973-74, MIT, 1974, 87, Rockefeller U., N.Y.C., 1988; cons. Inst. Theoretical Physics, Santa Barbara, Calif., 1979-80, 82, bd. dirs., 1979-83; assoc. Ctr. Internat./Strategic Affairs, UCLA, 1987—; cons. MITRE Corp., Aerospace Corp., Los Alamos Nat. Labs.; mem. dir's. adv. com. Lawrence Livermore Labs., 1991—; mem. Def. Sci. Bd., 1992—. Author: (with others) Academic Press Ency. of Science and Technology, other encys. and books; contbr. numerous articles to profl. jours. With. U.S. Army, 1956-58. Grantee NSF, NASA; NSF pre/postdoctoral fellow 1960-63, A.P. Sloan fellow, 1967-71. Mem. Am. Phys. Soc., Am. Geophys. Union, N.Y. Acad. Sci. Office: UCLA Dept Physics Los Angeles CA 90024

CORNWALL, KENT NEELEY, architect; b. Salt Lake City, Feb. 26, 1954; s. John Shril and Lenore Elizabeth (Neeley) C.; m. Susan Hodgkinson, June 19, 1979; children: Jason Spencer, Robert Kent, Kathryn Sue, Jeffery Melvin, Rachel Elizabeth, Sarah Lehn. BA cum laude, Calif. Polytechnic Inst., 1979. Lic. profl. architect, Calif. Draftsman Cornwall Assoc., Inc., Pasadena, Calif., 1975-86, architect, v.p., 1986-90; pres. Cornwall Assocs., Pasadena, Calif., 1991—; cons. in field, Monrovia, Calif., 1984—. Active Boy Scouts Am. Mem. AIA, Monrovia Preservation Soc., Nat. Hist. Trust. Republican. Mem. LDS Ch. Office: Cornwall Assocs Inc 234 N El Molino Ave Pasadena CA 91101

CORNYN, JOHN EUGENE, III, management consultant; b. Evanston, Ill., May 5, 1945; s. John Eugene and Virginia Ryder (Shannahan) C.; m. Patricia R. Benner, July 27, 1992; 1 child, Kelly. B.S. in Hotel and Restaurant Adminstrn., Okla. State U., 1968. Mgr. Indian Trail Restaurant, Winnetka, Ill., 1970-71; employee services mgr. Zenith Corp., Chgo., 1971-72; mgr. Red Lion Corp., Portland, Oreg., 1973; cons. Pannell, Kerr, Forster, Chgo., 1973-75; prin., ptnr. The Cornyn Fasano Group, Portland, 1976—; v.p. Seven Seas, Inc., Winnetka, Ill., 1978—, All Seas, Inc., Winneka, 1980—. Served to 1st lt. U.S. Army, 1968-70. Mem. Foodservice Cons. Soc. Internat. (chmn. mgmt. cons. com. 1983—), Inst. Mgmt. Cons. Republican. Club: Portland City. Home: 3350 NE Holladay St Portland OR 97232-2533 Office: The Cornyn Fasano Group 917 SW Oak St Ste 312 Portland OR 97205-2806

CORRADINI, DEEDEE, mayor. Student, Drew U., 1961-63; BS, U. Utah, 1965, MS, 1967. Adminstrv. asst. for public info. Utah State Office Rehab. Svcs., 1967-69; cons. Utah State Dept. Community Affairs, 1971-72; media dir., press sec. Wayne Owens for Congress Campaign, 1972; press sec. Rep. Wayne Owens, 1973-74; spl. asst. to N.Y. Congl. Rep. Richard Ottinger, 1975; asst. to pres., dir. community rels. Snowbird Corp., 1975-77; exec. v.p. Bonneville Assocs., Inc., Salt Lake City, 1977-80; pres. Bonneville Assocs., Inc., 1980-89, chmn., CEO, 1989-91; mayor Salt Lake City, 1992—. Bd. trustees Intermountain Health Care, 1980-92; bd. dirs., exec. com. Utah Symphony, 1983-92, vice chmn., 1985-88, chmn., 1988-92; dir. Utah chpt. Nat. Conf. Christians and Jews, Inc., 1988; bd. dirs. Salt Lake Olympic Bid Com., 1989—; chmn. image com. Utah Partnership for Edn. and Econ. Devel., 1989-92; active Sundance Inst. Utah Com., 1990-92; disting. bd. fellow So. Utah U., 1991; active numerous other civic orgns. and coms. Mem. Salt Lake Area C. of C. (bd. govs. 1979-81, chmn. City/County/Govt. com. 1976-86). Office: Office of the Mayor City & County Bldg 451 S State St Rm 306 Salt Lake City UT 84111

CORRICK, JAMES A., writer, editor; b. Astoria, Oreg., Sept. 12, 1945; s. James Adam and Harriet Moore (Perry) C.; m. Gay Miller, Nov. 26, 1982. BS, U. Tenn., 1967, MS, 1969, MA, 1971; PhD, U. Ariz., 1981. Grad. asst. Dept. English U. Tenn., Knoxville, 1970-73; grad. assoc. Dept. English U. Ariz., Tucson, 1973-81, tutor writing skills, 1981-82; writer Tucson, 1983-84; editor L5 News, Tucson, 1985-87, Space Frontier, Tucson, 1986-87, Space Advocate, Tucson, 1987; writer, editor Tucson, 1987-91; sci. writer Muscular Dystrophy Assn., Tucson, 1991-92; writer, editor Tucson, 1992—. Author: The Human Brain, 1983, Recent Revolutions in Chemistry, 1986, Recent Revolutions in Biology, 1987, Career Preparations, 1988, Double Your Pleasure, 1989, The World of Nature: Farm Animals, 1991, Mars, 1991, Muscular Dystrophy, 1992; contbr. 175 articles and short stories to profl. jours. Mem. Ariz. Sonora Desert Mus. Mem. Ariz. Hist. Soc., Tucson Book Pubs. Assn., So. Ariz. Arthropod Assn., Tucson Zool. Soc. Home and Office: 4402 E Cooper Circle Tucson AZ 85711

CORRIGAN, MARY KATHRYN, theatre educator; b. Mpls., July 11, 1930; d. Arthur Joseph Kolling and Hazel (Pierce) Colp; children: Michael Edward, Timothy Patrick. BA, U. Minn., Mpls., 1965, MA, 1967. Advisor, counselor Coll. Liberal Arts U. Minn., Mpls., 1964-65, instr. dept. theatre, 1966-69, asst. prof. dept. theatre, 1969-73; assoc. prof. dept. theatre Fla. State U., Tallahassee, 1973-75, U. Calif., San Diego, 1975-89, 92—; assoc. dir. U. Calif. Study Ctr. U.K., Ireland, 1989-91; master tchr. Brit. Am. Drama Acad., Balliol Coll., Oxford U., Eng., summers, 1987—, chair undergrad. & intermediate programs midsummer, 1992, 93. Actress nat. pub. radio Chopin, 1984, video film Ultrasonography, 1986. Mem. adv. com. United Ministeries, Mpls., 1968-73, Mpls. Sch. Bd., 1968-72. Recipient Tozier Found. award, Eng., 1967, Best Actress award Globe Theatre, San Diego, 1979, NEH award Folger Shakespeare Theatre, 1992-93; grantee Rockefeller Found., 1968, McMillan grantee U. Minn., Eng., 1968, U. Calif.-San Diego, 1982-87, NEH grantee Folger Inst., Washington, 1993-94. Mem. Am. Theatre Assn. (exec. com., v.p. performance tng. 1984-86), Voice and Speech Theater Assn. (bd. dirs. 1986-89). Democrat. Home: 2645 Gobat Ave San Diego CA 92122-3127 Office: U Calif San Diego Theatre Dept La Jolla CA 92093-0344

CORRIGAN, ROBERT ANTHONY, university president; b. New London, Conn., Apr. 21, 1935; s. Anthony John and Rose Mary (Jengo) C.; m. Joyce D. Mobley, Jan. 12, 1975; children by previous marriage: Kathleen Marie, Anthony John, Robert Anthony; 1 stepdau., Erika Mobley. A.B., Brown U., 1957; M.A., U. Pa., 1959, Ph.D., 1967. Researcher Phila. Hist. Commn., 1957-59; lectr. Am. civilization U. Gothenburg, Sweden, 1959-62, Bryn Mawr Coll., 1962-63, U. Pa., 1963-64; prof. U. Iowa, 1964-73; dean U. Mo., Kansas City, 1973-74; provost U. Md., 1974-79; chancellor U. Mass., Boston, 1979-88; pres. San Francisco State U., 1988—. Author: American Fiction and Verse, 1962, 2d edit., 1970, also articles, revs.; editor: Uncle Tom's Cabin, 1968. Vice chmn. Iowa City Human Rels. Commn., 1970-72, Gov.'s Commn. on Water Quality, 1983-84; mem. Iowa City Charter Commn., 1972-73; chmn. Md. Com. Humanities, 1976-78, Assn. Urban Univs., 1988-92; mem. Howard County Commn. Arts, Md., 1976-79; bd. dirs. John F. Kennedy Libr.; trustee San Francisco Econ. Devel. Corp., 1989-92, Modern Greek Studies Found., Found. of Spain and U.S., Adv. Coun. of Calif. Acad. Scis., Bishop Desmond Tutu South African Refugee Scholarship Fund, Calif. Historical Soc., 1989-92; co-chmn., bd. dirs. Calif. Compact, 1990—; exec. com. Campus Compact, 1991—. Smith-Mundt prof., 1959-60; Fulbright lectr., 1960-62; grantee Standard Oil Co. Found., 1968, NEH, 1969-74, Ford Found., 1969, Rockefeller Found., 72-75, Dept. State, 1977; recipient Clarkson Able Collins Jr. Maritime History award, 1956, Pa. Colonial Soc. Essay award, 1958, 59, William Lloyd Garrison award Mass. Ednl. Opportunity Assn., 1987; Disting. Urban Fellow Assn. Urban U., 1992. Mem. San Francisco C. of C. (bd. dirs.), San Francisco World Affairs Coun. (bd. dirs.), Private Industry Coun. (bd. dirs. 1992—), Boston World Affairs Coun. (1983-88), Greater Boston C. of C. (v.p. 1987-89), Fulbright Alumni Assn. (bd. dirs. 1978-80), Univ. Club, City Club, Phi Beta Kappa. Democrat. Office: San Francisco State U Office of Pres San Francisco CA 94132

CORRIGAN, WILFRED J., data processing, computer company executive; b. 1938. Divsn. dir. Motorola, Phoenix, 1962-68; pres. Fairchild Camera & Instrument, Sunnyvale, Calif., 1968-80; chmn. bd., CEO LSI Logic Corp., Milpitas, Calif., 1980—. Office: LSI Logic Corporation 1551 Mccarthy Blvd Milpitas CA 95035-7488*

CORRY, KATHRYN MARY, financial consultant; b. Springfield, Ohio, July 23, 1948; d. Stewart R. and Cleo J. (Kirk) C.; m. Harry F. Kempke. BS in Edn. cum laude, Ohio State U., 1971; MBA, U. Dayton, 1979. CPA, Ohio. Supr. cash control SCOA Industries, Inc., Columbus, Ohio, 1980-81, mgr. cash and debt, 1981-83, dir. cash mgmt., 1983-85, asst. treas., 1985-86; asst. treas. Ohio State U., Columbus, 1986; dir. treasury ops. Warner Cable Communications, Inc., Dublin, Ohio, 1986-88, asst. treas., 1988-90; asst. treas. Am. TV and Communications Corp., Englewood, Colo., 1990-92; ptnr. Kempcor Advisors, Littleton, Colo., 1993—. Mem. Assn. for Investment Mgmt. and Rsch. (chartered fin. analyst), Nat. Corp. Cash Mgmt. Assn. (cert. cash mgr.).

CORSINI, RAYMOND JOSEPH, psychologist; b. Rutland, Vt., June 1, 1914; s. Joseph August and Evelyn Carolyn (Lavaggi) C.; m. Kleona Rigney, Oct. 10, 1965; 1 dau., Evelyn Anne. B.S., CCNY, 1939, M.S. in Edn, 1941; Ph.D., U. Chgo., 1955. Prison psychologist Auburn (N.Y.) Prison, 1941-45, San Quentin Prison, 1945-47, Wis. Prison System, 1947-50; research assoc. U. Chgo., 1955-57; pvt. practice indsl. psychology Alfred Adler Inst., Chgo., 1957-63; assoc. prof. Ill. Inst. Tech., 1964-65, U. Calif. at Berkeley, 1965-66; pvt. practice psychology Honolulu, 1965-89; faculty research affiliate Sch. Pub. Health, U. Hawaii, 1970—; affiliate grad. faculty dept. psychology, U. Hawaii; founder, sr. counselor Family Edn. Centers Hawaii, 1966—. Author: Methods of Group Psychotherapy, 1957, Roleplaying in Business and Industry, 1961, Roleplaying in Psychotherapy, 1966, The Family Council, 1974, The Practical Parent, 1975, Role Playing, 1980, Give In or Give Up, 1981, Individual Psychology: Theory and Practice, 1982, Effective Discipline in the Home and the School, 1989, Five Therapists and One Client, 1990, Coping With Your Teenager, 1990; editor: Critical Incidents in Psychotherapy, 1959, Adlerian Family Counseling, 1959, Critical Incidents in Teaching, 1965, Critical Incidents in School Counseling, 1972, Critical Incidents in Nursing, 1973, Current Psychotherapies, 1973, 77, 83, 89, Current Personality Theories, 1977, Readings in Current Personality Theories, 1978, Great Cases in Psychotherapy, 1979, Alternative Educational Systems, 1979, Theories of Learning, 1980, Comparative Educational Systems, 1981, Handbook of Innovative Psychotherapies, 1981, Adolescence: The Challenge, Ency. of Psychology, 1984, Condensed Ency. of Psychology, 1987, Jour. Individual Psychology, 1974-76, Ency. of Aging, 1987. Bd. dirs. Hawaii chpt. John Howard Assn., 1966-68. Recipient James McKeen Cattell award psychology Psychol. Corp., 1944; Sertoma award, 1980. Mem. Am. Psychol. Assn. (Significant Profl. Contbn. award Hawaii chpt. 1985), N.Am. Soc. Adlerian Psychology. Club: Waikiki Yacht (Honolulu). Address: 140 Niuiki Circle Honolulu HI 96821

CORSON, KIMBALL JAY, lawyer; b. Mexico City, Sept. 17, 1941; came to U.S., 1942; s. Harland Jerry and Arleen Elizabeth (Jones) C.; m. Ann Dudley Wood, May 25, 1963 (div. Apr. 1978); 1 child, Claudia Ring; m. Joy Lorann Sligh, June 16, 1979; children: Bryce Manning, Jody Darlene. BA, Wayne State U., 1966; MA, U. Chgo., 1968, JD, 1971. Bar: Ariz. 1972, U.S. Dist. Ct. 1971, U.S. Supreme Ct. 1991. Assoc. Lewis & Roca, Phoenix, 1971-74, ptnr., 1974-90; ptnr. Horne Kaplan & Bistrow, Phoenix, 1990—. Co-author: (book) Document Control, Organization and Management, 1988; contbr. (book) Litigation Support Using Personal Computers, 1989. Co-fouder Desert Hills Improvement Assn., Phoenix, 1988—; mem. Tri-Village Long Range Planning Com., Phoenix, 1989—. With U.S. Army, 1961-64. Fellow Woodrow Wilson Found., 1966, 67. Mem. ABA (antitrust sect., civil practice and proc. 1988—, antitrust and litigation sects. 1984—), U.S. Trademark Assn. (USTA Speaker's award 1988), Maricopa County Bar Assn., Phi Beta Kappa. Home: Summit Ranch Stage II Box 1358 Black Canyon Desert Hills AZ 85027 Office: Horne Kaplan & Bistrow 40 N Central Ave # 2800 Phoenix AZ 85004

CORTINEZ, VERONICA, language and literature educator; b. Santiago, Chile, Aug. 27, 1958; came to U.S. 1979; d. Carlos Cortinez and Matilde Romo. Licenciatura en Letras, U. Chile, 1979; MA, U. Ill., Champaign, Ill., 1981, Harvard U., 1983; PhD, Harvard U., 1990. Teaching asst. U. Chile, Santiago, 1977-79, U. Ill., Champaign, 1979-80; teaching fellow Harvard U., 1982-86, instr., 1986-89; asst. prof. colonial and contemporary Latin Am. lit. UCLA, 1989—; fgn. corres. Caras, Santiago, 1987—. Editorial bd. Mester/Dept. Spanish and Portuguese of UCLA, 1989—; editor Plaza mag., 1981-89, Harvard Rev., 1983-89; contbr. articles to profl. jours. Recipient Award for Teaching Excellence, Danforth Ctr., Harvard U., 1982, 83, 84, 85, 86; Teaching prize, Romance Lang. Dept., Harvard U., 1986; Whiting fellow. Mem. Cabot House, Phi Beta Phi. Office: UCLA Dept Spanish and Portuguese 5310 Rolfe Hall Los Angeles CA 90024

CORTRIGHT, INGA ANN, accountant; b. Silver City, N.Mex., Sept. 30, 1949; d. Lester Richard and Claudia Marcella (Huckaby) Lee; m. Russell Joseph Cortright, June 25, 1987. BS in Acctg., Ariz. State U., 1976, MBA, 1978; postgrad., Walden U., 1991—. CPA, Ariz., Tex. Sole practice cert. pub. acctg. Ariz., 1981—; cons. in field. Mem. AICPA, Beta Alpha Psi. Republican. Episcopalian. Office: 9421 W Bell Rd Ste 108 Sun City AZ 85351

CORWIN, JACK B., holding company executive; b. N.Y.C., July 10, 1951; s. Howard Stanley and Sydelle (Friedman) C. BSBA, U. Md., 1978; M Pub. and Pvt. Mgmt., Yale U., 1980. Assoc. corp. fin. Advest, Inc., Hartford, Conn., 1980-82, Drexel Burnham, Lambert, N.Y.C., 1982-83; assoc. exec. corp. E.F. Hutton, N.Y.C., 1983-84; v.p. PruCapital, L.A., 1984-86; pres. Huntington Holdings, Inc., L.A., 1987—; chmn. Bianchi Holding, Temecula, Calif., 1987—; bd. dirs. FIPC Holding, Winston-Salem, N.C. Mem. Ketchum-Downtown YMCA (bd. dirs. 1991—), City Club Bunker Hill. Office: Huntington Holdings Inc 300 S Grand Ave Bldg 2425 Los Angeles CA 90071-3134 also: 99 Emerald Bay Laguana Beach CA 92651

CORWIN, KEVIN EDWARD, computer professional; b. Brockton, Mass., Feb. 14, 1947; s. Walter Whittier and Charlotte Evelyn (Gardner) C.; m. Constance Jean Hetman, May 9, 1987; children by previous marriage: Steven Scott, Timothy Tristan. AA in Data Processing, Denver C.C., 1976; BA in Bus. Adminstrn., Columbia Coll., Aurora, Colo., 1992. Computer systems mgr. USAF Acctg. and Fin. Ctr., Denver, 1970-81, Security Assistance Acctg. Ctr., Denver, 1981-91, Def. Fin. and Acctg. Svc., Denver, 1991-92, Def. Info. Tech. Svcs. Orgn., Denver, 1992—. Docent Raptor Edn. Found., Aurora. Sgt. USAF, 1966-70. Mem. Am. Mgmt. Assn., Data Processing Mgmt. Assn., Info. Tech. Coun. Intermountain States, Am. Soc. Mil. Comptrollers, Rocky Mountain R.R. Club, Sierra Club, Denver Zool. Found., Colo. R.R. Hist. Found., Nature Conservancy. Home: 966 S Ventura Way Aurora CO 80017 Office: Def Info Tech Svcs Orgn 6760 E Irvington Pl Denver CO 80279-8000

CORWIN, STANLEY JOEL, book publisher; b. N.Y.C., Nov. 6, 1938; s. Seymour and Faye (Agress) C.; m. Donna Gelgur; children: Alexandra, Donna, Ellen. AB, Syracuse U., 1960. Dir. subsidiary rights, v.p. mktg. Prentice-Hall, Inc., Englewood Cliffs, N.J., 1960-68; v.p. internat. Grosset & Dunlap, Inc., N.Y.C., 1968-75; founder, pres. Corwin Books, N.Y.C., 1975; pres., pub. Pinnacle Books, Inc., Los Angeles, 1976-79; pres. Stan Corwin Prodns. Ltd., 1980—; pres., chief exec. officer Tudor Pub. Co., N.Y.C. and Los Angeles, 1987-90; lectr. Conf. World Affairs, U. Colo., 1976, U. Denver, 1978, Calif. State U., Northridge, 1980, The Learning Annex; participant Pubmart Seminar, N.Y.C., 1977, UCLA, 1985; guest lectr. U. So. Calif., 1987—. Author: Where Words Were Born, 1977, How to Become a Best Selling Author, 1984, 2d edit., 1993; contbr. articles to L.A. Times, N.Y. Times, short stories to Signature Mag.; producer motion picture Remo Williams-The Adventure Begins, 1986; (golf video) Now to Golf with Jan Stephenson, 1987; exec. producer The Elvis Files TV Show, 1991, The Marilyn Files, 1993. Mem. Pres. Carter's U.S. Com. on the UN, 1977. Served with AUS, 1960. Nat. prize winner short story contest Writers' Digest, 1966. Mem. Assn. Am. Pubs., PEN. Home and Office: 9317 Burton Way Beverly Hills CA 90210-3605

CORY, ROLLAND WAYNE, business administrator; b. Camp Zama, Sagamihira, Japan, Feb. 7, 1957; s. Claude Charles Cory and Kyoko (Narasaki) Reibel; m. Victoria Athena Dale Plasting, Nov. 8, 1980. Assoc. Sci. in Transportation, Chaffey Coll., 1992. Crane tender Ameron Steel Producing Div., Etiwanda, Calif., 1976; structural fitter Kaiser Steel Fabricated Products Group, Fontana, Calif., 1976-81; retail camera salesman Fedco Inc., San Bernardino, Calif., 1981; elevator mechanic Exec. Elevator Co., Fontana, Calif., 1985; storekeeper TTX Co./Calpro div., Mira Loma, Calif., 1981-93; pres. United Steelworkers of Am. Local Union #8844, Mira Loma, 1992—; legis. educator United Steelworkers of Am. Local Union #8844, Mira Loma, 1985-91, safety chmn., 1983-88, recording sec., 1985-88. Recipient Cert. of Appreciation The Cousteau Soc., Norfolk, Va., 1982. Mem. Calif. Turtle and Tortoise club (treas. Inland Empire chpt. 1990-94, Plaque, 1991), Nichiren Shoshu of Am. (Cert. 1988), Nat. Geographic Soc. (Cert. 1982), Indsl. Rels. and Rsch. Assn. Democrat. Soka Gakkai of Am. Office: Calif Turtle & Tortoise Club PO Box 976 Fontana CA 92334-0976

CORZO, MIGUELANGEL, institute executive; b. Mexico City, Mar. 2, 1942; came to U.S., 1985; s. Miguel A. and Josefina (Melgar) C.; m. Liliane Monier, June 13, 1964; children: Liliane, Alexandre, Xavier Edward. BS, UCLA, 1967; MS, Nat. U. Mexico, Mexico City, 1970; DSc, Tech. U. Munich, Germany, 1974. Prof. Nat. U., Mexico City, 1967-74; dean acad. affairs Met. U., Mexico City, 1974-77; spl. adviser Mexican Ministry Urban Devel., Mexico City, 1977-80; sec. tourism Mexican Ministry Tourism, Mexico City, 1980-82; pres. Friends Arts of Mex., L.A., 1988-91; dir. spl. projects Getty Conservation Inst., L.A., 1986-88, dir., 1991—. Author: Engineering Design, 1971, Human Settlements, 1979 (gold award 1979); editor over 20 books. Fulbright fellow Harvard U., 1979. Office: Getty Conservation Inst 4503 Glencoe Ave Marina Del Rey CA 90292

COSGROVE, CAMERON, insurance executive; b. Arcadia, Calif., July 25, 1957; s. Joseph Patrick Jr. and Marion (Barrons) C.; m. Marilee Jane Mann, Feb. 12, 1980; children: Christopher Farley, Steven Patrick. BS in Mgmt., Calif. State U., Long Beach, 1980. Asst. v.p. Pacific Mut. Life Ins. Co., Newport Beach, 1982—. Co-author city ordnance Regulation of Ozone, Depleting Compounds, 1989-90; contbr. articles to newspaper. Fin. commr. City of Irvine, Calif., 1983-87, planning, commr. 1987-88, city councilman, 1988-90; bd. dirs. Irvine Transp. Authority, 1988-90; founding advisor Irvine Conservancy, advisor, 1986-88, Irvine Infrastructure Authority, 1988-90; founder San Joaquin Marsh Adv. Com., chair 1988-90. Recipient Sea and Sage Audubon Conservation award, 1990. Republican. Office: Pacific Mut Life Ins 700 Newport Center Dr Newport Beach CA 92660-6397

COSH, JOHN MORTON, bank executive; b. Mimico, Ont., Can., Dec. 28, 1924; s. George Morton and Margaret (Brown) C.; m. Marjorie Bernice Cosh, Apr. 20, 1952; children: George M., John Michael, Jayne Ann, Robert Alan. Cert. banking, U. Wis., 1971. Asst. cashier First Nat. Bank Vista, Calif., 1946-51; escrow officer, asst. mgr., mgr. security First Nat. Bank Vista, 1951-70; exec. v.p., pres., vice chmn. W. Coast Nat. Bank, 1970-77; pres. Palomar Ind. & Comml. Realtors Inc., 1977-83; v.p. Torrey Pines Bank, 1983—; apptd. to fee arbitration com. Calif. State Bar. Bd. dirs., past pres. Tri-City Hosp.; vice chmn. Oceanside Econ. Devel. Corp.; bd. dirs. Overall Econ. Devel. Commn. San Diego County; past pres. Greater San Luis Rey Council; past bd. dirs., chmn. guarantors fund North County Concert Assn.; vol. Vista Boys Club, founder, past. pres.; pres. Vista Boys Club Found.; life mem. San Luis Rey Council PTA's. Served with USAAF, 1943-46. Recipient Silver Keystone, Golden Boy, Bronze Medallion, Man Behind the Boy awards Boys Clubs Am.; named Distiing. Citizen Jaycees, Man of Yr. North County Associated C. of C.'s, 1965, Banker of Yr. Am. Bankers Assn., 1984, Hon. Officer Vista League Cancer Socs. Mem. Vista Hist. Soc., Vista C. of C. (bd. dirs.), Indsl. Devel. Bond Authority (past chmn.), Vista Econ. Devel. Assn. (past chmn.), Elks, Lions, Masons, Rotary. Republican. Presbyterian. Home: 1638 Alta Vista Dr Vista CA 92084-5708

COSSUTTA, RENÉE CLAIRE, graphic designer; b. N.Y.C., Oct. 6, 1955; d. Araldo Alfred and Thelma Claire (Bouchet) C. BA, Smith Coll., 1978; MFA, Yale U., 1982. Carl P. Rollins fellow Yale U. Printing Svc., New Haven, 1980-81; graphic designer Sussman Prejza, L.A., 1983-84; ptnr. Lausten/Cossutta Design, L.A., 1984—; mem. faculty graphic design dept. Calif. Inst. Arts; lectr. in field. Work published in Communication Arts Design Ann., 1990. Recipient award Am. Inst. Graphic Arts, 1985, Art Dirs. Club L.A., 1987, 88, Am. Mus. Assn., 1987. Office: 1724 Redcliff St Los Angeles CA 90026

COST, BETTYJO, art agent, gallery executive, print distributor; b. Merced, Calif., June 3, 1931; d. James Doyle Byrd and Ethel (Fondren) Root; m. James Peter Cost, Apr. 17, 1957 (div. Oct. 1989); children: Shelley Anne Cost Chaffee, Nancy Cost Loose; m. Ronald Gene Hansen, Sept. 3, 1992; 1 child, Tylor. Student, Monterey Peninsula Coll., 1964—, Calif. State U., Long Beach, 1963. Owner, mgr. James Peter Cost Gallery, Carmel, Calif., 1964-89, Cost Gallery, Carmel, 1991—; print distbr. Cost & Co., Carmel, 1970—. Fund raiser for candidate Calif. Assembly, Monterey County, 1982. Mem. Jr. League Monterey Peninsula. Republican. Christian Scientist. Office: PO Box 3638 Carmel CA 93921

COST, JAMES PETER, artist; b. Phila., Mar. 3, 1923; s. Peter and Rose (Perry) C.; children: Curtis, Shelley, Janet, Nancy. B.A., U. Calif. at Los Angeles, 1950; M.S., U. So. Calif., 1959. Tchr. art Los Angeles City Sch. Dist., 14 years; lectr. art Northwood Insts., Midland, Mich., Dallas, 1971; mem. faculty of art Principia Coll., 1975. One-man shows, Northwood Inst., Midland, 1971, R.W. Norton Gallery, Shreveport, La., 1971; exhibited in group shows at, Artists Guild Gallery Am., Carmel, 1961-63, James Peter Cost Gallery, (1964), Mus. Fine Arts, Springfield, Mass., 1965, 73, Nat. Arts Club, N.Y.C., 1966; represented in permanent collection, R.W. Norton Mus., Shreveport, also numerous pvt. collections; commd. 12 paintings for golf courses, Kobe, Osaka and Tokyo, Japan, 1986-87. Pres. Carmel Bus. Assn., 1970, Republican candidate for La. State Assembly, 1982. Served with USCGR, 1942-45. Recipient gold medal Franklin Mint, 1973. Republican. Christian Scientist. Studio: 27 Heaaula Pl Haiku HI 96708

COSTA, GUSTAVO, Italian language educator; b. Rome, Mar. 21, 1930; came to U.S., 1961; s. Paolo and Ida (Antonangelo) C.; m. Natalia Zalessow, June 8, 1963; 1 child, Dora L. Maturità Classica, Liceo Virgilio, Rome, 1948; D Philosophy cum laude, U. Rome, 1954. Asst. Istituto di Filosofia, Rome, 1957-60; instr. Italian Université de Lyon, Lyons, France, 1960-61; instr. Italian U. Calif., Berkeley, 1961-63, asst. prof., 1963-68, assoc. prof., 1968-72, prof., 1972-91, prof. emeritus, 1991—, chmn. dept. Italian, 1973-76, 88-91; vis. prof. Inst. Philosophy, U. Rome La Sapienza, 1992; reviewer RAI Corp., Rome, 1982-89. Author: La leggenda dei secoli d'oro nella lett. ital., 1972, Le antichità. germaniche nella cultura italiana, 1977; mem. edit. bd. Romance Philology, Nouvelles de la République des Lettres, New Vico Studies, Forum Italicum, L'anello che non tiene Cuadernos Sobre Vico. Istituto Italiano Studi Storici fellow, Naples, Italy, 1954-57, Guggenheim Meml. Found. fellow, N.Y.C., 1977; grantee French Govt., Paris, 1956, Belgian Govt., Brussels, 1956, Targa D'oro Apulia, Italy, 1990. Mem. MLA, Am. Assn. Tchrs. Italian, Am. Soc. for Eighteenth-Century Studies, Renaissance Soc. Am., Associazione Internazionale per gli Studi di Lingua e Letteratura Italiana, Dante Soc. Am., Faculty Club (Berkeley). Office: U Calif Dept of Italian Berkeley CA 94720

COSTALES, TROY EDWARD, state agency administrator; b. San Diego, June 18, 1964; s. Stanley Wayne Costales and Karen (Bechtold) Anderson; m. Laurie Jean Sams, Aug. 17, 1985; 1 child, Paul Ryan. BA in Mgmt. Human Resources, George Fox Coll., Newberg, Oreg., 1991. Community sch. coord. Salem-Keizer Sch. Dist., Salem, Oreg., 1982-86; asst. adminstr. Oreg. Traffic Safety Commn., Salem, 1987—; owner, cons. TLC Enterprises, Salem, 1987—; mem. transp. plan commn. Oreg. Dept. Transport, Salem, 1992, mem. accident data commn., 1992; mem. community sch. task force Salem-Keizer Sch. Dist., 1986. Editor Oreg. Hwy. Safety Plan, 1987-91, Oreg. Ann. Evaluation Plan, 1987-91. Mem. budget com. Mid-Willamette Valley United Way, Salem, 1991-92, campaign vol., 1985, 89; actor Pentacle Theatre, Salem, 1986. Recipient various awards. Mem. State Mgmt. Assn. Baptist. Home: 7132 35th Ave NE Salem OR 97303 Office: Oreg Traffic Safety Commn 400 State Library Bldg Salem OR 97310

COSTEA, ILEANA, educator, consultant, engineer, researcher; b. Bucuresti, Romania, May 20, 1947; came to U.S., 1973.; d. Paul and Ana (Ciumetti) Paunescu; m. Nicolas Vincent Costea, Apr. 20, 1973. MArch, Ion Mincu Inst., Bucuresti, 1972; MA in Indsl. Design, UCLA, 1974, PhD in Engring., 1982. Chief teaching asst. UCLA, 1981; scientist ground systems analysis sect. Hughes Aircraft Co., Fullerton, Calif., 1982; lectr. dept. mgmt. sci. Sch. Bus. Adminstrn. Calif. State U., Northridge, 1982-83; cons. CAE Office vehicle engring. div. Aerospace Corp., El Segundo, Calif., 1984; sr. scientist, cons. Perceptronics, Inc., Woodland Hills, Calif., 1985; asst. prof. dept. civil and indsl. engring. Calif. State U., Northridge, 1983-86; cons. Jet Propulsion Lab. Calif. Inst. Tech., Pasadena, 1986-87, assoc. prof. dept. civil and indsl. engring. and mechanics, 1986-89, prof. dept. civil and indsl. engring. and applied mech., 1989—; vis. prof. U. Calif., Davis, 1980, U. Metz, France, 1989-93, U. Claude Bermard, Lyon, France, U. Metz, U. Catholique de l'Quest, Angers. France, Inst. Français du Petrole, France, Rueil Malmaison, France, 1989-93, U. Milan, Italy, 1990-91; vis. researcher Social Sci. Rsch. Inst., U. So. Calif., 1982. Author: Artificial Intelligence/Expert Systems/CAD/CAM and Computer Graphics; contbr. articles to profl. jours.; reviewer for NSF and Computer jours. Recipient Merit award San Fernando Valley Engrs.' Coun., 1986. Mem. AAAS, IEEE, AAUP, AIAA, Computer Soc. of IEEE, Nat. Computer Graphics Assn., Assn. for Computing Machinery, Inst. Mgmt. Sci., Ops. Rsch. Soc. Am., Calif. Faculty Assn., Am. Inst. for Decision Scis., Women in Sci. and Engring., Am. Assn. Artificial Intelligence, European Assn. for Computer Graphics, Am. Inst. Indsl. Engrs., Computer and Automated Systems Assn., Soc. Women Engrs. Home: 3651 Terrace View Dr Encino CA 91436-4019 Office: Calif State U 18111 Nordhoff St Northridge CA 91330-0001

COSTELLO, DANIEL WALTER, bank executive; b. Mich., June 17, 1930; s. Walter William and Rose Angela (Dimond) C.; children: Michael Joseph, Colleen Marie. BS in Engring. Sci, Purdue U., 1952. Various sales, mktg. and real estate positions Shell Oil Co., 1955-63; dir. real estate and constrn., planning mgr. Ford Motor Co., U.S. and Can., 1963-71; dir. real estate devel. and constrn. Ford Land Devel. Corp., Dearborn, Mich., 1971-75; chmn. Am. Express Realty Mgmt. Co., N.Y.C., 1975—; corporate sr. v.p. real estate and gen. svcs. Am. Express Co. and subs., N.Y.C., 1975-82; exec. v.p. corp. real estate div. Bank of Am., San Francisco, 1982—. With U.S. Army, 1952-56; Korea. Mem. Nat. Assn. Rev. Appraisers (bd. dirs.), Internat. Real Estate Inst. (bd. govs.), Urban Land Inst., Nat. Assn. Corp. Real Estate Execs., San Francisco Real Estate Bd. (cert. master corp. real estate), Bldg. Owners and Mgrs. Assn., Meadow Club, Country Club, San Francisco Bankers Club, Theta Xi. Office: Bank Am Nat Trust & Savs Assoc Corp Real Estate Div 560 Davis St San Francisco CA 94111-1999

COSTELLO, STEVEN PATRICK, marketing professional; b. Corpus Christi, Tex., May 24, 1958; s. William and Patricia Ann (Mahoney) C. BS in Journalism, Boston U., 1980; MBA, Dartmouth Coll./Tuck Sch., 1987. Copy editor The Advocate, Stamford, Conn., 1980-81, reporter, editor, 1981-85; reporter, editor The AP, Hartford, Conn., 1985; asst. product mgr. Gen. Foods Corp., White Plains, N.Y., 1987-88, assoc. product mgr., 1988-89; assoc. mktg. mgr. Celestial Seasonings, Inc., Boulder, Colo., 1989-90, mktg. mgr., 1990—. Office: Celestial Seasonings 4600 Sleepytime Dr Boulder CO 80301-3292

COSTIN GUEST, JANET RAE, personnel training specialist; b. Santa Maria, Calif., Jan. 31, 1961; d. Boyd Ruter and Darlene Rae (Anderson) Costin; 1 child, Anna Rae. BS, Kans. State U., 1988. Rsch. asst. Kans. State U., Manhattan, 1985-88; adminstrv. sec. U. Wyoming, Laramie, 1988-90, program asst., 1990-92, also rep./chmn. staff coun., 1990-92, project dir. Total Quality Mgmt., 1992—. Mem. Wyo. Stock Growers Assn., Wyo. Agrl. Leadership Coun. Republican. Office: U Wyo PO Box 3314 Laramie WY 82071-3314

COTA, HAROLD MAURICE, educator; b. San Diego, Apr. 16, 1936. Educator engring. Calif. Poly. State U., Luis Obispo. Office: Calif Poly State U Dept Civil & Environ Engring San Luis Obispo CA 93407

COTCHETT, JOSEPH WINTERS, lawyer, author; b. Chgo., Jan. 6, 1939; s. Joseph Winters and Jean (Renaud) C.; children—Leslie F., Charles P., Rachael E., Quinn Carlyle, Camilla E. B.S. in Engring., Calif. Poly. Coll., 1960; LL.B., U. Calif. Hastings Coll. Law, 1964. Bar: Calif. 1965, D.C. 1980. Ptnr. Cotchett, Illston & Pitre, Burlingame, Calif., 1965—; mem. Calif. Jud. Coun., 1975-77, Calif. Commn. on Jud. Performance, 1985-89, Commn. 2020 Jud. Coun., 1991—, select com. on judicial retirement, 1993—. Author: (with R. Cartwright) California Products Liability Actions, 1970, (with F. Haight) California Courtroom Evidence, 1972, (with A. Elkind) Federal Courtroom Evidence, 1976, (with Frank Rothman) Persuasive Opening Statements and Closing Arguments, 1988, (with Stephen Pizzo) The Ethics Gap, 1991; contbr. articles to profl. jours. Chmn. San Mateo County Heart Assn., 1967; pres. San Mateo Boys Club, 1971; bd. dirs. U. Calif. Hastings Law Sch., 1980—. Served with Intelligence Corps, U.S. Army, 1960-61; col. JAGC, USAR, ret. Fellow Am. Bar Found., Am. Bd. Trial Advs., Am. Coll. Trial Lawyers, Internat. Acad. Trial Lawyers, Internat. Soc. of Barristers, Nat. Bd. Trial Advs. (diplomate civil trial adv.), State Bar Calif. (gov. 1972-75). Clubs: Commonwealth, Press (San Francisco). Office: 840 Malcolm Rd Burlingame CA 94010-1401 also: 12100 Wilshire Ste 1100 Los Angeles CA 90025

COTE, JOHN JOSEPH, secondary education educator; b. Omaha, Nov. 29, 1968; s. Laurence Joseph and LuCinda Kay (Scantlin) C. BS in Biology, Loyola Marymount U., L.A., 1991. Debate instr. Loyola Marymount U., 1991-92; tchr. biology Loyola High Sch., L.A., 1991-92, 92—, dir. of debate, 1991—. Nat. Lincoln-Douglas Debate champion, 1989. Mem. Nat. Forensic League, Sigma Xi, Eta Sigma Phi, Delta Sigma Phi. Roman Catholic. Home: 919 Main St # 104 El Segundo CA 90245 Office: Loyola High Sch 1901 Venice Blvd Los Angeles CA 90006

COTÉ, RALPH WARREN, JR., retired mining engineer, nuclear engineer; b. Berkeley, Calif., Oct. 5, 1927; s. Ralph Warren and Clara Maria (Neves) C.; m. Lois Lydia Maddox, Aug. 8, 1950; children: Ralph Warren III, Michele Marie. BSME, N.Mex. Inst. Mining and Tech., 1952. Registered profl. nuclear engr., Calif. Resident engr. Am. Smelting and Refining Co., Page, Idaho, 1952-54; shift boss Bunker Hill Co., Kellogg, Idaho, 1954-57, gen. mine foreman, 1958-60; project engr. Union Carbide Nuclear Co., Grand Junction, Colo., 1957-58; shift supr. GE, Richland, Wash., 1960-63; shift supr. GE, Vallecitos, Calif., 1963-66, maintenance mgr., 1966-67; start-up shift supr. GE, San Jose, Calif., 1967-71; project start-up mgr. Bechtel Power Corp., San Francisco, 1971-89, retired, 1989. Served to 2d lt. U.S. Army and U.S. N.G., 1946-50. Mem. Am. Nuclear Soc., VFW. Republican. Home: 14610 W Sky Hawk Dr Sun City West AZ 85375-5925 Office: Bechtel Power Corp 50 Beale St San Francisco CA 94105-1813

COTLIAR, GEORGE J., newspaper editor. Mng. editor Los Angeles Times. Office: Los Angeles Times Times Mirror Sq Los Angeles CA 90053

COTTEN, SAMUEL RICHARD, commercial fisherman; b. Juneau, Alaska, July 16, 1947; s. Samuel L. Cotten and Kathryn Russell; m. Martha Tillion, June 16, 1984; children: Samuel Tillion, Augustus O'Dwyer Russell. AA, U. Alaska, 1971. Rep. Alaskan Ho. Of Reps., Juneau, 1975-82, 85-90, speaker, 1989-91; senator Alaska State Senate, Juneau, 1991-93; chmn. Spl. Com. on Oil and Gas, chmn. Natural Resources, 1991-93; spl. advisor Intergovtl. Consultative Com. to North Pacific Fisheries Adv. Bd., 1989-92; mem. Internat. North Pacific Fisheries Commn., 1989-92; bd. dirs. Fire Lake Recreational Ctr., Eagle River, Alaska. Co-chmn. Alaska Criminal Code Revision Commn., Juneau, 1975-76; mem. Anchorage Planning and Zoning Commn., 1975-76. With USN, 1965-69, Vietnam. Recipient Nat. Def. award, 1965-69; named Outstanding Vietnam Vet. No Greater Love Found., 1976. Mem. Cook Inlet Seiners Assn., Navy League, Rotary, Elks, VFW (life), Anchorage Ski Club. Democrat. Home: PO Box 770296 Eagle River AK 99577-0296

COTTER, JOHN CATLIN, marketing consultant; b. Monterey Park, Calif., Apr. 3, 1950; s. Frank Cotter and Duncanne (Kilday) Tyson; children: Chris, Lisa. BS in Mktg., Ariz. State U., 1972. Promotion mgr. Gillcable, San Jose, Calif., 1982-85; mktg. dir. Stas. KSJO/KHTT, San Jose, 1985-87, Heritage Cablevision, San Jose, 1987-89; mktg. cons. The Cotter Media Group, San Jose, 1989—. Recipient Susan B. Murphy award San Jose Ad Club, 1986.

COTTER, LAWRENCE RAFFETY, management consultant; b. Albany, Calif., Aug. 13, 1933; s. Malcolm Thompson Cotter and Una Elyse Raffety. AA, U. Calif., Berkeley, 1953, BA in Astronomy, 1956; MS in Bus. Adminstrn., The George Washington U., 1967; PhD in Mgmt. Theory, UCLA, 1977. Commd. 2nd lt. USAF, 1956, advanced through grades to col., 1975, ret., 1982; orbital analyst, network controller Project Space Track USAF, Bedford, Mass., 1958-61; staff scientist Hdqs. N.Am. Air Def. Command, Colorado Springs, Colo., 1962-66, Hdqrs. USAF, Washington, 1967-70; dir. test and deployment DEF. Support program USAF, Los Angeles, 1975-76; commdr. detachment 1 Electronic Systems Div. USAF, Tehran, Iran, 1976-78; system program dir. Electronic Systems div. USAF, Bedford, Mass., 1978-79; dep. commdr. network plans and devel. AF Satellite Control Facility USAF, Sunnyvale, Calif., 1979-82; mgmt. cons. Berkeley, 1982—; adminstrv. asst. Arnold Air Soc., Washington, 1959-72. Co-author: The Arnold Air Soc. Manual, 1956; (computer program) SPACE, 1970; editor: The Arnold Air Soc. Manual 1964-72. Recipient Departmental Citation U. Calif. Berkeley, 1955, Citation of Honor, Arnold Air Soc., 1967. Mem. AF Assn., The Royal AF Club, Beta Gamma Sigma.

COTTINGHAM, SUSAN MARIE, infosystems specialist; b. Denver, July 14, 1950; d. Cyril Francis and Nancy Lee (Meyer) Kipp; m. Ronald Lynn Cottingham, Apr. 26, 1973. BFA, Colo. State U., 1972; postgrad., R.I. Sch. Design, 1972-73. Cert. in data processing Internat. Assn. for Cert. Computer Profls. Programmer Larimer County Govt., Ft. Collins, Colo., 1978-81, lead analyst, 1981-84, mgr., 1984—. Chmn. Larimer County Pension Bd., 1990—. Named Outstanding County Mgr. Bd. of Larimer County Commrs., 1989. Mem. Am. Mgmt. Assn., Data Processing Mgmt. Assn., Inst. Cert. Computer Profls. (cert., assoc.), Career Women's Roundtable (co-founder), Ft. Collins Potter's Guild (v.p. 1977-78), DAR. Republican.

COTTLE, CRAIG HANSEN, financial executive; b. Lewiston, Utah, July 11, 1943; s. Laurence Glen and Margaret (Hansen) C.; m. Sharon Elizabeth Dooley, June 25, 1969; children: Todd Alan, Sean Glen, Elizabeth Dawn, Jeremy Craig, Timothy Aaron, Darin Shea, Ayssa Shiree. BS, Weber State U., 1969; MBA, Utah State U., 1988. Cert. cash mgr. Tax acct. IRS, Ogden, Utah, 1967-69; staff acct. DelMonte Corp., San Francisco, 1969-71; fin. asst. to pres. Universal Distbg. Co., Sandy, Utah, 1971-72; staff acct. Hans Nievaard, CPA, Salt Lake City, Utah, 1972-73; contr. Master Lease, Inc., Salt Lake City, 1973-74; asst. treas. N.W. Energy Co., Salt Lake City, 1974-86; mgr. fin. resources Iomega Corp., Roy, Utah, 1986-87; asst. v.p. Key Bank of Utah, Salt Lake City, 1988; treas. Price Savers Wholesale Inc., Salt Lake City, 1989-91; pvt. practice fin. mgmt. cons. Kaysville, Utah, 1992—; exec. v.p., CFO VesCor Capital Corp., Ogden, Utah, 1992—. Aux. officer Utah Hwy. Patrol, Ogden, 1964-69; vol. fireman North Ogen Fire Dept., 1966-67; troop com. Boy Scouts of Am., Kaysville, 1978-88, explorer com. chmn., 1988-90. Mem. Treasury Mgmt. Assn. (bd. dirs. 1986-89, certification coun. 1980-89), Treasury Mgmt. Assn. Utah (founder, pres. 1984-86), Nat. Risk and Ins. Mgmt. Soc., Risk and Ins. Mgmt. Soc. of Utah. Republican. Mormon. Home: 293 Mourning Dove Cir Kaysville UT 84037

COTTON, CHESTER CHRISTIE, management educator; b. L.A., Nov. 17, 1939; s. Chester M. and Thelma (Lake) C.; m. Eileen Marie Giuffré, Apr. 3, 1971. BS, San Jose State U., 1962, MS, 1964; PhD, U. Oreg., 1974. Instr. Shasta Coll., Redding, Calif., 1965-67, U. Oreg., Eugene, 1967-70; asst. prof. mgmt. Calif. State U., Sacramento, 1970-72, Chico, Calif., 1972-77; assoc. prof. mgmt. Calif. State U., Chico, 1977-82, prof. mgmt., 1982—, assoc. dean bus., 1987-89; faculty fellow Agrl. Rsch. Svc. USDA, Washington, 1976-78; vis. prof. U. Guam, Mangilao, 1985-86. Contbr. articles to profl. jours. Mem. Acad. Mgmt., Decision Scis. Inst., So. Mgmt. Assn. (referee 1987—), Western Acad. Mgmt., Western Decision Scis. Inst. Office: Calif State U Dept Mgmt Chico CA 95929

COTTON, HERBERT LOUIS, telecommunications executive; b. Baton Rouge, Sept. 30, 1940; s. Arthur H. and Virginia (Watts) C.; m. Rosemary Amos, June 13, 1964; children: April, Timothy J. BS, So. U., Baton Rouge, 1962. Acct. Good Citizens Life Ins., New Orleans, 1962-64, RCA Svc. Co., Anchorage, 1966-69; mgr. rev. acctg. RCA Alascom, Anchorage, 1969-75; fin. analyst Alaska Fedn. of Natives, Anchorage, 1975-76; mgr. rev. acctg. Alascom, Inc., Anchorage, 1976-83, mgr. fin., treas., 1983-91, mgr. sales and customer svc., 1992—; trustee Humana Hosp. Alaska, Anchorage, 1989—. Officer Gideons Internat., Anchorage, 1969—; pres. Alaska Bapt. Conv., Anchorage, 1972-74. With U.S. Army, 1964-70. Mem. Alascom Mgmt. Assn. (pres. 1989-91). Home: 3389 Checkmate Dr Anchorage AK 99508-4923 Office: Alascom Inc 210 E Bluff Dr Anchorage AK 99501-1100

COUCH, JOHN CHARLES, diversified company executive; b. Bremerton, Wash., May 10, 1939; s. Richard Bailey and Frances Harriet (Gilmore) C. BS in Engring., U. Mich., 1963, MS, 1964; MBA, Stanford U., 1976. With Ingalls Shipbldg. div. Litton Industries, 1967-74; asst. to sr. v.p. engring. and marine ops. Matson Navigation Co. subs. Alexander and Baldwin., San Francisco, 1976-78; v.p. Matson Navigation Co., 1978-84; exec. v.p., chief operating officer Matson Navigation Co. subs. Alexander and Baldwin., San Francisco, 1984; pres., chief operating officer Matson Navigation Co., 1985, Alexander and Baldwin Inc., Honolulu, 1991—; pres., chief exec. officer Alexander and Baldwin, Inc., Honolulu, 1992—; bd. dirs. A&B Devel. Co., Calif., A&B Properties, Inc., East Maui Irrigation Co., Ltd., Kahului Trucking & Storage, Inc., McBryde Sugar Co., Ltd., Ohanui Corp., Princess Orchards, WDCI Inc., Calif. and Hawaiian Sugar Co., First Hawaiian Bank, First Hawaiian Inc., Hawaiian Sugar Transp. Co., Inc. Mem. Maui Econ. Devel. Bd., 1986—; mem. exec. bd. Aloha coun. Boy Scouts Am., 1986—; bd. dirs., mem. exec. com. Aloha United Way, 1988, campaign chmn., 1988, chmn. bd. dirs. Mem. Nat. Cargo Bur., Inc., Am. Bur. Shipping, Newcomen Soc. U.S., Hawaiian Sugar Planters' Assn. (chmn. bd. dirs. 1989-90, bd. dirs. 1985—), C. of C. of Hawaii (bd. dirs. 1986—), Hawaii Maritime Ctr. (vice-chmn. 1988-89, chmn. 1990), Honlulu Club, Oahu Country Club, Plaza Club. Office: Alexander & Baldwin Inc PO Box 3440 822 Bishop St Honolulu HI 96813-3925

COUCH, ROBERT FRANKLIN, military officer, geologist, environmental program manager; b. Kokomo, Ind., Feb. 15, 1947; s. Robert Franklin Sr. and Virginia Jean (Lorts) C.; m. Alice Ann Stemen, Jan. 1972 (div. Mar. 1979); m. Gloria Archuleta, Feb. 6, 1982. BS, Capital U., 1969; MS, Ohio State U., 1971. Commd. 2d. lt. USAF, 1969, advanced through grades to lt. col., 1985; spl. scientist and analyst DCS Devel. Plans Air Force Systems Command, Holloman AFB, N.Mex., 1971-73; nuclear weapons rsch. officer and geologist Air Force Weapons Lab., Kirtland AFB, N.Mex., 1973-74, chief earth phenomology, 1979-82; sect. chief microscopy lab. McClelland Central Lab., McClelland AFB, Calif., 1974-79; dir. nuclear surety and warhead integration Joint Cruise Missle Program, Crystal City, Va., 1982-84; program mgr. Def. Nuclear Agency Hdqs., Alexandria, 1984-87; dep. div. chief Strategic Nuclear div. Office of Asst. Sec. AF Acquisition, Pentagon, Washington, 1987-90; program mgr. PRC Environ. Mgmt., Inc., 1990—. Contbr. articles to profl. jours. Youth leader Luth. Ch., Roseville, Calif., 1974-79, Boy Scouts Am., Roseville, 1979; pastorial intern advisor Luth. Ch., Fairfax, Va., 1983-90. Mem. Kappa Iota Lambda. Republican. Home: 156 Desert Willow Rd Corrales NM 87048-7531 Office: 2021 Girard Blvd SE Ste 250 Albuquerque NM 87106

COUFAL, HANS JURGEN, physicist; b. Ruhla, Thuringen, Germany, Jan. 17, 1945; came to U.S., 1981; s. Hans Bernhard and Lore Mathilde (Hattich) C.; m. Lore Hedwig Bauer Harnisch, Dec. 7, 1973; children: Nicole G., Michelle A., Hans T. BS, Tech. U., Munich, 1966, MS, 1970, PhD, 1975. Asst. prof. Tech. U., Munich, 1975-77, assoc. prof., 1979-81; vis. prof. Free U., Berlin, 1977; vis. scientist IBM Rsch. Lab., San Jose, Calif., 1978-79, rsch. staff, 1981—; mem. IUPAC Commn. on Spectroscopy, 1989—. Author (with others) Physik-Gestern, Heute, Morgen, 1970, Physik--einmal anders. Moderne Aspekte einer Wissenschaft, 1976, Rare Gas Solids, Springer Tracts in Modern Physics, 1985; editor (with others) Liquid and Amorphous Metals, NATO ASI Series E, 1980, Photoacoustic Effect--Principles and Applications, 1984; editor Jour. Photoacoustics, 1981-84, Applied Physics, 1981—; contbr. articles to profl. jours. Mem. Am. Phys. Soc., German Phys. Soc. Office: IBM Rsch Div Almaden Rsch Ctr 650 Harry Rd San Jose CA 95120-6099

COUGHENOUR, JOHN CLARE, federal judge; b. Pittsburg, Kans., July 27, 1941; s. Owren M. and Margaret E. (Widner) C.; m. Gwendolyn A. Kieffaber, June 1, 1963; children: Jeffrey, Douglas, Marta. B.S., Kans. State Coll., 1963; J.D., U. Iowa, 1966. Bar: Iowa 1963, D.C. 1963, U.S. Dist. Ct. (we. dist.) Wash. 1966. Ptnr. Bogle & Gates, Seattle, 1966-81; vis. asst. prof. law U. Washington, Seattle, 1970-73; judge U.S. Dist. Ct. (we. dist.) Wash., Seattle, 1981—. Mem. Iowa State Bar Assn., Wash. State Bar Assn. Office: US Dist Ct 609 US Courthouse 1010 5th Ave Seattle WA 98104-1130

COUGHLIN, REV. BERNARD JOHN, university president; b. Galveston, Tex., Dec. 7, 1922; s. Eugene J. and Celeste M. (Ott) C. A.B., St. Louis U., 1946, Ph.L., 1949, S.T.L., 1956; M.S.W., U. So. Calif., 1959; Ph.D., Brandeis U., 1963. Joined S.J., Roman Cath. Ch., 1942, ordained priest, 1955; tchr., counselor chs. in Wis. and Kans., 1949-54; research asst. Los Angeles Juvenile Probation Project, 1959; social work ednl. cons. Guatemala City, summer 1960; mem. faculty St. Louis U., 1961-74; social work cons. Peru, Chile, 1967; Fulbright lectr. Colombia, 1970-71; prof. Sch. Social Service, 1970-74, dean, 1964-74; pres. Gonzaga U., Spokane, Wash., 1974—; mem. program com. Nat. Conf. Cath. Charities, 1964-68, mem. com. legislation social justice, 1973-80, bd. dirs., 1973-80, mem. com. study and study cadre, 1970-72; mem. adv. com. social welfare service Model Cities, St. Louis, 1967-68; council social work edn. Commn. Internat. Social Work Edn., 1968-81, adv. com. project on integrative teaching and learning, 1968-69, adv. com. population dynamics and family planning, 1969-71, structure rev. com., 1970-71; bd. dirs. Health and Welfare Council Met. St. Louis, 1968-74, Shearson Fundamental Value Fund, Inc.; chmn. task force community planning Child Welfare League Am., 1967-69; chmn. Conf. Deans Schs. Social Work, 1972-73; chmn. nominating com. U.S. com. Internat. Council Social Work, 1973-79; cons. in field, del. internat. confs.; mem. Assn. Governing Bds., 1980-81, Council for Postsecondary Edn., 1979-85. Author: Church and State in Social Welfare, 1965, also articles, revs., chpts. in books. Bd. dirs. United Way Spokane County, 1982-87; mem. Inland Empire council Boy Scouts Am., 1982—; mem. Nat. Conf. Cath. Charities, Washington Citizens' Commn. on Salaries for Elected Officials, 1987—; chmn. Northwest Citizens Forum Def. Waste, 1986-88; trustee St. Louis U., 1988—, Spokane Area Econ. Devel. Coun., 1991—; U.S. rep. to Internat. Coun. on Social Welfare, Study Commn. on Human Rights, Helsinki, Finland, 1968; mem. coun. on social work edn., Task Force on Structure and Quality in Social Work Edn., 1973-74; chmn. Northwest Citizens Forum on Nuclear Waste, 1986-88. Fulbright lectr. Colombia, 1970, 71; Grantee NIMH, 1963-68. Mem. Nat. Assn. Social Workers (chmn. cabinet div. profl. standards 1970-73), Internat. Assn. Schs. Social Work, Internat. Coun. Social Welfare, Nat. Conf. Social Welfare, Internat. Assn. Univ. Presidents (vice chmn. U.S. western regional coun. 1982—, mem. steering com. 1982—), Coun. Social Work Edn., Mo. Assn. for Social Welfare, Assn. Wash. Bus. (bd. dirs. 1991—), Spokane Area C. of C. (trustee 1979-81, vice chmn. 1987-88, chmn. 1988-89). Address: Gonzaga U East 502 Boone Ave Spokane WA 99258-0001

COUGHRAN, JAMES EUGENE, retired airline pilot; b. Whittier, Calif., Mar. 3, 1921; s. Samuel James and Elizabeth Rachel (Black) C.; m. Vivian Malaquias, Oct. 24, 1962 (dec. 1980); 1 child, Jodi; m. Elsie Emma Illenberg, Oct. 25, 1980. Grad. high sch., Fullerton, Calif. Lic. comml. pilot. Mgr. Anaheim (Calif.) Airport, 1938-42; flight instr. Ryan Aeronautical Sch., Hemet, Calif., 1942-45; airline dispatcher Western Airlines Inc., Fairbanks, Alaska, 1945; mgr. Coughran & Tester, Puente, Calif., 1945-46; chief pilot L.A. and R.E. Crow, Gen. Contractor, Elmonte, Calif., 1946-49; airport mgr. Corona (Calif.) Airport, 1949-50; inspector Pacific Air Motive Corp., Chimo, Calif., 1950-53; airline pilot, engr. TWA, Inc., N.Y.C. and L.A., 1953-83; aircraft maintenance cons. LaPalma, Calif., 1983—. With U.S. Army, 1942-46. Mem. OX5 Aviation Pioneers, Kiwanis Club (sgt. at arms, Kiwanian of Yr. 1989). Home: 5081 Sausalito Cir La Palma CA 90623

COULSON, ALAN STEWART, cardiothoracic surgeon; b. Leeds, Yorkshire, England, June 21, 1941; came to U.S., 19780; s. Charles Walter and Mary Gray (Aitkenhead) C.; m. Jan Coulson, June 9, 1979. MA, U. Cambridge, England, 1963; MA PhD, U. Cambridge, 1966, MB B Chir, 1969; LRCP, U. London, 1970; MD, U. Cambridge, 1976. Diplomate Am. Coll. Surgeons, Am. Coll. Physicians, Internat. Coll. Surgeons; Cert. thoracic surgery. Resident, fellow Stanford U. Med. Ctr., Palo Alto, Calif., 1971-77; pvt. prac. Stockton, Calif., 1978—. Contbr. articles to profl. jours. Mem. Internat. Heart Transplantation, Soc. Thoracic Surgery, North Am. Pacing and Electrophysiology, Western Thoracic Soc. Office: 2800 N California St Stockton CA 95204-3757

COULSON, NORMAN M., savings and loan executive; b. Hilt, Calif.; m. Helen; children—Virginia Coulson Bullard, Maria, Edward, Michael. BS, Long Beach State Coll., 1957; MBA, Pepperdine U., 1973; postgrad. exec. program, UCLA, 1973; postgrad. in exec. devel, U. Wash., 1973. With 1st Fed. Savs., San Pedro (Calif.), 1957-59; with Glendale (Calif.) Fed. Savs. and Loan Assn., 1959—, successively v.p., group v.p., exec. v.p., sr. exec. v.p. and gen. mgr. Calif. div., pres., chief executive officer, chmn., dir., 1984-92; vice-chmn., pres., chief exec. officer, GlenFed Inc., chmn., chief exec. officer, 1990—; instr. Inst. Fin. Edn., Community Coll. Accreditation. Mem. coun. communication div. Pepperdine U.; past chmn. adv. bd. Kennedy High Sch., Granada Halls, Calif.; bd. dirs. Citizens for Law and Order, Glendale, Glendale Adventist Med. Ctr. Found.; bd. govs. Inst. Fin. Edn., L.A.; bd. dirs., mem. exec. com., chmn. communications com. Am. Heart Assn., L.A. Served with USCG. Mem. Downey-Studio City C. of C. (bd. dirs.), Stonewood Mchts. Assn. (pres.), Calif. Savs. and Loan League (com. mem.), U.S. League Savs. Assn. (mem. savs. account adminstrn. com.), Nat. Coun. Savs. Instns. (state dir. 1984-85), Newcomen Soc. U.S. Clubs: Lakeside Country, Verdugo (Glendale); Rotary (Los Angeles). Office: GlenFed Inc 700 N Brand Blvd Glendale CA 91203-1238

COULTER, ANDREW, marketing executive; b. N.Y.C., Apr. 30, 1958; s. Harris Livermore Coulter and Natalie (Vergun) Grabar. BA, Columbia Coll., 1979; MBA, U. Brussels (Belgium), 1983. Ins. exec. Am. Internat. Group, N.Y.C., Paris, Brussels, 1979-84; banker Bankers Trust Co., N.Y.C., 1984-86; mgr. internat. sales O'Neill Inc., Santa Cruz, Calif., 1987-90; v.p. Body Glove Internat., Hermosa Beach, Calif., 1990—. Republican. Russian Orthodox. Home: 5987 Peacock Ridge Rd # 105 Palos Verdes Peninsula CA 90274 Office: Body Glove Internat 530 6th St Hermosa Beach CA 90254-4636

COUNELIS, JAMES STEVE, higher education educator; b. Streator, Ill., June 26, 1927; s. Steve and Mary (Drivas) C.; m. Anna Catherine Marakas, Nov. 25, 1962; children: Steven George, George James. AA, Chgo. City Jr. Coll., 1948; AM, U. Chgo., 1951, PhD, 1961. Cert. high sch., jr. coll. tchr., pub. sch. principal, Ill. High sch. tchr. Chgo. Pub. Schs., 1951-55; asst. prof. history and social scis. Chgo. City Jr. Coll., Woodrow Wilson br., 1955-62, dir. evening program, 1962-64; asst. prof. edn. Chgo Tchrs. Coll., 1964-66; assoc. prof. edn. Pa. State U., University Park, 1966-67; sr. adminstrv. analyst U. Calif., Berkeley, 1968-70; prof. edn. U. San Francisco, 1970—, dir. instl. studies and mgmt. info. systems, 1971-75, coord. evaluation Sch. Edn., 1986-90, chmn. orgn. and leadership program, 1989-91. Author, editor: To Be a Phoenix: The Education Professoriate, 1969; author: Higher Learning and Orthodox Christianity, 1990; contbr. articles, revs. and papers to profl. publs. pres., trustee Greek Orthodox Cathedral of the Ascension, Oakland, Calif., 1973; pres. Hellenic Am. Profl. Soc., San Francisco, 1974, 75; trustee tenure Hellenic Coll./Holy Cross, 1951-53, trustee, 1982-86; mem. Calif. Council on Criminal Justice, 1987; bd. dirs. Paul Wattson Lecture series, 1989. Served with Signal Corps, U.S. Army, 1946-47. Recipient Archon Chartoularius (honoris causa) award Ecumenical Patriarchate of Constantinople and New Rome, 1976, Norbert Wiener award The World Orgn. Gen. Systems and Cybernetics, 1978, Scholar U. Chgo., 1951, 52, 60-61, Pacific Sch. Religion, 1958; U. Calif., Berkeley grantee, 1962; Coolidge Research fellow Andover-Newton Theol. Sch., 1985, Wayne J. Doyle Rsch. award, 1986, Hellenic Coun. on Edn. award for Scholarship and Univ. Tching., 1991. Mem. AAAS, Am. Assn. Artificial Intelligence, Am. Assn. Higher Edn., Am. Assn. Instnl. Rsch., Am. Ednl. Rsch. Assn., Am. Ednl. Studies Assn., Internat. Soc. System Scis., Hellenic Am. Profl. Soc. (Axion award 1982), Hellenic Coun. on Edn. (award for Scholarship and University Teaching 1991), Orthodox Theol. Soc. Am., U. San Francisco Faculty Assn., Mensa, Gold Key, Phi Delta Kappa (U. San Francisco chpt. v.p. for programs 1990-91, pres. 1991-92). Office: U San Francisco Sch Edn San Francisco CA 94117-1080

COUNSIL, WILLIAM GLENN, electric utility executive; b. Detroit, Dec. 13, 1937; s. Glenn Dempsey and Jean Beverly (Rzepecki) C.; m. Donna Elizabeth Robinson, Sept. 10, 1960; children: Glenn, Craig. Student, U. Mich., 1955-56; B.S., U.S. Naval Acad., 1960; Advanced Mgmt. Program, Harvard U., 1991. Ops. supr., asst. plant supt.. sta. supt. N.E. Nuclear Energy Co., Waterford, Conn., 1967-76; project mgr., v.p. nuclear engring. and ops. N.E. Utilities, Hartford, Conn., 1976-80, sr. v.p. nuclear engring. and ops., 1980-85; exec. v.p. nuclear engring. and ops., electric-generating div. Tex. Utilities Generating Co., 1985-88; vice chmn. Tex. Utilities Electric Co., 1989-93; mng. dir. Wash. Pub. Power Supply System, Richland, 1993—. With USN, 1956-67. Recipient Outstanding Leadership award ASME, 1986. Republican. Presbyterian. Home: 3806 W 40th Pl Kennewick WA 99337-2603 Office: Wash Pub Power Supply System 300 George Washington Way Richland WA 99352-0968

COUNTRYMAN, CHARLES CASPER, retired chemist; b. N.Y.C., Oct. 6, 1913; s. Walter Guy and Clara (Casper) C.; m. Veronica Lenz, Oct. 3, 1953. BS in Chemistry, U. Mich., 1934, MS in Chemistry, 1935. Analytical chemist West End (Calif.) Chem. Co., 1935-40; rsch. chemist Truesdail Labs., L.A., 1940-45; mng. chemist William T. Thompson Co., L.A., 1945-50; analytical rsch. chemist Dart Industries, Inc., L.A., 1950-75; ret., 1975. Mem. Am. Chem. Soc., Pacific R.R. Soc., Magic Castle, Nat. Honor Soc. Republican. Roman Catholic. Home: 19404 Shelford Dr Cerritos CA 90701

COUNTRYMEN, CHRISTOPHER CHARLES, counselor; b. Ft. Belvoir, Va., Sept. 22, 1955; s. Charles Buddy and Dorothy May (Pence) C.; m. Susan Conrad, Apr. 5, 1980; 1 child, Ryan Christopher. AA, Phoenix Coll., 1976; BA in Edn. summa cum laude, Ariz. State U., 1980, M in Counseling, 1989. Spl. edn. tchr. Litchfield (Ariz.) Sch. Dist., 1980-82, LATCH Sch., Inc., Phoenix, 1982-84; spl. edn. tchr. Washington Sch. Dist., Phoenix, 1984-86, counselor, behavioral cons., 1986—; cons. Ariz. Dept. Edn., Phoenix, 1982-84, Ednl. Support Svcs., Phoenix, 1983-84; coord. summer program LATCH Sch. Inc., 1984. Vol. Ariz. Coalition Edn., Phoenix, 1989-90. Mem. Ariz. Counselors Assn., Ariz. Edn. Assn., Ariz. Flycasters, Saguaro Astronomy Club, Phi Kappa Phi. Home: 5940 E Gelding Dr Scottsdale AZ 85254-5516 Office: Desert Foothills Sch 3333 W Banff Ln Phoenix AZ 85023-4799

COUPE, JAMES WARNICK, lawyer; b. Utica, N.Y., Mar. 3, 1949; s. J. Leo and Helen Carbery (Brennan) C.; m. Andrea Jean Schaaf, Nov. 26, 1983; children: Helen Shriver, Benjamin Warnick, Charlotte Fitzgerald. AB, Hamilton Coll., 1971; JD, Vanderbilt U., 1974. Bar: N.Y. 1975, U.S. Dist. Ct. (so. and ea. dists.) N.Y. 1975, U.S. Ct. Appeals (2d cir.) 1975, Calif. 1981. Law clk. to judge U.S. Dist. Ct. (so. dist.) N.Y., N.Y.C., 1974-75; assoc. Donovan, Leisure, Newton & Irvine, N.Y.C., 1975-79, Phillips, Nizer, Benjamin, Krim & Ballon, N.Y.C., 1979-81; sr. atty. Atlantic Richfield Co., L.A., 1981-86; chief counsel Beverly Enterprises, Inc., Pasadena, Calif., 1986-88; gen. counsel Completion Bond Co., Inc., Century City, Calif., 1988—. Mem. State Bar Calif., Beverly Hills Bar Assn., Fed. Bar Coun. (asst. sec. 1977-79, trustee 1980-81). Republican. Roman Catholic. Office: Completion Bond Co Inc 2121 Avenue Of The Stars Los Angeles CA 90067-5010

COURNOYEA, NELLIE, government official; b. Aklavik, N.W.T., Canada, 1940; div.; 2 children: John, Maureen. Radio announcer, later regional mgr. CBC, Inuvik, N.W.T.; negotiator, Com. for Original People's Entitlement; mem. territorial legislature Yellowknife, 1984—; minister of renewable resources, and of culture and communications, 1983-85, minister various portfolios, from 1987, govt. leader, 1991—. Office: Government Leader, PO Box 1320, Yellowknife, NT Canada X1A 2L9

COURSER, LORI ANN, business executive; b. Grand Rapids, Mich., Feb. 10, 1956; d. Robert Daniel and Olive Norrine (Woodlock) C.; m. Frank Albin Beniche, Dec. 3, 1988. BA, Albion (Mich.) Coll., 1978. Customer svc. mgr. John F. Lawhon Furniture, Taylor, Mich., 1978-80; tchr. Cranbrook Theater Sch., Birmingham, Mich., 1981-83; market researcher PACE Mktg., Orchard Lake, Mich., 1983-84; promotional specialist Am. Motors Corp., Southfield, Mich., 1984-85; promotional coord. Concerts West, Beverly Hills, Calif., 1985-87; project mgr. Pacific Promotions, Laguna Hills, Calif., 1987—. Republican. Lutheran. Office: Pacific Promotions 24901 Avenida Bancal El Toro CA 92630

COURT, ARNOLD, climatologist; b. Seattle, June 20, 1914; s. Nathan Altshiller and Sophie (Ravitch) C.; m. Corinne H. Feibelman, May 27, 1941 (dec. Feb. 1984); children: David, Lois, Ellen; m. Mildred Futor Berry, Apr. 6, 1988. BA, U. Okla., 1934; postgrad., U. Wash., 1938, MS, 1949; PhD, U. Calif., Berkeley, 1956. Reporter and city editor Duncan (Okla.) Banner, 1935-38; observer, meteorologist U.S. Weather Bur., Albuquerque, Washington, Little Am., Los Angeles, 1938-43; chief meteorologist U.S. Antarctic Service, 1939-41; climatologist office Q.M. Gen. U.S. Army, Washington, 1946-51; research meteorologist U. Calif., Berkeley, 1951-56; meteorologist U.S. Forest Service, Berkeley, 1956-60; chief applied climatology, Cambridge Research Labs. USAF, Bedford, Mass., 1960-62; sr. scientist Lockheed-Calif. Co., Burbank, 1962-65; prof. climatology San Fernando Valley State Coll. (now Calif. State U.), Northridge, 1962-85, chmn. dept. geography, 1970-72, prof. emeritus, 1985—; part-time prof. Calif. State U., Northridge, 1986-87, UCLA, 1987-90. Editor: Eclectic Climatology, 1968; assoc. editor Jour. Applied Meteorology, 1978-88; chmn. editorial bd. Jour. Weather Modification, 1978-86; contbr. articles and revs. to profl. jours. Served to 1st lt. USAAF, 1943-46. Recipient Spl. Congl. medal, 1944. Fellow AAAS, Am. Meteorol. Soc., Royal Meteorol. Soc.; mem. Am. Geophys. Union (life), Am. Statis. Assn., Assn. Am. Geographers, Assn. Pacific Coast Geographers (pres. 1978-79), Calif. Geog. Soc., Weather Modification Assn. (trustee 1973-76), Western Snow Conf., Sigma Xi, Phi Beta Kappa. Home: 17168 Septo St Northridge CA 91325-1672 Office: Calif State U Dept Geography Northridge CA 91330

COURTNEY, RICHARD HOWARD, economist; b. Marion, Ohio, Jan. 2, 1938; s. Lawrence Eugene and Lyda Mae (Long) C.; m. Nancy Williams (div.); children: David Howard, Richard Craig; m. Victoria Black, Nov. 28, 1987. BSc, Ohio State U., 1963, MSc, 1964; PhD, U. Calif., Berkeley, 1968. CFP. Agrl. economist U. Calif. Agrl. Experiment Sta., Berkeley, 1968-74; assoc. prof. econs. U. Fla., Gainesville, 1974-75; economist Bank of Am., San Francisco, 1975—; instr. St. Mary's Coll. of Calif., Moraga, 1991—. Mem. steering com. Bay Area Econ. Forum, San Francisco, 1990—. Mem. Nat. Assn. Bus. Economists. Office: Bank of Am 555 California St San Francisco CA 94104

COURTNEY, VICTORIA BLACK (VICTORIA B. SPERRY), education educator, academic administrator; b. Mpls., Aug. 28, 1943; d. Raymond Delbert and Barbara Jean (Brewer) Black; m. June 15, 1965 (div. 1983); children: David Howard, Richard Craig; m. Richard Howard Courtney, Nov. 28, 1987; children: Lisa Catherine, William Donald. BS, Northwestern U., 1965; MA, San Jose State U., 1966; EdD, U. San Francisco, 1987. Cert. speech and language pathology, sch. audiometry, Calif. teaching educationally handicapped, adminstrn., supervision, speech correction and lipreading. Speech, lang. pathologist Children's Health Coun., Palo Alto, Calif., 1966-68; edn. diagnostician Diagnostic Sch. for Neurologically Handicapped, San Francisco, 1968-70; dir. speech, hearing Children's Hosp., Stanford, Calif., 1970-71; dir. Speech, Lang. and Learning Clinic, San Jose, Calif., 1970-72; adj. faculty U. Calif., Santa Cruz, 1972-79, Berkeley, 1977-84; asst. dean, faculty St. Mary's Coll. Calif., Moraga, 1987-89, acting dean, 1989-91, asst. dean, 1991-92; faculty mem., dir. Outreach program St. Mary's Coll., Moraga, 1992-93, faculty mem., 1993—; dir. Sperry Learning Cons., Palo Alto, Moraga, 1966-87; panel mem. Mental Retardation program, Calif. Health and Welfare Agy., 1967-72; adv. bd. mem. Calif. Sch. Learning Systems, 1970-76, Calif. Assn. Neurologically Handicapped Children, 1978-

80, Calif. Schs. in Pleasanton, Alameda, Contra Costa counties, Moraga Sch. Dist., Ctr. for Living Skills; chmn. program com. State Conf. Calif. Assn. for Neurophysically Handicapped Children, 1981-83; cons. spl. edn. Calif. Dept. Edn., 1988—. Author: (with others) Cognitive Learning and Perceptual Problems of the Educationally Handicapped, 1969; Of Course I Can: Auditory Skills, 1972, A Language Approach to Learning Disabilities, 1972, 74; also spl. edn directories, resource handbooks and fed. grant proposals. Pres. Moraga Newcomers Club, 1978-80; leader Brownie and Girl Scouts U.S., Moraga, 1978-85; bd. dirs. Moraga Care and Share, 1982-86; coord. tchr. tng. Orinda (Calif.) Community Ch., 1982-84; co-dir. Northwestern U. Alumni Coun., San Francisco, 1978-81. Recipient Rose Reese award, 1961, Edith Dillon award, 1965. Mem. AAUW (v.p. program, chair ednl. equity local chpt.), ASCD, Am. Speech, Lang. and Hearing Assn., Am. Assn. Counselor and Tchr. Educators, Nat. Assn. Women Deans, Adminstrs. and Counselors, Assn. Children with Learning Disabilities Calif., Calif. Coun. on Edn. Tchrs., Ind. Calif. Colls. and Univs. Coun. for the Edn. of Tchrs. (pres.), Sigma Alpha Eta. Office: St Mary's Coll PO Box 4350 Moraga CA 94575-4350

COUSINS, RICHARD FRANCIS, diversified financial services compay executive; b. Oceanside, N.Y., Feb. 11, 1955; s. Richard Felix and Hedwig (Kobierec) C.; m. Alice Annette Arant, Sept. 3, 1977; 1 child, Kathryn. BA, Georgetown U., 1977; MBA in Acctg., NYU, 1987. Project analyst European div. Citibank, N.Y.C., 1977-78, fin. analyst, 1978-79, fin. mgr., 1979-80, project leader, bus. mgr., 1980-83; dir. opns. Merrill Lynch Hubbard, N.Y.C., 1983-85; sr. grad. asst. NYU Grad. Sch. Bus., N.Y.C., 1985-86; sr. systems cons. Am. Express, N.Y.C., 1986-88; mgr. strategic opns. Am. Express, Phoenix, 1988-92, project advisor, 1992—. Home: PO Box 43438 Phoenix AZ 85080-3438 Office: Am Express 6225 N 24th St Phoenix AZ 85016-2028

COUTTS, ROBERT FRANCIS, educator; b. Ferndale, Mich., July 20, 1941; s. James Mortimer and Edith Kathleen (Lougheed) C.; m. Frances Joyce Fein, July 18, 1971. BA in Physics, Oakland U., 1963; MA, Calif. State U., Northridge, 1971. Cert. physics and math. tchr., Calif. Tchr. physics L.A. Unified Schs., 1963—; in-svc. leader U. Calif., L.A., 1984—; tchr., coord. UCLA, 1988; insvc. leader U. So. Calif., 1993; tchr. cons. UCLA Sci. Project, Calif. Sci. Project; lab instr. Pierce Coll., Woodland Hills, Calif. Woodrow Wilson Found. fellow Princeton U., 1986, L.A. Ednl. Partnership fellow, 1987, 88, Rsch. Corp. fellow, 1990-92. Mem. Am. Assn. Physics Tchrs. (resource agt.), United Tchrs. L.A., Nat. Sci. Tchrs. Assn.

COVALT, ROGER CALVIN, school system administrator, consultant; b. San Diego, Aug. 15, 1959; s. Elbert Milton and Ruth Elaine (Kraus) C.; m. Ericka Lynn Heinz, Aug. 16, 1990. AA in Applied Arts, San Diego Mesa Coll., 1980, AA in Bus. Mgmt., 1982; student, Santa Rosa Jr. Coll., 1987; BS in Bus. Adminstrn., Pacific Western U., L.A., 1990. Cert. in law enforcement. Acct. Poppleton CPA, San Diego, 1984-87; ptnr. Rogers Ventures, San Diego, 1984-86; ranger Nat. Park Svc., 1987-90; transp. supr. San Diego City Schs., 1990—. Rep. nominee Calif. State Assembly, 1990. Recipient Theodore Roosevelt award Young Ams. for Freedom, 1989, others. Mormon.

COVARRUBIAS, PATRICIA OLIVIA, small business owner, consultant, author, communications educator, public speaker; b. Mexico, Mex., Sept. 17, 1951; came to U.S., 1959; d. Alfredo Izaguirre and Carmen (Baillet) C.; m. Robert Elvin Smith, Sept. 11, 1982. BA in French, Calif. State U., Sacramento, 1973, MA in French, 1978; student, Clown Camp, LaCrosse, Wis., 1992. Tchr. d'anglais High Sch., Albi, France, 1973-74; instr. French Calif. State U., Sacramento, 1974-75; videotape editor Sta. KCRA-TV, Sacramento, 1977, news asst. assignment editor, 1978, news reporter, 1978-82; founder, exec. dir., instr. OCELOTL OCELOTL, Stockton, Calif., 1984—; guest speaker OCELOTL Speakers Bur., 1984—, Stockton Speakers Bur., 1985—; instr. lifelong learning program U. Pacific, Stockton, 1985—; instr. in community edn. San Joaquin Delta Coll., 1989—; cert. tutor Laubach Literacy Program, Stockton, 1984—. Author: Speaking Up with Style, 1985, Marketing Your Professional Self, 1986, Getting Good Press, 1988, The Speech Planner. . .Ten Steps to Successful Speaking, 1990; author video programs: Gear Up for Speaking English, 1987, Conversational English Made Easy, 1988, Make Presentations Work for You, 1993; columnist Clearly Speaking, 1990—; columnist for news jours.; contbr. articles to profl. jours. Child sponsor Feed the Children, Oklahoma City, 1986—; bd. dirs. San Joaquin County Arts Coun., Stockton, 1985-88, v.p., 1987; mem. Leadership Stockton, 1991-92. Mem. NAFE, Internat. Tng. in Communication (instr. 1985—, Florence Van Gilder award 1985), Stockton Women's Network, Lodi Writers Assn., Calif. Reading Assn., Pacific Delta Area Trainers, Greater Stockton C. of C. (liaison com. 1989—), Calif. State U. Alumni Assn. (bd. dirs. 1988—, pres. 1991-92, Rookie of Yr. 1988-89, Alumni Honors award 1991), Nat. Speakers Assn., Pi Delta Phi, Phi Kappa Phi. Home: 3144 Sea Gull Ln Stockton CA 95219-4603 Office: OCELOTL PO Box 7521 Stockton CA 95267-0521

COVEY, STEPHEN MERRILL RICHARDS, business consultant; b. Provo, Utah, Apr. 25, 1962; s. Stephen Richards and Sandra Renee (Merrill) C.; m. Jerolyn Shae Hutchings, Apr. 26, 1985; children: Stephen Hutchings, McKinlee Louise. BA magna cum laude, Brigham Young U., Provo, Utah, 1985; MBA, Harvard U., 1989. Leasing agt. Trammell Crow Co., Dallas, 1985-87; summer assoc. First Boston Corp., N.Y.C., 1988; v.p. corp. devel. Covey Leadership Ctr., Provo, 1987—, also bd. dirs. Mem. LDS Ch. Office: The Covey Leadership Ctr 3507 N University Ave Ste 100 Provo UT 84604-4479

COVINO, JOSEPH, JR., author; b. Phenix City, Ala., Jan. 24, 1954; s. Joseph Sr. and Eleanor Josephine (Bowen) C.; m. Elizabeth Perkins, June 1978 (div. Apr. 1981); 1 child, Michael John Perkins Covino. BA in Criminal Justice, U. West Fla., 1976, BA in Econs., 1979, BA in Internat. Studies, 1981; AS in Law Enforcement, Pensacola Jr. Coll., 1980. Cert. law enforcement, police tng. program. Social studies tchr. Cardinal Newman High, West Palm Beach, Fla., 1978-79. Author: And War For All, 1983, Lab Animal Abuse, 1990. Democrat. Roman Catholic. Office: The New Humanity Press PO Box 215 Berkeley CA 94701-0215

COWAN, GEORGE ARTHUR, chemist, bank executive, director; b. Worcester, Mass., Feb. 15, 1920; s. Louis Abraham and Anna (Listic) C.; m. Helen Dunham, Sept. 9, 1946. BS, Worcester Poly. Inst., 1941; DSc, Carnegie-Mellon U., 1950. Research asst. Princeton U., 1941-42, U. Chgo., 1942-45; mem. staff Columbia U., N.Y.C., 1945; mem. staff, dir. rsch. Los Alamos (N.Mex.) Sci. Lab., 1945-46, 49-88, sr. fellow emeritus, 1988—; teaching fellow Carnegie Mellon U., Pitts., 1946-49; chmn. bd. dirs. Los Alamos Nat. Bank, Trinity Capital Corp., Los Alamos; pres. Santa Fe Inst., 1984-91; mem. The White House Sci. Coun., Washington, 1982-85, cons., 1985-90, Air Force Tech. Applications Ctr., 1952-88; bd. dirs. Applied Tech. Assocs., Inc., Title Guaranty, Inc., Universal Properties, Inc. Contbr. sci. articles to profl. jours. Bd. dirs. Santa Fe Opera, 1964-79; treas. N.Mex. Opera Found., Santa Fe, 1970-79; regent N.Mex. Inst. Tech., Socorro, 1972-75; bd. dirs. N.Mex. Symphony Orch., N.Am. Inst., Santa Fe Inst. Recipient E.O. Lawrence award, 1965, Disting. Scientist award N.Mex. Acad. Sci., 1975, Robert H. Goddard award Worcester Poly. Inst., 1984, Enrico Fermi award, Presdl. Citation, Dept. Energy, 1990. Fellow AAAS, Am. Phys. Soc.; mem. Am. Chem. Soc., N.Mex. Acad. Sci., Cosmos Club(Washington), Sigma Xi. Home: 721 42D St Los Alamos NM 87544 Office: Santa Fe Inst 1660 Old Pecos Trl # A Santa Fe NM 87501-4768

COWAN, GEORGE LLEWELLYN, financial executive; b. Portland, Oreg., July 22, 1931; s. Irle L. Cowan and LaVerne (Lillie) Joys; m. Betty M. Knutson, June 30, 1954 (div. 1976); children: Richard, Steven, Jeanne, Cheryl. BA, Ea. Wash. U., 1954. Assoc. analyst methods Std. Oil Co. Calif., San Francisco, 1965-67; controller Bellevue (Wash.) C.C., 1967-75, mgr. fin. and bus., 1975-78; mgr. bus. Kuskokwin C.C., Bethel, Alaska, 1978-79, Inupiat U. of the Arctic, Barrow, Alaska, 1979-80; dir. fin. Ukpeagvik Inupiat Corp., Barrow, 1980-86, CFO, 1987—, also bd. dirs.; dep. dir. adminstrn. North Slope Borough, Barrow, 1986-87; bd. dirs. Piquniq Mgmt. Corp., Anchorage. Treas. Rep. Eileen P. MacLean, Barrow, 1988—. With USAF, 1951-52. Mem. Rotary Internat. Home: PO Box 824 Barrow AK 99723 Office: Ukpeagvik Inupiat Corp PO Box 427 Barrow AK 99723

COWAN, JAMES EDINGTON, banker; b. Knoxville, Tenn., Oct. 11, 1930; s. William Walker and Gertrude (Edington) C.; m. Barbra Ann Harrison, Apr. 15, 1953; children: Barbra, Cathy, Bob, Nanci. BS, U. Tenn., 1953; grad. Banking Sch., Rudgers U., 1984. Commd. 2d lt. USAF, 1953, advanced through grades to col., 1979; wing comdr. USAF, Warren AFB, Wyo., 1976-79; loan officer 1st Nat. Bank & Trust, Cheyenne, Wyo., 1979-80, v.p., 1980-81, sr. v.p., 1981-83; exec. v.p. Norwest Bank, Cheyenne, Wyo., 1983-86; pres. The Bank of Laramie, Laramie, Wyo., 1986—; bd. dirs. Am. Heritage Ctr., 1992-93. Bd. dirs. Wyo. Coun. Econ. Edn., Laramie, 1988-92; pres. bd. dirs. Laramie Jubliee Days, 1989-91; v.p. Ivinson Mem. Hosp. Found., Laramie, 1990, pres., 1992; pres. United Way Albany County, Laramie, 1990. Mem. Wyo. Banker Assn. (bd. dirs. 1991-92), Wyo. Mining Assn. (adv. coun. 1991-92), Rotary Internat. (bd. dirs. laramie chpt. 1989-93, pres. 1993). Methodist. Home: 1066 Granito Dr Laramie WY 82070-5025 Office: The Bank of Laramie 2835 E Grand Ave Laramie WY 82070-5276

COWAN, PENNEY LEE, association adminstrator; b. Pitts., June 23, 1948; d. C. Robert and M. Jean (Lang) Silknitter; m. H. Scott Cowan, July 20, 1968; children: Kimberly Ann, Scott Daniel. Cert. radiologist technician, Franklin Sch. Sci. & Art, 1968. Exec. dir., founder Am. Chronic Pain, Monroeville, Pa., 1980—. Author: Patient or Person Living with Chronic Pain, 1992; (workbook manual) American Chronic Pain Association Member's Manual, American Chronic Pain Association Workbook II: Maintaining your Wellness, American Chronic Pain Association Regional Director's Manual, ACPA Leaden's Manual. Mem. Am. Pain Soc. Office: Am Chronic Pain PO Box 850 Rocklin CA 95677

COWAN, STUART MARSHALL, lawyer; b. Irvington, N.J., Mar. 20, 1932; s. Bernard Howard and Blanche (Hertz) C.; m. Marilyn R.C. Toepfer, Apr., 1961 (div. 1968); m. Jane Alison Averill, Feb. 24, 1974 (div. 1989); children: Catherine R.L., Erika R.L., Bronwen P.; m. Victoria Yi, Nov. 11, 1989. BS in Econ., U. Pa., 1952; LLB, Rutgers U., 1955. Bar: N.J. 1957, Hawaii 1962, U.S. Supreme Ct., 1966. Atty., Greenstein & Cowan, Honolulu, 1961-70, Cowan & Frey, Honolulu, 1970-89, pvt. practice, 1989—; arbitration Fed. Mediation & Conciliation Svc., Honolulu, 1972—, Am. Arbitation Assn., Honolulu, 1978—, Hawaii Pub. Employee Rels. Bd., 1972—. Bd. dirs. Honolulu Symphony. Lt. USN, 1955-61. Mem. ABA, Hawaii Bar Assn., Am. Judicature Soc., Trial Lawyers Assn. of Am. (state committeeman for Hawaii 1965-69, bd. govs. 1972-75), Hawaii Trial Lawyers Assn. (v.p. 1972-78), Japan-Hawaii Lawyers Assn., Soc. Profls. in Dispute Resolution, Inter Pacific Bar Assn. Jewish. Clubs: Waikiki Yacht (Honolulu), Hawaii Yacht, San Francisco Comml., Hawaii Scottish Assn. (chieftain 1983-88), St. Andrews Soc., Caledonian Soc. (vice chieftain 1983-85), St. Francis Yacht, Honolulu Club, Honolulu Pipes and Drums (sec.-treas. 1985-90). Lodges: Masons, Pearl Harbor (master 1971, steward 1993), Masada, Elks. Home: 47-339 Mapumapu Rd Kaneohe HI 96744 Office: 1600 Grosvenor Ctr Towers 733 Bishop St Honolulu HI 96813-4022

COWAN, SUSAN ALISON, marketing professional; b. Pontiac, Mich., June 12, 1959; d. William Walker and Hester Anne Cowan. BS, U.S. Naval Acad., 1981; postgrad., U. Chgo., 1992. Commd. ensign USN, 1981; advanced through grades to lt. comdr. USNR, 1992; exec. officer USS Quapaw USN, Port Hueneme, Calif., 1983-85; exec. officer mobile diving unit USN, Pearl Harbor, Hawaii, 1985-88; resigned USN, 1988; asst. brand mgr. Kraft Gen. Foods, Glenview, Ill., 1988-89, assoc. brand mgr., 1989-91, brand mgr., 1991-93; mktg. mgr. All American Gourmet, Orange, Calif., 1993—. Mem. U.S. Naval Acad. Alumni Assn., Phi Kappa Phi. Office: All American Gourmet Ste 1100 1100 Town & Country Rd Orange CA 92668

COWARDIN, RICHARD MURREL, retired forester; b. San Diego, Apr. 28, 1930; s. Murrel Harvey and Edina Rose (Shaw) C.; m. Janet, May 8, 1977; children: Nanette, Susan, Kathleen; stepchildren: Cathy, Don, Robert. AA in Forestry, Lassen Community Coll., Susanville, Calif., 1951. Forest fireman Calif. Dept. Forestry, San Diego, 1946-50, fire capt., 1951-52, 56-57; forestry supr. Calif. Dept. Forestry, Butte County, Calif., 1957-60; state forest ranger Command Ctr. Calif. Dept. Forestry, Siskivou County, Calif., 1960-68; state forest ranger field Calif. Dept. Forestry, Siskivou County, 1968-74, profl. forester, 1974-84; CEO Cascade World Four Season Resort, Yreka, Calif., 1981—. With USAF, 1952-56. Mem. Nat. Ski Patrol, Yreka Metro. Patrol (dir.), Mount Ashland Patrol (dir.). Home and Office: 1019 North St Yreka CA 96097

COWART, BILL FRANK, academic administrator; b. San Benito, Tex., Aug. 5, 1932; m. Janet Marie Dube, Aug. 6, 1954; 1 child, Richard. B.S., Tex. A&I U., 1954; M.A., Stephen F. Austin State Coll., 1959; Ph.D., U. Tex., 1963. Asst. mgr. Brownie Butane, Inc., McAllen, Tex., 1956-57; office mgr. Cowart Cattle Co., Henderson, Tex., 1957-59; tchr. Tivy Jr. High Sch., Kerrville, Tex., 1959-61; dir. secondary teaching Tex. A&I U., Kingsville, 1963-66, dir. project Upward Bound, 1966-69; pres. Laredo State U., Tex., 1969-84; provost Western Oreg. State Coll., Monmouth, 1984—; mem. exec. council U. System of South Tex., 1969-84; mem. Commrs. Adv. Com. on Bi-Lingual Edn. State of Tex., 1974. Pres. United Fund of Laredo, 1980; chmn. Laredo Council for the Arts, 1980-84; chmn. Borderfest Steering Com., Laredo, 1980-83. Served to 1st lt. U.S. Army, 1954-56. Named Man of the Yr. Laredo Times, 1979; Exec. of the Yr. Colegio de Licenciados en Adminstrn. de Nuevo, 1981. Mem. Southwest Philosophy of Edn. Soc. (pres. 1970-71). Home: 350 Brightwood Ct Monmouth OR 97361-1707 Office: Western Oreg State Coll 345 Monmouth Ave N Monmouth OR 97361-1314

COWART, JIM CASH, venture capitalist; b. Hereford, Tex., July 1, 1951; s. Orville P. and Rosa Stratton (Cash) C.; m. Janet Carol Bergman, Aug. 24, 1973; 1 child, Jefferson Cash. BA in Computer Sci., Pomona Coll., 1973; MBA with honors, Harvard U., 1977. Computer analyst U.S. Ho. of Reps., Washington, 1973-74; asst. v.p. mktg. Amtrak, Washington, 1974-75; v.p. investment banking Kidder, Peabody & Co., N.Y.C., 1977-82; sr. v.p. investment banking Shearson Lehman, N.Y.C., 1982-87; pres. Shearson Venture Capital, N.Y.C., 1983-87; gen. ptnr. Capital Resource Ptnrs., Mission Viejo, Calif. and Boston, 1987-91, Aurora Ptnrs., Laguna Niguel, Calif., 1991—; chmn., CEO Aurora Electronics, Inc., Irvine, Calif., 1992—; bd. dirs. BE Aerospace, Inc., Santa Ana, Calif. Office: Aurora Electronics Inc Ste # 1120 2030 Main St Irvine CA 92714

COWART, R. GREG, sales executive; b. Woodville, Mar. 4, 1956; s. Raymon O. and Frances (Gregory) C. BBA Mktg., Stephen F. Austin St. U., 1986, BA in Psychology, 1986. Mgr. Angelina Sports, Lufkin, Tex., 1980-83; sales mgr. Angelina Health Spa, Lufkin, Tex., 1983-86, Hoffman LaRoche Inc., Nutley, N.J., 1986—; cons. in field. Football ofcl. Southwest Football Ofcls. Assn., Nacogdoches, 1983-89. Republican. Home: 2640-B W 235th St Torrance CA 90505

COWDEN, LOUIS FREDRICK, electronics executive, engineer; b. Hayden, Ariz., Nov. 11, 1929; s. Millard Martin and Lenore Eletha (Hedgepeth) C.; m. Ruth Norine Buchanan, May 13, 1953 (div. Sept. 1975); children: Mary Marguerite, Michael Millard, Timothy John; m. Anabel Joyce Tarantino, Nov. 19, 1976. BSEE, U. Ariz., 1957. Div. dir. Collins Radio Co., Newport Beach, Calif., 1957-75; pvt. ventures, 1976-76; mgr. GS engring. TRW, Redondo Beach, Calif., 1976-78; site mgr. TDRSS TRW, Las Cruces, N.Mex., 1981-83; staff mgr. TRW, Redondo Beach, 1983-89; div. mgr. Control Data Corp., Anaheim, Calif., 1979-80; regional mgr. WPL, Inc., 1989-90; site mgr. TDRSS Tracking Data Relay Satellite System GTE, Las Cruces, 1990—; asst. v.p. engring. Verilink Corp., San Jose, Calif., 1989. With U.S. Army, 1948-53. Mem. Am. Mgmt. Assn. Republican. Office: GTE Govt Systems Corp PO Box 235 Las Cruces NM 88004

COWEE, JOHN WIDMER, JR., architecture company executive; b. Madison, Wis., Jan. 23, 1949; s. John Widmer Cowee, Sr. and Annette (Oetking) C.; m. Marion Emiko Hironaka, Mar. 21, 1971; 1 child, Misa Melina. AB in Architecture, U. Calif., Berkeley, 1971, MA in Architecture, 1973. Assoc. architect Kaiser Engrs., Oakland, Calif., 1974-82; prin. Lundy, Ng & Cowee, Architects, Oakland, Calif., 1975-79; project mgr. ED2 Architects, San Francisco, 1982-84; assoc. Leo A. Daly Co. Architects, San Francisco, 1984-91; prin. Tecta Assocs., San Francisco, 1986-88; prin./owner Architectural Concepts, Albany, Calif., 1991—. Active El Cerrito, Calif. Redevel. Com., 1974-75, chmn. El Cerrito Design Review Bd., vice chmn. El Cerrito Planning Commn., 1975-79. Mem. El Cerrito Aquatic Masters. Democrat.

COWELL, ERNEST SAUL, lighting designer, consultant; b. Hollywood, Calif., Jan. 27, 1927; s. Ernest S. and Bernice Michael (Waterman) C.; m. Beverly Sue Bloom, Apr. 15, 1950 (div. May 1960); children: Steven Richard, Craig Wesley, Marilyn Tobiann. BA, UCLA, 1950; student, Moorpark Coll., 1971, Cerritos Jr. Coll., 1979. Regional mgr. Prentice Hall Inc., San Francisco, 1954-59; pvt. practice indsl. and govtl. sales L.A., 1959-70; area mgr. Philips Lighting, L.A., 1970-79; v.p. Coons & Cowell Lighting Unltd., Thousand Oaks, Calif., 1979-83; pres. Lighting Designs, L.A., 1983—; cons. City of Thousand Oaks, 1970—; crime prevention specialist L.A. Police Dept., 1991—. Mem. Rep. Presdl. Task Force, 1978—, gen. plan com. City of Thousand Oaks, 1967, gen. plan rev. com., 1984, 86, 88. Sgt. U.S. Army, 1943-46, PTO; with USNR, 1950-58, 70-91. Recipient Edison award Excellence in Lighting, Gen. Electric Corp., 1985, 86. Fellow Inst. Advancement Engring.; mem. Illuminating Engring. Soc. (bd. dirs. So. Calif. sect. 1977-85, nat. chmn. schs and colls. lighting standards com., residential lighting standards com., Internat. Illumination Design award 1983, 84, 85, 87, Disting. Svc. award), Internat. Assn. Lighting Designers, U.S. Nat. Com. to Internat. Commn. Illumination, Library Lighting Standards (nat. chmn. 1988-90), Designers Lighting Forum (bd. dirs. 1988—), Internat. Soc. Interior Designers (design affiliate), Navy League (pres. Hollywood/L.A. coun. 1993—), Roadway Lighting Forum (bd. dirs. 1988-90), Kiwanis (pres. Westlake Village club 1977-79).

COWEN, DONALD EUGENE, physician; b. Ft. Morgan, Colo., Oct. 8, 1918; adopted s. Franklin and Mary Edith (Dalton) C.; BA, U. Denver, 1940; MD, U. Colo., 1943; m. Hulda Marie Helling, Dec. 24, 1942; children: David L., Marilyn Marie Cowen Dean, Theresa Kathleen Cowen Cunningham Byrd, Margaret Ann Cowen Koenigs. Intern, U.S. Naval Hosp., Oakland, Calif., 1944; gen. practice medicine, Ft. Morgan, 1947-52; resident internal medicine U. Colo. Med. Ctr., Denver, 1952-54; practice medicine specializing in allergy, Denver, 1954-90, ret.; mem. staff Presbyn. Med. Ctr., Denver, Porter, Swedish hosps., Englewood, Colo.; clin. asst. prof. medicine U. Colo. Med. Center, 1964—; postgrad. faculty U. Tenn. Coll. Medicine, Memphis, 1962-82; cons. Queen of Thailand, 1973, 75, 77. Pres. Community Arts Symphony Found., 1980-82. Served to lt. M.C., USN, 1943-47. Fellow ACP, Am. Coll. Chest Physicians (vice chmn. com. on allergy 1968-72, 75-87, sec.-treas. Colo. chpt. 1971-77, pres. 1978-80), Am. Coll. Allergy and Immunology, Acad. Internat. Medicine, West Coast Allergy Soc., Southwest Allergy Forum, Am. Acad. Otolaryngic Allergy, Colo. socs. internal medicine, Colo. Allergy Soc. (past pres.), Ill. Soc. Opthalmology and Otolaryngology (hon.), Denver Med. Soc. (chmn. library and bldg. com. 1963-73), Arapahoe Med. Soc. (life emeritus mem.). Presbyterian (ruling elder 1956—). Club: Lions. Contbr. numerous articles to profl. jours. Home: Cherry Hills Village 1501 E Quincy Ave Englewood CO 80110

COWEN, SONIA SUE, university administrator; b. Wichita Falls, Tex., Sept. 30, 1952; d. Jackson Thompson and Shirley Isabel (Skerritt) C. BA magna cum laude, East Wash. U., 1973; MFA in Creative Writing, U. Mont., 1975; postgrad. U. Utah, 1981-82; EdD Gonzaga U., 1990. Grants adminstr. Eastern Wash. U., Cheney, 1978-81, 82, asst. to v.p. and provost, 1982-83, acad. projects adminstr., 1983-88, dir. acad. support svcs., 1988-90; dir. planning & programming, 1990-91; assoc. deputy commr. acad. affairs Mont. U. Systems; registered ski instr., 1985-92; instr. lt.'s profl. devel. program SAC, USAF, 1989-92; dir. Moving Ahead, 1985-86; mem. adj. faculty, 1979, exec. sec. N.W. Inst. for Advanced Study, 1978-81, 82; pres. Leadership Performance Group Co., 1990—; teaching asst. U. Mont., Missoula, 1974-75; instr., head journalism program Coll. of Siskiyous, Weed, Calif., 1975-76; spl. asst. in adminstrn. Ednl. Service Dist. 101, Spokane, Wash., 1976-78; teaching fellow U. Utah, Salt Lake City, 1981-82; freelance writer; cons. grants and contracts to hosps. and state govts.; speaker Internat. Conf. of Soc. Coll. and Univ. Planners, 1989; mem. exec. bd. Ctr. for the Book, Montana; reviewer Grants Program, Mont. Arts Coun., 1992—. Author: (with B. Mitchell and L. Triplett) Something About China, 1971; contbr. poems to various publs. Del. to Mont. State Land Use, 1974, Bend in the River Council, 1974-75; publicity chmn. Wash. State 4th Ann. Very Spl. Arts Festival for Handicapped Children and Adults, 1978, Nat. Theatre of Deaf Spokane Tour, 1978. Recipient Gov.'s Commendation, State of Wash., 1979, also named Outstanding Woman of Yr., 1979; recipient Leadership award YWCA, 1985; named Key Person, United Way of Spokane County, 1984; scholar Bread Loaf Writers Conf., 1973. Mem. LWV, NAFE (network dir. 1985-86), Nat. Council Univ. Research Adminstrs., Nat. Assn. Coll. and Univ. Bus. Officers, Nat. Assn. Univ. Women Deans, Adminstrs. and Counselors, Am. Assn. State Colls. and Univs., State Higher Edn. Exec. Officers, Profl. Ski Instrs. Am., Panhandle Yacht Club (bd. dirs.), Lake Coeur d'Alene Sailing Club. Home: PO Box 125 Helena MT 59624-0125 Office: Mont U Systems 2500 Broadway Helena MT 59620

COWHEY, PETER FRANCIS, international relations educator, consultant; b. Chgo., Sept. 28, 1948; s. Eugene F. and Vivien (High) C.; m. Mary Pat Williams, July 1973 (div. June 1978); m. M. Margaret McKeown, June 29, 1985; 1 child, Megan. BS in Fgn. Svc., Georgetown U., 1970; MA, PhD, U. Calif., Berkeley, 1976. Lectr. U. Calif., Berkeley, 1975-76; from asst. to assoc. prof. polit. sci. U. Calif. San Diego, La Jolla, 1976-88, prof. polit. sci. & internat. rels., 1989—; market planner AT&T Internat., Basking Ridge, N.J., 1985-86; advisor Telemation Assocs., Washington, 1987-88; mem. telecom. adv. bd. A.T. Kearney, Chgo., 1988-91; co-dir. project on internat. and security affairs U. Calif. San Diego, 1990—; rsch. scholar Berkeley Roundtable on the Internat. Economy, 1992—. Author: Problems of Plenty, 1985; co-author: Profit and the Pursuit of Energy, 1983, When Countries Talk, 1988, Managing the World's Economy, 1993; mem. editorial bd. Internat. Orgn., 1989—. Mem. adv. bd. Project Promothee, Paris, 1985—, Ctr. on Telecom. Mgmt., Lincoln, Nebr., 1989-92; com. mem. NRC, 1992-93. Rockefeller Found. internat. affairs fellow, 1984-87. Mem. Am. Polit. Sci. Assn., Coun. Fgn. Rels. (internat. affairs fellow 1985-86), Internat. Studies Assn., Assn. Comparative Econ. Studies. Democrat. Home: 1522 40th Ave Seattle WA 98122 Office: U Calif San Diego Grad Sch Internat Rels & Pacific Studies La Jolla CA 92093

COWINGS, EVERETT ALVIN, entertainment manager, film producer; b. Fresno, Calif., Feb. 11, 1963; s. Everett Alvin Cowings Sr. and Thelma Anita (Williams) Ricks. AA in Drama, Fresno C.C., 1984, AS in Engring., 1985; BS in Law, Western State U., Fullerton, Calif., 1989, student, Coll. of Law; student, Calif. Polytechnic U., Pomona. Owner, printing broker Agape Printing Brokerage, Pomona, 1986-88; mentor, pub. speaker, C.C. System Calif. Ednl. System, Glendorn, Calif., 1985-88; law clerk L.A. City Atty's Office, summer 1988; movie recruiter Nat. Rsch. Group, Hollywood, Calif., 1990-92; prin., entertainment mgr. The Everett Cowings Group, Burbank, Calif., 1992—. Author: (TV script) Homey Alone II, 1991; actor: Sunday Comics, Mancuso FBI, Days of Our Lives, 1987—; producer: Bach and Roll, Small World, Table of Dreams, 1992-93. Mem. NAACP, Fellow Nat. Soc. of Black Engrs., Calif. Lawyers for the Arts, Fellow Black Law Students, Black Filmaker Found., Alpha Phi Alpha. Democrat. Office: The Everett Cowings Group Empire Burbank Studios 1845 Empire Ave Ste 115 Burbank CA 91504

COWLES, DAVID WILLIAM, financial executive; b. San Francisco, Oct. 5, 1954; s. Thomas Richard and Martha (Lefler) C.; m. Karen Lynne Post, June 5, 1987. BS, Calif. State U., Chico, 1976; MS in Fin., Golden Gate U., 1991. CPA, Calif. Audit mgr. Coopers & Lybrand, San Francisco, 1976-88; v.p., chief fin. officer PacTel Products, Milpitas, Calif., 1988-91; v.p. fin. Creative Mktg. Incentives, San Francisco, 1991—. Mem. AICPA, Am. Assn. Individual Investors, Internat. Assn. for Fin. Planners, Calif. Soc. CPAs. Home: 13856 Campus Dr Oakland CA 94605-3830 Office: 120 Montgomery St Fl 5 San Francisco CA 94104-4302

COX, ARTHUR NELSON, astrophysicist, researcher; b. Van Nuys, Calif., Oct. 12, 1927; s. Arthur Hildreth and Sara (Nelson) C.; m. Clarice Wruck, Jan. 3, 1958 (div. 1973); children: Charles, Edward; m. Joan Frances Ellis, Oct. 21, 1973; children: Bryan, Kay, Sally. BS, Calif. Inst. Tech., 1948; AM, Ind. U., 1952, PhD, 1953, DSc (hon.), 1973. Staff mem. Los Alamos Sci. Lab., 1947-49, 53-57, 75-83, group leader, 1957-75, lab. fellow, 1983—; cons. Avco-Everett (Mass.) Rsch. Lab., 1960-61; vis. prof. UCLA, 1966; program advisor NSF, Washington, 1973-74. Sr. editor: The Solar Interior and Atmosphere, 1991. Fellow NSF, 1952-53, NATO, 1968; Fulbright scholar U. Liege, Belgium, 1968-69. Mem. AAAS, Am. Astron. Soc., Internat. Astron. Union (pres. com. 35, 1982-85), Sigma Xi. Office: Los Alamos Nat Lab PO Box 1663 Los Alamos NM 87545-0001

COX, CHARLES SHIPLEY, oceanography researcher, educator; b. Paia, Hawaii, Sept. 11, 1922; s. Joel Bean and Helen Clifford (Horton) C.; m. Maryruth Louise Melander, Dec. 23, 1951; children: Susan, Caroline, Valerie, Ginger, Joel. BS, Calif. Inst. Tech., 1944; PhD, U. Calif., San Diego, 1955. From asst. researcher to prof. U. Calif., San Diego, 1955—. Researcher in field. Fellow AAAS, Am. Geophys. Union (Maurice Ewing medal 1992), Royal Astron. Soc. Democrat. Office: U Calif San Diego Scripps Inst of Oceanography Dept Oceanograpay La Jolla CA 92093

COX, CHRISTOPHER, congressman; b. St. Paul, Minn., Oct. 16, 1952; s. Charles C. and Marilyn A. (Miller) C. BA, U. So. Calif., 1973; MBA, JD, Harvard U., 1977. Bar: Calif. 1978, D.C. 1980. Law clk. to judge U.S. Ct. Appeals (9th cir.), 1977-78; assoc. Latham & Watkins, Newport Beach, Calif., 1978-82, ptnr., 1985-86; sr. assoc. counsel to the Pres. The White House, Washington, 1986-88; mem. 101st-103rd congresses from 40th (now 47th) dist. Calif., Washington, DC, 1989—; mem. budget com., mem. govt. ops. com.; prin., founder Context Corp., St. Paul, 1984-86; lectr. bus. adminstrn. Harvard U., 1982-83. Editor Harvard Law Rev., 1975-77. Republican. Roman Catholic. Home: E Tower Ste 430 4000 MacArthur Blvd Newport Beach CA 92660 Office: US House of Representatives 206 Cannon Bldg Washington DC 20515-0547

COX, DOUGLAS CHARLES, museum executive; b. Pocatello, Idaho, July 24, 1944; s. Edwin Charles and Mary LaVerel (Sorensen) C.; m. Anne Bischoff, June 28, 1969; children: Robert Douglas, Kenneth Edwin, Jonathan Charles, Melissa Jane, Jenny Johanna, Trevor Dean. Assoc., So. Utah State, 1967; BS, Brigham Young U., 1968, PhD, 1976. Cert. secondary tchr. Utah, 1976. Secondary math. tchr. Dixon Sch. Provo Sch. Dist., 1976-77; mus. exec. Monte L. Bean Life Sci. Mus., Provo, 1978—. Scoutmaster local chpt. Boy Scouts of Am., 1985-89, chairperson scout com. 1989—. With U.S. Army, 1968-71. Mem. Mus. Edn. Round Table, Am. Assn. Mus. (edn. com.). Republican. Mem. LDS Ch. Office: Monte L Bean Life Mus Brigham Young Univ 290 MLBM Provo UT 84602

COX, DUANE L., academic administrator, consultant; b. Indpls., Feb. 17, 1940; s. Lee O. and Betty (Cupp) C.; m. Margaret Ann Cox, Aug. 19, 1962; children: Daren, Marci, Michelle. BTh, N.W. Christian Coll., 1966; post-grad., U. Oreg., 1966-67. Athletic dir., basketball coach N.W. Christian Coll., Eugene, Oreg., 1966-70; dir. ann. fund, alumni officer N.W. Christian Coll., Eugene, 1978-82; dir. devel. Nat. Benevolent Assn., Indpls., 1982-84, Luth. Social Svcs., Dayton, Ohio, 1984-85; v.p. devel. Tri-State U., Angola, Ind., 1985-91; pres. Arabian Horse Trust, Denver, 1991; v.p. Woodburn Assoc., 1991—; cons. Hosp. Found., Bloomington, Ind., 1988—; bd. dirs. Gilmore Found., Houston. Mem. strategic planning com. Cameron Community Hosp., Angola, 1990—. Mem. Nat. Soc. Fundraising Execs. (bd. dirs. 1990—), Ind. Coun. Fundraising Execs. (bd. dirs. Indpls. chpt. 1988—), Assoc. Colls. of Ind., Ind. Colls. and Univs. of Ind., Coun. for Advancement and Support of Edn., Ancola C. of C. Home: 195 Ln Big Otter Lk # 110 Fremont IN 46737 Office: 12000 Zuni St Denver CO 80234-2300

COX, GARY EVANS, aerospace company official, consultant; b. Ogden, Utah, July 4, 1937; s. Donald Evans and Maxine Louise (Altweis) C.; m. Carole Sue Brown, June 6, 1959; children: Theresa, Patrick, Colleen. BS in Indsl. Mgmt., U. Portland, 1961; MS in Pub. Adminstrn., Auburn UU., 1973. Commd. 2d lt. USAF, 1961, advanced through grades to col., 1982; pilot USAF, Europe, Korea, Vietnam, U.S., 1961-87; ret., 1987; program mgr. McDonnell Douglas Corp., Phoenix, 1987—; cons. McDonnell Douglas Corp., St. Louis, 1987. Pres. Holy Redeemer Sch. Bd., Tampa, Fla., 1976-78; scoutmaster Tampa coun. Boy Scouts Am., 1977-78; com. chmn. Hampton (Va.) Rep. Com., 1982. Decorated DFC, 20 Air medals; recipient Superior Svc. award Dept. Def., 1987. Mem. Air Force Assn., Ret. Officers Assn., Daedalian Soc. Roman Catholic. Home: 7733 W Villa Theresa Dr Glendale AZ 85308-8262 Office: McDonnell Douglas Tng Syst PO Box 218 Litchfield Park AZ 85340-0218

COX, GEORGE WYATT, biology educator; b. Williamson, W.Va., Feb. 10, 1935; s. Ira F. J. and Edna (Davis) C.; m. Carolyn Celena Kay, Dec. 21, 1958 (div. Apr. 1969); m. Darla Gail Bell, June 6, 1969; children: Daniel Robert, David William. BA, Ohio Wesleyan U., 1956; MS, U. Ill., 1958, PhD, 1960. Asst. prof. biology U. Alaska, Fairbanks, 1960-61, Calif. Western U., San Diego, 1961-62; from asst. prof. to prof. biology San Diego State U., 1962-69; vis. prof. biology Universidad Católica, Santiago, Chile, 1974; program dir. ecology NSF, Washington, 1978-79. Author: Laboratory Manual of General Ecology, 1967, Conservation Ecology: Biosphere and Biosurvival, 1992; co-author: Dynamic Ecology, 1973, Agricultural Ecology, 1979; editor: Readings in Conservation Ecology, 1969. Mem. Ecol. Soc. Am., Soc. Conservation Biology, Am. Soc. Mammologists, N.W. Sci. Assn., Am. Ornithologist's Union. Office: San Diego State U Dept Biology San Diego CA 92182-0057

COX, JOHN FREDERICK, protective services official; b. Denver, Mar. 9, 1955; s. Gerald Herman and Hellon Ann (Brewer) C.; m. Mary Beth Brown, Aug. 14, 1976; children: Christopher, Sarah, Rebekah. Student, Bethel Coll., St. Paul, 1973-75, Chadron State Coll., 1975, 76; BS, Internat. U., Independence, Mo., 1990; grad., FBI Nat. Acad., 1991. Cert. profl. peace officer, Wyo., law enforcement officer, Nebr. Police officer Chadron (Nebr.) Police, 1976-78; state patrolman Wyo. State Hwy. Patrol, Rock Springs, Wyo., 1978-79; dep. sheriff Converse County Sheriff's Office, Douglas, Wyo., 1980-81; police officer Douglas Police, 1981-82, patrol div. supr., 1982-87; chief of police Powell (Wyo.) Police, 1987—; bd. dirs. NW Drug Enforcement Team, 1988—; adv. bd. Wyo. Law Enforcement Acad., Douglas, 1989—; mem. Park County Child Protection Team, Cody, Powell, 1989—. Author: Small Departments and Community Policing, FBI Law Enforcement Bulletin, 1992. Bd. Dirs. Christian Broadcasting Inc., Douglas, 1984-87; mem. Powell Drug/Alcohol Coun., 1987-89. Named Outstanding Young Leo, Douglas Jaycees, 1985, one of Outstanding Young Men of Am., Jaycees, 1978, 85. Mem. Internat. Assn. Chiefs of Police, Wyo. Assn. Chief of Police, Wyo. Peace Officers Assn., NW Peace Officers. Republican. Baptist. Office: Powell Police 250 N Clark St Powell WY 82435-1950

COX, JOHN ROBERT, waste management consulting company executive; b. Kansas City, Mo., Nov. 17, 1945; s. Sherman R. and Marie S. (Souther) C.; m. Susan Gayle Hyland, Jan. 30, 1971; children: Bryna Christine, Shannon Sue. BS in Physics, Ctrl. Mo. State U., Warrensburg, 1974. Mgr. quality Dit-Mco Internat., Inc., Kansas City, Mo., 1974-83; dir. quality assurance MSE, Inc., Butte, Mont., 1983-85; group mgr. EG&G Idaho, Inc., Idaho Falls, 1985-90; gen. mgr. WASTREN, Inc., Idaho Falls, 1990—. Sgt. USMC, 1967-71, Vietnam. Mem. Idaho Falls C. of C. Republican. Lutheran. Home: 255 N 55th W Idaho Falls ID 83402-5451 Office: WASTREN Inc 956 Energy Dr Idaho Falls ID 83402

COX, JOSEPH WILLIAM, college president; b. Hagerstown, Md., May 26, 1937; s. Joseph F. and Ruth E. C.; m. Regina M. Bollinger, Aug. 17, 1963; children—Andrew, Matthew, Abigail. B.A., U. Md., 1959, Ph.D., 1967. Successively instr., asst. prof., assoc. prof., prof. history Towson (Md.) State U., 1964-81, dean evening, summer and minimester programs, 1972-75, acting pres., 1978-79, v.p. acad. affairs and dean of univ., 1979-81; prof. history, v.p. acad. affairs. No. Ariz. U.., Flagstaff, 1981-87; pres. So. Oregon Coll., Ashland, 1987—. Author: Champion of Southern Federalism: Robert Goodloe Harper of South Carolina, 1972, The Early National Experience: The Army Corps of Engineers, 1783-1812, 1979; mem. bd. editors Med. Hist. Mag., 1979-89; columnist S. Oreg. Hist. Mag.; contbr. articles to profl. jours. Bd. dirs. So. Oreg. Econ. Devel. Bd. Mem. AAUP, Am. Assn. Higher Edn., Am. Assn. State Colls. and Univs., Phi Kappa Phi, Omicron Delta Kappa. Episcopalian. Office: So Oreg State Coll 1250 Siskiyou Blvd Ashland OR 97520-2268

COX, KATHRYN CULLEN, nursing director, nursing consultant; b. Sedalia, Mo., June 29, 1943; d. Bernard Joseph and Ann (Matthews) Cullen; m. Paul John Cox, Oct. 3, 1964 (div. Sept. 1980); children: Donna, Eric. Diploma, St. John's Mercy Med. Ctr., 1964; BS, Coll. St. Francis, 1986. Staff RN Bapt. Med. Ctr., Kansas City, Mo., 1969-80, staff RN surgery, 1980-84; oper. rm. supr. Ctr. Eye Surgery, Kansas City, 1984-86; dir. nursing Hunkeler Eye Clinic, Kansas City, 1986-93; staff nurse Glendale (Calif.) Eye Med. Group, 1993—; cons. ophthalmology, Glendale, 1988—. Mem. Am. Soc. Ophthalmic Registered Nurses (pres. local chpt. 1984-86), Assn. Oper. Rm. Nurses, Am. Soc. Cataract & Refractive Surgery. Home: 25224 A Steinbeck Ave Stevenson Ranch CA 91381 Office: Glendale Eye Med Group & Surgery Ctr 607 N Central Glendale CA 91203

COX, MARILYN BUTLER, real estate company executive; b. Waltham, Mass., Mar. 27, 1946; d. Byron Clinton Butler and Helen Virginia (Bowser) Beach; m. Eugene Elwell Cox, May 1, 1971; children: Kimberly, Hillary. BA in Edn., Ariz. State U., 1969; grad. in Computer Programming, Ariz. Inst. Bus. & Tech., 1983. Lic. real estate broker, Ariz.; lic. real estate agt., Calif. Flight svc. Pan Am. World Airways, L.A., 1969-73; systems analyst A.M.S. Mgmt., Inc., Phoenix, 1983-85; pres. Maxi Storage Systems, Phoenix, 1986-87; propr. MBC Mgmt., Phoenix, 1986-87; pres. Cox Property Mgmt., Inc., Phoenix, 1988—. Pres. Florence Crittenton Svcs. Aux., Phoenix, 1978-80, pres., bd. dirs., 1984-85; bd. dirs. Child Welfare League of Am., Washington, 1986-92, sec., bd. dirs., 1993—; mem. Midtowners Bus. and Profl. Women, Phoenix, 1989-90. Named One of Top 25 Comml. Mgmt. Cos., Ariz. Bus. Jour., 1992. Mem. Cen. Ariz. Home Builders Assn., Better Bus. Bur., Inst. Real Estate Mgmt., Self Storage Assn., Women in Stock Edn. Republican. Episcopalian. Office: Cox Property Mgmt Inc 7321 N 16th St # 102 Phoenix AZ 85020

COX, MERIDITH BRITTAN, publishing executive, risk manager, consultant; b. Bklyn., Oct. 25, 1941; d. Vergil McLeod Cox and Elizabeth Joan (Maxey) Vautier. BA, Golden Gate U., 1974, MPA, 1975, postgrad., 1977-81. Exec. dir. Info. Ctr.-Hosp. Conf., San Francisco, 1967-69; rsch. adminstr. ASME, N.Y.C., 1970-72; field rep. Vis. Nurse Assn., San Francisco, 1972-73; cons. med. malpractice El Cerrito, Calif., 1973-76; adj. prof. Golden Gate U., San Francisco, 1977-89; risk mgmt. cons. Meridith B. Cox Assocs., El Cerrito, 1977-89, Billings, Mont., 1990-91; pres. Risk Mgmt. Resource Systems, Billings, Mont., 1992—; part-time instr. Sch. Mgmt., Ea. Mont. Coll., Billings, Mont., 1993—; pub., risk mgr. Cox Publs., El Cerrito, 1977-90. Author: Safety and Equipment Risks, 1991, Prevent Lawsuits, 1992, Standards of Care, 1984, (textbook) Risk Management for Department Head, 1991 (Nat. Fedn. Press Women award 1992); editor, pub. The Nurse, The Patient and The Law jour., 1977—. Commr. El Cerrito Appeals Bd., 1979-80, El Cerrito Parks and Recreation Commn., 1980-81, El Cerrito Safety Commn., 1981-82; mem. Subcom. on Cost Containment Health Care for Montanans, 1991-92. With USN, 1960-63. Recipient Teaching award JFK Univ., 1987. Mem. ASTD (Big Sky chpt.), Nat. League Nursing, Mont. League Nursing (chmn. legis. and pub. affairs 1991-93), Nat. Fedn. Press Women (Risk Mgmt. Textbook award 1992), Mont. Press Women (v.p. 1991-93, pres. 1993—), Mont. Assn. Female Execs. Episcopalian. Office: Cox Publs PO Box 20316 Billings MT 59104-0316

COX, RAYMOND WHITTEN, III, political science educator, academic director; b. Cambridge, Mass., Aug. 21, 1949; s. Raymond Whitten Cox Jr. and Louise Carolyn Holmes; m. Charlene Marie Sharp, Oct. 9, 1975 (div. Jan. 1981); 1 child, Geoffrey; m. Susan Jane Buck, Feb. 5, 1982 (div. 1988); m. Nancy Rose Foye, May 19, 1989. BA, Northeastern U., 1972; M in Pub. Adminstrn., Suffolk U., 1975; PhD, Va. Poly. Inst., 1983. Asst. dir. research Mass. Ho. of Reps., Boston, 1970-77; program dir. NSF, Washington, 1977-82; instr. Va. Poly. Inst., Blacksburg, 1982-83; asst. prof. Bemidji (Minn.) State U., 1983-85; dir. pub. adminstrn. programs No. Ariz. U., Flagstaff, 1985-87; assoc. prof., dir. MPA program N.Mex. State U., 1987-91; chief of staff to lt. gov. Office of the Lt. Gov. State Capitol Santa Fe, 1991—; cons. Beltrami County Welfare Office, Bemidji, 1984-85, Yuma (Ariz.) Econ. Devel. Corp., 1986, Voltaic Inst. Am., 1989-90, LaTuna facility U.S. Bur. Prison, Silver City, N.Mex., 1989-90. Contbr. articles to profl. jours. Exec. com. Beltrami County Dem. Farmer Labor Party, Bemidji, 1984-85; pres. Bemidji Campus United Ministries, 1984-85; mem. Dem. precinct com. Coconino County, Flagstaff, 1985-87; vice chmn. Coconino County Dems., 1987; ward com. chair Santa Fe Dems., 1992—; mem. N. Mex. Dem. State Ctrl. Com., 1993—; fund-raising com. No. Ariz. U. Campus Christian Ctr., Flagstaff, 1986-87. Recipient Outstanding Performance award Dept. of Def., Hartford, Conn., 1969; named one of Outstanding Young Men of Am., Jaycees, 1981. Mem. Am. Polit. Sci., Acad. Polit. Sci., Wester Polit. Sci. Assn. (chmn. membership com. 1986-89), Am. Soc. Pub. Adminstrn. (nat. council 1986-89, chmn. profl. devel. com., chmn. sect. on pub. adminstrn. edn.), Internat. City Mgmt. Assn. (mem. editorial bds. for 3 profl. jours.). Democrat. Episcopal. Home: 2760 Via Venado N Santa Fe NM 87505-6726 Office: Office of Lt Gov State Capitol Santa Fe NM 97503

COX, SUSIE, astrologer; b. Tucson, Ariz., June 17, 1949; d. William Francis and Beulah Marie (Schroeder) C.; m. Gary Clark Cramer, Feb. 14, 1980. Co-owner White Light Book Shop, Tucson, 1975-77, Aquarian Angels Pub., Tucson, 1977-80; astrologer Susie Cox, Inc., Tucson, 1971—; sales rep. Astrolabe Software, Brewster, Mass., 1986—; staff astrologer Canyon Ranch Resort, Tucson, 1982—; editor, pub. Internat. Directory of Astrologers, Tucson, 1992; internat. del. World Congress, Zurich, 1986, Lucern, 1989; speaker United Astrology Congress, San Diego, 1986, New Orleans, 1989; workshop presenter Susie Cox, Inc., N.Y.C., Calif., Ariz., others. Producer numerous video prodns. on astrology, 1985—, theatrical entertainment/award ceremonies, 1986—, astrol. mus. Birth and Death, 1988; author astrology column, 1977—. Chmn. bd. Superhealth Rehab., Tucson, 1980-89; bd. mem. Los Padrinos Hist. Soc., Tucson, 1990—. Mem. Tucson Astrologer's Guild (co-founder). Democrat. Roman Catholic. Home: 2920 E Monte Vista Tucson AZ 85716 Office: Canyon Ranch Resort 8600 Rockcliff Rd Tucson AZ 85716

COX, Z(AINAB) NAGÎN, space systems engineer; b. Bangalore, India, Mar. 25, 1965; d. Hajira (Begum) Ahmed; m. Earl Clyde Cox, Mar. 21, 1922. BA in Psychology and Ops. Rsch. Engring., Cornell U., 1986; M Space Ops. Engring., Air Force Inst. Tech., Wright-Patterson AFB, Ohio, 1990. Orbit systems engr. IBM, Santa Clara, Calif., 1992—. Vol. student work projects, Mex., 1985, Denmark and Germany, 1986, Suicide Prevention Ctr. Hotline, Dayton, Ohio, 1989-90. Officer USAF, 1986-92, mem. Res. Office: IBM/FSSC Bldg 952/2C203 3920 Freedom Circle Santa Clara CA 95054

COYLE, ROBERT EVERETT, federal judge; b. Fresno, Calif., May 6, 1930; s. Everett LaJoya and Virginia Chandler C.; m. Faye Turnbaugh, June 11, 1953; children—Robert Allen, Richard Lee, Barbara Jean. B.A., Fresno State Coll., 1953; J.D., U. Calif., 1956. Bar: Calif. Ptnr. McCormick, Barstow, Sheppard, Coyle & Wayte, 1958-82; chief judge U.S. Dist. Ct. (ea. dist.) Calif., 1982—; mem. exec. com. jud. coun. 9th Cir., chair space & security com. m. Calif. Bar Assn. (exec. com. 1974-79, bd. govs. 1979-82, v.p. 1981), Fresno County Bar Assn. (pres. 1972), 9th Cir. Dist. Judges Assn. (v.p.). Office: US Dist Ct 5116 US Courthouse 1130 O St Fresno CA 93721-2201

COZART, BERT C., lawyer, accountant; b. Concord, N.C., Mar. 17, 1965; s. Elbert Cordell and Carrie Alice (Miller) C. BSBA, U. N.C., 1987; JD, UCLA, 1992. Bar: Calif 1992; CPA, Calif. Sr. auditor Arthur Andersen and Co., Irvine, Calif., 1987; assoc. atty. Loeb and Loeb, L.A., 1992—. Student vol. Westside Legal Svcs., Santa Monica, Calif., 1989-91; mem. L.A. County Young Republicans, 1991—. Mem. ABA, AICPA, Calif. Soc. CPAs, L.A. County Bar Assn. (litigation sect.), Federalist Soc., Mensa Soc., Beta Gamma Sigma, Beta Alpha Psi. Home: 3724 Glendon Ave # 203 Los Angeles CA 90034

COZEN, LEWIS, orthopedic surgeon; b. Montreal, Canada, Aug. 14, 1911; came to U.S. 1922; AB, U. Calif., San Francisco, 1929, MD, 1934. Diplomate Am. Bd. Orthopedic Surgery. Intern San Francisco Hosp., 1933-34; resident orthopedic surgeon U. Iowa, 1934-35; resident and fellow orthopedic surgery San Francisco County Hosp., 1935-36, Children's Hosp. and Mass. Gen. Hosp., Boston, 1936-39; pvt. practice orthopedic surgery L.A., 1939-40, 45—; assoc. clin. prof. orthopedic surgery UCLA, 1965-93; assoc. clin. prof. emeritusLoma Linda Med. Sch., 1963—; attending orthopedic surgeon, emeritus Cedars Sinai Med. Ctr., 1939—, Orthopaedic Hosp., 1939—; chief orthopedic surgery City of Hope, 1948-67; sr. attending orthopedic surgeon, emeritus Unit One L.A. County Hosp., 1950-63; lectr. in field. Author: Office Orthopedics, 1955, 4th edit. 1973, Operative Orthopedic Clinics (with Dr. Avia Brockway), 1960, Atlas of Orthopedic Surgery, 1966, Difficult Orthopedic Diagnosis, 1972, Plannings and Pitfalls in Orthopedic Surgery, Natural History of Orthopedic Disease, 1993; mem. editorial bd. Resident & Staff Physician; contbr. numerous articles to profl. jours. Vol. physician Internat. Children's Program, Orthopedic Hosp., Mexicali, Mexico. Lt. col. U.S. Army, 1940-45. Fellow ACS, Internat. Coll. Surgeons; mem. Am. Rheumatism Assn., So. Calif. Rheumatism Assn. (pres. 1979), Am. Acad. Orthopedic Surgeons, WesternOrthopedic Assn., Phi Beta Kappa, Alpha Omega Alpha. Office: 6200 Wilshire Blvd #800 Los Angeles CA 90048

COZENS, RICHARD, upholsterer; b. Killeen, Tex., Oct. 21, 1952; s. Orman Roy and Betty Sue (Ward) C.; m. Kera Lynn Anderson, Apr. 30, 1988 (div. 1990); 1 child, Devon Killeen. BA, N.Mex. Highland U., 1975, MA, 1977. Apprentice upholsterer Don's Interiors, Las Vegas, N.Mex., 1977-79; owner/operator Blue Dart Ent., Las Vegas, 1979—. Home: 819 Highland Dr Las Vegas NM 87701-5024 Office: Blue Dart Ent 423 Railroad Ave Las Vegas NM 87701-3858

CRABB, CAROL ANN, library administrator, clergywoman; b. Buffalo, June 30, 1944; d. Howard F. and Estella G. (Zelie) Heavener; m. Lawson V. Crabb, Sept. 28, 1991. B.A. in Philosophy, SUNY, Buffalo, 1966; M.S. in Library Sci., Syracuse U., 1968; grad. Sacred Coll. Jamilian Theology and Div. Sch., 1976. Library trainee and research asst. SUNY, Med. Center, Syracuse, 1966-67; asst. editor SUNY Union List of Serials, Syracuse, 1967-68; readers services librarian, asst. prof. Jefferson Community Coll., Watertown, N.Y., 1968-75; ordained to ministry Internat. Community of Christ Ch., 1974; adminstr. public services dept. Internat. Community of Christ, Chancellery, Reno, 1975-84, dir. Jamilian Theol. Research Library, 1975—; mem. faculty Sacred Coll. Jamilian U. of the Ordained, Reno, 1979—, Jamilian Parochial Sch., Internat. Community of Christ, 1978—. Chmn. religious edn. com. All Souls Unitarian-Universalist Ch., Watertown, N.Y., 1970-71, treas., 1974-75; trustee North Country Reference and Research Resources Council, Canton, N.Y., 1974-75; dir. Gene Savoy Heritage Museum and Library, 1984—; violist Symphonietta, Reno, 1983—. Mem. ALA, Nev. Library Assn., Friends of Library Washoe County, Friends of Library U. Nev. Club: Coll. Women's. Contbr. articles on library sci. to profl. jours. Home: 16010 S Virginia St Reno NV 89511 Office: Internat Community of Christ Chancellory 643 Ralston St Reno NV 89503-4436

CRABB, PATRICK SHIA, art educator, ceramic artist; b. Shanghai, China, Oct. 12, 1947; came to U.S., 1955; s. William Ray and Lydia (Shia) C.; m. Vicki del Ridgway, Oct. 28, 1972; children: Kevin, Kenneth. BFA, U. Mass., 1970; MFA, U. Calif., Santa Barbara, 1976. Art instr. adult edn. Unified Sch. Dist., San Bernardino, Calif., 1973-74; asst. prof. art Utah State U., Logan, 1983; prof. art Rancho Santiago Coll., Santa Ana, Calif., 1976—; adj. prof. Calif. State U., Fullerton, 1982. Exhibited in 30 one-man shows, 175 group exbns.; lectr., workshop presenter; works represented in collections in U.S., Japan, New Zealand and Italy; published in Am. Craft mags., Ceramics Monthly mag., Am. Ceramics, exhbn. catalogs. Capt. USAF, 1970-76. Fulbright grantee, 1992; Rancho Santiago grantee, 1987, 92; recipient numerous art awards; named to Outstanding Young Men of Am., 1980. Mem. Am. Craft Coun., Am. Ceramic Soc., Nat. Coun. for Edn. of Ceramic Arts. Home: 2371 Silk Tree Tustin CA 92680 Office: Rancho Santiago Coll 17th and Bristol Sts Santa Ana CA 92706

CRABB, ROBERT JAMES, counselor; b. Madison, Wis., May 5, 1949; s. Jack Husting and Jean (Carey) C.; m. Maria Irene Warren, Oct. 11, 1980. BA, Whitman Coll., 1972; MEd, Ea. Wash. U., 1975. Cert. continuing level counselor; cert. provisional level secondary prin., Wash. Counselor Cheney (Wash.) High Sch., 1972-78; owner Grambo's Restaurant, Mt. Spokane, Wash., 1978-80; regional counselor Spokane Pub. Schs., 1980-87; counselor Joel E. Ferris High Sch., Spokane, 1987-91, Havermale Alternative Ctr., Spokane, 1991—. Named Young Educator of Yr., Wash. State Jaycees, 1975. Mem. Wash. State Coaches Assn. Roman Catholic. Home: 507 E Cooper Ln Colbert WA 99005-9302 Office: Havermale Alternative Ctr 1300 W Knox Ave Spokane WA 99205

CRABBS, ROGER ALAN, publisher, consultant, small business owner, educator; b. Cedar Rapids, Iowa, May 9, 1928; s. Winfred Wesley and Faye (Woodard) C.; m. Marilyn Lee Wescott, June 30, 1951; children: William Douglas, Janet Lee Crabbs Turner, Ann Lee Crabbs Menke. B.A. in Sci., State U. Iowa, 1954; M.B.A., George Washington U., 1965, D.B.A., 1973; M.Christian Leadership, Western Conservative Bapt. Sem., 1978. Commd. 2nd lt. USAF, 1950, advanced through grades to lt. col., 1968, Ret., 1972; prof. mgmt. U. Portland, Oreg., 1972-79; prof. bus. George Fox Coll., Newberg, Oreg., 1979-83; pres. Judson Bapt. Coll., The Dalles, Oreg., 1983-85; pres., assoc. pub. Host Pubs. Inc. doing bus. as Travelhost of Oreg. and S.W. Wash., 1985—; pres., chmn. various corps., 1974-86; cons. to various orgsn., corps. and agys. Author: The Infallible Foundation for Management-The Bible, 1978, The Secret of Success in Small Business Management-Is in the Short Range, 1983; co-author: The Storybook Primer on Managing, 1976. Bd. dirs. Christ Community Ch., English Speaking Union, Portland/Oreg. Visitors Assn., Oakhills Townhouse Assn. Decorated Air Force Commendation medal with oak leaf cluster, Meritorious Service medal Dept. Def.; rated Command Air Force Missileman; recipient regional, dist. and nat. awards SBA. Mem. Acad. Mgmt., Am. Arbitration Assn., Svc. Corps Ret. Execs./Active Corps of Execs., Air Force Assn., Portland Officers Club, Rotary (past pres.), Masons, Alpha Kappa Psi, Delta Epsilon Sigma. Republican. Office: Host Publs Inc 1075 NW Murray Rd Ste 173 Portland OR 97229-5501

CRABS, DONALD BENJAMIN, scenic and lighting designer, theater consultant; b. Puyallup, Wash., Oct. 29, 1926; s. Raymond D. Crabs and Dulcie (Bogie) Fullager; m. Clara Jane Kelly, Jan. 31, 1949; children: Kevin D., Krissy Ann., Shannon Maria. BA, U. Puget Sound, 1950; MA, Northwestern U., 1951. Asst. prof. Rutgers U., New Brunswick, N.J., 1951-65; prof. emeritus dept. theatre UCLA, L.A., 1965-91; cons. in field. Scenic, lighting designer including The House of Blue Leaves, The Rimers of Eldrich, No Place to be Somebody, Sleight of Hand, Mademoiselle Colombe, He Who Says, Yes, He Who Says, No., The Physicists, A Chorus Line, Ondine, U.S.A., Skin of Our Teeth, Troilus and Cressida, Sergeant Musgrave's Dance, The Measures Taken, Baal, Winterset; editor: California Theatre Index 1971: College & University Facilities, 1971; designer computer storage system for theatre facilities. With USN, 1944-46. Lecture and rsch. grantee U. Calif. Edn. Abroad Program, China, 1990. Mem. U.S. Inst. for Theater Tech. Methodist.

CRABTREE, GARVIN DUDLEY, horticulturist, educator; b. Eugene, Oreg., Nov. 29, 1929; s. Fred Wayne and Gertrude Ellen (Gum) C.; m. Priscilla Aileen Horning, Mar. 20, 1965; children: Melissa Ann, Andrew Douglas. BS, Oreg. State U., 1951; MS, Cornell U., 1955, PhD, 1958. Prof. horticulture Oreg. State U., Corvallis, 1958—; rsch. assoc. Mich. State U., East Lansing, 1975-76; vis. prof. Chung Hsing U. Taichung, Republic of China, 1989-90. Contbr. articles to profl. jours. Cpl. U.S. Army, 1951-53. Mem. Am. Soc. for Hort. Sci., Weed Sci. Soc. Am., Western Soc. Weed Sci., Oreg. Soc. Weed Sci. (sec. 1985—). Office: Oreg State U Dept Horticulture Corvallis OR 97331-7304

CRABTREE, VIVIAN SUCHER, nursing educator; b. N.Y.C., Mar. 29, 1923; d. Robert MacFarland and Helen Patrice (Merritt) Smith; m. Robert L. Sucher, Dec. 1, 1947 (div. Jan. 1959); children: Robert, Charles; m. Samuel Crabtree, Oct. 20, 1991. BS in Zoology, U. N.H., 1944; MSN, Yale U., 1946; MS in Med./Surg. Nursing, UCLA, 1962; cert. Gerontology Nursing, U. So. Calif., L.A., 1977; cert. nurse practioner, Calif. State U., Long Beach, 1978. RN, NP. Staff nurse N.Y. Hosp./Cornell Med. Ctr., N.Y.C., 1946-47; head nurse VA Hosp., Madison, Wis., 1953-57; asst. chief nurse Vets. Rsch. Hosp., Chgo., 1957-59; instr. Sch. of Nursing Seattle U., 1948-50; instr. in sci. Sch. of Nursing Milw. County Hosp., 1950-53; asst. prof. dept. nursing San Jose (Calif.) State U., 1969-61; prof. dept. nursing Calif. State U., Long Beach, 1962-90, prof. emeritus, 1990—; cons., prof. women's studies program Calif. State U., Long Beach, 1974-90, cons., prof. gerontology cert. program, 1978-90. Mem. Nat. Assn. for Mental Illness, 1980-90, Long Beach Assn. for Mental Illness. NIH grantee Calif. State U., 1976-80. Mem. Am. Soc. on Aging, Calif. Coun. Gerontology and Geriatrics, Calif. Coalition Nurse Practitioners, Geron. Soc. Am., Nat. League for Nursing (sec., treas. Long Beach chpt. 1965-75), NOW.

CRAFT, JOHN EDWARD, educator, media consultant; b. Hopedale, Ohio, Mar. 30, 1943; s. Clyde Edward and Mignon (Work) C.; m. Elizabeth Ann Harris, Dec. 18, 1965; children: Lauren, Jennifer. BFA in Dramatic Arts, Ohio U., 1966, MA in Radio and TV, 1972, PhD in Mass Communications, 1975. Dir. staging and lighting Sta. WOUB-TV, Athens, Ohio, 1965-66; dir. instructional TV Hancock County Schs., Weirton, W.Va., 1966-70; instructional TV coord. Ohio U., Athens, 1971-72; prof. Ariz. State U., Tempe, 1973—; analyst, Data for the Future, Phoenix, 1983-84; dir. video svcs., Samaritan Health Svcs., Phoenix, 1980-81; co-owner, Rich/Craft Prodns., Phoenix, 1974-75; field coord. Ednl. TV for S.E. Ohio, Athens, 1971-72; media cons. J. Craft, Cons., Tempe, 1969—; tech. staff mem., Ohio U. Theatre, Athens, 1964-65. Producer TV, Beauty of Individual Differences, 1990, Intervention Facilitator, 1983; producer, dir. TV, Staying Alive, 1981, The Cub, 1980, Princess and Tailor, 1966; appeared in plays, Ohio Valley Summer Theatre, 1963-65; contbr. articles to profl. publs. Bd. dirs. PAL Found., Mesa, Ariz., 1977. Recipient Outstanding Program award, Ariz. Med. Assn., Phoenix, 1981, Superior Achievement award, Internat. Radio & TV Soc., N.Y.C., 1985, Outstanding Program award, Alpha Epsilon Rho, Athens, 1964. Mem. NATAS (bd. dirs. 1973-76, 86—), AAUP, Internat. TV Assn. (pres. 1983-85), Broadcast Edn. Assn., Ariz. Cable TV Forum (treas. 1988—), Phi Kappa Phi. Democrat. Home: 218 E Carter Dr Tempe AZ 85282-6705 Office: Ariz State U Stauffer Hall Tempe AZ 85287

CRAFT, ROBBIE WRIGHT, artist; b. St. Louis, Feb. 22, 1951; d. Robert Edward and Irene (Tosch) Wright; m. Joseph Walter Epply III (div. 1978); 1 child, Joseph Walter IV; m. Raymond Wood Craft II, Feb. 14, 1987. Student, Casper Jr. Coll., 1969-71. Mgr. restaurant and bar Widow Browns, Crofton, Md., 1978-84; adminstrv. asst. U.S. Dept. Def., Andrews AFB, Md., 1974-75; illustrator, supr. U.S. Dept. Def., Cheyenne, Wyo., 1985-88, EEO counselor, 1987—, chief visual info., 1988—; ind. artist Maryland, Wyo., 1974—; ind. interior designer Wyo., 1985—. Lutheran. Home: 7223 Tumbleweed Dr Cheyenne WY 82009 Office: Visual Info Bldg 242 Cheyenne WY 82005

CRAGHEAD, JAMES DOUGLAS, civil engineer; b. Petersburg, Va., Nov. 27, 1950; s. William Douglas and Edith Marcia (Smith) C.; m. Vicki Lynn Taylor, June 5, 1970; 1 child, Jeffrey Taylor. BS, N.Mex. State U., Las Cruces, 1976. Design engr. Black & Veatch Cons. Engrs., Kansas City, Mo., 1976-77; engr. Frank Henri & Assocs., Las Cruces, N.Mex., 1977-78; sr. engr. Hughes Aircraft Co., Tucson, 1978-80, supr. engring., 1980-84, head environ. engr., 1985-90, sr. tech. specialist, 1990—. Inventor in field. Bd. dirs. Our Town Family Svcs., 1987-91. Sgt. U.S. Army, 1970-73. Scholar ROTC, 1969, N.Mex. Mil. Inst., 1969. Mem. ASCE, Am. Legion, Chi Epsilon. Republican. Episcopalian. Home: 8221 E Kenyon Dr Tucson AZ 85710-4225 Office: Hughes Aircraft Co PO Box 11337 Tucson AZ 85734-1337

CRAGUN, CALVIN, business owner; b. Salt Lake City, Nov. 14, 1940; s. Robert Wallace and Vivian (Parker) C.; m. Celestia Van Tussenbroek, Dec. 20, 1967; children: Marlayn, Caroline, David, Robert. BS, U. Utah, 1963, MS, 1966. Tchr. Utah Sch. for the Deaf, Ogden, 1966-72; from salesperson to mgmt. dept. Home Life of N.Y., Salt Lake City, 1972-82; with ins. sales dept. Standard of Oreg., Salt Lake City, 1982-84; owner Custom Benefits, Salt Lake City, 1984—, Rocky Mt. Brokerage, Salt Lake City, 1985-88, Ins. Designers, Salt Lake City, 1988—. Mem. Nat. Conf. for Autism, Salt Lake City, 1983; regional coord. Internat. Winter Spl. Olympics, Salt Lake City, 1985—; mem. Gov.'s Com. for Handicapped, Salt Lake City, 1983-84; vol. Jr. Achievement, 1991—; LUTC tchr., 1992—. Mem. Utah Coun. for Handicapped (v.p. 1982-83). Home and Office: 2686 Towne Dr Salt Lake City UT 84121-5146

CRAHAN, ELIZABETH SCHMIDT, librarian; b. Cleve., Oct. 6, 1913; d. Edward and Margaret (Adams) Schmidt; m. Kenneth Acker, 1938 (div. 1968); children: Margaret Miller, John Acker, Steven Acker, Charles Acker; m. Marcus E. Crahan, Dec. 16, 1968. Student Wellesley Coll., 1931-32; BArch, U. So. Calif., 1937, MLS, 1960. Reference libr. L.A. County Med. Assn., 1960-61, head reference libr., 1961-67, asst. libr., 1967-78, dir. libr. svcs., 1978-90, med. libr., 1990—. Founder Med. Libr. Scholarship Found., 1967; pres. Friends of the UCLA Libr., 1977-79; sec. Friends of the L.A. County Med. Assn. Libr., 1978—. Mem. Spl. Librs. Assn., Med. Libr. Assn., Med. Libr. Group, So. Calif. and Ariz., Med. Mus. Assn., Am. Inst. Wine Food.

CRAIG, CAROL MILLS, marriage, family and child counselor; b. Berkeley, Calif., May 7, 1952. BA in Psychology with honors, U. Calif., Santa Cruz, 1974; MA in Counseling Psychology, John F. Kennedy U., 1980; doctoral student, Calif. Sch. Profl. Psychology, Berkeley, 1980-87, Columbia Pacific U., San Rafael, Calif., 1987—. Psychology intern Fed. Correction Inst., Pleasanton, Calif., 1979-81, Letterman Army Med. Ctr., San Francisco, 1980-82; psychology intern VA Mental Hygiene Clinic, Oakland, Calif., 1981-82, Martinez, Calif., 1982-83; instr. Martinez Adult Sch., 1983, Piedmont Adult Edn., Oakland, 1986; biofeedback and stress mgmt. cons. Oakland, 1986—; dir. Buddies-A Nonprofit, Counseling Svc. for Persons in the Arts, Walnut Creek, Calif., 1986—; rsch. asst. Irvington Pubs., N.Y.C., 1979, Little, Brown and Co., Boston, 1983. Mem. Calif. Assn. Marriage and Family Therapists (clin.), Musicians Union Local 424, Calif. Scholarship Fedn. (life).

CRAIG, EDWARD CHARLES, computer programmer; b. El Paso, Tex., May 23, 1949; s. Charles Benjamin and Concepcion (Rivas) C.; m. Sally Lynne Dorman, June 18, 1988. AA in Bus. Adminstrn., L.A. Harbor Coll., 1977; BS in Acctg., Loyola Marmount U., L.A., 1980. From cost analyst to supr. cost control Western Airlines, L.A., 1980-87; contract focus programmer Oxford & Assocs., L.A., 1987; data base analyst First Interstate Bank, L.A., 1987-89; acctg. application programmer Taco Bell Corp., Irvine, Calif., 1989—. Sgt. USAF, 1968-72. Mem. Orange County Philharm. Soc., U.S. Power Squadrons, Delta Sigma Pi (sr.v.p. 1979-80). Republican. Roman Catholic. Office: Taco Bell Corp 17901 Von Karman Ave Irvine CA 92714-6212

CRAIG, EILEEN SISTERSON, human resources manager; b. Winnipeg, Manitoba, Can., Apr. 29, 1948; came to U.S., 1956; d. William G. and Kathleen (Dillon) Sisterson. BBA in Human Resources Mgmt., Nat. U., 1993. Cert. profl.in human resources, trainer skills for an empowered workplace. Dir. ops. CPT Calif., Inc., San Diego, 1980-85; bus. devel. mgr. Craig Horn Corp., San Diego, 1985-89; human resources mgr. Laidlaw Waste Sys Inc., Chula Vista, Calif., 1987—; cons. Advance Notice Consulting, San Diego, 1990—; co-instr. Dale-Carnegie, San Diego, 1990. Author: (manual) ADA Reference Manual, 1992, EEO Training Manual, 1990, Your Close Encounters, 1991. Grantee, Laidlaw Waste Sys Inc., 1990. Mem. EEOC, (legis com. 1991-92, census data chair 1992, v.p. EEO coun. 1993), Soc. for Human Resources Mgmt., Am. Payroll Assn. Office: Laidlaw Waste Systems 180 Otay Lakes Rd #200 Bonita CA 91902

CRAIG, GAIL HEIDBREDER, architect, educator; b. Balt., Jan. 20, 1941; d. Gerald August and Ora Henderson (Longley) Heidbreder; m. Val Dean Craig, Jan. 19, 1985; children: Laura Temple, John Temple. BA, Stanford U., 1966, postgrad., 1975-78. Registered architect, Calif. With various firms, 1969-85; owner Gail Craig, AIA-Architect, Porterville, Calif., 1985—; instr. architecture, constrn. and CADD, Coll. of Sequoias, Visalia, Calif., 1990—. Mem. AIA.

CRAIG, JAMES RALPH, university administrator; b. Great Falls, Mont., Mar. 24, 1938; s. Ralph Edward and Ruby Odessa (Allen) C.; m. Helen Marie Valach, Aug. 30, 1959; children: Jennifer Rae Craig Howe, Jeffrey Robert. BS, Mont. State U., 1960, MEd, 1961. Credit and loan officer Empire Savs. & Loan, Livingston, Mont., 1962-63, Wells Fargo Bank, San Francisco, 1963-66; dir. fin. aid svcs. Mont. State U., Bozeman, 1966—; mem. Adv. Com. on Student Fin. Assistance, Washington, 1988—, chair, 1988-91. Mem. City County Planning Bd., Bozeman, 1975-85, vice-chair, 1979-85. 1st lt. U.S. Army, 1961-62. Recipient Cert. of Merit U.S. Dept. Edn., 1985, Cert. of Recognition U.S. Dept. Edn., 1987. Mem. Nat. Assn. Fin. Aid Adminstrs. (v.p. 1972-73), Rocky Mountain Assn. Fin. Aid Adminstrs. (pres. 1972-73, Hall of Fame award 1988), Mont. Assn. Fin. Aid Adminstrs. (pres. 1969-70), Masons, Shrines, York Rite. Presbyterian. Home: 3312 Sundance Dr Bozeman MT 59715 Office: Mont State U Fin Aid Office Bozeman MT 59717

CRAIG, LARRY EDWIN, senator; b. Council, Idaho, July 20, 1945; s. Elvin and Dorothy Craig. B.A., U. Idaho; postgrad, George Washington U. Farmer, rancher Midvale area, Idaho; mem. Idaho Senate, 1974-80, 97th-101st Congresses from 1st Dist. Idaho, 1981-90; senator 102nd Congress from Idaho, 1990—, mem. com. agr., nutrition and forestry, com. energy and natural resources, spl. com. on aging, Sen. ethics com., ethics study commn.; chmn. Idaho Republican State Senate Races, 1976-78. Pres. Young Rep. League Idaho, 1976-77; mem. Idaho Rep. Exec. Com., 1976-78; chmn. Rep. Central Com. Washington County, 1971-72; advisor vocat. edn. in public schs. HEW, 1971-73; mem. Idaho Farm Bur., 1965-79. Served with U.S. Army N.G., 1970-74. Mem. NRA (bd. dirs. 1983—), Future Farmers of Am. (v.p. 1965). Methodist. Office: US Senate Offices of Senate Members Washington DC 20510

CRAIG, LEXIE FERRELL, career development specialist, guidance counselor, educator; b. Halls, Tenn., Dec. 12, 1921; d. Monroe Stancil and Hester May (Martin) Ferrell; m. Philip L. Craig, May 19, 1951; children: Douglas H., Laurie K., Barbara J. BS magna cum laude, George Peabody Coll., Vanderbilt U., 1944; MA with honors in Guidance Counseling Devel., Denver U., 1965; postgrad. Colo. U., 1972—, Colo. State U., 1964—, U. No. Colo., 1964—. Cert. vocat. adminstr., Colo., vocat. guidance specialist, vocat. bus. edn. specialist, vocat. home econs. specialist, reading specialist, nat. recreation dir. specialist. Danforth grad. fellow, counselor Mich. State U., East Lansing, 1944-46; nat. student counselor, field dir. dept. of univ. pastor and student work in the dept. of higher edn. Am. Bapt. Conv., summer svc. career projects dir. U.S. and Europe, 1946-51; coord. religious and career activities counselor, Colo. U., 1951-52; tchr. home econs., phys. edn., counseling, dist. 96, Riverside, Ill., 1952-54; substitute tchr., psychometrist, reading specialist part time, Deerfield, Ill., 1956-59; substitute tchr. Littleton (Colo.) Dist. VI, 1961-63, guidance and career counselor Littleton Pub. Schs., 1963-86, career devel. specialist, guidance counselor spl. assignments state and nat., Gov.'s Youth 2000 Task Force Com., 1988—, also mem. vocat. needs and assessment com., 1988-89, chmn. retirement workshops for educators in Littleton Pub. Schs., 1990, 91, 92; chmn. leadership AARP Works Employment Planning Team, Colo., 1989-91, state coodr. employment planning, 1988-93, pres. Greater Littleton (chartered chpt.), Colo., 1990-93; mem. Gov. of Colo. Older Workers Adv. Coun., 1989—; dir./counselor Job Corps, 1967-68; dir., counselor YWCA Extension Program, Job Corps, Denver, 1967-68; tchr. adult edn. home econs. (evening classes), 1963-66; mem. Colo. State Career Task Force, 1973-77; cons. vol. home econ. cons. Colo. State U extension office, 1988-89. Lay conf. rep. Meth. Ch. Pastor/Parish Commn.; vol. sr. citizens programs AARP, St. Andrew United Meth. Ch., Littleton Community Ctr., 1987-90, mem. nominating and personnel work area com.; youth work area chmn. membership com. St. Andrew United Meth. Ch. Women, 1989-92; mem. Greater Denver Friendship Force, 1972—; bd. dirs. Career Awareness Council Boy Scouts Am., Metro Denver, 1972—; also mem. Colo. Career Awareness Council, 1972—; mem. So. Suburban Recreation, Littleton Community Arts Ctr., mem. lit. book club; mem. Friends of Littleton Libr. and Mus.; charter mem. Littleton Townhall Music and Drama Ctr.; adv. council Powell PTO, 1981-84; adv. council SEMBCS area vocat. schs., 1969—; mem. local caucus com. Republican Party; mem. Dist. Environ. Sci. Council. Didcott scholar, Peabody/Vanderbilt Coll., 1942; mem. AVS adv. council Early Childhood Edn., Health Occupation, Restaurant Arts and Coop Career Devel., 1970—, Gov's. Older Workers Task Force, Pvt. Sector Adv. Coun., 1989—; chartered, pres. Colo. Career Devel. Assn., 1983-86, chmn., 1987-91; Colo. state vol., coord. employment planning program Colo. AARP/Works, 1989-91; pres. Greater Littleton chpt. AARP, 1990-93, Colo. Assn. Adult Devel. & Aging, 1989—; mem. youth area coun. St. Andrew's Meth. Ch., 1990-92. Danforth home econs. and leadership scholar, 1943, Danforth fellow, 1944-45 Danforth Found.; Am. Leadership Camp Found. scholar, Shelby, Mich., 1942-45; Hildegarde Sweet Scholar, 1983; recipient Sullivan award and grant, named outstanding grad., Geo. Peabody Coll., 1944; named Littleton Mother of Year, 1977, Colo. Vocat. Counselor of Yr., 1978, Colo. Vocat. Guidance Assoc. Counselor of Yr., 1984; recipient plaque for recruiting and career guidance Navy and Air Force, 1980, Clifford G. Houston Colo. Counselor award, 1985, Outstanding award Boy Scouts of Am. Career Awareness Council (Denver area), 1986, Recognition Gold Pin award United Meth. Ch. Women, 1988, Colo. Disting. Silver Svc. award, 1990, Gov.'s Silver Trophy award AARP, 1991, Nat. award, 1Plaque-Outstanding Vol. Svc. to Colo. Sr. Citizens award, 1991-92, Gov.'s Silver trophy for svc. and establishing AARP employment planning program for Colo., 1992. Mem. NEA, AAUW, Colo. Religious Values Assn. (mem. chmn. 1989), Colo. Edn. Assn., Littleton Edn. Assn., Am. Vocat. Assn., Colo. Vocat. Assn., Am. Assn. Counseling and Devel. (pres. 1990-91), Colo. Assn. for Adult Devel. and Aging (exec. bd., pres. 1991-92), Nat. Career Devel. Assn. (membership chmn.), Colo. Career Devel. Assn. (past pres., membership chmn.), Nat. Vocat. Guidance Assn. (Colo. rep.), Am. Assn. Retired Persons (charter mem., pres., v.p. Greater Littleton chpt. 1991—), Colo. Retired Sch. Employees Assn. (pres. 1990-92), Colo. Sch. Counselors Assn., Am. Field Service (pres. Littleton chpt.), Home Economists in Homemaking (Littleton and Bega, Australia clubs 1989—), Colo. Gerontol. Soc., Phi Delta Kappa, Delta Kappa Gamma Alpha Delta (past chpt. pres., Omega State DKG, state com. chmn. personal growth and svcs.), Order Eastern Star, Countryn Western Dance Club, Delta Pi Epsilon (past pres.), Pi Omega Pi (past pres.), Pi Gamma Mu (past pres.), Kappa Delta Pi (past pres.). Curriculum units in consumer edn., home econs., careers, parenting classes, AARP/Works Employment Planning Workshops. Office: 2655 S Sheridan Ct Denver CO 80227-4037

CRAIG, MAYADELLE DELL, psychotherapist; b. Wildrose, N.D., June 14, 1937; d. Willie O. and Olive May (Holland) Evenson; m. John Takas, 1979 (dec.); children: Cynthia, Joni. BA, U. Nev., Las Vegas, 1978; MA, Whitworth Coll., 1982; postgrad. Saybrook Inst. Cert. relapse prevention specialist. Cert. alcoholism counselor Wash. State Profl. Staff Soc., 1982. Counselor, group therapist Ct. Referral Services, Las Vegas, 1977-79; counselor, employee assistance program facilitator Southwest Community Alcohol Ctr., Seattle, 1979-81; pres. Dell Craig Therapists Inc., Des Moines, Wash., 1981-90, Joie, Inc., 1990—; developer, cons. employee assistance programs; franchiser catalyst plans on alcoholism recovery, organizational enhancement. Mem. Wash. State Council on Alcoholism, Am. Personnel and Guidance Assn., Psi Chi. Club: Toastmasters (Burien, Wash.). Office: Joie Inc 29507-1 Ave S Federal Way WA 98003

CRAIG, MICHAEL SCOTT, real estate executive, pharmacologist; b. Atlanta, Tex., Feb. 21, 1956; s. Hoyt Dean and Ellenda Claudia (Clements) C.; m. Angela Ruth Francisco, May 30, 1992. BS in Pharmacy, U. Tex., 1979, MBA in Real Estate/Fin., 1985. Registered pharmacist, Tex.; registered real estate broker, Calif. Pharmacist mgr. Script Shop Pharmacies, Austin, Tex., 1979-83; comml. loan credit mgr. Franklin Savs. & Loan, Austin, 1985-87; asset mgr. Continental Mgmt., Dallas, 1987-88; v.p. asset mgmt. Postal Mgmt. Svc. Corp., L.A., 1988-89, RRP Mgmt. Corp., L.A., 1989—; dir. Supermarket Video, Inc., L.A., 1988; cons. Assoc. U.S. Postal Svc. Lessors, L.A., 1989-93. Mem. Inst. Real Estate Mgmt., Beta Gamma Sigma.

CRAIG, ROBERT WALLACE, educational administrator; b. Long Beach, Calif., Sept. 16, 1924; s. Harold Fleming and Ellen Amelia (Stagg) C.; m. Carol Williams Gallun, Nov. 5, 1957; children: Kathleen Elizabeth, Jennifer Courtney, Michael Brian. BS, BA cum laude, U. Wash., 1949; MA, Columbia U., 1951. V.p., exec. dir. Aspen (Colo.) Inst. for Humanistic Studies, 1954-64; v.p. Unimark Internat. Design Inc., Aspen and Chgo., 1965-71; prin. Robert Craig & Assocs., 1965-73; ptnr. Genesis Inc., 1971-73, Rieben & Craig, Denver, 1973-75; pres., founder The Keystone (Colo.) Ctr., 1975—; mountain and cold weather tng. cons. U.S. Army, 1951-54; hon. trustee, co-founder Aspen Ctr. for Physics. Author: (with Charles Houston and Robert Bates) K-2, The Savage Mountain, 1954, Storm and Sorrow, 1978. Bd. dirs. Snake River Health Clinic, Keystone, Colo. Outward Bound, 1985, Santa Fe Inst., Jimmie Heuga Ctr.; mem. U.S. Antarctic Safety Rev. Panel NSF, Washington Inst. Fgn. Affairs. Lt. (j.g.) USNR, 1943-46, PTO. Democrat. Episcopalian. Clubs: Am. Alpine (pres. 1983-86), Century (N.Y.C.); Cactus (Denver); Bohemian (San Francisco). Office: Keystone Ctr PO Box 606 Dillon CO 80435-0606

CRAIG, STEPHEN WRIGHT, lawyer; b. N.Y.C., Aug. 28, 1932; s. Herbert Stanley and Dorothy (Simmons) C.; m. Margaret M. Baker, June 10, 1958 (div. 1984); children: Amelia Audrey, Janet Elizabeth, Peter Baker; m. Bette Piller, 1984. AB, Harvard U., 1954, JD, 1959. Bar: Maine 1959, Calif. 1960, Ariz. 1963. Reporter Daily Kennebec Jour., Augusta, Maine, 1956; with pub. rels. staff Am. Savoyards, 1957; atty. IRS, San Francisco, 1959-61; atty.-adviser U.S. Tax Ct., 1961-63; ptnr. Snell & Wilmer, Phoenix, 1963-78, Winston & Strawn (formerly Craig, Greenfield & Irwin), Phoenix, 1978-87, Brown & Bain, Phoenix and Palo Alto, Calif., 1989—; guest lectr. Amos Tuck Sch. Bus., Dartmouth U., 1962; lectr. Ariz. and N.Mex. Tax Insts., 1966-67; guest lectr. sch. law Ariz. State U., 1984, adj. prof. law, 1985-87. Chmn. Jane Wayland Child Guidance Ctr., 1968-70; mem. Maricopa County Health Planning Coun., chmn. mental health task force.; bd. dirs. Combined Met. Phoenix Arts, 1968, adv. bd., 1968-69; adv. bd. Ariz. State U. Tax Insts., 1968-70; bd. dirs. Phoenix Community Coun., 1970-73, Ariz. Acad. With AUS, 1954-56. Home: 5214 N 34th Pl Phoenix AZ 85018 Office: Brown & Bain 2901 N Central Ave Ste 2000 Phoenix AZ 85012-2740

CRAIG, THOMAS ALLEN, investor, developer; b. Brea, Calif., June 16, 1928; s. Edward and Ruth Mary (Gatchell) C.; m. Caroline Corbett Taylor, Jan. 26, 1957 (div. Sept. 1991); children: Patricia, David, Ted, Jane; m. Ellie Harris Black, Oct. 21, 1991. BA in Bus., Fresno (Calif.) State U., 1950. Various positions Calif.-Tex. Oil Co., India, 1952-64; resident dir. Calif.-Tex. Oil Co., Rhodesia, Zambia, 1964-68; dir. Calif.-Tex. Oil Co., Kenya, Uganda, Tanzania, 1969; v.p. various div. Clinton Oil Co., Wichita, Kans., 1970-76; dir. adminstrn. Cessna Jet Aircraft div., Wichita, 1977-82; mng. gen. ptnr. Craig Trusts Property div., Brea and Fresno, 1983—. Home and Office: Craig Trusts 577 E Mallard Cir Fresno CA 93720

CRAIGHEAD, FRANK COOPER, JR., ecologist; b. Washington, Aug. 14, 1916; s. Frank Cooper and Carolyn (Johnson) C.; m. Esther Melvin Stevens, Nov. 9, 1943 (dec. 1980); children: Frank Lance, Charles Stevens, Jana Catherine; m. Shirley Ann Cocker, July, 1987. AB, Pa. State U., 1939; MS, U. Mich., 1940, PhD, 1950. Sr. rsch. assoc. Atmospheric Scis. Rsch. Ctr., N.Y., 1967-77; wildlife biologist, cons. U.S. Dept. Interior, Washington, 1959-66; wildlife biologist U.S. Forest Svc., Washington, 1957-59; mgr. desert game range U.S. Dept. Interior, Las Vegas, 1955-57; cons. survival tng. Dept. Def., Washington, 1950-55; pres. Craighead Environ. Research Inst., Moose, Wyo., 1955—; research assoc. U. Mont., Missoula, 1959—, Nat. Geographic Soc., Washington, 1959—; lectr. in field. Author: Track of the Grizzly, 1979, A Field Guide to Rocky Mountain Wildflowers, 1963, Hawks, Owls and Wildlife, 1956, How to Survive on Land and Sea, 1943, Hawks in the Hand, 1937. Mem. Pryor Mountain Wild Horse Adv. Com., Dept. Interior, 1968; mem. Horizons adv. group Am. Revolution Bicentennial Commn., 1972. Recipient citation Sec. of Navy, 1947; recipient letter of commendation U.S. Dept. Interior, 1963, Disting. Alumnus award Pa. State U., 1970; alumni fellow Pa. State U., 1973; recipient John Oliver LaGorce Gold medal Nat. Geog. Soc., 1979, U. Mich. Sch. Natural Resources Alumni Soc. award for Disting. Service, 1984, Centennial award Nat. Geog. Soc., 1988. Mem. AAAS, Wilderness Soc., Wildlife Soc., Explorers Club, Phi Beta Kappa, Sigma Xi, Phi Sigma, Phi Kappa Phi. Home: PO Box 156 Moose WY 83012-0156 Office: Craighead Environ Rsch Inst PO Box 156 Moose WY 83012-0156

CRAIGHEAD, FRANK LANCE, conservation biologist, wildlife researcher; b. Jackson, Wyo., Aug. 8, 1947; s. Frank C. Jr. and Esther (Stevens) C.; m. April Charmaine Hudoff, Oct. 15, 1965. BA, Carleton Coll., 1969; MSc, U. Wis., 1977; postgrad., Mont. State U., 1992—. Marine biologist U.S. Peace Corps, Suva, Fiji, 1970-73; biologist, vol. Smithsonian Instn., Kathmandu, Nepal, 1973; biologist, contractor NOAA, Juneau, Alaska, 1975-76; raptor biologist, contractor U.S. Fish and Wildlife Svc., Fairbanks, Alaska, 1981; game biologist Alaska Dept. Fish and Game, Wrangell, 1982-83; biologist Wildlife-Wildlands Inst., Missoula, Mont., 1984-86; cons. biologist Alaska Biol. Rsch., Fairbanks, 1981—; cons. ecologist BioSystems Analysis Inc., Santa Cruz, Caif., 1992—; dir. Craighead Environ. Rsch. Inst., Moose, Wyo., 1978—; 1st v.p. No. Rockies Conservation Coop., Jackson, Wyo., 1987—; expert witness Greater Yellowstone Coalition, others, 1992. Author articles; cons. on 4 nature films. Mem. Soc. for Conservation Biology, Internat. Bear Assn., The Wildlife Soc., Sigma Xi. Home: Box 156 Moose WY 83012 Office: Craighead Environ Rsch Inst Box 156 Moose WY 83012

CRAIN, CHARLES ANTHONY, telephone company executive; b. Decatur, Ill., 1931. Grad., U. Ill., 1955. Formerly pres. Hawaiian Telephone Co., Honolulu; exec. v.p. Gen. Telephone Co. of Calif., Thousand Oaks, pres., 1989—, also bd. dirs. Office: GTE Calif Inc 1 Gte Pl Thousand Oaks CA 91362-3811 also: GTE Hawaiian Telephone Inc PO Box 2200 Honolulu HI 96841

CRAIN, CHESTER RAY, statistician, consultant; b. St. Louis, Apr. 17, 1944; s. Chester Raymond and Mary Louise (Landers) C.; m. Barbara Hope Fag .., Sept. 2, 1967; 1 child, Michelle Wigmore. AB, Knox Coll., 1965; MA, U. Calif., Riverside, 1967; PhD, U. N.Mex., 1974. Rsch. statistician Knoll Pharm. Co., Whippany, N.J., 1980; mgr. stats. McNeil Pharm., Spring House, Pa., 1980-81; sr. biostatistician Miles Pharms., West Haven, Conn., 1981-83; dir. statis. svcs. Boots Pharms., Shreveport, La., 1983-84; mgr. biometrics DuPont Co., Wilmington, Del., 1984-85, cons. dept. cen. R & D, 1985-90; dept. coord. Corp. Electronic Info. Security Com., 1987-90; sr. statistician Baxter Hyland Div., Glendale, Calif., 1990-91, Advanced Micro Devices, Sunnyvale, Calif., 1991-93; ind. cons., 1993—. Author: Scientific Computing Division's Enhanced Statistical Products Product Plan; contbr. articles to profl. jours. Mem. Am. Soc. Quality Control (cert. reliability engr.), Am. Statis. Assn., Soc. Clin. Trials, Biometric Soc., Phi Beta Kappa, Sigma Xi. Democrat. Unitarian. Home: 1038 Sandalwood Ln Milpitas CA 95035-3232

CRAIN, CULLEN MALONE, electrical engineer; b. Goodnight, Tex., Sept. 10, 1920; s. John Malone and Margaret Elizabeth (Gunn) C.; m. Virginia Raftery, Jan. 16, 1943; children—Michael Malone, Karen Elizabeth. B.S. in Elec. Engring, U. Tex., Austin, 1942, M.S., 1947, Ph.D., 1952. From instr. to asso. prof. elec. engring. U. Tex., 1943-57; group leader communications and electronics Rand Corp., Santa Monica, Calif., 1957-69; assoc. head and head engring. and applied scis. Rand Corp., 1969-88; cons. to govt., 1958—. Author numerous papers in field. Pres. Austin chpt. Nat. Exchange Club, 1954, Santa Monica chpt., 1975. Served with USNR, 1944-46. Recipient Disting. Grad. award U. Tex., 1987. Fellow IEEE (life); mem. Nat. Acad. Engring. Home: 463 17th St Santa Monica CA 90402-2235 Office: 1700 Main St Santa Monica CA 90401-3297

CRAIN, DANIEL RAYMOND, county official; b. Chgo., July 8, 1950; s. Lawrence John and Eileen Patricia (Lomasney) C.; m. Kathleen Mary Redoutey, Oct. 4, 1975; children: Anthony, Nicholas. BS in Social Svcs., Calif. State Polytech. U., 1973; MPA, U. So. Calif., 1979. Group counselor Verdemont Boys Ranch, San Bernardino, Calif., 1974-77; probation officer San Bernardino County Probation Dept., 1977-86; area dminstr. foster family agy., Redlands, Calif., 1986-88; adminstrv. asst. City of Highland, Calif., 1988-92; county drug program adminstr. San Bernardino County Office of Alcohol and Drug Programs, 1992—. Charter mem. Yucaipa Mcpl. Adv. Coun., 1981; mayor pro tem Yucaipa City Coun., 1992; mem. governing bd. Yucaipa Joint Unified Sch. Dist., 1981-92; Colton-Redlands-Yucaipa Regional Occupational Program bd. dirs., Redlands, 1981-92; pres. Yucaipa Sch. Bd., 1984-85, 88-89; exec. com. Homeless Coalition; mem. Gangs and Drugs Task Force, 1992—. Named to Outstanding Young Men of Am., 1986. Mem. Rotary, Calif. Assn. County Drug Program Adminstrs., Calif. Sch. Bd. Assn. (del. assembly, mem. legis. and fin. coms. 1981—). Democrat. Roman Catholic. Home: 35580 Vineyard St Yucaipa CA 92399 Office: San Bernardino County Office of Alcohol and Drug Programs 565 N Mount Vernon Ste 100 San Bernardino CA 92411

CRAIN, DANNY B., microbiologist; b. Lynwood, Calif., Feb. 2, 1964; s. John Dennis and Doreen Aglaie (LaPierre) C.; m. Deborah Kay Burisch, July 17, 1990; 1 child, Tiffany Nicole Burisch-Crain. BA, U. Nev., Las Vegas, 1986; PhD, NYU, 1989. Lab. asst. Bunyan Rsch., Inc., Dover, Eng., 1980-81, U. Nev., Las Vegas, 1982-85; owner, biologist Crain Environ.

Rsch., Las Vegas, 1987—; adj. cons. Space Biospheres, Tucson, 1989—; coord. Planetary Soc., Las Vegas, 1989-90; speaker Young Astronauts Nev., Las Vegas, 1990—, del. NASA Space Sta. Freedom Utilization Conf., 1993. Tchr. Jr. Girl Scouts Las Vegas, 1988-89. Recipient Hon. Young Astronaut award, cert. appreciation Young Astronauts Nev., Las Vegas, 1990; fellow Huntingdon (Eng.) Rsch. Inst., 1980; scholar Harry S Truman Scholar Found., Las Vegas, 1984. Mem. AAAS, Aris. Acad. Sci., Am. Inst. Biol. Scis., Nev. Acad. Sci., Am. Soc. Naturalists, N.Y. Acad. Scis.

CRAIN, RICHARD WILLSON, mechanical engineering educator; b. Denver, July 2, 1931; s. Richard Willson Sr. and Martha Emily (Lawver) C.; m. Carolee Ellen Thompson, June 20, 1955; children: Richard, Carolyn, Laura, Ruth, Andrew, David. BSME, U. Wash., 1953, MSME, 1955; PhD in Mech. Engring., U. Mich., 1965. Registered profl. engr., Wash. Instr. gen. engring. U. Wash., Seattle, 1954-55; instr., rsch. asst., teaching asst. U. Mich., Ann Arbor, 1961-65; from assoc. prof. to prof. mech. engring. Wash. State U., Pullman, 1965-76, chair mech. engring., 1976-83, acting dean Coll. of Engring., 1983-84, chair mech. and materials engring., 1984-87; sr. engr. Varian Assocs., Palo Alto, Calif., 1987-88; prof. mech. and materials engring. Wash. State U., Pullman, 1988—; summer faculty AEC, Battelle Pacific Northwest Lab., Richland , Wash., 1966, 67, summer faculty Lawrence Livermore Labs., Livermore, Calif., 1968. Scoutmaster Boy Scouts Am., Pullman, 1966—, coun. officer, Lewiston, Idaho, 1980-92. Lt. comdr. USN, 1955-61. Mem. ASME (accreditation bd. for engring. and tech. visitor 1977-83), Am. Soc. for Engring. Edn. Methodist. Home: NW 365 Janet Pullman WA 99163 Office: Wash State U Dept Mech and Materials Engring Pullman WA 99164-2920

CRAIR, BEVERLY ILENE, computer systems administrator; b. Paterson, N.J., Apr. 6, 1961; d. Morton Lowell and Ruth (Bloch) Crair; 1 child, Lorin Michelle. BA in Computer Sci., U. Calif., Santa Cruz, 1983; MBA, Pepperdine U., 1991. Systems programmer Unisys Corp., Irvine, Calif., 1983-86, project leader, 1986-88; tech. writer, analyst Unisys Corp., Pasadena, Calif., 1989-90; mgr. documentation Unisys Corp., Camarillo, Calif., 1990-91, mgr. systems software, 1992—. Mem. Sweet Adelines. Democrat. Jewish. Office: Unisys Corp 5155 Camino Ruiz Camarillo CA 93012

CRAKER, GILBERT LEONARD, college administrator; b. Emmett, Idaho, Feb. 10, 1940; s. Gilbert Donald and Lydia Alice (Malpass) C.; m. Nancy Helen Winholtz, Nov. 12, 1968; children: Robin, Tricia, Dale, Christina. BA, N.W. Nazarene Coll., Nampa, Idaho, 1963. Sports writer Decatur (Ill.) Herald, 1965-68, 69-70, World Herald, Omaha, 1968-69; news editor Herald, Decatur, 1970-71; copy editor Tri-City Herald, Kennewick, Wash., 1971-86, sports editor, asst. metro editor, 1972-73; dir. news and info. N.W. Nazarene Coll., Nampa, 1986—. Coord. 75th anniversary book, 1979; editor fall media guide, 1988, winter media guide, 1988-89, spring media guide, 1991 (best cover awards, 89, 91). Asst. dir. NAIA Men's Divsn. II Nat. Basketball Tournament, 1993. With U.S. Army, 1963-65. Mem. Idaho Press Club. Mem. Nazarene Ch. Office: NW Nazarene Coll 623 Holly Nampa ID 83686

CRALLEY, LESTER VINCENT, industrial hygienist, editor, retired; b. Carmi, Ill., Mar. 27, 1911; s. John W. Cralley and Martha Jones; m. Gertrude E. Wilson, Aug. 24, 1940; 1 child, Agnes D. BS, McKendree Coll., 1933; PhD, U. Iowa, 1942. Res. officer USPHS, Bethesda, Md., 1941-45; chief indsl. hygienist Aluminum Co. of Am., Pitts., 1945-67, mgr. environ. health svcs., 1968-74; mem. Sec. of Labor's Nat. Safety Adv. Com., Washington, 1969-70. Editor: Theory and Rationale of Industrial Hygiene Practice, 1985, In Plant Practices for Job Related Health Hazards Control, 1989, Health and Safety Beyond the Workplace, 1990. Mem. Am. Indsl. Hygiene Assn. (hon., treas. 1953-56, pres. 1956-57, Cummings Meml. award 1971), Am. Acad. Indsl. Hygiene, Internat. Commn. on Occupational Health, Planetary Soc., Wellness Soc. Home: 1453 Banyan Dr Fallbrook CA 92028-1105

CRAM, BRIAN MANNING, school system administrator,. AA, Dixie Jr. Coll., 1959; BA with honors, U. Utah, 1961; MA, Ariz. State U., 1962, EdS, 1964, EdD with Honors, 1967. Asst. prin. Clark (Nev.) High Sch., 1965-69, prin., 1969-73; asst. superintendent Clark County (Nev.) Sch. Dist., 1973-78; superintendentschs. Clark County (Nev.) Sch. Dist., 1989—; prin. Western High Sch., 1978-89; cons. Glendale Unified Sch. Dist., Whittier Sch. Dist., South Bay Union High Sch. Dist., Elk Grove Unified Sch. Dist., No. Ill. U., State of Hawaii; co-chairman Superintendent's Coun. Ednl. Tech., Coll. Prep Feasibility sub-com.; mem. Speakers Bureau Pay as You Go Bond Plan, Disting. Scholar's com., Extended Day com., In-Svc. com., State Attendence Audit, Spl. Assistance Team, Computer Mgmt. Project, Prin. Attendance adv. com., Prin.'s Math Curriculum com; speaker in field. Contbr. articles to profl. jours. Bd. dirs. Boulder Dam Area Coun. Boy Scouts Am., Las Vegas Council PTA, United Way, Clark County Sch. Dist. Articulation Com., Nev. Assn. Handicapped, Nev. Devel. Authority, Nev. Inst. Contemporary Art, Animal Found., Las Vegas Mus. Nat. History, Southwest Regional Ednl. Lab., Nat. Coun. Christians and Jews; adv. bd. U. Nev. Las Vegas Spl. Svcs., U. Nev. Sch. Medicine, Clark County Community Coll. Mem. Nev. Assn. Secondary Sch. Prins. (past sec.), Nev. Educator Awards Selection Com., Clark County Assn. Sch. Administrs. (chmn. negotiations, past exec. coun., past sec., past pres.), Ariz. State U. Alumni Assn. (past pres. So. Nevada chpt.), Greater Las Vegas C. of C., Latin C. of C., Nev. Black C. of C., Rotary, Phi Delta Kappa. Home: 417 S Wallace Dr Las Vegas NV 89107 Office: Clark County School District 2832 E Flamingo Rd Las Vegas NV 89121

CRAM, DONALD JAMES, chemistry educator; b. Chester, Vt., Apr. 22, 1919; s. William Moffet and Joanna (Shelley) C.; m. Jane Maxwell, Nov. 25, 1969. BS, Rollins Coll., 1941; MS, U. Nebr., 1942; PhD, Harvard U., 1947; PhD (hon.), U. Uppsala, 1977; DSc (hon.), U. So. Calif., 1983, Rollins Coll., 1988, U. Nebr., 1989, U. Western Ontario, 1990, U. Sheffield, 1991. Rsch. chemist Merck & Co., 1942-45; asst. prof. chemistry UCLA, 1947-50, assoc. prof., 1950-56, prof., 1956-90, S. Winstein prof., 1985—, univ. prof., 1988-90, univ. prof. emeritus, 1990—; chem. con. Upjohn Co., 1952-88, Union Carbide Co., 1960-81, Eastman Kodak Co., 1981-91, Technicon Co., 1984-92, Inst. Guido Donegani, Milan, 1988-91; State Dept. exch. fellow to Inst. de Quimica, Nat. U. Mex., 1956; guest prof. U. Heidelberg, Fed. Republic Germany, 1958; guest lectr. S. Africa, 1967; Centenary lectr. Chem. Soc. London, 1976. Author: From Design to Discovery, 1990, (with Pine, Hendrickson and Hammond) Organic Chemistry, 1960, 4th edit., 1980, Fundamentals of Carbanion Chemistry, 1965, (with Richards and Hammond) Elements of Organic Chemistry, 1967, (with Cram) Essence of Organic Chemistry, 1977; contbr. chpts. to textbooks, articles in field of host-guest complexation chemistry, carbanions, stereochemistry, mold metabolites, large ring chemistry. Named Young Man of Yr. Calif. Jr. C. of C., 1954, Calif. Scientist of Yr., 1974, Nobel Laureate in Chemistry, 1987, UCLA medal, 1993; recipient award for creative work in synthetic organic chemistry Am. Chem. Soc., 1965, Arthur C. Cope award, 1974, Richard Tolman medal, 1985, Willard Gibbs award, 1985, Roger Adams award, 1985, Herbert Newby McCoy award, 1965, 75, Glenn Seaborg award, 1989, award for creative rsch. organic chemistry Synthetic Organic Chem. Mfrs. Assn., 1965; Nat. Rsch. fellow Harvard U., 1947, Am. Chem. Soc. fellow, 1947-48, Guggenheim fellow, 1954-55. Fellow Royal Soc. (hon. 1989); mem. NAS (award in chem. scis. 1992), Am. Acad. Arts and Scis., Am. Chem. Soc., Royal Soc. Chemistry, Surfers Med. Assn., San Onofre Surfing Club, Sigma Xi, Lambda Chi Alpha. Office: UCLA Dept Chemistry Los Angeles CA 90024

CRAM, SCOTT WALTER, construction executive; b. Des Moines, Nov. 11, 1945; . Carroll Vigers and Eloise Grace (Sargent) C.; m. Elizabeth Sue Mettlin, Aug. 22, 1966; children: Bryan, Steven, Jordan. BArch, Iowa State U., 1969. Registered architect Iowa, Utah, Colo., Ariz. Architect Woodburn & O'Neil Architects, Des Moines, 1971-76; pres. CRSS Constructors, Inc., Denver, 1976—. Dir. Jr. Achievement Rocky Mountain, Inc., Denver, 1992—. Lt. jg USN, 1969-71. Mem. AIA, Constrn. Mgmt. Assn. Am. Office: CRSS Constructors Inc Ste 1700 216 16th St Denver CO 80202

CRAMER, DOUGLAS SCHOOLFIELD, broadcasting executive; b. Louisville, Aug. 22; s. Douglas Schoolfield and Pauline (Compton) C.; m. Joyce Haber, Sept. 25, 1966 (div. 1973); children: Douglas Schoolfield, III, Courtney Sanford. Student, Northwestern U., 1949-50, Sorbonne, Paris, 1951; B.A., U. Cin., 1953; M.F.A., Columbia U., 1954. Prodn. asst. Radio City Music Hall, N.Y.C., 1950-51; with script dept. Metro-Goldwyn-Mayer, 1952; mng. dir. Cin. Playhouse, 1953-54; instr. Carnegie Inst. Tech., 1955-56; TV supr. Procter & Gamble, 1956-59; broadcast supr. Ogilvy, Benson & Mather, 1959-62; v.p. program devel. ABC, 1962-66, 20th Century-Fox-TV, Los Angeles, 1966-68; exec. v.p. in charge prodn. Paramount TV, 1968-71; ind. producer, pres. Douglas S. Cramer Co., 1971—; exec. v.p. Aaron Spelling Prodns., 1976-87, vice-chmn., 1988-90; bd. dirs. Spelling Entertainment, Inc. Exec. producer: Bridget Loves Bernie, CBS-TV, 1972-73, QB VII, 1973-74, Dawn: Portrait of a Teenage Runaway, NBC-TV, 1976, Danielle Steel's Fine Things, Kalediscope, 1990, Changes, Daddy, Palomino, 1990-91, Secrets, 1991, Heart Beat, 1992, Star, Message to Nam, 1993; co-exec. producer: Love Boat, ABC, 1977-86, Vegas, ABC, 1978-81, Wonder Woman, ABC, 1975-77, CBS, 1977-78, Dynasty, 1981-89, Hotel, 1983-87, Trade Winds and Lake Success, 1993; author: (plays) Call of Duty, 1953, Love Is A Smoke, 1957, Whose Baby Are You, 1963. Pres., Mus. Contemporary Art, L.A., 1990-93, 1st vice-chair, 1993—; mem. bd. trustees and internat. Coun. Mus. Modern Art, N.Y.C.; pres. Douglas S. Cramer Found. With U.S. Army, 1954. Mem. Univ. Club of N.Y.C., Beta Theta Pi. Office: The Cramer Co 4605 Lankershim Blvd Ste 617 North Hollywood CA 91602-1818

CRAMER, OWEN CARVER, classics educator; b. Tampa, Fla., Dec. 1, 1941; s. Maurice Browning and Alice (Carver) C.; m. Rebecca Jane Lowrey, June 23, 1962; children—Alfred, Thomas, Ethan, Benjamin. A.B., Oberlin Coll., 1962; Ph.D., U. Tex., 1973. Spl. instr. U. Tex., Austin, 1964-65; instr. in classics Colo. Coll., Colorado Springs, 1965-69, asst. prof. classics, 1969-75, assoc. prof. classics, 1975-84, M.C. Gile prof. classics, 1984—; cons. humanist Colo. Humanities Program, Denver, 1982-83; vis. prof. U. Chgo., 1987-88. Editorial asst. Arion, 1964-65; contbr. papers, articles on Greek lang. and lit. to profl. publs., 1974—; contbr. classical music revs. to Colorado Springs Sun, 1984-86. Chorus tenor Colo. Opera Festival, Colorado Springs, 1976-82; mem. El Paso County Democratic Central Com., Colo., 1968-88; active ordained elder Presbyn. Ch., 1992. Hon. Woodrow Wilson fellow, 1962; univ. fellow U. Tex., Austin, 1962-64. Mem. Am. Philol. Assn. (campus adv. svc. 1989—, chmn. com. on smaller depts. 1979-80), Classical Assn. of Middle West and South, Modern Greek Studies Assn., Colo. Classics Assn., Phi Beta Kappa. Presbyterian. Club: Round Table (Colorado Springs). Home: 747 E Uintah St Colorado Springs CO 80903-2546 Office: Colo Coll Dept Classics Colorado Springs CO 80903

CRAMER, SANFORD WENDELL, III, photographer, business owner; b. Long Beach, Calif., Jan. 6, 1948; s. Sanford Wendell Cramer and Jeannette (Palmer) Rouleau; m. Maralene Hinton, May 25, 1968; 1 child, Heather Maralene. Student, Long Beach (Calif.) City Coll., 1970, Compton (Calif.) Jr. Coll., 1971-73, Santa Ana (Calif.) Jr. Coll., 1975. Lic. tax cons., preparer. Clk. L.A. County DPSS, Bell, Calif., 1970-76; intermediate clk. L.A. County DPSS, Hawaiian Gardens, Calif., 1976-78; asst. payroll clk. I L.A. County DPSS, Norwalk, Calif., 1978-80; supervising clk. L.A. County DPSS, Long Beach, 1980-81; warehouseman I L.A. County DPSS, Commerce, Calif., 1981; camp svc. mgr. L.A. County Probation, Malibu, Calif., 1981-89; co-owner Cramer & Cramer Enterprises, Garden Grove, Calif., 1987—; actor Garden Grove, 1979—, photographer, tax cons. and preparer. Author, copyright Anniversary Game Show, 1982; producer Garden Grove Community Theatre, 1979. Bd. mem. YSP Community Restitution Juveniles, Garden Grove, 1984. With USAF, 1966. Mem. AFTRA, Garden Grove C. of C., An Cloc Cosanta Soc., Am. Legion, Ctr. Entrepreneurial Mgmt., Merrill's Marauders Assn. Republican. Mem. Dutch Reformed Ch. Home and Office: 13241 Safford St Garden Grove CA 92643-2743

CRAMER, TIMOTHY JAMES, engineer, computer consultant; b. Wausau, Wis., Mar. 16, 1965; s. Michael James and Judith Agnes (Andraska) C.; m. Dana Jeanne Hanson, June 27, 1987. BS in Math. and Computer Sci., U. Wis., Eau Claire, 1987. Math scientist Lawrence Livermore (Calif.) Nat. Lab., 1987-88; sr. engr. Supercomputer Systems, Inc., Livermore, 1988-93, Sun Microsystems, Inc., Mountain View, Calif., 1993—; cons. in field, 1991—. Patentee in field. With USNG, 1987-92. Mem. Assn. for Computing Machinery. Home: 3117 Pawnee Way Pleasanton CA 94588 Office: Sun Microsystems Inc 2525 Garcia Dr MS12-40 Mountain View CA 94550

CRAMPTON, ESTHER LARSON, educator; b. Plainview, Nebr., Apr. 14, 1915; d. Charles W. and Anna Margrethe (Staugaard) Larson; m. Francis Asbury Crampton, Jan. 19, 1949 (dec.); children: Jacqueline, Edith. AB, Colo. Coll. of Edn., 1935; MA, U. Wis., 1937; PhD, Am. U., 1972. Observer, writer U.S. Weather Bur., Washington, 1942-48; interpreter Portuguese RFC Rubber Devel. Corp., Manaos, Brasil, 1943; tchr. Latin Glenn County High Sch., Willows, Calif., 1954-57; tchr. Latin/German Scottsdale (Ariz.) High Sch., 1957-62; tchr. Latin Natrona County High Sch., Casper, Wyo., 1962-64; tchr. social studies Bourgade High Sch., Phoenix, 1964-65; substitute tchr. Phoenix High Sch., 1965-66; instr. supr. We. N.Mex. U. Lab. Sch., Silver City, 1966-67; prof. sociology and polit. sci. Cochise C.C., Douglas, Ariz., 1967-77; adj. instr. Calif. Poly. State U., San Luis Obispo, 1991—. Sec., v.p., bd. dirs. Easter Seal Soc. of Santa Cruz, 1979-81; active Nat. Women's Polit. Caucus Br., Santa Cruz, 1979; tutor reading Literacy Coun., San Luis Obispo, 1988. Grantee Amazonia Rsch. Orgn. of Am. States, 1970, Am. Coun. of Learned Socs., 1941. Mem. AAUW (chair 1977-81, mem. at large internat. rels. group 1981—), Acad. of Polit. Sci., Wilson Ctr. Assocs., Rainforest Action Network.

CRAMPTON, GEORGE HARRIS, science educator, retired army officer; b. Spokane, Wash., Nov. 20, 1926. BS, Wash. State U., 1949, MS, 1950; PhD, U. Rochester, 1954. Enlisted U.S. Army Res., 1944; advanced through grades to col. U.S. Army M.S.C., 1970; ret. U.S. Army, 1971; prof. Wright State U., Dayton, Ohio, 1971-86, prof. emeritus, 1987—. Home: 1842 N Dawnview Terr Oak Harbor WA 98277

CRANDALL, KATHLEEN M., physics educator, writer; b. Lowell, Mass., Aug. 4, 1943; d. Kenneth J. and Anne Frances (Doonan) C.; m. Joseph Tomasulo (div. 1976); chilren: Michael A., Stephen J., Elizabeth A. BS in Biology, Chemistry, Tufts U., 1964; PhD, Columbia U., 1972; cert. in teaching, Calif. State U., 1986. Lectr. U. Calif., Irvine, 1974-79; assoc. dir. admissions Calif. Inst. Tech., Pasadena, 1979-82; tchr. physics Oakwood Sch., North Hollywood, Calif., 1983-85, L.A. Unified Sch. Dist., 1985—. Mem. Nat. Sci. Tchrs. Assn., Am. Assn. Physics Tchrs., Calif. Sci. Tchrs. Assn., L.A. Astron. Soc., Planetary Soc., Sierra Club. Office: LA Unified Sch Dist 11133 O'Melveny St San Fernando CA 91340

CRANDALL, LOREE YOKO YAMADA, mathematics educator; b. Ogden, Utah, Dec. 29, 1964; d. Masaru and Kiyoko (Kudo) Yamada; m. Wallace V. Crandall, Sept. 19, 1987. BS in Math. Edn., Utah State U., Logan, 1988, MS in Math., 1990. Teaching helper math. dept. Utah State U., Logan, 1985-88, teaching asst. math. dept., 1988-90, grad. teaching asst. math. dept., 1990; tchr. math. Rowland Hall/St. Mark's Sch., Salt Lake City, 1990-93; tutor Utah State U., Logan, 1985-90. Mem. Golden Key, Phi Kappa Phi. Home: 225 Medical Plz Salt Lake City UT 84112-1507

CRANDALL, ROBERT EARL, insurance company executive; b. Salt Lake City, Nov. 14, 1917; s. Earl M. and Tasy E. (Grace) C.; m. Evelyn Cockrell, June 23, 1949; children: Linda, Diane, Sandra, Nancy, John. BA, U. Utah, 1941; MBA, Harvard U., 1943. CLU. Spl. rep. The Lincoln Nat. Life Ins. Co., Ft. Wayne, Ind., 1947—; pvt. practice Salt Lake City, 1949-88; pres. Hawaii Mission LDS Ch., Honolulu, 1972-75; bd. dirs. BOMA Internat., Salt Lake City, 1987— (pres. Utah chpt. 1982-83). Voting dist. chmn. Salt Lake City Rep. Com., 1990; regional welfare agt. LDS Ch., 1989—. Lt. USNR, 1943-46. Home: 852 Le Grand St Salt Lake City UT 84108-1316 Office: Stanworth Burgess & Assoc 310 S Main St Ste 1310 Salt Lake City UT 84101-2172

CRANDELL, WILLIAM DEAN, geologist; b. Washington, June 13, 1950; s. William Palmer and Martha Josephine (Green) C.; m. Jennifer Naylor Schirmer, Dec. 20, 1972; children: Kimberly S., Allison S. BS in Geology, Clemson U., 1972. Dist. geologist Bur. of Land Mgmt., Ely, Nev., 1976-78, Spokane, Wash., 1978-85; phys. scientist U.S. Bur. of Mines, Spokane, Wash., 1985—. Author: Availability of Federally Owned Minerals for Exploration: Development in Western States-Nevada 1985, 1989, Availability of Federally Owned Minerals for Exploration: California Desert Conservation Area-1989, 1992. Lt. (j.g.) USNR, 1972-75. Mem. N.W. Mining Assn., Benjamin B. French Masonic, Spokane Valley Kiwanis. Republican. Episcopalian. Home: 2201 S Burns Rd Veradale WA 99037-9307 Office: US Bureau of Mines E 360 3rd Ave Spokane WA 99202

CRANE, DARLENE BARRIENTOS, project management consultant; b. Honolulu, Feb. 26, 1948; d. Henry Quiogue and Virginia Marie (Padilla) Barrientos; m. Steven Mayer Crane, May 29, 1976. BA, Pitzer Coll., Claremont, Calif., 1970; AM in East Asian Studies, U. Mich., 1974, Accredited Master Libr. Sci., 1974; MBA in Fin., Golden Gate U., 1986. Exec. dir. Project on Asian Studies in Edn., Ann Arbor, 1973; banking generalist Bank of Calif., San Francisco, 1974-78; tax acct. ITEL Leasing, San Francisco, 1979-81; project acct. GATX Leasing, San Francisco, 1981; asst. v.p. Bank of Am., San Francisco, 1981-89; pres. Crane Cons., Hayward, Calif., 1989—; vol. facilitator various non-profit orgns.; pub. speaker profl. orgns., Calif. and throughout U.S., 1988—. Contbr. articles on project mgmt. and systems devel. to profl. jours. Mem. Project Mgmt. Inst. (bd. mem. 1992), Assn. Systems Mgmt. (bd. mem. 1992-93), Assn. Computing Machinery SIG-CHI, Nat. Soc. Performance and Instrn.

CRANE, STEVEN, company executive; b. Los Angeles, Jan. 21, 1959; s. Roger D. and Violet (Heard) C.; m. Peggy Anne Gilhooly, Apr. 25, 1987; 1 child Allison Nicole. Grad. high sch. With Mobar Inc., Torrance, Calif., 1976-78; v.p. internat. Fluid Control Internat., Marina del Rey, Calif., 1978-79; pres. Energy Devel. Internat., Torrance, 1979-85; pres., chief exec. officer Kaempen USA, Inc., Anaheim, Calif., 1985-91; founding ptnr., chmn. Western Fin. Group, Inc., Hermosa Beach, Calif., 1991—; bd. dirs. Environ. Restoration, Inc., The Artist Network, MultiCultural Alliance; chmn. TRMC Bus. Devel. Group, 1992-93. Bd. dirs. Artist Network, Environ. Restoration, Inc. Mem. Office: Western Fin Group Inc 252 Pacific Coast Hwy Hermosa Beach CA 90254

CRANSTON, ALAN, former senator; b. Palo Alto, Calif., June 19, 1914; s. William MacGregor and Carol (Dixon) C.; children: Robin MacGregor (dec.), Kim Christopher. Student, Pomona Coll., 1932-33, U. Mexico, 1933; A.B., Stanford, 1936. Fgn. corr. Internat. News Service, Eng., Italy, Ethiopia, Germany, 1936-38; Washington rep. Common Council Am. Unity, Washington, 1940-41; chief fgn. lang. div. Office War Info., Washington, 1942-44; exec. sec. Council for Am.-Italian Affairs, Inc., Washington, 1945-46; partner bldg. and real estate firm Ames-Cranston Co., Palo Alto, Calif., 1947-58; controller State of Calif., 1959-67; pres. Homes for a Better America Inc., 1967-68; v.p. Carlsberg Financial Corp., Los Angeles, 1968; mem. U.S. Senate from Calif., 1969-93. Author: The Big Story, 1940, The Killing of the Peace, 1945. Mem. exec. com. Calif. Democratic Central Com., 1954-60; pres. Calif. Dem. Council, 1953-57. Served with AUS, 1944-45. Mem. United World Federalists (nat. pres. 1949-52). Club: Overseas Press Am. Home: 27020 Old Trace Ln Los Altos Hills CA 94022 Office: Gorbaegev Found USA Box 29434 The Presidio San Francisco CA 94129

CRANSTON, HOWARD STEPHEN, lawyer, management consultant; b. Hartford, Conn., Oct. 20, 1937; s. Howard Samuel and Agnes (Corvo) C.; m. Karen Youngman, June 16, 1962; children: Margaret, Susan. BA cum laude, Pomona Coll., 1959; LLB, Harvard U., 1962. Bar: Calif. 1963. Assoc. MacDonald & Halsted, L.A., 1964-68; ptnr. MacDonald, Halsted & Laybourne, L.A., 1968-82, of counsel, 1982-86; pres. Knapp Comm., L.A., 1982-87; pres. S.C. Cons. Corp., 1987—; bd. dirs. Wood Knapp Co., Boys Republic, Community Housing Svcs.; dir. Mental Health Assn. of L.A., 1st lt. U.S. Army, 1962-64. Mem. Assn. Corp. Growth, San Gabriel Country Club, Harvard Club (N.Y.). Republican. Episcopalian. Author Handbook for Creative Managers, 1987, Management Decision Mag., 1988—. Office: 1613 Chelsea Rd # 253 San Marino CA 91108-2453

CRAPO, MICHAEL DEAN, congressman, laywer; b. Idaho Falls, Idaho, May 20, 1951; s. George LaVelle and Melba (Olsen) C.; m. Susan Diane Hasleton, June 22, 1974; children: Michelle, Brian, Stephanie, Lara, Paul. BA Polit. Sci. summa cum laude, Brigham Young U., 1973; postgrad., U. Utah, 1973-74; JD cum laude, Harvard U., 1977. Bar: Calif. 1977, Idaho 1979. Law clk. to Hon. James M. Carter U.S. Ct. Appeals (9th cir.), San Diego, 1977-78; assoc. atty. Gibson, Dunn & Crutcher, L.A., 1978-79; ptnr. Holden, Kidwell, Hahn & Crapo, Idaho Falls, 1979-92; mem. Idaho State Senate from 32A Dist., 1984-93; asst. majority leader, 1987-88; pres. Pro Tempore, 1989-92; congressman U.S. House of Reps., Washington, 1992—, mem. commerce com.; precinct committeeman Dist. 29, 1980-85; vice chmn. Legislative Dist. 29, 1984-85; Mem. Health and Welfare Com., 1985-89, Resources and Environ. Com., 1985-90, State Affairs Com., 1987-92; Rep. Pres. Task Force, 1989. Leader Boy Scouts Am., Calif., Idaho, 1977-92; mem. Bar Exam Preparation, Bar Exam Grading; chmn. Law Day.; Bonneville County chmn. Phil Batt gubernatorial campaign, 1982. Named one of Outstanding Young Men of Am., 1985; recipient cert. of Merit Rep. Nat. Com., 1990, Guardian of Small Bus. award Nat. Fedn. of Ind. Bus., 1990, cert. of Recognition Am. Cancer Soc., 1990, Idaho Housing Agy., 1990, Idaho Lung Assn., 1985, 87, 89, Friend of Agr. award Idaho Farm Bur., 1989-90, medal of Merit Rep. Presdl. Tax Force, 1989, Nat. Legislator of Yr. award Nat. Rep. Legislators Assn., 1991. Mem. ABA (antitrust law sect.), Idaho Bar Assn., Rotary. Mormon. Office: US Ho of Reps 437 Cannon House Office Bld Washington DC 20515

CRAPO, RICHLEY H., anthropology educator; b. La Habra, Calif., Apr. 15, 1943; s. Leonard Owen and Ardys Maud (Moore) C.; m. Irma Christa Nielson (div.); children: David Owen, Stephen Christopher; m. Sharon Dale Burton, Aug. 8, 1980; children: Shannon Dale Cannon, Rhondda Denise Cannon, Torrie Ann Crapo, Andrew Burton Moore Crapo. BA, Calif. State U., Fullerton, 1967; MA, U. Utah, 1968, PhD, 1970. Asst. prof. anthropology Utah State U., Logan, 1970-76; assoc. prof. anthropology Utah State U., 1976-89, prof. anthropology, 1989—; Author: Cultural Anthropology, 2d edit. 1990, 3d edit. 1993, Big Smokey Valley Shoshoni, 1976; co-author: Bolivian Quechua Reader and Grammar/Dictionary, 1986, Cross-Cultural Perspectives in Indroductory Psychology, 1992. Author: Cultural Anthropology, 1987, 2d edit. 1990, Big Smokey Valley Shoshoni, 1976; co-author: Bolivian Quechua Reader and Grammar/Dictionary, 1986. Fellow Royal Anthropol. Inst.; mem. Am. Anthropol. Assn., Wenner-Gren Found. for Anthropol. Rsch., Soc. for Psychol. Anthropology, Utah Com. fo Corres. Mormon. Home: 654 E 1980 N Logan UT 84321-1933 Office: Utah State U Dept Sociology Logan UT 84322-0730

CRAPO, SHEILA ANNE, telecommunications company professional, artist; b. Elko, Nev., June 11, 1951; d. John Lewis and June Florene (Lani) C. BA, U. Nev., 1974. Various svc. positions Alltel-Nevada Inc., Elko, 1974-78, svc. rep., 1978-84, bus. office supr., 1984-87, bus. supr. Nev. office, 1987—; speaker in field; writer, artist, 1974—. Officer, organizer Freedom Com., Elko, 1984. Mem. AAUW (editor newsletter Elko 1980-82, v.p. programs 1991-93), Internat. Telephone Pioneers Assn., Northeastern Nev. Hist. Soc., Animal Relief Found., Ducks Unltd., Soroptimists Internat. of Elko (treas. 1992-93, sec. 1993-94). Office: Alltel-Nevada Inc 111 W Front St Elko NV 89801

CRAVEN, JAMES MICHAEL, economist, educator; b. Seattle, Mar. 10, 1946; s. Homer Henry and Mary Kathleen Craven; m. Aleyamma P. Thomas, Aug. 27, 1977. Student, U. Minn., 1966-68; BA in Sociology, U. Manitoba, Winnipeg, Can., 1971, BA in Econs., 1971, MA in Econs., 1974. Lic. pilot; cert. ground instr. Instr. econ. and bus. Red River C.C., Winnipeg, 1974-76; lectr. rsch. methods of stats. U. Manitoba, Winnipeg, 1977-78; instr. econ. and bus. Big Bend C.C., Moses Lake, Wash., 1980-81; planning analyst Govt. P.R., San Juan, 1984; prof. econs. and bus. Interam. U. P.R., Bayamon, 1984-85; instr. econs., lectr. history Green River C.C., Auburn, Wash., 1988-92; instr. econs. Clark Coll., Vancouver, Wash., 1992—; vis. prof. St. Berchman's U., Kerala, India, 1981, 83, 86, 91; instr. econs. Bellevue (Wash.) C.C., 1988-92; cons. Bellevue, 1988—. Text reviewer Harcourt Brace Jovanovich, San Diego, 1989—; inventor in field; contbr. articles to profl. jours. Platform com. mem. Wash. State Dem., Seattle, 1992; cons. Lowry for Gov. Campaign, Seattle, 1992. With U.S. Army, 1963-66. Fellow Govt. Can. 1973-74; recipient pilot wings FAA 1988-92. Mem. Assn. Northwest Econ. Educators, Assn. Nat. Security Alumni, Wash. Pilot Assn. Syrian Orthodox. Home: 125 108th SE Apt 14 Bellevue WA 98004 Office: Clark Coll Dept Econs 1800 E McLoughlin Blvd Vancouver WA 98663

CRAW, NICHOLAS WESSON, motor sports association executive; b. Governor's Island, N.Y., Nov. 14, 1936; s. Demas Thurlow Craw and Mary Victoria Wesson. BA, Princeton U., 1959; MBA, Harvard U., 1982. Dir. ops. Project Hope, Washington, 1960-68; dir. U.S. Peace Corps, Washington, 1970-74; pres., CEO Scorpio Racing, Washington, 1968-80, Sports Car Club Am., Englewood, Colo., 1983—; pres. Sports Car Club Am. Found, Englewood, 1986—; chmn. Nat. Motorsports Coun., 1992—. Office: Sports Car Club Am 9033 E Easter Pl Englewood CO 80112-2105

CRAWFIS, ROBERT P., lawyer; b. L.A., Jan. 11, 1950; s. Robert Leroy and Marie P. (Stewart) C.; m. Nancy Jo McDowell, May 25, 1974; children: Caroline, Anne, Julia. AB with honors, U. Calif., Riverside, 1972; JD, Willamette U., 1975. Bar: Calif. 1975; cert. tchr., real estate broker. Pvt. practice Huntington Beach, Calif., 1976-77, 1985—; assoc. Greenbaum & Greenbaum, Huntington Beach, 1977-78; managing lawyer Jacoby & Meyers, Huntington Beach, 1978-82; assoc. Banks, Leviton & Drass, Santa Ana, Calif., 1982-85; assoc. prof. law Coastline Community Coll., Fountain Valley, Calif., 1981—. Dir. Sunset Beach (Calif.) Sanitary Dist., 1978-80; pres. Sunset Beach Community Assn., 1977-78; candidate Huntington Beach City Coun., 1986; mem. Huntington Beach Tomorrow, 1988—. Russell Peters scholar, Willamette U. Coll. Law, Salem, Oreg., 1973. Mem. Calif. Tchrs. Assn., Orange County Bar Assn. Democrat. Office: 2134 Main St Ste 220 Huntington Beach CA 92648-6440

CRAWFORD, BRIAN LOUIS, air force officer, geography educator; b. Brownsville, Pa., Oct. 26, 1956; s. Louis Herschel and Dorothy Mae (Lowman) C.; m. Vicki Lynne Gregorini, Sept. 22, 1984; 1 child, Grant; stepchildren: Heidi Gregorini, Jason Bennett. BA, Indiana U. of Pa., 1982; MS, California U. of Pa., 1984. Enlisted U.S. Navy, 1976; commd. 2d lt. USAF, 1984, advanced through grades to capt., 1988; missile combat crew 91st Strategic Missile Wing, Minot, N.D., 1985-89; ICBM instr. 4315th Combat Crew Tng. Squadron, Vandenberg AFB, Calif., 1989-92, flight chief, 1992; chief plans br. 310 Tng. and Test Wing, Vandenberg AFB, Calif., 1992-93; wing quality advisor 30th Space Wing, Vandenberg AFB, Calif., 1993—; assoc. prof. geography Allan Hancock Coll., Santa Maria, Calif., 1992—. Pres. Peace Luth. Ch., Lompoc, Calif., 1991-93. Decorated Air Force Commendation medal. Mem. Assn. Am. Geographers, Nat. Coun. for Geographic Edn., Air Force Assn. Republican. Lutheran. Home: 503 Cedar St Vandenberg AFB CA 93437

CRAWFORD, GEORGE TRUETT, management systems company executive, consultat; b. Alcorn County, Miss., Mar. 13, 1936; s. Bascrum Claude and Louise K. (Killough) C.; m. Anne Craggs, June 8, 1975. Grad. high sch., Yuma, Ariz. Dir. food svcs. Food Dimensions, Inc., San Francisco, 1975-81; dir. food and nutrition Dominican Santa Cruz (Calif.) Hosp., 1981-90; pres. Diverse Mgmt. Systems, Half Moon Bay, Calif., 1990—; cons. Diverse Mgmt. Systems, 1987-89; bd. dirs. food tech. adv. bd. Cabrillo Coll., Santa Cruz. Contbr. articles to profl. jours. Pres. Calif. Hosp. Food Svc. Adminstrn., San Francisco, 1979. Mem. Food Svc. Cons. Soc. Internat., Am. Soc. Hosp. Food Svc. Adminstrn. No Calif. (sec. 1975-77, pres.-elect 1978, pres. 1979), Nat. Inst. Off Primis Catering (faculty). Republican. Baptist. Home: PO Box 322 Half Moon Bay CA 94019-0322

CRAWFORD, J. DOUGLAS, computer marketing professional; b. Winsor, Ont., Can., Mar. 17, 1948; came to U.S., 1951; s. Carmen Verne and Helen Louise Crawford; m. Karen E. Laurea, May 17, 1980; children: Jon A., Jacquelyn M., Justin A. Student, Wayne State U., 1971-72, Orange Coast Coll., 1976-78. Nat. accounts mgr. Uccel, Dallas, 1978-83; dir. OEM sales Original Equipment Mfr., Scottsdale, Mpls., Ariz., 1983-87; v.p. bus. devel. Wavefront Tech., Santa Barbara, Calif., 1987-91; v.p. mktg. and sales GTX Corp., Phoenix, 1991—; pres. CommuniVision, Santa Barbara, Calif., 1992-93. Bd. dirs. Ballet Pacifica, Laguna Beach, Calif., 1986. Sgt. U.S. Army, 1967-69. Home: 7256 Shepard Mesa Carpinteria CA 93013

CRAWFORD, JERRY LEROY, theatre arts educator, author, playwright; b. Whittemore, Iowa, Aug. 20, 1934; s. Roy Bert and Elizabeth Maxine (Riebhoff) C.; m. Patricia Lou Bunn, June 7, 1956; children: Mitchell Lee, Vali Elizabeth Crawford Borg, Keli Annalee. BFA, Drake U., 1956; MA, Stanford U., 1957; PhD, U. Iowa, 1964. Prof. theatre arts U. Nev., Las Vegas, 1962—; dir. literary seminars Utah Shakespeare Festival, Cedar City, Utah, 1987—; critic-at-large Am. Coll. Theatre Festival, Washington, 1970—. Author: Acting in Style and in Person, 4th edit., 1990, several plays; contbr. articles to profl. jours. Elected to Coll. of Fellows Am. Theatre, 1991. With U.S. Army, 1957-59. U. Nev.-Las Vegas Barrick Disting. scholar, 1983. Mem. Assn. Theatre in Higher Edn., Am. Coll. Theatre Festival (chmn. nat. playwriting com. 1981-82). Democrat. Home: 1016 Bonita Ave Las Vegas NV 89104-3154 Office: U Nev 4505 S Maryland Pky Las Vegas NV 89154-0002

CRAWFORD, JOHN EMERSON, communications educator; b. Omaha, July 10, 1943; s. Hugh E. Crawford and Bertha Z. (Faucette) Chilcott; m. Merrie E. Knight, July 14, 1972; 1 son, Justin E. B.A., Nebr. Wesleyan U., 1966; M.S., Calif. State U.-Sacramento, 1971; Ph.D., U. So. Calif., 1975. Mem. faculty Central Mich. U., Mt. Pleasant, 1974-76, U. Wyo., Laramie, 1976-80; prof. communication Ariz. State U., Tempe, 1980—; developer, pres. On Target Communication Systems, 1989—; cons. in field. Author: Communication, 1982, 2d edit., 1984; Communication Discovery, 1984. Mem. Western Speech Communication Assn., Speech Communication Assn., Internat. Communication Assn. Democrat. Methodist. Home: 6847 S Willow Dr Tempe AZ 85283-4137 Office: Ariz State U Tempe AZ 85281

CRAWFORD, JOYCE CATHERINE HOLMES, psychologist; b. Kansas City, Mo., May 30, 1918; d. Morton Henry and Lillian Catharine (Burton) Holmes; student Kansas City Jr. Coll., 1934-36; B.S. in Edn., U. Mo., 1938; M.A. in Guidance and Counseling, No. Ariz. U., 1957; Ph.D. in Ednl. Psychology, Ariz. State U., 1976; m. Merle Eugene Crawford, Dec. 18, 1938; children—Hal Wayne, Kent Holmes. Tchr., Sedona, Ariz., 1948-49, Verde Valley Sch., 1949-51, Cottonwood, Ariz., 1952-69; sch. psychologist, child study cons., Phoenix, 1971-75, Riverside Sch. Dist., 1972-74, Avondale Sch. Dist., 1971-83. Ranger-naturalist Tuzigoot Nat. Monument, U.S. Park Service, summers 1959-66; mem. Ariz. Gov.'s Adv. Com. on Mental Health, 1964-65, Ariz. Hosp. Survey and Constrn. Adv. Council, 1965-68; head start chmn. Cottonwood Neighborhood Council, 1967-69; sec. Yavapai County Head Start Policy Adv. Com., 1968-71; bd. dirs. Yavapai County Econ. Opportunity Council, 1967-70, sec., 1968-69; bd. dirs. Ariz. Assn. Mental Health, 1955-67, sec., 1961-64, founder Verde Valley chpt., 1956, pres., 1959-61; incorporating com. Verde Valley Community Guidance Clinic, 1965, bd. dirs., 1965-70; bd. dirs. No. Ariz. Comprehensive Guidance Center, 1967-69; bd. dirs., recreation chmn. Ariz. Congress Parents and Tchrs., 1954-55; bd. dirs. Westside Mental Health Services, 1980-87, pres., 1980, v.p., 1980-81; chmn. profl. referral com. Westside Children's Mental Health Service, 1983-87; bd. dirs. Southwest Community Network, 1985-87. Cert., lic. Ariz. Bd. Psychologist Examiners. Mem. Nat. Assn. Sch. Psychologists, Ariz. Assn. Sch. Psychologists (chmn. profl. standards com. 1980-81, pres. 1982-83, awards chmn. 1983-84, Keith Perkins Meml. award for Outstanding Achievement in Sch. Psychology 1988), Ariz. Psychol. Assn., Ariz. Edn. Assn. (mental health and spl. edn. com. 1961-67, chmn. 1964-65), Ariz. Assn. Children with Learning Disabilities, Psychologists for Social Responsibility, Planned Parenthood, Common Cause, ACLU, League of Women Voters of Tucson (edn. study com.). Democrat. Mem. Unitarian Universalist Ch. Home: 6770 E Carondelet Dr Apt 126 Tucson AZ 85710-2134

CRAWFORD, KEVAN CHARLES, nuclear engineer, educator; b. Salt Lake City, Utah, Jan. 26, 1956; s. Paul Gibson and Norma Irene (Christiansen) C. MS, U. Utah, 1983, PhD, 1986. Lic. Sr. reactor oper. U.S. NRC. V.p. Computer Mktg. Corp., Salt Lake City, 1977-81; sr. reactor engr. U. Utah Nuclear Engring. Lab., Salt Lake City, 1981-86; mgr. reactor ops. Tex. A&M U. Nuclear Sci. Ctr., College Station, Tex., 1986-88; prof. U. Utah, Salt Lake City, 1988—, Idaho State U., Pocatello, 1991—; ex officio mem. reactor safety com. U. Utah, Salt Lake City, 1981-91, Idaho State U., Pocatello, 1992—; mem. radiation safety com. U. Utah, 1988-91, Idaho State U., 1992—; cons. Envirocare of Utah, Inc., Salt Lake City, 1989, Westinghouse Idaho Nuclear, 1992—. Cadet Air Force Acad., 1974-75. Recipient S.S. Kisler scholarship U. Utah, Salt Lake City, 1975-78. Mem. Am. Nuclear Soc., Am. Soc. Engring. Educators, Phi Kappa Phi, Alpha Nu Sigma. Mormon. Office: Idaho State Univ Coll Engring Pocatello ID 83209 also: Univ Utah 3209 MEB Salt Lake City UT 84112

CRAWFORD, MICHAEL HOWARD, cardiologist, educator, researcher; b. Madison, Wis., July 10, 1943; s. William Henry and A. Kay (Keller) C.; m. Janis Raye Kirschner, June 23, 1968; children: Chelsea Susan, Dinah Jaye, Stuart Michael. AB, U. Calif., Berkeley, 1965; MD, U. Calif., San Francisco, 1969. Diplomate Am. Bd. Internal Medicine and sub-bd. Cardiovascular Disease. Med. resident U. Calif. Hosps., San Francisco, 1969-71; sr. med. resident Beth Israel Hosp., Boston, 1971-72; teaching fellow Harvard Med. Sch., Boston, 1971-72; cardiology fellow U. Calif. Hosps., San Diego, 1972-74; asst. prof. medicine U. Calif. Sch. Medicine, San Diego, 1974-76; asst. prof. medicine U. Tex. Health Sci. Ctr., San Antonio, 1976-78, assoc. prof. medicine, 1978-82, prof. medicine, 1982-89; Robert S. Flinn prof. cardiology U. N.Mex. Sch. Medicine, Albuquerque, 1989—; asst. dir. Ischemic Heart Disease Specialized Ctr. of Rsch., San Diego, 1975-76; adj. scientist S.W. Found. for Biomed Rsch., San Antonio, 1980-89; co-dir. div. cardiology U. Tex. Health Sci. Ctr., San Antonio, 1983-89; chief div. cardiology U. N.Mex. Sch. Medicine, Albuquerque, 1989—. Editor Clin. Cardiology Alert newsletter, 1990—; cons. editor (periodical) Cardiology Clinics, 1989—; editorial bd. Circulation jour., 1990—, Jour. Am. Coll. Cardiology, 1992—. Pres. Am. Heart Assn., San Antonio, 1981, Austin, Tex., 1987, chmn. coun. clin. cardiology, Dallas, 1989. Recipient Paul Dudley White award Assn. Mil. Surgeons of U.S., 1981, Merit Review grant Dept. VA, 1985; Rsch. Tng. grantee Nat. Heart Lung and Blood Inst., 1993—. Fellow Am. Coll. Cardiology, Am. Coll. Physicians; mem. Am. Soc. Echocardiography (bd. dirs. 1980-83), So. Soc. Clin. Investigation, Assn. Univ. Cardiologists, Western Assn. Physicians, Assn. Profs. Cardiology. Office: Univ NMex Hosp 2211 Lomas NE Albuquerque NM 87131

CRAWFORD, MURIEL LAURA, lawyer, author, educator; d. Mason Leland and Pauline Marie (Desllets) Henderson; m. Barrett Matson Crawford, May 10, 1959; children: Laura Joanne, Janet Muriel, Barbara Elizabeth. Student, U. Calif., Berkeley, 1958-60, 67-69; B.A. with honors, U. Ill., 1973; J.D. with honors, Ill. Inst. Tech., 1977; cert. employee benefit specialist U. Pa., 1989. Bar: Ill. 1977, Calif. 1991, U.S. Dist. Ct. (no. dist.) Ill. 1977, U.S. Dist. Ct. (no. dist.) Calif. 1991, U.S. Ct. Appeals (7th cir.) 1977, U.S. Ct. Appeals (9th cir.) 1991; CLU; chartered fin. cons. Atty., Washington Nat. Ins. Co., Evanston, Ill., 1977-80, sr. atty., 1980-81, asst. counsel, 1982-83, asst. gen. counsel, 1984-87, assoc. gen. counsel, sec., 1987-89, cons., employee benefit specialist, 1989-91; assoc. Hancock, Rothert & Bunshoft, San Francisco, 1991-92. Author: (with Beadles) Law and the Life Insurance Contract, 1989, 7th edit. 1993; co-author Legal Aspects of AIDS, 1990; contbr. articles to profl. jours. Recipient Am. Jurisprudence award Lawyer's Coop. Pub. Co., 1975, 2nd prize Internat. LeTourneau Student Med.-Legal Article contest, 1976, Bar and Gavel Soc. award Ill. Inst. Tech./Chgo.-Kent Student Bar Assn., 1977. Fellow Life Mgmt. Inst.; mem. ABA, Ill. Inst. Tech./Chgo.-Kent Alumni Assn. (bd. dir. 1983-89). Democrat. Congregationalist.

CRAWFORD, MYRON LLOYD, electronics engineer; b. Orem, Utah, Oct. 29, 1938; s. Carl A. and Thora L. C.; m. Marilyn L. Mott, Mar. 18, 1958; children: Myron S., Bryan V., Todd C., Russell D., Sharla A. BS in Maths., Brigham Young U., 1960; MSEE, U. Colo., 1968. Cert. electromagnetic compability engr. Nat. Assn. Radio and Telecommunications Engrs. Applied mathematician Nat. Bur. of Standards, Boulder, Colo., 1960-63, project engr., 1963-71, project leader, 1971-86, supervisory elec. engr., 1986—. Scoutmaster Boy Scouts Am., Boulder, 1965-80; bishop, priesthood leader LDS Ch., Boulder, 1980-85. Recipient Bronze medal U.S. Dept. of Commerce, 1984, Recognition award Soc. Automotive Engrs., 1987. Fellow IEEE; mme. EMC Soc. of IEEE (standards com. 1983-86, Cert. of Achievement 1979), Soc. of Automotive Engrs. (chmn. EMI com. 1977-87, Recognition award 1987), U.S. Tech. Adv. Group to ISO (chmn. 1982-86). Republican. Office: Nat Bur of Standards NIST 325 Broadway St Boulder CO 80303-3328

CRAWFORD, NATALIE WILSON, applied mathematician; b. Evansville, Ind., June 24, 1939; d. John Moore and Edna Dorothea (Huthsteiner) Wilson; BA in Math., U. Calif., Los Angeles, 1961, postgrad., 1964-67; m. Robert Charles Crawford, Mar. 1, 1969. Programmer analyst N.Am. Aviation Corp., El Segundo, Calif., 1961-64; mem. tech. staff Rand Corp., Santa Monica, Calif., 1964—, project leader, engring. tech., theater conflict and force employment programs, 1975—; dir. Theater Forces Program, 1988-90, Theater Force Employment Program, 1990-92, Force Structure and Force Modernization Program, 1992—; mem. Air Force Sci. Adv. Bd., 1988—, vice chmn., 1990—; cons., joint tech. coordinating group munition effectiveness. Named YWCA Woman of Yr., 1983. Mem. Am. Def. Preparedness Assn., USAF Assn., IEEE. Republican. Home: 20940 Big Rock Dr Malibu CA 90265-5316

CRAWFORD, PHILIP STANLEY, bank executive; b. Wichita, Kans., Nov. 30, 1944; s. Carson Eugene and Elizabeth Ellen (Childs) C.; m. Carolyn Louise Stephenson, June 10, 1989. BA, Sterling Coll., 1967; MBA, Baruch Coll., 1973. Programmer, analyst City of N.Y., 1968-72; planning analyst Fed. Reserve Bank, Boston, 1972-74; cons. Index Systems, Cambridge, Mass., 1974-79; sr. cons. Ernst & Whinney, Los Angeles, 1979; v.p. Union Bank, Los Angeles, 1979—. Mem. Mgmt. Info. Continuing Seminar (pres. 1985), Assn. Computing Machinery, Ops. Research Soc. Am., Inst. Mgmt. Sci. Republican. Office: Union Bank 445 S Figueroa St Los Angeles CA 90071-1602 Home: 3815 Olive Ave Long Beach CA 90807-3519

CRAWFORD, RICHARD EBEN, JR., investment advisor; b. Lake Forest, Ill., Dec. 24, 1930; s. Richard Eben Crawford and Alice B. (Appleton) Smith; m. Caroline Hellen Kelley, June 20, 1952 (div. 1980); children: Wes, John, J.D., Lindsay, Richard; m. Debbie Sum Chan, Feb. 1, 1985; children: Alexandra, Jessica. BA, Trinity Coll., Hartford, Conn., 1953; MBA, U. Pa., 1976. Various positions Minn. Natural Gas Co., St. Louis Park, Minn., 1957-69, pres., chief exec. officer, 1969-74; pres. Minn. Natural div. Minn. Gas Co., St. Louis Park, 1974-77; underwriter Conn. Gen. Life Ins. Co., Mpls., 1978-79; pres. Crawford Assocs., Tucson, 1980—, Crawford Meml. Cemetery, Emlenton, Pa., 1986-90. Area and state judge Career Devel. Conf. Ariz. Distbv. Edn. Clubs Am., 1986; vol. Mobile Meals program, Tucson, 1984-90; trustee St. Andrews Presbyn. Ch., Tucson, 1992—; Rep. committeeman, 1992—. Capt. USAF, 1955-57. Mem. SAR (treas. Tucson chpt. 1991, 2d v.p. 1992), Tucson C. of C. (com. mil. affairs 1983—), Pres.'s Club U. Ariz. Found., Skyline Country Club (tennis com. 1988-90), Wharton Club Ariz. (founder, pres. 1986—), Greater Tucson Econ. Coun. (agy. com. 1992), Toastmasters (pres. Aztec club 1984, 92, area gov. 1986-87, chmn. speechcraft com. 1987-88, Disting. Toastmaster), Rotary (dist. treas. 1988-89, chmn. various coms.), Alpha Delta Phi. Home: 6550 N St Andrews Dr Tucson AZ 85718-2616 Office: Crawford Assocs 5055 E Broadway Blvd Ste 214 Tucson AZ 85711-3640

CRAWFORD, RONALD LYLE, microbiology educator, consultant; b. Santa Anna, Tex., Sept. 28, 1947; s. Lester Crawford and Doris Delores (Smith) Crawford Norman; m. Onie Ann Thompson, Dec. 30, 1967; 1 child, Lisa Brooks. BA in Biology cum laude, Oklahoma City U., 1970; MS in Bacteriology, U. Wis.-Madison, 1972, PhD in Bacteriology, 1973. Rsch. assoc. U. Minn. St. Paul, 1973-74; rsch. scientist N.Y. State Dept. Health, Albany, 1974-75; asst. prof. microbiology U. Minn.-Twin Cities, 1975-79, assoc. prof., 1979-83, prof., 1983-86; prof. bacteriology and head dept. bacteriology and biochemistry, U. Idaho, Moscow, 1987-90, dir. Inst. Molecular and Agricultural Genetic Engring., 1988—, co-dir. Ctr. for Hazardous Waste Remediation Rsch., 1990—; mem. Idaho Higher Edn. Rsch. Coun., 1989-90; rsch. dir. Chem Waste Control, Wayzata, Minn., 1984-85; co-founder Innovative BioSystems, Inc., 1992; cons. to industry, 1975—; founder Innovative BioSystems, Inc., 1993. Author: Lignin Biodegradation and Transformation, 1981; also book chpts., numerous articles. Editor: (with R.S. Hanson) Microbial Growth on C1 Compounds, 1984; Applied and Environ. Microbiology, 1982-92. Weyerhauser fellow U. Wis.-Madison, 1970-73. Mem. AAAS, Am. Soc. Microbiology, Idaho Acad. Scis., Blue Key, Beta Beta Beta, Gamma Sigma Delta. Democrat. Avocations: playing guitar and banjo, long distance running.

CRAWSHAW, RALPH, psychiatrist; b. N.Y.C., July 3, 1921. A.B., Middlebury (Vt.) Coll., 1943; M.D., N.Y. U., 1947. Diplomate: Nat. Bd. Med. Examiners, Am. Bd. Psychiatry and Neurology. Intern Lenox Hill Hosp., N.Y.C., 1947-48; resident Menninger Sch. Psychiatry, Topeka, 1948-50, Oreg. State Hosp., Salem, 1950-51; practice medicine specializing in psychiatry Washington, 1954; staff psychiatrist C.F. Menninger Meml. Hosp., Topeka, 1954-57; asst. chief VA Mental Hygiene Clinic, Topeka, 1957-60; staff psychiatrist Community Child Guidance Clinic, Portland, Oreg., 1960-63; founder, clinic dir. Tualatin Valley Guidance Clinic, Beaverton, Oreg., 1961-67; pvt. practice medicine, specializing in psychiatry Portland, 1960—; mem. staff Holladay Park Hosp., 1961—; lectr. dept. child psychiatry Med. Sch. U. Oreg., 1961-63, clin. prof. dept. psychiatry, 1976; lectr. Sch. Social Work, Portland State U., 1964-67; founder Benjamin Rush Found., 1968, pres., 1968—; founder Friends of Medicine, 1969, Ct. of Man, 1970, Club of Kos, 1974, Oreg. Health Decisions, 1983, Am. Health Decisions, 1989, Health Vol. Overseas, 1984; Sonian Machanic vis. prof. South African Coll. Medicine, 1993. Contbr. editor: AMA Jour. of Socio-Econs, 1972-75; Columnist: Prism mag, 1972-76, The Pharos, 1972—, Portland Physician, 1975, Western Jour. Medicine, 1980—; Contbr. articles to med. jours. Cons. Bur. Hearings and Appeals, HEW, 1964-90; cons. Albina Child Devel. Center, Portland, 1965-75, HEW Region 8 Health Planning, 1979; mem. Inst. Medicine, Nat. Acad. Sci., 1978, Oreg. Health Coordinating Council, 1979; Mem. Gov.'s Adv. Com. on Mental Health, 1966-72; ad hoc com. Nat. Leadership Conf. on Am. Health Policy, 1976, Gov.'s Adv. Com. on Med. Care to Indigent, 1976—; trustee Millicent Found., 1964-67, Multnomah Found. for Med. Care, 1977; vis. scholar Center for Study Democratic Instns., 1969, Jack Murdock Charitable Trust, 1977, U.S.-USSR exchange scholar, 1973. Served with AUS, 1943-46; to lt., M.C. USN, 1951-54. Named Oreg. Dr./Citizen of Yr., 1978; U.S.-USSR rsch. scholar, 1973, 79; recipient I.N. Piragou medal for humanitarian Svcs., Russian Govt., 1992; Ralph Crawshaw Ann. Lectr. in Civic Medicine named in honor by Oreg. Found. for Med. Excellence, 1987. Fellow Am. Psychiat. Assn.; mem. AMA, APA, AAAS, Nat. Med. Assn., Oreg. Med. Assn. (trustee 1972—), Multnomah County Med. Soc. (pres. 1975), Royal Soc. Medicine, Inst. of Medicine of NAS, North Pacific Soc. Neurology and Psychiatry, Soc. for Psychol. Study Social Issues, Western European Assn. Aviation Psychology, Am. Med. Writers Assn., Portland Psychiatrists in Pvt. Practice (pres. 1971), Russian Acad. Natural Scis. (fgn. mem.), Alpha Omega. Address: 2525 NW Lovejoy St Ste 404 Portland OR 97210

CREACH, DAVID CLEO, retired tool designer, engineering draftsman; b. Carthage, Mo., June 23, 1918; s. Benjamin Russell and Libbye Florence (McCrory) C.; m. Phyllis Stone, 1948 (div. 1955); m. Muriel Pauline Reed, 1956 (div. 1965); 1 child, Douglas Jonathan; adopted children: Margaret, Timothy Michael. A in Structural Design, SUNY, Farmingdale, 1952. Machine tool operator Huntington Park, Calif., 1940-41, U.S. Steel, Gary, Ind., 1946-47; merchant seaman U.S. Freighters, Tankers, 1948-50; mem. surveyor crew Voohrees Engring. Co., Farmingdale, 1952-53; tool designer Douglas Aircraft Co., El Segundo, Calif., 1953-63; engring. draftsman McDonald Douglas Co., Huntington Beach, Calif., 1963-67; boiler tender Martin Bros. Lumber Mill, Portland, Oreg., 1973-79; ret., 1980. Sgt. U.S. Army Air Force, 1942-45, ETO. Home: 2950 Allane Ln Eugene OR 97402

CREAGER, CLIFFORD RAYMOND, editor; b. N.Y.C., Oct. 8, 1937; s. Clifford Henry and Catherine (Raymond) C.; m. Dorothy Ann Carlson, Dec. 18, 1965; children: Christopher, Curtis. AB, U. Mich., 1960. Reporter, wire editor, photographer Grand Haven (Mich.) Daily Tribune, 1960-61; reporter, photographer, city editor, editor Covina (Calif.) Sentinel, weekly, 1963-72; mng. editor Car Craft mag., Los Angeles, 1972-75, Motor Trend mag., Los Angeles, 1975-81; free-lance writer, editor, 1981-85; program dir. Safety Edn. Ctr., 1986-88; editor Profl. Counselor mag. and Adolescent Counselor mag., 1986—; v.p. A/D Communications Corp., Redmond, Wash., 1986-90, A/D Holding Corp., Redmond, Wash., 1990—. Trustee Wash. Coun. on Alcoholism and Drug Dependence. Served with AUS, 1961-63. Mem. U. Mich. Alumni Assn., Calif. Assn. Alcoholism And Drug Abuse Counselors, Calif. Assn. Drinking Driver Treatment Programs, Nat. Assn. Alcoholism and Drug Abuse Counselors.

CREAN, JOHN C., housing and recreational vehicles manufacturing company executive; b. Bowden, N.D., 1925; married. Founder Fleetwood Enterprises, Inc., Riverside, Calif., 1951, pres., 1952-70, chmn., chief exec. officer, 1970—, also dir. Served with USN, 1942; with U.S. Mcht. Marines, 1944-45. Office: Fleetwood Enterprises Inc 3125 Myers St PO Box 7638 Riverside CA 92523*

CREATH, KATHERINE, optical scientist; b. Wilmington, Del., Nov. 18, 1958; d. Donald Blades and Amelia (Gerhardt) C. BS, U. Rochester (N.Y.), 1980, MS, 1981; PhD, U. Ariz., 1985. Mem. tech. staff Bell Telephone Labs., Holmdel, N.Y., 1979, Aerospace Corp., El Segundo, Calif., 1980; teaching asst. U. Rochester, 1980-81; mem. tech. staff Hughes Aircraft Corp., El Segundo, 1981-85; optical engr. WYKO Corp., Tucson, 1985-91; asst. prof. Optical Scis. Ctr. U. Ariz., Tucson, 1991—; teaching assoc. U. Ariz., Tucson, 1983-85, adj. lectr., 1985-87, adj. asst. prof., 1987-90, asst. prof., 1991—. Author: (with others) Phase Measurement Interferometry, 1988, Optical Shop Testing, 2d edit., 1992; editor: Surface Characterization and Testing, 1986; contbr. articles to profl. jours. Mem. Am. Soc. Precision Engring, Optical Soc. Am. (pres. Tucson chpt. 1986-87), Internat. Soc. Optical Engrs., Soc. Exptl. Mechanics. Home: 4043 E Quiet Moon Dr Tucson AZ 85718-3427 Office: U Ariz Optical Scis Ctr Tucson AZ 85721

CREDE, ROBERT HENRY, physician, educator; b. Chgo., Aug. 11, 1915; s. William H. and Ethel (Starke) C.; m. Marjorie L. Lorain, Aug. 29, 1947; children: William, Victoria, Christina. A.B., U. Calif., Berkeley, 1937; M.D., U. Calif., San Francisco, 1941. Diplomate Am. Bd. Internal Medicine. Commonwealth fellow, instr. medicine U. Cin. Coll. Medicine, 1947-49; intern San Francisco City and County Hosp., 1941-42; asst. resident medicine U. Calif. Hosp., San Francisco, 1945-46; chief resident medicine U. Calif. Hosp., 1946-47; mem. faculty Sch. Medicine U. Calif., San Francisco, 1949—; prof. medicine Sch. Medicine U. Calif., 1960-86, vice chmn. dept., 1965-80, asso. dean, 1960-73, 79-89; chmn. div. ambulatory and community medicine Gen. Med. Clinic Sch. Medicine U. Calif. (Gen. Med. Clinic.), 1965-80, prof. emeritus, 1986—. Author articles in field. Served to capt., M.C. AUS, 1942-46. Recipient Guy K. Woodward prize internal medicine U. Calif. Sch. Medicine, 1941, Gold Headed Cane award, 1941. Mem. Am. Geriatrics Soc., Am. Fedn. Clin. Research, Soc. Gen. Internal Medicine, Am. Psychosomatic Soc., Calif. Med. Assn., San Francisco Med. Soc., Soc. Tchrs. Preventive Medicine. Office: Univ Calif Med Center PO Box 0410 San Francisco CA 94143-0410

CREECH, WILBUR LYMAN, air force officer; b. Argyle, Mo., Mar. 30, 1927; s. Paul and Marie (Maloney) C.; m. Carol Ann DiDomenico, Nov. 20, 1969; 1 son, William L. Student, U. Mo., 1946-48; B.S., U. Md., 1960; M.S., George Washington U., 1966; postgrad., Nat. War Coll., 1966. Commd. 2d lt. U.S. Air Force, 1949; advanced through grades to gen.; fighter pilot 103 combat missions USAF, North Korea, 1950-51; pilot USAF Thunderbirds, 1953-56; comdr., leader Skyblazers, Europe aerial demo team USAF, 1956-60; dir. Fighter Weapons Sch., Nellis AFB, Nev., 1960-61; advisor to comdr. Argentine Air Force, 1962; exec., aide to comdr. Tactical Air Command, 1962-65; dep. comdr. fighter wing, 177 combat missions in F-100 fighters and asst. dep. chief staff for ops. 7th Air Force, Vietnam, 1968-69; comdr. fighter wings USAF in Europe, Spain and W.Ger., 1969-71; dep. for ops. and intelligence Air Forces Europe, 1971-74; comdr. Electronic Systems Div., Hanscom AFB, Mass., 1974-77; asst. vice chief of staff HQS Air Force, Washington, 1977-78; comdr. Tactical Air Command, Langley AFB, Va., 1978—. Decorated D.S.M. with two oak leaf clusters, Silver Star medal, Legion of Merit with two oak leaf clusters, D.F.C. with three oak leaf clusters, Air Medal with 14 oak leaf clusters, Air Force Commendation medal with two oak leaf clusters, Army Commendation medal; Spanish Grand Cross of Aero. Merit with white ribbon. Mem. Air Force Assn., Order of Daedallans. Home: 20 Quail Run Rd Henderson NV 89014-2147

CREED, JOHN HENRY, international trade union representative; b. Mt. Kisco, N.Y., Apr. 15, 1940; s. Richard Francis and Edith Maude (Rea) C.; m. Linda Sue LeVesque. Feb. 14, 1983; children: John H., Sandra Jeanne. Grad. high sch., Pleasantville, N.Y. Driver AK Orient Van Svc., Anchorage, 1959-62, dispatcher, 1965-69; lobbyist, polit. analyst Internat. Brotherhood Teamsters, Anchorage, 1969—; polit. action com. dir. Internat. Brotherhood Teamsters, 1969—. Trustee Teamster Welfare Trust,

Anchorage, 1972—; pres. Anchorage Polit. Roundtable, 1979—, Alaska Hosp. and Med. Ctr., Anchorage, 1982-83, Security Title and Trust, Anchorage, 1983-89; mem. Dem. Nat. Com. Sgt. U.S. Army, 1962-65. Home: PO Box 240088 Douglas AK 99824 Office: Teamster Local #959 PO Box 102092 Anchorage AK 99510-2092

CREER, JAMES READ, financial officer; b. Ogden, Utah, Oct. 26, 1942; s. Harold and Geraldine (Jacobson) C.; m. Ann L. Curran, Aug. 7, 1964 (div. Aug. 1974); children: Wendy, Kellie, Mark, Jennifer; m. Carolyn Rudd, Jan. 11, 1985. BS in Acctg., U. Utah, 1968. CPA. Staff acct. PMM & Co., L.A., 1968-71; sr. acct. PMM & Co., Salt Lake City, 1971-72, Haynie, Tebbs & Smith, Salt Lake City, 1972-73; ptnr. Roberts & Creer, Salt Lake City, 1973-74; pvt. practice Salt Lake City, 1974-81; v.p., chief financial officer Johnstone Supply, Salt Lake City, 1981—, ACW Enterprises Inc., Salt Lake City, 1989—; acctg. instr. Utah Tech. Coll., Stevens-Henegar Coll. Bus., 1973-76. With USMC, 1960-63. Mem. Rotary (pres. so. Salt Lake City chpt. 1989-90, Paul Harris fellow 1988). Republican. Mem. LDS Ch. Office: Johnstone Supply 2940 S 300 W Salt Lake City UT 84115

CREGOR, JOHN MARSHALL, JR., lawyer; b. Indpls., Sept. 18, 1945; s. John M. and Janet Rose (Beach) C.; m. Heidi Alberta Penchansky, June 7, 1968; children: Conrad William, Carl J. AB, Columbia Coll., 1967; JD, Ind. U., 1970. Bar: Ind. 1970, U.S. Dist. Ct. (so. dist.) Ind. 1970, U.S. Ct. Mil. Appeals 1973, Ill. 1974, U.S. Dist. Ct. (no. dist.) Ill. 1974, U.S. Ct. Appeals (7th cir.) 1978, Hawaii 1983, U.S. Dist. Ct. Hawaii 1983, U.S. Ct. Appeals (9th cir.) 1987. Assoc. Foran Wiss & Schultz, Chgo., 1974-75, Defrees & Fiske, Chgo., 1976-83, Davis Reid & Richards, Honolulu, 1983-90; mng. atty., pvt. practice Honolulu, 1990—; arbitrator, mediator Am. Arbitration Assn., Honolulu, 1988—. Chmn. edn., trustee Waiokeola Congrl. Ch., Honolulu, 1988-92. Lt. USN, 1970-74, ret. Mem. ABA, Hawaii State Bar Assn., Ind. State Bar Assn., Chgo. Bar Assn., Obedience Tng. Club Hawaii, Dachshund Club Hawaii (bd. dirs.), Sigma Chi. Libertarian. Office: Six Waterfront Pla Ste 240 Honolulu HI 96813

CREIGHTON, DOUGLAS GEORGE, French educator; b. Toronto, Ont., Can., July 8, 1923; s. Henry Robinson and Marjorie (Douglas) C.; m. Margaret Ona West, Aug. 6, 1953; children—Geoffrey, Sheila, Rhonda. Instr. French, Brown U., Providence, 1947-49, U. Sask., Saskatoon, Can., 1950-53; asst. d'anglais Lycee Chaptal, Paris, 1953-54; asst. prof. Beloit Coll., Wis., 1955-59; asst. prof., assoc. prof., prof. French, U. Western Ont., London, 1959-89, prof. emeritus, 1989—. Author: Diderot's Refutation of Helvetius, 1952; J.-F. De Luc of Geneva and .....Rousseau, 1982. Editor: A Travers Les Siecles, 1967. Mem. Am. Assn. Tchrs. of French, Am. and Can. Socs. for 18th Century Studies. Avocation: philately. Home: 24 Longbow Pl, London, ON Canada N6G 1Y3

CREIGHTON, JOHN W., JR., forest products company executive; b. Pitts., Sept. 1, 1932; married; 3 children. BS, Ohio State U., 1954, JD, 1957; MBA, U. Miami, 1965. With Arthur Andersen and Co., 1957-59, Arvida Corp., 1959-66; exec. v.p. Mortgage Cons. Inc., 1966-70; gen. mgr. Shelter Group Weyerhaeuser Co., 1970, corp. v.p., 1970-85, exec. v.p., 1985-88, pres., dir., 1988—; pres., CEO Weyerhaeuser Real Estate Co.; chmn. bd. dirs. Fed. Home Loan Bank Seattle; bd. dirs. Nat. Corp. Housing Partnership, Puget Sound Bancorp, Mortgage Investments Plus, Inc., Am. Paper Inst. Trustee U. Puget Sound; bd. dirs. Chief Seattle Coun. Boy Scouts Am., King County United Way. With U.S. Army, 1954-56. Office: Weyerhaeuser Co 33663 Weyerhaeuser Way S Auburn WA 98001-9646*

CRESPIN, LESLIE ANN, artist; b. Cleveland, Ohio, Sept. 30, 1947; d. Edwin Creaver and Eunice Jane (Pierce) Ulrich; m. Raimondo J. Vinella; children: Greg, Chris, Tony. Student, Cleve. Art Inst., U. Capetown (S. Africa), Hiram (Ohio) U. Instr. Taos (N.Mex.) Sch. Fine Art; works in permanent collections at Johnson Humrick House Mus., Ohio, Harwood Found., Mus. Taos Art, Midland Savs. and Loan, Denver, Santa Fe Contract Design, Odessa, Tex., Monsanto Internat., N.Y.C., Carlsbad Fine Art Mus., Tubac Ctr. for the Arts, Rolm Corp., Dallas, Wichita Art Assn., Kans. Exhibits include Cleve. Mus. Art, Jewish Community Ctr., Cleve., Hiram U., U. Capetown, N.Mex. State U., Stables Art Gallrey, Taos, Roanoke (Va.) Fine Arts Mus., The New Gallery, Taos, 1981-84, Amarillo Art Ctr., 1983, Carlsbad Fine Arts Mus., 1984, Tracy Felix Artspace Gallery, Colorado Springs, 1985, Tubac Ctr. for Arts, Ariz., 1985, Erie (Pa.) Art Mus., 1986, Zanesville (Ohio) Art Ctr., 1987, Harwood Found. Mus. Taos Art, 1987, Fenix Gallery, N.Mex., 1990-91, J. Richards Gallery, Englewood, N.J., 1990-91, 92, 93, Sharon Blaustein, N.J. and N.Y., 1990, 91, 92, 93, Fenix Gallery, 1990, 91, 92, 93; represented in permanent collections Harwood Found., Maytag, Midland Savings and Loan, Santa Fe Contract Design, Marvin Buckles, Monsanto Internat., Carlsbad Fine Art Mus., Tubac Ctr. for the Arts, Bernard Ewell ASA, Rolm Corp., Johnson Humrick House Mus., N. Pajarola Museumstrasse, Switzerland, Carson County Square House Mus. Recipient numerous purchase awards; Masterfield award, North Coast Collage Soc., 1985, Grumbacher award, Beachwood Mus., Ohio, 1986, Master Field award, KennedyCtr. Gallery, 1987. Mem. Albuqueque United Artists, Soc. Artists in Multi-Media, North Coast Collage Soc., Nat. Mus. of Women in the Arts, Taos Seven. Home and Office: PO Box 357 Taos NM 87571-0357

CRESS, CHARLES R., pharmacology educator; b. Glendale, Calif., July 29, 1942; s. Harry M. and Delphina Pearl (Wical) C.; m. Gail Shiela Cress, Feb. 13, 1983; children: Kenneth, Peter, Heather, Loren. BS, Pacific Union Coll., 1965; PhD, Oreg. State U., 1970. Instr. pharmacology Loma Linda (Calif.) U.; asst. prof. pharmacology Loma Linda U.; assoc. prof. pharmacology —. Mem. Western Pharmacology Soc., Sigma Xi. Home: PO Box 6725 Crestline CA 92325-6725 Office: Loma Linda U Loma Linda CA 92350

CRESWELL, DONALD CRESTON, management consultant, marketing specialist; b. Balt., Mar. 28, 1932; s. Carroll Creston and Verna Moore (Taylor) C.; student Johns Hopkins U., 1951-52; MBA, U. Dayton, 1966; postgrad. bus. Stanford U., 1975; m. Terri Sue Tidwell, Dec. 27, 1958; 1 child, Creston Lee. Cons. engr. A.D. Ring & Assocs., Washington, 1956-58; sales and mktg. mgr. Ampex Corp., Redwood City, Calif., 1959-68; dir. mktg., magnetic products div. RCA Corp., N.Y.C., 1968-71; staff v.p. sales and advt. Pan Am. World Airways, N.Y.C., 1971-74; mktg. v.p. Rocor Internat., Palo Alto, Calif., 1975; v.p., chief oper. officer, gen. mgr., Am. AmBuCar Svcs., Inc., San Francisco, 1976; prin. mgmt. cons., dir. mktg. svcs. Stanford Rsch. Inst., Menlo Park, Calif., 1977-86 ; v.p. and gen. mgr. Strategic Decisions Group-Decision Systems, 1987—; mgr. R & D, dir. R & D strategy practice Decision Quality Assn., 1992—; bd. dirs. Rogerson Aircraft Controls, 1981-85; bd. dirs., mgrs. com. Jets Cybernetics, 1987—; lectr. planning and mktg. mgmt. Am. Mgmt. Assn., 1968-69; program chmn. Grad. Bus. Assn., 1965; rep. to Electronics Industries Assn., 1968-71, to Internat. Air Transport Assn., 1971-74. Bd. dirs. Peninsula Youth Soccer Club, 1981-82; nat. dir. referee assessment, mem. referee com. U.S. Soccer Fedn., 1986-88; regional chief referee San Carlos Am. Youth Soccer Orgn., 1981-85; State dir. assessment Calif. Soccer Assn., 1982-85 ; mem. L.A. Olympics Organizing Com., 1983-84, nat. referee assessor, 1987—; ofcl. N. Am. Soccer League, 1983-84. Mem. Am. Mktg. Assn. (exec. mem.), Am. Theatre Organ Assn. (bd. dirs. 1978-79), R&D Decision Quality Assn. (bd. dirs. 1992—), Nat. Intercollegiate Soccer Ofcls. Assn., Charles Lindbergh Fund, U.S. Soccer Fedn. (cert. soccer referee, nat. assessor), Wings Club, The Churchill Club, Stanford Jazz Com. Republican. Home: 8 Pyrola Ln San Carlos CA 94070-1532 Office: Strategic Decisions Group 2440 Sand Hill Rd Menlo Park CA 94025-6900

CRETARA, DOMENIC ANTHONY, artist, educator; b. Chelsea, Mass., Mar. 29, 1946; s. Anthony Mario and Carmella (Addivinola) C.; BFA magna cum laude, Boston U., 1968, MFA, 1970; m. Elizabeth Tarquinio, June 20, 1970; children: Jeanette, Anthony. One-man shows: Art Inst. Boston, 1976, Boston U., 1977, Camargo Found., Cassis, France, 1979, Helen Bumpus Gallery, Duxbury, Mass., 1980, Coll. William and Mary, 1980, U. Mass., 1980, Duxbury Art Complex Mus., 1982, First St. Gallery, N.Y.C., 1983, Segal Gallery, N.Y.C., 1984, 85, Koplin Gallery, L.A., 1987, Victor McNeil Gallery, N.Y.C., 1988, Alon Gallery, Brookling, Mass., 1989, 91, John Thomas Gallery, Santa Monica, Calif., 1991-93; group shows: Fitchburg (Mass.) Art Mus., 1973, Am. Embassy, Rome, 1975, Inst. Internat. Edn., N.Y.C., 1978, Boston Cyclorama, 1980, Drawing Ctr., N.Y.C., 1983, Weatherspoon Art Gallery, Greensboro, N.C., 1983, Sherry French Gallery, N.Y.C., 1987, L.A. Internat. Arts Fair, 1986, 88, Riverside (Calif.) Art Mus., 1989, Triton Mus. Art, Santa Clara, Calif., 1990, others; represented in permanent collections: Boston U., Art Inst. Boston, Met. Mus.; represented by John Thomas Gallery, Santa Monica, Calif., Alon Gallery, Boston; instr. painting DeCordova Mus. Sch., Lincoln, Mass., 1971-73, Fitchburg Art Mus., 1970-74; chmn. fine arts dept. Art Inst. Boston, 1972-78, instr. painting and drawing, 1970-83, assoc. prof. painting, 1983-86; prof. painting Calif. State U.-Long Beach, 1986—. Fulbright-Hays grantee, Italy, 1974-75; resident painter Camargo Found., Cassis, France, 1978-79; Boston-Padua Sister Cities grantee, 1984. Mem. Boston Visual Artists Union. Drawings and paintings reproduced in: Figure Drawing, 1976; The Art of Responsive Drawing, 1977, American Artist, 1992; Painting: Visual and Technical Fundamentals, 1979. Contbr. articles to The Artist's Mag., 1990, 91.

CREW, AUBREY TORQUIL, aerospace inspector; b. London, May 9, 1926; came to U.S. 1968; s. Thomas Alfred and Phyllis Sibil (Ibbetson) C.; m. Sally-Marie Thompson, Dec. 22, 1979; children: Clare Violet, Mark Ernest, Karen Audrey. Student, London Tech. Coll., 1956, Oslo State U., Norway, 1965-67. Marine radio officer Marchessini & Co., London, N.Y.C., 1956-57; flight radio officer Hunting Clan Aircraft Co., London, 1957-59; radio and TV engr. Radionette, Oslo, 1960-68; avionics tech. flight Lockheed Aircraft Co., Palmdale, Calif., 1971-82; aerospace inspector Rockwell Internat., Palmdale, 1983—. Appeared in film The Sundowners, 1959. Vol. blood donor Viking Group Charities, Beverly Hills, Calif., 1969—; capt. USAF Civil Air Patrol, 1978—. With Royal Navy, 1941-56. Fellow Royal Soc. St. George; mem. Air Force Assn. Republican. Episcopalian. Home: 1274 West Ave H-4 Lancaster CA 93534

CREWS, WILLIAM ODELL, JR., seminary administrator; b. Houston, Feb. 8, 1936; s. William O. Sr. and Juanita (Pearson) C.; m. Wanda Jo Ann Cunningham; children: Ronald Wayne, Rhonda Ann Crews Bolei. BA, Hardin Simmons U., 1957, HHD, 1987; BDiv, Southwestern Bapt. Theol. Sem., 1964; DD, Calif. Bapt. Coll., 1987. Ordained to ministry Bapt. Ch., 1953. Pastor Grape Creek Bapt. Ch., San Angelo, Tex., 1952-54, Plainview Bapt. Ch., Stamford, Tex., 1955-57, 1st Bapt. Ch., Sterling City, Tex., 1957-60, 7th St. Bapt. Ch., Ballinger, Tex., 1960-65, Woodland Heights Bapt. Ch., Brownwood, Tex., 1965-67, Victory Bapt. Ch., Seattle, 1967-72, Met. Bapt. Ch., Portland, Oreg., 1972-77; dir. communications Northwest Bapt. Conv., Portland, 1977-78; pastor Magnolia Ave Bapt. Ch., Riverside, Calif., 1978-86; pres. Golden Gate Bapt. Theol. Sem., Mill Valley, Calif., 1986—; pres. NW Bapt. Conv., Portland, 1974-76, So. Bapt. Gen. Conv. Calif., Fresno, 1982-84. Trustee Fgn. Mission Bd., Richmond, Va., 1973-78, Golden Gate Bapt. Theol. Sem., 1980-85, Marin Community Hosp. Found., 1992—; bd. dirs. Midway=Seatac Boys Club, Des Moines, 1969-72. Mem. Marin County C. of C. (bd. dirs. 1987—), Midway C. of C. (bd. dirs. 1968-72), Rotary (bd. dirs. San Rafael chpt. 1992—, pres. Portland club 1975-76, pres.-elect Riverside club 1984-85). Home: 10 Chapel Dr Mill Valley CA 94941-3109 Office: Golden Gate Bapt Theol Sem Strawberry Point Mill Valley CA 94941

CRICK, FRANCIS HARRY COMPTON, biologist, educator; b. June 8, 1916; s. Harry and Annie Elizabeth (Wilkins) C.; m. Ruth Doreen Dodd, 1940 (div. 1947); 1 son; m. Odile Speed, 1949; 2 daus. B.Sc., Univ. Coll., London; PhD, Cambridge U., Eng. Scientist Brit. Admiralty, 1940-47, Strangeways Lab., Cambridge, Eng., 1947-49; biologist Med. Rsch. Coun. Lab. of Molecular Biology, Cambridge, 1949-77; Kieckhefer Disting. prof. Salk Inst. Biol. Studies, San Diego, 1977—, non-resident fellow, 1962-73; adj. prof. psychology U. Calif., San Diego; vis. lectr. Rockefeller Inst., N.Y.C., 1959; vis. prof. chemistry dept. Harvard U., 1959, vis. prof. biophysics, 1962; fellow Churchill Coll., Cambridge, 1960-61; Korkes Meml. lectr. Duke U., 1960; Henry Sedgewick Meml. lectr. Cambridge U., 1963; Graham Young lectr., Glasgow, 1963; Robert Boyle lectr. Oxford U., 1963; Vanuxem lectr. Princeton U., 1964; William T. Sedgwick Meml. lectr. MIT, 1965; Cherwell-Simon Meml. lectr. Oxford U., 1966; Shell lectr. Stanford U., 1969; Paul Lund lectr. Northwestern U., 1977; Dupont lectr. Harvard U., 1979, numerous other invited, meml. lectrs. Author: Of Molecules and Men, 1966, Life Itself, 1981, What Mad Pursuit, 1988, The Astonishing Hypothesis: The Scientific Search for the Soul, 1994; contbr. papers and articles on molecular, cell biology and neurobiology to sci. jours. Recipient Prix Charles Leopold Mayer French Academies des Scis., 1961; (with J.D. Watson) Rsch. Corp. award, 1961, (with J.D. Watson & Maurice Wilkins) Nobel Prize for medicine, 1962, Gairdner Found. award, 1962, Royal Medal Royal Soc., 1972, Copley Medal, 1976, Michelson-Morley award, 1981, Benjamin P. Cheney medal, Spokane, Wash., 1986, Golden Plate award, Phoenix, 1987, Albert medal Royal Soc. of Arts, London, 1987, Wright Prize VIII Harvey Mudd Coll., Claremont, Calif., 1988, Joseph Priestly award Dickinson Coll., 1988. Fellow AAAS, Royal Soc.; mem. Acad. Arts and Scis. (fgn. hon.), Am. Soc. Biol. Chemistry (hon.), U.S. Nat. Acad. Scis. (fgn. assoc.), German Acad. Sci., Am. Philos. Soc. (fgn. mem.), French Acad. Scis. (assoc. fgn. mem.), Indian Acad. Scis. (hon. fellow), Order of Merit. Office: Salk Inst Biol Studies PO Box 85800 San Diego CA 92186-5800

CRIEL, LAURA VICTORIA, public affairs officer, education coordinator; b. Detroit, Apr. 11, 1933; d. William Ray Weible and Frieda Preshia (Lashley) Bradley; m. Harry Eugene Criel, June 13, 1953; children: Vicki Criel Fuchs, Bruce Harry, Todd Martin. Taxpayer svc. rep. IRS, Buffalo, 1974-77; aide U.S. Senator Harrison Schmitt, Albuquerque, 1978-80, taxpayer svc. rep., 1980-81, problem resolutions officer, 1981-82, revenue officer, 1982-84, pub. affairs officer, taxpayer edn. coord., 1984—. Mem. N.Mex. Bus. Assistance Coun. (chair Albuquerque chpt. 1990-91), Pub. Rels. Soc. Am. (bd. dirs., profl. edn. coord. 1992—), Albuquerque Press Club. Home: 326 Paint Brush Dr NE Albuquerque NM 87122-1415 Office: IRS 517 Gold Ave SW Albuquerque NM 87102-3156

CRILLY, EUGENE RICHARD, engineering specialist; b. Phila., Oct. 30, 1923; s. Eugene John and Mary Virginia (Harvey) C.; m. Alice Royal Roth, Feb. 16, 1952; ME, Stevens Inst. Tech., 1944, MS, 1949; MS, U. Pa., 1951; postgrad. UCLA, 1955-58. Sr. rsch. engr. N.Am. Aviation, L.A., 1954-57; sr. rsch. engr., Canoga Park and Downey, Calif., 1962-66; process engr. Northrop Aircraft Corp., Hawthorne, Calif., 1957-59; project engr., quality assurance mgr. HITCO, Gardena, Calif., 1959-62; sr. rsch. specialist Lockheed-Calif. Co., Burbank, 1966-74; engring. specialist N.Am. aircraft ops. Rockwell Internat., El Segundo, Calif., 1974-89. Author tech. papers. Served with USNR, 1943-46; comdr. Res. ret. Mem. Soc. for Advancement Material and Process Engring. (chmn. L.A. chpt. 1978-79, gen. chmn. 1981 symposium exhbn., nat. dir. 1979-86, treas. 1982-85, Award of Merit 1986), Soc. Mfg. Engrs. (sr.), Naval Inst., Am. Soc. for Composites, ASM Internat., Naval Res. Assn., VFW, Mil. Order World Wars (adj. San Fernando Valley chpt. 1985, 2d vice comdr. 1986, commdr. 1987-89, vice comdr. West, Dept Cen. Calif., 1988-89, comdr. Cajon Valley-San Diego chpt. 1990-92, adj./ROTC chmn. region XIV 1990-91, comdr. Dept. So. Calif. 1991-93, vice comdr. region XIV, 1992-93, dep. comdr. GSO region XIV 1993—, Disting. Chpt. Cmdr. Region XIV 1990-91), Former Intelligence Officers Assn. (treas. San Diego chpt. one 1990—), Ret. Officers Assn. (treas. Silver Strand chpt. 1992—), Navy League U.S., Naval Order U.S., Naval Intelligence Profls. Assn., Brit. United Svc. Club L.A., Marines' Meml. Club (San Francisco), Sigma Xi, Sigma Nu. Republican. Roman Catholic. Home and Office: 276 J Ave Coronado CA 92118-1138

CRIM, JACK C., diversified industry executive; b. 1930. B.S., Purdue U., 1954. With Economy Regulator, 1956-62; v.p. ops. Textron Inc., 1962-68; pres. Cuno div. AMF Inc., 1968-73, group v.p. exec. recreation vehicles, 1970-73; group v.p. Textron Inc., 1982-83, pres. Townsend div., 1981-82; exec. v.p., chief oper. officer Talley Industries Inc., 1982-83, pres., chief oper. officer, 1983—, also bd. dirs. Office: Talley Industries Inc 2702 N 44th St Phoenix AZ 85008-1500

CRIMINALE, WILLIAM OLIVER, JR., applied mathematics educator; b. Mobile, Ala., Nov. 29, 1933; s. William Oliver and Vivian Gertrude (Sketoe) C.; m. Ulrike Irmgard Wegner, June 7, 1962; children: Martin Oliver, Lucca. B.S., U. Ala., 1955; Ph.D., Johns Hopkins U., 1960. Asst. prof. Princeton (N.J.) U., 1962-68; asso. prof. U. Wash., Seattle, 1968-73; prof. oceanography, geophysics, applied math. U. Wash., 1973—, chmn. dept. applied math., 1976-84; cons. Aerospace Corp., 1963-65, Boeing Corp., 1968-72, AGARD, 1967-68, Lenox Hill Hosp., 1967-68, NASA Langley, 1990—; guest prof., Can., 1965, France, 1967-68, Germany, 1973-74, Sweden, 1973-74, Scotland, 1985, 89, 91, Eng., 1990, 91, Stanford, 1990, Brazil, 1992; Nat. Acad. exch. scientist, USSR, 1969, 72. Author: Stability of Parallel Flows, 1967; Contbr. articles to profl. jours. Served with U.S. Army, 1961-62. Boris A. Bakmeteff Meml. fellow, 1957-58, NATO postdoctoral fellow, 1960-61, Alexander von Humboldt Sr. fellow, 1973-74, Royal Soc. fellow, 1990-91. Mem. AAAS, Am. Phys. Soc., Am. Geophys. Union, Fedn. Am. Scientists, Soc. Indsl. and Applied Math. Home: 1635 Peach Ct E Seattle WA 98112-3428 Office: U Wash Dept Applied Math FS 20 Seattle WA 98195

CRINELLA, FRANCIS MICHAEL, neuropsychologist, science foundation director; b. Petaluma, Calif., Dec. 22, 1936; s. Marino Peter and Marian (Eleanor) C.; m. Terrie Kay Lynd, Sept. 19, 1959; children: Ramona, Gina, Peter, Andrew, Christina. BA, U. Notre Dame, 1958; MS, San Francisco State U., 1962; PhD, La. State U., 1969. Lic. clin. and exptl. psychologist, Calif. Psychology intern Alameda County (Calif.) Guidance Clinic, 1961-62, New Orleans, 1968-69; rsch. assoc. spl. edn. La. State U., Baton Rouge, 1966-69; staff psychologist Sonoma State Hosp., Eldridge, Calif., 1969-72, sr. psychologist, 1971-72, cons. program rev., 1972-77; research psychologist Brain Behavior Research Ctr., Eldridge, 1969-77; dir. Petaluma Hosp. Dist., 1971-76, treas., 1975; exec. dir. Fairview State Hosp., Costa Mesa, Calif., 1977-85; assoc. clin. prof. to clin. prof. psychiatry U. Calif., Irvine, 1977—, assoc. clin. prof. to clin. prof. phys. medicine, 1981—; dir. Devel. Research Insts., Costa Mesa, 1985—; pres. Rehab. Ctr. for Brain Dysfunction, Irvine, 1982—. Contbr. articles on neuropsychiatry to profl. jours. Bd. dirs. United Way Orange County, Calif., Orange County Epilepsy Soc., also pres., 1978—. Served to capt. USAF, 1962-66. Recipient Career Scientist award Rehab. Ctr. Brain Dysfunction Inc., 1983; grantee Nat. Inst. Child Health and Human Devel., 1972, Nat. Inst. Neurol. Diseases Communicative Disorders and Stroke, 1973, Nat. Inst. Aging, 1985, Nat. Inst. Mental Health, 1989. Mem. AAAS, Am. Psychol. Assn., Am. Acad. on Mental Retardation, Nat. Acad. Neuropsychologists, Western Psychol. Assn., Redwood Psychol. Assn. Republican. Roman Catholic. Club: Mesa Verde Country (Costa Mesa). Office: State Devel Rsch Insts 2501 Harbor Blvd Costa Mesa CA 92626-6179

CRIPPENS, DAVID LEE, broadcast executive; b. Nashville, Sept. 23, 1942; s. Nathaniel and Dorothy (Sharp) C.; m. Eloise Brown, Aug. 3, 1968; 1 child, Gerald Chinua. BA in Polit. Sci., Antioch U., 1964; MSW, San Diego State U., 1968. Assoc. dir. ednl. opportunities program San Diego State U., 1968-69; producer KPBS-TV, San Diego, 1969-71; staff producer, writer, newsperson WQED-TV, Pitts., 1971-73; dir. ednl. svc. KCET, L.A., 1973-77, v.p. ednl. svc., 1977-80, v.p., sta. mgr., 1980-83, v.p. nat. prodns., 1983-85, sr. v.p., 1985—. Exec. producer TV programs Straight Up, Watch Me Move, Yes, Inc., Fostering, Frederick Douglass: Slave and Statesman, Summer Faire, Inc., The New Americans, A Step in Time, Fair Play in Sports, Easier Done Than Said; prodn. exec. Blind Tom: The Story of Thomas Bethune, Day in the Country, Gold Boxes, Wilderness Journey, Neighbors, Olympic Arts Fesitval, Mr. Previn Comes to Town; contbr. articles to profl. publs. Trustee Antioch U., 1987—; bd. dirs. Calif. Found. on Employment and Disability, 1986—, Crittenton Ctr. Young Women and Infants; vol. Peace Corps, Nigeria, 1964-66. Recipient Excellence in Edn. Commendation award Calif. Poly. Black Faculty and Staff Assn., 1991, Prin.'s Orgn. award Sr. High Sch. Prins., 1991, honor Assn. Adminstrs. L.A., 1988, Calif. Coalition for Pub. Edn., 1987, Nat. Assn. Media Women, 1986, Calif. Assembly Legis. Com., 1971, San Diego State Black Student Coun., 1971, named One of Pitts.' Most Influential Blacks, Pitts. Post Gazette, 1973, Outstanding Ednl. Leadership award Phi Delta Kappa, 1992, Nat. Citation award, 1993, Positive Image Award Frank D. Parent PTA, 1992. Mem. AAAS (com. on pub. understanding of sci. and tech.), NCN (treas. nat. comm. network). Home: 5252 W 64th St Inglewood CA 90302-1016 Office: KCET 4401 W Sunset Blvd Los Angeles CA 90027-6090

CRISCUOLO, WENDY LAURA, lawyer, interior design consultant; b. N.Y.C., Dec. 17, 1949; d. Joseph Andrew and Betty Jane (Jackson) C.; m. John Howard Price, Jr., Sept. 5, 1970 (div. Apr. 1981); m. Ross J. Turner, July 23, 1988. BA with honors in Design, U. Calif., Berkeley, 1973; JD, U. San Francisco, 1982. Space planner GSA, San Francisco, 1973-79; sr. interior designer E. Lew & Assocs., San Francisco, 1979-80; design dir. Beier & Gunderson, Inc., Oakland, Calif., 1980-81; sr. interior designer Environ. Planning and Rsch., San Francisco, 1981-82; interior design cons. Hillsborough, Calif., 1982—; law clk. to Judge Spencer Williams U.S. Dist. Ct., San Francisco, 1983-84; atty. Ciros Investments, Hillsborough, 1984—. Author: (with others) Guide to the Laws of Charitable Giving, 3d rev. edit., 1983; staff mem. U. San Francisco Law Rev., 1983. Bd. dirs., v.p. and treas. Marin Citizens for Energy Planning, 1986-89; bd. dirs., pres. Calif. Ctr. for Wildlife, 1987-90; trustee Cayote Point Mus. for Environ. Edn., 1990-93. Mem. ABA, State Bar Calif., Queen's Bench (San Francisco), Calif. Women Lawyers, Nat. Environ. Leadership Coun., Commonwealth Club. Republican. Episcopalian.

CRISMAN, MARY FRANCES BORDEN, librarian; b. Tacoma, Nov. 23, 1919; d. Lindon A. and Mary Cecelia (Donnelly) Borden; m. Fredric Lee Crisman, Apr. 12, 1975 (dec. Dec. 1975). BA in History, U. Wash., 1943, BA in Librarianship, 1944. Asst. br. librarian in charge work with children Mottet br. Tacoma Pub. Libr., 1944-45, br. librarian, 1945-49, br. librarian Moore br., 1950-55, asst. dir., 1955-70, dir., 1970-74, dir. emeritus, 1975—; corp. libr. Frank Russell Co., 1985—; chmn. Wash. Community Library Council, 1970-72. Hostess program Your Library and You, Sta. KTPS-TV, 1969-71. Mem. Highland Homeowners League, Tacoma, 1980—, incorporating dir. 1980, sec. and registered agt., 1980-82. Mem. ALA (chmn. mem. com. Wash. 1957-60, mem. nat. library week com. 1965, chmn. library adminstrn. div. nominating com. 1971, mem. ins. for libraries com. 1970-74, vice chmn. library adminstrn. div. personnel adminstrn. sect. 1972-73, chmn. 1973-74, mem. com. policy implementation 1973-74, mem. library orgn. and mgmt. sect. budgeting acctg. and costs com. 1974-75), Am. Library Trustee Assn. (legis. com. 1975-78, conf. program com. 1978-80, action devel. com. 1978-80), Pacific N.W. (trustee div. nominating com 1976-77), Wash. Library Assn. (exec. bd. 1957-59, state exec., dir. Nat. Library Week 1965, treas., exec. bd. 1969-71, 71-73), Urban Libraries Council (editorial sec. Newsletter 1972-73, exec. com. 1974-75), Ladies Aux. to United Transp. Union (past pres. Tacoma), Friends Tacoma Pub. Library (registered agt. 1975-83, sec. 1975-78, pres. 1978-80, bd. dirs. 1980-83), Smithsonian Assocs., Nat. Railway Hist. Soc., U. Wash. Alumni Assn., U. Wash. Sch. Librarianship Alumni Assn. Roman Catholic. Club: Quota (sec. 1957-58, 1st v.p. 1960-61, pres. 1961-62, treas. 1975-76, pres. 1979-80) (Tacoma). Home: 6501 N Burning Tree Ln Tacoma WA 98406-2108 Office: Frank Russell Co Russell Bldg 909 S A St Tacoma WA 98402-5120

CRISPIN, JAMES HEWES, engineering and construction company executive; b. Rochester, Minn., July 23, 1915; s. Egerton Lafayette and Angela (Shipman) C.; m. Marjorie Holmes, Aug. 5, 1966. A.B. in Mech. Engring., Stanford U., 1938; M.B.A., Harvard U., 1941; grad., Army Command and Gen. Staff Sch., 1943. Registered profl. mech. engr., Calif. With C.F. Braun & Co. Alhambra, Calif., 1946-62; treas. Bechtel Corp., San Francisco, 1962-73, v.p., mem. fin. com., 1967-75, mgr. investment dept., 1973-75; retired, 1976; investment cons., Santa Barbara, Calif., 1978—. Lt. col. Ordnance Corps, AUS., 1941-46. Mem. Mil. Order World Wars, S.R., Soc. Colonial Wars, Colonial Wars Calif., Baronial Order Magna Carta, Mil. Order Crusades, Am. Def. Preparedness Assn., World Affairs Coun. No. Calif. (trustee 1968-75), Santa Barbara Mus. Art (trustee 1979-91, pres. 1986-88), Calif. Hist. Soc. (trustee 1979-86), Valley Club of Montecito (pres. 1987-90, bd. dirs. 1981-91), Calif. Club L.A., World Trade Club San Francisco (pres. 1977-78, bd. dirs. 1971-78), Beta Theta Pi. Republican. Home: 1340 E Mountain Dr Santa Barbara CA 93108-1215 Office: La Arcada Bldg 1114 State ST Ste 220 Santa Barbara CA 93101-2716

CRISPO, RICHARD CHARLES, artist, ethnologist, minister; b. Bklyn., Jan. 13, 1945; s. Frank C. and Irene M. (Lamont) C. M.F.A., Trinity Hall Coll., 1975; Ph.D., Collegii Romanii, Rome, 1976, Th.D., 1977. Instr. art Monterey Peninsula Coll., 1968-69, instr. ethnic studies, 1976; instr. art history Hartnell Coll.; coord. Arts in Corrections, Art Project, Soledad Prison, 1976-83; am. cultural specialist to Latin Am. for U.S.; vis. lectr. U. Calif., Santa Cruz, interdisciplinary studies dept. Porter Coll.; instr. pub. sch. art, Monterey, Calif., 1967-72; counselor Intrim, Inc., Monterey, 1976; founder Mus. on Wheels, 1973-74; founder World Folk Art Collection, Monterey, 1972; 53 murals and 63 one-man shows; executed half-mile-long mural at Soledad Prison; priest N. Am. Old Roman Catholic Ch. Recipient numerous awards including 1st prize Calif. State Fair, 1964; UNESCO award, 1971-73; Calif. Arts Council grantee. Mem. Artist Equity, Found. for the Community of Artists, Carmel Art Assn., Pacific Grove Art Center. Contbr. articles to art jours.

CRISTIANO, MARILYN JEAN, speech communication educator; b. New Haven, Jan. 10, 1954; d. Michael William Mary Rose (Porto) C. BA, Marquette U., 1975, MA, 1977; postgrad., Ariz. State U., 1977; EdD, Nova U., 1991. Speech comm. instr. Phoenix Coll., 1977-87, Paradise Valley C.C., Phoenix, 1987—; presenter at profl. confs., workshops and seminars. Author tng. manual on pub. speaking, 1991, 92; contbr. articles to profl. publs. Mem. Women in Higher Edn. in Ariz. (v.p., pres.), Am. Soc. Tng. and Devel., Speech Communication Assn., Western Speech Communication Assn., Ariz. Communication Assn. Office: Paradise Valley CC 18401 N 32d St Phoenix AZ 85032

CRISWELL, KIMBERLY ANN, public relations executive, dancer; b. L.A., Dec. 6, 1957; d. Robert Burton and Carolyn Joyce (Semko) C. BA with honors, U. Calif.-Santa Cruz, 1980; postgrad. Stanford U., 1993. Instr., English Lang. Services, Oakland, Calif., 1980-81; freelance writer Gambit mag., New Orleans, 1981; instr. Tulane U., New Orleans, 1981; instr., editor Haitian-English Lang. Program, New Orleans, 1981-82; instr. Delgado Coll., New Orleans, 1982-83; instr., program coord. Vietnamese Youth Ctr., San Francisco, 1984; dancer Khadra Internat. Folk Ballet, San Francisco, 1984-89; dir. mktg. communications Centram Systems West, Inc., Berkeley, Calif., 1984-87; communications coord. Safeway Stores, Inc., Oakland, 1985; dir. corp. communications TOPS, div. Sun Microsystems, Inc, 1987-88; pres. Criswell Communications, 1988—. Vol. coord. Friends of Haitians, 1981, editor, writer newsletter, 1981; dancer Komenka Ethnic Dance Ensemble, New Orleans, 1983; mem. Contemp. Art Ctr.'s Krewe of Clones, New Orleans, 1983, Americans for Nonsmokers Rights, Berkeley, 1985. Mem. Internat. Assn. Bus. Communicators, Sci. Meets the Arts Soc. (founding), NAFE, Dance Action, Bay Area Dance Coalition, Oakland Mus. Assn., Mus. Soc. Democrat. Avocations: visual arts, travel, creative writing. Office: 715 San Bruno Ave San Francisco CA 94107

CRITCHLOW, B. VAUGHN, research facility administrator, researcher; b. Hotchkiss, Colo., Mar. 5, 1927; s. Arthur Burtis and Nancy Gertrude (Lynch) C.; m. Janet Lee Howell, Mar. 1, 1987; children from previous marriage: Christopher, Eric, Jan, Carey. AA, Glendale Coll., 1946-49; BA, Occidental Coll., 1951; PhD, UCLA, 1957. Instr. to prof. anatomy, acting chmn. anatomy Baylor Coll. Medicine, Houston, 1957-72; prof., chmn. anatomy Oreg. Health Scis. U., Portland, 1972-82; mem. sci. adv. com. Oreg. Regional Primate Rsch. Ctr., Beaverton, 1973-82, mem. ad hoc adv. com., 1981-82, dir., 1982—; trustee Med. Rsch. Found. Oreg., 1982—; vis. investigator Nobel Inst. Neurophysiology, Karolinska Inst., Stockholm, 1961-62; invited speaker 2d Internat. Cong. Hormonal Steroids, Milan, Italy, 1966, 3d Internt. Cong. Endocrinology, Mexico City, 1968, others; mem. NIH reproductive biology study sects., 1969-73, 75-77. Contbr. numerous articles to profl. jours. Served with USN, 1945-46. NIH rsch. career devel. awardee, 1959-69; NIH rsch. grantee, 1958—. Mem. Am. Assn. Anatomists, Endocrine Soc., Soc. for Neurosci., Internat. Soc. Neuroendocrinology, Internat. Brain Rsch. Orgn. Office: Oreg Regional Primate Rsch Ctr 505 NW 185th Ave Beaverton OR 97006-3499

CRITES, RICHARD RAY, international franchising company executive; b. Rapid City, S.D., Aug. 29, 1952; s. Charles Dayton and Marcia Ann (Heil) C.; m. Randel E. Golobic, Dec. 27, 1980 (div. May 1988). B of Liberal Studies, U. Okla., 1975; MS, Stanford U., 1978; cert. sr. security checker, Advanced Orgn. L.A., 1987, cert. false purpose rundown auditor, 1988. Cert. staff status II, exec. status I, Am. St. Hill Orgn. Nat. sales trainer Continental Mktg. Corp., Detroit, 1975-76, regional sales mgr., 1976-80; pres., chief exec. officer Retail Packaging Specialists, Inc., San Mateo, Calif., 1982-86; owner, chief exec. officer Miracle Method of San Mateo, Inc., 1985-87, Miracle Method of Beverly Hills, Inc., L.A., 1987-90, Miracle Method of So. Calif., Inc., L.A., 1986-92, Miracle Method of No. Calif., Inc., L.A., 1988-89; v.p., treas., chmn. bd. Miracle Methods of the U.S., Inc., L.A., 1988-92; pres., chmn. bd. dirs. Miracle Method of the U.S., Inc., L.A., 1992—; pres., chmn. bd. Internat. Miracle Method Appearance Ctrs. Pacific, Inc., L.A., 1988-92, Internat. Miracle Method Ctrs. Equip. & Supply, Inc., L.A., 1989-92; exec. dir. full hat course Celebrity Ctr. Internat., 1992. Mem. Citizen's Commn. on Human Rights, Citizens for an Alternative Tax System. Mem. Internat. Assn. Scientologists (sponsor). Republican. Scientologist. Office: Miracle Method of the US Inc 3732 W Century Blvd Ste 6 Inglewood CA 90303-1108

CRIVELLO, SANDRA K., sales executive; b. Seattle, Apr. 26, 1960; d. Wilbur A. and Beatrice C. (Koch) Bender. Student, Scottsdale (Ariz.) C.C., Scottsdale C.C., 1990-92, U. Phoenix, 1991. Salesperson Ashton-Tate, Torrance, Calif., 1982-91, Tech. Source Consulting, Phoenix, 1992—; founding mem. Ashton-Tate, Torrance, 1982. Author: The Crystal Cathedrals, 1993. Mem. Data Processing Mgmt. Assn., Ariz. Software Assn. Democrat. Home: 10912 E Yucca St Scottsdale AZ 85259 Office: Tech Source Consulting 6619 N Scottsdale Rd Scottsdale AZ 85250

CROCKER, J. A. FRAZER, JR., minister, social worker; b. Detroit, Oct. 4, 1935; s. J. A. Frazer, Sr. and Marjorie Olievia (May) C.; m. Jaqueline Fairchild Arnold, Apr. 15, 1961 (div. Aug. 1972); children: John A. F. III, Matthew M.; m. Diana Worden, June 4, 1977; 1 stepchild, Colin E. Brayton. AB, Kenyon Coll., Gambier, Ohio, 1957; MDiv, Ch. Div. Sch. of the Pacific, Berkeley, Calif., 1960; MSW, U. Utah, 1974; DMin, Grad. Theol. Found., 1992. Lic. clin. social worker; ordained to ministry Episcopal Ch. as deacon then priest, 1960. Asst. min. Trinity Cathedral, Davenport, Iowa, 1960-61; priest in charge St. Paul's Ch., Sioux City, Iowa, 1961-64; assoc. rector Grace Ch., Jamaica, N.Y., 1964-67; rector St. Mary's Ch., Provo, Utah, 1967-72; program dir. Utah State Prison Alcohol Treatment Program, Draper, 1974-81; pvt. practice Salt Lake City, 1981-83; dir. mental health Family Health Plan, Salt Lake City, 1983-88; bishop's canon Episcopal Diocese Utah, Salt Lake City, 1988—; protestant chaplain Utah State Prison, 1968-74; asst. chaplain St. Mark's Hosp., Salt Lake City, 1983; exec. dir. Episcopal Social and Pastoral Ministries, 1990—. Pres. Utah Mental Health Assn., Salt Lake City, 1970-72; flotilla comdr. USCG Aux., Salt Lake City, 1980; bd. dirs. Family Support Ctr., Salt Lake City, 1989—, pres., 1991-93; bd. dirs. Olympus View Hosp., Salt Lake City, 1992—, United Episcopal Charities, 1993—; mem. coun. Our Lady of the Mountains Retreat House, 1992—. Mem. Great Salt Lake Yacht Club (bd. dirs. 1980-82). Office: Episcopal Diocese Utah PO Box 3090 Salt Lake City UT 84110-3090

CROCKER, KENNETH FRANKLIN, data processing consultant; b. Centralia, Wash., July 29, 1950; s. Earl Thomas and Mary Jane (Hamil) C.; m. Mary Louise Underwood, June 15, 1974 (div. Dec. 1987); children: Matthew A., Benjamin F., Jonathan C.; m. Sally Marlene Gammelgard, Dec. 21, 1987. AS in Computer Programming and System Design, Control Data Inst., Long Beach, Calif., 1972. Programmer City of Greenville, S.C., 1973; computer operator Winn Dixie Stores, Greer, S.C., 1973-75; programmer Piedmont Industries, Greenville, S.C., 1975-78; systems engr. Micro-Systems, Greenville, 1978; sr. programmer Reeves Bros., Lyman, S.C., 1978-80; systems analyst Cryovac div. W.R. Grace Co., Duncan, S.C., 1980-84; sr. cons. Cap Gemini Am., San Francisco, 1984-85; prin. mem. tech. staff Citibank-FSB Calif., Oakland, 1985-91; adv. software engr. Lucky Stores Inc., Dublin, Calif., 1991—. Umpire Contra Costa Umpires Assn., 1990—. Republican. Baptist. Home: 301 Livorna Heights Rd Alamo CA 94507-1326

CROCKER, MYRON DONOVAN, judge; b. Pasadena, Calif., Sept. 4, 1915; s. Myron William and Ethel (Shoemaker) C.; m. Elaine Jensen, Apr. 26, 1941; children—Glenn, Holly. A.B., Fresno State Coll., 1937; LL.B., U. Calif. at Berkeley, 1940. Bar: Calif. bar 1940. Spl. agt. FBI, 1940-46; practiced law Chowchilla, Calif., 1946-58; asst. dist. atty. Madera County, Calif., 1946-51; judge Chowchilla Justice Ct., 1952-58, Superior Ct. Madera County, 1958-59; U.S. judge Eastern Dist. Calif., Sacramento, 1959—. Mem. Madera County Republican Central Com., 1950—. Named Outstanding Citizen Chowchilla, 1960. Mem. Chowchilla C. of C. (sec.). Lutheran. Club: Lion. Office: US Dist Ct US Dist Courthouse 1130 O St Fresno CA 93721-2201

CROCKER, RHONDA DEE, information systems specialist; b. Longmont, Colo., Nov. 13, 1957; d. Robert Carl and Irene Marie (Stahlecker) Aschenbrenner; m. Tillman Hans Crocker, July 18, 1976; children: Heather Christina Marie, Desirae Jolene. AAS in EDP, Aims C.C., 1983; postgrad., Ea. N.Mex. U., 1990—. Student systems mgr. Campus Am., Inc., Roswell, N.Mex., 1984-92; sr. sytems oper. Transportation Mfg. Corp., Roswell, 1992—; community advisor ENMU-R, Roswell, 1991—. Mem. Am. Assn. Collegiate Registrars Admissions Officers, Nat. Assn. Student Fin. Aid Adminstrs., Decus, Phi Theta Kappa. Democrat. Lutheran. Home: 3741 Crossroads Roswell NM 88201

CROCKER, SYLVIA FLEMING, psychotherapist, writer; b. Live Oak, Fla., Apr. 10, 1933; d. Tom and Lydia (Compton) Fleming; divorced; children: Sarah Lydia, Trena Elizabeth. AA, Stephens Coll., 1951; BA, U. Mo., 1957, PhD, 1969; MA, Northwestern U., Evanston, Ill., 1958; MS, U. Wyo., 1987. Lic. prof. counselor, Wyo. Grad. asst. in philosophy U. Mo., Columbia, 1960-63; asst. prof. philosophy Marquette U., 1966-70; lectr. in philosophy Calif. State U., San Bernardino, 1972-75, U. Wyo., 1975-76; pvt. practice Laramie, Wyo., 1980—. Mem. Assn. Advancement of Gestalt Therapy (steering com., chair of com. for Gestalt rsch. and theoretical devel.). Episcopalian. Home and Office: 2115 E Hancock St Laramie WY 82070-2935

CROCKER, TILLMAN HANS, computer analyst; b. Schweinfurt, Bavaria, West Germany, Feb. 10, 1956; s. Lloyd Tillman and Waltraud Christina (Korn) C.; m. Rhonda Dee Aschenbrenner, July 18, 1975; children: Heather, Desirae. AAS, CIS, ENMU, Roswell, N.Mex., 1986. System tech. ENMU-R, Roswell, N.Mex., 1986-87; product specialist Campus Am., Roswell, N.Mex., 1987-89; dir./comp. serv. ENMU-R, Roswell, N.Mex., 1989—. Computer cons., Sr. Olympics, Roswell, N.Mex., 1990. Republican. Mem. New Apostolic.

CROFFORD, HELEN LOIS, accountant; b. Mesa, Ariz., Sept. 1, 1932; d. Elmer Earl and Lillian Irene (Williams) C.; grad. Lamson Bus. Coll., Phoenix, 1952. Acct., Bob Fisher Enterprises, Inc., Holbrook, Ariz., 1964-78; office mgr. for physician, Holbrook, 1978-79; office mgr. Trans Western Services, Inc., Holbrook, 1979; acct., Northland Pioneer Coll., Holbrook, 1980—. Squadron comdr. CAP, 1965-67, mission coordinator, 1970-79, group comdr., 1972-77, mem. regional staff, 1977-79, wing. historian, 1984—; mem. Navajo Fair Commn., 1966-75; mem. Navajo County Natural Resource Conservation Dist., 1970—, sec.-treas., 1971-81, chairperson, 1981-88; chmn. Navajo County Emergency Service Council, 1984-87; co-chmn. Navajo County Local Emergency Planning Com., 1987-88; troop com. sec. Boy Scouts Am., 1989. Mem. Ariz. Assn. Conservation Dists. (exec. bd. 1977-78, sec., 1979-80, v.p. 1981-82, pres. 1983-84, past pres. 1985), Nat. Assn. Conservation Dists. (past pres., edn. com. 1981-84), DAR, Nat. Assn. Search and Rescue. Democrat. Home: PO Box 36 Woodruff AZ 85942-0036 Office: 1200 E Hermosa Dr Holbrook AZ 86025

CROISSANT, ANN BAILEY, science, curriculum educator; b. Maytown, Ky., Jan. 24, 1940; d. William Taulbee and Prova Julia (Bowman) Bailey; m. Gerald LeRoy Croissant, June 20, 1961; children: Brian David, Polly Kay, Carol Renee. BA, U. No. Colo., 1961; MS, U. Wis., 1968; PhD, U. So. Calif., 1991. Cert. secondary, elem., C.C. tchr., Calif. Tchr. various pub. and pvt. schs., colls. and univs., 1960-78; lectr. Calif. State Poly. U., Pomona, 1978-87; instr. Mt. San Antonio C.C., Walnut, Calif., 1984-87; prof. edn. Azusa (Calif.) Pacific U., 1984—; sci. curriculum cons. L.A. and San Bernadino County Schs., 1978—; environ. impact reports/cons., L.A. County, 1987—. Author: Taxonomy: Key to Organization, 1978, Plants: The Green Machines, 1978, Ecology/Pollution/Energy, 1978. Pres. Glendora (Calif.) PTA, 1977-78, 79-80, 81-82; sci. cons. Girl Scouts U.S.A., Glendora, 1980-87; campaign chair City Coun. Election, Glendora, 1981-82; pres. Glendora Ednl. Found., 1983-84; sec. Mayor's Blue Ribbon Conservancy Adv. Com., Glendora, 1989; pres., founder Glendora Community Conservancy, 1991—. NSF fellow, 1962; recipient Friend of Edn. award Glendora Tchr.'s Assn., 1987, Spl. Achievement award Glendora Sch. Bd., 1983, Hon. Svc. award Glendora PTA, 1982, Women of Achievement award YWCA, 1991, Outstanding Teaching award Alpha Chi, 1991, Exemplary Teaching Forum award Am. Assn. Higher Edn., 1992. Mem. ASCD, Nat. Sci. Tchrs. Assn., Calif. Native Plant Soc., So. Calif. Botanists, Gifted Children's Assn. (bd. dirs. 1978—), Am. Ednl. Rsch. Assn. Republican. Baptist. Home: 1323 E Bennett Ave Glendora CA 91740 Office: Azusa Pacific U PO Box APU Azusa CA 91702

CROKER, DAVID CARL, air force officer, energy management consultant; b. Kingston, N.Y., July 22, 1957; s. William Leslie and Helen (Bendert) C.; m. Cynthia Jo Cook, July 15, 1978; 1 child, Amber Noelle. Grad. pvt. sch., Seneca Falls, N.Y. Enlisted man USAF, 1970, advanced through grades to E-6; aircraft maintenance man 22d BMW, Riverside, Calif., 1977-80; alarm technician 416th Civil Engring. Div., Rome, N.Y., 1980-84; elec. foreman 5073d Air Base Group, Shemya, Alaska, 1984-85; energy mgmt. system technician and operator 22d Civil Engring. Div., Riverside, 1985—. Contbr. articles to profl. publs. Office: 22d CES/DEMCS March AFB Riverside CA 92518

CROMLEY, BRENT REED, lawyer; b. Great Falls, June 12, 1941; s. Arthur and Louise Lilian (Hiebert) C.; m. Dorothea Mae Zamborini, Sept. 9, 1967; children: Brent Reed Jr., Giano Lorenzo, Taya Rose. AB, Dartmouth Coll., 1963; JD, U. Mont., 1968. Bar: Mont. 1968, U.S. Dist. Ct. Mont. 1968, U.S. Ct. Appeals (9th cir.) 1968, U.S. Supreme Ct. 1978, U.S. Ct. Claims 1988, U.S. Ct. Appeals (D.C. cir.) 1988. Law clk. to presiding justice U.S. Dist. Ct. Mont., Billings, 1968-69; assoc. Hutton & Sheehy and predecessor firms, Billings, 1969-77, ptnr., 1977-78; ptnr. Moulton, Bellingham, Longo & Mather, P.C., Billings, 1979—, also bd. dirs. Contbr. articles to profl. jours. Mem. Yellowstone Bd. Health, Billings, 1972—; chmn. Mont. Bd. Pers. Appeals, 1974-80; mem. Mont. Ho. of Reps., 1991-92. Mem. ABA, ACLU, Internat. Assn. Def. Counsel, Mont. Bar Assn., Mont. Def. Trial Lawyers Bd., Yellowstone County Bar Assn. (various offices), Christian Legal Soc., Internat. Brotherhood of Magicians, Kiwanis. Home: 235 Parkhill Dr Billings MT 59101-0660 Office: Moulton Bellingham Longo & Mather PC 1900 Sheraton Pla Billings MT 59101

CRONE, RICHARD ALLAN, cardiologist, educator; b. Tacoma, Nov. 26, 1947; s. Richard Irving and Alla Marguerite (Ernst) C.; m. Rita Louzetta Mitchell, June 9, 1972 (div. Oct. 1981); m. Mika Jane Hinkle, Feb. 12, 1983 (div. Aug. 1991). BA in Chemistry, U. Wash., 1969, MD, 1973. Intern Madigan Army Med. Ctr., Tacoma, 1973-74, resident in medicine, 1974-76, fellow in cardiology, 1977-79; commd. med. officer U.S. Army, Tacoma, Denver, San Francisco, 1972; advanced through grades to lt. col. U.S. Army, 1981; dir. coronary care unit Fitzsimons Army Med. Ctr., Denver, 1979-81; practice medicine specializing in cardiology Stevens Health Clinic, Edmonds, Wash., 1981—, also dir. coronary care unit, cardiac catheter lab, 1982—; clin. asst. prof. medicine U. Wash., Seattle, 1983—. Fellow Am. Coll. Angiology; mem. AMA, Am. Coll. Cardiology, Am. Heart Assn., Seattle Acad. Internal Medicine, Wash. State Soc. Internal Medicine, Wash. State Med. Assn. Republican. Roman Catholic. Home: 10325 66th Pl W Mukilteo WA 98275-4559 Office: 21701 76th Ave W Ste 100 Edmonds WA 98026-7537

CRONIN, MICHAEL JOHN, research scientist; b. L.A., Nov. 19, 1949; m. Anna Marie Schneider, Feb. 24, 1979; children: Kevin John, Daniel Patrick, Pater Michael. BS in Biology, Loyola U. L.A., 1971; PhD in Physiology, U. So. Calif., 1976; postdoctoral, U. Calif., San Francisco, 1979. PHS postdoctoral fellow, 1976-79; asst. prof. physiology U. Va. Sch. Medicine, Charlottesville, 1979-82, assoc. prof., 1983-87, tenured, 1984; sr. scientist Genentech, Incorp., South San Francisco, 1987—, also dir. endocrin rsch. dept.; adj. prof. physiology and biophysics dept. U. So. Calif. Sch. Medicine, L.A., 1988—; speaker in field. Mem. editorial bd. Endocrinology, Neuroendorcrinology; contbr. numerous articles to profl. jours.; co-patentee in field. Asst. scout master troop 363 Boy Scouts Am., 1970-71, leader, 1991. Scholar NSF, 1980-84, DuPont, 1983-87; grantee NIH, NSF, DOA, Am. Heart Assn., Jeffries Found. Va. VA, PEW Scholars, Alberta Heritage Found. Med. Rsch., Montreal Children's Hosp., MRC Can. Office: Genentech Incorp 460 Point San Bruno Blvd South San Francisco CA 94080

CRONIN, ROBERT HILLSMAN, musical instrument maker; b. Houston, Feb. 9, 1943; s. Thomas Dillon and Anne Catherine (Heyck) C. BA, Rice U., 1964, BSME, 1965; MS in Applied Mechanics, Stanford U., 1966, PhD in Applied Mechanics, 1972. Rsch. engr. SRI Internat., Menlo Park, Calif., 1972-77; R & D engr. Stanford (Calif.) U., 1978-80; tech. staff KLA Instruments, Santa Clara, Calif., 1981-86; owner RHC Hist. Instruments, Menlo Park, 1981—. Author: Evolution of the Bassoon Bore, 1981. Mem. Bicycle Adv. Com., 1991-92. Mem. Internat. Double Reed Soc., Hist. Brass Soc. Am. Musical Instrument Soc., San Francisco Early Music Soc. Home and Office: 360 Marmona Dr Menlo Park CA 94025

CRONK, MILDRED SCHIEFELBEIN (MILI CRONK), special education consultant; b. Waverly, Iowa, May 29, 1909; d. Emil August and Nettie Marie (Berger) Schiefelbein; m. Dale Cronk, July 20, 1930; children: Barbara Cronk Burress, Bruce, Margaret, Michael. Student, Wartburg Coll., Waverly, 1927, Tampa (Fla.) U., 1944-45, Los Angeles City Coll., 1957; BA in Psychology, Calif. State U., 1960, MA in Spl. Edn. Supervision, 1971. Aircraft communicator, weather observer CAA, Fla. and Calif., 1942-49; dir. Parkview Nursery Sch., L.A., 1956-57; tchr. trainable mentally retarded Hacienda-LaPuente United Sch. Dist., LaPuente, Calif., 1961-74; cons. spl. edn. La Mirada, Calif., 1975—; in-svc. trainer for tchrs.; mem. Spl. Olympics S.E. L.A. County com., 1977—; mem. Internat. Very Spl. Arts Festival Com., 1981; mem. adv. com. Very Spl. Arts Festival, Orange County, 1976—, chmn., 1986-87; treas. Very Spl. Arts Calif., 1986-87, bd. dirs., 1986—. Author: Create with Clay, 1976, Vocational Skills Taught through Creative Arts, 1978, Attitude Change toward Trainable Mentally Retarded Students—Mainstreaming in Reverse, 1978, Career Education for Trainable Mentally Retarded Students—It's for Life!, 1982, also others. Mem. Am. Assn. on Mental Deficiency (bd. dirs. region II, editor Newsette, 1975-77, chmn. publicity com., 1977-79, presenter ann. confs.), Coun. for Exceptional Children (bd. dirs. Calif., editor Calif. State Fedn./Coun. for Exceptional Children Jour., 1977-80, past pres. San Gabriel Valley chpt. 538, mem.-at-large So. Calif. div. mental retardation 1976-79, pres. Calif. div. mental retardation 1980-81, sec. 1988-89, chmn. com. on officers' handbook, nat. coun., div. mental retardation, 1977-78, liaison, 1986—, mem. Orange County chpt., bd. dirs. 1987—, presentation coord. internat. conf. 1989, spl. recognition awards, 1976, 77, 78, 79, 89), Nat. Assn. for Retarded Citizens (rec. sec. 1980-81), Nat. Soc. Autistic Children (nat., state, local orgns.), Nat. Ret. Tchrs. Assn. (nat., state, local orgns.), Am. Ceramic Soc. (design div.), Smithsonian Instn., Wilderness Soc., Psi Chi. Democrat. Home and Office: 13116 Clearwood Ave La Mirada CA 90638-1814

CRONKLETON, THOMAS EUGENE, physician; b. Donahue, Iowa, July 22, 1928; s. Harry L. and Ursula Alice (Halligan) C.; BA in Biology, St. Ambrose Coll., 1954; MD, Iowa Coll. Medicine, 1958; m. Wilma Agnes Potter, June 6, 1953; children: Thomas Eugene, Kevin P., Margaret A., Catherine A., Richard A., Robert A., Susan A., Phillip A. Diplomate Am. Bd. Family Practice. Rotating intern St. Benedict's Hosp., Ogden, Utah, 1958-59; Donahue, Iowa, 1959-61, practice family medicine, Davenport, Iowa, 1961-66, Laramie, Wyo., 1966—; asso. The Davenport Clinic, 1961-63, partner, 1963-66; active staff St. Luke's Hosp., Mercy Hosp., Davenport; staff physician U. Wyo. Student Health Service, 1966-69, 70-71, 74-75, 76—, acting dir., 1988-89; staff physician outpatient dept. VA Hosp., Iowa City, 1969-70: staff physician outpatient dept. VA Hosp., Cheyenne, Wyo., 1971-74, chief outpatient dept., 1973-74; dir. Student Health Service Utah State U., Logan, 1975-76; physician (part-time) dept. medicine VA Hosp., Cheyenne, 1976-81. Active Long's Peak council Boy Scouts Am., 1970—, scout chaplain Diocese of Cheyenne, 1980—, mem. Diocesan Pastoral Council, 1982-85. Served with USMC, World War II, Korea. Recipient Dist. Scouter award Boy Scouts Am., 1974, St. George Emblem, Nat. Cath. Scouter award, 1981. Recipient 5, 10, and 15-yr. service pins Boy Scouts Am. Fellow Am. Acad. Family Practice; mem. Wyo. State Med. Soc., Albany County (Wyo.) Med. Soc., Iowa Med. Soc., Johnson County (Iowa) Med. Soc. Democrat. Roman Catholic. Club: K.C. (4 deg.). Home: 2444 Overland Rd Laramie WY 82070-4808 Office: U Wyo Student Health Svc Laramie WY 82071

CROOK, GAINES MORTON, electrical engineer; b. Ellisville, Miss., May 7, 1923; s. Harry Hunter and Annie Virginia (Jones) C.; m. Bettie Ruth Benson, Nov. 15, 1947; children: Gaines Mark, David Elliot, Joel Hunter, Joshua Conrad Lee. BSEE, U. S.C., 1952; postgrad., UCLA, 1958-62, Pierce Coll., 1962, Calif. Poly. Inst., 1975. Registered profl. engr., Calif. Owner Gaines M. Crook & Assocs./GMC Labs., Chatsworth, Calif., 1972—; elec. engr. Miller Electric Co., Aiken, S.C., 1951-53; instrument engr. E.I. duPont de Nemours & Co., Aiken, 1953-56; design engr., group leader missiles div. Douglas Aircraft Co., Inc., Santa Monica, Calif., 1956-58; mem. tech. staff, sect. head, dept. mgr., sr. staff engr. Ramo-Wooldridge/Space Tech. Labs./TRW Systems, Redondo Beach, Calif., 1959-72; prin. investigator Office Sci. and Tech., NASA; cons. German Govt. Space Agy.; mem. tech. forecasting team TRW Future Probe; expert witness for Pacific Bell Telephone Co. Contbr. articles, paper to profl. publs., chpts. to books; patentee in field. Cpl. U.S. Army, 1943-46. Mem. IEEE (sr.), Calif. Soc. Profl. Engrs. (past pres. San Fernanco Valley chpt.). Republican. Mormon. Office: GMC Labs 9625 Cozycroft Ave # D Chatsworth CA 91311-5118

CROOK, SEAN PAUL, aerospace systems engineering manager; b. Pawtucket, R.I., July 6, 1953; s. Ralph Frederick and Rosemary Rita (Dolan) C.; m. Mary Wickman, June 10, 1978; children: Kimberly Anne, Kelly Dolan, Erin Webster, Mary Katherine. BSME, U.S. Naval Acad., 1975; MBA, U. So. Calif., 1991. Commd. ensign USN, 1975, advanced through grades to lt., 1979, resigned, 1981; sr. systems engr. space div. Gen. Electric Co., Springfield, Va., 1982-84; sr. aerospace systems engr. Martin Marietta Aero. Def. Systems, Long Beach, Calif., 1984-87; sr. aerospace system engring. mgr. Martin Marietta Aero Def. Systems, Long Beach, Calif., 1987—. Commdr. USNR, 1992—. Mem. Am. Mgmt. Assn. Home: 23565 Via Calzada San Juan Capistrano CA 92691 Office: Martin Marietta Aerospace 1501 Hughes Way Ste 300 Long Beach CA 90810-1865

CROOKE, STANLEY THOMAS, pharmaceutical company executive; b. Indpls., Mar. 28, 1945; m. Nancy Alder (dec.); 1 child, Evan; m. Rosanne M. Snyder. BS in Pharmacy, Butler U., 1966; PhD, Baylor Coll., 1971, MD, 1974. Asst. dir. med. rsch. Bristol Labs., N.Y.C., 1975-76, assoc. dir. med. rsch., 1976-77, assoc. dir. R&D, 1977-79, v.p. R&D, 1979-80; v.p. R&D Smith Kline & French Labs., Phila., 1980-82; pres. R&D Smith Kline Beckman, Phila., 1982-88; chmn. bd., chief exec. officer ISIS Pharms., Inc., Carlsbad, Calif., 1989; cons. Enzytech, Cambridge, Mass., 1988, Bachem Biosci., Phila., 1988, Centocor, Malvern, Pa., 1988, BCM Techs., Houston, 1988; chmn. bd. dirs. GES Pharms., Inc., Houston, 1989-91; adj. prof. Baylor Coll. Medicine, Houston, 1982, U. Pa., Phila., 1982-89; bd. dirs. Cytel Corp., San Diego, GeneMedicine, Houston, Biotech. Industry Orgn., Calif. Healthcare Inst., Indsl. Biotech. Assn., Washington, 1993; mem. sci. adv. bd. SIBIA, La Jolla, Calif.; adj. prof. pharmacology UCLA, 1991. Editor: Anti Cancer Drug Design, 1984; mem. editorial adv. bd. Molecular Pharmacology, 1986, Jour. Drug Targeting; patentee in field. Trustee Franklin Inst, Phila., 1987-89; bd. dirs. Mann Music Ctr., Phila., 1987-89; children's com. Children's Svcs., Inc., Phila., 1983-84; adv. com. World Affairs Coun., Phila. Recipient Disting. Prof. award U. Ky., 1986, Julius Sterner award Phila. Coll. Pharmacy and Sci., 1981, Outstanding Lectr. award Baylor Coll. Medicine, 1984. Mem. AAAS, Am. Assn. for Cancer Rsch. (state legis. com.), Am. Soc. for Microgiology, Am. Soc. Pharmacology and Exptl. Therapeutics, Am. Soc. Clin. Pharmacology and Therapeutics, Am. Soc. Clin. Oncology, Indsl. Biotech. Assn. (bd. dirs. 1992-93), Biotech. Industry Orgn., Calif. Healthcare Inst. Office: ISIS Pharms Inc 2280 Faraday Ave Carlsbad CA 92008-7208

CROOKS, JOHN A., management consultant; b. Sydney, N.S.W., Australia, May 20, 1936; s. Alan William and Ida Linda (Kohnke) C.; m. Shirley Jean Foote, Dec. 22, 1961; children: Madeline Linda, Peter John. Student, Met. Coll., Sydney, Australia, 1954-57, U. of Alaska, 1960-62; SE, MIT, 1977. Sr. v.p. Wells Fargo Bank, San Francisco, 1959-83; pres., chief exec. officer Computer Systems Design, Inc., San Francisco, 1983-86; pres. Technologix, Inc., Walnut Creek, Calif., 1986—. With U.S. Army, 1960-62. Mem. Systems Cons. Consortium. Republican. Presbyterian. Office: Technologix Inc PO Box 104 Walnut Creek CA 94597-0104

CROSA, JORGE HOMERO, bacterial geneticist, educator, consultant; b. Buenos Aires, Mar. 1, 1941; came to U.S., 1972; s. Ismael and Manuela (Merino) C.; m. Lidia Marta Coscia, Sept. 1968; children: Giselle Annette, Nicholas Alexander, Paul Christopher. MS, U. Buenos Aires, 1967, PhD in Chemistry, 1974. Lectr. U. Buenos Aires, 1967-72; sr. fellow Walter Reed Army Inst. Rsch., Washington, 1972; rsch. assoc. U. Wash., Seattle, 1973-80; asst. prof. bacterial genetics Oreg. Health Scis. U., Portland, 1981-82, assoc. prof., 1983-87, prof., 1988—; mem. study sect. NIH, 1986—. Mem. editorial bd. Jour. Bacteriology, 19866, Infection and Immunity, 1986—; contbr. numerous articles to various profl. jours., chpts. to books. Mem. Am. Soc. Microbiology (lectr. div. genetics and molecular biology, 1983, Donald B. Slocum award 1986). Office: Oreg Health Sci U 3818 SW Sam Jackson Park Rd Portland OR 97201-3013

CROSBY, DONALD ALLEN, philosophy educator; b. Mansfield, Ohio, Apr. 7, 1932; s. Edmund Bevington Crosby and Mary Lou (Bogan) Foster; m. Charlotte Mae Robinson, Sept. 15, 1956; children: Colleen Judith Davis, Kathleen Bridgett Carnahan. BA, Davidson Coll., 1953; BD, Princeton Sem., 1956, ThM, 1959; PhD, Columbia U., 1963. Minister Christiana (Del.) Presbyn. Ch., 1956-59; asst. minister First Congregational Ch., Norwalk, Conn., 1959-62; asst. prof. philosophy and religion Centre Coll., Danville, Ky., 1962-65; prof. philosophy Colo. State U., Ft. Collins, 1965—. Author: Horace Bushnell's Theory of Language, 1975, Interpretive Theories of Religion, 1981, The Specter of the Absurd, 1988; mem. editorial bd. and exec. com. Am. Jour. Theology and Philosophy. Dist. capt. Larimer County (Colo.) Dem. Party, 1969-70. Recipient Excellence in Grad. Rsch. and Teaching award, 1989; named Honors Prof., 1981; Presbyn. Grad. fellow Presbyn. Ch. USA, 1961-62. Mem. Am. Philos. Assn., Am. Acad. Religion (bd. dirs.), Highlands Inst. for Am. Religious Thought (bd. dirs.), Soc. Philosophy of Religion, N.Am. Soc. for Social Philosophy, Internat. Soc. for the Study of Human Ideas on Ultimate Reality and Meaning (bd. dirs.). Home: 3517 Canadian Pky Fort Collins CO 80524-1368 Office: Colo State U Dept Philosophy Fort Collins CO 80523

CROSBY, GLENN ARTHUR, chemistry educator; b. nr. Youngwood, Pa., July 30, 1928; s. Edwin Glenn and Bertha May (Ritchey) C.; m. Jane Lichtenfels, May 29, 1950; children: Brian, Alan, Karen. B.S., Waynesburg Coll., 1950; Ph.D., U. Wash., 1954. Research assoc. Fla. State U., Tallahassee, 1955-57; vis. asst. prof. physics Fla. State U., 1957; asst. prof. chemistry U. N. Mex., Albuquerque, 1957-62; assoc. prof. chemistry U. N. Mex., 1962-67; prof. chemistry and chem. physics Wash. State U., Pullman, 1967—; chmn. chem. physics program Wash. State U., 1977-84; mem. adv. com. Rsch. Corp., Tucson, 1981-88, 90-92; vis. prof. phys. chemistry U. Tübingen, Fed. Republic Germany, 1964; vis. prof. physics U. Canterbury, Christchurch, N.Z., 1974; Humboldt sr. scientist, vis. prof. phys. chemistry U. Hohenheim, Fed. Republic Germany, 1978-79; mem. commn. on life scis. NRC, 1991—. Author: Chemistry: Matter and Chemical change, 1962; also numerous sci. and sci.-related articles. Recipient U.S. Sr. Scientist award Humboldt Found., Fed. Republic Germany, 1978-79, Catalyst award Chem. Mfrs. Assn., 1979, Disting. Alumnus award Waynesburg Coll., 1982, Faculty Excellence award Wash. State U., 1984, Pub. Svc. award Wash. State U., 1989, Disting. Prof. award Wash. State U. Mortar Bd., 1990; named Prof. of Yr., U. N.Mex., 1967; NSF fellow U. Wash., Seattle, 1953-54; Research Corp. venture grantee, 1960; Fulbright fellow, 1964. Fellow AAAS; mem. Am. Chem. Soc. (numerous activities including chmn. div. chem. edn. 1982, vice chmn. com. on edn. 1984-88, chmn. com. on edn. 1990-91, Western Conn. sect. Vis. Scientist award 1981, nat. award in chem. edn. 1985), Am. Phys. Soc., Inter-Am. Photochem. Soc., Nat. Sci. Tchrs. Assn., Wash. Sci. Tchrs. Assn. (Outstanding Coll. Sci. Tchr. award 1975), Sigma Xi, Phi Kappa Phi, Sigma Pi Sigma. Home: 1825 NE Valley Rd Pullman WA 99163-4628 Office: Wash State U Dept Chemistry Pullman WA 99164-4630

CROSBY, JOHN O'HEA, conductor, opera manager; b. N.Y.C., July 12, 1926; s. Laurence Alden and Aileen Mary (O'Hea) C. Grad., Hotchkiss Sch., 1944; BA, Yale U., 1950, DFA (hon.), 1991; LittD (hon.), U. N.Mex., 1967; MusD (hon.), Coll. of Santa Fe, 1968, Cleve. Inst. Music, 1974; LHD (hon.), U. Denver, 1977. pres. Manhattan Sch. Music, 1976-86. Accompanist, opera coach, condr., N.Y.C., 1951-56, gen. dir., mem. conducting staff, Santa Fe Opera, 1957—; guest condr. various opera cos. in, U.S. and Can., 1967—; condr.: U.S. stage premiere Daphne, 1964, Friedenstag, 1988; world premiere Wuthering Heights, 1958. Served with inf. AUS, 1945-46, ETO. Recipient Nat. Medal of Arts, 1991, Verdienstkreuz 1st klasse Bundesrepublik, Deutschland, 1992. Roman Catholic. Clubs: Metropolitan Opera (N.Y.C.), Century Assn. (N.Y.C.), University (N.Y.C.). Office: Santa Fe Opera PO Box 2408 Santa Fe NM 87504-2408

CROSBY, LA RHONDA SMITH, health educator; b. Oakland, Calif., Dec. 31, 1960; d. Johnny and Irma Mae (Johnson) Smith; m. Darwin Jrome Crosby, Dec. 31, 1981 (div. 1987); 1 child, Raymar Jrome. BSW, San Francisco State U., 1984. Benefits coord. Diablo Systems, Xerox Co., Hayward, Calif., 1980-84; pregnancy counselor Planned Parenthood, Oakland, 1981-82, client svc. specialist, 1982-84, asst. mgr., 1984-85, health educator, 1985-88; office mgr. 1st AME Ch., Oakland, 1988-90; health educator West Oakland Health Ctr., 1990—; also program dir. Imani House, 1993—; trainer, ind. cons. various health and social svc. agys. Office: West Oakland Health Ctr 700 Adeline St Oakland CA 94607

CROSS, CARLA JEAN, sales and real estate educator, management speaker; b. Lebanon, Oreg., Dec. 20, 1941; d. Robert and Eleanora (Christiansen) Garrison; m. Richard B. Cross, May 23, 1970; 1 child, Christopher Robert. BA, U. Oreg., 1964, MA, 1967; grad., Grad. Realtors Inst., Seattle, 1979. Cert. real estate broker, 1986. With real estate sales Quadrant Corp., Bellevue, Wash., 1974-76; real estate sales agt. John L. Scott, Inc., Bellevue, 1976-81, real estate mgr., 1981-88; real estate educator Windermere Real Estate, Seattle, 1988—; sr. faculty instr. nat. mgmt. classes Cert. Real Estate Brokers. Contbr. numerous real estate articles to profl. jours.; speaker state and nat. convs. Mem. Nat. Assn. Realtors (Nat. Realtor Educator 1991), Wash. Assn. Realtors (bd. dirs. 1987-89, co-chmn. conv. 1988, chmn. edn. com. 1987-88, Wash. Realtor Educator of Yr. 1990), Nat. Speakers Assn. Home: 1070 Idylwood Dr SW Issaquah WA 98027-4521 Office: Windermere Real Estate 8401 35th Ave NE Seattle WA 98115-4818

CROSS, CHRISTOPHER CHARLES, lawyer; b. Morgantown, W.Va., Sept. 11, 1952; s. Aureal T. and Aleen (Teyssier) C.; children: Nicholas, Connor. BA, Denison U., Granville, Ohio, 1974; JD, U. Denver, 1979. Bar: Colo. 1979, U.S. Dist. Ct. Colo. 1979, U.S. Ct. Appeals (10th cir.) 1992. Dep. dist. atty. Denver Dist. Atty.'s Office, 1979-84; assoc. Roath & Brega, P.C., Denver, 1984-86; pvt. practice Denver, 1986—. Named Outstanding Young Man of Am., Outstanding Young Men of Am., 1989. Mem. Colo. Bar Assn. (bd. govs. 1989-91, 93—), Denver Bar Assn., Colo. Criminal Def. Bar, Assn. Trial Lawyers Am., Colo. Trial Lawyers Assn. Office: 2303 E Dartmouth Ave Englewood CO 80110

CROSS, GLENN LABAN, engineering company executive, development planner; b. Mt. Vernon, Ill., Dec. 28, 1941; s. Kenneth Edward and Mildred Irene (Glenn) C.; m. Kim Lien Duong, Aug. 30, 1968 (div. Oct. 1975); m. Tran Tu Thach, Dec. 26, 1975; children: Cindy Sue, Cristy Luu, Crystal Tu, Cassandra Caitlynn; BA, Calif. Western U., 1981, MBA, 1982. Hosp. adminstr. pub. health div. USAID, Dept. State, Washington, 1966-68; pers. mgr. Pacific Architects and Engrs., Inc., L.A., 1968-70, contract adminstr., 1970-73, mgr. mgmt. svcs., 1973-75; contracts adminstr. Internat. Svcs. div., AVCO, Cin., 1975-77; sr. contract adminstr. Bechtel Group, Inc., San Francisco, 1977-80, Arabian Bechtel Co. Ltd.; contract adminstrv. supr. Bechtel Civil, Inc., Jubail Industrial City, Saudi Arabia, 1980-85; cons. Bechtel Western Power Corp., Jakarta, Indonesia, Pacific Engrs. and Constructors, 1985-90, prin. contract adminstr. Ralph M. Parsons Co., Pasadena, Calif., 1990-93, contract adminstr. Parsons-Brinckerhoff, Costa Mesa, Calif., 1993—. Author: Living With a Matrix: A Conceptual Guide to Organizational Variation, 1983. Served as sgt. 1st spl. forces group, airborne, AUS, 1962-65; Okinawa, Vietnam. Decorated Combat Infantryman's Badge. Mem. Nat. Contract Mgmt. Assn., Construction Mgmt. Assn. Am., Internat. Pers. Mgmt. Assn., Assn. Human Resource Systems Profls., Human Resource Planning Soc., Assn. MBA Execs., Am. Mgmt. Assn., Am. Arbitration Assn., Internat. Records Mgmt. Coun., Adminstrv. Mgmt. Soc. Republican. Avocations: swimming, reading. Home: 25935 Faircourt Ln Laguna Hills CA 92653-7517 Office: Parsons-Brinckerhoff 345 Clinton St Costa Mesa CA 92626-6011

CROSS, HERBERT JAMES, psychologist; b. Ashland, Va., Mar. 18, 1934; s. Charles Richard and Virginia (Purnell) C.; m. Betty Gene Thompson, Mar. 20, 1954 (div. 1973); children: Charles, Catherine; m. Sharon Willard, Jan. 17, 1993. BA, Randolph-Macon Coll., 1958; MA, U. Richmond, 1960; PhD, Syracuse U., 1965. Asst., assoc. prof. U. Conn., Storrs, 1965-72; prof. Wash. State U., Pullman, 1972-75, dir. human rels. ctr., 1975-89, dir. clin. tng., 1989—. Co-leader Vietnam Vets. self-help Group, Moscow, Idaho, 1984—; with U.S. Army, 1954-56. Mem. APA, NRA, Wash. Psychol. Assn., Western Psychol. Assn., Ea. Psychol. Assn., Rocky Mountain Psychol. Assn., Assn. Dirs. Psychol. Tng. Clinics (chmn. exec. bd. 1985-91), VFW. Office: Wash State Univ Pullman WA 99164

CROSS, KATHRYN PATRICIA, education educator; b. Normal, Ill., Mar. 17, 1926; d. Clarence L. and Katherine (Dague) C. BS, Ill. State U., 1948; MA, U. Ill., 1951, PhD, 1958; LLD (hon.), SUNY, 1988; DS (hon.), Loyola U., 1980, Northeastern U., 1975; DHL (hon.), De Paul U., 1986, Open U., The Netherlands, 1989. Math. tchr. Harvard (Ill.) Community High Sch., 1948-49; rsch. asst. dept. psychology U. Ill., Urbana, 1949-53, asst. dean of women, 1953-59; dean of women then dean of students Cornell U., Ithaca, N.Y., 1959-63; dir. coll. and univ. programs Ednl. Testing Svc., Princeton, N.J., 1963-66; vis. prof. U. Nebr., 1975-76; rsch. educator Ctr. Rsch. and Devel. in Higher Edn. U. Calif., Berkeley, 1966-77; rsch. scientist, sr. rsch. psychologist, dir. univ. programs Ednl. Testing Svc., Berkeley, 1966-80; prof. edn., chair dept. adminstrn., planning & social policy Harvard U., Cambridge, Mass., 1980-88; Elizabeth and Edward Conner prof. edn. U. Calif., Berkeley; del. to Soviet Union, Seminar on Problems in Higher Edn., 1975; vis. scholar Miami-Dade Community Coll., 1987; mem. sec. adv. com. on automated personal data systems Dept. HEW, 1972-73; speaker, cons. in field. Author: Beyond the Open Door: New Students to Higher Education, 1971, (with S.B. Gould), Explorations in Non-Traditional Study, 1972, (with J.R. Valley and Assocs.) Planning Non-Traditional Programs: An Analysis of the Issues for Postsecondary Education, 1976, Adults as Learners, 1981, (with Thomas A. Angelo) Classroom Assessment Techniques, 1993; contbr. articles, monographs to profl. publs., chpts. to books; mem. editorial bd. to several ednl. jours.; cons. editor ednl. mag. Change, 1980—. Trustee Coun. for Advancement of Exptl. Learning, 1982-85, Bradford Coll., Mass., 1986-88, Antioch Coll., Yellow Springs, Ohio, 1976-78; mem. nat. adv. bd. Nat.Ctr. of Study of Adult Learning, Empire State Coll.; mem. nat. adv. bd. Okla. Bd. Regents; mem. higher edn. rsch. program Pew Charitable Trusts. Mem. Am. Assn. Higher Edn. (bd. dirs. 1987—, chair 1989-90), Am. Assn. Community and Jr. Colls. (vice chair commn. of future of community colls.), Carnegie Found. Advancement of Teaching (adv. com. on classification of colls. and univs.), Nat. Ctr. for Devel. Edn. (adv. bd.), New Eng. Assn. Schs. and Colls. (commn. on instns. higher edn. 1982-86), Am. Coun. Edn. (commn. on higher edn. and adult learner 1986-88). Office: U Calif Sch Edn 3531 Tolman Hall Berkeley CA 94720

CROSS, PAUL EDWARD, pearl cultivation company executive, researcher; b. Bremerton, Wash., Apr. 9, 1948; s. Byron Kent Cross and Leah West Wear. Student, U. Hawaii, 1969-71, Haliburton Sch. Engring., 1972. Seaman MSTS, Hono, Hawaii, 1966-69; jewelry designer Hono, 1969-75; pres. Tyrex Petroleum, Monroe, La., 1976-85; pres., chief exec. officer Cross Pacific Pearls, Inc., Vancouver, B.C., Can., 1985—; head researcher Cross Pacific Pearls, Inc., Woodland Hills, Calif., 1985—.

CROSS, ROBERT LOUIS, real estate agent, writer; b. Alton, Ill., Aug. 9, 1937; s. Louis William and Marion (Hanna) C.; m. Paula Sutton, June 8, 1958 (div. June 1970); children: Britomart, Christopher, Amoret; m. Carolee Sharko, May 5, 1990. BA, U. Kans., 1959, MA, 1961; grad., UCLA, 1969, Realtors Inst., L.A., 1980. Lectr. English lang. U. Kans., Lawrence, 1959-60, Washburn U., Topeka, Kans., 1960-61; editorial-mktg. rep. Prentice-Hall, Inc., Englewood Cliffs, N.J., 1962-64; mgr. pub. info. Forest Lawn Meml. Pk., Glendale, Calif., 1964-66; account exec. pub. rels. J. Walter Thompson, L.A., 1968-70; sr. account exec. pub. rels. Botsford Ketchum, L.A., 1970-71, Harsh, Rotman & Druck, L.A., 1971-72; pres. Crossroads Combined Communications, L.A., 1973-80; real estate agt. Carmel (Calif.) Bd. Realtors, 1979—; gen. ptnr. Crossroads Design Ltd., Big Sur, Calif., 1990—; cons. Watts Mfg. Corp., L.A., 1970-73, U.S. Office Edn., Washington, 1971, U.S. Dept. Interior, Washington, 1972, Calif. State Coastal Commn., San Francisco, 1980-85. Author: Henry Miller: The Paris Years, 1991; assoc. editor Calif. Life Mag., 1976; contbr. IN Monterey Mag., 1977; real estate editor Monterey Life Mag., 1978. Pres., dir. Big Sur Hist. Soc., 1980-90, Coastlands Mut. Water Co., Big Sur, 1984—; co-founder Dialogue for Big Sur, 1984; dir. Big Sur Natural History Assn., 1984-86; founding doscent Dept. Pks. and Recreation, Big Sur, 1987; With U.S. Army, 1961-63. Mem. Archeol. Inst. Am., Nat. Assn. Realtors, Nat. Assn. Real Estate Appraisers (cert.), Calif. Assn. Realtors, Carmel Bd. Realtors (Multiple Listing Svc. Sales award 1980), Carmel Multiple Listing Svc., Big Sur Grange, Coast Property Owners Assn., Environ. Assessment Assn. (cert.). Home: PO Box 244 Coastlands Rd Big Sur CA 93920 Office: Crossroads Design Ltd. PO Box 244 Big Sur CA 93920

CROSS, TRAVIS, foundation administrator; b. Salem, Oreg., Mar. 23, 1927; s. Henry Alexander and Belvie Loutisha (Gilbert) C.; m. Beverly Jean Briggs, Oct. 30, 1949; children: Craig, Jennifer, Sara, Paul. BA, Stanford U., 1949; D Pub. Svc. (hon.), Willamette U., 1969. Dir. info. and alumni affairs Willamette U., Salem, 1949-50; chancellor's staff Oreg. System Higher Edn., Eugene, 1950-57; asst. to sec. of state State of Oreg., Salem, 1957-59, asst. to gov., 1959-66; pres. Travis Cross & Assocs., Salem, 1966-69; v.p. univ. rels. U. Calif., Berkeley, 1969-71; v.p. exec. rels. Beverly Enterprises, Pasadena, Calif., 1971-75; asst. adminstr. St. Vincent Hosp. & Med. Ctr., Portland, Oreg., 1975-88, asst. to adminstr., 1988-92; trustee Meyer Meml. Trust, Portland, 1982—; cons. in field. Transition officer Oreg. Gov.-Elect, Salem, 1966, 79; spl. asst. Romney for Pres., Lansing, Mich., 1967-68; exec. dir. St. Vincent Med. Found., Portland, 1975-81; chmn. Oreg. Commn. Pub. Broadcasting, Portland, 1979-82; mem. Oreg. Jud. Fitness Commn., Portland, 1982-84. Recipient Disting. Svc. award City of Salem. 1968. Home: 12444 SW 55th Pl Portland OR 97219-7113 Office: Meyer Meml Trust 1515 SW 5th Ave Portland OR 97201

CROSSLER, JOHNNIE CHARLES, fisheries biologist, outdoor supplies salesman; b. Moscow, Idaho, May 12, 1954; s. Johnnie M. and Marilyn Lenore (Czyhold) C. BA, U. Idaho, 1983, MS, 1978; postgrad., Wash. State U., 1979-83. Rsch. asst. U. Idaho, Moscow, 1975-77, acad. advisor, 1976-82, rsch. technician, 1975-83; fisheries biologist U.S. Dept. Sports Fisheries, Moscow, 1984-86, Idaho Fish and Game, Lewiston, 1986; permanently disabled, 1986; owner Aardwolf Enterprises, Moscow, 1982—; del. Bus. Today VIII, Princeton U., Dallas, 1982; asst. student chair Borah Symposium, U. Idaho, 1980. Author: Letters from a Small Town, 1993; editor: Physical Site Survey, 1991; contbg. editor: Women and Children First, 1992. Precinct coord. Young Reps., no. Idaho, 1972-74; chair Moscow Transit, 1991-92. Mem. NRA, Nat. Assn. Pvt. Providers, Audubon Soc., Natural History Soc., Nature Conservancy. Quaker. Home: PO Box 9392 Moscow ID 83843-0118

CROSSMAN, JOHN SHERMAN, government official; b. Parsons, Kans., Aug. 12, 1943; s. Celian Cook and Barbara Lee (Acord) C.; m. Jerilee Ann Murphy, June 7, 1969; children: Sarah Ann, Elizabeth Erin. BA, Ea. Wash. U., 1969; PhD in Zoology, Va. Poly. Inst. and State U., Blacksburg, 1973. Mgr. environ. scis. Teledyne-Brown Engring., Huntsville, Ala., 1973-75; environ. scientist Tenn. Valley Authority, Muscle Shoals, Ala., 1975-76; mgr. reg. water quality prog. Tenn. Valley Authority, 1976-79, asst. Washington rep., 1979-80; policy analyst Tenn. Valley Authority, Knoxville, 1980-88; environ. coord. U.S. Bur. Reclamation, Denver, 1988—; cons. in field. Contbr. articles to profl. jours. Participant, Nat. Environ. Leadership Coun., Washington, 1990. With USN, 1962-66. Recipient Phi Sigma award, Va. Poly. Inst. and State U., 1972, Bronze Medal award, EPA, 1990. Mem. Ecol. Soc. Am., N. Am. Lake Mgmt. Soc., Water Pollution Control Fedn., AAAS, Toastmasters (area gov. 1988, pres. 1987), Sigma Xi. Presbyterian. Home: 5825 S Bellflower Dr Littleton CO 80123-2709 Office: US Bureau of Reclamation PO Box 25007 Denver CO 80225-0007

CROSSON, ALBERT J., food products executive; b. 1934. With Beatrice/Hunt-Wesson (formerly Beatrice Grocery Group Inc.), 1956-69, 74—, Arden-Mayfair Inc., L.A., 1969-74, to present; exec. v.p. sales Beatrice/Hunt-Wesson Inc., from 1978, now pres., also dir. Office: Beatrice/Hunt-Wesson Foods 1645 W Valencia Dr Fullerton CA 92633-3899

CROSSON, JOHN ALBERT, advertising executive; b. L.A., Oct. 5, 1961; s. Albert J. and Virginia (Kienzle) C. BABA, Loyola U., 1983; MBA, U. So. Calif., L.A., 1984. V.p., mgmt. supr. Dailey & Assocs. Advt., L.A., 1984—; lectr. Loyola Marymount U., L.A., 1986—.

CROTEAU, DENIS, bishop; b. Thetford Mines, Que., Can., Oct. 23, 1932. Ordained priest Roman Cath. Ch., 1947, titular bishop of Mons, aux. bishop of MacKenzie-Ft. Smith, 1986. Bishop Diocese MacKenzie/Ft. Smith, Yellowknife, N.W.T., Can., 1986—. Office: Diocese MacKenzie-Ft Smith, 5111 53d St Bag 8900, Yellowknife, NT Canada X1A 2R3*

CROTTI, JOSEPH ROBERT, aviation executive; b. Azzio, Italy, June 11, 1923; came to U.S., 1924; s. John Roberto and Teresa (Tabacchini) C. Student, U. Calif., Berkeley, 1960-91; grad., Delahanty Inst. Fire Adminstrn., 1953. Accredited airport executive 1964. Dep. chief Merced (Calif.) Fire Dept., 1946-59; airport mgr./city mgr. pro tem Merced, 1959-67; dir. aeronautics State of Calif., Sacramento, 1967-74; dep. dir. Calif. Dept. Transp., Sacramento, 1974-75; exec. dir. Calif. Air Tankers Assn., Sacramento, 1975-79; cons. Pan Am. World Svc., Teterboro, N.Y., 1979-80; western region rep. Aircraft Owners & Pilots Assn., Frederick, Md., 1981—; v.p. Calif. Fire Chief's Assn., Merced, 1958-59, Calif. Assn. Airport Execs., Merced, 1967; vice chmn. Gov.'s Aerospace-Aviation Task Force, Sacramento, 1970; pres. No. Calif. Div. of CD, Merced, 1963; accident prevention counselor FAA, Sacramento, 1980—; mem. Calif. Divsn. Aeronautics Advisory Coun., Sacramento, 1988—. Contbr. numerous manuals and plans for airport regulations and safety. Scout master Boy Scouts Am. Air Explorers, Merced, 1954-65; gen. chmn. Mercy Hosp. Bldg., Merced, 1959; bd. dirs. United Givers, Merced, 1962; chmn. County Heart Fund Drive, Merced, 1967; v.p. Sacramento Youth Band, 1969. Recipient Nat. Flight Safety award, Nat. Fire Protection Assn., 1957-58, Harris Aviation Safety award, Western States Assn. Sheriff's Air Squadron, 1970, Bronzemedal, Am. Meteorol. Soc., 1972, CD Commendation, Office of Emergency Svcs., 1986, Paul Harris Fellow, Rotary Internat., 1990, Gen. Aviation Sharples award, 1988. Mem. Am. Assn. Airport Execs., Nat. Assn. State Aviation Officials (pres. 1972),Profl. Helicopter Pilots Assn., Aircraft Owners and Pilots Assn., Calif. Assn. Airport Execs., Calif. State Sheriffs Assn., Am. Legion, Cameron Park Rotary Club(pres. 1980), Delta Marina Yacht Club (commodore 1989). Office: Joe R Crotti & Assocs PO Box 549 Shingle Springs CA 95682

CROW, EDWIN LOUIS, mathematical statistician, consultant; b. Browntown, Wis., Sept. 15, 1916; s. Frederick Marion and Alice Blanche (Cox) C.; m. Eleanor Gish, June 13, 1942; children: Nancy Rebecca, Dorothy Carol Crow-Willard. B.S. summa cum laude, Beloit Coll., 1937; Ph.M., U. Wis., 1938, Ph.D., 1941; postgrad., Brown U., 1941, 42, U. Calif.-Berkeley, 1947, 48, Univ. Coll., London, 1961-62. Instr. math. Case Sch. Applied Sci., Cleve., 1941-42; mathematician Bur. Ordnance Dept. Navy, Washington, 1942-46, U.S. Naval Ordnance Test Sta., China Lake, Calif., 1946-54; cons. statistics Boulder Labs., U.S. Dept. Commerce, Boulder, Colo., 1954-73, Nat. Telecommunications and Info. Adminstrn., Boulder, Colo., 1974—; statistician Nat. Ctr. Atmospheric Research, Boulder, Colo., 1975-82; instr. math. extension div. UCLA, China Lake, 1947-54; adj. prof. math. U. Colo., Boulder, 1963-81; lectr. stats. Met. State Coll., Denver, 1974. Co-author: Statistics Manual, 1960; co-editor: Lognormal Distributions, 1988; assoc. editor: Communications in Statistics, 1972—, Jour. Am. Statis. Assn., 1967-75, Current Index to Stats., 1981—; contbr. articles to profl. jours. Survey statistician Boulder Valley Sch. Dist., 1971-72; founder, pres. Boulder Tennis Assn., 1967-69, pres., 1982. Recipient Outstanding Publ. award Nat. Telecommunications and Info. Adminstrn., 1980, 82; Bronze medal U.S. Dept. Commerce, 1970, Editor's award Am. Meteorol. Soc., 1987. Fellow Royal Statis. Soc., Am. Statis Assn. (coun. mem. 1959-60, 68-69, Outstanding Chpt. mem. 1989), AAAS; mem. Am. Math. Soc., Math. Assn. Am., Inst. Math. Stats., Bernoulli Soc. for Math. Stats. and Probability, Soc. Indsl. and Applied Math., U.S. Tennis Assn., Sigma Xi, Phi Beta Kappa. Democrat. Unitarian. Clubs: Colo. Mountain, Harvest House Sporting Assn. (Boulder). Home: 605 20th St Boulder CO 80302-7714 Office: Nat Telecommunications and Info Adminstrn ITS N3 325 Broadway Boulder CO 80303-3328

CROW, KENNETH ARTHUR, pathologist; b. Boise, Idaho, July 16, 1938; s. Arthur Holbeach and Blanche Aleen (Tate) C.; m. Roberta Monroe, June 12, 1965; children: Jonathan and Jason (twins), Justin. AA, Boise Jr. Coll., 1958; BS, U. Utah, 1960; MD, U. Wis., 1964. Diplomate Am. Bd. Pathology. Rotating intern Denver Gen. Hosp., 1964-65; pathologist Albany (Oreg.) Gen. Hosp., 1973—; resident in pathology U. Colo. Med. Ctr., 1969-73; chief of pathology, clin. lab. Albany (Oreg.) Gen. Hosp., 1991—. Lt. USN, 1965-67. Fellow Am. Soc. Clin. Pathologists, Coll. Am. Pathologists; mem. AMA, Oreg. Med. Assn., Oreg. Pathologists Assn. Home: 1500 12th Ave SW Albany OR 97321 Office: Albany Gen Hosp 1046 6th Ave SW Albany OR 97321

CROW, NANCY REBECCA, lawyer; b. Ridgecrest, Calif., Nov. 3, 1948; d. Edwin Louis and Eleanor Elizabeth (Gish) C.; 1 child, Rebecca Ann Carr; m. Mark A.A. Skrotzki, Apr. 4, 1987. BA, Antioch Coll., 1970; JD, U. Colo., 1974; LLM in Taxation, NYU, 1977. Bars: Colo. 1974, Calif. 1977. Atty., advisor IRS, N.Y.C., 1975-77; assoc. Brawerman & Kopple, Los Angeles, 1977-80; prof. Sch. Law, U. Denver, 1980-81; of counsel Krendl & Netzorg, Denver, 1981-84; ptnr. (shareholder) Krendl & Krendl, Denver, 1984-92; shareholder Pendleton & Sabian, Denver, 1992—. Editor estate and trust forum Colorado Lawyer, 1992-93, bd. editors, 1993—; contbr. chpts. to books. Mem. ABA (chmn. Welfare Benefits subcom. of personal svcs. orgns. com., tax sect.), Colo. Bar Assn. (exec. coun. tax sect. 1990-93, sec. tax sect. 1993-94), Colo. Women's Bar Assn. (chmn. pub. policy com. 1982-83), Denver Bar Assn., Denver Tax Assn., Denver Tax Inst. Planning Com., Alliance of Profl. Women (publs. com.), Sierra Club. Democrat. Unitarian. Club: Colo. Mountain. Home: 637 Jackson St Denver CO 80206-4544 Office: Pendleton & Sabian 303 E 17th Ave Ste 1000 Denver CO 80203-1262

CROW, TIMOTHY ALAN, engineer; b. Seattle, May 31, 1962; s. Richard and Marilyn Jane (Sankela) C. AA in Liberal Studies, Seattle Ctrl. Community Coll., 1984; AAA in Music and Video, Art Inst. of Seattle, 1987. Jr. site mgr. Software Unltd. DBA Software Pipeline, Tukwila, Wash., 1987-89; warehouse sales assoc. Mack V Technologies, Kent, Wash., 1989; jr. ptnr. CE Enterprises, Kent, Wash., 1989-90; asst. audio engr. Lackey Sound and Light/1990 Goodwill Games, Seattle, 1990; supplies, communications transfer coord. Muzak Ltd. Partnership, Seattle, 1990-91, environ. channel submaster engr., 1991—; assoc. video producer, cons. Muzak Ltd. Partnership, Seattle, 1991—. Recipient Cert. of Merit, Wash. State Rep. Com., 1984, Employee of the Month nominee Muzak Ltd. Partnership, 1991. Home: 2552 28th Ave W Seattle WA 98199-3318 Office: Muzak Ltd Partnership 400 N 34th St Ste 200 Seattle WA 98103

CROWDER, DAVID LESTER, historian, educator; b. American Falls, Idaho, Jan. 5, 1941; s. Lester J. and E. Louise (Curtis) C.; m. JoAnne Russell, Sept. 1, 1960; children: Linda, Carolyn, Rebecca, William, Ethan, Heather, Johnathan. Student, Boise Jr. Coll., 1962-63; BA, Idaho State U., 1965, MA, 1966; PhD, U. Utah, 1972. Prof. history Ricks Coll., Rexburg, Idaho, 1966-87; dir. Idaho State Hist. Soc., Boise, Idaho, 1987-91; tchr. Garden Valley (Idaho) High Sch., 1991—; adj. prof. history Idaho State U., Pocatello, 1967-87, Boise State U., 1987—. Author: Tendoy: Chief of the Lemhis, 1969, James W. Webster: Upper Snake River Valley Pioneer, 1979, Tales of Eastern Idaho, 1981, Rexburg, Idaho: The First One Hundred Years, 1883-1983, 1983; contbr. articles to profl. jours. Commr. Idaho Centennial Commn., Boise; v.p. PTA, Rexburg; scoutmaster Boy Scouts Am., Rexburg. With USN, 1958-62. Research fellow U. Utah, 1971-72. Mem. Am. Assn. for State and Local History (Cert. of Commendation 1986), Nat. Hist. Adminstrs., Nat. Conf. State Hist. Preservation Officers, Idaho Geog. Names Adv. Com., Lewis and Clark Trails Com., Kiwanis (pres. Rexburg chpt. 1977-78), Phi Kappa Phi.

CROWE, CHRISTOPHER EVERETT, English language educator, writer; b. Danville, Ill., May 28, 1954; s. Richard Everett and Ruth Anne (Christensen) C.; m. Elizabeth Ann Foley, July 28, 1973; children: Christy Anne, Jonathan Everett, Carrie Elizabeth, Joanne Ruth. BA, Brigham Young U., 1976; MEd, Ariz. State U., 1980, EdD, 1986. English tchr. Weber High Sch., Ogden, Utah, 1977, McClintock High Sch., Tempe, Ariz., 1977-83, 84-87; asst. supr. Himeji (Japan) Bd. Edn., 1983-84; asst. prof. English Himeji Dokkyo U., 1987-89, Brigham Young U.-Hawaii, Laie, 1989-93; assoc. prof. English Brigham Young U., Provo, Utah, 1993—; adj. instr. Mesa (Ariz.) C.C., 1980-83, 85; book reviewer Assn. for Lit. Adolescents, 1991—, Kliatt Paperback Book Guide, 1990—; columnist Latter-day Sentinel, Phoenix, 1981-88, Chandler Arizonan, 1983. Author: What Americans Don't..., 1990; contbr. articles to profl. jours. Recipient citation of excellence Tchrs. USA, 1989. Mem. Nat. Coun. Tchrs. English, Nat. Collegiate Honors Soc., Associated Writing Programs, Hawaii Coun. Tchrs. English, Hawaii Lit. Arts Coun., Phi Kappa Phi (chpt. pres. 1990-92, disting. svc. & leadership award 1992). Republican. Mem. LDS Ch. Home: 660 S Canyon Rd Springville UT 84663 Office: Brigham Young U Dept English 3146 JKH8 Provo UT 84602

CROWE, JOHN T., lawyer; b. Cabin Cove, Calif., Aug. 14, 1938; s. J. Thomas and Wanda (Walston) C.; m. Marina Protopapa, Dec. 28, 1968; 1 child, Erin Aleka. BA, U. Santa Clara, 1960, JD, 1962. Bar: Calif. 1962, U.S. Dist. Ct. (no. dist.) Calif. 1964, U.S. Dist. Ct. (ea. dist.) Calif. 1967. Practiced in Visalia, Calif., 1964—; ptnr. firm Crowe, Mitchell & Crowe, 1971-85; referee State Bar Ct., 1976-82; gen. counsel Sierra Wine, 1986—. Bd. dirs. Mt. Whitney Area Coun. Boy Scouts Am., 1966-85, pres., 1971, 72; bd. dirs. Visalia Associated In-Group Donors (AID), 1973-81, pres., 1978-79; mem. Visalia Airport Commn., 1982-90. 1st lt. U.S. Army, 1962-64; brig. gen. Res. Decorated Meritorious Svc. Medal with 3 oak leaf clusters, Army Commendation Medal; named Young Man of Yr., Visalia, 1973; Senator, Jr. Chamber Internat., 1970; recipient Silver Beaver award Boy Scouts Am., 1983. Mem. ABA, Tulare County Bar Assn., Nat. Assn. R.R. Trial Counsel, State Bar Calif., Visalia C. of C. (pres. 1979-80). Republican. Roman Catholic. Clubs: Rotary (pres. 1980-81); Downtown (Fresno, Calif.). Home: 3939 W School Ave Visalia CA 93291-5514

CROWE, RICHARD ALLAN, astronomy educator; b. Montreal, Que., Can., Feb. 12, 1952; came to U.S., 1984; s. William Holsworth and Erna Gertrude (Ohlke) C.; m. Debra Anne Craig, Dec. 22, 1985; children: Ginger Catherine, Jasmine Miranda. BSc, U. West Ontario, London, Can., 1974, MSc, 1977; grad., Royal Conservatory Music, Toronto, Can., 1983; PhD, U. Toronto, Toronto, 1984. Teaching asst. U. We. Ontario, London, 1973-76; resident observer Las Campanas Observatory, La Serena, Chile, 1977-79; teaching asst., lectr. U. Toronto, Toronto, 1979-83; resident astronomer Can.-France-Hawaii Telescope, Kamuela, Hawaii, 1984-87; asst. prof. Astronomy U. Hawaii, Hilo, 1987-92, assoc. prof. Astronomy, 1992—; sec. curriculum com. U. Hawaii, Hilo, 1990-91, rep. natural sci. faculty admissions, 1991-92, faculty sen., 1990—, chmn. dept. Physics/Astronomy, 1992—. Editor 7 newsletters, 1984-87; contbr. 24 articles to profl. jours. Organist Waikoloa (Hawaii) Community Ch., 1986-87; clarinetist Hawaii County Band, Hilo, 1988—. Gulf (Can.) Oil Scholar, 1970-74, Ontario Grad. scholar govt. of Ontario, Toronto, 1979-83; Univ. Rsch. Coun. Seed-Money grantee U. Hawaii, 1991-92; Fujio Matsuda fellow, 1991-92. Mem. Can. Astron. Soc., Com. for the Scientific Investigation of Claims of the Paranormal (Astrology subcom. 1990—), Sigma Xi (pres.-elect 1990-91, pres. 1991-92, sec. 1992—). Office: U Hawaii Dept Physics & Astronomy 523 W Lanikaula St Hilo HI 96720

CROWELL, MICHAEL EARL, diver, chemical engineer, chemist; b. Mpls., Nov. 16, 1949; s. Harold Earl and Elizabeth Anne (Kripps) C.; m. Constance Wilson Church, Feb. 19, 1987. Student, Augsburg Coll., 1966, Coll. of San Mateo (Calif.), 1967-69; BS in Chemistry, U. Calif., Berkeley, 1971; BSChemE, Calif. State U., Long Beach, 1982; postgrad., Calif. State U., 1981, Western State U., 1982, Coll. Redwoods, 1984-90. Pilot plant tech. Ortho div. Chevron Chem. Co., Richmond, Calif., 1973-77; chemist Martin Metals, L.A., 1978-79, Platinum Group Process Ind., Sante Fe Springs, Calif., 1979-80; student engr. Fractionation Rsch. Inc., South Pasadena, Calif., 1980-82; comml. diver F/V Lost Dutchman, Fort Bragg, Calif., 1986—; founder Mass Energy Control Corp., Fort Bragg, 1992. Author: Sea Farms, 1990, Basic Artificial Intelligence, 1992, System Universal, 1992, Secrets of the Universe, 1992. Recipient Lab. Sci. award Bank of Am., Mendocino, Calif., 1967. Mem. AICE, Am. Chem. Soc. (most outstanding chemistry student award 1966), Am. Acad. Scis., Calif. Urchin Producers Assn., L-5 Soc., Orgn. for Advancement of Space Industrialization and Settlement, Fort Bragg Urchin Drivers Assn. (sec. 1991-92), The Planetary Soc. Home: 18300 Georges Lane Fort Bragg CA 95437 Office: Mass Energy Control Corp PO Box 1914 Fort Bragg CA 95437

CROWLEY, CHRISTINA, production company executive; b. Detroit, July 31, 1945; d. Patrick Joseph and Alice (Murray) C.; m. Peter Michael Hobe, Oct. 19, 1974; children: Daniel, Michael, Hobe. BA cum laude, Newton Coll., Mass., 1967. Assoc. producer KQED-TV, San Francisco, 1970-72; script spr. Lucas Film, Ltd., San Rafael, Calif., 1972; editor/cameraperson Boston, 1972-73; editor/cameraperson San Francisco, 1973-77, producer/dir., 1977-86; exec. producer The Kenwood Group, San Francisco, 1986-88, pres., 1988-91, prin. owner, 1991—; v.p. One Pass Film & Video, San Francisco, 1987-91. Dir. film: Teenage Suicide, 1980, Violence Behind Closed Doors, 1977 (Silver Award, N.Y. Film Festival, Special Jury Award, San Francisco Film Festival), Deck the Halls (Cine Golden Eagle 1980), In Need of Special Attention, 1982 (Cine Golden Eagle 1983). Mem. Assn. Visual Communicators, San Francisco Film-Tape Coun. Office: The Kenwood Group 139 Townsend St Ste 505 San Francisco CA 94107

CROWLEY, DANIEL JOHN, anthropologist; b. Peoria, Ill., Nov. 27, 1921; s. Michael Bartholomew and Elsie Magdalene (Schnebelin) C.; m. Pearl Rita Ramcharan, Feb. 4, 1958; children: Peter Mahendranath, Eve Lakshmi, Magdalene Lilawati. AB, Northwestern U., 1943, PhD, 1956; MA, Bradley U., 1948. Instr. art history Bradley U., Peoria, 1948-50; tutor in anthropology U. West Indies, St. Augustine, Trinidad, 1953-56; instr. in anthropology Northwestern U., Evanston, Ill., 1956-57; asst. prof. U. Notre Dame., Ind., 1958-59; from asst. prof. to prof. U. Calif., Davis, 1961-93 ret.; vis. rsch. prof. Inst. African Studies U. Ghana, Legon, 1969-71; vis. prof. U. West Indies, 1973-74, Latrobe U., Bundoora, Australia, 1990. Author: I Could Talk Old-Story Good, 1966; editor African Folklore in the New World, 1977; contbg. editor African Arts, 1966—, Research in African Lits., 1973-90, Jour. African Studies, 1976—; translator (book) Congolese Sculpture, 1982; contbr. articles to profl. jours. Active U.S. Nat. Commn. for UNESCO, Washington, 1972-78. Served to lt. (j.g.) USN, 1942-46, PTO. Fellow Ford Found., 1959-60, Fulbright, 1978-79; grantee Indo-U.S. Commn., 1985; recipient Centennial Citation U. Calif. Santa Cruz, 1968, Archer Taylor Meml. lectr. U. Calif. Folklore Soc., 1986. Fellow Am. Folklore Soc. (life, pres. 1969-71, Stafford prize 1952), Am. Anthropol. Assn., Calif. Folklore Soc. (pres. 1980), African Studies Assn.; mem. Southwestern Anthropol. Assn., Sigma Xi. Democrat. Roman Catholic. Home: 726 Peach Pl Davis CA 95616-3218 Office: U Calif Dept Anthropology Davis CA 95616

CROWLEY, JOHN CRANE, real estate developer; b. Detroit, June 29, 1919; s. Edward John and Leah Helen (Crane) C.; m. Barbara Wenzel Gilfillan, Jan. 12, 1945; children: F. Alexander, Leonard, Philip, Eliot, Louise, Sylvia. BA, Swarthmore Coll., 1941; MS, U. Denver, 1943. Asst. dir. Mcpl. Finance Officers Assn., Chgo., 1946-48; So. Calif. mgr. League Calif. Cities, Los Angeles, 1948-53; mgr. City of Monterey Park, Calif., 1953-56; founder, exec. v.p. Nat. Med. Enterprises, L.A., 1968; pres. Ventura Towne House (Calif.), 1963—; mem. faculty U. So. Calif. Sch. Pub. Adminstrn., 1950-53; bd. dirs. Regional Inst. of So. Calif., The L.A. Partnership 2000, Burbank-Glendale-Pasadena Airport Authority. Contbr. articles to profl. jours. Mem. State Adv. Coun. on Retirement Housing, 1965-68, L.A. County Com. on Affairs of Aging, 1966—; Mayor City of Pasadena, 1986-88; city dir. Pasadena, 1979-91; bd. dirs. Nat. Mcpl. League, 1986-92, Pacificulture Found. and Asia Mus., 1971-76, pres., 1972-74; bd. dirs. Pasadena Area Liberal Arts Ctr., 1962-72, pres., 1965-68; trustee Pacific Oaks Friends Sch. and Coll., Pasadena, 1954-57, 92—; chmn. Pasadena Cultural Heritage Commn., 1975-78; pres. Pasadena Civic Improvement Corp., 1985-89; bd. mgrs. Swarthmore Coll., 1986—; bd. dirs. Western Justice Ctr., 1992—. Sloan Found. fellow, 1941-43. Mem. Internat. City Mgmt. Assn., Nat. Mcpl. League (nat. bd. 1980-92, Disting. Citizen award, 1984), Inst. Pub. Adminstrn. (sr. assoc.), Phi Delta Theta. Democrat. Unitarian. Home: 615 Linda Vista Ave Pasadena CA 91105-1122

CROWLEY, JOSEPH NEIL, university president; b. Oelwein, Iowa, July 9, 1933; s. James Bernard and Nina Mary (Neil) C.; m. Johanna Lois Reitz, Sept. 9, 1961; children: Theresa, Neil, Margaret, Timothy. BA, U. Iowa, 1959; MA, Calif. State U., Fresno, 1963; PhD (Univ. fellow), U. Wash., 1967. Reporter Fresno Bee, 1961-62; asst. prof. polit. sci. U. Nev., Reno, 1966-71, asso. prof., 1971-79, prof., 1979—, chmn. dept. polit. sci., 1976-78, pres., 1978—; bd. dirs. Citibank Nev., Channel 5 Pub. TV; policy formulation officer EPA, Washington, 1973-74; dir. instl. studies Nat. Commn. on Water Quality, Washington, 1974-75; cons. in field. Author: Democrats, Delegates and Politics in Nevada: A Grassroots Chronicle of 1972, 1976, Notes From The President's Chair, 1988; editor: (with Robert Roelofs and Donald Hardesty) Environment and Society, 1973. Mem. Commn. on Colls., 1980-87; mem. adv. commn. on mining and minerals rsch. U.S. Dept. Interior, 1985-91; mem. coun. NCAA, 1987-92, mem. pres.'s commn., 1991-92, pres., 1993—; bd. dirs., campaign chmn. No. Nev. United Way, 1985-90. Recipient Thornton Peace prize U. Nev., 1971, Humanitarian of Yr. award NCCJ, 1986, Alumnus of Yr. award Calif. State U., 1989; Nat. Assn. Schs. Public Affairs and Adminstrn. fellow, 1973-74. Mem. Rotary. Roman Catholic. Home: 1265 Muir Dr Reno NV 89503-2629 Office: U Nev Office of Pres Reno NV 89557-0095

CROWLEY, THOMAS B., marine transportation company executive; b. 1914; married. With Crowley Maritime Corp., San Francisco, 1935—, chmn., formerly pres., dir. Recip. Vice-Admiral Jerry Land Medal, Soc. Naval Architects and Marine Engrs., 1985. Office: Crowley Maritime Corp 155 Grand Ave Oakland CA 94612-3758

CROWSER, LINDA ANN, research chemist; b. Gardena, Calif., Mar. 27, 1969; d. Mervin Eugene and Barbara Mae (Sill) C. BS in Chemistry and Math., Azusa Pacific U., 1990. Lab. technician Glendora (Calif.) Employment Agy., 1989-90; rsch. chemist Avery Dennison CPD, Covina, Calif., 1991—. Vol. Sta. KCET, L.A., 1991-92. Office: Avery Dennison 777 E Foothill Blvd # 4 Azusa CA 91702

CROWSON, DAN MICHAEL, electrical engineer, company executive; b. Tulsa, Aug. 1, 1953; s. Bobby Earl and Virginia Marie (Stoops) C.; m. Brenna Leigh Gentry, Oct. 16, 1982; children: Bobby Christopher, Chelsea Ann. AS in Elec. Engring. Tech., Okla. State U., 1975, BS in Engring. Tech., 1976. Engr. Xerox Corp., Oklahoma City, 1977-81, Phillips Petroleum, Dallas, 1981-82, H.P. Smith Paper Co., Chgo., 1982-83; engr., designer Stearns-Catalytic World Corp., Denver, 1984-87; electrical engr. mgr. Master Palletizer Systems, Inc., Denver, 1987-89; specialist S.W. regional automation Telemecanique Inc., Denver, 1989—; specialist Telemecanique Inc., Raleigh, N.C., 1992—; computer cons., Denver, 1985—. Office: Telemecanique Inc Hwy 64E Knightdale NC 27545

CRUE, BENJAMIN LANE, JR., neurosurgeon; b. Rahway, N.J., May 22, 1925; s. Benjamin Lane and Grace J. (Cornish) C.; m. Beverly Marie Malyon, Sept. 22, 1943; children: Benjamin III, Catherine, Elizabeth, B. Jane. BS, U. Chgo., 1946, MD, 1948. Diplomate Am. Bd. Neurological Surgery. Chmn. clin. neurology City of Hope Nat. Med. Ctr., Duarte, Calif., 1960-80; prof. nuerosurgery, co-chmn. Calif. Coll. Medicine, L.A., 1962-63; clin. prof. neurosurgery U. So. Calif. Sch. Medicine, L.A., 1964-85, clin. prof. neurosurgery emeritus, 1985—; bd. trustees San Gabriel (Calif.) Community Hosp., 1977-80, chief med. staff, 1980; bd. trustees Albambia Community Hosp., 1983-84; chief med. staff LaPlata Community Hosp., Durango, Colo., 1987. Contbr. numerous articles to profl. jours. Capt. USNR, 1943-79. Grantee NIH, 1961. Fellow ACS; mem. AMA, So. Calif. Neurosurgery Soc. (pres. 1973), L.A. Soc. Neurology (pres. 1979), Am. Pain Soc. (pres. 1980), Am. Acad. Pain Medicine (pres. 1984). Republican. Mormon. Home: 580 Oakcrest Dr Durango CO 81301-6905 Office: 1130 Main Ave Durango CO 81302

CRUICKSHANK, DUNCAN REDFORD, nursing home administrator; b. Aberdeen, Scotland, U.K., Dec. 31, 1965; came to U.S., 1982; s. William James and Margaret (McIntosh) C. BA in Psychology, U. N.Mex., 1987, MBA, 1990. Adminstr. Sunrise Healthcare, Cathlamet, Wash., 1992—. Vol. fire and ambulance dept. Mem. Am. Coll. Healthcare Adminstrs. Home: PO Box 233 Cathlamet WA 98612

CRUICKSHANK, JAMES DAVID, bishop; b. Vancouver, B.C., Can., June 10, 1936; s. James Cruickshank and Florence Mary (Mitchell) Bell; m. Susanne Margrot Nickelson, May 17, 1989 (seperate); children: Jason Robert, Anna Dorthy. BA, U. Minn., Duluth, 1959; LTh with distinction, Coll. Emmanuel and St. Chad, Saskatoon, Sask., Can., 1962; DRel, Chgo. Theol. Sem., 1970. Vicar Upper Fraser Mission Anglican Ch., Cariboo Diocese, 1962-65; dir. Sorrento (B.C.) Lay Tng. Ctr., 1965-73; vice prin., prof. pastoral theology Vancouver Sch. Theology, 1973-83; dean, rector Christ Ch. Cathedral, Vancouver, 1983-92; bishop Cariboo Diocese Anglican Ch. Can., Kamloops, B.C., 1992—; chancellor bd. govs. Vancouver Sch. Theol., 1989—; mem. nat. ministry com. Anglican Ch., 1981-83, doctrine and worship com., 1986-92, nat. exec. coun., 1992—. Mem. Vancouver Club. Office: Cariboo Diocese, # 5 618 Tranquille Rd, Kamloops, BC Canada V2A 3H6

CRUMBLEY, JOHN DAVID, counselor; b. Mpls., Feb. 17, 1951; s. Thornton Askew and Janet Catherine (Christley) C.; m. Cheryl Anne Nelson, July 28, 1989; children: Kelda Elizabeth Barnum, Holly Lorraine Barnum. BA, Harvard Coll., 1973; MS, U. Oreg., 1982, PhD, 1989. Lic. profl. counselor. Paraprofl. therapist Boston State Hosp., 1973-74; vol. VISTA, Ashland, Oreg., 1975-76; founding dir. Jackson County Foster Grandparent Program, Medford, Oreg., 1976-78; grad. teaching fellow U. Oreg., Eugene, 1979-84, 85-86; asst. prof. U. Nev., Reno, 1984-85, assoc. prof., 1987; counselor Lane County Dept. Youth Svcs., Eugene, 1980—; pres. CAF Assoc. Inc, Eugene, 1993—; cons. Puyallup Tribe of Indians, Tacoma, Wash., 1986, Nat. Ctr. Juvenile Justice, Pitts., 1991. Mem. Nat. Student Mobilization, Cambridge, Mass., 1971-73; bd. mem. Community Skills Bank, Ashland, Oreg., 1976-78. Mem. AACD, Nat. Juvenile Justice Trainers Assn., Oreg. Counseling Assn., Oreg. Soc. Individual Psychology (treas. 1978-80, v.p. 1981-83). Democrat. Methodist. Office: Lane County Dept Youth Svcs 2411 Centennial Blvd Eugene OR 97401

CRUMP, GERALD FRANKLIN, lawyer; b. Sacramento, Feb. 16, 1935; s. John Laurin and Ida May (Banta) C.; m. Glenda Roberts Glass, Nov. 21, 1959; children: Sara Elizabeth, Juliane Kathryn, Joseph Stephen. A.B., U. Calif.-Berkeley 1956, JD, 1959; MA, Baylor U., 1966. Bar: Calif. 1960. Dep. county counsel L.A. County, 1963-73, legis. rep., 1970-73; chief pub. works div. L.A. County Counsel, 1973-84, sr. asst. county counsel, 1984-85, chief asst. county counsel, 1985—; lectr. Pepperdine U., 1978, U. Calif., 1982. V.p. San Fernando Valley Girl Scout Coun. Served to capt. USAF, 1960-63; to maj. gen. USAFR, 1963—, mobilization asst. to the judge adv. gen. Mem. ABA, State Bar of Calif. (del.), Los Angeles County Bar Assn. (past chmn., trustee govtl. law sect., past mem. exec. com. litigation sect.), Am. Judicature Soc., Am. Acad. Polit. and Social Sci., Res. Officers Assn., Air Force Assn., Phi Alpha Delta, Delta Sigma Phi. Home: 4020 Camino De La Cumbre Sherman Oaks CA 91423-4522 Office: 648 Hall of Adminstrn Los Angeles CA 90012

CRUMP, JULIANNE JUANITA, eligibility technician, graphologist; b. Chgo., Jan. 25, 1950; d. Samuel and LaVergne Harriet (Bassmire) Millard; m. Richmond Alexander White, July, 1970 (div. Mar. 1975); 1 child, Zacharias Joseph; m. Lee Roy Crump Jr., Mar. 24, 1979. Cert. graphology, Inst. Graphic Sci., 1987; student, Cabrillo Coll., 1992—. Office mgr. Tect Electronics Corp., Concord, Calif., 1974-75; freelance bookkeeper Santa Cruz, Calif., 1975-79; account clk. II County of Santa Cruz, 1979-84, eligibility worker, 1984-88, quality control analyst, 1988-89, eligibility III technician, 1989—; pvt. practice graphologist Santa Cruz, 1988—. Mem. Food Stamp Corrective Action Com., Santa Cruz, 1987. Mem. Inst. Graphological Sci., Svc. Employees Inter Union.

CRUMP, SPENCER, publisher, business executive; b. San Jose, Calif., Nov. 25; s. Spencer M. and Jessie (Person) C.; m. Cynthia Fink, 1992; children by previous marriage: John Spencer, Victoria Elizabeth Margaret. B.A., U. So. Calif., 1960, M.S. in Edn, 1962, M.A. in Journalism, 1969. Reporter Long Beach (Calif.) Ind., 1945-49; freelance writer Long Beach, 1950-51; travel columnist, picture editor Long Beach Ind.-Press-Telegram, 1952-56; pres. Crest Industries Corp., Long Beach, 1957-58; editor suburban sects. Los Angeles Times, 1959-62; editorial dir. Trans-Anglo Books, Los Angeles, 1962-73, pub., 1973-81; pub. Zeta Pubs. Co., Corona Del Mar, Calif., 1981—; mng. dir. Person-Crump Devel. Co. (formerly Person Properties Co.), Justiceburg, Tex., 1951—; chmn. dept. journalism Orange Coast Coll., 1966-82; chmn. bd. Zeta Internat., 1976—; cons. Queen Beach Press, 1974-87, Flying Spur Press, 1976—, So. Pacific Transp. Co., 1979-80, Interurban Press/Trans-Anglo Books, 1981-87; bd. dirs. Zeta Britain, Zeta Internat.; chmn. bd. T & S Publs. Group, Inc., Canyon Lake, Calif., 1988-89. Author: Ride the Big Red Cars, 1962, Redwoods, Iron Horses and the Pacific, 1963, Western Pacific-The Railroad That was Built Too Late, 1963, California's Spanish Missions Yesterday and Today, 1964, Black Riot in Los Angeles, 1966, Henry Huntington and the Pacific Electric, 1970, Fundamentals of Journalism, 1974, California's Spanish Missions—An Album, 1975, Suggestions for Teaching the Fundamentals of Journalism in College, 1976, The Stylebook for Newswriting, 1979, Newsgathering and Newswriting for the 1980s and Beyond, 1981, Riding the California Western Skunk R.R., 1988, Durango to Silverton by Narrow Gauge Rail, 1990, Riding the Cumbres & Toltec Railroad, 1992. Mem. Los Angeles County Democratic Central Com., 1961-62. Mem. Book Pubs. Assn. So. Calif., Fellowship Reconciliation, Soc. Profl. Journalists. Unitarian-Universalist. Office: Zeta Pubs Co PO Box 38 Corona Del Mar CA 92625-3060

CRUMPTON, EVELYN, psychologist, educator; b. Ashland, Ala., Dec. 23, 1924; d. Alpheus Leland and Bernice (Fordham) Crumpton. AB, Birmingham So. Coll., 1944; MA, UCLA, 1953, PhD in Psychology, 1955. Lic. psychologist, Calif.; diplomate Am. Bd. Profl. Psychology. Rsch. psychologist VA Hosp., Brentwood, L.A., 1955-77; asst. chief psychology svc., dir. clin. tng. VA Adminstrn. Med. Ctr. West Los Angeles, 1977-88; clin. prof. dept. psychology UCLA, assoc. rsch. psychologist dept. psychiatry, UCLA Sch. Med., 1957—; cons. chief of staff Brentwood div., VA Adminstrn. Med. Ctr. Contbr. numerous articles to profl. jours. Recipient Profl. Svc. award, Assn. Chief Psychologists VA, 1979. Fellow Soc. Personality Assessment; mem. APA, Western Psychol. Assn., Sigma Xi.

CRUSA, MICHAEL CHARLES, political and public affairs consultant; b. Carthage, Mo., Sept. 17, 1947; s. Robert Lewis and Wonivere Joy (Matthews) C.; m. Jody Marie Thurston, Nov. 18, 1989; 1 child, Michael Jr. Adminstrv. asst. Tucson City Coun., 1973-76; spl. asst. state affairs U.S. Senator Dennis De Concini, Phoenix, 1976-83; state dir. U.S. Senator Dennis De Concial, Phoenix, 1988-91; pres. The Summit Group, Phoenix, 1991—; govt. rels. rep. Ariz. Nuclear Power Project, Phoenix, 1983-86; pol. cons. First Tuesday/Roots Devel., Phoenix, 1986-88. Chmn. Phoenix Parks and Recreation Commn., 1985-90; bd. dirs. Ariz. Close-up Found., Phoenix, 1983—, Valley Leadership, Inc., Phoenix, 1986-89, 93-, Phoenix Substance Abuse Comsn., 1993-; pres. Valley Leadership Alumni Assn., Phoenix, 1983-86. Mem. Jaycees (Outstanding Young Men of Am. 1980, 81). Democrat. Baptist. Office: 400 W Camelback Rd Ste 121 Phoenix AZ 85013

CRUSE, ALLAN BAIRD, mathematician, computer scientist, educator; b. Birmingham, Ala., Aug. 28, 1941; s. J. Clyde and Irma R. Cruse. AB, Emory U., 1959-62, PhD, 1974; postgrad. (Woodrow Wilson fellow) U. Calif.-Berkeley, 1962-63, MA, 1965; teaching fellow Dartmouth Coll., 1963-64. Instr., U. San Francisco, 1966-73, asst. prof. math., 1973-76, assoc. prof., 1976-79, prof., 1979—, chmn. math. dept. 1988-91; vis. instr. Stillman Coll., summer 1967; vis. assoc. prof. Emory U., spring 1978; prof. computer sci. Sonoma State U., 1983-85; cons. math edn. NSF fellow, 1972-73. Mem. Am. Math. Soc., Math. Assn. Am., Assn. Computing Machinery, U. San Francisco Faculty Assn., Sigma Xi (Dissertation award 1974). Author: (with Millianne Granberg) Lectures on Freshman Calculus, 1971; research, publs. in field. Office: U San Francisco Harney Sci Ctr San Francisco CA 94117

CRUSE, C(LYDE) LANSFORD, III, manufacturing company marketing executive; b. Middletown, Ohio, June 20, 1956; s. Clyde Lansford and Ruth Marie (Gillespie) C.; m. Stephanie Ann Wedig, Oct. 25, 1980; children: Clyde Lansford IV, Holly Corrine, Reid August. BSME, U. Cin., 1979; MBA, U. Tex., 1980. Asst. to v.p. Armco Nat. Supply, Houston, 1980-83; corp. acquisitions The Coleman Co., Wichita, Kans., 1983-85; dir. engring. Soniform Inc., Coleman, San Diego, 1985-86, v.p. fin., 1986-87, gen. mgr., 1987-88; pres., gen. mgr. Coleman Spas Inc., Chandler, Ariz., 1988-90; gen. mgr. spl. products div. Sulzer Bingham Inc., Portland, Oreg., 1990-91, gem. mgr. mktg., 1991—. Bd. dirs., strategic planning United Way, Gulf Coast, 1982-83. Home: 31 Partridge Ln Lake Oswego OR 97035 Office: Sulzer Bingham Pumps Inc 2800 NW Front Ave Portland OR 97210

CRUSE, DENTON W., marketing and advertising executive, consultant; b. Washington, May 21, 1944; s. Denton W. Sr. and Frances Rankin (Moore) C.; m. Susan Costello, June 11, 1988. BS, Va. Commonwealth U., 1966; MBA, So. Ill. U., 1977. Media supr. Procter & Gamble Co., Cin., 1967-73; assoc. media dir. Ralston Purina Co., St. Louis, 1973-78; dir. advt. Armour-Dial Co., Phoenix, 1978-81; mktg. dir. Valentine Greeting Inc., Phoenix, 1981-82; dir. mktg. svcs. J. Walter Thompson/USA, L.A., 1982-83; cons. L.A., 1983-86; dir. advt. svcs. Mattel Inc., L.A., 1986-88; cons. C and O Assocs., L.A., 1988—; instr. UCLA, L.A., 1986—. Editor-in-chief: Cobblestone, 1965. Marathon monitor L.A. Olympic Organizing Com., 1984; bd. dirs. Old Hometown Fair. Mem. Mktg. Club L.A., Beta Gamma Sigma, Pi Sigma Epsilon. Republican. Presbyterian.

CRUTCHFIELD, ALEXANDER, investment banker, venture capitalist; b. Tucson, Dec. 12, 1958; s. Alec Randall and Virginia Cushing (Smith) C. BA, Claremont (Calif.) Men's Coll., 1980; MBA, Columbia U., 1984. Assoc. RRY Ptnrs., Buckingham, Pa., 1984-86; exec. v.p. Am. Water Devel., Denver, 1986-87, vice chmn., 1987—; pres. Crutchfield & Co., Denver, 1988—; prin. RRY Ptnrs., 1986-87, mng. dir., 1988; chmn. ATFAB Corp., Boca Raton, Fla., 1986—; bd. dirs., vice chmn. First Colo. Corp., Denver; gen. ptnr. Oasis Ptnrs., N.Y., 1990—; vice chmn. bd. dirs. Am. Water Devel., Denver; bd. dirs. Baca Minerals, Inc. Mem. Nat. Cattleman's Assn., Econs. Club N.Y., Denver Petroleum Club, Denver Club. Home: 1880 Arapahoe St Denver CO 80202-1855 Office: Crutchfield & Co Ste 2350 1099 18th St Denver CO 80202-1929

CRUTCHFIELD, JAMES PATRICK, physicist; b. San Francisco, June 30, 1955; s. James Patrick C. and Marilyn Grether. BA in Physics and Math., U. Calif., Santa Cruz, 1979, PhD in Physics, 1983. Post doctoral fellow Miller Inst. for Basic Rsch. U. Calif., Berkeley, 1983-85; post doctoral fellow in solid state physics IBM Fellowship Program, U. Calif., Berkeley, 1986; rsch. physicist, physics dept. U. Calif., Berkeley, 1983—; external prof. Santa Fe (N.Mex.) Inst., 1990—; cons. IBM Rsch. Ctr., San Jose, Calif., 1977, Xerox Rsch. Ctr., Palo Alto, Calif., 1980, Los Alamos (N.Mex.) Nat. Lab., 1982—; disting. vis. rsch. prof. Beckman Inst. U. Ill., Champaign-Urbana. Author several films and videos; contbr. articles to profl. jours. Mem. N.Y. Acad. of Scis. Office: U Calif Physics Dept Berkeley CA 94720

CRUZE, DEBORAH KAYE, city judge; b. Scottsbluff, Nebr., Aug. 5, 1957; d. Eugene Morgan and Caroline Mae (Hartwig) Hughes; m. Gary Lee Cruze, June 14, 1980; children: Melissa Anne, Aaron Griffith, Rebecca Danielle. BS, No. Ariz. U., 1978; postgrad., Washington & Lee U., 1978-79; JD, Ariz. State U., 1981. Bar: Ariz. 1981. Legis. intern Ariz. State Senate, Phoenix, 1978; asst. atty. gen. Ariz. Atty. Gen.'s Office, Phoenix, 1981-82; adj. faculty Rio Salado Community Coll., Phoenix, 1985, Glendale (Ariz.) Community Coll., 1986-90, Ariz. State U., 1991; judge pro tempore Magistrate Ct. City of Glendale, 1990-91, judge, 1991—; congl. intern U.S. Senate, Washington, summer, 1978; law clk. Mangum, Wall, Stoops & Warden, Flagstaff, Ariz., summer 1979, Samaritan Health Svc., Phoenix, summer, 1990. Participant, coord. Glendale Leadership and Devel. Program, 1985-86; chairperson Housing Authority Commn., City of Glendale, 1985-91, Faith United Meth. Presch. Bd., 1987-92; speaker Law Day Drug Edn. Program, Phoenix, 1988; mem. Alternative Expenditure Limitation Com., Glendale, 1989, Campaign Com. to Re-elect Mayor Renner, Glendale, 1989, edn. com. Christ's Community Ch., 1982-83; chairperson Parent Enrichment Program,

1984-86; active Faith United Meth. Presch. Bd., 1987-92, chairperson, 1989-91, Community Ch. of Joy, 1993—; speaker in field. Mem. Ariz. Bar Assn., Ariz. Women Lawyer's Assn. (mem. mother's forum 1990—), Ariz. Magistrates Assn., Maricopa Bar Assn. (mem. bench/bar rels. com. 1992—), Alpha Delta Pi (Dorothy Shaw Leadership award 1978), Phi Alpha Delta, Phi Kappa Phi (v.p. 1977-78, grad. fellow 1978), Phi Kappa Phi, P.E.O. Democrat.

CRUZ-URIBE, EUGENE DAVID, assistant college dean; b. Green Bay, Wis., Dec. 22, 1952; s. Antonio and Lillian Mae (Hasseler) Cruz-U.; m. Kathryn Allwarden, Dec. 12, 1981; children: Alicia, Mariana. BA, U. Chgo., 1975, MA, 1977, PhD, 1983. Project Egyptologist Seattle Art Mus., 1978; curatorial asst. Met. Mus. Art, N.Y.C., 1978-79; membership sec. Oriental Inst., Chgo., 1979-81; asst. editor Demotic Dictionary U. Chgo., 1981-83; asst. prof. Egyptology Brown U., Providence, 1983-88; asst. dean Coll. Social and Behavioral Scis. No. Ariz. U., Flagstaff, 1989—. Editor Serapis, Am. Jour. Egyptology, 1978-88; contbr. articles to profl. jours. Trustee's fellow U. Chgo., 1975-78; grantee NEH, 1985-87, NSF, 1991—, M. Schiff Giorgini Found., 1992, Serapis Rsch. Inst., 1988, Am. Philos. Soc., 1986, access/rsch. grantee, 1986, travel grantee, 1985. Mem. Am. Rsch. Ctr. in Egypt, Internat. Assn. Egyptologists, Soc. for Study of Egypt Antiquities (bd. dirs. 1992—), Egyptological Seminar N.Y., Egypt Exploration Soc. (London). Democrat. Roman Catholic. Home: 3175 W Brenda Loop Flagstaff AZ 86001-0906 Office: Northern Ariz Univ PO Box 15700 Flagstaff AZ 86011-1570

CRYDEN, DAVID WILLIAM, financial planner; b. Chgo., July 25, 1955; s. Joseph and Joan (Lewinson) C.; m. Allyson Lynne Krugh, Nov. 24, 1989; children: Stephen August Hiltscher, Tanner Joseph. BA in Media Studies, Sonoma State U., 1977. CFP. Sales mgr. Sta. KVEC, San Luis Obispo, Calif., 1977-84; fin. planner, v.p. Blakeslee & Blakeslee, San Luis Obispo, 1984—; instr. fin. planning Cuesta C.C., San Luis Obispo, Hancock C.C., Santa Maria, Calif., 1989—; host fin. talk show local radio, 1992—. Founder Widowed Persons Outreach, San Luis Obispo, 1988—, San Luis Obispo July 4th Parade, 1988; bd. dirs. EOC Family Planning Clinic, San Luis Obispo, 1989-91; adv. bd. Women's Shelter Program, San Luis Obispo, 1991—. Home: 327 McCarthy Ave Oceano CA 93445 Office: Blakeslee & Blakeslee 1110 California Blvd San Luis Obispo CA 93401

CRYER, CLIFFORD LOPER, real estate appraiser; b. Balt., July 27, 1948; s. William Clinton and Jean Elaine (Loper) C.; m. Mary Carol Clark, Apr. 22, 1972; children: Chad Michael Townsend, William Clark Clifford. BSBA, U. Denver, 1970. Real estate appraiser Knapp & Co., Denver, 1971-73, Arnold & Assocs. Corp., Denver, 1973-74; pres. Cryer & Co. Appraisers, Inc., Denver, 1974-89, Cryer & Assocs., Appraisers, Englewood, Colo., 1989—. Author: ERC's Relocation Appraisal Guide, 1989; contbr. articles to profl. jours. Soccer coach YMCA, Littleton, Colo., 1985, 89, Cherry Creek Soccer Assn., Englewood, 1989, 92; instr. Emily Griffin Opportunity Sch., U. Colo., Denver, 1974-92. Recipient Outstanding Svc. award SREA-Denver #9, 1987, Pres.'s award Employee Relocation Coun., 1989, Meritorious Svc. award, 1989, Pres.'s award, 1990, Disting. Svc. award, 1990. Mem. Appraisal Inst., Employee Relocation Coun. Episcopalian.

CRYER, RODGER EARL, educational administrator; b. Detroit, Apr. 2, 1940. AB in Fine Arts, San Diego State U., 1965; MA in Edn. Adminstrn., Stanford U., 1972; PhD in Psychol. Services Counseling, Columbia-Pacific U., 1985. Cert. tchr., N.J., Calif.; cert. gen. adminstrn., Calif. Spl. asst. to commissioner N.J. State Dept. Edn., Trenton, 1967-68; cons. N.J. Urban Sch. Devel., Trenton, 1969-70; mgmt. cons. Rodger E. Cryer, Co., Pinole, Calif., 1970-73; adminstrv. asst. Franklin McKinley Sch. Dist., San Jose, Calif., pres. Chief Exec. Tng. Corp., San Jose, 1981-82; prin. McKinley Sch., 1986-91, prin. Hellyer Sch., 1991—; ptnr. Guided Learning Enterprises; bd. dirs., Commonwealth Cen. Credit Union, 1989—. Mem. Nat. Sch. Pub. Rels. Assn. (sec. 1975—), Calif. Sch. Pub. Rels. Assn. (pres.). Contbr. articles to profl. jours. Commr. Home: PO Box 21917 San Jose CA 95151-1917 Office: Hellyer Sch 725 Hellyer Ave San Jose CA 95111-1523

CRYSTALL, JOSEPH N., communications company executive; b. Bklyn., Dec. 19, 1922; s. Samuel H. and Frances (Eiten) C.; m. Martha Jane Ladson, Feb. 23, 1957; 1 child, Bonnie Leigh. Student, Bklyn. Coll., 1939-42, U. Pitts., 1942-43. Radio performer Sta. KOPO, Tucson, 1951-54; advt. agy. exec. The Wiener Co., Tucson, 1955-59; sta. mgr., TV performer Sta. KOLD-AM-TV, Tucson, 1959-69; gen. mgr. Sta. KOPO, Tucson, 1969-73, Stas. KEVT, KWFM, Tucson, 1974-81; pres., gen. mgr. Sta. KGVY, Green Valley, Ariz., 1981—; pres. Crystal Sets, Inc., Tucson, 1981—; instr. U. Ariz., Tucson, 1968-69. Contbr. articles, TV scripts, short stories to various publs., 1955—. Pres. Better Bus. Bur. So. Ariz., Tucson, 1983. Served as 1st lt. USAF, 1943-45, ETO, MTO. Decorated DFC, Air medal with three clusters. Mem. Ariz. Broadcasters Assn. (pres. 1966-67), Tucson Broadcasters Assn. (pres. 1971-72), Nat. Assn. Broadcasters, Tucson Advt. Club (pres. 1968-69, 73-74, named to Advt. Hall of Fame 1987), Am. Advt. Fedn. (recipient Silver medal 1989), Green Valley C. of C. (bd. dirs., v.p. 1988—), Sigma Delta Chi. Clubs: Tucson Press (pres. 1967, 71, 72, named Broadcaster of Yr. 1981). Lodges: Elks, Lions (pres. 1974-75), Rotary (pres. 1989—). Home: 3147 E Pima St Tucson AZ 85716-3131 Office: Sta KGVY PO Box 767 Green Valley AZ 85622-0767

CSENDES, ERNEST, chemist, corporate and financial executive; b. Satu-Mare, Romania, Mar. 2, 1926; came to U.S., 1951, naturalized, 1955; s. Edward O. and Sidonia (Littman) C. m. Catharine Vera Tolnai, Feb. 7, 1953; children: Audrey Carol, Robert Alexander Edward. BA, Protestant Coll., Hungary, 1944; BS, U. Heidelberg (Ger.), 1948, MS, PhD, 1951. Rsch. asst. chemistry U. Heidelberg, 1950-51; rsch. assoc. biochemistry Tulane U., New Orleans, 1952; rsch. fellow chemistry Harvard U., 1952-53; rsch. chemist organic chems. dept. E. I. Du Pont de Nemours and Co., Wilmington, Del., 1953-56, elastomer chems. dept., 1956-61; dir. rsch. and devel. agrl. chems. div. Armour & Co., Atlanta, 1961-63; v.p. corp. devel. Occidental Petroleum Corp., L.A., 1963-64, exec. v.p. rsch., engrng. and devel., mem. exec. com., 1964-68; chief operating officer, exec. v.p., dir. Occidental Rsch. and Engrng. Corp., L.A., London, Moscow, 1964-68; mng. dir. Occidental Rsch. and Engrng. (U.K.) Ltd., London, 1964-68; pres., chief exec. officer TRI Group, London, Amsterdam, Rome and Bermuda, 1968-84; chmn., chief exec. officer Micronic Techs., Inc., L.A., 1981-85; mng. ptnr. Inter-Consult Ltd., Pacific Palisades, Calif., 1984—; internat. con. on tech., econ. feasibility and mgmt., 1984—. Contbr. 250 articles to profl. and trade jours., studies and books; achievements include 29 patents; research in area of elastomers, rubber chemicals, dyes and intermediates, organometallics, organic and biochemistry, high polymers, phosphates, plant nutrients, pesticides, process engineering, design of fertilzer plants, sulfur, potash and phosphate ore mining and metallurgy, coal burning and acid rain, coal utilization, methods for aerodynamic grinding of solids, petrochemicals, biomed. engrng., consumer products, also acquisitions, mergers, internat. fin. related to leasing investment and loans, trusts and ins.; regional devel. related to agr. and energy resources. Recipient Pro Mundi Beneficio gold medal Brazilian Acad. Humanities, 1975; Harvard U. fellow, 1953. Fellow AAAS, Am. Inst. Chemists, Royal Soc. of Chemistry (London); mem. AIAA, Am. Chem. Soc., German Chem. Soc., N.Y. Acad. Sci., Am. Inst. Chem. Engrs., Am. Concrete Inst., Acad. Polit. Sci., Global Action Econ. Inst., Am. Def. Preparedness Assn., Sigma Xi. Home: 514 N Marquette St Pacific Palisades CA 90272-3314

CUBIN, BARBARA LYNN, state legislator, public relations consultant; b. Salinas, Calif., Nov. 30; d. Russell G. and Barbara Lee (Howard) Sage; m. Frederick William Cubin, Aug. 1; children: William Russell, Frederick William III. BS in Chemistry, Creighton U., 1969. Chemist Wyo. Machinery Co., Casper, Wyo., 1973-75; mem. Wyo. Ho. Reps., 1987-92, Wyo. Senate, 1993—; pres. Spectrum Promotions and Mgmt., Casper, 1993—; mem com. Nat. Coun. State Legislators, San Francisco, 1987—, Lexington, Ky., 1990—. Mem. steering com. Exptl. Program to Stimulate Competitive Research (EPSCOR); mem. Coun. of State Govts.; active Gov.'s Com. on Preventive Medicine, 1992; vice chmn. Cleer Bd. Energy Coun., Irving, Tex., 1993—; chmn. Wyo. Senate Rep. Conf., Casper, 1993—; mem. Wyo. Rep. Party Exec. Com., 1993. Toll fellow Coun. State Govts., 1990. Mem. Am. Legis. Exch. Coun., Rep. Women. Episcopalian. Office: Wyo State Senate Capitol Bldg Cheyenne WY 82001

CUCINA, VINCENT ROBERT, management and financial consultant, educator; b. Balt., Mar. 31, 1936; s. Anthony James and Josephine (Lazzaro) C.; m. Rosemary Warrington, Apr. 24, 1965; children: Victor, Gregory, Russell. BS in Acctg., Loyola Coll., Balt., 1958; MS in Fin. Mgmt., George Washington U., 1967. Cert. profl. cons.; CPA, Calif., Md. Auditor Deloitte & Touche, Balt., 1958, 61-63; acctg. mgr. books and reports Chesapeake & Potomac Telephone Co., Cockeysville, Md., 1964-68; mgr. fin. controls ITT, N.Y.C., 1968; contr. ITT World Directories, N.Y.C., 1969-70; v.p. fin. analysis and planning Dart Industries, Inc., L.A., 1970-82; v.p., chief fin. officer Epson Am., Inc., Torrance, Calif., 1984-87; cons. Westlake Village, Calif., 1988—; v.p., chief fin. officer, cons. Phoenix Furniture Co., L.A., 1988-89; cons. Universal Studios Tours, L.A., 1988, Smithline Audio, L.A., 1990, FMS Prodns., Carpinteria, Calif., 1990; lectr. planning & fin. Calif. Luth. U., 1991—. Capt. U.S. Army, 1959-60, USAR, 61-64. Mem. AICPA, Fin. Execs. Inst., Acad. Profl. Cons. and Advisors. Roman Catholic. Home and Office: 32305 Blue Rock Rdg Westlake Village CA 91361-3912

CUDMORE, WYNN WATSON, biologist, educator; b. Winchester, Mass., Sept. 12, 1955; s. Lemuel Ralph and Jane Ellen (Robinson) C.; m. Carla Jean Eaton, Dec. 22, 1984; children: Calin Elizabeth, Alyssa Anne, Rebecca Jean. BS in Biology, Northeastern U., 1978; PhD in Ecology, Ind. State U., 1983. Postdoctoral rsch. assoc. Wash. State U., Pullman, 1984-85; life sci. instr. Chemeketa Community Coll., Salem, Oreg., 1985—; cons. U.S. Forest Svc., Blue River, Oreg., 1985. Contbr. articles to profl. jours. Invited speaker UN Assn., Salem, 1992, Native Plant Soc., Salem, 1992; bd. dirs. Earth Kids, Salem, 1991-92. Mem. Am. Soc. Mammalogists, Ind. Acad. Sci. (chair zoology 1984), N.W. Scientific Assn., Sigma Xi, Phi Kappa Phi. Home: 14860 Orchard Knob Dallas OR 97338 Office: Chemeketa Community Coll Life Sci PO Box 14007 Salem OR 97309

CUKIERSKI, MATTHEW JOHN, pharmaceutical toxicologist; b. Hempstead, N.Y., Dec. 12, 1958; s. Alphonse Julian and Mary Alice (Flanagan) C.; m. Deborah Marie Strasser, July 11, 1981; 1 child, Alison Marie. BS in Biol. Scis., SUNY, Stony Brook, 1981; PhD in Anatomical Scis., SUNY, Buffalo, 1986. Postdoctoral rsch. morphologist, dir. electron microscopy facility primate rsch. ctr. U. Calif., Davis, 1986-88; staff scientist ALZA Corp., Palo Alto, Calif., 1988—; mem. computers users steering com. ALZA Corp., 1990—. Vice pres. Hyde Park Homeowners Assn., Pleasanton, Calif., 1989-91, pres., 1991-92. N.Y. State Regents scholar, 1977-81. Mem. AAAS, Am. Assn. Anatomists, N.Y. Acad. Scis., Electron Microscopy Soc. Am., Teratology Soc. (local arrangements com. 1987), Soc. Toxicology (No. Calif. chpt.), West Coast Teratology Soc. Republican. Roman Catholic. Office: ALZA Corp 950 Page Mill Rd Palo Alto CA 94304-1080

CULBERT, READ SHEPHARD, securities broker; b. Phoenix, Apr. 23, 1966; s. Wickham Shephard and Avis (Read) C. BS in Corp. Fin., U. Ariz. Comml. real estate appraiser Burke Hansen, Inc., Tucson, 1988-91, Dietrich and Hawkins, Ltd., Tucson, 1991; fin. cons. D.E. Frey & Co., Inc., Mesa, Ariz., 1992—. Mem. Rotary Internat., Shito-Ryu, Itosu Kai.

CULBERTSON, JAMES THOMAS, psychologist; b. Scranton, Pa., Dec. 25, 1911; s. Walter Edwards and Katharine (Evans) C.; m. Jean Herman, Nov. 1, 1941; children—Elizabeth, Hazel, Jamie, Samuel. B.A., Yale U., 1934, Ph.D., 1940. Sterling Research fellow Yale U., 1941; research assoc. in math. and biology U. Chgo., 1946-49; prof. philosophy U. So. Calif., Los Angeles, 1949-51; math. rsch. assoc. Rand Corp., Santa Monica, Calif., 1951-53; prof. math. and computer sci. Calif. Poly. State U.-San Luis Obispo, 1953-65, chmn. philosophy dept., 1968-78; rsch. prof. psychology UCLA, 1965-68; freelance theoretical brain rschr., San Luis Obispo, 1978—. Author: Consciousness and Behavior, 1950; Mathematics and Logic for Ditigal Devices, 1958; A Student's Survey of the Mind-Body Problem, 1960; The Minds of Robots, 1963; Sensations, Memories and the Flow of Time, 1976; Consciousness: Natural and Artificial, 1982; Achievements include contributions to early work on neural nets and designs for any input-output; helped develop RAND robots; contbr. book chpts. and articles to profl. jours. Mem. nat. bd. advisers Inst. Advanced Philos. Research. Mem. IEEE (life), AAAS, Am. Math. Soc., Am. Philos. Assn., Philosophy of Sci. Assn., Soc. Philosophy and Psychology. Mind Assn. Home: 115 Del Norte Way San Luis Obispo CA 93405-1507

CULL, CHRIS ALAN, operations executive; b. Las Cruces, N.Mex., Jan. 3, 1947; s. William Roy Cull and Doris Jean (Compton) Morgan; m. DuAnne Elizabeth Diers King, July 26, 1967 (div. 1979); children: Joey Lynn, Jamie Ayn, Brandon Alan. BS, N.Mex. State U., 1976. Lab./field technician N.Mex. State U., Las Cruces, 1973-76; research soil scientist Mont. State U., Bozeman, 1976-77; reclamation supr. Western Energy Co., Colstrip, Mont., 1977-80; mgr. ops. permitting Western Energy Co., Billings, Mont., 1980-85; asst. project mgr. En Tech Inc., Butte, Mont., 1985-86; mgr. ops. Spl. Resource Mgmt. Inc., Billings, 1986-87; owner EnviroChek Inc., Billings, 1987-88; dir. environ. svcs. Western Tech. Inc., Tucson, 1988-90; dir. regulatory affairs Western Tech. Inc., Golden, Colo., 1990-91; mgr. regulatory affairs Sergent, Hauskins & Beckwith, Lakewood, Colo., 1991-92; mgr. regulatory svcs. Morrison-Maierle Environ., Billings, Mont., 1992, Morrison-Maierle Environ. Corp., Billings, 1992—. Contbr. articles to profl. jours. Mem. Am. Indsl. Hygiene Assn., Nat. Asbestos Coun., Nat. Assn. Environ. Profls., Soil Conservation Soc. Am. (chmn. surface mine reclamation com. 1978-80, mem. univ. and coll. rels. com. 1977-78, spl. task force surface mine reclamation div. 1977-79, pres. Mont. chpt. 1980-82), Mont. Coal Coun. (cochmn. environ./tech. com. 1983-85), Mining and Reclamation Coun. Am. (tech. com. 1983-85), Am. Coun. on Sic. and Health, SME Inc., N.W. Mining Assn., Mont. Mining Assn. Home: 3221 Banff Ave # 2 Billings MT 59102 Office: Morrison-Maierle Einviron Corp 2020 Grand Ave Billings MT 59102

CULLEN, ROBERT JOHN, publishing executive, financial consultant; b. York, Pa., Feb. 14, 1949; s. John Joseph and Florence Susanne (Staab) C.; m. Elizabeth Maule, Oct. 20, 1984; 1 child, Michael Joseph. BA, Winona (Minn.) State U., 1972. CFP; registered investment advisor. Editor-in-chief Overseas Life, Leimen, Fed. Republic of Germany, 1978-80; feature editor L.A. Daily Commerce, 1980-83; pres. HighTech Editorial, L.A., 1983—; fin. planner Cullen Fin. Svcs., Rancho Cucamonga, Calif., 1989—; computer editor Plaza Communications, Irvine, Calif., 1984-91. With U.S. Army, 1974-78, ETO. Mem. Internat. Assn. Fin. Planners, Calif. Advs. Nursing Home Reform. Episcopalian.

CULLER, DAVID ETHAN, educator; b. Santa Barbara, Calif., Nov. 12, 1959; s. Glen Jacob and Susanne (Kreith) C.; m. Sara Chie Mayeno, May 20, 1983; 1 child, Ethan. BA, U. Calif., Berkeley, 1980; MS, MIT, 1985, PhD, 1989. Programmer Culler-Harrison Inc., Santa Barbara, 1976, UCSD Chemistry Dept., La Jolla, Calif., 1976-78; logic designer CHI Systems Inc., Santa Barbara, 1979; math. programmer Lawrence Berkeley Lab., Berkeley, 1980; systems programmer Nat. Magnetic Fusion Energy Computer Ctr., Livermore, Calif., 1980-82; rsch. asst. MIT Lab. Computer Sci., Cambridge, 1982-89; co-founder, chief systems architect A.I. Architects Inc., Cambridge, 1986-88; asst. prof. U. Calif., Berkeley, 1989—. Inventor, patentee in field. Named NSF Presdl. Young Investigator, 1990, Presdl. faculty fellow, 1992; jr. faculty rsch. grantee, 1990; regents jr. faculty fellow, 1990. Mem. IEEE, Assn. Computing Machinery, Sigma Xi. Office: U Calif Divsn Computer Sci Berkeley CA 94720

CULP, GARY, military officer, engineer; b. Columbus, Ohio, Mar. 14, 1940; s. Chester Harold and Alice May (Cole) C.; m. Caryl Ann Miller, June 7, 1962; children: Meredith Lynn, Mackinley Leigh. BS in Physics, U. Ark., 1962; MS in Engrng. Space Physics, Air Force Inst. Tech., Dayton, Ohio, 1964; MS in Engrng. Mgmt., Northeastern U., Boston, 1968. Commd. 2d lt. USAF, 1962, advanced through grades to col., 1980, ret., 1988; rsch. physicist Cambridge Rsch. Labs. USAF, Boston, 1964-68; program mgr. Office of Sec. of Def. USAF, Saigon, Republic of Vietnam, 1968-69; project officer Tech. Applications Ctr. USAF, Alexandria, Va., 1969-72; hdqrs staff officer USAF, Washington, 1973-77; program dir. Space Div. USAF, L.A., 1978-84; comdr. Systems Command Inspection Ctr. USAF, Ft. Walton Beach, Fla., 1984-86, Fgn. Tech. Div. USAF, Dayton, 1986-88; program mgr. Space Systems div. Rockwell Internat., Seal Beach, Calif., 1990—; lectr. U. Ark., Fayetteville, 1982-86, Air Command and Staff Coll., USAF, Montgomery, Ala., 1982-84, Defense Systems Mgmt. Coll., Ft. Belvoir, Va., 1993; cons. USAF Systems Command, Washington, 1984-86. Contbr. articles, papers to physics jours. Life mem. Rep. Nat. Com., Washington, 1971—; mem. No. Va. Coun. Big Bros. Am., Alexandria, 1974-78; bd. dirs. Internat. Decathlon Acads., Costa Mesa, Calif., Precious Life Shelter, Los Alamitos, Calif., Vol. Ctr. of Orange County West, Huntington Beach, Calif. Decorated Legion of Merit, 1985, 88; recipient Superior Mgmt. award Sec. of Def., Washington, 1982. Mem. AIAA (sr.), Am. Phys. Soc. (life), Armed Forces Communications and Electronics Assn. (life), Air Force Assn. (life, Sr. Officer of Yr., Air Power chpt. 147, L.A., 1984), Nat. Mgmt. Assn., Sigma Pi Sigma. Republican. Presbyterian. Home: 6106 Jeffrey Mark St Cypress CA 90630-3934 Office: Rockwell Internat Space Systems Div Seal Beach CA

CULP, MILDRED LOUISE, corporate executive; b. Ft. Monroe, Va., Jan. 13, 1949; d. William W. and Winifred (Stilwell) C. BA in English, Knox Coll., 1971; AM in religion and literature, U. Chgo., 1974, PhD The Com. on History of Culture, 1976. Mem. faculty, adminstr. Coll., 1976-81; dir. Exec. Résumés, Seattle, 1981—; pres. Exec. Directions Internat., Inc., Seattle, 1985—; speaker in field. Columnist Seattle Daily Jour. Commerce, 1982-88; featured on TV and radio; contbr. articles and book revs. to profl. jours.; presenter Workwise Report, KIRO Radio, 1991—, WorkWise registered 1992. Admissions advisor U. Chgo., 1981—; mem. Nat. Alliance Mentally Ill, 1984—, bd. dirs., 1987, adv. bd., 1988; mem. A.M.I Hamilton County, 1984—; founding mem. People Against Telephone Terrorism and Harassment, 1990. Recipient Alumni Achievement award Knox Coll., 1990, 8 other awards. Mem. Nat. Assn. Radio Talk Show Hosts, U. Chgo. Puget Sound Alumni Club (bd. dirs. 1982-86), Knox Coll. Alumni Network. Office: Exec Directions Internat Inc 3313 39th Ave W Seattle WA 98199-2530

CULPEPPER, ROBERT SAMMON, retired investment executive; b. Farmington, N.Mex., Aug. 23, 1927; s. Charles C. Culpepper and Ethelwyn (Hart) Sammon; m. Mary Eleanor Hancock, Nov. 14, 1953; children: Charles, Mary, Robert. BS, N.M. A&M, 1951. Entomologist Edmunds Chem., Albuquerque, 1951-54; v.p. ins. Farmington Investment, 1954-72; pres., owner Culpepper Ins., Farmington, 1972-88; ptnr. C-P-N Ins., Farmington, 1988-90; cons. Wolcott Investment Co., Farmington, 1990-91; ret., 1991; vice chmn. bd. First Nat. Bank, Farmington, 1982—. Councilman City of Farmington, 1970-78, mayor, 1978-82; trustee N.M. Mus. Nat. Hist., Albuquerque, 1991—; mem. N.Mex. Arts Com., 1970-82; vice chmn. Farmington Pub. Utility Commn., Farmington, 1984—; dir., past pres. San Juan Coll. Found., 1984—; past pres., life mem. N.M. Mcpl. League, Santa Fe. Mem. N.M. Inst. Agts. (past pres.), Elks (past pres.), Lions, Rotary. Democrat. Episcopalian. Home: 5703 Woodland Ct Farmington NM 87402-4832

CULTON, PAUL MELVIN, therapist, educator, interpreter; b. Council Bluffs, Iowa, Feb. 12, 1932; s. Paul Roland and Hallie Ethel Emma (Paschal) C. BA, Minn. Bible Coll., 1955; BS, U. Nebr., 1965; MA, Calif. State U., Northridge, 1970; EdD, Brigham Young U., 1981. Cert. tchr., Iowa. Tchr. Iowa Sch. for Deaf, Council Bluffs, 1956-70; ednl. specialist Golden West Coll., Huntington Beach, Calif., 1970-71, dir. disabled students, 1971-82, instr., 1982-88; counselor El Camino Coll., Via Torrance, Calif., 1990-93, acting assoc. dean, 1993—; interpreter various state and fed. cts., Iowa, Calif., 1960-90; asst. prof. Calif. State U., Northridge, Fresno & Dominguez Hills, 1973, 76, 80, 87-90; vis. prof. u. Guam, Agana, 1977; mem. allocations task force, task force on deafness, trainer handicapped students Calif. Community Colls., 1971-81. Editor: Region IX Conf. for Coordinating Rehab. and Edn. Svcs. for Deaf proceedings, 1970, Toward Rehab. Involvement by Parents of Deaf conf. proceedings, 1971; composer Carry the Light, 1986. Bd. dirs. Iowa NAACP, 1966-68, Gay and Lesbian Community Svcs. Ctr., Orange County, Calif., 1975-77; founding sec. Dayle McIntosh Ctr. for Disabled, Anaheim and Garden Grove, Calif., 1974-80; active Dem. Cent. Com. Pottawattamie County, Council Bluffs, 1960-70. League for Innovation in Community Coll. fellow, 1974. Mem. Registry of Interpreters for Deaf, Congress Am. Instrs. Deaf, Am. Deafness and Rehab. Assn., Calif. Assn. Postsecondary Educators Disabled, Am. Fedn. Tchrs., Nat. Assn. Deaf. Home: 2567 Plaza Del Amo 203 Torrance CA 90503-7327 Office: El Camino Coll Spl Resource Ctr 16007 Crenshaw Blvd Torrance CA 90506-0001

CUMMINGS, BARTON, musician; b. Newport, N.H., July 10, 1946; s. C. Barton and Ruth (Ricard) C.; m. Florecita L. Lim, July 23, 1983;. BS in Music Edn., U. N.H., 1968; MusM, Ball State U., Muncie, Ind., 1973. Dir. music Alton (N.H.) Pub. Sch., 1971-72; lectr. San Diego State U., 1974-79; instr. music Point Loma Coll., San Diego, 1976-79; instr. San Diego Community Coll. Dist., 1977-79, Delta State U., Cleveland, Miss., 1979-82; supr. Clarksdale Separate Sch. Dist., 1982-84; dir. music Walnut (Calif.) Creek Concert Band, 1985—, Richmond Unified Sch. Dist., 1988—, Golden Hills Concert Band, 1990—; condr. Devil Mountain Symphony, 1991—; tuba player Vallejo Symphony Orch., 1988—, Concord Pavilion Pops Orch., 1985—, Brassworks of San Francisco, 1985—, Solano Dixie Jubilee. Author: The Contemporary Tuba, 1984, The Tuba Guide, 1989, Teaching Techniques for Brass Instruments, 1989; composer over two dozen pub. compositions; recorded on Capra, Coronet and Crystal labels. Mem. ASCAP, NACUSA, T.U.B.A., Am. Fedn. of Musicians, Conductor's Guild, Phi Mu Alpha Sinfonia. Home: 550 Cambridge Dr Benicia CA 94510-1316

CUMMINGS, DANIEL O'DONNELL, computer software company executive; b. Tacoma, Feb. 23, 1954; s. Donald Frances and Dorothy Ann (O'Donnell) C.; m. Diane Louise Ritter, June 1979 (div. June 1982); m. Meredith Lynn Phelps, July 23, 1983; 1 child, Sarah Emelissa. BS in Pharmacy, U. Wash., 1978, postgrad., 1980-82. Pharmacist St. Joseph Hosp. Pharmacy, Tacoma, 1978-80; systems analyst U. Wash., Seattle, 1980-82; Boeing analyst-in-charge Cray Rsch. Inc., Seattle, 1982-83; NASA analyst-in-charge Cray Rsch. Inc., Mountainview, Calif., 1983-84; mgr. IOS software Cray Rsch. Inc., Mendota Hts., Minn., 1984-89; strategic mgr. tech. planning Cray Rsch. Inc., Mpls., 1987-88; software architect Tera COmputer Co., Seattle, 1988-90; pres. The Cummings Group, Seattle, 1990—; cons. in field. V.p. Vashon Food Bank, 1992—. Rsch. grantee NSF, 1977. Mem. IEEE, Acad. Computing Machinery, Kiwanis. Office: The Cummings Group 1008 Western Ave Ste 307 Seattle WA 98104

CUMMINGS, DAROLD BERNARD, aircraft engineer; b. Batavia, N.Y., June 27, 1944; s. Bernard Laverne and Doris Helen (Klotzbach) C.; children from a previous marriage: Carla, Bret; m. Karen Jean Cacciola, Dec. 19, 1992. BS in Indsl. Design, Calif. State U., Long Beach, 1967. Engr. aircraft design Rockwell Internat., Los Angeles, 1967-82; chief engr. trainer aircraft Rockwell Internat., El Segundo, Calif., 1988—; chief designer advanced design Northrop Corp., Hawthorne, Calif., 1982-88; lectr. Calif. State U., Long Beach, 1969-73; pres. Matrix Design, Hawthorne, 1967—. Author: What Not to Name Your Baby, 1982; cons., actor movie Search for Solutions, 1979. Advisor aero engrng. dept. Calif. Polytech. Coll., Pomona, 1985—. Mem. Air Force Assn. Republican. Home: 5320 W 124th Pl Hawthorne CA 90250-4154 Office: Rockwell Internat El Segundo CA 90245

CUMMINGS, DAVID, geophysicist, engineering geologist; b. N.Y.C., Feb. 11, 1932. BS, CCNY, 1957; MS, U. Tenn., 1959; PhD, Mich. State U., 1962. Registered geologist, geophysicist, engrng. geologist. Engrng. geologist U.S. Geol. Survey, Denver, and Flagstaff, Ariz., 1962-67, Dames & Moore, L.A., 1973-74; pres., chief exec. officer Ryland-Cummings Inc., Pasadena, Calif., 1979-83; dir. geophysics div. Leighton & Assocs., Inc., Irvine, Calif., 1985-88; sr. geophysicist SAIC, Denver, 1988—; assoc. prof. Occidental Coll., L.A., 1967-85. Author: Environmental Geology, 1983; contbr. numerous articles to profl. jours. With U.S. Army, 1953-55. Fellow Geol. Soc. Am., Am. Geophys. Union, Assn. of Engrng. Geologists, Am. Assn. Petroleum Geologists, Am. Inst. Profl. Geologists. Office: SAIC 14062 Denver West Pky # 255 Golden CO 80401-3121

CUMMINGS, D(ONALD) W(AYNE), English language educator, dean; b. Seattle, May 21, 1935; s. Oliver Warren Cummings and Mildred Marie (Thayer) Smith; m. Carol Frances Feuling, Aug. 10, 1956; children: Daniel, Lon, Jody. BA in English, U. Washington, 1958, MA in English, 1964, Phd in English, 1965. Instr. English Ctrl. Wash. U., Ellensburg, 1989-93; asst. prof. English Cen. Wash. U., Ellensburg, 1964-66, assoc. prof. English, 1966-71, prof. English, 1971—, dir. acad. skills ctr., 1966-90, chair English dept., 1984-87, dean coll. of letters, arts and scis., 1989—; tchr. English Newport High Sch., Bellevue, Washington, 1971-72. Co-author: (with J. Herum) Writing, Plans, Drafts, Revisions, 1971; co-author, editor Tempo: Life,

Work, and Leisure, 1973; author Basic Speller for Older Students, 1988, American English Spelling, 1988. Home: 2313 Hannah Rd Ellensburg WA 98926-9402 Office: Ctrl Wash U Dept English Coll Letters Arts/Sci Ellensburg WA 98926

CUMMINGS, GREGG ALEX, civil engineer; b. Oakland, Calif., May 18, 1963; s. Garth Ellis and Shirley Elaine (Wolfe) C.; m. Donna Marie Cavalieri, May 24, 1986. BCE, U. Calif., Berkeley, 1985; MCE, San Jose State U., 1989. Registered profl. engr., Calif. Staff engr. Metcalf & Eddy, Palo Alto, Calif., 1986-89; project engr. Dames & Moore, San Francisco, 1989—. Mem. ASCE, Am. Pub. Works Assn., Water Pollution Control Fedn., Chi Epsilon. Home: 53 Gladys St San Francisco CA 94110-5427

CUMMINGS, NICHOLAS ANDREW, psychologist; b. Salinas, Calif., July 25, 1924; s. Andrew and Urania (Sims) C.; m. Dorothy Mills, Feb. 5, 1948; children—Janet Lynn, Andrew Mark. AB, U. Calif., Berkeley, 1948; MA, Claremont Grad. Sch., 1954; PhD, Adelphi U., 1958. Chief psychologist Kaiser Permanente No. Calif., San Francisco, 1959-76; pres. Found Behavioral Health, San Francisco, 1976—; chmn., chief exec. officer Am. Biodyne, Inc., San Francisco, 1985-93; chmn., CEO Kendron Internat., Ltd., Reno, Nev., 1993—, Reno, 1992—; co-dir. South San Francisco Health Ctr., 1959-75; pres. Calif. Sch. Profl. Psychology, Los Angeles, San Francisco, San Diego, Fresno campuses, 1969-76; chmn. bd. Calif. Community Mental Health Ctrs., Inc., Los Angeles, San Diego, San Francisco, 1975-77; pres. Blue Psi, Inc., San Francisco, 1972-80, Inst. for Psychosocial Interaction, 1980-84; mem. mental health adv. bd. City and County San Francisco, 1968-75; bd. dirs. San Francisco Assn. Mental Health, 1965-75; pres., chmn. bd. Psycho-Social Inst., 1972-80; dir. Mental Rsch. Inst., Palo Alto, Calif., 1979-80; pres. Nat. Acads. of Practice, 1981-93. Served with U.S. Army, 1944-46. Fellow Am. Psychol. Assn. (dir. 1975-81, pres. 1979); mem. Calif. Psychol. Assn. (pres. 1968). Office: Kendron Internat Ltd 561 Keystone Ave Ste 212 Reno NV 89503

CUMMINGS, ROGER DAVID, power coatings consultant, sales executive; b. Topeka, May 7, 1944; s. Edwin David and Genevieve Mildred (Russell) C.; m. Helen Spidell, Nov. 30, 1963; children: Kenneth David, Keith Roger, Kevin Daniel. BA in Math., Washburn U., 1967. Indsl. engr. Kaiser Steel, Fontana, Calif., 1967-71; shift supt. Jeffco Mfg., Golden, Colo., 1971-72; shift supr. Ball Metal Cont., Williamsburg, Va., 1972-74; gen. foreman, asst. plant mgr. Nat. Can, Millis, Mass., 1974-75, Hoover-Ugine, Bridgeman, Mich., 1975-77; prodn. supt. Armstrong Products, Warsaw, Ind., 1977-78; mgr. tech. svc. Morton Power Coating, Warsaw, 1978-85, devel. sales specialist, 1985-90; cons. Power Coating Techniques, Davis, Calif., 1990-93; area sales mgr. H.B. Fuller Co., Vadnais Heights, Minn., 1993—. Co-author: User's Guide to Powder Coating, 1985. Mem. Powder Coating Inst., Chem. Coaters Assn., Am. Consultants League, Assn. Finishing Processes of the Soc. Mfg. Engrs. (com. mem. 1983-85). Republican. Presbyterian. Home: 4036 El Macero Dr Davis CA 95616 Office: H B Fuller Co 3200 Labore Rd White Bear Lake MN 55110

CUMMINGS, RUSSELL MARK, aerospace engineer, educator; b. Santa Cruz, Calif., Oct. 3, 1955; s. Gilbert Warren and Anna Mae (Phillips) C.; m. Cherilyn Suzanne Parsons, Mar. 25, 1985 (div. 1990). BS, Calif. Poly. State U., 1977, MS, 1985; PhD, U. So. Calif., 1988. Mem. tech. staff Hughes Aircraft Co., Canoga Park, Calif., 1979-86; prof., chmn. Calif. Poly. State U., San Luis Obispo, 1986-91; prof. aerospace engring. Calif. Poly. State U., San Luis Obispo, Calif., 1991—; dept. chmn. aero. engring. dept. Calif. Poly. State U., 1992—; cons. Steiner and Assocs., San Luis Obispo, 1989-90. Contbr. chpt. to book: Numerical and Physical Aspects of Aerodynamic Flows, 1990; contbr. articles to profl. jours. Asst. scoutmaster Boy Scouts Am., San Luis Obispo, 1978-79. Howard Hughes fellow, 1984, Hughes Engring. fellow, 1980; NASA grantee, 1986-93; named Eagle Scout Boy Scouts Am., 1970; recipient Group Achievement awards NASA, 1989, 90. Fellow AIAA (assoc.); mem. Am. Soc. Engring. Educators, Sigma Xi, Sigma Gamma Tau. Republican. Mem. Evangelical Christian Ch. Office: Calif Poly State U Dept Aero Engring San Luis Obispo CA 93407

CUMMINGS, SPANGLER (MELINDA JOHNSON), art dealer, artist; b. L.A., Dec. 27, 1936; d. Clyde Lewis and Lena Glyde (Spangler) Cummings; m. Richard Johnson, Nov. 25, 1955; children: Edward, Jeanne, Lisa. BA, Chatham Coll., Pitts., 1978; postgrad., Carnegie-Mellon U., Pitts., 1979-80. Founding pres., dir. Artists in Action, Pitts., 1981-82; founder, owner, operator Spangler Cummings Galleries, Columbus, Ohio, 1985-87; owner Spangler Cummings-Twentieth Century Art, Malibu, Calif., 1989—. Community rep. Artist/Lecture Series Cypress, Calif., 1973; mem. exec. bd. Three Rivers Art Festival Pitts., 1980; docent Columbus Mus. Art, 1985-87; docent Mus. Contemporary Art, L.A., 1989, mem. curator's coun., 1990-93. Named Best of Show by Cypress Cultural Arts Assn., 1967; finalist Internat. Soc. Artists, N.Y.C., 1979. Mem. SAG, So. Calif. Community Artists (pres. 1972-73); charter mem. Internat. Soc. Artists; assoc. mem. Am. Watercolor Soc.; mem. Pitts. Soc. Artists (bd. dirs. 1980-81); Columbus Art League (bd. dirs. 1983-85). Democrat. Home and Office: 11926 White Water Ln Malibu CA 90265-9724

CUMMINS, CHARLES FITCH, JR., lawyer; b. Lansing, Mich., Aug. 19, 1939; s. Charles F. Sr. and Ruth M. Cummins; m. Anne Warner, Feb. 11, 1961; children: Michael, John, Mark. AB in Econs., U. Mich., 1961; LLB, U. Calif., Hastings, 1966. Bar: Calif. 1966, Mich. 1976. Assoc. Hall, Henry, Oliver & McReavy, San Francisco, 1966-70, 1971-75; ptnr. Cummins & Cummins, Lansing, Mich., 1976-82, Pitto & Ubhaus, San Jose, Calif., 1982-85; prin. Law Offices Charles F. Cummins Jr., San Jose, 1985-87; ptnr. Cummins & Chandler, San Jose, 1987-92; prin. Law Offices of Charles F. Cummins, Jr., San Jose, 1992—. Bd. dirs., officer various civic orgns., chs. and pvt. schs. Lt. USNR, 1961-63. Mem. Kiwanis. Office: Law Offices of Charles F Cummins Jr 4 N 2nd St Ste 1230 San Jose CA 95113-1307

CUMMINS, JOHN STEPHEN, bishop; b. Oakland, Calif., Mar. 3, 1928; s. Michael and Mary (Connolly) C. A.B., St. Patrick's Coll., 1949. Ordained priest Roman Catholic Ch., 1953; asst. pastor Mission Dolores Ch., San Francisco, 1953-57; mem. faculty Bishop O'Dowd High Sch., Oakland, 1957-62; chancellor Diocese of Oakland, 1962-71; rev. monsignor, 1962, domestic prelate, 1967; exec. dir. Calif. Cath. Conf., Sacramento, 1971-77; consecrated bishop, 1974; aux. bishop of Sacramento, 1974-77; bishop of Oakland, 1977—; Campus minister San Francisco State Coll., 1953-57, Mills Coll., Oakland, 1957-71; Trustee St. Mary's Coll., 1968-79. Home: 634 21st St Oakland CA 94612-1691 Office: Oakland Diocese 2900 Lakeshore Ave Oakland CA 94610-3697*

CUMMINS, NANCYELLEN HECKEROTH, electronics engineer; b. Long Beach, Calif., May 22, 1948; d. George and Ruth May (Anderson) Heckeroth; m. Weldon Jay, Sept. 15, 1987; stepchildren: Tracy Lynn, John Scott, Darren Elliott. Student avionics, USMC, Memphis, 1966-67. Tech. publ. engr. Lockheed Missile and Space Div., Sunnyvale, Calif., 1973-76, engring. instr., 1977; test engr. Gen. Dynamics, Pomona, Calif., 1980-83; quality assurance test engr. Interstate Electronics Co., Anaheim, Calif., 1983-84; quality engr., certification engr. Rockwell Internat., Anaheim, 1985-86; sr. quality assurance programmer Point 4 Data, Tustin, Calif., 1986-87; software quality assurance specialist Lawrence Livermore Nat. Lab., Yucca Mountain Project, Livermore, Calif., 1987-89, software quality mgr., 1989-90; sr. constrn. insp. EG&G Rocky Flats, Inc., Golden, Colo., 1990, sr. quality assurance engr., 1991, engr. IV software quality assurance, 1991-92, instr., developer environ. law and compliance, 1992—; customer engr. IBM Gen. Systems, Orange, Calif., 1979; electronics engr. LDS Ch. Exhibits Div., Salt Lake City, 1978; electronics repair specialist Weber State Coll., 1977-78. Author: Package Area Test Set, 6 vols., 1975, Software Quality Assurance Plan, 1989. Vol., instr. San Fernando (Calif.) Search and Rescue Team, 1967-70; instr. emergency preparedness and survival, Clairmont, Calif., 1982-84, Modesto, Calif., 1989; mem. Lawrence Livermore Nat. Lab. Employees Emergency Vols., 1987-90, EG&G Rocky Flats Bldg. Emergency Support Team, 1990—. Mem. NAFE, NRA, Nat. Muzzle Loading Rifle Assn., Am. Soc. Quality Control, Job's Daus. (majority mem.). Republican. Mem. LDS Ch. Home: PO Box 334 2282 Country Rd Jamestown CO 80455-0334 Office: EG&G Rocky Flats Inc PO Box 464 Golden CO 80402-0464

CUNDALL, KATHLEEN FOY, drug and alcohol counselor; b. Douglas, Wyo., Aug. 6, 1948; d. Leo John and Anne Theresa (Egging) Foy; m. Richard Dan Cundall, Dec. 27, 1967; children: Shane Patrick, Danielle JoAnn. AS, Front Range Community Coll., Westminster, Colo., 1989; BS Human Svcs. magna cum laude, Met. State Coll., 1990-92. Sec., receptionist Rural Electric Co., Wheatland, Wyo., 1970-71, billing clk., 1971-72; seamstress Powderhorn Mountaineering, Jackson, Wyo., 1974-76, Bananna Equipment, Estes Park, Colo., 1977-79; pvt. practice upholstery bus. Pinewood Springs, Colo., 1979-86; head seamstress Latok Mountaineer, Lyons, Colo., 1986-88; on-call attendant counselor Boulder County Dept. Health, Boulder, Colo., 1988-89, attendant counselor, 1989-90. Coord. Chem. People Task Force (Drug and Alcohol), Estes Park, 1983-86, Estes Park Hotline, 1984-87; vol. Pinewood Springs VFD, 1984-91, Alcohol Recovery Ctr., Boulder, 1985-88; sponsor Mid. Sch. Just Say No Club, Estes Park, 1989. Met. State Coll. Presdl. scholar, 1990, Colo. scholar Front Range Community Coll., 1987-89. Mem. Human Svc. Edn. Orgn., Golden Key Nat. Honor Soc., Phi Theta Kappa, Alpha Delta Omega. Democrat. Roman Catholic.

CUNEO, DENNIS CLIFFORD, lawyer, corporate executive; b. Ridgway, Pa., Jan. 12, 1950; s. Clifford Francis and Erma Theresa (Nissel) C.; m. Bonnie Frances Mish, Aug. 18, 1972; children: Corinne, Kyle, James. BS, Gannon U., 1971; MBA, Kent State U., 1973; JD, Loyola U., New Orleans, 1976. Bar: D.C. 1977. Trial atty. U.S. Dept. Justice, Washington, 1976-80; assoc. Arent, Fox, Kintner, Plotkin & Kahn, Washington, 1980-84; gen. counsel New United Motor Mfg. Inc. joint venture GM-Toyota, Fremont, Calif., 1984-88, v.p. legal and govt. affairs, 1988-90, v.p. corp. planning and legal affairs, 1990-92, v.p. corp. planning and external affairs, 1992—; chmn. New United Motors Pub. Policy Com., Fremont, 1986—; chmn. New United Motors Strategic Bus. Com., 1988—; chmn. Calif. Workside Rsch. Com., Sacramento, 1988—; lectr. exec. program U. Calif., Davis, 1988—; lectr. orientation in Am. law program U. Calif., 1990—; campaign chmn. United Way, Alameda County, 1993. Vice chmn. Alameda County Econ. Devel. Bd., Oakland, 1990—; bd. visitors Loyola Law Sch., 1987—; sec.-treas. Moraga-Orinda-Lafayette Football League, Moraga, Calif., 1989—; bd. dirs. Californians for Compensation Reform, Sacramento, 1988—, mem. select com. on jud. retirement, 1993; mem. steering com. Bay Area Coun. San Francisco, 1990—; mem. environ. rev. com. Town of Moraga, 1991-93; mem. steering com. Bay Area Dredging Coalition, San Francisco, 1991—. Mem. ABA, Am. Corp. Counsel Assn. (select com. judicial retirement 1993), Calif. Mfrs. Assn. (bd. dirs. 1993—). Office: New United Motor Mfg Inc 45500 Fremont Blvd Fremont CA 94538-6368

CUNNANE, PATRICIA S., medical facility administrator; b. Clinton, Iowa, Sept. 7, 1946; d. Cyril J. and Corinne Spain; m. Edward J. Cunnane, June 19, 1971. AA, Mt. St. Clare Coll., Clinton, Iowa, 1966. Mgr. Eye Med. Clinic of Santa Clara Valley, San Jose, Calif. Mem. Med. Adminstrs. Calif. Polit. Action Com., San Francisco, 1987. Mem. Med. Group Mgmt. Assn., Am. Coll. Med. Group Adminstrs. (nominee), Nat. Notary Assn., NAFE, Exec. Women Internat. (v.p. 1986-87, pres. 1987—), Profl. Secs. Internat. (sec. 1979-80), Am. Soc. Ophthalmic Adminstrs., Women Health Care Execs., Healthcare Human Resource Mgmt. Assn. Calif. Roman Catholic. Home: 232 Tolin Ct San Jose CA 95139-1445 Office: Eye Med Clinic of Santa Clara Valley 220 Meridian Ave San Jose CA 95126-2903

CUNNINGHAM, PAUL BERNARD, strategic planner, researcher; b. San Fancisco, Jan. 10, 1943; s. Forrest Eugene and Lois Berdeen (Caster) C.; m. Patricia Lynn Jewett, Oct. 21, 1971; children: Erin, Dara. BS, Humbolt State U., 1970; MS, Calif. State U., Arcata, 1979. Research biologist Alaska Dept. Fish and Game, King Salmon, 1971-73; arctic area biologist Alaska Dept. Fish and Game, Nome, 1973-76; dep. dir. Alaska Dept. Fish and Game, Juneau, 1979-81; mgmt. biologist Quinault Indian Nation, Taholah, Wash., 1978; planner, demographer Alaska Dept. Community and Regional Affairs, Juneau, 1981-91; ret., 1991. Chmn. Luth. Ch. council, Juneau, 1983-86, mem. adv. com. City of Nome, 1974-76; mem. Iditarod Trail Race Com., Nome, 1973-76. Served with U.S. Army, 1961-64, Korea. Mem. AAAS, Alaska Assn. for Advancement of Sci. and Engring., Am. Planning Assn., Am. Fisheries Soc., Appraisers and Measures Soc. (charter). Lutheran.

CUNNINGHAM, RANDY, congressman; b. L.A., Dec. 8, 1941; m. Nancy Jones; 3 children. BA, U. Mo., MA; MBA, Nat. U. Mem. 102nd-103rd Congresses from Calif. dist. 44 (now 51), 1991—; mem. armed svcs. com., mem. edn. and labor com., mem. merchant marine and fisheries com. Republican. Baptist. Office: US House of Representatives 117 Canon Washington DC 20515-0551*

CUNNINGHAM, ROBERT STEPHEN, computer science educator, writer, consultant; b. Springfield, Mo., June 28, 1942; s. Robert Cyril and Helen Marian (Platte) C.; m. Ruth Ann Pyle, Jan. 25, 1964; children: Robert Andrew, Richard Stephen. BA, Drury Coll., 1964; MA, U. Oreg., 1966, PhD, 1969; MS, Oreg. State U., 1982. Asst. prof. math. U. Kans., Lawrence, 1969-74; assoc. prof. computer sci. Birmingham (Ala.)-So. Coll., 1974-82; prof. computer sci. Calif. State U. Stanislaus, Turlock, 1982—; conf. co-chair Internat. Fedn. for Info. Processing, 1991. Author: Programming the User Interface, 1989; editor: Visualization in Teaching and Learning Mathematics, 1991, Computer Graphics Using Object-Oriented Programming, 1991, Interactive Learning Through Visualization, 1992; contbr. articles to profl. jours. Recipient traineeship NSF, 1969, Instructional Sci. Improvement grant, 1976, Local Course Improvement grant, 1978, Sci. Faculty Profl. Devel. grant, 1980, Instructional Lab. Improvement grant, 1987. Mem. Computer Soc. of IEEE, Eurographics, Math. Assn. Am. (bd. govs. Washington 1990—), Assn. Computing Machinery, Spl. Interest Group for Graphics of Assn. Computing Machinery (edn. com. chair 1984-90, educators' program chair 1991, dir. for publs., bd. dirs. 1991—), Spl. Interest Group for Computer Sci. Edn. (bd. dirs. 1991-93). Office: Calif State U Stanislaus 801 W Monte Vista Ave Turlock CA 95380-0299

CUNNINGHAM, ROGER ALAN, meteorologist; b. Fresno, Calif., May 1, 1951; s. Albert William and Marjorie Alice (Harrison) C. AB, U. Calif., Berkeley, 1973, MBA, 1980. Climatologist Vallejo, Calif., 1974-78, Golden West Meteorology, Vallejo, Florence, Oreg., 1978—; weather observer Nat. Weather Svc., Eugene, Oreg., 1992—, Redwood City, Calif., 1983-92. Contbr. articles to profl. jours. Mem. Am. Meteorol. Assn., Assn. Am. Weather Observers, Skywatchers Club Calif., Phi Beta Kappa. Republican. Home and Office: 240 Munsel Creek Loop Florence OR 97439

CUNTZ, MANFRED ADOLF, astrophysicist, researcher; b. Landau, Rheinland-Pfalz, Fed. Republic of Germany, Apr. 21, 1958; came to U.S., 1988; s. Gerhard Hermann and Irene Emma (Messerschmitt) C.; m. Anne-Gret Vera Friedrich, Sept. 19, 1988; 1 child, Heiko Benjamin. Diplom in Physics, U. Heidelberg, Fed. Republic of Germany, 1985, PhD in Astronomy, 1988. Postdoctoral, rsch. assoc. Joint Inst. Lab. Astrophysics-U. Colo., Boulder, 1989-91; postdoctoral, rsch. assoc. High Altitude Obs. div. Nat. Ctr. Atmospheric Rsch., Boulder, 1992—. Contbr. articles to Astrophys. Jour., Astronom. Jour., Astronomy and Astrophysics. Grantee German Rsch. Found., NASA, NSF, Dutch Nat. Sci. Orgn. Mem. Internat. Astron. Union (com. 36), Am. Astron. Soc., Deutsche Astronomische Gesellschaft, Deutsche Physikalische Gesellschaft, Vereinigung der Sternfreunde. Office: High Altitude Obs 3450 Mitchell Ln Boulder CO 80301

CUPERY, ROBERT RINK, manufacturing executive; b. Beaver Dam, Wis., Apr. 5, 1944; s. Rink Eli and Ruby Elizabeth (Haima) C.; m. Kathleen Gonzalez. Airframe and Powerplant, Northrop U., 1967; BSBA, U. Redlands, 1978. Aircraft mechanic Northwest Airlines, Mpls., 1968-69; corp. flight engr. Northrop Corp., Hawthorne, Calif., 1969-76, engr., 1976-79, sr. staff customer relations, 1979-82, internat. quality mgr., 1982-84; pres., chief exec. officer Aircraft Window Repairs, Torrance, Calif., 1984—, Cupery Corp., Torrance, Calif.; bd. advisers Northrop Rice Aviation Sch., 1992; lectr. throughout U.S. and Europe, 1986, 89, 90. Contbr. articles to profl. jours. Served as staff sgt. USAF, 1962-66. Mem. Profl. Aviation Maintenance Assn. (corp.), Can. Aviation Mech. Engring., Nat. Bus. Aircraft Assn., Aero Club So. Calif. (bd. dirs. 1992). Republican.

CURCIO, CHRISTOPHER FRANK, city official; b. Oakland, Calif., Feb. 3, 1950; s. Frank William and Virginie Theresa (Le Gris) C. BA in Speech/Drama, Calif. State U., Hayward, 1971; MBA in Arts Adminstrn., UCLA, 1974; MPA in Pub. Policy, Ariz. State U., 1982. Intern John F. Kennedy Ctr. for Arts, Washington, 1973; gen. mgr. Old Eagle Theatre, Sacramento, 1974-75; cultural arts supr. Fresno (Calif.) Parks and Recreation Dept., 1975-79; supr. cultural and spl. events Phoenix Parks, Recreation and Libr. Dept., 1979-87, budget analyst, 1987, mgmt. svcs. adminstr., 1987—; mgmt. and budget analyst City of Phoenix, 1985, grants panelist Phoenix Arts Comm., 1987, Ariz. Commn. on Arts, 1987-88; voter Zony Theatre Awards, 1991—; freelance theater critic, 1987-89. Active Valley Leadership Program, Phoenix, 1987—, Valley Big Bros./Big Sisters, 1980—; chair allocation panel United Way, 1990-92; sec. Los Olivos Townhome Assn., Phoenix, 1986-92. Mem. Am. Soc. Pub. Adminstrn., Nat. Recreation and Park Assn., Am. Theatre Critics Assn., Ariz. Park and Recreation Assn., Herberger Theater Ctr. Assocs., Rosson House-Heritage Square Found. Republican. Office: Phoenix Dept Parks Recreation & Libr 2333 N Central Ave Phoenix AZ 85004-1324

CURD, JOHN GARY, physician, scientist; b. Grand Junction, Colo., July 2, 1945; s. H. Ronald and Edna (Hegested) C.; m. Karen Wendel, June 12, 1971; children: Alison, Jonathan, Edward, Bethany. BA, Princeton U., 1967; MD, Harvard U., 1971. Diplomate Am. Bd. Internal Medicine, Am. Bd. Rheumatology, Am. Bd. Allergy and Immunology. Rsch. assoc. NIH, Bethesda, Md., 1973-75; fellow in rheumatology U. Calif., San Diego, 1975-77; fellow in allergy-immunology Scripps Clinic, La Jolla, Calif., 1977-78, asst. mem. rsch. inst., 1978-81, mem. div. rheumatology, 1981-91, head div. rheumatology, vice chmn. dept. medicine, 1989-91; pres. med. staff Green Hosp., La Jolla, 1988-90; clin. dir. Genentech Inc., South San Francisco, Calif., 1991—. Author numerous. sci. papers in field. Med. dir. San Diego Scleroderma Found., 1983-91; sec. San Diego Arthritis Found., 1986-87. Lt. comdr. USPHS, 1973-75. Mem. Princeton Club No. Calif. Republican. Home: 128 Reservoir Rd Hillsborough CA 94010 Office: Genentech Inc 460 Point San Bruno Blvd South San Francisco CA 94080

CURETON, BENJAMIN, JR., landscape architect; b. Vallejo, Calif., July 13, 1947; s. Benjamin Sr. and Jeanette (Singer) C. AS, Vallejo Community Coll., 1968. With Janitorial Svcs., Fairfield, Calif., 1962-65, Comml. Lawn Svc., Pasadena, Calif., 1965-67, Ben Cureton Lawn Svc., 1969-81, Met. Home Design Inc., Vallejo, Calif., 1982—; decorator, painter, interior designer Vallejo, 1982—; musician, Vallejo, 1972—. Mem. NAACP, Vallejo, 1980, Rep. Nat. Com., Washington, 1987, Global Exch., San Francisco, 1988, Overseas Devel. Network, San Francisco, 1989. Fellow Am. Poetry Assn., Am.'s Best and Brightest Young Business Men, Vallejo C. of C., L.A. Links, Golfer's Getaway Club, El Segundo (Calif.) Key Club. Baptist. Home: 336 Phelan Ave Vallejo CA 94590-6461

CURLEE, RICHARD FREDERICK, speech and hearing sciences educator, consultant; b. Charlotte, N.C., July 21, 1935; s. Fred H. and Wilma Eve (Ferris) C.; m. Dorsia Jenrose Hodge, June 1, 1958. BA, Wake Forest Coll., 1961; MA, U. So. Calif., 1965, PhD, 1967. Cert. of clin. competence in speech-lang. pathology. Adj. asst. prof. U. So. Calif., L.A., 1967-71; assoc. sec. for rsch. and sci. affairs Am. Speech-Lang. Hearing Assn., Bethesda, Md., 1971-75; assoc. prof. speech and hearing scis. U. Ariz., Tucson, 1975-80, prof., 1980—, assoc. dean Grad. Coll., 1984-87; editor-in-chief Seminars in Speech and Lang., Thieme Med. Pubs., N.Y.C., 1991—; sr. scientist Bahill Intelligent Computer Systems, Inc., Tucson, 1989—; editorial cons. Jour. Speech and Hearing Rsch., 1981-92, Jour. Fluency Disorders, 1989—. Author, editor: Stuttering and Related Disorders of Fluency, 1992; co-editor Nature and Treatment of Stuttering, 1984; contbr. chpts. to books, articles to profl. jours. Bd. dirs. Disability Resource Ctr. of Tucson, 1988-92, pres., 1990. Fellow Am. Speech-Lang. Hearing Assn.; mem. Ariz. Speech and Hearing Assn. (pres. 1978-89, honors 1980), Internat. Fluency Assn., Phi Beta Kappa, Sigma Xi, Phi Kappa Phi. Office: U Ariz Dept Speech and Hearing Sci Tucson AZ 85721

CURLEY, JACK R., foundation administrator; b. San Francisco, May 12, 1928; s. Clyde J. and Mary Margaret (Lamb) C.; m. Norma Jeanne Elkington, Dec. 8, 1949 (div. June 1977); children: Jean Catherine, John Richard, James Norman, Janis Margaret; m. Elva Emily Bennetts, Feb. 29, 1980; stepchildren: Elva Doris Harding, Bradley Miles Harding, Edward James Harding. BS, U. Calif., 1949; postgrad., Mpls.-Minn. Coll. Law, 1955-57; cert. of grad., UCLA Grad. Sch. Bus. Exec. Program, 1968. Budget and control mgr. Montgomery Ward & Co., Oakland, Calif. and Chgo., 1949-54; rsch. sec. Mpls. Star & Tribune Co., Mpls., 1954-57; asst. contr. Pacific Sci. Co., San Francisco, 1957-60; contr. E-H Rsch. Labs., Oakland, 1960; v.p., gen. mgr. San Fernando Valley Times, North Hollywood, Calif., 1960-64, Orange Coast Daily Pilot, Costa Mesa-Newport Beach, Calif., 1964-81; exec. officer Pacific Area Newspaper Pubs. Assoc., Melbourne, Australia, 1981-82; owner, developer Pier 31 Warehouse Self-Storage, San Francisco, 1982—; treas., chief fin. officer Koret Found., San Francisco, 1985—; founder, vice chmn. bd. Citizens Bank Costa Mesa, 1971-74. First pres. Harbor Area United Way, Newport Beach-Costa Mesa, 1971-72. Lt. U.S. Army, 1952-54. Mem. Calif. Newspaper Pubs. Assn. (sec. Orange County unit), Preeminent Albert's Field Internat. Tennis Club, Mala Lahaina Boat Club (vice-commodore). Home: 5 Lido Ln San Rafael CA 94901-4311 Office: Koret Found 33 New Montgomery St Ste 1090 San Francisco CA 94105-4509

CURLEY, JONATHAN EDWARD, small business owner; b. Atlanta, Sept. 10, 1953; s. Paul David and Margaret (Bryne) C.; m. Laura Ann Lay, June 20, 1975(div. Aug. 1985); m. Jo Ann Moran, Aug. 25, 1985; child, Kevin Francis. BA, Coll. the Holy Cross, Worcester, Mass., 1975; postgrad., Clark U., 1977-78. CLU; Chartered fin. cons. Sales mgr. Paul Revere Life Ins. Co., Worcester, Mass., 1975-81; pres. Jonathan E. Curley Inc., Hudson, Mass., 1981-82; tng. dir. The New Eng., Boston, 1982-83; sales mgr. The New Eng., Seattle, 1983-86, gen. agent, 1986; gen. agent The New Eng., Portland, Oreg., 1986-90; v.p. MCM Fin., Seattle, 1990-92; prin. Curley & Assocs, Seattle, 1992—. Found. bd. dirs. Bellevue C.C., 1992—. Mem. Gen. Agts. and Mgrs. Assn. (bd. dirs. 1988—), Nat. Assn. Life Underwriters, Am. Soc. CLU and Chartered Fin. Cons., Estate Planning Coun. East King County, Internat. Assn. Fin. Planning, Wash. Athletic Club Seattle, Sahalee Country Club (Redmond. Wash.). Republican. Roman Catholic. Office: Curley & Assocs 411 108 Ave NE Ste 1630 Bellevue WA 98004

CURNUTTE, JOHN TOLLIVER, III, pediatric hematologist, oncologist, researcher; b. Dixon, Ill., Sept. 9, 1951; s. John Tolliver and Elizabeth Ann (Mueller) C.; m. Karen Diane Northrop, June 21, 1975; children: Jacqueline, John IV, Margaret. A.B. magna cum laude in Biochemistry, Harvard U., 1973; M.D., Harvard Med. Sch., 1979; Ph.D. in Biol. Chemistry, Harvard U., 1980. Diplomate Nat. Bd. Med. Examiners, Am. Bd. Pediatrics. Pediatric resident Mass. Gen. Hosp. and Harvard Med. Sch., Boston, 1979-81; fellow pediatric hematology/oncology Dana Farber Cancer Inst. and Harvard Med. Sch., Boston, 1981-83; asst. prof. pediatrics U. Mich. Med. Sch., Ann Arbor, 1983-86; assoc. mem. with tenure Dept. Molecular and Exptl. Medicine, Scripps Rsch. Inst., La Jolla, Calif., 1986—. est. investigator Am. Heart Assn., 1986-91. Contbr. articles to profl. jours. NIH Neutrophil Research grantee, 1983—, Soc. Pediatric Research Starter Research grantee, 1984-85; recipient Young Investigator award First Internat. Congress on Inflammation. Mem. Am. Soc. Clin. Investigation, Am. Soc. Cell Biology. Roman Catholic. Club: Aesculapian (Boston). Avocations: football, mountain climbing. Home: 1434 Victoria Glen Escondido CA 92025 Office: The Scripps Rsch Inst Divsn Hematology CAL 1 10666 N Torrey Pines Rd La Jolla CA 92037-1027

CUROTTO, RICKY JOSEPH, lawyer, corporate executive; b. Lomita Park, Calif., Dec. 22, 1931; s. Enrico and Nora M. (Giusso) C.; m. Lynne Therese Ingram, Dec. 31, 1983; children: Dina L., John F., Alexis J. BS cum laude, U. San Francisco, 1953, JD, 1958. Bar: Calif. 1959. Assoc. Peart, Baraty & Hassard, San Francisco, 1958-60; sr. counsel, asst. sec. BHP Minerals Internat. Inc.(formerly BHP-Utah Internat. Inc.), San Francisco, 1960—; of counsel Curotto Law Offices, Oakland and Sacramento, Calif., 1984—; sec. AOFR, Inc., BHP Engineering Inc., BHP Instruments Inc., Austgen-Biojet Inc., EcoScience Inc.; bd. dirs. Fathom Mgmt. Corp., Newco Trading Corp., Inc., Broken Hill Proprietary (U.S.A.) Inc., BHP Securities Inc., BHP Transport USA Inc., BHP Internat. Marine Transport Inc., Garden Hotels Investment Co., Family Housing and Adult Resources Inc. Contbr. articles to law revs. Trustee emeritus U. San Francisco; dir. and v.p. Shorebird Homeowners Assn. 1st lt. U.S. Army, 1954-56. Named to U. San Francisco Athletic Hall of Fame, 1985, Alumnus of Yr. U. San Francisco, 1989; recipient Bur. Nat. Affairs award, 1958, Disting. Svc. award U. San

Francisco, 1981. Mem. ABA, State Bar Calif., San Francisco Bar Assn., Am. Arbitration Assn. (nat. panel arbitrators), Am. Corp. Counsel Assn., Commonwealth Club of Calif. Republican. Roman Catholic. Office: BHP Minerals Internat Inc 550 California St Ste 500 San Francisco CA 94104

CURRAN, DANIEL RICHARD, environmental and mechanical engineer, consultant; b. Providence, Dec. 1, 1961; m. Roberta Ann Curran; children: Brittany April, Brandon Edward. BSME, U. R.I., 1983; MS in Engring. Mechanics, Pa. State U., 1985; MS in Theoretical and Applied Mechanics, U. Ill., 1987. Structural analyst Naval Underwater Systems Ctr., Newport, R.I., 1983; rsch. analyst Applied Rsch. Lab., University Park, Pa., 1983-85; rsch. engr. Nat. Ctr. for Composite Materials Rsch., Urbana, Ill., 1985-87; project engr. Northrop Corp., Pico Rivera, Calif., 1987-89; sr. scientist Lockheed Corp., Burbank, Calif., 1989-90; tech. cons. environ. and mech. engring. West Hollywood, Calif., 1990—. Contbr. articles to profl. jours. Recipient Jefferson Cup award AIAA, New Orleans, 1982. Mem. ASME.

CURRAN, JOHN ROGER, neurologist; b. Newark, July 7, 1934; s. John Henry and Marion (Law) C.; m. Anne Robinson, Sept. 1, 1956; children: Patrick, Christopher, Andrew, Julia. BS in Pharmacy, U. Mich., 1956; MD, Temple U., 1967. Diplomate Am. Bd. Psychiatry and Neurology. Intern U. Mich., 1967-68, resident in neurology, 1968-71; neurologist Nampa, Idaho, 1973—; bd. dirs. MRI Ctr. Idaho, Boise, Med. Ventures, San Diego. Maj. USAF, 1971-73. Mem. AMA, Am. Acad. Neurology, Am. EEG Soc., Idaho Med. Assn., Alpha Omega Alpha. Republican. Presbyterian.

CURRAN, MARCELLA JOYCE, astronomy educator; b. Cheyenne, Wyo., May 30, 1953; d. Walter Lloyd and Charlotte Eileen (Burnside) Flint; m. Martin D. Curran, June 29, 1992. BS, U. Wyo., 1975. Instr. astronomy Laramie County C.C., Cheyenne, 1989—; contbg. editor Cheyenne Newspapers, Inc., 1990—. Author: Wyoming Skies, 1990; editor newsletter Cosmic Babbler, 1986—. Mem. Cheyenne Astron. Soc. (bd. dirs., sec., editor 1986—). Home: 6614 N College Dr Lot G Cheyenne WY 82009

CURRAN, MARK ALBERT, investment banker; b. St. Louis, May 6, 1954; s. William Henry and Esther A. (Borgwald) C.; m. Kristine Charnowski, June 1, 1985. BA in Polit. Sci., U. Calif., Berkeley, 1976; M in Urban Planning, San Jose State U., 1979. Adminstrv. asst. to city mgr. City of Foster City (Calif.), 1977-78; sr. v.p. City Bond & Mortgage Corp., Oakland, Calif., 1978-85; sr. v.p. Sutro & Co., San Francisco, 1985-90, mng. dir. pub. fin., 1990—; lectr. pub. fin. San Jose State U., Berkeley, 1980—; dir. Calif. City Mgmt. Found., Sacramento, 1988—. Mem. Pacific Securities Assn., Calif. City Mgmt. Found. (dir., treas. 1988—), Calif. Mcpl. Forum, San Francisco Bond Club. Roman Catholic. Home: 1976 Manzanita Dr Oakland CA 94611-1138 Office: Sutro & Co 201 California St San Francisco CA 94111-5002

CURRIE, CHRISTOPHER CLYDE, telecommunications professional; b. Denver, June 28, 1966; s. Clyde and Ann Marie (Glenn) C. BS in Computer and Infosystems, Regis Coll., 1988; MBA, Colo. U., 1991. Emergency med. technician Regis Coll., Denver, 1985-88; cons., acct. exec. US West Communications, Dnever, 1991—. Mem. African-Am. Leadership Inst. Office: US West Communications 1801 California St Denver CO 80202

CURRIE, MADELINE ASHBURN, business administration educator; b. Rankin, Tex., Sept. 28, 1922; d. Herman and Ivan G. Vinson; BS, Tex. Woman's U., 1962; MA, Calif. State U., 1967; EdD, UCLA, 1974; m. Gail G. Currie; children: Robb Ashburn, Mark Ashburn, Michael Ashburn. Tchr., Edgewood High Sch., West Covina, Calif., 1962-69 ; instr. Rio Hondo Coll., Whittier, Calif., 1968-69; prof., grad. dir. Coll. Bus. Adminstrn., Calif. State Poly. U., Pomona, 1969-88, prof. emerita, 1988—. Recipient award Alpha Lambda Delta, Prof. Emerita award 1988, Exceptional Merit award, Meritorious Service awards Calif. State Poly. U., 1984. Mem. Grad. Sch. Edn., UCLA. Mem. Calif. Bus. Edn. Assn. (Recognition award), Tex. Woman's U. Alumnae Assn., Women in Mgmt., Rotary Internat. (Upland club, bd. mem.) Delta Pi Epsilon, Pi Lambda Theta, Delta Kappa Gamma, Delta Mu Delta. Home: 9749 Coca St Alta Loma CA 91737

CURRIE, MALCOLM RODERICK, scientist, aerospace and automotive executive; b. Spokane, Wash., Mar. 13, 1927; s. Erwin Casper and Genevieve (Hauenstein) C.; m. Sunya Lofsky, June 24, 1951; children: Deborah, David, Diana; m. Barbara L. Dyer, Mar. 5, 1977. A.B., U. Calif. at Berkeley, 1949, M.S., 1951, Ph.D., 1954. Research engr. Microwave Lab., U. Calif. at Berkeley, 1949-52, elec. engring. faculty, 1953-54; lectr. U. Calif. at Los Angeles, 1955-57; research engr. Hughes Aircraft Co., 1954-57, v.p., 1965-66; head electron dynamics dept. Hughes Research Labs., Culver City, Calif., 1957-60; dir. physics lab. Hughes Research Labs., Malibu, Calif., 1960-61, asso. dir., 1961-63, v.p., dir. research labs., 1963-65, v.p., mgr. research and devel. div., 1965-69; v.p. research and devel. Beckman Instruments, Inc., 1969-73; undersec. research and engring. dept. Office Sec. Def., Washington, 1973-77; pres. missile systems group Hughes Aircraft Co., Canoga Park, Calif., 1977-83, exec. v.p., 1983-88, chief exec. officer, chmn. bd., 1988—, also bd. dirs.; pres., chief exec. officer Delco Electronics Corp., 1986-88; chmn., chief exec. officer Hughes Aircraft Co., 1988-92, chmn. emeritus, 1992—; bd. dirs. Unocal Corp., Investment Co. Am., LSI Logic Corp.; mem. Def. Sci. Bd. Contbr. articles to profl. jours.; patentee in field. Mem. adv. bd. U. Calif., Berkeley, UCLA; trustee U. So. CAlif., 1989—, Howard U., 1989-92, UCLA Found.; bd. dirs. western region United Way, 1987; coord., head U.S. Savs. Bond Dr., So. Calif., 1991. With USNR, 1944-47. Decorated comdr. Legion of Honor France; named Nation's Outstanding Young Elec. Engr. Eta Kappa Nu, 1958, one of 5 Outstanding Young Men of Calif. by Calif. Jr. C. of C., 1960; recipient Nat. Achievement medal Am. Elec. Assn. 1992, Goddard Astronautics award AIAA, Chester Nimitz award U.S. Navy League, 192, Thomas White award USAF, 1992. Fellow IEEE, AIAA (pres.-elect, Goddard Astronautics award); mem. NAE, Am. Phys. Soc., Berkeley Fellows, Commn. on Competitiveness, Calif. Coun. on Sci. and Tech. (co-chair project Calif.), Phi Beta Kappa, Sigma Xi, Lambda Chi Alpha. Club: Cosmos. Home: 28780 Wagon Rd Agoura Hills CA 91301-2732 Office: Hughes Aircraft Co 7200 Hughes Terr Los Angeles CA 90045

CURRY, DANIEL FRANCIS MYLES, filmmaker; b. N.Y.C., Sept. 22, 1946; s. John Joseph Jr. and Florence Cecelia (Rattler) C.; m. Ubolvan Chaiwatana, July 27, 1972; children: Devin, Daniel. BA, Middlebury Coll., 1968; MFA, Humboldt State U., 1979. Vol. community devel. U.S. Peace Corps, Khon Kaen, Thailand, 1969-71; writer-dir. ednl. TV Ministry of Edn., Govt. of Thailand, Bangkok, 1971-72; freelance filmmaker/artist/designer various clients Bangkok, 1972-74; instr. fine arts Cape Cod Community Coll., West Barnstable, Mass., 1974-77; instr. film and theatre Humboldt State U., Arcata, Calif., 1977-79; visual effects artist Universal Studios Hartland Facility, North Hollywood, Calif., 1979-80; art dir. Modern Film Effects, Hollywood, Calif., 1980-85; v.p., dir. creative svcs. Cinema Rsch. Corp., Hollywood, 1985-88; visual effects supr.-dir. Star Trek, the Next Generation, Paramount Pictures, Hollywood, 1987—; pres. O.M.R. Prodns., Manhattan Beach, Calif., 1989—. Supr., title designer Star Trek IV, Top Gun, Flash Dance, Fatal Attraction, Cujo, The Blob, Rocky IV, Cobra, Staying Alive, Tootsie, Risky Business, Amadeus, The Right Stuff, Mommie Dearest, Uncommon Valor, Pure Luck, Back to School, Raging Bull, Class, Cool World, Captured, Christine, Body Double, Flashpoint, Tiger Town, Invasion U.S.A., Fast Forward, Bolero, Wild Thing, Pray for Death, Days of Thunder, Indiana Jones & The Temple of Doom; visual effects prodr. 6th season Star Trek, The Next Generation (best spl. visual effects Emmy award 1992). Recipient Emmy award for spl. visual effects Acad. TV Arts and Scis., 1992, nominations, 1989, 90. Mem. Acad. TV Arts and Scis., Soc. Motion Picture and TV Engrs., Am. Film Inst. Office: Paramount Pictures Star Trek Next Generation 5555 Melrose Ave Los Angeles CA 90038-3197

CURRY, JAMES TRUEMAN, JR., retired mining company executive; b. Nevada City, Calif., June 12, 1936; s. James Trueman and Nancy (Sherwin) C.; m. Barbara Hartman, June 21, 1958; children: James Trueman, Jennifer, Steven John. BS in Civil Engring, U. Calif. at Berkeley, 1959; MBA, Stanford, 1962. With Utah Internat. Inc., San Francisco, 1962-87, adminstrv. asst. to pres., 1962-65; asst. to mgr. Navajo (N.Mex.) Mine, 1965-66, adminstrv. mgr., 1966-68; adminstrv. mgr. Australian operations Utah Devel. Co. subs., 1969-70; treas. Utah Internat. Inc., 1970-72, v.p., treas., 1972-75, fin. v.p., 1975-82; pres., mng. dir. Utah Devel. Co. subs., 1982-85, exec. v.p., 1985-87, also bd. dirs.; chief exec. officer minerals group Broken Hill Pty. Ltd., Melbourne and San Francisco, 1987-91; bd. dirs. Broken Hill Pty. Ltd., Melbourne and San Francisco. Trustee Calif. Acad. Scis., 1992—. With AUS, 1959-60. Mem. Calif. Acad. Scis. (bd. dirs. 1992—). Clubs: Burlingame Country, Pauma Valley Country, Bohemian, Pacific Union, Melbourne, Queensland.

CURRY, MICHAEL BRUCE, community college dean, coach; b. Logan, W.Va., Mar. 18, 1938; s. Albert Bruce and Mary Naomi (Shugert) C.; m. Maryanne Davis, Dec. 21, 1976; children: Michael Davis, Daniel Patrick. BS, Wheeling Coll., 1960; M Math., Utah State U., 1970. Cert. C.C. math. tchr., Ariz. Math. tchr. Logan County Schs., 1962-65, Holtville (Calif.) Unified Sch. Dist., 1965-68; math. instr. Utah State U., Logan, 1968-70; math. instr. Pima C.C., Tucson, 1970-89, assoc. dean instrn., 1989—, men's tennis coach, 1973—. Author: Algebra I, 1974. Bd. dirs. Pima Fed. Credit Union, Tucson, 1976—. Mem. NEA, Ariz. Edn. Assn., Ariz. C.c. Assn., Nat. Assn. Jr. Coll. Coaches. Office: Pima CC 2202 W Anklam Rd Tucson AZ 85709

CURRY, WILLIAM SIMS, procurement manager; b. Mt. Vernon, Washington, Feb. 6, 1938; s. Eli Herbert Curry and Winona Geraldine (Davis) Mickelson; m. Kirsten Inge Arms, May 20, 1970; children: William II, Kevin, Randal, Kim Cannova, Derek. BS in Bus. Mgmt., Fla. State U., 1967; MBA, Ohio State U., 1968. Cert. profl. contracts mgr. Asst. purchasing officer Stanford (Calif.) Linear Accelerator Ctr., 1977-80; subcontract adminstr. Lockheed Missiles & Space Co., Sunnyvale, Calif., 1980-81; materials mgr. Altus Corp., San Jose, Calif., 1981-86; purchasing mgr. Litton Electron Devices, San Carlos, Calif., 1986—; bd. dirs. Industry Coun. for Small Bus. Devel., Sunnyvale, 1992—, v.p. programs, 1992—. Contbr. articles to profl. jours. Capt. USAF, 1955-77. Decorated Meritorious Svc. medal with one oak leaf cluster, USAF, 1977. Fellow Nat. Contract Mgmt. Assn.; mem. Am. Mensa, Ltd., Beta Gamma Sigma. Republican. Home: 8289 Del Monte Ave Newark CA 94560-2129 Office: Litton Electron Devices 960 Industrial Rd San Carlos CA 94070-4194

CURTIN, MICHAEL DANIEL, financial planner; b. N.Y.C., Feb. 8, 1938; s. Michael Daniel and Mary (Smarz) C.; m. Mary Elizabeth Davidson, Oct. 9, 1962; children: Rebecca Ann, Laura Lee. BS, Lafayette Coll., 1959; MS, Carnegie Mellon U., 1961. CFP. Group brand mgr. Procter & Gamble, Cin., 1960-72; v.p. Miracle White Co., Div. Beatrice Foods, Inc., Chgo., 1972-77; asst. to exec. v.p. Beatrice Foods, Inc., Chgo., 1977; exec. v.p., dir. Brookside Winery, Inc., Div. Beatrice Foods, Inc., Guasti, Calif., 1977-82; v.p., dir. Daelco, Inc., Commerce, Calif., 1982-84; pres. Michael Curtin CFP & Assoc., Upland, Calif., 1985—; bd. dirs. Estate Planning Coun., Inc., Claremont, Calif., Redco II, Inc., North Hollywood, Calif.; bd. dirs., v.p. Inst. CFPs, Inc., Pomona, Calif., Weite, Inc., Upland. Patentee in field. Bd. dirs. Boy Scouts Am., Inc., Ontario, Calif., 1988—. Recipient Pres.'s Honor award Waddell & Reed, Inc., 1986. Mem. Claremont Club, Pilgrim Place Endowment Bd. (advisor 1991—), San Antonio Hosp. Endowment Bd. (advisor), Lafayette Coll. (alumni advisor 1988—), Upland C. of C. Office: Michael Curtin CFP & Assoc PO Box 1829 Upland CA 91785-1829

CURTIN, THOMAS LEE, ophthalmologist; b. Columbus, Ohio, Sept. 9, 1932; s. Leo Anthony and Mary Elizabeth (Burns) C.; m. Constance L. Sallman; children: Michael, Gregory, Thomas, Christopher. BS, Loyola U., L.A., 1954; MD, U. So. Calif., 1957. Intern, Ohio State U. Hosp., 1957-58; resident in ophthalmology U.S. Naval Hosp., San Diego, 1961-64; practice medicine specializing in ophthalmology, Oceanside, Calif., 1967—; mem. staff Tri City, Palomar Meml., Scripps Meml. Mercy hosps.; sci. adv. bd. So. Calif. Soc. Prevention Blindness, 1973-76; cons. in field. Trustee, Carlsbad (Calif.) Unified Sch. Dist., 1975-83, pres., 1979, 82, 83. Served as officer M.C., USN, 1958-67. Diplomate Am. Bd. Ophthalmology. Mem. Am., Calif. med. assns., San Diego County Med. Soc., Am. Acad. Ophthalmology, Aerospace Med. Assn., San Diego Acad. Ophthalmology (pres. 1979), Calif. Assn. Ophthalmology (dir.), Carlsbad Rotary, El Camino Country Club. Republican. Roman Catholic. Home: 2304 Back Nine St Oceanside CA 92056 Office: 3231 Waring Ct Ste S Oceanside CA 92056-4561

CURTIS, GEORGE DARWIN, research scientist; b. Galveston, Tex., Apr. 30, 1928; m. Jean Allen, July 23, 1988. Sr. scientist western div. LTV Rsch. Ctr., Honolulu, 1961-64, asst. dir., prin. investigator, 1965-67; staff specialist Control Data Corp., Honolulu, 1967-68, systems dir., 1969-70; systems engring. cons., lectr. U. Hawaii, Honolulu, 1970—, instr. engring., 1988—, resarcher Joint Inst. for Marine and Atmospheric Rsch., 1979—, tech. coord. Hawaii Natural Energy Inst., 1981-87; cons. State of Hawaii, 1976-86, County of Honolulu, 1981-85; lectr. USN Post-Grad. Sch. Contbr. essays, chpts to books in field; pub. (jour.) Sci. of Tsunami Hazards, 1982—. Dir. ARC, Honolulu, 1978; squadron comdr. CAP, Honolulu, 1982-84. Grantee IR Scanner Program, 1987-88. Mem. IEEE (sr., program and publ. chmn. Ocean Electronics Symposium 1966, chmn. Hawaii sect. 1978-79), Acoustical Soc. Am., Nat. Assn. Environ. Profls., Tsunami Soc. (pres. 1985-88), Marine Tech. Soc., Sigma Xi (pres. Univ. Hawaii chpt., 1993—). Home: Box 237 Honomu HI 96728 Office: U Hawaii 1000 Pope Rd MSB 312 Honolulu HI 96822

CURTIS, GLEN RUSSELL, program manager; b. Ogden, Utah, Oct. 17, 1947; s. Von R. and Barbara (Fougler) C.; m. Nancy Norr, Dec. 1, 1971; children: Tamara, Brian, Cathy, Angie, Julie, Jared. BS in Journalism and Polit. Sci., Weber State Coll., Ogden, 1972; MBA, U. Phoenix, 1992. Bus. mgr. Signpost, Ogden, 1970-72; prin. various bus., Tremonton, Utah, 1975-87; pub. The Leader, Tremonton, 1976-87; proposal mgr. Thiokol Corp., Brigham City, Utah, 1987-90, project mgr., 1990—. Scoutmaster, commr. Silver Beaver Lake Bonneville coun. Boy Scouts Am., Ogden, 1976—; chmn. state rules com. Rep. County Com., Salt Lake City, 1976-86; bd. dirs. Headstart, Area Aging Coun., Alcohol and Drug Bd., Logan, Utah, 1983-87; campaign dir. Wolthius for Congress, Ogden, 1972; county commr. Box Elder County, Brigham City, 1983-87. 1st lt. USAF, 1972-75. Decorated Commendation medal; recipient Outstanding Svc. to Mental Health award Intermountain Assn. Mental Health, 1985, Outstanding Svc. to Job Tng. Utah Assn. Pvt. Industry Couns., 1987, Andy Rytting Community Svc. award Bear River Valley C. of C. 1988. Mormon. Home: 564 S 600 W Tremonton UT 84337-1745 Office: Thiokol Corp Space Ops PO Box 707 Brigham City UT 84302-0707

CURTIS, JESSE WILLIAM, JR., retired federal judge; b. San Bernardino, Calif., Dec. 26, 1905; s. Jesse William and Ida L. (Seymour) C.; m. Mildred F. Mort, Aug. 24, 1930; children: Suzanne, Jesse W., Clyde Hamliton, Christopher Cowles. A.B., U. Redlands, 1928, LL.D., 1973; J.D., Harvard U., 1931. Bar: Calif. 1931. Pvt. practice, 1931-35; mem. firms Guthrie & Curtis, San Bernardino, 1935-40, Curtis & Curtis, 1946-50, Curtis, Knauf, Henry & Farrell, 1950-53; judge Superior Ct. of Calif., 1953-62; judge U.S. Dist. Ct. (cen. dist.) Calif., 1962-90, ret., 1990; with Jud. Arbitration and Mediations Svc., L.A., 1990—; rep. dist. ct. on Jud. Council U.S., 1972-74. Chmn. San Bernardino Sch. Bd., 1942-46, mem., 1946-49; mem. Del Rosa Bd. Edn., 1950-53; chmn. San Bernardino County Heart Fund; dir., past pres. YMCA; bd. dirs. GoodWill Industries, Crippled Children's Soc., Arrowhead United Fund; adv. bd. Community Hosp. Mem. ABA, Calif. State Bar, Orange County Bar Assn., Am. Judicature Soc., Am. Law Inst., Newport Harbor Yacht Club, Phi Delta Phi. Democrat. Congregationalist. Home: 305 Evening Star Ln Newport Beach CA 92660-5704

CURTIS, LINDA JENARIE, genealogist; b. Bend, Oreg., June 4, 1941; d. Joel Howard and Elnora H. (Allgood) Clift; m. Robert P. Temple, Dec. 27, 1959 (div. 1968); children: Steven, Laura Mazzella; m. Roger Ward Curtis, Apr. 5, 1969; children: Benjamin, Brian. Grad. high sch., Pendleton, Oreg. 1st v.p. Colo. Coun. Geneal. Socs., Denver, 1988-89. Editor (jour.) Allgood Ancestry, 1988. Mem. Nat. Geneal. Soc., Assn. Profl. Genealogists, Colo. Assn. Profl. Genealogists, Colo. Geneal. Soc. (instr., edn. coord. 1992), Aurora Geneal. Soc. (pres. 1988, 89, instr., genealogist 1992—). Home: 3709 S Mission Pkwy Aurora CO 80013-2405

CURTIS, LYNNE KATHERINE, legal investigator, consultant, writer; b. Buffalo, Mar. 4, 1950; d. Ralph Joseph and Theresa K. (Szymakowski) C. Student, Okla. City U., 1964, Robert Morris Jr. Coll., 1965, Stanford U., 1968. Cert. legal investigator; lic. race track trainer. Horse trainer, 1968-82, free-lance writer, 1974—; chief legal investigator Holland & Hart, Boise, Idaho, 1983-88; legal investigator, cons., speaker Posner & Houghton, San Francisco, 1988—; computer cons., San Francisco, 1992—. Author: (chpt.) Litigation in the 21st Century, 1991; contbr. articles to profl. jours. Bd. dirs. Idaho Vols. in Corrections, Boise, 1980-81. Mem. Nat. Assn. Legal Investigators (cert. com. chmn. 1990—, regional dir. 1987), Mystery Writers of Am., San Francisco Personal Computer Users Group (products review 1992—), Mensa. Office: Posner and Houghton 1230 Market St # 420 San Francisco CA 94102

CURTIS, MARIE THERESE DODGE, executive assistant; b. Niagara Falls, N.Y., May 1, 1935; d. Edward Francis and Agnes Anne (Dell) Dodge; m. Charles R. Curtis, July 30, 1967 (div. 1979). Cert., Katharine Gibbs Sch., N.Y.C., 1956. Corp. sec., dir. Topa Equities, Ltd., L.A., 1964—; corp. sec., dir. Ace Beverage Co., L.A., 1964—, Paradise Beverages, Inc., Honolulu, 1980—, West Indies Corp., Saint Thomas, U.S. Virgin Islands, 1982—. Office: Topa Equities Ltd 1800 Avenue Of The Stars # 1400 Los Angeles CA 90067-4220

CURTIS, PAUL NELSON, computer technology executive; b. San Francisco, Feb. 1, 1944; s. Claude Hamilton and Kathleen Geralda (Starr) C.; m. Mary Louise Parchen, July 6, 1986; children: Sharon K. Harris, Teresa Marie Curtis. Student, Calif. State U., L.A., 1964-68. Ptnr. Coast Computer Tech., Anaheim, Calif., 1986—; pres. Intercomm, Newport Beach, Calif., 1991—; adv. bd. Lotus World, Cambridge, Mass., 1991—, PC World, San Francisco, 1992. With USN, 1961-64. Mem. Rotary Internat., Assn. of PC User Groups (bd. dirs. Washington 1990—).

CURTIS, WILLIAM SHEPLEY, radiologist; b. St. Louis, Sept. 11, 1915; s. Edward Glion and Isabel (Wallace) C.; m. Frances Lois Elmer, Jan. 3, 1942; children: William Shepley Jr., David Jennings, Anne Goodson Curtis Curfman. AB, Dartmouth Coll., 1936; MD, Washington U., St. Louis, 1940. Diplomate Am. Bd. Radiology. Intern St. Luke's Hosp., St. Louis, 1940-41; resident St. Louis Maternity Hosp., 1941, Mallinkrodt Inst. Radiology, 1945-48; radiologist Wasson and Bouslog, Denver, 1948-52; radiologist, ptnr. Boulder (Colo.) Med. Ctr., 1953-83; cons. Wardenburg Student Health Ctr. U. Colo., Boulder, 1953-91; past trustee Colo. Blue Shield, Denver, cons. Past chmn. Colo. Found. Med. Care, Denver, Boulder County Health Com.; mem. Colo. Health Occupations Adv. Com., Denver; bd. dirs. Boulder Day Nursery. Lt. col. M.C., U.S. Army, 1941-46. Recipient U. Colo. medal, 1992. Fellow Am. Coll. Radiology (emeritus, past councilor); mem. Radiol. Soc. N.Am., Colo. Radiol. Soc. (past pres.), Colo. Med. Soc. (past pres., del.), Boulder County Med. Soc. (past pres.), Boulder Town and Gown, Rotary (past pres. Boulder chpt.). Unitarian. Home and Office: 3151 6th St Boulder CO 80304-2507

CURTISS, ELDEN F., bishop; b. Baker, Oreg., June 16, 1932; s. Elden F. and Mary (Neiger) C. B.A., St. Edward Sem., Seattle, M.Div., 1958; M.A. in Ednl. Adminstrn, U. Portland, 1965; postgrad., Fordham U., U. Notre Dame. Ordained priest Roman Catholic Ch., 1958; campus chaplain, 1959-64, 65-68; supt. schs. Diocese of Baker (Oreg.), 1962-70; pastor, 1968-70; pres./rector Mt. Angel Sem., Benedict, Oreg., 1972-76; mem. bd. regents Mt. Angel Sem., Benedict, 1990—; bishop of Helena (Mont.), 1976—; mem. priests senate Archdiocese of Portland, 1974-76; mem. ecumenical ministries State of Oreg., 1972; mem. pastoral services com. Oreg. State Hosp., Salem, 1975-76; bishop Diocese Helena, Mont., 1976—; mem. adminstrv. bd. Nat. Conf. Cath. Bishops, 1976-80, 89—; mem. pro-life com., 1977-89, chmn. com. on vocations, 1989—, mem. com. on priestly formation, also mem. com.. Nat. Cath. News Svc., bd. dirs. Cath. Mut. Relief Soc., 1977—, Mont. Cath. Conf., 1976—, Mont. Cath. Social Svcs., Inc.; mem. N.W. Assn. Bishops and Major Religious Superiors, 1976—, Mont. Assn. Chs., 1976—, bd. regents U Portland, bishops and pres's com ednl. dept. U.S. Cath. Conf.; chancellor Carroll Coll., Helena. Mem. Nat. Cath. Ednl. Assn. (Outstanding Educator 1972, bishops and pres's com. coll. dept.). Office: PO Box 1729 515 N Ewing Helena MT 59624-1729*

CURWIN, NORMA PAULINE, geriatrics, medical/surgical nurse; b. Pomona, Calif., Nov. 16, 1937; d. Norman Valentine and Leona Pauline (Johnson) Unroe; m. Robert L. Curwin Dec. 21, 1957 (div. 1983); children: Cathleen A. Curwin McGrath, Steven S., Kenneth R. (dec.), Christine M. Curwin Carter. Student, Pomona Coll., Claremont, Calif., 1955-58; AS with high honors, McHenry County Coll., Crystal Lake, Ill., 1980; BSN, Elmhurst (Ill.) Coll., 1983. Cert. in oncology. Staff nurse Royal Terrace, McHenry, Ill.; staff nurse med./cardiac unit North Chicago (Ill.) VA Hosp.; staff nurse med./surg./oncology unit Good Shepherd Hosp., Barrington, Ill.; nurse Woodstock (Ill.) Residence; staff nurse med. unit Brea (Calif.) Community Hosp.; staff nurse Crystal Pines Health Care Ctr., Crystal Lake, Seminole (Fla.) Nursing Pavillion. Home: 131 NW 20th #D Newport OR 97365

CUSANOVICH, MICHAEL ANTHONY, biochemistry educator; b. Los Angeles, Mar. 2, 1942; s. Lucian Anthony and Ruth Elizabeth (McElroy) C.; m. Carol Owens, June 15, 1963 (div. May 1973); children: Kurt Michael, Carrie Elizabeth; m. Marilyn Jean Wainio, Mar. 31, 1980; 1 child, Darren Anthony. BS, U. Pacific, 1963; PhD, U. Calif., San Diego, 1967, postgrad., 1967-68; postgrad., Cornell U., 1968-69. Asst. prof. biochemistry U. Ariz., Tucson, 1969-74, assoc. prof., 1974-79, prof., 1979—, acting vice-dean grad. coll., 1987-88, v.p. rsch., dean grad. coll., 1988—, interim provost, 1992; program dir. NSF, Washington, 1981-82; cons. Univ. Patents, Inc., Westport, Conn., 1983-88. Contbr. articles to profl. jours. Fellow NIH, 1968-69; recipient Career Devel. award NIH, 1975-80. Mem. Am. Soc. Biol. Chemists, Am. Chem. Soc., Am. Photobiology Soc. Republican. Office: U Ariz Dept Biochemistry Tucson AZ 85721

CUSHMAN, JOHN PALMER, management consultant; b. Canton, Ohio, Feb. 9, 1932; s. John Kenneth and Kathryn (Palmer) C.; m. Jacqueline Ann Harris, Sept. 2, 1960; children: Pamela, Susan, JoAnn, Karen. AB, Franklin and Marshall Coll., 1955; BCE, Rensselaer Poly. Inst., 1955; MSME, San Diego State U., 1965; MBA, Pepperdine U., 1974. Registered profl. engr., Calif. Design engr. Gen. Dynamics, San Diego, 1959-67; chief project engr., design engr. Northrop Corp., Newbury Park, Calif., 1967-91; founder, mgmt. cons. Tech. Interface Consulting, Thousand Oaks, Calif., 1992—; co-developer Concurrent Engring. workshops, seminars U. Calif.-Santa Barbara and Nat. Technol. U., 1992. Contbr. articles, book revs. to profl. publs. Organizer assessment dist. Thousand Oaks, 1970s. Capt. USAF, 1955-58. Mem. Inst. Mgmt. Cons., Soc. Concurrent Engring. (v.p. programs), Toastmasters Internat. (div. gov. 1992-93, area gov. of yr. 1992-92). Office: 1336 La Granada Dr Thousand Oaks CA 91362

CUSUMANO, JAMES ANTHONY, chemical company executive, former recording artist; b. Elizabeth, N.J., Apr. 14, 1942; s. Charles Anthony and Carmella Madeline (Catalano) C.; m. Jane LaVerne Melvin, June 15, 1985; children: Doreen Ann, Polly Jean. BA, Rutgers U., 1964, PhD, 1967; grad. Exec. Mktg. Program, Stanford U., 1981, Harvard U., 1988. Mgr. catalyst rsch. Exxon Rsch. and Engring. Co., Linden, N.J., 1967-74; pres., chief exec. officer, founder Catalytica Inc., Mountain View, Calif., 1974-85, chmn., 1985—, also bd. dirs.; lectr. chem. engring. dept. U. Stanford U., 1978; advisor to Inst. Internat. Edn. Fulbright Scholar Program; lectr. Rutgers U., 1966-67; Charles D. Hurd lectr. Northwestern U., 1989-90; speaker to chem. and physics grads. U. Wis., 1992; mem. NSF Com. on Catalysts and Environment; exec. briefings with Pres. George Bush and Cabinet mems., 1990, 92; fellow Churchill Coll., Cambridge U., 1992—. Author: Catalysis in Coal Conversion, 1978, (with others) Critical Materials Problems in Energy Production, 1976, Advanced Materials in Catalysis, 1977, Liquid Fuels from Coal, 1977, Kirk-Othmer Encyclopedia of Chemical Technology, 1979, Chemistry for the 21st Century, Perspectives in Catalysis, 1992; contbr. articles to profl. jours., chpts. to books; founding editor Jour. of Applied Catalysis, 1980; rec. artist with Royal Teens and Dino Take Five for ABC Paramount, Capitol and Jubilee Records, 1957-67; single records include Short Shorts, Short Shorts Twist, My Way, Hey Jude, Rosemarie, Please Say You Want Me, Lovers Never Say Goodbye; albums include The Best of the Royal Teens, Newies But Oldies; appeared in PBS TV prodn. on molecular engring., Little by Little, 1989. Recipient Surface Chemistry award Continental Oil Co., 1964; Henry Rutgers scholar, 1963, Lever Bros. fellow, 1965, Churchill Coll. fellow Cambridge Univ., 1992. Mem. Am. Chem. Soc., Am. Inst. Chem. Engrs., Am. Phys. Soc., N.Y. Acad. Sci., Am. Mus. Natural History, Pres.'s Assn., Smithsonian Assocs., Sigma Psi, Phi Lambda

Upsilon (hon.). Republican. Roman Catholic. Home: 3111 Bandera Dr Palo Alto CA 94304-1341 Office: Catalytica Inc 430 Ferguson Dr Bldg 3 Mountain View CA 94043-5215

CUTINO, BERT PAUL, chef, restaurant owner; b. Carmel, Calif., Aug. 7, 1939; m. Bella Manigiapane; children: Marc, Michele, Bart. AA in Bus., Monterey Peninsula Coll., 1964; D of Culinary Arts (hon.), Johnson and Wales Coll., 1988. Various restaurant positions Monterey, Calif.; owner Sardine Factory, Monterey, Calif., 1968—; co-founder Cannery Row Co.; comml. real estate developer, Pacific Hospitality, Inc., 1983—; protocol chmn. 1992 USA Nat. Culinary Team; formation of Western Region Culinary Team to 1988 Culinary Olympics, Frankfurt; founder Culinary Arts Program at local community coll., 1981; hospitality amb. internat. teams to Am. Culinary Classic, 1991; speaker and lectr. in field. Contbr. articles for hospitality industry publs. and profl. jours. Food chmn. Calif. Wine Festival, 1977—, March of Dimes, 1985-89; chmn. Taste of Monterey, 1987-89; co-chmn. Easter Week Brunch for Alliance on Aging, March of Dimes, Monterey County, 1987-89, Jumpin Pumpkins money raiser for local pub. schs., 1984-87, African Relief Fund, 1985; v.p. Monterey Peninsula C. of C., 1984-88; mem. Sheriff's Adv. Com., Monterey County; hon. judge March of Dimes Gourmet Gala, 1985-92; dir. Found. to Support Monterey Peninsula Schs., 1984-86. With USNR, 1959-67. Recipient numerous awards including Travel Holiday, Mobil Guide, Nat. Restaurant News Hall of Fame, Calif. Top 10 Restaurants, Town and Country; one of 50 restaurants in Am. selected to serve at Pres. Reagan's Inauguration, 1981, 85; recipient Alumni award Calif. C.C., 1982, Antonin Careme Soc. medal Chefs Assn. of Pacific Coast, 1987, Medal of Honor, Escoffier Soc., 1986, Presdl. Medallion, Les Toques Blanches Internat., 1989, 1st Soviet-Am. Culinary Exchange Medallion, 1988, Medallion of World Trade Ctr., Moscow, 1988; named Chef of Yr., Monterey Peninsula Chefs Assn., 1983. Mem. Am. Culinary Fedn. (life, cert. exec. chef, western region v.p. 1985-89, bd. dirs. The Chef and the Child Found. 1989, nat. membership com. 1982, western regional coord. 1983, nat. accreditation team 1987, Nat. Chef of Yr. 1988, Pres.'s medal 1982, 89), Am. Acad. Chefs, Am. Acad. of Restaurant Scis., Am. Inst. of Wine and Food (founding), Knights of Vine (master knight), Wine Inst., Soc. for Am. Cuisine (founding), Calif. Restaurant Assn. (Chef of Yr., 1984), Nat. Restaurant Assn., Guild of Sommeliers Eng., Am. Inst. Food and Wine, Les Amis d'Escoffier Soc. N.Y. (amb.-at-large), Internat. Assn. Cooking Profls., Soc. Advancement of Food Svc. Rsch., Italian Restaurant Soc., Calif. Culinary Acad. (adv. bd. 1990—), L'Ordre Mondial Des Gourmets Degustateurs (spl. medal of honor, 1991), Confrerie de la Chaine Des Rotisseurs (vice chancelier-argentie, Bronze medal, 1990), Assn. Des Maitres Conseils en Gastronomie Francaise (comdr.), Les Toques Blanches Internat. Club (founder Monterey chpt., mem. internat. bd., Presdl. Medallion), Calif. Travel Industry Assn. (F. Norman Clark Entrepreneur award 1992), Monterey Peninsula C. of C. (v.p.). Office: Restaurants Central 765 Wave St Monterey CA 93940-1018

CUTLER, HOWARD ARMSTRONG, economics educator, chancellor; b. Webster City, Iowa, Apr. 27, 1918; s. Harry O. and Myrtle (Armstrong) C.; m. Enid Ellison, Jan. 2, 1943; children: Cheryl Varian, Kristen Ellison, Sherwood Thor. A.B., U. Iowa, 1940, M.A., 1941; grad. certificate, Harvard U., 1943; Ph.D., Columbia U., 1952. Instr. econs. U. Iowa, 1946; asst. to economist Irving Trust Co., N.Y.C., 1946-47; instr. econs. U. Ill., Urbana, 1948-50; asst. prof. U. Ill., 1950; asst. to dean U. Ill. (Coll. Commerce), 1949-51; asst. prof. econs. Pa. State U., 1951-53, assoc. prof., 1953-56, prof., 1956-62, head dept., 1953-58, dir. gen. edn., 1957-62, asst. to v.p. academic affairs, 1958-61, asst. to pres., 1961-62; acad. v.p., prof. econs. U. Alaska, 1962-66, chancellor, 1976-81, chancellor emeritus, 1983—, Regents' prof. econs., 1981-83, Regents' prof. emeritus, 1983—; exec. v.p. Inst. Internat. Edn., N.Y.C., 1966-76; vis. prof. U. Chgo., 1955-56. Editor: Jour. Gen. Edn, 1960-62. Mem. Martin Luther King, Jr., Fellowship Selection Com., 1968-70; mem. pub.-at-large Ednl. Commn. for Fgn. Med. Grads., 1970-85; mem. chancellor's panel on univ. purposes State U. N.Y., 1970-72; mem. Nat. Liaison Com. Fgn. Student Admissions, 1968-75; mem. adv. com. Carl Duisberg Soc., 1968-75; bd. dirs. Nat. Council for Community Services to Internat. Visitors, 1971-75, Internat. Schs. Services, 1971-75, Axe-Houghton Found., 1970-85, bd. dirs. Alaska Council on Economic Edn., 1977—. Served to lt. USNR, 1942-46. Recipient Disting. Alumnus Achievement award U. Iowa, 1989. Mem. Phi Beta Kappa, Beta Gamma Sigma, Pi Gamma Mu, Omicron Delta Epsilon. Office: U Alaska Dept Econs Fairbanks AK 99775-0580

CUTLER, KENNETH ROSS, pension funds investment counsel; b. Tacoma, Mar. 5, 1920; s. Clarence William and Matilda Roxanne (Ross) C.; m. Pat Virginia Reinecke, Aug. 6, 1943; children—Geoffrey William, Craig Lee, Brooke Roxanne. Student U. Chgo., 1941-42, UCLA, 1945. Broker, William R. Staats & Co., 1945-47, Dempsey-Tegeler & Co., Los Angeles, 1950-53; pres. Calif. Fund, Los Angeles, 1953-62; investment counsel, Van Nuys, Calif., 1962-66; broker Dean Witter & Co., Century City, Calif., 1966-72; mgr. spl. accounts dept. Paine Webber, Los Angeles, 1972-77; chmn. Cutler & Co., Inc., Medford, Oreg., 1977—; trustee Cutler Trust, 1992—. Mem. Phi Delta Theta. Republican. Presbyterian. Clubs: Balboa Bay (Newport Beach); Rogue Valley Country; University (Medford). Home: 4300 Livingston Rd PO Box 1411 Jacksonville OR 97530 Office: Cutler & Co Inc 503 Airport Rd Medford OR 97504-4159

CUTLER, LORRAINE MASTERS, interior designer, facilities manager; b. Indpls., Oct. 19, 1943; d. James Mark and Dorothy Aileen (DeLawter) Masters; m. Albert B. Cutler III, June 3, 1965 (div.); children: Valina Dawn, Anthony Bret. BFA, Ariz. State U., 1974, BA, 1974; MA, U. Phoenix, 1989. Intern Walsh Bros., Phoenix, 1973, jr. designer, 1973-74, staff designer, 1978-80; dir. interior design Dick & Fritsche Design Group, Phoenix, 1980-84; dir. interior design and space planning HNC Inc., Phoenix, 1984-87; mgr. advanced facilities planning PCS, Inc., Scottsdale, Ariz., 1987-89; cons. Cons. Mgmt. Systems, 1989—; asst. prof. interior design and facility mgmt. Ariz. State U., Tempe, 1991—. Participant Interior Design Efforts for Ariz. Legis., Phoenix, 1986-87; bd. dirs. Southwest Builds, 1985-88, chmn. fin. com., 1987-88. Recipient Presdl. Citation Am. Soc. Interior Designers, 1984. Mem. Inst. Bus. Designers (profl., acad. liaison 1991-93, pres. 1985-87, v.p. programs 1983-85, sec. 1981-83, Cert. Appreciation, 1981), Internat. Facility Mgmt. Assn. (profl., treas.). Home: 4034 E Yowy St Phoenix AZ 85044-1527 Office: Ariz State U Coll Architecture and Environ Design Tempe AZ 85287-2105

CUTLER, RICHARD BRUCE, lawyer; b. Portland, Maine, July 15, 1931; s. Shepard Hugh and Dena Cutler; m. Felice Reinitz, June 7, 1959; children: Stephen, Laura. BS, U. Utah, 1953; LLB, Yale U., 1959. Bar: Maine 1959, Calif. 1961. Assoc. Berman, Berman, Wernick et al, Portland, Maine, 1959-60; atty. Calif. Ct. Appeals, L.A., 1960-61; assoc. Ward, Ryan et al, 1961-62, Louis Lee Abbott, L.A., 1962-65; atty./prin. Cutler & Cutler, L.A., 1965-90, 92—; ptnr. Dilworth, Paxson et al, L.A., 1990-91. Home: 10601 Wilshire Blvd Apt 19W Los Angeles CA 90024-4521

CUTRIGHT, FRANCES LARSON, marriage and family therapist; b. Visalia, Calif., July 11, 1935; d. Francis Oscar and Faye (Sawyer) Larson; m. Forest F. Cutright, June 30, 1962 (div. 1982); children: Melinda, Forest F. BA, U. Calif., Berkeley, 1958, MA, 1982; PhD, Profl. Sch. Psychol. Studies, San Diego, 1986. Lic. marriage and family therapist, Calif. Group therapist in alcohol and drug dependence program VA Hosp., La Jolla, Calif., 1982-85; mem. staff Psychotherapy Inst. of San Diego, 1982-87; co-founder, v.p. Ctr. for Healing Group, San Diego, 1987-92; psychotherapist in pvt. practice San Diego, 1992—; instr. drugs and alcohol U. Calif., San Diego, 1988—; adj. faculty The Union Inst., San Diego, 1984—. Contbr. articles to mags. Educator, trainer San Diego AIDS Project, 1989-91, Oasis, Serenity House Counselling Staffs, Escondido, Calif., 1987-89; developer, trainer adolescent and family groups Fellowship House, 1987-89. Mem. Am. Assn. Marriage and Family Therapists (clin. mem.), Calif. Assn. Marriage and Therapy Therapists (clin. mem.), San Diego Assn. Marriage and Family Therapists (clin. mem.), Nat. Assn. for Children of Alcoholics, Am. Orthopsychiatric Assn. (clin. mem.), Am. Group Psychotherapy (clin. mem.). Office: 5230 Carroll Canyon Ste 220 San Diego CA 92121

CUTTER, REGINALD, financial and tax consultant; b. Savannah, Ga., Dec. 28, 1951; s. Jason Jr. and Ruthie (Arnett) C.; m. Teresa M. Lucas, July 13, 1970; children: Regina M., Jennifer L., Reginald W. Student, Savannah State Coll., 1969-71, American River Coll., Sacramento, 1977-81, Sacramento City Coll., 1982, Consumes River Coll., Sacramento, 1989. Tax cons., tax preparer Cutter Fin. Svcs., Sacramento, 1984—; life and disability agt. Bolden Fin. Svcs., Sacramento, 1982—; mng. gen. ptnr. Investors Dedicated Econ. Advancement, Sacramento, 1989—, Capital Youth Group Home, Sacramento, 1990—. Coord., cons. Glen Elder Anti-Drug Sports Festival, Sacramento, 1991-92; youth group leader Murph Emanuel AME Ch., Sacramento, 1992. Sgt. USAF, 1971-77. Named to Outstanding Young Men in Am., 1986, 89. Mem. Masons (jr. steward 1991-92). Home: 2713 Tiffany West Way Sacramento CA 95827

CVAR, DUANE EMIL, marketing professional; b. Cleve., May 11, 1944; s. Emil Frank and Marge Evelyn (Kuehl) C.; m. Roberta Kay Kastler, Oct. 14, 1966 (div. Feb. 1974); children: David, Tamra; m. Phyllis Boardman, Jan. 24, 1976; children: David, Brian, Scott, Michael, Jason. AA in Mktg., Cuyahoga Community Coll., 1966; BA in Mktg., Cleve. State U., 1969. Sales mktg. rep. Union Paper & Twine Co., Cleve., 1968-77; dist. sales mgr. Modern Maid, Inc., Cin., 1977-79; sales mktg. mgr. Butler Paper Co., Denver, 1979-80; dist. sales mgr. Hammermill Papers Group, San Francisco, 1980-84; gen. mgr. Jim Walter Papers, Phoenix, 1984-86; v.p. western divsn. Star Forms, Inc., San Diego, Calif., 1986—; cons. Philip Kendall Indsl. Products, Denver, 1979-80, Hotel St. Claire, San Jose, Calif., 1982. Leader Indian Guides, Cleve., 1976; coach Little League, Cleve., 1976-77; mem. coun. Lyndhurst (Ohio) Luth. Ch., 1966-74; parent advisor debate team Bellevue (Wash.), High Sch., 1987-88. Staff sgt. U.S. Army, 1965-72. Named Mead Dynamo Winner, Mead Corp., 1972-76. Mem. Nat. Bus. Forms Assn., Western Bus. Systems Assn., Coll. Bookstore Assn. (Sales Mgr. of Yr. 1987), Western Forms Caravan, Nat. Office Products Assn. Republican. Lutheran. Home: 7537 Navigator Cir Carlsbad CA 92009 Office: Star Forms Inc 674 Via DeLa Valle # 221 Solana Beach CA 92075

CZAPLEWSKI, RAYMOND LAWRENCE, forestry scientist, consultant, educator; b. Chgo., Feb. 2, 1949; m. Vicki Sue Rothwell, Aug. 20, 1976; 1 child, Glen. BA, Northwestern U., 1970; MS, U. Wyo., 1972; PhD, Colo. State U., 1986. Strategic planner Wyo. Game & Fish Dept., Cheyenne, Wyo., 1976-79, Bighorn Nat. Forest, Sheridan, Wyo., 1979-82; math. statistician Rocky Mountain Forest and Range Exptl. Sta., USDA Forest Svc., Ft. Collins, Colo., 1982—; affiliate prof. and lectr. Colo. State U., 1987—; cons. Nat. Forests Timber Mgmt., Washington, Pacific N.W. and Rocky Mountain regions, 1989—, EPA, Las Vegas RTP, 1989—, UN Food and Agr. Argn., Rome, 1989-90, Dept. Conservation and Environ., Melbourne, Australia. Contbr. articles to profl. jours. Bd. dirs. Wyo. Wildlife Soc., 1980-81. Home: 2012 Huntington Cir Fort Collins CO 80526-1510 Office: USDA Forest Svc 240 W Prospect Rd Fort Collins CO 80526-2098

CZARNECKI, GERALD MILTON, banker; b. Phila., Mar. 22, 1940; s. Casimir M. and Rose-Mary (Grajek) C.; m. Lois Rae DiJoseph, July 9, 1965; 1 dau., Robin Alexandra. B.S., Temple U., Phila., 1965; M.A., Mich. State U., 1967. C.P.A., Ill., Tex. With Continental Bank, Chgo., 1968-79, v.p., operating gen. mgr. trust ops. and gen. mgr. corp. services, 1971-78; pres. Fla. Computing Services, 1979; exec. v.p. Houston Nat. Bank, 1979-82; sr. v.p. fin. Republic Bank Corp., 1982-83, exec. v.p., 1983-84; pres., chief exec. officer Altus Bank, 1984-87; chmn., chief exec. officer Bank of Am. Hawaii, Honolulu, 1987-93; sr. v.p. human resources and adminstrn. IBM Corp., Armonk, N.Y., 1993—; mem. faculty DePaul U., Chgo., 1975-78; adj. prof. econs. Houston Bapt. U., 1980-82; mem. faculty Bank Adminstrn. Inst., 1978-85, Grad. Sch. Banking, U. Wis., 1979-86; chmn. bd. dirs. Inroads, Inc./Chgo., 1977-79, Inroads, Inc./Houston, 1981 vis. prof. Jones Sch. Bus., Rice U., 1980; adj. prof. policy and strategy So. Methodist U., 1983-84; mem. adv. com. Banking Center, Tex. So. U., 1980-82; chmn. securities processing sub-com. Am. Nat. Standards Inst., 1974-79, mem. Tuskegee Inst. State Adv. Council, 1984-87; treas., mem. exec. com., bd. dirs. Nat. Council Savs. Instns., 1984-90; pres. thrift adv. council Fed. Res. Bd., 1986-90. Contbr. articles to profl. publs. Bd. dirs., treas. Hawaii Theatre Ctr., 1988-93; bd. dirs. Honolulu Econ. Devel. Corp., 1988-93, Nature Conservancy Hawaii, 1988-93, U. Hawaii Pres.' Coun., 1988-93, Aloha United Way, 1988-93; mem. Bus. Roundtable of Hawaii, 1989-93; chmn. Mil. Affairs Coun., 1992-93. Mem. AICPA, Am. Bankers Assn. (chmn. securities processing com. 1974-77, trust ops. com. 1978, mem. exec. com. ops. and automation div. 1980-83, rsch. com.), Am. Econ. Assn., Tex. Soc. CPAs, Fin. Execs. Inst., Consumer Bankers Assn. (bd. dirs. 1986-89), N. Am. Soc. Corp. Planners (bd. dirs. Dallas Chpt. 1982-83), Assn. for Corp. Growth, Hawaii C. of C. (bd. dirs. 1988-89, chmn. bd. 1990-92), Omicron Delta Epsilon, Alpha Delta Phi.

CZARTOLOMNY, PIOTR ANTONI, librarian; b. Kutno, Poland, June 10, 1946; came to U.S., 1984; s. Piotr Mikolai and Barbara Danuta (Galkowska) C.; m. Janina Stanislawa Janas, Feb. 16, 1971; children: Piotr Olaf, Sara Zofia. M Polish Philology, Poznan (Poland) U., 1970. Asst. prof. Inst. Polish Lit. Poznan U., 1970-76; mng. editor Solidarity Regional Pub. House, Poznan, 1980-81; archivist Boise (Idaho) State U., 1984-85; clk. Idaho Dept. Transp., Boise, 1985-86; lit. coord. Haynes Trane Svcs., Denver, 1987—; manuscript reader various pub. houses, Poland, 1970-84; lit. cons. City Theatre,Bielsko Biala, Poland, 1977. Lit. and art critic, Poland, 1970-80; contbr. articles to various publs. Mem. regional com. Solidarity, Poland, 1980-81. Mem. Union Solidarity Journalists (exec. pres. 1981). Roman Catholic. Office: Haynes Trane 5654 Greenwood Plaza Blvd Englewood CO 80111-2310

CZIPOTT, PETER VICTOR, physicist, researcher; b. Alhambra, Calif., Feb. 5, 1954; s. Akos Zoltan and Ilona (Jurassa) C.; m. Jenene Jo Allison, Jan. 2, 1983 (div. Jan. 1992). BA in Physics, U. Calif., San Diego, 1975, PhD in Physics, 1983. Staff scientist Phys. Dynamics, Inc., La Jolla, Calif., 1984-90; v.p. SQM Tech., Inc., San Diego, 1990—. Contbr. articles to profl. jours. Regents fellow U. Calif., San Diego, 1976; NSF Grad. fellow, 1977-79. Mem. AAAS, Internat. Assn. for Phys. Scis. of the Ocean (working group, sea ice commn.), Am. Geophys. Union, Nat. Assn. Corrosion Engrs., Am. Phys. Soc., San Diego Symphony Orch. Assn., U. Calif. San Diego Alumni Assn. Office: SQM Tech Inc Ste 314 11545 Sorrento Valley Rd San Diego CA 92121

DADISMAN, LYNN ELLEN, marketing executive; b. L.A., Mar. 1, 1946; d. Orlan Sidney and Erna Lou (Harris) Friedman; m. Kent Dadisman, May 1973 (div. 1974). Student UCLA, 1963-65, 71-72, Willis Bus. Coll., 1965-66, Fin. Schs. Am., 1982, Viewpoints Inst., 1970-71. Office mgr. Harleigh Sandler Co., L.A., 1965-67; customer svc. Investors Diversified Svcs., West L.A., Calif., 1968-76; exec. sec. McCulloch Oil Corp., West L.A., 1976; mgr. publs. Security 1st Group, Century City, Calif., 1976-80; office mgr. Morehead & Co., Century City, 1980-81; dir. mktg., mgr. customer svc. Ins. Mktg. Services, Santa Monica, Calif., 1981-82; v.p. Decatur Petroleum Corp., Santa Monica, 1982-83; asst. v.p., broker svcs., dir. Angeles Corp., L.A., 1984-87; asst. to pres. Pacific Ventures, Santa Monica, 1988-90; La Grange Group, West L.A., 1990—. Mem. Nat. Assn. Securities Dealers, Migi Car Am. Club (sec., newsletter editor). Fin. and ins. writer; contbr. poetry to UCLA Literary Mag., 1964. Home: 3442 S Centinela Ave Apt 15 Los Angeles CA 90066-1851

DADO, ARNOLD EMMETT, financial and insurance consultant; b. Petaluma, Calif., Mar. 17, 1938; s. Emmett Stephen and Madeline Lenore (Ouzts) D.; m. Frances Clark, June 10, 1958 (div. June, 1970); children: Alan, Sharlyn, Melanie; m. Susan Carol Forbes, June 9, 1990. Student, U. San Francisco, 1956-61. CLU, chartered fin. cons. Sales rep. ins. industry, 1962-67; asst. mgr. Mut. of N.Y., Oakland, Calif., 1967-71; tng. asst. mgr. of N.Y., N.Y.C., 1971; mgr. Mut. of N.Y., San Rafael, Calif., 1971-73, field sales dir. western region, 1973; mgr. Mut. of N.Y., Santa Rosa, Calif., 1973-80; pvt. practice fin. planning Santa Rosa, 1980—; expert witness for Tech. Adv. Svc. for Attys., 1990—, U.S. Dept. Justice, 1991; lectr. in field. Organizer Spl. Olympics, Santa Rosa, 1975—. Sgt. U.S. Army, 1960-64. Mem. Am. Soc. CLU and Chartered Fin. Cons. (past pres., chmn. continuing edn. com.), Redwood Empire Assn. Life Underwriters (chmn. ethics com., former bd. dirs.), Estate Planning Coun. (former bd. dirs.), Elks Club. Democrat. Roman Catholic. Office: 2300 Bethards Dr Ste J Santa Rosa CA 95405-8568

DAEMEN, JAAK JOSEPH K., mining and geotechnical engineering educator; came to the U.S., 1967; Degree in mining engring., U. Leuven, Belgium, 1967; PhD in Geol. Engring., U. Minn., 1975. Registered profl. engr., Ariz. Rsch. asst., then rsch. assoc. U. Minn., Mpls., 1967-75; rsch. engr. explosives products divsn. E.I. DuPont de Nemours & Co., Martinsburg, W.Va., 1975-76; asst. prof., then assoc. prof. mining and geol. engring. U. Ariz., Tucson, 1976-90; prof., dept. chair U. Nev., Reno, 1990—. Mem. ASCE, AIME, Internat. Soc. for Rock Mechanics, Am. Underground Space Assn., Am. Geophys. Union, Internat. Soc. Explosives Engrs., Internat. Soc. for Soil Mechanics and Found. Engring., Royal Flemish Engring. Soc., Royal Belgium Assn. of Engrs. and Industrialists. Home: 2620 Pioneer Dr Reno NV 89509 Office: U Nev Dept of Mining Engring Reno NV 89557-0139

DAGGETT, ROBERT SHERMAN, lawyer; b. La Crosse, Wis., Sept. 16, 1930; s. Willard Manning and Vida Naomi (Sherman) D.; m. Lee Sullivan Burton, Sept. 16, 1961; children: Ann Daggett McCluskey, John Sullivan; m. Helen Hosler Ackerman, July 20, 1976. A.B. with honors in Polit. Sci. and Journalism, U. Calif.-Berkeley, 1952, J.D., 1955. Bar: Calif. 1955, U.S. Supreme Ct. 1967. Assoc. firm Brobeck, Phleger & Harrison, San Francisco, 1958-66, ptnr., 1966—; counsel, Reapportionment Lit. Calif. Senate, 1972-73; adj. prof. evidence and advocacy Hastings Coll. Law, 1982—; instr. No. Dist. Fed. Practice Program, 1982—, mem. teaching com., 1983—; demonstrator-instr. Nat. Inst. for Trial Advocacy, 1981—; demonstrator-instr. Hastings Ctr. for Trial and Appellate Advocacy, 1981-88, mem. adv. bd., 1983-88; vol. pro tem judge San Francisco Mcpl. Ct., 1981-88, San Francisco Superior Ct., 1990—; evaluator Fed. Early Neutral Evaluation Program, 1983-88, arbitrator and pvt. comml. arbitrator, 1984—; occasional host Face to Face, Sta. KQID-TV. Bd. editors Calif. Law Rev., 1953-55; contbr. articles and lectures to profl. jours. Bd. dirs. San Francisco Legal Aid Soc.; bd. visitors U. Calif., Santa Cruz. 1st lt. JAGC, U.S. Army, 1958-62. Walter Perry Johnson scholar, 1953. Fellow Am. Bar Found.; mem. ABA, State Bar Calif., San Francisco Bar Assn. (past dir.), Fed. Bar Assn. (pres. San Francisco chpt. 1992—), Am. Judicature Soc., Am. Law Inst., Order Golden Bear, Bohemian Club, Commonwealth Club, Comml. Club (bd. dirs. 1989—, pres. 1993), Phi Delta Phi, Theta Xi. Republican. Office: Brobeck Phleger & Harrison Spear St Tower 1 Market Pla San Francisco CA 94105

DAHEIM, MARY RENE, writer; b. Seattle, Nov. 7, 1937; d. Hugh Emery and Monica Mary (Dawson) Richardson; m. David Charles Daheim, Dec. 18, 1965; children: Barbara, Katherine, Magdalen. BA in Communications, U. Wash., 1960. Mng. editor Anacortes (Wash.) Am. Bull., 1960; mgr. Pacific NW Bell Tel. Co., Seattle, 1960-66; reporter, columnist Port Angeles (Wash.) Evening News, 1966-69; pub. rels. cons. Pacific N.W. Bell, U.S. West, Seattle, 1969-86; writer Seattle, 1983—. Author: Love's Pirate, 1983, Destiny's Pawn, 1984, Pride's Captive, 1986, Passion's Triumph, 1988, King's Ransom, 1990, Improbable Eden, 1991, Just Desserts, 1991, Fowl Prey, 1991, Holy Terrors, 1992, Gypsy Baron, 1992, Alpine Advocate, 1992, Dune to Death, 1993, Alpine Betrayal, 1993, Bantam of the Opera, 1993, The Alpine Christmas, 1993. Mem. Romance Writers Am., Mystery Writers Am., Authors Guild. Roman Catholic.

DAHL, ALAN RICHARD, toxicologist; b. Ottawa, Ill., Feb. 24, 1944; married, 1982; 5 children. AB, Princeton (N.J.) U., 1966; MS, U. Colo., 1970, PhD in Inorganic Chemistry, 1971. Rsch. assoc. chemist U. Munich, 1971-72, Tex. Tech U., Berlin, 1972-73, Northwestern U., 1973-74; sr. scientist toxicology Lovelace Inhalation Toxicol. Rsch. Inst., 1977—, prin. investigator, 1978—; mem. toxicol. study sect. NIH, 1987-91; cln. prof. U. N.Mex. Sch. Pharm., 1986—. Mem. AAAS, Am. Chem. Soc., Am. Soc. Pharm. and Exptl. Therapy, Soc. Toxicology, Internat. Soc. Study Xenobiotics. Office: Lovelace Inhalation Toxicol Rsch Inst PO Box 5890 Albuquerque NM 87185-5890

DAHL, DONALD DOUGLAS, newswriter; b. Savage, Mont., Mar. 25, 1920; s. Alfred Kristian and Elsie (McDonell) D.; m. Helen Copeland, Oct. 6, 1946 (div. 1978); children: Christine Dahl, Karen McKenzie. BA, U. N.D., 1941; MS, Columbia U., 1950. Supr. Fed. Writers Project, Bismarck, N.D., 1941; extension editor U. N.H., Durham, 1946-49; reporter Journal Bulletin, Providence, 1950; correspondent United Press, Manila, The Philippines, 1951-53; copy editor, wire editor, news editor The Albuquerque Tribune, 1954-82. Lt. USNR, 1942-46, PTO. Mem. Beta Theta Pi. Presbyterian. Home: 1305 Girard Blvd SE Albuquerque NM 87106

DAHL, GARDAR GODFREY, JR., geologist, consultant; b. Hood River, Oreg., May 27, 1946; s. Gardar Godfrey Sr. and Margaret Jean (North) D.; m. Margarette Yvonne Beryyman Goodwin. BS in Geol. Engring., Mont. Coll. Mineral Sci. and Tech., 1969, MS in Geol. Engring., 1971. Registered profl. geologist. Asst. geologist Burlington No., St. Paul, 1971-72; mining geologist Burlington No., Seattle, Wash. and Billings, Mont., 1972-75; mgr. coal exploration and devel. Burlington No., Billings, 1975-79; dir. resource devel. Peabody Coal Co., Flagstaff, Ariz., 1979-81; chief geologist Cyprus Coal Co., Englewood, Colo., 1981-85, mgr. geology, 1985-88; mgr. tech. services Cyprus Shoshone Coal Co., Hanna, Wyo., 1988-90; sr. cons. geologist Cyprus Coal Co., Englewood, Colo., 1990-92; contract geologist Dahl & Assocs., 1992—; mng. dir. MEC Resources, Ltd., 1993—; prin. Internat. Mining Cons., 1993—. Mem. AIME, AAAS, Internat. Assn. Math. Geology, Rocky Mountain Coal and Mining Inst., Am. Assn. Profl. Geologists, Mont. Mining Assn., Colo. Mining Assn., Wyo. Profl. Geologists, Denver Coal Club. Lutheran. Home and Office: 8008 South Newport Ct Englewood CO 80112

DAHL, LOREN SILVESTER, federal judge; b. East Fairview, N.D., Mar. 1, 1921; s. William T. and Maude (Silvester) D.; m. Luana Siler, Apr. 5, 1942 (dec.); children: Candy Dahl, Walter Ray. AA, Coll. of Pacific, 1940; LLB, JD, U. Calif., San Francisco, 1949. Bar: Calif., 1950, U.S. Supreme Ct., 1957. Pvt. practice law Sacramento, 1950; sr. ptnr. Dahl, Hefner, Stark & Marois, Sacramento, 1950-80; chief judge U.S. Bankruptcy Ct. (ea. dist.) Calif., Sacramento, 1980, 86—; chmn. Conf. Ch. Judges, 9th cir., 1992. Pres. Golden Empire Coun. Boy Scouts Am., Sacramento, 1955-56, chmn. bd. trustees, 1956, exec. com. region 12, 1958, regional chmn. 1968-70, nat. exec. bd. 1968-70; Sacramento County Juvenile Justice Commn.; mem. bd. visitors McGeorge sch. law U. Pacific, 1987—; bd. dirs. Salvation Army, Sacramento, 1954-57; Sacramento Symphony Assn., 1958-59, Sacramento Safety Coun. With USAAF, 1942-46. Recipient Disting. Svc. award Jaycees, 1957, Silver Beaver award, Boy Scouts Am., 1957, Silver Antelope award, Boy Scouts Am., 1963, Disting. Eagle Scout award, Boy Scouts Am., Judge of Yr. award Sacramento County Bar Assn., 1993. Mem. U. of Pacific Alumni Assn. (pres. 1974-78, bd. regents 1980—, Disting. Alumnus award 1979), ABA, Calif. Bar Assn. (lectr. bankruptcy, continuing edn.), Am. Judicature Soc., Phi Delta Phi. Club: Del Paso Country. Lodge: Masons, Shriners, Lions (dir. Sacramento club 1952-53). Home: 842 Lake Oak Ct Sacramento CA 95864-6154 Office: US Bankruptcy Ct 650 Capitol Mall 8308 US Courthouse Sacramento CA 95814

DAHL, TERRENCE CURTIS, pharmaceutical scientist, researcher; b. Valley City, N.D., Sept. 5, 1954; s. Erling Andrew and Jean Ardist (Schneekloth) D. BS in Pharmacy, N.D. State U., 1977; PhD in Phys. Pharmacy, U. Iowa, 1983. Lic. pharmacist, N.D., Mont., Iowa, Calif. Staff pharmacist Holy Rosary Hosp., Miles City, Mont., 1977-78; rsch. pharmacist E. R. Squibb & Sons, New Brunswick, N.J., 1980; staff researcher I Syntex Corp., Palo Alto, Calif., 1983-85, staff researcher II, 1985-91, sr. staff researcher, 1991—; vis. scientist Pharm. Mfr.'s Assn., Washington, 1989-91. Mem. Am. Assn. Pharm. Sci., Acad. Pharm. Sci., Controlled Release Soc., Rho Chi. Roman Catholic. Home: 1646 Kennewick Dr Sunnyvale CA 94087-4130 Office: Syntex 3401 Hillview Ave # R1-145 Palo Alto CA 94304-1397

DAHLBERG, RICHARD CRAIG, nuclear energy company executive; b. Astoria, Oreg., July 23, 1929; s. Walfred Andrew and Ruth (Slotte) D.; m. Patricia Harriet Ravage, June 2, 1957; children: Robin Lee, Julia Ann, Andrea Craig. Student, Reed Coll., 1947-48; BS in Physics, U. Oreg., 1951; MS in Physics, U. Mich., 1953; PhD in Nuclear Sci., Rensselaer Poly. Inst., 1964. Registered profl. engr., Calif. Mgr. nuclear engring. Knolls Atomic Power Lab., Schenectady, N.Y., 1957-64; mgr. nuclear engring. Gen. Atomic, San Diego, 1964-70, dir. fuel div., 1970-83, dir. advanced projects, 1983—. Author: (drama) Next Year Will Be Better, 1983. Pres. La Jolla (Calif.) Shores Assn., 1970-80, La Jollans Inc., La Jolla, 1975-80. Fellow Am. Nuclear Soc.; mem. Sigma Xi, Phi Beta Kappa. Democrat. Home: 7733

Esterel Dr La Jolla CA 92037-3520 Office: PO Box 85608 San Diego CA 92186-5608

DAHLBERG, THOMAS ROBERT, columnist, screenwriter, author; b. Pitts., Nov. 28, 1961; s. J. Robert and Patricia Ann (McSweeney) D.; m. Teresa Marie Dorr, Aug. 21, 1981 (div. 1989); 1 child, Mary Katherine; m. Jeanne Marie Henderson, July 19, 1992. BS, Pa. State U., 1984, postgrad, 1982-84; MS, Georgetown U., 1986; JD, U. Notre Dame, 1987. Legis. asst. U.S. Senate, Washington, 1985; dir. fin. Ctr. Judical Studies, Washington, 1986; fgn. svc. officer U.S. Dept. State, Reston, Va., 1987-88; assoc. various firms, 1988-90; columnist, screenwriter, author Sacramento, 1991—. Author: Drug Crazy, 1993, Literary Transaction Guide, 1993, (screenplay) Sequential Monogamy, 1992, (screenplay) Spooks and Loggers, 1992, (screenplay) Whippers and Slippers, 1992, (screenplay) Trauma Drama, 1993; editor Benchmark, Washington, 1986-87; Notre Dame Law Sch. editorial group, Harvard Jour. Law & Public Policy, editor, 1985-86, sr. editor, 1986-87; contbr. articles to profl. jours. and mags. speaker Sacramento AIDS Found., 1991-92. Capt. USAR, 1979-90, Ctrl. Am., Europe. Nominee Pulitzer Prize for Disting. Commentary, 1993. Mem. Federalist Soc. for Law and Pub. Policy Studies (past pres. Notre Dame chpt. 1985-87), Assn. Trial Lawyers Am., Natl. Assn. Criminal Defense Lawyers (com. on presecutorial misconduct, com. to free the innocent imprisoned, death penalty project), Writers Guild Am. (west), Amnesty Internat. (lawyer's com.), Mensa. Office: Ste 145 5960 S Land Park Dr Sacramento CA 95822

DAHLEN, LAUREL JUNE, artist, educator; b. L.A., June 17, 1949; d. Charles Richard and Eunice Helen (Melander) Leef; m. Noel Dahlen, July 2, 1972; children: Jenny Marie, Julie Ana, Peter Duane, Joy Christine. AA, L.A. Harbor Coll., Wilmington, Calif., 1969; BA, U. Calif., San Barbara, 1971. Owner Laurel's Handiwork, Santa Ana, 1982-85; owner, artist Divine Design, Santa Ana, 1986—; tchr. pvt. art lessons, 1985—. Chmn. Calvery Chapel Visual Arts Fellowship, Santa Ana, 1991—. Mem. Am. Soc. Interior Designers. Republican. Office: Divine Design 610 S Mohawk Dr Santa Ana CA 92704

DAHLHEIMER, DONALD JOSEPH, consumer products manufacturing executive; b. St. Louis, Apr. 23, 1931; s. Joseph Adam and Marie Barbara (Fraum) D.; m. Adelma Mae Gresham, Apr. 1, 1937; children: Mark, Dona, Philip, Craig. Student, St. Louis U., 1953-54, Washington U., 1960-62. Region supr. Campbell Soup Co., Detroit, 1953-64; gen. mktg. mgr. PET, Inc., St. Louis, 1964-69; v.p. mktg. Borden Co., Coral Gables, Fla., 1969-71; exec. v.p. Lindsay Internat., San Mateo, Calif., 1971-76; pres. Dahlheimer & Assocs., Belmont, Calif., 1976-85, Trident Products, Hayward, Calif., 1985-87; chmn., CEO Super Brands, Inc., Henderson, Nev., 1987—; lectr. Washington U., St. Louis, 1969-71, U. Calif., Davis, 1975-76, Princeton Rsch. Inst., Scottsdale, Ariz., 1977-87. Patentee in field. Ky. Col. apptd. by Gov. Louie B. Nunn, 1971. Sgt. USMC, 1950-52, Korea. Roman Catholic. Office: Super Brands Inc 8251 Gallagher Crest Henderson NV 89014

DAHLIN, DENNIS JOHN, landscape architect; b. Ft. Dodge, Iowa, June 12, 1947; s. Fred E. and Arlene (Olson) D.; m. Jeanne M. Larson, Mar. 2, 1969 (div. 1990); 1 child, Lisa. BA, Iowa State U., 1970; M in Landscape Architecture, U. Calif., Berkeley, 1975. Lic. landscape architect. Assoc. planner San Luis Obispo County, Calif., 1971-73; prin. Dennis Dahlin Assocs., Modesto, Calif., 1975-90; v.p. WPM Planning Team, Inc., Modesto, 1991—; v.p. El Porvenir Found., Sacramento, Calif., 1991—. Contbg. author: The Energy Primer, 1976. Bd. dirs. Ecology Action Ednl. Inst., Modesto, 1984-85, Econ. Conversion Coun., San Diego, 1988-89; pres. San Joaquin Habitat for Humanity, Stockton, Calif., 1986-87. Ferrand fellow U. Calif., 1974, Kearney fellow Harvard U., 1975. Mem. Am. Planning Assn., Am. Soc. Landscape Architects, Assn. Environ. Profls. Congregationalist. Office: WPM 1200 G St # 1B Modesto CA 95354

DAHLQUIST, GREGORY EDWARD, physician; b. Denver, Nov. 22, 1957; s. Jerry Edward and Jeanine Marie (Eldien) D.; m. Cecile Duc-Than, Feb. 10, 1990. AS, Santa Rosa (Calif.) Jr. Coll., 1978; BA, U. Calif., San Diego, 1980; MD, U. Calif., L.A., 1984. Diplomate Am. Bd. of Family Practice. Resident family practice Ventura County (Calif.) Med. Ctr., 1984-87; family Practitioner Buenaventura Med. Clinic, Ventura, 1987—; pres., bd. dirs. Buenaventura Med. Clinic, Inc., 1990—. Home: 1700 Isabella Ct Ventura CA 93004 Office: Buenaventura Med Clinic 2705 Loma Vista Rd Ventura CA 93003

DAHLSTEN, DONALD LEE, enviromental biology, forest entomology educator; b. Clay Center, Nebr., Dec. 8, 1933; s. Leonard Harold and Shirley B. (Courtright) D.; m. Reva D. Wilson, Sept. 19, 1959 (div.); children: Dia Lee, Andrea; m. Janet Clair Winner, Aug. 7, 1965; stepchildren: Karen Rae, Michael Allen. BS, U. Calif., Davis, 1956; MS, U. Calif., Berkeley, 1960, PhD, 1963. Asst. prof. Los Angeles State Coll., 1962-63; asst. entomologist U. Calif., Berkeley, 1963-65, lectr., 1965-68, asst. prof., 1968-69, assoc. prof., 1969-74, prof. entomology, 1974—, chmn. div. Biol. Control, 1980-88, 1993—, chmn. dept. cons. and rsch. studies, 1989-91; vis. prof. Yale Sch. Forestry and Environ. Studies, 1980-81, Integrated Pest Mgmt. Team People's Republic China, 1980, 81.. Mem. AAAS, Am. Inst. Biol. Scis. (vis. prof., lectr. 1970-71), Entomol. Soc. Am., Entomol. Soc. Can., Soc. Am. Foresters. Office: U Calif Div Biol Control Berkeley CA 94720

DAHLSTEN, SHIRLEY ANNETTE, artist, educator; b. Salina, Kans., Jan. 11, 1940; d. William Woodrow and Clara Lenora (Kunau) Hudson; m. John Wendell Dahlsten, Dec. 28, 1959; 1 child, James Michael. Student, Kans. State U., 1962, Cloud County C.C., Concordia, Kans., 1966, Clatsop C.C., Astoria, Oreg., 1970; BA in Painting, Portland State U., 1984. Artist. asst. to Stan Wanlass, Astoria, 1977-78; ct. room artist Sta. KATU, Portland, Oreg., 1978; tchr. art Cannon (Oreg.) Beach Artist Group, 1988-89; instr. art Tillamoon Bay C.C., Manzanita, Oreg., 1987, Clatsop C.C., 1975—; owner Dahlsten Studio Gallery, Astoria, 1990—; chmn., developer Art Reigns Gallery, Astoria, 1990—. One-woman shows include The Edge Gallery, Astoria, 1987, On The Edge Gallery, Salem, Oreg., 1988, Michael's Gallery, Astoria, 1989; group exhbns. include Ariel Gallery, N.Y.C., 1989-90, Hilton Gallery, Portland, 1988-89, Victoria Mann Gallery, Sun River, Oreg., 1989, Bill Dodge Gallery, Carmel, Calif., 1989, Attic Gallery, Portland, 1990; represented in permanent collections Health Link Corp, Portland, Hudson Concrete Corp., Livermore, Calif., Bruno Rubeo Collection, Hollywood, Calif.; works represented in Ency. Living Am. Artists, 3d edit., 1988, Internat. Catalog Contemporary Artists, 1989, Manhattan Arts mag., 1990. Chmn. Astoria Arts Celebration, 1990-91, co-chmn., 1991-92, Astoria Downtown Arts Project, 1990—; pres. coun. 1st Luth. Ch., Astoria, 1991-92. Mem. P.E.O. (sec. chpt. DL 1991-92). Democrat. Home and Studio: 3909 Franklin Ave Astoria OR 97103

DAHLSTROM, GRANT RUSSELL, hotel management professional; b. Pocatello, Idaho, Mar. 2, 1954; s. Hubert Mark and Leota (Sorensen) D.; m. Luci Ribeiro Campanella, Mar. 3, 1976; children: Jenefer, Josiah, Andy, Tony, Luciana. Grad. high sch., Pocatello. Tchr. English Rio de Janeiro, 1976-78; sales rep. Mr. Mac Clothier, Pocatello, 1975; thin film technician Am. Microsystems, Inc., Pocatello, 1979; field underwriter Met. Life Ins., Pocatello, 1979; sales rep. Satterfield Realty, Pocatello, 1980-81; co-owner, mgr. Cordon's Pies, Pocatello, 1981-83; field underwriter N.Y. Life Ins. Co., Pocatello, 1983-85; mgmt. trainee Pizza Hut, Pocatello, 1985; from front desk clk. to gen. mgr. Best Western Cotton Tree Inn, Pocatello, 1985—. Bd. dirs. Pocatello Sports Com., 1987-93, Time Max Inc., 1992; active Pocatello strategic planning for econs. devel., 1987—. Mem. Pocatello C. of C. (chmn. com. on travel and tourism 1986-91, bd. dirs. 1987-90, chamber pres. 1992-93). Mormon. Home: 1656 Shasta Pocatello ID 83201-2214 Office: Best Western CottonTree Inn 1415 Bench Rd Pocatello ID 83201-2499

DAIGLE, RONALD ELVIN, medical imaging scientist, researcher; b. Lake Charles, La., Oct. 14, 1944; s. Elvin and Dorothy Helen (Mayo) D.; m. Ann Jean Lassman, Dec. 30, 1966; children: Janah Wryn, Jon Kim. BA in Physics, U. Calif., Santa Barbara, 1967; MSEE, Colo. State U., 1971, PhD in Physiology and Biophysics, 1974. Rsch. assoc. dept. physiology and biophysics Colo. State U., Ft. Collins, 1974; postdoctoral fellow cardiovascular tng. program Ctr. for Bioengring., U. Wash., Seattle, 1974-75; rsch. assoc. Ctr. for Bioengring., U. Wash., 1975-76; sr. engr. cen. rsch. Varian Assocs., Palo Alto, Calif., 1976-81; dir. advanced devel. Advanced Tech. Labs., Bothell, Wash., 1981-86, sr. scientist, 1986-88, chief sr. tech. staff, 1988-89, dir. advanced products, 1990—, lectr. Doppler physics, 1987—, tech. fellow in perpetuity, 1988—; cons. in cardiovascular instrumentation NASA, Houston, 1987—; mem. microsensor rev. bd. Wash. Tech. Ctr., Seattle, 1987—. Mem. editorial bd. Jour. Cardiovascular Ultrasonography, 1983—; contbr. articles to profl. jours., chpts. to books; patentee in field. Recipient IR-100 award Indsl. Rsch. mag., 1978; Nat. Inst. Heart and Lung grantee, 1976. Mem. Am. Inst. Ultrasound in Medicine, Amiga Users Group (pres. 1988-89). Democrat. Home: 22126 NE 62d Pl Redmond WA 98053 Office: Advanced Tech Labs PO Box 3003 Bothell WA 98041-3003

DAIGNAULT, DAVID WILLIAM, insurance company executive; b. Spencerport, N.Y., Oct. 25, 1939; s. Louis Joseph and Marian Agnes (VanGeison) D.; m. Lynn Grace Crossan, Nov. 11, 1961; children: Chari Lynn, Melanie Danielle, Jacqulyn, Leigha Rene. BA, Alfred U., 1961; MS in System Mgmt., U. So. Calif., 1976. Commd. 2d lt. U.S. Army, 1961, advanced through grades to lt. col., 1978, ret., 1983; mng. dir. ERA Magnum Properties, Aiea, Hawaii, 1983-84; ops. mgr. T.I. of Hawaii Inc., Honolulu, 1984-86, exec. v.p., 1986-92; pres. Communicative Pubs., Inc., 1986-91; gen. mgr. The Title Group, Inc., Boulder, Colo., 1992—; bd. dirs. ERA Beacan, Pearl City, Hawaii, 1985—; market mgmt. coll. instr. Mem. Kaneohe (Hawaii) Neighborhood Bd., 1985-87, chmn. 1986-87; mem. Small Bus. Hawaii Polit. Action Com., Honolulu, 1985-86; pres. bd. dirs. Hawaii Philharm., Honolulu, 1985-86. Decorated Bronze Star, Legion of Merit. Mem. Yacht Club Terrace Owner's Assn. (pres. 1984-87), Caledonian Soc. (vice chieftan 1988-91), Hawaiian Scottish Assn. (chieftain 1988-89, chmn. Scottish Heritage Week, Hawaii 1989), St. Andrew Soc. (pres. 1989-92), Rotary (treas. 1991-92). Republican. Office: The Title Group Inc 4770 Base Line Ste 310 Boulder CO 80303

DAILEY, FRED WILLIAM, hotel executive; b. Aurora, Ill., Feb. 3, 1908; s. Louis A. and Frances (McCoy) D.; m. Elizabeth Murphy, Apr. 22, 1946; children: Michael K., Pam Sue Hinman. Builder, operator tourist resorts, 1933-42; builder, So. Calif., 1946-52; pres. Mokuleia Assos., Mokuleia Polo Farms, Inc., Waikiki Corp., Adv. bd. Hawaii, Army; past mem. Honolulu Bd. Water Supply. Served as maj. AUS, World War II. Decorated Purple Heart, Bronze Star; named Hon. Col. 111th Cav. Mem. U.S. Air Force Assn., C. of C., Am. Hotel Assn. (past dir.), Hawaii Hotel Assn. (past pres.), Hawaii Horse Show Assn. (past pres.), Hawaii Polo and Racing Assn. (pres.), U.S. Polo Assn. (past gov.). Clubs: L.A. Athletic; Hawaii Polo (Honolulu); Santa Barbara Polo. Author: Blood, Sweat and Jeers; One Man's Meat, Polo Is A Four Letter Word, Memories. Address: 2003 Kalia Rd Apt 1-H Honolulu HI 96815 Address: Mokuleia Polo Farm Inc Gahu HI 96815

DAILY, RICHARD W., lawyer; b. Boulder, Colo., Nov. 10, 1945; s. L. Donald and Lois W.; m. Patricia A. Cronin, June 30, 1986; 1 child, Samuel. BA, Antioch Coll., 1968; JD, Harvard U., 1971. Bar: Colo. 1971, U.S. Dist. Ct. Colo. 1971, U.S. Ct. Appeals (10th cir.) 1973, Fed. Cir. 1983. Assoc. Hodges, Kerwin, Otten & Weeks, Denver, 1972-73; assoc. Davis, Graham & Stubbs, Denver, 1973-79, ptnr., 1979-91; spl. counsel Burns, Wall, Smith & Mueller, P.C., Denver, 1991. Counsel Colo. Dem. Party, Denver, 1987-93; bd. dirs. Goodwill Industries Denver, 1981-87; mem. Colo. Coun. on Arts and Humanities, 1983-89. Capt. USAR, 1971-77. Mem. ABA, Colo. Bar Assn., Denver Bar Assn. Office: Burns Wall Smith & Mueller 303 E 17th Ave Ste 800 Denver CO 80203-1261

DAKIN, KARL JONATHAN, lawyer; b. Sugar Creek Twp., Kans., June 2, 1954; s. John R. and Vera (Stockabrand) D.; m. Darla Anne Click, Nov. 29, 1986; children: Tara Nicole, Emma Ariel. BBA, WAshburn U., 1976, JD, 1979. Bar: Colo. 1980. Legal counsel Educo Corp., Arvada, Colo., 1979-81; jr. ptnr. Corporon & Keene, Englewood, Colo., 1981-83; sr. assoc. Berkowitz, Berkowitz & Brady, Denver, 1985-86; pres. Karl J. Dakin & Assocs., P.C., Englewood, 1983-84, Karl J. Dakin, P.C., Englewood, 1986—; adj. prof. U. Denver, 1983-85, 93, Met. State Coll., Denver, 1989, 90. Author: (seminar) Trade Secrets, 1985; co-author: Computer Law, 1990, Technology Transfer, 1991. Mem. Colo. Tech. Action Consortium. Mem. Tech. Transfer Soc. (pres. Colo. chpt. 1992-93), Licensing Execs. Soc., Rocky Mountain Inventors and Entrepreneurs Congress. Office: 5445 DTC Pkwy Ste 1000 Englewood CO 80111

DAKOFSKY, ANDREW ERIC, computer scientist; b. Bklyn., Apr. 4, 1960; s. Lawrence B. Dakofsky and Rhoda Weintraub. BS, U. N.Mex., 1993. Coop. engring. student Los Alamos (N.Mex.) Nat. Lab., 1980; student aide N.Mex. Engring. Rsch. Inst., Albuquerque, 1981; mech. engr. I trainee Eg&g Energy Measurements, Albuquerque, 1981-82, systems programmer 1, 1982-84, systems programmer, 1984-86; systems programmer 3, project engr. EG&G Energy Measurements, Las Vegas, N.Mex., 1986-90; systems programmer, project engr. Eg&g Energy Measurements, Albuquerque, 1990—; team mem. Sandia Nat. Lab. and Dept. Energy-Internat. Conf., Pembroke, Can., 1992; mem. installation team Dept. Energy, Tokai, Japan, 1991. Author tech. papers in field. Mem. IEEE, Digital Equopment Computer User Soc., Assn. Computing Machinery. Republican. Home: 10209 Jiles Dr NE Albuquerque NM 87111-1934 Office: EG&G Energy Measurements PO Box 4339 Sta A Albuquerque NM 87196

DALE, BEVERLY ANN, biochemist, educator; b. Detroit, Oct. 19, 1942; d. Paul H. and Elsie May (Liggett) Goodell; m. Philip Dale (div. 1990); children: Jonathan, Jessica. BS, U. Mich., 1964, PhD, 1968. Postdoctoral fellow U. Wash., Seattle, 1968-70, rsch. asst. prof., then rsch. assoc. prof. Sch. Dentistry, 1972-86, rsch. prof. Sch. Dentistry, 1988-90, prof. dept. oral biology, 1990—; dir. dentist scientist tng. program Sch. Dentistry, Seattle, 1990—; mem. NIH study sect., Nat. Inst. Arthritus, Musculo-skeletal and Skin, Bethesda, Md., 1989—. Recipient Merit award Nat. Inst. Dental Rsch. Mem. AAAS, Am. Assn. Dental Rsch., Soc. Investigative Dermatology, Am. Soc. Cell Biology. Office: Univ Wash Dept Oral Biology SB 22 Seattle WA 98195

DALE, DENVER THOMAS, III, retired military officer, educator; b. Santa Barbara, Calif., July 30, 1931; s. Denver Thomas Jr. and Ethel Helen (Squire) D.; m. Elizabeth Ann Donleavy, Nov. 17, 1956 (div. Oct. 1978); children: Denver Thomas IV, Matthew J., Jeffrey N.; m. Peggy Frances Altice, Nov. 19, 1982. Student Va. Mil. Inst., 1948-52; BA, San Francisco State U., 1959; MS, Cen. Conn. State U., 1969. Cert. secondary educator, Calif. Enlisted USMC, 1952, advanced through grades to lt. col., 1975; comdg. officer Co. K., 3d Bn., 4th Marine Regt., Kaneohe Bay, Hawaii, 1961-64; manpower mgmt. officer 1st Marine Aircraft Wing, Iwakuni, Japan and Danang, Vietnam, 1964-65; exec. officer, comdg. officer 3d Bn., 5th Marine Regt., An Hoa, Vietnam, 1969-70; head officer force mgmt. unit Hdqrs. U.S. Marine Corps, Washington, 1970-73; exec. officer, comdg. officer, assoc. prof. naval sci. NROTC Unit, Rice U., Houston, 1973-75; ret., 1975; project mgr. Telemedia, Inc., Teheran, Iran, 1978; sr. marine instr. Marine Corps jr. ROTC unit, Portage High Sch., Ind., 1979-81, North High Sch., Bakersfield, Calif., 1981-92, chmn. dept. mil. sci., 1981-92, high sch. varsity boys tennis coach, 1983-86; prin. speaker at numerous civic, frat., vets., high sch. and coll. groups, 1965—. Asst. scoutmaster Boy Scouts Am., 1970-73. Decorated Bronze Star with V device, Comdt. U.S. Marines commendation; Vietnamese Cross of Galantry. Mem. Marine Corps Assn., VFW, VMI Alumni Assn. Republican. Lodge: Masons. Home: 8127 Running Deer Ln Roanoke VA 24019

DALE, FRANCIS LYKINS, foundation executive, former performing arts officer, former sports executive, lawyer, former newspaper publisher, diplomat; b. Urbana, Ill., July 13, 1921; s. Charles Sherman and Sarah (Lykins) D.; m. Kathleen Hamlin Watkins, Mar. 20, 1947; children: Mitchell Watkins, Myron Lykins, Kathleen Hamlin, Holly Moore. AB, Duke U., 1943; LLB, U. Va., 1948; cert., Acad. Internat. Law, The Hague, 1958; LLD (hon.), Eastern Ky. U., U. Cin., Ohio Wesleyan U., Salmon P. Chase Coll. of Law, Bloomfield Coll., Pepperdine Sch. of Bus., Whittier Coll. Bar: Ohio 1948. Assoc. Frost & Jacobs, Cin., 1948-53, ptnr., 1953-65; asst. sec. Cin. Enquirer, Inc., 1952-65, pres., pub., 1965-73; pres. The Cin. Reds, Inc., 1967-73, vice-chmn., 1973-76; pub. L.A. Herald Examiner, 1977-85; commr. Major Indoor Soccer League, 1985-86; pres. The Music Ctr. of L.A. County, 1986-88, Maureen and Mike Mansfield Found., 1988-90; sr. assoc. Moxham, Carver & Assocs., Pasadena, Calif., 1990—; bd. dirs., pres. Citizens for Water and Power for N.Am., Pasadena, Calif., 1991—; chmn. Nat. Coun. Crime and Delinquency, 1973-74, vice chmn., 1975-91; chmn. Commn. White House fellows, 1973-74; U.S. ambassador and rep. to European Office of UN and other internat. orgns., Geneva, 1974-76; spl. asst. to asst. sec. state, 1976; spl. adviser U.S. del. 31st Gen. Assembly; bd. dirs. ICN Biomeds., New Economy Fund, Coachman Inc., Smallcap World Fund; pres. Rep. Assocs. Active United Appeal, Cin., L.A.; bd. dirs. Goodwill Industries, Cin., v.p., 1968; bd. dirs., mem. exec. com. Cin. area chpt. ARC; bd. dirs. Boys Clubs' Am., Bethesda Hosp., Boys' Club Cin., Taft Inst., Cin. Natural History Mus., also symphony, opera, ballet cos.; trustee Am. U., 1982-87, Occidental Coll., 1977-92, Claremont Sch. Theology, 1983—; chmn. bd. councilors U. So. Calif. Coll. Continuing Edn.; bd. councilors Sch. Internat. Rels. and Sch. Bus.; assoc. Calif. Poly. U., bd. dirs. Los Angeles chpt. ARC, Central City Assn., 1978-84, Meth. Hosp. So. Calif. Found., 1980—, Huntington Meml. Research Inst., 1985—, Operating Co.-Music Center, 1982-86, Los Angeles World Affairs Coun., Los Angeles chpt. NCCJ, Town Hall Calif., Greater Los Angeles Visitors and Conv. Bur.; bd. dirs., pres. Los Angeles Area council Boy Scouts Am., 1983-84, mem. nat. adv. bd., 1984—; bd. dirs. Coun. Am. Ambssadors; mem., vice-chmn. So. Calif. Salvation Army; v.p. USAIM; assoc. chmn. World Media Assn. With USNR, World War II. Named Outstanding Young Man of Year Cin., 1951; recipient Gov.'s award for adding prestige Ohio, 1968, Superior Honor award State Dept., 1976, Freedoms Found. award, 1976, Silver Beaver award Boy Scouts Am., 1969, Disting. Citizen's award U.S. Olympic Com., 1984; named to Wisdom Hall of Fame, 1987. Fellow ABA; mem. Ohio Bar Assn. (pres. 1961-62), L.A. C. of C. (v.p., bd. dirs. 1961-63), Coun. Chs. Greater Cin. (pres. 1959-61), Frat. of Friends (v.p. 1986-88), Order of Coif, Phi Kappa Psi, Sigma Nu Phi. Methodist (dist. lay leader 1958-64; mem. bd. publs. 1977-82). Clubs: Lincoln, Rotary; Comml. (Cin.); Annandale Golf (Los Angeles), Calif. (Los Angeles); Bohemian (San Francisco); Valley Hunt (Pasadena).

DALE, LEON ANDREW, business administrator, educator; b. Paris, May 9, 1921; m. Arlene R. Dale; 1 child, Melinda Jennifer. B.A., Tulane U., 1946; M.A., U. Wis., 1947, Ph.D., 1949. Grad. asst. in econs. U. Wis., 1946-48; Asst. prof. labor econs. U. Fla., 1949-50; internat. economist AFL, Paris, 1950-53; AFL rep. at nat. labor convs. Greece, 1951, Naples, Italy, 1951, Switzerland, Sweden, Norway, Belgium, Austria, Luxembourg, Gt. Britain, 1950-53; cons. U.S. Govt., 1954-56; internat. economist U.S. Dept. Labor, Washington, 1956-59; prof., chmn. dept. mgmt. and indsl. rels., dir. internat. ctr., coord. courses for fgn. students U. Bridgeport, Conn., 1960-69; chief union task force Coll. Bus. Admstrn. Calif. State Poly. U., Pomona, 1980, coord. internat. activities Sch. Bus. Adminstrn., 1969-77, prof. mgmt. and human resources, 1969-91, prof. emeritus, 1991—, also, acting chmn. bus. mgmt. dept., summer 1973; chief Coll. Bus. Adminstrn. Calif. State U., Pomona, 1981; lectr. Internat. Conf. Tree Trade Unions Summer Sch., Wörgl, Austria, 1951; lectr. on Am. labor UN, Stockholm, 1952; lectr. U. Wis., Milw., 1960; seminar leader Mgmt. Ctr, Cambridge, 1962-63; vis. prof. Columbia U., 1966, 67, Bernard Baruch Sch. Bus. and Pub. Adminstrn., 1966-69; cons., arbitrator, fact-finder State of Conn., 1964-69; Am. del., speaker 3d Internat. Symposium on Small Bus., Washington, 1976, 4th Internat. Symposium on Small Bus., Seoul, Korea, 1977, 5th Internat. Symposium on Small Bus., Anaheim, Calif., 1978, 6th Internat. Symposium on Small Bus., Berlin, 1979; also mem. U.S. steering com. Internat. Symposium on Small Bus.; chief union task force Coll. Bus. Adminstrn. Calif. State Poly. U., Pomona, 1980; sr. cons. Am. Grad. U., Covina, Calif., 1981-82; adj. prof. econs. Nat. U., San Diego, 1981-90, Pepperdine U., 1986; discussion leader Calif. Inst. Tech. Internat. Conf. on Combining Best of Japanese and U.S. Mgmt., Anaheim, 1981; lectr. on indsl. rels. to execs. Miller Brewing Co., Irwindale, Calif., 1983; cons. Agy. Internat. Devel., N'Djamena, Republic of Chad, 1987; cons. to Minister for Planning, Republic of Chad; cons., instr. behavior courses U. Chad.; instr. mgmt. French-speaking African Students internat. ctr. Calif. State Poly. U., 1988; participant Ea. Europe and the West: Implication for Africa, So. Calif. Consortium on Internat. Studies conf., Pomona, 1990; lectr. confs. on leadership in fund, Dakar, Senegal, 1990; seminar tchr. on leadership and mgmt. Citibank of N.Y., Dakar, Senegal, 1991. Author: Marxism and French Labor, 1956, A Bibliography of French Labor, 1969; (video tape) Industrial Relations and Human Resources, 1982, Labor Relations in Crisis, 1989; originator Liberté (first French newspaper published in liberated France, 1944); contbr. articles to profl. jours. Served with U.S. Army, 1942-45. Recipient U. Bridgeport Faculty rsch. grantee, 1962; U. Wis. fellow, 1949; named one of Outstanding Educators of Am., 1972, 73. Mem. Indsl. Rels. Rsch. Assn., Am. Acad. Polit. and Social Sci., Soc. Profls. Dispute Resolution (charter) Racing Club de France. Home and Office: 30 S La Senda Dr Laguna Beach CA 92677-3342

DALE, SHARON R., special education educator; b. Niagara Falls, N.Y., Feb. 27, 1955; d. Eldon L. and Phyllis M. (Haines) Frailey; m. Joel Dale, July 28, 1984; children: Lauren, Jonathan. BS, SUNY, Buffalo, 1977, MS, 1980. Cert. CCC, speech/lang. pathology, speech correctionist, Type D sch. adminstr., Type E spl. svcs., Colo.; cert. speech and hearing handicapped; pvt. practice lic. for speech pathology, N.Y. Program supr. Autistic Svcs., Inc., Buffalo; speech/lang. specialist Niagara Falls Bd. Edn., Cherry Creek Sch. Dist., Denver, Denver Pub. Schs. Developed program for severely lang. impaired students and lang. expansion program at secondary level. Mem. ASCD, Am. Speech and Hearing Assn., Colo. Assn. Sch. Execs., Buffalo State Coll. Alumni Assn., Colo. Assn. Sch. Execs., Phi Delta Kappa. Home: PO Box 441491 Aurora CO 80044

DALESIO, WESLEY CHARLES, former aerospace educator; b. Paterson, N.J., Mar. 26, 1930; s. William James and Sarah (Sheets) Delison; m. Dorothy May Zellers, Nov. 17, 1951; children: Michael Kerry, Debra Kaye Dalesio Weber. Student, Tex. Christian U., 1950, U. Tex., Arlington, 1957. Enlisted USAF, 1948, advanced through grades to sr. master sgt., 1968; aircraft engine mech., mgmt. analyst USAF, worldwide, 1948-70; ins. agt. John Hancock Ins., Denver, 1970-71; office mgr. Comml. Builder, Denver, 1972-73; aerospace educator Sch. Dist. 50, Westminster, Colo., 1973-93; dir. aerospace edn. CAP, Denver, 1982-86. Bd. dirs. Crimestoppers, Westminster, 1988-91; mem. Police and Citizens Teamed Against Crime, Westminster, 1992—. Maj. CAP, 1983—. Mem. Nat. Assn. Ret. Mil. Instrs. (charter mem.), Westminster Edn. Assn. Episcopalian. Home: 2537 W 104th Cir Westminster CO 80234

D'ALESSANDRO, MARY PATRICIA, poet, photographer, writer; b. Washington, Pa., Apr. 7, 1924; d. Battista and Rosaria (Valitutti) D'A.; children: Christopher Lee, Timothy Evance, Daniel Peter. BS in Human Relations/Orgnl. Behavior, U. San Francisco, 1982. Sec. FBI, Washington, 1942-45; adminstrv. asst. to dist. sales mgr. Trans World Airlines, San Francisco, 1946-55; travel counselor Stanford and Bungey Travel, Palo Alto, Calif., 1963-66; adminstrv. asst. to psychologist Menlo Park (Calif.) Sch. Dist., 1966-68; adminstrv. asst. to dean residential edn. Stanford (Calif.) U., 1971-76; adminstrv. asst. to v.p., gen. mgr. Levi Strauss and Co., San Francisco, 1977-82; adminstrv. asst. Internat. Women's Health Coalition, N.Y.C., 1985—. Campaigner Dem. Cen. Com., San Francisco, 1971-82; bd. dirs. Menlo-Atherton (Calif.) High Sch., 1964-68, Coun. Arts Palo Alto, 1968-74; active Friends of N.Y. Pub. Library, Internat. Ctr. Photography, N.Y.C. Recipient 1st Place award for poetry Calif. Writers, 1975, Honor's award U. San Francisco, 1983, Judges award for photography City of N.Y., 1988. Mem. Inst. for Design and Experimental Art (bd. dirs., sec.), Soroptimist Internat., MATRIX Gallery.

DALEY, ARTHUR STUART, retired humanities educator; b. Osceola, N.Y., Sept. 16, 1908; s. Kieran A. and Mary (Adams) D.; m. Jean Abendroth, Aug. 29, 1942; 1 child, Arthur Stuart. AB with honors in English, Syracuse U., 1932; postgrad., Harvard U., 1932-33; PhD, Yale U., 1942. Instr. English Syracuse (N.Y.) U., 1935-37, Ind. U., 1946-47, UCLA, 1947-49; asst. prof. English U. Nev., 1949-54; prof., chmn. dept. Coe Coll., 1954-59; prof. Drake U., Des Moines, 1959-76, chmn. dept., 1959-67, coord. humanities div., 1967-75, prof. emeritus, 1976—. Co-author: Private Charity in England, 1747-1757, 1938; contbr. articles especially on Shakespeare to profl. jours.; contbr. articles to rev. Norton crit. edit. Wuthering Heights (Emily Brontë). Served to lt. col. AUS, 1941-46, 51-53; lt. col. AUS ret. Decorated Bronze Star; mem. by right Ancient and Hon. Arty. Co. Mass. Mem. MLA, Renaissance Soc. Am., Soc. Mayflower Descendants, Shakespeare Assn., Brontë Soc., Theta Alpha Phi, Sigma Nu. Home: 2705 Barnson Pl San Diego CA 92103-6103

DALEY, RICHARD HALBERT, foundation executive; b. Centralia, Ill., Oct. 8, 1948; s. Richard Glen D.; m. Lucy C. Costen, Nov. 27, 1976. Student, Lake Forest (Ill.) Coll., 1966-67; BS, Colo. State U., 1970, MS, 1972. Instr. Colo. State U., Ft. Collins, 1972; from dir. biol. svcs. to dir. programs Mo. Bot. Garden, St. Louis, 1973-84; exec. dir. Mass. Hort. Soc., Boston, 1984-91, Denver Botanic Gardens, 1991—; instr. Environ. Ethics Denver U., 1991—. Editorial com. mem. Am. Mus. Natural History, N.Y.C., 1983-92. Mem. Am. Assn. Bot. Gardens, Hort. Club Boston. Office: Denver Botanic Gardens 909 York St Denver CO 80206-3799

DALIS, IRENE, mezzo-soprano, opera company administrator, music educator; b. San Jose, Calif., Oct. 8, 1925; d. Peter Nicholas and Mamie Rose (Boitano) D.; m. George Loinaz, July 16, 1957; 1 child, Alida Mercedes. AB, San Jose State Coll., 1946; MA in Teaching, Columbia U., 1947; MMus (hon.), MS (hon.), San Jose State Coll., 1957; studied voice with, Edyth Walker, N.Y.C., 1947-50, Paul Althouse, 1950-51, Dr. Otto Mueller, Milan, Italy, 1952-72; MusD (hon.), Santa Clara U., 1987. Prin. artist Berlin Opera, 1955-65, Met. Opera, N.Y.C., 1957-77, San Francisco Opera, 1958-73, Hamburg (Fed. Republic Germany) Staatsoper, 1966-71; prof. music San Jose State U., Calif., 1977—; founder, gen. dir. Opera San Jose, 1984—; dir. Met. Opera Nat. Auditions, San Jose dist., 1980-88. Operatic debut as dramatic mezzo-soprano Oldenburgisches Staatstheater, 1953, Berlin Staedtische Opera, 1955; debut Met. Opera, N.Y.C., 1957, 1st Am.-born singer, Kundry Bayreuth Festival, 1961, opened, Bayreuth Festival, Parsifal, 1963; commemorative Wagner 150th Birth Anniversary; opened 1963 Met. Opera Season in Aida; premiered: Dello Joio's Blood Moon, 1961, Henderson's Medea, 1972; rec. artist Parsifal, 1964 (Grand Prix du Disque award); contbg. editor Opera Quarterly, 1983. Recipient Fulbright award for study in Italy, 1951, Woman of Achievement award Commn. on Status of Women, 1983, Pres.'s award Nat. Italian Am. Found., 1985, award of merit People of San Francisco, 1985, San Jose Renaissance award for sustained and outstanding artistic contbn., 1987, Medal of Achievement Acad. Vocal Arts, 1988; named Honored Citizen City of San Jose, 1986; inducted into Calif. Pub. Edn. Hall of Fame, 1985, others. Mem. Beethoven Soc. (mem. adv. bd. 1985—), San Jose Arts Round Table, San Jose Opera Guild, Am. Soc. Univ. Women, Arts Edn. Week Consortium, Phi Kappa Phi, Mu Phi Epsilon. Office: Opera San Jose 12 S 1st St Ste 207 San Jose CA 95113-2404

DALRYMPLE, GARY BRENT, research geologist; b. Alhambra, Calif., May 9, 1937; s. Donald Inlow and Wynona Edith (Pierce) D.; m. Sharon Ann Tramel, June 28, 1959; children: Stacie Ann, Robynne Ann, Melinda Ann. AB, Occidental Coll., 1959; PhD, U. Calif., Berkeley, 1963; DSc, Occidental Coll., Los Angeles, 1993. Registered geologist, Calif. Rsch. geologist U.S. Geol. Survey, Menlo Park, Calif., 1963-81, 84—, asst. chief geologist, 1981-84; vis. prof. Stanford U., 1971-72, cons. prof., 1983-85, 90—. Author: Potassium-Argon Dating, 1969, Age of Earth, 1991; contbr. over 150 papers to profl. jours. Fellow AAAS, Am. Inst. Phys. (bd. govs. 1991-94), Am. Geophys. Union (pres. elect 1988-90, pres. 1990-92), Nat. Acad. Scis., Am. Acad. Arts Scis., Geol. Soc. Am. Fellow AAAS, Am. Inst. Phys. (bd. govs. 1991-94), Am. Geophys. Union (pres. elect 1988-90, pres. 1990-92), Am. Acad. Arts Scis., Geol. Soc. Am.; mem. Nat. Acad. of Scis., 1993. Office: US Geol Survey Br Isotope Geology 345 Middlefield Rd Menlo Park CA 94025-3591

DALTON, CLAIR EUGENE, realtor, consultant, educator; b. Iowa City, Apr. 12, 1939; s. William Lawrence and Carol Belle (Lake) D.; m. Anita LeCain, Sept. 17, 1989; children from previous marriage: Jack, Maureen. BA, Wash. State U., 1966; MBA, U. Wash., 1968; MPA, U. Alaska, 1976; PhD, Kennedy Western, 1986. Info. systems specialist Douglas United Nuclear, Richland, Wash., 1966-68; mgr. manpower systems & plans Boeing Corp., Seattle, 1968-70; asst. v.p. Nat. Bank Alaska, Anchorage, 1970-72; fin. mgmt. specialist Municipality of Anchorage, 1972-86, mgr. fin. & adminstrn., 1986-89; realtor Coldwell Banker, Anchorage, 1989—; adj. prof. U. Alaska, Anchorage, 1970-80. Mem. Citizens Budget Adv. Com., Anchorage, 1970-72; advisor Sch. Budget Adv. Com., Anchorage, 1972-75. With U.S. Army, 1957-60. Mem. Anchorage Bd. Realtors, Kiwanis (pres. 1975). Home and Office: 8442 Jupiter Anchorage AK 99507

DALTON, PAMELA YVONNE WERTON, education educator; b. Waynesburg, Pa., Jan. 25, 1943; d. Willis Alexander and Margaret Mary (Ryan) Werton; m. Michael Joseph Dalton Sr., Oct. 10, 1975; 1 child, Michael Joseph Jr. BA, Marian Coll., 1971; MEd, Ball State U., Muncie, Ind., 1973, EdD, 1975. Cert. tchr. elem. and early childhood edn., Oreg. Tchr. elem. sch. Archidiocese of Indpls., 1962-73; postdoctoral fellow Ball State U., 1973-75; asst. prof. edn. U. Tex., San Antonio, 1975-78; with Linfield Coll., McMinnville, 1978, prof. edn., dir. grad. program, 1982-90, chairperson dept. edn., 1985-88; dir. child care resource ctr. U. Tex., 1977-78. Author several books; contbr. articles to profl. jours. Tex. Dept. Pub. Welfare grantee, 1977, Jr. League grantee, 1977, Levi Strauss Co., 1977, Tex. Dept. Human Resources grantee, 1978, CETA grantee Mid-Valley Manpower Consortium, 1978-81. Mem. Nat. Assn. for Edn. Young Children (validator early childhood com. 1986—, mentor 1988—, cons., presenter), Oreg. Assn. for Edn. Young Children, Phi Delta Kappa (v.p. 1979-83, pres. 1983-84), Kappa Delta Pi (counselor, editorial staff 1992—). Democrat. Roman Catholic. Home: 920 E 1st St McMinnville OR 97128-4403 Office: Linfield Coll Potter Hall McMinnville OR 97128-6505

DALTON, PHYLLIS IRENE, library consultant; b. Marietta, Kans., Sept. 25, 1909; d. Benjamin Reuben and Pearl (Travelute) Bull; m. Jack Mason Dalton, Feb. 13, 1950. BS, U. Nebr., 1931, MA, 1941; MA, U. Denver, 1942. Tchr. city schs., Marysville, Kans., 1931-40; reference libr. Lincoln Pub. Libr., Nebr.; libr. U. Nebr., Lincoln, 1941-48; libr. Calif. State Libr., Sacramento, 1948-57, asst. state libr., 1957-72; pvt. libr. cons., Scottsdale, Ariz., 1972—. Author: Library Services to the Deaf and Hearing Impaired Individuals, 1985, 91 (Pres.' Com. Employment of Handicapped award 1985); contbr. chpt., articles, reports to books and publs. in field. Mem. exec. bd. So. Nev. Hist. Soc., Las Vegas, 1983-84; mem. So. Nev. Com. on Employment of Handicapped, 1980-89, chairperson, 1988-89; mem. adv. com. Nat. Orgn. on Disability, 1982—; mem., sec. resident coun. Forum Pueblo Norte Retirement Village, 1990-91, pres. resident coun., 1991—; bd. dirs. Friends of So. Nev. Libraries; trustee Univ. Library Soc., U. Nev.-Las Vegas; mem. Allied Arts Council, Pres.' Com. on Employment of People with Disabilities, mem. emeritus 1989—; Ariz. Gov.'s Com. on Employment of People with Disabilities, 1990—; Scottsdale Mayor's Com. on Employment of People with Disabilities, 1990—. Recipient Libraria Sodalitas, U. So. Calif., 1972, Alumni Achievement award U. Denver, 1977, Alumni Achievement award U. Nebr., Lincoln, 1983. Mem. LWV, ALA (councilor 1963-64, exceptional svc. award 1981), Am. Assn. U. Women, Assn. State Librs. (pres. 1964-65), Calif. Libr. Assn. (pres. 1969), Nev. Libr. Assn. (hon.), Internat. Fedn. Libr. Assns. and Instns. (chair working group on libr. svc. to prisons, mem. standing com. Sect. Librs. Serving Disadvantaged Persons 1987—), Nat. League Am. Pen Women (Las Vegas chpt. 1988—, parliamentarian Scottsdale chpt. 1989—, v.p. 1992—), Pilot Internat. (mem.-at-large). Republican. Presbyterian. Home: 7090 E Mescal St Apt 261 Scottsdale AZ 85254-6125

DALTON, THOMAS GEORGE, social worker, legal consultant; b. Hoonah, Alaska, Mar. 14, 1940; s. George and Jessie K. (Starr) D.; m. Hazel Hope, Nov. 1960 (div. Sept. 1965); children: Roderick O., Rhoeda J. Garcia, Pamela Vasquez; m. Kathy Pelan, Sept. 1972 (div. Feb. 1980); children: Deirdra J. (dec.), Thomas L., Michael G. AAS, Shoreline Community Coll., Seattle, 1981; BA, Seattle Pacific U., 1985. Social work intern Pub. Defender's Assn., Seattle, 1983-85; client advocate in criminal justice system Seattle, 1985—; legal cons., Seattle. Elder United Presbyn. Ch., Hoonah, 1973—; pres. Alaska Native Brotherhood, Seattle, 1984—; sec. Nat. Am. Community Coun., Seattle, 1990—; mem. Seattle chpt. Tlinget and Haida Indians Alaska. Recipient Founder's award Alaska Native Brotherhood, 1989. Democrat. Home: 7009 10th Ave NW Seattle WA 98117-5242 Office: 8th Fl 810 3rd Ave Central Bldg Seattle WA 98104

DALVESCO, REBECCA, industrial designer; b. Pa., Jan. 9, 1962; d. Rudy and Kathryn Ann (Homol) D. BFA, Ariz. State U., 1985, MS, 1993. Info. specialist Nelson Fine Arts Ctr., Ariz. State U., Tempe, 1989—, Scottsdale (Ariz.) Ctr. for Arts, 1988-89; indsl. designer Works Night Club, Scottsdale, 1989—. Mem. Semiotic Soc. Am. Democrat. Home: PO Box 1176 Tempe AZ 85280

DALY, JIM ROY, artist; b. Holdenville, Okla., Oct. 18, 1940; s. Joe and Barbara Pauline (Nelms) D.; m. Ellen Marie Grabau, Nov. 24, 1958 (div.); children: John, Joe, Dan, Jerry; m. Carole Louise, Apr. 24, 1976; 1 child, Mike. Student, Art Ctr. Coll. of Design, L.A., 1964-68. Artist Eugene, Oreg., 1967—; instr. Scottsdale (Ariz.) Artist Sch. With U.S. Army, 1958-61. Recipient Shorty Shope Peoples Choice award Western Rendezvous of Art, Helena, Mont., 1981, Millpond Press award, 1981, Peoples Choice award, 1989, Merit award, 1989, Western Heritage award Favell Mus., 1993; inductee U.S. Art Hall of Fame, 1992. Mem. N.W. Rendezvous Group. Home and Studio: 2355 Bailey Hill Rd Eugene OR 97405

DALY, PAUL SYLVESTER, technical university chancellor; b. Belmont, Mass., Jan. 8, 1934; s. Matthew Joseph and Alice Mary (Hall) D.; m. Maureen Teresa Kenny, May 25, 1957; children: Judith Mary, Paul S. Jr., Susan Marie, John Joseph, Maureen H. BS in Engring. Sci., Naval Post-grad. Sch., 1968; MBA, U. W. Fla., 1971. Commd. ensign USN, 1955; coll. dean Embry-Riddle Aero. U., Daytona Beach, Fla., 1979-81; advanced through grades to capt. Embry-Riddle Aero. U., 1979, chancellor, 1981—; lectr. seminars, 1977-85; cons. British Aerospace, 1979-84, McDonnell Douglas, 1979-84, IBM, 1983-84; sr. faculty U. Phoenix, 1983-86. Bd. dirs. Yavapai Regional Med. Ctr., Prescott, Ariz., 1983-86, Ariz. Hosp. Fedn., Prescott C. of C., 1982-84; chmn. Ariz. State Bd. Pvt. Postsecondary Edn., Phoenix, 1982—, Interactive Health Corp.; pres. Ind. Coll. and Univs. of Ariz., Phoenix, 1982—; pres., founder West Yavapai County Am. Heart Assn. Chpt., chmn. affiliate of Am. Heart Assn./Ariz. Decorated Legion of Merit. Mem. Ariz. Airport Assn., Retired Officers Assn., Ariz. Town Hall, USAF Assn. Republican. Roman Catholic. Office: Embry-Riddle Aero U 3200 Willow Creek Rd Prescott AZ 86301-3721

DALY, TIMOTHY PATRICK, lawyer; b. Laramie, Wyo., May 11, 1959; s. Joseph Crinion and Jeanette Marie (Tyrrell) D.; m. Melanie Lynne Baker, may 19, 1984; 1 child, John Joseph. Student, U. Wyo., 1977-79; BA, San Diego State U., 1982; JD, George Washington U., 1988; postgrad., Colo. Inst. for Leadership Tng., 1991. Bar: Colo. 1988, U.S. Ct. Appeals (10th cir.). Dir. outreach Community Action Laramie County, Cheyenne, Wyo., 1983-84; exec. dir. Wyo. Dem. Party, Casper, 1984-85; assoc. atty. Kutak Rock, Denver, 1988-93; dep. legal counsel to Gov. Ray Romer, Colo., 1993—; mem. mgmt. com. Kutak Rock, Denver, 1991-93; spl. prosecuting atty. Denver City Atty., 1990. Mem. collaborative decision-making com. Gove Mid. Sch., Denver, 1991; chair elect Downtown Dem. Forum, Denver, 1992; counsel Colo. Inst. for Leadership Tng., 1993. Mem. ABA, Colo. Bar Assn., Denver Bar Assn., Phi Sigma Alpha. Roman Catholic. Home: 1037 St Paul Denver CO 80206 Office: State Capitol Office of Gov Rm 136 Denver CO 80203

DAMEWOOD, RACHEL WANG, environmental engineer; b. Taiwan, Republic of China, Feb. 6, 1952; came to U.S., 1976; d. Chien-Chang and Shu-Feng (Chang) Wang; m. Bruce H. Damewood; 1 child, Jeffrey T. BS, Nat. Chung-Hsing U., Taiwan, 1975; MBA, Idaho State U., 1984, postgrad., 1990—. Mgmt. specialist Fortmore, Ltd., Taiwan, 1975-76; program coord. Idaho State U., Pocatello, 1978-80; records specialist Idaho Dept. Health and Welfare, Pocatello, 1980-83; fin. analyst, sr. adminstr. EG&G Idaho, Inc., Idaho Falls, 1984-90, ops. cons., prin. adminstr., 1990-92, environ. program and project engr., 1992—. Mem. NAFE, Assn. MBA Execs., Internat. Tng. in Communications (past coun., pres.), Project Mgmt. Inst. (past cert. chair Ea. Idaho chpt.), Phi Kappa Phi, Beta Gamma Sigma. Home: 15319 W Lacey Rd Pocatello ID 83202-5020 Office: EG&G Idaho PO Box 1625 Idaho Falls ID 83415-3103

D'AMICO, MICHAEL, architect, urban planner; b. Bklyn., Sept. 11, 1936; s. Michael and Rosalie (Vinciguerra) D.; BArch, U. Okla., 1961; postgrad. So. Meth. U. Sch. Law, 1962-63, Coll. Marin, 1988-89; m. Joan Hand, Nov. 26, 1955; children: Michael III, Dion Charles. Supr. advanced planning sect. Dallas Dept. City Planning, 1961-63; designer, planner in charge Leo A. Daly Co., San Francisco, 1963-66; project planner Whisler, Patri Assos., San Francisco, 1966-67; architect, urban planner D'Amico & Assocs., San Francisco, N.Y., Guam, 1967-73, pres. D'Amico & Assocs., Inc., Mill Valley and San Francisco, Calif., and Guam, 1973—; pres. Jericho Alpha Inc., 1979-82; cons. architect, planner City of Seaside (Calif.), 1967-72, 79-81, 89—; cons. urban redevel. Eureka (Calif.), 1967-82; cons. planner, Lakewood, Calif.; redevel. cons. to Daly City (Calif.), 1975-77; redevel. adviser to Tamalpais Valley Bus. Assn., 1975-77; archtl. and hist. analyst to Calif. Dept. Transp., 1975-77; agt. for Eureka, Calif. Coastal Commn., 1977-79; devel. cons. City of Scotts Valley, 1988—, City of Suisun, 1988-89, City of Union City, 1989-91. Mem. steering com. San Francisco Joint Com. Urban Design, 1967-72. Recipient Community Design award AIA, 1970; First prize award Port Aransas (Tex.) Master Plan Competition, 1964; Design award Karachi Mcpl. Authority, 1987, Merit award St. Vincent's/Silveira. Mem. AIA (inactive), Am. Inst. Cons. Planners, Am. Planning Assn., Calif. Assn. Planning Cons. (sec., treas. 1970-72), World Future Soc., Solar Energy Soc. Am. Office: 525 Midvale Way Mill Valley CA 94941-3706

DAMON, JAMES CHRISTIAN, communications engineer; b. Ft. Belvoir, Va., Oct. 30, 1951; s. John Charles and Alice Darlene (Hays) D. ASET, Grantham Sch. Engring., Washington, 1972. Lic. FCC 1st class radiotelephone with radar endorsement. Sr. engring. asst. Lockheed Missiles and Space, San Diego, to 1986; owner and prin. Signal Scis., Flagstaff, Ariz., 1986—; licensee, prin. KMJ-TV 6, Flagstaff, Ariz., 1991—; permittee KDR-TV 20, San Luis Obispo, Calif., 1991—. Designer programmable channel deletion filter, designer, builder RRCS com. CATV system for Rough Rock, Ariz. Precinct committeeman, Coconino County Rep. Party, Flagstaff, 1987-89; speaker, Sunshine Rescue Mission, Flagstaff, 1988. Mem. IEEE, Soc. Cable TV Engrs., Soc. Broadcast Engrs. Republican. Home: PO Box 1890 Flagstaff AZ 86002-1890 Office: Signal Sciences 508 S Fountaine St Ste B Flagstaff AZ 86001-5822

DAMON, MICHAEL, systems design and marketing executive; b. L.A., Oct. 29, 1962; s. Richard Allen and Gloria Elizabeth (Fox) Olson. Student, San Diego State U., 1986, Pacific Western U., 1988. Lic. real estate broker, Calif.; credentials of ministry, Calif. Ptnr. MDO Investments, San Diego, 1981-84; sales dir. Promotional Concept, Inc., San Diego, 1984-85; sr. acct. exec. T.J. Carr Investment Co., La Jolla, Calif., 1985-88; sales dir. Discover The Bahama's Ltd., San Diego, 1988-90, Creative Mktg. Systems, San Diego, 1990-92; pres. Live to Win, La Jolla, 1989—; dir. system design and mktg. Nat. Response Media, San Diego, 1992—. Republican. Home: #145 5580 La Jolla Blvd La Jolla CA 92037 Office: National Response Media #210 San Diego CA 92108

DAMPHOUSSE, VINCENT, professional hockey player; b. Montreal, Ont., Can., Dec. 17, 1967. Left wing/center Edmonton (Can.) Oilers. Shares NHL All-Star single-game record for most goals (4), 1991. Office: Edmonton Oilers, Northlands Coliseum, Edmonton, AB Canada T5B 4M9

DAMRON, CHARLES FRANKLIN, minister; b. Pulaski, Va., Dec. 18, 1948; s. Noah Ralph and Sallie (Painter) D.; m. Martha Ellen Owen, Aug. 21, 1970; children: Benjamin Edward, Gwyndolyn Spring, Sallie Faye. BA, SUNY, Albany, 1976; MDiv with honors, Midwestern Bapt. Theol. Sem., 1989, M in Religious Edn. with highest honors, 1990. Ordained minister Bapt. Ch., 1989. Tchr.'s aide U.S. DOD, Fort Stewar., Ga., 1986-87; chaplain Mo. Bapt., Platte City, 1988-90; pastor Valley Drive Bapt. Ch., Miles City, Mont., 1991—, Prairie Bapt. Ch., Terry, Mont., 1991—; chaplain VA Med. Ctr., Miles City, 1992—. Vol. chaplain Miles City Police Dept.; active Family Issues Forum, Miles City, 1991-92; active Miles City Ministeral Assn., 1990—, treas., 1992—; chmn. time and space com. Mont. So. Bapt. Fellowship, 1993; mem. campus ministry com. Miles C.C., 1993-94, chmn., 1994-95. Mem. So. Bapt. Bivocational Mins., Mont. Pastoral Care Assn., Big Sky Assn. (dir. Sunday sch. 1991—, exec. com. 1991—, discipleship tng. dir. 1993—), Salvation Army, Am. Legion, DAV, Lions. Home: 802 S Earling Miles City MT 59301-5018 Office: Valley Drive Bapt Ch 1004 N Sewell PO Box 687 Miles City MT 59301-0687

DAMSBO, ANN MARIE, psychologist; b. Cortland, N.Y., July 7, 1931; d. Jorgen Eiener and Agatha Irene (Schenck) D. B.S., San Diego State Coll., 1952; M.A., U.S. Internat. U., 1974, Ph.D., 1975. Diplomate Am. Acad. Pain Mgmt. Commd. 2d lt. U.S. Army, 1952, advanced through grades to capt., 1957; staff therapist Letterman Army Hosp., San Francisco, 1953-54, 56-58, 61-62, Ft. Devers, Mass., 1955-56, Walter Reed Army Hosp., Washington, 1958-59, Tripler Army Hosp., Hawaii, 1959-61, Ft. Benning, Ga., 1962-64; chief therapist U.S. Army Hosp., Ft. McPherson, Ga., 1964-67; ret. U.S. Army, 1967; med. missionary So. Presbyterian Ch., Taiwan, 1968-70; psychology intern So. Naval Hosp., San Diego, 1975; pre-doctoral intern Naval Regional Med. Ctr., San Diego, 1975-76, postdoctoral intern, 1975-76, chief, founder pain clinic, 1977-86; chief pain clinic, 1977-86; adj. tchr. U. Calif. Med. Sch., San Diego; lectr., U.S., Can., Eng., France, Australia; cons. forensic hypnosis to law enforcemnt agys. Contbr. articles to profl. publs., chpt. to book. Tchr. Sunday sch. United Meth. Ch., 1945—; Rep. Nat. Candidate Trust Pres. adv. com.; mem. Lonta Internat. Presdl. Adv. Com. Fellow Am. Soc. Clin. Hypnosis (psychology mem. at large, exec. bd. 1989—); mem. San Diego Clin. Hypnosis (pres. 1980), Am. Phys. Therapy Assn., Calif. Soc. Clin. and Hypnosis (bd. govs.), Am. Soc. Clin. Hypnosis Edn. Rsch. Found. (trustee 1992-94), AAUW, Internat. Platform Assn., Am. Soc. Clin. Hypnosis (exec. bd.) Ret. Officers Am., Retired Officers Assn. (rep. presdl. task force, pres. adv. com.), Toastmasters (local pres.), Job's Daus. Republican. Home and Office: 1062 W 5th Ave Escondido CA 92025-3802

DAMSKY, ROBERT PHILIP, communications executive; b. Boston, May 19, 1921; s. Mark and Ann (Wisser) D.; m. Rose Hollender, Jan. 18, 1955 (div. 1985); children: Marla Markley, Lori Diana. Cert., MIT, 1939, Tex. A&M U., 1944; diploma, Spartan Sch. Aero., Tulsa, 1946. Indsl. editor Spartan Aircraft Co., Tulsa, 1946-47; with Transocean Airlines, Hartford, Conn., 1947; chief pilot MIT, Beverly, Mass., 1947-48; sr. check pilot Civil Air Patrol, Beverly, 1948; airport mgr. Hartport, Inc., Bellfontaine, Ohio, 1948-49; airline pilot Slick Airlines and U.S. Overseas Airlines, Burbank, Calif. and Wildwood, N.J., 1949-55; founder Flight Edn. Assn., Santa Ana, Calif., 1955-80; pres., dir., chief pilot Aeromedia Nat. Syndicate, L.A., 1980—. Aviation editor: Beverly News, Gen. Aviation News. With U.S. Army Air Corps, 1940-45. Decorated Purple Heart, 1941. Mem. Airline Pilots Assn., Aircraft Owners and Pilots Assn., Silver Wings, VFW, Am. Legion, Pearl Harbor Survivors Assn. Home: PO Box 2704 Costa Mesa CA 92628-2704

DANA, CHARLES HAROLD, JR., computer science educator; b. San Jose, Calif., Oct. 13, 1950; s. Charles Harold and Delvina Anna (Malatesta) D. BA, U. Calif., Santa Barbara, 1972, MS, 1974, PhD, 1981. Assoc. prof. Calif. Poly. State U., San Luis Obispo, 1982-88, prof. computer sci., 1988—. Mem. IEEE, Assn. Computing Machinery. Roman Catholic. Home: 1609 Royal Way San Luis Obispo CA 93405 Office: Calif Poly State U Computer Sci Dept San Luis Obispo CA 93407

DANA, HUGH RICHARD, internist, educator; b. Balt., May 28, 1950; s. Edward Runkle and Lilian Lorraine (Kirschner) D. BS, U. N.C., 1973; MD, U. So. Calif., 1978. Diplomate Am. Bd. Internal Medicine. Intern in medicine St. Mary's Hosp.-UCLA, Long Beach, 1978-79; rsch. in hematology Mayo Clinic, Rochester, Minn., 1979-80; resident in internal medicine U. Calif.-Irvine program VA Hosp., Long Beach, 1980-82, physician ambulatory care clinic, 1983-89; staff physician Kaiser Permanente, Bellflower, Calif., 1989-91, Family Health Plan Inc., Hawaiian Gardens, Calif., 1991—; asst. clin. prof. U. Calif.-Irvine Sch. Medicine, Orange, 1989—. Mem. ACP, AMA. Home: 5595 E 7th St Apt 297 Long Beach CA 90804

DANA-DAVIDSON, LAOMA COOK, English language educator; b. Herndon, W.Va., Nov. 23, 1925; d. Virgil A. and Latha (Shrewsbury) Cook; m. William J. Davidson, Apr. 1946 (div. 1971); 1 child, Deborah Davidson Bollom. BE, Marshall U., 1956; MA in Adminstrn., Azusa U., 1981. Cert. tchr., Calif. Tchr. Cajon Valley Union Sch. Dist., El Cajon, Calif., 1958—; master tchr. to 30 student tchrs. Author: Reading series used in dist., 1968. Former 1st v.p. El Cajon Rep. Women Federated, pres., 1992—; candidate Cajon Valley Sch. Bd., 1986; mem. El Cajon Hist. Assn. Recipient sabbatical to study British Schs. Cajon Valley Union Sch. Dist., 1977-78. Mem. AAUW (pres. 1964-65, edn. com., public policy com., women's issues com.), Grossmont Concert Assn., Delta Kappa Gamma. Home: 1552 S Camino Real Apt 229 Palm Springs CA 92264-8878 Office: 609 Ecken Rd El Cajon CA 92020-7312

DANCE, FRANCIS ESBURN XAVIER, communication educator; b. Bklyn., Nov. 9, 1929; s. Clifton Louis and Catherine (Tester) D.; m. Nora Alice Rush, May 1, 1954 (div. 1974); children: Clifton Louis III, Charles Daniel, Alison Catherine, Andrea Frances, Frances Sue, Brendan Rush; m. Carol Camille Zak, July 4, 1974; children: Zachary Esburn, Gabriel Joseph, Caleb Michael, Catherine Emily. BS, Fordham U., 1951; MA, Northwestern U., 1953, PhD, 1959. Instr. speech Bklyn. Adult Labor Schs., 1951; instr. humanities, coordinator radio and TV U. Ill. at Chgo., 1953-54; instr. Univ. Coll., U. Chgo., 1958; asst. prof. St. Joseph's (Ind.) Coll., 1958-60; asst. prof., then assoc. prof. U. Kans., 1960-63; mem. faculty U. Wis., Milw., 1963-71, prof. communication, 1965-71, dir. Speech Communication Center, 1963-70; prof. U. Denver, 1971—; partner Helix Press, Shorewood, Wis., 1970-71; cons. in field. Author: The Citizen Speaks, 1962, (with Harold P. Zelko) Business and Professional Speech Communication, 1965, 2d edit., 1978, Human Communication Theory, 1967, (with Carl E. Larson) Perspectives on Communication, 1970, Speech Communication: Concepts and Behavior, 1972, The Functions of Speech Communication: A Theoretical Approach, 1976, Human Communication Theory, 1982, (with Carol C. Zak-Dance) Public Speaking, 1986; editor: Jour. Communication, 1962-64, Speech Tchr, 1970-72; adv. bd.: Jour. Black Studies; editorial bd.: Jour. Psycholinguistic Research; Contbr. articles to profl. jours. Bd. dirs. Milw. Mental Health Assn., 1966-67. 2d lt. AUS, 1954-56. Knapp Univ. scholar in communication, 1967-68; recipient Outstanding Prof. award Standard Oil Found., 1967; Master Tchr. award U. Denver, 1985, University Lectr. award U. Denver, 1986. Fellow Internat. Communication Assn. (pres. 1967); mem. Speech Communication Assn. (pres. 1982), Psi Upsilon. Office: U Denver Dept Human Comm Studies Univ Of Denver CO 80208

DANDO, HOWARD C., theatre and television producer; b. Phila., Aug. 22, 1943; s. Howard C. Sr. and Ann (Durkin) D.; m. Hilda Morales, Aug. 24, 1971 (div. Jan. 1979). BA, LaSalle U., 1966; MA, Temple U., 1969; postgrad., So. Ill. U. Dir. Phila. Arts Festival, 1970-71; producer Am. Dance Festival, Phila., 1973; dir. Stars of Am. Ballet, N.Y.C., 1974-80; arts dir. New World Festival of the Arts, Miami, 1980-83; producer, dir. Cintel TV, L.A., N.Y.C., 1983—; prof. Moore Coll. of Art, Phila., 1970-71, Lab. Inst. of Merchandising Coll., N.Y.C., 1976-80; adj. prof. CUNY, 1972-77, West L.A. Coll., 1989—. Producer (broadway play) Tommy, 1971-73, Sargents Pepper's Lonely Hearts Club Band, 1972-74. Bd. dirs. Miami Coun. on Arts and Edn., 1980-82; mem. Miami Performing Arts Bldg. Com., 1980-82. Grantee NEA, 1974; named Best Dir. Pa. State Theatre Festival, 1973. Fellow Nat. Assn. of Profl. TV Execs., Nat. Tchr. Assn. Home: 8180 Manitoba St Playa Del Rey CA 90293

DANFORTH, ELIZABETH TURNER, artist, librarian; b. Rockford, Ill., Nov. 16, 1953; d. Herman Leonard and Ruth Marie (Gelpi) D. BA in Anthropology cum laude, Ariz. State U., 1976; postgrad., Scottsdale C.C., 1979-86. Freelance illustrator, writer Phoenix, 1976—; art dir., producer, dir., mag. editor Flying Buffalo, Inc., Scottsdale, Ariz., 1978-85; asst. libr. Phoenix Pub. Libr., 1985—. Editor, developer (with Michael Stackpole) Mage's Blood and Old Bones, 1992, also various gamebooks; writer, game designer computer games Wasteland, 1987 (Best Adventure Game of Yr., Computer Gaming World 1988, Gold cert. Software Pub. Assn. 1991), Tunnels & Trolls: Crusaders of Khazan, 1989, Star Trek: 25th Ann. Game, 1991; contbr. short stories to anthologies. Treas. Ariz. Visionary Alternative, Phoenix, 1989—. Recipient various awards from sci. fiction conventions, including Best of Show, Tus-Con 17, 1990; Artist Guest of Honor regional sci. fiction conventions. Mem. Assn. Sci. Fiction Artists, Acad. Game Critics (charter), Acad. Gaming Arts and Design (awards com. 1989—), Sci. Fiction Writers Am. Episcopalian. Office: PO Box 64082 Phoenix AZ 85082-4082

DANFORTH, JACK TIMOTHY, engineer; b. Fayetteville, Ark., Sept. 29, 1946; s. Jack Glidden and Margaret Jean (Silver) D.; m. Suzan Dell Dickey, June 26, 1981; children: Timothy, Scott, Candace Dawn. BSEE, U. Idaho, 1969. Registered profl. engr. Electrical engr. Pacific Power and Light, Portland, Oreg., 1972-75; dist. mgr. Portland Gen. Electric, 1975-79; conservation mgr. Snohomish Pud, Everett, Wash., 1979-80; utilities dir. City Kissimmee, Fla., 1980-82; gen. mgr. Elmhurst Power and Light, Tacoma, Wash., 1982-87; asst. dir. Wash. State Energy Office, Olympia, 1987-88; pres. ANCO Cons. Group, Milw., 1988-92; regional mgr. A&C Enercom, Redmond, Wash., 1993—; mng. dir. Power Smart (USA); bd. dirs. Northwest Trek, Eatonville, Wash., 1985-87. Author: (software) Alliance 2000, 1991. Lt. USN, 1968-72. Mem. Wash. Assn. Bldg. Officals, Electric Power and Light Assn., Norwest Pub. Power Assn., Pierce County C. of C. (pres. 1986-87), Pierce County Club (pres. 1985-87). Episcapal. Home: 20347 NE 34th Ct Redmond WA 98053-4319 Office: A&C Enercom 22845 NE 8th St Ste 311 Redmond WA 98053-7299

DANG, MARVIN S.C., lawyer; b. Honolulu, Feb. 11, 1954; s. Brian K.T. and Flora (Yuen) D. BA with distinction, U. Hawaii, 1974; JD, George Washington U., 1978. Bar: Hawaii 1978, U.S. Dist. Ct. Hawaii 1978, U.S. Ct. Appeals (9th cir.) 1979. Atty. Gerson, Steiner & Anderson and predecessor firms, Honolulu, 1978-81; owner, atty. Law Offices of Marvin S.C. Dang, Honolulu, 1981—; bd. dirs. Foster Equipment Co. Ltd., Honolulu; sr. v.p., bd. dirs. Rainbow Fin. Corp., Honolulu; hearings officer (per diem) Adminstrv. Drivers License Revocation Office, Honolulu, 1991—. Chmn., vice-chmn., mem. Manoa Neighborhood Bd. Honolulu, 1979-82, 84-87; pres., v.p., mem., Hawaii Coun. on Legal Edn. for Youth, Honolulu, 1979-86; state rep., asst. minority floor leader Hawaii State Legislature, Honolulu, 1982-84; mem. Hawaii Bicentennial Commn. of U.S. Constitution, Honolulu, 1986-88. Recipient Cert. of Appreciation award Hawaii Speech-Language-Hearing Assn., Honolulu, 1984. Mem. ABA (standing com. on law and electoral process 1985-89, spl. com. on youth edn. for citizenship, 1979-85, 89-92, Hawaii membership chmn. 1981—, exec. coun. young lawyers div. 1986-88), Hawaii State Bar Assn. (bd. dirs. young lawyers div. 1990), Hawaii State Jaycees (Ten Outstanding Young Persons of Hawaii 1983), Hawaii Fin. Svcs. Assn. (bd. dirs. 1990—, sec. 1991, treas. 1992, v.p. 1992), Plaza Club of Hawaii. Republican. Office: PO Box 4109 Honolulu HI 96812-4109

DANIEL, GARY WAYNE, communications and music industry executive; b. Wendall, Idaho, June 22, 1948; s. Milan Chauncey Daniel and Ila Fay (Cox) Harkins; m. Jeanne Laurane Blandford, July 1969 (div. Aug. 1972); 1 child, Kelly Jean; m. Sandra Kay Modey, July 26, 1974; 1 child, Marcus Chauncey. AA, Boise Bus. Coll., 1969. Cert. master practitioner Neuro Linguistic Programming. Program dir. Sta. KSKI, Sun Valley, Idaho, 1967-68, Sta. KYME, Boise, Idaho, 1968-69; gen. mgr. Sta. KSPD, Boise, 1969-72; radio personality Sta. KBBK-FM, Boise, 1972-74; account exec. ABC-TV, Nampa, Idaho, 1974-77; nat. sales dir. Agri-Steel Corp., Boise, 1977-79; mgmt. ptnr. Agri. Devel. Corp., Caldwell, Idaho, 1979-82; owner, prin. Video Magic Amusement Co., Caldwell, 1982-85; pres., chief exec. officer Victory Media Group, Santa Rosa, Calif., 1985—; gen. mgr. Victory Record Label, 1986—, also bd. dirs.; bd. dirs. Bay City Records, San Francisco; pres. Lightforce Music Pub., Santa Rosa, 1987—; mktg. cons. Firenze Records, San Francisco, 1987—, Capital Bus. Systems, Napa, Calif., 1986-91, Plum, Inc., Napa, 1985-86. Author: Concert Operations Manual, 1987; devel. of the Neuro Achievement System. Recipient Most Humorous TV Comml. award Boise Advt. Club, 1975, Most Creative TV Comml. award Boise Advt. Club, 1976; named Top Radio Personality Idaho State Broadcasters Assn., 1971. Mem. ASCAP, NARAS, Video Software Dealer Assn., Ind. Record Mfg. and Distbrs., Gospel Music Assn., Am. Coun. of Hypnotist Examiners, Hypnotist Examiners Coun. Calif., Am. Assn. Behavioral Therapists, Internat. Assn. of NLP, Time Line Therapy Assn., Internat. Platform Assn. Republican. Office: Neuro Achievement Ctr Ste 844 55 Maria Dr Petaluma CA 94954-5368

DANIELS, CHARLES WILLIAM, airline pilot; b. Havre, Mont., July 31, 1945; s. Charles Albert and Else (Bydeley) D.; m. Joy Suzanne Rogneby, Dec. 16, 1967; children: Sherri Lin, Treena Joy. BSME, Mont. State U., 1968; MS in Human Resource Mgmt., Gonzaga U., 1977. Commd. 2nd lt. U.S. Air Force, 1968; advance through grades to lt. col., 1984; instr. pilot USAF, various locations, 1970-74; pilot, instr. USAF, Fairchild AFB, Wash., 1974-79; test pilot USAF, Edwards AFB, Calif., 1980-84, Seattle, 1984-89; pilot Delta Air Lines, Seattle, 1989—. Chair protestant parish coun. Edwards Chapel, 1983; chair fin. com. Auburn (Wash.) 1st United Meth. Ch., 1985, 93, lay leader, 1986, 87, chair adminstrv. bd., 1988, 89, 90, chair trustees com., 1991. Decorated Meritorious Svc. medal with 2 oak leaf clusters, Air Force Commendation medal. Mem. AIAA (sr. mem.), Soc. Exptl. Test Pilots. Home: 16907 SE 309th St Auburn WA 98002 Office: Delta Air Lines Sea Tac Airport Seattle WA 98158

DANIELS, HUGH ALLAN, inn executive, consultant; b. Pasadena, Calif., Feb. 26, 1952; s. Edward K. and Elizabeth P. (Cornwell) D. BS, Calif. State Poly. U., Pomona, 1978, MBA, 1983; profl. cert., UCLA, 1979. Cert. med. ICU paramedic; cert. instr., trainer Nat. Hwy. Traffic Safety Adminstrn. Operator Lamb Ambulance Co., Pasadena, 1970-72; med. ICU paramedic City of Pasadena, 1973-77, coordinating med. ICU paramedic, 1977-82, chief med. ICU paramedic, 1982-83; pres., gen. mgr. The Old Miners' Lodge, Inc., Park City, Utah, 1983—; mem. faculty Pasadena City Coll., 1977, Mt. San Antonio City Coll., 1976-82; cons. H.A. Daniels Bus. Svcs., Park City, 1980—. Mem. editorial bd. Innsider mag., 1989-91. Ops. comdr. emergency med. svcs. City of Pasadena/Tournament of Roses, 1977-82; mem. rev. bd. Utah Dept. Health, Salt Lake City, 1989-90; bd. dirs., treas. Park City Balloon Festival, Inc., 1989—; mem. del. Salt Lake City Olympic Bid Com., 1991; mem. County of L.A. EMS Commn. Hist. renovation grantee City of Park City, 1988. Mem. Profl. Assn. Innkeepers Intrnat. (nat. speaker 1989—), Bed and Breakfast Inns. Utah (founding pres. 1985-91), Park City Area Lodging Assn. (trustee 1991—), Utah Tourism Industry Coalition (vice chmn. 1988-89), Utah Hotel and Motel Assn., Utah Ski Assn., Calif. State Poly. U. Alumni Assn., Park City Area C. of C. (treas., exec. com. 1987-91, pres. 1991-92). Office: The Old Miners' Lodge Inc PO Box 2639 Park City UT 84060-2639

DANIELS, JAMES ARTHUR, electronics sales company executive; b. Indpls., Feb. 1, 1937; s. Arthur Weldon and Helen Marie (Collins) D.; m. Beverly Ann Monfreda, Aug. 25, 1956; children: Kristina, Rebecca, Kevin, Caroline, Bryan, Bret, Susan, Erica. AB in Sociology, U. Notre Dame, 1958; MBA, U. So. Calif., 1966. Engr. Ralph M. Parsons, Pasadena, Calif., 1960-61; sales engr. Dressen Barnes, Pasadena, Calif., 1961-64; sales mgr. Burton Mfg., Van Nuys, Calif., 1964-66; productmgr. Leach Relay, L.A., 1966-67; sales mgr. Bourns Trimpot Products, Riverside, Calif., 1967-74; pres. D2 Sales Inc., Solana Beach, Calif., 1974—; bd. dirs. San Diego Elec. Shows & Meeting Inc., 1985—. Mem. Elec. Rep. Assn. (pres. 1974, 75, dir. 1981-84, white pin 1983), Elec. VIPs, KC. Roman Catholic. Home: 662 Nardo Ave Solana Beach CA 92075 Office: D2 Sales Inc PO Box 1311 Solana Beach CA 92075

DANIELS, LORI S., insurance agent; b. Burlingame, Calif., Nov. 5, 1955; d. Robert William and Sue Ann (McCowen) McCroskey; m. Stephen L. Daniels, June 19, 1976 (div. June 1980). Student, Ariz. State U., 1973-76. CLU. Trainer Campus Crusade for Christ, San Bernardino, Calif., 1977-79; with instalment loans dept. Ariz. Bank, Mesu, 1979-80; agt. State Farm Ins., Gilbert, Ariz., 1980—; bus. cons. Jr. Achievement, Mesu, 1987-92. V.p. Valley of Sun United Way, Phoenix, 1990—. Recipient Small Bus. Person of Yr. award Gilbert C. of C., 1989. Mem. Chandler C. of C. (v.p. 1991—, Pres.'s award 1990, Chamber cup 1992). Republican. Home: 941 W Detroit Chandler AZ 85224

DANIELS, LYDIA M., health care administrator; b. Louisville, Dec. 21, 1932; d. Effort and Gladys T. (Turner) Williams; student Calif. State U., Hayward, 1967, 69-72; BA, Golden Gate U., 1992, MS, 1993; cert. Samuel Merritt Hosp. Sch. Med. Record Adminstrs., 1959; student Cen. State Coll., Ohio, 1950-52; children by previous marriage: Danny Winston, Jeffrey Bruce, Anthony Wayne. Sec. chemistry dept. Cen. State Coll., Wilberforce, Ohio, 1950-52; co-dir. Indian Workcamp, Pala Indian Reservation, Pala, Calif., 1956-58; clk.-typist Camarillo (Calif.) State Hosp., 1956-58; student med. record adminstr. Samuel Merritt Hosp., Oakland, Calif., 1958-59, asst. med. record adminstr., 1962-63, asst. chief med. record adminstr., 1965, chief med. record adminstr., 1965-72; med. record adminstr. Albany (Calif.) Hosp., 1964-65; asst. med. record adminstr. Children's Hosp., San Francisco, 1960; co-dir. interns in community svc. Am. Friends Svc. Com., San Francisco, 1960-61; med. record adminstr. Pacific Hosp., Oakland, Calif., 1963-64; med. record cons. Tahoe Forest Hosp., Truckee, Calif., 1969-73; chief med. record adminstr. Highland Gen. Hosp., Oakland, Calif., 1972-74; dir. med. record svcs. U. Calif. San Francisco Hosps. and Clinics, 1975-82; mgr. patient appointments, reception and registration Kaiser-Permanente Med. Ctr., 1982-88; dir. ambulatory adminstrv. svcs., 1988—; adj. prof. mgmt., office automation Golden Gate U., 1978—; pres. Daniels Consultation Svcs., 1988—. Leader Girl Scouts Am. Oakland area council, 1960-62; sunday sch. tchr. Soc. of Friends, Berkeley, Calif., 1961-63, mem. edn. com., 1965-68; mem. policy and adv. bd. Far West Lab. Demonstration Sch., Oakland, 1973-75. Recipient Mgmt. Fellowship award U. Calif., San Francisco, 1979-80. Mem. Am. Med. Record Assn., Calif. Med. Record Assn. (editorial bd. 1976-77, pres. 1974-75), East Bay Med. Record Assn. (chmn. edn. com. 1971-72, pres. 1969-70), Assn. Systems Mgmt., Am. Mgmt. Assn., San Francisco Med. Records Assn. (pres.-elect 1982-83, pres. 1983-84). Author: Health Record Documentation: A Look at Cost, 1981; Inservice Training as a Tool in Managing the Changing Environment in the Medical Record Department, 1983; the Budget as a Management Tool, 1983. Issues editor Topics in Health Record Management, Parts I and II, 1983. Home: 545 Pierce St Apt 1105 Albany CA 94706-1048 Office: Kaiser-Permanente Med Ctr 280 W Macarthur Blvd Piedmont CA 94611-5693

DANIELS, PHILIP BLISS, psychology educator; b. Annabella, Utah, Nov. 9, 1928; s. William Bliss and Lavern (Hawley) D.; m. Patsy Unger, July 3, 1951; children: Matt, Darsi, Jamie, Drew, Patrick. BS, Brigham Young U., 1954, MS, 1957; PhD, Harvard U., 1962. Prof. Brigham Young U., Provo, Utah, 1961-92; assoc. Nat. Tng. Lab., Washington, 1965-75; CEO Behavioral Sci. Resources, Provo, 1972—; cons. pvt. practice, Provo, 1965—. Co-author: manual Management Profiling, 1975, 4 mgmt. profiling instruments, 1972, 1981, 1985, 1986. Capt. USAF, 1954-56. Recipient rsch. grant U.S. Office of Edn., 1964. Mormon. Home: 1814 N 1500 E Provo UT 84604-5750 Office: BSR PO Box 411 Provo UT 84603

DANIELS, RICHARD MARTIN, public relations executive; b. Delano, Calif., Feb. 24, 1942; s. Edward Martin and Philida Rose (Peterson) D.; m. Kathryn Ellen Knight, Feb. 28, 1976; children: Robert Martin, Michael Edward. A.A., Foothill Coll., 1965; B.A., San Jose State U., 1967; M.A., U. Mo., 1971. News reporter Imperial Valley Press, El Centro, Calif., summers 1963-66, San Diego (Calif.) Evening Tribune, 1967-68, Columbia Daily Tribune (Mo.), 1969-70; nat. news copy editor Los Angeles Times, 1966-67; staff writer San Diego Union, 1971-74, real estate editor, 1974-77; v.p. pub. relations Hubbert Advt. & Pub. Relations, Costa Mesa, Calif., 1977-78; ptnr. Berkman & Daniels Mktg. Communications, San Diego, 1979-91; prin. Nuffer, Smith, Tucker, Inc., 1991—; lectr. various bus. groups and colls., Chmn. bd. dirs. March of Dimes San Diego County, 1984-87; bd. dirs. Nat. Coun. Vols., 1983—. Served with USN, 1959-62. Mem. Pub. Rels. Soc. Am., Counselors Acad. (accredited), Bldg. Industry Assn. San Diego County. Republican. Home: 2261 Ritter Pl Escondido CA 92029-5608 Office: 3170 Fourth Ave San Diego CA 92103

DANIELSEN, KAREN CHRISTINE, botanist; b. Santa Monica, Calif., Oct. 24, 1958; d. Berne Eugene and Jean Frazier (MacNee) D.; m. Dale Andrew Thomas, June 3, 1989. BA in Population Ecology, U. Calif. San Diego, La Jolla, 1980; MS in Plant Ecology, Calif. State U., L.A., 1990. Botanist Channel Islands Nat. Pk., Ventura, Calif., 1985-90, Vandenberg AFB, Calif., 1990-92, Los Padres Nat. Forest, Goleta, Calif., 1992—. Recipient Pres.'s Undergrad. fellowship U. Calif., San Diego, 1980, Rsch. grant Quercus Fund, 1986. Mem. Ecol. Soc. Am., Calif. Native Plant Soc. (rsch. grantee 1986), Calif. Bot. Soc., Soc. for Ecol. Restoration, The Nature Conservancy, Phi Kappa Phi, Sigma Xi. Office: Los Padres Nat Forest 6144 Calle Real Goleta CA 93117

DANIELSON, GORDON DOUGLAS, dentist; b. Everett, Wash., Nov. 11, 1942; s. Marvin and Elanor (Weers) D.; m. Jamie Lynn Waters, Jan. 9, 1977. BS with honors, U. Oreg., 1968; postgrad., MIT, 1968-69; MA in Molecular Biology, U. Calif., 1974, BS in Med. Sci., DDS, 1975. DDS. Pvt. practice Larkspur, Calif., 1975—; exec. v.p. Atmospheric Rsch. Tech., Sacramento, Calif., 1984-85; cons. Freeport Fin. Svcs., Denver, 1985-87; pres. Lynmar Enterprises Inc., Rno, 1987—; bd. dirs. Freeport Venture Fund. MIT fellow, 1968-69; U. Calif., Berkeley fellow, 1969-71; U. Calif., San Francisco fellow, 1973-75, pres. fellow, 1973-75. Mem. U. Calif. Dental Alumni Assn., U. Oreg. Alumni Assn., Marin County Dental Soc. (chmn. emergency care 1975-81), St. Francis Yacht Club (mem. com. 1973—), Aircraft Owners and Pilots Assn., Assoc. Pilots Bay Area, Marin Rowing Club, Omicron Kappa Upsilon. Republican. Office: 5 Bon Air Rd Ste 114 Larkspur CA 94939-1135

DANIHER, JOHN M., retired engineer; b. LaJunta, Colo., Aug. 2, 1926; s. Gerald and Mary Isabelle (Manly) D.; m. Edna Erle Hoshall, Sept. 4, 1948; children: Lyn Mari, Suzanne Laurie, Patricia Gail, Jerome Matthew, Michael Kevin. AB, Western State Coll., Gunnison, Colo., 1948; postgrad. Idaho State U., 1957-74, U. Idaho, 1974-76. High sch. tchr., Grand Junction, Colo., 1948-52; salesman Century Metalcraft, Denver, 1952-53; chem. plant supr. U.S. Chem. Corps., Denver, 1953-56; sr. engr. instrument and controls Phillips Petroleum Co., Idaho Falls, 1956-76; project engr. E G & G Idaho, Idaho Falls, 1976-85, engring. specialist, 1985-91; adv. Eastern Idaho Vocat. Tech. Sch., 1975-80. Cubmaster, Boy Scouts Am., 1970-75, asst. scoutmaster, 1975-80. Recipient Cub Man of Yr., Boy Scouts Am., 1973. Mem. Am. Nuclear Soc. Roman Catholic. Club: K.C. (state dep. 1979-81, Supreme council 1981-84) Home: 250 12th St Idaho Falls ID 83404-5370

DANIS, PETER G., JR., office products company executive; b. St. Louis, Jan. 20, 1932; s. Peter Godfrey and Katherine (Kramer) D.; m. Ann Wilmot, Apr. 14, 1934; children: Cathy, Peter, David, Mark, Laura. B.S., St. Louis U., 1953, M.B.A., 1958; postgrad., Columbia U., 1975. Sales mgr. Crown Zellerbach, San Francisco, 1955-68; gen. mgr. Boise Cascade, San Francisco, 1968-69; regional mgr. Boise Cascade, 1969-70; v.p., div. mgr. Boise Cascade, Chgo., 1976-80; dist. v.p. Boise (Idaho) Cascade, 1981—, sr. v.p., 1981-89, exec. v.p., 1989—. Bd. dirs. Woodlands Acad. Served to 1st lt. U.S. Army, 1953-55. Mem. Nat. Forest Products Assn., Am. Forest and Paper Assn., Springs Club, Hillcrest Country Club, Arid Club, Onwentsia Club, Mid-Am. Club. Republican. Roman Catholic. Office: Boise Cascade Corp 1 Jefferson Sq Boise ID 83728-0202

DANKANYIN, ROBERT JOHN, business executive; b. Sharon, Pa., Sept. 4, 1934; s. John and Anna (Kohlesar) D.; m. Dorothy Jean Kuchel, Aug. 9, 1958 (div. June 1975); children: Douglas John, David Jay, Dana Jean; m. Georgia C. Oleson, Apr. 2, 1988 (dec. Sept. 1990). BS, Pa. State U., 1956; MBA, U. So. Calif., 1961; M in Engring., UCLA, 1963. From mgr. mobile ICBM systems engring. dept. to mgr. space system lab. Hughes Aircraft Co., Culver City, Calif., 1956-68, asst. mgr. for U.S. Roland program, Canoga Pk., Calif., 1975-77, asst. div. mgr. missile devel. div., Culver City, 1977-84, div. mgr. land combat systems div., 1984-86, group v.p. missile systems group, 1986-87; v.p., asst. group exec. missle systems group Canoga Park, Calif., 1987-88; v.p., asst. group exec. space and communication group, El Segundo, Calif. Hughes Aircraft Co., Culver City, Calif., 1988-89; corp. sr. v.p. diversification Hughes Aircraft Co., L.A., 1989-92, sr. v.p. bus. devel., 1992-93; program mgr. Litton Industries, Beverly Hills, Calif., 1968-70; sr. v.p., pres. Hughes Indsl. Electronics Co., L.A., 1993—; group exec. Whittaker Corp., Westwood Village, Calif., 1973-75; pres., chmn. bd. Whittaker Community Devel. Corp., Englewood, Colo., Knoxville, Tenn., Westwood Village, Calif., 1973-75; chmn. Hughes Program Mgr. Devel. Course, L.A., 1976-88; chmn., bd. dirs. Light Valve Products, Inc., 1988-92, Hughes/Japan Victor Tech. Inc., 1992—; bd. dirs. Hughes Micro Electronics Ltd., Scotland, Hughes Environ. Systems, Inc., Hughes España, Aero Systems, Inc., Hughes Europa; dir. several wholly owned subs.; lectr., guest speaker on tech. mgmt., orgn., bus. ventures, fgn. mktg. and entrepreneurship. Editor Inter Fraternity/Sorority Newsletter Pa. State U., 1955-56. Chmn. indsl. and profl. adv. coun. Coll. Engring. Pa. State U. Voted Ordo Honorium by Kappa Delta Rho Fraternity, 1991, outstanding Engr. of the Yr. by Pa. State U., 1991; honored as outstanding engineering alumnus, 1992. Mem. Am. Def. Preparedness Assn. (bd. dirs. 1986—, chmn. fin. com. 1990—), Hughes Mgmt. Club, Aero Club So. Calif., Marina City Club, Riviera Country Club. Republican. Roman Catholic. Home: 1 Catamaran St Marina Del Rey CA 90292-5707 Office: Hughes Aircraft Co PO Box 45066 Hughes Ter Los Angeles CA 90045-0066

DANNEMAN, EDWARD CARL, insurance company executive; b. Fairfield, Calif., Jan. 1, 1959; s. Robert E. and Joye M. (MacDowell) D.; m. Patricia A. Gutierrez, Sept. 17, 1983; children: Steven Earl, Aaron James, Shannon Nicole. Student, Lewis and Clark Coll., 1977-79, U. Oreg., 1979-82; BS, SUNY, Albany, 1983. Office mgr. Beneficial Fin. Co., Olympia, Wash., 1982-86; v.p. Capital Savs. Bank, Olympia, 1986-87; adminstrv. officer, loan trainer Gt. Am. Bank, Federal Way, Wash., 1987-89; rep. Century Cos. of Am., Seattle, 1989-90; loan officer Boeing Employees Credit Union, Tukwila, Wash., 1991-92; rep. Horace Mann Ins., Vancouver, 1993—. Home: 2719 B Neals Ln Vancouver WA 98661 Office: Horace Mann Companies 10700 SW Beaverton Hillsdale Hwy Beaverton OR 97005

DANNEMEYER, WILLIAM EDWIN, congressman; b. South Gate, Calif., Sept. 22, 1929; s. Henry William and Charlotte Ernestine (Knapp) D.; m. Evelyn Hoemann, Aug. 27, 1955; children: Bruce, Kim, Susan. B.A., Valparaiso U., 1950; J.D., U. Calif., 1952. Bar: Calif., U.S. Supreme Ct. Individual practice law Fullerton, Calif., 1957-79; asst. city atty. City of Fullerton, 1959-62; mem. Calif. Assembly, 1963-66, 77-78; judge pro tem Mcpl. Ct., 1966-76, Superior Ct., 1966-76; mem. 96th-102nd Congresses from 39th Calif. dist., 1979—. Author: Shadow in the Land: Homosexuality in America, 1989. Bd. dirs. Orange County Luth. High Sch., 1972-78; bd. dirs. Luth. Ch.-Mo. Synod, So. Calif. Dist.; spl. gifts chmn. Capital Fund drive Boy Scouts Am. Served with U.S. Army, 1950-52. Mem. Orange County Bar Assn. (dir.), Orange County Criminal Justice Council. Republican. Office: 2234 Rayburn Washington DC 20515

DANNEMILLER, EDWARD PAUL, air conditioning executive; b. Akron, Ohio, July 15, 1934; s. Lawrence Martin and Francis Claire (Auseon) D.; m. Delphine Mary Penote, Sept. 15, 1962; children: John, Joan, Denise, Eddie. BSME, Case Western Res. U., 1957. Engr. Carrier Corp., Cleve., 1957-59; project engr. United Air Conditioning, L.A., 1959-61; sales engr. Fred Griswold Co., Santa Barbara, Calif., 1961-69; project mgr. ACCO, Santa Barbara, 1969-72; pres. San Bar Air Inc., Santa Barbara, 1972—. Allocation com. mem. United Way, 1986; century club mem. YMCA, 1990; active San Roque Ch. With USAR. Mem. SMACNA (Bd. dirs.), ACCA (pres. 1991—), LaCumbre Country Club (bd. dirs. 1984-87). Republican. Roman Catholic. Home: 820 Willowglen Rd Santa Barbara CA 93105-2442 Office: San Bar Air Inc 528 N Quarantina St Santa Barbara CA 93103-3177

DANNER, PAUL KRUGER, III, communications executive; b. Cin., Aug. 20, 1957; s. Paul Kruger Jr. and Phyllis Jean (Speak) D.; m. Cynthia Lee Hurst, May 5, 1984; children: Catherine Hurst, Elizabeth Speak, Caroline Tyree. BS, Colo. State U., 1979; MBA, Old Dominion U., 1986. Mktg. rep. Control Data Corp., Denver, 1985-86; dist. mgr. NEC Home Electronics (U.S.A.), Inc., Denver, 1987-88; regional mgr. NEC Home Electronics, Inc. subs. NEC Corp. (Tokyo), L.A., 1988-89, v.p. NEC Techs., Inc. subs., 1989-91; v.p. sales and mktg. Command Communications, Aurora, Colo., 1991—. Lt. USN, 1979-85; Lt.comdr. USNR, 1985—. Mem. Navy League of U.S., U.S. Naval Inst., NRA, Ducks Unltd., Met. Club, Castle Pines Country Club. Republican. Home: 503 Providence Dr Castle Rock CO 80104-9018

D'ANNUNZIO, ELEONORA See RAFN, ELEANOR YOLANDA

DANO, GARTH LOUIS, lawyer; b. Ellensburg, Wash., Dec. 20, 1953; s. Harrison K. and Dorothy (Koenigs) D.; m. Karen Lynne McPherson, Aug. 14, 1976; children: Nicole, Garrett, Kellen. BA, Santa Clara U., 1976; JD, Gonzaga U., 1979. Atty. Dano Law Firm, Moses Lake, Wash., 1980—; atty. Grant County Pro-Bono Coun., Moses Lake, 1986—. Campaign chmn. Sid Morrison Election Com., Grant County, 1980. Mem. Wash. State Bar Assn. (pres. 1989-90), Wash. State Trial Lawyers Assn., Wash. State Crim. Def. Assn., Grant County Bar Assn. (chmn.), Phi Delta Theta. Roman Catholic. Office: Dano Law Firm 100 E Broadway PO Box 1159 Moses Lake WA 98837

DANOFF, DUDLEY SETH, surgeon, urologist; b. N.Y.C., June 10, 1937; s. Alfred and Ruth (Kauffman) D.; m. Hevda Amrani, July 1, 1971; children: Aurele Alfie, Doran. BA summa cum laude, Princeton U., 1959; MD, Yale U., 1963. Diplomate Am. Bd. Urology. Surg. intern Columbia-Presbyn. Med. Ctr., N.Y.C., 1963-64; resident in surgery Yale New Haven Med. Ctr., 1964-65; resident in urologic surgery Squier Urologic Clinic, Columbia-Presbyn. Med. Ctr., 1965-69; NIH trainee Francis Delafield Hosp., N.Y.C., 1969; asst. in urology Columbia U.-Columbia-Presbyn. Hosp., N.Y.C., 1969; cons., surgeon New Orleans VA Hosp., 1970; asst. surgeon Tulane U., New Orleans, 1970; pvt. practice urologic surgery L.A., 1971—; attending urologic surgeon Cedars-Sinai Med. Ctr., L.A., Midway Hosp., L.A., Century City Hosp., L.A., VA Hosp., L.A., Beverly Hills Med. Ctr., L.A.; attending urologic surgeon, clin. faculty UCLA. Author: Superpotency, 1993, Research: Laparoscopic Urologic Procedures; contbr. articles to profl. jours. Bd. dirs. Tel-Hashomer Hosp., Israel, Christian Children's Fund, Beverly Hills Edn. Found.; trustee Anti-Defamation League; mem. profl. adv. bd. The Wellness Community; mem. nat. exec. bd. Gesher Found.; mem. adv. com., past pres. Med. div. L.A. Jewish Fedn. Coun.; mem. nat. leadership cabinet United Jewish Appeal; chmn. Am. Friends of Assaf Harofeh Med. Ctr., Israel. Maj. USAF, 1969-71. Fellow ACS; mem. AMA, Internat. Coll. Surgeons, Israeli Med. Assn., Am. Fertility Soc., Soc. Air Force Clin. Surgeons, Am. Urologic Assn., Societe International d'Urologie, Transplant Soc. So. Calif., Los Angeles County Med. Assn., Soc. for Minimally Invasive Surgery, Am. Technion Soc., Profl. Men's Club of L.A. (past pres.), Princeton Club So. Calif., Yale Club So. Calif., Hillcrest Country Club, Phi Beta Kappa, Sigma Xi, Alpha Omega Alpha, Phi Delta Epsilon (past pres., mem. exec. com.). Jewish. Office: Cedars-Sinai Med Ctr Towers 8631 W 3d St # 915E Los Angeles CA 90048

DANOS, ROBERT MCCLURE, oil company executive; b. New Orleans, Dec. 9, 1929; s. Joseph A. and Muriel R. (McClure) D.; m. Barbara Umbach, Apr. 30, 1955; children: Robert M., Sally C., Susan M., Julie A., Richard F., Renee R. B.S. in Geology, Tulane U., 1950; M.S., La. State U., 1952. Geologist Texaco, Inc., New Orleans, 1955-67; staff geologist Texaco, Inc., Houston, 1967; div. geologist Texaco, Inc., Tulsa, 1968-70; exploration mgr. Texaco, Inc., Denver, 1970-80; sr. v.p. K N Energy, Inc., Lakewood, Colo., 1980-83; pres., chief exec. officer Midlands Energy Co., Lakewood, 1983-84; pres. McMoRan-Midlands Oil Co., New Orleans, 1984-86; pres., chief ops. officer McMoRan Oil & Gas Co., New Orleans, 1986-89; pres. Plains Petroleum Oper. Co., Lakewood, Colo., 1989—. Served to 1st lt. U.S. Army, 1954. Mem. Am. Assn. Petroleum Geologists (del.), New Orleans Geologists Soc. (v.p. 1965-67), Rocky Mountain Assn. Geologists, Rocky Mountain Oil and Gas Assn., Rocky Mountain Natural Gasmen's Assn., In. Petroleum Assn. Am., Cherry Hills Country Club, Essex Club, Pickwick Club, Denver Petroleum Club. Home: 124 High St Denver CO 80218-4018 Office: 12596 W Bayaud Ave Ste 400 Lakewood CO 80228-2019

D'ANTONI, HECTOR LUIS, paleoecologist; b. Ensenada, Argentina, Oct. 9, 1943; came to U.S., 1989; s. Hector and Adelina Clelia (Cagnacci) D'A.; m. Susana Mabel Lasta, Jan. 29, 1971; children: Pablo Luis, Leonardo. BS, Nat. Coll., La Plata, Buenos Aires, Argentina, 1962; MS in Anthropology, U. La Plata, Buenos Aires, Argentina, 1969; Specialist Modern/Quaternary Palynology, U. Amsterdam, Netherlands, 1971; Dr of Natural Scis, Nat. Sci. U. La Plata, Buenos Aires, Argentina, 1976. Instr. U. of La Plata, Argentina, 1970-72, asst. researcher, 1972-75; rsch. assoc. U. Ariz., Tucson, 1975-78; vis. scientist U. Hohenheim, West Germany, 1978-80; ind. researcher Commn. of Sci. Rsch., La Plata, Argentina, 1982-90; full prof. Nat. U. Mar del Plata, Argentina, 1980-89; sr. rsch. scientist NASA Ames Rsch. Ctr., Moffet Field, Calif., 1989—; chair biol. commn., Argentina Nat. Rsch. Coun., Buenos Aires, 1988-89, assesor, 1984-89; pres. bd. trustees Inst. Botanica Darwinion, San Isidro, Buenos Aires, 1987-89; dir. dept. biology U. Mar del Plata, 1984-86. Author: (monography) Structural Palynology, 1983 (Prize 1983), (project) Paleoecology Method, 1992 (Grant 1992-93). Grantee NASA, 1992, Stiftung-Volkswagenwerk, 1985; recipient Rsch. associateship Nat. Rsch. Coun., 1989, Humboldt fellowship, 1978, Guggenheim fellowship, 1975. Mem. Am. Assn. Stratigraphic Palynologists, Assn. Paleontologica Argentina. Office: NASA Ames Rsch Ctr Mail Stop 242-4 Moffett Field CA 94035-1000

DANTZIG, GEORGE BERNARD, applied mathematics educator; b. Portland, Oreg., Nov. 8, 1914; s. Tobias and Anja (Ourisson) D.; m. Anne Shmuner, Aug. 23, 1936; children—David Franklin, Jessica Rose, Paul Michael. A.B. in Math., U. Md., 1936; M.A. in Math., U. Mich., 1937; Ph.D. in Math., U. Calif.-Berkeley, 1946; hon. degree, Technion, Israel, Linkoping U., Sweden, U. Md., Yale U., Louvain U., Belgium, Columbia U., U. Zurich, Switzerland, Carnegie-Mellon U. Chief combat analysis br. Statis. Control Hdqrs. USAAF, 1941-46, math. advisor, 1946-52; research mathematician Rand Corp., Santa Monica, Calif., 1952-60; prof., chmn. Ops. Research Ctr., U. Calif.-Berkeley, 1960-66; C.A. Criley prof. ops. research and computer sci. Stanford U., Calif., 1966—; chief methodology Internat. Inst. Applied System Analysis, 1973-74; cons. to industry. Author: Linear Programming and Extensions, 1963; co-author: Compact City, 1973; contbr. articles to profl. jours.; assoc. editor Math. Programming, Math. of Ops. Research, others. Recipient Exceptional Civilian Svc. medal War Dept., 1944, Nat. medal of Sci., 1975, Von Neumann theory prize in ops. rsch., 1975, award Nat. Acad. Scis., 1975, Harvey prize Technion, 1985, Silver Medal Operational Rsch. Soc., Gt. Britain, 1986, Coors Am. Ingenuity award, 1989. Fellow Am. Acad. Arts and Scis., Econometric Soc., Inst. Math. Stats.; mem. Nat. Acad. Scis., Nat. Acad. Engring., Ops. Research Soc. Am., Am. Math. Soc., Math. Programming Soc. (chmn. 1973-74), Inst. Mgmt. Sci. (pres. 1966), Phi Beta Kappa, Sigma Xi, Phi Kappa Phi, Pi Mu Epsilon. Home: 821 Tolman Dr Stanford CA 94305-1025 Office: Stanford Univ Ops Research Dept Stanford CA 94305

DANZEISEN, RHONDA LEIGH, secondary education educator; b. Williston, N.D., Feb. 4, 1967; d. Rodney Lowell and Karen Marie (Stecker) D. BA in Spanish, Colo. State U., 1989; MAEd in Counseling, U. Phoenix, Aurora, Colo., 1992. Cert. secondary Spanish tchr., Colo. Residence hall program advisor Colo. State U., Ft. Collins, 1987-88; tchr. Spanish Aurora Pub. Schs., 1990—. Named Hot Shot Most Valuable Tchr., Denver Nuggets and Denver Post, 1992, Tchr. of Yr., 1990-91. Mem. NEA, Colo. Edn. Assn., Aurora Edn. Assn., Colo. Congress Fgn. Lang. Tchrs. Republican. Christian.

DANZIG, ROBERT JAMES, newspaper executive; b. Troy, N.Y., Nov. 18, 1932; s. David and Irene (Forman) D.; m. Patricia Brady, Aug. 17, 1957; children: Mary Beth, Marsha, Darcy, Matthew, Stephen. BA cum laude, Siena Coll., 1962; postgrad., Am. Press Inst., 1965, Columbia U., 1969, Stanford U., 1969. With Albany (N.Y.) Times Union, 1950-61, 68-69, advt. salesman, 1952-61, adminstrv. asst., to exec. editor, 1968; asst. advt. mgr. Capital Newspapers, Albany, 1961-64, asst. bus. mgr., 1964-68, pub., 1969-76; gen. mgr. Schenectady (N.Y.) Union-Star, 1969; v.p., gen. mgr. newspapers Hearst Corp., N.Y.C., 1977, also bd. dirs.; dir. UPI, N.Y.C., 1980-84. Trustee Albany Med. Coll., Siena Coll., Russell Sage Coll., St. Peter's Hosp., Sunnyview Hosp.; bd. dirs. Saratoga Performing Arts Ctr. With USN, 1954-56. Mem. Am. Newspaper Pubs. Assn., N.Y. State Pubs. Assn. (pres.), Newspaper Advt. Bur. Roman Catholic. Office: Hearst Corp 959 8th Ave New York NY 10019-3737

DANZIGER, JERRY, broadcasting executive; b. N.Y.C., Jan. 23, 1924; s. Harry and Lillie (Lacher) D.; m. Zelda Bloom, Dec. 26, 1948; children: Sydney, Alan, Lee. Grad. high sch. With Sta. WTTV, Bloomington, Ind., 1950-53; ops. mgr. Sta. WTTV, Indpls., 1953-57; program mgr. Sta. WTSK-TV, Knoxville, Tenn., 1953; pres. Sta. KOB-TV, Albuquerque, 1957-88, v.p., 1983-88, pres., 1988-93, vice-chmn., 1993—; mem. Gov. N.Mex. Commn. for Film Entertainment, 1970-71. Bd. dirs. KIPC All Indian Pueblo Coun., 1975-88, Albuquerque Little Theatre, Albuquerque Pub. Broadcast, Albuquerque Jewish Welfare Fund, Albuquerque Econ. Devel. 1989—, Albuquerque Conv. and Visitors Bur., 1990—; v.p. for TV AP Broadcasting, 1980-88, Goodwill Industries N.Mex., 1980, bd. dirs., 1991—; me. Albuquerque Econ. Forum. Recipient Compadre award Am. Women in Radio and TV, 1978, 80. Mem. N.Mex. Broadcasters Assn. (pres. 1972-73, Broadcaster of Yr. award , 1976, 78), Press Club, Advt. Club, Albuquerque Country Club. Office: Sta KOB-TV PO Box 1351 Albuquerque NM 87103-1351

DAPPLES, EDWARD CHARLES, geologist, educator; b. Chgo., Dec. 13, 1906; s. Edward C. and Victoria (Gazzolo) D.; m. Marion Virginia Sprague, Sept. 2, 1931; children—Marianne Helena, Charles Christian. B.S., Northwestern U., 1928, M.S., 1934; M.A., Harvard, 1935; Ph.D., U. Wis., 1938. Geologist Ziegler Coal Co., 1928; geologist Truax-Traer Coal Co., 1928-32, mine supt., 1932; instr. Northwestern U., 1936-41, asst. prof., 1941, asso. prof., 1942-50, prof. geol. scis., 1950-75, prof. emeritus, 1975—; geologist Ill. Geol. Survey, 1939, Sinclair Oil Co., 1945-50, Pure Oil Co., 1950; dir. Evanston Exploration Corp., 1954-84; sr. vis. scientist U. Lausanne, Switzerland, 1960-61; vis. prof. U. Geneva, Switzerland, 1970. Author: Basic Geology for Science and Engineering, 1959, Atlas of Lithofacies Maps, 1960. Fellow Geol. Soc. Am., Soc. Econ. Geologist; mem. Am. Inst. Mining Engrs. (Legion of Honor), Assn. Petroleum Geologists, Internat. Assn. Sedimentologists, Soc. Econ. Paleontologists and Mineralogists (pres. 1970, hon. mem. 1974), Am. Inst. Profl. Geologists (pres. Ill.-Ind. sect. 1979, pres. Ariz. 1982, hon. mem. 1986), Assn. Engring. Geologists. Home: 13035 98th Dr Sun City AZ 85351

D'AQUILA, JAMES ANTHONY, financial investment executive; b. Hibbing, Minn., June 10, 1960; s. Carl Mario and Dolores Mae (Casagrande) D'A.; m. Bonnie R. Manhan. BBA, Notre Dame U., 1982. Assoc. E.F. Hutton & Co., N.Y.C., 1982-84, Drexel Burnham, N.Y.C., 1984-86; v.p., dir. Drexel Burnham, Beverly Hills, Calif., 1986-88; mng. dir., ptnr. Columbia Savings, Beverly Hills, Calif., 1989; exec. v.p., chief fin. officer WSGP Ptnrs., L.P., L.A., 1990-92; mng. dir. Dain Bosworth, Mpls., 1992—; bd. dirs. Threadneedle, Inc., Boca Raton, Fla. Founder Dig Deep; mem. Am. Heart Assn., Minn. Mem. Minn. Horse and Hunt Club, Mesabi C.C. Republican. Roman Catholic. Home: 5611 Seaview Dr Malibu CA 90265 Office: WSGP Ptnrs LP 1800 Century Park E Los Angeles CA 90067-1501

DARBY, JOHN WILLIAM, computer software company executive; b. Espanola, Ont., Can., Aug. 5, 1953; came to U.S., 1978; s. John Flockhart and Marjorie Alma (Wilson) D.; m. Mary Eileen Hatzl, Mar. 1, 1980; 1 child, Graham William. Dir. MIS-West Coast Sheraton Corp., L.A., 1980-85; mgr. customer svcs. ECI Computer Corp., Santa Ana, Calif., 1986-87, mgr. product devel., 1988-89; pres. Wetherly Internat., Langley, Wash., 1990—. Author: ACCESS Cookbook, 1985, Random ACCESS, 1987; co-designer (software) ECI/UX Property Management System, 1989. Office: 602 1st St Langley WA 98260

DARBY, WESLEY ANDREW, minister, educator; b. Glendale, Ariz., Sept. 19, 1928; s. Albert Leslie and Beulah E. (Lamb) D.; student Bible Inst. L.A., 1946, No. Ariz. U., 1946-47, Rockmont Coll., Denver, 1948-50, Ariz. State U., 1965, St. Anne's Coll., Oxford (Eng.) U., 1978; m. Donna Maye Bice, May 29, 1947; children: Carolyn Darby Eymann, Lorna Dale, Elizabeth Darby Bass, Andrea Darby Perdue. Ordained to ministry Bapt. Ch., 1950; pastor Sunnyside Bapt. Ch., Flagstaff, Ariz., 1947-48, First Bapt. Ch. of Clifton, Ariz., 1950-55, West High Bapt. Ch., Phoenix, 1955-90; pastor emeritus, 1990—; dep. assessor Greenlee County, 1951-55; instr. English lit. and pastoral subjects Southwestern Conservative Bapt. Bible Coll., Phoenix, 1961-87. Chmn. bd. Conservative Bapt. Found. Ariz., 1974-83, Gospel Wings, 1960-88; v.p. Ariz. Bapt. Conf., 1976-83; pres. Ariz. Alcohol-Narcotic Edn. Assn., 1968—. Recipient God, Family and Country award Freeman Inst., 1981. Mem. Evang. Philos. Soc., Greater Phoenix Assn. Evangelicals (pres. 1960-63, 91—), Ariz. Breakfast Club, (chaplain 1969—). Contbr. articles to profl. jours. Republican. Home: 5628 N 11th Dr Phoenix AZ 85013-1714 Office: 3301 N 19th Ave Phoenix AZ 85015

DARBYSHIRE, ROBYN WILLEY, forester; b. Hannibal, Mo., Mar. 29, 1958; d. Richard Lee and Elsie (Miller) Willey; m. Jerry L. Darbyshire, Aug. 11, 1979; children: Jane Emily, Benjamin Lee. BS in Forest Resources, U. Idaho, 1979; MS in Forest Sci., Oreg. State U., 1982; postgrad., U. Goettingen, 1982-83. Cert. silviculturist. Forestry trainee Bur. Land Mgmt., Coeur d'Alene, Idaho, 1976-77; forestry rsch. intern Weyerhauser Co., Centralia, Wash., 1978; forestry rsch. asst. Oreg. State U., Corvallis, 1983-87; silviculturist U.S. Forest Svc., Sweet Home, Oreg., 1987-89, Brookings, Oreg., 1989—. Team parent City Youth Soccer League, Brookings, 1992. Mem. Soc. Am. Foresters. Office: Chetco Ranger Dist 555 5th Ave Brookings OR 97415

D'ARCANGELO, MARIA TERESE, radio producer; b. Melrose, Mass., Mar. 16, 1963; d. Anthony Joseph and Mary Lillian (Renda) D'A. BS, Emerson Coll., 1985. Talent exec. asst. CAA, Beverly Hills, Calif., 1986-88; talent mgr. M.C.E.G., Santa Monica, Calif., 1988-90; pres., owner Arc Angel Mgmt., L.A., 1990—; radio producer KROQ-FM, Burbank, Calif., 1991—; nat. alumni bd. Emerson Coll., Boston, 1986—. Recipient Star award Emerson Coll., 1991. Mem. Nat. Acad. TV Arts & Svcs., Italian Ams. in Communications, Nat. Alumni Bd., So. Calif. Alumni Assn. (v.p. 1986-91). Office: KROQ-FM 3500 W Olive #900 Burbank CA 91505

DARKEY, KERMIT LOUIS, association executive, lawyer; b. Berea, Ohio, Oct. 11, 1930; s. Louise Anna (Watts) D.; m. Barbara Jean Rufer, Aug. 17, 1957; children: Kathryn Ann, Susan Lynn, Scott Rufer. AB, Ohio Wesleyan U., 1952; JD, U. Colo., 1957. Bar: Colo. 1957. Mem. labor rels. staff Mountain States Employers Coun., Denver, 1957-64, dir. labor rels., 1964-70, v.p., 1970-80, pres., 1980—; bd. dirs. Norwest Colo., Inc., Archway Cookies, Inc., Battle Creek, Mich., RMO, Denver. Chmn. Winter Park (Colo.) Recreation Assn., 1978—, St. Joseph Hosp., Denver, 1984-86, R.M.O., Denver, Mile Hi chpt. ARC, Metro Denver Boys & Girls Clubs. Capt. USAF, 1952-54. Mem. Colo. Bar Assn., Denver Bar Assn., Denver Met. Exec. Club (pres. 1980), Univ. Club Denver. Office: Mountain States Employers PO Box 539 Denver CO 80201-0539

DARLING, SCOTT EDWARD, lawyer; b. Los Angeles, Dec. 31, 1949; s. Dick R. and Marjorie Helen (Otto) D.; m. Cynthia Diane Harrah, June 1970 (div.); 1 child, Smokie; m. Deborah Lee Cochran, Aug. 22, 1981; children: Ryan, Jacob. BA, U. Redlands, 1972; JD, U.S.C., 1975. Bar: Calif. 1976, U.S. Dist. Ct. (cen. dist.) Calif. 1976. Assoc. atty. Elver, Falsetti, Boone & Crafts, Riverside, 1976-78; ptnr. Falsetti, Crafts, Pritchard & Darling, Riverside, 1978-84; sr. ptnr. Darling, Miller & King, Riverside, 1984—; grant reviewer HHS, Washington, 1982-88; judge pro tem Riverside County Mcpl. Ct., 1980, Riverside County Superior Ct., 1987-88; bd. dirs. Tel Law Nat. Legal Pub. Info. System, Riverside, 1978-80. Author, editor: Small Law Office Computer Legal System, 1984. Bd. dirs. Youth Adv. Com. to Selective Svc., 1968-70, Am. Heart Assn. Riverside County, 1978-82, Survival Ministries, 1986-89; atty. panel Calif. Assn. Realtors, L.A., 1980—; pres. Calif. Young Reps., 1978-80; mem. GI Forum, Riverside, 1970-88; presdl. del. Nat. Rep. Party, 1980-84; asst. treas. Calif. Rep. Party, 1981-83; Rep. Congl. candidate, Riverside, 1982; treas. Riverside Sickle Cell Found., 1980-82, recipient Eddie D. Smith award; pres. Calif. Rep. Youth Caucus, 1980-82; v.p. Riverside County Red Cross, 1982-84; mem. Citizen's Univ. Com., Riverside, 1978-84, World Affairs Council, 1978-82, Urban League, Riverside, 1980-82. Calif. Scholarship Fedn. (life). Named one of Outstanding Young Men in Am., U.S. Jaycees, 1979-86. Mem. ABA, Riverside County Bar Assn., Speaker's Bur. Riverside County Bar Assn., Riverside Jaycees, Riverside C. of C. Lodge: Native Sons of Golden West. Office: Darling Miller & King 3697 Arlington Ave Riverside CA 92506-3938

DARLINGTON, RONALD LAWRENCE, English language educator; b. Lethbridge, Alta., Can., Apr. 30, 1936; came to U.S. 1967; s. Joseph Lawrence and Lois Mary (Ashcroft) D.; m. Joanne Patricia Green, Sept. 26, 1959; children: Kimberley, Ronald II. BSc, Mont. State U., 1963, postgrad., 1966—. Tchr. Lethbridge Sch. Dist., 1963-64, Cranbrook (B.C.) Sch. Dist., 1965-66; tchr. English/writing Del Norte Unified Sch. Dist., Crescent City, Calif., 1967—; co-developer field study course of history of Modoc War and geology of Lava Beds area. Co-author: Modoc - We Walk Through Time, 1990-91. Mem. NEA, Calif. Tchrs. Assn. Home: 361 Dillman Rd Crescent City CA 95531-8839

DARMSTAETTER, JAY EUGENE, secondary education educator; b. Altadena, Calif., Nov. 30, 1937; s. Eugene Jamison and Virginia (Fagans) D. AA, L.A. City Coll., 1958; BA, L.A. State Coll., 1960, MA, 1962; postgrad., U. So. Calif., 1962-65. Cert. secondary edn. tchr., secondary adminstr. Tchr. L.A. Unified Schs., 1960—, master tchr., 1983-84; announcer L.A. Unified Schs., 1970—, CIF/So. Section, Artesia, Calif., 1964-85, State CIF, Fullerton, Calif., 1970-85. Soloist Christian Sci. Chs., L.A., 1958—; mem. Citizens Community Planning Coun., L.A. County, 1989—. Recipient Nat. Def. Edn. Assn. award Dept. of Edn., L.A., 1968. Mem. NEA, Calif. Tchrs. Assn., United Tchrs. L.A., Phi Mu Alpha Sinfonia. Republican. Office: Wilson High/LA Schools 4500 Multnomah St Los Angeles CA 90032-3799

DARNALL, ROBERTA MORROW, university official; b. Kemmerer, Wyo., May 18, 1949; d. C. Dale and Eugenia Stayner (Christmas) Morrow; m. Leslie A. Darnall, Sept. 3, 1977; children: Kimberly Gene, Leslie Nicole. BS, U. Wyo., Laramie, 1972. Tariff sec., ins. adminstr. Wyo. Trucking Assn., Casper, 1973-75; asst. clerical supr. Wyo. Legislature, Cheyenne, 1972-77; congl. campaign press aide, 1974; pub. relations dir. in Casper, Wyo. Republican Central Com., 1976-77; asst. dir. alumni relations U. Wyo., 1977-81, dir. of alumni, 1981—. Mem. Council Advancement and Support Edn. (membership com.), Higher Edn. Assn. Rockies, Am. Soc. Assn. Execs., Laramie C. of C. (acad. instns. com.), PEO (former courtesy com., officer), Sigma Delta Chi. Republican. Episcopalian. Home: 15 Snowy View Laramie WY 82070-5358 Office: Box 3137 University Sta Laramie WY 82071

DARNELL, CATHERINE MARGARET, anatomy and physiology educator; b. Oak Park, Ill., Aug. 29, 1957; d. Jon Nicholas and Violet Henderson (Low) Rougas; m. Gene Edwin Darnell, June 18, 1983; children: John Charles, Justin Lee, Ryan James. BS in Biology, Sioux Falls (S.D.) Coll., 1980; BS in Secondary Edn., MS in Zool. and Physiology, U. Wyo., 1988. Adj. prof. Laramie County Community Coll., Cheyenne, Wyo., 1989—. Contbr. articles to profl. jours. Home: 4315 Rose Ct Cheyenne WY 82009-5558 Office: Laramie County CC 1400 E College Dr Cheyenne WY 82007-3295

DARNELL, ROBERT CARTER, small business owner, anthropologist, linguist; b. Cuyahoga Falls, Ohio, June 6, 1927; s. Robert Carter Sr. and Georgia Eleanor (Jackson) D.; m. Mary Lucy Tunison, Dec. 27, 1949; children: Leonard, Allan, Kenneth. PhD, U. Mich., 1970. Editor N000, 1960-65; pres. Mid. East Coll., Beirut, 1959-60, Mid. East Union, Beirut, 1970-77; prof. Loma Linda (Calif.) U., 1977-82; owner Hanif Tower, Loma Linda, 1982—. Past editor Call to Health mag. Home and Office: 11652 Welebir St Loma Linda CA 92354-3634

DA ROZA, VICTORIA CECILIA, human resource administrator; b. East Orange, N.J., Aug. 30, 1945; d. Victor and Cynthia Helen (Krupa) Hawkins; m. Thomas Howard Kaminski, Aug. 28, 1971 (div. 1977); 1 child, Sarah Hawkins; m. Robert Anthony da Roza, Nov. 25, 1983. BA, U. Mich., 1967; MA, U. Mo., 1968. Contract compliance mgr. City of San Diego, 1972-75; v.p. personnel Bank of Calif., San Francisco, 1975-77; with human resources Lawrence Livermore (Calif.) Nat. Lab., 1978-86; pvt. cons. Victoria Kaminski-da Roza & Assocs., 1986—; lectr. in field; videotape workshop program on mid-career planning used by IEEE. Contbr. numerous articles to profl. jours. Mem. social policy com. City of Livermore, 1982. Mem. Am. Soc. Tng. and Devel., Western Gerontol. Soc. (planning com. Older Worker Track 1983), Gerontol. Soc. Am. Home and Office: 385 Borica Dr Danville CA 94526-5457

DARRAH, JOAN, mayor. Mayor City of Stockton, Calif. Office: City of Stockton 425 N El Dorado St Stockton CA 95202-1997

DARRIN, DAVID KEVIN, special agent; b. San Jose, Calif., Apr. 29, 1956; s. Patrick Lanier D. and Laura (Musso) Mann; m. Marina A. Speciale, Aug. 27, 1988; 1 child, Andrew. AA, Diablo Valley Coll., Pleasant Hill, Calif., 1977; BS, San Jose State U., 1979. Police sgt. Foster City (Calif.) Police Dept., 1979-85; criminal inspector Office Dist. Atty. Santa Clara County, San Jose, 1985-88; spl. agt. office of The Atty. Gen. State of Calif., San Jose, 1988—. Mem. Internat. Police Assn., Calif. Narcotic Officers Assn., Phi Kappa Phi.

DARROW, GEORGE F., natural resources company owner, consultant; b. Osage, Wyo., Aug. 13, 1924; s. George Washington and Marjorie (Ord) D.; m. Elna Tannehill, Oct. 23, 1976; children by previous marriage: Roy Stuart, Karen Josanne, Reed Crandall, John Robin. AB in Econs., U. Mich., 1945, BS in Geology, 1949. Geologist Amerada Petroleum Corp., Billings, Mont., 1949-50; v.p. Northwest Petroleum Co., 1951-58; resource cons. Resource Consultants, Billings, 1959-78; pres., CEO Crossbow Corp., Billings, 1962—; v.p. Kootenai Galleries, Bigfork, Mont., 1976—; sr. ptnr. Crossbow Assocs., resource mgrs.; chmn. Mont. Environ. Quality Coun., Helena, 1971-73; bd. dirs. Ord Ranch Corp., Lusk, Wyo., Mont. Pvt. Capital Network. Contbr. articles on resource mgmt. and econs. to various publs. Elected mem. Mont. Ho. of Reps., 1967-69, 71-73, Mont. Senate, 1973-75; bd. dirs. Bigfork Ctr. Performing Arts, 1980—. Lt. (j.g.) USNR, 1943-46, PTO. Mem. Am. Assn. Petroleum Geologists (past pres. Rocky Mountain sect.), Am. Inst. Profl. Geologists (charter), Mont. Geol. Soc. (founding mem., charter), Billings Petroleum Club. Home and Office: Crossbow Corp 2014 Beverly Hills Blvd Billings MT 59102-2314 also: Paladin Farms 924 Chapman Hill Dr Bigfork MT 59911

DART, JOHN SEWARD, religion news writer; b. Peekskill, N.Y., Aug. 1, 1936; s. Seward Homer and Vella Marion (Haverstock) D.; m. Gloria Joan Walker, Aug. 31, 1957; children—Kim, John W., Randall, Christopher. B.A., U. Colo., 1958. Staff writer UPI, Indpls. and Los Angeles, 1961-65; sci. writer Calif. Inst. Tech., Pasadena, 1966-67; religion writer Los Angeles Times, 1967—. Author: The Laughing Savior, 1976, The Jesus of Heresy and History, revised, expanded edit., 1988. Served with U.S. Army, 1958-61. Recipient Supple Meml. award Religion Newswriters Assn., 1980, Merrell Meml. award Jim Merrell Religion Liberty Found., 1980, William F. Leidt award Episcopal Ch., 1980, Angel award Religion in Media, 1985; NEH fellow Stanford U., 1973-74, First Amendment Ctr. fellow Vanderbilt U., 1992-93. Mem. Soc. Prof. Journalists (chpt. pres. 1976), Religion Newswriters Assn. (pres. 1990-92), Soc. Bibl. Lit. (mem.-at-large exec. com. Pacific Coast region 1990—). Democrat. Office: Los Angeles Times 20000 Prairie St Chatsworth CA 91311

DARVAS, ENDRE PETER, artist; b. Kisvadra, Sz-Szatmar, Hungary, July 18, 1946; came to U.S., in 1957; s. Bela and Maria (Filtczer) Darvas. BFA, U. Tex., 1969. Pres. Studio Arts and Frames, Inc., South Lake Tahoe, Calif., 1974-78; owner Darvas Studio, South Lake Tahoe, 1969—. One-man shows include San Angelo, Tex., 1963, Taos, N.Mex., 1971, Carmel, Calif., 1975, San Carlos, Mex., 1987, Galerias del Pacifico, Sonora, Mex., 1989, Studio Retrospective, Lake Tahoe, 1990; represented in permanent collections Sierra Gallery, Sierra Galleries, Lake Tahoe, Rosequist Gallery, Tucson. Recipient numerous awards from art exhibits. Mem. Soc. Am. Impressionists, Southwestern Watercolor Soc. Office: Darvas Studio PO Box 711 South Lake Tahoe CA 96156-0711

DASCALOS, DANIELLE MERRIE, marketing professional; b. Louisville, Dec. 25, 1960; d. Maurice Stanford Richey and Verna Lydia (Seidel) Hogberg; m. James Dascalos, Sept. 14, 1985. BA in Journalism, Met. State U., 1983. Reporter Mountain Bell, Denver, 1982-83; spl. events dir. Falk & Co., Denver, 1983-85; pres., owner Communications Unlimited, Denver, 1985-91; mktg. exec. Denver Mus. Natural History, 1989—; dir. mktg. Concierge Internat. Travel Card, Denver, 1988-91. Author, editor: Silence Isn't Golden, 1989, Talk To Your Kids About Sex, 1991, Communications is Everything, How to Talk To Your Kids About Drugs, 1990. Organizer, promoter Coats 4 Colo., Denver, 1986—. Mem. Denver Advt. Fedn. (Alfie award 1986-87), Jr. League Denver (chair, mem. Hall Life coms. 1989—). Democrat. Office: Mus Natural History Hall Life 2001 Colorado Blvd Denver CO 80205-5798

DASCHBACH, CHARLES CLARK, medical educator; b. Pasadena, Calif., Oct. 23, 1948; s. Albert Charles and Catharine Clark (MacDonald) D. MD, U. Ariz., 1980; MPH, Harvard U., 1984. Resident internal medicine St. Joseph's Hosp., Phoenix, 1980-83; fellow gen. internal medicine Harvard Sch. Pub. Health, Boston, 1983-84; assoc. dir. med. edn. St. Joseph's Hosp., Phoenix, 1984-87; dir. med. edn. St. Joseph's Hosp. and Med. Ctr., Phoenix, 1987—. Office: St Josephs Hosp PO Box 2071 Phoenix AZ 85001-2071

DASGUPTA, DIPANKAR, spacecraft payload engineer; b. Calcutta, India, Oct. 23, 1952; came to U.S., 1983; s. Manik and Sadhana (Sen) D.; m. Sharmila Banerjee, Jan. 24, 1982; children: Deborshi, Rajorshi. BS with honors, Maulana Azad Coll., Calcutta, 1970; BTech, Inst. Radio Physics Electronics, Calcutta, 1973, MTech, 1975. Lectr., rsch. assoc., sr. rsch. fellow Inst. Radiophysics and Electronics, 1982; engr. Comm. Satellite Corp., El Segundo, Calif., 1983-90; sr. engr. Comm. Satellite Corp., Palo Alto, Calif., 1990—.

DASH, HARVEY DWIGHT, artist; b. Bklyn., June 28, 1924; s. Irving Edward and Ann (Walters) D.; B.F.A., also B.S. in Edn., Temple U., 1948, M.F.A., 1949; m. Ruth Strom, May 30, 1946 (dec. 1975); children—Stefanie (Mrs. Jon Marvel), Eric, Stuart; m. 2d, Beverly Saraby, 1976. Supr. art public schs. Bound Brook, N.J., 1949-51; dir. Dash Sch. Art, Plainfield, N.J., 1951-54, 70-78, founder, dir. Lighthouse Sch. Art, Upper Grandview, N.Y., 1967-79; instr. adult evening schs. Bergen and Union counties, N.J., 1950-67; head dept. art Tenafly High Sch., N.J., 1950-57; dir. creative arts Paramus High Sch., N.J., 1957-67; pres. Lighthouse Galleries, Inc., Nyack, N.Y., 1967-70, Lighthouse Art Gallery, Nyack, N.Y., 1967-70; curator gallery Five, Grandview, N.Y.; one-man shows Melbourne Gallery, N.Y.C., 1960, Aker Gallery, N.Y.C., 1961; exhibited group shows Pa. Acad., Temple U., Fairleigh-Dickinson U., Brighton Gallery, others; cons., lectr. in field. Served with AUS, 1942-43. Berley grantee, 1964, Paramus Sch. System grantee, 1965. Mem. Bergen County (pres. 1962-63), Eastern, Nat. art edn. assns., Mod. Artists Guild, Rockland Council Arts, Internat. Platform Assn. Address: 16345 Bassett Ct Ramona CA 92065

DASHEN, ROGER FREDERICK, physics educator, consultant; b. Grand Junction, Colo., May 5, 1938; m. Mary Kelleghan; children: Monica, Melissa. AB summa cum laude, Harvard U., 1960; PhD, Calif. Inst. Tech., 1964. Rsch. assoc. Calif. Inst. Tech., Pasadena, 1964-65, asst. prof., 1965-66, prof. theoretical physics, 1966-69; prof. Inst. for Advanced Study, Princeton, N.J., 1969-86; prof. U. Calif. San Diego, La Jolla, 1986—, chmn. dept. physics, 1988—; mem. JASON, 1966—, Def. Sci. Bd. Panel on Anti-Submarine Warfare and SSBN Security, 1980-88; mem. planning and steering adv. com. of the advanced tech. panel Dept. of the Navy, 1984—; mem. adv. bd. Applied Physics Lab., U. Wash., Seattle, 1987-91; cons. Los Alamos Sci. Lab., 1975—; rsch. cons. Schlumberger, 1978-83; advisor Alfred P. Sloan Found., 1985-91; Amos de Shalit lectr. Weizmann Inst. Sci., Israel, 1981. Contbr. 115 articles to profl. jours. Fellow Alfred P. Sloan Found., 1966-73; Green Scholar Scripps Instn. Oceanography, 1977. Mem. NAS, Am. Acad. Arts and Scis. Office: U Calif San Diego Dept Physics 0354 9500 Gilman Dr La Jolla CA 92093-0354

DASSANOWSKY-HARRIS, ROBERT VON, writer, editor, educator; b. N.Y.C., N.Y., Jan. 28, 1956; s. Leslie Harris de Erendred and Elfriede von Dassanowsky. Grad., Am. Acad. Dramatic Arts; BA with honors, UCLA, 1985, MA, 1988, PhD, 1992. Actor, dir. L.A., N.Y.C., 1975-82; asst. prof. of German UCLA, 1992-93; asst. prof. of German and Humanities U. Colo., 1993—; TV writer, researcher, L.A., 1990—. Author: (plays) The Birthday of Margot Beck, 1980, Briefly Noted, 1981, Vespers, 1982 (Beverly Hills Theatre Guild award 1984), Tristen in Winter, 1986, Songs of a Wayfarer, 1986, Coda, 1991; founding editor Rohwedder: Internat. Jour. Lit.and Art, 1986—; editor New German Rev., 1987-92, PEN CNT mag., 1992—; contbg. editor Osiris, 1992—, Rampike (Can.), 1992—; author numerous poems; contbr. articles, reviews and essays to jour. Mem. Pan Europa Union, Munich, Vienna, 1982—, Accademia Culturale d'Europa, Italy, 1988—. Recipient Residency award Karolyi Found., France, 1979, Man of Achievement award, U.K., 1986, Accademico Honoris Causa Diploma, Accademia Culturale d'Europa, Italy, 1989. Mem. PEN (West bd. dirs. L.A. 1992—), Dramatists Guild, Authors League, Poets and Writers, Modern Lang. Assn. Home: 4346 Matilija Ave Apt 27 Sherman Oaks CA 91423-3626

DATTAR, KARL SHREEPAD, information systems executive; b. Calcutta, India, Aug. 17, 1965. BS in Bus., Acctg., Sch. of the Ozarks, 1988. EDP acct. Zuercher, Sturmann & Co., CPA's, Branson, Mo., 1988-89; systems specialist, staff acct. Calif. Sch. Profl. Psychology, San Francisco, 1989-90; systems mgr. Seamodal Transport Corp., San Francisco, 1990—. Home: 1833 Filbert St #6 San Francisco CA 94123 Office: Seamodal Transport Corp 221 Main St # 765 San Francisco CA 94105

DAUBEN, WILLIAM GARFIELD, chemist, educator; b. Columbus, Ohio, Nov. 6, 1919; s. Hyp J. and Leilah (Stump) D.; m. Carol Hyatt, Aug. 8, 1947; children: Barbara, Ann. AB, Ohio State U., 1941; AM, Harvard U., 1942, PhD, 1944; PhD (hon.), U. Bordeaux, France, 1980. Edward Austin fellow Harvard U., 1941-42, teaching fellow, 1942-43, research asst., 1943-45; instr. U. Calif. at Berkeley, 1945-47, asst. prof. chemistry, 1947-52, assoc. prof., 1952-57, prof., 1957—; lectr. Am.-Swiss Found., 1962; mem. med. chem. study sect. USPHS, 1959-64; mem. chemistry panel NSF, 1964-67; mem. Am.-Sino Sci. Cooperation Com., 1973-76; NRC, 1977-80. Mem. bd. editors Jour. of Organic Chemistry, 1957-62; mem. bd. editors Organic Syntheses, 1959-67, bd. dirs., 1971—; editor in chief Organic Reactions, 1967-83, pres., 1967-84, bd. dirs. 1967—; mem. edit. bd. Steroids, 1989—; contbr. articles profl. jours. Recipient citation U. Calif., Berkeley, 1990; Guggenheim fellow, 1951, 66, sr. fellow NSF, 1957-58, Alexander von Humboldt Found. fellow, 1980. Fellow Royal Soc. Chemistry, Swiss Chem. Soc.; mem. NAS (chmn. chemistry sect. 1977-80), Am. Chem. Soc. (chmn. div. organic chemistry 1962-63, councilor organic div. 1964-70, mem. coun. publ. com. 1965-70, mem. adv. com. Petroleum Research Fund 1974-77, award Calif. sect. 1959, Ernest Guenther award 1973, Arthur C. Cope scholar 1990), Am. Acad. Arts and Scis., Pharm. Soc. Japan (hon.), Phi Beta Kappa, Sigma Xi, Phi Lambda Upsilon, Phi Eta Sigma, Sigma Chi. Club: Bohemian. Home: 20 Eagle Hl Kensington CA 94707-1408 Office: U Calif Berkeley Dept Chemistry Berkeley CA 94720

DAUBER, IRA MITCHELL, cardiologist; b. N.Y.C., Sept. 23, 1952; s. Jack Simon and Shirley Frances (Meyer) D.; m. Sylvia Louise Brice, Mar. 4, 1989; children: Hannah Elizabeth, Benjamin David. BS, Cornell U., 1973, MD, 1977. Intern U. Colo. Med. Ctr., Denver, 1977-78; resident N.Y. Hosp., N.Y.C., 1978-79; fellow U. Colo. Med. Ctr., Denver, 1979-81, resident, 1982-83, chief resident, 1983-84, cardiology fellow, 1984-86, asst. prof. medicine and cardiology, 1986-91, clin. asst. prof. cardiology & medicine, 1991—; rsch. assoc. Denver VA Med. Ctr., 1986-90; assoc. dir. heart failure and cardiac transplant U. Colo. Med. Ctr., 1990-91, South Denver Cardiology Assocs., 1991—. Contbr. articles to profl. jours. VA grantee, 1986. Fellow Am. Coll. Cardiology, Am. Coll. Chest Physicians; mem. Am. Heart Assn. (grantee 1987), ACP, AM. Fedn. for Clin. Rsch., N.Y. Acad. Scis., AAAS. Office: 950 E Harvard Ave Ste 100 Denver CO 80210-7007

DAUGHADAY, DOUGLAS ROBERT, computer engineer; b. Highland Park, N.J., Mar. 13, 1954; s. Robert Owings and Mary (Kirkpatrick) D.; m. Ilene D. Eichel, Feb. 14, 1987; 1 child, Brian Douglas. BSEE cum laude, W.Va. Inst. Tech., 1976; MSEE, U. So. Calif., 1979. Mem. tech. staff Hughes Aircraft Co., Culver City, Calif., 1977-79; sr. engr. Litton G&CS, Woodland Hills, Calif., 1979-80; lab. engr. Garrett Airesearch, Torrance, Calif., 1980-84; mem. tech. staff The Aerospace Corp., El Segundo, Calif., 1984-87, mgr., 1987—. Mem. IEEE, Assn. Computing Machinery, Soc. Am. Magicians (2d v.p. assembly # 22), Nat. Assn. Underwater Instrs. (instr.), U. S.C. Alumni Assn. (life mem.), Eta Kappa Nu (life mem.). Democrat. Home: 2385 Roscomare Rd Los Angeles CA 90077 Office: The Aerospace Corp 2350 E El Sequndo Blvd El Segundo CA 90245

DAUGHERTY, CHARLES EDWARD, accountant, military officer; b. Minden, La., Oct. 25, 1945; s. Ruel Jack and Iru (Smith) D.; m. Linda Kay Bryant. BS, McNeese U., 1967; MS in Systems Mgmt., U. So. Calif., 1974. CPA. Commd. 2d lt. USAF, 1967, advanced through grades to col., 1988, various acctg. assignments, 1967—; instr. U. So. Miss. USAF, Hattiesburg, 1978-81; budget analyst USAF, Omaha, 1981-83, Montgomery, Ala., 1983-89; dir. acctg. and fin. Pacific Air Forces, Hickam AFB, 1989—; dep. commandant Profl. Military Comptroller Sch., Maxwell AFB. Mem. AICPA, Tex. Soc. CPA's, Assn. Govt. Accts. Republican. Mem. Assembly of God Ch. Home: 106 Beard Ave Honolulu HI 96818-5119 Office: USAF HQPACAF/FMF Hickam AFB HI 96818

DAUGHERTY, DENNIS ALAN, nutritionist, consultant, cattle rancher; b. Chico, Calif., July 29, 1952; s. Herman Thomas and Opal Lucile (Wood) D.; m. Denise René Barber, June 29, 1973; children: Todd Alan, Tara Anne. BS, Calif. Poly. State U., 1975; MS, Oreg. State U., 1978, PhD, 1981. With weights and measures div. County Agr. Commn., Red Bluff, Calif., 1975-76; rsch. asst. Oreg. Agrl. Rsch. Ctr., Burns, Oreg., 1977-80; nutrition cons. Loper Systems, Corona, Calif., 1980-82, Turlock, Calif., 1982-86; nutritionist, owner Pine Creek Nutrition Svc., Turlock, 1986—; gen. co-owner Pine Creek Cattle Co., Chico, Calif., 1986—; organizer, lectr. dairy tour and seminar for Japanese dairymen, Modesto and Stockton, Calif., 1987-89; guest lectr. Japanese Feed Industry, Tokyo, 1992; mem. steering com. Calif. Animal Nutrition Conf., 1992—. Contbr. articles to profl. jours. Dir. Turlock Volleyball Club, 1991—, chmn., 1992—. Wrasse scholar Calif. Poly. State U., 1970. Mem. Am. Soc. Animal Sci., Am. Dairy Sci. Assn., Am. Registry Profl. Animal Scientists, Calif.-Nev. chpt. Am. Registry Profl. Animal Scientists (chmn. nominating com., bd. dirs. 1989-90), Valley Nutritionists, NRA, Calif. Poly. State U. Alumni Assn., Oreg. State U. Alumni Assn. Republican. Office: Pine Creek Nutrition Svc 259 N Palm St Turlock CA 95380-4028

DAUGHERTY, DUKE EDWIN, insurance company marketing official; b. Dayton, Ohio, Feb. 20, 1966; s. Larry Ray and Carole Jean (Krimm) D.; m. Kimberly Joy Love, July 6, 1985; children: Ashley Clay, Brittany Joy. Student, Pikes Peak C.C., Colorado Springs, Colo., 1991-93, U. Colo., Colorado Springs, 1993—. Crew trainer McDonald's, Dayton, 1982-83; sales assoc. Galenkamp Shoe Corp., Dayton, 1983-85; ins. underwriter Progressive Ins. Cos., Colorado Springs, 1985-86, tech. trainer, 1986-88, customer svc. rep., 1988, corp. trainer, 1988-90, mktg. assoc., 1990—. Mem. ASTD (treas. Pike's Peak chpt. 1987-92, v.p. fin. region VI conf. 1990-92). Republican. Nazarene. Home: 8050 Freemantle Dr Colorado Springs CO 80920

DAUGHERTY, JAMES ROBERT, nutrition educator; b. Reading, Pa., July 26, 1949; s. John Seiders and Elizabeth Jane (Lengel) D.; m. Arlen Anne Deubler, June 9, 1972; 1 child, Ryan James. BS, Ariz. State U., Tempe, 1975, MS, 1979. Registered dietitian. Clin. dietitian CIGNA Health Plan of Ariz., Phoenix, 1980-83, mgr., 1983-87; instr. Glendale (Ariz.) Community Coll., 1987-89, asst. dept. chair, 1989—; co-chmn. Coll. Tech. Com. Glendale Comunity Coll., 1992—, Faculty senator, 1992—; mem. Deer Valley High Sch. Home Econs. adv. com., Glendale, 1989, chmn., 1990. Mem. Internat. Diabetic Athletes (bd. dirs. 1987-89), Ariz. Pub. Health Assn. (bd. dirs. 1986-88), Ind. Order Foresters (high chief ranger 1985—, Man of Yr. 1985), Mensa, Irish Am. Social Club. Home: 5614 W Mariposa St Phoenix AZ 85031-1024 Office: Glendale Community Coll 6000 W Olive Ave Glendale AZ 85302-3090

DAUGHERTY, ROBERT MELVIN, JR., university dean, medical educator; b. Kansas City, Mo., May 2, 1934; s. Robert Melvin and Mildred Josephine (Johnson) D.; m. Sandra Allison Keller, Aug. 10, 1957; children—Robert Melvin III, Allison, Christopher. B.A., U. Kans., 1956, M.D., 1960; M.S., U. Okla., 1963, Ph.D., 1964. Intern Jefferson Davis Hosp., Houston, 1960-61; resident U. Okla. Med. Center, Oklahoma City, 1961-64; asst. prof. physiology and medicine U. Okla. Med. Sch., Oklahoma City, 1964-66; asso. prof. physiology and medicine Mich. State U. Coll. Human Medicine, East Lansing, 1966-69; prof., dir. Office Curriculum Implementation, 1969-76; prof. physiology and medicine U. Wyo. Coll. Human Medicine, Laramie, 1976-78; dean U. Wyo. Coll. Human Medicine, 1976-78; prof. physiology and medicine Ind. U. Sch. Medicine, Indpls., 1978-81; asso. dean Ind. U. Sch. Medicine, 1978-81, dir. continuing med. edn., 1978-81; dean Sch. Medicine, U. Nev., 1981—; teaching scholar Am. Heart Assn., 1970-75. Mem. AMA (coun. med. edn. 1991—), Am. Physiol. Soc., Am. Heart Assn., Central Soc. for Clin. Investigation. Presbyterian. Home: 820 Marsh Ave Reno NV 89509-1945 Office: U Nev Sch Medicine Reno NV 89557

DAUGHTON, DONALD, lawyer; b. Grand River, Iowa, Mar. 11, 1932; s. F.J. and Ethel (Edwards) D.; m. Sally Daughton; children by previous marriage: Erin, Thomas, Andrew, J.P. BSC, U. Iowa, 1953, JD, 1956. Bar: Iowa, 1956, Ariz., 1958. Assoc. Browder & Daughton, 1964-65, Browder, Gillenwater & Daughton, 1967-72, Daughton Feinstein & Wilson, 1972-86, Daughton, Hawkins & Bacon P.C., 1986-87, Bryan, Cave, McPheeters and McRoberts, 1988-92, Daughton, Hawkins, Brockelman & Guinan, Phoenix, 1992—; judge Superior Ct. Ariz., 1965-67; asst. county atty. Polk County, 1958-59 chmn. Phoenix Employees Relations Bd., 1976. Pres. Maricopa County Legal Aid Soc., 1971-73. 1st lt. JAG, USAF, 1956-58. Fellow Am. Bar Found., Ariz. Bar Found. (founder); mem. ABA (bd. govs. 1989-92, exec. com. 1991-92), State Bar Ariz. (chmn. pub. rels. com. 1980-84, jud. evaluation poll com. 1984—), Iowa State Bar, Maricopa County Bar Assn. (bd. dirs. 1962-64), 9th Crct. Jud. Conf. (lawyer rep. 1981-84, 88), Ariz. Acad. Arbitrators, Nat. Acad. Arbitrators, Univ. Club. Home: 6021 N 51st Pl Paradise Valley AZ 85253 Office: Daughton Hawkins Brockelman & Guinan 40 N Central Ave Ste 2500 Phoenix AZ 85004

DAUM, JOHN BRADFORD, reinsurance broker; b. Princeton, N.J., Nov. 3, 1957; s. Robert William and Lois Audrey (Bischoff) D. BA, Boston Coll., 1980. Reins. broker Sedgwick Payne, London, 1980-83, AON Corp., Old Bridge, N.J., 1987-89, E. W. Blanch Co., San Francisco, 1989—; reins. underwriter Gen. Reins. Co., Stamford, Conn., 1983-87. Republican. Episcopalian. Home: 1980 Washington St # 108 San Francisco CA 94109 Office: E W Blanch Co 201 California St San Francisco CA 94111-5002

DAUNT, JACQUELINE ANN, lawyer; b. Flint, Mich., Dec. 2, 1953; d. Henry Thomas and Germaine Mary (Vanwayenbergh) D.; m. Ronald Glenn Decker, June 21, 1986. Student, Open U. Brussels, 1978-79; BA in Econs., U. Mich., 1975, JD, 1978. Bar: Calif. 1978, Mich. 1979. Assoc. Bronson, Bronson & McKinnen, San Francisco, 1979-81; assoc. Fenwick & West, Palo Alto, Calif., 1981-85, ptnr., 1986—; bd. dirs. Assn. Software Design, Palo Alto, 1991—. Author: (booklets) Venture Capital: A Strategy for High Tech Companies, 1989, Internat. Technology Distribution Agreements, 1990; co-author: (booklets) Corporate Partnering: A Strategy for High Tech Companies, 1991, Structuring Effective Earnouts, 1991, Entering the U.S. Market: A Strategy for High Tech Companies, 1992. Mem. ABA, Calif. Bar Assn., Mich. Bar assn., No. Calif. Venture Capital Assn. (co-chmn. 1991—). Office: Fenwick & West Two Palo Alto Sq Ste 800 Palo Alto CA 94306

DAVE, SHASHI BHAISHANKER, engineer; b. Jharia, Bihar, India, Apr. 13, 1931; came to U.S., 1957; s. Bhaishanker O. and Daya Dave; m. Saroj Dave, Jan. 15, 1963; children: Sonal, Sanjay. BSc with honors, Gujarat U., Ahmedabad, India, 1955; BS, U. Tenn., 1959, MS, 1960. Rsch. engr. Gaylorad Assocs., Newark, 1960-66. Patentee in field. Recipient rsch. fellow Celite Corp., 1966—. Mem. ASTM, Am. Chem. Soc., India Assn. (pres. Denver chpt. 1986). Hindu. Office: Celite Corp 2500 Miguelito Rd Lompoc CA 93436-9798

DAVENPORT, ALFRED LARUE, JR., manufacturing company executive; b. Upland, Calif., May 6, 1921; s. Alfred Larue and Nettie (Blocker) D.; m. Darrow Ormsbee Beazlie, May 16, 1950 (div. 1953); m. Jean Ann Given, June 21, 1957; children: Lawrence, Terisa, Lisa, Nancy. Student, Chaffey Jr. Coll., Ontario, Calif., 1940; BE in Indsl. Engring., U. So. Calif., 1943. Weight engring. Lockheed Aircraft, Burbank, Calif., 1940-41; ptnr. Pacific Traders, L.A., 1946-48; founder, pres. Pactra Industries, Inc., L.A., 1947-79; owner Davenport Internat., Ltd., Van Nuys, Calif., 1979—; pres., founder Trans Container, Inc., Upland, Calif., 1970-79; pres., owner Pactra Hobby, Inc., Van Nuys, 1983—, Davenport Export-Import, Inc., Encino, Calif., 1982—; cons. Plasti-Kote, Inc., Medina, Ohio, 1985—; pres. Pactra Coatings Inc., Hobby Div., Upland, 1985-89; mgr. craft div. Plasti-Kote Inc., Medina, Ohio, 1989—; dir. R.C. Dudek, Inc., Westlake, Calif., 1978—, Aerosol Info. Assn., L.A., 1974-79. Lt. USN, 1943-46. Recipient Blue Key, U. So. Calif., L.A., 1942. Mem. So. Calif. Hobby Industry Assn. (sec. 1959-62), Hobby Industry Assn. Am. (dir. 1961-64), Young Pres. Orgn. (L.A. chpt.), World Bus. Coun., Woodland Hills Country Club (treas. 1981-83), Sigma Phi Epsilon (v.p. 1954-81, alumni bd. dirs. 1955-75, Disting. Bro. award 1979, Alumni of Yr. award 1975). Republican. Presbyterian. Home: 4650 Hayvenhurst Ave Encino CA 91436-3252 Office: Plasti-Kote Inc 14540 Haynes St Van Nuys CA 91411-1612

DAVENPORT, JANET LEE, real estate saleswomen, small business owner; b. Napa, Calif., Dec. 10, 1938; d. George Perry and Stella Dolores (Ramalho) Gomez; m. Bingo George Wesner, Aug. 4, 1957 (July 1978); children: Bing George, Diane Estelle; m. Marvin Eugene Davenport, Jan. 13, 1979. Student, U. Calif., Davis, 1956-57, Nat. Jud. Coll., 1975-79. Co-owner, operator Bar JB Ranch, Benicia, Calif., 1960-71, Lovelock, Nev., 1971-78; owner, mgr. Wesner Bookkeeping Svc., Lovelock, 1973-78; chief tribal judge Ct. Indian Offenses, Lovelock, 1975-79; justice of peace, coroner County of Pershing, Lovelock, 1975-79; paralegal, legal sec. Samuel S. Wardle, Carson City, Nev., 1979; dep. ct. adminstr. Reno Mcpl. Ct., Reno, 1979-81; co-owner horse farm Reno, 1979—, freelance real estate investor, 1979—; real estate saleswoman Merrill Lynch Realtors, Sparks, Nev., 1981-82; realtor, farm and ranch div. mgr. Copple and Assocs., Realtors, Sparks, 1982-91; real estate saleswoman Vail and Assocs. Realty, Reno, Nev., 1991—; co-owner, operator Lovelock (Nev.) Merc. Co., 1988—; sec. Nev. Judges Assn., 1977-78. Dir. Pershing County Drug and Alcohol Abuse Council, Lovelock, 1976-78. Mem. Reno/Sparks Bd. Realtors, Nat. Assn. Realtors, Nev. Assn. Realtors, Am. Quarter Horse Assn. Republican. Roman Catholic. Home: 4805 Sinelio Dr Reno NV 89502-9510 Office: Vail and Assocs Realty 1700 S Virginia St Reno NV 89502

DAVENPORT, L. SCOTT, software technician; b. Bismarck, N.D., Apr. 28, 1959; s. Lance Eugene and Adeline Marianne (Keck) D. Grad. high sch., Sweet Home, Oreg. Sales clk. Anderson's Sporting Goods, Albany, Oreg., 1978, Webfoot Sports Ctr., Vancouver, Wash., 1980; forest technician U.S. Forest Svc., Sweet Home, 1979; live-in attendant Adult and Family Svc., Corvallis, Oreg., 1989-81; mail clk. Hewlett-Packard Co., Corvallis, 1981-82, adminstrv. support clk., 1984-87, adminstrv. specialist, 1987-90, adminstrv. and systems support specialist, 1990-92, software technician, 1992—. Mem. Airplane Owners and Pilots Orgn. Office: Hewlett-Packard Co 1000 NE Circle Blvd Corvallis OR 97330

DAVENPORT, ROGER LEE, research engineer; b. Sacramento, Calif., Oct. 27, 1955; s. Lee Edwin and Ada Fern (Henderson) D.; m. Becky Alice Youtz, Dec. 31, 1977 (div. Apr. 1992). AB Physics, U. Calif., Berkeley, 1977; MSME, U. Ariz., 1979. Assoc. engr. Solar Energy Rsch. Inst., Golden, Colo., 1979-82; cons. Darmstadt, Fed. Republic Germany, 1982-84; missionary Eastern European Sem., Vienna, Austria, 1984-87; staff researcher Sci. Applications Internat. Corp., San Diego, 1987—. Mem. Am. Solar Energy Soc., Wycliffe Assocs., Sierra Club, Phi Beta Kappa. Home: 19076 W 59th Dr Golden CO 80403 Office: SAIC 15000 W 6th Golden CO 80401

DAVENPORT, WILLIAM HAROLD, mathematics educator; b. Jackson, Tenn., Dec. 21, 1935; s. John Heron and Mary (Troutt) D.; m. Mary Janice Johnson, Mar. 18, 1960; children—Mark Edson, Amber Yvette; m. Sandra Elaine Holloway, July 30, 1973; children—William Harold II, David Carleton, Bennett John Joseph. B.S., U. Tenn., 1962; M.S., Tex. A&M U., 1966; Ph.D. in Math., U. Ala., 1971. Aerospace technologist NASA Manned Spacecraft Ctr., Houston, 1962-64; research mathematician Brown Engring. Co., Huntsville, Ala., 1966-67; teaching fellow, instr. math. U. Ala., University, 1967-71; mathematician U.S. Army Missile Command, Huntsville, 1971-72; asst. prof. math. U. Petroleum and Minerals, Dhahran, Saudi Arabia, 1972-77, Columbus Coll., Ga., 1977-81; assoc. prof. U. Ark., Little Rock, 1981-87, Northwestern State U., Natchitoches, La., 1987-88, Mesa State Coll., Grand Junction, Colo., 1988—. Served with USN, 1954-58. Mem. Am. Math. Soc., Math. Assn. Am., Sigma Pi Sigma, Phi Kappa Phi, Pi Mu Epsilon. Roman Catholic. Avocation: tennis.

DAVID, GEORGE, psychiatrist, economic theory lecturer; b. N.Y.C., Feb. 19, 1940; s. Norman and Jennie (Danziger) D. BA, Yale U., 1961; MD, NYU, 1965. Intern Children's Hosp., San Francisco, 1965; resident in psychiatry Colo. Psychiat. Hosp., Denver, 1965-66; practice medicine specializing in psychiatry San Francisco; staff Mt. Zion Hosp., San Francisco, 1966-67, San Mateo County (Calif.) Mental Health Svcs., 1968-71; lectr. on application of econ. theory to personal decision making. Mem. San Francisco Clin. Hypnosis (v.p. 1973-74). Libertarian. Home: 2334 California St San Francisco CA 94115-2705 Office: 3527 Sacramento St San Francisco CA 94118-1846

DAVID, LEON THOMAS, judge, educator, former army officer; b. San Francisco, Aug. 25, 1901; s. Leon Kline and Ella Nancy (Thomas) D.; m. Henrietta Louise Mellin, May 22, 1927; children: Carolyn L. Eskra, Leon Colby. A.B., Stanford, 1924, J.D., 1926; M.S. in Pub. Adminstrn., U. So. Calif., 1935, Dr. Pub. Adminstrn., 1957. Bar: Calif. 1926, U.S. Supreme Ct. 1932. City editor Vallejo (Calif.) Times, 1920-21; free-lance journalist, 1921-26, pvt. practice law; mem. Malcolm & David, Palo Alto, Calif., 1926-31; dep. and acting city atty. Palo Alto, 1926-31; mem. faculty Sch. Law, U. So. Calif., 1931-34, Sch. Pub. Adminstrn., 1934-41, 1947-67; sr. asst. city atty. L.A., 1934-41, 46-50; spl. counsel L.A. Harbor Commn., 1939-41; judge Municipal Ct., L.A. Jud. Dist., 1950-53; judge Superior Court, 1953-67, with appellate dept., 1958-60, ret., 1967; assoc. justice pro tem Calif. Ct. Appeal, 1969-73. Author: Municipal Liability for Tortious Acts and Omissions, 1936; Administration of Public Tort Liability in Los Angeles, 1939; Tort Liability of Public Officers, 1940; Law and Lawyers, 1950; Role of the Lawyer in Public Administration, 1957; Law of Local Government, 1966; Old 89, My Horse, and Other Tales, Essays and Verse, 1974; History of State Bar of California, 1979; also articles in field of municipal law, ct. procedure and practice, legal history, legal aid, pub. adminstrn. Mem. Calif. Gov.'s Adv. Com. Law Enforcement, 1959-67. Chmn. legal aid com. State Bar Calif. intermittently to 1950, chmn. state bar com. history of law, 1975-78; founder, past pres. L.A. Legal Aid Found.; mem. World Affairs Council, San Francisco, 1987—; mem. Gov. Alameda County Colony Mayflower Descendents, 1989-90. Served from 2d lt. to maj. F.A.-O.R.C., 1924-42; from lt. col. to col., AUS, 1942-61; comdt. U.S. Army Sch. for Spl. Pers. Svcs., 1942-43, chief Spl. Svcs., N. Africa and Mediterranean theaters of operation, 1943-45; col. AUS (ret.), 1961; elder, mem. laws and regulations com. Presbyn. Ch., mem. social edn. and action com. L.A. Presbytery, 1965-69). Decorated Legion of Merit (U.S.), Hon. Officer Order Brit. Empire, Medaille d'Honneur d'Or (France), Medalha do Guerra (Brazil), Comdr. Crown of Italy; recipient Reginald Heber Smith medal for distinguished legal aid svc. to indigent, 1962. Mem. L.A. Bar Assn., Contra Costa County Bar Assn., Am. Legion (past comdr.), Calif. Judges Assn. (life), Stanford, U. Calif., U. So. Calif. Alumni assns., Calif. Hist. Soc., 9th Jud. Cir. Hist. Soc., Mt. Diablo Amateur Radio Club, Soc. Mayflower Descendants, Mason (K.T., 32d degree, Shriner), DeMolay Legion of Honor (life), Commonwealth Club, Kiwanis (pres. Palo Alto 1931, L.A. 1962, lt. gov. Div. 1 Calif.-Nev.-Hawaii dist. 1967, internat. rels. com. 1957-58), Order of Coif (life), Phi Alpha Delta, Phi Kappa Phi, Pi Sigma Alpha, Sigma Alpha Iota. Home: The Waterford # 2107 1840 Tice Creek Pky Walnut Creek CA 94595

DAVID, ROBERT PORTER, health care executive; b. Walnut Creek, Calif., Dec. 2, 1956; s. Richard Lawrence and Virginia Lee (Porter) D.; m. Mary Jo Adair, Oct. 14, 1989. BA, U. Calif., Berkeley, 1979. Account exec. Corroon & Black, San Francisco, 1980-83; sr. underwriter Fairmont Ins. Co., San Francisco, 1983-85; mgr. payor rels. Tokos Med. Corp., Santa Ana, Calif., 1985-88; dir. managed care Healthdyne, Inc., Garden Grove, Calif., 1988-92; dir. nat. accounts Sutter Corp., San Diego, 1992—. Apptd. mem. Calif. Health Care Adv. Com., Sacramento, 1987-92. Mem. Young Exec. Am., Calif. Alumni Assn. (life). Republican. Presbyterian. Home: 34 Vassar Aisle Irvine CA 92715 Office: Sutter Corp 9425 Chesapeake Dr San Diego CA 92123

DAVID, RONALD SIGMUND, psychiatrist; b. L.A., Feb. 3, 1940; s. Sam and Beatrice Yvonne (Fertig) D.; m. Eloise Nadine Jensen, June 15, 1969; children: Diana Kirsten, Samuel Sherman. BA, Stanford U., 1962, MD, 1967. Bd. cert. in psychiatry. Resident Albert Einstein Coll. Medicine, N.Y.C., 1974, fellow adminstrv. psychiatry, 1975; dir. adult outpatient svcs. Soundview-Throgs Neck Community Mental Health Ctr., Bronx, N.Y., 1975-77; lectr. dept. psychiatry Albert Einstein Coll. Medicine, Bronx, 1975-77; dir. adult outpatient sect. So. Ariz. Mental Health Ctr., Tucson, 1977-79; asst. prof. U. Ariz., Tucson, 1977-79, lectr., 1979—; med. dir. Ctr. for Family and Individual Counseling, Tucson, 1979—; chmn. Tucson Mental Illness Awareness Week Coalition, 1988, 89, So. Ariz. Com. for the Chronically Mentally Ill, Tucson, 1977-79; med. dir. St. Mary's Day Treatment Program, Tucson, 1979-82; cons. Family Counseling Agy., Tucson, 1986—. Co-author: Financing Planning F-2 Committee, 1978. Pres. Colonia Solana Neighborhood Assn., Tucson, 1981-82, 86-88; mem. Broadway Corridor Planning Com., Tucson, 1986-88; founding bd. mem. COPE, Tucson, 1977-83. Capt. USAR, 1968-71. Fellow Am. Psychiat. Assn., Am. Orthopsychiat. Assn., Ariz. Psychiat. Soc. (chair ins. com. 1987-88, chair pub. affairs 1988—, chair program com. 1989—), Tucson Psychiat. Soc. (sec.-treas. 1986-87, pres. 1987-89), Am. Assn. for Social Psychiatry. Jewish. Office: Ctr for Family and Individual Counseling 430 N Tucson Blvd Tucson AZ 85716-4755

DAVIDS, KENNETH HAWLEY, English language educator; b. Chgo., May 9, 1937; s. Walter Charles and Evelyn Rose (Faber) D.; m. Elizabeth Davis, June 1959 (div. 1967). BA, Northwestern U., 1959; MA, U. Calif., Berkeley, 1961. Teaching asst. U. Calif., Berkeley, 1960-62; from. inst. to assoc. prof. Calif. Coll. Arts and Crafts, Oakland, 1965-67, 70-84, dean extended studies, 1976-80, v.p. acad. affairs, 1980-87, prof. English and gen. studies, 1984—, dir. div. humanities and scis., 1987-91; instr. in English U. Hawaii, Honolulu, 1968-69; part-time instr. in English Laney Coll., Oakland, 1970-78. Author: Softness on the Other Side of the Hole, 1968, 2d edit., 1976, Coffee, 1976, 4th edit., 1992, The Coffee Book, 1980; translator poetry for various periodicals, 1970-73; contbr. articles to profl. publs. Mem. World History Assn. Home: 367 Moraga Ave Piedmont CA 94611 Office: Calif Coll Arts and Crafts 5212 Broadway Ave Oakland CA 94618

DAVIDSON, BILL (WILLIAM JOHN DAVIDSON), entertainment journalist, author; b. Jersey City, Mar. 4, 1918; s. Louis J. and Gertrude (Platt) D.; m. Muriel Roberts, May 21, 1960 (dec. Sept. 1983); 1 child, Carol; m. Maralynne Beth Nitz, July 27, 1986. BA, NYU, 1939. Assoc. editor Collier's mag., N.Y.C., 1946-56; contbg. editor Look mag., N.Y.C., 1956-61; editor-at-large Saturday Evening Post, N.Y.C., 1961-69; radio commentator NBC, N.Y.C., 1968-71; TV writer Universal Studios, Universal City, Calif., 1971-76; contbg. editor TV Guide, Radnor, Pa., 1971-90; chmn. alumni communications com. NYU, 1959-64. Author: The Real and the Unreal, Six Brave Presidents, 1962, Indict and Convict, 1971, (with Sid Caesar) Where Have I Been?, 1982, Spencer Tracy: Tragic Idol, 1988, Jane Fonda: An Intimate Biography, 1990, (with Danny Thomas) Make Room for Daddy, 1991. Mem. N.Y. County Dem. com., N.Y.C., 1948-50. Served as sgt. U.S. Army, 1941-45, ETO. Recipient Disting. Reporting award Sigma Delta Chi, 1951, 53, Albert Lasker Med. Journalism award, 1953, Disting. Journalism award Family Service Assn. Am., 1963. Mem. Writers Guild Am. West. Democrat. Home: 13225 Morrison St Sherman Oaks CA 91423-2156

DAVIDSON, DENNIS MICHAEL, preventive cardiologist; b. Detroit, May 30, 1939; s. Ralph Cornell and Amy Ernstine (Ray) D. BS, U.S. Naval Acad., 1960; MD, U. Mich., 1971; MA, U. Calif., Irvine, 1987; MDiv, Grad. Theol. Union, 1992. Ordained to ministry Unitarian Universalist Ch., 1992. Commd. ensign USN, 1960, advanced through grades to capt., 1991; asst. prof. naval sci. U. So. Calif., L.A., 1964-66; exec. officer Naval Support Activity, Quinhon, Vietnam, 1966; med. resident USN Hosp., San Diego, 1971-74; med. dir., refugee camp Marine Corps Base, Camp Pendleton, Calif., 1975; staff internist USN, Camp Pendleton, 1974-77; cardiology fellow Stanford (Calif.) U., 1977-79, asst. prof. medicine, 1979-81; dir. preventive cardiology UCLA, 1981-83, U. Calif., Irvine, 1983-92; assoc. prof. medicine U. Calif., San Francisco, 1992—; dir. cardiology clinic San Francisco Gen. Hosp., 1992—. Author: Preventive Cardiology, 1991. Recipient Preventive Cardiology Acad. award NIH, 1984, Clin. Cardiology Teaching award Am. Heart Assn., 1986. Fellow Am. Heart Assn. Epidemiology Coun.; mem. Soc. for Preventive Cardiology (pres. 1989-90).

DAVIDSON, EDWIN DOW, JR., geologic sample control and quality assurance specialist; b. Ft. Worth, Aug. 12, 1953; s. Edwin Dow Davidson Sr. and Edra Zoe (Austin) McElahney; m. Mary Alliene Schwarz, May 26, 1973; children: Brockett Dow, Austin Erich Graham, Angèle Dominique. Student, U. Hawaii, Honolulu, 1976. Curator Tex. Bur. Econ. Geology, Austin, 1978-80, quality assurance specialist, 1980-85, asst. coord. quality assurance program, 1985-86; curator Yucca Mountain Project, dep. mgr. Sci. Applications Internat. Corp., Las Vegas, Nev., 1986-89; project dir., archaeologist Bernice Bishop Mus., Honolulu, 1989-90; prin. cons.

Curatorial Sci. Cons., Austin, Tex., 1990—. U.S. Govt. grantee, 1972. Mem. Am. Assn. Petroleum Geologists (assoc., conf. on preservation of samples and cores 1982-85).

DAVIDSON, ERIC HARRIS, developmental and molecular biologist; b. N.Y.C., Apr. 13, 1937; s. Morris and Anne D. B.A., U. Pa., 1958; Ph.D., Rockefeller U., 1963. Research asso. Rockefeller U., 1963-65, asst. prof., 1965-71; asso. prof. devel. molecular biology Calif. Inst. Tech., Pasadena, 1971-74; prof. Calif. Inst. Tech., 1974—, Norman Chandler prof. cell biology, 1981—. Author: Gene Activity in Early Development, 3d edit. 1986. NIH grantee, 1965—; NSF grantee, 1972—. Mem. Nat. Acad. Scis. Office: Calif Inst Tech Div Biology Mail Code 156 29 Pasadena CA 91125

DAVIDSON, JAMES MADISON, III, engineer, technical manager; b. San Antonio, Feb. 24, 1930; s. James Madison Jr. and Ella Louise (Wehmeyer) D.; m. Geneva Upchurch, Aug. 28, 1949; children: Robert John, William Allen, James Brian. BS, S.W. Tex. State U., 1951. Registered profl. engr., Wash. Engr., then sr. engr. GE Co., Richland, Wash., 1951-65; mgr. fast flux test facility, materials and tech. dept. Battelle-Pacific N.W. Lab., Richland, 1965-67, sr. adviser to lab. dir., 1967-72; mgr. office nat. security tech. Battelle-Pacific N.W. Lab., 1972-89; staff mem. Los Alamos (N.Mex.) Nat. Lab., 1989-90, acting group leader, 1990-91, group leader, 1992—; tech. adviser Coordinating Com. on Munitions, Paris, 1987—. Exec. bd. Boy Scouts Am., 1970-75. Recipient Silver Beaver award Boy Scouts Am., 1972. Home: 18 W Wildflower Dr Santa Fe NM 87501

DAVIDSON, JAMES MICHAEL, hydrogeologist, consultant; b. Melrose, Mass., Sept. 28, 1962; s. Joseph John and Jean Mary (Rice) D.; m. Gloria N. Davidson, Nov. 11, 1989. BS in Geology, U. Mass., 1985; MS in Geology, Colo. State U., 1988. Hydrogeologist Geologic Svcs. Corp., Hudson, Mass., 1985-86, Shell Oil Co., Houston, 1988-89; sr. hydrogeologist Water, Waste & Land, Inc., Ft. Collins, Colo., 1989-90; pres. Alpine Environ., Inc., Ft. Collins, 1990—; manuscript reviewer Jour. Groundwater, 1988—. Author: Investigating Hydrocarbon Spills: A Practical Guideline to Delineating Subsurface Contamination, 1991. Mem. Assn. Groundwater Scientists and Engrs., Assn. Engring. Geologists (assoc.). Office: Alpine Environ Inc 1048 Driftwood Dr Ste 3 Fort Collins CO 80525

DAVIDSON, JOHN ROBERT JAY, computer company executive; b. L.A., Mar. 30, 1950; s. John Robert Davidson and Carolyn Rose Monson Wiederanders; m. Kristina Maria Jonson, Dec. 29, 1978; children: Joshua Kingseley, Michelle Maria. BSME, U. N.D., 1972; postgrad., AMP Corp. Leadership Coll., 1990. Engr. Dow Chem. Co., Pauls Valley, Okla., 1972-74; investor Mpls., 1974-77; account exec. AMP Inc., Boulder, Colo., 1977-83; mkt. mgr. AMP Inc., Harrisburg, Pa., 1983-86; dist. mgr. AMP Inc., Denver, 1986-90, nat. mgr., 1990—; dir./cons. Am. State Bank, Williston, N.D., 1988—. Supporter Jr. League of Denver; mem. Rep. Nat. Com. Mem. Masons. Home: 4845 S Dillon Way Aurora CO 80015 Office: AMP 5299 DTC Blvd #1020 Englewood CO 80015

DAVIDSON, JULI, artist, writer, entrepreneur, publisher; b. Houston, Aug. 23, 1960; d. Martin J. Davidson and Ruth Carol Rosenberg. Diploma, Park Sch., Brooklandville, Md., 1978; Cert., Richmond Coll., Surrey, Eng., 1978; student, Austin Coll., U. N.Mex, others, 1978-84. Cert. med. terminology and transcription, 1981. Pres. Surrenderings, Inc., Albuquerque, 1989-93; owner, artist Juli Davidson Studio Gallery, Albuquerque, 1987-89; freelance writer, editor, photographer Albuquerque, 1985-86; med. word processor Lovelace Med. Ctr., Albuquerque, 1989-90; exec. adminstr. Albuquerque Art Bus. Assn., 1989; bd. sec. Albuquerque United Artists, 1988. Contbr. to various publs. and is subject of various art revs. Recipient 2d and 3d place photography awards Churches in N.Mex. Exhibit, 4th place Colorfest Human Interest Category, Colo. Mem. Garden Writers Assn. Am. (award for handmade booklet on dividing and multiplying potted plants), N.Mex. Organic Growers and Assocs. Studio: PO Box 21669-WW Albuquerque NM 87154-9903

DAVIDSON, MARK, writer, educator; b. N.Y.C., Sept. 25, 1938; m. Elizabeth Browne, May 29, 1989. BA in Polit. Sci., UCLA, 1958; MS in Journalism, Columbia U., 1960. Sci. writer U. So. Calif., L.A., 1980-90; assoc. prof. comm. Calif. State U., Dominguez Hills, Carson, 1985—; freelance writer. Former feature writer, columnist for met. newspapers and wire svc., byliner for nat. mags.; producer-host for TV talk show, L.A.; scriptwriter for mag. and variety shows (Emmy award 1978-79); corr. Sci. Digest; med. writer City of Hope Nat. Med. Ctr.; author: Uncommon Sense, 1983, Watchwords, 1992, Techniques of Thought Control, 1993; mem. editorial bd. PEN Ctr. U.S.A. West, L.A., 1992—. Mem. Am. Soc. Journalists and Authors, Nat. Assn. Sci. Writers, Am. Med. WRiters Assn., Authors Guild, Writers Guild Am., Calif. Faculty Assn. (v.p. Dominguez Hills chpt. 1992—). Home: 195 Malcolm Dr Pasadena CA 91105 Office: Calif State U 1000 E Victoria St Carson CA 90747

DAVIDSON, ROBERT WILLIAM, association executive; b. Colfax, WA, Sept. 18, 1949; s. William Martin and Lena (Soli) D.; m. Molly Evoy, Apr. 16, 1977; children: Ford Patrick, Matthew Harpur, Marshall Andrew. AB, Harvard U., 1971. Exec. dir. Sabre Found., Cambridge, Mass., 1971-72; adminstrv. asst. Congressman Joel Pritchard, Washington, 1973-79; asst. sec. state State of Wash., Olympia, 1979-80; pres. Frayn Fin. Printing, Seattle, 1982-87, Frayn Printing Co., Seattle, 1985-87; exec. dir. Woodland Park Zool. Soc., Seattle, 1987-93, pres., 1993—; mem. adv. com. Wash. State Software Ind. Devel. Bd., 1984-85. Chmn. pub. funding com. Mayor's Zoo Commn., Seattle, 1984-85; pres. Sacred Heart Sch. Bd., 1988-91; dir. Discovery Inst., 1992—; mem. King County Bond Oversight Com., 1986-93. Mem. N.W. Devel. Officers Assn. (pres.-elect 1993—), Roundtable Club, Downtown Rotary Club, Wash. Athletic Club. Republican. Roman Catholic. also: Woodland Park Zool Soc PO Box 31665 Seattle WA 98103

DAVIDSON, TERESA D., lawyer. BA with distinction, U. Va.; JD with honors, U. Tenn. Ptnr. Johnston, Maynard, Grant & Parker, Phoenix, 1992—; chmn. Subcom. on Uniform Comml. Code Act 2A, Phoenix, 1988—. Mem. ABA (divsns. taxation, bus. law, probate, real property), Ariz. Bar Assn. (securities, real estate and bus. com.), Maricopa County Bar Assn. (bd. dirs. corp. counsel divsn.). Episcopalian. Office: Johnston, Maynard et al 3200 N Central Ave 2300 Great American Tower Phoenix AZ 85345

DAVIDSON, THOMAS FERGUSON, chemical engineer; b. N.Y.C., N.Y., Jan. 5, 1930; s. Lorimer Arthur and Elizabeth (Valentine) D.; m. Nancy Lee Selecman, Nov. 11, 1951; children: Thomas Ferguson, Richard Alan, Gwyn Ann. BS in Engring., U. Md., 1951. Sr. project engr. Wright Air Devel. Ctr., Dayton, Ohio, 1951-58; dep. dir. Solid Systems Div., Edwards, Calif., 1959-60; mgr. govt. ops. Thiokol Chem. Corp., Ogden, Utah, 1960-64; dir. aerospace mktg. Thiokol Chem. Corp., Bristol, Pa., 1965-67; dir. tech. mgmt. Thiokol Chem. Corp., Ogden, 1968-82; v.p. tech. Morton Thiokol Inc., Chgo., 1983-88, Thiokol Corp., Ogden, 1989-90; cons. Ogden, 1990—; mem. subcom. lubrications and wear NACA, Washington, 1955-57; chmn. Joint Army, Navy, NASA, Air Force exec. com., 1959-60. Editor: National Rocket Strategic Plan, 1990; contbr. articles to profl. jours. Chmn. bd. Wesley Acad., Ogden, 1990—; mem. Utah State Bd. Edn., 1993—; trustee Family Counselling Svc., Ogden, 1991—; dir. Habitat for Humanity Internat.; mem. Rep. Presdl. Task Force, Washington, 1987-92, Am. Security Coun., Washington, 1975—; vice moderator SHARED Ministry Utah. Lt. USAF, 1951-53. Fellow AIAA (assoc.) (sect. chmn. 1979-80, chmn. AIAA rocket propulsion com. 1987-90, mem. AIA aerospace tech. coun. 1987-90, AIAA Wyld Propulsion award 1991); mem. Am. Newcomers Soc., Smithsonian Instn., Exchange Club, Ogden Golf and Country Club. Republican. Methodist. Home: 4755 Banbury Ln Ogden UT 84403-4484

DAVIES, DARREN ALLEN, banker; b. Yerington, Nev., June 15, 1961; s. Arthur Allen and Virginia Louise (Aydelotte) D. Student, Ft. Lewis Coll., Durango, Colo., 1979, Adams State Coll., Alamosa, Colo., 1980-81; 2d yr. degree, Western States Sch. Banking, Albuquerque, 1990. Bookkeeper Rio Grande County Bank, Del Norte, Colo., 1984-87, asst. cashier, 1987-89, cashier, 1989—, v.p., 1991—. Chmn., bd. dirs. Rio Grande County (Colo.) Tourism Bd., 1988-91; EMT, treas. Del Norte Community Ambulance, 1991-92. Mem. Del Norte C. of C. (pres. 1988-90). Presbyterian. Home: 505 8th St Del Norte CO 81132 Office: Rio Grande County Bank 505 Grande Ave Del Norte CO 81132

DAVIES, GRANT WILLIAM, physical education educator; b. Helper, Utah, July 16, 1937; s. Charlie William and Alice (Bartlett) D.; m. Diana Kay Kirby, Aug. 22, 1968; children: Marcia Joy, Alesa Kay, Jeffrey Grant, Chad William, Daniel Alan. BS, Brigham Young U., 1964, MS, 1965. Cert. intramural dir., cert. intercollegiate bowling coach/instr., water safety instr. ARC. Instr. Portland (Oreg.) Community Coll., 1965—, intramural dir., 1965-75, coach softball, 1966-85, coach bowling, 1966-91, coach volleyball, 1967-81, acting dept. chair, 1969-70; pres. pacific Energy Cons., Portland, 1985-90, Davies Vending Co., 1990—, Davies Computer Bus. Svc., 1992—. Aquatics dir. summer camp Portland YMCA, 1969, Riverside Country Club, Portland, 1970; pres. Oreg. Collegiate Bowling Conf., 1980-89 (Bowling Coach of Yr. 1980). Mem. Nat. Intramural Recreation Sports Assn., Oreg. Assn. Phys. Edn. (conf. registration dir. 1984), Nat. Collegiate Bowling Coaches Assn. (treas. 1985-91). Republican. Mormon. Office: Portland Community Coll 12000 SW 49th Ave Portland OR 97219-7197

DAVIES, HUGH MARLAIS, museum director; b. Grahamstown, South Africa, Feb. 12, 1948; came to U.S., 1956; s. Horton Marlais and Brenda M. (Deakin) D.; children: Alexandra, Dorian; m. Lynda Forsha; 1 stepdaughter, Mackenzie Forsha Fuller. AB summa cum laude, Princeton U., 1970, M.F.A., 1972, PhD, 1976. Dir., Univ. Gallery, U. Mass., Amherst, 1975-83, Mus. of Contemporary Art, San Diego (formerly La Jolla Mus. Contemporary Art,) Calif., 1983—; vis. prof. fine arts Amherst Coll., 1980-83; mem. mus. com. Rose Art Mus., Brandeis U., 1981-83; mem. adv. coun. dept. art and archeology Princeton U., 1989, panel mem. fed. adv. com. internat. exhbns., 1990—; mem. Art in Public Places Profl. Adv. Com., Met. Dade County, 1980—; panel mem. Mass. Bay Transit Authority, Artist Selection Panel, 1990. Author: Francis Bacon: The Early and Middle Years: 1928-58; co-author: Sacred Art in a Secular Century: 20th Century Religious Art, 1978, Francis Bacon (Abbeville), 1986. Nat. Endowment Arts fellow, 1982. Mem. Am. Assn. Mus., Coll. Art Assn., Assn. Art Mus. Dirs., Am. Fedn. Arts (trustee). Office: Mus Contemporary Art San Diego 700 Prospect St La Jolla CA 92037-4291

DAVIES, JACK LLOYD, vintager, consultant; b. Cin., June 19, 1923; s. John Lloyd and Celia (Davis) D.; m. Jamie Peterman; children: Bill, John, Hugh. Student, Northwestern U., 1942, Stanford U., 1946-68; MBA, Harvard U., 1950. Prodn. mgr. Avalon Desk Mfg., L.A., 1950-52; planning analyst Kaiser Aluminum, Oakland, Calif., 1952-55; assoc. McKinsey & Co., San Francisco, 1955-60; v.p. mktg. Fibreboard Corp., San Francisco, 1960-63; v.p. devel. Ducommun Inc., L.A., 1963-65; pres. Schramsberg Vineyards, Calistoga, Calif., 1965—, Schramsberg Assocs. Internat., Calistoga, 1989—, Caves Transmontanas LDA, Alijo, Portugal, 1989—. Sgt. USAF, 1942-46, ETO. Mem. Bohemian Club, Knights of St. John. Office: Schramsberg Vineyards Calistoga CA 94515

DAVIES, JOHN G., federal judge; b. 1929. BA, U. Mich., 1953; postgrad., U. Sydney, 1956-57; LLB, UCLA, 1959. Assoc. Hagenbaugh, Murphy & Davies, L.A., 1961-72, Rosenfeld, Meyer & Susman, Beverly Hills, Calif., 1972-86; dist. judge U.S. Dist. Ct., L.A., 1986—; L.A. Ct. Arbitrator; Inns of Ct. Winner Gold medal in swimming 1952 Olympic Games, Helsinki, Finland. Mem. ABA, Internat. Acad. Trial Lawyers, Am. Coll. Trial Lawyers, Am. Bd. Trial Advocates, State Bar Calif., L.A. County Bar Assn. Office: US Dist Ct US Courthouse Rm 1006 Los Angeles CA 90012

DAVIES, JOHN TUDOR, physicist; b. Pontypridd, Wales, Eng., May 9, 1937; s. Herbert John and Catherine Mary Davies; m. Kay Dierst, Aug. 4, 1964; children: Gwen, Ceri, Rhodri. BA, Oxford (Eng.) U., 1959, MA, 1963, DPhil, 1963. Rsch. assoc. U. Pitts., 1962-65; lectr. U. Wales, Swansea, 1965-78; tech. devel. mgr. Gasonics/IPC, San Jose, Calif., 1978—. Mem. Am. Vacuum Soc., Semicondr. Equipment and Materials Inst. Methodist.

DAVIES, KENNETH, research physicist; b. Merthyr Tydfil, Wales, Jan. 28, 1928; came to U.S., 1955; s. William Rees and Hannah Elizabeth (Broad) D.; m. Joyce Alice Demerchant, Feb. 20, 1958; children: Russell, Elizabeth, Kenneth. BSc, U. Wales, 1949, PhD, 1953. Physicist Defence Research Bd., Ottawa, Can., 1952-55; asst. prof. Brown U., Providence, 1956-58; physicist Dept. Commerce, Boulder, Colo., 1958-85, sr. scientist, 1985-90; guest prof. Wuhan U., 1988—; vis. prof. Kyoto U., 1990-91. Author: Ionospheric Radio Propagation, 1965, Ionospheric Radio Waves, 1969, Phase and Frequency Instabilities, 1970, Ionospheric Radio, 1990; contbr. over 130 articles to profl. jours. Chmn. Plan Boulder County; pres. Boulder Council for Internat. Visitors. Webster fellow U. Queensland, Brisbane, Australia, 1975-76; recipient A.V. Humbolt award Max-Planck Inst., Germany, 1991-92. Fellow AAAS, IEEE. Office: SEL/ERL/NOAA 325 Broadway Boulder CO 80303-3328

DAVIES, LINDA, teacher; b. Denver, Jan. 27, 1963; d. Lyle Allen Petersen and Susie (Mae) Horning, m. Stephen DAvies, June 18, 1989. BA, U. Denver, 1985. Rsch. asst. U. Denver, 1983-85; secondary tchr. Sierra High Sch., Colorado Springs, Colo., 1985–. Recipient Sierra Pride award Sierra High Sch., 1989. Mem. Nat. Edn. Assn., Phi Beta Kappa. Home: 412 Yucca Dr Colorado Springs CO 80906

DAVIES, MERTON EDWARD, planetary scientist; b. St. Paul, Sept. 13, 1917; s. Albert Daniel and Lucile (McCabe) D.; AB, Stanford, 1938, postgrad., 1938-39; m. Margaret Louise Darling, Feb. 10, 1946; children: Deidra Louise Stauff, Albert Karl, Merton Randel. Instr. math. U. Nev., 1939-40; group leader Math. Lofting, Douglas Aircraft Co., El Segundo, Calif., 1940-48; sr. staff Rand Corp., Santa Monica, Calif., 1948-59, 62—, liaison USAF, Washington, 1959-62. U.S. observer inspected stas. under terms Antarctic Treaty, 1967; TV co-investigator Mariner Mars, 1969, 71, Mariner Venus/Mercury 1973 Mission, Voyager Mission, Galileo Mission, Magellan Mission, Mars Observer Mission. Fellow AIAA (assoc.); mem. Am. Soc. Photogrammetry, AAAS. Author: (with Bruce Murray) The View from Space, 1971; (with others) Atlas of Mercury, 1978. Patentee in field. Home: 1414 San Remo Dr Pacific Palisades CA 90272-2737 Office: RAND 1700 Main St Santa Monica CA 90407-2138

DAVIES, PAUL LEWIS, JR., real estate executive; b. San Jose, Calif., July 21, 1930; s. Paul Lewis and Faith (Crummey) D.; m. Barbara Bechtel, Dec. 22, 1955; children: Laura (Mrs. Segundo Mateo), Paul Lewis III. AB, Stanford U., 1952; JD, Harvard U., 1957. Bar: Calif. 1957. Assoc. Pillsbury, Madison & Sutro, San Francisco, 1957-63, ptnr., 1963-89; gen. counsel Chevron Corp., 1984-89; pres. Lakeside Corp., San Francisco, 1989—; bd. dirs. FMC Corp, FMC Gold Co., Sumitomo Bank Calif. Hon. trustee Calif. Acad. Scis., trustee, 1970-83, chmn., 1973-80; pres. Herbert Hoover Found.; bd. overseers Hoover Instn., chmn. 1976-82, 91—; hon. regent U. of Pacific, regent, 1959-90. Lt. U.S. Army, 1952-54. Mem. Bohemian Club, Pacific-Union, Villa Taverna, World Trade (San Francisco), Claremont Country, Lakeview (Oakland, Calif.), Cypress Point (Pebble Beach, Calif.), Sainte Claire (San Jose, Calif.), Collectors, Explorers, Links (N.Y.C.), Met., 1925 F St. (Washington), Chgo. Club, Phi Beta Kappa, Phi Sigma Alpha. Republican. Office: 50 Fremont St Ste 3520 San Francisco CA 94105-2239

DAVIES, WILLIAM RALPH, service executive; b. Santa Barbara, Calif., Aug. 17, 1955; s. Ralph Emmett and Georgann Marie (Cordingly) D.; m. Karen L. Blake, May 12, 1984. AA in Real Estate, Am. River Coll., 1978; BS in Fin., Ins. and Real Estate, Calif. State U., Sacramento, 1980; postgrad. in Internat. Bus., Golden Gate U., 1982-84. Real estate assoc. Kiernan Realtors, Sacramento, 1975-77; co-owner real estate firm Sacramento, 1977, pvt. practice real estate cons., property mgr., 1978-80; broker assoc. MBA Bus. Brokers, Sacramento, 1980-85, pres., 1985—; pres. WRD Group, Sacramento, 1984—; bd. dirs. WRD, Inc., Sacramento. Mem. Internat. Bus. Brokers Assn., No. Calif. Assn. Bus. Intermediaries (bd. dirs.), Sacramento C. of C., World Wildlife Fund, Internat. Bus. Club Grad Sch. Republican. Office: 1555 River Park Dr Sacramento CA 95815

DAVIN, JANA MCCULLOUGH, pharmacist; b. Branson, Mo., May 31, 1951; d. John Cleo McCullough and Edna Lea Chase; div.; children: Janice, Robert. AA in History, Cuesta Coll., 1972; MS in Pharmacy, U. N.Mex., 1982. Part-time tchr. pharmacology San Juan Coll., Farmington, New Mexico; clin. pharmacist Presbyn. Med. Svc., Farmington, N.Mex., 1982-85; prin. Mill St. Drug Store, Bayfield, Colo., 1985—. Mem. Bayfield Planning Commn., 1986—. Roman Catholic. Office: Mill St Drug Store Mill & Church Bayfield CO 81122

DAVIS, ALFRED AUSTIN, entrepreneur; b. Calvert, Tex., July 7, 1940; s. Bud Gwines and Eula Mae (Hammond) Davis; m. Mable Dean Johnson, Sept. 18, 1962 (div. 1978); children: Romelda, Demont, Danita, Dewitt, Deanna. AA, Pasadena Coll., 1972; BA, Calif. State U., L.A., 1975. Dish washer J.W. Robinson, Pasadena, Calif., 1959-60; mail rm. clk. Mobil Oil Co., Santa Fe Springs, Calif., 1960-65; R & D technician Sterling Motors Co., L.A., 1965-69; sales clk. Emils Clothing Store, Pasadena, 1969-75; ins. underwriter Safeco Ins. Co., Panarama City, Calif., 1975-77; head underwriter United Pacific Ins. Co., L.A., 1977-79, Aim Ins. Brokers, L.A., 1979-80; CEO, owner C & A Comml. Inst., Beverly Hills, Calif., 1980—; pres., owner Electric Dist. Co./Night Club Restaurant, Pasadena, 1990—; organizer Calif. Minority Janitorial Assn., Monrovia, Calif., 1981-82; bus. cons. Walkers Electronics, Pasadena, 1988—; gen. ptnr. Creative Entertainment, Pasadena, 1990—; bd. pres. 199 East Colorado Ptnrs., Pasadena, 1990—. Author: Poems of Inspirations, 1984; columnist in field. Youth dir. City Election Campaign, Pasadena, 1969; office mgr. Black Reps. for Nixon, Pasadena, 1972; bd. dirs. NAACP, Pasadena, 1970. Recipient Cert. of Merit, Rep. Presdl. Task Force, 1986, Medal of Merit, 1987, Flag & Cert., Pres. Ronald Regan, 1987. Mem. L.A. C. of C., Pasadena C. of C., U.S. C. of C., L.A. Raiders NFL Booster. Republican. Home: 2717 Santa Rosa Altadena CA 91001

DAVIS, ALLEN, professional football team executive; b. Brockton, Mass., July 4, 1929; s. Louis and Rose (Kirschenbaum) D.; m. Carol Segall, July 11, 1954; 1 son, Mark. Student, Wittenberg Coll., 1947; A.B., Syracuse U., 1950. Asst. football coach Adelphi Coll., 1950-51; head football coach Ft. Belvoir, Va., 1952-53; player-personnel scout Baltimore Colts, 1954; line coach The Citadel, 1955-56, U. So. Calif., 1957-59; asst. coach San Diego Chargers, 1960-62; gen. mgr., head coach Oakland Raiders (now Los Angeles Raiders), 1963-66, owner, mng. gen. ptnr., 1966—; former mem. mgmt. council and competition com. Nat. Football League. Served with AUS, 1952-53. Named Profl. Coach of Year A.P., Profl. Coach of Year U.P.I., Profl. Coach of Year Sporting News, Profl. Coach of Year Pro-Football Illustrated, 1963; Young Man of Yr. Oakland, 1963; only individual in history to be an asst. coach, head coach, gen. mgr., league commr. and owner. Mem. Am. Football Coaches Assn. Office: Los Angeles Raiders 332 Center St El Segundo CA 90245-4098*

DAVIS, ARTHUR DAVID, psychology educator, musician; m. Gladys Lesley Joyce, Dec. 29, 1965; children: Kimaili, Mureithi. Student, Manhattan Sch. Music, 1953-56, Juilliard Sch. Music, 1953-56; BA suma cum laude, CUNY, 1973; MA, City Coll., N.Y.C., 1976, NYU, 1976; PhD with distinction, NYU, 1982. Lic. sch. psychologist. Musician various worldwide tours, 1962—, NBC-TV Staff Orch., N.Y.C., 1962-63, Westinghouse TV Staff Orch., N.Y.C., 1964-68, CBS-TV Staff Orch., N.Y.C., 1969-71; prof. Manhattan Community Coll., N.Y.C., 1971-86, U. Bridgeport, Conn., 1978-82; psychologist Lincoln Med. and Mental Health Ctr., Bronx, 1982-85; sch. psychologist, cons. Lakeside Union Free Sch. Dist., Spring Valley, N.Y., 1985-86; psychologist, tchr. N.Y. Med. Coll., Valhalla, 1982-87; prof. Orange Coast Coll., Costa Mesa, Calif., 1987—, Calif. State U., Fullerton, 1988-90; U. Calif.-Irvine, 1993—; psychologist Cross Cultural Ctr., San Diego, 1986-91; cons. Head Start, Bklyn., 1981-82, Orange County Minority AIDS, Santa Ana, Calif., 1987-88, Orange County Fair Housing, Costa Mesa, 1988, Sickle Cell Anemia Assn., Santa Ana, Calif., 1987-88, Human Rels. Orange County City, Costa Mesa, 1988-89, William Grant Still Mus., L.A., 1988—; musician various symphonies Radio City Music Hall Orch. Nat. Symphony, Symphony of the Air, N.Y. Philharmonic, Met. Opera Orch., John Coltrane, others, 1960—. Author: The Arthur Davis System for Double Bass, 1976; record composer Interplay, 1980, ARKIMU, 1985, Soulnote, 1987. Composer, condr., mem. coun. Diaglogue, Costa Mesa, 1988; mgr. Little League of Cortlandt, N.Y., 1979-82; pack master Cub Scouts Am., Cortlandt and Croton, N.Y., 1979-80, dist. chmn., 1980-81; bd. dirs. Local 47 Musicians Union, Hollywood, Calif., 1993—, Orange County Urban League, Inc., 1992—; bd. dirs. Local 47 Musicians' Union, Hollywood, Calif., 1993—; chmn. Better Advantages for Students and Soc., Corona del Mar, Calif., 1993. NIMH grantee, 1976-77; named World's Foremost Double Bassist IBA, 1969—; recipient Lion award Black MBA Assn., 1985, Chancellor's Disting. Lectr.'s award U. Calif., Irvine, 1991-92; Ann. Dr. Art Davis Scholarships established in his honor Dr. Art Davis Fan Club. Mem. APA, ASCAP, N.Y. Acad. Scis., Astron. Soc. of the Pacific (charter), Orange County Psychol. Assn., Assn. of Black Psychologists, Planetary Soc. (charter), Am. Hort. Soc., Nat Trust for Hist. Preservation Soc., Rec. Musicians Assn., Stanford U. Alumni Assn., NYU Alumni Assn., CCNY Alumni Assn., Sierra Club. Republican. Office: ARKIMU 3535 E Coast Hwy Ste 50 Corona Del Mar CA 92625-2404

DAVIS, BETTY JEAN BOURBONIA, real estate investment executive; b. Ft. Bayard, N.Mex., Mar. 12, 1931; d. John Alexander and Ora M. (Caudill) Bourbonia; BS in Elem. Edn., U. N.Mex., 1954; children: Janice Cox Anderson, Elizabeth Ora Cox. Gen. ptnr. BJD Realty Co., Albuquerque, 1977—. Bd. dirs. Albuquerque Opera Guild, 1977-79, 81-83, 85-86, 86-87, membership co-chmn., 1977-79; mem. Friends of Art, 1978-85, Friends of Little Theatre, 1973-85, Mus. N.Mex. Found.; mem. grand exec. com. N.Mex. Internat. Order of Rainbow for Girls; mem. Hodgin Hall Preservation com. U. N.Mex. Recipient Matrix award for journalism Jr. League. Mem. Albuquerque Mus. Assn., N.M. Hist. Soc., N.Mex. Symphony Guild, Jr. League Albuquerque, Alumni Assn. U. N.Mex. (dir. 1973-76), Mus. N.Mex. Found., Alpha Chi Omega (Beta Gamma Beta chpt., adv., bldg. corp. 1962-77), Tanoan Country Club, Order Eastern Star, Order Rainbow for Girls (past grand worthy adv. N.Mex., past mother adv. Friendship Assembly 50, state exec. com. N.Mex. Order 1989, chair pub. rels. com., co-chair gen. arrangements com. 1990-93). Republican. Methodist. Home: 9505 Augusta Ave NE Albuquerque NM 87111-5820

DAVIS, BETTYE JEAN, academic administrator, state official; b. Homer, La., May 17, 1938; d. Dan and Rosylind (Daniel) Ivory; m. Troy J. Davis, Jan. 21, 1959; children: Anthony Benard, Sonja Davis Wade. Cert. nursing, St. Anthony's, 1961; BSW, Grambling State U., 1971; postgrad., U. Alaska, 1972. Psychiat. nurse Alaska Psychiat. Inst., 1967-70; asst. dir. San Bernardino (Calif.) YWCA, 1971-72; child care specialist DFYS Anchorage, 1975-80, soc. worker, 1980-82, foster care coordinator, 1982-87; dir. Alaska Black Leadership Edn. Program, 1979-82; bd. dirs. Anchorage Sch. Dist., 1982-89; mem. Alaska Legislature, 1990—. Pres. Anchorage Sch. Bd., 1986-87; bd. dirs. Blacks in Govt., 1980-82, March of Dimes, 1983-85, Anchorage chpt. YWCA, 1989-90, Winning with Stronger Edn. Com., 1991, Alaska 2000, Anchorage Ctr. for Families, 1992—, active Anchorage chpt. of NAACP, bd. dirs. 1978-82. Named Woman of Yr., Alaska Colored Women's Club, 1981, Child Care Worker of Yr. , Alaska Foster Parent Assn., 1983, Social Worker of Yr., Nat. Foster Parents Assn., 1983, Outstanding Bd. Mem, Assn. Alaska Sch. Bds., 1990,; recipient Outstanding Achievement in Edn. award Alaska Colored Women's Club, 1985, Outstanding Women in Edn. award Zeta Phi Beta, 1985, Boardsmanship award Assn. Alaska Sch. Bds., 1989, Woman of Achievement award YWCA, 1991, Outstanding Leadership award Calif. Assembly, 1992. Mem. LWV, Nat. Sch. Bd. Assn., Nat. Caucus of Black Sch. Bd. Mems. (bd. dirs. 1986-87), Alaska Black Caucus (chair 1984—), Alaska Women's Polit. Caucus, Alaska Black Leadership Conf. (pres. 1976-80), Alaska Women Lobby (treas.), Women Legislators Lobby, Women's Action for New Directions, North to Future Bus. and Prof. Women (pres. 1978-79, 83), Delta Sigma Theta (Alaska chpt. pres. 1978-80). Democrat. Baptist. Club: North to Future Bus. and Profl. Women (past pres.). Home: 2240 Foxhall Dr Anchorage AK 99504-3350

DAVIS, CAROLYN LEIGH, Episcopal priest, psychotherapist; b. Houston, Mar. 18, 1936; d. William Harvey Speight and Veral Audra (Nunn) Speight Poole; m. John C. Rogers, June 22, 1957 (div. Nov. 1970); children: Elizabeth Leigh Porterfield, Rena Kathleen Stephan, John; m. L.B. Davis Sept. 14, 1972. Diploma in nursing, U. Houston, 1956; MSW, U. Denver, 1981; MDiv, Iliff Sch. Theology, 1990; cert. individual theol. studies, Episcopal Theol. Sem. of S.W., 1990. RN, Tex., Colo.; lic. clin. social worker,

Colo.; cert. alcohol, drug counselor, Colo.; ordained to ministry Episcopal Ch. as deacon, 1990, as priest, 1990. Therapist Bethesda Mental Health Ctr., Denver, 1972-73; supr. emergency alcoholism services Denver Gen. Hosp., 1973-74; dir. alcoholism services Jefferson County Health Dept., Lakewood, Colo., 1974-78; pvt. practice psychotherapy Lakewood, Colo., 1981—; curate St. Joseph's Episc. Ch., Lakewood, 1991, interim rector, 1991-92, rector, 1992—. Author: The Most Important Nine Months of Your Child's Life: Fetal Alcohol Syndrome, 1976. Mem. Nat. Assn. Social Workers. Democrat. Office: St Joseph Episcopal Ch 11202 W Jewell Ave Lakewood CO 80232

DAVIS, CHARLES ARTHUR, psychiatrist; b. Greensboro, N.C., Nov. 14, 1921; s. Charles Arthur and Ann Ethel D. BS, Columbia Union Coll., Takoma Park, Md., 1950; MD, Loma Linda U., 1953. Diplomate Am. Bd. Psychiatry and Neurology, Am. Bd. Forensic Psychiatry. Chief addiction svc. USPHS Hosp., Ft. Worth, Tex., 1956-58; med. dir. Kings View Hosp., Reedley, Calif., 1958-73; clin. dir. Kings View Corp., Fresno, Calif., 1970-75; exec. dir. Kings County Mental Health, Hanford, Calif., 1975-91; lectr. U. Calif., San Francisco, 1980—; program adminstr. Calif. State Prison, Corcoran, 1992—; ct.'s examiner Superior Cts. of Fresno, Madera, Tulare & King Counties, 1960—; vis. prof. U. Guadalajara, Mexico, 1979-81. Pres. Fresno County Mental Health Adv. Bd., 1986-88. Lt. comdr. USPHS, 1955-58. Fellow Am. Psychiat. Assn. (life, Gold award 1970); mem. AMA, Cen. Calif., Psychiat. Soc. (pres. 1970), Calif. Med. Assn. (del. 1985-86), Kings County Med. Soc. (governing bd. 1981-87, pres. 1985), Calif. Conf. Local Mental Health Dirs., Am. Acad., Psychiatry and Law. Home: 4400 Ave 428 Reedley CA 93654 Office: 4400 Ave 428 Reedley CA 93654

DAVIS, CHRIS MARK, broadcast executive; b. Riverside, Calif., Jan. 7, 1954; s. Malcomb Ray and Anna Dana (Walker) D.; m. Kathryn Ann Ryan, Dec. 3, 1983; children: Michael Selmi, David Selmi. Program dir. KTRT, Truckee, Calif., 1977-79; air personality KGLR-KOZZ, Reno, 1979-82, KGB, San Diego, 1982-83; news dir. KZAP-KNCI, Sacramento, 1983—; news dir. KZAP-KNCI, Sacramento, 1983—; pub. address announcer Sacramento Surge World League of Am. Football, Sacramento, 1991—. Recipient numerous broadcast awards. Mem. Radio TV News Dir. Assn. (pres. 1990—), Sacramento Valley Broadcasters Assn. (pres. 1991—). Office: KNCI 298 Commerce Circle Sacramento CA 95815

DAVIS, COLEEN COCKERILL, educator; b. Pampa, Tex., Sept. 20, 1930; d. Charles Clifford and Myrtle Edith (Harris) Cockerill; m. Richard Harding Davis, June 22, 1952 (div. Dec. 1984); children: David Christopher, Denis Benjamin (dec. 1979). BS, U. Okla., 1951; MS, UCLA, 1952; postgrad. U. So. Calif., Whittier Coll., UCLA. Cert. tchr., Calif. Chmn, dept. home econs., tchr. Whittier Union High Sch. Dist., Calif., 1952-85; substitute tchr., 1985—; home tchr., 1985—, cons. 1986—; owner CoHost Am.'s Bed & Breakfast, Whittier, 1983—, also founder, pres., exec. dir. Contbr. articles to newspapers. Founder Children of Murdered Parents, Whittier, 1984, Whistle Ltd., Whittier, 1984, Coalition of Orgns. and People, Whittier, 1984, chpt. leader Parents of Murdered Children, Whittier, 1984, Southeast/Long Beach: mem. citizens' adv. bd. Fred C. Nelles Sch. Mem. NAFE, NEA, Calif. Tchrs. Assn., Internat. Tour Mgmt. Inst., Whittier C. of C. (ambassador). Republican. Episcopalian. Avocation: volunteer worker. Office: CoHost Am's Bed & Breakfast PO Box 9302 Whittier CA 90608

DAVIS, DARRELL L., automotive executive; b. Sharon, Pa., Aug. 8, 1939; s. Paul Darrell and Dorothy Jane (Snyder) D.; m. Jacqueline Donna Pain, July 18, 1986; children: Paul Darrell II, Robert Tod. BS, Youngstown State U., 1963; cert., Stanford U., 1987. Svc. rep., warranty mgr., dist. mgr., asst. zone mgr. Chrysler Motors Corp., Orlando, Fla., 1966-77; zone mgr. Chrysler Motors Corp., Omaha, 1977-78, Troy, Mich., 1978-79; nat. distbn. mgr., regional mgr., gen. mgr. import export ops., gen. sales mgr. Chrysler Motors Corp., Detroit, 1979-88; pres., chief exec. officer Alfa Romeo Distbrs. N. Am., Orlando, 1988-91; gen. sales mgr. Chrysler Corp., Orange, Calif., 1991—. Lt. U.S. Army, 1963-65. Republican.

DAVIS, DENNIS ALBERT, college president; b. Westport, Oreg., Jan. 4, 1934; s. George J. and Gertrude C. (Hibbard) D.; m. Nancy Ree Friend, July 20, 1956; 1 child, Jeffrey Dennis. BA, N.W. Coll., Kirkland, Wash., 1956. Pastor Assembly of God, Rainier, Oreg., 1956-57; evangelist Assemblies of God, over 200 crusades, 1957-61; pastor First Assembly of God, Pacific Grove, Calif., 1961-67, The People's Ch., Salem, Oreg., 1967-87; state supt. Oreg. Dist. Assemblies of God, Salem, 1987-90; pres. N.W. Coll., 1990—. Bd. dirs. ARC Polk, Marion Counties, 1980-86; mem. Salem Meml. Hosp. Instl. Review Com., Salem, 1984-87. Mem. Salem Ministerial Assn., Rotary (pres. East Salem Club 1976-77, recipient Paul Harris award 1980), Delta Epsilon Chi. Republican. Office: NW Coll 5520 108th Ave NE Kirkland WA 98033-7523

DAVIS, DONALD RUSSELL, educator; b. San Francisco, Apr. 7, 1932; s. Maynard D. Davis and Lauralee (Baker) DeMello; m. BettyLou Matson, Sept. 8, 1952 (div. 1967); children: Mark, Gregg, Louis, Jan, Cheryl, Rod; mem. Marie E. Roelle, Feb. 21, 1968 (div. 1989); 1 child, Evan; m. Emy Gonzaga, June 4, 1991; 1 child, Donelle. AA, City Coll. of San Francisco, 1968; BA, San Francisco State U., 1970, MBA, 1971. Cert. tchr., Calif. Tchr. Modesto (Calif.) Jr. Coll., 1974—; owner DaMar Mktg., Modesto, 1977—. Author (newspaper column) Marketing, 1980. LDS. Office: Modesto Jr Coll Dept Bus 435 College Ave Modesto CA 95350-5800

DAVIS, ELISA ELAINE, social services organization director; b. Mesa, Ariz., May 1, 1963; d. Ellis Eugene and Emma (Magana) D. BS, Sul Ross State U., 1985, MPA, 1985; Cert., Dept. Def., Richmond, Va., 1987, U. Colo./Nat. Leadership, Inst. on Aging, 1990. Human resource planner West Ariz. Coun. of Govts., Yuma, 1986-87; spl. agt. DOD Def. Investigative Svc., Phoenix, 1987-89; dir. Western Ariz. Coun. of Govts., Yuma, 1989—; tchr. Ariz. Western Coll., Yuman, 1992; real estate agt., Roadrunner Realty, Yuma, 1989—. Bd. dirs. Big Bros./Big Sisters, Yuma, 1989—; vol. various aging-related svcs., Yuma, 1989—, various children-related svcs., Yuma, 1986—. Named to Young Women of Am., 1991; recipient various scholarships Sul Ross State U., Alpine, Tex., 1981-85. Republican. Baptist.

DAVIS, ERIC KEITH, professional baseball player; b. L.A., May 29, 1962; m. Erica D. Outfielder Cin. Reds (Nat. League), 1986-91, L.A. Dodgers (Nat. League), 1992—. Mem. Nat. League All-Star Team, 1987. Office: Los Angeles Dodgers Dodger Stadium Los Angeles CA 90012

DAVIS, GENE, state legislator; b. Salt Lake City, July 2, 1945; s. John A. Davis and Glenna (Cameron) Moffat; m. Penny L. Hansen, Mar. 9, 1971; children: James, Pamela. Student, Radio Operational Enging. Sch., Burbank, Calif., 1963, LaSalle Extension U., 1971-74. Broadcaster KDXV Radio, St. George, KPGE, Page, Ariz., KNAK Radio, Salt Lake City, KALL/KLCY, Salt Lake City; dir. pub. rels. Valley Mental Health; disc jockey, prodn. and continuity dir.; mem. Utah Ho. of Reps., Salt Lake City, 1987—. Bd. dirs. State Alliance for Health Access, Minn., East county Recreation; chmn. Sugar House Community Coun., Salt Lake City, 1983-86; mem. adv. bd. Salt Lake County Aging Svc. Democrat. Mem. LDS Ch. Home: 865 Parkway Ave Salt Lake City UT 84106-1704 Office: Ho of Reps Salt Lake City UT

DAVIS, J. ALAN, lawyer; b. N.Y.C., Nov. 7, 1961. Student, Marlborough Coll., Eng., 1979; BA, So. Meth. U., 1983; JD with honors, U. Tex., 1987. Bar: Calif. 1988. Assoc. O'Melveny & Myers, L.A., 1987-89, Rosenfeld, Meyer & Susman, Beverly Hills, Calif., 1989-90. Mem. ABA, Calif. Bar Assn., Internat. Bar Assn., Beverly Hills Bar Assn. Office: 8585 Walnut Dr Los Angeles CA 90046

DAVIS, JAMES IVEY, laboratory administrator; b. Repton, Ala., Apr. 9, 1937; s. James Ivey and Jewel Francis (Straughn) D.; m. Susan Elizabeth Endres, June 15, 1965 (div. Dec. 1980); 1 child, Melinda Cynthia; m. Roberta Claire Venerdi, Mar. 9, 1990. BS, Calif. Inst. Tech., 1962; MS, UCLA, 1965, PhD, 1969. Staff physicist Hughes Aircraft Co., Culver City, Calif., 1962-66; lectr. U. Ghana, Kumasi, 1966-67; dept. mgr. Hughes Aircraft Co., Culver City, Calif., 1970-74; assoc. dir. Lawrence Livermore (Calif.) Nat. Lab., 1974—; cons., investor JIDCO, Danville, Calif., 1985—. Mem. The Commonwealth Club, San Francisco, 1987. With U.S. Army, 1953-56. Fellowship, Hughes Aircraft, 1963, NSF, 1969. Mem. AAAS, Am. Phys. Soc. Home: 4114 Sugar Maple Dr Danville CA 94506-4639 Office: Lawrence Livermore Nat Lab PO Box 808 Livermore CA 94551-0808

DAVIS, JAMES LUTHER, retired utilities executive, lawyer; b. Memphis, May 8, 1924; s. Luther and Sarah (Carter) D.; m. Natalie Young, Jan. 26, 1947; children: James Luther, Fred C., Peggy E. BBA, U. Ariz., 1946, LLB, 1949. Bar: Ariz. 1949. Sole practice Tucson, 1949-52, asst. city atty., 1952-53, city mgr., 1953-55; with Tucson Gas & Electric Co. (now Tucson Electric Power Co.), 1955—; exec. v.p., 1958-59, pres., 1959-76, also bd. dirs., 1961-89, emeritus, 1989—, chmn. bd., 1967-88; bd. dirs. El Paso br. Fed. Res. Bd., Dallas, 1974-77, chmn. 1976-77. Mem. charter rev. com. City of Tucson, 1965-71; bd. dirs. Tucson Airport Authority, 1957-62, 64-70, pres., 1965; bd. dirs. Tucson Med. Ctr., 1955-58, 59-65, pres., 1957-58; mem. Tucson Indsl. Devel. Bd., 1959-64; bd. dirs. Ariz. Town Hall, 1962-74, 78-82, Health Planning Coun. Tucson, 1964-71, Tucson Regional Plan, 1966-89, United Way, 1985-88; bd. dirs. Green Fields Sch., 1964-69, chmn. bd., 1964-66; bd. dirs. U. Ariz. Found., 1985-92, dir. emeritus, 1992—. Mem. Nat. Assn. Mfrs. (bd. dirs. 1960-62), Tex. Bar Assn., Ariz. Bar Assn., Pacific Coast Gas Assn. (bd. dirs. 1958-60), Pacific Coast Elect. Assn. (bd. dirs. 1972-86, pres. 1978-79), Western Energy and Supply Assn. (bd. dirs. 1964-76), Tucson C. of C. (bd. dirs. 1958-60, 64-66, 80-90, chmn. 1987-88), So. Ariz. Water Resources Assn. (bd. dirs. 1982-88, pres. 1987), Blue Key, Phi Gamma Delta, Alpha Kappa Psi, Phi Delta Phi, Tucson Country Club. Home: 6781 N Altos Primero Tucson AZ 85718-2054

DAVIS, JEFFREY STUART, retail executive; b. Syracuse, N.Y., Nov. 7, 1942; s. Seymour William and Evelyn (Etkin) D. BA in English, U. Colo., 1965. Vol. Peace Corps, Ankara, Turkey, 1965-68; dist. retail sales mgr. Almar Music Merchandisers of Colo., Ltd., Denver, 1968-75; unit supr. Hatch's Bookstore #3, Englewood, Colo., 1975-80; store mgr. Baldwin Printing, Inc., Littleton, Colo., 1981-83; office mgr. mktg. and lobbyist Oxford Recycled Aggregates, Inc., Englewood, 1984-87; bookstore mgr. Denver Univ. Law Bookstore, Inc., 1988—; featured mgr. in Coll. Store Exec. mag., 1991; interviewed in Little, Brown Law, 1992. Editor Penny Poetry Weekly, 1963-65. Mem. Cinderella City Promotional Com., Englewood, 1973-74; mem. Englewood Pub. Libr. Bd., 1990-93. Republican. Jewish. Office: Denver Univ Law Bookstore 7150 Montview Blvd Denver CO 80220-1878

DAVIS, JEREMY MATTHEW, chemist; b. Bakersfield, Calif., Aug. 5, 1953; s. Joseph Hyman and Mary (Pavetto) D.; m. Bernadette Sobkiewicz, Aug. 28, 1976; children: Andrew Jeremy, Christopher Peter. BS in Biol. Scis., U. Calif., Irvine, 1974; M in Pub. Adminstrn., Calif. State U., Long Beach, 1983. Chemist I, II, Orange County Water Dist., Fountain Valley, Calif., 1977-84, chemist supr., 1984—. Papers in field. Adult leader Cub Scouts, Boy Scouts Am. Named Lab. Person of Yr., Calif. Water Pollution Control Assn., Santa Ana River Basin, 1984. Mem. Am. Chem. Soc., Am. Water Works Assn., Calif. Water Pollution Control Assn. (bd. dirs. Santa Ana River Basin chpt. 1984), Toastmasters Internat. (sec., treas. Watermeisters Club 1993). Office: Orange County Water Dist PO Box 8300 Santa Ana CA 92728-8300

DAVIS, JOEL ALLEN, lawyer; b. L.A., Apr. 10, 1956; s. Donald S. and Anita (Levenback) D.; m. Diane E. Kerr, July 22, 1989; children: Erin R., Alexander L. BA, UCLA, 1978; JD, U. Calif., Davis, 1983. Bar: Calif. 1983; U.S. Dist. Ct. (ea. and cen. dists.) Calif., U.S. Ct. Appeals (9th cir.), U.S. Supreme Ct. Assoc. Weinstein, Shelley & Proctor, Pasadena, Calif., 1984-85; dep. atty. gen. Calif. Dept. Justice, Office of Atty. Gen., L.A., 1985—; arbitrator L.A. County Superior Ct., L.A., 1989—. Author: (with others) California Government Tort Liability Practice, 3d edit., 1992. Vol. atty. Bet Tzedek Legal Svcs., L.A., 1987—. Mem. Calif. State Bar, L.A. County Bar Assn. Office: Calif Dept Justice 300 S Spring St Los Angeles CA 90013

DAVIS, JOHN AARON, JR. (JACK DAVIS), retired university administrator; b. Oak Park, Ill., Sept. 30, 1928; s. J. Aaron and M. Corinne (Carroll) D.; m. Nina Maxine Tucker, Dec. 23, 1951; children: Shelby June, Michael Crit, Jacquelyn Carroll. BA, U. Iowa, 1951, MA, 1954; postgrad. Pa. State U., 1955-59; PhD, Syracuse U., 1964. Music dir. Sta. WSUI, U. Iowa, Iowa City, 1953-54; motion picture technician U. Iowa, Iowa City, 1954-55, vis. prof., 1965; instr. Pa. State U., University Park, 1958-59; assoc. prof. SUNY, Geneseo, 1959-61, prof., dir. Audio Visual Ctr., 1961-65, dir. instructional resources, 1965-66; dir. instructional media svcs. Wash. State U., Pullman, 1966-90; coord. faculty devel., 1990-93; chmn. various standing coms. on faculty senate Wash. State U., Pullman, 1985-89; pres. Wesley Found. at Wash. State U., Pullman, 1990-93; communications cons. various univs. Contbg. author: Educational Media Yearbook, 1978, International Encyclopedia of Education, 1985, Video Copyright Permissions, 1989. Mem. conf. rules com. United Meth. Conf. Comm. Commn., 1988-92; citizen amb. People-to-People Internat., Australia, N.Z., 1988. Bandsman U.S. Army, 1950-52. Mem. Assn. Ednl. Comm. and Tech. (bd. dirs. 1974-75, contbg. author Code of Professional Ethics 1976, Standards for College and University Learning Resources Programs 1983), Wash. Assn. Ednl. Communications and Tech. (bd. dirs. 1973-76, pres. 1974-75), Coun. Mgmt. Ednl. Tech., N.W. Coll. and U. (Outstanding Svc. award 1989, bd. dirs. 1987-92), Phi Delta Kappa. Home: SW 810 Cityview Pullman WA 99163

DAVIS, JOSEPH EDWARD, retired supermarket chain executive; b. Los Angeles, May 7, 1926; s. Joseph Edward and Myrtle Dorothy (Longstreet) D.; m. Marjorie Ann Mier, Mar. 27, 1953; children: Theresa, Sally, Victoria, Joseph. B.A., Occidental Coll., Los Angeles, 1949; M.B.A., U. Calif., Berkeley, 1951. C.P.A., Calif. Staff acct. Arthur Andersen & Co., C.P.A.s, Los Angeles, 1951-59; with Alpha Beta Co., La Habra, Calif., 1959-83; controller Alpha Beta Co., 1961-69, v.p., 1969-83, v.p. fin., 1973-83; v.p. fin. Stater Bros. Markets, Colton, Calif., 1983-92. Treas. Museum Assn. North Orange County, 1975-83, Fullerton-Morelia Sister City Assn., 1975-85. Served with AUS, 1945-46. Mem. Am. Inst. C.P.A.s, Calif. Soc. C.P.A.s, Fin. Execs. Inst., Alta Vista Country Club, Hacienda Golf Club. Republican. Presbyterian.

DAVIS, JOSEPH LA ROY, horticulturist, educator; b. Pasadena, Calif., June 6, 1932; s. Reading LaRoy and Beulah May (Noble) D.; (dec. Feb. 22, 1988); children: Melissa, Michele, Michael, Myles. BS, Calif. Poly. U., 1958. Lic. pest control advisor. Owner, dir. Joseph L. Davis Cons. Horticulturist, Sierra Madres, Calif., 1958—; prof. Napa (Calif.) Valley Coll., 1975—; cons. Horticulture, Pest Mgmt., Napa, 1958—, expert witness, 1965—. Author: Horticulture Dictionary, 1988. Apptd. Tree Commn., Napa, 1982-90, Pks. & Recreation Commn., Napa, 1988-90. MSgt. USAFR, 1974-92, Korea. Named Prof. Emeritus, Napa Valley Coll., 1991. Mem. Calif. Agrl. Prodn. (chpt. pres. 1984-85, state dir. 1985-91), Calif. Assn. Nurseryman, Calif. Land Contractors Assn., Internat. Growth Regulator Soc., Am. Soc. Enologists, Pest Control Operators of Calif., Napa County Farm Bur. Episcopalian. Office: Consulting Horticulturist 1944 Trinity Way Napa CA 94558

DAVIS, JOSEPH SAMUEL, retired department store executive, consultant; b. Chgo., Jan. 27, 1930; s. Joseph and Elizabeth (Cowen) D.; m. Martha Louise Gries, June 18, 1955; children: Elizabeth Louise, Katherine Ann, Mark Bennett, James Lincoln. B.A., Columbia U., 1951; M.B.A., Harvard U., 1953. From mgmt. trainee to buyer May D & F Co., Denver, 1956-61; from asst. div. mdse. mgr. to exec. v.p. Kaufmann's, Pitts., 1961-75; pres. G. Fox and Co., Hartford, Conn., 1975-79; pres., chief exec. officer M. O'Neil Co., Akron, Ohio, 1979-83; pres., chief exec. officer May D&F, Denver, 1983-89, chief exec. officer, 1989-90, pres., chief exec. officer, 1990-93; cons. dir. Banc-Ohio Nat. Bank, Akron, 1980-83; dir. Ohio Edison, 1982-83; adv. bd. Sch. Bus., U. Conn., 1977-79; bd. dirs. Colo. Nat. Bank; spl. vis. prof., exec.-in-residence Coll. and Grad. Sch. Bus. and Adminstrn., U. Colo., Denver, 1993—. Bd. dirs. Hartford Symphony Soc., 1977-79, Downtown Denver, Inc., 1983-86; bd. dirs. Nat. Jewish Ctr., 1984—, chmn. bd., 1990-92; bd. dirs. Greater Denver C. of C., 1987-90, Greater Denver Corp., 1988—; adv. bd. Akron Symphony, 1980-83, Jr. League Akron, 1979-83; trustee Akron Gen. Med. Center, 1980-83, Akron Art Mus., 1980-83, Akron Regional Devel. Bd., 1980-83, Denver Art Mus., 1984-87, Colo. Alliance Bus., 1985-88; mem. pres.'s bus. coun. U. Colo., 1986—. Served as officer USN, 1953-56. Mem. Denver C. of C. (bd. dirs. 1987-90), Harvard Bus. Sch. Club Colo. Clubs: Denver (bd. dirs. 1990-92), Brown Palace. Office: May D & F 16th St at Tremont Pl Denver CO 80202

DAVIS, LANCE EDWIN, economics educator; b. Seattle, Nov. 3, 1928; s. Maurice L. and Marjorie Dee (Seibert) D.; m. Susan Elizabeth Gray, Dec. 2, 1977; 1 child, Maili. BA, U. Wash., Seattle, 1950; PhD (Ford Found. dissertation fellow summer 1956), Johns Hopkins U., 1956. Teaching asst. U. Wash., 1950-51, 52-53; teaching asst., then instr. Johns Hopkins U., 1953-55; from instr. to prof. econs. Purdue U., 1955-62; mem. faculty Calif. Inst. Tech., Pasadena; prof. econs. Calif. Inst. Tech., 1968—, Mary Stillman Harkness prof., 1980—; research assoc. Nat. Bur. Econ. Research, 1979—. Author: The Growth of Industrial Enterprise, 1964; co-author: The Savings Bank of Baltimore, 1956, American Economic History: The Development of a National Economy, 2d rev. edit, 1968, Institutional Change and American Economic Growth, 1971, Mammon and the Pursuit of Empire: The Political Economy of British Imperialism, 1860-1912, 1987; co-editor: American Economic Growth: An Economist's History of the United States, 1971; mem. bd. editors Jour. Econ. History, 1965-73, Explorations in Economic History, 1984-88, THESIS, Theory, and History of Econ. and Social Instns. and Structures, with Society and Western Scholars, 1991—. Served with USNR, 1945-48, 51-52. Recipient Arthur Cole prize Econ. History Assn., 1966; Ford Found. Faculty fellow, 1959-60; Guggenheim fellow, 1964-65; fellow Ctr. for Advanced Study in Behavioral Scis., 1985-86. Fellow Am. Acad. Arts and Scis.; mem. Coun. 1 Rsch. Econ. History (chmn. 1973-74, 75-76), Econ. History Assn. (pres. 1978-79, trustee 1980-82), Anglo-Am. Hist. Assn. (gov. 1978-80), Econs. Inst. (policy and adv. bd. 1984-87), Cliometric Soc. (trustee 1993-97). Home: 1746 Grevelia St South Pasadena CA 91030-2753 Office: Calif Inst Tech Humanities and Social Scis Div Pasadena CA 91125

DAVIS, LAURENCE RICHARD, retired military officer, transit executive; b. Santa Cruz, Calif., June 10, 1934; s. Laurence Ritchie and Henrietta Jean (Steiner) D.; m. JoAnn Kendall, Dec. 3, 1966; children: Valerie, Deirdre, Andrea, Colin, Kyle. BS, U. Calif., 1956; MS, U. Okla., 1962; grad., Air War Coll., 1975. Col. USAF, 1956-79; dir. maintenance L.A. County Met. Transp. Authority, 1979—; mem. Transp. Rsch. Bd., Washington, 1986— I-Time Task Force U.S.-Can. Mass Transit 1990—; advisor Fed. Transit Adminstrn., U.S. Dept. Transp., Washington, 1991—; speaker, program presenter on alternate fuels, etc. various profl. meetings. Mem. adv. coun. L.A. Town Hall, 1983-89. Decorated Legion of Merit USAF, 1979; recipient "Thank You", U.S. Olympic Com., 1984, Adminstrs. award U.S. Dept. Transp., Washington, 1991, Tranny award, Calif. Transit Found., 1992. Fellow Inst. for Advancement Engrng.; mem. Am. Pub. Transit Assn. (chmn. mech. administrv. com. 1982-85, chmn. bus equipment and maintenance com. 1986-89, mem. environ. task force 1989—). Methodist. Home: 17822 Cardiff Cir Huntington Beach CA 92649 Office: So Calif Rapid Transit 900 Lyon St Los Angeles CA 90012

DAVIS, LINDA JACOBS, marketing, development professional; b. Miami, July 10, 1955; d. Martin Jacque and Doris Harriet (Stucker) Jacobs; m. John Joseph Mantos, Jan. 1, 1984 (dec. 1988); m. Perry Davis, June 4, 1989; children: Aaron, Jacob. Student, U. South Fla., 1977. Mgr., cons. Werner Erhard & Assocs., San Francisco, 1978-82, program leader, 1979-90; asst. exec. dir. The Breakthrough Found., San Francisco, 1982-88; owner Mantagaris Galleries, San Francisco, 1988-92; dir. mktg. devel. Marin Child Care Coun., San Rafael, Calif., 1992—; profl. fund-raiser. Vol. The Hunger Project, Fla., 1977-78; bd. dirs. Marin Child Care Coun. Recipient Outstanding Young Women Am. Mem. NOW (pres. local chpt.). Democrat. Jewish. Home: 75 Milland Dr Mill Valley CA 94941-4910 Office: Marin Child Care Coun 828 Mission Ave San Rafael CA 94901

DAVIS, MARK, professional baseball player; b. Livermore, CA, Oct. 19, 1960. Pitcher Phila. Phillies, Phila., 1979-82, San Francisco Giants, San Francisco, 1983-87, San Diego Padres, San Diego, Calif., 1987—. Recipient Cy Young Award, 1989; mem. Nat. League All-Star Team, 1988-89. Office: San Diego Padres PO Box 2000 San Diego CA 92112-2000

DAVIS, MARVIN, petroleum company executive, entrepreneur; b. Newark, Aug. 28, 1925; s. Jack Davis; m. Barbara Davis; 5 children. BSCE, NYU, 1947. Gen. ptnr. Davis Oil Co., Denver; co-owner 20th Century-Fox, 1981-85. Office: Davis Oil Co 410 17th St Ste 1610 Denver CO 80202-4472

DAVIS, PEGGY MCALISTER, director budget and finance, accountant; b. Coos Bay, Oreg., June 9, 1950; d. Calvin Earl and Verna Eugenie (Pundt) McAlister; m. Paul K. Davis, Oct. 5, 1990. BA, U. Oreg., 1971; MBA, Calif. State U., Fresno, 1990. CPA, Calif. Acct., auditor Hood and Strong, CPAs, San Francisco, 1975-77; dir. budget and fin. Fresno Pacific Coll., 1984—. Treas. Fig Garden Bible Ch., 1984-86; comm. coord. ARC, Fresno, 1987—. Mem. ACLU (sec. Fresno chpt. 1991—), Nat. Assn. Accts., Phi Beta Kappa. Democrat. Office: Fresno Pacific Coll 1717 S Chestnut Ave Fresno CA 93702-4798

DAVIS, RANDALL SCOTT, public relations executive; b. Ottumwa, Iowa, July 26, 1952; s. Donald Dale and Marguaritte Louise (Maier) D.; m. Ruthe Eugena Forbriger, Nov. 21, 1976; 1 child, Ryan Scott. BA, Calif. State U., L.A., 1974. Dir. merchandising and advt. Capitol Records, Hollywood, Calif., 1975-82; mktg. svcs. mgr. Walt Disney Home Video, Burbank, Calif., 1982-83; account exec. Berkhemer & Kline Pub. Rels., L.A., 1983-85; v.p. ops. Jensen Communications, Burbank, 1985-86; pres. The Creative Svc. Co., La Crescenta, Calif., 1986—. Freelance writer various mags., newspapers and pub. rels. agys., L.A., 1970—. Recipient CLIO, N.Y.C., 1981. Mem. The Hemingway Found.

DAVIS, RANDY L., soil scientist; b. L.A., Nov. 23, 1950; s. Willie Vernon and Joyce Catherine (Manes) D. AA, Yuba Community Coll., 1972; BS in Soils and Plant Nutrition, U. Calif., Berkeley, 1976. Vol. soil scientist U.S. Peace Corps, Maseru, Lesotho, 1976-79; soil scientist Hiawatha Nat. Forest, Sault Saint Marie, Mich., 1979-86; forest soil scientist Bridger-Teton Nat. Forest, Jackson, Wyo., 1986—; detailed soil scientist Boise (Idaho) Nat. Forest, 1989, 92. Editor Soil Classifiers newsletter; contbr. articles to profl. jours. Pres. Sault Community Theater, Sault Saint Marie, 1984-86. Mem. Am. Chem. Soc., Soil Sci. Soc. Am., Soil and Water Conservation Soc. Am. (bd. dirs. 1991-92, chpt. pres. 1993), Internat. Soc. Soil Sci., Soc. for Range Mgmt. Methodist. Home: PO Box 7795 Jackson WY 83001-7795 Office: Bridger-Teton Nat Forest PO Box 1888 Jackson WY 83001-1888

DAVIS, RHONDA SUE, accountant, children's entertainer; b. Kittanning, Pa., June 27, 1967; d. Christopher George Kough and Patti Anne (Traister) Logan; m. Brian Dee Davis, Aug. 22, 1988. Grad. high sch., El Paso, Tex. Soloist Friendship, Colorado Springs, Colo., 1984-85, instr. in puppetry, 1985-86, drama dir., 1985-87, program writer, 1984-87; from crew mem. 2d asst. Burger King, Olympia, Wash., 1987-89; from crew person to staff asst. McDonald's, Olympia, 1989-91; puppet dir. Imagine Nation, Olympia, 1989—; acct. dept. revenue State of Wash., Olympia, 1991—. Producer local TV programs; appearances include Sta. TCTV.

DAVIS, RICHARD ANTHONY, college creative arts division chairman; b. Renton, Wash., Mar. 20, 1941; s. Thomas J. and Rena Mae (Hodder) D.; m. Beverly Jean Morse, May 11, 1963; children: Wyndeth Victoria, Michael Edward David. BA, Cen. Wash. State, 1963; MA, U. Wash., 1964, PhD, 1976. Prof. Western Oreg. State Coll., Monmouth, 1964—, costume designer over 100 plays, 1968-88, chmn. div. creative arts, 1989—, dir. numerous theatrical prodns., 1965—; bd. dirs. N.W. Drama Conf., 1986-93, pres., 1986-88; chief regional officer ATA Region IX, 1984-86, mem. nat. bd.; adjudicator Am. Coll. Theatre Festival, Region IX, 1982-88. Theatre columnist Md. Valley Arts Newsletter, 1985-86; contbr. poetry to Calapooya Collage, 1968-77. Recipient Melba Day Sparks award Oreg. Thespians, 1986, ACTF Amoco award of excellence, 1984. Mem. NW Drama Conf. (bd. dirs., Pres.'s award 1991), Oreg. Theatre Arts Assn., Nat. Honor Soc., Alpha Psi Omega, Kappa Delta Pi. Democrat. Presbyterian. Home: 310 Willow Way E Monmouth OR 97361-1105 Office: Western Oreg State Coll Creative Arts Monmouth OR 97361

DAVIS, RICHARD CALHOUN, dentist; b. Manhatten, Kans., Jan. 4, 1945; s. William Calhoun and Alison Rae (Wyland) D.; Danna Ruth Ritchel,

June 13, 1968; 1 child, Darin Calhoun. Student, Ariz. State U., 1963-65, BA, 1978; BA, U. Ariz., 1966; DDS, U. of Pacific, 1981. Retail dept. head Walgreens, Tucson, 1965-66; mgmt. trainee Walgreens, Tucson, San Antonio, 1967-70; asst. store mgr. Walgreens, Baton Rouge, 1970-72; field rep. Am. Cancer Soc., Phoenix, 1972-74; dept. head Lucky Stores, Inc., Tempe, Ariz., 1976-78; practice dentistry specializing in gen. dentistry Tucson, 1981—; bd. dirs. Home Again, Inc. Chmn. bd. Capilla Del Sol Christian Ch., Tucson, 1984. Mem. ADA, Acad. Gen. Dentists, Am. Straight Wire Orthodontic Assn., N.W. Dental Study Club, Optimists (past pres. N.W. club), Elks. Republican. Mem. Disciples of Christ Ch. Office: 2777 N Campbell Ave Tucson AZ 85719-3101

DAVIS, RICHARD ERNEST, engineer; b. San Francisco, Nov. 20, 1936; 1 child, Richard Jr.; m. Sharon L. Buss, Aug. 26, 1961; children: Dawn, Michelle. BS in Engring., Calif. State Poly. U., San Luis Obispo, 1967. Facilities engr., energy conservation engr. Naval Weapons Ctr., China Lake, Calif., 1967-77; solar program coordinator U.S. Dept. Energy, Oakland, Calif., 1977-78; program mgr. Solar Energy Research Inst., Golden, Colo., 1978-80; engring. specialist Holmes & Narver, Mercury, Nev., 1980-90; engring. specialist nuclear waste Nev./Yucca Mountain Project Raytheon Svcs., Mercury, 1990-93; prin. project engr. Fluor Daniel, Inc., Las Vegas, 1993—. Contbr. articles to profl. jours. Served with USAF, 1954-62. Home: HCR 69 Box 495 Amargosa Valley NV 89020 Office: Fluor Daniel Inc 101 Convention Ctr Dr Las Vegas NV 89109

DAVIS, ROBERT EUGENE, JR., computer company executive; b. Pasadena, Calif., July 17, 1956; s. Robert Eugene and Estelle Martin (Beall) D. BA, U. Calif., Santa Barbara, 1979; MBA, U. Calif., Irvine, 1990. Software engr. Interstate Electronics, Anaheim, Calif., 1980-82; sr. engr. Intermetrics, Huntington Beach, Calif., 1982-86; software mgr. Tau Corp., Long Beach, Calif., 1986-92, Loral Electro-Optical, Pomona, Calif., 1992—. Active L.A. County Mus. Art, 1981—, Newport Harbor Art Mus., Newport Beach, Calif., 1987—, World Affairs Coun. of Orange County, 1991—. Mem. Assn. Computing Machinery, IEEE Computer Soc. Office: Loral Electric-Optical 600 Terrace Dr San Dimas CA 91773

DAVIS, ROBERT WAYNE, broadcasting executive; b. Snohomish, Wash., May 9, 1947; s. Hugh Edward and Lorraine Mae (Tronsrud) D.; m. Joan Carol Miller, June 21, 1969; children: Emily Lyn, Alison Kay. BBA, U. Wash., 1969. sales rep. Sta. KNDO-TV, Yakima, Wash., 1969-74; acct. exec., Simpson/Reilly & Assoc., Seattle, 1974-77, Sta. KOMO-TV, Seattle, 1977-81; pres., gen. mgr. Sta. KMTR-TV, Eugene, Oreg., 1981—. Mem. Oreg. Assn. of Broadcasters (bd. dirs. 1987-90), Arbitron TV Adv. Coun. (bd. dirs. 1987-90, chmn. 1990), Nat. Assn. Broadcasters (TV bd. 1990-92), NBC-TV Affiliates (com. congl. rels.), Wash. Athletic (Seattle), Rotary. Office: KMTR Inc PO Box 7308 Eugene OR 97401-0208

DAVIS, RON LEE, clergyman, author; b. Carroll, Iowa, Oct. 17, 1947; s. David Clarence and Elizabeth Regina (Thompson) D.; m. Shirley Louise O'Connor, Aug. 31, 1973; children: Rachael LeeAnn, Nathan Paul. BA cum laude, Tarkio (Mo.) Coll., 1969; MDiv cum laude, Dubuque (Iowa) Theol. Sem., 1971; DDiv, Bethel Theol. Sem., St. Paul, 1977. Ordained to ministry Presbyn. Ch., 1971. Chaplain Minn. Vikings, Mpls., 1975-80; assoc. pastor Hope Presbyn. Ch., Mpls., 1971-80; sr. pastor First Presbyn. Ch., Fresno, Calif., 1981-86, Community Presbyn. Ch., Danville, Calif., 1986-91; tchr. Bible Oakland (Calif.) A's, 1990-91; writer, 1983—; real estate loan cons. Danville Fin. Group, Calif., 1992—; invited speaker at gen. sessions and confs. and on TV. Author: Gold in the Making, 1983, A Forgiving God in an Unforgiving World, 1984, Healing Life's Hurts, 1986, A Time for Compassion, 1986, Courage to Begin Again, 1988, Mistreated, 1989, Becoming a Whole Person in a Broken World, 1990, Mentoring, 1990. Mem. pres.'s adv. coun. Fellowship of Christian Athletes; bd. dirs. Youth for Christ, cen. Calif., 1982-85, Fresno Pacific Coll., 1983-84. Recipient award for outstanding leadership State Bar; named to Outstanding Young Men of Am. Home: 3513 Canfield Danville CA 94526

DAVIS, RONALD, artist, printmaker; b. Santa Monica, Calif., June 29, 1937. Student, U. Wyo., 1955-56, San Francisco Art Inst., 1960-64. Announcer, Sta. KVWO, Cheyenne, Wyo., 1958-59; instr. U. Calif., Irvine, 1966. Represented in permanent collections: Albright-Knox Gallery, Buffalo, Los Angeles County Mus., Mus. Modern Art, N.Y.C., Mus. Contemporary Art, Los Angeles, TateGallery, London, San Antonio Mus. Art, San Francisco Mus. Art, Whitney Mus., N.Y.C., Va. Mus., Richmond, Walker Art Ctr., Minn. and other internat. pub. collections; 57 one-man shows include Leo Castelli, N.Y.C., Nicholas Wilder Gallery, Los Angeles, BlumHelman Los Angeles, Asher/Faure, Los Angeles, John Berggruen, San Francisco, Kasmin Gallery, London, Mirvish Gallery, Toronto, N.Y. Acad. Scis., N.Y.C., Sedona Arts Ctr., Ariz., Oakland (Calif.) Mus., retrospective, 1976, numerous others; also numerous nat. and internat. group shows. Yale-Norfolk Summer Sch. Music and Art grantee, 1962, Nat. Endowment Arts grantee, 1968. Studio: PO Box 276 Arroyo Hondo NM 87513

DAVIS, STANFORD MELVIN, engineering executive, publishing consultant; b. Camden, N.J., June 12, 1941; s. Winford and Rose Marie (Rich) D.; m. Pamela Davis, Nov. 25, 1967 (div. 1980); children: Peter, Shawna; m. Laura A. Rudolph, Feb. 21, 1987. AB, BSEE, Rutgers U., 1964; postgrad., UCLA, 1967; MBA, U. Portland, 1984. Elec. engr. RCA, Van Nuys, Calif., 1966-68; project engr. Tek, Wilsonville, Oreg., 1968-79; S/W mgr. Tektronix, Wilsonville, 1979-81, mgr. mktg., 1981-83; founder, v.p. engring. Concept Technologies, Portland, 1983-86; mgr. engring. program INTEL, Hillsboro, Oreg., 1986-87; product line mgr. INTEL, Hillsboro, 1987-88; engring. mgr. Graphic Printing div. Textronix, Wilsonville, Oreg., 1989—. Patentee in field. Served to capt. U.S. Army, 1964-66. Recipient Outstanding Product award Datapro, Delran, N.J., 1985. Mem. Assn. of Computing Machinery, IEEE. Home: 7320 SW 103d Ave Beaverton OR 97005

DAVIS, STERLING EVAN, television executive; b. Mpls., Feb. 10, 1941; s. Lyman Eugene and Ruby Elizabeth (Larson) D.; m. Bonnie S. Taylor, Jan. 15, 1977; children: Evan, Emily, Robin. BA, Taylor U., 1963; postgrad., U. So. Calif., L.A., 1968-70. Chief engr. Metrotape, Hollywood, Calif., 1974-78; v.p. ops. The Vidtronics Co., Hollywood, 1978; chief engr. Telemation Prodns., Seattle, 1978-82; dir. ops. Sta. KTVU, Inc., Oakland, Calif., 1982—. Bd. dirs. Post Adoption Ctr. for Edn. & Rsch., Easter Seal Soc. of Alameda County, Oakland. Lt. USN, 1963-67, Vietnam. Mem. IEEE, Soc. Motion Picture & TV Engrs., Audio Engring. Soc., Soc. Broadcast Engrs. Office: Sta KTVU PO Box 22222 Oakland CA 94623-2222

DAVIS, SUZY, information center owner; b. Duncan, Okla., July 19, 1936; d. Elmer Arvin and Reba Dorril (Johnson) Gilstrap; m. Francis Jerome Dillard, Jan. 22, 1955 (div. May 1975); children: Jeri S., Lawrance A., Joe P., Marie E.; m. William Thomas Davis, Dec. 20, 1984 (dec.). Grad. high sch., Newman, Calif., 1954. Guest lectr. Calif. State U., Long Beach, 1986, 89; model Calif. State U., Riverside, 1988, San Bernardino, 1988—; model Community Coll., San Bernardino, 1988—, Robert E. Wood Watercolor Workshop, Palm Springs, Calif., 1990, Cheyenne (Tex.) Community Coll., 1993; owner, operator Nudist Info. Ctr., North Las Vegas, Nev., 1984-92, NIC, North Las Vegas, 1984-92; bd. dirs. Beachfront USA, Moreno Valley; prodn. coord. Heritage Video, Las Vegas, Nev., 1992. Bd. dirs. Callen-Davis Meml. Fund, Moreno Valley, Calif., 1988—, Western Sunbathing Assn., Studio City, Calif., 1989-92; active adopt-a-hwy. Western Sunbathing Assn., Victorville, Calif., 1990-92, Earth Week (city clean-up), Daggett, 1990. Named as part of Family of Yr., Western Sunbathing Assn., 1986, for Membership Increase by Percentage, Am. Sunbathing Assn., 1986, Woman of the Yr., Am. Sunbathing Assn., 1992; recipient Glen Eden award Am. Sunbathing Assn., 1986. Mem. Silver Valley Sun Club.

DAVIS, TERI LYNN, naturopathic physician, biology educator; b. Corvallis, Oreg., Sept. 1, 1951; d. Monte Vincent and Betty Lou (Morton) D.; m. Thomas Charles DiMaggio, Mar. 9, 1985; 1 child, Thomas Dylan. BS, Kans. Newman Coll., Wichita, 1976; D of Naturopathic Medicine, Nat. Coll. Naturopathic Medicine, Portland, Oreg., 1978. Cert. secondary edn. tchr. in biology. Naturopathic physician in pvt. practice Tucson, 1978—; tutor Casey Family Program, Tucson, 1991—; cons. in field. Contbr. articles to profl. jours. Mem. Am. Assn. Naturopathic Physicians (conv. mgr. 1991—), Ariz. Naturopathic Med. Assn. (sec. 1979-81, v.p. 1981-82, conv. mgr. 1980—), Profl. Conv. Mgrs. Assn.

DAVIS, TERRY LEE, communications systems engineer; b. Enid, Okla., Aug. 18, 1950; s. Walter Joseph and Bessie Lee (McDaniel) D.; m. Jennie Sue Petrik, Jan. 21, 1972; children: Mistie Rae, Brandon Scott. BSCE, Okla. State U., 1972. Registered profl. engr., Okla., Colo., Wash. Civil engr. U.S. Army Corps of Engrs., Webbers Falls, Okla., 1973, Omaha, 1974; water resources engr. U.S. Bur. Reclamation, Grand Junction, Colo., 1974-75, Amarillo, Tex., 1974-75, Montrose, Colo., 1976; water resources engr. U.S. Bur. Reclamation, AID, Dubai, United Arab Emirates, 1977-78; communication and control systems engr. Western Area Power Adminstrn., U.S. Dept. Energy, Loveland, Colo., 1979-84, Boeing, Seattle, 1984—. Mem. Issaquah (Wash.) Devel. Commn., 1987—, Issaquah Rivers and Streams Bd., 1985-86, Issaquah Basin Planning Team, 1990-92. Mem. Masons (jr. warden lodge 108 1993—), Order Eastern Star (chaplain century chpt. 66). Republican. Office: Boeing Computer Svcs PO Box 3707 Seattle WA 98124-2207

DAVIS, THOMAS PAUL, pharmacology and biochemistry educator; b. L.A., Jan. 13, 1951; s. Joseph Jefferson and Margaret Catherine (Moran) D.; m. Alecia Anne Kiehn, June 19, 1971; children: Melissa, Rebecca, Ryan. BS, Loyola U., 1973; MS, U. Nev., 1975; PhD, U. Mo., 1978. Cert. profl. chemist. Biochemist Abbott Labs. Inc., Chgo., 1978-80; asst. prof. Coll. of Medicine U. Ariz., Tucson, 1981-86, assoc. prof. Coll. of Medicine, 1986-91, prof. Coll. of Medicine, 1991—; cons. Biomeasure Inc., Milford, Mass., 1990—; dir. quality assurance Hansens Beverage Co., Anaheim, Calif.; speaker in field. Contbr. articles to profl. jours., chpts. to books. Speaker Optimists, Tucson, 1987, Soc. for Med. Technologists, Tucson, 1988; mem. faculty U.S. Fed. Judiciary Def. Lawyers Drug Course, Phoenix, 1989. Nat. Inst. on Aging grantee, 1983, Robert S. Flynn Found. grantee, 1985, Nat. Cancer Inst. grantee, 1981—, NIH grantee, 1985—, NIDA grantee, 1986—. Fellow Am. Inst. Chemists; mem. Am. Physiol. Soc., Am. Soc. for Pharmacology and Exptl. Therapeutics, Internat. Brain Rsch. Orgn., Internat. Soc. Psychoneuroendocrinology, Soc. for Neurosci., Sigma Xi. Democrat. Roman Catholic. Office: U Ariz Coll of Medicine Dept of Pharmacology Tucson AZ 85724

DAVIS, THOMAS RONALD, computer company executive; b. Memphis, Mar. 23, 1949; s. T.H. Davis and Mary Lou Stroud; m. Jan Allison Lee, Jan. 16, 1970; children: Jeremy Lee, Benjamin Levi, Allison Elizabeth. Student, La. State U., 1960-70, Phoenix Coll., 1971-74, Ariz. State U., 1980-83; teaching cert., Ariz. C.C., 1987. Programmer analyst Am. Express, Phoenix, 1970-73, sr. systems analyst, 1973-78; br. software mgr. Digital Equipment Corp., Phoenix, 1978-82, dist. mktg. mgr., 1982-86, strategic acct. mgr., 1986-88; corp. acct. mkt. mgr. Microsoft, Redmond, Wash., 1988-91, dir. sales tng., 1991—. Chair Fiesta Bowl Com., Phoenix, 1986; pres. North Phoenix Little League Assn., 1988; instr. Ariz. Mountaineer Club, Phoenix, 1988; strategist mayoral election com., Remond, 1991. Named Top Solo Performer in the French Quarter musicians poll, New Orleans, 1969. Home: 16217 NE 45th Ct Redmond WA 98052

DAVIS, WANDA ROSE, lawyer; b. Lampasas, Tex., Oct. 4, 1937; d. Ellis DeWitt and Julia Doris (Rose) Cockrell; m. Richard Andrew Fulcher, May 9, 1959 (div. 1969); 1 child, Greg Ellis; m. Edwin Leon Davis, Jan. 14, 1973 (div. 1985). BBA, U. Tex., 1959, JD, 1971. Bar: Tex. 1971, Colo. 1981, U.S. Dist. Ct. (no. dist.) Tex. 1972, U.S. Dist. Ct. Colo. 1981, U.S. Ct. Appeals (10th cir. 1981, U.S. Supreme Ct. 1976. Atty. Atlantic Richfield Co., Dallas, 1971; assoc. firm Crocker & Murphy, Dallas, 1971-72; prin. Wanda Davis, Atty. at Law, Dallas, 1972-73; ptnr. firm Davis & Davis Inc., Dallas, 1973-75; atty. adviser HUD, Dallas, 1974-75, Air Force Acctg. and Fin. Ctr., Denver, 1976-92; co-chmn. regional Profl. Devel. Inst., Am. Soc. Mil. Comptrollers, Colorado Springs, Colo., 1982; chmn. Lowry AFB Noontime Edn. Program, Exercise Program, Denver, 1977-83; mem. speakers bur. Colo. Women's Bar, 1982-83, Lowry AFB, 1981-83; mem. fed. ct. liaison com. U.S. Dist. Ct. Colo., 1983; mem. Leaders of the Fed. Bar Assn. People to People Del. to China, USSR and Finland, 1986. Contbr. numerous articles to profl. jours. Bd. dirs. Pres.'s Coun. Met. Denver, 1981-83; mem. Lowry AFB Alcohol Abuse Exec. Com., 1981-84. Recipient Spl. Achievement award USAF, 1978; Upward Mobility award Fed. Profl. and Adminstrv. Women, Denver, 1979. Mem. Fed. Bar Assn. (pres. Colo. 1982-83, mem. nat. coun. 1984—, Earl W. Kintner Disting. Svc. award 1983, 1st v.p. 10th cir. 1986—), Colo. Trial Lawyers Assn., Bus. and Profl. Women's Club (dist. IV East dir. 1983-84, Colo. pres. 1988-89), Am. Soc. Mil. Comptrollers (pres. 1984-85), Denver South Met. Bus. and Profl. Women's Club (pres. 1982-83), Denver Silver Spruce Am. Bus. Women's Assn. (pres. 1981-82; Woman of Yr. award 1982), Colo. Jud. Inst., Colo. Concerned Lawyers, Profl. Mgrs. Assn., Fed. Women's Program (v.p. Denver 1980), Colo. Woman News Community adv. bd., 1988—, Dallas Bar Assn., Tex. Bar Assn., Denver Bar Assn., Altrusa, Zonta, Denver Nancy Langhorn Federally Employed Women. (pres. 1979-80). Christian.

DAVIS, WILLIAM ROSS, JR., health club owner; b. San Francisco, Mar. 16, 1953; s. William Ross Sr. and Julie (Weatherby) D.; m. Nancy Jane Hurley, June 11, 1976; children: Adam Neil, Amanda Erin. Grad. high sch., Pocatello, Idaho. Apprentice G&W Flooring, Pocatello, 1974-78; owner Bill Davis Custom Flooring, Pocatello, 1978-86; agt., salesperson A.L. Williams, Pocatello, 1982-88, regional v.p., 1988-90; owner Fitness Inc. Health Club, Pocatello, 1990—; ins. agt. State Dept. Ins., Boise, Idaho, 1982-90; securities agt. SEC, Boise, 1985-90, securities prin., 1989-90. With U.S. Army, 1971-74. Roman Catholic. Home: 538 Hiawatha Pocatello ID 83204 Office: Fitness Inc Health Club 1800 Garrett Way Pocatello ID 83201

DAVIS-BANKS, PHYLLIS EILEEN, retired city official; b. Shelby County, Ind., May 6, 1918; d. Acy Earl and Grace V. (Crane) Lancaster; m. Charles M. Davis, July 2, 1937 (div. 1963); children: Linda Ann Scott, Randal Lee; m. Hal N. Banks, Dec. 24, 1971. Student, Long Beach (Calif.) City Coll., 1959-61, Art Inst. San Miguel de Allende, San Miguel, Mexico, 1970. Legal sec. Bingham & Bingham, Indpls., 1935-36; sec. Herff Jones, Indpls., 1936-37, Ind. PTA, Indpls., 1937-41; acct. Curtis Wright, Indpls., 1941-42; cashier Fed. Housing Adminstrn., San Diego, 1943; legal sec. Kelly Svcs./Western Girl, Long Beach, Calif., 1960-63; sec., acting dir. Alaska Heart Assn., Anchorage, 1965-68; adminstrv. asst. Greater Anchorage Area Community Action, 1968-71; dep. clk. Municipality of Anchorage, 1973-79, clk., 1979-80. Editor newsletter Alaska Presbyn., 1966-80; author: Cocahnia, 1969, Anchorage Fun Book, 1967; editor newsletter Artist's Action Line, 1981-91; contbr.a rticles to profl. jours.; one woman show The Gallery, Anchorage, 1975, 4 person show, 1976; exhibited in group shows at Anchorage Fine Arts Mus., 1986, El Paso (Tex.) Mus., 1989. Mem. Roswell Fine Arts League (pres. 1987-90), Taos Art Assn., N.Mex. Watercolor Soc., Alaska Watercolor Soc. (signature mem.). Presbyterian. Home: 1016 Crescent Dr Roswell NM 88201-3220

DAVIS-KIMBALL, JEANNINE, archaeology educator; b. Driggs, Idaho, Nov. 23, 1929; d. Elmer Jacob and Cora (Kimball) Davis; m. Wayne Elbert Hargett, Nov. 23, 1946 (div. 1980); children: Teresa, Mary Patrice, Stephen, John Eric, Christopher, Leslie Ann; m. Warren B. Matthew, Dec. 27, 1987. Lic. vocat. nurse, Sacred Heart Hosp., Idaho Falls, Idaho, 1958; BA, Calif. State U., Northridge, 1978; MA, Goddard Coll., 1980; PhD, U. Calif., Berkeley, 1988. Curatorial asst. Los Angeles County Mus. Art, L.A., 1976-80; project dir. Calif. Indian libr. collections U. Calif., Berkeley, 1992—; exec. dir. Kazakh-Am. Rsch. Project, Berkeley, 1989—, dir. archaeol. excavations, Kazakhstan, Russia, 1991—; participant Silk Road dialogue UNESCO, Paris, 1991, 92. Contbg. author: Arts and Cultures of the Sun God, 1992; tech. editor Catalogue Raisonne of Alaska Commercial Collection, 1993; editor: Guides to the California Indian Library Collections, 1993; contbr. articles to profl. jours. Active various polit. campaigns, Berkeley, 1989—. Mem. Archaeol. Inst. Am. (sec.-treas. 1986—), Assn. for Cen. Asian Studies (editor ACASIA 1990-93). Office: Kazakh/Am Rsch Project Inc 1607 Walnut St Berkeley CA 94709

DAVISON, ARTHUR LEE, engineer, scientific instrument manufacturing company executive; b. Burlington, Iowa, May 8, 1936; s. John Earl and Helen Medera (Jones) D.; m. Dorothea Ellen Jones, June 14, 1958; children: Ken, Ron, Greg. BA, Monmouth Coll., 1958; MS, Purdue U., 1960. Registered profl. engr., Calif. R & D engring. physicist Baird Corp., Bedford, Mass., 1960-65; rsch. engr. Bethlehem (Pa.) Steel, 1965-69; project engring. mgr. Applied Rsch. Labs., Sunland, Calif., 1969-79; sr. v.p., gen. mgr. Applied Rsch. Labs., Valencia, Calif., 1985-91; dir. engring. Berkey Colortron, Burbank, Calif., 1979-80; pres., chief exec. officer Labtest Equipment Co., L.A., 1981-85; pres. Kevex Instruments, San Carlos, Calif., 1991-92; pres. X-ray div. Fisons Instruments, Santa Clarita, Calif., 1992—. Bd. dirs. Valencia Indsl. Assn., 1988—; vol. worker Boy Scouts Am., various youth groups. Mem. Am. Optical Soc., Am. Phys. Soc., Soc. Applied Spectroscopy. Democrat. Methodist. Office: Kevex Instruments 24911 Avenue Stanford Valencia CA 91355

DAVISON, HELEN IRENE, educator, counselor; b. Oskaloosa, Iowa, Dec. 19, 1926; d. Grover C. and Beulah (Williams) Hawk; m. Walter Francis Davison, June 20, 1953 (div.); 1 child, Linda Ellen. BS in Zoology, Iowa State U., 1948; MS in Biol. Sci., U. Chgo., 1951; MA in Ednl. Psychology and Counseling, Calif. State U., Northridge, 1985. Med. rsch. technician U. Chgo. Med. Sch., 1951-53; tchr. sci. Lane High Sch., Charlottesville, Va., 1953-55; med. rsch. asst. U. Va. Med. Sch., Charlottesville, 1955-56, U. Mich., Ann Arbor, 1956-60; tchr. sci. Monroe High Sch., Sepulveda, Calif., 1966—, chmn. sci. dept., 1990-91; rsch. technician Los Alamos Sci. Labs., summer 1954; part-time counselor psychotherapy Forte Found., Encino, Calif., 1987-92, Tarzana, Calif., 1993—. V.p. San Fernando Valley chpt. Am. Field Svc., 1980-81; vol. counselor Planned Parenthood Am., L.A., 1982-88. NSF fellow, 1985-86. Mem. Calif. Tchrs. Assn., Calif. Assn. Marriage and Family Therapists, Iowa Acad. Sci. (assoc.), AAUW. Home: 17425 Vintage St Northridge CA 91325-1538 Office: James Monroe High Sch 9229 Haskell Ave Sepulveda CA 91343-3199

DAVY, WOODS, sculptor; b. Washington, Oct. 6, 1949; s. Walter Woodward and Barbara (Barley) D.; m. Kathleen Dantini, Nov. 14, 1985; children: Doniella, Veronica. BFA, U. N.C., 1972; MFA, U. Ill., 1975. represented in permanent collections at L.A. County Mus. Art, LaJolla Mus. Art, Palm Springs Desert Mus., Laguna Beach Mus. Art, Calif. State U.-Long Beach, Fed. Res. Bank San Francisco, Tishman West Inc., L.A., United Bank, Houston, Met Life, L.A.; large-scale outdoor sculpture commns. include W.O.D.O.C., Beverly Hills, 1990, U. So. Calif., L.A., 1988, Cranston Securities, Washington, 1987, IBM, Gaithersburg, Md., 1987, Edward J. DeBartolo Corp., Palm Springs, Calif., 1986, Sterling Drug Co., Collegeville, Pa., 1992, Xerox Corp., N.Y.C., 1992;. one man shows at Works Gallery, Long Beach, Calif., 1990, Thomas Babeor Gallery, LaJolla, 1989, Tortue Gallery, Santa Monica, 1987, 85, McIntosh/Drysdale Gallery, Washington, 1984, 85, 86, Hunsaker/Schlesinger & Assocs., 1983, Security Pacific Plaza, 1980; exhibited group shows at Works Gallery, 1989, Tortue Gallery, 1986, 87, McIntosh/Drysdale Gallery, 1986, Otis Art Inst., L.A., 1984, Cirrus Gallery, L.A., 1984, Roy Boyd Gallery, Chgo., L.A., 1984, Koplin Gallery, L.A., Babeor Gallery, 1983. Named Morehead scholar U. N.C. Home and studio: 562 San Juan Ave Venice CA 90291

DAWDY, DORIS OSTRANDER, writer; d. Archie and Lydia (Matz) Ostrander; m. David R. Dawdy, Feb. 21, 1951; 1 child, Barbara Dahl. Student music, MacPhail Sch. Music, Mpls. cons. in field of writing. Composer: I Keep Telling Myself, 1947; author: Artists of the American West, vols. I, II, III, reprinted 1987, Congress in its Wisdom: The Bureau of Reclamation and the Public Interest, 1989, George Montague Wheeler: The Man and the Myth, 1993; editor: A Voice in Her Tribe, 1980, 3d edit. 1984, The Wyant Diary/An Artist with the Wheeler Survey, 1980, others. Mem. Western History Assn., The Westerners, Mus. Soc. San Francisco.

DAWES, DOUGLAS CHARLES, military officer; b. Detroit, Nov. 24, 1952; s. Carl Joseph and Margaret Elisabeth (Ingalls) D.; m. Belle Ann Black, May 22, 1978 (div. Feb. 1986); m. Theresa Neel, June 9, 1990. BBA in Mgmt., Loyola U., New Orleans, 1974; grad. with honors, Command and Gen. Staff Coll., 1987; MA in Procurement and Acquisition Mgmt., Webster U., St. Louis, 1990. Field artillery officer U.S. Army, various locations, 1974-80; asst. fin. officer U.S. Army, Ft. Sill, Okla., 1980-82; deputy fin. and acctg. officer U.S. Army, Fed. Republic of Germany, 1982-86, Ft. Carson, Colo., 1986-87; comdr. and fin. officer U.S. Army, Ft. Carson, 1987-88, budget officer, asst. div. comptr., 1988-90, div. comptr., 1990-91; chief joint pay operation Joint Svc. Software, Def. Fin. and Acctg. Svc., Denver, 1991—. Vol., water safety instr. trainer, life guard instr.-trainer ARC; vol. chmn. health and safety com. Ft. Carson sta. ARC. Mem. Blazers Ski Club (treas. 1988-90), Pikes Peak Road Runners Club, Delta Sigma Pi (life, chancellor Delta Nu chpt. 1973, 1st v.p. 1974). Republican. Home: 17523 E Caspian Pl Aurora CO 80013-4172 Office: DFAS-DE Denver CO 80279-8000

DAWSON, DOUG, artist, educator; b. Oak Park, Ill., Aug. 23, 1944; s. Joseph P. and Sara (Dove) D.; m. Susanne Lyall Kemper, Nov. 1965; children: Nathan, Jenny. BS, Macalester Coll., St. Paul, 1966; postgrad., Drake U., Des Moines, 1969. Tchr. Denver pub. schs., 1969-75; art instr. Colo. Inst. Art, Denver, 1978—, Denver Art Students League, 1986—; profl. artist Wheat Ridge, Colo., 1975—; instr. workshop Acad. Art/Hatterman Inst. Art, Suriname, S.Am., 1989, Mus. Don Quixote, Guanajuato, Mex., 1990; instr. Axton Inst., So. Ill. U., Carbondale, 1990. One man show at Frye Mus., Seattle, 1989, Saks Gallery, Denver, Ventana Gallery, Santa Fe, 1992, Hensley Gallery of S.W., Taos, N.Mex., Cacciola Gallery, N.Y.C.; author: Capturing Light and Color With Pastel, 1991. Founding bd. dirs. Denver Art Students League, 1986-89. Pastel Soc. Am. (award 1990), Am. Watercolor Soc., Pastel Soc. of S.W. (Roe award 1982), Knickerbocker Artists. Home and Studio: 8622 W 44th Pl Wheat Ridge CO 80033

DAWSON, FRANCES EMILY, nurse, poetess; b. Augsburg, Fed. Republic Germany, Dec. 7, 1952; d. Emmett C. Jr. and B. Louise (Boddie) D. BS in Nursing, Pa. State U., 1974. RN, D.C. Staff nurse Howard U. Med. Ctr., Washington, 1974-75, charge nurse, 1975-77. Author: Live for Today, 1986, With You In Mind, 1987, Reflections, 1988. Active Disabled Resource Ctr., Lupus Found. Am., Calif. Assn. Physically Handicapped. Recipient Golden Poetry award, 1985, 86, 87, 88, 89, 90, 91, 92, Excellence in Lit. award Pinewood Poetry, 1987, 88, 89. Mem. Walt Whitman Guild, Broadcast Music Inc., Pa. State U. Alumni Assn. Democrat. Baptist. Home: 6477 Atlantic Ave Apt 308S Long Beach CA 90805-2391

DAWSON, GILBERT EDWARD, II, systems engineer; b. New Orleans, July 15, 1945; s. Gilbert Edward and Helen Mabel (Fisher) D. BA, Rice U., 1968; MS in Computer Sci., U. So. Calif., 1973. Sr. systems analyst Telos Computing, Santa Monica, Calif., 1974-78, mktg. mgr., 1978-80; cognizant design engr. Jet Propulsion Lab., Pasadena, Calif., 1980-85; telemetry systems supr. Jet Propulsion Lab., Pasadena, 1985-87, sr. systems engr., 1987—. Sec. Great Am. Yankee Freedom Band, West Hollywood, Calif., 1980. Capt. USAF, 1968-72. Democrat. Home: 3828 Toland Way Los Angeles CA 90065 Office: Jet Propulsion Lab 4800 Oak Grove Dr Pasadena CA 91109

DAWSON, JOHN ALAN, artist; b. Joliet, Ill., Sept. 12, 1946; s. Thomas Allan and Margaret C. (McRoberts) D.; m. Linda Kay Williams, June 2, 1947 (div. 1989); m. Shirley Ann Bader, Mar. 1993. BFA, No. Ill. U., 1969; MFA, Ariz. State U., 1973. works in permanent collections at Western N.Mex. U., Ariz. State U., El Paso Mus. Art, Phoenix Art Mus., Scottsdale Ctr. for the Arts, Okla. Art Ctr., Ark. Art Center, Little Rock, U. P.R., Sheldon Meml. Art Gallery, Lincoln, Nebr., Ulrich Mus. Art, Wichita, Kans., Tucson Mus. Art, others. One man shows at Meml. Union Gallery, Tempe, Ariz., 1973, Del Mar Coll., 1974, Elaine Horwitch Gallery, Scottsdale, 1975, 76, 78, 80, 82, 84, Segal Gallery, N.Y.C., 1986, Ratliff-Williams Gallery, Sedona, Ariz., 1989, 91, 92, Benjamin Mangel Gallery, Phila., 1982, 85, 90, C.G. Rein Gallery, Santa Fe. 1988, 89, 90, many others; group shows include McCray Gallery, N.Mex., 1974, Phoenix Art Mus., 1975, Huntsville (Ala.) Mus. Art, 1981, Fine Arts Ctr. Tempe, 1984, others. Democrat. Home and Office: 10246 E Brown Rd Mesa AZ 85207-4516

DAWSON, LAWRENCE, plastics manufacturing company executive; b. Akron, Ohio, June 9, 1953; s. John James and Dorothy Ana (Sokol) D.; m. Kathleen Ann Rett, Apr. 17, 1982; 1 child, Jonathan. BS in Math., U.S. Naval Acad., Annapolis, Md., 1975; M Nuclear Engring., Postgrad. Naval Sch., Idaho Falls, Idaho, 1977; postgrad., Pepperdine U., Irvine, Calif., 1990—. Supr. mfg. Am. McGaw of Am. Hosp. Supply Corp., Milledgeville, Ga., 1980-82; supt. plastic processing Kendall McGaw, Irvine, Calif., 1982-85, dir. purchasing, 1985-88; plant mgr. Continental Plastic Containers of Continental Can, Santa Ana, Calif., 1989-90; v.p. ops. Plaxicon Co., Rancho Cucamonga, Calif., 1990—. Treas. Homeowners Assn., Laguna Niguel,

Calif., 1989—. Lt. USN, 1975-80. Office: Plaxicon Co 10660 Acacia St Rancho Cucamonga CA

DAWSON, LELAND BRADLEY, dentist; b. Princeton, Ill., Jan. 30, 1950; s. Harold Bradley and Frances Emilia (Strandholm) D.; m. Debra Hjort. BA, Pacific Luth. U., 1972; DDS, U. Ill., Chgo., 1976. Dentist Group Health Dental, Burien, Wash., 1976-78; pvt. practice dentistry Kent, Wash., 1978—; clin. instr. dental asst. program Highline Community Coll., Kent, 1978-85. Deacon Kent Covenant Ch., 1983-89. Mem. ADA, Pacific Luth. U. Alumni Assn., Seattle-King County Dental Soc., Q Club of Pacific Luth. U. Mem. Evang. Covenant. Home: 14224 SE 270th Pl Kent WA 98042-8001 Office: 13210 SE 240th St Ste 1B Kent WA 98042-5182

DAWSON, MARK H., university administrator. Chancellor U. Nev. system, 1987—. Office: U Nev 2601 Enterprise Rd Reno NV 89512-1608*

DAWSON, MARTHA MORGAN, minister, writer; b. Anderson, Ind., Aug. 30, 1908; d. Earl R. and Elena (Hill) Morgan. Student, Colo. U.; D. in Div. Sci. (hon.), Brooks Divinity Coll., 1986. Ordained to ministry, 1982. Sales profl., owner Denver, 1959-68; copywriter Maginot Advt. Co., Denver, 1968-71; travel host Middle East, 1971-84; instr. Brooks Divine Sci. Coll., 1979-91. Columnist: Aspire, 1978-81; contbr. articles, stories, poems to religious and gen. publs. Mem. Colo. Poetry Soc. (pres. 1977-79), Altrusa, Denver Woman's Press Club (pres. 1973-74).

DAWSON, MELISSA JANE, business manager; b. Waltham, Mass., Apr. 2, 1963; d. John Richard and Rebecca Anne (Varney) D. AAS, Edmonds C.C., Lynnwood, Wash., 1986; BS, Seattle Pacific U., 1987. Acctg. clk. I Shoreline Savings Bank, Seattle, 1981-82; asst. bookkeeper Sleep-Aire Co., Seattle, 1982-83; editorial sec. Hundman Publishing, Edmonds, 1983-84; exec. asst. Actionline, Inc., Seattle, 1985-86; bookkeeper Kelly Svcs., Inc., Seattle, 1986-87; lead bookkeeper Picture Source, Inc., Seattle, 1987-89; bus. mgr. The Tacher Co., Inc., Seattle, 1989—; cons. for events All the Arrangements, Seattle, 1989—. Rep. campaign worker, Seattle, 1980—; advisor, role model Big Sisters of King County, Seattle, 1988—; vol. Seattle Commons Project, 1992. Mem. Am. Inst. of Profl. Bookkeepers. Episcopalian. Office: The Tacher Co 211 Sixth Ave N Ste 200 Seattle WA 98109

DAWSON, THERESA MARIE, speech pathologist; b. Lexington, Ky., Feb. 28, 1959; d. P.V. and Phoebe (McCabe) Tanedo; m. Robert C. Dawson, July 5, 1985. BS, U. Cin., 1981; MS, Vanderbilt U., 1983. Cert. ins. rehab. specialist, 1990. Speech/lang. pathologist Rancho Los Amigos Med. Ctr., Downey, Calif., 1984-86; program case mgr. Alamitos-Belmont Hosp., Long Beach, Calif., 1986-88, NeuroCare, Pasadena, Calif., 1988-90; ind. contractor case mgmt. and speech pathology L.A., 1990—; seminar chair 5th Ann. Transitional Living Conf., Arrowhead, Calif., 1989; case mgr. LINC, Pasadena, Calif., 1990—; lectr. and presenter in field; profl. adv. bd. So. Calif. Head Injury Found., 1988-90; symposium chair So. Calif. Head Injury Found., 1991. Recipient South Bay Community Achievement award, 1992. Mem. Am. Speech Lang. Hearing Assn., Nat. Head Injury Found., Case Mgmt. Soc. Am. (co-chmn. ann. conf. 1992, 93, bd. dirs. 1992—, So. Calif. chpt. bd. dirs. 1991-93), Rehab. Nurses Soc., Ind. Case Mgmt. Assn., Panhellenic Assn., Alpha Chi Omega (advisor, UCLA chpt. bd. dirs. 1989—, v.p. alumni chpt. 1989-93).

DAY, ANN, state legislator; b. EL Paso, Tex.. Former tchr., counselor; mem. Ariz. Senate. Republican. Home: Box 64276 Tucson AZ 85726 Office: Arizona State Senate 5115 N Campana Circle Tucson AZ 85718

DAY, ARTHUR GROVE, author, educator; b. Phila., Apr. 29, 1904; s. Arthur Sinclair and Clara T. (Hogeland) D.; m. Virginia Teresa Molina, July 2, 1928. A.B. in English, Stanford U., 1926, M.A., 1942, Ph.D., 1944. Mem. Faculty Tchrs. Coll., 1926-27; Mem. Faculty Stanford U., 1932-36, asst. dir. engring., sci. and mgmt. war tng., 1943-44; mem. faculty U. Hawaii, 1944-69, sr. prof. English, 1961-69, prof. emeritus, 1969—, chmn. dept., 1948-53; propr. White Knight Press, Honolulu, 1946-90; ret., 1990; chmn. pub. com. 10th Pacific Sci. Congress, 1961; Fulbright sr. research fellow, Australia, 1955; Smith-Mundt vis. prof. Am. studies U. Barcelona, Spain, 1957-58; Fulbright vis. prof. Am. studies U. Madrid, 1961-62. Author: (with F.J. Buenzle) Bluejacket, 1936, 2d edit., 1986, Coronado's Quest: The Discovery of the Southwestern States, 1940, The Sky Clears: Poetry of the American Indians, 1951, (with James A. Michener) Rascals in Paradise, 1957, Hawaii and Its People, 3d edit, 1968, Hawaii, Fiftieth Star, 1960, 69, The Story of Australia, 1960, (with R.S. Kuykendall) Hawaii, A History, 2d edit, 1961, They Peopled the Pacific, 1964, James A. Michener, 1964, 77, Louis Becke, 1966, Explorers of the Pacific, 1967, Coronado and the Discovery of the Southwest, 1967, Pirates of the Pacific, 1967, Adventurers of the Pacific, 1969, Jack London in the South Seas, 1971, Pacific Islands Literature, One Hundred Basic Books, 1972, (with Edgar C. Knowlton) V. Blasco Ibáñez, 1972, Robert D. FitzGerald, 1973, Eleanor Dark, 1976, Books About Hawaii, 1977, Captain Cook and Hawaii, 1977, (with Amos P. Leib) Hawaiian Legends in English, 1979, History Makers of Hawaii: A Biographical Dictionary, 1984, Mad About Islands: Novelists of a Vanished Pacific, 1987, Hawaii and Points South: True Pacific Tales, 1992; editor: (in Spanish) Despatches from Mexico by Fernando Cortes, 1935; (with Carl Stroven) The Spell of the Pacific: An Anthology of Its Literature, 1949, (with W.F. Bauer) The Greatest American Short Stories, 1953, (with Carl Stroven) A Hawaiian Reader, 1959, (with Carl Stroven) Best South Sea Stories, 1964, Stories of Hawaii (Jack London), 1965, Mark Twain's Letters from Hawaii, 1966, 75, True Tales of the South Seas, 1966, (with Virginia M. Day) The Spanish in Sydney, 1793, 1967, South Sea Supercargo (Louis Becke), 1967, (with Carl Stroven) The Spell of Hawaii, 1968, Melville's South Seas, 1970, The Art of Narration: The Short Story, 1971, The Art of Narration; The Novella, 1971, Robert Louis Stevenson's Travels in Hawaii, 1973, Modern Australian Prose, 1901-1975, 1980; (with Bacil F. Kirtley) Horror in Paradise, 1986, The Lure of Tahiti, 1986; Great California Stories, 1991, Hawaii and Points South, 1992; editor in chief: Pacific Science, 1947-49. Recipient Hawaii State award lit., 1979. Mem. MLA, Authors Guild, Adventurers Club (Honolulu), Phi Beta Kappa. Club: Adventurers (Honolulu). Home: 1434 Punahou St Apt 1223 Honolulu HI 96822-4748 Office: care The Univ Press of Hawaii 2840 Kolowalu St Honolulu HI 96822-1830

DAY, DAVID JOHN, communications executive; b. Waterloo, Lancs, Great Britain, May 10, 1932; came to U.S. 1970; s. Joseph Thomas and Lady Violet Alberta (Howe) D.; m. Monica Margery Banks, 1965; children: Fiona, Victoria, Margery. MCh, Manchester (Eng.) U. Med. cons. Lancashire, Cumberland, Barrow County Couns., Eng.; founder Internat. Facsimile Assn., Lake Havasu City, Ariz., 1986. Author: Facsimile Facts and Figures, 1990, Facsimile Corporate Report, 1992, Just The Fax... Charts and Analysis, The PC Fax Report, 1992. Lt. RAF, 1951-53. Recipient Paul Ziller trophy, French Alpine, 1962. Office: Internat Facsimile Assn 4023 Lakeview Rd Lake Havasu City AZ 86403-4517

DAY, DENNIS GENE, communications educator; b. Gary, Ind., Oct. 14, 1936; s. Dennis Manley and Irene Ellen (Johnson) D.; m. Priscilla Dean Guezec, 1958; children: Dennis Emil, Michael Alan. AA, Bakersfield (Calif.) Coll., 1956; BA, Coll. of the Pacific, 1958; MA, U. Ill., 1960, PhD, 1961. Prof. communications San Diego State U., 1961-63, U. Wis., Madison, 1963-66, San Francisco State U., 1966-91; prof. emeritus San Diego State U., 1991—; parliamentarian acad. senate, faculty San Francisco State U., 1978-91; cons. in field. Contbr. articles to profl. jours. U. Ill. grad. fellow, 1958-60, Inst. Communications Rsch. fellow, 1960-61; recipient Meritorious Performance and Profl. Promise award, San Francisco State U., 1990. Mem. Kenneth Burke Soc. (founder 1990, pres. Western chpt. 1990—, planning com. 1990—), Western Speech Communication Assn., Speech Communication Assn. Home: 3530 23rd St San Francisco CA 94110-3011 Office: San Francisco State Univ 1600 Holloway Ave San Francisco CA 94132-1722

DAY, JANICE ELDREDGE, cosmetic company executive; b. New Bedford, Mass., Sept. 26, 1919; d. Wendell Tripp and Lucy Forbush (Houghton) Eldredge; m. Frank Perrett, Apr. 22, 1949; 1 child, Janna. BA in English, Middlebury Coll., 1941, LittD (hon.), 1990. Publicity writer A.H. Handley, Boston, 1941-42; sec. media Ladies Home Jour., Boston, 1942-45, McCann, Erickson, N.Y.C., 1945; sec. Cambridge U. Press, MacMillan Co., N.Y.C., 1945-46; exec. sec. Fort Monroe, Va., 1946-47, Stone & Webster Engring., 1947-49; mgr. sales Collier Co., San Francisco, 1947-48; unit mgr. Stanley Home Products, L.A., 1949-51; dist. sales mgr. Beauty Creators Cosmetics, L.A., 1951-56; co-founder, v.p. sales and mktg. Jafra Cosmetics, Inc., Malibu, Calif., 1956-76, chmn. bd., 1976-87, pres. Jan and Frank Day Scholarship Fund, 1978. Recipient Alumni Achievement award Middlebury Coll., 1983. Mem. Direct Selling Assn. (dir.), DAR. Republican. Episcopalian. Office: Jafra Cosmetics Inc Westlake Village CA 91361

DAY, JOHN DENTON, retired company executive, cattle and horse rancher, trainer; b. Salt Lake City, Jan. 20, 1942; s. George W. and Grace (Denton) Jenkins; m. Susan Hansen, June 20, 1971; children: Tammy Denton Wadsworth, Jeanett B, Lloyd. Student, U. Utah, 1964-65; BA in Econs. and Bus. Adminstrn. with high honors, Westminster Coll., 1971. Riding instr., wrangler Uinta wilderness area U-Ranch, Neola, Utah, 1955-58; stock handler, driver, ruffstock rider Earl Hutchinson Rodeo Contractor, Idaho, 1959; YMCA Camp Rodger U-Ranch, Kamas, Utah; with Mil. Data Cons., Inc., L.A., 1961-62, Carlseon Credit Corp., Salt Lake City, 1962-65; sales mgr. sporting goods Western Enterprises, Salt Lake City, 1965-69; founder Rockin d Ranch, Millcreek, Utah, 1969; Western rep. PBR Co., Cleve., 1969-71; dist. sales rep. Crown Zellerbach Corp., Seattle and L.A., 1971-73; pres., founder Dapco paper, chem., instl. food and janitorial supplies, Salt Lake City, 1973-79; owner, founder, pres. John D. Day, mfrs. reps., 1972—; dist. sales mgr. Surfonics Engrs., Inc., Woods Cross, Utah, 1976-78, Garland Co., Cleve., 1978-81; rancher Heber, Utah, 1976-90, horse tng. facility and ranch, Temecula, Calif., 1984-90, St. George, Utah, 1989—; sec. bd. Acquadyne, 1974, 75. Contbr. articles to jours. Group chmn. Tele-Dex fund raising project Westminster Coll. With AUS, 1963-64. Recipient grand nat. award Internat. Custom Car Show, San Diego, 1962, Key to City, Louisville, 1964, Champion Bareback Riding award, 1957, Dally team roping heading and heeling champion, 1982. Mem. Internat. Show Car Assn. (co-chmn. 1978-79), Am. Quarter Horse Assn. (high point reining champion 1981), Intermountain Quarter Horse Assn. (sr. reining champion 1981, champion AMAT reining 1979-81), Utah Quarter Horse Assn. (trained working cowhorse and rider champion 1982, champion AMAT reining 1979, 80, AMAT barrel racing 1980, bd. dir. 1992—), Profl. Cowhorseman's Assn. (world champion team roping, heeling 1986, 88, high point rider 1985, world champion stock horse rider 1985-86, 88, world champion working cowhorse 1985, PCA finals open cutting champion, 1985-88, PCA finals 1500 novice champion 1987, PCA finals all-around champion 1985-88, inducted into Hall of Fame 1988, first on record registered Tex. longhorn cutting contest, open champion, PCA founder, editor newsletter 1985-89, pres. 1984-88), World Rodeo Assn. Profls. (v.p. Western territory 1989—). Home and Office: PO Box 55 Saint George UT 84771-0055 also: 1876 E 2450 S Daylark Ln Saint George UT 84771

DAY, JOSEPH DENNIS, librarian; b. Dayton, Ohio, Sept. 23, 1942; s. John Albert and Ruth (Pearson) D.; m. Mary Louise Herbert, Oct. 10, 1964; children: Cindy, Jeff, Chris, Steve, Tom. B.A., U. Dayton, 1966; M.L.S., Western Mich. U., 1967; degree in Libr. Mgmt., U. Miami, 1975. Community libr. Dayton-Montgomery Pub. Libr., 1967-70; dir. Troy-Miami County Pub. Libr., Troy, Ohio, 1970-76, Salt Lake City Pub. Libr., 1976—; chmn. Miami Valley Library Orgn., 1971-73; pres. Ohio Library Assn., 1975-76; project dir. planning and constrn. first solar powered library in world, 1973-76; exec. devel. program Miami, Ohio, libr., 1975. Pres. Troy Area Arts Coun., 1973-74; v.p. SLC Salvation Army Bd., 1986-91. Recipient Disting. Community Service award Troy C. of C., 1974; John Cotton Dana award, 1975, 77, 83, 85; AIA-ALA architecture award, 1977. Mem. ALA (chmn. intellectual freedom com. 1981-84, exec. bd. 1987-93, rep. to Internat. Fedn. Libr. Assn. 1989-97), Utah Libr. Assn. (pres. 1979-80, Disting. Svc. award 1985), Am. Soc. Pub. Adminstrn., Mountain Plains Libr. Assn. (pres. 1990-91), Freedom to Read Found. (treas. 1984-86, pres. 1986-87), Kiwanis Club (pres. Troyp 1975-76, Disting. Svc. award Troy, 1973, pres. Salt Lake-Foothill 1979-80). Address: Salt Lake City Pub Libr 209 E 5th St S Salt Lake City UT 84111

DAY, JULIAN CHARLES, management consultant; b. Scarborough, Eng., May 14, 1952; came to U.S., 1987; s. Stephen Bradshaw and Gwendoline (Adams) D.; m. Kathleen Lynn Healy. BA, Oxford (Eng.) U., 1974, MA, 1979; MSc in Bus. Adminstrn., London U., 1979. Mgr. new bus. deve. Smiths Industries, London, 1974-77; cons. McKinsey & Co., London, 1980-85; v.p. Chase Manhattan Bank, London, 1985-87; ind. mgmt. cons. San Francisco, 1988—. Office: 369 Pine St Ste 700 San Francisco CA 94010

DAY, KEVIN ROSS, pomologist, researcher, consultant, farmer; b. Dinuba, Calif., Aug. 2, 1960; s. Ronald Keith and Dolores Ione (Unruh) D. AA, Reedley (Calif.) Coll., 1980; BS magna cum laude, Calif. State U., Fresno, 1983, MS with honors, 1985. Cert. tchr., Calif. Lectr. Calif. State U., Fresno, 1984-85; postgrad. rschr. U. Calif., Davis, 1985-88, rsch. assoc., 1988-91; farm advisor U. Calif., Berkeley, 1991—; mng. ptnr. Day Orchards, Dinuba, 1981—; cons. K.R. Day Hort. Cons., Dinuba, 1988—. Editor, author newsletter Orchard Notes, 1991—; contbr. chpt. to book, articles to profl. jours. Announcer Dinuba High Sch. Football and Baseball, 1988—. Calif. Agrl. Tech. Inst. fellow, 1984. Mem. Am. Soc. for Hort. Sci., Am. Pomological Soc., Dinuba Lions Club (bd. dirs. 1992—), Phi Kappa Phi. Republican. Presbyterian. Home: 41139 Road 70 Dinuba CA 93618 Office: U Calf Agrl Bldg Ag Bldg County Civic Ctr Visalia CA 93291-4584

DAY, L. B., management consultant; b. Walla Walla, Wash., Sept. 16, 1944; s. Frank Edmond and Geraldine Eloise (Binning) D. BS, Portland State Coll., 1966; MBA, George Washington U., 1971. Design mktg. cons. Leadership Resources Inc., Washington, 1971-76; faculty mem. USDA Grad. Sch. of Spl. Programs, Washington, 1971-76; mgr. Office of Employee Devel. Oreg. Dept. Transp., Salem, 1972-75; prin. Day-Henry Assoc. Inc., Portland, Oreg., 1975-78, Day-Floren Assocs. Inc., Portland, Oreg., 1978—; cons. Allergan (U.S., Italy), Am. Bankers Assn., Arthur Andersen & Co., AMD, John Fluke Mfg. Co. (U.S. and Holland), Intel Corp. (U.S., Eng., France, Malaysia, P.R.), Sequent Computer Systems, Inc., Vitesse Semiconductor, Sun Microsystems, VLSI Tech., Inc., U.S. Nat. Bank Oreg., U.S. Army Corps Engrs., others; faculty Am. Bankers Assn., Bank Trainers Sch., 1981-84, Grad. Personnel Sch., 1982; adj. prof. Willamette U. Grad. Sch. Adminstrn., Salem, 1978. Author: The Supervisory Training Program, 1977; co-author: Preparing for Supervision, 1979, Performance Management, 1981, Team-Oriented Management, 1989; contbr. articles to profl. jours. With U.S. Army, 1967-70. Scottish Rite fellow George Washington U., 1970. Mem. Am. Soc. Tng. and Devel. (chmn. Transp. Spl. Interest Group 1977, cert. of appreciation). Office: Day-Floren Assocs Inc 806 SW Broadway Fl 11 Portland OR 97205-3333

DAY, LUCILLE ELIZABETH, educator, author; b. Oakland, Calif., Dec. 5, 1947; d. Richard Allen and Evelyn Marietta (Hazard) Lang; m. Frank Lawrence Day, Nov. 6, 1965; 1 child, Liana Sherrine; m. 2nd, Theodore Herman Fleischman, June 23, 1974; 1 child, Tamarind Channah. AB, U. Calif., Berkeley, 1971, MA, 1973, PhD, 1979. Teaching asst. U. Calif., Berkeley, 1971-72, 75-76, research asst., 1975, 77-78; tchr. sci. Magic Mountain Sch., Berkeley, 1977; specialist math. and sci. Novato (Calif.) Unified Sch. Dist., 1979-81; instr. sci. Project Bridge, Laney Coll., Oakland, Calif., 1984-86; sci. writer and mgr. precollege edn. programs, Lawrence Berkeley (Calif.) Lab., 1986-90, life scis. staff coord., 1990-92, mgr. Hall of Health, Berkeley, Calif., 1992—. Author numerous poems, articles and book reviews; author: (with Joan Skolnick and Carol Langbort) How to Encourage Girls in Math and Science: Strategies for Parents and Educators, 1982; Self-Portrait with Hand Microscope (poetry collection), 1982. NSF Grad. fellow, 1972-75; recipient Joseph Henry Jackson award in lit. San Francisco Found., 1982. Mem. AAAS, No. Calif. Sci. Writers Assn., Nat. Assn. Sci. Writers, Women in Communications, Phi Beta Kappa, Iota Sigma Pi. Home: 1057 Walker Ave Oakland CA 94610-1511 Office: Hall of Health 2230 Shattuck Ave Berkeley CA 94704

DAY, MARILYN LEE, nutritionist; b. Denver, Mar. 16, 1949; d. George Miller Day and Jeanette (Hufman) Day Stanton. BS in Pub. Health, UCLA, 1985; MS in Human Nutrition, Colo. State U., 1987. Registered dietitian, Colo. Grad. teaching asst. Colo. State U., Ft. Collins, 1985-87; nutritionist Denver Sporting Club, Englewood, Colo., 1987-88; nutritionist drs. office Englewood, 1988; co-dir. pediatric preventive cardiology, nutritionist Children's Hosp., Denver, 1988—; nutritionist Pulse Aerobics & Fitness Ctr., Ft. Collins, 1986-87, Health Mark Ctrs., Inc., Englewood, 1987. Co-author: Popular Diets, 1987; compiler, author Denver Metro Area Referrl Directory, 1988. Bd. dirs. Denver-Met. chpt. Am. Heart Assn., 1990—, slim-for-life instr., 1981, chmn., 1989-92; mem. health and safety com. Boy Scouts Am., Denver, 1989—. Scholar U. Calif., 1981-82, Colo. Dietetic Assn., 1987. Mem. Am. Dietetic Assn. (corp. scholar 1985, 86), Sports and Cardiovascular Nutritionists, Pediatric Practice Group, Denver Dietetic Assn. Home: 6710 Montview Blvd Denver CO 80207-4013 Office: Childrens Hosp Pediatrics 1056 E 19th Ave Denver CO 80218-1088

DAY, PIETRINA ANN, therapist; b. Milw., Oct. 29, 1943; d. Peter Bernard and Bernadina (Campanelli) Sara; m. Steven Homer Day, Sept. 13, 1971 (div. Feb. 1983); 1 child, Sara Lynn Hunt; m. Barry Carr Sanborn, Feb. 14, 1987. BS, Nat. U., 1983, M of Counseling Psychology, 1984. Intern Vol. of Am., San Diego, 1984, Dr. Anne Evans, San Diego, 1984-89; alcoholism specialist The Landing Zone Alcohol Recovery Ctr., San Diego, 1985-88; pvt. practice marriage and family therapy San Diego, 1989—. Mem. Calif. Assn. Marriage and Family Therapists, Nat. U. Alumni Assn. (life), Vietnam Vets. of S.D. (assoc., appreciation award 1988). Democrat. Roman Catholic. Office: 4024 Ibis St Ste B San Diego CA 92103

DAY, RICHARD EDWARD, casino executive; b. Bayonne, N.J., Aug. 21, 1960; s. James William and Carol Marie (Sutphen) D. BA in Econs., Rutgers U., 1982. Mktg. clk. Riviera Hotel and Casino, Las Vegas, Nev., 1983-84, casino mktg. analyst, 1984-85, casino ops. asst., 1985-89, dir. casino programs, 1989—. Republican. Home: 2050 S Magic Way Trlr 88 Henderson NV 89015-8640 Office: Riviera Inc 2901 Las Vegas Blvd S Las Vegas NV 89109-1931

DAY, RICHARD SOMERS, author, editorial consultant; b. Chgo., June 14, 1928; s. Milo Frank and Ethel Mae (Somers) D.; m. Lois Patricia Beggs, July 8, 1950; children: Russell Frank, Douglas Matthew, Gail Leslie. Student, Ill. Inst. Tech., 1946, U. Miami, 1947. Promotion writer, editor Portland Cement Assn., Chgo., 1958-62, promotion writer, 1963-66; editor Am. Inst. Laundering, Joliet, Ill., 1962-63; freelance writer, Monee, Ill., 1966-69, Palomar Mountain, Calif., 1969-87; cons. editor home and shop Popular Sci. mag., N.Y.C., 1966-89; editorial cons. St. Remy Press, Montreal, Que., Can., 1987—; pres., exec. producer Vi-Day-O Prodns., Inc., Palomar Mountain, Calif., 1991—. Author numerous home improvement & repair books including: Patios and Decks, 1976, Automechanics, 1982, Do-It-Yourself Plumbing--It's Easy with Genova, 1987, Building Decks, Patios, and Fences, 1992 (Nat. Assn. Home and Workshop Writers Stanley Tools Do-It-Yourself Writing award 1992); editor: (newspaper) Powderlines, 1958; (mag.) Concrete Hwys. and Pub. Improvements, 1958-62, (mag.) Soil-Cement News, 1960-62; (mag.) Fabric Care, 1962-63. Contbr. chpts. to books. Bd. dirs. Land Use Council, San Diego, 1977, Palomar Mountain Planning Orgn., 1984-91. Mem. Nat. Assn. Home and Workshop Writers (mng. editor newsletter 1982—, bd. dirs. 1974—, pres. 1984-85). Home: PO Box 10 Palomar Mountain CA 92060-0010

DAY, ROBERT HUGH, marine ecologist; b. Carrollton, Ohio, June 7, 1952; s. Morris Eugene and Betty Violet (Parsons) D.; m. Karen Anne Stevens Schrader, Apr. 10, 1991; stepchildren: Lloyd, Michael. BA, Antioch Coll., 1974; MS, U. Alaska, 1980, PhD, 1992. Biol. tech. U.S. Fish and Wildlife Svc., Adak, Alaska, 1975-76; teaching asst. U. Alaska, Fairbanks, 1976-79, lab. asst., 1980-83, rsch. asst., 1983-87; ind. cons. Fairbanks, 1987-89; sr. scientist Alaska Biol. Rsch., Inc., Fairbanks, 1989—. Contbr. articles to profl. jours. and books. Named Alfred P. Sloan scholar Alfred P. Sloan Found., Antioch Coll., 1970-74, Angus Gavin fellow Angus Gavin Found., U. Alaska, 1985-86. Mem. Am. Ornithologists' Union (life mem., co-chair annual meeting 1993), Assn. Field Ornithologists (life), British Ornithologists' Union (life), Cooper Ornithol. Soc. (life), Wilson Ornithol. Soc. (life), African Seabird Group, Colonial Waterbird Group, Ornithol. Soc. New Zealand, Pacific Seabird Group, Royal Australian Ornithologists' Union, Soc. Western Field Ornithologists, South African Ornithol. Soc., Sigma Xi (bd. dirs. Alaska chpt. 1988-89). Home: PO Box 81931 Fairbanks AK 99708 Office: Alaska Biol Rsch Inc PO Box 81934 Fairbanks AK 99708

DAY, ROBERT WINSOR, research administrator; b. Framingham, Mass., Oct. 22, 1930; s. Raymond Albert and Mildred (Doty) D.; m. Jane Alice Boynton, Sept. 6, 1957 (div. Sept. 1977); m. Cynthia Taylor, Dec. 16, 1977; children: Christopher, Nathalia. Student, Harvard U., 1949-51; MD, U. Chgo., 1956; MPH, U. Calif., Berkeley, 1958, PhD, 1962. Intern USPHS, Balt., 1956-57; resident U. Calif., Berkeley, 1958-60; research specialist Calif. Dept. Mental Hygiene, 1960-64; asst. prof. sch. medicine UCLA, 1962-64; dep. dir. Calif. Dept. Pub. Health, Berkeley, 1965-67; prof., chmn. dept. health services Sch. Pub. Health and Community Medicine, U. Wash., Seattle, 1968-72, dean, 1972-82, prof., 1982—; dir. Fred Hutchinson Cancer Rsch. Ctr., Seattle, 1981-91, pres., 1991—; mem. Nat. Cancer Adv. Bd., 1992—; cons. in field. Pres. Seattle Planned Parenthood Ctr., 1970-72. Served with USPHS, 1956-57. Fellow Am. Pub. Health Assn., Am. Coll. Preventive Medicine; mem. Am. Soc. Clin. Oncology, Soc. Preventive Oncology, Assn. Schs. Pub. Health (pres. 1981-82), Am. Assn. Cancer Insts. (bd. dirs. 1983-88, v.p. 1984-85, pres. 1985-86, chmn. bd. dirs., 1986-87). Office: Fred Hutchinson Cancer Rsch Ctr LY-301 1124 Columbia St Seattle WA 98104

DAY, THOMAS BRENNOCK, university president; b. N.Y.C., Mar. 7, 1932; s. Frederick and Alice (Brennock) D.; m. Anne Kohlbrenner, Sept. 5, 1953; children: Erica, Monica, Mark, Kevin, Sara, Timothy, Jonathan, Patrick, Adam. B.S., U Notre Dame, 1953; Ph.D., Cornell U., 1957. Prof. U. Md., College Park, 1964-78, vice chancellor for acad. planning and policy, 1970-77, spl. asst. to pres., 1977-78, vice chancellor for acad. affairs Baltimore County, 1977-78; pres. San Diego State U., 1978—; cons. Bendix Corp., IBM Corp., Digital Equipment Corp.; vis. physicist Brookhaven Nat. Lab., 1963; cons. Argonne Nat. Lab., Ill., 1967; vice chair Nat. Sci. Bd.; bd. dirs. Scripps Clinic and Research Found. Contbr. articles to profl. jours. Mem. Am. Phys. Soc., Sigma Xi, Phi Kappa Phi. Republican. Roman Catholic. Lodge: Rotary. Office: San Diego State U Office of Pres San Diego CA 92182-0711 also: NSF Nat Sci Bd 1800 G St NW Washington DC 20550

DAYALA, HAJI FAROOQ, real estate broker; b. Karachi, Pakistan, Dec. 1, 1948; came to U.S., 1969; s. Haji Razzak and Hamida H. (Bai) D.; m. Susanna WK. Cheung, Aug. 25, 1973; children: Sabrina R., Ryan M. BS in Indsl. Engring., Calif. Poly. State U., 1972; M in Sci. and Adminstrn., Calif. State U., Dominguez Hills, 1979. Cert. GRI Calif. Assn. Realtors. Mgr. plant Thomas & Betts Corp., L.A., 1977-82, 84-86; v.p. ops. Prime Cir. Tech., San Jose, Calif., 1982-84; real estate agt. Merrill Lynch Realty, Diamond Bar, Calif., 1987-88; broker, co-owner Realty World-Ampak, Diamond Bar, Calif., 1988-90; real estate broker, assoc. SNS Realtors, Diamond Bar, Calif., 1990-93, The Prudential Calif. Realty, Diamond Bar, Calif., 1993—. Mem. Nat. Notary Assn., Diamond Bar Realtor Bd. Home: 24324 E Knoll Ct Diamond Bar CA 91765-4308 Office: The Prudential Calif Realty 1200 S Diamond Bar CA 91765

DAYDAY, HENRY, mayor. Formerly alderman City of Saskatoon, Sask., elected mayor, 1988. Office: Office of Mayor, City Hall, Saskatoon, SK Canada S7K 0J5*

DAY-GOWDER, PATRICIA JOAN, association executive, consultant; b. Lansing, Mich., Apr. 9, 1936; d. Louis A. and Johanna (Feringa) Whipple; m. Duane Lee Day, Jan. 7, 1961 (div.); children: Kevin Duane, Patricia Kimberley; m. William A. Gowder, Nov. 30, 1986. BA, Mich. State U., 1958; MA, Lindenwood (Mo.) Coll., 1979; postgrad. U. So. Calif., 1982-83. Cert. secondary tchr., Calif. Health edn. asst. YWCA, Rochester, N.Y., 1958-59; tchr. jr. high schs., Flint, Mich., 1959-61; tchr. Brookside Acad., Montclair, N.J., 1963-68; adult program dir. YMCA, Long Beach, Calif., 1968-73; community edn. dir. Paramount (Calif) Unified Sch. Dist., 1973-78; exec. dir. counseling ctr., Arcadia, Calif., 1978-80; sr. citizens program dir. City of Burbank (Calif.), 1981-83; div. dir. Am. Heart Assn., L.A., 1983-87 ; exec. dir. Campfire Orgn., Pasadena, 1987-89; exec. dir. greater L.A. chpt. Nat. Found. of Ileitis and Colitis, 1989-90; mgr. sr. citizens mktg. dept. Meth. Hosp. So. Calif., 1990—; cons. community edn. State Dept. Edn., Fed. Office Community Edn., L.A. County Office Edn. Bd. dirs., v.p. Children's Creative Ctr., Long Beach, Calif., 1969-73, Traveler's Aid Soc., 1969-72; vice-chmn. Cerritos YMCA, 1968-73. Mott Found. fellow, 1977-78. Mem. AAUW, Western Gerontology Assn., Nat. Assn. Female Execs., Calif.

Community Edn. Assn. (sec.-treas., 1974-77), LWV. Democrat. Congregationalist. Avocations: tennis, hiking, bicycling, painting, reading. Home: 170 Oak Forest Circle Glendora CA 91740 Office: Meth Hosp So Calif 300 W Huntington Dr Arcadia CA 91007

DAY-LYON, KAREN, nurse, medical reimbursement consultant; b. Columbus, Ohio, Dec. 1, 1951; d. Walter Hans Jr. and Julia Faye (Andre) Day; m. Thomas Nicholas Lyon, Dec. 9, 1978; children: Heather Deanne, Kristin Alicia, Erin Colleen. ADN, Victor Valley Coll., Victorville, Calif., 1983. RN, Calif. Unit svc. coord. III, UCLA Med. Ctr., 1973-77; nurse II, charge nurse San Bernardino County Med. Ctr., San Bernardino, Calif., 1983-85; coord. quality assurance St. Mary Desert Valley Hosp., Apple Valley, Calif., 1989-91; mng. ptnr., med. reimbursement cons. Lyon Enterprises, Victorville, 1978—. Republican. Mem. Assembly of God. Home and Office: 14253 Brentwood Dr Victorville CA 92392

DAYTON, DOUGLAS EMORY, computer marketing consultant; b. Lakewood, N.J., Sept. 17, 1951; s. Samuel S. and Estelle Dayton. BA, San Diego State U., 1973; postgrad., U. Calif., San Diego, 1974-75, U. Wash., 1976. Mktg. rep. IBM, Seattle, 1981-82; mgr. original equipment mfr. sales and contract support Microsoft Corp., Seattle, 1982-85; founder, pres. Dayton Assocs., Seattle, 1985—, Client-Centered Tng., Inc., Seattle, 1991—. Author: Computer Solutions for Business, 1988; contbr. articles to profl. jours. Mem. Wash. State Software Assn. Office: Dayton Assocs 477 123rd Pl NE Bellevue WA 98005-8419

DE, SUKLA, hazardous materials specialist; b. Calcutta, India; came to U.S., 1972; d. Nirendra K. and Maya (Chakraborty) Majunder; m. Jayanta B. De, June 11, 1968; children: Sona, Shampa. MS in Chemistry, Calif. State U., Hayward, 1985. Mgr. organic chemistry lab. Trace Analysis Lab., Hayward, 1981-85; pub. health chemist County of San Mateo, San Mateo, Calif., 1985-87; hazardous materials specialist Newark (Calif.) Fire Dept., 1987—; sec. Alameda County Hazardous Materials Subcom., Pleasanton, Calif., 1988—. Mem. Am. Chem. Soc., Am. Indsl. Hygiene Assn., No. Calif. Fire Prevention Officers. Office: Newark Fire Dept 37101 Newark Blvd Newark CA 94560

DEACON, ROBERT THOMAS, economics educator; b. Tacoma, Sept. 10, 1944; s. Robert Thomas Sr. and Bernice Evelyn (Anderson) D.; m. Charmien Rae Carrier, Sept. 21, 1965; children: Michael Gregory, Juliet Renee. BA in Econs., U. Wash., 1968, MA in Econs., 1971, PhD in Econs., 1972. Asst. prof. U. Calif., Santa Barbara, 1972-78, assoc. prof., 1978-82, prof., 1982—; vis. assoc. prof. U. Wash., Seattle, 1980-81. Co-author: Taxing Energy, 1990; editor: Forestlands Public and Private, 1985; contbr. articles to profl. jours. Hoover Inst. Nat. fellow Stanford U., 1975-76, Gilbert F. White fellow Resources for the Future, 1989-90. Mem. Am. Econ. Assn., Assn. for Environ. and Resource Economists, Western Econ. Assn., European Assn. Environ. and Resource Economists. Office: U Calif Dept of Economics Santa Barbara CA 93106

DEADRICH, PAUL EDDY, lawyer, real estate broker, retired; b. Lakeport, Calif., Jan. 30, 1925; s. John Adolph and Grace Estelle (Jackson) D.; m. Violet Ann Walls, Oct. 29, 1962 (div. 1982); children: Marjanne Robinson, Nancy Wolfer, Dianne Deadrich-Rogers, Betianne Buck, John Fredrick, Daniel David; m. Irene Eloise Banks, Dec. 11, 1982 (div. 1992); m. Constance Artice Washburn, Sept. 8, 1992. AA, U. Calif., Berkeley, 1946; JD, U. Calif., San Francisco, 1949. Bar: Calif. 1950. Sales assoc. Deadrich Real Estate, San Leandro, Calif., 1947-50; pvt. practice San Leandro, 1950-61; pvt. practice law, real estate and ins. Twain Harte, Calif., 1961-73; pvt. practice Loomis, Calif., 1973-75, Cameron Park, Calif., 1975-78; missionary Apostolic Alliance, Gibi, Liberia, West Africa, 1978-82; pvt. practice law and real estate San Leandro, 1982-92; pvt. practice law Santa Clarita, Calif., 1993—; judge Tuolumne County Justice Ct., Calif., 1964-66; instr. phys. edn., coach Mother Lode Christian Sch., Tuolumne, 1969-73; adminstr., coach, tchr. Loomis Christian Sch., 1974-75. Bd. dirs. Alameda Contra Costa Transit Dist., Oakland, Calif., 1956-61, Calif. Conservatory Theater, 1988-90. Decorated Bronze Star, Purple Heart, Badge of Bastogne. Mem. Gospel Businessmen's Fellowship (pres. San Leandro chpt. 1988-90), Clowns of Am., Internat. Golden Gate Alley #80 and Bay Area Fun Makers (sec. 1987-89), Tuolumne County Bd. Realtors (pres. 1973), Kiwanis, Rotary (chpt. pres. 1966-67), Broadmoor Men's Club (pres. 1958). San Leandro Breakfast Club (pres. 1985-86), Masons, Order Ea. Star. Republican. Home and Office: 26516 Cockleburr Way Santa Clarita CA 91351-2337

DEAL, LYNN EATON HOFFMANN, interior designer; b. Atlantic City, N.J., Nov. 7, 1953; d. Ralph Eaton and Helen P. Hoffmann; m. James A. Deal, Sept. 19, 1981. Diploma Environmental & Interior Design, U. Calif.-Irvine, 1989. Prin. Lynn Deal and Assocs., Newport Beach, Calif., 1982—; adv. bd. U. Calif. Irvine, 1984—; bd. dirs. Am. Soc. Interior Designers, Orange County, Calif., 1988—. chmn. Philhormonic Showcase House, 1992. Mem. Am. Soc. Interior Designers (recipient chpt. award 1991, Pres.'s award, 1992, author introductory video Orange County chpt.), Internat. Furnishings and Design Assn., Interior Educators Coun. Republican. Episcopalian. Home: 218 Via Palermo Newport Beach CA 92663

DEAL, TERRY DEAN, marketing executive; b. Lyons, Kans., Sept. 27, 1948; s. Willis Clifton and Geneva G. (Gamble) D.; m. Diana Kathlene Gerstner, Feb. 14, 1970; 1 child, M. Shane. BS Agricultural Bus., Ft. Hays Kans. State U., 1971. Area sales mgr. Senvita Products Inc., Seneca, Kans., 1971-73, total sales mgr., 1973-74; unit sales mgr. Agri-Distbrs. and Leasing, Abilene, Kans., 1974-75; gen. mgr. Agri-Distbrs. and Leasing, Abilene, 1975-76; terr. mgr. Owatonna (Minn.) Mfg. Co., 1976-84, regional sales mgr., 1984-87; dir. mktg. Impulse Hydraulics Inc., San Diego, 1987-90; product specialist ESCO Corp., Portland, Oreg., 1990—; pres. Agri-Distbrs. and Leasing, 1974-85. Bd. dirs. Persimmon Homeowners Assn., 1989—, Owatonna Swimming Assn., 1985-86; mem. Owatonna Little Theatre, 1984-88. Mem. NRA (presdl. transition com. 1989), Sertoma (bd. dirs. 1982-83), Elks, Tau Kappa Epsilon. Republican. Methodist. Office: ESCO Corp 2141 NW 25th Ave Portland OR 97210-2597

DEAN, BRITTEN, history educator; b. Syracuse, N.Y., May 27, 1935; s. Phillips Vose and Emily Mae (Britten) Dean; children: Dana Adams Dean, Cecilia Gratian Dean; m. Kayoko Ishizaki, Apr. 8, 1977; 1 child, Sophia Emily Dean. BA, Brown U., 1957; MA, Columbia U., 1962, PhD, 1969. Asst. prof. Calif. State U. Stanislaus, Turlock, 1967-70, assoc. prof., 1970-75, prof., 1975—, history dept. chmn., 1976-78, 91—. Author: China and Great Britain, 1974; contbr. articles to profl. jours.; translator: (Chinese fiction) The Piano Tuner, 1989, The Banker, 1992. Fgn. Lang. fellow U.S. Govt., Columbia U., 1961-62, Fulbright fellow U.S. Govt., Republic of China, 1966-67, Rsch. fellow Social Sci. Rsch. Coun., Republic of China, 1972, Profl. fellow Japan Found., 1980-81; sabbatical leave grantee Calif. State U. Stanislaus, 1973, 80-81, 89. Mem. Assn. for Asian Studies, AAUP, NEA, Calif. Faculty Assn. Office: Calif State U 801 W Monte Vista Ave Turlock CA 95382-0299

DEAN, CAROLYNN LESLIE, health science technological administrator; b. Oak Park, Ill., Mar. 30, 1952; d. Robert Lee and Jeane Kathleen (Kenitz) D. Student, U. Hawaii, 1970-73; BS, Solano County Regional, Occupational Program, 1983. Registered vascular technologist, Calif. Cardiopulmonary and multi-phasic technologist Family Doctor Med. Group, Vallejo, Calif., 1976-78; non-invasive vascular technologist Alta Bates Hosp., Berkeley, Calif., 1979-80; cardiovascular technologist Herrick Hosp. Health Ctr., Berkeley, Calif., 1978-81; supr., dir. non-invasive vascular lab. St. Mary's Hosp., San Francisco, 1981--; ptnr. Cardiovascular Lab. Assocs., San Francisco, 1983--; sr. ptnr. Vascular Imaging Svcs., Vallejo, 1983; RVT Children's Hosp., San Francisco, 1988—; cons. in field. Contbr. articles to profl. jours. Mem. Soc. Non-Invasive Vascular Tech., Am. Registry Diagnostic Med. Sonographers, Am. Inst. Ultrasound in Medicine. Home: 113 Compass Ct Vallejo CA 94590-4028 Office: Vascular Lab St Marys Hosp and Health Ctr 450 Stanyan St San Francisco CA 94117-1079

DEAN, MICHAEL ANTHONY, lawyer; b. San Diego, Jan. 16, 1942; s. Roy Otis and Opie (Gray) D.; m. Eula Goossen, Aug. 11, 1962; children: Matthew, Taggart. AB, San Jose (Calif.) State Coll., 1964; JD, U. Calif., Berkeley, 1967. Bar: Calif. 1967, U.S. Dist. Ct. (9th dist.), U.S. Ct. Appeals (9th cir.). Sr. ptnr. Wendel, Rosen, Black, Dean and Levitan, Oakland, Calif., 1967-91, mng. exec. ptnr., 1991—; lectr. Calif. Continuing Edn. of Bar, Berkeley, 1978—. Bd. dirs. Oakland Conv. Ctr., 1987—, Oakland Community Devel. Adv. Commn., 1980-87; bd. dirs. Oakland Symphony, 1988-90, pres. 1990; bd. dirs. Lincoln Child Ctr., Oakland, 1987-90, pres., 1990—. Mem. Calif. State Bar Assn., Internat. Coun. Shopping Ctrs., Nat. Assn. Indsl. Office Parks, Internat. Assn. Corp. Real Estate Execs., Calif. Bus. Properties Assn. (legal affairs com. 1988), Lakeview Club (bd. govs.). Democrat. Home: 239 Bannister Ct Alameda CA 94501-7739 Office: Wendel Rosen Black et al 1221 Broadway Ste 20 Oakland CA 94612-1836

DEAN, RICHARD ALBERT, mathematics educator; b. Columbus, Ohio, Oct. 9, 1924; s. Lindley Richard and Belle Wierman (Bream) D.; m. Dorothy Green, Sept. 5, 1948 (div. Mar. 1979); 1 child, Jason; m. Carol Kipps, Mar. 31, 1979. BS, Calif. Inst. Tech., 1945; AB, Denison U., 1947; MA, Ohio State U., 1948, PhD, 1953; DSc (hon.), Denison U., 1973. Instr. math. Middlebury (Vt.) Coll., 1947; from Bateman rsch. fellow to prof. Calif. Inst. Tech., Pasadena, 1954-86, prof. emeritus, 1987—; cons. Nat. Security Agy., Washington, 1955-63, Sch. Math. Study Group, Palo Alto, Calif., 1958, 66-67, Calif. State Dept. Edn., Sacramento, 1960—. Author: Elements of Abstract Algebra, 1966, Arithmetic and Calculators, 1978, Classical Abstract Algebra, 1990; contbr. articles to profl. jours. Lt. USN, 1943-46, 52-54. Mem. Am. Math. Soc., Math. Assn. Am. Home: 6349 Stone Bridge Rd Santa Rosa CA 95409-5859

DEANE, DEBBE, journalist, editor, consultant; b. Coatesville, Pa., July 30, 1950; d. George Edward and Dorothea Alice (Martin) Mays; widowed; children: Theo, Vonisha, Lorise, Voniece. AA in Psychology, Mesa Coll., 1989; BA Psychology, San Diego State U., 1993. News dir. Sta. KLDR, Denver, 1976-78; host, reporter Sta. KMGH-TV, Denver, 1978-81; news anchor, editor Sta. KHOW, Denver, 1978-79; news & pub. affairs dir. Sta. KLZ, Denver, 1979-80, Sta. KCBQ, San Diego, 1980-82; news anchor Sta. KOGO, San Diego, 1983-84; news anchor, reporter Sta. KCST-TV, San Diego, 1984-87; dir. comm. Omni Corp., San Diego, 1987—; news anchor Sta. KFI, L.A., 1990-91; media liaison United Negro Coll. Fund, San Diego, 1990-92; dir. comm. United Chs. of Christ, San Diego, 1989-92; cons. San Diego Assn. Black Journalists, 1985-92, San Diego Coalition Black Journalists, 1985-92. Campaign fin. analyst San Diego County Registrar of Voters, San Diego, 1990; cons. San Diego County Office Disaster Preparedness, 1990-91, Nu Way Youth Ctr. & Neighborhood House, Inc., San Diego, 1991-92; counselor Project STARRT, San Diego, 1991-92. Recipient San Diego Black Achievement award Urban League, 1989, Best News Show & Spot News award San Diego Press Club, 1985, Golden Mike award So. Calif. Broadcast Assn., L.A., 1986; named one of Top 25 Businesswomen Essence Mag., 1978, Outstanding Humanitarian Worldvision, 1993, Outstanding Humanities Alumna Mesa Coll., 1993. Mem. AFTRA, APA, Am. Women in Radio & TV, Women in Comm., Black Students Sci. Orgn. (sec. 1989-91), Africana Psychol. Soc. (media coord. 1990-92), Psi Chi. Democrat. Home: 1335 S Woodman St # 3 Paradise Hills CA 92139

DEANS, DAVID HENRY, telecommunication company executive; b. London, Aug. 10, 1954; came to U.S., 1978; s. James Giffin and Velia Maria (DeCupis) D.; m. Dylania Andrea Fernández; children: Vanessa, Kassandra. BSME, Poplar Coll., London, 1973. Engr. ITT Worldcom, London, 1975-79; project mgr. Quotron Systems Inc., L.A., 1979-83; product mgr. Allied-Bunker Ramo, Trumbull, Conn., 1983-85; sr. cons. Northern Telecom, Dallas, 1985-86; product mgr. Ericsson Inc., Dallas, 1986-87; dir. market devel. AG Comm. Systems-GTE, Phoenix, 1987-91; sr. ptnr. Deans & Assocs., Phoenix, 1991—; seminar leader Texpo '89 Conf., San Francisco. Author, editor: Solutions in Action, 1989 (Mktg. Achievement award, 1989). Mem. Am. Mktg. Assn. (exec., communications com. mem. 1989), Nat. Centrex Users Group (assoc., advisor to bd. dirs. 1989).

DEARDORF, DAVID A., semiconductor company executive; b. Terre Haute, Ind., Oct. 29, 1937; s. Norman O. and Laura E. (Creasey) D.; m. Eileen Walters, Feb. 17, 1962; children: Darcia, Daniel, Dena. AA in Engring., Ventura Coll., 1957; BSEE, U. Calif., Berkeley, 1960. Engr. Electronic Systems Devel., 1960-61; project mgr. Westinghouse Electric Corp., 1961-65; v.p., gen. mgr. Rho Electronics Glass Corp., 1965-67; plant mgr., prodn. Fairchild Camera & Instrument Co., Mt. View, Calif., 1967-75; v.p., gen. mgr. Raytheon Semiconductor Div., Mt. View, 1975—; dir. Santa Clara (Calif.) County Mfg. Group, 1987—, Silicon Valley Devel., Santa Clara, 1985—. Mem. IEEE. Office: Raytheon Semiconductor Div 350 Ellis St Mountain View CA 94043-2237

DEARMOND, M. KEITH, chemistry educator, researcher; b. Ft. Wayne, Ind., Dec. 10, 1935; s. Murray M. and Alice M. (Stetler) DeA.; m. Anna Hofmanova, Jan. 23, 1985; children: Dominique, Thea. BA, DePauw U., Greencastle, Ind., 1958; PhD, U. Ariz., 1963. Asst. prof. N.C. State U., Raleigh, 1964-69; assoc. prof. N.C. State U., 1969-75, prof., 1975-80, asst. dept. head, 1979-82; prof., head N.Mex. State U., Las Cruces, 1988-91; vis. prof. U. Bologna, Italy, 1976; vis. disting. prof. U. Paris, 1987. Contbr. articles to profl. jours. Rector scholar DePauw U., 1954-57, Sherwin Williams scholar, 1958. Mem. Am. Chem. Soc., N.Am. Photochem. Soc. Office: N Mex State U Las Cruces NM 88003

DEASY, DONALD WAYNE, real estate broker; b. Yakima, Wash., Dec. 27, 1938; s. Wayne Delbert and Louise Anita (Nocchi) D.; m. E. Jane England, Sept. 23, 1961; children: Kimberly, Deanne, Matthew, Joseph. BA, U. Wash., 1961. Salesman IBM, Seattle, L.A., 1963-66; v.p. Pacific Nat. Bank of Wash., Seattle, 1966-77; sales assoc. Windermere Real Estate Co., Seattle, 1977-80; pres. Windermere Real Estate/East Inc., Bellevue, Wash., 1980—; cons. Windermere Svcs. Co., Seattle, 1983—. Pres. Bellevue (Wash.) Breakfast Rotary, 1989-90. 1st lt. U.S. Army, 1961-63. Mem. Rotary Internat. (Paul Harris fellow 1990), Bellevue Athletic Club, Lakes Club. Home: 6216 129th Pl SE Bellevue WA 98006

DEASY, JOHN BERCHMANS, environmental health specialist; b. San Francisco, Mar. 7, 1911; s. Thomas A. and Katherine G. (Conway) D.; m. Minna Lou Cangelosi, Apr. 16, 1947; 1 child, Yvonne A. Deasy-Gowdey. BS, U. San Francisco, 1933; grad., U.S. Army Command and Gen. Staff Coll., 1964. Registered environ. health specialist; cert. tchr. Gen. clerk City and County of San Francisco, 1934-48; insp. San Francisco Tax Office, 1948-54; insp., sr. insp., and prin. insp. San Francisco Dept. Health, 1954-72; pres. John Mulhern Co., San Francisco, 1981-83; tchr. San Francisco Gen. Hosp., Laguna Honda Hosp., 1973-74. Scoutmaster Boy Scouts Am., 1930-34, dist. commr., 1954-56, troop committeeman and scouting coord., 1974—; bd. dirs. U. San Francisco Health Profl. Soc. Lt. Col. U.S. Army, 1942-64, ETO, Korea. Decorated Bronze Star; recipient Silver Beaver award Boy Scouts Am. Mem. Young Men's Inst. (Outstanding Mem. award 1970, various offices), Res. Officers Assn. chpt. 90 (Man of Yr. award 1984, various offices), Ret. Officers Assn., San Francisco Ret. City Employees Assn., Sons in Retirement (Big Sir 1978, various offices), 86th Chem. Mortar Bd. Assn. (founder, adj.), Vets. Battle of Bulge (treas.), U. San Francisco Alumni Assn. (past bd. govs.), Am. Legion (life). Democrat. Roman Catholic. Home: 1830 30th Ave San Francisco CA 94122-4227

DEATHERAGE, PHILIP ROY, computer company executive; b. Little Rock, Ark., Mar. 22, 1948; s. Argil Roy and Ethel Allen (Fowler) D.; m. Christina Helen Scherer (div. 1985); m. Linda Louise Guckert, Dec. 23, 1986; children: Kacey Jones, Kelly Jones. BS, Calif. Poly., 1978. Cert. data processor. Pres., CEO Symcas, Inc., Rancho Cucamonga, Calif. Pub. (newsletter) SYMNEWS, 1991—, Cucamonga Legin News, 1991—. With U.S. Army, 1966-69. Mem. ASCE, City and County Engrs. Assn., Indep. Computer Cons. Assn., Am. Legion (comdr. 1992-93). Office: Symcas Inc 9229 Utica Ave Ste #140 Rancho Cucamonga CA 91730

DEATON, ROBERT LESTER, educator, consultant; b. Beaumont, Tex., July 21, 1936; s. Robert Lee and Elinor Louise (Prentice) D.; m. June Sanders, Aug. 18, 1958 (div. 1963); m. Lucy Carol Carlson, Apr. 29, 1966; children: Travis, Tricia. AB, Scarritt Coll., 1958; MSW, U. Utah, 1964; EdD, U. Nev., 1981. Child welfare social worker Utah Dept. Family Svcs., Salt Lake City, 1964-66, supr., 1966-67, tng. specialist, project dir., 1967-69; mem. faculty dept. social work U. Mont., Missoula, 1969—, asst. prof., 1969-76, assoc. prof., 1976-82, prof., 1982—; cons. in field. Contbr. articles to profl. jours. Sgt. U.S. Army, 1960-62. Recipient Disting. Svc. award Missoula Rural Fire Dept., 1988, Mont. Social Worker of Yr. award 1991; Mont. Dept. Family Svcs. and Health and Human Svcs. grantee, 1974-84. Mem. Missoula Exch. Club (dist. chmn. child abuse prevention 1989—, pres. 1993-94). Home: 2710 Mulberry Ln Missoula MT 59801-5102 Office: U Mont Dept Social Work Rankin Hall Missoula MT 59812

DEAVER, PHILLIP LESTER, lawyer; b. Long Beach, Calif., July 21, 1952; s. Albert Lester and Eva Lucille (Welton) D. Student, USCG Acad., 1970-72; BA, UCLA, 1974; JD, U. So. Calif., 1977. Bar: Hawaii 1977, U.S. Dist. Ct. Hawaii 1977, U.S. Ct. Appeals (9th cir.) 1978, U.S. Supreme Ct. 1981. Assoc. Carlsmith, Wichman, Case, Mukai & Ichiki, Honolulu, 1977-83, ptnr., 1983-86; mng. ptnr. Bays, Deaver, Hiatt, Kawachika & Lezak, Honolulu, 1986. Contbr. articles to profl. jours. Mem. ABA (forum com. on the Constrn. Industry), AIA (affiliate Hawaii chpt.), Am. Arbitration Assn. (arbitrator). Home: 2471 Pacific Heights Rd Honolulu HI 96813-1029 Office: Bays Deaver Hiatt Kawachika & Lezak PO Box 1760 Honolulu HI 96806

DEB, SATYEN K., research physicist; b. Sylhet, India, Mar. 1, 1932; came to U.S., 1962; s. Surendra K. and Monomohini Deb; m. Sima Mukherjee, Sept. 15, 1956; children: Sharmila Sen, Shummita Bose. BS, Dacca (Bangladesh) U., 1953, MS, 1955; PhD, Cambridge (Eng.) U., 1960. Sci. officer Nat. Rsch. Coun., Ottawa, Ont., Can., 1960-62; various rsch. positions Am. Cyanamid Co., Stamford, Conn., 1963-72; dir. rsch. Optel Corp., Princeton, N.J., 1973-78; mgr. solid state rsch. Solar Energy Rsch. Inst., Golden, Colo., 1978—; vis. scientist CNRS Lab., Grenoble, France, 1972-73; cons. LTT, French tel. co., Paris, 1972-73. Contbr. over 100 articles to sci. jours., chpts. to books; inventor electrochromic phenomenon; numerous patents in field. Fellow Am. Phys. Soc.; mem. Electrochem. Soc. Home: 4322 Peachway Boulder CO 80301 Office: Solar Energy Rsch Inst 1617 Cole Blvd Golden CO 80401

DEBARD, ROGER, investment executive; b. Cleve., Nov. 10, 1941; d. Victor and Margaret Ann (Henderson) DeB.; m. Janet Marie Schulz, July 3, 1965; children: Eila Burns, Ryan Alexander. BS, Bowling Green State U., 1963; MBA, Case Western Res. U., 1968; MA, Claremont McKenna Coll., 1978, PhD, 1981. Asst. v.p. A.G. Becker & Co., L.A., 1972-76; sr. portfolio mgr. Scudder Stevens & Clark, L.A., 1976-81; v.p. Crocker Investment Mgmt., L.A., 1981-85; exec. v.p. Olympic Trust, L.A., 1985—; prin. Hotchkis and Wiley, L.A., 1985—; adj. prof. Pepperdine U., L.A., 1981-85; guest Fin. News Network, L.A., 1981—. Mem. L.A. World Affairs Coun., 1988—, L.A. Libr. Assn., 1976—, pres. 1980-81. Recipient First Pl. Pub. award Investment Dealers Digest, 1971, Outstanding Svc. award City of L.A., 1980; grad. fellow Rand Grad. Inst., 1974-76. Mem. L.A. Bd. Bond Club (sec./dir. 1986-89), L.A. Soc. Fin. Analysts, Yosemite Assoc., California Club, Bel-Air Bay Club, Sigma Chi. Republican. Episcopalian. Home: 48 Haldeman Rd Santa Monica CA 90402-1004 Office: Hotchkis and Wiley 800 W 6th St Los Angeles CA 90017-2704

DEBARTOLO, EDWARD JOHN, JR., professional football team owner, real estate developer; b. Youngstown, Ohio, Nov. 6, 1946; s. Edward J. and Marie Patricia (Montani) DeB.; m. Cynthia Ruth Papalia, Nov. 27, 1968; children: Lisa Marie, Tiffanie Lynne, Nicole Anne. Student, U. Notre Dame, 1964-68. With Edward J. DeBartolo Corp., Youngstown, Ohio, 1960—, v.p., 1972-75, exec. v.p., 1975—, pres., chief adminstrv. officer, 1979; owner, mng. ptnr. San Francisco 49ers, 1977—. Trustee Youngstown State U., 1974-77; mem. nat. adv. coun. St. Jude Children's Rsch. Hosp., 1978—, local chmn., 1979-80; local chmn. fund drive Am. Cancer Soc., 1975—, City of Hope, 1977; mem. Nat. Cambodia Crisis Com., 1980—; chmn. 19th Ann. Victor awards City of Hope, 1985; apptd. adv. coun. Coll. Bus. Adminstrn. U. Notre Dame, 1988; adv. coun. Nat. Assn. People with AIDS, 1992; bd. dirs. Cleve. Clinic Found., 1991. Served with U.S. Army, 1969. Recipient Man of Yr. award St. Jude Children's Hosp., 1979, Boy's Town of Italy in San Francisco, 1985, Sportsman of Yr. award Nat. Italian Am. Sports Hall of Fame, 1991; Salvation Army Citation of Merit, 1982. Mem. Internat. Council of Shopping Ctrs. Roman Catholic. Clubs: Tippecanoe Country, Fonderlac Country, Dapper Dan (dir. 1980—). Office: Edward J DeBartolo Corp PO Box 3287 Youngstown OH 44513-6085 also: care San Francisco 49ers 4949 Centennial Blvd Santa Clara CA 95054

DEBAS, HAILE T., gastrointestinal surgeon, physiologist, educator; b. Asmara, Eritrea, Ethiopia, Feb. 25, 1937; came to U.S., 1980; s. Tesfaye and Keddes (Gabre) D.; m. Ignacia Kim Assing, May 23, 1969. BS in Biology, U. Coll., Addis Ababa, Ethiopia, 1958; MD,CM, McGill U., Montreal, Que., Can., 1963. Intern Ottawa (Ont.) Civic Hosp., Can., 1963-64; resident in surgery U. B.C., Vancouver, Can., 1964-69, asst. prof. surgery, 1970-76, assoc. prof., 1976-79; fellow in gastrointestinal physiology UCLA, 1972-74, assoc. prof. surgery, 1979-81, prof., 1981-85; chief gastrointestinal surgery U. Wash., Seattle, 1985-87; prof., chmn. dept. surgery U. Calif., San Francisco, 1987—; key investigator Ctr. for Ulcer Rsch. and Edn., UCLA, 1980—; cons. NIH, Bethesda, Md., 1983-87, Bd. Med. Quality Assurance, Calif., 1983-85; bd. dirs. Am. Bd. Surgery. Mem. editorial bd. Am. Jour. Physiology, Am. Jour. Surgery, Jour. Surg. Rsch., Western Jour. Medicine, Gastroenterology; contbr. over 250 articles and abstracts to jours. and chpts. to books. Recipient Merit awards, Va., 1981-87; fellow Med. Rsch. Coun. of Can., 1972-74; rsch. grantee NIH, 1976—. Fellow ACS, Royal Coll. Physicians and Surgeons Can.; mem. AAAS, Am. surg. Assn., Am. Gastroent. Assn., Am. Assn. Endocrine Surgeous, Collequium Internat and Chirugiae Digestivae, Soc. Univ. Surgeons, Soc. Surgeons Alimentary Tract (trustee 1985-89), Inst. Medicine NAS, Inst. Medicine, Am. Acad. Arts and Scis., Internat. Hepato-Biliary Pancreatic Assn. (pres. 1991-92), Assn. Minority Acad. Physicians (pres. 1993—). Office: Univ Calif Dept Surgery 505 Parnassus Ave # 320S San Francisco CA 94143-0001

DEBENHAM, RAY GENE, electric supply company executive; b. Salt Lake City, Oct. 1, 1935; s. Shirley R. and Lillian (Greguhn) D.; m. Rita J. Peterson, Aug. 14, 1959; children: Debra, Julie, Michael, Shaun. BS, Alaska Pacific U., 1972; OPM, Harvard U., 1987. CEO Debenham Alaska Investments, Anchorage, 1960—, Taku Enterprises, Anchorage, 1988—; pres. Debenham Electric Supply, Anchorage, 1968-91, CEO, 1968—; chmn. bd. dirs. Profl. Botanicals, Ogden, Utah, 1979-80; bd. advisers SBA, Washington, 1983-88, Philips Lighting, 1990-92, Cuttler Hammer, 1989-90. Mem. bd. advisors Alaska Pacific U., 1992—. Mem. Nat. Assn. Elec. Distbrs. (chmn. utility com. 1981-85), Nat. Assn. Disbtrs., Am. Legion. Mormon.

DEBLASE, ANTHONY FRANK, publishing company executive, biology educator, consultant; b. South Bend, Ind., Apr. 3, 1942; s. Stephan and Ida (Macri) D.; m. Alyce Mae Myers, Aug. 19, 1969 (dec. Mar. 1976). A.B., Earlham Coll., 1964; Ph.D. in Zoology, Okla. State U., 1971. Asst. dir. museums Earlham Coll., dir. Conner Prairie Mus. (now Conner Prairie Pioneer Settlement), Noblesville, Ind., 1964-66; chief of security and visitor services Field Mus. of Natural History, Chgo., 1970-78; assoc. prof. biology Roosevelt U., Chgo., 1969-78; pres., pub. Desmodus Publs., Inc., Chgo., 1978-86; v.p. pub. Desmodus, Inc, San Francisco, 1986-88, pres. 1988-92; editor emeritus Desmodus Inc, 1992—. Named expdn. co-mammalogist W.S. & J.K. Street Expdn. to Iran, Field Mus. Natural History, 1968, Bus. Person of Yr. The Leather Jour., 1990. Mem. Am. Soc. of Mammalogists (life), Nat. Leather Assn. (mem. exec. com., dir. resource ctr., Man of Yr. 1987), Leather Archives and Mus. (treas.). Club: CHC (Chgo.). Author (with Robert E. Martin & Ronald Pine) A Manual of Mammalogy (3d edit.), 1993; author tech. publs., short stories; contbr. articles to profl. jours. Office: Desmodus Inc PO Box 410390 San Francisco CA 94141-0390

DE BODE, OLEG, information systems administrator; b. San Cristobal, Venezuela, Oct. 26, 1956; came to U.S., 1963; s. Konstantine de Bode and Olga (Zavadsky) Kennedy. BS in Math. and Computer Sci., UCLA, 1978. Programmer Electronic Data Systems, Torrance, Calif., 1979-80; programmer/analyst EDS, Torrance, Calif., 1980-85; data processing mgr. Dep Corp., Rancho Dominguez, Calif., 1985-90, dir. mgmt. info. systems, 1990—. Instr. St. George Pathfinders, L.A., 1975—. Mem. COMMON, Focus, Data Processing Mgrs. Assn., Assn. Systems Mgmt. Republican.

DE BOLT, DONALD WALTER, insurance claims administrator; b. Oakland, Calif., Mar. 30, 1952; s. Walter Kenneth and Carol Dolores (Gregory) De B.; m. Eva Janette Lavio, Sept. 18, 1976; children: Katie Lee, James Scott. AA, Ohlone Coll., 1974. Agt. Gygax, Fremont, Calif., 1974-76;

owner, mgr. M & W, Alameda, Calif., 1977-85; property claims estimator State Farm Ins., Fremont, 1985—. Contbr. articles to profl. jours. Mem. Newark (Calif.) Commn. Vols., 1986-90, Sch. Dist. Advisor Com., Fremont, 1990—; dep. chmn. San Francisco Bay Area Coun. Jr. C. of C., 1985. Mem. Calif. Tigers, Fremont Jaycees (pres. 1979-89). Republican. Office: State Farm Ins PO Box 5019 Newark CA 94560-5519

DEBOLT, VIRGINIA FAYE, English language educator; b. LaJunta, Colo., Mar. 21, 1941; d. Virgil Verne and Faye Nellie (Butler) DeBolt; m. William F. Pike Sr., Mar. 15, 1961 (div. 1988); children: William F. Jr., Elizabeth. AA, Otero Jr. Coll., LaJunta, Colo., 1961; BA, Adams State Coll., 1965; MA, U. Northern Colo., 1969. Tchr. Manzanola, Colo., 1963-65, Loveland, Colo., 1965-69, Hobbs, N.Mex., 1969-72, Loving, N.Mex., 1976-81, Carlsbad, N.Mex., 1981-93. Author: Write! Cooperative Learning and the Writing Process, 1993; contbr. articles to profl. jours. Mem. AAUW (officer). Methodist. Home: 1603 W Blodgett Apt G Carlsbad NM 88220-9531

DEBREE, SUSAN KIDDER, pastor; b. Norwalk, Conn., Oct. 25, 1943; d. John Faus Kidder and Barbara (Johnson) Larson; m. Roger Lawrence Towne, 1965 (div. 1970); m. Kenneth Ralph DeBree, July 25, 1971; children: Angel, Charmain, Gretchen, Frederick, Veronica, Barbara. BA, U. Mont., 1965; MDiv, Ilif Sch. of Theology, 1990. Tchr. Bur. of Indian Affairs, Selawik, Alaska, 1966-68, Blackfeet Res., Heart Butte, Mont., 1970-71, Trinity Sch. Dist., Canyon Creek, Mont., 1971-73; health educator Lewis & Clark City County Health, Helena, Mont., 1975-87; assoc. pastor United Meth. Ch., Cheyenne, Wyo., 1990—; coord. DUI task force, Helena, 1984-87. Author, illustrator (book) Tell Me, Ahna, 1975. Bd. dirs. Needs Inc., Cheyenne, 1992, Comea Shelter, Cheyenne, 1992; coord. Crop Walk, Cheyenne, 1991, 92. Recipient Women, Infants, Children (WIC) Svc. award USDA, 1984. Mem. Zonta Internat. (bd. dirs.). Democrat. United Methodist. Home: 3401 Luckie Rd Cheyenne WY 82001 Office: 1st United Meth Ch 108 E 18th St Cheyenne WY 82001

DEBREU, GERARD, economics and mathematics educator; b. Calais, France, July 4, 1921; came to U.S., 1950, naturalized, 1975; s. Camille and Fernande (Decharne) D.; m. Françoise Bled, June 14, 1945; children: Chantal, Florence. Student, Ecole Normale Supérieure, Paris, 1941-44, Agrégé de l'Université, France, 1946; DSc, U. Paris, 1956; Dr. Rerum Politicarum honoris causa, U. Bonn, 1977; D. Scis. Economiques (hon.), U. Lausanne, 1980; DSc (hon.), Northwestern U., 1981; Dr. honoris causa, U. des Scis. Sociales de Toulouse, 1983, Yale U., 1987, U. Bordeaux I, 1988. Rsch. assoc. Centre Nat. De La Recherche Sci., Paris, 1946-48; Rockefeller fellow U.S., Sweden and Norway, 1948-50; rsch. assoc. Cowles Commn., U. Chgo., 1950-55; assoc. prof. econs. Cowles Found., Yale, 1955-61; fellow Ctr. Advanced Study Behavioral Scis., 1960-61; vis. prof. econs. Yale U., fall 1961; prof. econs. U. Calif., Berkeley, 1962—, prof. math., 1975—, univ. prof., 1985—; Guggenheim fellow, vis. prof. Ctr. Ops. Rsch. and Econometrics, U. Louvain, 1968-69, vis. prof., 1971, 72, 88; Erskine fellow U. Canterbury, Christchurch, New Zealand, 1969, 87, vis. prof., 1973; Overseas fellow Churchill Coll., Cambridge, Eng., 1972; vis. prof. Cowles Found. for Rsch. in Econs., Yale U., 1976; vis. prof. U. Bonn, 1977; rsch. assoc. CEPREMAP, Paris, 1980; faculty rsch. lectr. U. Calif., Berkeley, 1984-85, univ. prof., 1985—, Class of 1958 Chair, 1986—; vis. prof. U. Sydney, Australia, 1987. Author: Theory of Value, 1959, Mathematical Economics: Twenty Papers of Gerard Debreu, 1983; assoc. editor Internat. Econ. Rev., 1959-69; mem. editorial bd. Jour. Econ. Theory, 1972—, Games and Econ. Behavior, 1989—, Econ. Theory, 1991; mem. adv. bd. Jour. Math. Econs., 1974—. Served with French Army, 1944-45. Decorated chevalier Légion d'Honneur; recipient Nobel Prize in Econ. Scis., 1983, Commandeur de l'Ordre du Merite, 1984; sr. U.S. Scientist awardee Alexander von Humboldt Found. Fellow AAAS, Econometric Soc. (pres. 1971), Am. Econ. Assn. (disting. fellow 1982, pres.-elect 1989, pres. 1990); mem. NAS (com. human rights 1984—, chair class V behavioral and social scis. 1989—), Am. Philos. Soc., French Acad. Scis. (fgn. assoc.). Office: U Calif Dept Econs Berkeley CA 94720

DEBROECK, DENNIS ALAN, design engineer; b. Van Nuys, Calif., Jan. 29, 1957; s. Justin Bernard and Janice Arlene (Buzzell) DeB.; m. Kathi Lynn Cole, June 17, 1978; children: Katie Lynn, Daniel Alan. Grad. high sch. with honors, Milton-Freewater, Oreg., 1975. Cons. Hanford Nuclear Plant, Richland, Wash., 1983, Oreg. D.E.Q., Portland, 1984; design engr. 3-D Tank & Petroleum Equipment, Milton-Freewater, 1975-86, DTEK Corp., Milton-Freewater, 1986—. Deacon Ch. of Christ, 1989-90. Office: DTEK Corp 3475 Powerline Rd Walla Walla WA 99362

DEBUS, ELEANOR VIOLA, retired business management company executive; b. Buffalo, May 19, 1920; d. Arthur Adam and Viola Charlotte (Pohl) D.; student Chown Bus. Sch., 1939. Sec., Buffalo Wire Works, 1939-45; home talent producer Empire Producing Co., Kansas City, Mo., sec. Owens Corning Fiberglass, Buffalo; public relations and publicity Niagara Falls Theatre, Ont., Can.; pub. rels. dir. Woman's Internat. Bowling Congress, Columbus, Ohio, 1957-59; publicist, sec. Ice Capades, Hollywood, Calif., 1961-63; sec. to contr. Rexall Drug Co., L.A., 1963-67; bus. mgmt. acct. Samuel Berke & Co., Beverly Hills, Calif., 1967-75; Gadbois Mgmt. Co., Beverly Hills, 1975-76; sec., treas. Sasha Corp., L.A., 1976-92; former bus. mgr. Dean Martin; pres. Tempo Co., L.A., 1976-92. Mem. NAFE, Nat. Notary Assn., Am. Film Inst. Republican. Lodge: Order Ea. Star. Contbr. articles to various mags.

DECARIA, MICHAEL DEE, psychologist; b. Ogden, Utah, Dec. 2, 1946; s. Victor and LaVera Ellen (Drysdale) DeC.; m. Carol Diane Bruderer, Aug. 3, 1991; children: Kiyoko, Aaron. BS in Psychology cum laude, Weber State Coll., Ogden, 1970; MS in Clin. Psychology, U. Utah, 1975, PhD in Clin. Psychology, 1977. Lic. psychologist, Utah. Clin. psychologist Salt Lake County Alcoholism & Drugs, 1976-90; pvt. practice Salt Lake City, 1981—; clin. psychologist Salt Lake County Pre-Trial Svcs., 1990—. Mem. Am. Psychol. Assn., Utah Psychol. Assn. (sec., treas. 1980-82). Office: Salt Lake County Pre-Trial Svcs 424 E 500 S Ste 200 Salt Lake City UT 84111-3337

DECHARIO, TONY HOUSTON, symphony orchestra executive; b. Girard, Kans., Sept. 25, 1940; s. Tony and Enid Eulalia (Frogue) D.; m. Rachel Dennisse Kennedy, Apr. 12, 1963 (div. Dec. 1974); children: Samuel Paul, Rachel Christina, Mary Rebecca; m. Mary Gill Roby, Dec. 29, 1974; 1 child, Toni Elizabeth; stepchildren: Edmund Kidd II, Kenneth Hamilton Kidd, Todd Roby Kidd. Student, U. Wichita, 1958-61; MusB, performer's cert., Eastman Sch. Music, U. Rochester, 1962, MusM, 1963. 2d trombone Kansas City (Mo.) Philharm. Orch., 1963-64; prin. trombone Dallas Symphony Orch., 1964-65; 2d trombone Rochester (N.Y.) Philharm. Orch., 1965-75, personnel mgr., 1972-75, gen. mgr., 1975-84, exec. dir., 1984-85, pres., chief exec. officer, 1985-88. Exec. dir. Honolulu Symphony Soc., 1991—. Mem. Am. Symphony Orch. League. Home and Office: Honolulu Symphony Orch 1441 Kapiolani Blvd Honolulu HI 96814-4401

DECHELLIS, MICHAEL ANTHONY, architectural illustrator, designer; b. L.A., June 26, 1940; s. Romeo Joseph and Josephine Betty (D'Ambrosio) DeC.; m. Louise Lee Stadlemeir, July 21, 1961 (div. Jan. 1973); children: Deborah Lynn DeChellis Brannen, Michael B., Jefferey A. AA, Pasadena City Coll., 1960; cert. arts, Art Ctr. Sch., L.A., 1964. Illustrator, designer Qvale-Archtl. Arts, L.A., 1964-71; prin. Michael DeChellis Illustrations, L.A., 1971-73, 76—; scenic artist CBS TV City, Hollywood, Calif., 1973-76; illustrator, designer Gruen Assocs. Architects, L.A., 1979-92. Illustrator Angeles mag., 1990. Mem. Assn. Archtl. Perpectivist U.S.A. Home and Office: 747 N Hayworth Ave Los Angeles CA 90046-7141

DECHERT, PETER, photographer, writer, foundation administrator; b. Phila., Dec. 17, 1924; s. Robert and Helen Hope (Wilson) D.; m. Phoebe Jane Booth; children: Sandra, Robin Booth, Caroline. BA, U. Pa., 1948, MA, 1950, Ph.D., 1955. Owner, Peter Dechert Assocs., Bryn Mawr, Pa., 1956-68; asst. dir. Sch. of Am. Rsch., Santa Fe, 1968-71; pres. Indian Arts Fund, Santa Fe, 1971-72; pres. Southwest Found. for Audio-Visual Resources, Santa Fe, 1973-77; self-employed writer, photographer, Santa Fe; tchr., cons. photog. communications, 1964—. Author: Canon Rangefinder Cameras, 1933-68, 1985, The Contax Connection, 1990, Olympus Pen SLR Cameras, 1989, Canon SLR Cameras, 1959-91, 1992, The Contax S Camera Family, 1991, Los Alamos Ranch Book of Rosters, 1991; contbg. editor Shutterbug mag., other photographic periodicals; contbr. articles on history and design of miniature cameras and other photog. topics to profl. publs. Bd. dirs. St. Vincent Hosp. Found. (pres. 1981-83, v.p. 1983-84); pres. Indian Arts Fund, 1971-72. Served with AUS, 1943-46. Mem. N.Mex. Poetry Soc. (pres. 1969-74), Am. Soc. Mag. Photographers, SAR, Southwest Assn. Indian Affairs, N.Mex. Jazz Workshop, Don Quixote Club, Phi Beta Kappa, Delta Psi. Address: PO Box 636 Santa Fe NM 87504-0636

DECIUTIIS, ALFRED CHARLES MARIA, medical oncologist, television producer; b. N.Y.C., Oct. 16, 1945; s. Alfred Ralph and Theresa Elizabeth (Manko) de C.; m. Catherine L. Gohn. B.S. summa cum laude, Fordham U., 1967; M.D., Columbia U., 1971. Diplomate Am. Bd. Internal Medicine, Am. Bd. Med. Oncology. Intern N.Y. Hosp.-Cornell Med. Ctr., N.Y.C., 1971-72, resident, 1972-74; fellow in clin. immunology Meml. Hosp.-Sloan Kettering Cancer Ctr., N.Y.C., 1974-75, fellow in clin. oncology, 1975-76, spl. fellow in immunology, 1974-76; guest investigator, asst. physician exptl. hematology Rockefeller U., N.Y.C., 1975-76; practice medicine, specializing in med. oncology Los Angeles, 1977—; host cable TV shows, 1981—; med. editor Cable Health Network, 1983—, Lifetime Network, 1984—; mem. med. adv. com. 1984 Olympics; co-founder Meditrina Med. Ctr., free outpatient surg. ctr., Torrance, Calif. Syndicated columnist Coast Media News, 1980's; producer numerous med. TV shows; contbr. articles to profl. jours.; author first comprehensive clin. description of chronic fatique syndrome as a neuro-immunologic acquired disorder. Founder Italian-Am. Med. Assn., 1982. Served to capt. M.C., U.S. Army, 1972-74. Leukemia Soc. Am. fellow, 1974-76. Fellow ACP; mem. AMA, Am. Soc. Clin. Oncology, N.Y. Acad. Sci. (life), Calif. Med. Assn., Los Angeles County Med. Assn., AAAS, Am. Soc. Hematology, Nature Conservancy, Nat. Wildlife Fedn. Home: 32062 1/2 Lobo Canyon Rd Agoura Hills CA 91301-3423

DECKARD, IVAN LOWELL, pilot; b. Vincennes, Ind., Mar. 24, 1928; s. Leonard Zon and Edna Dean (Graham Wodsok) D.; m. Marian Annis Keller, Aug. 19, 1950 (div. Dec. 1980); children: Randall Lee, Kimberely Sue, John Gregory. Grad. high sch., Germania Gardens, N.J. pilot; ATP; cert. flight instr. Guerrilla advisor, solider Anastasio Somoza Garcia's Nat. Guard, Managua, Nicaragua, 1946-48; mil. ad./arms supplier, solider Batista's revolt against Pre. Prio Socarra, Havana, Cuba, 1952; arms supplier, soldier 26th of July Movement, Havana, 1955-57, Liberal Party, Bogota, Colombia, 1966-68, Nat. Front, Bogota, 1968; guerrilla/arms supplier M-19 Guerrilla Group, Bogota, 1969; guerrilla, arms supplier APRA/PAP/Shining Path, Lima, Peru, 1970-72, 76-79, 1979-83; fin. supporter, advisor Shining Path, Lima, 1983—; arms and fin. supporter Sandinistas, Managua, Nicaragua, 1966-83, M-19S, Bogota, 1966-79, Shining Path, Lima, 1979. With USN, 1948-49. Mem. Mensa. Democrat. Jewish. Home: 3817 S Hampton Pl Terre Haute IN 47802-9999 Office: Box 7 880 Front St Rm B-S-10 San Diego CA 92188-1003

DECKER, GEORGE JOHN, litigation photographer; b. Wilkes-Barre, Pa., May 29, 1955; s. George John and Henrietta (Towarnicki) D.; m. Margaret Helen Sharp, May 3, 1986. BA, Yale U., 1977; JD, U. Ariz., 1980; cert. of graduation in profl. photography, N.Y. Inst. of Photography, 1993. Bar: Calif. 1984, Ariz. 1980, Nev. 1984. Land atty. Amselco Exploration Inc., Reno, Nev., 1981-84; atty. Haase, Harris and Morrison, Reno, 1984-86, Gordon and Rees, San Francisco, San Diego, 1986-91; owner George J. Decker, JD, Litigation Photography, San Diego, 1991—. Contbr. articles to profl. jours. Mem. Mus. Photog. Arts. Mem. Profl. Photographers Am., Assn. of Profl. Videographers, State Bar Calif., State Bar Ariz., State Bar Nev., San Diego County Bar Assn., Evidence Photographers Internat. Coun. Democrat. Episcopalian. Home and Office: 11035 Poblado Rd San Diego CA 92127-1349

DECKER, JOHN ALVIN, JR., technology company executive; b. Columbia, Mo., Oct. 25, 1935; s. John Alvin and Mildred Evaline (Harrington) D.; m. Linda Louise McCullough, Dec. 30, 1957; children: Trigg Harrington (dec.), Sarah Louise. BS in Aero. Engring., Aero. Engring. Profl. Degree, MIT, 1958; PhD in Plasma Physics, Cambridge U., 1965; postgrad., Boston Coll. Sch. Bus., 1967-69, Episcopal Theol. Sch., 1971-73. Rsch. physicist Sperry Rand Rsch. Lab., Bedford, Mass., 1965-67; dir. physics Comstock & Wescott, Inc., Cambridge, Mass., 1967-70; pres. Spectral Imaging, Inc., Concord, Mass., 1971-77; rsch. and tech. mgr. vacuum div. Varian Co., Lexington, Mass., 1977-79; mgr. strategic plans SPIRE, Inc., Bedford, Mass., 1979-80; mng. dir. AVCO Everett Rsch. Labs, Puunene, Hawaii, 1981-82; pres. Kuau Tech., Ltd., Puunene, 1982—; cons. John A. Decker, Jr., Cons., Puunene, 1982—. Contbr. numerous articles to profl. pubs.; patentee in field. Mem. coun. Episc. Diocese Hawaii, Honolulu, 1985-86; jr. warden Good Shepherd Ch., 1990-92, sr. warden, 1992—; chmn. Episc. Hawaii Cursillo, 1987-88, Maui Cath. Charities, 1988-90. Capt. USAF, 1962-65. Recipient IR.100 award Indsl. Rsch. mag., 1972, award of Excellence, Soc. Plastics Industry's Composites Inst., 1991, 92; alumni scholar MIT, 1954. Mem. Instrument Soc. Am. (sr.), Am. Phys. Soc., Optical Soc. Am., Catgut Acoustical Soc., Guild Am. Luthiers, Soc. Applied Spectroscopy, Am. Model Yacht Assn., Rotary (pres. Paia, Maui 1989-90). Home: 307 S Alu Rd Wailuku HI 96793-1509 Office: Kuau Tech Ltd PO Box 1031 Puunene HI 96784-1031

DECKER, PURLEY JOHN, computer educator; b. Sandpoint, Idaho, July 8, 1947; s. Leroy Alfred Decker and Beryl Ann (Bennett) Morgan; m. Rita Kay Martin, July 4, 1970; children: Shane Neil, Neil Allan, Lyle Thomas, Shannon Louise Ann. BS in Bus., Troy State U., 1988; MS in Info. Systems with distinction, Hawaii Pacific U., 1990. Surveyor asst. U.S. Forest Svc., Sandpoint, 1967-68; enlisted U.S. Army, 1968, served in Vietnam, 1969-70, advanced through grades to master sgt., retired, 1992; contract educator Pierce Coll., Tacoma, Wash., 1992—; computer troubleshooter Madigan Army Med. Ctr., Tacoma, 1992—, computer educator, 1992—. Mem. PTA, Lake City, Wash., 1991-92. Decorated Bronze Star, Army Commednation medal, Meritorious Svc. medals. Mem. IEEE Computer Soc., Assn. Computing Machinery. Home: 12806 Lakeholme Rd SW Tacoma WA 98498

DECKER, RICHARD JEFFREY, lawyer; b. Manhasset, N.Y., Aug. 26, 1959; s. Alan B. and Shelley T. (Belkin) D.; m. Carrie Ann Gordon, Aug. 13, 1989. BA, Union Coll., Schenectady, N.Y., 1981; JD, Boston U., 1984. Bar: N.Y. 1985, Calif. 1985, Mass. 1985, U.S. Dist. Ct. (cen. dist.) Calif. 1985. Assoc. Turner, Gesterfeld, Wilk & Tigerman, Beverly Hills, Calif., 1985-86, Shapiro, Posell & Close, L.A., 1986-90, Katten, Muchin, Zavis & Weitzman, L.A., 1990-93, Ginsburg, Stephen, Oringher & Richman, L.A., 1993—. Mem. Los Angeles County Bar Assn., Beverly Hills Bar Assn., Century City Bar Assn. Office: Ginsburg Stephen et al Ste 800 10100 Santa Monica Blvd Los Angeles CA 90067-2901

DECKER, RICHARD KELSEY, equipment distribution company executive; b. Monrovia, Calif., Dec. 31, 1927; s. Raymond Grant and Dorothy Irene (Heady) D.; m. Barbara Carolyn Carlson, 1956; children—Richard Brian, Carolyn Ann Decker Johnson. B.S., U. So. Calif., 1952. Cost. acct. S.W. Products Co., Monrovia, 1953-55; controller Scotsman Refrigeration Inc., Monterey Park, Calif., 1955-64; with Scotsman Distbrs. of Los Angeles, Inc., La Verne, Calif., 1964—, retired, 1991; pres., chief exec. officer, 1976—. Served with USN, 1945-47. Mem. Alpha Kappa Psi (pres.), Beta Gamma Sigma.

DECKER, SUELYN, accountant; b. Alameda, Calif., Apr. 29, 1948; d. Richard McNeal and Lucille (Nahhas) Cudabac; m. Clarence Eugene Decker (div. Sept. 1990); children: David Eugene, Kimberlie Anne. Ops. mgr. Data Processing Svcs., Findlay, Ohio, 1979-81; with credit/collection A.B. Dick Co., Oakland, 1981-82; acct., treas., Christian Counseling Svs., San Mateo, Calif., 1984-86; acct. D.E. Staal, CPA, Fremont, Calif., 1986-88; staff acct. Evergreen Oil, Inc., Newark, Calif., 1988—. Office: Evergreen Oil Inc 6880 Smith Ave Newark CA 94560

DECKER SLANEY, MARY TERESA, Olympic athlete; b. Bunnvale, N.J., Aug. 4, 1958; d. John and Jacqueline Decker; m. Ron Tabb (div. 1983); m. Richard Slaney, June 1, 1985; 1 child, Ashley Lynn. Student, U. Colo., 1977-78. Amateur runner, 1969—, holder several world track and field records, 1980—; winner 2 gold medals at 1500 and 3000 meters World Track and Field Championship, Helsinki, Finland, 1983; mem. U.S. Olympic teams, 1980, 84; cons. to CBS Records, Timex, Eastman Kodak. Recipient Jesse Owens Internat. Amateur Athlete award, 1982, Sullivan award AAU, 1982; named Amateur Sportswoman of the Yr., Women's Sports Found., 1982, 83, Top Sportswoman A.P. Europe, 1985. Address: 2923 Flintlock St Eugene OR 97401-4660

DECKERT, CURTIS KENNETH, management and technical consultant; b. Whittier, Calif., Jan. 3, 1939; s. Arlen Peter and Ruth Kathrine Deckert; m. Janet Kay Newsom, June 18, 1964; children: Denise Joy, Juliet Kay. AA, Fullerton Coll., 1958; BSME, U. Ariz., 1960; MSME, U. So. Calif., 1962, MBA, 1968; PhD, Calif. Coast U., 1989. Cert. mgmt. cons. Sr. engr. Nortronics, Anaheim, Calif., 1960-66, ITT, Los Angeles, 1966; mem. tech. staff Calif. Computer Products, Anaheim, 1966-70; mgr. research and devel. Universal Graphics, Irvine, Calif., 1971; pvt. practice mgmt. cons., 1971-72; research and devel engr. Ford Aerospace, Newport Beach, Calif., 1972-75; sr. devel. engr. Abbott Labs., Cerritos, Calif., 1975-76; pres. Curt Deckert Assocs., Inc., Santa Ana, Calif., 1976—. Contbr. articles to profl. jours. Bd. dirs. Alpha Ctr., Placentia, Calif., 1982-85; chmn. Calvary Ch., Placentia, 1978-85, elder, 1973-75, 78-88. Mem. ASA, PDMA, Inst. of Mgmt. Cons. (bd. dirs. L.A. chpt. 1981-88, pres. 1986-87), Internat. Soc. Optical Engring., Optical Soc. Am., Am. Arbitration Assn., Soc. Photographic and Instrumentation Engrs. Republican. Home and Office: Curt Deckert Assocs Inc 18061 Darmel Pl Santa Ana CA 92705

DECKERT, HARLAN KENNEDY, JR., manufacturing company official; b. Evanston, Ill., May 22, 1923; s. Harlan Kennedy Sr. and Lady Otey (Hutton) D.; BS, U. Calif., Berkeley, 1949; MBA, U. So. Calif., 1962; m. Mary Emma Eldredge, Nov. 27, 1971; children: Mary Adrienne, Christine Ann, Daniel Gregory, Deborah Alice. Systems analyst Northrop Corp., Hawthorne, Calif., 1949-53, supr. engring. adminstrv. svcs., 1953-57, adminstrv. systems engr., 1957-59; with AiResearch Indsl. div. Garrett Corp., Torrance, Calif., 1959-88, systems svc. adminstr., 1962-72, mgr. adminstrv. svcs., 1972-75, adminstr. internat. ops., 1975-80, sr. staff advisor Garrett Automotive Group Allied-Signal, Inc., 1980-88, ret., 1988. Patron L.A. County Mus. Art, Director's Guild and Docent; Greater L.A. Zoo Assn.; mem. L.A. County Mus. Natural History, San Luis Obispo zoological Soc., Exotic Cat Breeding Compound, African Wildlife Found., Friends Cabrillo Marine Mus., Assn. Zoo & Aquarium Docents; supporting mem. Living Desert. With USAAF, 1943-46, CBI, capt. USAFR, 1946-57. Mem. Am. Assn. Zoo Keepers, Am. Assn. Zool. Parks and Aquariums, Nat. Parks & Conservation Assn., Nat. Wildlife Fedn., San Diego Zool. Soc. (Diamond Club), World Wildlife Fund, Nat. Audubon Soc. Nature Conservancy, Wildlife Waystation. Home: 2509 20th St Santa Monica CA 90405-2705

DE CONCINI, DENNIS, senator, lawyer; b. Tucson, May 8, 1937; s. Evo and Ora (Webster) DeC.; m. Susan Margaret Hurley, June 6, 1959; children: Denise, Christina, Patrick Evo. B.A., U. Ariz., 1959, LL.B., 1963. Bar: Ariz. 1963. Mem. firm Evo DeConcini, Tucson; ptnr. DeConcini & McDonald, Tucson, 1968-73; dep. Pima County atty. Sch. Dist. 1, 1971-72, county atty., 1972-76; U.S. Senator from Ariz., 1977—; mem. Appropriations com.; chmn. subcom. on Treasury, Postal Svc. and Gen. Govt.; mem. subcom. on Def., subcom. on Energy and Water Devel., subcom. on Fgn. Ops.,subcom. on Interior Related Agys.; mem. Jud. com.; chmn. subcom. on Patents, Copyrights and Trademarks; mem. subcom. on Antitrust, Monopolies and Bus. Rights, subcom. on the Constitution, com. on Rules and Adminstrn., com. on Vets. Affairs; chmn. select com. on Intelligence; chmn. Commn. on Security and Cooperation in Europe; mem. Internat. Narcotics Control Caucus, We. Coalition of Senators; former pres., now dir. Shopping Ctrs., Inc., select com. Indian Affairs. Chmn. legis. com. Tucson Community Council, 1966-67; mem. major gifts com., devel. fund drive St. Joseph's Hosp., 1970, mem. devel. council, 1971-73; mem. major gifts com. Tucson Mus. and Art Center Bldg. Fund, 1971; adminstr. Ariz. Drug Control Dist., 1975-76; precinct committeeman Ariz. Democratic Party, 1958—; mem. Pima County Dem. Central Com., 1958-67, Dem. State Exec. Com., 1958-68; state vice chmn. Ariz. Dem. Com., 1964-66, 70-72; vice chmn. Pima County Dem. Com., 1970-73. Served to 2d lt. JAG U.S. Army, 1959-60. Named Outstanding Ariz. County Atty., 1975. Mem. Am., Ariz., Pima County bar assns., Nat. Dist. Attys. Assn., Ariz. Sheriffs and County Attys. Assn., Am. Judicature Soc., Ariz. Pioneer Hist. Soc., NAACP, U. Ariz. Alumni Assn., Tucson Fraternal Order Police, Phi Delta Theta, Delta Sigma Rho, Phi Alpha Delta. Roman Catholic. Clubs: Nucleus (Tucson), Old Pueblo (Tucson), Pres.'s U. Ariz. (Tucson), Latin Am. (Tucson), Latin Am. Social (Tucson). Office: US Senate 328 Hart Senate Bldg Washington DC 20510

DECOURTEN, FRANK L., earth science educator; b. Los Angeles, Jan. 14, 1950; s. Frank Dominic and Angel DeCourten; m. Cynthia Yvonne Estrada, Apr. 14, 1973. B.S., U. Calif.-Riverside, 1973, M.S. in Geol. Sci., 1976; postgrad. U. Utah, 1980. Lectr. geology Calif. State U.-Chico, 1974-76; research paleontologist Mus. No. Ariz., Flagstaff, 1974-75; chief curator, assoc. instr. U. Utah, Salt Lake City, 1978—; cons. geologist R&M Cons., Salt Lake City, 1980-82. Editor: Earth Essays, 1984. Contbr. articles to profl. jours. Mem. Geol. Soc. Am., Nat. Assn. Geology Tchrs. Roman Catholic. Home: 2566 Wellington St Salt Lake City UT 84106-4010 Office: Utah Mus of Nat History U Utah Presidents Circle Salt Lake City UT 84112

DECUIR, JOSEPH CHARLES, electronics engineer, business executive; b. Pasadena, Calif., Oct. 2, 1950; s. Laurence E. and Leota D. (Miller) D.; m. Elizabeth Clare Strauss, Apr. 30, 1982; children: Michael, Matthew, Margaret. BSEE, U. Calif., Berkeley, 1972, MSEE, 1974, postgrad., 1979-81. Engr. Nat. Med. Engring., Corte Madera, Calif., 1973-74; rsch. asst. Insts. Med. Scis., San Francisco, 1974-75; systems engr. Atari, Inc., Sunnyvale, Calif., 1975-79; dir. engring. Standard Technologies Corp., Berkeley, 1979-83; cons. Amiga, Santa Clara, Calif., 1983-84; ptnr. Teledesign, Berkeley, 1984-86; v.p. Cygnet div. Everex Systems Inc., Berkeley, 1986—. Nine patents in data processing field. Mgr. computer club Marin Sch. PTA, Albany, Calif., 1989—; den leader cub scouts Boy Scouts Am., Albany, 1990—. Mem. IEEE, Telecomm. Industry Assn. (chmn. facsimile digital interfaces tech. stds. com., editor fax stds.). Democrat. Roman Catholic. Office: Everex Systems Inc 901 Page Fremont CA 94538

DEDANAAN, LLYN PATTERSON, anthropology educator; b. Springfield, Ohio, Oct. 13, 1942; d. William Homer and Doris (May-Davis) Patterson; 1 child, Ricardo Patterson. BA cum laude, Ohio State U., 1966; MA, U. Wash., 1968; PhD, Union Grad. Sch., 1985. Mem. faculty Evergreen State Coll., Olympia, Wash., 1971—, dean, 1973-76; bd. dirs. Wash. Protection and Advocacy; cons. Pugallup Tribe of Indians. Reviewer Choice and Asian Theatre Jour.; contbr. numerous articles to profl. jours. Bd. dirs. extensive cons. in mental health spl. programs, N.W. Ctr. for Visual Anthropology, 1979-83, Family Planning, Olympia, 1985-90, Mental Health Adv., Olympia, 1988—, exec. com. consumer/survivor rsch. & policy rev. Fellow Am. Anthrop. Assn.; mem. Soc. for Disability Studies, N.W. Women's Studies, Anthropology and Gerontology, Soc. for Lesbian and Gay Anthrops., Phi Beta Kappa. Office: Evergreen State Coll Olympia WA 98505

DEDEAUX, PAUL J., orthodontist; b. Pass Christian, Miss., Feb. 22, 1937; s. Mack and Harriet D.; m. Janet Louise Harter, June 29, 1971; children: Michele, Kristen, Kelly. BA, Dillard U., 1959; DDS, Howard U., 1963; MS, Fairleigh Dickinson U., 1975. Pvt. practice, Washington, 1967-69, Santa Ana, Calif., 1976—; instr. Howard U., Washington, 1967-69; dental dir. Dr. Martin Luther King Health Ctr., Bronx, N.Y., 1969-70, dentist, 1970-76; instr. Howard U., Washington, 1967-69; cons. Hostos C.C., Bronx, 1971-76; mem. adv. panel Dental Econs. mag., 1976; adj. assoc. prof. Columbia U., N.Y.C., 1970-72. Contbr. articles to profl. jours. Capt. U.S. Army, 1963-67, col. USAR, 1975—. Mem. Am. Assn. Orthodontists, Pacific Coast Soc. Orthodontists, ADA, Calif. Dental Assn., Assn. Mil. Surgeons of U.S. Democrat. Methodist. Home: 12181 Anzio St Garden Grove CA 92640-4644 Office: 1125 E 17th St Ste W119 Santa Ana CA 92701-2201

DEDHIA, NAVIN SHAMJI, electrical engineer; b. Bombay, Dec. 25, 1940; came to U.S., 1966; s. Shamji Pancharia and Devkaben Shamji (Furia) D.; m. Neelam Navin, Feb. 2, 1971; children: Nivita, Neha. BEE, U. Bombay, 1963; MSEE, Tenn. Technol. U., 1968; MBA, Golden Gate U., 1983. Registered profl. engr., Calif. Engr. Polychem Ltd., Bombay, 1963-66; design engr. Consol. Comstock Co., Pitts., 1967; mfg. engr. IBM, East Fishkill, N.Y., 1968-76; quality engr. IBM, San Jose, Calif., 1976-83, adv. engr., 1983—. Editor Quality World newsletter, 1982—. Pres. Mid-Hudson India

Assn., Poughkeepsie, N.Y., 1973-74, Jain Ctr. No. Calif., Fremont, 1987-88. Fellow Am. Soc. for Quality Control (cert. reliability and quality engr., chmn. Internat. chpt. 1984—, Santa Clara Valley chpt. 1987-88, chmn. cert. mech. inspector certification program 1986-92, mem. E.J. Lancaster award com. 1986-90, Vol. of Month award Milw. 1988); mem. Brazilian Assn. for Quality Control (hon.). Jain. Home: 5080 Bougainvillea Dr San Jose CA 95111-3905 Office: IBM ADSTAR 791-501 5600 Cottle Rd San Jose CA 95193

DEDINI, ELDON LAWRENCE, cartoonist; b. King City, Calif., June 29, 1921; s. Grutly Stefano and Oleta Regina (Loeber) D.; m. Virginia DeSales Conroy, July 15,1944; 1 son, Giulio. A.A., Hartnell Coll., Salinas, Calif., 1942; grad., Chouinard Art Inst., Los Angeles, 1942-44. Staff cartoonist: Salinas Morning Post, 1940-41; staff story dept., Walt Disney Studios, Burbank, Calif., 1944-46; staff cartoonist: Esquire mag, Chho., 1946-50, New Yorker mag, N.Y.C., 1950—, Playboy mag, Chgo., 1960—; Author: cartoon album The Dedini Gallery, 1961, A Much, Much Better World, 1985; anthologies of New Yorker, Playboy cartoons. Recipient ann. award for best color Cartoon Playboy, 1978. Mem. Nat. Cartoonists Soc. (Best Mag. Cartoonist award 1958, 61, 64, 89), Cartoonists Guild Inc (2d v.p. N.Y.C. 1970). Address: Box 1630 Monterey CA 93942

DEDONA, FRANCIS ALFRED, technology industry executive; b. Buffalo, N.Y., Apr. 29, 1924; s. Henry Joseph and Angela Agnes (Maggio) D.; m. Jacquelin Dalton, Apr. 14, 1956; children: Gregory Philip, Paul Francis, Andrea Grace, Daniela Angela. BS, U. Calif., Berkeley, 1949; DSc (hon), Northrop U., 1987. Engr. Northrop Aircraft Corp., Hawthorne, Calif., 1951-52; dir. fin. planning analysis Hughes Aircraft Co., Culver City, Calif., 1952-56; asst. dir., computer systems labs Litton Industries, Inc., Beverly Hills, Calif., 1956-61; exec. v.p., co-founder The Scionics Corp., Northridge, Calif., 1961-69; exec. v.p. U.S. Electro-Optical Systems Corp., L.A., 1969-72; pres., chief exec. officer The Scionics Corp, L.A., 1972-78; pres. Arrowsmith Industries, Inc., L.A., 1978-86; pres., owner Nortel and Nortel PTE, LTD, Sherman Oaks, Calif., 1970—; pres. Nortel Consultancy, import-export, Sherman Oaks, Calif., 1970—; dir. Pertron Controls Corp., Chatsworth, Calif., 1978—, AFCOA Corp., Chatsworth, 1968-69, Nat. Security Indsl. Assn., L.A., 1979—. Inventor in technology field. Trustee, chmn. devel. com., Northrop U., L.A., 1981—; fund raiser, advisor Boy Scouts Am., L.A., 1960—. Lt. (j.g.), naval aviator USN, 1943-46. Mem. NSPE, Inst. Mgmt. Cons., Indsl. Devel. Rsch. Coun., Dist. Export Coun. (US Dept. of Commerce), Export Mgrs. Assn. of Calif., Nat. Security Indsl. Assn., Am. Defense Preparedness Assn., Am. Ordnance Assn., Soc. of Mfg. Engrs., Am. Metal Stamping Assn., Nat. Machine Tool Builder's Assn., Nat. Tool and Spl. Machine Assn., ASME-UCLA Engring. Adv. Coun., Inst. Mgmt. Scis., Nat. Soc. Profl. Engr. Railway Progress Inst., Assn. Computing Machinery, Assn. Corp. Growth, The Newcomen Soc., Univ. Tech. Transfer, Inc (v.p.), The Regency Club, Los Angles Athletic Club. Republican. Home: 3553 Scadlock Ln Sherman Oaks CA 91403-4317 Office: PO Box 5747 Sherman Oaks CA 91413-5747

DEDRICK, KENT GENTRY, retired physicist, researcher; b. Watsonville, Calif., Aug. 9, 1923; s. Frederick David and Matilda (Redman) D.; 1 child, Susan Marie. BS in Chemistry and Physics, San Jose (Calif.) State U., 1946; MS in Phys. Scis., Stanford U., 1949, PhD in Theoretical Physics, 1955. Rsch. assoc. U. Mich., Ann Arbor, 1954-55, Stanford U., 1955-62; math. physicist Stanford Rsch. Inst., Menlo Park, Calif., 1962-75; cons. scientist Atty. Gen.'s Office State of Calif., Sacramento, 1976-80; with marine tech. safety dept. State Lands Commn., Sacramento, 1980-81, rsch. specialist, 1981-92; cons. scientist phys. and environ. scis., 1992—. Contbr. articles to profl. jours.; composer instrumental and vocal works, 1978—. Pres. Com. for Green Foothills, Palo Alto, Calif., 1972-74; founding co-chmn. So. Crossing Action Team, San Francisco Bay area, 1970-72, chmn. Bayfront com. Sierra Club, Palo Alto, 1967-72. Mem. Am. Phys. Soc., Am. Geophys. Union, Soc. Wetland Scientists, Sigma Xi. Home: 1360 Vallejo Way Sacramento CA 95818-3450

DEE, MICHAEL, food service executive, restaurant manager; b. Santa Cruz, Bolivia, Oct. 24, 1964; came to the U.S., 1988; s. Jorge and Ilse (Ortiz) D.; m. Stephanie A. Palenque, Oct. 31, 1992; stepchildren: Patricia Maher, Susan Maher, Melissa Eaker. BS in Sci. Comm., U. Santa Cruz, 1985, cert. in acctg., 1986; cert. in cooking, Morris County Adult Sch., 1990. Bank teller Banco Boliviano-Americano, Santa Cruz, 1985; owner, chef Coconuts Bar and Restaurant, Santa Cruz, 1985-88; chef Tragaras Restaurant, Balt., 1988-89, Jean Pierre, Washington, 1989; chef, manager The Green Village (N.J.) Deli, 1989-93; owner Jaime's Place, Sacramento, 1993—; cons. Sacramento Culinary Arts Sch., 1993—. Author: Your Guide to Bolivian Cuisine, 1988, 101 Ways to Serve Meat and Rice, 1989, Hot! Hot! Hot!, 1990, Home Cooking with Saltaneas and Cuniapae, 1992, The Chicken Smells Good, 1993. Recipient Svc. and Hospitality Excellence award Sacramento C. of C., 1993. Mem. Sacramento Restaurant and Hotel Assn. Republican. Roman Catholic. Office: Werick Towers 3517 Marconi Ave Ste 211 Sacramento CA 95821

DEEMS, ANDREW WILLIAM, health facility administrator; b. Corpus Christi, Tex., Sept. 19, 1946; s. Ralph Francis and Ruth Frances (Pfister) D.; m. Glenda Jean Wyma, Apr. 6, 1968; children: Leslie, Matthew. BA with honors, Occidental Coll., 1968; MPH, U. Calif., Berkeley, 1972. Asst. adminstr. Merle West Med. Ctr., Klamath Falls, Oreg., 1972-77, Alta Bates Hosp., Berkeley, 1977-79; exec. v.p. Mt. Zion Hosp. and Med. Ctr., San Francisco, 1979-84; exec. v.p. St. Mary's Hosp. and Med. Ctr., San Francisco, 1984-88, pres., chief exec. officer, 1988-92; pres., CEO Palomar Pomerado Health System, Escondido, Calif., 1992—; pres. San Francisco Sect. Hosp. Coun., 1990-92, West Bay Hosp. Conf., 1990-92; bd. dir. Hosp. Coun. No. and Cen. Calif., 1990-92. Bd. dirs. United Way, 1993—, Hosp. Coun. San Diego and Imperial Counties, 1993—. Lt. (j.g.) USN, 1968-69. Recipient W. Glenn Ebersole award Hosp. Forum Mag., 1972. Fellow Am. Coll. Healthcare Execs.; mem. West Bay Hosp. Conf. (pres., bd. dirs. 1990-92), Hosp. Coun. No. and Cen. Calif. (bd. dirs. 1990-92), Hosp. Coun. San Diego and Imperial Counties (bd. dirs. 1993—). Republican. Presbyterian.

DEERING, FRED ARTHUR, insurance company executive; b. Winfield, Kans., Jan. 12, 1928; s. Frederick A. and Lucile (Phillips) D.; m. Isabell Staufenberg, June 14, 1949; m. Elizabeth Kimball MacMillan, Apr. 12, 1979; children: Anne Deering Buchanan, Kate. BS, U. Colo., 1951, LLB, 1951; LHD (hon.), Loretto Heights Coll., 1984. Bar: Colo. 1951. Assoc. firm Gorsuch, Kirgis, Campbell, Walker & Grover, Denver, 1951-54, ptnr., 1954-62; v.p., gen. counsel Security Life of Denver, 1962-66, pres., chief exec. officer, 1966-82, chmn., chief exec. officer, 1982-89, chmn., 1989—; chmn. chief exec. officer, dir. Midwestern United Life Ins. Co., 1983-89, Halifax Life Ins. Co., Toronto, 1985-88; vice chmn. bd. Inveseo Fin. Funds Group, chmn., 1968-90; bd. dirs. NN Fin. Co. of Can.; instr. Am. Inst. Banking, 1953-57; guest lectr. Colo. Sch. Law, 1958-59. Editor-in-chief Rocky Mountain Law Rev. Trustee Loretto Heights Coll., 1968-88, chmn. bd. dirs., 1968-84, chmn. emeritus, 1984-88; bd. dirs. Wallace Village for Children, 1968-78, Met. United Fund, 1969-71, Porter Hosp., 1970-79, U. Colo. Found., 1972-75; mem. adv. com. Met. Assn. for Retarded Children, Denver, 1970-71, Denver Rsch. Inst., 1972-76; trustee Huebner Found., 1980-85, St. Mary's Acad., Denver, 1989—; bd. dirs. Inst. Internat. Edn., Denver, 1986-92, Nat. Western Stock Show, 1990—, Global Health Scis. Fund. With U.S. Army, 1946-47. Named Colo. Businessman of Yr. Alpha Kappa Psi, 1977, Disting. Law Alumnus, U. Colo., 1982. Mem. ABA, Colo. Bar Assn., Denver Bar Assn., Am. Judicature Soc., Colo. Life Conv., Life Office Mgmt. Assn. (dir. 1977-81, 82-85, chmn. 1983-84), Denver C. of C., Met. Denver Execs. Club (pres. 1970-71), Old Baldy Club, Cherry Hills Country Club (bd. dirs. 1973-76, pres. 1975-76), Wigwam Club, Indian Creek Club, Mission Valley Country Club, Univ. Club, Order of Coif, Sigma Alpha Epsilon.

DEERING, MARK STEPHEN, computer operations manager; b. San Francisco, Nov. 7, 1966; s. Denis Paul and Patricia Anne (Murphy) D. BA in Stats., U. Calif., Berkeley, 1989. Computer ops. mgr. Saint Vincent's Day Home, Oakland, Calif., 1988—, Holy Family Day Home, San Francisco, 1988—. Home: 487 29th St San Francisco CA 94131 Office: Saint Vincents Day Home 1086 8th St Oakland CA 94607

DEFAZIO, LYNETTE STEVENS, dancer, choreographer, educator, chiropractor; b. Berkeley, Calif., Sept. 29; d. Honore and Mabel J. (Estavan) Stevens; student U. Calif., Berkeley, 1950-55, San Francisco State Coll., 1950-51; D. Chiropractic, Life-West Chiropractic Coll., San Lorenzo, Calif., 1983, BA in Humanities, New Coll. Calif., 1986; children—Joey H. Panganiban, Joanna Pang. Diplomate Nat. Sci. Bd.; eminence in dance edn., Calif. Community Colls. dance specialist, standard services, childrens ctrs. credentials Calif. Dept. Edn. Contract child dancer Monogram Movie Studio, Hollywood, Calif., 1938-40; dance instr. San Francisco Ballet, 1953-64; performer San Francisco Opera Ring, 1960-67; performer, choreographer Oakland (Calif.) Civic Light Opera, 1963-70; fgn. exchange dance dir. Academie de Danses-Salle Pleyel, Paris, France, 1966; dir. Ballet Arts Studio, Oakland, 1960—; teaching specialist Oakland Unified Sch. Dist.-Childrens Ctrs., 1968-80; instr. Peralta Community Coll. Dist., Oakland, 1971—, chmn. dance dept., 1985—; cons., instr. extension courses UCLA, Dirs. and Suprs. Assn., Pittsburg Unified Sch. Dist., Tulare (Calif.) Sch. Dist., 1971-73; researcher Ednl. Testing Services, HEW, Berkeley, 1974; resident choreographer San Francisco Childrens Opera, 1970—, Oakland Civic Theater; ballet mistress Dimensions Dance Theater, Oakland, 1977-80; cons. Gianchetta Sch. Dance, San Francisco, Robicheau Boston Ballet, TV series Patchwork Family, CBS, N.Y.C.; choreographer Ravel's Valses Nobles et Sentimentales, 1976. Author: The Opera Ballets; A Choreographic Manual, Vols. I-V, 1986. Recipient Foremost Women of 20th Century, 1985, Merit award San Francisco Children's Opera, 1985, 90. Mem. Profl. Dance Tchrs. Assn. Am. Author: Basic Music Outlines for Dance Classes, 1960, rev., 1968; Teaching Techniques and Choreography for Advanced Dancers, 1965; Basic Music Outlines for Dance Classes, 1965; Goals and Objectives in Improving Physical Capabilities, 1970; A Teacher's Guide for Ballet Techniques, 1970; Principle Procedures in Basic Curriculum, 1974; Objectives and Standards of Performance for Physical Development, 1975. Assoc. music arranger Le Ballet du Cirque, 1964, Techniques of a Ballet School, 1970, rev., 1974; assoc. composer, lyricist The Ballet of Mother Goose, 1968; choreographer: Valses Nobles Et Sentimentales (Ravel), Transitions (Kashevaroff), 1991, The New Wizard of Oz, 1991, San Francisco Children's Opera (Gingold); Canon in D for Strings and Continuo (Pachelbel), 1979. Home and Office: 4923 Harbord Dr Oakland CA 94618-2506

DEFAZIO, PETER A., congressman; b. Needham, Mass., May 27, 1947; m. Myrnie Daut. BA in Econs. and Polit. Sci., Tufts U., 1969; postgrad., U. Oreg., 1969-71, MS in Pub. Adminstrn./Gerontology, 1977. Aide to U.S. Rep. Jim Weaver, 1977-82; sr. issues specialist, caseworker, dist. field office U.S. rep. Jim Weaver, 1977-78, legis. asst. Washington office, 1978-80, dir. constituent services, 1980-82; mem. commn. representing Springfield Lane County (Oreg.) Commn., 1982-86; mem. 100-103rd Congresses from 4th Oreg. dist., Washington, D.C., 1987—; mem. natural resources com., mem. pub. works and transp. com. Mem. Lane County Econ. Devel. com., Intergovtl. Relations com.; bd. dirs. Eugene-Springfield Met. Partnership; Lane County Dem. precinct person, 1982—. Served with USAFR. Mem. Assn. of Oreg. Counties (legis. com.), Nat. Assn. of Counties (tax and fin. com.). Office: US Ho of Reps 1233 Longworth Washington DC 20510-3704*

DEFEO, JOHN EUGENE, communications executive; b. Phila., Sept. 26, 1946; married; 3 children. A of Tech. in Elec. Engring., Temple U., 1967, BBA, 1970. Mktg., sales, engring. and mfg. mgmt. positions Schaevitz Engring., Pennsauken, N.J., 1966-70, Air-Shields, Inc., Hatsboro, Pa., 1970-74; product mgr. nuclear instruments Abbott Lab., North Chicago, Ill., 1974-76; program gen. mgr. nuclear diagnostics GE, Milw., 1976-78; mgr. mktg. programs mobile communications div. GE, Lynchburg, Va., 1978-81; v.p. mktg., exec. v.p. U S West NewVector Group, Inc., Bellevue, Wash., 1986, chmn. bd. dirs., CEO, 1987-88, pres., CEO, 1991—; pres., CEO U S West Spectrum Enterprises, Bellevue, 1990-91, pres., 1991—; bd. dirs. U.S. West Advanced Techs., Mobilink; guest lectr. U. Wash., U. Oreg., various other univs., Seattle area; chmn. Nuclear Imaging Sector. Chmn. bd. Ind. Colls. Wash.; bd. dirs. Seattle Symphony, Seattle U. Bus. Sch.; mem. exec. com. Ctr. Retail and Distbn. Mgmt.; active in MBA mentor program Seattle U. Mem. NEMA (bd. dirs. diagnostic imaging and therapy div.), Cellular Telecommunications Industry Assn. (bd. dirs.), Found. for Ind. Higher Edn. (trustee). Office: US West NewVector Group Inc 3350 161st Ave SE PO Box 7329 Bellevue WA 98008-1329

DEFLYER, JOSEPH EUGENE, college dean; b. Whitefish, Mont., Nov. 9, 1943; s. George Samuel and Alice Irene (Hellman) DeF.; m. Janet Lee Maresh, Oct. 29, 1971; children: Erika Ann, Elizabeth Ruth, David Joseph. BA, Carroll Coll., 1966; PhD, U. Nebr., 1974. Instr. U. Nebr., Lincoln, 1970-76; from asst. prof. to assoc. prof. McMurry Coll., Abilene, Tex., 1976-80; from asst. prof. to assoc. prof. U. N.D., Grand Forks, 1980-90, dept. chair, 1984-88; assoc. dean acad. affairs Oreg. Inst. Tech., Klamath Falls, 1990-91, dean Sch. Health and the Arts and Scis., 1991—. Contbr. articles to profl. jours.; author revs.; author correspondence course. Mem. Lions Club, Grand Forks, 1987-90; deacon Federated Ch., Grand Forks, 1986-90; mem. Dem. Party, Tex., N.D., Oreg., 1976—; mem. Sierra Club, 1982—, group leader, 1988, chpt. del., 1990; mem., conf. sect. chair Rocky Mountain MLA, 1976-90; mem., leader Citizens Against Toxic Waste, N.D., 1987-88. NDEA Title fellow U. Nebr./U.S. Govt., 1967-70; presdl. scholar Carroll Coll., 1961-65. Mem. MLA (occasional conf. sect. chair 1976-90), Assn. for Study of Am. Indian Lit. (conf. presenter 1976—). Democrat. Home: 146 Hillside Ave Klamath Falls OR 97601 Office: Oreg Inst Tech 3201 Campus Dr Klamath Falls OR 97601

DE FONVILLE, PAUL BLISS, historic organization administrator; b. Oakland, Calif., Mar. 3, 1923; s. Marion Yancey and Charlotte (Bliss) de F.; m. Virginia Harpell, June 17, 1967. Student, Calif. Poly. U., 1942-44, Michael Chekhov Group, 1947-52. Founder, pres. Cowboy Meml. and Libr., Caliente, Calif., 1969—; tchr. outdoor edn. Calif. State U., Bakersfield, 1980. Life mem. Presdl. Task Force, Washington, 1984—, Rep. Senatorial inner circle, Washington, 1989—, Nat. Rep. Congl. Com., Washington, 1990—, Rep. Nat. Com., 1987—, U.S. Senatorial Club, 1988—, Rep. Senatorial Commn., 1991, Presdl. Election Registry, 1992. Recipient Slim Pickens award Calif. State Horsemen, 1980, Marshall-Working Western award Rose Parade, Pasadena, 1980, recognition Kern County, 1984, proclamations Mayor of Bakersfield, 1984, 85, Govt. of Calif., 1984, resolution Calif. Senate, 1988, Calif. Assembly, 1990, Presdl. Order of Merit, 1991, Congl. Cert. of Merit, 1992, Rep. Presdl. Legion of Merit award, 1992, document Gov. of Calif., 1993. Mem. SAG, NRA, Calif. State Horsemen (life), Equestrian Trails (life), Forty Niners (life), Calif. Rep. Assembly, Heritage Found., Cowboy Turtles Assn. (life), Rodeo Cowboys Assn. (life), Pro Rodeo Cowboys Assn. (life), Internat. Platform Assn. Baptist. Home: 40371 Cowboy Ln Caliente CA 93518-1405

DE FOREST, EDGAR LESTER, actor, poet, educator; b. Hull, Mass.; s. Edgar Leonard and Ellen Marian (Huntington) De F.; m. Beulah Mary Ingalls, Nov. 21, 1940; children: Peter, Stephen, David, Richard. Diploma, Leland Powers Sch. of Theatre, Boston, 1937; BS, Boston U., 1940; MA, U. So. Calif., 1941; EdD, Columbia U., 1954. Cert. elem. tchr., Calif. (life); cert. secondary tchr., Calif. (life); cert. sch. adminstr., Calif. Dir. reading Mich. State U. (formerly Mich. State Coll.), East Lansing, 1945-48, asst. dir. summer program, 1954-57; dir. students Suffolk U., Boston, 1948-52; assoc. survey research Columbia U., N.Y.C., 1952-53; acting dean instruction Ventura (Calif.) Coll., 1957-60; prof. Coll. Desert, Palm Desert, Calif., 1962-78, prof. emeritus, 1979—; dean of ship U. Seven Seas, Whittier, Calif., 1964-65. Author various poems; appeared in plays Man of La Mancha, 1982, Death of a Salesman, 1983, Homage to Dali, 1988, Becket, The Fantastiks, Booth Majority of One, The King and I. Mem. Mayor's cultural planning 2000 com., Palm Desert, 1985-86; pres. Friends of the Library Coll. of the Desert, Palm Desert, 1983-85. Named Ideal Citizen of the Age of Enlightenment, World Govt. for the Age of Enlightenment, 1971. Mem. Mich. Reading Assn. (founder, pres. 1954-55), Lambda Chi Alpha. Democrat. Home: 220 Pinyon Crest Mountain Center CA 92561-9756

DEFREESE, VERNON LEE, JR., air force officer; b. Kittery, Maine, Sept. 29, 1962; s. Vernon Lee Sr. and Velma Jean (Glover) DeF.; m. Karen Lee Nagle, Feb. 14, 1987; children: Adrianna Corrin, Danielle Lee, Alexis Maria. BS in Bus. Adminstrn., Norwich U., Northfield, Vt., 1984; MS in Adminstrn., Ctrl. Mich. U., Mt. Pleasant, 1992. Commd. 2d lt. U.S. Air Force, 1984, advanced through grades to capt., 1988; with 91 Ops. Group U.S. Air Force, Minot AFB, 1985-90; missile staff officer Hdqrs. 15th Air Force U.S. Air Force, March AFB, Calif., 1990-91; missile staff officer 20th Air Force Hdqrs. U.S. Air Force, Vandenberg AFB, Calif., 1991—. Decorated Air Force Commendation medal (2). Mem. Missile Boosters Assn. (chmn. philanthropy 1992—), Air Force Assn. (life), Kuk Sool Won Assn., San Diego Zool. Soc. Republican. Lutheran. Home: 427 Aspen Vandenberg AFB CA 93437-1319 Office: 20 AF/DOMM 747 Nebraska Ave Ste 15 Vandenberg AFB CA 93437-6275

DE GALI, ERNESTO, news editor; b. Havana, Cuba, Nov. 7, 1939; came to U.S. 1965; s. Manuel and Concepcion De G.; m. Nory, Nov. 10, 1964; 1 child, Vicente. Student, Havana U., Cuba, L.A. City Coll. News editor/commentator KTNQ Spanish Radio, L.A., 1979-86, KKHJ Spanish Radio, L.A., 1986—. Honored by U.S. Congress for svc. to Spanish Community. Office: Liberman Communication 5724 Hollywood Blvd Hollywood CA 90028

DEGEORGE, GAIL, special education educator; b. Englewood, N.J., Nov. 27, 1950; d. Frank Anthony and Bertha (Zwienzska) DeG.; m. Georges Melhim Mouchantaf, May 7, 1981 (div. Jan. 1985). BA, Ariz. State U., Tempe, 1977, MEd, 1986, postgrad., 1988—. Cert. elem. edn., spl. edn. tchr., prin., Ariz. Spl. edn. tchr. Ariz. Boys' Ranch (Ariz.)-Helamen House, 1977-80, Ariz. State Hosp., Phoenix, 1980-82, Mesa (Ariz.) Pub. Schs., 1982-84; tng. supr. Am. West Airlines, Tempe, 1984-86; spl. edn. tchr. Phoenix Union High Sch., 1986—. Mem. NEA, Ariz. Ednl. Assn., Profl. Women in Edn., Wine Taster's Guild. Republican. Roman Catholic. Home: 2402 E San Miguel Phoenix AZ 85016 Office: Camelback High Sch 4612 N 28th St Phoenix AZ 85016

DE GETTE, DIANA LOUISE, lawyer, state legislator; b. Tachikawa, Japan, July 29, 1957; came to U.S., 1957; d. Richard Louis and Patricia Anne (Rose) De G.; m. Lino Sigisnmondo Lipinsky de Orlov, Sept. 15, 1984; 1 child, Raphaela Anne. BA magna cum laude, The Colo. Coll., 1979; JD, NYU, 1982. Bar: Colo. 1982, U.S. Dist. Ct. Colo. 1982, U.S. Ct. Appeals (10th cir.) 1984, U.S. Supreme Ct. 1989. Dep. state pub. defender Colo. State Pub. Defender, Denver, 1982-84; assoc. Coghill & Goodspeed, P.C., Denver, 1984-86; sole practice Denver, 1986-92; of counsel Feiger, Collison & Killmer, Denver, 1992—; mem. Colo. Ho. of Reps., 1992—, mem. judiciary, local govt., legal svcs. coms. Editor: (mag.) Trial Talk, 1989-92. Mem. Mayor's Mgmt. Rev. Com., Denver, 1983-84; resolutions chair Denver Dem. Party, 1986; bd. dirs. Root-Tilden Program, NYU Sch. Law, N.Y.C., 1986-92; bd. trustees, alumni trustee Colo. Coll., Colorado Springs, 1988—. Recipient Root-Tilden scholar NYU Sch. Law, N.Y.C., 1979, Vanderbilt medal, 1982. Mem. Colo. Bar Assn. (bd. govs. 1989-91), Colo. Trial Lawyers Assn. (bd. dirs., exec. com. 1986-92), Colo. Women's Bar Assn., Denver Bar Assn., Phi Beta Kappa, Pi Gamma Mu. Office: Feiger Collison & Killmer 551 16th St #300 Denver CO 80202

DE GOFF, VICTORIA JOAN, lawyer; b. San Francisco, Mar. 2, 1945; d. Sidney Francis and Jean Frances (Alexander) De G.; m. Peter D. Coppelman, May 2, 1971 (div. Dec. 1978); m. Richard Sherman, June 16, 1980. BA in Math. with great distinction, U. Calif., Berkeley, 1967, JD, 1972. Bar: Calif. 1972, U.S. Dist. Ct. (no. dist.) Calif. 1972, U.S. Ct. Appeals 1972, U.S. Supreme Ct. 1989. Rsch. atty. Calif. Ct. Appeal, San Francisco, 1972-73; Reginald Heber Smith Found. fellow San Francisco Neighborhood Legal Assistance Found., 1973-74; assoc. Field, De Goff, Huppert & McGowan, San Francisco, 1974-77; pvt. practice Berkeley, Calif., 1977-80; ptnr. De Goff and Sherman, Berkeley, 1980—; lectr. continuing edn. of bar, Calif., 1987, 90-92, U. Calif. Boalt Hall Sch. Law, Berkeley, 1981-85, dir. appellate advocacy, 1992; cons. California Civil Practice: Procedure, Bancroft Whitney, 1992. Author: (with others) Matthew Bender's Treatise on California Torts, 1985. Appointed to adv. com. Calif. Jud. Coun. on Implementing Proposition 32, 1984-85; mem. adv. bd. Hastings Coll. Trial and Appellate Adv., 1984-92; expert 20/20 vision project, commn. on future of cts. Jud. Coun. Calif., 1992; appointed to appellate standing adv. com. to Calif. Jud. Coun., 1993. Fellow Woodrow Wilson Found., 1967-68. Mem. Calif. Trial Lawyers Assn. (bd. govs. 1980-88, amicus-curiae com. 1981-87, editor-in-chief assn. mag. 1980-81, Presdl. award of merit 1980, 81), Calif. Acad. Appellate Lawyers (sec./treas. 1989-90, 2d v.p. 1990-91, 1st v.p. 1991-92, pres. 1992-93), Edward J. McFetridge Am. Inn of Cts. (counsellor 1990-91, edn. chmn. 1991-92, social chmn. 1992-93, v.p. 1993—), Boalt Hall Sch. Law U. Calif. Alumni Assn. (bd. dirs. 1989-92), Order of Coif. Jewish. Office: 1916 Los Angeles Ave Berkeley CA 94707-2496

DEGRASSI, LEONARD RENE, art historian, educator; b. East Orange, N.J., Mar. 2, 1928; s. Romulus-William and Anna Sophia (Sannicolo) DeG.; m. Dolores Marie Welgoss, June 24, 1961; children: Maria Christina, Paul. BA, U. So. Calif., 1950, BFA, 1951, MA, 1956; postgrad., Harvard U., 1953, Istituto Centrale del Restauro di Roma, 1959-60, U. Rome, 1959-60, UCLA, 1970-73. Tchr. art Redlands (Calif.) Jr. High Sch., 1951-53, Toll Jr. High Sch., Glendale, Calif., 1953-61, Wilson Jr. High Sch., Glendale, 1961; mem. faculty Glendale Coll., 1962—, prof. art history, 1974-92, chmn. dept., 1972, 89, prof. emeritus, 1992—. Prin. works include: (paintings) high altar at Ch. St. Mary, Cook, Minn., altar screen at Ch. St. Andrew, El Segundo, Calif., 1965-71, 14 Stas. of the Cross Ch. St. Mary, Cook, Minn., altar screen at Ch. of the Descent of the Holy Spirit, Glendale, 14 Stas. of the Cross at Ch. of St. Benedict, Duluth, Minn; also research, artwork and dramatic work for Spaceship Earth exhbn. at Disney World, Orlando, Fla., 1980. Decorated knight Grand Cross Holy Sepulchre, 1974, knight St. John of Jerusalem, 1976, knight Order of Merit of Republic of Italy, 1973, Cross of Merit, 1984, 89; named First Disting. Faculty, 1987. Mem. Art Educators Assn., Glendale Art Assn., Egypt Exploration Soc. London, Am. Research Ctr. Egypt, Tau Kappa Alpha, Kappa Pi, Delta Sigma Rho. Office: 1500 N Verdugo Rd Glendale CA 91208-2894

DEGRAW, STEPHEN TODD, marketing executive; b. Long Beach, Calif., Apr. 14, 1956; s. Fredrick and Roseanne (Bertleshofer) DeG.; m. Juli Sage McGee, Feb. 23, 1991; 1 child, Devin Sage. BS in Pharmacology, U. Calif., Santa Barbara, 1979; MBA in Mktg., San Diego State U., 1988. Investigator, sr. rsch. assoc. Am. McGaw, Irvine, Calif., 1980-84; rsch. assoc. molecular biology dept. Scripps Clinic and Rsch. Found., La Jolla, Calif., 1984-87; grad. rsch. asst. San Diego State U., 1987-88; mktg. mgmt. cons. Am. Innovision, San Diego, 1988-89, biomed. product mgr., nat. sales mgr., 1989-92; product mgr. ONCOR Inst. Systems, 1992—. Contbr. articles to profl. jours.; co-patentee cooled low light color video camera. Recipient silver medal Osaka (Japan) Dragon Boat Championship, 1989, Penang (Malaysia) Dragon Boat Championship, 1990, gold medal World Invitational Dragon Boat Championship, Singapore, 1990. Mem. San Diego Internat. Dragonboat Racing Assn. (pres. 1991—), Hano Hano Outrigger Canoe Club. Office: ONCOR Instrument Systems 9581 Ridgehaven Ct San Diego CA 92123

DEGREIF, LARRY LEE, hospital official; b. Independence, Iowa, Nov. 25, 1941; s. Eldon C. DeGreif; m. Nancy L. McClain, Dec. 2, 1962; children: Timothy, Anthony, Penelope. AA, Chapman Coll., 1976, MS, 1984; BA, SUNY, Albany, 1980. Enlisted ensign USN, 1961, advanced through grades to master chief hosp. corpsman, 1980, preventive medicine technician, 1968-80; ret., 1980; asst. dir. environ. svcs. Mercy Hosp. and Med. Ctr., San Diego, 1981-88; mgr. environ. svcs. Hillside Hosp., San Diego, 1988-92; supr. environ. svcs. Children's Hosp. & Health Care Ctr., San Diego, 1992—; instr. San Diego City Coll., 1984-88. Mem. sch. site coun. Santana High Sch., Santee, Calif., 1982-86; pres. Santana High Sch. Parent-Tchr.-Student Assn., 1983-84; mem. adv. bd. San Diego C.C., 1985—; mem. Rep. Presdl. Task Force. Mem. Nat. Exec. Housekeepers Assn. (registered, speakers bur. 1984—), Am. Soc. Healthcare Environ. Svcs., VFW, Mensa. Office: Childrens Hosp & Health Ctr 3020 Children's Way San Diego CA 92123

DE GROUCHY, ROBERT TRAVIS, JR., regional manager; b. Abington, Pa., Jan. 17, 1953; s. Robert Travis Sr. and Marie (Teefy) de G.; m. Milagros Inocencio, Apr. 30, 1977; children: Efren John Echebaria, Robert Travis III. Student, St. Mary's (Md.) Coll., 1971-74; BSBA, City U., 1980, MBA, 1989. Retail mgr. Tandy Corp., Tacoma, 1985; team leader VSE Corp., Seattle, 1985-87; site mgr. ICT Corp., Seattle, 1987-89, N.W. regional mgr., 1989—. Lt. S.C., USN, 1974-84.

DEHAVEN, KENNETH LE MOYNE, retired physician; b. The Dalles, Oreg., Mar. 28, 1913; s. Luther John and Dora (Beeks) DeH.; m. Ledith Mary Ewing, Jan. 11, 1937; children: Marya LeMoyne DeHaven Keeth, Lisa

Marguerite DeHaven Jordan, Camille Suzanne DeHaven. BS, North Pacific Coll. Oreg., 1935; MD, U. Mich., 1946. Intern USPHS Hosp., St. Louis, 1947; intern Franklin Hosp., San Francisco, 1947-48, resident, 1949; clinician Dept. Pub. Health, City San Francisco, Dept. V.D., 1949-51; practice gen. medicine, Sunnyvale, Calif., 1955-87; mem. staff El Camino Hosp., Mt. View, Calif., San Jose (Calif.) Hosp. Pres. Los Altos Hills Assn. Served to capt., USAF, 1952-55. Fellow Am. Acad. Family Practice; mem. Calif. Med. Assn., Santa Clara Couty Med. Soc., Astron. Soc. Pacific, Sunnyvale C. of C. (bd. dirs. 1955-56), Book Club (San Francisco), Masons, Alpha Kappa Kappa. Republican. Home: 9348 E Casitas Del Rio Dr Scottsdale AZ 85255-4313

DEHGHAN, ELIZABETH IRENE, waste management administrator; b. Pasadena, Calif., May 15, 1951; d. William Klein and Laurie Louise (Aslin) Reif; m. Ahmad Dehghan, July 19, 1972 (div. Feb. 1979); children: Mehrdad Irme, Nader Wenton; m. Rodger H. Thomas, Dec. 31, 1988. ASBA, Allen Hancock Coll., Santa Maria, Calif., 1977; BSBA in Info. Systems, Calif. State U., 1980. Bookkeeper, computer cons. Dehghan Mgmt. Svcs., Baldwin Park, Calif., 1976-82; computer cons. Lizzy's Computer Help, Portales, N.Mex., 1982—; dir. tng. Acropolis Info. Systems, Ada, Okla., 1983-84; mgr. Tandy Corp./Radio Shack, Oklahoma City, 1984-85; mgr., salesperson Tandy Corp./Radio Shack, Clovis, N.Mex., 1987-91, mgr., 1985-87; computer mapping specialist City of Clovis (N.Mex.) Pub. Work Dept., 1987—, solid waste mgmt. coord., 1990—; mem. Environ. Dept. Recycling and Reduction Task Force, Santa Fe, N.Mex., 1991—; exec. coord. Beautiful Clovis, A Keep Am. Beautiful Affiliate, 1992—; mem. High Plains Solid Waste Assn., Clovis, 1991—. Author: Street Map of Clovis, 1988-92; editor: O&M Manual for Clovis WWTP, 1990; author: (computer aided drafting) City of Clovis Construction Standards Drawings, 1992. Leader Campfire Girls, Portales, N.Mex., 1982-84; cub master Boy Scouts Am., Ada, Okla., 1984-85. Recipient Environ. Leadership award N.Mex. Environ. Dept., Sante Fe, 1992. Mem. NAFE, Urisa. Office: Clovis Pub Works Dept PO Box 760 Clovis NM 88102

DEHMELT, HANS GEORG, experimental physicist; b. Germany, Sept. 9, 1922; came to U.S., 1952, naturalized, 1962; s. Georg Karl and Asta Ella (Klemmt) D.; 1 child from previous marriage, Gerd; m. Diana Elaine Dundore, Nov. 18, 1989. Grad., Graues Kloster, Berlin, Abitur, 1940; D Rerum Naturalium, U. Goettingen, 1950; D Rerum Naturalium (hon.), Ruprecht Karl-Universitat, Heidelberg, 1986; DSc (hon.), U. Chgo., 1987. Postdoctoral fellow U. Goettingen, Germany, 1950-52, Duke U., Durham, N.C., 1952-55; vis. asst. prof. U. Wash., Seattle, 1955; asst. prof. physics U. Wash., 1956, asso. prof., 1957-61, prof., 1961—; cons. Varian Assocs., Palo Alto, Calif., 1956-76. Contbr. articles to profl. jours. Recipient Humboldt prize, 1974, award in basic research Internat. Soc. Magnetic Resonance, 1980, Rumford prize Am. Acad. Arts and Scis., 1985, Nobel prize in Physics, 1989; NSF grantee, 1958—. Fellow Am. Phys. Soc. (Davisson-Germer prize 1970); mem. Am. Acad. Arts and Scis., Nat. Acad. Scis. Home: 1600 43d Ave E Seattle WA 98112 Office: U Wash Physics Dept FM 15 Seattle WA 98195

DEICHMAN, SHANE DANIEL, physicist; b. Paw Paw, Mich., July 28, 1967; s. Daniel James Mulrenin and Marguerite Judith (Haywood) Deichman. BS in Physics, U. Calif., Berkeley, 1989; postgrad., U.S. Naval War Coll., 1992—. Pneumatic system tech. Stanley-Bostitch, Alameda, Calif., 1984-87; student rsch. asst. Lawrence Livermore (Calif.) Nat. Labs., 1987-89, physicist, 1989-90; scientist rsch., devel., test & evaluation divsn. Naval Command, Control and Ocean Surveillance Ctr., San Diego, 1990—; coord. new profl. program Naval Ocean Systems Ctr., San Diego, 1990-92. Active Calif. Rep. Cen. Com., Sacramento, 1989—. Named one of Outstanding Young Men Am., 1989. Mem. Am. Phys. Soc. (assoc. zone councillor 1989-90), Armed Forces Comm. and Electronics Assn. (Regional Young AFCEAN rep. 1992—, v.p. programs 1993—, Disting. Young AFCEAN 1992), Arms Control Assn., U.S. Naval Inst., Naval Submarine League, Mensa, Delta Sigma Phi.

DEIHL, RICHARD HARRY, savings and loan association executive; b. Whittier, Calif., Sept. 8, 1928; s. Victor Francis and Wilma Aileen (Thomas) D.; m. Billie Dantz Beane, Mar. 24, 1952; children: Catherine Deihl Hamilton, Michael, Victoria Deihl Dresch, Christine Deihl Brant. A.B., Whittier Coll., 1949; postgrad., UCLA, 1949, U. Calif.-Berkeley, 1949-50. With Nat. Cash Register Co., Pomona, Calif., 1955-59; trainee Rio Hondo Savs. & Loan, Calif., 1959-60; loan cons. Home Savs. & Loan Assn. (now Home Savs. Am., A Fed. Savs. & Loan Assn.), Los Angeles, 1960-63; loan agt., supr., v.p. Home Savs. & Loan Assn., 1964, loan service supr., 1964, v.p. ops., v.p. loans, 1965, exec. v.p., 1966, pres., 1967-84, chief exec. officer, 1967—, chmn., 1984—, also dir.; chief exec. officer, dir. H.F. Ahmanson Co., 1984-92, chmn., 1986—; bd. dirs. Atlantic Richfield, FHLB, San Francisco, vice chmn., 1992. Contbr. articles to profl. jours. Trustee Whittier Coll.; bd. dirs. Good Samaritan Hosp. 1st lt. USAF, 1951-55. Decorated D.F.C., Air medal with three clusters. Republican. Club: Fairbanks Ranch Country (Rancho Santa Fe). Office: H F Ahmanson & Co 4900 Rivergrade Rd Irwindale CA 91706-1438

DEINES, HARRY J., agricultural and livestock company executive; b. Loveland, Colo., Nov. 5, 1909; s. John and Mary (Maseka) D.; B.M.E., U. Colo.; grad. Advanced Mgmt. Program, Harvard; m. Eleanor Vrooman, 1932; children: Gretchen Deines Langston, Mark, Katrina, Stephen. Advt. mgr. Gen. Electric Co., 1930-45; v.p. Fuller & Smith & Ross, 1945-49; gen. advt. mgr. Westinghouse Electric Corp., 1949-53; v.p. J. Walter Thompson, N.Y.C., 1953-56, Fuller & Smith & Ross, N.Y.C., 1956-59; exec. v.p., dir. Campbell, Mithun, Inc., Mpls., 1959-71; mng. partner Deines Agr. & Livestock Co., Ft. Collins, Colo., 1971—; pres. Collectors' Books Ltd. Home and Office: 1852 Edna Pl NW Bainbridge Is WA 98110-2627

DEIOTTE, CHARLES EDWARD, computer software company executive; b. Gary, Ind., Jan. 31, 1946; s. Raymond Louis and Dorothy Jane (Paulson) D.; A.A., Skagit Valley Jr. Coll., 1966; student Wash. State U., 1970; m. Margaret Williams Tukey, Sept. 11, 1971; children—Raymond, Karl, Ronald. Programmer, Wash. State U., Pullman, 1969-70; project dir. AGT Mgmt. Systems, Renton, Wash., sr. tech. cons., sect. mgr. McDonnell-Douglas Automation, Bellevue, Wash., 1972-73; sr. engr. Boeing Computer Services, Seattle, 1973-75, computer based instrn. specialist, Tng. div., 1975-79; mgr. microprocessor design support center Boeing Aerospace Co., Kent, Wash., 1979-80; mgr. concept research Federal Express Corp., Colorado Springs, Colo., 1980-81, mgr. microprocessor support group, 1981-82; pres. Deitron Systems, Inc., Auburn, Wash., 1976-81; pres., chmn. bd. Logical Systems Inc., Colorado Springs, 1981-87; chmn., CEO Cedsys Inc., 1987-91, sr. software engr., cons. LinCom Corp., 1992-93; software systems specialist, MCI Corp., 1993—; chmn. bd. Summit Med. Systems, Inc., 1985-86 . Neighborhood commr. Chief Seattle council Boy Scouts Am., 1971-72; v.p. REACT alert, Seattle, 1974; advisor Jr. Achievement, Colorado Springs, 1980; coach Odyssey of the Mind, 1991-92. Recipient Boeing Aerospace Co. Cert. of Achievement, 1979. Mem. Assn. Computing Machinery, IEEE, AAAS, Data Processing Mgmt. Assn., Am. Mgmt. Assn., Gamma Sigma Epsilon. Home: 16955 Vollmer Rd Colorado Springs CO 80908 Office: 5526 N Academy Colorado Springs CO 80918

DEISENROTH, CLINTON WILBUR, electrical engineer; b. Louisville, Aug. 9, 1941; s. Clifton Earl and Nell (Pierce) D.; B.E.E., Ga. Inst. Tech., 1965; m. Lisbeth D. Isaacs, May 10, 1974; 1 dau., Susan Michelle. With Raytheon Co., 1966-81, div. mgr. Addington Labs., Inc., solid state products div., Santa Clara, Calif., 1975-77, program mgr. electromagnetic systems div., Goleta, Calif., 1977-79, dir. surface navy electronic warfare systems, 1979-81; sr. v.p. systems div. Teledyne-MEC, 1981-84; pres. Teledyne CME, 1984-90; exec. v.p., gen. mgr. Aerospace Products div. G&H Tech., Inc., 1990-92; v.p. bus. devel. Whittaker Electronic Systems, 1992—. Mem. IEEE, Am. Mgmt. Assn., Am. Def. Preparedness Assn., Navy League. Home: 518 Oak Hampton Ct Thousand Oaks CA 91361 Office: Whittaker Electronic Systems 1785 Voyager Ave Simi Valley CA 93063-3349

DEITER, NEWTON ELLIOTT, clinical psychologist; b. N.Y.C., Dec. 12, 1931; s. Benjamin and Anna (Leibowitz) D. BS, UCLA, 1957; MS, Leland Stanford, 1960; PhD in Clin. Psychology, U. Chgo., 1965. Cert. in clin. psychology. Pvt. practice clin. psychology L.A., 1965-90; exec. dir. Nat. Family Planning Coun., L.A., 1965-76, Gay Media Task Force, L.A., 1976—; staff cons. Aaron Spelling Prodns., L.A., 1980-90, spl. cons. NBC, L.A., 1970-79, cons. broadcast standards dept. CBS, L.A., 1968-82, cons. City Coun., City of L.A., 1975-85. Columnist Bottomline Mag., 1992—. Mem. Dem. Cen. Com., L.A., 1972-76; bd. dirs. Gay Community Svcs. Ctr., L.A., 1970-75, Am. Cancer Soc., L.A., 1972-77, Palm Springs Gay Tourism Coun., 1993—; commr. L.A. Probation Commn., 1977-85; bd. advisors San Francisco Sheriffs Dept., 1969-79; pres. Internat. Gay Travel Assn., 1991-92. Lt. col. USAFR, 1950-75. Mem. Acad. TV and Scis., Press Club L.A., Internat. Gay Travel Assn. (bd. dirs. 1986-93, pres. 1991-92), Desert Bus. Assn. (v.p. 1993, bd. dirs. 1992), Air Force Assn., Am. Mensa, Masons. Home: 71426 Estellita Dr Rancho Mirage CA 92270-4215 Office: Rancho Mirage Travel 71-428 Hwy 111 Rancho Mirage CA 92270

DEITRICH, RICHARD ADAM, pharmacology educator; b. Monte Vista, Colo., Apr. 22, 1931; s. Robert Adam and Freda Leona (Scott) D.; m. Mary Margaret Burkholder, Jan. 29, 1954; children: Vivian Gay, Leslie Lynn, Lori Christine. BS, U. Colo., 1953, MS, 1954, PhD, 1959. Postdoctoral fellow, then instr. Johns Hopkins U., Balt., 1959-63; asst. prof., then assoc. prof. U. Colo., Denver, 1963-76, prof. pharmacology, 1976—, sci. dir. Alcohol Rsch. Ctr., 1977—; vis. prof. U. Berne, Switzerland, 1973-74. Editor: Development of Animal Models, 1981, Initial Sensitivity to Alcohol, 1990; contbr. over 100 articles to sci. publs. Pres. Mile High Coun. on Alcoholism, Denver, 1972-73; moderator 1st Universalist Ch., Denver, 1979. With U.S. Army, 1954-56. Grantee Nat. Inst. Alcoholism, 1977—, Nat. Inst. Communicative Disease and Stroke, 1963, numerous others. Mem. Rsch. Soc. on Alcoholism (pres. 1981-83), Internat. Soc. Biomed. Rsch. on Alcoholism (treas. 1986—), Am. Soc. Pharmacology, Am. Soc. Biol. Chemistry. Office: Univ Colo 4200 E 9th Ave Denver CO 80262-0001

DEJONG, BRUCE ALLEN, architect; b. Sully, Iowa, June 17, 1946; s. Floris Donald and Margaret (Van Roeckel) DeJ. BArch, Iowa State U., 1969. Registered architect Minn., Calif. Architect Charles Herbert & Assocs., Des Moines, 1968-70, Parker Klein Assocs., Mpls., 1970-71; v.p., project architect Perrenoud Architects Inc., Mpls., 1971-81; prin. Frederick Bentz, Milo Thompson, Robert Rietow, Inc., Mpls., 1981-91; v.p., chief architect Ellerbe Becket, Inc., Santa Monica, Calif., 1991—. Mem. arts adv. com. Met. Coun., St. Paul, 1986-89. Mem. AIA (v.p. 1988, pres. 1989, dir. Mpls. chpt. 1977-79, 88, 90-91, chmn. annual conf. 1985-87, L.A. chpt. 1991—), Am. Arbitration Assn., Constrn. Specifications Inst. Home: 2145 Mayview Dr Los Angeles CA 90027-4635

DEKKER, GEORGE GILBERT, literature educator, literary scholar, writer; b. Long Beach, Calif., Sept. 8, 1934; s. Gilbert J. and Laura (Barnes) D.; m. Linda Jo Bartholomew, Aug. 31, 1973; children by previous marriage: Anna Allegra, Clara Joy, Ruth Siobhan, Laura Daye. B.A. in English, U. Calif.-Santa Barbara, 1955; M.A. in English, 1958; M.Litt., Cambridge U. (Eng.), 1961; Ph.D. in English, U. Essex (Eng.), 1967. Lectr. U. Wales, Swansea, 1962-64; lectr. in lit. U. Essex, 1964-69, reader in lit., 1969-72, dean Sch. Comparative Studies, 1969-71; assoc. prof. English Stanford (Calif.) U., 1972-74, prof., 1974—, chmn. dept., 1978-81, 84-85, Joseph S. Atha prof. humanities, 1988—, dir. program in Am. Studies, 1988-91, assoc. dean grad. policy, 1993—. Author: Sailing After Knowledge, 1963, James Fenimore Cooper the Novelist, 1967; Coleridge and the Literature of Sensibility, 1978, The American Historical Romance, 1987; editor: Donald Davie: The Responsibilities of Literature, 1983. Nat. Endowment Humanities fellow, 1977; Inst. Advanced Studies in Humanities fellow U. Edinburgh (Scotland), 1982. Mem. MLA. Democrat. Office: Stanford U Dept English Stanford CA 94305

DE KRUIF, JACK H., manufacturing executive; b. Grand Rapids, Mich., Mar. 5, 1921; s. Angus Alton and Lois Grace (Bailey) deK.; m. Dolores Sue Rossi; 1 child: Lisa-Nicole. AB, Mich. State U., 1948; LLB, Ind. U., 1951. Atty. Bendix Corp., South Bend, Ind., 1951-53; group atty. Bendix Corp., Teterboro, Mich., 1953-55; gen. counsel NWL, Kalamazoo, Mich., 1955-58; dir. mktg. semi-conductor div. Hughes Aircraft, Newport Beach, Calif., 1958-60; pres., chief exec. officer Aseco, Inc., Novi, Mich., 1960-68, W-K Mfg. Co., Mt. Clemens, Mich., 1968-75; sole practice cons. Newport Beach, Calif., 1975-84; chmn., chief exec. officer Wayne Corp., Richmond, Ind., 1984; chmn., chief exec. officer Richmond Transp., Newport Beach, Calif., 1984—, also bd. dirs.; bd. dirs. Wayne Corp., Richmond, Inc. Pres. Big Bros./Big Sisters of Orange County, Tustin, Calif., 1987; dir., trustee Newport Harbor Art Mus., 1978-83; mem. Nat. Head Start Assn. Corp. Bd. With USAC, 1942-45, ETO. Mem. Ind. Bar Assn., Detroit Athletic Club, Ctr. Club, Balboa Bay Club. Episcopalian. Office: Richmond Transp Corp 4931 Birch St Newport Beach CA 92660-2166

DELA CRUZ, JOSE SANTOS, chief justice; b. Saipan, Commonwealth No. Mariana Islands, July 18, 1948; s. Thomas Castro and Remedio Sablan (Santos) Dela C.; m. Rita Tenorio Sablan, Nov. 12, 1977; children: Roxanne, Renee, Rica Ann. BA, U. Guam, 1971; JD, U. Calif., Berkeley, 1974; cert., Nat. Jud. Coll., Reno, 1985. Bar: No. Mariana Islands, 1974, U.S. Dist. Ct. No. Mariana Islands 1978. Staff atty. Micro. Legal Svcs. Corp., Saipan, 1974-79; gen. counsel Marianas Pub. Land Corp., Saipan, 1979-81; liaison atty. CNMI Fed. Laws Commn., Saipan, 1981-83; ptnr. Borja & Dela Cruz, Saipan, 1983-85; assoc. judge Commonwealth Trial Ct., Saipan, 1985-89; chief justice Supreme Ct. No. Mariana Islands, 1989—; Mem. Conf. of Chief Justices, 1989, Adv. Commn. on Judiciary, Saipan, 1980-82; chmn. Criminal Justice Planning Agy., Saipan, 1985—. Mem. Coun. for Arts, Saipan, 1982-83; chmn. Bd. of Elections, Saipan, 1977-82; pres. Cath. Social Svcs., Saipan, 1982-85. Mem. No. Marianas Bar Assn. (pres. 1984-85). Roman Catholic. Office: Commonwealth Supreme Ct Civic Ctr Saipan MP 96950

DE LA GARZA, RAY, systems analyst; b. L.A., Oct. 25, 1958; s. Ray and Dorothy (Sackett) de la G.; m. Nancy Carol Kahn, Nov. 14, 1981; children: Brett Michael, Bree Carol. BA in Liberal Scis., U. Calif., Riverside, 1981; BS in Computer Sci., Coleman Coll., 1983. Programmer, analyst Data Planning & Control Systems, Newport Beach, Calif., 1983-85; mgr. mgmt. info. systems Jaycor, San Diego, 1985—. Contbr. articles to profl. jours. Mem. San Diego Pick User Group, Orange County Pick Users. Home: 12561 Dormouse Rd San Diego CA 92129

DELANCEY, SCOTT CAMERON, linguistics educator; b. Rochester, N.Y., June 22, 1949; s. Robert Winks and Margaret Campbell (McKellar) DeL.; m. Kathryn Ann Rumsey, July 15, 1975; children: Robert Gilroy, Blaine Michael, Laura McKellar DeLancey. BA, Cornell U., 1972; PhD, Ind. U., 1980. Asst. prof. U. Colo., Boulder, 1980-82; asst. prof. U. Oreg., Eugene, 1982-85, assoc. prof., 1985-92, prof. linguistics, 1992—, head linguistics dept., 1985-90. Contbr. articles to profl. jours. NSF grantee, 1984—, NEH grantee, 1986-87. Mem. Am. Oriental Soc., Soc. for the Study of the Indigenous Langs. of the Americas, Linguistic Soc. Am., Nepal Studies Assn. Office: U Oreg Dept of Linguistics Eugene OR 97403

DELANEY, HERBERT WADE, JR., lawyer; b. Leadville, Colo., Mar. 30, 1925; s. Herbert Wade and Marie Ann (Garbarino) DeL.; m. Ramona Rae Ortiz, Aug. 6, 1953; children: Herbert Wade III, Paula Rae, Bonnie Marie Manshel. BSBA, U. Denver, 1949, LLB, 1951. Bar: Colo. 1951, U.S. Supreme Ct. 1959. Pvt. practice, Denver, 1953-64, 1965-91; mem. firm DeLaney and Sandven, P.C., 1992—; faculty U. Denver, Colo., 1960-61, 89; ptnr. DeLaney & West, Denver, 1964-65. Capt. JAG's Dept., USAF, 1951-53. Mem. ABA, Colo. Trial Lawyers Assn., Assn. Trial Lawyers of Am., Colo. Bar Assn., Denver Bar Assn., Am. Legion, Masons, Elks, Phi Alpha Delta. Office: 50 S Steele St Denver CO 80209-2805

DELANEY, MARION PATRICIA, advertising agency executive; b. Hartford, Conn., May 20, 1952; d. William Pride Delaney Jr. and Marian Patricia (Utley) Murphy. BA, Union Coll., Schenectady, N.Y., 1973. Adminstrv. asst. N.Y. State Assembly, Albany, 1973-74; account exec. Foote, Cone & Belding, N.Y.C., 1974-78; sr. account exec. Dailey & Assocs., L.A., 1978-81; pub. rels. cons. NOW, Washington, 1981-83; account supr. BBDO/West, L.A., 1983-85; v.p. Grey Advt., L.A., 1985-87, San Francisco, 1987-89; sr. v.p. McCann-Erickson, San Francisco, 1989—. Del. Dem. Nat. Conv., San Francisco, 1984; bd. dirs. JED Found., Hartford, Conn., 1989—. Mem. NOW (v.p. L.A. chpt. 1980-83, pres. 1984, advisor 1985-87). Congregationalist. Home: 11 Gary Way Fairfax CA 94930-1002

DELANEY, MATTHEW SYLVESTER, educator, academic administrator; b. Ireland, Nov. 26, 1927; s. Joseph C. and Elizabeth M. (Berrigan) D.; came to U.S., 1947, naturalized, 1952; student St. John's Coll., 1947-51; BA, Immaculate Heart Coll., L.A., 1958; MS, Notre Dame U., 1960; PhD, Ohio State U., 1971. Ordained priest Roman Cath. Ch., 1951; assoc. pastor L.A. Cath. Diocese, 1951-55; instr. math., physics Pius X High Sch., Downey, Calif., 1955-58, vice prin., 1960-62; instr. math. Immaculate Heart Coll., L.A., 1962-65, asst. prof., 1965-72, assoc. prof., 1972-76, prof., 1976—; asst. acad. dean, 1973-78; dean acad. devel. Mt. St. Mary's Coll., L.A., 1978-82, acad. dean, 1978-91; prof. mathematics, 1991—. NSF grantee, 1959-60, 61. Mem. Am. Math. Soc., Math. Assn. Am., Am. Conf. Acad. Deans, N.Y. Acad. Scis.. Democrat. Contbr. articles to math. publs. Home: 13700 El Dorado Dr # 32C Seal Beach CA 90740 Office: Mt St Mary's Coll 12001 Chalon Rd Los Angeles CA 90049-1597

DELANGE, GEORGE NOEL, science educator; b. Long Beach, Calif., Nov. 1, 1940; s. George Noel and Laurine (Pitts) deL.; m. Audrey Maxine Holland, Nov. 12, 1937; children: John Noel, James Edward. BS in Social Studies, Grand Canyon U., Phoenix, 1972; MA in Edn./Adminstrn., No. Ariz. U., Flagstaff, 1991. Cert. tchr., sci., math., social studies, sch. adminstrn. Agt. Farmers Ins. Co., Phoenix, 1978-82; tchr. Laveen (Ariz.) Sch. Dist., 1982-86, Phoenix Union High Sch. Dist., 1986—; Co-author deep space database on computer The Arizona Database. Recipient Newmast award Nat. Sci. Tchrs. Assn. and NASA, Washington, 1987. Republican. Mem. LDS Ch. Office: Maryvale High Sch 3415 N 59th Ave Phoenix AZ 85033-4699

DE LANGE, ROBERT J., biological chemistry educator; b. Richfield, Utah, Mar. 30, 1937; s. Talmage Young and Selena Mae (Taylor) De Lange; m. Verlie Gaye Dayton, May 27, 1960; children: Robert Lance, Michael Dayton, Thayne Clarke, Eric Paul, Stephanie Gae, Tyler Cameron. AS, Weber Coll., 1957; BS, Brigham Young U., 1961; PhD, U. Wash., 1965. Postdoctoral scholar dept. biol. chemistry UCLA, 1965-67, asst. prof. dept. biol. chemistry, 1967-71, assoc. prof. dept. biol. chemistry, 1971-77, prof. dept. biol. chemistry, 1977—; vis. prof. dept. immunology and microbiology U. Calif., Berkeley, 1987-88; study sect. mem. physiol. chemistry NIH, Bethesda, 1985-88; invited expert analyst Chemtracts-Biochemistry and Molecular Biology, N.Y.C., 1990—. Author: Chemical Modification of Proteins, 1975; editorial bd. Jour. Biol. Chemistry, 1976-81; reviewer sci. jours.; co-author (with others) books; contbr. articles to profl. jours. Merit badge counselor, institutional rep. Boy Scouts Am., Canoga Park, Calif., Woodland Hills, Calif., 1970—. Recipient award in biochemistry Eli Lilly Co., 1965; fellow Guggenheim Found., U. Sussex, Eng., 1973; NSF grantee UCLA, USPHS grantee UCLA. Mem. Am. Soc. for Biochemistry and Molecular Biology. Republican. Mormon. Office: U Calif Dept Biol Chemistry Sch Medicine Los Angeles CA 90024-1737

DE LANY, WILLIAM HURD, radio broadcasting executive; b. Birmingham, Ala., June 5, 1943; s. William H. Jr. and Margaret (Mauney) DeL.; m. Rebecca Fowler; children: Kathleen Lynn, James Eliot, Jeffrey Martin, Scott Douglas. Student, U. Miami (Fla.), 1961-62. Mktg. dir. Teleprompter, St. Petersburg, Fla., 1975-77; regional mktg. dir. Teleprompter, Lakeland, Fla., 1977-80; gen. mgr. Group W (MDS System), Tampa, Fla., 1980-83, ABC, N.Y.C., 1983-84; v.p. mktg. Rite Communications Co., Miami, 1984-86; sr. v.p. network ops. Home Shopping Network, Clearwater, Fla., 1986-87; sr. v.p. adminstrn. Shop TV Network, Hollywood, Calif., 1987-88; pres. Digital Radio Channel, Carson, Calif., 1988—. Republican. Home: 2022 Marshallfield Ln Redondo Beach CA 90278-4214

DELAQUIS, NOEL, bishop; b. Notre-Dame de Lourdes, Man., Can., Dec. 25, 1934; s. Louis and Therese (Hebert) D. B.A., U. Man., 1954; B.Th., U. Laval, 1958; J.C.L., Latran, Rome, 1962. Ordained priest Roman Catholic Ch., 1958; asst. priest Christ the King Parish, St. Vital, Man., 1958-60; prof. canon law St. Boniface Sem., Man., 1962-68; chancellor Archdiocese of St. Boniface, Man., 1965-73; bishop of Gravelbourg, Sask., Can., 1974—. Address: CP 690, Gravelbourg, SK Canada S0H 1X0*

DE LA TORRE, DAVID JOSEPH, art museum director; b. Santa Barbara, Calif., June 14, 1948; s. Joseph Raymond and Jacqueline (Ator) de la T.; m. Georgianna M. Lagoria, May 15, 1982. BA in Polit. Sci., U. San Francisco, 1970; MA in Museology, John F. Kennedy U., 1982. Intern, Mexican Mus., San Francisco, 1976-77; curatorial asst. Fine Arts Mus. San Francisco, 1977-79; dir. devel. Triton Mus. Art, Santa Clara, Calif., 1979-84; exec. dir. Mexican Mus., San Francisco, 1984-89; chief planning cons. The Latino Mus., 1989-91; assoc. dir. Honolulu Acad. of the Arts, 1991—; panelist NEA, 1984-92, Calif. Arts Coun., 1985-87, Met. Life Found., 1986-89, Hawaii State Found. Culture and Arts 1993. Bd. dirs., regional v.p. Calif. Confedn. Arts, 1983-89; bd. dirs. Cultural Coun. Santa Clara County, 1981-84; chmn. Cultural Arts Alliance Santa Clara County, 1981-84. Democrat. Roman Catholic. Office: Honolulu Acad Arts 900 S Beretania St Honolulu HI 96814-1495

DELCOUR, DAVID WILLIAM, business executive; b. St. Louis, Dec. 27, 1943; s. W.T. and Mary F. (Eiermann) D.; m. Susan K.J. Delcour, Nov. 27, 1970; 1 child, Michael. BA, U. Colo., 1965, JD, 1968. Bar: Colo. 1968. Law clk. to presiding justice 10th Cir. Ct., Denver, 1968-69; adminstrv. asst. Congressman Don Brotzman, Washington, 1969-74; lawyer Amax, Inc., Denver, 1975-77, dir. environ. affairs, 1986-90; dir. govt. affairs Climax Molybdenum Co., Denver, 1978, dir. external affairs, 1979-85; pres. Amax Resource Conservation Co., Denver, 1991—. Chmn. pub. lands com. Am. Mining Congress, Washington, 1981-92; mem. Nat. Pub. Lands adv. coun., Washington, 1986-91; trustee Rocky Mountain Mineral Law Found., 1987-93. Mem. Colo. Assn. Commerce and Industry (bd. dirs., chmn. 1990), Colo. Mining Assn. (bd. dirs., chmn. 1986). Office: Amax Resource Conservation 1626 Cole Blvd Golden CO 80401

DELEAR, RICHARD HENRY, personnel consultant; b. Wichita, Kans., Dec. 19, 1927; s. Ernest C. Delear and Clara M. Boberg; m. Helen J. Clark, Jan. 8, 1950; children: Cherie, Cindy, Kimberly, Kirkland, Dianne, Michelle. Student, Hiedleburg U., Germany, 1946-47, San Jose St. U., 1959-60. Cert. hypnotherapist. Enlisted U.S. Army, 1944, advanced through grades to m/sgt., 1952, ret., 1959; entrepreneur Calif., 1960-74; human resources cons. Success Thru Humaneering, Scotts Valley, Calif., 1974—. Author: Leadership Strategies, 1988. Pres. Exchange club, Scotts Valley, 1978-79. Decorated two Bronze Stars, two Purple Hearts, Silver Star. Republican. Roman Catholic. Office: Success Thru Humaneering 202 Burlwood Dr Scotts Valley CA 95066-3704

DELEUR, ROBBIE LYNN, university program director; b. Ada, Okla., Oct. 14, 1956; d. Ralph Owren and Beverly Jane (Ferguson) Randles; children: Raymond A. Jr., John Robert. A of Bus. Adminstrn., Casper Coll., 1986; BS in Gen. Bus. Mgmt., U. Wyo., 1989. Sec., adminstr. Equipment Renewal Co., Rock Springs, Wyo., 1979-80; sr. clk. Brown & Root, Rock Springs and Green River, Wyo., 1980-82; unemployment eligibility reviewer Wyo. Employment Security Commn., Evanston and Rock Springs, Wyo., 1983-84; asst. money room mgr. Cent. Wyo. Fair and Rodeo, Casper, 1983—; fin. aid specialist Casper Coll., 1986-89; dir. fin. aid. Western Wyo. Community Coll., Rock Springs, 1989—. Sec.-treas., bd. dirs. YWCA, Rock Springs, 1990. Mem. Nat. Assn. Student Fin. Aid Adminstrs., Wyo. State Assn. Student Fin. Aid. (sec., treas. 1990-92), Rocky Mountain Assn. Student Fin. Aid. Adminstrs. (prof. deve. com. 1992—, chmn. legis. response com. 1992-93, Disting. Svc. award 1992-93), Bus. and Profl. Women's Club Sweetwater County (chmn. scholarship com. 1988—, pres. 1991-92, dir. dist. IV, chmn., Young Career Women award 1989, 91). Democrat. Baptist. Home: 2012 Johnson St Rock Springs WY 82901-4455 Office: Western Wyo Community Coll 2500 College Dr Rock Springs WY 82901-5802

DELGADO, SHARON LEE, nursing administrator, psychotherapist; b. Denver, Aug. 7, 1945; d. Francis Leon Frederick and Martha Jane (Burback) Simpson; m. William G. Delgado, May 21, 1966 (div. May 1987); children: Frank William, Christina Marie. AA in Nursing, Fullerton (Calif.) Jr. Coll., 1965; BSN, Calif. State U., Fullerton, 1984, MS in Counseling, 1986. RN, Calif.; lic. marriage, family and child counselor, Calif.; cert. pub. health nurse, Calif. Staff nurse St. Jude Hosp., Fullerton, 1965-69, Saddleback Community Hosp., Laguna Hills, Calif., 1977-87; office nurse T.A. Ross, M.D., Mission Viejo, Calif., 1970-71; nurse mgr. Beech Street-Managed

Health Care, Irvine, Calif., 1987—; sch. counselor Irvine Unified Sch. Dist., 1985-87; community mental health therapist Ctr. for Creative Alternatives, Mission Viejo, 1986-87; pvt. practice psychotherapy Inst. Self-Esteem, Laguna Niguel, Calif., 1987—; assoc. home health nurse Vis. Nurses Assn., Orange, County, Calif., 1984; assoc. occupational health nurse employee assistance program, cons. Hoag Meml. Hosp., Newport Beach, Calif., 1984; mem. staff Capistrano By Sea Hosp., Dana Point, Calif., CPC Laguna Hills Hosp. Vol. youth dir. Presbyn. Ch. of Master, Mission Viejo, 1982-85; vol. nurse Laguna Beach (Calif.) Community Clinic, 1984; instr. CPR and first aid ARC, Orange County, 1983-85. Mem. Calif. Assn. Marriage and Family Therapists, Assn. for Play Therapy, Nat. Mental Health Assn. (coalition for prevention). Republican. Office: Inst Self-Esteem Ste 280 30131 Town Center Dr Laguna Niguel CA 92677

DELLAS, ROBERT DENNIS, investment banker; b. Detroit, July 4, 1944; s. Eugene D. and Maxine (Rudell) D.; m. Shila L. Clement, Mar. 27, 1976; children—Emily Allison, Lindsay Michelle. B.A. in Econs., U. Mich., Ann Arbor, 1966; M.B.A., Harvard U., Cambridge, 1970. Analyst Burroughs Corp., Detroit, 1966-67, Pasadena, Calif., 1967-68; mgr. U.S. Leasing, San Francisco, 1970-76; pres., dir. Energetics Mktg. & Mgmt. Assn., San Francisco, 1978-80; sr. v.p. E.F. Hutton & Co., San Francisco, 1981-85; prin. founder Capital Exchange Internat., San Francisco, 1976—; gen. ptnr. Kanland Assocs., Tex., 1982, Claremont Assocs., Calif., 1983, Lakeland Assocs., Ga., 1983, Americal Assocs., Calif., 1983, Chatsworth Assocs., Calif., 1983, Walnut Grove Assocs., Calif., 1983, Somerset Assocs., N.J., 1983, One San Diego Assocs., Calif., 1984; bd. dirs. CYMAK Techs., Inc. Bd. dirs., treas. Found. San Francisco's Archtl. Heritage. Mem. U.S. Trotting Assn., Calif. Harness Horse Breeders Assn. (Breeders award for Filly of Yr. 1986, Aged Pacing Mare, 1987, 88, Colt of Yr. 1990), Calif. Golf Club San Francisco. Home: 1911 Sacramento St San Francisco CA 94109-3419 Office: One Sansome St #3800 San Francisco CA 94104

DELLIQUANTI, JAMES, financial consultant; b. Long Beach, Calif., Sept. 14, 1963; s. Peter James and Mildred Marie (Hughes) D.; m. Julie Ann Newman, June 25, 1989; 1 child, Blue Jean. BA, Calif. State U., Long Beach, 1989. Investment exec. Paine Webber, Inc., Long Beach, 1989-90, account v.p., 1990-91, 1st v.p., 1991-92; fin. cons., 1st v.p. Shearson Lehman Bros., Costa Mesa, Calif., 1992—. With USN, 1984-87. Mem. Jr. C. of C. Office: Shearson Lehman Bros 650 Town Ctr Dr Ste 100 Costa Mesa CA 92626

DELLIS, DEBORAH RUTH, assistant corporate secretary; b. Phoenix, Aug. 29, 1960; d. Horace Alan and Eleanor Ann (Ellison) D.; m. Michael Patrick Feeley, Oct. 13, 1984 (div. Apr. 1987). BS in Journalism, Ariz. State U., 1982. Pub. rels. intern Phoenix Suns Profl. Basketball Club, 1982-83; promotion asst. Sta. KPNX-TV/Gannett Co. Inc., Phoenix, 1983; community rels. rep. Salt River Project, Phoenix, 1983-91, asst. corp. sec., 1991—. Contbr. articles to profl. jours. Chmn. environ. expo com. Valley Forward Assn., Phoenix, 1990-92; mem. comm. com. Am. Cancer Soc., Phoenix, 1990-92; environ. com. Valley Citizens League. Mem. Meeting Planners Internat. (co-chair comm. com. 1988-89, co-chmn. program com., bd. dirs. 1989-90, sec. 1990-91), Friends of COMPAS. Congregationalist. Office: Salt River Project PO Box 52025 Phoenix AZ 85072-2025

DELLUMS, RONALD V., congressman; b. Oakland, Calif., Nov. 24, 1935; m. Leola Roscoe Higgs; 3 children. A.A., Oakland City Coll., 1958; B.A., San Francisco State Coll., 1960; M.S.W., U. Calif., 1962. Psychiat. social worker Calif. Dept. Mental Hygiene, 1962-64; program dir. Bayview Community Ctr., San Francisco, 1964-65; from assoc. dir. to dir. Hunters Point Youth Opportunity Ctr., 1965-66; planning cons. Bay Area Social Planning Coun., 1966-67; dir. concentrated employment program San Francisco Econ. Opportunity Coun., 1967-68; sr. cons. Social Dynamics, Inc., 1968-70; mem. 92nd-103rd Congresses from 9th Calif. Dist., 1971—; chmn. house com. on D.C., 1979—, mem. armed svcs. com., chmn. house armed svcs. subcom. on rsch. and devel., 1989—, mem. permanent select com. on intelligence; lectr. San Francisco State Coll., U. Calif., Berkeley; mem. U.S. del. North Atlantic Assembly; former chmn. Congl. Black Caucus, Calif. Dem. Congl. Del., Dem. Study Group. Author: Defense Sense: The Search For A Rational Military Policy, 1983. Mem. Berkeley City Coun., 1967-71. With USMCR, 1954-56. Democrat. Office: US House of Representatives 2108 Rayburn House Office Washington DC 20515-0509*

DELLWO, DENNIS A., state legislator; b. Washington, Aug. 31, 1945; s. Robert D. and Madeline (Maguire) D.; m. Jeannine Dellwo; children: Allison, Julia. BA, Gonzaga U., 1967; JD, Ariz. State U., 1971. Bar: Wash. 1971, U.S. Dist. Ct. Wash. 1973. With Winston & Cashatt Law Offices, Spokane, Wash.; mem. Wash. State Ho. Reps., Olympia, 1983—. Home: W 2636 Riverview Dr Spokane WA 99205 Office: Winston & Cashatt 1900 Seafirst Financial Ctr Spokane WA 99201

DELLWO, ROBERT DENNIS, lawyer; b. Polson, Mont., Dec. 10, 1917; s. Dennis Aloysius and Mary Grace (Cassidy) D.; m. Madeline Maguire, June 7, 1941; children: Rosemary, Kathleen, Dennis, Gerard, Joan, Madeline, Robert, Joseph. PhB, Gonzaga U., 1940, JD, 1942. Bar: Wash. 1943, U.S. Dist. Ct. 1948, U.S. Supreme Ct. 1954. Farmer Charlo, Mont.; spl. agt. Fed. Bur. of Investigations, Washington, 1942-48; part time investigator CIA, 1954-64; sr. ptnr. Dellwo, Roberts and Scanlon, Spokane, Wash., 1948-93; mayor pro tem Spokane (Wash.) City, 1986-92; adj. prof. Gonzaga Univ. Contbr. articles to profl. jours. Active in civic affairs. Mem. ABA, Spokane Bar Assn. (past pres.), Wash. Bar Assn., Fed. Bar Assn., Am. Indian Law Bar Assn., Judicature Soc., Spokane City Club, Spokane Elks and Moose. Democrat. Roman Catholic. Home: 1021 S Primrose Ln Spokane WA 99204-2005 Office: City of Spokane 808 W Spokane Falls Blvd Spokane WA 99201-3333

DELMERICO, GEORGE ANTHONY, publications executive; b. Dobbs Ferry, N.Y., Aug. 23, 1945; s. Patrick A. and Helen (Jordan) D. BFA in Visual Comm., Pratt Inst., 1967. Asst. art dir. N.Y. mag., N.Y.C., 1968-70; art dir. The Herald, N.Y.C., 1971, Newsday, Garden City, N.Y., 1972-74, N.Y. Times, N.Y.C., 1974-76; design dir. Village Voice, N.Y.C., 1976-85; assocl pub. design Santa Barbara (Calif.) News and Rev., 1986; creative dir. Santa Barbara Ind., 1986-90; dir. publs. U. Calif., Santa Barbara, 1990—; instr. Sch. Visual Arts, N.Y.C., 1972-85, Santa Barbara City Coll., 1987-90, U. Calif., Santa Barbara Extension, 1989—; cons. N.Y. Times Co., Santa Rosa, Calif., 1986. Recipient Bronze medal Coun. for Advancement and Support of Edn., 1992. Home: 5544 Baseline Ave Santa Ynez CA 93460 Office: U Calif Publs Santa Barbara CA 93106

DEL MORAL, ROGER, botany educator, wetland consultant; b. Detroit, Sept. 13, 1943; married; children: Sara, Andrea. BA, U. Calif., Santa Barbara, 1965, MA, 1966, PhD, 1968. Cert. sr. ecologist. Asst. prof. U. Wash., Seattle, 1968-74, assoc. prof., 1974-83, prof., 1983—; prin. del Moral & Assocs., Seattle, 1984—; Contbr. articles to profl. jours. Mem. Wash. State Noxious Weed Control Bd., 1987-88. NSF rsch. grantee, 1971, 75, 79, 81, 82, 84, 87, 89, 90, 91, 93. Mem. Ecol. Soc. Am., Bot. Soc. Am. (sec. 1983-86), Brit. Ecol. Soc., Internat. Union Vegetation Scientists, Tokyo Bot. Soc. (editorial bd.). Home: 2002 42nd Ave E Seattle WA 98112-2714 Office: U Wash Dept Botany KB 15 Seattle WA 98195

DELOACH, ROBERT EDGAR, corporate executive; b. Daytona Beach, Fla., Jan. 6, 1939; s. Ollie Newman and Sally Gertrude (Schrowder) DeL. Student U. Alaska-Anchorage, 1967-69, Alaska Meth. U., 1970, Pacific Luth. U., 1972. Lic. elec. engr. and adminstr., Alaska, 1979; lic. pvt. pilot, real estate broker, ins. agt. Former chmn. bd. Alaska Stagecraft, Inc., Anchorage; pres. BG Systems Co., BG Tax & Acctg., Inc., The Electric Doctor, Inc., Apollo, Inc.; former pres. Coastal Electronics, Inc.; former owner-mgr. Bargain Towne, Anchorage. Active Anchorage Community Theatre, Anchorage Theater Guild. Mem. Assn. Ind. Accts., Internat. Assn. Theatrical Stage Employees and Moving Picture Machine Operators U.S. (pres. local 770), Ind. Elec. Contractors Assn., Internat. Assn. Elec. Insps. Home: 1207 W 47th Ave Anchorage AK 99503-6917 Office: 7910 King St Anchorage AK 99502

DELONG, CHARLES COGGESHAIL, psychiatrist; b. Gary, Ind., Mar. 14, 1936; s. Charles Wallace and Katherine (Coggeshail) DeL.; m. Karin Swanson, June 18, 1959 (div. 1977); children: James Swanson, Lisa Marie. BA, Carleton Coll., 1958; MD, Northwestern U., 1962. Diplomate Am. Bd. Psychiatry and Neurology. Intern U. Vt., Burlington, 1962-63; resident U. Cin., 1963-66; pvt. practice psychiatry Palo Alto, Calif., 1968—. Lt. comdr. USNR, 1966-68. Office: 701 Welch Rd # 318 Palo Alto CA 94304

DE LORCA, LUIS L., educational administrator, educator; b. L.A., Oct. 18, 1959; s. Patricia Jean Clougher Harvey; m. Lori Ann Vanzant, Mar. 23, 1991. AA, Rio Hondo Jr. Coll., Whittier, Calif., 1983; BA, Calif. State Poly. U., 1989. High sch. football coach various high schs., So. Calif., 1980; pub. rels. dir. Calif. Poly Pomona Music Dept., 1987-89; pres. Exclusive Concepts, L.A., 1987-89; lifeguard L.A. City Recreation Dept., 1980-87; tchr. English Cathedral High Sch., L.A., 1989-90; tchr., rsch. specialist Whittier (Calif.) Union High Sch., 1990; founder, dir. The Learning Advantage Ctr., Whittier, 1991—. Active Big Bros. of Am., Fair Housing, Greenpeace. Mem. Whittier C. of C., Cousteau Soc. Democrat. Unity Ch. Home: 9427 Tarryton Ave Whittier CA 90605 Office: The Learning Advantage Ctr 13710 Whittier Blvd #206 Whittier CA 90605

DELOREAN, JOHN ZACHARY, manufacturing executive, engineer, inventor; b. Detroit, Jan. 6, 1925; s. Zachary R. and Katharine (Pribak) DeL.; children: Zachary Thomas, Kathryn Ann. BS in Indsl. Engring., Lawrence Inst., Detroit, 1948; MS in Automotive Engring., Chrysler Inst., Detroit, 1952; MBA, U. Mich., Detroit, 1952. Registerd profl. engr., Utah. Dir. R & D Packard Motor Co., Detroit, 1952-56; dir. advanced engring. Pontiac (Mich.) div. GM, 1956-59, asst. chief engr., 1959-60, chief engr., 1961-65; v.p., gen. mgr. Pontiac (Mich.) div. Gen. Motors Corp., 1965-69, Cheverolet div. GM, Detroit, 1969-72; group v.p., mgr. car and truck divs. GM, Detroit, 1972-73; pres. Nat. Alliance Bus., Washington, 1973-74; chmn. DeLorean Motor Co., N.Y.C., 1975-87, Logan (Utah) Mfg. Co., 1979—; Co-dir. New Start in Life Ctr., San Diego, 1985—. Author: On A Clear Day You Can See GM, 1976, DeLorean, 1985; inventor 47 patents. With U.S. Army, 1943-45. Mem. N.Y. Acad. Sci. Mem. Evang. Ch.

DELORENZO, DAVID A., food products executive; b. 1947. Colgate U.; MBA, U. Pa. With Dole Food Co., Inc., Westlake Village, Calif., 1970—, exec. v.p., 1990—, pres., 1991—. Office: Dole Food Co Inc 31355 Oak Crest Dr Westlake Village CA 91361*

DE LORY, PETER, photographer, educator; b. Fall River, Mass., Oct. 2, 1948; s. James Lawrence and Eileen (Buckley) D.; m. Martha Jane Heavenston, Aug. 19, 1989. BFA, San Francisco Art Inst., 1971; student, Ctr. of the Eye Sch., Photography, Aspen, Colo., 1968-72; MFA, U. Colo., 1974. Faculty San Jose State U., Calif., 1986-93; various teaching positions to faculty The Sch. of the Art Inst. of Chgo., 1979-80, 84-85; lectr. numerous univs. including San Diego (Calif.) State U., 1989, Sonoma State Univ., Calif., 1988, San Francisco City Coll., 1988, U. So. Oreg., Ashland, 1987, San Jose (Calif.) State U., 1986, U. So. Maine, 1983, others; lectr. various insts. in field including Seattle Mus. of Art, 1987, Cleve. Art Inst., 1983, Chgo. Inst. Design, 1983, others. One man-shows include: Kneeland Gallery, Ketchum, Idaho, 1991, Sandy Carson Gallery, Denver, 1991, Santa Monica Coll., Calif., 1988, Sandra Berler Gallery, Chevy Chase, Md., 1988, Scheinder Mus. of Art, Ashland, Oreg., 1987, Magic Theatre, San Francisco, 1986, Gallery Interform, Osaka, Japan, 1986, others; group exhbns. include The Art Ctr./faculty seminar exhbn., Pasadena, Calif., 1990, U. Oreg. Mus. of Art, Eugene, 1990, Sun Valley (Idaho) Ctr. Photographers Reunion, 1990, Etherston/Stern Gallery, Tucson, Ariz., 1993, numerous others. Recipient award of Merit for book "The Wild and the Innocent", Am. Art Mus. Publ. Competition, 1988, artist fellowship in photography, Calif. Arts Coun., 1990, photographer fellowship, Calif. Mus. of Photography, Riverside, 1987, Nat. Endowment for the Arts, 1979, artist fellowship Western States Art Found., 1976. Office: 333 5th St # F San Francisco CA 94107-1033

DEL PAPA, FRANKIE SUE, state official; b. 1949. BA, U. Nev.; JD, George Washington U., 1974. Bar: Nev. 1974. Staff asst. U.S. Senator Alan Bible, Washington, 1971-74; assoc. Law Office of Leslie B. Grey, Reno, Nev., 1975-78; legis. asst. to U.S. Senator Howard Cannon, Washington, 1978-79; ptnr. Thornton & Del Papa, 1979-84; pvt. practice Reno, 1984-87; sec. of state State of Nev., Carson City, 1987-91; atty. gen. State of Nev., 1991—. Mem. Sierra Arts Found. (bd. dirs.), Trust for Pub. Land (adv. com.), Nev. Women's Fund. Democrat. Office: Office of Atty Gen Heroes Meml Bldg Capitol Complex Carson City NV 89710*

DEL RAZO, ERICK SILVA, automotive mechanic; b. L.A., Nov. 6, 1967; s. Sergio Pacheco and Candelaria (Silva) Del R. Grad. high sch., Rosemead, Calif., 1986; cert. brakes and front end, Valley Trade Tech., 1988. Cert. Automotive Svc. Excellence, brake adjuster, Calif. Asst. mgr. Midas Corp., Rosemead, 1988-89, Chief Auto Parts, Inc., San Gabriel, Calif., 1989-90. Awarded Doctor of Motors, Dana Corp., Calif., 1988. Republican. Home: 3785 Strang Ave Rosemead CA 91770-2160

DEL SANTO, LAWRENCE A., retail merchandising company executive; b. 1934; married. B.S., U. San Francisco, 1955. With Household Merchandising Inc., Des Plaines, Ill., from 1957, with advt. dept. subs. Vons Grocery Co., 1957-58, asst. advt. mgr., 1958-61, advt. mgr., 1961-68, mgr. sales and mdse., 1968-71, sr. v.p., 1971-73, pres., chief exec. officer, 1973-75, corp. sr. v.p., 1975-79, exec. v.p., from 1979, also bd. dirs.; exec. v.p. Lucky Stores Inc., Dublin, Calif., to 1986, pres., 1986—, now also chmn., chief exec. officer, also bd. dirs. Served with U.S. Army, 1955-57. Office: Lucky Stores Inc 6300 Clark Ave PO Box BB Dublin CA 94568

DEL SOLAR, DANIEL, broadcasting executive; b. N.Y.C., June 13, 1940; s. Daniel del Solar and Luisa Garcia. BA cum laude, Harvard U., 1964. Regional health care planner Health Care Research Inc., San Jose, Calif., 1974-75; community resources coordinator Open Studio Sta. KQED-TV, San Francisco, 1975-76; dir. tng. and devel. Corp. for Pub. Broadcasting, Washington, 1976-80; freelance writer NAACP, N.Y.C., 1980-82; instr. Hunter Coll., N.Y.C., 1982-84; fgn. corr. in Cen. Am. and Mexico, 1984-85; gen. mgr. Sta. KALW-FM, San Francisco, 1985-92, Sta. WYBE-TV, Phila., 1992—. Producer: (radio feature) Introspection Towards the Future, (radio series) Readings from the Congressional Record, 1975; originating producer for radio: Music from the Pacific Basin Nations, 1987; writer, co-producer for TV: I Was Born a Chilean, 1980. Recipient Radio Meritorious Achievement award Media Alliance San Francisco, 1987. Mem. Union for Democratic Communications, Nat. Fedn. for Community Broadcasters.

DELUCA, DIANA MACINTYRE, academic administrator; b. Brighton, Eng., Aug. 15, 1943; d. H.R.C. and Mary Winifred (Fairbairn) M.; m. Charles John DeLuca, Mar. 21, 1962; 1 child, David Edward Charles. BA with honors, U. Hawaii, 1966, MA, 1967; PhD, U. Wash., 1981. Instr. English U. Hawaii, Honolulu, 1967-72; instr. English Windward C.C., Kaneohe, Hawaii, 1972-84, asst. dean, 1984-87; asst. to pres. U. Hawaii, 1986-93, interim v.p. for univ. rels., 1990; pres. Macintyre Comm. Svcs., Golden, Colo., 1993—; organizer Creativity & Sci. conf., 1984, Perceiving Nature conf., 1986; pres. Hawaii Coun. of Tchr.'s of English, 1984-85. Author (book) Pacific Marine Life, 1976; editor (books) Essays on Creativity & Science, 1985, Essays on Perceiving Nature, 1988, Toward a National Health Care Strategy: The Dukakis Lectures. Sec. Gov.'s Congress on Hawaii's Internat. Role, Honolulu, 1988. Fellow Renaissance Soc. Am. Home and Office: 16000 W 76th Ave Golden CO 80403

DELUCCA, GREGORY JAMES, wine industry executive; b. Milw., June 2, 1937; s. Anthony James and Irene Eleanor (Linski) DeL.; BS in Chem. Engring., U. Wis., 1959, MBA, 1962; m. Carol L. Enrico, Apr. 8, 1967; children: Alison, Ashley. Mgr. mktg. Pacific Coca-Cola Bottling Co., Seattle, 1967-71, mgr. ops. Western area Coca-Cola U.S.A., Burlingame, Calif., 1971-73, mgr. ops. engring. The Coca Cola Co., Atlanta, 1973-77; v.p., gen. mgr. Sterling Vineyards, Calistoga, Calif., 1977-82, pres., 1982-84; owner Gregory J. DeLucca Co. Wine Cons., 1985; pres. Lyeth Vineyard and Winery, Ltd., 1985-87, Chateau St. Jean Vineyards and Winery, 1987-90, Cru Industries, 1990-92, owner Gregory J. DeLucca Wine Consulting Co., 1992—. Served to capt. USAR, 1959-67. Mem. Napa Valley Vintners (pres.), Sonoma County Wineries Assn. (bd. dirs.). Republican. Roman Catholic. Home: PO Box 1937 Sonoma CA 95476-1937 Office: PO Box 1937 Sonoma CA 95476-1937

DELUCCHI, GEORGE PAUL, accountant; b. Richmond, Calif., Apr. 20, 1938; s. George Carl and Rose Caroline (Golino) D. BA, San Jose State U., 1959. CPA, Calif. Ptnr. Delucchi, Swanson & Co., Santa Clara, Calif., 1968-74, Delucchi, Swanson & Sandival, Santa Clara, 1974-76, Delucchi, Sandoval & Co., Santa Clara, 1976-77, Wolf & Co., San Jose, Calif., 1977-78; v.p. Lautze & Lautze, San Jose, 1978-82, also bd. dirs.; sr. ptnr. G.P. Delucchi & Assocs. (name changed to Delucchi, Robinson, Streit & Co., Santa Clara, 1982—. Treas. Crippled Children Soc., San Jose, 1967-71, San Jose Catholic Charities, 1984-90, F. Schmidt Found. for Youth; bd. dirs. Serra Med. Found., Mission City Community Fund; pres. Santa Clara Police Activity League, 1977-78; bd. fellows Santa Clara U., 1975—; chair pioneer dist. Santa Clara coun. Boy Scouts Am. Served to lt. U.S. Army, 1959-62. Mem. AICPA, Calif. Soc. CPA's, Silicon Valley Capital Club, Serra Club, Elks (Santa Clara exalted ruler 1969-70), Rotary (pres.-elect, bd. dirs. 1986-89), Knights of Malta (invested, Knight of Magistral Grace). Republican. Roman Catholic. Home: 774 Circle Dr Santa Clara CA 95050-5927 Office: 2075 De La Cruz Blvd Santa Clara CA 95050-3035

DE LUMEN, BENITO O., science educator; b. Taytay, Philippines, July 28, 1940; came to U.S., 1965; s. Amado S. and Soledad O. de Lumen; m. Helen Z. de Lumen; children: Karmina, Paul. BS, U. Philippines, 1962; MS, U. Mo., 1968; PhD, U. Calif., Davis, 1971. Grad. biochemist U. Calif., Davis, 1971-72; sr. rsch. chemist Campbell Inst. Sci. and Tech., Camden, N.J., 1972-78; asst. prof. in nutritional scis. U. Calif., Berkeley, 1978-82, assoc. prof., 1982—; mem. editorial bd. Jour. Agrl. Food Chemistry, 1984-87. Mem. AAAS, Am. Soc. Plant Physiologists, Internat. Soc. Plant Molecular Biologists, Am. Inst. Nutrition, Inst. Food Technologists, Vols. for Internat. Tech. Assistance. Office: U Calif Nutritional Scis Dept Berkeley CA 94720

DELUZE, JAMES ROBERT, physician; b. L.A., Sept. 14, 1948; s. James Vierea and Jean Ruth (Hanna) DeL. BA, U. Hawaii, 1974; student, Andrews U., 1980-82; DO, U. Health Scis., Kansas City, 1987. Product specialist Hanna Enterprise, Kailua, Hawaii, 1972-74; pres. Ecol. Engring., Honolulu, 1976-79; intern Kirksville (Mo.) Osteo. Med. Ctr., 1987-88; pvt. practice medicine Kailua, 1988-89; physician Mental Health Systems, San Diego, 1989-90; pvt. practice Waialua, Hawaii, 1991—. Rep. candidate U.S. Ho. of Reps., 1992; pres. Waialua Rep. Precinct, 1992; del. Rep. State Conv., Honolulu, 1992. Mem. Am. Assn. Clin. Anatomists, Am. Coll. Occupational and Environ. Medicine, Am. Osteo. Assn. (del. 1992), Hawaii Assn. Osteo. Physicians and Surgeons (v.p. 1991-92, pres. 1992-93), Nat. Space Soc., U.S. C. of C. Republican. Seventh Day Adventist. Home and Office: 67-365 Waialua Beach Rd Waialua HI 96791

DELVOYE, JACQUES VICTOR, bank executive; b. Lille, France, May 10, 1947; came to U.S., 1976; s. Victor Edouard and Jeanne Emilie (Gilleron) D.; m. Terry Davidowitz, Ma. 2, 1975; children: Eric, Stefan. BA, Ecole St. Genevieve, Versailles, France, 1966; MBA, Ecole des hautes Etudes Comml., Paris, 1969; MA, U. Paris, U. Caen, 1970; postgrad., U. Calif., San Diego, 1969-71. Trust dept. portfolio mgr. Credit Lyonnais, Paris, 1972-76; asst. v.p. Credit Lyonnais, L.A., 1976-78; v.p. Credit Lyonnais, N.Y.C., 1978-81, L.A., 1981-84; v.p., mgr. corp. banking Banque Indosuez, L.A., 1984-86; mgr. Western U.S. Banca Nazionale dell'Agricoltura, L.A., 1987—. Author: (internal pub.) Etude de la Conjoncture Economique a la Banque de France. Treas. Italy-Am. C. of C., L.A., 1990. Fullbright scholar U. Calif. San Diego, 1969, U. Calif. fellow, 1969. Mem. Internat. Bankers Assn. in Calif., Beverly Hills Country Club, La Canada Flintridge Country Club. Home: 2247 S Beverly Dr Los Angeles CA 90034-1005 Office: Banca Nazionale dell Agricoltura 633 W 5th St Ste 2530 Los Angeles CA 90071-2045

DELZEIT, LINDA DORIS, physical education educator; b. Toronto, Ont., Can., June 20, 1954; d. George C. and Doris L. (McEwan) Whitehead; m. James R. Delzeit, Aug. 13, 1977; children: Christy, Melissa. BA in Phys. Edn., Calif. State U., Long Beach, 1977, MA in Phys. Edn., 1980, postgrad., 1988-91. Instr. phys. edn. El Camino Coll., Torrance, Calif., 1977—, Harbor Jr. Coll., 1991—; Calif. dir. Nat. Pub. Telecomputing Network, Cypress, Calif., 1990-91, dir. edn., dir. Acad. 1 project, 1991—; instr., trainer ARC, L.A., 1984—; presenter at numerous aquatics and fitness confs. Author: Swimming Made Easy and Fun, 1988; contbg. author: Aquatic Fitness Manual, 1990; columnist Westminster Jour., 1987, 88; inventor foot paddles. Mem. AAHPERD (aquatic coun.), Aquatic Exercise Assn. (instr. trainer 1989-93), Commodore Longfellow Soc., Coun. Nat. Cooperation in Aquatics, Am. Swimming Coaches Assn. (level 1 cert.). Office: Successful Water 6330 Lincoln Ave Cypress CA 90630-5879

DEMAAR, NATALIE SHANA, federal agency administrator; b. Balt., July 8, 1950; d. Paul and Vera Rebecca (Abrams) Rosenbaum; m. Verrell Leon Dethloff Jr., June 2, 1974 (div. 1987); children: Daniel, Joseph; m. Michael Henry deMaar, June 4, 1988; 1 child, Michael Henry deMaar Jr.; stepchildren: Alexander, Peter, Andrew. BA, Simmons Coll., 1972; JD with honors, U. Md., Balt., 1976. Bar: Md. 1976, U.S. Ct. Appeals (4th & 10th cirs.) 1977, U.S. Dist. Ct. Md. 1977, U.S. Ct. Appeals (5th cir.) 1985, U.S. Supreme Ct. 1981. With HHS, Seattle, 1976—, regional adminstr. family support adminstrn. div., 1987-90, asst. regional adminstr. children and families, 1991—; speaker in field. Contbr. articles to profl. jours. Mem. Wash. Commn. for Humanities, Alliance for Children, Youth & Families, Nat. Child Support Advocacy Coalition. Mem. NAFE, Md. Bar Assn., Northwest Women's Bar Assn., Seattle-King County Bar Assn., Am. Assn. Pub. Welfare Attys., Am. Pub. Welfare Assn., Am. Soc. Pers. Adminstrn., Opera Guild, Campfire, City Club, Simmons Coll. Alumnae Assn. (pres. Seattle chpt.). Office: Adminstrn Children and Families 2201 6th Ave Seattle WA 98121-1832

DE MACARTY, PETER CHARLES RIDGWAY, market research professional; b. Holyoke, Mass., July 9, 1952; s. Pierre Cormac and Lotta Henrietta (Kennedy) de MaC.; m. Norma Rejalde Rayala, July 30, 1983; 1 child, Anne. Student, Williams Coll., 1971-72, 74-75; BFA, San Francisco Art Inst., 1977; MA, Lone Mountain Coll., 1978; PhD, The Fielding Inst., Santa Barbara, Calif., 1985. Lic. marriage, family and child counselor, Calif. Conscientious objector Christian Sci. Benevolent Assn., Chestnut Hill, Mass., 1972-74; marriage, family and child counselor intern Community Inst. for Psychotherapy, San Rafael, Calif., 1977-79; clin. psychology intern Marin County Community Mental Health, Point Reyes Station, Calif., 1979-80; resident mgr. Marin Emergency Housing Program, San Rafael, 1979-81; clin. psychology intern St. Vincent's Sch. for Boys, San Rafael, 1980-82; market rsch. project mgr. Hewlett-Packard Co., Cupertino, Calif., 1985—. Mem. Sierra Club, Audubon Soc., Environ. Def. Fund, Natural Resources Def. Coun., Common Cause. Calif. Grad. Fellow State of Calif., 1977-85; Beinecke Meml. Scholar The S&H Found., N.Y.C., 1971-77. Mem. Am. Mktg. Assn. Democrat. Home: 1124 87th St Daly City CA 94015-3524 Office: Hewlett Packard Co 19483 Pruneridge Ave Cupertino CA 95014-0781

DE MAIO, VICTORIA ANTOINETTE, corporate professional; b. Napa, Calif., Dec. 9, 1947; d. Nicholas Albert and Rose Marie (Bertolini) DeM. BA, U. Calif., Irvine, 1970. Cert. secondary tchr., 1971, elem. tchr., 1976. Tchr. L.A. (Calif.) City Schs., 1971-72, Newport-Mesa Unified Sch. Dist., Newport Beach, Calif., 1972-79; mktg. asst. Orange County Transit Dist., Garden Grove, Calif., 1980-82; sales rep. Prin. Fin. Group, Newport Beach, 1982-85; asst. adminstrv. mgr. Lee & Sakahara AIA, Costa Mesa, Calif., 1985-87; fin. asst. Digital Equipment Corp., Irvine, Calif., 1987-88; owner Victoria & Co., Newport Beach, 1989—; account exec. Tiffany and Co., Costa Mesa, Calif., 1991—; speaker misc. assns. and groups including O.C. Bus. and Career Conf., So. Calif. Conf. on Women, Anaheim, 1989; instr. Coastline Community Coll., Fountain Valley, Calif., 1989—. Bd. dirs., womens div. Newport Harbor C. of C., Newport Beach, 1982-85, AAUW, Profl. Womens Assn., Santa Ana, Calif., 1983-84. Mem. Nature Conservancy, Nat. Audubon Soc., Environ. Def. Fund, Ctr. Marine Conservancy, Greenpeace. Democrat. Office: Victoria & Co PO Box 9481 Newport Beach CA 92658-9481

DE MARANVILLE, NANCY JOAN, educator; b. Sioux City, Iowa, Jan. 20, 1932; d. Harry Thurl and Esther Sophia (Dobbert) De M.; m. Edward Feigenbaum, Oct. 4, 1958 (div. 1974); children: Janet Denise Feigenbaum, Carol Leonora Feigenbaum. BS, UCLA, 1956, MEd, 1962. Tchr. Coll. San Mateo, Calif., 1974-78, San Francisco C.C., 1980-81, OICW Job Tng. Program, Menlo Park, Calif., 1984-86, John Swett High Sch., Crockett,

Calif., 1986—. Mem. Calif. Tchrs. Assn., Berkeley Watercolor Soc. Democrat. Home: 401 Monte Vista Ave # 206 Oakland CA 94611 Office: John Swett High Sch 1098 Pomona St Crockett CA 94525

DEMARCHI, ERNEST NICHOLAS, aerospace engineering administrator; b. Lafferty, Ohio, May 31, 1939; s. Ernest Costante and Lena Marie (Cireddu) D.; B.M.E., Ohio State U., 1962; M.S. in Engring., UCLA, 1969; m. Carolyn Marie Tracz, Sept. 17, 1960; children—Daniel Ernest, John David, Deborah Marie. Registered profl. cert. mgr. With Space div. Rockwell Internat., Downey, Calif., 1962—, mem. Apollo, Skylab and Apollo-Soyuz missions design team in electronic and elec. systems, mem. mission support team for all Apollo and Skylab manned missions, 1962-74, mem. Space Shuttle design team charge elec. systems equipment, 1974-77, in charge Orbiter Data Processing System, 1977-81, in charge Orbiter Ku Band Communication and Radar System, 1981-85, in charge orbitor elec. power distbr., displays, controls, data processing, 1984-87, in charge space based interceptor flt. exper., 1987-88, kinetic energy systems, 1988-90, ground based interceptor program, 1990—. Recipient Apollo Achievement award NASA, 1969, Apollo 13 Sustained Excellent Performance award, 1970, Astronaut Personal Achievement Snoopy award, 1971; Exceptional Service award Rockwell Internat., 1972, Outstanding Contbn. award, 1976; NASA ALT award, 1979; Shuttle Astronaut Snoopy award, 1982; Pub. Service Group Achievement award NASA, 1982; Rockwell Pres.'s award, 1983, 87; registered profl. engr., Ohio. Mem. AIAA, ASME, Nat. Mgmt. Assn., Varsity O Alumni Assn. Home: 25311 Maximus St Mission Viejo CA 92691 Office: 12214 Lakewood Blvd Downey CA 90241

DEMARCO, RALPH JOHN, real estate developer; b. N.Y.C., Mar. 22, 1924; s. Frank and Mary (Castriota) DeM.; m. Arlene Gilbert, July 1, 1945; children: Sheryl DeMarco Grahn, Stephen, Laura DeMarco Wilson. BA, Claremont Men's Coll., 1956. Assoc. John B. Kilroy Co., Riverside, Calif., 1960-64, also mgr. ops. Riverside, San Bernardino counties, 1960-64; v.p. Marcus W. Meairs Co., 1964-67; pres. Diversified Properties, Inc., Riverside, 1967-72; v.p. Downey Savs. & Loan Assn. (Calif.), 1972-75; exec. v.p. DSL Svc. Co., 1972-75; pres. Interstate Shopping Ctrs., Inc., Santa Ana, Calif., 1975-87; exec. dir. comml. devel. Lewis Homes Mgmt. Corp., Upland, Calif., 1987-89; pvt. practice, San Diego, Calif., 1989—. Mem. City of Riverside Planning Commn., 1955-59, Airport Commn., 1960-70; mem. Urban Land Inst. 1st lt. USAF, 1942-45. Mem. Internat. Coun. Shopping Ctrs. Home: 5295 Wainwright Ct Riverside CA 92507 Office: 1403 Scott St Ste 201 San Diego CA 92106

DE MASSA, JESSIE G., media specialist. BJ, Temple U.; MLS, San Jose State U., 1967; postgrad., U. Okla., U. So. Calif. Tchr. Palo Alto (Calif.) Unified Sch. Dist., 1966; librarian Antelope Valley Joint Union High Sch. Dist., Lancaster, Calif., 1966-68, ABC Unified Sch. Dist., Artesia, Calif., 1968-72; dist. librarian Tehachapi (Calif.) Unified Sch. Dist., 1972-81; also media specialist, free lance writer, 1981—. Contbr. articles to profl. jours. Mem. Statue of Liberty Ellis Island Found., Inc.; charter supporter U.S. Holocaust Meml. Mus., Washington; supporting mem. U.S. Holocaust Meml. Coun., Washington. Fellow Internat. Biog. Assn.; mem. Calif. Media and Libr. Educators Assn., Calif Assn. Sch. Librs. (exec. coun.) AAUW (bull. editor chpt., assoc. editor state bull., chmn. publicity, 1955-68), Nat. Mus. Women in Arts. (charter), Hon. Fellows John F. Kennedy Libr. (founding mem.), Women's Roundtable of Orange County, Nat. Writer's Club. Home: 9951 Garrett Cir Huntington Beach CA 92646-3604

DEMELLO, AUSTIN EASTWOOD, astrophysicist, concert artist, poet, writer; b. New Bedford, Mass., Oct. 15, 1939; s. Manuel and Dora (Eastwood) De M; 1 child, Adragon Eastwood De Mello. BA in English, UCLA, 1974; MSc in Physics and Astronomy, Met. Coll. Inst., London, 1977, DSc in Theoretical Astrophysics, 1981. Engring. writer Raytheon Co., Santa Barbara, Calif., 1982; dir. research and sci. publs. Cosmosci. Research Inst., Sunnyvale, Calif., 1983—. Author: Black Night Poetry, 1960, Tengu, 1962, (record) El Duende Flamenco, 1965, The Metagalactic System, 1969, The Four States of Man, 1971, Early Development of the Scientific Mind, 1981, Theory of Cosmodynamics, 1983, The Cosmotorsion Effect, 1984, James Bay Missionaries, 1986, The Origin and Influence of Flamenco Music on the Classics, 1992, Offenbach and the Can-Can Dance, 1993, Adragon: The Youngest Scholar, 1993, Legacy of Poetry and Philosophy, 1993, The Magic Formula, 1993, Views of Chaos, 1993. Acad. Merit scholar UCLA, 1972-74. Mem. AIAA, AAAS, N.Y. Acad. Sci., Am. Astronautical Soc., Mensa Internat. Home: PO Box 461 Moss Landing CA 95039-0461 Office: CSR Inst 663 S Bernardo Ave Sunnyvale CA 94087-1020

DE MENT, JACK (ANDREW), research chemist, author; b. Portland, Oreg., Feb. 6, 1920; s. Andrew Thomas and Bernadine (Michaels) De M. Student, Reed Coll., 1938-41; D.Sc. (hon.), Western States Coll., 1955. Diplomate in nuclear physics Am. Bd. Bio-Analysts. Chemist and metallurgist Mont. Assay Office, 1941; asst. spectroscopist Charlton Labs., Portland, 1941-42; research chemist, assoc. editor Mineralogist Mag., Portland, 1940-51; rsch. chemist and head De Ment Labs., Portland, 1941-91; research asst. Sch. Dentistry, Oreg. Health Scis. U., 1948-50, research cons. biophysics and pharmacology, 1961-66; co-investigator USPHS, 1953-58; pres. Polyphoton Corp., 1955—; sci. editor Prevue Mag., 1958-65; rsch. cons. Ultra-Violet Products, Inc., L.A., 1942-50; Cons. Sec. of War (Project Crossroads) (spent 2 mos. at Bikini atomic bomb tests), 1946; mem. Pres.' Conf. Tech. Distbn. Rsch., 1957; del. 1st Nat. Laser Safety Seminar, Orlando, Fla., 1966; reviewer NSF, 1979-80; formerally enunciated First Law of Flourescence (Lommel-DeMent Absorption Law), new tests for uranium and ores; invented explotron new weapons, radiol. directed energy, new methods for radioactive decontamination; several hundred discoveries and inventions described in over 300 papers in sci. jours.; U.S. and fgn. patents granted on new laser systems; 100 patents held or filed, assigned two dozen to AEC. Author: (with H.C. Dake) Fluorescent Light and Its Applications, 1941, Uranium and Atomic Power, 1941 (rev. edit., 1945), Fluorescent Chemicals and Their Applications, 1942, Ultraviolet Light and Its Applications, 1942, Fluorochemistry, 1945, Rarer Metals, 1946 (Brit. edit. 1949), Handbook of Uranium Minerals, 1947, rev. edit., 1949, Handbook of Fluorescent Minerals, 1947, New Horizons in Cancer Control, 1954; prize essay Gravity Research Found., 1951; contbr. to other books and encys. Recipient Wisdom Award of Honor, 1970, commendation Joint Com. AEC, 1957. Mem. Profl. Execs. Hall of Fame, Sigma Xi, Chi Beta Phi. Home: 11325 NE Weidler St # 44 Portland OR 97220-1999

DEMEO, EDGAR ANTHONY, energy researcher; b. Yonkers, N.Y., Jan. 14, 1942; s. Peter Christopher and Lucia (Goldthorp) DeM.; m. Linda Loring Whitney, May 4, 1968; children: Tracy, Jonathan. BEE, Rensselaer Poly. Inst., 1963; ScM, Brown U., 1965, PhD, 1968; postgrad., Northeastern U., 1980. Mem. tech. staff Bell Labs., Holmdel, N.J., 1963; officer instr. U.S. Naval Acad., 1967-69; rsch. asst. prof. Brown U., Providence, 1969-75, rsch. assoc. prof., 1975-76; project mgr. Electric Power Rsch. Inst., Palo Alto, Calif., 1976-80, program mgr., 1980-90, sr. program mgr., 1990—; mem. adv. com. Solar Energy Rsch. Inst., Golden, Colo., 1982-86; mem. steering com. Photovoltaics for Utility-Scale Applications, San Ramon, Calif., 1986—; coord. Utility Wind Interest Group, Palo Alto, 1989—; chmn. steering com. U.S. Windpower Turbine Devel. Consortium, Livermore, Calif., 1989—. Contbr. articles to profl. jours., chpts. to book; inventor optical sensing device. Bd. dirs. Friends Chamber Music, Providence, 1970-76; pres., bd. dirs. Palo Alto Girls' Softball League, 1982-88; mem. Futurecast Planning Coun., Palo Alto, 1986-87. Lt. USN, 1967-69. Mem. Internat. Solar Energy Soc., Sigma Xi. Office: Electric Power Rsch Inst 3412 Hillview Ave Palo Alto CA 94304

DEMEREE, GLORIA See **LENNOX, GLORIA**

DEMETRESCU, MIHAI CONSTANTIN, computer company executive, scientist; b. Bucharest, Romania, May 23, 1929; s. Dan and Alina (Dragosescu) D.; M.E.E., Poly. Inst. of U. Bucharest, 1954; Ph.D., Romanian Acad. Sci., 1957; m. Agnes Halas, May 25, 1969; 1 child, Stefan. Came to U.S., 1966. Prin. investigator Research Inst. Endocrinology Romanian Acad. Sci., Bucharest, 1958-66; research fellow dept. anatomy UCLA, 1966-67; faculty U. Calif.-Irvine, 1967-83, asst. prof. dept. physiology, 1971-78, assoc. researcher, 1978-79, assoc. clin. prof., 1979-83; v.p. Resonance Motors, Inc., Monrovia, Calif., 1972-85; pres. Neurometrics, Inc., Irvine, Calif., 1978-82; pres. Lasergraphics Inc., Irvine, 1982-84, chmn., chief exec. officer, 1984—. Mem. com. on hon. degrees U. Calif.-Irvine, 1970-72. Postdoctoral fellow UCLA, 1966. Mem. Internat. Platform Assn., Am. Physiol. Soc., IEEE (sr.). Republican. Contbr. articles to profl. jours. Patentee in field. Home: 20 Palmento Way Irvine CA 92715-2109 Office: 20 Ada Irvine CA 92718-2303

DE MICHELE, O. MARK, utility company executive; b. Syracuse, N.Y., Mar. 23, 1934; s. Aldo and Dora (Carno) De M.; m. Faye Ann Venturin, Nov. 8, 1957; children: Mark A., Christopher C., Michele M., Julianne; m. Barbara Joan Stanley, May 22, 1982; 1 child, Angela Marie. BS, Syracuse U., 1955. Mgr. Seal Right Co., Inc., Fulton, N.Y., 1955-58; v.p., gen. mgr. L.M. Harvey Co. Inc., Syracuse, 1958-62; v.p. Niagara Mohawk Power, Syracuse, 1962-78; v.p. Ariz. Pub. Svc., Phoenix, 1978-81, exec. v.p., 1981-82, pres., chief exec. officer, 1982—, also bd. dirs.; bd. dirs. Am. West Airlines; dir. Pinnacle West Capital Corp. Pres. Jr. Achievement, Syracuse, 1974-75, Phoenix, 1982-83, United Way of Cen. N.Y., Syracuse, 1978, Ariz. Opera Co., Phoenix, 1981-83, Phoenix Symphony, 1984-86, United Way of Phoenix, 1985-86, Ariz. Mus. Sci. and Tech., 1988-90; pres. Childrens Action Alliance, 1989—; chmn. Valley of Sun United Way, 1984-86, Phoenix Commn. on Ednl. Excellence, 1987—, Ariz. Arts Stabilization Fund, 1991, Greater Phoenix Econ. Coun. Named Outstanding Young Man of Yr. Syracuse Jaycees, 1968, Phoenix Man of Yr., Phoenix Ad Club, 1992. Mem. Phoenix C. of C. (chmn. bd. 1986-87). Republican. Clubs: Phoenix Country, Ariz. (Phoenix). Home: 5620 N Wilkinson Rd Paradise Vly AZ 85253-5234 Office: Ariz Pub Svc Co 400 N 5th St Phoenix AZ 85004-3902

DEMOFF, MARVIN ALAN, lawyer; b. L.A., Oct. 28, 1942; s. Max and Mildred (Tweer) D.; m. Patricia Caryn Abelov, June 16, 1968; children: Allison Leigh, Kevin Andrew. BA, UCLA, 1964; JD, Loyola U., L.A., 1967. Bar: Calif. 1969. Asst. pub. defender Los Angeles County, 1968-72; ptnr. Steinberg & Demoff, L.A., 1973-83, Craighill, Fentress & Demoff, L.A. and Washington, 1983-86; of counsel Mitchell, Silberberg & Knupp, L.A., 1987—. Mem. citizens adv. bd. Olympic Organizing Com., L.A., 1982-84; bd. trustees Curtis Sch., L.A., 1985—, chmn. bd. trustees, 1988—; sports adv. bd. Constitution Rights Found., L.A., 1986—; bd. dirs. 4A Found., 1988—. Mem. ABA (mem. forum com. on entertainment and sports), Calif. Bar Assn., UCLA Alumni Assn., Phi Delta Phi. Office: Mitchell Silberberg & Knupp Los Angeles CA 90064

DE MONTE-CAMPBELL, ALPHA, novelist; b. Munich; came to U..S, 1960; d. Philippe and Vicky (von May-Menzinger) de Monte; m. Robert James Campbell, Dec. 24, 1968. Student, Convent and U. Munich. Author (novels): It Began in Cannes, 1956, O'Hara, 1963, She Followed Him to Ireland, 1965, In Return for..., 1983; (novelette) The Doll and the Old Man, 1985. Roman Catholic.

DEMPSEY, BARBARA MATTHEA, medical/surgical nurse, critical care nurse; b. The Netherlands, July 27, 1943; d. Petrus Antonius and Hendrika Petronella (Kemp) Petersen; m. James D. Dempsey, June 13, 1981; children: Jennifer, Daniel. AA, Santa Monica (Calif.) Coll., 1970; cert. lactation educator, UCLA, 1982. Staff nurse med./surg. Santa Monica Hosp., 1967-72; surg. intensive care nurse VA Wadsworth Hosp., L.A., 1973-77; staff nurse med./surg. Community Hosp., Santa Rosa, Calif., 1988-90; staff nurse Redwood Nurses Registry, Santa Rosa, 1990—, Norrell Healthcare, Santa Rosa, Calif., 1990—. Office: Norrell Health Care 350 College Ave Santa Rosa CA 95404

DEMPSEY, JAMES HAROLD, court executive officer; b. Long Beach, Calif., Nov. 21, 1953; s. John William and Gloria June (Finchum) D.; 1 child, Melissa. BA in Polit. Sci., Calif. State U., Fullerton, 1976; MPA in Pub. Adminstrn., U. So. Calif., 1978. Adminstrv. analyst Lane County Cir. and Dist. Cts., Eugene, Oreg., 1978-80; asst. ct. adminstr. Santa Cruz (Calif.) County Mcpl. Ct., 1980-82; ct. mgmt. analyst Adminstrv. Office of the Cts., San Francisco, 1982-83; chief adminstrv. officer Marin County Mcpl. Ct., San Rafael, 1983-88, Santa Clara County Mcpl. Ct., San Jose, Calif., 1988-91; exec. officer, clk., jury commr. L.A. Superior Ct., 1991—; mem. trial ct. funding adv. com. Jud. Coun. Calif., San Francisco, 1991—, mem. fin. reporting and automation performance standards com., 1991—, mem. ethics com., 1991—; mem. ct. adminstrs. adv. com. Judicial Coun. Calif., San Francisco, 1993. Recipient Resolutions of Commendation, Marin County Bd. Suprs., 1988, Santa Clara County Bd. Suprs., 1991; named Outstanding Ct. Adminstr., Calif. Trial Lawyers, 1991. Mem. Nat. Conf. Met. Cts., Calif. Assn. Superior Ct. Adminstrs., County Clks. Assn. Calif., Met. Superior Cts. Assn., So. Calif. Trial Ct. Adminstrs. Assn., Los Angeles County Bar Assn. (state cts. com. 1991-92, jud. resources com. 1991-92), L.A. C. of C. (law and justice com. 1991-92). Office: LA Superior Ct 111 N Hill St Rm 105E Los Angeles CA 90012

DEMPSEY, MARGARET A., broadcasting executive; b. La Junta, Colo., Apr. 9, 1950; d. Oliver James and Elisabeth Ann (Clevenger) Cuddy. BA in Communications, Loyola U., New Orleans, 1971; MBA in Mktg. and Econs., U. Wash., 1977. Continuity dir. Sta. KALB, Sta. KSLI-FM, Alexandria, La., 1972-73; merchandise and promotion dir. Sta. KTAC, Sta. KBRD-FM, Seattle, Tacoma, Wash., 1977-78; account exec. Sta. KTAC, Seattle, Tacoma, 1978-80, gen. sales mgr., 1980-83; gen. sales mgr. Sta. KTAC, Sta. KBRD-FM, Seattle, Tacoma, 1983-84; v.p., gen. mgr. Sta. KMFY, Sta. WAYL-FM, Mpls., 1984—. Mem. Mpls. Advt. Fedn. Office: WEZX-FM 3876 Bridge Way N Seattle WA 98103

DEMPSEY, PAUL STEPHEN, law educator; b. Aug. 27, 1950. BA in Journalism, U. Ga., 1972, JD, 1975; LLM in Internat. Law summa cum laude, George Washington U., 1978; DCL cum laude, McGill U., Montreal, Canada, 1986. Bar: Colo., Ga., D.C. Atty., advisor Office Proceedings Interstate Commerce Comm., Wash., D.C., 1975-77; legal advisor to chmn. Interstate Commerce Comm., 1981-82; atty., advisor Office Gen. Counsel Civil Aeronautics Bd., 1977-79; asst., assoc. prof. Coll. Law U. Denver, 1979-85, prof. Coll. Law, 1986—, Hughes Rsch. prof. Coll. Law, 1985-86, 89-91; prof. law distinguished vis. DePaul U., Chgo., 1989-90; Hughes prof. law, dir. transp. law program U. Denver, 1993—; Dir. U. Denver Transp. Law Program, 1979—; appeared on ABC Evening News with Peter Jennings, MacNeil-Lehrer News Hour, ABC World Bus. Report, NBC Today, CNN Crossfire, Nat. Pub. Radio, CBS Radio, NBC Mutual Radio and other news broadcasting programs; host Your Right to Say It, KWGN-TV, 1986—. Author: Airline Deregulation & Laissez Faire Mythology, 1992, Flying Blind: The Failure of Airline Deregulation, 1990, The Social and Economic Consequences of Deregulation, 1989, Law and Foreign Policy in International Aviation, 1987, Aviation Law and Regulation, 2 vols., 1993; author: (with William Thoms) Law and Economic Regulation in Transportation, 1986; (with others) The Law of Transnational Business Transactions; editor: Transp. Law Jour.; contbr. articles to profl. jours; has appeared on numerous TV shows including Mac Neil-Lehrer News Hour, ABC News, NBC News. Fulbright fellow, 1986-87; Canadian Institutional Rsch. grantee, 1989-90, Econ. Policy Inst. grantee, 1989, Hughes Foun. Rsch. grantee, 1987-88, 82, Rocky Mountain Minearl Law Inst. Rsch. grantee, 1987; U. Denver Burlington No. Foun. Outstanding scholar, 1987; recipient Transp. Lawyers Assn. Distinguished Svc. award 1986, Cert. Claims Profl. Accreditation Coun. Outstanding Svc. award 1983. Mem. ABA (vice chmn. transp. com. of adminstrv. law sect. 1988-91), Assn. Am. Law Schs. (chmn. air and space law 1989-90), Cert. Claims Profl. Accreditation Coun. (chmn. bd. dirs. 1981-83), Am. Arbitration Assn. (bd. arbitrators 1987—), Citizens Responsible Transp. (pres. bd. dirs. 1984-86), Internat. Aerospace Inst. (bd. dirs. 1982-86). Office: U Denver Coll Law 1900 Olive St Denver CO 80220-1879

DEMPSTER, STUART ROSS, trombonist/composer, music educator; b. Berkeley, Calif., July 7, 1936; s. Fred Harper and Kathryn Emlyn (Shepardson) D.; m. Renko Carolyn Ishida, Dec. 19, 1964; children: Brian Komei, Loren Kiyoshi. BA in Performance, San Francisco State Coll., 1958, MA in Composition, 1967. Part-time instr. San Francisco Conservatory of Music, 1961-66; part-time asst. prof. Calif. State U., Hayward, 1963-66; prof. U. Wash., Seattle, 1968—; prin. trombone Oakland (Calif.) Symphony, 1962-66; performer in field. Author: The Modern Trombone, 1979. Bd. dirs. Artist Trust, Seattle, 1986-89. With U.S. Army, 1958-60. Recipient Performance award Martha Baird Rockefeller Fund for Music, 1971; U. Ill. fellow, 1971-72, Nat. Endowment for the Arts fellow, 1978, 79, Guggenheim Found. fellow, 1981; Fulbright-Hays grantee Govt. of Australia, 1973. Mem. Internat. Trombone Assn., ASCAP. Office: U Wash Sch of Music Seattle WA 98195

DEMUTH, ALAN CORNELIUS, lawyer; b. Boulder, Colo., Apr. 29, 1935; s. Laurence Wheeler and Eugenia Augusta (Roach) DeM.; m. Susan McDermott; children: Scott Lewis, Evan Dale, Joel Millard. BA magna cum laude, U. Colo., 1958, LLB, 1961. Bar: Colo. 1961, U.S. Dist. Ct. Colo. 1961, U.S. Ct. Appeals (10th cir.) 1962. Assoc. Akolt, Turnquist, Shepherd & Dick, Denver, 1961-68; ptnr. DeMuth & Kemp, 1968—. Conf. atty. Rocky Mountain Conf. United Ch. of Christ, 1970—; bd. dirs. Friends of U. Colo. Library, 1978-86; bd. dirs., sponsor Denver Boys Inc., 1987—, sec., 1988-89, v.p., 1989-90, pres. 1992—; bd. advisors Metro Denver Salvation Army, 1988—. Mem. ABA, Colo. Bar Assn., Denver Bar Assn., Am Judicature Soc., Rotary, Phi Beta Kappa, Sigma Alpha Epsilon, Phi Delta Phi. Republican. Mem. United Ch. of Christ. Office: DeMuth & Kemp 1600 Broadway Ste 1660 Denver CO 80202-4916

DE NARAY, ANDREW THOMAS, environmental planner; b. Budapest, Hungary, July 3, 1942; came to U.S., 1949; s. Andrew and Maria (Sashalmi) de N.; m. Nicole Dee Fairlamb, May 25, 1974; 1 child, Andrew John. BA, U. Ill., 1965. Environ. health specialist U.S. Army, 1965-77; environ. protection specialist region V EPA, Chgo., 1977-84; environ. coord civil engring. USAF, Mountain Home AFB, Idaho, 1984-86, Peterson AFB, Colo., 1986—. Chmn. Greensprings, Colorado Springs, Colo., 1989—; chmn. beautification bd., Mountain Home, 1985-86; mem. steering com. Partnership for Community Design, Colorado Springs, 1989—; mem. Clean Air Campaign, Colorado Springs, 1987—, forestry adv. com. Park and Recreation Dept., Colorado Springs, 1990—. Recipient Cert. Appreciation City of Mountain Home, 1986, Leadership 2000 Cert. Citizen's Goals, 1990. Mem. Sierra Club (Pikes Peak chpt.), Colo. Mountain Club (Pikes Peak chpt., Cert. Appreciation 1988), Springs Area Beautiful Assn., Pikes Peak Camera Club, Soli Deo Gloria Chorale, Colorado Springs Racquet Club, Hort. Arts Soc. (bd. dirs. 1987-89). Roman Catholic. Home: 1322 Wynkoop Dr Colorado Springs CO 80909-3244

DENBOER, JAMES DREW, university official, writer; b. Sheboygan, Wis., Aug. 21, 1937; s. Jacob and Jeannette G. (Verhulst) DenB.; m. Leah G. Zeff, Mar. 1, 1986; children: Megali Stuart DenBoer Havens, Joshua Reeve. BA, Calvin Coll., Grand Rapids, Mich., 1960; MA, U. Calif., Santa Barbara, 1969. Writer, editor USPHS, Washington, 1962-67; dep. dir. Unicorn Press, Santa Barbara, 1968-70; dep. dir. Office Spl. Events, White House Conf. on Children, Washington, 1970-71; freelance writer, Tacoma and Santa Barbara, 1971-73, Los Gatos, Calif., 1976-85; adminstrv. analyst U. Calif., Santa Barbara, 1973-76; mktg. dir. U. Calif., Santa Cruz, 1985—. Author: Learning the Way, 1968 (Internat. Poetry Forum award 1968), Trying To Come Apart, 1970 (Nat. Coun. on Arts award 1970), Nine Poems, 1973, Olson/DenBoer: a Letter, 1976, Lost in Blue Canyon 1981. Grantee Authors League Am., 1972, Carnegie Fund for Authors, 1972, PEN Ctr., N.Y., 1973, Nat. Endowment for Arts, 1976, Nat. Inst. Arts and Letters, 1976. Home: 156 McKay Rd Aptos CA 95003 Office: U Calif Ext 740 Front St Rm 155 Santa Cruz CA 95060

DENHOLM, THOM W., software engineer; b. Coeur D'Alene, Idaho, May 1, 1966; s. Thomas Richard and Helen Jean (Hempel) D. BS in Computer Sci. and Math., Gonzaga U., 1989. Software engr. Attachmate Corp., Bellevue, Wash., 1989—. Mem. Seattle Bach Choir, 1990—, Seattle Peace Chorus, 1992. Mem. Assn. Computing Machinery. Home: 4314 Winslow Pl N # 101 Seattle WA 98103 Office: 3617 131st Ave SE Bellevue WA 98006

DENISON, WILLIAM CLARK, mycologist, educator; b. Rochester, N.Y., June 1, 1928; s. Glenn M. and Rhoda T. (Torrance) D.; m. Margaret R. Mellinger, Sept. 11, 1948; children: Robert Ford, Thomas C., Glenn T., Rebecca S. Denison Johnston. BA, Oberlin (Ohio) Coll., 1950, MA, 1952; PhD, Cornell U., 1956. Apprentice millwright Eastman Kodak Co., Rochester, 1944-46; co-dir. Kanawauke Regional Mus., Bear Mtn. (N.Y.) Park, summer 1947; preparator Dept. Preserved Materials Gen. Biol. Supply House, Chgo., 1948-49; teaching asst. Dept. of Botany Oberlin Coll., 1950-52; teaching asst. Dept. of Plant Pathology Cornell U., 1952-55; asst. prof. Dept. of Biology Swarthmore (Pa.) Coll., 1955-66; assoc. prof. Dept. of Botany & Plant Pathology Oreg. State U., Corvallis, 1966—, curator, 1966—; vis. asst. prof. Dept. of Botany U. N.C., Chapel Hill, 1958-59; pres., sr. scientist Northwest Mycological Cons., Inc., Corvallis, 1985—; rsch. in field. Contbr. articles to numerous profl. jours. Co-organizer, counselor Corvallis Draft Info. Ctr., 1968-72; chmn. North Benton County Citizen's Adv. Com., 1974-78; charter mem., firefighter Adair Rural Fire Protection Dept., Adair Village, Oreg., 1975-83; foster parent Children's Svcs. Div. Oreg. Dept. HHS, 1976-79; citizen mem. representing Benton County Benton Govt. Com., 1978-80; pres. Friends of Benton County, 1978-88; founding mem. First Alternative Coop., Corvallis; bd. dirs. Willamette Inst. Biol. Control. Grantee NSF, Am. Philos. Assn. Mem. Internat. Lichenological Assn., AAUP, AAAS, Mycological Soc. Am., Oreg. Natural Resources Coun., Oreg. Pub. Employee Union (assoc.). Home: 37043 Belden Creek Rd Corvallis OR 97330-9358 Office: Oreg State Univ Dept Botany Corvallis OR 97331

DENKE, PAUL HERMAN, aircraft engineer; b. San Francisco, Feb. 7, 1916; s. Edmund Herman and Ella Hermine (Riehl) D.; m. Beryl Ann Lincoln, Feb. 10, 1940; children: Karen Denke Mottaz, Claudia Denke Tesche, Marilyn Denke Dunn. BCE, U. Calif.-Berkeley, 1937, MCE, 1939. Registered profl. engr., Calif. Stress engr. Douglas Aircraft Co., Santa Monica, Calif., 1940-62, mgr. structural mechanics Long Beach, Calif., 1962-65, chief sci. computing, 1965-71, chief structures engr. methods and devel., 1972-78, chief scientist structural mechanics, 1979-84, staff mgr. MDC fellow, 1985—; mem. faculty dept. engring. UCLA, 1941-50. Assoc. fellow AIAA; mem. Soc. Automotive Engrs. (Arch T. Colwell Merit award 1966, IAE Outstanding Engr. Merit award 1985), Sigma Xi, Chi Epsilon, Tau Beta Pi. Democrat. Pioneered and developed finite element method of structural analysis; author numerous technical papers. Home: 1800 Via Estudillo Palos Verdes Peninsula CA 90274-1908

DENKENBERGER, JOHN DAVID, engineer; b. Ellenville, N.Y., Mar. 2, 1963; s. Edward Francis and Kazuko Mitzuko (Akamine) D. BS, U. Buffalo, 1985; postgrad., U. Puget Sound, 1992—. Assoc. engr. Grumman Corp., Bethpage, N.Y., 1986-88; engr. Gen. Dynamics, Ft. Worth, Tex., 1988-91; specialist engr. Boeing Co., Seattle, 1991—. Coord. Renew St. Patrick's Cathedral, Ft. Worth, 1989-91; chmn. Adopt-A-Family Christmas Fund, Ft. Worth, 1989-91; cons. Jr. Achievement, Ft. Worth, 1990. Republican. Roman Catholic. Home: 31500 33d Pl SW # D204 Federal Way WA 98023 Office: Boeing Co M/Z 6H-CJ Seattle WA 98124

DENLEA, LEO EDWARD, JR., insurance company executive; b. N.Y.C., Mar. 7, 1932; s. Leo Edward Sr. and Teresa (Carroll) D.; m. Nancy Burkley, Aug. 16, 1959; children: Leo Edward III, Thomas, Gregory, Kathryn, Nancy, Rita, Philip. B.S. in Econs., Villanova U., 1954; M.B.A., U. Pa., 1959. Group v.p. fin. services Internat. Basic Economy Corp., N.Y.C., 1966-74; v.p., treas. Pacific Lighting Corp., Los Angeles, 1974-81; sr. v.p. fin. Farmers Group, Inc., Los Angeles, 1981-85, pres., 1985—, chief operating officer, 1985-86, chief exec. officer, chmn. bd., 1986—, also bd. dirs.; Bd. dirs. Alexander and Baldwin, Inc., B.A.T. Industries PLC. Served to lt. (j.g.) USN, 1954-57. Club: California; Wilshire Country. Office: Farmers Group Inc 4680 Wilshire Blvd Los Angeles CA 90010-3807

DENNETT, NOLAN ALMA, dancer, dance and theater educator; b. Ontario, Oreg., Mar. 23, 1950; s. David Lawrence and Myla (Hunsaker) D. BA, Brigham Young U., 1973; MA, Western Wash. U., 1981. Dir. dance St. Louis Conservatory for Arts, 1974-78; artist-in-residence Chgo. Moving Co., 1978-81; mem. movement faculty Goodman Sch. Drama, Chgo., 1980-81; mem. faculty U. Calif., Santa Barbara, 1981-88; prin. dancer Repertory-West Dance Co., Santa Barbara, 19981-88; assoc. prof. San Jose (Calif.) State U., 1988-89; prin. dancer San Francisco Moving Co., 1988-89; mem. faculty Western Wash. U., Bellingham, 1989—; dir. Dance Gallery, Bellingham, 1990—; panelist in dance Wash. State Arts Coun., Olympia, 1991. Author: A Place of Shelter, 1993; contbr. articles to profl. jours.; prodr., dir. (video) Lucas Hoving, Choreographer, 1986. Choreographic fellow Mo. Arts Coun., 1976; Chmn.'s grantee Chgo. Arts Coun., 1979; video grantee Found. for Community Cable TV, 1986; recipient Choreographic award Am. Coll. Dance Festival, 1985. Office: Theatre Arts Dept Western Wash U Bellingham WA 98225

DENNEY, DORIS ELAINE, pharmacist; b. Norwalk, Conn., Sept. 5, 1940; d. Harry Taylor and Mary Matilda (Lobeda) D. BS in Pharmacy, U. Conn., 1962; MBA, Boise State U., 1990. Registered pharmacist, Conn., Idaho, Mass. Retail pharmacist Gilbert Pharmacy, Noroton Heights, Conn., 1963-64; sr. pharmacist Children's Hosp. Med. Ctr., Boston, 1964-68; pharmacist Project Hope, Colombia, 1968-70; adminstrv. intern Denver Gen. Hosp., 1972; dir. pharmacy svcs. Terry Reilly Health Svcs., Nampa, Idaho, 1973—; cons. (Bolivia) Mgmt. Scis. for Health, Cambridge, Mass., 1976. Bd. dirs. Payada drug abuse orgn., Boise, 1983-88; mem. health adv. com. Idaho State U., Boise, 1988-89; bd. dirs., mem. Boise Master Chorale, pres., 1992—. Named Preceptor of Yr. Syntex Labs., 1987; recipient McKesson Leadership award McKesson-Robbins, 1987, Pharmacy Leadership award Nat. Assn. Retail Druggists, 1987. Mem. Idaho State Pharm. Assn. (pres. 1987-88), Am. Pharm. Assn., Am. Pub. Health Assn. (cons. 1978), Am. Soc. of Hosp. Pharmacists, Lambda Kappa Sigma. Democrat. Lutheran. Home: 1519 N 19th St Boise ID 83702-0702 Office: Terry Reilly Health Svcs 1515 3rd St N Nampa ID 83687-4097

DENNING, MICHAEL MARION, computer company executive; b. Durant, Okla., Dec. 22, 1943; s. Samuel M. and Lula Mae (Waitman) D.; m. Suzette Karin Wallance, Aug. 10, 1968 (div. 1979); children: Lila Monique, Tanya Kerstin, Charlton Derek; m. Donna Jean Hamel, Sept. 28, 1985; children: Caitlin Shannon, Meghan O'Donnell. Student, USAF Acad., 1963; BS, U. Tex., 1966, Fairleigh Dickinson U., 1971; MS, Columbia U., 1973. Mgr. systems IBM, White Plains, N.Y., 1978-79; mgr. svc. and mktg. IBM, San Jose, Calif., 1979-81; nat. market support mgr. Memorex Corp., Santa Clara, Calif., 1979-81, v.p. mktg., 1981-82; v.p. mktg. and sales Icot Corp., Mountain View, Calif., 1982-83; exec. v.p. Phase Info. Machines Corp., Scottsdale, Ariz., 1983-84, Tricom Automotive Dealer Systems Inc., Hayward, Calif., 1985-87; pres. ADS Computer Svcs., Inc., Toronto, Ont., Can., 1985-87, Denning Investments, Inc., Palo Alto, Calif., 1987—, Pers. Solutions Group, Inc., Menlo Park, Calif., 1990—. With USAF, 1962-66; Vietnam. Mem. Rotary, English Speaking Union, Phi Beta Kappa, Lambda Chi Alpha (pres. 1965-66). Republican. Methodist. Home: H-2140 Camino de los Robles Menlo Park CA 94025 Office: Denning Investments Inc 1010 El Camino Real Ste 200 Menlo Park CA 94025-4306

DENNIS, BERT R., electrical engineer, educator; b. Suffern, N.Y., Mar. 23, 1932; m. Ramona Shirley McNerl, Aug. 15, 1953; children: Roberta C., Janet R., Marilyn J. BSEE, Fairleigh Dickenson U., 1959; MS in Nuclear Engring., U. N.Mex., 1964. Instrument engr. Los Alamos (N.Mex.) Nat. Lab., 1959-65, sect. leader, 1965-69, project engr., 1969-76, project mgr. energy rsch., 1976—; cons. com. on planetary lumar explorations NAS, Woods Hole, Mass., 1981; cons. Joint Oceanographic Inst., College Station, Tex., 1984-89, Salton Sea Sci. Drilling Project, El Centro, Calif., 1983-87. Contbr. articles to profl. jours. Scholar Blonder Tongue Found., 1958. Mem. Soc. Profl. Well Log Analysts, Lions (pres. Los Alamos 1989-90). Methodist. Home: 106 Sherwood Blvd White Rock NM 87544 Office: Los Alamos Nat Lab MS D4448 PO Box 1663 Los Alamos NM 87545

DENNIS, DENNIS MICHAEL, corporate psychologist; b. Buffalo, Apr. 18, 1949; s. Warren Arthur and Valerie Ann (Pokorski) D.; m. Louise Ivanov, Mar. 17, 1970 (div. Dec. 1978); children: Tami Louise, Heather Anne; m. Cheryl Renee Heinrich, Feb. 17, 1989. BA with honors, SUNY, Buffalo, 1971, BS, 1972; MS, Purdue U., 1976, PhD, 1980. RN; lic. psychologist. Intern Seattle VA Med. Ctr., 1979-80; asst. prof. Purdue U., West Lafayette, Ind., 1980-82; program coord. Seattle VA Med. Ctr., 1982-84; asst. prof. Cen. Wash. U., Ellensburg, 1984-88; consulting psychologist FHPS, Seattle, 1986—; founding ptnr., consulting psychologist First Hill Psychol. Svcs., Seattle, 1986—; pres. Organizational Rsch. and Cons. Assocs., Issaquah, 1991; adv. bd. United Backcare, Bellevue, Wash., 1990—; adj. faculty Cen. Wash. U., 1989—, U. Wash., 1991—. Bd. dirs. Seattle Crisis Clinic, Lafayette Crisis Clinic; Lt. USN, 1971-73. Mem. Am. Psychol. Assn., Am. Psychol. Soc., Soc. for Indsl. & Orgnl. Psychology, Wash. State Psychol. Assn. (pres. 1989, treas. 1985-86), Greater Seattle C. of C. Office: ORCA 1420 NW Gilman Blvd Ste 2728 Issaquah WA 98027-7001

DENNIS, EVIE, school system administrator. BS, St. Louis U., 1953; MA, U. Colo., 1971; postgrad., U. Denver, 1964-66; EdD, Nova U., 1976. Hosp. attendant St. Louis City Infirmary Hosp., 1947-52; lab. technician hypertension divsn. dept. internal medicine Sch. Medicine Washington U., St. Louis, 1952-55, rsch. asst. hypertension divsn. dept. internat medicine Sch. Medicine, 1955-58; rsch. asst. allergy rsch. lab. Jewish Hosp., St. Louis, 1956-58; rsch. asst. children's asthma rsch. inst. and hosp. Jewish Nat. Home for Asthmatic Children, Denver, 1958-63, rsch. assoc. children's asthma rsch. inst. and hosp., 1963-66; counselor, tchr. Lake Jr. High Sch. Denver Pub. Schs., 1966-71, community specialist, 1971-76, adminstrv. asst. to supt., 1976-77, dir. office human rels. and student adv. svcs., 1977-80, exec. dir. dept. human rels. and student adv. svcs., 1980-84, exec. dir. II ednl. and profl. devel. and svcs., 1984-86, exec. dir. II sch./community affairs, 1986-88, dep. supt., 1988-90, supt., 1990—; vis. prof. Met. State Coll., 1974-75, We. State Coll., 1977, Atlanta U., 1978, lectr. U. Colo., Denver, 1990, 91, 92, U. Denver, 1993; cons. North Ctrl. Assn. Colls. and Secondary Schs., 1972, Denver Vocat. Guidance Inst., 1972, Vibrations for Understanding, Inc., 1973, Denver Pub. Schs. Human Rels. Workshops, 1974-93, Kent State U. KEDS, 1978, U. No. Colo., 1978; presenter Leadership Denver, 1971, 85; participant Colo. Human Rights Symposium, 1974, 82; advisor Colo. Women's Coll. Women and Bus. Conf., 1979; keynote speaker Utah Dept. Edn. Adminstrs. Seminar, 1984. Active Nat. Adv. Allergy and Infectious Diseases Coun., 1979-82, Denver Bd. Health and Hosps., 1981-91, chmn., 1984-87; bd. dirs. Lupus Found. Am., Inc., 1982-87, exec. v.p., 1985-86, pres., 1986-87; mem. Nat. Arthritis and Musculoskeletal and Skin Diseases Adv. Coun., 1987-91; mem. Joseph Robichaux Meml. Found. Com., 1972-75; mem. finance com. women's track and field, chmn. region 10 womens track and field Amateur Athletic Union U.S.A., 1970-75, team mgr. womens track and field, 1973, nat. chmn. womens track and field, 1976-79, mem. exec. com. 1976-82, 2nd v.p. 1979-80; chmn. girls and womens track and field Rocky Mountain Assn., Amateur Athletic Union, 1970-73, mem. exec. com., 1973-84, v.p., 1976-79, 92-93, pres., 1980-82; mem. U.S. Women's Track and Field Team Com., 1973-80, mgr., 1976, 80; mem. internat. sect. Women's Track and Field, 1973-79; interim pres. The Athletics Congress/ U.S.A., 1978-79, acting pres., 1979, v.p., 1980, nat. chmn. women's track and field, 1979-84, bd. dirs. 1979-92; mem. Gov.'s Coun. on Phys. Fitness, 1975-78, 80-82; mem. exec. com. U.S. Olympic Com., 1976-92, v.p., 1981-88, spl. asst. to pres., 1989-93; chief del. U.S. Team World Cup II, 1979, U.S. Olympic Team, Seoul, Korea, 1988; San Juan women's adminstr. Pan Am. Games, 1979, bd. dirs., 1985-87, chief. Cuba del., 1991; chief del. U.S. Nat. Track and Field Team, Tokyo, Peking, 1980; bd. dirs. L.A. Olympic Organizing Com., 1982-84; chief del. U.S. Pan Am Team, Caracas, 1983; team leader U.S. Taekwondo Team, Seoul, 1985; bd. visitors U.S. Sports Acad., 1984-91, bd. trustees, 1992—; U.S. del. Internat. Amateur Athletic Fedn., 1980-84, 90—, alt. del., 1986—; U.S. Del. Pan. Am. Sports Orgn., 1982-89; mem. tech. commn. Assn. Nat. Olympic Coms., 1987-92; bd. dirs. Colo. Sports Coun., 1990—; bd. dirs., mem. exec. com. U.S.A. Track & Field, Inc., 1993—; mem. State Equal Ednl. Opportunity Com., 1972-75, vice chmn., 1973-74; mem. Dem. State Equal Rights Commn., 1973-74, Dept. Navy Recruiting Dist. Assistance Coun., 1974-78, Mayor's Commn. on Youth, 1977-79, Denver Clean Air Task Force, 1978-85, Denver Pvt. Industry Com., 1978-88, Denver Community Devel. Adv. Com., 1980-83, Denver Child Car Adv. Com., 1986-87, Denver Area Schs. Supts. Coun., 1990—, U.S. Def. Adv. Com. on Svc. Acad. Athletic Programs, 1992—; mem.-at-large Assn. Ednl. Alumni and Friends, U. Colo. Boulder Sch. Edn., 1979-82; bd. dirs. Nortnver Youth Svcs. Bur., 1973-75, 79-82, Colo. Career Info. System, 1979-81, Denver Met. YMCA, 1981—, Pub. Edn. Coalition, 1990—, Metro Denver Gives, 1990-91; bd. dirs. Women's Forum Colo., 1978-80, sec., 1979; bd. mgrs. Colo. Congress Parents and Tchrs., Inc., 1974-75; mem. exec. bd. Coun. Great City Schs., 1992—; vice-chmn. Denver Pan Helenic Coun., 1959-60, chmn., 1961-63; chmn. State Guidance Liason Com, 1972-73, chmn. membership Colo. Pers. and Guidance Assn., 1971-73; chmn. schs. and solicitation United Negro Coll. Fund, 1971; v.p. North City Park Civic Assn., 1976-79; Dem. Precinct Committeewoman, 1971-82. Recipient award People Let's Unite for Schs., 1975, NOW, 1975, Northeast Denver Optimist, 1975, Oustanding Adminstr. award Black Educators, 1977, Community Svc. award VFW, Woman of Yr. award Delta Sigma Theta, 1978, Operation Push award, 1979, Edn. award S.Y.L. Found., 1979, Sportswomen Pioneer award, 1979, Disting. Svc. award Denver Regional Coun. Govts., 1979, Pres.'s award Athletics Congress U.S.A., 1980, Salute to Women Sports award Big Sisters Colo., 1980, Congl. Gold Medal award U.S. Olympic Team, 1980, Colo. Black Women for Polit. Action award, 1981, Appreciation award Mayor's Adv. Coun., 1982, 83, Joseph Robichaux Meml. award, 1983, Honor Fellow award Nat. Assn. for Girls and Women in Sports, 1983, Pres.'s award, 1987, Spl. award Denver Pub. Schs. Hall Fame, 1983, Denver Community Devel. Agy. award, 1983, Robert Giegengack award Athletic Congres, 1985, Oustanding Achievement and Svc. award Colo. Gospel Music Acad., 1986, Oustanding Community Svc. and Leadership award, 1991, Appreciation cert. Colo. Alliance Bus., 1987, U.S. Collegiate Sports Coun., 1987, Racial Justice award YWCA, 1988, Outstanding Alumni Yr. award Nova U., 1988, Outstanding Contbn. Am. and Israel award Am.-Israel Friendship League, 1989, Contbn. to Sports award Sportswomem Colo., 1989, Spl. citation Colo. Sports Hall Fame, 1989, Citizen of Yr. award Denver Alumni chpt. Kappa Alpha Psi, 1989, Woman That Has Made a Difference award Internat. Women's Forum, 1990, Image award Joint Effort Community Sports Program, 1991, Oustanding Humanitarian Svcs. award Denver NAACP, 1991, Olympic Order award Internat. Olympic Com., 1992, Daniel Payne award Shorter COmmunity African Meth. Episc. Ch., 1993, Achievement in Edn. award Optimists, 1993, Women in Action award Syrian Ct. # 40 Daus. Isis, 1993. Mem. Nat. Assn. Black Sch. Educators, Adminstrs. and Suprs. Assn., Black Adminstrs. and Suprs. Assn., Denver Area Sch. Supts. Coun., We. Athletic Conf. (charter 1983—, Stan Bates award), Nova U. Alumni Assn., Rocky Mountain Assn. (amateur athletic union), Denver Rotary, DenCo Track Club (pres. 1974-79), Mile High Denver Track Club (pres. 1972-73), Denver Allstars Track Club (pres. 1965-72), Alpha Kappa Alpha (pres. Epsilon Nu Omega chpt. 1962-65, 72-73). Office: Denver County SD 1 900 Grant St Denver CO 80203-2996*

DENNIS, HOWARD WILLIS, oil company executive; b. Denver, June 23, 1927; s. Willis J. and Grace (Hammond) D.; m. Sylvia Reisewitz, Nov. 13, 1954; children: Vance F., Heather Ellen, Adam H. BS, U. Nebr., 1952; MA, U. Denver, 1967; PhD, U. Ga., 1971. Asst. prof. Ind. State U., Terre Haute, 1970-73; regional mgr. Applied Sci. and Resource Planning, Denver, 1973-74; environ. and geology cons. Dennis Assocs., Denver, 1974-88; v.p. exploration and new devel. McKenzie Petroleum Co., Denver, 1988—; keynote speaker Dept. Energy Natural Gas Conf., Morgantown Energy Tech. Ctr., 1992. Editor: (internat. newsletter) Computer Oriented Geological Soc. Letter, 1986-89, (trade assn. newsletter) Flowline, 1991—; contbr. articles to profl. jours. Precinct committeeman, twp. capt. Rep. Party, Terre Haute, 1970-73. With U.S. Army, 1945-47. Recipient fellowship Nat. Def. Edn. Act, U. Ga., 1967-70, grants NSF, 1967, 72. Mem. Internat. Assn. Energy Economists (dir. 1989-90), Colo. Oil and Gas Assn. (dir. 1989—), Sigma Xi. Episcopalian. Office: McKenzie Petroleum Co 1625 Broadway Ste 2580 Denver CO 80202

DENNIS, JAMES M., university administrator; s. Roy and Maryjane (Mercer) D.; m. Leslie Dennis; children: Jeff, Brian. BA, Occidental Coll., L.A., 1966; PhD, U. So. Calif., 1971; postgrad., The Claremont Colls., Pomona, Calif., 1978. With dept. health, phys. edn. and recreation U. So. Calif., L.A., 1966, asst. prof., 1971-77, assst. dir. athletics, 1973-80, exec. dir. ednl. clinics, 1970-80, asst. v.p. student affairs, 1978-81, v.p. student affairs, 1981—; lectr. throughout U.S.; presented papers at nat. convs. Bd. mem. Calif. Mus. Sci. and Industry; bd. govs. Occidental Colls. Mem. Inter-Assn. Task Force on Intercollegiate Athletics, U.S. Dept. Edn. Network on Colls. and Univs. Committed to Elmination of Drug and Alcohol Abuse, Am. Assn. Student Pers. Adminstrs., Western Assn. Schs. and Colls. Accrediting Commn. Team, Exec. Commn. for Nat. Youth Sports Program. Office: U So Calif Student Union 201 Los Angeles CA 90089-4891

DENNIS, LARRY WALTER, management trainer; b. Poplar Bluff, Mo., Nov. 8, 1939; s. Joe Dennis and Velma (Geer) Stokes; m. Donna Lee, June 23, 1962; children: Larry Jr., Barry A., Loren Lee. BS, John Wesley, 1975. Gen. mgr. Ralph Nichol Corp., Detroit, 1966-75; owner Dale Carnegie Franchise, Rockford, Ill., 1975-76, Portland, Oreg., 1976-81; v.p. mktg. Internat. Trading Group, San Francisco, 1981-83; v.p. regional Penn Corp., Portland, 1983-85; pres. Turbo Mgmt. Systems, Portland, 1985—. Inventor video process; author: Repbat Business, 1992; columnist. Campaign mgr. U.S. Congress, Portland, 1980; candidate County Bd., Rockford, Ill., 1976; bd. dirs. Rockford Hosp. Planning, 1975; bd. com. mem. Portland C. of C., 1977-78; bd. advisor Warner Pacific Coll., Portland, 1989—; bd. dirs. John Wesley Coll., 1974-76; bd. dirs. Unity Ch., Portland, 1987-89. With U.S. Army, 1960-62. Mem. Sales and Mktg., Portland Speakers Burrow, Portland Speakers Assn. Republican. Home: 5036 SW Hilltop Ln Portland OR 97221 Office: Turo Mgmt Systems Ste 340 5440 SW Westgate Portland OR 97221

DENNIS, SONYA RENEÉ, television station official; b. Silver Springs, Md., May 9, 1965; d. James Richard and Sandra Diane (Lewis) D. BA, U. Nev., Las Vegas, 1989; cert. of completion, Inst. Children's Lit., Las Vegas, 1991. Master control prodn. and traffic coord. Sta. KBLR-TV, Las Vegas, 1989-91; traffic coord. and asst. Sta. KVBC-TV3, Las Vegas, 1991—. Recipient Brotherhood Week award K.O. Knudson Jr. High Sch., 1991. Office: Sta KVBC-TV 1500 Foremaster Ln Las Vegas NV 89101

DENNIS, WINSTON ROBERT, JR., educational administrator; b. Mason City, Iowa, July 18, 1941; s. Winston Robert and Ruth Virginia (Fredrickson) D.; m. Carolyn Jeanne Smith, June 5, 1961 (div. May 1973); children: Winston Robert III, Walter Rudyard; m. Carole Lee Travelstead, Dec. 19, 1973; stepchildren: Catherine Denise Ballard, Grady Stanton Hall. BS in Music Edn., Pacific Union Coll., Angwin, Calif., 1962; MMus, U. Redlands, 1969; EdS, Loma Linda U., 1987, EdD, 1989. Tchr., band dir. Loma Linda (Calif.) Acad., 1962-71, vice prin., 1970-79; prin. San Diego Acad., National City, Calif., 1979-82, Fresno (Calif.) Adventist Acad., 1984-87; pres. Friends San Diego Acad., 1982-84; grad. asst. Loma Linda U., Riverside, Calif., 1987-88; prin. Pacific Union Coll. Prep. Sch., 1989—. Bd. dirs. Paradise Valley Hosp., National City, 1979-84; mem. Napa County Grand Jury, Napa, Calif., 1991-92. Mem. ASCD, Nat. Assn. Secondary Sch. Prins., Rotary. Republican. Adventist. Home: 1726 Crinella Dr Saint Helena CA 94574 Office: Pacific Union Coll Prep Sch McKibbin Hall Angwin CA 94508

DENNISH, GEORGE WILLIAM, III, cardiologist; b. Trenton, N.J., Feb. 14, 1945; s. George William and Mary Ann (Bodnar) D.; m. Kathleen Macchi, June 28, 1969; children: Andrew Stuart, Brian George, Michael John. AB magna cum laude, Seton Hall U., 1967; MD, Jefferson Med. Coll., 1971. Diplomate Nat. Bd. Med. Examiners, Am. Bd. Internal Medicine (sub. specialty cert. in cardiovascular diseases). Intern Naval Hosp., Phila., 1971-72, jr. asst. resident, 1972-73, sr. asst. resident, 1973-74; fellow cardiovascular diseases Naval Regional Med. Ctr., San Diego, 1974-76, dir. coronary care unit, 1977-78; pvt. practice cardiology, San Diego, 1978—; v.p. Splty. Med. Clinic, La Jolla and San Diego, 1982—; staff cardiologist Naval Regional Med. Ctr., Faculty Medicine, San Diego, 1976—; dir. spl. care units Scripps Meml. Hosp., La Jolla, 1981-88, chmn. cardiology div., 1987—; chief medicine Scripps-Encinitas Hosp., 1983-87; co-editor Cardiac CATV, 1987—; adj. asst. prof. of medicine Baylor Coll., Houston; assoc. clin. prof. medicine U. Calif., San Diego, 1976—. Bd. dirs. San Diego County Heart Assn.; founder, pres., Cardiovascular Inst., La Jolla. Lt. comdr. USNR, 1971—. Decorated Knight of Holy Sepulchre; recipient Physician's Recognition award AMA, 1974-77. Fellow ACP, Am. Coll. Cardiology, Am. Heart Assn. (clin. coun.), Am. Coll. Chest Physicians, Am. Coll. Angrology mem. Am. Soc. Internal Medicine, AAAS, Am. Coll. Clin. Pharmacology, N.Y. Acad. Scis., Am. Fedn. Clin. Rsch., N.Am. Soc. Pacing and Electrophysiology, Soc. for Cardiac Angiography, Soc. for Cardiac Angiography and Intervention, Old Mission Players Club, K.C. Roman Catholic. Contbr. articles to med. jours. Home: 13063 Caminito Pointe Del Mar Del Mar CA 92014-3854 Office: 351 Santa Fe Dr Ste 200 Encinitas CA 92024-5197 Address: 9844 Genesee Ave Suite 400 La Jolla CA 92037

DENNISON, ANNA NASVIK, artist; b. St. Paul; d. Peter Olson and Hattie Mathilda (Swenson) Nasvik; m. Roger Bennett, Nov. 7, 1936; children: Lynne, Kristin. Student, Coll. of St. Catherine, St. Paul, 1925, St. Paul Sch. of Art, 1927, Art Student's League, 1932. Tchr. art St. Joseph's Acad., St. Paul, 1926-30; freelance fashion illustrator N.Y.C., 1930-64; artist syndicated page The Fashion Syndicate, N.Y.C., 1934-38; mem. nat. art bd. Nat. League Am. Pen Women, 1990-92. One woman shows include Colbert Galleries, Sherbrooke St., Mont., Can., 1979, Gallery Milhalis, Sherbrooke St., Mont., 1984, T. Eaton Foyer des Arts, Mont., 1982-87, Venable-Neslage Gallerie, Washington, 1979-84, Lido Galleries, Scottsdale, Ariz., 1988, Hilltop Galleries, Nogales, Ariz. (top painting award, People's Choice award), Maiden Ln. Gallery, San Francisco, 1991; represented Newman Galleries, Scottsdale, Ariz. Named Woman of Art, Foyer des Arts, 1982; winner 3 top awards Ariz. juried show, Nat. League Am. Pen Women, 1989; recipient 3 People's Choice award Hilltop Galleries, 1991. Mem. Santa Cruz Valley Art Assn., Lakeshore Assn. of Art, Nat. League of Pen Women (3 Top awards 1989, nat. bd. dirs. 1990—), Pen Women Sonora Desert. Home and Office: 231 W Paseo Adobe Green Valley AZ 85614-3462

DENNISON, GEORGE MARSHEL, academic administrator; b. Buffalo, Ill., Aug. 11, 1935; s. Earl Fredrick and Irene Gladys (McWhorter) D.; m. Jane Irene Schroeder, Dec. 26, 1954; children: Robert Gene, Rick Steven. AA, Custer County (Mont.) Jr. Coll., 1960; BA, U. Mont., 1962, MA, 1963; PhD, U. Wash., 1967. Asst. prof. U. Ark., Fayetteville, 1967-68; vis. asst. prof. U. Wash., Seattle, 1968-69; asst. prof. Colo. State U., Fort Collins, 1969-73, assoc. prof., 1973-77, assoc. dean Coll. Arts, Humanities and Social Sci., 1976-80, prof., 1977-87, acting acad. v.p., 1980-82, acting assoc. acad. v.p., 1982-86, assoc. acad. v.p., 1987; provost, v.p. acad. affairs Western Mich. U., Kalamazoo, 1987-90; pres. U. Mont., Missoula, 1990—; cons. U.S. Dept. Justice, 1976-84; bd. Community Med. Ctr, Missoula, 1st Bank, Missoula, Inst. Medicine and Humanities, Missoula. Author: The Dorr War, 1976; contbr. articles to jours. in field. Bd. dirs. Kalamazoo Ctr. for Med. Studies, 1989-90. With USN, 1953-57. ABA grantee, 1969-70; Colo. State U. grantee, 1970-75, Nat. Trust for Hist. Preservation grantee, 1976-78; U.S. Agy. for Internat. Devel. grantee, 1979—; Colo. Commn. on Higher Edn. devel. grantee, 1985. Mem. Am. Hist. Assn., Orgn. Am. Historians, Am. Assn. Higher Edn., Am. Soc. for Legal History. Office: U Montana Office of Pres Missoula MT 59812

DENNISON, JACK LEE, religion educator; b. Ft. Wayne, Ind., July 7, 1951; s. Lawrence Caldwell and Barbara Jean (Stilwell) D.; m. Janice Louise Hoffman, Apr. 17, 1971; children: Stephen, David. BA, Biola U., 1976; MDiv, Talbot Sch. Theology, 1980; D Ministry, Fuller Theol. Sem., 1989; postgrad., Western Bapt. Sem., 1989—. Ordained to ministry Bapt. Ch., 1981. Assoc. pastor Whittier (Calif.) Hills Bapt. Ch., 1978-80, 1st Bapt. Ch., Yakima, Wash., 1980-82; sr. pastor Northlake Bapt. Ch., Longview, Wash., 1982-88; grad. prof. Multnomah Sch. of Bible, Portland, Oreg., 1988—; cons. David C. Cook Pub. Co., Wash., 1981; ch. cons. Ch. Growth Network, San Bernardino, Calif., 1989. Maj. USAR, 1968—. Home: 408 SE 18th St Troutdale OR 97060 Office: Multnomah Sch of Bible 8435 NE Glisan St Portland OR 97220

DENNISON, RONALD WALTON, engineer; b. San Francisco, Oct. 23, 1944; s. S. Mason and Elizabeth Louise (Hatcher) D.; children: Ronald, Frederick. BS in Physics and Math., San Jose State U., 1970, MS in Physics, 1972. Physicist, Memorex, Santa Clara, Calif., 1970-71; sr. engr. AVCO, San Jose, Calif., 1972-73; advanced devel. engr. Perkin Elmer, Palo Alto, Calif., 1973-75; staff engr. Hewlett-Packard, Santa Rosa, Calif., 1975-79; program gen. mgr. Burroughs, Westlake Village, Calif., 1979-82; dir. engring., founder EIKON, Simi Valley, Calif., 1982-85; sr. staff technologist Maxtor Corp., San Jose, 1987-90; dir. engring. Toshiba Am. Info. Systems, 1990—; materials. Author tech. publs. Served to sgt. USAF, 1963-67. Mem. IEEE, Am. Vacuum Soc., Internat. Soc. Hybrid Microelectronics, Internat. Disk Drive Equipment and Materials Assn. Republican. Methodist. Mem. Aircraft Owners and Pilots Assn., Internat. Comanche Soc. Home: 2217 Yosemite Dr Milpitas CA 95035-6649

DENNISTON, MARTHA KENT, business owner, author; b. Phila., Feb. 8, 1920; d. Samuel Leonard and Elizabeth (Cryer) Kent; m. Edward Shippen Willing, May 14, 1942 (div. 1972); children: Peter, Matthew, Thomas, Stephen; m. George C. Denniston, July 5, 1974. BA, Bryn Mawr (Pa.) Coll., 1941; MA, U. Wash., Seattle, 1965. Clinic dir. Population Dynamics, Seattle, 1973-84; pvt. practice investor, 1950—; resort owner Ecologic Pl., Port Townsend, Wash., 1972—; sec. bd. dirs. Population Inst., Washington, 1980-83, Ctr. for Population Communications, N.Y.C., 1983-86. Author: Beyond Conception, Our Children's Children, 1971. Bd. dirs. Population Action Coun., Washington, 1977-80. Mem. Nat. Soc. Colonial Dames Am., Am. Farmlands Trust, Sigma Xi. Office: Population Dynamics 2442 NW Market St Seattle WA 98107-4177

DENNY, JAMES CLIFTON, tree farm administrator, forestry consultant; b. Palo Alto, Calif., Aug. 3, 1922; s. James Milton and Alma May (Siler) D.; m. Ann Elliott, Oct. 31, 1948; children: Christine, Stuart, James, Matthew, Katharine. BS, U. Calif., Berkeley, 1948. Registered profl. forester, Calif. Forest fire dispatcher Calif. Div. Forestry, Redding, 1948-50, asst. forest technician, 1950-53, forest technician, 1953-59, sr. forest technician, 1959-62; asst. dep. state forester Calif. Div. Forestry, Sacramento, 1962-71, Santa Rosa, Calif., 1971-75; chief resource mgmt. Calif. Dept. Forestry, Sacramento, 1975-80; forestry cons., 1980—; bd. dirs., sec. Forest Landowners of Calif., Sacramento, 1989—. 1st lt. USAF, 1942-46, ETO. Mem. Soc. Am. Foresters. Republican. Presbyterian. Home and Office: 8996 Ritts Mill Rd Shingletown CA 96088

DENSON, NANCY RAE, healthcare management consultant; b. Bellingham, Wash., Nov. 17, 1951; d. Fred Denson and Ruth (Lifendahl) Bovee; m. Nick Stemm. Assoc. degree, Everett Community Coll., 1977; BA in Polit. Sci. magna cum laude, U. Wash., 1987, MHA in Health Svcs. Adminstrn., 1989. RN. RN Group Health Coop., Redmond, Wash., 1978-85; healthcare rev. coord. Profl. Rev. Orgn., Seattle, 1985-88; cons. Found. for Healthcare Quality, Seattle, 1989; mgr. bus. adv. svc. Arthur Andersen & Co., Seattle, 1989-92; mgr. payment policy adminstrn. Group Health Coop., Seattle, 1992—; mem. Healthcare Fin. Mgmt., Chgo., 1990—. Asst. coord. Wash. State Rural health Commn., Olympia, 1989—. Mem. Phi Beta Kappa. Office: Arthur Andersen & Co 801 2d Ave Ste 900 Seattle WA 98104

DENT, ERNEST DUBOSE, JR., pathologist; b. Columbia, S.C., May 3, 1927; s. E. Dubose and Grace (Lee) D.; m. Dorothy McCalman, June 16, 1949; children: Christopher, Pamela; m. 2d, Karin Frehse, Sept. 6, 1970. Student, Presbyn. Coll., 1944-45; M.D., Med. Coll. S.C., 1949. Diplomate clin. pathology and pathology anatomy Am. Bd. Pathology. Intern U.S. Naval Hosp., Phila., 1949-50; resident pathology USPHS Hosp., Balt., 1950-54; chief pathology USPHS Hosp., Norfolk, Va., 1954-56; assoc. pathology Columbia (S.C.) Hosp., 1956-59; pathologist, dir. labs. Columbia Hosp., S.C. Baptist Hosp., 1958-69; with Straus Clin. Labs., L.A., 1969-72; staff pathologist Hollywood (Calif.) Community Hosp, St. Joseph Hosp., Burbank, Calif., 1969-72; dir. labs. Glendale Meml. Hosp. and Health Ctr., 1972—; bd. dirs. Glendale Meml. Hosp. and Health Ctr. Author papers nat. med. jours. Mem. Am. Cancer Soc., AMA, L.A. County Med. Assn. (pres. Glendale dist. 1980-81), Calif. Med. Assn. (councillor 1984-90), Am. Soc. Clin. Pathology, Coll. Am. Pathologists (assemblyman S.C. 1965-67; mem. publs. com. bull. 1968-70), L.A. Soc. Pathologists (trustee 1984-87), L.A. Acad. Medicine, S.C. Soc. Pathologists (pres. 1967-69). Lutheran. Home: 1526 Blue Jay Way Los Angeles CA 90069-1215 Office: S Central and Los Feliz Aves Glendale CA 91225-7036

DENTON, WILLIAM LEWIS, performing arts company administrator; b. San Diego, July 25, 1932; s. D. Lewis and Ruth Virginia (Goodbody) D. BA, San Diego State U., 1957. Mng. dir. Atlanta Symphony, 1968-70, Nat. Symphony, Washington, 1970-77; exec. dir. Ill. Arts Coun., 1977-78; gen. mgr. San Diego Symphony, 1964-68, 80-82; exec. dir. Midsummer Mozart Festival, San Francisco, 1986—; adj. prof. Gov's. State U., Springfield, Ill., 1976-78. With USAF, 1950-54. Fisher fellow, N.Y., 1971-75. Mem. Am. Symphony League (treas. 1972-74), Marines Meml. Democrat. Office: Midsummer Mozart Festival World Trade Ctr Ste 280 San Francisco CA 94111

DEPAOLIS, POTITO UMBERTO, food company executive; b. Mignano, Italy, Aug. 28, 1925; s. Giuseppe A. and Filomena (Macchiaverna) deP.; Vet. Dr., U. Naples, 1948; Libera Docenza, Ministero Pubblica Istruzione (Rome, Italy), 1955; m. Marie A. Caronna, Apr. 10, 1965. Came to U.S., 1966, naturalized, 1970. Prof. food service Vet. Sch., U. Naples, Italy, 1948-66;

retired, 1966; asst. prof. A titre Benevole Ecole Veterinaire Alfort, Paris, France, 1956; vet. inspector U.S. Dept. Agr., Omaha, 1966-67; sr. research chemist Grain Processing Corp., Muscatine, Iowa, 1967-68; v.p., dir. product devel. Reddi Wip, Inc., Los Angeles, 1968-72; with Kubro Foods, Los Angeles, 1972-73, Shade Foods, Inc., 1975—; pres. Vegetable Protein Co., Riverside, Calif., 1973—, Tima Brand Food Co., 1975—, Dr. Tima Natural Foods, 1977—. Fulbright scholar Cornell U., Ithaca, N.Y., 1954; British Council scholar, U. Reading, Eng., 1959-60; postdoctoral research fellow NIH, Cornell U., 1963-64. Mem. Inst. Food Technologists, Italian Assn. Advancement Sci., AAAS, Vet. Med. Assn., Biol. Sci. Assn. Italy, Italian Press Assn., Greater Los Angeles Press Club. Contbr. articles in field to prol. jours. Patentee in field. Home: Bel Air 131 Groverton Pl Los Angeles CA 90077 Office: 8570 Wilshire Blvd Beverly Hills CA 90211-3133 also: 6878 Beck Ave North Hollywood CA 91605

DEPAOLO, DONALD JAMES, earth science educator; b. Buffalo, Apr. 12, 1951; s. Dominic James and Lorraine Marie (Nassiff) DeP.; m. Geraldine Sue Adler, Apr. 14, 1973 (div. Oct. 1984); 1 child, Tara Michelle; m. Bonnye Lynn Ingram, Aug. 24, 1985; 1 child, Daniel James. BS in Geology, SUNY, Binghamton, 1973; PhD in Geology, Calif. Inst. Tech., 1978. Asst. prof. geology UCLA, 1978-81, assoc. prof., 1981-83, prof., 1983-88; prof. geology, dir. Berkeley Ctr. for Isotope Geochemistry U. Calif., Berkeley, 1988—, chmn. dept. geology and geophysics, 1990-93; mem. various research coms. NRC, 1983—; mem. sci. adv. com. DOSECC, 1985-87. Contbr. articles to profl. jours. Fellow Am. Geophys. Union (chmn. award coms., Macelwane award 1983), Mineral. Soc. Am. (award 1987); mem. AAAS, Geol. Soc. Am. (Clarke medal 1978), Nat. Acad. Scis., Geochem. Soc. (chmn. awards coms.). Office: U Calif Dept Geology & Geophysics Berkeley CA 94720

DE PASSE, DERREL BLAUVELT, electronics industry executive; b. Bronxville, N.Y., Jan. 17, 1950; d. Alfred Bernard and Josephine Martha (Weyland) De P. BA, U. Tex., 1971, MPA, 1973. Mgr. pub. affairs Container Corp. Am., Chgo., 1974-75; regional mgr. pub. affairs Container Corp. Am., Phila., 1976-78; dir. fed. pub. affairs Container Corp. Am., Washington, 1979-83; spl. asst. to dir. U.S. Peace Corps, Washington, 1984-85; dir. govt. affairs Varian, Palo Alto, Calif., 1985-90, v.p. govt. rels., 1990-92; v.p. worldwide govt. rels. Varian, Palo Alto, 1992—; vice chmn. industry sector adv. com. on electronics and instrumentation U.S. Dept. Commerce, Washington, 1987—; commr. Calif. state World Trade Com., 1992—. Trustee San Jose/Cleve. Ballet; commr. Parks and Recreation Commn., San Mateo County, Calif.; state co-chmn. Pro-Wilson, Calif. Mem. Pub. Affairs Coun. (exec. com. bd. dirs. 1990—), Calif. Coun. for Internat. Trade (exec. com., bd. dirs. 1989—), Lincoln Club No. Calif. (exec. com.). Office: Varian 3050 Hansen Way Palo Alto CA 94304-1000

DE PASSE, SUZANNE, record company executive; m. Paul Le Mat. Student, Manhattan Community Coll. Former talent coordinator Cheetah Disco, N.Y.C.; creative asst. to pres. Motown Prodns., Los Angeles, 1968-81, pres., from 1981; now c.e.o. de Passe Entertainment, L.A. Acts signed and developed for Motown include The Commodores, The Jackson Five, Frankie Valli and the Four Seasons, Lionel Richie, Thelma Houston, Billy Preston, Teena Marie, Rick James, Stephanie Mills; co-author screenplay for film Lady Sings the Blues (Acad. award nomination); exec. producer: (TV miniseries) Lonesome Dove, (TV series) Motown on Showtime, Nightlife starring David Brenner, Motown Revue starring Smokey Robinson, Motown Returns to the Apollo (Emmy award, NAACP Image award), (TV spl.) Motown 25: Yesterday, Today, Forever (Emmy award, NAACP Image award); writer: (TV spls.) Happy Endings, Jackson 5 Goin' Back to Indiana, Diana; creative cons: Git on Broadway-Diana Ross & The Supremes & Temptations, TCB-Diana Ross & The Supremes & Temptations. Office: de Passe Entertainment Ste 610 5750 Wilshire Blvd Los Angeles CA 90036

DE PATER, IMKE, astronomy educator; b. Hengelo, The Netherlands, Mar. 28, 1952; came to U.S., 1980; d. Cornelis and Lucie (Holterman) de P.; m. Fool Bull, Aug. 10, 1976; 1 child, Floris. PhD, Leiden U., The Netherlands, 1980. Rsch. asst. Leiden U., 1976-80; rsch. assoc. Lunar and Planetary Lab., Tucson, 1980-83; asst. prof. U. Calif., Berkeley, 1983-87, assoc. prof., 1987—; mem. editorial bd. Icarus; mem. coun. Space Telescope Inst. Contbr. articles to profl. publs. Sloan Found. fellow. Mem. Union Radio Sci. Internat. (John Howard Gold medal), Am. Astron. Soc., Am. Geophys. Union, Internat. Astron. Union. Office: U Calif Astronomy Dept 601 Campbell Hall Berkeley CA 94720

DEPEW, MARIE KATHRYN, retired educator; b. Sterling, Colo., Dec. 1, 1928; d. Amos Carl and Dorothy Emelyn (Whiteley) Mehl; m. Emil Carlton DePew, Aug. 30, 1952 (dec. 1973). BA, U. Colo., 1950, MA, 1953. Post grad. Harvard U., Cambridge, Mass., 1962; tchr. Jefferson County Pub. Schs., Arvada, 1953-73; mgr. Colo. Accountability Program, Denver, 1973-83; sr. cons. Colo. Dept. Edn., Denver, 1973-85, ret., 1985. Author: (pamphlet) History of Hammil, Georgetown, Colorado, 1967; contbr. articles to profl. jours. Chmn. Colo. State Accountability Com., Denver, 1971-75. Fellow IDEA Programs, 1976-77, 79-81. Mem. Colo. Hist. Assn., Jefferson County Edn. Assn. (pres. 1963-64), Colo. Edn. Assn. (bd. dirs. 1965-70), Ky. Colonels (hon. mem.), Phi Beta Kappa. Republican. Methodist. Home: 920 Pennsylvania St Denver CO 80203-3157

DEPEW, WILLIAM EARL, logistics engineer; b. Lyons, N.Y., Sept. 25, 1948; s. Bela Earl DePew and Cora (Teeter) Craine; m. Debra Ann Bailey, Sept. 26, 1992; 1 child, Carey Anne Mills. Grad. high sch., Red Creek, N.Y.; student, Union Coll., Schenectady, N.Y., 1966-67. Mgr. bar and restaurant facilities Am. Legion Post 52, Sierra Vista, Ariz., 1971-75; prodn. control indsl. ops. directorate U.S. Army, Ft. Huachuca, Ariz., 1975-76, quality assurance engr., 1976-83, logistics mgr., 1983-87, contracts team chief, 1987-89, DISA logistics mgr., 1989—; expert for tng. in subject matter Ft. Gordon, Ga. Signal Ctr., 1985; mem. Network Working Group Def. Communications Agy., Washington, 1988. Served with U.S. Army, 1968-71, Vietnam. Mem. Def. Contract Mgmt. Assn., Soc. Logistics Engrs., Armed Forces Comm. Elecrronics Assn., Am. Legion (hon. life, post comdr. 1976-77, dist. comdr. 1980-81), VFW, Masons, Shriners, Elks (exalted ruler Sierra Vista 1987-88), Moose. Democrat. Methodist. Home: 1711 Cottonwood Sierra Vista AZ 85635 Office: Joint Interoperability Test Ctr TCACB Fort Huachuca AZ 85613-7020

DEPINTO, JOSEPH ANTHONY, social worker; b. N.Y.C., Sept. 5, 1951; s. Marco John and Frances Rose (Barbaro) DeP.; m. Judith Ann Paris, Apr. 30, 1976 (div. 1984); children: Marco. BA, Ariz. State U., 1973, MSW, 1978. Cert. ind. social worker, cert. addictions counselor. Counselor Jane Wayland Ctr., Phoenix, 1975-78; caseworker Valley Big Bros., Phoenix, 1978-79; social worker Child Protective Svcs., Phoenix, 1979, Bostrom Alternative Ctr., Phoenix, 1979—; therapist Treatment Assessment Screening Ctrs., Phoenix, 1985-90, Youth Evaluation Treatment Ctrs., Phoenix, 1990-91; instr. Rio Salado Community Coll., Phoenix, 1990—; cons. DePinto & Assocs., Mesa, 1989—. Mem. NEA, Nat. Assn. Social Workers, Ariz. Grp. Psychotherapy Soc., Ariz. Edn. Assn. Democrat. Office: Bostrom Alternative Ctr 3535 N 27th Ave Phoenix AZ 85017-5015

DEPINTO, RONALD DUNCAN, business owner; b. Chgo., Aug. 28, 1932; s. Angus Jacque and Margaret (Bensema) DeP.; m. Nancy West, Aug. 21, 1954 (div. 1972); children: Debora, Steven, Christopher; m. Lee Allen, Sept. 15, 1976. BS in Radio/TV, Northwestern U., 1954. Promotion mgr. KPHO-TV, Phoenix, 1955-57; owner, mgr. Hi-Fidelity House, Phoenix, 1958-60; v.p. Recording Ctr., San Diego, 1960-63; sales tng. specialist Ampex Corp., Sunnyvale, Calif., 1963-66; nat. sales mgr. TV Rsch. Internat., Palo Alto, Calif., 1967-69, Convergence Corp., Irvine, Calif., 1970-73; mktg. cons. Interquest, Fountain Valley, Calif., 1974-79; bus. owner New Video Exch., Fountain Valley, Calif., 1980—; owner Electrotek: R & D & Mktg. Cons., Fountain Valley, 1985—. Author: Short Stories, 1954 (Schuman award 1954), (manual) Professional Salesmanship, 1965, (radio script) CBS Radio Network, 1957. Recipient Best In-House Publication award, 1956. Mem. Tiger Moth Club of Great Britain, Acad. Model Aeronautics, Soc. Motion Picture & TV Engrs., Soc. Broadcast Engrs., Phi Kappa Sigma Frat. Episcopalian. Office: New Video Exch 9550 Warner Ste 250 Fountain Valley CA 92708

DEPREIST, JAMES ANDERSON, conductor; b. Phila., Nov. 21, 1936; s. James Henry and Ethel (Anderson) De P.; m. Betty Louise Childress, Aug. 10, 1963; children: Tracy Elisabeth, Jennifer Anne; m. Ginette Grenier, July 19, 1980. Student, Phila. Conservatory Music, 1959-61; BS, U. Pa., 1958, MA, 1961, LHD (hon.), 1976; LHD (hon.), Reed Coll., 1990; MusD (hon.), Laval U., Quebec City, Can., 1980, Linfield Coll., 1986; DFA (hon.), U. Portland, 1983, Pacific U., 1985, Willamette U., 1987, Drexel U., 1989, Oreg. State U., 1990; Doctor of Arts and Letters (hon.), St. Mary's Coll., Moraga, Calif., 1985; HHD (hon.), Lewis and Clark U., 1986; DFA (hon.), Drexel U., 1989; LHD (hon.), Reed Coll., 1990; DFA (hon.), Oregon State U., 1990; MusD (hon.), Juilliard, 1993. Am. specialist music for State Dept., 1962-63; condr.-in-residence Bangkok, 1963-64; condr. various symphonies and orchs., 1964—. Condr.: Am. debut with N.Y. Philharm., 1964, asst. condr. to Leonard Bernstein, N.Y. Philharm. Orch., 1965-66, prin. guest condr. Symphony of New World, 1968-70, European debut with Rotterdam Philharm., 1969; Helsinki Philharm., 1993; assoc. condr. Nat. Symphony Orch., Washington, 1971-75, prin. guest condr. Nat. Symphony Orch., 1975-76; music dir. L'Orchestre Symphonique de Que., 1976-83, Oreg. Symphony, 1980—, prin. guest condr. Helsinki Philharmonic, 1993, Mus. Dir. Monte Carlo Philharm., 1994; appeared with Phila. Orch., 1972, Chgo. Symphony, 1973, 90, Boston Symphony, 1973, Cleve. Orch., 1974; condr.: Am. premiere of Dvorak's First Symphony, N.Y. Philharm., 1972; prin. condr.: Malmö Symphony, 1991; author: (poems) This Precipice Garden, 1987, The Distant Siren, 1989. Trustee Lewis and Clark Coll., 1983—. Recipient 1st prize gold medal Dimitri Mitropoulos Internat. Music Competition for Condrs., 1964, Merit citation City of Phila., 1969, medal of City of Que., 1983; grantee Martha Baird Rockefeller Fund for Music, 1969. Fellow Am. Acad. Arts and Scis. Offices: Oreg Symphony Ste 200 711 SW Alder St Portland OR 97205

DEPUY, CHARLES HERBERT, chemist, educator; b. Detroit, Sept. 10, 1927; s. Carroll E. and Helen (Plehn) DeP.; m. Eleanor Burch, Dec. 21, 1949; children: David Gareth, Nancy Ellen, Stephen Baylie, Katherine Louise. B.S., U. Calif., Berkeley, 1948; A.M., Columbia U., 1952; Ph.D., Yale U., 1953. Asst. prof. chemistry Iowa State U., 1953-59, asso. prof., 1959-62, prof., 1962-63; prof. chemistry U. Colo., Boulder, 1963-92, prof. emeritus, 1992—; vis. prof. U. Ill., summer 1954, U. Calif., Berkeley, summer 1960; NIH sr. postdoctoral fellow U. Basel, Switzerland, 1969-70; cons. A.E. Staley Co., 1956-80, Marathon Oil Co., 1964-89. Author: (with Kenneth L. Rinehart) Introduction to Organic Chemistry, 1967, rev. edit., 1975, (with Orville L. Chapman) Molecular Reactions and Photochemistry, 1970, (with Robert H. Shapiro) Exercises in Organic Spectroscopy; contbr. articles profl. jours. Served wih AUS, 1946-47. John Simon Guggenheim fellow, 1977-78, 86-87; Alexander von Humboldt fellow, 1988-89. Fellow AAAS; mem. Am. Chem. Soc. (exec. com. organic div., chmn. Colo. sect., mem. adv. bd. jour. 1987-92, gold medal), Sigma Xi. Home: 1509 Cascade Ave Boulder CO 80302-7631 Office: U Colo Boulder Dept Chemistry & Biochemistry Campus Box 215 University Of Colorado CO 80309

DERAAD, BRENT EUGENE, public relations executive; b. Ottumwa, Iowa, Sept. 4, 1966; s. Eugene Wayne and Marilyn Ann (Mleynek) DeR.; m. Beth Ann Skul, Aug. 4, 1990. BA in Journalism, Ariz. State U., 1989, MA in Mass Comm., 1991. Sports info. asst. Ariz. State U., Tempe, 1986-89; sports info. grad. asst. Ariz. State U., 1989; asst. dir. pub. rels. Fiesta Bowl, Tempe, 1989-90; dir. pub. rels. Fiesta Bowl, 1990—; media coord. U.S.A. vs. USSR Wrestling, Tempe, 1988, USA vs Holland Men's Volleyball, 1989; adj. faculty Ariz. State U., Tempe, 1993—; cons. in field. Editor Fiesta Bowl Newsletter/Fiesta Bowl Media Guide, 1989—; editor various recruiting brochures. Mem. Coll. Sports Info. Dirs. Am., Phoenix Press Box Assn. Republican. Methodist. Office: Fiesta Bowl 120 S Ash Ave Tempe AZ 85281-2832

DERBY, JILL T., anthropologist, educator, consultant; b. Lovelock, Nev., Apr. 19, 1940; d. Thomas R. and Helen Margaret (Moody) D.; m. Stephen C. Talbot, June 2, 1973; children: Ryan, Tobyn. BS, U. Calif., San Francisco, 1962; BA, U. Nev., Las Vegas, 1970; MA, U. Calif., Davis, 1974, PhD, 1988. Lic. dental hygienist, Calif., Nev. Dental hygienist Berkeley, Oakland, Calif., 1962-65; lectr., clin. instr. U. Calif., San Francisco, 1965-66; health educator, tng. coord. Aramco, Dhahran, Saudi Arabia, 1966-69; dental hygienist Berkeley, Lake Tahoe, 1971-80; part-time instr. Western Nev. C.C., Carson City, 1974-76, Sierra Nev. Coll., Incline Village, 1977-79; dir. D & R Assocs., Genoa, Nev., 1982-90; regent Univ. and C.C. System Nev., Reno, 1989—; cons., lectr. Derby Enterprises, Gardnerville, Nev., 1980-92; conf. speaker, lectr. over 100 orgns., Nev., Calif., 1980-92. Contbr. articles to profl. jours. State chair Nev. Women's Polit. Caucus, 1979-81, mem. nat. steering com., Washington, 1979-82; appointee Judicial Selection Commn. State of Nev., Carson City, 1986, Supreme Ct. Gender Bias Task Force, Carson City, 1987—; mem. leadership team Bi-State Coalition for Peace. Grad. scholar U. Calif., Nat. Episcopal Ch., 1972-77; recipient Woman Helping Women award Soroptimists Internat., 1988, Woman of Distinction award, 1990. Mem. Western Social Sci. Assn., Assn. Governing Bds., Assn. C.C. Trustees (state rep. 1991—), Assn. Jr. and C.C. Trustees, Rural Sociol. Soc., Phi Kappa Phi. Democrat. Episcopalian. Home: 1298 Kingsbury Gardnerville NV 89410 Office: Univ & CC System Nev 2601 Enterprise Rd Reno NV 89512

DERBY, MARK GARALD, trust company executive, consultant; b. Eugene, Oreg., Apr. 12, 1965; s. Gerald Wayne and Patricia Arlene (Stever) D.; m. Shannon Lynn Purtle, July 18, 1987; children: Justin Robert, Kristine Lynn. Student, Lane Community Coll., Eugene, 1984-85. Ins. salesman MGD Enterprises, Eugene, 1985—; pres., owner Trust Adminstrs., Inc., Cottage Grove, Oreg., 1989—; cons., lobbyist Ind. Contractors Assn., Eugene, 1989—. Mem. Ind. Small Bus. Owners Assn., Lane County Basketball Ofcls. Assn. (bd. control 1987-89), The Dorena Grange. Democrat. Home: 1790 Pritchett Pl Cottage Grove OR 97424-1226 Office: Trust Adminstrs Inc 19 N 6th St Cottage Grove OR 97424-2012

DERDENGER, PATRICK, lawyer; b. L.A., June 29, 1946; s. Charles Patrick and Drucilla Marguerite (Lange) D.; m. Jo Lynn Dickins, Aug. 24, 1968; children: Kristin Lynn, Bryan Patrick, Timothy Patrick. BA, Loyola U., L.A., 1968; MBA, U. So. Calif., 1971, JD, 1974; LLM in Taxation, George Washington U., 1977. Bar: Calif. 1974, U.S. Ct. Claims 1975, Ariz. 1979, U.S. Ct. Appeals (9th cir.) 1979, U.S. Dist. Ct. Ariz. 1979, U.S. Tax Ct. 1979, U.S. Supreme Ct. 1979; cert. specialist in tax law. Trial atty. honors program U.S. Dept. Justice, Washington, 1974-78; ptnr. Lewis & Roca, Phoenix, 1978—; adj. prof. taxation Golden Gate U., Phoenix, 1983-87; mem. Ariz. State Tax Ct. Legis. Study Commn. Author: Arizona State and Local Taxation, Cases and Materials, 1983, Arizona Sales and Use Tax Guide, 1990, Advanced Arizona Sales and Use Tax, 1987, Arizona State and Local Taxation, 1989, Arizona Sales and Use Tax, 1988. Pres., bd. dirs. North Scottsdale Little League. Served to capt. USAF, 1968-71. Recipient U.S. Law Week award Bur. Nat. Affairs, 1974. Mem. ABA (taxation sect., various coms.), Ariz. Bar Assn. (taxation sect., various comms., vice chair sect. taxation, former treas., chmn. state and local tax com., chmn. continuing legal edn. com.), Maricopa County Bar Assn., Inst. Property Taxation, Inst. Sales Taxation, Phoenix Met. C. of C., Ariz. C. of C. (tax com.), U. So. Calif. Alumni Club (pres., bd. dirs.), Phi Delta Phi. Home: 9501 N 49th Dr Paradise Valley AZ 85253-1503 Office: Lewis & Roca 2 Renaissance Plz 40 N Central Phoenix AZ 85004-4429

DERFLER, EUGENE L., real estate broker; b. Portland, Oreg., May 24, 1924; s. Leo and Jessie E. (Tatom) D.; m. Thelma M. Brekke, Aug. 14, 1944; children: Judith Lynne, Dennis Gene, Richard Henry. Mgr. Firestone Tire & Rubber Co., Tillamook, Oreg., 1946-52; owner Nico Furniture & Appliance Co., Salem, Oreg., 1952-81; broker Coldwell Banker, Salem, 1982—. Pres. Transit System fpr Salem, 1981-84; chmn. Marion County Juvenile Service Commn., Salem, 1983-87; bd. dirs. YMCA, Salem, 1984-85. Lt. USN, 1943-46. Republican. Home: 1408 34th Ave NW Salem OR 97304-2211 Office: Coldwell Banker Mountain West 1011 Commercial St NE Salem OR 97301-1019

DERICKSON, JEFFREY CLINE, dentist; b. Tucson, Ariz., Apr. 15, 1950; s. Philip Gregg and Doris Anna (Cline) D.; m. Celaine Gay Bartow, June 23, 1973; children: Deborah Anne, Dana Christine, Darcy Lynne. BS, U. Ariz., 1972, MS, 1973; DDS, U. So. Calif., 1978. Pvt. practice Tucson, 1978—. Mem. ADA, Ariz. State Dental Assn. (del. 1981-87), So. Ariz. Dental Soc., Nat. Soc. Dental Practitioners, So. Ariz. Bushmasters (pres. 1990), Wildcat Club, Bobcat Alumni Club (v.p. 1992—), Rotary (pres. Catalina Club 1989-90, dist. gov.'s drp. dist. 5500 1990-91, dist. chmn. membership retention dist. 5500 1991-93, dist. chmn. world community svc. dist. 5500 1993—, chmn. World Community Svc. 1991-93), Phi Gamma Delta. Republican. Presbyterian.

DE ROE DEVON, THE MARCHIONESS See **DEVONTINE, JULIE E(LIZABETH) J(ACQUELINE)**

DE ROO, REMI JOSEPH, bishop; b. Swan Lake, Man., Can., Feb. 24, 1924; s. Raymond and Josephine (De Pape) De R. Student, St. Boniface (Man.) Coll.; STD, Angelicum U., Rome, Italy.; LLD (hon.), U. Antigonish, N.S., 1983, U. Brandon, Man., 1987; DD (hon.), U. Winnipeg, Man., 1990; LLD (hon.), U. Victoria, B.C., 1991. Ordained priest Roman Catholic Ch., 1950; curate Holy Cross Parish, St. Boniface, 1952-53; sec. to archbishop of St. Boniface, 1954-56; diocesan dir. Cath. action Archdiocese St. Boniface, 1953-54; exec. sec. Man. Cath. Con., 1958; pastor Holy Cross Parish, 1960-62; bishop of Victoria, B.C., Can., 1962—; Canadian Episcopal rep. Internat. Secretariat Apostleship Sea, 1964-78, Pontifical Commn. Culture, 1984-87; chairperson Human Rights Commn. B.C., 1974-77; mem. social affairs commn. Can. Conf. Cath. Bishops, 1973-87, 91—; pres. Western Cath. Conf. Bishops, 1984-88; mem. theology commn. Can. Conf. Cath. Bishops, 1987-91. Hon. fellow Ryerson Poly. Inst., 1987. Address: 4044 Nelthorpe St # 1, Victoria, BC Canada V8X 2A1

DEROSA, FRANCIS DOMINIC, chemical company executive; b. Seneca Falls, N.Y., Feb. 26, 1936; s. Frank and Frances (Bruno) DeR.; m. Vivian DeRosa, Oct. 24, 1959; children: Kevin, Marc, Terri. Student, Rochester Inst. Tech., 1959-61; BS, Chadwick U., MBA; PhD, City U. L.A. Cert. med. photographer. Chief exec. officer Advance Chem. & Equipment Co. Inc., Mesa, Ariz., 1974—, Pottery Plus Ltd., Mesa, 1984—, Advance Tool Supply Inc., Mesa, 1989—. Vice chmn. bd. adjustments City of Mesa, 1983-89, bd. dirs. dept. parks and recreation, 1983-86; pres. Christ the King Mens Club, 1983-84; bd. dirs. Mesa C. of C., 1983-88. Mem. Ariz. Sanitary Supply Assn. (pres. 1983-84), Internat. Sanitary Supply Assn. (Coordinator Ariz. chpt. 1987-89, dist. dir. 1989-91), Gilbert, Ariz. C. of C. (bd. dirs., v.p. 1992-93), Gilbert Heights Owners Assn. (pres. 1992—), Mesa Country Club, Santa Monica (Calif.) Yacht Club, Rotary (pres. Mesa Sunrise chpt. 1987-88, Paul Harris fellow 1988), Masons (pres. 1973), Sons of Italy (pres. 1983-84). Home: 513 E Horseshoe Ave Gilbert AZ 85234-6899 Office: Advance Chem & Equipment Co Inc 33 W Broadway Mesa AZ 85210-1505

DERR, JOHN SEBRING, geophysicist, seismologist; b. Boston, Nov. 12, 1941; s. Thomas Sieger and Mary Ferguson (Sebring) D.; children: Alex, Mary, Nathan. BA, Amherst Coll., 1963; MA, U. Calif., Berkeley, 1965, PhD, 1968. Geophysicist Pan Am. Petroleum Corp., Midland, Tex., 1964; research assoc. MIT, Cambridge, 1968-70; research scientist Martin-Marietta Aerospace Corp., Denver, 1970-74; chief ops. Nat. Earthquake Info. Service U.S. Geol. Survey, Golden, Colo., 1974-79; chief tech. reports U.S. Geol. Survey, Menlo Park, Calif., 1980-83; chief spl. seismol. analysis project U.S. Geol. Survey, Golden, Colo., 1983-89; global seismological networks U.S. Geol. Survey, Albuquerque, N.Mex., 1989—. Contbr. articles to profl. jours. Mem. AAAS, Am. Geophys. Union, Seismol. Soc. Am., Soc. Sci. Exploration (councilor 1986—), Sigma Xi. Office: Albuquerque Seismological Lab Albuquerque NM 87115

DERR, KENNETH T., oil company executive; b. 1936; m. Donna Mettler, Sept. 12, 1959; 3 children. BME, Cornell U., 1959, MBA, 1960. With Chevron Corp. (formerly Standard Oil Co. of Calif.), San Francisco, 1960—, v.p., 1972-85; pres. Chevron U.S.A., Inc. subs. Chevron Corp., San Francisco, 1978-84; head merger program Chevron Corp. and Gulf Oil Corp., San Francisco, 1984-85; vice-chmn. Chevron Corp., San Francisco, 1985-88, chmn., chief exec. officer, 1989—; bd. dirs. Citicorp. Trustee Cornell U., The Conf. Bd. Mem. The Bus. Coun., Calif. Bus. Roundtable, Am. Petroleum Inst. (dir.), Nat. Petroleum Coun. (vice chmn.), Bus. Roundtable, Bus. Coun. Sustainable Devel., San Francisco Golf Club, Orinda Country Club, Pacific Union Club. Office: Chevron Corp PO Box 7137 225 Bush St San Francisco CA 94104-4207

DERR, MARY LOUISE, freelance writer; b. Binghamton, N.Y., May 19, 1917; d. Ralph Oscar and Jessie Birdsall (Sherwood) Van Atta; m. Vernon Ellsworth Derr, Mar. 6, 1943; children: Michael, Katherine, Louise, Carol. BA, Mary Baldwin Coll., Staunton, Va., 1940. Proofreader Vail Ballou Press, Binghamton, 1940-42; cyptographic clk. U.S. Signal Corps, Washington, 1942-44; reporter Fairchild Publs., Orlando, Fla., 1966; feature writer Town & Country Rev., Boulder, Colo., 1970-76; assoc. editor Weaver's Jour., Boulder, 1978-86; feature writer Boulder Courier, 1988. Mem. Soc. Childrens Book Writers, Colo. Archaeol. Soc. (treas. 1988), Colo. Tennis Assn., Boulder Tennis Assn., Sr. Citizens Ctr., Boulder Writers Club (pres. 1992-93). Democrat. Episcopalian. Home: 3410 Everett Dr Boulder CO 80303

DERRICK, WILLIAM DENNIS, physical plant administrator, consultant; b. San Diego, Feb. 7, 1946; s. Charles Woodrow and Catherine Elizabeth (McCormick) D.; m. Lynda Ray Adams, June 15, 1964 (div. 1971); children: Tod Sean, Shannon Kay, Nicole Dione, Johnathon Robert; m. Frances C. Bouck, Nov. 19, 1979; children: Kaila June Warner, Bryan Charles. Student, U. Nebr., 1971-72, 73-74, U. Mont., 1974-76, Internat. Corr., 1966-67, 81, Battelle Meml. Inst., 1985. Elec. draftsman City of Lincoln (Nebr.) Light Dept., 1964-65; asst. engr. to adjutant gen. Nebr. N.G. State of Nebr., Lincoln, 1965-66; owner, mgr., archtl. draftsman Lumberman's Plan Svc., Inc., Lincoln, 1966-70; owner, mgr. Lenny's Lounge, Missoula, Mo., 1978-80; engring. technician USDA/Helena (Mont.) Nat. Forest, 1980-83; project mgr. pub. office bldgs. div. City and County of Denver, 1984-86; supt. bldgs. and grounds Denver Pub. Libr., 1986-91; dir. phys. plant Red Rocks C.C., Lakewood, Colo., 1991—. Elected commr. Local Govt. Study Commn., Stevensville, Mont., 1974; appointed bd. dirs. Lewis & Clark County Fair Bd., Helena, Mont., 1979-83. With U.S. Army, 1967-70, Korea. Mem. Project Mgmt. Inst. (cert. project mgr. profl., v.p. programs Denver chpt. 1988-89, pres. 1990-91). Democrat. Home: 4400 S Utica St Denver CO 80236-3421 Office: Red Rocks CC 13300 W 6th Ave Lakewood CO 80401-5398

DERROUGH, NEIL E., television executive; b. Milo, Iowa, Jan. 31, 1936; s. James L. and Nell (Donehue) D.; m. Lois Sharron Lovejoy, July 4, 1981; children: Carolyn, Rebecca Gene, Althea. B.A., San Jose State U. With CBS, 1962-86; v.p., gen. mgr. KCBS Radio CBS, San Francisco, 1967-71; v.p., gen. mgr. WCBS Radio CBS, N.Y.C., 1971-73, WBBM-TV, Chgo., 1974-77, WCBS-TV, N.Y.C., 1978-80; pres. CBS TV Stas., N.Y.C., 1981-86; pres., gen. mgr. Sta. KSBY-TV, San Luis Obispo, Calif., 1986-88; v.p. broadcasting West Coast region, Gillett Group, 1988—; pres., gen. mgr. Sta. KNSD-TV, San Diego, 1988—; bd. dirs. TV Bur. of Advt., N.Y.C. Mem. broadcast adv. com. Congl. Subcom. on Communications, 1977-78; mem. San Diego Communications Coun., 1988—; bd. dirs. Ronald McDonald House, N.Y.C., Old Globe Theatre, 1988—, San Diego Consortium and Pvt. Industry Coun.; bd. dirs. San Diego chpt. Am. Cancer Soc., 1988—, pres., 1992. Mem. Nat. Assn. Industry-Edn. Cooperation (bd. dirs.), N.Y. State Broadcasters Assn. (past pres.), San Diego C. of C. (bd. dirs.). Home & Office: Sta KNSD-TV 8330 Engineer Rd San Diego CA 92111-2493

DERSHEM, STEPHEN MICHAEL, chemist; b. San Diego, Dec. 1, 1954; s. William Aaron and Helen Maureen (Ullery) D.; m. Amanda Margaret Smith, Apr. 19, 1980. BS, San Diego State U., 1978, MA, 1981; PhD, Miss. State U., 1986. Chemist Johnson Matthey, Inc., San Diego, 1980-83; rsch. mgr. Quantum Materials Inc., San Diego, 1986—, cons., 1985-86; cons. Johnson Matthey, Inc., San Diego, 1983-84. Contbr. articles to profl. jours. Mem. Am. Chem. Soc., Calif. Scholarship Fedn. (life). Republican. Home: 9097 Truman St San Diego CA 92129-3629 Office: Quantum Materials Inc 9938 Via Pasar San Diego CA 92126

DERSHIMER, HAROLD H., elementary education educator; b. Darby, Pa., July 4, 1961; s. John Francis Xavier and Patricia Ann (McGinnis) D.; m. Kathryn Marion Melot, Aug. 10, 1985; children: Andrew Charles, Jennifer Lauren. BFA in Drama, U. So. Calif., 1986; student, Calif. State U.,

Dominguez Hills, 1991. Cert. tchr., Calif. Actor, dancer Gt. Am. Melodrama and Vaudeville, Bakersfield, Calif., 1986; credit mgr. Paris Blues Sportswear, L.A., 1987; acct. Grayson Freight Svc., Torrance, Calif., 1988-89; tchr. 4th grade Washington Sch., Hawthorne (Calif.) Sch. Dist., 1989—, dist. arts mentor tchr., 1993—. Mem. Actors' Repertory Theatre at Courtyard Playhouse, Palos Verdes, Calif., 1988—, v.p., 1991-92, pres., 1992—. Recipient scholarships U. So. Calif., 1982-86.

DERUBERTIS, PATRICIA SANDRA, software company executive; b. Bayonne, N.J., July 10, 1950; d. George Joseph and Veronica (Lukaszewich) Uhl; m. Michael DeRubertis, 1986. BS, U. Md., 1972. Account rep. GE, San Francisco, 1975-77; tech. rep. Computer Scis. Corp., San Francisco, 1977-78; cons., pres. Uhl Assocs., Tiburon, Calif., 1978-81; cons. mgr. Ross Systems, Palo Alto, Calif., 1981-83; COO, exec. v.p. Distributed Planning Systems, Calabasas, Calif., 1983-92; pres. DeRubertis & Assocs., Thousand Oaks, Calif., 1992—. Troop leader San Francisco council Girl Scouts U.S., 1974; participant Women On Water, Marina Del Rey, Calif., 1983. Mem. NAFE, Delta Delta Delta. Democrat.

DERVAN, PETER BRENDAN, chemistry educator; b. Boston, July 28, 1945; s. Peter Brendan and Ellen (Comer) D.; m. Jackqueline K. Barton; children: Andrew, Elizabeth. BS, Boston Coll., 1967; PhD, Yale U., 1972. Asst. prof. Calif. Inst. Tech., Pasadena, 1973-79, assoc. prof., 1979-82, prof. chemistry, 1982-88, Bren prof. chemistry, 1988—; adv. bd. ACS Monographs, Washington, 1979-81. Mem. adv. bd. Jour. Organic Chemistry, Washington, 1981—; mem. editorial bd. Bioorganic Chemistry, 1983—, Chem. Rev. Jour., 1984—, Nucleic Acids Res., 1986—, Jour. Am. Chem. Soc., 1986—, Acct. Chem. Res., 1988—, Bioorg. Chem. Rev., 1988—, Bioconjugate Chemistry, 1989—, Jour. Med. Chemistry, 1991—, Tetrahedron, 1992—, Biorganic and Med. Chemistry, 1993—, Chemical and Engineering News, 1992—; contbr. articles to profl. jours. A.P. Sloan Rsch. fellow, 1977; Camille and Henry Dreyfus scholar, 1978; Guggenheim fellow, 1983; Arthur C. Cope Scholar award 1986. Fellow Am. Acad. Arts and Scis.; mem. NAS, Am. Chem. Soc. (Nobel Laureate Signature award 1985, Harrison Howe award 1988, Arthur C. Cope award 1993, Willard Gibbs medal, 1993). Office: Calif Inst Tech 1201 E California Blvd Pasadena CA 91125-0001

DESAI, CHANDRAKANT S., civil engineering and engineering mechanics educator; b. Nadisar, Gujarat, India, Nov. 24, 1936; came to U.S., 1964, naturalized, 1973; s. Sankalchand P. and Kamala M. (Kothari) D.; m. Patricia L. Porter, Apr. 28, 1969; children: Maya C., Sanjay C. B.Engring., U. Bombay, 1959; M.S. (Ideal Cement Co. fellow 1964), Rice U., Houston, 1966; Ph.D. (Am. Petroleum Inst. fellow 1966), U. Tex., Austin, 1968. Registered profl. engr., Miss. Civil engr. govt. and pvt. agencies India, 1959-64; research civil engr. USAE Wayerways Expt. Sta., Vicksburg, Miss., 1968-74; prof. civil engring., dir. computational methods group Va. Poly. Inst. and State U., Blacksburg, 1974-81; prof., dir. engring. mechanics, geomech. and structural mechanics program dept. civil engring. and engring. mechanics U. Ariz., Tucson, 1981-87, prof. civil engring. and engring. mechanics, 1987-89, Regent's prof., 1989—, head dept., 1987-91; Erskine prof. U. Canterbury, Christchurch, N.Z., 1980, 91. Author: Elementary Finite Element Method, 1979; co-author: Introduction to Finite Element Method, 1972, Constitutive Laws of Engineering Materials, 1983; co-editor, co-author: Numerical Methods in Geotechnical Engineering, 1977; Mechanics of Engineering Materials, 1984; gen. editor: Internat. Jour. Numerical and Analytical Methods in Geomechs; mem. editorial bds. profl. jours. Trustee Deep Founds. Inst., 1978-80; chmn./vice chmn. 1st, 2d, 4th, 5th, 6th, 7th Internat. Conf. Numerical Methods Geomechanics. Recipient Meritorious Civilian Svc. award C.E., U.S. Army, 1972, Alexander von Humboldt award German Govt., 1976, Theodore Cooke Meml. prize U. Bombay, 1958, Meritorious Contbns. medal Czech Acad. Scis., 1992; grantee NSF, Dept. Transp., C.E. Fellow ASCE (chmn. computer and numerical methods com. GT div. 1976-81); mem. ASTM, Inst. Structural Engrs. (Wallace Premium prize 1963), Internat. Soc. Soil Mechanics and Found. Engring., Earthquake Rsch. Inst., Am. Acad. Mechanics, Am. Soc. Engring. Edn., Internat. Assn. Computer Methods and Advances in Geomechanics (pres. 1991—, Outstanding Contbns. medal 1991). Home: 5110 N Calle La Cima Tucson AZ 85718-5815 Office: U Ariz Dept Civil Engring and Engring Mechanics Tucson AZ 85721

DE SAINT-ERNE, NICHOLAS JOHN, veterinarian; b. Wichita, Kans., Dec. 12, 1958; s. Philip George and Gladys May (Fitzgerald) de S.-E. BS, Kans. State U, 1982, DVM, 1984. Accredited veterinarian, Nev. Veterinarian Lake Mead Animal Hosp., Las Vegas, Nev., 1984-87, Exotic Pet Hosp., Las Vegas, 1987-89, Animal Med. Hosp., Las Vegas, 1989-92, Park Animal Hosp., Las Vegas, 1992—; bd. dirs. Wild Wing Project, Las Vegas. Author: Chinese Linking Rings, 1981; editor: The Berg Book, 1983. Mem. Am. Vet. Med. Assn., Internat. Brotherhood Magicians (pres. 1984-85). Republican. Roman Catholic. Home: 441 Inglewood Cir Las Vegas NV 89123 Office: Park Animal Hosp 7380 S Eastern # 110 Las Vegas NV 89123

DE SANTOS, ROBIN KING, manufacturing executive; b. Columbus, Ohio, Nov. 3, 1958; s. Robert Lawrence de Santos and Martha Jean (King) Veitch; m. Cynthia Marie Walters, Sept. 20, 1986. Student, Ohio State U., 1974-76, 79-80, MIT, 1976-77. Cert. mfg. technologist. Patient svcs. coord. Ohio State U. Hosp., Columbus, 1977-81; project engring., N.Am. aircraft ops. Rockwell Internat., Columbus, 1981-85, supr. planning, 1985-87, artificial intelligence program leader, 1987-88; DNC project mgr. Rocketdyne Div. Rockwell Internat., Canoga Park, Calif., 1988-89, productivity engr., leader, 1989-90; material handling engring. leader Rockwell Internat., Canoga Park, Calif., 1990-92; ind. cons., 1992—. Mem. Rep. Nat. Com., Washington, 1980—. Mem. Astron. League (sec. 1984, 1985), AAAS, Soc. Mfg. Engrs. Republican. Lutheran. Office: Saint Software Inc 44025 4th St E Lancaster CA 93535-3612

DE SEIGNE, PASCAL (LAWRENCE), writer, art appraiser; b. Paris, France; came to U.S., 1981; s. Antoine and Jeanne (de Fumel) de S. MPhil, Sorbonne U., Paris, 1967, M in Ethnology, 1970, cert. art appraisal, 1972. Pres. Gallery de Thezan, Nice, France, 1973-84; mgr. Gallery de Thezan, Beverly Hills, Calif., 1985—. Author: Sculptures of Buddahs, 1975, Martial Arts, 1980, Au Nom de Ma Horde, 1992 (European bestseller 1992). Capt., commdg. officer spl. forces Airborne, 1967-72, commdr. Biafra, Laos. Democrat. Roman Catholic. Home and Office: 1440 Veteran Ave # 540 Los Angeles CA 90024

DESMOND, TIMOTHY JUSTICE, educator; b. Madera, Calif., Mar. 18, 1946; s. Jack Griffen and Nelle Gilette (Justice) D.; m. Linda C. Ledford Thach, May 29, 1965 (div. Mar. 1971); children: Shaun Maurice, Timilia Kindell, Mary Renelle; m. Barbara Lee Barker, July 22, 1971; children: William Dotson, Lauren Mullins. BA, Calif. State U., 1974. Cert. secondary edn. tchr., Calif., single subject credential community coll. credential. Retail mgr. Regal Petroleum Co., San Leandro, Calif., 1967-68; engr.'s aide City of Madera (Calif.), 1968-69; male nurse aide Sierra Hosp. Inc., Fresno, Calif., 1971-75; sci. tchr. Madera Unified Sch. Dist., 1975-85; freelance artist/writer Fresno, 1964—; biology tchr. Firebaugh (Calif.) High Sch., 1985—; instr. physiology West Hills Community Coll., Coalinga, Calif., 1990—; tchr. in space app. State of Calif., Madera, 1984-86. Author: World War Four, 1984. Com. mem. Madera County Substance Abuse, 1984-85, Madera Unified Sci. Curriculum, 1983-85, Calif. Dept. Edn., Sacramento, 1988-89; mem. Nat. Sci. Tchrs. Assn., Washington, 1979, Calif. Sci. Tchr.'s Assn., Sacramento, 1985, Nat. Rifle Assn., Washington, 1987, Calif. Rifle and Pistol Assn., Garden Grove, Calif., 1988. Grantee Madera Unified Schs., 1984, Firebaugh-Las Deltas, 1987; recipient 1st place award Fresno Fair Photography, 1989. Mem. Firebaugh Tchrs. Assn. (treas. 1989—), Calif. Tchrs. Assn.; Nat. Educators Assn., Fresno Rifle & Pistol Club, Fresno High Power Rifle. Republican. Lutheran.

DE SOLA, RALPH, author, editor, educator; b. N.Y.C., July 26, 1908; s. Solomon and Grace (von Geist) DeS.; m. Dorothy Clair, Dec. 24, 1944. Student, Columbia U., 1927, 29, 31, Swarthmore Coll., 1928. Collector N.Y. Zool. Soc., N.Y.C., 1928-29, 30-33, Am. Mus. Natural History, N.Y.C., 1930, Tropical Biology Soc., Miami, Fla., 1933-34; zool. editor Fed. Writers Project, N.Y.C., 1935-39; tech. dir. U.S. Microfilm Corp., N.Y.C., 1939-49; hist. dir. Travel U.S. 90 and Mex. Border Trails Assn., Del Rio, Tex., 1951-54; publs. editor Convair div. Gen. Dynamics Corp., San Diego, 1955-68; instr. tech. English San Diego Unified Colls., 1962-88. Author: (with Fredrica De Sola) Strange Animals and Their Ways, 1933, Microstat Technicians Handbook, 1943, Microfilming, 1944, Worldwide What and Where, 1975; compiler Abbreviations Dictionary, 1991, Crime Dictionary, 1982, rev. edit., 1990, (booklet) Great Americans Discuss Religion, 1963, (booklet) Quotations from A to Z for freethinkers and other skeptics, 1985, (with Dorothy De Sola) A Dictionary of Cooking, 1969; Great Americans Examine Religion, 1983; editor: International Conversion Tables, 1961; compiler-editor Whitman books, specializing in zool. juveniles, 1937-41, Abbreviations Dictionary, 8th edit., augmented internat. 7th, edit., 1991; translator: Beethoven-by-Berlioz, 1975, World Wide What and Where Geographic Glossary and Traveller's guide, 1975; editor in chief The Truth Seeker, 1988-89; cons. on microfilming to USN, on abbreviations to Dept. Def.; contbr. articles to Copeia, 1928-32, revs. to classical records and concerts to Freeman, Del Rio News-Herald, San Diego Engr., Downtown. Home: 1819 Puterbaugh St San Diego CA 92103-2714

DESORRENTO, JAMES, cable television company executive; b. Troy, N.Y., Feb. 20, 1943; s. Anthony John and Emily (Whelan) DeS.; m. Karen Graham, Nov. 4, 1972; children: Suraya, Justin. BA in English Lit., St. Michael's Coll., 1964. Dir. mktg. and regional mgr. Viacom Internat., San Francisco, Cleve., 1970-75; dir. mktg. U.S. Computer Systems, Sacramento, 1975-76; v.p. brokerage/investment banking Daniels & Assocs., Denver, 1976-80; v.p. corp. devel. U.S. Cable Corp., Barrington Hills, Ill., 1980-82; chmn. CEO Triax Comm. Corp., Denver, 1982—. Capt. USMC, 1964-67. Mem. Community Antenna TV Assn. (chmn. bd. 1990—), Ohio Cable TV Assn. (pres. 1974), Nat. Cable TV Assn. (mem. pres.'s com. 1974), Entrepreneurs Club (N.Y.C.), Denver Athletic Club, Rolling Hills Country Club (Denver). Office: Triax Comm Corp 100 Fillmore St #600 Denver CO 80206

DESOTO, ROBERT LEE, state official; b. Pueblo, Colo., Jan. 9, 1949; s. Jess P. Soto and Margaret Guerrero; m. Denice Lian Waterhous, May 31, 1988; 1 child, Jesse Severiano. Student, San Jose State U., 1973-77. Design liaison engr. asst. Lockheed Missiles & Space Co., Sunnyvale, Calif., 1971-73; crew supr. Ctr. for Solar Energy Applications, San Jose, Calif., 1975-77; tech. planner Solar Planning Office-West, Dept. Energy, Denver, 1977-78; project mgr. Solar Energy Rsch. Inst., Golden, Colo., 1978-81; pvt. cons. Encon Energy Inc. and SunMas Inc., Denver, Boulder, Colo., 1981-84; supr. field svcs. Colo. Div. Housing, Denver, 1984—. Co-author: Simplified Solar Sizing Workbook, 1980, Residential Conservation Service Auditor/Inspector Manual, 1980. With U.S. Army, 1969-71, Vietnam. Recipient outstanding state monitor award Dept. Energy, 1989, tng. grantee, 1987. Mem. ASHRAE. Democrat. Home: 12772 W 7th Dr Golden CO 80401

DESPOL, JOHN ANTON, former state deputy labor commissioner; b. San Francisco, July 22, 1913; s. Anton and Bertha (Balzer) D.; m. Jeri Kaye Steep, Dec. 7, 1937, (dec. 1986); children—Christopher Paul, Anthony John. Student, U. So. Calif., 1931, Los Angeles Jr. Coll., 1929-30. Sec.-treas., council Calif. CIO, Los Angeles, 1950-58, gen. v.p. Calif. Labor Fedn. AFL-CIO, San Francisco, 1958-60; internat. rep. United Steelworkers Am., Los Angeles, 1937-68; with Dempsey-Tegeler & Co., Inc., 1968-70; rep. Bache & Co., 1970-71; commr. Fed. Mediation and Conciliation Services, Los Angeles, 1972-73; indsl. relations cons., 1971-76; dep. labor commr. State of Calif., 1976-89; cons., 1989—; mem. Nat. Steel Panel Nat. War Labor Bd., 1944-45; chmn. bd. trustees Union Mgmt. Ins. Trust Fund, Los Angeles, 1948-68. Mem. Calif. Def. Council, 1939-41, 10th Regional War Manpower Commn., 1942-46; bd. dirs. So. Calif. region NCCJ, 1960-68; bd. dirs. Los Angeles Community Chest, Los Angeles World Affairs Council, 1951-80, Braille Inst. of Am., 1961—; del. Nat. Democratic Conv., 1948, 52, 56, 60; mem. Los Angeles County Dem. Com., 1942-44; mem. exec. com. Calif. Dem. Com., 1952-56; chmn. Calif. Congl. dist., 1954-56; mem. Calif. Legislative Adv. Commn. to State Legislature, 1956-59; del. Nat. Republican Conv., 1968; bd. dirs. Los Angeles World Affairs Council, 1953-81, Braille Inst. Am., 1961—; bd. govs. Town Hall, Los Angeles, 1941-44, 67-70, chmn. econ. sect., 1964-65; mem. Los Angeles Coun. Fgn. Rels., 1946—; mem. Calif. Job Tng. and Placement Coun., 1967-68. Mem. Indsl. Relations Research Assn., Inst. Indsl. Relations, Assn. Calif. State Attys. and Administrv. Law Judges, Soc. Profl. Dispute Resolution. Home and Office: 916 Via Vido Soud Newport Beach CA 92663

DESROSIERS, JOHN JOSEPH, software company executive; b. Quebec City, Que., Sept. 26, 1959; came to U.S., 1990; s. Francois Xavier and Bibiane D. Degree in Pure & Applied Scis., Dawson Coll., Montreal, 1978; BSc in Computer Sci., U. Montreal, 1983. Software engr. Philips Data Systems/Micom, Montreal, 1978-80; pres. Interactive Software Rsch., Montreal, 1980-82; ind. cons. Montreal, 1982-85; v.p. Soft Horizons, N.Y.C., 1985—; Author: (computer software) Now! Disk Accelerator, 1987, Emulaser Print Enhancer, 1992; co-author: (computer software) SPACEMANager for DOS 6, 1993; inventor and patentee in field. Mem. Assn. for Computing Machinery.

DEST, LEONARD RALPH, aerospace engineer, telecommunications specialist; b. Northampton, Pa., Oct. 31, 1949; s. Philip P. and Pauline (Michalgyk) D.; m. Beverly J. Teel, May 12, 1979. BS, Lehigh U., 1971, MS, 1973. With Fairchild Space/Electronics, Germantown, Md., 1973-74; engr. RCA Global Comm., Princeton, N.J., 1974-75; analyst COMSAT, Washington, 1975-78; sr. engr., supr. INTELSAT, Washington, 1978-82; mgr. spacecraft engring. INTELSAT, El Segundo, Calif., 1982-91; chief scientist Hughes Aircraft Co., El Segundo, Calif., 1991—. Mem. AIAA. Republican. Lutheran. Home: 1709 Club View Dr Los Angeles CA 90024-5311 Office: Hughes Space and Comm PO Box 92919 Los Angeles CA 90009

DETEMPLE, WILLIAM CHARLES, technology executive; b. Vancouver, B.C., Can., Sept. 4, 1953; s. James Clemmens and Mary Clare (Lipp) DeT.; m. Ethel Eileen Congdon, Aug. 30, 1975 (div. 1987); children: Renee Lynn, Ryan William; m. Wendy Rae Duggan, Nov. 19, 1988; 1 child, Joshua Donn Kelley. Grad. high sch., Port Coquitlam, B.C. Technician Can. Telephone and Supplies, Burnaby, B.C., 1973-75; sales mgr. Internat. Promotions, Inc., Edmonton, Alta., Can., 1975-78; pres. Aggressive Mktg., Inc., Coquitlam, B.C., 1978-84, Spectra Automotive Supplies, Rancho Cucamonga, Calif., 1985-87, Rest Mfg., Inc., Rancho Cucamonga, 1987-89, Pine Ridge Consulting, Upland, Calif., 1989—; v.p. mktg./sales Gen. Power Corp., Anaheim, Calif., 1991—. Patentee remote electronic shelf edge label. Mem. North Vancouver Jaycees, 1977-80; active Vancouver Big Bros., New Westminister, B.C., 1979-83; sec.-treas. Coquitlam Kiwanis, 1984. Mem. So. Calif. Tech. Exec. Network, Orange County Venture Group. Home: 1759 3d Ave Upland CA 91786 Office: Gen Power Corp 955 E Ball Rd Anaheim CA 92805

DETHLEFSEN, ROLF, engineer; b. Niebuell, Schleswig, Germany, Aug. 30, 1934; s. Andreas and Clara Dethlefsen; m. Ingrid Baars, July 30, 1961; children: Olaf, Stefan, Karin, Tanja. Diplom Engr., Tech. U. Braunschweig, Fed. Republic Germany, 1961; MS, MIT, 1962, DSc, 1965. Lab. asst. MIT, Cambridge, 1962-65; staff scientist Gen. Dynamics Convair, San Diego, 1965-67; dept. mgr. Allis Chalmers, Milw., 1967-72; consulting engr. ITE/Gould Inc., Greensburg, Pa., 1972-79; sr. project engr. Brown Boveri Electric, Chalfont, Pa., 1979-83; prin. engr. Maxwell Labs., San Diego, 1983—. Patentee in field. Fellowship NATO, MIT, 1961-62. Mem. IEEE (sr.), AIAA, Electromagnetic Launch Assn. (sec. 1989-90), Am. Radio Relay League, N.Y. Acad. Scis., Verein Deutscher Ingenieure. Office: Maxwell Labs 8888 Balboa Ave San Diego CA 92123-1506

DETLOR, JOHN SYDNEY, security executive; b. Summerside, P.E.I., Can., Sept. 1, 1940; came to U.S., 1952; s. W. Lyall and Margaret A. (Baxter) D.; m. Cecile A. Foy, June 9, 1962 (dec. Jan. 1968); m. Jeanette L. Duncan, Apr. 26, 1969; children: William, Susan. BA, Whitworth Coll., 1962; JD, Willamette U., 1964. Spl. agt. FBI, Albuquerque, 1964-65, L.A., 1965-68, Seattle, 1968-89; dir. security Costco Wholesale, Kirkland, Wash., 1989—. Elder Rose Hill Presby. Ch., 1991—. Mem. Am. Soc. Indsl. Security, Soc. of Former Spl. Agts. of the FBI (sec. 1992-93, treas. 1991-92). Home: 11415 Juanita Dr NE Kirkland WA 98034-3423 Office: Costco Wholesale 10809 120th Ave NE Kirkland WA 98033-5030

DETTERMAN, ROBERT LINWOOD, financial planner; b. Norfolk, Va., May 1, 1931; s. George William and Jeanneille (Watson) D.; m. Virginia Armstrong; children: Janine, Patricia, William Arthur. BS in Engring., Va. Poly. Inst., 1953; PhD in Nuclear Engring., Oak Ridge Sch. Reactor Tech., 1954, postgrad., 1954; cert. in fin. planning, Coll. Fin. Planning, Denver, 1986. Registered investment advisor, Calif. Engring. test dir. Foster Wheeler Co., N.Y.C., 1954-59; sr. research engr. Atomics Internat. Co., Canoga Park, Calif., 1959-62; chief project engr. Rockwell Internat. Co., Canoga Park, Calif., 1962-68, dir. bus. devel., 1968-84, mgr. internat. program, 1984-87; pres. Bo-Gin Fin., Inc., Thousand Oaks, Calif., 1987—; owner Bo-Gin Arabians, Thousand Oaks, 1963—; nuclear cons. Danish Govt., 1960, Lawrence Livermore Lab., Calif., 1959. Trustee, mem. exec. com. Morris Animal Found., Denver, 1984—, chmn., 1984-88; treas., trustee Arabian Horse Trust, Denver, 1979—; pres. Rolling Oaks Homes Assn., Thousand Oaks, Calif., 1980-82; chmn. Cal Bred Futurity. Mem. Nat. Assn. Personal Fin. Advisers, Internat. Assn. Fin. Planners, Inst. Cert. Fin. Planners, Am. Nuclear Soc., Atomic Indsl. Forum, Acad. Magical Arts, Am. Horse Shows Assn., Am. Horse Coun., Magic Castle Club, Internat. Arabian Horse Assn. Club, Tau Beta Phi, Eta Kappa Nu, Phi Kappa Phi. Republican. Office: Bo-Gin Fin Inc Ste 220 3625 E Thousand Oaks Blvd Thousand Oaks CA 91362-3626

DETTMAN, GERALDINE LOUISE, biologist; b. Evanston, Ill., Aug. 28, 1943; d. Walter Fred and Almyra Emelia (Hasse) D. BS in Biology, No. Ill. U.; PhD in Biology, U. Calif., Irvine, 1972. Asst. rsch. biologist U. Calif., Irvine, 1972-73, asst. adj. prof., 1973-79; asst. prof. med. scis. Brown U., Providence, R.I., 1980-83, radiation safety officer, 1980-85, biosafety officer, 1983-85; founder, pres. Viro Rsch. Internat., Inc., Durango, Colo., 1985—. Contbr. articles to profl. jours. NSF fellow, 1968-72. Office: 178 Bodo Dr Unit C Durango CO 81301

DETTMER, SCOTT C., lawyer. BA, U. Calif., Santa Barbara, 1978; JD, U. So. Calif., L.A., 1982. Assoc. Cooley, Godward, Castro, Huddleson & Tatum, San Francisco, 1982-89; ptnr. Cooley, Godward, Castro, Huddleson & Tatum, Palo Alto, Calif., 1989-90, Brobeck, Phleger & Harrison, Palo Alto, 1990—. Exec. editor Computer/Law Jour., 1981-82. Bd. dirs. North of Market Child Devel. Ctr., San Francisco, 1985-87, Marin Conservation Corps, 1984-90. Mem. ABA, Calif. State Bar, Bar Assn. of San Francisco, Order of Coif. Office: Brobeck Phleger & Harrison Embarcadero Pl 2200 Geng Rd Palo Alto CA 94303-0913

DEUBLE, JOHN L., JR., environmental science and engineering services consultant; b. N.Y.C., Oct. 2, 1932; s. John Lewis and Lucille (Klotzbach) D.; m. Thelma C. Honeychurch, Aug. 28, 1955; children: Deborah, Steven. AA, AS in Phys. Sci., Stockton Coll., 1957; BA, BS in Chemistry, U. Pacific, 1959. Cert. profl. chemist, profl. engr., environ. inspector; registered environ. profl., registered environ. assessor. Sr. chemist Aero-Gen Corp., Sacramento, Calif., 1959-67; asst. dir. rsch. Lockheed Propulsion Co., Redlands, Calif., 1968-73; asst. div. mgr. Systems, Sci. and Software, La Jolla, Calif., 1974-79; gen. mgr. Wright Energy Nev. Corp., Reno, Nev., 1980-81; v.p. Engergy Resources Co., La Jolla, 1982-83; dir. hazardous waste Aerovironment Inc., Monrovia, Calif., 1984-85; environ. cons. Encinitas, Calif., 1986-88; sr. program mgr. Ogden Environ. and Energy Svcs., San Diego, 1989—. Contbr. articles profl. jours. With USAF, 1951-54. Recipient Tech. award Am. Ordnance Assn., 1969, Cert. of Achievement Am. Men and Women of Sci., 1986, Envrion. Registry, 1992. Fellow Am. Inst. Chemists; mem. ASTM, Am. Chem. Soc., AM. Inst. Chem. Engrs., Am. Meteorol. Soc., Am. Nuclear Soc., Am. Def. Preparedness Assn., Air and Waste Mgmt. Assn., Calif. Inst. Chemists, Hazardous Materials Control Rsch. Inst., N.Y. Acad. Scis., Environ. Assessors Assn. Republican. Lutheran. Home: 369 Cerro St Encinitas CA 92024-4805 Office: Ogden Environ & Energy Svcs 5510 Morehouse Dr San Diego CA 92121-3720

DEUEL, DAVID CHARLES, theology educator; b. Johnstown, N.Y., Sept. 23, 1952; s. Roger Warren and Doris Marie (Mosher) D.; m. Nancy Ruth Van Duren, Aug. 12, 1978; children: Rebekah, Joanna, Michael. AA, Bapt. Bible Coll., Clarks Summit, Pa., 1976, B in Religious Edn., 1976; postgrad., Inst. Holy Land Studies, Jerusalem, 1981; postgrad, Dropsie Coll., 1982-84; postgrad., U. Pa., 1982-84; ThM summa cum laude, Grace Theological Seminary, Winona Lake, Ind., 1982, MDiv., 1983; MA, Cornell University, 1986; PhD, Cornell U. Tchr.'s asst. Grace Theological Seminary, Winona Lake, 1979-82; instr. Cornell U., Ithaca, N.Y., 1983-87; prof. The Master's Seminary, Sun Valley, Calif., 1987—; bd. dirs. Accent Books, Denver, Children's Hosp., L.A., North L.A. Regional Ctr., Direct Link for the Disabled, Solvang, Calif., Crisis Pregnancy Ctr., L.A.; cons. Bible transl. Contbr. articles to profl. jours., books. Tchr. jr. high Sunday sch.; coord. Parents of Children with Down Syndrome. Mem. Nat. Assn. Fgn. Student Affairs, Evang. Theol. Soc., Nat. Assn. Profs. Hebrew, Soc. Bibl. Lit., L.A. Down Syndrome Assn.

DEUKMEJIAN, GEORGE, lawyer, former governor; b. Albany, N.Y., June 6, 1928; s. C. George and Alice (Gairdan) D.; m. Gloria M. Saatjian, 1957; children: Leslie Ann, George Krikor, Andrea Diane. BA, Siena Coll., 1949; JD, St. John's U., 1952. Bar: N.Y. 1952, Calif. 1956, U.S. Supreme Ct. 1970. Mem. Calif. Assembly, 1963-67; mem. Calif. Senate, 1967-79, minority leader; atty. gen. State of Calif., 1979-82, gov., 1983-91; former dep. county counsel Los Angeles County.; partner Sidley & Austin, 1991—. Served with U.S. Army, 1953-55. Republican. Episcopalian. Office: Sidley & Austin 555 W 5th St 40th Fl Los Angeles CA 90013-1010

DE URIOSTE, GEORGE ADOLFO, IV, software company executive; b. San Francisco, June 25, 1955; s. George Adolfo Sr. and Janet Germaine (Bruzzone) de U. BS, U. So. Calif., L.A., 1978; MBA, U. Calif., Berkeley, 1980. CPA, Calif. Auditor, cons. Deloitte Haskins & Sells, San Francisco, 1980-83; sr. fin. analyst Genstar Corp., San Francisco, 1983-85, Rolm Mil-Spec Computers, Inc., San Jose, Calif., 1986-88; mgr. fin. planning and analysis Ask Computer Systems, Inc., Mountain View, Calif., 1988-90; CFO TeamOne Systems, Inc., Sunnyvale, Calif., 1990-92; v.p. of fin. Remedy Corp., Mountain View, Calif., 1992—. Pres. Commerce Assocs., San Francisco, 1988-89. Mem. AICPAs, Calif. Soc. CPAs, Blue Key, Churchill Club (bd. dirs., vice chmn. Palo Alto, Calif. 1989—). Home: 282 Walker Dr Mountain View CA 94043-2108 Office: Remedy Corp 1965 Landings Dr Mountain View CA 94043-2108

DEUTSCH, BARRY JOSEPH, management development company executive; b. Gary, Ind., Aug. 10, 1941; s. Jack Elias and Helen Louise (La Rue) D.; B.S., U. So. Calif., 1969, M.B.A. magna cum laude, 1970; m. Gina Krispinsky, Feb. 20, 1972. Lectr. mgmt. U. So. Calif., L.A., 1967-70; pres., founder The Deutsch Group, Inc., mgmt. cons. co. tng. upper and middle mgmt., L.A., 1970—, chmn. bd., 1975—; founder, chief exec. officer, chmn. bd. Investment Planning Network, Inc., 1988—; dir. Red Carpet Corp. Am., 1975-77, United Fin. Planners, 1984-86. Chmn. bd. govs. Am. Hist. Ctr., 1980—. With M.I., U.S. Army, 1964-66. Mem. Am. Mgmt. Assn., Am. Soc. Bus. and Mgmt. Cons.'s, Am. Soc. Tng. and Devel., Internat. Mgmt. by Objectives Inst. Author: Leadership Techniques, 1969, Recruiting Techniques, 1970, The Art of Selling, 1973, Professional Real Estate Management, 1975, Strategic Planning, 1976, Employer/Employee: Making the Transition, 1978, Managing by Objectives, 1980, Conducting Effective Performance Appraisal, 1982, Advanced Supervisory Development, 1984, Managing A Successful Financial Planning Business, 1988, How to Franchise Your Business, 1991. Home: 4509 Candleberry Ave Seal Beach CA 90740-3026

DEVANEY, DONALD EVERETT, law enforcement official; b. Providence, Nov. 21, 1936; s. William Francis and Elizabeth Florence (Hill) D.; m. Tokiko Yoshida, May 19, 1960; 1 child, George Y. AA in Edn., El Paso Community Coll., 1973; BA, SUNY, Albany, 1979. Cert. healthcare protection adminstr. Internat. Healthcare Safety and Security Found. Sgt. maj. U.S. Army, 1954-83; customs inspector U.S. Customs Svc., Honolulu, 1983-84; provost marshal Tripler Army Med. Ctr., Honolulu, 1984—; regional chair Europe and Asia, 1989—; Pacific rep. Chief of Staff Retiree Coun. Fin. donor Okinawa Cultural Ctr., Waipahu, Hawaii, 1987-89. Recipient Disting Svc. award Hawaii Joint Police, 1977, 86, George Washington Honor medal Freedom's Found., 1973; decorated Legion of Merit. Mem. Hawaii Joint Police Assn. (pres. 1985), U.S. Army CID Command, Rotary (pres. Pearl Harbor chpt. 1991-92, dir. community svc. dist. 5000, 1992-93), KC.

Roman Catholic. Home: 98-911 Ainanui Loop Aiea HI 96701 Office: Office Provost Marshal Tripler Army Med Ctr Honolulu HI 96859

DEVENOT, DAVID CHARLES, human resource executive; b. Indpls., May 27, 1939; s. Charles Joseph and Pearl (Geodfry) D.; m. Mary Jennifer Bateman, July 7, 1970; children: Daniel, Mark. BBA, U. Hawaii, 1962. Dir. indsl. rels. USP Corp subs. Consol. Foods, Sara Lee, San Jose, Calif., 1964-70; dir. human resource svcs. Hawaii Employers Coun., Honolulu, 1970—. Bd. dirs. Hawn Humane Soc., Honolulu, 1975—, Lanikila Rehab. Ctr., Honolulu, 1985—, Am. Cancer Soc., Honolulu, 1989—. Mem. Santa Clara Valley Pers. Assn. (pres. 1968-69), Soc. Human Resource Mgmt., Indsl. Rels. Rsch. Assn. Home: 46-141 Nahiku St Kaneohe HI 96744 Office: Hawaii Employers Coun 2682 Wai Wai Loop Honolulu HI 96820

DEVENS, JOHN SEARLE, college president, mayor; b. Shickshinny, Pa., Mar. 31, 1940; s. John Ezra and Laura (Bulkley) D.; m. Sharon I. Snyder (div. 1979); children: John, Jerilyn, James, Janis. BS, Belmont Coll., 1964; MEd, Emory U., 1966; PhD, Wichita State U., 1975. Dir. speech and hearing Columbia (S.C.) Coll., 1967-70; head dept. audiology Inst. Logopedics, Wichita, Kans., 1970-71; supr. audiology State of Alaska, Fairbanks, 1971-73; asst. prof. U. Houston, Victoria, 1975-77; pres. Prince William Sound Community Coll., Valdez, Alaska, 1977-92; dir. Valdez Hearing and Speech Ctr., 1977—; mayor City of Valdez, 1985-89; mem. Valdez City Council, 1980-89. Producer films on hearing problems; contbr. articles to profl. jours. Nat. chmn. adv. com. Horsemanship for Handicapped, 1964-67; mem. Alaska Gov.'s Coun. for Handicapped, 1980-82; pres. Valdez chpt. Alaska Visitors Assn., 1980; mem. small cities adv. coun. Nat. League Cities, 1983-87, internat. econ. devel. task force; mem. Nat. Export Coun.; bd. dirs. Resource Devel. Coun.; former mayor Valdez; Dem. nominee U.S. Ho. of Reps., 1992 and 1992; hosted internat. conf. on oil spills for mayors. Mem. Am. Speech-Lang. Hearing Assn. (cert. clin. competence in audiology and speech and lang. pathology), Am. C. of C.. in Korea, Valdez C. of C., Alaska Mcpl. League (bd. dirs. 1984-89), Elks, Eagles. Democrat. Methodist. Home: PO Box 730 Valdez AK 99686-0730 Office: 1200 I St # 205 Anchorage AK 99501

DEVENS, MICHAEL WILLIAM, construction, contract disputes consultant; b. Tacoma, Oct. 12, 1961; s. John Wellington and Carol Christine (Cambio) D.; m. Lorraine Downes Dunn, Apr. 8, 1989; children: Michael William Jr., John Wellington II. BCE, Va. Mil. Inst., Lexington, 1983. Lt., platoon leader U.S. Army Corps Engrs., Karlsruhe, Fed. Republic Germany, 1983-84, Lt., logistics officer, 1984-86; Capt., intelligence officer U.S. Army Corps Engrs., Ft. Carson, Colo., 1987-88; staff engr. William H. Gordon Assocs., Woodbridge, Va., 1988; contract adminstr. Excell Inc., Colorado Springs, Colo., 1988-89, sr. contract adminstr., 1989-91, program dir., 1991-92, sr. program dir., 1992—. Capt. U.S. Army, 1983-88. Mem. Nat. Contract Mgmt. Assn., Soc. Am. Mil. Engrs. Republican. Roman Catholic. Home: 7060 Native Cir Colorado Springs CO 80919-5003 Office: Excell Inc 5475 Mark Dabling Blvd Ste 300 Colorado Springs CO 80918-3865

DEVER, DANIEL, academic administrator. Supt. of schs. Roman Cath. Diocese of Honolulu. Office: Cath Schs Dept 6301 Pali Hwy Kaneohe HI 96744-5224

DEVERAUX, TSENRE LISETTA POMPEO, travel consultant; b. Santa Fe, Apr. 28, 1959; d. Ernest and Betty Lou (Wilton) Pompeo; m. Michael Allen Deveraux, May 25, 1985; children: Amber Michelle, Lauren Alisse. BS in Edn., U. N.Mex., 1982. Office clk. Auto Trading Post, Santa Fe, 1981; bus. tchr. Albuquerque Vocat. Schs., 1981-82; travel agt. Small World Travel, Santa Fe, 1983-85; customer svc. rep. Continental Airlines, Denver, 1985; asst. mgr. Master Travel, Denver, 1985-87; sales rep. MTI Vacations, Denver, 1987-88; travel cons., sales mgr. Northglenn (Colo.) Travel, 1988—; cons., mgr. Capital Travel, Denver, 1987-88. Mem. Chi Omega, Pi Gamma. Republican. Office: The Traveler's Choice 6570 W 120th Ave Broomfield CO 80020

DEVEREL, STEVEN JOHN, hydrologist; b. Augusta, Calif., Mar. 7, 1952; s. Warren Lee and Adele Ruth (Christensen) D.; m. Maria Teresa Oliveira, July 16, 1977; children: Nicholas, Clarissa. BA, U. Calif., Berkeley, 1974; BS, U. Calif., Davis, 1978, MS, 1980, PhD, 1983. Tech. salesman Dow Chem. Co., Sao Paulo, Brazil, 1974-77; rsch. aide U. Calif., Davis, 1978-79, staff rsch. assoc., 1979-82, rsch. asst., 1982-84, teaching asst., postgrad. researcher, 1982-84; rsch. chemist U.S. Geol. Survey, Sacramento, Calif., 1984-91, supervisory hydrologist, 1991—; assoc. in experiment sta. U. Calif., Davis, 1988-91, lectr., 1988-90. Contbr. articles to profl. jours. and chpts. to books. Coach Davis Little League, 1988-89, Am. Youth Soccer, Davis, referee, 1988-93. Mem. Am. Geophys. Union, Am. Soc. Agronomy. Home: 2107 Bueno Dr Davis CA 95616 Office: US Geol Survey 2800 Cottage Way Sacramento CA 95825

DEVERMAN, JERONE NELSON, computer systems consultant; b. Pekin, Ill., July 4, 1938; s. Wilmer Henry Gerhardt and Elizabeth Augusta (Reich) D.; m. Wona Annette Dodge, Sept. 4, 1960; children: James Dodge, John Henry. BS, Purdue U., 1960, MS, 1962, PhD, 1969. Mem. tech. staff Sandia Nat. Labs., Livermore, Calif., 1968-69, 70-73; sr. statistician BDM Inc., Albuquerque, 1969-70; sr. rsch. statistician Dikewood Inds., Albuquerque, 1973-77; prin. cons. Med. Data Systems, Albuquerque, 1977—; owner, founder Med. Data Systems, 1977—; speaker in field. Dir. Purdue Alumni Assn., West Lafayette, Ind., 1981-84, pres. coun. Capt. U.S. Army, 1966-68. Lutheran. Office: Med Data Systems PO Box 11879 Albuquerque NM 87192

DEVGAN, ONKAR DAVE N., technologist, consultant; b. Lahore, Panjab, India, Oct. 11, 1941; came to U.S., 1967; s. Thakar Dass Devgan and Sohag Wati Sharma; m. Veena Devgan, July 20, 1969; children: Sanjay, Pooja. BS, Panjab U., 1960; MS, Vikham U., 1963, PhD, 1966; MBA, Temple U., 1975. Instr., rsch. assoc. U. Pa., Phila., 1970-73; scientist C.E. Glass, Pennsauken, N.J., 1973-76; cons., vis. prof. U. Tex., Dallas, 1976-78; mgr. material devel., sr. engr. Tex. Inst., Dallas, 1978-83; engring. mgr. Fairchild Semiconductor, Palo Alto, Calif., 1983-84, 88; program mgr. Varian Assocs., Palo Alto, 1984-86; dir. microelectronics Northrup Corp., L.A., 1986-88; dir. tech. and ops. Polylithics Inc., Santa Clara, Calif., 1989-90; tech. and mgmt. cons. Devgan Assocs., Sunnyvale, Calif., 1991—; co-chmn. Semi GaAs Com., Mt. View, Calif., 1984-85; mem. Semi Automation Com., Mt. View, 1984-86; advisor Semi Equipment Uptime Com., Mt. View, 1985-86; presenter high tech. presentations to various corps., 1975-91. Contbr. articles to tech. and bus. jours. PhD fellow Govt. of India, 1963-66, Coun. of Sci. and Indsl. Rsch. sr. fellow, 1966-67; NIH postdoctoral fellow, 1967-70. Mem. IEEE, Am. Chem. Soc. Home and Office: 161 Butano Ave Sunnyvale CA 94086-7025

DEVIN, RONALD BOYD, theatre educator; b. Heppner, Oreg., Mar. 13, 1933; s. Harlan Justus Devin and Lorah Irene (Hiatt) VanSchoiack; m. Carroll Jeanne Ferguson, Mar. 16, 1957; children: Hillary Jeanne, Scott Ferguson. BS, U. Oreg., 1959, MS, 1961; EdD, Wash. State U., 1971. Instr. Everett (Wash.) Jr. Coll., 1960-69; from asst. prof. to prof. Eastern Wash. U., Cheney, 1969—, chmn. dept. theatre, 1970-77, 83-86. Dir. over 120 plays and musicals. Staff sgt. USAF, 1952-56. Named one of Outstanding Educators of Am., 1973-74, for Dept. of Def. Best Play on Tour, 1971, 84. Mem. NEA, Phi Delta Kappa. Democrat. Episcopalian. Home: 1608 4th St Cheney WA 99004-1917 Office: Eastern Wash U MS 80 Cheney WA 99004

DEVINE, EMILY ELIZABETH, pharmacist, educator; b. Oak Park, Ill., May 18, 1955; d. Sylvanus John and Emily Jane (Davies) D.; m. Robert A. Arntsen, Dec. 27, 1975 (div. Sept. 1985). Student, U. Pacific, 1973-75, PharmD, 1978. Pharmacy resident VA Med. Ctr., Palo Alto, Calif., 1978-79; staff pharmacist HPI-Health Care Svcs., Inc., Los Gatos, Calif., 1979-85; asst. dir. pharmacy HPI-Health Care Svcs., Inc., Los Gatos, 1985-87, regional clin. coord., 1984-87, quality assurance coord., 1985-87; quality assurance, spl. projects coord. AMI-Sierra Vista Med. Ctr., San Luis Obispo, Calif., 1987-90; asst. clin. prof. U. Calif., San Francisco, 1990—; clin. coord. pharm. svcs. Mt. Zion Med. Ctr./U. Calif., San Francisco, 1993—; mem. Am., Calif. Pharmacists Assn., 1975-80, Lambda Kappa Sigma, 1975-78 (sec. 1978), Delta Delta Delta, 1974-78. Lectr. in field. Vol. usher San Luis Obispo County Symphony, 1988-90, San Luis Obispo Mozart Festival, 1988-90; vol. pharmacist The Flying Samaritans to Baja, 1988-90; coord. Poison Prevention Week, San Luis Obispo, 1989. Named Toastmaster of the Yr. Toastmasters of San Luis Obispo, 1989. Mem. AAUW, Am. Soc. Hosp. Pharmacists, Am. Soc. Parenteral/Enteral Nutrition, Calif. Soc. Hosp. Pharmacists (bd. dirs. 1990-93, sec. Quatra chpt. 1980, pres. Cuestra chpt. 1988-90, coun. organizational affairs 1989, nominations com. 1990, pharmacist of Yr. award 1990), Calif. Soc. Hosp. Pharmacists (pres.-elect 1993, pres. 1994). Office: UCSF Div Clin Pharmacy 521 Parnassus C-152 PO Box 622 San Francisco CA 94143-0001

DEVITO, CARL LOUIS, mathematics educator; b. N.Y.C., Oct. 21, 1937; s. Salvatore and Rose (Giossi) DeV.; m. Marilyn Jane Zink, Aug. 26, 1965; 1 child, Stephanie Lee. BS, CUNY, 1959; PhD, Northwestern U., 1967. Computer programmer North Hills Electronic Co., Garden City, N.Y., 1959-60; instr. in maths. DePaul U., Chgo., 1965-66, asst. prof. maths., 1966-67; asst. prof. maths. U. Ariz., Tucson, 1967-71, assoc. prof. maths., 1971-85, 1988—; invited speaker 41st Congress of Internat. Astronautical Fedn., Dresden, Germany, 1990; adj. prof. maths. Naval Postgrad. Sch., Monterey, Calif., 1985-87; cons. dept. elec. engring. U.Ariz., summer 1979, 1983; vis. scholar Calif. Inst. Tech., Pasadena, 1981. Author: Functional Analysis, 1979, Functional Analysis and Linear Operator Theory, 1990. NSF fellow, 1962, 64; Naval Postgrad. Sch. Found. Rsch. grantee, 1987-88, 88-89, Rsch. Corp. grantee, 1989-90. Mem. Am. Math. Soc., Math. Assn. Am. Office: U Ariz Dept Math Tucson AZ 85721

DEVITT-GRASSO, PAULINE VIRGINIA, civic volunteer, nurse; b. Salem, Mass., May 13, 1930; d. John M. and Mary Elizabeth (Cologey) Devitt; m. Frank Anthony Grasso, Oct. 26, 1968; 1 stepson, Christopher Anthony. BSN, Boston Coll., 1952; student, Boston U., 1954-55, Boston State Tchrs. Coll., 1953-54. RN. Staff nurse J.P. Kennedy Jr. Meml. Hosp., Brighton, Mass., 1952-53; head nurse, day supr. J.P. Kennedy Jr. Meml. Hosp., Brighton, 1953-54, day supr., 1955, clin. instr., 1955-58, adminstrv. asst., 1968, dir. nursing edn., 1958-68; vis. instr. Boston Coll., Mass. State Coll., Meml. Hosp. Sch. Nursing, Newton, Mass. Meml. Hosp. Sch. Nursing, 1955-68, CUA S of N, 1990. Pres. Project H.O.P.E., Manhattan Beach, Calif., 1982; pres. adv. coun. Meals on Wheels, Salvation Army, 1989, 90, 91, bd. dirs. Redondo Beach, 1992—; cons. Manhattan Beach Housing Found., 1986—, Manhattan Beach Case Mgr., 1982—; mem. adv. coun. South Bay Sr. Svcs., Torrance, Calif., 1986—; sr. advocate City of Manhattan Beach, 1982; bd. dirs. Ret. Sr. Vol. Program, Torrance, 1986-90, Behavioral Health Svcs., 1992—; neighborhood chair Girl Scouts U.S.; mem. Beach City Coun. on Aging, 1983-91; mem. Salvation Army Ladies Aux.; mem. adv. bd. Salvation Army Corps, Redondo Beach. Recipient Cert. of Appreciation, County of L.A., 1988, Vol. of the Yr. award City of Manhattan Beach, 1988, Award of Honor County of L.A., 1989, State of Calif. Senate Rules Com. Resolution Commendation, 1988; named Outstanding Vol. Cath. Daus. of Am., 1986, Vol. of Yr. City Manhattan Beach, 1986-87; Rose and Scroll award Manhattan Beach C. of C., 1989, Art Michel Meml. Community Svc. award Manhattan Beach Rotary Club, 1989, Cert. of Appreciation KC's Queen of Martyers Coun., 1989, Redondo Beach Lila Bell award Salvation Army, 1989, others, Manhattan Beach Vol. Appreciation award, 1982, 83, 84, 85, 86, 88, 90, 91, 92, 93, cert. South Bay Centinela Credit Union, 1990; nominated for Pres's. Vol. Action award Project H.O.P.E., 1987. Mem. AARP, Am. Martyrs Altar Soc. (pres. 1983, coun. mem.-at-large 1992), Cath. U. Am. Nat. Alumni Assn. (hon.), Cath. U. Am. Sch. Nursing Alumni Assn. (hon.), Boston Coll. Alumni Assn., Manhattan Beach Sr. Citizens Club (pres. 1985-86, 88-89), Lions (Citizen of Yr. award Manhattan Beach club 1986), DAV (comdr.'s club 1990, 91, 92), Equestrian Order of Holy Sepulchre of Jerusalem. Democrat. Roman Catholic. Home: 329 3D St Manhattan Beach CA 90266

DEVIVI, CARMINE WILBUR, fine artist, designer, sculptor; b. Rural Valley, Pa., June 27, 1929; s. Carmine and Vienna (Spera) DeV.; m. Patricia J. Dolecki; 1 child, Skye Patricia. BFA, U. of Arts, Phila., 1960; MFA, U. Pa., 1961. Instr. Phila. Mus. Coll. Art, 1956-60; chair art dept. Hill Sch., Pottstown, Pa., 1961-65, Athenian Sch., Danville, Calif., 1966-71; lectr., prof. art Calif. Coll. of Arts and Crafts, Oakland, 1969-71; dir. summer program Art Inst., Cuernavaca, Mex., 1968-71; prin. Carmine DeVivi Gallery, Danville, 1972—; art appraiser, cons. One Man Shows: Studio Gallery, Stoning, Conn., 1965, Gallery 252, Phila., Pa., 1966, Sheradin Gallery, Kutztown State Coll., Pa, 1966, Porter Garnett Gallery, Carnegie-Mellon Univ., Pitts., Pa., 1967, Hewlett Gallery, Carnegie-Mellon Univ., Pitts., Pa., 1968, Paley Library, Temple Univ., Phila., Pa., 1968, Moore Galleries, Inc., San Francisco, 1968, Galeria Trini, Cuernavaca, Mexico, 1969, Galeria Misrachi, Mexico City, Mexico, 1970, Galeria Trini, Cuernavaca, Mexico, 1970, Reflections Gallery, Oakland, Ca., 1970, Gallery on Victorian Row, Oakland, Ca., 1973, Galeria Akari, Cuernavaca, Mexico, 1974, Galeri Clemons, Hjerring, Denmark, 1974, The Village Theatre Gallery, Danville, Ca., 1990, Los Medanos Coll, Pittsburg, Ca., 1991, Coriel Gallery, Albuquerque, N.Mex., 1993; Juried Shows: Freida Kahlo Comm. Exhibition, Albuquerque, N.Mex., 1992, Fine Crafts in Corrages, N. Mex., 1993, Albuquerque Festival of the Arts, 1993. Founder, participant ann. Christmas tree lighting ceremony Town of Danville, 1979—; mem. fine arts fundraising com. San Ramon Valley High Sch., Danville, 1986, presenter DeVivi award to art students, 1987-90. Staff sgt. USAF, 1950-54. Home and Office: PO Box 2113 4146 Corrales Rd Corrales NM 89748

DEVOE, KENNETH NICKOLAS, food service executive, assistant mayor; b. Mineola, N.Y., Sept. 13, 1944; s. Kenneth Pettit and Wykiena (Bos) D.; m. Linda Faye Mizer, May 7, 1965; children: Andrea W., Christina L., Kenneth C., Paula A. Student, Merced Coll., 1970-75. Police sgt. Merced (Calif.) Police Dept., 1966-75; sheriff sgt. Mariposa (Calif.) County Sheriff, 1975-81; pk. mgr. Am. Campgrounds Inc., Bellevue, Wash., 1981-83; owner DeVoe Enterprises, Atwater, Calif., 1983—. Chmn. Merced County Assn. Govts., 1990—, Atwater 4th of July Com., 1983—; asst. mayor City of Atwater, 1987—. With U.S. Air Force, 1962-66. Mem. Atwater C. of C. (dir. 1991, dir.-at-large 1983-86, Citizen of Yr. 1987), Merced Trade Club (dir. 1991—), Castle Air Force Base Cols. Club., Kiwanis, Masons. Republican. Home: 2381 Crestview Dr Atwater CA 95301 Office: Devoe Enterprises 1898 Bellevue Rd Atwater CA 95301

DEVOE, ROBERT CARL, artist; b. Canyonville, Oreg., July 21, 1933; s. Perry Jean and Clarice Azalea (Totten) DeV.; m. Donna Gayel McCullough, Sept. 12, 1952 (div. 1975); children: Robert W., John L., Mark D., Laura M.; m. Kathryn Carol Griffith McNair, Dec. 15, 1975. BA, So. Oreg. State Coll., 1960; MA, U. Calif., Berkeley, 1962. Asst. to assoc prof. So. Oreg. State Coll., Ashland, 1964-85; pvt. practice artist Ashland, 1985—; dir. writing programs English dept. So. Oreg. State Coll., Ashland, 1965-80. Staff sgt. USAF, 1953-57. Recipient Art Assn. and Galleries award N.W. Watercolor Soc., 1983, Cash and Purchase awards S.W. Mo. Mus. Assn., Springfield, 1984. Mem. Am. Watercolor Soc. (High Winds medal 1984), Nat. Watercolor Soc. (Walter Bronson Crandall Meml. award 1981), West Coast Watercolor Soc., Watercolor USA Honor Soc. Democrat. Home and Office: 380 Taylor St Ashland OR 97520

DEVONTINE, JULIE E(LIZABETH) J(ACQUELINE) (THE MARCHIONESS DE ROE DEVON), systems analyst, consultant; b. Edmund, Wis., Jan. 7, 1934; d. Clyde Elroy and Matilda Evangeline Knapp; m. Roe (Don Davis) Devon Gerringer-Busenbark, Sept. 30, 1968 (dec. Dec. 1972); student Madison Bus. Coll., 1952, San Francisco State Coll., 1953-54, Vivian Rich Sch. Fashion Design, 1955, Dale Carnegie Sch., 1956, Arthur Murray Dance Studio, 1956, Biscayne Acad. Music, 1957, L.A. City Coll., 1960-62, Santa Monica (Calif.) Jr. Coll., 1963; attended Hastings Coll. of Law, 1973, Wharton Sch., U. Pa., 1977, London Art Coll., 1979; Ph.D., 1979; attended Goethe Inst., 1985. Bar: Calif., 1965. Actress, Actors Workshop San Francisco, 1959, 65, Theatre of Arts Beverly Hills (Calif.), 1963, also radio; cons and systems analyst for banks and pub. accounting agys.; artist, poet, singer, songwriter, playwright, dress designer. Pres., tchr. Environ Improvement, Originals by Elizabeth; atty. Dometrik's, JIT-MAP, San Francisco, 1973—; steering com. explorations in worship, ordained min. 1978. Author: The Cardinal, 1947, Explorations in Worship, 1965, The Magic of Scents, 1967, New Highways, 1967, The Grace of Romance, 1968, Happening - Impact-Mald, 1971, Seven Day Rainbow, 1972, Zachary's Adversaries, 1974, Fifteen from Wisconsin, 1977, Bart's White Elephant, 1978, Skid Row Minister, 1978, Points in Time, 1979, Special Appointment, A Clown in Town, 1979, Happenings, 1980, Candles, 1980, Votes from the Closet, 1984, Wait for Me, 1984, The Stairway, 1984, The River is a Rock, 1985, Happenings Revisited, 1986, Comparative Religion in the United States, 1986, Lumber in the Skies, 1986, The Fifth Season, 1987, Summer Thoughts, 1987, Crimes of the Heart, 1987, Toast Thoughts, 1988, The Contrast of Russian Literature Through the Eyes of Russian Authors, 1988, A Thousand Points of Light, 1989, The Face in the Mirror, 1989, Voices on the Hill, 1991, It's Tough to Get a Matched Set, 1991, Equality, 1991, Miss Geranium Speaks, 1991, Forest Voices, 1991, Golden Threads, 1991, Castles in the Air, 1991, The Cave, 1991, Angels, 1991, Real, 1991, An Appeal to Reason, 1992, We Knew, 1992, Like It Is, 1992. Mem. Assn. of Trial Lawyers of Am. Address: 1500 El Camino Ave # 382 Sacramento CA 95833

DEVORE, CHARLES STUART, aerospace industry executive; b. Seattle, May 20, 1962; s. Jerome Dean DeVore and Sharron Lorreen (Wheeler) Gill; m. Diane Mary Rappa, Jan. 9, 1988; 1 child, Jennie. Student, Am. U. in Cairo, Egypt, 1984-85; BA in Strategic Studies with honors, Claremont McKenna Coll., 1985. Intelligence officer U.S. Army, Ft. Huachuca, Ariz., 1985; campaign mgr. J.F. Chadband for Congress, Idaho Falls, Idaho, 1986; spl. asst. for fgn. affairs Office of Assn. Sec. of Def. for Legis. Affairs, Washington, 1986-88; pub. liaison Christopher Cox for Congress, Newport Beach, Calif., 1988; sr. asst. Congressman Christopher Cox, Newport Beach, Calif., 1989-90; intelligence officer U.S. Army, Ft. Irwin, Calif., 1991; mgr. mktg. Steven Myers & Assocs., Newport Beach, Calif., 1991—. Mem. Orange County Rep. Ctrl. Com., 1993—; commr. City of Irvine, 1991—; bd. dirs. Jewish Nat. Fund of Orange County, 1989-92; pres. Corona del Mar Rep. Assembly, 1990-91. Capt. U.S Army N.G., 1992. Decorated Army Achievement medal with two oakleaf clusters. Republican. Home: 327 Deefield Irvine CA 92714 Office: 1301 Dove St Ste 720 Newport Beach CA 92660

DEVOSS, DAVID ARLEN, journalist; b. Dallas, Aug. 4, 1947; s. Hugh Arlen and Barbara Helen (Cooper) DeV.; m. Elizabeth Ann Rushton; children: Thomas Arlen, Matthew Richard. BA, U. Tex., 1968. Corr. Time Mag., N.Y.C., 1968-81, bur. chief, 1981-85; spl. reporter L.A. Times, 1985-89; sr. corr. East-West News Svc., L.A., 1990—; Americas editor Asia, Inc., 1992—. Author: Day in the Life of California, 1988, Day in the Life of China, 1989, Insider's Guide to Indonesia, 1993. Recipient Unity award in Media, Lincoln U., 1989; recipient Best Mag. Sports Story award Sporting News, 1986, Best Sports Story award Assoc. Press, 1986. Mem. Inst. for Democracy in Vietnam (bd. dirs.), Fgn. Corr. Club Hong Kong (bd. dirs. 1978-81), Fgn. Corr. Club Thailand (bd. dirs. 1981-83). Mem. Anglican Ch. Office: East-West News Svc 4159 Stansbury Ave Sherman Oaks CA 91423-4621

DE VOTO, TERENCE ALAN, radio station executive; b. San Francisco, Aug. 2, 1946; s. Albert Anthony and Virginia Louise (Kohnke) De V.; m. Christine McKannay, Jan. 24, 1976; children: Tommy, Mark, Julie, Carolyn. BBA in Mktg., Gonzaga U., 1968. V.p. trading Birr, Wilson & Co., San Francisco, 1968-74; account exec. Sta. KFOG Radio, San Francisco, 1974-78, Sta. KSFO Radio, San Francisco, 1978-81; nat. sales mgr. Sta. KYUU Radio, San Francisco, 1981-83, gen. sales mgr., 1983-84, gen. mgr., 1984-88; v.p. Fuller-Jeffrey Broadcasting, Santa Rosa, Calif., 1989-91; pres. radio divsn. Americom, San Francisco, 1991—. Pres. Marin Assn. for Retarded Citizens, 1988—. Mem. The Olympic Club, The Guardsmen. Republican. Roman Catholic. Home: 295 Oak Ave San Anselmo CA 94960-2741 Office: Americom 350 California St Ste 1450 San Francisco CA 94104

DE VRIES, KENNETH LAWRENCE, mechanical engineer, educator; b. Ogden, Utah, Oct. 27, 1933; s. Sam and Fern (Slater) DeV.; m. Kay M. DeVries, Mar. 1, 1959; children—Kenneth, Susan. AS in Civil Engring., Weber State Coll., 1953; BSME, U. Utah, 1959, PhD in Physics, Mech. Engring., 1962. Registered profl. engr., Utah. Rsch. engr. hydraulic group Convair Aircraft Corp., Fort Worth, 1957-58; prof. dept. mech. engring. U. Utah, Salt Lake City, 1962—, mem. faculty, 1969-76, prof. dept. mech. and indsl. engring., 1976-81, Disting. prof., 1991—, chmn. dept., 1970-81, assoc. dean rsch. Coll. Engring., 1983—; program dir. div. materials rsch. NSF, Washington, 1975-76; materials cons. Browning, Morgan, Utah, 1972—; cons. 3M Co., Mpls., 1985—; tech. adv. bd. Emerson Electric, St. Louis, 1978—; mem. Utah Coun. Sci. and Tech., 1973-77; trustee Gordon Rsch. Conf., 1989—, chair, 1992-93. Co-author: Analysis and Testing of Adhesive Bonds, 1978; contbr. chpts. to numerous books, articles and abstracts to profl. publs. Fellow ASME, Am. Phys. Soc.; mem. Am. Chem. Soc. (polymer div.), Soc. Engring. Scis. (nat. officer), Adhesion Soc. (nat. officer). Mem. LDS Ch. Office: U Utah 2220 Merrill Engring Bldg Salt Lake City UT 84112

DEVROEDE, PETER JOHN, software engineer, computer scientist; b. Ft. Wayne, Ind., Apr. 12, 1960; s. Charles and Margeretha Elizabeth (Van Werden-Poelman) deV. AB in Physics, U. Calif., 1983; postgrad., San Francisco State U., 1986-87, U. Calif., Berkeley, 1987-88. Rsch. asst. Lawrence Berkeley (Calif.) Labs., 1982-83; dir. engring. Cubicomp Corp, Berkeley, 1983-88; mem. sr. tech. staff Adobe Systems, Mountain View, Calif., 1988-89; mgr. engring. Xaos, San Francisco, 1989-90; cons. Digital F/X, BioCad, Disney, 1990-91; mgr. engring. Macromedia, San Francisco, 1991—. Dir. short film; author computer-generated image. Local group organizer Amnesty Internat., Berkeley, 1982-83. Mem. Assn. for Computing Machinery (spl. interest group on graphics), Soc. Motion Picture and TV Engrs. Office: Macromedia 144 Frisbie St Oakland CA 94611

DEVYLDER, EMIL RAYMOND, investment executive; b. Kamsack, Sask., Can., July 16, 1930; s. Raymond Adolph and Rose (Cleutinx) DeV.; m. Marjorie Skrepnechuk, June 30, 1956. Student, Vancouver (Can.) Vocat., 1952; AS, Community Coll. So. Nev., 1981. Cert. single engine land pilot, 1971. Offset press operator Capital News, Kelowna, B.C., Can., 1948-51; field engr. Finning Tractor, Vancouver, 1952-56; owner, operator Starview Motel, Boulder City, Nev., 1957-78, Stagecoach Saloon, Boulder City, 1975-78; pres. Star-D-Inc. Investments, Boulder City, 1973—; mgr. electronics Community Coll. Southern Nev. (formerly Clark County Community Coll.), Las Vegas, 1981—; bd. dirs. PAI-D-Inc., Boulder City; band leader Country & Western Fiddler, Kelowna, B.C., 1948-51. Inventor pick-pocket proof wallet. Mem. Elks, Phi Lambda Alpha. Democrat. Episcopalian. Home: 1243 Tamarisk Ln Boulder City NV 89005-2629 Office: Clark County Community Coll 3200 E Cheyenne Ave North Las Vegas NV 89030-4228

DEW, THOMAS RODERICK, museum librarian; b. N.Y.C., Dec. 16, 1940; s. Thomas Roderick and Sarah Montague (Caperton) D. BA, Yale U., 1963; MA in Librarianship, U. Denver, 1970, MA in History of Art, 1976. Asst. libr. Colorado Springs (Colo.) Fine Arts Ctr., 1977-78, libr., 1979—. Editorial adv. bd. Native Peoples mag. With U.S. Army, 1965-67. Mem. Art Librs. Soc. N.Am., Descendents of the Signers of the Declaration of Independence. Home: 1124 N Hancock Colorado Springs CO 80903 Office: Colorado Springs Fine Arts Ctr 30 W Dale Colorado Springs CO 80903

DEW, WILLIAM WALDO, JR., bishop; b. Newport, Ky., Dec. 14, 1935; s. William Waldo and Thelma (Dittus) D.; m. Mae Marie Eggers, Jan. 5, 1958; children: Linda Dew-Hiersoux, William, Marilyn. BA, Union Coll., Barbourville, Ky., 1957; MDiv, Drew Theol. Sch., 1961; PhD (hon.), Rust Coll., 1991, Union Coll., 1992. Ordained to ministry United Meth. Ch. as deacon, 1958, as elder, 1963. Pastor Springville (Calif.) United Meth. Ch., 1961-64, Lindsay (Calif.) United Meth. Ch., 1964-67, Meml. United Meth. Ch., Clovis, Calif., 1967-72, Epworth United Meth. Ch., Berkeley, Calif., 1972-79; dist. supt. Cen. Dist. Calif.-Nev. Annual Conf., Modesto, Calif., 1979-84; pastor San Ramon Valley United Meth. Ch., Alamo, Calif., 1984-88; bishop United Meth. Ch., Portland, Oreg., 1988—; lectr. Pacific Sch. Religion, Berkeley, 1976-79. Trustee Willamette U., Salem, Oreg., 1988—, Alaska Pacific U., Anchorage, 1988—. Paul Harris fellow Rotary Internat., 1988. Democrat. Office: United Meth Conf Ctr 1505 SW 18th Ave Portland OR 97201-2599

DEWALL, KAREN MARIE, marketing consultant; b. Phoenix, May 31, 1943; d. Merle C. and Agnes M. (Larson) Feller; m. Charles E. DeWall, Sept. 3, 1963 (div. Feb. 1988); 1 child, Leslie Karen. A.A., Phoenix Coll., 1969. Media buyer Wade Advt., Sacramento, 1964-66; media dir., Harwood

Advt., Phoenix, 1967-71; co-owner, account exec. DeWall & Assocs. Advt. Co., 1971-87; dir. advt. Auto Media, Inc./Automotive Investment Group, Phoenix, 1987—; bd. dirs. Phoenix Festivals, Inc.; sustaining mem. Jr. League of Phoenix. Named Ad-2 Advt. Person of Yr., Phoenix, 1984. Mem. Am. Women in Radio and TV (achievement award 1986). Republican. Club: Phoenix Country. Home: 10847 N 11th St Phoenix AZ 85020-5836 Office: Automotive Investment Group 1220 E Camelback Rd Phoenix AZ 85014-3309

DE WEERDT, MARK MURRAY, judge; b. Cologne, Germany, May 6, 1928; arrived in Can., 1949.; s. Hendrik Eugen and Ina Dunbar (Murray) deW.; m. Linda Anne Alden Hadwen, March 31, 1956; children: Simon André, Murray Hadwen, Daved Lockhart, Charles Dunbar. MA, Glasgow (Scotland) U., 1949; LLB, B.C. U., 1955. Cert. barrister and solicitor, B.C. 1956, N.T. 1958. Assoc. solicitor Cross & O'Grady, Victoria, B.C., 1956-57; adv. coun. Can. Dept. Justice, Ottawa, 1957-58; Crown Atty. Yellowknife, N.W.T., 1958-63; sr. counsel Can. Dept. Justice, Vancouver, 1976-79, gen. counsel and dir., 1979-81; barrister, solicitor deWeerdt, Searle, Finall et al., Yellowknife, N.W.T., 1958-71; magistrate and juvenile ct. judge N.W.T. Magistrate's Ct., Yellowknife, N.W.T., 1971-73; gen. solicitor Ins. Corp. B.C., Vancouver, 1974-76; justice N.W.T and Yukon Supreme Cts., Yellowknife and Whitehouse, 1981—, N.W.T and Yukon Cts. Appeals, 1981-; chairperson judicial coun. N.W.T., Yellowknife, 1981—; dir. Canadian Judges' Conf., 1982-89; alternating mem. Can. Judicial Coun., 1985-7, 89-91, 93—. Author profl. papers. Vice-chmn. Yellowknife Sch. Dist. #1, 1964-68. Apptd. to Queen's Coun., Canada, 1968. Mem. Can. Bar Assn., Can. Inst. Administrn. Justice (life), N.W.T. Bar Assn. (pres. 1961-71), MacKenzie River and N.W.T. Progressive Conservation Assn. (pres. 1959-71). Office: Court House, PO Box 1439, Yellowknife, NT Canada X1A 2PI

DEWEESE, MALCOLM LESLIE, JR., social sciences educator; b. Moultrie, Ga., Nov. 11, 1935; s. Malcolm Leslie DeWeese Sr. and Mary Katherine (Harryman) Harper; m. Catherine Marie McGuern, Jan. 28, 1963 (div. 1984); 1 child, Abraham. AA, Valley Coll., 1957; BA cum laude, U. Ariz., 1965; PhD, U. Wash., 1973, MBA, 1979. Sr. research investigator Wash. State Hosp. Commn., Olympia, 1979-81; sci. systems programmer U. Wash., Seattle, 1981-89; bus. mgr. Christ the King Parish, Seattle, 1989—; prin. investigator Prospective Reimbursement Program, Health and Human Services, Washington, 1979-81; cons. Geriatric Studies, Seattle, 1981—, Inst. on Aging, U. Hosp., Seattle, 1981-84; vis. faculty The Evergreen State Coll., Olympia, 1986—. Author: (software program) Electragrade, 1986; contbr. articles to profl. jours. Served with U.S. Army, 1958-60. Grantee U. Wash., 1970; Ford Found. fellow, 1965. Fellow Am. Math. Assn.; mem. Am. Econ. Assn., Nat. Assn. Bus. Economists, Nat. Econometric Assn., Medieval Acad. Am. Democrat. Roman Catholic. Home: 11526 Phinney Ave N Seattle WA 98133 Office: 405 N 117th St Seattle WA 98133-8609

DEWELL, MICHAEL, theater executive, writer, producer, translator; b. West Haven, Conn., Mar. 21, 1931; s. Mansfield Humphrey and Minnie (Dwy) D.; m. Nina Foch, Oct. 31, 1967 (div. Aug. 1993). BA, Yale U., 1952; diploma, Royal Acad. Dramatic Arts, London, 1954. Stage mgr. Cherry Lane Theatre, N.Y.C., 1954-56; writer-producer Sta. WRAMC-TV, Dept. Def., Washington, 1956-58; producer Nat. Phoenix Theatre, N.Y.C., 1958-60; founder, producer Nat. Repertory Theatre, N.Y.C., 1961-68; pres. Nat. Repertory Theatre Found., L.A., 1969—; producer Nat. Repertory Theatre at Ford's Theatre, Washington, 1967-68; bd. dirs., mem. exec. com. Am. Nat. Theatre and Acad., N.Y.C., 1960-68; adviser N.Y. State Arts Council, Albany, 1962-64; trustee Company Theatre Found., L.A., 1968-71; founder, producer, trustee, mem. exec. com. Free Shakespeare Festival, L.A., 1973, 74; founder, producer, pres. L.A. Free Pub. Theatre Found., 1974. Producer: Broadway plays, musicals including The Crucible, 1964, The Seagull, 1964, Tonight at 8:30, 1967, A Touch of the Poet, 1967, The Imaginary Invalid, 1967; opera The Turn of the Screw, Am. premier at Am. Festival, Boston, 1961; touring plays Mary Stuart, 1958-59, 61-62, Once Upon a Mattress, 1959-60, Ring Round the Moon, 1963-64, Elizabeth the Queen, 1961-62, Hedda Gabler, 1963-64, Liliom, 1963-64, The Trojan Women, 1965-66, The Madwoman of Chaillot, 1964-65; Los Angeles prodns.: As You Like It, 1973, Macbeth, 1974, Comedy of Errors, 1974; tour dir. Calif. Uprooted, 1978, Blood Wedding, 1985; nat. TV prodns. Mary Stuart, 1960 Play of The Week, CBS All-Star Gala, Inaugural Night at Ford's, 1968; authorized translator: (with Carmen Zapata) plays by Federico García Lorca: Blood Wedding, 1979; Yerma, 1981 (Drama-Logue award 1981), House of Bernarda Alba, 1982, The Shoemaker's Prodigious Wife, 1985, Mariana Pineda, 1988, Dona Rosita, The Spinster, 1990; pub. Lorca: The Rural Trilogy, 1991, Three Plays by Lorca, 1993; co-author (libretto) Lorca, Child of the Moon, 1986-91 (commd. by Nat. Endowment for the Arts); contbr. articles on theater to newspapers and mags., N.Y. Herald Tribune, Dallas News, Washington Post, Boston Globe; editor: short-story anthology Hell and High Water, 1956; asst. editor, Yale Rev., 1950-52; editorial asst.: Time and Tide, London, 1953-54; mng. editor: Man's Mag., Challenge Mag., N.Y.C., 1954-56; author: narration for compilation film Olé Hollywood, 1981. Trustee, mem. exec. com. El Pueblo Park Assn., L.A., 1983—, pres. 1988-90, sec. 1990-91; trustee Bilingual Found. of Arts, L.A., 1977-85, sec., 1982-83, v.p., 1982-85 ; trustee El Hogar de los Ninos, Tijuana, Mex., 1984-86; founder, project dir. Nat. Play Award, 1978—; project dir. Humanities and Arts Computer Consortium, 1982—. Recipient Antoinette Perry award Am. Theatre Wing, N.Y.C., 1965, Outer Circle award Nat. Critics Circle N.Y.C., 1959, 65, El Angel award Bilingual Found. of the Arts, L.A., 1986. Office: Nat Repertory Theatre Found PO Box 71011 Los Angeles CA 90071-0011

DEWEY, DONALD ODELL, university dean; b. Portland, Oreg., July 9, 1930; s. Leslie Hamilton and Helen (Odell) D.; m. Charlotte Marion Neuber, Sept. 21, 1952; children—Leslie Helen, Catherine Dawn, Scott Hamilton. Student, Lewis and Clark Coll., 1948-49; B.A., U. Oreg., 1952; M.S., U. Utah, 1956; Ph.D., U. Chgo., 1960. Mng. editor Condon (Oreg.) Globe-Times, 1952-53; city editor Ashland (Oreg.) Daily Tidings, 1953-54; asst. editor, assoc. editor The Papers of James Madison, Chgo., 1957-62; instr. U. Chgo., 1960-62; asst. prof., assoc. prof., prof. Calif. State U.-Los Angeles, 1962—, dean Sch. Letters and Sci., 1970-84, dean Sch. Natural and Social Sci., 1984—. Author: The Continuing Dialogue, 2 Vols, 1964, Union and Liberty: Documents in American Constitutionalism, 1969, Marshall versus Jefferson: The Political Background of Marbury v. Madison, 1970, Becoming Informed Citizens: Lessons on the Constitution for Junior High School Students, 1988, Invitation to the Dance: An Introduction to Social Dance, 1991. Recipient Outstanding Prof. award Calif. State U., 1976. Mem. Am. Hist. Assn. (exec. coun. Pacific Coast br. 1971-74), Orgn. Am. Historians, Am. Soc. Legal History (adv. bd. Pacific Coast br. 1972-75), Gold Key, Phi Alpha Theta, Pi Sigma Alpha, Phi Kappa Phi, Sigma Delta Chi. Office: Calif State U Dept History 5151 State University Dr Los Angeles CA 90032

DEWEY, DONALD WILLIAM, magazine editor and publisher, writer; b. Honolulu, Sept. 30, 1933; s. Donald William and Theckla Jean (Engeborg) D.; m. Sally Rae Ryan, Aug. 7, 1961; children: Michael Kevin, Wendy Ann. Student, Pomona Coll., 1953-55. With Pascoe Steel Corp., Pomona, Calif., 1955-56, div. Reynolds Aluminum Co., Los Angeles, 1956-58, Switzer Panel Corp., Pasadena, Calif., 1958-60; sales and gen. mgr. Western Pre-Cast Concrete Corp., Ontario, Calif., 1960-62; editor, pub. R/C Modeler Mag., Sierra Madre, Calif., 1963—, Freshwater and Marine Aquarium Mag., Sierra Madre, 1978—; pres., chmn. bd. R/C Modeler Corp., Sierra Madre, 1963—. Author: Radio Control From the Ground Up, 1970, Flight Training Course, 1973, For What It's Worth, Vol. 1, 1973, Vol. 2, 1975; contbr. articles to profl. jours. Sustaining mem. Rep. Nat. Com., 1981—; charter mem. Nat. Congl. Club, 1981—; mem. Rep. Presdl. Task Force, 1981—, U.S. Senatorial Club, 1983—, 1984 Presdl. Trust, Conservative Caucus, Nat. Tax Limitation Com., Nat. Conservative Polit. Action Com.; assoc. Meth. Hosp. of Southern Calif. Served with Hosp. Corps, USN, 1951-53. Mem. Am. Aquarium Socs., Am. Philatelic Soc., Am. Topical Assn., Am. Wildlife Fedn., Am. Radio Relay League, Am. Revenue Assn., Am. Air Mail Soc., Am. Fedn. Police, Marine Aquarium Soc., Acad. Model Aeronautics, Nat. Aeronautic Assn., Nat. Assn. Sport Flyers Assn., Exp. Aircraft Assn., Radio Amateurs, Am. Radio Relay League, APS Writers Unit 30, Heritage Found., Am. First Day Cover Soc., United Postal Stationery Soc., Confederate Stamp Alliance, Bur. Issues Assn., C.Z. Study Group, Pitcairn Island Study Group, Am. Ctr. Law & Justice; Claremont Inst., Found. Endowment, Rutherford Inst., Heritage Found., Calif. State Sheriff's Assn., Ven Order Michael the Archangel (hon. knight.). Republican. Lutheran. Home: 410 W Montecito Ave Sierra Madre CA 91024-1716 Office: 144 W Sierra Madre Blvd Sierra Madre CA 91024-2435

DEWEY, MICHAEL LEE, wood technologist; b. Spokane, Wash., Nov. 9, 1944; s. Leland Sullivan and Lorraine Margaret (Kofmehl) D.; m. Beverly Jean Thompson, Dec. 30, 1967; children: Cheryl, Michelle, Marci, Monica. BS in Wood Tech., U. Idaho, 1968, BS in Chemistry, 1969; AA in Acctg., Mendocino Community Coll., 1980, AA in Bus. Adminstrn., 1980. Chemist, U.S. Plywood, Lebanon, Oreg., 1969-70; wood chemist Koppers Co., Orrville, Ohio, 1971-76; process engr. Masonite Co., Ukiah, Calif., 1976-79, sr. process engr., 1979-82, cost acct., fin. analyst, 1982-83, acctg. mgr., 1983-92, controller Retech Inc., 1992—. Served with USNR, 1966-70. Mem. Am. Chem. Soc., Am. Mgmt. Assn., Forest Products Research Soc., Soc. Wood Sci. and Tech., Am. Legion, Alpha Phi Omega. Republican. Lodges: Elks (officer 1985-90), Lions (Ukiah treas. 1986-88). Home: 650 Chablis Ct Ukiah CA 95482-3206 Office: Retech Inc PO Box 997 Ukiah CA 95482-3498

DEWEY, ROGER WILLIAM, state official; b. Chgo., May 15, 1928; s. Allan Manzer and Carolyn (Elander) D.; m. Emma Catherine Beaird, Aug. 31, 1957; children: Linda Catherine, Jill Elaine. Student, Denison U., Granville, Ohio, 1946-48. With Continental Assurance Co., 1948-62, Gen. Am. Life Ins. Co., 1962; account exec. J.P. Cleaver Co., Princeton, N.J., 1962-66; dir. mktg. Nat. Ben Franklin Life Ins., Chgo., 1966-68; broker Rich Port Realtor, LaGrange, Ill., 1968-70; prin. Mgmt. Progs. Inc., Glen Ellyn, Ill., 1970-78, Roger Dewey & Assocs., Boulder, Colo., 1978-82; v.p. Rocky Mt. Energy/Union Pacific, Broomfield, Colo., 1982-87; dir. Dept. of Audit, State Wyo., Cheyenne, Wyo., 1989—; bd. dirs. Diversified Environ. Holdings, Dewey Ins. Agy., LaGrange, Ill. Bd. dirs. Ucross Found., 1987-91; pres. Colo. Music Festival, Boulder, 1986-88; chmn. task force Wyo. Futures Project, 1986-88; chmn. coal com. Western Reg. Coun.; prog. exec. com. Com. for Energy Awareness; exec. com. Alliance for Clean Energy; mem. Wyo. Coal Info. Com. Mem. Uranium Producers of Am. (bd. dirs., v.p.), Am. Mining Congress, Alliance for Acid Rain Control (dir.), Am. Nuclear Energy Coun., Atomic Indsl. Forum, Nat. State Auditors Assn. Baptist. Home: 2504 Oneil Ave Cheyenne WY 82001-3016 Office: Department of Audit Herschler Bldg Cheyenne WY 82002

DEWHURST, WILLIAM GEORGE, physician, psychiatrist, educator, researcher; b. Frosterley, Durham, Eng., Nov. 21, 1926; came to Can., 1969; s. William and Elspeth Leslie (Begg) D.; m. Margaret Dransfield, Sept. 17, 1960; children—Timothy Andrew, Susan Jane. B.A., Oxford U., Eng., 1947, B.M., B.Ch., 1950; MA, Oxford U., 1961; D.P.M. with distinction, London U., 1961. House physician, surgeon London Hosp., 1950-52, jr. registrar, registrar, 1954-58; registrar, sr. registrar Maudsley Hosp., London, 1958-62, cons. physician, 1965-69; lectr. Inst. Psychiatry, London, 1962-64, sr. lectr., 1965-69; assoc. prof. psychiatry U. Alta., Edmonton, Can., 1969-72, prof., 1972-92, prof. emeritus, 1992—, Hon. prof. pharmacy and pharm. scis., 1979—, chmn. dept. psychiatry, 1975-90, dir. emeritus neurochem. rsch. unit, 1990—, hon. prof. oncology, 1983—, chmn. med. staff adv. bd., 1988-90; mem. Atty. Gen. Alta. Bd. Rev., 1991, N.W.T. Bd. Rev., 1992; pres.'s coun. U. Alta. Hosps., 1988-90, quality improvement coun., 1988-90, ethics consultative com., 1984-88, planning com. Vision 2000, 1985-87, hosps.' planning com. and joint conf. com., 1971, 80, 87-90; cons. psychiatrist Royal Alexandra Hosp., Edmonton, Edmonton Gen. Hosp., Alberta Hosp., Ponoka, Ponoka Gen. Hosp.; chmn. med. coun. Can. Test Com., 1977-79, Royal Coll. Text Com. in Psychiatry, 1971-80, examiner, 1975-83. Co-editor: Neurobiology of Trace Amines, 1984, Pharmacotherapy of Affective Disorders, 1985; also conf. procs. Referee Nature, Can. Psychiat. Assn. Jour., Brit. Jour. Psychiatry; mem. editorial bd. Neuropsychobiology, Psychiat. Jour. U. Ottawa. Contbr. articles to profl. jours. Chmn. Edmonton Psychiat. Svcs. Steering Com., 1977-80; chmn. Edmonton Psychiat. Svcs. Planning Com., 1985-90; mem. Provincial Mental Health Adv. Coun., 1973-79, Mental Health Rsch. Com., 1973, Edmonton Bd. Health, 1974-76; Can. Psychiat. Rsch. Found., 1985— (also bd. dirs.); bd. dirs. Friends of Schizophrenics, 1980—, Alta., 1988; grant referee Health & Welfare Can., Med. Rsch. Coun. Can., Ont. Mental Health Found., Man. Health Rsch. Coun., B.C. Health Rsch. Found. Capt. Royal Army M.C., 1952-54. Fellow Can. Coll. Neuropsychopharmacology (pres. 1982-84, Coll. medal 1993), Am. Psychopathol. Assn., Am. Coll. Psychiatrists, Am. Psychiat. Assn., Royal Coll. Psychiatrist; mem. AAAS, Alta. Psychiat. Assn. (pres. 1973-74), Can. Psychiat. Assn. (pres. 1983-84), Alta Coll. Physicians and Surgeons, Alta. Med. Assn., Child and Adolescent Assn. (bd. dirs., v.p. 1992), Assn. for Acad. Psychiatry, Brit. Med. Assn., Faculty Club. Anglican. Office: U Alta Dept Psychiatry, 1E1 01 Mackenzie Ctr, Edmonton, AB Canada T6G 2B7

DEWHURST, WILLIAM HARVEY, psychiatrist; b. Huntington, W.Va., July 23, 1929; s. Richard Joseph and Grace Evelyn (Hollandsworth) D.; m. Katharine Ann Grigg, Apr. 2, 1955 (div. 1973); children: Cynthia, Katharine, Angela, William Richard; m. Blanca Maria Peres, Nov. 22, 1974 (div. 1993); 1 child, Neil; m. Joan Diemer Wesley, July 3, 1993. BS, Marshall U., 1950, W.Va. U., 1952; MD, Med. Coll. of Va., 1954. Diplomate Am. Bd. Psychotherapy, Am. Bd. Psychiatry and Neurology; cert. med. examiner, Calif. Intern Med. Coll. of Va. Hosps., Richmond, 1954-55; jr./intermediate resident in psychiatry St. Elizabeth's Hosp./George Washington U., Washington, 1955-56; intermediate/sr. resident in psychiatry Brentwood VA/UCLA and Mt. Sinai Hosps., L.A., 1958-60; pvt. practice Redondo Beach, Calif., 1960-72; pres. Torrance (Calif.) Mental Health Group, 1972-75, Dewhurst Med. Corp., Torrance, 1975—; chief of staff Del Amo Hosp., Torrance, 1972-76; med. dir. Charter Baywood Hosp., Long Beach, Calif., 1980-82; clin. instr. psychiatry, Univ. Calif., 1968-72; asst. clin. prof. psychiatry UCLA, 1972-91; clin. dir. alcohol and substance abuse svcs. Del Amo Hosp., 1975-78, eating disorders unit San Pedro Hosp., L.A., 1989-90; acting clin. dir. San Pedro Hosp., 1990; med. dir. Rivendell Ky. Hosp., 1991-92, chief of staff, 1992-93. Lt. USNR, 1956-68. Recipient Silver Bowl award Charter Med. Corp., Long Beach, 1982, awards in field. Mem. AMA, South Bay Psychiat. Soc. (pres. 1967-68), Ky. Med. Assn., Barren County Med. Assn., Am. Psychiat. Assn., Ky. Psychiat. Soc., So. Calif. Psychiat. Soc. (councilor 1972-75), Am. Acad. Psychiatrists in Alcoholism and Addictions, others. Republican.

DEWINE, PAUL ROBERT, educator; b. Springfield, Ohio, Jan. 3, 1957; s. Dennis Paul and Patricia (Hannon) DeW. BA, U. Toledo, 1980; MA, Bowling Green (Ohio) State U., 1982. Asst. dean Purdue U., West Lafayette, Ind., 1982-87, assoc. dean, 1987-89; leadership coord. U. Calif., San Diego, 1989—. Mem. nat. steering com. Am. Youth Found.'s Internat. Leadership Conf., 1992-93. Mem. Nat. Assn. Student Pers. Adminstrs., Assn. Fraternity Advisors (nat. pres. 1989-90. Office: U Calif 9500 Gilman Dr La Jolla CA 92093-0078

DEWITT, GERRY, councilman, broadcast commentator; b. Pontiac, Mich., Mar. 20, 1952; s. Richard Herbert and Jane (Hansen) DeW.; div. BA in Econs., Sociology, U. Calif., Santa Barbara, 1974. Urban planner Santa Barbara Planning Task Force, 1974-75; broadcast journalist Sta. KTYD, Santa Barbara, 1975-81, broadcast host, 1975—; planning commr. City of Santa Barbara, 1979-81, councilman, 1981-93; program dir. Sta. KTMS, 1992—; mayor pro tem, 1985, 89, 93; chmn. ordinance com., 1983, 86, 90, 92. Producer, host: radio program The 60's Revisited, 1975— (top rating 1981—); co-host Head to Head, 1992—. Named Best Local Politician Santa Barbara Independent readers' poll, 1985-92. Mem. League of Calif. Cities. Democrat. Office: City of Santa Barbara PO Box 1990 Santa Barbara CA 93102-1990

DEWITT, JOHN BELTON, conservation executive; b. Oakland, Calif., Jan. 13, 1937; s. Belton and Florence Jeffery D.; m. Karma Lee Sowers, Sept. 17, 1960. BA in Wildlife Conservation, U. Calif., Berkeley, 1959. With forest svc. El Dorado Nat. Forest, 1955-56; ranger naturalist Nat. Park Svc., Yosemite Nat. Park, 1957-58, Mt. Rainer Nat. Park, 1959, Death Valley Nat. Monument, 1960; land law examiner, info. officer, land appraiser Bur. of Land Mgmt., Sacramento, 1960-64; asst. sec. Save-the-Redwoods League, 1964-71; dir. No. Calif. chpt. Nature Conservancy, 1976-77; dir. Tuolumne River Preservation Trust, 1981-85; exec. dir., sec. Save-the-Redwoods League, 1971—; adv. coun. Trust for Pub. Land, 1975-78, Anza Borrego Desert Com., 1983-93; advisor to U.S. Sec. Interior, 1964-92. Author: California Redwood Parks and Preserves, 1982, 2d rev. edit., 1985. Recipient Nat. Conservation award DAR, 1982, Golden Bear award Calif. State Park & Recreation Commn., 1982, Gulf Oil conservation award, 1985; named Hon. Calif. State Park Ranger, 1985. Mem. Sierra Club (conservation com. 1953-63), Am. Forestry Assn., Nat. Parks Assn., Wilderness Soc., Nat. Audubon Soc. Office: Save the Redwoods League 114 Sansome St Ste 605 San Francisco CA 94104-3814

DEWITT-ROGERS, JOHARI MARILYN, community college administrator; b. Montgomery, Ala., Jan. 28, 1950; d. Rufus Birchard and Mary Lease (Borders) DeWitt; m. Paul Sabu Rogers, Dec. 21, 1976; children: Malachi Omari, Kofi Ayinde. BS, Howard U., Washington, 1971, MEd, 1973; postgrad., U. So. Calif., 1980-83. Abstractor APA, Washington, 1971-72; media technician San Diego Unified Schs., 1974-75; media coord. L.A. Regional Family Planning, 1975-79; asst. producer KABC TV News, 1979-80; dir. audio visual svcs. U. So. Calif. Dental Sch., 1979-81; dir. media Pasadena (Calif.) City Coll., 1987—; cons. City of Pasadena, 1991-92. Author: (play) All That Glitters, 1989. Sec. Linda Vista PTA, 1991, v.p., 1992; pres. Sch. Site Coun., 1992, 93. Recipient Paragon award Nat. Coun. Mktg. and Pub. Rels., New Orleans, 1990, Pro award Calif. Assn. C.C., 1990. Mem. Am. Assn. Women in Colls. and Jr. Colls. (pres. 1992-93), Assn. Calif. Community Coll. Adminstrs. (mentor program 1992, chapt. pres. 1992-93), Dirs. Ednl. Tech. in Calif. Higher Edn., Delta Sigma Theta. African Methodist Episcopal. Office: Pasadena City Coll 1570 E Colorado Blvd Pasadena CA 91106

DEWOLFE, FRED STANLEY, social science educator, consultant; b. Seattle, Jan. 7, 1928; s. Tom E. and Mary (Chamberlain) DeW.; m. Brigitte Stolwitzer, Feb. 10, 1955; children: Andrew, Christopher. BA, Lewis & Clark Coll., 1954; MA, Portland U., 1960, Reed Coll., 1963. Mgr. speakers bur. Southwestern Oreg. Community Coll., Coos Bay, Oreg., 1962-63; chmn. faculty assn. Clackamas Community Coll., Oregon City, Oreg., 1968-70; film lectr., N.W. Film Studies Ctr. Clackamas Community Coll., Oregon City, 1970's, chmn. social sci. dept., 1967—; tv. cons./discussant on war and architecture, various TV stas., Portland, 1970—. Author: Impressions of Portland, 1970, Old Portland, 1973, Portland West, 1976, Portland Tradition Buildings and People, 1980; staff writer Northwest Examiner Newspaper, Portland; contbr. articles to profl. jours. Dir. S.W. Hills Residential League, 1989. With U.S. Army, 1951. Decorated Purple Heart. Mem. Multnomah Athletic Club. Home: 2752 SW Roswell Ave Portland OR 97201-1664 Office: Clackamas Community Coll 19600 S Molalla Ave Oregon City OR 97045-9049

DE WOODY, CHARLES, lawyer; b. Chgo., Oct. 18, 1914; s. Charles and Oneta (Ownby); student U. Fla., 1931-33, U. Mich., 1933-35, Columbia U., 1935-36, Western Res. U., 1936-38; m. Nancy Tremaine, June 15, 1940; children—Charles, Nancy. Office atty. Oglebay, Norton & Co., Cleve., 1939-43; ptnr. Arter, Hadden, Wykoff & Van Duzer, 1943-61; sole practice, 1961—; dir. Nat. Extruded Metal Products Co., Ferry Cap and Set Screw Co., Meteor Crater Enterprises, Inc.; gen. partner Bar-T-Bar Ranch, Mem. Am., Ohio, Cleve. bar assns., Cleve. Law Library Assn. Clubs: Rancho Santa Fe Tennis; Chagrin Valley Hunt (Gates Mills, Ohio). Home: El Mirador Box 1169 Rancho Santa Fe CA 92067

DE WYS, EGBERT CHRISTIAAN, geochemist; b. Soerabaja, Netherlands East Indies, Apr. 9, 1924; came to U.S., 1925; s. Gerard H. L. and Agnita (Versteegh) de W.; m. Sheila Naulty, Dec. 12, 1973; children: Wendy, Tanya, Mark, Matthew. BA, Miami U., 1950, MA, 1951; PhD, Ohio State U., 1955. Scientist Owens-Corning Fiberglass Co., Newark, Ohio; sr. physicist, mgr. process control IBM, San Jose, Calif.; sr. scientist Jet Propulsion Lab., Pasadena, Calif.; prof. Tex. Tech. U., Lubbock; geologist Oasis Oil Co., Tripoli, Libya, Amoco Prodn. Co., Denver; v.p. Coastal Congo Corp., Point Noire, Congo; dep. dir. ESRI, Columbia, S.C.; pres. Exploration Geochemists, Santa Rosa, Calif., 1983—; adj. prof. San Jose U., U. Tripoli. Contbr. articles to profl. jours.; patentee in field. Sgt. maj. Royal Netherland East Indies Army; lt. Armee Secrete Belgium; paratrooper U.S. Army. Bownacker Scholar, Ohio State U. Fellow Am. Mineral. Soc., JPL (sr. fellow); mem. Sigma Xi, Sigma Gamma Epsilon, Phi Sigma, Pi Delta Phi, Delta Phi Alpha. Office: Exploration Geochemists 3600 Aaron Dr Santa Rosa CA 95404-1505

DEXTER, LELAND RUSSELL, geologist, earth scientist, educator; b. L.A., July 20, 1946; s. Wilbur Henry and Lillian Pearl (Sonenstahl) D.; m. Kristine Anne Borg, Jan. 14, 1977 (div. 1987); m. Nancy Elaine Rayner, July 14, 1990. BS, No. Ariz. U., 1969, MS, 1981; PhD, U. Colo., 1986. Prin. Alpineer Ltd., Flagstaff, Ariz., 1971-87; asst. prof. Calif. State U., San Bernadino, 1987-89; assoc. prof. No. Ariz. U., Flagstaff, 1989—. Contbr. articles to profl. jours. With U.S. Army, 1969-71. Recipient W.A. Tarr award Sigma Gamma Epsilon, 1969. Mem. Am. Assn. Geographers, Geol. Soc. Am., Sigma Xi. Office: No Ariz U Dept Geography PO Box 15016 Flagstaff AZ 86011

DEXTER, RAYMOND ARTHUR, social services administrator; b. Hartford, Conn., Dec. 11, 1923; s. Lyman Arthur and Mona Vera (Major) D.; m. Kathleen Eleanor Ferguson, Aug. 8, 1975. BS, MS, MIT, 1947; EdD, Stanford U., 1962. Math. instr. Trinity Coll., Hartford, 1947-49; field officer Salvation Army, San Francisco, 1955-57, edn. officer, 1957-69; state commdr. Salvation Army, Honolulu, 1969-73; social svc. dir. Salvation Army, San Francisco, 1973-74; adminstr. Clitheroe Ctr. Salvation Army, Anchorage, 1977—; chaplain coord. Alyeska Pipeline Svc. Co., Fairbanks, Alaska, 1974-77; v.p. Alaska Alcohol Drug Abuse Cert. Bd., Anchorage, 1982-87, 90—; sec. State Manpower Devel. Com., Anchorage, 1979-82; active U. Alaska Annual Sch. of Addiction Studies Adv. Com., Anchorage, 1983—. Bd. dirs. Anchorage Opera, 1984-90, 92—, Out North Theater Co., 1989-92. Lt. USN, 1942-46. Decorated Meritorious Service medal; named Administr. of Yr. Ctr. for Alcohol and Addiction Studies U. Alaska, 1987; Nat. Inst. Alcohol Abuse and Alcoholism grantee, 1988. Mem. Ret. Officers Assn. (v.p. 1992—), Res. Officers Assn. (state chaplain 1985—), Substance Abuse Dirs. Assn. of Alaska (v.p. 1987—), Rotary, Sigma Xi. Democrat. Episcopalian. Home: 2440 Laird Cir Anchorage AK 99516-2658 Office: Salvation Army Clitheroe Ctr PO Box 190567 Anchorage AK 99519-0567

DEY, CAROL RUTH, logistics manager; b. N.Y., Mar. 9, 1943; d. Robert Lewis Adelson and Anne Millman; m. John Peter Dey, Feb. 9, 1968 (div. Feb. 1978). AA, San Bernardino Valley Coll., 1965; BA, Calif. State U., Sacramento, 1969; MBA, Calif. State U., San Bernardino, 1983. Sec. U.S. Dept of Interior, USAF, Retail Industry, San Bernardino, Sacramento, Calif., 1960-80; logistics mgr. USAF, San Bernardino, 1980—. Dancer Coppélia, San Bernardino, Calif., 1984; mem. St. Anne's Ch., San Bernardino, 1978—. Mem. Am. Bus. Women's Assn. (Calif. State Coll. scholar), Nat. Contract Mgmt. Assn., Smithsonian Inst., AF Assn., Alumni Assn. Calif. State U. San Bernardino. Republican. Roman Catholic.

DEYOUNG, JANE KEARNEY, interior designer; b. St. Louis, May 16, 1935; d. James Robert Kearney and Barbara (Berger) McLaughlin; m. Patrick Lyons DeYoung (div.); children: Torrey Ann Binion, Athene Garfield, Paget Mitchell, Patrick Jr. BA, Scripps Coll., 1957; cert. interior design, No. Va. C.C., Leesburg, 1980. Nursery sch. tchr. All Saints Episcopal Ch., Santa Barbara, Calif., 1959-60; head start tchr. Ventura, Calif., 1959; 2d grade tchr. Colegio Nueva Granda, Bogata, Colombia, 1975-76; interior designer, prin. DeYoung Designs, Santa Barbara, 1986—. Bd. dirs. Hospice of Santa Barbara, 1985-93, hospice vol., 1993; active Music Acad. of the West, Santa Barbara; mem. Jr. League, Santa Barbara Fgn. Rels. Com. Republican. Home and Office: 4426 Via Alegre Santa Barbara CA 93110

DEZEEUW, GLEN WARREN, insurance agent; b. LeMars, Iowa, Jan. 2, 1948; s. Gerrit and Dina (Van de Berg) DeZ.; m. Carolyn J. Van deGriend, June 12, 1968; 1 child, Christian Marc. BS, Iowa State U., 1969. CLU. Agt./mgr. Northwestern Mutual Life Ins. Co., Milw., 1970—. Pres. Poudre Valley Hosp. Found., Ft. Collins, Coll., 1990-91. Mem. Larimer County Assn. Life Underwriters (pres. 1987-88, Englestad Mem. award 1991), Rotary Internat. (bd. dirs. Ft. Collins club 1991—), Northwestern Mutual Life Dist. Agts.' Assn. (western region zone bd. dirs. 1991—). Home: 3101 Conestoga Ct Fort Collins CO 80526-2715 Office: Northwestern Mutual Life 375 E Horsetooth Rd Fort Collins CO 80525-3155

DEZERN, GERARD EDWARD, construction projects executive; b. St. Louis, Oct. 1, 1955; s. Thomas Edward and Loraine Elizabeth (Eckhoff) DeZ. B. in Environ. Design, U. Kans., 1979, BS in Archtl. Engring., 1979; MBA, So. Ill. U., Edwardsville, 1990. Project mgr. West Port Assocs., Inc., St. Louis, 1979-82; v.p. Team CM, Inc., St. Louis, 1982-87; mgr. facilities engring. Thomas J. White Co., St. Louis, 1987-90; constrn. projects mgr. CMR Constrn., Inc., Santa Monica, Calif., 1990—. Bd. pres. Hosea House, St. Louis, 1989-90. Mem. Constrn. Specifications Inst., Design and Constrn. Quality Inst. Roman Catholic. Office: CMR Constrn Inc 8500 Eager Rd Saint Louis MO 63144

DHOLLANDE, LAURENT R., corporate finance manager; b. Amiens, France, Apr. 19, 1960; came to U.S., 1986; s. René and Paule (Carlier) D.; m. Lisa Anne McDonald, Mar. 25, 1984. MBA, U. Calif., Berkeley, 1988. Jr. profl. UN, Dar es Salaam, Tanzania, 1983-84; fin. analyst Credit Lyonnais Bank Nederland, Rotterdam, The Netherlands, 1984-86; founder Paris Direct, Oakland, Calif., 1986-87; sr. treasury analyst Hewlett-Packard Corp., Palo Alto, Calif., 1988-90, project mgr. real estate acquisitions, 1990—; pres. A.V.E.N.I.R., Paris, 1980-83. Office: Hewlett-Packard Corp 3000 Hanover St Palo Alto CA 94304-1112

DHRUV, HARISH RATIBHAI, textile chemist, colorist; b. Ahmedabad, India, Mar. 14, 1946; came to U.S., 1970, naturalized, 1978; s. Ratilal Chhaganial and Shantaben HaripRasad (Dave) D.; m. Kaumudini Vasudev Vyas, June 21, 1971; children: Nirav H., Niraj H. BS in Chemistry, St. Xavier's Coll., Gujarat U., India, 1966; diploma in textile chemistry, M.S. U., Baroda, India, 1967; BS in Textile Chemistry, Phila. Coll. Textiles and Sci., 1972. Trainee supr. Mafatlal Fine Mills, Ahmedabad, 1967-68; supr. Calico Mills, Ahmedabad, 1969-70; quality control and processing mgr. fashion prints U.S. Industries Co., Allentown, Pa., 1972-77; print supt., v.p. mfg. Pacific Fabric Printers, Vernon, Calif., 1977-80; owner textiles importing, converting and printing bus. Vernon, Calif., 1980—. Pres. India Assn. of Lehigh Valley, 1974, 75, 76; active Indo Am. Polit. Assn., 1991—; sec. Overseas Friend of Bharatiya Janata Party, 1992—; mem. Gujarati Cultural Soc. So. Calif., 1977—. Recipient Bicentennial medal for pub. service to community City of Allentown, 1977. Mem. Am. Assn. Textile Chemists and Colorists, Am. Chem. Soc., Assn. Western Furniture Suppliers (sec.), West Coast Furniture Fabric Club (sec. 1984, treas. 1985, v.p. 1986, pres. 1987—), Bharatiya Cultural Soc. (pres. 1976). Democrat. Hindu. Home: 269 St Albans Ave South Pasadena CA 91030-3561

DIAMOND, AVIVA, communications consultant; b. New York, May 14, 1953; d. Herbert and Lynne D. Student, Hebrew U., 1972-73; BA in French and English with honors, Wellesley Coll., 1974; MS in Journalism, Columbia U., 1976. Anchor, producer, reporter Sta. WAAB Radio, Worcester, Mass., 1974-75; staff reporter The Miami Herald, Fla., 1976-77; mgmt. trainee Westinghouse Broadcasting, Boston, 1977-78; reporter, anchor Sta. WRAL-TV, Raleigh, N.C., 1978-79; med. reporter Sta. KTVI, St. Louis, 1979-82; corr. ABC Network News, L.A., 1982-84; anchor, reporter Sta. KATV, Little Rock, 1985-87; v.p. Ready for Media, L.A., 1988-90; pres. Blue Streak A Communications Co., L.A., 1990—. Recipient Emmy award, 1980, Emmy nominations 1981, 82, Feature Reporting award Sigma Delta Chi, 1985, RTNDA Regional award Spot News, 1979; Wellesley Coll. scholar, 1974; Columbia U. Internat. fellow, 1975-76. Mem. Pub. Rels. Soc. Am. Office: Blue Streak A Communications Co 1817 Hillcrest Rd Ste 42 Los Angeles CA 90068-3150

DIAMOND, BERNIE RICHARD, management and training company executive; b. Salt Lake City, May 21, 1922; s. Harry and Anna (Erlich) D.; m. Verbena Mae Brostrom, Jan. 31, 1940; children: Richard, Judie, Susan. Student, Weber State U., 1946. Exec. dir. Ogden (Utah) C. of C., 1952-62; dir. customer rels. Thiokol Corp., Ogden, 1962-80; v.p. spl. svcs. Mgmt. & Tng. Corp., Ogden, 1980—, also bd. dirs. Mem. Ogden City Coun., 1962-66; asst. mayor City of Ogden, 1966; nat. dir. community rels. OEO, Washington, 1967. Staff sgt. AUS, 1943-46, ETO. Named Outstanding Young Man in Community, Ogden Jr. C. ov C., 1960, Outstanding Alumni, Weber State U., 1986. Home: 4045 Bona Villa Dr Ogden UT 84403

DIAMOND, CARL IRWIN, insurance company executive; b. St. Paul, July 18, 1950; s. Jack and Rose (Gotlieb) D. AA, Long Beach City Coll., 1990. Lic. ins. agt. Sales mgr. Long Beach (Calif.) Honda Motorcycles, 1979-90; owner C. Diamond Ins. Agy., Long Beach, 1990—. Contbr. articles to profl. jours. Recipient History scholarship Long Beach City Coll., 1990. Mem. Am. Motorcyclist Assn., Gold Wing Road Riders Assn., Am. Brotherhood Aimed Toward Edn. Democrat. Jewish. Home and Office: 53 W Home St Long Beach CA 90805

DIAMOND, JOSEF, lawyer; b. L.A., Mar. 6, 1907; s. Michael and Ruby (Shifrin) D.; m. Violett Diamond, Apr. 2, 1933 (dec. 1979); children: Joel, Diane Foreman; m. Ann Dulien, Jan. 12, 1981 (dec. 1984); m. Muriel Bach, 1986. B.B.A., U. Wash., 1929, J.D., 1931. Bar: Wash. 1931, U.S. Dist. Ct. (we. dist.) Wash. 1932, U.S. Ct. Appeals (9th cir.) 1934, U.S. Supreme Ct. 1944. Assoc. Caldwell & Lycette, Seattle, 1931-35; ptnr. Caldwell, Lycette & Diamond, 1935-45; ptnr. Lycette, Diamond & Sylvester, 1945-80, Diamond & Sylvester, 1980-82, of counsel, 1982-88; of counsel Short, Cressman & Burgess, 1988—; chmn. bd. Diamond Parking Inc., Seattle, 1945-70; cons. various businesses. Bd. dirs. Am. Heart Assn., 1960; chmn. Wash. Heart Assn., 1962. Col. JAGC U.S. Army, World War II. Decorated Legion of Merit. Mem. Assn. Trial Lawyers Wash., Wash. Bar Assn., Seattle Bar Assn., The Beavers, Mil. Engrs. Soc., Wash. Athletic Club, Bellevue Athletic Club, Harbor Club, Seattle Yacht Club, Rainier Club.

DIAMOND, MARIA SOPHIA, lawyer; b. Portland, Oreg., Aug. 29, 1958; d. Harry and Nitsa (Fotiou) D. BA in Eng. cum laude, U. Wash., 1980; JD, U. Puget Sound, 1983. Bar: Wash. 1983, U.S. Dist. Ct. (we. dist.) Wash. 1983, U.S. Ct. Appeals (9th cir.) 1985. Ptnr. Levinson, Friedman, Vhugen, Duggan & Bland, Seattle, 1990—. Named to Nat. Order of the Barristers U. Puget Sound, 1983. Mem. ABA, Fed. Bar Assn., Assn. Trial Lawyers Am., Wash. State Trial Lawyers Assn. (mem. bd. govs., editor-in-chief Trial News 1992—), Seattle-King County Bar Assn., Women's Fisheries Network, U. Wash. Alumni Assn., Alpha Gamma Delta Alumni Assn. Office: Levinson Friedman Vhugen Duggan & Bland 600 University St Ste 2900 Seattle WA 98101-4156

DIAMOND, MICHAEL SHAWN, science educator, computer consultant; b. St. Louis, Jan. 26, 1960; s. Robert Dale Diamond and Jean Marie (Reutner) White. BSChemE, U. Mo., 1982; MEd, Hyles-Anderson Coll., 1989. Cert. engr.-in-tng.; lic., ordained to ministry Bapt. Ch., 1989; cert. tchr. Nuclear engr. Charleston (S.C.) Naval Shipyard, Nuclear Engring. Dept., 1983-88, asst. shift test engr., 1983-85, asst. shift refueling engr., 1985-88; systems mgr. and sci. tchr. Faith Bapt. Ch. and Schs., Canoga Park, Calif., 1989-90, sci. tchr., 1989-90; sci. dept. chmn. Gethsemane Bapt. Christian Sch., Long Beach, Calif., 1990-92, sci., math., computer tchr.; programming asst., cons. Peterson Rsch., Costa Mesa, Calif., 1989-92; adj. instr. transfer chemistry and engring. Trident Tech. Coll., North Charleston, S.C., 1993—; contract computer instr. Tng. Alliance, North Charleston, 1993—. Sunday sch. tchr. Gethsemane Bapt. Ch., Long Beach, 1990-92, choir mem. Trident Bapt. Ch., Charleston, S.C., 1993—. Mem. NSPE, Am. Nuclear Soc., Pi Kappa Alpha (house mgr. 1979-80), U.S. Judo Assn. (Winner's Cir. award 1987, 88, 89). Republican. Home: 404 Mendenhall St Summerville SC 29483-5226 Office: Trident Tech Coll Dept Arts and Scis 7000 Rivers Ave North Charleston SC 29411

DIAMOND, ROCHELLE ANNE, biologist; b. Phoenix, Aug. 9, 1951; d. Harold and Helen (Garfinkle) D.; m. Clifford L. Sailor Jr., July 6, 1976 (div. 1985). BA in Molecular Biology, U. Calif., Santa Barbara, 1974. Technician U. So. Calif., L.A., 1974-77; rsch. technician City of Hope Nat. Med. Ctr., Duarte, Calif., 1978-81; assoc. biologist UCLA, 1981-82; rsch. biologist Calif. Inst. Tech., Pasadena, 1982-91, chief opr., tech. applications specialist cell sorting facility, 1984—, mem. profl. staff, 1991—. Guest editor Methods, 1991; contbr. articles to profl. jours. Com. mem. AIDS Project L.A. Med. Advisory Com., 1985-87. Mem. AAAS, Am. Chem. Soc., Nat. Orgn. Gay and Lesbian Scientists and Tech. Profls. (chmn. 1985—), N.Y. Acad. Sci., L.A. Gay and Lesbian Scientists (co-chmn. 1984—), Internat. Soc. Analytical Cytology, Athenaeum. Democrat.

DIAMOND, STANLEY JAY, lawyer; b. Los Angeles, Nov. 27, 1927; s. Philip Alfred and Florence (Fadem) D.; m. Lois Jane Broida, June 22, 1969; children: Caryn Elaine, Diana Beth. B.A., UCLA, 1949; J.D., U. So. Calif., 1952. Bar: Calif. 1953. Practiced law Los Angeles, 1953—; dep. Office of Calif. Atty. Gen., Los Angeles, 1953; ptnr. Diamond & Tilem, Los Angeles, 1957-60, Diamond, Tilem & Colden, Los Angeles, 1960-79, Diamond & Wilson, Los Angeles, 1979—; lectr. music and entertainment law UCLA; Mem. nat. panel arbitrators Am. Arbitration Assn. Bd. dirs. Los Angeles Suicide Prevention Center, 1971-76. Served with 349th Engr. Constrn. Bn. AUS, 1945-47. Mem. ABA, Calif. Bar Assn., Los Angeles County Bar Assn., Beverly Hills Bar Assn., Am. Judicature Soc., Calif. Copyright Conf., Nat. Acad. Rec. Arts and Scis., Zeta Beta Tau, Nu Beta Epsilon. Office: 12304 Santa Monica Blvd 3d Fl Los Angeles CA 90025

DIAMOND, STEPHEN EARLE, investor, consultant, inventor; b. San Francisco, Dec. 2, 1944; s. Earl Conrad and Sally (Gonzales) D. Pvt. study music and drama, 1956-65; grad., Ft. Sam Houston (Tex.) Army Med. Sch., 1964. Exec. dir. Gondia Corp., San Francisco, 1973-76, exec. chmn., 1976-78; chief exec. officer G.C.I. C'ies, San Francisco, 1978-80, chief adminstrv. officer, 1980-85; owner S.E. Diamond Founds., San Francisco, 1985-86, S.E. Diamond Assn., San Francisco, 1986—. Patentee in field. Leader 5th Congl. dist. Strategic Def. Initiative; active Am. Inst. for Cancer Rsch., 1981—, Ronald Reagan Rep. Ctr., Washington, 1987, Stanford (Calif.) U. Libr., 1987; state advisor U.S. Congl. adv. bd., Washington and San Francisco, 1983-86; hon. chater mem. St. Mary's Hosp., San Francisco, 1988; friend San Francisco Symphony Orch., 1980—; founding mem. Am. Space Frontier Com., Falls Ch., 1984-86, Challenger Space Ctr., 1987—; sponser and producer Concerned Women for Am., 1984—. Recipient merit award Rep. Nat. Com., 1984, merit award Rep. Party, 1985, Achievement award United Inventors and Scientists, L.A., 1975. Mem. Nat. Small Bus. Assn., Nat. Taxpayers Union, Statue of Liberty and Ellis Island Found. (charter), Presdl. Task Force (charter), Clan Morrison Soc. (Life), North Shore Animal League. Republican. Home: Oxford 248 San Francisco CA 94134 Office: PO Box 640238 San Francisco CA 94164-0238 also: PO Box 246 South Lake Tahoe CA 96156 also: PO Box 4361 Zephyr Cove NV 89499

DIAS, ANTONIO RAINHA, electrical engineer; b. Porto, Portugal, June 18, 1948; came to U.S. 1975; s. Eduardo A. and Maria R. Dias; m. Marta L. Alexandre, Aug. 3, 1972; children: Antonio, Jose, Marta, Joao. BEE, Oporto U., Portugal, 1971; MSc in EE, Stanford U., 1977, PhD in EE, 1980. Lectr. Oporto U., 1971-75; rsch. asst. Stanford U., 1976-80; rsch. engr. E.R.I.M., Ann Arbor, Mich., 1980-84; staff engr. Litton-Applied Tech., Sunnyvale, Calif., 1984-86; mgr. Optivision, Inc., Palo Alto, Calif., 1986-91; pres. Dias Assocs., Sunnyvale, 1991—, LusEuropa Corp., Sunnyvale, 1991—. Sr. mem. IEEE; mem. Soc. Photo-optical Instrumentation Engrs., Optical Soc. Am. Office: LusEuropa Corp 1307 S Mary Ave Ste 102 Sunnyvale CA 94087

DIAZ, GEORGE EDWARD, electrical engineer; b. San Lorenzo, Honduras, Nov. 24, 1964; s. Luis Tomas and Norma D. BSEE, U. So. Calif., L.A., 1986. Unit commanding officer Navy Reserve Ctr., Tucson, 1992—. Lt. USN, 1986-90. Decorated Navy Achievement medal; Navy ROTC 4-Yr. scholar USN, 1982. Mem. Soc. Am. Mil. Engrs., Am. Prodn. and Inventory Control Soc., Soc. Hispanic Profl. Engrs., Res. Officers Assn. Home: 6312 N Camino Los Mochis Tucson AZ 85718-3516

DIAZ, RAMON VALERO, judge; b. Manila, Oct. 13, 1918; came to Guam, 1951; s. Vicente and Bibiana (Valero) D.; m. Josefina Dela Concepcion, July 3, 1945; children: Carlos, Marilu, Mariles, Maribel, Marilen, Maryann, Anthony, Vincent, Ramon, Maricar. PhB, U. St. Tomas, Manila, 1940, LLB, 1941; grad. U.S. Army J.A.G. Sch., 1945; Diploma Jud. Skills, Am. Acad. Jud. Edn., 1984. Bar: Philippines 1941, Guam 1956, U.S. Ct. Appeals (9th cir.) 1966, High Ct. of Trust Territories 1977, No. Marianas 1985. Assoc. Diokno Law Office, Manila, 1943-44; pvt. practice, Guam, 1960-80; judge Superior Ct. of Guam, Agana, 1980—; mem. U.S. Selective Service Bd. Appeals, Guam, 1950-62. Permanent deacon Roman Catholic Ch. Judge Adv. Gen.'s Svc., Philippine Army, 1941-51. Mem. ABA, Am. Judges Assn., Nat. Council Juvenile and Family Ct. Judges, VFW. Survivor Bataan Death March, 1942. Home: 114 Manga Ct Dedano GU 96912 Office: Superior Ct Guam Judicial Ctr Agana GU 96910 also: PO Box AR Agana GU 96910

DIAZ-ZUBIETA, AGUSTIN, nuclear engineer, executive; b. Madrid, Spain, Mar. 24, 1936; came to U.S., 1953; s. Emilio Diaz Cabeza and Maria Tereza Zubieta Atucha; m. Beth Lee Fortune, Sept. 6, 1958; children: Walter Austin, Michael Joel, Anthony John. B, U. Madrid, 1953; BSc in Physics, U. Tenn., 1958; MSc in Mech. Engring., Duke U., 1960; PhD in Nuclear Engring., U. Md., 1981. Nuclear engr. Combustion Engring., Tenn., 1954-58; instr. engring. Duke U., Durham, N.C., 1958-60; nuclear physicist Allis Chalmers Co., Washington, 1960-64; country mgr. South Africa Allis Chalmers Co., 1964-66; mgr. internat. power generation projects GE, N.Y.C., 1966-69, mgr. Europe and Middle East strategic planning, 1969-71; dir. internat. constrn. planning GE, Westport, Conn., 1971-75, dir. constrn., 1975-83; chief exec. officer GE Affiliate, Westport, 1983-87; v.p. internat. sales, devel. Internat. Tech. Corp., L.A., 1987—; mng. dir. IT Italia S.P.A., IT Spain, S.A. Author: Measurement of Subcriticality of Nuclear Reactors by Stocastic Processes, 1981. Pres. Fairfield (Conn.) Assn. Condo Owners, 1983-87. Named Astronomer of Yr. Barnard Astronomical Soc., Chattanooga, 1957; fgn. exchange scholar U.S. Govt., 1953, 54-58; grantee, NSF, 1958-60, U.S. Office of Ordinance Rsch. U.S. Army, 1958-60. Mem. Am. Nuclear Soc., Am. Soc. Mech. Engrs., Am. Soc. Profl. Engrs., Sigma Xi. Republican. Roman Catholic. Home: 47 Country Meadow Rd Rolling Hills Estates CA 90274-5774 Office: Internat Tech Corp 23456 Hawthorne Blvd Torrance CA 90505-4716

DIBALLA DE LOPEZ, SUSAN, chiropractor; b. Pitts., May 24, 1958; d. John Paul and Joan Margaret (Kelleher) D.; m. Raymond F. Lopez, Jr., Aug. 27, 1988; children: Velia Brianna, Antonio John. BS, Santa Clara U., 1981; D. Chiropractic, Cleve. Chiropractic Coll., L.A., 1990. Chiropractor Thousand Oaks (Calif.) Chiropractic, 1990—. Mem. Soroptomist Club, Santa Paula, Calif., 1991. Mem. Calif. Chiropractic Assn., Ventura County Profl. Women's Assn., Internat. Chiropractor's Assn. Office: Thousand Oaks Chiropractic 1489 E Thousand Oaks Blvd # 5 Thousand Oaks CA 91362

DIBARTOLOMEO, DENNIS, data acquisition and process control engineer; b. N.Y.C., Aug. 21, 1949; s. Carl and Leona (Spallone) DiB. BS in Astronomy, Calif. Inst. Tech., 1971; MA in Psychology, U. Calif., Berkeley, 1974; postgrad., City Coll. San Francisco, 1977-78. Rsch. technician Lawrence Berkeley Lab., 1978-84, sr. rsch. assoc., 1984-89, prin. rsch. assoc., 1989—. Contbr. articles to profl. jours. Mem. Internat. Soc. for Study Subtle Energies and Energy Medicine, Parapsychology Rsch. Group, Union Concerned Scientists, Inst. Noetic Sciences. Buddhist. Home: 747 Elm St El Cerrito CA 94530 Office: Bldg 90 Rm 3111 Lawrence Berkeley Lab Berkeley CA 94720

DIBLE, ROSE HARPE MCFEE, special education educator; b. Phoenix, Apr. 28, 1927; d. Ambrose Jefferson and Laurel Mabel (Harpe) McFee; m. James Henry Dible, June 23, 1951 (div. Jan. 1965); 1 child, Michael James. BA in Speech Edn., Ariz. State U., Tempe, 1949; MA in Speech and Drama, U. So. Calif., L.A., 1950; fellow, Calif. State U., Fullerton, 1967. Cert. secondary tchr., spl. edn. tchr. English and drama tchr. Lynwood (Calif.) Sr. High Sch., 1950-51, Montebello (Calif.) Sr. High Sch., 1952-58; tchr. English and Social Studies Pioneer High Sch., Whittier, Calif., 1964-65; spl. edn. tchr. Bell Gardens (Calif.) High Sch., 1967-85, spl. edn. cons., 1985-90. Mem. DAR, Daus. Am. Colonists, Whittier Christian Woman Assn., La Habra Womans Club, Eastern Star Lodge, Kappa Delts, Phi Delta Gamma. Republican. Presbyterian. Home: 1201 N Russell St La Habra CA 90631 Office: Montebello Unified Sch Dist 123 Montebello Blvd Montebello CA 90640-4729

DICK, BARCLAY L., airport executive; b. Tucson, Ariz., June 30, 1948; s. Gamble C. and Betsey (Lay) D.; m. Susan F. Schmidt, May 17, 1973; children: Aaron B., Adam M., Logan A. Cert. airport exec. Safety engr. Tucson Airport Authority, 1970-72, supr., 1972-76, constrn. supr., 1976-79, project dir., 1979-86, mgr. terminal ops., 1986—. Bd. dirs. Tucson Children's Mus., 1991, Leadership Alumni, Tucson, 1991, Met. Tucson Conv. and Visitors Bur.; mem. Tucson Unified Sch. Dist. Bonds Projects Com., 1991. Mem. Ariz. Airports Assn. (pres. 1992-93), Am. Assn. Airport Execs (pres.-elect 1992-93), Rotary (bd. dirs. Old Pueblo chpt. 1991). Office: Tucson Airport Authority 7005 S Plumer Ave Tucson AZ 85706-6990

DICK, BERTRAM GALE, JR., physics educator; b. Portland, Oreg., June 12, 1926; s. Bertram Gale and Helen (Meengs) D.; m. Ann Bradford Volkmann, June 23, 1956; children—Timothy Howe, Robin Louise, Stephen Gale. B.A., Reed Coll., 1950; B.A. (Rhodes scholar), Wadham Coll., Oxford (Eng.) U., 1953, M.A., 1958; Ph.D., Cornell U., 1958. Research assoc. U. Ill., 1957-59; mem. faculty U. Utah, 1959—, prof. physics, 1965—, Univ. prof., 1979-80, chmn. dept., 1964-67, dean grad. sch., 1987-93; cons. Minn. Mining and Mfg. Co., 1960-67; vis. prof. Technische Hochschule, Munich, 1967-68; vis. scientist Max Planck Institut für Festkörperforschung, Stuttgart, Fed. Republic Germany, 1976-77; faculty Semester at Sea, fall 1983, 86. Mem. Alta Planning and Zoning Commn., 1972-76; pres. Chamber Music Salt Lake City, 1974-76; bd. dirs. Citizen's Com. to Save Our Canyons, 1971—, Coalition for Utah's Future Project 2000, 1989—. Served with USNR, 1944-46. Fellow Am. Phys. Soc.; mem. AAAS, Am. Alpine Club, Sierra Club, Phi Beta Kappa, Sigma Xi. Home: 1377 Butler Ave Salt Lake City UT 84102-1803 Office: U Utah Dept Physics Salt Lake City UT 84112

DICK, PAUL DOUGLAS, sales and marketing executive; b. Salem, Oreg., June 12, 1956; s. Ken David and Patricia Ann (Bramble) D. BS, Oreg. State U., 1978. Sales mgr. Farmcraft, Tigard, Oreg., 1979-80; sales rep. Velsicol Chem. Co., Portland, Oreg., 1980-86; mktg. mgr. Sandoz Crop Protection, Chgo., 1986-88; mktg. dir. Sandoz Crop Protection, Denver, 1988-90; dir. sales and mktg. BIOSYS, Palo Alto, Calif., 1990—; pres. Oreg. Agrl. Chem. Assn., Portland, 1985-86; state chmn. Western Agrl. Chem. Assn., Sacramento, 1986-87. Big bro. Big Bros. & Sisters, Chgo., 1987; varsity asst. Oreg. State Basketball, Corvallis, 1978—. Republican. Lutheran. Home: 737 Mediterranean Dr Redwood City CA 94065 Office: BIOSYS 1057 E Meadow Circle Palo Alto CA 94303

DICKENS, WILLIAM THEODORE, economics educator; b. Chgo., Dec. 31, 1953; s. William James and Estelle Geraldine (Schmidt) D.; m. Maureen Ellen Finegan, June 18, 1982; 1 child, Christopher James. BA, Bard Coll., 1976; PhD, MIT, 1981. Econometric computing cons. MIT, Cambridge, Mass., 1978-80, vis. asst. prof., 1985-86; asst. prof. econ. U. Calif., Berkeley, 1980-85, assoc. prof. econ., 1986—; cons. World Bank, Washington, 1987-88, Calif. State Employers Assn., Oakland, Calif., 1988-89; sr. economist, pres. Coun. Econ. Advisors, 1993—. Editor, author: Dynamics of Trade and Employment, 1988, Labor and an Integrated Europe, 1993; author: The U.S. Labor Market Effects of European Economic Integration, 1993; contbr. articles to profl. jours. Graduate fellow NSF, 1976, numerous grants. Mem. Am. Econs. Assn., Econometrics Soc., U. Calif. Flying Club. Democrat. Home: 1500 Barth Ave San Pablo CA 94806-4214 Office: U Calif Dept Econs Berkeley CA 94720

DICKERSON, BARBARA ANN RANSOM, educator, consultant; b. Jackson, Miss., Apr. 18, 1952; d. Jimmie Lee and Marie Eunice (West) Ransom; m. Mark Steven Dickerson, Dec. 30, 1978; children: Amber Tiffany, Christopher Ryan. BS, Grand Canyon Coll., 1974; MA, Ariz. State U., 1976, PhD, 1987. Tchr. Pendergast Elem. Dist., Tolleson, Ariz., 1974-76; reading clin. S. Mountain High Sch. Dist., Phoenix, 1976-80; instr. High Sch. Drop Out Program, Phoenix, 1978, Mesa (Ariz.) Community Coll., 1978; reading specialist Deer Valley Sch. Dist., Phoenix, 1980-82; asst. dir. Honors Coll. Ariz. State U., Tempe, 1984-87, asst. prof. edn., 1988-89; faculty mem. Grand Canyon Coll., Phoenix, 1987-88; dean Coll. Arts and Sci. Grand Canyon U., 1991—; cons. Rising Star, Phoenix, 1987—. Pres. Valley Christian Ctrs., Phoenix, 1984-89; youth instr. First Bapt. Ch., Phoenix, 1987-88; active Foster Care Rev. Bd., Ariz., Ariz. Adoption Spl. Kids. Greater Phoenix Area Writing Project fellow, 1979. Mem. Ariz. Tchrs. of Reading, Ariz. English Tchrs. Assn., Assn. for Curriculum and Devel., Delta Sigma Theta (sec., v.p. 1977—). Democrat. Home: 8533 N 50th Pl Paradise Valley AZ 85253-2006 Office: Grand Canyon U 3300 W Camelback Rd Paradise Valley AZ 85253-5113

DICKERSON, COLLEEN BERNICE PATTON, artist, educator; b. Cleburne, Tex., Sept. 17, 1922; d. Jennings Bryan and Alma Bernice (Clark) Patton; m. Arthur F. Dickerson; children: Sherry M., Chrystal Charmine. BA, Calif. State U., Northridge, 1980; studied with John Pike. One woman shows include Solo Show, Morro Bay Comunity Blgd.; exhibited in group shows at Aquarius Watercolor Show, Brushctrokes Oil Show, Great Western Painting Show, Morro Bay Monthly Show; represented in permanent collections at Polk Ins. Co., San Luis Obispo, Med. Ctr. MDM Ins. Co., L.A.; demonstrations at Cayucos Art Assn., Morro Bay Art Assn., El Camino Real Art Assn. Mem. Cen. Coast Watercolor Soc. (pres. 1986-87), Art. Ctr., Oil Acrylic Pastel Group (chmn., co-chmn. 1989—), Morro Bay Art Assn., Les Arts, San Luis Obispo Art Ctr. Home and Studio: 245 Hacienda San Luis Obispo CA 93401

DICKERSON, CYNTHIA ROWE, marketing firm executive, consultant; b. Cin., Apr. 14, 1956; d. Richard Emmett and Frances Jeanette (Ellwanger) Rowe; m. Mark Alan Dickerson, Oct. 24, 1981; children: Shannon Gayle, Meredith Lynne. BSBA, U. So. Calif., 1979. Mgmt. asst. Computer Scis. Corp., Pasadena, Calif., 1974-78; rsch. asst. Dailey & Assocs., L.A., 1978-79; account exec. Young & Rubicam, L.A., 1979-81, Rowley & Linder Advt., Wichita, Kans., 1981-82, Chiat/Day Inc. Advt., San Francisco, 1983-85; product mgr. Sun-Diamond Growers of Calif., Pleasanton, 1985-88; mktg. cons. San Francisco, 1988-90; sr. bus. mgr. Del Monte Foods, San Francisco, 1990—. Named Outstanding Youth Women of Am., Jr. C. of C., 1985. Mem. Am. Rose Soc. Republican. Office: Del Monte Foods One Market Plaza San Francisco CA 94119

DICKERSON, ERIC DEMETRIC, professional football player; b. Sealy, Tex., Sept. 2, 1960; s. Helen Dickerson. Student, So. Meth. U. Running back Los Angeles Rams, 1983-87; running back Indianapolis Colts, 1987-91, L.A. Raiders, 1992, Atlanta Falcons, 1993—. Author: (with Richard Graham Walsh) Eric Dickerson's Secrets of Pro Power, 1989. Named NFL Player of Yr., 1983, Pro Football Writers Rookie of Yr., 1983; played in Pro Bowl 1984-88; set single season rushing yardage record, 1984; led NFL in rushing 1983-84, 86. Office: Atlanta Falcons 2745 Burnett Rd Suwanee GA 30174

DICKERSON, WILLIAM ROY, lawyer; b. Uniontown, Ky., Feb. 15, 1928; s. Banjamin Franklin and Honor Mae (Staples) D. BA in Acctg., Calif. State U., 1952; JD, UCLA, 1958. Bar: Calif. 1959. Dep. atty., ex-officio city prosecutor City of Glendale, Calif., 1959-62; assoc. James Brewer, Los Angeles, 1962-68, LaFollette, Johnson, Schroeter & DeHaas, Los Angeles, 1968-73; sole practice, Los Angeles, 1973—; arbitrator Los Angeles Superior Ct; judge pro tem Los Angeles Mcpl. Ct., Small Claims Ct., Traffic Ct.; lectr. and speaker in field. Bd. dirs. LosFeliz Improvement Assn., 1986-88, Zoning Commn.; co-chmn. Streets and Hwys. Commn. Mem. ABA, Calif. Bar Assn., Los Angeles County Bar Assn., Soc. Calif. Accts., Fed. Bar Assn., Am. Film Inst., Internat. Platform Assn. Home and Office: 813 N Doheny Dr Beverly Hills CA 90210-3528

DICKEY, GARY ALAN, minister; b. Santa Monica, Calif., Jan. 25, 1946; s. Charles Harry and Audrey W. (White) D.; m. Tamara Jean Kimble, Jan. 11, 1976. BA, UCLA, 1968; MDiv, Fuller Theol. Sem., Pasadena, 1972; DMin, Sch. Theology, Claremont, Calif., 1974. Assoc. pastor Magnolia Pk. United Meth. Ch., Burbank, Calif., 1974-78; sr. pastor St. James United Meth. Ch., Pasadena, 1978-90, First United Meth. Ch. of Canoga Park, 1990—; exec. com. mem. Calif.-Pacific Ann. Conf. Bd. of Ordained Ministry, 1980-88; chmn. Pasadena Dist. Com. on Ordained Ministry, 1978-90; supervising pastor Bd. Higher Edn., Nashville, 1978—. Recipient Polonia Restituta, Polish Peoples Republic, 1990. Mem. Soc. Colonial Wars, Soc. War of 1812 (chaplian 1989—), Soc. of Sons of Am. Revolution (chaplain 1988—, Outstanding Citizenship award 1990), Soc. of Sons of the Revolution, Descendants of Soldiers of Valley Forge, Soc. Sons Am. Colonists, Soc. Sons. Vets. Civil War, Vet. Corps Artillery State N.Y., United Empire Loyalists Assn. (Can.), Royal Soc. St. George (Eng.), Rotary (pres. 1989-90, Paul Harris fellow 1986). Republican. Methodist. Home: 22167 Bryant St

Canoga Park CA 91304-2306 Office: First United Meth Ch 22700 Sherman Way Canoga Park CA 91307-2396

DICKEY, GLENN ERNEST, JR., sports columnist; b. Virginia, Minn., Feb. 16, 1936; s. Glenn Ernest and Madlyn Marie (Emmert) D.; m. Nancy Jo McDaniel, Feb. 25, 1967; 1 son, Kevin Scott. B.A., U. Calif., Berkeley, 1958. Sports editor Watsonville (Calif.) Register-Pajoronian, 1958-63; sports writer San Francisco Chronicle, 1963-71, sports columnist, 1971—. Author: The Jock Empire, 1974, The Great No-Hitters, 1976, Champs and Chumps, 1976, The History of National League Baseball, 1979, The History of American League Baseball, 1980, (with Dick Berg) Eavesdropping America, 1980, America Has a Better Team, 1982, The History of Professional Basketball, 1982, The History of the World Series, 1984, (with Jim Tunney) Impartial Judgment: The Dean of NFL Referees Calls Football As He Sees It, 1988, San Francisco Forty-Niners: The Super Year, 1989; (with Bill Walsh) Building a Champion, 1990; Just Win, Baby, Al Davis and His Raiders, 1991; Sports Hero Kevin Mitchell (juvenile), 1993, Sports Hero Jerry Rice (juvenile), 1993; contbr. stories to Best Sports Stories, 1962, 68, 71, 75, 76. Home: 120 Florence Ave Oakland CA 94618-2249 Office: Chronicle Pub Co 901 Mission St San Francisco CA 94103-2988

DICKEY, ROBERT MARVIN (RICK DICKEY), property manager; b. Charleston, S.C., Dec. 3, 1950; s. John Lincoln II and Ruth (Marvin) D.; m. Teresa Ann Curry, Dec. 19, 1969 (div. 1979); 1 child, Gena Lynette. A of Computer Sci., USMC Degree Program, Washington, 1975. Cert. apt. property supr. Nat. Apt. Assn., Wash., occupancy specialist Nat. Ctr.for Housing Mgmt., Wash. Enlisted USMC, 1968, advanced through grades to staff sgt., 1968-78; shop mgr., bookkeeper Amalgamated Plant Co., Las Vegas, Nev., 1978-79; supr. constrn. Joseph Yousem Co., Las Vegas, 1979-80; apt. mgr. Robert A. McNeil Corp., Las Vegas, 1980, comml. bldg. mgr., leasing agt., 1980-82; asst. v.p., regional property mgr. Westminster Co., Las Vegas, 1982-87, Weyerhaeuser Mortgage Co., Las Vegas, 1988-89; pres., ptnr. Equinox Devel., Inc., Las Vegas, 1989-91; residential dept. mgr. R.W. Robideaux & Co., Spokane, Wash., 1991—. Contbr. articles to profl. jours. Mem. Inst. Real Estate Mgmt. (accredited residential mgr., legis. chmn. 1987-88,Accredited Residential Mgr. award 1985, 86, 90), Nev. Apt. Assn. (v.p. 1985, pres. 1988—, bd. dirs.), So. Nev. Homebuilders Assn., Las Vegas Bd. Realtors (mgmt. legis com. 1988).

DICKEY, ROBERT PRESTON, author, educator, poet; b. Flat River, Mo., Sept. 24, 1936; s. Delno Miren D. and Naomi Valentine (Jackson) D.; children: Georgia Rae, Shannon Ezra, Rain Dancer. BA, U. Mo., 1968, MA, 1969; PhD, Walden U., 1975. Instr. U. Mo., 1967-69; asst. prof. English and creative writing U. So. Colo., 1969-73; assoc. mem. faculty Pima Coll., Tucson, 1975-78. Author: (with Donald Justice, Thomas McAfee, Donald Drummond) poetry Four Poets, 1967, Running Lucky, 1969, Acting Immortal, 1970; Concise Dictionary of Lead River, Mo., 1972, The Basic Stuff of Poetry, 1972, Life Cycle of Seven Songs, 1972, McCabe Wants Chimes, 1973, Admitting Complicity, 1973; opera librettos Minnequa, 1976, The Witch of Tucson, 1976; Jimmie Cotton!, 1979, Way Out West, 1979, The Poetica Erotica of R.P. Dickey, 1989, The Little Book on Racism and Politics, 1990; contbr. poetry to popular mags., Poetry, Saturday Rev., Commonweal, Prairie Schooner; founder, editor: The Poetry Bag quar., 1966-71; poetry editor: So. Colo. Standard, 1973-74. With USAF, 1955-57. Recipient Mahan award for poetry U. Mo., 1965-66. Home: PO Box 4072 Taos NM 87571-9998

DICKEY, WILLIAM (HOBART DICKEY), humanities educator, poet; b. Bellingham, Wash., Dec. 15, 1928; s. Paul Condit and Anne Marie (Hobart) D. B.A., Reed Coll., 1951; M.A. (Woodrow Wilson fellow), Harvard, 1955; M.F.A., U. Iowa, 1956; postgrad., Jesus Coll. U. Oxford, Eng., 1959-60. Instr. Cornell U., Ithaca, N.Y., 1956-59; asst. prof. English Denison U., 1960-62; asst. prof. San Francisco State U., 1962-65, assoc. prof., 1966-69, prof. English and creative writing, 1970-91, prof. emeritus, 1991—, chmn. creative writing, 1974-77; vis. prof. English U. Hawaii, 1972. Author: Of the Festivity, 1959, Interpreter's House, 1964, Rivers of the Pacific Northwest, 1969, More Under Saturn, 1971, The Rainbow Grocery, 1978 (Juniper prize), The Sacrifice Consenting, 1981, Six Philosophical Songs, 1983, Joy, 1983, Brief Lives, 1985, The King of the Golden River, 1986, Metamorphoses, 1991, Night Journey, 1992. Recipient Union League prize Poetry mag., 1961, Commonwealth Club of Calif. medal, 1972, Juniper prize U. Mass. Press, 1978, Creative Writing award Am. Inst. Arts and Letters, 1980, Poetry award Bay Area Book Reviewers, 1986; fellow Fulbright Found., 1959-60, NEA, 1978-79. Mem. Calif. Assn. Tchrs. English (Classroom Excellence award 1985), Philol. Assn. Pacific Coast, MLA, (del. assembly 1974-76), PEN Am. Ctr., Phi Beta Kappa. Home: 1476 Willard St San Francisco CA 94117-3721

DICKINSON, ANN, fundraiser; b. Topeka, Sept. 12, 1961; d. Jacob Alan II and Ruth (Curd) D.; m. Michael James Mahoney, May 29, 1993. AB in History, Grinnell Coll., 1983; postgrad., McGill U., Montreal, Quebec, Can., 1985. Analyst, corp. fin. dept. E.F. Hutton & Co., Inc., N.Y.C., 1983-85; pres., owner The Dark Side, N.Y.C., 1985-87; asst. dir. individual giving Meml. Sloan-Kettering Cancer Ctr., N.Y.C., 1987-88, dir. spl. gifts, 1988-91; assoc. dir. devel. Sch. Humanities and Scis. Stanford (Calif.) U., 1991—; devel. asst. regional office Brandeis U., N.Y.C., 1987. Vol. interviewer Grinnell Coll., N.Y.C., San Francisco, 1983—; vol. Tom Huening for Congress, Palo Alto, Calif., 1992. Mem. Nat. Soc. Fund Raising Execs. Republican. Episcopalian. Home: 15 Hoffman Ave San Francisco CA 94114 Office: Stanford U Bldg One Stanford CA 94305

DICKINSON, DONALD CHARLES, library science educator; b. Schenectady, N.Y., June 9, 1927; s. Charles William and Stella Barney (Sheldon) D.; m. Colleen Eleanor Schindler, Aug. 7, 1954; children: Ann, Jean, Ellen, Mary, Kathleen, Sheila. AB, SUNY, Albany, 1949; MLS, U. Ill., 1951; PhD, U. Mich., 1964. Ref. librarian Cen. Mo. State Coll., Warrensburg, 1951-53, Eastern Mich. U., Ypsilanti, 1953-56; asst. acquisitions U. Kans., Lawrence, 1956-58; head librarian Bemidji (Minn.) State Coll., 1958-66; dir. reader service U. Mo., Columbia, 1966-69; dir. grad. library sch. U. Ariz., Tucson, 1969-78, prof. grad. library sch., 1979—. Author: Bio-bibliography Langston Hughes, 1967, 2d edit., 1972, Hellmut Lehmann-Haupt, 1975, Dictionary of American Book Collectors, 1986, George Watson Cole, 1990. Grantee Am. Philos. Assn., 1969; Andrew W. Mellon fellow Henry E. Huntington Libr., 1989. Mem. ALA (coun. 1972-73, travel grantee 1960), Bibliographic Soc. Am., Ariz. Libr. Assn. (pres. 1978-79), Grolier Club (N.Y.C.). Democrat. Office: Univ Ariz Sch Libr Sci 1515 E First St Tucson AZ 85719

DICKINSON, JACOB JOHN LOUIS, mechanical engineer; b. Honolulu, Dec. 17, 1957; s. Jacob Alan and Ruth (Curd) D.; m. Janis Miyeko Kibe, Feb. 25, 1983; children: Jacob Carl Toshiro, Ellen Tamiko, Alexander Seiji. Student, Deep Springs Coll., 1976-78, Washburn U., 1979; BSME, U. Wash., 1982; cert. advanced program in Artificial Intelligence, UCLA, 1988. Cert. knowledge engr. Sr. engr. Douglas Aircraft, Long Beach, Calif., 1983-87; engr., scientist specialist McDonnell Douglas Astronautics, Huntington Beach, Calif., 1987-89; lead engr. avionics software artificial intelligence group McDonnell Douglas Space Systems Co., Huntington Beach, Calif., 1989—. Chmn. decade fundraising Deep Springs Coll. Mem. AAAS, Am. Assn. for Artificial Intelligence.

DICKINSON, JAMES GORDON, editor; b. Melbourne, Australia, Nov. 13, 1940; came to U.S., 1974, naturalized, 1983; s. David Rushbrook and Lorna Aida (Anderson) D.; m. Carol Rosslyn McBurnie, Sept. 7, 1963; children: Craig, Peter (dec.), Samantha; m. Sheila Laraine Ferguson McManus, Aug. 20, 1982. Student Melbourne U., 1960-63. Cadet reporter Hobart Mercury, 1957-59, Melbourne Age, 1959-63; reporter Melbourne Herald, 1963-64, TV Channel O, Melbourne, 1964-66; cons. Internat. Public Relations Pty. Ltd., 1966-68; editor, pub. Australian Jour. Pharmacy, 1968-74; asst. exec. dir. Am. Pharm. Assn., Washington, 1975; sr. editor FDC Reports Inc., Washington, 1975-78; founder, editor Washington Drugwire, 1978-79; Washington bur. chief Drug Topics, Med. Econs. Co., 1978-83; Washington corr. Scrip, Clinica World Med. Device News, Animal Pharm World Vet. News (U.K.), 1978-85, Pharm. Tech., Pharm. Exec., 1977-89, N.Z. Pharmacy, Brit. Pharm. Jour., Drug News & Perspectives mag. (Spain), Med. Device and Diagnostic Industry mag., Med. Mktg. & Media, 1990—; pres., chief exec. officer Ferdic Inc., 1982—; editor, pub. Dickinson's FDA and Dickinson's PSAO industry newsletters, 1985—, VixeNews, 1989-90, Dickinson's Pharmacy newsletter, 1989—, Dickinson's FDA Inspection newsletter, 1992—; columnist syndicated all state pharm. jours., 1986—; cons. to drug industry; pres. Australian Monthly Newspapers and Periodicals Assn., 1972-74; founding sec. Melbourne Press Club, 1971-74. Editor: Weekly Pharmacy Reports, 1975-78. Mem. Australian Liberal Party, 1971-74; pres. Lee Forest Civic Assn., 1977-79. Mem. Periodical Corrs. Assn., Am. Pub. Health Assn. Club: Nat. Press (Washington). Office: PO Box 367 Las Cruces NM 88004-0365

DICKINSON, JANET MAE WEBSTER, relocation consulting executive; b. Cleve., Oct. 2, 1929; d. Richard and Gizella (Keplinger) Fisher; m. Rodney Earl Dickinson, June 18, 1965 (div. 1976); 1 child, Kimberly Cae. Grad., Larson Coll. for Women, New Haven; student, Portland State Coll. Lic. broker, Oreg. Pub. rels./promotion dir. KPTV-Channel 27, Portland, Oreg., 1951-54; exec. dir. Exposition-Recreation Commn., Portland, 1954-58; v.p. Art Lutz & Co., Realtors, Portland, 1975-79, Lutz Relocation Mgmt., Portland, 1977-79; corp. relocation mgr. Ga. Pacific Corp., Portland, 1979-82; pres., broker Ga. Pacific Fin. Co., Portland, 1980-82; pres., chief exec. officer The Dickinson Cons. Group, Beaverton, Oreg., 1982—; pres. Wheatherstone Press, Lake Oswego, Oreg., 1983—, The Relocation Ctr., Beaverton, 1984—; cons. in field; lectr. in field; conductor workshops/seminars in field. Author: The Complete Guide to Family Relocation, The International Move, Building Your Dream House, Obtaining the Highest Price for Your Home, Having a Successful Garage Sale, Moving with Children, My Moving Coloring Book, The Group Move, Counseling the Transferee, Games to Play in the Car, Portland (Oreg.) Facts Book, Welcome to the United States, many others; contbr. articles to profl. jours. Mem. Pres.'s Com. to Employ Physically Handicapped, Oreg. Prison Assn.; established Women's Aux. for Waverly Baby Home; bd. dirs. Columbia River coun. Girl Scouts U.S.A., Salvation Army; active various polit. orgns.; chmn. ways and means com. Oreg. Symphony Soc., Portland Art Mus., Assistance League, Portland Jr. Symphony, March of Dimes, others. Mem. Employee Relocation Coun., City Club, Multnomah Athletic Club, Tualatin Valley Econ. Devel. Assn. (dir. 1988—). Republican. Episcopalian. Home: 20 Wheatherstone Lake Oswego OR 97035-1916 Office: The Dickinson Cons Group Lincoln Ctr 10250 SW Greenburg Rd Ste 125 Portland OR 97223-5460

DICKINSON, J(EROLD) THOMAS, physics educator, materials science researcher; b. Detroit, Mar. 9, 1941; s. Jerold R. and Jean Alta (Flanagan) D.; m. Ruthellen Carol Pugh, 1965 (div.); 1 child, Jennifer Anne; m. Diane Louise Allison, July 8, 1980. BA in Physics, Math, Western Mich. U., 1963; MS in Physics, U. Mich., 1964, PhD, 1968. Asst. prof. physics Wash. State U., Pullman, 1968-74, assoc. prof. physics, chem. physics, 1974-79, prof., 1979—, prof. materials sci., 1990—, mem. grad. faculty mech. and materials engring., 1990—; acting dir. Ctr. for Materials Rsch., Wash. State U., Pullman, 1989—. Contbr. numerous articles to profl. jours. Fellow Am. Vacuum Soc. (chmn. Pacific N.W. 1993-95); mem. Am. Phys. Soc., Am. Ceramics Soc., Am. Chem. Soc. Democrat. Unitarian. Office: Wash State U Dept Physics Pullman WA 99164-2814

DICKINSON, LEE GEORGE, retired systems test engineer; b. Seattle, Nov. 27, 1935; s. Lee Edwin Dickinson and Georgina Evelyn (Hedges) Rushworth; m. Grace Janet Leach, Dec. 21, 1956; children: L. Gordon, Nancy A., Daniel B. BS in Meterology and Climatology, U. Wash., Seattle, 1957, MS in Atmospheric Scis., 1963; MBA in Fin. Planning, Golden Gate U., 1987; postgrad., U. Wis., 1967-70. Rsch. asst. U. Wash., 1957-58; commd. 2d lt. USAF, 1958, advanced through grades to lt. col., ret., 1979; systems test engr. specialist Lockheed Missles & Space Co., Sunnyvale, Calif., 1979-92; ret. Missles & Space Co., Sunnyvale, Calif., 1992; rep. Waddell & Reed, San Jose, Calif., 1988-89. Mem. Am. Meterol. Soc., Am. Geophys. Union, Nat. Weather Assn. (charter), Assn. Am. Weather Observers, Oreg. Small Woodlands Assn.

DICKINSON, RANDOLPH PAUL, chemist; b. Glendale, Calif., Sept. 23, 1945; s. Paul Bruce and Fern (Barrett) D.; m. Loretta Sue Meeks-Smith, Nov. 27, 1971 (div. 1984); children: Paul, Taryn; m. Lori Jo Dresselhaus, July 23, 1988; stepchildren: Elizabeth Keesling, James Keesling. BS, Calif. Inst. Tech., 1967; MS, U. Calif., San Diego, 1970. Rsch. assoc. U. So. Calif. Med. Sch., L.A., 1971-74, Hyland Diagnostics, Costa Mesa, Calif., 1974-79; sr. rsch. chemist Beckman Instruments, Brea, Calif., 1979-84; mgr. new reagent devel. Internat. Immunology Corp., Murrieta, Calif., 1984-86, dir. R&D, 1986-89, v.p. R&D, 1989—. Mem. Am. Assn. Clin. Chemistry, Mensa. Office: Internat Immunology Corp 25549 Adams Ave Murrieta CA 92562

DICKINSON, RITA HARKINS, educational consultant; b. Long Beach, Calif., Sept. 19, 1949; d. Joseph Marr and Dorothy Lucille (Gentry) Harkins; m. Thomas Wood Dickinson, June 4, 1977; 1 child, Joseph Harkins Dickinson. BS in Edn., No. Ariz. U., 1972, B Music Edn., 1972, MA in Edn., 1973. Cellist Flagstaff (Ariz.) Symphony Orch., 1967-72, Long Beach (Calif.) Symphony Orch., 1970; head tchr. Prescott (Ariz.) pub. schs., 1973-75; spl. edn. dir. Cave Creek Sch. Dist., Ariz., 1975-79; instr. Rio Salado Community Coll., Phoenix, 1978-83; pres. A.M. Pubs., Phoenix, 1983-88; pub.'s rep. Charlesbridge Pub., Watertown, Mass., 1980-92; ednl. cons. McDougal, Littell and Co., Evanston, Ill., 1992—. Co-author: Creatures and Features of the Desert, 1980, Creatures and Features of the Zoo, 1982, Creatures and Features of the Seashore, 1984, others. Bd. dirs. Ariz. Spl. Olympics, 1970—; mem. Ariz. Dept. Edn. Task Force, 1987-88, Madison Sch. Bd., Phoenix, 1989-93 (pres. 1991-92); participant Ariz. Town Hall ON Edn., Prescott, 1989; active Jr. League of Phoenix, 1985-93. Mem. Ariz. Acad., Valley Leadership Alumni Assn. (bd. dirs., treas. 1991-92, 93—), Ariz. Ednl. Rep. Assn., Phoenix Panhellenic Assn. (pres. 1985-86), Nat. Sch. Bd. Assn. (fed. rels. network), Malibou Lake Mountain Club, Gamma Phi Beta. Democrat. Congregationalist. Home: 2002 E Rancho Dr Phoenix AZ 85016-2702

DICKINSON, ROBERT EARL, atmospheric scientist, educator; b. Millersburg, Ohio, Mar. 26, 1940; s. Leonard Earl and Carmen L. (Ostby) D.; m. Nancy Mary Mielinis, Jan. 5, 1974. AB in Chemistry and Physics, Harvard U., 1961; MS in Meteorology, MIT, 1962, PhD in Meteorology, 1966. Rsch. assoc. MIT, Cambridge, 1966-68; scientist Nat. Ctr. Atmospheric Rsch., Boulder, Colo., 1968-73, sr. scientist, 1973-90, head climate sect., 1975-81, dep. dir. A.A.P. div., 1981-86, acting dir., 1986-87; prof. atmospheric physics U. Ariz., 1990—; mem. climate rsch. com. NRC, Washington, 1985-90, chmn., 1987-90, com. earth sci., 1985-88, global change com., 1985-92; mem. WCRP sci. steering group GEWEX, 1988-92; UNU steering com. Climatic, Biotic and Human Interactions in Humid Tropics, 1984-88, steering com. Internat. Satellite Land Surface Climatology project, 1984-89. Editor: The Geophysiology of Amazonia, 1986; contbr. articles to profl. jours. Fellow AAAS, Am. Meteorol. Soc. (chmn. com. biometeorol. and aerobiol. 1987-89, Meisinger award 1973, Editors award 1976, Jule Charney award 1987), Am. Geophys. Union (com. earth as a system 1986-88, pres.-elect. 1988-90, pres. 1990-92); mem. NAS, Internat. Assn. Meteorol. and Atmospheric Physics (sec. climate commn. 1983-87). Democrat. Home: 9290 N Yorkshire Ct Tucson AZ 85741-9357 Office: U Ariz Inst Atmospheric Physics Tucson AZ 85721

DICKINSON, WILLIAM RICHARD, geologist, educator; b. Nashville, Oct. 26, 1931; s. Jacob McGavock and Margaret Adams (Smith) D.; m. Margaret Anne Palmer, 1953 (div. 1968); children: Ben William, Edward Ross; m. Jacqueline Jane Klein, Feb. 20, 1970. BS in Petroleum Engring., Stanford U., 1952, MS in Geology, 1956, PhD in Geology, 1958. Prof. geology Stanford U., Palo Alto, Calif., 1958-79; prof. geoscis. U. Ariz., Tucson, 1979-91; retired, 1991. Contbr. and editor articles to profl. jours. Lt. USAF, 1952-54. Fellow Guggenheim Meml. 1965. Fellow Geol. Soc. Am. (Penrose medal 1991); mem. Am. Geophys. Union, Am. Assn. Petroleum Geologists, Nat. Acad. Sci., Nat. Assn. Geology Tchrs., Soc. for Sedimentary Geology.

DICKS, NORMAN DE VALOIS, congressman; b. Bremerton, Wash., Dec. 16, 1940; s. Horace D. and Eileen Cora D.; m. Suzanne Callison, Aug. 25, 1967; children: David, Ryan. BA, U. Wash., 1963, JD, 1968; LLD (hon.), Gonzaga U., 1987. Bars: Wash. 1968, D.C., 1978. Salesman, Boise Cascade Corp., Seattle, 1963; labor negotiator Kaiser Gypsum Co., Seattle, 1964; legis. asst. to Senator Warren Magnuson of Wash., 1968-73, adminstrv. asst., 1973-76; mem. 95th-103rd Congresses from 6th Wash. dist., Washington, D.C., 1977—. Mem. U. Wash. Alumni Assn., Sigma Nu. Democrat. Lutheran. Office: US Ho Reps 2467 Rayburn House Office Bldg Washington DC 20515*

DICKSON, FRANK WILSON, geologist, educator; b. Oplin, Tex., Nov. 28, 1922; s. William Elmer and Annie May D.; m. Elizabeth Rose Broggi, Sept. 30, 1945; children: Frank Woodrow, Elizabeth Elaine, Bruce William, Leslie Anne, Donald George. BA in Geology, UCLA, 1950, BS in Chemistry, 1959, PhD in Geology, 1956. Registered geologist Calif. Rsch. geologist Shell Devel. Co., Houston, 1955-56; prof. geology U. Calif., Riverside, 1956-69, Stanford U., Palo Alto, Calif., 1969-79; rsch. scientist Oak Ridge (Tenn.) Nat. Lab., 1979-84; adj. prof. and rschr. Mackay Sch. Mines, U. Nev., Reno, 1984—. Home: 110 E Sky Ranch Blvd Sparks NV 89436

DICKSON, ROBERT LEE, lawyer; b. Hot Springs, Ark., Sept. 3, 1932; s. Constantine John and Georgia Marie (Allen) D.; m. Christina Farrar, Oct. 29, 1978; children—Robert Lee, Geoffrey, Alexandra, Christopher, George, John. B.B.A., U. Tex., 1959, LL.B., 1960. Bar: Tex. 1960, Calif. 1965, U.S. Dist. Ct. (no. dist.) Tex. 1960, U.S. Dist. Ct. (ea. dist.) Wis. 1979, U.S. Supreme Ct. 1980, U.S. Dist. Ct. (ea. dist.) Calif. 1983, U.S. Ct. Appeals (7th cir.) 1983, U.S. Dist. Ct. (no. and so. dists.) Calif. 1984, U.S. Ct. Appeals (9th cir.) 1987, U.S. Ct. Appeals (1st and 10th cirs.) 1989. Assoc. to ptnr. Eplen, Daniel & Dickson, Abilene, Tex., 1960-65; assoc. to sr. ptnr. Haight, Dickson, Brown & Bonesteel, Santa Monica, Calif., 1965-88; sr. ptnr. Dickson, Carlson & Campillo, Santa Monica, 1988—; bd. advisors UCLA Sch Nursing. Contbr. articles to profl. jours. Fellow Am. Coll. Trial Lawyers; mem. Ind. Bar Com., Def. Rsch. Inst. (steering com. of drug and device litigation com.), Fedn. Ins. and Corp. Counsel (chmn. pharm. liability litigation sect. 1984-87, v.p. 1986-89, bd. dirs. 1989—, sec./treas. 1991-92, pres.-elect 1992-93), Am. Bd. Trial Advocates, Assn. So. Calif. Def. Counsel (pres. 1976). Republican. Am. Baptist. Club: Bel Air Bay (Pacific Palisades). Home: 14952 Alva Dr Pacific Palisades CA 90272-4401 Office: Dickson Carlson & Campillo 120 Broadway 3d Fl PO Box 2122 Santa Monica CA 90407-2122

DICKSON, STEWART PRICE, graphics programmer; b. Cooperstown, N.Y., July 16, 1956; s. Frederick Stoever III and Jean Stewart (Price) D.; m. Rebecka DeAnn Yaeger, Oct. 2, 1981; children: Price Alexandra, Nathaniel Stewart. BEE, U. Del., 1981. Janitor Rollins Broadcasting Sta. WAMS, Wilmington, Del., 1973-77; rsch. asst. Dept. Elec. Engring. and Physics, U. Del., Newark, 1978-79; devel. engr. Western Electric Co., Lisle, Ill., 1980-84, AT&T Technologies, Inc., Naperville, Ill., 1980-84; dir. computer-generated imagery Goldsholl Design and Film, Inc., Northfield, Ill., 1984-87; 3D graphics programmer The Post Group, Inc., Hollywood, Calif., 1988—; cons., lectr. Calif. Inst. of the Arts, Valencia, 1989—; cons., artist Wolfram Rsch., Inc., Champaign, Ill., 1990—. Contbr./illustrator articles to profl. jours.; profl. sculptor, 1981—; patentee in field. Mem. Am. Mensa, Ltd., Assn. for Computing Machinery (spl. project grant 1990 graphics spl. interest group), Internat. Sculpture Ctrs., Artists Using Sci. and Tech., Internat. Soc. for the Arts, Scis. and Tech. Home: 1105 Burtonwood Ave Thousand Oaks CA 91360 Office: The Post Group 6335 Homewood Ave Los Angeles CA 90028

DICKSTEIN, HAROLD DAVID, lawyer; b. Bisbee, Ariz., Mar. 31, 1929; s. Joseph Louis and Sara Rebecca (Brown) D.; m. Dolores Feldman, Mar. 9, 1952 (div. Mar. 1977); children: Paul Warren, Dawn Carol; m. Marion Yvonne Blumenthal, May 22, 1977. BSEE, U. Ariz., 1951; MS in Engring., U. Calif., San Diego, 1959; JD, U. San Diego, 1968. Bar: Calif. 1969. Electronic sci. staff Navy Electronics Lab, San Diego, 1951-53; group supr. Gen. Dynamics, San Diego, 1953-59, design specialist, 1965-69; group supr. Cubic Corp., San Diego, 1959-61, 63-65; chief engr. TEMEC div. Cubic Corp., L.A., 1961-63; pvt. practice law San Diego, 1969-70; gen. ptnr. Millsberg & Dickstein, San Diego, 1970-82; sr. ptnr. Dickstein, Truxaw, Tannenberg, San Diego, 1982-92, Dickstein & Truxaw, San Diego, 1992—. Contbr. articles on electronics to profl. publs. Pres. Temple Emanuel, San Diego, 1969-71. Mem. Calif. State Bar, San Diego County Bar, San Diego Family Law Specialists, Kiwanis, Masons, Shriners. Office: Dickstein & Truxaw Ste 101 438 Camino Del Rio S San Diego CA 92108

DIEDERICH, J(OHN) WILLIAM, financial consultant; b. Ladysmith, Wis., Aug. 30, 1929; s. Joseph Charles and Alice Florence (Yost) D.; m. Mary Theresa Klein, Nov. 25, 1950; children: Mary Theresa Diederich Evans, Robert Douglas, Charles Stuart, Michael Mark, Patricia Anne Diederich Irelan, Donna Maureen (dec.), Denise Brendan, Carol Lynn Diederich Weaver, Barbara Gail, Brian Donald, Tracy Maureen, Theodora Bernadette, Tamara Alice, Lorraine Angela. PhB, Marquette U., Milw., 1951; MBA with high distinction, Harvard U., 1955. With Landmark Comm., Inc., Norfolk, Va., 1955-90, v.p., treas., 1965-73, exec. v.p. fin., 1973-78, exec. v.p. community newspapers, 1978-82, exec. v.p., CFO, 1982-90, fin. cons., 1990—; chmn. bd. dirs. Landmark Community Newspapers, Inc., 1977-88; pres. Exec. Productivity Systems, Inc., 1982-88, LCI Credit Corp, 1991—, Landmark TV, Inc., 1991—, LTM Investments, Inc., 1991—; instr. Boston U., 1954, Old Dominion U., 1955-59. Bd. dirs. Landmark Commn., Inc., Telecable Corp., Trader Pub. Landmark Found. Lt. col. USMC, 1951-53, USMCR, 1953-71 (ret.). Mem. SAR, Nat. Assn. Accts., Am. Numismatic Assn., Nat. Geneal. Soc., Wis. Geneal. Soc., Pa. Geneal. Soc., Sigma Delta Chi. Roman Catholic. Home and Office: PO Box 7334 1466 Glarus Ct Incline Village NV 89452-7334

DIEDRICK, GERALDINE ROSE, nurse; b. Chgo.; d. Milton Edward and Rose Agnes (Michalski) Goodman; R.N., Mt. San Antonio Coll., Walnut, Calif., 1963; BS, Calif. State U., L.A., 1966; MS, UCLA, 1968; divorced; 1 son, Scott Wesley. Nurse, State of Calif., 1960-83, dir. nursing Met. State Hosp., Norwalk, 1977-83; cons. in mental health, devel. disabilities. Recipient Letter of Commendation, State of Calif., 1974-77. Mem. Am. Nurses Assn., Nat. League Nursing, Am. Assn. Devel. Disabilities, Calif. Nurses Assn. (svc. awards), Am. Hosp. Assn., World Future Soc., Town Hall Calif. Democrat. Lutheran. Contbr. to profl. jours.

DIEHL, DIGBY ROBERT, journalist; b. Boonton, N.J., Nov. 14, 1940; s. Edwin Samuel and Mary Jane Shirley (Ellsworth) D.; m. Kay Beyer, June 6, 1981; 1 dau., Dylan Elizabeth. A.B. in Am. Studies (Henry Rutgers scholar), Rutgers U., 1962; M.A. in Theatre Arts, UCLA, 1966, postgrad., 1966-69. Editor Learning Center, Inc., Princeton, N.J., 1962-64; dir. research Creative Playthings, Los Angeles, 1964-66; editor Coast mag., Los Angeles, 1966-68, Show mag., Los Angeles, 1968-69; book editor Los Angeles Times, 1969-78; v.p., editor-in-chief Harry N. Abrams, Inc., N.Y.C., 1978-80; book editor LA. Herald Examiner, 1981-86; movie critic, entertainment editor Sta. KCBS TV, Los Angeles, 1986-88; book columnist Playboy mag., Pasadena, Calif., 1988—; instr. journalism UCLA, 1969-78; jurist Nat. Book Awards, 1972, Internat. Imitation Hemingway Contest, 1978—; mem. nominating com. Nat. Medal for Lit., 1972-75; v.p. Nat. Book Critics Cir., 1975-78, bd. dirs., 1981-87; jurist Am. Book Awards, 1981-85, v.p. programming, 1984-86; lit. columnist IBM/Prodigy, 1987—; columnist Modern Maturity, Long Beach, Calif., 1987—. Author: Supertalk: Extraordinary Conversations, 1974, Front Page, 1981. Trustee KPFK-Pacifica Found. Recipient; Irita Van Doren award, 1977. Mem. AAUP, PEN (pres. L.A. Ctr. 1987, v.p. treas. 1988—), AFTRA, Am. Soc. Journalists and Authors, Writers Guild Am., Phi Beta Kappa, Phi Sigma Delta. Home: 788 S Lake Ave Pasadena CA 91106-3948

DIEHL, SHARON FAY, geologist; b. Mesa, Ariz., Apr. 21, 1951; d. Roy Francis and Shirley Ann (Favre) D.; m. Michael Peter Chornack, Sept. 27, 1985. BA, U. Colo., 1974; postgrad., Colo. Sch. Mines, 1977-84; M in Basic Sci., U. Colo., 1988. Geologist Homestake Mining Co., San Francisco, 1974-75, Power Resources, Denver, 1976; phys. sci. tech. U.S. Geol. Survey, Denver, 1976-81, geologist, 1981—; petrologic cons. water resources div. U.S. Geol. Survey, 1988-91, Bur. of Reclamation, Denver, 1992. Contbr. articles to profl. jours. Speaker Outreach U.S. Geol. Survey, 1989—. Mem. Colo. Scientific Soc., Geol. Soc. Am., Soc. for Sedimentary Geology, Sigma Xi. Democrat. Home: 830 32d St Boulder CO 80303 Office: US Geol Survey MS 966 Box 25046 Denver Fed Ctr Denver CO 80225

DIEMER, EMMA LOU, composer, music educator; b. Kansas City, Mo., Nov. 24, 1927; d. George Willis and Myrtle (Casebolt) D. MusB, Yale U., 1949, MusM, 1950; PhD, Eastman Sch. Music, 1960. Composer-in-residence Arlington (Va.) Schs., 1959-61; composer, cons. pub. schs., Arlington and Balt., 1964-65; prof. theory and composition U. Md., College Park, 1965-70; prof. emerita theory and composition U. Calif., Santa Barbara, 1971-91; organist Ch. of the Reformation, Washington, 1962-71, Ch. of Christ, Santa Barbara, 1973-84, 1st Presbyn. Ch., Santa Barbara, 1984—. Composer of over 100 choral and instrumental compositions including Music for Woodwind Quartet, 1976, Four Poems of Alice Meynell for Soprano and Chamber Ensemble, 1977, Symphony No. 2, 1980, Suite for Orchestra, 1981, Suite of Homages, 1985, Church Rock, 1986, Variations for Piano, 4 Hands, 1987, String Quartet No. 1, 1987, Serenade for String Orch., 1988, Concerto for Marimba, 1990, Concerto fo Piano, 1991, Sextet, 1992, Four Biblical Settings for Organ, 1992; composer-in-residence Santa Barbara Symphony, 1990—. Fulbright scholar, 1952-53; grantee Ford Found. Young Composers, 1959-61, Kindler Found. Commn., 1963, Nat. Endowment Arts, 1980-81; Kennedy Ctr. Friedham award, 1992. Mem. Am. Guild Organists, Internat. League Women Composers, Am. Women Composers, ASCAP (ann. awards 1962—), Am. Music Ctr., Mu Phi Epsilon. Democrat. Presbyterian.

DIENER, ROYCE, corporate director, retired health care services company executive; b. Balt., Mar. 27, 1918; s. Louis and Lillian (Goodman) D.; m. Jennifer S. Flinton; children: Robert, Joan, Michael. BA, Harvard U.; LLD, Pepperdine U. Comml. lending officer, investment banker various locations to 1972; pres. Am. Med. Internat., Inc., Beverly Hills, Calif., 1972-75, pres., chief exec. officer, 1975-78, chmn., chief exec. officer, 1978-85, chmn. bd., 1986-88, chmn. exec. com., 1986-89; bd. dirs. Calif. Econ. Devel. Corp., Acuson, Inc., Advanced Tech. Venture Funds, Am. Health Properties, AMI Health Svcs., plc., Consortium 2000. Author: Financing a Growing Business, 1966, 3d edit., 1978. Bd. visitors Grad. Sch. Mgmt., UCLA; mem. governing bd., UCLA Med. Ctr.; mem. vis. com. Med. Sch. and Sch. Dental Medicine, Harvard U.; bd. dirs. L.A. Philharm. Assn., L.A. chpt. ARC, Heritage Sq. Mus., Santa Monica. Served to capt. USAF, 1942-46, PTO. Decorated D.F.C. with oak leaf cluster. Mem. L.A. C. of C. (bd. dirs.), Calif. C. of C. (bd. dirs.), Calif. Bus. Round Table (bd. dirs.), Harvard Club, Regency Club, Calif. Yacht Club, Riviera Country Club (L.A.), Marks Club (London).

DIEPHOLZ, DANIEL RAY, real estate consultant, accountant; b. Hemet, Calif., Aug. 25, 1964; s. Eugene L. and Ruby J. (Forsch) D. BSBA in Acctg., Valparaiso U., 1985; MS in Real Estate with acad. honors, NYU, 1990. CPA, Calif.; lic. real estate broker, Calif. Auditor Blue Cross Calif., Woodland Hills, 1986-87; corp. fin. assoc., v.p. Bateman Eichler, Hill Richards Inc., L.A., N.Y.C., 1987-89; real estate cons. Price Waterhouse, L.A., 1990—; chmn. bd. Taos Palms Inc., L.A., 1990—. Mem. Nat. Assn. Accts. (bd. dirs. 1990—). Republican. Mem. LDS Ch. Home: 270 N Canon Dr # 1140 Beverly Hills CA 90210-5323 Office: Price Waterhouse 1880 Century Park E Los Angeles CA 90067-1600

DIERICKX, MARY FAHY, historian, researcher; b. San Diego, June 1, 1941; d. Phil Arthur and Elizabeth (Fahy) D.; m. Alvin Lyle Cox, Aug. 30, 1959 (div. Sept. 1981); children: Elizabeth, Fred, Georgiana, Hilary, Ian, Julia, Kelly, Loring, Megan. AA, Pierce Coll., L.A., 1974; BA, San Francisco State Coll., 1980. Founder Mansion Memoirs, House Histories, San Francisco, 1985—; lectr. Magic Castle, Hollywood, Calif., 1984, 86, Calif. Hist. Soc., San Francisco, 1989-91, Browning Soc., San Francisco, 1988-91, Found. for San Francisco's Archtl. Heritage, 1986, City Guides, San Francisco, 1990, 92, various sr. citizen ctrs., San Francisco, 1991—. Contbr. articles to profl. jours.; contbr. Guidelines, 1981—. Docent Calif. Hist. Soc., San Francisco, 1978-91. Recipient Golden Scissors award NAAFA, Inc., 1992. Mem. Acad. Magical Arts, St. Vincent de Paul Soc. (pres. 1990—). Democrat. Roman Catholic. Home: 149 1/2 Prentiss St San Francisco CA 94110-5729

DIETHRICH, EDWARD BRONSON, heart institute executive, cardiovascular surgeon; b. Toledo, Aug. 6, 1935; m. Gloria Baldwin, June 17, 1956; children: Lynn, Edward Bronson II. A.B., U. Mich., 1956, M.D., 1960. Diplomate: Am. Bd. Surgery, Am. Bd. Thoracic Surgery. Intern. St. Joseph Mercy Hosp., Ann Arbor, Mich., 1960-61; resident in surgery St. Joseph Mercy Hosp. and U. Mich. Med. Ctr., Ann Arbor, 1961-62, 64-65, Henry Ford Hosp., Detroit, 1963-64; resident in thoracic and cardiovascular surgery Baylor Coll. of Medicine Hosp., Houston, 1965-66; instr. Baylor Coll. of Medicine Hosp., 1966-67, asst. prof. surgery, 1967-71; med. dir. Ariz. Heart Inst., Phoenix, 1971—; pres. Ariz. Heart Inst. Found., Phoenix, 1971—; dir., chmn. dept. cardiovascular services, dir. and chief cardiovascular surgery and heart,lung transplantation, Healthwest Regional Med. Ctr., 1987—. Author: Heart Test, 1981; editor: Noninvasive Cardiovascular Diagnosis, 197i, 80, Noninvasive Assessment of the Cardiovascular System, 1982, Women and Heart Disease, 1992. Mem. Pres.'s Council for Phys. Fitness and Sports. Recipient U. Mich. Regents Alumni Honor award, 1953-54; recipient Med. Research award St. Joseph Mercy Hosp., 1963, 64, San Francisco Film Festival 1st prize, 1967, Cardiovascular Surgery Adv. Panel citation Ethicon, Inc., 1976. Fellow Am. Coll. Cardiology, Am. Coll. Chest Physicians (merit cert 1970, Outstanding Film award 1973, 77); mem. AMA (Hektoen Gold Medal award 1970), Am. Coll. Angiology, ACS, Am. Fedn. for Clin. Research, Am. Heart Assn. (council on cardiovascular diseases), Am. Trauma Soc., Assn. for Acad. Surgery, Denton A. Cooley Cardiovascular Surg. Soc. (exec. com. 1977-78), Frederick A. Coller Surg. Soc. (award 1963), Internat. Cardiovascular Soc., Michael E. DeBakey Internat. Cardiovascular Soc., Samson Thoracic Surg. Soc., Surg. Soc. Chile, Soc. for Vascular Surgery, Soc. Thoracic Surgeons, Soc. Acad. Surgeons, Southwestern Surg. Congress, Jordanian Surg. Soc., Nu Sigma Nu. Office: Ariz Heart Inst 2632 N 20th St Phoenix AZ 85006

DIETRICH, WILLIAM ALAN, reporter; b. Tacoma, Sept. 29, 1951; s. William Richard and Janice Lenore (Pooler) D.; m. Holly Susan Roberts, Dec. 19, 1970; children: Lisa, Heidi. BA, Western Wash. U., 1973. Reporter Bellingham (Wash.) Herald, 1973-76, Gannet News Svc., Washington, 1976-78, Vancouver (Wash.) Columbian, 1978-82, Seattle Times, 1982—. Author: The Final Forest, 1992. Recipient Paul Tobenkin award Columbia U., 1986, Pulitzer prize Columbia U., 1990; Nieman fellow Harvard U., 1987-88. Office: Seattle Times PO Box 70 Seattle WA 98111-0070

DIETTERICH, THOMAS GLEN, computer scientist, educator; b. South Weymouth, Mass., Nov. 23, 1954; s. Paul Merritt and Charlotte Eleanor (Jones) D.; m. Carol Jane Rivin, Apr. 28, 1985; children: Noah Albert, Hannah Rose. AB, Oberlin Coll., 1977; MS, U. Ill., Champaign, 1979; PhD, Stanford U., 1984. Asst. prof. Oreg. State U., Corvallis, 1985-88, assoc. prof., 1988—; sr. scientist Arris Pharm. Corp., South San Francisco, Calif., 1992—. Editor: Readings in Machine Learning, 1990; editor Jour. Machine Learning, 1989—, exec. editor, 1992—; contbr. articles to profl. jours. Trustee Oberlin Coll., 1977-80. Recipient grad. fellowship IBM, 1982, 83, 4 rsch. grants NSF, 1 rsch. grant NASA; named Presdl. Young Investigator NSF, 1987. Mem. AAAS, Computer Soc. of IEEE, Assn. Computing Machinery, Am. Assn. Artificial Intelligence (program co-chair 1990, councilor 1990—), Am. Statis. Assn., Cognitive Sci. Soc., Internat. Neural Networks Soc., Phi Beta Kappa, Sigma Xi. Office: Oreg State U Dept Computer Sci 303 Dearborn Hall Corvallis OR 97331

DIETZ, DAVID, physicist, mathematician; b. Bklyn., Mar. 10, 1946; s. Charles and Beatrice (Harris) D.; m. Sandra Louise Chesler, Aug. 28, 1966; children: Alysa, Elana, Sara. BS, UCLA, 1966; MS, Ind. U., 1969, AM, 1970, PhD, 1975. Assoc. instr. Math & Physics Depts., Ind. U., Bloomington, 1970-73; physicist U.S. Naval Fleet Analysis Ctr., Corona, Calif., 1973-76, U.S. Naval Weapons Evaluation Facility, Albuquerque, 1976-80; rsch. physicist U.S. Air Force Test/Evaluation Ctr., Albuquerque, 1980-82, U.S. Air Force Weapons Lab./Phillips Lab., Albuquerque, 1982—; lectr. depts. math. and physics U. N.Mex., Albuquerque, 1980-91; adj. asst. prof. Embry Riddle Aeronautical U., Albuquerque, 1992—; participating guest Lawrence Livermore Nat. Lab., 1988-90; guest scientist Los Alamos Nat. Lab., 1990—. Contbr. articles to profl. jours. Dow Chem. Co. scholar, 1963-66; NDEA fellow, 1966-69, NSF trainee, 1969-70. Mem. Am. Math. Soc., Am. Phys. Soc., Soc. for Indsl. and Applied Math., Sigma Xi. Home: 4916 Camino De Monte NE Albuquerque NM 87111-2931 Office: USAF Phillips Lab High Energy Plasmas Div-WSP Kirtland A F B NM 87117

DIETZ, JAMES LOWELL, economics educator, author; b. Chgo., June 11, 1947; s. James Lowell and Edna Barbara (Maclean) D.; m. Lydia E. Vélez, Aug. 24, 1981; 1 child, Jaime Antonio Dietz-Vélez. BS, Calif. Poly. Inst., Pomona, 1969; MA, U. Calif., Riverside, 1970, PhD, 1974. Prof. econs. Calif. State U., Fullerton, 1973—; vis. prof. U. Calif., Irvine, 1977-78. Author: Economic History of Puerto Rico, 1986; editor: Latin America's Economic Development, 1987, Progress Toward Development in Latin America, 1990. Recipient Outstanding Prof. award Calif. State U. Sch. Bus. Adminstrn. and Econs., 1987. Mem. Assn. for Evolutionary Econs. (bd. dirs. 1988-91), Latin Am. Studies Assn., Mystery Writers Am. Roman Catholic. Office: Calif State U Econs Dept Fullerton CA 92634

DIETZ, PATRICIA ANN, city administrator; b. L.A., Nov. 30, 1958; m. Frank Raymond Dietz, July 1, 1978; children: Lindy K., Frank R. Jr. BA in Polit. Sci., U. Colo., 1983; MA in Psychology, Pepperdine U., 1993; Paralegal Cert., U. San Diego, 1988. Investment broker 1st Investors Corp., Colorado Springs, Colo., 1986-88; paralegal Law Offices of Ben Williams, Santa Monica, Calif., 1988-89; mgmt. analyst Bur. of Engring., City of L.A., 1989—; camp commandant Operation Safe Harbor-Haitian Humanitarian Relief Effort, 1992. Mem. Parent Tchr. Student Assn., Rosamond, Calif., 1992. Capt. USAR, 1986—. Nat. Urban fellow, 1991. Mem. Civil Affairs Assn., Res. Officers Assn., Engrs. and Architects Assn. Republican.

DIETZ, ROBERT ELDON, physicist; b. Joplin, Mo., May 8, 1931; s. Alvah Eldon and Julia Lucille (McKenna) D.; m. Florence Harriett Chinn, Mar. 31, 1956; children: Tamara, Benjamin. BS, Tex. Tech U., 1956; PhD, Northwestern U., 1960. Mem. tech. staff AT&T Bell Labs., Murray Hill, N.J., 1959-85, disting. mem. tech. staff., 1985-87; sr. prin. engr. Boeing, Seattle, 1987—. Contbr. over 50 rsch. articles on solid state physics to profl. jours. Sgt. U.S. Army, 1951-54. Home: 10725 Marine View Dr SW Seattle WA 98146

DIETZ, ROBERT SINCLAIR, retired geology educator; b. Westfield, N.J., Sept. 14, 1914; s. Louis Andrew Dietz and Bertha Staiger; m. Nanon Grinstead, 1954 (div. 1974); children: Drew Loren, Robert Rex. BS, U. Ill., 1937, MS, 1939, PhD, 1941; DSc (honoris causa), Ariz. State U., 1988. With USN Electronic Lab., 1946-54. 59-63; asst. dir. Office Naval Rsch., London, 1954-59; with U.S. Coast and Geodetic Survey, 1963-70, Nat. Oceanic and Atmospheric Adminstrn., 1970-77; prof. geology Ariz. State U., Tempe, 1977-85, prof. emeritus, 1985—; vis. prof. U. Ill., 1974, Wash. State U., 1975, Washington U., 1976, Farleigh Dickenson U., 1976, Tuebingen U., Fed. Republic Germany, 1978, U. Tokyo, 1980; adj. prof. Scripps Inst. Oceanography, 1949-53, U. Miami, 1963-73. Author about 250 sci. papers and articles and 4 books, including ((with Jacques Piccard) Seven Miles Down: Story of Bathyscaph Trieste, 1961, Creation/Evolution Satiricon: Creationism Bashed, 1987; co-author Present State of Plate Tectonics, 1977. Patron Nat. Ctr. for Sci. Edn., Berkeley, Calif., 1987—. Lt. col. USAF, 1941-45. Decorated World War II, 5 medals; recipient Superior Civilian Svc. award USN, 1960, Antarctic Svc. medal Navy-Byrd Expedition, 1946-47, Outstanding Sci. Paper award U.S. Coast and Geodetic Survey, 1968, Gold medal U.S. Dept. Commerce, Alexander von Humboldt prize Fed. Republic Germany, 1978, Francis P. Shepard medal Soc. Econ. Paleontologists and Mineralogists, 1979, Barringer medal and prize, 1985, Founders of Plate Tectonics award Tex. A&M, 1988, Sigma Xi Spl. award for integrity of sci., 1986, Disting. Achievement award Ariz. State U., 1990. Fellow Geol. Soc. Am. (Penrose medal 1988), Geol. Soc. London (hon.), Am. Geophys. Union (Walter H. Bucher medal 1971), Mineralogical Soc. Am., Meteoritical Soc. (v.p. 1970-72); mem. Phi Beta Kappa. Home: 1314 W University Dr Apt 31 Tempe AZ 85287-0001 Office: Ariz State U Dept Geology Tempe AZ 85287-1404

DIETZ, RUSSELL SCOTT, communications company executive; b. Freeport, N.Y., Mar. 1, 1963; s. Russell N. and Mary E. (Sattler) D.; m. Carla R. Cadwell, June 4, 1983. BS in Computer Sci., SUNY, Stony Brook, 1985. Computer system mgr. Shoreham Wading River Schs., Shoreham, N.Y., 1979-81; sr. computer programming RMS Data Svcs., Hicksville, N.Y., 1981-83; bd. dirs. Technically Elite Concepts Inc., Hermosa Beach, Calif.; sr. systems programmer/analyst Bendix Field Engring. Corp., St. Inigoes, Md., 1983-84; system implementation specialist Magnavox Electronic Systems Co., Ashburn, Va., 1984-87; prin. software specialist Digital Equipment Corp., Landover, Md., 1987-88; v.p. systems devel. Technically Elite Concepts Inc., Hermosa Beach, Calif., 1988—; cons. Cedars-Sinai Med. Ctr., L.A., 1988-90. Contbr. articles to profl. jours. Mem. Digital Equipment Corp. User Soc., DC VAX Local Users Group (chmn. 1985-87). Republican. Lutheran. Office: Technically Elite Concepts Inc 2615 Pacific Coast Hwy 322 Hermosa Beach CA 90254-2225

DIETZ, VIDA LEE, utility company executive; b. Brawley, Calif., July 2, 1952. BSBA, U. Nev., 1975. Spl. asst. Sierra Pacific Co., Reno, 1976-78, asst. analyst, 1978-79, adminstr. extension agreement, 1979-83, adminstr. speaker's bur. and sch. programs, 1983-85, rep. community info., 1985-87; dir. spl. events, adminstr. charitable foundation Sierra Pacific Power Co., Reno, 1988—. Bd. dirs., 1st v.p. Sierra Nev. coun. Girl Scouts U.S., Reno, 1984-90, mem. nominating com., 1991-93; chmn. pub. rels. com. Jr. League Reno, 1986, chmn. ways and means, trustee, 1990-91; chmn. meetings and events com. United Way No. Nev., 1987, mem. pub. rels. and spl. events com., 1988—; mem. individual sessions com. Nev. Gov.'s Conf. Women, 1989; mem. Sierra Arts Found., Nev. Women's Fund Scholarship Selection Com., 1989; bd. dirs. Western Nev. Clean Communities, 1990—, Nev. Women's Fund, 1992—; vol. pub. TV Sta. KNPB. Mem. AAUW (program v.p. 1986), Reno Women in Advt. (ednl. chmn. 1986), Western Indsl. Nev., Reno-Sparks C. of C. (ednl. com. 1986-87), U. Nev. Coll. Bus. Alumni Assn. (bd. dirs., treas. 1989-90, pres.-elect 1993-94), U. Nev. Reno Alumni Coun. (treas. 1992—), Meeting Planners Internat. Office: Sierra Pacific Power Co 6100 Neil Rd BO Box 10100 Reno NV 89520

DIFALCO, JOHN PATRICK, arbitrator, lawyer; b. Steubenville, Ohio, Nov. 24, 1943; s. Pat John and Antoinette (Ricci) DiF.; m. Carolyn L. Otten, June 11, 1977; children: Elizabeth Ann, Jennifer Ann, Kevin John. BA, Ohio State U.; MA, U. No. Colo.; JD, Ohio State U. Bar: Ohio 1968, Colo. 1972, U.S. Dist. Colo. 1972, U.S. Ct. Appeals Colo. 1972, U.S. Supreme Ct. 1972, U.S. Ct. Appeals (fed. cir.) 1986, D.C. 1989. Atty., hearing officer, dir. U.S. Postal Svc., Washington, 1970-77; labor rels. specialist City and County of Denver, 1977-80; city atty. City of Greeley, Colo., 1980-87; pvt. practice Greeley, 1987—; prin. John P. DiFalco & Assocs., P.C., Ft. Collins, Colo., 1987—; instr. Regis U., Denver, U. Phoenix, Denver, Aims Community Coll., Greeley, Arapahoe Community Coll., Littleton, Colo., Pikes Peak Community Coll., Colo. Springs, Tri-State Coll., Angola, Ind.; arbitrator, 1980—; speaker in field. Contbr. Postmaster Advocate mag., also articles to profl. jours. Named an Outstanding City Atty. Colo., 1986. Mem. ABA (com. on pub. employee bargaining), Colo. Bar Assn. (labor law sect., Spl. Achievement award 1987), Fed. Bar Assn. (coms. on pub. sector labor rels., arbitration and office mgmt.), Colo. Trial Lawyers Assn., Indsl. Rels. Rsch. Assn., Nat. Pub. Employer Labor Rels. Assn., Am. Arbitration Assn., Nat. Inst. Mcpl. Law Officers (com. on law office mgmt.), Larimer County Bar Assn., Colo. Mcpl. League (chmn. attys. sect., mcpl. govt. issues and open meeting coms.), Met. Denver City Attys. Assn. (pres.), Ohio State U. Pres.'s Club, Rotary. Republican. Roman Catholic. Office: 1136 E Stuart St Ste 4102 Fort Collins CO 80525-1194

DIGBY, JAMES FOSTER, research engineer; b. Farmerville, La., Aug. 11, 1921; s. Sebe Lee and Maud Eloise (McLees) D.; m. Mary Jane Bruck, Dec. 5, 1959; children: Ward McLees, Drew James, Leslie Jane. BS, La. Tech., 1941; MA, Stanford (Calif.) U., 1942. Editor Watson Labs., USAF, Eatontown, N.J., 1946-47, def. planner, 1947-79; rsch. engr. The Rand Corp., Santa Monica, Calif., 1949-55, dept. head, 1956-58, program mgr. internat. studies, project leader, 1959-86, cons., 1986—; exec. dir. Calif. Seminar, Santa Monica, 1976-90; cons. Pres.'s Sci. Adv. Com., Washington, 1959-73, Commn. on Long Term Strategy, Washington, 1986-88; vice dir. Pan Heuristics, Marina del Rey, Calif., 1986-88; v.p. Am. Inst. for Strategic Coop., L.A., 1986-90; bd. dirs. European Am. Inst. for Security Rsch., L.A., 1976—. Author: (monograph) Precision-Guided Weapons, 1976. 1st lt. USAF, 1942-46, ETO. Mem. Internat. Inst. for Strategic Studies. Democrat. Home: 20773 Big Rock Dr Malibu CA 90265-5311 Office: The Rand Corp 1700 Main St Santa Monica CA 90407-2138

DI GIACINTO, SHARON, artist, educator; b. Chula Vista, Calif., Apr. 13, 1960; d. Vendal J. and Virginia J. Di G.; m. Richard K. Hillis, Aug. 1983; children: Tiffany Di Giacinto, Nikos Di Giacinto-Hillis, Gino Di Giacinto-Hillis. BFA, Ohio U., 1981; MFA, Tex. Woman's U., 1983. Teaching asst. art Stephen F. Austin State U., Nacogdoches, Tex., 1981, Tex. Woman's U., Denton, 1982-83; art instr. Phoenix Coll., 1983-84, Glendale (Ariz.) C.C., 1985-88; ind. artist Peoria, Ariz. One-woman shows include Scottsdale (Ariz.) C.C., 1989, Sun Cities Art Mus., 1989, Phoenix Visual Arts Gallery, 1990; group exhbns. include 2-person exhbn. Chandler (Ariz.) Ctr. for Arts, 1991. Co-chair Peoria Arts Commn., 1988-91. Mem. Coll. Art Assn. Am., Phoenix Art Mus., Phoenix Zoo. Democrat. Roman Catholic. Home: 6741 W Cholla Peoria AZ 85345

DIGIROLAMO, RUDOLPH GERARD, microbiologist, oceanographer, educator; b. Bklyn., Jan. 26, 1934; s. Carmine Francis and Carmella Josephine (Maresca) DiG.; m. Patricia Anne Doneen, July 3, 1964 (dec. 1977); 1 child, Christopher Robert. BS in Biology, Mount St. Mary Coll., Emmitsburg, Md., 1955; postgrad., St. John's U., Jamaica, N.Y., 1955-57, U. Rome, 1957-63; PhD in Ocean Sci., U. Wash., 1969. Prof., chmn. biology Coll. Notre Dame, Belmont, Calif., 1970-80; dir. Marine Rsch. Ctr. Coll. Notre Dame, 1973-80; prof. biology/microbiology Los Rios Community Coll. Dist., Sacramento, 1980—; prof. oceanography Nat. U. Sacramento, 1983—; cons. Marine Resources Ctr., Sacramento, 1980—; rsch. assoc. Nat. U., 1989-90; mem. NIH Sci. Rev. Group, 1985—. Author: Field Guide: Intertidal Invertebrates of San Mateo County, 1985; Some Experiments in Microbiology, 1986, 4th edit. 1992; contbr. chpts. to books, articles to profl. jours. Cons. San Francisco Bay Area Govts. Viral Pollution in San Francisco Bay, 1975—; mem. spl. pub. health com. San Francisco Bay Mussel Quarantine Policy, 1975—. Pfizer rsch. fellow, 1958; USPHS shellfish sanitation fellow, 1959-64; recognized as marine pollution expert, food virology expert, WHO of UN. Mem. N.Y. Acad. Sci., AAAS, Am. Fisheries Soc., Am. Soc. Microbiology, Internat. Oceanographic Soc. Home: 1 Shoal Ct Apt 112 Sacramento CA 95831-1446

DIJEAU, EDWARD FRANCIS, electric construction and manufacturing engineering; b. Alameda, Calif., Dec. 8, 1946; s. George Edward and Joyce (Merrill) D.; m. Shirley Kurniahardja, Dec. 12, 1987. Cert., U.S. Army Acad., Ft. Knox, Ky., 1967, Joint Apprenticeship Tng. Com., Oakland, Calif., 1972. Apprentice wireman IBEW S95, Oakland, Calif., 1968-72; inside wireman IBEW 595, Oakland, 1972-73; foreman Barber Electric, Oakland, 1973-76, Standard Electric & Engring., South San Francisco, Calif., 1976—. With U.S. Army, 1966-68, Vietnam. Mem. Fremont Coin Club (life). Office: Standard Electric & Engring 930 Linden Ave South San Francisco CA 94080-6811

DILBECK, CHARLES STEVENS, JR., real estate company executive; b. Dallas, Dec. 2, 1944; s. Charles Stevens Sr. and Betty Doris (Owens) D.; m. Lennie Jean Routledge, Apr. 29, 1964 (div. Aug. 1970); 1 child, Stephen Douglas. BS, Wichita State U., 1968; MS, Stanford U., 1969, postgrad., 1970-71. Engr. United Tech. Ctr., Sunnyvale, Calif., 1971-72; cons. Diversicom, Inc., Santa Clara, Calif., 1972-73; engr. Anamet Labs., San Carlos, Calif., 1973-75; cons. real estate investment Cert. Capital Corp., San Jose, Calif., 1975-82; pvt. practice in real estate, San Jose, 1981—; prin. Am. Equity Investments, San Jose, 1982—; mem. Los Gatos (Calif.) Rent Adv. Com., 1988. Mem. Nat. Apt. Assn., San Jose Real Estate Bd., Tri-County Apt. Assn., Gold Key Club, Tau Beta Pi (pres. 1968), Sigma Gamma Tau. Republican. Home: 301 Alta Loma Ln Santa Cruz CA 95062-4620 Office: Am Equity Investments 455 Los Gatos Blvd Ste 103 Los Gatos CA 95032

DILIBERTO, HELEN BRATNEY, librarian, retired educator; b. Newark, June 9, 1920; d. Leon and Julia (Spilchak) Bratney; m. Stephen Peter Diliberto, June 29, 1943 (div. 1972); children: Nina Diliberto Marlowe, Stephen Paul, Michael Lucio, James J. BA, N.J. Coll. for Women, 1943, U. Calif., Berkeley, 1961. Cert. tchr., N.J., Calif. Libr. League of Nations, Princeton, N.J., 1943-45; tchr. elem. grades Berkeley (Calif.) Unified Sch. Dist., 1961-65, libr., media specialist, 1965-72; libr., media specialist U.S. Overseas Dependency Schs., Yokosuka, Japan, 1980-82; now ret.; chmn. Berkeley Libr. Adv. Com., 1969-70; bd. dirs. Berkeley Educator's Assn., 1974-75; mem. Berkeley Supt.'s Edn. and Grade Com., 1974-75; mem. membership com. Overseas Educators Assn., Yokosuka, 1981; developer playwriting and puppetry program for children, 1972-76; cons. on audio-visual and book materials. Actress, Oreg. Barnstormers, Grants Pass, 1979, Yokosuka Drama Group, 1980-82; docent Oakland (Calif.) Mus., 1988-91; mem. choir Unitarian Universalist Ch., Berkeley, 1977—. Mem. LWV, NEA, AAUW, El Cerrito Hist. Soc., Grey Panthers. Democrat. Unitarian. Home: 769 Balra Dr El Cerrito CA 94530-3302

DILITKANICH, KENNETH RODGER, pharmaceutical company executive; b. Chgo., Aug. 17, 1954; s. John and Doris Mae (Bertenshaw) D.; m. Donna Marie Deichmann, Oct. 1, 1977; children: David Kenneth, Laura Kathryn. BA, Augustana Coll., Rock Island, Ill., 1976; postgrad., Calif. State U., San Bernardino, 1992—. Group mgr. Salkin and Linoff, Inc., Moline, Ill., 1976-78; from pers. project analyst to hdqrs. pers. mgr. Campus Crusade for Christ, San Bernardino, Calif., 1978-86, assoc. pers. dir., 1986-89, dir. human resources, 1989-91, dir. human resources, nat. ministries, 1991-93; pharm. sales rep. 3M Co., 1993—; co-founder, bd. dirs. Alliance Human Resource Mgmt., Highland, Calif., 1985-89. Campaigner, John Paul Stark for Congress, San Bernardino, 1980, 84; coach Little League. Named to Outstanding Young Men of Am., 1987. Mem. Pers. and Indsl. Rels. Assn. (dr. 1990-91, dist. chair 1990). Republican. Mem. Reformed Ch. in Am.

DILL, LADDIE JOHN, artist; b. Long Beach, Calif., Sept. 14, 1943; s. James Melvin and Virginia (Crane) D.; m. Ann Cathrine Thornycroft, Jan. 13, 1976 (div. 1992); children: Ariel, Jackson Caldwell. B.F.A., Chouinard Art Inst., 1968. lectr. painting and drawing UCLA, 1975-88. Exhbns. include: San Francisco Mus. Modern Art, 1977-78, Albright Knox Mus., Buffalo, 1978-79, Charles Cowles Gallery, N.Y.C., 1983-85, The First Show, Los Angeles; represented in permanent collections: Mus. Modern Art, N.Y.C., Laguna Mus. Art, Los Angeles County Mus., Mus. Contemporary Art, Los Angeles, Santa Barbara Mus., San Francisco Mus. Modern Art, Seattle Mus., Newport Harbor Art Mus., Oakland Mus., Smithsonian Instn., IBM, Nat. Mus., Seoul, Republic of Korea, San Diego Mus. Art, La. Mus., Denmark, Am. Embassy, Helsinki, Finland, Corcoran Gallery Art, Washington, Chgo Art Inst., Greenville County (S.C.) Mus., Palm Springs Desert Mus., Phoenix Art Mus., William Rockhill Nelsen Mus., Kansas City, Phillips Collection. Nat. Endowment Arts grantee, 1975, 82; Guggenheim Found. fellow, 1979-80; Calif. Arts Council Commn. grantee, 1983-84.

DILLARD, JOHN MARTIN, lawyer, pilot; b. Long Beach, Calif., Dec. 25, 1945; s. John Warren and Clara Leora (Livermore) D.; student U. Calif., Berkeley, 1963-67; B.A., UCLA, 1968; J.D., Pepperdine U., 1976; m. Patricia Anne Yeager, Aug. 10, 1968; children: Jason Robert, Jennifer Lee. Instr. pilot Norton AFB, Calif., 1973-77. Bar: Calif., 1976. Assoc. Magana, Cathcart & McCarthy, L.A., 1977-80, Lord, Bissell & Brook, L.A., 1980-85; of counsel Finley, Kumble, Wagner, 1985-86, Schell & Delamer, 1986—, Law Offices of John M. Dillard, 1986—, v.p., gen. counsel, dir. Resort Aviation Svcs, Inc., Calif., 1988—; mng. ptnr. Natkin & Weisbach, So. Calif., 1988-89. Active Am. Cancer Soc. Capt. USAF, 1968-73, Vietnam. Mem. Am. Trial Lawyers Assn. (aviation litigation com.), Am. Bar Assn. (aviation com.), Orange County Bar Assn., Fed. Bar Assn., L.A. County Bar Assn. (aviation com.), Century City Bar Assn., Internat. Platform Assn., Res. Officers Assn., Orange County Com. of 100, Sigma Nu. Home: 19621 Verona Ln Yorba Linda CA 92686-2847 Office: 313 N Birch St Santa Ana CA 92701-5264

DILLARD, MARILYN DIANNE, property manager; b. Norfolk, Va., July 7, 1940; d. Thomas Ortman and Sally Ruth (Wallerich) D.; m. James Conner Coons, Nov. 6, 1965 (div. June 1988); 1 child, Adrienne Alexandra Coons (dec.). Studied with Russian prima ballerina, Alexandra Danilova, 1940's; student with honors at entrance, UCLA, 1958-59; BA in Bus. Adminstrn. with honors, U. Wash., 1962. Modeling-print work Harry Conover, N.Y.C., 1945; ballet instr. Ivan Novikoff Sch. Russian Ballet, 1955; model Elizabeth Leonard Agy., Seattle, 1955-68; retail worker Frederick & Nelson, Seattle, 1962, I. Magnin & Co., Seattle, 1963-64; property mgr. Seattle, 1961—; antique and interior designer John J. Cunningham Antiques, Seattle, 1968-73; owner, interior designer Marilyn Dianne Dillard Interiors, 1973—; mem.

rsch. bd. advisors Am. Biog. Inst., Inc., 1990—. Author: (poetry) Flutterby, 1951, Spring Flowers, 1951; contbr., asst. chmn. (with Jr. League of Seattle) Seattle Classic Cookbook, 1980-83. Charter mem., pres. Children's Med. Ctr., Maude Fox Guild, Seattle, 1965—, Jr. Women's Symphony Assn., 1967-73, Virginia Mason Hosp. Ctr. and Med. Found. Soc., 1990—, Nat. Mus. of the Am. Indian, Smithsonian Instn., Washington, 1992; assoc. Seattle Jr. Club, 1962-65, property mgr. Seattle Jr. Club, 1962-65; bd. dirs. Patrons N.W. Civic, Cultural and Charitable Orgns. (chmn. various coms.), Seattle, 1976—, prodn. chmn., 1977-78, 84-85, auction party chmn., 1983-84, exec. com., 1984-85, chmn. bd. vols., 1990-91, adv. coun., 1991—; mem. U. Wash. Arboretum Found. Unit, 1966-73, pres., 1969; bd. dirs. Coun. for Prevention Child Abuse and Neglect, Seattle, 1974-75; v.p., mem. various coms. Seattle Children's Theatre, 1984-90, asst. in lighting main stage plays, 1987—, mem. adv. coun., 1993—; Bathhouse Theatre, 1987—, asst. in lighting main stage plays, 1987-90; adv. bd. N.W. Asian Am. Theatre, 1987—, Co-Motion Dance Co., 1991—; organizer teen groups Episcopal Ch. of the Epiphany, 1965-67; provisional class pres. Jr. League Seattle, 1971-72, next to new shop asst. chmn., 1972-73, bd. dirs. admissions chmn., 1976-77, exec. v.p., exec. com., bd. dirs., 1978-79; charter mem. Jr. Women's Symphony Assn., 1967-73; mem. Seattle Art Mus., 1975-90, Landmark, 1990—, Corp. Coun. for the Arts, 1991—; founding dir. Adrienne Coons Meml. Fund, 1985, v.p., 1985-92, pres. 1992—; mem. steering com. Heart Ball Am. Heart Assn., 1986, 87, auction chmn., 1986; mem. steering com. Bellevue Sch. Dist. Children's Theatre, 1983-85, pub. rels. chair, 1984, asst. stage mgr., 1985. Named Miss Greater Seattle, 1964. Mem. AFTRA, Am. Biographical Inst., Seattle Tennis Club, U. Wash. Alumnae Assn. (life), Pacific Northwest Ballet Assn. (charter), Progressive Animal Welfare Soc., Associated Women (student council U Wash. 1962), Alpha Phi. Republican. Episcopalian. Home and Office: 2053 Minor Ave E Seattle WA 98102-3513

DILLEHAY, RONALD CLIFFORD, psychology educator; b. Malvern, Iowa, Nov. 2, 1935; s. Clifford Marvin and Lela May (Raines) D.; m. Valerie Ruth Sherbourne, Dec. 22, 1954; children: Pamela Ann, Ronald Clifford Jr., Darin Raines. Student, Calif. State U.-Fresno, 1953-55; A.B., U. Calif.-Berkeley, 1957, Ph.D., 1962; postgrad. in law U. Ky., 1976. Research behavioral scientist, lectr. U. Calif.-Berkeley, 1960-64; from asst. prof. to assoc. prof. dept. behavioral sci. and psychology U. Ky., Lexington, 1964-66, assoc. prof., 1969-71, prof., 1971-90, chmn. dept. psychology, 1973-80; assoc. prof. dept. psychology Tex. Christian U., Ft. Worth, 1966-69; rsch. assoc. Social Welfare Rsch. Inst., 1970-73; assoc. dean grad. sch., prof. U. Nev., Reno, 1990—; cons. pub. health agys., Calif. and Ky., 1960-70, various pvt. legal firms and pub. agys., Ky., Calif., Oreg., Ga., Ala., Md., S.C., 1978—. Author: (with John P. Kirscht) Dimensions of Authoritarianism, 1967; (with Michael T. Nietzel) Psychological Consultation in the Courtroom, 1985. Contbr. chpts. to books, articles and papers to profl. publs. Fulbright-Hays sr. fellow La Pontificia Universidad Católica, Lima, Peru, 1973-74; fellow James McKeen Cattell Found., 1980-81, fellow U.S.-Spanish Joint Com. Cultural Ednl. Cooperation, La Universidad Autonoma, Madrid, 1988-89. Fellow Am. Psychol. Soc., Am. Psychol. Assn., Soc. for Psychol. Study Social Issues; mem. Western Psychol. Assn., Soc. Exptl. Social Psychology, Sociedad Interamericana de Psicología, Internat. Soc. Pol. Psychology, Ky. Kickers Soccer Club (bd. dirs. 1983-85, coach 1984-87) (Lexington), Sigma Xi. Home: 3425 Southampton Dr Reno NV 89509-3867 Office: U Nev-Reno Grad Sch 239 Getchell Reno NV 89557-0035

DILLEY, WILLIAM GREGORY, aviation company executive; b. Sterling, Colo., June 6, 1922; s. William Gregory and Ethel Marie (Chandler) D.; m. M. Jean McCarthy, May 14, 1944; children: Gregory Dean, Karen Kay. BEng, U. Colo., 1951. Founder Spectra Sonics, Ogden, Utah, 1963—; cons., lectr. in field; investigator USAF Directorate of Flight Safety Rsch.. Contbr. over 300 articles to profl. jours.; patentee in field. Organizing mem. Minutemen. With USAF, Colo. Air N.G. Recipient Disting. Engring. Alumnus award U. Colo., 1977; named one of prominent engrs. in U.S. Sci. and Tech. div. Libr. of Congress; fellow Audio Engring. Soc., 1970. Fellow Audio Engring. Soc.; mem. Soc. Broadcast Engrs. (sr.). Office: Spectra Sonics 3750 Airport Rd Ogden UT 84405-1531

DILLINGHAM-EVANS, DONNA FAYE, college official; b. Nashville, Nov. 28, 1948; d. John Thomas and Geneva Mae (Williams) Dillingham; m. Keith Harry Evans, Sept. 15, 1972; children: Hal, Micah, Keith Ayn, Bonita, Daniel. BA in Chemistry, Austin Peay State U., Clarksville, Tenn., 1970; secondary cert., So. Utah U., 1982; MEd in Post Secondary Edn., U. Nev., Las Vegas, 1989; postgrad., Utah State U., 1991, No. Ariz. U.C.C., 1993—. Cert. in toxicology, chemistry and math. tchr., Utah. Rsch. assoc. Vanderbilt U., Nashville, 1970-71, Calbiochem, La Jolla, Calif., 1973-74; toxicologist Poison Lab., San Diego, 1974-76, Smith Kline Labs., Claremont, Calif., 1976-80; instr. math. Dixie Coll., St. George, Utah, 1982—, dir. Acad. Support Ctr., 1988—; cons. S.W. Mental Health, St. George, 1982—; pres. math. and sci. network So. Utah. Author: (poetry) Stump, 1982; Golden Rules for Rulers, 1986. Judge Regional Sci. Fair, South Utah, 1986—; bd. dirs. Non-denominational Prodns., St. George, 1990—; v.p. Utah Gov.'s Task Force on Drug Use, 1986. Fellow Rotary Internat. Mem. Assn. Suprs., Assn. Women in Jr. and Community Colls. (leadership award 1989, regional rep. 1992—), Assn. Spl. Programs in Region Eight, Dixie Coll. Faculty Assn. (bd. dirs. 1989), Phi Delta Kappa. Republican. Home: PO Box 1636 Saint George UT 84771 Office: Dixie Coll 225 South 700 East Saint George UT 84770

DILLON, FRANCIS PATRICK, human resources executive, management/personnel sales consultant; b. Long Beach, Calif., Mar. 15, 1937; s. Wallace Myron and Mary Elizabeth (Land) D.; B.A., U. Va., 1959; M.S., Def. Fgn. Affairs Sch., 1962; M.B.A., Pepperdine U., 1976; m. Vicki Lee Dillon, Oct. 1980; children: Cary Randolph, Francis Patrick Jr., Randee, Rick. Traffic mgr., mgr. pers. svcs. Pacific Telephone Co., Sacramento and Lakeport, Calif., 1966-69; asst. mgr. manpower planning and devel. Pan-Am. World Airways, N.Y.C., 1969-71; mgr. pers. and orgn. devel. Continental Airlines, L.A., 1971-74; dir. human resources Bourns, Inc., Riverside, Calif., 1974-80; dir. employee and community relations MSI Data Corp., 1980-83; pres. Pavi Enterprises, 1983—; cons. mgmt. Pers. Outplacement Counseling/Sales/Mgmt., fin. svcs./mortgage reductions 1983-90; pres., chief exec. officer Pers. Products & Svcs., Inc., 1984-91; pres. Meditrans Inc. Bd. dirs. Health Svcs. Maintenance Orgn., Inc., Youth Svcs. Ctr., Inc.; vol. precinct worker. Served to lt. comdr. USN, 1959-66; asst. naval attaché, Brazil, 1963-65. Recipient Disting. Svc. award Jaycees, 1969; Jack Cates Meml. Vol. of Year award Youth Svc. Ctr., 1977. Mem. Assn. Internal Mgmt. Cons.'s, Am. Soc. Personnel Adminstrn., Personnel Indsl. Relations Assn., Am. Soc. Tng. and Devel., Am. Electronics Assn. (human resources com., chmn. human resources symposium). Republican. Episcopalian. Clubs: Mission Viejo Sailing, YMCA Bike, Mission Viejo Ski, Caving, Toastmasters (pres. 1966-67), Have Dirt Will Travel. Office: Pavi Enterprises 27331 Via Amistoso Mission Viejo CA 92692-2410

DILLON, GEORGE CHAFFEE, manufacturing company executive; b. Kansas City, Mo., Oct. 29, 1922; s. Edward J. and Mary (Coon) D.; m. Joan Alamo Kent, Sept. 11, 1948; children: Kent, Courtney, Emily. BS, Harvard U., 1944, MBA, 1948. Adminstrv. asst. J. A. Bruening Co., Kansas City, Mo., 1948-51; with Butler Mfg. Co., Kansas City, Mo., 1951-86, treas., from 1960, v.p., 1961-63, exec. v.p., 1963-67, pres., 1967-78, chmn. bd., chief exec. officer, 1978-86; chmn. Manville Corp., Denver, 1986-91; bd. dirs. Johns Manville Corp., Phelps Dodge Corp., Newhall Land and Farming Co., Astec Industries, Chattanooga; chmn. oversight com. Nat. Renewable Energy Lab. Past. chmn. bd. trustees Midwest Research Inst., Kansas City, Mo.; trustee Mayo Found., Rochester, Minn., Children's Mercy Hosp., Kansas City, Mo.; bd. overseers Harvard U., 1980-86. Lt. USNR, 1943-46. Home: 5049 Wornall Rd Kansas City MO 64112-2423 Office: Manville Corp 5045 Wornall Rd PO Box 5108 Denver CO 80127

DILLON, GREGORY RUSSELL, hotel executive; b. Chgo., Aug. 26, 1922; s. Gregory Thomas and Margaret Moore (Russell) D.; m. Nancy Jane Huntsberger, Nov. 8, 1969; children: Michael Gregory, Patricia Jean, Margaret Esther, Richard Thomas, Daniel Russell. Student, Elmhurst Coll., Ill., 1941-43, 45-46; JD, DePaul U., Chgo., 1948. Bar: Ill. Sole practice Chgo.; ptnr. Friedman Mulligan Dillon & Urist, Chgo., 1950-63; asst. to pres. Hilton Hotels Corp., Beverly Hills, Calif., 1963-65, v.p., asst. sec., 1965-71, sr. v.p., asst. sec., 1971-80, exec. v.p., 1980-90, also bd. dirs., 1977—; vice-chmn., 1990—; pres. Conrad Internat. Hotels, 1986-90, vice chmn., 1990—, also bd. dirs., 1980—; bd. dirs. Jupiters Ltd., Surfer's Paradise, Queensland, Australia. Served to 1st lt. USAAF, 1943-46, ETO. Mem. Urban Land Inst. (trustee 1980—, trustee found. 1981—), ABA, Ill. Bar Assn., Chgo. Bar Assn., Am. Hotel and Motel Assn. Republican. Roman Catholic. Clubs: Chicago Athletic (Chgo.); Bel-Air Country (Los Angeles); Marco Polo (N.Y.C.). Office: Hilton Hotels Corp 9336 Civic Center Dr Beverly Hills CA 90210-3964

DILLON, RAY WILLIAM, engineering technician; b. China Lake, Calif., Aug. 8, 1954; s. Duane L. and Audrey J. (Amende) D.; m. Kathy M. Shrum , Sept. 3, 1980; 1 child, Stephanie. Student, U. Okla., 1976-78, Oklahoma City Comm. Coll., 1986; BA, So. Nazarene U., Bethany, Okla., 1987. Cert. level IV Nat. Inst. for Certification in Engring. Techs. Technician B&B Fire Protection, Oklahoma City, 1977-78; lead technician Grinell Fire Protection Systems, Oklahoma City, 1978-80; gen. mgr. A.L. Fire Protection, Inc., Oklahoma City, 1980-87, exec. v.p., 1989-90; store mgr. Master Systems Ltd., Oklahoma City, 1987-89; region mgr. Casteel Automatic Fire Protection, Oklahoma City, 1990-92; gen. mgr. Allied Rubber & Gasket Co., Dillon, Colo., 1992—; instr. Okla. State U., 1990-91. Mem. Nat. Inst. Cert. Engring. Technicians (cert.), Oklahoma City IBM-PC Users Group, Okla. Fire Protection Contractors Assn. (sec. 1986-87, chmn. 1987, sec. 1990-91), Nat. Fire Protection Assn., Soc. of Fire Protection Engrs. Republican. Baptist. Home: PO Box 399 Silverthorne CO 80498

DILWORTH, CHARLES DEWEES, architect; b. Princeton, N.J., Feb. 11, 1956; s. Joseph Richardson and Elizabeth (Cushing) D.; m. Lucienne Felice Geber, Mar. 15, 1986; children: Jessica Logan, Elizabeth Caroline. BA, Yale U., 1979, MArch, 1983. Registered architect, Calif. Designer Frank O. Gehry & Assoc., Venice, Calif., 1985-86, MBT Assocs., San Francisco, 1986-87; project architect Tanner & Vandine Architects, San Francisco, 1987-88; studio dir. Studios Architecture, San Francisco, 1988—. Mem. AIA. Office: Studios Architecture 99 Green St San Francisco CA 94111

DIMAIO, VIRGINIA SUE, gallery owner; b. Houston, July 6, 1921; d. Jesse Lee and Gabriella Sue (Norris) Chambers; AB, U. Redlands, 1943; student U. So. Calif., 1943-45, Scripps Coll., 1943, Pomona Coll., 1945; m. James V. DiMaio, 1955 (div. 1968); children: Victoria, James V. Owner, dir. Galeria Capistrano, San Juan Capistrano and Santa Fe, N.Mex., 1979—; founder Mus. Women in Arts, Washington; cons., appraiser Southwestern and Am. Indian Handcrafts; lectr. Calif. State U., Long Beach; established ann. Helen Hardin Meml. scholarship for woman artist grad. Inst. Am. Indian Art, Santa Fe, also ann. Helen Hardin award for outstanding artist at Indian Market, S.W. Assn. on Indian Affairs, Santa Fe; bd. dirs. Mus. of Man, San Diego, 1989; mem. Intertribal Coun. U. Calif., Irvine, 1990. Author: (forward to Mus. of Man exhibit catalogue) Paths Beyond Tradition. Recipient Bronze Plaque Recognition award Navajo Tribal Mus., 1977. Mem. Inst. Am. Indian Art (founder, bd. dirs.), Indian Arts and Crafts Assn., S.W. Assn. Indian Affairs, Heard Mus., San Juan Capistano C. of C. Republican. Roman Catholic. Office: 31892 Camino Capistrano San Juan Capistrano CA 92675-3216

DIMARTINO, SANTO JOHN, physician assistant; b. N.Y.C., May 13, 1946; s. Thomas Frank and Katharine (Cascio) DiM. BS, Long Island U., 1978. Physician asst. Health Ins. Group of Greater N.Y., Queens, 1978-88, U.S. Navy, Honolulu, 1989—; physician asst. Alpha Plasma Ctr., Honolulu, 1987-89. Fellow Am. Acad. Physician Assts., Washington Acad. Physician Assts.; mem. Hawaii Acad. Physician Assts. (pres. 1989-90, v.p. 1990-91), Masons (32 deg.), Shriners. Office: Med Clinic Naval Air Sta Barbers Point Ewa Beach HI 96706

DIMMICK, CAROLYN REABER, federal judge; b. Seattle, Oct. 24, 1929; d. Maurice C. and Margaret T. (Taylor) Reaber; m. Cyrus Allen Dimmick, Sept. 10, 1955; children: Taylor, Dana. BA, U. Wash., 1951, JD, 1963; LLD, Gonzaga U., 1982, CUNY, 1987. Bar: Wash. Asst. atty. gen. State of Wash., Seattle, 1953-55; pros. atty. King County, Wash., 1955-59, 60-62; sole practice Seattle, 1959-60, 62-65; judge N.E. Dist. Ct. Wash., 1965-75, King County Superior Ct., 1976-80; justice Wash. Supreme Ct., 1981-85; judge U.S. Dist. Ct. (we. dist.) Wash., Seattle, 1985—. Recipient Matrix Table award, 1981, World Plan Execs. Council award, 1981, others. Mem. ABA, Am. Judges Assn. (gov.), Nat. Assn. Women Judges, World Assn. Judges, Wash. Bar Assn., Am. Judicature Soc., Order of Coif (Wash. chpt.), Wash. Athletic Club, Wingpoint Golf and Country Club, Harbor Club. Office: US Dist Ct 911 US Courthouse 1010 5th Ave Seattle WA 98104-1130

DIN, GILBERT C., history educator; b. Holtville, Calif., Nov. 11, 1932; s. John Khair and Isabel (Chavarria) D.; m. Judy Lynn Sutliff, Sept. 20, 1988; 1 child, Alexander; children from a previous marriage: Frederic, Gregory. AB, U. Calif., Berkeley, 1957; MA, U. Calif., 1958; PhD, U. Madrid, Spain, 1960. Instr. history Imperial Valley Coll., Imperial, Calif., 1961-65; prof. history Ft. Lewis Coll., Durango, Colo., 1965-90; ind. researcher Albuquerque, N. Mex. Author: Louisiana in 1776, 1977, Getting to Know Latin America, 1978, The Canary Islanders of Louisiana, 1988, Francisco Bouligny: A Bourbon Soldier in Spanish Louisiana, 1993; co-author: The Imperial Osages, 1983; contbr. articles to profl. jours. With USAF, 1951-55. Del Amo Found. fellow, 1959; Am. Philos. Soc. grantee, 1978; recipient award for best publication, L. Kemper Williams, 1988. Mem. Am. Hist. Assn., La. History Assn., Conf. on Latin Am. Home: 2518 Gen Bradley NE Albuquerque NM 87112

DINEL, RICHARD HENRY, lawyer; b. L.A., Sept. 16, 1942; s. Edward Price and Edith Elizabeth (Rheinstein) D.; m. Joyce Ann Korsmeyer, Dec. 26, 1970; children: Edward, Alison. BA, Pomona Coll., 1964; JD, Stanford U., 1967. Bar: Calif. Owner Richard H. Dinel, A Profl. Law Corp., L.A., 1971-79; ptnr. Richards, Watson & Gershon, L.A., 1979-92, of counsel, 1992—; pres. R. H. Dinel Investment Counsel, Inc., 1992—; bd. dirs. The Price Co., 1990-92. Chmn. bd. Pomona Coll. Assocs., 1987-89; ex-officio trustee Pomona Coll., 1987-89; arbitrator Chgo. Bd. Options Exch., 1978—, Pacific Stock Exch., 1979—; bd. govs. Western Los Angeles County counsel Boys Scouts Am., 1993—. Mem. Securities Ind. Assn. (speaker compliance and legal div. 1978-92), Pomona Coll. Alumni Assn. (chmn. alumni fund and continuing edn. com. 1972-73), Nat. Assn. Securities Dealers (mem. nat. bd. arbitrators 1978-90), City Club on Bunker Hill, Bond Club L.A. Office: 11661 San Vicente Blvd Ste 400 Los Angeles CA 90049-5112

DING, JONATHAN ZHONG, professional society administrator; b. Chong Qing, Peoples Republic of China, Sept. 26, 1952; came to the U.S., 1982; s. Long-Yi and Guang-Qiong (Zhou) D.; m. Sheila Yuemei Luo. BA, Sichuan U., 1981; MA, Ohio U., 1984, U. So. Calif., 1987; PhD, U. So. Calif., 1990. Researcher U. So. Calif., L.A., 1984-89; dir. internat. tech. transfer Comparator Systems Corp., Irvine, Calif., 1989-91; chief exec. officer China Infinity Tech. Inc., Irvine, 1990-91; chmn. Citec Am. Holdings Ltd., Anaheim, Calif., 1991—; founder, chief exec. officer Am.-China Bus. Soc., Laguna Hills, Calif., 1991—; cons. tech. transfer numerous corps. and govts., Peoples Republic of China, 1984—; bus. cons. E.F. Hutton, 1986, Gen. Motors, 1986, Hill & Knowlton, Beijing, 1987, GTE, 1986, China Expo, 1989, AT&T, 1987, Sci. Applications Internat. Corp., Pacific Rim Ventures, 1990-92; speaker ABA, Chgo., N.Y.C., 1992. Producer: (documentary) China Comes to Ohio, 1983. Annenberg doctoral fellow U. So. Calif., 1984-88; acad. rsch. grantee UNESCO, 1986; Young Chinese scholar China Times and Nat. Chengchi U., 1990. Mem. Chinese Assn. USA (sec. gen. 1988—), Acad. Mgmt., Acad. Internat. Bus. Home: 414 S Manchester Apt 143 Anaheim CA 92802 Office: Am China Bus Soc 20271 Acacia St Ste 200 Santa Ana Heights CA 92707

DING, KUNG-HAU, physicist, researcher; b. Taipei, Taiwan, Republic of China, Oct. 28, 1956; came to the U.S., 1981; s. Shao-Yun and Yueh-Hsueh (Sun) D.; m. Shwu-Ing Fan, June 7, 1981; 1 child, Tiffany. BS in Physics, Nat. Tsing-Hua U., Taiwan, 1978; MS, U. Wash., 1984, MEE, 1985, PhD, 1989. Rsch. assoc. phys. sci. lab. N.Mex. State U., Las Cruces, 1989—. Contbr. chpts. to books and articles to profl. jours. Mem. IEEE, Optical Soc. Am., Sigma Xi. Home: 937 Dorado Ct Las Cruces NM 88001 Office: NMex State U Phys Sci Lab Las Cruces NM 88003

DING, MAE LON, employee compensation consultant; b. Norwalk, Calif., May 7, 1954; d. Lock Gee and Ruth (Tang) D.; m. Stephen M. Batcheller, Nov. 30, 1985 (div. Mar. 1992). BA, UCLA, 1976; MBA, U. So. Calif., 1979. Cons. Forum Corp., Boston, 1978, Wyatt Co., Boston, 1978-81; sr. cons. R. A. Smith & Assoc., Mission Viejo, Calif., 1981-83; mgr. compensation Allergan Pharms., Irvine, Calif., 1983-85; pres. Pers. Systems Assoc., Newport Beach, Calif., 1985—; instr. U. Calif., Irvine, 1988-89, Calif. State U., Long Beach, 1988-90, Calif. State Coll., Pomona, 1987-88, Chapman Coll., Orange, Calif., 1991; speaker in field. Author: Survey Sources, 1991, 3rd rev. edit. 1993; contbr. articles to profl publs. Mem. Charter 100, Corona del Mar, Calif., 1990—. Mem. Assn. Profl. Cons. (bd. dirs. 1989—, pres. 1993-94), Am. Compensation Assn. (instr. 1984—), Orange County Compensation Assn., Orange County Ski Club (bd. dirs. 1990). Office: Pers Systems Assoc 2282 Aspen St Tustin CA 92680

DINGES, RICHARD ALLEN, entrepreneur; b. Englewood, N.J., June 17, 1945; m. Kathie A. Headley; children: Kelly, Courtney. Grad., Jersey City State Coll., 1967; MEd, U. Hawaii, 1972; postgrad., William Peterson Coll., 1974-79. Cert. sch. adminstr.; cert. sch. spl. services dir., N.J., Ariz., Hawaii. Pres. Def. Industry Assocs., Sierra Vista, Ariz., 1979—, Fed. Career Cons., Sierra Vista, Ariz., 1985; dir. Nat. Scholarship Locators, Sierra Vista, 1985—. Editor: Guide to U.S. Defense Contractors, 1985, 87, 10 Step Guide to College Selection, Salary Negotiations for Military, How to Survive the Job Interview. Vice prin. Little Egg Harbor Primary Sch. Mem. Cochise County Merit Commn. (vice-chmn.), Platform Soc. Speakers' Assn. Office: 2160 E Fry Blvd Ste 400 Sierra Vista AZ 85635-2709

DINI, JOSEPH EDWARD, JR., state legislator; b. Yerington, Nev., Mar. 28, 1929; s. Joseph and Elvira (Castellani) D.; m. Jeanne Marion Demuth, Sept. 22, 1949; children: Joseph, George, David, Michael. BSBA, U. Nev., Reno, 1951. Mem. Nev. State Assembly, Carson City, 1967-93; majority leader Nev. State Assembly, 1975; speaker Nev. State Assembly, Carson City, 1977, 87, 89, 91-93; minority leader Nev. State Assembly, 1982, 85; interim fin. com. mem., 1985-92, speaker pro tem, 1973, chmn. water policy com. Western Legis. Conf., 1993-94; pres. Dini's Lucky Club Casino, Yerington, Nev., 1972—. Recipient Outstanding Citizen award Nev. Edn. Assn., 1973, Friend of Edn. award Nev. State Edn. Assn., 1986, Citizen of Yr. award Nev. Judges Assn., 1987, Dedicated and Valued Leadership award Nat. Conf. State Legislatures, 1989, Excellence in Pub. Svc. award Nev. Trial Lawyers Assn., 1990, Silver Plow award Nev. Farm Bur., 1991; named Conservation Legislator of Yr. Nev. Wildlife Fedn., 1991. Mem. Mason Valley C. of C. (pres.), Rotary (pres. Yerington 1989), Lions (pres. Yerington chpt. 1975), Masons, Shriners, Gamma Sigma Delta. Home: 104 N Mountain View St Yerington NV 89447-2239 Office: Dini's Lucky Club Inc 45 N Main St Yerington NV 89447-2230

DINKELSPIEL, PAUL GAINES, investment banking and public financial consultant; b. San Francisco, Feb. 12, 1935; s. Edward Gaines and Pauline (Watson) D. A.B., U. Calif., Berkeley, 1959. Gen. ptnr. Stone & Youngberg, San Francisco, 1961-71; 1st v.p. Shearson Lehman Hutton and predecessor firms, San Francisco, 1971-79; pres., chmn. bd. dirs. Dinkelspiel, Belmont & Co., Inc., San Francisco; investment banking and pub. fin. cons., 1979—; bd. dirs. Gemstone Investors Assurance Corp., N.Y.C. With AUS, 1959-60. Mem. Govt. Fin. Officers Assn., Am. Water Works Assn., San Francisco Mcpl. Forum, Calif. Pub. Securities Assn. (public fin. com.), San Francisco Comml. Club, Commonwealth Club of Calif., Mcpl. Bond Club, N.Y. World Trade Club, Calif. Waterfowl Assn., Ducks Unltd., Sigma Chi. Home: PO Box 727 Stinson Beach CA 94970-0727 Office: 101 California St Fl 37 San Francisco CA 94111-5802

DINNER, MARIE BERNICE, social services program administrator; b. Bolton, Eng., Mar. 3, 1947; came to U.S., 1958; d. Philip and Sarah (Reich) Myers; m. Bruce Jon Dinner, June 18, 1967; childen: Alec W., Tara Lea. BA, U. Denver, 1971, MA, 1973; PhD, U. Colo., 1981. Cert. clin. competence-audiology. Audiologist Rose Med. Ctr., Denver, 1973-76; clin. supr. U. Colo. Comm. Disorders Clinic, Denver and Boulder, Colo., 1977-81; audiologist Pfenninger Inst., Wheat Ridge, Colo., 1982-84; dir. of cochlear implants Childrens Deafness Found., Denver, 1984-88, exec. dir., 1987-88; pres. Hear Now, Denver, 1988—. Bd. dirs. Allied Jewish Fedn., Denver, 1990—; pres. Beth Joseph Congregation, Denver, 1989-91. Mem. Sertoma, Am. Speech, Hearing, Lang. Assn., Acad. of Audiology, Cochlear Implant Club Internat. (adv. bd. 1990—, bd. dirs. 1992—). Democrat. Office: Hear Now 4001 S Magnolia Way Denver CO 80237

DINSDALE, GRACE KATHERINE, nursery executive; b. Hillsboro, Oreg., Feb. 15, 1957; d. James Huber Dinsdale and Sara (Rankin) Dinsdale-Auel. BA in Psychology with honors, Portland State U., 1977; BS in Botany with honors, Oreg. State U., 1981. Equipment operator Dinsdale Custom Haying, Ft. Rock, Oreg., 1976-77; rschr. Oreg. Gov.'s Commn. for Women, Salem, 1977-78; mgr. produce market Blue Heron Farm, Salem, 1978-81; mgr., owner Blooming Nursery Inc., Cornelius, Oreg., 1982—. Mem. Perennial Plant Assn., Oreg. Assn. Nurserymen, Profl. Plant Growers Assn., Hardy Plant Soc. Democrat. Office: Blooming Nursery Inc 3839 SW Golf Course Rd Cornelius OR 97113

DINSMORE, PHILIP WADE, architect; b. Gilroy, Calif., Nov. 4, 1942; s. Wilbur Allen and Elizabeth Eleanor (Hill) D.; m. Mary Kathryn Mead; children—Robert Allen, Kerry Philip. B.Arch., U. Ariz., 1965. Registered architect, Ariz., Calif., Nev., N.C., Nat. Coun. Archtl. Registration Bds. Designer, William L. Pereira & Assocs., Los Angeles, 1965-67; assoc. CNWC Architects, Tucson, 1967-69; prin., ptnr. Architecture One Ltd., Tucson, 1970-90; ptnr. Roberts/Dinsmore Assoc., Phoenix, 1990—. Mem., chmn. Archtl. Approval Bd., City of Tucson, 1974-75, 77. Fellow AIA (nat. bd. dirs. 1981-84, nat. sec. 1984-88, Ariz. Architects Medal 1985, Western Mountain Region Citation award 1973, 76, 78, Award of Honor 1983); mem. Am. Archtl. Found. (bd. regents 1988-92), Constrn. Specifications Inst., Ariz Soc. Architects (citation 1977, 78, 79, 80, 89). Recipient Tucker award Bldg. Stone Inst., 1986. Republican. Presbyterian. Office: Roberts/Dinsmore Assoc 450 W Paseo Redondo Ste 130 Tucson AZ 85701

DIONISIO, WILLIAM PASQUALE, history educator, academic administrator; b. Sacramento, Calif., Jan. 20, 1933; s. Samuel Eugene and Mary Helen (Azzara) D.; m. Gladys J. Butz, Jan. 20, 1957; children: David, Carolyn, Patricia, Thomas. BA in History, U. Calif., Davis, 1957; MA in History, U. San Francisco, 1971. Cert. secondary educator, Calif.; adminstrv. svcs. credential. Tchr. history Luther Burbank High Sch., Sacramento, Calif., 1962-77; student activities advisor Luther Burbank High Sch., Sacramento, 1972-77; dean of students C.K. McClatchy High Sch., Sacramento, 1977-82; dist. hearing officer Cen. Office, Sacramento, 1982-84; vice prin. Hearing Office, SCUSD, Sacramento, 1983-84; prin. John Still Mid. Sch., Sacramento, 1984-87, C.K. McClatchy High Sch., Sacramento, 1987—; instr. history Sacramento City Coll., 1964—. Sgt. USAF, 1951-53. Mem. Sacramento City Adminstrs. Assn. (pres. 1984-85). Democrat. Roman Catholic. Home: 6899 Ewing Way Sacramento CA 95828-3911 Office: CK McClatchy High Sch 3066 Freeport Blvd Sacramento CA 95818-4397

DIPALMA, DANIEL, library consulting executive; b. Buffalo, Feb. 10, 1958; s. John and Mickey (Pangallo) DiP. BS, Canisius Coll., 1980. Sales rep. Am. Tobacco Co., Denver, 1980-83, Rsch. Inst. Am., Denver, 1983-89; pres. United Profl. Svcs., Inc., Denver, 1989—. Mem. Colo. Assn. Law Librs. Republican. Presbyterian. Home: 4089 S Nucla Way Aurora CO 80013-2913 Office: United Profl Svcs Inc 1120 Lincoln St Ste 200 Denver CO 80203-2136

DI PALMA, JOSEPH ALPHONSE, company executive, lawyer; b. N.Y.C., Jan. 17, 1931; s. Gaetano and Michela May (Ambrosio) Di P.; m. Joycelyn Ann Engle, Apr. 18, 1970; children: Joycelyn Joan, Julianne Michelle. BA, Columbia U., 1952; JD, Fordham U., 1958; LLM in Taxation, NYU, 1959. Bar: N.Y. 1959. Tax atty. CBS, N.Y.C., 1960-64; v.p. tax dept. TWA, N.Y.C., 1964-74; pvt. practice law N.Y.C., 1974-87; investor, exec. dir. Di Palma Family Holdings, L.A. and N.Y.C., 1987—; cons. in field; head study group Comprehensive Gaming Study, N.Y.C. and Washington, 1990—; think tank exec. dir. Di Palma Position Papers. Contbr. articles to profl. jours.; author: Di Palma Postion Papers. Bd. dirs. Friends of the Henry St. Settlement, N.Y.C., 1961-63, Outdoor Cleanliness Assn., N.Y.C., 1961-65; chmn. Air Transport Assn. Taxation Com., 1974. With U.S. Army, 1953-54. Recipient Disting. Svc. and Valuable Counsel commendation award Air Transport Assn., 1974. Mem. Internat. Platform

Assn., N.Y. State Bar Assn., N.Y. Athletic Club. Roman Catholic. Home: 3111 Bel Air Dr Apt 21B Las Vegas NV 89109-1506 Office: PO Box 72158 Las Vegas NV 89170-2158 also: 930 Fifth Ave # 4J New York NY 10021 also: 10535 Wilshire Blvd # 1504 Los Angeles CA 90024 also: 7870 E Camelback Rd # 311 Scottsdale AZ 85251

DIPIETRO, ANGELA LEE, administrative assistant; b. Canoga Park, CAlif., Aug. 7, 1967; d. Leon Frank and Elaine Eleanor (Echelberger) DiP. AA, U. Md., 1989; BA in Psychology magne cum laude, Master's Coll., 1992. Data engry clk. Bankhardt Ins. Co., Reseda, Calif., 1989-90; adminstrv./advt. asst. Advance Mktg., Saugus, CAlif., 1990; adminstrv. asst. Children Internat., Canhon Country, Calif., 1991; retail sales clk. The Gift Horse, Saugus, 1992. Sgt. U.S. Army, 1986-89. Republican.

DIPPREY, DUANE FLOYD, aerospace engineer; b. Mpls., Dec. 22, 1929; s. Floyd Daniel and Dena Levina (Larson) D.; m. Ingrid Linnea Carlson, Oct. 11, 1953; children: Neil Floyd, Ellen Linnea. Student, Gustavus Adolphus Coll., 1947-48; BS, U. Minn., 1951, MS, 1953; PhD, Calif. Inst. Tech., 1961. Registered profl. engr., Calif. Sr. devel. engr. Jet Propulsion Lab./Calif. Inst. Tech., Pasadena, 1953-60, engring. group supr., 1960-62, asst. sect. mgr., 1962-64, sect. mgr., 1964-74, dep. divsn. mgr., 1974-78, divsn. mgr., 1978-86, asst. lab. dir., 1986-91, assoc. dir., 1991-93; lectr. jet propulsion systems U. So. Calif., L.A., 1963-65. Co-author: Chemistry in Space Research, 1972. Bd. dirs. YMCA, La Canada, 1989—. Recipient Outstanding Leadership medal NASA, 1985. Fellow AIAA (assoc., chmn. liquid rockets tech. com. 1965); mem. Sigma Xi. Office: Jet Propulsion Lab 4800 Oak Grove Dr Pasadena CA 91109

DIRKS, DAVID MCCORMICK, accounting executive, consultant; b. Indpls., June 29, 1941; s. George Herman and Vera Louise (Brizius) D.; m. Laura Lee McClure, Aug. 20, 1966; Children : Anne Marie, Michael David, Katherine Lee. BA, DePauw U., Greencastle, Ind., 1963; MBA, Ind. U., 1965. CPA, Colo. Staff acct. Arthur Andersen & Co., Indpls., 1965-65; mgr. Arthur Andersen & Co., Denver, 1969-78; pvt. practice David M. Dirks, CPA, Denver, 1978-80; shareholder Tanner, Dirks & Co., Inc., Denver, 1980 —. Contrib. articles to profl. jours. Bd. dirs., pres. Karis, Inc., Denver; pres., bd. dirs. Human Services; trustee, treas. Mile High United Way. Capt. USAF, 1965-69. Decorated Bronze Star, Air Force Commendation medal; recipient Selectee award Leadership Denver. Fellow AICPA (coun. 1989-90, 91—), Colo. Soc. CPAs (pres. 1990-91); mem. Greater Denver C. of C. (bd. dirs.). Republican. Episcopalian. Office: Tanner Dirks & Co Inc 999 Jasmine St Ste 300 Denver CO 80220-4576

DIRKS, LAURA MCCLURE, marketing educator; b. Chgo., Nov. 30, 1946; d. Roy Earl and Therese Marie (Roberts) McC.; m. David McCormick, Aug. 20, 1966; children: Anne, Michael, Katherine. Student, Ind. U., 1964-66; BS, U. Colo., 1968, MBA, 1975. Bank officer United Bank of Denver, 1968-72; mktg. officer Am. Security & Trust Co., Washington, 1972-73; rsch. asst. U. Colo., Boulder, 1974-75; mem. adj. faculty U. Colo., Denver, 1979-88; cons. L.M. Dirks & Assocs., Denver, 1973-89; ptnr. Dirks & Daniel Cos., Denver, 1989—; mem. adj. faculty Regis U., Denver, 1991—; nat. mktg. cons. various businesses and nonprofits nat. seminars, 1973—. Co-author: Marketing Without Mystery-Playbook, 1990, Marketing Without Mystery, 1991; mng. co-editor: A Colorado Kind of Christmas, 1993; columnist Small Bus. Rev., 1992; contbr. articles on mktg. to profl. jours. Mem. Jr. League Denver, 1978—, bd. mem., 1986; bd. mem. The Children's Mus., Denver, 1987-89, Denver Ballet Guild, 1992—; mktg. com. Mile High United Way, Denver, 1990—; Denver dir. Nat. Jr. Tennis League, 1972. Mem. Colo. Author's League, Beta Gamma Sigma. Episcopalian. Office: Dirks & Daniel Cos 5950 E 10th Ave Denver CO 80220

DIRUSCIO, LAWRENCE WILLIAM, advertising executive; b. Buffalo, Jan. 2, 1941; s. Guido Carmen and Mabel Ella (Bach) DiR.; m. Gloria J. Edney, Aug. 19, 1972; children: Lawrence M., Lorie P., Darryl C., Teresa M., Jack D. With various broadcast stas. and instr., adminstr. Bill Wade Sch. Radio and TV, San Diego, San Francisco, Los Angeles, 1961-69; account exec. Sta. KGB Radio, San Diego, 1969, gen. sales mgr., 1970-72; pres. Free Apple Advt., San Diego, 1972—, Fin. Mgmt. Assocs., Inc., San Diego, 1979-84, Self-Pub. Ptnrs., San Diego, 1981—, Media Mix Assocs. Enterprises, Inc., 1984-86; pres. Press-Courier Pub. Co., Inc., 1985-86; pres. Media Mix Advt. and Pub. Relations, 1985—, Taking Care of Bus. Pub. Co., 1990—; pres. Formula Mktg. Co., 1993. Chmn. bd. Quicksilver Enterprises, Inc., A Public Corp., 1992-93; lectr., writer on problems of small bus. survival. Served with USN, 1958-60. Five Emmy nominations for T.V. commercial writing and prodn. Mem. Nat. Acad. TV Arts and Scis. Democrat. Roman Catholic. Office: Free Apple Advt 726 W Kalmia St San Diego CA 92101-1311

DISALVO, BEVERLY JANE, English language educator; b. Oakland, Calif., May 11, 1952; d. Robert Desimone and Ruth Marie (Buntain) Rhien; m. Dick Saverio DiSalvo, Aug. 7, 1976 (Dec. 1986); children: Samuel Scott, Steven Thomas, Evelyn Eileen. BA, U. of the Pacific, 1972; MA, U. Calif., Davis, 1975. Cert. community coll. tchr., Calif. Instr. English as a second lang. Merced (Calif.) Coll., 1975-76, coord. English as a second lang., 1976-88, instr. English as a second lang. and devel. writing, 1988—; mem. curriculum com. Merced Coll., 1990—; cons. English as a second lang. Merced County Schs., Merced, 1979; advisor Phi Theta Kappa, 1992—. Coun. mem. Shepherd of the Valley Luth. Ch., Merced, 1987-90; com. mem. pack 127 Boy Scouts Am., Merced, 1989-93, advancements chmn. troop 88, 1992—, com. mem. troop 88, 1991—. Mem. Tchrs. English to Speakers of Other Langs., Calif. Tchrs. English to Speakers of Other Langs. Republican. Office: Merced Coll 3600 M St Merced CA 95348-2898

DISMUKES, VALENA BROUSSARD, educator; b. St. Louis, Feb. 22, 1938; d. Clobert Bernard and Mary Henrietta (Jones) Broussard; m. Martin Ramon Dismukes, June 26, 1965; 1 child, Michael Ramon. AA in Edn., Harris Tchrs. Coll., 1956; BS in Phys. Edn., Washington U., St. Louis, 1958; MA in Phys. Edn., Calif. State U., L.A., 1972; BA in TV and Film, Calif. State U., Northridge, 1981. Cert. phys. edn. tchr., standard svcs. supr. Phys. edn. tchr., coach St. Louis Pub. Schs., 1958-60; phys. edn. tchr., coach L.A. Unified Sch. Dist., 1960-84, health and sci. tchr., mentor tchr., 1984—; coord. Chpt. I, 1989-92; mem. sch. based mgmt. team, 1990-93. Editor parent newsletter, 1975-80; photographs exhibited in one-woman shows include The Olympic Spirit, 1984, L.A.-The Ethnic Place, 1986; contbr. articles to profl. jours. Mem. adv. com. Visual Comm., L.A., 1980; bd. dirs. NACHES Found., Inc., L.A., 1985-86; mem. Community Consortium, L.A., 1986-87; mem. adv. com. L.A. Edn. Partnership, 1986-87. Recipient Honor award L.A.-Calif. Assn. Health, Phys. Edn. and Recreation, 1970; photography grantee L.A. Olympic Organizing Com., 1984, Teaching grantee L.A. Edn. Partnership, 1987-89; Marine Educators fellow, 1992. Mem. ACLU, Am. Fedn. Tchrs., United Tchrs. of L.A., Sierra Club. Home: 3800 Stocker St # 1 Los Angeles CA 90008 Office: 32d St/USC Magnet Sch 822 W 32d St Los Angeles CA 90007

DISNEY, MICHAEL GEORGE, financial services executive; b. Harvey, Ill., Nov. 30, 1955. Grad. high sch., Harvey, Ill.; grad., Life Underwriters Tng. Coun. Sales mgr. Met. Life Ins. Co., Naperville, Ill., 1979-84; regional dir. Firemens Fund Ins. Co., San Diego, 1984-85; owner, mgr. Disney Fin., Inc., El Cajon, Calif., 1985—. Mem. Nat. Assn. Life Underwriters, Life Underwriters Tng. Council (moderator-cons. 1986-87), Million Dollar Round Table (coord., chmn. San Diego chpt. 1987-89), La Mesa (Calif.) C. of C., San Diego C. of C., El Cajon C. of C., LaMesa C. of C., Toastmasters. Home: 3910 Dorsie Ln La Mesa CA 91941-7335 Office: 7863 LaMesa Blvd La Mesa CA 91941

DISNEY, ROY EDWARD, broadcasting company executive; b. Los Angeles, Jan. 10, 1930; s. Roy Oliver and Edna (Francis) D.; m. Patricia Ann Dailey, Sept. 17, 1955; children: Roy Patrick, Susan Margaret, Abigail Edna, Timothy John. B.A., Pomona Coll., 1951. Guest relations exec. NBC, Hollywood, Calif., 1952; apprentice film editor Mark VII Prodns., Hollywood, 1942; asst. film editor, cameraman prodn. asst., writer, producer Walt Disney Prodns., Burbank, Calif., 1954-77, dir., 1967—; pres. Roy E. Disney Prodns. Inc., Burbank, 1978—; chmn. bd. dir. Shamrock Broadcasting Co., Hollywood, 1979—; chmn. bd. dir., founder Shamrock Holdings Inc., Burbank, 1980—; trustee Calif. Inst. Arts, Valencia, 1967—; vice chmn. Walt Disney Co., Burbank. Author: novelized adaptation of Perri; producer (film) Pacific High, Mysteries of the Deep (TV show) Walt Disney's Wonderful World of Color, others; exec. producer Cheetah; writer, dir., producer numerous TV prodns. Bd. dirs. Big Bros. of Greater Los Angeles; mem. adv. bd. dirs. St. Joseph Med. Ctr., Burbank; mem. U.S. Naval Acad. Sailing Squadron, Annapolis, Md.; fellow U. Ky. Recipient Acad. award nomination for Mysteries of the Deep. Mem. Dirs. Guild Am. West, Writers Guild Am. Republican. Clubs: 100, Confrerie des Chevaliers du Tastevin, St. Francis Yacht, Calif. Yacht, San Diego Yacht, Transpacific Yacht, Los Angeles Yacht. Office: Walt Disney Co 500 S Buena Vista St Burbank CA 91521-0001

DISSANAYAKE, CHANDRA, orthopedic surgeon; b. Colombo, Sri Lanka. BS, MB, Faculty of Medicine, Colombo, 1965; MD, Downstate U., 1974. Diplomate Am. Bd. Orthopedic Surgery. Orthopedic surgeon So. Calif. Permanente Med. Group, Harbor City, 1983—, chief dept. orthopedics, 1988-93. Fellow Am. Acad. Orthopedic Surgeons. Office: So Calif Permanente Med Grp 25825 Vermont Ave Harbor City CA 90710-3599

DISSE, DIANE MARIE, writer, educator; b. Detroit Lakes, Minn., Mar. 11, 1943; d. Arthur Raymond and Luella Martha (Schultz) D.; m. Charles Kowalski, Sept. 15, 1966 (div. 1973); 1 child, Stephanie Diane; m. James Joseph Murphy, Aug. 17, 1985. BS in English, Moorhead State U., 1965; MA in Mass Communication, Calif. State U., Northridge, 1973. Info. officer Western Ins. Info. Svc., Santa Ana, Calif., 1974-78; freelance editor, 1978-79; mgr. corp. communications Republic Airlines, Mpls., 1979-80; dir. communications and mktg. U. St. Thomas, St. Paul, 1980-86; info. officer Minn. Hist. Soc., St. Paul, 1986-88; exec. dir. Mpls. Citizens Com. Pub. Edn., 1988-90; dir. publs. Sci. Mus. Minn., St. Paul, 1990-92; instr. writing, student media adviser Western Oreg. State Coll., Monmouth, 1992—; adv. bd. Heritage Cinemas, Fairfax, Calif., 1991—. Contbr. poetry to anthologies. Vol. Children's Home Soc., St. Paul, 1990-92. Mem. Soc. Profl. Journalists, Women in Communication (Crystal Clarion award 1991), Coun. Advancement and Support Edn. (Publs. award 1983), Pub. Rels. Soc. Am. (sec.-treas. 1976, Protos award 1977). Home: 2510 Dune Ave SW Lincoln City OR 97367

DISTEFANO, PETER ANDREW, insurance executive; b. N.Y.C., Nov. 26, 1939; s. Peter Julian and Marie Antoinette (Onorato) D.; children: Diane, Daniel, Donald. Student, City Coll. San Francisco, 1965, Costa Mesa (Calif.)-Orange Coast Coll., 1975; cert. enrolled employee benefits, Wharton Sch., U. Pa., 1980. Cert. profl. ins. agt., 1987; registered profl. disability and health ins. underwriter. Agt. Mut. N.Y., San Francisco, 1971-73; regional mgr. Hartford Ins. Group, Santa Ana, Calif., 1972-77; v.p. Lachman & Assos., Inc., Lafayette, Calif., 1977-80; pres., owner Distefano Ins. Svcs., Benicia, Calif., 1980-92; lectr., cons. risk mgmt., employee benefits. . Past pres. Contra Costa/Solano County Easter Seal Soc. With USNR, 1957-62. Recipient various ins. sales awards, Cert. Profl. Ins. Agt. Designation award, 1987. Fellow Acad. Producer Ins. Studies; mem. Nat. Assn. Health Underwriters, Nat. Assn. Life Underwriters, Soc. Registered Profl. Health Underwriters, Nat. Assn. Security Dealers, Internat. Found. Employee Benefit Plans, Profl. Ins. Agts. Calif./Nev. Soc. (cert.), Oakland/East Bay Assn. Life Underwriters. Greek Orthodox.

DITCHIK, ROBERT ANDREW, biochemist, consultant, small business owner; b. N.Y.C., Mar. 29, 1958; s. Philip M. Ditchik and Harriet A. (Lane) Shpiner. BS in Biochemistry, Calif. Polytech. U., 1980; MBA, Ariz. State U., 1982. Bus. analyst, purchasing agt. TRW, Inc, Redondo Beach, Calif., 1982-84; sr. price/cost analyst TRW, Inc, Redondo Beach, 1984-87; div. bus. mgr. PRC, Inc., Camarillo, Calif., 1990-92; owner, mgr. DNA Bus. Ops. Consulting Svcs., Encino, Calif., 1992—. Mem. Rep. Nat. Com. Recipient scholarship Ariz. State U., Tempe, 1981-82. Office: DNA Bus Ops Consulting Svcs 16000 Ventura Blvd Ste 500 Encino CA 91436

DITMANSON, DENNIS L., national monument superintendent; b. Webster, S.D., June 17, 1947; s. Arnold H. and Evelyn (Burns) D.; m. Barbara Jean Buekhart, Aug. 15, 1970; children: Ethan James, Rebecca Jean, Kevin Jon. BS in Edn., U. S.D., 1972. Seasonal ranger Custer Battlefield Nat. Monument, Crow Agency, Mont., 1971, 72, supt., 1987—; ranger Lyndon B. Johnson N.H.S., Johnson City, Tex., 1973, Sanjuan Island N.H.P., Ferry Harbor, Wash., 1973-75; chief Fort Clark Nat. Monument, Asbrig, Oreg., 1975-77, Bent's Old Fort N.H.S., La Junta, Wyo., 1977-81; mgr. Jewel Cave Nat. Monument, Custer, S.D., 1981-86. Leader Cub Scouts Am., Custer, 1985-86, Odessy of the Mind, Custer, 1985-86; com. mem. Hardin Area C. of C. and Agrl., Hardin, Mont., 1987—. Mem. Assn. Nat. Park Rangers (bd. dirs.), Nat. Park Service Employees and Alumni Assn., Council on Am. Military Past., Rotary, Kiwanis, Elks. Office: Custer Battlefield Nat Monument PO Box 39 Crow Agency MT 59022-0039

DITTMAN, DEBORAH RUTH, real estate broker; b. Sacramento, Apr. 15, 1932; d. Charles Harwood and Ruth (Potter) Kinsley; m. John Alvin Cardoza, Sept. 1950 (div. 1964); children: Harold Cardoza, Nancy Jongeward, John Allan Cardoza, Gregory Cardoza, Janice Boswell; m. Edgar Marshall Dittman, Jan. 22, 1967 (dec. Jan. 6 1982); m. Philip George Vrieling, July 7, 1990. Student Humprey's Coll., Stockton, Calif., 1966; grad. real estate sales Anthony Schs., 1978; cert. in real estate San Joaquin Delta Coll., 1977. Lic. real estate broker, Calif., 1978, real estate sales assoc., 1974-78; cert. residential specialist. Sec. Calif. Dept. Water Resources, Patterson and Tracy, 1966-72; hostess Welcome Wagon, Tracy, 1973-74; assoc. realtor Reeve Assocs., Tracy, 1975-80; broker Allied Brokers, Tracy, 1980-83; ptnr. real estate Putt, Fallavena, Willbanks & Dittman, Tracy, 1983—; mem. adv. bd. Tracy Fed. Bank(formerly Tracy Savings & Loan), 1989—, Women's Coun. Realtors, 1990—. Mem. Residential Sales Coun., 1989, Women's Coun. Realtors, 1990. Mem. Tracy Bd. Realtors (pres. 1981, 85, dir. 1976, 77, 80-83, 85-86), Calif. Assn. Realtors (dir. 1980-81, 85), Cert. Real Estate Specialists (v.p. no. Calif. chpt. 1990, pres. 1991), Nat. Assn. Realtors, Tracy Assn. Realtors, So. Alameda Assn. Realtors, Tracy C. of C. (bd. dirs. 1988-90). Presbyterian. Home: 12134 Midway Dr Tracy CA 95376-9113 Office: 1045 Tracy Blvd Tracy CA 95376-3726

DIU, CHIN KEE, mechanical engineer; b. China, July 23, 1952; came to U.S. 1973; s. Siu Wang and Yuk ying (Chan) D. BS, SUNY, Buffalo, 1976, MS, 1978, PhD, 1982. Asst. prof. John Brown U., Silver Spring, Ark., 1982-84; adv. engr. IBM, San Jose, 1984—. Mem. ASME (assoc. mem., tech. dir. 1990-91). Office: IBM Corp A74/124 5600 Cottle Rd San Jose CA 95193-0001

DIVELEZ, GILBERT JULIAN, machinery erectors executive; b. Saltillo, Coahuila, Mexico, Jan. 9, 1950; s. Gilberto Velez Gonzalez and Maria (Trujillo) De Velez; children: Ray, Jorrel, Johanna. Student, U. Colo., 1986; A in Gen. Studies, Pikes Peak C.C., Colorado Springs, Colo., 1992. Cert. human resource mgmt. and bus. Machinist "A" Internat. Assn. Machinery and Aerospace, Chgo. and L.A., 1970-76; journey man working jurisdiction Colo./Wyo. Millwright-Machinery Erector, Denver, 1976—; chmn., bus. mgr., CEO Occ. Mech. Contractors, Colorado Springs, 1986-89. Patentee in field. Bd. mem. Orgn. of West Side Neighbors, Colorado Springs, 1985. Mem. Colo. Springs Area Labor Coun. (del. 1992), Millwright Labor Union 2834 (so. dist. coun. 1986—), Phi Theta Kappa. Home: 1115 W Kiowa Colorado Springs CO 80904

DIVINE, CHARLES HAMMAN, telecommunications industry executive; b. Mishawaka, Ind., June 16, 1945; s. Gail Kenneth and Maxine (Roebuck) D.; m. Carol Evelyn Ash, Feb. 14, 1970; children: Craig Eric, Bradley Ryan. BSEE, Rose-Hulman Inst., 1967; MSEE, Stanford U., 1968, PhD, 1972; MBA, Pepperdine U., 1988. Mem. tech. staff Bell Telephone Labs., Denver, 1971-76; supr. software devel. Am. Telecom, Inc., Anaheim, Calif., 1976-77, mgr. software devel., 1977-78, sr. mgr. devel., 1978-81, dir. exploratory devel., 1981-83, dir. product mktg., 1983-84; v.p. R & D Toshiba Am. Info. Systems, Inc., Irvine, Calif., 1984-90, v.p. strategic and bus. planning, 1990-92; v.p. engring. and customer support Applied Digital Access, Inc., San Diego, Calif., 1992—. Mem. dean's adv. bd. Pepperdine U. Sch. Bus. Mgmt., Malibu, 1989—; co-chmn. Young Life Area Com. S. Orange County, Calif., 1987-90. Mem. IEEE, Eta Kappa Nu, Tau Beta Pi. Baptist. Office: 6175 Lusk Blvd San Diego CA 92121

DIVINE, JAMES ROBERT, chemical engineer; b. Stockton, Calif., Mar. 11, 1939; s. Eli Jackson and Ida Caroline (Schmid) D.; m. Kay Ellen Giezentanner, Mar. 1, 1974; children: David A., Amanda N. BS with honors, U. Calif.-Berkeley, 1961; PhD, Oreg. State U., 1965. Registered profl. engr., Wash., Alaska; cert. corrosion specialist. Engr., Western Regional Research Lab., U.S. Dept. Agr., Albany, Calif., summer 1961; sr. engr. Battelle-N.W., Richland, Wash., 1965-74, 78-83, staff engr., 1983-86, mgr. corrosion and metallurgy sect., 1986-90; chief engr. ChemMet, Ltd., P.C., West Richland, Wash., 1991—; sr. engr. Westinghouse-Hanford, Richland, 1974-78. Staff officer Tri-Cities squadron CAP, Richland, 1981—. NDEA fellow Oreg. State U., 1961-64. Mem. NSPE, Am. Inst. Chem. Engrs., Nat. Assn. Corrosion Engrs., Sigma Xi, Tau Beta Pi, Phi Lambda Upsilon. Office: ChemMet Ltd PC PO Box 4068 Richland WA 99352-0017

DIVINE, THEODORE EMRY, electrical engineer; b. Hailey, Idaho, May 27, 1943; s. Theodore Clyde and Muriel Juanita (Kirtley) D.; BSEE, U. Wash., Seattle, 1966, MBA, 1970; m. Roberta Louise Erickson, Mar. 19, 1966; children: Timothy Shannon, Brianna Kristine, Rachel Melissa. Engr., Gen. Telephone Co. of N.W., 1968-69; mem. tech. staff NW ops. Computer Scis. Corp., 1970-72; research engr. Battelle Pacific N.W. Labs., Richland, Wash., 1973—, research sect. mgr., 1978, staff engr., def. programs, 1980-89; program mgr., special programs Idaho Nat. Engr. Lab., 1989—, mgr. Nat. Security Programs Office, 1992—. Pres., Mid-Columbia Sci. Fair Assn., 1975-76; ruling elder First Presbyn. Ch., Prosser, Wash., 1982-84. Served as officer Signal Corps, USAR, 1966-84; Vietnam, 1967. Decorated Bronze Star. Mem. IEEE, Am. Def. Preparedness Assn., Assn. of U.S. Army, Am. Soc. Agrl. Engrs. (com. chmn. 1977-78, 82-83, chmn. nat. conf. on electronics in agr. 1983), Beta Gamma Sigma. Mem. editorial adv. bd. Internat. Jours. Computers & Electronics in Agr., Elsevier, The Netherlands, 1983—.

DIVINSKY, NATHAN JOSEPH, mathematician, educator; b. Winnipeg, Man., Can., Oct. 29, 1925; s. Abraham David and Rose (Polonsky) D.; children: Judith, Miriam, Pamela. BSc, U. Man., 1946; MS, U. Chgo., 1947, PhD, 1950. Asst. prof. Ripon Coll, Wis., 1950-51; asst. prof., then assoc. prof. U. Man., Winnipeg, 1951-59; assoc. prof., then prof. math., U. B.C., Vancouver, 1959—, asst. dean sci., 1968-76; mem. NSF Insts. U. Oreg., 1960-69; vis. prof. U. London, Queen Mary Coll., 1957, 65, 72, 85. NRC grantee 1963-72, Can. Coun. postdoctoral grantee, 1972. Author: Around the Chess World in Eighty Years, 1961, Rings & Radicals, 1965, (with R. Keene) Warriors of the Mind, 1988, also articles; editor: Chess Chat, 1959—; reviewer Zentralblatt, 1965—; editor in chief Batsfords Chess Ency., 1990; referee Australian Math. Soc. Jour. 1965—. Mem. Am. Math. Soc. (referee jour. 1965—), Can. Math. Congress (referee jour. 1965—), London Math. Soc., Math. Assn. Am., Chess Journalists World (v.p. 1969—), Commonwealth Chess Assn. (pres. 1990—), Can. Chess Fedn. (v.p. 1953-54, pres. 1993—), Am. Contract Bridge League (life master 1967), Sigma Xi. Office: Dept Math U BC, #121-1984 Mathematics Rd, Vancouver, BC Canada V6T 1Y4

DIVOLA, JOHN, artist; b. Santa Monica, Calif., June 6, 1949; s. John M. and Marion (Foster) D. BA, Calif. State U., Northridge, 1971; MA, UCLA, 1973, MFA, 1974. Instr. Calif. Inst. of the Arts, Valencia, 1978-88; prof. U. Calif., Riverside, 1988—. Fellowship John Simon Guggenheim, 1987, Nat. Endowment for the Arts, 1973, 76, 79, 90. Home: 245 Ruth Ave Venice CA 90291-2711 Office: U Calif Art Dept 1107 Olmstead Hall Riverside CA 92521-0320

DIXON, ERNEST H., computer programmer; b. L.A., Jan. 28, 1952; s. Alfred A. and H. Adelaide (Russum) D. Student, Brigham Young U. Programmer self-employed, 1970-75; teaching asst. Brigham Young U., Computer Sci. Dept., Provo, Utah, 1973-74; programmer United Computing Corp., L.A., 1974-75, Transaction Technology Inc., L.A., 1975-76; customer rels. mgr., programmer Sphere Corp., Salt Lake City, 1976-77; programmer The Computer Rm., Salt Lake City, 1977; programmer,. systems analyst LDS Hosp., Salt Lake City, 1977-80; lead programming analyst Blue Cross & Blue Shield of Utah, Salt Lake City, 1980—; chair Wasatch Front Group-1 Users, Salt Lake City, 1989-92. Bd. dirs. Greater Aves. Community Coun., Salt Lake City, 1988—; cen. com. Utah State Rep. Party, 1991-93; basketball and softball official Utah High Sch. Activities Assn., 1986—. Recipient Readibility Improvement Leadership award U.S. Postal Svc., 1991. Mem. Salt Lake City Postal Customer Coun. (exec. bd. 1991—), Greater Aves. Community Coun. (bd. dirs. 1988—). Republican. Mem. LDS Ch. Home: 77 C St Salt Lake City UT 84103-2369 Office: Blue Cross & Blue Shield 2455 Parleys Way Salt Lake City UT 84109-1299

DIXON, JULIAN CAREY, congressman; b. Washington, Aug. 8, 1934; m. Betty Lee; 1 son, Cary Gordon. B.S., Calif. State U., Los Angeles, 1962; LL.B., Southwestern U., Los Angeles, 1967. Mem. Calif. State Assembly, 1972-78; mem. 96th-103rd Congresses from Calif. 28th (now 32nd) Dist., 1979—; mem. House Appropriations Com. 96th-102nd Congresses from Calif. 28th Dist.; chmn. subcom. of D.C., mem. subcom. on Def.; mem. Congl. Black Caucus 96th-102d Congresses from Calif. 28th Dist.; mem. appropriations com., mem. intelligence com., me. house Democrats steering and policy com.; bd. dirs. CBC Found., Inc. Served with U.S. Army, 1957-60. Mem. NAACP, Urban League, Calif. Arts Commn. Democrat. Office: House of Representatives 2400 Rayburn Washington DC 20515-0532

DIXON, LYNN DIANE, retail executive; b. Bellingham, Wash., Sept. 26, 1947; d. Russell Edward Riemann and Doris Ann Sommer; m. Ronald Edward Dixon, May 30, 1970; children: Elizabeth, Steven, Nicholas. Student, Alaska Meth. U., 1966; BA, Linfield Coll., 1969; postgrad., U. Alaska, 1970. Store mgr. Book Cache, Anchorage, 1970-71, store managerial asst., 1977-80, buyer, 1980-83, mng. dir., 1983-89, exec. dir., 1989-93; owner Cook Inlet Book Co. Inc., Anchorage, 1993—; v.p. Alaska News Agy., Inc., Anchorage, 1977, also bd. dirs.; bd. dirs. Alaska Ctr. for the Book, 1992-93. Neighborhood chairperson Girl Scouts Am., 1983; neighborhood coord. Boy Scouts Am.; mem. Community Concert Band, 1987-89. Mem. Am. Mgmt. Assn., Am. Assn. Female Execs., Am. Booksellers Assn., N.W. Booksellers Assn., Alaska Ctr. for the Book, Anchorage Conv. and Visitors Bur., Anchorage Downtown Assn., C. of C., Mu Phi Epsilon. Democrat. Roman Catholic. Home: 7530 Labrador Cir Anchorage AK 99502-4191 Office: Book Cache 325 W Potter Dr Anchorage AK 99518-1142

DIXON, MICHAEL WAYNE, designer, writer; b. Honolulu, Hawaii, May 3, 1942; s. Gordon Alvin and Terry (Mendes) D.; m. Janis Marie Travis, Jan. 4, 1963 (div. 1977); children: Kimberlee Ann, Gregory Page, Morgan Ashley. Tech. illustrator Rockwell Internat., Anaheim, Calif., 1962-66, Western Gear Corp., Lynwood, Calif., 1966-69; owner Unisex Clothing Store, Norwalk, Calif., 1969-71; mgr. Am. Health Industries, Downey, Calif., 1971-72; police officer Vernon Police Dept., L.A. Police Dept., 1972-81; designer, pres. Dornaus and Dixon Enterprises, Inc., Huntington Beach, Calif., 1979-88; freelance writer Huntington Beach, 1986—. Inventor firearm safety devices; 10mm auto cartridge; Just'n Case police holster; MAWB cutter police bullet; author: Bren Ten Owner's Manual, 1982, BodyShaping, 1985, BodyQuest, 1993, BodySense, 1993, BodyLanguage, 1993, Courtroom Rapport, 1993. With USN, 1959-62. Mem. N.Y. Acad. Scis., Am. Film Inst., Rsch. Coun. Scripps Clinic and Rsch. Found., Smithsonian Instn., Los Angeles County Mus. Art, Linus Pauling Inst. Sci. and Medicine.

DIXON, RICHARD B, county official; b. San Diego, Apr. 17, 1937; s. Beecher and Vivienne (Alspaugh) D.; m. Marilyn Tams, Dec. 20, 1957 (div. 1969); children: Louise M. Webb, John P.; m. Susan C. Widman, Dec. 26, 1974, John P. Santee, Jeffrey S. Santee (stepsons). BA, Pomona (Calif.) Coll., 1957; grad., UCLA. County mgmt. and staff various depts. State of Calif., 1958-78; asst. chief budget divsn. L.A. County, 1974-78, chief budget divsn., chief adminstrv. officer, 1978-84, treas., tax collector, 1984-87, chief adminstrv. officer, 1987—; Mem. bd. adv. The Public's Capital, mem. editorial bd. Municipal Finance Jour.; mgmt. instr. east L.A. C.C., Pepperdine U. Grad. Program. Vice chmn. Union Rescue Mission, 1989-92, sec. L.A. County Employees Retirement Assn. Bd. Investments, 1984-87, chair L.A. Unified Sch. Dist. Annuity Reserve Bd., 1984-87, dir. Courts and Records Fed. Credit Union, 1968-78, sec. Credit Com., 1964-68, corp. dir. L.A. United Way, chmn. L.A. County Adminstrv. Coms. of Thrift, Savings, and Deferred Compensation Plans, mem. Nat. Bd. Dirs. Privatization Coun. Recipient Top Ten Pub. Treas. award Instl. Investor, 1986, Outstanding County Exec. award City & State, 1988, Emery E. Olson award So. Calif.

Personnel Mgmt. Assn., 1989, Benjamin M. Watson award So. Calif. Emergency Svcs. Assn., 1991, Outstanding Public Servant award N.Y. Municipal Forum, 1992, Fed. Emergency Mgmt. Agency Dir's. Outstanding Pub. Svc. award, 1992. Mem. ASPA (Nat. Conf. chmn.), Govt. Fin. Officers Assn. (past pres., exec. bd., Cash mgmt. com.), L.A. County Econ. Devel. Corp. (bd. dirs., exec. com.), L.A. chpt. ASPA (exec. bd.), UCLA Graduate Sch. Bus. (adv. bd.), Workforce L.A. Exec. Coun., Nat. Assn. Counties Taxation and Fin. Steering Com., San Francisco Mcpl. Forum (hon.). Republican. Home: 3320 Viewcrest Dr Burbank CA 91504 Office: LA County 500 W Temple St Los Angeles CA 90012

DIXON, WILLARD MICHAEL, artist; b. Kansas City, Mo., Mar. 31, 1942; s. Willard Watson and Elizabeth (O'Gorman) D.; m. Gertrude Butler, Apr. 8, 1963 (dec. July 1969); children: Anne Butler, Willard Christopher; m. Pamela Tompkins, June 20, 1970; children: Ezra Hueter, Sophia Souther. Student, Art Students League, 1959, Cornell U., 1960-61, Bklyn. Mus. Sch.; MFA, San Francisco Art Inst., 1969. painting and drawing instr. Calif. State U., Hayward, 1971-72, Calif. Coll. of Arts and Crafts, Oakland, 1973-74, 76, Acad. of Art Coll., San Francisco, 1974-76; painting instr. San Francisco State U., 1989-90; sem. leader San Francisco Art Inst., 1975. One-man shows include William Sawyer Gallery, San Francisco, 1972, 73, 75, 76, 78, 79, 81, 84, 86, 89, Tortue Gallery, L.A., 1979-80, Fischbach Gallery, N.Y., 1982, 83, 85, 87, 90, 92, Harris Gallery, Houston, 1984, Earl McGrath Gallery, L.A., 1987, 88, 91, Contemporary Realist Gallery, San Francisco, 1992, 93; group showsJoslyn Mus., Omaha, 1974, Expo 74, Spokane, Wash., Robert Schoelekopf Gallery, N.Y.C., 1989; permanent collections Met. Mus. Art, N.Y.C., San Francisco Mus. Modern Art. Fellowship Nat. Endowment for the Arts, 1989. Soto Zen Buddhist.

DIXON-BALSIGER, NANCY MARIE, publisher, editor, television production assistant; b. Ogden, Utah, May 9, 1958; d. Clarence Alfred and Dorothy Elaine (Rasmussen) Dixon; m. David Wayne Balsiger, Oct. 12, 1991. Student, Weber State Coll., 1977-79; flight attendant tng., Frontier Airlines, 1979; student, Jones Real Estate Coll., 1983, Mike Jones' Sch. Real Estate, 1990. Lic. ins. agt. Office asst., jr. loan processor Admiral Fin. Svcs., Mission Viejo, Calif., 1986-87; title rep. Commerce Title Co., Santa Ana, Calif., 1987; escrow rep. Burrow Escrow Co., Irvine, Calif., 1987-88; rep. to div. mortgage loans Am. Family Mortgage Credit Union Svcs., Orange, Calif., 1988-89; title rep. Southland Title Ins., Santa Ana, Calif., 1989-90; ins. agt. Primerica, Irvine, Calif., 1990-91; co-founder, pub., assoc. editor Christian Singles Connection Mag., Costa Mesa, Calif., 1991—; exec. dir. Christian Datemate Connection, Costa Mesa, 1991—; co-owner Sport Fotos, 1991—; co-prodr., co-host Christian Singles Connection radio broadcast; sec. Christian Singles Connection Inc., Costa Mesa, 1992—. Prodn. asst. CBS TV network spl. Ancient Secrets of the Bible, The Incredible Discovery of Noah's Ark, Ancient Secrets of the Bible II. Mem. fundraising com. Living Well Med. Clinic, Santa Ana, Calif., 1988-89; bd. dirs. Nat. Citizens Action Network, Costa Mesa, 1991—. Mem. Irvine Bd. Realtors (affiliates com. 1987-91, Home Restoration-Handicapped award 1987, 1st Pl. award golf tournament 1989), Singles Press Assn., Toastmasters (dir. membership 1989-90). Republican.

D'JAVID, ISMAIL FARIDOON, surgeon; b. Rasht, Iran, Apr. 10, 1908; arrived in Germany, 1926; came to U.S., 1946; s. Youssef and Khadidja D'Javid. Grad. high sch., Iran; MD, Friedrich Wilhelm U., Berlin, 1937, PhD, 1941. Diplomate Am. Bd. Surgery. Intern and resident Urban-Krankenhous, Robert-Koch Krankenhous and Charite, Berlin, 1938-41; physician Imperial Iranian Embassy, Berlin, 1938-41; appointed by Shah as surgeon 500-bed hosp. Mash-had, Iran, 1941; chief surgeon Army Hdqrs., Tehran, 1941-43; surgeon-in-chief Iranian 4th Army, Kordestan, Iran; pvt. practice surgery Tehran, 1941-46; intern, resident various hosps., 1947-49, chief resident in thoracic and abdominal surgery, 1950-63; major, surgeon U.S. Army M.C., 1953-55; pvt. practice specializing in surgery N.Y.C., 1957-78. Contbr. numerous articles to profl. jours.; patentee in field. Recipient Physician's Recognition award, AMA, 1977-80, 83. Life fellow Acad. Sci., Assn. Mil. Surgeons of U.S., Am. Soc. Abdominal Surgeons, Am. Physician's Art Assn.; fellow Assn. Am. Physicians and Surgeons, Am. Coll. Gastroenterology; mem. AMA, Coll. Surgeons, Deutsche Gesellschaft fur Chrirurgie (Surg. Soc. Greater Germany) (life), German Plastic Surg. Soc., Pan-Am. Med. Assn., Med. Soc. D.C., Calif. Med. Soc., World Med. Assn., N.Y. County Med. Soc., N.Y. State Med. Soc., Rudolf-Wirchow Med. Soc. Home: VOC 230 Fairway Oaks Dr Sedona AZ 86336-8823

DJAWAD, SAID TAYEB, paralegal; b. Kandahr, Afghanistan, Feb. 27, 1958; came to U.S., 1986; s. Mir Hussain and zakia Shah; m. Shamin Rahman, Nov. 16, 1986. Student, Kabul (Afghanistan) U., 1976-80; postgrad., Wilhelms U., Muenster, Germany, 1984-86, Long Island U., 1986. Paralegal Lehnardt & Bauman, N.Y.C., 1988-89, Steefel, Levitt & Weiss, San Francisco, 1989—. Editor weekly newspaper OMAID; pub. Modern Dictatorship, Occupation of Wakhan, Soviets Exapnsion to the South, Fundamentalism in Central Asia; contbr. articles to profl. jours. Dir. Afghanistan Cultural Soc., Fremont, Calif., 1990—; mem. Internat. Soc. for Human Rights, Frankfort, Germany, 1986—; mem. nat. adv. bd. Info. Am., Atlanta, 1991—. Home: 4279 Merced Circle Antioch CA 94509

DJERASSI, CARL, chemist, educator, writer; b. Vienna, Austria, Oct. 29, 1923; s. Samuel and Alice (Friedmann) D.; m. Norma Lundholm (div. 1976); children: Dale, Pamela (dec.); m. Diane W. Middlebrook, 1985. A.B. summa cum laude, Kenyon Coll., 1942, D.Sc. (hon.), 1958; Ph.D., U. Wis., 1945; D.Sc. (hon.), Nat. U. Mex., 1953, Fed. U., Rio de Janeiro, 1969, Worcester Poly. Inst., 1972, Wayne State U., 1974, Columbia, 1975, Uppsala U., 1977, Coe Coll., 1978, U. Geneva, 1978, U. Ghent, 1985, U. Man., 1985, Adelphi U., 1993. Research chemist Ciba Pharm. Products, Inc., Summit, N.J., 1942-43, 45-49; asso. dir. research Syntex, Mexico City, 1949-52; research v.p. Syntex, 1957-60; v.p. Syntex Labs., Palo Alto, Calif., 1960-62; v.p. Syntex Research, 1962-68, pres., 1968-72; pres. of Zoecon Corp., 1968-83, chmn. bd., 1968-86; prof. chemistry Wayne State U., 1952-59, Stanford (Calif.) U., 1959—; D.Sc. (hon.); bd. dirs. Quidel, Inc., Affymax, N.V., Cortech, Inc.; pres. Djerassi Found. Resident Artists Program. Author: The Futurist and Other Stories, (novel) Cantor's Dilemma, The Bourbani Gambit, (poetry) The Clock Runs Backward, (autobiography) The Pill, Pygmy Chimps, and Degas' Horse, also 9 others; mem. editorial bd. jour. Organic Chemistry, 1955-59, Tetrahedron, 1958-92, Steroids, 1963—, Proc. of NAS, 1964-70, Jour. Am. Chem. Soc., 1966-75, Organic Mass Spectrometry, 1968-91; contbr. numerous articles to profl. jours., poems, memoirs and short stories to lit. publs. Recipient Intrasci. Rsch. Found. award, 1969, Freedman Patent award Am. Inst. Chemists, 1970, Chem. Pioneer award, 1973, Nat. Medal Sci. for first synthesis of oral contraceptive, 1973, Perkin medal, 1975, Wolf prize in chemistry, 1978, John and Samuel Bard award in sci. and medicine, 1983, Roussel prize, Paris, 1988, Discovers award Pharm. Mfg. Assn., 1988, Esselen award ACS, 1989, Nat. Medal Tech. for new approaches to insect control, 1991, Nev. medal, 1992; named to Nat. Inventors Hall of Fam. Mem. NAS (Indsl. Application of Sci. award 1990), NAS Inst. Medicine, Am. Chem. Soc. (award pure chemistry 1958, Baekeland medal 1959, Fritzsche award 1960, award for creative invention 1973, award in chemistry of contemporary tech. problems 1983, Priestley medal 1992), Royal Soc. Chemistry (hon. fellow, Centenary lectr. 1964), Am. Acad. Arts and Scis., German Acad. (Leopoldina), Royal Swedish Acad. Scis. (fgn.), Royal Swedish Acad. Engring. Scis. (fgn.), Am. Acad. Pharm. Scis. (hon.), Brazilian Acad. Scis. (fgn.), Mexican Acad. Sci. Investigation, Bulgarian Acad. Scis. (fgn.), Phi Beta Kappa, Sigma Xi, Phi Lambda Upsilon (hon.). Office: Stanford U Dept Chemistry Stanford CA 94305-5080

DJURDJEVIC, ROBERT SLOBODAN, computer company executive; b. Belgrade, Serbia, Yugoslavia, June 3, 1945; m. Honor Nivin, June 29, 1974; two children. BS, U. Belgrade, 1968. Mgr. IBM Can., Toronto, 1970-78; pres. Annex Rsch., Toronto, 1978-83, Phoenix, 1983—; pub. speaker in field. Columnist computer jours.; translator (Yugoslavian drama) The Professional, 1990; author short stories, 1986-90. Republican. Office: Annex Rsch 5110 N 40th St Phoenix AZ 85018-2126

DMYTRYSHYN, BASIL, historian, educator; b. Poland, Jan. 14, 1925; came to U.S., 1947, naturalized, 1951; s. Frank and Euphrosinia (Senchak) Dmytryshyn; m. Virginia Roehl, July 16, 1949; children: Sonia, Tania. B.A., U. Ark., 1950; M.A., U. Ark, 1951; Ph.D., U. Calif.-Berkeley, 1955. Asst. prof. history Portland State U., Oreg., 1956-59; assoc. prof. Portland State U., 1959-64, prof., 1964-89, prof. emeritus, 1989—, assoc. dir. Internat. Trade and Commerce Inst., 1984-89; vis. prof. U. Ill., 1964-65, Harvard U., 1971, U. Hawaii, 1976, Hokkaido U., Sapporo, Japan, 1978-79. Author books including: Moscow and the Ukraine, 1918-1953, 1956, Medieval Russia, 900-1700, 3d edit., 1990, Imperial Russia, 1700-1917, 3d edit., 1990, Modernization of Russia Under Peter I and Catherine II, 1974, Colonial Russian America 1817-1832, 1976, A History of Russia, 1977, U.S.S.R.: A Concise History, 4th edit., 1984, The End of Russian America, 1979, Civil and Savage Encounters, 1983, Russian Statecraft, 1985, Russian Conquest of Siberia 1558-1700, 1985, Russian Penetration of the North Pacific Archipelago, 1700-1799, 1987, The Soviet Union and the Middle East, 1917-1985, 1987, Russia's Colonies in North America, 1799-1867, 1988; contbr. articles to profl. jours. U.S., Can., Yugoslavia, Italy, South Korea, Fed. Republic Germany, France, Eng., Japan, Russia. State bd. dirs. PTA, Oreg., 1963-64; mem. World Affairs Council, 1965-92. Named Hon. Rsch. Prof. Emeritus, Kyungnam U., 1989—; Fulbright-Hays fellow W. Germany, 1967-68; fellow Kennan Inst. Advanced Russian Studies, Washington, 1978; recipient John Mosser award Oreg. State Bd. Higher Edn., 1966, 67; Branford P. Millar award for faculty excellence Portland State U., 1985. Mem. Am. Assn. Advancement Slavic Studies (dir. 1972-75), Am. Hist. Assn., Western Slavic Assn. (pres. 1990-92), Can. Assn. Slavists, Oreg. Hist. Soc., Nat. Geog. Soc., Conf. Slavic and East European History (nat. sec. 1972-75), Am. Assn. for Ukrainian Studies (pres. 1991—), Ctr. Study of Russian Am. (hon.), Assn. Study Nationalities, Czechoslovak Soc. Arts and Scis., Soc. Jewish-Ukraine Contacts. Home: 2745 S Via Del Bac Green Valley AZ 85614-1071

DO, TAI HUU, mechanical engineer; b. Quang Binh, Vietnam, May 31, 1942; came to U.S., 1975; s. Mau Do and Thi Hai Nguyen; 1 child, Frederick Quan. BSME, U. Paris, 1970, MS, 1971. Rsch. engr. Soc. Automobile Engrs., Paris, 1970-71; test engr. Yanmar Diesel Co., Ltd., Osaka, Japan, 1971-72; prodn. mgr. Vietnam Products Co., Ltd., Saigon, Vietnam, 1972-75; chief engr. European Parts Exchange, Irvine, Calif., 1975-77; project mgr. Fairchild Fastener Group, Santa Ana, Calif., 1977—. Co-author: Literary Dissident Movement in Vietnam; editor: Khai Phong Mag.; patentee in field; contbr. articles to profl. jours. Mem. Soc. Automotive Engrs., Soc. Mfg. Engrs. Buddhist. Office: Fairchild Fastener Group 3130 W Harvard St Santa Ana CA 92704-3999

DO AMARAL, LUIZ HENRIQUE DE FILIPPIS DE STEFANO REZENDE, building designer, interior designer, construction company executive; b. Rio De Janeiro, Oct. 18, 1952; came to U.S., 1964; s. Jefferson R. and Erminia D. Do Amaral. BArch, U. Calif., Berkeley, 1975. Lic. gen. contractor. Sr. ptnr. Do Amaral, Brower & Stewart, Santa Clara, Calif., 1976-77, Do Amaral & Stewart, Santa Clara, 1977-78; prin. Do Amaral Assocs., Santa Clara, 1978-80, Do Amaral Assocs. Definitive Environments & Arch-West Constrn. Co., Los Gatos, Calif., 1980-82; pres., chief exec. officer Amalgamated Devel. Enterprises, Inc., Los Gatos, 1982—. Charles M. Marshall Found. scholar, 1972. Mem. Am. Inst. Bldg. Design (cert. bldg. designer, bd. dirs. 1978-79, chpt. v.p. 1979-80), Internat. Conf. Bldg. Officials, Constrn. Specifications Inst., Pi Lambda Phi, Alpha Mu Gamma. Roman Catholic. Office: Amalgamated Devel Enterprises 61 E Main St Ste C Los Gatos CA 95032-6907

DOBBEL, RODGER FRANCIS, interior designer; b. Hayward, Calif., Mar. 11, 1934; s. John Leo and Edna Frances (Young) D.; m. Joyce Elaine Schnoor, Aug. 1, 1959; 1½ child, Carrie Lynn. Student, San Jose State U., 1952-55, Chouinard Art Inst., L.A., 1955-57. Asst. designer Monroe Interiors, Oakland, Calif., 1957-66; owner, designer Rodger Dobbel Interiors, Piedmont, Calif., 1966—. Pub. in Showcase of Interior Design, Pacific edit., 1992; contbr. articles to mags. and newspapers. Decorations chmn. Trans. Pacific Ctr. Bldg Opening, benefit Oakland Ballet, and various other benefits and openings, 1982—; chmn. Symphonic Magic, Lake Marritt Plaza., Opening of Oakland Symphony Orch. Season and various others, 1985—; cons. An Evening of Magic, Oakland Hilton Hotel, benefit Providence Hosp. Foudn., bd. dirs., 1991. Recipient Cert. of Svc., Nat. Soc. Interior Designers, 1972, 74; recipient Outstanding Contbn. award, Oakland Symphony, 1986, Nat. Philanthropy Day Disting. Vol. award, 1991. Mem. Nat. Soc. Interior Designers (profl. mem. 1960-75, v.p. Calif. chpt. 1965, edn. found. mem. 1966—, nat. conf. chmn. 1966), Am. Soc. Interior Designers , Claremont Country, Diabetic Youth Found. Democrat. Roman Catholic.

DOBBS, CHARLES M., university administrator, history educator; b. N.Y.C., Mar. 4, 1950; s. Harry N. Dobbs and Lily R. (Weissman) Lane; m. Ann Raber, Jan. 4, 1975; children: Hannah Elizabeth, Jonathan Nevin. BA, U. Conn., 1972; AM, Ind. U., 1974, PhD, 1978. Instr. Ind. U., Bloomington, 1975-76; asst. prof. history Met. State Coll. Denver, 1977-81, assoc. prof. history, 1981-85, prof. history, 1985—, asst. to pres., 1989—; mem. adv. bd. Nat. Ctr. Freshman Yr. Studies, Columbia, S.C., 1989—; grants adviser Iowa Spl. Olympics, Des Moines, 1990—. Author: The Unwanted Symbol, 1981, The U.S. and East Asia Since 1945, 1990, Getting Grants, 1991; contbr. articles to profl. jours. Mem. Ogrn. Am. Historians, Am. Assn. Higher Edn., Assn. Can. Studies in U.S., Soc. Historians Am. Fgn. Rels., Western Social Sci. Assn. Home: 10438 Ronald Ln Denver CO 80234 Office: Met State Coll Denver PO Box 173362 Denver CO 80217

DOBELIS, GEORGE, manufacturing company executive; b. July 31, 1940; s. John and Dorothy Dobelis; m. Dolores Ann Nagle, Dec. 2, 1972; children: Sally Ann Berg, Christian Eric Berg, Kurt Conrad Berg. AA in Engring., Santa Monica Coll., 1963; student, Control Data Inst., 1970. Engring. Masterite Ind., Torrance, Calif., 1969-70; engring. mgr. Elco Corp., El Segundo, Calif., 1964-76, mgr. new products, 1976-77; pres. Connector Tech. Inc., Anaheim, Calif., 1977—. Patentee in field; contbr. articles to profl. jours. Served as sgt. N.G., 1963-69. Mem. IEEE. Republican.

DOBROVOLNY, KENNETH RAY, state official; b. Denver, July 8, 1947; s. Milton Joseph and Maxine (Shay) D.; m. Jacqueline Lea Davis, May 30, 1970. BA in English, U. Colo., 1970; MA in Pub. Adminstrn., U. No. Colo., 1978, MA in Psychology and Counseling, 1982. Agt. N.Y. Life Ins. Co., Denver, 1974-75; adminstrv. officer Nat. Coll. of Bus. Ext., Denver, 1975-79; vocat. counselor Dept. Labor and Employment, Boulder and Denver, 1979-82; vocat. counselor Job Corps Dept. Labor and Employment, Denver, 1982-83; tng. officer Colo. Dept. Pers., Denver, 1983-84; dir. performance appraisal Colo. Dept. Personnel, Denver, 1984—. Publs. editor Western Region Br. Assembly, 1989-91. Bd. dirs. French Quarter Condominium Assn., Denver, 1981-83. 1st lt. USMC, 1970-74. Mem. ACA, Colo. Counseling Assn. (pres. 1985-86, treas. 1992—), Am. Soc. Quality Control, Assn. for Quality and Participation (treas. 1992—), Colo. Career Devel. Assn., Wellshire-Kennedy Men's Golf Club (pres. 1986-87). Democrat. Home: 6492 E Mississippi Ave Denver CO 80224-1455 Office: State of Colo Personnel Dept. 1313 Sherman St Denver CO 80203-2236

DOBSON, BRIDGET MCCOLL HURSLEY, television executive and writer; b. Milw., Sept. 1, 1938; d. Franklin McColl and Doris (Berger) Hursley; m. Jerome John Dobson, June 16, 1961; children: Mary McColl, Andrew Carmichael. BA, Stanford U., 1960, MA, 1964; CBA, Harvard U., 1961. Assoc. writer General Hospital ABC-TV, 1965-73, head writer General Hospital, 1973-75; producer Friendly Road Sta. KIXE-TV, Redding, Calif., 1972; head writer Guiding Light CBS-TV, 1975-80, head writer As the World Turns, 1980-83; creator, co-owner Santa Barbara NBC-TV, 1983—, head writer Santa Barbara, 1983-86, 91, exec. producer Santa Barbara, 1986-87, 91, creative prodn. exec. Santa Barbara, 1990-91. Author, co-lyricist: Slings and Eros, 1993. Recipient Emmy award, 1988. Mem. Nat. Acad. TV Arts and Scis. (com. on substance abuse 1986-88), Writers Guild Am. (award for Guiding Light 1977, for Santa Barbara 1991), Am. Film Inst. (mem. TV com. 1986-88). Office: Fl 656 2121 Avenue of the Stars Los Angeles CA 90067-5023

DOBSON, DOROTHY GRACE, teacher, reading consultant; b. Seattle, Feb. 11, 1928; d. Harold Thomas and Marjorie Rose (Wilson) D.; children: Janet Miller, Catherine Stephens. BA in English and Polit. Sci., Pomona Coll., 1949; postgrad., Claremont Grad. Sch., 1949-50, L.A. State Coll., 1955-58, U. Calif., 1973-74; MS in Elem. Edn., Reading, So. Oreg. State Coll., 1980. Cert. elem. edn., secondary edn., reading specialist, Calif., Oreg., Mo. Tchr. chemistry Girls' Collegiate High Sch., Claremont, Calif., 1947-50, tchr. reading, English, 1957-64; tchr. grade 4 Pomona (Calif.) Sch. Dist., 1950-53; tchr. Claremont (Calif.) Sch. Dist., 1953-54; dir. Claremont Pre-Sch., 1955-57; reading specialist Palo Alto (Calif.) Sch. Dist., 1964-65; title I learning disabled tchr. San Dimas (Calif.) Schs., 1966-70; reading coord. The Principia, St. Louis, Mo., 1974-77; title I tchr. Ashland (Oreg.) Schs., 1977-78; reading specialist Ontario (Oreg.) High Sch., 1980-81; reading cons. Sch. Dist. 24J, Oreg. Reading Ctr., Salem, Oreg., 1982-93; dir., tchr. Oreg. Reading Ctr.; developed reading program Girl's Collegiate High Sch., 1957-64; learning disability and reading cons., Ventura, Calif., 1970-74, Ashland and Salem, Oreg., 1978-81; reading cons. in field. Vol. Brownie leader Girl Scouts Am., 1959-64; teen advisor Adventure Unltd., 1977-81; vol. recreation dir. Chemeketa Found. Fountain Ct., Salem, 1986-92; vol. Community TV, Salem, 1991-92. Mem. Camerata, Friends of Salem Orch., Chemeketa Found. Home: 235 Candalaria Blvd S Salem OR 97302

DOBSON, TERRANCE JAMES, banker; b. Odessa, Wash., Aug. 16, 1940; s. Leon C. and Dorothy (Armstrong) D.; m. Judith Kaye Blaesi, June 12, 1965; children: Terrance James Jr., Tad Jeremy. BA, Wash. State U., 1964; MBA, Mich. State U., 1969. Venture analyst Gen. Mills, Mpls., 1969-71; v.p., mgr. First Nat. Bank of Mpls., 1971-77; v.p. First Bank System, Inc., Mpls., 1977-78; exec. v.p. Old Nat. Bank of Wash., Spokane, 1978-87; sr. v.p. U.S. Bancorp, Portland, Oreg., 1987, exec. v.p., 1987-90; exec. v.p. West One Bank, Boise, Idaho, 1990—. Chmn. YMCA Inland Empire, Spokane, 1979-86; mem. bus. adv. coun. Wash. State U., 1980—; mem. Wash. State U. Found. Bd., 1990—; bd. dirs. Sisters of Holy Names, 1983-87. Capt. USAF, 1964-68. Mem. Am. Automobile Assn. (bd. dirs. 1978-88), Hayden Lake County Club (bd. dris. 1986-87), Crane Creek Country Club. Home: 2393 N Cliffview Way Boise ID 83702-6511 Office: West One Bank 101 S Capital PO Box 8247 Boise ID 83733-0001

DOCKSON, ROBERT RAY, savings and loan executive; b. Quincy, Ill., Oct. 6, 1917; s. Marshall Ray and Letah (Edmondson) D.; m. Katheryn Virginia Allison, Mar. 4, 1944; 1 child, Kathy Kimberlee. A.B., Springfield Jr. Coll., 1937; B.S., U. Ill., 1939; M.S. in Fgn. Service, U. So. Calif., 1940, Ph.D., 1946. Lectr. U. So. Calif., 1940-41, 45-46, prof., head dept. mktg., 1953-59; dean U. So. Calif. (Sch. Bus. Adminstrn.); and prof. bus. econs., 1959-69; vice chmn. bd. Calif. Fed. Savs. & Loan Assn., Los Angeles, 1969-70; pres. Calif. Fed. Savs. & Loan Assn., 1970-77, chmn., 1977-88, chief exec. officer, 1973-83; chmn. CalFed Inc., 1984-88, chief exec. officer, 1984-85, also dir.; instr. Rutgers U., 1946-47, asst. prof., 1947-48; dir. Bur. Bus. and Econ. Research, 1947-48; economist Western home office Prudential Ins. Co., 1948-52, Bank of Am., San Francisco, 1952-53; econ. cons., 1953-57; bd. dirs. IT Corp., Computer Scis. Corp. Am. specialist for U.S. Dept. State; mem. Town Hall, 1954—, bd. govs., 1963-65, hon. bd. govs., 1965—, pres., 1961-62; trustee John Randolph Haynes and Dora Haynes Found., Com. for Econ. Devel., Calif. Council for Econ. Edn.; chmn. bd. Rose Hills Meml. Park Assn., 1990-92; trustee, pres. Orthopedic Hosp.; bd. councilors Grad. Sch. Bus. Adminstrn., U. So. Calif.; bd. regents, chmn. univ. bd. Pepperdine U.; chmn. housing task force Calif. Roundtable, Commn. on the Future of the Calif. Cts., 1991-92. Served from ensign to lt. USNR, 1942-44. Decorated Star of Solidarity Govt. of Italy.; Recipient Asa V. Call Achievement award; Disting. Community Service award Brandeis U.; Whitney M. Young Jr. award Urban League, 1981, Albert Schweitzer Leadership award; Man of Yr. award Nat. Housing Conf., 1981; Industrialist of Yr. award Calif. Mus. Sci. and Industry, 1984. Mem. Am. Arbitration Assn., Newcomen Soc. N.Am., Hugh O'Brian Youth Found., Calif. C. of C. (pres. 1980, bd. dirs. 1981-86), L.A. C. of C. (bd. dirs.), Phi Kappa Phi (Diploma of Honor award 1984), Beta Gamma Sigma, Bohemian Club, Calif. Club, L.A. Country Club, One Hundred Club, Birnam Wood Golf Club, Thunderbird Country Club. Office: CalFed Bank 5700 Wilshire Blvd Ste 530 Los Angeles CA 90036-3659

DOCKSTADER, JACK LEE, electronics executive; b. Los Angeles, Dec. 14, 1936; s. George Earl and Grace Orine (Travers) D.;m. Kerry Jo King, Oct. 24, 1987; children: Travis Adam Mayer, Bridget Olivia Mayer. student UCLA, 1960-70. Rate analyst Rate Bur., So. Pacific Co., Los Angeles, 1954-57; traffic analyst traffic dept. Hughes Aircraft Co., Fullerton, Calif., 1957-58, Culver City, Calif., 1958-59, traffic mgr. Hughes Research Labs., Malibu, Calif., 1959-70, material mgr., 1970-75; material mgr. Hughes Aircraft Co., Culver City, 1975-80, prodn. material mgr. Electro-Optical and Data Systems Group, El Segundo, Calif., 1980-84, mgr. material total quality 1984-85, mgr. cen. material ops. and property mgmt. 1987-88, mgr. group property mgmt., 1988—, mgr. electro optical systems, property mgmt., aerospace and def. sector, 1993—. Mem. adv. council transp. mgmt. profl. designation program UCLA, 1966-80, mem. Design for Sharing Com., 1977-82; adv. com. transp. program Los Angeles Trade Tech. Coll., 1970-80. Served with USNR, 1954-76. Mem. Nat. Property Mgmt. Assn. (pres. L.A. chpt. 1992, 93), UCLA Alumni Assn., Nat. Contracts Mgmt. Assn., Naval Enlisted Res. Assn., Hughes Aircraft Co. Mgmt. Club, Delta Nu Alpha (pres. San Fernando Valley chpt. 1965-66, v.p. Pacific S.W. region 1969-71, region man of year 1971). Republican. Presbyn. Home: PO Box 3156 Redondo Beach CA 90277-1156 Office: PO Box 902 El Segundo CA 90245-0902

DOCKTOR, WILLIAM JAY, pharmacist, educator; b. Jamestown, N.D., Apr. 19, 1951; s. Alvin M. and Grace K. (Ellis) D.; m. Paulette K. Reuther, Aug. 26, 1972; children: Lisa Ann, Paul Jay. BS, N.D. State U., 1974; D in Pharmacy, U. Mich., 1977. Cert. pharmacotherapy specialist. Intern pharmacist Osco Drug, Elkhart, Ind., 1974-75; pharmacist Osco Drug, Grand Forks, N.D., 1975; assoc. in clin. pharmacy Wash. State U., Pullman, 1975-76; asst. prof. U. Mont., Missoula, 1977-83, assoc. prof., 1983—; cons. Mont. Mental Disablitites Bd. Visitors, Helena, 1977—; U.S. Forest Svc., Missoula, Mont., 1980—; clin. cons. St. Patrick Hosp., Missoula, 1988—, acting clin. coord. pharmacy, 1991-92; presenter continuing edn. programs, 1977—. Author: (with others) various books and manuals; editor drug info. column Mont. Pharmacist, 1989—, also articles. Soccer coach YMCA, Missoula, Mont., 1979-82; judge Mont. State Sci. Fair, Missoula, 1979-86, 90—; sec.-treas. Lorraine South County Water Dist., Missoula, 1985—; pres. ch. coun. Atonement Luth. Ch., Missoula, 1986-89. Named one of Outstanding Young Men Am., U.S.Jaycees, 1982. Mem. Am. Coll. Clin. Pharmacy, Am. Soc. Hosp. Pharmacists, Mont. Soc. Hosp. Pharmacists (continuing edn. and publicity chair 1982-83, program chair 1983-84, 1988-89, pres. 1984-85, bd. dirs. 1983-86), Mont. State Pharm. Assn. Lutheran.

DOCTORIAN, SAM EMMANUEL, JR., banker; b. Beirut, Dec. 7, 1962; came to U.S., 1975; s. Samuel B. and Naomi (Pashgian) D. BA, Point Loma Nazarene Coll., San Diego, 1985; postgrad., UCLA, 1990—. Teller Highland Fed. Bank, FSB, L.A., 1986-87, VIP teller, new accounts counselor, 1987, savs. supr., 1987-88, ops. officer, 1988-89, acting br. mgr., 1989, br. mgr., 1989—. Youth dir. Glendale (Calif.) Ch. of Nazarene. Mem. L.A. C. of C. (bd. dirs.), Kiwanis (com. mem. Glendale). Republican. Home: 2020 Kinclair Dr Pasadena CA 91107-1018 Office: Highland Fed Bank FSB 3355 Glendale Blvd Los Angeles CA 90039-1839

DOCTORS, SAMUEL I., management educator; b. Phila., July 1, 1936; s. Abraham and Celia (Lakoff) D.; divorced, 1973; children: Eric, Rachel, Rebecca. BS, U. Miami, 1956; JD, Harvard U., 1967, DBA, 1969. Bar: Mass. 1967. Assoc. engr. Westinghouse Electric Corp., Balt., 1956-58; sr. math. analyst AC Sparkplug div. Gen. Motors, El Segundo, Calif., 1958-59; sr. devel. engr., work dir. aero. div. Honeywell, St. Petersburg, Fla., 1961-64; cons. tech., mgmt., econs. various orgns., 1968-81; project mgr. N. Lawndale Econ. Devel. Corp. & NUGSM, 1971-73; assoc. prof. Northwestern U., Evanston, Ill., 1969-73; faculty advisor, dir. Mgmt. Asst. Clinic, Northwestern U., Chgo., 1969-73; prof. U. Pitts., 1974-84, co-prin. investigator, project monitor, 1977-79; project mgr. Allegheny County Energy Study, 1977; prin. investigator Urban Tech. System Evaluation, NSF, 1978-81, Small Bus. Adminstrn. and Dept. Energy, Washington, 1979-80; prof., adminstrn. Calif. State U., Hayward, 1982—, founder, dir. Ctr. for Bus. & Environ. Studies, 1991—; lectr. Harvard U. Bus. Sch., 1968-69; chmn. R & D workshop task force on minority bus. edn. and tng. U.S. Office Edn., 1972-73; bus. advisor David Community Devel. Corp., Ky., 1973-76; bd. dirs. Energy Policy Inst., U. Pitts., 1979-81; vis. prof. U. Calif. Sch. Bus., Berkeley, 1980-82; tech. advisor Western Gerontol. Soc., 1984—; prof. bus. adminstrn. Calif. State U. Hayward, 1983—; mem. steering com. Harvard Bus. Sch. Community Ptnrs; dir. Ctr. Bus. & Environ. Studies, Calif. State U., Hayward, 1991—. Author books (9) and over 40 articles on management. V.p., bd. dirs. Sr. Citizens Service Corp., Pitts.; chairperson Energy Outlook '78, Allegheny County Air Pollution Control Bd. Sponsoring Agy.,

San Francisco Community Recyclers. Mem. ABA, Am. Polit. Sci. Assn., Am. Econ. Assn., Nat. Assn. Community Devel., AAAS, Nat. Council Small Bus. Devel., Nat. Acad. Mgmt. (sounding bd. manpower div.), Pitts. C. of C. Office: Calif State U Hayward Mgmt Scis Dept Hayward CA 94542

DODD, DEBBIE LYNN, religious studies educator, missionary; b. Portland, Oreg., July 2, 1959; d. Douglas James and Muriel Irene (Potts) Henderson; m. Peter Daniel Dodd, Aug. 10, 1991. BA in Psychology and Religion, Whitworth Coll., 1980; MDiv, Western Sem., Portland, 1988, ThM, 1990. Tchr. Bethania High Sch., Palau, Micronesia, 1982-84; youth dir. Vernon Presbyn. Ch., Portland, 1985-90; prof. Western Sem., 1990—; missionary Liebenzell Mission, Palau, 1982-84, Conservative Bapt. Fgn. Missions Soc., Wheaton, Ill., 1993—. Author: Simplified Theological Dictionary, 1990. Mem. Evang. Theol. Soc. Baptist. Office: Western Sem 5511 SE Hawthorne Portland OR 97215

DODD, JOE DAVID, safety engineer, consultant, administrator; b. Walnut Grove, Mo., Jan. 22, 1920; s. Marshall Hill and Pearl (Combs) D.; m. Nona Bell Junkins, Sept. 17, 1939; 1 dau. Linda Kay Dodd Craig. Student S.W. Mo. State U., 1937-39, Wash. U., 1947-55. Cert. profl. safety engr. Calif. Office asst. retail credit co., Kansas City, Mo., 1939-42; bus driver City of Springfield (Mo.), 1945-47; ops., engring., and personnel positions Shell Oil Co., Wood River (Ill.) Refinery, 1947-66; health and safety dept. mgr. Martinez Mfg. Complex, Calif., 1966-83, retired 1983; exec. dir. Fire Protection Tng. Acad., U. Nev.-Reno; rep. Shell Oil Co., Western Oil and Gas Assn., 1970-81. Mem. Republican Presdl. Task Force. Served with USMC, 1942-45. Decorated Presdl. Citation. Mem. Western Oil and Gas Assn. (Hose Handler award 1972-81, Outstanding mem. award), Am. Soc. Safety Engrs., Veterans Safety, State and County Fire Chiefs Assn., Peace Officers Assn., Nat. Fire Protection Assn. Presbyterian (elder). Established Fire Protection Tng. Acad., U. Nev.-Reno, Stead Campus.

DODDS, DALE IRVIN, chemicals executive; b. Los Angeles, May 3, 1915; s. Nathan Thomas and Mary Amanda (Latham) D.; m. Phyllis Doreen Kirchmayer, Dec. 20, 1941; children: Nathan E., Allan I., Dale I. Jr., Charles A. AB in Chemistry, Stanford U., 1937. Chem. engr. trainee The Texas Co., Long Beach, Calif., 1937-39; chemist Standard Oil of Calif., Richmond, 1939-41; chief chemist Scriver and Quinn Interchem., L.A., 1941-46; salesman E.B. Taylor and Co. Mfg. Rep., L.A., 1947-53, Burbank (Calif.) Chem. Co., 1953-57, Chem. Mfg. Co./ICI, L.A., 1957-68; pres., gen. mgr. J.J. Mauget Co., L.A., 1969—. Inventor: Systemic Fungicide, 1976; patentee in field; contributed to devel. Microinjection for Trees. Fellow Am. Inst. Chemists; mem. Am. Chem. Soc., L.A. Athletic Club, Sigma Alpha Epsilon Alumni (pres. Pasadena, Calif. chpt. 1973, 90). Republican. Christian Scientist. Office: JJ Mauget Co 2810 N Figueroa St Los Angeles CA 90065-1500

DODDS, J. ALLAN, educator, plant pathologist; b. Sunderland, England, June 29, 1947; came to U.S., 1976; s. Henry B. and Dorothy (Nelson) D.; m. Carol Jackson, Aug. 9, 1969; 1 child, Claire Dodds. BSc with honors, Leeds U., Eng., 1969; MSc, McGill U., Montreal, Can., 1972, PhD, 1974. Postdoctoral fellow U. B.C., Vancouver, 1974-76; asst. plant pathologist Conn. Agrl. Experiment Sta., New Haven, 1976-80; asst. prof. U. Calif., Riverside, 1980-82, assoc. prof., 1982-88, prof., 1988—; cons. Salk Inst. Biotechnological Indsl. Assocs., La Jolla, Calif., 1990-92. Contbr. chpts. to books and numerous articles on plant viruses to profl. jours. Grantee NSF, 1982-85, USDA, 1982-90, Calif. Commodity Bds., 1980—. Mem. Am. Phytopathol. Soc., Can. Phytopathol. Soc., Am. Soc. Virology, Internat. Soc. of Citrus Virologists. Office: Dept Plant Pathology U Calif Riverside CA 92521

DODGE, DOUGLAS STUART, federal agency administrator; b. Van Nuys, Calif., May 26, 1951; s. John Marvin and Barbara Jean (McMillan) D.; m. Leslie Ann Condron, Apr. 24, 1982; children: Sarah Elizabeth, Gwendolyn Marie. BA in History, U. Calif., Davis, 1975. Outdoor recreation planner Bur. Land Mgmt., U.S. Dept. Interior, Yuma, Ariz., 1976-80; dist. recreation planner Bur. Land Mgmt., U.S. Dept. Interior, Salt Lake City, Utah, 1980-83, dist. archeologist, 1983-88; supervisory resource mgmt. specialist Bur. Land Mgmt., U.S. Dept. Interior, Bishop, Calif., 1989—. Softball umpire Am. Softball Assn., U.S. Slow-pitch Softball Assn., So. Calif., Mcpl. Athletic Fedn., Calif., Ariz., Utah, 1976—. Mem. Utah Profl. Archeologist Coun., Roundalab Internat. Tchrs. Assn. (ednl. com. 1987-88), Utah Round Dance Assn. (pres. 1988-89), Utah Round Dance Tchrs. Assn. (chmn. 1983-85), Lions. Home: 131 Mountain Rd Big Pine CA 93513-9730 Office: Bur Land Mgmt 787 N Main St Ste P Bishop CA 93514-2430

DODGEN, JAMES, engineering company executive; b. Anniston, Ala., Sept. 15, 1921. BSChemE, Ga. Tech., 1943; postgrad., Wayne State U., 1947, George Washington U., 1952, U. Utah, 1962, Stanford U., 1964, U. Wash., 1967, UCLA, 1967. Registered profl. engr., Colo., Calif., N.Mex. Comdr. U.S. Navy, 1943-46, 51-68; prin. engr. Penn Walt, 1946-51; program mgr. Lockheed, 1968-69; product dir. Olin Corp., 1969-72; program mgr. Aerojet, 1972-74; pres. Dodgen Engring. Co., Colorado Springs, Colo., 1974—. Prin. works include design of facilities for the research, development, production and test and evaluation of all types of high energy materials including propellants and explosives. Mem. Am. Mgmt. Assn., AICHE, ADPA, ACS, AUSA. Office: Dodgen Engring Co 2902 W Colorado Ave Colorado Springs CO 80904-2478

DODS, WALTER ARTHUR, JR., bank executive; b. Honolulu, May 26, 1941; s. Walter Arthur Sr. and Mildred (Phillips) D.; m. Diane Lauren Nosse, Sept. 18, 1971; children: Walter A. III, Christopher L., Peter D., Lauren S. BBA, U. Hawaii, 1967. Mktg. officer 1st Hawaiian Bank, Honolulu, 1969, asst. v.p. mktg. div., 1969-71, v.p., chmn. mktg. and rsch. group, 1971-73, sr. v.p. mktg. and rsch. group, 1973-76, exec. v.p. retail banking group, 1976-78, exec. v.p. gen. banking group, 1978-84, pres., 1984-89, chmn., ceo, 1989—; chmn., pres., CEO First Hawaiian, Inc., 1989-90, chmn., CEO, 1989—; chmn., CEO First Hawaiian Creditcorp., 1989-92; bd. dirs. First Hawaiian Inc., 1st Hawaiian Bank, First Hawaiian Creditcorp Inc., First Hawaiian Leading, Inc., Alexander & Baldwin Inc., A&B-Hawaii Inc., Duty Free Shoppers Adv. Bd., Matson Navigation Co. Inc., 1st Ins. Co. Hawaii Ltd., GTE Calif., GTE Hawaiian Telephone Co., GTE Northwest, Grace Pacific Corp., Oceanic Cablevision Inc., Pacific Guardian Life Ins. Co., Princeville Adv. Group, RHP, Inc., Restaurant Suntory USA, Inc., Suntory Resorts, Inc. Bd. dirs. Ahahui Koa Anuenue, East-West Ctr. Found.; past sec., treas. The Rehab. Hosp. of the Pacific; exec. bd. mem. Aloha Coun., Boy Scouts Am.; trustee, past chmn., trustee Blood Bank Hawaii; past chmn. bd. Aloha United Way; past chmn. Bd. Water Supply; bd. govs., v.p. fin. Ctr. for Internat. Comml. Dispute Resolution; bd. dirs., treas. Coalition for Drug-Free Hawaii; trustee Contemporary Mus. co-chmn. corp. campaign com.; mem. Duty Free Shoppers Adv. Bd.; past chmn. Gubernatorial Inauguration, 1974, 82; bd. govs. Hawaii Employers Coun.; trustee Hawaii Maritime Ctr; mem. Gov.'s Adv. Bd. Geothermal/Inter-Island Cable Project, Gov.'s Blue Ribbon Panel on the Future of Healthcare in Hawaii; dir., past chmn. Hawaii Visitors Bur.; exec. com. Hawaiian Open; past spl. dir. Homeless Kokua Week; bd. gov. Honolulu Country Club, Japanese Cultural Ctr. Hawaii, Pacific Peace Found.; trustee Japan-Am. Inst. Mgmt. Sci., The Nature Conservancy Hawaii, Punahou Sch.; Hawaii chmn. Japan-Hawaii Econ. Coun.; chmn., dir. Pacific Internat. Ctr. for High Tech. Rsch.; past co-chmn., chmn. bldg. fund St. Louis High Sch.; treas. The 200 Club; dir. World Cup Honolulu 1994. Named Outstanding Jaycee in Nation, 1963, Outstanding Young Man Am. from Hawaii, 1972, Marketer of Yr., Am. Mktg. Assn., 1987; recipient Riley Allen Individual Devel. award, 1964, Hawaii State Jaycees 3 Outstanding Young Men award, 1971, Am. Advt. Fedn. Silver medal, 1977, St. Louis High Sch.'s Outstanding Alumnus award, 1980. Mem. Am. Bankers Assn., Bank Mktg. Assn., Hawaii Bankers Assn., Hawaii Bus. Roundtable, C. of C. of Hawaii, Honolulu Press Club. Office: 1st Hawaiian Bank PO Box 96813 165 S King St Honolulu HI 96813-3501

DODSON, CHRISTOPHER THOMAS, bank regulator; b. Rantoul, Ill., Dec. 3, 1964; s. John Thomas and Aselean Sheila (Davis) D. BS, Western N.Mex. U., Silver City, 1987. Resident dormitory dir. Western N.Mex. U.-Housing, 1985-87; asst. buyer Am. Stores, Inc., Anaheim, Calif., 1987-89; fed. regulator FDIC, L.A., 1989—; bank trust specialist, computer trainer FDIC, Pasadena, Calif., 1990—. Vol. Spl. Olympics, L.A., 1988-90, Rep. Hdqrs., Pasadena, 1990—. Mem. Western N.Mex. U. Alumni Assn. Home: 762 E Orange Grove # 4 Pasadena CA 91104 Office: FDIC 25 Ecker St Ste 2300 San Francisco CA

DODSON, DAVID PHILIP, university dean; b. Logansport, Ind., Dec. 25, 1939; s. D.S. and Frances (Fullenwider) D.; m. Stephanie Ginn, Apr. 4, 1971; children: Chad, Bret, Channing. BA, Linfield Coll., McMinnville, Oreg., 1962; BD, Berkeley Bapt. Div. Sch., Calif., 1966; PhD, Grad. Theol. Union, Berkeley, 1972. Asst. chaplain, residence dir. Colgate U., Hamilton, N.Y., 1964-65; campus min. 1st Congl. Ch., Berkeley, 1966-69; preceptor Grad. Theol. Union, 1969-70; instr., asst. prof., assoc. prof. philosophy Chapman Coll., Orange, Calif., 1970-81, dean student devel., 1977-81; dean students U. Puget Sound, Tacoma, 1981-93. Contbg. author: (monograph series) Private Dreams and Shared Visions: Student Affairs Work in Small Colleges, 1986, The Role of Student Affairs in Involving Colleges, 1991. Sec. Push-Excel Parent Adv. Bd., Tacoma, 1989—; bd. dirs. Tacoma Urban League, 1991—; mem. Tacoma Schs. B.E.S.T. Ptnrs., 1990—. Mem. Nat. Assn. Student Pers. Adminstrs., Am. Assn. for Higher Edn., Am. Coll. Pers. Assn., N.W. Coll. Pers. Assn.

DODSON, DON CHARLES, academic adminstrator; b. Los Alamos, N.Mex, Dec. 30, 1944; s. Richard Wolford and Mary Ellen (Stout) D.; m. Barbara Judy Termin, Sept. 7, 1969; children: Rebecca Jane, Rachel Anne, Benjamin James. BA, Haverford Coll., 1966; MA, Stanford U., 1967, Northwestern U., 1968; PhD, U. Wis., 1974. Acting asst. prof. Stanford (Calif.) U., 1971-74, asst. prof., 1974-77; spl. asst. to v.p. Santa Clara (Calif.) U., 1977-78, dir. various programs, 1978-83, asst. v.p. for acad. affairs, 1983-86, assoc. v.p. for acad. affairs, 1986—, acting v.p. for acad. affairs, 1990-91, assoc. prof., 1991—; vis. scholar Stanford U., 1991-92. Contbr. articles to profl. jours. Grantee Exxon Edn. Found., 1985-86, U. Wis., 1971, Stanford U., 1972; Melville Jacoby fellow Stanford U., 1966-67, Univ. fellow Northwestern U., 1967-68; NSF traineeship U. Wis., 1968-71. Mem. Am. Assn. Higher Edn., Assn. Am. Colls., Internat. Communication Assn. Office: Santa Clara U Santa Clara CA 95053

DODSON, JOHN PAUL, tax executive; b. Memphis, Nov. 1, 1938. BS in Acctg., U. Tenn., 1970; MBA, Middle Tenn. State U., 1972. Acct. Sandoz Pharms., Hanover, N.J., 1960-66; tax acct. Genesco, Inc., Nashville, Tenn., 1966-72; acctg. instr. Mid. Tenn. State U., Murfreesboro, 1972-74; tax mgr. excise Weyerhaeuser Co., Tacoma, 1974-91; sr. mgr. tax Ernst & Young, Seattle, 1991-92; tax refund auditor Bogle & Gates, Seattle, 1993—. With USN, 1956-59. Mem. Inst. Mgmt. Accts., Inst. Property Taxation (cert. sales tax mem.), Evergreen Maltese Club (bd. dirs. 1985-92). Home: 32803 2nd Ave SW Federal Way WA 98023 Office: Bogle & Gates 2 Union Sq 601 Union St Seattle WA 98101-2346

DODWORTH, ALLEN STEVENS, art appraiser, consultant, curator; b. Long Beach, Calif., Nov. 19, 1938; s. Ralph Harper and Margaret (Funk) D.; m. Melissa Lloyd, June 1967 (div.); m. Julie Axelsen, Apr. 18, 1980; stepchildren: Joshua Seare, Susannah Seare. AB in Fine Art, Stanford U., 1962; postgrad., Portland State U., 1968-69, U. Utah, 1981. Art dir. Sullivan Assocs./Sullivan Press, Los Altos, Calif., 1962-67, The Clarke Press, Portland, Oreg., 1967-68; coord. exhibits White Gallery, Portland State U., 1968-69; dir. Boise (Idaho) Gallery Art (now Boise Art Mus.), 1969-76, Salt Lake Art Ctr., Salt Lake City, 1976-81, Western Colo. Ctr. for Arts, Grand Junction, 1981-85; art appraiser, owner Allen Dodworth Fine Arts Appraisal, Salt Lake City, 1985—; cons. Western States Arts Found., Santa Fe, 1981-82; bd. dirs. art design Salt Lake City, 1992—; art adv. com. Salt Lake County, 1992—. Assoc. editor Idaho Heritage mag., 1975-76; curator over 200 art exhbns., 1968—, including Am. Masters in West, 1974, The Grand Beehive Exhbn., 1980. Mem. coms. and panels Utah Arts Coun., Salt Lake City, 1978-79, 90—, Colo. Coun. on Arts and Humanities, Denver, 1982-84; bd. dirs. Salt Lake City Arts Coun., 1977-79, 87-89, Utah Lawyers for Arts, 1987—; vice chmn. Sta. KPRN, pub. radio, Grand Junction, 1983-85. Mus. profl. fellow Nat. Endowment for Arts, 1973. Mem. Am. Soc. Appraisers (candidate mem., bd. dirs. Salt Lake chpt. 1989—), Utah State Bar Assn. Fee Arbitration Com. (lay mem.), Western Assn. Art Mus. (trustee 1973-79), Salt Lake Art Dealers Assn. (pres. 1988-90), Stanford Club Idaho (pres. 1974-75). Democrat. Office: 1013 S 13th E Salt Lake City UT 84105-1549

DOE, RICHARD PHILIP, physician, educator; b. Mpls., July 21, 1926; s. Richard Harding and Ruth Elizabeth (Schoen) D.; m. Shirley Joan Cedarleaf, Sept. 15, 1950; children—Nancy Jean, Charles Jeffrey, Robert Bruce. B.S., U. Minn., 1949, M.B., 1951, M.D., 1952, Ph.D., 1966. Intern Oakland (Cal.) Hosp., 1951-52; resident internal medicine Mpls. VA Hosp., 1952-54, fellow in endocrinology, 1954-55, chief chemistry sect., 1956-60, chief metabolic endocrine sect., 1960-69, endocrine staff, 1976-88; head metabolic endocrine sect. U. Minn. Hosp., 1969-76; faculty U. Minn. Med. Sch., Mpls., 1955-88; prof. medicine U. Minn. Med. Sch., 1969-88, prof. emeritus, 1988—; pres. MEMC Corp., Carmel, Calif., 1988—. Served with USNR, 1944-46. UPSHS grantee, 1958-88. Mem. Am. Soc. Clin. Investigation, Minn. Soc. Internal Medicine, Central Soc. Clin. Research, Endocrine Soc., Am. Fedn. Clin. Research. Home and Office: MEMC Corp Box 86 Corona Rd Carmel CA 93923-9610

DOELLING, HELLMUT HANS, geologist; b. N.Y.C., July 25, 1930; s. Otto Johannes and Emma Camilla (Hartmann); m. Gerda Anna Scherwinski, May 25, 1960; children: David, Barbara, Jedediah, Doris, Peggy, Teresa, Matthew. BS, U. Utah, 1956, PhD, 1964. Staff geologist Utah Geol. and Mineral Survey, Salt Lake City, 1959-64, econ. geologist, 1966-73, sr. econ. geologist, 1973-83, sr. mapping geologist, 1983—; asst. prof. geology Midwestern U., Wichita Falls, Tex., 1964-66. Author: Coal in Utah, 1972; author bulletins Utah County studies, 1975, 80, 89. Cpl. U.S. Army, 1951-53. Mem. AAAS, Soc. Econ. Geologists, Utah Geol. Assn. (pres. 1990), Sigma Xi. Mem. LDS Ch. Office: Utah Geol Survey 2363 S Foothill Dr Salt Lake City UT 84109-1491

DOERFLING, HANK, aerospace engineer; b. San Pedro, Calif., Nov. 3, 1936; s. Laurence Howard and Julia Margret (Rusbarsky) D.; B.S. in Physics, Oreg. State U., 1958, M.S., 1963; M.Pub. Adminstrn., Pepperdine U., 1975; m. Elaine Carole; children: Howard, Carrie, Cassie, Tony, Evon. Analyst, No. Am. Aviation Co., Downey, Calif., 1963-64; mem. tech. staff TRW Systems Redondo Beach, Calif., 1964-66, adminstrv. and project mgr. Logicon, San Pedro, Calif., 1966-77; sr. scientist, engr. advanced digital communication program systems sector Hughes Aircraft Co., El Segundo, Calif., 1977—. Mem. Hermosa Beach Improvement Commn., 1970-72, chmn., 1971-72; mem. City of Hermosa Beach City Coun., 1972-80, mayor, 1973-74, 79-80; pres. South Bay Cities Assn., 1975-76; commr. South Coast (Calif.) Regional Coastal Commn., 1977-80, Calif. Coastal Commn., 1978-80. With USN, 1958-61. Mem. Hermosa Beach C. of C. (bd. dirs. 1970-71), League Calif. Cities, Sigma Pi Sigma. Home: 1011 2d St Hermosa Beach CA 90254 Office: Hughes Aircraft Co 650 N Sepulveda Blvd El Segundo CA 90245-3419

DOERNER, MARTIN DAVID, school system administrator; b. Terre Haute, Ind., May 13, 1960; s. John William and Mary Jane (Flaherty) D. BA in English Lit., Okla. U., 1983. Mombusho English fellow Japan Ministry of Edn., Tochigi, 1983-85; instr. in English Kanrisha Yosei Gakko, Fujinomiya, Japan, 1985-86; chief instr. Sony Lang. Lab., Inc., Fukuoka, Japan, 1986-87; asst. mgr. Kumon Ednl. Inst., Torrance, Calif., 1987-89; mgr. Kumon Ednl. Inst., Burlingame, Calif., 1989-90; gen. mgr. Kumon S.W. Inc., Phoenix, 1990—. Refugee vol. Cath. Social Svcs. Mem. Japan-Am. Soc., World Wildlife Soc. Democrat. Roman Catholic. Home: 13816 N 31st Ave Phoenix AZ 85023-5708 Office: Kumon SW Inc 8055 N 24th Ave Ste 101 Phoenix AZ 85021-4865

DOERPER, JOHN ERWIN, food writer; b. Wuerzburg, Fed. Republic of Germany, Sept. 17, 1943; came to U.S., 1963, permanent resident, 1973; s. Werner and Theresia (Wolf) D.; m. Victoria McCulloch, Dec. 2, 1970. BA, Calif. State U., Fullerton, 1968; MA/ABD, U. Calif., Davis, 1972. Food writer/author Seattle, 1984—; food columnist Washington, Seattle, 1985-88, Seattle Times, 1985-88; food editor Wash.-The Evergreen State Mag., Seattle, 1988-89, Pacific Northwest mag., 1989—, Seattle Home and Garden, 1989-91; pub., editor, founder Pacific Epicure, Quarterly Jour. Gastronomy, Bellingham, Wash., 1988—; dir. Annual N.W. Invitational Chef's Symposium. Author: Eating Well: A Guide to Foods of the Pacific Northwest, 1984, The Eating Well Cookbook, 1984, Shellfish Cookery: Absolutely Delicious Recipes from the West Coast, 1985; contbr. articles to profl. jours. Recipient Silver medal, White award for city and regional mags. William Allen White Sch. Journalism, U. Kans. Mem. Oxford Symposium Food and Cookery (speaker 26th Ann. Pacific Northwest Writer's Conf. 1982, 92). Home: 111 Old Mill Village Bellingham WA 98226

DOGLIONE, ARTHUR GEORGE, data processing executive; b. Bklyn., May 24, 1938; s. Francis and Georgia (Smith) D.; m. Maryann Laurette Bonfanti, Sept. 3, 1960; children: Dana Ann, Arthur Todd, Lora Michele. AA, Scottsdale (Ariz.) Community, 1978; AAS, Maricopa Tech. Coll., Phoenix, 1984; BS, Ariz. State U., 1985. Salesman Columbus Realty Co., Trenton, N.J., 1962-65; appraiser J.H. Martin Appraisal Co., Trenton, 1965-68; office mgr. Mcpl. Revaluations, Avon-by-the-Sea, N.J., 1968-69; pres., broker Area Real Estate Agy., Wall, N.J., 1969-76; property appraiser Ariz. Dept. Revenue, Phoenix, 1976-78; investment appraiser Continental Bank, Phoenix, 1978-79; appraisal systems specialist Ariz. Dept. Revenue, Phoenix, 1979-80; project dir. Ariz. Dept. Adminstrn., 1980-83; pres. Logical Models, Scottsdale, Ariz., 1983—; founder Genus Tech., Scottsdale, 1989—; tax assessor Upper Freehold Twp., N.J., 1974-75, Borough of Bradley Beach, N.J., 1975; lectr. in field. Author various software. Counselor SCORE, SBA, Mesa, Ariz., 1986-90. Mem. Phi Theta Kappa. Republican. Roman Catholic. Office: Logical Models 2828 N 74th Pl Scottsdale AZ 85257-1506

DOHERTY, ALFRED EDWARD, engineer, consultant; b. Shaker Heights, Ohio, Nov. 11, 1929; s. Alfred Edward and Florence (Pylick) D.; m. Jeannette Smith, Dec. 31, 1931 (dec. Feb. 1981); children: James Edward, Thomas Vincent, George Michael; m. Virginia Dolores Meza. BS, Calif. Coast U., 1987. Registered profl. engr.; cert. mech. engr. Methods devel. Douglas Aircraft Co., Torrance, Calif., 1954-59; mgr. advanced materials Aerojet Gen. Corp., Downey, Calif., 1959-69; v.p. Electro-Form, Inc., Ft. Worth, 1969-78; pres. A&T Engring., A&T Mfg., Ft. Worth, 1978-84; plant mgr. Leland Southwest, Ft. Worth, 1984-87; v.p. and gen. mgr. formed products Explosive Fabricators, Inc., Louisville, Colo., 1987—. Contbr. technical papers to profl. jours.; patentee in field. Sgt. U.S. Army, 1948-54, Korea. Mem. Soc. Mech. Engrs., Elks. Lutheran. Home: 4955 Cornwall Dr Boulder CO 80301-4103

DOHERTY, CORNELIUS GREGORY, software engineer; b. St. Louis, Oct. 3, 1962; s. Cornelius and Bobbie Ann (Rogers) D. BA, U. Calif., Berkeley, 1987. Mem. tech. staff Ingres Corp., Alameda, Calif., 1985-86; software engr. Altos Computer Systems, San Jose, Calif., 1986-88; sr. software engr. Pyramid Tech., Mountain View, Calif., 1988-90, mgr. database engring., 1990-91; dir. database engring. Pyramid Tech., San Jose, 1992; mgr. RDBMS devel. Oracle Corp., Redwood Shores, Calif., 1992—. Mem. IEEE, Assn. for Computing Machinery. Home: 1531 Oak St San Francisco CA 94117 Office: Oracle Corp 500 Oracle Pky 659414 Redwood City CA 94065

DOHERTY, GEORGE WILLIAM, counselor, researcher, consultant; b. N.Y.C., Oct. 18, 1941; s. William George and Catherine Marguerite (Nierenhausen) D. BS, Pa. State U., 1964; MS, Miss. State U., 1977. Cert. Nat. Acad. Cert. Clin. Mental Health Counselors; lic. profl. counselor; psychol. tech. cert., Wyo. Program coord., dir. youth devel. program Econ. Opportunities Advancement Corp., Waco, Texas, 1968-71; psychol. counselor parent tng., parenting cons. Counseling or Referral Assistance Svcs., Phila., 1973-75; psychologist III, Rural Clinics Community Counseling Ctr., Ely, Nev., 1980-85; researcher, cons. O'Dochartaigh Rsch. and Cons., Laramie, Wyo., 1985—; clinician/evaluator San Luis Valley Comprehensive Community Mental Health Ctr., Alamosa and Monte Vista, Colo., 1987-88; lead therapist adolescent treatment program Cen. Wyo. Counseling Ctr., Casper, Wyo., 1989; psychol. technician, team leader counseling program Wyo. State Tng. Sch., Lander, 1990; adj. instr. No. Nev. Community Coll., Ely, 1980-85. Co-chmn. human rights com. Blue Peaks Devel. Ctr., Alamosa, 1988; mem. Wyo. Civil Air Patrol; vol. Alumni admissions program Pa. State U. Capt. USAF, 1964-68, USAFR, 1968-75. Mem. AAAS, APA (assoc., program reviewer div. 27 program presentations for ann. meetings 1991, 92), Western Psychol. Assn., Wyo. Psychol. Assn. (assoc.), Intern-Am. Soc. Psychology, Internat. Assn. Applied Psychology, Assn. Behavior Analysis, Assn. Counselor Edn. and Supervision (chmn. task force and interest group community counseling 1984-85)), Western Assn. Counselor Edn. and Supervision, Assn. Measurement Edn. and Guidance, Am. Mental Health Counselors Assn., Air Force Assn., World Future Soc., Planetary Soc., Pa. State U. Alumni Assn., Smithsonian Assocs., Irish-Am. Cultural Inst., O'Dochartaigh Family Rsch. Assn., Am. Legion, Wilderness Soc., Nat. Audobon Soc. Democrat. Home and Office: 2845 Fort Saunders Dr Laramie WY 82070

DOHERTY, JOELENE GIORGIS, elementary educator; b. Rock Springs, Wyo., June 29, 1950; d. Joseph and Constance Ellen (Lucas) Giorgis; m. John Joseph Doherty, Aug. 14, 1975 (div. Aug. 1990); children: Caitlin Anne, Ryanne Elizabeth. BA in Elem. Edn., U. Wyo., 1972. Cert. elem. tchr., Wyo. Elem. tchr. Sweetwater Sch. Dist. 1, Rock Springs, 1988-92, tchr. liaison computer test scoring, 1992—, coord. computer dept., 1993-94; elem. student coun. sponsor. V.p. Sweetwater Dem. Women's Club, Rock springs, 1988-90; instr.-mem. drug prevention com. Sweetwater Sch. Dist. #1. Named Wife of Yr., Wyo. N.G., 1988. Mem. Sweetwater Edn. Assn. (bldg. rep. 1972-73), VFW Aux., Am. Legion Aux. (pres., dist. pres. Rock Sprinigs 1978-80), Eagles Aux. (sec. Rock Springs 1980-81), Lions Aux. (sec. Superior, Wyo. 1985-88). Episcopalian. Home: 1307 Wyoming St Apt A Rock Springs WY 82901 Office: Sweetwater Sch Dist 1 PO Box 1089 Rock Springs WY 82902-1089

DOHR, RONALD MICHAEL, human resources executive, management consultant; b. St. Louis, Mar. 9, 1951; s. Nickalaus Michael and Catherine Edyth (Jarvis) D.; m. Mary Anne Klein, Aug. 9, 1975; children: Michelle Briann, Jesse Douglas. BS in Psychology, Portland State U., 1973, MS in Orgn. Communicatons, 1975; PhD in Orgn. Communications, U. Wash., 1982. Instr. U. Wash., Seattle, 1975-78; portfolio mgr. Seafirst, Seattle, 1978-79, tng. svcs. officer, 1979-82, sr. manpower planning analyst, 1982-83, asst. v.p. mgmt. devel., 1983-84; v.p. human resources devel. West-One Bank, Boise, Idaho, 1985-86; tng. mgr. NC Machinery, Seattle, 1984-85, dir. tng. and orgn. devel., 1986-91, dir. quality and edn., 1991—; bus. spokesperson Private Initiatives in Pub. Edn., 1982-84; prof. Chapman Coll. Bellevue Campus (Tchr. of Yr. 1988). Bd. dirs. NC Found., Seattle, 1989-92; speaker, bd. dirs. Wash. Bus. Week, 1989-92. Mem. Wash. Private Industry Coun. (bd. dirs.). Home: 17626 157th Ave SE Renton WA 98058 Office: NC Machinery 17035 W Valley Hwy Seattle WA 99188-5519

DOI, LOIS, psychiatric social worker; b. Honolulu, Oct. 24, 1951; d. James Masato and Thelma Kimiko Miyamoto; m. Brian Doi, May 26, 1972; children: Michael, Lorian. BS, U. Hawaii, 1974, MSW, 1978. Lic. clin. social worker, Calif. Psychiat. social worker, child specialist Desert Community Mental Health Ctr., Indio, Calif., 1979-92, coordinator children's day treatment program, 1982-91; pvt. practice psychiat. social worker 1-2-1 Counseling, Palm Springs, Calif., 1983—; psychiat. social worker, adult case mgr. Desert Community Mental Health Ctr., Palm Springs, Calif., 1992-93; expert examiner, bd. of commr. Behavioral Sci. Examiners for Licensed Clin. Social Workers in Calif., 1987—. Vol. advisor Community Recreation Ctr. Youth Group, Hawaii, 1967-69; vol. interviewer ARC Food Stamp Program, Hawaii, 1973; vol. asst. YWCA Programs Young Mothers and Teens, Hawaii, 1973; vol. group leader YWCA Juvenile Delinquent Program, Hawaii, 1973; placement counselor Vols. In Service to Am., L.A., 1975; VISTA counselor L.A. Urban League, 1975-76. Mem. Nat. Assn. Social Workers. Office: 1-2-1 Counseling 400 S Farrell Ste # B116 Palm Springs CA 92262

DOI, MARY ELLEN, research chemist, laboratory administrator; b. Memphis, Mo., Jan. 15, 1933; d. Earl Edward and Beulah Mae (Leach) Tucker; m. Minoru Doi, June 16, 1962; 1 child, Paul Edward. BS, Northeast Mo. State U., 1953. Cert. med. technologist, 1957. Tchr. chemisty, biology Princeton (Mo.) High Sch., 1953-54; tchr. sci. Evans Jr. High Sch., Ottumwa, Iowa, 1954-56; lab. technician Shelby County Hosp., Shelbyville, Ill., 1957-58; med. chemist Barnes Hosp., St. Louis, 1958-60; research chemist Monsanto Chem. Co., St. Louis, 1960-63; chief chemist, dir. lab. Nutrition Lab. Svcs., Tolleson, Ariz., 1963—. Active Rep. campaign, 1976. Mem. Am. Chem. Soc., Assn. Official Analytical Chemists, Ariz.

Assn. Cert. Labs. Republican. Methodist. Club: Bus. and Profl. Women (Maryvale, Glendale, Ariz.) (past sec.-treas., v.p., pres., Woman of Yr. 1974, 79). Home: 5963 W Hazelwood St Phoenix AZ 85033-2115 Office: Nutrition-Lab Svcs PO Box 237 Tolleson AZ 85353-0237

DOI, ROY HIROSHI, biochemist, educator; b. Sacramento, Mar. 26, 1933; s. Thomas Toshiteru and Ima (Sato) D.; m. Joyce Takahashi, Aug. 30, 1958 (div. 1992); children: Kathryn E., Douglas A.; m. Joan M. Saul, Feb. 14, 1992. AB in Physiology, U. Calif., Berkeley, 1953, AB in Bacteriology, 1957; MS in Bacteriology, U. Wis., 1958, PhD in Bacteriology, 1960. NIH postdoctoral fellow U. Ill., Urbana, 1960-63; asst. prof. Syracuse (N.Y.) U., 1963-65; asst. prof. U. Calif., Davis, 1965-66, assoc. prof., 1966-69, prof. biochemistry, 1969—, chmn. dept. biochemistry and biophysics, 1974-77, coord. for biotech., 1989-92; cons. NIH, Bethesda, Md., 1975-79, 82-84, Syntro Corp., San Diego, 1983-88; treas. Internat. Spores Conf., Boston, 1980-89; mem. recombinant DNA adv. com. NIH, 1990—. With U.S. Army, 1953-55. Fellow NSF, 1971-72; recipient Sr. Scientist award, von Humboldt Found, Munich, 1978-79, vis. scholar award Naito Found, Tokyo. Fellow AAAS; mem. AAUP, Am. Soc. Biochem. Molecular Biology, Am. Soc. Microbiology, Sigma Xi. Democrat. Unitarian. Office: U Calif Dept Biochemistry and Biophysics Davis CA 95616

DOIDA, STANLEY Y., dentist; b. Kalamath Falls, Calif., Dec. 15, 1944; s. Sam S. and Mae M. (Nakao) D.; m. Eileen M. Crilly; children: Stanley Jr., Scott Samuel. Student, Knox Coll., 1965-67; DDS, Northwestern U., 1970. Asst. prof. Sch. Dentistry Northwestern U., Chgo., 1970-71; pres. Midtown Dental, Denver, 1971—; instr. U. Colo. Dental Sch., Denver, 1972-74. Mem. ADA, Acad. Operative Dentistry, Acad. Gold Foil Operators, Glenmoor Country Club. Home: 4700 E 6th Ave Denver CO 80220-5032 Office: Midtown Dental 1800 Vine St Denver CO 80206-1122

DOIG, IVAN, writer; b. White Sulphur Springs, Mont., June 27, 1939; s. Charles Campbell and Berneta (Ringer) D.; m. Carol Dean Muller, Apr. 17, 1965. BJ, Northwestern U., 1961, MS in Journalism, 1962; PhD in History, U. Wash., 1969; LittD (hon.), Montana State U., 1984, Lewis and Clark Coll., 1987. Editorial writer Lindsay-Schaub Newspapers, Decatur, Ill., 1963-64; asst. editor The Rotarian, Evanston, Ill., 1964-66. Author: (memoir) This House of Sky, 1978; (non-fiction) Winter Brothers, 1980; (novels) The Sea Runners, 1982, English Creek, 1984, Dancing at the Rascal Fair, 1987, Ride With Me, Mariah Montana, 1990, Heart Earth, 1993. Sgt. USAFR, 1962-69. Recipient Gov.'s Writers Day award, 1979, 81, 85, 88, Pacific N.W. Booksellers award for lit. excellence, 1979, 81, 83, 85, 88, Disting. Achievement award Western Lit. Assn., 1989; NEA fellow, 1985. Mem. Authors Guild, PEN Am. Ctr., Forest History Soc.

DOIRON, DIANE BOETTIGER, insurance sales professional, estate planner; b. Glen Ridge, N.J., Dec. 22, 1942; d. Russell William Boettiger and Elaine (Nelson) Hibbard; children: Neil Royster, Stephen. BA in Sociology, U. of the Pacific, 1965. CLU. Prin. Doiron Fin. Group, Santa Barbara, Calif., 1974—. Pres., bd. dirs., Endowment Com. United Way, Santa Barbara, 1988—; bd. dirs. Santa Barbara Estate Planning Coun. Named Endowment Vol. of Yr., United Way, 1986. Mem. Channel City Club, Santa Barbara Life Underwriters Assn. (bd. dirs. 1987—), Santa Barbara Planning Giving Round Table (pres. 1988-90), Million Dollar Round Table (mem. Ct. of the Table 1992). Office: Doiron Fin Assocs 1018 Garden Ste 108 Santa Barbara CA 93101

DOKUZOGUZ, SUSAN WEBER, computer software applications analyst; b. Paterson, N.J., Sept. 1, 1942; d. Bruce Orin and Francis (Keeney) Weber; m. H. Zafer Dokuzoguz, May 29, 1964. BS, N.C. State U., 1964. Sr. programmer N.C. Dept. Adminstrn., Raleigh, 1966-69; sr. systems analyst Babcock & Wilcox, Lynchburg, Va., 1969-70, 75-85, Barberton, Ohio, 1973-74; applications analyst Control Data, GmbH, Frankfurt, Germany, 1970-73; computer scientist Computer Scis. Corp., Las Vegas, Nev., 1986—. Reach to recovery vol. Am. Cancer Soc., Las Vegas, 1986—. Named among Top 100 Profls., Fed, Computer Week, 1992. Mem. Assn. for Computer Machinery, Assn. Systems Mgmt. Home: PO Box 80535 Las Vegas NV 89180 Office: Computer Scis Corp 2801 S Westwood Las Vegas NV 89109

DOLAN, ANDREW KEVIN, lawyer; b. Chgo., Dec. 7, 1945; s. Andrew O. and Elsie (Grafner) D.; children: Andrew, Francesca, Melinda. BA, U. Ill., Chgo., 1967; JD, Columbia U., 1970, MPH, 1976, DPH, 1980. Bar: Wash. 1980. Asst. prof. law Rutgers-Camden Law Sch., N.J., 1970-72; assoc. prof. law U. So. Calif., L.A., 1972-75; assoc. prof. pub. health U. Wash., Seattle, 1977-81; ptnr. Bogle & Gates, Seattle, 1988-93. Commr. Civil Svc. Commn., Lake Forest Park, Wash., 1981; mcpl. judge City of Lake Forest Park, 1982—. Russell Sage fellow, 1975. Mem. Order of Coif, Rainier Club, Washington Athletic Club. Office: 2200 Columbia Ctr 701 5th Ave Seattle WA 98104-7091

DOLAN, MARYANNE MCLORN, small business owner, writer, educator, lecturer; b. N.Y.C., July 14, 1924; d. Frederick Joseph and Kathryn Cecilia (Carroll) McLorn; m. John Francis Dolan, Oct. 6, 1951; children: John Carroll, James Francis McLorn, William Brennan. B.A., San Francisco State U., 1978, M.A., 1981. Tchr. classes and seminars in antiques and collectibles U. Calif., Berkeley, Davis, Santa Cruz, Coll. of Marin, Kentfield, Calif., Mills Coll., Oakland, St. Mary's Coll., Moraga, 1969-90, Solano C.C., 1969-90; tch. writing Dolan Sch., 1969-90; owner antique shop, Benicia, Calif., 1970—; lectr. Nat. Assn. Jewelry Appraisers Symposium, Tucson; mem. Vintage Fashion Expo., Oakland. Author: Vintage Clothing, 1880-1960, 1983, Collecting Rhinestone Jewelry, 1984, Old Lace and Linens, 1989, Commonsense Collecting, 1991, 300 Years of American Sterling Silver Flatware, 1992; weekly columnist The Collector, 1979-88; contbr. articles to profl. jours. Mem. AAUW, Antique Appraisal Assn. Am. Inc., Costume Soc. Am., New Eng. Appraisers Assn., Questers, Women's Nat. Book Assn. Inc., Nat. Assn. Jewelry Appriasers, Internat. Soc. Appraisers (lectr. ann. meeting), Internat. Platform Assn., Calif. Writers Club. Republican. Roman Catholic. Home: 138 Belle Ave Pleasant Hill CA 94523-4640 Office: 191 W J St Benicia CA 94510-3143

DOLAN, THOMAS JAMES, nuclear engineer, researcher; b. Urbana, Ill., July 23, 1939; s. Thomas James and Virginia Bess (Fisher) D.; m. Charlotte Louise Baker, Dec. 23, 1966; children: Zak Edward, Dan Hennessy, Meg Eileen. Student, USN Chem. Warfare Def. Sch., 1961; BS in Nuclear Engring., U. Ill., 1961, MS in Nuclear Engring., 1965, PhD in Nuclear Engring., 1970. Registered profl. engr., Idaho. Rsch. asst. U. Ill., Urbana, 1964-69; postdoctoral rschr. Internat. Rsch. and Exchs. Bd., Novosibirsk, USSR, 1970-71; prof. dept. nuclear enging. U. Mo., Rolla, 1971-89; prin. project physicist Phillips Petroleum Co., Bartlesville, Okla., 1987-88; sci. specialist EG&G Idaho, Idaho Falls, 1988-89, prin. scientist, 1989—; cons. Phillips Petroleum Co., Bartlesville, 1981-87; program co-chair Nuclear Tech. for Space Exploration Conf., Jackson, Wyo., 1992. Author: (textbook) Fusion Research, 1982; contbr. articles to profl. jours. Lt. USN, 1961-63. NSF fellow, 1968-69. Mem. NSPE, Am. Nuclear Soc. (sec. Idaho chpt. 1991-92), Am. Phys. Soc. (lifetime), Am. Soc. Engring. Edn., Tau Beta Pi. Home: 1748 Charlene St Idaho Falls ID 83402 Office: EG&G Idaho/Idaho Nat Engring Lab PO Box 1625 Idaho Falls ID 83415-3880

DOLAN, THOMAS PATRICK, insurance company executive; b. LaSalle, Ill., Mar. 13, 1936; s. Francis Henry and Josephine (Quigley) D.; 1 child, Elizabeth. BSBA, U. Ill., 1960. Asst. dept. mgr. Transamerica Life Cos., L.A., 1960-69, systems coord., 1969-72, dept. mgr., 1972-78, asst. v.p., sub div. mgr., 1978-86, 2d v.p., div. mgr., 1986—. Fellow Life Mgmt. Inst. Home: 14 Bonita Ln Palm Desert CA 92260-1626 Office: Transamerica Occidental 1149 S Olive St Los Angeles CA 90015-2208

DOLAN, WILLIAM MARK, retired newspaper executive; b. Ely, Nev., Apr. 2, 1923; s. Mark and Muriel (Fletcher) D.; m. Dorothy Fendrich, Nov. 5, 1945; children: Susan Jeanne, Lowrey Trent. BA in Journalism, U. Nev., 1950. Prin. Cherry Creek (Nev.) Sch., 1950-54; reporter, photo editor Nev. Appeal, Carson City, 1957-60, advt. mgr., 1962-66; editor Nev. Graphic Mag., Carson City, 1965-69, Carson Chronicle, 1970-85; bus. editor Nev. Appeal, 1976-86, entertainment editor, 1970-85. Mem. Carson City Fourth of July Com., 1978-85, Nev. 125th Anniversary Commn., 1989-91; bd. dirs. Nev. Day Com., Carson City, 1970-91. With AUS, 1942-45, ETO. Mem. Nat. Press Assn. (Silver Rule award 1987), Lions (pres. 1960-62, editor and pub. dist. 4-N newspaper 1989-93), Elks, Toastmasters (area gov. 1959-61), Sigma Delta Chi. Home: 1621 Molly Dr Carson City NV 89706-2641

DOLBERG, DAVID SPENCER, business executive, lawyer, scientist; b. L.A., Nov. 28, 1945; s. Samuel and Kitty (Snyder) D.; m. Katherine Blumberg, Feb. 22, 1974 (div. 1979); 1 child, Max; m. Sarah Carnochan, May 23, 1992. BA in Biology with honors, U. Calif., Berkeley, 1974; PhD in Molecular Biology, U. Calif., San Diego, 1980; JD, U. Calif., Berkeley, 1989. Bar: Calif. 1989, U.S. Dist. Ct. (no. dist.) Calif. 1989, U.S. Patent and Trademark Office, 1990. Staff biologist, postdoctoral fellow Lawrence Berkeley Lab. U. Calif., 1980-85; assoc. Irell & Manella, Menlo Park, Calif., 1989-91; v.p. EROX Corp., Menlo Park, Calif., 1991-92; v.p. sci. and patents Pherin Corp., Menlo Park, Calif., 1992—; speaker in field. Contbr. articles to Jour. Gen. Virology, Jour. Virology, Nature, Science. Home: 360 Summit Dr Redwood City CA 94062-3330 Office: 535 Middlefield Rd Ste 240 Menlo Park CA 94025-3444

DOLGOW, ALLAN BENTLEY, consulting company executive; b. N.Y.C.; BIE, NYU, 1959, MBA, 1972; postgrad. Hunter Coll., 1976, U. Calif., 1991; m. Nina Kim; children: Nicole, Marc, Ginger, Kimbie. with, Republic Aviation Corp., Farmingdale, N.Y., 1959-60; mgr. Internat. Paper Co., N.Y.C., 1960-73; project mgr. J.C. Penney Co. Inc., N.Y.C., 1973-76; dir. mfg. and planning Morse Electro Products, N.Y.C., 1976-77, exec. mgr. Morse Electrophonic Hong Kong Ltd., 1976-77; internat. project mgr. Revlon Inc., Edison, N.J., 1977-79; cons. SRI Internat., Menlo Park, Calif., 1979—. With U.S. Army, 1954-56, Germany. Office: 333 Ravenswood Ave Menlo Park CA 94025-3493

DOLIBER, DARREL LEE, design engineer, consultant, laboratory manager; b. Mpls., June 19, 1940; s. Russell Clifford Doliber and Helen Carol (Homa) Price; m. Ethel Lorraine Dzivi, June 17, 1962; children: Wendy Lorraine, Heather Leigh; m. Helga Renate Miggo, Oct. 31, 1986. AA, Palomar Coll., 1973. Prodn. engr. Hughes Aircraft Co., Carlsbad, Calif., 1969-74; sr. engr. I.T.T., Roanoke, Va., 1974-77; dir. mfg. Gainsboro Elec. Mfg. Co., Inc., Roanoke, Va., 1977-78; mfg. engr. Litton Industries, Tempe, Ariz., 1978-82; sr. engr. Datagraphix, Inc., San Diego, 1982-84; lab. mgr. S.A.I.C., San Diego, 1984—. Contbr. articles in field; patentee in field. Mem. Soc. Photo-Optical and Instrumentation Engrs. Roman Catholic. Home: 2952 Victoria Dr Alpine CA 91901 Office: Sci Applications Internat Corp 4161 Campus Point Ct San Diego CA 92121-1595

DOLICH, ANDREW BRUCE, professional baseball team administrator; b. Bklyn., Feb. 18, 1947; s. Mac and Yetta (Weiselter) D.; m. Ellen Andrea Fass, June 11, 1972; children: Lindsey, Caryn, Cory. B.A., Am. U., 1969; M.Ed., Ohio U., 1971. Adminstrv. asst. to gen. mgr. Phila. 76ers, NBA, 1971-74; v.p. Md. Arrows Lacrosse, Landover, 1974-76; mktg. dir. Washington Capitals, NHL, Landover, 1976-78; exec. v.p., gen. mgr. Washington Diplomats Soccer, 1978-80; exec. v.p. Oakland A's Baseball, Calif., 1980—; nat. fundraising chair sports adminstrs. program Ohio U., Athens, dir. 1978-82; dir. Maj. League Baseball Properities; lectr. sports mktg. U. Calif. Extension; bd. dirs. Greenfields. Bd. dirs. Bay Area Sports Hall of Fame, 1982—, Celebrate Oakland Com., No. Calif. Food Industries Cir.; chmn. Oakland Sports and Spl. Events Commn. Recipient Alumni of Yr. award Ohio U. Sports Adminstrs. Program, Athens, 1982; recipient Clio award Am. Advt. Fedn., 1982. Office: Oakland A's Baseball Oakland Coliseum Oakland CA 94621

D'OLIER, H(ENRY) MITCHELL, lawyer; b. Chgo., June 10, 1946; s. Henry and Helen Elizabeth (Mitchell) D'O.; m. Barbara Ann Miller, June 12, 1971; children: Jason Mitchell, Justin Frank, Jordan Henry. BA in English and Gen. Sci., U. Iowa, 1968, JD with distinction, 1972. Bar: Iowa 1972, Hawaii 1972. Assoc. tax Goodsill, Anderson, Quinn & Stifel, Honolulu, 1972-77; ptnr. tax, health, mgmt. com. Goodsill, Anderson, Quinn & Stifel, Honolulu, 1977—; bd. dirs. Reyn's Men's Wear Inc., Kamuela, Hawaii. Note and comment editor Iowa Law Rev., 1971. Chmn., co-chmn. Friends of Fred Hemmings, Honolulu, 1984, 86, 88, 90; chmn., vice-chmn. profl. div. campaign Aloha United Way, 1982-84; clk., deacon Cen. Union Ch., 1983-85, bd. dirs., 1989—; bd. dirs. Boys' and Girls' Club Honolulu, 1977—, pres., 1988-89, vice-chmn., 1990—. Mem. ABA (tax and health law sects.), Nat. Health Lawyers Assn., Am. Coll. Hosp. Attys., Hawaii State Bar Assn. (tax sect.), Plaza Club (Honolulu), Order of Coif, Rotary (bd. dirs. Honolulu club 1988, v.p., pres.-elect 1990—), Omicron Delta Kappa. Home: 1704 Kumakani Loop Honolulu HI 96821-1326 Office: Goodsill Anderson Quinn & Stifel PO Box 3196 Honolulu HI 96801

DOLL, LINDA A., artist, educator; b. Bklyn., May 5, 1942; d. William James Harrington and Ann B. (Casey) Cook; m. William John Doll, Feb. 4, 1962; children: Patricia, William Jr. AA, Palomar Coll., 1974; BA, San Diego State U., 1976. chairperson Arts Adv. Com. to Congressman Jim Bates, 1983-84; U.S. Coast Guard Artist, 1985—. Exhibited in group shows with Am. Watercolor Soc., 1985-91 (selected for one yr. nat. travel show, Elsie and David Ject-key award 1988) N.Y.C., 1986, 87, 88, Canton, Ohio, 1985, Nat. Watercolor Soc., Brea, Calif., 1984-89, Watercolor West Annual, Riverside, Calif., 1982, 84-88 (E. Gene Crain Purchase Selection award 1985, Second Place Jurors award 1982), Rocky Mountain Nat., Golden, Colo., 1984-85, Midwest Annual, Davenport, Iowa, 1983, 85, Nat. Watercolor Soc., Riverside, 1985 (selected for one yr. nat. travel show) 88, Canton Ohio, 1985, Watercolor Internat., San Diego, 1978-79, 82-88 (selected for one yr. nat. travel show 1983-84), Watercolor Okla., 1982-84 (Harry Hulett Jr. award 1984), Pa. Soc. Watercolor Painters, Harrisburg, 1988, 1982 (hon. mention); represented in permanent collections including E. Gene Crain Collection, Scripps Hosp., La Jolla, Calif., Redlands Community Hosp., Riverside, Campbell River Community Art Council, Can., Simpact Assocs. Inc., San Diego. Mem. San Diego Watercolor Soc. (past pres., life), Nat. Watercolor Soc., Knickerbocker Artists, Am. Watercolor Soc. (chmn. of assocs. 1985—). Office: PO Box 270017 San Diego CA 92198-2017

DOLLARHYDE, GREGORY GENE, food service executive; b. Santa Monica, Calif., Nov. 3, 1952; s. Theodore E. and Virginia Louise (Richardson) D.; m. Jackie O. Oxley, Apr. 28, 1984; children: Kate, Trent. BS with distinction, Cornell U., 1980, MBA, 1981. Gen. ptnr. Harvest Moon Restaurant, Tahoe City, Calif., 1972-75; gen. mgr. Vintage Mgmt. Co., San Francisco, 1975-77; dir. adminstrn. TGI Fridays, Inc., Dallas, 1981-83, v.p. fin., 1983-85, CFO, exec. group v.p., 1985-86; CFO Rusty Pelican Restaurant, Inc., Irvine, Calif., 1986-88; v.p. acquisitions Pizza Hut/PepsiCo, Wichita, Kans., 1988-90; pres., CEO Rusty Pelican Restaurant, Inc., San Juan Capistrano, 1990—; prin. JKG Enterprise Group, Laguna, Calif., 1987-91; bd. dirs. Exel Fin. Assocs., Newport Beach, Calif., 1991—. Adv. dir. Nova U., Fla., 1990—. Mem. Am. Beverage Inst. (bd. dirs.). Republican. Home: 30 Glastonbury Pl Laguna Niguel CA 92677-5310

DOLLIVER, JAMES MORGAN, state supreme court justice; b. Ft. Dodge, Iowa, Oct. 13, 1924; s. James Isaac and Margaret Elizabeth (Morgan) D.; m. Barbara Babcock, Dec. 18, 1948; children: Elizabeth, James, Peter, Keith, Jennifer, Nancy. BA in Polit. Sci. with high honors, Swarthmore Coll., 1949; LLB, U. Wash., 1952; D in Liberal Arts (hon.), U. Puget Sound, 1981. Bar: Wash. 1952. Clk. to presiding justice Wash. Supreme Ct., 1952-53; sole practice Port Angeles, Wash., 1953-54, Everett, Wash., 1961-64; adminstrv. asst. to Congressman Jack Westland, 1955-61, Gov. Daniel J. Evans, 1965-76; justice Supreme Ct. State of Wash., 1976—, chief justice, 1985-87; 2d v.p. conf. Chief Justices, 1985-86; adj. prof. U. Puget Sound Sch. Law, 1988—. Chmn. United Way Campaign Thurston County, 1975, pres., 1976, mem. exec. bd., 1977—; chmn. Wash. chpt. Nature Conservancy, 1981—; pres. exec. bd. Tumwater Area coun. Boy Scouts Am., 1972-73, Wash. chpt. The Nature Conservancy, 1981-83, mem. 1979—, Wash. State Capital Hist. Assn., 1976-80, 85—, also trustee, 1983-84; trustee Deaconess Children's Home, Everett, 1963-65, U. Puget Sound, 1969—, chair exec. com., 1990—, Wash. 4-H Found., 1977-84, also v.p., 1983—, Claremont (Calif.) Theol. Sem., assoc. mem., Community Mental Health Ctr., 1977-84; bd. mgrs. Swarthmore Coll., 1980-84; bd. dirs. Thurston Mason Community Health Ctr., 1977-84, Thurston Youth Svcs. Soc., 1969-84, also pres., 1983, mem. exec com. 1970-84, Wash. Women's Employment and Edn., 1982-84; mem. jud. coun. United Meth. Ch., 1984-92, gen. cong., 1970-72, 80—, gen. bd. ch. and soc., 1976-84; adv. coun. Ret. Sr. Vol. program, 1979-83; pres. Wash. Ctr. Law-related Edn., 1987-89, bd. dirs. 1987—; bd. dirs. World Assn. for Children and Parents, 1987—; trustee U. Wash. Law Sch. Found., 1982-90, Olympic Park Inst., 1988—; mem. bd. visitors U. Wash. Sch. Social Work, 1987—; chair bd. visitors U. Puget Sound Sch. Law, 1988-90, bd. visitors, 1988—. With USN, 1943-45; ensign USCG, 1945-46. Recipient award Nat. Council Japanese Am. Citizens League, 1976; Silver Beaver award, 1971; Silver Antelope award, 1976. Mem. Am., Wash. bar assns., Am. Judges Assn., Am. Judicature Soc., Pub. Broadcast Found. (bd. dirs. 1982—), Masons, Rotary, Phi Delta Theta, Delta Theta Phi. Office: Supreme Ct PO Box 40929 Temple of Justice Olympia WA 98504-0929

DOLMAT, ELIZABETH, writer, consultant; b. N.Y.C., Aug. 2, 1937; d. Michael and Mary (Kardish) D. BA, U. Calif., San Diego, 1973; MA, UCLA, 1976. Mgr. spl. projects Cross Access, Santa Clara, Calif., 1991; ind. mktg. writing cons., Calif.; ind. writer, 1991—. Mem. World Future Soc.

DOLOWITZ, DAVID AUGUSTUS, otolaryngologist, educator; b. N.Y.C., Nov. 3, 1913; s. Alexander and Florence Reda (Levine) D.; m. Frances Marie Fleisher, May 6, 1937 (dec. 1967); children: David S., Julia Louise, Wilma Florence, Susan Reda, Fridolyn Gimble; m. Emma Ruth Halvorsen, June 11, 1968. AB, Johns Hopkins U., 1933; MD, Yale U., 1937; MA, U. Utah, 1951, ScD (hon.), 1978.Intern, Morristown (N.J.) Meml. Hosp., 1937-38, Albany (N.Y.) Hosp., 1938-39; resident Johns Hopkins Hosp., Balt., 1939-43; practice medicine, specializing in otolaryngology, Salt Lake City, 1946-78; asst. otolaryngology Johns Hopkins U., Balt., 1938-39, instr., 1942-43; instr. U. Utah, Salt Lake City, 1943-48, assoc. clin. prof., 1948-58, assoc. prof., chief otolaryngology, 1958-67, clin. prof. otolaryngology, 1967-83, emeritus prof., 1983—; instr. biology Dixie Coll., St. George, Utah, 1987-93; staff Holy Cross Hosp., VA Hosp., Salt Lake City, U. Utah Med. Hosp., Primary Children's Hosp., Salt Lake City, all 1946-78; councilman, treas. Town of Toquerville (Utah), 1982-87, mayor, 1987-90. Chmn. bd. Pioneer Craft House, Salt Lake City, 1965-84; mem. gov.'s com. study exceptional children, Utah, 1967; mem. Com. for Endowment of the Humanities, 1988—; mem. otolaryngologic del. to China, People to People, 1986. Served with M.C., U.S. Army, 1943-46. NIH fellow, U. Lund, Sweden, 1959-60; Merit of Honor award Emeritus Alumni Assn. Univ. Utah, 1993. Fellow ACS; mem. AMA, Utah Med. Assn. (editorial bd. 1991—), Am. Bd. Otolaryngology, Am. Acad. Otolaryngology, Am. Bd. Clin. Allergy, Am. Otol. Soc., Deafness Research Found., Soc. Univ. Otolaryngologists (adv. com. pulmonary-allergy drugs 1973-78), Am. Laryngology, Rhinology and Otolaryngology Soc., Barany Soc., C. of C. Democrat. Jewish. Author: Basic Otolaryngology, 1964; editor: Allergy in Otolaryngologic Practice: The Otolaryngologic Clinics of North America, 1971; Transactions of Am. Soc. Ophthalmologic and Otolaryngologic Allergy, 1973-78; contbr. articles to profl. jours. Home: PO Box 189 Toquerville UT 84774-0189

DOLSEN, DAVID HORTON, mortician; b. Durango, Colo., Feb. 27, 1940; s. Donald B. and Florence I. (Maxey) D.; BA, Southwestern Coll., 1962; Mortuary Sci. Degree, Dallas-Jones Coll. Mortuary Sci., 1963; m. Jo Patricia Johnson, Dec. 23, 1962; children: Wendy, Douglas. Apprentice, Davis Mortuary, Pueblo, Colo., 1963-64; bus. mgr. George F. McCarty Funeral Home, Pueblo, 1964-65; owner Dolsen Mortuary, Lamar, Colo., 1965-72; pres., gen. mgr., dir. Almont, Inc., Pueblo, 1972-92; sec. Dolsen, Inc., 1967—; pres. Wilson Funeral Dirs. Inc., gen. ptnr. Let's Talk Travel, Ltd. Mem. Lamar City Council, 1969-73; mayor City of Lamar, 1971-73. Bd. dirs. Lamar Community Coll., 1967-73, Prowers County Hist. Soc., 1966—, San De Cristo Arts and Conf. Center, 1979-85; bd. dirs., sec. Pueblo Met. Mus. Assn., 1975-79; chmn. council on fin. and adminstrn. Rocky Mountain Conf. United Meth. Ch., 1976—, del. Gen. Conf., 1979, 80, 84, 88, 92; mem. Pres.'s Council Nat. Meth. Found., 1978—, Iliff Sch. Theology, 1986-88; trustee, mem. exec. com. Southwestern Coll., Winfield, Kans., 1979—; dist. chmn. Boy Scouts Am., 1981-88; treas., mem. exec. com. Girl Scouts USA, 1981-88; mem. council on fin. and adminstrn. Western Jurisdiction, United Meth. Ch., 1980-88; trustee, gen. council on fin. and adminstrn. United Meth. Ch., 1980-88, gen. coun. on mininstries, mem. gen. bd. of higher edn. and ministries; trustee Meth. Corp., 1988—, United Meth. Ch. Ins. Trust, 1982-88, Iliff Sch. Theology, 1992—; mem. World Service Commn., Meth. Episcopal Ch., 1980-88; mem. gen. council on adminstrn., bd. adminstrn. Ch. of United Brethren in Christ, 1980-88; trustee Sunny Acres Retirement Community, 1986, bd. dirs.; trustee Africa U., Mutare, Zimbabwe. Mem. Nat. Funeral Dirs. Assn., Nat. Selected Morticians, Cremation Assn. Am., Monument Builders N.Am., Colo. Funeral Dirs. Assn., Masons, Shriners, Elks, Rotary (bd. dirs., pres. 1990—, Paul Harris fellow), Pi Sigma Eta, Pi Kappa Delta, Pi Gamma Mu. Home: 3503 Morris Ave Pueblo CO 81008-1345 Office: 401 Broadway Ave Pueblo CO 81004-2127

DOMAN, MARGARET HORN, city council member; b. Portland, Oreg., July 28, 1946; d. Richard Carl and Dorothy May (Teepe) Horn; m. Steve Hamilton Doman, July 12, 1969; children: Jennifer, Kristina, Kathryn. BA, Willamette U., 1968; postgrad., U. Wash., 1968-69, 72. Cert. tchr. Tchr. jr. high Bellevue (Wash.) Sch. Dist., 1969-70, subs. tchr., 1990-91; tchr. jr. high University City (Mo.) Sch. Dist., 1970-71; employment counselor employment security dept. State of Wash., Seattle, 1971; planning commn. mem. City of Redmond, Wash., 1980-83, chmn., 1982-83; city coun. mem. City of Redmond, 1983-91, pres., 1990-91; exec. dir. Eastside Human Svcs. Coun., Redmond, Wash., 1992; employment specialist Wash. State Dept. Employment Security, 1993—; cons. land policy, decision analysis Redmond, 1993—; Redmond rep. Puget Sound. Coun. of Govt., Seattle, 1984-91, vice chmn., 1988, 90, chmn. transp., 1986-88, exec. bd., 1987, mem. standing com. on transp., 1986-91; bd. dirs., pres. Eastside Human Svcs. Coun., Bellevue, 1983-91, pres., 1990. Bd. dirs. Redmond YMCA, 1985-86; mem. state exec. com. Nat. History Day, Olympia, Wash., 1986; vol. Bellevue Sch. Dist., 1977—; bd. dirs. Camp Fire, Eastside br., Bellevue, 1992—. Mem. Suburban Cities Assn., Eastside Transp. Com. Republican. Unitarian. Home: 2104 180th Ct NE Redmond WA 98052

DOMANTAY, NORLITO VALDEZ (LITO DOMANTAY), communications executive; b. Manila, Oct. 28, 1946; came to U.S. 1970.; s. Juan and Felicidad (Valdez) D.; m. Deborah Anne Huffman, Aug. 25, 1980. BSC, AB, De La Salle U., Manila, 1968; MBA, Columbia U., 1971. Brand mgr. Procter & Gamble, Cin., 1971-80; v.p. mktg. Fed. Express Corp., Memphis, 1980-82; v.p. brand mgmt. Brown & Williamson Tobacco, Louisville, 1982-84; exec. v.p. Simon Mktg., Inc., L.A., 1984—; pres. Peninsula Communications, L.A., 1990—; bd. dirs. Express Data Svcs., Anaheim, Nobel Med. Ctr., L.A. Contbr. articles to profl. jours. Cons. Skid Row Devel., L.A., 1987, Cultural Found., L.A., 1986. Anheuser-Busch fellow, 1971. Mem. Promotion Mktg. Assn. Am. Republican. Home: 9420 Eden Dr Beverly Hills CA 90210-1309 Office: Simon Mktg Inc 1900 Ave of the Stars Los Angeles CA 90067-4301

DOMARADZKI, JULIAN ANDRZEJ, physics educator; b. Szczecin, Poland, June 7, 1951; came to U.S., 1981; s. Julian Domaradzki and Zofia Wukowicz; m. Anna Teresa Kulesza, Feb. 11, 1979; children: Mateusz Barnaba, Julia Jagna. MS, U. Warsaw, Poland, 1974; PhD, U. Warsaw, 1978. Asst. prof. U. Warsaw, 1978-80; von Humboldt fellow Essen (Germany) U., 1980-81; rsch. staff Princeton (N.J.) U., 1981-83; rsch. assoc. MIT, Cambridge, Mass., 1983-84; rsch. scientist Flow Industries, Inc., Kent, Wash., 1984-87; asst. prof. U. So. Calif., L.A., 1987-91, assoc. prof. aerospace engring., 1991—. Recipient Sr. Rsch. award Alexander von Humboldt Found., Bonn, Germany, 1992. Mem. AIAA, Am. Phys. Soc., Soc. Indsl. and Applied Math. Office: U So Calif Aerospace Engring U Park Los Angeles CA 90089-1191

DOMBROWER, MARIO, civil engineer; b. LaPaz, Bolivia, June 26, 1941; came to U.S., 1953; s. William and Jenny (Gotthelf) Feigenblatt; m. Beatriz Horowitz, Oct. 30, 1965; children: Michael, Shirley. BS in Engring., Calif. State U., L.A., 1966; M in Pub. Adminstrn., Calif. State U at Dominquez, Carson, 1985. registered Civil Engr. Calif., Real Estate Broker, Calif. Student profl. worker County of L.A., 1961-65; civil engr. Pub. Works Dept. of Engring., L.A., 1965—; mem., bd. gov's. Engrs. & Architects Assn., L.A., 1982-88, 92—. Recipient Oustanding Scholarship award, Mayor of N.Y., 1959, Pub. Works Supr. of Month, Bd. Pub. Works City of L.A., 1990; named: mem. nat. Engr. Honor Soc., Tau Beta Pi, 1966, mem. Nat. Honor Soc., Pi Alpha Alpha, 1985. Mem. Am. Soc. of Civil Engrs. Democrat.

Home: 6215 Rustling Oaks Dr Agoura Hills CA 91301-1638 Office: City L.A. Dept Public Works 650 S Spring St Ste 1200 Los Angeles CA 90014

DOMBU, SIVERT ROLF, printing company executive; b. Rjukan, Telemark, Norway, June 17, 1938; came to U.S., 1952; s. Martin and Gunvor (Fredriksen) D.; m. Adis S. Suarez, Aug. 4, 1973. BS, Tulane U., 1961; B. in Chemistry, U. Minn., 1967. Corp. quality control Procter & Gamble, Cin., 1967-71; pvt. practice gaming industry Las Vegas, Nev., 1971-83; owner CQP Printing, Las Vegas, 1983—. Author: Rules of Poker, 1983; editor (newsletter) LVBA, 1977-93. 1st lt. USAF, 1961-64. Mem. Nat. Assn. Quick Printers, Nat. Assn. Bridge Tchrs., Am. Contract Bridge League (life, unit pres. 1978-79, 80-81, bd. dirs. 1977-82). Office: CQP Inc 3883 Spring Mountain Rd Las Vegas NV 89102

DOMENICI, PETE (VICHI DOMENICI), senator; b. Albuquerque, May 7, 1932; s. Cherubino and Alda (Vichi) D.; m. Nancy Burk, Jan. 15, 1958; children: Lisa, Peter, Nella, Clare, David, Nanette, Helen, Paula. Student, U. Albuquerque, 1950-52; BS, U. N.Mex., 1954, LLD (hon.); LLB, Denver U., 1958; LLD (hon.), Georgetown U. Sch. Medicine; HHD (hon.), N.Mex. State U. Bar: N.Mex. 1958. Tchr. math. pub. schs. Albuquerque, 1954-55; ptnr. firm Domenici & Bonham, Albuquerque, 1958-72; chmn., ex-officio mayor Albuquerque, 1967; mem. U.S. Senate from N.Mex., 1972—; city commr. Albuquerque, 1966-68; mem. energy and natural resources com., chmn. subcom. on energy research and devel.; mem. com. on environ. and public works; chmn. budget com.; mem. spl. com. on aging; mem. Presdl. Adv. Com. on Federalism. Mem. Gov.'s Policy Bd. for Law Enforcement, 1967-68; chmn. Model Cities Joint Adv. Com., 1967-68. Recipient Nat. League of Cities award Outstanding Performance in Congress; Disting. Svc. award Tax Found., 1986, Legislator of Yr. award Nat. Mental Health Assn., 1987. Mem. Nat. League Cities, Middle Rio Grande Council Govts. Home: 120 3rd St NE Washington DC 20002-7314 Office: US Senate 434 Dirksen Senate Office Bldg Washington DC 20510-3101*

DOMINGO, CYNTHIA GARCIANO, human services specialist; b. Killeen, Tex., Dec. 14, 1953; d. Nemesio Dagdagan and Adelina (Garciano) D.; m. Garry Wade Owens, Apr. 7, 1990; children: Malik Silme Domingo Owens, Jamil Nemesio Domingo Owens. BA in Asian-Am. Studies, U. Wash., 1976; MA in Philippine History, Goddard-Cambridge U., 1977. Nat. coord. Com. for Justice for Domingo and Viernes, Seattle, 1981-91; program dir. human svcs. Cen. Area Motivation Program, Seattle, 1986—. Sec. bd. dirs Ch. Coun. Greater Seattle, 1986-92; co-chair Asia Pacific Task Force, Seattle, 1987—; v.p. Inst. for Global Security Studies, Seattle, 1988—; treas. N.W. Labor and Employment Law Office, Seattle, 1991—. Democrat. Office: Cen Area Motivation Program 722 18th Ave Seattle WA 98122

DOMINOSKI, RONALD ALAN, real estate agent; b. Aberdeen, Wash., Jan. 9, 1948; s. Stanley Richard and Audrey Laura (Hamm) D.; m. Margaret Jean Baumann, May 17,1969 (div. 1989); children: Sean, Terry. BBA, U. Puget Sound, 1970. Sales mgr. Sears, western Wash., 1970-85; real estate agt. Century 21, Seattle, 1986—. Home: 8120 NE 113th St Kirkland WA 98034 Office: Century 21 Real Estate Ctr 19720 W 44th Ave Ste T Lynnwood WA 98036

DOMMER, ALLISON ELIZABETH, sales executive; b. Yuba City, Calif., Apr. 17, 1967; d. Bernice (Foad) Dommer. BS in Agrl. Edn., U. Calif., Davis, 1990. Tech. sales asst. ICI Ams., Roseville, Calif., 1990; sales rep. Merck Ag Vet div. Merck & Co. Inc., Woodbridge, N.J., 1991—. Mem. Calif. Agrl. Prodn. Cons. Assn. (v.p. 1992, pres. 1993, chpt. bd. dirs.), Calif. Women for Agr. (chair consumer edn. 1991-92, chair speakers bur. 1992, state sec. 1993), Young Farmers and Ranchers, Toastmasters Internat. Republican. Roman Catholic.

DOMNIE, SCOTT HAROLD, real estate investor, country club operator; b. Milw., Jan. 19, 1954; s. Harold G. and Pearl (Watters) D.; m. Robin Castle, Sept. 27, 1986; 1 child, Adam Scott, Katherine Alyce. Student, U. Wis., Menomonie, 1972-74. V.p. ops. Breakers Restaurants, Inc., Calif., 1975-80; with real estate devel. dept. Calif. Brokers, 1981-84; investment broker Fed. Investors Corp., Fla., 1984-88; gen. mgr. Belmont Country Club, Fresno, Calif., 1988—; cons. to country clubs, Tampa, Fla., 1985-88; seminar presenter, Fla., 1986. Contbr. articles to profl. jours. Mem. Calif. Wine Soc. (bd. dirs. 1990—), Club Mgrs. Assn. Am., Nat. Restaurant Assn., Internat. Wine Soc., Sonoma County Enology Assn. Republican. Lutheran. Home: 1017 Matador Rd Pebble Beach CA 93953-2711

DOMONDON, OSCAR, dentist; b. Cebu City, Philippines, July 4, 1924; Came to U.S., 1954, naturalized, 1956.; s. Antero B. and Ursula (Maglasang) D. ; m. Vicky Domondon. children—Reinelda, Carolyn, Catherine, Oscar. DMD, Philippine Dental Coll., 1951; DDS, Loma Linda U., 1964. Dentist Manila Sanitarium and Hosp., 1952, U.S. Embassy, Manila, 1952-54; pvt. practice dentistry Long Beach, Calif., 1964—; Dentist, Children's Dental Health Center, Long Beach, part-time, 1964-68; past mem. Calif. State Bd. Dental Examiners. Past pres., Filipino Community Action Services, Inc. With AUS, 1946-49, U.S. Army, 1954-60. Fellow Acad. Dentistry International, Acad. Gen. Dentistry, Internat. Inst. Community Service, Acad. Internat. Dental Studies, Internat. Coll. Dentists, Am. Coll. Dentists, Acad. Continuing Edn.; mem. ADA, Am. Soc. Dentistry Children, Am. Acad. Oral Radiology (award 1964), Internat. Acad. Orthodontists, Am. Soc. Clin. Hypnosis, Am. Endodontic Soc., Western Conf. Dental Examiners and Dental Sch. Deans, Fedn. of Assns. of Health Regulatory Bds., Calif. Assn. Fgn. Dental Grads. (past pres.), Filipino Dental Soc. (past pres.), Philippine Tech. and Profl. Soc. (v.p.), Am. Acad. Dentistry for Handicapped, Am. Assn. Dental Examiners, Nat. Assn. Filipino Dentists in Am. (past pres.), Pierre Fauchard Acad., Knights of Rizal (comdr.), Lions (past pres.), Elks (past chmn. rangers), Masons. Republican. Home: 3570 Aster St Seal Beach CA 90740-2801 Office: 3714 Atlantic Ave Long Beach CA 90807-3490

DOMSKY, IRA MICHAEL, environmental planning manager; b. Washington, Dec. 1, 1951; s. Bernard Maxwell and Charlotte Anne (Janet) D.; m. Carol Lee Campbell, Nov. 1, 1980; children: Mira Lee, Ezra Mendel, Simon Garreth. BA, Lycoming Coll., 1973; MS, Ariz. State U., 1977, postgrad., 1983—. Rsch. & statistics analyst Ariz. Dept. Health Svcs., Phoenix, 1977-78, 79-81, environ. planner, 1984-86; health planner, implementer S.W. Wash. Health System Agy., Olympia, 1978-79; environ. planner Indian Dev. dist. of Ariz., Phoenix, 1981-84; environ. planning mgr. Ariz. Dept. Environ. Quality, Phoenix, 1986—. Contbg. author: Managing Water in a Water Scarce State, 1985; contbr. articles to profl. jours. Newsletter editor Mitchell Park Neighborhood Assn., Tempe, Ariz., 1988-89. EPA Fellow, 1986-87. Mem. Air & Waste Mgmt. Assn. (newsletter editor Ariz. chpt. 1989-92, bd. dirs. Grand Canyon sect. 1992—), Am. Statis Assn., Western Social Sci. Assn., State Bar Ariz. (natrual resource & environ. law sect.), Ariz. Statis Assn. (sec., v.p. 1981-82), Pi Alpha Alpha. Home: 1225 S Judd St Tempe AZ 85281-5431 Office: Ariz Dept Environ Quality PO Box 600 3033 N Central Phoenix AZ 85001-0600

DONAHOO, STANLEY ELLSWORTH, orthopaedic surgeon; b. St. Joseph, Mo., Dec. 3, 1933; s. Charles Ellsworth and Opal (Cole) D.; m. Cheryl R. Donahoo; children: Shan Maureen, Brian Patrick, Mary Kathleen, Jane Eileen; stepchildren: Trina Person, Kevin. MD, U. Wash., 1963. Resident, Duke U., Durham, N.C., 1967-68, U.S. Naval Hosp., Oakland, Calif., 1963-67; commd. lt., U.S. Navy, 1963 advanced through grades to lt. comdr. (orthopaedic surgeon), 1971; practice medicine, specializing in orthopaedic surgery, Roseburg, Oreg., 1971—; chief surgery Mercy Hosp., Roseburg, 1973-74; chief surgery Douglas Community Hosp., Roseburg, 1973, chief of staff, 1974—; cons. Guam Meml. Hosp., co-dir. rehab. unit, 1970-71; cons. orthopaedic surgery VA Hosp., Roseburg, 1971—; chmn. Douglas County (Oreg.) Emergency Med. Services Com., 1973-74. Trustee Douglas Community Hosp., 1975. Served with AUS, 1952-55. Diplomate Am. Bd. Orthopaedic Surgery. Fellow Am. Acad. Orthopaedic Surgeons (admissions com. region 14), North Pacific Orthopaedic Assn. (v.p. 1984-85, trustee 1991—); mem. Piedmont Orthopaedic Soc., Oreg. Med. Assn. (mem. sports medicine com., med. rev. com. 1981), Guam Med. Soc. (pres. 1970), Am. Trauma Soc. (founding mem.), Roseburg C. of C. (bd. govs. 1978—). Home: 173 Songbird Ct Roseburg OR 97470 Office: 1813 W Harvard Blvd Ste 100 Roseburg OR 97470-2792

DONAHUE, DENNIS DONALD, foreign service officer; b. Indpls., May 31, 1940; s. George Robert and Lucille Kathryn (Tannrath) D.; m. Gretchen Jane Siedling, Sept. 21, 1963 (dec. 1987); children: Mauree Denise, Megan Jane, Benjamin Josef; m. Diane Burdette Obenchain, Mar. 25, 1990. BA, Marian Coll., 1962; student, Ind. U., 1962-63; MA, Am. U., 1980, postgrad., 1981—. With USIA, 1967—; asst. cultural officer Am. Consultate Gen., Calcutta, India, 1969-70; asst. publs. officer Am. Embassy, New Delhi, 1970-72; publs. officer Am. Embassy, Saigon, Republic of Vietnam, 1973-75; cultural affairs officer Am. Embassy, Wellington, New Zealand, 1975-78; country/program officer East Asia/Pacific Office, Washington, 1979-81, 83-84; East Asia policy officer Voice of Am., Washington, 1982-83; program chief Am. Embassy, Tokyo, 1984-88; advisor U.S. Pacific Command, Honolulu, 1988-90; counselor for pub. affairs Am. Embassy, Singapore, 1990—; adj. lectr. polit. sci. Temple U. Japan, Tokyo, 1986. Mem. Am. Fgn. Svc. Assn., Internat. Communication Assn., Internat. House Japan, Phi Kappa Phi. Roman Catholic. Office: US Info Svc Am Embassy Singapore, 30 Hill St, Singapore 0617, Singapore

DONAHUE, DONALD JORDAN, mining company executive; b. Bklyn., July 5, 1924; s. John F. and Florence (Jordan) D.; m. Mary Meyer, Jan. 20, 1951 (dec. June 1990); m. Carol Ann Pascal, Sept. 16, 1992; children: Mary G., Judith A., Donald Jordan, Thomas, Nicholas P. BA, Georgetown U., 1947; MBA, NYU, 1951. With Chem. Corn Exch. Bank, N.Y.C., 1947-49, Am. Metal Climax Inc. (name changed to AMAX, Inc.), N.Y.C., 1949-75; treas. Am. Metal Climax Inc. (name changed to AMAX, Inc.), 1957-67, v.p., 1963-65, exec. v.p., 1965-69, pres., 1969-75, also dir., 1964-75; vice chmn. Continental Can Co., Inc. (name changed to Continental Group, Inc.), N.Y.C., 1975-84; chmn. KMI Continental Can Co., Inc. (formerly Continental Group, Inc.), 1987, Magma Copper Co., San Manuel, Ariz., 1987—; bd. dirs. N.E. Utilities, Inc., Counsellors Cash Res. Fund, Counsellors Tandem Securities Fund, Finevest Foods, Inc., Greenwall Fedn. With AUS, 1943-46. Mem. Greenwich Country Club, Blind Brook Country Club, University (N.Y.C.), Jupiter Hills (Fla.) Golf Club, Loblolly Pines Golf Club. Home: Meads Point Greenwich CT 06830 Office: Magma Copper Co Inc 99 Indian Field Rd Greenwich CT 06830-7200

DONAHUE, JAMES J., JR., corporate executive, consultant, retired; b. Pueblo, Colo., Dec. 16, 1919; s. James John and Sarah Evelyn (Bryden) D.; m. Laura L. Sherman, Sept. 7, 1968 (div. 1981); m. Priscilla Arlene Mourning, Apr. 11, 1982; children: James J. III, Thomas M. Donahue, David, Paul, Lisa, Nancy Berg. Student, Lawrence U., 1938-40, U. Minn., 1940-41, U. Md., Am. U., George Washington U., 1957-63; AA, Nat. Def. U. Salesman Am. Brass Co., Mpls., 1938-40; salesman, advt. mgr. United Van Lines, Skellet Van & Storage, Co., Mpls., 1947-50; dir. rsch., devel. Conwed Corp., St. Paul, 1967-71; v.p., gen. mgr. Anderson Machine Co., Inc., Chaska, Minn., 1971-73; exec. v.p., treas., dir. U.S. Bedding Co., St Paul, 1973-80; bus. cons., realtor Calhoun Realty Co., Edina, Minn., 1980-82; faculty mem. Command & Gen. Staff Coll., Ft. Leavenworth, KS., 1953-57; nuclear specialist, Dept. of Army Staff, SHAPE (NATO), Joint Chiefs of Staff, 1958-66. Contbr. articles to profl. jours. Bd. dirs. seven companies, Jr. C. of C., Rotary Internat., United Fund, ARC. Col. U.S. Army, 1942-46, 51-66. Decorated Legion of Merit, Joint Services Commendation medal, Bronze Star with three oak leaf clusters, Air medal. Mem. Nat. Def. Exec. Reserve Retired Officers Assn., Advt. Club, Traffic Club, Nat. Treas. Assn., Mason (32 degree), Cottonwood Golf Club. Republican. Home: 26221 S Howard Dr Sun Lakes AZ 85248-7231

DONAHUE, LAURI MICHELE, lawyer; b. Phoenix, Oct. 7, 1961; d. Gerald Michael Donahue and Janet Leatrice (Fischer) Stevens. BA, Boston U., 1983; JD, Harvard U., 1986. Bar: Calif. 1987, U.S. Dist. Ct. (no. dist.) Calif., U.S. Ct. Appeals (9th cir.). Asst. corp. counsel Atari Corp., Sunnyvale, Calif., 1989-90; atty. Khourie, Crew & Jaeger, San Francisco, 1990-92; program dir. LAWS Internat. Law Ctr. Project, 1992—. Mem. Harvard Law Sch. Assn. of No. Calif. (pres. 1989, 91-92), Harvard Club (bd. dirs. 1989, 91-92), Ivy Club.

DONAHUE, RICHARD KING, athletic apparel executive, lawyer; b. Lowell, Mass., July 20, 1927; s. Joseph P. and Dorothy F. (Riordan) D.; m. Nancy Lawson, Sept. 19, 1953; children: Gail M., Timothy J., Michael R., Nancy C., Richard K., Daniel J., Alicia A., Stephen J., Christopher P., Tara E., Philip A. A.B., Dartmouth Coll., 1948; J.D., Boston U., 1951. Bar: Mass. 1951. Ptnr. Donahue & Donahue, Attys., P.C., Lowell, Mass., 1951-60, 63-90; pres., COO, Nike, Inc., 1990— ; asst. to Pres. Kennedy, Washington, 1960-63. Served with USNR. Recipient Herbert Harley award Am. Judicature Soc., 1981. Mem. Am. Bd. Trial Advs., ABA (gov., ho. of dels. 1972—), Am. Coll. Trial Lawyers, Mass. Bar Assn. (past pres., Gold medal 1979), New Eng. Bar Assn. (past pres.). Clubs: Union League (Boston); Vesper Country (Tyngsboro, Mass.); Fed. City (Washington); Yorick (Lowell). Office: Nike Inc 1 Bowerman Dr Beaverton OR 97005*

DONALD, IAN, wood products company executive. Formerly pres. Crown Forest Industries Ltd., Vancouver, B.C., Can.; pres. Forest Products Ltd. (now Fletcher Challenge Can. Ltd.), Vancouver, B.C., Can., 1987—. Office: Fletcher Challenge Can Ltd, 700 W Georgia St, Vancouver, BC Canada V7Y 1J7

DONALDSON, DEIRDRE HUNTER, neurologist, researcher; b. New Haven, May 23, 1953; d. E. Talbot Donaldson and Christine Hamilton (Hunter) Hutchison. BA, Yale U., 1974; PhD, U. Calif., Berkeley, 1983; MD, Vanderbilt U., 1986. Instr. U. Colo. Health Sci. Ctr., Denver, 1990—; rsch. assoc. Eleanor Roosevelt Inst., Denver, 1992—. Contbr. articles to profl. jours. Bd. dirs. Muscular Dystrophy Assn., Denver, 1989—. Recipient Physician-Scientist award Nat. Inst. on Aging/NIH, 1990-94. Mem. AAAS, ACP (assoc.), Am. Chem. Soc., Am. Acad. Neurology, Soc. for Neurosci., Sigma Chi. Office: Dept Neurology B-129 U Colo Health Sci Ctr 4200 E 9th Ave Denver CO 80262-0001

DONALDSON, GEORGE BURNEY, chemical company executive; b. Oakland, Calif., Mar. 16, 1945; s. George T. and L.M. (Burney) D.; m. Jennifer L. Bishop, Feb. 16, 1974; children: Dawn Marie, Matthew George. AS in Criminology, Porterville Coll., 1972. Police officer City of Lindsay (Calif.), 1966-67; distbn. mgr. Ortho div. Chevron Chem. Co., Lindsay, 1967-73; safety specialist Wilbur-Ellis Co. Fresno, Calif., 1973-77, safety dir., 1977-79, dir. regulatory affairs, 1979—; industry rep. to White House Inter-Govtl. Sci. Engring., and Tech. Adv. Panel, Task Force on Transp. of Non-Nuclear Hazardous Materials, 1980; industry rep. Transp. Rsch. Bd.'s Nat. Strategies Conf. on Transp. of Hazardous Materials and Wastes in the 1980's, NAS, 1981, Hazardous Materials Transp. Conf., Nat. Conf. of State Legislatures, 1982. speaker and moderator in field; dir. Western Fertilizer and Pesticide Safety seminar, Sacramento, 1979; speaker Southeastern Agrl. Chem. Safety seminar, Winston-Salem, N.C., 1986. Chmn. industry/govt. task force for unique on-site hazardous waste recycling, devel. task force for computerized regulatory software and data base system, devel. task force modifying high expansion foam tech. for fire suppression; hazardous materials adviser, motor carrier rating com. Calif. Hwy. Patrol, 1978-79. With U.S. Army, 1962-65. Mem. Western Agrl. Chems. Assn. (past chmn. transp., distbn. and safety com., outstanding mem. of year 1981, govtl. affairs com., trustee polit. action com.), Nat. Agrl. Chems. Assn. (past chmn. transp. and distbn. com., occupational safety and health com., environ. mgmt. com., state affairs com., moderator spring conf. 1989), Am. Soc. Safety Engrs., Calif. Fertilizer Assn. (transp. and distbn. com., environ. com.), Fresno City and County C. of C. (agrl. steering com., govt. affairs com.), Calif. C. of C. (environ. policy com.), Am. Legion, Elks. Republican. Office: 191 W Shaw Ave Ste 107 Fresno CA 93704-2876

DONALDSON, JOHN RILEY, physics educator; b. Dallas, Nov. 24, 1925; s. John Riley and Marguerette Hoover (Atkinson) D.; m. Shirley Jean Brown, June 30, 1951; children: Nancy Gullett, Dorothy Chaffee, Jack Donaldson, Jane Hollingsworth. BS, Rice U., 1945, MA, 1947; MS, Yale U, 1949; PhD, 1951. Physicist Calif. R & D, Livermore, 1950-53; assoc. prof. U. Ariz., 1953-54; physicist U.S. Army, Frederick, Md., 1954-56; asst. prof. then assoc. prof. Calif. State U., Fresno, 1956-67, prof., 1967-91, chmn. dept. physics, 1983-91, prof. emeritus, 1991—; vis. prof. Swiss Fed. Inst. Tech., Zurich, 1967-68, 82-83. Choir dir. Coll. Community Congl. Ch., Fresno, 1956—, moderator, 1960-61; elected supr. Fresno County, 1973-80. Mem. AAAS, Am. Phys. Soc., Am. Assn. Physics Tchrs. Democrat. Mem. United Church of Christ. Home: 4559 N Dewitt Ave Fresno CA 93727-7160 Office: Calif State U Fresno Shaw and Cedar Aves Fresno CA 93740-0037

DONALDSON, LESLIE ALLAN, molecular biologist; b. Albuquerque, Feb. 28, 1958; s. George Howard and Barbara Jean (Gaddis) D.; m. Sandra Yvonne Contreras, Aug. 2, 1985. BS, U. N.Mex., 1982. Mgr. G. F. Devel., Albuquerque, 1979-82; lab. technician Lovelace Hosp., Albuquerque, 1982-84; teaching asst. U. N.Mex., Albuquerque, 1984-87; rsch. technologist Lovelace Med. Found., Albuquerque, 1987—; lab. asst. Lovelace Hosp., 1988—. Contbr. articles to profl. jours. Fund raiser United Way, 1990-92. Grad. Rsch. grantee, 1985. Libertarian. Presbyterian. Office: Lovelace Med Found 2425 Ridgecrest SE Albuquerque NM 87108

DONALDSON, LESLIE ANNE, television news producer; b. Pitts., Feb. 19, 1955; d. John Hammond and Marjory (Sharp) D. BA, U. Calif., Santa Cruz, 1977; postgrad., San Francisco State U., 1978-79. Film and tape editor KTVU-TV/Cox Broadcasting, Oakland, Calif., 1978-86; bur. videotape editor NBC-TV, Burbank, Calif., 1986; freelance producer Oakland, 1987; news and documentary producer KTVU-TV/Cox Broadcasting, Oakland, 1988—; film instr. San Francisco State U., 1978. Producer, editor documentaries including Angel of Death, Fox Network, 1987. Recipient Emmy award San Francisco NATAS, 1979, Best Mini-Series award AP, 1988, Gold medal, Internat. Film and TV Festival N.Y., 1988. Mem. NATAS (bd. dirs. San Francisco chpt. 1980-84). Office: KTVU TV 2 Jack London Sq Oakland CA 94607-3727

DONALDSON, MARY KENDRICK, nurse; b. Tifton, Ga., June 25, 1937; d. Howard Story and Trudy (Donalson) Marlin; m. Harvey Kendrick Sr., Apr. 13, 1953 (dec. 1965); children: Jerome, Micheal, Harvey Jr., Merry, Sheila, Larry; m. Isaac Hargett, Feb. 16, 1985. AA, Compton (Calif.) Coll., 1969; BS, Pepperdine U., 1972, MA, 1976; diploma in nursing, SW Coll., Los Angeles, 1984. Staff nurse St. Francis Hosp., Lynwood, Calif., 1965-67; pvt. duty nurse Profl. Nurse's Registry, Los Angeles, 1967-82; elem. tchr. Compton Sch. Dist., Calif., 1975-80; caseworker, clk. Los Angeles County Probation Dept., 1980-90, dep. probation officer, 1990—; pediatric, nurse companion Personal Care Health Service, Torrance, Calif., 1984—; home economist Dept. Welfare, Compton, 1970-72; asst. dir. Century Plaza Hotel, Century City, Calif., 1971-72. Chairperson Com. To Elect Garland Hardeman For Councilman, Inglewood, Calif., 1987. Exec. Housekeeping scholarship Century Plaza Hotel, Los Angeles, 1971. Mem. Fellow Am. Home Econs. Assn., Pepperdine Alumni Assn., Pepperdine's Kappa-Kappa Sorority, Am. Nurse's Assn. Democrat. Home: 4540 Orange Ave Apt 308 Long Beach CA 90807-2377 Office: L A County Probation Dept 1601 Eastlake Ave Los Angeles CA 90033-1094

DONALDSON, MICHAEL THOMAS, sales executive; b. Port Jefferson, N.Y., May 8, 1957; s. Gerald Peter and Patricia Elizabeth (Hoppenstedt) D.; m. Denise Van Acker, June 19, 1981; children: Kelly, Sarah. Student, Calif. State U., Long Beach, 1976-79. Sales rep. Glaxo Pharms., Santa Barbara, Calif., 1980-82; sales mgr. Glaxo Pharms., Conn., 1982-89, Astra Pharms., Irvine, Calif., 1989—. Republican. Roman Catholic. Home: 18 Coldbrook Irvine CA 92714

DONALDSON, WILBURN LESTER, property management corporation executive; b. St. Augustine, Fla., Mar. 2, 1938; s. Chester Campbell and Dovie (Pratt) D.; m. Patricia Lilias Babcock, Sept. 11, 1956; children: John Randolph, David Chester, James Robert. BA, San Francisco State U., 1968, MBA, 1971. Transp. clk. Armour Food Co., San Francisco, 1958-60, transp. mgr., 1960-65, product mgr., 1965-70; So. Calif. sales mgr. Armour Food Co., L.A., 1970-73; tng. mgr. Armour Food Co., Phoenix, 1973-77, nat. mktg. mgr., 1977-80; region sales mgr. Armour Food Co., Pitts., 1980-83; nat. tng. mgr. Armour Food Co., Phoenix, 1983-84; pres. Allied Investment Mgrs., Inc., Phoenix, 1984—. Author: How To Use Psychological Leverage, 1978, Conversational Magic, 1978, Behavioral Supervision, 1980, Human Resource Development, 1986. Mem. Nat. Real Estate Assn. Republican. Home: 350 E Deepdale Rd Phoenix AZ 85022-4229 Office: Allied Investment Inc 1121 E Missouri Ave # 123S Phoenix AZ 85014-2713

DONATH, FRED ARTHUR, geologist, geophysicist; b. St. Cloud, Minn., July 11, 1931; s. Arnold C. and Elizabeth (Crary) D.; m. Mavis Eleanor Hagen, July 19, 1952; children: Robert William, Deborah Ann. B.A., U. Minn., 1954; M.S., Stanford U., 1956, Ph.D., 1958. Mem. faculty San Jose (Calif.) State Coll., 1957-58; mem. faculty Columbia U., N.Y.C., 1958-67; prof. geology Columbia U., 1966-67, U. Ill., Urbana, 1967-80; head dept. geology U. Ill., 1967-77; cons. U.S. Nuclear Regulatory Commn., 1977-80; pres. CGS, Inc., Urbana, 1980-83; dir., prin. geoscientist The Earth Tech. Corp., Long Beach, Calif., 1983-85; v.p. geoscis., dir. research The Earth Tech. Corp., 1985-86, v.p. R&D, 1987-88, sr. cons., 1988-90; exec. dir. Inst. for Environ. Edn., Geol. Soc. Am., 1990—; advisor Office Sci. and Tech. Policy, 1978-79; mem. U.S. Nat. Com. Rock Mechanics, 1978-81; advisor U.S. Dept. of Energy, 1992—; rschr. in exptl. high pressure geophysics, dynamic structural geology, deep geol. disposal of nuclear waste. Editor: Ann. Rev. Earth and Planetary Scis., 1970-80; assoc. editor: Geol. Soc. Am., 1963-73; acting editor, 1964; mem. editorial bd.: Engring. Geology, 1964-83, Tectonophysics, 1964-77; contbr. numerous articles on geology and geophysics to sci. jours. Recipient Semicentennial Medallion Rice U., 1962. Fellow Geol. Soc. Am., Geol. Soc. London, AAAS; mem. Am. Geophys. Union (sec. tectonophysics sect. 1964-68, vis. lectr. 1967-72), Am. Assn. Petroleum Geologists (lectr. continuing edn. program 1965-78), Phi Beta Kappa, Sigma Xi.

DONATONI, PAUL J., pharmacist; b. L.A., Dec. 4, 1957; s. Jerry and Stella D. BA in Biology, UCLA, 1980; PharmD, U. Calif., San Francisco, 1986. Pharmacy resident NIH, Bethesda, Md., 1986-87; pharmacist UCLA Med. Ctr., 1987—. Mem. Am. Soc. Hosp. Pharmacists, So. Calif. Soc. Hosp. Pharmacists (com. mem.), Phi Delta Chi. Office: UCLA Med Ctr 10833 Le Conte Ave Los Angeles CA 90024-1707

DONE, ALAN KIMBALL, physician; b. Salt Lake City, Sept. 23, 1926; s. Willard Vivian and Alice June (Kimball) D.; m. Winifred Kessler, 1946 (div. 1972); m. Georgia Polson Scott, 1973 (div. 1984); m. Carol Black, Dec. 14, 1985; children: Gregory, Jeffrey, Scot, Kathryn, Gary. BA in Biology, U. Utah, 1950, MD, 1952. Diplomate Am. Bd. Pediatrics, Am. Bd. Med. Toxicology. Intern, resident and fellow in pediatrics Salt Lake County Gen. Hosp., 1953-56; instr. to ast. prof. of pediatrics U. Utah, Salt Lake City, 1956-58, prof. pediatric, 1960-62; assoc. prof. pediatrics Stanford U., Palo Alto, Calif., 1958-60; dir. pediatric pharmacology FDA, Rockville, Md., 1972-75; prof. pediatrics and pharmacology Wayne State U., Detroit, 1975-83; pvt. cons. Salt Lake City, 1984—; adj. prof. pharmacology U. Utah, 1960-72; dir. div. of clin. pharmacology and toxicology Childrens Hosp. of Mich., Detroit, 1975-82, dir. intermountain regional poison control ctr. U. Hosp., Salt Lake City, 1960-72, chief-of-staff, 1962; dir. poison control ctr. Salt Lake County Gen. Hosp., 1954-58; cons. Nat. Clearinghouse for Poison Control Ctrs., USPHS, Washington, 1960-68, 75-77; expert FDA, Washington, 1975-77. Author: LaTriviata, Fun, Folly and Facts for Opera Lovers, 1992. Coord. poisoning Div V, Emergency Med. Svcs., U.S. Dept. Health, Edn. and Welfare, Detroit, 1979-81; adv. panel mem. Utah State Div. of Health, Salt Lake City, 1969-72. Recipient Ross award for Pediatric Rsch. Western Soc. for Pediatric Rsch., 1959, Joint Recognition award Am. and Can. Acads. of Clin. Toxicology, 1980, Rsch. Career Devel. award USPHS, 1961-66, Physicians Recognition award AMA, 1971. Fellow Am. Acad. of Pediatrics (specialty cert.), Am. Acad. of Clin. Toxicology; mem. Soc. for Pediatric Rsch., Am. Assn. of Poison Control Ctrs. (exec. com. 1966-68), Am. Bd. Med. Toxicology (assoc. chmn. 1980-82), Trial Lawyers for Pub. Justice. Republican. Home and Office: 6337 Highland Dr #2054 Salt Lake City UT 84121

DONE, ROBERT STACY, criminal investigative specialist, consultant; b. Tucson, Apr. 7, 1965; s. Richard Avon Done and Nancy Jane (Meeks) Underwood; m. Michele Renae Barwick, May 17, 1987 (div. Mar. 1990); m. Elizabeth Evans Robinson, Feb. 20, 1993. AS in Law Enforcement, Mo. So. State Coll., 1987, BS in Criminal Justice Adminstrn., 1987; MPA, U. Ariz., 1992. Lic. realtor, Ariz., pvt. investigator, Ariz. Criminal investigator Pima County, Tucson, 1988—; pres. Data Methods Corp., Tucson, 1984—. Mem. Am. Soc. for Pub. Adminstrn., Ariz. Mcpl. Mgmt. Assts. Assn. Republican.

Home: 7549 N Oliver Ave Tucson AZ 85741-1726 Office: Pima County Pub Defender 2225 E Ajo Way Tucson AZ 85713-6295

DONELSON, IRENE W., property manager; b. Placerville, Calif., Mar. 5, 1913; d. John H. and Emma Marie (Frechette) Witmer; m. Kenneth Wilber, July 25, 1937; children: Carol Korb, Richard Kenneth. AA, U. Calif., Berkeley, 1932; postgrad., Sacramento City Coll., 1934, U. of the Pacific, 1951. Advt. copywriter Hale's Dept. Store, Sacramento, 1934-37, Breuner's Home Furnishings, Sacramento, 1939-41; law office mgr., legal asst. Kenneth W. Donelson, Sacramento, 1951—; property mgr. The Law Bldg., Sacramento, 1986—. Co-author: (with Kenneth Donelson) When You Need a Lawyer, 1964, How to Handle Your Legal Problems, 1965, revised edits., 1968, 71, Married Today, Single Tomorrow: Marriage Breakup and the Law, 1969; contbr. articles to nat. mags. Recipient Woman With a View award Sacramento Union, 1972. Mem. NAFE, Calif. Writers' Club (pres. 1962-63, 76-77, dir. 1978-79, Jack London award 1979), Sacramento Book Collectors Club. Republican. Office: 708 10th St Ste 150 Sacramento CA 95814-1806

DONELSON, KENNETH LAVERN, English language educator; b. Holdrege, Nebr., June 16, 1927; s. Lester Homer Irving and Minnie Irene (Lyons) D.; m. Virginia Juanita Watts (div. 1970); children: Sheryl Lynette George, Kurt Allen; m. Marie Elizabeth Smith, May 30, 1983; 1 child, Jeanette. BA, U. Iowa, 1950, MA, 1951, PhD, 1963. English tchr. Glidden (Iowa) High Sch., 1951-56, Thomas Jefferson High Sch., Cedar Rapids, Iowa, 1956-63; asst. prof. English Edn. Kans. State U., Manhattan, 1963-65; asst. prof. English Ariz. State U., Tempe, 1965-67, assoc. prof. English, 1967-71, prof. English, 1971—. Co-author: Literature for Today's Young Adults, 1980, 4th edit., 1993; author: The Student's Right to Read, 1972. With USN, 1945-46. Mem. Nat. Coun. Tchrs. English (chmn. conf. on English edn. 1974-76, Award for Outstanding Contbn. to the Field of Adolescent Lit. 1983, pres. adolescent lit. assembly 1980-81, co-editor English Jour. 1980-87). Democrat. Episcopalian.

DONER, JOHN ROLAND, hospital administrator; b. Ontario, Oreg., May 6, 1949; s. L. L. and Majorie R. (Robinson) D.; m. Kathleen M. Lang, Mar. 6, 1970; children: J. R., Erica C. BBA, Boise (Idaho) State U., 1971. Lic. nursing home adminstr., Idaho. Disability claims adjucator Idaho Disability Determinators Unit, Boise, 1972-74, quality assurance specialist, 1974-76, unit mgr., 1976-78; mgmt. and fin. cons. Idaho Dept. Health & Welfare, Boise, 1978-81; asst. adminstr. Idaho State Sch. & Hosp., Nampa, 1981-92, adminstrv. dir., 1993—. Sec., treas. bd. dirs. Idaho Spl. Olympics, Boise, 1985-92; vice chmn. Nampa Community Work Release Ctr. Bd., 1987—; mem. adv. bd. Bogus Basin Recreation Assn. Inc., Boise, 1987—; mem., bd. dirs. Archie B. Teater Fund for Handicapped, Inc., 1991—; vol. driver, judge Am. Water Ski Assn. Mem. Profl. Ski Instrs. Am. (cert.). Home: 10341 Shiloh Dr Boise ID 83704-2736 Office: Idaho State Sch & Hosp 3100 11th Ave N Nampa ID 83687-3447

DONGES, SAMUEL ARNOLD (SAM), process control engineer; b. Ashland, Ohio, Oct. 9, 1958; s. George H. and Cathleen (Vanosdal) D. BSEE, Metro State U., 1971. Quality control Martin Co., Denver, 1960-61; water commr. City of Frisco (Colo.), 1961-65; contract adminstr. MSI of Tenn., Huntsville, Ala., 1966-68; svc. mgr. BCS Assocs., Orlando, Fla., 1968-69; prodn. supr. Honeywell, Denver, 1969-70; process control engr. Denver Autometrics Inc., Boulder, Colo., 1970—. With USN, 1956-60. Mem. Instrument Soc. Am., Elks, Masons, Scotish Rite, York Rite. Office: Denver Autometrics Inc 6235 Lookout Rd Boulder CO 80301-3335

DONISTHORPE, CHRISTINE ANN, state senator; b. Christina, Mont., May 31, 1932; d. Lambert A. and Ludmilla (Hruska) Benes; m. Oscar Lloyd Donisthorpe, 1951; children—Paul, Karen, Bruce, Brian. Student U. Mont., 1951-53, San Juan Coll., N.Mex. Real Estate Sch., 1958-70. Pres. Bd. of Edn., Bloomfield, N.Mex., 1975-81; mem. N.Mex. State Senate, 1979—, mem. edn. com., 1979, fin. com., 1980, edn. study com., 1981; mem. Bd. Realtors San Juan County, 1978-81. Adv. bd. Salvation Army, 1970-75; active C. of C. Recipient U.S. Soil and Water Conservation award, 1967; Hon. State Future Farmers Adv. award, 1975. Mem. N.Mex. Hay Growers Assn. Republican. Methodist. Home: PO Box 746 Bloomfield NM 87413-0746

DONKER, RICHARD BRUCE, health association administrator; b. Modesto, Calif., Sept. 29, 1950; s. Luverne Peter and Ruth Bernice (Hoekenga) D.; m. Susan Gail Content, May 3, 1986; 1 child, Elizabeth Anne. AA, Modesto Jr. Coll., 1970; BS, Calvin Coll., Grand Rapids, Mich., 1972; MA, Calif. State Coll., Turlock, 1978; EdD, U. Pacific, 1980. Grant dir. Yosemite Community Coll. Dist., Modesto, 1975-77; dir. flight ops. Meml. Hosps. Assn., Modesto, 1980-85, adminstrv. coord., 1985-87, v.p. bus. systems, 1987-89; v.p. clin. svcs. Meml. Hosp. Assn., Modesto, 1989-92; mng. dir. Global Bus. Network, Emeryville, Calif., 1992—; exec. dir. MediPLUS Health Plans, Inc., Modesto, 1986-92; pres. Calif. Aeromed. Rescue and Evacuation, Inc., Modesto, 1985; lectr. Am. Hosp. Assn., Chgo., 1984—; bd. dirs. Synergistic Systems, Inc.; cons. in field, 1984—. Author: Emergency Medical Technician Outreach Training, 1977, (with others) The Hospital Emergency Department: Returning to Financial Viability, 1987, Restructuring Ambulatory Care, A Guide to Reorganization, 1990, The Hospital Emergency Department, 1992. Bd. dirs. Stanislaus Paramedic Assn., Modesto, 1978-82, Head Rest, Inc., Modesto, 1980; bd. dirs. regional occupational program Stanislau County Dept. Edn., 1980; del. People-to-People Citizen Amb. Program, People's Republic of China, 1988. Mem. Am. Acad. Med. Adminstrs., Nat. Acad. Scis. Inst. Medicine (com. pediatric emergency med. svcs. 1991-92), Phi Delta Kappa, Commonwealth Club. Presbyterian. Home: 1322 Edgebrook Dr Modesto CA 95354-1537 Office: Meml Hosps Assn 1700 Coffee Rd Modesto CA 95355-2869

DONLON, WILLIAM CHRISTOPHER, maxillofacial surgeon, educator, author, editor; b. N.Y.C., Oct. 17, 1952; s. William Aloyisius and Margaret Mary (O'Donovan) D.; m. Marianne Patricia Truta, May 28, 1983; 1 child, Sean Liam Riobard. BA, Hofstra U., 1974, MA, 1975; DMD, Tufts U., 1979. Diplomate Am. Bd. Oral Maxillofacial Surgery. Resident Mt. Sinai Med. Ctr., N.Y.C., 1979-81, chief resident, 1981-82; asst. clin. prof. U. Pacific, San Francisco, 1982-88, assoc. clin. prof., 1988—; prin. surgeon Peninsula Maxillofacial Surgery, South San Francisco, Calif., 1982—, Burlingame, Calif., 1988—; Redwood City, Menlo Park, Calif., 1990—; dir. Facial Pain Rsch. Ctr., San Francisco, 1986—; lectr. in field. Editor: Headache and Facial Pain, 1990; contbr. articles to profl. jours., chpts. to books. Fellow Am. Dental Soc. Anesthesiology, Am. Assn. Oral Maxillofacial Surgeons (chmn. com. on hosp. affairs 1992-95, chmn. reference com., House of Dels., 1992—), Am. Coll. Oral Maxillofacial Surgeons; mem. AMA, ADA, Am. Soc. TMJ Surgeons, Western Soc. Oral Maxillofacial Surgeons (bd. dirs. 1993—), European Assn. Craniomaxillofacial Surgery, Internat. Assn. Maxillofacial Surgery, Calif. Dental Assn., No. Calif. Oral Maxillofacial Surgeons (bd. dirs. 1986-88, sec.-treas. 1990-91, pres. 1992-93), Calif. Assn. Oral Maxillofacial Surgeons (bd. dirs. 1991-94), Soc. of Med. Friends Wine, Tufts Dental Alumni Assn. (v.p. Calif. chpt. 1984—). Office: Peninsula Maxillofacial Surgery 1860 El Camino Real Ste 300 Burlingame CA 94010-3114

DONNELLY, DONALD FRANK, mathematics educator, computer consultant; b. San Diego, Nov. 23, 1928; s. George Dewey and Helen Mabel (Jones) D.; m. Barbara Gay Moore, Nov. 22, 1952 (div. Aug. 1964); m. Mary Ruth Hutchinson, June 1, 1974; children: Kathleen Alice, Michael Patrick, Christiane, Kelley Ann, Kerry Colleen. BA, San Diego State Coll., 1954; MA, Calif. Western U., 1964; EdS, Point Loma Coll., 1983; EdD, No. Ariz. U., 1986. Tchr., coach William S. Hart Sch. Dist., Newhall, Calif., 1955-56, San Diego City Schs., 1956-72, Grossmont Union High Sch. Dist., El Cajon, Calif., 1972-88; instr. math. Grossmont C.C., El Cajon, 1988—. Actor Old Globe Theatre, San Diego, 1966-76, San Diego Opera Co., 1973-81, SAG, San Diego, 1981—. With U.S. Army, 1950-52, Korea. Mem. AFTRA, VFW, Am. Legion, Old Mission Beach Athletic Club, San Diego Aerospace Mus., San Diego State U. Aztec Varsity Club (membership chair 1991—), Aztec Athletic Found., Elks, Phi Delta Kappa (historian 1984-86). Democrat. Roman Catholic. Home: 391 Aldwych Rd El Cajon CA 92020-2201 Office: Grossmont CC 8800 Grossmont Coll Dr El Cajon CA 92020

DONNELLY, JOHN, philosophy educator; b. Worcester, Mass., Mar. 30, 1941; s. Donald Smith and Viola Frances (Norton) D.; m. Joyce Marie Mattress, June 10, 1967; children: Colin, Maria. BS, Holy Cross Coll., 1963; MA, Boston Coll., 1965; AM, Brown U., 1967, PhD, 1969. Prof. U. San Diego, 1976—. Editor: Suicide: Right or Wrong, 1990, Reflective Wisdom, 1989, Language, Metaphysics and Death, 1978, Logical Analysis and Contemporary Theism, 1972, Conscience, 1973; editorial bd. Internat. Philos. Quar., N.Y.C., 1972-76. Recipient award NEH, 1980. Mem. Am. Philos. Assn., Soc. Christian Philosophers, Am. Acad. Religion, Soren Kierkegaard Soc. (v.p. 1988, pres. 1989). Democrat. Roman Catholic. Home: 7890 Hummingbird Ln San Diego CA 92123 Office: U San Diego Alcala Park San Diego CA 92110-2429

DONNELLY, TIMOTHY CHRISTOPHER, chemist, educator; b. Oakland, Calif., June 11, 1947. BS in Chemistry, Calif. State U., Hayward, 1970, MS, 1972; PhD, U. Calif., Davis, 1977. Lectr. Calif. State U., Hayward, 1971-72; rsch. assoc. U. Calif., Davis, 1972-77; rsch. chemist Clorox Corp., Pleasanton, Calif., 1977-79; prof. chemistry U. Calif., Davis, 1979—; pres. TiDon Rsch. Inst., Vacaville, Calif., 1976—. Contbr. articles to profl. jours.; inventor super hot sauce, laser medicine technique, all temp ski wax. Mem. Am. Chem. Soc. (div. chem. edn., small chem. bus. div.), Air and Space Assn., Nat. Air Racing Assn., Sigma Xi. Office: U Calif Dept Chemistry Davis CA 95616

DONNER, NEAL ARVID, educator; b. Wernigerode, Germany, Aug. 17, 1942; came to U.S., 1946; s. Otto Richard Gustav Donner and Jane Esch; m. Carol Anne Linnell, May 4, 1968 (div. Dec. 1981); children: Erich, Rebecca. BA, Oberlin, 1964; MA, U. Mich., 1968; PhD, U. B.C., Vancouver, Can., 1976. Tchr. Peace Corps, Ethiopia, 1964-66; scholar-in-residence Cimarron Zen Ctr., L.A., 1978-79; violin tchr. L.A., 1981—; vis. asst. prof. U. Va., Charlottesville, 1976-78. Translator: Entrepreneur and Gentleman, 1976, History of Hindu-Buddhist Thought, 1977, The Legacy of Pythagoras, 1993, The Great Calming and Contemplation of Chih-i, 1993. Libertarian candidate Calif. State Assembly, Santa Monica, 1984, 86; vice-chair Libertarian Party of Calif., 1989. Mem. Suzuki Music Assn. Calif. (pres. L.A. br. 1988-90). Buddhist. Home and Office: 2739 S Westgate Ave Los Angeles CA 90064-3527

DONNICI, PETER JOSEPH, lawyer, law educator, consultant; b. Kansas City, Mo., Sept. 5, 1939; s. Albert H. and Jennie (Danubio) D.; m. Diane DuPlantier, July 27, 1985; children—JuliaAnn Donnici Clifford, Joseph A., Joann Donnici Powers. B.A., U. Mo.-Kansas City, 1959, J.D., 1962; LL.M., Yale U., 1963. Bar: Mo. 1963, U.S. Supreme Ct. 1966, Calif. 1969. Asst. prof. law U. San Francisco, 1963-65, assoc. prof., 1965-68, prof., 1968-91; assoc. Law Offices Joseph L. Alioto, San Francisco, 1967-72; sole practice, San Francisco, 1974—; ptnr. Donnici & LuPo, San Francisco, 1982-92, Donnici, Kerwin, Phillips & Donnici, San Francisco, 1993—; asst. prosecutor Jackson County Prosecutor's Office, Mo., 1963; cons. to Office of Mayor of San Francisco, 1968-72; No. Calif. bd. dirs. Coun. on Legal Ednl. Opportunity, San Francisco, 1969-70; conciliator for housing discrimination cases HUD, San Francisco, 1976; cons. Calif. Consumer Affairs' Task Force on Electronic Funds Transfer, Sacramento, 1978-79; dir. DHL Corp., interim chmn. bd. dirs. 1988-89; dir. Air Micronesia, Inc., 1987—, dir. DHL Internat., Ltd, Bermuda, 1992—; spl. counsel and del. to internat. confs. Commonwealth of No. Mariana Islands, 1983-84; faculty adviser U. San Francisco Law Rev., 1966-91. Editor in chief U. Mo.-Kansas City Law Rev., 1961-62; contbr. articles to profl. jours., 1964—. Lawyers' Com. for Urban Affairs, San Francisco, 1965-68. Wilson scholar U. Mo.-Kansas City, 1956-62; Sterling fellow Law Sch., Yale U., 1962-63. Mem. Bench and Robe, Phi Delta Phi. Democrat. Roman Catholic. Home: 190 Cresta Vista Dr San Francisco CA 94127 Office: One Post St Ste 2450 San Francisco CA 94104

D'ONOFRIO, MARY ANN, medical transcription company executive; b. Detroit, Jan. 24, 1933; d. Charles Henry and Cecilia Rose (Levan) Clifford; m. Dominic Armando D'Onofrio, Apr. 19, 1958; children: Margaret Clement, Anthony, Elizabeth, Maria Spurgeon. BA, Marygrove Coll., 1954; MLS, U. Mich., 1955. Cert. med. transcriptionist. Reader's advisor Detroit Pub. Libr., 1955-58; cataloger Willow Run (Mich.) Pub. Libr., 1959-61, St. Thomas Grade and High Sch., Ann Arbor, Mich., 1968-72; med. record analyst Chelsea (Mich.) Community Hosp., 1972-79; pres. Meditranscript Svc., Ann Arbor, 1979-81; asst. office mgr. Dr. Maxfield, D.O., Tucson, 1981-82; quality assurance analyst, utilization rev. Tucson (Ariz.) Gen. Hosp., 1983-86; exec. asst. Dr. McEldoon M.D., Tucson, 1986-88; pres. Meditranscript Svc., Tucson, 1986-88; co-owner Med-Comm Assocs., Tucson, 1989—. Co-author: Psychiatric Words & Phrases, 1990; contbr. articles to profl. jours; co-developer Cross-Search. Block leader Infantile Paralysis Assn., Ann Arbor, 1975-80, Easter Seal Assn., Tucson, 1983-86; capt. Tucson chpt. Am. Cancer Soc., 1992. Mem. NAFE, Am. Assn. for Med. Transcription (parliamentarian Sonora Desert chpt. 1984-86, 90—, compiler/editor booklet AAMT Annotated Bibliography, 1981, named disting. mem. 1984, treas. Sonora Desert chpt. 1987, jour. columnist 1982-86), Ednl. Honor Soc., Pi Lambda Theta (life).

DONOHUE, GEORGE L., mechanical engineer; b. Wichita, Kans., July 8, 1944; s. George Edward and Dorothy Mae (Cunningham) Custer; m. Andreana Grillis, June 7, 1969; children: Carmen, Kathleen, Georgiana, Caroline. Student, Ga. Inst. Tech., Atlanta, 1962-64; BSME, U. Houston, 1967; MS, Okla. State U., 1968, PhD, 1972. Coop student NASA, Clear Lake, Tex., 1963-67; postdoctoral fellow Naval Undersea Ctr., Pasadena, 1972-73; br. head Naval ocean Sys. Ctr., San Diego, 1973-76; prog. mgr. DARPA, Arlington, Va., 1976-77; div. head Naval Ocean Sys. Ctr., San Diego, 1977-79; v.p. Dynamics Tech. Inc., Torrance, Calif., 1979-84; prog. mgr. The Rand Corp., Santa Monica, Calif., 1984-88; office dir. Def. Adv. Rsch. project Agy., Arlington, 1988-89; v.p. The Rand Corp., Santa Monica, 1989—; mem. profl. adv. com. Aerospace Engring. dept. Pa. State U., 1988-91. Contbr. articles to profl. jours.; patentee in field. Adult advisor Girl Scouts U.S.A., Torrance, 1987-88; treas. YMCA Girls Gymnastics Team, San Pedro, Calif., 1983. Dept. Def. Merit Civil Svc. medal, 1977; NRC fellow, 1972; NDEA fellow, 1967. Fellow AIAA (assoc., policy com. 1990—); mem. Internat. Inst. Strategic Studies, Elks, Tau Beta Pi, Sigma Xi, Omicron Delta Kappa, Pi Tau Sigma. Roman Catholic.

DONOHUE, PATRICIA JEAN, college official, media relations consultant; b. San Francisco, Aug. 27, 1947; d. Robert Cooper and Thelma Louise Vandevort; m. James H. Donohue, July 11, 1977 (div. Jan. 1988). BA in English and Biology, San Francisco State U., 1971, postgrad., 1971-72, secondary credential, 1973. Tchr. Oakland (Calif.) Unified Sch. Dist., 1974-76; sec. grad. div. San Francisco State U., 1976-77; community liaison for pres. Sonoma State U., Rohnert Park, Calif., 1977-78; owner, pub. Times Star & Blank Pub. Co., Middletown, Calif., 1979-83; tchr. English and journalism Middletown Unified Sch. Dist., 1984-86; computer svc. operator, proofreader Drager & Mount Typographers, Mountain View, Calif., 1988-89; tchr. journalism Contra Costa County Regional Occupation Program, Walnut Creek, Calif., 1989-90; real estate editor Contra Costa Times, Walnut Creek, 1990; dir. pub. rels. Holy Names Coll., Oakland, 1991—. Mem. Lake County Bd. Edn., Lakeport, Calif., 1979-83; mem. 49th Dist. Agrl. Assn., 1980-81; mem. Oakland steering com. World Affairs Coun., 1991—. Office: Holy Names Coll 3500 Mountain Blvd Oakland CA 94619

DONOHUGH, DONALD LEE, physician; b. Los Angeles, Apr. 12, 1924; s. William Noble and Florence Virginia (Shelton) D.; m. Virginia Eskew McGregor, Sept. 12, 1950 (div. 1971); children: Ruth, Laurel, Marilee, Carol, Greg; m. Beatrice Ivany Redick, Dec. 3, 1976; stepchildren: Leslie Ann, Andrea Jean. BS, U.S. Naval Acad., 1946; MD, U. Calif., San Francisco, 1956; MPH and Tropical Medicine, Tulane U., 1961. Diplomate AM. Bd. Internal Medicine. Intern U. Hosp., San Diego, 1956-57; resident Monterey County Hosp., 1957-58; dir. of med. svcs. U.S. Depart. Interior, Am. Samoa, 1958-60; instr. Tulane U. Med. Sch., New Orleans, 1960-63; resident Tulane Svcs. V.A. and Charity Hosp., New Orleans, 1961-63; cons. Internat. Ctr. for Rsch and Tng., Costa Rica, 1961-63; asst. prof. medicine & preventive medicine La. State U. Sch. Medicine, 1962-63; assoc. prof., 1963-65; vis. prof. U. Costa Rica, 1963-65; faculty advisor, head of Agy. Internat. Devel. program U. Costa Rica Med. Sch., 1965-67; dir. med. svcs. Med. Ctr. U. Calif. (formerly Orange County Hosp.), Irvine, 1967-69; assoc. clin. prof. U. Calif., Irvine, 1967-79, clin. prof., 1980-85; pvt. practice Tustin, Calif., 1970-80; with Joint Commn. on Accreditation of Hosps., 1981; cons. Kauai, Hawaii, 1981—. Author: The Middle Years, 1981, Practice Management, 1986, Kauai, 1988, 3d edit., 1990; co-translator; Rashomon (Ryonosuke Akutagawa), 1950; also numerous articles. Lt. USN, 1946-52, capt. USNR, 1966-84. Fellow Am. Coll. Physicians (life); mem. Delta Omega. Republican. Episcopalian. Home: 4890 Lawai Rd Koloa HI 96756

DONOVAN, CHARLES STEPHEN, lawyer; b. Boston, Feb. 28, 1951; s. Alfred Michael and Maureen (Murphy) D.; m. Lisa Marie Dicharry, Apr. 21, 1979; children: Yvette, Martine, Neal. BA, Haverford Coll., 1974; JD, Cornell U., 1977. Bar: Mass. 1977, La. 1977, Calif. 1982, U.S. Supreme Ct. 1988. Atty. Phelps, Dunbar, Marks, Claverie & Sims, New Orleans, 1977-81, Dorr, Cooper & Hays, San Francisco, 1981-84, Walsh, Donovan, Lindh & Keech, San Francisco, 1984—; instr. maritime law Calif. Maritime Acad., Vallejo, 1982—; spl. advisor U.S. State Dept., 1993—. Contbr. numerous articles to profl. jours. Recipient Gustavus H. Robinson prize Cornell Law Sch., 1977. Mem. ABA (chmn. admiralty and maritime law com., Chgo. 1989-90), Internt. Bar Assn., Maritime Law Assn. U.S., Tulane Admiralty Inst. (permanent adv. bd.), Marine Exch. Club (bd. dirs. San Francisco Bay region 1993—). Office: Walsh Donovan Lindh & Keech 595 Market St Ste 2000 San Francisco CA 94105-2831

DONOVAN, JOHN ARTHUR, lawyer; b. N.Y.C., Apr. 11, 1942; children: Lara, Alex. AB, Harvard U., 1965; JD, Fordham Law Sch., 1967. Bar: N.Y. 1967, U.S. Tax Ct. 1968, U.S. Ct. Appeals (2nd cir), 1968, U.S. Dist. Ct. (so., no. dists.) N.Y. 1969, U.S. Supreme Ct. 1971, U.S. Ct. Appeals (10th cir.) 1972, U.S. Ct. Appeals (9th cir.) 1976, Calif. 1982, U.S. Dist. Ct. (so., no. dists.) Calif. 1982, U.S. Ct. Appeals (5th cir.) 1983. Assoc. Hughes, Hubbard & Reed, N.Y.C., 1967-74; ptnr. Hughes, Hubbard & Reed, N.Y.C., L.A., 1974-85, Skadden, Arps, Slate, Meagher & Flom, L.A., 1985—; adj. faculty law sch. U. So. Calif., L.A., 1986-87. Office: Skadden Arps Slate Meagher et al 300 S Grand Ave Fl 34 Los Angeles CA 90071-3109

DONOVAN, JOHN JOSEPH, JR., real estate broker and developer; b. Oakland, Calif., Mar. 10, 1916; s. John Joseph and May Ella (Coogan) D.; Ph.B., Santa Clara U., 1938; postgrad. Stanford U., 1938-40, Harvard U., 1942; m. Margaret Mary Abel, June 7, 1941; children: John Joseph III, Mary Margaret Donovan Szarnicki, Patricia Anne Donovan Jelley, Eileen Marie, Marian Gertrude Donovan Corrigan, George Edwin, Timothy Christopher, Michael Sean. Sales mgr. Universal Window Co., Berkeley, Calif., 1940-41, v.p., 1946-49, pres., chmn. bd., 1949-66; real estate broker and developer, 1966—. Mem. aluminum window mfrs. adv. com. NPA, 1951-52; chmn. pace setters com., commerce and industry div. Alameda County United Crusade, 1961. Mem. Republican small businessmen's com., Alameda County, Calif., 1946. Bd. dirs. Providence Hosp., 1970-80, also Found., 1980-82; bd. dirs. Apostleship of the Sea Ctr., 1968-85, Hanna Boy's Ctr., Sonoma County, 1976-79; mem. Oakland Mayor's Internat. Welcoming Ctr., 1972-77; trustee, treas. Serra Internat. Found., 1980-87, pres., 1981-82; mem. Serra Bicentennial Commn., 1983-86; mem. membership enrollment maj. div. San Francisco Bay Area council Boy Scouts Am., 1984—; mem. bd. Jesuit Sch. Theology, Berkeley, 1982-85, Grad. Theol. Union, Berkeley, 1982-85; bd. regents Santa Clara U., 1990—; trustee Flax Trust, Ireland, 1990. Served from ensign to lt. Supply Corps, USNR, 1940-46; in U.S.S. General Ballou; capt. Res. Decorated knight St. Gregory the Gt., Pope John XXIII, 1962 (pres. Oakland diocese 1970—); Knights of Malta, (Cross of Comdr. Merit, 1978, Cross of Comdr. of Merit with swords Order of Malta, Rome, 1981; named grand officer of merit, Order of Malta with swords, 1983, Knight Grace and Devotion, Order of Malta, 1987, Knight of Obedience, Order of Malta, 1988, Cross of Merit 1991, trustee Holy Family Hosp., Bethlehem, Israel 1991); invested and decorated Knight of Grace, Sacred Mil. Constantinian Order of St. George, 1988. Mem. Am. Legion, Western Archtl. Metal Mfrs. Assn. San Francisco (dir. 1956-65, exec. com. 1958-65, pres. 1959-60), Aluminum Window Mfrs. Assn. N.Y.C. (dir. 1950-58, 1st v.p. 1955-56), Newcomen Soc. N.Am., Naval Order U.S., Navy Supply Corps Assn. San Francisco Bay Area (2d v.p. 1970—), Father Junipero Serra 250th Anniversary Assn. (v.p., sec.), Internat. Coun. Shopping Ctrs., AIM (pres.'s coun.), Naval Res. Assn., VFW. Roman Catholic. Clubs: Berkeley Serra (charter mem.), Comml., Commonwealth, Pacific-Union (San Francisco), Monterey Peninsula Country (Pebble Beach, Calif.), Claremont Country (Oakland, Calif., bd. dirs. 1988-90), Army-Navy (Washington). Home: 2 Lincolnshire Dr Oakland CA 94618-1726 Office: PO Box 11100 Oakland CA 94611

DONOVAN, MICHAEL RICHARD, program manager, engineer; b. Bay Village, Ohio, May 12, 1952; s. George Patrick and Doris Ruth (Eimicke) D.; m. Christine Simony, May 8, 1976; children: Peter Michael, Elizabeth Anne. BS, U.S. Naval Acad., 1974; MS, MIT, 1975. Registered profl. engr., Calif., Va. Commd. ensign USN, 1974, advanced through grades to lt. comdr., res., 1983; program mgr. Solar Turbines Inc., San Diego, 1983—; Block capt. Neighborhood Watch, Coronado, Calif., 1983-89; mem. Coronado Hist. Soc., 1987—. Comdr. USNR, 1983—. Block capt. Neighborhood Watch, Coronado, Calif., 1983-89; mem. Coronado Hist. Soc., 1987—. Mem. ASME (gas turbine marine com. 1988—), Am. Soc. Naval Engrs. (chmn. San Diego chpt. 1988-89, nat. bd. dirs. 1990—), Soc. Naval Architects and Marine Engrs., San Diego C. of C. (commerce mil. affairs com. 1987—). Republican. Roman Catholic. Home: 928 A Ave Coronado CA 92118-2629 Office: Solar Turbines Inc 2200 Pacific Hwy San Diego CA 92101-1773

DONOVAN, STEVEN ROBERT, institute executive; b. Chgo., Aug. 28, 1941; s. Robert Anderson and Vera (Southwell) D.; m. Alexandra Corson, June 28, 1967 (div. Feb. 1972); 1 child, Kristen Clea; m. Anita Eubank Donovan, June 2, 1988. BA, Hobart Coll., 1963; MBA, Columbia U., 1967. Sales rep. IBM, Rochester, N.Y., 1964-66; fin. analyst Cummins Engine Co., Inc., Columbus, Ind., 1967-72; owner Donovan Assocs., San Francisco, 1973-86; pres. Esalen Inst., Big Sur, Calif., 1985—, trustee, 1979—; bd. dirs. Peet's Coffee & Tea Co., Emeryville, Calif. Co-author: The Physical and Psychological Effects of Meditation, 1987. Office: Esalen Inst Big Sur CA 93920

DONOVAN, WALTER EDGAR, retired mayor; b. Santa Ana, Calif., Mar. 7, 1926; s. Walter Raymond and Pretoria (Garver) D.; m. Diane Gertrude Mead, Mar. 28, 1948; children: Walter M., Thomas J., Victoria. Student, U. Oreg., 1945-47. Sales rep. So. Calif. Edison Co., Long Beach, Calif., 1950-55; mayor City of Garden Grove, Garden Grove, Calif., 1988-92; area mgr. So. Calif. Edison Co., Garden Grove, Calif., 1965-80, Cypress and Garden Grove, Calif., 1980-86; councilman City of Garden Grove, 1972-80, 1984-88, mayor, 1988-92.; bd. dirs. Garden Grove Hosp.-Med. Ctr., 1982-90; commr. Orange County (Calif.) Waste Mgmt. Commn., 1984-92. Recipient Community Americana Garden Grove award Cypress Coll., 1980. Mem. Rotary (pres. 1962-63), Masons, Shriners, Elks. Republican.

DONTIGNY, RICHARD LOUIS, physical therapist; b. Havre, Mont., Aug. 9, 1931; s. Theodore Emil and Helen Estelle (Halverson) D.; m. Josephine Virginia Faltrino, June 15, 1957; children: Debra Jo, Laura Jean, Richard Emil, Julie Ann. BS, Mont. State Coll., 1954; cert. in phys. therapy, U. Iowa, 1958. Staff therapist St. Francis Hosp., Colorado Springs, Colo., 1958-60, chief therapist, 1960-61; staff therapist No. Pacific Beneficial Assn., Missoula, Mont., 1961-63; chief therapist Sacred Heart Hosp., Havre, Mont., 1963-74, Deaconess Hosp., Havre, 1963-74, No. Mont. Hosp., Havre, 1974-83; staff therapist Havre Clinic, 1983-86; pvt. practice DonTigny Phys. Therapy, Havre, 1986—; mem. Mont. Bd. Phys. Therapy Examiners, 1984-87; book, manuscript reviewer Jours. Phys. Therapy, Arlington, Va., 1978—. Contbr. articles to profl. publs., chpt. to book. With U.S. Army, 1954-56. Mem. Am. Phys. Therapy Assn. (pres. Mont. chpt. 1970-74, subject matter expert orthopedic specialty coun. 1987). Home: 66 15th St W Havre MT 59501-2514 Office: DonTigny Phys Therapy 115 2D St W Havre MT 59501

DONZE, JERRY LYNN, electrical engineer; b. Wauneta, Nebr., June 12, 1943; s. John Henry and Virgina May (Francis) D.; m. Marilyn Grace Bascue, Feb. 22, 1964 (div. May. 1980); children: Scott. L., Michele A.; m. Sandra Kay Morris, July 25, 1981. Cert. technician, Denver Inst. Tech., 1964; BSEE, U. Colo., 1972; postgrad., Advanced Metaphysics Inst. Religios Sci., 1986. Electronic technician A.B.M. Co., Lakewood, Colo., 1964-71; computer programmer Nat. Bur. Standards, Boulder, Colo., 1971-72; electronic engr. Autometrics Co., Boulder, Colo., 1972-76, Gates Research and Devel., Denver, 1976-77; devel. engr. Emerson Electric Co., Lakewood, 1977; engring. mgr. Storage Tech., Louisville, Colo., 1977—; cons. Sun Co., Arvada, Colo., 1974-75. Patentee in field. Mem. IEEE Student Soc. (treas. 1971-72), Eta Kappa Nu. Republican. Religious Scientist. Home: 12021 W

54th Ave Arvada CO 80002-1907 Office: Storage Tech 2270 S 88th St Louisville CO 80028-0002

DOOLEY, CALVIN MILLARD, congressman; b. Visalia, Calif., Jan. 11, 1954. BS, U. Calif., Davis; MA, Stanford U. Mem. 102nd-103rd Congresses from Calif. Dist. 17(now 20th), 1991—; mem. agriculture com., mem. natural resources com., mem. banking, fin. and urban affairs com. Democrat. Methodist. Office: House of Representatives 1227 Longworth Washington DC 20515

DOOLITTLE, JOHN TAYLOR, congressman; b. Glendale, Calif., Oct. 30, 1950; s. Merrill T. and Dorothy Doolittle; B.A. in History with honors, U. Calif., Santa Cruz, 1972; J.D., McGeorge Sch. Law, U. Pacific, 1978; m. Julia Harlow, Feb. 17, 1979; 1 son, John Taylor Jr. Bar: Calif. 1978. Mem. Calif. State Senate, 1980—; mem. 102nd-103rd Congresses from Calif. 4th dist., 1991—; mem. agriculture com., natural resources com. Republican. Mormons. Mem. Sacramento Safari Club, Native Sons of Golden West. Office: House of Representatives 1524 Longworth Washington DC 20515*

DOOLITTLE, RUSSELL FRANCIS, biochemist, educator; b. New Haven, Jan. 10, 1931; s. Russell A. and Mary Catherine (Bohan) D.; m. Frances Ann Tynan, June 6, 1931; children: Lawrence Russell, William Edward. BA, Wesleyan U., 1952; MA, Trinity Coll., 1957; PhD, Harvard U., 1962. Instr. biochemistry Amherst (Mass.) Coll., 1961-62; asst. research biologist U. Calif.-San Diego, La Jolla, 1964-65, asst. prof. biochemistry, 1965-67, assoc. prof., 1967-72, prof., 1972—, chmn. dept. chemistry, 1981-84. Author of Urfs and Orfs, 1987; contbr. articles to profl. jours. Served as sgt. U.S. Army, 1952-54. Guggenheim fellow, 1984-85, Non-Resident fellow Salk Inst., 1990—. Fellow AAAS; mem. NAS, Am. Soc. Biol. Chemistry, Am. Acad. Arts and Scis., Am. Philos. Soc. (Paul Ehrlich prize 1989, Stein and Moore award 1991). Office: Univ Calif San Diego Ctr Molecular Genetics La Jolla CA 92093

DOOLITTLE, WILLIAM LAWRENCE, management consultant; b. Burlington, Vt., Aug. 15, 1959; s. William Hotchkiss and Arvilla Jean (Boswell) D.; m. Marsha Lynn Williams, June 9, 1991; children: Geoffrey Lawrence, Allison Nicole. BBA, U. Alaska, 1984; MBA, Claremont Grad. Sch., 1987. Cert. data processor. Firefighter, security guard U. Alaska, Fairbanks, 1978-84; systems coord. On-line Computer Libr. Ctr., Claremont, Calif., 1985-86; mgr. The Warner Group, Woodland Hills, Calif., 1987—. Mem. Info. Systems Security Assn., Assn. Pub. Safety Comms. Officers. Republican. Home: 3617 Barry Ave Los Angeles CA 90066-3201 Office: The Warner Group Ste 600 5950 Canoga Ave Woodland Hills CA 91367

DOOT, TIMOTHY ALLAN, communications company executive; b. Detroit, Dec. 7, 1957; s. Lewis Herman and Beatrice Mary (Frank) D.; m. Catherine Frances Foley, July 7, 1981; children: Jared, Sarah, Timothy, Anna. BMus, U. Mich., 1982; MMus, U. Tex., 1984, MBA, 1987. Recording engr. U. Tex., Austin, 1983-86; prodn. mgr. Sound Recorders, Inc., Austin, 1986-89, gen. mgr., 1989-90; v.p. audio prodn. Bonneville Comms., Salt Lake City, 1990—. Composer various musical compositions. Campaign vol. Rep. Party, State of Mich., 1980. U. Mich. acad. and music scholar, 1977-82, U. Tex. acad. and music scholar, 1983-86; Loise Smith Peterson Found. grantee, 1976, 87; recipient Tex. Ex-Student award Tex. Ex Student Assn., 1986-87. Mem. Austin C. of C. (mem. music com. 1989-90). LDS. Office: Bonneville Communications 130 Social Hall Ave Salt Lake City UT 84111

DORAN, CHRISTOPHER MILLER, psychiatrist; b. Albany, N.Y., Aug. 2, 1946; s. Kenneth Thompson and Kathleen (Miller) D.; m. Maureen Imelda O'Keefe, June 27, 1971; children: Alison, Meghan. BS, Boston Coll., 1968; postgrad., Cornell U., 1968-69; MD, Yale U., 1973. Diplomate Am. Bd. Psychiatry and Neurology. Intern Mary Imogene Bassett Hosp., Cooperstown, N.Y., 1973-74; resident Dept. Psychiatry, U. Colo. Health Sci. Ctr., Denver, 1974-78; psychiatrist Colo. State Hosp., Pueblo, 1976-77; chief resident U. Hosp., Denver, 1977-78; psychiatrist Aurora (Colo.) Community Mental Health Ctr., 1979-81; unit cons. Mt. Airy Psychiat. Ctr., Denver, 1981-86; med. staff Presbytn., St. Lukes Med. Ctr., Denver, 1981—; med. staff Columbine Psychiat. Ctr., Littleton, Colo., 1986—, clin. dir. adult svcs., 1987-91; pvt. practice Englewood, Colo., 1978—; cons. Colo. Dept. Insts., Canon City, 1980-81, Colo. West Mental Health Ctr., Grand Junction, 1991, U.S. VA, Denver and Cheyenne, Wyo., 1991—, Health Care Fin. Adminstrn. Dept. Health Human Svcs., Washington, 1988—; dir. psychopharmacology Columbine Psychiat. Ctr., Littleton, 1992, pres. med. staff, 1993; asst. clin. prof. psychiatry U. Colo. Health Sci. Ctr., Denver, 1979—; pres. med. staff Mt. Airy Psychiat. Ctr., Denver, 1984; speaker, lectr. in field. Bd. dirs. Mt. Airy Hosp., Denver, 1983-87; coach youth basketball and softball Cath. Youth Recreation Assn., Denver, 1986. Named Man of Yr. Vincentian Inst., Albany, 1964. Mem. Am. Psychiat. Assn., Colo. Psychiat. Soc. Office: 384 Inverness Dr S Ste 120 Englewood CO 80112

DORAN, VINCENT JAMES, steel fabricating company consultant; b. Ephrata, Wash., June 13, 1917; s. Samuel Vincent and Sarah Anastasia (Fitzpatrick) D.; B. Phil., Gonzaga U., Spokane, 1946; m. Jean Arlene Birrer, Jan. 15, 1949; children: Vincent James, Mollie Jean, Michele Lee, Patrick Michael. Mgr., Flying Service, Coulee Dam, Wash., 1947-48; mgr. constrn. Morrison-Knudsen Co., Wash. and Alaska, 1953-60; co-owner C.R. Foss Inc., constrn., Anchorage, 1961-64; mgr. Steel Fabricators, Anchorage, 1965-86. Inventor method of reducing and dewatering sewage sludge. Active Boy Scouts Am.; co-founder, pres. Chugach Rehab. Assn., 1962; mem. Alaska Gov.'s Rehab. Adv. Bd., 1962-63; mem. CAP. Served with USAAF, 1943-45, USAF, 1949-50. Decorated Air medal with 4 clusters. Mem. Welding Inst. Alaska (co-organizer, dir. 1977-78), 34th Bomb Group Assn., Am. Arbitration Assn. Roman Catholic. Club: Toastmasters. Compiler, pub. home owners' and builders' guide to sun's positions in N.Am. during solstices and equinoxes, designer packaged water, sewage treatment plants and water collection systems Arctic communities. Home: 3811 Knik Ave Anchorage AK 99517-1047 Office: Steelfab 3243 Commercial Dr Anchorage AK 99501

DORAY, ANDREA WESLEY, corporate communication specialist, writer; b. Monte Vista, Colo., Oct. 4, 1956; d. Dant Bell and Rosemary Ann (Kassap) D. BA, U. No. Colo., 1977. Cert. post secondary tchr. Asst. advt. mgr. San Luis Valley Publ. Co., Monte Vista, 1977-78; mktg. dir. Stuart Scott & Assocs. (formerly Philip Winn & Assocs.), Colorado Springs, Colo., 1978-80; sr. v.p. Heisley Design & Advt., Colorado Springs, Colo., 1980-85; pres., creative dir. Doray Doray, Monument, Colo., 1985—; account svcs. dir. Praco Ltd., Advt., Colorado Springs, 1987-88; dir. corp. community rels. Current, Inc., Colorado Springs, 1988-90; creative writer greeting cards, children's books, 1990—; artist in residence The Childrens Mus., Colorado Springs, Colo.; instr. part-time Pikes Peak Community Coll., Colorado Springs, 1983-86, 92, mem. mktg. adv. coun., 1985-93; guest lectr. Colo. Mountain Coll., 1982-84, U. So. Colo., 1983, Pikes Peak Community Coll., 1983-87, U. Colo., Colorado Springs, 1988—. Author: The Other Fish, 1976, Oil Painting Lessons, 1986, Coming to Terms, 1986, Roger Douglas, 1987, Sunshine and the Very First Christmas, 1991, The Wonderful Birthday Star, 1991, Too-Late Tiffany and the Little Shepherd, 1991, If Only It Would Snow, 1992, The Year There Could Be No Christmas, 1992, Boris Bear Remembers His Manners, 1992, The Day Daisy Found Christmas, 1992, Friends, 1993; editor: Current Impressions, 1988-90; contbg. editor Colorado Springs Bus. Mag., 1984-86; creative writer World Cycling Fedn. Championships, 1986; speaker in field. Chmn. Colorado Springs Local Advt. Rev. Program, 1985; chmn., mem. exec. com. advt. and pub. rels. task force U.S. Olympic Hall of Fame, 1986; mem. State Legis. Alert and Action Coalition, 1985-87; mem. project bus. cons. Jr. Achievement, Colorado Springs, 1985-87; trustee Citizen's Goals Colorado Springs, 1988-89; speaker Nat. Coun. Community Rels., Orlando, Fla., 1988; grad. Leadership 2000, 1988; commencement speaker Yuma (Colo.) High Sch., 1987; social styles trainer Producing Results with Others. Named One of Colorado Springs Leading Women, Colorado Springs Gazette Telegraph, 1984, One of Women of 90s, 1989; Outstanding Young Alumna, U. No. Colo., 1987. Mem. Am. Advt. Fedn. (chmn. dist. 12 legis. com. 1985-87, pub. rels. com. 1986, Silver medal award 1986), Pikes Peak Advt. Fedn. (pres. 1984-86, Advt. Person of Yr. award), Colorado Springs C. of C. (advt. roundtable, speaker small bus. coun. 1986—, communications task force 1989-90, speaker woman in bus. conf.). Office: Current Inc PO Box 2559 Colorado Springs CO 80901-2559

DORE, FRED HUDSON, retired state supreme court chief justice; b. Seattle, July 31, 1925; s. Fred Hudson and Ruby T. (Kelly) D.; m. Mary Therese Shuham, Nov. 26, 1956; children: Margaret, Fred Hudson, Teresa, Tim, Jane. BS in Fgn. Svc., Georgetown U., 1946, JD, 1949. Bar: Wash. 1949. Pvt. practice Seattle, 1949-77; mem. Wash. Ho. of Reps., 1953-59; state senator from Wash., 1959-74; judge Wash. State Ct. Appeals, 1977-80; justice Wash. State Supreme Ct., Olympia, 1981-93; chief justice Wash. State Supreme Ct., Olympia, 1991-93; ret., 1993.

DORER, FRED HAROLD, chemistry educator; b. Auburn, Calif., May 3, 1936; s. Fred H. and Mary E. (Fisher) D.; m. Marilyn Pearl Young, Sept. 6, 1958; children: Garrett Michael, Russell Kenneth. B.S., Calif. State U.-Long Beach, 1961; Ph.D., U. Wash., 1965; postgrad., U. Freiburg, (Germany), 1965-66. Rsch. chemist Shell Devel. Co., Emeryville, Calif., 1966-67; prof. chemistry Calif. State U., Fullerton, 1967-75; assoc. program dir. chem. dynamics NSF, Washington, 1974-75; chmn., prof. chemistry San Francisco State U., 1975-81; dean natural sci. Sonoma State U., Rohnert Park, Calif., 1981-82, provost, v.p., 1982-84; acad. v.p. Calif. State U., Bakersfield, 1984—. Contbr. articles to profl. jours. Served with USMC, 1954-57. Grantee Research Corp., 1968; grantee NSF, 1969-75, Petroleum Research Fund, 1978, 80; fellow NSF, 1965. Mem. AAAS, Am. Assn. Higher Edn., Am. Chem. Soc. Home: 2809 English Oak Dr Bakersfield CA 93311-1729 Office: Calif State U 9001 Stockdale Hwy Bakersfield CA 93311

DORFMAN, STEVEN DAVID, space and communications company executive; b. Bklyn., Sept. 26, 1935; s. Murray Dorfman and Eleanor Judith (Blitzer) Pisani; m. Georgina Breckenridge (divorced): 1 child, Jennifer; m. Beverly Joan Pain, Dec. 28, 1965; children: Lorraine, Gene, Lynn. BSEE, U. Fla., 1957; MSEE, U. So. Calif., 1959. Mgr. adv. programs Hughes Aircraft Co., El Segundo, Calif., 1967-72, mgr. Pioneer Venus, 1972-78, assoc. mgr. NASA Systems Div., 1978-82, mgr. NASA Systems Div., 1983; pres., chief exec. officer Hughes Communications Inc. subs. Hughes Aircraft Co., L.A., 1983-86; corp. v.p., pres. space and communications group, mem. policy bd. Hughes Aircraft Co., L.A., 1986-92; pres., CEO Hughes Space & Comm. Co., L.A., 1992—; chmn. comml. space transp. adv. com. (COMSTAC) Washington Dept. Transp., 1987—; mem. space systems tech. adv. com. NASA, Washington, 1982—; mem. U.S. Info. Agy. TV/Telecom Adv. Coun., Washington, 1985-90. Contbr. articles to profl. jours.; patentee in field. State Senate scholar, Fla., 1955-56; recipient Disting. Pub. Svc. medal NASA, 1980. Mem. NAE. Home: 517 Veteran Ave Los Angeles CA 90024 Office: Hughes Aircraft Co PO Box 92919 Los Angeles CA 90009-2919

DORIUS, EARL FREDRIC, legal counsel; b. Salt Lake City, Mar. 26, 1947; s. Earl Nelson and Ruth Lapriel (Damron) D.; m. Katherine Bean, Sept. 4, 1968; children: Jennifer, Dawn, Ashley, Amanda, Joshua, Adam. BS, U. Utah, 1971, JD, 1973. Bar: Utah 1973, U.S. Supreme Ct. 1976. Asst. atty. gen. Utah Atty. Gen., Salt Lake City, 1973-89; legal counsel Utah Alcoholic Beverage Control, Salt Lake City, 1989—; chief govt. affairs Utah Atty. Gen., Salt Lake City, 1983-89, chief criminal appeals, 1982-89; legal counsel U. Utah/Weber State, Salt Lake City, 1981; extradition counsel Gov. of Utah, Salt Lake City, 1973-89. Author: Utah Extradition Manual, 1990, Capital Punishment, 1980, Utah Justice of Peace, 1976. Mem. Alcoholic Beverage Control Task Force, Salt Lake City, 1988-89, Gov.'s Task Force on Corrections, Salt Lake City, 1974-76, Utah Task Force on Insanity Def., Salt Lake City, 1982-83; instr. Utah Corrections Acad., Salt Lake City, 1974-80; mem. Adv. Bd. on Criminology, U. Utah, 1975. Mem. Assn. Govt. Attys. in Capital Litigation (pres. 1980-81), Nat. Assn. Extradition Ofcls. (pres. 1988-89), Nat. Assn. Attys. Gen. Commn. on Habeas Corpus, Utah Supreme Ct. Adv. Commn. on Criminal Procedure, Utah Peace Officer Standards & Tng. Coun. LDS. Office: Utah Alcohol Beverage 1625 S 900 W Salt Lake City UT 84104

DORLAND, FRANK NORTON, art conservator; b. Peru, Nebr., Oct. 11, 1914; s. Frank Norton and Marion Hope (Abbot) D.; student Calif. Christian Coll., 1931-33; San Diego State Coll., 1933-38; m. Mabel Vyvyan Jolliffe, July 29, 1938. Artist preliminary design engring. Convair Co., San Diego, Calif., 1938-49; pvt. practice as art conservator, La Jolla, Calif., 1949-59, San Francisco, 1959-63, Mill Valley, Calif., 1963-73, Santa Barbara, Calif., 1973-85; formerly engaged in authentication and classification art objects; cons. art assns. galleries, museums, collectors, churches. Author: Holy Ice: The Story of Electronic Quartz Crystal, 1992. Mem. Internat. Inst. for Conservation, Internat. Coun. Museums, Am. Mus. Assn. Pioneer in use of spl. waxes in painting; inventor oil and water mix wax mediums; engaged in research and devel. waxes and resins and properties and usage of electronic quartz crystals, also pioneer biocrystallographer, researcher on crystals and the human mind. Home: PO Box 6233 San Luis Obispo CA 93412-6233

DORMAN, ALBERT A., consulting engineer, architect; b. Phila., Apr. 30, 1926; s. William and Edith (Kleiman) D.; m. Joan Bettie Heiten, July 29, 1950; children: Laura Jane, Kenneth Joseph, Richard Coleman. BS, Newark Coll. Engring., 1945; MS, U. So. Calif., 1962. Registered profl. engr., Calif., N.Y., Ill., Oreg., Ariz., Hawaii, Pa., Nev., La. registered architect, Calif., Oreg. Owner firm Albert A. Dorman, Hanford, Calif., 1954-66; v.p. Daniel, Mann, Johnson & Mendenhall, Los Angeles, 1967-73; pres., chief oper. officer Daniel, Mann, Johnson & Mendenhall, 1974-77, pres., chief exec. officer, 1977-84, chmn., chief exec. officer, 1984—; chmn., chief exec. officer AECOM Tech. Corp., L.A., 1988-91, chmn., 1991-92; chmn. Holmes & Narver, Inc., Orange, Calif., 1984-91; chmn. chief exec. officer Frederic R. Harris, Inc., N.Y.C., 1988-91; chmn. Consoer, Townsend and Assocs., Inc., Chgo., 1988-91; pres., chmn. bd. dirs. Hanford Savs. & Loan Assn., 1963-72; pres. Hanford Svc. Co., Inc. Contbr. articles to profl. jours. Pres. Community Concerts Assn., 1962-64; mem. bd. councilors Sch. Urban and Regional Planning, U. So. Calif.; trustee Harvey Mudd Coll., J. David Gladstone Found., 1988—, Nat. Found. Advancement in Arts, 1988—; bd. overseers N.J. Inst. Tech., 1989—; vice chmn. Los Angeles County Earthquake Fact-Finding Commnm., 1980. With AUS, 1945-47. Recipient Civil Engring. Alumnus award U. So. Calif., 1976, Edward F. Weston medal N.J. Inst. Tech., 1986, Golden Beaver Engring. award, 1991. Fellow AIA, (hon. mem.) ASCE (Harland Bartholomew award 1976, Parcel-Sverdrup Civil Engring. Mgmt. award 1987, pres. L.A. sect. 1984-85), NCCJ; mem. Real Estate Constrn. Industries (Humanitarian award 1986), Am. Pub. Works Assn., Cons. Engrs. Assn. Calif. (bd. dirs. 1982-88, pres. 1985-86), Am. Water Works Assn., Water Pollution Control Fedn., Calif. C. of C. (bd. dirs. 1986—), L.A. Area C. of C. (bd. dirs. 1983-88, exec. com. 1985-87), Calif. Club, Met. Club, Kiwanis (pres. 1962), Tau Beta Pi, Chi Epsilon. Office: Daniel Mann Johnson Mendenh 3250 Wilshire Blvd Los Angeles CA 90010

DORMAN, THOMAS PATRICK, marketing professional, consultant; b. LaPorte, Ind., June 24, 1950; s. James Thomas and Edith Helen (Harris) D.; m. Mary Elizabeth Lapp, Aug. 20, 1976; 1 child, Matthew James. Student, Ind. U., 1968-71. Freelance musician Los Angeles, 1971-76; mgr. sales adminstrn. Franciscan Dinnerware, Los Angeles, 1976-79; mgr. nat. field mktg. Internat. Gold Corp., N.Y.C., 1979-83; exec. dir. Gold Filled Assn., N.Y.C., 1983-85; dir. investor products Engelhard Corp, Iselin, N.J., 1985-87; dir. mktg. Krementz and Co., Newark, 1987—; exec. dir. Am. Gem Soc. Mem. 24 Karat Club So. Calif., Boston Jewelers Club, Providence Jewelers Club. Republican. Congregationalist. Office: American Gem Society 5901 W 3d St Los Angeles CA 90036

DORMER, JAMES THOMAS, art educator; b. Morristown, N.J., Nov. 11, 1934; s. Edward Vincent and Elizabeth (Bensley) D.; m. Carol Jean Lombardi, Nov. 18, 1960; children: Elizabeth, James, Jennifer. BA, William Paterson Coll., 1961; MA, Pa. State U., 1964, U. Iowa, 1969. Designer Seneca Textiles, N.Y., 1952-54, Kniep Assocs., Dover, N.J., 1958-60; pub. rels. Binney and Smith, N.Y., 1963-67; prof. Colo. State U., Ft. Collins, Colo., 1969—; chmn. Art Dept. Colo. State U., 1985—. Exhibited in group shows at Newark Art Mus., 1964, Trenton Art Mus., 1966, Montclair Art Mus., 1964, Dallas Mus. of Art, 1969, Seattle Art Mus., 1971, Denver Art Mus., 1970, Smithsonian Instn., Washington, 1965, numerous other juried and invitational nat. and internat. exhibitions. Sgt. U.S. Army NG, 1953-60. Office: Colo State U Art Dept Fort Collins CO 80523

DORN, EDWARD MERTON, poet, educator; b. Villa Grove, Ill., Apr. 2, 1929. Student, U. Ill., Black Mountain Coll. Vis. prof. Am. lit., Fulbright lectr. U. Essex, 1965-68; vis. poet U. Kans., 1968-69; mem. faculty Idaho State U., Northeastern Ill. U., U. Colo., 1977—; sr. editor Rolling Stock mag., Boulder, Colo., 1981—. Author: What I See in the Maximus Poems, 1960, The Newly Fallen: Poems, 1961, Hands Up!, 1964, From Gloucester Out, 1964, (with M. Rumaker and W. Tallman) Prose I, 1964, The Rites of Passage: A Brief History, 1965, rev. edit. as By the Sound, 1971, Idaho Out, 1965, Geography, 1965, The Shoshoneans: The People of the Basin-Plateau, 1966, North Atlantic Turbine, 1967, Gunslinger Book I, 1968, Gunslinger Book II, 1969, Twenty Four Love Songs, 1969, The Midwest is That Space Between the Buffalo Statler and the Lawrence Eldridge, 1969, The Cosmology of Finding Your Spot, 1969, Songs: Set Two, A Short Count, 1970, Spectrum Breakdown: A Microbook, 1971, A Poem Called Alexander Hamilton, 1971, The Cycle, 1971, Some Business Recently Transacted in the White World, 1971, The Hamadryas Baboon at the Lincoln Park Zoo, 1972, Gunslinger Book II: The Winterbook Prologue to the Great Book IV Kornerstone, 1972, Recollections of Gran Apacheria, 1973, Gunslinger, Books I, II, III, IV, 1975, Collected Poems of Edward Dorn, 1975, 1984, Hello, La Jolla, 1978, Views, Interviews, 1978, Selected Poems, 1978, Yellow Lola, 1981, Captain Jack's Chaps, 1983, Abhorrences, 1990; By the Sound, 1991, Way West, 1992; translator Images of the New World, 1979, (with G. Brotherston) Tree Between the Two Walls, 1969, Our World: Guerilla Poems from Latin America, 1968, Selected Poems by Vallejo, 1976, (with Jennifer Dunbar) Manchester Square, 1975. Nat. Endowment for Arts grantee, 1966, 68; D.H. Lawrence fellow, 1969. Office: U Colo Campus Box 226 Boulder CO 80309

DORN, MARIAN MARGARET, educator, sports management administrator; b. North Chicago, Ill., Sept. 25, 1931; d. John and Marian (Petkovsek) Jelovsek; m. Eugene G. Dorn, Aug. 2, 1952 (div. 1975); 1 child, Bradford Jay. B.S., U. Ill., 1953; M.S., U. So. Calif., 1961. Tchr., North Chicago Community High Sch., 1954-56; tchr., advisor activities, high sch., Pico-Rivera, Calif., 1956-62; tchr., coach Calif. High Sch., Whittier, 1962-65; prof. phys. edn., chmn. dept., coach, asst. chmn. div. women's athletic dir. Cypress (Calif.) Coll., 1966—; men's golf coach; mgr. Billie Jean King Tennis Ctr., Long Beach, Calif., 1982-86; founder King-Dorn Golf Schs., Long Beach, 1984; pres. So. Calif. Athletic Conf., 1981; curriculum cons. Calif. Dept. Edn., 1989-92. Recipient cert. of merit Cypress Elem. Sch. Dist., 1976; Outstanding Service award Cypress Coll., 1986. Mem. Calif. (v.p. So. dist.), San Gabriel Valley (pres.) assns. health, phys. edn. and recreation, So. Calif. Community Coll. Athletic Council (sec., dir. pub. relations), NEA, Calif. Tchrs. Assn., AAHPERD, Ladies Profl. Golf Assn. Republican. Conglist. Author: Bowling Manual, 1974. Office: 9200 Valley View Cypress CA 90630

DORNAN, ROBERT KENNETH, congressman; b. N.Y.C., Apr. 3, 1933; s. Harry Joseph and Gertrude Consuelo (McFadden) D.; m. Sallie Hansen, Apr. 16, 1955; children: Robin Marie, Robert Kenneth II, Theresa Ann, Mark Douglas, Kathleen Regina. Student, Loyola U., Westchester, Calif., 1950-53. Nat. spokesman Citizens for Decency Through Law, 1973-76; mem. 95th-97th Congresses from 27th Calif. dist., 1977-83, 99th-103rd Congresses from 38th (now 46th) Calif. dist., 1985—; chmn. Ho. Rep. Study Commn. 99th-102d Congresses from 38th Calif. dist., 1989-91, 103d Congress from 46th Calif. dist. Host TV polit. talk shows in Los Angeles, 1965-73; host, producer: Robert K. Dornan Show, Los Angeles, 1970-73; combat photographer/broadcast journalist assigned 8 times to Laos-Cambodia-Vietnam, 1965-74; originator POW/MIA bracelet. Served to capt. as fighter pilot USAF, 1953-58, as fighter pilot and amphibian rescue pilot USAFR, 1958-75. Mem. Am. Legion, Navy League, Air Force Assn., Res. Officers Assn., AMVETS, Assn. Former Intelligence Officers, AFTRA. Republican. Roman Catholic. Lodge: K.C. Office: Rm 2402 Rayburn House Office Bldg Washington DC 20515*

DORNBUSCH, SANFORD MAURICE, sociology and biology educator; b. N.Y.C., June 5, 1926; s. Meyer and Gertrude (Weisel) D.; m. Barbara Anne Farnham, Feb. 28, 1950; children: Jeffrey Neil, Steven Samuel. A.B., Syracuse U., 1948; M.A., U. Chgo., 1950, Ph.D., 1952. Instr. sociology Syracuse U., 1948-49, U. Ill., 1950-51, Ind. U., 1950- 52; research assoc. U. Chgo., 1951-52; asst. prof. U. Wash., 1952-54, assoc. prof., 1958-59; asst. prof. Harvard, 1955-58; head dept. sociology Stanford U., 1959-64, prof., 1959—, Reed-Hodgson prof. human biology, 1978—, prof. edn., 1977—, assoc. dean Sch. Humanities and Scis., 1961-62, dir. freshman seminars, 1967-69, chmn. senate acad. council, 1970-71, research assoc. Center for Research and Devel. in Teaching, 1968-78, dep. dir. Stanford Ctr. for the Study of Families, Children and Youth, 1980-87, dir., 1987—, chmn. adv. bd., 1991—; Ford vis. prof. sociology U. Ibadan, Nigeria, 1966-67; cons. Social Sci. Research Council; mem. behavioral scis. fellowship panel NIH, 1961-67; editorial cons. Sociometry, 1957-60, Rev. Religious Research, 1980-84, Devel. and Behavioral Pediatrics, 1982—; advisor to Office Ednl. Research and Improvement U.S. Dept. Edn., 1987—; mem. panel on high risk youth Commn. on Behavioral and Social Scis. and Edn., NRC, 1989—; mem. nat. adv. panel Ctr. on Families, Communities, Schs. and Children's Learning, 1990—. Author: A Primer of Social Statistics, 1955, Popular Religion, 1958, Evaluation and the Exercise of Authority, 1975, Toward Reform of Program Evaluation, 1980, Teacher Evaluative Standards and Student Effort, 1984; editor: Feminism, Children, and the New Families, 1988; cons. editor sociology, McGraw-Hill Book Co., 1958-62. Chmn. regional selection com. Woodrow Wilson Nat. Fellowship Found., 1963-66; founder Stanford-Midpeninsula Urban Coalition, 1968; mem. bd. maternal, child and family health NRC; mem. Pres.'s Commn. on Mental Health, Task Panel on Community Support Systems, 1977-78; mem. evaluation task force Nat. Inst. Child Health and Human Devel., 1977-79, mem. mental retardation research com., 1977-81; mem. nat. adv. panel Ctr. on Families, Communities, Schs., and Children's Learning, 1990—; bd. dirs. Urban Arts Found. Served as pvt. AUS, 1943-44; with USCG, 1944-45; with USNR, 1945-46. Grantee NSF, NIH, Ford Found., Russell Sage Found., Boys Town, Hewlett Found., Irvine Found., Bank Am. Found., Spencer Found., Carnegie Found., Grant Found., Drown Found.; fellow Center Advanced Study Behavioral Scis., 1954-55; faculty research fellow Social Sci. Research Council, 1958-59; hon. univ. fellow U. Chgo., 1949-50; recipient Walter J. Gore award for Excellence in Teaching Stanford U., 1984. Fellow Am. Sociol. Assn. (chmn. methodology sect., social psychology sect., sociology of edn. sect.), African Studies Assn.; mem. AAUP (chpt. pres. 1968-69), Pacific Sociol. Assn. (pres. 1963-64), Am. Statis. Assn., Internat. Orgn. for Study Human Devel. (coun. 1970-84), Soc. for Rsch. in Child Devel., Soc. for Rsch. on Adolescence (pres. 1992—), Ednl. Press Assn. Am. (Disting. Achievement award 1989). Home: 841 Pinehill Rd Palo Alto CA 94305-1094

DORNBUSH, VICKY JEAN, medical billing systems executive; b. Willowick, Ohio, Aug. 12, 1951; d. Charles W. and Josephine H. (Palumbo) Rader; m. Eric D. Erickson, Oct. 22, 1972 (div. June 1974); m. Thomas Dornbush, Dec. 29, 1979 (div. 1987); 1 child, Dana. Student, Kent State U., 1969-72, San Jose State U., 1982-84. Accounts receivable clk. MV Nursery, Richmond, Calif., 1975-76; accounts receivable and computer supr. Ga. Pacific, Richmond, 1976-78; acct. Ga. Pacific, Tracy, Calif., 1978-79, Crown-Zellerbach, Anaheim, Calif., 1979-80; acct. Interstate Pharmacy Corp., San Jose, Calif., 1981-83, contr., 1983-85; gen. ptnr. Med. Billing Systems, San Jose, 1984-89; seminar trainer Systems Plus, Mountain View, Calif., 1987-89, MD Solutions, 1989—. Mem. San Jose Civic Light Opera, 1987—, San Jose Repertory Co., 1986-90; pres., bd. dirs. San Jose Stage Co., 1990—. Mem. AGPAM, Exec. Sales Women, Nat. Soc. Pub. Accts., Women in Bus. Republican. Methodist. Office: MD Solutions 4960 Almaden Expway Ste 266 San Jose CA 95118

DORNEMAN, ROBERT WAYNE, manufacturing engineer; b. Oaklawn, Ill., Nov. 13, 1949; s. Robert John and Julia (Vorchenia) D.; M. Katrina Holland, July 30, 1977; children: Tamara, Tiana. BA in Biol. Sci., Calif. State U., Fullerton, 1974. Mfg. engr. Gen. Telephone Co., Anaheim, Calif., 1974-77, Xerox/Century Data, Anaheim, 1977-80; advance mfg. engr. MSI Data, Costa Mesa, Calif., 1980-83; sr. mfg. engr. Parker Hannifin, Irvine, Calif., 1983-86; sr. advanced mfr. engr. Western Digital, Irvine, 1986-89, mgr. advanced mfg. engring., 1989-91; mfg. engr. Pairgain Tech., Cerritos, Calif., 1991-93, mgr. mfg. engring., 1993—; specialist automated assembly of circuits; cons. Base 2, Fullerton, 1980; developer surface mount tech. for computer mfg. industry; set up computer assemble plants internat. Devel. and implimented environ. safe mfg. process for computer bd. industry; contbr. articles in 3M-Alert to profl. jours. Mem. Nat. Assn. Realtors (broker), N. Orange County Bd. Realtors (broker), Calif. Assn. Realtors, Internat. Platform Assn., Internat. Soc. Hybrid Mfg., Phillips Ranch Assn., Tau Kappa Epsilon. Republican. Home: 56 Meadow View Dr Phillips

Ranch Pomona CA 91766 Office: Pairgain Tech 12921 E 166th St Cerritos CA 90701-2104

DORNETTE, RALPH MEREDITH, church organization executive, educator, minister; b. Cin., Aug. 31, 1927; s. Paul A. and Lillian (Bauer) D.; m. Betty Jean Pierce, May 11, 1948; 1 child, Cynthia Anne Dornette Orndorff. AB, Cin. Bible Coll., 1948. Ordained to ministry Christian Ch., 1947. Min. Indian Creek Christian Ch., Cynthiana, Ky., 1946-51; assoc. prof. Cin. Bible Coll., 1948-51; sr. min. First Christian Ch., Muskogee, Okla., 1951-57; founding min. Bellaire Christian Ch., Tulsa, 1957-59; exec. dir. So. Calif. Evangelistic Assn., Torrance, Calif., 1959-62, 68-77; sr. min. Eastside Christian Ch., Fullerton, Calif., 1962-68; dir. devel., prof. ministries Cin. Bible Coll. & Sem., 1977-79; exec. dir. Ch. Devel. Fund, Inc., Fullerton, 1986-77, CEO, 1979—; sr. preaching minister 1st Christian Ch., Downey, Calif., 1971, 91; pres. So. Calif. Christian Mins. Assn., Fullerton, 1975. Author: Bible Answers to Popular Questions, 1954, Walking With Our Wonderful Lord, 1955, Bible Answers to Popular Questions II, 1964. Pres. Homeowners Assn., Anaheim, Calif., 1980-81. Named Churchman of Yr. Pacific Christian Coll., Fullerton, 1973. Mem. N.Am. Christian Conv. (conv. com. Cin. chpt. 1963, chair nat. registration 1963, v.p. 1972, exec. com. 1963, 70-72, 80-82). Office: Ch Devel Fund Inc 905 S Euclid St Fullerton CA 92632-2808

DORNHELM, MARILYN CELIA, computer consultant, owner; b. Bklyn., Dec. 20, 1945; d. Jacob and Ella Landau; m. Richard Baruch Dornhelm, Dec. 31, 1969; children: Rachel, Ethan. BS in Math., SUNY, Binghamtom, N.Y., 1966. Trainee, programmer AT&T, N.Y.C., 1966-67; programmer, systems analyst Fireman's Fund, San Francisco, 1967-69, ZIM, Haifa, Israel, 1970-72, UCLA, 1973-75; computer cons. self-employed Eureka, Calif., 1984-85; owner Dornhelm Consulting, Walnut Creek, Calif., 1986—. Bd. dirs. Temple Beth El, Eureka, 1980-84, Hebrew sch. prin., 1978-84; exec. bd. mem. B'nai Shalom Sisterhood, Walnut Creek, 1987—; steering com. mem. San Francisco Youth Orch., 1980-92; bd. dirs. Friends of the Oakland (Calif.) Youth Orch., 1988-89. Mem. East Bay Database Users Group. Office: Dornhelm Consultants 975 Tumwater Ct Walnut Creek CA 94598

DORR, ROBERT THOMAS, pharmacologist; b. Jacksonville, N.C., Mar. 1, 1951; s. William Raymond and Lorena Bee (Daly) D.; m. Cynthia Marie Gray, June 5, 1971; children: Kerry Michelle, Robert William. AA, Bakersfield (Calif.) Jr. Coll., 1971; BS in Pharmacy, U. Ariz., 1975, MS in Hosp. Pharmacy, 1978, PhD in Pharmacology/Toxicology, 1984. Registered pharmacist, Ariz., Calif. Staff hosp. pharmacist Univ. Hosp., Tucson, 1974-78; asst. prof. pharm. practice Coll. of Pharmacy, U. Ariz., Tucson, 1977-79; grad. rsch. asst. Coll. Medicine, U. Ariz., 1980-84, rsch. asst. prof., 1984-89, assoc. prof. medicine and pharmacology, 1989—; Contbr. articles to profl. jours.; inventor in field. Mem. Am. Assn. Cancer Rsch., Am. Soc. Clin. Oncology. Republican. Office: Univ of Ariz Cancer Ctr 1515 N Campbell Ave Tucson AZ 85724-0001

DORSETT, CHARLES BARCLAY, SR., architect; b. San Francisco, Oct. 14, 1927; s. Ralph John and Helen Elizabeth (Waters) D.; m. Dorothy Marion Brandlein, July 1, 1951; children: Charles Barclay, Jr., Robert John, Catherine Jeanne, John Andrew. MA in Architecture, U. Calif., Berkeley, 1955. Registered architect, Calif. Architect Anshen & Allen, San Francisco, 1955-64, Botsai Overstreet Assoc., San Francisco, 1964-68, self-employed, San Francisco, 1968-70, Elbasani Logan Severin, Berkeley, Calif., 1970-75, Wudtke Watson Davis, San Francisco, 1975-79, Anshen & Allen, San Francisco, 1979-85, Richardson Voinovich Inc., Pleasant Hill, Calif., 1985-88, self-employed, Walnut Creek, Calif., 1988—; free-lance film and stage actor, San Francisco, 1968—; cons. to pres. U. Calif. Berkeley, 1978—. Contbr. articles to profl. jours. With USN, 1945-46. Recipient Pres. award Constrn. Specification Inst., 1987, Cert. Merit Appreciation west region 1990; Wakefield Champion Nat. Free Flight Soc, 1990. Mem. Acad. Model Aeronautics, Nat. Aeronautics Assn., Screen Actors Guild (pres. San Francisco branch 1984, nat. bd. 1984-89, 6th nat. v.p. 1989—), AFTRA, Actors Equity Assn., San Francisco Labor Coun., Theta Xi (trustee 1965—). Democrat. Home and Office: 2645 San Benito Dr Walnut Creek CA 94598

DORSEY, JULIE ANN, accountant; b. Oconto, Wis., Jan. 16, 1961; d. Arthur Louis and Carol Winona (Funk) L. AA, U. Wis., Marinette, 1982; BS in Acctg., U. Wis., Green Bay, 1985. Cert. tax practioner, Wash. Acct. Haines & Co., Bellevue, Wash., 1986-87; fin. analyst Korry Electronics, Seattle, 1987-88; acctg. supr. Seamar Community Health Ctr., Seattle, 1988-89; pres. Lynnwood (Wash.) Acctg. Ctr., Inc., 1989-92; self employed, 1992—. Named Outstanding First Yr. Jaycee, Kirkland, Wash., 1987. Mem. Wash. State Tax. Profl. (sec. 1991), Snohomish County Women Bus. Owners Assn. (treas. 1991).

DORST, HOWARD EARL, entomologist; b. Pomeroy, Ohio, Sept. 19, 1904; s. Otto Henry and Clara Barbara (Kautz) D.; m. Martha Hauserman, Aug. 1, 1931; 1 child, Ronald Valison. AB, U. Kans., 1929, MA, 1930; DHL (hon.), Westminster Coll., 1984. Jr. entomologist USDA, Richfield, Utah, 1929; asst. entomologist USDA, Salt Lake City, 1930-36; commd. 2d lt. USAR, 1932; assoc. entomologist USDA, Logan, Utah, 1936-41;, 1932; advanced through grades to col. USAR, 1954; commd. capt. SN Corps, 1941; retired USAR, 1964; ret. lt. col. MSC, 1946; sr. entomologist USDA, Logan, Utah, 1946-65, ret., 1965; emeritus prof. zoology Utah State U., Logan, 1966. Contbr. articles to Jour. Econ. Entomology, Proceedings Am. Soc. Sugar Beet Tech. Chmn. Am. Cancer Soc. Cache County, Logan, 1967-71, ARC Cache County, Logan, 1985-86; moderator Presbytery Utah, Logan, 1980. Served to col. Med. Svc. Corps. USAR, 1964. Recipient Presdl. Citation award Utah State U., 1988; named to Old Main Soc., Utah State U., 1990. Republican. Presbyterian. Home: 1679 E 1030 N Logan UT 87321

DOSS, JAMES DANIEL, electrical engineer, writer; b. Reading, Pa., Mar. 9, 1939. BS in Maths., Ky. Wesleyan Coll., 1964; MSEE, U. N.Mex., Albuquerque, 1969. Mem. staff Los Alamos (N.Mex.) Nat. Lab., 1964—; adj. instr. in radiology and surgery U. N.Mex. Sch. of Medicine. Author: Engineer's Guide to High Temperature Superconductivity, 1989, (novel) The Shaman Sings, 1993; contbr. numerous articles to profl. jours. Mem. IEEE. Episcopalian. Office: Los Alamos Nat Lab IT-3 B230 Los Alamos NM 87545

DOSSETT, LAWRENCE SHERMAN, professional services company official; b. Santa Ana, Calif., May 11, 1936; s. Wheeler Sherman and Eunice Elizabeth (Bright) D.; student U. Ariz., 1957-58, U. Calif., Irvine, 1973-75, Loyola Marymount Coll., 1974; m. Joanne Kallisch; children: Todd Sherman, Garrick Robert (dec.), Dana Shelene, Ryan William. Engring. draftsman Hughes Aircraft Co., Tucson, 1955-57, John J. Foster Mfg. Co., Costa Mesa, Calif., 1958, Standard Elec. Products, Costa Mesa, 1959; engring. mgr. Electronic Engring. Co., Santa Ana, 1959-79; product quality mgr. Farwest Data Systems, Irvine, Calif., 1979-82; dist. mgr. profl. svcs., nat. cons. mgr., sr. industry cons. Comserv/MSA/DBSoftware, 1982-92, sr. manufacturing industry cons., 1992-93; mfg. cons. Marcam Corp., 1993—. Mem. Western Electronic Mfrs. Assn., Am. Prodn. and Inventory Control Soc., 1976-82, Computer Mfrs. Conf., 1980. Cert. in mgmt. Am. Mgmt. Assn., 1968. Mem. Am. Prodn. and Inventory Control Soc. Author: MRPXXI Asset/Liability Management System, 1993; co-author patent reel spindle, 1972.

DOSTART, PAUL JOSEPH, lawyer, professional investor and director; b. Riceville, Iowa, Nov. 12, 1951; s. Leonard Atchison and Lois Marie Dostart; m. Joyce Alene Sicking, Aug. 14, 1976; children: Zachariah Paul, Samuel Paul. BS, Iowa State U., 1973; JD, U. Houston, 1977; LLM in Taxation, NYU, 1978. Bar: Tex, 1977, Calif. 1978; CPA, Ill. From assoc. to ptnr., chmn. tax and employee benefits dept. Gray, Cary, Ames & Frye, San Diego, 1978-92; founder, ptnr. Monroe & Dostart, San Diego, 1992—; adj. prof. U. San Diego, 1986-90; assoc. Econ. Policy Seminar Series U. Calif., San Diego, 1984-86, lect.r, 1985; mem. U. Calif. Inst. Global Conflict and Coop.; bd. dirs. various companies, 1990—. Editor Houston Law Rev.; contbr. articles to profl. jours. Founder U. Houston Tax Law Soc.; dir. Christian Exec. Officers, 1988-91, pres., 1989-90; mem. Pres. Club, Nat. Assn. Evang., 1986—. Lasker scholar, NYU, Nat. Merit scholar, Iowa State Merit scholar; recipient Cert. of Merit U. Houston Student Bar Assn. Fellow Am. Bar Found.; mem. ABA (chmn. various subcoms. sect. taxation 1982—, exempt orgns. com. 1977—), Calif. Bar Assn. (tax and bus. sects.), San Diego County Bar Assn. (chmn. tax sect. 1989), San Diego Soc. Pension Attys., San Diego Tax Practitioners Group, Am. Electronics Assn (San Diego coun. exec. com. 1993—), World Trade Assn. (bd. dirs.), Western Pension Conf., Order of Barons (chancellor), Phi Delta Phi (magister Hutcheson Inn). Presbyterian. Office: Monroe & Dostart 9191 Towne Centre Dr Ste 270 San Diego CA 92122-1228

DOTO, IRENE LOUISE, statistician; b. Wilmington, Del., May 7, 1922; d. Antonio and Teresa (Tabasso) D. BA, U. Pa., 1943; MA, Temple U., 1948, Columbia U., 1954. Engring. asst. RCA-Victor, 1943-44; research asst. U. Pa., 1944; actuarial clk. Penn Mut. Life Ins. Co., 1944-46; instr. math. Temple U., 1946-53; commd. sr. asst. health services officer USPHS, 1954, advanced through grades to dir., 1963; statistician Communicable Disease Ctr., Atlanta, 1954-55, Kansas City, Kans., 1955-67; chief statis. and publ. services, ecol. investigations program Ctr. for Disease Control, Kansas City, 1967-73, chief statis. services, div. hepatitis and viral enteritis, Phoenix, 1973-83; statis. cons., 1984—; mem. adj. faculty Phoenix Ctr., Ottawa U., 1982—. Mem. Am. Statis. Assn., Biometrics Soc., Am. Pub. Health Assn., Ariz. Pub. Health Assn., Ariz. Council Engring. and Sci. Assn. (officer 1982—, pres. 1988-89), Primate Found. Ariz. (mem. animal care and use com. 1986—), Bus. and Profl. Women's Club Phoenix, Sigma Xi, Pi Mu Epsilon. Office: PO Box 22197 Phoenix AZ 85028-0197

DOTSON, GERALD RICHARD, biology educator; b. Brownsville, Tex., Sept. 8, 1937; s. Jasper William and Mary Agnes (Courtney) D.; m. Rose Dolores Gonzales; children: Roberta Ana, Deborah Irene, Matthew Charles. BS, Coll. Santa Fe (N.Mex.), 1960; MS, U. Miss., 1966; PhD, U. Colo., 1974; postgrad., Loyola U., New Orleans, U. Tex., Loyola U. New Orleans, El Paso, 1960-61. Sci. tchr. Cathedral High Sch., El Paso, Tex., 1959-61; sci./math./music tchr. St. Paul's High Sch., Covington, La., 1961-62; sci./math./Spanish tchr. Christian Bros. Sch., New Orleans, 1962-63; sci. tchr., chmn. Hanson High Sch., Franklin, La., 1963-67; biology instr. Coll. Santa Fe (N.Mex.), 1967-69, U. Colo., Boulder, 1969-70, Community Coll. Denver, 1970-77; prof. biology and chmn. sci. Front Range Community Coll., Westminster, Colo., 1977—; cons. in field; mem. com. for teaching excellence FRCC in Westminster, 1988—. Reviewer biology text books, 1970—; contbr. articles to profl. jours. Mem. recreation dept. City of Westminster, 1971—. Named Master Tchr. of the Yr., Front Range Community Coll., 1985-86. Mem. Am. Microscopical Soc., Am. Soc. Limnology and Oceanography, Nat. Assn. Biology Tchrs., Nat. Sci. Tchrs. Assn. (reg. sec. 1965), Eagles, K.C. (3rd and 4th deg.), Elks, Sigma Xi, Phi Sigma. Roman Catholic. Home: 8469 Otis Dr Arvada CO 80003-1241 Office: Front Range Community Coll 3645 W 112th Ave Westminster CO 80030-2199

DOTY, DALE DOUGLAS, state official; b. Fairbanks, Alaska, Apr. 13, 1962; s. Dale Patrick and Emma Marie (Porter) D. AA, Dawson Coll., Glendive, Mont., 1982; BS, Ea. Mont. Coll., 1985, MS, 1988. Cert. EMT. Behavior specialist Billings (Mont.) Tng. Industries, 1986-88; tng. and contract mgr. Mont. Devel. Disabilities Div., Miles City, 1988-90, Missoula, 1990-91, Billings, 1991—; chmn. Statewide Tng. Curriculum Com., Helena, Mont., 1991-92, mem., 1992—; conf. presenter Alheimer's Disease and the Aging Downs Syndrome Adult, 1987.. Mem. Mont. Coyote Growers Assn. (pres. 1983—), Montanans for Choice. Office: Devel Disabilities Div 1211 Grand Ave Billings MT 59102

DOTY, HORACE JAY, JR., theater administrator, arts consultant; b. St. Petersburg, Fla., May 25, 1924; s. Horace Herndon and Mabel (Bruce) D.; student Sherwood Music Sch., Chgo., 1942-43; BA in Music, Pomona Coll., 1950; cert. La Verne Coll., 1969; MA in Edn., Claremont Grad. Sch., 1972; cert. in Bus. Adminstrn., 1984; m. Wanda L. Flory, Dec. 27, 1947; 1 child, Janet. Propr. Jay Doty's Inc., Claremont, 1960-68; concert mgr. Claremont Colls., 1968-73, supr. Garrison Theater, U. Ctr. Box Office, dir. Auditorium, theater events, coordinator programs, 1973-79, 81-90; exec. dir. Flint Ctr. for Performing Arts, Cupertino, Calif., 1979-81. Mem. blue ribbon com. Fox Theater Restoration, Pomona, Calif., 1982; mem. Claremont Bicentennial Com. for Performing Arts, 1975-76; mem. touring adv. panel, cons. and site visitor Calif. Arts Council; mem. exec. bd., Calif. Presenters. Served with inf. AUS, 1943-46. NEA fellow, 1986. Mem. Assn. Coll., Univ. and Community Arts Adminstrs. (dir. 1983-86), Western Alliance Arts Adminstrs. (pres. 1975-77), Internat. Assn. Auditorium Mgrs., Claremont C. of C. (pres. 1965-66). Office: Jay Doty Arts Cons 4145 Oak Hollow Rd Claremont CA 91711-2329

DOTY, J.E., real estate executive; b. Oakland, Calif., Nov. 12, 1941; s. Abraham Richard and Frances Edith (Bishop) D.; m. Nancy McCann, May 27, 1984; children: Elizabeth Ann, John Joseph, Alexandra M. Student, U. Calif., 1963. Assoc. property mgr. Milton Meyer and Co., San Francisco, 1968-69; dir. property mgmt. Hanford, Freund and Co., San Francisco, 1969-71; exec. v.p. Best, Schuman and Doty Co., San Francisco, 1971-75; pres. J.E. Doty and Assocs., San Francisco, 1976-81, Metro Pacific Corp., San Francisco, 1981—; developer numerous residential real estate projects. Pres. Lower Nob Hill Property Owners Assn.; active Rep. Com., San Francisco, 1989, Mayor's Fiscal Task Force, San Francisco, 1984; mem. receiving code envorcement program City of San Francisco. Presbyterian. Office: Metro Pacific Corp 952 Sutter St San Francisco CA 94109-8412

DOUDNA, MARTIN KIRK, English language educator; b. Louisville, June 4, 1930; s. Arthur Bundy and Ruth Edson (Dewey) D.; m. Dorothy Jane Williams, Sept. 15, 1962; children: Jennifer Anne, Ellen Ruth, Sarah Corinne. AB in English, Oberlin (Ohio) Coll., 1952; postgrad., Princeton (N.J.) U., 1952-53; MA in English, U. Louisville, 1959; PhD in Am. Culture, U. Mich., 1971. Writer USAF, Washington, 1959-66; asst. prof. English Mackinac Island (Mich.) Coll., 1966-69; assoc. prof. English U. Hawaii, Hilo, 1971-78, prof. English, 1978—; sec. Hawaii Com. for the Humanities, Honolulu, 1986-88. Author: Concerned About the Planet, 1977; editor: Greene, Transcendentalism (1849), 1981; author: (play) Have You Any Room for Us?, 1975; contbr. articles to profl. jours. With U.S. Army, 1953-55. Rackham fellow U. Mich., 1970; Nat. Endowment for the Humanities, 1976, 83, 88. Mem. Modern Lang. Assn., Thoreau Soc., Phi Beta Kappa. Home: 181 S Wilder Rd Hilo HI 96720-1443 Office: U Hawaii Hilo HI 96720-4091

DOUGAL, JEROLD LYNN, architect; b. Boise, Idaho, May 5, 1953; s. Jerold R. and Maxine (Jones) D.; m. Deborah Lynn Boman, Jan. 23, 1975; children: Brian, Brent, Rebecca. AS, Boise State U., 1975; BS, Brigham Young U., 1981. Registered architect, Idaho, Oreg., Calif., Utah. Art dir. Hewlett-Packard, Boise, Idaho, 1975-77; draftsman Albertsons Archtl., Boise, Idaho, 1978-85, architect, 1985-88; architect, sr. project mgr. The Nadel Partnership, Costa Mesa, Calif., 1988-91, architect, assoc. ptnr., 1991-92, architect, prodn. mgr., 1992—; instr. U. Calif., Irvine, 1991; guest lectr. U. So. Calif., L.A., 1991. Author: Master Specification for Small Scale Commercial Buildings, 1992. Scout master Boy Scouts of Am., Boise, 1986, chmn. scout com., Yorba Linda, Calif., 1990. Mem. AIA, Constrn. Specifiers Inst., BYU Constrn. Mgmt. Soc. of Orange County (organizing head 1991). Republican. LDS. Office: The Nadel Partnership Inc 1760 Creekside Oaks Dr Sacramento CA 95833

DOUGHERTY, BARBARA LEE, artist, writer; b. L.A., Apr. 25, 1949; d. Cliff and Muriel Tamarra (Rubin) Beck; m. Michael R. Dougherty, Feb. 10, 1970; children: Jessie, Luke, Elvi. BFA, N.Y. State Coll., 1975. Staff writer South Coast Community Newspapers, Santa Barbara, Calif., 1988-90; mktg. editor Art Calendar, Great Falls, Va., 1991—; instr. art programs, 1975—; mem. City Adv. Bd.-Art, Santa Barbara, 1979-89, chmn., 1991—; prodr. KCTV, Santa Barbara, 1990—. Author, artist: In Search of a Sunflower, 1992, Harvest California, 1990; prodr. 4 videos on art, 1990—; contbr. articles in Mktg. Art, 1991-92. Fundraiser Boys and Girls Club of Am., Carpinteria, Calif., 1977—. Recipient Best of Show award Hosp. Aux., Boulder, Nev., 1991, 1st place award Death Valley 49ers Club, 1989, 2d place award, 1990. Democrat. Roman Catholic. Home and Office: Harvest Am PO Box 152 Carpinteria CA 93014

DOUGHERTY, CELIA BERNIECE, educator; b. Toronto, Ohio, Aug. 7, 1935; d. Ernest Merle and Dorthy Grace (Erwin) Putnam; student Ohio U., 1953-54; BA, Calif. State U., Fullerton, 1971, MS, 1974; postgrad. U. So. Calif., 1980-83; m. William Vincent Dougherty, May 14, 1955; children: Marie Collette, Michael Charles. Reading specialist Anaheim (Calif.) Union High Sch. Dist., 1972-78, asst. prin. jr. high, 1978-80; asst. prin. jr. high Orange (Calif.) Unified Sch. Dist., 1980-88, elem. prin., 1988—; trustee Anaheim City Sch. Dist., 1985—. Leader, Girl Scouts, 1968-71; mem. alumni council Calif. State U., Fullerton. Scholar Ohio U., 1953-54. Mem. Orange County Reading Assn. (bd. dir. 1978-85, pres. 1982-83), Calif. Reading Assn., Internat. Reading Assn., Assn. Calif. Sch. Adminstrs., Calif. Sch. Bd. Assn., Assn. Supervision and Curriculum Devel., Educare. Phi Kappa Phi, AAUW, Phi Alpha Theta. Democrat. Home: 860 S Cardiff St Anaheim CA 92806-4804 Office: 1829 N Cambridge St Orange CA 92665-1032

DOUGHERTY, JOHN JAMES, computer software company executive, consultant; b. Phila., Aug. 15, 1924; s. John James Sr. and Hilda Margaret (Belmont) D.; m. Marjorie Theresa Coyle, June 28, 1947; children: John J., Moira A., Marjorie T., Brian P., Hilda M., Eileen M., Ann J. BSEE, Villanova (Pa.) U., 1950. Registered profl. engr., Pa. Jr. engr. Phila. Electric Co., 1951-53, engr., 1953-56, sr. engr., 1956-62, engr. in charge, 1972-75; div. dir. Electric Power Rsch. Inst., Palo Alto, Calif., 1975-79, v.p., 1979-86; cons. Electric Power Rsch. Inst. 1986—, Forensic Techs. Inc., San Francisco, 1986—; bd. dirs. Geoworks, Berkeley, Calif. Lt. USN, 1943-46. Fellow IEEE (Herman Halpern award 1988). Roman Catholic. Home: 4766 Calle De Lucia San Jose CA 95124-4848

DOUGHERTY, MICHAEL JOSEPH, oil company executive; b. Olympia, Wash., May 17, 1949; s. Joseph John and Thelma Christine (Holthusen) D.; m. Paula Marie Fournier, June 26, 1971; children: Ronald C., Brian A., Jennifer A. BS in Chemistry, Oreg. State U., 1971; MS in Environ. Sci., Calif. State U., Fullerton, 1977; postgrad., Harvard U., 1989. Rsch. chemist Union Oil, Brea, Calif., 1971-77; coord. environ. control Union Oil, L.A., 1977-80, mgr. environ. control, 1980-86; mgr. state govt. rels. Unocal, L.A., 1986—. Chmn. petroleum com. Air Pollution Control Assn., Pitts., 1978-81; chmn. air pollution rsch. adv. com. Coord. Rsch. Coun., Atlanta, 1985-86; leader Boy Scouts Am., Placentia, Calif., 1989—; mem. Orange (Calif.) Diocese Cath. Com. on Scouting. 1990—. Republican. Roman Catholic. Home: 668 Highlander Ave Placentia CA 92670-3229 Office: Unocal 1201 W 5th St Los Angeles CA 90017-1461

DOUGHERTY, RALEIGH GORDON, manufacturer's representative; b. Saginaw, Mich., Aug. 19, 1928; s. Raleigh Gordon and Helen Jean (McCrum) D.; 1 child, Karen Kealani. Salesman, H.D. Hudson Mfg. Co., Chgo., 1946-48; field sales rep. Jensen Mfg. Co., Chgo., 1948-50; field sales mgr. Regency Idea, Indpls., 1950-54; mgr. Brenna & Browne, Honolulu, 1954-56; owner, pres. Dougherty Enterprises, Honolulu, 1956—. With U.S. Army, 1950-52. Mem. Hawaii Hotel Assn., Internat. Home Furnishings Reps. Assn., Air Force Assn., D.A.V. (life), Am. Soc. Interior Designers (industry found.), Navy League U.S., Am. Legion, Hawaii Restaurant Assn., Nat. Fedn. Ind. Bus., Korean Vet. Small Bus. of Hawaii, Historic Hawaii Found., Hawaii Visitors Bur., Elks (past trustee Hawaii), Kani Ka Pila Golf Club. Republican. Methodist. Home and Office: 7715 Waikapu Loop Honolulu HI 96825-2129

DOUGHERTY, ROBERT CHARLES, rubber company executive, consultant; b. Elizabeth, N.J., Apr. 29, 1929; s. Joseph Howard and Marie Louise (Zusi) D.; m. Mary Cecelia Tolbert, June 25, 1956 (div. May 1972); children: Mary, Robert; m. Judy Ann Martinson, June 22, 1972; children: Michael, Shawn, Erin. Student, Stevens Inst. Tech., Hoboken, N.J., 1947-50; BSME, U. Md., 1952, postgrad.; postgrad., George Washington U., CCNY, Am. Univ. Sr. engr., supr. Melpar, Inc., Falls Church, Va., 1954-56; lab. mgr. Emerson Rsch. Lab., Silver Spring, Md., 1956-59; gen. mgr. Materials Testing Co., Bethesda, Md., 1959-65; chief engr. R.E. Darling Co. Inc., Tucson, 1965-75; v.p., gen. mgr. Durodyne, Inc., Tucson, 1975—. Patentee for 17 inventions in field. Pres. St. Pius X Sch., Bethesda, 1964-69; v.p. Washington Montessori Inst., 1962-69. Capt. USAF, 1954-59. Recipient Apollo Achievement award NASA, Washington, 1969. Mem. Optimists (pres. Tucson chpt. 1985). Republican. Roman Catholic. Office: Durodyne Inc PO Box 11740 Tucson AZ 85734-1740

DOUGHERTY, RONALD JARY, owner, accountant; b. Washington, Ind., Aug. 19, 1936; s. Paul Jesse and Mary Eunice (Gaither) D.; m. Carol S. Anderson, Dec. 24, 1980; children: Dawn, Erin, Paula, Jeffery. BS in Acctg., Ind. U., 1971. Acct. Internat. Harvester Co., Indpls., 1960-71; comptr. Standard Forms Co., Phoenix, 1971-82; ptnr., CEO R & C Acctg. Svc., Inc., Phoenix, 1979—; ptnr. Bene-Facts of Ariz., 1990. Office: R & C Acctg Svc Inc 5150 N 16th St Ste 161C Phoenix AZ 85016-3925

DOUGHTY, JOHN ROBERT, mechanical engineer, consultant; b. Clarksburg, W.Va., July 30, 1936; s. Merrill Newton and Margaret Clara (Watson) D.; m. Betty Jeanette Smith, June 5, 1970; children: Donna, Marc, John, Denise, James, Dawn. BSME, U. N.Mex., 1958; PhD, U. Ariz., 1971. Registered profl. engr., Calif., N.Mex. Commd. 2d lt. USAF, 1958, advanced through grades to lt. col., 1975; sect. head Air Force Weapons Lab., Kirtland AFB, N.Mex., 1970-75; div. chief Air Force Space Div., L.A. Air Force Sta., 1975-79; ret., 1979; mem. tech. staff Gen. Rsch. Corp., El Segundo, Calif., 1979-80; sect. head space and tech. group TRW, Redondo Beach, Calif., 1980-85; vis. lectr., researcher Ben Gurion U., Beersheva, Israel, 1985-86; cons. engr. Doughty Rsch. Engring., Huntington Beach, Calif., 1986-88, Albuquerque, 1988—; adj. profl. Emory-Riddle Aero. U., Kirtland AFB Ext., 1990—. Contbr. articles to profl. jours. Mem. exec. com. Am. Assocs. Ben Gurion U., Orange County, Calif., 1984-88; sec. Christian Missionary Pilots, Newport Beach, Calif., 1983-85; v.p. Albuquerque Bible Coll., 1989-91, pres., 1991—; sec.-treas. Christian Sci. Fellowship N.Mex., Albuquerque, 1990—; pilot N.Mex. Wing, CAP, 1991—. Mem. AIAA, ASME. Republican. Home and Office: 532 Calle De Los Hijos NW Albuquerque NM 87114-2039

DOUGLAS, CHARLES WESLEY, insurance sales executive; b. Phoenix, Aug. 10, 1933; s. Marvin Wesley and Nellora Almeda (Wright) D.; m. Nancy Carol Melton, May 26, 1955; children: Lori Ann Douglas Lass, Evan Wesley. BS, Ariz. State U., 1955. CLU. Salesman Prudential Ins. Co., Phoenix, 1957-62, asst. sales mgr., 1962-67; salesman Kansas City Life Ins. Co., Phoenix, 1967—; v.p., sec. Douglas Capital Commitments and Ins. Inc., Phoenix, 1982—. Chmn. bd. congl. devel. Desert SW Conf. Meth. Ch., Phoenix, 1991—; pres. Found. Cross Desert Ch., Phoenix, 1986-91; lay mem. ann. conf. Desert SW Conf. Meth. Ch., Phoenix, 1989-92. Lt. U.S. Army, 1955-57. Mem. CLU/ChFC (Phoenix chpt.), Million Dollar Round Table, Elks. Office: 1250 E Missouri Phoenix AZ 85014

DOUGLAS, DIANE MIRIAM, museum director; b. Harrisburg, Pa., Mar. 25, 1957; d. David C. and Anna (Barron) D.; m. Steve I. Perlmutter, Jan. 23, 1983; 1 child, David Simon. BA, Brown U., 1979; MA, U. Del., 1982. Oral history editor Former Members of Congress, Washington, 1979-80; assoc. curator exhibitions John Michael Kohler Arts Ctr., Sheboygan, Wis., 1982-83; dir. arts ctr. Lill Street Gallery, Chgo., 1984-88; exec. dir. David Adler Cultural Ctr., Libertyville, Ill., 1988-91; dir., chief curator Bellevue (Wash.) Art Mus., 1992—; program chair, exec. bd. nat. Coun. for Edn. in Ceramic Arts, Bandon, Oreg., 1990-93; nat. adv. bd. Friends of Fiber Art, 1992; artists adv. com. Pilchuck Glass Sch., 1993—. Office: Bellevue Art Mus 301 Bellevue Sq Bellevue WA 98004

DOUGLAS, GARY, mergers and acquisitions entrepreneur; b. Hamtramck, Mich., Sept. 15, 1945; s. Richard and Zosia (Dombrzalski) Dembowski; m. Debra McKay, June 28, 1980; children: Amy, Kelly. BBA, Walsh Coll. of Accountancy, 1977. Registered investment advisor. Stock broker Paine, Webber Inc., Troy, Mich., 1968-73; pres., owner Am. Auto Care Corp., Toledo, 1974-79; ptnr. Douglas & Douglas, Inc., Newport Beach, Calif., 1980-82; pres. Geneva Learning Systems, Inc., 1983-90, H. Roman & Co. subs. Hambros Bank London, L.A., 1990-92; mem. adv. bd. Davstar Corp., Toronto, Ont., Can., 1990. Author: Zero Base Budgeting and Sunset Laws, 1977 (William T. Creed Acctg. Writing award 1977). Co-founder Fair Share 502, Newport Beach, 1990; pres. West Newport Bridge Assn., 1989. Mem. Balboa Bay Club, Laguna Artist's Assn. (pres. 1985). Home: 21 Balboa Cove Newport Beach CA 92663-3226

DOUGLAS, JAMES FRANKLIN, employee benefit company executive; b. L.A., Apr. 11, 1963; s. Ernest Walter and Barbara Jean (Bond) D.; m.

Cynthia Lee Kikuchi, Sept. 20, 1988. BS in Fin. cum laude, U. So. Calif., 1986, MBA in Fin., 1987. CLU; ChFC. Asst. dist. mgr. The Equitable, Irvine, Calif., 1987-89; v.p. Merrill Lynch, Yorba Linda, Calif., 1989-92; pres. Bebefits Inc., Irvine, Calif., 1992—; pres. Benefits Inc., Irvine; lectr. Stanford U. Inst. Mktg., Calif., 1987. Contbr. articles to profl. jours. Vol. The Soup Kitchen, Costa Mesa, Calif., 1990—; mem. Rep. Nat. Com., Washington, Lincoln Club, Newport Beach., Calif. Mem. Nat. Assn. Watch Collectors. Episcopalian. Home: 191 Streamwood Irvine CA 92720 Office: Word & Brown 721 S Parker Ste 300 Orange CA 92668

DOUGLAS, MARION JOAN, labor negotiator; b. Jersey City, May 29, 1940; d. Walter Stanley and Sophie Frances (Zysk) Binaski; children: Jane Dee, Alex Jay. BA, Mich. State U., 1962; MSW, Sacramento State Coll., 1971; MPA, Calif. State U.-Sacramento, 1981. Owner, mgr. Linkletter-Totten Dance Studios, Sacramento, 1962-68, Young World of Discovery, Sacramento, 1965-68; welfare worker Sacramento County, 1964-67, welfare supr., 1968-72, child welfare supr., 1972-75, sr. personnel analyst, 1976-78, personnel program mgr., 1978-81, labor relations rep., 1981-89; cons. State Dept. Health, Sacramento, 1975-76; cons. in field. Author/editor: (newsletter) Thursday's Child, 1972-74. Presiding officer Community Resource Orgn., Fair Oaks, Calif., 1970-72; exec. bd. Foster Parent's Assn., Sacramento, 1972-75; organizer Foster Care Sch. Dist. liaison programs, 1973-75; active Am. Lung Assn., 1983-87; rep. Calif. Welfare Dirs. Assn., 1975-76; county staff advisor Joint Powers Authority, Sacramento, 1978-81; mem. Mgmt. Devel. Com., Sacramento, 1979-80; vol., auctioneer sta. KVIE Pub. TV, Sacramento, 1970-84, 88-90; adv. bd. Job and Info. Resource Ctr., 1976-77; spl. adv. task force coordinator Sacramento Employment and Tng. Adv. Council, 1980-81; vol. leader Am. Lung Assn., Sacramento, 1983-86 Calif. Dept. Social Welfare ednl. stipend, 1967-68, County of Sacramento ednl. stipend, 1969-70. Recipient Achievement award Nat. Assn. Counties, 1981. Mem. Mgmt. Women's Forum, Indsl. Relations Assn. No. Calif., Indsl. Relations Research Assn., Nat. Assn. Female Execs., Mensa. Republican. Avocations: real estate, nutrition. Home: 7812 Palmyra Dr Fair Oaks CA 95628-3423

DOUGLAS, SALLY JEANNE, publishing executive; b. San Francisco, Jan. 25, 1964; d. Harvey James III and Georgette Ruth (Steiger) Price; m. Alan Lloyd Douglas, May 1, 1988. BA in Comm. cum laude, Calif. State U., Chico, 1986. Technical writer Info World Mag., Menlo Park, Calif., 1986-89; technical writer Software Profl's., Inc., San Mateo, Calif., 1989-91, assoc. editor of tech. publs., 1991—.

DOUGLAS, STEPHEN, publishing company exective; b. Glendale, Calif., Apr. 20, 1954. Grad. cum laude in Telecom., Harvard U., 1978. Founder, pres. Redheads Internat., Corona del Mar, Calif., 1981—; exec. dir., prodr. USA Petites. Author: The Redhead Dynasty, 1986. Democrat. Deist. Office: 537 Newport Center Dr Newport Beach CA 92660-6900 also: Redheads Internat PO Box 2000 Corona Del Mar CA 92625-0020

DOUGLAS, STEWART, publishing executive, rancher; b. Brockton, Mass., July 16, 1918; s. Percy Tylor and Edith (Grant) Burtt; m. Ann Adriance, June 3, 1950 (div. Nov. 1965); children: Vincent, Tracie Lynn; m. Julie A. Mallow, June 22, 1975. Student, Colo. A&M U., 1941, Washington and Lee U., 1945, So. Calif. Coll. Bus., 1955, Tex. Tech. U., 1946. Owner Stewart Douglas Photography, Hollywood, Calif., 1945—; pres., pub. Fine Art Lithographs, Santa Ana, Calif., 1945—; owner, radio actor, TV prodr. Calif. Caravan, 1945-47; pres. Rantra Phonograph Rcords, Santa Ana, 1959—; mfr. picture frames, furniture Santa Ana, 1959-65; owner Homestead Cattle Ranches, Calif., Nev, Ariz., 1969-85; co-owner, pres. Thermography by Computer, Tustin, Calif., 1984-86; co-owner Homestead Fine Art Carpet Sculpture, La Mesa, Calif., 1991—; dir. Ice Vendors Manufacture, Tustin, 1974-80; dir. fin. Your Community Fund-Speed Riggs, Fullerton, Calif., 1978-85; co-owner Spectrums of Living Light Art (merged with Ohio Tourist Ctr.), 1978—; chmn. bd. dirs. Am. Minerals Internat., 1985-86, Minerals, Mining, Energy Pub. Corp., Denver, 1980-86. Author: Beef Animals and Natural Feeding, 1975; pub.: U.S. Marine Catalog, 1965; prodr. TV and Radio commls., new approaches to fine art; author nutritional papers for humans and animals; newspaper editor Army Air Force Cryptographer. Actor Kosloff Drama, Beverly Hills, Calif., 1940-41; founder Golden West Lecture Group, Tustin, 1969—; mem. Rep. Nat. Com., Washington, 1972—. With U.S. Army Air Force, 1942-45. Recipient Cert. of Merit award Dictionary of Internat. Biography (Eng.), 1973. Methodist. Home and Office: 8130 La Mesa Blvd 100 La Mesa CA 91941

DOUGLASS, DONALD ROBERT, banker; b. Evanston, Ill., Oct. 7, 1934; s. Robert William and Dorothy (Gibson) D.; m. Susan Douglass. BBA, U. N.Mex., 1959, MBA, 1966. With Security Pacific Nat. Bank, Los Angeles, 1961—, mgmt. trainee, 1962-63, asst. mgr. Vernon (Calif.) br., 1963-64, asst. mgr. Whittier (Calif.), 1964, asst. v.p., 1965, asst. v.p., credit officer regional adminstrn., Los Angeles, 1966-69, v.p., San Francisco, 1969-74, mgr. corp. accounts credit adminstrn. No. Calif. Corp. Banking, 1974-77; group v.p. Annco Properties, Burlingame, Calif., 1977-79; v.p., sr. loan officer Borel Bank and Trust Co., San Mateo, Calif., 1979-83, sr. v.p., 1983-84, exec. v.p. mortgage banking div. comml. property sales, Los Altos, 1984-87 ; ptnr. Key Equities, Inc., San Mateo, 1987—; ptnr., broker Centre Fin. Group, Inc., San Mateo, 1987—, Centre Fin. Group South Inc., Menlo Park, 1987—; instr. Am. Inst. Banking, 1963, Coll. San Mateo, 1982—. Served with AUS, 1954-56. Mem. U. N.Mex. Alumni Assn., Sigma Alpha Epsilon, Delta Sigma Phi. Republican. Presbyterian. Home: 745 Celestial Ln San Mateo CA 94404-2771

DOUGLASS, ENID HART, oral history educational program director; b. L.A., Oct. 23, 1926; d. Frank Roland and Enid Yandell (Lewis) Hart; m. Malcolm P. Douglass, Aug. 28, 1948; children: Malcolm Paul Jr., John Aubrey, Susan Enid. BA, Pomona Coll., 1948; MA, Claremont (Calif.) Grad. Sch., 1959. Research asst. World Book Ency., Palo Alto, Calif., 1953-54; exec. sec., asst. dir. oral history program Claremont Grad. Sch., 1963-71, dir. oral history program, 1971—, history lectr., 1977—; mem. Calif. Heritage Preservation Commn., 1977-85, chmn. 1983-85. Contbr. articles to hist. jours. Mayor pro tem City of Claremont, 1980-82, Mayor, 1982-86; mem. planning and rsch. adv. coun. State of Calif., mem. city coun., Claremont, 1978-86; founder Claremont Heritage, Inc., 1977-80, bd. dirs., 1986—; bd. dirs. Pilgrim Pla., Claremont; founder steering com., founding bd. Claremont Community Found., 1989—, pres., 1990—. Mem. Oral History Assn. (pres. 1979-80), Southwest Oral History Assn. (founding steering com. 1981, J.V. Mink award 1984), Nat. Council Pub. History, LWV (bd. dirs. 1957-59, Outstanding Svc. to Community award, 1986). Democrat. Home: 1195 N Berkeley Ave Claremont CA 91711-3842 Office: Claremont Grad Sch Oral History Program 1027 N Dartmouth Ave Claremont CA 91711-6163

DOUGLASS, JOHN MICHAEL, internist; b. Takoma Park, Md., Apr. 13, 1939; s. Jones All and Helen Louise D.; BA, Columbia Union Coll., Takoma Park, 1959; MD (Salutatorian), U. So. Calif., 1964; DPh Pacific West U., 1986; PhD Clayton U., 1987. m. Sue Nan Peters, May 15, 1962; children: Dina Lynn, Lisa Michele. Rotating intern Los Angeles County, U. So. Calif. Med. Ctr., 1964-65, resident internal medicine, 1965-67, home care physician, 1965-68; practice medicine specializing in internal medicine, Cin., 1968-70, L.A., 1970-91; physician Pasadena Emergency Ctr., 1965-68, Deaconess Hosp., 1968-70; postdoctoral fellow automobile safety and trauma rsch. UCLA, 1967-68, med. cons. Emergency Med. Svcs. Project, 1970-71; commd. officer USPHS, 1968, advanced through grades to comdr., sr. surgeon USPHS Res. 1982—, asst. sci. adviser injury control program ECA, Cin., 1968-69, med. specialities cons. Office Product Safety, FDA, 1969-70; internal medicine cons. East End Neighborhood Community Health Ctr. Cin., 1968-70, Hollywood Sunset Free Clinic, 1971-72; sr. med. cons. multidisciplinary hwy. accident investigation unit U. So. Calif., 1971-73; staff internist, coordinator health improvement service Kaiser Found. Hosp., L.A., 1970-92; instr. biomedical engring. course UCLA, 1968, sr. med. cons., assoc. sci. advisors, 1970—, instr. internal medicine, 1971-74; instr. internal medicine U. Cin. Sch. Medicine, 1968-70; instr. kinesthesiology, traumatic anatomy and head injury U. So. Calif., 1971-74, instr. foodstyle and lifestyle, 1977—; mem. med. adv. bd. Dominican Sisters of Sick Poor, 1969; traffic safety cons. Countywide Conf. on Emergency Med. Svcs., 1972; mem. nutrition council Las Virgenes Sch. Dist., 1977. Active mgmt. devel. program Boy Scouts Am. Execs., 1966; bd. dirs. Calif. Assn. Pvt. Schs. and Colls., 1967, Coronary Club (adult jogging program), 1967-68; co-organizer Oriental rug exhibit Pacificulture Mus., Pasadena, Calif., 1973; v.p. L.A. Med. Milk Commn. Diplomate Nat. Bd. Med. Examiners, Am. Bd. Internal Medicine. Fellow ACP; mem. AMA, Calif. Med. Assn., L.A.County Med. Assn., Am. Soc. Internal Medicine, Calif. Soc. Internal Medicine, L.A. Soc. Internal Medicine, Am. Assn. Automotive Medicine (exec. com. Western chpt. 1977-82), Am. Cancer Soc. (profl. edn. com., nutrition subcom.), Internat. Hajji Baba Soc., Decorative Arts Council, L.A. Mus. Art, Sierra Club, Phi Delta Epsilon, Alpha Omega Alpha, Phi Kappa Phi. Author: The Lost Language; contbr. over 100 articles to profl. jours.

DOUPE, ROBERT N., children's protective services specialist; b. Seattle, May 4, 1941; s. William A. and Eva Arlys (Craig) D.; widowed; children: Robert A., Michael T. BA, U. Wash., 1963; MSW, U. B.C., 1967. Cert. social worker. Supr. Dept. Public Assistance, Everett, Wash., 1963-69; cons. medical social work Div. Vocat. Rehab., Seattle, 1969-73; regional planner Dept. Social & Health Svcs., Seattle, 1971-73; welfare adminstr. Bellevue (Was.) Community Svc. Office, 1973-76; dir. social svcs. Echo Glen Children's Ctr., Snoqualmie, Wash., 1976-85, dir. mental health, 1988-91; dir. program standards Div. Juvenile Rehab., Olympia, Wash., 1985-88; area mgr. children's protective svcs. Region 4 Div. Children and Family Svcs., Seattle, 1991—; bd. dirs. Horizen Provisional Devel. Inst., Seattle, Friends of Youth, Renton, Wash.; chmn. Wash. Human Rsch. Rev. Bd., Olympia, 1984-90. Recipient Presidential Svc. award Wash. Assn. Social Workers, 1979. Mem. NASW (pres. 1975-79), Acad. Cert. Social Workers, Am. Correctional Assn. Office: Region 4 Div Children & Family Svcs 2809 26th Ave S Seattle WA 98144

DOUTT, JEFFREY (THOMAS), marketing and management specialist, university dean; b. Oakland, Calif., Mar. 30, 1947; s. Richard L. and Lucinda M. (Killian) D.; B.S., U. Calif.-Berkeley, 1968, M.S., 1970, Ph.D., 1976. Assoc. in bus. adminstrn. U. Calif.-Berkeley, 1974; asst. prof. mgmt. Sonoma (Calif.) State U., 1974-78, assoc. prof., 1978-83, prof., 1983—, chmn. dept. mgmt. studies, 1976-80, dean Sch. Social Scis., 1980-86, dean Sch. Bus. and Econs., 1986—; prin. assoc. Mgmt. Devel. Internat.; cons. mktg. and mgmt. Recipient Internat. Exchange award Rotary Found., 1979; Giannini Found. fellow, 1968-70. Mem. Am. Mktg. Assn., Acad. Mktg. Sci., Acad. Internat. Bus., Western Mktg. Educators Assn., Phi Beta Kappa. Democrat. Club: Rotary. Contbr. articles to profl. jours. Home: 5130 Gilchrist Rd Sebastopol CA 95472-6321 Office: 1801 E Cotati Ave Rohnert Park CA 94928-3609

DOVE, DONALD AUGUSTINE, city planner, educator; b. Waco, Tex., Aug. 7, 1930; s. Sebert Constantine and Amy Delmena (Stern) D.; m. Cecelia Mae White, Feb. 9, 1957; children—Angela Dove Gaddy, Donald, Monica, Celine, Austin, Cathlyn, Dianna, Jennifer. B.A., Calif. State U.-Los Angeles, 1951; M.A. in Pub. Adminstrn., U. So. Calif., 1966. Planning and devel. cons. D. Dove Assocs., Los Angeles, 1959-60; supr. demographic research Calif. Dept. Pub. Works, Los Angeles, 1960-66, environ. coordinator, Sacramento, 1971-75; dir. transp. employment project State of Calif., Los Angeles, 1966-71, chief Los Angeles Region transp. study, 1975-84; chief environ. planning Calif. Dept. Transp., Los Angeles, 1972-75; dir. U. So. Calif. Praetors, Los Angeles, 1984-87; panelist, advisor Pres. Conf. on Aging, Washington, 1970—, Internat. Conf. on Energy Use Mgmt., 1981; guest lectr. univs. western U.S., 1969—. Author: Preserving Urban Environment, 1976; Small Area Population Forecasts, 1966. Chmn. Lynwood City Planning Commn., Calif., 1982—; pres. Area Pastoral Council, Los Angeles, 1982-83; mem., del. Archdiocesan Pastoral Council, Los Angeles, 1979-86, Compton Community Devel. Bd., Calif., 1967-71; pres. Neighborhood Esteem/Enrichment Techniques Inst., 1992—. Served to cpl. U.S. Army, 1952-54. Mem. Am. Planning Assn., Am. Inst. Planners (transp. chmn. 1972-73), Calif. Assn. of Mgmt. (pres. 1987-88), Am. Inst. Cert. Planners, Assn. Environ. Profls. (co-founder 1973), Optimists (sec. 1978-79), K.C., Knights of Peter Claver. Democrat. Roman Catholic. Home: 11356 Ernestine Ave Lynwood CA 90262-3711 Office: Calif Dept Transp 120 S Spring St Los Angeles CA 90012-3606

DOVE, JAMES LEROY, architect; b. Brigantine, N.J., July 18, 1960; s. Warner Dove and Florence Elizabeth (Miller) Grimshaw; m. Lili Francis Schwarz, Aug. 28, 1988; children: Phillip Walker, Ella Mae. BA, Montclair State Coll., 1983; MArch, UCLA, 1990. Adminstrv. asst. N.J. Dept. Commerce and Econ. Devel., Trenton, 1983-85; archtl. designer Gwynne Pugh & Assocs., AIA, Santa Monica, Calif., 1988-89, Architecture 2000, P.C., Denver, 1990—. Mem AIA. Home: 2270 Bellaire St Denver CO 80207

DOW, FREDERICK WARREN, management educator; b. Boston, Aug. 2, 1917; s. Frederick Vincent and Marcia (McMahon) D.; m. Patricia Rathbone, Oct. 2, 1943; children: Frederick Warren, Bradford Rathbone, Martha Trevelen Dow Lewis. B.S. in Chemistry, Boston Coll., 1940; M.S. in Physical Chemistry, U. Mass., 1942; A.M. in Ednl. Psychology, Yale, 1950, Ph.D. in U. Adminstrn, 1955. Various mgmt. positions Dow Chem. Co., 1950-67; mng. dir. Dow Chem. Co., France, 1963-66; gen. mgr. Latin Am., Pacific, Office of Asso. Cos., Midland, Mich., 1966-67; Hayes Healy prof. mktg. Grad. Sch. Bus., U. Notre Dame, 1967-77; Univ. prof. internat. mgmt. U.S. Internat. U., San Diego, 1977—, dean Sch. of Bus., 1986-89; chmn. bd. Kestrel Inc., N.Y.C.; Mem. sci. adv. com. Italian Ministry of Tourism, 1969-89. Served to maj. U.S. Army, 1942-46. Decorated Air medal, Bronze Star.; Sr. Fulbright scholar Ecuador, 1973. Fellow Royal Soc. Art; mem. Am. Chem. Soc., Sigma Xi, Phi Kappa Phi. Clubs: Union League (N.Y.C.); Travelers (Paris). Home: 5080 Carlsbad Blvd Carlsbad CA 92008-4353 Office: US Internat U Coll Bus Adminstrn San Diego CA 92131

DOW, MARY ALEXIS, financial executive; b. South Amboy, N.J., Feb. 19, 1949; d. Alexander and Elizabeth Anne (Reilly) Pawlowski; m. Russell Alfred Dow, June 19, 1971. BS with honors, U. R.I., 1971. CPA, Oreg. Staff acct. Deloitte, Haskins & Sells, Boston, 1971-74; sr. acct. Price Waterhouse, Portland, Oreg., 1974-77, mgr., 1977-81, sr. mgr., 1981-84; chief fin. officer Copeland Lumber Yards Inc., Portland, 1984-86; ind. cons. in field, 1986—; bd. dirs. Longview Fibre Co. Treas. Oreg. Mus. Sci. and Industry; past chmn. bd., exec. com. Oreg. Trails chpt. ARC, N.W. Regional Blood Svcs.; treas. Portland chpt. Fin. Execs. Inst. Mem. AICPA, Am. Woman's Soc. CPAs, Oreg. Soc. CPAs, Fin. Execs. Inst. Roman Catholic. Clubs: City (bd. govs.), Multnomah Athletic. Contbr. articles to profl. publs.

DOW, ROBERT STONE, neurologist; b. Colo., Jan. 4, 1908; s. Simon Stone and Mary Edna (Sisson) D.; m. Margaret Willetta Leever, July 9, 1934; children: Margreita, Barbara. BS, Linfield Coll., 1929; MA, MD, U. Oreg., Portland, 1934, PhD, 1935; DSc (hon.), Linfield Coll., 1963. Diplomate Am. Bd. Neurology. From asst. prof. to assoc. prof. Anatomy U. Oreg., Portland, 1939-46, clin. instr. Nuerology, 1940-46, asst. clin. prof. Neurology, 1946-52, assoc. clin. prof. Neurology, 1952-66, clin. prof. Neurology, 1966; intern Wis. Gen. Hosp., Madison, 1935-36; fellow Dept. of Physiology Yale U., New Haven, 1936-37; adj. prof. Northwestern Coll. of Law, Lewis and Clark Coll., 1986-88. Co-author (book) Physiology & Pathology of Cerebellum, 1958. Fellow Belgium-Am. Found., 1937-38, Rockefeller Inst., 1938-39; recipient Disting. Svc. award Western Inst. on Epilepsy, 1979, Ann. Svc. award Multnomah County med. Soc., 1978, Aubney R. Watzek award Lewis and Clark Coll., 1986, Discovery award Med. Rsch. Found. of Oreg., 1988; named Alumnus Of Yr. Linfield Coll., 1982. Fellow Am. Acad. of Neurology; mem. ACP, AMA, Am. Assn. of Anatomists, Am. EEG Soc. (pres. 1958, Am. Neurolog. Soc., Am. Physiol. Soc., Am. Assn. Neurolog. Surgeons, Am. Epilepsy Soc. (pres. 1965), Oreg. Med. Assn., Soc. of Neurosci., Sigma Xi, Alpha Omega Alpha, Univ. Club. Republican. Home: 2221 SW First Ave Portland OR 97201 Office: Good Samaritan Hosp/Med Ctr 1015 NW 22d Ave Portland OR 97210

DOWDEN, ANNE OPHELIA, botanical illustrator, writer; b. Denver, Sept. 17, 1907; d. James Campbell and Edith Belinda (Brownfield) Todd; m. Raymond Baxter Dowden, Apr. 1, 1934 (dec. Jan. 1982). BA, Carnegie Inst. Tech., Pitts., 1930; student, Art Students League, N.Y.C., 1930-32; DFA (hon.), Moore Coll. of Art, Phila., 1988. Instr. art Pratt Inst., Bklyn., 1930-33; freelance textile designer N.Y.C., 1935-52; head art dept. Manhattanville Coll., N.Y.C., 1932-53; bot. illustrator, author N.Y.C., 1952-90, Boulder, Colo., 1990—. Author-illustrator: The Secret Life of the Flowers, 1964, Roses, 1965, Look at a Flower, 1963, Wild Green Things in the City: A Book of Weeds, 1972, The Blossom on the Bough: A Book of Trees, 1975, State Flowers, 1977, From Flower to Fruit, 1984, This Noble Harvest: A Chronicle of Herbs, 1979, The Clover and the Bee: A Book of Pollination, 1990; illustrator Shakespeare's Flowers, 1969, The Golden Circle, 1977, Wildflowers and the Stories Behind Their Names, 1977, The Lore and Legends of Flowers, 1982, Consider the Lilies, 1986, Plants of Christmas, 1987; contbr. numerous articles to mags. Recipient Am. Inst. Graphic Arts, Children's Book Show award, 1973, ALA, Notable Children's Books, 1963, 75, 77, 82, Children's Book Coun., Showcase Selection, Sch. Library Jour., Best Books award, Nat. Sci. Tchrs. Assn., Outstanding Sci. Books for Children awards; recipient fellowship, Tiffany Found., L.I., N.Y., 1929, 30, 31. Mem. Bklyn. Botanic Garden, N.Y. Bot. Garden, Denver Botanic Garden. Home: 350 Ponca Pl Boulder CO 80303-3828

DOWDLE, PATRICK DENNIS, lawyer; b. Denver, Dec. 8, 1948; s. William Robert and Helen (Schraeder) D.; m. Eleanor Pryor, Mar. 8, 1975; children: Jeffery William, Andrew Peter. BA, Cornell Coll., Mt. Vernon, Iowa, 1971; JD, Boston U., 1975. Bar: Colo. 1975, U.S. Dist. Ct. Colo. 1975, U.S. Ct. Appeals (10th cir.) 1976, U.S. Supreme Ct. 1978. Acad. dir. in Japan Sch. Internat. Tng., Putney, Vt., 1974; assoc. Decker & Miller, Denver, 1975-77; ptnr. Miller, Makkai & Dowdle, Denver, 1977—; designated counsel criminal appeals Colo. Atty. Gens. Office, Denver, 1980-81; guardian ad litem Adams County Dist. Ct., Brighton, Colo., 1980-83; affiliated counsel ACLU, Denver, 1980—. Mem. Colo. Bar Assn., Denver Bar Assn. (various coms.), Porsche Club of Am. Democrat. Home: 3254 Tabor Ct Wheat Ridge CO 80033-5367 Office: Miller Makkai & Dowdle 2325 W 72d Ave Denver CO 80221

DOWELL, TIMOTHY JOHN, educator; b. Chgo., Aug. 9, 1947; s. Clyde I. and Emma (Wollan) D.; m. Bonnie G. Dowell, May 30, 1970; children: Eric, Rebecca. BS, Western Ill. U., 1970. Educator Kalispell, Mont., 1972-92. Chmn. United Way, Kalispell, 1985; vice chair Hockaday Art Ctr., Kalispell, 1985-87; del. White House Conf. on Small Bus., Washington, 1986; bd. trustees Big Bros. and Sisters, Kalispell, 1990—. Democrat. Home: 46 Westview Dr Kalispell MT 59901

DOWLIN, CHARLES EDWIN, librarian; b. Laird, Colo., June 3, 1933; s. Ross Everett and Fern May (Peterson) D.; m. May Nichol, Sept. 5, 1960; children: Patrick Edwin, Kerry Anne. BS in Bus., U. Colo., 1955, MPS, 1956; MA, U. Denver, 1963; PhD, U. Pitts., 1980. Quality control clk. Sunstrand Aviation, Denver, 1960-62; city librarian Provo (Utah) City Corp., 1963-67; head libr. devel. State Libr. of Ohio, Columbus, 1967-70; state librarian N.Mex. State Libr., Santa Fe, 1970-77; sr. rsch. scientist Applied Mgmt. Scis., Inc., Silver Spring, Md., 1978-80; dir. sch. libr. sci. Sam Houston State U., Huntsville, Tex., 1980-85; dir. Golden Libr., Ea. N.Mex. U., Portales, 1985—. Bd. dirs. N.Mex. Outdoor Drama Assn., 1989-92. With U.S. Army, 1956-59. Mem. ALA, Sci. Fiction Rsch. Assn., N.Mex. Libr. Assn. (Librarian of the Yr. 1977), N.Mex. Coun. of Acad. Libraries (bd. dirs. 1989-91), Rotarian. Presbyterian. Home: 508 E 17th Ln Portales NM 88130 Office: Eastern New Mexico Univ Golden Library Station #32 Portales NM 88130

DOWLIN, KENNETH EVERETT, librarian; b. Wray, Colo., Mar. 11, 1941; s. Ross Everett and Fern Mae (Peterson) D.; m. Janice Marie Simmons, Mar. 11, 1961; children: Kevin Everett, Kristopher Everett. BA, U. Colo., 1963, MPA, 1981; MA, U. Denver, 1966. Bookmobile libr., libr. asst. Adams County Public Libr., Westminster, Colo., 1961-63; libr. asst. II Denver Pub. Libr., 1962-64; head libr. Arvada Public Libr., Colo., 1964-68; adminstrv. asst. Jefferson County Pub. Libr., Colo., 1969; dir. Natrona County Pub. Libr., Casper, Wyo., 1969-75, Pikes Peak Regional Libr. Dist., Colorado Springs, Colo., 1975-87; city libr. San Francisco Pub. Libr., 1987—; instr. Casper Coll., 1971-73; chmn. Colo. Librs. in Coop., 1975-76, Colo. Ad-hoc Com. Networking, 1976; libr. City of San Francisco, 1987; mem. Western Interstate Commn. Higher Edn. Libr. Network Task Force; past trustee Wyo. Dept. Libr., Archives and History; mem. Libr. of Congress Commn. on Book of Future; bd. dirs. Satellite Libr. Info. Network; vis. instr. U. Denver, 1980, 81, vis. faculty U. Calif., Berkeley, 1993; cons. in cable TV. Editorial bd. Microcomputers for Info. Mgmt., Libr. Hi Tech., Elec. Libr. Mem. adv. bd. for series on tech. WNET, N.Y.C., 1981-83; active San Francisco Mayor's com. on Juveniles in Detention; bd. dirs. Citizens Goals for Colorado Springs, 1981-85; bd. govs. Colo. Tech. Coll., 1982-85. With USMCR, 1959-65. Recipient Disting. Alumni award U. Denver Grad. Sch. for Libr. and Info. Mgmt. Mem. ALA (coun. mem. 1985-89, commn. on equality and freedom access to info. 1984-85, chmn. awards com. 1985-86, pres.'s com. on preservation 1990—, ad hoc com. on MARC licensing, chair local arrangements com. for 1992, 1989-92, pres.'s com. on preservation policy 1989-90, Hammond Inc. Libr. Award Jury 1968), ALA Libr. and Info. Tech. Assn. (long range planning com. 1981-82, pres. 1983-84, com. mem. Gaylord Awards), Mountain Plains Libr. Assn., Calif. Libr. Assn. (fin. com., coun. mem. 1989—), Colo. Libr. Assn. (pres. 1968-69), Denver Coun. Govts. (chmn. librs. com. 1966), Colo. Mcpl. League (chmn. librs. sect. 1967), Bibliog. Ctr. Rocky Mountains (pres. 1972-74), Pikes Peak Area C. of C. (chmn. cultural affairs com. 1976-77). Home: 359 Melrose Ave San Francisco CA 94127-2395 Office: San Francisco Pub Libr Civic Ctr San Francisco CA 94102

DOWLING, ELLEN CATHERINE, training executive; b. Bayshore, N.Y., Dec. 15, 1948; d. John Philip and Patricia Mary (McGovern) D.; m. William Weldon, July 15, 1977 (div. Oct. 1992); 1 child, Brando Weldon. BS in Edn., N.Mex. State U., Las Cruces, 1970, MA in English, 1973; PhD in English, U. N.Mex., 1977. Asst. prof. Tex. A&M U., College Station, 1977-83; instr. Communication Strategies, Inc., Albuquerque, 1983-84; v.p. Communication Strategies, Inc., Corrales, N.Mex., 1984—; prin. The Profl. Tng. Co., Corrales, 1984—; alternate sr. faculty rep., communications area chair U. Phoenix, Albuquerque, 1987—. Author: Presentation Strategies, 1984; editor: Verbal Judo, 1984; contbr. articles to Tng. and Devel. Jour. Bd. mem. Stage Ctr. Community Theater, Bryan, Tex., 1975-77; designer orientation slide show Greater Albuquerque C. of C., 1986; keynote speaker United Way of Albuquerque, 1988. Named Leader of Yr., Leads Club, Albuquerque, 1987. Mem. Am. Soc. Tng. and Devel. (asst. regional dir. 1991-92, pres. 1990, Outstanding Mem. of Yr. 1991), Orgn. Devel. Network, Nat. Soc. Performance and Instrn. Democrat. Office: Profl Tng Co PO Box 2578 Corrales NM 87048-2578

DOWNER, ALAN SEYMOUR, government executive; b. Princeton, N.J., Nov. 29, 1949; s. Alan Seymour and Florence Marsha (Walsh) D.; m. Kahtryn Marie Shaw, June 19, 1971; children: Charles Macready, Jillian Caroline. BS in Geology, Allegheny Coll., 1971; MA in Anthropology, U. Mo., 1978, PhD in Anthropology, 1989. Mgr. trainee Friendly Ice Cream Corp., Livingston, N.J., 1974-75; asst. mgr. Friendly Ice Cream Corp., Columbia, Md., 1975-77; grad. asst. anthropology U. Mo., Columbia, 1975-78, rsch. specialist, 1978; coord. archaeol. preservation Historic Sites div. Ill. Dept. Conservation, Springfield, 1978-79, acting chief archaeologist, 1979-82, sr. archaeologist, 1982-83; sr. archaeologist Fed. Adv. Coun. on Historic Preservation, Golden, Colo., 1983-86; dir. Historic Preservation dept. Navajo Nation, Window Rock, Ariz., 1986—. Co-editor: Historic Preservation on the Reservation, 1990. Head referee Gallup (N.Mex.) Soccer League, 1989-91; pres. Gallup Aquatics Assn., 1988-91. Mem. Soc. for Am. Archaeology (com. mem. govt. rels. 1986—, chmn. com. pub. archaeology 1980-83, assoc. editor 1983-86), Preservation Forum, Keepers of the Treasures (treas. 1990-91). Democrat. Office: Navajo Nation Hist Preserva Morgan Blvd Window Rock AZ 86515

DOWNES, BRYAN TREVOR, public affairs educator; b. Vancouver, B.C., Can., Sept. 22, 1939; s. Trevor Gordon and Jessie Lillian (Stephenson) D.; m. Sharon Elizabeth Lenahan, Feb. 15, 1963; children: Laura Elizabeth, Alexander Bryan. BS, U. Oreg., 1962, MS, 1963; PhD, Washington U., St. Louis, 1966. Asst. prof. San Francisco State Coll., 1966-67; asst. prof. Mich. State U., East Lansing, 1967-70, assoc. prof., 1970-71; assoc. prof. U. Mo., St. Louis, 1971-76; assoc. prof. U. Oreg., Eugene, 1976-78, prof. pub. affairs, 1978—; exec. dir. Pacific Northwest Can. Studies Consortium, Eugene, 1986—; panel organizer various profl. orgns. Author, editor: Cities and Suburbs: Selected Readings in Local Politics and Public Policy, 1971; author: Politics, Change and the Urban Crisis, 1976. Mem. bd. YMCA, Vol. Action Ctr., Joint Social Svcs. Adv. Commn., Housing and Community Svcs. Adv. Commn., Lane County, University City, Mo. Bd. Edn. Recipient Outstanding Vol. of Yr. award Lane County Vol. Action Ctr., 1989; Fulbright scholar Coun. for Internat. Exchange of Scholars, New Zealand, 1989-90.

Mem. ASPA, Western Social Sci. Assn. (exec. dir. 1990—, cert. of recognition 1989), Assn. Can. Studies in U.S. (exec. coun. 1992—). Home: 195 Coachman Dr Eugene OR 97405-4811 Office: U Oreg Dept Planning Pub Policy and Mgmt Eugene OR 97403

DOWNEY, JAMES EDGAR, manufacturing executive; b. Spartanburg, S.C., Sept. 29, 1950; s. Vernon P. and Lu Vera (McGraw) D.; m. Jean Lucille Gallo, May 24, 1980; 1 child, Jeana Marie. BBA, U. Phoenix, 1987; postgrad., Golden Gate U., 1992—. Draftsman Pacific Rolling Door Co., San Lorenzo, Calif., 1970-74; prodn. mgr. Pacific Rolling Door Co., San Lorenzo, 1975-87, v.p. mfr., 1988—. Instr. ARC, Hayward, Calif., 1968-80, bd. dirs., 1983-87, vice chmn. disaster svcs., Solano County, Calif., 1980-90. With USAFR, 1970-91. Republican. Presbyterian. Office: Pacific Rolling Door Co 15900 Worthley Dr San Lorenzo CA 94580-1844

DOWNIE, PAMELA, career counselor; b. Chester, Calif., Dec. 1, 1954; d. William John and June (De La Mont) D. BA, Widener U., 1980; MS, Villanova U., 1985; postgrad., U. So. Calif. Counselor Del. County Community Coll., Media, Pa., trainer, educator; counselor, educator New Beginnings, Media; teaching asst. U. So. Calif., 1989-91, instr. practicum, 1991, psychol. intern., 1991-93. Mem. APA (student), NAFE, AACD, Am. Mental Health Coun. Assn., Assn. for Multicultural Counseling, Pa. Counselors Assn., Assn. for Specialists in Group Work, Assn. for Coun. Edn. and Supervision. Home: PO Box 660582 Arcadia CA 91066-0582

DOWNING, DOUGLAS ALLAN, economics educator, writer; b. Seattle, Oct. 11, 1957; s. Robert Allan and Marguerite Louise (Hayland) D. BS, Yale U., 1979, MPhil, 1982, PhD in Econs., 1987. Acting instr. Yale U., New Haven, Conn., 1981-83; asst. prof. Seattle Pacific U., 1983-91, assoc. prof., 1991—. Author: Calculus the Easy Way, 1982, Algebra the Easy Way, 1983, Trigonometry the Easy Way, 1984; co-author: Dictionary of Computer Terms, 1986, and 7 others. Mem. State Com. on Teenage Parents, Olympia, Wash., 1986-88; witness Wash. State Legis., Olympia, 1991-92; vol. legis. compaign, Wenatchee, Wash., 1992. Austin Howard grad. fellow Yale U., 1979. Mem. Am. Econ. Assn., Seattle Economist Club, Yale Assn. Western Wash. (treas. 1987—), Phi Beta Kappa. Presbyterian. Home: 9012 12th Ave NW Seattle WA 98117 Office: Seattle Pacific U McKenna Hall Seattle WA 98119

DOWNS, DOUGLAS WALKER, sculptor; b. Pomona, Calif., May 30, 1945; s. Walker and Dorothy (Spoor) D.; m. Anne Venables, Jan. 15, 1971; 1 child, Devon. BA, Whittier Coll., 1967; postgrad., Claremont Grad. Sch., 1968-69, Ariz. State U., 1969-70. Prin. works include bronze commn. Hawk on Rock, 1979 (Tor House award), Daughter of Wind, 1987 (Juror's Choice award); exhbns. include New Am. Masters May Gallery, Scottsdale, 1986, 91, Scottsdale Ctr. for Arts, 1990, Carmel Art Assn, 1990, 92; represented in permanent collections L.I. Chess Mus. Mem. Pacific Grove (Calif.) Heritage Soc., 1979—. Recipient 1st prize Gallery La Luz, N.Mex., 1989, 90, 91, Painters and Sculptors Soc. Washington, 1989, 90, 91, Ga. Miniature Art Soc., 1991. Mem. Carmel Art Assn. (treas., bd. dirs. 1983-84, v.p. 1993).

DOWNS, KATHLEEN JOAN, purchasing supervisor; b. Chgo., Aug. 16, 1950; d. Joseph C. and Joan Ida (Godfrey) D.; div.; 1 child, Marsha Leigh Hill. BBA, Nat. U., 1987, MBA in Fin., 1989. Buyer Rush-Presbyn. St. Luke's Med. Ctr., Chgo., 1972-74, Loyola U. Med. Ctr., Maywood, Ill., 1979-85; adminstrv. asst. U. Calif. San Diego Med. Ctr., 1986-91; purchasing supr. San Diego C.C. Dist., 1991—. Bd. dirs. Loyola U. Employees' Fed. Credit Union, Maywood, 1983-85. Mem. Parents Without Ptnrs. (1st v.p. San Diego chpt. 1989, pres. 1990). Unitarian. Office: San Diego CC Dist 3375 Camino del Rio S San Diego CA 92108

DOWNS, WILLIAM FREDRICK, geochemist; b. Santa Maria, Calif., Aug. 4, 1942; s. William Nielson and Lotus (Mankins) D.; m. Karen Mona Farnsworth, July 15, 1967; 1 child, William Ross. BA, U. Colo., 1965, MS, 1974; PhD, Pa. State U., 1977. Registered geologist, Calif., Idaho. Reseach assoc. Pa. State U., University Park, Pa., 1974-77; scientist Idaho Nat. Engring. Lab., Idaho Falls, Idaho, 1977-88; geochemist Jacobs Engring. Group, Albuquerque, 1988-92; sr. assoc. Hart Crowser Inc., Seattle, 1992—; adj. prof. U. Idaho, Idaho Falls, 1979-90, Idaho State U., Idaho Falls, 1984-90. Mem. tech. adv. bd. N.Mex. Waste Edn. & Rsch. Consortium; mem. dept. adv. bd. dept. geoscis. U. Colo., 1991—. Lt. USNR, 1966-69, Vietnam. Mem. Geochem. Soc., Geol. Soc. Am., Civitan (pres. Idaho Falls chpt. 1986-87), Am. Legion (commander Idaho Falls 1980-81). Home: 9825 232d SW Edmonds WA 98020

DOXEY, GORDON EARL, physical therapist; b. Ogden, Utah, July 5, 1954; s. George Rhodes and R'Lene (Paul) D.; m. Nina Droubay, July 8, 1977; children: Rebecca, Rachael, Lindsay. BS in Zoology, Weber State U., 1973; BS in Phys. Therapy, U. Utah, 1981, MS in Exercise Physiology, 1986. Lic. phys. therapist, Utah. Staff phys. therapist St. Benedict's Hosp., Ogden, Utah, 1981-86; indsl. phys. therapist McKay Dee Hosp., Ogden, Utah, 1986-87; asst. mgr. phys. therapy St. Benedict's Hosp., Ogden, Utah, 1988-90, mgr. phys. therapy, 1990-91, mgr. rehab. svcs., 1991—, instr. quality mgmt., 1993; exercise cons. Weber State U. Ogden, 1983-86; pres. Utah Chpt. Allied Arthritis Health Profls., Salt Lake City, 1985; health cons. Newgate Mall Walkers Club, Ogden, 1981-92; team mem. Holy Cross Rehab. Svcs. Line Quality and Strategic Planning Teams, 1993. Contbr. articles to profl. jours. Instr. Adult Sunday Sch., LDS Ch., Clinton, Utah, 1981-87, pres. elders quorum, Roy, Utah, 1992; vol. missionary in Eng., 1973-75. Mem. Am. Phys. Therapy Assn. LDS. Office: Saint Benedict's Hosp 5475 S 500 E Ogden UT 84405

DOYEL, DAVID ELMOND, archaeologist, museum director; b. Lindsay, Calif., Aug. 24, 1946; s. Lester Levi Doyel and Jewell Mae (Hill) Burney; m. Sharon S. Debowski, Apr. 23, 1983. BA, Calif. State U., Chico, 1969, secondary teaching credential, 1971, MA, 1972; PhD, U. Ariz., 1977. Archaeologist Ariz. State Mus., Tucson, 1972-79; dir. Archaeology and Mus. Div., Window Rock, Ariz., 1979-82; mgr. Soil Systems, Inc., Phoenix, 1982-83; dir. Pueblo Grande Mus., City of Phoenix, 1984-89; cons. Estrella Cultural Rsch., Phoenix, 1990—; dir., cons. rsch. projects for govt. agys., Indian tribes, others. Contbr. articles to profl. publs. Bd. dirs. San Juan County Mus., Farmington, N.Mex., 1993. Named Outstanding Surp., Navajo Nation, Window Rock, 1980. Mem. Soc. Am. Archaeology, Ariz. Archaeol. and Hist. Soc. (exec. coun. 1976), Mus. Assn. Ariz., Planetary Soc., Ariz. Archaeol. Coun. (pres. 1982), Sigma Xi. Office: PO Box 60474 Phoenix AZ 85082-0474

DOYLE, HARLEY JOSEPH, health products executive; b. Springfield, Ohio, Oct. 10, 1942; s. William Cecil and Norma Louise Doyle. Grad. high sch., Springfield, Ohio. With Quick Mfg., Springfield, Ohio, 1963-64, Hugo Bosco, Springfield, 1964-65, Boise Cascade, Springfield, 1965-68, Robbins & Myers, Springfield, 1968-70, Wm. Bayley Co., Springfield, 1970-73, Frigidaire, Dayton, Ohio, 1973-78; sr. lab. prep. specialist Alpha Therapeutics, L.A., 1979—. With Air Nat. Guard, 1963-68. Mem. Mamie Van Doren Fan Club (pres. 1986—). Home: 8340 Rush St Rosemead CA 91770-3617

DOYLE, JACK DAVID, microbial ecologist; b. Bisbee, Ariz., Aug. 9, 1952; s. Jack Delmont Doyle and Betty Mae Hossler Embrey; m. Sandra Lee Hartwell, Dec. 24, 1972 (div. 1979); m. Suzannah Leigh Pratt, Jan. 20, 1990; children: Ariana Yoryhn (dec.), Rylan Cai; 1 stepchild, Lyris Kyla Cooper. AA, Cochise Coll., Douglas, Ariz., 1972; BS, U. Ariz., 1976, MS, 1981, PhD, 1985. With J.C. Penney Co., Bisbee and Tucson, Ariz., 1970-73; nurse tech. St. Mary's Hosp., Tucson, 1973-80; rsch. asst. II U. Ariz., Tucson, 1980-81, assoc. investigator, 1981-83, rsch. asst. III, 1984-85, rsch. assoc., 1985-87; assoc. rsch. scientist NYU, 1987-89; project scientist ManTech Environ. Tech., Inc., Corvallis, Oreg., 1989—; cons. Dames & Moore, Phoenix, 1986; part-time faculty Linn-Benton Community Coll., Albany, Oreg., 1990-93. Editor Fertility Awareness Svcs., Corvallis, 1989-92; contbr. articles to profl. jours. Vol. Project Literacy PLUS, Tucson, 1987. U. Ariz. resident acad. scholar, 1972-73, grad. acad. scholar, 1983-85. Mem. Am. Soc. Agronomy, Am. Soc. Microbiology, Internat. Soc. Soil Sci., Internat. Assn. Water Pollution Rsch. and Control, Soil Ecology Soc., Soil Sci. Soc. Am., Williamette Kayak & Canoe Club (ad hoc mem. exec. bd.), Sigma Xi. Democrat. Office: ManTech Environ Tech 200 SW 35th St Corvallis OR 97333

DOYLE, MICHAEL JAMES, educational administrator, organist; b. Bell, Calif., Aug. 24, 1939; s. Joseph Edward and Irma Louise (Smith) D.; m. Mina Katherine Martensen, Feb. 8, 1964; children: Michael James II, Mary Katherine, Matthew John. BA, Whittier Coll., 1961, MEd, 1971. Tchr. El Rancho Unified Sch. Dist., Pico Rivera, Calif., 1961-79, dept. chmn., 1967-74, acting prin., 1979; tchr., asst. prin. Alta Loma (Calif.) Sch. Dist., 1979-86, summer sch. prin., 1985, prin., 1986—; organist, dir. various Luth. chs. in So. Calif., 1955-86; organist St. Paul's Luth. Ch., Pomona, Calif., 1986—; mem. Calif. State Program Rev., 1982-83; assoc. mem. Calif. Sch. Leadership Acad., Ontario, 1986—; v.p. So. Calif. Luth. Music Clinic, 1978-81. Clk. Zion. Luth. Sch. Bd. Edn., Maywood, Calif., 1962-64, chmn., 1966-67; mem. Downey (Calif.) City Water Bd., 1977-78; mem. Luth. High Personnel Commn., La Verne, Calif., 1988—. Named Outstanding Tchr. of Yr., Burke Jr. High Sch. PTA, Pico Rivera, 1973; recipient hon. svc. award Jasper Sch. PTA, Alta Loma, 1983, continuing svc. award, 1988; employee recognition award Alta Loma Sch. Dist., 1985. Mem. Assn. Calif. Sch. Adminstrs., Assn. West End Sch. Adminstrs., Calif. Tchrs. Assn., Am. Guild ORganists, Downey Hist. Soc., Cucamonga Hist. Soc., Casa de Rancho (Cucamonga, Calif.), Phi Delta Kappa (pres. Mt. Baldy chpt. 1993, found. chmn. 1991-93). Democrat. Lutheran. Home: 2085 N Palm Ave Upland CA 91786-1476 Office: Jasper Sch 6881 Jasper St Alta Loma CA 91701

DOYLE, MICHAEL NORBERT, training consultant, business owner; b. Vancouver, B.C., Can., Apr. 27, 1948; s. Francis Anthony and Genevieve Rose (Daly) D.; m. Barbara Elizabeth Harris, Oct. 16, 1970 (div. Dec. 1987); children: Judith, Aidan, Stephen. BA, U. B.C., 1973; MEd, U. Victoria, B.C., 1982. Cert. tchr., B.C., 1975. Tchr. Maple Ridge (B.C.) Sch. Dist., 1975-79; coll. adminstr. Camosun Coll., Victoria, 1980-85; tng. cons., pres. Doyle Tng. Ltd. and Doyle Tng. Co., Victoria, B.C. and Everett, Wash., 1986—. Pub. Developing Training Manuals, 1991. Mem. Am. Soc. Tng. and Devel., Tng. and Devel. Soc. B.C. (v.p., mem. svcs. 1991-92), Inst. Cert. Mgmt. Consultants B.C. Office: Doyle Tng Co 1812 Hewitt Ave Everett WA 98201

DOYLE, PETER THOMAS, accountant, realtor; b. Chgo., Nov. 22, 1928; s. Peter Vincent and Elizabeth Mary (Maguire) D.; m. Mary Leontina Ulrath, Jan. 17, 1953. BA in Acctg. cum laude, Claremont McKenna Coll., 1955; postgrad., UCLA, 1962-63. CPA, Calif.; realtor, Calif. Staff auditor Price Waterhouse & Co., L.A., 1955-59; asst. treas. Pardee Contrn. Co., L.A., 1959-64; treas. Provident Mortgage Corp., Pasadena, Calif., 1964-67; contr. William L. Pereira Assocs., L.A., 1967-72, Hosp. of Good Saaritan, L.A., 1972-73; contr., treas. ArchiSystems Internat., Van Nuys, Calif., 1973-79; v.p., fin., dir. McClellan/Cruz/Gaylord & Assocs., Inc., Pasadena, 1979-85; v.p., sec. dir. Doyle Properties, Inc., 1975—; dir. Brandeis Constrn., Inc., Brandeis Property and Facilities Mgmt. Co., Inc., The Bannister Group, Romaine Devel. Corp. Bd. dirs. Sunset Mesa Property Owners Assn., 1973-75; mem. Town Hall Calif. With U.S. Army, 1946-48. Mem. AICPAs, Calif. Soc. CPAs, Nat. Assn. Accts., Calif. Assn. Realtors, Nat. Assn. Realtors, Simi Valley Bd. Realtors. Republican. Home: 3430 Cloudcroft Dr Malibu CA 90265-5632 Office: 10345 W Olympic Blvd Los Angeles CA 90064-2524

DOYLE, WILLIAM EDWARD, advertising professional; b. Hazel Green, Wis., Dec. 1, 1951; s. Bernard E. and Isabelle M. (Leahy) D.; m. Wendy Carol Prokosch, Sept. 5, 1986; children: Patrick Liam, Kevin Charles. BA, U. Wis., 1983. Media analyst Campbell-Mithun-Esty, Mpls., 1984-85, media planner, 1985-86; media supr. Young & Rubicam SF, San Francisco, 1986-89, v.p. assoc. media dir., 1989—. Office: Young & Rubicam SF 100 1st St San Francisco CA 94105

DOZIER, FLORA GRACE, civil and human rights activist, entrepreneur; b. Pineland, Tex., Apr. 5, 1937; d. Whitto G. and Agather (Price) Grace; m. Robert Alan Dozier, Dec. 16 1962 (div. Jan. 1967); 1 child, Martine Denise. AA in Real Estate, 1979; BA in Polit. Sci., Calif. State U., 1985. Various positions Fed. Civil Svc., 1964-84; real estate saleswoman, 1971-77. Author poems. Mem. Merritt Coll. Community Ctr. Literacy Task Force; bd. dirs. Black Cowboys Assn.; advisory bd. Nat. Youth Sports Program. Recipient Golden Poet award World of Poetry, 1992, Franam Scholarship for Black Women San Francisco State U., 1992-93. Mem. NAACP, NAFE, NCNW, Internat. Black Writers Assn., Ctr. for Black Concerns, Internat. Platform Assn., Oakland Black Writers Guild, Black United Front for Edn. Reform, Nat. Assn. of Black Reading and Lang. Educators (membership sec. Bay Area chpt.), Help Abolish Legal Tyranny. Democrat. Baptist. Home: 408-13th St Ste 437 Oakland CA 94612

DRACHNIK, CATHERINE MELDYN, art therapist; b. Kansas City, Mo., June 7, 1924; d. Gerald Willis and Edith (Gray) Weston; m. Joseph Brennan Drachnik, Oct. 6, 1946; children: Denise Elaine, Kenneth John. BS, U. Md., 1945; MA, Calif. State U., Sacramento, 1975. Lic. family and child counselor; registered art therapist. Art therapist Vincent Hall Retirement Home, McLean, Va., Fairfax Mental Health Day Treatment Ctr., McLean, Arlington (Va.) Mental Health Day Treatment Ctr., 1971-72, Hope for Retarded, San Jose, Calif., Sequoia Hosp., Redwood City, Calif., 1972-73; supervising tchr. adult edn. Sacramento Soc. Blind, 1975-77; ptnr. Sacramento Div. Mediation Svcs., 1981-82; instr. Calif. State U., Sacramento, 1975-82, Coll. Notre Dame, Belmont, Calif., 1975—; art therapist, mental health counselor Psych West Counseling Ctr. (formerly Eskaton Am. River Mental Health Clinic), Carmichael, Calif., 1975—; instr. U. Utah, Salt Lake City, 1988—; lectr. in field. One woman shows throughout Calif., East Coast and abroad; group juried shows in Calif. and Orient. Active various charitable orgns. Mem. Art Therapy Assn. (hon. life, pres. 1987-89), No. Calif. Art Therapy Assn. (hon. life), Calif. Coalition Rehab. Therapists, Nat. Art Edn. Assn., Am. Assn. Marriage and Family Therapists, Kappa Kappa Gamma Alumnae Assn. (pres. Sacramento Valley chpt. 1991-92), Alpha Psi Omega, Omicron Nu. Republican. Home: 4124 American River Dr Sacramento CA 95864-6025 Office: Psych West Counseling Ctr 6127 Fair Oaks Blvd Carmichael CA 95608-4818

DRAGGON, RODNEY WINSTON, minister; b. Conway, S.C., Sept. 13, 1956; s. Leonard and Anestine (Sumpter) D.; m. Linda Holmes, July 2, 1956; 1 child, Alesia. BA, Oakwood Coll., 1980; MA, Andrews U., 1984. Salesman S.W. Region Conf., Dallas, 1983-84; youth counselor Southeastern Conf., Riverside, Calif., 1984; pastor Cen. States Conf., Colorado Springs, 1985-86, Omaha, 1986-89; pastor Wash. Conf., Tacoma, 1989—; chmn. Youth for Drug Free, Tacoma, 1991-92, Tobacco Free Sch., Tacoma, 1992; bd. dirs. Nat. Com. for Prevention Alcoholism and Drug, Wash., 1992. Spokesperson Black Coalition Wash., Tacoma, 1991. Mem. Youth to Youth. Democrat. Seventh Day Adventist. Home: 517 190 Shot Ct E Spanaway WA 98387-8364

DRAGON, WILLIAM, JR., footwear and apparel company executive; b. Lynn, Mass., Dec. 1, 1942; s. William and Anne (Stavru) D.; m. Suzanne Gail Behlmer, Feb. 24, 1968; children: Todd Christopher, Heather Anne. B.S. in Engring. Mgmt., Norwich U., Northfield, Vt., 1964; M.S. in Mgmt. Scis., Rensselaer Poly. Inst., Troy, N.Y., 1965. With mfg., sales and mktg. staff Gen. Electric Co., Mass. and Ky., 1967-73; dir. product planning and design Samsonite div. Beatrice Corp., Denver, 1973-75, dir. mktg. Samsonite div., 1975-78; v.p. mktg. and sales Buxton div. Beatrice Corp., Springfield, Mass., 1978-81; gen. mgr. Johnston & Murphy Div. Genesco Inc., Nashville, 1981-85, exec. v.p., pres. U.S. Footwear Group, 1985-88, also dir.; pres. Avia Group Internat. Inc., Portland, Oreg., 1989-92. Promotion Products Inc., Portland, 1992—; dir. Deja, Inc., Portland, 1993-. Bd. dirs. Nashville Youth Hockey League, 1983-85, Two/Ten Charity Found., 1988—; vice-chmn. Nashville United Way, 1985; mem. men's adv. bd. Cumberland Valley council Girl Scouts U.S.A., 1985-86; mem. adminstrv. bd. Brentwood United Meth. Ch., 1986. Served to 1st lt. U.S. Army, 1965-67, Vietnam. Decorated Bronze Star medal. Recipient Superior Achievement Recognition award Genesco Inc., 1984. Methodist.

DRAGUTSKY, HOWARD WILLIAM, estate planner; b. Bklyn., Apr. 18, 1941; s. Joseph and Marcia (Kramer) D.; m. Paula Alpren, Dec. 1, 1968 (div. Feb. 1978); 1 child, Nancy Gayle; m. Judith Anne Iger, May 7, 1978; children: Lauren Jane, Jordan Neil. AB in History, Boston U., 1962, LLM in Taxation, 1966; JD, Fordham U., 1965. Bar: N.Y. 1966, Calif. 1992; CPA, Calif., N.Y.; lic. life ins. agt., Calif., N.Y., Fla. Jr. acct., sr. acct. Haskins & Sells, N.Y.C., 1966-69; tax supr. Clarence Rainess & Co., N.Y.C., 1969-72; tax mgr. Friedman, Alpren & Green, N.Y.C., 1972-74; tax ptnr. Weber, Lipshie & Co., N.Y.C., 1974-78, Rashba & Pokart, N.Y.C., 1979-84, Edward Isaacs & Co., N.Y.C., 1984-85, Weber, Lipshie & Co., Beverly Hills, Calif., 1985-90; estate planner L.A., 1990—. Officer, bd. trustees Park Ave. Synagogue, N.Y.C., 1974-81; mem. budget and fin. com. Stephen S. Wise Temple, L.A., 1987—; bd. dirs. Fashion Industries Guild Cedars Sinai Med. Ctr., 1986—. Jewish. Office: Ste 500 1901 Ave of the Stars Los Angeles CA 90067

DRAKE, DAVID ANDERSON, electrical engineer, business analyst; b. Paterson, N.J., June 27, 1952; s. William Martin and Doris (Anderson) D.; m. Virginia Irene Pighetti, Feb. 26, 1984. BSEE, Calif. Inst. Tech., 1974. Staff engr. Jet Propulsion Lab., Pasadena, Calif., 1974-79; mem. advanced tech. group Oak Industries, Rancho Bernardo, Calif., 1979-81; mgr. engring. Oak Adec Inc., Santa Ana, Calif., 1981-85; bus. cons. Digital Equipment Corp., San Diego, 1985-93. Patentee in field. Planning commr. City Escondido, Calif., 1988-93; bd. dirs. San Diego County Water Authority, 1989-93. Soc. Exptl. Test Pilots scholar, 1971-74. Mem. AAAS, IEEE (1st Pl. Nat. Design award 1976), EE Times, Planetary Soc. Home: 3019 Hypoint Ave Escondido CA 92027 Office: Digital Equipment Co 5471 Kearny Villa Rd San Diego CA 92123

DRAKE, E MAYLON, college chancellor; b. Nampa, Idaho, Feb. 8, 1920; s. Austin Henry and Daisy Naomi (Smith) D.; m. Lois Elloise Noble, Oct. 12, 1940; children: E. Christopher, Cameron Lee. BS, U. So. Calif., Los Angeles, 1951, MS, 1954, EdD, 1963. Mgr. Frederick Post Co., San Francisco, 1943-47; asst. supt. Baldwin Park (Calif.) Schs., 1947-51; supt. Duarte (Calif.) Schs., 1951-64, Alhambra (Calif.) City Schs., 1964-70; dep. supt. Los Angeles County Schs., 1970-78; dir. Acad. Ednl. Mgmt., Los Angeles, 1978-80; pres. L.A. Coll. Chiropractic, Whittier, 1980-90, chancellor, 1990-93, chancellor emeritus, 1993—; adj. prof. U. So. Calif., 1964-90, bd. councilors, 1991—. Author Attaining Accountability in Schools, 1972; contbr. articles to profl. jours. Pres. Industry-Ednl. Council So. Calif., 1978; dir. United Way 1970; dir. Greater Los Angeles Zoo Bd., 1970. Recipient Am. Educator's medal Freedom Found.; named Educator of Yr. Los Angeles Chiropratic Soc., 1981. Mem. Coun. on Chiropractic Edn. (pres. 1988-90), Rotary (pres. Duarte 1954-56, bd. dirs. Alhambra 1964-70). Republican. Presbyterian. Home: Brookview 83 1201 Monument Blvd Concord CA 94520 Office: LA Coll Chiropractic 16200 E Amber Valley Dr B 1166 Whittier CA 90609-1166

DRAKE, FRANK DONALD, astronomy educator; b. Chgo., May 28, 1930; s. Richard Carvel and Winifred (Thompson) D.; m. Elizabeth Bell, Mar. 7, 1953 (div. 1977); children: Stephen, Richard, Paul; m. Amahl Zekin Shakhashiri, Mar. 4, 1978; children: Nadia, Leila. B in Engring. Physics, Cornell U., 1952; MA in Astronomy, Harvard U., 1956, PhD in Astronomy, 1958. Astronomer Nat. Radio Astron. Obs., Green Bank, W.Va., 1958-63; sect. chief Jet Propulsion Lab., Pasadena, Calif., 1963-64; prof. Cornell U., Ithaca, N.Y., 1964-84; dir. Nat. Astron. and Ionospace Ctr., Ithaca, 1971-81; dean natural sci. dept. U. Calif., Santa Cruz, 1984-88, prof., 1984—. Author: Intelligent Life in Space, 1962, Murmurs of Earth, 1978, Is Anyone Out There, The Scientific Search for Extraterrestrial Intelligence, 1992. Lt. USN, 1947-55. Fellow AAAS, Am. Acad. Arts and Scis.; mem. Nat. Acad. Scis., Internat. Astron. Union (chair U.S. nat. com.), Astron. Soc. Pacific (pres. 1988-90), Seti Inst. (pres. 1984—). Office: U Calif Obs Santa Cruz CA 95064

DRAKE, HAROLD ALLEN, history educator; b. Cin., July 24, 1942; s. Morris N. and Mollie N. (Cooperstein) D.; mn. Kathleen Ann Senica, May 31, 1969; children: Susan Jennifer, Katherine Jessica. AB, U. So. Calif., L.A., 1963; MA, U. Wis., 1966, U. Wis., 1969; PhD, U. Wis., 1970. Staff reporter UPI, L.A., 1962-65; teaching asst. U. Wis., Madison, 1965-68; lectr. U. Calif., Santa Barbara, 1970-71, asst. prof., 1971-76, assoc. prof., 1977-82, prof. history, 1982—, chmn. dept., 1987-90; NEH fellow Inst. Advanced Study, Princeton, N.J., 1976-77; fellow Annenberg Rsch. Inst., Phila., 1991-92. Author: In Praise of Constantine, 1976; co-author: Eudoxia & the Holy Sepulchre, 1980; editor for Roman history Classical Antiquity, Berkeley, 1986—. Ford fellow U. Wis., 1968-69; Annenberg Rsch. Inst. fellow, 1991-92. Mem. Calif. Lambda, Phi Beta Kappa (pres. 1986-88), Phi Alpha Theta (internat. councillor 1982-84), Phi Kappa Phi, Sigma Delta Chi. Democrat. Roman Catholic. Home: 423 Los Verdes Dr Santa Barbara CA 93111-1505 Office: U Calif Dept History Santa Barbara CA 93106-9410

DRAKE, LUCIUS CHARLES, JR., school administrator, university consultant; b. Tacloban, Philippines, June 29, 1946; s. Lucius Charles and Victoria (Badiles) D. BA, Fisk U., 1968; EdM, Temple U., 1970. Cert. sch. adminstr.; cert. guidance counselor. Math. tchr. Sch. Dist. of Phila., 1968-70, Gary (Ind.) City Schs., 1970-72, Dept. Defense Dependents Sch., Fed. Republic Germany and Okinawa, 1972-77; elemtary tchr. Dept. Defense Dependents Sch., Philippines, 1977-79; guidance counselor Dept. Defense Dependents Sch., Japan and Korea, 1979-83; asst. prin. Dept. Defense Dependents Sch., Seoul and Taegu, Korea, 1983-886; univ. cons. U. No. Colo., 1988-89; employment counselor Ft. Collins, Colo., 1989-90; asst. prin. Misawa, Japan, 1990-91, Philippines, 1991-92; chmn. math dept. Sayre Jr. High Sch., Phila., 1969-70; math. curriculum rev. com., Dept. Defense Dependents Schs., Karlsruhe, Fed. Republic Germany, 1972-73; dir. Far East Basketball Tourney, Taegu, Korea, 1984-86; mem. regional mgmt. council, Dept. Defense Dependents Schs., Okinawa, 1985-86. Chairperson human rels. commn. Ft. Collins City Coun., 1990. Recipient Disting. Educator award IDEA Acad. Fellows, Denver, 1985. Fellow Am. Bd. Master Educators (disting.); mem. ASCD, Assn. Am. Sch. Adminstrs., Nat. Assn. Secondary Sch. Prins., Nat. Assn. Elem. Sch. Prins., Internat. Educator's Inst., Phi Delta Kappa, Alpha Phi Alpha (edn. sec. Seoul chpt. 1984-85). Democrat. Baptist. Home: 3318 Hickok Dr Unit B Fort Collins CO 80526-2502 Office: Bob Hope Primary Sch APO AP 96368-0005

DRAKE, ROBERT ARTHUR, packaging executive; b. Rochester, N.Y., Dec. 20, 1924; s. Claude Howell and Clara (Doser) D.; B.S. in Mech. Engring., Purdue U., 1948; postgrad. in Bus. Law, Shurtcliff Coll., 1950; postgrad. in Bus. Adminstrn., A. Hamilton Inst., 1953; Ph.D. in Mech. Engring., Southwestern U., 1982; m. Marjorie Steck, Oct. 27, 1945; children—Linda Sue, Deborah Lisa Drake Hoglund. Research and devel. engr., mgr. Olin Mathieson Corp., East Alton, Ill., 1948-55; research and devel. mgr., asst. plant mgr., plant mgr. Ball Bros. Co., Muncie, Ind., 1955-63; planning and design engr. Del Monte Corp., San Francisco, 1963-65; new product mgr., facility mgr., gen. factories mgr. internat. Owens-Ill., U.S., Eng., Can., 1965-71; gen. factories mgr. Chattanooga Glass, 1971-73; mgr. engring. Anchor Hocking, Lancaster, Ohio, 1973-77; v.p. tech. Glass Packaging Inst., Washington, 1977-84; pres. D and A Inc., 1983—; pres. Glass Tech. Inst., 1984—; cons. on glass industry. Pres. PTA, Muncie, 1957-59; chmn. United Fund, Mundelein, 1960-63, zoning commr., 1960-63. Served with USNR, 1941-46. Recipient leadership award Am. Mgmt. Assn., 1973, award Sales Analysis Inst., 1976. Mem. Air Pollution Control Assn., Glass and Ceramic Soc., ASME, Brit. Light Aircraft Pilots Assn. Republican. Methodist. Clubs: Westwood Country, Masons, Blue Lodge, Shrine. Contbr. chpt. to textbook, writings in field to profl. publs.; speaker, expert witness in field; govt. regulations expert.

DRAY, TEVIAN, mathematics educator; b. Washington, Mar. 17, 1956; s. Sheldon and Margaret D.; m. Corinne Alison Manogue, Mar. 29, 1986; children: Alyssa Whitby Manogue Dray, Colan Skye Manogue Dray. BS in Math., MIT, 1976; MA in Math., U. Calif., Berkeley, 1977, PhD in Math., 1981. Tutor Inst. für Theorie der Elementarteilchen Freie Universität Berlin, 1981-83; wetenschappelijk medewerker Inst. voor Theoretische Fysica Rijksuniversiteit Utrecht, The Netherlands, 1984-85; mem. sch. math. Inst. for Advanced Study, Princeton, N.J., 1984-85; rsch. fellow dept. math. Univ. of York, U.K., 1986-87; asst. prof. dept. math. Oreg. State U., Corvallis, 1988-90, assoc. prof., 1990—; sr. mem. Math Scis. Rsch. Inst., Berkeley, 1991. Contbr. articles to profl. jours. NATO postdoctoral fellow, Berlin, 1982-83, Indo-U.S. fellow Coun. Internat. Exch. of Scholars, Washington, Madras and Bombay, 1987-88; Stipendiat Deutscher Akademischer Austauschdienst, Bonn, Munich, 1978-79. Mem. Am. Math. Soc., London Math. Soc., Internat. Soc. Gen. Relativitiy an Gravitation, Indian Assn. Gen. Relativity and Gravitation. Office: Oreg State Univ Dept Math Corvallis OR 97331

DRAZNIN, JULES NATHAN, journalism and public relations educator, consultant; b. Chgo., May 14, 1923; s. Charles G. and Goldie (Malach) D.; m. Shirley Bernstein, Apr. 9, 1950; children: Dean, Jody, Michael. Student, Wright City Coll., Chgo., 1941; BA in Journalism, Calif. State U., Northridge, 1978, MA in Higher Edn., 1984. Various journalism positions Chgo., 1941; with promotions & publicity Balaban & Katz Theaters, Chgo., 1941-43; asst. dir pub. rels. Combined Jewish Appeal, Chgo., 1944; prin. J.N. Draznin Assocs., Chgo., 1945-50; account supr. Olian & Bronner Advt. Agy., Chgo., 1951-53; dir. advt. Chgo. Defender Robert S. Abbott Pub. Co., 1953-55; freelance cons. Chgo., 1955-60; pub. rels. dir. Abel and Lamensdorf Properties, Chgo., 1960-62; editor-in-chief, assoc. pub. Indsl. News Bender Publs., Calif., 1962-64; labor editor, spl. features writer Valley News and Green Sheet, Calif., 1964; ind. ins. agt. Calif., 1965-74; tch. pub. rels. UCLA and Calif. State U., L.A.; prof. journalism & pub. rels. L.A. Trade Tech. Coll., 1976—; chair lang. arts dept., 1984-90; tchr. journalism & pub. rels. L.A. City Coll., L.A. Pierce Coll., L.A. Southwest Coll., East L.A. Coll., L.A. Mission Coll.; guest lectr. Calif. State U., Northridge. Mem. Assn. for Edn. in Journalism and Mass Communication, Soc. Profl. Journalists. Office: LA Trade Tech Coll 400 W Washington Blvd Los Angeles CA 90015

DREA, EDWARD JOSEPH, pharmacist; b. Springfield, Ill., Jan. 24, 1954; s. Edward Francis and Doris Mae (Reynolds) D.; m. Lori Ann Urban, Dec. 6, 1985; children: Brandon Christopher, Bradley Joseph. BS in Pharmacy, U. Iowa, 1977, D in Pharmacy, 1986. Pharmacist The Pharmacy, Taylorville, Ill., 1977-84; rsch. assoc. U. Iowa Coll. Pharmacy and Medicine, Iowa City, 1985-86; dir. pharmacy St. Vincent Meml. Hosp., Taylorville, 1986-88; coord. clin. svcs. Meml. Med. Ctr., Springfield, Ill., 1988-92; asst. clin. prof. U. Ill. Coll. Pharmacy, Chgo., 1990-92; dir. clin. pharmacy svcs. CIGNA Healthplan Ariz., Phoenix, 1992—, HPI Health Care Svcs., Inc., 1992—; cons., Phoenix, 1990—. Assoc. editor book, 1990. Rsch. grantee The Uphjohn Co., 1988, Schering/Key Pharms, 1990, Xoma Corp., 1990. Mem. Am. Coll. Clin. Pharmacy, Am. Soc. Hosp. Pharmacists, Am. Pharm. Assn., Ill. Pharmacists Assn., Ariz. Pharmacy Assn., Acad. Managed Care Pharmacy. Home: 15613 N 7th Dr Phoenix AZ 85023 Office: CIGNA Healthplan Ariz 8826 N 23d Ave Phoenix AZ 85021

DRECHSEL, EDWIN JARED, retired magazine editor; b. Bremen, Germany, Apr. 17, 1914; came to U.S., 1924, naturalized, 1935; s. William A. and Estelle Laura D.; m. Ilona Bolya, Aug. 12, 1972; children: John M., Barbara A. Grad., Dartmouth Coll., Amos Tuck Sch. Bus. Adminstrn., 1936. With Standard Oil Co., N.J., 1936-43; with U.S. News and World Report, 1943-79; regional editor, editorial ombudsman U.S. News and World Report, San Francisco, 1976-79. Author shipping company histories and fleet lists, catalogs of ship mail postal markings, including A Century of German Ship Posts, 1886-1986, 1987, Norddeutscher Lloyd, Bremen 1857-1970. Former chmn. Reed Sch. Bd., Marin County, Calif.; lay reader, former vestryman St. Stephen's Episcopal Ch., Belvedere, Calif., former mayor, City of Belvedere. Club: San Francisco Press. Home: 170 Hillcrest Rd Berkeley CA 94705-2846

DRECHSLER, RANDALL RICHARD, resort management company executive; b. Red Bank, N.J., Dec. 17, 1945; s. John Henry and Maura (Turner) D.; m. Roxanne Pinkerton, Dec. 22, 1984; children: Courtney Autumn, Whitney Anne. Student, UCLA, 1963-64, Calif. State U., Northridge, 1964-68, San Fernando Coll. Law, 1968-69. Asst. v.p. Gt. Western Cities, Inc., L.A., 1968-72; pres., owner Internat. Registration Svc., Denver, 1972-73, R.D. Whitcor, Inc., Reno, 1984—; exec. v.p. R.J.B. Devel. Co., Reno, 1973-89; pres. Plaza Resort Club, Inc., Reno, 1980-83; chief exec. officer, owner Bosley/Turner/Finch Advt., Reno, 1984-89; pres., bd. dirs. Plaza Resort Club Assocs., Reno, 1980— ; expert witness various bankruptcy cases, Las Vegas, Nev., 1988-89; v.p. Vacation Resorts Internat., Laguna Hills, Calif., 1989—. Staff mem. Robert F. Kennedy Presdl. Campaign Com., Washington, 1968. Mem. Am. Resort Devel. Assn., Resort Condominiums Internat., Aircraft Ownes and Pilots Assn., greater Reno C. of C., Reno Flying Club. Democrat. Home: 26591 Via Manolete Mission Viejo CA 92691 Office: Vacation Resorts Internat 23212 Mill Creek Dr Laguna Hills CA 92653

DRECHSLER-PARKS, DEBORAH MARIE, research physiologist; b. Lakewood, Ohio, Apr. 27, 1952; d. Albert Carl and Dorothea Marie (Angersbach) Drechsler; m. Edward Parks, Oct. 29, 1983. AB, Westmont Coll., 1974; MA, U. Calif., Santa Barbara, 1976; PhD, Pa. State U., 1981. Postdoctoral fellow U. Calif., Santa Barbara, 1981-85, asst. research physiologist, 1985-91, assoc. rsch. physiologist, 1991—. Contbr. articles to publs. Bd. dirs. Santa Barbara Chpt. Am. Heart Assn., 1991—. Health Effects Inst. grantee, 1983-85, EPA grantee, 1986-89, NIH grantee, 1991—. Mem. AAAS, N.Y. Acad. Scis., Am. Physiol. Soc., Air and Waste Mgmt. Assn. Orthodox Presbyterian. Office: U Calif Neuroscience Rsch Inst Santa Barbara CA 93106-5060

DREIER, DAVID TIMOTHY, congressman; b. Kansas City, Mo., July 5, 1952; s. H. Edward and Joyce (Yeomans) D. BA cum laude, Claremont McKenna Coll., 1975; MA in Am. Govt., Claremont Grad. Sch., 1976. Dir. corp. rels. Claremont McKenna Coll., 1975-78; dir. mktg. and govt. rels. Indsl. Hydrocarbons, San Dimas, Calif., 1978-80; mem 97th-103rd Congresses from 33rd (now 28th) Calif. dist., 1980—; v.p. Dreier Devel. Co., Kansas City, Mo., 1985—; mem. rules com., ranking Rep. rules of the house subcom., chmn. task force on fgn. policy, mem. task force on POW/MIAs; mem. spl. task force on the devel. of parliamentary instns.; mem. U.S.-Mex. Interparliamentary Caucus; bd. dirs. Nat. Rep. Inst. for Internat. Affairs, Internat. Rep. Inst.; vice co-chmn. joint com. on orgn. of Congress; vice chmn. GOP Calif. Congl. Del.; asst. regional whip; mem. task force on fed. mandates. Recipient Golden Bulldog award Watchdogs of the Treasury, 1981-92, Taxpayers Friends award Nat. Taxpayers Union, 1981-92, Clean Air Champion award Sierra Club, 1988. Office: US Congress House of Representatives Washington DC 20515

DREISBACH, JOHN GUSTAVE, investment banker; b. Paterson, N.J., Apr. 24, 1939; s. Gustave John and Rose Catherine (Koehler) D.; m. Janice Lynn Petitjean; children: John Gustave Jr., Cassandra Michelle, Niklas Philip, Christopher Erik. BA, NYU, 1963. With Shields & Co., Inc., 1965-68, Model, Roland & Co., Inc., N.Y.C., 1968-72, F. Eberstadt & Co., Inc., N.Y.C., 1972-74; v.p. Bessemer Trust Co., 1974-78; pres. Community Housing Capital, Inc., 1978-80; chmn., pres. John G. Dreisbach, Inc., Santa Fe, N.Mex., 1980—; JGD Housing Corp., 1982—; bd. dirs., pres. The Santa Fe Investment Conf., 1986—; assoc. Sta. KNME-TV; active U. N.Mex. Anderson Schs. Mgmt. Affiliate Program. Mem. Santa Fe Community Devel. Commn. Served with USAFR, 1964. Mem. Internat. Assn. for Fin. Planning, NYU Alumni Assn., Venture Capital Club N.Mex., N.Mex. First, Friends of Vieilles Maisons Francaises Inc., NYU Alumni Assn., Mensa, Santa Fe C. of C. Republican. Episcopalian. Clubs: St. Bartholomew's Community, Essex, Hartford, Amigos del Alcalde. Home: 730 Camino Cabra Santa Fe NM 87501-5924 Office: 1800 Old Pecos Trail Ste O Santa Fe NM 87501-4759

DRELL, SIDNEY DAVID, physicist, educator; b. Atlantic City, N.J., Sept. 13, 1926; s. Tulla and Rose (White) D.; m. Harriet Stainback, Mar. 22, 1952; children: Daniel White, Persis Sydney, Joanna Harriet. AB, Princeton U., 1946; MA, U. Ill., 1947, PhD, 1949, DSc (hon.), 1981. Rsch. assoc. U. Ill., 1949-50; instr. physics Stanford U., 1950-52, assoc. prof., 1956-60, prof., 1960-63, Lewis M. Terman prof. and fellow, 1979-84; co-dir. Stanford U. Ctr. for Internat. Security and Arms Control, 1983-89; prof. Stanford Linear Accelerator Ctr., 1963—, dep. dir., 1969—, exec. head theoretical physics, 1969-86; research assoc. MIT, 1952-53, asst. prof., 1953-56, adv. bd. Lincoln Lab., 1985-90; vis. scientist Guggenheim fellow CERN Lab., Switzerland, 1961, U. Rome, 1972; vis. prof., Loeb lectr. Harvard U., 1962, 70; vis. Schrodinger prof. theoretical physics U. Vienna, 1975; cons. Office Sci. and Tech., 1960-73, Office Sci. and Tech. Policy, 1977-82, ACDA, 1969-81, Office Tech. Assessment U.S. Congress, 1975-91, House Armed Svcs. Com., 1990—, Senate Select Com. on Intelligence, 1990—, NSC, 1973-81; mem. high energy physics adv. panel Dept. Energy, 1973-86, chmn., 1974-82, mem. energy rsch. adv. bd., 1978-80; mem. Jason, 1960—; Richtmyer lectr. to Am. Assn. Physics Tchrs., San Francisco, 1978; vis. fellow All Souls Coll., Oxford, 1979; Danz lectr. U. Wash., 1983, Hans Bethe lectr. Cornell U., 1988; I.I. Rabi vis. prof. Columbia U., 1984; mem. Carnegie Commn. on Sci., Tech. and Govt., 1988—; chmn. U.C. pres. coun. on nat. labs., 1992—; chmn. internat. adv. bd. Inst. Global Conflict and Cooperation, U. Calif., 1990—; adj. prof. engring., pub. policy Carnegie Mellon U., 1989—. Author 6 books; contbr. articles to profl. jours. Trustee Inst. Advanced Study, Princeton, 1974-83; bd. govs. Weizmann Inst. Sci., Rehovoth, Israel, 1970—; bd. dirs. Ann. Revs., Inc., 1976—; mem. Pres. Sci. Adv. Com., 1966-70. Recipient Ernest Orlando Lawrence Meml. award and medal for research in theoretical physics AEC, 1972, Alumni award for distinguished service in engring. U. Ill., 1973, Alumni Achievement award, 1988; MacArthur fellow, 1984-89. Fellow Am. Phys. Soc. (pres. 1986, Leo Szilard award for physics in the public interest 1980); mem. Nat. Acad. Scis., Am. Acad. Arts and Scis. (Hilliard Roderick Prize in Sci., Arms Control, Internat. Security, 1993), Am. Philo. Soc., Arms Control Assn. (bd. dirs. 1978—), Council on Fgn. Relations, Aspen Strategy Group (emeritus 1991). Home: 570 Alvarado Row Palo Alto CA 94305-8501 Office: Stanford Linear Accelerator Ctr PO Box 4349 Palo Alto CA 94309-4349

DRENNAN, MICHAEL ELDON, banker; b. Yakima, Wash., June 24, 1946; s. George Eldon and Jane (Nilsson) D.; m. Alice Marie Seabolt, May 13, 1972; children: Brian, David. BS in Fin., U. Oreg., 1968; grad., Pacific Coast Banking Sch. U. Wash., 1981. Ops. officer First State Bank, Aloha, Oreg., 1972-73; ops., loan officer First State Bank, Portland, Oreg., 1973-74; asst. mgr. First State Bank, Milwaukie, Oreg., 1974-76; asst. v.p. Citizens Bank, Corvallis, Oreg., 1976-80, v.p., 1980-81; pres., chief exec. officer Bank of Corvallis, 1981-87; v.p. dist. mgr. U.S. Bank, Corvallis, Oreg., 1987; sr. v.p. market area mgr. U.S. Bank, Bend, Oreg., 1988—; bd. dirs. Cascades W. Fin. Svcs. Bd. dirs. United Way Benton County, 1984-88; trustee Good Samaritan Hosp. Found., 1984-88; bd. dirs. Jr. Achievement of Benton County, 1983-85, treas. 1984-85, mem. exec. bd., 1984-85; mem. budget comm. Corvallis Sch. Dist., 1987; bd. dirs. Benton County Family YMCA, 1978-80, sec. 1979, mem. fin. com., 1978-80, mem. personnel com. 1979, active sustaining membership dr.; bd. dirs. Community Club, 1978-83, pres., 1978, treas. 1979-80; active Corvallis Ambassadors, 1976-88; mem. mgmt. com. Corvallis Conv. and Vis. Bur., 1982-85; fund. raising chmn. Com. City Improvemnt Levy, 1980; mem. exec. com. Pack 17 Boy Scouts Am., 1984-87, treas. 1984-87; mem. adv. bd. Cen. Oreg. Econ. Devel. Corp., 1988-90, bd. dirs., exec. bd., treas., 1991-93, v.p., 1993—; bd. dirs. Regional Arts Coun. of Cen. Oreg., treas. 1989-92; bd. dirs. Cen. Oreg. Air Svc. Task Force, 1989—, chmn. airline rels. com., 1990; mem. Bend Bus. Assistance Team, 1989-90, United Way Deschutes county, chmn. Loaned exec. recruitment, 1992; mem. planning com. St. Charles Med. Ctr. Found., 1993, dir. adminstrn. capital fund drive, 1993—; mem. adv. bd. Deschutes County Fair, 1993—. Lt. USN, 1968-71. Named Jr. First Citizen, Corvallis, 1980. Mem. Bend C. of C. (chmn. mem. dir. task force 1988, chmn. mem. svcs. coun. 1989, chmn. chamber forums com. 1990, Outstanding Leadership award 1989), Corvallis C. of C. (v.p. fin. 1980-83, pres. 1985-86, chmn. bd. dirs. 1986-87, Econ. Devel. award 1978, Chmn. of Bd. award 1979, George award 1980-81, Devel. award 1983), Am. Inst. Banking (cert.), Rotary (bd. dirs. Corvallis club 1981-87, Bend 1988—), Chi Phi, Alpha Kappa Psi, Beta Gamma Sigma. Home: 21725 Eastmont Dr Bend OR 97701-9541 Office: US Bank PO Box 911 Bend OR 97709-0911

DRESKIN, STEPHEN CHARLES, immunologist; b. Chgo., Aug. 11, 1949; s. E. Arthur and Jeanet (Steckler) D.; m. June Inuzuka, May 8, 1982; children: Andrea T., Samuel M., Lauren F. BA, U. Pa., 1970; PhD, Emory U., 1975, MD, 1977. Diplomate Am. Bd. Internal Medicine. Intern U. Calif., Davis, 1977-78, resident, 1978-80; med. staff fellow NIH, Bethesda, Md., 1981-85; guest researcher NIH, 1985-87, expert, 1987-88; asst. prof. dept. immunology U. Colo. Health Scis. Ctr., Denver, 1989—. Contbr. articles to profl. jours. Recipient investigator award Arthritis Found., 1985-88, developing investigator award Gouroughs Wellcome Found., 1990—; rsch. grantee Arthritis Found., 1985-88, NIH, 1991—. Mem. Am. Acad. Allergy and Immunology, Am. Fedn. Clin. Investigation, AAAS. Office: Univ Colo Health Sci Ctr PO Box 164B Denver CO 80262-0001

DRESSER, JESSE DALE, real estate investor; b. San Diego, May 5, 1906; s. Charlwood Fessenden and Ora (Evans) D.; m. Mary A. Goldsworthy, June 9, 1934; children—Dennis T., Brian D., Linda A. Ed. pub. schs. Trainee Union Title Ins. Co., San Diego, 1926; sr. title examiner, chief title officer, v.p. So. Title & Trust Co., San Diego, 1937-51; v.p., chief title officer Security Title Ins. Co., San Diego, 1951-54; asst. to pres. San Diego Fed. Savs. & Loan Assn., 1954-55, v.p., sec., 1955-56, exec. v.p., dir., 1956-70; v.p., dir. Calif. Gen. Mortgage Service, Inc., 1967-70, San Diego Federated Ins. Agy., Inc., 1967-70; real estate investments La Mesa, Calif., 1970-86; ret., 1986. Home: 3833 Acacia Ave Bonita CA 91908-0418

DRESSER, MILES JOEL, physicist, educator; b. Spokane, Wash., Dec. 19, 1935; s. Lloyd Joel and Stella Christine (Nelson) D.; m. Muriel Louise Hunt, June 7, 1959; children: Don Joel, Marilyn Louise, Laura Jill. BA, Linfield Coll., 1957; PhD, Iowa State U., 1964. Research asst. Ames (Iowa) Lab. AEC, 1959-64; asst. prof. Wash. State U., Pullman, 1964-70, assoc. prof. physics, 1970-93, assoc. chair physics, 1993—; vis. physicist Nat. Bur. Standards, Washington, 1972, Pacific Northwest Labs., Batelle, Wash., 1991-93; vis. prof. physics U. Pitts., 1984-88—; mem. exec. council Wash. State U. Resident Instrs. Staff, 1983—; prof. short course Wash. State U., 1981-84. Contbr. articles to profl. jours. Bd. dirs. Pullman United Way, 1972-75, Common Ministry, Wash. Stte U., 1980-84, 90. Mem. Am. Phys. Soc., Am. Assn. Physics Tchrs. (pres.-elect Wash. sect. 1992-93), Am. Vacuum Soc., Pacific Northwest Assn. Coll. Physics (bd. dirs. 1991—), Sigma Xi. Baptist.

DRESSLER, ALAN MICHAEL, astronomer; b. Cin., Mar. 23, 1948; s. Charles and Gay (Stein) Dressler. BA in Physics, U. Calif., Berkeley, 1970; PhD in Astronomy, U. Calif., Santa Cruz, 1976. Carnegie Instn. of Washington fellow Hale Obs., Pasadena, Calif., 1976-78, Las Campanas fellow, 1978-81; mem. sci. staff Mt. Wilson and Las Campanas Obs. (formerly Hale Obs.), Pasadena, 1981—; acting assoc. dir. Obs. of Carnegie Instn. (formerly Mt. Wilson and Las Campanas Obs.), Pasadena, 1988-89. Contbr. to sci. jours. Fellow AAAS; mem. Am. Astron. Soc. (councilor 1989-91, Pierce prize 1983), Internat. Astron. Union. Office: Obs of Carnegie Inst 813 Santa Barbara St Pasadena CA 91101-1232

DREVER, RICHARD ALSTON, JR., consulting architect; b. Kearny, N.J., Feb. 9, 1936; s. Richard A. and Dorothy L. (Farrer) D.; m. Ellen M. Cornell, Dec. 21, 1957 (div. Oct. 1978); children—Richard A. III, Diana J., Beverly K.; m. Jane L. Cash, June 1, 1981. A.B., Columbia U., 1957, B.Arch., 1963, M.Arch., 1963. Registered architect, Calif., Alaska, Ariz., Nev., Nat. Council Archtl. Registration Bds. Intern, Frederick Frost & Assocs., N.Y.C., 1961, 63; with Allen-Drever-Lechowski, Architects, San Francisco, 1963-85, pres., 1983-85; cons. architect in pvt. practice, 1985—; officer, dir. Medos Corp., San Francisco, 1979-81. Author profl. articles. Bd. dirs. Tamalpais Community Services Dist., Marin County, Calif., 1970-75; mem. Tamalpais Parks and Recreation Commn., 1968-70. Lt. USNR, 1957-59. Mem. AIA, The Hosp. Forum (chmn. architects sect. 1983-84), The Forum for Health Care Planning. Home and Office: 314 Vista De Valle Mill Valley CA 94941-4017

DREW, CHARLES MILTON, chemist; b. McKinney, Tex., Feb. 13, 1921; s. Andrew Everett and Lutie Lella (Weger) D.; divorced; children: Darrell Everett, Donna Lee, Carl Allen. BS, U. Tex., 1943. Supr. chemist Columbia Southern, Corpus Christi, Tex., 1943-47; research scientist Naval Weapons Ctr., China Lake, Calif., 1947-70; cons. U. Ariz., Tucson, 1980—. Author: Principles of Gas Chromatography, 1959; contbr. articles to profl. jours.; patentee in field. Mem. Rsch. Soc. Am., Soaring Soc. Am., Colo. West Soaring Club, Glider Club (pres. China Lake, Calif. chpt. 1967-70), Rockhounds Club (pres. local chpt. 1949-50), Sigma Xi. Home: 1420 Walker View Rd Wellington NV 89444-9326 Office: Glass By Charles Parachute CO 81635

DREW, SHARON LEE, social worker; b. L.A., Aug. 11, 1946; d. Hal Bernard and Helen Elizabeth (Hammond) D.; children: Keith, Charmagne. BA, Calif. State U., Long Beach, 1983; postgrad., Calif. State U., Dominguez Hills, 1988—. Clerical support Compton (Calif.) Unified Sch. Dist., 1967-78; case worker L.A. County Dept. Pub. Social Svcs., 1978—. Den mother Boy Scouts Am., Compton, 1971-72; employee vol. Dominguez Sr. High Sch., Compton, 1972-73; project coord. Tomorrow-Parent Edn. Leadership Devel. Project, Compton, 1989-90. Recipient cert. Calif. tomorrow-Parent Edn. Leadership Devel. Project, 1990. Mem. Am. Statis. Assn. (so. Calif. chpt.), Internat. Soc. Teaching Alternatives, Calif. Sociological Assn. (1st gov. at large grad. students 1990-91), Dominguez Hills Gerontology Assn. (chairperson 1990-91), Sociology of Edn. Assn., Alpha Kappa Delta (Xi chpt. treas. 1992—). Home: 927 N Chester Ave Compton CA 90221-2105

DREXLER, CLYDE, professional basketball player; b. New Orleans, June 22, 1962. Student, U. Houston, 1980-83. Basketball player Portland (Oreg.) Trailblazers, 1983—; mem. U.S. Olympic Basketball Team (received Gold medal), 1992. Mem. NBA All-Star Team, 1986, 88-93; mem. all-NBA first team, 1992; mem. All-NBA second team, 1988, 91; mem. All-NBA third team, 1990. Office: Portland Trailblazers Lloyd Bldg 700 NE Multnomah St Ste 950 Portland OR 97232-4109

DREXLER, KENNETH, lawyer; b. San Francisco, Aug. 2, 1941; s. Fred and Martha Jane (Cunningham) D.; BA, Stanford U., 1963; JD, UCLA, 1969. Bar: Calif. 1970. Assoc., David S. Smith, Beverly Hills, Calif., 1970, McCutchen, Doyle, Brown and Enersen, San Francisco, 1970-77; assoc. Chickering & Gregory, San Francisco, 1977-80, ptnr., 1980-82; ptnr. Drexler & Leach, San Rafael, Calif., 1982—. Served with AUS, 1964-66. Mem. Calif. State Bar (resolutions com. conf. of dels. 1979-83, chmn. 1982-83, adminstrn. justice com. 1983-89, chmn. 1987-88), Marin County Bar Assn. (bd. dirs. 1985-87), Bar Assn. San Francisco (dir. 1980-81), San Francisco Barristers Club (pres. 1976, dir. 1975-76), Marin Conservation League (bd. dirs. 1985—). Office: 1330 Lincoln Ave Ste 300 San Rafael CA 94901-2143

DREXLER, KIM ERIC, researcher, author; b. Oakland, Calif., Apr. 25, 1955; s. Allan Barry and Hazel Edna (Gassmann) D.; m. Christine Louise Peterson, June 18, 1981. BS in Interdisciplinary Sci., MIT, 1977, MS in Engring., 1979, PhD in Molecular Nanotech., 1991. Researcher, author, lectr., inventor Cambridge, Mass., 1980-85; researcher, author, lectr., cons. Palo Alto, Calif., 1985—; rsch. affiliate MIT Space Lab, Cambridge, 1980-86, MIT Artificial Intelligence Lab, Cambridge, 1986-87; sr. rsch. fellow Inst. for Molecular Mfg., 1991—; vis. scholar Stanford (Calif.) U. Computer Sci. Dept., 1986-92; bd. dirs., pres. The Foresight Inst., Palo Alto, 1986—. Author: Engines of Creation, 1986, Nanosystems, 1992 (Assn. Am. Pubs. Best Computer Science Book, 1992); co-author: Unbounding the Future, 1991; contbr. articles to profl. jours.; inventor high performance solar sail, method for processing and fabricating metals in space. Sec. bd. dirs. L5 Soc., Tucson, 1981, bd. dirs., 1979-86, advisor, 1979-86, co-editor jour., 1983-84; bd. dirs. Nat. Space Soc., 1986—. Grad. fellow NSF, MIT, 1977; recipient Space Pioneer award for Scientist/Engr., Nat. Space Soc., 1991, Kilby Young Innovator award Kilby Found., Dallas, 1993. Mem. AAAS, Am. Assn. Artificial Intelligence, Am. Chem. Soc., Authors Guild. Office: The Foresight Inst PO Box 61058 Palo Alto CA 94306-6058

DREXLER, PAUL, multimedia director; b. N.Y.C., Dec. 8, 1947; s. Julien and Shirley (Stern) D.; m. Julie Marsh, Apr. 1988; children: Lily Marsh, Michelle Marsh. BS in Labor Rels., Cornell U., 1968. Owner Paul's Old Time Furniture, Amherst, Mass., 1972-78; owner, dir. Art Dreco Inst., San Francisco, 1979-81; pres. Drexler Communications, San Francisco, 1981-86; cons., writer-producer Apple Computer, Cupertino, Calif., 1987-88; tng. cons. Rolm Corp., Santa Clara, Calif., 1988-89; creative dir. The SoftAd Group, Sausalito, Calif., 1989—; ptnr. Drexler/Marsh Multimedia, 1990-91; prin. InterWorks, San Francisco, 1991—. Writer videotapes; contbr. articles to profl. jours. Bd. dirs. Mus. Moder Mythology, San Francisco, 1982-84, Unknown Mus., Mill Valley, 1984—, Art Dreco Inst., Amherst, Mass., San Francisco, 1978—. Mem. Internat. Interactive Communications Soc., Internat. TV Assn. (bd. dirs. 1987-88). Jewish. Home: 1709 Sanchez St San Francisco CA 94131-2740 Office: Art Dreco Inst 1713 Sanchez St San Francisco CA 94131-2740

DRIESSEL, KENNETH RICHARD, applied mathematician; b. Milw., 1940; s. Richard H. and Margaret (Otto) D. BS, U. Chgo., 1962; MS Oreg. State U., 1965, PhD, 1967. Asst. prof. U. Colo., Denver, 1967-71; research scientist Amoco Research, Tulsa, 1971-85; vis. lectr. Clemson U., 1986-87. Mem. Am. Math. Soc., Soc. for Indsl. Applied Math., Math. Assn. Am. Avocation: bicycling. Office: Math Dept Idaho State U Pocatello ID 83209

DRINKWATER, HERBERT R., mayor; m. Jackie Drinkwater; 2 children. Asst. bus. mgr. Phoenix Union High Sch. and Jr. Coll. System; owner, oper. ind. bus., 1964; mem. Scottsdale (Ariz.) City Coun., 1970-78, chmn. fin. com.; mem. Design Rev. Bd. City of Scottsdale, vice mayor, 1972-73, 76, mayor, 1980—; apptd. to Phoenix adv. coun. U.S. Bur. Land Mgmt.; chmn. Regional Pub. Transit Authority; ex-officio mem. Fiesta Bowl Com.; bd. dirs. No. Trust Co. of Ariz., Mayor's Com. on Employment of Persons with Disabilities. Bd. dirs. Ariz. Heart Inst., Lucky 13 Edn. and Rehab. Ctr., Scottsdale Boys Club, Found. for Handicapped, Ch. of the Beatitudes, Scottsdale Symphony Orch.; co-vice chmn. govt. div. Valley of the Sun campaign United Way; past mem. Scottsdale Adv. Bd., Hospice of the Valley; active Ariz. Acad., Ariz. Sr. Olympics Gold Medal Adv. Group, Camelback Mental Health Found., Scottsdale Sister Cities. Named Nationwide Retailer of Yr., 1968; named Outstanding Young Man, City of Scottsdale, 1972; recipient Disting. Achievement award Ariz. State U. Coll. Pub. Programs, 1986, Disting. Citizen award Boy Scouts Am. Mem. U.S. Conf. Mayors (arts, culture and recreation, energy and environ. standing coms.), League Ariz. Cities and Towns (treas., exec., resolution coms.), Ariz. Mcpl. Water Users Assn., Scottsdale Charros, Ariz. Wildlife Fedn., Paralyzed Vets. Assn. (life mem. Ariz. chpt.), Jaycees (pres. and exec. bd. Scottsdale chpt., internat. senate, adv. bd. Parada Del Sol 1970-74), Lions, Rotary (hon.). Office: Office of Mayor 3939 N Civic Center Blvd Scottsdale AZ 85251-4468*

DRISCOLL, EDWARD CARROLL, JR., medical device company executive; b. Phila., Aug. 24, 1952; s. Edward Carroll and Nancy (Bell) D.; m. Susan Learned, May 28, 1976; children: Adam, Laura. BA, U. Pa., 1974; MA, Harvard U., 1977, MLA, 1978; PhD, Stanford U., 1985. Mgr. R&D Internat. Imaging Systems, Milpitas, Calif., 1978-84; v.p. engring. Identix, Sunnyvale, Calif., 1984-88; v.p. corp. tech., chief tech. officer Diasonics, Milpitas, 1988-92; sen. v.p. Focal Surgery, Inc., Milpitas, 1992—. Author: (with others) Digital Image Processing Technology, 1983; author tech. papers; inventor, patentee fingerprint image recognition. Chmn. Planning Commn., Town of Fortola Valley, Calif., 1991—; chmn. ANSI standards com. Internat. Biometrics Assn., Washington, 1986-89; mem. Architecture and Site Control Commn., Portola Valley, 1987-88, chmn., 1989-90. Mem. IEEE, Assn. for Computing Machinery. Home: 11 Sandstone Way Portola Valley CA 94028 Office: Diasonics 1565 Barber Ln Milpitas CA 95035

DRISCOLL, MICHAEL P., bishop; b. Long Beach, Calif., Aug. 8, 1939. Grad., St. John's Sem., Camarillo, Calif.; student, U. So. Calif. Ordained priest Roman Cath. Ch., 1965, titular bishop of Massita. Aux. bishop Orange, Calif., 1990—. Office: Chancery Office 2811 Villa Real Dr Orange CA 92667*

DROEGE, HARRISON DAVID, auditor, consultant; b. San Francisco, Dec. 20, 1961; s. Harrison Albert and Donna Marie (Largent) D. BS in Acctg., Ind. U., 1984, JD, 1987; MA in Polit. Sci., St. John's U., Springfield, La., 1988; MM/MS, West Coast U., 1990; MBA, Calif. State U., Northridge, 1992. CPA, Va.; cert. mgmt. acct., fin. planner, pension cons., data mgr., systems programmer, quality assurance, CPCU. Auditor Keller, Miller & Jerman, CPAs, Indpls., 1978-83, Sears Bus. Systems Ctr., Indpls., 1983-85, Guchini & Levine, CPAs, Modesto, Calif., 1985-86, Weinstein, Goldstein & Weisman, CPAs, Los Gatos, Calif., 1986-87; project acct. Turner Construction Co., L.A., 1987-88; auditor Def. Contract Audit Agy., Oxnard, Calif., 1988—; cons. TKS, Inc., Moorpark, Calif., 1987—, Bus. Solutions, Inc., San Francisco, 1987—; chief exec. officer US Comercio, Sao Paulo, Brazil, 1987—; sr. v.p. fin. Montreu Internat., Switzerland, 1988—, v.p. U.S. Ops., Fontainebleau (France) Informatique, 1988—, LDA Paradisio, Milan, Italy, 1988—. Author: Symphony Business Models, 1989, Lotus Business Models, 1989, DBase III Business Models, 1987, (with others) Advanced DOS Techniques, 1987. Vol. Internat. Red Cross, 1980—. Capt. U.S. Army, 1979-85. Mem. AICPA, Am. Mgmt. Assn., Inst. Mgmt. Accts., Va. Soc. CPAs, Inst. Internal Auditors, Assn. Govt. Accts., EDP Auditors Assn., Jaycees, Kiwanis, Lions. Republicn. Home: 827 Tamlei Ave Thousand

Oaks CA 91362-2337 Office: Def Contract Audit Agy 300 Esplanade Dr Ste 300 Oxnard CA 93030-1246

DROHOJOWSKA-PHILP, HUNTER, liberal arts department chair; b. Schenectady, N.Y., Sept. 5, 1952; d. Richard Arlington and Carol Creps Gleason. BFA, Inst. San Miguel de Allende, Guanajuato, Mex., 1976. Film critic Japan Times, Tokyo, 1978; art editor L.A. Weekly, 1981-84; art and architecture editor L.A. Style, 1984-86; arts reporter L.A. Herald Examiner, 1984-87; chair dept. liberal arts and scis. Otis Sch. Art and Design, L.A., 1987—; west coast corr. Art News Mag. Author: Peter Shire-Rizzoli, 1990; contbr. Art Issues Mag. Mem. Internat. Assn. Art Critics, Coll. Art Assn., Found. Advanced Critical Studies (bd. dirs.). Office: Otis 2401 Wilshire Blvd Los Angeles CA 90057-3398

DROWN, EUGENE ARDENT, national park service official; b. Ellenburg, N.Y., Apr. 25, 1915; s. Frank Arthur and Jessie Kate D.; BS, Utah State U., 1938; postgrad. Mont. State U., 1939-40; PhD in Pub. Adminstrn., U. Beverly Hills, 1979; m. Florence Marian Munroe, Mar. 5, 1938; children: Linda Harriett Oneto, Margaret Ruth Lunn. Park ranger Nat. Park Svc., Yosemite Nat. Park, 1940-47; forest ranger U.S. Forest Svc., Calif. Region, 1948-56; forest mgr. and devel. specialist U.S. Bur. Land Mgmt., Calif., 1956—; forest engring. cons., 1970—; R&D coord. U.S. Army at U. Calif., Davis., 1961-65. Mem. adv. bd. Sierra Coll., Rocklin, Calif., 1962—; active Boy Scouts Am.; instr. ARC, 1954—. With AUS, 1941-45. Decorated Bronze Star, Silver Star; registered profl. engr., profl. land surveyor, profl. forester, Calif. Recipient Nat. Svc. medal ARC, 1964. Mem. Nat. Soc. Profl. Engrs., Soc. Am. Foresters, Am. Inst. Biol. Scientists, Ecol. Soc. Am., Res. Officers Assn. U.S., NRA, Internat. Rescue and First Aid Assn., Internat. Platform Assn., Bulldog Sentinels of Superior Calif, Masons, Shriners. Methodist. Home: 5624 Bonniemae Way Sacramento CA 95824-1402

DROZD, LEON FRANK, JR., lawyer; b. Victoria, Tex., Sept. 11, 1948; s. Leon Frank and Dorothy Lucille (Smith) D.; BBA, Tex. A&M U., 1971; J.D., U. Denver, 1979. Bar: Colo., Calif., U.S. Dist. Ct. Colo. U.S. Dist. Ct. (no. dist.) Calif., U.S. Ct. Appeals (9th and 10th cirs.). Legis. asst. U.S. Ho. of Reps., also Dem. Caucus, Washington, 1971-74, chief clk. com. on sci. and tech., 1974-75; asst. to dean for devel. Coll. Law, U. Denver, 1975-79; v.p. Braddock Publs., Inc., Washington, 1975-79; land and legal counsel Chevron Shale Oil Co., Chevron Resources Co., 1980-87, ins. div., 1987-88; assoc. counsel Chevron Corp. Law Dept. 1987—, Chevron Overseas Petroleum and White Nile Petroleum Co. Ltd. (Sudan), 1983, Colo. elector Anderson/Lucey Nat. Unity Campaign, 1980. Mem. ABA, Colo. Bar. Assn., San Francisco Bar Assn., Fed. Bar Assn., Am. Trial Lawyers Assn., Internat. Assn. Corp. Real Estate Execs., Denver C. of C. (steering com. 1981-82). Office: Chevron Corp Law Dept PO Box 7141 555 Market St San Francisco CA 94105-7141

DRUCKER, PETER FERDINAND, writer, consultant, educator; b. Vienna, Austria, Nov. 19, 1909; came to U.S., 1937, naturalized, 1943; s. Adolph Bertram and Caroline D.; m. Doris Schmitz, Jan. 16, 1937; children: Kathleen Romola, J. Vincent, Cecily Anne, Joan Agatha. Grad., Gymnasium, Vienna, 1927; LL.D., U. Frankfurt, 1931; 21 hon. doctorates. Economist London Banking House, 1933-37; Am. adviser for Brit. banks, Am. corr. Brit. newspapers, 1937-42; cons. maj. bus. corps. U.S., 1940—; prof. philosophy, politics Bennington Coll., 1942-49; prof. mgmt. NYU, 1950-72, chmn. mgmt. area, 1957-62; Clarke prof. social sci. Claremont Grad. Sch. (Calif.), 1971—; prof. dept. art Pomona Coll., Calif., 1979-85; mem. Govs. Coun. Econ. Policy Adv., Calif., 1993—. Author: The End of Economic Man, 1939, The Future of Industrial Man, 1941, Concept of the Corporation, 1946, 2nd edit., 1993, The New Society, 1950, Practice of Management, 1954, America's Next Twenty Years, 1957, The Landmarks of Tomorrow, 1959, Managing for Results, 1964, The Effective Executive, 1966, The Age of Discontinuity, 1969, new edit., 1992, Technology; Management and Society, 1970, Men, Ideas and Politics, 1971, Management: Tasks, Responsibilities, Practices, 1974, The Unseen Revolution: How Pension Fund Socialism Came to America, 1976, People and Performance, 1977, Management, An Overview, 1978, Adventures of a Bystander, 1979, new. edit., 1991, Managing in Turbulent Times, 1980, Toward the Next Economics and Other Essays, 1981, (essays) The Changing World of the Executive, 1982, Innovation and Entrepreneurship, 1985, The Frontiers of Management, 1986, The New Realities, 1989, Managing the Non-Profit Organization, 1990, (essays) Managing for the Future, 1992, (essays) The Ecological Vision, 1992, Post Capitalist Society, 1993; (fiction) The Last of All Possible Worlds, 1982, The Temptation to Do Good, 1984; producer: movie series The Effective Executive, 1969, Managing Discontinuity, 1971, The Manager and the Organization, 1977, Managing for Tomorrow, 1981; producer 25 audiocassette series The Non-Profit Drucker, 1988. Recipient gold medal Internat. U. Social Studies, Rome, 1957; Wallace Clark Internat. Mgmt. medal, 1963; Taylor Key Soc. for Advancement Mgmt., 1967; Presdl. citation NYU, 1969; CIOS Internat. Mgmt. gold medal, 1972; Chancellor's medal Internat. Acad. Mgmt., 1987. Fellow AAAS (council), Internat., Am., Irish Acads. Mgmt., Brit. Inst. Mgmt. (hon.), Am. Acad. Arts and Scis.; mem. Soc. for History Tech. (pres. 1965-66), Nat. Acad. Pub. Adminstrn. (hon.), Peter F. Drucker Found. Non Profit Mgmt. (founder, chmn).

DRUMHELLER, GEORGE JESSE, motel and hotel chain owner; b. Walla Walla, Wash., Jan. 30, 1933; s. Allen and Ila Margaret (Croxdale) D.; student Wash. State U., 1951-52, Whittier Coll., 1955-58; m. Carla Rene Cunha, May 4, 1965 (div. 1985). Asst. mgr. Olympic Hotel, Seattle, 1959; jr. exec. Westin Hotels, Seattle, 1959-63; founder, pres. George Drumheller Properties, Inc., motel holding co., Pendleton, Oreg., 1963—; founder, chmn. bd. Dalles Tapadera, Inc., motel and hotel holding co., The Dalles, Oreg., 1964-77; founder, pres. Lewiston Tapadera, Inc. (Idaho), motel holding co., 1970-77; founder, pres. Yakima Tapadera, Inc. (Wash.), 1971-77; founding ptnr. Drumheller & Titcomb (Tapadera Motor Inn), Ontario, Oreg., 1972-84; merger with Tapadera motel holding cos. and George Drumheller Properties, Inc., 1978—, founder Tapadera Budget Inns, Kennewick and Walla Walla, Wash., 1981-85, also merged with George Drumheller Properties, Inc., 1986; engaged in farming, eastern Wash., 1958-80; bd. dirs. Privacy Fund Wash. State PAC, 1991-92. With USCG, 1952-55. Mem. Am. Hotel and Motel Assn. (nat. dir. 1980-84, pres.'s exec. com. 1983-84), Oreg. Hotel Motel Assn. (dir. 1974-78), Wash. State Lodging Assn. (dir., v.p. 1976-84), Spokane Club, Walla Walla Country Club, Washington Athletic Club, J.D. Shea Club, LaJolla Beach and Tennis Club. Home: 244 Marcus St Walla Walla WA 99362 also: 7960 Sunset Dr Neah-Kah-Nie OR 97131 Office: George Drumheller Properties Inc PO Box 1234 Walla Walla WA 99362-0023

DRUMHELLER, JOHN EARL, physics educator; b. Walla Walla, Wash., Dec. 19, 1931; s. J. Earl and Geraldine L. (Gollehon) D.; m. Patricia L. Weiss, Dec. 15, 1956; children: John Earl III, Kristen L., Susan H. BS, Wash. State U., 1953; MS, U. Colo., 1958, PhD, 1962; postgrad., U. Zurich, Switzerland, 1962-64. Rsch. assoc. U. Zurich, 1962-64; asst. prof. Mont. State U., Bozeman, 1964-67, assoc. prof., 1967-72, prof. physics, 1972—; dean Coll. Letters and Sci., Mont. State U., 1991—. Contbr. articles to sci. jours. Active U.S. Ski Patrol. 1st lt. USAF, 1954-56. Office: Mont State U Dept Physics Bozeman MT 59717

DRUMMER, DONALD RAYMOND, financial services executive; b. Binghamton, N.Y., Oct. 10, 1941; s. Donald Joseph and Louise Frances (Campbell) D.; AS, Broome Community Coll., 1962; BS, U. Colo., 1972; MBA, Regis U., 1981; m. Rita Kovac, May 22, 1965; children: Shelley Rita, Adam Donn. With, Lincoln First Bank, Binghamton, N.Y., 1962-69; asst. comptr. Adams & Horne, Denver, 1969; with Colo. State Bank, Denver, 1969-87, v.p., 1972-81, comptr., 1972-87, sr. v.p., 1981-87; sr. v.p., CFO Wyo. Nat. Bancorp. (formerly Affiliated Bank Corp. of Wyo.), Casper, 1987-91; v.p., contr. Crop Hail Mgmt., Kalispell, Mont., 1991-92, sr. v.p., CFO, 1992; treas. Rural Community Ins, 1992; sr. v.p., CFO Wyo. Nat. Bank, Casper, Cheyenne, 1987-91; bd. dirs. Wyo. Nat. Bank, Lovell and Kemmerer, 1987-88; corp. sec. Wyo. Nat. Bancorp. (formerly Affiliated Bank Corp. of Wyo.), 1987-91; sr. v.p. finance Am. Nat. Bank, Cheyenne, 1993—; bd. dirs. Wheatland Ins. Agency, 1989-91; CFO, exec. com. Am. Bankers Assn., 1989-91; adj. faculty Regis Coll., mem. grad. edn. task force, 1986-87. Editor: Chronicle, 1980-81. Bd. dirs. Girl's Club of Casper, 1988. Mem. Nat. Assn. Accts. (dir. 1975-79, v.p. 1977-79), Am. Acctg. Assn., Am. Taxation Assn., Denver Sertoma Club (past pres.), City Club (v.p., dir. 1979-83). Office: 1912 Capitol Ave Cheyenne WY 82001

DRUMMOND, GERARD KASPER, minerals company executive, lawyer; b. N.Y.C., Oct. 9, 1937; s. John Landells and Margaret Louise (Kasper) D.; m. Donna J. Mason, Sept. 14, 1957 (div. 1976); children: Alexander, Jane, Edmund; m. Sandra Hamilton, Aug. 31, 1985. B.S., Cornell U., 1959, LL.B. with distinction, 1963. Bar: Oreg. 1963. Assoc. Davies, Biggs, Strayer, Stoel & Boley, Portland, Oreg., 1963-64; assoc., ptnr. Rives, Bonyhadi, Drummond & Smith, Portland, 1964-77; pres. Nerco, Inc., Portland, from 1977-87, chmn. bd. dirs., 1987—; mem. corp. policy group PacifiCorp, 1979—, exec. v.p., 1987—, also bd. dirs.; bd. dirs. Willamette Industries Inc., 1991—; bd. dirs. Pacific Telecom. Pres. Tri-County Met. Transit Dist., Portland, 1974-86, bd. dirs., 1974-86; Oreg. Investment Coun., 1987—, chmn., 1990—; trustee Reed Coll., 1982—; bd. dirs. Oreg. Symphony, 1987—, pres., 1990-92; community bd. dirs. Providence Hosp., 1986—, chmn. 1993; mem. adv. coun. Cornell U. Law Sch., 1991—; bd. dirs. Oreg. Shakespeare Festival Assn., 1992—, Oregon chpt. Nature Conservancy, 1992—; chmn. bd. dirs. N.W. Bus. Comm. for Arts, 1992—. 1st lt. USAR, 1959-67. Mem. ABA, Oreg. Bar Assn., Am. Mining Congress (bd. dirs. 1986-92), Arlington Club, Univ. Club. Home: 28815 S Needy Rd Canby OR 97013-9526 Office: Nerco Inc 500 NE Multnomah Ste 1600 Portland OR 97232

DRUMMOND, MARSHALL EDWARD, business educator, university administrator; b. Stanford, Calif., Sept. 14, 1941; s. Kirk Isaac and Fern Venice (McDeritt) D. BS, San Jose State U., 1964, MBA, 1969; EdD, U. San Francisco, 1979. Adj. prof. bus. and edn. U. San Francisco, 1975-81; adj. prof. bus. and info. systems San Francisco State U., 1981-82; prof. MIS, Ea. Wash. U., Cheney, 1985—, exec. dir. info. resources, 1988, assoc. v.p. adminstrv. svcs., chief info. officer, 1988-89, v.p. adminstrv. svcs., 1989-90, exec. v.p., 1990, pres., 1990—; cons. Sch. Bus., Harvard Coll., U. Ariz. Contbg. editor Diebold Series; contbr. articles to profl. jours. Democrat. Methodist. Home: PO Box 187 Cheney WA 99004-0187 Office: Ea Wash U Mail Stop 130 Cheney WA 99004

DRUMMOND, MARTHA MASON (MOLLY DRUMMOND), oncology social worker, lecturer; b. Summit, N.J., Oct. 23, 1958; d. John III and Mary Ann (McClements) Mason; m. David Porter Drummond, May 25, 1985; 1 child, John Mason. BSW, U. Vt., 1980; MSW, San Diego State U., 1985. Lic. clin. social worker, Calif. Women's health counselor Imperial Beach (Calif.) Community Clinic, 1982-85; crisis counselor Am. Cancer Soc., San Diego, 1985-87, asst. dir. patient svcs., 1987-89, dir. patient svcs., 1989-90; oncology social worker Green Cancer Ctr. Scripps Clinic and Rsch. Found., La Jolla, Calif., 1990-92; dir. spl. programs Community Hospice Care, San Diego, 1992—; lectr. in field, 1987—; adj. prof. Sch. Social Work, San Diego State U., 1992—. Co-author When a Loved One Dies...A Family Guide to Helping Children Cope, 1988. Chairperson 9th ann. symposium San Diego Health Coun., 1987, San Diego Oncology Social Work Group, 1988-89, 93—. Nat. Charity League scholar, 1984. Mem. NASW, Nat. Assn. Oncology Social Workers, San Diego Oncology Social Work Groups (chairperson 1988-89). Democrat. Home: 5137 Abuela Dr San Diego CA 92124 Office: Community Hospice Care 8880 Rio San Diego Dr Ste 950 San Diego CA 92108

DRUMMOND, WILLIAM JOE, journalism educator; b. Oakland, Calif., Sept. 29, 1944; s. Jack Martin and Mary Louise (Tompkins) D.; m. Faye M. Drummond, June 22, 1962 (div. 1986); children: Tammerlin Roxanne, Sean Regan. BA, U. Calif.-Berkeley, 1965; MS, Columbia U., 1966. White House fellow AP Sec. to Pres. Jimmy Carter, Washington, 1976-77; staff writer The Courier-Jour., Louisville, 1966-67; corres. L.A. Times, 1967-79, Nat. Pub. Radio, Washington, 1979-83; prof. journalism U. Calif., Berkeley, 1983—; spl. corr. Christian Sci. Monitor, 1992—. Producer radio documentary: Vale of Tears (with others), 1986 (Sidney Hillman Found. award), Las Vegas: Mississippi of the West or Promised Land?, 1991 (Nat. Journalism award Scripps-Howard Found.). Recipient Nat. Press Club Found. award, 1980, Chancellor's Disting. Lectr., U. Calif., Berkeley, 1982, Edwin M. Hood award for Excellence in diplomatic corres., 1983, award of Excellence for outstanding coverage of blk. condition, Nat. Assn. Blk. Journalists, 1989. Mem. Nat. Assn. Black Journalists, Soc. Profl. Journalists. Office: Sch Journalism 121 N Gate Hall Berkeley CA 94720

DRUTCHAS, GERRICK GILBERT, investigator; b. Detroit, Sept. 23, 1953; s. Gilbert Henry and Elaine Marie (Rutkowski) D.; 1 child, Gilbert Henry II. BA, Mich. State U., 1975; postgrad., U. Redlands, 1983-85. Pres. Argentum Publs., Los Angeles, 1986—. Dir. Childrens Welfare Found. Sgt. USAR, 1981-85. Named Baron, Royal House of Alabona-Ostrogojsk, 1992. Mem. K of P (past chancellor 1983-84), Order of the Swan (chevalier), Delta Sigma Phi. Unitarian. Home: 601 E California Blvd Pasadena CA 91106-3852 Office: Sterling Guaranty Ltd Pasadena CA 91106

DRYDEN, ROBERT EUGENE, lawyer; b. Chanute, Kans., Aug. 20, 1927; s. Calvin William and Mary Alfreda (Foley) D.; m. Jetta Rae Burger, Dec. 19, 1953; children: Lynn Marie, Thomas Calvin. AA, City Coll., San Francisco, 1947; BS, U. San Francisco, 1951, JD, 1954. Bar: Calif. 1955; diplomate Am. Bd. Trial Advocates. Assoc. Barfield, Dryden & Ruane (and predecessor firm), San Francisco, 1954-60, jr. ptnr., 1960-65, gen. ptnr., 1965-89; sr. ptnr. Dryden, Margoles, Schimaneck, Hartman & Kelly, San Francisco, 1989—; lectr. continuing edn. of the bar, 1971-77; evaluator U.S. Dist. Ct. (no. dist.) Calif. Early Neutral Evaluation Program; master atty. San Francisco Am. Inn of Ct. Served with USMCR, 1945-46. Fellow Am. Coll. Trial Lawyers, Am. Bar Found., Internat. Acad. Trial Lawyers; mem. ABA (product liability adv. coun.), San Francisco Bar Assn., Assn. Def. Counsel (bd. dirs. 1968-71), Def. Rsch. Inst., Internat. Assn. Ins. Counsel, Fedn. Ins. Counsel, Am. Arbitration Assn., U. San Francisco Law Soc. (exec. com. 1970-72), U. San Francisco Alumni Assn. (bd. govs. 1977), Phi Alpha Delta. Home: 1320 Lasuen Dr Millbrae CA 94030-2846 Office: Dryden Margoles Schimaneck Hartman & Kelly 1 California St Ste 3100 San Francisco CA 94111-5483

DRYER, CLAYTON CHRISTOPHER, software quality engineer; b. Grand Island, Nebr., Oct. 25, 1951; s. Clayton George and Glada Mae (Pritchett) D. BA in Chemistry, U. No. Colo., 1973. Scientist GA Technologies Inc, San Diego, 1980-84; sr. software quality engr. Gen. Atomics, San Diego, 1984-92; sr. process engr. System Quality Cons., Inc., San Diego, 1992—; cons. Colandrea & Assocs., Inc., San Diego, 1989—. Tchr. U.S. Peace Corps, Kenya, 1973-76. Mem. Am. Soc. for Quality Control (cert. quality engr.), Soc. for Software Quality (chmn. standards com. 1988-90, v.p. 1990-91, pres. 1991-92, bd. dirs. 1992—). Office: System Quality Cons 7373 University Ave Ste 213 La Mesa CA 91941

DRYFOOS, MICHAEL G., software engineer; b. San Francisco, Mar. 26, 1959; s. David M. and Jeanne D. BA in Biology, Reed Coll., 1981. Software engr. Control-C Software Inc., Portland, 1981-85; instr. Mt. Hood Community Coll., Gresham, Oreg., 1984-85; software engr. Microsoft Corp., Redmond, Wash., 1986—. Precinct chair Multnomah County Dem. Party, Portland, 1984; bd. dirs. Alliance for Social Change, Portland, 1984-85. Mem. AAAS, IEEE Computer Soc., Assn. Computing Machinery, Gamelan Pacifica. Office: Microsoft Corp 1 Microsoft Pl Redmond WA 98052

DRYSDALE, GEORGE MARSMAN, venture capitalist, lawyer; b. Manila, Sept. 16, 1954; (parents Am. citizens); s. George Williams and Anne (Marsman) D.; m. Diane Elizabeth Rogers, Aug. 17, 1991; 1 child, Catherine Elizabeth. BS in Engring., Harvey Mudd Coll., 1976; MBA, Stanford U., 1980, JD, 1980. Bar: N.Y., Calif. Cons. Braxton Assocs., Boston, 1980; lawyer Davis Polk & Wardwell, N.Y.C., 1981-83; gen. ptnr. Hambrecht & Quist Venture Ptnrs., San Francisco, 1983-87; asst. to sec. USDA, Washington, 1987-88; mng. gen. ptnr. Westar Capital, Costa Mesa, Calif., 1988-91; pres. Drysdale Enterprises, Newport Beach, Calif., 1991—; vice chmn. Marsman-Drysdale Group, Manila, Philippines, 1992—; bd. dirs. H&Q Ventures, Marsman Group Plantations, Skyvision, Pepsi Mktg., Upside Pub., Internat. Wireless Comm., Philippine Wireless. Mem. guardsmen, San Francisco, 1985; exec. dir. Nat. Adv. Coun. Small Bus., 1991; bd. trustees Harvey Mudd Coll. Mem. Western Assn. Venture Capitalists (bd. dirs.), Pacific Club, N.Y. Athletic Club, Bahia Corinthian Yacht Club. Republican. Office: Drysdale Enterprises 620 Newport Ctr Dr Ste 1100 Newport Beach CA 92660

DUARTE, RAMON GONZALEZ, nurse; b. San Fernando, Calif., Jan. 5, 1948; s. Salvador Revelez and Juanita (Gonzalez) D.; m. Sophia Constant Garabedian, Apr. 17, 1983; children: David Ramon, John Robert. AA in Nursing, Los Angeles Valley Coll., 1972; student, Calif. State U., Los Angeles, 1972-76. RN; Cert. Bd. Nephrology Examiners. Staff nurse hemodialysis unit U. So. Calif. Med. Ctr., L.A., 1971-75; charge nurse self care hemodialysis unit Kaiser Found. Hosp., L.A., 1976, Culver City (Calif.) Dialysis Svcs., Inc., 1981-82; adminstrv. head nurse hemodialysis unit Valley Presbyn. Hosp., Van Nuys, Calif., 1976-78; adminstrv. head nurse Kidney Dialysis Care Units, Lynwood, Calif., 1980-81; ind. nursing contractor Nursing Svcs. in Nephrology, Van Nuys and Santa Barbara, 1982—; clin. instr., rschr. Nursing Svcs. in Nephrology, Santa Barbara, 1980—, dir. rsch., 1988—; coord. clin. rsch. Valley Dialysis Assocs., Inc., Van Nuys, 1978-80; mem. rsch. com. Valley Presbyn. Hosp. Rsch.; founder, pres. Dialysis Mus. Coun., chmn. So. Calif. Dialysis Earthquake Preparedness Commn.; mem. coun. nephrology nurses and technicians, mem. allied profl. adv. com., chmn. allied health profl. rsch. grant com. Nat. Kidney Found., Inc.; mem. sci. adv. coun. Nat. Kidney Found. So. Calif.; coord. Airlift Armenia Dialysis Emergency Svcs.; team coord. Armenian Relief Soc. Editorial bd. Dialysis and Transplantation mag.; pubr., editor: Dialysis and the Earthquake Connection; contbr. articles to med. publs.; patentee biologicals. Founder Mus. Hope, Van Nuys; coord. Airlift Armenia, Armenia Relief Soc., 1988. Recipient Dedicated Svc. award Hemodialysis Found., 1976; named Allied Health Profl. of Yr., Nat. Kidney Found. So. Calif., 1986; scholar Am. G.I. Forum, 1966, 40 and 8, L.A. Valley Coll. Assoc. Students; grantee Santa Barbara Cottage Hosp., 1993. Mem. AACCN, Am. Assn. Artificial Internal Organs, Am. Assn. Nephrology Nurses and Technician, Am. Soc. Nephrology, N.Y. Acad. Scis. (cert.), Kidney Found. So. Calif., Ind. Nurses Assn., Nat. Assn. Patients on Hemodialysis and Transplantation Inc. Democrat. Roman Catholic. Home and Office: 3770 Torino Dr Santa Barbara CA 93105-4433

DUBA, DARCIE ANN, speech-language pathologist, consultant; b. Van Nuys, Calif., July 22, 1965; d. Robert Jerome and Marie Eugene D. BS, U. Nev., 1987, MS, 1989. Cardiology technician Washoe Med. Ctr., Reno, Nev., 1985-89; speech-lang. pathologist Alameda Hos, 1992—. Mem. Alpha Chi Omega (chmn. membership devel., sec. 1991-92). Republican. Home: 367 MacArthur Blvd Oaklanda CA 94610 Office: Alameda Hosp 2070 Clinton Ave Alameda CA 94501

DUBOFF, LEONARD DAVID, legal educator; b. Bklyn., Oct. 3, 1941; s. Rubin Robert and Millicent Barbara (Pollach) DuB.; m. Mary Ann Crawford, June 4, 1967; children: Colleen Rose, Robert Courtney, Sabrina Ashley. JD summa cum laude, Bklyn. Law Sch., 1971. Bars: N.Y. 1974, Oreg. 1977, U.S. Dist. Cts. (so. and ea. dists.) N.Y. 1974, U.S. Ct. Appeals (2d cir.) 1974, U.S. Ct. Appeals (9th cir.) 1990, U.S. Customs Ct. 1975, U.S. Supreme Ct. 1977, U.S. Fed. Dist. Ct. 1990. Teaching fellow Stanford (Calif.) U. Law Sch., 1971-72; mem. faculty Lewis & Clark Coll. Northwestern Sch. Law, Portland, Oreg., 1972—, prof. law, 1977—; of counsel Cooney & Crew, P.C.; instr. Hastings Coll. Law Coll. Civil Advocacy, San Francisco, summers 1978, 79. Founder, past pres. Oreg. Vol. Lawyers for Arts; mem. lawyers' com. ACLU, 1973-78, bd. dirs. Oreg., 1974-76; mem. Mayor's Adv. Com. Security and Privacy, 1974; bd. dirs. Portland Art Mus. Asian Art Council, 1976-77, Internat. Assn. Art Security, N.Y.C., 1976-80; pres. Arts Commn. of Tigard Tualatin and Sherwood, 1990-92; Gov. Oreg. Com. Employment of Handicapped, 1978-81; cons., panelist spl. projects Nat. Endowment for Arts, 1978-79; mem. Mayor's Adv. Com. on Handicapped, 1979-81; mem. Wash. State Atty. Gen's. Com. to Reorganize Maryhill Mus.; Oreg. Commn. for Blind; Oreg. Com. for Humanities, 1981-87. Recipient Bklyn. Law Sch. Stuart Hirschman Property, Jerome Prince Evidence, Donald W. Matheson Meml. awards, 1st scholarship prize; Hofstra U. Lighthouse scholar 1965-71; recipient Hauser award, 1967, Howard Brown Pickard award, 1967-69, Oreg. Govs. Arts award, 1990. Mem. Am. Soc. Internat. Law, Assn. Alumni and Attenders of Hague Acad. Internat. Law, Assn. Am. Law Schs. (standing com. sect. activities 1975, chmn. sect. law and arts 1974-80, 91-93, spl. com. on disabilities 1989-91), ABA, N.Y. State Bar Assn., Oreg. Bar Assn., Delta Kappa Phi, Sigma Pi Sigma, Sigma Alpha. Spl. columnist on craft law, The Crafts Report; editor, contbr. materials to legal and art textbooks; author textbooks and articles for legal and art jours. Office: Lewis & Clark Law Sch 10015 SW Terwilliger Blvd Portland OR 97219-7799

DUBOIS, FRANK A., III, state agency official, agriculturist; b. Lynwood, Calif., May 29, 1947; s. Frank A. and Wanda Eileen (McCarey) DuB.; m. Sharon Rose Chesher, May 24, 1973; children: Frank Austin, Sevon Nicole. BA in Agri. and Extn. Edn., N.M. State U., 1973, MA in Agri. and Extn. Edn., 1987. Insp. N.Mex. Dept. Agriculture, Albuquerque, 1973-74; agrl. programs specialist N.Mex. Dept. Agri., Las Cruces, 1979-81, asst. dir., 1983-87, dir., sec., 1988—; legis. asst. U.S. Senator Pete V. Domenici, Washington, 1974-76; spl. asst. field office U.S. Senator Pete V. Domenici, Las Cruces, 1976-79; dep. asst. sec. land and water resources U.S. Dept. Interior, 1981-83; mem. Water Quality Control Commn., N.M., 1988—, Western States Water Council, 1987—, Interstate Oil Compact Commn., 1987—. Contbr. articles to profl. jours. Mem. N.Mex. Cattle Growers Assn., N.Mex. Wool Growers Assn., Nat. Assn. State Depts. Agriculture, Western Assn. State Depts. Agriculture, Western U.S. Agrl. Trade Assn. (pres.), Mil Gracias Assn. (pres. 1986-88), N.Mex. Businessman's Team Roping Assn., Las Cruces C. of C. Republican. Methodist. Office: NMex Dept Agr Dept 3189 PO Box 30005 Las Cruces NM 88003-8005

DUBOSE, FRANCIS MARQUIS, clergyman; b. Elba, Ala., Feb. 27, 1922; s. Hansford Arthur and Mayde Frances (Owen) DuB.; BA cum laude, Baylor U., 1947; MA, U. Houston, 1958; BD, Southwestern Bapt. Sem., 1957, ThD, 1961; postgrad. Oxford (Eng.) U., 1972; m. Dorothy Anne Sessums, Aug. 28, 1940; children: Elizabeth Anne Parnell, Frances Jeannine Stevens, Jonathan Michael, Celia Danielle. Pastor Bapt. chs., Tex., Ark., 1939-61; supt. missions. So. Bapt. Conv., Detroit, 1961-66; prof. missions Golden Gate Bapt. Sem., 1966—, dir. World Mission Ctr., 1979—; lectr., cons. in 115 cities outside U.S., 1969-82; v.p. Conf. City Mission Supts., So. Bapt. Conv., 1964-66; trustee Mich. Bapt. Inst., 1963-66; mem. San Francisco Inter-Faith Task Force on Homelessness. Mem. Internat. Assn. Mission Study, Am. Soc. Missiology, Assn. Mission Profs. Co-editor: The Mission of the Church in the Racially Changing Community, 1969; author: How Churches Grow in an Urban World, 1978, Classics of Christian Missions, 1979, God Who Sends: A Fresh Quest for Biblical Mission, 1983, Home Cell Groups and House Churches, 1987; contbr. to Toward Creative Urban Strategy; Vol. III Ency. of So. Baptists, also articles to profl. jours. Home: 2 Carpenter Ct San Francisco CA 94124-4429 Office: Golden Gate Bapt Sem Mill Valley CA 94941

DUBRIN, STANLEY, physician, hand surgeon, director medical clinics; b. N.Y.C., June 3, 1928; s. Leonard B. and Claire (Lehman) DuB.; m. Magda Arruda, Dec. 31, 1976; children: Dean, Skipper, Richard, Kathleen. AB, Ohio U., 1944; postgrad., Columbia U., 1944; AB, BS, Denison U., 1946; MD, U. Calif., Irvine, 1962. Developer, mem. bd. dirs. Woodland Pk. Community Hosp., Canoga Park, Calif., 1957-62; chief of staff Van Nuys (Calif.) Community Hosp., 1964-72; med. dir. MD Med. Clinics, Anaheim, Calif., 1980—. Author: Acupuncture and Your Health, 1974. Lt. USNR, 1942-46. Mem. AMA, Calif. Med. Assn., Orange County Med. Assn. Republican. Roman Catholic. Office: MD Med Clinics 1300 N Kraemer Blvd Anaheim CA 92806 Other Office: 2630 S Harbor Blvd Santa Ana CA 92704 also: 2620 E Katella Ave Anaheim CA 92806 also: 4711 Schaefer Ave Chino CA 91710

DUBROVAY, JAESON, financial executive; b. Mexico City, Mexico, July 16, 1955; s. E. and Julia D. BA, U. Wash., 1977; MBA, Santa Clara U., 1989. CPA. Sr. acct. Arthur Andersen & Co., Seattle, 1977-80, Squibb Corp., N.Y.C., 1980-81; mgr. fin. controls Charles of the Ritz Group Ltd., N.Y.C., 1981-83; contr. Holland Am. Line, Inc., Seattle, 1983-88; v.p./treas. HAL Investments, Inc., Seattle, 1990—. Mem. AICPA, Nat. Assn. Accts. (dir. meetings 1979), Wash. Soc. CPAs, Beta Gamma Sigma. Office: HAL Investments Inc Columbia Ctr 701 5th Ave Ste 6600 Seattle WA 98104

DUCHNOWSKI, EDWARD MARTIN, airline executive; b. Johnstown, Pa., Apr. 22, 1942; s. Henry Edward and Mary Frances (Grachek) D.; m. Mildred Bernice Long, June 14, 1964, (div. Nov. 1984); children: David Martin, Daniel Paul; m. Janet Kay Turner, May 17, 1985. BS, Pa. State U., 1964; MBA, Auburn U., 1974. Asst. mine engr. Gouverneur (N.Y.) Talc

Co., 1964; C-141 instr. pilot USAF, McChord AFB, Wash., 1965-69; C-141 flight examiner USAFR, McChord AFB, 1970-82, asst. dir. ops., 1982-84, chief safety, 1984-85; aviation safety inspector FAA, Seattle, 1985-87, prin. ops. inspector, 1987-91; dir. flight standards, safety Alaska Airlines, Inc., Seattle, 1991—; spl. asst. to wing commdr. USAFR, McChord AFB, 1987-90. Contbr. articles to profl. jours. Mem. Rep. Nat. Com., Seattle, 1978-93. Col. USAFR, 1964-91. Mem. Res. Officer's Assn., Air War Coll. Alumni Assn. Republican. Roman Catholic. Office: Alaska Airlines Inc PO Box 68900 Seattle WA 98168-0900

DUCKER, JAMES HOWARD, planner; b. Rochester, N.Y., July 24, 1950; m. Brenda A. Theyers; 1 child, Allison Marie. BA, Villanova U., 1972; PhD, U. Ill., 1980. Author: Men of the Steel Rails: Workers on AT&SF Railroad, 1983; editor Alaska History, 1985—. Recipient Cert. commendation Am. Assn. for State and Local History, 1989. Mem. Orgn. Am. Historians, Western Hist. Soc. (bd. mem. 1988-91), Alaska Hist. Soc., Cook Inlet Hist. Soc.

DUCKLES, SUE PIPER, pharmacology educator; b. Oakland, Calif., Mar. 1, 1946; d. Carl Frank and Joan (Brashares) Piper; m. Lawrence Taylor Duckles, Mar. 20, 1968; children: Ian Muir, Galen Vincent. BA, U. Calif., Berkeley, 1969; PhD, U. Calif., San Francisco, 1973. Postdoctoral fellow UCLA, 1973-76, asst. prof. in residence, 1976-79; asst. prof. Dept. Pharmacology U. Ariz., Tucson, 1979-83, assoc. prof., 1983-85, , U. Calif., Irvine, 1985-88, prof., 1988—, chair acad. senate 1990-92; councillor Am. Soc. Pharmacology and Exptl. Therapeutics, Bethesda, Md., 1992—. Contbr. articles to profl. jours.; assoc. editor Life Scis., 1980-85; field editor Jour. Pharmacology and Exptl. Therapeutics, Bethesda, Md., 1983—. Mem. Am. Soc. Pharmacology and Exptl. Therapeutics, Am. Heart Assn., Soc. for Neurosci., Western Pharmacoloy Soc. (pres., 1991-92), Phi Beta Kappa. Office: U Calif Dept Pharmacology Irvine CA 92717

DUCKWORTH, GUY, musician, educator; b. L.A., Dec. 19, 1923; s. Glenn M. and Laura (Lysle) D.; m. Ballerina Maria Farra, May 23, 1948. BA, UCLA, 1951; MusM, Columbia U., 1953, PhD, 1969. Piano soloist Metro Goldwyn Mayer Studios, 1936-41, Warner Bros. Studios, 1936-41, Sta. KFI, L.A., 1938, Sta. KNX, L.A., 1939, Sta. KHJ, L.A., 1940; artist Columbia Concerts, 1942-49; asst. prof. music. U. Minn., Mpls., 1955-60, assoc. prof., 1960-62; prof. piano, fellow Northwestern U., Evanston, Ill., 1962-70; chmn. dept. preparatory piano Northwestern U., 1962-70; prof. music U. Colo., Boulder, 1970-88; prof. emeritus U. Colo., 1988, originator, coordinator masters and doctoral programs in mus. arts; piano concert tours in U.S., Can., Mexico, 1947-49; condr. various music festivals, U.S., 1956—; dir. Walker Art Children's Concerts, Mpls., 1957-62; nat. piano chmn. Music Educators Nat. Conf., 1965-71; vis. lectr., scholar 96 univs., colls. and conservatories, U.S. and Can., 1964—; cons. to Ill. State Dept. Program Devel. for Gifted Children, 1968-69; vis. prof. U. Colo., 1988-90. Author: Keyboard Explorer, 1963, Keyboard Discoverer, 1963, Keyboard Builder, 1964, Keyboard Musician, 1964, Keyboard Performer, 1966, Keyboard Musicianship, 1970, Guy Duckworth Piano Library, 1974, Guy Duckworth Musicianship Series, 1975, Keyboard Musician: The Symmetrical Keyboard, 2 vols., 1987-88, Keyboard Musician: The Symmetrical Keyboard, 1988, rev. edit., 1990; contbr. to over 6 books, 23 articles on pedagogy of music to various jours.; producer, performer video tapes on piano teaching; producer, writer (film) The Person First: A Different Kind of Teaching, 1984. Served with U.S. Army, 1943-46. Recipient All-Univ. Teaching award for excellence, U. Colo., 1981; named Pioneer Pedagogue Nat. Corp. Piano Pedagogy, Princeton U. Retrospective, 1992. Mem. Music Tchrs. Nat. Assn., Colo. State Music Tchrs. Assn., Coll. Music Soc., Music Educators Nat. Conf., Music Teachers Assn. Calif., Phi Mu Alpha, Pi Kappa Lambda. Home: 720 Camino De La Reina San Diego CA 92108-3225 Office: U Colo Boulder CO 80302

DUCKWORTH, KIM PELTO, marketing executive; b. Fresno, Calif., Dec. 15, 1956; d. William Armos and Marjorie Mae (Haninger) Pelto; m. David Paul Duckworth, Aug. 16, 1986; children: Heather Ann, Angela Marie, Claire Louise. BA in Communications, Stanford U., 1978. Asst. dir. membership club Westin Internat. Hotel, San Francisco, 1978; mktg. trainee IBM, Palo Alto, Calif., 1978-79, mktg. rep., 1979-82; account mktg. rep. IBM, San Francisco, 1982-83; with advt. staff IBM, White Plains, N.Y., 1983-85; mgr. mktg. IBM, Sunnyvale, Calif., 1985-88; regional mktg. mgr. software IBM, San Jose, Calif., 1989-91; CMR KidSoft, Inc., Los Gatos, Calif., 1992—. Mem. Young Reps. Los Gatos; precinct leader United Way, Palo Alto, 1985, vol. canvasser White Plains, 1984; vol. Am. Heart Assn., March of Dimes, Los Gatos, Calif., 1988—. Mem. NAFE, Stanford Alumni Assn., Roundhill Country Club. Republican. Episcopalian. Clubs: Stanford (Los Gatos), Los Gatos Athletic. Office: KidSoft Inc 718 University Ave Ste 112 Los Gatos CA 95030-3313

DUCKWORTH, WALTER DONALD, museum executive, entomologist; b. Athens, Tenn., July 19, 1935; s. James Clifford and Vesta Katherine (Walker) D.; m. Sandra Lee Smith, June 17, 1955; children: Clifford Monroe, Laura Lee, Brent Cullen. Student, U. Tenn., 1953-55; BS, Middle Tenn. State U., 1955-57; MS, N.C. State U., 1957-60, PhD, 1962. Entomology intern Nat. Mus. Nat. History, Washington, 1960-62, asst. curator, 1962-64, assoc. curator, 1964-75, entomology curator, 1975-78, spl.asst. to dir., 1975-78; spl. asst. to asst. sec. Smithsonian Inst., Washington, 1978-84; dir. Bishop Mus., Honolulu, 1984-86, pres., dir., 1986—; trustee Sci. Mus. Va., Richmond, 1982-86, bd. dirs. 1982-84; bd. dirs. Hawaii Maritime Mus., Honolulu, 1984—; mem. Sci. Manpower Commn., Washington, 1982-84. Co-editor: Amazonian Ecosystems, 1973; Am. editor: Dictionary of Butterflies and Moths, 1976; author, co-author numerous monographs and jour. articles in systematic biology. Pres. Social Ctr. for Psychosocial Rehab., Fairfax, Va., 1975. N.C. State U. research fellow, 1957-62; recipient numerous grants NSF, Am. Philos. Soc., Smithsonian Research Found. Assn., Exceptional Service awards Smithsonian Inst., 1973, 77, 80, 82, 84, Disting. Alumnus award Middle Tenn. State U., 1984. Mem. Am. Inst. Biol. Scis. (pres. 1985-86, sec. treas. 1978-84), Entomol. Soc. Am. (pres. 1982-83, governing bd. 1976-85, Disting. Svc. award 1981), Assn. Tropical Biology (exec. dir. 1971-84, sec. treas. 1976-71), Hawaii Acad. Sci. (coun. 1985—), Arts Coun. Hawaii (legis. com. 1986-87), Assn. Sci. Mus. Dirs., Social Sci. Assn., Assn. Systematic Collections (v.p. 1988-89, pres. 1990-91), Pacific Sci. Assn. (pres. 1987-91, pres. Pacific Sci. Congress, Honolulu 1991). Democrat. Presbyterian. Lodges: Rotary, Masons, Order Eastern Star. Office: Bishop Mus PO Box 190000A Honolulu HI 96817-9291

DUDICS-DEAN, SUSAN ELAINE, interior designer; b. Perth Amboy, N.J., Oct. 22, 1950; d. Theodore W. and Joyce M. (Ryals) D.; m. Rick Dean, Apr. 30, 1989; 1 child, Merissa Joyce. BS in Sociology, W.Va. U., 1972; postgrad. Rutgers U., 1975-78, U. Calif., Irvine, 1979-81, Can. Coll., 1981-89. Programmer Prudential Life, Newark, 1972-73; sr. systems analyst Johnson & Johnson, New Brunswick, N.J., 1973-78, Sperry Univac, Irvine, Calif., 1978-80; sr. systems analyst, project leader Robert A. McNeil, San Mateo, Calif., 1981-83; dist. design dir. TransDesigns, Woodstock, Ga., 1982—. Contbr. articles to profl. jours. High sch. mentor Directions, San Francisco, 1985—. Mem. Women Entreprenuers (membership com., treas. 1983-87), Cen. N.J. Alumni Assn. Delta Gamma (assoc. sec., founder, pres.), San Francisco C. of C., Nat. Assn. of Profl. Saleswomen, Am. Soc. Interior Designers (allied mem. 1989—), Delta Gamma. Recipient awards TransDesigns, Woodstock, Ga., 1984, 85, 86, 87, 89, 90, 91. Avocations: skiing, sewing, scuba diving, ballet, hand crafts.

DUDIS, JOHN BETZ, lawyer; b. Chgo., Nov. 6, 1946; s. John A. and Dorothy (Geiger) D.; m. Rhonda Marie Pettinato, July 30, 1977; children: Amanda Robin, Allison JoHanna. BA in Bus., Econs. summa cum laude, Rocky Mountain Coll., 1969; JD, U. Mont., 1972; LLM in Taxation, U. Mo., 1974. Law clk. to chief justice Mont. Supreme Ct., Helena, 1972-73; assoc. law Murphy, Robinson, Heckathorn & Phillips, P.C., Kalispell, Mont., 1974—; bd. mem. Mont. Bd. Realty Regulation, Dept. of Commerce, State of Mont., 1983-86, chmn., 1986-91; speaker tax and estate planning continuing edn. ins. licensees, real estate licensees, bankers, ABA, gen. pub., Mont., 1974—. Assoc. editor, contbr. Mont. Law Rev., 1970-72. Mem. Mont. Arts Coun., Helena, 1991; chmn. Flathead County Red Cross Chpt., Kalispell, Mont., 1981; mem. adv. bd. State of Mont. Blood Svcs. ARC, Gt. Falls, 1983-90; bd. dirs. Salvation Army, Kalispell, 1991, United Way, Flathead County, Kalispell, 1982-91; pres. Kalispell Tastmasters Club, 1979; com. chmn. Job Svc. E mployers com., Kalispell, 1989-91; sec., bd. mem. Bigfork (Mont.) Ctr. for Performing Arts, 1981—; fin. chmn. Glacier dist. Boy Scouts am., Kalispell, 1992, Eagle Scout, 1963. Recipient Testimonial of Appreciation, Mont. Assn. Realtors, 1991; named Boss of Yr., Flathead Valley Legal Secs. Assn., Kalispell, 1985; Phi Delta Phi scholar U. Mont. Law Sch., 1971-72. Mem. ABA, Mont. Bar Assn., NW Mont. Bar Assn., Elks. Republican. Roman Catholic. Office: Murphy Robinson et al 431 1st Ave W Kalispell MT 59901

DUDLEY, CLYDE BERTRAM (BERT DUDLEY), insurance specialist, educator; b. Boise, Idaho, Jan. 20, 1948; s. Orie Leslie and Bertha Clara (Bertram) D.; m. Laurie Ann Buchman, Aug. 23, 1986. BA with honors, U. Wash., 1970, MA in Econs., 1971. CLU, ChFC, CPCU. Teaching and rsch. asst. U. Wash., Seattle, 1970-75; agt. Farmers Ins. Group, Seattle, 1976-77; ins. instr. SAFECO Ins. Group, Seattle, 1977—; cert. employee benefits instr. U. Wash., 1984—. Author: Group Insurance Basics, 1986, How to Value an Independent Insurance Agency, 1988. Chairperson SAFECO campaign United Way, 1980. Fellow Life Mgmt. Inst.; mem. Life Office Mgmt. Assn. (mem. adminstrn. com. 1984-88), Phi Beta Kappa, Omicron Delta Epsilon. Office: SAFECO Ins Cos SAFECO Plz 0-1 Seattle WA 98185

DUDLEY, LONNIE LEROY, information scientist; b. Belding, Mich., Mar. 3, 1948; s. Edmond LeRoy and LuLa Madeline (Sloan) D. Student, Mich. State U., 1966-67, LaSalle Extension U., Chgo., 1968-69. Encoder III, inventory buyer, acctg. clk. III Brotman Med. Ctr., Culver City, Calif., 1984-88; materiels mgmt. system coord., dir. data processing Chino (Calif.) Community Hosp., 1988-91, dir. materials mgmt., 1988-91, dir. info. systems/materials mgmt./data processing, 1972-75. Scout master Boy Scouts Am., Dowagiac, Mich., 1972-75; adv. Order of the Arrow, Dowagiac, 1972-75, Med. Explorer Post, Dowagiac, 1972-75, Four-H, Dowagiac, 1975-79, Iven C. Kincheloe Jr. Chpt. Order of Demolay, Dowagiac, 1975-79. With USN, 1967-71. Mem. F&AM, Masons, Kincheloe Jr. Chpt. Order of Demolay (scribe and fin. adv., Lmp of Knowledge 1973).

DUENSING, CAROL JANET, corporate professional; b. Bellflower, Mo., Apr. 14, 1937; d. Charles Donald and Mary Lois (Drewer) Buermann; m. George Herman Duensing, Aug. 26, 1967; children: Mary Theresa, Julie Ann. Student, Suburba Sch. Music. Office mgr. Dempsey Tegeler, Corpus Christi, Tex., 1960-62; sec. Goldman Sachs Investment Co., Los Angeles, 1962-63; sec., treas. Music Systems Enterprises Inc., Orange, Calif., 1966—; owner Straw Hat Pizza, Palm Desert, Calif. Mem. Grand Jury Orange County, 1989-90, 91-92. Recipient Community Service award Tustin (Calif.) Schs., 1976. Mem. Pacific Coast Buckskin Horse Assn. (sec. 1980—). Republican. Home: 18901 Valley Dr Orange CA 92667-2839 Office: Music Systems Enterprises Inc PO Box 1744 935 N Main Orange CA 92668 Also: Straw Hat Pizza 73-155 Hwy III Palm Desert CA 92260

DUERR, ALFRED, mayor. Formerly alderman City of Calgary, Alta., Can., elected mayor, 1989. Office: City of Calgary, Po Box 2100 Sta M, Calgary, AB Canada T2P 2M5

DUESLER, DAVID MAYNARD, air force officer; b. Fairbanks, Alaska, Dec. 5, 1947; s. Donald Barton and Mary Jean (Nelson) D. BA, U. Iowa, 1969; MA, Ball State U., 1975. Commd. 2d lt. U.S. Air Force, 1969, advanced through grades to col., 1991; logistics and other assignments U.S. Air Force, U.K., Thailand, Korea, Japan, others; logistics staff Hdqrs. Pacific Air Forces, Hickam AFB, Hawaii, 1992—. Recipient King's Guard badge Kingdom of Thailand, 1984, Gold medal in swimming Aloha State Games, 1991, 92; named to Outstanding Young Men of Am., 1979. Mem. Air Force Assn. Office: Hdqrs Pacific Air Forces Hickam AFB HI 96853

DUFF, JAMES GEORGE, financial services executive; b. Pittsburg, Kans., Jan. 27, 1938; s. James George and Camilla (Vinardi) D.; m. Linda Louise Beeman, June 24, 1961 (div.); children: Michele, Mark, Melissa; m. Beverly L. Pool, Nov. 16, 1984. B.S. with distinction (Sunray Mid-Continent Scholar; Bankers Scholar), U. Kans., 1960, M.B.A., 1961. With Ford Motor Co., Dearborn, Mich., 1962—; various positions fin. staff Ford Motor Co., 1962-71; dir. product, profit, price, warranty Ford of Europe, 1972-74; controller Ford Div., 1974-76, controller car ops., 1976, controller car product devel., 1976-80; exec. v.p. Ford Motor Credit Co., 1980-88, bd. dirs.; pres., chief operating officer U.S. Leasing Internat. Inc., San Francisco, 1988-89, pres., chief exec. officer, 1990-91, chmn., chief exec. officer, 1991—, also bd. dirs.; bd. dirs. USL Securities Corp., U.S. Fleet Leasing Inc., Airlease Mgmt. Svcs.; mem. Conf. Bd., 1990—. Mem. adv. bd. U. Kans. Sch. Bus., 1980—; bd. dirs. Bay Area Coun., 1990—; trustee San Francisco Mus. Modern Art, 1990—; chmn. bus. devel. unit United Found., 1980-85, chmn. edn. and local govt. unit, 1986-88. Mem. San Francisco C. of C. (bd. dirs. 1990-91). Home: 7 Russian Hill Pl San Francisco CA 94133-3605 Office: US Leasing Internat 733 Front St San Francisco CA 94111-1980

DUFFIN, RICHARD ALLEN, environmental engineer, consultant; b. Chgo., Oct. 17, 1946; s. Robert Warren and Ruth Lee (Williams) D.; m. Shari Lynn Anderson (div. 1975); 1 child, Timothy Bryant; m. Dianne Lee Saibini (div. 1985). BS, Calif. State U., Sacramento, 1974; postgrad., U. Nev., 1975-78. Registered environ. assessor, Calif.; registered Nat. Registry Environ. Profls. Resources planner grants and statewide studies div. Calif. Dept. Parks and Recreation, Sacramento, 1971-74; rsch. asst. Remote Sensing Lab., Coll. Agr., U. Nev. Knudsten Sch. Renewable Natural Resources, Reno, 1975-76; dep. dir. edn. Nat. Coun. on Gene Resources, Sacramento, Berkeley, Calif., 1980-81; nat. resources conservationist Bur. Indian Affairs, U.S. Dept. Interior, Eagle Butte, S.D., 1982-84; environ. protection specialist U.S. Army Hdqs. and 7th Inf. Div., Ft. Ord, Calif., 1985-87; environ. cons. Rad-Environ. Engring./Planning, Capitola, Calif., 1986-89; environ. engr. Marine Corps Air Sta.-El Toro, Santa Ana, Calif., 1989—. Home: PO Box 156 East Irvine CA 92650 Office: El Toro FMD-1AU.20 El Toro FMD-1JG-20 Marine Corps Air Sta Santa Ana CA 92709

DUFFY, BARBARA JEAN, managment, education consultant, publisher; b. Colorado Springs, Colo., Dec. 13, 1938; d. Eugene Hagaman and Ruth Mae (Sills) Vannest; m. William M. Campbell (div.); children: Holli Denise Campbell Dowell, Heidi Diane Campbell; m. Donald D. Duffy (div.). BS, Cen. State U., Edmond, Okla., 1972; MEd, U. Okla., 1974, EdD, 1983. From clk. to acctg. dept. Continental Oil Co., Ponca City, Okla., 1959-65; sec. Apco Oil Co, Oklahoma City, 1966-70; libr. media specialist Putnam City West High Sch., Oklahoma City, 1973-80; curriculum coord. Okla. State Dept. Edn., Oklahoma City, 1980-89; cons./publisher Bayview Assocs., San Mateo, Calif., 1989-90; grants dir., profl. svcs. assoc. Assn. Calif. Sch. Adminstrs., Burlingame, Calif., 1992; mgr. schs. libr. Sonoma County Office Edn., Santa Rosa, Calif, 1992—; ind. cons., advisor, 1992—. Editor: One of a Kind, 1983, 86; author, producer: video tape Magical Mix, 1985. Mem. Edmond Women's Polit. Caucus, 1980; chair Gov.'s Speak-out on Librs., 1977. Mem. ASCD (dir. clearinghouse on learning teaching styles and brain behavior 1986-90), Assn. for Edn. Communications and Tech. (pres. div. ednl. media mgmt. 1990-91, chair long range planning com. 1986-88), Internat. Visual Literacy Assn. (bd. dirs. 1987-89), Okla. Libr. Assn. (chair libr. devel. com. 1975-76). Democrat. Mem. Unity Ch. Home: 112 Airport Blvd E Santa Rosa CA 95403 Office: Sonoma County Office Edn 5340 Skylane Blvd Santa Rosa CA 95403

DUFFY, BERNARD KARL, educator; b. Bremen, Fed. Republic Germany, Apr. 27, 1948; came to U.S., 1953; s. Bernard E. and Elfriede G. (Loenecker) D.; m. Susan Jacobelli, Aug. 14, 1976; 1 child, Elizabeth. BA with great distinction, San Jose State Coll., 1970, MA, 1971; PhD, U. Pitts., 1976. Asst. prof. Hiram (Ohio) Coll., 1976-79; asst. prof. Clemson (S.C.) U., 1979-84, assoc. prof., 1984-87, prof., 1987-88; prof. Calif. Poly. State U., San Luis Obispo, 1988—, dept. chair, 1988-91. Author: (with Martin Jacobi) The Politics of Rhetoric: Richard M. Weaver and the Conservative Tradition, 1993; editor: (with Halford Ryan) American Orators of the Twentieth Century, 1987, American Orators Before 1900, 1987; series advisor Great American Orators, 1989—; contbr. articles to profl. jours. NEH Summer Seminar grantee, 1981, 84. Mem. Speech Communication Assn., Western Speech Communication Assn., Phi Kappa Phi. Democrat. Episcopalian. Office: Calif Poly State U Speech Communication Dept San Luis Obispo CA 93407

DUFFY, LAWRENCE KEVIN, biochemist, educator; b. Bklyn., Feb. 1, 1948; s. Michael and Anne (Browne) D.; m. Geraldine Antoinette Sheridan, Nov. 10, 1972; children: Anne Marie, Kevin Michael, Ryan Sheridan. BS, Fordham U., 1969; MS, U. Alaska, 1972, PhD, 1977. Teaching asst. dept. chemistry U. Alaska, 1969-71, research asst. inst. arctic biology, 1974-77; postdoctoral fellow Boston U., 1977-78, Roche Inst. Molecular Biology, 1978-80; research asst. prof. med. br. U. Tex., 1980-82; asst. prof. neurology (biol. chemistry) Med. Sch. Harvard U., Boston, Mass., 1982-87, adv. biochemistry instr. Med. Sch., 1983-87; instr. gen. and organic chemistry Roxbury Community Coll., Boston, 1984-87; prof. chemistry and biochem. U. Alaska, Fairbanks, 1992—, coord. program biochem and molecular biology, summer undergrad. res. in chemistry and biochem., 1987—. Bd. dirs. Alzheimer Disease Assn. of Alaska, 1988—; mem. instnl. rev. bd. Fairbanks Meml. Hosp., 1990. Lt. USNR, 1971-73. NSF trainee, 1971; J.W. McLaughlin fellow, 1981; W.F. Milton scholar, 1983; recipient Alzheimers Disease and Related Disorders Assoc. Faculty Scholar award, 1987. Mem. Am. Soc. Neurochemists, Am. Soc. Biol. Chemists, N.Y. Acad. Sci., Am. Chem. Soc. (Analytical Chemistry award 1969), Internat. Soc. Toxicologists, Sigma Xi (pres. 1991— Alaska club), Phi Lambda Upsilon. Roman Catholic. Office: U Alaska Inst Arctic Biology Fairbanks AK 99775

DUFFY, SUSAN WENGER, journalist; b. Columbus, Ohio, June 23, 1945; d. Roy Emerson and Florence Edith (Heineman) Wenger; m. Patrick Edward Duffy, May 11, 1979; children: Keough Clare, Mariah Eleanor. BA in History, Earlham Coll., Richmond, Ind., 1967; MAT, Antioch-Putney Coll., Yellow Springs, Ohio, 1970; postgrad., U. Mont., 1976-78. Cert. tchr. Tchr. Phila. Pub. Schs., 1969-70, Holton-Arms Acad. for Girls, Bethesda, Md., 1970-72; ednl. cons. Adv. for Open Edn., Cambridge, Mass., 1972-74; writer Visual Edn. Corp., Princeton, N.J., 1974-75; copy editor Procs. Nat. Acad. Scis., Washington, 1979-80; media coord. Pat Williams for Congress, Helena, Mont., 1980; writer, parent liaison Mont. U. Affiliated Program, Missoula, 1982-85, Co-Teach, Missoula, 1985-86; tech. writer Rural Inst. on Disabilities, Missoula, 1991-92; parent adv. Family Support Network, 1992—. Editor, co-author: Acceptance Is Only the First Battle, 1983, Robbie, 1985, We're All In This Together, So Let's Talk, 1992; editor The Missoulian, 1983-91. Mem. Gov.'s Coun. on Devel. Disabilities, Helena, 1984-86, U. Utah Project on Tech. Dependent Children, Salt Lake City, 1987-90, Mountain States Regional Genetic Svcs. Network, Denver, 1989—, Region 5 Coun. on Devel. Disabilities, We. Mont., 1982-86, 91—; bd. dirs. Comprehensive Devel. Ctr., 1992—. Recipient Tom McMaster Vol. award Mont. Assn. Retarded Citizens, 1987. Mem. Coun. Exceptional Children, Assn. for Care of Children's Health. Democrat. Mem. Soc. of Friends. Home: 620 Woodworth Ave Missoula MT 59801

DUFFY, WAYNE EDWARD, lawyer; b. Boise, Idaho, Dec. 28, 1920; s. Charles Edward and Lorena Essie (Buxton) D.; m. Florence A. Reichel, Apr. 27, 1951 (div. Apr. 1968); 1 stepchild, James Michael Moore; m. Ruth Seville Leonard, Sept. 3, 1983; stepchildren: Deborah, Diane. BA, Coll. of Idaho, 1947; MS, U. Idaho, 1948; postgrad., N.Y. Coll. of Forestry, 1950; JD, Lincoln U., 1972. Bar: Calif. 1973, U.S. Patent Office 1981. Supr. mass spectrom Am. Cyanamid, Phillips Petroleum, NRTS (name now INEL), Idaho Falls, Idaho, 1951-55; sr. engr., lab. supr. Westinghouse-Bettis, Pitts., 1956; sr. rsch. engr. Atomics Internat., Canoga Park, Calif., 1956-59; mgr. mass Spectrom Gen. Electric, Pleasanton, Calif., 1959-68; sr. staff engr. Martin-Marietta, Denver, 1969-70; pvt. practice law Fresno, Calif., 1976-82; dep. county coun. Fresno County Coun., Fresno, 1974-76; pvt. practice law Santa Ana, Calif., 1982-83; pvt. practice patent atty., chem. cons. Nampa, Idaho, 1983—; cons. EG&G, San Ramon, Calif., 1969, Denver Rsch. Inst. U. Denver, 1970, Nyssa-Nampa Beet Growers Assn., Nyssa, Oreg., 1988—. Inventor patented Chem. Process; asst. editor Lincoln Law Rev., 1971, 72; contbr. articles to profl. jours. 1st Sgt. U.S. Army, 1943-46. Fellow Am. Inst. Chemists; mem. U.S. Patent Bar. Republican. Home and Office: 107 Central Kings Rd Nampa ID 83687-3653

DUFRESNE, ARMAND FREDERICK, management and engineering consultant; b. Manila, Aug. 10, 1917; s. Ernest Faustine and Maude (McClellan) DuF.; m. Theo Rutledge Schaefer, Aug. 24, 1940 (dec. Oct. 1986); children: Lorna DuFresne Turnier, Peter, m. Lois Burrell Klosterman, Feb. 21, 1987. BS, Calif. Inst. Tech., 1938. Dir. quality control, chief product engr. Consol. Electrodynamics Corp., Pasadena, Calif., 1945-61; pres., dir. DUPACO, Inc., Arcadia, Calif., 1961-68; v.p., dir. ORMCO Corp., Glendora, Calif., 1966-68; mgmt., engring. cons., Duarte and Cambria, Calif., 1968—; dir., v.p., sec. Tavis Corp., Mariposa, Calif., 1968-79; dir. Denram Corp., Monrovia, Calif., 1968-70, interim pres., 1970; dir., chmn. bd. RCV Corp., El Monte, Calif., 1968-70; owner DUFCO, Cambria, 1971-82; pres. DUFCO Electronics, Inc., Cambria, Calif., 1982-86, chmn. bd. 1982-92; pres. Freedom Designs, Inc., Simi Valley, Calif., 1982-86, chmn. bd. dirs., 1982—; owner DuFresne Consulting, 1992—; chmn. bd., pres. DUMEDCO,Inc., 1993—. Patentee in field. Bd. dirs. Arcadia Bus. Assn., 1965-69; bd. dirs. Cambria Community Services Dist., 1976, pres., 1977-80; mem., chmn. San Luis Obispo County Airport Land Use Commn., 1972-75. Served to capt. Signal Corps, AUS, 1942-45. Decorated Bronze Star. Mem. Instrument Soc. Am. (life), Arcadia (dir. 1965-69), Cambria (dir. 1974-75) C. of C., Tau Beta Pi. Home: 901 Iva Ct Cambria CA 93428-2913

DUGAN, WALTER JAMES, supply company executive; b. Troy, N.Y., Mar. 20, 1922; s. Walter James and Deborah Dorothy (Faden) D.; m. Grace Mary Kennedy, July 13, 1946; children: Lynn Dugan Schaefer, Robert Michael, Pamela Dugan Ryan. BSChemE, Rensselaer Poly. Inst., 1943, MSChemE, 1946. Instr. chem. engring. Rensselaer Poly. Inst., Troy, 1946-48; engr. and mktg. cons. silicone Products dept. GE, Waterford, N.Y., 1948-61, gen. mgr., 1969-73; mktg. mgr. chem. materials dept. GE, Pittsfield, Mass., 1961-66, gen. mgr. plastics dept., 1966-69; gen. mgr. GE Supply Co., Chgo., 1973-83; v.p., gen. mgr. GTE Supply Co., Salt Lake City, Utah, 1983-88, ret.; chmn., pres. W.J. Dugan Assoc. Cons., Salt Lake City, 1988—. Contbr. GE newsletter, GTE newsletter. Bd. dirs. United Way, 1963-73, Community Nursing Assn., 1984-89. Lt. (jg) 1943-46, PTO. Mem. Willow Creek Country Club, Sigma Xi. Home: 3000 Connor St # 23 Salt Lake City UT 84109

DUGAN GINDHART, ANDREA CLAIRE, marketing manager; b. DuBois, Pa., Jan. 29, 1961; d. Paul John and Olga Taeresa (Burns) Dugan; m. Richard Thomas Gindhart Jr., Oct. 26, 1986; children: Austin Michael, Cole Thomas. BS in Psychology, BA in Bus. Mgmt., Calif. State U., Chico, 1983; MBA, Golden Gate U., 1989. Sales rep. Wyeth Labs., 1984-86; sales, mktg. staff Jerran Enterprises, 1986-87; sales exec. R.J. Reynolds/Nabisco, 1987-89; salesperson Planter/Lifesavers, 1990—; ins. sales, adminstr. Pacific Nat., 1991—; CEO nat. network, internat. mktg. Galaxy Enterprises, 1992—. Recipient Top Sales award Wyeth Labs. Mem. NAFE, Nat. Assn. Profl. Sales, Young Entrepreneurs Assn., Profl. Reps. of Sacramento, Criminal Justice Club, Am. Mktg. Assn., Sigma Kappa Sorority, Tau Kappa Epsilon Frat. Roman Catholic. Home: 8104 Eagle Peakway Sacramento CA 95842 Office: 117 Main St Roseville CA 95661

DUGAW, JOHN EDWARD, JR., family practice physician; b. Seattle, June 12, 1945; s. John Edward and Marjorie (McNiven) D.; m. Virginia Ingram, Feb. 3, 1975; children: John Ingram Baker, Charles Sherman Baker. BSc, U. Portland, 1967; MD, Creighton U., 1971. Diplomate Am. Bd. Family Practice. Resident in pediatrics U. Nebr., Omaha, 1971-72; resident in family practice U. Calif.-Davis, Scenic Gen. Hosp., Modesto, 1975-77; staff physician Gross Clinic, Sedro-Woolley, Wash., 1977-79; pvt. practice N. Skagit Family Practice, Inc., Sedro-Woolley, 1979—; sec. Skagit (county) Family Physicians, 1990—; del. Wash. Acad. Family Physicians, Seattle, 1990—. Sr. Warden St. James Episcopal Ch., Sedro-Woolley, 1988-89; bd. dirs. Washington State Med. Polit. Action Com., Seattle, 1982-86. Lt. comdr. USNR, 1972-75. Recipient Disting. Svc. award Skagit March of Dimes, 1984. Fellow Am. Acad. Family Practice; mem. AMA, Wash. State Med. Assn., Am. Geriatrics Soc., Sedro-Woolley C. of C. (pres. 1987), Wash. Athletic Club, Rotary. Republican. Home: 1327 Railroad Ave Sedro Woolley WA 98284-9748

DUGGAN, JOSEPH JOHN, university dean, educator; b. Phila., Sept. 8, 1938; s. Bartholomew James and Mary Elizabeth (Boyce) D.; m. Mary Kay Conyers, Mar. 19, 1962 (div. 1979); children: Marie Christine, Kathleen Maura; m. Annalee Claire Rejhon, June 20, 1981; 1 child, Joseph Rejhon. AB in French, Fordham U., N.Y.C., 1960; PhD in Romance

Langs., Ohio State U., 1964. Lectr. French U. Calif., Berkeley, 1964-65, asst. prof. French and comparative lit., 1965-71, assoc. prof., 1971-77, prof. French, comparative lit., romance philology, 1977—, chmn. dept. comparative lit., 1980-84, assoc. dean grad. div., 1987—. Author: The Song of Roland, 1973, A Guide to Studies on the Song of Roland, 1976, A Fragment of Les Enfances Vivien, 1986, The Cantar de mio Cid: Poetic Creation in its Economic and Social Contexts, 1989. Fellow Woodrow Wilson Found., Princeton, N.J., 1960, 64, John Simon Guggenheim Found., N.Y.C., 1979. Office: U Calif Dept Comparative Lit Berkeley CA 94720

DUGMORE, KENT CLYDE, lawyer; b. Price, Utah, Oct. 14, 1939; s. William Clyde and Anna (Stringham) D.; m. Joylynne Johnson, June 9, 1962; children: Pamela Kay, Steven Kent. BS, U. Utah, 1961, JD, 1964; LLM, George Washington U., 1971. Bar: Utah 1964, U.S. Dist. Ct. Utah 1964, U.S. Supreme Ct. 1970. Judge adv. USAF, 1965-85; sr. atty. The Boeing Co., Seattle, 1985-87; v.p., gen. counsel ITT Corp. Gilfillan Div., Van Nuys, Calif., 1988--. Mem. ABA, Utah Bar Assn. Office: ITT Corp Gilfillan Div 7821 Orion Ave PO Box 7713 Van Nuys CA 91409

DUHL, LEONARD, psychiatrist, educator; b. N.Y.C., May 24, 1926; s. Louis and Rose (Josefsberg) D.; m. Lisa Shippee; children: Pamela, Nina, David, Susan, Aurora. B.A., Columbia U., 1945; M.D., Albany Med. Coll., 1948; postgrad., Washington Psychoanalytic Inst., 1956-64. Diplomate: Am. Bd. Psychiatry and Neurology (examiner 1977, 85). With USPHS, 1951-53, 54-72, med. dir., 1954-72; fellow Menninger Sch. Psychiatry Menninger Sch. Psychiatry, Winter VA Hosp., Topeka, 1949-51, resident psychiatry, 1953-54; asst. health officer Contra Costa County (Calif.) Health Dept., 1951-53; with USPHS, 1949-51, 53-54; psychiatrist profl. svcs. br., chief office planning NIMH, 1954-66; spl. asst. to sec. HUD, 1966-68; cons. Peace Corps, 1961-68; assoc. psychiatry George Washington Med. Sch., 1961-63, asst. clin. prof., 1963-68, assoc. prof., 1966-68; prof. public health Sch. Pub. Health U. Calif., Berkeley, 1968—; prof. city planning Coll. Environ. Design U. Calif., Berkeley, 1968-92; dir. dual degree program in health and med. scis. U. Calif., Berkeley, 1971-77; clin. prof. psychiatry U. Calif., San Francisco, 1969—; pvt. practice psychiatry Berkeley; sr. assoc. Youth Policy Inst., Washington; mem. sci. adv. coun. Calif. Legislature, 1970-73, sr. cons. Assembley Office of Rsch., 1981-85; cons. Healthy Cities Program, Environ. Health, WHO, UNICEF, ICDC, Florence, Global Forum of Parliamentarians and Spiritual Leaders, 1989—, Ctr. for Fgn. Journalists, 1987—; bd. dirs. Calif. Inst. of Integral Studies, 1990—. Author: Approaches to Research in Mental Retardation, 1959, The Urban Condition, 1963, (with R.L. Leopold) Mental Health and Urban Social Policy, 1969, Health Planning and Social Change, 1986, Social Entrepreneurship of Change, 1990, The Urban Condition-25 Years Later, 1992, Health and the City, 1993; bd. editors Jour. Community Psychology, 1974—, Jour. Community Mental Health, 1974—, Jour. Mental Health Consultation and Edn, 1978—, Jour. Prevention, 1978—; contbr. articles to tech. lit. Trustee Robert F. Kennedy Found., 1971—; bd. dirs. Citizens Policy Ctr., San Francisco, 1975-85, New World Alliance, 1980-84, Calif. Inst. for Integral Studies, 1991—, Ptnrs. for Dem. Change, 1990—; chair Calif. Healthy Cities Project conf. 1993; exec. trustee Nat. Inst. for Citizen Participation and Negotiation, 1988-90. Fellow Am. Psychiat. Assn. (life), Am. Coll. Psychiatry, No. Calif. Psychiat. Soc. (life), Group for Advancement in Psychiatry (chmn. com. preventive psychiatry 1962-66). Home: 639 Cragmont Ave Berkeley CA 94708-1329 Office: U Calif Sch Pub Health 410 Warren Hall Berkeley CA 94720

DUHNKE, ROBERT EMMET, JR., aerospace engineer; b. Manitowoc, Wis., Jan. 28, 1935; s. Robert Emmet and Vivian Dorothy (Abel) D.; m. Patricia R. Ebben, 1956 (div. 1972); children: Kim Marie, Lori Ann, Dawn Diane, Robert III, Mary Lynn; m. Judy Anne Lind, Feb. 14, 1978. B of Aero. Engring., Purdue U., 1957. Engr. Convair/Aerodyns. Group, Pomona, Calif., 1957-58; engr., instr. Boeing Co., Seattle, 1964-66, 72-84, engr. instr., 1990—, engr., analyst mil. div., 1984-90; flight navigator Flying Tigers, San Francisco, 1966-68; salesman various real estate and ins. cos., Seattle, 1968-72. Author poems in English, German and Spanish. Sponsor World Vision, Pasadena, Calif.; mem. Citizens Against Govt. Waste. Capt. USAF, 1958-64. Recipient Hon. Freedom Fighter award Afghan Mercy Fund, 1987. Mem. Inst. Navigation, Air Force Assn., Wild Goose Assn. Mem. United We Stand Party. Home: 1219 30th St NE Auburn WA 98002-2471

DUKE, DONALD NORMAN, publisher; b. Los Angeles, Apr. 1, 1929; s. Roger V. and Mabel (Weineger) D. BA in Ednl. Psychology, Colo. Coll., 1951. Comml. photographer Colorado Springs, Colo., 1951-53; pub. relations Gen. Petroleum, Los Angeles, 1954-55; agt. Gen. S.S. Corp., Ltd., 1956-57; asst. mgr. retail advt., sales promotion Mobil Oil Co., 1958-63; pub. Golden West Books, Alhambra, Calif., 1964—; dir. Pacific R.R. Publs., Inc., Athletic Press; pub. relations cons. Santa Fe Ry., 1960-70. Author: The Pacific Electric—A History of Southern California Railroading, 1958, Southern Pacific Steam Locomotives, 1962, Santa Fe... Steel Rails to California, 1963, Night Train, 1961, American Narrow Gauge, 1978, RDC: The Budd Rail Diesel Car, 1989, The Brown Derby, 1990, Camp Cajon, 1991, Fred Harvey: Civilizer of the American West, 1992; editor: Water Trails West, 1977, Branding Iron, 1988-91. Recipient Spur award for Trails of the Iron Horse Western Writers Am., 1975. Mem. Ry. and Locomotive Hist. Soc. (dir. 1944—), Western History Assn., Newcomen Soc., Lexington Group of Transp. History, Western Writers Am., P.E.N. Internat. (v.p. 1975-77), Authors Guild Am., Book Pubs. Assn. So. Calif. (dir. 1968-77), Cal. Writers Guild (dir. 1976-77), Calif. Book Pubs. Assn. (dir. 1976-77), Westerners Internat. (hon., editor Branding Iron 1971-80, 88-91), Hist. Soc. So. Calif. (dir. 1972-75), Henry E./Arabella Huntington Soc., Kappa Sigma (lit. editor Caduceus 1968-80). Home: PO Box 80250 San Marino CA 91118-8250 Office: Golden West Books 525 N Electric Ave Alhambra CA 91801-2032

DUKE, GARY PHILIP, architect, developer, broker; b. Chgo., July 25, 1957; s. Godfrey Lawrence and Audrey Louise (Huey) D.; m. Jan Alison Mosteller, May 14, 1983. BS in Architecture, Calif. Polytechnic U., 1979, MBA, 1980. Licensed architect, real estate broker, Calif. Architect Godfrey L. Duke A.I.A., San Diego, 1980-83; facility planner Hotel del Coronado, San Diego, 1983-85; architect, developer Duke Ptnrs., Deerfield, Ill., 1985-88; comml. real estate broker Cushman & Wakefield, L.A., 1988-89; real estate investor Duke Properties, Inc., L.A., 1989—. Mem. Big Brothers Am., San Luis Obispo, Calif., 1977-80. Recipient First Place award So. Calif. Art Exposition, San Diego, 1975. Mem. Am. Inst. of Architects (pres. assoc. student chpt. San Luis Obispo, Calif., 1979), Calif. Scholarship Found. (life mem.), Culver City C. of C., Toastmasters Club Internat., Kiwanis Club (v.p. Coronado, Calif. 1982-83).

DUKE, PAMELA RUTH, reading specialist; b. Salt Lake City, Feb. 14, 1945; d. Carson Bailey Duke and Ruth (Jones) Stafford. BA, Calif. State U., Chico, 1966; MA, Chapman U., 1973. Tchr. Murray Sch. Dist., Dublin, Calif., 1967-69; tchr. Lompoc (Calif.) Unified Schs., 1969-72, math specialist, 1972-86, reading specialist, 1986—; math fellow Tri-County Math. Project, Santa Barbara, 1985; fellow Impact II, Santa Barbara, 1987—. Grantee Impact II Santa Barbara, 1988, 90; recipient PTA scholarships, Calif. State PTA, L.A., 1992. Mem. PTA, Santa Maria Kennel Club, Calif. Tchrs. Assn., Reading Specialists Calif., Internat. Reading Assn., Calif. Reading Assn., Atari Fed. Office: Fillmore Elementary School 1211 E Pine Ave Lompoc CA 93436

DUKE, WILLIAM EDWARD, petroleum company executive; b. Bklyn., July 18, 1932; m. Leilani Kamp Lattin, May 7, 1977; children by previous marriage, William Edward, Jeffrey W., Michael R. BS, Fordham U., 1954. City editor Middletown (N.Y.) Record, 1956-60; asst. state editor Washington Star, 1961-63; exec. asst. to U.S. Senator from N.Y. State, Jacob K. Javits, Washington, 1963-69; dir. pub. affairs Corp. Pub. Broadcasting, Washington, 1969-72; dir. fed. govt. rels. Atlantic Richfield Co., Washington, 1973-78, mgr. pub. affairs, L.A., 1978-90; mgr. external affairs We. States Petroleum Assn., 1993—; lectr. U. So. Calif. Grad. Sch. Journalism, 1988—; cons. in field. Community trustee Greater Washington Ednl. Telecommunications Assn., WETA-TV-FM, chmn. radio com., exec. com., 1976-78; Fellow Pub. Rels. Soc. Am. (bd. dirs. pub. affairs sec.), Am. Petroleum Inst. Clubs: Nat. Press, Internat., Capitol Hill, Los Angeles Athletic. Office: We States Petroleum Assn 505 N Brand Blvd Glendale CA 91203

DUKER, LAURA THOMPSON, anthropologist, retired; b. Honolulu, Jan. 23, 1905; d. William and Maud (Balch) Thompson; m. John Collier, 1943 (div.); m. Sam Duker, 1963. BA, Mills Coll., 1927; PhD, U. Calif., Berkeley, 1933; LLD (hon.), Mills Coll., 1974. Asst. ethnologist Bishop Mus., Honolulu, 1929-34; social scientist Edn. Ter. Hawaii, Honolulu, 1940-41; coord. Indian Edn., Washington, 1946-54; prof. anthropology CCNY, 1954-56; vis. prof. anthropology U. N.C., Chapel Hill, 1957-58; vis. prof. N.C. State Coll., Raleigh, 1959-60; disting. vis. prof. Pa. State U., University Park, 1961; prof. anthropology U. So. Ill., Carbondale, Ill., 1961-62, San Francisco State U., 1962-63; lectr. CCNY, Bklyn., 1964; cons. U.S. Naval Govt. Guam, 1938-40, U.S. Office of Indian Affairs, Washington, 1942-44, Hutterite Socialization Project, Pa. State U., 1962-65; rep. Nat. Indian Inst., Mex., 1942, advisor plicy bd., Washington, 1946-54. Author: Fijian Frontier, 1940, Culture in Crisis, 1950, Guam and its People, 1941, The Secret of Culture, 1968, Beyond the Dream a Search for Meaning, 1991; author: (with A. Joseph) The Hopi Way, 1941. Mem. AAUW, Soc. for Applied Anthropology (founder). Home: 1434 Punahou St Honolulu HI 96822

DUKES, JOAN, state legislator; b. Tacoma, Wash., 1947; 3 children. BA, Evergreen State Coll. Mem. Oreg. State Senate, Dist. 1, 1987—. Democrat. Home: Rte 2 Box 503 Astoria OR 97103 Office: State Capitol S-210 Salem OR 97310

DUKES, LAJENNE MARIE, chiropractic physician; b. Chadron, Nebr., Sept. 12, 1931; d. James Ellsworth and LuRena Mary (Malsi) Phillips; m. Henry Benard Dukes, May 19, 1951 (div. Apr. 1985); children: Christine Dukes Creigh, Catherine Dukes Lucchesi, Craig, Cheryl. AAS in Retail/Mktg., Bus./Midmgmt., AA, Clark County Community Coll., 1980; D of Chiropractic, Western States Chiropractic, Portland, Oreg., 1983. Diplomate Nat. Bd. Chiropractic Examiners. Dictaphone sec. Las Vegas Conv. Bur., 1963-64, part-time registration convs. and housing, 1963-76; typist-clk. housing bur. Las Vegas Conv. Visitors Authority, 1976-78; svc. rep. Cen. Telephone Co., Las Vegas, 1978-80; casino security guard Stardust Hotel and Casino, Las Vegas, 1981; intern/preceptorship Chiropractic Physicians Ctr., Las Vegas, 1983-85; owner Spring Valley Chiropractic Ctr., Las Vegas, 1985—; prof., lectr. Americana Leadership Coll., Inc. Contbr. articles to mags. Mem. Am. Chiropractic Assn., Nev. State Chiropractic Assn., Oreg. Chiropractic Physicians Assn., Parker Chiropractic Rsch. Found., Toastmasters Internat., Women's Coun. C. of C., Coop. Assn. Chiropractic Physicians, Calif. Chiropractic Assn., David Singer Enterprises (chiropractic cons.), Found. Chiropractic Edn. and Rsch., Las Vegas Success Network, Las Vegas C. of C., Clark County Women's Dem. Club, Beta Sigma Phi. Democrat. Roman Catholic. Office: Spring Valley Chiropractic # 109 3233 W Charleston Blvd Las Vegas NV 89102-1923

DULBECCO, RENATO, biologist, educator; b. Catanzaro, Italy, Feb. 22, 1914; came to U.S., 1947, naturalized, 1953; s. Leonardo and Maria (Virdia) D.; m. Guiseppina Salvo, June 1, 1940 (div. 1963); children: Peter Leonard (dec.), Maria Vittoria; m. Maureen Muir; 1 dau., Fiona Linsey. M.D., U. Torino, Italy, 1936; D.Sc. (hon.), Yale U., 1968, Vrije Universiteit, Brussels, 1978; LL.D., U. Glasgow, Scotland, 1970. Asst. U. Torino, 1940-47; research asso. Ind. U., 1947-49; sr. research fellow Calif. Inst. Tech., 1949-52, asso. prof., then prof. biology, 1952-63; sr. fellow Salk Inst. Biol. Studies, San Diego, 1963-71; asst. dir. research Imperial Cancer Research Fund, London, 1971-74; dep. dir. research Imperial Cancer Research Fund, 1974-77; disting. research prof. Salk Inst., La Jolla, Calif., 1977—, pres., 1989-92; pres. emeritus Salk Inst., La Jolla, 1993—; prof. pathology and medicine U. Calif. at San Diego Med. Sch., La Jolla, 1977-81, mem. Cancer Ctr.,; vis. prof. Royal Soc. G.B., 1963-64, Leeuwenhoek lectr., 1974; Clowes Meml. lectr. Atlantic City, 1961; Harvey lectr. Harvey Soc., 1967; Dunham lectr. Harvard U., 1972; 11th Marjory Stephenson Meml. lectr., London, 1973, Harden lectr., Wye, Eng., 1973, Am. Soc. for Microbiology lectr., L.A., 1979; mem. Calif. Cancr Adv. Coun., 1963-67; mem. vis. com. Case Western Res. Sch. Medicine; adv. bd. Roche Inst., 1968-71, Inst. Immunology, Basel, Switzerland, others. Trustee LaJolla Country Day Sch. Recipient John Scott award City Phila., 1958; Kimball award Conf. Pub. Health Lab. Dirs., 1959; Albert and Mary Lasker Basic Med. Research award, 1964; Howard Taylor Ricketts award, 1965; Paul Ehrlich-Ludwig Darmstaedter prize, 1967; Horwitz prize Columbia U., 1973; (with David Baltimore and Howard Martin Temin) Nobel prize in medicine, 1975; Targa d'oro Villa San Giovanni, 1978; Mandel Gold medal Czechoslovak Acad. Scis., 1982, Via de Condotti prize, 1990; Cavaliere di Gran Croce Italian Rep., 1991; named Man of Yr. London, 1975; Italian Am. of Yr. San Diego County, Calif., 1978; hon. citizen City of Imperia (Italy), 1983; Guggenheim and Fulbright fellow, 1957-58; decorated grand ufficiale Italian Republic, 1981; hon. founder Hebrew U., 1981. Mem. NAS (Selman A. Waksman award 1974, com. on human rights), Am. Assn. Cancer Rsch., Internat. Physicians for Prevention Nuclear War, Am. Philos. Soc., Accademia Nazionale del Lincel (fgn.), Accademia Ligure di Scienze e Lettre (hon.), Royal Soc. (fgn. mem.). Home: 7525 Hillside Dr La Jolla CA 92037-3941

DULEY, CHARLOTTE DUDLEY, vocational counselor; b. Lincoln, Nebr., Oct. 2, 1920; d. Millard Eugene and Inez Kathryn (Miller) Dudley; student U. Nebr., 1938-41; M.A. in Guidance Counseling, U. Idaho, 1977; B.S., Lewis and Clark State Coll., 1973; m. Phillip D. Duley, Mar. 28, 1942; (dec. Sept. 1984); children: Michael Dudley (dec.), Patricia Kaye; m. P. Fredrik Nordgaard, Sep.1, 1990. Tchr., Nebr. schs., 1951-56; with Dept. of Employment, Lewiston, Idaho, 1958-81, local office counselor handling fed. tng. programs, 1958-81; ind. job cons.; counselor; rep. Avon, Lewiston; part-time counselor, tester, 1981—. Pres., bd. dirs. Civic Arts, Inc., 1972-81; mem. women's svc. league Wash.-Idaho Symphony Orch., 1972—; bd. dirs. YWCA, 1980-88, treas., 1981-88; mem. adv. bd. Salvation Army, 1980—; dir. artist series Lewis and Clark State Coll., 1984-90. Recipient Altrusa Woman of Achievement award, 1984. Mem. Am., Idaho pers. guidance Assns., Idaho State Employees Assn., Internat. Assn. Employees in Employment Security, Am. Assn. Counseling & Devel., Idaho State Employment Counselors Assn. (pres. 1979-80), Stateline Guidance and Counseling Assn. (sec.-treas. 1964, 76-77), Lewiston Community Concert Assn. (bd. dirs., pres. 1980—), Greater Lewiston C. of C. (chmn. conv. and tourism com. 1984-87), Altrusa (bd. dirs.), Elks (pres. 1986-87, exec. bd. 1985-88, election bd. chmn. 1986—, 1st v.p., 1993—). Baptist. Home: 1819 Ridgeway Dr Lewiston ID 83501-3890

DULUDE, GARY JOSEPH, copywriter; b. Abilene, Tex., June 29, 1966; s. Ronald Joseph and Patricia Lillian (Earle) D. BA, Angelo State U., 1987. Copywriter Mark Anderson Assocs., Scottsdale, Ariz., 1988—; asst. to bd. officers Tech. Mktg. Assn., Phoenix, Ariz., 1991—. Contbr. articles to profl. jours. Republican. Baptist. Office: Mark Anderson Assocs 8700 E Via De Ventura Ste 235 Scottsdale AZ 85258-4500

DUMAINE, R. PIERRE, bishop; b. Paducah, Ky., Aug. 2, 1931; student St. Joseph Coll., Mountain View, Calif., 1945-51, St. Patrick Sem., Menlo Park, Calif., 1951-57; Ph.D., Cath. U. Am., 1962. Ordained priest Roman Cath. Ch., 1957; asst. pastor Immaculate Heart Ch., Belmont, Calif., 1957-58; mem. faculty dept. edn. Cath. U. Am., 1961-63; tchr. Serra High Sch., San Mateo, Calif., 1963-65; asst. supt. Cath. schs., Archdiocese of San Francisco, 1965-74, supt., 1974-78; ordained bishop, 1978, bishop of San Jose, Santa Clara, Calif., 1981—; dir. Archdiocesan Ednl. TV Ctr., Menlo Park, Calif., 1968-81. Mem. Pres.'s Nat. Adv. Council on Edn. of Disadvantaged Children, 1970-72; bd. dirs. Cath. TV Network, 1968-81, pres., 1975-77; bd. dirs. Pub. Service Satellite Consortium, 1975-81. Mem. Nat. Cath. Edn. Assn., Assn. Cath. Broadcasters and Allied Communicators, Internat. Inst. Communications, Assn. Calif. Sch. Adminstrs. Office: Diocese of San Jose 900 Lafayette St Ste 301 Santa Clara CA 95050-4966*

DUMAS, LOUISE ISABELLE, elementary school educator; b. Greensboro, Ala.; d. Walter James and Alise (Collins) Outland; m. Andrew Alexander Dumas, July 8, 1962; children: Andrew A. Jr., Cassandra Alise. BS, Ala. State U., 1956; Hon. PhD, Faith Coll., Birmingham, Ala., 1993. Tchr. Hale Country Elem. Sch., Greensboro, Ala., 1956-66, Muroc Unified Sch. Dist., Edwards, Calif., 1967—. Mem. Antelope Valley Alpha Charter Guild of Antelope Valley Hosp.; v.p. A.V. Juliettes, Lancaster, Calif., 1986-89. Mem. NEA, AAUW (scholarship com.), Muroc Edn. Assn. (bldg. rep. 1971-73), Calif. Elem. Edn. Assn., Calif. Tchrs. Assn., Delta Sigma Theta, Delta Kappa Gamma. Republican. Methodist. Home: 43636 Devyn Ln Lancaster CA 93535-5804

DUMITRESCU, DOMNITA, educator, researcher; b. Bucharest, Romania; came to U.S., 1984; d. Ion and Angela (Barzotescu) D. Diploma, U. Bucharest, 1966; MA, U. So. Calif., L.A., 1987, PhD, 1990. Asst. prof. U. Bucharest, 1966-74, assoc. prof., 1974-84; asst. lectr. U. So. Calif., 1985-89; asst. prof. Calif. State U., L.A., 1987-90, assoc. prof., 1990—. Author: Gramatica Limbii Spaniole, 1976, Indreptar Pentru Traducerea Din Limba Romana in Limba Spaniola, 1980; translator from Spanish lit. to Romanian; contbr. articles to profl. jours. Fulbright scholar, 1993—. Mem. MLA, Am.-Romanian Acad. Arts and Scis., Am. Assn. Tchrs. Spanish, Linguistic Soc. Am., Internat. Assn. Hispanists, Assn. Linguistics and Philology of Latin Am., Spanish Linguistics Soc., Am. Assn. Tchrs. Spanish and Portuguese (pres. So. Calif. chpt.). Office: Calif State U 5151 State University Dr Los Angeles CA 90032-4221

DUNAGAN, JAMES ALAN, radio announcer, broadcasting educator; b. Astoria, Oreg., Jan. 28, 1954; s. Archie Frederick and Jocelyn Arlene (Poston) D.; m. Sharon Lea Rose, Aug. 18, 1979 (div. Aug. 1988). Student, Linfield Coll., 1976. Announcer, program dir. Sta. KBMY, Billings, Mont., 1978-80; announcer, music dir. Sta. KUUY, Cheyenne, Wyo., 1980-82; announcer, music and program dir. Wyomedia Inc. (Sta. KTAG & KTRS), Cody and Casper, Wyo., 1982-84; announcer, music dir. Sta. KZLS, Billings, 1984-87; instr. May Sch. of Broadcasting, Billings, 1985-87; announcer Sta. KPLZ, Seattle, 1987—; instr. Conn. Sch. of Broadcasting, Bellevue, Wash., 1990—. Methodist.

DUNAWAY, DAVID R., construction executive, business owner; b. Kansas City, Kans., Apr. 20, 1939; s. Raymond John and Martha Cathryn (Whittelsey) D. BA in Sociology, Duke U., 1971; postgrad., U. Nev., 1979-81. Tight end Green Bay (Wis.) Packers, 1966-68, Atlanta Falcons, 1969, N.Y. Giants, N.Y.C., 1969-72; owner, gen. contractor Custom Home Builder, L.A., 1973-79; gen. contractor, owner restaurant, bar, lounge and casino, Custom Home Builder, Las Vegas, Nev., 1979—. Mem. spl. events com. Am. Cancer Soc., Las Vegas, 1980-82; counselor nutrition and weight tng. Child SuperStar Program, L.A., 1977—; mem. Make-A-Wish Found., Las Vegas, 1989—, Rep. Senatorial Inner Circle, 1988, Athletes Internat. Ministries, Phoenix, St. Jude's Ranch, We Can Child Abuse, United Cerebral Palsy Assn. Named to Nat. Football Found. Hall of Fame. Mem. NFL Players Assn., NFL Alumni Assn. Presbyterian. Home: 335 Greenbriar Townhouse Way Las Vegas NV 89121-2421

DUNAWAY, MARGARET ANN (MAGGIE DUNAWAY), consultant; b. Fresno, Calif., Feb. 10, 1943; d. Joseph John and Anna Frances (Dice) Cumero; children from previous marriage, Christian Anthony Freitag, Erika Lynn Bullard; m. Michael Earl Babcoke, Oct. 6, 1990; 1 stepchild, Jason Earl Babcoke. Student, U. Calif., Davis, 1960-62, U. Calif., Berkeley, 1962-63. Supr. Gov's Office, Sacramento, 1969-72; office mgr. State Health and Welfare Agy., Sacramento, 1972-73; analyst regulations devel. Calif. State Depts. Health and Social Svcs., Sacramento, 1974-84, cons. adult and children's svcs., 1984-90, rep. adult svcs., 1984-90, with food drive com., 1987-88, rep. ind. living program com., 1989-90; community program specialist Calif. State Dept. Devel. Svcs., Sacramento, 1990—; project coord. SDSS study L.A. County Children's Svcs. Caseload, 1989-90. Active Southpark Homeowner's Assn., Sacramento, 1974-78; presenter Adult Svcs. Ann. Asilomar Conf., 1987. Office: Calif Dept Devel Svcs 1600 9th St Rm 320 Sacramento CA 95814

DUNAWAY, ROBERT LEE, sales and marketing executive; b. Indpls., Sept. 26, 1942; s. Robert Lee and Rosemary Ellen (McInturf) D.; m. Mary Catherine Peterson, Oct. 15, 1988; children: Robert III, Kirk E., Darcy L. BS in Mech. Engring., Purdue U., 1966; postgrad., U. Utah. Sales engr. Fisher Controls Co., Marshalltown, Iowa, 1966-73; sales mgr., owner, pres. Controls, Valves, Instrumentation Inc., Salt Lake City, 1973-87; regional sales mgr. Conax Florida Corp., L.A., 1987-89; regional sales and application mgr. Circle Seal Controls Co., Anaheim, Calif., 1989-91; sales and mktg. mgr. Crane Aerospace Corp., Burbank, Calif., 1991-93; cons. Aerospace/Indsl. Conversion, Calif. Bd. dirs. Marshalltown Community Theatre. Recipient Martha Ellen Tye award, 1970. Mem. Instrument Soc. Am. (sr. mem., sect. pres. 1975-76), Kappa Kappa Psi. Republican. Episcopalian. Home: PO Box 6543 Thousand Oaks CA 91359-6543

DUNBAR, MAURICE VICTOR, English language educator; b. Banner, Okla., May 24, 1928; s. Moyer Haywood and Louise Edna (Curry) D.; m. Carol Ann Cline, July 28, 1948 (div. 1963); children: Kurt, Karl, Karla, Karen. AA, Compton Jr. Coll., 1948; BA, U. Calif., Berkeley, 1952; MA, Calif. State U., Sacramento, 1965. Tchr. elem. sch. Lone Tree Sch., Beale AFB, Calif., 1962-64; prof. English De Anza Coll., Cupertino, Calif., 1962—; tchr. jr. high sch. Anna McKenney, Marysville, Calif., 1964-66; tchr. high sch. Yuba City (Calif.) High Sch., 1966-67; instr. jr. coll. Foothill Coll., Los Altos Hills, Calif., 1967-82. Author: Fundamentals of Book Collecting, 1976, Books and Collectors, 1980, Collecting Steinbeck, 1983; contbr. articles to profl. jours. With U.S. Army, 1948-58, PTO. Mem. Masons, Shriners. Republican. Office: De Anza Coll Cupertino CA 95014-5797

DUNBAR, PATRICIA LYNN, new product development consultant; b. St. Louis, Feb. 11, 1953; d. William R. and Beryl Ione Noland (Ferrand) Dunbar; m. Michael R. Jeffrey, Oct. 2, 1950. BS, Northwestern U., 1973, MFA, 1975. With NBC-TV, Chgo., 1975-79; regional sales/mktg. mgr. Home Box Office, Chgo., 1979-81; sr. product mgr. Bank of Am., San Francisco, 1981-82, v.p., 1982-84; interactive communications services cons., 1984—. Mem. Women in Cable (1st pres. Chgo. chpt. 1981), Jr. League Seattle. Episcopalian. Patentee on child's chair, 1973.

DUNBAR, RICHARD PAUL, sales manager; b. Watertown, S.D., Aug. 28, 1951; s. Earl Paul and Leona Matilda (Clausen) D. Student, S.D. State U., 1969-71; BSBA, U. Ariz., 1981. Account mgr. bus. forms and supplies div. Nat. Cash Register, Phoenix, 1981-83; sales cons. Compugraphic Corp., Phoenix, 1983-84; sales rep. constrn. products div. W.R. Grace and Co., Phoenix and Tucson, 1985-87; sales rep. constrn. products div. for Ariz., so. Nev., N.Mex., El Paso (Tex.) region Pleko SW, Inc., Tempe, Ariz., 1987-92, S.W. regional sales mgr., 1992—. Mem. Jaycees (treas. 1977-78, recipient Outstanding Jaycee award, Pres.'s award, Jaycee of Month award), Constrn. Specifications Inst. (chmn. tech. documents com. Tucson chpt. 1987, program chmn. Phoenix chpt. 1988-89, Chpt. Pres'. Cert. award 1988, 90, 91, 92, dir. Phoenix chpt. 1989-90, Outstanding Indsl. award 1989, editor monthly newsletter Phoenix chpt. 1990-91, Inst. Publs. Commendation award 1990, 91, Gem award 1990, 1st v.p. Phoenix chpt. 1991, rep. Ariz. Constrn. Industries Coalition 1991—, chmn. S.W. region publs. 1992, pres.-elect Phoenix chpt. 1992, chmn. nominating com. 1992, CCPR inst. rev. com. 1992, region dir. citation 1992, S.W. region cert. thanks 1992, pres. Phoenix chpt., 1993, Individual Appreciation award 1991), Constrn. Products Mfrs. Coun. (treas. 1986), Alpha Mu Alpha. Republican. Congregational. Office: Pleko SW Inc 1824 E 6th St Tempe AZ 85281-2950

DUNCAN, ANDREW MALCOLM, engineer; b. London, May 27, 1960; came to U.S., 1965; s. Glen Malcolm and Eleanor Jane (Watson) D.; m. Gabriella Clementine Borsay, Aug. 23, 1986 (div. Oct. 1987). BS in Engring., Calif. Inst. Tech., 1983; MA in Pure Math, U. Calif., Santa Cruz, 1989. Physics tchr. Pasadena (Calif.) Sch. Dist., 1983-84; programmer Cerwin-Vega, Simi Valley, Calif., 1984-86, 89; cons. E-mu Systems, Scotts Valley, Calif., 1987-88; engr. MAMA Found., Studio City, Calif., 1990-92; sr. engr. Philips Interactive Media, L.A., 1992—. Developer zebra bd. synthesizer, 1991. Mem. Audio Engring. Soc. (committeeman 1990-92, publ. award 1989), Am. Math. Soc. (jour. rev. bd. 1993—). Home: 641 Las Lomas Ave Pacific Palisades CA 90272-3355 Office: Philips Interactive Media 11050 Santa Monica Blvd Los Angeles CA 90025-7511

DUNCAN, ANSLEY MCKINLEY, aerospace company executive; b. Homer City, Pa., Jan. 25, 1932; s. William McKinley and Marion Melissa (Davis) D. Student, U. Denver, 1955-57, Pa. State U., 1957-59. Engring. adminstr. RCA, Van Nuys, Calif., 1959-61; program evaluation coord. N.Am. Aviation, Anaheim, Calif., 1961-66; mfg. supr., Rockwell Internat., Anaheim Calif., 1966-70, program adminstr., 1970-76, program controls mgr., 1976-81, plans/schedule advisor, 1981-89; ret., 1989.With USN, 1951-55. Home: 12600 Willowood Ave Garden Grove CA 92640-4245

DUNCAN, DORIS GOTTSCHALK, information systems educator; b. Seattle, Nov. 19, 1944; d. Raymond Robert and Marian (Onstad) D.; m. Robert George Gottschalk, Sept. 12, 1971 (div. Dec. 1983). B.A., U. Wash., Seattle, 1967, M.B.A., 1968; Ph.D., Golden Gate U., 1978. Cert. data processor, systems profl., data educator. Communications cons. Pacific NW Bell Telephone Co., Seattle, 1968-71; mktg. supr. AT&T, San Francisco, 1971-73; sr. cons., project leader Quantum Sci. Corp., Palo Alto, Calif., 1973-75; dir. co. analysis program Input Inc., Palo Alto, 1975-76; dir. info. sci. dept. Golden Gate U., San Francisco, 1982-83, mem. info. systems adv. bd., 1983-85; lectr. acctg. and info. systems Calif. State U., Hayward, 1976-78, assoc. prof., 1978-85, prof., 1985—; cons. pvt. cos., 1975—; speaker profl. groups and confs. Author: Computers and Remote Computing Services, 1983; contbr. articles to profl. jours. Loaned exec. United Good Neighbors, Seattle, 1969; nat. committeewoman, bd. dirs. Young Reps., Wash., 1970-71; adv. Jr. Achievement, San Francisco, 1971-72; mem. nat. bd. Inst. for Certification of Computer Profls. Edn. Found., 1990—; mem. Editorial Rev. bd. Journal Info. Systems Edn., 1992—; bd. dirs. Computer Repair Svcs., 1992—. Mem. Data Processing Mgmt. Assn. (1982, Meritorious Service award, Bronze award 1984, Silver award 1986, Gold Award 1988, Emerald award 1992, Nat. grantee, 1984. dir., edn. chmn. San Francisco chpt. 1984-85, sec. and v.p. 1985, pres. 1986, assn. dir. 1987, by-laws chmn. 1987; nat. bd. dirs. spl. interest group in edn. 1985-87), Am. Inst. Decision Scis., 1982-83, Western Assn. Schs. and Colls. (accreditation evaluation team, 1984-85), Assn. Computing Machinery, 1984—. Club: Junior (Seattle). Subspecialties: Information systems (information science). Current work: curriculum development, professionalism in data processing field, professional certification, industry standards, computer literacy and user education, design of data bases and data banks. Office: Calif State U Sch of Bus and Econs Hayward CA 94542

DUNCAN, IRMA WAGNER, retired biochemist, museum educator; b. Buffalo, Jan. 30, 1912; d. Carl R. and Emily (Leue) Wagner; m. David R.L. Duncan, Mar. 21, 1937 (dec. Aug. 1972); children: David L., Paul R. BS, U. Buffalo, 1933; MS, U. Chgo., 1935, PhD, 1950. Prof. sci. Colo. Women's Coll., Denver, 1944-48; assoc. prof. chemistry U. Denver, 1951-59; rsch. chemist Arctic Health Rsch. Ctr., HEW, USPHS, Anchorage, Alaska, 1960-67, Fairbanks, Alaska, 1967-74; rsch. chemist Ctrs. for Disease Control, USPHS, Atlanta, 1974-82; docent N.Mex. Mus. Nat. History and Sci., Albuquerque, 1984—, Maxwell Mus. Anthropology, U. N.Mex., Albuquerque, 1984—. Editor work books; contbr. articles to prof. jours. Mem. Am. Assn. Ret. Persons, Gray Panthers, Nature Conservancy, Sierra Club, Sigma Xi (emeritus). Home: 1620 Francisca Rd NW Albuquerque NM 87107

DUNCAN, JAMES BYRON, research engineer; b. Georgetown, Tex., Aug. 10, 1947; s. Joseph Dewitt and Oma Faye (Darby) D.; m. Billie Jeanne Latson, Aug. 22, 1970 (div. May 1973); 1 child, Douglas Brian; m. Joanne Patricia Cleveland, Feb. 14, 1984. BS, U. Ark., 1970; MS, Tex. Tech. U., 1972, PhD, 1985. Head, advanced chem. tech. group Eastman Kodak Co., Rochester, N.Y., 1986-91; staff scientist Batelle, Pacific NW Labs., Richland, Wash., 1991-92; prin. engr. Westinghouse Hanford Co., Richland, Wash., 1992—; cons. Tex. Vet. Labs., Ludbock, 1976-79, U.S. Army Mobility and Energy R & D Labs., Ft. Belvoir, Va., 1981-84; lectr. Wash. State U., Richland, 1992—. Co-inventor of membrane to separate tritiated water from water. Maj. U.S. Army, 1980-85, USAR, 1985—. Mem. Chi Epsilon, Sigma Xi. Home: 2507 S Jefferson Ct Kennewick WA 99337

DUNCAN, JAMES RICHARD, broadcast engineer; b. Little Rock, June 3, 1948; s. James Richard and Mary (Bond) D. BA in Geography, U. Calif., Berkeley, 1969; postgrad. in mass comms., Denver U., 1970. Profl. broadcast engr. Cons. self-employed San Jose, Calif., 1972-90; broadcast engr. Nationwide Comms., San Jose, Calif., 1985-90; corp. engr. Kool Comms., San Jose, Calif., 1990—; cons. Ohlone Community Coll., Fremont, Calif., 1990—. Mem. Soc. Broadcast Engrs., Am. Coun. for Arts, Studio Ballet Theater, Santa Clara Ballet, No. Calif. Frequency Coord. Comm. Home: 380 Blossom Way Scotts Valley CA 95066 Office: KUFX Radio Sta 1589 Schallenberger Rd San Jose CA 95131

DUNCAN, JOHN WILEY, mathematics and computer educator, retired air force officer; b. San Francisco, Aug. 8, 1947; s. Vernon Alexander and Nellie May (Shaw) D.; m. Trudy Rae Hirsch, Feb. 25, 1967; children: Amber Rose, John Anthony. BS in Math. and Physics, N.W. Mo. State U., 1969; MBA, So. Ill. U., 1973; MS in Computer Sci., U. Tex., San Antonio, 1982. Tchr. Savannah (Mo.) High Sch., 1969; enlisted USAF, 1969, advanced through grades to maj.; aeromed. officer 9AES USAF, Clark Air Base, The Philippines, 1978-80; student UTSA, San Antonio, 1981-82; systems implementation team leader Sch. of Health Care Scics., Sheppard AFB, Tex., 1982-83; asst. chief med. systems Hdqrs. Air Tng. Command, Randolph AFB, Tex., 1983-86; chief med. systems Hdqrs. Pacific AF, Hickham AFB, Hawaii, 1986-89, 15 Med. Group, Hickham AFB, Hawaii, 1989; tchr. Kapiolani Community Coll., Honolulu, 1989—; computer cons., 1983—; instr. Tex. Luth. Coll., Seguin, 1984-86, Hawaii Pacific Coll., Honolulu, 1987-89, Leeward Community Coll., 1989-91. Cons. Ronald McDonald House, San Antonio, 1986. Presbyterian. Home: 4486 Luapele Pl Honolulu HI 96818-1983

DUNCAN, KATE CORBIN, art historian, educator; b. Mesa, Ariz., Aug. 16, 1942; d. Gordon M. and Anne (Maulsby) Corbin. BA, U. N.Mex., Albuquerque, 1964, MA, 1967; PhD, U. Wash., Seattle, 1982. Lectr. U. Alaska, Fairbanks, 1970-71, 74, U. Wash., 1981, 83-85; asst. prof. dept. fine arts Seattle U., 1985-90, chair dept. fine arts, 1985-88; asst. prof. Sch. of Art Ariz. State U., Tempe, 1991-92, assoc. prof. Sch. of Art, 1992—; cons. in field. Author: Northern Athapaskan Art, 1989 (Davenport Publ. award 1991); co-author: A Special Gift, 1988, Out of the North, 1989; contbr. articles to profl. jours. Smithsonian Instn. fellow, 1978-79, Getty Trust fellow, 1985-86; grantee Can. Ethnology Svc., 1982, Wenner Gren Found., 1982, 84, Am. Philos. Soc., 1985, Can. Consulate, 1993. Mem. Costume Soc. Am. (bd. dirs.), Am. Anthrop. Assn., Coun. for Mus. Anthrop., Coll. Art Assn., Alaska-Siberia Rsch.Inst., Native Am. Art Studies Assn., Soc. Bead Rschrs. Office: Ariz State Univ Sch of Art Tempe AZ 85287-1505

DUNCAN, STEVEN MERLE, construction company manager, philosophy educator; b. Seattle, Jan. 12, 1954; s. Merle Albert and Lydia (Herrera) D. BA, U. Wash., 1976, PhD, 1987; MA, U. Utah, 1978. Teaching fellow U. Utah, Salt Lake City, 1976-78, U. Mo., Columbia, 1978-79, U. Wash., Seattle, 1979-84; philos. instr. Pierce Coll., Tacoma, Wash., 1987-88; security specialist First Interstate Bank of Wash., Seattle, 1989-90; office mgr. Higrade Construction Asphalt, Inc., Puyallup, Wash., 1990—; part-time instr. Green River C.C., Auburn, Wash., 1982-83, Highline C.C., Seattle, 1986; vis. prof. Western Wash. U, Bellingham, 1983. Active St. Martin of Tours Parish, Fife, Wash.; mem. Metro Transit Citizens Adv. Panel, Seattle, 1984-86, St. James Cathedral Parish, Seattle, 1979-90. Gregory scholar U. Mo., 1979. Mem. Am. Philos. Assn., U.S. Chess Fedn., Wash. Chess Fedn., U. Wash. Alumni Assn. Roman Catholic. Home: 111 Meridian E Puyallup WA 98372

DUNCAN, VERNE ALLEN, university dean; b. McMinnville, Oreg., Apr. 6, 1934; s. Charles Kenneth and S. La Verne (Robbins) D.; m. Donna Rose Nichols, July 11, 1964; children: Annette Marie Kirk, Christine Lauree Didway. B.A., Idaho State U., 1960; M.Ed., Univ. Idaho, 1964; Ph.D., U. Oreg., 1968; M.B.A., U. Portland, 1976. Tchr. Butte County (Idaho) Pub. Schs., 1954-56, prin., 1958-63, supt. schs., 1963-66; rsch. asst. U. Oreg., 1966-68, asst. prof. ednl. adminstrn., 1968-70; supt. Clackamas County (Oreg.) Intermediate Edn. Dist., 1970-75; elected supt. pub. instrn. State of Oreg., 1975-89, re-elected, 1978, 82, 86; dean Sch. Edn. U. Portland, Oreg., 1989—; chmn. commn. on ednl. credits and credentials Am. Coun. on Edn.; commr. Gov's Commn. on Futures Rsch.; mem. Edn. Commn. of States. Author numerous articles on ednl. adminstrn. Trustee Marylhurst Coll.; mem. gov. bd. Fund for Improvement & Reform of Schs. & Teaching U.S. Dept. Edn.; mem. Idaho Ho. of Reps., 1962-65, chmn. econ. affairs com.; mem. interim com. Oreg. Legis. Assembly Improvements Com. With U.S. Army, 1956-58. Mem. Am. Assn. Sch. Adminstrs., Council Chief State Sch. Officers (pres. 1987-89), Res. Officers Assn., Nat. Forum Edn. Leaders, Sons and Daughters of Oreg. Pioneers (state pres. 1993—), Phi Delta Kappa (Educator-Statesman of Yr. award 1977). Republican. Presbyterian. Home: 16911 SE River Rd Portland OR 97267-5502 Office: U Portland 5000 N Willamette Blvd Portland OR 97203-5750

DUNCAN, WILLIAM LOUIS, photographer, educator; b. Salt Lake City, Nov. 17, 1945; s. Louis William and Mae U. (Jeppsen) D.; m. Marilyn Bardsley, Apr. 1, 1968; children: Cindy Kay, Gay Linn, LeAnn Dawn. Student, U. Utah, 1964-68, Famous Artists Sch., Westport, Conn., 1969; M Photography, Profl. Photographers Am., New Orleans, 1989. Advt. artist Ross Jurney Advt. Agy., Salt Lake City, 1967-71; artist, prodn. lithographer Blaine Hudson Printing Co., Salt Lake City, 1971-73; artist, prodn. cameraman Rocky Mountain Bank Note Co., Salt Lake City, 1973-74; artist, photographer Skaggs Cos. Inc., Salt Lake City, 1974-76; owner, mgr. Duncan Photography Studio, Salt Lake City, 1976—; photographer Hercules Aerospace Co., Magna, Utah, 1984-90; tchr. photography high schs., Salt Lake City, 1976, 77, 78, profl. photog. orgns., Miss., Salt Lake City, Wash., Denver, Idaho, Ga., 1985—, bus. and comml. orgns., Salt Lake City, 1987, 88; photog. supr. div. exhbn. Utah State Fair. Contbr. illustrated articles to profl. pubis. Photog. judge Utah Fair Expns., 1978-88; supr. Utah State Fair Photog. Exhibit, 1991. Recipient award Hallmark Color Labs., 1982, award of excellence Kodak Gallery, 1988, 89, 91, Best of Show award Utah Div. Expns., 1981, 82, 83, Utah State Fair Assn., 1982, 88, also numerous awards from photog. assns. Mem. Profl. Photographers Am. (cert., nat. photog. judge 1982—, numerous awards), Wedding Photographers Internat. (life, awards 1973—, award of excellence 1989), Rocky Mountain Profl. Photographers Assn. (conv. bd. 1987), Intermountain Profl. Photographers Assn. (bd. dirs. 1980-86, program dir., conv. dir. 1985-86), Photog. Soc. Am. (instr. 1986—). Republican. Mormon. Office: 4915 S 3200 W Salt Lake City UT 84118-2931

DUNCKER, MICHAEL CHARLES, dentist; b. Montebello, Calif., Dec. 30, 1950; s. Charles Montiel and Helen (Hunick) D.; m. Marie DeLeon, 1975 (div. 1985); 1 child, Vanessa Leann. BA, U. So. Calif., L.A., 1976; DDS, UCLA, 1980. Sr. staff dentist Community Health Found., East L.A., 1980-86; dentist/owner Cali Family Dental Ctr., Huntington Park, Calif., 1986—; pvt. practice Downey, Calif., 1993—. With U.S. Army, 1970-72. Mem. Latin Am. Dental Assn. (pres. 1991-92), Kiwanis (bd. dirs. 1991-92). Office: 11411 Brookshire Ave Ste 405 Downey CA 90241

DUNFORD, MAX PATTERSON, biology educator; b. Bloomington, Idaho, June 17, 1930; s. George Osmond and Venna (Patterson) D.; m. Katie Pearl Thornhill, Sept. 1, 1954; children: Mark L., Steven O., Keith M., Thomas M., Karen, Allen R. A.S., Snow Coll., 1950; B.S., Brigham Young U., 1954, M.S., 1958; Ph.D., U. Calif., Davis, 1962. Faculty U. Calif., Santa Barbara, 1961-62, Mills Coll., Oakland, Calif., 1962-63; faculty biology dept. N.Mex. State U., Las Cruces, 1963—; asst. chmn. biology dept. N.Mex. State U., 1992—; asst. chmn. dept. biology N.Mex. State U., Las Cruces, 1992—. Contbr. articles to profl. jours. Served with U.S. Army, 1954-56. NSF grantee, 1966-68, 75, 77, 78, 79, 81. Fellow AAAS (exec. officer Southwestern and Rocky Mountain div. 1973-78, pres. SWARM 1981-82, mem. council, com. for council affairs 1973-79); mem. Bot. Soc. Am., Am. Genetic Assn. Mem. Ch. of Jesus Christ of Latter-day Saints. Home: 205 Capri Rd Las Cruces NM 88005-3726

DUNGWORTH, DONALD L., veterinary educator, consultant; b. Hathersage, Derbyshire, Eng., July 16, 1931; came to U.S., 1957; s. Lawrence and Alice (Dearnaley) D.; m. Margaret Alice Begg, July 28, 1961; children: Dawn Lesley, Duncan Lawrence. BVSc, Liverpool U., Eng., 1956; PhD, U. Calif., Davis, 1961. Lectr. U. Bristol, Eng., 1961-62; from asst. prof. to prof., dept. veterinary med. pathology U. Calif., Davis, 1962—, chmn., 1969—; cons. pulmonary path and inhalation toxicology, Internat. Agy. for Rsch. on Cancer and various nat. and internat. insts., 1980—. Author, editor books. Lt. Brit. Army, 1949-51. Recipient Sr. award Von Humboldt Found., 1990-91; WHO fellow, 1968-69, Fulbright fellow Fulbright-Hays Program, 1976-77. Mem. Royal Coll. of Vet. Surgeons, Am. Assn. Pathologists, Am. Coll. Toxicology, Internat. Acad. Pathology, Am. Coll. Vet. Pathologists (diplomate, pres. 1977-78). Office: U Calif Davis School Vet Med Dept Vet Pathology Davis CA 95616

DUNHAM, GLEN CURTIS, materials scientist, consultant; b. Grand Forks, N.D., Nov. 3, 1956; s. Vern Kenneth and Mary Jean (Larsen) D.; m. Cheryl Renee Daehlin, July 7, 1979; children: Kari, Erik, Isak, Joshua. BS in Physics cum laude, Pacific Luth. U., 1980, BA in Chemistry cum laude, 1980; MS in Materials Sci., Wash. State U., 1983. Rsch. engr. U. Wash., Richland, 1983-89; rsch. scientist Wash. State U., Richland, 1989-92, Battelle Pacific Northwest Lab., 1992—; cons. Failure Analysis Assocs., Redmond, Wash., 1989-92, Matrix Scis., Richland, 1989-92, Advanced Imaging Systems, Richland, 1991, Siemens Quantum, Kirkland, Wash., 1992, Diagnostic Devices Group, Bellevue, Wash., 1992, Eastman Kodak, Rochester, N.Y., 1992; judge high sch. writing contest Soc. Tech. Communication, Richland, 1984—. Contbr. papers on photovoltaic rsch. to profl. publs. Organizer Jr. Solar Sprint, Richland, 1992. Mem. Assembly of God Ch. Home: 32003 Reata Rd Kennewick WA 99337 Office: Battelle Pacific Northwest Lab PO Box 999 Richland WA 99352

DUNIGAN, PAUL FRANCIS XAVIER, JR., federal agency administrator; b. Richland, Wash., June 22, 1948; s. Paul Frances Xavier Sr. and Eva Lucille (Reckley) D.; m. Elizabeth Anne Henricks, Apr. 8, 1978; children: Katherine Anne, Theresa Anne. BS in Biology, Gonzaga U., 1970; MS in Environ. Sci., Washington State U., 1973. Tech. program mgr. ERDA, AEC, Richland, 1972-75; environ. biologist U.S. Dept. Energy, ERDA, Richland, 1975-81; waste mgmt. engr. U.S. Dept. Energy Waste Mgmt., Richland, 1981-84; civilian program mgr. Surplus Facilities Mgmt. Program U.S. Dept. Energy, Richland, 1984-87, environ. biologist, 1987—; also compliance officer Nat. Environ. Policy Act. Contbr. articles to profl. jours. Mem. AAAS, Water Pollution Control Fedn., Pacific Northwest Pollution Control Fedn. Roman Catholic. Home: 1612 Judson Ave Richland WA 99352-2944 Office: US Dept Energy PO Box 550 Richland WA 99352-0550

DUNIPACE, IAN DOUGLAS, lawyer; b. Tucson, Dec. 18, 1939; s. William Smith and Esther Morvyth (McGeorge) D.; m. Janet Mae Dailey, June 9, 1963; children: Kenneth Mark, Leslie Amanda. BA magna cum laude, U. Ariz., 1961, JD cum laude, 1966 Bar: Ariz. 1966, U.S. Supreme Ct. 1972. Reporter, critic Long Branch (N.J.) Daily Record, 1963; assoc. firm Jennings, Strouss, Salmon & Trask, Phoenix, 1966-69, Jennings, Strouss & Salmon, 1969-70, ptnr., 1971—. Reporter Phoenix Forward Edn. Com., 1969-70; mem. Phoenix Arts Commn., 1990—, chmn., 1992-93; bd. mgmt. Downtown Phoenix YMCA, 1973-80, chmn., 1977-78; bd. dirs. Phoenix Met. YMCA, 1976-87, 88—, chmn., 1984-85; bd. mgmt. Paradise Valley YMCA, 1979-82, chmn., 1980-81; bd. mgmt. Scottsdale/Paradise Valley YMCA, 1983, mem. legal affairs com. Pacific Region YMCA, 1978-81; chmn. YMCA Ariz. State Youth and Govt. Com., 1989—; bd. dirs. The Schoolhouse Found., 1990—, pres., 1990—, Kids Voting, 1990—, Beaver Valley Improvement Assn., 1977-79, Pi Kappa Alpha Holding Corp., 1968-72, The Heard Mus. 1993—; trustee Paradise Valley Unified Sch. Dist. Employee Benefit Trust, 1980-93, chmn., 1987-93; trustee First Meth. Found. of Phoenix, 1984-93; mem. Greater Paradise Valley Community Coun., 1985-87; bd. dirs. Heard Mus. Coun., pres. 1993-94, Heard Mus., 1993—. Capt. AUS, 1961-63. Mem. State Bar Ariz. (securities regulation sect. 1970—, chmn., 1991-92, mem. com. unauthorized practice of law 1972-84, chmn. 1975-83, mem. bus. law sect. 1981—, chmn., 1984-85), Am., Fed. (pres. Ariz. chpt. 1980-81), Maricopa County bar assns., Ariz. Zool. Soc., U. Ariz. Law Coll. Assn. (bd. dirs. 1983-90, pres. 1985-86), Smithsonian Assn., U. Ariz. Alumni Assn. (bd. dirs. 1985-86), Phi Beta Kappa, Phi Kappa Phi, Phi Delta Phi, Phi Alpha Theta, Sigma Delta Pi, Phi Eta Sigma, Pi Kappa Alpha (nat. counsel 1968-72). Democrat. Methodist (mem. met. Phoenix commn. 1968-71, lay leader 1975-78, trustee 1979-81, pres. 1981; mem. Pacific S.W. ann. conf. 1969-79, lawyer commn. 1980-85, chancellor Desert S.W. ann. conf. 1985—). Clubs: Renaissance. Lodges: Masons, Kiwanis (pres. Phoenix 1984-85, disting. lt. gov. 1986-87, SW dist. community service chmn. 1987-88, dist. activity com. coord. 1988-89, dist. laws and regulation chmn. 1989-90, 92-93, asst. to dist. gov. for club svcs. 1990-91, field dir. 1991-92, dist. conv. chmn., 1993—, mem. internat. com. on Project 39, 1988-89, internat. com. On to Anaheim 1990-91, internat. com. on leadership tng. and devel. 1991-92, 93—, trustee SW dist. found. 1987-92, 1st v.p. 1990-92). Comments editor Ariz. Law Rev., 1965-66. Home: 4147 E Desert Cove Phoenix AZ 85028-3514 Office: Jennings Strouss & Salmon 2 N Central 1 Renaissance Sq Phoenix AZ 85004-2393

DUNLAP, BURNIE HAROLD, computer systems executive, consultant; b. San Diego, June 3, 1943; s. Burnie H. Dunlap and Marie L. (Alvarado) Parks; m. Jacqué D. Dunlap, Oct. 7, 1967; children: Mark C., Jennifer M. BA, San Diego State U., 1967; MA and Cert. in Exec. Mgmt., Claremont (Calif.) Coll., 1988; PhD, Newport (Calif.) U., 1989. With Pacific Bell, 1967-87; mktg. mgr. Pacific Bell, Orange County, Calif., 1984-85; exec. dir. Pacific Bell, L.A., 1985-87; v.p. mktg. sales Communique Telecommunications, Ontario, Calif., 1987-88; gen. mgr. Volt Info. Scis., Orange, Calif., 1988-90; v.p. sales Delta Resources, Inc., Orange, 1990-91; pres. Dunlap Resources, Brea, Calif., 1991—; mem. faculty So. Calif. Inst., San Diego, So. Calif. Inst., Orange County. Pres. Brea (Calif.) Sister City Assn., 1988-89; bd. dirs. La Mesa (Calif.) Lions, 1971-78, San Diego Cen. City Assn., 1979-81; mayor pro tem City of Brea, 1990-91, mayor 1992-93. 1st lt. Calif. NG, 1961-74. Mem. Fellow Rotary Internat. (bd. dirs. 1987-90); mem. Am. Mktg. Assn. (exec.), San Diego State U. Alumni Assn., Claremont Coll. Grad. Sch. Alumni Assn., MENSA, Psi Chi. Home: 122 S Starflower St Brea CA 92621-4739 Office: City of Brea 1 Civic Center Cir Brea CA 92621

DUNLAP, JACK STUART, financial investigator; b. Mullens, W.Va., Jan. 6, 1930; s. James Edward and Mary Katherine (Carpenter) D.; m. Harriett June Foglesong, Sept. 27, 1952 (div. Apr. 1977); children: Katherine Gaye, James Edward, Jack Carter; m. Linda Sue Hayes, May 1, 1978. BSBA, Concord Coll., 1958; postgrad., Saddelback Coll., 1985-90. Lic. pvt. investigator, Calif. Spl. agt. U.S. Treasury Dept., IRS, Toledo, 1959-64, 65-67, Charleston, W.Va., 1964-65, San Diego, 1967-72, 77-80, L.A., 1972-75, Santa Ana, Calif., 1975-77; pvt. practice Dunlap Investigations, El Cajon, Calif., 1980-84, San Clemente, Calif., 1984—; pres. Intelligence Investigations, Inc., San Diego, 1982-85; expert witness, 1980—. Coach Singing Hills Little League, El Cajon, 1969-72; asst. scoutmaster Boy Scouts Am., Mullens, 1950-59. Sgt. U.S. Army, 1951-53. Named Eagle Scout Boy Scouts Am., 1946. Mem. Calif. Assn. Lic. Investigators, Nat. Assn. Pub. Accts., Calif. Assn. Enrolled Agts., San Diego County Investigators Assn., Nat. Assn. Cert. Fraud Examiners (cert.). Democrat. Baptist. Home: 2985 Calle Frontera San Clemente CA 92673-3051 Office: Dunlap Investigations PO Box 4328 San Clemente CA 92674-4328

DUNLAP, JAMES RILEY, SR., former financial executive, credit manager; b. Portland, Oreg., May 21, 1925; s. William Gates and Laura (Riley) D.; m. Betty Towe; children: James R. Jr., Brian Jay, William David. BSBA, U. Oreg., 1950; postgrad., Portland State Coll., 1963-65. Sales rep. Hyster Co., Portland, 1950-61; br. asst. mgr. Reynolds Metals Co., Portland, 1961-71; corp. credit mgr. Burns Bros. Inc., Portland, 1971-79, sec.-treas., 1979-89. Contbr. articles on credit and fin. mgmt. to profl. jours. With USAAF, 1943-46. Mem. Nat. Assn. Credit Mgmt. (past pres., bd. dirs.), Internat. Assn. Credit Mgmt. (past pres., bd. dirs., Disting. Svc. award 1985, Herb Barnes Meml. award 1987), Portland Retail Credit Assn. (past pres., bd. dirs.), Oreg. State Cons. Credit Assn. (past pres., lifetime bd. dirs.), Portland J. C. of C., Oreg. Motor Supply Credit Assn. (past pres., bd. dirs.), Consumer Counseling Svc. Oreg. (exec. com. 1979—), Am. Contract Bridge League (past pres. Portland chpt., life master), Lions (past pres. local club), Masons, Elks, Delta Tau Delta Alumni Assn. (past pres.).

DUNLOP, LAURENCE JAMES, educator; b. Adelaide, Australia, Jan. 7, 1939; came to U.S., 1980; s. Walter James and Jean Wilson (Eardley) D. Licentiate in Theology, Gregorian U., Rome, 1966; Licentiate in Scripture, Pontifical Bibl. Inst., Rome, 1967, Doctorate in Scripture, 1970. Lectr. Sacred Heart Monastery, Canberra, Act, Australia, 1964-65; lectr. St. Paul's Nat. Sem., Sydney, N.S.W., Australia, 1970-79, rector, 1975-79; asst. prof. Loyola U., Chgo., 1981-83; assoc. prof. Marymount Coll., Rancho Palos Verdes, Calif., 1983—. Author: The Happy Poor, 1975, Patterns of Prayer in the Psalms, 1981; contbr. articles to profl. jours. Roman Catholic. Office: Marymount Coll 30800 PV Dr E Rancho Palos Verdes CA 90274

DUNN, DAVID CAMERON, entrepreneur, business executive; b. Juneau, Alaska, Dec. 8, 1941; s. Robert Charles and Kay (Watson) D.; m. Karen Ann Leonard, Jan. 17, 1970 (div. 1990); children: David Cameron Jr., Paige. BA, Stanford U., 1963; MBA, U. Pa., 1968. Account exec. J. Walter Thompson, N.Y.C., 1968-70; product mgr. Gen. Foods, White Plains, N.Y., 1970-73; dir. mktg. Heublein, San Francisco, 1973-77; exec. v.p. Perelli-Minetti Winery, San Francisco, 1977-79; sr. v.p. Valchris Farms, Modesto, Calif., 1980-84, DFS Advt., San Francisco, 1984-87; pres. Thomas-Rahm Advt., Oakland, Calif., 1987-89, Mktg. Communs. Assocs., Oakland, 1990—; co-founder Re-Con Systems (OTC) 1968; bd. dirs. PC Guardian, San Rafael, Calif. Trustee Oakland Symphony, 1989-90, Orinda (Calif.) Edn. Found., 1986-87. 1st lt. U.S. Army, 1964-66, Germany. Mem. Napa Valley Conv. Bur., Oakland Athletic Club, Oakland C. of C. (Small Bus. of Yr. 1991), Commonwealth Club. Republican. Roman Catholic. Office: Mktg Communs Assocs 40 Jack London Sq Oakland CA 94607

DUNN, DAVID JOSEPH, financial executive; b. Bklyn., July 30, 1930; s. David Joseph and Rose Marie (McLaughlon) D.; BS, U.S. Naval Acad., 1955; MBA, Harvard U., 1961; m. Marilyn Percaccia, June 1955 (div.); children: Susan, Steven, Linda; m. Marilyn LaMarsh, June 1976 (div.); m. Kathryn Alari, Apr. 1986 (div.). Investment banker G.H. Walker & Co., N.Y.C., 1961-62; ptnr. J.H. Whitney & Co., N.Y.C., 1962-70; mng. ptnr. Idanta Ptnrs., San Diego, 1971—; chmn. bd. Iomega Corp., Munchkin Bottling, Inc., Van Nuys, Calif.; bd. dirs. Visionary Design Systems, Inc., Mountain View, Calif. Mem. Univ. Club (N.Y.C.), San Diego Yacht Club, LaJolla (Calif.) Country Club, Pauma Valley Country Club. With USMC, 1950-51, 55-59. Home: 9776 LaJolla Farms Rd La Jolla CA 92037

DUNN, GORDON HAROLD, physicist; b. Montpelier, Idaho, Oct. 11, 1932; s. Jesse Harold and Winifred Roma (Williams) D.; m. Donetta Dayton, Sept. 25, 1952; children: Jesse Lamont, Randall Dayton, Michael Scott, Brian Eugene, David Edward, Susan, Harold Paul, Richard Elzo. BS in Physics, U. Wash., 1954, PhD in Physics, 1961. NRC postdoctoral rsch. assoc. Nat. Bur. Standards, Washington, 1961-62; physicist Nat. Bur. Standards/Join Inst. for Lab. Astrophysics, Boulder, Colo., 1962-77, chief quantum physics div., 1977-85; sr. scientist Nat. Inst. Standards/Join Inst. for Lab. Astrophysics, Boulder, 1985—; lectr. dept. physics U. Colo., Boulder, 1964-74, adj. prof., 1974—; commerce sci. fellow Commn. on Sci. & Tech., U.S. Ho. of Reps., Washington, 1975-76; chmn. com. on atomic molecular & optical sci. NRC, Washington, 1990—, vice-chair, 1989-90, mem. com., 1983-86; mem. NRC Panel on Instruments and Facilities, Washington, 1983-84, NRC Panel on Ion Storage Rings for Atomic Physics, 1985-88; mem. gen. com. Internat. Conf. on Physics of Electron & Atomic Collisions, 1969-73, mem. program com., 1974-75; chmn. Gaseous Electronics Conf., 1968-69, com. mem., 1966-70, sec., 1967-68; chmn. Atomic Processes in High Temperature Plasmas, 1980-81, com. mem., 1977-81, co-sec., 1978-79; co-organizer NATO Advanced Study Inst., 1984-85, U.S.-Japan Workshop, 1985-86; bd. editors Jour. Phys. & Chem. Reference Data, 1990—. Editor, author: Electron-Impact Ionization, 1985; contbr. over 85 articles to profl. jours. Scoutmaster Boy Scouts Am., Boulder, 1967-72, 87-88; coach, league pres. Little League, Boulder, 1966-71, 76-77; pres. Parent-Tchr. Orgns., Boulder, 1973, 75; bishop LDS Ch., Boulder, 1977-82. Recipient Gold medal U.S. Dept. Commerce, 1970. Fellow Am. Phys. Soc. (chmn. div. atomic & molecular physics 1989-90, vice-chair 1988-89, mem. exec. com. 1969, 85-88, 91, Davisson-Germer prize 1984), Joint Inst. for Lab. Astrophysics. Office: U Colo Joint Inst Lab Astrophysics Campus Box 440 Boulder CO 80309-0440

DUNN, GUY WESLEY, air force officer; b. Honolulu, Sept. 3, 1960; s. William John Jr. and Sandra Lynn (Bixby) D.; m. Stacey Ann Dalzell, Feb. 1, 1992. BA in Acctg., U. Puget Sound, 1982, MBA, 1983. Commd. 2d lt. USAF, 1983, advanced through grades to capt., 1987; officer 323d Flight Tng. Wing USAF, Mather AFB, Calif., 1983-92; officer 92d Bomb Wing USAF, Fairchild AFB, Wash., 1985—. Ski instr. for blind and mentally retarded students. Mem. Air Force Assn., Assn. Old Crows, Profl. Ski Instrs. Am., Kappa Sigma. Presbyterian. Home: 14214 SE 270th Pl Kent WA 98042

DUNN, JACK HIBBARD, neurological surgeon; b. Clayton, N.Y., Apr. 5, 1944; s. Jack K. and Helen (Hibbard) D.; m. Rosemary Moroney, May 1, 1980; children: Erica Rose, Allison Marie. BA, Yale U., 1967; MD, Wayne State U., 1971. Diplomate Am. Bd. Med. Examiners, Am. Bd. Neurol. Surgery. Clin. instr. surgery NYU, N.Y.C., 1971-72, clin. instr.

neurosurgery, 1974-79; asst. chief physiol. neurosurgery West Chester County Med. Ctr., N.Y.C., 1980; asst. prof. surgery, neurosurgery U. Ariz., Tucson, 1980-82; v.p. Western Neurosurgery, Tucson, 1982—; chief of surgery El Dorado Med. Ctr., St. Joseph's Med. Ctr., 1988. Lt. M.C., USN, 1972-74. Mem. Pima County Med. Soc. (pres. 1991). Home and Office: 2100 N Rosemont Blvd Ste 110 Tucson AZ 85712-2161

DUNN, JENNIFER BLACKBURN, congresswoman; b. Seattle, Wash., July 29, 1941; d. John Charles and Helen (Gorton) Blackburn; div.; children: Bryant, Reagan. Student, U. Wash., 1960-62; BA, Stanford U., 1963. Former chmn. Rep. Party State of Wash.; now mem. 103rd Congress from 8th Wash. dist., Washington, D.C., 1993—. Del. Rep. Nat. Conv., 1980, 84, 88; active Nat. Trust for Hist. Preservation. Mem. Gamma Phi Beta. Office: US Ho Reps Office Ho Mems Washington DC 20515

DUNN, MARY PRICE, management consultant; b. Albuquerque, Oct. 17, 1952; d. Linden Harrison and Norma (Davies) Price; m. Leo Kevin Dunn, Nov. 21, 1973; children: Molly Jo, Michael Kevin. BS in Edn., U. N.Mex., 1974, MBA, 1990. Educator Archdiocese of Santa Fe, Albuquerque, 1974-75; paralegal Sutin, Thayer & Browne, P.C., Albuquerque, 1975-83; mgmt. cons. Dunn Consulting Group, Albuquerque, 1991—. Contbr. articles to profl. jours. Selected mem. Leadership Albuquerque, 1992-93; v.p., dir. Peppertree/Royal Oak Residents Assn., Albuquerque, 1991-93; mem. exec. com. Shared Vision, chairperson community planning caucus. Mem. ASTD (chairperson conf. promotions). Office: Dunn Consulting Group 5700 Elderberry Ct NE Albuquerque NM 87111

DUNN, MICHAEL JOSEPH, system engineer; b. Bellingham, Wash., Jan. 29, 1951; s. Edgar Payne and Betty Jean (Markworth) D. BSc in Aero., U. Wash., 1972, MSc in Aero., 1973, M of Aero. and Astronautics, 1974. Engr. Boeing Aerospace & Electronics, Kent, Wash., 1974-76; optical engr. McGhan Med./3M, Goleta, Calif., 1976-78; propulsion engr. Boeing Aerospace & Electronics, Kent, 1978-82, system engr., 1982—. Author: (with others) Defending A Free Society, 1984; editor, author: (newsletter) American Defense, 1982-86; inventor, patentee in field. Chief justice Libertarian Party of Wash. State, Seattle, 1983-91. Mem. AIAA, U.S. Naval Inst., Am. Def. Preparedness Assn., U.S. Strategic Inst. Home: 3933 S 326th Pl Auburn WA 98001-9639

DUNN, ROBERT ALAN, marketing consultant, training company executive; b. Wilmar, Calif., Aug. 22, 1941; s. Evans DeWitt and Olive Marie (Canning) D.; m. Diane Karen Jensen, Sept. 21, 1963; children: Paul Harold, Timothy Alan, Thomas Robert. BS in Forestry, Oreg. State U., 1963; MBA, U. Oreg., 1970, PhD, 1974. Asst. prof. Cen. Wash. U., Ellensberg, 1972-75, Pacific Luth. U., Tacoma, 1975-78; mktg. and sales mgr. Internat. Paper Co., N.Y.C., 1978-82; v.p. mktg. Shakertown Corp., Winlock, Wash., 1982-85; exec. v.p. Std. Structures, Inc., Santa Rosa, Calif., 1985-87; owner Action Mgmt. Co., Santa Rosa, Calif., 1987—; ptnr. Action Seminars Inc., Houston, 1992—; lectr. U. Calif., Berkeley, 1990—, San Francisco State U., 1986-90, Shanghai (People's Republic of China) U., 1989. Author: Sales Forecasting Using Lotus, 1992, Power Marketing Using Lotus, 1992, Sales Force Management with Lotus, 1991; co-author: Management Science, 1980. Mem. San Francisco-Shanghai Sister City Com., 1989-90. Capt. U.S. Army, 1963-68. Mem. Am. Mktg. Assn. (del. Dr. consortium 1971), Rotary (Santa Rose Sunrise pres. 1988-89, bd. dirs. 1985-87, dist. sec. 1992—), Beta Gamma Sigma. Republican. Lutheran. Home and Office: Action Mgmt Co 1385 Quail Ct Santa Rosa CA 95404

DUNN, STEVEN ALLEN, chemist; b. Laurens, Iowa, May 1, 1948; s. Lloyd and Avis (Nelson) D.; m. Diana R. Epply, Jan. 11, 1986; children: Mark William, Jeffrey Allen. BS in Phys. Sci., Peru (Nebr.) State Coll., 1980. Electronics technician Gen. Communications Co., Omaha, 1971-76; math. tutor, maintenance worker Peru State Coll., 1976-80; chemist power generation sect. Colo.-Ute Electric Assn., Hayden, 1980-92; sr. chemist power generation sec. Pub. Svc. Co. Colo., Hayden, 1992—. With USCG, 1967-71. Mem. Lions (sec. Hayden club 1986-87, pres. 1988). Democrat. Office: Pub Svc Co of Colo PO Box C Hayden CO 81639

DUNN, STUART THOMAS, graphic designer, consultant; b. Rock Island, Ill., Aug. 27, 1940; s. Paul Thomas and Peggy (Boltinghaus) D.; m. Rosemary Meehan (div.); 1 child, Angela; m. Patrice Wagner, Oct. 28, 1986. BS, Missoura Sch. of Mines, 1962; MS, Okla. State U., 1963, PhD, 1965. Research assoc. Nat. Bur. Standards, Silver Springs, Md., 1964-65; pres. Dunn Assocs., Silver Springs, 1965-67, Digilab, Cambridge, Mass., 1967-73; v.p. EOCOM Corp., Newport Beach, Calif., 1974-76; pres. Dunn Tech., Inc., Vista, Calif., 1976—; chmn. bd. Dunn Tech., Inc. Japan, Tokyo, 1986—; chmn. Vendor Tech. Subcommittee, Reston, Va., 1986—, Lasers in Graphics Conf. Vista, Calif., 1978—, Electronic Printing Systems Conf., Vista, Calif., 1984—, Electronic Design in Print Conf., Vista, Calif., 1988. Author: Electronic Design Systems, 1985, Direct Digital Color Proofing, 1986, Color Electronic Prepress Systems, 1988, Computer to Plate Technology, 1988. Recipient Craftsman of Yr. award nat. Assn. Printers and Lithographers, 1986, InterTech Tech. award Graphic Arts Tech. Found., 1987. Mem. Tech. Assn. Graphic Arts (bd. dirs. 1985-88), Internat. Prepress Assn., Rsch. Engring. Council, Printing Industries Am., Japan Assn. Graphic Arts Tech. Republican. Roman Catholic. Office: Dunn Tech Inc 1855 E Vista Way Vista CA 92084-3315

DUNN, THOMAS GUY, biology educator, university administrator; b. Livingston, Mont., Jan. 31, 1935; s. Thomas L. and E. Gretchen (Gibson) D.; m. Nancy Jane Murphy, Aug. 6, 1960; children: T. James, Michael M. BS, Mont. State Coll., 1962; MS, U. Nebr., 1965; PhD, Colo. State U., 1969. Asst. prof. animal sci. Purdue U., West Lafayette, Ind., 1968-70; asst. prof. animal physiology U. Wyo., Laramie, 1970-73, assoc. prof., 1973-77, prof., 1977—, dean Grad. Sch., 1984—; acting dean Coll. Agr. U. Wyo., Laramie, 1983-84; vis. prof. Colo. State U., Ft. Collins, 1979. Refereed sci. jours.; contbr. articles to profl. jours., chpts. to books. Trustee Mus. of Rockies, Bozeman, Mont., 1986-89. Served with U.S. Army, 1956-58. Grantee NIH, FDA, USDA, Human Growth Found., Nat. Assn. Animal Breeders. Mem. AAAS, Am. Soc. Animal Sci., Soc. Study of Reprodn., Endocrine Soc. Republican. Home: PO Box 4268 Laramie WY 82071-4268 Office: U Wyo Grad Sch PO Box 3108 Laramie WY 82071-3108

DUNNE, JAMES MICHAEL, travel company executive; b. Pitts., May 26, 1942; s. Michael Joseph and Agnes Geraldine (Smith) D.; children: Michael, Kelly, Kathy, Patrick, Sandy, Tony. BA, Duke U. Corr., 1959. Rsch. engr. Hughes Aircraft Co., L.A., 1959-62; ind. bus. pilot San Francisco, 1977-80; pres. Lifetime Adventures, L.A., 1980—. Author: Guerrilla Warriors in the 20th Century, 1974. Activist Reagan Reelection, San Francisco, 1983. With USMC, 1955-59, lt. col. U.S. Army, 1962-77. Recipient award Vietnam Vets. Assn., Culver City, Calif., 1992. Republican. Office: Lifetime Adventures 8033 W Sunset Blvd Bldg 15B Los Angeles CA 90046

DUNNE, THOMAS, geology educator; b. Prestbury, U.K., Apr. 21, 1943; came to U.S., 1964; s. Thomas and Monica Mary (Whitter) D. BA with honors, Cambridge (Eng.) U., 1964; PhD, Johns Hopkins U., 1969. Research assoc. USDA-Agrl. Research Service, Danville, Vt., 1966-68; research hydrologist U.S. Geol. Survey, Washington, 1969; asst. prof. McGill U., Montreal, Que., Can., 1969-73; from asst. prof. to prof. U. Wash., Seattle, 1973—, chmn. dept., 1984-89; vis. prof. U. Nairobi, Kenya, 1969-71; cons. in field, 1970—. Author (with L.B. Leopold) Water in Environmental Planning. Fulbright scholar 1984; grantee NSF, NASA, Rockefeller Found., 1969—; named to NAS. 1988, Guggenheim fellow, 1989-90. Fellow Am. Geophys. Union, Am. Acad. Arts and Scis.; mem. AAAS, NAS, Geol. Soc. Am., Brit. Geomorphological Rsch. Grup, Sigma Xi. Office: U Wash Dept Geol Scis AJ-20 Seattle WA 98195

DUNNEBACKE-DIXON, THELMA HUDSON, research biologist; b. Nashville, Dec. 23, 1925; d. Frederick Charles and Allie Thelma (Hudson) D.; m. Jonathan Stanton Dixon, June 9, 1954; children: James Dunnebacke, Lindsay Ann, Frederick Charles. AB, Washington U., St. Louis, 1947, MA, 1949, PhD, 1954. Instr. Zoology dept. Smith Coll., Northampton, Mass., 1949-50; rsch. staff Virus Lab. U. Calif., Berkeley, 1954-76, instr., 1974-76; rsch. scientist Viral and Rickettsial Disease Lab. Calif. Dept. Health Svcs., Berkeley, 1976—. Contbr. numerous articles to profl. jours. Vol. resource scientist to schs., mus., Berkeley, Oakland, Calif. Mem. AAAS, Fedn. Am. Biologists, Tissue Culture Assn., Am. Soc. for Cell Biology, Electron Microscope Soc. Am., Soc. Protozoologists, Sigma Xi. Home: 2326 Russell St Berkeley CA 94705 Office: Calif Dept Health Svcs Viral & Rickettsial Disease Lab 2151 Berkeley Way Berkeley CA 94704

DUNNETT, DENNIS GEORGE, state official; b. Auburn, Calif., Aug. 5, 1939; s. George DeHaven and Elizabeth Grace (Sullivan) D. AA in Elec. Engring., Sierra Coll., 1959; AB in Econs., Sacramento State Coll., 1966. Engring. technician State of Calif., Marysville, 1961-62; data processing technician State of Calif., Sacramento, 1962-67, EDP programmer and analyst, 1967-74, staff services mgr. and contract adminstr., 1974-76, hardware acquisition mgr., 1976-86, support services br. mgr., information security officer, 1986-90, chief Office Security and Operational Recovery, 1990-92, spl. projects mgr., 1992—; instr. Am. River Coll., 1972; cons. to state personnel bd. on data processing testing, 1983. Mem. Data Processing Mgmt. Assn. (certs.), Calif. State U. Sacramento Alumni Assn. (life), Assn. Computing Machinery, IEEE Computer Soc., Assn. Inst Cert. of Computer Profls., Intergovtl. Council on Tech. of Info. Processing, The Mus. Soc., San Francisco Opera Guild. Home: 729 Blackmer Cir Sacramento CA 95825-4704 Office: Teale Data Ctr 2005 Evergreen St Sacramento CA 95815

DUNNIGAN, MARY ANN, former educational administrator; b. St. Maries, Idaho, Sept. 7, 1915; d. William Henry and Mary Ellen (Kelly) D.; BA, Holy Names Coll., Spokane, 1942; MA, Gonzaga U., Spokane, 1957; postgrad. U. Idaho, UCLA. Tchr. rural schs. Bonner County, 1936-41, elem. schs., 1941, 45-59, high sch., 1942, 45, coordinator elem. edn., 1959-78; prin. kindergarten Sch. Dist. 271, Coeur d'Alene, Idaho, 1978-81; tchr. extension classes U. Idaho; curriculum chmn. Gov.'s Conf. on Edn.; adv. council Head Start. Adv. council Council for Aging; mem. N. Idaho Mus., Community Council, Community Concerts, Community Theater, N. Idaho Booster Club, Mayor's Com. on Handicapped; mem. task force and diocesan bd. Catholic Edn. of Idaho, 1969-74; mem. Coeur d'Alene U.S. Constitution Bicentennial Com., 1986-91. Bd. dirs. Coeur d'Alene Tchrs. Credit Union, 1958-87, pres., treas., 1976-89; hist. chmn. Coeur d'Alene Centennial, 1986-89, chmn. hist. com., 1988, mem. state centennial com. for Koetenai county, 1990. Named Citizen of Yr. N. Idaho Coll., 1974, Idaho Cath. Dau. of Year, 1968; named to Idaho Retired Tchr.'s Hall of Fame, 1987; recipient Hon. Alumnus award N. Idaho Coll., 1987, Nat. Community Svc. award AARP/NRTA, 1989. Mem. Idaho Edn. Assn., NEA, Idaho Ret. Tchrs. Assn. (state chmn. preretirement 1985-92), Kootenai County Ret. Tchrs. Assn. (pres. 1983-87), Delta Kappa Gamma (charter, past pres Zeta chpt 1947-92). Club: Cath. Daus. Am. (state regent 1956-62). Home: 720 N 9th St Coeur D Alene ID 83814-4259

DUNNING, KENNETH LAVERNE, research physicist; b. Yale, Iowa, Sept. 24, 1914; s. Howard Grant and Gertrude Estelle (Dygert) D.; m. Ruth Ellen Pyle, Sept. 2, 1941; children: David M., Jane B., John K., Marion Leigh. BEE, U. Minn., 1938; MS in Physics, U. Md., 1950; PhD in Physics, Cath. U. Am., 1968. Engr. Western Union, N.Y.C., 1938-41; physicist U.S. Naval Research Lab., Washington, 1945-80; cons. Port Ludlow, Wash., 1981—. Contbr. articles to profl. jours. Pres. Highland Greens Condominium Assn., Port Ludlow, 1983-84, v.p. 1984-85. Served to maj. U.S. Army, 1941-45. Recipient Research Pub. award Naval Research Lab., 1971. Mem. IEEE, Am. Phys. Soc., Coll. Club Seattle, Sigma Xi, Tau Beta Pi, Eta Kappa Nu. Home and Office: 10 Foster Ln Port Ludlow WA 98365-9611

DUNN-RANKIN, PETER, psychology educator, writer; b. Hackensack, N.J., Nov. 16, 1929; s. Frederic Alonzo and Helen Lindsey (Schoonmaker) Dunn-Rankin; m. Patricia Ann Cummins, May 28, 1955; children: Denise, Derek, Dean. BS in Edn., Fla. State U., 1953, MS in Lang. Arts, 1954; MA in Math., La. State U., 1963; EdD, Fla. State U., 1965. Asst. researcher Edn. R & D Ctr., Honolulu, 1965-69, assoc. researcher, 1969-72; postdoctoral fellow U.S. Office of Edn. Bell Telephone Lab., Murray Hill, 1969-70; assoc. prof. Coll. of Edn. U. Hawaii, Honolulu, 1972-74, chmn. dept. ednl. psychology, 1976-80, assoc. dean grad. studies Coll. of Edn., 1981-84, acting dean Coll. of Edn., 1984-86, prof., 1974—; dir. eye tracker lab. Coll. Edn., U. Hawaii, 1987—. Author: Scaling Methods; contbr. numerous articles to profl. jours. Lt. USN, 1954-57. Disting. Educator's award Fla. State U., 1985. Mem. Am. Ednl. Rsch. Assn., Hawaii Ednl. Rsch. Assn. (pres. 1980-82), Sigma Delta Psi. Home: 517 Kawaihae St Honolulu HI 96825-1204 Office: U Hawaii Coll of Edn 1776 University of Hawaii Honolulu HI 96822

DUNSTAN, JAMES ROSCOE, provincial official; b. Gilbert Plains, Man., Canada, Aug. 5, 1927; s. Thomas Edward and Maglen Matilda (Presley) D.; m. Katherine Reinheimer, May 25, 1948; children: James Brian, Brent Donald. Mgr. Richardson Securities Can., Alta.; officer U. Lethbridge, Alta.; chmn. Electric Energy Mktg. Agy. Alta.; mem. Pub. Utilities Bd. Alta., Lethbridge; bd. dirs. art gallery. Alderman City of Lethbridge; mem. Lethbridge Police Commn., Lethbridge Mcpl. Planning Commn., Lethbridge Community Svcs. Adv. Bd. Mem. Lethbridge C. of C. (past pres.), Gideons Internat. Can. (life), Kiwanis. Home: 1819 14th Ave S, Lethbridge, AB Canada T1K 0V2 Office: Pub Utilities Bd Alta, Rm 1:10 Ct House, 320 4th St S, Lethbridge, AB Canada T1V 1Z8

DUNSTAN, LARRY KENNETH, insurance company executive; b. Payson, Utah, May 26, 1948; s. Kenneth Leroy Dunstan and Verna Matilda (Carter) Taylor; m. Betty K. Limb, Sept. 23, 1966 (div. June 1975); children: Tamara, Thane; m. Jacqueline Lee Darron, Oct. 7, 1975; children: Tessa, Matthew, Bennett, Spencer, Adam. CLU, CPCU, chartered fin. cons., registered health underwriter, life underwriter tng. council fellow. Mgr. Diamond Bar Inn Ranch, Jackson, Mont., 1972-73; agt. Prudential Ins. Co., Missoula, Mont., 1973-77; devel. mgr. Prudential Ins. Co., Billings, Mont., 1977-78; div. mgr. Prudential Ins. Co., Gt. Falls, Mont., 1978-83; pres. Multi-Tech Ins. Services, Inc., West Linn, Oreg., 1983—; agy. mgr. Beneficial Life Ins. Co., Portland, Oreg., 1983-88. Mem. planning commn. City of West Linn, Oreg., 1986; mem. bishopric Ch. Jesus Christ of Latter Day Sts., West Linn, 1984-86, exec. sec. Lake Oswego Oreg. Stake, 1987-89; scouting coordinator Boy Scouts Am., West Linn, 1984-86, scoutmaster various troops; pres. West Linn Youth Basketball Assn., 1991—, West Linn/Wilsonville Youth Track Club, 1993—. Named Eagle Scout Boy Scouts Am., 1965, recipient Heroism award 1965. Fellow Life Underwriter Tng. Coun. (bd. dirs. 1980-81); mem. Gen. Agts. and Mgrs. Assn. (bd. dirs. 1981-82), Am. Soc. CLU (pres. 1982-83). Republican. Home: 19443 Wilderness Dr West Linn OR 97068-2005 Office: Multi-Tech Ins Svcs 19125 Willamette Dr West Linn OR 97068

DUNWICH, GERINA, magazine editor, author; b. Chgo., Dec. 27, 1959; d. W. E. Novotny and Teri Enies (LoMastro) D. Freelance writer, 1975—; editor, pub. Aquarius Poetry Anthology, Downers Grove, Ill., 1986; editor, pub. Golden Isis mag., Granada Hills, Calif., 1980-86, Salem, Mass., 1986-91, West Hills, Calif., 1991—; research advisor Am. Biog. Inst., Raleigh, N.C., 1986—. Author: Candlelight Spells, 1988, The Magick of Candleburning, 1989, Circle of Shadows, 1989, The Concise Lexicon of the Occult, 1990, WICCA Craft, 1991, Secrets of Love Magick, 1992; editor, pub. The Liberated Voice, 1987, Coven, 1987, Evil Genius Poetry Journ, 1987-88; contbr. numerous articles and poems to jours. and newsletters. Mem. Wiccan Pagan Press Alliance. Office: PO Box 4862 Chatsworth CA 91313-4862

DU PEN, EVERETT GEORGE, sculptor, educator; b. San Francisco, June 12, 1912; s. George E. and Novelle (Freeman) DuP.; m. Charlotte Canada Nicks, July 1, 1939; children: Stuart, Destia, Novelle, William, Ninia, Marguerite. Student, U. So. Calif., 1931-33, Chouinard Art Sch., Los Angeles, summer 1932, Harvard Sch. Architecture, summer 1933; B.F.A. (scholar), Yale, 1937; B.F.A. European traveling fellow, 1937-38. Teaching fellow Carnegie Inst. Tech. Sch. Art, 1939-39; teaching asst. sculpture Washington U. Sch. Art, St. Louis, 1939-42; marine draftsman and loftsman Sausalito Shipbldg. Corp., Calif., 1942-45; instr. sculpture U. Wash. Sch. Art, Seattle, 1945-47; asst. prof. U. Wash. Sch. Art, 1947-54, assoc. prof. sculpture, 1954-60, prof. art, 1960-82, prof. emeritus, 1982—, chmn. sculpture div. One man shows include Seattle Art Mus., 1950, Bon Marche Nat. Gallery, Seattle, 1970, Fred Cole Gallery, Seattle, 1973, Pacific Luth. U., Tacoma, 1975, Wash. Mut. Savs. Bank, Seattle, 1979-80; exhibited Prix de Rome Exhbn., Grand Central Gallery, N.Y.C., 1935-37, 39, St. Louis Mus. Ann., 1939-42, N.A.D., N.Y.C., 1943, 49, 53-55, 57-58, Seattle Art Mus. Ann., 1945-59, Pa. Acad. Art, Phila., 1950-52, 55-58, Ecclesiastical Sculpture competition, 1950, Sculpture Ctr., N.Y.C., 1951, 53, 54, Pa. Acad. Fine Arts, 1954-58, Detroit Mus. Art, 1958, N.W. Inst. Sculpture, San Francisco Art Assn., 1959, Mainstreams, 1972, Marietta Coll., 1972, Holt Galleries, Olympia, Wash., 1980, Martin & Zambotti Gallery, Seattle, 1991-92, Freemont Art Gallery, Seattle, 1991-92, Ellensburg, Wash. Community Art Gallery, 1988, Bellevue, Wash. Invitational, Bellevue Art Mus., 1988, NAD, 1989, Wash. State Art Centennial Exhbn., Tacoma Art Mus., 1990; represented in permanent collections Wash. Mut. Savs. Bank, Seattle, Bell Telephone Co., Seattle, Nat. Acad. Design, N.Y.C. (Saltus Medal 1954), Seattle Art Mus., Safeco Ins. Co., U. Wash., also sculptures in pvt. collections; creator garden figures and portrait heads, small bronze, terra cotta, hardwood sculptures, archtl. medallions, sculpture panels for comml. bldgs. and theatres, figures and wood carvings various chs., relief panels, U. Wash. campus, 1946, 83, bronze fountain, Wash. State Library, Olympia, 1959; Du Pen Fountain; bronze fountain, Coliseum Century 21, Seattle World's Fair, 2 walnut screens, Mcpl. Bldg., Seattle, 8 large sculpture commns. Seattle chs., 1957-64; wood carving Risen Christ, St. Pius X Cath. Ch., Montlake Terrace, Wash., 1983, 3 foot wood carving St. Joseph and Mary, 1985; 6 foot wood carving Ascension, St. Elizabeth Seton Ch., Bothell, Wash., 1986, Elizabeth and Mary, 5 foot mahogany for Visitation Ctr., Fed. Way, Wash., 1990; two figure group for Dallas, 1982; bronze figure Edmonds, Wash., 1983-84, bronze sculpture of Charles Odegaard, Pres. U. Wash., 1973, pvt. commns. Mem. U. Wash. Senate, 1952-55, exec. com., 1954-55; v.p. Allied Arts Movement for Seattle; mem. Seattle Municipal Art Commn., 1958-63. Recipient Saltus gold medal NAD, 1954, 1st prize for sculpture Bellevue (Washington) Arts and Crafts Fair, 1957; U. Wash. research grantee for creative sculpture, 1953-54. Fellow Nat. Sculpture Soc. (hon. mention Henry Herring competition); mem. Artists Equity Assn. (bd. Seattle chpt.), Nat. Acad. Design, Puget Sound N.W. Painters Group (bd.), N.W. Inst. Sculpture (pres. 1957), Allied Artists Am., U. Wash. Research Soc., Northwest Stone Sculptors, Seattle (bd. dirs. 1989—). Home: 1231 20th Ave E Seattle WA 98112-3530

DUPONT, COLYER LEE, television and film producer, video and film distributing company executive; b. Golden, Colo., Oct. 23, 1957; s. Alfred Lee and Frances Dudley (Smith) D. BA, More U., 1980. Advt. mgr. Magical Blend mag., San Francisco, 1981-83; owner, mgr. Newave Co., San Francisco, 1983; mktg. dir. Venture Rsch., Inc., San Francisco, 1983-84; assoc. producer Left Coast Prodns., San Francisco, 1984-86; owner, mgr. Cinemagic Prodns., San Francisco, 1986—. Writer, producer, dir. TV spl. Computer Magic, 1987; videoworks exhibited Mus. Modern Art, N.Y.C., Nat. Mus. Natural History, Smithsonian Inst., Washington, N.Y. Hall of Sci., Corona, Fine Arts Mus. L.I., Hempstead, N.Y.; inventor belt-attached carrier. Recipient Chris award 34th Columbus (Ohio) Internat. Film and Video Festival, 1986, Silver medal Internat. Film and TV Festival N.Y., 1986, Joey award of merit Profl. Media Network, 1986, Golden Eagle award Coun. for Internat. Non-theatrical Events, 1987, Gold Electra award Birmingham (Ala.) Internat. Edn. Film Fetival, 1987, Silver plaque Chgo. Internat. Film Festival, 1987. Mem. Bay Area Video Coalition, Ind. Filmmakers No. Calif. (founder), Film Arts Found., Visual Communicators Calif., San Francisco Advt. Club (Excellence award 1987). Office: Cinemagic Prodns 537 Jones St Ste 898 San Francisco CA 94102-2007

DUQUETTE, DIANE RHEA, library director; b. Springfield, Mass., Dec. 15, 1951; d. Gerard Lawrence and Helen Yvette (St. Marie) Morneau; m. Thomas Frederick Duquette Jr., Mar. 17, 1973. BS in Sociology, Springfield Coll., 1975; MLS, Simmons Coll., 1978. Libr. asst. Springfield City Libr., 1975-78; reference libr. U. Mass., Amherst, 1978-81; head libr. Hopkins Acad., Hadley, Mass., 1980; instr. Colo. Mountain Coll., Steamboat Springs, 1981-83; libr. dir. East Routt Libr. Dist., Steamboat Springs, 1981-84; agy. head Solono County Libr., Vallejo, Calif., 1984; dir. libr. svcs. Shasta County Libr., Redding, Calif., 1984-87; dir. librs. Kern County Libr., Bakersfield, Calif., 1987—; chmn. San Joaquin Valley Libr. System, 1988. Contbr. articles to profl. jours. Recipient John Cotton Dana Spl. Pub. Rels. award, 1989. Mem. ALA, Calif. Libr. Assn. (mem. coun. 1987—), Calif. County Librs. Assn. (pres. 1990). Democrat. Roman Catholic. Home: PO Box 6595 Pine Mountain Club Frazier Park CA 93222 Office: Kern County Libr 701 Truxtun Ave Bakersfield CA 93301-4800

DURAI-SWAMY, KANDASWAMY, company executive; b. Thondipatti, Tamil Nadu, India, Sept. 28, 1945; came to U.S., 1968; s. Mutha Gounder and Kaliammal (Muthuswamy) Kandaswamy; m. Vijayalaakshmi Diraviam, Dec. 27, 1971; 1 child, Kumaran Nambi. BE in Chem. Engring., Annamalai U., Tamil Nadu, 1967; MSChemE, Bucknell U., 1969; M Engring. Adminstrn., U. Utah, 1971, PhD, 1973. Registered profl. engr., Calif. Rsch. engr. Garrett R&D Co. (Occidental), La Verne, Calif., 1973-75; mem. tech. staff TRW Energy Systems, McLean, Va., 1975-77; group leader, prin. engr. Occidental Rsch. Corp. (OXY), Irvine, Calif., 1977-83; mgr. Foster Wheeler Devel. Corp., Livingston, Calif., 1983-85; v.p. west coast ops. and tech. devel. Mfg. & Tech. Conv. Internat., Santa Fe Springs, Calif., 1985—; also bd. dirs. Mfg. & Tech. Conv. Internat., Columbia, Md.; Thermo Chem Inc., Santa Fe Springs, Calif., 1992—; bd. dirs. ThermoChem, Inc., Columbia; mem. adj. faculty chem. engring. dept. Calif. State Poly. U., Pomona, 1978-80, Calif. State U., Long Beach, 1983. Contbr. articles to profl. jours.; numerous patents in field. Elder Hope Chapel, Torrance, Calif., 1990—. Mem. AICE, TAPPI, Am. Chem. Soc., Phi Kappa Phi. Home: 4812 Konya Dr Torrance CA 90503 Office: Thermo Chem Inc 13080 Park St Ste #B Santa Fe Springs CA 90670

DURAN, MICHAEL CARL, bank executive; b. Colorado Springs, Colo., Aug. 27, 1953; s. Lawrence Herman and Jacqueline Carol (Ward) D. BS magna cum laude, Ariz. State U., 1980. With Valley Nat. Bank Ariz., Phoenix, 1976—, corp. credit trainee, 1984-85, comml. loan officer, 1985-86, br. mgr., asst. v.p., 1986-90, comml. banking officer, asst. v.p., 1990—; cons. various schs. and orgns., 1986—; incorporator Avondale Neighborhood Housing Svcs., 1988. Mem. Cen. Bus. Dist. Revitalization Com., Avondale, Ariz., 1987-88, Ad-Hoc Econ. Devel. Com., 1988; coord. Avondale Litter Lifters, 1987-88; vol. United Way, Phoenix, 1984; bd. dirs. Jr. Achievement, Yuma, Ariz., 1989—; yokefellow 1st So. Bapt. Ch. of Yuma, 1990—. Recipient Outstanding Community Svc. award City of Avondale, 1988. Mem. Robert Morris Assocs., Ariz. State U. Alumni Assn. (life), Toastmasters, Kiwanis (local bd. dirs. 1986-88), Beta Gamma Sigma, Phi Kappa Phi, Phi Theta Kappa, Sigma Iota Epsilon. Democrat. Home: 5430 E Charter Oak Rd Scottsdale AZ 85254-4218

DURANTE, SALVATORE (RUSTY DURANTE), broadcast executive; b. Passaic, N.J., Nov. 4, 1946; s. Frank Anthony and Tillie (Formica) D.; m. Jeanie A. Durante, June 28, 1969; 1 child, Natalie A. Attended, Univ. Nev., Las Vegas, 1966-68. Part time runner, cameraman Sta. KHBV-TV, Henderson, Nev., 1968-69, film editor, 1969-71; mgr. film dept. Sta. KVVU-TV, Henderson, Nev., 1971-73, prodn. mgr., 1973-74, operation mgr., 1974-75, program dir., 1975-78, sta. mgr., 1978-79, VP & GM, 1979—; mem. NATPE, TVB, NAB, NV Broadcasters Assn., L.A., 1977—. Bd. dirs. Henderson C. of C., 1989—, chmn. of bd. Nev. Child Seekers, 1992—, bd. dirs. 1991-92. Office: Sta KVVU-TV 25 TV 5 Dr Henderson NV 89014

DURAZO, GUILLERMO, JR., protective services company executive; b. Chula Vista, Calif., Jan. 17, 1952; s. Guillermo Bustamante Durazo and Alicia (Niebla) Hernandez; m. Joy Eva Estrada, May 25, 1974; children: Monique Andrea, Natasha Monet, Guillermo III. Student, U. Utah, 1971-72, Mesa Jr. Coll., 1973, Nat. U., 1980-81. Editor newsletter Naval Supply Ctr., San Diego, 1980-83; corrections officer Met. Correctional Ctr., San Diego, 1975-78; insp. U.S. Customs, Calexico, Calif., 1978-79; owner, mgr. Precision Investigations, San Diego, 1981-83, Durazo Security Patrol, San Diego, 1983-84; pres., chief exec. officer Dugazo, Inc., Chula Vista, 1980—, Agencia Internacional de Seguridad Durazo, Tijuana, Mex., 1989-91; mem. San Diego Equal Employment Coun., 1980-83, Hispanic Employment Com., San Diego, 1980-83. Co-chmn. Padre Hidalgo Community Ctr., 1973-78; active Mex. and Am. Found., San Diego, 1979-90; v.p. Chula Vista Pop-Warner Football League, 1986; founder, pres. Southbay Young Republicans, 1986, pres. San Diego County Nat. Rep. Hispanic Assembly, 1988, nat. committeeman. Served with U.S. Army, 1969-72, Vietnam. Named Caballero of Distinction Mex. and Am. Found., 1981, Entrepreneur of Month U.S. SBA, 1986, 89, One of Outstanding Young Men of Am., 1985. Mem. VFW. Roman Catholic.

DURBETAKI, N. JOHN, software company executive; b. Rochester, N.Y., Oct. 7, 1955; s. Pandeli and Elisabeth (Megerle) D.; m. Jeanne Feng, June 16, 1984; children: Lee Daniel, Mark John. BEE, Ga. Inst. Tech., 1977. Product engr. Nat. Semiconductor, Santa Clara, Calif., 1977-78; product engr. Intel, Aloha, Oreg., 1978-80, test engr., 1980-83; cons. Intel, Hillsboro, Oreg., 1983-84; chmn. bd., pres. OrCAD Systems Corp., Hillsboro, 1984-86, chmn. bd., chief exec. officer, 1986-89; chief exec. officer OrCAD L.P. and predecessors, 1989-91; bd. dirs., v.p. R&D OrCAD, Inc., 1991—. Mem. ACM, IEEE, Oreg. Software Assn. (bd. dirs. 1991-92). Republican. Lutheran. Office: 3175 NW Aloclek Dr Hillsboro OR 97124-7135

DURDY, JAMES DIRK, marketing professional; b. Denver, Nov. 24, 1957; s. James G. and Elizabeth (Collins) D. BA in Biol., Colo. State U., 1980. Cert. emergency med. technician, in CPR. and as a CPR instr. Founder, mgr. firewood service, 1974-75; owner/operator DD and Y Springling System, 1978-81, summers; pres., dir., chief ops. officer Mt. Experience Inc., Littleton, Colo., 1982—; advt. exec. Saatchi & Saatchi Advt., N.Y.C., 1988-89; sr. account dir. Young & Rubicam Advt., Adelaide, Australia, 1989-90; pres. Global Inc. U.S.A./Australia, 1991—; cons. Roo Mark, Victoria, Australia, 1986—. Tchr. CPR and emergency first aid Red Cross throughout Colo., mem. Idaho Mt. Search and Rescue Team. Named Outstanding Young Man in Am., 1985. Republican. Roman Catholic. Home: 6010 S Detroit St Littleton CO 80121-2810

DURFLINGER, JEFFREY DUANE, plastics engineer, manager; b. Oakland, Calif., Mar. 15, 1961; s. Laurence Duane and Patricia Etta (Cord) D.; m. Kelly Denise Evans, June 24, 1989. BS in Polymer Tech., Calif. State U., Chico, 1986; MS in Ops. Mgmt., Golden Gate U., 1993. Cert. sr. indsl. technologist. Prodn. devel. mgr. Omni Sci., Martinez, Calif., 1986-87; process engr. Alza Corp., Palo Alto, Calif., 1987-89, Vacaville, Calif., 1989—; cons. Polytex Cons., Sacramento, 1989—. Mem. Soc. Plastic Engrs. (pres. 1985-86), Soc. for Advancement of Material and Process Engring. (chmn. 1986). Republican. Methodist. Office: Alza Corp 700 Eubanks Dr Vacaville CA 95688-9470

DURHAM, BARBARA, state supreme court judge; b. 1942. BSBA, Georgetown U.; JD, Stanford U. Bar: Wash. 1968. Former judge Wash. Superior Ct., King County; judge Wash. Ct. Appeals; assoc. justice Wash. Supreme Ct., 1985—, acting chief justice. Office: Wash Supreme Ct Temple of Justice PO Box 40929 Olympia WA 98504-0929

DURHAM, CHRISTINE MEADERS, state supreme court justice; b. L.A., Aug. 3, 1945; d. William Anderson and Louise (Christensen) Meaders; m. George Homer Durham II, Dec. 29, 1966; children: Jennifer, Meghan, Troy, Melinda, Isaac. A.B., Wellesley Coll., 1967; J.D., Duke U., 1971. Bar: N.C. 1971, Utah 1974. Sole practice law Durham, N.C., 1971-73; instr. legal medicine Duke U., Durham, 1971-73; adj. prof. law Brigham Young U., Provo, Utah, 1973-78; ptnr. Johnson, Durham & Moxley, Salt Lake City, 1974-78; judge Utah Dist. Ct., 1978-82; justice Utah Supreme Ct., 1982—. Pres. Women Judges Fund for Justice, 1987-88. Fellow Am. Bar Found.; mem. ABA (edn. com. appellate judges' conf.), Nat. Assn. Women Judges (pres. 1986-87), Utah Bar Assn., Am. Law Inst. (coun. mem.), Nat. Ctr. State Courts (bd. dirs.). Home: 1702 Yale Ave Salt Lake City UT 84108-1836 Office: Utah Supreme Ct 332 State Capitol Salt Lake City UT 84114-1181

DURHAM, HARRY BLAINE, III, lawyer; b. Denver, Sept. 16, 1946; s. Harry Blaine and Mary Frances (Oliver) D.; m. Lynda L. Durham, Aug. 4, 1973; children: Christopher B., Laurel A. BA cum laude, Colo. Coll., 1969; JD, U. Colo., 1973. Bar: Wyo. 1973, U.S. Tax Ct. 1974, U.S. Ct. Appeals (10th cir.) 1976. Assoc., Brown, Drew, Apostolos, Massey & Sullivan, Casper, Wyo., 1973-77; ptnr. Brown & Drew, 1977—. Permanent class pres. Class of 1969, Colo. Coll.; bd. dirs. Casper Amateur Hockey Club, 1970-77, sec. 1974-77; bd. dirs. Casper Symphony Assn., 1974-88, v.p., 1979-82, pres., 1983-87; bd. dirs., sec. Wyo. Amateur Hockey Assn., 1974-85, pres., 1985-88; bd. dirs. Natrona County United Way, 1974-76, pres., 1975-76; mem. City of Casper Parks and Recreation Commn., 1985—, vice chmn., 1987—. Mem. ABA, Wyo. Bar Assn., Natrona County Bar Assn., Nat. Assn. Railroad Trial Counsel, Phi Beta Kappa. Republican. Articles editor U. Colo. Law Rev., 1972-73. Home: 3101 Hawthorne Ave Casper WY 82604-4929 Office: 123 W First St Ste 800 Casper WY 82609-1916

DURHAM, WALTER ALBERT, JR., investment planning manager; b. Portland, Oreg., July 6, 1910; s. Walter Albert and Vesta Velona (Broughton) D.; m. Elizabeth Cram, Apr. 14, 1934; children: Eleanor Francis, Lawrence Edward (dec.). BA, Reed Coll., 1932; MA, Clark U., 1933; MS, U. Denver, 1940. CFP. Rschr. Brookings Instn., Denver, 1940; economist Bonneville Power Adminstrn., Portland, Oreg., 1940-42; mem. Nat. War Labor Bd. Lumber Commn., Portland, 1942-46; mgr. Lumbermen's Indsl. Rels. Coun., Portland and Seattle, 1947-61; compensation svcs. mgr. Tektronix, Inc., Beaverton, Oreg., 1961-67; securities rep. ITT Fin. Svcs. (and predecessor cos.), Lake Oswego, Oreg., 1963-75; br. mgr. Interpacific Investor Svcs., Inc., Lake Oswego, 1975-91, Columbia Pacific Securities, Inc., Lake Oswego, 1991—. Contbr. articles to profl. jours. Chmn. City of Lake Oswego (Oreg.) Project Policy Adv. Com., 1979-81. Grad. fellowship in Govt. Mgmt., Alfred P. Sloan Found., 1938; named First Citizen, Lake Oswego C. of C., 1981. Mem. Multnomah Athletic Club. Congregationalist. Office: Columbia Pacific Securities Inc 311 B #212 Lake Oswego OR 97034

DURINGER, JACOB CLYDE, project engineer, researcher; b. Calexico, Calif., Oct. 18, 1956; s. Jacob Clyde Sr. and Stella Marie (Pippin) D.; m. Catherine Ann Grecich, Sept. 20, 1986 (div. Feb. 1988); 1 child, Irena Mauve; m. Mary Helen Montes, May 27, 1989; 1 child, Trint Jacob. AA in Electronics, Electronic Tech. Inst., 1978. Staff engr. Mitsubishi Electronics, Santa Ana, Calif., 1978-81; sr. technician Efratom, Irvine, Calif., 1981-82, MCT Electronics, Carpinteria, Calif., 1982-83; project engr. Parker Bertea Aerospace, Irvine, 1985—. Inventor monolithic two dimensional keyboard. Mem. Nat. Assn. Music Mchts. Mem. Christian Ch. Home: 23341 La Glorieta # E Mission Viejo CA 92691-6844

DURON, SUSAN BUDDE, research corporation executive; b. Chgo., Mar. 17, 1947; d. Earl Leslie and Ivy May (Smith) Budde; m. Guillermo Duron, June 27, 1981. BA, Ill. State U., 1969; MEd, No. Ill. U., 1975; PhD, So. Ill. U., 1978. Cert. tchr., ednl. adminstr. Tchr. West Aurora (Ill.) Pub. Schs., 1969-72, coord. bilingual program, 1972-76; instr. So. Ill. U., Carbondale, 1976-78; evaluations cons. Ill. State Bd. Edn., Chgo., 1978-81; sr. program analyst Advanced Tech., Inc., Indpls., 1982-83; rsch. assoc. N.W. Regional Ednl. Lab., Denver, 1983-85; owner, pres. META Assocs., Littleton, Colo., 1985—; v.p., regional officer dir. RMC Rsch. Corp., Denver, 1988—. Author: Student Study Skills, 1987; contbr. articles to profl. pubs.; editor cons. handbook. Grantee World Congress Spl. Edn., 1978, Bur. Edn. of Handicapped, 1988. Mem. Am. Edn. Rsch. Assn., Nat. Assn. Bilingual Edn., Coun. Computer Users Edn., Coun. Exceptional Children, Greenpeace Club, Valley Racquet Club, Kappa Delta Pi. Democrat. Congregationalist. Home: 16 Holly Oak Littleton CO 80127-4330 Office: RMC Rsch Corp 1512 Larimer St Ste 540 Denver CO 80202-1620

DURYEE, DAVID ANTHONY, management consultant; b. Tacoma, Wash., July 29, 1938; s. Schuyler L. and Edna R. (Muzzy) D.; m. Anne Getchell Peterson, Nov. 26, 1966; children: Tracy Anne, Tricia Marie. BA in Bus., U. Wash., 1961, MBA, 1969; diploma, Pacific Coast Banking Schs., Seattle, 1973. Cert. fin. planner. Lending officer Seattle 1st Nat. Bank, 1964-68, v.p., trust officer, 1970-80; cons., chmn. Mgmt. Adv. Svcs., Inc., Seattle, 1980—; bd. dirs. Lafromboise Newspapers, Inc., Seattle; lectr. in field; expert witness Wash., N.Y., Md., Calif., Mass., Ind., Fla. Contbr. articles to profl. jours. Capt. U.S. Army, 1962-64. Mem. Am. Soc. Appraisers, Internat. Assn. Fin. Planners, Inst. for Cert. Planners, Inst. Bus. Appraisers (speaker), Am. Bankers Assn., Nat. Retail Jewelers, Nat. Moving and Storage assn., Pacific N.W. Bankers Assn., Internat. Assn. for Fin. Planning, Estate Planning Coun. Seattle, Washington Bar Assn., Wash. State Trial Lawyers Assn., Wash. State Automobile Dealers Assn., Ky./Mo. Auto Dealers Assn., Motor Dealers Assn. B.C., Nat. Office Products Assn., Mayflower Warehousemen's Assn., Can. Movers Assn., Fedn. of Automobile Dealer Assns. of Can., Seattle Tennis Club, Wash. Athletic Club, Seattle Yacht Club, Rotary. Home: 3305 E John St Seattle WA 98112-4938 Office: Mgmt Adv Svcs 2401 4th Ave Fl 3D Seattle WA 98121-1438

DUSHANE, PHYLLIS MILLER, nurse; b. Portland, Oreg., June 3, 1924; d. Joseph Anton and Josephine Florence (Eicholtz) Miller; m. Frank Maurice Jacobson, Mar. 13, 1945 (dec. 1975); children: Karl, Kathleen, Kraig, Kirk, Karen, Kent, Krista, Kandis, Kris, Karlyn; m. Donald McLelland DuShane, July 21, 1979 (dec. 1989); stepchildren: Diane DuShane Bishop, Donald III. BS in Biology, U. Oreg., 1948; BS in Nursing, Oreg. Health Scis. U., 1968. R.N., Oreg. Pub. health nurse Marion County Health Dept., Salem, Oreg., 1968-77; pediatric nurse practitioner Marion County Health Dept., Salem, 1977-91, Allergy Assocs., Eugene, Oreg., 1979-89; mem. allied profl. staff Sacred Heart Gen. Hosp., Eugene, 1979—. Named Oreg. Pediatric Nurse Practitioner of Yr., 1991. Mem. P.E.O., Oreg. Pediatric Nurse Practioners Assn. (v.p. Salem chpt. 1977-78), Am. Nurses Assn., Oreg. Nurses Assn., Nat. Assn. Pediatric Nurse Assocs. and Practitoners, Am. Acad. Nurse Practitioners, Nurse Practitioners Spl. Interest Group, Salem Med. Aux. (sec. 1968), Oreg. Republican Women, Delta Gamma Alumni (v.p. 1979), Rep. Rubicon Soc. Presbyterian. Home: 965 E 23d Ave Eugene OR 97405-3074 Office: Clinic For Children & Young Adults 755 E 11th Ave Eugene OR 97401 also: Oakway Pediatrics P C 465 Oakway Rd Eugene OR 97401 also: Eugene Pediatric Assocs 1680 Chambers St Eugene OR 97402

DUSTON, JENNIFER, performing arts association administrator; b. Ipswich, Mass., Apr. 8, 1954; d. Joseph Richard and Ruth Evelyn (Duston) Coupal; m. Horst Ludwog Kloss, Jan. 3, 1976 (div. Sept. 1983). Diploma, Boston Conservatory, 1974; BA with highest honors, Wellesley Coll., 1986. Ops. mgr. Elgin (Ill.) Symphony Orch., 1985-86; conservatory mgr. Elgin Community Coll., 1985-86; gen. mgr. Napa Valley (Calif.) Symphony Assoc., 1986-90; exec. dir. Marin Symphony Orch., San Rafael, Calif., 1990—. Exhibited photographs in pub. shows, 1984. Mem. AAUW, Symphony Orch. League (finalist mgmt. fellow 1984), Assn. Calif. Symphony Orchs. (panelist 1987, 88). Office: Marin Symphony Orch 4172 Redwood Hwy San Rafael CA 94903-2618

DUTHLER, CHARLES DIRK, industrial technologist, environmental specialist; b. St. Paul, Oct. 12, 1956; s. Richard Gorden and Nancy (Elam) D.; m. Suzanne Klaas, Oct. 4, 1981; children: Michael, Elizabeth, Michelle. BS in Indsl. Tech., U. Wis.-Stout, Menomonee, 1979. Supr. mfg. engring. Despatch Indsl. Inc., Lakeville, Minn., 1979-86; ops. mgr. ICI Composites Inc., Tempe, Ariz., 1986—. Mem. Soc. Mfg. Engrs., Am. Inst. Plant Engrs. Office: ICI Composites Inc 2055 E Technology Cir Tempe AZ 85284

DUTKOWSKI, MICHAEL MIECZYSLAW, fiberglass manufacturing company executive; b. Slubice, Gorzow, Poland, Sept. 13, 1946; came to U.S., 1983; s. Piotr Mieczyslaw and Kazimiera (Piasecka) D. M. in Econs., U. Trade, Warsaw, Poland, 1974. Ops. mgr. Regional Dairy Products Wholesale, Warsaw, 1974-79; planning mgr. KDO, Zremb, ZMD, Warsaw, 1979-82; acct. J. Miller Industries Inc., Santa Ana, Calif., 1983-85, contr., 1985-91, v.p. fin., 1992—. Dep. chmn. Solidarity Trade Union, co. unit, Warsaw, 1980-81; pres. Solidarity Calif., Orange, 1986-92; v.p. Polish Am. Congress, So. Calif. divsn., L.A., 1988-92, pres., 1992—. Mem. Polish Am. Bus. and Profl. Club, KC (charter grand knight 1987-88). Republican. Roman Catholic. Home: 904 E Palmyra Ave Orange CA 92666-2421 Office: J Miller Industries Inc 3330 W Castor St Santa Ana CA 92704

DUTTON, GUY G. S., chemistry educator; b. London; came to Can., 1949; BA, Cambridge U., 1943; MS, U. London, 1952; PhD, U. Minn., 1955. Conf. coordinator B.C. Acad. Scis., 1952-53, conf. chmn., 1953; lectr. U. B.C., Vancouver, 1949-50, asst. prof., 1950-59, assoc. prof., 1959-64, prof., 1964-88, prof. emeritus, 1988—; chmn. 28th Internat. Union of Pure and Applied Chem. Congress, Vancouver, 1981, 11th Internat. Carbohydrate Symposium, Vancouver, 1982. NATO fellow, 1966; Killam fellow, 1975, 84. Fellow Chem. Inst. Can. (exec. Vancouver sect. 1956-58, chmn. 62d conf. 1979, v.p. 1987-88, pres. 1988-90, Montreal medal 1986), Can. Soc. Chemistry (Labatt award 1989). Office: U BC Dept Chemistry, 2036 Main Mall, Vancouver, BC Canada V6T 1Z1

DUTTON, PAULINE MAE, fine arts librarian; b. Detroit, July 15; d. Thoralf Andreas and Esther Ruth (Clyde) Tandberg; B.A. in Art, Calif. State U., Fullerton, 1967; M.S. in Library Sci., U. So. Calif., 1971; m. Richard Hawkins Dutton, June 21, 1969. Elem. tchr., Anaheim, Calif., 1967-68, Corona, Calif., 1968-69; fine arts librarian Pasadena (Calif.) Public Library, 1971-80; art cons., researcher, 1981—. Mem. Pasadena Librarians Assn. (sec. 1978, treas. 1979-80), Calif. Library Assn., Calif. Soc. Librarians, Art Librarians N.Am., Nat. Assn. Female Execs., Am. Film Inst., Am. Entrepreneurs Assn., Gilbert and Sullivan Soc., Alpha Sigma Phi. Club: Toastmistress (local pres. 1974).

DUVALL, ROBERT F., university president. Pres. Pacific U., Forest Grove, Oreg. Office: Pacific U 2043 College Way Forest Grove OR 97116-1797

DUVIVIER, KATHRYN SHELLEY, real estate development and construction executive; b. Long Beach, Calif., Aug. 30, 1952; d. Dennis Ambrose and Jane (Claypool) Shelley; m. Charles Girault DuVivier, Sept. 22, 1973; children: Edward, David. BA, Antioch Coll., 1974. Owner-operator Whistling Winds Farm, Readstown, Wis., 1974-82; owner, v.p. DuVivier Co., Inc., Encinitas, Calif., 1983—. Founding dir. Pleasant Ridge Sch., Viroqua, Wis., 1977-81; pres. Rhoades Sch. Found., Encinitas, 1987-88; pres., founding dir. San Dieguito Heritage Mus., Encinitas, 1989-93; bd. dirs., sec., 3d v.p. Community Resource Ctr., Encinitas, 1990-92; bd. dirs. No. Coast San Diego LWV, San Diego, 1986-87, Carlsbad Religious Sci. Ch., 1989—. Mem. Bldg. Industry Assn. Democrat. Religious Scientist. Office: DuVivier Co Inc 285 N El Camino Real # 212 Encinitas CA 92024

DUXBURY, ALYN CRANDALL, oceanography educator; b. Olympia, Wash., Dec. 1, 1932; s. Maynard Clair and Lona Mae (Crandall) D.; m. Alison Beatrix Saunders, Dec. 20, 1956; children: Andrew Saunders, Alison Jean, Alexander Ramsay. BS in Oceanography, U. Wash., 1955, MS in Phys. Oceanography, 1956; PhD in Phys. Oceanography, Tex. A&M U., 1963. Rsch. assoc. faculty mem. Bingham Oceanographic Lab., Yale U., New Haven, 1960-64; mem. rsch. faculty Sch. Oceanography, U. Wash., Seattle, 1964—, mem. rsch. faculty Sch. Marine Affairs, 1978-92, prof. emeritus, 1992—; dir. ops. Sch. Oceanography, U. Wash., 1972-77, asst. dir. sea grant program, 1972-88. Advisor to state and local environ. mgmt. agys. With C.C., U.S. Army, 1956-58. Mem. AAAS, Am. Geophys. Union, Am. Soc. Limnology and Oceanography, The Explorers Club, Sigma Xi. Home: 3823 44th Ave NE Seattle WA 98105-5448

DUZAN, STEPHEN ANDREW, biotechnology company executive; b. Prineville, Oreg., May 9, 1941; s. Lynn Leslie and June Irene (Yancey) D.; m. Mary Elizabeth David, Oct. 13, 1962 (div. Jan. 1986); children: Elizabeth Lynn, Melissa Lynn; m. Barbara Gail French, Sept. 4, 1986. Student, Dartmouth Coll., 1959, U. Washington, Seattle, 1960-63, U. Washington, Seattle, 1963. Account exec. Marsh & McClennan, Inc., Seattle, 1964-66; various positions Fred S. James & Co., Inc., Seattle, 1966-69, Leckenby Co., Seattle, 1969-75; pres., chief exec. officer, bd. dirs. Cello Bag Co., Inc., Tukwila, Washington, 1975-80; exec. v.p., chief operating officer, bd. dirs. North Star Ice Equipment Corp., Seattle, 1980-81; co-founder, chief exec. officer, chmn. bd. dirs. Immunex Corp., Seattle, 1981—; bd. dirs. Commerce Bank, Seattle, Neopath Inc., Bellevue, Wash., Targeted Genetics Corp., Seattle; chmn. adv. com. Wash. State Biotech. Targeted Sector, 1990-91. Mem. Forward Thrust of King County, Seattle, 1967-69; mem. vis. com. U. Washington Sch. of Medicine, Seattle, 1985-89; exec. com., bd. dirs. SeaFair of Seattle, 1973-75; bd. dirs. Big Bros., Seattle, 1982-84, Downtown Seattle Assn., 1986-89, A Contemporary Theater, Seattle, 1987-89; chmn. bd. trustees Corp. Coun. of Arts, Seattle, 1988-89; co-chairperson task force on taxation and bus. climate Small Bus. Improvement Council, Seattle, 1984-85; bd. of govs. Griffin Coll., Seattle, 1983-87; bd. of overseers Whitman Coll., Walla Walla, Washington, 1986-91; trustee Fred Hutchinson Cancer Rsch. Ctr., Seattle, 1989—. Mem. Indsl. Biotech. Assn. (bd. dirs. 1988—, chmn. 1992—), Greater Seattle C. of C. (bd. dirs. 1986-88), Columbia Tower Club, City Club, U. Wash. Pres.'s Club, Rainier Club, Univ. Club, Overlake Golf and Country Club, San Juan Golf Club. Office: Immunex Corp 51 University St Seattle WA 98101-2936

DÜZGÜNES, NEJAT A., biophysicist; b. N.Y.C., Feb. 28, 1950; s. Orhan and Zeliha (Uygurer) D. BS, Mid. East Tech. U., Ankara, Turkey, 1972; PhD, SUNY, Buffalo, 1978. Postdoctoral fellow U. Calif., San Francisco, 1978-81, asst. rsch. biochemist, 1981-87, asst. adj. prof., 1985-87, assoc. rsch. biochemist, 1987—, assoc. adj. prof., 1987—; assoc. prof., chmn. Dept. Microbiology U. Pacific, San Francisco, 1990—; vis. prof. Kyoto (Japan) U., 1988. Editor: Membrane Fusion in Fertilization Cellular Transport and Viral Infection, 1988, Mechanisms and Specificity of HIV Entry into Host Cells, 1991, Membrane Fusion Techniques, Methods in Enzymology, 1993. Vol. AFS Internat. Intercultural Programs, N.Y.C., 1969-86. Co-recipient Orgn. award U.S.-Japan Binat. Seminar on Membrane Fusion, NSF, 1992; Japan Soc. Promotion of Sci. fellow, 1988; grantee Am. Heart Assn., 1983-87, U. Calif. Univ. Wide AIDS Rsch. Program, 1986-90, 92—, NIAID/NIH, 1988—. Mem. Am. Soc. Cell Biology, Am. Soc. Microbiology, Internat. Soc. Antiviral Rsch., Internat. AIDS Soc., Am. Assn. Dental Schs., Am. Assn. Dental Rsch., Biophysics Soc. Office: U of Pacific Dept Microbiology 2155 Webster St San Francisco CA 94115-2399

DVORAK, RAY P., insurance company official; b. Center, N.D., Sept. 24, 1931; s. Stanley Joseph and Katherine (Schimpf) D.; m. Deanna Ellen Kern, June 1961 (div. 1974); children: Mitchell Scott, Lara Suzanne; m. Delores Marie Davis, Mar. 12, 1975 (dec. Jan. 1990). BS, U. Oreg., 1953; LLB, LaSalle Extension U., Chgo., 1964. CLU; CPCU; charter fin. cons. Claim rep. State Farm Ins. Co., Salem, Oreg., 1957-67; claim supt. State Farm Ins. Co., Medford, Oreg., 1967—. With USAF, 1953-55, lt. col. Res. ret. Mem. Soc. CPCU, Am. Soc. CLU's. Republican. Methodist. Home: PO Box 188 840 S Oregon St Jacksonville OR 97530 Office: State Farm Ins Co PO Box 757 Medford OR 97501-0055

DWIGHT, DONALD STEARNS, artist, retired military officer; b. Cin., Aug. 25, 1921; s. Harold Stearns and Rosalind Dell (Vail) D.; m. Nancy Bartron, Oct. 22, 1949; 1 child, Jennifer. Grad., Cen. Acad. Comm. Art, Cin., 1942. Commd. 2d lt. U.S. Army Air Corps, 1943; advanced through grades to lt. col. USAF, ret., 1966; dist. sales mgr. L.L. Sams & Sons, Waco, Tex., 1966-76; ind. artist Colorado Springs, Colo., 1977—. Exhbns. of watercolors include Rocky Mountain Nat. Watermedia, Golden, Colo., 1980, 81, 86, Watercolor West, Redlands, Calif., 1986, 87, 88, Madison (Wis.) Nat., 1986, 87, 88, N.Mex. Watercolor Soc., Albuquerque, 1987, 88, 89, Southwestern Watercolor Soc., Dallas, 1987, 92, Georgia Watercolor Soc., Atlanta, 1988, 89, 92, Tex. Watercolor Soc., San Antonio, 1988, Ky. Watercolor Soc., Louisville, 1988, Kans. Watercolor Soc., Wichita, 1989, 91, Nat. Watercolor Soc., Fullerton, Calif., 1990, Midwest. Recipient Grumbacker Gold Medal for Color, 1987, Betsy Crooks award North Fla. Watercolor Soc., 1990, George Sponable award Adirondacks Nat., 1992. Mem. Watercolor West, Ga. Watercolor Soc. (Atlanta Artists Club award 1992), N.Mex. Watercolor Soc., Kans. Watercolor Soc., Tex. Watercolor Soc., Knickerbocker Artists Assn., Am. Watercolor Soc. (Bronze medal 1992). Home: 46 Upland Rd Colorado Springs CO 80906

DWORKOSKI, ROBERT JOHN, headmaster; b. Hackensack, N.J., July 9, 1946; s. Alexander George and Pauline Mary (Jurgaitis) D.; m. Amy Walsh, Nov. 22, 1975 (div. 1991); 1 child, Kathryn Louise; m. Kristin Okey, Dec. 24, 1991; 1 child, Hillary Anne. BA in Polit. Sci., George Washington U., 1964-68; AM in History, NYU, 1970; MA in History, Columbia U., 1971, PhD, 1978. Adj. instr. history Bklyn. Coll., 1976, N.Y. Inst. Tech., N.Y.C., 1976-78, Essex County Coll., Newark, N.J., 1976-78; tchr. history Woodmere (N.Y.) Acad., 1978-80, chair social studies, 1979-80; head upper sch. Harvard Sch., North Hollywood, Calif., 1980-86; headmaster Viewpoint Sch., Calabasas, Calif., 1986—. Contbr. articles to profl. jours. Bd. dirs. Will Geer Theatrium Botanicum, Topanga, Calif., 1993; mem. com. for satellite mus. L.A. County Natural History Mus., L.A., 1988. Fullbirght scholar, 1983; grantee NEH, 1993. Mem. Nat. Assn. Coll. Admissions Counselors, Calif. Assn. Ind. Schs. Office: Viewpoint Sch 23620 Mullholland Hwy Calabasas CA 91302

DWYER, GARY COLBURN, artist; b. Denver, Oct. 1, 1943; s. Alfred William and Alice Richardson (Power) D.; children: Heather Allyson, Chelsea K. BSLA/BFA, Syracuse U., 1967; BLA, NYU, 1967; MFA, U. Denver, 1970; postgrad., Akademie for bildende Kunst, Austria, 1980. Landscape architect Roark Assocs. Architects, Denver, 1972-73; prof. dept. landscape arch. Calif. Poly. State U., San Luis Obispo, Calif., 1973—; design cons. Gary Dwyer & Assocs., San Luis Obispo, 1981—; environ. artist San Luis Obispo, 1981—; adv. bd. design art prog. Nat. Endowment for the Arts, Washington, 1983. Contbr. articles to profl. jours.; author video: German National Television, 1985. Nat. Endowment for Humanities fellow, 1984; recipient Communication Design award, Am. Soc. Landscape Architects, 1988. Mem. AIA (assoc.), Sigma Lambda Alpha. Home: 415 Dana St Apt 5 San Luis Obispo CA 93401-3403 Office: Calif Poly State Univ Dept Landscape Architecture San Luis Obispo CA 93407

DWYER, WILLIAM L., judge; b. Olympia, Wash., Mar. 26, 1929; s. William E. and Ila (Williams) D.; m. Vasiliki Asimakopulos, Oct. 5, 1952; chldren: Joanna, Anthony, Charles. BS in Law, U. Wash., Seattle, 1951; JD, NYU, 1953. Bar: Wash. 1953, U.S. Supreme Ct., U.S. Ct. Appeals (9th cir.). Law clk. Supreme Ct. Wash., Olympia, 1957; ptnr. Culp, Dwyer, Guterson & Grader, Seattle, 1957-87; judge U.S. Dist. Ct. (we. dist.) Wash., Seattle, 1987—. Author: The Goldmark Case, 1984 (Gavel award ABA 1985, Gov.'s award Wash. 1985). 1st lt. U.S. Army, 1953-56. Recipient Outstanding Svc. award U. Wash. Law Rev., 1985, Helen Geisness Disting. Svc. award Seattle-King County Bar Assn., 1985. Fellow Am. Coll. Trial Lawyers, Am. Bar Found., Hon. Order of Coif; mem. ABA, Inter-Am. Bar Assn., Am. Judicature Soc., Supreme Ct. Hist. Soc., 9th Cir. Hist. Assn. Office: US Dist Ct 502 US Courthouse 1010 5th Ave Seattle WA 98104-1130

DYADKIN, LEV JOSEPH, computer programmer; b. Oktiabrsky, USSR, Nov. 18, 1955; came to U.S. 1989; s. Iosif G. and Valentina (Artamonova) D.; m. Tatiana Smirnova, Feb. 14, 1976; children: Sofia L., Anna L. M.Physics, Kalinin State U., Russia, 1978. Mathematician Geophys. Trust, Kimri, Russia, 1978-88; computer engr. Inst. Applied Math., Kalinin, 1988; programmer Golden Dawn Computer Sys., Salt Lake City, 1989; software engr. Lahey Computer Sys., Incline Village, Nev., 1989—. Mem. ACM. Home: Southwood Blvd #63 PO Box 7741 Incline Village NV 89452-7741 Office: Lahey Computer Systems PO Box 6091 Incline Village NV 89450

DYCK, ANDREW ROY, philologist; b. Chgo., May 24, 1947; s. Roy H. and Elizabeth (Beck) D.; m. Janis Mieko Fukuhara, Aug. 20, 1978. BA, U. Wisc., 1969; PhD, U. Chgo., 1975. Sessional lectr. U. Alberta, Edmonton, Can., 1975-76; vis. asst. prof. UCLA, 1976-77, asst. prof., 1978-82, assoc. prof., 1982-87, prof., 1987—, chair dept. classics, 1988-91; asst. prof. U. Minn., Mpls., 1977-78. Editor: Epimerismi Homerici, 1983, Essays on Euripides and George of Pisidia and on Heliodorus and Achilles Tatius (Michael Psellus), 1986. Alexander von Humboldt-Stiftung fellow, Bonn, Fed. Republic of Germany, 1980-89; NEH fellow, 1991-92. Mem. Am. Philol. Assn., Calif. Classical Assn., Byzantine Studies Conf., Soc. for Promotion Byzantine Studies, U.S. Nat. Com. on Byzantine Studies, Mommsen-Gesellschaft. Office: UCLA Classics Dept 405 Hilgard Ave Los Angeles CA 90024-1301

DYER, ALICE MILDRED, psychotherapist; b. San Diego, July 4, 1929; d. William Silas Cann and Louise Lair (Addenbrooke) Vaile; divorced; children: Alexis Dyer Guagnano, Bryan, Christine Dyer Morales; m. James Vawter, Dec. 26, 1972. BA, Calif. State U., Fullerton, 1965, MA, 1967; PhD, U.S. Internat. U., 1980. Coord., counselor Brea (Calif.)-Olinda High Sch., 1968-72; sch. psychologist Cypress (Calif.) Sch. Dist., 1972-86; instr. North Orange County Community Coll., Fullerton, 1975-77; pvt. practice ednl. psychology Long Beach and Fountain Valley, Calif., 1978—; pvt. practice marriage and family therapy Fullerton and Brea, Calif., 1979—; psychologist, cons. Multiple Sclerosis Soc. Orange County, 1986—; facilitator adult mental health La Habra (Calif.) Community Hosp., 1988-89. Bd. dirs., officer, pres. Friends of Fullerton Arboretum, 1974—; pres., bd. dirs. Fullerton Beautiful, 1987-88, Brea Ednl. Found., 1988-89; therapist Orange County Juvenile Connection Project, 1988—. Recipient Appreciation award Gary Ctr., La

Habra, 1975, Multiple Sclerosis Soc. Orange County, 1987. Mem. Calif. Assn. Marriage and Family Therapists, Assn. for Children and Adults with Learning Disabilities (cons. 1970—, bd. dirs., facilitator), AAUW, Am. Bus. Women's Assn., Soroptomists (health chmn. Brea chpt. 1987-88). Republican. Unitarian. Office: Brea Mental Health Assocs PO Box 1688 Brea CA 92622-1688

DYER, CAROLYN PRICE, artist, writer; b. Seattle, Dec. 19, 1931; d. Herbert Frederick and Evelyn Ida (Nelson) Price; m. M. Clark Dyer, Sept. 7, 1954; children: Philip Nelson, Paul Clark, Andrew Mark Price. Student, U. Wash., 1949-50; BA, Mills Coll., Oakland, Calif., 1953; MA, Mills Coll., 1955. Coll. level teaching credential, Calif. Owner Stone Ct. Gallery Contemporary Art, Yakima, Wash., 1958-65; prin. Carolyn Dyer Textiles, Pasadena, Calif., 1965—; mem. faculty L.A. Community Coll., 1970-78, Pasadena Art Mus. Art Workshops, 1971-73; freelance writer art and travel publs., 1976—; juror N.W. Craftsmen's Exhbn., Seattle, 1964, Fiber Structure Nat., Downey, Calif., 1983; curator So. Calif. Galleries, 1974, Blue Heron Ctr. for Arts, Vashon, Wash., 1991. One-woman shows inlcude The Kennedy Douglas Ctr. for the Arts, Florence, Ala., 1992; two-woman shows include Monrovia (Calif.) Arts Ctr., 1985, Blue Heron Ctr. for Arts, 1988; major exhibitions in group shows include Fullerton (Calif.) Mus. Ctr., 1985, Cortland (N.Y.) Arts Coun. Gallery, 1985, Brea (Calif.) Mcpl. Art Gallery, 1987, Mills Coll., 1987, Laguna Art Mus., Laguna Beach, Calif., 1988, Oreg. Sch. Arts and Crafts, Portland, 1985, 89, 90, Mariposa Gallery, Santa Fe, 1990, Frye Art Mus., Seattle, 1991, Wignall Mus. and Gallery, Rancho Cucamonga, Calif., 1991, Maude Kerns Art Ctr., Eugene, Oreg., 1991, Blue Heron Ctr. for Arts, 1991; represented in numerous pvt. and corp. collections; contbg. editor Fiberarts mag., 1978—; editor (newsletter) Lineup, 1978—. Bd. dirs. Pasadena Art Alliance, 1981-87, Pasadena Arts Coun., 1977-79. Recipient Gold Crown award Pasadena Arts Coun., 1982; Trustee scholar Mills Coll., 1950-53, Grad. fellow, 1953-55. Mem. Am. Craft Coun., Pasadena Soc. Artists, Tapestry Artists of Puget Sound, Textile Mus. Assocs., Textile Arts Coun.

DYER, MICHAEL RODNEY, psychotherapist, consultant; b. Singapore, May 9, 1949; s. Clarence Herbert Dyer and Gwene Phylis Berkholst Olney; m. Dona Gail Johnson, June 1, 1980 (div. 1988); m. Sandra Lynn Johnson, May 24, 1992; children: Lindsay, Shannon, Michael. BA, Calif. State Coll., San Bernardino, 1976, MS, 1983. Lic. marriage and family counselor, Calif. Civilian counselor North AFB - Social Actions, San Bernardino, 1972-78; psychologist asst. Dr. Shearer, San Bernardino, 1977-82; project coord. West End Family Counseling, Upland, Calif., 1983-85; project coord. Family Svc. Assn., Riverside, Calif., 1980-86, clin. supr., 1987-89; sr. family therapist Loma Linda (Calif.) Pediatric Med. Ctr., 1988—; clin. supr. Family Stress Program, San Bernardino, 1988—; psychotherapist Hospitality Family Therapy, San Bernardino, 1988—. Chmn. Domestic Violence Intervention Consortium, San Bernardino, 1989—; mem. Domestive Violence Task Force, San Bernardino, 1990—; bd. dirs. Alternatives to Domestic Violence, Riverside, 1991. With U.S. Army, 1968-70. Mem. Calif. Assn. Marriage and Family Therapists. Office: Hospitality Family Therapy 1849 Commercenter E "B" San Bernardino CA 92408

DYER, TIM ALAN, aerospace engineer; b. Missoula, Mont., Oct. 13, 1958; s. Gilbert Ronald and Melissa Ellen (Murphy) D. AS in Engring. Design Tech., U. Nev., 1978; BSME, Northrop U., Inglewood, Calif., 1988. Engr. E-3 Lear Fan Ltd., Stead, Nev., 1982-85; adj. prof. Northrop U., Inglewood, Calif., 1988-90; engring. specialist Northrop Corp., Hawthorne, Calif., 1985—. Mem. Soc. for Advancement of Material and Processes Engring., AIAA Engring. Soc., Pi Tau Sigma, Tau Beta Pi. Office: Northrop Aircraft Division One Northrop Ave Hawthorne CA 90250

DYESS, EDWIN EARL, academic administrator; b. Roswell, N.Mex., Apr. 23, 1949; s. Marion and Johnnie Lorea (Murray) D.; m. Delila Ann Frazier, May 12, 1973; 1 child, Tyler Christopher. BBA, Ea. N.Mex. U., 1971. Supt. grounds Ea. N.Mex. U., Roswell, 1972-78, N.Mex. Mil. Inst., Roswell, 1978—; sec. S.W. Phys. Plant Suprs. Assn., Albuquerque, N.Mex., 1980-81. Named Outstanding Young Man of Am., 1982. Mem. N.Mex. Irrigation Assn., Delta Sigma Pi. Republican. Baptist. Home: 1005 Hamilton Dr Roswell NM 88201-1132 Office: NMex Mil Inst 101 W College Blvd Roswell NM 88201-5174

DYGERT, HAROLD PAUL, JR., cardiologist; b. Rochester, N.Y., June 21, 1919; s. Harold Paul and Elsie Viola (Howe) D.; m. Helen Adelaine Nelson, Apr. 22, 1944; children: Harold Paul III, William Nelson, Peter Howe. BA, U. Rochester, 1941; postgrad., Alfred U., 1942-43; MD, Syracuse U., 1950. Diplomate Am. Bd. Internal Medicine. Intern Receiving Hosp., Detroit, 1950-51, resident internal medicine, 1951-53, chief resident, 1953-54; instr. medicine Wayne State U., Detroit, 1954-55; mem. staff VA Hosp., Vancouver, Wash., 1955-59; practice medicine specializing in cardiology and internal medicine Vancouver, 1959—; chmn. Health Care Consortium, 1974-87. Pres. Wash. State Med., Ednl. and Research Found., 1971-73; bd. dirs. Wash.-Alaska Regional Med. Program, 1966-72; participant Manhattan Project, 1943-46. Served with AUS, 1943. Fellow ACP, Am. Coll. Cardiology; mem. AMA (del. 1976-77), Am. Fedn. Clin. Research, Wash. State Med. Assn. (pres. 1973-74), Portland Heart Club (pres. 1975-77), Wash. State Soc. Internal Medicine (trustee 1976-80). Home: 8407 SE Evergreen Hwy Vancouver WA 98664-2335 Office: 2101 E Mcloughlin Blvd Vancouver WA 98661

DYKES, FRED WILLIAM, retired nuclear scientist; b. Pocatello, Idaho, Jan. 20, 1928; s. Fred Elmer and Lina Estelle (Dutton) D.; m. Peggy True, Oct. 8, 1950; children: Mark William, James Fred. BS in Chemistry, Idaho State U., 1952. Jr. chemist Am. Cyanamid Co., Idaho Falls, Idaho, 1952-53; chemist Phillips Petroleum Co., Idaho Falls, 1953-66, Idaho Nuclear Corp., Idaho Falls, 1966-71; engr. specialist Allied Chem. Corp., Idaho Falls, 1971-79; sr. scientist Exxon Nuclear Idaho Co., Idaho Falls, 1979-84; fellow scientist Westinghouse Idaho Nuclear Co., Idaho Falls, 1984-93; ret., 1993. Co-author: Progress in Nuclear Energy, Volume 10, 1972; contbr. U.S. Govt. reports and articles to profl. jours. Leader Boy Scouts Am., Pocatello, 1955-78. Sgt. U.S. Army, 1946-48, Korea. Mem. Idaho Hist. Soc., Oreg.-Calif. Trail Assn. (Idaho bd. dirs. 1990—). Home: 964 Wayne Ave Pocatello ID 83201-3612

DYKSTRA, DAVID CHARLES, accountant, management consultant, author, educator; b. Des Moines, July 10, 1941; s. Orville Linden and Ermina (Dunn) D.; m. Ello Paimre, Nov. 20, 1971; children: Suzanne, Karin, David S. BSChemE, U. Calif., Berkeley, 1963; MBA, Harvard U., 1966. CPA, Calif. Corp. contr. Recreation Environs., Newport Beach, Calif., 1970-71, Hydro Conduit Corp., Newport Beach., 1971-78; v.p. fin. and adminstrn. Tree-Sweet Products, Santa Ana, Calif., 1978-80; pres., owner Dykstra Cons., Irvine, Calif., 1980-88, Long Beach, 1991—; pres. Easy Data Corp., 1981-88; pub. Easy Data Computer Comparisons, 1982-87; sr. mgr. Deloitt & Touche, Costa Mesa, Calif., 1988-90; pres., owner Golden West Personnel, Long Beach; prof. mgmt. info. systems Nat. U., Irvine, 1984—; pub. Dykstra's Computer Digest, 1984—. Author: Manager's Guide to Business Computer Terms, 1981, Computers for Profit, 1983; contbr. articles to profl. jours. Chmn. 40th Congl. Dist. Tax Reform Immediately, 1977-80; mem. nat. com. Rep. Com.; vice-chmn. Orange County Calif. Rep. Assembly, 1979-80; bd. dir. Corona Del Mar Rep. Assembly, 1980—, v.p., 1980-87, pres. 1987—. Mem. AICPA, Am. Mgmt. Assn., Calif. Soc. CPA's, Data Processing Mgmt. Assn., Am. Prodn. and Inventory Control Soc., Ind. Computer Cons. Assn., Internat. Platform Assn., Data Processing Mgmt. Assn., Orange County C. of C., Newport Beach C. of C., Harvard U. Bus. Sch. Assn. Orange County (bd. dir. 1984—, v.p 1984-86, 87-88, pres. 1986-87, 91-92), Harvard U. Bus. Sch. Assn. So. Calif. (bd. dirs. 1986-87, 91-92, v.p. 1992—), Town Hall, John Wayne Tennis Club, Lido Sailing Club, Rotary (bd. dirs. 1984-86). Home: 3857 Birch St Apt 541 Newport Beach CA 92660 Office: 3505 Long Beach Rd # 2-E Long Beach CA 90807

DYKSTRA, PHILIP ROUSE, manufacturing company executive; b. Corvallis, Oreg., May 12, 1929; s. Theodore Peter and Myrtle Marie (Rouse) D.; m. Martha Lou Hierholzer, Sept. 12, 1953 (div. Oct. 1990); children: Joan, Robert, John, Mark, Ann, Mary, Karen; m. Nancy Ruth Heal, Oct. 10, 1990. BSChemE, La. State U., 1949, MSChemE, 1950. Rocket engr. USAF, Dayton, Ohio, 1950-53, U.S. Army, Huntsville, Ala., 1953-58; program mgr., minuteman Thiokol Corp., Brigham City, Utah, 1958-62; program mgr., 156 segmented Thiokol Corp., 1962-64, dir. program mgmt., 1964-82, v.p., asst. gen. mgr. Wasatch div., 1982-85, v.p., gen. mgr. strategic ops., 1985-88, v.p., gen. mgr. advance launch vehicles, 1988-89; v.p. strategic planning Thiokol Corp., Ogden, Utah, 1989—. With U.S. Army, 1953-55. Office: Thiokol Corp 2475 Washington Blvd Ogden UT 84401-2300

DYKSTRA-ERICKSON, ELIZABETH ANN, computer researcher; b. Peoria, Ill., Nov. 9, 1954; d. Wayne Harold and Edith Pearl (Christoff) Dykstra; m. Michael Aaron Gottlieb, Jan. 31, 1988 (div. June 1989); m. David Wayne Erickson, Dec. 14, 1991; 1 child, Rianneke Pearl. BA, Ind. U., 1974, MS, 1976; MS, San Jose State U., 1991. Mgr. Levi Strauss & Co., San Francisco, 1979-80; analyst Pacific Bell, San Francisco, 1980-88; cybernetician Pacific Bell, San Ramon, Calif., 1988-90, human-computer interaction rschr., 1990—; mem. tech. staff U.S. West Advanced Techs., 1992—; mem. adj. faculty San Jose (Calif.) State U., 1988, U. San Francisco, 1991—; rschr., cons. U. Amsterdam, The Netherlands, 1989-90; cons. XenoSys, San Francisco, Amsterdam, 1988—; chmn. supervisory com. Pacific Tel. Co. Credit Union, San Francisco, 1983-89. Contbg. author: Addenda and Errata, 1990, CSCW and Groupware, 1991; mng. editor Gen. Systems Yearbook, 1988. Mem. Am. Soc. for Cybernetics, Assn. for Computing Machinery, Human Factors Sci., Internat. Soc. Systems Scis., Ctr. for Innovation and Coop. Tech. (U. Amsterdam), Women in Telecom. (internat. bd. dirs. 1983-86), Bay Computer Human Interaction. Democrat. Mem. LDS Ch. Home: 1630-30th # 468 Boulder CO 80301-1000

DYM, CLIVE LIONEL, engineering educator; b. Leeds, England, July 15, 1942; came to U.S., 1949, naturalized, 1954; s. Isaac and Anna (Hochmann) D.; children: Jordana, Miriam. B.C.E., Cooper Union, 1962; M.S., Poly. Inst. Bklyn., 1964; Ph.D., Stanford U., 1967. Asst. prof. SUNY, Buffalo, 1966-69; assoc. professorial lectr. George Washington U., Washington, 1969; research staff Inst. Def. Analyses, Arlington, Va., 1969-70; assoc. prof. Carnegie-Mellon U., Pitts., 1970-74; vis. assoc. prof. TECHNION, Israel, 1971; sr. scientist Bolt Beranek and Newman, Inc., Cambridge, Mass., 1974-77; prof. U. Mass., Amherst, 1977-91, head dept. civil engring., 1977-85; Fletcher Jones prof. engring. design Harvey Mudd Coll., Claremont, Calif., 1991—; vis. sr. rsch. fellow Inst. Sound and Vibration Rsch., U. Southampton, Eng., 1973; vis. scientist Xerox PARC, 1983-84; vis. prof. civil engring. Stanford U., 1983-84, Carnegie Mellon U., 1990; cons. Bell Aerospace Co., 1967-69, Dravo Corp., 1970-71, Salem Corp., 1972, Gen. Analytics Inc., 1972, ORI, Inc., 1979, BBN Inc., 1979, Avco, 1981-83, 85-86, TASC, 1985-86; vice chmn. adv. bd. Amerinex Artificial Intelligence, 1986-88. Author: (with I.H. Shames) Solid Mechanics: A Variational Approach, 1973, Introduction to the Theory of Shells, rev. edit. 1990, Stability Theory and Its Applications to Structural Mechanics, 1974, (with A. Kalnins) Vibration: Beams, Plates, and Shells, 1977, (with E.S. Ivey) Principles of Mathematical Modeling, 1980, (with I.H. Shames) Energy and Finite Element Methods in Structural Mechanics, 1985, (with R.E. Levitt) Knowledge-Based Systems in Engineering, 1990; editor: Applications of Knowledge-Based Systems to Engineering Analysis and Design, 1985, Artificial Intelligence for Engring. Design Analysis and Mfg., 1986—; contbr. articles and tech. reports to profl. publs. NATO sr. fellow in sci., 1973. Fellow Acoustical Soc. Am., ASME, ASCE (Walter L. Huber research prize 1980); mem. AAAS, Am. Assn. for Artificial Intelligence, Computer Soc. of IEEE, ASEE (Western Electric Fund award 1983). Jewish. Office: Harvey Mudd Coll Engr Dept 301 East 12th St Claremont CA 91711

DYMALLY, MERVYN MALCOLM, retired congressman, international business executive; b. Cedros, Trinidad, W.I., May 12, 1926; s. Hamid A. and Andreid S. (Richardson) D.; m. Alice M. Gueno; children: Mark, Lynn. BA in Edn., Calif. State U., 1954; MA in Govt., Calif. State U., Sacramento, 1970; PhD in Human Behavior, U.S. Internat. U., 1978; JD (hon.), Lincoln U., Sacramento, 1975; LLD (hon., U. W. L.A., 1970, Calif. Coll. Law, L.A., City U., L.A., 1976, Fla. Meml. Coll., 1987, Lincoln U., San Francisco, 1984; HLD (hon.), Shaw U., N.C., 1981; PHD (hon.), Calif. Western. U., 1982. Cert. elem., secondary and exceptional children tchr. Tchr. L.A. City Schs., 1955-61; coord. Calif. Disaster Office, 1961-62; mem. Calif. Assembly, 1962-66, Calif. Senate, 1967-74; lt. gov. Calif., 1975-79; mem. 97th-102nd Congresses from 31st Calif. dist., 1981-92; pres. Dymally Internat. Group Inc., Inglewood, Calif., 1992—; mem. Com. on Fgn. Affairs and its subcoms. on Internat. Ops., chmn. subcom. on Africa, 1989—; mem. Com. on D.C. and chmn. subcom. on judiciary and edn., 1981—; chmn. Congl. Task Force on Minority Set Asides, 1987—; chmn. Senate Majority Caucus, Senate Select Com. on Children and Youth; chmn. Senate coms. on mil. and vets affairs, social welfare, elections and reapportionment, subcom. on med. edn. and health needs; chmn. joint coms. on legal equality for women, on revision of election code; chmn. assembly com. on indsl. rels.; current mem. Congl. Hispanic Caucus, Congl. Caucus Women's Issues, Congl. Human Rights Caucus, Congl. Black Caucus and chmn. of its task force on Caribbean; chmn. Caribbean Action Lobby, Caribbean Am. Rsch. Inst.; founder Congl. Inst. for Space, Sci. and Tech., chmn. adv. bd.; past chmn. Calif. Commn. Econ. Devel., Commn. of Califs. (U.S, Baja Calif., Calif. Sur, Mex.); past vice chmn, Nat. Conf. Lt. Govs.; former Gov.'s designee U.S. Border States Commn.; past mem. State Lands Commn., others; lectr. Claremont (Calif.) Grad. Sch., Golden Gate U., Sacramento, Pepperdine U., L.A., Pomona (Calif.) Coll., U. Calif., Davis, Irvine, Whittier (Calif.) Coll., Shaw U., Raleigh, N.C.; Disting. prof. Ctrl. State U. Author: The Black Politician-His Struggle for Power, 1971; co-auhtor: (with Dr. Jeffrey Elliot) Fidel Castro: Nothing Can Stop the Course of History, 1986, also articles; former editor:The Black Politician (quar.). Chmn. Congl. Caucus on Sci. and Tech.; chmn. bd. Caribbean Action Lobby; mem. Los Angeles County Water Appeals Bd. Recipient numerous awards including Chaconia Gold medal Govt. Trinidad and Tobago, Adam Clayton Powell award Congl. Black Caucus, Dr. Solomon P. Fuller award Black Psychiatrists of Am., others from Golden State Med. Assn., United Tchrs. L.A., Bd. Suprs. L.A., L.A. City Coun., various univs., colls., orgns. Mem. AAUP, NAACP, Am. Acad. Polit. Sci., Am. Polit. Sci. Assn., Am. Acad. Polit. and Social Sci., ACLU, Urban League, Phi Kappa Phi, Kappa Alpha Psi. Office: Dymally Internat Group Inc 9111 S La Cienega Blvd Ste 204 Compton CA 90220

DYNDA, ERNEST FRANCIS, marketing and governmental consultant; b. Chgo., June 20, 1934; s. Stanley John and Alice Clara Dynda; m. Carole Ann Gebhard, Dec. 20, 1964; 1 child, Allison Amy Dynda Sain. BS in Bus., U. Ill., 1959. Mgr. Thrifty Drug Stores, L.A., 1959-62; sales rep. Internat. Harvester, L.A., 1962-68; sales rep., account mgr. AC-Delco, GM, Calif., 1968-88; ret., 1988; sales cons. Kay Automotive Distbrs., Van Nuys, Calif., 1988—; govt. cons., Calif., 1988—; columnist Agoura (Calif.) Valley News, 1976-80. Pres. Las Virgenes Cityhood Com., Agoura, 1978-82, United Orgn. Taxpayers, L.A., 1987—; charter mem. City of Agoura Hills (Calif.) City Coun., 1982-87. With U.S. Army, 1955-57. Named One of Top 10 Newsmakers, Dail News, L.A., 1983. Mem. Las Virgenes C. of C. (bd. dirs. 1977-80), Masons (steward). Republican. Office: United Orgns Taxpayers PO Box 1378 Agoura Hills CA 91376

DZIECIOL, GEORGE, software engineer; b. Warsaw, Poland, Nov. 10, 1960; came to U.S., 1989; s. Wieslaw and Jolanta (Filipowicz) D.; m. Christine Kwasniak, Apr. 6, 1991. MSEE, Warsaw Tech. U., 1984. Software engr. Inst. Computer Scis., Warsaw, 1984-89; software devel. engr. PC Dynamics, Westlake Village, Calif., 1989-91; sr. software engr. Teleprocessing Products, Inc., Simi Valley, Calif., 1991—; asst. lectr. Polish Acad. Scis., Warsaw, 1988-89. Roman Catholic. Office: Teleprocessing Products Inc 4565 E Industrial St Ste 7K Simi Valley CA 93010

EAKIN, CHARLES GILLILAN, music educator, composer; b. Pitts., Feb. 24, 1927; s. Charles Thornton and Ruth Clare (Gillilan) E.; m. Shirley Peterson, Dec. 28, 1957 (div. 1969); children: Nancy, George, Charles; m. Jo Anne Morgan (div. 1990). B. Music, Manhattan Sch. Music, 1950; M. Music, Carnegie Mellon U., 1955; PhD, U. Minn., 1964. Double bassist Houston Symphony, 1950-52, New Orleans Symphony, 1953; tchr. Baylor U., Waco, Tex., 1960-64; prof. U. Colo., Boulder, 1964—. Composer Capriccii for all orchestral instruments, 3 string quartets, 2 operas, songs, electronic music, chamber & symphony works. Recipient Hans Kindler award for chamber music Hans Kindler Soc., Washington, 1977, Violin Concerto award Nat. Endowment for the Arts, 1979, Spontaneities for Jazz Group and Orch. award Nat. Endowment for the Arts, 1977. Home: 830 20th St Boulder CO 80302-7724

EAKIN, MARGARETTA MORGAN, lawyer; b. Ft. Smith, Ark., Aug. 27, 1941; d. Ariel Thomas and Oma (Thomas) Morgan; m. Harry D. Eakin, June 7, 1959; 1 dau., Margaretta E. B.A. with honors, U. Oreg., 1969, J.D., 1971. Bar: Oreg. 1971, U.S. Dist. Ct. Oreg. 1973, U.S. Ct. Appeals (9th cir.) 1977. Law clk. to chief justice Oreg. Supreme Ct., 1971-72; Reginald Heber Smith Law Reform fellow, 1972-73; house counsel Hyster Co., 1973-75; assoc. N. Robert Stoll, 1975-77; mem. firm Margaretta Eakin, P.C., Portland, Oreg., 1977—; tchr. bus. law Portland State U., 1979-80; speaker; mem. state bd. profl. responsibility Oreg. State Bar, 1979-82. Mem. bd. visitors U. Oreg. Law Sch., 1986—, vice chair, 1989-91; chair, 1991-93; mem. ann. fund com. Oreg. Episc. Sch., 1981, chmn. subcom. country fair, 1981; sec. Parent Club Bd., St. Mary's Acad., 1987; mem. Oreg. State. Bar Com. on Uniform State Laws, 1989-93. Paul Patterson fellow. Mem. ABA, Assn. Trial Lawyers Am., Oreg. Trial Lawyers Assn., Oreg. Bar Assn., Multnomah County Bar Assn., 1000 Friends of Oreg. Land Use Attys. (jud. selection com. 1992—). Democrat. Club: City (cooperating atty.). Office: 30th Fl Pacwest Ctr 1211 SW 5th Ave Portland OR 97204-3730

EAKINS, JOEL KENNETH, archaeology and Old Testament educator, pediatrician; b. Ozark, Mo., Feb. 22, 1930; s. Alvin Homer and Pearl Annie (Meadows) E.; m. Marian LaNette McInnes, Aug. 14, 1949 (dec. Aug. 1990); children—Douglas Gene, Nancy Lynn, Sheri Lee, Laurie Lane. B.S., Wheaton Coll., 1952; B.S., U. Ill., 1954, M.D., 1956; B.D., So. Baptist Theol. Sem., 1967, Ph.D., 1970. Diplomate Am. Bd. Pediatrics. Rotating intern Akron Gen. Hosp., Ohio, 1956-57; pediatric resident Akron Children's Hosp., 1957-59; pediatric hematology fellow Children's Hosp., Columbus, Ohio, 1961-62; practice medicine specializing in pediatrics, Thomasville, Ga., 1962-63; part-time pediatric practice Kaiser Hosp., Oakland, Calif., 1971-88 ; prof. archaeology and O.T., Golden Gate Bapt. Sem., Mill Valley, Calif., 1970—; osteologist Tell-el-Hesi expdn., Israel, 1977—. Contbr. articles to profl. jours. Flutist, Community Band, Marin County, Calif., 1977—. Served as capt. U.S. Army, 1959-61. Mem. Nat. Assn. Profs. Hebrew (v.p. 1982-89, pres. 1989-91), Am. Schs. Oriental Research (ann. prof. appointment, 1983), Soc. Bibl. Lit., Paleopathology Assn. Democrat. Baptist. Home: 78 Labrea Way San Rafael CA 94903-3066 Office: Golden Gate Bapt Sem Mill Valley CA 94903

EAMER, RICHARD KEITH, health care company executive, lawyer; b. Long Beach, Calif., Feb. 13, 1928; s. George Pierce and Lillian (Newell) E.; m. Eileen Laughlin, Sept. 1, 1951; children: Brian Keith, Erin Maureen. B.S. in Acctg., U. So. Calif., 1955, LL.B., 1959. Bar: Calif. 1960; C.P.A., Calif. Acct. L. H. Penney & Co. (C.P.A.s), 1956-59; assoc. firm Ervin, Cohen & Jessup, Beverly Hills, Calif., 1959-63; partner firm Eamer, Bell and Bedrosian, Beverly Hills, 1963-69; chmn. bd., chief exec. officer Nat. Med. Enterprises, Inc., Los Angeles, 1969—; also dir. Nat. Med. Enterprises, Inc.; dir. Union Oil Co. Calif., Imperial Bank. Mem. Am. Bar Assn., Am. Inst. C.P.A.s, Calif. Bar Assn., Los Angeles County Bar Assn. Republican. Clubs: Bel Air Country, Bel Air Bay; California. Office: Nat Med Enterprises Inc 11620 Wilshire Blvd Los Angeles CA 90025*

EAMES, EDWIN JACOB, educator; b. N.Y.C., Mar. 7, 1930; s. Morris Aron and Anna (Korn) Eisenberg; m. Phyllis Edelstein, Sept. 9, 1951 (div. Mar. 1987); children: Mona, David, Lori; m. Toni Ann Gardiner, June 14, 1987. BS, CCNY, 1951; PhD, Cornell U., 1965. Asst. to assoc. prof. Temple U., Phila., 1956-70; from assoc. prof. to prof. Baruch Coll., CUNY, N.Y.C., 1970-88; adj. prof. Calif. State U., Fresno, 1988—; cons. Ford Found., Fgn. Fellowship program, N.Y.C., 1972-75. Co-author: Urban Poverty, 1972, Anthropology of the City, 1977, Cultural Anthropology, 1982, A Guide to Guide Dog Schools, 1986; contbr. articles to profl. jours. Chair FAX-ADA Adv. Com., Fresno, Calif., 1990—; co-chair NFB of Calif. Guide Dog Com., Fresno, 1989; mem. Assistance Dog Consumer Coun., Fresno, 1992—. Rsch. grant World Inst. on Disability, 1989-90, Indian Govt. (Indo-Am. fellowship), 1980-81, Ford Found., 1953-55, NIMH, U.K., 1969-70. Fellow Am. Anthropol. Assn., Phi Delta Kappa, Sigma Xi. Jewish. Home: 3376 N Wishon Fresno CA 93704

EARLE, JULIUS RICHARD, JR., child, adolescent and family psychiatrist; b. Columbus, Ohio, July 6, 1954; s. Julius Richard Sr. and Myrtle Vivian (Corbett) E.; m. Carmen Elaine McCall, Aug. 8, 1981; children: Taylor Corbett, Merritt Kelley. BS, Clemson U., 1975; MD, Am. U. Caribbean, 1981. Diplomate psychiatry and child and adolescent psychiatry, Am. Bd. Psychiatry and Neurology. Pvt. practice child, adolescent and family psychiatry Billings, Mont., 1987-91; pres. Profl. Health Resources, Billings, 1988-90, treas., 1990; clin. dir. child and adolescent psychiatry Billings Deaconess Med. Ctr., 1991—; cons. Billings area office Indian Health Svc., 1987-91; cons. Yellowstone Treatment Ctrs., Billings, 1987-90, med. dir., 1989-90; cons. youth partial hospitalization program Deaconess Psychiat. Ctr., 1987-91. Mem. AMA, Am. Psychiat. Assn., Am. Acad. Child and Adolescent Psychiatry (pres. Big Sky regional coun. 1992—), Mont. Med. Assn., Mont. Psychiat. Assn. (pres.-elect 1990-91, pres. 1991—). United Methodist. Office: Deaconess Behavioral Health Clinic 550 N 31st St Ste 502 Billings MT 59101

EARLE, SYLVIA ALICE, research biologist, oceanographer; b. Gibbstown, N.J., Aug. 30, 1935; d. Lewis Reade and Alice Freas (Richie) E. BS, Fla. State U., 1955; MA, Duke U., 1956, PhD, 1966, PhD (hon.), 1993; PhD (hon.), Monterey Inst. Internat. Studies, 1990, Ball State U., 1991, George Washington U., 1992; DSc (hon.), Duke Univ., 1993. Resident dir. Cape Haze Marine Lab., Sarasota, Fla., 1966-67; research scholar Radcliffe Inst., 1967-69; research fellow Farlow Herbarium, Harvard U., 1967-75, researcher, 1975—; research assoc. in botany Natural History Mus. Los Angeles County, 1970-75; research biologist, curator Calif. Acad. Scis., San Francisco, from 1976; research assoc. U. Calif., Berkeley, 1969-75; fellow in botany Natural History Mus., 1989—; chief scientist U.S. NOAA, Washington, 1990-92, advisor to the adminstr., 1992-93; founder, pres., CEO, bd. dirs. Deep Ocean Tech., Inc., Oakland, Calif., 1981-90; founder, pres., CEO Deep Ocean Engring., Oakland, 1982-90, bd. dirs., 1992—. Author: Exploring the Deep Frontier, 1980; editor: Scientific Results of the Tektite II Project, 1972-75; contbr. 80 articles to profl. jours. Trustee World Wildlife Fund U.S., 1976-82, mem. coun., 1984—; trustee World Wildlife Fund Internat., 1979-81, mem. coun., 1981—; trustee Charles A. Lindbergh Fund, pres., 1990—; trustee Ctr. Marine Conservation, 1992—, Perry Found., chmn., 1993—; mem. coun. Internat. Union for Conservation of Nature, 1979-81; corp. mem. Woods Hole Oceanographic Inst.; mem. Nat. Adv. Com. on Oceans and Atmosphere, 1980-94. Recipient Conservation Service award U.S. Dept. Interior, 1970, Boston Sea Rovers award, 1972, 79, Nogi award Underwater Soc. Am., 1976, Conservation service award Calif. Acad. Sci., 1979, Lowell Thomas award Explorer's Club, 1980, Order of Golden Ark Prince Netherlands, 1980, David B. Stone medal New Eng. Aquarium, 1989, Gold medalist Soc. of Women Geographers, medal Radcliffe Coll., 1990, Pacon Internat. award, 1992, Dirs. award Natural Resources Coun. Am., 1992; named Woman of Yr. L.A. Times, 1970, Scientist of Yr., Calif. Mus. Sci. and Industry, 1981. Fellow AAAS, Marine Tech. Soc., Calif. Acad. Scis., Explorers Club, Calif. Acad. Sci.; mem. Internat. Phycological Soc. (sec. 1974-80), Phycological Soc. Am., Am. Soc. Ichthyologists and Herpetologists, Am. Inst. Biol. Scis., Brit. Phycological Soc., Ecol. Soc. Am., Internat. Soc. Plant Taxonomists, Explorers Club (fellow, bd. dirs. 1989—). Home: 12812 Skyline Blvd Oakland CA 94619-3125 Office: Deep Ocean Engring 1431 Doolittle Dr San Leandro CA 94577

EARLY, JAMES MICHAEL, electronics research consultant; b. Syracuse, N.Y., July 25, 1922; s. Frank J. and Rhoda Gray E.; m. Mary Agnes Valentine, Dec. 28, 1948; children: Mary Beth Early Dehler, Kathleen, Joan Early Farrell, Rhoda Early Alexander, Maureen Early Mathews, Rosemary Early North, James, Margaret Mary Early Staton. B.S., N.Y. Coll. Forestry, Syracuse, N.Y., 1943; M.S., Ohio State U., 1948, Ph.D., 1951. Instr., research assoc. Ohio State U., Columbus, 1946-51; dir. lab. Bell Telephone Labs., Murray Hill, N.J., 1951-64, Allentown, Pa., 1964-69; dir. research and devel. Fairchild Semicondr. Corp., Palo Alto, Calif., 1969-83, sci. advisor, 1983-86; research cons., 1986—. Contbr. over 20 papers to profl. jours. Served with U.S. Army, 1943-45. Fellow AAAS, IEEE (numerous coms., John Fritz Medal bd. of award); mem. IEEE Electron Device Soc. (J.J. Ebers award 1979), Am. Phys. Soc., Internat. Platform Assn. Roman Catholic. Home and Office: 708 Holly Oak Dr Palo Alto CA 94303-4142

EARLY, ROBERT JOSEPH, magazine editor; b. Indpls., Sept. 22, 1936; s. Robert Paul and Helen Theresa (Schluttenhofer) E.; m. Gail Louise Horvath, Sept. 6, 1958; children: Mary Jane, Joseph Robert, Jill Ann. BA, U. Notre Dame, 1958. Reporter Indpls. Star, 1958-61; reporter The Ariz. Republic, Phoenix, 1961-66, asst. city editor, 1966-69, city editor, 1969-77, asst. mng. editor, 1977-78, mng. editor, 1978-82; pres. Telesource Communication Svcs. Inc., Phoenix, 1982-90; editor Phoenix Mag., 1985-89, Ariz. Hwys., Phoenix, 1990—. Chmn. Victims Bill of Rights Task Force, Phoenix, 1989. Recipient Virg Hill Newsman of Yr. award Ariz. Press Club, 1976. Mem. Soc. Profl. Journalists. Republican. Roman Catholic. Office: Ariz Hwys 2039 W Lewis Ave Phoenix AZ 85009-2893

EARNER, WILLIAM ANTHONY, JR., naval officer; b. Pitts., Nov. 2, 1941; s. William Anthony and Marie Veronica (Ward) E.; m. Jennifer Elizabeth Laurence, Dec. 11, 1971; children: William Andrew, John Laurence. BS, U.S. Naval Acad., 1963; MS, U.S. Naval Postgrad. Sch., 1969; DBA, Harvard U., 1973. Commd. ensign USN, 1963, advanced through grades to rear adm., 1990; 1st lt. USS Blue USN, Yokosuka, Japan, 1963-65; weapons officer USS Black USN, San Diego, 1965-67; ops. officer River Sect. 534 USN, Vietnam, 1967-68; weapons officer USS Dale USN, Mayport, Fla., 1973-75, exec. officer USS Luce, 1975-77; prof. Naval War Coll. USN, Newport, R.I., 1977-78, fellow strategic studies group, 1987-88; commanding officer Office Chief Naval Ops. USN, Washington, 1978-81; comdg. officer USS Deyo USN, 1981-83; mil. asst. to dir. NET assesment Office of Sec. Def. USN, Washington, 1983-85, comptr. naval air systems, 1988-90; comdr. Destroyer Squadron Four USN, Charleston, S.C., 1985-87; comdr. naval surface group mid-Pacific USN, Pearl Harbor, Hawaii, 1990-92; budget officer Dept. Navy, 1992—; instr. Harvard Grad. Sch. Edn., Cambridge, Mass., 1972-73; adj. prof. Bryant Coll., Smithfield, R.I., 1977-78. Dir. Aloha United Way, Honolulu, 1990-91; active Hawaii Bus. Roundtable. Decorated Legion of Merit, Bronze Star with V device. Mem. U.S. Naval Inst., Am. Soc. Mil. Comptrs., U.S. Naval Acad. Alumni Assn., Harvard Bus. Sch. Club. Office: Dir Budget and Reports Pentagon 4C736 Dept Navy Washington DC 20350-1100

EASLEY, GEORGE WASHINGTON, construction executive; b. Williamson, W.Va., Mar. 14, 1933; s. George Washington and Isabel Ritchie (Saville) E.; student U. Richmond, 1952-56; children: Bridget Bland, Kathy Clark, Saville Woodson, Marie Alexis, Isabell Roxanne, George Washington, Laura Dean, Dorothy Elizabeth. m. Bettyrae Fedje Hanner, Sep. 15, 1990. Hwy. engr. Va. Dept. Hwys., Richmond, 1956-62; dep. city mgr. City of Anchorage, 1962-68; prin. assoc. Wilbur Smith & Assos., Los Angeles, 1969-70; commr. pub. works State of Alaska, Juneau, 1971-74; exec. v.p. Burgess Internat. Constrn. Co., Anchorage, 1974, pres., 1975; pres., chmn. bd. George W. Easley Co., Anchorage, 1976-86 ; pres. Alaska Aggregate Corp., Fairbanks Sand & Gravel Co., 1986-90; constrn. mgr. Alyeska Pipeline Svc. Co., 1990—; bd. dirs. Totem Ocean Trailer Express, Inc. Recipient commendations City of Anchorage, 1966, Greater Anchorage, Inc., 1969, Ketchikan C. of C., 1973, Alaska State Legis., 1974, Gov. of Alaska, 1974; named one of Outstanding Young Men, Anchorage Jaycees, 1964. Registered profl. engr., Calif. Mem. U.S. C. of C. (nat. com. on small bus.), Alaska C. of C. (dir. 1978—, chmn. 1982-83), Anchorage C. of C. (sec.-treas. 1976, v.p. 1977, pres.-elect 1978, pres. 1979-80, dir. 1982-88, Gold Pan award 1969, 77), Hwy. Users Fedn. Alaska (dir. 1972—, treas. 1974—), Orgn. Mgmt. of Alaska's Resources (past dir.), Am. Pub. Works Assn., Anchorage Transp. Commn. (past chmn.), Associated Gen. Contractors (dir. Alaska chpt. 1978—, chpt. treas. 1980-81, sec. 1981, pres. 1984, nat. com. labor relations, Hard Hat award, 1985), Am. Mil. Engrs. (v.p. Alaska chpt. 1978), Ak. Trucking Assn. (bd. dirs. 1986—), Inst. Mcpl. Engrs., Inst. Traffic Engrs., Internat. Orgn. Masters, Mates and Pilots (hon.), Common Sense for Alaska (past pres.), Commonwealth North (charter). Democrat. Presbyterian. Club: San Francisco Tennis. Lodge: Rotary. Home: 4921 Sportsman Dr Anchorage AK 99502-4193 Office: 3601 C St # 6088 Anchorage AK 99503-5925

EASLEY, LOYCE ANNA, painter; b. Weatherford, Okla., June 28, 1918; d. Thomas Webster and Anna Laura (Sanders) Rogers; m. Mack Easley, Nov. 17, 1939; children: June Elizabeth, Roger. BFA, U. Okla., 1943; postgrad., Art Students League, N.Y.C., 1947-49; 1977; postgrad., Santa Fe Inst. Fine Arts, 1985. Tchr. Pub. Sch., Okmulgee, Okla., 1946-47, Hobbs, N.Mex., 1947-49; tchr. painting N.Mex. Jr. Coll., Hobbs, 1965-80; tchr. Art Workshops in N.Mex., Okla., Wyoming. Numerous one-woman shows and group exhbns. in mus., univs. and galleries, including Gov.'s Gallery, Santa Fe, Selected Artists, N.Y.C., Roswell (N.Mex.) Mus., N.Mex. State U., Las Cruces, West Tex. Mus., Tex. Tech U., Lubbock; represented in permanent collections USAF Acad., Colorado Springs, Colo., Roswell Mus., Carlsbad (N.Mex.) Mus., Coll. Santa Fe, N.Mex. Supreme Ct, also other pvt. and pub. collections; featured in S.W. Art and Santa Fe mag., 1981, 82. Named Disting. Former Student, U. Okla. Art Sch., 1963; nominated for Gov.'s award in Art, N.Mex., 1988. Mem. N.Mex. Artists Equity (lifetime mem. 1963). Democrat. Presbyterian. Home: 10909 Country Club Dr NE Albuquerque NM 87111-6548

EAST, BRENDA KATHLEEN, author; b. Dartford, Kent, Eng., June 18, 1937; came to U.S., 1955; d. Charles Ernest and Kathleen Edith (Wilkinson) E.; m. Ronald Grant Bierer, Mar. 12, 1955 (div. 1983); children: Grant Keith, Carolyn Joy Bierer-Carlisle, Ronda Lynn Bierer-Atwell, Heber Jay, Janet Ray Bierer-Thorning, David East Bierer. Student, Gravesend (Kent) Coll. Art, 1951-52; grad., Inst. Children's Lit., Conn., 1992. Contbr. articles to profl. jours. and mags. Recipient Short Story Lit. awards Mont. Mother's Assn., 1990, Am. Morther's Assn., 1991, Am. Mother's Inc., 1992, Article Lit. award Am. Mother's Inc., 1992, Short Story award Mont. Mother's, 1993, Article Lit. award Mont. Mother's, 1993. Home: 1423 Hwy 93N Victor MT 59875-9770

EAST, DON G., computer engineer, archaeologist; b. Carlisle, Ind., Mar. 7, 1935; s. Omer R. and Gladys A. (Jarrel) E.; m. Lilliam M. Tim, Aug. 11, 1957; children: Donald A., Lynne, M., Eric T. BS in Physics, U. Ariz., 1970, BS in Engring. Physics, 1970; cert. in field archaeology, Pima Coll., 1982. Field engr. IBM, Tucson, 1961-64; sr. assoc. engr. IBM, Poughkeepsie, N.Y., 1964-67, staff engr., 1967-70, adv. engr., 1970-74, sr. engr., 1974-78; sr. engr. IBM, Tucson, 1978-91; prin. Synchromy Co., Tucson, 1991—; cons. Ctr. for Archaeol. Field Studies, Tucson, 1988—. Patentee in field. Bd. dirs. Tucson Assn. for the Blind, 1986-92, chmn. tech. com., 1990-92; musician USAFE Band, 1957-61; mem. Ariz.-Sonora Desert Mus., Nature Conservancy. With USAF, 1957-61. Mem. IEEE (assoc.), Earthwatch. Mem. Reformed Ch. Home: 3610 W Cobbs Pl Tucson AZ 85745-9653

EAST, DONALD ROBERT, civil engineer; b. Kimberley, South Africa, June 2, 1944; came to U.S., 1985; s. Robert George and Gladys Enid (Macintyre) E.; m. Diana Patricia Ruske, Dec. 21, 1968 (div. Mar. 1993); children: Lisa Ann, Sharon Margaret. BSCE, U. Cape Town, 1969; MSc in Found. Engring., U. Birmingham, England, 1971. Jr. engr. Ninham Shand & Ptnrs., Cape Town, South Africa, 1968-71; mgr. Civilab Ltd., Johannesburg, South Africa, 1972-74; ptnr. Watermeyer, Legge, Piesold & Uhlmann, Johannesburg, 1975-85, Knight Piesold & Co., Denver, 1985—; Contbr. articles to profl. jours. Fellow South Africa Instn. Civil Engrs. (chmn. 1979-85); mem. ASCE, Soc. Mining Engrs. (com. mem. 1988-89). Home: 7902 E Iowa Ave Denver CO 80231 Office: Knight Piesold & Co 1600 Stout St Ste 800 Denver CO 80202-3107

EASTIN, DELAINE ANDREE, state legislator; b. San Diego, Aug. 20, 1947; d. Daniel Howard and Dorothy Barbara (Robert) Eastin; m. John Stuart Saunders, Sept. 17, 1972. BA in Polit. Sci., U. Calif., Davis, 1969; MA in Polit. Sci., U. Calif., Santa Barbara, 1971. Instr. Calif. Community Colls., various locations, 1971-79; acctg. mgr. Pacific Bell, San Francisco, 1979-84; corp. planner Pacific Telesis Group, San Francisco, 1984-86; assemblywoman Calif. State Legis., Sacramento, 1986—. Bd. dirs. CEWAER, Sacramento, 1988—; commr. Commn. on Status of Women, Sacramento, 1990—; mem. coun. City of Union City, Calif., 1980-86; chair Alameda County Libr. Commn., Hayward, Calif., 1981-86; planning commr. City of Union City, 1976-80; mem., pres. Alameda County Solid Waste Mgmt. Authority, Oakland, Calif., 1980-86. Named Outstanding Pub. Ofcl. Calif. Tchrs. Assn., 1988, Cert. of Appreciation Calif. Assn. for Edn. of Young Children, 1988-92, Legislator of the Yr. Calif. Media Libr. Educators, 1991, Calif. Sch. Bd. Assn., 1991, Ednl. Excellence award Calif. Assn. Counseling and Devel., 1992. Mem. Am. Bus. Women's Assn. (Outstanding Bus. Woman 1988), The Internat. Alliance (21st Century award 1990), World Affairs Coun., Commonwealth Club. Democrat. Home: 2140 Spring Water Dr Fremont CA 94539 Office: House of Representatives 2140 Springwater Dr Fremont CA 94539

EASTIN, KEITH E., lawyer; b. Lorain, Ohio, Jan. 16, 1940; s. Keith Ernest and Jane E. (Heimer) E. A.B., U. Cin., 1963, M.B.A., 1964; J.D., U. Chgo., 1967. Bar: Ill. 1967, Tex. 1974, Calif. 1975, U.S. Supreme Ct. 1975, D.C. 1983. Atty. Vedder, Price, Kaufman & Kammholz, Chgo., 1967-73; v.p., sec., gen. counsel Nat. Convenience Stores, Inc., Houston, 1973-79; ptnr. Payne, Eastin & Widmer, Houston, 1977-83; dep. under sec. U.S. Dept. Interior, 1983-86; prin. dep. asst. sec. USN, 1986-88; ptnr. Hopkins & Sutter, Washington, 1989-91; sr. v.p. Guy F. Atkinson Co., San Francisco, 1991-92; pres. Infrastructure Group, Incline Village, Nev., 1992—; sr. v.p., gen. counsel Guy F. Atkinson Co., 1991-92; dir. Nat. Money Orders Inc., Feast & Co., Inc., Kempco Petroleum Co., Bertman Drilling Co., Pacific Options, Inc., Del Rey Food Svcs., Inc., Stratford Feedyards, Inc. Bd. dirs. Theatre Under the Stars, Houston, Statue of Liberty-Ellis Island Found.; mem. exec. com. Harris County Republican Party, 1976-83. Mem. ABA, Ill. Bar Assn., Tex. Bar Assn., D.C. Bar Assn., State Bar Calif., Beta Gamma Sigma, Phi Delta Phi, Beta Theta Pi. Clubs: University (Houston); Capitol Hill (Washington). Office: PO Box 5163 Incline Village NV 89450

EASTMAN, RICHARD DARE (DOC HOLLIDAY, JR.), radio personality, writer, actor; b. Portland, Maine, June 18, 1936; s. Ross Elliot and Dorothy Edith (Dare) E.; m. Kay C. McLeod, Sept. 4, 1955 (div. 1975); children: Adair, Glen, Brian. Grad., Boston Sch. Fine & Applied Art, 1951, Neighborhood Playhouse Sch. Theater, 1953; BA, UCLA, 1958, MFA, 1967; PhD, Pacific Western U., 1991. Asst. mgr. bus. affairs CBS-TV Network, Hollywood, Calif., 1964-68; v.p. Martin Advt. Inc., Anaheim, Calif., 1968-69; creative dir. Irvine (Calif.) Co., 1969-71; instr. Santa Ana (Calif.) Coll., 1972-73; prof. Calif. State U. System, 1975-80; pres. Eastman Imagineering, Newport Beach, Calif., 1980-88; talkshow host KCIN-Radio, Victorville, Calif., 1989—. Author: Dramatronics, 1980, Speakwrite, 1985, (screenplay, novel) Solaricus, 1990. Capt. USMC, 1953-58, PTO. Mem. Nat. Audio Visual Assn. (Gold Eagle awards), Ind. Film Producers Assn., Am. Assn. Advt. Agys. Home: 19188 Palo Verde Dr Apple Valley CA 92308 Office: Island Broadcasting Corp Box 1428 Victorville CA 92393

EASTMAN, ROGER HERBERT, philosophy educator, author; b. N.Y.C., June 7, 1931; s. Herbert Henry and Ella (Coghlan) E.; m. Gloria Jean Byram, Dec. 29, 1962; children: Carolyn, Jennifer. BA, San Jose (Calif.) State U., 1954; MA, Stanford (Calif.) U., 1961. Prof. philosophy Kings River Col., Reedley, Calif., 1958-89. Editor: Coming of Age in Philosophy, 1973, The Ways of Religion, 1975, 2d edit., 1993. Cpl. USMC, 1954-57. NEH fellow, 1972.

EASTON, DAVID, political science educator; b. Toronto, Can., June 24, 1917; m. Sylvia Johnstone, Jan. 1, 1942 (dec. 1990); 1 child, Stephen Talbot. BA, U. Toronto, 1939, MA, 1943; PhD, Harvard U., 1947; LLD (hon.), McMaster U., Can., 1970, Kalamazoo Coll., 1972. Andrew MacLeish Disting. Svc. prof. dept. polit. sci. U. Chgo., 1947-82, prof. emeritus; Sir Edward Peacock prof. Queen's U., Can., 1971-80; disting. prof. U. Calif., Irvine, 1981—; cons. Brookings Inst., Mass., 1953, mental health inst. U. Mich., Ann Arbor, 1955-56, Royal Commn. Biculturalism/Bilingualism, Can., 1965-67; commn. examiners, grad. rec. exam polit. sci. Ednl. Testing Svc., Princeton, N.J., 1966-68; Ford prof. govt. affairs Ford Found., N.Y., 1960-61; pres. Internat. Com. Social Sci. Documentation, 1969-71; chair bd. trustees Acad. Ind. Scholars, 1979-81; co-chair Internat. Com. Devel. Polit. Sci., 1988—. Author: The Political System: An Inquiry into the State of Political Science, 1953, A Framework for Political Analysis, 1965, A Systems Analysis of Political Life, 1965, The Analysis of Political Structure, 1990; co-author: Children in the Political System: Origins of Political Legitimacy, 1969; editor: Varieties of Political Theory, 1966; co-editor: Divided Knowledge: Across Disciplines, Across Cultures, 1991, The Development of Political Science, 1991. Fellow ctr. advanced study behavioral scis. Stanford U., 1957-58. Fellow Am. Acad. Arts and Sci. (v.p. 1984-89, co-chair Western Ctr. 1984-89), Royal Soc. Can.; mem. Am. Polit. Sci. Assn. (pres. 1968-69). Office: U Calif Dept Politics & Society 667 Social Scis Tower Irvine CA 92717

EASTON, ROBERT (OLNEY), author, environmentalist; b. July 4, 1915; s. Robert Eastman and Ethel (Olney) E.; m. Jane Faust, Sept. 24, 1940; children: Joan Easton Lentz, Katherine Easton Renga (dec.), Ellen Easton Brumfiel, Jane. Student, Stanford U., 1933-34, postgrad., 1938-39; B.S., Harvard U., 1938; M.A., U. Calif., Santa Barbara, 1960. Ranch hand, day laborer, mag. editor, 1939-42; co-pub., editor Lampasas (Tex.) Dispatch, 1946-50; instr. English Santa Barbara City Coll., 1959-65; writing and pub. cons. U.S. Naval Civil Engring. Lab., Port Hueneme, Calif., 1961-69. Author: The Happy Man, 1943, (with Mackenzie Brown) Lord of Beasts, 1961, (with Jay Monaghan and others) The Book of the American West, 1963, The Hearing, 1964, (with Dick Smith) California Condor: Vanishing American, 1964, Max Brand: The Big Westerner, 1970, Black Tide: The Santa Barbara Oil Spill and Its Consequences, 1972, Guns, Gold and Caravans, 1978, China Caravans: An American Adventurer in Old China, 1982, This Promised Land, 1982, Life and Work, 1988, Power and Glory, 1989, (with Jane Faust Easton) Love and War, 1991; editor: Max Brand's Best Stories, 1967, (with Mackenzie Brown) Bullying the Moqui, 1968, (with Jane Faust Easton) Max Brand's Best Poems, 1992, (with Jane Faust Easton) Max Brand: Collected Stories, 1993; contbr. to numerous mags. including Atlantic and N.Y. Times mag.; also anthologies including Great Tales of the American West. Co-chmn. Com. for Santa Barbara, 1973-81; trustee Santa Barbara Mus. Natural History, 1975-78, rsch. assoc., 1980-83; trustee Santa Barbara Community Environ. Coun., 1974-79; co-founder Sisquoc Sanctuary for Calif. Condor, 1937, also first wilderness area established under Nat. Wilderness Act, Los Padres Nat. Forest, Calif., 1968. Served to 1st lt. inf. U.S. Army, World War II. Recipient Honor award Calif. Conservation Coun., 1975. Home: 2222 Las Canoas Rd Santa Barbara CA 93105-2113

EASTON, ROGER DAVID, art history educator; b. Douglaston, N.Y., Jan. 4, 1923; s. Spencer Garnet and Ruth Natalie (Albright) E.; m. June Marcella Healy, Dec. 21, 1953. BS, SUNY, 1949; MA, State U. Iowa, 1951; EdD, U. Denver, 1958; postgrad., U. Rochester, Fogg Mus., Harvard U. Cert. tchr., N.Y., Colo. Fellow U. Iowa, Iowa City, 1950-51; instr. to assoc. prof. SUNY, Cortland, 1951-58; prof. Ball State U., Muncie, Ind., 1958-85, ret., 1985. One-man shows include S.W. Savs. and Loan, Green Valley, Ariz., 1989; exhibited in group shows at Smithsonian Instn. Crafts Invitational Nat. Traveling Exhibit, 1960-62, Ball State U. Art Gallery, 1977-80, 80-81, Sheldon Swope Art Gallery, Terre Haute, Ind., 1979-80, 83, Ft. Wayne Mus. Art, 1981-82, Tubac Ctr. of the Arts, 1989, 90, Santa Cruz Valley Art Assn., Tubac, Ariz., 1990, 93, Kessel-Long Gallery, Scottsdale, Ariz., 1990, So. Ariz. Watercolor Guild, 1991, 92, 93, Ariz. Aqueous, 1992, So. Ariz. Art Guild, 1993 and numerous others; contbr. articles to profl. jours. Mem. Nat. Watercolor Soc., So. Ariz. Watercolor Guild, Santa Cruz Valley Art Assn., Ariz. Watercolor Assn., Nat. Art Edn. Assn., Ariz. Art Edn. Assn. Home: 3371 Placita Esconces Green Valley AZ 85614

EASTWOOD, GLEN WAYNE, conductor, educator; b. Pine Bluff, Ark., Dec. 24, 1946; 1 child, Bill; m. Gail Farnes Eastwood, June 4, 1992. BMus, North Tex. State U., 1969, MMusEd, 1970; PhD, U. North Tex., 1989. Dir. choirs Angelo State U., San Angelo, Tex., 1986-88; dir. choirs Idaho State U., Pocatello, 1988—, chair elect faculty senate, 1991—. Contbr. articles to profl. jours. Title V grantee Dept. of Energy, 1970, Idaho State U. faculty rsch. grantee, 1990-91. Mem. Music Educators Nat. Assn., Am. Choral Dirs. Assn., Tex. Music Edn. Assn., Idaho Music Educators Assn. (higher edn. chair 1991—).

EATON, ANGELA, systems and user interface analyst, writer; b. Ft. Bragg, N.C., Jan. 19, 1953; d. Richard John and Patricia (Baldwin) E. BS in Govt., George Mason U., 1976. Ballet dancer, tchr. Fairfax Ballet Co., Arlington, Va., 1974-76; asst. dir. Pa. Dance Theatre, State College, 1976-81; dancer Colo. State Ballet, Denver, 1981-85; prin. Eaton Enterprises, Evergreen, Colo., 1986—; cons. Western Occupational Rsch. Corp., Denver, 1982-84, Multi-List, Lakewood, Colo., 1984-86, U.S. Dept. Energy, Denver, 1986-91, US West, Littleton, Colo., 1990-91, Argonne Nat. Lab., Denver, 1991—. Pres. Search & Rescue Dogs Colo., 1990—; bd. dirs. Alpine Rescue Team, Evergreen, 1989-91. Home: 1521 Hwy 74 Evergreen CO 80439 Office: Eaton Enterprises 1521 Hwy 74 Evergreen CO 80439

EATON, GEORGE WESLEY, JR., oil company executive; b. Searcy, Ark., Aug. 3, 1924; s. George Wesley and Inez (Roberson) E.; m. Adriana Amin, Oct. 28, 1971; 1 child, Andrew. BS in Petroleum, U. Okla., 1948. Registered profl. engr. Tex., N.Mex. Petroleum engr. Amoco, Longview, Ft. Worth, Tex., 1948-54; engring. supr. Amoco, Roswell, N.Mex., 1954-59; dist. engr. Amoco, Farmington, N.Mex., 1959-70; constrn. mgr. Amoco Egypt Oil Co., Cairo, 1970-81; ops. mgr. Amoco Norway Oil Co., Stavanger, 1981-84; petroleum cons. G.W. Eaton Cons., Albuquerque, 1984—; adj. prof. San Juan Coll., Farmington, 1968-70. Bd. dirs. Paradise Hills Civic Assn., Albuquerque, 1986-89; elder Rio Grande Presbyn. Ch., Albuquerque, 1987-90; mem. Rep. Nat. Com., Washington, 1986-92. Mem. N.Mex. Soc. Profl. Engrs. (bd. dirs. 1967-70), Soc. Petroleum Engr. (sr.), Egyptian Soc. Petroleum Engrs. (chmn. 1980-81). Home: 5116 Russell NW Albuquerque NM 87114

EATON, HENRY TAFT, forest products executive, consultant; b. N.Y.C., Aug. 29, 1918; s. Henry Taft and Ina (Kissel) E.; m. Gladys Foote, June 12, 1938 (dec.); children: Penelope, Wendy; m. Phyllis Elaine Thompson, Oct. 13, 1989; stepchildren: Vaile, Danny, Terry, Theresa. Student, Harvard U., 1941. Pres. Eaton-Young Lumber Co., Eugene, Oreg., 1948-68, Henry Eaton & Co., Eugene, 1969-78; owner Henry Eaton & Co., Bend, Oreg., 1979—; pres. Veneer Products Singapore-U.S.A. div., Eugene, 1969-74; v.p. Persis Corp, Honolulu, 1977-79; cons. Bunnings Bros. Pty. Lty., Perth, West Australia, 1982-90, Persis Corp., 1980—. Author: (tech. manual) Tropical Hardwood Plywood, 1972; inventor The Time Wheel. Chmn. Eugene Airport Commn., 1960-67; comdr. CAP, Eugene, 1964-66; mem. mktg. adv. coun. U. Oreg., Eugene, 1965-67. 1st lt. inf. U.S. Army, World War II, ETO. Decorated Purple Heart. Mem. Bend Golf Country Club, South Cowichan Lawn Tennis Club. Republican. Home and Office: 60648 Thunderbird Ct Bend OR 97702-9653

EATON, PAULINE, artist; b. Neptune, N.J., Mar. 20, 1935; d. Paul A. and Florence Elizabeth (Rogers) Friedrich; m. Charles Adams Eaton, June 15, 1957; children: Gregory, Eric, Paul, Joy. BA, Dickinson Coll., 1957; MA, Northwestern U., 1958. Lic. instr., Calif. Instr., Mira Costa Coll., Oceanside, Calif., 1980-82, Idyllwild Sch. Music and Arts, Calif., 1983—; juror, demonstrator numerous art socs. Recipient award Haywood (Calif.) Area Forum for the Arts, 1986. Exhibited one-woman shows Nat. Arts Club, N.Y.C., 1977, Designs Recycled Gallery, Fullerton, Calif., 1978, 80, 84, San Diego Art Inst., 1980, Spectrum Gallery, San Diego, 1981, San Diego Jung Ctr., 1983, Marin Civic Ctr. Gallery, 1984, R. Mondavi Winery, 1987; group shows include Am. Watercolor Soc., 1975, 77, Butler Inst. Am. Art, Youngstown, Ohio, 1977, 78, 79, 81, NAD, 1978; represented in permanent collections including Butler Inst. Am. Art, St. Mary's Coll., Md., Mercy Hosp., San Diego, Sharp Hosp., San Diego, Redlands Hosp., Riverside, 1986; work featured in books: Watercolor, The Creative Experience, 1978, Creative Seascape Painting, 1980, Painting the Spirit in Nature, 1984, Exploring Painting (Gerald Brommer); author: Crawling to the Light, An Artist in Transition, 1987. Trustee San Diego Art Inst., 1977-78, San Diego Mus. Art, 1982-83. Mem. Nat. Watercolor Soc. (exhibited traveling shows 1978, 79, 83, 85), Rocky Mountain Watermedia Soc. (Golden award 1979, Mustard Seed award 1983), Nat. Soc. Painters in Acrylic and Casein (hon.), Watercolor West (Strathmore award 1979, Purchase award 1986), Soc. Experimental Artists (pres. 1989-92, Nautilus Merit award 1992), Marin Arts Guild (instr. 1984-87), San Diego Watercolor Soc. (pres. 1976-77, workshop dir. 1977-80), Artists Equity (v.p. San Diego 1979-81), San Diego Artists Guild (pres. 1982-83), Western Fedn. Watercolor Socs. (chmn. 1983, 3d prize 1982, Grumbacher Gold medal 1983), West Coast Watercolor Soc. (exhbns. chmn. 1983-86, pres. 1989-92), Eastbay Watercolor Soc. (v.p. 1988-90), Soc. Layerists in Multi-Media (bd. dirs. 1992—). Democrat. Home: 68 Hop Tree Trail Corrales NM 87048

EATON, PERRY ALAN, geophysicist; b. Leadville, Colo., Mar. 1, 1959; s. Bruce Clifford Eaton and Winifred Claire Grimshaw; m. Mollie Marie Uhl, Mar. 2, 1991. BS, Colo. Sch. of Mines, 1981; MS, U. Utah, 1984, PhD, 1987. Geophysicist Newmont Exploration Ltd., Denver, 1988-90, sr. geophysicist, 1991—. Mem. Soc. of Exploration Geophysicists (assoc.), European Assn. of Exploration Geophysicists (assoc.), Sigma Xi. Office: Newmont Exploration Ltd 1700 Lincoln St Denver CO 80203

EATON, THOMAS CLARK, insurance and financial consultant; b. Fresno, Calif., Nov. 24, 1952; s. Robert Louis and Polly (Gregory) E.; m. Deborah Thomason, Nov. 19, 1983; children: Jonathan, Elisabeth. BA, Pacific U., 1976. Salesman Fred S. James & Co., Portland, Oreg., 1974-75; v.p., treas. Eaton & Eaton Ins. Brokers, Fresno, 1976-84; mgr. truck ins. div. Marsh & McLennan, San Francisco, 1984-85; chmn., pres. Wyndham Ins. Svcs. Ltd., Burlingame, Calif., 1985-91; ind. cons. Fresno, Calif., 1991—; chmn. bd. Wyndham Cons. Svcs., Burlingame, Calif., 1985-91. Dir. San Mateo (Calif.) County Vol. Ctr., 1987—. Mem. Ind. Ins. Agts. and Brokers, Fedn. Afro Asian Insurors and Reinsurors, Sunnyside Country Club, Green Hills Country Club. Republican. Office: 5555 N West # 150 Fresno CA 93711

EATON, THOMAS G., environmental engineer; b. Vincennes, Ind., Jan. 11, 1953; s. Robert Edwin and Peggy Delores (Carter) E.; m. Cynthia Mary Monge, Aug. 11, 1979; 1 child, David. BSCE, Purdue U., 1976; postgrad., Ill. Inst. Tech. Cert. environ. program mgr. San. engr. EPA, 1977-79; san. engr. Wash. State Dept. Ecology, Lacey, 1979-83, dist. supr. environ. enforcement and permitting, 1983-86, acting mgr. solid and hazardous waste program, 1986-87, supr. hazardous waste sect., 1987, mgr. solid and hazardous waste program. Home: 1205 Eastside NE Olympia WA 98506 Office: Wash Stae Dept Ecology ROWE6 Bldg 4 PV-11 4224 6th Ave Olympia WA 98504

EAVES, MARY MARIE, utility executive; b. Wichita Falls, Tex., June 30, 1939; d. James Pinckney Hines and Mary Edna (Hughes) Harvey; m. John H. Dendahl, June 11, 1983 (div. 1987); children: Christie Jo, Lea Ann. Student, U. Colo., 1978, U. Mich., 1980. Pres. MED Tankers, Inc., Farmington, N.Mex., 1970-78; v.p. Chaparral Oil & Gas Co., Aztec, N.Mex., 1970—; adminstrv. asst. to pres. Gas. Co. N.Mex., Santa Fe, 1975-82; dir. govt. affairs So. Union Co., Washington, Santa Fe, 1982-85, Pub. Svc. Co. N.Mex., Santa Fe, Albuquerque, Washington D.C., 1985—. Vice chairwoman N.Mex. State Dems., 1967-74; mem. Dem. Nat. Com., Washington, 1967-73, del. nat. conv., 1968, mem. charter com., 1972-74; bd. dirs. Santa Fe Community Coll. Found., 1987—, Santa Maria El Mirador, 1985—, sec., 1986-91. Named Outstanding Young Woman of Am., 1969-70; recipient appreciation award N.Mex. State Dems., 1974, Santa Maria El Mirador, 1991. Mem. N.Mex. Oil & Gas Assn., Tex. State Soc., Daughters ofthe Nile. Presbyterian. Home: 1345 Don Gaspar Ave Santa Fe NM 87501 Office: Pub Svc Co NMex 224 W Manhattan Santa Fe NM 87501

EBAUGH, WILLIAM LEE, insurance company executive; b. L.A., Mar. 10, 1930; s. Robert M. and Edith Leona (Means) E.; m. Lu Anne Slavik, Feb. 15, 1972 (div. Aug. 1987); children: Linda L., Lawrence G., William C., Lee W., Launa L. M Psychology, Met. U., 1963; LLD (hon.), London Inst., 1973. V.p., corp. sec. Water Supply Analysts, Inc., San Gabriel, Calif., 1952-56; det. comdr. City of Baldwin Park (Calif.) Police Dept., 1956-60; agt. Aetna Life Ins. Co., Pasadena, Calif., 1960-62; group supr. Phoenix Mutual Life Ins. Co., Tarzana, Calif., 1962-85; exec. v.p. George Washington Underwriters, Tarzana, 1985-88; pres. Trans-Pacific Diversified Ins. Co., Redondo Beach, Calif., 1988—. Republican. Episcopalian. Home: 1806 Belmont Ln Redondo Beach CA 90278-4120

EBEL, ALFRED RICHARD, clergyman, educator; b. Alamosa, Colo., June 21, 1942; s. Paul Otto and Mabel Irene (Reinwold) E.; m. Nancy Irene Seim, June 17, 1966; children: Robert Paul, Thomas James, Susan Myra. BS, Concordia Coll., Seward, Nebr., 1964, MA, 1978; MA, Azusa (Calif.) Pacific U., 1979; Colloque, Concordia Theol. Sem., Ft. Wayne, Ind., 1988. Ordained to ministry Luth. Ch.-Mo. Synod, 1988. Tchr., youth dir. Our Savior Luth. Ch. and Sch., Lake Worth, Fla., 1964-68; tchr., missionary Luth. Ch.-Mo. Synod, Papua New Guinea, 1968-78; Indian counselor Concordia Coll., 1979-85; pastor Messiah Luth. Ch., Ewa Beach, Hawaii, 1987—; tchr. Luth High Sch. Hawaii, Honolulu, 1991—, chmn. bd. dirs.,

1988—. Bd. dirs. Balob Tchr.'s Coll., Papua New Guinea, 1975-78, Cornhusker United Way, Crete, Nebr., 1980-84. Mem. Ewa Ministerial Assn. (sec., treas. 1989—). Republican. Home and Office: 91-325 Pupu Pl Ewa Beach HI 96706

EBEL, DAVID M., judge; b. 1940. BA, Northwestern U., 1962; JD, U. Mich., 1965. Law clk. assoc. justice Byron White U.S. Supreme Ct., 1965-66; pvt. practice Davis, Graham & Stubbs, Denver, 1966-88; judge U.S. Ct. Appeals (10th cir.), Denver, 1988—. Mem. Am. Coll. Trial Lawyers, Colo. Bar Assn. (v.p. 1982). Office: C-530 US Courthouse 1929 Stout St Denver CO 80294

EBERENZ, JON G., business consultant; b. Corning, N.Y., July 14, 1942; s. John G. and Marion (Rienwald) E.; m. Heidi C. Batenburg, June 26, 1965; children: Katherine, Karen. BS in Mgmt., Syracuse U., 1964. Gen. mgr., v.p. Foodmart Inc., Corning, 1965-77; pres. Orange Enterprises, Phoenix, 1977-79, CDIM, Inc., Phoenix, 1979-81; ceo Impac Internat., Phoenix, 1981-92; sr. cons. Mgmt. Action Programs, Phoenix, 1992—; adv. bd. Reality Execs., Phoenix, 1986—; bd. dirs. Eberenz Corp., Corning; mem. Internat. Mergers/Acquisitions, Phoenix, 1989—; founder Merger/Acquisition Roundtable, Phoenix, 1991—. Pres. Phoenix Local Devel. Corp., 1982-84. Named Outstanding Citizen Corning Jaycees, 1969. Mem. Ariz. Licensor/Franchisor Assn., Phoenix Inst. Mgmt. Cons., Phoenicians. Mem. United Ch. of Christ. Home: 8249 N 1st Dr Phoenix AZ 85021

EBERHART, STEVE A., federal agency administrator, research geneticist; b. S.D., Nov. 11, 1931; m. Laurel Lee Hammond, July 19, 1953; children: Lyndl Schuster, Paul Eberhart, Sally Cooley, Sue May. BS, U. Nebr., 1952, MS, 1958, DSc (hon.), 1988; PhD, N.C. State U., 1961. Rsch. geneticist USDA, Agrl. Rsch. Svc. Iowa State U., Ames, 1961-64, 69-75, U.S. Agy. for Internat. Devel./USDA, Agrl. Rsch. Svc., Kitale, Kenya, 1964-68; assoc. dir. rsch. Funk Seeds Internat., Bloomington, Ill., 1975-78, v.p. rsch., 1978-83, v.p. internat. tech., 1984-87; dir. Nat. Seed Storage Lab. USDA Agrl. Rsch. Svc., Ft. Collins, Colo., 1987—. Contbr. articles to profl. jours. 1st lt. USAF, 1952-56. Recipient Arthur S. Fleming award D.C. Jaycees, 1970. Fellow Am. Soc. Agronomy, Crop Sci. Soc. Am. (pres. 1990), Nat. Coun. Comml. Plant Breeders (1st v.p. 1986); mem. Sigma Xi. Office: USDA Agrl Rsch Svc Nat Seed Storage Lab 1111 S Mason St Fort Collins CO 80521-4500

EBERLE, PETER RICHARD, abbot; b. Silverton, Oreg., June 29, 1941; s. Valentine Anthony and Kathryn Theresa (Moffenbeier) E. Licentiate in theology, St. Paul U., Ottawa, Can., 1972; S.T.D., Accademia Alfonsiana, Rome, 1979. Ordained priest in Roman Cath. Ch., 1968. Professed as a monk Mt. Angel Abbey, St. Benedict, Oreg., 1961—, prior of monastery, 1980-88, elected abbot of monastery, 1988—. Home and office: Mount Angel Abbey Saint Benedict OR 97373

EBERWEIN, BARTON DOUGLAS, construction company executive, consultant; b. Balt., Aug. 19, 1951; s. Bruce George and Thelma Joyce (Cox) E. BS, U. Oreg., 1974, MBA, 1988. Sales mgr. Teleprompter of Oreg., Eugene, 1974-75; pres., owner Oreg. Images, Eugene, 1975-80; mktg. mgr. Clearwater Prodns., Eugene, 1980-82; sales mgr. Western Wood Structures, Portland, Oreg., 1982-84, mktg. coordinator, 1984-85, mktg. dir., 1985-89; dir. bus. devel. Hoffman Constrn. Co., Portland, 1989—; chmn. Forest Products Com., Portland, 1984—, Am. Inst. Timber Constrn., Denver, 1985—; cons. Dept. Econ. Devel., Oregon City, 1984—, Oreg. Forest Industry, Salem, 1985—. Editor: (jour.) Why Wood, 1984; prod. video Vault of Man, 1984. Bd. dirs. N.W. Youth Corps, Eugene, 1984—, Police Activity League, 1991; vol. Portland Marathon Com., 1984—, Portland Festival Arts, 1986—; vol. Clackamas County (Oreg.) Econ. Devel., 1985—. Recipient Johnny Horizen award U.S. Dept. Interior Bur. Land Mgmt., 1978; named Mktg. Firm of Yr., Portland C. of C., 1984. Mem. Soc. Mktg. Profl. Svcs., Am. Mktg. Assn., Univ. Club, Founders Club, Riverside Athletic Club, Oreg. Road Runners Club. Democrat. Presbyterian. Home: 5639 SW Menefee Dr Portland OR 97201-2781 Office: Hoffman Constrn Co 1300 SW 6th Ave Portland OR 97201-2781

EBIE, TERESA HAYES, museum registrar; b. Jackson, Tenn., Apr. 29, 1957; d. Charles J. and Gretchen (Wall) Hayes; m. William Dennis Ebie, June 10, 1989. BA, Union U., 1983; MA, Memphis State U., 1987. Registrar Art Gallery Memphis State U., 1984-87, Roswell (N.Mex.) Mus., 1987—. Contbr. articles to profl. jours. Mem. Am. Assn. Mus. (registrar com., exec. bd. 1988-90), Nat. Assn. Mus. Exhibition, Mountain Plains Mus. Assn. (chair registrar com. 1988-90, vice chair 1991—, pub. editor 1992—), N.Mex. Assn. Mus. (membership chmn. 1988-90, S.E. regional rep. 1990—), N.Mex. Art History Conf. (sec. 1992-93). Episcopalian. Office: Roswell Mus & Art Center 100 W 11th St Roswell NM 88201-4998

EBIE, WILLIAM D., museum director; b. Akron, Ohio, Feb. 7, 1942; s. William P. and Mary Louise (Karam) E.; m. Gwyn Anne Schumacher, Apr. 11, 1968 (div. Jan. 1988); children: Jason William, Alexandra Anne; m. Mary Teresa Hayes, June 10, 1989. BFA, Akron Art Inst., 1964; MFA, Calif. Coll. of Arts and Crafts, 1968. Graphic artist Alameda County Health Dept., Oakland, Calif., 1967-68; instr. painting Fla. A&M U., Tallahassee, 1968-69; instr. photography Lawrence (Kans.) Adult Edn. Program, 1969-70; asst. dir. Roswell (N.Mex.) Mus. & Art Ctr., 1971-87, dir., 1987—; juror various art exhbns., 1971—; panelist N.Mex. Arts Div., Santa Fe, 1983—; field reviewer Inst. for Mus. Svcs., 1988. Chmn. Roswell Cultural Arts Com., 1981-82, Roswell Cultural Affairs Com., 1983-85; mem. Roswell Conv. and Vis. Bur., 1983. Mem. Am. Assn. of Mus., Mountain Plains Mus. Assn., N.Mex. Assn. of Mus. Democrat. Office: Roswell Mus & Art Ctr 100 W 11th St Roswell NM 88201-4998

EBI-KRYSTON, KRISTIE LEE, epidemiologist, consultant; b. Detroit, Nov. 17, 1950; d. Albert R. and Dorothy (Wicen) Ebi; 1 child, Katherine M. Kryston. BS, MIT, 1977; MPH, U. Mich., 1983, PhD, 1985. Biochem. rsch. asst. Upjohn Co., Kalamazoo, 1973-74; toxicologist Equitable Environ. Health, Inc., Rockville, Md., 1977-78; indsl. toxicologist GM, Detroit, 1978-81; rsch. fellow London Sch. Hygiene and Tropical Medicine, 1985-87; rsch. asst. Med. Coll. of St. Bartholomew's Hosp., London, 1988-90; sr. scientist Failure Analysis Assocs., Inc., Menlo Park, Calif., 1990—. Contbr. articles to sci. jours. Mem. Am. Coll. Epidemiology, Soc. for Epidemiologic Rsch., Internat. Epidemiologic Assn., Soc. Toxicology (assoc.), Mortar Bd. Office: Failure Analysis Assocs Inc 149 Commonwealth Dr Menlo Park CA 94025-1122

EBINER, ROBERT MAURICE, lawyer; b. Los Angeles, Sept. 2, 1927; s. Maurice and Virginia (Grand) E.; m. Paula H. Van Sluyters, June 16, 1951; children—John, Lawrence, Marie, Michael, Christopher, Joseph, Francis, Matthew, Therese, Kathleen, Eileen, Brian, Patricia, Elizabeth, Ann. J.D., Loyola U., Los Angeles, 1953. Bar: Calif. 1954, U.S. dist. ct. (cen. dist.) Calif. 1954. Solo practice, West Covina, Calif., 1954—; judge pro tem Los Angeles Superior Ct., 1964-66, arbitrator, 1979—; judge pro tem Citrus Mcpl. Ct., 1966-70; mem. disciplinary hearing panel Calif. State Bar, 1968-75. Bd. dirs. West Covina United Fund, 1958-61, chmn. budget com. 1960-61; organizer Joint United Funds East San Gabriel Valley, 1962, bd. dirs. 1961-68; bd. dirs. San Gabriel Valley Cath. Social Services, 1969—, pres., 1969-72; bd. dirs. Region II Cath. Social Service, 1970—, pres. 1970-74; trustee Los Angeles Cath. Welfare Bur. (now Cath. Charities), 1978—; charter bd. dirs. East San Gabriel Valley Hot Line, 1969-74, sec., 1969-72; charter bd. dirs. N.E. Los Angeles County unit Am. Cancer Soc., 1973-78, chmn. by-laws com. 1973-78; bd. dirs. Queen of the Valley Hosp. Found., 1983-89; organizer West Covina Hist. Soc., 1982—; active Calif. State Dem. Cen. Com., 1963-68; mng. meet dir. Greater La Puente Valley Spl. Olympics, 1985-88, Bishop Amat Relays, 1981-93; mem. MSAC Relays com., 1978-88; campaign mgr. Congressman Ronald B. Cameron, 1964. With U.S. Army, 1945-47. Recipient Los Angeles County Human Relations Commn. Disting. Service award, 1978, Thomas A. Kiefer Humanitarian award, 1993. Named West Covina Citizen of Yr., 1986, San Gabriel Valley Daily Tribune's Father of Yr., 1986. Mem. ABA, Calif. Bar Assn., Los Angeles County Bar Assn., Fed. Ct. So. Dist. Calif. Assn., Los Angeles Trial Lawyers Assn., Eastern Bar Assn. Los Angeles County (pres. Pomona Valley 1965-66), West Covina C. of C. (pres. 1960), Am. Arbitration Assn. Clubs: K.C., Bishop Amat High Sch. Booster (bd. dirs. 1973—, pres. 1978-80), Kiwanis (charter West Covina, pres. 1976-77, lt. gov. div. 35 1980-81, Kiwanian of Yr. 1978, 82, Disting. Lt. Gov. 1980-81, bd. dirs. Cal-Nev-Ha Found. 1986—). Avocations: collector of historical olympic and political memorabilia. Office: 1000 E Garvey Ave # 365 West Covina CA 91790-2708

EBITZ, DAVID MACKINNON, art historian, museum director; b. Hyannis, Mass., Oct. 5, 1947; s. Robert White Creeley and Ann (MacKinnon) Kucera; m. Mary Ann Stankiewicz, Jan. 1, 1983; children: Rebecca Aemilia, Cecilia Charlotte. BA, Williams Coll., 1969; AM, Harvard U., 1973, PhD, 1979. Teaching fellow, then head teaching fellow dept. fine arts Harvard U., Cambridge, Mass., 1975-78; asst. prof., then assoc. prof. dept. art U. Maine, Orono, 1978-87, interim dir. galleries, curator univ. art collection, 1986-87; head dept. edn. and acad. affairs J. Paul Getty Mus., Santa Monica, Calif., 1987-92; dir. John and Mable Ringling Mus. Art, Sarasota, Fla., 1992—; vis. faculty Bangor (Maine) Theol. Sem., 1981; lectr. in field; presenter workshops. Author exbhn. revs., book revs.; contbr. articles to arts publs., exhbn. catalogues. Heritage Found. fellow, 1968. Mem. Assn. Art Mus. Dirs., Coll. Art Assn., Nat. Art Edn. Assn., Am. Assn. Museums (mus. edn. com.), Medieval Acad. Am., Internat. Ctr. Medieval Art, Am. Soc. Aesthetics, Phi Beta Kappa.

EBRIGHT, PEGGY LINDEN SHORT, theatre community relations executive; b. Cin., Sept. 8, 1928; d. Robert Justin and Mildred Dorothea (Schmid) Short; m. James Newton Ebright, Mar. 17, 1951 (div. 1978); children: Don H. II, Douglas Justin. BA, Coll. Wooster, 1950. Sec. to Sec. of State of Ohio, Columbus, 1951-52; artist Calif., 1960—; set designer San Marino Players, 1970-85; artist, dir. community rels. Pasadena (Calif.) Playhouse, 1985—; sec., chmn. bd. trustees Pasadena Playhouse Assn., 1965-69; pres. Pasadena Theatre Acad., 1969-85. Treas., bd. dirs., v.p. Jr. League of Pasadena, 1965-69; bd. dirs. Pasadena Arts Coun., 1969-73, 75-78, sec., 1993—; pres. Dionysians, Pasadena, 1968, San Marino Players, Pasadena, 1979-85; vol. Jr. League Akron, 1955-60, Jr. League Pasadena, 1960—; bd. dirs. Pasadena Humane Soc., 1991—. Recipient Tenth Muse award Pasadena Arts Coun., 1976, Keeper of Flame award Pasadena Playhouse Alumni & Assocs., 1975, Spl. Friends award Friends of Pasadena Playhouse, 1991-92. Mem. Pasadena Playhouse Alumni & Assoc. Republican. Methodist. Home: 1635 Bedford Rd San Marino CA 91108-2029 Office: Pasadena Playhouse 39 S El Molino Ave Pasadena CA 91101-2023

EBY, FRANK SHILLING, research scientist; b. Kansas City, Mo., Apr. 6, 1924; s. Frank Shilling and Irene (Trissler) E.; m. Nancy Rea Vinsonhaler, Sept. 2, 1958; children: Elizabeth, Susan, Carl. BS, U. Ill., 1948, MS, 1949, PhD, 1954. Group leader fusion research Lawrence Livermore (Calif.) Nat. Lab., 1954-58, group leader, 1958-66, div. head, 1967-72, sr. scientist, 1973—. Inventor classified mil. weaponry. Served to 1st lt. USAAF, 1942-46, PTO. Recipient Intelligence Community Seal medallion, 1992. Mem. AAAS. Home: 27 Castlewood Dr Pleasanton CA 94566 Office: Lawrence Livermore Nat Lab Dept Spl Projects Livermore CA 94550

EBY, MICHAEL JOHN, marketing research and technology consultant; b. South Bend, Ind., Aug. 3, 1949; s. Robert T. and Eileen Patricia (Holmes) E.; m. Judith Alyson Gaskell, May 17, 1980; children: Elizabeth, Katherine. Student, Harvey Mudd Coll., 1969-70; BS in Biochemistry with high honors, U. Md., 1972, MS in Chemistry, 1977; postgrad., IMEDE, Lausanne, Switzerland, 1984. Product mgr. LKB Instruments Inc., Rockville, Md., 1976-79; mktg. mgr. LKB-Produkter AB, Bromma, Sweden, 1979-87; strategic planning mgr. Pharmacia LKB Biotech. AB, Bromma, 1987-88; dir. mktg. Am. Bionetics, Hayward, Calif., 1988-89; pres. PhorTech Internat., Belmont, Calif., 1989—. Author: The Electrophoresis Explosion, 1988, Electrophoresis in the Nineties, 1990; contbr. articles to profl. jours. Fin. chair The Carey Sch. Festival, San Mateo, Calif., 1991. Mem. Am. Chem. Soc., Am. Electrophoresis Soc., Internat. Electrophoresis Soc., Spirit of LKB Internat. Assn., U. Md. Alumni Assn., Belmont C. of C. Episcopalian. Office: PhorTech Internat 2844 Wemberly Dr Belmont CA 94002

ECCLES, SPENCER FOX, banker; b. Ogden, Utah, Aug. 24, 1934; s. Spencer Stoddard and Hope (Fox) E.; m. Cleone Emily Peterson, July 21, 1958; children: Clista Hope, Lisa Ellen, Katherine Ann, Spencer Peterson. B.S., U. Utah, 1956; M.A., Columbia U., 1959; degree in Bus. (hon.), So. Utah State Coll., 1982; LLB (hon.), Westminster Coll., Salt Lake City, 1986. Trainee First Nat. City Bank, N.Y.C., 1959-60; with First Security Bank of Utah, Salt Lake City, 1960-61, First Security Bank of Idaho, Boise, 1961-70; exec. v.p. First Security Corp. Salt Lake City, 1970-75, pres., 1975-86, chief operating officer, 1980-82, chmn. bd. dirs., chief exec. officer, 1982—; dir. Union Pacific Corp., Anderson Lumber Co., Zions Corp., Merc. Instn.; mem. adv. council U. Utah Bus. Coll. Served to 1st lt. U.S. Army. Recipient Pres.'s Circle award Presdl. Commn., 1984, Minuteman award Utah N.G., 1988; Named Disting. Alumni U. Utah, 1988. Mem. Am. Bankers Assn., Assn. Bank Holding Cos., Assn. Res. City Bankers, Salt Lake Country Club, Alta Club. Office: 1st Security Corp 79 S Main St PO Box 30006 Salt Lake City UT 84130*

ECHOHAWK, LARRY, lawyer; b. Cody, Wyo., Aug. 2, 1948; m. Terry Pries; children: Jennifer, Paul, Mark, Matthew, Emily, Michael. Grad., Brigham Young U., 1970; JD, U. Utah, 1973; postgrad., Stanford U. Bar: Utah 1973, Calif. 1974, Idaho 1979. With Calif. Indian Legal Svcs., Oakland; pvt. practice law Salt Lake City; chief gen. counsel Shoshone-Bannock Tribes, 1977-85; mem. Idaho Ho. of Reps., 1982-86; former prosecutor Bannock County, Idaho; now atty. gen. State of Idaho; inaugurated Idaho's 30th atty. gen. on Jan. 7, 1991, the 1st Native Am. in U.S. history to be elected to that office. Active Idaho Bd. Land Commrs.; mem. exec. com. Conf. Western Attys. Gen.; active Idaho Elder Care Coalition; mem. exec. bd. Ore-Ida Boy Scout Coun.; past chmn. Idaho Job Tng. Coun.; past vice-chmn. Idaho Commn. for Children and Youth; speaker Dem. Nat. Conv., 1992; mem. steering com. Dem. Policy Commn., 1985-87. With USMC. Recipient Martin Luther King medal George Washington U., 1991. Mem. ABA, Calif. Bar Assn., Utah Bar Assn., Idaho Bar Assn. (Outstanding Svc. award 1986, mem. Attys. Against Hunger Project), Nat. Assn. Attys. Gen. (mem. exec. com.), Pawnee Tribe, Phi Delta Kappa (Friend of Edn. award 1985). Office: State House Office of Atty Gen Rm 210 Boise ID 83720*

ECHOLS, HORACE RICHARD, sales executive; b. Tucumcari, N.Mex., June 28, 1942; s. Horace and Edith (Toon) E.; m. Rita Louise Smith, June 14, 1965 (div. 1976); 1 child, Amy Lynn Echols White; m. Susan Lynn Harris, June 24, 1978; children: Christopher Alan, Stephanie Lee. B in Music Edn., Ea. N.Mex. U., 1964, MA, 1965. Jr. high band dir. Seminole (Tex.) Jr. High Sch., 1965-66, Gattis Jr. High Sch., Clovis, N.Mex., 1966-76; zone mgr., sales person Henco, Inc., Albuquerque, 1976-78; area mgr., sales person Henco, Inc., Denver, 1978-85; regional sales mgr. Henco, Inc., Las Vegas, Nev., 1985-91, Cherrydale Farms, Inc., Las Vegas, 1991-92. Named N.Mex. Outstanding Young Educator, N.Mex. Jaycee Internat., Clovis, 1971. Mem. Nat. Assn. Product Fund Raisers. Republican. Baptist. Home: 2400 La Luna Dr Henderson NV 89014

ECK, CHARLES PETER, electronics executive; b. Pensacola, Fla., Sept. 15, 1944; s. William Leighton and Florence (Klewin) E.; m. Mary English, Feb. 21, 1967 (div. Aug. 1987); children: Christine M., Jacqueline D.; m. Paula Baynar, Aug. 28, 1988. BS in Bus. Mgmt., York Coll. of Pa., 1976. Asst. to sec. Pa. Dept. of Revenue, Harrisburg, 1976-81; dep. exec. dir. Pa. Lottery, Harrisburg, 1981-82; dep. dir. Wash. Lottery, Olympia, 1982-83; bus. cons. CPE Consultants, Eulees, Tex., 1983-86, 87-88; v.p. ops. The Arnold Corp., Akron, Ohio, 1986-87; staff cons. U. of Medicine and Dentistry of N.J., Newark, 1988-90; dir. network planning Nintendo of Am., Inc., Redmond, Wash., 1990—; pres. CPE Consultants, Redmond, 1983—; mem. Adv. Com. to Gov. on Cash Mgmt., Harrisburg, 1978-79. Contbr. articles to profl. jours. Vice chmn. Nat. Assn. Tax Adminstrn., Washington, 1978, chmn., 1979; assn. mem. Nat. Assn. of State & Provincial Lotteries, Washington, 1983-88. Recipient Army Commendation medal Dept. of Def., 1991, Meritorious Svc. medal Dept. of Def., 1990, Nat. Def. Svc. medal Dept. of Def., 1968, 91. Mem. Nat. Assn. State & Provincial Lotteries, Nat. Guard Assocs. of U.S. Roman Catholic. Office: Nintendo of Am Inc 4820 150th Ave NE Redmond WA 98052

ECK, DENNIS K., supermarket chain executive; b. 1942. Exec. v.p. Am. Stores Co., 1983-90, COO, chmn. bd., 1988-90; pres., COO, vice chmn. bd. Vons Cos. Inc., 1990—. Office: Vons Cos Inc PO Box 3338 618 Michillinoa Arcadia CA 91007*

ECK, DOROTHY FRITZ, state senator; b. Sequim, Wash., Jan. 23, 1924; d. Ira Edward and Ida (Hokanson) Fritz; B.S. in Secondary Edn., Mont. State U., 1961, M.S. in Applied Sci., 1966; m. Hugo Eck, Dec. 16, 1942 (dec. Feb. 1988); children: Laurence, Diana. Mgr. property mgmt. bus., 1955—; conf. coord. Am. Agrl. Econs. Assn., 1967-68; state-local coord. Office of Gov. Mont., Helena, 1972-77; mem. Mont. State Senate, 1981—; mem. Mont. Environ. Quality Council, 1981-87. Bd. dirs. Methodist Youth Fellowship, 1960-64, Mont. Council for Effective Legislature, 1977-78, Rocky Mountain Environ. Council, 1982—; del., Western v.p. Mont. Constl. Conv., 1971-72; chmn. Gov.'s Task Force on Citizen Participation, 1976-77; mem. adv. com. No. Rockies Resource and Tng. Center (now No. Lights Inst.), 1979-81. Recipient Outstanding Alumna award Mont. State U., 1981, Centennial Equity award, 1989. Mem. LWV (state pres. 1967-70), Common Cause, Nat. Women's Polit. Caucus. Democrat.

ECK, MICHAEL JOHN, marketing professional; b. L.A., Mar. 21, 1956; s. Frank T. and Joan F. (Lustig) E.; m. Nancy Ann Furlong, Aug. 17, 1976; 1 child, Kathryn Denise. BS in Fin., U. Nev., 1978. Diagnostic salesman Abbott Diagnostics U.S. Orgn., Seattle, 1982-83, product specialist, 1983-85; worldwide product mgr. infectious disease bus. unit Abbott Diagnostics U.S. Orgn., Chgo., 1985-87; strategy mgr. European area Abbott Diagnostics Europe Physican Office Bus. Devel., Wiesbaden, Fed. Republic of Germany, 1987-88; mktg. mgr. European area Abbott Diagnostics Europe, Middle East & Africa, Wiesbaden, 1988-91; dir. mktg. Quidel Corp., San Diego, 1991—. Coach youth basketball Frankfurt Internat. Sch., 1989—. Capt. U.S. Army, 1978-82. Mem. Biomed. Mktg. Assn., Am. C. of C. Republican. Roman Catholic. Home: 10165 Mckellar Ct San Diego CA 92121-4201

ECKARDT, CHARLES LINCOLN, accountant; b. Phila., Feb. 2, 1930; s. George Herbert and Lillian Louisa (Marsden) E.; m. Eillean Jeannie Young, Mar. 16, 1957. BA in Bus. Adminstrn., Franklin & Marshall, 1977; MDiv., Phila. Theol. Sem., 1977. Pastor Third Reformed Presbyn. Ch., Phila., 1956-65; contr. Quarryville (Pa.) Presbyn. Home Inc., 1965-74; fin. dir. World Presbyn. Missions, Inc., Wilmington, Del., 1974-83; contr. Tri Mark, Inc., New Castle, Del., 1983-91; asst. contr. Medco Rsch., Inc., L.A., 1992-93; bus. mgr. Pacific Oaks Coll., Pasadena, Calif., 1993—. Mem. The Inst. Mgmt. Accts. (dir. West L.A. chpt. 1991-92). Republican. Mem. Reformed Church in America.

ECKELMAN, RICHARD JOEL, engineering specialist; b. Bklyn., Mar. 25, 1951; s. Leon and Muriel (Brietbart) E.; m. Janet Louise Fenton, Mar. 21, 1978; children: Christie, Melanie, Erin Leigh. Student, Ariz. State U., 1988-91. Sr. engr., group leader nondestructive testing Engring. Fluor Corp., Irvine, Calif., 1979-83; sr. engr. nondestructive testing McDonnell Douglas Helicopter Co., Mesa, Ariz., 1983-91; engring. specialist Convair div. Gen. Dynamics, San Diego, 1991—. Mem. Am. Soc. Nondestructive Testing (nat. aerospace com. 1987—, sec. Ariz. chpt. 1987-88, treas. 1988—, sect. chmn. 1989—, sect. bd. dirs. 1990-91), Am. Soc. Quality Control, Soc. Mfg. Engrs., Porsche Owners Club Am., Val Vista Lakes Club. Home: 4084 Santa Nella Pl San Diego CA 92130 Office: Gen Dynamics Convair Div San Diego CA 92100

ECKER, ANTHONY JOSEPH, orthodontist; b. Denver, Colo., Apr. 9, 1937; s. Anthony Joseph and Esther (Rizzi) E.; m. Doris Lee Shafer, June 14, 1958; children: Anthony Joseph III, John Michel, Robert Daniel. Student, U. Ariz.; DDS, Washington U., St. Louis, 1961, MS in Orthodontics, 1966. Diplomate Am. Bd. Orthodontics. Orthodontist pvt. practice Camarillo, Calif., 1966—. Lt. USN, 1961-64,. Mem. Am. Dental Assn., Am. Assn. of Orthodontists, Pacific Coast Soc. Orthodontists, Santa Barbara-Ventura County Dental Assn., Coll. Diplomates Am. Bd. Orthodontics. Office: 450 Rosewood Ave Ste 100 Camarillo CA 93010

ECKERMAN, ROY EMMANUEL, clergyman; b. Grantsburg, Wis., July 12, 1921; s. Carl Adolph and Esther (Carlson) E.; m. Evelyn Mae Tarasenko, Nov. 1, 1944; children: Arva Dell Mae Eckerman Seltzer, Ginger Sue Eckerman Kent. BA, Union Coll., 1944; MEd, Ind. U., 1965. Ordained clergyman, Adventist Ch., 1948. Clegyman Iowa Conf., Spencer, 1944-49, S.D. Conf., Aberdeen, 1949-51, Mich. Conf., Pt. Huron, Escanaba, 1951-56, Ind. Conf., Bloomington, 1956-63, Upper Columbia Conf., Coeur d'Alene, Idaho, 1963-68; dir. pub. rels. Upper Columbia Conf., Spokane, Wash., 1968-73; dir. found. and corp. rels. Loma Linda (Calif.) U., 1973-84; pres., trustee Opportunity With Legacy Found., Salinas, Calif., 1977—. State conf. exec. com. Lansing, Mich., 1952-55, Spokane, 1964-69; treas. Ministeral Assn., Coeur d'Alene, 1966-67. Republican. Home: 25199 Casiano Dr Salinas CA 93908-8956 Office: Opportunity With Legacy Found 25199 Casiano Dr Salinas CA 93908-8956

ECKERMANN, GERALD CARLTON, writer, corporate executive; b. Covina, Calif., Feb. 10, 1934; s. Carlton Herman and Ethel Marie (Argue) E.; m. Gwendolyn Wegeforth, Feb. 10, 1990; children: G. Kevin, Darci Lee, Darin Allen. BBA, UCLA, 1956. Personnel specialist Gen. Dynamics/Astronautics, San Diego, Calif., 1960-65; dir. personnel Computer Scis. Corp., El Segundo, Calif., 1965-66; internal cons. ITT, N.Y.C., 1966-71; v.p. personnel Kaiser Industries, Oakland, Calif., 1971-75; cons. prin. Exec. Mgmt. Cons., Walnut Creek, Calif., 1975-77; dir. personnel Lawrence Livermore Labs., Livermore, Calif., 1977; dir. regional practice compensation A.S. Hensen, L.A., 1978-81; gen. mgr. Security Corp. of Am., Westlake Village, Calif., 1981-82; mgmt. cons. Coopers & Lybrand CPAs, L.A., 1982-83, Grant-Thorton CPAs, L.A., 1983-86, Legal Info. Tech. Group, L.A., 1986-90; pres. Marina Bus. Svcs., 1990-92; CFO Laser Care, 1992—; dir. Transp. Scis. Corp., L.A., 1979—. Author: Price of Ambition, 1986, Forgotten Man, 1988, Amethyst Idol, 1989, Echos from the Past, 1990, Women Ask...Men Answer, 1991. Vice chmn. bd. trustees West Coast U., L.A., 1979-89; nat. rep. Boy Scouts Am., 1973; v.p. Mt. Diablo Coun., 1974-75; bd. dirs. Mt. Diablo Rehab. Ctr., Alameda County Counseling Ctr., 1973-76. With USN, 1956-62; commdr. USNR. Mem. Am. Compensation Assn., Am. Soc. Pers. Adminstrs., Res. Officers Assn., Naval Res. Assn. (v.p. Jack London chpt. 1976), Jonathan Club, Calif. Yacht Club (chmn. yachting luncheons 1989, pub., editor in chief Breeze 1990, 91). Republican. Home: 486 Carroll Ave Marina Del Rey CA 90291-4641

ECKERSLEY, DENNIS LEE, professional baseball player; b. Oakland, Calif., Oct. 3, 1954; m. Nancy O'Neill; 1 child, Mandee. Pitcher Cleve. Indians, 1975-77, Boston Red Sox, 1978-84, Chgo. Cubs, 1984-86, Oakland A's, 1987—. Recipient Cy Young award Baseball Writers Assn. Am., 1992; mem. Am. League All-Star Team, 1977, 82, 88, 90-92; named Fireman of Yr. The Sporting News, 1988, 91, Am. League Rookie Pitcher of Yr., 1975; pitched no-hit game, 1977. Office: Oakland As PO Box 2220 Oakland CA 94621-0120

ECKERSLEY, NORMAN CHADWICK, banker; b. Glasgow, Scotland, June 18, 1924; came to U.S., 1969; s. James Norman and Beatrice (Chadwick) E.; m. Rosemary J. Peters, May 23, 1986, 1 child, Anne. D Laws Strathclyde U., Scotland. With Chartered Bank, London and Manchester, 1947-48; acct., Bombay, 1948-52, Singapore, 1952-54, Sarawak, 1954-56, Pakistan, 1956-58, Calcutta, 1958-59, Hong Kong, 1959-60, asst. mgr. Hamburg, 1960-62, mgr. Calcutta, 1962-67, Thailand, 1967-69; pres. Chartered Bank London, San Francisco, 1964-74, chmn., chief exec., 1974-79; chmn. Standard Chartered Bancorp, 1978-81; dep. chmn. Union Bank, L.A., 1979-82; chmn., chief exec. officer The Pacific Bank, San Francisco, 1982—, chmn. emeritus, 1993; chmn. Scottish Am. Investment Com., U. Strathclyde Found. With RAF, 1940-46. Decorated D.F.C.; comdr. Order Brit. Empire. Mem. Overseas Banks Assn. Calif. (chmn. 1972-74), Calif. Coun. Internat. Trade, San Francisco C. of C., World Trade Assn., Royal and Ancient Club, Royal Troon Golf Club (Scotland), World Trade Club, San Francisco Golf Club, Pacific Union Club (San Francisco). Mem. Ch. of Scotland. Home: 401 El Cerrito Ave Hillsborough CA 94010-6819 Office: Pacific Bank 351 California St San Francisco CA 94104-2412

ECKERT, GERALDINE GONZALES, language professional, educator, entrepreneur; b. N.Y.C., Aug. 5, 1948; d. Albert and Mercedes (Martinez) Gonzales; m. Robert Alan Eckert, Apr. 1, 1972; children: Lauren Elaine, Alison Elizabeth. BA, Ladycliff Coll., Highland Falls, N.Y., 1970; student, U. Valencia, Spain, 1968; MA, N.Y.U., 1971; student, Instituto de Cultura Hispanica, Madrid, 1970-71. Tchr. Spanish Clarkstown High Sch. N. (N.Y.), 1971-73, Rambam Torah Inst., Beverly Hills, Calif., 1973-75; translator City of Beverly Hills, 1976-83; edn. cons. Los Angeles County of Calif. Dept. Forestry, Capistrano Beach, 1982-84; lang. services and protocol Los Angeles Olympic Organizing Com., 1983-84; pension adminstr. Pension Architects, Inc., Los Angeles, 1984-87; instr. El Camino Coll., Torrance, Calif., 1987-88, Santa Monica (Calif.) Coll., 1975-89; owner, pres. Bilingual Pension Cons., L.A., 1987-89; bd. dirs. Institute for Hispanic Cultural Studies, Los Angeles; spl. asst. to Internat. Olympic Com., Lausanne, Switzerland, 1983—. V.p. Notre Dame Acad. Assoc., West L. A., 1987—; mem. L.A. March of Dimes Ambassadors Group, 1987; co-founder, pres. Blind Cleaning Express, L.A., 1989—; bd. dirs. Inst. Hispanic Cultural Studies, L.A., 1984-89; spl. asst. to pres. Internat. Olympic Com. Lausanne, Switzerland, 1983—. Democrat. Roman Catholic. Clubs: Five Ring, Los Angeles, Friends of Sport, Amateur Athletic Found., Los Angeles. Office: 3728 Overland Ave Los Angeles CA 90034-6387

ECKHARDT, ROGER LEE, military officer; b. Mendota, Ill., July 21, 1963; s. Eugene Ralph and Evelyn Amelia (Stevenson) E. Enlisted USAF, 1981, advanced through grades to tech. sgt., 1990; mem. load crew 31st Aircraft Generation Squadron, Homestead AFB, Fla., 1981-83; custodian tech. order account 50th Aircraft Generation Squadron, Hahn AFB, W. Germany, 1983-85; load crew team chief 27th Tactical Air Support Squadron, George AFB, Calif., 1986-88; loading standardization crew team chief 27th Tactical Air Support Squadron, George AFB, 1988-90; flightline weapons expeditor 35th Aircraft Generation Squadron, George AFB, 1990-92; officer 57th Sortie Generation Squadron, Nellis AFB, Nev., 1992—. Mem. NRA, Am. Legion, Elks. Republican. Office: USAF 57th Sortie Generation Sq Nellis AFB NV 89191

ECONOMIDES, FLOYD A., city councilman; b. New Orleans, June 25, 1928; s. Basile J. and Susie M. (Uhle) E.; m. Belle M. Hebert, Dec. 1, 1948; 1 child, Curtis. Grad. high sch., New Orleans. Profl. baseball catcher Evangeine League, La., 1948, Rio Grande League, Tex., 1949, Gulf Coast League, Tex., 1950, Big State League, Tex., 1951; welder Navajo Refinery, Artesia, N.Mex., 1962-64, electrician, 1966-85, transp. supr., 1985-90; councilman City of Artesia, 1964-84, 88—. V.p. Crime Stoppers, 1985-90. With USMCR, 1952-54. Recipient Disting. Svc. award Artesia Jr. Jaycees, 1962, Big Guy award Coll. Artesia, 1967. Mem. KC (grand knight 1986-88, 90—), Elks (sec. 1982-90). Democrat. Roman Catholic. Home: 1505 W Briscoe Ave Artesia NM 88210-2217

EDBERG, STEPHEN J., astronomer; b. Pasadena, Calif., Nov. 3, 1952; m. Janet Greenstein, 1979; children: Aaron, Shanna, Jordan. BA, U. Calif., Santa Cruz, 1974; MA, UCLA, 1976. Observer San Fernando Observatory, 1978-79; astronomer Jet Propulsion Lab., Pasadena, Calif., 1979—; asst. sci. coord. Jet Propulsion Lab., 1979-81; discipline specialist Internat. Halley Watch, 1981-88; investigation scientist CRAF Project, 1986-92; sci. coord. Galileo Project, 1989—; investigation scientist Cassini Project, 1992—; trustee Corp. for Rsch. Amateur Astronomy; exec. dir. Riverside Telescope Makers Conf. Author: books; contbr. articles to profl. jours. Recipient G. Bruce Blair medal Western Amateur Astronomers, profl. award Astron. Assn. No. Calif.; minor planet named (3672) Stevedberg. Mem. Am. Astron. Soc. Home: 163 Starlight Crest Dr La Canada Flintridge CA 91011-2836

EDBLOM, DALE CLARENCE, city official; b. Belle Plaine, Minn., Aug. 25, 1934; s. Clarence Edwin and Emma Bertha (Leikam) E.; m. Leona Mae Evenson, July 6, 1957; children: Terri, Todd. AA, San Diego Jr. Coll., 1960. Apprentice carpenter City of San Diego, 1952-54, 56-58, carpenter, 1958-60, carpenter supr., 1960-62, bldg. maintenance supr., 1962-70, sr. bldg. maintenance supr., 1970-90. With USMC, 1954-56. Mem. Eagles, Am. Legion. Democrat. Home: 5745 Lodi St San Diego CA 92117

EDDY, HOWARD N., county official. BA in Mgmt., U. Redlands. Registered environ. assessor, Calif.; cert. advanced P.O.S.T. Dep. Kern County Sheriff's Office, Bakersfield, Calif.; investigator Kern County Dist. Atty.'s Office, Bakersfield; coord. Kern Hazardous Materials Task Force, Bakersfield. Contbr. articles on environ. to various publs. Mem. Calif. Rep. Com., Kern County Rep. Cen. Com.; mem., bd. dirs. various local civic orgns. Mem. Calif. Hazardous Materials Investigators Assn. (past pres.), Calif. Peace Officers Assn., Calif. Robbery Investigators Assn., Calif. Fraud Investigators Assn., NRA (life), Calif. Aire Eagles. Office: Kern County Office Dist Atty 1215 Truxtun Ave Bakersfield CA 93301

EDDY, LYNNE JONES, physiologist, pharmacologist; b. New Haven, July 2, 1944; d. Richard Langston and Marion Lyon (Jones) E. BA, Kalamazoo (Mich.) Coll., 1966; PhD, U. Ala., Birmingham, 1972; BS, U. South Ala., 1987. Lic. phys. therapist. Asst. prof. Fla. State U., Tallahassee, 1974-75; asst. prof. U. South Ala., Mobile, 1975-83, assoc. prof., 1983-86; assoc. prof. U. So. Calif., L.A., 1986-90; cons. Amgen Inc., Thousand Oaks, Calif., 1991; clin. project mgr. Alpha Therapeutic Corp., L.A., 1991—. Author: Physical Theraphy Pharmacology, 1992; contbr. articles to profl. jours. Mem. Am. Physiol. Soc., Am. Heart Assn., Sigma Xi. Office: Alpha Therapeutic Corp 5555 Valley Blvd Los Angeles CA 90032

EDDY, ROBERT PHILLIP, retired mathematician; b. Indpls., Nov. 19, 1919; s. Myron Elmer and Hazel Marguerite (Merrill) E. m. Consuelo Sanz, June 26, 1948; children: Robert A., James M. BS, Beloit Coll., 1941; postgrad., U. Wis., 1941-42; MS, Brown U., 1948. Staff mathematician aeroballistic div. Naval Ordnance Lab., White Oak, Md., 1948-52; head engring. applications br. Applied Math. Lab. David Taylor Model Basin, Carderock, Md., 1953-57; staff mathematician, analyst Computation and Math. Dept. Naval Ship Rsch. and Devel. Ctr., Bethesda, Md., 1958-80; ret. Naval Ship Rsch. and Devel. Ctr., Bethesda, 1980. With AUS, 1943-46. Mem. Am. Math. Soc., Soc. Indsl. and Applied Math., Phi Beta Kappa. Home: 2902 Flintridge Sq Colorado Springs CO 80918-4202

EDEL, (JOSEPH) LEON, biographer, educator; b. Pitts., Sept. 9, 1907; s. Simon and Fannie (Malamud) E.; m. Roberta Roberts, Dec. 2, 1950 (div. 1979); m. Marjorie P. Sinclair, May 30, 1980. MA, McGill U., 1928, LittD, 1963; D.ès.L., U. Paris, 1932; DLitt, Union Coll., 1963; D.Litt., U. Sask., 1982; DLitt, Hawaii Loa Coll., 1988. Writer, journalist, 1932-43; vis. prof. N.Y. U., 1950-52, assoc. prof. English, 1953-54, prof. English, 1955-66, Henry James prof. English and Am. letters, 1966-73, emeritus, 1973; citizens prof. humanities U. Hawaii, 1971-78, emeritus, 1978—; mem. faculty Harvard U., summer 1952, vis. prof., 1959-60; Centenary vis. prof. U. Toronto, 1967; Gauss seminar lectr. Princeton U., 1952-53; vis. prof. Ind. U., 1954-55, U. Hawaii, summer 1955, 69-70; Alexander lectr. U. Toronto, 1956; Westminster Abbey address Henry James Meml., 1976; vis. prof. Center Advanced Study, Wesleyan U., 1965; vis. fellow Humanities Rsch. Ctr., Canberra, Australia, 1976; Vernon prof. biography Dartmouth Coll., 1977; Bollingen Found. fellow, 1958-61. Author: Henry James: Les années dramatiques, 1932, The Prefaces of Henry James, 1932, James Joyce: The Last Journey, 1947, The Life of Henry James, 5 vols. (The Untried Years, 1953, The Conquest of London and The Middle Years, 1962, The Treacherous Years, 1969, The Master, 1972), Henry James, A Life, 1985; (with E.K. Brown) Willa Cather, A Critical Biography, 1953; The Psychological Novel, 1955, revised, 1959, Literary Biography, 1957; (with Dan H. Laurence) A Bibliography of Henry James, 1957, revised edit., 1985; Henry D. Thoreau, 1970, Henry James in The Abbey, The Address, 1976, Bloomsbury, A House of Lions, 1979, Stuff of Sleep and Dreams, Experiments in Literary Psychology, 1982, Writing Lives, Principia Biographica, 1984, Some Reminiscences of Edith Wharton, 1993, Some Memories of Edith Wharton, 1993. Editor: (writings of Henry James) The Complete Plays, 1949, revised edit., 1990, Ghostly Tales (reissued as Tales of the Supernatural, 1970), rev. edit., 1990, Selected Fiction, 1954, Selected Letters, 1955, American Essays, 1956, revised edit., 1990, The Future of the Novel: Critical Papers, 1956; (with Gordon N. Ray) James and H.G. Wells, Letters, 1958; Complete Tales, 12 vols., 1962-64, HJ: Letters, 4 vols., 1974-84; (with Mark Wilson) Complete Criticism, 2 vols., 1984; (with Lyall H. Powers) The Complete Notebooks, 1987; Henry James Reader, 1965, Selected Letters, 1987. Editor (other authors) Edmund Wilson Papers, 4 vols., 1972-86, Literary History and Literary Criticism, 1965, The Diary of Alice James, 1964. Mem. adv. com. edn. Met. Mus. Centenary, 1969-70; mem. ednl. adv. com. Guggenheim Found., 1967-80. Served as lt. AUS, World War II; dir. Press Agy. 1945-46, U.S. zone Germany. Decorated Bronze Star; recipient Pulitzer prize in biography, 1963; Nat. Book award for non-fiction, 1963; Nat. Book Critics Circle award for biography, 1985; medal of lit. Nat. Arts Club, 1981; Nat. Inst. Arts and Letters grantee, 1959; elected to Am. Acad. Arts and Letters, 1972; Gold medal for biography Acad.-Inst., 1976; Hawaii Writers award, 1977; Guggenheim fellow, 1936-38, 65-66; Nat. Endowment for Humanities grantee, 1974-77. Fellow Am. Acad. Arts and Scis., Royal Soc. Lit. (Eng.); mem. Nat. Inst. Arts and Letters (sec. 1965-67), W.A. White Psychoanalytic Soc. (hon.), Am. Acad. Psychoanalysis (hon.), Soc. Authors (Eng.), Authors Guild (mem. council, pres. 1969-71), P.E.N. (pres. Am. Center 1957-59), Hawaii Lit. Arts Council (pres. 1978-79), Century Club (N.Y.C.). Address: 3817 Lurline Dr Honolulu HI 96816

EDELMAN, GERALD MAURICE, biochemist, educator; b. N.Y.C., N.Y., July 1, 1929; s. Edward and Anna (Freedman) E.; m. Maxine Morrison, June 11, 1950; children: Eric, David, Judith. B.S., Ursinus Coll., 1950, Sc.D., 1974; M.D., U. Pa., 1954, D.Sc., 1973; Ph.D., Rockefeller U., 1960; M.D. (hon.), U. Siena, Italy, 1974; DSc (hon.), Gustavus Adolphus Coll., 1975, Williams Coll., 1976; DSc Honoris Causa, U. Paris, 1989; LSc Honoris Causa, U. Cagliari, 1989; DSc Honoris Causa, U. degli Studi di Napoli, 1990, Tulane U., 1991. Med. house officer Mass. Gen. Hosp., 1954-55; asst. physician hosp. of Rockefeller U., 1957-60, mem. faculty, 1960-92, assoc. dean grad. studies, 1963-66, prof., 1966-74, Vincent Astor disting. prof., 1974-92; mem. faculty and chmn. dept. neurobiology Scripps Rsch. Inst., La Jolla, Calif., 1992—; mem. biophysics and biophys. chemistry study sect. NIH, 1964-67; mem. Sci. Council, Ctr. for Theoretical Studies, 1970-72; assoc., sci. chmn. Neurosciences Research Program, 1980—, dir. Neuroscis. Inst., 1981—; mem. adv. bd. Basel Inst. Immunology, 1970-77, chmn., 1975-77; non-resident fellow, trustee Salk Inst., 1973-85; bd. overseers Faculty Arts and Scis., U. Pa., 1976-83; trustee, mem. adv. com. Carnegie Inst., Washington, 1980-87; bd. govs. Weizman Inst. Sci., 1971-87, mem. emeritus; researcher structure of antibodies, molecular and devel. biology. Author: Neural Darwinism, 1987, Topobiology, 1988, The Remembered Present, 1989, Bright Air, Brilliant Fire, 1992. Trustee Rockefeller Bros. Fund., 1972-82. Served to capt. M.C. AUS, 1955-57. Recipient Spencer Morris award U. Pa., 1954, Ann. Alumni award Ursinus Coll., 1969, Nobel prize for physiology or medicine, 1972, Albert Einstein Commemorative award Yeshiva U., 1974, Buchman Meml. award Calif. Inst. Tech., 1975, Rabbi Shai Shacknai meml. prize Hebrew U.-Hadassah Med. Sch., Jerusalem, 1977, Regents medal Excellence, N.Y. State, 1984, Hans Neurath prize, U. Washington, 1986, Sesquicentennial Commemorative award Nat. Libr. Medicine, 1986, Cécile and Oskar Vogt award U. Dusseldorf, 1988, Disting. Grad. award U. Pa., 1990, Personnalité de l'année, Paris, 1990, Warren Triennial Prize award Mass. Gen. Hosp., 1992. Fellow AAAS, N.Y. Acad. Scis., N.Y. Acad. Medicine; mem. Am. Philos. Soc., Am. Soc. Biol. Chemists, Am. Assn. Immunologists, Genetics Soc. Am., Harvey Soc. (pres. 1975-76, Am. Chem. Soc., Eli Lilly award biol. chemistry 1965), Am. Acad. Arts and Scis., Nat. Acad. Sci., Am. Soc. Cell Biology, Acad. Scis. of Inst. France (fgn.), Japanese Biochem. Soc. (hon.), Pharm. Soc. Japan (hon.), Soc. Developmental Biology, Council Fgn. Relations, Sigma Xi, Alpha Omega Alpha. Office: Scripps Rsch Inst Dept Neurobiol SBR-14 10666 N Torrey Pines Rd La Jolla CA 92037

EDELMAN, NORMA LOU, health care administrator; b. Denver, Nov. 22, 1939; d. Nate and Lottie E. (Cohn) Bernstone; m. Howard S. Edelman; children: Sherri, Andrea, Devra, Brian. Student, Pa. State U., 1957-59, U. Colo., 1959-60. Med. technologist Children's Med. Ctr., Denver, 1961-67; sec., v.p., pres. Nat. Coun. Jewish Women, Denver, 1962-80; state pub. affairs rep. for Colo. Nat. Coun. Jewish Women, 1980-84; program coord. juvenile justice staff Dept. Inst., Denver, 1980-81; exec. dir. Colo. Commn. on Children and Family, Denver, 1982-84; program mgr. child health screening Colo. Dept. Health, Denver, 1985—, tng. officer Early and Periodic Screening Diagnosis and Treatment, 1991—; prof., rsch. assoc., cons. in community child devel. program Med. Sch., U. Colo., Denver, 1987—; cons. Child Find-Denver Pub. Schs., 1991—, Denver Family Opportunity, 1990—. Author: (manual) A Handbook for Screeners, 1986; co-author: (manual) Denver II Developmental Screening Test, 1990. Treas., sec., v.p., pres. Inter-Neighborhood Coop., 1986—; grants chairperson Neighborhood Cultures of Denver, 1991—; legis. liaison Colo. Advs. for Children, 1976-84; legis. liaison, bd. dirs. Colo. Juvenile Coun., 1981-86; Dem. candidate for state legislature, Denver, 1982, 84; community dir. Family Violence Task Force-Jewish Fedn., Denver, 1990-92. Named Outstanding Child Adv., Colo. Advs. for Children, 1981. Mem. Colo. Pub. Health Assn. (v.p., bd. dirs. 1986-90), Leadership Denver Assn. Democrat. Jewish. Office: Colo Dept of Health Well Child/Early and Periodic SDT 4300 Cherry Creek So Dr Denver CO 80222

EDELSTEIN, JEROME MELVIN, bibliographer; b. Balt., July 31, 1924; s. Joseph and Irene (Schwartz) E.; m. Eleanor Rockwell, Nov. 5, 1950; children: Paul Rockwell, Nathaniel Benson. A.B. cum laude (teaching fellow 1946-49), Johns Hopkins U., 1947, postgrad., 1947-49; M.L.S., U. Mich., 1953. Italian Govt. fellow, Fulbright grantee U. Florence, Italy, 1949-50; reference librarian rare book div. Library of Congress, 1955-62; bibliographer Medieval and Renaissance studies UCLA, 1962-64; librarian spl. collections N.Y. U., 1964-66; humanities bibliographer, lectr. bibliography UCLA, 1966-72; chief librarian Nat. Gallery Art, Washington, 1972-86; sr. bibliographer, resource coordinator Getty Ctr. for History of Art and Humanities, Santa Monica, Calif., 1986—; lectr. rare book librarianship Cath. U. Am., Washington, 1975-83. Author: A Bibliographical Checklist of Thornton Wilder, 1959; editor, contbr. A Garland for Jake Zeitlin, 1967, The Library of Don Cameron Allen, 1968, Wallace Stevens: A Descriptive Bibliography, 1974; contbr. articles, revs. to profl. jours. Pres. bd. trustees Crossroads Sch., Santa Monica, Calif., 1970-72, hon. mem. bd. trustees ex officio, 1972—; bd. advisers Ctr. for Book Arts, N.Y.C., Franklin Furnace, N.Y.C. With AUS, 1943-46. Herzog August Bibliothek fellow, Wolfenbüttel, Fed. Republic Germany, 1985; Guggenheim Meml. fellow, 1986-87. Mem. Am. Antiquarian Soc., Ateneo Veneto, Bibliog. Soc. Am. (notes editor 1964-81), Assn. Internat. de Bibliophilie, Wallace Stevens Soc. (cons. editor jour. 1976-90), Am. Printing History Assn., Art Libraries Soc. N.Am., Jargon Soc. (dir. 1976-85), Phi Beta Kappa. Clubs: Grolier (N.Y.C.), Century Assn. (N.Y.C.); Cosmos (Washington); Rounce and Coffin, Zamorano (L.A.).

EDEM, BENJAMIN G., computer company executive; b. Syracuse, N.Y., Apr. 20, 1952; s. Charles H. and Beulah R. Edem. BS in Astrophysics, U. Rochester, 1974; diploma in Christian studies, Regent Coll., Vancouver, British Columbia, 1976; MS in Computer Sci., Johns Hopkins U., 1980. Programmer U. Rochester, N.Y., 1974-75; programmer/analyst Computer Scis. Corp., Greenbelt, Md., 1976-82; programmer IBM Corp., Fed. Systems Co., Gaithersburg, Md., 1982-84, mgr. software devel., 1984-87; systems engr. IBM Corp., Fed. Systems Co., Santa Clara, Calif., 1987-88, mgr. system engring., 1988-90, subcontract program mgr., 1990—. Republican. Mem. Bible Ch. Home: 772 Maplewood Ave Palo Alto CA 94303-4708 Office: IBM Corp PO Box 58183 Santa Clara CA 95052-8183

EDENFIELD, T(HOMAS) KEEN, JR., real estate developer; b. Chattanooga, May 8, 1943; s. Thomas Keen Sr. and Francis (Love) E.; m. Ann Louise Goodney, Jan. 24, 1976; children: Thomas Keen III, Andrew Ward, Stuart Douglas, Curtis Arthur. BS in Econs., Emory U., 1967; MBA, Oxford Sch. Econs., London, 1969. Capt. Saudi Arabian Airlines, 1976-78, Air Jamaica, 1978-80; owner, pres. Mountain Hospitality, Inc., Albuquerque, 1982-86, Lamb Realty & Investment, Albuquerque, 1980—; pres. Seeganex Internat. Ltd., London, 1984—; chmn. Seeganex Am., Albuquerque; CIA aviation operative, Washington, 1974-85. Contbr. articles to profl. jours. Decorated Turkish Civilian Wings award; recipient Nicaraguan Civilian Humanitarian award, 1984. Mem. Albuquerque Country Club, Wings Club of Arabia (pres. 1978-79). Office: Lamb Realty & Investment PO Box 26026 Albuquerque NM 87125-6026

EDENS, GARY DENTON, broadcasting executive; b. Asheville, N.C., Jan. 6, 1942; s. James Edwin and Pauline Amanda (New) E.; m. Hannah Suellen Walter, Aug. 21, 1965; children: Ashley Elizabeth, Emily Blair. BS, U. N.C., 1964. Account exec. PAMS Prodns., Dallas, 1965-67; account exec. Sta. WKIX, Raleigh, N.C., 1967-69; gen. mgr. Sta. KOY, Phoenix, 1970-81; sr. v.p. Harte-Hanks Radio, Inc., Phoenix, 1978-81, pres., chief exec. officer, 1981-84; chmn., chief exec. officer Edens Broadcasting, Inc., 1984—; dir. Gt. Western Bank & Trust Ariz., 1975-86, Citibank Ariz., 1986—. Bd. dirs. Valley Big Bros., 1972-80, Ariz. State U. Found., 1979—, COMPAS, 1979—, Men's Arts Coun., 1975-78. Named One of Three Outstanding Young Men, Phoenix Jaycees, 1973; entrepreneurial fellow U. Ariz., 1989. Mem. Phoenix Execs. Club (pres. 1976), Nat. Radio Broadcasters Assn. (dir. 1981-86), Radio Advt. Bur. (dir. 1981—), Young Pres.'s Orgn. (chmn. Ariz. chpt. 1989-90), Chief Execs. Orgn., 1992—, Phoenix Country Club, Univ. Phoenix Club. Republican. Methodist. Office: 840 N Central Ave Phoenix AZ 85004-2096

EDENS, GLENN THOMAS, engineering executive; b. Cin., Nov. 17, 1952; s. Asa and Janine (Divivue) E. Student, Calif. Poly. Inst., Pomona, 1970-72. Mgr. advanced devel. Xerox Corp., Palo Alto, Calif., 1971-76; dir. engring. Nat. Semicondr. Corp., Santa Clara, Calif., 1976-79; mgr. product mktg. Apple Computer, Cupertino, Calif., 1979-80; v.p. devel., co-founder Grid Systems Corp., Mountain View, Calif., 1980-84; v.p., gen. mgr. NBI, Boulder, Colo., 1984-86; co-founder, pres., chief exec. officer WaveFrame Corp., Boulder, 1986-88; co-founder, pres. Set Tech., Boulder, 1988-89; co-founder, chief tech. officer, v.p. engring. Vantage Point Video, Boulder, 1989—; cons., Boulder, 1988—. Co-patentee grid portable computer; designer grid computer, portable computer. Vol. Boulder Hist. Soc., 1989; pres. Boulder Philharm. Orch., 1989—; co-chmn. Esprit Entrepreneur Program, Boulder, 1988; mem. adv. bd. Boulder County Ptnrs., 1990. Recipient gold record for Tangerine Dream, 1988. Mem. IEEE, Assn. for Computing Machinery, Am. Symphony Orch. League. Presbyterian. Home: 3232 Sixth St Boulder CO 80304

EDGAR, JAMES MACMILLAN, JR., management consultant; b. N.Y.C., Nov. 7, 1936; s. James Macmillan Edgar and Lilyan (McCann) E.; B. Chem. Engring., Cornell U., 1959, M.B.A. with distinction, 1960; m. Judith Frances Storey, June 28, 1958; children: Suzanne Lynn, James Macmillan, Gordon Stuart. New product rep. E.I. duPont Nemours, Wilmington, Del., 1960-63, mktg. services rep., 1963-64; with Touche Ross & Co., 1964-78, mgr., Detroit, 1966-68, ptnr., 1968-71, ptnr. in charge, mgmt. services ops. for No. Calif. and Hawaii, San Francisco, 1971-78, ptnr. Western regional mgmt. services, 1978; prin. Edgar, Dunn & Co., San Francisco, 1978—; mem. San Francisco Mayor's Fin. Adv. Com., 1976—, mem. exec. com., 1978—, Blue Ribbon com. for Bus., 1987-88; mem. Alumnae Resources adv. bd., 1986—, mem. San Francisco Planning and Urban Research Bd., 1986-89, mem. adv. bd., 1989—; mem. alumni exec. council Johnson Grad. Sch. Mgmt. Cornell U., 1985—, Cornell Coun., 1970-73; mem. steering com. Bay Area Coun., 1989—; chmn. San Francisco Libr. Found., 1990—. Recipient Award of Merit for outstanding pub. service City and County of San Francisco, 1978; Honor award for outstanding contbns. to profl. mgmt. Johnson Grad. Sch. Mgmt., Cornell U., 1978. CPA, cert. mgmt. cons. Mem. Assn. Corp. Growth (v.p. membership San Francisco chpt. 1979-81, v.p. programs 1981-82, pres. 1982-83, nat. bd. dirs. 1983-86), AICPA, Calif. Soc. CPAs, Inst. Mgmt. Cons. (regional v.p. 1973-80, dir. 1975-77, bd. v.p. 1977-80), Profl. Services Mgmt. Assn., San Francisco C. of C. (bd. dirs. 1987-89, 91—, mem. exec. com. 1988-89, 91—, chmn. mktg. San Francisco program 1991-92, membership devel. 1993, chmn. elect, bd. dirs. 1994), Libr. Found. San Francisco (chmn. 1989—), Tau Beta Pi. Clubs: Pacific Union, Commonwealth of San Francisco, Marin Rod and Gun. Patentee nonwoven fabrics. Home: 10 Buckeye Way San Rafael CA 94904-2602 Office: Edgar Dunn & Co Inc 847 Sansome St San Francisco CA 94111-1529

EDGAR, ROBERT WILLIAM, clergyman, former congressman; b. Phila., May 29, 1943; s. Leroy Raymond and Marion Louise (Fish) E.; m. Merle Louise Deaver, Aug. 29, 1964; children: Robert William, Thomas David, Andrew John. BA in History and Religion, Lycoming Coll., 1965; MDiv, Drew U., 1968; cert. in pastoral psychology, Hahnemann Med. Coll. and Hosp., 1967. Ordained to ministry Methodist Ch., 1968. Pastor chs. Pa., 1962-71, Lansdowne United Meth. Ch., Pa., 1972-74; mem. 94th-99th congresses from 7th Dist. Pa.; mem. pub. works and transp. com. on its sub-coms.; econ. devel., water resources, surface transp.; mem. vets. affairs com.; exec. com. for house enviro House Select Com. Assassinations, 1976-78; exec. dir. Com. for Nat. Security, 1988-90; pres. Sch. Theology at Claremont, Calif., 1990—; vis. prof. social change Swarthmore (Pa.) Coll., 1987; chmn. N.E.-Midwest Congl. Coalition, 1978-82; chmn. Congl. Clearinghouse on the Future, 1982-86; mem. clergy unit Phila. Police Dept., 1972; United Protestant chaplain Drexel U., 1971-74. Organizer, first pres. Human Rels. Com. of East Falls, Phila., 1968-71. Recipient Most Effective Mem. Congress award Nat. Com. for Effective Congress, 1978, Outstanding Young Man award Pa. Jaycees, 1978, Conservation award Sierra Club, 1978, Disting. Conservation award Am. Rivers Council, 1979, Bread for World awards, 1979, Smaller Mfrs. Council award, 1980. Democrat. Office: Sch Theology at Claremont 1325 N College Ave Claremont CA 91711-3199

EDGETT, STEVEN DENNIS, transportation consultant; b. Indpls., June 3, 1948; s. Robert Neil and Elizabeth Catherine (Hatch) E.; m. Catherine Ann Bartel, June 19, 1971; children: Jeffrey Steven, Christopher Steven. Student, N. Mex. State U., 1965-67, U. Cin., 1967-68, Grossmont Coll., 1971-72, San Diego State U., 1974-75. Lead designer U.S. Elevator Corp., San Diego, 1970-76; safety engr. State Calif., San Diego, 1976-78; assoc. Skidmore, Owings & Merrill, San Francisco, 1978-86; pres. Edgett Williams Cons. Group, Inc., Mill Valley, Calif., 1986—. Mem. Constrn. Specifications Inst., ASCE Coun. Tall Bldgs. Home: 541 Shasta Way Mill Valley CA 94941-3726 Office: Edgett Williams Cons Group Inc 100 Shoreline Hwy Ste 250A Mill Valley CA 94941-3645

EDLIN, JAMIE ANN, television and commerical producer, writer; b. St. Louis, Apr. 13, 1950; d. Joseph J. and Miriam (Steinberg) E. Student, Carnegie-Mellon U., 1970. Prodn. assoc. Sta. WPGH-TV, Pitts., 1969-70, Sta. WTTW (PBS)-TV, Chgo., 1970-71; assoc. prodr. Maritz-Communico, USIA, Casablanca Filmworks, McDonough-Jones, 1972-81; spl. projects Lifetime Cable Network, L.A., 1982-85; exec. producer Brooktree Prodns., L.A., 1985-87; ptnr., exec. producer Square One, L.A., 1988—; cons. Eagle Comm., Toronto, Can., L.A., 1988, numerous commls., TV prodns., L.A., 1977—; voice-over announcer numerous commls., L.A., 1978-90. Rec. artist, lead singer Tuxedo Junction, 1978; painter, designer decorative and practical artworks, 1990—; exec. prodr., creator Missing Children, 1993, The Video Catalogue, 1993. PSA announcer Am. Cancer Found., L.A., 1978; vol. Amanda Found., L.A., 1980-83; vol., speaker AIDS Project L.A., 1992; program devel. vol. Missing Children HELP Ctr., L.A. 1992. Harris Found. fellow PBS, 1971. Home: 8153 W 4th St Los Angeles CA 90048

EDMISTON, JOSEPH TASKER, state official; b. Monterey Park, Calif., Oct. 27, 1948; s. Tasker Lee and Beula Viola (Bates) E.; m. Pepper Salter Abrams, 1985; children: William Tasker, Charles Henry. AA, East Los Angeles Coll., 1968; AB, U. So. Calif., 1970. Mgr. of ct. process Roy Rottner & Associates, Hollywood, Calif., 1970-73; So. Calif Coastal coord. Sierra Club, L.A., 1973-76, energy coord., Sacramento, Calif., 1976-77; dir. State of Calif. Santa Monica Mountains Land Acquisition Program, 1979-80; exec. dir. Santa Monica Mountains Comprehensive Planning Commn., L.A., 1977-79; exec. dir. Santa Monica Mountains Conservancy, State of Calif., 1980— . Pres. Associated Students, East L.A. Coll., 1968. Recipient Weldon Heald Conservation award Sierra Club, 1970; Hollywood Heritage, Inc. (bd. dirs.). Mem. Marine Tech. Soc. (dir. L.A. region sect. 1975-77), Coastal Soc., Am. Planning Assn. (vice dir. policy L.A. Sect. 1989-90), Phi Rho Pi, Delta Sigma Rho, Tau Kappa Alpha. Democrat. Office: 3700 Solstice Canyon Rd Malibu CA 90265-9502

EDMONDS, CHARLES HENRY, publisher; b. Lakewood, Ohio, Sept. 4, 1919; s. Howard H. and Mary Frances (Galena) E.; student Woodbury Bus. Coll., 1939-40; m. Ruth Audrey Windfelder, Nov. 4, 1938; children: Joan Dickey, Charles Henry, Carolyn Anne, Dianne Marie. Owner, Shoreline Transp. Co., L.A., 1946-58; mgr. transp. Purity Food Stores, Burlingame, Calif., 1958-61; supr. Calif. Motor Express, San Jose, 1961-64; account exec. Don Wright Assos., Oakland, Calif., 1964-65; sales mgr. Western U.S., Shippers Guide Co., Chgo., 1965-70; pub. No. Calif. Retailer, San Jose, 1970-83; v.p. Kasmar Publs., 1983-88; pub. Retail Observer, 1990—. Recipient journalism awards various orgns. Republican. Roman Catholic. Contbr. articles to profl. jours. Home: 1442 Sierra Creek Way San Jose CA 95132-3618

EDMONDS, IVY GORDON, writer; b. Frost, Tex., Feb. 15, 1917; s. Ivy Gordon and Delia Louella (Shumate) E.; student pub. schs.; m. Reiko Mimura, July 12, 1956; 1 dau., Annette. Freelance writer; author books including: Ooka the Wise, 1961; The Bounty's Boy, 1963; Joel of the

Hanging Gardens, 1966; Trickster Tales, 1966; Taiwan—the Other China, 1971; The Magic Man, 1972; Mao's Long March, 1973; Motorcycling for Beginners, 1973; Micronesia, 1974; Pakistan, Land of Mystery, Tragedy and Courage, 1974; Automotive Tuneups for Beginners, 1974; Ethiopia, 1975; The Magic Makers, 1976; The Shah of Iran, 1976; Allah's Oil: Mid-East Petroleum, 1976; Second Sight, 1977; Motorcycle Racing for Beginners, 1977; Islam, 1977; Buddhism, 1978; The Mysteries of Troy, 1977; Big U Universal in the Silent Days, 1977; D.D. Home, 1978; Bicycle Motocross, 1979; Girls Who Talked to Ghosts, 1979; The Magic Brothers, 1979; (with William H. Gebhardt) Broadcasting for Beginners, 1980; (with Reiko Mimura) The Oscar Directors, 1980; The Mysteries of Homer's Greeks, 1981; The Kings of Black Magic, 1981; Funny Car Racing for Beginners, 1982; The Magic Dog, 1982; author textbooks: (with Ronald Gonzales) Understanding Your Car, 1975, Introduction to Welding, 1975; also author pulp and soft cover fiction and nonfiction under names of Gene Cross and Gary Gordon and publishers house names; pub. relations mgr. Northrop Corp., Anaheim, Calif., 1968-79, indsl. editor, Hawthorne, Calif., 1979-86. Served with USAAF, 1940-45, USAF, 1946-63. Decorated D.F.C., Air medals, Bronze Star. Home: 5801 Shirl St Cypress CA 90630-3326

EDMONDSON, SCOTT THOMAS, urban and regional planner, policy analyst; b. Ithaca, N.Y., June 22, 1955; s. James Thomas and Helvi Karennina (Selkee) E.; m. Marie Jean Summers, June 4, 1978; 1 child, Chloe Ming-Hwa Summers. BA in Internat. Devel. Stds., U. Calif., Berkeley, 1979; postgrad. in pub. policy analysis, U. Rochester, N.Y., 1980-81; MA in Urban Planning, UCLA, 1983, postgrad., 1984-85. Policy analyst, intern Dept. of Waste Disposal Planning, N.Y.C., 1981; rsch. asst., assoc. Higher Edn. Rsch. Inst., UCLA, 1982-83, 84-85; stagiare, cons. Orgn. for Econ. Coop. & Devel., Paris, 1983-84; jr. planner Marin County Planning Dept., San Rafael, Calif., 1986; planner-economist EIP Assocs., San Francisco, 1986-89; lead facilities planner Kaiser Found. Health Plan, Inc., Oakland, Calif., 1989-91; sr. planner-economist EIP Assocs., San Francisco, 1991—; exec. dir., founder Sustainable Futures Project, San Francisco, 1992—. Mem. Am. Inst. Cert. Planners, Am. Planning Assn., Econ. Devel. Divsn. of Am. Planning Assn., Am. Alpine Club. Democrat.

EDMONDSON, W(ALLACE) THOMAS, limnologist, educator; b. Milw., Apr. 24, 1916; s. Clarence Edward and Marie (Kelley) E.; m. Yvette Hardman, Sept. 26, 1941. BS, Yale U., 1938, PhD, 1942; postgrad., U. Wis., 1938-39; DSc (hon.), U. Wis., Milw., 1987. Research assoc. Am. Mus. Natural History, 1942-43, Woods Hole Oceanographic Instn., 1943-46; lectr. biology Harvard U., Cambridge, Mass., 1946-49; mem. faculty U. Wash., Seattle, 1949—, prof., 1957-86, prof. emeritus, 1986—, Jessie and John Danz lectr., 1987; R.E. Coker Meml. lectr. U. N.C., 1977; Brode lectr. Whitman Coll., 1988. Editor: Freshwater Biology (Ward and Whipple), 2d edit, 1959; contbr. articles to profl. jours. Recipient Einar Naumann-August Thienemann medal Internat. Assn. Theoretical and Applied Limnology, 1980, Outstanding Pub. Svc. award U. Wash., Seattle, 1987, commendation State of Wash., 1987; NSF sr. postdoctoral fellow Italy, Eng. and Sweden, 1959-60, Wilbur Lucius Cross medal Yale U. Grad. Sch. Alumni Assn., 1993. Mem. NAS (Cottrell award 1973), AAAS, Am. Soc. Limnology and Oceanography (G. Evelyn Hutchinson medal 1990), Internat. Assn. Limnology, Ecol. soc. Am. (eminent Ecologist award 1983), Yale Grad. Sch. Alumni Assn. (Wilbur Lucius Cross medal 1993). Office: U Wash Dept Zoology NJ-15 Seattle WA 98195

EDRICH, LESLIE HOWARD, physician, surgeon; b. Bklyn., Dec. 31, 1953; s. Eugene and Ruth (Jacobs) E. BA, Franklin and Marshall Coll., Lancaster, Pa., 1975; MD, NYU, N.Y.C., 1980. Diplomate Am. Bd. Surgery. Intern NYU Med. Ctr., N.Y.C., 1980-81, resident, 1981-82; resident U. Calif. Irvine, Orange, 1982-85; surgeon Meml. Med. Ctr., Long Beach, Calif., 1986—; dir. trauma svc., chief gen. & vascular surgery Long Beach Meml. Med. Ctr., 1992—. Mem. AMA, Calif. Med. Assn. Office: 2880 Atlantic Ave Ste 200 Long Beach CA 90806-1716

EDSON, WILLIAM ALDEN, electrical engineer; b. Burchard, Nebr., Oct. 30, 1912; s. William Henry and Pearl (Montgomery) E.; m. Saralou Peterson, Aug. 23, 1942; children: Judith Lynne, Margaret Jane, Carolyn Louise. B.S. (Summerfield scholar), U. Kans., 1934, M.S., 1935; D.Sc. (Gordon McKay scholar), Harvard U., 1937. Mem. tech. staff Bell Telephone Labs., Inc., N.Y.C., 1937-41; supr. Bell Telephone Labs., Inc., 1943-45; asst. prof. elec. engring. Ill. Inst. Tech., Chgo., 1941-43; prof. physics Ga. Inst. Tech., Atlanta, 1945-46; prof. elec. engring. Ga. Inst. Tech., 1946-51, dir. sch. elec. engring., 1951-52; vis. prof., research asso. Stanford U., 1952-56, cons. prof., 1956; mgr. Klystron sub-sect. Gen. Electric Microwave Lab., Palo Alto, Calif., 1955-61; v.p., dir. research Electromagnetic Tech. Corp., Palo Alto, 1961-62; pres. Electromagnetic Tech. Corp., 1962-70; sr. scientist Vidar Corp., Mountain View, Calif., 1970—71; asst. dir. Radio Physics Lab., SRI Internat., Menlo Park, Calif., 1971-77; sr. prin. engr. Geosci. and Engring. Ctr., SRI Internat., 1977—; cons. high frequency sect. Nat. Bur. Standards, 1951-64; dir. Western Electronic Show and Conv., 1975-79. Author: (with Robert I. Sarbacher) Hyper and Ultra-High Frequency Engineering, 1943, Vacuum-Tube Oscillators, 1953. Life fellow IEEE (chmn. San Francisco sect. 1963-64, com. standards piezoelectricity 1950-67); mem. Am. Phys. Soc., Sigma Xi, Tau Beta Pi, Sigma Tau, Phi Kappa Phi, Eta Kappa Nu, Pi Mu Epsilon. Home: 23350 Sereno Ct # 29 Cupertino CA 95014-6507 Office: SRI Internat 333 Ravenswood Ave Menlo Park CA 94025-3493

EDWARDS, ALISON EDITH, advertising executive; b. Torrance, CA, Sept. 29, 1952; d. Holly Carl and Norma Marie Edwards; m. Robert Lee Schuchard, Sept. 9, 1978; 1 child, Andrew Edwards. BA, Stanford U., 1974; MS, San Jose State U., 1978; MBA, UCLA, LA, 1985. Copywriter Bergthold, Fillhardt and Wright, San Jose, Calif., 1976-78; tech. writer The Wiggins Co., Redondo Beach, Calif., 1978-80; asst. v.p. First Interstate Bank, L.A., 1980-84; pres. Alison Edwards Communications, L.A., 1984—; dir. L.A. Advt. Women, L.A., 1979-82. Author: Lessons in Professional Liability: A Notebook for Certified Public Accountants, 1990; editor: Lessons in Professional Liability: A Notebook for Design Professionals, 1987. Recipient Pilot Program Mem. Womens Network for Entrepreneurial Training, Small Bus. Adminstrn. Mem. Stanford Profl. Women Dir. Office: Alison Edwards Communications 1590 D Rosecrans Ave Ste 150 Manhattan Beach CA 90266

EDWARDS, ARDIS LAVONNE QUAM, elementary education educator, retired; b. Sioux Falls, S.D., July 30, 1930; d. Norman and Dorothy (Cade) Quam; m. Paul Edwards, Apr. 18, 1953 (dec. Sept. 1988); children: Kevin (dec. 1980), Kendall, Erin, Sally, Kristin, Keely. Teaching credentials, Augustana Luth. Coll., Sioux Falls, 1949; provisional teaching credentials, San Jose State Coll., 1953. Lic. pvt. pilot, FAA, 1984. Mgr. The Cottage Restaurant, Sioux Falls, 1943-50; one-room sch. tchr. Whaley Sch., Colman, S.D., 1949-50, East Sioux Sch., Sioux Falls, 1950-51; recreation dir. City of Albany, Calif., 1951-52; first grade tchr. Decoto (Calif.) Sch. Dist., 1952-58. Author Health Instrn. Unit Study Packet for Tchrs. Bible sch. tchr. eAst Side Luth. Ch., Sioux Falls, S.D., 1945-58, Sunday sch. tchr., 1945-51, Christian Week Day Sch. tchr., 1970, 87, ch. historian, 1986—, other offices; treas. PTA, Hayward, Calif., 1959, mem., 1959-76; pres. Luth. Women's Missionary League, 1976; charter mem., historian Our Savior Luth Ch., Fremont, Calif., 1964—, mem. choir; chmn. OSLC Blood Bank, 1968—; edn. officer, fraternal communicator Luth. Brotherhood, respecteen officer. Recipient Spl. Svc. award Girl Scouts U.S., 1971, Arthritis Found., Fremont, 1974, 75, Spl. Commendation March Fong Eu, 1954. Mem. NAFE, Republic Airlines Retired Pilots Assn., Retired Airline Pilots Assn., Aircraft Owners and Pilots Assn., Southwest Airways Pilots Wives Assn., AARP, Concerned Women for Am., Am. Heart Assn., Am. Cancer Soc., Arthritis Found., March of Dimes, others. Republican.

EDWARDS, BRUCE GEORGE, ophthalmologist, naval officer; b. Idaho Springs, Colo., Apr. 6, 1942; s. Bruce Norwood and Evelyn Alice (Kohut) Edwards. BA, U. Colo., 1964; MD, U. Colo., Denver, 1968. Diplomate Am. Acad. Ophthalmology. Commd. ensign USN, 1964; advanced through grades to capt. U.S. Naval Hosp., 1980; intern U.S. Naval Hosp., San Diego, 1968-69; USN med. officer USS Long Beach (CGN-9), 1969-70; gen. med. officer U.S. Naval Hosp., Taipei, Taiwan, 1970-72, U.S. Naval Dispensary Treasure Island, San Francisco, 1972-73; resident in ophthalmology U.S. Naval Hosp., Oakland, Calif., 1973-76, U. Calif., San Francisco, 1973-76; mem. opthalmologist staff Naval Hosp., Camp Pendleton, Calif., 1976-83; ophthalmologist, chief of med. staff Naval Hosp., Naples, Italy, 1983-85; ophthalmology head Camp Pendleton Naval Hosp., Camp Pendleton, 1985—; dir. surg. svcs. Camp Pendleton Naval Hosp., 1990-92, dir. physician advisor quality assurance, 1985-86; vol. Internat. Eye Found., Harar, Ethiopia, 1975. Fellow Am. Acad. Ophthalmology; mem. AMA, Calif. Med. Assn., Calif. Assn. Ophthalmologists, Am. Soc. Contemporary Ophthalmologists, Assn. U.S. Mil. Surgeons, Pan Am. Assn. Ophthalmology, Order of DeMolay (Colo. DeMolay of Yr. 1961, Idaho Springs Chevalier, Colo. State sec. 1961-62). Republican. Methodist. Office: US Naval Hosp Ophthalmology Dept Camp Pendleton CA 92055

EDWARDS, CHARLES CORNELL, physician, research administrator; b. Overton, Nebr., Sept. 16, 1923; s. Charles Busby and Lillian Margaret (Arendt) E.; m. Sue Cowles Kruidenier, June 24, 1945; children: Timothy, Charles Cornell, Nancy, David. Student, Princeton U., 1941-43; B.A., U. Colo., 1945, M.D., 1948; M.S., U. Minn., 1956; L.L.D. (hon.), Phila. Coll. Pharmacy and Sci.; L.H.D. (hon.), Pa. Coll. Podiatry, U. Colo. Diplomate: Am. Bd. Surgery. Intern St. Mary's Hosp., Mpls., 1948-49; resident surgery Mayo Found., 1950-56; pvt. practice medicine specializing in surgery Des Moines, 1956-61; mem. surg. staff Georgetown U., Washington, 1961-62; also cons. USPHS; dir. div. socio-econ. activities A.M.A., Chgo., 1963-67; v.p., mng. officer health and sci. affairs Booz, Allen & Hamilton, 1967-69; commr. FDA, Washington, 1969-73; asst. sec. for health HEW, Washington, 1973-75; sr. v.p., dir. Becton, Dickinson & Co., 1975-77; pres. Scripps Clinic and Research Found., La Jolla, Calif., 1977-91; pres., CEO Scripps Insts. Medicine and Sci., La Jolla, 1991—; bd. dirs. Bergen Brunswig Corp., Biomagnetic Techs., Inc., Molecular Biosystems, Inc., Nova Pharm. Corp.; bd. regents Nat. Libr. Medicine, 1981-85; mem. Nat. Leadership Commn. on Health Care, 1986—; bd. govs. Hosp. Corp. Am., 1986-89. Served to lt. M.C. USNR, 1942-46. Mem. Inst. Medicine, Nat. Acad. Scis. Clubs: Chevy Chase, Princeton; La Jolla Country, La Jolla Beach and Tennis; Fairbanks Ranch Country. Office: Scripps Inst Medicine & Sci 4275 Campus Point Ct San Diego CA 92121

EDWARDS, CHARLES RICHARD, printing equipment and supplies company executive; b. South Bend, Ind., July 16, 1931; s. Bernard Stuart and Mary Irene (Chamberlaine) E.; student pub. schs.; m. Joanne Wood, Dec. 15, 1950; children—Timothy Stuart, Terry Lynne, David Bryan. Pressman, Toastmasters Internat., Santa Ana, Calif., 1954-60; with 3M Co., 1960-69, Salesman, Western U.S. tech. service and nat. market mgr., St. Paul, 1966-69; chief exec. officer, sec., chief fin. officer, co-owner Graphic Arts Supplies, Inc., Orange, Calif., 1969-86; owner, operator Edwards Bus. Services, 1987—; bus. and trade cons., 1986-92; instr., cons. in field. Bd. dirs. treas. #1 Network, Inc., Chgo., 1982-86. Served with USAF, 1950-54; Korea. Mem. Nat. Assn. Lithographic Clubs (chpt. co-founder, officer, dir.), Nat. Assn. Printing House Craftsmen (past chpt. pres., regional officer), Toastmasters, Hobo Golf Assn. (pres. 1985—). Republican. Home: 7221 Judson Ave Westminster CA 92683-6109

EDWARDS, DANIEL WALDEN, lawyer; b. Vancouver, Wash., Aug. 7, 1950; s. Chester W. Edwards and Marilyn E. Russell; m. Joan S. Heller, Oct. 18, 1987; children: Nathaniel, Matthew, Stephen. BA in Psychology magna cum laude, Met. State Coll., Denver, 1973, BA in Philosophy, 1974; JD, U. Colo., 1976. Bar: Colo. 1977, U.S. Dist. Ct. Colo. 1977. Dep. pub. defender State of Colo., Denver, 1977-79, Littleton, 1979-81, Pueblo, 1981-86; head office pub. defender State of Colo., Brighton, 1987-89; mem. jud. faculty State of Colo., 1988-91; sole practitioner Denver, 1991—; instr. sch. of law U. Denver, 1988-91, adj. prof., 1991—, coach appellate advocacy team, 1991—; adv. coun. Colo. Legal Svcs., 1989—; adj. mem. Colo. Supreme Ct. Grievance Com., 1991—. Mem. visual arts com. City Arts III, 1989-90, com. chmn., mem. adv. coun., 1991; bd. dirs. Metropolitan State Coll. Alumni Assn., 1991-92; vol. lectr. CSE Thursday Night Bar Pro Se Divorce Clinic, 1991—. Named Pub. Defender of Yr. Colo. State Pub. Defender's Office, 1985, Outstanding Colo. Criminal Def. Atty., 1989. Mem. ABA, Assn. Trial Lawyers Am., Colo. Bar Assn., Adams County Bar Assn., Denver Bar Assn., Met. State Coll. Alumni Assn. (bd. dirs. 1991—). Home: 2335 Clermont St Denver CO 80207-3134 Office: 1888 Sherman Ste 600 Denver CO 80203

EDWARDS, DON, congressman; b. San Jose, Calif., Jan. 6, 1915; s. Leonard P. and Clara (Donlon) E.; m. Edith B. Wilkie; children—Leonard P., Samuel D., Bruce H., Thomas C., William D. A.B., Stanford, 1936; student, Law Sch., 1936-38. Bar: Calif. Agt. FBI, 1940-41; mem. 88th-93d Congresses from 9th Calif. Dist., 94th-102nd Congresses from 10th Calif. Dist., 103rd Congress from 16th Calif. Dist., 1963—; Nat. chmn. Americans for Democratic Action, from 1965. Served to lt. USNR, 1941-45. Democrat. Unitarian. Office: US House of Representatives 2307 Rayburn House Office Washington DC 20515*

EDWARDS, ERNEST GRAY, pathologist, artist; b. Va., Dec. 1, 1927; s. Clifford Ernest and Flora Lee (Gray) E.; m. Consuelo N. Mercé, Dec. 26, 1960; children: Teresa, James. BS, Coll. William and Mary, 1949; MD, Med. Coll. Va., 1953. Diplomate Am. Bd. Pathology. Intern U.S. Naval Hosp., Phila., 1953-54; resident in internal medicine and pathology San Francisco VA Hosp., 1957-59; fellow in surg. pathology and ophthalmic pathology Med. Coll. Va., Richmond, 1959-61; resident in clin. pathology Santa Clara Med. Ctr., San Jose, Calif., 1961-62; assoc. pathologist all hosps., Santa Cruz, Calif., 1962-65; co-dir. labs. San Bernardine Hosp., San Bernardino, Calif., 1965-70; chmn. dept. pathology Santa Ana (Calif.) Community Hosp., 1970-80; asst. clin. prof. pathology U. Calif., Irvine, 1969-83; chmn. dept. pathology Santa Ana-Tustin Community Hosp., 1970-80; cons. pathologist, Santa Ana and Mallorca, Spain, 1980—; portrait artist, Santa Ana and Valencia, Spain, 1985—. Lt. M.C., USNR, 1953-55. Fellow Coll. Am. Pathologists (emeritus); mem. Orange County Soc. Pathologists (pres. 1974-76, v.p. 1978). Republican. Home: 1391 Faren Dr Santa Ana CA 92705

EDWARDS, F(LOYD) KENNETH, journalist, educator, management consultant, marketing executive; b. Salina, Kans., Sept. 29, 1917; s. Floyd Altamus and Grace Frances (Miller) E.; AB, Fort Hays State U., 1940; MS, 1970; m. Virginia Marie Lewark, Sept. 10, 1970; children: Elaine Patricia, Diana, Kenneth, John Michael, Melody, Daniel J. Ins. sales exec., Denver, 1947-50; reporter Sterling (Colo.) Daily Jour., 1950, editor, 1950-52; editor Waverly (Iowa) Newspapers, 1953-55; editor, pub. Edina (Minn.) Courier Newspapers, 1955-56; v.p., editor Mpls. Suburban Newspapers, Hopkins, Minn., 1956-65; editor, gen. mgr. Valley of the Sun Newspapers, Tempe, Ariz., 1968; instr. Mankato (Minn.) State U., 1970-72, asst. prof., 1972-73; assoc. prof. U. Ala., 1973-80, prof., 1980; vis. prof. communications U. Portland (Oreg.), 1981-83, Western Wash. U., 1987-88; mktg. and sales dir. C.C. Publs., Tualatin, Oreg., 1983-86; pres. GoodLife Publs., Bellingham, Wash., 1988—; cons. on newspaper mgmt., mktg., pub. rels. Pres. Calhoun-Harriet Home Owners Assn., Mpls., 1958-60; bd. dirs. Hennepin County Assn. for Mental Health, 1959-60, S.W. Activities Council, 1960-61, S.W. High Sch. PTA, Mpls., 1960-61. With USN, World War II. Grantee Ford Found., 1976, U. Ala., 1977. Recipient awards for community svc. and editorial writing. Mem. AARP (Wash. state media specialist 1989-92, mem. nat. bd. publicity 1991—), Nat. Conf. of Editorial Writers. Republican. Contbr. articles to profl. jours., chpts. to books; author newspaper profit planning and management manual. Home: 15709 Sentinel Dr Sun City West AZ 85375

EDWARDS, JACK A., state agency professional; b. Riverside, Calif., Nov. 17, 1948; s. Douglas Eugene and Billie Sue (Pruitt) E.; m. Donna Lee Klahr, Dec. 20, 1968 (div. Mar. 1973); m. Carolyn Ann Strause, May 7, 1983 (div. Jan. 1993); m. Tracey M. Moreno, Feb. 21, 1993. Student, Riverside City Coll.; BS in Zoology, U. Calif., Davis, 1975; postgrad., Calif. State U., Sacramento. Horseshoer Riverside, Calif., 1972-75; park ranger asst. Sacramento Parks and Recreation, 1975-77; game warden Calif. Dept. Fish and Game, Half Moon Bay, Calif., 1977-81; game warden Calif. Dept. Fish and Game, Sacramento, 1981-86, patrol capt., statewide hunter edn. coordinator, 1986-93, dep. chief, 1993—. Co-author, editor: Defense Tactics and Arrest Techniques, 1985; author: Wildlife Protection Computer Database for California Fish and Game. Mem. South Sacramento Planning Com., 1985-86. Served to staff sgt. USAF, 1968-72. Mem. Calif. Fish and Game Warden's Protective Assn. (treas. 1981-86, pres. 1986—), N.Am. Wildlife Officers Assn. Republican. Home: 7288 Gardner Ave Sacramento CA 95828-3812

EDWARDS, JOHN HENRY, manufacturing company executive; b. Washington, Mar. 14, 1930; s. George Allan and Carole Marie (Boots) E.; m. Joanne Marcsisak, Jan. 13, 1952; 1 child, Jay Marc. BBA, Calif. Western U., 1962. Logistics rep. Gen. Dynamics Convair, San Diego, 1956; contract analyst Gen. Dynamics Astronautics, San Diego, 1957, contract rep., 1958, contract adminstr., 1959-61, chief of contracts, 1962-66; chief of contracts Gen. Dynamics Convair Div., San Diego, 1967-80; mgr. contracts Gen. Dynamics Svc. Co., San Diego, 1981-83, Gen. Dynamics Space System, San Diego, 1984—; adj. prof. Nat. U., San Diego, 1981-83. Drafter/negotiator numerous govt. contracts. Pres. Little League, San Diego, 1977. With USN, 1950-53, Korea. Mem. Nat. Mgmt. Assn., Nat. Contract Mgmt. Assn. (pres. San Diego chpt. 1969-70). Republican. Home: 7921 Blue Jay Pl San Diego CA 92123-3311

EDWARDS, JOHN STUART, zoology educator, researcher; b. Auckland, N.Z., Nov. 25, 1931; came to U.S., 1962; s. Charles Stuart Marten and Mavis Margaret (Wells) E.; m. Ola Margery Shreeves, June 21, 1957; children—Richard Charles, Duncan Roy, Marten John, Andrew Zachary. B.Sc., U. Auckland, 1954, M.Sc. with 1st class honors, 1956; Ph.D., U. Cambridge, Eng., 1960. Asst. prof. biology Western Res. U., 1963-67, assoc. prof., 1967; assoc. prof. zoology U. Wash., Seattle, 1967-70, prof., 1970—, dir. biology program, 1982-88. Recipient Alexander von Humboldt award, 1981; Guggenheim fellow, 1972-73; vis. fellow Gonville and Caius Coll., Cambridge U., Eng., 1989-90. Fellow Royal Entomol. Soc., AAAS; mem. Soc. Neurosci., Am. Soc. Zoologists, Western Apicultural Soc. (v.p. 1983). Home: 5747 60th Ave NE Seattle WA 98105-2035 Office: U Wash Dept Zoology NJ 15 Seattle WA 98195

EDWARDS, JOHN WESLEY, JR., urologist; b. Ferndale, Mich., Apr. 9, 1933; s. John W. and Josephine (Wood) E.; m. Ella Marie Law, Dec. 25, 1954; children: Joella, John III. Student, Alma Coll., 1949-50; BS, U. Mich., 1954; postgrad., Wayne State U., 1954-56; MD, Howard U., 1960. Internship Walter Reed Gen. Hosp., 1960-61, surg. resident, 1962-63, urol. resident, 1963-66; asst. chief urology Tripler Army Med. Ctr., 1966-69; comdr. 4th Med. Battalion, 4th Infantry Div., Vietnam, 1969; chief profl. svcs., urology 91st Evacuation Hosp., Vietnam, 1969-70; urologist Straub Clinic, Inc., 1970-74; pvt. practice, 1974—; v.p. med. staff. svcs. Queen's Med. Ctr., Honolulu, 1993—; chief Dept. Surgery, Straub Clinic and Hosp., 1973; asst. chief Dept. Surgery Queen's Med. Ctr., 1977-79, chief, 1989-93; cons. in urology; chief Dept. Clin. Svcs., Kapiolani Women's and Children's Med. Ctr., 1981-83; clin. assoc. prof. U. Hawaii Sch. of Medicine. Contbr. articles to profl. jours. Bd. dirs. Am. Cancer Soc., Honolulu unit, 1977-79, Hawaii Med. Svc. Assn., 1979-85, Hawaii Heart Assn., 1977-79, Hawaii Assn. for Physicians Indemnification, 1980-86; commr. City and County of Honolulu Liquor Commn., 1986-89; mem. reorgn. commn. City and County of Honolulu, 1990-91. Recipient Howard O. Gray award for Professionalism, 1988, Leaders of Hawaii award, 1983. Fellow ACS (sec.-treas. Hawaii chpt. 1980-81, gov.-at-large 1986-92); mem. AMA, NAACP, Am. Urol. Assn. (alt. del. Western sect. 1991-92, gen. chmn. Western sect. 56th ann. meeting 1980, exec. com. 1983-84, del. dist. 1 1985-86, gen. chmn. 63d ann. meeting 1987, pres. 1989-90), Am. Coll. Physician Execs., Nat. Med. Assn., Hawaii Urol. Assn., Hawaii Med. Assn., Surgicare of Hawaii (v.p. 1983-86), Alpha Phi Alpha, Chi Delta Mu, Alpha Omega Alpha. Office: The Queen's Med Ctr 1301 Punch Bowl St Honolulu HI 96813

EDWARDS, KENNETH NEIL, chemist, consultant; b. Hollywood, Calif., June 8, 1932; s. Arthur Carl and Ann Vera (Gomez) E.; children: Neil James, Peter Graham, John Evan. BA in Chemistry, Occidental Coll., 1954; MS in Chem. and Metall. Engring., U. Mich., 1955. Prin. chemist Battelle Meml. Inst., Columbus, Ohio, 1955-58; dir. new products rsch. and devel. Dunn-Edwards Corp., L.A., 1958-72; sr. lectr. organic coatings and pigments dept. chem. engring. U. So. Calif., L.A., 1976-80; bd. dirs. Dunn-Edwards Corp., L.A.; cons. Coatings & Plastics Tech., L.A., 1972—. Contbr. articles to sci. jours. Mem. Am. Chem. Soc. (chmn. divisional activities 1988-89, exec. com. div. polymeric materials sci. and engring. 1963—), Alpha Chi Sigma (chmn. LA.A profl. chpt., 1962, pacific dist. counselor 1967-70, grand profl. alchemist nat. v.p. 1970-76, grand master alchemist nat. pres. 1976-78, nat. adv. com. 1978—). Home: 2926 Graceland Way Glendale CA 91206-1331 Office: Dunn Edwards Corp 4885 E 52d Pl Los Angeles CA 90040

EDWARDS, KIRK LEWIS, real estate company executive; b. Berkeley, Calif., July 30, 1950; s. Austin Lewis and Betty (Drury) E.; m. Barbara Lee Preston, Oct. 21, 1983; children: Elliott Tyler, Jonathan Bentley. BA in Rhetoric and Pub. Address, U. Wash., Seattle, 1972; postgrad., Shoreline Coll., 1976. From salesperson to mgr. Rede Realty, Lynnwood, Wash., 1973-77; br. mgr. Century 21/North Homes Realty, Lynnwood, Wash., 1977-79, Snohomish, Wash., 1979-81; pres., owner Century 21/Champion Realty, Everett, Wash., 1981-82, Champion Computers, Walker/Edwards Investments, Everett, 1981-82; br. mgr. Advance Properties, Everett, 1982-87; exec. v.p. Bruch & Vedrich Better Homes & Garden, Everett, 1987-88, dir. career devel., 1988-90; pres., chief exec. officer Century 21/Champion Realty, Everett, 1991—. Mem. Snohomish County Camano Bd. Realtors (chmn. 1987-88), Snohomish County C. of C., Hidden Harbor Yacht Club. Republican. Home: 20210 107th Ave NE Bothell WA 98011 Office: Century 21/Champion Realty Ste 201 C 12811 8th Ave W Everett WA 98204-6300

EDWARDS, LUCY HADINOTO, mathematics educator; b. Malang, East Java, Indonesia, Feb. 27, 1963; came to U.S., 1981; d. Usman and Justina Hadinoto; m. Oliver D. Edwards IV, July 9, 1986; 1 child, Keith Alan. BS in Math., Baldwin-Wallace Coll., 1984; MS, Carnegie-Mellon U., 1985. Career cons. Pleasanton, Calif., 1986-88; cost analyst, contract mgmt. NISH, Livermore, Calif., 1988-91; mgr. Discovery Toys, Livermore, 1991—; math. instr. Las Positas Coll., Livermore, Calif., 1988—. Sun. sch. com. mem. St. Bartholomew's Ch., Livermore, 1991-92.

EDWARDS, LYDIA JUSTICE, state official; b. Carter County, Ky., July 9, 1937; d. Chead and Velva (Kinney) Justice; m. Frank B. Edwards, 1968; children: Mark, Alexandra, Margot. Student, San Francisco State U. Began career as acct., then Idaho state rep., 1982-86; treas. State of Idaho, 1987—; legis. asst. to Gov. Hickel, Alaska, 1967; conf. planner Rep. Gov.'s Assn., 1970-73; mem. Rep. Nat. Commn., 1972, del. to nat. conv., 1980. Mem. Rep. Womens Fedn. Congregationalist. Office: State Treas's Office State Capital Bldg Rm 102 Boise ID 83720*

EDWARDS, MARIE BABARE, psychologist; b. Tacoma; d. Nick and Mary (Mardesich) Babare; B.A., Stanford, 1948, M.A., 1949; m. Tilden Hampton Edwards (div.); 1 son, Tilden Hampton Edwards III. Counselor guidance center U. So. Calif., Los Angeles, 1950-52; project coordinator So. Calif. Soc. Mental Hygiene, 1952-54; pub. speaker Welfare Fedn. Los Angeles, 1953-57; field rep. Los Angeles County Assn. Mental Health, 1957-58; intern psychologist UCLA, 1958-60; pvt. practice, human rels. tng., counselor tng. Mem. Calif., Am., Western, Los Angeles psychol. assns., AAAS, So. Calif. Soc. Clin. Hypnosis, Internat. Platform Assn. Author: (with Eleanor Hoover) The Challenge of Being Single, 1974, paperback edit., 1975. Office: 6100 Buckingham Pky Culver City CA 90230-7237

EDWARDS, MARK ROBERT, marketing professional; b. Modesto, Calif., Apr. 4, 1948; s. George Robert and Mary (Bomberger) E.; m. Ann Ewen, Jan. 2, 1993; 1 child, Sarah. BS in Mech. Engring., U.S. Naval Acad., 1970; MBA in Mktg., Ariz. State U., 1972, PhD, 1978. Personnel dir. Greyhound Corp., Phoenix, 1972-76; pres. TEAMS, Inc., Tempe, 1976—; prof. Ariz. State U., Tempe, 1978—. Author: Culture Change Sourcebook, 1991; contbr. articles to profl. jours. Recipient numerous awards for work with handicapped, 1976—. Republican. Presbyterian. Office: Team Evaluation Mgmt System 438 E Southern Ave Tempe AZ 85282-5203

EDWARDS, MICHAEL DAVID, business executive; b. Iromagawa, Japan, Aug. 19, 1955; came to U.S., 1957.; s. John Robert and Virginia (Pemberton) E.; 1 child, Kimberly C. BBA, U. Miami, 1976, MBA, 1977. Stock broker AG Edwards & Sons, Denver, 1979-81; v.p. of investment Drexel Burnham Lambert, Denver, 1981-86; pres., chief exec. officer Pure Bred Co. Inc., Denver and Los Angeles, 1986—; fin. advisor City of Denver, 1986. Vol.

Am. Cancer Soc., 1985, Big Brothers, Miami, 1976. Republican. Presbyterian. Office: Purebred Co Inc PO Box 37122 Denver CO 80237-0122

EDWARDS, PATRICIA BURR, small business owner, counselor, consultant; b. Oakland, Calif., Feb. 19, 1918; d. Myron Carlos and Claire Idelle (Laingor) Burr; m. Jackson Edwards, Nov. 14, 1942; children: Jill Forman-Young, Jan Kurzweil. AB, U. So. Calif., 1939, MSEd, 1981. Prin. Constructive Leisure, L.A., 1968—; speaker, lectr. in field; writer, prodr. counseling materials for career, leisure and life planning. Author: You've Got to Find Happiness: It Won't Find You, 1971, Leisure Counseling Techniques: Individual and Group Counseling Step-by-Step, 1975, 3d edition, 1980; contbr. articles to profl. jours., mags. and books. Active media com. L.A. County Task Force to Promote Self-Esteem and Personal and Social Reponsibitlity, 1988—; chmn. L.A. County Foster Families 50th Anniversary, 1962-64, Hollywood Bowl Vols., L.A., 1952—. Mem. Am. Counseling Assn., Calif. Assn. for Counseling and Devel., Nat. Recreation and Park Assn., Assn. for Adult Devel. and Aging, Trojan League, Travellers Aid Soc. L.A., Jr. League L.A., First Century Families of L.A., Delta Gamma. Republican. Episcopalian.

EDWARDS, PATRICK MICHAEL, sales consultant; b. Burbank, Calif., Sept. 20, 1947; s. Kenneth Charles and Thelma Kay (Allen) E. BS, Calif. Poly State U., 1975. Med. salesperson Burroughs Wellcome Co., Research Triangle Park, N.C., 1975-79; sr. cons. G.D. Searle & Co., Chgo., 1979—. Author photo essay in Ford Times mag., 1989. With USCG, 1968-72. Mem. Assn. of Pharm. Reps. (pres. 1986). Republican. Home and Office: 5341 Parejo Dr Santa Barbara CA 93111

EDWARDS, PAUL ROBERT, writer, speaker; b. Kansas City, Mo., Apr. 11, 1940; s. Milton Willard and Ida Rae Edwards; m. Sarah Anne Glandon, Apr. 24, 1965; 1 child, Jon Scott. BA, U. Mo., Kansas City, 1962, JD, 1965. Bar: Mo. 1965. Assoc. Hutson & Van Horn, Kansas City, 1965-66; pvt. practice Kansas City, 1966-68; coord. intergovtl. rels. Jackson County, Kansas City, 1968-69; urban specialist Inst. Community Studies, Kansas City, 1969-70; pres., CEO Environ. R&D Found., Kansas City, 1970-74; prin. Pub. Affairs Assistance, Kansas City, 1974-76; ptnr. Paul & Sarah Edwards, L.A., 1976—; adminstr. Working From Home Forum, CompuServe Info. Svc., 1983—. Co-author: Working From Home, 1985, 87, 90, The Best Home Businesses for the 90's, 1991, Getting Business to Come to You, 1991, Making It On Your Own: Surviving and Thriving on the Ups and Downs of Being Self-Employed, 1991; contbr. articles to profl. jours.; contbg. editor Home Office Computing mag., 1988—; co-host home office show Bus. Radio Network, Colorado Springs, 1988—. Sec. Citizens Assn., Kansas City, 1973; pres. Westport Community Coun., Kansas City, 1969-71. Named Mo. Outstanding Young Man Mo. Jaycees, 1972; recipient Disting. Svc. award Kansas City Jaycees, 1972. Mem. Computer Press Assn., Mo. Bar (governing coun. young lawyers sect. 1967-68). Office: 2607 2d St Ste 3 Santa Monica CA 90405

EDWARDS, PHYLLIS MAE, accountant, graphologist; b. Wichita, Kans., June 25, 1921; d. William Noble and Nettie Mae (Riggs) Merry; m. Joseph Andrew Edwards, Sept. 19, 1945 (dec.); children: Joseph Noble (dec.), James Richard, Robert Andrew, Jacqueline Merry. Student, Bus. Preparatory Sch., Wichita, Kans., 1939; BA in Journalism, Wichita State U., 1944; grad. advanced graphologist, Sampson Inst. Graphology, 1967; cert. of proficiency, Tao Acupuncture, 1975; D of Graphology Sci., Rocky Mountain Graphology, 1978. Cert. profl. graphologist. Sec., bookkeeper Healy & Co., Wichita, 1939-42, Wichita State U., 1942-43; acct. Moberly & West, Pub. Accts., Wichita, 1943-45, McQuain, Edwards, & Teffs, Oakland, Calif., 1952-55; acct., graphologist Rocky Mountain Graphology Sch., Denver, 1972-81; prin. Multi-Pro Svcs., Denver, 1976—; acct. Indsl. Hard Chrome Plating Co., Denver, 1957—; expert witness for all levels of ct., Colo., Wyo., 1976—; pub. and pvt. speaker, Colo., Wyo., 1976—; sec., treas. Indsl. Hard Chrome Plating Co., Denver, 1990—. Den mother Aurora (Colo.) Cub Scout Troop, 1956-59; asst. troop leader Girl Scouts U.S., Denver, 1960-64; charity fund raiser various churches, schs., and non-profit orgns., 1967—. Mem. AAUW (Denver br. treas. 1975-77, bull. editor 1980-81, 92-93, sec. 1986-88, roster/circulation editor, pres.-elect 1988-90, pres. 1990-92, chair interbr. coun. 1991-92), Am. Handwriting Analysts Found. (Rocky Mountain chpt.), Am. Assn. Handwriting Analysts, Coun. Graphological Socs., Rocky Mountain Graphology Assn. (treas. 1972-81), U. Denver Women's Libr. Assn. Home: 2986 S Fairfax St Denver CO 80222-6841 Office: Indsl Hard Chrome Plating 919 Santa Fe Dr Denver CO 80204-3936

EDWARDS, RALPH M., librarian; b. Shelley, Idaho, Apr. 17, 1933; s. Edward William and Maude Estella (Munsee) E.; m. Winifred Wylie, Dec. 25, 1969; children: Dylan, Nathan, Stephen. B.A., U. Wash., 1957, M.Library, 1960; D.L.S., U. Calif.-Berkeley, 1971. Libr. N.Y. Pub. Libr., N.Y.C., 1960-61; catalog libr. U. Ill. Libr., Urbana, 1961-62; br. libr. Multnomah County Libr., Portland, Oreg., 1964-67; asst. prof. Western Mich. U., Kalamazoo, 1970-74; chief of the Central Libr. Dallas Pub. Libr., 1975-81; city librarian Phoenix Pub. Libr., 1981—. Author: Role of the Beginning Librarian in University Libraries, 1975. U. Calif. doctoral fellow, 1967-70; library mgmt. internship Council on Library Resources, 1974-75. Mem. ALA, Ariz. Library Assn., Pub. Library Assn. Democrat. Home: 4839 E Mulberry Dr Phoenix AZ 85018-6520 Office: Phoenix Pub Libr 12 E Mcdowell Rd Phoenix AZ 85004-1684

EDWARDS, TIMOTHY ERNEST, electronics engineer; b. Sioux City, Iowa, Nov. 8, 1942; s. Robert Ward and Shirley Phyliss (Plummer) E.; m. Ruth Frances Grose, June 29, 1963; children: Robert Sean, Karen Lynn. Electronics engr. S.A.I. Technology, San Diego, 1975-92; enlisted USN, 1960, electronics technician, 1960-74, resigned, 1974. Mem. San Diego Computer Soc. (chmn. Timex/Sinclair group 1984-90), Planetary Soc., Nat. Space Soc./L5.

EDWARDS, WALTER MEAYERS, editor, photographer; b. Leigh-on-Sea, Essex, Eng., July 21, 1908; came to U.S., 1930, naturalized, 1936; s. Walter James and Lillian Emma (Meayers) E.; m. Mary Woodward Worrall, Feb. 11, 1937. Student, Lindisfarne Coll., Westcliff, Essex, Eng., 1917-26. Staff Paris bur. N.Y. Times-Wide World Photos, 1926-27; with Topical Press Agy., London, 1927-29, Harris & Ewing, photographers, Washington, 1930-31; sec.-treas. Pioneer Air Transport Operators Assn., N.Y.C., Washington, 1931-33. Mem. illustrations staff Nat. Geog. mag., 1933-54, illustrations editor, 1955-58, mem. fgn. editorial staff, 1958-62, chief pictorial rsch. div., 1963-73; contbr. articles to Nat. Geog. mag.; contbr. color photographs for Great American Deserts, 1972, America's Beginnings, 1974. Recipient Americanism medal DAR, 1968, Picture of Yr. award Nat. Press Photographers Assn., 1969, 72. Mem. Explorers Club (N.Y.C.), Masons. Christian Scientist. Home: PO Box 1631 Sedona AZ 86339-1631

EDWARDS, WILLIAM MARTIN, computer engineer; b. Fort Hood, Tex., Sept. 2, 1951; s. William M. and Betty Jane (Savage) E.; m. Seiko Endo, Sept. 5, 1972; 1 child, Michiko Ann. BS in Computer Sci./Engring., San Jose State U., 1986. Field svc. engr. BTI Computer Sys., Sunnyvale, Calif., 1979-84; sustaining engr. BTI Computer Sys., 1984-85; mfg. engr. Momentum Computer Sys., Fremont, Calif., 1985; applications engr. Mitsubishi Internat. Corp., Fremont, 1985-88; engring. mgr. Tescon America, Inc., Milpitas, Calif., 1988—. With USAF, 1970-79. Office: Tescon American Inc 1597 Mccandless Dr Milpitas CA 95035-8001

EDWARDSEN, KENNETH ROBERT, administrator; b. Bklyn., Mar. 23, 1934; s. Erling Christian and Hulda (Samuelson) E.; m. Henrietta Day, June 7, 1981. BA, Western Mich. U.; postgrad., Mich. State U. Exec. dir. United Cerebral Palsy of Akron and Summit County, Ohio, 1969-72; dir. resources Lung Assn., L.A., 1972-74; dir. devel. and pub. rels. Hawthorne (Calif.) Communtiy Hosp., 1974-81; dir. devel. Medic Alert Found. Internat., Turlock, Calif., 1981-82; dir. devel. Sansum Med. Rsch. Found., Santa Barbara, Calif., 1982-83, exec. dir., 1983—; radio announcer Sta. WMUS AM/FM, Muskegon, Mich. Writer, photographer, corr. Akron (Ohio) Beacon Jour. Min. Empire Meth. Ch., Empire and Traverse City, Mich.; publicity dir. March of Dimes, Wooster, Ohio; dir. youth svcs. for summers YMCA, bd. dirs., bd. mental health; speaker fund-raising seminars and confs. Recipient Svc. award-Community Leader of Am. award YMCA, 1969-70. Mem. NEA, Mich. Edn. Assn., Ohio Edn. Assn., Nat. Schs. Pub. Rels. Assn., N.Y. Inst. of Photography, Assn. of Profl. Workers, Rotary Internat., Calif. Soc. of Fund Raising Execs., Nat. Soc. of Fund Raising Execs. (cert., pres. Santa Barbara/Ventura counties chpt., Outstanding Fund Raiser of Yr. 1987), So. Calif. Pub. Health Assn., Nat. and State Assn. of Hosp. Devel. Dirs., Elks, Cen. Calif. Assn. of Fundraising Execs. (pres.), L.A. Press Club, Hollywood Press Club, Nat. Assn. of Rsch. Affiliates, Nat. Vol. Assn., Nat. Assn. of Non-Profits, Tau Kappa Alpha (pres.). Home: 227 Remington Ventura CA 93003 Office: Sansum Med Rsch Found 2219 Bath St Santa Barbara CA 93105-4321

EFFORD, MICHAEL ROBERT, police administrator, educator; b. L.A., July 22, 1950; s. Robert Victor and Mary (Athens) E.; m. Jolene Lynn Buttner, Mar. 20, 1976 (dec. Jan. 1980); m. Patricia Ann Jones, Feb. 2, 1985; children: Stacy Anne, Ashley Elizabeth. AA in Criminal Justice, Western Nev. Community Coll., 1976; BA in Bus., Calif. Coast U., 1990, postgrad., 1990-92. Trooper Nev. Hwy. Patrol, Las Vegas, 1976-80; law instr. Western Nev. Community Coll., Carson City, 1980—; adminstrv. lt. Carson City Sheriff's Dept., 1972—; instr. Reno Police Acad., 1980—, Nev. Hwy. Patrol Acad., Carson City, 1980—. Editor C.C.S.S.A. newsletter, 1989—. Pres. Carson City Labor Coalition, 1992—, planning commr. Regional Planning Commn., Carson City, 1989—; chmn. Mainstreet/Redevelopment Authority Carson City, 1991—; mem. Nev. Day com., Carson City, 1985—, 4th of July com., Carson City, 1985—, Gov.'s Ball com., Carson City, 1985—. Sgt. U.S. Army, 1970-73. Recipient Svc. award Carson City Bd. Suprs., 1984. Mem. AFL-CIO Police Assn. (pres. 1989—), Sertoma. Democrat. Roman Catholic. Home: 1839 Panaca Dr Carson City NV 89701

EFIMOV, VITALY, physics educator; b. St. Petersburg, Russia, Dec. 10, 1938; came to U.S., 1989; s. Nicholas and Nina (Lifshits) E.; m. Betsy Rappoport, Jan. 22, 1966 (div. July 1975); 1 child, Inna; m. Albina Kuznetsova Shabelsky, Nov. 18, 1983; 1 child, Vladislav Shabelsky. BS in Radio Engring. with honors, Leningrad Elec. Engring. Inst., 1962; PhD in Theoretical Physics, Ioffe Physico-Tech. Inst., Leningrad, 1966; D Theoretical Physics, Leningrad Nuclear Physics Inst., 1976. Cert. theoretical and math. physics sr. scientist. Jr. scientist Ioffe Physico-Tech. Inst., 1962-71; sr. scientist Leningrad Nuclear Physics Inst., 1971-89; vis. prof. U. Minn., Mpls., 1989-90; sr. rsch. fellow Calif. Inst. Tech., Pasadena, 1990; lectr. physics, scientist U. Wash., Seattle, 1990—; lectr. Soc. for Dissemination Sci. Knowledge, St. Petersburg, 1977-84; mem. coun. Sci. Coun. on Nuclear Physics, Acad. Sci., Moscow, 1981-89. Contbr. articles to sci. jours. Mem. Am. Phys. Soc. Home: 1210 NE 41st St # D Seattle WA 98105 Office: U Wash Dept Physics FM-15 Seattle WA 98195

EGAN, CHERYL COBB, advertising executive; b. San Francisco, Oct. 30, 1960; d. Howard Jeff and Anne (Morris) Cobb; m. David Tureman Egan II, Apr. 19, 1986; children: Beverly Anne, Samuel David. BA in TV and Radio, San Francisco State U., 1982. Prodn. coord. DJMC Advt., San Francisco, 1982-83, prodn. mgr., 1984-85; dir. prodn. svcs. DBC Advt., San Francisco, 1985—, account supr., 1990—. Producer: (TV commls.) McDonald's "Nice Randy Cross", 1985 (Addy 1985), Toyota Dealers "Wrap It Up", 1986 (Addy 1986), L.A. Earthquake Preparedness, 1986-87 (Joey award 1986, Houston Internat. Film Fest award 1986, Internat. Film and TV Festival, N.Y., 1986, Nat. Telly, 1986), Northwest Toyota Dealers"4x4s", 1987 (Nat. Telly 1988), Marine World Africa USA "Journey/Calling/Balls, 1988 (Internat. Film and TV Festival, N.Y., 1988), Marine World Africa USA/commls., 1988 (Nat. Telly awards 1989). Mem. San Francisco Ad Club, Film Arts Found., Bay Area Video Coalition, Bay Area S.T.A.R., Advt. Print Prodn. Assn., P.E.O., Alphi Chi Omega. Office: DBC Advt 731 Market St Fl 6 San Francisco CA 94103-2002

EGAN, JAMES TIMOTHY, regulatory-environmental management executive; b. Milw., Nov. 5, 1946; s. James Herbert and Dorothy Elenor (Krause) E.; m. Rosemary Elaine Cunningham, July 17, 1971; children: Ryan James, Erin Elizabeth. BSCE, U. Wis., Platteville, 1969; MSCE, Loyola U., L.A., 1975. Registered profl. engr., water and waste water operator, Calif., Colo. Civil and sanitary engr. City of L.A., 1969-79; div. supt. Wastewater Divsn., Utilities Dept., Colorado Springs, Colo., 1979-91; pres. Regulatory Mgmt., Inc., Colorado Springs, 1991—. Author: Regulatory Management, 1991; co-author: Toxic Substances in Municipal Wastewater, 1992; contbg. author: Handbook of Cholorination, 1986. Del. water pollution control del. to China, People to People Internat., 1986. Mem. Water Environ. Fedn. (com. chair rsch. coun. 1989—), Calif. Water Pollution Control Assn. (Gerson Chanin award 1977), Rocky Mountain Water Pollution Control Assn., Am. Acad. Environ. Engrs. (diplomate). Office: Regulatory Mgmt Inc 6190 Lehman Dr Ste 106 Colorado Springs CO 80918

EGAN, JOHN TINNERMAN, rancher; b. Cleve., May 18, 1948; s. Robert Brooks and Elisabeth Neubauer (Tinnerman) E.; children: Joseph Clinton, Elisabeth Lindsay Jane; m. Deborah Anne Montoya, Oct. 12, 1986. BA, Loretto Heights Coll., 1973; BA (hon.), Coll. Santa Fe, 1982. Pres., gen. mgr. Rancho Encantado, Santa Fe, 1968-83, owner, mgr., 1983—; chmn. Encantado Mgmt., Santa Fe, 1985-92. Author: The Present, 1973. Bd. dirs. Symphony Santa Fe, 1986-88; pres. N.Mex. North, Santa Fe, 1982; mem. 375th Anniversary Commn., Sante Fe City Coun. Dist. 2, 1986-90. Named One of Outstanding Young Men of Am., U.S. Jaycees, 1984, Outstanding New Mexican, N.Mex. Jaycees, 1988. Mem. Santa Fe Lodgers Assn. (pres. 1981), N.Mex. Amigos, Santa Fe C. of C. (pres. 1986—, Dir. Yr. award 1982). Republican. Methodist. Club: Santa Fe Country. Lodge: Eagles. Office: Rancho Encantado Inc RR 4 Box 57C Santa Fe NM 87501-9804

EGAN, SISTER M. ELLENE, nursing educator; b. San Francisco, July 3, 1946; d. James Leo and Thelma (Hennig) E. BA, Russell Coll., 1969; BS, U. San Francisco, 1971; MS, Loma Linda U., 1979; EdD, U. San Francisco, 1989. RN, Calif.; cert. Pub. Health Nurse; joined Sisters of Mercy, Roman Catholic Ch., 1964. Staff nurse Mercy Hosp. & Med. Ctr., San Diego, 1971-72, staff developer, 1972-75, nursing supr., 1975-77; prof. nursing U. San Francisco, 1979—. Bd. dirs. Mercy Hosp., Bakersfield, Calif. 1980-83, Mercy Retirement and Care Ctr., Oakland, Calif., 1983-89. Mem. ANA, Calif. Nurses Assn. (del. 1983—, bd. dirs. region 12 1981, 86, 90—, bylaws and awards com. 1987-89, 1990-92, Cert. Appreciation, 1978, 89, 91), Univ San Francisco Faculty Assn. (treas. 1988—), Sigma Theta Tau (treas. Beta Gamma chpt. 1986-88), Sisters of Mercy. Republican. Home: 3250 19th Ave San Francisco CA 94132 Office: Univ San Francisco Ignatian Heights San Francisco CA 94117-1080

EGAN, SUSAN CHAN, security analyst; b. Manila, Feb. 11, 1946; came to U.S., 1969; d. Mariano Sui Ming and Rita Patricia (Quejong) Chan; m. Ronald Christopher Egan, Mar. 22, 1971; 1 child, Louisa. BA in Chinese Lang. and Lit., U. Wash., 1970; MBA, Boston U., 1981; MA in Comparative Lit., U. Wash., 1971. Chartered Fin. Analyst. Bus. counselor Local Devel. Corp. of South End, Boston, 1973-74; cons. Boston, 1974-76; dir. edn. and tng. Mass. Dept. Commerce and Devel., Boston, 1976-79, program devel. cons., 1979-81; trust investment officer State St. Bank and Trust Co., Boston, 1981-83, sr. trust investment officer, 1983-86, v.p., 1986-87; v.p. Scudder, Stevens & Clark, L.A., 1987—. Author: Coping With Utility Bills and Other Enegry Costs, 1971, How to Do Business with the State, 1980, New Business, 1981, A Latterday Confucian, 1987, Hung Yeh Chuan, 1992. Mem. Assn. for Investment Mgmt. and Rsch., L.A. Soc. Fin. Analysts. Home: 921 W Campus Ln Santa Barbara CA 93117-4341 Office: Scudder Stevens & Clark 333 S Hope St Los Angeles CA 90071-3003

EGER, MARILYN RAE, artist; b. Offett A.F.B., Nebr., Jan. 2, 1953; d. John W. and Joyce Faye (Carpenter) Shaver, stepmother Myrle I. MAsoner; m. Darrell W. Masoner, Feb. 28, 1971 (div. Sept. 1977); children: William Matthew, Melissa Rae; m. Gerard J. Eger, Jan. 30, 1982. BA, Calif. State U., Turlock, 1987. Cert. art tchr. 1990, Calif., lang. devel. specialist, 1993. Freelance artist oil painting Gibson Greetings Inc., Cin.; tchr. art and ceramics Bear Creek High Sch., Stockton, Calif.; tchr. art privately. One-woman shows include Stockton Fine Arts Gallery, 1984-88, Accurate Art Gallery, Sacramento, 1989-90, Sharon Gile Gallery, Isleton, Calif., 1988-91, Le Galerie, Stockton, 1989-91, Masterpiece Gallery, Carmel, Calif., 1991—, Alan Short Gallery, Stockton, 1991; represented in permanent collections Gulf Oil Chemicals, Kaiser Permanent, Masterpiece Gallery; prints published in Mus. Edits. West. Bd. dirs. Lodi Art Ctr., 1988-91, chmn. 1989. Recipient award of Excellence, Unitarian Fall Art Festival, 1990, Bank Stockton award & H.M. Haggin Mus., 1989, U.S. Nat. Collegiate Art Merit award, 1988, Lodi 31st Annual, 1st Oils, 1988, award of Excellence Oils Unitarian Fall Art Festival, 1992, award of Excellence Pastel Haggin Mus., 1992, 1st Oils and Don Morrell Meml. award CCAL Gallo Show, 1993. Mem. C.A.E.A., Stockton Art League, Nat. League Am. Pen. Women, West Coast Pastel Soc., Calif. Art League, Ctrl. Calif. Art League. Republican. Methodist.

EGGERS, RICHARD HOWELL, consumer products executive; b. N.Y.C., Sept. 12, 1938; s. William Richard and Evelyn Louise (Howell) E.; m. Linda Ada, June 30, 1962; children: Carolyn Baiden, Diane Elizabeth. BA, Williams Coll., 1960; MBA, Columbia U., 1962. Account exec. BBDO Advt. Agy., N.Y.C., 1962-65, Norman, Craig & Kummel Advt., N.Y.C., 1966-67; group product dir. Warner-Lambert Co., Morris Plains, N.J., 1967-75; v.p. mktg., gen. mgr. Shulton Internat. div. Am. Cyanamid, Wayne, N.J., 1976-83, gen. mgr. Lederle Pharm. Internat. div., 1984-88; v.p., gen. mgr. Internat. div., mem. exec. bd. Teledyne Waterpik Co., Fort Collins, Colo., 1988—. Treas., vestryman St. Davids Ch., Kinnelon, N.J., 1971-74; bd. dirs. Smoke Rise Community Club, Kinnelon, 1980-81. With U.S. Army, 1962-68. Lutheran. Office: Teledyne Water Pik 1730 E Prospect Rd Fort Collins CO 80525-1334

EGGERT, KAREN MCMAHAN, army officer; b. Elizabethtown, Ky., Sept. 23, 1959; d. Ernest and Virginia Lee (Coakley) McMahan; m. Steven F. Eggert, Nov. 23, 1988. B. Gen. Sci., U. Ky., 1983; postgrad., Golden Gate U., 1985—. Commd. 2d lt. U.S. Army, 1983, advanced through grades to capt., 1987; intelligence officer 501st Mil. Intelligence Bn., Yongsan, Seoul, Republic of Korea, 1985-86; spl. security officer 25th infantry divsn. (L), Schofield Barracks, Hawaii, 1986-88; counterintelligence officer 45th Support Group, Schofield Barracks, 1988-90; bn. S3 officer 902d Mil. Intelligence Bn., Presidio of San Francisco, Calif., 1991-92; detachment exec. officer 902d Mil. Intelligence Detachment, Presidio of San Francisco, 1992—. Vol. Nat. Park Svc., Presidio of San Francisco, 1991—, Gov.'s Coun. on Litter Control, Honolulu, 1988-90; reporter Indsl. Security Adv. Com., San Jose, Calif., 1991—; mem. Tiburon (Calif.) Bapt. Ch., 1991—. Decorated Army Commendation medal, Army Achievement medal. Mem. Am. Soc. for Indsl. Security. Republican. Office: 902d Mil Intelligence Bn (CI) (S) Bldg 1201 The Presidio San Francisco CA 94129

EGGERT, ROBERT JOHN, SR., economist; b. Little Rock, Dec. 11, 1913; s. John and Eleanora (Fritz) Lapp; m. Elizabeth Bauer, Nov. 28, 1935; children: Robert John, Richard F., James E. BS, U. Ill., 1935, MS, 1936; candidate in philosophy, U. Minn., 1938; LHD (hon.), Ariz. State U., 1988. Research analyst Bur. Agrl. Econs., U.S. Dept. Agr., Urbana, Ill., 1935; prin. marketing specialist War Meat Bd., Chgo., 1943; research analyst U. Ill., 1935-36; rsch. analyst U. Minn., 1936-38; asst. prof. econs. Kans. State Coll., 1938-41; asst. dir. marketing Am. Meat Inst., Chgo., 1941-43; economist, assoc. dir. Am. Meat Inst., 1943-50; mgr. dept. marketing research Ford div. Ford Motor Co., Dearborn, Mich., 1951-53; mgr. program planning Ford div. Ford Motor Co., 1953-54, mgr. bus. research, 1954-57, mgr. marketing research marketing staff, 1957-61; mgr. marketing research Ford div. Ford Motor Co. (Ford div.), 1961-64, mgr. internat. marketing research marketing staff, 1964-65, mgr. overseas marketing research planning, 1965-66; mgr. marketing research Ford div. Ford Motor Co. (Lincoln-Mercury div.), 1966-67; dir. agribus. programs Mich. State U., 1967-68; staff v.p. econ. and marketing research RCA Corp., N.Y.C., 1968-76; pres., chief economist Eggert Econ. Enterprises, Inc., Sedona, Ariz., 1976—; lectr. mktg. U. Chgo., 1947-49; adj. prof. bus. forecasting No. Ariz. U., 1976—; mem. econ. adv. bd. U.S. Dept. Commerce, 1969-71, mem. census adv. com., 1975-78; mem. panel econ. advisers Congl. Budget Office, 1975-76; interim dir. Econ. Outlook Ctr. Coll. Bus. Adminstrn. Ariz. State U., Tempe, 1985-86, cons., 1985—; mem. Econ. Estimates Commn. Ariz., 1979—; apptd. Ariz. Gov.'s Commn. Econ. Devel., 1991—; bd. trustees Marcus J. Lawrence Med. Ctr. Found., 1992—. Contbr. articles to profl. lit.; editor: monthly Blue Chip Econ. Indicators, 1976—; exec. editor Ariz. Blue Chip, 1984—, Western Blue Chip Econ. Forecast, 1986—. Elder Ch. of Red Rocks. Recipient Econ. Forecast award Chgo. chpt. Am. Statis. Assn., 1950, 60, 68; Seer of Yr. award Harvard Bus. Sch. Indsl. Econs., 1973. Mem. Coun. Internat. Mktg. Rsch. and Planning Dirs. (chmn. 1965-66), Am. Mktg. Assn. (dir., v.p. 1949-50, pres. Chgo. chpt. 1947-48, v.p. mktg. mgmt. div. 1972-73, nat. pres. 1974-75), Am. Statis. Assn. (chmn. bus. and econ. stats. sect. 1957—, pres. Chgo. chpt. 1948-49), Fed. Stats. Users Conf. (chmn. trustees 1960-61), Conf. Bus. Economists (chmn. 1973-74), Am. Quarter Horse Assn. (dir. 1966-73), Nat. Assn. Bus. Economists (coun. 1969-72), Alpha Zeta, Ariz. Econ. Roundtable, Am. Econs. Assn., Phoenix Econ. Club (hon.), Ariz. C. of C. (bd. dirs.). Republican. Club: Poco Diablo Country. Office: Eggert Econ Enterprises Inc PO Box 2243 Sedona AZ 86339-2243

EGGERTSEN, FRANK THOMAS, research chemist; b. Provo, Utah, Mar. 26, 1913; s. Burton Simon and Anne (Thomas) E.; m. Beth Marie Krueger, Dec. 29, 1939; children: Karl F., Thomas K., Grace Ann. BA, U. Utah, 1934; PhD, U. Minn., 1939. Rsch. chemist Sherwin-Williams Co., Chgo., 1939-43, Shell Devel. Co., Emeryville, Calif., 1943-72; prin. rsch. scientist Calif. Ink Co. div. Flint Ink Corp., Berkeley, Calif., 1973-90; cons. Flint Ink Corp., Berkeley, 1990—. Contbr. articles to profl. jours.; patentee in field. Shevlin fellow U. Minn., 1938-39. Mem. Am. Chem. Soc., Sigma Xi, Phi Lambda Upsilon, Phi Kappa Phi. Democrat. Mormon. Home: 3710 W 6800 S Spanish Fork UT 84660

EGGMAN, JACK RAY, artist; b. Tucson, Ariz., Nov. 5, 1954; s. Arthur Dale and Joyce Mae (Glascock) E.; m. Barbara Ann Boscoe, Jan. 1, 1986 (div. Feb. 1987). Student, Pima C.C., Tucson, 1975-78. Artist (mono prints) Phoenix Art Press, 1982-85, Telo's Graphic's Pubs., Tempe, Ariz., 1985-87, 89—, Orgins Press Pubs., Tucson, 1986-89; artist (painter) Impression Gallery, Tucson, 1986-91; Exhibited in group shows at L.A. Art Expo, 1989, 90, N.Y. Art Expo, N.Y.C., 1990, 91; artist invention copper inlay mono print Copper Ponys, 1983. With U.S. Army, 1972-75. Home: 3307 N Flanwil Blvd Tucson AZ 85716

EGLEY, THOMAS ARTHUR, computer services executive, accountant; b. Aberdeen, S.D., June 23, 1945; s. Ralph Joseph and Cora Ellen (Wade) E.; m. Cecelia K. Kuskie, Feb. 22, 1985. BBA, U. Mont., 1967, postgrad., 1973-75. CPA, Mont. Programmer, analyst Comml. Data, Missoula, Mont., 1973-77; data processing mgr. John R. Daily, Inc., Missoula, 1977-78; ptnr. Egley & White CPA's, Missoula, 1978-84, Egley & White Computer Services, Missoula, 1978-85; pres. Able Fin., Inc., Missoula, 1984—, PC Software, Inc., 1987—, E & W Computer Services, Inc., 1983—; lectr., Missoula, 1973—. Bd. dirs. Missoula Children's Theater, 1975-82. Served to sgt. U.S. Army, 1968-71. Mem. Am. Inst. CPAs, Mont. Soc. CPAs, Inst. Mgmt. Accts., Phi Sigma Kappa Alumni Club (pres. 1973—). Republican. Lutheran. Lodge: Elks. Home and Office: E&W Computer Svcs Inc PO Box 2729 Missoula MT 59806-2729

EGUCHI, YASU, artist; b. Japan, Nov. 30, 1938; came to U.S., 1967; s. Chihaku and Kiku (Koga) E.; m. Anita Phillips, Feb. 24, 1968. Student, Horie Art Acad., Japan, 1958-65. Exhibited exhbns., Tokyo Mus. Art, 1963, 66, Santa Barbara Mus. Art, Calif., 1972, 73, 74, 85, Everson Mus. Art, Syracuse, N.Y., 1980, Nat. Acad. Design, N.Y.C., 1980—, one-man shows, Austin Gallery, Scottsdale, Ariz., 1968-87, Joy Tash Gallery, Scottsdale, 1989—, Greyston Galleries, Cambria, Calif., 1969, 70, 72, Copenhagen Galleries, Calif., 1970-78, Charles and Emma Frye Art Mus., Seattle, 1974, 84, Hammer Galleries, N.Y.C., 1977, 79, 81, 93, City of Heidenheim, W. Ger., 1980, Artique Ltd., Anchorage, 1981—; pub. and pvt. collections, Voith Gmbh, W. Ger., City of Giengen and City of Heidenheim, Fed. Republic Germany, represented, Deer Valley, Utah, Hunter Resources, Santa Barbara, Am. Embassy, Paris, Charles and Emma Frye Art Mus., Seattle, Nat. Acad. Design, N.Y.C.; author: Der Brenz Entlang, 1980; contbr. to jours in field. Active Guide Dogs for the Blind, San Raphael, Calif., 1976; active City of Santa Barbara Arts Council, 1979, The Eye Bank for Sight Restoration, N.Y., 1981, Anchorage Arts Council, 1981, Santa Barbara Mus. Natural History, 1989. Recipient Selective artist award Yokohama Citizen Gallery, 1965; recipient Artist of Yr. award Santa Barbara Arts Council, 1979, Hon. Citizen award City of Heidenheim, 1980, The Adolph and Clara Obrig prize NAD, 1983, Cert. of Merit NAD, 1985, 87. Home: PO Box 30206 Santa Barbara CA 93130-0206

EHLE, ROBERT CANNON, music educator; b. Lancaster, Pa., Nov. 7, 1939; s. George Escott and Betty Ruth (Cannon) E.; m. Linda Kay Caudle, July 19, 1965; 1 child, Robert Todd. MusB, Eastman Sch., 1961; MusM, U. North Tex., 1970, PhD, 1970. Teaching asst. U. North Tex., Denton, 1965-70; instr. Denver Inst. Tech., 1970-71; prof. music U. No. Colo., Greeley, 1971—. Sgt. U.S. Army, 1961-64. Mem. ASCAP (Composition awards 1971—). Home: 2107 26th Avenue Ct Greeley CO 80631-6618 Office: U No Colo Sch of Music Greeley CO 80639

EHLER, KENNETH WALTER, chemist; b. Chgo., June 9, 1946; s. Walter Max and Irma Mae (Stout) E. BS summa cum laude, Ariz. State U., 1968; PhD, U. Ariz., 1972. Rsch. assoc. Swiss Fed. Inst. Tech., Zurich, Switzerland, 1972-73, ICN Nucleic Acid Rsch. Inst., Irvine, Calif., 1973-74, The Salk Inst., San Diego, 1974-76; organic chemist U. Calif., San Francisco, 1976-77; rsch. assoc. U. Nev., Reno, 1977-83; rsch. asst. prof. U. Nev. Sch. Medicine, Reno, 1983-86; rsch. assoc. U. Ariz., Tucson, 1986-88, Carnegie Mellon U., Mellon Inst., Pitts., 1988-89; chemist Molecular Probes Inc., Eugene, Oreg., 1989—; vol. science tchr. Jamilian Parochial Sch., Reno, 1979-84. Contbr. articles to profl. jours. Vol. fund raiser Pub. radio Sta. KUNR, Reno, 1985-86, vol. announcer, 1986; vol. fund raiser Pub. radio, TV KUAT, Tucson, 1986-88, pub. radio stas. KWAX, KLCC, Eugene, 1990—. Predoctoral fellow NIH, U. Ariz., 1968-72; postdoctoral fellow NIH, Zurich, 1972-73; rsch. grantee Epilepsy Found. Am. U. Nev. Sch. Medicine, 1984-85. Mem. Am. Peptide Soc., Action Linkage. Democrat. Office: Molecular Probes Inc 4849 Pitchford Ave Eugene OR 97402-0414

EHLER, LESTER ERVIN, entomology educator; b. Slaton, Tex., Jan. 3, 1946. BS, Tex. Tech U., 1968; PhD, U. Calif., Berkeley, 1972. Asst. prof. Tex. A&M U., College Station, 1972-73; asst. prof. U. Calif., Davis, 1973-79, assoc. prof., 1979-85, prof., 1985—. Office: U Calif Dept Entomology Davis CA 95616

EHLER, RICHARD LEE, advertising executive, publisher, consultant; b. Holywood, Kans., July 11, 1930; s. John and Katie Anna (Schmidt) E.; m. Sharon K. DePue, 1959 (div. Apr. 1981); 1 child, Quinton John; m. Barbara J. Decker (div. May 1984). BS in Tech. Journalism, Kans. State U., 1952. Mgr. tech. communications GE, 1955-63; supr. tech. communications Motorola, Phoenix, 1963-64; account exec. Lennen & Newell Inc., San Francisco, 1964-65; v.p. Chace Co. Advt. Inc, Santa Barbara, Calif., 1965-72; account exec. Larson/Bateman Inc., Santa Barbara, 1972-79; owner Richler & Co., Santa Barbara, 1979—. Author: The Print Media Planning Manual, 1991, Directory of Print Media Advertising Resources, Print Media Analysis Tools, Checklists for Print Media Advertising Planning and Buying, 1991. Staff sgt. U.S. Army, 1952-54. Mem. Internat. Assn. of Ind. Pubs., Pubs. Mktg. Assn., Santa Barbara Advt. Club (bd. dir. 1970), Soc. of Tech. Communications (sr., nat. 1963-72), Screenwriters Assn. of Santa Barbara, Toastmasters Internat. (ATM cert. 1984), Elks. Republican. Mem. Unity Ch.

EHLERS, ELEANOR MAY COLLIER (MRS. FREDERICK BURTON EHLERS), civic worker; b. Klamath Falls, Oreg., Apr. 23, 1920; d. Alfred Douglas and Ethel (Foster) Collier; BA, U. Oreg., 1941; secondary tchrs. credentials Stanford, 1942; m. Frederick Burton Ehlers, June 26, 1943; children: Frederick Douglas, Charles Collier. Tchr., Salinas Union High Sch., 1942-43; piano tchr. pvt. lessons, Klamath Falls, 1958—. Mem. Child Guidance Adv. Coun., 1956-60; mem. adv. com. Boys and Girls Aid Soc., 1965-67; mem. Gov.'s Adv. Com. Arts and Humanities, 1966-67; bd. mem. PBS TV Sta. KSYS, 1988-92, Friends of Mus. U. Oreg., 1966-69, Arts in Oreg., 1966-68, Klamath County Colls. for Oreg.'s Future, 1968—; co-chmn. Friends of Collier Park, Collier Park Logging Mus., 1986-88, sec. 1988—; chpt. pres. Am. Field Svc., 1962-63; mem. Gov.'s Com. Governance of Community Colls., 1967; bd. dirs. Favell Mus. Western Art and Artifacts, 1971-80, Community Concert Assn., 1950—, pres., 1966-74; established Women's Guild at Merle West Med. Ctr., 1965, sec. bd. dirs, 1962-65, 76-90, bd. dirs., 1962—, mem. bldg. com. 1962-67, mem. planning com., chmn. edn. and rsch. com. hosp. bd., 1967—; pres., bd. dirs. Merle West Med. Ctr., 1990-92, vice chmn., 1992—. Named Woman of Month Klamath Herald News, 1965; named grant to Oreg. Endowed Fellowship Fund, AAUW, 1971; recipient greatest Svc. award Oreg. Tech. Inst., 1970-71, Internat. Woman of Achievement award Quota Club, 1981, U. Oreg. Pioneer award, 1981. Mem. AAUW (local pres. 1955-56), Oreg. Music Tchrs. Assn. (pres. Klamath Basin dist. 1979-81), P.E.O. (Oreg. dir. 1968-75, state pres. 1974-75, trustee internat. Continuing Edn. Fund 1977-83, chmn. 1981-83), Friends of Collier State Park Logging Mus. (sec. 1988—), Pi Beta Phi, Mu Phi Epsilon, Pi Lambda Theta. Presbyterian. Home: 1338 Pacific Terr Klamath Falls OR 97601

EHLERS, WILLIAM ALBERT, psychiatrist; b. Marshall, Minn., Feb. 2, 1942; s. Millard Earl and Doris Sylva (Wall) E. BA cum laude, St. Olaf Coll., 1964; MD, U. Chgo., 1968. Rotating intern U. Oreg. Med. Sch., Portland, 1968-69; resident in psychiatry U. B.C. Med. Sch., Vancouver, Can., 1971-72, U. Oreg. Med. Sch., Portland, 1972-75; pvt. practice, Portland, 1975-86; staff psychiatrist Western State Hosp., Ft. Steilacoom, Wash., 1986—; past cons. mental health ctrs. Mem. ch. coun. Trinity Luth. Ch., Tacoma, Wash., 1989-91. Mem. AAAS, Am. Psychiat. Assn., Am. Acad. Child Psychiatry, Audubon Soc., Tacoma Astron. Soc., Cornell Lab. Ornithology, Mensa. Office: Western State Hosp 9601 Steilacoom Blvd SW Fort Steilacoom WA 98494

EHRHART, STEVEN E., professional sports team executive; m. Mary Ehrhart; children: Ryan, Brandon. BS, Colo. Coll., 1969; JD, U. Colo., 1972. Bar: Colo. Sports atty., 1972-82; off counsel Chrisman, Bynum & Johnson, Boulder, Colo.; legal counsel then exec. dir. U.S. Football League, 1982-84, pres., gen. mgr., co-owner Memphis Showboats franchise, 1984; now pres. Colo. Rockies Profl. Baseball Team, Denver; asst. football coach U. Colo.; commr. World Basketball League; bd. dirs. Liberty Bowl; active Colo. Fed. Jud. Selection Commn. Bd. dirs. Memphis YMCA, Memphis Devel. Found., chmn. Long Range Planning com.; former bd. dirs. Memphis Boys Club, Memphis Conv. and Visitors Bur.; chmn. Leadership Memphis; mem. selection bd. Boettcher Found., Denver. Recipient NCAA Scholar-Athlete Post-grad. scholarship U. Colo. Sch. Law. Mem. Colo. Coll. Alumni Assn. Office: Colorado Rockies 1700 Broadway Ste 2100 Denver CO 80290

EHRHORN, JEAN HELEN, library administrator; b. Cottage Grove, Oreg., Sept. 2, 1943; d. Wayne M. and Grace A. (Grimes) Monroe; m. Charles A. Ehrhorn, June 18, 1965; 1 child, Ericka J. BA, U. Oreg., 1965, MLS, 1968; MBA, U. Hawaii, 1986. Catalog libr. Cornell U., Ithaca, N.Y., 1972-74; head reprography U. Hawaii Libr., Honolulu, 1974-78, asst. to univ. libr., 1978-87, assoc. univ. libr., 1987—. Mem. ALA, Women in Acad. Adminstrn., Libr. Adminstrs. and Mgmt. Assn. Office: U Hawaii Libr 2550 The Mall Honolulu HI 96822

EHRINGER, ANN GRAHAM, business executive, real estate broker, management consultant; b. Cass City, Mich., Aug. 14, 1938; d. John Lakin Zemke and Madelyn Mary (Muck) Beaudry; m. Otis L. Graham, Jr., Sept. 9, 1959 (div. June 1981); children: Lakin Graham Crane, Wade Livingston Graham; m. Albert Thomas Ehringer Jr., Aug. 27, 1986. BA, U. Hawaii, 1960; MA, Stanford U., 1967; Owner Pres. Mgmt. Program, Harvard U., 1982; PhD, U. So. Calif., 1992. Real estate broker, Calif. V.p. Greentree Realty, Inc., Santa Barbara, Calif., 1976-78, The Littlestone Co., Santa Barbara, 1978-80; pres., chief exec. officer Montec, Inc., Santa Barbara, 1980-82; pres., chief oper. officer Grand Am. Inc., Santa Monica, Calif., 1982-85, vice chmn., 1985—, also bd. dirs.; exec. group chmn. The Exec. Com., San Diego, 1990—; bd. dirs. Ocean Park Restaurant Corp., Santa Monica. Contbr. articles to profl. publs. Mem. exec. com. Pepperdine U. Assoc. Bd., Malibu, Calif., 1988-92; bd. dirs. Mountains Restoration Trust, Malibu, 1989—, Malibu Rd. Property Owners Assn., Malibu, 1990—, Cabal Malibu, 1990—; mem. Malibu Twp. Coun. Grad. fellow Danforth Found., 1965-67. Mem. Jr. League Santa Barbara, Harvard Club L.A., Stanford Club L.A. Democrat. Home: 24402 Malibu Rd Malibu CA 90265 Office: Grand Am Inc 2929 Washington Blvd Marina Del Rey CA 90292

EHRINGER, MARTHA LUCY MILLER, public relations executive; b. Decatur, Ill., Dec. 16, 1940; d. Robert Archie and Kathryn Mae (Reinhart) Miller; m. John Currie Schwarm, Nov. 24, 1962 (dec. 1969); children: Walter Palmer, Carl Robert; m. William Joseph Ehringer, Oct. 31, 1973. BA, Northwestern U., 1962; student, Coll. of William & Mary, 1958-60. Owner San Francisco Bay Co., San Francisco, La Jolla, Calif., 1975-81; placement coord. and housing dir. Calif. Western Sch. of Law, San Diego, 1986-88, asst. dir. devel., 1988-89, dir. pub. rels., 1989—; profl. mime, San Diego, San Francisco, 1981—. Mem. com. San Diego Zoo Ritz Benefit, 1990—; bd. dirs. Las Patronas, San Diego, 1983-87, adv. mem., 1988—; bd. dirs. Fair Housing Coun. of San Diego, The Support Ctr., 1992—; vice chair San Diego County Fair Housing Task Force, 1991; pres. 3's Co., 1990-91; vol. Mingei Internat. Mus.; charter mem. Achievement Rewards for Coll. Scientists (ARCS) San Diego chpt. Mem. Pub. Rels. Club San Diego, Nat. Soc. Fund Raising Execs. (bd. dirs. 1992—). Home: PO Box 2934 La Jolla CA 92038-2934 Office: Calif Western Sch Law 350 Cedar St San Diego CA 92101-3113

EHRLICH, GRANT C(ONKLIN), business consultant; b. Chgo., Aug. 16, 1916; s. Howard and Jenese (Conklin) E.; m. Gretchen Woerz, Sept. 14, 1940; children: Galen Wood, Gretel Ehrlich. B.S. in Adm. Engring. and Mech. Engring., Cornell U., 1938. Sales and engring. mgr. New Eng. Tape Co., Hudson, Mass., 1938-44; pres. Resin Industries, Inc., Santa Barbara, Calif., 1944-56, Industrial de Resinas. S.A., Mexico City, 1953-85; chmn. Templock Corp., Carpinteria, Calif., 1977—; chief exec. officer Flow Gen. Inc., McLean, Va., 1983-85, chmn., 1983-88. Chmn. Young Republicans of Calif., 1950. Club: Valley Club of Montecito (treas., dir. 1980-82). Office: 5464 Carpinteria Ave Ste 212 Carpinteria CA 93013-1475

EICHINGER, MARILYNNE H., museum executive; m. Martin Eichinger; children: Ryan, Kara, Julia, Jessica, Talik. AB in Anthropology and Sociology magna cum laude, Boston U., 1965; MA, Mich. State U. With emergency and outpatient staff Ingham County Mental Health Ctr., 1972; founder, pres., exec. dir. Impression 5 Sci. and Art Mus., Lansing, Mich., 1973-85; pres. Oreg. Mus. Sci. and Industry, Portland, 1985—; instr. Lansing (Mich.) Community Coll., 1978; ptnr. Eyrie Studio, 1982-85; conductor numerous workshops in interactive exhibit design, adminstrn. and fund devel. for schs., orgns., profl. socs.; bd. dirs. Assn. Sci. Tech. Ctrs., 1980-84, 88—; mem. adv. bd. Portland State U. Author: (with Jane Mack) Lexington Montessori School Survey, 1969, Manual on the Five Senses, 1974; pub. Mich. edit. Boing mag. Founder Cambridge Montessori Sch., 1964; mem. pres.'s adv. coun. Portland State U., 1986—; bd. dirs. Lexington Montessori Sch., 1969, Mid-Mich. South Health Systems Agy., 1978-81, Community Referral Ctr., 1981-85, Sat. WKAR-Radio, 1981-85; active Lansing "Riverfest" Lighted Boat Parade, 1980; mem. state Health Coordinating Coun., 1980-82; mem. pres.' adv. bd. Portland State U., 1987—. Recipient Diana Cert. Leadership, YWCA, 1976-77, Woman of Achievement award, 1991, Community Svc. award Portland State U., 1992. Mem. Am. Assn. Mus., Oreg. Mus. Assn., Assn. Sci. and Tech. Ctrs. (bd. dirs. 1980-84), Portland C. of C., City of Portland Club, Internat. Women's Club, Rotary. Club: City of Portland, Internat. Womens Club. Lodge: Zonta (founder, bd. dirs. East Lansing club 1978), Rotary (Portland). Office: Oreg Mus Sci and Industry 1945 SE Water Ave Portland OR 97214

EIFLER, CARL FREDERICK, retired psychologist; b. Los Angeles, June 27, 1906; s. Carl Frederick and Pauline (Engelbert) E.; m. Margaret Christine Aaberg, June 30, 1963; 1 son, Carl Henry; 1 adopted son, Byron Hisey. BD, Jackson Coll., 1956; Ph.D., Ill. Inst. Tech., 1962. Insp. U.S. Bur. Customs, 1928-35, chief insp., 1936-37, dep. collector, 1937-56; bus. mgr. Jackson Coll., Honolulu, 1954-56, instr., 1955-56; grad. asst. instr., research asst. Ill. Inst. Tech., Chgo., 1959-62; psychologist Monterey County Mental Health Services, Salinas, Calif., 1964-73; ret., 1973. Contbg. author Psychon. Sci., vol. 20, 1970; co-author: The Deadliest Colonel; author, pub.: Jesus Said. Served with U.S. Army, 1922-23, 40-47; col. ret. Decorated Combat Infantryman's Badge, Legion of Merit with 2 oak leaf clusters, Bronze Star medal, Air medal, Purple Heart; named to Military Intelligence Corps Hall of Fame, 1988. Mem. AAUP, Am. Psychol. Assn., Western States Psychol. Assn., Calif. Psychol. Assn., Res. Officers Assn. (Hawaii pres. 1947), Assn. Former Intelligence Officers (bd. govs., Western coord.), Pearl Harbor Survivors, 101 Assn., Assn. U.S. Army Vets. of OSS (past bd. govs., Western coord., v.p.), Ret. Officers Assn., Masons, KT, Shriners, Elks, Nat. Sojourners, Psi Chi. Home: 22700 Picador Dr Salinas CA 93908-1116

EIGLER, DONALD MARK, physicist; b. L.A., Mar. 23, 1953; s. Irving Baer and Evelin Muriel (Baker) E.; m. Roslyn Winifred Rubesin, Nov. 2, 1986. BA, U. Calif., San Diego, 1975, PhD in Physics, 1984. Rsch. assoc. U. Köln (Fed. Republic Germany), 1975-76; rsch. assoc. U. Calif., San Diego, 1977-84, postdoctoral rsch. assoc., 1984, assoc. rsch. physicist dept. physics, 1986; postdoctoral mem. tech. staff AT&T Bell Labs., Murray Hill, N.J., 1984-86; mem. rsch. staff IBM, San Jose, Calif., 1986-93, IBM fellow, 1993—. Office: IBM Almaden Rsch Ctr 650 Harry Rd San Jose CA 95120-6099

EIGSTI, ROGER HARRY, insurance company executive; b. Vancouver, Wash., Apr. 17, 1942; s. Harry A. and Alice E. (Huber) E.; m. Mary Lou Nelson, June 8, 1963; children: Gregory, Ann. BS, Linfield Coll., 1964. CPA, Oreg., Wash. Staff CPA Touche Ross and Co., Portland, Oreg., 1964-72; asst. to controller Safeco Corp., Seattle, 1972-78, controller, 1980; controller Safeco Life Ins. Co., Seattle, 1978-80; pres. Safeco Credit Co., Seattle, 1980-81, Safeco Life Ins. Co., Seattle, 1981-85; exec. v.p., chief fin. officer Safeco Corp., Seattle, 1985—. bd. dirs. Ind. Colls. of Wash., Seattle, 1981-87, bus. dir. Seattle Repertory Theatre, 1981—, bd. dirs. 1981—. Mem. Am. Inst. CPA's, Life Office Mgmt. Assn. (bd. dirs. 1983—), Seattle C. of C. (chmn. metro budget rev. com. 1984—). Republican. Clubs: Mercer Island (Wash.) Country (treas., bd. dirs. 1981-84); Central Park Tennis. Home: 11701 NE 36th Pl Bellevue WA 98005-1234

EIKENBERRY, ARTHUR RAYMOND, service executive, researcher, writer; b. Sebring, Fla., June 5, 1920; s. Leroy Albertus and Vernie Cordelia (Griffin) E.; m. Carol Jean Parrott, June 10, 1955; children: Robin Rene, Shari LaVon, Jan Rochelle, Karyn LaRae, Kelli Yvette. Student, Pasadena (Calif.) Jr. Coll., 1939, Kunming U., China, 1944-45. MSgt. Army Air Corps, 1941-45, re-enlisted in grade of TSgt., 1947; advanced through grades to SMSgt. USAF, 1968; ret., 1973, mgmt., pers., adminstrv. and security insp.; mgr. inventory control TR Devel. Co., Englewood, Colo., 1973-74; real estate agt. The Pinery, Parker, Colo., 1974-75; mgr., patient acctg. dept. Univ. Colo. Health Scis. Ctr., Denver, 1975-89. Author: Investment Strategies for the Clever Investor, 1989, LOTTO GURU (Omni-Personal Selection Systems & Strategies), 1989. Charter mem. U.S. Congl. Adv. Bd. Fellow Internat. Biog. Ctr. (hon. life patron, dep. dir. gen.); mem. Am. Biog. Inst. (life, dep. gov., nat. adviser), World Inst. of Achievement (disting.), Masons, Royal Order of the Amaranth. Address: The Lakes 8524 W Sahara Ave # 174 Las Vegas NV 89117

EIKENBERRY, KENNETH OTTO, state attorney general; b. Wenatchee, Wash., June 29, 1932; s. Otto Kenneth and Florence Estelle E.; m. Beverly Jane Hall, Dec. 21, 1963. BA in Polit. Sci., Wash. State U., 1954; LLB, U. Wash., 1959. Bar: Wash. 1959. Spl. agt. FBI, 1960-62; dep. pros. atty. King County (Wash.), Seattle, 1962-67; with firm Richey & Eikenberry, 1967-68, Clinton, Andersen, Fleck & Glein, Seattle, 1968-73; legal counsel King County Council, 1974-76; chmn. Wash. Republican party, 1977-80; atty. gen. State of Wash., 1981-93; chmn. Wash. State Rep. Party, Seattle, 1993—; judge pro tem Seattle Mcpl. Ct., 1979-80; mem. Pres.'s Task Force on Victims of Crime, 1982, Pres.'s Child Safety Partnership, 1986, State Criminal Justice Tng. Commn., 1980-93, State Corrections Stds. Bd., 1980-85; mem. Legis. Exch. Coun., 1986. Chmn., King County Rep. Conv., 1974, 78; mem. Wash. Ho. of Reps., 1970-76. Served with AUS, 1954-56. Named Legislator of Year, Young Americans for Freedom/Wash. Conservative Union, 1974, Rep. Man of Year, Young Men's Rep. Club King County, 1979. Mem. Wash. Bar Assn., Nat. Gov.'s Assn./Nat. Assn. Attys. Gen. Task Force on Fed. Facilities (co-chair 1989-90), Western Conf. Attys.-Gen. (chmn. 1983-84), Soc. Former Spl. Agts. FBI, Nat. Assn. Attys. Gen. (pres. 1991-92, chmn. energy com. 1983-84, sub-com. on RICO issues 1984-86, criminal law com. 1987-89, crime victims adv. com. 1984-86, working group on model patient abuse legis. 1986-87, mem. consumer protection com. 1986-93, environ. control com. 1988-93, asbestos coordination com. 1988-90, Indian affairs working group 1988-91). Clubs: Kiwanis, Rainrunners. Office: Wash State Rep Party 16400 South Ctr Pkwy # 200 Seattle WA 98188

EILENBERG, LAWRENCE IRA, theater educator, artistic director; b. Bklyn., May 26, 1947; s. Jerome and Dorothy Vera (Natleson) E.; m. Diane Marie Eliasof, Nov. 25, 1973 (dec. Dec. 1984); children: David Joseph, Benjamin Alan; m. Judith Heiner, Nov. 10, 1990. BA, Cornell U., 1968; MPhil, Yale U., 1971, PhD, 1975. Jr. fellow Davenport Coll., Yale U., New Haven, 1971-72; asst. prof. theatre dept. Cornell U., Ithaca, N.Y., 1972-75; vis. asst. prof. in theatre U. Mich., Ann Arbor, 1975-77; asst. prof., then assoc. prof. U. Denver, 1977-82, 83; prof. San Francisco State U., 1983—, chmn. theatre arts dept., 1984-92; artistic dir. Magic Theatre, San Francisco, 1992—; theatre corr. Sta. KCFR (NPR), Denver, 1979-82; literary mgr. Denver Ctr. Theatre Co., 1981-83; artistic dir. San Francisco New Vaudeville Festival, 1985-89; dramaturg One Act Theatre Co., San Francisco, 1986-88; bd. dirs. Theatre Bay Area, San Francisco, 1985—, pres., 1987-89; speaker, lectr. in field. Editor Stage/Space mag., 1981-83; contbr. articles, book and theater revs. to profl. publs. U.S. del. Podium Festival of USSR, Moscow, 1989. Grantee Lilly Found., 1981, Idaho Humanities Assn., 1983, 84, 85, NEA, 1986, Calif. Arts Coun., 1987, 88; recipient Best Broadcast award Colo. Broadcasters Assn., 1982. Mem. Literary Mgrs. and Dramaturgs Am. (v.p. 1989-90), Nat. Assn. Schs. of Theatre (bd. accreditation, 1990-91, evaluator 1986—). Home: 1568 Columbus Ave Burlingame CA 94010-5512 Office: San Francisco State U Theatre Arts Dept 1600 Holloway Ave San Francisco CA 94132-1722

EILERMAN, BETTY JEAN, marriage and family counselor; b. Phila., Nov. 1, 1942; d. Frank Irving and Elizabeth Marquerite (Lennon) Gunsauls; m. Jerome Louis Eilerman, Dec. 15, 1969. BA, Rosemont Coll., 1964; M.Rel.Ed., Loyola U., Chgo., 1970; PhD, Calif. Pacific U., 1980; MA, U. San Francisco, 1984. Lic. marriage and family therapist, Calif., Minn. Instr. Maria Goretti High Sch., Phila., 1964-66, Bishop McDavitt High Sch., Wyncote, Pa., 1966-68; assoc. editor George A. Pflaum Pub., Dayton, Ohio, 1968-69; instr. Acad. of Our Lady of Peace, San Diego, 1970, The Bishop's Schs., LaJolla, Calif., 1970-80; ptnr. Write Right!, LaJolla, 1979-81; counselor Ctr. Creative Consciousness, Santa Rosa, Calif., 1982; intern Clin. Cognitive Inst., Santa Rosa, 1982-83; counselor Cath. Community Svc., Santa Rosa, 1983-84; pvt. practice Santa Rosa, 1983-88, Fargo, N.D., 1988—; bereavement counselor Home Hospice, Santa Rosa, 1983-85; hypnotherapist, Santa Rosa and Fargo, 1985—; co-facilitator Rebuilding: Divorce Workshops, Santa Rosa, 1986-88; co-dir. Reconnections, Santa Rosa, 1987-88, Counselor Employee Support Systems, Santa Rosa, 1987-88; founder Crossings, Fargo, 1988—, Bridge House, Santa Rosa, 1993—. Pres. Profl. Women's Group, Phila., 1966-67, Newcomers Club, Santa Rosa, 1982; dir. Svc. League, LaJolla, 1970-80. Honoree Nat. Disting. Svc. Registry for Counseling and Devel., 1990. Mem. Am Assn. Marriage & Family Therapy, Calif. Assn. Marriage & Family Therapy, Assn. Humanistic Psychology, Assn. Transpersonal Psychology, Am. Mental Health Counselors Assn., Am. Assn. Counseling and Devel., Am. Assn. Pastoral Counselors, Delta Epsilon Sigma. Office: 1211 Pacific Ave Santa Rosa CA 95401

EINHORN, BRUCE JEFFREY, judge, lawyer, historian; b. Orlando, Fla., Dec. 7, 1954; s. Arthur and Iris Joan (Maller) E.; m. Terri Jan Schneider, Mar. 9, 1980; children: Lee Michael, Matthew Mitchell. BA magna cum laude, Columbia U., 1975; JD, NYU, 1978. Bar: D.C. 1980, U.S. Dist. Ct. D.C. 1980, U.S. Ct. Appeals (D.C. cir.) 1980, U.S. Supreme Ct. 1983, U.S. Ct. Appeals (9th cir.) 1984, Pa. 1986, N.Y. 1987. Law clk. to assoc. judge D.C. Ct. Appeals, Washington, 1978-79; sr. trial atty. office spl. investigations U.S. Dept. Justice, Washington, 1979-87, dep. dir. litigation office spl. investigations, 1988-90; judge U.S. Immigration Ct., L.A., 1990—; adj. prof. law Pepperdine U., Malibu, Calif., 1991—; ann. judge law sch. Moot Ct. competition George Washington U., Washington, 1983-90. Sr. fellow Am.-Israel Pub. Affairs Com., Washington, 1986; chair civil rights com. Anti-Defamation League of B'nai B'rith, 1992—. Mem. ABA (internat. law sect. and litigation), Assn. of Holocaust Educators, Phi Beta Kappa, Columbia U. Club (Washington). Democrat. Jewish. Office: US Immigration Ct 300 N Los Angeles St Ste 2001 Los Angeles CA 90012-3308

EINSTEIN, STEPHEN JAN, rabbi; b. L.A., Nov. 15, 1945; s. Syd C. and Selma (Rothenberg) E.; m. Robin Susan Kessler, Sept. 9, 1967; children: Rebecca Yael, Jennifer Melissa, Heath Isaac, Zachary Shane. AB, UCLA, 1967; B.H.L., Hebrew Union Coll., L.A., 1968; M.A.H.L., Hebrew Union Coll., Cin., 1971. Ordained rabbi. Rabbi Temple Beth Am, Parsippany, N.J., 1971-74; rabbi Temple Beth David, Westminster, Calif., 1974-76, Congregation B'nai Tzedek, Fountain Valley, Calif., 1976—; bd. dirs. Heritage Pointe, Coll. Jewish Studies Orange County. Co-author: Every Person's Guide to Judaism, 1989; co-editor: Introduction to Judaism, 1983. Pres., trustee Fountain Valley (Calif.) Sch. Bd., 1984-90; mem. Personnel Commn. Fountain Valley Sch. Dist., 1991--. Honored for Maj. Contributions to Jewish Learning, Orange County (Calif.) Bur. Jewish Edn., 1986; recipient Micah Award for Interfaith Activities, Am. Jewish Com., 1988. Mem. Ctrl. Conf. Am. Rabbis (exec. bd. 1989-91), Pacific Assn. Reform Rabbis (exec. bd. 1987-91), Orange County Bd. Rabbis (pres., sec.-treas. 1974-79), Jewish Educators Assn. Orange County (pres. 1979-81), Orange County Bur. Jewish Edn. (v.p. 1982-84, 92—). Democrat. Office: Congregation Bnai Tzedek 9669 Talbert Ave Fountain Valley CA 92708

EIRMAN, THOMAS FREDRICK, music festival manager; b. N.Y.C., July 8, 1947; s. Fredrick Joseph E. AA, Queensborough Coll., 1972; postgrad., SUNY, Queens, 1972-75. Tech. dir. Western Opera Theatre, San Francisco, 1982-83; asst. lighting designer Portland (Oreg.) Opera, 1985-87; prodn. mgr. Pacific Ballet Theater, Portland, 1985-87; gen. mgr. Aspen Music Festival, N.Y.C. Office: Music Assocs Aspen PO Box AA Aspen CO 81612

EISELE, MILTON DOUGLAS, viticulturist; b. N.Y.C., Apr. 2, 1910; s. Charles Francis and Helen Agnes (Dolan) E.; B.A., U. Calif.-Berkeley, 1933; grad. San Francisco Stock Exch. Inst., 1938; m. Barbara Lois Morgan, July 26, 1941; children: Helen Frances Eisele Osthimer, Barbara Glennis, William Douglas. Investment cashier Wells Fargo Bank, San Francisco, 1934-39; coordinator cement sales Permanente Corp., 1940-41, constrn. supt., 1941-43; mgr. refractory div. Kaiser Aluminum, 1943-47, mgr. regional sales, Chgo., 1947-50, mgr. foil div., 1950-55, mgr. prodn., 1955-60, mgr. market and prodn. devel., 1960-65, mgr. investments, 1966-71; ret., 1971; former owner, operator Eisele Vineyards, Napa Valley, Calif., 1969-89. Dir., former pres. Napa Valley Found., 1981-85; bd. dirs., past chmn. Vintage Hall, Inc., 1973-85; bd. dirs., pres. Napa Valley Heritage Fund, 1973—; past pres., bd. dirs. Upper Napa Valley Assocs., 1976-80; mem. adv. coun. Napa County Land Trust, 1976-79; mem. Napa County Grand Jury, 1988-89, hon. co-chmn. 150th anny. planting first grapes. Mem. Am. Soc. Enologists, Napa Valley Grape Growers Assn. (dir.), Calif. Assn. Wine Grape Growers (dir., former sec., chmn. 1986-87), Calif. Vintage Wine Soc., Agrl. Coun. of Napa County, Wine and Winegrape Mktg. Order State of Calif. (dir. 1984), Napa Valley Growers and Vinters (chmn. bd. dirs., mktg. and promotion com. 1985—), Kappa Alpha Order. Republican. Episcopalian (vestryman, sr. warden 1966-69). Home and Office: 1865 St Helen Hwy PO Box 687 Rutherford CA 94573

EISEMANN, KURT, director computer center, mathematics educator; b. Nuremberg, Germany, June 22, 1923; came to U.S., 1948; s. Lazarus and Lina (Bacharach) E.; m. Marlene K. Cross, June 22, 1969 (div. Oct. 1988); children: Jamin, Caroline. BA in Math., Yeshiva U., 1950; MS in Applied Math., MIT, 1952; PhD in Applied Math., Harvard U., 1962. Sr. mathematician IBM, N.Y.C., 1952-56; rsch. mathematician IBM, 1956-61; mgr. math. rsch. Univac Div. Sperry Rand Corp., Washington, 1961-63; dir. computer ctr., assoc. prof. Sch. Engring. Cath. U. Am., Washington, 1963-66; tech. dir. Comput Usage Devel. Corp., Boston, Mass., 1966-68; dir. acad. computer svc., prof. computer sci. Northeastern U., Boston, 1968-74; dir. computer svc., prof. math and computer sci. U. Mo. Kansas City, Kansas City, 1974-82; dir. univ. computer ctr., prof. math. and computer sci. San Diego State U., 1982-92, prof. emeritus, 1992—; lectr. Yeshiva U., 1953-55, Cath. U. Am., 1962-63. Office: San Diego State U Math Dept San Diego CA 92182-0314

EISENBERG, RONALD LEE, radiologist; b. Phila., July 11, 1945; s. Milton and Betty (Klein) E.; m. Zina Leah Schiff; 2 children. AB, U. Pa., 1965, MD, 1965. Diplomate Am. Bd. Radiology. Staff radiologist VA Med. Ctr., San Francisco, 1975-80; prof. and chmn. dept. radiology La. State U., Shreveport, 1980-91; chmn. dept. radiology Highland Hosp., Oakland, Calif., 1991—. Author: Gastrointestinal Radiology, 1982, Diagnostic Imaging in

Internal Medicine, 1985, Diagnostic Imaging in Surgery, 1986, Atlas of Differential Diagnoses, 1988, Radiology: An Illustrated History, 1992, others; contbr. over 70 articles to profl. jours. Maj. U.S. Army, 1971-73. Named Man of the Yr., Am. Physicians Fellowship, Boston, 1987. Mem. Radiol. Soc. N.Am., Am. Roentgen Ray Soc., Assn. of Univ. Radiologists, Soc. for Gastrointestinal Radiology, So. Med. Assn., Am. Coll. Radiology, Ark-La-Tex Radiol. Soc. Office: Highland Hosp Dept Radiology 1411 E 31st St Oakland CA 94602

EISENHARDT, (EMIL) ROY, science academy executive; b. 1939; m. Auban Slay, 1965 (div. 1976); m. Elizabeth Haas, 1978; children: Sarah, Jesse. BA, Dartmouth Coll., 1960; LLB, U. Calif., Berkeley, 1965. Bar: Calif. 1966. With firm Farella, Braun and Martel, San Francisco; vis. prof. U. Calif. Boalt Hall Sch. Law, Berkeley, from 1974; pres. Oakland A's, Am. League, Calif., 1980-88; exec. v.p. Oakland A's, Am. League, From 1988; exec. dir. Calif. Acad. of Scis., San Francisco; former coach U. Calif. rowing crew. Served with USMC, 1960-62. Address: Calif Acad of Sciences Golden Gate Park San Francisco CA 94118

EISENHAUER, JOHN ALLEN, software developer, consultant; b. Seattle, June 3, 1959; s. Philip Lynn and Patricia Joan (Patterson) E.; m. M. Dee Hermes; children: Emma Lynn, Karen Rose. BS in Math., Rocky Mountain Coll., Billings, Mont., 1980. Tech. svcs. mgr. Terminal Brokers, Inc., Marina del Rey, Calif., 1980-82; mgr. data processing BDT Products, Inc., Irvine, Calif., 1982-84; mgr. systems engring. The Byte Shops, Seattle, 1984; pres. A Bit Better Software Pub., Tacoma, 1985—. Democrat. Mem. United Ch. of Christ. Office: A Bit Better Software Pub 1551 Broadway Ste 300 Tacoma WA 98402

EISENHAUER, SCOTT ALBERT, military officer; b. Watertown, N.Y., Dec. 18, 1962; s. Wesley Earl Jr. and Donna Jean (Wilson) E.; m. Melissa Joy Manday, Jan. 14, 1989. BSCE, U.S. Mil. Acad., 1985. Commd. U.S. Army, 1985, advanced through grades to co. comdr., 1985. Mem. Am. Fedn. Herpeculturists, Soc. Am. Mil. Engrs. Home: 122 B Iliamna Ave Fort Richardson AK 99505 Office: C Co 1st Bn 501st IN ABN Bldg 628 Fort Richardson AK 99505

EISERLING, FREDERICK ALLEN, microbiologist, educator; b. San Diego, May 8, 1938; s. Allen Frederick and Nancy Lucille (Simpson) E. B.A., UCLA, 1959, Ph.D., 1964. Postdoctoral U. Geneva, 1964-66; asst. prof. UCLA, from 1966, assoc. prof., to 1981, prof., chmn. dept. microbiology, 1981-87, dean life scis., 1987—, dir. undergrad. program Howard Hughes Med. Inst., 1992—; cons. USPHS, NSF, Washington, 1968-83. Contbr. articles to sci. jours. Rsch grantee NIH, NSF, Howard Hughes Med. Inst. Mem. Am. Soc. Microbiology, Am. Soc. Virology, AAAS, Fedn. Am. Scientists. Office: UCLA Dept Microbiology & Molecular Geneticw Los Angeles CA 90024-1489

EISLER, DAVID LEE, university dean, music educator; b. Camden, N.J., Nov. 15, 1951; s. Jacob and Sarah Elizabeth (Korman) E.; m. Patricia Ann Johnson, Jan. 6, 1973; children: Heather Leigh, Lindsay Suzanne. Mus.B., U. Mich., 1972; Mus.M., Yale U., 1975; D.M.A., U. Mich., 1978. Teaching fellow Yale U., New Haven, 1974-75; instr. music Troy State U. (Ala.), 1975-77, asst. prof., 1978-85, assoc. prof., 1985-89, prof., 1989-90, asst. dean Sch. Fine Arts, 1982-90, coord. instrumental music, dir. grad. studies in music, 1978-90; dean coll. fine arts, prof. music Eastern N.Mex. U., 1990—; teaching fellow U. Mich., Ann Arbor, 1977-78; exec. dir. Southeastern U.S. Band Clinic. Mem. dean's adv. bd. Yale U., 1974-75. Boston Symphony fellow, 1972; cons. Girl Scouts U.S.A. Pres. Roosevelt County United Way. Mem. Coll. Band Dirs. Nat. Assn., Internat. Clarinet Soc., Nat. Assn. Coll. Wind Percussion Instrs., N.Mex. Music Educators Assn., Music Educators Nat. Conv., Tex. Bandmasters, Internat. Coun. Fine Arts Dean (pres.), Nat. Band Assn., Pi Kappa Lambda, Kappa Kappa Psi, Phi Mu Alpha, Tau Beta Sigma. Methodist. Lodge: Rotary. Author: A Bass Clarinet Orchestral Excerpt Book, 1972. Office: Eastern NMex U Coll Fine Arts Sta # 16 Portales NM 88130

EISLER, ROBERT DAVID, engineer; b. N.Y.C., June 7, 1952; s. Leo and Lillian (Gottlieb) E.; m. Fern Robin Eisler, Aug. 1, 1982; children: Lee William, Neal Alan. BA, Colgate U., 1974; BS, Columbia U., 1980, MS, 1981, profl. engring. degree, 1982. Cert. engr., N.Y. Respiratory therapist Norwalk (Conn.) Hosp., 1970-76; pres., gen. mgr. Fillow Flower Co., Inc., Westport, Conn., 1976-78; biomed. rsch. assoc. Norwalk (Conn.) Hosp., 1978-80; rsch. assoc. Columbia U. Guggenheim Inst. for Flight Structures, N.Y.C., 1980-82, Argonne Nat. Lab., Idaho Falls, 1980; program mgr., prin. investigator McDonnell Douglas Astronautics Co., Huntington Beach, Calif., 1982-85; leader structural mechs. group Mission Rsch. Corp., Costa Mesa, Calif., 1985—; U.S. del. to NATO for close combat ops.; mem. Joint Army Navy NASA Air Force Com. Design and Analysis of Composite Rocket Motor Cases. Contbr. articles to profl. jours. Recipient McDonnell Douglas Corp. award for contbns. to the Strategic Def. Initiative, 1982; Dept. of Energy fellow Argonne Nat. Lab., 1980. Mem. AIAA (sr.), ASME (exec. com. 1983-86), Soc. Advancement of Materials and Process Engring., Materials Rsch. Soc., Internat. Assn. Wound Ballistics, Mil. Ops. Rsch. Soc.

EISNER, HARVEY BRIAN, controller, tax consultant; b. L.A., May 7, 1958; s. Donald Laurence and Lillian (Israel) E.; m. Linda McDougall, June 18, 1989. BS, U. Nev., Las Vegas, 1981. CPA, Nev. Staff acct. Laventhol & Horwath, Las Vegas, Nev., 1981-83; sr. acct. Laventhol & Horwath, Tucson, 1983; acctg. and reporting supr. Holiday Casino, Holiday Corp., Las Vegas, 1983-87; tax and acctg. mgr. Harrah's Holiday Corp., Reno, 1987; contr. Desert Radiologists, Las Vegas, 1987—. Mem. Nat. Acctg. Assn., Nev. Soc. CPA's. Democrat. Office: Desert Radiologists 2020 Palomino Ln Ste 100 Las Vegas NV 89106

EISNER, MICHAEL DAMMANN, motion picture company executive; b. Mt. Kisco, N.Y., Mar. 7, 1942; s. Lester and Margaret (Dammann) E.; m. Jane Breckenridge; children: Breck, Eric, Anders. BA, Denison U., 1964. Began career in programming dept. CBS; asst. to nat. programming dir. ABC, 1966-68, mgr. spls. and talent, dir. program devel.-East Coast, 1968-71, v.p. daytime programming, 1971-75, v.p. program planning and devel., 1975-76, sr. v.p. prime time prodn. and devel., 1976; pres., chief operating officer Paramount Pictures, 1976-84; chmn., chief exec. officer Walt Disney Co., Burbank, Calif., 1984—. Bd. dirs. Denison U., Calif. Inst. Arts, Am. Film Inst., Performing Arts Coun., L.A. Music Ctr. Office: Walt Disney Co 500 S Buena Vista St Burbank CA 91521-0001*

EISNER, RONALD RICHARD, anesthesiologist; b. Bklyn., Mar. 21, 1933; s. M.A. and Mae Eisner. BS, William and Mary Coll., 1954; MD, Chgo. Med. Sch., 1958. Diplomate Am. Bd. Anesthesiology. Am. Bd. Med. Examiners. Anesthesiologist Albert Einstein Med. Ctr., Phila., 1961-72, Kaiser Found. Hosp., Oakland, Calif., 1972—; asst. prof. Temple U. Sch. Medicine and Dentistry, Phila., 1965-72. Mem. AMA, Am. Soc. Anesthesiologists, Am. Soc. Critical Care Anesthesiologists, Am. Coll. Anesthesiologists. Office: Kaiser Found Hosp Broadway-W MacArthur Blvd Oakland CA 94611

EITNER, LORENZ EDWIN ALFRED, art historian, educator; b. Brunn, Czechoslovakia, Aug. 27, 1919; came to U.S., 1935, naturalized, 1943; s. Wilhelm and Katherina (Thonet) E.; m. Trudi von Kathrein, Oct. 26, 1946; children: Christy, Kathy, Claudia. A.B., Duke U., 1940; M.F.A., Princeton U., 1948, Ph.D., 1952. Research unit head Nuremberg War Crimes Trial, 1946-47; from instr. to prof. art U. Minn., Mpls., 1949-63; chmn. dept. art, dir. mus. Stanford U., Calif., 1963—; organizer exhbn. works of Gericault for museums of Los Angeles, Detroit and Phila., 1971-72. Author: The Flabellum of Tournus, 1944, Gericault Sketchbooks in the Chicago Art Institute, 1960, Introduction to Art, 1951, Neo-Classicism and Romanticism, 1969, Gericault's Raft of the Medusa, 1972, Gericault, His Life and Work, 1983 (Mitchell prize 1984, C.R. Morey award 1985), An Outline of 19th Century European Painting from David through Cezanne, 1987; (with others) The Arts in Higher Education, Stanford Mus. Art, The Drawing Collection, 1993; contbr. articles to profl. jours. Mem. Regional Arts Council San Francisco Bay Area. Served as officer OSS, AUS, 1943-46. Fulbright grantee, Belgium, 1952-53; Guggenheim fellow, Munich, Federal Republic Germany, 1956-57; recipient Gold Medal for Meritorious Service to Austrian Republic, 1990. Mem. AAAS, Am. Acad. Arts and Scis., Coll. Art Assn. Am. (bd. dirs., past v.p.), Phi Beta Kappa. Home: 684 Mirada Ave Palo Alto CA 94305-8475 Office: Stanford U Art Dept Stanford CA 94305-2018

EKONG, RUTH J., nursing administrator; b. St. Thomas, V.I.; d. Rufus and Ruby (Maduro) Norman; m. Eno A. Ekong. Commr. spl. edn., nurse cons., dir. nurses, nurse gerontology specialist; ethnic food cons.; developer Tantie Ruth Corp. Developer Original African Salad Dressings, Tantie Ruth Foods, Vzimi cooking, (TV show) Tantie Ruth.

ELA, PATRICK HOBSON, museum director, consultant, educator; b. Oakland, Calif., June 20, 1948; s. Benjamin W., Jr., and Jeanette (Lamoreau) E. B.A., Occidental Coll., 1970; postgrad. in Art History, UCLA, 1970-71, M.B.A., 1973. Curator Gemini Graphics Edits., Ltd., Los Angeles, 1970-71; edn. intern Alta Pinakothek, Munich, W.Ger., 1972; asst. dir. Kohler Arts Ctr., Sheboygan, Wis., 1973-74; edn. specialist Los Angeles County Mus. Art, 1974-75; adminstrv. dir. Craft and Folk Art Mus., Los Angeles, 1975-82, exec. dir., 1982—; prin. Crown Internat. Travel Inc.; mgmt. cons.; instr. Occidental Coll., Calif. State U.-Fullerton; mem. faculty mus. studies program John F. Kennedy U. Vice pres., pres. alumni bd. govs. Occidental Coll., 1979-80; bd. dirs. R.M. Schindler House, Scott Newman Ctr., 1986-91. Mem. Calif. Assn. Mus. (founding bd. 1980-81). Office: Craft and Folk Art Mus 5800 Wilshire Blvd Los Angeles CA 90036-3695

ELAINE, KAREN, musician, educator; b. San Jose, Calif., Nov. 6, 1965; d. Gaston Ortega and Alice Lee (Ray) Sanders. Diploma in music, Curtis Inst. of Music, Phila., 1987; studies with Karen Tuttle, Michael Tree, Curtis Inst. Music, 1987; studies with Louis Kievman, L.A., 1988-90. Solo viola New Am. Chamber Orch., Detroit, 1986-87; prin. viola San Diego Symphony Orch., 1987-90; string specialist Sch. Creative & Performing Arts, San Diego, 1987-90; pvt. instr. Studio of Karen Elaine, San Diego, 1987—; violist Rinaldi String Quartet, San Diego, 1988-91; prin. viola Internat. Symphony Orch. Tijuana, Mex., 1988—; viola prof. Chanterelle Music Festival, Pouidoux, Switzerland, 1989—; adj. prof. viola San Diego State U., 1989—; featured on TV program Reflections in Music, San Diego, El Cajon, Calif., 1990; solo viola Delos Internat. Records, Paraiba Symphony Orch., Brazil, 1988, Laurel Records, London Symphony Orch., 1990, Harmonia Mundi, City of London Sinfonia, 1990; guest soloist and lectr. 19th Internat. Viola Congress, 1991, solo recitalist throughout U.S.; guest speaker Sta. KFSD-FM, Sta. KPBS-FM; solo tour Austria, 1993. Commissions include Concert Piece for Viola, David Baker, 1989, Cinnabar Concerto for Viola and Strings, David Ward-Steinman, 1991, Concerto for Viola and Orch., Gordon Kerry, 1993, Sounds for Solo Viola, John Naples, 1992, Li'l Phrygian Rondo for Karen, Katrina Wreede, 1992; contbg. editor Mythos to Melos; Greek Tragedy in Opera, 1992-93; contbr. articles to Jour. of Internat. Viola Soc. Donor World Wildlife Fund, Washington, 1989—. Recipient 1st Pl. award Bruno Giurana Internat. Viola Competition, Brazil, 1988; winner numerous solo competitions Musical Merit of San Diego, 1988, 89, Rio Hondo Symphony Young Artists' Solo Competition, 1989, S.E. L.A. Young Artists Solo Competition, 1990, Nat. Assn. Negro Musicians Young Artists Solo Competition, 1992. Mem. Am. Viola Soc., Musicians Union (local 325). Democrat. Home: 208 Welling Way San Diego CA 92114-5947

ELDER, CURTIS HAROLD, geologist; b. Laramie, Wyo., Mar. 30, 1921; s. Cecil and Agnes Christine (Miller) E.; m. Wiese Wild, Jan. 2, 1948; children: George W., Christian N., Robin T., Melody C. Student, U. Mo., 1939-43, BS in Geology, 1951, postgrad., 1951-52. Grad. asst. U. Mo., Columbia, 1950-52; jr. rsch. engr. Pan Am. Petroleum Corp., Tulsa, 1952-56; intermediate geologist Pan Am. Petroleum Corp., Salt Lake City, 1956-59; geologist Pan Am. Petroleum Corp., Denver, 1959-63; ind. cons. geologist pvt. practice, Denver, 1963-65; geologist U.S. Bur. Mines, Pitts., 1965-82, U.S. Dept. Interior, Pitts., 1982-88; pvt. practice Evergreen, Colo., 1988—. Conservation chmn. Denver Area coun. Boy Scouts Am.; assoc. dir. Allegheny Soil and Water Conservation Dist., 1966-81. Recipient Silver Beaver award Allegheny Trails coun. Boy Scouts Am. Fellow Geol. Soc. Am. (sr.); mem. Am. Inst. Profl. Geologists (cert.), Soc. Econ. Paleontologists and Mineralogists, Mineralogical Soc. Am., Rocky Mountain Assn. Geologists, Tulsa Geol. Soc., Pitts. Geol. Soc., Kappa Sigma. Republican. Presbyterian. Home: 33172 Lynx Ln Evergreen CO 80439-6823

ELDER, GREGORY DEAN, military officer; b. Munich, Dec. 7, 1956; s. Thomas R. and Anna (Juhaz) E.; m. Ann E. Volz, June 5, 1979; children: Jonathan M. Elder, William L. Elder. BS, USAF Acad., 1979; MS, Wright State U., 1986; postgrad., Ariz. State U., 1990—. Commd. 2d lt. USAF, 1979, advanced through grades to maj.; computer systems devel. officer Air Force Data Systems Design Ctr., Montgomery, Ala., 1979-81; microprocessor tech. project mgr. Air Force Small Computer/Office Automation Svc. Orgn., Gunter AFB, Ala., 1981-83; data base mgr. Info. Systems Tech. Ctr., Wright-Patterson AFB, Ohio, 1983-84; dep. div. chief Info. Cen. Div., Wright-Patterson AFB, 1984-87; asst. prof. U. Nebr., Lincoln, 1987-88; instr. Mil. Studies Dept., USAF Acad., Colo., 1988-89; dep. chief Ednl. Tech. Div., USAF Acad., Colo., 1989-90. Developer (software) Dial-A-Log, 1983; contbr. articles to profl. jours. Mem. Meal on Wheels, Montgeromy, Ala., 1981-83, Co. Grade Officers Com., 1979-88. Mem. IEEE Computer Soc., Assn. for Computing Machinery, Air Force Assn., Am. Assn. for Artificial Intelligence, Computer Sci. Grad. Student Assn. (editor), Upsilon Pi Epsilon.

ELDERKIN, PHILIP LEROY, journalist, consultant; b. Marlboro, Mass., May 5, 1926; s. Augustus and Dorothy (Brigham) E.; m. Barbara Stormont Cummings, Apr. 10, 1953; children: John, Jean Elderkin, Mark. Student, Boston U., 1944, Northeastern U., 1945. Cub reporter Christian Sci. Monitor, Boston, 1948-49, makeup editor, 1950-54, sports writer, 1955-59, sports columnist, 1960-89, sports editor, 1970-74; sports editor So. Calif. Mag., Riverside, 1993—; freelance writer Claremont, Calif., 1990-93. Author: Phil Elderkin on Sports, 1975. Recipient Best Column award U.S. Basketball Writers, 1964, Headliner's award Nat. Headliner's Club, 1975, Best News Story award Basketball Writers Assn., 1976, Best Story award Press Club So. Calif., 1991, Collegiate Baseball Mag. award, 1991. Mem. Baseball Writers Assn. Am. Office: So Calif Mag 3769 Tibbetts Ave Riverside CA 92506

ELDRIDGE, BRUCE FREDERICK, entomology educator, researcher; b. San Jose, Calif., Mar. 26, 1933; s. Arthur Julius and Ruth Myrtle (Pracht) E.; m. Shirley Jean Tate, Apr. 20, 1957; children: Deborah, Stuart, Kenneth. AB, San Jose (Calif.) State U., 1954; MS, Wash. State U., 1956; PhD, Purdue U., 1965. Commd. 2nd lt. U.S. Army, 1956, advanced through grades to col., 1975; med. entomologist 2d lt., 1956-77; ret., 1977; prof. entomology, chmn. dept. Oreg. State U., Corvallis, 1978-86; prof., dir. univ.-wide mosquito rsch. program U. Calif., Davis, 1986—. Contbr. over 80 articles to profl. jours. Fellow AAAS; mem. Am. Mosquito Control Assn. (pres. 1988), Entomol. Soc. Am. (editor jours. 1969-79, governing bd. 1980-83), Am. Soc. Tropical Medicine and Hygiene. Office: U Calif Dept Entomology Davis CA 95616

ELEANDO, MONA LISA, public agency official; b. Whiteriver, Ariz., June 20, 1960; d. Rencher Sr. and Theresa (Johnson) Paxson; m. Johnsen Jay Eleando, Feb. 4, 1983; children: Gracie Renee, Rosie Marie. AA, Cen. Ariz. Coll., 1982; student, Ariz. State U., 1984, Mesa C.C., 1985. Counselor Tribal Office, Whiteriver, 1982; tchr. asst. Dist. # 20, Whiteriver, 1983-85; liaison Tribal Office, Whiteriver, 1987-90, dir., 1990; eligibility interviewer Dept. Econ. Security, Whiteriver, 1992—. Mem. Linda Lupe Ms. Indian Am., Whiteriver, 1987-89; chairperson classroom Whiteriver Headstart, 1985; advocate Cen. Ariz. Coll., 1980. Named one of Outstanding Young Women, 1981. Republican. Lutheran. Home: PO Box 741 Whiteriver AZ 85941

ELECCION, MARCELINO, marketing executive, editor, writer, lecturer, artist; b. N.Y.C., Aug. 22, 1936; s. Marcelino G. and Margaret J. (Krcha) E.; m. Marcia L. Smith, June 6, 1962; 1 child, Mark Eaton; m. Naomi E. Kor, Jan. 5, 1978; 1 child, Jordan Kai. BA, NYU, 1961; postgrad. Courant Inst. Math. Scis., 1962-64; AS, Coll. San Mateo, 1988; postgrad. San Jose State U., 1988-91. Electromech. draftsman Coll. Engring., NYU, Bronx, 1954-57, chief designer dept. elec. engring., 1957-60, tech. editor lab. for electrosci. research, 1960-62, editor publs. Sch. Engring. and Scis., 1962-67; asst. editor IEEE Spectrum, N.Y.C., 1967-69, assoc. editor, 1969-70, staff writer, 1970-76, contbg. editor, 1976—; dir. adminstrn. Internat. Bur. Protection and Investigation, Ltd., N.Y.C., 1976-78; account exec. Paul Purdom & Co., pub. relations, San Francisco, 1978-81, creative dir., 1981-83; dir. mktg. communications Am. Info. Systems, Palo Alto, 1983-85; dir. engring. Tech. Cons., Palo Alto, 1986—; cons. tech. artist, 1953—; music orchestration cons., 1956-70; cons. Ency. Britannica, 1969-70, Time-Life Books, 1973; spl. guest lectr. Napa Coll., 1979—. Recipient Mayor's commendation award N.Y.C., 1971. Mem. IEEE (sr.), N.Y. Acad. Scis., Am. Math. Soc., AAAS, Optical Soc. Am., Smithsonian Assocs., Am. Numis. Assn., Nat. Geog. Soc., U.S. Judo Fedn., Athletic Congress, AAU. Fedn. Home: 3790 El Camino Real # 2004 Palo Alto CA 94306-3389

ELGIN, GITA, psychologist; b. Santiago, Chile; came to U.S., 1968, naturalized 1987; d. Serafin and Regina (Urízar) Elguin; BS in biology summa cum laude, U. Chile, Santiago, DPs, 1964; PhD in Counseling Psychology, U. Calif., Berkeley, 1976; m. Bart Bödy, Oct. 23, 1971; children: Dio Christopher Károly, Alma Ilona Raia Julia. Clin. psychologist Barros Luco-Trudeau Gen. Hosp., Santiago, 1964-65; co-founder, co-dir. Lab. for Parapsychol. Rsch., Psychiat. Clinic, U. Chile, Santiago, 1965-68; rsch. fellow Found. Rsch. on Nature of Man, Durham, N.C., 1968; researcher psychol. correlates of EEG-Alpha waves U. Calif., Berkeley, 1972-76; originator holistic method of psychotherapy Psychotherapy for a Crowd of One, 1978; co-founder, clin. dir. Holistic Health Assos., Oakland, Calif., 1979—; lectr. holistic health Piedmont (Calif.) Adult Sch., 1979-80; hostess Holistic Perspective, Sta. KALW-FM, Nat. Public Radio, 1980. Author: (video documentary) Taking the Risk: Sharing the Trauma of Sexual & Ritualistic Abuse in Group Therapy, 1992. Lic. psychologist, Chile, Calif. Chancellor's Patent Fund grantee U. Calif., 1976, NIMH fellow, 1976. Mem. Am. Psychol. Assn., Am. Holistic Psychol. Assn. (founder 1985—), Alameda County Psychol. Assn., Calif. State Psychol. Assn., Montclair Health Profls. Assn. (co-founder, pres. 1983-85), Sierra Club, U. Calif. Alumni Assn. Contbr. articles in clin. psychology and holistic health to profl. jours. and local periodicals. Presenter Whole Life Expo, 1986. Office: Montclair Profl Bldg 2080 Mountain Blvd Ste 203 Piedmont CA 94611-2817

ELGIN, RON ALAN, advertising executive; b. Milw., Sept. 15, 1941; s. Carl John and Vivian Elaine (Phillips) E.; m. Bonnie Kay Visintainer, Dec. 3, 1968; 1 child, Alison. BA in Advt., U. Wash., 1965. With Cole & Weber, Seattle, 1965-81; pres. Elgin Syferd, Seattle, 1981—; chmn. Elgin Syferd, Boise, Idaho, 1987—; pres. DDB Needham Retail, 1990-93; bd. dirs. Kunath, Karren, Rinne & Atkins, Seattle, 1987—; chmn. Hornall Anderson Design Works, Seattle, 1982-91; ptnr. Christiansen & Fritsch Direct, Seattle, 1988—. Bd. dirs. Pacific N.W. Ballet, Seattle, 1988—, Big Bros., Seattle, 1986—, Ronald McDonald House, Seattle, 1984—, Spl. Olympics, Seattle, 1987-90, Poncho, Seattle, 1991—; mem. adv. bd. U. Wash., Wash. State U. Lt. U.S. Army, 1965-69. Mem. AICPA, Mich. Assn. CPAs, AAA Mich. (bd. dirs.), Country Club (Bloomfield Hills, Mich.), Orchard Lake (Mich.) Country Club, Lost Tree Club (Palm Beach, Fla.), Jupiter (Fla.) Hills Club, Everglades Club (Palm Beach). Republican. Office: DDB Needham Worldwide Inc Elgin Syferd/DDB Needham 1008 Western Ave Seattle WA 98104

ELIAS, SHEILA, artist; b. Chgo., June 30. MA, Calif. State U., Northridge, 1975; BFA, Columbus Coll. Art & Design, 1973; student, Art Inst. of Chgo., 1963-73. One-woman shows include Alex Rosenberg, N.Y.C., 1987, U. N.C., Chapel Hill, 1987, Gallery 99, Bay Harbor, Fla., 1988, Paula Allan Gallery, N.Y.C., 1987-89, Ratner Gallery, Chgo., 1990, others: group exhbns. include Louvre, Paris, 1987, Valerie Miller Fine Arts, Palm Springs, Calif., 1988, Otis Parsons Sch. of Design, L.A., 1988, Anne Jaffe Gallery, Bay Harbor, 1989, Santa Monica (Calif.) Heritage Mus., 1991, Ft. Lauderdale Mus., 1991, New England Mus. of Contemporary Art, 1993, Art and Cultural Ctr. of Hollywood, 1993; pub. collections include Bklyn. Mus. Art, Chase Manhattan Bank, N.Y.C., First L.A. Bank, Exec. Life Ins., L.A., Security Pacific Bank, L.A., Paramount Pictures, L.A., Laguna Beach Mus. Art, Kinsan Contemporary Mus., Korea. Address: 9188 W Pico Blvd Los Angeles CA 90035

ELIAS, THOMAS SAM, botanist, author; b. Cairo, Ill., Dec. 30, 1942; s. George Sam and Anna (Clanton) E.; m. Barbara Ana Boyd (dec.); children: Stephen, Brian. BA in Botany, So. Ill. U., 1964, MA in Botany, 1966; PhD in Biology, St. Louis U., 1969. Asst. curator Arnold Arboretum of Harvard U., Cambridge, Mass., 1969-71; adminstr., dendrologist Cary Arboretum, N.Y. Botanical Garden, Millbrook, 1971-73, asst. dir., 1973-84; dir., chief exec. officer Rancho Santa Ana Botanic Garden, Claremont, Calif., 1984—; chmn., prof. dept. botany Claremont Grad. Sch., 1984—; lectr. in extension Harvard U., 1971; adj. prof. Coll. Environ. Science and Forestry, Syracuse, N.Y., 1977-80; coord. U.S.A/U.S.S.R. Botanical Exch., Program for U.S. Dept. of Interior, Washington, 1976—, U.S.A./China Botanical Exch., Program for U.S. Dept. of Interior, 1988—. Editor: Extinction is Forever, 1977 (one of 100 Best Books in Sci. and Tech. ALA 1977), Conservation and Management of Rare and Endangered Plants, 1987; author: Complete Trees of North America, 1980 (one of 100 Best Books in Sci. and Tech. ALA 1980), Field Guide to Edible Wild Plants of North America (one of 100 Best Books in Sci. and Tech. ALA 1983). Recipient Cooley award Am. Soc. Plant Taxonomist, 1970, Disting. Alumni award So. Ill. U., 1989. Home: 2447 San Mateo Ct Claremont CA 91711-1652 Office: Rancho Santa Ana Botanic Garden 1500 N College Ave Claremont CA 91711-3157

ELIAS, ZIAD MALEK, engineering educator; b. Syria, Mar. 29, 1934; came to U.S., 1959; s. Malek R. and Laurice Y. (Chedid) E.; m. Ralda Camille Saleh, Aug. 15, 1973; children: Maria, Laila, Paul. ScD, MIT, 1963; Ingenieur, Ecole Centrale, Paris, 1958. Asst. prof. engring. MIT, Cambridge, Mass., 1963-68; vis. assoc. prof. engring. Am. U. of Beirut, 1968-69; assoc. prof. engring. U. Wash., Seattle, 1969-74, prof. civil. engring., 1974—. Author: Theory and Methods of Structural Analysis, 1986; contbr. articles to profl. jours. Home: 23307 14th Pl W Bothwell WA 98021 Office: U Wash FX-10 Seattle WA 98195

ELIASON, ALAN LEWIS, computer scientist, educator; b. St. Paul, Dec. 27, 1939; s. Robert Garfield and Lurene Elizabeth (Nelson) E.; m. Millicent Jane Hayhoe, Feb. 11, 1965; children: Edward Andrew, Brian James. Student, Gustavus Adolphus Coll., St. Peter, Minn., 1957-59; MBE, U. Minn., 1962, MBA, 1965, PhD, 1970. Product devel. engr. E.I. duPont deNemours, Buffalo, 1962-63; pers. asst. U. Minn., Mpls., 1964-65, instr., 1967-70; asst. prof. Calif. State Poly. U., San Luis Obispo, 1965-67; assoc. prof. U. Oreg., Eugene, 1970-77, 79—, U. Calgary, Alta., Can., 1977-79; cons. Eliason and Assocs., Eugene, Oreg., 1979—, Sci. Rsch. Assocs., Inc., Chgo., 1985—. Author numerous books and case studies, 1974—; series editor Prentice-Hall, Inc., 1989—. NDEA fellow, 1968. Mem. Am. Product Inventory Control Soc. (bd. dirs.), Willamette Ski Club (bd. dirs.), South Eugene Soccer Club (bd. dirs.). Democrat. Home: 2520 Charnelton St Eugene OR 97405-3216 Office: U Oreg Dept Computer Sci Eugene OR 97403

ELIASSEN, JON ERIC, utility company executive; b. Omak, Wash., Mar. 10, 1947; s. Marvin George and Helen Grace (Meyer) E.; m. Valerie A. Foyle, Aug. 14, 1971; 1 child, Michael T. BA in Bus., Wash. State U., 1970. Staff acct. Wash. Water Power Co., Spokane, 1970-73, tax acct., 1973-76, fin. analyst, 1976-80, treas., 1980-86, v.p. fin., chief fin. officer, 1986—; bd. dirs. Spokane Capital Mgmt. Co., Itron Corp., Pentzer Corp., Nova NW Utility Funding, I. Trustee Wash. State Univ. Found., Pullman, 1987—, Spokane Symphony, 1989—, treas., 1990—. Mem. Pacific Coast Gas Assn. (past chmn. adminstrv. svcs. com.), Edison Electric Inst. (fin. com. 1986—), Fin. Exec. Inst. (bd. dirs., sec., past pres. Inland N.W. chpt. 1983—). Episcopalian. Office: Wash Water Power Co PO Box 3727 Spokane WA 99220-3727

ELIE, MEHRDAD, mortgage banking executive; b. Tehran, Iran, July 26, 1959; came to U.S., 1976; s. Jamshid and Esther E. BS in Aero. Engring., San Jose State U., 1980; MBA in Real Estate, Golden Gate U., 1987. Cert. mortgage banking. Dir. mktg. Internat. Mktg. Group, Burlingame, Calif., 1982-87; pres. Am. Residential Svcs., Burlingame, 1987-90; CEO, pres. Alliance Bancorp, Millbrae, Calif., 1990—. Mem. Nat. Assn. Mortgage Brokers, Calif. Assn. Mortgage Brokers, Calif. Assn. Residential Lenders,

Mortgage Bankers Assn. Office: Alliance Bancorp 800 El Camino Rd Millbrae CA 94030

ELIEN, MONA MARIE, air transportation professional; b. Atwood, Kans., June 13, 1932; d. Lawrence Wallace Berry and Adele Rosina (Gulzow) Wright; m. R.J. Wright, Jan. 1952 (div. 1957); m. J.P. Kobus, Nov. 1968 (div. 1991); m. Robert Louis Tour, Oct. 3, 1992. BS, U. Ariz., 1961; grad., Swiss Mountain Climbing Inst., Rosenalui, 1963; postgrad., No. Ariz. U., 1966-67, Ariz. State U., 1967-69, 86-87; MPA, Ariz. State U., 1981. Customer rels. rep. Ariz. Pub. Svc. Co., Casa Grande, Flagstaff, Ariz., 1961-67; owner/operator Mona's Clipping Svc., Phoenix, 1969-74; various positions City of Phoenix, 1974—; contract mgr. Phoenix CETA/PSE/PNP, 1978-81; planning and devel. asst. Phoenix Sky Harbor Internat. Airport, 1986—; staff asst. 1988 Citizens Bond Com. for Aviation, Phoenix, 1987-88. Compiler, editor: Aviation Acronyms and Abbreviations, 1987, 2d rev. edit., 1992; editor, writer (newsletter) Rapsheet, 1972-75; author profl. columns, 1961-67. Pres. state home econs. occupations adv. bd. Ariz. State U., 1983-84; mem. City Mgr.'s Women's Issues com., Phoenix, 1989-91, Zonta Internat., 1962-65; pres.-elect, Tri-City (Ariz.), 1964-65; vol. speaker's bur. Phoenix Community Alliance and Prep. Acad. Partnership, 1992—; mem. exec. com. Svc. Fund Dr., Phoenix, 1984-86; precinct com. Yuma County, Ariz., 1958; employee-of-yr. com. mem. City of Phoenix Aviation Dept., 1993, 94. Recipient Recognition Pub. Svc. award Ariz. Dept. Econs. Security, 1975, Heart and Soul award Barry M. Goldwater Terminal 4, 1990, PHXcellence award, 1993; named one of Outstanding Young Women of Am., 1966. Mem. APSA (life; Phoenix chpt. awards banquet com. 1991, 92, nat. com. 1990-91), Am. Home Econs. Assn. (life), Ariz. Home Econs. Assn. (pres. no. region 1965-67), Sinagua Soc. Museum No. Ariz., Satisfied Frog Gold Mountain Club, Flagstaff C. of C. (chmn. Indian princesses, retail mchts. sect. 1965-67), So. Ariz. Hiking Club, Desert Bot. Gardens, Swinging Stars Square Dance Club, Delta Delta Delta. Republican. Lutheran. Home: 2201 E Palmaire Ave Phoenix AZ 85020-5633 Office: Phoenix Sky Harbor Internat Airport 3400 E Sky Harbor Blvd Phoenix AZ 85034-4403

ELINGER, WAYNE JOHN, engineering educator; b. Toledo, Sept. 7, 1943; s. John Charles and Florence (Berry) E.; m. Janet Louise Lehnherr, June 24, 1967; children: Joan Louise, Lisa Anne. BS in Indsl. Edn., Stout State U., 1967, MS in Edn., 1970. Instr. in structural arch. Larson, Playter, Smith, Green Bay, Wis., 1967-72; curriculum specialist N.W. Wis. Tech. Inst., Green Bay, 1972-76, instr. in constrn. tech., 1976-82; instr. in engr.-computer aided design Cen. Wyo. Coll., 1982-84; owner CAD West Computer Cons. and Tng., Riverton, Wyo., 1984-85; asst. dir. spokane computer aided design Spokane C.C., 1985-89, assoc. dean mfg. engring., 1989—, dir. applied tech. ctr., 1991—. Author: Applying AUTOSketch, 1990, 2d edit., 1992. Sec.-treas. Wash. Coalition for ATC, 1992; mem. edn. com. Econ. Devel. Ctr., Spokane, 1991-92; ednl. rep. SIRTI, Spokane, 1989-92, Tech. Prep., Spokane, 1990-92. Mem. Alliance Mfg. Productivity (exec. chair 1990-92), Soc. Mfg. Engrs., Nat. Fluid Power Soc. Home: 6108 N Parkview Ln Spokane WA 99205 Office: Spokane CC 1810 N Greene St MS 2013 Spokane WA 99207

ELINSON, HENRY DAVID, artist, language educator; b. Leningrad, USSR, Dec. 14, 1935; came to U.S., 1973; s. David Moses and Fraida Zelma (Ufa) E.; m. Ludmila Nicholas Tepina, Oct. 7, 1955; 1 child, Maria Henry. Student, Herzen State Pedagogical U., Leningrad, 1954-57; BA, Pedagogical Inst., Novgorod, USSR, 1958; MA, Pedagogical Inst., Moscow, 1963. Cert. educator. Spl. edn. tchr. Leningrad Sch. Spl. Edn., 1961-64; supr. dept. speech therapy Psychoneurological Dispensary, Leningrad, 1964-73; instr. Russian lang. Yale U., New Haven, Conn., 1975-76, Def. Lang. Inst., Presidio of Monterey, Calif., 1976—. One-man shows include The Light and Motion Transmutation Galleries, N.Y.C., 1974, Thor Gallery, Louisville, 1974, Monterey (Calif.) Peninsula Art Mus., 1977, U. Calif. Nelson Gallery, Davis, 1978, Nahamkin Gallery, N.Y.C., 1978, Nahamkin Fine Arts, N.Y.C., 1980, Gallery Paule Anglim, 1981, 85, 87, Gallery Paule Anglim, San Francisco, 1991, 93, Dosfoevsky's Mus., St. Petersburg, Russia, 1992; exhibited in group shows at Bklyn. Coll. Art Ctr., 1974, CUNY, 1974, Galleria II Punto, Genoa, Italy, 1975, New Art From the Soviet Union, Washington, 1977, Gallery Hardy, Paris, 1978, Mus. of Fine Art, San Francisco, 1979, and numerous others; represented in permanent collections Mus. Fine Arts, San Francisco, Yale U. Art Gallery, Monterey Mus. Art, U. Calif. Art Mus., Berkeley, Bochum Mus., West Germany, Check Point Charlie Mus., West Berlin, State Russian Mus., Leningrad; participant Nonconforminst Art Exhbns., St. Petersburg, 1960; contbr. articles to profl. jours. Mem. Underground Anti-Soviet Govt. Students' Orgn., 1957. Recipient Gold medal Art Achievement City of Milan, 1975. Home: 997 Benito Ct Pacific Grove CA 93950-5333

ELION, HERBERT A., optoelectronics and bioengineering executive, physicist; b. N.Y.C., Oct. 16, 1923; s. Robert and Bertha (Cohen) E.; m. Sheila Thall, June 16, 1945; children: Gary Douglas, Glenn Richard, Jonathon Lee, Maxine Yael Gold. BSME, CCNY, 1945; MS, Bklyn. Poly. Inst., 1949, grad. in physics, 1954; grad. cert. X-ray Microanalysis, MIT, 1960; PhD (hon), Hamilton State U., 1973; cert., Cambridge U., Eng., U. Bordeaux, France, Pa. State U., Rutgers U., M.I.T., Northeastern U.; MA, U. Calif., Santa Barbara, San Francisco and Davis; postgrad., Coll. of Marin, Calif., Revere Acad. Jewelry Arts, San Francisco; cert., MacDowell Labs., Aldie, Va. Registered profl. engr., Mass., Pa., N.Y.; MacDowell Labs. VA Cert. Group leader RCA, Camden, N.J., 1957-59; pres. Elion Instruments, Inc., Burlington, N.J., 1959-64; assoc. dir. space sci. GCA Corp., Bedford, Mass., 1965-67; mng. dir. electro-optics Arthur D. Little Inc., Cambridge, Mass., 1967-79; pres., chief exec. officer Internat. Communications and Energy, Inc., Framingham, Mass., 1979—; pres. Aetna Telecommunications Cons., Centerville, Mass., 1981-85; also ptnr. Aetna Telecommunications Cons., Hartford, Conn., 1981-85; pres., chief exec. officer Internat. Optical Telecommunications, Mill Valley, Calif., 1981—; co-founder Kristallchemie M & Elion GmbH, Meudt, Fed. Fepublic Germany, 1961-64; lectr. on communications to Japanese, French, Can., Korean and Brazilian govts., 1970—; lectr. on optical communication to govt. depts. in Japan, France, Can., Korea, Brazil, 1970—; cons. on data communications Exec. Office of Pres., Washington, 1978-79; cons. Ministry Internat. Trade and Industry, Tokyo, 1975-88; chmn. internat. conf. European Electro-optics Conf., Heeze, The Netherlands, 1972-78; Mont. amb. Clean Coal Energy com., 1990—; internat. lectr. in field. Author, editor 27 books including 11 on lightwave info. networks; co-editor: Progress in Nuclear Energy in Analytical Chemistry Series, 1964-75; mem. adv. bd. Photonics Mag.; several Japanese and internat. world records in geothermal energy devel. activities in clean energy by GeoGas (R) process and clean air by elimination of methane and carbon dioxide gases and econ. prodn. of methyl alcohol from geothermal gases and econ. prodn. of methyl alcohol from geothermal gases; devel. supervision in 100% high strength organically biodegradable or smokeless burning plastic; contbr. articles to profl. jours. Pres. Elion Found., Princeton, N.J., 1960-67; founder Rainbow's End Camp, Ashby, Mass., 1960; elder Unitarian Ch., Princeton, 1963-64, Wellesley Soc. of Friends, 1970. With USN, 1944-46. Decorated Chevalier du Tastevin (France); recipient Presdl. awards Arthur D. Little Inc. Fellow Am. Phys. Soc.; mem. AAAS, IEEE (life mem., sr.), Optical Soc. Am., Soc. Photo Instrumentation Engrs., Am. Vacuum Soc., Nat. Security Industrial Assn., Soc. for Nondestructive testing, Am. Chem. Soc., Geothermal Resources Coun., Sigma Xi, Epsilon Nu Gamma, United Fedn. of Doll Clubs. Office: Internat Comms and Energy PO Box 2890 Sausalito CA 94966-2890 also: Box 789 Chatham MA 02633

ELKIND, MORTIMER MURRAY, biophysicist, educator; b. Bklyn., Oct. 25, 1922; s. Samuel and Yetta (Lubarsky) E.; m. Karla Annikki Holst, Jan. 27, 1960; children—Sean Thomas, Samuel Scott, Jonathan Harald. B.M.E., Cooper Union, 1943; M.M.E., Poly. Inst. Bklyn., 1949; M.S. in Elec. Engring, Mass. Inst. Tech., 1951, Ph.D. in Physics, 1953. Asst. project engr. Wyssmont Co., N.Y.C., 1943; project engr. Safe Flight Instrument Corp., White Plains, N.Y., 1946-47; head instrumentation sect. Sloan Kettering Inst. Cancer Research, 1947-49; physicist Nat. Cancer Inst. on assignment to Mass. Inst. Tech., 1949-53; on assignment to Donner Lab., U. Calif. at Berkeley, 1953-54; physicist Lab. Physiology, Nat. Cancer Inst., Bethesda, Md., 1954-67; sr. research physicist Lab. Physiology, Nat. Cancer Inst., 1967-69; sr. biophysicist biology dept. Brookhaven Nat. Lab., Upton, L.I., N.Y., 1969-73; guest scientist MRC exptl. radiopathology unit Hammersmith Hosp., London, 1971-73; sr. biophysicist, div. biol. and med. research Argonne (Ill.) Nat. Lab., 1973—, asst. dir., 1976-78, head mammalian cell biology group, 1978-81; prof. radiology U. Chgo., 1973-81; prof., chmn. dept. radiology and radiation biology Colo. State U., 1981-89, U. Disting. prof. dept. radiological health scis., 1986—; mem. radiation study sect. NIH, 1962-66, molecular biology study sect., 1970-71; mem. developmental therapeutics com. Nat. Cancer Inst., 1975-77. Author monograph. Served with USNR, 1944-46. Recipient E.O. Lawrence award AEC, 1967, Superior Service award HEW, 1969, L.H. Gray medal Internat. Com. Radiation Units and Measurements, 1977, E.W. Bertner award M.D. Anderson Hosp. and Tumor Inst., 1979, A.W. Erskine award Radiol. Soc. N. Am., 1980, Albert Soiland Meml. award Albert Soiland Cancer Found., 1984, 1st Henry S. Kaplan Disting. Scientist award Internat. Assn. Radiation Research, 1987, Charles F. Kettering prize Gen. Motors Cancer Rsch. Found., 1989, Honor Scientist award Colo. State U. chpt. Sigma Xi, 1991; Outstanding Investigator grantee Nat. Cancer Inst., 1988; Nat. Cancer Inst. Spl. fellow, 1972-74. Fellow Am. Coll. Radiology (hon.); mem. AAAS, Biophys. Soc., Radiation Research Soc. (council 1965-66, assoc. editor jour. 1965-68, pres.-elect and pres. 1980-81, G. Failla Meml. award 1984), Am. Assn. Cancer Research (assoc. editor jour. 1980-81), Am. Soc. Therapeutic Radiology and Oncology (gold medalist 1983), Tau Beta Pi. Office: Colo State U Dept Radiol Health Scis Fort Collins CO 80523

ELKINS, GLEN RAY, service company executive; b. Winnsboro, La., May 23, 1933; s. Ceicel Herbert and Edna Mae (Luallen) E.; m. Irene Kay Hildebrand, Aug. 25, 1951; children: Steven Breen, Douglas Charles, Karen Anne, Michael Glen; m. Diane Hodgson, Mar. 2, 1992. AA in Indsl. Mgmt, Coll. San Mateo, 1958. Successively mgr. production control, mgr. logistics, plant mgr., asst. v.p. ops. Aircraft Engring. and Maintenance Co. (Aemco), 1957-64; successively mgr. field ops., v.p. ops., exec. v.p., pres. Internat. Atlas Svcs. Co., Princeton, N.J., 1964-85; sr. v.p. Atlas Corp., Princeton; chmn., chief exec. officer, dir. Global Assocs., 1973-85; pres. Global Assocs. Internat. Ltd., 1975-84; pres., chief exec. officer Triad Am. Svcs. Corp., 1985—; pres. Pacific Mgmt. Svcs. Corp., TASC Enterprises Inc., dba Gottschall Engraving Co., 1993—. Area chmn. Easter Seals drive, 1974; bd. dirs. Utah Children's Mus. With USN, 1950-54. Mem. Nat. Mgmt. Assn., Electronic Industries Assn. Clubs: Lakeview, Willow Creek Country (Salt Lake City). Home: 1445 Harvard Ave Salt Lake City UT 84105-1917 Office: 45 W Senior Way Salt Lake City UT 84115

ELKINS, ROLAND LUCIEN, marketing executive; b. Coral Gables, Fla., Aug. 8, 1945; s. George Meyer and Leona (Wolfson) E.; m. Ruth Binder, Apr. 1, 1967; children: Eric Seth, Sarah Lynn, Karen Rachel. BA, Am. U., 1967. Prodn. mgr. Am. Aviation Pub., Washington, 1968-69, Govt. Exec. Mag., Washington, 1969-72; advt. scheduling mgr. Army Times Pub. Co., Washington, 1972-75; prodn. mgr. Colo. Mag., Denver, 1975-80; gen. mgr. Guest Informant, Beverly Hills, Calif., 1980-82; exec. v.p. Williams Printing Inc., Colorado Springs, Colo., 1983-88; chief exec. officer Automobile Quar., 1988-89; dir. adminstrn. Eagle Direct, Denver, 1989—; cons. Western Pub. Assn., Los Angeles, 1980-82. Recipient 1st Pl. awards Colorado Springs Classic, 1983, Valley Ralley, 1983, Gleneagle (Colo.) Balloon Regatta, 1984, Grand Junction (Colo.) Balloon Rodeo, 1990, 92. Mem. Nat. Assn. Printers and Lithographers (top mgmt. award 1984), Ballooning Soc. of Pike's Peak (Colorado Springs) (pres. 1986-88, v.p. 1989-90). Jewish. Club: Ballooning Soc. of Pike's Peak (Colorado Springs) (pres. 1986—). Office: Eagle Direct 5105 E 41st Ave Denver CO 80216-4420

ELLAM, GUNNAR, architect, planner; b. Tallinn, Estonia, July 25, 1929; came to U.S., 1950; s. Hanno and Erika (Siirak) E.; m. Renate Sternberg, June 7, 1959 (div. 1984); 1 child, Inger. BA in Architecture, U. Calif., Berkeley, 1955, MA in Architecture, 1963. Registered architect, Calif. Head. archtl. dept. Soule Steel Co., San Francisco, 1959-63; chief architect CSB Constrn., Inc., Oakland, Calif., 1963-83; prin. Gunnar Ellam Architect, Oakland, 1983—. Prin. works include Pacific Gas and Electric Co. Offices, Merced, Calif. (City of Merced archtl. commendation award 1969), March Metalfab Co. Facility, Hayward, Calif., 1971 (Hayward C. of C. 1st award for archtl. design), Milne Trucking Co. Facility, San Leandro, Calif., 1975 (City of San Leandro archtl. design award), DiSalvo Trucking Co. Facility, Oakland, 1969, South San Francisco, Calif., 1978 (award Archtl. Record and Fleet Owner mag.), Centennial Bank Bldg., San Leandro, 1981 (City of San Leandro comml. devel. design award), Yellow Cab Office and Maintenance Facility, San Francisco (Calif. Systems Builders Assn. 1st honor award 1987, Systems Builders Assn. nat. honor award 1988). Capt. with USAF, 1956-59, USNG. Mem. AIA, Estonian League West Coast (v.p. 1992—), Estonian Soc. San Francisco (v.p. 1986-87, pres. 1988-91). Democrat.

ELLEGOOD, DONALD RUSSELL, publishing executive; b. Lawton, Okla., June 21, 1924; s. Claude Jennings and Iva Claire (Richards) E.; m. Bettie Jane Dixon, Dec. 11, 1947; children—Elizabeth Nemi, Francis Hunter, Kyle Richards, Sarah Helen. B.A., U. Okla., 1948, M.A., 1950. Asst. editor U. Okla. Press, 1950-51; editor Johns Hopkins Press, 1951-54; dir. La. State U. Press, 1954-63, U. Wash. Press, Seattle, 1963—. Contbr. articles to profl. jours. Served to 1st lt. USAAF, 1943-46. Decorated Air medal, D.F.C. Mem. Am. Univ. Pubs. Group London (dir.), Am. Assn. Univ. Presses (pres.), Phi Beta Kappa. Home: 17852 49th Pl NE Seattle WA 98155-4312 Office: U Wash Press PO Box 50096 Seattle WA 98145-5096

ELLER, GREGORY WILLIAM, human resources manager; b. Winston-Salem, N.C., Mar. 21, 1957; s. Vernon Gilbert Jr. and Bettye Jo (Lovette) E.; m. Jennifer Maria Guzzardi, Apr. 28, 1989. BA in Bus., U. N.C., Charlotte, 1979. Assoc. dir. pers. Am. Red Cross, Charlotte, N.C., 1979-80; pers. rep. Jack Eckerd Drug Co., Charlotte, 1980-83; dir. human resources Hilton Hotels, Miami, Fla., Myrtle Beach, S.C., Beverly Hills, Calif., 1983-89; corp. dir. human resources L'Ermitage Hotels Corp., W. Hollywood, Calif., 1988-89; mgr. divsn. human resources Vitro Vidrio Plano Am., Placentia, Calif., 1989—; mgmt. trustee Hotel Emplyees Trust Fund, L.A., 1987-89, Glazier's & Glassworkers Trust Fund, San Francisco, 1992—. Adv. bd. mem. Mecklenburg County, Charlotte, 1982-83. Mem. Sigma Phi Epsilon. Republican. Baptist. Office: VVP Am 231-A Lakeview Ave Placentia CA 92670

ELLER, THOMAS JULIAN, aerospace company executive, astronautical engineer, computer scientist; b. Pelham, Ga., Oct. 19, 1937; s. Eugene Robert and Frances Elizabeth (Greer) E.; m. Beverly Anne Lafitte, June 7, 1963; children: Julie Anne Eller Schake, Elizabeth Jean, Robert Lafitte. Student, Furman U., 1955-57; BS in Engring. Scis., USAF Acad., 1961; MS in Aero. and Astronautics, Purdue U., 1969; PhD in Aerospace Engring., U. Tex., 1974. Commd. 2nd lt. USAF, 1961, advanced through grades to col., 1981, pilot, 1961-69; prof., asst. dean faculty USAF Acad., Colorado Springs, Colo., 1969-78, comdr. 2nd group, 1978-79, prof., head dept. astronautics and computer sci., 1979-81; ret. USAF, 1981; program mgr. Internat. Tng. & Edn. Co., Boston, 1981-82; chief contracts requirements Martin Marietta Aerospace, Denver, 1982-85; bus. devel. mgr. Kaman Scis. Corp., Colorado Springs, 1985-86, space applications and astrodynamics mgr., 1986—; chmn. Mil. Space Doctrine Symposium USAF Acad., 1981; mem. space adv. com. Colo. 5th U.S. Congl. Dist., 1987—, chmn. 1992—. Contbr. articles on astronautics to profl. jours. Trustee Colorado Springs Fine Arts Ctr., 1986—; bd. dirs. The Falcon Found., Colorado Springs, 1983—, Acad. Rsch. and Devel. Inst., Colorado Springs, 1986—; founder, pres. Colo. Vietnam Vets. Leadership Program, Denver, 1983-84. Decorated D.F.C. (2), Airman's medal, Air medal (6), Vietnamese Cross of Gallantry with palm. Fellow AIAA (assoc.), chmn.-elect astrodynmic com. 1991-92, chmn. 1992—, astrodynamics standards com. 1991—), Accreditation Bd. Engring. and Tech. (engring. visitor 1981—), Assn. Grads. of USAF Acad. (v.p. 1975-79, bd. dirs. 1969-75, pres., chmn. 1979-83). Republican. Presbyterian. Office: Kaman Scis Corp PO Box 7463 Colorado Springs CO 80933-7463

ELLERMAN, CURTIS HOWELL, academic administrator; b. Lancaster, Calif., Sept. 6, 1959; s. Donald Roscoe Howell and Carol Elizabeth (Ellerman) Burns; m. Jana Stuart, Nov. 26, 1988; 1 child, Justin Stuart. AB, Occidental Coll., 1981; JD, Loyola Law Sch., 1986. Bar: Calif. 1986, U.S. Ct. Appeals (9th cir.) 1987. Adminstrv. analyst City of Glendale, Calif., 1980-83; dir. devel. Coro Found., L.A., 1983-86; pvt. practice law Pasadena, Calif., 1986-91; exec. asst. to pres. Occidental Coll., L.A., 1991—, adj. assoc. prof. politics, 1991—. Facilitator/editor: Of Excellence and Equity, 1991. Pres. Internat. Visitors Coun. L.A., 1992. Democrat. Presbyterian. Office: Occidental Coll Office of Pres Los Angeles CA 90041

ELLICOTT, HAROLD CHRISTIANSEN, retail company executive; b. Portland, Oreg., July 23, 1918; s. Randall M. and Dorthea A. (Christiansen) E.; m. Mary M. Mulkey, Aug. 10, 1941 (dec. Mar. 1975); children: Kristi, Randall; m. Irene M. Saloum, Mar. 13, 1976; children: Nicholas, Mark. BS, U. Oreg., 1941. Mgr. Honolulu Jr. C. of C., 1946-50; pers. mgr. Willamette Nat. Lumber Co., Sweet Home, Oreg., 1950-51; advt. dir. Malarkey Forest Products, Portland, 1951-55; advt. and promotions mgr. Ga.-Pacific Corp., Portland, 1955-70, dir. corp. comm., 1970-76, dir. industry affairs, 1977-80; dir. corp. comm. La.-Pacific Corp., Portland, 1976-77; pres. Easy Street Corp., Portland, 1980—. Precinct committeeman Rep. Com. Oreg., Portland, 1991. 2d lt. USAAF, 1943-45. Mem. Am. Wood Coun. (nat. pres. 1976-78), Nat. Forest Products Assn. (nat. bd. dirs. 1976-80), Am. Hardboard Assn. (nat. pres. 1975), Am. Plywood Assn. (chmn. promotion com. 1974-75). Office: Easy Street Corp 16337 SW Bryant Rd Oswego OR 97035

ELLINGS, RICHARD JAMES, research institution executive; b. Santa Barbara, Calif., Jan. 7, 1950; s. George MacMachan and Barbara Marie (Kollin) E.; m. Marta Anna Korduba; children: Katherine Nicole, John William. AB, U. Calif., Berkeley, 1973; MA, U. Wash., 1976, PhD, 1983. Lectr. Calif. Poly. State U., San Luis Obispo, 1980-81; lectr. U. Wash., Seattle, 1982-83, assoc. dir. Henry M. Jackson Sch. Internat. Studies, 1986-89; legis. asst. U.S. Senate, Washington, 1984-85; exec. dir. Nat. Bur. Asian Rsch., Seattle, 1989—; also bd. dirs.; participant Continuing N.W. Regional Colloquim on Internat. Security, 1982—; dir. George E. Taylor Fgn. Affairs Inst., Seattle, 1986-89; lectr. USIA, 1992; cons. in field. Author: Embargoes and World Power, 1985; co-author: Private Property and National Security, 1991; (monograph) Asia's Challenge to American Strategy, 1992. Del. Rep. Party State Conv., Tacoma, Wash., 1988; mem. state adv. group U.S. Senator Slade Gorton, Wash., 1989—; advisor Explorers, Seattle, 1992—. Grantee Dept. Def., 1990—. Mem. Am. Polit. Sci. Assn., Western Polit. Sci. Assn., Internat. Studies Assn. Home: PO Box 95673 Seattle WA 98145 Office: Nat Bur Asian Rsch 715 Safeco Plz Seattle WA 98185

ELLINGTON, JAMES WILLARD, mechanical design engineer; b. Richmond, Ind., May 26, 1927; s. Oscar Willard and Leola Lenora (Sanderson) E.; m. Sondra Elaine Darnell, Dec. 6, 1952; children: Ronald, Roxanna. BSME summa cum laude, West Coast U., L.A., 1978. Designer NATCO, Richmond, Ind., 1954-67; design engr. Burgmaster, Gardena, Calif., 1967-69; sr. mfg. engr. Xerox Co., El Segundo, Calif., 1969-84; cons. mem. engring. staff Xerox Co., Monrovia, 1984-87; staff engr. Photonic Automation, Santa Ana, Calif., 1987-88; sr. mech. engr. Optical Radiation Co., Azusa, Calif., 1988; sr. staff engr. Omnichrome, Chino, Calif., 1988—. With USN, 1945-52. Mem. Soc. Mfg. Engrs. (sec. 1984), West Coast U. Alumni Assn. (bd. dirs. 1988—, v.p. budget and fin.). Republican. Baptist. Office: Omnichrome 13580 5th St Chino CA 91710-5113

ELLIOTT, DARRELL KENNETH, minister, legal researcher; b. Inglewood, Calif., Apr. 19, 1952; s. Lloyd Kenneth and Marjorie (Myers) E. BA, Biola Coll., La Mirada, Calif., 1975; M Div., Talbot Theol. Sem., La Mirada, 1980; cert. in legal assistantship, U. Calif., Irvine, 1986; MS in Taxation, Northrop U., L.A., 1988; postgrad., U. Strasbourg, France, 1979, Western State U., Fullerton, Calif., 1988—, Simon Greenleaf Sch. of Law, 1990—. Ind. legal researcher, businessman Buena Park, Calif., 1970—; Simon Greenleaf U.; rep. Am. Soc. Internat. Law, 1984. Co-founder, assoc. minister Faith Community Ch., Cypress, Calif., 1972; assoc. minister Village Ch., Burbank, Calif., 1978; traveled throughout the country with Campus Crusade for Christ, 1980-81. Calif. State scholar, 1970-75, fellow 1975-80. Mem. Christian Legal Soc., Concerned Women for Am., The Rutherford Inst., Western Ctr. Law and Religious Freedom. Republican. Baptist. Home: 7839 Western Ave # B Buena Park CA 90620-2626

ELLIOTT, DOUGLAS CHARLES, chemist; b. Great Falls, Mont., Aug. 2, 1952; s. Walter Allen and Phyllis Marion (Daughters) E.; m. Nancy Lee Reynolds, July 21, 1973; children: Geoffrey Reynolds, Matthew Douglas, Christopher Allen. BS, Mont. State U., 1974; MBA, U. Wash., 1980. Scientist to staff Battelle-N.W., Richland, Wash., 1974—. Contbr. articles to profl. jours.; patentee in field. Recipient Fed. Lab. Consortium Tech. Transfer award, 1989, R&D 100 award, 1989, 91. Mem. Am. Chem. Soc. Home: 1130 Catskill St Richland WA 99352-2112 Office: Battelle NW PO Box 999 Richland WA 99352-0999

ELLIOTT, GORDON JEFFERSON, English language educator; b. Aberdeen, Wash., Nov. 13, 1928; s. Harry Cecil and Helga May (Kennedy) E.; m. Suzanne Tsugiko Urakawa, Apr. 2, 1957; children: Meiko Ann, Kenneth Gordon, Nancy Lee, Matthew Kennedy. AA, Grays Harbor Coll., 1948; BA, U. Wash., 1950; Cert. Russian, Army Lang. Sch., Monterey, Calif., 1952; MA, U. Hawaii, 1968. Lifetime credential, Calif. Community Coll. System. English prof. Buddhist U., Ministry of Cults, The Asia Found., Phnom Penh, Cambodia, 1956-62; English instr. U. Hawaii, Honolulu, 1962-68; dir., orientation English Coll. Petroleum and Minerals, Dhahran, Saudi Arabia, 1968-70; asst. prof., English/linguistics U. Guam, Mangilao, 1970-76; tchr., French/English Medford (Oreg.) Mid High Sch., 1976-77; instr., English Merced (Calif.) Coll., 1977—; cons. on Buddhist Edn., The Asia Found., San Francisco, Phnom Penh, Cambodia, 1956-62; cons. on English Edn., Hawaii State Adult Edn. Dept., Honolulu, 1966-68; conf. on English Edn. in Middle East, Am. U., Cairo, Egypt, 1969; vis. prof. of English, Shandong Tchrs. U., Jinan, China, 1984-85. Co-author: (textbooks, bilingual Cambodian-English) English Composition, 1962, Writing English, 1966, (test) Standard English Recognition Test, 1976; contbr. articles to profl. jours. Mem. Statue of Liberty Centennial Commn., Washington, 1980-86, Heritage Found., Washington, Lincoln Inst., Am. Near East Refugee Aid, Washington, Sgt. U.S. Army Security Agy., 1951-55. Tchr. Fellowship, U. Mich., Ann Arbor, 1956; recipient summer seminar stipend, Nat. Endowment For Humanities, U. Wash., Seattle, 1976, travel grants, People's Rep. of China, Beijing, 1984-85. Mem. NRA, Collegiate Press (editorial adv. bd.), Merced Coll. Found., Am. Assn. Woodturners, Elks. Republican. Home: 680 Dennis Ct Merced CA 95340-2410 Office: Merced Coll 3600 M St Merced CA 95348-2806

ELLIOTT, HAROLD MARSHALL, geography educator; b. Sebring, Fla., Jan. 4, 1943; s. Vernon G. and Elise (Marshall) E.; m. Anna J. Lang, Jan. 24, 1975; children: Dora Louise, Sarah Ariel; 1 child from previous marriage, Laura Diane. BA, San Francisco State U., 1964, MA, 1970; PhD, U. Okla., 1978. Instr. Coll. San Mateo, Calif., 1969, Cameron U., Lawton, Okla., 1970-72, Fla. Internat. U., Miami, 1977-78; from asst. prof. to assoc. prof. Weber State U., Ogden, Utah, 1979-88, prof. geography, 1988—; cartographer Thomas Bros. Maps, L.A., 1977; asst. planner Coral Gables (Fla.) City Planning Dept., 1978. Contbr. numerous articles to profl. jours. including Geog. Analysis, Econ. Geography, Urban Geography, Jour. Geography, Profl. Geographer. Del. Weber County Dem. Conv., 1980-83. 1st lt. U.S. Army, 1964-67. Mem. ACLU, Assn. Am. Geographers, Assn. Pacific Coast Geographers, Am. Mensa. Home: 4834 Van Buren Ave Ogden UT 84403-4255

ELLIOTT, JAMES HEYER, fine arts consultant; b. Medford, Oreg., Feb. 19, 1924; s. Bert R. and Marguerite E. (Heyer) E.; m. Judith Ann Algar, Apr. 23, 1966 (div.); children—Arabel Joan, Jakob Maxwell. BA, Willamette U., Salem, Oreg., 1947, DFA (hon.), 1978; AM, Harvard U., 1949; DFA (hon.), San Francisco Art Inst., 1991. James Rogers Rich fellow Harvard U., 1949-50; Fulbright grantee Paris, 1951-52; art critic European edit. N.Y. Herald-Tribune, 1952-53; curator, acting dir. Walker Art Center, Mpls., 1953-56; asst. chief curator, curator modern art Los Angeles County Mus. Art, 1956-63, chief curator, 1964-66; dir. Wadsworth Atheneum, Hartford, Conn., 1966-76; dir. Univ. Art Mus., Berkeley, Calif., 1976-88, chancellor's curator, 1989-90, dir. emeritus, 1990—; adj. prof. Hunter Coll., N.Y.C., 1968, U. Calif., Berkeley, 1976-90; commr. Conn. Commn. Arts, 1970-76; fellow Trumbull Coll., Yale U., 1971-75; mem. mus. arts panel Nat. Endowment Arts, 1974-77; bd. dirs. San Francisco Art Inst., 1980-90; art adv. com. Exploratorium, 1982-91; adv. com. Artists TV Access, 1987-90. Author: Bonnard and His Environment, 1964, James Lee Byars: Notes Towards a Biography, 1990. Trustee Marcia Simon Weisman Found., 1991—, 23--5 Found., San Francisco, 1993—; mem. adv. bd. Artspace San Francisco, 1989—. With USNR, 1943-46. Mem. Internat. Council Mus., Am. Assn. Mus., Coll. Art Assn., Assn. Art Mus. Dirs. (sec., trustee 1980-

81), Artists Space N.Y. (dir. 1980-84). Club: Arts (Berkeley). Home: 5 Sunset Way Sausalito CA 94965-9757

ELLIOTT, JEANNE MARIE KORELTZ, transportation executive; b. Virginia, Minn., Mar. 9, 1943; d. John Andrew and Johanna Mae (Tehovnik) Koreltz; m. David Michael Elliott, Apr. 30, 1983. Student, Ariz. State U., 1967, U. So. Calif. Cert. aviation safety inspector. Tech. asst. Ariz. State U., Tempe, 1966-68; from supr. to mgr. inflight tng./in-svc. programs Northwest Airlines Inc. (formerly Republic Airlines, Hughes Airwest, Air West Inc.), Seattle, 1968—; air carrier cabin safety specialist Flight Standards Service, FAA, Washington, 1975-76; cons. Interaction Research Corp., Olympia, Wash., 1982—. Contbg. editor Cabin Crew Safety Bull., Flight Safety Found., 1978—. Recipient Annual Air Safety award Air Line Pilots Assn., Washington, 1971, Annual Safety award Ariz. Safety Council, Phoenix, 1972; first female to hold FAA cabin safety inspector's credential, 1976. Mem. Soc. Air Safety Investigators Internat., Survival and Flight Equipment Assn., Assn. Flight Attendants (tech. chmn. 1968-85), Soc. Automotive Engrs. (assoc., chmn. cabin safety provisions com. 1971—), Teamsters Local 2000 (chairperson Nat. Safety & Health). Republican. Roman Catholic. Home: 16215 SE 31st St Bellevue WA 98008-5704 Office: NW Airlines Inc Inflight Svcs Dept Seattle-Tacoma Internat Airport Seattle WA 98158 also: IBT Minneapolis MN 55425

ELLIOTT, JOHN GREGORY, aerospace design engineer; b. Surabaya, Dutch East Indies, Nov. 9, 1948; came to U.S., 1956; s. Frans Jan and Charlotte Clara (Rosel) E.; m. Jennifer Lee Austin, May 7, 1988. AA, Cerritos Coll., 1974; BS, Calif. State U., Long Beach, 1978. Design engr. Douglas Aircraft Co., Long Beach, 1978-82, lead engr., 1983-89, sect. mgr. elect. installations group, 1989—. With USN, 1969-73. Mem. So. Calif. Profl. Engring. Assn., Douglas Aircraft Co. Tennis Club, Douglas Aircraft Co. Surf Club, Douglas Aircraft Co. Mgmt. Club. Republican. Presbyterian. Office: Douglas Aircraft Co Internal Mail Code 2-91 3855 N Lakewood Blvd Long Beach CA 90846-0001

ELLIOTT, KATHLEEN ADELE, director of publications; b. Chgo., June 21, 1956; d. Patrick Frank and Martha Lou (Dick) E. Student, U. Kans., 1974-75; AA with honors, Johnson County Community Coll., Overland Park, Kans., 1987; student, Ottawa U., 1991—. Graphic artist The Pica Den, Overland Park, 1987-89; dir. publs., advisor student publs. Ottawa (Kans.) U., 1989-93; graphics dir. MPCO Graphics & Printing, Boulder, Colo., 1993—. Mem. Ottawa Area C. of C. (chairperson com. 1991—, Leadership award 1990, 91), Ottawa Country Club, Jaycees. Democrat. Baptist. Office: MCPO 607 F S Broadway Boulder CO 80303

ELLIOTT, LEROY, flea market owner; b. Wasco, Calif., Feb. 16, 1944; s. James Albert and Blanche Marie (Murphy) E.; m. Linda Smith, 1965 (div. 1977); m. Cheryl Lynn Duncan, July 9, 1979; 1 child, Christina Lynn. Grad. high sch., Bakersfield, Calif. Machine operator Owens/Ill. Glass Factory, Oakland, Calif., 1962-64; constrn. worker various cos., Bakersfield, 1964-82; owner Tires-R-Us, Bakersfield, 1982-85; owner Rags to Riches Second Hand, Tehachapi, Calif., 1985-86, Oroville, Calif., 1986-91; owner Rags to Riches Flea Market/Auction, Oroville, 1991—. Republican. Baptist. Office: Rags to Riches Flea Market Hwy 70 Palermo Rd Oroville CA 95965

ELLIOTT, ODUS VERNON, higher education organization administrator; b. Nacogdoches, Tex., July 19, 1940; s. Odus Vernon and Mary Opal (Lewis) E.; m. Diana Beverly Scarbrough, Oct. 8, 1965; children: Lara Evelyn, Devin Odus. BA in History, Stephen F. Austin U., 1962; MA in Govt., U. Ariz., 1966, PhD in Edn. Adminstrn. and Govt., 1973. Assoc. dir. student housing U. Ariz., Tucson, 1966-77; acad. planning analyst Ariz. Bd. Regnets, Phoenix, 1977-79, asst. dir. acad. programs, 1979-83, assoc. dir. acad. programs, 1983-91; program officer Fund for the Improvement of Post-secondary Edn., Washington, 1992—. Mem. adjustment bd. City of Mesa, Ariz., 1981-82, mem. planning and zoning bd., 1982-88, mem. bond adv. com., 1981, mem. long range planning commn., 1982. Mem. Am. Assn. for Higher Edn., Alpha Chi, Phi Delta Kappa. Presbyterian. Home: 2205 S Las Flores Mesa AZ 85202

ELLIOTT, ROBERT JAMES, mathematician; b. Swanwick, Derby, Eng., June 12, 1940; s. James Alfred and Marjorie Jane (Hilditch) E.; m. Ann Beardsley, Aug. 29, 1962; children—Jane Ann, Catherine Louise. B.A., Oxford U., 1961, M.A., 1964; Ph.D., Cambridge U., 1965, Sc.D., 1983. Lectr. U. Newcastle, Eng., 1964-65; instr. Yale U., 1965-66; fellow, lectr. Oriel Coll. and Oxford U., 1966-69; sr. research fellow Warwick U., England, 1969-72; prof. Hull U., Eng., 1973-76, G.F. Grant prof., 1976-86; prof. U. Alberta, Can., 1986—; vis. prof. Northwestern U., 1972-73, U. Toronto, 1972, U. Alberta, 1985-86, Australian Nat. U., 1983; disting. vis. prof. U. Alta., 1984-85. Author: Stochastic Calculus, 1982. Co-author: Values in Differential Games, 1972, also articles. Mem. Am. Math. Soc., Soc. for Indsl. and Applied Math., Math. Assn. Am. Avocation: music. Office: U Alberta, Dept Statis and Applied Probability, 434 CAB, Edmonton, AB Canada T6G 2G1

ELLIOTT, ROSS COX, insurance company executive; b. Orem, Utah, June 9, 1948; s. Grant Hansen and Pauline (Cox) E.; m. Mynon Hayes, Apr. 23, 1970; children: Edgar M., James W., Rosann. BS in Bus. Mgmt., Brigham Young U., 1972. Regional sales mgr. ADP Dealer Svcs., Denver, 1975-76, regional customer svc. mgr., 1976-78; dir. tng. Automatic Data Processing-Dealer Svcs., Portland, Oreg., 1979-85; dir. ins. svcs. Larry H. Miller Group, Murray, Utah, 1986—; chief oper. officer Landcar Life Ins. Co., Murray, 1986—, Landcar Agy., Murray, 1986—, Landcar Ins. Co. Colo., Murray, 1990—. Chmn. Murray City Gang Task Force, 1992—. Mem. Ins. Acctg. and Systems Adminstrn., Utah Life and Disability Ins. Guaranty Assn. (bd. dirs. 1990—, Murray City C. of C. (bd. dirs. 1992). Republican. Mem. LDS Ch. Home: 5865 Holstein Way Murray UT 84107 Office: Larry H Miller Group 5650 S State St Murray UT 84107

ELLIOTT, STEPHAN CHARLES, marketing executive; b. Houston, Oct. 26, 1948; s. Donald James and Ethel Genevieve (Mayfield) E.; m. Linda Jo Blackmon, May 2, 1985 (div.); children: Andrew, Nicklaus; m. Christine Habib, July 18, 1986; children: Amy, Annie. BS, U. Houston, 1970. Store mgr. Met. Paint Co., Arlington, Va., 1970-71; div. mgr. Handy Dan Home Improvement, San Antonio, 1971-76, Atlanta, 1976-79; gen. merchant mgr. Bonanza Bldg. Cts., San Jose, Calif., 1979-82, Omalley's Bldg. Ctrs., Phoenix, 1982-87; v.p. mktg. PK Lumber Co., Dayton, Ohio, 1987-89, City Mill Co. Ltd., Honolulu, 1990—. Sponsor Adopt a Classroom, Dayton, 1987-89, Honolulu, 1990-92, Easter Seals Soc., Honolulu, 1991-92. Recipient Advt. Excellence award Nat. Home Ctr. mag., 1982. Mem. Nat. Home Ctr. Inst. (coun. mem.), Rotary Club. Republican. Mem. Ch. of LDS. Home: 6772 Pukoo St Honolulu HI 96825 Office: City Mill Co Ltd 660 N Nimitz Hwy Honolulu HI 96817

ELLIOTT, THOMAS JOSEPH, English language educator; b. Boston, Jan. 25, 1941; s. Thomas Joseph and Anne Teresa (Regan) E.; m. Eugenia Marie Coleman, June 18, 1966; 1 child, Christine. AB, Boston Coll., 1963, MA, 1967; PhD, U. Mich., 1970. High sch. English and Latin instr. St. Dominic Savio Coll. Prep. Sch., East Boston, 1963-67; teaching fellow U. Mich., Ann Arbor, 1968-69; asst. prof. to prof. Calif. State Poly. U., Pomona, 1970—; vis. scholar U. Kent, Canterbury, England, 1984. Translator: A Medieval Bestiary, 1971; contbr. articles to profl. jours. Fellow Southeastern Ctr. for Medieval and Renaissance Studies, Duke U., 1976. Mem. MLA, New Chancer Soc. Democrat. Roman Catholic. Home: 982 W Richmond Dr Claremont CA 91711-3348 Office: Calif Poly U, Dept English 3801 W Temple Ave Pomona CA 91768-2557

ELLIOTT, W. NEIL, systems engineer; b. St. Louis, Mar. 7, 1948; s. Warren Harry and Virginia Elmira (Wagner) E.; m. Marcia Schiffra Lind (div. 1984); m. Rose Ann Polsky, Feb. 12, 1992. BA in English Lit., Duke U., 1970; PhD in Linguistics, CUNY, 1981. Sales promotion JC Penny Co., Inc., N.Y.C., 1970-72, advt. copywriter, 1972-75; lectr., rsch. specialist U. Calif., Irvine, 1983-90; systems engr. PacTel Meridian Systems, Cypress, Calif., 1990—; vis. scientist MIT, Cambridge, Mass., 1980-83. Contbr. articles to profl. jours. Dir. Rose Polsky and Dancers, L.A., 1985—. Mem. L.A. County Mus. Art, Dance Resource Ctr. L.A. Office: PacTel Meridian Systems 5785 Corp Ave #200 Cypress CA 90630

ELLIOTT, WARD EDWARD YANDELL, political science educator; b. Cambridge, Mass., Aug. 6, 1937; s. William Yandell and Mary Louise Ward; m. Myrna Joy Victoria Krahn; children: William Yandell, Christopher David. AB, Harvard U., 1959, AM, PhD, 1968; LLB, Va. Law Sch., 1964. Bar: D.C. 1964, Va. 1964; ordained to ministry Universal Life Ch., 1969. Assoc. Covington & Burling, Washington, 1964; prof. polit. sci. Claremont (Calif.) McKenna Coll., 1968—. Author: The Rise of Guardian Democracy, 1975. Served to 1st lt. U.S. Army, 1959-61. Fellow NIH, 1975, Earhart, 1975, 83, NEH, 1985; Haynes grantee NEH, 1988; recipient Roy C. Crocker prize Claremont McKenna Coll., 1984. Mem. AAAS. Republican. Clubs: Claremont McKenna Coll. East Coast (faculty sponsor), Pumpkin Papers Irregulars. Home: 875 N College Ave Claremont CA 91711-3923 Office: Claremont McKenna Coll Dept Govt 850 N Columbia Ave Claremont CA 91711-6420

ELLIS, AARON EDMUND, public affairs manager; b. Richland, Wash., Mar. 13, 1954; s. Sam Theodore Ellis and Mary Victoria (Newmaster) Mitchell; m. Debora Tims, Dec. 14, 1984. BS in Journalism, U. Oreg., 1977, MS in Journalism, 1986. Photographer Kennell-Ellis Studios, Inc., Eugene, Oreg., 1974-77; dir. Kennell-Ellis Studios, Inc., Eugene, 1978-86; pub. rels. exec. Capener/Walcher PR, San Diego, 1987-88, McKellar, Inc. PR, Salem, Oreg., 1988; correspondent Statesman Jour., Salem, 1988-89; pub. affairs mgr. Oreg. Mus. Sci. and Industry, Portland, 1989-91, Port of Portland, 1991—. Photographer numerous portraits. Chmn. Assoc. Profl. Photographers Lane County, 1983-85. Mem. Pub. Rels. Soc. Am., N.W. Writers, Inc., Kappa Tau Alpha. Democrat. Home: 2822 SE 19th Ave Portland OR 97202-2227 Office: Port of Portland PO Box 3529 Portland OR 97208

ELLIS, BIRK WOLFGANG, marketing professional, consultant; b. San Jose, Calif., June 29, 1966; s. Kenneth LeRoy, Jr. and Kim Darlene (Brinton) E. Grad. high sch., San Jose, Calif. Sales rep. Periodical Pubs. Svc. Bur., Los Gatos, Calif., 1984-85; unit sales mgr. Periodical Pubs. Svc. Bur., 1985-87; mktg. rep. 1st Nationwide Mortgage, San Jose, Calif., 1987; asst. br. mgr. Periodical Pubs. Svc. Bur., Los Gatos, Santa Clara, 1987-90; br. mgr. Profl. Readers Svc., Inc., Carmichael, Calif., 1990-92; franchisee/owner Profl. Readers Svc., Inc., Carmichael, 1992—; cons. pvt. practice, Carmichael, Calif., 1990—. Named 1st Place Best of Show Campbell Unified Sch. Dist. Art Show, Blackford High Sch., 1983, Br. of Yr. Periodical Pubs. Svc. Bur., 1989. Republican.

ELLIS, CARLTON CASE, managed futures trading specialist; b. Chgo., May 18, 1954; s. John Ogborn and Amanda Sophronia (Rogers) E.; m. Donna Lynn Sirjord, Oct. 12, 1985; children: Arthur John, Michael Stewart. AAS, Paul Smiths Coll., 1974; BS, Cornell U., 1976; M. Forestry, Oreg. State U., 1979. Cons. forester Sanders Cronk & Holmes, Portland, Oreg., 1979-81; mgmt. trainee Holman Transfer, Portland, 1981-82; pres. Mescan, Inc., Seattle, 1982-84; assoc. v.p. Prudential Securities, Seattle, 1984—. Mem. Managed Futures Assn., Cornell Club of Western Wash. (treas. 1990—, membership dir. 1989—, pres. 1992—), Wash. Athletic Club. Office: Prudential Securities 1201 3d Ave Ste 3500 Seattle WA 98101

ELLIS, ELDON EUGENE, surgeon; b. Washington, Ind., July 2, 1922; s. Osman Polson and Ina Lucretia (Cochran) E.; BA, U. Rochester, 1946, MD, 1949; m. Irene Clay, June 26, 1948 (dec. 1968); m. Priscilla Dean Strong, Sept. 20, 1969 (dec. Feb. 1990); children: Paul Addison, Kathe Lynn, Jonathan Clay, Sharon Anne, Eldon Eugene, Rebecca Deborah; m. Virginia Michael Ellis, Aug. 22, 1992. Intern in surgery Stanford U. Hosp., San Francisco, 1949-50, resident and fellow in surgery, 1950-52, 55; Schilling fellow in pathology San Francisco Gen. Hosp., 1955; ptnr. Redwood Med. Clinic, Redwood City, Calif., 1955-87, med. dir., 1984-87; semi-ret. physician, 1987—; med. dir. Peninsula Occupational Health Assocs., San Carlos, Calif., 1991—; dir. Sequoia Hosp., Redwood City, 1974-82; asst. clin. prof. surgery Stanford U., 1970-80. Pres. Sequoia Hosp. Found., 1983-92, bd. dirs.; pres., chmn. bd. dirs. Bay Chamber Symphony Orch., San Mateo, Calif., 1988-91; mem. Nat. Bd. of Benevolence Evang. Covenant Ch., Chgo., 1988-93; mem. mgmt. com. The Samarkand Retirement Community, Santa Barbara, Calif.; pres. Project Hope Nat. Alumni Assn.; med. advisor Project Hope, Russia CIS, 1992. Served with USNR, 1942-46, 50-52. Named Outstanding Citizen of Yr., Redwood City, 1987. Mem. San Mateo County (pres. 1961-63), Calif. (pres. 1965-66), Am. (v.p. 1974-75) heart assns., San Mateo Med. Soc. (pres. 1969-70), San Mateo County Comprehensive Health Planning Coun. (v.p. 1969-70), Calif., Am. med. assns., San Mateo, Stanford surg. socs., Am. Coll. Chest Physicians, Calif. Thoracic Soc., Cardiovascular Council. Republican. Mem. Peninsula Covenant Ch. Club: Commonwealth. Home: 3621 Farm Hill Blvd Redwood City CA 94061-1230 Office: Peninsula Occupational Health Assocs 1581 Industrial Rd San Carlos CA 94070-4111

ELLIS, EUGENE JOSEPH, cardiologist; b. Rochester, N.Y., Feb. 23, 1919; s. Eugene Joseph and Violet (Anderson) E.; m. Ruth Nugent, July 31, 1943; children: Eugene J., Susan Ellis Renwick, Amy Ellis Miller. AB, U. So. Calif., L.A., 1941; MD, U. So. Calif., 1944; MS in medicine, U. Minn., 1950. Diplomate Am. Bd. Internal Medicine and Cardiovascular Diseases. Intern L.A. County Hosp., 1944, resident, 1946; fellowship Mayo Clinic, Rochester, Minn., 1947-51; dir. dept. cardiology St. Vincent's Hosp., L.A., 1953-55; dir. dept. cardiology Good Samaritan Hosp., L.A., 1955-84; ret., ret., 1984; prof. emeritus medicine U. So. Calif., 1984—; Mem. Med. Bd. of Calif., 1984-91; pres., 1988; pres. Div. of Med. Quality, State of Calif., 1985-89; exec. com. trustees U. Redlands, 1976-86. Lt. USN, 1944-46. Contbr. articles to profl. jours. Lt. USN, 1944-46. Mem. L.A. Country Club, Pauma Valley Country Club (dir. 1980-83), Birnfim Wood Country Club. Republican. Home: 450 Eastgate Ln Santa Barbara CA 93108

ELLIS, EVA LILLIAN, artist; b. Seattle, June 4, 1920; d. Carl Martin and Hilda (Persson) Johnson; m. Everett Lincoln Ellis, May 1, 1943; children: Karin, Kristy, Hildy, Erik. BA, U. Wash., 1941; MA, U. Idaho, 1950; M in Painting (h.c.), U. delle Arti, 1983. Assoc. dir. art Best & Co., Seattle, 1943; dir. Am. Art Week, Idaho, 1949-55; mem. faculty dept. art U. Idaho, 1946-48; dir., tchr. Children's Art Oreg., 1966-71; mem. faculty aux. bd. U. Wash., Seattle, 1987—, faculty chair, 1988—; freelance artist, 1943-46; lectr. in art, New Zealand, 1971-73. Author: A Comparison of the Use of Color of Old and Modern Masters, 1950; works include: Profilo d'Artisti Contemporanei Premio Centauro D'Oro, 1982; exhbns. shows include Henry Gallery, U. Wash., 1941, Immanuel Gallery, N.Y.C., 1943-46, Rackham Gallery, U. Mich., 1956-64, Detroit Inst. Art, 1959, Kresge Gallery, 1959-64, Portland Art Mus., 1967, Corvallis Art Ctr., Oreg., 1966, U. Idaho, 1946-56, U. Canterbury, N.Z., 1979, Boise Mus., 1949-55, CSA, 1972, 79, small gallery, Sydney, Australia, 1971-73, Survey of New Zealand Art, 1979, Shoreline Mus., Seattle, 1981, N.Z. Embassy, London, 1979, Karlshamn Art Soc., Sweden, 1979, Italian Acad. Art, 1982, Palos Verdes (Calif.) Art Ctr., 1982, Swedish Embassy, 1982, Aigantighe Gallery, N.Z., 1983; represented in permanent collections U. Calif.-Berkeley, U. Wash., Calif. Forest Products Lab., 1991; portrait commns. U.S.A. and Japan; pvt. commns. Wash., Calif., N.Y., Engl., Sweden, 1986-92; guest appearances on NBC-TV, N.Y.C. Counselor Cancer Soc.; active Girl Scouts U.S., People to People Friendship Worldwide, 1943-90, Art in Embassies Abroad Program, U.S., 1980-90; elected to Acad. of Europe, 1980; mem. sister com. Christ Ch., New Zealand and Seattle, 1981-83; chair '41 Class Reunion U. Wash.; chmn. scholarship drive for fgn. students U. Wash., Seattle, 1992; mem. Painting Commns. U.S. and Japan. Recipient awards Acad. Art and Sci., 1958-66, Ann Arbor Women Painters, diploma with gold medal, Italian Acad. Art, 1980, hon. diploma fine art, 3 Nat. awards Nat. League Profl. Artists, N.Y.C.; World Culture prize, 1984; Internat. Peace award in Art, 1984; Internat. Art Promotion award, 1986, others. Fellow I.B.C. (Cambridge, Eng. chpt.); mem. Mich. Acad. Art and Sci., Nat. League Am. Pen Women, Nat. Mus. Women in Arts (charter mem.), Royal Overseas League (London), Fine Arts Soc. Idaho, Canterbury Soc. Art New Zealand, Copley Soc. Fine Arts (Boston), Inst. D'Arte Contemporanea Di Milano (Italy), Nat. Slide Registry of Artists (New Zealand and Australia), Alpha Omicron Pi. (featured in nat. mag.), Scandinavian Club (pres. 1977—), Faculty Wives Club (pres. 1979). Address: 19614 24th Ave NW Seattle WA 98177

ELLIS, GEORGE EDWIN, JR., chemical engineer; b. Beaumont, Tex., Apr. 14, 1921; s. George Edwin and Julia (Ryan) E.; B.S. in Chem. Engring., U. Tex., 1948; M.S., U. So. Calif., 1958, M.B.A., 1965, M.S. in Mech. Engring., 1968, M.S. in Mgmt. Sci., 1971, Engr. in Indsl. and Systems Engring., 1979. Research chem. engr. Tex. Co., Port Arthur, Tex., 1948-51, Long Beach, Calif., Houston, 1952-53, Space and Information div. N.Am. Aviation Co., Downey, Calif., 1959-61, Magna Corp., Anaheim, Calif., 1961-62; chem. process engr. AiResearch Mfg. Co., Los Angeles, 1953-57, 57-59; chem. engr. Petroleum Combustion & Engring. Co., Santa Monica, Calif., 1957, Jacobs Engring. Co., Pasadena, Calif., 1957, Sesler & Assos., Los Angeles, 1959; research specialist Marquardt Corp., Van Nuys, Calif., 1962-67; sr. project engr. Conductron Corp., Northridge, 1967-68; information systems asst. Los Angeles Dept. Water and Power, 1969-92. Instr. thermodynamics U. So. Calif., Los Angeles, 1957. Served with USAAF, 1943-45. Mem. ASTM, ASME, Nat. Assn. Purchasing Mgmt., Nat. Contract Mgmt. Assn., Am. Inst. Profl. Bookkeepers, Am. Soc. Safety Engrs., Am. Chem. Soc., Am. Soc. for Metals, Am. Inst. Chem. Engrs., Am. Electroplaters Soc., Inst. Indsl. Engrs., Am. Prodn. and Inventory Control Soc., Am. Soc. Quality Control, Am. Inst. Plant Engrs., Am. Soc. Engring. Mgmt., Inst. Mgmt. Accts., Soc. Mfg. Engrs., Assn. Proposal Mgmt. Profls., Assn. Finishing Processes, Pi Tau Sigma, Phi Lambda Upsilon, Alpha Pi Mu. Home: 1344 W 20th St San Pedro CA 90732-4408

ELLIS, GEORGE RICHARD, museum administrator; b. Birmingham, Ala., Dec. 9, 1937; s. Richard Paul and Dorsie (Gibbs) E.; m. Sherroll Edwards, June 20, 1961 (dec. 1973); m. Nancy Enderson, Aug. 27, 1975; 1 son, Joshua. BA, U. Chgo., 1959, MFA, 1961; postgrad., UCLA, 1971. Art supr. Jefferson County Schs., Birmingham, 1962-64; asst. dir. Birmingham Mus. Art, 1964-66; asst. dir. UCLA Mus. Cultural History, 1971-81, assoc. dir., 1981-82; dir. Honolulu Acad. Arts, 1981—. Author various works on non-western art, 1971—. Recipient Ralph Altman award UCLA, 1968; recipient Outstanding Achievement award UCLA, 1980; fellow Kress Found., 1971. Mem. Pacific Arts Assn. (v.p. 1985-89, exec. bd. 1989—), Hawaii Mus. Assn. (v.p. 1986-87, pres. 1987-88), Assn. Art Mus. Dirs., Am. Assn. Mus., L.A. Ethnic Arts Coun. (hon.), Friends of Iolani Palace (bd. dirs. 1989—), Pacific Club. Office: Honolulu Academy of Arts 900 S Beretania St Honolulu HI 96814-1495

ELLIS, JANICE RIDER, nursing educator, consultant; b. Sioux City, Iowa, Mar. 13, 1939; d. Evert Alvin and Lillian June (Hanson) Rider; m. Ivan R. Ellis, Aug. 3, 1959; children: Mark Allen, Anne Grace Ellis Wiley. BSN, U. Iowa, 1960; MN, U. Wash., 1971; Phd, U. Tex., 1990. RN, Iowa, Wash., Tex. Camp nurse Marrowstone Music Festival, Seattle; staff nurse various hosps., Wash., Oreg., Iowa; prof., acting dir. Shoreline Community Coll., Seattle, prof., dir. nursing edn.; rschr. in field. Contbr. to textbooks and profl. jours. Mem. ANA, Nat. League Nursing, Wash. State Nurses Assn., Sigma Theta Tau, Phi Kappa Delta. Home: 16229 14th Ave NE Seattle WA 98155-6345 Office: Shoreline C C 16101 Greenwood Ave N Seattle WA 98133-5696

ELLIS, JOHN W., professional baseball team executive, utility company executive; b. Seattle, Sept. 14, 1928; s. Floyd E. and Hazel (Reed) R.; m. Doris Stearns, Sept. 1, 1953; children: Thomas R., John, Barbara, Jim. B.S., U. Wash., 1952, J.D., 1953. Bar: Wash. State bar 1953. With firm Perkins, Coie, Stone, Olsen & Williams, Seattle, 1953-70; with Puget Sound Power & Light Co., Bellevue, Wash., 1970—, exec. v.p., 1973-76, pres., chief exec. officer, 1976-87, also dir., chmn., chief exec. officer, 1987-92, chmn. bd., 1992—; dir., chmn. Seattle br. Fed. Res. Bank of San Francisco, 1982-88; chief exec. officer Seattle Mariners, 1992—; mem. Wash. Gov.'s Spl. Com. Energy Curtailment, 1973-74; mem. Wash. Gov.'s Coun. on Edn., 1991—; chmn. Pacific N.W. Utilities Coordinating Com., 1976-82; bd. dirs. Wash. Mut. Savs. Bank, Seattle, SAFECO Corp., Nat. Energy Found., 1985-87, FlowMole Corp., Assoc. Electric & Gas Ins. Svcs. Ltd.; chmn. Electric Power Rsch. Inst., 1984—; chmn., CEO, The Baseball Club of Seattle, L.P.; regent Wash. State U., 1992—. Pres. Bellevue Boys and Girls Club, 1969-71, Seattle/King County Econ. Devel. Council, 1984—; mem. exec. dirs. Seattle/King County Boys and Girls Clubs, 1972-75; bd. dirs. Overlake Hosp., Bellevue, 1974—, United Way King County, 1977—, Seattle Sci. Found., 1977—, Seattle Sailing Found., Evergreen Safety Council, 1981, Assn. Wash. Bus., 1980-81, Govs. Adv. Council on Econ. Devel., 1984—; chmn. bd. Wash. State Bus. Round Table, 1983; pres. United for Washington; adv. bd. Grad. Sch. Bus. Adminstrn. U. Wash., 1982—, Wash. State Econ. Ptnrship., 1984—; chmn. Seattle Regional Panel White Ho. Fellows, 1985—; trustee Seattle U., 1986—. Mem. ABA, Wash. Bar Assn., King County Bar Assn., Nat. Assn. Elec. Cos. (dir. 1977-79), Edison Electric Inst. (dir. 1978-80, exec. com. 1982, 2d vice chmn. 1987, 1st vice chmn. 1988, now chmn.), Assn. Edison Illuminating Cos. (exec. com. 1979-81), Seattle C. of C. (dir. 1980—, 1st vice chmn. 1987-88, chmn. 1988—), Phi Gamma Delta, Phi Delta Phi. Clubs: Rainier (Seattle) (sec. 1972, v.p. 1984, pres. 1985), Seattle Yacht (Seattle), Corinthian Yacht (Seattle); Meydenbauer Bay Yacht (Bellevue), Bellevue Athletic. Lodge: Rotary (Seattle). Office: Seattle Mariners PO Box 4100 411 First Ave South Seattle WA 98104 Home: 901 Shoreland Dr SE Bellevue WA 98004-6738 Office: Puget Sound Power & Light Co Puget Power Bldg PO Box 97034 Bellevue WA 98009-9734

ELLIS, LEE, publisher, editor; b. Medford, Mass., Mar. 12, 1924; s. Lewis Leeds and Charlotte Frances (Brough) E.; m. Sharon Kay Barnhouse, Aug. 19, 1972. Child actor, dancer, stage, radio, movies, Keith-Albee Cir., Ea. U.S., 1927-37; announcer, producer, writer, various radio stas. and CBS, Boston and Miami, Fla., 1946-50; TV dir. ABC; mem. TV faculty Sch. Journalism U. Mo., Columbia, 1950-55; mgr. Sta. KFSD/KFSD-TV, San Diego, 1955-60, GM Imperial Broadcasting System, 1960-62; v.p., dir. advt., Media-Agencies-Clients, Los Angeles, 1962-66; v.p., dir. newspaper relations Family Weekly (name now USA Weekend), N.Y.C., 1966-89; pres., owner, editor Sharlee Publs., 1989—; voice of Nat. Date Festival, 1990—; lectr. gen. semantics and communications Idaho State U., Utah State U., San Diego State U. Served with USN, 1941-44, PTO. Mem. San Diego Press Club, Indio C. of C. Republican. Methodist. Home and Office: 47-800 Madison St #53 Indio CA 92201

ELLIS, LEO H., management consultant, project analyst; b. San Francisco, Oct. 22, 1925; s. John Herbert and Gretchen (Stucken) E.; m. Ella Mary Thorp, Dec. 17, 1949; children: Steven Lee, David Dunham, Patrick William. BS in Engring., U. Calif., Berkeley, 1949, MA in Econs., 1975. Registered profl. engr., Calif.; cert. tchr., Calif. Field engr., designer Kaiser Engrs., Oakland, Fontana, Calif., 1950-55; project engr. Kaiser Engrs., Oakland, 1956-60; engring. mgr. Kaiser Engrs., Argentina, 1961-63; mgr. Kaiser Engrs., L.A., 1964-67; project mgr. Bechtel Corp., San Francisco, 1968-75; market analyst Bechtel, San Francisco, 1975-78, econs. mgr., 1975-80; v.p. Overseas Behtel Inc., Buenos Aires, 1981-85; mgmt. cons., project analyst Berkeley, 1986—. Creator board game Exploitation, 1979. Bd. dirs. Fulbright Commn., Argentina, 1985; cons. Greenpeace, San Francisco, 1987, Internat. Exec. Svc. Corps, Jordan, Egypt, Poland, Russia, 1988, 91, 92, 93, Trade and Devel. Program, Venezuela, India, Bulgaria, 1989-92. With USNR, 1943-46, PTO. Mem. IEEE, SANE, Amnesty Internat., Sierra Club, Commonwealth Club. Democrat. Home and Office: 1438 Grizzly Peak Blvd Berkeley CA 94708-2202

ELLIS, LORETTA BUSBY, social worker; b. Danville, Va., Dec. 13, 1958; d. Lonnie Vernon and Dora Mae (Swift) Busby; m. Robert Daniel Ellis, Aug. 7, 1982; children: Christopher Todd, Sara Elizabeth. AA in Liberal Arts, Danville Community Coll., 1979; BSW, Longwood Coll., Farmville, Va., 1981; MSW, Norfolk (Va.) State U., 1990. Dir. social svcs. Riverside Health Care Ctr., Danville, 1984-85; social worker Onslow County Social Svcs., Jacksonville, N.C., 1985-86, 86-89; social svcs. asst. Army Community Svcs., Okinawa, Japan, 1986. Fellow NASW; mem. Phi Kappa Phi. Home: 1815B Bennett Cir Irvine CA 92714-8036

ELLIS, ROBERT HARRY, retired television executive, university administrator; b. Cleve., Mar. 2, 1928; s. John George Ellis and Grace Bernice (Lewis) Ellis Kline; m. Frankie Jo Lanter, Aug. 7, 1954; children: Robert Harry Jr., Kimberley Kay Ellis Murphy, Shana Lee Ellis Stout. BA, Ariz. State U., 1953; MA, Case Western Res. U., 1962. Newswriter, announcer Sta. KOY, Phoenix, 1953-55, continuity dir., 1955-61; dir., radio ops. Ariz. State U., Tempe, 1959-61; gen. mgr. Sta. KAET-TV, Tempe, 1961-87; assoc. v.p. Ariz. State U., Tempe, 1986-90; exec. com. bd. dirs. Pub. Broadcasting

Svc., Washington, 1972-77, 80-86; founder Pacific Mountain Network, Denver, 1972, pres., 1973-75; mem. ednl. telecomm. com. Nat. Assn. Ednl. Broadcasters, Washington, 1973-77, 80-86. Mem. Sister City, Tempe, Tempe Ctr. For the Handicapped, East Valley Mental Health Alliance, Mesa, Ariz., Ariz. Acad., State Ariz. Behavior Health Bd. of Examiners, 1991-92. Bd. Govs. award Pacific Mountain Network, 1987. Mem. Nat. Assn. TV Arts and Scis. (life, v.p., bd. trustees 1969-70, bd. dirs. Phoenix chpt. 1986, silver circle award 1992), Nat. Assn. Pub. TV Stas. (bd. dirs. 1988—), Tempe C. of C. (diplomate, bd. dirs. 1987-90), Sundome Performing Arts Assn. (bd. dirs. 1986-90), Ariz. Zool. Soc. (bd. dirs., sec. 1984-90), Ariz. State U. Alumni Assn. (life), Ariz. State U. Retirees Assn. (founder, pres. 1991-92), Tempe Conv. and Visitors Bur., Tempe Sports Authority, ASU Faculty Emeritus Orgn. (pres. 1992-93). Methodist. Office: Ariz State U Univ Rels Tempe AZ 85287-2503

ELLIS, ROBERT MALCOLM, artist, foundation administrator; b. Cleve., Apr. 14, 1922; s. Harry Franklin and Mary B. (Leonard) E.; m. Barbara Currie, Mar. 15, 1958 (div. 1984); stepchildren: Derek Shannon, Wendy Shannon; m. Caroline Lee, Dec. 22, 1990. Student, Western Res. U., 1940-42; grad., Cleve. Sch. Art, 1948; BA, Mexico City Coll., 1949; MFA, U. So. Calif., 1952. Curator edn. Pasadena (Calif.) Art Mus., 1956-64; prof. dept. art and art history U. N.Mex., Albuquerque, 1964-87, prof. emeritus, 1987—, asst. dir., then dir. art mus., 1964-71; dir. The Harwood Found., Taos, N.Mex., 1990—; mem. panel visual arts Nat. Endowment for Arts, Washington, 1976. One-man shows include Occidental Coll. Gallery, L.A., 1958, Pasadena Art Mus., 1961, Esther Robles Gallery, L.A., 1962, Hollis Gallery, San Francisco, 1964, Jonson Gallery, Albuquerque, 1964, James Yu Gallery, N.Y.C., 1975, White Oak Gallery, Albuquerque, 1977, Hills Gallery, Santa Fe, 1977, David Stuart Gallery, L.A., 1978, Wildine Gallery, Albuquerque, 1981, Kauffman Galleries, Houston, 1986, Philip Bareiss Contemporary Exhbns., Taos, 1991, Caroline Lee Gallery, Taos, 1991, retrospective exhbn. U. N.Mex. Art Mus., 1991, others; exhibited in group shows at Long Beach (Calif.) Mus. Art, 1958, Mus. Fine Arts, Santa Fe, 1973, 76, 83, Hills Gallery, 1976, Packard Gallery, Akron, Ohio, 1977, Mus. Albuquerque, 1978, 79, Santa Barbara (Calif.) Mus. Art, 1979, Jill Youngblood Gallery, L.A., 1984, Kron/Reck Gallery, Albuqerque, 1985, Kimo Gallery, Albuqerque, 1988, numerous others; represented in permanent collections Mus. Albuquerque, Mus. Fine Arts, Santa Fe, Mus. Fine Arts U. Utah, U. N.Mex. Art Mus., Albuqerque Pub. Libr., Roswell (N.Mex.) Art Mus., Herbert F. Johnson Mus., Cornell U., others; also in numerous pvt. collections; designer: (book) The Painter and the Photograph, 1974 (design award Western Books Assn. 1990); author catalogues. Bd. dirs. Internat. Folk Art Found., Santa Fe, 1974-78; founding bd. dirs. Artspace, Southwestern Contemporary Arts Mag., Albuquerque, 1977-82. Recipient Friends of the Friends award Friends of Art, U. N.Mex. Art Mus., 1987. Mem. Contemporary Arts Soc. (founding bd. dirs. 1987), Taos Art Assn. (bd. dirs. 1988-91). Address: The Harwood Foundation Univ NM PO Box 4080 Taos NM 87571

ELLIS, ROBERT PAUL, microbiologist; b. Ogden, Utah, June 28, 1944; s. Robert Walter and Anita Irene (Darnell) E. BS, U. Wyo., 1966; MS, Purdue U., 1969, PhD, 1972. Asst. to assoc. prof. dept. vet. sci. S. Dakota State U., Brookings, 1971-77; assoc. prof. to prof. dept. microbiology Colo. State U., Fort Collins, 1978—, head. bacteriology sect. vet. diagnostic lab., 1989-92; adj. prof. dept. vet. sci. U. Wyo., Laramie, 1989—; cons. various vet. biol. firms, 1975—; exec. dir. Conf. of Rsch. Workers in Animal Disease, Ft. Collins, 1987—; biosafety officer Colo. State U., 1986-89; lectr. in field. Patentee in field; contbr. articles to profl. jours.; reviewer med. publs. Mem. com. on biomed. regulations, Colo. Dept. Health, Denver, 1987-89; cons., expert witness, Colo. Legis., Denver, 1988-89. Recipient grants USDA, 1986, 89. Mem. Am. Soc. Microbiology (councillor 1990-92), Am. Soc. Microbiology (treas., v.p., pres. Rocky Mountain br., 1980-84), AAAS, Am. Assn. Vet. Lab. Diagnosticians, Am. Assn. Small Ruminant Practitioners, Livestock Conservation Inst., others. Office: Colo State U Dept Microbiology Fort Collins CO 80523

ELLIS, VICTOR SEIGFRIED, civil engineer, chemical engineer; b. L.A., June 11, 1955; s. Elias E. and Ursula (Charlotte) E. Student, Colo. U., 1976-79. Registered profl. engr. Colo., Calif. Sr. engr. Westernaires, Golden, Colo., 1980—. Jewish. Home: 6195 Everett St Arvada CO 80004

ELLIS, VIVIAN ELIZABETH, obstetrician-gynecologist; b. Biloxi, Miss; d. James A. and Aida (Fernande) E. BA with spl. honors, U. TEx., 1973; DO, Tex. Coll. of Osteopathic Med., 1978. Diplomate Am. Bd of Ob-Gyn. Commd. ensign USN, 1977, advanced through grades to comdr., 1987; intern Naval Regional Med. Ctr., Portsmouth, Va., 1978-79; gen. med. officer Miramar Naval Air Station, San Diego, Calif., 1979-80; resident ob-gyn Naval Regional Med. Ctr., San Diego, 1980-83, chief resident, 1983; attending staff Naval Regional Med. Ctr., Okinawa, Japan, 1983-84, Camp Pendleton, Calif., 1984-86; resigned, 1986; staff Scripps Clinic and Rsch. Found., La Jolla, Calif., 1987—. Comdr. USNR, 1986—. Recipient Teaching award, Family Practice Residents, Camp Pendleton, Calif., 1986. Fellow Am. Coll. Ob-Gyn.; mem. AMA, Calif. Med. Assn., San Diego County Med. Soc. (young physicians com., north county physicians com.), Am. Assn of Gynecologic Laparoscopists, San Diego Gynecol. Soc., Am. Inst. Of Ultrasound Medicine, N.Y. Acad. of Scis., Am. Fertility Soc., Am. Women's Med. Soc. Office: Scripps Clinic & Rsch Found 10666 N Torrey Pines Rd La Jolla CA 92037-1027

ELLISON, CYRIL LEE, publisher; b. N.Y.C., Dec. 11, 1916; s. John and Rose (Ellison) E.; m. Anne N. Nottonson, June 4, 1942. With Watson-Guptill Publs., 1939-69, v.p., advt. dir., 1939-69, assoc. pub. Am. Artist mag.; exec. v.p. Communication Channels, Inc., N.Y.C., 1969-88; pub. emeritus Fence Industry, Access Control, Pension World, Trusts and Estates, Nat. Real Estate Investor, Shopping Center World; pres. Lee Communications, Rsch. & Communications Co. Cons., 1980—; assoc. Kids Countrywide, Inc.; cons. Mark Clements Rsch. N.Y., Inc.; pub. cons. Mag. Rsch. Mktg. Co. Pres. Westbury Hebrew Congregation, 1954, chmn. bd. trustees, 1955. Served with USAAF, 1942-46, PTO. Named Gray-Russo Advt. Man of Year Ad Men's Post Am. Legion, 1954; recipient Hall of Fame award Internat. Fence Industry Assn., 1985. Mem. Am. Legion (life, comdr. advt. men's post 1954, 64). Home: 6839 N 29th Ave Phoenix AZ 85017-1213 Office: Lee Communications 5060 N 19th Ave Phoenix AZ 85015-3210

ELLIS-VANT, KAREN MCGEE, elementary and special education educator; b. La Grande, Oreg., May 10, 1950; d. Ellis Eddington and Gladys Vera (Smith) McGee; m. Lynn F. Ellis, June 14, 1975 (div. Sept. 1983); children: Megan Marie, Matthew David; m. Jack Scott Vant, Sept. 6, 1986; children: Kathleen Erin, Kelli Christine (dec.). BA in Elem. Edn., Boise State U., 1972, MA in Spl. Edn., 1979; postgrad. studies in curriculum and instruction, U. Minn., 1985—. Tchr. learning disabilities resource room New Plymouth Joint Sch. Dist., 1972-73, Payette Joint Sch. Dist., 1973, diagnostician project SELECT, 1974-75; cons. tchr. in spl. edn. Boise Sch. Dist., 1975-90; tchr. 1-2 combination, 1990-91, team tchr. 1st grade, 1991-92, chpt. 1 program cons., 1992—; mem. profl. Standards Commn., 1983-86. Bd. dirs. Hotline, Inc., 1979-82; mem. Idaho Coop. Manpower Commn., 1984-85. Recipient Disting. Young Woman of Yr. award Boise Jaycettes, 1982, Idaho Jaycettes, 1983; Coffman Alumni scholar U. Minn., 1985-86. Mem. NEA (mem. civil rights com. 1983-85, state contact for peace caucus 1981-85, del. assembly rep., 1981-85), NSTA, ASCD, Internat. Reading Assn., NCTE, Internat. Coop. Learning Assn., Idaho Edn. Assn. (bd. dirs. region VII 1981-85, pres. region VII 1981-82), Boise Edn. Assn. (v.p. 1981-82, 84-85, pres. 1982-83), Nat. Council Urban Edn. Assn., World Future Soc., Council for Exceptional Children (pres. chpt. 1978-79), Nat. Coun. Tchrs. English, Minn. Coun. for Social Studies, Calif. Assn. for Gifted, Assn. for Grad. Edn. Students. Contbr. articles to profl. jours.; editor, author ednl. texts and communiques; conductor of workshops, leadership tng. and coop. learning. Office: Boise Pub Schs Adminstrn Bldg 1207 Fort St Boise ID 83702

ELLNER, CAROLYN LIPTON, university dean, consultant; b. N.Y.C., Jan. 17, 1932; d. Robert Mitchell and Rose (Pearlman) Lipton; m. Richard Ellner, June 21, 1953; children: D. Lipton, Alison Lipton. AB cum laude, Mt. Holyoke Coll., 1953; A.M., Columbia Tchrs. Coll., 1957; PhD with distinction, UCLA, 1968. Tchr., prof., adminstr., N.Y. and Md., 1957-62; prof. dir. tchr. edn., assoc. dean Claremont Grad. Sch. (Calif.) 1967-82; prof., dean sch. edn. Calif. State U., Northridge, 1982—. Co-author: School-making, 1977; Studies of College Teaching (Orange County Authors award 1984), 1983. Trustee Ctr. for Early Edn., Los Angeles, 1968-71, Oakwood Sch., Los Angeles, 1972-78, Mt. Holyoke Coll., South Hadley, Mass., 1979-84; commr. Economy and Efficiency Com., Los Angeles, 1974-82, Calif. Commn. Tchr. Credentialing, 1987-90; bd. dirs. Found. for Effective Govt., Los Angeles, 1982, Calif. Coalition for Pub. Edn., 1985-88, Valley Hosp. Found., 1992—, Mt. Holyoke Alumnae Assn., 1993—; founding dir. Decade of Edn., 1990; bd. dirs., chair edn. com. Valley Industry and Commerce Assn., 1990—; mem. coun. trustees L.A. Alliance for Restructing Now, 1992—. Ford Found. fellow, 1964-67, fellow Ednl. Policy Fellowship Program, 1989-90; recipient Office of Edn. award U.S. Office of Edn., 1969-72; W. M. Keck Found. grantee, 1983. Mem. Am. Edn. Rsch. Assn., Am. Assn. Colls. for Tchr. Edn., Assn. for Supervision and Curriculum Devel., Nat. Soc. for Study of Edn. Office: Calif State U Sch of Edn 18111 Nordhoff St Northridge CA 91330-0001

ELLRAM, LISA MARIE, management educator; b. Robbinsdale, Minn., Dec. 18, 1960; d. Ergav Nils and Aime (Magiste) E. BS in Acctg., U. Minn., 1982, MBA, 1987; MA in Logistics, Ohio State U., 1989, PhD in Bus. Adminstrn., 1990. CPA; cert. mgmt. acct., cert. purchasing mgr. Cost acct. prepared dough div. Pillsbury Co., Mpls., 1982-83, fin. analyst, 1985-86, acctg. supr. Green Giant, 1983-85; mgr. acctg. and planning U.S. Food Group Pillsbury Co., 1986-87; grad. asst. Ohio State U., Columbus, 1988-90; asst. prof. Ariz. State U., Tempe, 1990—; pvt. practice employee tng. Chandler, Ariz., 1991—. Contbr. articles to profl. jours. Mem. Desert Bot. Garden Soc., 1990—, Soc. for the Arts, Scottsdale, 1992—; vol. Reach, Mpls., 1986-87. Mem. NAFE, NOW, Inst. Mgmt. Sci., Decision Scis. Inst., Mensa, Pueblo Grande Mus., Nat. Assn. Purchasing Mgmt., Inst. Mgmt. Acctg. Home: 12026 S 44th St Phoenix AZ 85044 Office: Ariz State U Coll Bus Tempe AZ 85287

ELLSAESSER, ADRIENNE SUE, environmental health specialist; b. Washington, Oct. 29, 1956; d. Hugh Walter and Lois Merel (McCaw) Ellsaesser; m .Kenneth Morris Jones, Nov. 21, 1981; children: Brenna Hayley Ellsaesser Jones, Kyle Collin Ellsaesser Jones. BS in Entomology, U. Calif., Davis, 1980. Registered environ. health specialist. Agrl. field insp. Stanislaus County Agrl. Dept., Modesto, Calif., 1981-86; environ. health specialist Stanislaus County Environ. Health Dept., Modesto, 1986—.

ELLSAESSER, HUGH WALTER, retired atmospheric scientist; b. Chillicothe, Mo., June 1, 1920; s. Charles Theobald and Louise Minerva (Bancroft) E.; m. Lois Merle McCaw, June 21, 1946; children: Corbin Donald, Adrienne Sue. AA, Bakersfield (Calif.) Jr. Coll., 1941; SB, U. Chgo., 1943, PhD, 1964; MA, UCLA, 1947. Commd. 2d lt. USAF, 1943, advanced through grades to lt. col., 1960; weather officer USAF, Washington, Fla., Eng., 1942-63; ret., 1963; physicist Lawrence Livermore (Calif.) Nat. Lab., 1963-86, guest scientist, 1986—. Editor: Global 2000 Revisited, 1992; contbr. numerous articles to profl. jours. Mem. Am. Meteorol. Soc., Am. Geophysics Union. Republican. Presbyterian. Home: 4293 Stanford Way Livermore CA 94550-3463 Office: Lawrence Livermore Nat Lab PO Box 808 Livermore CA 94551-0808

ELLSTRAND, NORMAN CARL, plant genetics, horticulture and evolution educator; b. Elmhurst, Ill., Jan. 1, 1952; s. Edwin August and Beverly (Singer) E.; m. Tracy Lynn Kahn, July 2, 1983, 1 child, Nathan. B.S., U. Ill., 1974; Ph.D., U. Tex., 1978. Assoc., Duke U., 1978-79; asst. prof. genetics U. Calif.-Riverside, 1979-86, assoc. prof., 1986-91, prof. 1991—. Contbr. articles to profl. jours. Grantee NSF, Dept. Agr., named Mid-Career Fellow, 1992; named Researcher of Yr. Calif. Rare Fruit Growers Assn., 1984, Eminent Ecologist, W.K. Kellog Biological Sta., 1988; recipient Honor award Calif. Cherimoya Assn., 1992; Fullbright grantee, 1993. Mem. Soc. Study Evolution, Ecol. Soc. Am., Am. Soc. Naturalists, Internat. Soc. Plant Population Biologists, Am. Fedn. Tchrs., Phi Beta Kappa, Phi Kappa Phi. Office: U Calif Dept Botany and Plant Scis Riverside CA 92521

ELLSWORTH, RICHARD GERMAN, psychologist; b. Provo, Utah, June 23, 1950; s. Richard Grant and Betty Lola (Midgley) E.; BS, Brigham Young U., 1974, MA, 1975; PhD, U. Rochester (N.Y.), 1979; postgrad. UCLA, 1980-84; PhD, Internat. Coll., 1983; m. Carol Emily Osborne, May 23, 1970; children: Rebecca Ruth, Spencer German, Rachel Priscilla, Melanie Star, Richard Grant, David Jedediah. Cert. Am. Bd. Med. Psychotherapy, 1986 (fellow), Am. Bd. Sexology, 1988. Instr. U. Rochester, 1976-77; rsch. assoc. Nat. Tech. Inst. for Deaf, Rochester, 1977; instr. West Valley Coll., Saratoga, Calif., 1979-80, San Jose (Calif.) City Coll., 1980; psycholinquist UCLA, 1980-81; rsch. assoc. UCLA, 1982-85; psychologist Daniel Freeman Meml. Hosp., Inglewood, Calif., 1981-84, Broderick, Langlois & Assocs., San Gabriel, Calif., 1982-86, Beck Psychiat. Med. Group, Lancaster, Calif., 1984-87, Angeles Counseling Ctr., Arcadia, Calif., 1986-89, Assoc. Med. Psychotherapists, Palmdale, Calif., 1988—; cons. LDS Social Svcs. Calif. Agy., 1981—, Antelope Valley Hosp. Med. Ctr., 1984—, Palmdale Hosp. Med. Ctr., 1984—, Treatment Ctrs. of Am. Psychiat. Hosps., 1985-86. Scoutmaster, Boy Scouts Am., 1976-79. UCLA Med. Sch. fellow in psychiatry, 1980-81. Mem. Am. Psychol. Assn., Am. Assn. Sex Educators, Counselors and Therapists, Assn. Mormon Counselors and Psychotherapists, Am. Soc. Clin. Hypnosis, Psi Chi. Contbr. articles to profl. jours. Office: 1220 East Ave S Ste A Palmdale CA 93550

ELMETS, DOUGLAS GREGORY, oil industry executive; b. Des Moines, Iowa, Feb. 16, 1958; s. Harry Barnard and Charlotte Irene (Musin) E.; m. Pamela Lynne Koehler, July 7, 1984; children: Lauren Elizabeth, Andrew Koehler. BA with honors, U. Iowa, 1980. Speechwriter The White House Polit. Affairs, Washington, 1981-82; presidential spokesman The White House Media Relations, Washington, 1982-83; exec. asst. White House Office of Communications, Washington, 1983-84; spl. asst. Reagan-Bush Presidential Campaign, Washington, 1984; exec. asst. White House Presidential Personnel, Washington, 1984-85, U.S. Sec. Energy, Washington, 1985-86; dep. asst. sec., press sec. U.S. Dept. of Energy, Washington, 1986-89; dir. media and pub. affairs Atlantic Richfield Co., L.A., 1989-91, mgr. govt. rels., 1991—; bd. dirs. KVIE-TV, Make-A-Wish Found. Asst. editor, researcher: (book) Ronald Reagan: A Record of Communications 1981 to 1984, 1984. vol. George Bush for Pres., 1979, Ronald Reagan for Pres., 1980. Mem. Pub. Relations Soc. Am., PBS-KVIE TV (bd. dirs.), Make-a-Wish Found. (bd. dirs.), River Oak Ctr. for Children (bd. dirs.). Republican. Office: Atlantic Richfield Co 1201 K St Ste 1990 Sacramento CA 95814

ELMORE, TIMOTHY SCOTT, clergyman; b. Indpls., Nov. 22, 1959; s. Clifford Lee and Sally Gay (Smith) E.; m. Pamela Jean Hobson, June 20, 1981; children: Bethany Jean, Jonathon Christopher. BA, Oral Roberts U., 1983; MDiv, Azusa Sch. Theology, 1989; postgrad., Fuller Sem., 1992—. Ordained elder Wesleyan Ch., 1987. Itinerant lectr. Student Discipleship, Internat., Tulsa, 1979-83; pastor Assemblies of God Ch., Sand Springs, Okla., 1979-83, Skyline Wesleyan Ch., San Diego, 1983—; itinerant speaker Kingdom Bldg. Ministries, Denver, 1988—; prison minister, Christian Svc. Coun., Tulsa, 1978-79; homeless/st. minister Eagles Nest, Tulsa, 1978-80. Author: Caring for the Called, 1984, What's Gotten Into You, 1986, Being Used by God, 1990, Soul Provider, 1992; polit. cartoonist Four Newspaper Syndicate, Okla., 1981-83, Pacific Beach Newspaper Syndicate, San Diego, 1992—. Mem. Kiwanis Internat. Republican. Office: Skyline Wesleyan Ch 1345 Skyline Dr Lemon Grove CA 91945

ELMQUIST, DONNA LOIS, special education educator, consultant, writer, researcher; b. Sturgis, S.D., July 4, 1948; d. Donald Phillip Hines and Lois Elaine (Morrill) Watson. BA in English, Augustana Coll., 1970; MS in Spl. Edn., U. Utah, 1977; PhD in Spl. Edn., Utah State U., 1992. Cert. edn. adminstrn. and supervision, learning disabled and behavioral disorders tchr., spl. edn. resource tchr., secondary English and speech tchr., Utah. Rsch. asst. U. Utah, Salt Lake City, 1975-77; tchr. Granite Sch. Dist., Salt Lake City, 1977-87; rsch. assoc. Utah State U., Logan, 1987-91; sr. ptnr., co-founder Terrel Bell and Assocs., Salt Lake City, 1991—; cons. Swiss Fed. Inst. Tech., Zurich, 1992, United Arab Emirates U., Al Ain, 1990-91, Office for Substance Abuse Prevention, Balt., 1990; founder, nat. commr. Nat. Acad. League; presenter in field. Author: How To Shape Up Our Nation's Schools, 1991; contbr. articles to profl. jours. Mem. Utah State Course of Study, Utah State Textbook Commn. in Lang. Arts and Spl. Edn., Coun. for Exceptional Children. Office: Terrel Bell and Assocs 9 Exchange Pl Ste 311 Salt Lake City UT 84111

ELMSTROM, GEORGE P., optometrist, writer; b. Salem, Mass., Dec. 11, 1925; s. George and Emily Irene (Wedgwood) E.; grad. So. Calif. Coll. Optometry, 1951; m. Nancy DePaul, Apr. 29, 1973; children—Pamela, Beverly, Robert. Pvt. practice optometry, El Segundo, Calif., 1951—; mem. staff So. Calif. Coll. Optometry, 1951—; book cons. Med. Econs. Books, 1970—; instrument and forensic editor Jour. Am. Optical Assn.; comml. airplane and balloon pilot, 1968—. Served with U.S. Army, World War II. Decorated Silver Star; named Writer of Year, Calif. Optometric Assn., 1957, Man of Year, El Segundo, 1956; recipient spl. citation Nat. Eye Found., 1955. Fellow Am. Acad. Optometry, AAAS, Southwest Contact Lens Soc., Disting. Service Found. of Optometry, Internat. Acad. Preventive Medicine; mem. Am. Optometric Assn., Assn. for Research in Vision, Am. Soc. Ultrasonography, Am. Pub. Health Assn., Optometric Editors Assn., Assn. Research in Vision, Internat. Soc. Ophthalmic Ultrasound, Profl. Airshow Pilots Assn., Flying Optometrists Assn. Am., Beta Sigma Kappa, So. Calif. Coll. Optometry Alumni (pres. 1955-56). Author: Optometric Practice Management, 1963; Legal Aspects of Contact Lens Practice, 1966; Advanced Management for Optometrists, 1974; Modernized Management, 1982; mgmt. editor Optometric Monthly, 1973. Home: 484B Washington St Monterey CA 93940-3050 Office: PO Box S-3061 Carmel CA 93921-3061

ELPERIN, LOUIS SOLOMON, physician; b. L.A., June 8, 1958; s. Harry and Dina (Budgor) E.; m. Beth Ann Cyrlin, June 27, 1982; children: Dina Tiffany and Jason Michael. BA in Biology magna cum laude, UCLA, 1980; MD, Loma Linda U., 1986. Diplomate Am. Bd. Internal Medicine. Intern Loma Linda (Calif.) U. Med. Ctr., 1986-87, resident, 1987-89; attending physician Kaiser Permanante, Woodland Hills, Calif., 1989—; mem. pharmacy and therapeutics com. Kaiser Permanete, Woodland Hills, 1990—, imaging guideline com., med. records com., 1991—, internal medicine compensation com. 1992—, internal medicine residency program coord., 1993—. Contbr. articles to profl. jours. Mem. Temple Beth Kodesh, West Hills, Calif., 1989—, Mulwood Homeowners' Assn., Woodland Hills, 1990—. Mem. Am. Coll. Physicians, Phi Eta Sigma, Alpah Omega Alpha. Democrat. Jewish. Office: Kaiser Permanente 5601 DeSoto Ave Woodland Hills CA 91365

EL-RUBY, MOHAMED HASSAN, data processing company professional; b. Cairo, Egypt, Nov. 27, 1956; came to U.S., 1986; s. Hassan Mohamed El-Ruby and Rafiha Hassan Riad. BScEE, Mil. Tech. Coll., Cairo, 1979; MSc in Systems and Computer Engring., Al-Azhar U., Cairo, 1986; PhD in Computer Sci., Ill. Inst. Tech., 1990. Project mgr. No. Telecom, Cairo, 1982-84; instr. Signal Corps Inst., Egypt, 1979-80, Mil. Tech. Coll., Egypt, 1980-87; devel. staff mem. DB2 devel. IBM, Santa Teresa Lab., San Jose, Calif., 1990—. Contbr. articles to profl. publs. Major Signal Corps, Egyptian Armed Forces, 1974-90. Mem. IEEE, Assn. for Computing Machinery. Home: 5450 Blossom Garden Cir San Jose CA 95123 Office: IBM 555 Bailey Ave San Jose CA 95141

ELSBERRY, SUSAN DAVISE, computer-aided manufacturing engineer; b. Lincoln, Nebr., Oct. 27, 1953; d. Leo Herbert and Genevieve (Richards) Bischof; m. Terence Ray Elsberry, Aug. 9, 1986. BS, Brigham Young U., 1985, MS, 1992. CAM engr. Northrop, Hawthorne, Calif., 1986-91; owner, tng. instr. mine safety Safety First, 1993—. Mem. Westec Adv. Com., 1987-90. named Whirlpool Corp. fellow, 1984-86. Fellow Inst. for Advancement of Engring. Democrat. Roman Catholic. Home: 1555 W Highsmith Dr Tucson AZ 85746-3308

ELSBREE, LANGDON, English language educator; b. Trenton, N.J., June 23, 1929; s. Wayland Hoyt and Miriam (Jenkins) E.; m. Aimee Desiree Wildman, June 9, 1952; 1 child, Anita. BA, Earlham Coll., 1952; MA, Cornell U., 1954; PhD, Claremont Grad. Sch., 1963. Instr. in English Miami U., Oxford, Ohio, 1954-57, Harvey Mudd Coll., Claremont, Calif., 1958-59; instr. in humanities Scripps Coll., Claremont, Calif., 1959-93; instr., prof. Claremont McKenna Coll., 1960—; mem. grad. faculty Claremont Grad. Sch., 1965—; part-time lectr. Calif. State U., L.A., 1968-70; vis. prof. Carleton Coll., 1987. Author: The Rituals of Life, 1982, Ritual Passages and Narrative Structures, 1991; co-author: Heath College Handbook, 6th-12th edits., 1967-90; guest editor D.H. Lawrence Rev., 1975, 87. Bd. dirs. Claremont Civic Assn., 1964-66; mem. founding com. Quaker Studies in Human Betterment, Greensboro, N.C., 1987. Fulbright Commn. lectr., 1966-67; grantee NEH, 1975, Claremont McKenna Coll., 1980, 82, 87. Mem. AAUP, MLA, Friends Assn. Higher Edn., D.H. Lawrence Soc. (exec. bd. 1990), Virginia Woolf Soc., Coll. English Assn., Sci. Fiction Rsch. Assn., Phi Beta Kappa. Democrat. Mem. Soc. of Friends. Office: Claremont McKenna Coll Bauer Ctr 890 N Columbia Ave Claremont CA 91711-6400

ELSE, CAROLYN JOAN, library system administrator; b. Mpls., Jan. 31, 1934; d. Elmer Oscar and Irma Carolyn (Seibert) Wahlberg; m. Floyd Warren Else, 1962 (div. 1968); children—Stephen Alexander, Catherine Elizabeth. B.S. Stanford U., 1956; M.L.S., U. Wash., 1957. Cert. profl. librarian, Wash. Librarian Queens Borough Pub. Library, N.Y.C., 1957-59, U.S. Army Special Services, France, Germany, 1959-62; info. librarian Bennett Martin Library, Lincoln, Neb., 1962-63; br. librarian Pierce County Library, Tacoma, Wash., 1963-65, dir., 1965—. Bd. dirs. Campfire, Tacoma, 1984-92; mem. study commn. Wash. State Local Governance, 1985-88; mem. Higher Edn. Coun. South Puget Sound, 1988-92. Mem. Wash. Library Assn. (v.p. 1969-71), Pacific Northwest Library Assn. (sec. 1969-71), ALA. Club: City (Tacoma), Tacoma Rotary #8. Office: Pierce County Libr Dist 3005 112th St E Tacoma WA 98446-2215

ELSER, DANNY RAY, financial planner; b. Butte, Mont., June 22, 1953; s. Duane Donald and Edith N.H. (Tam) E.; m. Janet L. Bottom, Dec. 1, 1974; children: Sara E., Katie V., Andrew J., Patrick M. BS, Colo. St. U., 1976. CLU. Mgr. Coll. Life, Bloomington, Ind., 1976-82, Prin. Fin. Group, Bloomington, 1982-86; prin. Fin. Strategies Corp., Bloomington, 1986-88; mgr. No. Colo. Prin. Fin. Group, 1988-89, Prin. Fin. Group, Billings, Mont., 1989—. Bd. dirs. Community Svc. Coun., Bloomington, 1982-85; mem. Young Reps., Bloomington, 1982-86; mission chmn. Evang. Community Ch., Bloomington, 1985-86, missions com. Faith Evang. Ch., Ft. Collins, Colo, 1987-88, 91—, mem. ch. coun., 1991—; bd. dirs. working com. Mont. Found. Consumer Ins. Edn. Bd. Mem. Nat. Assn. Life Underwriters (Nat. Quality and Sales Achievement award 1980-88, Outstanding Young Man of Am., 1983-85), Ind. State Assn. Life Underwriters (Bloomington chpt. bd. dirs. 1980-84, state bd. dirs. 1985-86), S.E. Mont. Assn. Life Underwriters (sec., prog. chmn., v.p. 1989-92, pres. 1992-93), Internat. Assn. Fin. Planning, Nat. Assn. Security Dealers (registered rep.), So. Ind. Estate Planning Forum, Million Dollar Round Table, Bloomington C. of C. (chmn. leadership Bloomington 1982-86), Ft. Collins C. of C. (bus. excellence com.), No. Rocky Mountain Chpt. CLU (sec., treas. 1988, bd. dirs. chartered fin. cons. 1988), Mont. Gen. Agts.-Mgrs. Assn. (bd. dirs. 1989—, Nat. Mgmt. award 1989, 90, 91, pres.-elect 1990, past pres. 1991-92), Mont. Soc. CLU and Chartered Fin. Cons., Bloomington Jaycees (pres. 1982-86), ECC Club (mission chmn. 1985-86). Republican. Office: Prin Fin Group 401 N 31st St Ste 950 Billings MT 59101-1200

ELSOM, CLINT GARY, credit union executive; b. Spokane, Wash., May 7, 1946; s. Joseph Logan and Louise Catherine (Worster) E.; m. Teresa Ellen Coe, Sept. 2, 1967; children: Tonya, Travis. AA in Data Processing, Seattle Community Coll., 1971; BA in Bus., U. Wash., 1973. Mgmt. trainee Sears Roebuck & Co., Seattle, 1967-68; data processing clk. King County, Seattle, 1969-70, EDP coordinator, 1970-71, programmer analyst, 1972-73, asst. supr. data processing, 1974-75, mgr. elections, 1976-80; pres., chief exec. officer King County Credit Union, Seattle, 1981—; mem. bd. Fed. Election Com., Washington, D.C., 1977-80. Northwest chmn. Nat. Inhancement-Fiserve, San Diego, 1983—. Recipient Disting. Svc. award Fed. Election Com., 1978. Mem. Wash. Share Guarantee Assn. (bd. dirs. 1984—, v.p.), Wash. Assn. County Ofcls. (pres. 1977-80, Disting. Svc. award 1980). Republican. Christian Scientist. Office: King County Credit Union 801 2d Ave Ste 100 Seattle WA 98104

ELSTNER, RICHARD CHESNEY, structural engineer; b. Pitts., Jan. 23, 1924; s. Richard Alfred and Marguerite (Chesney) E.; m. Elizabeth Ann Smith, Sept. 19, 1947; children—Richard Graham, Dwight Smith, Charles William. B.S. in Civil Engring., Rose Poly. Inst., 1947; M.S. in Theoretical and Applied Mechanics, U. Ill., 1953; Dr. Engring. (hon.), Rose-Hulman Inst. Tech., 1992. Registered profl. engr., Ill., Iowa, Ind., Miss., Calif.,

Hawaii, Wash. Instr. Rose Poly., Terre Haute, Ind., 1947-48, U. Hawaii, Honolulu, 1948-50; rsch. assoc. U. Ill., Urbana, 1950-53; devel. engr. Portland Cement Assn., Skokie, Ill., 1953-59; prin. Wiss, Janney, Elstner, Northbrook, Ill., 1960-78, br. mgr., Honolulu, 1979-88; bd. dirs. Insulating Glass Certification Coun., Chgo., 1975—. Served with U.S. Army, 1943-46; PTO. Fellow Am. Concrete Inst. (bd. dirs., Wason medal 1955); mem. ASCE (hon., sect. pres. 1983), Structural Engrs. Assn. Hawaii (pres. 1989), Structural Engrs. Assn. Ill. (life), Cement and Concrete Products Industry of Hawaii (hon.).

ELSTON, LESTER CHARLES, management consultant; b. Flint, Mich., Sept. 22, 1929; s. Alfred Samuel and Elizabeth Catherine (Nankervis) E.; m. Marilyn Joyce Anderson, July 12, 1952; children: David, Arthur, Nancy, Karen. Student, U. Mich., Flint, 1947-48, So. Ill. U., 1948-49; profl. cert., Ariz. State U., 1972, degree in mgmt., 1976. Cert. profl. contract mgr. Design engr. Bendix Aviation, South Bend, Ind., 1949-55; sr. design engr. Electric Boat div. Gen. Dynamics, Groton, Conn., 1955-59; sr. devel. engr. AiResearch Mfg. Co. of Ariz., Phoenix, 1959-68; mgr. of contracts Garrett Turbine Engine co., Phoenix, 1968-88; dir. contracts and quotations Allied Signal Aerospace Co., Phoenix, 1988-90; cons. in domestic and internat. contracting affairs, 1990. Cpl. U.S. Army, 1951-53. Mem. Machinery and Allied Products Inst., Nat. Contract Mgmt. Assn., El Zariba Shrine, Vasa (master Ariz. dist. 1988-90). Republican. Lutheran. Home: PO Box 358 Rimrock AZ 86335-0358

ELVANDER, PATRICK EDWARD, biology educator; b. San Mateo, Calif., Feb. 26, 1950; s. Herbert Eldred and Catherine Marie (Wren) E. BA, Pomona Coll., 1972; MS, U. Wash., 1975, PhD, 1979. Rsch. assoc. U.S. Forest Svc., Wenatchee, Wash., 1979-80; lab. asst., lectr. biology U. Calif., Santa Cruz, 1981—; vis. lectr. U. Calif., 1980, acting asst. prof. U. Wash., Seattle, 1980, vis. asst. prof. Oreg. State U. Corvallis, 1981; cons. NUS Corp., Bellevue, Wash., 1979, U. Calif. Jepson Herb., Berkeley, 1983-89, Herbarium U. Ariz., Tucson, 1988-91, Mo. Botanical Garden, St. Louis, 1991—. Contbr. articles to profl. jours. Singing mem. San Francisco Gay Men's Chorus, 1983—. Mem. Am. Soc. Plant Taxonomists, Calif. Botanical Soc. (1st v.p. 1985-86), Phi Beta Kappa (selection com. 1989-92), Sigma Xi. Office: U Calif Dept Biology Santa Cruz CA 95064

ELWAY, JOHN ALBERT, professional football player; b. Port Angeles, Wash., June 28, 1960; s. Jack Elway; m. Janet Elway; 2 daughters: Jessica Gwen, Jordan Marie. BA in Econs., Stanford U., 1983. Quarterback Denver Broncos, 1983—. Mem. Mayor's Council on Phys. Fitness, City of Denver; chmn. Rocky Mountain region Nat. Kidney Found. Played Super Bowl XXII, 1988, XXIV, 1990; named to Sporting News Coll. All-Am. team, 1980, 82, Sporting News NFL All-Pro team, 1987, Pro Bowl team, 1986, 87, 89, 91. Office: Denver Broncos 13655 Broncos Pky Englewood CO 80112-4150

ELY, BETTY JO, school system educational consultant; b. Oakland, Calif., June 28, 1947; d. Levi and Betty (Turner) E.; m. Joseph Dettling, July 15, 1967 (div.); 1 child, Aiyana A. BA, San Diego State U., 1969; postgrad., U. Calif.-San Diego, La Jolla, 1971-74, U. Hawaii, 1973; PhD in Clin. Psychology, Cambridge Grad. Sch. Psychology, L.A., 1991; L.A., 1991. Cert. tchr., learning handicapped tchr., spl. edn. tchr., Calif. Tchr. Carlsbad (Calif.) Unified Sch. Dist., 1970-74; resource specialist The Learning Ctr., Jackson, Wyo., 1977-78; dir. Carlsbad Montessori Sch., 1979-81; learning handicapped specialist Del Amo Hosp., Torrance, Calif., 1982-87; owner, dir. Ely Edn., San Pedro, Calif., 1983—; resource specialist Torrance Unified Sch. Dist., 1987-92, program specialist, 1992—; speaker, cons. in field; instr. U. Wyo., Laramie, 1978, Loyola Marymount U., L.A., 1985. Author: Interface, 1987; interviewee TV, radio and profl. publs. Mem. Nat. Abortion Rights Action League. Recipient PTA Hon. Svc. award, 1991. Mem. So. Coast Bot. Garden Found., Sierra Club, Nat. Assn. for the Edn. of Young Children, NEA, AAUW. Democrat. Office: Ely Edn 322 S Miraleste Dr Unit 179 San Pedro CA 90732-3037

ELY, MARICA MCCANN, interior designer; b. Pachuca, Mex., May 2, 1907 (parents Am. citizens); d. Warner and Mary Evans (Cook) McCann; m. Northcutt Ely, Dec. 2, 1931; children: Michael and Craig (twins), Parry Haines. B.A., U. Calif.-Berkeley, 1929; diploma Pratt Inst. of Art, N.Y.C., 1931. Free-lance interior designer, Washington and Redlands, Calif., 1931—; lectr. on flower arranging and fgn. travel, 1931—; prof. Sogetsu Ikebana Sch., Tokyo, 1972. Art editor (calendar) Nat. Capital Garden Club League, 1957-58. Pres. Kenwood Garden Club, Md.; bd. dirs. Nat. Libr. Blind, Washington; mem. adv. bd. George C. Marshall Home Preservation Fund, Inc. Leesburg, Va.; v.p. bd. dirs. Washington Hearing and Speech Soc., 1969; co-founder Delta Gamma Found. Pre-Sch. Blind Children, Order of Delta Gamma Rose. Finalist Nat. Silver Bowl Competition, Jackson-Perkins Co., 1966; garden shown on nat. tour Am. Hort. Soc., 1985. Mem. Calif. Arboretum Found., Redlands Hort. and Improvement Soc. (bd. dirs. 1982—), Redlands Panhellenic Soc., Yucaipa Valley Garden Club, Redlands Country Club, Chevy Chase Club (D.C.), Delta Gamma.

ELZEY, JAMES ALAN, mechanical engineer, consultant; b. Burien, Wash., June 27, 1964; s. Michael Bartlett and Lorretta Jean (Ormiston) E.; m. Lisa Joy Heiner, Dec. 20, 1986; children: Crystal, Priscilla, Dominique, Ashley, Ryan, Tyler, Colton, Emi. BSME, Brigham Young U., 1989, MSME, 1991. Project engr. Frito-Lay, Pulaski, Tenn., 1988-89, maintenance supr., 1989-90; maintenance cons. Bushman Press, Provo, Utah, 1990—; project engr. Orbit Underground Sprinklers, Bountiful, Utah, 1991—. Ch. LDS. Home: 2725 E Sunset Dr Layton UT 84040

ELZINGA, PETER, Canadian government official; b. Edmonton, Alta., Can., Apr. 6, 1944; m. Patricia Nanninga, May 28, 1965; children—Gregory, Roger, Peter Burl. Grad., Alta. Sch. Econ. Sci. M.P. from Pembina, Alta., 1974-86; exec. mem. Alta. Progressive Conservative Assn.; mem. nat. exec. com. Progressive Conservative Assn. Can., Ottawa, Ont.; pres. Progressive Conservative Assn. Can., 1983-86; chmn. Leadership Conv., 1983; minister of agriculture Province of Alta., Edmonton, 1986-89, minister econ. devel. and trade, 1989-92, chmn. communications com., min. of fed. and intergovtl. affairs, min. for govt. reorganization secretariat, 1993—; mem. following Cabinet coms.: Priorities, Treasury Bd.,Econ. Planning, Agriculture and Rural Economy, Energy; past. sec. Alta. Progressive Conservative Caucus, Progressive Conservative Caucus on Govt. Ops. Recipient Kinsmen of Yr. award, 1972-73. Mem. Can.-U.S. Inter-Parliamentary Group, Can. NATO Parliamentary Assn., Commonwealth Parliamentary Assn., Can. Wildlife Fedn., Heritage Can., Royal Can. Legion (hon. Sherwood Park br. 177 chpt.), Full Gospel Businessmen's Fellowship (Sherwood Park chpt.), Assoc. Can. Travellers, C. of C. Mem. Christian Ref. Ch. Clubs: Toastmasters (Klondike)(past sec.); Sherwood Park Kinsmen (exec.). Office: Deputy Premier, 404 Legislature Bldg, Edmonton, AB Canada T5K 2B6

EMBERSON-NASH, WALLY, marketing company executive; b. Newcastle Upon Tyne, Eng., Aug. 26, 1937; came to U.S., 1982; s. Herbert Henry Nash and Ellen (Murray) Robinson; m. Geraldine Ann Thane, Mar. 15, 1963 (div. Aug. 1973); children: Amber Fern, Jason Adam; m. Susan Alice Remley, Dec. 23, 1982. Student pub. schs., County Durham, Eng. Mgr. trainee John Lewis Partnership, Newcastle, Eng., 1954-55; sales rep. IBM, Leeds, Eng., 1960-62; from personal asst. to mng. dir. Ring Enterprises, Newcastle, 1962-67; pres. Bo-Nash Inc., Eng., Auburn, Wash., 1989—. Author: Wok Cooking Recipes and Instructions, 1991, Pressure Plus: Pressure Cooker Instructions and Recipes, 1992, Bamboo Steamer Cookbook, 1992. With RAF, 1955-60. Home: 33707 170th Ave SE Auburn WA 98002 Office: Bo-Nash Inc Box 1797 Auburn WA 98071

EMBLETON, TOM WILLIAM, horticultural science educator; b. Guthrie, Okla., Jan. 3, 1918; s. Harry and Katherine (Smith) E.; m. Lorraine Marie Davidson, Jan. 22, 1943; children: Harry Raymond (dec.), Gary Thomas, Wayne Allen, Terry Scott, Paul Henry. BS, U. Ariz., 1941; PhD, Cornell U., 1949; Diploma de Honor al Ingeniero Agronomo, Coll. Engring. Agronomy, Santiago, Chile, 1991. Jr. sci. aide Bureau Plant Industry USDA, Indio, Calif., 1942, horticulturist Bureau Plant Industry, 1942, 1946; asst. horticulturist Wash. State Coll., Prosser, 1949-50; asst. horticulturist to prof. hort. sci. U. Calif., Riverside, 1950-86, prof. hort. sci. emeritus, 1987—; cons. in field, 1973—. Contbr. over 200 articles to profl. jours. Leader Riverside Boy Scouts of Am., 1952-74. Recipient Citrograph Rsch. award, Citrograph Mag., 1965, Award of Honor, Lemon Men's Club, 1987, Calif. Avocado Soc., 1987, Chancellor's Founders' award U. Calif, 1990, Honor award Am. Soc. Agronomy, 1993. Fellow AAAS, Am. Soc. Hort. Sci. (Wilson Popenoe award 1985, chmn. western region 1958-59); mem. U. Calif. Riverside Faculty Club (pres. 1958), Sigma Xi (pres. Riverside chpt. 1981-82), others. Home: 796 Spruce St Riverside CA 92507-2501 Office: U Calif Dept Botany & Plant Scis Riverside CA 92521-0124

EMBLEY, DAVID WAYNE, education educator; b. Salt Lake City, Oct. 30, 1946; s. Wayne R. and Barbara (Calder) E.; m. Ann Fenton, June 8, 1970; children: Jeanine, Jennifer, Kristin, Angela, Jason, Matthew, Melinda, Sonya, Janelle, Mark, Michael, Ryan, Jared, Eric. BA, U. Utah, 1970, MS, 1972; PhD, U. Ill., 1976. Asst. prof. U. Nebr., Lincoln, 1976-80, assoc. prof., 1980-82; assoc. prof. Brigham Young U., Provo, Utah, 1982-84, prof., 1984—. Author: Object-Oriented Systems Analysis: A Model-Driven Approach, 1992; contbr. articles to profl. jours. Grantee NSF, 1980-84.

EMBRY, DENNIS DAVID, psychologist; b. Great Bend, Kans., Nov. 21, 1948; s. H. Herbert and Ruth Elizabeth (Gregory) E.; m. Lynne A. Haggarty, Aug. 21, 1971 (div. 1990). BA, U. Kans., 1972, MA, 1979, PhD, 1981. Lic. psychologist, Ariz. Dir. Curriculum and Instrn. Survey, Lawrence, Kans., 1969-72; rsch. asst. Dept. Human Devel., Lawrence, Kans., 1974-75; instr. Dept. Western Civilization, U. Kans., Lawrence, 1975-77; asst. rsch. dir. Early Childhood Rsch. Inst., Lawrence, 1977-79; pres. Circle Inst., Lawrence, 1979-82; sr. fellow Nat. Rsch. Adv. Coun., Wellington, N.Z., 1983-86; rsch. assoc. U. Kans., Lawrence, 1981-83, 84-87; pres. Quality Time, Inc., Tucson, 1987-91, Heartsprings, Inc., Tucson, 1991—; cons. Pentagon Family Policy/USAF, Washington, 1991—; dir. Tucson Children's Mus., 1991—; team leader Pathways to Resiliency Nat. Coalition, Tucson, 1992—; exec. dir. Project ME, Inc., Tucson, 1990—. Author six book series: Reunion: I'm Coming Home, 1991; two book series: Someone in my Family Went to Middle East, 1990; 6 book series: Safe Playing, 1981, 85, 87; author: I Play Creatively, 1991, I Help Build Peace, 1992. Designer Plan for FEMA Mental Health Response to L.A. Riots, Tucson, 1992; witness Senate Vets. Affairs Com., Washington, 1991; mem. Mayor's Task Force on Children's Mental Health, Tucson, 1990-91; founder Nat. Effort to Help Mil. Children in Gulf War, Tucson, 1990-91. Recipient Cert. of Appreciation U.S. Dept. Def., 1991, Desert Storm Bronze Coin 7th Army Germany, 1991; named Outstanding Community Contbr. 836th Davis Monthan AFB, Tucson, 1991. Mem. APA (task force on trauma response 1991—), Assn. for Behavior Analysis. Methodist. Office: Heartsprings Inc PO Box 12158 Tucson AZ 85732

EMBRY, RONALD LEE, physician, diagnostic radiologist; b. Louisville, May 19, 1947; s. Rodney Y. Sr. and Velma F. (Davis) E.; m. Rosemarie Brockman, 1968 (div. 1985); m. Cynthia Jane Chung Ai, Oct. 15, 1988. B of Gen. Studies, U. Ky., 1974, MS in Pharmacology, MD, 1978. Diplomate Am. Bd. Radiology. Intern in categorical diagnostic radiology Tripler Army Med. Ctr., 1978-79, resident in diagnostic radiology, 1979-82; diagnostic radiologist Hilo Radiologic Assocs., Ltd., 1985-90; diagnostic radiologist, dept. radiology Tripler Army Med. Ctr., Honolulu, 1990—. Contbr. articles to profl. jours. Instr., trainer BCLS, Hawaii Heart Assn., Honolulu, 1979-84. Maj. U.S. Army, 1978-85. Mem. AMA, Honolulu County Med. Soc. (bd. govs. 1990—), Am. Cancer Soc. (bd. dirs. Hawaii Pacific div. 1989—), Hawaii Med. Assn. (chmn. com. legis. issues, mem. com. health econs., mem. com. med., moral, ethical, and legal issues), Hawaii Radiol. Soc. (pres. 1992—, sec./treas. 1991-92), Am. Coll. Radiology, Radiol. Soc. North Am., Phi Beta Kappa. Republican. Office: Dept Radiology PO Box 11477 Honolulu HI 96828

EMCH, RENÉ-DIDIER GUILLAUME, sales executive; b. Geneva, Feb. 26, 1963; came to U.S., 1964, naturalized, 1985; s. Gérard and Antionette (Dériaz) E.; m. Tina Michele Roberts, July 6, 1991. BS in Agronomy, U. Wis., 1985. Sales rep. Ferry-Morse Seed Co., Modesto, Calif., 1986-88; regional sales mgr. Sunseeds Ltd. L.P., Morgan Hill, Calif., 1988—. Mem. Nat. Onion Assn., N.E. Colo. Onion Assn., Wash. State Vegetable Assn. Office: Sunseeds Ltd LP 18640 Sutter Blvd Morgan Hill CA 95037-2825

EMENHISER, JEDON ALLEN, political science educator, academic administrator; b. Clovis, N.Mex., May 19, 1933; s. Glen Allen and Mary Opal (Sasser); m. Patricia Ellen Burke, Jan. 27, 1954; 1 child, Melissa Mary Emenhiser Westerfield. Student, Am. U., 1954; BA, U. Redlands, 1955; PhD, U. Minn., 1962. Cert. community coll. adminstr., Calif. Instr. to prof. polit. sci. Utah State U., Logan, 1960-77, acting dean, 1973-74; prof. Humboldt State U., Arcata, Calif., 1977—, dean, 1977-86; acting v.p. Humboldt State U., Arcata, 1984; prof. Jr. Statesmen Summer Sch., Stanford U., 1989—; vis. instr. U. Redlands, Calif., 1959-60; vis. prof. U. Saigon, Vietnam, 1964-65; asst. dean. Colgate U., Hamilton, N.Y., 1972-73; staff dir. Utah Legislature, Salt Lake City, 1967, cons., 1968-77; dir. Bur. Govt. and Opinion Rsch., Logan, 1965-70; cons. USCG, McKinleyville, Calif., 1982; v.p. Exch. Bank, New Franklin, Mo., 1970-76; reader advanced placement exam. U.S. Govt. Coll. Bd., 1990—. Author: Utah's Governments, 1964, Freedom and Power in California, 1987; editor, contbr. Dragon on the Hill, 1970, Rocky Mountain Urban Politics, 1971; producer, dir. TV broadcasts The Hawks and the Doves, 1965-66; contbr. articles to profl. jours. Sec. Cache County Dem. Party, Logan, 1962-63; chmn. Mayor's Commn. on Govt. Orgn., Logan, 1973-74; campaign mgr. various candidates and issues, Logan, 1965-75; bd. dirs. Humboldt Connections, Eureka, Calif., 1986—, pres., 1989-92; elder Presbyn. ch. Sr. Fulbright-Hays lectr. Com. Internat. Exchange of Persons, Vietnam, 1964-65; Adminstrv. fellow Am. Council Edn., Colgate U., 1972-73. Mem. Am. Polit. Sci. Assn., Western Polit. Sci. Assn., Am. Studies Assn. Presbyterian. Home: PO Box 250 Bayside CA 95524-0250 Office: Humboldt State U Dept Polit Sci Arcata CA 95521

EMERICK, JUDSON JOHNSON, art historian; b. Kingston, N.Y., July 3, 1941; s. Benjamin Cutter and Betty Carhart (Johnson) E.; m. Betsy Ann Kruizenga, Aug. 24, 1963. BA, Hope Coll., Holland, Mich., 1963; MA in Art History, U. Mich., 1965; PhD in Art History, U. Pa., 1975. Instr. Pomona Coll., Claremont, Calif., 1973-75; prof. Pomona Coll., 1975-81, prof. art history, 1981—, chmn. dept. art, 1981-87; chmn. writing com. Pomona Coll., 1983-87, chmn. rsch. com., 1990-91. Co-author (with C. Davis-Weyer) Monograph, Early 6th Century Frescoes of S. Martino ai Monti, Rome, 1984; contbr. articles to profl. jurs. Penfield scholar, U. Pa., 1970-71, Samuel H. Kress Found. fellow, 1971-73, NEH fellow, 1981. Mem. Coll. Art Assn. Am., Soc. Archtl. Historians, Internat. Ctr. Medieval Art, Art Historians of So. Calif. (pres. 1979-80, 1989-90). HOme: 1421 Guadalajara Pl Claremont CA 91711-3516 Office: Pomona Coll 333 N College Way Claremont CA 91711-6328

EMERSON, ALTON CALVIN, physical therapist; b. Webster, N.Y., Sept. 29, 1934; s. Homer Douglas and Pluma (Babcock) E.; m. Nancy Ann Poarch, Dec. 20, 1955 (div. 1972); children: Marcia Ann, Mark Alton; m. Barbara Irene Stewart, Oct. 6, 1972. BS in Vertibrate Zoology, U. Utah, 1957; cert. phys. therapy, U. So. Calif., 1959. Staff phys. therapist Los Angeles County Crippled Children's Services, 1958-65; pvt. practice phys. therapy Los Angeles, 1966—; cons. City of Hope, Duarte, Calif., 1962-72; trustee Wolcott Found. Inc., St. Louis, 1972-86, chmn. bd. trustees, 1980-85. Recipient Cert. of Achievement, George Washington U., Washington, 1986. Mem. Aston Martin Owners Club, Masons (pres. Temple City High Twelve Club 1971, master Camellia 1973, pres. Calif. Assn. High Twelve Clubs 1986, internat. pres. High Twelve 1990-91, mem. High Twelve Internat., Pasadena Scottish Rite Bodies, Legion Merit), Royal Order Scotland, Al Malaikah Temple, Ancient Arabic Order Nobles Mystic Shrine, DeMolay Legion of Honor, Order of DeMolay (hon. internat. supreme coun.). Home and Office: 287 W Avenida De Las Flores Thousand Oaks CA 91360-1808

EMERSON, RICHARD CLARK, priest, business administrator; b. L.A., Mar. 9, 1945; s. George Heins and Irma Furney (Sorter) E.; m. Katharine Ann Lawrence, June 27, 1980; children: Cynthia, Holly, Angela, William, Richard. BA, San Jose State U., 1966; MDiv, Ch. Divinity Sch. the Pacific, 1972. Cert. secondary tchr., Calif. Comml. tchr. Middletown (Calif.) High Sch., 1967-69; asst. to rector St. Francis Ch., Palos Verdes, Calif., 1972-76; adminstr. Power Transistor Co., Torrance, Calif., 1977-85; priest assoc. St. John's Ch., L.A., 1976-85; adminstr. Richard B. Belli Accountancy, Cupertino, Calif., 1988-92; priest assoc. St. Luke's Ch., Los Gatos, Calif., 1985—. Contr. St. John's Well Child Ctr., L.A., 1985. Republican. Episcopalian.

EMERT, GEORGE HENRY, biochemist, academic administrator; b. Tenn., Dec. 15, 1938; s. Victor K. Emert and Hazel G. (Shultz) Ridley; m. Billie M. Bush, June 10, 1967; children: Debra Lea Lipp, Ann Lanie Taylor, Laurie Elizabeth, Jamie Marie. BA, U. Colo., 1962; MA, Colo. State U., 1970; PhD, Va. Tech. U., 1973. Registered profl. chem. engr. Microbiologist Colo. Dept. Pub. Health, Denver, 1967-70; post doctoral fellow U. Colo., Boulder, 1973-74; dir. biochem. tech. Gulf Oil Corp., Merriam, Kans., 1974-79; prof. biochemistry, dir. biomass rsch. ctr. U. Ark., Fayetteville, 1979-84; exec. v.p. Auburn (Ala.) U., 1984-92; pres. Utah State U., Logan, 1992—; adj. prof. microbiology U. Kans., Lawrence, 1975-79. Editor, author: Fuels from Biomass and Wastes, 1981; author book chpt.; contbr. articles to profl. jours. Mem. So. Tech. Coun., Raleigh, N.C., 1985-92; dir. Ala. Supercomputer Authority, Montgomery, 1987-92. Capt. U.S. Army, 1963-66, Vietnam. Named to Educators Hall of Fame, Lincoln Meml. U., 1988. Fellow Am. Inst. Chemists; mem. Auburn Arts Assn., Rotary (Paul Harris fellow, pres., v.p. 1989-90). Republican. Office: Utah State Univ Old Main Logan UT 84322

EMERY, PHILIP ANTHONY, geologist; b. Neodesha, Kans., Oct. 20, 1934; s. Vincent A. and Whilomena B. (Kempker) E.; m. Janet L. Emery, Apr. 13, 1960; 1 child, David A. BS in Geology, Kans. U., 1960, MS in Geology, 1962. Project chief U.S. Geol. Survey, Alamosa, Colo., 1966-70; subdist. chief U.S. Geol. Survey, Pueblo, Colo., 1970-72; project chief U.S. Geol. Survey, Lincoln, Nebr., 1972-74; ground water specialist U.S. Geol. Survey, Menlo Park, Calif., 1974-75; dist. chief U.S. Geol. Survey, Louisville, Colo., 1975-81; dist. chief U.S. Geol. Survey, Anchorage, 1981-89, Alaska dir.'s rep., 1985-89; ground water cons., 1990—; assoc. instr. Mohave Community Coll., 1991—. Contbr. articles to profl. jours. Served as sgt. U.S. Army, 1954-57. Recipient Superior Performance award Dept. Interior, 1984, Meritorious Svc. award Dept. Interior, 1988. Fellow Geol. Soc. Am.; mem. Am. Inst. Hydrology, Am. Inst. Profl. Geologists. Home: 2910 Star Dr Lake Havasu City AZ 86403-8566

EMIGH, ELIZABETH EVELYN, retired educator; b. Schenectady, N.Y., Oct. 2, 1924; d. Howard Pleasant and Vivian Stuart (Townsend) Bish; m. Charles Robert Emigh, Apr. 14, 1946; children: Robert Alan, Ted Howard, David Andrew. BS in Social Adminstrn., Ohio State U., 1946. Sec. Los Alamos (N.Mex.) Schs., 1962-66, tchr. 4th and 5th grades, 1967-88. Bd. dirs. LWV, Los Alamos, 1954-58; sec. missions bd. United Ch., Los Alamos, 1984-86; chmn. Books for Babies Literacy Program, 1990—. Mem. AAUW (chpt. pres. 1960-62, treas. 1990-93), Delta Delta Delta (collegiate officer 1944-46, Santa Fe-Los Alamos alumnae sec.-treas. 1986-90), Sigma Alpha Sigma, Delta Kappa Gamma (chpt. v.p. 1978-80, treas. 1986-88, 1st v.p. 1990-92, pres. 1992—). Republican. Presbyterian. Home: 215 Barranca Rd Los Alamos NM 87544-2409

EMLET, RICHARD BOND, marine biologist; b. Pensacola, Fla., July 20, 1955; s. John Richard and Ruth Winslow (Slocumb) E.; m. Patricia Maren Mace, Apr. 26, 1986; 1 child, Logan. BS, Duke U., 1977; PhD, U. Wash., 1985. Postdoctoral fellow Smithsonian Instn., Washington, 1985-86, U. Calif., Berkeley, 1986-89; rsch. assoc. L.A. County Mus. of Natural History, L.A., 1989—; asst. prof. marine biology U. So. Calif., L.A., 1989-92, U. Oreg., Eugene, 1992—. Contbr. articles to profl. jours. Recipient Presdl. Young Investigator award NSF, 1990—. Mem. AAAS, Am. Soc. Zoologists, Soc. for Studyof Evolution, Western Soc. Naturalists, Am. Soc. Limnology and Oceanography. Office: Inst of Marine Biology 4619 Boat Basin Dr Charleston OR 97420

EMMANOUILIDES, GEORGE CHRISTOS, physician, educator; b. Drama, Greece, Dec. 17, 1926; came to U.S., 1955; s. Christos Nicholas and Vassiliki (Jordanopoulos) E.; married; children: Nicholas, Elizabeth, Christopher, Martha, Sophia. MD, Aristotelion U., 1951; MS in Physiology, UCLA, 1963. Diplomate Am. Bd. Pediatrics (pediatric cardiology and neonatal-perinatal medicine). Asst. prof. UCLA, 1963-69, assoc. prof., 1969-73, prof., 1973—; chief div. pediatric cardiology Harbor UCLA Med. Ctr., Torrance, Calif., 1963—; chief div. neonatology, 1963-69. Co-author: Practical Pediatric Electrocardiography, 1973; co-editor (2nd ed.) Heart Disease in Infants, Children and Adolescents, 1977, Moss' Heart Disease in Infants, Children and Adolescents, 3d edit., 1983, 4th edit., 1989, Neonatal Cardiopulmonary Distress, 1988; contbr. more than 70 articles in field to profl. jours. Served as 2d lt. M.C., Greek Army, 1953-55. Recipient Sherman Mellincoff award UCLA Sch. Medicine, 1982; several research awards Am. Heart Assn., 1965-83. Fellow Am. Acad. Pediatrics (cardiology section, chmn. 1978-80), Am. Coll. Cardiology; mem. Am. Pediatric Soc., Soc. for Pediatric Research, Hellenic-Am. Med. Soc. (pres.). Democrat. Greek Orthodox. Clubs: Hellenic Univ. (Los Angeles) (bd. dirs.). Home: 4619 Browndeer Ln Rolling Hills Estates CA 90274 Office: Harbor-UCLA Med Ctr 1000 W Carson St Torrance CA 90502-2004

EMMANUEL, JORGE AGUSTIN, chemical engineer, environmental consultant; b. Manila, Aug. 28, 1954; came to U.S., 1970; s. Benjamin Elmido and Lourdes (Orozco) E.; 1 child, Andres Layanglawin. BS in Chemistry, N.C. State U., 1976, MSChemE, 1978; PhD in Chem. Engring., U. Mich., 1988. Registered profl. engr., Calif., environ. profl.; cert. hazardous materials mgr. Process engr. Perry Electronics, Raleigh, N.C., 1973-74; rsch. asst. N.C. State U., Raleigh, 1977-78; rsch. chem. engr. GE Corp. R & D Ctr., Schenectady, N.Y., 1978-81; Amoco rsch. fellow U. Mich., Ann Arbor, 1981-84; sr. environ. analyst TEM Assocs., Inc., Emeryville, Calif., 1988-91; pres. Environ. & Engring. Rsch. Group, Hercules, Calif., 1991—; environ. cons. to the Philippines, UN Devel. Program, 1992; rsch. assoc. U. Calif., Berkeley, 1988-90. Contbr. articles to profl. jours. Mem. Assn. for Asian Studies, Ann Arbor, 1982-88; sec. Alliance for Philippine Concerns, L.A., 1983-91; assoc. Philippine Resource Ctr., Berkeley, 1988-92; bd. dirs. Arms Control Rsch. Ctr., San Francisco, 1990—. N.C. State U. grantee, 1976, Phoenix grantee U. Mich., 1982. Mem. NSPE, AAAS, Air and Waste Mgmt. Assn., Calif. Acad. Scis., N.Y. Acad. Sci., Filipino-Am. Soc. Architects and Engrs. (exec. sec. 1989-90, Svc. award 1990). Office: The Environ & Engring Rsch Group PO Box 5544 Hercules CA 94547

EMMELUTH, BRUCE PALMER, investment banker; venture capitalist; b. Los Angeles, Nov. 30, 1940; s. William J. and Elizabeth L. (Palmer) E.; children: William J. II (dec.), Bruce Palmer Jr., Carrie E.; m. Canda E. Samuels, Mar. 29, 1987. Sr. investment analyst, corp. fin. dept. Prudential Ins. Co. Am., L.A., 1965-70; with Seidler Amdec Securities, Inc., 1970-90, sr. v.p., mgr. corp. fin. dept., 1974-90, also bd. dirs.; pres., bd. dirs. SAS Capital Corp., venture capital subs. Seidler Amdec Securities, 1977-90; mng. dir. corp. fin., mgr. corp. fin. dept., mem. exec. com. Van Kasper & Co., L.A., 1990—, also bd. dirs.; bd. dirs. Denar Corp., Yes Clothing Co.; allied mem. N.Y. Stock Exch., Inc.; bd. advisors Entrepreneurial Studies Program, Grad. Sch. Mgmt. UCLA, 1985—, past. bd. dirs. With Army NG, 1965-71. Mem. Assn. for Corp. Growth (pres. L.A. chpt. 1979-80), Los Angeles Venture Assn., Beta Gamma Sigma. Republican. Presbyterian. Club: Jonathan. Home: 17146 Palisades Cir Pacific Palisades CA 90272-2141 Office: Van Kasper & Co Ste 709 11661 San Vicente Blvd Los Angeles CA 90049-5115

EMMONS, RICHARD WILLIAM, physician, health facility administrator, ; b. N.Y.C., Oct. 21, 1931; s. Chester W. and Florence (Hall) E.; m. Barbara Joan Voorhees, Aug. 30, 1959; children: Christopher Earl, Anna Marie, Esther Joan, Stephen Wilson, Mari Mai, Maria Song Hee, Toki Song Mee. BA, Earlham Coll., 1953; MD, U. Pa., 1957; DTM and Hygiene, London Sch. Hygiene/Trop. Med., 1961; MPH, U. Calif., Berkeley, 1962, PhD in Epidemiology, 1965. Diplomate Am. Bd. Preventive Medicine. Pub. health med. officer Calif. State Dept. Pub. Health, Berkeley, 1965-78; chief, viral and rickettsial disease lab. Calif. State Dept. Health Svcs., Berkeley, 1978—. Co-editor: (scientific reference book) Diagnostic Procedures for Viral, Rickettsial and Chlamydial Infections, 1989; editorial bd. Jour. Clin. Microbiology, 1974-86. Medical officer USPHS, 1958-60. Mem. Am. Pub. Health Assn., Am. Soc. Tropical Medicine & Hygiene, Am. Soc. Microbiology, Delta Omega. Quakers. Office: Calif State Dept Health Svc 2151 Berkeley Way Berkeley CA 94704-1011

EMPEY, GENE F., real estate executive; b. Hood River, Oreg., July 13, 1923; BS in Animal Husbandry, Oreg. State U., 1949; M. of Tech. Journalism Iowa State U., 1950; m. Janet Halladay, Dec. 27, 1950; children: Stephen Bruce, Michael Guy. Publs. dir. U. Nev., Reno, 1950-55; mgr.

Zephyr Cove Lodge Hotel, Lake Tahoe, Nev., 1955-65; owner Empey Co., real estate agy., Carson City and Tahoe, Nev., 1964—; land developer, owner investment and brokerage firm. Mem. Nev. Planning Bd., 1959-72, chmn., 1961-66; mem. Nev. Tax Commn., 1982—. Capt., inf. U.S. Army, 1943-47; PTO. Grad. Realtors Inst. Mem. Nat. Assn. Realtors, (cert. comml. investment mem.; pres. Nev. chpt. 3 terms), Tahoe Douglas C. of C. (pres. 1962, dir.), Carson City C. of C., Carson-Tahoe-Douglas Bd. Realtors, Capital City Club, Rotary, Heavenly Valley Ski (pres. 1968) Club, The Prospector's Club. Republican. Home: PO Box 707 Zephyr Cove NV 89448-0707 Office: 512 S Curry St Carson City NV 89703-4614

ENDER, RICHARD LOUIS, information systems educator, consultant; b. Chippewa Falls, Wis., Nov. 4, 1945; s. Arnold Louis and Colleen Marie (Baldwin) E.; m. Joyce Eileen Ehlers, June 9, 1968; children: Matthew, Beth. BA, Kearney (Nebr.) State Coll., 1967; PhD, SyracuseU., 1977; student Am. Assembly Collegiate Sch. Bus, MIS Inst., 1989, 90. Intern/contractor Agy. for Internat. Devel., Lahore, Pakistan, 1969; rsch. coord. Ctr. for Opinion Rsch., Syracuse, N.Y., 1972-74; asst. prof. polit. sci. U. Alaska, Anchorage, 1974-78, assoc. prof. polit.sci., 1978-83, prof. pub. policy methods, 1983-87, prof. mgmt. info. systems, 1987—, chair computer info. & office systems dept., 1991—; dir. Anchorage Urban Conservatory, 1977-83; pres. Policy Analysts, Ltd., 1978—; cons. Alaska Jud. Coun., Anchorage, 1982-89; bd. dirs. Alaska Housing Fin. Corp., 1989-91, Anchorage Telephone Utility, 1992—. Co-author: (book chpts.) Reapportinment Politics, 1981, Energy Resources Development: Politics and Policies, 1987, Public Opinion and Political Attitudes in Alaska, 1987, Crisis Management: A Casebook, 1988, Managing Disaster: Strategies and Policy Perspectives, 1988; editor (jour.) Current Issues in Energy Policy, 1984; contbr. articles to profl. jours. Mem. Anchorage Population Comm., 1977—, Mcpl. Data Processing ReviewComm., 1982, Gifted and Talented, Anchorage Sch. Dist., 1983-86; cons. Anchorage mayoral campaigns, 1981, 1984, gubernatorial campaign, 1990. NSF grantee, 1983-84. Mem. Internat. Acad. for Info. Mgmt., Assn. for Computing Machinery, Decision Scis. Inst., Data Processing Mgmt. Assn. (scholarship chair, conf. treas. 1989—, bd. dirs. 1992—). Republican. Congregationalist. Office: U Alaska Sch Bus 3211 Providence Dr Anchorage AK 99508-4614

ENDERUD, WILBUR DONALD, JR., data processing executive; b. Pueblo, Colo., Nov. 4, 1945; s. Wilbur Donald and Loretta Faye (Jackson) E.; BA in Math., San Diego State U., 1967; MBA, Calif. State U., Long Beach, 1972; children: Cynthia. From programmer to project leader Mattel, Inc., Hawthorne, Calif., 1967-72; dir. mgmt. info. systems Audio-Magnetics Corp., Gardena, Calif., 1972-75; founder, 1975, since owner, prin. cons. Don Enderud & Assocs. (now Mgmt. Info. Solutions, Inc.), Diamond Bar, Calif.; founding ptnr. New Century Leasing, Diamond Bar, 1978—. Served with USAR, 1968-69; Vietnam. Decorated Army Commendation medal. Mem. Assn. Computing Machinery, Aircraft Owners and Pilots Assn. Republican. Lutheran. Office: PO Box 4237 Diamond Bar CA 91765-0237

ENDICOTT, WILLIAM F., journalist; b. Harrodsburg, Ky., Aug. 26, 1935; s. William O. and Evelyn E.; m. Mary Frances Thomas, Dec. 27, 1956; children: Gene, Fran, Greg. Student, Am. U., 1955; B.A. in Polit. Sci., Transylvania U., 1957. With Lexington (Ky.) Leader, 1957; sports writer Louisville Courier-Jour., 1958-62; reporter Tulare (Calif.) Advance-Register, 1963; reporter, city editor Modesto (Calif.) Bee, 1963-66; city editor Sacramento Union, 1966-67; with Los Angeles Times, 1968-85; Capitol bur. chief Sacramento Bee, 1985—; Hearst vis. profl. U. Tex., 1993. Served with USMCR, 1957-58. Recipient various journalism awards Disting. Alumnus award Transylvania U., 1980. Episcopalian. Office: 925 L St Ste 1404 Sacramento CA 95814-3704

ENDO, AMY ARAKAWA, optometric technician; b. Wahiawa, Hawaii, May 21, 1961; d. Wally and Keiko (Suganuma) Arakawa; m. Edwin Yoshio Endo, June 23, 1984; 1 child, Edwin Yoshio III. BBA, U. Hawaii, 1983. Registered optometric technician, Hawaii; Diplomate Am. Bd. Opticianry. Optometric technician Edwin Y. Endo, 1985—. Fellow Nat. Acad. Opticianry; mem. Am. Optometric Assn. (paraoptometric sect., Nat. Paraoptometric of Yr. award 1993), Hawaiian Paraoptometric Assn. (pres. 1992—), Hawaii Dispensing Opticians Assn., Hawaii Ophthamalic Assts. Soc., Opticians Assn. Am. Office: Edwin Endo 98-1247 Kaahumanu St # 105 Aiea HI 96701

ENFIELD, D(ONALD) MICHAEL, insurance executive; b. L.A., Jan. 24, 1945; s. Fred Donald Jr. and Suzanne Arden (Hinkle) E.; m. Roseanne Burke, Dec. 29, 1978; children: Susan Ann, Michael David, Peter Christian. BA in Polit. Sci., U. San Francisco, 1967. Mgmt. trainee Marsh & McLennan, Inc., San Francisco, 1967-70, acct. exec., 1970-77, asst. v.p., 1977-79, v.p., 1979-81, sr. v.p., 1981-82, mng. dir., 1982-89; chmn., CEO Frank B. Hall & Co. of No. Calif., San Francisco, 1989-92; founder, chmn., CEO Metro/Risk, Inc., San Francisco, 1992—; cons. in field. Contbr. articles to profl. publs. Bd. dirs. Ronald McDonald House, San Francisco, 1989—; chmn. bd. dirs. Midsummer Mozart Festival, San Francisco, 1985—. Mem. San Francisco C. of C. (dir. bus./arts coun. 1987—), Soc. Calif. Pioneers (county v.p. 1974—), Lotos Club of N.Y., City Club of San Francisco, Olympic Club of San Francisco. Home: 18 Palm Ave San Francisco CA 94118-2514

ENG, LAWRENCE FOOK, biochemistry educator, neurochemist; b. Spokane, Wash., Feb. 19, 1931; s. On Kee and Shee (Hue) E.; m. Jeanne Leong, Aug. 30, 1957; children: Douglas, Alice, Steven, Shirley. BS in Chemistry, Wash. State U., 1952; MS in Chemistry, Stanford U., 1954, PhD in Chemistry, 1962. Chief chemistry sect. lab. svc. VA Med. Ctr., Palo Alto, Calif., 1961—; rsch. assoc. dept. pathology Sch. of Medicine Stanford (Calif.) U., 1966-70, sr. scientist dept. pathology Sch. of Medicine, 1970-75, adj. prof., 1975-82, prof. dept. pathology Sch. of Medicine, 1982—; mem. ad hoc neurol. sci. study sect. and neurology B study sect. NIH, 1976-79, mem. neurol. sci. study sect., 1979-83; mem. adv. bd. VA Office of Regeneration Rsch. Program, 1985-89; mem. VA Merit Rev. Bd. for Neurobiology, 1987-90; mem. Nat. Adv. Neurol. Disorders and Stroke Coun., 1991—. Mem. editorial bd. Neurobiology, 1970-75, Jour. of Neurochemistry, 1978-85, Jour. of Neuroimmunology, 1980-83, Molecular and Chem. Neuropathology, 1982—, Glia, 1987—, Jour. for Neurosci. Rsch., 1991—, Neurochemical Rsch., 1993—. Capt. USAF, 1952-57. Mem. Am. Soc. for Neurochemistry (coun. 1979-83, 85-87, 93—, sec. 1987-93), Am. Soc. Biochemistry and Molecular Biology, Internat. Soc. for Neurochemistry, Soc. for Neurosci. Office: VA Med Ctr Lab Svc 3801 Miranda Ave Palo Alto CA 94304-1207

ENGAR, RICHARD CHARLES, insurance executive, dentist, educator; b. Salt Lake City, Apr. 2, 1953; s. Keith Maurice and Amy Kathryn (Lyman) E.; m. Elizabeth Ann Willardson, June 21, 1978; children: Robert Keith, Thomas William, Julia Elizabeth. BA in Psychology, U. Utah, 1976; DDS, U. Wash., 1980. Resident gen. practice Sinai Hosp., Detroit, 1980-81; pvt. practice Salt Lake City, 1981-91; cons. Profl. Ins. Exch., Salt Lake City, 1990-91, atty.-in-fact, 1991—; clin. instr. dept. pathology, dental gen. practice residency program U. Utah Med. Ctr., Salt Lake City, 1988—. Author: Dental Treatment of the Sensory Impaired Patient, 1977. Dist. trainer Spring Creek Dist., Great Salt Lake coun. Boy Scouts Am., 1989-92. Fellow Acad. Gen. Dentistry (regional dir. 1991—), Pierre Fauchard Acad., Utah Acad. Gen. Dentistry (pres. 1987); mem. ADA, Salt Lake Dist. Dental Soc. (treas. 1986-88), Utah Dental Assn., Sugar House Rotary (bull. chair 1992-93), No. Utah Plastic Modelers Assn. (v.p. 1992), Phi Beta Kappa, Phi Kappa Phi. Mem. LDS Ch. Home: 1806 Glenbrook Cir Salt Lake City UT 84121-1213 Office: Profl Ins Exch Ste 130 445 E 4500 S Salt Lake City UT 84107

ENGEL, JEROME, JR., neurologist, neuroscientist, educator; b. Albany, N.Y., May 11, 1938; s. Jerome and Pauline (Feder) E.; m. Catherine Margaret Lambourne, Feb. 26, 1967; children: Sean, Jesse, Anasuya. BA, Cornell U., 1960; MD, Stanford U., 1965, PhD in Physiology, 1966. Diplomate Nat. Bd. Med. Examiners, Am. Bd. Qualification in EEG, Nat. Bd. Psychiatry and Neurology. Intern in medicine Ind. U., Indpls., 1966-67; resident in neurology Albert Einstein Coll. Medicine, Bronx, N.Y., 1967-68, 70-72; resident in EEG Nat. Hosp. Nervous and Mental Disease Queen Sq., London, 1971, Maudsley Hosp., London, 1972; attending neurologist, dir. electroencephalography labs. Bronx Mcpl. Hosp. Ctr., Hosp. Albert Einstein Coll. Medicine, 1972-76; attending neurologist, chief of epilepsy, clin. neurophysiology UCLA Hosp. and Clinics, 1976—; assoc. investigator lab. nuclear medicine of Lab. Biomed. and Environ. Scis. UCLA Med. Ctr., 1981—; staff assoc. NINDS NIH Lab. of Perinatal Physiology, San Juan, P.R., vis. asst. prof. dept. physiology and biophysics Sch. Medicine U. P.R., 1968-69, Lab. of Neural Control, Bethesda, Md., 1969-70; asst. prof. neurology Albert Einstein Coll. Medicine, Bronx, 1972-76, neuroscience 1974-76; assoc. prof. neurology Sch. Medicine UCLA, 1976-80, anatomy, 1977-80, prof. neurology, anatomy and cell biology, 1980—; assoc. investigator Lab. Nuclear Medicine Lab. Biomedical and Environ. Scis., 1981—; chmn. Internat. and Coop. Projects Study Sect. NIH, 1989-90, mem. Biomed. Scis. Study Sect., 1985-89, chmn. 1988-89; vis. prof. dept. anatomy Sydney U., 1984. Author: Epilepsy and Positron CT, Clinical Relevance for Diagnosis of Epilepsy, 1985, Surgical Treatment of the Epilepsies, 1987, Seizures and Epilepsy, 1989, Surgical Treatment of Epilepsies, 1993, (with others) Neurotransmitters, Seizures and Epilepsy II, 1984, Neurotransmitters, Seizures and Epilepsy III, 1986, The Epileptic Focus, 1987, Fundamental Mechanisms of Human Brain Function, 1987, Clinical Use of Emission Tomography in Focal Epilepsy, Current Problems in Epilepsy, Vol. 7, 1990, Neurotransmitters in Epilepsy, 1992, Molecular Neurobiology and Epilepsy, 1992; contbr. over 77 chpts. to books including Functional Brain Imaging, 1988, Anatomy of Epileptogenesis, 1989, EEG Handbook, rev. series vol. 4, 1990, Comprehensive Epileptology, 1990, Generalized Epilepsy, 1990, Neurotransmitters in Epilepsy, Epilepsy Research (Supplement), 1992, Molecular Neurobiology and Epilepsy; contbr. over 440 articles to profl. jours. including, New Issues in Neuroscis., Neurology, Jour. Neurosurg., Jour. Epilepsy, Epilepsia, Can. Jour. Neurol. Sci., Radiology, Jour. Cerebral Blood Flow Metabolism, Acta Neurochirugica, Jour. Clin. Psychiatry; chief editor Advances in Neurobiology of Epilepsy, 1989-91; assoc. editor Jour. Clin. Neurphysiology, 1983—, Epilepsy Rsch., 1985—, Epilepsy Advances, 1985-87, Brain Topography, 1990—. Active profl. adv. bd. Epilepsy Found. Am., 1979-87; chmn. organizing com. Workshop on Neurobiology of Epilepsy Internat. League Against Epilepsy, 1988-91. Lt. comdr. USPHS, 1968-70. Recipient N.Y. State Regents scholarship, 1956-60, NIH traineeship, summer 1962, predoctoral fellowship, 1964, postdoctoral fellowship, 1965-66, career devel. award 1972-76, Epilepsy Found. Am. award, 1963, Stiftung Michael prize, 1982; named Fulbright scholar, 1971-72, fellow in neurology Sch. Medicine Stanford U., 1965-66, Lab. Applied Neuophysiology, C.N.R.S., Marseilles, France, 1966, Dagan Lectr. Winter Conf. on Brain Rsch., 1981, John Guggenheim fellow, 1983-84, Hanna lectr. Case-Western Reserve, 1983, First Aird lectr. U. Calif. San Francisco, 1985, First Cox lectr. Albert Einstein Coll. Medicine, 1985, First Vaajasalo lectr. and award, Kuopio, Finland, 1987, Aring lectr. U. Cin. Med. Ctr., 1987, First Hans Berger lectr. Internat. Congress of EEG and Clin. Neurophysiology, 1990. Fellow Am. Acad. Neurology (self assessment epilepsy task force chair 1990—); mem. AAAS, Am. EEG Soc. (or 1984-87, chmn. rsch. fellowship com. 1988-91, pres. elect 1991-92, pres. 1992-93), Am. Epilepsy Soc. (sec. 1979-82, 2nd v.p. 1982-83, 1st v.p. 1983-84, pres. 1984-85, councillor 1985-86, v.p. to Internat. League Against Epilepsy 1990—, William G. Lennox lectr. 1990), Am. Neurol. Assn. (mem. program com. 1987-90), Am. Physiol. Soc., Internat. Brain Rsch. Orgn., Internat. Fedn. EEG and Clin. Neurophysiology Socs. (program com. 1988-90, chmn. com. on guidelines for long-term monitoring for epilepsy 1989—), Internat. League Against Epilepsy (program com. 1986-88, commn. on epilepsy surgery 1988—, chmn. commn. on neurobiology of epilepsy 1989—, amb. for epilepsy award 1991), Internat. Soc. Cerebral Blood Flow and Metabolism, Ea. Assn. Electroencephalographers, Nat. Assn. Epilepsy Ctrs. (bd. dirs. 1988—, treas. 1990—), Soc. for Neurosci. (neurobiology of disease workshop organizing com 1989—), Australian Assn. Neurologists (hon.), Western Electroencephalography Soc. Home: 791 Radcliffe Ave Pacific Palisades CA 90272-4334 Office: UCLA Sch Medicine Reed Neurol Rsch Ctr # 1250 710 Westwood Plz Los Angeles CA 90024-1769

ENGEL, LINDA JEANNE, mining executive; b. Denver, Aug. 24, 1949; d. Thomas Mintor and Irene Evelyn (Esbenson) Kelley; m. William Stephen Engel, May 6, 1972; children: Kacey, Ryan. BA in Polit. Sci. and Econs., U. Colo., 1975. Statis. researcher Martin Marietta, Waterton, Colo., 1971; asst. dir. Fed. Drug Abuse Program, Denver, 1972-74; corp. sec./treas. Grayhill Exploration Co., Arvada, Colo., 1981-84; controller Western Internat. Gold-Silver, Westminster, Colo., 1985-86; investor rels. dir. and corp. sec. Canyon Resources Corp., Golden, Colo., 1986—. Dem. campaign mgr., Mayor of Boulder, Colo., 1970. Mem. NAFE, Am. Mgmt. Assn., Am. Soc. Corp. Secs., Nat. Investor Rels. Inst., Women in Mining, Fellowship Christian Athletes, Delta Delta Delta. Republican.

ENGELHARDT, ALBERT GEORGE, physicist; b. Toronto, Ont., Can., Mar. 17, 1935; came to U.S., 1957, naturalized, 1965; s. Samuel and Rose (Menkes) E.; m. Elzbieta Szajkowska, June 14, 1960; children—Frederick, Leonard, Michael. B.A.Sc., U. Toronto, 1958; M.S., U. Ill., 1959, Ph.D. (grad. fellow), 1961. Research asst. elec. engring. U. Ill., Urbana, 1958-61; staff research and devel. center engr. Westinghouse Electric Co., Pitts., 1961-70; mgr. Westinghouse Electric Co., 1966-69, fellow scientist, 1969-70; sr. research scientist, group leader Hydro-Que. Research Inst., Varennes, Can., 1970-74; mem. staff Los Alamos Sci. Lab., 1974-86; adj. prof. elec. engring. Tex. Tech. U., Lubbock, 1976—; pres., chief exec. officer, founder Enfitek, Inc., Los Alamos, N.Mex., 1982—; vis. prof. U. Que., 1970-77. Contbr. articles to profl. jours. Group leader Boy Scouts Can., 1972-74. Mem. IEEE Nuclear and Plasma Scis. Soc., Am. Phys. Soc. Home and Office: 549 Bryce Ave Los Alamos NM 87544-3607

ENGELHARDT, JERRY M., pipeline company executive, musician; b. Rockford, Ill., July 17, 1942; s. Elzo Michael and Mabel Victoria (Peterson) E.; m. Lynda Marie Turner, Sept. 6, 1969. BS in Civil Engring., Purdue U., 1966, MS in Indsl. Adminstrn., 1967. Various engring. and ops. positions to tech. supt. Shell Oil, Shell Pipe Line and Shell Internat., various locations, 1966-79; gen. mgr., v.p. MacMillan Ring-Free Oil, L.A., 1979-83; v.p. Santa Fe Pacific Pipelines, L.A., 1983—; v.p., bd. dirs. Ind. Liquid Terminal Assn., Washington, 1986-90; mem. Calif. State Fire Marshal's Pipeline Adv. Com., 1990. Congregation pres. Lutheran Ch., 1982-84, 1991—; active in Canine Companions for Independence. Mem. Am. Petroleum Inst. (various coms. 1986—), Western States Petroleum Assn. (pres. 1993, past chmn. pipeline com.), Western Pipe Liners Club (sec.-treas. 1991-92), L.A. Athletic Club, L.A. Petroleum Club, Jonathan Club. Lutheran. Home: 1349 Empire St Anaheim CA 92804 Office: Santa Fe Pacific Pipelines 888 S Figueroa Los Angeles CA 90017

ENGELKING, PAUL CRAIG, chemistry educator; b. Glendale, Calif., May 11, 1948; s. Fred Carl and Gladys M. (Nicol) E.; m. Patricia Donaldson, Aug. 2, 1975; children: Kirstin, Gwynne. BS, Calif. Inst. Tech., 1971; MPhil, Yale U., 1974, Ph.D., 1976. Rsch. asst. Joint Inst. Lab. Astrophysics, Boulder, Colo., 1976-78; asst. prof. chemistry U. Oreg., Eugene, 1978-84, assoc. prof., 1984-91, prof., 1991—; vis. fellow Joint Inst. Lab. Astrophysics, Boulder, 1985-86. Contbr. articles to profl. jours. Mem. city coun., Lowell, Oreg., 1983-84. Alfred P. Sloan fellow, 1982. Mem. Am. Chem. Soc., Am. Phys. Soc. Democrat. Home: PO Box 236 Lowell OR 97452-0236 Office: Dept Chemistry U Oreg Eugene OR 97403

ENGER, KARI JO, publications coordinator; b. Dickinson, N.D., June 22, 1965; d. John E. and Joan G. (Jonas) E.; m. Bruce B. LeCaptain, Aug. 22, 1992. BA, Augustana Coll., 1988. Editor Moonsinger Mktg. & Design, Cody, Wyo., 1988-89; publs. coord. Rocky Mountain Coll., Billings, Mont., 1989—; freelance graphic artist Enger, Ink., Billings, 1990—; cons. Mary Kay Cosmetics, Billings, 1992—. Democrat. Lutheran. Home: 240 Alderson Ave Billings MT 59101 Office: Rocky Mountain Coll 1511 Poly Dr Billings MT 59102

ENGERBRETSON, DAVID LANCE, writer, photographer, educator; b. Tracy, Minn., Feb. 18, 1936; s. A. M. and Marcella J. (Rawlings) E.; m. Shirley A. Goodsell, July 3, 1981; children: Eric, Jeff; stepchilden: Don, Jennifer. BS, Macalester Coll., 1958; MS, U. Ill., 1962; PhD, Pa. State U., 1969. Tchr. Two Harbors (Minn.) High Sch., 1958-59; membership sec. Downtown YMCA, St. Paul, Minn., 1959-60; asst. prof. Northeastern U., Boston, 1962-65; assoc. prof. Macalester Coll., St. Paul, 1969-72, Wash. State U., Pullman, 1972—. Author: The Human Muscle System, 1983, Tight Lines, Bright Water, 1986; western editor Fly Fisherman mag.; contbr. numerous mag. and profl. jour. articles. Recipient Don Harger award Fedn. Fly Fishers, Yellowstone, Mont., 1984; named Sportsman of Yr., North Idaho Hall of Fame, 1988, numerous other awards and grants. Mem. AAHPERD, Am. Coll. Sports Medicine, Outdoor Writer's Assn. of Am., N.W. Outdoor Writers' Assn. Home: 1272 Highland Dr Moscow ID 83843 Office: Wash State U Dept Phys Edn Sports and Leisure Study 120 PEP Pullman WA 99164-1400

ENGFER, SUSAN MARVEL, zoological park executive; b. Mpls., Dec. 6, 1943; d. Frederick Paul and Dorothy M. Engfer. BS, Albion Coll., 1965; MS, U. Wyo., 1968; postgrad., U. Calif., Santa Barbara, 1975-76; dipl., Sch. Profl. Mgmt. Devel. for Zoo and Aquarium Pers., 1981. Ranger, naturalist Grand Teton Nat. Park, Moose, Wyo., 1967; cancer rsch. technician U. Calif., Santa Barbara, 1967-68; zoo keeper Santa Barbara Zool. Gardens, 1968-70, edn. curator, 1970-72, asst. dir., 1972-88; pres., CEO Cheyenne Mountain Zool. Park, Colorado Springs, Colo., 1988—; cons. oiled bird rehab. Union Oil and Standard Oil Co., 1968-70; master plan cons. Moorpark (Calif.) Coll., 1986-88; instr., bd. regents Sch. Profl. Mgmt. Devel. Zoo and Aquarium Pers., Wheeling, W.V., 1984-87. Author: North American Regional Studbook, Asian Small-Clawed Otter (Aonyx cinerea), 1987—. Profl. fellow Am. Assn. Zool. Parks and Aquariums (bd. dirs. 1987-90, mem. accreditation commn. 1990—); mem. Internat. Union Dirs. Zool. Gardens, Internat. Union Conservation of Nature and Natural Resources (mem. otter specialist group), Soc. Conservation Biology, Internat. Coun. Bird Preservation, Colo. Women's Forum, Rotary. Office: Cheyenne Mountain Zool Park 4250 Cheyenne Mountain Zoo Rd Colorado Springs CO 80906-5755

ENGILES, JIM GEORGE, marketing professional; b. Giessen, Germany, Sept. 17, 1947; came to U.S., 1947; s. Martin Herbert and Sophia (Bolaska) E.; m. Anita Edwards, Dec. 26, 1969 (div. 1984). BS, Oreg. State U., 1969; MLS, U. Oreg., 1975, MA, 1977. Mktg. engr. Intel Corp., Hillsboro, Oreg., 1982-84, mgr. mktg., 1990-91; mgr. mktg. Intel GmbH, Munich, 1984-86; mgr. European mktg. communications Intel-Europe, Paris, 1986-89; mgr. mktg. communications Tektronix Corp., Wilsonville, Oreg., 1991—; prin. Graphicommentary, Portland, 1990-92. Mem. Nat. Fund for Hist. Preservation. Capt. U.S. Army, 1969-73, Korea. Mem. ACLU. Home: 414 NW 22d Ave Portland OR 97210

ENGLADE, KENNETH FRANCIS, writer; b. Memphis, Oct. 7, 1938; s. Joseph George and Sara (Schneider) E.; m. Sharon Flynn, Nov. 27, 1960 (div. Feb. 1971); children: Dennis Alan, Michelle Suzanne, Mark Andrew; m. Sara Elizabeth Crews, Feb. 29, 1980 (div. Sept. 1991). BA in Journalism, La. State U., 1960. Reporter LaFourche Comet, Thibodaux, La., 1960-63; reporter, bur. mgr., corr. UP Internat., Baton Rouge, 1963-64, New Orleans, 1964-67, Edinburgh, Tex., 1967-68, Albuquerque, 1968-71, N.Y.C., 1971-72, Saigon, Vietnam, 1972-73, Hong Kong, 1973-75, Dallas, 1975-77; freelance writer, 1977-79, 81—. Author: (non-fiction) Cellar of Horror, 1989, Murder in Boston, 1990, Beyond Reason, 1990, Deadly Lessons, 1991, A Family Business, 1992; (fiction) Hoffa, 1992. Mem. Am. Soc. Journalists and Authors, Mystery Writers of Am. Democrat. Roman Catholic. Office: PO Box 27800 Albuquerque NM 87125-7800

ENGLAND, ALPHONSE, financial analyst; b. Houston, Oct. 10, 1961; s. William and Eugenia (Coleman) E. BA in Econs., Princeton U., 1986. Fin. analyst Drexel Burnham Lambert, Beverly Hills, Calif., 1987-89; analyst Prudential Bache, L.A., 1989—. Chmn. Young Reps., Brentwood, Calif. Mem. Brentwood Country Club, Phi Beta Kappa. Home: 6709 La Tijera Blvd # 401 Los Angeles CA 90045

ENGLAND, SHARON E., social worker; b. Gary, Ind., Mar. 22, 1939; d. Leo Charles and Elizabeth (Schamer) E.; m. Ronald W. Ohlson, Sept. 5, 1964 (div. 1970); m. Bernard S. Super, Aug. 20, 1989. BA cum laude, Whitworth Coll., Spokane, 1964; MSW, U. Wash., 1972. Diplomate Assn. Clin. Social Workers; cert. social work, marriage and family counseling. Counselor Presbyn. Counseling Svc., Seattle, 1972-85; social worker Children's Hosp., Seattle, 1972-80; supr. Tumor Inst.-Swedish Hosp., Seattle, 1984-89; psychotherapist pvt. practice, Bellevue, Wash., 1980-93; realtor assoc. Prudential Preferred Properties, 1993—. Producer video Exercise for Cancer Patients, 1988. Mem. Nat. Assn. Social Workers, Acad. Cert. Social Workers (clin. mem.), Am. Assn. Marriage and Family Therapists (clin. mem.). Democrat. Presbyterian. Home: 18906 SE 44th Pl Issaquah WA 98027-9713 Office: 11016 NE 2nd Pl Bellevue WA 98004-5830

ENGLE, HOWARD EUGENE, JR., law educator; b. Lewiston, Idaho, Aug. 28, 1935; s. Howard Eugene and Alma (Norbo) E.; m. Diane Dalyrmple, June 3, 1963; children: Joseph Carlos, Lara Karin, Desiree Anne, Eric Crispin, Madeleine Diane. BA, Wash. State U., 1957; student, Harvard, 1957-58, LLM, 1968; JD, U. Wash., 1961. Bar: Wash. 1961, Calif. 1962. Acct. Egan, Sites & Lala, CPA's, Seattle, 1958-59; estate tax examiner IRS, Seattle, 1961-62, San Diego, 1962-66; prof. law Willamette U., Salem, Oreg., 1966-67; assoc. Goodis, Greenfield, Narin & Mann, Phila., 1968-69; prof. law U. Toledo, Ohio, 1969-71; prof. McGeorge Sch. Law U. Pacific, Sacramento, 1971—. Mem. ABA, Wash. Bar Assn., Calif. Bar.. Democrat. Home: PO Box 51367 Pacific Grove CA 93950 Office: U Pacific McGeorge Sch Law 3200 5th Ave Sacramento CA 95817

ENGLE, KENNETH WILLIAM, information management executive; b. Hazleton, Pa., Feb. 1, 1937; s. Ishmael Charles and Margaret Elizabeth (Bond) E.; m. Jeanne Mae Davis, June 3, 1961; children: Kenneth Richard, Jonathan Edward. BA, George Washington U., 1964; MA, Am. U., 1970; MS, Colo. State U., 1984—. Intelligence officer USAF, 1955-59, 64-82; research analyst Sci. Applications Internat., Denver, 1982-85, cons., 1985-88; v.p. mgmt. svcs. Hosp. Svc., Inc. Health Plans, Ft. Collins, Colo., 1985—; pres. KKJ Cons., Ft. Collins, Colo., 1991—. Contbr. articles to profl. jours. Named Outstanding Colo. State U. Mgmt. Infosystems Grad., Denver Bus. Mag., 1984-85. Mem. Ret. Officers Assn. (2d v.p. 1986-88, pres. 1988-90, bd. dirs. 1990-92). Republican. Presbyterian. Home: 2018 Rollingwood Dr Fort Collins CO 80525-1224 Office: HSI Health Plans Inc PO Box 2367 200 S Coll Ave Fort Collins CO 80522

ENGLE, RAY, graphic designer; b. Calgary, Alta., Can., June 6, 1934; s. Ely and Lilian (Belkin) E.; m. Anne Mary Jiry, Mar. 24, 1960 (div.); children: Elysa, Shaena. BA, Art Ctr. Coll., 1959; MA, UCLA, 1973. Designer Porter & Goodman, Los Angeles, 1959-60; cons. McCann-Erickson, Inc., Los Angeles, 1960-63; pres. Ray Engle & Assocs., Los Angeles, 1963—; mem. faculty Art Ctr. Coll. Design, Pasadena, Calif., 1960-87; mem. adv. bd. Noland Paper Co., Los Angeles, 1963-65, Los Angeles Trade Tech. Coll., 1975—; cons. Hughes Electronics, 1993—. Film documentary for Cannes Film Festival, 1960. Recipient Design award Internat. Ctr. Typographic Arts, Italy, 1965, U.S. Dept. Commerce, 1965. Mem. Art Ctr. Alumni (pres. 1963-64), Am. Inst. Graphic Arts, Graphic Arts Guild, Flings (bd. dirs. 1965-67), Los Angeles Advt. Club (recipient Belding award 1968), Pub. Relations Soc. Am. (recipient Prism award 1987), Del Rey Yacht Club. Home: 4726 La Villa Marina Marina Del Rey CA 90292

ENGLE, ROBERT IRWIN, music educator, musician, composer, writer; b. New Kensington, Pa., Feb. 11, 1945; s. Dale Clair Engle and Rosalyn Imogene (Timblin) Erickson. BS in Music Edn., U. Cin., 1967; postgrad., Stanford U., 1967-68, Ind. U., 1969, U. So. Calif., 1969-71; MA in Music, U. Hawaii, 1973; postgrad. in music edn., U. Wash., 1991—. Cert. tchr. music grades K-12, Calif., Wash. Choral instr. Terminal Island Prison, San Pedro, Calif., 1969-71; choral music tchr. Palos Verdes (Calif.) High Sch., 1968-72; dir. music Makiki Christian Ch., Honolulu, 1978-84, 1st United Meth. Ch., Honolulu, 1986-88; tchr. music and French Redemption Acad., Kailua, Hawaii, 1988-91; dir. music Kapiolani Community Coll., Honolulu, 1975—; con. Performing Arts Abroad, Kalamazoo, 1979—, Pacific Basin Choral Festival in Hawaii, Berkeley, Calif., 1989—; tchr. music theory, piano, S. Seattle C.C., 1993—. Author: Taking Note of Music, 1988, Piano Is My Forte, 1989; composer: Tatalo A Le Alii, 1984 (3d pl. state competition); composer, recording artist: Pese Pa'ia, 1988; profl. recording Christmas Aloha; contbr. articles to profl. jours. Founder E Himeni Kakou Colls. Choral Festival, Honolulu, 1976—; founder, dir. Maile Aloha Singers, Honolulu, 1973—, Carols at the Centerstage Festival, Honolulu, 1989—, Lokahi Choral Festival, Honolulu, 1989—. Dir. mus. group representing Hawaii, Cultural Office for Territorial Activity, Papeete, Tahiti, 1982, World U. Games, 1983, Casa De La Cultura, Southeastern Mex., 1984, La. World EXPO, 1984, EXPO '86, Vancouver, Hawaiian Airlines, 1987, Goodwill Tour Am. Samoa, 1989, Artists in the Schs. Auckland, N.Z., 1991; dir. mus.

group representing U.S.A., U.S. Dept. State, EXPO '85, Tsukuba, Japan, 1985; dir. 2d pl. group Collegiate Showcase, Chgo., 1988. Mem. AAUP, Am. Choral Dirs. Assn. (Hawaii chpt. 1978—, editor newsletter 1987-89, state pres. 1989-91), U. Hawaii Profl. Assembly, Samoa Fealofani Club, Delta Tau Delta (life). Republican. Mem. Pentecostal Ch. Home: 2901 Numana Rd Honolulu HI 96819-2904 Office: Kapiolani Community Coll 4303 Diamond Head Rd Honolulu HI 96816-4496

ENGLEMAN, DAVID S., diversified financial services executive; b. 1937. CFO, exec. v.p. Mortgage Guarantee & Ins. Corp., Milw., 1962-74; mgmt. cons., 1962-79; founder, pres. Fin. Am. Network, San Diego, 1983-87; dir. Comml. Fed. Savings & Loan, Omaha, 1979—; chmn. bd., pres., CEO Union Fed. Savings Bank, 1991—, Unionfed Fin. Corp., Brea, Calif. Office: Unionfed Fin Corp 330 E Lambert Rd Brea CA 92621-4112*

ENGLER, MARY B., physiologist, educator, nurse, researcher; b. Washington. AAS, Marymount U., 1975; BS, Am. U., 1978, MS, 1981; PhD in Physiology, Georgetown U., 1988. RN, Calif., Md. Critical care nurse Suburban Hosp., Bethesda, Md., 1975-80; clin. nurse cardiovascular NIH, Nat. Heart, Lung and Blood Inst., Bethesda, 1980-88; asst. prof. dept. physiol. nursing U. Calif., San Francisco, 1988—; cons., educator in field. Contbr. rsch. papers to profl. jours. Recipient Clin. Nursing Rsch. award Am. Heart Assn., 1989-90. Mem. Am. Physiol. Soc., N.Y. Acad. Scis., Fedn. Am. Soc. Exptl. Biology, Am. Assn. Critical Care Nurses, Am. Heart Assn. (coun. basic sci. circulation, nursing, arteriosclerosis), Soc. for Preventive Cardiology, AAAS, Western Inst. for Nursing, Sigma Theta Tau. Office: U Calif San Francisco 3d and Parnassus N611Y San Francisco CA 94143-0610

ENGLISH, DONALD MARVIN, loss control representative; b. Raleigh, N.C., July 31, 1951; s. Marvin Lee and Lois (Woodard) E.; m. Rebecca Pritchard, Sept. 3, 1970 (div. 1977). Student, Miami U., Oxford, Ohio, 1969-70, 73-74, U. Cin., 1977-78, Calif. State U., Fresno, 1980—; AA, Fresno City Coll., 1991. Ins. inspector Comml. Services, Cin., 1974-78, Ohio Casualty Ins. Co., Fresno, 1978-93; owner Loss Control Systems, Renton, Wash., 1993—. Served with U.S. Army, 1970-73. Mem. Am. Soc. Safety Engrs., Soc. CPCU (cert.), Ins. Inst. Am. (assoc. in loss control mgmt. 1990—), East Fresno Exch. Club (pres. 1984-85). Home and Office: 14023 SE 177th St # L303 Renton WA 98058-9258

ENGLISH, GERALD MARION, otolaryngologist; b. Caldwell, Idaho, Feb. 14, 1931; s. Marion L. and Opal V. (Sackett) E.; m. Carol Katherine Baker, Aug. 23, 1953; children: Elizabeth Katherine, Margaret Susan, Gerald Marion Jr. Student, Coll. of Idaho, 1949-52; MD, Tulane U., New Orleans, 1956. Diplomate Am. Bd. of Otolaryngology. Intern, resident in pathology The Charity Hosp. of La., New Orleans, 1956-58; resident in gen. surgery, otolaryngology U. Colo. Med. Ctr., Denver, 1965-66, 66-69; staff Pathology Health Rsch. Lab., Los Alamos Sci. Lab., 1958-59; pvt. gen. practice medicine Denver, 1960-65, pvt. practice otolaryngology, 1974—; asst. prof. div. otolaryngology dept. gen. surgery U. Colo., Denver, 1969-73; assoc. prof. otolaryngology U. Colo., 1973-74, clin. assoc. prof. otolaryngology, 1974-79, clin. prof. otolaryngology, 1979—; cons. otolaryngology Nat. Jewish Hosp., Denver, 1969-82, VA Hosp., Denver, 1969—, Fitzsimons Army Med Ctr., 1977—; attending physician Gen. Rose Meml. Hosp., St. Luke's Hosp., St. Anthony's Hosp., Luth. Med. Ctr., Presbyn. Med. Ctr., Swedish Med. Ctr./Porter Meml. Hosp.; attending physician Denver Children's Hosp., bd. dirs., 1985-86; bd. med. advisers Listen Found., Denver, 1977-81; bd. dirs. Ctr. Hearing, Speech and Lang., Denver, 1989—; lectr. in field. Author: Otolaryngology-A Textbook, 1976; editor-in-chief Otolaryngology, 1974—; editorial bd. Outpatient Surgery, 1985—; contbr. numerous articles to profl. jours., chpts. to books. Bd. dirs. Colo. Speech and Hearing Ctr., Denver, 1988—; vestry St. Johns Episcopal Cathedral, Denver, 1987-90, mem. forward planning com., 1985-90, chmn. organ com., 1987-90. Comdr. USPHS, 1958-60. Fellow Am. Acad. Otolaryngology, ACS; mem. AMA, Am. Soc. Head and Neck Surgery, Am. Coun. Otolaryngology, Am. Bd. Otolaryngology, Colo. Med. Soc., Clear Creek Valley Med. Soc., Arapahoe County Med. Soc., Colo. Otolaryngology Maxillo Facial Soc., Soc. Univ. Otolaryngologists, Physicians of Am., Triologic Soc., Orders and Medal Soc. Am., U.S. Naval Inst., Korean Vets. Assn., Am. Soc. Mil. Insignia Collectors, Alpha Omega Alpha. Republican. Episcopalian. Office: 601 E Hampden Ave Ste 390 Englewood CO 80110-2769 also: Colo Otolaryngology 601 E Hampden Ave #390 Englewood CO 80110

ENGLISH, H. ELWOOD, lawyer, county commissioner; b. Greybull, Wyo., Aug. 3, 1945; s. W. Lincoln and Leona Elizabeth (Easley) E.; m. Margaret Jane Sprigg, June 15, 1968 (div. July 1981); 1 child, Gillian Diane. BA, Ottawa U., 1967; JD, Harvard U., 1973. Bar: D.C. 1974, Mont. 1974, U.S. Dist. Ct. Mont. 1974, U.S. Ct. Appeals (9th cir.) 1977. Assoc. Crowley, Haughey, Hanson, Toole, Dietrich, Billings, Mont., 1974-78; ptnr. English & Lee, Billings, 1979-86, 1983-86; chief legal counsel Mont. Sec. State, Helena, 1986-87; pvt. practice Billings, 1989-91; commr. Yellowstone County Commn., Billings, 1991—; pres. Yellowstone Regional Devel. Co.; instr. Eastern Mont. Coll., Billings, 1981-83, 86, Rocky Mountain Coll., Billings, 1976, 83-85; commr. Yellowstone County, Mont., 1991-93. Campaign mgr. Angell for U.S. Senate, Topeka, 1978, Ramirez for Gov., Billings, 1980; ops. dir. Williams for U.S. Senate, Billings, 1978, campaign mgr. Burns, Billings, 1988; alt. Rep. Nat. Conv., Dallas, 1984; sec. Mont. Reps., 1986-91. Lt. USN, 1969-71. Named one of Outstanding Young Men in Am., Outstanding Young Men of Am., 1978. Mem. Unitarian Ch. Office: PO Box 275 Billings MT 59103

ENGLISH, KARAN, state senator; b. Berkeley, Calif., Mar. 23, 1939. Formerly Arizona State Rep., now State Senator. Democrat. Home: PO Box 272 Flagstaff AZ 86002-0272 Office: US Representatives House of Representatives Washington DC 20515

ENGLISH, ROBERT JACKSON, communications company executive, consultant; b. Travis AFB, Calif., July 26, 1951; s. Paul Jackson and Olga (Ward) E.; children: Travis, Lacey. BSc in Journalism, U. Tex., 1973. Program dir. Sta. KCUB, Tucson, 1973-77; program dir. Sta. WUBE, Cin., 1977-79, gen. mgr., 1979-83; gen. mgr. Broadcast Programming Inc., Seattle, 1983-87; gen. sales mgr. Sta. KXRX, Seattle, 1987-92, Wash. Transit Advt., Seattle, 1992—; mktg. cons. Mem. Am. Advt. Fedn. (1st place award for govt. rels. and edn. 1991), Puget Sound Radio Broadcasters, Wash. Assn. Broadcasters, Seattle Advt. Fedn. (v.p. 1989-90, pres. 1990-91, chmn. 1991-92). Office: Wash Transit Advt 1601 5th Ave Ste 1100 Seattle WA 98101

ENGORON, EDWARD DAVID, food service consultant, television and radio broadcaster; b. Los Angeles, Feb. 19, 1946; s. Leo and Claire (Gray) E.; m. Charlene Scott, Oct. 7, 1970 (div. July 1982). BArch., U. So. Calif., 1969, MBA, 1973, PhD, 1974; MA, Cordon Bleu, Paris, 1975. Art dir. ABC, L.A., 1964-67, Paramount Pictures, L.A., 1967-68, Warner Bros. Pictures, Burbank, Calif., 1968-69; mktg. dir. Lawry's Foods Inc., Burbank, 1969-74; v.p. Warehouse Restaurants, Marina del Rey, Calif., 1968-72; pres. Perspectives, San Francisco, 1974-82, Perspectives Comm. Syndicated Talk Shows, L.A., 1986—, China Rose Inc., Dallas, 1982-86; exec. v.p. T.G.I. Fridays Inc., Dallas, 1986-87; pres., chief exec. officer, bd. dirs. Guilt Free Goodies, Ltd., Vancouver, B.C., Can., 1986-90, Sugarless Co., L.A., 1986-90; cons. Southland Corp., Dallas, 1982-86, Pizza Hut Inc., Wichita, Kans., 1975-87, Frank L. Carney Enterprises, Wichita, 1982-87, Safeway Stores, Inc., Freemont, Calif., Romacorp, Dallas, Bel-Air Hotel Co., L.A., Capital Cities-ABC, Hollywood, Nestle Foods, White Plains, Screiber Foods, Green Bay, Rich's Food Products, Buffalo, Taco Bell, Inc., Irvine, Calif., Basic Am., Inc. San Francisco, Nat. Super Markets, St. Louis, Wok Fast, Inc., L.A., The Vons Cons., L.A., 1989—; pres. Sweet Deceit, Inc., Guilt-Free Goodies, Ltd.; co-host nationally syndicated radio talk show The Super Foodies, ABC. Author: (cookbook) Stolen Secrets, 1980; patentee pasta cooking sta., 1981, micro-wave controller, 1982. Bd. govs. Los Angeles Parks, 1971-74; mem. Fine Arts Commn., Tiburon, Calif., 1974-76. Mem. Foodsvc. Cons. Soc. Internat., Soc. Motion Picture Art Dirs., Food, Wine and Travel Writers Assn., Internat. Assn. Culinary Profls., Masons. Republican. Office: 11030 Santa Monica Blvd Ste 301 Los Angeles CA 90025-3594

ENNIS, THOMAS MICHAEL, health foundation executive; b. Morgantown, W.Va., Mar. 7, 1931; s. Thomas Edson and Violet Ruth (Nugent) E.; m. Julia Marie Dorety, June 30, 1956; children: Thomas John, Robert Griswold (dec.). Student, W.Va. U., 1949-52; AB, George Washington U., 1954; JD, Georgetown U., 1960. With Gov. Employees Ins. Co., Washington, 1956, 59, Air Transport Assn. Am., Washington, 1959-60; dir. ann. support program George Washington U., 1960-63; nat. dir. devel. Project HOPE, People to People Health Found., Inc., Washington, 1963-66; nat. exec. dir. Epilepsy Found. Am., Washington, 1966-74; exec. dir. Clinton, Eaton, Ingham Community Mental Health Bd., Lansing, Mich., 1974-83; nat. exec. dir. Alzheimer's Disease and Related Disorders Assn., Inc., Chgo., 1983-86; exec. dir., pres. French Found. for Alzheimer Rsch., Los Angeles, 1986—; clin. inst. dept. community medicine and internat. health Georgetown U., 1967-74; adj. assoc. prof. dept. psychiatry Mich. State U., 1975-84; lectr. Univ. Ctr. for Internat. Rehab., 1977; cons. health and med. founds., related orgns.; cons. Am. Health Found., 1967-69, Reston, Va.-Georgetown U. Health Planning Project, 1967-70. Contbr. articles on devel. disabilities, mental health and health care to profl. jours. Mem. adv. bd. Nat. Center for the Law and the Handicapped, 1971-74; advisor Nat. Reye's Syndrome Found.; mem. Nat. Com. for Research in Neurol. Disorders, 1967-72; mem. nat. adv. bd. Developmental Disabilities/Tech. Assistance System, U. N.C., 1971-78; nat. trustee Nat. Kidney Found., 1970-74, mem. exec. com. and bd. Nat. Capitol Area chpt., pres., 1972-74; bd. dirs. Nat. Assn. Pvt. Residential Facilities for Mentally Retarded, 1970-74; bd. dirs., mem. exec. com. Epilepsy Found. Am., 1977-84, Epilepsy Center Mich., 1974-83; nat. bd. dirs. Western Inst. on Epilepsy, 1969-72; bd. dirs., pres. Mich. Mid-South Health Systems Agy., 1975-78; sec. gen. Internat. Fedn. Alzheimer's Disease and Related Disorders, 1984-86; mem. panel mem. Alzheimer's Disease Edn. and Referral Ctr., 1990—. World Rehab. Fund fellow Norway, 1980. Mem. Nat. Epilepsy League (bd. dirs. 1977-78), Mich. Assn. Community Mental Health (pres. 1977-79), Nat. Coalition Rsch. Neurological Disorders (dir. at large 1991-92), Phi Alpha Theta, Phi Kappa Psi. Office: French Found Alzheimer Rsch 11620 Wilshire Blvd Ste 820 Los Angeles CA 90025-1793

ENNIS, WILLIAM LEE, physics educator; b. Houston, Aug. 10, 1949; s. Arthur Lee and Helen Ruth Ennis; m. Constance Elizabeth Livsey, July 20, 1991. BS, Auburn (Ala.) U., 1974, BA, 1978. Rsch. tech. Nat. Tillage Lab., Auburn, Ala., 1974-76; tchr. Stanford Jr. High Sch., Hillsborough, N.C., 1979-81; physics tchr. East High Sch., Anchorage, 1981—; curriculum devel. sci. cons. Copper River Schs., Anchorage, 1991; sci. cons. Imaginarium, Anchorage, 1987—. Fermi Lab scholar U.S. Dept. Energy, 1991. Fellow N.Y. Acad. Scis.; mem. AAAS, Am. Assn. Physics Tchrs., Am. Phys. Soc., Nat. Sci. Tchrs. Assn., Alaska Sci. Tchrs. (life). Office: East High Sch 4025 E Northern Lights Blvd Anchorage AK 99508

ENNISS, LEONARD FRANKLIN, religious educator; b. Kankakee, Ill., Oct. 30, 1955; s. Leonard Franklin and Elsie Irene (Lamb) E.; m. Sharon Diane Stanfield, July 17, 1976; 1 child, Clairessa Mary Fern. ThB, Western Evang. Sch. Theology, Phoenix, 1980, MEd, 1981, PhD, 1984; BA in Religion magna cum laude, Ottawa U., Phoenix, 1992. Pres. Western Evang. Sch. Theology, Phoenix, 1981-90; provost and master regent S.W. Christian U., Phoenix, 1990—; assoc. Nat. Inst. for Certification of Engring. Tech., Alexandria, Va., 1986—. Contbr. articles to profl. jours. Mem. Soc. of Christian Philosophers. Libertarian. Pentecostal Ch. Home: 5807 W Osborn Phoenix AZ 85031 Office: Southwest Christian Univ PO Box 23805 Phoenix AZ 85063

ENOKI, DONALD YUKIO, curriculum specialist; b. Hilo, Hawaii, Sept. 27, 1937; s. Charles Tetsuo and Doris Kiyoko (Funai) E.; children: Dayna Yukie, Donn Kiyomi. BEd, U. Hawaii, 1959, postgrad., 1967-70; MA, Columbia U., 1966; PhD, Wayne State U., 1974. Tchr. Hawaii Pub. Schs., Hilo, 1960-64; dist. resource tchr. Dept. Edn. Gifted and Talented Program, State of Hawaii, Hilo, 1964-66; curriculum writer, planner Dept. Edn., U. Hawaii, Honolulu, 1966-71; dir. Project Follow Through, State of Hawaii, Honolulu, 1971-73; dist. ednl. specialist Dept. Edn., Honolulu Sch. Dist., 1974—; ednl. cons. Multicultural Resource Ctr., Am. Samoa, 1985-86, Yap State, FS Micronesia, 1980-85, Reka Daigaku, Okayama, Japan, 1977—; lectr., presenter U. hawaii, 1965—; cons. in field; lectr. in field. Contbr. articles to profl. jours. Pres. Pacific Rsch. Ctr. Hawaii, Honolulu, 1985, Aloha Ki-Aikido Ctr., Oahu, 1987; chief instr. Noelani Ki-Aikido Soc., Honolulu, 1985; chmn. supervisory com. Oahu Ednl. Employees Fed. Credit Union, Honolulu, 1993; rep. Japanese Cultural Ctr. Hawaii, 1992—. Columbia U. fellow, 1965; Wayne State U. scholar, 1973; Title VII Bilingual Edn. grantee, 1980-83. Mem. Am. Ednl. Rsch. Assn., Teaching English as a Second Lang., Internat. Reading Assn., Hawaii Orgn. Whole Lang. Tchrs. (pres. 1991—), Am. Assn. for Asian and Pacific Am. Edn., Am. Assn. Sch. Adminstrs., Assn. Supervision and Curriculum Devel., Hawaii State Ednl. Officers Assn., Nat. Assn. Adminstrs. of State and Fed. programs, Nat. Assn. Elem. Sch. prins., Nat. Assn. Secondary Sch. Prins., Nat. Coun. Tchrs. English. Buddhist. Home: Apt 4C 60 N Kuakini St Honolulu HI 96817 Office: Honolulu Sch Dist Dept Edn 4967 Kilauea Ave Honolulu HI 96816

ENRIGHT, CYNTHIA LEE, illustrator; b. Denver, July 6, 1950; d. Darrel Lee and Iris Arlene (Flodquist) E. BA in Elem. Edn., U. No. Colo., 1972; student, Minn. Sch. Art and Design, Mpls., 1975-76. Tchr. 3d grade Littleton (Colo.) Sch. Dist., 1972-75; graphics artist Sta. KCNC TV, Denver, 1978-79; illustrator No Coast Graphics, Denver, 1979-87; editorial artist The Denver Post, 1987—. Illustrator (mag.) Sesame St., 1984, 85; illustrator, editor "Tiny Tales" The Denver Post, 1991—. Recipient Print mag. Regional Design Ann. awards, 1984, 85, 87, Phoenix Art Mus. Biannual award, 1979. Mem. Mensa. Democrat. Home: 1210 Ivanhoe St Denver CO 80220-2640 Office: The Denver Post 1560 Broadway Denver CO 80202-5133

ENRIGHT, STEPHANIE VESELICH, investment company executive; b. L.A., Mar. 24, 1929; d. Stephen P. and Violet (Guthrie) Veselich; m. Robert James Enright (dec. Sept. 1982); children: Craig James, Brent Stephen, Erin Suzanne, Kyle Stephen. BA, U. So. Calif., 1952, MS, 1975. Fin. and engring. cons. Orange County, Santa Ana, Calif., 1976-79; fin. cons. The Sim-Ehrflo Group, Newport Beach, Calif., 1979-81; pres. Enright Fin. Cons., Torrance, Calif., 1981—; fin. columnist Copley Newspapers, 1987—; adj. faculty mem., UCLA, U. So. Calif.; pres. Pacific Home Builders. Contbr. articles to profl. jours. Mem. Com. Assn. of the Peninsula, Palos Verdes, Calif., 1986; found. dir. Little Co. of Mary Hosp., Torrance; bd. dirs. local chpt. YWCA; dir. endowment com. Pa. Art Assn.; housing bd. Assistance League; bd. dirs. Pa. Symphony Soc., 1991. Mem. Internat. Assn. Fin. Planning (bd. dirs., officer 1982-84, Planner of Month award 1984), Inst. Cert. Fin. Planners, Nat. Assn. Women Owners, Nat. Assn. Fin. Edn., Registry Profl. Planners, Torrance C. of C., Assistance League (bd. dirs. South Bay), Women in Constrn., Trojan Club and League (bd. dirs. 1978-79, 91—). Republican. Roman Catholic. Office: Union Bank Tower Ste 1000 21515 Hawthorne Blvd Torrance CA 90503

ENRIGHT, WILLIAM BENNER, judge; b. N.Y.C., July 12, 1925; s. Arthur Joseph and Anna Beatrice (Plante) E.; m. Bette Lou Card, Apr. 13, 1951; children—Kevin A., Kimberly A., Kerry K. BA, Dartmouth, 1947; LLB, Loyola U. at L.A., 1950. Bar: Calif. 1951; diplomate: Am. Bd. Trial Advs. Dep. dist. atty. San Diego County, 1951-54; ptnr. Enright, Levitt, Knutson & Tobin, San Diego, 1954-72; judge U.S. Dist. Ct. (so. dist.) Calif., San Diego, 1972—; Mem. adv. bd. Joint Legis. Com. for Revision Penal Code, 1970-72, Calif. Bd. Legal Specialization, 1970-72; mem. Jud. Council, 1972; Bd. dirs. Defenders, 1965-72, pres., 1972. Served as ensign USNR, 1943-46. Recipient Honor award San Diego County Bar, 1970; Extraordinary Service to Legal Professions award Mcpl. Ct. San Diego Jud. Dist., 1971. Fellow Am. Coll. Trial Lawyers, Am. Bar Found.; mem. ABA, San Diego County Bar Assn. (dir. 1963-65, pres. 1965), State Bar Calif. (gov. 1967-70, v.p. 1970, exec. com. law in a free soc. 1970—), Dartmouth Club San Diego, Am. Judicature Soc., Alpha Sigma Nu, Phi Delta Phi. Club: Rotarian. Office: US Dist Ct 940 Front St San Diego CA 92189-0010

ENRIQUEZ, CAROLA RUPERT, museum director; b. Washington, Jan. 2, 1954; d. Jack Burns and Shirley Ann (Orcutt) Rupert; m. John Enriquez, Jr., Dec. 30, 1989. BA in history cum laude, Bryn Mawr Coll., 1976; MA, U. Del., 1978, cert. in mus. studies, 1978. Personnel mgmt. trainee Naval Material Command, Arlington, Va., 1972-76; teaching asst. dept. history, U. Del., Newark, 1976-77; asst. curator/exhibit specialist Hist. Soc. Del., Wilmington, 1977-78; dir. Macon County Mus. Complex, Decatur, Ill., 1978-81; dir. Kern County Mus., Bakersfield, Calif., 1981—; pres. Kern County Mus. Found., 1991—; advisor Kern County Heritage Commn., 1981-88; chmn. Historic Records Commn., 1981-88; sec.-treas. Arts Council of Kern, 1984-86, pres. 1986-88; county co-chmn. United Way, 1981, 82; chmn. steering com. Calif. State Bakersfield Co-op Program, 1982-83; mem. Community Adv. Bd. Calif. State Bakersfield, Anthrop. Soc., 1986-88; bd. dirs. Mgmt. Council, 1983-86, v.p., 1987, pres. 1988; bd. dirs. Calif. Council for Promotion of History, 1984-86, v.p., 1987-88. pres., 1988-90; mem. community adv. bd. Calif. State U.-Bakersfield Sociology Dept., 1986-88; mem. women's adv. com. Girl Scouts U.S., 1989-91. Hagley fellow Eleutherian Mills-Hagley Found., 1977-78; Bryn Mawr alumnae regional scholar, 1972-76. Mem. Calif. Assn. Mus. (regional rep. 1991—, v.p. legis. affairs 1992—), Am. Assn. for State and Local History (chair awards com. Calif. chpt. 1990—). Unitarian Universalist. Office: Kern County Museum 3801 Chester Ave Bakersfield CA 93301-1395

ENRIQUEZ, FRANCISCO JAVIER, immunologist; b. Mexico City, June 24, 1955; came to U.S., 1982; s. Camilo Javier and Maria de Lourdes (Serralde) E.; m. Lisa Barricklow, May 30, 1987; 1 child, Alesi Brie. Diploma, London Sch. Hygiene & Tropical, 1984; MD, La Salle U., Mexico City, 1979; PhD, Cornell U., 1986. Clinician Santa Fe Hosp., Mexico City, 1979-81; asst. prof. Sch. of Medicine La Salle U., 1980-82; med. researcher Ministry of Health, Mexico City, 1980-82; postdoctoral fellow U. Ariz., Tucson, 1987-88, dir. hybridoma tech., 1988—; cons. NIH, Bethesda, Md., 1989—, Health Corp., 1992—, NCR, Washington, 1990—; sci. cons. Aegeria Inc., 1992—, Igx Inc., 1992—, Bristol Meyers, Squibb, Mead Johnson, 1992—. Author: (novel) Las Primas Segundas, 1991, (short stories) La evolucion del Pensamiento, 1992; editorial reviewer sci. jours., 1991—. Home: 339 E University Blvd Tucson AZ 85705-7848 Office: U Ariz Ariz Health Scis Ctr Tucson AZ 85724

ENSIGN, RICHARD PAPWORTH, transportation executive; b. Salt Lake City, Jan. 20, 1919; s. Louis Osborne and Florence May (Papworth) E.; m. Margaret Anne Hinckley, Sept. 5, 1942; children: Judith Ensign Lantz, Mary Jane Ensign Hofmeister, Richard L., James R., Margaret. B.S., U. Utah, 1941. With Western Air Lines, 1941-70, v.p. in-flight service, 1963-70, v.p. passenger service, 1970; v.p. passenger service Pan Am. World Airways, 1971, sr. v.p. field mgmt., 1973-74, sr. v.p. mktg., 1974-79; exec. v.p. Western Airlines, 1980-82; pres. R.P. Ensign & Assocs., 1982—; spl. asst. to pres. Marriott-Host, Marriott Corp., 1990-91; spl. asst. to chmn. Caterair Internat. Corp.; chmn. Utah Nat. Adv. Coun., 1984-86; bd. dirs. Western Airlines, 1980-81, Pacific Area Travel Assocs., 1976-81, Marriott Airport Svc. Co., Osaka, Japan, 1986-92, Marriott Internat. Corp., Seoul, People's Republic of Korea. Nat. fund raising chmn. U. Utah, 1982-83, 83-84. Recipient Disting. Service award Fla. Internat. U., 1973; named Disting. Alumnus U. Utah, 1976, 86, recipient merit award of honor, 1985. Mem. Nat. Aeros. Assn. Republican. Mormon. Club: Lochinvar. Home: 3848 Malibu Country Dr Malibu CA 90265-4717 Office: PO Box 566 Malibu CA 90265-0566

ENSMINGER, MARK DOUGLAS, chemist; b. Escondido, Calif., Oct. 11, 1955; s. Douglas Lloyd and Mary Theresa (Barron) E.; m. Marsha Lynn Westerhold, Dec. 20, 1980. BA, BS, U. Calif., Santa Barbara, 1977; AM, U. Ill., 1979, PhD, 1982. Rsch. chemist Chevron Oil Field Rsch. Co., La Habra, Calif., 1982-86; cons. Getty Conservation Inst., Marina Del Rey, Calif., 1986-87; engring. specialist Aircraft Div. Northrop Corp., Hawthorne, Calif., 1987-91; engring. specialist B-2 div. Northrop Corp., Pico Rivera, Calif., 1991—. Contbr. articles to profl. jours. Mem. Am. Chem. Soc., Am. Phys. Soc., Optical Soc. Am., Soc. for Applied Spectroscopy, Sigma Xi. Mem. Evangelical Free Ch. Home: 8141 Andora Dr La Mirada CA 90638 Office: Northrop Corp B-2 Div Dept W691/62 8900 E Washington Blvd Pico Rivera CA 90660-3737

ENSSLIN, THEODORE GUSTAV, insurance agent; b. Porterville, Calif., June 24, 1927; s. Theodore G. Ensslin Sr. and Pearl (Jackson) Penning; m. Dorothy Elizabeth Campbell; children: Marti, Steven, Lisa, Jeri, Mia, David. AA, Porterville Coll., 1947; BA in Phys. Edn. and Bus. Adminstrn., U. Nev., 1949. CLU; ChFC; CFP; cert. tchr. adult edn. Fin. agr. mgr. Anderson Clayton Co., 1951-57; agt., registered rep. N.Y. Life Ins. Co., 1958—; coach all sports Lander County High Sch., Battle Mountain, Nev., 1949-50; lectr. in ins. field. Contbr. articles to profl. jours. Mayor, City of Porterville, 1977-82, 89-91; mem. Porterville City Coun., 1985-89; mem. taxation and legis. coms. League of Calif. Cities, 1979-81; chmn. redevel. com., City of Porterville, 1989-91; mem. com. Tulare County Assn. Gov.; past bd. dirs. Porterville Hist. Mus.; bd. dirs. Porterville Coll. Found.; various other city, county and state coms.; chmn. Nat. Decathlon Com., 1971, 73; past. rep. AAU Masters, Calif. and Nev. Inducted into Porterville Coll. Athletic Hall of Fame, 1991. Mem. Calif. State Bar (assoc.), Nat. Assn. Life Underwriters, Million Dollar Round Table (life), Tulare Kings Counties Assn. Life Underwriters (past pres.), ASCAP, Univ. Nev. Alumni Assn. (past bd. dirs.), Hospice Assn. Am. (bd. dirs.), Hist. Archeology Soc. of U.S., Alpha Tau Omega. Republican. Home: 143 N Carmelita Porterville CA 73257 Office: 195 W Putnam Porterville CA 93257

ENSTAD, GALE SINCLAIR, county official; b. McVille, N.D., May 18, 1932; s. Severin Peter and Gladys M.A. (Nelson) E.; m. LaNora Steinberger, Feb. 20, 1960; children: Aaron P., Mark O., Lorena J. BS, Calif. State Polytech., 1960. Adminstrv. asst. State Assemblyman William M. Ketchum, Sacramento, Calif., 1966-68; budget analyst County of Kern, Bakersfield, Calif., 1968-73, asst. county clk., 1973-79, county clk., 1979-82, county clk. recorder, 1982—. Chmn. bd. Bethany Svcs.-Operating Bakersfield Homeless Ctr., 1991-92. Named Layman of Yr., Kiwanis Club, 1986. Mem. County Clks. Assn. Calif. (pre. 1989-91). Republican. Baptist. Home: 1210 Davis Cup Ct Bakersfield CA 93306 Office: County of Kern 1415 Truxtun Ave Bakersfield CA 93301

ENTRIKEN, ROBERT KERSEY, management educator; b. McPherson, Kans., Jan. 15, 1913; s. Frederick Kersey and Opal (Birch) E.; m. Elizabeth Freeman, May 26, 1940 (div. Nov. 1951); children—Robert Kersey, Jr., Edward Livingston Freeman, Richard Davis; m. Jean Finch, June 5, 1954; 1 child, Birch Nelson. B.A., U. Kans. 1934; M.B.A., Golden Gate U., 1961; postgrad. City Univ. Grad. Bus. Sch., London, 1971-73. C.P.C.U. Ins. broker, Houston, Tex. and McPherson, Kans., 1935-39; asst. mgr. Cravens, Dargan & Co., Houston, 1939-42; br. mgr. Nat. Surety Corp., Memphis and San Francisco, 1942-54; v.p. Fireman's Fund Ins. Co., San Francisco. 1954-73; adj. prof. Golden Gate U., San Francisco, 1953-73, prof. mgmt., 1974-89; resident dean Asia Programs, Singapore, 1987-88; prof. emeritus 1989—, underwriting mem. Lloyd's of London, 1985—. Contbr. articles to trade and profl. jours. Bd. dirs., sec., treas. Northstar Property Owners Assn., Calif., 1982-86. Served to capt. USNR, 1944-73, ret., 1973. Mem. Ins. Forum San Francisco (pres. 1965, trustee 1975-78, 84-88), Surety Underwriters Assn. No. Calif. (pres. 1956), CPCU Soc. (pres. No. Calif. chpt. 1957, Ins. Profl. of Yr., San Francisco chpt. 1981, bd. dirs., 1989-93), Chartered Ins. Inst., Ins. Inst. London, Musicians' Union Local No. 6 (life), U.S. Naval Inst., Assn. Naval Aviation, Phi Delta Theta. Episcopalian. Clubs: University, Marines' Meml. (San Francisco); Commonwealth. Lodge: Naval Order U.S. Office: 109 Minna St Ste 525 San Francisco CA 94105

ENZI, MICHAEL BRADLEY, accountant, state legislator; b. Bremerton, Wash., Feb. 1, 1944; s. Elmer Jacob and Dorothy (Bradley) E.; m. Diana Buckley, June 7, 1969; children: Amy, Bradley, Emily. BBA, George Wash. U., 1966; MBA, Denver U., 1968. Pres. NZ Shoes, Inc., Gillette, Wyo., 1969—, NZ Shoes of Sheridan, Inc., Wyo., 1983-91; acctg. mgr. Dunbar Well Svc., Inc., Gillette, 1985—; mem. Wyo. Ho. of Reps., Cheyne, 1987-91, Wyo. State Senate, Cheyne, 1991—; chmn. bd. dirs. First Wyo. Bank, Gillette; bd. dirs. N.Y. Stock Exch. Black Hills Corp., Rapid City, S.D.; chmn. Senate Revenue Com., 1992—. Mayor City of Gillette, 1975-82; pres. Wyo. Assn. Mcpls., Cheyenne, 1980-82. Sgt. Wyo. Air NG, 1967-73. Mem. Wyo. Order of DeMolay (master councilor 1963-64), Wyo. Jaycees (state pres. 1973-74), Masons (Sheridan and Gillette lodges), Scottish Rite, Shriners, Lions. Republican. Presbyterian. Home: 431 Circle Dr Gillette WY 82716 Office: Dunbar Well Svc Inc PO Box 1209 Gillette WY 82717-1209

EPCAR, RICHARD MICHAEL, actor, writer, director; b. Denver, Apr. 29, 1955; s. George Buck and Shirley (Learner) E.; m. Ellyn Jane Stern, Aug. 15, 1982; children: Jonathan Alexander, Jacqueline Elizabeth. BFA in Performing Arts, U. Ariz., 1978; postgrad., U. So. Calif., L.A., 1980, U.

Calif., L.A., 1981, Am. Film Inst., 1982. Pres. Trouble Shooter Prodns., L.A., 1986—. Actor (films) including Memoirs of an Invisible Man, D.C. Collins, Incident of War, Street Hawk, Escape to Love, Not of This World, (TV series) Beverly Hills 90210, Cheers, General Hospital, Guns of Paradise, Matlock, Who's the Boss?, Sonny Spoons, Moonlighting, Highway to Heaven, Amazing Stories, Fast Times, Crazy Like a Fox, Hell Town, Stir Crazy, Santa Barbara, (on stage) Why a Hero, Dracula, An Evening With Lincoln, Real Inspector Hound, Richard II; actor, writer (play) (on stage) Take My Wife...Please!, 1980; wrote and directed English adaptation of Acad. award winning Cinema Paradiso, Women on the Verge of a Nervous Breakdown (Acad. award nomination); dir. (for TV) A Cowboy Christmas. Mem. L.A. Zoo Assn., 1983-90, 91, Natural History Mus., L.A., 1989-91, Earth Save, L.A., 1990, L.A. Mus. Art, 1991; host fall festival Sta. KCET-Pub. TV, L.A., 1980; active Am. Cancer Soc. Recipient Haldeman Found. scholarship, U. Ariz., 1973-78; named Nat. Best Actor of Yr., Nat. Players, 1977, CPC Repertory Group, 1980; recipient Irene Ryan Soloist award, 1978. Office: Trouble Shooter Prodns PO Box 5429 North Hollywood CA 91616-5429

EPPELE, DAVID LOUIS, columnist; b. Jersey City, Apr. 4, 1939; s. Joseph Anton and Lena Marie (Tadlock) E.; m. Gladys Emily Padilla (div. 1975); children: David D., Joseph E.; m. Geneva Mae Kirsch, July 7, 1977. Student, N.Mex. State U., 1958, U. N.Mex., 1966, U. Portland, 1972. Field botanist SW Deserts and Mex., 1947-92, N.Mex. Cactus Rsch., Belen, 1953-62; dir. Ariz. Cactus and Succulent Rsch., Bisbee, 1984—; editor Ariz. Cactus News, 1984—; columnist Western Newspapers, 1987—. Author (newspaper column) On the Desert, 1986—; author: On the Desert, 1991; editor: Index of Cactus Illustrations, 1990, Desert in Bloom, 1989. Mem. Mule Mountain Dem. Party, Bisbee, 1978—. With USN, 1958-59. Mem. AAAS, Cactus and Succulent Soc. of Am., N.Mex. Acad. Sci., Bisbee C. of C. Home and Office: Ariz Cactus 8 Mulberry Ln Bisbee AZ 85603

EPPERSON, BRYAN KEITH, research geneticist; b. Fresno, Apr. 25, 1957; s. Edward Leo and Marianne (Schmall) E.; 1 child, Joseph Keith Epperson. BS, U. Calif., 1979, Phd, 1983. Postdoctoral assoc. U. Ga., Athens, 1983-84; postdoctoral geneticist U. Calif., Riverside, 1984-91, asst. rsch. geneticist, 1992—; Reviewer Princeton U. Press, 1992—, Grant Proposals for NSF, 1983—, over 14 jours., 1983—. Contbr. articles to profl. jours. Nat. merit scholar, 1975, Alumni scholar U. Calif., 1975, Calif. state scholar, 1975-79, Herbert-Kraft Meml. scholar, 1978, Jastro-Shields grad. rsch. fellow U. Calif., 1980; NIH grantee, 1993-96. Mem. European Soc. Evolutionary Biology, Soc. for the Study of Evolution, Genetics Soc. of Am., Nature Conservancy, Sigma Xi, Xi Sigma Pi. Office: U Calif Dept Botany & Plant Scis Riverside CA 92521

EPPERSON, ELEANOR LOUISE, retired educator; b. Longmont, Colo., July 15, 1916; d. Fred and Anna Weir (Smith) Dormann; m. John Ira Epperson, July 22, 1944; children: Dirk Alan, Kent John, Glen Scott. BA, U. Denver, 1938, MA, 1978. Cert. diagnostic tchr. Tchr. Denver Pub. Schs., 1938-81. Author: (young teen book) Timberjack and the Chief, 1984; contbr. articles to profl. jours. Legis. rep., state legis. chmn. Delta Kappa Gamma, Denver, 1983-88, active leadership devel. retreat, 1988 (Cert. of Merit 1989, Tribute 1989). Mem. Alpha Gamma Delta (ARC pin 1961). Home: 1615 Holly St Denver CO 80220-1442

EPPERSON, ERIC ROBERT, financial executive; b. Oregon City, Oreg., Dec. 10, 1949; s. Robert Max and Margaret Joan (Crawford) E.; m. Lyla Gene Harris, Aug. 21, 1969; 1 child, Marcie. B.S., Brigham Young U., 1973, M.Acctg., 1974; M.B.A., Golden Gate U., 1977, J.D., 1981. Instr. acctg. Brigham Young U., Provo, Utah, 1973-74; supr. domestic taxation Bechtel Corp., San Francisco, 1974-78; supr. internat. taxation Bechtel Power Corp., San Francisco, 1978-80; mgr. internat. tax planning Del Monte Corp., San Francisco, 1980-82, mgr. internat. taxes, 1982-85; internat. tax specialist Touche Ross & Co., San Francisco, 1985-87; dir. internat. tax Coopers & Lybrand, Portland, 1987-89; exec. v.p., chief fin. officer Epperson Dayton Sorenson Prodns., Inc., Salt Lake City, 1989-90, Epperson Prodns., 1990-92; exec. dir. The Oreg. Trail Found., Inc., Oregon City, 1992—. Author: (with T. Gilbert) Interfacing of the Securities and Exchange Commission with the Accounting Profession: 1968 to 1973, 1974; exec. producer (motion picture) Dream Machine, 1989. Scoutmaster, Boy Scouts Am., Provo, 1971-73, troop committeeman, 1973-74, 83—; mem. IRS Vol. Income Tax Assistance Program, 1972-75; pres. Mut. Improvement Assn., Ch. Jesus Christ of Latter-day Saints, 1972-74, pres. Sunday sch., 1977-79, tchr., 1974-80, ward clk., 1980-83, bishopric, 1983-87; bd. dirs. Oreg. Art Inst. Film Ctr., Oreg. Trail Coordinating Coun., Hist. Preservation League of Oreg.; vice chmn. ranch devel. com. Boy Scouts Am., Butle Creek. Mem. World Affairs Coun., Japan/Am. Soc., Internat. Tax Planning Assn., Internat. Fiscal Assn., Oreg. Trail Coordinating Coun. (exec. bd.), Oreg. Hist. Soc., U.S. Rowing Assn., Oreg. Calif. Trail Assn., Commonwealth Club. Republican. Home: 1051 SW Ardmore Ave Portland OR 97205

EPSTEIN, ALEXANDER MAXIM, filmmaker; b. N.Y.C., Jan. 26, 1963; s. Howard Michael and Cynthia (Fuchs) W. BA, Yale Coll., 1985; MFA, UCLA, 1990. V.p. prodn. Arama Entertainment, Tarzana, Calif., 1990—. Writer, dir. films including Leaving Pasadena, 1987, Santa Fe, 1990; assoc. prodr. Warriors, 1993. Democrat. Home: 1277 Barry Ave Apt 5 Los Angeles CA 90025-1729

EPSTEIN, ERVIN HAROLD, JR., dermatologist, educator, researcher; b. Oakland, Calif., Mar. 6, 1941; s. Ervin Harold Sr. and Selma E.; m. Sally Ann Fain, Aug. 11, 1963; children: Adam, Stephanie, Emily. AB, Harvard Coll., 1962; MD, U. Calif., San Francisco, 1966. Diplomate Am. Bd. Dermatology. Intern Barnes Hosp., Washington U., St. Louis, 1966-67; resident in dermatology Harvard U., Cambridge, Mass., 1967-68; clin. assoc. dermatol. br. NIH, Bethesda, Md., 1968-70, resident fellow in biochemistry, 1970-71; resident in dermatology NYU Med. Sch., 1971-72; asst. to clin. prof. dept. dermatology U. Calif. Med. Sch., San Francisco, 1972—, asst. to rsch. dermatologist, 1972—; prin. investigator various rsch. grants NIH, Bethesda, 1972—, mem. gen. medicine study sect., 1987-91, mem. adv. coun. Nat. Inst. AMS, 1993—. Co-editor: Skin Surgery, 1977, 3rd edit., 1988; editor: Progress in Dermatology, 1982-87; assoc. editor: (audio tape) Dialogues in Dermatology, 1977-84; author numerous rsch. papers, 1966—. Lt. USPHS, 1968-70. Mem. Soc. Investigative Dermatology (sec.-treas. 1984-89, pres.-elect 1990-91, pres. 1991-92), Dermatology Found. (trustee 1981-83, 84-91), Am. Dermatol. Assn. (treas. 1992—), Harvard Club San Francisco (v.p.). Jewish. Office: San Francisco Gen Hosp Bldg 100 Rm 269 1001 Potrero St San Francisco CA 94110

EPSTEIN, JONATHAN AKIBA, publishing executive; b. Seattle, Dec. 8, 1963; s. Charles Joseph and Lois (Barth) E. BA in Phys. Scis., Harvard Coll., 1986. Editorial asst. Ziff-Davis Pub. Co., Boston, 1985; contbg. editor Ziff-Davis Pub. Co., 1985-86; dir. ops. Digital News Pub. Co., Boston, 1986; dir. research Digital News Pub. Co., 1987; southwest regional mgr. Digital News Pub. Co., Irvine, Calif., 1987-89; western sales mgr. Digital News Pub. Co., 1989-90; dir. spl. projects Digital News Pub. Co., Boston, 1990-91; pub. Multimedia World Mag. PC World Comms., Inc., San Franciso, 1991—. Editor: Guided Tour of Multimedia; contbr. articles to profl. publs. Bd. dirs. Pierian Found., Cambridge, Mass., 1986—. Mem. Internat. Interactive Comm. Soc., San Francisco Multimedia Devel. Group. Jewish. Office: Multimedia World 501 2d St #201 San Francisco CA 94107

ERATH, EDWARD HYDE, investment management company executive; b. Chgo., Dec. 23, 1929; s. George Glennon and Edith (Benson) E.; widowed; 1 child, Edward L. BS in Liberal Arts, Northwestern U., 1954; MS in Physics, UCLA, 1957, PhD in Physics, 1961. Physicist Hughes Rsch. Labs., Malibu, Calif., 1955-61; dir. rsch. Electronics Investment Mgmt. Corp., San Diego, 1961-64; asst. dir. corp. devel. Douglas Aircraft co., Santa Monica, Calif., 1964-66; pres., dir., founder Tech. Svcs. Corp., L.A., 1966-74; advisor to chmn. So. Calif. Gas Co., L.A., 1975-81; chmn., CEO, founder Ctr. for Commercialization of Advanced Tech., L.A., 1990—; advisor to mayor City of L.A., 1966-71; cons. to sec. of bus. State of Calif., 1976-78, advisor to gov., Sacramento, 1985-93. Contbr. articles to profl. jours., chpts. to books; patentee cryogenic refrigeration. Co-organizer L.A. Traffic Action Coun., 1967-69; mem. com. United Way, L.A., 1969-71, West Point Fund Com. U.S. Mil. Acad., 1978-84, L.A. County Economy and Efficiency Commn., 1986-91; trustee Ctr. for Tech. Svcs., San Diego, 1975-80; bd. dirs. Fgn. Policy Rsch. Inst., Phila., 1979-85. Recipient Spl. Commendation Mayor City of L.A., 1965, County of L.A. Bd. Suprs., 1991; Hughes Doctoral fellow Hughes Aircraft, Co., Culver City, Calif., 1958-61. Mem. Calif. Club. Home: 538 S Flower St Los Angeles CA 90071 Office: Ctr for Commercialization of Advanced Tech 16000 Ventura Blvd # 500 Los Angeles CA 90071

ERBST, LAWRENCE ARNOLD, lawyer, consultant; b. N.Y.C., Oct. 5, 1930; s. Ben Erbst and Rose (Farbish) Levy; m. Eileen Sheila Frohman, July 29, 1956; children: Leslie Charles, Allison Carol, Jonathan Stuart. ABcum laude, Harvard Coll., 1952, LLB, 1955. Bar: N.Y. 1956. Assoc. Sylvester and Harris, N.Y.C., 1958-59; atty. NBC, N.Y.C., 1959-62, Screen Gems, Inc., N.Y.C., 1962-65; assoc. Regan, Goldfarb, Powell and Quinn, N.Y.C., 1965-69; assoc. to ptnr. Krause, Hirsch and Gross, N.Y.C., 1969-72; ptnr. Pryor, Cashman, Sherman and Flynn, N.Y.C., 1972-80; v.p. United Artists Corp., Culver City, Calif., 1980-82, Lorimar, Culver City, 1982-84; pvt. practice fin. and bus. cons. L.A., 1984—; bd. dirs., v.p. L.A. Venture Assn. With U.S. Army, 1955-57. Mem. ABA, L.A. Copyright Soc. Democrat. Jewish. Home: 4818 Mary Ellen Ave Sherman Oaks CA 91423-2120

ERBURU, ROBERT F., media and information company executive; b. Ventura, Calif., Sept. 27, 1930. BA, U. So. Calif., 1952; JD, Harvard U. Law Sch., 1955. Chmn. bd., chief exec. officer Times Mirror Co., L.A., also bd. dirs.; bd. dirs. Tejon Ranch Co. Trustee Huntington Ahmanson Found. Library, Art Collections and Bot. Gardens, 1981—, chmn. 1990, Flora and William Hewlett Found., bd. trustees, 1980—, Brookings Instn., 1983—, Tomas Rivera Ctr., 1985—, Carrie Estelle Doheny Found., Fletcher Jones Found., 1982—, Pfaffinger Found., 1974—, J. Paul Getty Trust; bd. dirs., 1987—, chmn. Times Mirror Found., 1962—; bd. dirs. Independent Coll's. of Southern Calif., Los Angeles Festival, 1985—, Ralph M. Parsons Found., 1985—; mem. Nat. Gallery of Art Trustees Council, 1985—. Mem. Newspaper Assn. Am. (bd. govs., exec. bd., exec. com., bd. dirs. 1980—, officer 1988-92, chmn. 1991-92), Coun. of Fgn. Rels. (bd. dirs.), Calif. Bus. Foundtable, Bus. Coun., L.A. World Affairs Coun. (vice chmn. bd. dirs. 1987—). Home: 1518 Blue Jay Way Los Angeles CA 90069-1215 Office: Times Mirror Co Times Mirror Sq Los Angeles CA 90012-3816

ERDAL, BRUCE ROBERT, program manager; b. Albuquerque, June 15, 1939; s. Selmer Clifford and Louise Marion (Hubbell) E.; m. Jean Elizabeth Davis, June 25, 1970. Student, U. N.Mex., Albuquerque, 1961; PhD, Washington U., St. Louis, 1966. Rsch. assoc. Brookhaven Nat. Lab., L.I., 1967-69; vis. scientist CERN, Geneva, 1970-71; asst. physicist Ames (Iowa) Lab., 1971-72; mem. staff Los Alamos (N.Mex.) Nat. Lab., 1972-80, dep. group leader, 1980-82, project officer, 1980-82, assoc. div. leader, 1982-87, program mgr. environ. techs., 1987—. NSF fellow, 1969-70. Fellow Am. Inst. Chemists; mem. AAAS, Am. Chem. Soc. (sec. div. nuclear chem. tech. 1983-86, chmn. 1991—), Am. Geophys. Union, Materials Rsch. Soc., Phi Kappa Phi, Sigma Xi. Home: 577 Todd Loop Los Alamos NM 87544-3543 Office: Los Alamos Nat Lab Inc Environ Techs MS-J515 Los Alamos NM 87545

ERDMANN, JOACHIM CHRISTIAN, physicist; b. Danzig, June 5, 1928; s. Franz Werner and Maria Magdalena (Schreiber) E.; doctorate Tech. U. Braunschweig (Germany), 1958; m. Ursula Maria Wedemeyer, Aug. 24, 1957; children—Michael Andreas, Thomas Christian, Maria Martha Dorothea. Physicist, Osram Labs., Augsburg, Germany, 1954-60; sr. research scientist Boeing Sci. Research Labs., Seattle, 1960-72; sr. research scientist Boeing Aerospace Co., Seattle, 1972-73; prin. engr. Boeing Comml. Airplane Co., Seattle, 1973-81, sr. prin. engr., 1981-84; sr. prin. engr. Boeing Aerospace, Seattle, 1984—; vis. prof. Max Planck Inst. for Metals Research, Stuttgart, Germany, 1968-69; lectr. Tech. U. Stuttgart, 1968-69; pres. Optologics Inc., Seattle, 1973—. Mem. Am. Phys. Soc., Optical Soc. Am., Soc. Photo Optical Instrumentation Engrs. Author: Heat Conduction in Crystals, 1969. Contbr. articles to profl. jours. Research in cryogenics, statis. physics and opto electronics. Home: 14300 Trillium Blvd SE Apt 8 Bothell WA 98012-1313 Office: Boeing Def and Space Group PO Box 3999 Seattle WA 98124-2499

ERIACHO, BELINDA PEARL, environmental scientist; b. Ft. Defiance, Ariz., May 28, 1963; d. Tony Leopoldo Eriacho Sr. and Irene Rosalyn Lewis. BS, Ariz. State U., 1986; postgrad., U. N.Mex., 1988-89; MPH, U. Hawaii, 1990; postgrad., U. Mich., 1992. Adminstrv. asst. health educator Maricopa County Health Svcs., Phoenix, 1986-87; health educator Navajo Dept. Health, Window Rock, Ariz., 1987-88; tng. coord. Navajo Nation Family Planning Corp., Window Rock, Ariz., 1988-89; extern Navajo Area Indian Health Svc., Window Rock, Ariz., 1989-90, jr. health adminstrv. officer, 1990; environ. scientist III Ariz. Pub. Svc. Co., Phoenix, 1991—; pub. speaker mth, engring., sci. achievement, Phoenix, 1992, Window Rock High Sch., 1992. Co-chairperson Native Am. Heritage Com., Phoenix, 1992. Recipient scholarship Navajo Nation, 1990, Nat. Action Coun. for Minorities in Engring., 1981-82, Indian Health Svc., 1984-85. Mem. APHA, Am. Indian Sci. and Engring. Soc., Am. Indsl. Hygiene Assn., Ariz. Indsl. Hygiene Assn., Ariz. State U. Alumni, Ariz. State NativeAm. Alumni Assn. (bd. dirs. 1988-89), Environ. Auditing Roundtable, U. Hawaii Pub. Health Alumni Assn., Delta Omega. Office: Ariz Pub Svc Co PO Box 53999 Sta 9386 Phoenix AZ 85072-3999

ERICKSON, ARTHUR CHARLES, architect; b. Vancouver, B.C., Can., June 14, 1924; s. Oscar and Myrtle (Chatterson) E. Student, U. B.C., Vancouver, 1942-44; B.Arch., McGill U., Montreal, Que., Can., 1950; LL.D. (hon.), Simon Fraser U., Vancouver, 1973, U. Man., Winnipeg, Can., 1978, Lethbridge U., 1981; D.Eng. (hon.), Novia Scotia Tech. Coll., McGill U., 1971; Litt.D. (hon.), U. B.C., 1985. Asst. prof. U. Oreg., Eugene, 1955-56; assoc. prof. U. B.C., 1956-63; ptnr. Erickson-Massey Architects, Vancouver, 1963-72; prin. Arthur Erickson Architects, Vancouver, 1972-91, Toronto, Ont., Can., 1981-91, Los Angeles, 1981-91; prin. Arthur Erickson Archtl. Corp., Vancouver, 1991—. Prin. works include Can. Pavilion at Expo '70, Osaka (recipient first prize in nat. competition, Archtl. Inst. of Japan award for best pavilion), Robson Square/The Law Courts (honor award), Mus. of Anthropology (honor award), Eppich Residence (honor award), Habitat Pavilion (honor award), Sikh Temple (award of merit), Champlain Heights Community Sch. (award of merit), San Diego Convention Ctr., Calif. Plz., L.A., Fresno City Hall; subject of Time mag. cover article and New Yorker profile; contbr. articles to profl. publs. Mem. com. on urban devel. Coun. of Can., 1971; bd. dirs. Can. Conf. of Arts, 1972; mem. design adv. coun. Portland Devel. Commn., Can. Coun. Urban Rsch.; trustee Inst. Rsch. on Pub. Policy. Capt. Can. Intelligence Corps., 1945-46. Recipient Molson prize Can. Coun. Arts, 1967, Triangle award Nat. Soc. Interior Design, Royal Bank Can. award, 1971, Gold medal Tau Sigma Delta, 1973, residential design award Can. Housing Coun., 1975, August Perret award Internat. Union Archiects Congress, 1975, Chgo. Architecture award, 1984, Gold medals Royal Archtl. Inst. Can., 1984, French Acad. Architecture, 1984, Pres. award excellence Am. Soc. Landscape Architects, 1979; named Officer, Order of Can., 1973, Companion Order of Can., 1981. Fellow AIA (hon., Pan Pacific citation Hawaiian chpt. 1963, gold medal 1986), Royal Archtl. Inst. Can. (recipient award 1980); mem. Archtl. Inst. B.C., Royal Can. Acad. Arts (academician), Heritage Can., U. B.C. Faculty Club. Office: Arthur Erickson Archtl Corp, 1672 W 1st Ave, Vancouver, BC Canada V6J 1G1

ERICKSON, CALVIN HOWARD, computer systems engineer; b. Worcester, Mass., June 18, 1946; s. Stanley Howard and Mae Harriet (Wivagg) E.; m. Radmila Frencic, June 5, 1970; children: Jennifer Joy, Melissa Mae. Student, Clark U., 1975-77; ABS in Computer Sci., Quinsigamond Community Coll., Worcester, 1971; cert. Unix System Mgmt. and Adminstrn., U. Calif., Santa Cruz, 1991. Sr. systems programmer Datatrol Inc., Hudson, Mass., 1972-76; tech. support mgr. Keane Inc., Wellesley, Mass., 1976-81; software support specialist Data Gen. Corp., Westboro, Mass., 1981-87; computer systems engr. Loral Rolm-Mil Spec Computers, San Jose, Calif., 1987-92; co devel. support engr. Adobe Systems, Mountain View, Calif., 1992—. Author: AOS/VS Internals Manual, 1986. With USN, 1965-71. Mem. Nat. Geog. Soc., San Francisco Zool. Soc., Golden Gate Nat. Park Assn., The Friends of Photography (sustaining), Smithsonian (assoc.), Alpha Nu Omega. Home: 34786 Comstock Common Fremont CA 94555-2820 Office: Adobe Systems 1585 Charleston Rd Mountain View CA 94039

ERICKSON, CAROL ANN, psychotherapist; b. Worcester, Mass., Dec. 26, 1933; d. Milton Hyland and Helen (Hutton) E.; m. Jean LaRue Barnes, Mar. 20, 1952 (div. Sept. 1962); children: Stephanie Free, Suzanne Hackett, Paul, Sandra Smith, Larry, Cynthia Baker. BS, Ariz. State U., 1964; MSW, Calif. State U., Fresno, 1977. Social worker Los Angeles County, 1964-83; pvt. practice psychotherapy Berkeley, Calif., 1977—; exec. dir. Erickson Inst., Berkeley, 1981—; adj. faculty U. Calif., Berkeley; adj. faculty Vermont Coll. San Francisco, 1986—. Co-writer, composer Deep Self Appreciation, 1983, Self-Hypnosis, A Relaxing Time Out, 1984, Natural Self Confidence, 1985, Deep Sleep and Sweet Dreams, 1989, Rapid Pain Control, 1989, Easy Enhanced Learning, 1989, Quick Stress Busters, 1990. Bd. dirs. YWCA, Torrance, Calif., 1981-83. Mem. Internat. Soc. Hypnosis, No. Calif. Soc. Clin. Hypnosis, So. Calif. Soc. Clin. Hypnosis, Calif. Assn. Marriage and Family Therapists (cert.), Soc. Clin. and Exptl. Hypnosis, Soc. Clin. Social Workers, Nat. Assn. Social Workers (cert.), AAUW, NOW, Phi Kappa Phi. Democrat. Office: Erickson Inst PO Box 739 Berkeley CA 94701-0739

ERICKSON, CHARLES JOHN, government official; b. Chgo., Sept. 4, 1931; s. Charles Gustave and Alice (Wackenfeldt) E.; m. Roberta Anne Moose, Jan. 6, 1953 (div. Dec. 1990); children: Kristina, Kirsten, Karin; m. Patricia Ann Miller, Dec. 22, 1990. AB, U. Chgo., 1952, AM, 1954. Assoc. social scientist Rand Corp., Santa Monica, Calif., 1955-56; sr. human factors engr. Northrop Aircraft Corp., Hawthorne, Calif., 1956-59; human factors specialist Systems Devel. Corp., Santa Monica, 1959-60; systems analyst Stanford Rsch. Inst., Menlo Park, Calif., 1960-62; supr. life systems N.Am. Aviation, Downey, Calif., 1962-64, Apollo crew systems engr., 1964-65; mgr. med. systems N.Am. Rockwell, Anaheim, Calif., 1965-70; assoc. dir. health systems Office R & D, Indian Health Svc., Tucson, 1970-80, dep. assoc. dir. Office Health Program R&D, 1980—; cons. Peace Corps, Calif. State U., L.A., 1968; mem., chmn. systems panel L.A. Mental Health Assn., 1968-70; rural health cons. Egyptian Ministry Health, Cairo, 1978, 79; guest lectr. UCLA Sch. Pub. Health, 1970-73. Contbr. articles to profl. jours. Mem. Wiche Com. on Improving Mental Health, Tucson, 1972, Pima County Health Planning Coun., Tucson, 1973-76, Health Systems Agy. So. Ariz., Tucson, 1976-79; mem. bd. Christian edn. Congl. Ch., Tucson, 1990-91; moderator Rincon Congl. Ch., 1992. Recipient Superior Performance award HEW, 1974, Dir.'s award for excellence Indian Health Svc., 1988, Sec.'s Sr. Mgmt. citation HHS, 1983. Fellow Soc. for Applied Anthropology; mem. AAAS, Human Factors Soc. (pres. L.A. chpt. 1969-70), Human Factors Soc. (book reviewer 1974-75), Soc. for Gen. Systems Rsch. (paper referee 1983-84), Am. Anthrop. Assn., N.Y. Acad. Scis. Home: 10700 N La Reserve Dr Tucson AZ 85737-9199 Office: Indian Health Svc Office Health Program R & D 7960 S J Stock Rd Tucson AZ 85746-7012

ERICKSON, CHRISTOPHER ANDREW, economics educator; b. St. Helens, Oreg., Oct. 18, 1957; s. Kenneth S. and Valerie I. (Williams) E.; m. Laura Vanyo, Feb. 27, 1982; children: Andrew S., Mischelle I. BA, Willamette U., 1980; PhD, Ariz. State U., Tempe, 1989. Bus. analyst Dun & Bradstreet, Seattle, 1981-83; analyst Criterion Inc., Phoenix, 1985-86; asst. prof. econs. N.Mex. State U., Las Cruces, 1987—. Precinct committeeman Dem. Party, Warren, Oreg., 1978-80; chmn. Sykes for County Commr. campaign, Columbia County, Oreg., 1980. Mem. Am. Econ. Assn., Western Econ. Assn., So. Econ. Assn., Assn. Borderland Scholars. Democrat. Office: NMex State U Dept Econs 30001/3CQ Las Cruces NM 88003-0001

ERICKSON, DONALD ARTHUR, education educator; b. Saskatoon, Can., June 27, 1925; s. Joseph Arthur and Pearl Ada (Stephenson) E.; m. Phyllis Gladys Mundt, Nov. 19, 1947 (div. Aug. 1983); 1 child, Roddy Wayne; m. Raquel Hernandez Awad, Sept. 8, 1991. AB, Bob Jones U., 1954; AM, U. Chgo., 1960, PhD, 1962. Asst. prof. Fla. State U., Tallahassee, 1962-63; asst. prof. to assoc. prof. to prof. U. Chgo., 1963-64; prof. Simon Fraser U., Burnaby, B.C., Can., 1974-77, U. San Francisco, 1977-81; prof. UCLA, 1981-93, prof. emeritus, 1993—; cons. Pres. Commn. on Sch. Fin., Washington, 1968-70, Legis. Commn. in Ill., N.Y., Mass., S.D., Mich., 1970—, State Depts. of Edn., B.C., Australia, 1968-81. Author 3 books; contbr. over 100 articles to profl. jours. Grantee Pres. Commn., Ill. Elem. and Secondary Non-Pub. Schs. Study Commn., Office of Econ. Opportunity, Nat. Inst. of Edn., Spencer Found., B.C. Ministry of Edn. Office: UCLA 405 Hilgard Ave Los Angeles CA 90024

ERICKSON, ERIC DOUGLAS, chemist; b. Astoria, Oreg., July 31, 1955; s. Douglas Leon and Patricia (Thiebes) E.; m. Barbara Marie Davenport, Sept. 3, 1977; children: Ivy Marie, Benjamin Clark. BS in Chemistry, Oreg. State U., 1977; Cert. of Proficiency Indsl. Hygiene, San Diego City Coll., 1980; PhD in Chemistry, Mich. State U., 1989. Chemist AMTECH Labs., San Diego, 1977-80, Naval Weapons Ctr., China Lake, Calif., 1980-84; teaching/rsch. asst. Mich. State U., East Lansing, 1984-89; chemist Naval Weapons Ctr., China Lake, 1989-92; chemist weapons div. Naval Air Warfare Ctr., China Lake, 1992—. Contbr. articles to profl. jours. Scout leader Cub Scouts/Boy Scouts Am., Ridgecrest, Calif., 1990—, sci. explorer, post advisor, 1992—. Mem. Am. Chem. Soc. (treas. 1990-92), Am. Soc. Mass Spectroscopists, Sigma Xi (v.p. 1990, pres. 1991). Office: Naval Air Warfare Ctr Weapons Div Code CO2353 China Lake CA 93555

ERICKSON, JAMES GARDNER, retired artist, cartoonist; b. International Falls, Minn., Apr. 11, 1925; s. Albin Edwin and Edna Lucille (Thomas) E. Student, Hundredmark Art Sch., Mpls., 1946-47. Comml. artist Pillsbury Co., Mpls., 1947-50; sign painter Tri-State Display Ctr., Mpls., 1950-64, Displaymasters, Inc., Mpls., 1964-80, Signdesign, Inc., St. Paul, 1980-90; ret., 1990. Contbr. cartoons to numerous publs. including Daily Worker, 1949-67. With U.S. Army, 1943-46, MTO. Decorated Inf. Combat Badge. Mem. ACLU, 36th Divsn. Assn. (life). Home: 1848 Hwy 28 Hot Springs MT 59845-9704

ERICKSON, JAMES H., academic administrator; b. Oak Park, Ill., May 18, 1939; s. Chester E. and Ethyl M. (Jackson) E.; m. Janet Jean Selberg, June 24, 1966; children: Michael James, Richard James. BS, Bradley U., 1961, MA, 1966; EdD, Ind. U., 1970. Reporter UPI, Chgo., 1960-61; cons. Lambda Chi Alpha Frat., Inc., Indpls., 1961-63; dir., pub. info. Bradley U., Peoria, Ill., 1963-69, asst. to pres. and chancellor, 1970-78, dean of student svcs., 1978-82, assoc. v.p., 1982-85; dir. news bur. Ind. U., Bloomington, 1969-70; vice chancellor for univ. rels. and devel. U. Calif., Riverside, 1985—; adj. prof. Bradley U., Peoria, 1969-84; fundraising cons. for colls. and charitable orgns., Ill. and Calif., 1980-90; commencement speaker for high schs., Ill., 1970-85. Editor: Assn. Urban Univs. Nat. Jour., 1965-70. Pres. Tri-County Urban League, Peoria, 1974-76, bd. mem., Disting. Svc award, 1981; v.p. Salvation Army Adv. Bd., Peoria, 1980, bd. mem.; bd. mem. Symphony Bd. Dirs., Econ. Devel. Coun.; Pres. Greater Riverside Area Urban League, 1993—. Sgt. USAR, 1962-68. Recipient United Way, Ill., 1980; named Man of Yr. City of Peoria, 1970, Outstanding Young Man Ill. Jr. C. of C., 1971, Riverside Citizen of Yr. award Greater Riverside C. of C., 1993. Mem. Raincross club. Methodist. Home: 6275 Appian Way Riverside CA 92506-4506 Office: U Calif 4108 Hinderaker Hall Bldg Riverside CA 92521

ERICKSON, LEIF B., judge; b. Helena, Mont., June 10, 1942; s. Leif B. and Huberta (Brown) E.; m. Carole I. Hedlund, Dec. 30, 1967; children: Kristin J., Leif Trenton. BA, U. Mont., 1964, JD, 1967. Bar: Mont. 1967, U.S. Dist. Ct. Mont. 1967. Dep. county atty. Lewis and Clark County, Mont., 1970-75; pvt. practice Whitefish, Mont., 1975-85; judge State Dist. Ct., Kalispell, Mont., 1985-92; U.S. Magistrate judge U.S. Dist. Ct., Missoula, Mont., 1992—. Past bd. dirs. Big Bros. and Sisters, North Valley Hosp., Whitefish Kiwanis, Hockaday Ctr. for Arts, Am. Cancer Soc., Whitefish Winter Carnival; past bd. dirs. or commr. Whitefish City Bd. Adjustments, Whitefish City-County Planning Bd., Mont. Dept. Family Svc.-Juvenile Justice Com., Mont. Bar Assn.-Criminal Procedure Commn. Mem. Mont. Bar Assn. Office: Federal Bldg PO Box 7219 200 E Broadway Missoula MT 59801-7219

ERICKSON, RICHARD BEAU, life insurance company executive; b. Chgo., May 14, 1952; s. Charles Arthur and Carole Annette (Beaumont) E.; m. Pamela J. Sievers, Aug. 20, 1977. BS, U. Ky., 1974, MBA, 1975. CLU. Sales rep. Met. Life and affiliated cos., Chgo. Hgts., Ill., 1975-78; sales mgr. Met. Life and affiliated cos., Flossmoor, Ill., 1978-80; mktg. specialist Met. Life and affiliated cos., Aurora, Ill., 1980-81; branch mgr. Met. Life and affiliated cos., Orland Park, Ill., 1981-84; corp. dir. Met. Life Gen. Ins. Agy.

Inc., N.Y.C., 1984-86; regional sales mgr. Met. Life Gen. Ins. Agy. Inc., L.A., 1986-89, agy. v.p., sr. mktg. and sales exec., 1989—, agy. v.p., 1989; rep. (Midwest) Sales Mgr. Adv., N.Y.C., 1979; dir. South Cook County Assn. Life Underwriters, Chgo., 1983. Author: Met. Manpower Development, 1981, Met. Manpower Development: A Guideline for Success, 1986. Sponsor UCLA Soccer, 1986—. Mem. Nat. Assn. Securities Dealers, Life Underwriters Tng. Counsel, Chartered Life Underwriters, U. Ky. Alumni Assn., Nat. Assn. Life Underwriters, Gen. Agts. & Mgrs. Assn., Nat. Rifle Assn., Sierra Club, Sigma Nu. Republican. Office: Met Life 801 N Brand Blvd #245 Glendale CA 91203

ERICKSON, ROBERT ALLEN, English literature educator; b. Fargo, N.D., Apr. 1, 1940; s. Allen Gerald and Ruth Dorothy (Dahl) E.; m. Liisa Raatikainen, Nov. 21, 1966; children: Martin, Stephen, Annalisa. AB, Boston U., 1962; MA, Yale U., 1964, PhD, 1966. Asst. instr. in English Yale U., New Haven, 1965; asst. prof. of English U. Calif., Santa Barbara, 1966-73, lectr. in English with security, 1973-77, assoc. prof. of English, 1977-85, prof. English, 1985—. Author: Mother Midnight, 1986, (with others) The History of John Bull, 1976; contbr. articles to profl. jours. Woodrow Wilson fellowship, 1962-63, Fulbright fellowship, U.S. Govt., 1965-66; Augustus Howe Buck scholarship Boston U., 1958-60. Mem. AAUP, Am. Soc. for Eighteenth Century Studies. Home: 2517 Medcliff Rd Santa Barbara CA 93109-1819 Office: U Calif Dept English 2607 S Hall Santa Barbara CA 93106

ERICKSON, ROBERT L., cellular company executive, minister; b. Englewood, Colo., May 19, 1938; s. Albert Sanford and Margaret Mae (Weese) E.; m. Sara Ruth Dunlap, Dec. 22, 1958 (div. 1969); 1 child, Virginia Ruth McLaughlin; m. Linda Louise Carlson, June 22, 1988; children: Tawni Lynn Latter, Douglas Quinn Starcevich. Dist. engr. Harris Corp., Wash., 1967-87; mktg. mgr. AANSR Co., Wash., 1985-86; exec. United Cellular Assocs., Hawaii, 1985—; owner Big E Computers, Wash., 1987—; dir. His Truth Ministries, Wash., 1987—; chmn. RSA A-3, Wash., 1993—. With USAF, 1959-63. Home: 7855 124th Ave NE Kirkland WA 98033-8228 Office: His Truth Ministries 12505 116th St NE A26 Kirkland WA 98033-8228

ERICKSON, RUSSELL JOHN, pediatrician; b. Sauk Center, Minn.; s. Russell John and Valerie Jeanette (Rose) E.; m. Patricia Ann Parker, June 22, 1958; children: Karen Michelle, Kevin David, Keith Lawrence. AB in Chemistry cum laude, Occidental Coll., 1957; MD, U. Calif., San Francisco, 1961; cert. in acupuncture, UCLA, 1990. Intern, resident and fellow in Pediatrics U. Calif., San Francisco, 1961-63; resident and fellow U. Wash., Seattle, 1963-65; pediatrician, asst. chief pediatrics Kaiser-Permanente, Oakland, Calif., 1965-66, 68-72; chief pediatrics Kaiser-Permanente, Richmond, Calif., 1972-88, chief quality assurance, 1978-84, chief med. edn., 1980-82, sr. cons., 1988—; clin. instr. U. Calif. Med. Sch., San Francisco, 1965-66, 68-72; chair manpower com. No. Calif. Acad. Pediatrics, 1976-78; mem. State Pediatric Healthplan Com., Calif., 1979. Contbr. articles to med. jours. Founder, bd. dirs. Moraga (Calif.) Park and Recreation Dept., 1968-76; bd. dirs. Moraga Community Assn., 1970-74; pres. Saddleridge Homeowners, Pleasant Hill, Calif., 1990-93; sec. Sunrise Hills II Homeowners, Calif., 1993; trustee Am. Found. Med. Acupuncture, 1993—. Capt. U.S. Army, 1966-68. Fellow Am. Acad. Pediatrics; mem. AMA, Am. Acad. Med. Acupuncture, Sierra Club (life), Sons of Norway. Office: Kaiser-Permanente Med 901 Nevin Ave Richmond CA 94801

ERICKSON, STACI KENNEDY, public radio administrator; b. Spokane, Wash., May 8, 1969; d. Marvin M. and Linda L. (Humiston) Murphy; m. Kenneth J. Erickson, Feb. 10, 1989; children: Alexander, Jacob. Student, Falls C.C., Spokane, 1987-90. Membership dir. KPBX-Spokane Pub. Radio, 1987—. Office: Spokane Pub Radio 2319 N Monroe Spokane WA 99205

ERICKSON, TIMOTHY ERIC, mathematics educator; b. Palo Alto, Calif., July 29, 1954; s. William E. and Melba (Moss) E.; m. Margaret A. Holmberg; 1 child, Anne Katherine. BS, Calif. Inst. Tech., 1975; MA, U. Calif., Berkeley, 1977, PhD, 1987. Engr. Jet Propulsion Lab., Pasadena, Calif., 1979-82; curriculum developer EQUALS Program, Berkeley, 1983-92; ind. cons. Epistemological Engring., Oakland, Calif., 1987—; asst. prof. Mills Coll., Oakland, 1988-89. Author: Off and Running, 1986, Desktop Publishing with Microsoft Word, 1988, Get It Together, 1989. Mem. ASCD, Math. Assn. Am., Calif. Math. Coun.

ERICKSON, VIRGINIA BEMMELS, chemical engineer; b. Sleepy Eye, Minn., June 19, 1948; d. Gordon Boothe and Marion Mae (Rieke) Bemmels; m. Larry Douglas Erickson, Sept. 6, 1969; children: Kirsten Danielle, Dean Michael. Diploma in Nursing, Swedish Hosp. Sch. Nursing, 1969; BSChemE, U. Wash., 1983, MChemE, 1985. RN. Asst. head nurse N. Meml. Hosp., Mpls., 1970-73; intensive care RN Swedish Med. Ctr., Seattle, 1973-83; research asst. U. Wash., Seattle, 1983-85; instrumentation and control engr. CH2M Hill, Bellevue, Wash., 1985—, mgr. dept., 1988—; cons. instrumentation and control engr. Mem. editorial adv. bd. Control. Leader Girl Scouts U.S., Seattle, 1985; supt. Seattle Ch. Sch., 1983; rep. United Way, 1986—. Recipient Cert. Achievement, Soc. Women Engrs., 1983, Teenfeed, 1990. Mem. AICE, NAFE, Instrument Soc. Am., Tau Beta Pi. Democrat. Mem. United Methodist Ch. Home: 6026 24th Ave NE Seattle WA 98115-7009 Office: CH2M Hill 777 108th Ave NE PO Box 91500 Bellevue WA 98009-2050

ERICKSON, WILLIAM HURT, state supreme court justice; b. Denver, May 11, 1924; s. Arthur Xavier and Virginia (Hurt) E.; m. Doris Rogers, Dec. 24, 1953; children: Barbara Ann, Virginia Lee, Stephen Arthur, William Taylor. Degree in petroleum engring., Colo. Sch. Mines, 1947; student, U. Mich., 1949; LLB, U. Va., 1950. Bar: Colo. 1951. Pvt. practice law Denver; justice Colo. Supreme Ct., 1971—, chief justice, 1983-85; faculty NYU Appellate Judges Sch., 1972-85; mem. exec. Commn. on Accreditation of Law Enforcement Agys., 1980-83; chmn. Pres.'s Nat. Commn. for Rev. of Fed. and State Laws Relating to Wiretapping and Electronic Surveillance, 1976. With USAAF, 1943. Recipient Disting. Achievement medal Colo. Sch. Mines, 1990. Fellow Internat. Acad. Trial Lawyers (former sec.), Am. Coll. Trial Lawyers, Am. Bar Found. (chmn. 1985), Internat. Soc. Barristers (pres. 1971); mem. ABA, (bd. govs. 1975-79, former chmn. com. on standards criminal justice, former chmn. coun. criminal law sect., former chmn. com. to implement standards criminal justice, mem. long-range planning com., action com. to reduce ct. cost and delay), Colo. Bar Assn. (award of merit 1989), Denver Bar Assn. (past pres., trustee), Am. Law Inst. (coun.), Practising Law Inst. (nat. adv. coun., bd. govs. Colo.), Freedoms Found. at Valley Forge (nat. coun. trustees, 1986—), Order of Coif, Scribes (pres. 1978). Home: 10 Martin Ln Englewood CO 80110-4820 Office: Colo Supreme Ct 2 E 14th Ave Denver CO 80203-2116

ERICSON, DAVID PAUL, philosophy of education educator; b. Kansas City, Mo., Oct. 29, 1949; s. Paul Jacob and Jane Marie (Miller) E.; m. Bonnie Lynn Chrlund, May 28, 1971; children: Kristin Elisabeth, Marisa Jane. BA cum laude, St. Olaf Coll., 1971; MA in Philosophy, Syracuse U., 1973; postgrad., U. London, 1974-75; PhD, Syracuse U., 1976. Asst. prof. Va. Tech., Blacksburg, Va., 1977-79; asst. prof. UCLA, 1979-86, assoc. prof., 1986—; prof., chair dept. curriculum and instrn. Coll. Edn. U. Hawaii at Manoa, Honolulu, 1992—; researcher Pacific Rim Ctr., U. Calif., L.A., 1989—; cons. Nichinoken Inst., Yokahama, Japan, 1989—. Co-author: Predicting the Behavior of the Education System, 1980; editor-in-chief: Studies in Philosophy and Education, 1989—. Grantee Spencer Found., 1981-86, Pacific Rim Ctr., U. Calif., 1989—. Fellow Philosophy of Edn. Soc.; mem. ACLU, Am. Edn. Rsch. Assn., Calif. Assn. for Philosophy of Edn. (pres. 1980-81). Democrat. Office: U Hawaii at Manoa Coll Edn Dept Curriculum and Instrn Wist Annex 2 Honolulu HI 96822

ERICSON, FRITSI HANCOCK, fund executive; b. Reno, Apr. 24, 1938; d. Melville Davis and Gretchen Louise (Mock) Hancock; m. Harry Richard Ericson; children: Heidi, Gretchen, Jon, Brook. BEd, U. Nev., Reno, 1961. Elem. tchr. Washoe County Sch. Dist., Reno, 1961, 63; dist. Congl. aide U.S. Rep., Reno, 1972-82; pres., CEO Nev. Women's Fund, Reno, 1984—. Contbr. articles to profl. jours. Trustee Nev. State Mus. and Hist. Soc.; mem. adv. coun. Truckee Meadows C.C.; mem. adv. coun. Ctr. for Dispute Resolution; mem. fund distbn. com. United Way of No. Nev. and the Sierra. Recipient Silver Flame award Sierra Sage Camp Fire Coun., 1985, Women Helping Women award Soroptimist Internat., 1991, Mae Carvell award, 1992. Mem. Nat. Soc. Fund Raising Execs. (pres. Sierra chpt.). Home: 3175 Idlewild Dr Reno NV 89509 Office: Nev Women's Fund PO Box 50428 Reno NV 89513

ERICSON, JOHN, actor, painter; b. Detroit, Sept. 25, 1926; s. Carl Frederick and Ellen (Wilson) Meibes; m. Karen Huston, Mar. 31, 1974; children: Nicole McPhie, Brett Ericson. Grad. Newton high sch., Elmhurst, N.Y. Starred in motion pictures: Teresa, Rhapsody, Bad Day at Black Rock, Pretty Boy Floyd, Forty Guns, Day of the Bad Man, The Student Prince, 7 Faces of Dr. Lao, Return of Jack Slade, Alien Zone, The Money Jungle, The Destructors, Oregon Passage, Slave Queen of Babylon, Heads or Tails, Bedknobs and Broomsticks, Under Ten Flags and many others; in tv Honey West, RFK the Man, House on the Rue Riviera, Space, Hog Wild, Bounty Man, Police Woman, Hunters Moon, Murder, She Wrote, Fantasy Island, FBI, Ironside, Police Story, Bonanza, Magnum P.I., General Hospital, Airwolf, Knight Rider, Mannix, Gunsmoke, One Day at a Time and many others; on Broadway Stalag 17; starred in regional theatre prodns.: Camelot, A Streetcar Named Desire, I Do, I Do, Mr. Roberts, On a Clear Day, Richard II, Funny Girl, others; cited in published book: Actors as Artists, 1992. Pvt. U.S. Army, 1945. Recipient nomination Laurel award, N.Y.C., 1952, Star on Hollywood Walk of Fame, Hollywood (Calif.) C. of C., 1960's. Mem. Acad. Motion Picture Arts and Scis. Democrat.

ERICSON, JONATHON EDWARD, environmental science educator, researcher; b. Bronx, N.Y., May 22, 1942; s. Erling and Ruth Cecila (Kleinberger) E.; m. Glenda Prince Ericson, Dec. 19, 1987; 1 child from previous marriage, Burke Evan. AB in Exploration Geophysics, UCLA, 1970, MA in Anthropology, 1973, PhD in Anthropology, 1977. Conservation chemist L.A. County Mus. Art, 1976-78; assoc. prof. dept. anthropology Harvard U., Cambridge, Mass., 1978-83; asst. prof. program in social ecology U. Calif., Irvine, 1983-85, assoc. prof. Dept. Environ. analysis and Design, 1985-91, assoc. prof. dept. anthropology, 1987-91, prof. depts. environ analysis and design, anthropology, 1991—; chair Irvine divsn. edn. reward com. U. Calif., Irvine, 1991—; cons. NASA-Ames, Moffett Field, Calif., 1983, Keith Co./Irvine Co., 1988-93; designer Ctr. for Archaeol. Rsch. and Devel., Harvard U., 1978-80. Co-editor: Exchange Systems in Prehistory, 1977, Contexts of Prehistorical Exchange, 1982, Prehistoric Quarries and Lithic Production, 1984, Exchange Systems in N. American Prehistory, 1993. Mem. Orange County Quincentenary Com., 1988-93; v.p. Mus. Natural History and Sci., Aliso Viejo, Calif., 1988-91; asst. scout master Boy Scouts Am., Dana Point, Calif., 1990—. Fulbright Hayes scholar, 1980, 91; NASA fellow, 1983; NSF grantee, 1984-86. Fellow Sigma Xi; mem. AAAS, Soc. Am. Archaeology, Soc. Archaeol. Scis. (pres. 1981-82). Episcopalian. Office: U Calif Irvine Dept Environ Analysis and Design Irvine CA 92717

ERICSON, MARK FREDERICK, investment analyst; b. Colorado Springs, Colo., June 28, 1957; s. Frederick Walter and Eleanor Joan (Juraska) E. BS in Civil Engring., U. Colo., 1979, MBA, 1986. Registered profl. engr., Colo. Project mgr. JR Engring. Ltd., Englewood, Colo., 1982-86; cons. Kirkham Michael & Assocs., Greenwood Village, Colo., 1988-89, Merrick & Co., Aurora, Colo., 1989—; pres. Ericson Investors, Aurora, 1986—. Author: Follow the Crowd and Be Contrary, 1991. Mem. ASCE, Am. Assn. Individual Investors, Chi Epsilon. Republican. Home: 2068 S Pitkin St Aurora CO 80013

ERNST, ELDON GILBERT, religion educator, seminary dean; b. Seattle, Jan. 27, 1939; s. Kenneth G. and Bydell N. (Painter) E.; m. Joy S. Skoglund, June 12, 1959; children: Michael P., David G., Peter J., Samuel F., Rachel J. BA, Linfield Coll., 1961; BD, Colgate Rochester Divinity Sch, 1964; MA, Yale U., 1965, PhD, 1968. Prof. Am. Bapt. Sem. of the West, Berkeley, Calif., 1967-82, Grad. Theol. Union, Berkeley, 1983-90; prof., dean Am. Bapt. Sem. of the West, Berkeley, 1990—; rep. No. Calif. Ecumenical Coun., 1985-88; mem. Bapt. Peace Fellowship of North Am., 1970—. Author: Moment of Trust for Protestant America, 1974, Without Help or Hindrance, 1977, 87, Pilgrim Progression, 1993; author: (with others) Religion and Society in the American West, 1987; contbr. articles to profl. jours. Rsch. grantee Lilly Endowment, U. Calif., Santa Barbara, 1989-92. Mem. Am. Acad. Religion (pres. West regional chpt. 1985-86), Am. Soc. Ch. History, Am. Hist. Assn., Calif. Hist. Soc., Pacific Coast Theol. Soc., Sierra Club. Democrat. Home: 1855 San Antonio Ave Berkeley CA 94707-1617 Office: Am Bapt Sem of the West 2606 Dwight Way Berkeley CA 94704-3097

EROKAN, DENNIS WILLIAM, magazine publisher; b. Istanbul, Turkey, Aug. 20, 1950; came to U.S., 1955; s. Don H. and Athena (Caragianis) E.; m. Lori Engelfried, Dec. 18, 1976; children: Lane Katharine, Darcy Beth, William Bruce, Miranda Louise. Grad. high sch., San Jose, Calif., 1968. Bassist Green Catherine band, San Francisco and N.Y.C., 1973-74; mgr. Peter's Plum Restaurant, Boston, 1974-75; nat. sales mgr. Dean Markley Strings, Santa Clara, Calif., 1975; chief exec. officer Bam Publs., Pleasant Hill and Los Angeles, Calif., 1976—; Exec. producer, founder Bay Area Music awards, San Francisco, 1978-; pres., founder Bay Area Music Archives, San Francisco, 1979-86; concert producer, Hollywood, 1983, San Francisco, 1978-83; bd. dirs. San Francisco Rock and Roll Mus., 1986-88. Editor, pub. (mag.) The Mix, 1977-78, BAM, 1976— (Maggie award 1984, 86, 87, 89), MicroTimes, 1984— (2 Maggie awards 1986), Drive!, 1991—; exec. producer TV shows: The 1981 Bammies, 1981, A San Francisco Celebration, 1986; contbr. articles to mags. Auctioneer Sta. KQED Fundraiser, San Francisco, 1978-87. Mem. Nat. Acad. Songwriters (bd. dirs. 1983-88), Freedom Found. (bd. dirs. 1980-83). Episcopalian. Office: BAM Publs 3470 Buskirk Ave Pleasant Hill CA 94523-4316

ERPELDING, CURTIS MICHAEL, furniture designer; b. Ft. Dodge, Iowa, Nov. 29, 1950; s. Clarence Peter and Catherine Angela (Swirzcynski) E. BS in English Edn., U. Colo., 1972. Designer, prin. Curtis Erpelding Furniture Design, Seattle, 1977—; bd. dirs. Northwest Gallery Fine Woodworking, Seattle. Subject (videotape): Radial Arm Saw Joinery, 1985; contbr. articles to profl. publs.; one man shows at Oreg. Sch. Arts and Crafts, 1982, North West Gallery Fine Woodworking, 1983; exhibited in group show at Am. Craft Mus., 1986-88. NEA grantee, 1980-81. Mem. Am. Craft Coun. Office: Curtis Erpelding Furniture Design 756 Broadway E Apt 405 Seattle WA 98102-4677

ERQUIAGA, ELISA PIPER CAFFERATA, planner; b. Portland, Oreg., May 10, 1962; d. Harold Treat and Patricia Anne (Dillon) Cafferata; children: Brendan Manuel Cafferata Erquiaga, Morgan Joan Erquiaga. BA in Communications, Mills Coll., 1984; MBA, U. Nev., Reno, 1991. Orgn. dir. Uucanovich for Congress, Reno, 1986; exec. dir. Washoe County Rep. Party, Reno, 1987-88, Nev. Opera, Reno, 1988-91; owner The Art of Strategy, Reno, 1991-93; program dir. quality of life Truckee Meadows Regional Planning Agy., Reno, 1993—; letter of appt. Univ. Nev., Reno, 1991-93. Mem. planning com. City 2000 Arts Commn., Reno, 1990—; vol. Mills Coll. Alumnae, Oakland, Calif., 1990—; dir. Com. to Aid Abused Women, Reno, 1992—; mgr. Beekun for Assembly Campaign, Reno, 1992. Mem. Beta Gamma Sigma. Republican. Office: Truckee Meadows Regional Planning Agy 1400 A Wedekind Rd Reno NV 89512

ERSKINE, JOHN MORSE, surgeon; b. San Francisco, Sept. 10, 1920; s. Morse and Dorothy (Ward) E. BS, Harvard U., 1942, MD, 1945. Diplomate Am. Bd. Surgery. Surg. intern U. Calif. Hosp., San Francisco, 1945-46; surg. researcher Mass. Gen. Hosp., Boston, 1948; resident in surgery Peter Bent Brigham Hosp., Boston, 1948-53; George Gorham Peters fellow St. Mary's Hosp., London, 1952; pvt. practice in medicine specializing in surgery San Francisco, 1954—; asst. clin. prof. Stanford Med. Sch., San Francisco, 1956-59; asst., assoc. clin. prof. U. Calif. Med. Sch., San Francisco, 1959—; surg. cons. San Francisco Vets. Hosp., 1959-73. Contbr. articles to profl. jours., chpts. to books. Founder No. Calif. Artery Bank, 1954-58, Irwin Meml. Blood Bank, San Francisco, commr., pres., 1969-74; bd. dirs. People for Open Space-Greenbelt Alliance, 1984—; chmn. adv. coun. Dorothy Erskine Open Space Fund. Capt. with U.S. Army, 1946-48. Fellow ACS; mem. San Francisco Med. Soc. (bd. dirs. 1968-72), San Francisco Surg. Soc. (v.p. 1984), Pacific Coast Surg. Soc., Am. Cancer Soc. (bd. dirs. San Francisco br. 1965-75), Calif. Med. Assn., Olympic Club, Sierra Club. Democrat. Unitarian. Home: 233 Chestnut St San Francisco CA 94133-2452 Office: 2340 Clay St San Francisco CA 94115-1932

ERSKINE, ROBIN RICHARDSON, newspaper printing executive; b. Coral Gables, Fla., July 26, 1963; s. Stewart McDowell and Margaret (Richardson) E.; m. Arminda Angelica Quintanar, July 5, 1986; 1 child, Zasha Alexandria. AAS, DeVry Inst. Tech., Kansas City, Mo., 1983, BS in Electronics Engring. Tech., 1985. Tech. sales rep. Equinox Systems, Inc., Miami, Fla., 1985-86; field svc. engr. Genlink Corp., Miami, 1986-87, Quipp Systems, Inc., Miami, 1987-89; asst. prodn. coord. San Francisco Newspaper Agy., 1989—. Mem. IEEE (sec.-treas. student br. 1983-85). Office: San Francisco Newspaper Agy 925 Mission St San Francisco CA 94103

ERVIN, PATRICK FRANKLIN, nuclear engineer; b. Kansas City, Kans., Aug. 4, 1946; s. James Franklin and Irma Lee (Arnett) E.; m. Rita Jeanne Kimsey, Aug. 12, 1967; children: James, Kevin, Amber. BS in Nuclear Engring., Kans. State U., 1969, MS in Nuclear Engring., 1971; postgrad., Northeastern U., 1988. Registered profl. engr., Ill., Colo., Calif., Idaho, Wash.; cert. paleontology paraprofl., Colo. Reactor health physicist Dept. Nuclear Engring. Kans. State U., Manhattan, 1968-69, rsch. asst. Dept. Nuclear Engring., 1969-72, sr. reactor operator, temp. facility dir. Dept. Nuclear Engring., 1970-72; system test engr. Commonwealth Edison Co., Zion, Ill., 1972-73, 73-74; shift foreman Commonwealth Edison Co., Zion, 1973, shift foreman with sr. reactor operator lic., 1974-76, prin. engr., 1976-77, acting operating engr., 1977; tech. staff supr. Commonwealth Edison Co., Byron, Ill., 1977-81; lead test engr. Stone & Webster Engring. Corp., Denver, 1982-83, project mgr., 1982—, ops. svcs. supr., 1982-86, asst. engring. mgr., 1986-89, consulting engr., 1989—. Contbr. articles to profl. jours. Served with U.S. Army N.G., 1971-77. Mem. Am. Nuclear Soc. (Nat. and Colo. chpts., chmn. reactor ops. div.), Am. Nat. Standards Inst. (working group on containment leakage testing). Republican. Roman Catholic. Home: 2978 S Bahama St Aurora CO 80013-2340 Office: Stone & Webster Engring Corp PO Box 5406 Denver CO 80217-5406

ERVING, CLAUDE MOORE, JR., military career officer, pilot; b. St. John's, N.F., Can., Sept. 10, 1952; s. Claude Moore Sr. and Ingeborg (Mauss) E.; m. Donna Lee Mathis, June 17, 1978; children: Zachary C., Allyson B., Michael J. M. BS in Geography, USAF Acad., 1975. Commd. 2d lt. USAF, 1975, advanced through grades to lt. col., 1979; check pilot, instr. 85th Flying Tng. Squadron, Laughlin AFB, Tex., 1976-80; flight examiner, instr. pilot, flight comdr. 460th Fighter Interceptor Tng. Squadron, Peterson AFB, Colo., 1980-82; flight comdr. 49th Fighter Interceptor Squadron, Griffiss AFB, N.Y., 1982-85; chief of tng. 18th Tactical Fighter Squadron, Eielson AFB, Alaska, 1985-86; chief of flight safety, asst. chief of safety 343d Tactical Fighter Wing, Eielson AFB, Alaska, 1986-88; chief ops. plans div. and exec. officer to dep. comdr. ops. for 11th Air Force and Alaskan NORAD region Hdqrs. Alaskan Air Command, Elmendorf AFB, 1988-92; comdr. 94th airmanship tng. squadron USAF Acad., Colo., 1992—; aircraft accident investigator USAF, worldwide, 1986—. Mem. CAP (flight comdr. 1990-93). Republican. Home: 4112 Douglass Loop U S A F Academy CO 80840

ERWIN, DONALD CARROLL, plant pathology educator; b. Concord, Nebr., Nov. 24, 1920; s. Robert James and Carol (Sexson) E.; m. Veora Marie Endres, Aug. 15, 1948; children: Daniel Erwin, Myriam Erwin Casey. Student, Wayne State (Nebr.) Tchrs.Coll, 1938-39; BSc, U. Nebr., 1949, MA, 1950; PhD, U. Calif.-Davis, 1953. Jr. plant pathologist U. Calif., Riverside, 1953-54; asst. plant pathologist U. Calif., 1954-60, assoc. plant pathologist, 1960-66, prof. plant pathology, 1966—, emeritus prof., 1991. Editor: Phytophthora: Its Biology, Taxonomy, Ecology and Pathology, 1983; contbr. articles to profl. jours. With U.S. Army, 1942-46; ETO. Nathan Gold fellow, 1949, Guggenheim fellow, 1959. Fellow Am. Phytopathol. Soc.; mem. Mycological Soc. Am., Sigma Xi. Democrat. Roman Catholic. Office: U Calif Dept Plant Pathology Riverside CA 92521

ERWIN, JAMES C., x-ray technician, educator; b. Rockford, Ill., Sept. 12, 1927; s. James H. and Addie (Covington) E.; m. (dec. 1979); 1 child, Julie Anne Hernandez. Diploma, x-ray, Swedish Am. Hosp., 1962; diploma, mgmt., Crafton Jr. Coll; credentials teaching, UCLA. Cert. ARRT, CRT. X-ray tech. Northweaster Hosp., Chgo., Dr. Bateman & Stanley, Escondido, Hemit Valley (Calif.) Hosp., Hosp. St. Bernadine, San Bernadino, Calif., Patton State Hosp., San Bernadino, Calif., Calif. Inst. for Women, Frontera, Calif.; sen. x-ray tech. Calif. Men's Colony, San Luis Obispo; instr. Ctrl. Calif. Schs., San Luis Obispo. With USN, 1944-56. Presbyterian. Home: 3860 S Higuera D-7 San Luis Obispo CA 93401

ERYSIAN, BILL MYRON, international relations educator; b. Fresno, Calif., Nov. 12, 1957; s. Myron and Vera (Ellezian) E. BA, Calif. State U., Fresno, 1980; postgrad. diploma, London Sch. Econs./Polit. Sci., 1983. News dir. KVPR-FM, Fresno, 1981-82; internat. rsch. specialist ABC News, London, 1983-84; pub. affairs mgr. Brit. Telecom, Tymnet, San Jose, Calif., 1984-87; pres. Erysian Communications, Fresno and San Jose, 1987-90; lectr. dept. journalism Calif. State U., Fresno, 1990—; dir. instl. rels. San Joaquin Coll. Law, Fresno, 1990—. Mem. Nat. Assn. Fgn. Student Advisers, World Affairs Coun., Pub. Rels. Soc. Am., Calif. Sch. Pub. Rels. Assn., Fresno C. of C. (mem. com. in internat. trade 1992), Sigma Delta Chi. Office: San Joaquin Coll Law 3385 E Shields Fresno CA 93726

ERZURUMLU, H. CHIK M., engineering educator; b. Istanbul, Turkey, Mar. 7, 1934; m. H. Ulku Erzurumlu, 1963. Profl. degree in civil engring., Istanbul Tech. U., 1957; MS in Civil Engring., U. Tex., 1962, PhD in Civil Engring., 1970. Registered profl. engr., Oreg. Rsch. engr. civil engring. dept. U. Tex., Austin, 1960-62; instr. engring. Portland (Oreg.) State U., 1962-65, asst. prof. engring., 1962-68, assoc. prof. engring., 1968-72, prof. civil engring., 1972—, head civil engring. dept., 1975-79, dean engring., 1979—; engring. cons., 1965—; tech. reviewer NSF, 1972—, DOE, 1972—. contbr. articles to profl. jours. Coun. mem. Oreg. Mus. Sci. and Industry, Portland, 1987—; mem. Oreg. Art Inst., Portland, 1970—, City Club Portland, 1984—. Ford Found fellow, 1968-70. Fellow ASCE (pres. Oreg. sect. 1980-81, tech. reviewer 1972—, sec. com. on bridges 1978-88, chmn. com. on bridges 1988-93); mem. NSPE, Am. Soc. Engring. Edn., Am. Soc. Engring. Mgmt., Structural Engrs. Assn. Oreg. Office: Portland State U Sch of Engring PO Box 751 Portland OR 97207-0751

ESAU, JOHN NICHOLAS, design engineer, software engineering consultant; b. Chgo., Oct. 27, 1944; s. Jacob Nick and Barbara Thieadora (Goetz) E.; m. Linda Dorthia Clowser (div. 1969); m. Ingrid Christa Bratke, June 3, 1973; children: Warren, Sean Brady, Christopher. BS, DeVry Inst. Tech., Chgo., 1972; Asst. in Computer Sci., Bellevue (Wash.) C.C., 1991. Test engr. Memorex Corp., Santa Clara, Calif., 1972-74, Watkins-Johnson, Palo Alto, Calif., 1974-78; cons. Gould-Modicon, Boston, 1978-79; sr. engr. GTE-Sylvania, Mountain View, Calif., 1979-82; sr. test engr. Fairchild Hybrid, Mountain View, 1982-84; responsible equipment engr. Lockheed Austin, Tex., 1984-86; prin. design engr. Boeing Aircraft, Seattle, 1986—; pres. EEBEE Software, Bellevue, 1987—. Asst. leader Boy Scouts Am., Bellevue, 1987—. Mem. Am. Legion. Democrat. Lutheran. Home: 6102 139th Pl SE Bellevue WA 98006-4384 Office: Boeing Comml Airplane PO Box 3707 M/S 0T-23 Seattle WA 98124

ESCHENBACH, ARTHUR EDWIN, human factors engineer; b. N.Y.C., Jan. 31, 1918; s. Karl Godfried and Magdelena (Rupert) E.; m. Maria Louise Perez, June 22, 1968; children: Mary Patricia, Karl, Deborah, Charmion, Roxanne. AB, Cornell U., 1947; MA, U. Fla., 1949, PhD, 1955. Lic. psychologist, Fla. Commd. 2nd lt. USAF, 1943, advanced through grades to lt. col., 1965; scientist, human engr. USAF, NASA, U.S., Republic of Korea, 1951-66; ret. USAF, 1966; assoc. prof., dept. head Jacksonville (Fla.) U., 1966-86; pvt. cons., 1986—. Contbr. articles to profl. jours. Home: PO Box 163 Teton Village Jackson WY 83025

ESCOVER, THOMAS FRANK, accountant, small business owner; b. San Jose, Calif., May 29, 1947; s. Frank Robert and Grace Monica (Goularte) E.; m. Jean A. Melle, June 6, 1970 (div. 1976); m. Harriette R. Grooh, Nov. 2, 1990. AA in Bus. Adminstrn., Gavilan Jr. Coll., Gilroy, Calif., 1965-67; BS in Acctg., Fresno (Calif.) State U., 1967-70; postgrad., Sonoma State U., 1992. Lic. tax preparer, Calif. Cost acct. GTE Lenkurt, San Carlos, Calif., 1970-73, Data Products, Sunnyvale, Calif., 1973-76; sr. cost acct. Eimac/Varian, San Carlos, Calif., 1976-78, mgr., gen. acctg., 1978-81; mgr., product rsch. Lazorlite Parts Importers, Palo Alto, Calif., 1981-86; pvt. practice Novato, Calif., 1987—; pres. Escover Motorsports Mgmt., Sonoma, Calif.,

1990-91. Mem. Newark Hazardous Waste Com., Newark, Calif., 1984-85, Marin County Hazardous Waste Mgmt. Adv. Com., San Rafael, Calif., 1987-88; treas. Hillside Homeowners Assn., Novato, 1990—. Calif. Soc. Accts. scholar, 1967. Mem. Nat. Assn. Accts. (dir. mktg. Oakland chpt. 1988-89), British Auto Racing Club, Sports Car Club Am. Republican. Office: Escover Motorsports Mgmt 9 Paper Mill Creek Ct Novato CA 94949-6635

ESHELMAN, ENOS GRANT, JR., prosthodontist; b. Birmingham, Ala., Oct. 18, 1943; s. Enos Grant and Kathleen Marie (Lokey) E.; m. Mary Darlene Duncan, Nov. 22, 1975; children: Duncan Grant, Hunter Nicholas, Parker Jacob. AB, Franklin and Marshall Coll., Lancaster, Pa., 1965; DDS, Columbia U., 1969; MS, U. Mo., 1980. Commd. 2d lt. USAF, advanced through grades to col., 1969-86; gen. dental officer USAF, Lackland AFB, Tex., 1969-72; asst. base dental surgeon, oral surgeon, dental officer USAF, Korat Air Base, Thailand, 1972-73; asst. base dental surgeon, prosthodontics and lab. officer USAF, Sembach Air Base, Germany, 1973-78; chief prosthodontics USAF, Norton AFB, Calif., 1980-83; prosthodontics tng. officer USAF Hosp., Davis Monthan AFB, Ariz., 1983-89; chief prosthodontics, dental lab. officer 36 TFW Hosp., Bitburg Air Base, Germany, 1989-93; tng. offcr. prosthodontics USAF Hosp., Langley AFB, Va., 1993—; asst. prof. Loma Linda (Calif.) U. Sch. Dentistry, 1981-83; prosthodontics cons. Jerry Pettis Vets. Hosp., Loma Linda, 1982-83, Vets. Affairs Med. Ctr., Tucson, 1983-89; pres. Fed. Svcs. Regional Dental Conf., Davis Monthan AFB, Ariz., 1983-85. Pres. Jr. Officers Coun., Korat Air Base, Thailand, 1973; asst. coach Sabino Little League Baseball, Tucson, 1988-89. Rinehart Found. rsch. grantee U. Mo. Sch. Dentistry, 1978; decorated Meritorious Svc. medal. Mem. ADA, Am. Coll. Prosthodontics, Fedn. Prosthodontic Orgns., Internat. Coll. Dentists, Air Force Assn., Psi Omega. Home: 7141 E River Canyon Rd Tucson AZ 85715-2111

ESHELMAN, JOHN D., academic administrator. Dean bus. Seattle U., until 1987, exec. v.p., 1987-89, provost, 1989—. Office: Seattle U Office of Provost Seattle WA 98122

ESHOO, ANNA GEORGES, congresswoman; b. New Britain, Conn., Dec. 13, 1942; d. Fred and Alice Alexandre Georges; children: Karen Elizabeth, Paul Frederick. AA with honors, Cañada Coll., 1975. Chmn. San Mateo County Dem. Ctrl. Com., Calif., 1978-82; chair Human Rels. Com., 79-82; former mem. Calif. State Dem. Ctrl. Exec. Com.; mem. Dem. Nat. Com., 103rd Congress from 14th Calif. dist., 1993—. Active League of Women Voters. Roman Catholic. Office: US House of Representatives Office of House Mems Washington DC 20515

ESKEW, CATHLEEN CHEEK, social services administrator; b. Oklahoma City, Oct. 20, 1953; d. John Dasherman and Nancy Lucile (Gray) Cheek; m. Bruce Lynn Eskew, Aug. 23, 1986; children : William Michael amd Matthew James (twins), Anna Elaine. BA in Math., Whitworth Coll., 1976; MST, Fuller Sem., Pasadena, Calif., 1984; postgrad., U. Colo., Colorado Springs, Inst. Children's Lit., 1989-91. Cert. secondary tchr., Colo. Tchr., adminstrv. asst. The Colorado Springs Sch., 1976-78; recruiter, trainer Young Life, Colorado Springs, 1978-82; mem. publs. and stats. staff Young Life Internat., Port-au-Prince, Haiti, 1982-83; documentation specialist Compassion Internat., Colorado Springs, 1984-85, program adminstr., 1986-88. Elder Presbyn. Ch., 1992, growth commn., 1993. Named Outstanding Young Woman in Am., 1981. Mem. Assn. Evang. Relief and Devel. Orgn., Whitworth Coll. Alumni Assn. (coun. person 1978-81). Democrat. Home: 1365 Oak Hills Dr Colorado Springs CO 80919-4803

ESKOFF, RICHARD JOSEPH, life insurance company executive. Formerly v.p., chief exec. officer Transamerica Life Ins. & Annuity Co., L.A., now chmn. bd., pres., chief exec. officer. Office: Transamerica Life Ins & Annuity Co 1150 S Olive St Los Angeles CA 90015-2211

ESLER, JOHN KENNETH, artist; b. Pilot Mound, Man., Can., Jan. 11, 1933; s. William John and Jennie Mae (Thompson) E.; m. Annemarie Schmid, June 26, 1964; children—William Sean, John Derek. B.F.A., U. Man., B.Ed., 1962. Mem. faculty dept. art Alta. Coll. Art, 1964-68; mem. faculty U. Calgary, Alta., Can., 1968-80; chmn. Print and Drawing Council Can., 1976-78. One man exhbn., Gallery Moos, Toronto, Ont., 1978; represented in permanent collections, Victoria and Albert Mus., London, Eng., Albright Knox Gallery, Buffalo,N.Y., Mus. Modern Art, N.Y.C., Nat. Gallery Can., Ottawa, Ont; Author: Printing in Alberta. Life mem. Print and Drawing Coun. Can. Address: Box 2 Site 7, SS 1, Calgary, AB Canada T2M 4N3

ESLER, TIKA AMELIA, academic administrator; b. Moron, Cuba, June 5, 1949; came to U.S., 1962; d. Oscar Angel and Berta Angela (Gallinat) Hernandez; m. Michael Arthur Esler, June 8, 1968; 1 child, Lisa. AA, Shoreline C.C., 1969; BA, Evergreen State Coll., 1975. Fin. aid asst. Shoreline C.C., Seattle, 1968-73; fin. aid counselor U. Wash., Seattle, 1973-78; dir. fin. aid Seattle Cen. C.C., 1978-92; assoc. dean enrollment svcs. and ednl. planning Bellevue (Wash.) C.C., 1992—; cons. Mgmt. Adv. Group, Portland, Oreg., 1987—; trainer Nat. Assn. Student Fin. Aid Adminstrs., Washington, 1989, 90, 91, Western Assn. Student Fin. Aid Adminstrs., Calif., 1990. Fund raiser Seattle Art Mus., 1988, Seattle YMCA, 1989; auction chair Kenmore Elem. PTA, Bothell, Wash., 1989; state dir. Miss Nat. Pre-Teen Pageant, Lehigh, Fla., 1990—. Mem. Am. Assn. Women in Community and Jr. Colls. (v.p. profl. devel. 1990-92, pres.-elect. 1992, pres. 1993—), Nat. Assn. Student Fin. Aid Adminstrs. (bd. dirs. 1989-91), WEstern Assn. Student Fin. Aid Adminstrs. (sec. 1987-88, summer inst. faculty 1992), Wash. Fin. Aid Assn. (pres. 1988-89). Democrat. Office: Bellevue CC 3000 Landerholm Cir Bellevue WA 98002

ESMERIA, VIRGILIO REYES, accountant; b. Manila, May 17, 1946; came to U.S., 1975; s. Rodrigo Espaldon and Crispina (Reyes) E.; m. Anita Ilano, Sept. 4, 1976; children: Norimel, Virgilio Jr., Ann Maree. BS in Commerce, San Sebastian Coll., Manila, 1968. Chief acct. Philippine Century Resorts, Philippines, 1974-75; acct., adminstr. Trans-Asia Engring., Guam, 1976-77; acct. Vertex Distbg., Inc., Calif., 1978-79, acctg. supr., 1979-80, contr., 1981; staff mem. CPA firm, Calif., 1982-86; pvt. practice as CPA Calif., 1987—. Scholar Cath. Charities Orgn., 1964-68. Mem. AICPA, Calif. Soc. CPA. Home: 16303 Binney St Hacienda Heights CA 91745

ESPALDON, ERNESTO MERCADER, former senator, plastic surgeon; b. Sulu, Philippines, Nov. 11, 1926; arrived in Guam, 1963; s. Cipriano Acuna Espaldon and Claudia (Cadag) Mercader); m. Leticia Legaspi Virata, May 31, 1952; children: Arlene Espaldon Ramos, Vivian Espaldon Wolff, James, Diane, Karl, Ernesto Jr. AA, U. Philippines, Manila, 1949; MD, U. Santo tomas, Manila, 1954; postgrad., Washington U., St. Louis, 1961. Diplomate Am. Bd. Plastic Surgery. Resident in gen. surgery U. Okla. Med. Ctr., Oklahoma City, 1959; gen. and plastic surgeon Guam Meml. Hosp., Agana, 1963—, chief surgery, 1965-69; pres., plastic surgeon Espaldon Clinic, Agana, 1969—; mem. Guam Legislature, Agana, 1974-80, 86-92, chmn. Com. on Health, Welfare and Ecology and Com. on Ethics and Standards, 1986-92; vis. prof. Bicol Med. and Edn. Ctr., Legaspi City, The Philippines, 1980—. Pres., founder Guam Balikbayan Med. Mission, Agana, 1974—; organizer, co-founder Aloha Med., Mission, Honolulu, 1982—; pres. PTA Acad. Our Lady Guam, Agana, 1969-71; bd. dirs. Am. Cancer Soc., Agana, 1969-82, ARC, Agana, 1969-82, Vocat. Rehab., Agana, 1969-82, Guam Meml. Hosp., 1969-82. Guerrilla comdr. Sulu (Philippines) Area Command, 1943-46, 2d lt. Philippine Army, 1946-47. Recipient Thomas Jefferson award for pub. svc., Am. Inst. Pub. Svc., Washington, and Honolulu Advertiser, 1983; named Outstanding Filipino Overseas Philippine Govt. and Philippine Jaycees, 1982, Most Outstanding Alumni U. Santo Tomas, 1981, Outstanding Community Leader of Guam Philippine-Am. Community, 1979, Outstanding Community Leader of Guam Jaycees, 1982. Fellow Am. Coll. Surgeons, Philippine Coll. Surgeons; mem. AMA, Guam Med. Soc. (pres. 1970-72, chief del. to AMA 1973-76), KC. Republican. Roman Catholic. Home: PO Box Ce Agana GU 96910-8982 Office: GCIC Bldg Ste 709 Agana GU 96910

ESPAÑA, CAROLINE SOPHIE, computer company executive; b. Mexico City, Oct. 24, 1965; d. Roger Henri and Marie Christiane (Jaques D'Hont) E. BA in Advt., UDEC, Mexico City, 1983-87. Adminstrv. asst. C. Steel & Co., Phoenix, 1982-83; sub dir. Ashton Internat. de Mexico, Mexico City, 1987-88; v.p. fin. Ashton Internat., S.A. de C.V., Mexico City, 1988-90, pres., 1990—; bd. dirs. Sources S.A. de C.V., Mexico City, Ashton Internat. Corp., Chula VistaCalif.; v.p. LDVI Corp., Chula Vista, 1992—; sec./treas. IOEC Corp., Chula Vista, 1989—, AI-AI-AI, S.A. de C.V., Mexico City, 1991—. Roman Catholic. Office: LDVI Corp PO Box 1175 Chula Vista CA 91912-1175

ESPANA, JEAN PHILIPPE, computer company executive; b. Mexico City, July 4, 1961; s. Roger Henri and Marie Christiane (Jaques D'Hont) E. BA, Inst. Technologico Autonomo De Mexico, Mexico City, 1984. Asst. mgr. Christian De Paris, S.A., Mexico City, 1975-81; asst. analyst Banco de Mexico, Mexico City, 1981-82, economist, 1982-84; import/export mgr. Schlumberger/Flopetrol Internat., Mexico City, 1984-85; econs. analyst Suma Consultores, Mexico City, 1985-87; econs. specialist Consejo Coordinador Empresarial, Mexico City, 1987-88; v.p. mktg. Ashton Internat., Chula Vista, Calif., 1988-92; pres. Sources, Chula Vista, 1991-92; v.p. mktg. LDVI, Chula Vista, 1991-92. Author: Computers: Practical Guide, 1992. Recipient Econ. grant Mexican Bankers Assn., Mexico City, 1981. Mem. Instituto de Capacitacion Politica/Partido Revolucionario Institucional. Roman Catholic. Office: LDVI Corp PO Box 1175 Chula Vista CA 91912-1175

ESPANDER, WILLIAM ROBERT, mechanical engineer; b. Colorado Springs, Feb. 23, 1947; s. Robert Leslie and Helen Ida (McCombs) E.; m. Marcia Kay Williams, Nov. 29, 1969; children: Christopher Robert, Geoffrey Brian. BS, Colo. State U., 1969, MS, 1971, PhD, 1974. Mem. tech. staff The Aerospace Corp., El Segundo, Calif., 1974-77; staff engr. Logicon/RDA, Albuquerque, 1977—. Contbr. articles to profl. jours. Mem. AIAA, ASME, IEEE, U.S. Soccer Fedn., Nat. Fedn. Interscholastic Officials Assn. Home: 632 La Jolla Pl NE Albuquerque NM 87123-2410 Office: Logigon/RDA 2600 Yale Blvd SE Albuquerque NM 87106-4217

ESPINO, DAVID RAMIREZ, financial services executive; b. L.A., Oct. 8, 1963; s. Samuel R. and Grace R. Espino; m. Tammy M. Espino, Dec. 12, 1987. AS in Drafting/Design, Don Bosco Tech. Inst., 1982. Drafting technician Magnaflux Corp., L.A., 1981-82, City of L.A./Bur. of Engring., 1982-87; regional mgr. Primerica Fin. Svs., Pasadena, Calif., 1986—; owner Espino and Assocs., Pico Rivera, Calif., 1985-89. Mem. Trinity Luth. Ch., Whittier, Calif., 1991—. Republican. Office: Primerica Fin Svcs 253 San Gabriel Blvd Pasadena CA 91107

ESPINOSA, JUDITH M., state agency administrator; b. Albuquerque, N.Mex.; d. Severo B. and Elma (Triviz) E.; 1 child, Madalena C. Salazar. BS in Nursing, Univ. N.Mex., 1972; M in Pub. Health Adminstrn., Univ. Calif., L.A., 1974; JD, Univ. N.Mex., 1980. Bar: N.Mex., 1980. Owner Health Rsch. Svcs. and Analysis, Inc., Calif., N.Mex.; leader transp. institutional/intergovernmental program, Waste Isolation Divsn. Westinghouse Electric Corp.; sec. transp. State of N.Mex., sec. environ., 1991—; mem. N.Mex. Radioactive Waste Consultation Task Force, Gov's. Job-Tng. Coun., N.Mex. Finance Authority, U.S. Environ. Protection Agy., Nat. Adv. Coun. on Environ. Policy and Tech., Waste Mgmt. Edn. and Rsch.; adv. bd. Southwest Ctr. for Environ. Rsch. and Policy; dir. Vehicle Pollution Mgmt. Divsn. Environ. Health Dept.; chair N.Mex. Emergency Mgmt. Task Force; Gov's rep. Nat. Assn. of Hwy. Safety Adminstrs., Western Interstate Energy Bd. High Level Waste Com.; cons. Battelle Meml. Inst., Columbus, Ohio, Dept. Energy Joint Integration Office Westinghouse Electric Corp., Albuquerque; apptd. mem. President's Coun. Sustainable Devel., 1993. Prodr. Cambio, Sta. KOAT-TV, 1990. Asst. to the Chmn. N.Mex. Democratic Party, 1985-86. recipient U.S. Pub. Health Svc. Health Sci. fellow, N.Mex. Senate Meml. Recognizing Work in Air Quality, 1990; named Friend of the Environ., 1989, Woman on the Move, YMCA, 1990. Mem. N.Mex. First (charter), Hispanic Women's Coun., Inc. of N.Mex. (founder, past pres.), N.Mex. Hispanic Cultural Found. (bd. dirs.), N.Mex. Bar Assn., N.Mex. Conservation Voters Alliance (steering com.). Home: 1190 St Francis Dr PO Box 26110 Santa Fe NM 87502 Office: Environment Dept PO Box 26110 Santa Fe NM 87502

ESPINOSA, PAULA MARIA, writer; b. Boston, Jan. 6, 1939; d. Robert Marcus and Maxine Judd (Silver) Cronbach; m. Mario Espinosa, Nov. 16, 1962 (div. 1965); 1 child, Carmen Espinosa; m. Walter Selig, Feb. 1978. BS, Columbia Sch., N.Y.C., 1960; MA, San Francisco State U., 1981. Cert. adult tchr., Calif. Tchr. ESL San Francisco Bay Area Adult Schs., 1968-78; various teaching positions, 1968-87; tchr. New Coll. of Calif., San Francisco, 1987-90, Pima C.C., Tucson, 1991. Author: (novel) Longing, 1986, (poems) Love Feelings, 1967, Night Music, 1969, (translator) Lelia, 1978; contbr. articles to profl. jours. Mem. Bay Area Poets Coop., Pen West. Buddhist. Home and Office: 3396 Orchard Valley Ln Lafayette CA 94549

ESQUER, DEBORAH ANNE, elementary educator; b. Omaha, Oct. 28, 1950; d. Thomas Ross and Carolyn Mae (Wright) Woods; m. Mario H. Esquer, Aug. 21, 1971 (div. Apr. 1991); children: Mario, Michael. BA, Ariz. State U., 1972, MA in Edn., 1972, 78; postgrad., Ottawa U., Phoenix, 1990-92. Cert. elem. tchr., spl. edn. Tchr. Paradise Valley Sch. Dist., Phoenix, 1972—. Mem. Phoenix Children's Theater, 1987-89, Phoenix Community Forum, 1992—. Tchr. venture grantee, Phoenix, 1988. Mem. NEA, Ariz. Edn. Assn., Paradise Valley Edn. Assn., Paradise Valley Reading Coun., Phoenix Art Mus., Ariz. Hist. Soc., Paradise Valley Jr. Women's Club (corr. sec. 1991-92), Alpha Delta Kappa (pres. 1986-88, ctrl. dist. treas. 1986-88, corr. sec. 1992—), Alpha Phi. Democrat. Methodist. Office: Desert Springs 6010 E Acoma Scottsdale AZ 85254

ESQUEVIN, CHRISTIAN RAYMOND, library director; b. Marseille, France, Aug. 11, 1948; came to U.S., 1953; s. Edmond Louis Esquevin and Genevieve Juliette (Lambert) Mathieu; m. Sydney Jean Stanley, Sept. 24, 1977. BA, Calif. State U., L.A., 1971; MS in Libr. Sci., U. So. Calif., 1975. Reference libr. San Diego County Libr., San Diego, 1976-78, regional reference libr., 1979-82, regional ctr. dir., 1982-84, community librs. dir., 1985-88; dir. libr. svcs. Coronado (Calif.) Pub. Libr., 1988—; chairperson Serra Coop. Libr. System, 1991—. Chairperson libr. centennial steering com. City of Coronado, 1989-90. Mem. ALA (chairperson fundraising and fin. devel. sect. 1991-92, LAMA nominating com. chair 1993), Calif. Libr. Assn. (pres.-elect Calif. Coun. City Librs.), Pub. Libr. Assn. (chairperson collection devel. com. 1990-91, bd. dirs.), Optimists (bd. dirs. Coronado club 1992-93). Home: 960 A Ave Coronado CA 92118-2629 Office: Coronado Pub Libr 640 Orange Ave Coronado CA 92118-2296

ESSA, LISA BETH, educator; b. Modesto, Calif., Nov. 19, 1955; d. Mark Newyia and Elizabeth (Warda) Essa. B.A., U. Pacific-Stockton, 1977, M.A. in Curriculum and Instrn. Reading, 1980. Cert. tchr. elem., multiple subject and reading specialist, Calif. Tchr. primary grades Delhi (Calif.) Elem. Sch. Dist., 1978-80; reading clinic tutor San Joaquin Delta Community Coll., Stockton, Calif., 1980; tchr. primary grades Hayward (Calif.) Unified Sch. Dist., Supr., San Francisco host com. Dem. Nat. Conv., 1984. Femmes Club scholar, 1973; U. Calif. Optometry Alumni Assn. scholar, 1973; Jobs Daughters scholar, 1974. Mem. Internat. Reading Assn., Calif. Tchrs. Assn., Hayward Unified Tchrs. Assn., San Francisco Jr. C. of C., Jr. League San Francisco. Democrat. Episcopalian. Home: 1960 Clay St Apt 109 San Francisco CA 94109-3435

ES-SAID, OMAR SALIM, metallurgy educator; b. Cairo, Egypt, Apr. 3, 1952; came to U.S., 1981; s. Salim Asim and Haifa Aref (El-Imam) E. BS, Am. U., Cairo, 1976, MS, 1979; PhD, U. Ky., 1985. Bilingual tng. tchr Arabian Am. Oil Co., Dharan, Saudi Arabia, 1979-81; grad. rsch. asst. U. Ky., Lexington, 1981-85; asst. prof. mech. engring. Loyola Marymont U., L.A., 1985-92, assoc. prof., 1992—, dir. mech. engring. grad. program, 1986-90. Contbr. articles to profl. jours. Mem. Islamic Catholic Com., L.A., 1986—. Grantee NSF, 1986, Soc. Mech. Engrs., 1987, Dept. of Engery, 1988. Mem. AAUP, ASME, AIME, Am. Soc. Metals, Internat. Assn. Sci. and Tech. for Devel., Am. Soc. Engring. Edn., Alpha Sigma Mu. Home: 8155 Manitoba St # 9 Playa Del Rey CA 90293 Office: Loyola Marymont U Loyola Blvd at W 80th St Los Angeles CA 90045

ESTEBAN, MANUEL ANTONIO, university administrator, educator; b. Barcelona, Spain, June 20, 1940; came to U.S., 1970; s. Manuel and Julia Esteban; m. Gloria Ribas, July 7, 1962; 1 child, Jacqueline. BA with 1st class honors in French, U. Calgary, Can., 1969, MA in Romance Studies, 1970; PhD in French, U. Calif., Santa Barbara, 1976. From asst. prof. to prof. French and Spanish langs. and lit. U. Mich., Dearborn, 1973-87, assoc. dean, 1984-86, acting dean coll. arts, scis., and letters, 1986-87; dean arts and scis. Calif. State U., Bakersfield, 1987-90; provost, v.p. acad. affairs Humboldt State U., Arcata, Calif., 1990—; pres., prof. French and Spanish Calif. State U., Chico; mem. Calif.-Catalonia Sister State Task Force, Sacramento, 1988—. Author: Georges Feydeau, 1983; contbr. books revs. and articles to profl. publs. Bd. dirs. Mercy Hosp., Bakersfield, 1989-90. Woodrow Wilson fellow, 1969, doctoral fellow U. Calif., Santa Barbara, 1970-73, Can. Coun doctoral fellow, Govt. Can., 1970-73; Rackham grantee U. Mich., 1979, fellow, 1982-83. Mem. Coun. Colls. Arts and Scis. (bd. dirs. 1988-90), N.Am. Catalan Soc. (bd. dirs. 1984—), MLA. Office: Humboldt State U Calif State U Chico CA 95929-0150

ESTERLY, LEONARD JOHN, JR., military officer; b. Reading, Pa., Apr. 3, 1958; s. Leonard John and Bertha Minerva (Althouse) E.; m. Wasana Kaitkow, July 15, 1983. BSEE, The Citadel, 1980; MS in Mgmt., U. So. Calif., L.A., 1988. Commd. 2d lt. USAF, 1980, advanced through grades to maj., 1992; undergrad. navigator tng. 323rd Flight Tng. Wing, Mather AFB, Calif., 1980-81; B-52G student navigator 328th Bomb Wing, Castle AFB, Calif., 1981-82, 441st Bomb Squadron, Mather AFB, 1982-84; student FB-111 tng. 380th Bomb Wing, Plattsburgh AFB, N.Y., 1984-85; FB-111 instr. navigator 528th Bomb Squadron, Plattsburgh AFB, 1985-87; FB-111 target officer 380th Bomb Wing, Plattsburgh AFB, 1987-88; FB-111 evaluator navigator 529th Bomb Squadron, Plattsburgh AFB, 1988-89; DSCS II crew comdr. 3rd Space Ops. Squadron, Falcon AFB, Colo., 1989-90; satellite ops. flight comdr. 3rd Space Ops. Squadron, Falcon AFB, 1990-92; detachment comdr. 750 Space Group USAF Space Command, Diego Garcia BIOT, 1992-93; crew comdr., staff officer J30 U.S. Space Command, Cheyenne Mountain AFB, 1993—. Vol. fire fighter Lincoln Park Fire Dept., Shillington, Pa., 1974-80; mem. Young Reps., Charleston, 1978-80. Mem. U.S. Space Found., Assn. of Citadel Men. Home: 1690 Dublin Blvd Apt 111 Colorado Springs CO 80918 Office: SPACE Surveillance Ctr J30-CM Cheyenne Mountain AFB Colorado Springs CO 80914-5000

ESTES, MARK WAYNE, corporate communications writer, editor; b. Phoenix, Feb. 19, 1955; s. Wilbur Calvin and Mary Rose Elizabeth (Filchak) E.; m. Odilia Ana Altamirano, Aug. 6, 1983; children: Anna Christina, Matthew, Samuel, Roseanne. Student, No. Ariz. U., 1973-76; BA, U. Ariz., 1978; postgrad., Gateway Community Coll., Phoenix, 1989. Reporter The Ariz. Republic, 1972-73; adminstrv. reporter The Lumberjack, Flagstaff, Ariz., 1974-75; assoc. editor The Voice, Flagstaff, 1975; reporter Flagstaff News, 1975-76; assoc. editor Tucson Sports Mag., 1981; pub. rels. advisor Am. Chiropractic Assn., Tucson, 1981; staff writer Salt River Project, Phoenix, 1981-87, sr. staff writer, 1987—, internal projects editor, 1989—, fin. publs. editor, 1991—, fin. projects editor; mem. Svc. Quality Task Force Salt River Project, Phoenix, 1990, Substance Abuse Task Force Salt River Project, Phoenix, 1984-85. Contbr. numerous articles to local newspapers. Fundraiser St. Daniel's Home and Sch., Scottsdale, Ariz., 1983-89; dep. registrar Pima County Rep. Party, Tucson, 1979-80; dist. gov. Circle K. Internat., Ariz., N.Mex., Tex., 1975-76, lt. gov., Ariz., N.Mex., 1974-75; publicity chair Ariz. Vocat. Indsl. Clubs Am. Industry Coun.; bd. dirs. St. Theresa Sch.; coach, bd. dirs. Arcadia Scottsdale United Soccer Club, 1991-93; active Xavier Coll. Prep. Parents' Assn. Recipient Merit award Utility Comm. Internat., 1990, News Reporting 1st Place Editor's Forum, 1989, award Utility Communicators Assn., 1989, award of excellence Awards for Publs. Excellence, 1991, 92, award of merits Ann. Reports. Mem. Internat. Assn. Bus. Communicators (programs com. 1990, v.p. profl. devel., v.p. ednl. svcs., accreditation chair, accredited 1990, Silver Quill award of Merit Dist. 5 1988, Copper Quill award of merit Phoenix chpt. 1984, 88, 89, 92, Pres. award, award of excellence Dist. 5), Salt River Project Polit. Involvement Com. Home: 8233 E Edgemont Ave Scottsdale AZ 85257-1730 Office: Salt River Project PO Box 52025 Phoenix AZ 85072-2025

ESTES-JACKSON, JANE ELIZABETH, geologist; b. Huntsville, Ala., Oct. 24, 1964; d. Glen Dale and Mary Malone (Wyche) E. BS, U. Southwestern La., 1987; MS, Colo. Sch. Mines, 1992. Geotechnician RPI Internat., Inc., Boulder, Colo., 1989; asst. geologist Coyote Geologic Svcs., Boulder, 1990-91; asst. geologist Gerrity Oil & Gas, Denver, 1992, ops. geologist, 1992—. Mem. Am. Assn. Petroleum Geologists. Home: 18258 W 58th Pl #1 Golden CO 80403-1078

ESTRUTH, JERRY THOMAS, financial professional; b. San Jose, Calif., Feb. 6, 1943; s. Thomas and Thelma Jeannette (Harter) E.; m. Margo Linn Spencer, Jan. 1, 1990; children: Jeannette Alden, Molly Kristen, Thomas Douglas. BA, Stanford U., 1964; CFP, Coll. Fin. Planning, Denver, 1985; cert., Dean Witter Mgmt. Tng., N.Y.C., 1985. Account exec., v.p. Dean Witter Reynolds, San Jose, 1969—; computer cons. Dean Witter Reynolds, 1982—, asst. mgr., 1986—. Columnist Sr. Times, 1987-88. Vol. Peace Corps, Colombia, 1964-67, mem. staff, 1967-69; mem. city coun. City of San Jose, 1979-84, vice-mayor, 1980; reader for Spanish-speaking blind Variety Audio and Peninsula Blind Ctr., San Jose and Palo Alto, Calif., 1974, 84; pres. Santa Clara unit Am. Cancer Soc., 1988; chair Open Space Com., Santa Clara County, 1988-90, Yes on Tobacco Tax com. Santa Clara County, 1990. Recipient Am. Field Svc. scholarship, 1959. Mem. Silicon Valley Capital Club (founder, mem. exec. com. 1990—), Masons (lodge trustee, Hiram award 1988). Democrat. Episcopalian. Home: 1254 University Ave San Jose CA 95126 Office: Dean Witter Reynolds PO Box 1239 San Jose CA 95108

ETCHEMENDY, NANCY ELISE HOWELL, graphic designer, writer; b. Reno, Nev., Feb. 19, 1952; d. Fredrick Lewis Howell and Barbara Fay (Nelson) Murdock; m. John William Etchemendy, Apr. 14, 1973; 1 child, Matthew Xavier. BA, U. Nev., 1974. Lithographer Western Indsl. Parts, Reno, 1970-75, Sutherland Printing, Reno, 1975-76; art dir. W.H. Barth Corp., Sunnyvale, Calif., 1976-79; pvt. practice Menlo Park, Calif., 1979—. Author: The Watchers of Space, 1980, Stranger from the Stars, 1983, The Crystal City, 1985; author short stories, 1983—. Mem. Soc. Children's Book Writers, Sci. Fiction Writers of Am. Democrat.

ETHERINGTON, LARRY ROBERT, entrepreneur, consultant; b. Mankato, Minn., Mar. 31, 1956; s. Robert LeRoy and LaVon Etta (Parry) E. BA in History, U. Minn., 1978, BA in Internat. Rels., BA in Chinese, 1985; M in Internat. Mgmt., Am. Grad. Sch. Internat. Mgmt., Glendale, Ariz., 1986. Indsl. waterproofer Hines Co., Mpls., 1979-80; bar mgr. Bombay Bicycle Co., Blaine, Minn., 1980-83; lead bar supr. S A Cattle Co., Fridley, Minn., 1983-84; dir. beverage ops. Registry Hotel Corp., Bloomington, Minn., 1984-86; dir. internat. mktg. U-Haul Internat., Phoenix, 1987-88; pres. Utilities Auditing Svcs., Phoenix, 1990—, UAS Publs., Inc., Phoenix, 1991—; bd. dirs. Global Objectives, Inc., Phoenix, Sophmar Inc., Phoenix. Author: How to Save Money On Your Electric, Gas, Water & Telephone Bills!, 1992. Mem. Internat. Assn. Ind. Pubs., Pubs. Mktg. Assn., Phoenix C. of C. Republican.

ETHRIDGE, FRANK GULDE, geology educator, consultant; b. Meridian, Miss., Dec. 21, 1938. BS, Miss. State U., 1960; MS, La. State U., 1966; PhD, Tex. A&M U., 1970. Prodn. geologist Chevron Oil Co., New Orleans, 1965-67; asst. prof. So. Ill. U., Carbondale, 1970-74, assoc. prof., 1974-75; assoc. prof. Colo. State U., Ft. Collins, 1975-81, prof., 1981—, acting head dept. earth resources, 1989; cons. in field, Ft. Collins, 1977—. Co-editor: Recent and Ancient Nonmarine Depositional Environments: Medals for Exploration, 1981, Fluvial Sedimentology, 1987. 1st Lt. U.S. Army, 1960-63. Fellow Tex. A&M U., 1967, 68, grad. fellow 1970, Halbouty scholar, 1969; faculty devel. grantee Colo. State U., 1986. Mem. Internat. Assn. Sedimentologists, Am. Assn. Petroleum Geologists (assoc. editor 1983—), Soc. Sedimentary Geologists (Rocky Mountain sect. sec. 1977-78, v.p. 1978-79, pres. 1983-84), Rocky Mountain Assn. Geologists, Sigma Xi. Roman Catholic. Office: Colo State U Dept Earth Resources Fort Collins CO 80523

ETT, ALAN PAUL, composer; b. Detroit, Mar. 2, 1952; s. Seymour and Florence (Lesan) E. BA in Psychology, U. N.C., 1972; MM, New Eng. Conservatory, 1978. Faculty Berklee Coll. Music, Boston, 1976-79; internat. concert performer W. Europe, North Am., 1979-83; composer, producer various groups, L.A., 1983—; musical dir. in field; master classes W. German

Kulturamt, 1979-83. Composer music for TV shows including 227, Who's the Boss, 1987-89, Unsolved Mysteries, 1989-91, Wild & Crazy Kids, Why Didn't I Think of That, 1992, TV's Funniest Commercials, 1992, Shame on You, 1993, How'd They Do That, 1993; films including Fourth War, Cold Feet, Mob Boss, Madhouse, 1988-90, Pacific Heights, Thelma & Louise, Madonna-Truth or Dare; videos including Kareem-Reflections, 1989 (Golden Globe award). Mem. Broadcast Music Inc., Am. Fedn. Musicians. Home: 13112 Valleyheart Dr Apt 203 Studio City CA 91604-1983 Office: Alan Ett Music 3500 W Olive Ave Ste 1470 Burbank CA 91505-4628

ETTEDGUI, ALAIN MICHAEL, mortgage and insurance broker; b. Casablanca, Morocco, July 1, 1963; came to U.S., 1967; s. Louis Armand and Simone (Amsellem) E. BS, U. S. Calif., 1985; MBA, UCLA, 1990. Real estate mgmt. exec. Etton Enterprises, Westlake Village, Calif., 1981-85; fin. planner Beverly Hills, Calif., 1985—. Campaign aid Congressman Barry Goldwater Jr., 1981; mem. CARE (Homeless and Starving in Africa, 1986—, Chabad Temple, 1978—; donor ARC, 1980—. Mem. Million Dollar Round Table, Life Ins. Leaders Round Table, Nat. Assn. Life Underwriters, Internat. Assn. Fin. Planners, MONY Fin. Svc. (pres.'s coun. 1986), Nat. Eagle Scout Assn. Republican. Jewish. Office: PO Box 63 Beverly Hills CA 90210

ETTLING, BRUCE VINCENT, fire consultant; b. Detroit, Feb. 1, 1930; s. Arthur James and Alice Estelle (Kayser) E.; m. Carlyse Alyne Cole, Apr. 11, 1959; children: Steven V., Daniel W., Allen S. BS, Wayne State U., Detroit, 1951, MS, 1954; PhD, Wash. State U., 1958. Chemist U.S. Rubber Co., Detroit, 1951-53, Phillips Petroleum Co., Bartlesville, Okla., 1958-59, Wash. State U., Pullman, 1959-76; cons. Tech Fire Investigation Svcs., Vancouver, Wash., 1976—. Mem. Am. Chem. Soc., Internat. Assn. Arson Investigators (chmn. S.W. Wash. dist. 1978, editor 1986-88), Soc. Fire Protection Engrs., Nat. Fire Protection Assn.

ETTLINGER, ROBERT EMIL, physician; b. N.Y.C., Aug. 14, 1947; s. Hans A. and G. Ettlinger; 1 child, Adrian Leonidas. BA, Queens Coll., N.Y.C., 1968; MD, SUNY, Syracuse, 1972. Cert. in rheumatology Am. Bd. Internal Medicine. Intern, resident U. Oreg., Portland, 1972-75; fellow Mayo Clinic, Rochester, Minn., 1975-78, assoc. cons., 1977-78; instr. Mayo Grad. Sch. Medicine, Rochester, 1977-78; pvt. practice rheumatology Tacoma, Wash., 1978—; affiliate clin. prof. U. Puget Sound, Tacoma, 1990; clin. researcher various pharm. firms, 1982—. Contbr. articles on rheumatology to profl. jours. Bd. dirs. Western Wash. chpt. Arthritis Found., Seattle, 1989—. P. Kahler Hench scholar Mayo Clinic, 1977. Fellow Am. Coll. Physicians, Am. Coll. Rheumatology (founding); mem. Wash. State Med. Assn., Pierce County Med. Assn., Tacoma Acad. Internal Medicine (pres. 1983-84), Tacoma Orthopedic Soc. Office: 1901 S Cedar St Tacoma WA 98405-2308

ETZEL, L. A., construction company executive; b. Clarion, Pa., July 21, 1947; s. Frank William and Evelyn Mae (Hoover) E.; m. Ellen J. Clark, Aug. 23, 1975; children: Paula, Kimberly, Susan, Michael. Student, Pa. State U., 1967. Constrn. engr. Procter & Gamble Co., Cin., 1967-72; project mgr. Scott-Buttner Corp., Oakland, Calif., 1972-80; mgr. regional ops. Swinerton & Walberg, San Francisco, 1980—. Mem. Contra Costa County Coalition Labor and Bus., 1990, Contra Costa County Coun. Mem. No. Calif. Coord. Assn., Comml. Club San Francisco. Office: Swinerton & Walberg 580 California St San Francisco CA 94104

ETZLER, MARILYNN EDITH, biochemist, educator; b. Detroit, Oct. 30, 1940; d. Elmer Ellsworth and Doris (Tegge) E. BS, BA, Otterbein Coll., Westerville, Ohio, 1962; PhD, Washington U., St. Louis, 1967. Asst. prof. biochemistry U. Calif., Davis, 1969-75, assoc. prof. biochemistry, 1975-79, prof. biochemistry, 1979—. Contbr. articles to sci. publs. Grantee NIH, 1970—, NSF, 1981—. Mem. Am. Soc. Biochemistry and Molecular Biology, Am. Soc. Cell Biology, Complex Carbohydrate Soc., Am. Soc. Plant Physiology, Protein Soc. Office: U Calif Dept Biochemistry/Biophyics Davis CA 95616

EU, MARCH KONG FONG, state official; b. Oakdale, Calif., Mar. 29, 1922; d. Yuen and Shiu (Shee) Kong; children by previous marriage: Matthew Kipling Fong, Marchesa Suyin Fong; m. Henry Eu, July 30, 1973; stepchildren: Henry, Adelina, Yvonne, Conroy, Alaric. Student, Salinas Jr. Coll.; B.S., U. Calif.-Berkeley; M.Ed., Mills Coll., 1951; Ed.D., Stanford U., 1956; postgrad., Columbia U., Calif. State Coll.-Hayward; LL.D., Lincoln U., 1984. Chmn. div. dental hygiene U. Calif. Med. Center, San Francisco; dental hygienist Oakland (Calif.) Pub. Schs.; supr. dental health edn. Alameda County (Calif.) Schs.; lectr. health edn. Mills Coll., Oakland; mem. Calif. Legislature, 1966-74, chmn. select com. on agr., foods and nutrition, 1973-74; mem. com. natural resources and conservation, com. commerce and pub. utilities, select com. med. malpractice; sec. state State of Calif., 1975—, chief of protocol, 1975-83, sec. of state; chmn. Calif. State World Trade Commn., 1982-87; spl. cons. Bur. Intergroup Relations, Calif. Dept. Edn.; ednl., legis. cons. Sausalito (Calif.) Pub. Schs., Santa Clara County Office Edn., Jefferson Elementary Union Sch. Dist., Santa Clara High Sch. Dist., Santa Clara Elementary Sch. Dist., Live Oak Union High Sch. Dist.; mem. Alameda County Bd. Edn., 1956-66, pres., 1961-62, legis. adv., 1963. Mem. budget panel Bay Area United Fund Crusade; mem. Oakland Econ. Devel. Council; mem. tourism devel. com. Calif. Econ. Devel. Commn.; mem. citizens com. on housing Council Social Planning; mem. Calif. Interagy. Council Family Planning; edn. chmn., mem. council social planning, dir. Oakland Area Baymont Dist. Community Council; charter pres., hon. life mem. Howard Elementary Sch. PTA; charter pres. Chinese Young Ladies Soc., Oakland; mem., vice chmn. adv. com. Youth Study Centers and Ford Found. Interagy. Project, 1962-63; chmn. Alameda County Mothers' March, 1971-72; bd. councillors U. So. Calif. Sch. Dentistry, 1976; mem. exec. com. Calif. Democratic Central Com., mem. central com., 1963-70, asst. sec.; del. Dem. Nat. Conv., 1968; dir. 8th Congl. Dist. Dem. Council, 1963; v.p. Dems. of 8th Congl. Dist., 1963; dir. Key Women for Kennedy, 1963; women's vice chmn. No. Calif. Johnson for Pres., 1964; bd. dirs. Oakland YWCA, 1965. Recipient ann. award for outstanding achievement Eastbay Intercultural Fellowship, 1959; Phoebe Apperson Hearst Disting. Bay Area Woman of Yr. award; Woman of Yr. award Calif. Retail Liquor Dealers Inst., 1969; Merit citation Calif. Assn. Adult Edn. Adminstrs., 1970; Art Edn. award; Outstanding Woman award Nat. Women's Polit. Caucus, 1980; Person of Yr. award Miracle Mile Lions Club, 1980; Humanitarian award Milton Strong Hall of Fame, 1981; Outstanding Leadership award Ventura Young Dems., 1983; Woman of Achievement award Los Angeles Hadassah, 1983, Outstanding Leadership award Filipino-Am. C. of C., 1985, CARE award, 1985, Disting. Svc. award Republic of Honduras, 1987, Polit. Achievement award Calif Dem. Party Black Caucus, 1988, JFK Am. Leadership award Santa Ana Dem. Club, 1989, L.A. County Good Scout award, Boy Scouts Am., 1989; named Woman of Yr., Democrats United, San Bernadino, 1989, Woman of Distinction, Soroptimist Internat., Monterey Park, 1987, Woman of Achievement, Santa Barbara Legal Secs. Assn. and County Bar Assn., 1987, one of Am.'s 100 Most Important Women, Ladies Home Jour., 1988; recipient Community Leadership award Torat-Haijun Hebrew Acad., 1990, Special Appreciation U. Vietnamese Student Assns. So. Calif., 1990, Nat. Assn. Chinese-Am. Bankers, 1990, Orange County Buddhist Assn., 1990, Internat. Bus. award, West Coast U., 1992. Mem. Am. Dental Hygienists Assn. (pres. 1956-57), No. Calif. Dental Hygienists Assn., Oakland LWV, AAUW (area rep. in edn. Oakland br.), Calif. Tchrs. Assn., Calif. Sch. Bd. Assn., Alameda County Sch. Bd. Assn. (pres. 1965), Alameda County Mental Health Assn., So. Calif. Dental Assn. (hon.), Bus. and Profl. Women's Club, Chinese Retail Food Markets Assn. (hon.), Delta Kappa Gamma. Office: Sec of State State of Calif 1230 J St Sacramento CA 95814-2924*

EULAU, MARTIN FRANK, accountant; b. Manila. BA in Econs., Pomona Coll., 1959; MBA, U. Calif., Berkeley, 1961. CPA, Calif.; cert. personal fin. specialist. Self-employed Ventura, Calif., 1966—; former instr. acctg. Ventura Coll., U. La Verne, Ventura County. Mem. AICPA, Calif. Soc. CPAs (mem. state com. on personal fin. planning), Greater Ventura C. of C., Lions (bd. dirs., former officer), Channel City Club, Beta Alpha Psi. Office: 2419 E Main St Ventura CA 93003-2603

EURE, WERDNA WAYLAND, JR., physician, radiation oncologist; b. Balcksburg, Va., Mar. 31, 1952; s. Wernda Wayland and Margaret Amanda (Yowell) E.; m. Kris Susan Kershaw, Oct. 13, 1979; children: Andrew Carter, Maxwell Christopher. BS, Coll. of William & Mary, 1974; MD, U. Va., 1978. Diplomate Am. Bd. Radiology. Intern U. Va. Hosp., Charlottesville, 1978-79, resident, 1979-82; owner, physician Radiation Therapy Med. Group, Riverside, Calif., 1982—; govt. rels. com. Am. Coll. Radiology, 1992—; pres. Assn. Freestanding Radiation Oncology Ctrs., 1991—. Med. adv. bd. Hospice, Riverside, Calif., 1986—. Am. Cancer Soc. fellow Charlottesville, Va., 1980-81; fellow Loma Linda U. Med. Ctr., 1982. Mem. AMA, Am. Soc. Clin. Oncologists, Am. Soc. Therapeutic Radiology and Oncology (fed. legis. oversight com. 1992—), Am. Coll. Radiation Oncology, Am. Coll. Radiology, Calif. Radiol. Soc., So. Calif. Radiol. Soc., Calif. Med. Assn., Calif. Radiation Oncology Soc., L.A. Radiol. Soc., Assn. Ind. Radiologists and Oncologists of Russia. Office: Radiation Therapy Med Group 6939 Palm Ct Riverside CA 92506

EVANGER, ARDEN EIDE, pathologist; b. Camas, Wash., Nov. 16, 1933; s. Andrew John and Sierio Martha (Eide) E.; div.; children: Andrew J., Bradley L., James R., Heidi A. BA, U. Wash., 1957, MD, 1960. Intern USPHS, Staten Island, N.Y., 1960-61; resident U. Wash., 1961-65; pathologist VA Hosp., Portland, Oreg., 1968-70; pvt. practice Yakima, Wash., 1970-75, Missoula, Mont., 1975—. Capt. U.S. Army, 1965-68. Fellow Am. Soc. Clin. Pathologists, Coll. Am. Pathologists. Home: 710 Highland Park Dr Missoula MT 59803 Office: St Patrick Hosp 500 W Broadway Missoula MT 59802

EVANKOVICH, GEORGE JOSEPH, labor union administrator; b. Butte, Mont., Jan. 27, 1930; s. Joseph and Lubja (Broze) E.; m. Nevada Murray, Aug. 16, 1969; children: Karen, Lucy, Joseph, Janna. Student, U. Mont., 1954-57; BA, U. San Francisco, 1958. Miner Anaconda Co., Butte, 1946-50, Ind. Lease Mining, Helena, Mont., 1957-60; sec., treas. local 261 Laborers Internat. Union, San Francisco, 1960-68, bus. mgr., 1968-87, pres., 1987—; mem. bd. govs. dept. indsl. rels. Occupational Safety and Health Standards Bd. State of Calif., Sacramento, 1990—; pres. Calif. region Pub. Employee Coun. AFL-CIO, 1973—; pres. No. Dist. Coun. of Laborers, 1977—; bd. dirs., trustee Laborer's Trust Funds, Inc., San Francisco. Dir. labor studies program San Francisco City Coll., 1978—; chmn. San Francisco Housing Authority, 1972-76; advisor various senatorial, congl. and mayoral campaigns, 1966—; sustained mem. Rep. Nat. Com., 1980—. With inf. U.S. Army, 1951-54, Korea. Mem. Laborers Polit. Action Com. (bd. dirs.), Commonwealth Club of San Francisco. Roman Catholic. Office: Laborers Union Local #261 3271 18th St San Francisco CA 94110-1996

EVANO, DENNIS CHARLES, novelist; b. Hammond, Ind., July 10, 1946; s. Joseph Thomas and Helen Marie Christ; m. Gloria Jean Siedelmann, June 22, 1968 (div. Sept. 1980); children: Rachel, Daniel, Mary Ann. Student, Truman City Coll., Chgo., 1989. Electrician Tri-City Electric Co., Hammond, Ind., 1972-75; gen. contractor Classic Builders, Demotte, Ind., 1975-79; electrical foreman Allstate Energy, Inc., Phoenix, 1980-84; project supt. Arthur Greene Constrn., Vernon Hills, Ill., 1986-89; fitness instr., novelist Phoenix, 1989—; mem. Ariz. State Bd. Realtors, 1980-81. Author: His Chosen, 1992. Mem. Planetary Soc. Home: 3801 E Larkspur Dr Phoenix AZ 85032

EVANS, ANTHONY HOWARD, university president; b. Clay County, Ark., Sept. 24, 1936; s. William Raymond and Thelma Fay (Crews) Romine; m. Lois Fay Kirkham, Aug. 29, 1959. BA, East Tex. Bapt. Coll., Marshall, 1959; MA, U. Hawaii, 1961; PhD, U. Calif.-Berkeley, 1966. Program officer Peace Corps, Seoul, Korea, 1970-72; chief program planning Peace Corps, Washington, 1972-73, dir. planning office, 1973-75; asst. to pres. Eastern Mich. U., Ypsilanti, 1975-76, 1976-79, acting pres., 1978-79, provost, v.p. acad. affairs, 1979-82; pres. Calif. State U., San Bernardino, 1982—. Mem. Orgn. Am. Historians, Phi Kappa Phi. Home: 664 E Parkdale Dr San Bernardino CA 92404-1731

EVANS, BERNARD WILLIAM, geologist, educator; b. London, July 16, 1934; came to U.S., 1961, naturalized, 1977; s. Albert Edward and Marjorie (Jordan) E.; m. Sheila Campbell Nolan, Nov. 19, 1962. B.Sc., U. London, 1955; D.Phil., Oxford U., 1959. Asst. U. Glasgow, Scotland, 1958-59; departmental demonstrator U. Oxford, 1959-61; asst. research prof. U. Calif., Berkeley, 1961-65; asst. prof. U. Calif., 1965-66, assoc. prof., 1966-69; prof. geology U. Wash., Seattle, 1969—; chmn. dept. geol. scis. U. Wash., 1974-79. Contbr. articles to profl. jours. Recipient U.S. Sr. Scientist award Humboldt Found., Fed. Republic Germany, 1988-89. Mem. Geol. Soc. Am., Mineral. Soc. Am. (award 1970), Geochem. Soc., Geol. Soc. London, Mineral. Soc. Gt. Britain, Swiss Mineral. Soc. Home: 8001 Sand Point Way NE Apt 55C Seattle WA 98115-6399 Office: Dept Geol Scis AJ-20 U Wash Seattle WA 98195

EVANS, BEVERLY ANN, school administrator, state legislator; b. Tod Park, Utah, Jan. 26, 1944; d. Elias Wilbur and Geraldine Vilate (Rigby) Cook; m. Stephen R. Evans, July 31, 1965; children: Lorie Ann, James. MA, Utah State U, 1968. Tchr. Duchesne (Utah) Sch. Dist., 1965-70; instr. Uintah Basin Applied Tech. Ctr., Roosevelt, Utah, 1970-73, adminstr., 1973—; instr. Utah State U., Logan, 1968—; rep. Utah Legislature, Salt Lake City, 1986—; cons. Utah State U., 1980—. Recipient Award of Merit, Nat. Safety Coun., Chgo., 1985-87, Alumni award Nat. 4-H, 1989, Bus. Woman of Yr award Utah BPW, 1990, Pub. Servant award Duchesne County C. of C., 1993. Republican. Mem. LDS Ch. Home: HC 65 Box 36 Altamont UT 84001-9801

EVANS, BURTIS ROBBINS, physician; b. Salt Lake City, Dec. 7, 1925; s. Alldridge N. and Thelma (Robbins) E.; m. Janeth Jensen, June 5, 1953; children: Vicki, Scott, Cathie, Elizabeth, Mary, Alan, Margaret, Richard. Student, U. Utah, 1946-47; MD, Temple U., 1951. Intern LDS Hosp., Salt Lake City, 1951-52; resident Cleve. Clinic, 1952-55; asst. clin. prof. medicine U. Utah, Salt Lake City, 1956—, team physician, 1956—; prin. Drs. Evans, Evans & Evans, Salt Lake City, 1956—; pres. Physicians Care Corp., 1986—; bd. dirs. CARE Enterprises, Tustin, Calif. Bd.dirs. Utah Symphony, Salt Lake City, 1976—; trustee Salt Lake Visitors and Conv. Bur., Salt Lake City, 1986—. Home: 2879 Sherwood Dr Salt Lake City UT 84108-2540

EVANS, CATHERINE LEE, social worker, researcher; b. San Diego, May 17, 1965; d. Robert John and Hazel Lorene (McEwen) E. BA in Psychology, San Diego State U., 1987, MSW, 1992. Cert. in recovery svcs., alcohol and drug social work. Grad. asst. San Diego State Found., 1991-92; social work intern Options for Recovery, Chula Vista, Calif., 199o-91, Naval Air Sta. Miramar/Family Svc. Ctr., San Diego, 1991—. Named to Outstanding Young Women of Am., 1987. Mem. Nat. Assn. Social Workers, Nat. Assn. Pub. Health Policy, Calif. Coun. on Alcohol Policy. Republican. Evangelical Christian.

EVANS, DON A., healthcare company executive; b. Jerome, Ariz., June 22, 1948; s. Rulon Cooper and Berniece (Ensign) E.; m. Susan Dahl, June 3, 1972; children: Emily, Austin, Adrienne, Alan. BS, Ariz. State U., Tempe, 1972; MS, U. Colo., 1974. Asst. adminstr. Nat. Jewish Hosp., Denver, 1974-80; asst. adminstr. LDS Hosp., Salt Lake City, 1980-84, chief operating officer, 1984-88; chief exec. officer Luth. Healthcare Network, Mesa, Ariz., 1988—; adj. prof. U. Minn., 1985-86; bd. dirs. Advanced Home Health, Mesa. Fellow Am. Coll. Healthcare Execs.; mem. Ariz. Hosp. Assn. (bd. dirs.), Am. Heart Assn. (bd. dirs., treas.), Rotary. Republican. Office: Lutheran Healthcare Network 500 W 10th Pl Mesa AZ 85201-3216

EVANS, JAMES HANDEL, university president, architect, educator; b. Bolton, Eng., June 14, 1938; s. Arthur Handel and Ellen Bowen (Ramsden) E.; m. Carol Mulligan, Sept. 10, 1966; children: Jonathan, Sarah. Diploma of Architecture, U. Manchester, Eng., 1965; MArch, U. Oreg., 1967; postgrad., Cambridge (Eng.) U., 1969-70. Registered architect, Calif., U.K.; cert. NCARB. Assoc. dean. prof. architecture Calif. Poly. State U., San Luis Obispo, 1967-78; prof. art San Jose (Calif.) State U., 1979—, assoc. exec. v.p., 1978-81, interim exec. v.p., 1981-82, exec. v.p., 1982-91, interim pres., 1991-92, pres., 1992—; cons. Ibiza Nueva, Ibiza, Spain, 1977-80; vis. prof. Ciudad Universitaria, Madrid, 1977; vis. lectr. Herriott Watt U., Edinburgh, 1970; mem. adv. com. Army Command Staff Coll., Ft. Leavenworth, Kans., 1988. Trustee Good Samaritan Hosp., San Jose, 1987-90; bd. dirs. San Jose Shelter, 1988-90. Sci. Rsch. Coun. fellow Cambridge U., 1969-70. Fellow AIA; mem. Royal Inst. Brit. Architects, Assn. Univ. Architects. Office: San Jose State U One Washington Sq San Jose CA 95129-0002

EVANS, JAMES LOUIS, mathematics and science educator; b. Washington, June 29, 1935; s. Felton Jasper and Nellie (Brown) E.; m. Ada Earley, Aug. 10, 1957; children: Kevin, Kyle, Cheryl, Shawna. BEE, Cath. U. Am., 1957; MEE, Air Force Inst. Tech., Dayton, Ohio, 1968; MS in Secondary Edn., Eastern N.Mex. U., 1984. Enlisted USAF, 1958, advanced through grades to maj., navigator, 1958-80, ret., 1980; tech. instr. Eastern N.Mex. U., Pontales, 1980—; tchr. Muleshoe (Tex.) Ind. Sch. Dist., 1987-89, Tucumcar (N.M.) Mcpl. Schs., 1989—. Mem. NEA, Masons (dep. grand master N.Mex. dist.). Home: 1708 Courtland Cir Clovis NM 88101-3925 Office: Tucumcar Mcpl Schs 1100 S 7th St Tucumcar NM 88401

EVANS, JAMES WILLIAM, metallurgical educator; b. Dobcross, Yorkshire, Eng., Aug. 22, 1943; came to U.S., 1970; s. James Hall and Alice Maud (Dransfield) E.; m. Beverley Lynn Connor, July 22, 1967 (div. 1978); 1 child, James; m. Sylvia Marian Johnson, Jan. 5, 1985; children: Hugh Edmund, Claire Meredith. BS, Univ. Coll., London, 1964; PhD, SUNY, Buffalo, 1970. Tech. adviser Internat. Computers Ltd., London, 1964-65; chemist Can. Cyanamid, Niagara Falls, Ont., Can., 1965-67; engr. Ethyl Corp., Baton Rouge, 1970-72; from asst. prof. to prof. U. Calif., Berkeley, 1972—, chmn. dept., 1986-90. Co-author: Gas-Solid Reactions, 1976, Mathematical and Physical Modeling of Primary Metals Processing, 1988, The Production of Inorganic Materials, 1991; contbr. over 100 articles to profl. jours. Mem. AICE, Minerals, Metals and Materials Soc. (bd. dirs. 1985-89, Extractive Metallurgy Sci. award 1973, 83, Champion H. Mathewson Gold medal 1984), Electrochem. Soc., Iron and Steel Inst. Japan. Democrat. Office: U Calif Dept Matls Sci & Mineral Eng Berkeley CA 94720

EVANS, JED REEDER, retired librarian; b. L.A., Nov. 3, 1929; s. Leland Hayes and Marion Graham (Reeder) E. AB in Edn., U. Wash., 1952; MLS, Emporia State U., Kans., 1954. Catalog libr. Orange County Library, Santa Ana and Orange, Calif., 1954-67; catalog libr. Nev. Ctr. Coop. Libr. Svcs., Carson City, 1967-69, acting dir., 1967-68; asst. catalog libr. Calif. State U. Libr., Chico, 1969-70; catalog libr. Mont. State U. Libr., Bozeman, 1972-73; head of tech. process, cataloger Rocky Mountain Libr., Billings, Mont., 1973-74; asst. cataloger Tulare County Libr., Visalia, Calif., 1975-78; Shipmates libr. Solana Beach (Calif.) Presbyn. Ch., Calif., 1984-92; sr. asst. Solana Beach (Calif.) Presbyn. Ch., 1992—. Mem. ALA, Calif. Libr. Assn., So. Calif. Tech. Process Group, Sierra Club. Home: 235 27th St Del Mar CA 92014-2026 Office: Solana Beach Presbyn Ch 120 Stevens Ave Solana Beach CA 92075-2039

EVANS, JERRY LEE, state school superintendent; b. Cascade, Idaho, Sept. 6, 1931; s. Ivan Lee Evans and Verna Luella (McCoy) Scovel; m. Phyllis Noreen, Apr. 13, 1952; children—Andrew, Catherine, Vicki. B.S. in Edn., U. Idaho, Moscow, 1953; M.S. in Gen. Sci., Oreg. State U., Corvalis, 1962. Tchr., coach Sch. Dist. 422, Cascade, Idaho, 1953-54, tchr., prin., supt., 1956-69; dist. supt. Sch. Dist. 132, Caldwell, Idaho, 1969-75; dept. state supt. Dept. Edn., Boise, Idaho, 1975-78, state supt. pub. instrn., 1979—; bd. dirs. Agy. for Instrnl. Tech., 1989. Mem. Idaho Library Bd., Boise, 1979; bd. dirs. Blue Cross Idaho Health Svcs., Boise, 1978. Served to 1st lt. USAF, 1954-56. Named to Idaho Republican Hall of Fame, Rep. Party, 1982. Mem. Idaho Bd. Edn., Edn. Commn. of States, Northwest Regional Lab. (bd. dirs. 1980), Council Chief State Sch. Officers. Methodist. Office: Dept Edn Len B Jordan Bldg 650 W State St Boise ID 83720-0001

EVANS, LARRY MELVYN, newspaper columnist, chess expert; b. N.Y.C., Mar. 22, 1932; s. Harry and Bella (Shotl) E.; m. Ingrid Carla Hamann, Sept. 15, 1968; children—Karin Louise, Michael Charles, Gary Dean. B.A. with honors, Coll. City N.Y., 1954. Columnist Denver Post, 1971—; columnist Chgo. Tribune, 1972, Washington Post, 1975—; commentator World Chess Tournament ABC-TV, 1972; mem. U.S. Olympic chess team, 1950, 1968, 1970, 76; European chess tour for U.S. State Dept., 1956. Author: Trophy Chess, 1956, New Ideas in Chess, 1958, Modern Chess Openings, 1965, Chess: Beginner to Expert, 1967, Modern Chess Brilliancies, 1970, Chess Catechism, 1970, What's the Best Move? 1973, Evans on Chess, 1974, World Championship: Fischer v. Spassky, 1972, The Chess Opening for You, 1975, An Unbeatable White Repertoire, 1988; contbg. editor: Chess Life and Rev, 1950—, Chess Digest, 1970—, Americana Ann, 1972—, Games, 1979. Recipient Internat. Chess Grandmaster award, 1957. Mem. U.S. Chess Fedn., Friends of U.S. Chess Fedn. (chmn. 1990). Office: PO Box 1182 Reno NV 89504-1182

EVANS, LAWRENCE JACK, JR., lawyer; b. Oakland, Calif., Apr. 4, 1921; s. Lawrence Jack and Eva May (Dickinson) E.; m. Marjorie Hisken, Dec. 23, 1944; children: Daryl S. Kleweno, Richard L., Shirley J. Coursey, Donald B. Diplomate Near East Sch. Theology, Beirut, 1951; MA, Am. U. Beirut, 1951; PhD, Brantridge Forest Sch., Sussex, Eng., 1968; JD, Ariz. State U., 1971; grad. Nat. Jud. Coll., 1974. Bar: Ariz. 1971, U.S. Dist. Ct. Ariz. 1971, U.S. Ct. Claims 1972, U.S. Customs Ct., 1972, U.S. Tax Ct. 1972, U.S. Ct. Customs and Patent Appeals 1972, U.S. Ct. Appeals (9th cir.) 1972, U.S. Supreme Ct. 1975. Enlisted U.S. Navy, 1938-41, U.S. Army, 1942-44, commd. 2d lt. U.S. Army, 1944, advanced through ranks to lt. col., 1962; war plans officer, G-3 Seventh Army, 1960-62, chief, field ops. and tactics div., U.S. Army Spl. Forces, 1963, chief spl. techniques div., U.S. Army Spl. Forces, 1964, unconventional warfare monitor, U.S. Army Spl. Forces, 1964-65; assigned to Command and Gen. Staff Coll., 1960; ops. staff officer J-3 USEUCOM, 1965-68; mem. Airborne Command Post Study Group, Joint Chiefs of Staff, 1967; ret., 1968; mem. faculty Ariz. State U., 1968; sole practice law, cons. on Near and Middle Eastern affairs, Tempe, Ariz., 1971-72, 76—; v.p., dir. Trojan Investment & Devel. Co., Inc., 1972-75; active Ariz. Tax Conf., 1971-75; mem. adminstrv. law com., labor mgmt. relations com., unauthorized practice of law com. Ariz. State Bar. Author: Legal Aspects of Land Tenure in the Republic of Lebanon, 1951, International Constitutional Law, (with Helen Miller Davis) Electoral Laws and Treaties of the Near and Middle East, 1951; contbr. articles to mags., chpts. to books. Chmn. legal and legis. com. Phoenix Mayor's Com. To Employ Handicapped, 1971-75; active Tempe Leadership Conf., 1971-75; chmn. Citizens Against Corruption in Govt., 1976-92; mem. Princeton Council on Fgn. and Internat. Studies, 1968. Decorated Silver Star, Legion of Merit, Bronze Star, Purple Heart; named Outstanding Adminstrv. Law Judge for State Service for U.S., 1974; named to U.S. Army Ranger Hall of Fame, 1981. Fellow Coll. of Rites of U.S.A.; mem. Ranger Bus. Assn. World War II (life), Tempe Rep. Mens Club (v.p., bd. dirs. 1971-72, U.S. Army Airborne Ranger Assn. (life), Mil. Order Purple Heart (life), NRA (official referee, life), Masons, Masonic Order of the Bath, BL (past master Rsch. Lodge # 1, twice past master Thuderbird lodge # 48 Phoenix), Order Ky. Colonels, Sovereign Mil. Order of Temple of Jerusalem (Chevalier 1989), Fraternal Order of Medieval Knighthood, Internat. (sovereign venerable master Ariz. Coll. 1988-93, supreme sovereign grand master 1991), YR (past high priest, past thrice illustrious master, twice eminent past comdr., Knight Templar Cross of Honor, 1988, SR (32, ritual dir.), Chief Adept Ariz. Coll. Socs. Rosicruceana (In Civitatibus Foederatis VIII 1988-93), Grand Commandery of Knights Templar of Ariz. (grand insp. gen. 1990-91), Knight Mason of U.S.A., Order of Secret Monitor, So. Calif. Rsch. Lodge, Royal Order of Scotland, Phi Delta Phi, Delta Theta Phi. Episcopalian. Home: 539 E Erie Dr Tempe AZ 85282-3712

EVANS, MAX ALLEN, writer, artist; b. Ropes, Tex., Aug. 29, 1924; s. W. B. and Hazel (Swafford) E.; m. Helene Caterlin, June 10, 1942 (divorced); 1 child, Sharon; m. Patsy Jo James, Aug. 4, 1949; children: Charlotte and Sharon (twins). Student pub. schs., N.Mex., Tex. Pres. Solar Metals, Inc., Taos, N.Mex., 1954-59; v.p. Evans Minerals, Inc., Taos, 1955-57; dir. Taos Minerals, Inc.; v.p. Taos Rodeo Assn., 1955-57; founding dir. N.Mex. State Film Commn., Santa Fe, 1969-73; hon. lifetime mem. bd. chancellors U. Tex. System, 1969—; founding dir. N.M. Farm and Ranching Inst. N.Mex. State U., Las Cruces, 1986—; bd. dirs. Cowboy Culture Inst. Tex. Tech. U., 1989—; mem. Gov.'s 1st N.M. Film Commn., 1967. Author: Southwest Wind, 1958, Long John Dunn of Taos, 1959, The Rounders, 1960, The Hi Lo Country, 1961, The One-Eyed Sky, 1963, The Mountain of Gold, 1965, The Shadow of Thunder, 1969, My Pardner, 1972 (L.A. Commendation award 1975), Sam Peckinpah - Master of Violence, 1972, Bobby Jack Smith

You Dirty Coward, 1974, The White Shadow, 1977, The Great Wedding, 1984, Xavier's Folly and Other Stories, 1984, Super Bull and Other True Escapades, 1986, Rounders 3 - A Trilogy, 1990; (novellas) The Orange County Cowboys, 1987 (Golden Spur award for best short fiction 1988), Candles in the Bottom of the Pool, 1988, The Wild One -- The New Frontier Anthology, 1989, Old Bum, 1993; (artist) produced over 300 water color and oil for public and private collections, shown in juried shows inluding The Harwood Found., Taos, Mus. of N.Mex., Sante Fe; (films) The Rounders (also TV series), 1965, The Ballad of Cable Hogue, 1972, The Wheel, 1973, documentaries include Every Man's Mountain, Fred Martin-Out of the West, Rio Grande-River of Legends. With U.S. Army, 1942-45, ETO. Recipient Golden Spur award Western Writers of Am., Inc., 1983, Nat. Cowboy Hall of Fame Wrangler award, 1984, Levi Straus Golden Saddleman award for Lifetime Achievement, 1990, State of N.Mex.'s Ann. Rounders' award Gov. N.Mex. and Sec. Agr., Lifetime Achievement Culture award Nat. Cowboy Symposium, 1993; Max Evans Day named in his honor Hobbs, N.Mex., 1968, Albuquerque, 1985. Home: 1111 Ridgecrest Dr SE Albuquerque NM 87108

EVANS, MAX JAY, historical society director; b. Lehi, Utah, May 11, 1943; s. Karl Robinson and Lucile (Johnson) E.; m. Mary Wheatley, June 16, 1967; children: David Max, Joseph Michael, Katherine Anne, Laura, Emily. BS, U. Utah, 1968; MS, Utah State U., 1971. Archivist Mormon Ch. Hist. Dept., Salt Lake City, 1971-75, asst. ch. librarian, archivist, 1975-77; dep. state archivist State Hist. Soc. Wis., Madison, 1977-86, library dir., 1986; dir. Utah State Hist. Soc., Salt Lake City, 1986—; acting dir. Utah State Archives, Salt Lake City, 1986-88; archival cons. N.Y. State Archives, Albany, 1981, Wyo Dept. Archives and Hist., Cheyenne, 1982. Co-author: MARC for Archives and Manuscripts: A Compendium of Practice, 1985 (SAA Coker award 1986); articles in field. Trustee Middleton (Wis.) Pub. Libr., 1974-86; exec. sec. Utah Statewood Centennial Commn., 1988-93; bd. dirs. Rsch. Librs. Group, 1991-92. Fellow Soc. Am. Archivists; mem. Utah State Hist. Soc. Mem. LDS Ch. Office: Utah State Hist Soc 300 Rio Grande St Salt Lake City UT 84101-1182

EVANS, PAUL M., retail executive; b. Kansas City, Kans., Dec. 10, 1954; s. John Paul and Mary H. (Sackuvich) E.; m. Pamela Ann Porter, Oct. 6, 1979; children: Paige Marie, John Paul. AA, Kansas City Community Coll., 1974; BA in Archtl. Design, Kansas City Art Inst., 1976; student, GE Lighting Inst., Cleve., 1989—. Printing apprentice Raden-C Auto Step Photography, Kansas City, 1972-73; freelance landscape designer Kansas City, 1973-74, freelance display artist, cons., 1974-75; city display mgr. K-G Men's Stores, Kansas City, 1975-77, advtg./visual regional supr., 1977-82; dir., store planning K-G Retail Stores Inc., Engelwood, Colo., 1983-89; v.p. store planning/visual merchandising K-G Retail Stores Inc., Denver, 1989—; design cons. NB Assocs., Englewood, 1985, Dover Elevator Co., Denver, 1985-86; store planning cons. Underworld Ltd., Boulder, Colo., 1986; dir. archtl. Control Dakota Sta. Littleton, Co., 1989-92. Designer Barrel-B-Que Grill, 1985. T-ball coach, Littleton (Colo.) YMCA, 1986; bd. dirs. design control com. Dakota Sta. Subdivision, Littleton, 1985-86, 89—. Republican. Roman Catholic. Home: 9409 W Nichols Dr Littleton CO 80123-5184 Office: K-G Retail Stores Inc 2 Denver Highlands 10065 E Harvard Ave Ste 700 Littleton CO 80231

EVANS, PAUL VERNON, lawyer; b. Colorado Springs, Colo., June 19, 1926; s. Fred Harrison and Emma Hooper (Austin) E.; m. Frances Irene Pool, Sept. 7, 1947 (div. Jan. 1964); m. Patricia Gwyn Davis, July 27, 1964; children—Bruce, Paula, Mike, Mark, Paul. B.A. cum laude, Colo. Coll., 1953; J.D., Duke U., 1956. Bar: Colo. 1956, U.S. Dist. Ct. Colo. 1956, U.S. Supreme Ct. 1971, U.S. Ct. Appeals (10th cir.) 1974. Field mgr. Keystone Readers Service, Dallas, 1946-50; sole practice, Colorado Springs, 1956-60; ptnr. Goodbar, Evans & Goodbar, 1960-63; sr. ptnr. Evans & Briggs Attys., Colorado Springs, 1963—; city atty. City of Fountain, Colo., 1958-62, City of Woodland Park, Colo., 1962-78; atty. Rock Creek Mesa Water Dist., Colorado Springs, 1963—. Author instruction materials. Precinct com. man Republican Com., Colorado Springs, 1956-72. Served with USNR, 1944-46, PTO. Recipient Jr. C. of C. Outstanding Achievement award, 1957. Mem. Colo. Mining Assn., Am. Jud. Soc., ABA, Colo. Bar Assn. (com. chmn. 1966-67, 84), El Paso County Bar Assn. (com. chmn. 1956—), Assn. Trial Lawyers Am., Colo. and Local Trial Lawyers, Tau Kappa Alpha (pres.), Phi Beta Kappa. Republican. Club: Optimist (pres. 1966-67). Home: 244 Cobblestone Dr Colorado Springs CO 80906-7624 Office: Evans & Briggs 532 S Weber St Colorado Springs CO 80903-3942

EVANS, PAULINE D., physicist, educator; b. Bklyn., Mar. 24, 1922; d. John A. and Hannah (Brandt) Davidson; m. Melbourne Griffith Evans, Sept. 6, 1950; children: Lynn Janet Evans Hannemann, Brian Griffith. BA, Hofstra Coll., 1942; postgrad., NYU, 1943, 46-47, Cornell U., 1946, Syracuse U., 1947-50. Jr. physicist Signal Corps Ground Signal Svc., Eatontown, N.J., 1942-43; physicist Kellex Corp. (Manhattan Project), N.Y.C., 1944; faculty dept. physics Queens Coll., N.Y.C., 1944-47; teaching asst. Syracuse U., 1947-50; instr. Wheaton Coll., Norton, Mass., 1952; physicist Nat. Bur. Standards, Washington, 1954-55; instr. physics U. Ala., 1955, U. N.Mex., 1955, 57-58; staff mem. Sandia Corp., Albuquerque, 1956-57; physicist Naval Nuclear Ordnance Evaluation Unit, Kirtland AFB, N.Mex., 1958-60; programmer Teaching Machines, Inc., Albuquerque, 1961; mem. faculty dept. physics Coll. St. Joseph on the Rio Grande (name changed to U. Albuquerque 1966), 1961—, assoc. prof., 1965—, chmn. dept., 1961—. Mem. AAUP, Am. Phys. Soc., Am. Assn. Physics Tchrs., Fedn. Am. Scientists, Sigma Pi Sigma, Sigma Delta Epsilon. Achievements include patents on mechanical method of conical scanning (radar), fluorine trap and primary standard for humidity measurement Home: 730 Loma Alta Ct NW Albuquerque NM 87105-1220 Office: U Albuquerque Dept Physics Albuquerque NM 87140

EVANS, RANDALL DAVID, radio engineering director; b. Casper, Wyo., Sept. 1, 1951; s. Jack Conrad Evans and Emma Jean (Wunder) Rapack; m. Brenda Novotny Evans, Apr. 11, 1981. Cert. electronics comm. technician, Navy ETA and ETC Schs., Great Lakes, Ill., 1969-71. Sr. field engr. Burroughs, Casper, 1976-77; regional technician Go Wireline Svcs., Casper, 1977-79; pres., gen. mgr. Best Impressions, Inc., Casper, 1979-87; chief engr. Sta. KTWO-AM, KMGW-FM, Casper, 1987—, dir engring., 1987—; operational area chair Wyo. State Emergency Comm. Com., Casper, 1990—, state chair, 1992—; chair Casper Emergency Broadcast System, 1990—. With USN, 1969-75. Recipient Achievement award Nat. Emergency Tng. Ctr., Fed. Emergency Mgmt. Agy., 1992. Republican. Methodist. Office: Sta KTWO 150 N Nichols Casper WY 82601

EVANS, RICHARD LLOYD, financial services company executive; b. Seattle, Oct. 16, 1935; s. Lloyd Herman and Dorleska L. (Rotta) E.; m. Judith Anne Sahlberg, Dec. 20, 1958; children: Dallas J., Douglas L., Daniel A., Marjorie A., Rebecca M. BA in Bus. Adminstrn., U. Wash., 1957. CLU; chartered fin. cons. Agt. Phoenix Mut. Life Ins. Co., Seattle, 1960-69; pres. R.L. Evans Co. Inc., Seattle, 1969—, mng. prin.; speaker on ins. and fin. planning to numerous orgns., 1975—. Mem. exec. bd. Chief Seattle coun. Boy Scouts Am., 1976—; chmn. N.W. Theol. Union, Seattle, 1984-88. Lt. USN, 1957-59. Recipient award of merit Chief Seattle coun. Boy Scouts Am., 1984. Mem. Am. Soc. CLU, Am. Soc. Chartered Fin. Cons., Nat. Assn. Life Underwriters, Wash. State Assn. Life Underwriters (bd. dirs. 1973-79, pres. 1977-78), Seattle Assn. Life Underwriters (v.p. 1972-73), Assn. Advanced Underwriting, Million Dollar Round Table, Estate Planning Coun. Seattle, Rainier Club, Masons, Rotary (dir.). Republican. Presbyterian. Home: 4001 Hunts Point Rd Bellevue WA 98004 Office: 1210 Plaza 600 Bldg Seattle WA 98101

EVANS, ROBERT DARYLD, air force officer; b. San Francisco, Feb. 9, 1962; s. Thomas Oscar and Marilyn Mae (Colony) E.; m. Suzanne Elizabeth Waldo, Aug. 16, 1986; 1 child, Trevor Thomas. BS in Mech. Engring. Tech., Calif. State U., Sacramento, 1986; MS in Computer Info. Systems, Boston U., 1991. Commd. 2d lt. USAF, 1986, advanced through grades to capt., 1990; instr., weapon systems officer, weapons and tactics officer 48th Fighter Wing, Lakenheath, Eng., 1988-91; instr., nav. 455 Flying Tng. Squadron, Mather AFB, Calif., 1991-92; weapon systems officer 461 Fighter Squadron, Luke AFB, Ariz., 1992, 391 Fighter Squadron, Mountain Home (Idaho) AFB, 1992—. Decorated Air medal with 3 oak leaf clusters. Mem. Air Force Assn. (life), Aircraft Owners and Pilots Assn., Assn. for Computing Machinery. Republican.

EVANS, ROBERT JOHN, retired biochemistry educator, researcher; b. Logan, UT, Mar. 18, 1909; s. Robert James and Alice Hazel (Stallings) E.; m. Alice Pugmire, Aug. 14, 1941 (dec.); children: Patricia Alice Evans Leavitt, Robert P. Student, Brigham Young U., 1929; BS, Utah State U., 1934, MS, 1936; PhD, U. Wisc., 1939. Instr. Carbon Coll., Price, UT, 1939-40; assoc. chemist Washington Agrl. Expt. Sta., Pullman, Wash., 1940-47; prof. Biochemistry Mich. State U., East Lansing, Mich., 1947-77; prof. emeritus Mich. State U., East Lansing, 1977—; vis. prof. Cambridge U., England, 1963-64, U. Edinburgh, Scotland, U. Coll. London, England, 1971, Rowett Rsch. Inst., Aberdeen, Scotland, 1971, Cambridge U., 1971. Contbr. articles to profl. jours. Active Boy Scouts Am., East Lansing, PTA, Lansing, Mich., Citizens Mich., Lansing. Recipient Rsch. Achievement award Poultry and Egg Nat. Bd., 1958, rsch. grants Nat. Inst. Health, 1963-75. Fellow Am. Assn. Advancement Sci.; mem Am. Chem. Soc., Am. Inst. Nutrition., Poultry Sci. Assn. Mem. LDS Ch. Home: 760 Polk Ave Ogden UT 84404-5255

EVANS, ROBERT VINCENT, engineering executive; b. Mobile, Ala., Sept. 21, 1958; s. William Alexander Evans and Katherine Barbara (Doerr) Davidson; m. Debra Marie Winters, July 27, 1984; children: James Vernon, Chelsea Marie. BS in Computer Info. Systems, Regis U., Denver, 1987, BS in Tech. Mgmt., 1987. Electrician Climax (Colo.) Molybdenum Co., 1978-82; applications engr. Honeywell, Inc., Englewood, Colo., 1982-83, sales engr., 1983-87; systems engr. Apple Computer, Inc., Seattle, 1987-88; regional systems engring. mgr. Apple Computer, Inc., Portland, Oreg., 1988—. Author: Anthology of American Poets, 1981. Dir. Operation Lookout, Seattle, 1989; mem. Rep. Nat. Com. Recipient USMC Blues award, Marine Corps Assn. Leatheanger award, 1977, Denver Post Outstanding Svc. award, 1983, N.Y. Zool. Soc. Hon. medal. Mem. Am. Mgmt. Assn., Mensa. Republican. Mem. Vineyard Ch. Office: Apple Computer Inc 10210 NE Points Dr Ste 310 Kirkland WA 98033

EVANS, RONALD ALLEN, lodging chain executive; b. Louisville, Apr. 5, 1940; s. William Francis and Helen Maxine (Hart) E.; m. Lynne Anne Ingraham, Aug. 25, 1979; children: Nicole Louise, Michele Lynne, Christopher Hart. B.S. in Mgmt., Ariz. State U., 1963. Vice pres. Electronic Data Systems, Dallas, 1969-73; vice pres. First Fed. Savs., Phoenix, 1973-77, Community Fin. Corp., Scottsdale, Ariz., 1977-78; pres. Evans Mgmt. Services, Inc., Phoenix, 1978-84; pres., CEO Best Western Internat., Inc., Phoenix, 1979—. Served to lt. USNR, 1963-66. Decorated Bronze Star. Republican. Episcopalian. Lodges: Masons (32 deg.), KT, Shriner. Office: Best Western Internat Inc PO Box 10203 Phoenix AZ 85064-0203

EVANS, STEPHEN ARTER, aerospace executive; b. Phila., Aug. 17, 1941; s. Stephen Arter and Ethel Rae (Reed) E.; m. Sheila Marie Maloney, July 8, 1963; children: Jane-Marie Evans Bilman, Diana Lynne. SB, MIT, 1963, SM, 1965; ME, UCLA, 1972. Rsch. engr. Rocketdyne div. Rockwell Internat., Canoga Park, Calif., 1965-75, program mgr., 1975-80, dir. new bus., 1980-90, dir. advanced tech., 1990—; advisor Space Sci. and Tech. Adv. Com., Washington, 1985-92, Propulsion Engring. Rsch. Ctr., State College, Pa., 1985—, Space Propulsion Synergy Group, Washington, 1990—, AIA Tech. for 90's, Washington, 1985-90. Author manuals, publs. in field. Vice chmn. MIT Ednl. Coun.-L.A., 1980—. Oak Ridge Inst. Nuclear Studies fellow, 1963. Mem. AIAA, Nat. Space Soc., Santa Monica Yacht Club. Office: Rocketdyne div Rockwell Int 6633 Canoga Ave Canoga Park CA 91303

EVANS, THOMAS DOWLING, hotel executive; b. Cleve., May 12, 1942; s. John Eugene and Charlotte Pauline (Dowling) E.; m. Kathleen Diane Torrez, Aug. 31, 1952; children: Mary Elizabeth, Jennifer Suzanne. BS, Calif. Polytech., 1969. Employment mgr. ALCOA, Corona, Calif., 1970-71; v.p., dir. human resources So. Calif. 1st Bank, San Diego, 1971-72; sr. v.p. human resources Gt. Am. Savings Bank, San Diego, 1972-78; sr. v.p. adminstrn. Watt Industries, Santa Monica, Calif., 1978-85, Am. Diversified Cos., Costa Mesa, Calif., 1985-87; pres., CEO TDE Enterprises, Costa Mesa, 1987-89; pres., CEO Vagabond Inns, Inc., San Diego, 1989—, bd. dirs. Exec. com. Children's Hosp., San Diego, 1992—. Mem. Am. Hotel and Motel Assn.(pres.'s acad. ednl. found., cert. hotel administr.), Calif. Hotel and Motel Assn. (bd. dirs. 1989—), San Diego C. of C. Republican. Roman Catholic. Office: The Vagabond Inns 9605 Scranton Dr San Diego CA 92121

EVANS, THOMAS EDGAR, JR., title insurance agency executive; b. Toronto, Ohio, Apr. 17, 1940; s. Thomas Edgar and Sarah Ellen (Bauer) E.; BA, Mt. Union Coll., 1963; m. Cynthia Lee Johnson, Feb. 23; children: Thomas Edgar, Douglas, Melinda, Jennifer. Tchr. Lodi, Ohio, 1963-64; salesman Simpson-Evans Realty, Steubenville, Ohio, 1964-65, Shadron Realty, Tucson, 1965-67; real estate broker, co-owner Double E Realty, Tucson, 1967-69; escrow officer, br. mgr., asst. county mgr., v.p. Ariz. Title Ins., Tucson, 1969-80; pres. Commonwealth Land Title Agy., Tucson, 1980-82, also dir.; pres. Fidelity Nat. Title Agy., 1982-90; bd. govs. Calif. Land Title Assn., 1990—; exec. v.p. Fidelity Nat. Title Ins. Co., 1990-92; v.p. Inland Empire Divsn. Fidelity Nat. Title, 1992—; bd. dirs. Western Fin. Trust Co., Fidelity Nat. Fin. Inc., Fidelity Nat. Title Ins. Co., Fidelity Nat. Title Agy. Pinal, The Griffin Co.; bd. dirs., chmn. bd. Cochise Title Agy., TIPCO; v.p., dir. A.P.C. Corp. Named Boss of Year, El Chaparral chpt. Am. Bus. Women's Assn., 1977. Mem. So. Ariz. Escrow Assn., So. Ariz. Mortgage Bankers Assn. (bd. dirs. 1982-85), Ariz. Mktg. Bankers Assn., Old Pueblo Businessmen's Assn. Tucson, Tucson Bd. Realtors, Ariz. Assn. Real Estate Exchangors (bd. dirs. 1968-69), Land Title Assn. Ariz. (pres. 1984), So. Ariz. Homebuilders Assn., Blue Key, Sigma Nu. Republican. Methodist. Clubs: Old Pueblo Courthouse, La Paloma, Ventana Country, Centre Court, Elks, Pima Jaycees (dir. 1966), Sertoma (charter pres., chmn. bd. Midtown sect. 1968-70); Tucson Real Estate Exchangors (pres. 1968); Sunrise Rotary; Old Pueblo. Home: 28861 Glen Ridge Mission Viejo CA 92692 Office: 2100 Main St Ste 400 Irvine CA 92714-6240

EVANS, TIMOTHY MONROE, natural resource company executive; b. Vallejo, Calif., July 3, 1945; s. Wayne Ross and Delphine (Rodgers) E.; m. Clarisse Ann Kulievan, Feb. 27, 1970; children: Wayne Ross II, Peter Monroe. Title officer Title Ins. and Trust Co., Santa Rosa, Calif., 1963-71; mgr. lands Pacific Energy Corp., Santa Rosa, Calif., 1971-73; v.p., land Republic Geothermal, Inc., Santa Fe Springs, Calif., 1973-85, chmn., chief exec. officer, 1985—. Mem. Am. Assn. Profl. Landmen. Republican. Office: Rep Geothermal Inc 11823 E Slauson Ave Ste 5 Santa Fe Springs CA 90670

EVANS, WILLIAM NEAL, pediatric cardiologist; b. Bakersfield, Calif., Aug. 14, 1950; s. William Ed and June Marie (Anderson) E.; m. Stefani Broudy, Aug. 28, 1977; children: Adrianna, Erica. BS cum laude, U. Calif., Irvine, 1972; MD, U. Calif., 1976. Diplomate Am. Bd. Pediatrics. Intern Children's Hosp. L.A., 1976-77, resident, 1977-78, pediatric cardiology fellow, 1978-80; owner Pediatric Cardiovascular Cons., Las Vegas, 1980—; asst. clin. prof. pediatrics U. Nev. Sch. Medicine, 1980—, UCLA, 1980—; chief pediatrics Humana Hosp. Sunrise, 1987-89; mem. staff Univ. Med. Ctr. So. Nev., Women's Hosp. Las Vegas, Valley Hosp. Bd. dirs. Discovery, The Children's Mus. Fellow Am. Acad. Pediatrics, Am. Coll. Cardiology, Las Vegas Pediatric Soc. (pres., founder), Nev. State Med. Soc., Clark County Med. Soc., Alpha Omega Alpha. Presbyterian.

EVANS, WILLIAM THOMAS, physician; b. Denver, Aug. 21, 1941; s. Alfred Lincoln and Marian Audrey (Biggs) E.; m. Lucy Fales. BA, U. Colo., 1963; MD, Baylor U., 1967; grad., Chinese Coll. U.K.; Licentiate Acupuncture, Oxford, Eng., 1976. Intern Mary Fletcher Hosp., Burlington, Vt., 1967; physician Villages of Kodiak Island and Lake Iliamna, 1968-70; founder, dir. emergency dept. St. Elizabeth Hosp., Yakima, Wash., 1970-75; practice medicine specializing prevention and conservative treatment of spine injuries Denver; founder, dir. Colo. Back Sch., Denver, 1979-89; assoc. med. dir. Ctr. for Spine Rehab., 1989—. Dir. Colo. High Sch. Think First Program for Prevention of Head and Spinal Cord Injuries; Friends of Earth del. Limits to Medicine Congress, 1975; initiator Colo. Sun Day, 1978. Lt. comdr. Indian Health Svc., USPHS, 1968-70. Mem. Rocky Mountain Traumatological Soc. (pres.), Arapahoe County Med. Soc., Colo. Med. Soc. (workmen's compensation com.), N.Am. Spine Soc., Am. Coll. Occupational Medicine Asns., Rocky Mountain Acad. Occupational Medicine (past pres.), AMA, Am. Coll. Sports Medicine, Traditional Acupuncture Soc. Home: PO Box 174 Littleton CO 80160-0174 Office: 125 E Hampden Ave Englewood CO 80110-2546

EVANS LE BLANC, CANDACE KAY, bank executive; b. Shafter, Calif., Sept. 22, 1958; d. Reeves Robert and Margaret (Hildebrand) Evans; m. Richard Francis Le Blanc, June 5, 1982, (div.); 1 child, Courtney Rae. BS in Pub. Adminstrn., U. So. Calif., L.A., 1980. Feature writer Sierra Madre (Calif.) News, 1974-77; with U. So. Calif., 1979-84, asst. to dir. News Svc., 1981-82, sr. bus. adminstr. Sch. Fine Arts, 1982-84; bus. banking officer Bank of Am., N.T. & S.A., Commerce, Calif., 1984-87, asst. v.p., team leader, 1987-89, v.p., 1989-91; v.p., comml. real estate developer lending Bank of Am., L.A., 1991-92; v.p., exec. credit adminstr. BOFA, Oreg., 1992—; mentor devel. program Bank of Am., L.A., 1985—, mentee, 1987-89. Republican. Congregationalist.

EVELAND, LAVERNE KENT, microbiology educator; b. Waverly, Iowa, Oct. 7, 1940; s. Carlton Derald and Grace Johanna (Harris) E. BS, State U. Iowa, 1964; MS, U. Iowa, 1968, PhD, 1968. Instr. SUNY-Downstate Med. Ctr., Bklyn., 1968-70, asst. prof., 1971-75, assoc. prof., 1976-82, dir. clin. parasitology, 1973-84, prof., 1983-84; dir. clin. immunology King's County Hosp., Bklyn., 1979-84; prof. and chmn. microbiology Calif. State U., Long Beach, 1984—. Editor Am. Soc. Parasitologists Newsletter, 1981-91; editorial bd. Exptl. Parasitology, 1978—; contbr. articles to profl. jours. Grantee Rockefeller Found., 1973-76, Edna McConnell Clark Found., 1977-80, NIH/NIAID, 1981-84. Fellow Am. Acad. Microbiology, Royal Soc. Tropical Medicine and Hygiene; mem. Am. Soc. Microbiology, Am. Soc. Parasitology, Helminthological Soc. of Washington, N.Y. Soc. Tropical Medicine, So. Calif. Soc. Parasitologists, Sigma Xi (chpt. pres. 1989-91). Office: Calif State Univ 1250 Bellflower Blvd Long Beach CA 90840

EVENSON, S. JEANNE, small business owner; b. Wheeler County, Tex., Oct. 17, 1938; d. Glynn Edward and LaVerne (Bailey) Pugh; m. A. Berniel Evenson, May 31, 1957; children: Tara Jean Harper, Troy Berniel. BA in Secondary Edn., Coll. Great Falls, 1972. Tchr. East Jr. High Sch., Great Falls, 1972-78; owner, operator Cattail Lawn Svc., Great Falls, 1976-80, B-J Pac-A-Part, Great Falls, 1976—. Methodist. Home: 410-25 Avenue S Great Falls MT 59405

EVERDING, ROBERT GEORGE, humanities educator, dean; b. St. Louis, Apr. 25, 1945; s. R.G. and Elizabeth Jane (Lehman) E.; m. Sarah Page Monroe, June 1, 1968; children: Brian, Julia. BA, U. Mo., 1967; MA, U. Minn., 1969, Stanford U., 1972; PhD, Stanford U., 1976. Cert. secondary tchr., Mo., Calif. Dir., prof. Sch. of Humanities and Arts U. Houston, Clear Lake, Tex., 1976-84; dir. Sch. of Art and Architecture U. Southwestern La., Lafayette, 1984-88; dean, prof. Coll. Visual and Performing Arts Humboldt State U., Arcata, Calif., 1988-91, prin. investigator Redwood Arts Project, 1991—, dir., 1992—; artistic dir. Houston Shaw Festival, Houston, 1978-84; reviewer U. Mo., Kansas City, 1987; outside reviewer Kalyani U., West Bengal, India, 1989—. Contbr. articles to profl. jours. Mem. Mayor's Blue Ribbon Task Force on Arts, Lafayette, 1986; bd. dirs. Humboldt Arts Coun., Eureka, Calif.,1 988-91; reviewer Design Assistance Com. City of Arcata, 1988—, chair, 1991—. Mem. Internat. Coun. Fine Arts Deans, Coun. Arts and Sci. Deans, Acadiana Arts Coun. (chmn., bd. dirs., chmn. arts-in-edn. com. 1987-88), Off Main St. Theatre (bd. dirs., v.p.), Bernard Shaw Soc., Stanford Alumni Club, Phi Beta Kappa Soc., Phi Kappa Phi (sec.), Omicron Delta Kappa. Home: 2711 Hilltop Ct Arcata CA 95521-5220 Office: Humboldt State U Theater Arts Dept Arcata CA 95521

EVERETT, EUGENIA ZINK, sculptor, educator; b. Loveland, Colo., Nov. 11, 1908; d. Charles Henry and Ruby Olivia (Giddings) Zink; m. Richard Henry Everett, Apr. 2, 1932 (dec. Dec. 1975); children: Jane Carolyn, Fredric Richard. AB, Mt. St. Mary's, L.A., 1929; grad., Claremont Coll., 1958-59; postgrad., Am. U., 1960. Sculptor WPA - FAP, Calif., 1934-38; tchr. Ventura (Calif.) Coll., 1960-69, Sedona (Ariz.) Art Ctr., 1971-92; Author: (poems) Between Silences, 1990. Mem. Internat. Friends Transformative Art, Audubon Soc., Nature Conservancy, Sedona Art Ctr., Sierra Club. Home: 170 Navajo Trail Sedona AZ 86336

EVERETT, HOBART RAY, JR., engineer, naval officer, consultant, researcher, inventor; b. Charleston, S.C., Nov. 29, 1949; s. Hobart Ray and Ruth (Humphreys) E.; m. Rachael Patricia Lewis, Dec. 30, 1971; children: Todd Ashley, Rebecca Nicole. BEE, Ga. Inst. Tech., 1973; MS in Mech. Engring., Naval Postgrad. Sch., 1982. Commd. ensign U.S. Navy, 1973, advanced through grades to comdr., 1988; asst. engr. USS Nitro, 1975-77; engring. recruiter for officer programs, Montgomery, Ala., 1977-80; robotics coordinator Naval Sea Systems Command, Washington, 1983-84, dir. Office of Robotics and Autonomous Systems, 1984-86; autonomous systems project officer Naval Ocean Systems Ctr., San Diego, 1986-88, chief engr. USMC teleoperated vehicle program, 1988-89, assoc. div. head advanced systems div., 1988—; founder DoD Robotics and Artificial Intelligence Database; Navy rep. to tri-svc. Joint Tech. Panel for Robotics, 1984-86; guest lectr. in robotics U. Md., U. Pa., 1983-86, U. Calif., San Diego, 1988; robotics researcher Naval Ocean Systems Ctr., prin. tech. cons. U.S. Army Mobile Detection Assessment and Response System interior program, 1990-93; tech. dir. Joint Army-Navy Mobile Detection Assessment and Response System interior and exterior program, 1993—. Contbg. author Robotics Age mag., 1982-86, Sensors mag., 1987—; mem. editorial bd., contbg. author Robotics and Autonomous Systems mag.; contbr. 50 tech. publs.; inventor 1st autonomous sentry robot; patentee in field. Decorated Navy Commendation; recipient Naval Sea Systems Command award for Acad. Excellence, 1983, Woelful award for Acad. Excellence, Naval Sea Systems Command, 1983, Gen. Dynamics award for Acad. and Mil. Accomplishment, 1973. Mem. Soc. Mfg. Engrs. (sr.), Robotics Inst. Am., Nat. Svc. Robot Assn. (bd. dirs. 1991—), Sigma Xi. Office: Naval Command Control & Ocean Surveillance Ctr RDT & E Divsn Code 5303 53400 Woodward Rd San Diego CA 92152-7381

EVERETT, HOWARD CHESTON, civil engineer; b. Pelahatchee, Miss., Feb. 12, 1909; s. Looney Newton and Loretta Adela (Moore) E.; m. Maude Evelyn Rockefeller, May 29, 1929; 1 child, Howard Cheston (dec.). BSc in Civil Engring., U. Houston, 1950, postgrad., 1950-52; postgrad. U. Calif.-San Francisco, 1960-61, Coll. San Mateo, 1959-60, postgrad. Colo. Tech. Coll., 1987. Registered profl. engr. Tex., Calif., Colo. Numerous engring. positions with United Gas and other cos. in petroleum industry, Tex., La., 1928-45; asst. prof. civil engring. U. Houston, 1950-51; pres. Everett-Heinen Corp., Houston, 1948-50; pres. Fairfield Park Corp., Houston, 1951-52; chief draftsman, structural engr. Holly Sugar Corp., San Mateo, Calif. and Colorado Springs, Colo., 1955-74; chief engr. Schloss & Shubart, Denver, 1974-80; instr. engring. Menlo (Calif.) Coll., 1960-63; designer machinery for city water supply Schloss Engineered Machinery Co., 1986; cons. and lectr. in field. Mem. Colo. Soc. Profl. Engrs., Calif. Soc. Profl. Engrs., Masons, Shriners, Tau Beta Pi, Phi Kappa Phi.

EVERETT, JAMES JOSEPH, lawyer; b. San Antonio, May 7, 1955. BA, St. Mary's U., San Antonio, 1976; JD, Tex. So. U., 1980. Bar: U.S. Dist. Ct. Ariz. 1987, U.S. Tax Ct. 1980, U.S. Ct. Appeals (9th cir.) 1988. Sr. trial atty. IRS, Phoenix, 1980-87; ptnr. Brnilovich & Everett, Phoenix, 1987-89; of counsel Broadbent, Walker & Wales; pvt. practice Law Offices of James J. Everett, Phoenix, 1987—. Mem. ABA, Tex. Bar Assn., Ariz. Bar Assn., State Bar Ariz. (cert. tax specialist 1988—), Assn. Trial Lawyers Am., Maricopa County Bar Assn., Ariz. Tax Controversy Group, Valley Estate Planners (Phoenix), Cen. Ariz. Estate Planners. Office: 3101 N Central Ave Ste 1500 Phoenix AZ 85012-2638

EVERETT, PAMELA IRENE, legal management company executive, educator; b. L.A., Dec. 31, 1947; d. Richard Weldon and Alta Irene (Tuttle) Bunnell; m. James E. Everett, Sept. 2, 1967 (div. 1973); 1 child, Richard Earl. Cert. Paralegal, Rancho Santago Coll., Santa Ana, Calif., 1977; BA, Calif. State U.-Long Beach, 1985; MA, U. Redlands, 1988. Owner, mgr. Orange County Paralegal Svc., Santa Ana, 1979-85; pres. Gem Legal Mgmt. Inc., Fullerton, Calif., 1986—; co-owner Bunnell Pubs., Fullerton, Calif., 1992—, Edn. and Pub. Inc., Raleigh, N.C.; instr. Rancho Santiago Coll., 1979-90, chmn. adv. bd., 1980-85; instr. Coastline C.C., Costa Mesa, Calif.,

1980-82, Fullerton Coll., 1989—, Rio Hondo Coll., Whittier, Calif., 1992—; advisor Nat. Paralegal Assn., 1982—, Saddleback Coll., 1985—, North Orange County Regional Occupational Program, Fullerton, 1986—, So. Calif. Coll. of Bus. and Law, Pacific Coll. Bus.; bd. dirs. Nat. Profl. Legal Assts. Inc., editor PLA NEWS. Author: Legal Secretary Federal Litigation, 1986, Legal Secretary Bankruptcy, 1987, Going Independent-Business Planning Guide, Fundamentals of Law Office Management, 1993. Republican. Office: 406 N Adams Ave Fullerton CA 92632-1605

EVERETT, STEPHEN EDWARD, advertising and communications educator, researcher; b. Tulsa, Feb. 5, 1958; s. George A. and Sandra J. (Stephens) E.; m. Shu-Ling Chen, Apr. 7, 1988. PhD, U. Tenn., 1989. Announcer Sta. KWHO, Salt Lake City, 1977-78, Sta. WUOT U. Tenn., Knoxville, 1978-85; disk jockey Sta. WOKI, Oak Ridge, Tenn., 1978-82; program dir. Sta. WUAL, U. Ala., Tuscaloosa, 1983-84; account exec. Sta. WBMK, Knoxville, 1985; adminstrv. asst. U. Tenn., 1985-88; asst. prof. U. Colo., Boulder, 1988—; rsch. cons., Denver, 1988—, Colo. Alliance for Mentally Ill, 1990, Colo. Dept. of Revenue, 1992, office of contbns. United Ch. of Christ, Colo. Springs Gazette Telegraph and KOAA-TV opinion polls. Contbr. articles to profl. jours. Vol. rsch. cons. Mile High United Way, Denver, 1988. Mem. Am. Acad. Advt., Assn. Edn. Journalism & Mass Communication, Am. Assn. Pub. Opinion Rsch., Midwest Assn. Pub. Opinion Rsch. (exec. bd.). Home: 7441 Old Mill Trl Boulder CO 80301-3909 Offce: U Colo Journalism Mass Communication CB 287 Boulder CO 80309-0287

EVERHART, LEON EUGENE, retired air force officer; b. Abilene, Kans., Jan. 14, 1928; s. Charles Francis and Florence Etta (Amess) E. BS with distinction, Ariz. State U., 1957; postgrad., U. Tenn., 1965. Commd. 2d lt. USAF, 1952, advanced through grades to col., 1970, ops. officer Berlin Air Safety Ctr., 1961-63; project officer Missile Devel. Ctr. USAF, Holloman AFB, N.Mex., 1963-65, chief spl. projects div. Missile Devel. Ctr., 1965-66; tactical fighter pilot, flight commander USAF, South Vietnam, 1967-68; system program dir. Aero. Systems Div. USAF, Wright Patterson AFB, Ohio, 1968-72; dir. test engring. Devel. and Test Ctr. USAF, Eglin AFB, Fla., 1973-78; comdr. Air Force Western Test Range USAF, Vandenberg AFB, Calif., 1978-82; ret. USAF, 1982; cons. in field. Speaker on big-game hunting in Africa and wildlife conservation for various civic and ednl. orgns. Mem. Amateur Trapshooting Assn. Ohio, NRA. Home: 1285 Oak Knolls Rd Santa Maria CA 93455-4302

EVERHART, THOMAS EUGENE, university president, engineering educator; b. Kansas City, Mo., Feb. 15, 1932; s. William Elliott and Elizabeth Ann (West) E.; m. Doris Arleen Wentz, June 21, 1953; children—Janet Sue, Nancy Jean, David William, John Thomas. A.B. in Physics magna cum laude, Harvard, 1953; M.Sc., UCLA, 1955; Ph.D. in Engring., Cambridge U., Eng., 1958. Mem. tech. staff Hughes Research Labs., Culver City, Calif., 1953-55; mem. faculty U. Calif., Berkeley, 1958-78, prof. elec. engring. and computer scis., 1967-78, Miller research prof., 1969-70, chmn. dept., 1972-77; prof. elec. engring., Joseph Silbert dean engring. Cornell U., Ithaca, N.Y., 1979-84; prof. elec. and computer engring., chancellor U. Ill., Urbana-Champaign, 1984-87; prof. elec. engring. and applied physics, pres. Calif. Inst. Tech., Pasadena, 1987—; fellow scientist Westinghouse Rsch. Labs., Pitts., 1962-63; guest prof. Inst. Applied Physics, U. Tuebingen, Germany, 1966-67, Waseda U., Tokyo, Osaka U., 1974; vis. fellow Clare Hall, Cambridge, U., 1975; chmn. Electron, Ion and Photon Beam Symposium, 1977; cons. in field; mem. sci. and ednl. adv. com. Lawrence Berkeley Lab., 1978-85, chmn., 1980-85; mem. sci. adv. com. GM, 1980-89, chmn., 1984-89, bd. dirs., 1989—; bd. dirs. Hewlett Packard Corp., 1991—; tech. adv. com. R.R. Donnelly & Sons, 1981-89. NSF sr. fellow, 1966-67, Guggenheim fellow, 1974-75. Fellow IEEE, AAAS, Royal Acad. Engring.; mem. NAE (ednl. adv. bd. 1984-88, mem. com. 1984-89, chmn. 1988—, coun. 1988—), Microbeam Analysis Soc. Am., Electron Microscopy Soc. Am. (coun. 1970-72, pres. 1977), Coun. on Competitiveness (vice-chmn. 1990—), Assn. Marshall Scholars and Alumni (pres. 1965-68), Athenaeum Club, Sigma Xi, Eta Kappa Nu. Home: 415 S Hill Ave Pasadena CA 91106-3407 Office: Calif Inst Tech Office of Pres 1201 E California Blvd Pasadena CA 91125-0001

EVERINGHAM, HARRY TOWNER, editor, publisher; b. Memphis, Aug. 14, 1908; s. William Kirby and Ida Pauline (Towner) E.; m. Margaret Sophia Johnson, May 1, 1934; children: Martha Meister, Barbara Miller, Richard Kirby. Student, Christian Bros. Coll., Memphis, 1919-20, Northwestern U., Evanston, Ill., 1936-39, U. Chgo., 1940. Radio writer, producer Miles Lab., Chgo., 1934-35, Wade Advt. Agy., Chgo., 1934-35; v.p. Sehl Advt. Agy., Chgo., 1936-41; broadcasting Henry C. Lytton & Co., Chgo., 1936-41; film producer, lectr. Employers Assn., Chgo., 1942; pub. rels. dir. Ingalls-Shepard Div. Wyman Gordon Co., Harvey, Ill., 1943-45; editor, pub. The Fact Finder, Chgo., 1942-65, Phoenix, 1965-89, Scottsdale, Ariz., 1989—; Founder, pres. We, the People - United, 1978—. Editor, pub. U.S.A.-Beyond the Crossroads, Chgo., 1952, The Am. Patriot, 1959—. Vice pres. Greater Chgo. Churchmen, 1946-47. Mem. Publicity Club Chgo. (founder 1942), Ariz. Breakfast Club (pres., founder Phoenix 1969—). Republican. Office: We the People UNITED Box A Scottsdale AZ 85252

EVERITT, CHERYL ANNE, marketing professional; b. Colon, Panama, Nov. 16, 1948; came to the U.S., 1950; d. Marvin Lee Salmon and Mary Ellen (Bennett) Wenzlick; m. William M. Everitt, Dec. 30, 1972. BA, U. Md., 1976; legal asst., El Paso Community Coll., 1978; MBA, U. Colo., 1988. Product analyst Shepard's/McGraw Hill, Colorado Springs, 1984-86, product mgr., 1986-87, sr. product mgr., 1986-87, mgr. products mgmt., 1987-90, market mgr. electronic pub., 1990-92, market mgr. topical pub., 1992—; guest lectr. U. Colo., Colorado Springs, 1988-90; mktg. cons., 1989—. Mem. Am. Mktg. Assn. Republican. Methodist. Home: 17055 W Goshawk Rd Colorado Springs CO 80908

EVERT, JOHN ANDREW, JR., surgeon; b. Brainerd, Minn., Oct. 31, 1917; s. John A. and Pearl Alma (Nash) E.; m. Nora Staael, May 10, 1980. BS, Haverford (Pa.) Coll., 1938; MD, Harvard U., 1942; MS in Surgery, U. Minn., 1946. Diplomate Am. Bd. Surgery. Pvt. practice surgery St. Paul, 1947-53, Missoula, Mont., 1955—; dir. Health Svc. Assn., St. Paul, 1975-90. Chmn. Montpac, Mont., 1962-64.Capt. U.S. Army 1953-55. Fellow in Surgery Mayo Found., Rochester, N.Y., 1943-46. Fellow ACS; mem. Am. Soc. Colon and Rectal Surgeons (assoc. fellow), Western Mont. Med. Soc. Home: 1925 Alvina Dr Missoula MT 59802 Office: 900 N Orange St Missoula MT 59802

EVETT, MALCOLM, chemistry educator; b. Chgo., June 20, 1942; s. Arthur Floyd and Esther (Mann) E. BS, U. Ill., 1964; PhD, U. Calif., Berkeley, 1968. Postdoctoral fellow U. Alta., Can., 1968-70; chemistry researcher U. Calif., 1971-76; cons. Airesearch, 1976—; instr. San Jose (Calif.) City Coll., 1991—. Mem. AAAS, ASHRAE, Phi Beta Kappa, Phi Kappa Phi.

EVRIGENIS, JOHN BASIL, obstetrician-gynecologist; b. Athens, Greece, Feb. 23, 1929; came to U.S., 1951; s. Basil I. and Maria (Soteriou) E.; m. Sophia M. Goritsan, June 22, 1952; children: Maryellen, E. Debbie, W. Gregory, John Jr. BA, U. Athens, 1947, MD, 1951. Diplomate Am. Bd. Ob-Gyn. Intern Providence Hosp., Portland, Oreg., 1951-52, resident in gen. practice medicine, 1952-53; resident in ob-gyn Emanuel Hosp. and U. Oreg. Med. Sch., Portland, 1953-56; pvt. practice specializing in ob-gyn Sacramento, 1956—; assoc. clin. prof. ob-gyn Med. Sch., U. Calif., Davis, 1975—; chief ob-gyn dept. Mercy Hosp., Sacramento, 1972-73. Mem. AMA, Am. Fertility Soc., Pan-Am. Med. Soc., Royal Soc. Medicine, Royal Soc. Health, Sacramento County Med. Soc., Calif. Med. Assn., So. Calif. Ob-Gyn Assembly, Am. Soc. Gynecol. Laproscopists, Am. Soc. Abdominal Surgeons, No. Calif. Ob-Gyn Soc. (pres. 1975-76), Dynamis Club, Ahepa, Del Paso Country Club, Northridge Country Club, Sutter Club, Sacramento Club, Lions, Elks, Masons. Eastern Orthodox. Home: 3615 Winding Creek Rd Sacramento CA 95864 Office: 3939 J St # 360 Sacramento CA 91819

EWBANK, HENRY LEE, communication educator; b. Albion, Mich., Mar. 26, 1924; s. Henry Lee Sr. and Rachel Angelique (Belt) E.; m. Jane Brickbauer, Jan. 15, 1948 (div. 1972); children: Kimberley, S. Heller, Mark Michael; m. Barbara Ann Harris, Dec. 24, 1972. AB, U. Wis., 1947, AM, 1948, PhD, 1952. Instr. U. Wis., Milw., 1947-49; instr., dir. forensics U. Hawaii, Honolulu, 1949-51; asst. prof., dir. forensics Ea. Ill. State Coll., Charleston, 1951-53; from asst. prof. to prof. comm. Purdue U., West Lafayette, Ind., 1953-78; prof. comm. U. Ariz., Tucson, 1978—; vis. assoc. prof. U. Hawaii, Honolulu, 1963-64; asst. to dir. coop. ext. Purdue U., West Lafayette, 1967-73. Author: Meeting Management, 1968; editor (newsletter) CAPP News, 1976-88, (ann. rsch. vol.) Free Speech Yearbook, 1982-85; contbr. over 30 articles to profl. jours. Mem. exec. com., moderator Off the Record debate soc., Tucson, 1988—; moderator Continental Comment, PBS, West Lafayette, 1968-71. With USNR, 1943-46. Mem. AAUP (pres. Purdue chpt. 1961-63, pres. Ind. Conf. 1963, pres. Ariz. chpt. 1986-89, mem. nat. coun. 1967-70), Delta Sigma Rho, Phi Kappa Phi. Office: Dept Comm U Ariz Tucson AZ 85721

EWELL, MIRANDA JUAN, journalist; b. Beijing, Apr. 25, 1948; d. Vei-Chow and Hsien-fang Yolanda (Sun) J.; m. John Woodruff Ewell Jr., Feb. 20, 1971; children: Emily, David, Jonah. BA summa cum laude, Smith Coll., 1969; postgrad., Princeton U., 1971, U. Calif., Berkeley, 1981-82. Staff writer The Montclarion, Oakland, Calif., 1982-83, San Jose (Calif.) Mercury News, 1984—. Recipient Elsa Knight Thompson award Media Alliance, San Francisco, 1984, George Polk award L.I. U., N.Y., 1989, Heywood Brown award Newspaper Guild, Washington, 1989. Mem. Asian-Am. Journalists Assn.

EWELL, P. LAMONT, fire department chief. Fire chief Oakland (Calif.) Fire Dept. Office: Oakland Fire Dept 1605 Martin Luther King Jr Way Oakland CA 94612*

EWERS, ANNE, opera company director. Gen. dir. Boston Lyric Opera, 1984-89, Utah Opera, Salt Lake City, 1990—; panelist Nat. Endowment for Arts; freelance stage dir. San Francisco Opera, N.Y.C. Opera, Can. Opera Co., Minn. Opera, Vancouver Opera, numerous others. Dir. nearly fifty opera prodns. including La Giaconda, Un Ballo in Maschera, La Rondine, The Merry Widow, Ring Cycle, Salome, Dialogues des Carmelites, Eugene Onegin; dir. Dame Joan Sutherland's North American Farewell, Dallas Opera. Bd. dirs. Opera Am., 1993—. Office: Utah Opera 50 W 2d St Salt Lake City UT 84101

EWERT, ALAN, government official; b. Wausau, Wis., Nov. 22, 1949; s. Walter Arthur and Florence Ann (Allen) E.; m. Alison Voight, Aug. 17, 1984; children: Alyssa, Alanna. BS, U. Wis., Stevens Point, 1972; MS, Ea. Wash. U., Cheney, 1977; PhD, U. Oreg., 1982. Asst. prof. Ohio State U., Columbus, 1984-86; dir. profl. devel. Outward Bound, Santa Monica, Calif., 1986-87; supervisory rsch. scientist forest svc. USDA, Riverside, Calif., 1987-90, br. chief recreation, wilderness, forestry rsch., forest svc., 1990—; asst. prof. Appalachian State U., Boone, N.C., 1983; survival instr. USAF, 1973-77. Author: Outdoor Adventure Pursuits: Theories and Models, 1989. Mem. Moreno Valley (Calif.) Multi-Use Trails Com., 1990—. With USAF, 1973-77. Decorated Air medal. Mem. Soc. of Rsch. Adminstrs., Am. Alpine Club, Nat. Recreation and Park Assn., Sierra Club. Office: USDA Forest Svc 14th and Independence Ave SW Washington DC 20250

EWING, DEAN EDGAR, veterinarian; b. Ft. Wayne, Ind., Aug. 15, 1932; s. Theodore Harris and Mildred Wavel (Hennon) E. BS, Mich. State U., 1954, DVM, 1956; MS, U. Rochester, 1962; diploma, U. So. Calif., 1973. Lic. veterinarian, Colo., Oreg., Calif. Veterinarian Dept. Agr., Calif., 1956-58; commd. 1st lt. USAF Vet. Corp., 1958, advanced through grades to lt. col., 1971, retired, 1979; prop. Vet. Housecall Svc., San Diego, 1979—, The Bird Doctor, San Diego, 1981—, Birdlife Products, San Diego, 1981—, Bird Ctr./Morena Pet Hosp., San Diego, 1986-89; dir. Ctr. for Care and Study of Birds, Manitou Springs, Colo., 1986—; cons. Birdworks, Jamul, Calif., 1989—; chmn. vet. and animal care seminars, San Diego, 1981-84. Chmn. Symposium on Sci., Philosophy and Religion, Albuquerque, 1967, 70, also several conservation groups, 1965, 80. Fellow Explorers Club; mem. Assn. Avian Veterinarians (exec. bd. 1981-83), Am. Vet. Med. Assn., San Diego Vet. Med. Assn. (bd. dirs. 1984-88), Calif. Vet. Med. Assn., Am. Fedn. Aviculture. Home and Office: 5128 Neeper Valley Rd Manitou Springs CO 80829

EWING, JACK ROBERT, accountant; b. San Francisco, Feb. 14, 1947; s. Robert Maxwell and Blanche Julia (Diak) E.; m. Joan Marie Coughlin Ewing, Nov. 25, 1967; children: Theresa Marie Ewing, Christina Ann Ewing. BS, U. Mo., 1969. CPA. Staff acct. Fox & Co., St. Louis, 1969-70; radio station opr. USAF, Mountain Home, Idaho, 1970-72; internal auditor Air Force Audit Agy., Warren, Wyo., 1972-74; supr. auditor Fox & Co., St. Louis, 1974-79; audit mgr. Erickson, Hunt & Spillman, P.C., Ft. Collins, Colo., 1979-82; stockholder, owner Hunt, Spillman & Ewing, P.C., Ft. Collins, Colo., 1982-93. Mem., pres. Parent Adv. Bd., Beattie Elem. Sch., 1982-83, 86-87; mem. Entrepreneur of Yr. Selection Com., Ft. Collins, Colo., 1989-92, Suicide Task Force Larimer County, Ft. Collins, Colo., 1992, bd. dirs.; mem. Leadership Ft. Collins-Class of 1992; dir. treas. One West Contemporary Art Ctr., 1989—, Ctr. for Diversity in Work Place, 1991—; adv. bd. Larimer County Mental Health Ctr., 1992. Mem. Am. Inst. CPAs, Colo. Soc. CPAs, Eye Openers Kiwanis Club. Office: 3112 Meadowlark Ave Fort Collins CO 80526

EWING, RICHARD EDWARD, mathematics, chemical and petroleum engineering educator; b. Kingsville, Tex., Nov. 24, 1946; s. Floyd Ford and Olivia Clara (Henrichson) E.; m. Rita Louise Williams, Aug. 8, 1970; children: John Edward, Lawrence Alan, Bradley William. BA, U. Tex., 1969, MA, 1972, PhD, 1974. Asst. prof. Oakland U., Rochester, Mich., 1974-77; asst. prof. Ohio State U., Columbus, 1977-80, assoc. prof., 1980-81; sr. rsch. mathematician Mobil R & D Corp., Dallas, 1980-82, assoc. mathematician, 1982-83; prof. math., petroleum and chem. engring. U. Wyo., Laramie, 1983-92, J.E. Warren dist. prof. energy and environ., 1984-92, dir. Enhanced Oil Recovery Inst., 1984-92, dir. Inst. for Sci. Computation, 1986-92, dir. Ctr. for Math. Modeling, 1986-92, Wold Centennial chair in energy, 1991-92; dean Coll. Sci. Tex. A&M U., College Station, 1992—, prof. math. and engring., 1992—, dir. Inst. for Sci. Computation, 1992—, dist. rsch. chair, 1992—; disting. rsch. chair TEES, 1992—; adj. prof. Rice U., Houston, 1980-84; cons. oil cos., Norway, Wyo., Tex., Calif., Colo., 1982—; adv. Res. Inst. for Petroleum, Beijing, 1987—; mem. steering com. Ctr. for Fluid Dynamics and Geoscis., Columbia, S.C., 1987—; hon. prof. Shandong (People's Republic China) U., 1987; adv. bd. Interdisciplinary Ctr. Computational Sci., Heidelberg, Germany, 1992—, Instit. Biosci. Tech., Houston, 1992—; exec. com. Partnership Computational Scis., Oak Ridge Nat. Lab., 1991—. Author: The Mathematics of Reservoir Simulation, 1983, Mathematical Modeling in Energy and Environmental Sciences, 1988; contbr. articles to sci. jours., chpts. to books. Cubmaster Boy Scouts Am., Dallas, 1981, Webelos leader, 1982, asst. scoutleader,Laramie, 1984. Recipient numerous rsch. grants NSF, Dept. Energy, NRC, oil cos., others, 1978—. Mem. Soc. Petroleum Engrs., Soc. Indsl. and Applied Math. (trustee 1986—), Am. Math. Soc., Math. Assn. Am., Internat. Assn. for Math. and Computers in Simulation, Internat. Assn. Computer Mech. (trustee 1991—), Inst. for Advancement Sci. Computing (trustee 1987—), Geoscis. Inst. (bd. dirs. 1988-92). Democrat.

EWING, RUSSELL CHARLES, II, physician; b. Tucson, Aug. 16, 1941; s. Russell Charles and Sue M. (Sawyer) E.; m. Louise Anne Wendt, Jan. 29, 1977; children: John Charles, Susan Lenore. BS, U. Ariz., 1963; MD, George Washington U., 1967. Intern, Los Angeles County-U. So. Calif. Med. Ctr., Los Angeles, 1967-68; gen practice medicine and surgery, Yorba Linda, Calif. and Placentia, Calif., 1970—; mem. staff St. Judes Hosp., Fullerton, Calif., 1970—; mem. staff Placentia Linda Community Hosp., 1972—, vice chief staff, 1977-78, chief staff, 1978-80; sec., dir. Yorba Linda Med. Group, Inc., 1974-90; dir. Western Empire Savs. & Loan Assn. (Calif.). Bd. dirs. Yorba Linda YMCA, 1973-88, pres., 1973-74, 81; bd. dirs. Placentia Linda Community Hosp., 1974-81. Served with USN, 1968-70. Diplomate Am. Bd. Family Practice. Fellow Am. Acad. Family Practice; mem. AMA, Calif. Med. Assn. (house of del. 1978-90, trustee 1990—), Orange County Med. Assn. (bd. dirs. 1983—, pres. 1988-89). Republican. Episcopalian. Home: 9212 Smoketree Ln Villa Park CA 92667-2219 Office: 603 Valencia Ave Ste 204 Brea CA 92621-6300

EYER, BRUCE JARRETT, school district administrator; b. Kelso, Wash., Oct. 29, 1941; s. Carman James and Thelma Laura (West) E.; m. Martha Patricia Ann Husa, Feb. 9, 1962; children: Allison, Angela. AA, Lower Columbia Coll., 1961; BA, Wash. State U., 1964; MEd, Cen. Wash U., 1969. High sch. tchr. math. Yakima (Wash.) Pub. Schs., 1964-69, dir. learning resources, 1969—. Contbr. articles to Medium mag. Pres. Sta. KYVE-TV, Yakima, 1975-78; bd. dirs. Yakima Valley Mus., 1985-90, pres. 1988-90, 91-92. Recipient Disting. Svc. award Yakima Edn. Assn., 1977. Mem. ALA, Assn. for Ednl. Communications and Tech., Wash. Libr. Media Assn. (treas. 1976-83, Pres.'s award 1989), Optimist Club (pres. Yakima chpt. 1980-81, named Disting. Pres. 1981), Phi Delta Kappa (Outstanding Educator award Yakima club 1977). Methodist. Office: Yakima Pub Schs 104 N 4th Ave Yakima WA 98902-2636

EYER, MICHAEL JOHN, materials specialist; b. Portland, Oreg., Apr. 21, 1947; m. Jeanette L. Roper, Feb. 3, 1973; 1 child, Dawn M. BS cum laude, Oreg. State U., 1969; MBA, Portland State U., 1979. Cert. hazardous materials mgr., K-12 tchr., Oreg. Dist. insp. Bur. Explosives, Portland, 1976-87; coord. hazardous materials Oreg. Dept. Environ. Quality, Portland, 1987-90; hazardous materials specialist Oreg. Pub. Utility Commn., Portland, 1990—; mem. Wash. Hazardous Materials Adv. Bd., Olympia, 1984-89; asst. chmn. Hanford Adv. Panel, Seattle, 1983-87; com. chmn. U.S.-Can. Spill Adv. Group, Juneau, Alaska, 1989—. Author: Portland Restaurants, 1986; editor video series on chemistry, response of various chems., 1988—; also numerous articles. Team leader Metro Crisis Intervention Svc., Portland, 1982—; elder Presbyn. Ch. Staff sgt. USAF, 1969-73, Vietnam. Recipient Patriotic Civilian Svc. award U.S. Army, 1981; fellow Ctr. for Codification Human Behavioral Laws, 1974. Mem. Acad. Hazardous Materials Mgmt. (bd. dirs. 1990—), Inst. Hazardous Materials Mgmt. (founding pres. Oreg. chpt. 1988—), Oreg. Assn. Hazardous Materials Teams (vice chmn. 1988-90), N.W. Hazardous Materials Transp. Inst. (pres. 1987—), Am. Contract Bridge League (event mgr. Portland 1980-87, asst. dist. dir. 1981-87). Office: Oreg Pub Utility Commn 12345 N Martin L. King Jr Blvd Portland OR 97207

EYRE, R(EGINALD) JOHN, marketing specialist; b. Ogden, Utah, Oct. 10, 1931; s. Reginald D. and Lucille Augusta (Hoyt) E.; m. Joan Carbine, Dec. 21, 1953; children: Steven John, David Bradley, Gregg Evan, Reginald Ian, Sean Richard, Kristopher Ivan. BA in Polit. Sci, U. Utah, 1955; MA in Polit. Sci., U. N.Mex., 1957; PhD in Polit. Sci., U. Colo., 1966. Lic. series 3 Commodities Futures Trading Commn. Tchr. Mesa (Ariz.) High Sch., 1956-59; grad. teaching asst. U. Colo., Boulder, 1959-62; regional dir. Fgn. Policy Assn., N.Y.C., 1962-66; prof., chmn. govt. dept., dir. govt. rsch. inst. Idaho State U., Pocatello, 1967-77, v.p. adminstrn., 1967-80; bd. dirs. Forex, Inc., Utah, Calif., 1985-91; cons. Escondido, Calif., 1991—; cons. Triad Communications Group, San Diego, 1986—, Kaes-San Diego, Inc., 1986—. Author: (book) The Colorado Primary System, 1967; co-author: (book) Political Dynamiting, 1971; contbr. articles to profl. jours. Pres. Young Dems. Colo., Denver, 1961-62, Adult Edn. Assn. Colo., Denver, 1962; rep. Idaho State Legislature, Boise, 1972-74; advisor Idaho Assn. Cities and Counties, Boise, 1974-76. Fellow Citizenship Clearing House, 1960-61; grantee Lincoln Inst. Land Policy, Cambridge, Mass., 1977, S.E. Idaho Coun. Govts., Pocatello, 1972. Mem. Rotary. Mormon. Home and Office: 2176 Oro Verde Rd Escondido CA 92027-4812

EYRICH, HENRY THEODORE, environmental planning executive, geologist; b. Potlatch, Idaho, Dec. 5, 1933; s. Frederick Jacob Martin and Fleta Lucile (Craven) E.; m. Mary Lucille Livesay, Dec. 5, 1959 (dec. Dec. 1987); children: Jennifer Lucille (dec.), Heidi Lee Duncan; m. Jaime Kathleen Gaskin, Jan. 14, 1989. BS in Geology, U. Idaho, 1955; postgrad., Wash. State Coll., 1957-58, 64-66; PhD in Geology, Wash. State U., 1969. Registered geologist, Ariz. Exploration geologist Union Carbide Corp., Spokane, Wash., 1961-64; regional mgr. exploration Cyprus Mines Corp., Tucson, 1967-71; regional exploration mgr. Minerals Exploration Co., Tucson, 1971-74, Spokane, Wash., 1974-76; mgr. of exploration Lindgren Exploration Co., Wayzata, Minn., 1976-78; minerals exploration cons. Tucson, 1978-80, 85-86; v.p. mining Continental Materials Corp., Tucson, 1980-85; phys. planning mgr. Pima Assn. of Govts., Tucson, 1986—. Pres. NW Mining Assn., Spokane, 1976; prs. Ariz. sect. Am. Water Resources Assn., Tucson, 1988; home care vol. Hospice, Tucson, 1989-91; membership chmn. Commn. on the Ariz. Environment, Phoenix, 1990-91, chmn. air, energy, transp. com, 1992; mem. Pima County Wastewater Adv. Com., Tucson, 1986—. With USN, 1955-57. Mem. So. Ariz. Water Resources Assn. (water quality com. chmn. 1988-90). Office: Pima Assn of Govt Ste 405 177 N Church Tucson AZ 85701

EYSSELELN, VIKTOR ERNST, gastroenterologist; b. Ansbach, Bavaria, Germany, June 16, 1951; came to U.S. 1988; s. Ernst and Dorothea (Gross) E.; m. Zoi Anastasopoulou, Sept. 30, 1978. MD, U. Wurzburg, Germany, 1978. Resident/fellow U. Essen, Germany, 1979-81, 83-88; rsch. fellow UCLA/CURE, 1981-83; assoc. prof. U. Essen, 1988; vis. assoc. prof. Harbor-UCLA Med. Sch., Torrance, Calif., 1988-91, chief div. gastroenterology, 1991—. Recipient Physician/Scientist award NIH, 1988. Mem. ACP, Am. Gastroenterol. Assn., So. Calif. Soc. Gastrointestinal Endoscopy, Western Soc. for Clin. Investigation, German Soc. Digestive Diseases (Thannhauser award 1987), German Rsch. Soc. (Heisenberg award 1989). Home: 17110 Palisades Cir Pacific Palisades CA 90272 Office: Harbor-UCLA Med Ctr 1000 W Carson St Torrance CA 90509

EZRA, DAVID A., district judge; b. 1947. BBA magna cum laude, St. Mary's U., 1969, JD, 1972. Law clk. Office of Corp. Counsel City and County Honolulu, 1972; mem. firm Greenstein, Cowen & Frey, 1972-73, Anthony, Hoddick, Reinwald & O'Connor, 1973-80, Ezra, O'Connor, Moon & Tam, 1980-88; dist. judge U.S. Dist. Ct. Hawaii, 1988—; adj. prof. law Wm. S. Richardson Sch. Law, 1978—. Co-editor, author: Hwaii Construction Law - What to Do and When, 1987; editor: Hawaii Collection Practices Manual. 1st lt. USAR 1971-77. Daugherty Fund scholar, 1971, San Antonio Bar Assn. Aux. scholar, 1972. Mem. ABA, Hawaii State Bar, Am. Arbitration Assn., Delta Epsilon Sigma, Phi Delta Phi. Office: US Dist Ct PO Box 50128 Honolulu HI 96850-0001

EZZELL, BEN ROACH, publisher, author; b. Seymour, Tex., Oct. 31, 1943; s. Ben R. and Nancy Catherine (Morgan) E.; m. Mary Meaders Brown, Jan. 26, 1966. BA in Computer Sci., Nat. Tech. Schs., 1980. Pub. Dragon Tree Press, Boulder, Colo., 1981—; freelance system analyst L.A., 1986-89; columnist Sextant Mag., Washington, 1987-89, Inside Turbo Pascal, Louisville, 1989-90; cons. Electronic U./Inst. for Tech. Edn., Eugene, Oreg., 1990-91; dir. devel. Gem Internat. Network, Inc., 1991-92. Author, programmer: I-Ching, 1987; author: Programming the IBM User Interface, 1988, Graphics Programming in Turbo C, 1989, Programming OS/2 Resident Utilities, 1989, Japanese transl., 1991, Object-Oriented Programming in Turbo Pascal 5.5, 1989, Turbo C++ Programming, 1990, Portuguese transl., 1991, Graphics Programming in Turbo C++, 1990, Portuguese transl., 1991, Turbo Debugger & Tools 2.0, 1991, The Complete Turbo Pascal, 1991, Borland C++ 2.0 Programming, 1991; contbr. to PC Mag. Windows Graphics Programming, 1992. With USN, 1963-72. Fellow Legion of Chaos. Buddhist. Office: 2851 Ironwood Eugene OR 97401-6508

FAATZ, JEANNE RYAN, state legislator; b. Cumberland, Md., July 30, 1941; d. Charles Keith and Myrtle Elizabeth (McIntyre) Ryan; B.S., U. Ill., 1962; postgrad. (Gates fellow) Harvard U. Program Sr. Execs. in state and local Govt., 1984; M.A., U. Colo.-Denver, 1985. children: Kristin, Susan. Instr. Speech Dept., Met. State Coll., Denver, 1985—; sec. to majority leader Colo. Senate, 1976-78; mem. Colo. Ho. Reps. from Dist. 1, 1978—, asst. majority leader. Past pres. Harvey Park (Colo.) Homeowners Assn., Southwest Denver YWCA Adult Edn. Club; Southwest met. coord. UN Children's Fund, 1969-74; mem. citizens adv. coun. Ft. Logan Mental Health Center; bd. mgrs. Southwest Denver YMCA. Mem. Bear Creek Rep. Women's Club. Home: 2903 S Quitman St Denver CO 80236-2208 Office: State Capitol Denver CO 80203

FABIAN, JOHN MCCREARY, non-profit company executive, astronaut; b. Goosecreek, Tex., Jan. 28, 1939; s. Felix Monroe and Amy Blanchard (Seip) F.; m. Donna Kay Buboltz, Sept. 18, 1961; children: Michael Kenneth, Amy Louise. BS, Wash. State U., 1962; MS, Air Force Inst. Tech., Dayton, Ohio, 1964; PhD, U. Wash., 1974. Commd. 2d lt. USAF, 1962, advanced through grades to col., 1982; engr. Air Logistics Command, San Antonio, 1964-65; pilot SAC, Oscoda, Mich., 1967-71; assoc. prof. USAF Acad., Colorado Springs, Colo., 1974-78; astronaut NASA-Johnson Space Ctr., Houston, 1978-86; dir. space USAF, Washington, 1986-87; ret., 1987; pres., CEO,

ANSER, Arlington, Va., 1987-91, pres., chief exec. officer, 1991—. Contbr. articles to profl. jours. Bd. dirs. Phi Sigma Kappa Found., Indpls., 1983—, Wash. State U. Found., Pullman, 1984—. Decorated Legion of Merit, Air medal; Legion of Honor (France), King Abdul Aziz medal (Saudi Arabia); recipient Disting. Alumnus award Wash. State U., 1983, Kamarov diploma Fedn. Aeros. Internat. Fellow AIAA (assoc.); mem. Internat. Acad. Astronautics (corr.), Am. Astron. Soc. (corp. rep.), Assn. Space Explorers (v.p. 1988-89, pres. 1989—). Home: 3303 Circle Hill Rd Alexandria VA 22305 Office: Assn Space Explorers USA 35 White St San Francisco CA 94109-2609

FABIAN, LEONARD JAY, economic development specialist; b. Middletown, Conn., Sept. 13, 1946; s. Samuel T. and Bessie (Manevitz) F.; m. Maria Isabel Linares, Sept. 24, 1988; 1 child, Eva Rebeca. BA in Govt. and Philosophy, Boston U., 1969; MA in Polit. Sci., Trinity Coll., Hartford, Conn., 1975. Jr. planner Hartford Redevel. Agy., 1969-74; planner II Imperial Valley Assn. Govts., El Centro, Calif., 1975-76; sr. planner Imperial County Planning Dept., El Centro, 1976-84; adminstr. Imperial County Div. Community Econ. Devel., El Centro, 1984-86; econ. devel. specialist Regional Econ. Devel., Inc./Pvt. Ind. Coun. Imperial County, El Centro, 1986—; rsch. asst. Coun. on Econ. Priorities, San Francisco, 1975; lectr. San Diego State U., Calexico, Calif., 1980-81, mem. adv. bd., 1986-89; mem. regional bd. Calif. Regional Water Quality Control Bd., Colo. River Basin, Palm Desert, 1979-83. Bd. dirs. Imperial County Arts Coun., 1983-90, chmn. granting com., 1986-91; bd. dirs. Imperial Valley Coll. Mus. Soc., El Centro, 1978-80; mem. adv. bd. Small Bus. Devel. and Internat. Trade Ctr., Southwestern Coll., 1991—; mem. adv. com. Imperial Valley coll. Bus. Div., 1990—; mem. adv. bd. bus. div. San Diego State U., 1991—. Office: Regional Econ Devel Inc 1411 State St El Centro CA 92243-2816

FACKLER, DONALD A., JR., finance company owner; b. Moline, Ill., Sept. 27, 1955; s. Donald A. and Barbara J. (Young) F.; m. Vicki Rae Notick, Apr. 7, 1990. AAS, Black Hawk Jr. Coll., Moline, 1975; BS, So. Ill. U., 1977. Sales rep. Burroughs Corp., Peoria, Ill., 1977-78, br. mgr., 1978-83; dist. sales mgr. Burroughs Corp., Jacksonville, Fla., 1983-85, Stanton, Calif., 1985-87; regional product mgr. F & E Hedman Co., L.A., 1987-88; acctg. exec. Maverick Microsystems, Seattle, 1988-89; owner Facs Fin. Systems, Costa Mesa, Calif., 1989—. Mem. Masons, Moose. Republican. Home: 1808 Alaska Ave Costa Mesa CA 92626-2009 Office: Facs Fin Systems 2973 Harbor Blvd # 466 Costa Mesa CA 92626-3934

FACKLER, MARTIN L(UTHER), surgeon; b. York, Pa., Apr. 8, 1933; s. Martin Luther and Naomi Dorcas (Gibbs) F.; m. Nancy Aleen Gray, Sept. 29, 1964. AB magna cum laude, Gettysburg Coll., 1955; MD, Yale U., 1959. Diplomate Am. Bd. Surgery. Enlisted USN, 1960, advanced through grades to col., 1976; intern U. Oreg. Med. Sch. Hosp., 1959-60; resident in gen. surgery U.S. Naval Hosp., Boston, 1961-65; resident in plastic surgery U.S. Naval Hosp., Bethesda, Md., 1966-67; staff surgeon NSA Hosp., DaNang, Socialist Republic of Vietnam, 1967-68, USN Hosp., Yokosuka, Japan, 1969-71; chief dept. surgery USN Hosp., Memphis, 1972-74; intersvc. transfer U.S. Army chief dept. surgery 2d Gen. Hosp., Landstuhl, Republic of Germany, 1975-80; chief dept. surgery U.S. Army Hosp., Ft. Carson, Colo., 1980-81; dir. wound ballistics lab. Presidio, San Francisco, 1981-91; ret. U.S. Army, 1991; tech. adv. Assn. Firearm and Toolmark Examiners, 1984—; adv. forensic sci. grad. sch. U. Calif., Berkeley, 1985-91; speaker on war surgery, wound ballistics, weapons effects; expert witness, cons. to various state, city and nat. law enforcement agys. and criminalistics labs.; appointed steering com. on devel. less-than-lethal weapons for law enforcement use Nat. Inst. Justice, 1986—; mem. of Can. Gen. Standards Bd. Com. on Police Ammunition, 1989—, FBI symposium on wound ballistics, 1987, 93; mem. adv. coun. on soft body armor U.S. Office Tech. Assessment, 1991-92; apptd. permanent mem. exam. jury wound ballistics, U. Marseille, France, 1993, vis. prof. wound ballistics faculty forensic medicine, U. Marseille, France, 1993—. Editor in chief Wound Ballistics Rev., 1990—; contbr. articles to profl. jours. Decorated Legion of Merit, Meritorious Svc. medal; recipient Commendation 2d Gen. Hosp., Landstuhl, 1981. Fellow ACS (com. on trauma); mem. Internat. Wound Ballistics Assn. (pres. 1990—), Nat. Rifle Assn. (life), Phi Beta Kappa. Home: RR 4 Box 264 Hawthorne FL 32640

FACTOR, MAX, III, lawyer, investment advisor; b. L.A., Sept. 25, 1945; s. Sidney B. and Dorothy (Levinson) F.; BA in Econs. magna cum laude, Harvard Coll., 1966; JD, Yale U., 1969. Bar: Calif. 1970, U.S. Ct. Appeals (6th cir.) 1971, U.S. Dist. Ct. (cen. dist.) Calif. 1971. Law clk. U.S. Ct. Appeals (6th cir.), 1969-71; exec. dir. Calif. Law Ctr., Los Angeles, 1973-74; dir. Consumer Protection Sect., Los Angeles City Atty., 1974-77; pres. MF Capital Ltd., Beverly Hills, Calif., 1978-86; ptnr. Cooper, Epstein & Hurewitz, Beverly Hills, Calif., 1986—; expert witness numerous state and fed. bds., 1974-78; guest lectr. UCLA, U. So. Calif., Los Angeles County Bar Assn., Calif. Dept. Consumer Affairs, 1974-76; hearing examiner City of Los Angeles, 1975. Contbr. articles to profl. jours. Bd. dirs. Western Law Ctr. for the Handicapped, Los Angeles, 1977-79, Beverly Hills Unified Sch. Dist., 1979-83; pres. Beverly Hills Bd. Edn., 1983; bd. councilors U. So. Calif. Law Ctr., Los Angeles, 1983—; chmn. Beverly Hills Visitors Bur., 1989-90. Recipient scholarship award Harvard Coll., 1965; Max Factor III Day proclaimed in his honor Beverly Hills City Council, 1979; recipient Disting. Service to Pub. Edn. award Beverly Hills Bd. Edn., 1979. Mem. Los Angeles County Bar Assn. (chmn. various coms. 1976-78), Beverly Hills C. of C. (pres. 1987-88), Beverly Hills Edn. Found. (pres. 1977-79). Democrat. Jewish. Office: Cooper Epstein & Hurewitz Ste 200 345 N Maple Dr Beverly Hills CA 90210-3855

FADDEN, DELMAR MCLEAN, electrical engineer; b. Seattle, Nov. 10, 1941; s. Gene Scott and Alice Elizabeth (McLean) F.; m. Sandra Myrene Callahan, June 22, 1963; children: Donna McLean, Lawrence Gene. BSEE, U. Wash., 1963, MSEE, 1975. Lic. comml. pilot, Wash. With Boeing Comml. Airplane Co., Seattle, 1969—, chief engr. 737/757 avionics/flight systems, 1990—. Contbr. articles to IEEE Proceedings. Capt. USAF, 1963-69. Mem. AIAA, IEEE, Human Factors Soc., Soc. Automotive Engrs. (vice chmn. G-10 com. 1981-91, chmn. systems integration task group 1990—), Mountaineers (pres. 1984-85). Republican. Home: 5011 298th Ave SE Preston WA 98050 Office: Boeing Comml Airplane Co PO Box 3707 M/S 9R-28 Seattle WA 98124-2207

FADELEY, EDWARD NORMAN, state supreme court justice; b. Williamsville, Mo., Dec. 13, 1929. A.B., U. Mo., 1951; J.D., U. Oreg., 1957. Bar: Oreg. 1957, U.S. Supreme Ct. 1968. Practice law Eugene, Oreg., 1957-88; mem. Oreg. Ho. of Reps., 1961-63; mem. Oreg. Senate, 1963-87, pres., 1983-85; justice Oregon Supreme Ct., 1989—; mem. jud. working group Internat. Water Tribunal, Amsterdam, The Netherlands; invitee Rio Environ. Conf., 1992, Indigenous Peoples of World Conf., New Zealand, 1993; adj. prof. law U. Oreg. Chmn. Oreg. Dem. party, 1966-68; chmn. law and justice com. Nat. Conf. Legislators, 1977-78; adv. com. to State and Local Law Ctr., Washington; participants com. Washington Pub. Power Supply System, 1984-88; candidate for nomination for gov., 1986; bd. dirs. Wayne Morse Hist. Park. Lt. USNR, 1951-54. Recipient First Pioneer award U. Oreg., 1980, Assn. Oreg. Counties award for reform of state ct. system, 1982. Mem. ABA (internat. law, pub. utility law, judicial administrn.), Oreg. State Bar Assn. (chmn. uniform laws com. 1962-64), Order of Coif, Alpha Pi Zeta, Phi Alpha Delta. Democrat. Methodist. Office: Oreg Supreme Ct Supreme Ct Bldg Salem OR 97310

FAGELSON, HARVEY J., emergency physician, dermatologist, educator; b. Chgo., June 19, 1938; s. Lawrence Larry and Eva (Stein) F.; m. Rosalie Schwartz, July 12, 1964; children: James E., Nancy E., Robert E. Student, U. Ill., Chgo., 1958, MD, 1962. Diplomate Am. Bd. Dermatology. Intern St. Francis Hosp., Evanston, Ill., 1962-63; resident in dermatology U. Ill. Rsch. and Ednl. Hosps., Chgo., 1963-66; med. dir. emergency clinic L.A. County-U. So. Calif. Med. Ctr., L.A., 1969—; asst. prof. emergency medicine U. So. Calif., L.A., 1973—. Capt. USAF, 1966-68. Fellow Am. Acad. Dermatology. Office: LAC-USC Med Ctr 1200 N State St Box 211 Los Angeles CA 90033

FAGERBERG, DIXON, JR., retired accountant, weather observer; b. Prescott, Ariz., Mar. 20, 1909; s. Dixon and Amy (Nelson) F.; m. Mary Jergens, June 21, 1933 (div. Aug. 1980); children: Dick, Mary, Nelson; m. Lorraine Brenn, Sept. 22, 1980. AB in Econs. summa cum laude, Stanford U., 1931. CPA, Ariz. Valuation engr. Calif. R.R. Commn., San Francisco, 1931-32; acct. Harmon Audit Co., Prescott, 1933-34; owner, mgr. Dixon Fagerberg, Jr., CPA, Flagstaff, Kingman, Phoenix, Ariz., 1935-57; ptnr.-in-charge Peat, Marwick, Mitchell & Co., Phoenix, 1957-71; RET., 1971; vol. cons. Internat. Exec. Svc. Corps, Guatemala City, Guatemala, 1975. Co-author: 108 Sedona Westerner Trail Walks, 1979; author: Boyhood Recollections of Prescott, Arizona, 1983, Dix's Almanac of Weather and Climate, 1989; columnist Practitioner's Forum, 1954-56. Bd. dirs. Phoenix Libr., 1960-65; mem. Coconino County Planning and Zoning Commn., Flagstaff, 1973-76; councilman City of Sedona, 1988. Lt. USNR, 1944-46. Recipient medal of merit U. Ariz., 1960, Outstanding CPA award Mountain States Acctg. Conf., 1966. Mem. AICPA (nat. v.p. 1955-56), Ariz. Soc. CPAs (pres. 1938-39, columnist The Oasis 1972—), Am. Soc. Mining Engrs., Assn. Am. Weather Observers, Sedona Westerners (trail boss 1973-74), Pinewood Country Club (Munds Park, Ariz.), Poco Diablo Tennis Club, Masons.

FAGG, RUSSELL, lawyer, state legislator; b. Billings, Mont., June 26, 1960; s. Harrison Grover and Darlene (Bohling) F.; m. Karen Barclay, Feb. 15, 1992. BA, Whitman Coll., 1983; JD, U. Mont., 1986. Law clerk Mont. Supreme Ct., Helena, Mont., 1986-87; atty. Sandall Law Firm, Billings, Mont., 1987-89; city prosecutor City of Billings, 1989-91; dep. atty. Yellowstone County, Billings, 1991—; state legislator Mont., Helena, 1991—; dir. Midland Empire Pachyderm Club, 1988—, pres. 1990-91; chmn. judiciary com. House of Reps., 1993-94. Republican. Home: 221 Ave E Billings MT 59101 Office: PO Box 176 Billings MT 59103

FAGIN, DAVID KYLE, natural resource company executive; b. Dallas, Apr. 9, 1938; s. Kyle Marshall and Frances Margaret (Gaston) F.; m. Margaret Anne Hazlett, Jan. 22, 1959; children—David Kyle, Scott Edward. B.S. in Petroleum Engring, U. Okla., 1960; postgrad., Am. Inst. Banking, So. Meth. U. Grad. Sch. Bus. Adminstrn. Registered profl. engr., La., Okla., Tex. Trainee Magnolia Petroleum Co., 1955-56; jr. engr., engr., then partner W.C. Bednar (petroleum cons.), Dallas, 1958-65; petroleum engr. NationsBank (formerly First Nat. Bank Dallas), Dallas, 1965-68; v.p. Rosario Resources Corp., N.Y.C., 1968-75; pres. Alamo Petroleum Corp., 1968-82; exec. v.p. Rosario Resources Corp., N.Y.C., 1975-77; dir. Rosario Resources Corp., 1975-80, pres., 1977-82; v.p. AMAX Inc. (merged with Rosario Resources Corp. 1980), N.Y.C., 1980-82; chmn., dir., pres., chief exec. officer Fagin Exploration Co., Denver, 1982-86; pres., COO, bd. dirs. Homestake Mining Co., San Francisco, 1986-91; Golden Star Resources (merged with S.Am. Goldfields 1992); chmn., CEO, bd. dirs. Golden Star Resources, Ltd., Denver, 1992—; bd. dirs. several T. Rowe Price mut. funds, Balt., Mineral Info. Inst., The Keystone Ctr. Past mem. bd. dirs. Bay Area coun. Boy Scouts Am. Mem. AIME (chmn. Dallas sect. 1975, chmn. investment fund 1979-82), Soc. Petroleum Engrs., Soc. Mining Engrs., Denver Petroleum Club. Office: Golden Star Resources Ltd Ste 1950 1700 Lincoln St Denver CO 80203

FAGUNDO, ANA MARIA, creative writing and Spanish literature educator; b. Santa Cruz de Tenerife, Spain, Mar. 13, 1938; came to U.S., 1958; d. Ramón Fagundo and Candelaria Guerra de Fagundo. BA in English and Spanish, U. Redlands, 1962; MA in Spanish, U. Wash., 1964, PhD in Comparative Lit., 1967. Prof. contemporary lit. of Spain and creative writing U. Calif., Riverside, 1967—; vis. lectr. Occidental Coll., Calif., 1967; vis. prof. Stanford U., 1984. Author 8 books of poetry include Invention le la Luz, 1977 (Carabela de Oro poetry prize Barcelona, Spain 1977), Obra Poetica: 1965-90, 1990, (poetic anthology) Isla En Si, 1992; founder, editor: (literary jour.) Alaluz, 1969—. Grantee Creative Arts Inst., 1970-71, Humanities Inst., 1973-74; Summer faculty fellow U. Calif., 1968, 77; Humanities fellow, 1969. Mem. Am. Assn. Tchrs. Spanish and Portuguese, Sociedad Gen. de Autores de Espana. Roman Catholic. Home: 5110 Caldera Ct Riverside CA 92507-6002 Office: U Calif Spanish Dept Riverside CA 92521

FAIN, KAREN KELLOGG, history and geography educator; b. Pueblo, Colo., Oct. 10, 1940; d. Howard Davis and Mary Lucille (Cole) Kellogg; m. Sept. 1, 1961; divorced; 1 child, Kristopher. Student, U. Ariz., 1958-61; BA, U. So. Colo., 1967; MA, U. No. Colo., 1977; postgrad., U. Denver, 1968, 72-93, Colo. State U., 1975, 91, U. No. Ill., 1977, 83, Ft. Hayes State Coll., 1979, U. Colo., 1979, 86-87, 92, Ind. U., 1988. Cert. secondary tchr., Colo. Tchr. history and geography Denver Pub. Schs., 1967—; tchr. West High Sch., Denver, 1992—, 1992—; area adminstr., tchr. coord. Close Up program, Washington, 1982-84; reviewer, cons. for book Geography, Our Changing World, 1990. Vol., chmn. young profls. Inst. Internat. Edn. and World Affairs Coun., Denver, 1980—; mem. state selection com. U.S. Senate and Japan Scholarship Com., Denver, 1981-89, Youth for Understanding, Denver; mem. Denver Art Mus., 1970—; vol. Denver Mus. Natural History, 1989—; bd. overseas Dept. Def. Dependents Sch., Guantanamo Bay, Cuba, 1990-91. Fulbright scholar Chadron State Coll., Pakistan, 1975; Geog. Soc. grantee U. Colo., 1986; recipient award for Project Prince, Colo. U./Denver Pub. Schs./Denver Police Dept., 1992. Mem. Colo. Coun. Social Studies (sec. 1984-86), Nat. Coun. Social Studies (del. 1984), World History Assn., Fulbright Assn., Am. Forum for Global Edn., Rocky Mountain Regional World History Assn. (steering com. 1984-87), Colo. Geographic Alliance (steering com. 1986), Gamma Phi Beta. Democrat. Episcopalian. Home: 12643 E Bates Circle Aurora CO 80014 Office: West High Sch 951 Elati St Denver CO 80204

FAIR, RODNEY DALE, optometrist; b. San Antonio, Apr. 12, 1956; s. Ron G. and Patricia Ann (Shenkle) F.; m. Ella Monica Leyba, Sept. 19, 1992. BA in Biology, Hastings Coll., 1978; BS in Visual Sci., So. Calif. Coll. Optometry, 1982, OD, 1982. Resident in pediatric eye care SUNY, N.Y.C., 1983; pvt. practice optometry Brighton (Colo.) Vision Clinic, 1983—; adj. clin. prof. optometry U. Houston, 1986-87; bd. dirs. Colo. Optometric Ctr., Denver, 1987-93; bd. dirs. Platte Valley Med. Ctr. Found., 1988—; lectr. in field. Contbr. articles to profl. publs. Precinct capt., state conv. del., 1988—; vol. Denver Rescue Mission, 1988—; bd. fine arts at cultural arts orgns., Brighton, 1991-93. Fellow Am. Acad. Optometry; mem. Am. Optometric Assn. (Optometric Continuing Edn. Recognition award 1988—), Colo. Optometric Assn. (Young Optometrist of Yr. 1987, med. adv. coun. 1992—, vice chmn. legis. com. 1987-88, dist. rep. bd. trustees 1990-92), Brighton C. of C. (bd. dirs. 1985-87, treas. 1988), Hastings Coll. Alumni Assn. (sec.-treas. Denver chpt. 1989—), Kiwanis (pres. Brighton club 1985-86, Disting. Svc. award 1990). Republican. Presbyterian. Home: 1562 Brighton Dr Brighton CO 80601 Office: Brighton Vision Clinic 105 Bridge St Brighton CO 80601

FAIRBAIRN, STEPHEN CARL, air force officer; b. Freeport, Ill., Jan. 9, 1960; s. Carl Owen and Neenah Pearl (Hughes) F.; m. Margaret Walsh, May 31, 1985. BS, MIT, 1981, MS, 1982. Lic. comml. instrument pilot. Commd. USAF, 1982, advanced through grades to capt., 1985; served as pilot, flight Ld 492 Tac Fighter Squadron, RAF Lakenheath, U.K., 1984-86, instr. pilot, 1986-87; instr. pilot 389 Tac Fighter Tng. Squadron, Mountain Home AFB, Idaho, 1988-89, chief acads., 1990; flight comdr. 389 Tac Fighter Tng. Squadron, Mountain Home AFB, 1990-91; student USAF Test Pilot Sch., Edwards AFB, Calif., 1991-92; adj. prof. Embry-Riddle Aero. U., Mountain Home AFB, 1989-90. Mem. ASME, Daedalian Mil. Pilot Fraternity.

FAIRBANKS, MARY KATHLEEN, data analyst, researcher; b. Manhattan, Kans., June 4, 1948; d. Everitt Edsel and Mary Catherine (Moran) F. BS, St. Norbert Coll., 1970; postgrad., Calif. Family Study Ctr., 1981-82. Neuropsychology researcher U.S. VA Hosp., Sepulveda, Calif., 1970-76; mgr. print shop Charisma In Missions, City of Industry, Calif., 1976-77; neuropsychology researcher L.A. County Women's Hosp., 1977-79; mem. tech. staff Computer Scis. Corp., Ridgecrest, Calif., 1979-81; systems programmer Calif. State U., Northridge, 1982-84; bus. systems analyst World Vision, Monrovia, Calif., 1984-86; configuration analyst Teledyne System Co., Northridge, 1986-87; applications system analyst Internat. Telephone and Telegraph/Fed. Electric Corp., Altadena, Calif., 1987-88; supr. data analysts OAO Corp., Altadena, 1988—. Co-author, contbr.: Serotonin and Behavior, 1973, Advances in Sleep Research, vol. 1, 1974. Mem. OAO Mgmt. Assn., So. Calif. Application System Users Group, Digital Equipment Computer Users Soc. Roman Catholic. Home: 37607 Lasker Ave Palmdale CA 93550-7721 Office: OAO Corp 787 W Woodbury Rd Ste 2 Altadena CA 91001-5368

FAIRCHILD, ARVID PERSHING, travel agency executive; b. Turlock, Calif., Jan. 6, 1925; s. Clarence Frank and Maybelle (Dunagan) F.; B.S. in Civil Engring., U. Miami (Fla.), 1955; m. Grace M. Stewart, June 20, 1943; children—Jack W., Jean A. Fairchild Gartner. Dir. ops. Interocean Airways, Luxembourg, 1961-63; flight instr. United Airlines, 1963-64; check pilot Japan Air Lines, 1964-74; pres., chmn. bd. Island Air Tours, Kilohana World Travel (formerly Scenic Island Travel), Honolulu, 1974-85; v.p. Horizon Airlines/Trans Nat. Airlines; v.p. Pacific Air Express, 1982-87; v.p., dir. Care-All Aviation, 1987—, dir. ops. UN airlift for Congo, 1962, Hawaii Pacific Air, 1990—; capt. Seaboard Western Airlines, 1955-62. Served with USN, 1940-53, USNR 1953-62. Decorated Air medal (3), Purple Heart, Army Disting. Service medal with oak leaf clusters. Mem. Nat. Assn. Businessmen. Republican. Presbyterian. Clubs: Masons, Shriners, Order Eastern Star. Author: Instrument Flight Technique; also articles in aviation publs. Home: 44-133 Hako St Kaneone HI 96744 Office: 3031 Aolele St Honolulu HI 96819-1801

FAIRLEIGH, KAREN EVELYN, college official; b. Madison, Ind., Aug. 29, 1965; d. James Parkinson and Marlane (Paxson) F. BA in Comm., U. Ala., Tuscalosa, 1986. Dir. mktg. and promotions union programs U. Ala., 1984-85, dir. cultural and fine arts, 1985; dir. group sales and mktg. Wool Warehouse Dinner Theater, Albuquerque, 1986-87; mktg. mgr. Home Club, Inc., Glendale, Ariz., 1987-89; coord. community svcs., dir. performing arts seriesa Mohave C.C., Bullhead City, Ariz., 1989—; TV host Cityline, Bullhead City, 1991-92. Facilitator Bullhead City Town Hall, 1991. J. Kelly Sisk scholar U. Ala., 1983; grantee Ariz. Commn.. on Arts, 1989-92, United Way, 1989-90. Mem. AAUW, Bus. and Profl. Women, Rotary (v.p. Bullhead City 1991-92), Kappa Tau Alpha. Republican. Presbyterian. Office: Mohave CC 3400 Hwy 95 Bullhead City AZ 86442

FAIRWEATHER, EDWIN ARTHUR, electronics company executive; b. London, July 21, 1916; came to U.S., 1967; s. Arthur Henry and Elizabeth (Dawson) F.; m. Joan Barbara Branson, Sept. 14, 1946; children: David Martin, Janet Elizabeth Fairweather Nelson. BSME, London Poly., 1940. Quality engr. Lucas-Rotex, Toronto (Ont., Can.) and Birmingham (Eng.), 1951-58; mfg. engr. Flight Refuelling Co., Dorset, Eng., 1958-62, Spar Aerospace, Toronto, 1962-67, Sperry Flight Systems, Phoenix, 1967-71; engr. research and devel. Ford Aerospace Co., Palo Alto, Calif., 1971-85; founder, pres., chief engr. Fairweather & Co., Sunnyvale, Calif., 1980—. Patentee in field. Served with RAF, 1940-46. Home and Office: 1442 S Wolfe Rd Sunnyvale CA 94087-3669

FALARDEAU, ERNEST RENE, clergyman, theologian; b. Holyoke, Mass., Nov. 14, 1928; s. Wilfrid Peter and Alboma (Roy) F. STD, Pontifical Gregorian U., Rome, 1959; MLS, Western Res. U., 1963. Ordained priest, Roman Catholic Ch., 1956. Prof. classical langs. Eymard Prep. Sem., Hyde Park, N.Y., 1959-61; prof. liturgical and spiritual theology Blessed Sacrament Sem., Cleve., 1961-67; rector Eymard Prep Sem., 1967-73; pres. Dutchess County (N.Y.) Interfaith Coun., 1972-74; clergy Congregation of the Blessed Sacrament, Barre, Mass., 1949—; pres. Dutchess Interfaith Coun., Poughkeepsie, N.Y., 1972-74; mem. commn. for ecumenical and interreligious rels. diocese of Cleve., 1978-79; dir. Office of Ecumenical and Interreligious Affairs, Archdiocese of Santa Fe, N.Mex., 1979—, dir. ecumenical staff Blessed Sacrament Congregation, 1981—; chmn. faith and order task force N.Mex. Conf. of Chs., 1981-87. Mem. ALA, N.Am. Acad. of Ecumenists (bd. dirs. 1986—, v.p., pres.-elect 1989-91, pres. 1991-93), Nat. Assn. of Diocesa Ecumenical Officers (regional rep. region XIII S.W. 1981-89), co-chairperson, standing com. 1983-88), del. for ARC/USA 1984-88, treas. 1982-83, v.p. 1983-89, pres. 1989-92), Nat. Assn. of Ecumenical Staff, Cath. Theol. Soc. of Am., N.Am. Acad. of Ecumenists, Beta Phi Mu. Home and Office: 1818 Coal Pl SE Albuquerque NM 87106-4025

FALCO, CHARLES MAURICE, physicist, educator; b. Fort Dodge, Iowa, Aug. 17, 1948; s. Joe and Mavis Margaret (Mickelson) F.; m. Dale Wendy Miller, May 5, 1973; children: Lia Denise, Amelia Claire. BA, U. Calif., Irvine, 1970, MA, 1971, PhD, 1974. Trainee NSF, 1970-74; asst. physicist Argonne (Ill.) Nat. Lab., 1974-77, physicist, 1977-82, group leader superconductivity and novel materials, 1978-82; prof. physics and optical scis., research prof. U. Ariz., Tucson, 1982—, dir. lab. x-ray optics, 1986—; vis. prof. U. Paris Sud, 1979, 86, U. Aachen, 1989; lectr., 1974—; mem. panel on artificially structured materials NRC, 1984-85; co-organizer numerous internat. confs. in field, 1978—; mem. spl. rev. panel on high temperature superconductivity Applied Physics Letters, 1987—; mem. panel on superconductivity Inst. Def. Analysis, 1988—; researcher on artificial metallic superlattices, X-ray optics, auperconductivity, condensed matter physics, electronic materials. Editor: Future Trends in Superconductive Electronics, 1978, Materials for Magneto-Optic Data Storage, 1989; contbr. articles to profl. jours.; patentee in field. Mem. divsn. condensed matter physics Exec. Com. Arts, 1992—. Alexander vo Humboldt Found. sr. disting. grantee, 1989. Fellow Am. Phys. Soc. (counselor 1992-94, exec. com. div. condensed matter physics 1992-94); mem. IEEE (sr.), Am. Vacuum Soc., Materials Research Soc., Sigma Xi. Home: 6301 N Caravan Ln Tucson AZ 85704-2802 Office: U Ariz Dept Physics 1118 E 4th St Tucson AZ 85721

FALCONE, ALFONSO BENJAMIN, physician; b. Bryn Mawr, Pa.; s. B. and Elvira (Galluzzo) F.; m. Patricia J. Lalim, Oct. 22, 1955; children: Christopher L., Steven B. AB in Chemistry with distinction, Temple U., 1944, MD with honors, 1947; PhD in Biochemistry, U. Minn., 1954. Diplomate Am. Bd. Internal Medicine subspecialty bd. endocrinology and metabolism. Intern Phila. Gen. Hosp., 1947-48, resident in internal medicine, 1948-49; teaching fellow internal medicine U. Hosps., U. Minn., 1949-51; asst. clin. prof. medicine U. Wis., Madison, 1956-59, assoc. clin. prof., 1959-63, asst. prof. Inst. Enzyme Research, 1963-66, vis. prof., 1966-67; practice medicine specializing in endocrine and metabolic diseases Fresno, Calif., 1968—; mem. staff Fresno Community Hosp., chmn. dept. medicine, 1973; mem. staff St. Agnes Hosp., Fresno, Valley Med. Ctr., Fresno; sr. corr. Ettor Majorana Ctr. for Sci. Culture, Erice, Italy. Contbr. articles to profl. jours. Served with AUS, 1944-46; served to lt. comdr. M.C., USNR, 1954-56. NIH postdoctoral fellow, 1951-53; NIH research grantee, 1958-68. Fellow ACP; mem. AMA, AAAS, Am. Soc. Biochemistry and Molecular Biology, Cen. Soc. Clin. Rsch., Am. Fedn. Clin. Rsch., Am. Chem. Soc., Am. Soc. Internal Medicine, Am. Assn. for Study Liver Disease, Am. Diabetes Assn., Assn. Acad. Excellence, U. Calif. Fresno Com., Fresno County Assn. for U. Calif. Campus, Archeol. Inst. Am., Calif. Acad. Medicine, Sigma Xi, Phi Lambda Epsilon. Office: 2240 E Illinois Ave Fresno CA 93701-2191

FALCONE, CARMINE, oil industry executive; b. Oct. 14, 1946. BSChemE, McGill U., 1968. With Shell Canada, Calgary, Alta., Can., 1968—; sr. project engr. Shell Canada, Calgary, Alta., 1973-76; mgr. heavy oils dept., mgr. process engring. Shell Canada, Montreal, Que., 1976-80; tech. mgr. head office Shell Canada, Toronto, Ont., 1980-82, mgr. strategy devel., corp. strategies dept., 1982-83, v.p. corp. strategies, 1983-86, v.p. western complex, 1986-90; exec. v.p. products Shell Canada, Calgary, 1990-93; head strategy divsn.-mfg. Shell Internat. Maatschappij B.V. (SIPM), The Hague, Netherlands, 1993—. Dir. West Island Coll. Mem. Can. Petroleum Products Inst. (bd. dirs.), Assn. Profl. Engrs., Geologists and Geophysicists Alta. Office: Shell Internat Maatschappij BV (SIPM), Post Bus 162 2501 AN, The Hague Netherlands

FALCONE, PHILIP FRANCIS, computer engineer; b. Bethlehem, Pa., Jan. 20, 1929; s. Dominic Thomas and Mary Elizabeth (Beresh) F.; m. Kathryn Frances Buck, Sept. 9, 1950; children: Teresa Marie Holley, Philip Thomas. Student, Lehigh U., 1948-50, U. Cin., 1957-59, Ariz. State U., 1968, 70, 72. With Roller-Smith Corp., Bethlehem, 1950-55; nuclear engring. designer Gen. Electric. Co., Cin., 1955-60; supr. engring., drafting Honeywell, Phoenix, 1960-67, computer systems analyst, 1967-82, mgr. computer aided engring., 1982-89; ret., 1989; mem. internat. steering com. Honeywell Computer Aided Design, 1982-89. Rep. Sunburst Farms Home Owners Assn., Phoenix and Glendale, Ariz., 1969-75; leader horses Maricopa County 4-H Program, Phoenix, 1970-77; eucharistic minister Our Lady of the Valley parish, Phoenix, 1984—. With U.S. Army, 1946-48. Mem. Italian-Am. Wine Promoters Assn. (pres. Phoenix chpt. 1985—), Mensa, Moose (mem. exec. com. 1954-55). Democrat. Roman Catholic. Home: 4701 W Country Gables Dr Glendale AZ 85306-3509

FALERO, FRANK, forensic economist, educator; b. N.Y.C., Dec. 22, 1937; s. Frank and Lydia Maria (Camis) F.; m. Verna D. Whittier, Nov. 22, 1990; children: Lisa Ann, Sara Francine. AA, St. Petersburg Jr. Coll., 1962; BA, U. of S. Fla., 1964; MS, Fla. State U., 1966, PhD, 1967. Research economist Fed. Res. Bank, Richmond, Va., 1967-68; Fulbright prof. Peru, 1968-69; asst. prof. econs. Va. Poly. Inst. and State U., Blacksburg, 1967-72; prof. econs. and fin. Calif. State U., Bakersfield, Calif., 1972—; v.p. fin. Am. Wind, Tehachapi, Calif., 1981-85; ind. cons., Bakersfield, 1972. Author: Monetary History of Honduras, 1970; contbr. numerous articles to profl. jours. Served with U.S. Army, 1955-58. NDEA Title IV fellow 1964-67; recipient Golden Mike award Associated Press TV Radio Announcers, 1985. Home: 40144 Balch Park Rd Springville CA 93265 Office: Calif State U 9001 Stockdale Hwy Bakersfield CA 93311-1022

FALEY, ROBERT LAWRENCE, instruments company executive; b. Bklyn., Oct. 13, 1927; s. Eric Lawrence and Anna (Makahon) F.; B.S. cum laude in Chemistry, St. Mary's U., San Antonio, 1956; postgrad. U. Del., 1958-59; m. Mary Virginia Mumme, May 12, 1950; children: Robert Wayne, Nancy Diane. Chemist, E.I. Dupont de Nemours & Co., Inc., Wilmington, Del., 1956-60; sales mgr. F&M Sci., Houston, 1960-62; pres. Faley Assos., Houston, 1962-65; sales mgr. Tech. Inc., Dayton, Ohio, 1965-70; biomed. mkt. mgr. Perkin-Elmer Co., Norwalk, Conn., 1967-69; mktg. dir. Cahn Instruments, Los Angeles, 1970-72; pres. Faley Internat., El Toro, Calif., 1972—. Internat. speaker in field; dir. Whatman Lab. Products Inc., 1981-82, Status Instrument Corp., 1985-87; tech. mktg. cons. Whatman Ltd., Abbott Labs., OCG Tech., Inc., Pacific Biochem., Baker Commodities, Bausch & Lomb Co., Motorola Inc., Whatman Inc., Filtration Scis. Corp., PMC Industries. Mem. adv. com. on Sci., tech., energy and water U.S. 43d Congl. Dist., 1985-87. With USMS, 1944-47, 1st lt. USAF, 1948-53. Charter mem. Aviation Hall Fame. Fellow Am. Inst. Chemists, AAAS; mem. ASTM, Am. Chem. Soc. (sr.), Instrument Soc. Am. (sr.), Inst. Environ. Scis. (sr.), Aircraft Owners and Pilots Assn., U.S. Power Squadrons, Delta Epsilon Sigma. Club: Masons. Contbr. articles on technique of gas chromatography to profl. jours. Home: 27850 Espinoza San Juan Capistrano CA 92692-2156 Office: PO Box 520 Lake Forest CA 92630-0520

FALGIANO, VICTOR JOSEPH, electrical engineer, consultant; b. San Francisco, Nov. 25, 1957; s. Victor Anthony and Frances Mary Falgiano; m. Linda Maxine Owens, July 24, 1982; children; Gregory Joseph, Nicholas Rexford. BS in Elec. Engring. Tech. magna cum laude, Cogswell Coll., 1989, BS in Computer Engring. magna cum laude, 1989. Sr. design engr. Amdahl Corp., Sunnyvale, Calif., 1978-93; mem. steering com. System Design and Integration Conf., Santa Clara, Calif.; mem. acad. adv. com. Cogswell Coll., Cupertino, Calif., 1991. Advisor to high sch. students Jr. Achievement. Mem. IEEE (sr.), Assn. Computing Machinery.

FALICK, ABRAHAM JOHNSON, printing company executive; b. Chgo., Oct. 11, 1920; s. Simon Falick and Ellen Martina (Johnson) Sherwood; m. Carolyn Weber, Dec. 11, 1947; 1 child, Leslie Carol Falick Koplof. BA, Ind. U., 1947; MBA, U. Chgo., 1951; MA, UCLA, 1967, PhD, 1970. Cert. pub. planner. Commd. ensign USNR, 1941, advanced through grades to lt. comdr., 1941-46, ret., 1967; mgr. sales/mktg. Webb-Linn Printing Co., Chgo., 1948-56; pres., chief exec. officer Murray and Gee, Inc., Culver City, Calif., 1956-60; planning economist City of Los Angeles, 1967-75; pres., chief exec. officer AJ Falick Assocs., Los Angeles, 1960-67, Navigator Press, Inc., Los Angeles, 1975—. Contbr. transp. research articles to profl. jours. Chmn. Coalition Rapid Transit, Los Angeles, 1978—, Friends of Geography UCLA, 1989—; v.p. Westwood Dem. Club, 1988—; chair L.A. Bus./Profl. Dem. Club, 1992—. Mem. Am. Econ. Assn., Am. Planning Assn., Am. Inst. Cert. Planners (counselor 1972-74). Democrat. Jewish. Office: Navigator Press Inc 516 N Fair Oaks Ave Pasadena CA 91103

FALICOV, LEOPOLDO MAXIMO, physicist, educator; b. Buenos Aires, June 24, 1933; came to U.S., 1960, naturalized, 1967; s. Isaias Felix and Dora (Samoilovich) F.; m. Marta Alicia Puebla, Aug. 13, 1959; children: Alexis, Ian. Licenciado in chemistry, Buenos Aires U., 1957; Ph.D. in Physics, Cuyo U. Instituto J. A. Balseiro, Argentina, 1958, Cambridge U., 1960; Sc.D., Cambridge U., 1977. Rsch. assoc. dept. physics Inst. Study Metals, U. Chgo., 1960-61, instr. physics, 1961-62, asst. prof. physics, 1962-65, assoc. prof., 1965- 68, prof., 1968-69; prof. physics U. Calif., Berkeley, 1969—; Miller rsch. prof. U. Calif., 1979-80, chmn. dept. physics, 1981-83; cons. in field. Author: Group Theory and Its Physical Applications, 1966, La Estructura Electronica de los Solidos, 1967; contbr. articles to profl. jours. Alfred P. Sloan Found. fellow, 1964-68; vis. fellow Fitzwilliam Coll., Cambridge, Eng., 1966; Fulbright fellow, 1969; OAS vis. prof. Argentina, 1970; Nordita vis. prof. U. Copenhagen, 1971-72, 87; Fulbright lectr. Spain, 1972; Guggenheim fellow, 1976-77; vis. fellow Clare Hall, Cambridge, Eng., 1976-77; exchange prof. U. Paris, 1977, 84. Fellow Third World Acad. Scis.; mem. NAS, Royal Danish Acad. Scis. and Letters (fgn.). Home: 90 Avenida Dr Berkeley CA 94708-2146 Office: U Calif Dept Physics Berkeley CA 94720

FALKENBERG, WILLIAM STEVENS, architect, contractor; b. Kansas City, Mo., July 21, 1927; s. John Joseph and Maraba Elizabeth (Stevens) F.; m. Janis Patton Hubner, Apr. 13, 1951; children: Ruth Elizabeth, Christopher Joseph, Charles Stevens. BS in Archtl. Engring., U. Colo., 1949. Pres. Falkenberg Constrn. Co., Denver, 1951-71, 74-84, devel. cons., 1984—; broker Hogan & Stevenson Realty, Denver, 1971-74. Chmn. constrn. Archdiocesan Housing Com., Inc.; chmn. restoration 9th Street Hist. Park; chmn. bldg. comm. Four Mile House Hist. Park; chmn. Housing Trust Coun., Denver, 1986-90; chmn. Rocky Mountain Better Bus. Bur., 1965-67; pres. Denver Friends Folk Music, 1966. Lt. (j.g.) USNR, 1945-51. Mem. AIA (bd. dirs. Denver chpt. 1978-81, treas. 1981), Home Builder Assn. Met. Denver, Colo. Hist. Soc. Found. (trustee, sec. 1987—), Serra Internat. (pres. 1971, dist. gov. 1973), Nat. Assn. Atomic Vets., Colo. Archeol. Soc., Denver Athletic Club, Equistrian Order of Holy Sepulchre, Cactus Club. Home and Office: 430 Marion St Denver CO 80218-3930

FALKNER, JAMES GEORGE, treasurer; b. Spokane, Wash., Dec. 24, 1952; s. Albert Andrew and Amanda Rosalia (Reisinger) F.; m. Joleen Rae Ann Brown, June 22, 1974; children: James Jr., Jayson, Jerin, Jarret. BS in Acctg., U. Wash., 1975. CPA, Wash. CPA LeMaster & Daniels, Spokane, 1975-80; treas. Dominican Sisters Spokane, 1980—; bd. dirs. Dominican Network, Spokane, Dominican Health Svcs.; mem. Bishop's Fin. Coun. Spokane Diocese, 1990—. Bd. dirs. sch. bd. St. Mary's Ch., Veradale, Wash., 1986-89, 90—, sch. found., 1987—; active acctg. adv. com. Spokane Falls Community Coll., 1989—. Mem. Healthcare Fin. Mgmt. Assn. (bd. dirs. 1982-85), AICPA, Wash. State Soc. CPAs, Conf. Religious Treas., Nat. Assn. Treas. Religious Insts., Nat. Notary Assn. Office: Dominican Sisters Spokane 3102 W Ft George Wright Dr Spokane WA 99204-5297

FALKOW, STANLEY, microbiologist, educator; b. Albany, N.Y., Jan. 24, 1934; s. Jacob and Mollie (Gingold) F.; children from previous marriage: Lynn Beth, Jill Stuart; m. Lucy Stuart Thompkins, Dec. 3, 1983. BS in Bacteriology cum laude, U. Maine, 1955, DSc (hon), 1979; MS in Biology, Brown U., 1960, PhD, 1961. Asst. chief dept. bacterial immunity Walter Reed Army Inst. Rsch., Washington, 1963-66; prof. microbiology Med. Sch. Georgetown U., 1966-72; prof. microbiology and medicine U. Wash., Seattle, 1972-81; prof., chmn. dept. med. microbiology Stanford (Calif.) U., 1981-85; Karl H. Beyer vis. prof. U. Wis., 1978-79; Sommer lectr. U. Oreg. Sch. Medicine, 1979, Kinyoun lectr. NIH, 1980; Rubbro orator Australian Soc. Microbiology, 1981; Stanhope Bayne-Jones lectr. Johns Hopkins U., 1982; mem. Recombinant DNA Molecule Com, task force on antibiotics in animal feeds FDA, microbiology test com. Nat. Bd. Med. Examiners. Author: Infectious Multiple Drug Resistance, 1975; editor: Jour. Bacteriology, Jour. Infection and Immunity, Jour. Infectious Diseases. Recipient Ehrlich prize, 1981. Fellow Am. Acad. Microbiology; mem. Infectious Disease Soc. Am. (Squibb award 1979), am. soc. Microbiology, Genetics Soc. Am., AAAS, Sigma Xi. Home: 8 Longspur Portola Valley CA 94028 Office: Stanford U Dept Med Microbiology & Immunology Stanford CA 94305

FALLETTA, JO ANN, musician; b. N.Y.C., Feb. 27, 1954; d. John Edward and Mary Lucy (Racioppo) F.; m. Robert Alemany, Aug. 24, 1986. BA in Music, Mannes Coll. Music, N.Y.C., 1976; MA in Music, Juilliard Sch., N.Y.C., 1982; PhD in Musical Arts, Juilliard Sch., 1989; Honorary Doctorate, Marian Coll., Wis., 1988. Music dir. Queens Philharmonic, N.Y.C., 1978-91, Den. Chamber Orch., Colo., 1983-92; assoc. condr. Milw. Symphony, Wis., 1985-88; music dir. Women's Philharmonic, San Francisco, 1986—, Long Beach Symphony, Calif., 1989—, Va. Symphony, Norfolk, 1991—. Stokowski Conducting Competition, Toscanini Conducting award. Office: Long Beach Symphony Orch 555 E Ocean Blvd Ste 106 Long Beach CA 90802

FALTIN, BRUCE CHARLES, hotel executive; b. Cin., Mar. 7, 1947; s. Charles F. and Meryl (Gunther) F.; m. H. Ann Walker: children: Sharon, Laura, John. BS, Cornell U., 1969. Mgr. Winegardner & Hammons Inc., Cin., 1969-78; ptnr. Idahotels Ltd., Boise, Idaho, 1978—; pres. Mountain States Mgmt. Inc., Boise, 1978—, also bd. dirs; trustee Rodeway Inns Advt. Fund, Phoenix, 1985—; chmn. Rodeway Inns Owner's Council, Phoenix, 1986-88. Co-founder, dir., pres. Idaho Hospitality Edn. Found., 1990-91. Mem. Am. Hotel and Motel Assn. (state dir. 1983-84), Nat. Restaurant Assn., Idaho Innkeepers Assn. (bd. dirs. 1974-86, 88—, pres. 1979, treas. 1988-91), Greater Boise C. of C. (bd. dirs. 1987), Choice Hotels Brands Adv. Coun., Idaho Hospitality Edn. Found. (pres. 1990-91). Home: 2423 Hillway Dr Boise ID 83702-0933 Office: Rodeway Inn of Boise 1115 N Curtis Rd Boise ID 83706-1298

FAN, HUNG Y., virology educator, consultant; b. Beijing, Oct. 30, 1947; s. Hsu Yun and Li Nien (Bien) F. BS, Purdue U., 1967; PhD, MIT, 1971. Asst. research prof. Salk Inst., San Diego, 1973-81; asst. prof. U. Calif., Irvine, 1981-83, assoc. prof., 1984-88, prof., 1988—, dir. Cancer Rsch. Inst., 1985—, acting dean Sch. Biol. Scis., 1990-91. Contbr. more than 80 articles to profl. jours. NIH, Am. Cancer Soc. research grantee, 1973—, grant review coms., 1973—; Woodrow Wilson Found. grad. fellow, 1967, Helen Hay Whitney Found. postdoctorate fellow, 1971. Fellow Am. Acad. Microbiology; mem. AAAS, Am. Soc. Microbiology, Am. Soc. Virology. Office: U Calif Cancer Rsch Inst Sch Biol & Scis Irvine CA 92717

FANCHER, MICHAEL REILLY, newspaper editor, newspaper publishing executive; b. Long Beach, Calif., July 13, 1946; s. Eugene Arthur and Ruth Leone (Dickson) F.; m. Nancy Helen Edens, Nov. 3, 1967 (div. 1982); children: Jason Michael, Patrick Reilly; m. 2d Carolyn Elaine Bowers, Mar. 25, 1983; Katherine Claire, Elizabeth Lynn. BA, U. Oreg., 1968; MS, Kans. State U., 1971; MBA, U. Wash., 1986. Reporter, asst. city editor Kansas City Star, Mo., 1970-76, city editor, 1976-78; reporter Seattle Times, 1978-79, night city editor, 1979-80, asst. mng. editor, 1980-81, mng. editor, 1981-86, exec. editor, 1986—, vice pres., 1989—; bd. dirs. Walla Walla Union-Bulletin, Yakima Herald Rep. Ruhl fellow U. Oreg., 1983. Mem. Am. Soc. Newspaper Editors, Associated Press Mng. Editors (bd. dirs. 1985—), Soc. Profl. Journalists, Nat. Press Photographers Assn. (Editor of Yr. 1986). Office: Seattle Times Fairview Ave N & John St PO Box 70 Seattle WA 98111-0070

FANDRICH, LAMONT H., accountant; b. Bismarck, N.D., Oct. 10, 1951; s. Roy and Lucille Clara (Schuh) F. BA cum laude, Minot State Coll., 1973; MBA, Calif. Luth. U., 1989. CPA, N.D.; accredited tax advisor Coun. Accountancy & Taxation. Acctg. supr. Collins Foods Internat., Los Angeles, 1976-77; gen. ledger supr. Sambos Restaurants, Inc., Carpintera, Calif., 1977-79; asst. v.p. fin. Amfac Garden Products, Fallbrook, Calif., 1979-84; dir. fin. Twyford Plant Labs., Santa Paula, Calif., 1984-86; v.p. fin. Oreg. Garden Products, Hillsboro, 1986-88, L.F. Enterprises, Ventura, Calif., 1987—. Contbg. author: Portfolio of Accounting Systems for Small and Medium-Sized Businesses. Served to 1st lt. USMCR, 1973-76. Mem. AICPAs, Nat. Assn. Accts., Calif. Soc. CPAs (chmn. microcomputer com. Channel Islands chpt.), Calif. Assn. Ind. Accts., Nat. Assn. Pub. Accts., Greater Ventura C. of C., Kiwanis (bd. dirs.). Home: PO Box 7588 Ventura CA 93006-7588

FANGMEIER, DELMAR DEAN, agriculture and biosystems engineering educator, researcher; b. Hebron, Nebr., Oct. 27, 1932; s. August Henry and Louise Marie F.; m. Margaret-Ann Wagner, June 21, 1969; children: Kurt Joseph, Kristin Louise. BSA, U. Nebr., 1954, BS in Agrl. Engring., 1960, MS in Agrl. Engring., 1961; PhD in Engring., U. Calif., Davis, 1967. Registered profl. engr., Ariz., Calif. Agrl. engr. Agrl. Rsch. Svc., USDA, Lincoln, Nebr., 1960-61; asst. prof. U. Wyo., Laramie, 1966-68; assoc. prof. U. Ariz., Tucson, 1968-72, prof., 1972—; cons. Colombian Cotton Growers, Bogota, 1987, SunCor Devel. Corp., Phoenix, 1990. Author: World Book Encyclopedia; contbg. author: Irrigation; also articles. Mem. coms. Sch. Dist., Tucson, 1980-87; pres. Homeowners' Assn., Tucson, 1987-88. Lt. U.S. Army, 1954-56. Rsch. grantee NSF, 1979, USDA, 1980, 87, U.S. Water Cons. Lab. Mem. ASCE, Am. Soc. Agrl. Engrs. (paper award 1980), Am. Soc. for Engring. Edn., Guayule Rubber Soc. (pres. 1987). Home: 3635 E Calle Alarcon Tucson AZ 85716-5018 Office: U Ariz Dept Agrl & Biosystems Enging Tucson AZ 85721

FANNIN, WILLIAM RICHARD, dean; b. Ithaca, N.Y., July 4, 1951; s. Bob Meredith and Martha Ellen (Stewart) F.; m. Valerie Kay Foster, May 21, 1988; children: Addley Coffee, Stewart Powell. BA, U. Tex., 1973, MBA, 1976; PhD, Tex. A&M U., 1980. Asst. prof. U. Maine, Orono, 1980-83; asst. prof. U. Houston-Clear Lake, 1983-85, assoc. v.p., 1985-88; assoc. dean coll. bus. Idaho State U., Pocatello, 1988-89, dean, 1989—; bd. dirs. Internat. Bus. Ctr. Idaho Dept. Commerce, Boise, Idaho Innovation Ctr., Idaho Falls, Boise Dist. U.S. Small Bus. Adminstrn., Bannock Devel. Corp., Pocatello. Contbr. articles to profl. jours. Bd. dirs. Idaho State Symphony, Pocatello, 1990-91. Mem. Rotary, Beta Gamma Sigma, Phi Kappa Psi. Presbyterian. Home: 2686 Castle Peak Way Pocatello ID 83201-2625 Office: Idaho State U Coll Bus Campus Box 8020 Pocatello ID 83209

FANNY-DELL (FANNY-DELL HENDRICKS), artist, sculptor, educator; b. Trinidad, Colo., May 30, 1939; d. Troy Stephen and Madelene Leona (Ball) Swift; div. first husband; children: Dennis Howard, Kim Renee, Terry Don, Laura Beth Wigley; m. Cecil Gene Hendricks, Dec. 10, 1979; stepchildren: Richard, Elizabeth, Russell, K. Renee, Beverly. Student, South Oklahoma City Jr. Coll., 1978, Highline Community Coll., Seattle, 1980, Bellevue Community Coll., 1982-84. Freelance illustrator, 1978—; owner, artist Fannytastics, Seattle, 1983—; asst. instr. Bellevue (Wash.) Community Coll., 1984-90; vol. archaeol. field excavations, Okla., 1977-80; sec. to Okla. state archaeologist, Norman, 1977-78; exhibit preparer and coord. Spiro Mounds, Okla. State Park Visitor Ctr. Exhibits, 1978; asst. art lab. South Okla. City Jr. Coll., 1979; docent Cowboy Hall of Fame, Oklahoma City, 1979; artist, craftsman Bringloe Hist. Figures, Seattle, 1980-81. Shows include Bellevue (Wash.) Community Coll. Art Faculty Shows, 1986, 87, 88, 89, 90, St. David Religious and Fine Art Show, Lynwood, Mass., 1986, 87, 89, 93 (Best of Show cash award), Mercer Island Visual Arts League Summer Arts Festival, Mercer Island, Wash., 1982, 83, 85, 86, The Best and the Brightest, Scottsdale, Ariz., 1991; represented in permanent collections Pacific N.W. Mus. of Flight, Seattle, Okla. SPIRO Archaeol. State Park Interpretive Ctr., Stoval Mus. Okla. U., Norman; producer (videotapes) Wax Sculpture, 1988, Lost Wax Sculpture, 1988; commd. portraits for pvt. collectors. Recipient 2d place award Art X 5 Show, Oklahoma City, 1979, lst place medal SeaTac Visual Arts Olympics, 1984. Mem. Internat. Sculpture Ctr., Women in Arts, Sculpture Source and Artist Trust, Western Art Assn., Exptl. Aircraft Assn. (historian 1982-88), 99's, Aircraft Owners and Pilots Assn. Office: Fannytastics 4735 S 158th St Seattle WA 98188

FANSLOW, JULIA EARLEEN, oncology nurse specialist, nursing educator; b. Ellensburgh, Wash., Nov. 8, 1939; d. Wayne Wendall Corum and Mary Christina (Van Wagoner) Dunkle; m. William Christian Fanslow, Jr. Apr. 16, 1960; children: William III, Brett, Heidi. AD in Nursing, San Diego City Coll., 1973; BSN, U. Tex., Ft. Worth, 1976; MSN, U. Tex., Arlington, 1978; EdD, Gonzaga U., 1983. Oncology cert. nurse, advanced cardiac life support cert. Supr. emergency svcs. Campbell Meml. Hosp.r., Weatherford, Tex., 1974-76; dir. emergency svcs. Harris Hosp., Ft. Worth, 1976-78; asst. prof. nursing Tarleton State U., Stephenville, Tex., 1978-79; RN emergency dept. Sacred Heart Hosp., Spokane, 1979-85; assoc. prof. Intercollegiate Ctr. for Nursing Edn., Spokane, 1979-85; pvt. practice counselor Tacoma, 1982—; home health nurse Good Samaritan Home Health Hospice, Puyallup, Wash., 1985—; assoc. prof. Sch. Nursing Pacific Luth. U., Tacoma, 1985-90, 92—; oncology nurse specialist St. Joseph Cancer Ctr., Tacoma, 1989—; cons. Narrows Glen Retirement Ctr., 1990-91, Lakewood (Wash.) Gen. Hosp., 1988; case cons. Larson & Larson Attys.-at-Law, Tacoma, 1988, Williams, Kastner and Givvs, Seattle, 1991—; rsch. cons. MCH Dept., St. Joseph Hosp., Tacoma, 1990—; accreditation site visitor Nat. League for Nursing, 1986-90, 92—; mem. bd. rev. Oncology Nursing Forum, Home Health Care Nurse. Author: Pain Management, 1991; contbr. articles to profl. jours. Mem. Profession Ednl. Adv. Bd. for Widowed Info. and Cons. Svcs., Tacoma, 1987—; mem. state com. Wash. State Cancer Pain Initiative, State Sch. Nurses Adv. Com., Olympia, Wash., 1987-90; mem. adv. bd. Good Samaritan Home Health Hospice, Puyallup, 1985—; bd. dirs. Pierce County Am. Cancer Soc., Tacoma, 1986—. Recipient Vol. Leadership award Am. Cancer Soc., 1989; Am. Cancer Soc. scholar, 1987; Joan Ashley Fiffick award in Oncology Nursing, 1993. Mem. Am. Pain Soc., Internat. Assn. for Study of Pain, Puget Sound Oncology Nursing Soc., Nat. League for Nursing, Internat. Soc. Nurses in Cancer Care, Sigma Theta Tau. Mem. Christian Ch. Home: 6004 12th St NE Tacoma WA 98422-3855 Office: Pacific Luth U Sch of Nursing Tacoma WA 98447

FARAH, TAWFIC ELIAS, political scientist; b. Nazareth, Palestine, Aug. 12, 1946; came to U.S., 1965; s. Elias Tawfic and Itaf Fahim F.; BA, Calif. State U., Fresno, 1970, MA, 1971; PhD, U. Nebr., 1975; m. Linda Maxwell, Apr. 24, 1969; children—Omar Lee, Aliya Jane. Market researcher Xerox Corp., Lincoln, Nebr., 1974-75; asst. prof. polit. sci. Kuwait U., 1975-79; pres. Merg Analityca, 1979—; vis. asso. prof. UCLA, summers 1978-83, fellow Center for Internat. and Strategic Affairs, 1980-81, Ctr. for Near Eastern Studies, 1986; Fulbright scholar, 1983. Toyota Found. grantee, 1985. Mem. Am. Polit. Sci. Assn., Middle East Studies Assn. Greek Orthodox. Coauthor: Research Methods in the Social Sciences, 1977; A Dictionary of Social Analysis, 1980; author: Aspects of Modernization and Consociationalism: Lebanon as an Exploratory Test Case, 1975, 77; co-editor: Palestinians Without Palestine: Socialization of Palestinian Children, 1979; Learning to Become Palestinians, 1985; editor Political Behavior in the Arab States, 1983; Pan Arabism and Arab Nationalism: The Continuing Debate, 1986, Political Socialization in the Arab States, 1987, Survey Research in the Arab World, 1987; editor Jour. Arab Affairs, 1981—.

FARANDA, JOHN PAUL, college administrator; b. Orange, Calif., Feb. 21, 1957; s. Paul L. and Kay S. (Wilson) F. BA cum laude, Claremont McKenna Coll., 1979. Staff liaison L.A. County Bar Assn., 1979-80; spl. programs adminstr. L.A. County Med. Assn., 1980-85; dir. corp. rels. Claremont (Calif.) McKenna Coll., 1985-87, dir. campaign and devel. svcs., 1987-89, dir. devel., 1989—. Contbr. articles to profl. jours. Campaign chmn. United Way, Mt. Baldy Region, Ontario, Calif., 1987-90; bd. govs. Faculty Ho. of the Claremont Colls., pres., 1993—. Recipient Gold award Mt. Baldy United Way, 1988, 91. Mem. L.A. County Bar Assn. (com. on arbitration), Coun. for Advancement and Support of Edn. (USX award 1986), Univ. Club L.A. Office: Claremont McKenna Coll Bauer Ctr #320 500 E 9th St Claremont CA 91711-6400

FARBER, BERNARD, sociologist, educator; b. Chgo., Feb. 11, 1922; s. Benjamin and Esther (Axelrod) F.; m. Annette Ruth Shugan, Dec. 21, 1947 (div. 1970); children—Daniel, Michael, Lisa, Jacqueline; m. Rosanna Bodanis, June 10, 1971 (dec. June 1988); 1 dau., Tanya. A.B., Roosevelt U., Chgo., 1943; A.M., U. Chgo., 1949, Ph.D., 1953. Research asso. U. Chgo., 1951-53; asst. prof. Henderson State Tchr. Coll., Arkadelphia, Ark., 1953-54; mem. faculty U. I., 1954-71, prof. sociology, 1964-71; asso. dir. Inst. Research Exceptional Children, 1967-69; prof. Ariz. State U., 1971-92, prof. emeritus, 1992—, chmn. dept. sociology, 1971-75, 90-92; vis. prof. U. Tex., Austin, 1974-75, U. Ill., Chgo., 1988—; cons. in field, 1957—. Author: Family: Organization and Interaction, 1964, Mental Retardation: Its Social Context and Social Consequences, 1968, Kinship and Class, 1971, Guardians of Virtue, 1972, Family and Kinship in Modern Society, 1973, Conceptions of Kinship, 1981; editor Sociol. Perspectives, 1985-89. Mem. mental retardation research com. Nat. Inst. Child Health and Human Devel., 1971-75. Served with AUS, 1943-46. Recipient E.W. Burgess award Nat. Council on Family Relations, 1975; Disting. Research award Ariz. State U., 1980. Mem. Am. Sociol. Assn. (council mem. family sect. 1966-69), Ill. Sociol. Assn. (founding pres. 1965-66), Pacific Sociol. Soc. (pres. 1986-87). Jewish. Home: 7949 E Montebello Ave Scottsdale AZ 85250-6108 Office: Ariz State U Dept Sociology Tempe AZ 85287-2101

FARBER, PAUL LAWRENCE, historian, educator, academic administrator; b. N.Y.C., Mar. 7, 1944; s. Charles and Helen (Shapiro) F.; m. Vreneli Regula Marti, Aug. 27, 1966; children: Benjamin, Channah. BS, U. Pitts., 1965; MS, Ind. U., 1968, PhD, 1970. Prof. history of sci., chmn. dept. gen. sci. Oreg. State U., Corvallis, 1983-91, chmn. history dept., 1991—; vis. prof. U. Wash., Seattle, 1974, Imperial Coll., London, 1978, U. Cambridge, Eng., 1989. Author: The Emergence of Ornithology, 1982; co-editor: Religion, Science, and Worldview, 1985. Bd. dirs. Corvallis Sch. Bd. Dist. 509J, 1986-88. Mem. AAAS (nominating com.), History of Sci. Soc. (exec. coun. 1978-81), Coumbia History of Sci. Soc. (pres. 19850. Home: 3655 NW Jackson Ave Corvallis OR 97330-4944 Office: Oreg State U Dept History Corvallis OR 97331-5104

FARBER, STEVEN GLENN, lawyer; b. Phila., July 20, 1946; s. Isadore Irving and Sylvia (Galperin) F.; m. Barbara Nobel, Dec. 12, 1972 (div. 1983); children: Jamie, Daniel; m. Pamela Messer, Mar. 16, 1986; children: Zoey, Avi. BBA, Temple U., 1968, JD, 1972. Bar: Pa. 1972, U.S. Dist. Ct. (ea. dist.) Pa. 1972, U.S. Dist. Ct. Appeals (3d cir.) 1972, N.Mex. 1975, U.S. Dist. Ct. N.Mex. 1975, U.S. Ct. Appeals (10th cir.) 1979, U.S. Supreme Ct. 1980. Asst. defender Pub. Defender Assn. Phila., 1972-74; acting dist. pub. defender State of N.Mex., Santa Fe, 1975-76, asst. atty. gen., 1976-78; pvt. practice Santa Fe, 1978—; mem. N.Mex. Bd. Legal Specialization, 1986-90, chmn. 1991—. Elected city councilor, City of Santa Fe, 1992—. Mem. Nat. Assn. Criminal Def. Lawyers (vice chair continuing legal edn. com. 1990-91), N.Mex. Lawyers Guild (pres. 1980-81), N.Mex. State Bar Assn. (bd. dirs. criminal law sect. 1980-83, chmn. 1981-82), N.Mex. Criminal Def. Lawyers Assn. (bd. dirs. 1991). Democrat. Jewish. Office: 409 Hillside Ave Santa Fe NM 87501-2248

FARHAT, CAROL S., motion picture company executive; b. Santa Monica, Calif.; d. Annis Abraham and Jacklin (Thomas) F.; divorced; 1 child, Michael. AA, Santa Monica Coll., 1967; student, Inst. Audio Rsch., 1976-78, Otis Parsons Inst., 1980-84, UCLA, 1984-90; BA in Bus., Music, Antioch U., 1992. Recording studio mgr. The Village Recorder, L.A., 1972-78; audio engr. The Village Recorder Studio, L.A., 1978-79; music adminstr. 20th Century Fox Film Corp., Beverly Hills, Calif., 1980-82, music supr., 1983-86, music dir., 1986-92; supr. internat. music 20th Century Fox Film Corp., Tokyo, 1993; music prodr. Scopus Films, England, 1987-89; songwriter Music Experts Ltd., Santa Monica, Calif., 1989-90. Author: China Diary, 1992; composer (music book) Children's Songbook, 1991; songwriter (for film) Rockin' Reindeer, 1990. Mem. BMI, NATAS, Women in Film, Am. Film Inst., Pacific Composers Forum. Office: 20th Century Fox Film Corp PO Box 900 Beverly Hills CA 90213

FARHAT, VINCE LEE, real estate executive, consultant; b. Santa Monica, Calif., June 15, 1966; s. Ernie Annis and Janet (Bisbing) F. BA in Internat. Studies, Am. U., 1987; MBA, Pepperdine U., 1991. Lic. real estate broker, Calif. Broker assoc. The Prudential Stevenson, Glendale, Calif., 1987-91; sales assoc. Sanjo Investments, Marina Del Rey, Calif., 1985-87, v.p., 1991—; devel. cons. FDC, Inc., L.A., 1990—. Vice chair Calif. Selective Svc. Bd., West Los Angeles, 1989—; bd. dirs. Assocs. Friends of Child Advocates, Pasadena, Calif., 1990—; mem. L.A. World Affairs, Coun., 1988—; presentation leader The Hunger Project, L.A., 1990—; mem. Calif. State Republican Com., 1990—. Named to Outstanding Young Men of Am., 1988. Mem. Am. Indsl. Real Estate Assn., Young Execs. Am., Am. Mgmt. Assn. Roman Catholic. Office: Sanjo Investments 4040 Del Rey Ave # 1 Marina Del Rey CA 90292

FARIN, LISA SCHULKE, graphic designer, business owner; b. San Francisco, Mar. 4, 1958; d. Russell E. and Helen (Joyce) Schulke; m. Federico M. Farin, Nov. 8, 1980. BS, U. Calif., Davis, 1980. Advt. mgr. Omega N.W., Bellevue, Wash., 1980-81; designer, typographer Northgate Printing & Graphics, Seattle, 1981-84; owner Farin Design Group, Seattle, 1984—. Recipient Halo award Seattle Advt. Fedn., 1989, Award of Excellence, Soc. Tech. Com.. Publs., 1991, Award of Merit, N.W. Classics, Internat. Assn. Bus. Comm., 1992. Mem. Am. Inst. Graphic Arts (bd. dirs. Seattle chpt.), Women Bus. Owners, Greater Seattle C.of C. Office: Farin Design Group 2326 N Pacific St Seattle WA 98103

FARIS-STOCKEM, DEBBIE ANNE, architectural sheet metal executive; b. Portland, Oreg., Jan. 6, 1955; d. Ernest Duane and Elizabeth Anne (McCullough) Faris; m. Robert A. Stockem, Oct. 18, 1975 (div.); children: Melissa Gene, Cassandra Lynn. Office mgr. Faris Sheet Metal, Inc., Portland, 1975-84, v.p., 1984-88, pres., 1988—. Mem. Nat. Assn. Women in Constrn. (bd. dirs. Portland chpt. 1987—, pres. 1990-91). Republican. Office: Faris Sheet Metal Inc 102 SE 99th Ave Portland OR 97216-2397

FARKAS, ABRAHAM KRAKAUER, urban developer, educator; b. Dunkirk, N.Y., Oct. 31, 1947; s. Louis Ari and Hedy (Krakauer) F.; m. Pamela Ann Price, June 15, 1970; children: Madeleine, Uri, Jacob. BA in Polit. Sci., Purdue U., 1969, MA in Am. Studies, 1971; PhD in Am. Studies, U. Minn., 1976. Asst. prof. housing and pub. policy U. Tenn., Knoxville, 1976-80; dir. community devel. and planning City of Ft. Wayne, Ind., 1980-83; mgr. econ. devel. City of Seattle, 1983-85; exec. dir. planning and devel. City of Eugene, Oreg., 1985—; me. bd. advisors for housing and mktg. Oreg. State U., Corvallis, 1990—. Editor Housing and Society, 1980; contbr. articles to profl. jours. Bd. dirs. Temple Beth Israel, Eugene, 1990-91. Lilly fellow, 1979; Tenn. Endowment for Humanities grantee, 1978. Mem. Urban Land Inst., Nat. Community Devel. Assn. (bd. dirs. 1982), Coun. for Urban Econ. Devel. (treas. N.W. chpt. 1986-87). Jewish. Office: City of Eugene 72 W Broadway Eugene OR 97401

FARLAND, EUGENE HECTOR, retired educator; b. Woonsocket, R.I., Aug. 20, 1918; s. Joseph and Alma (Cayer) F.; m. Felice Ursala Paquin, Dec. 20, 1944 (div. 1967); children: Julien H., Linda F. Student, U. Calif., 1976-78. Cert. edn.-aeronautics. Mcpl. field engr. Woonsocket, 1939-40; ind. ins. broker R.I., Mass., 1946-55; ins. claims br. mgr. Portland, Maine, 1955-57; bush pilot Nome, Alaska, 1961-66; flight instr. Alaska, 1964-66; instr. flight and aircraft mechanics Community Coll., San Francisco, 1966-79; cons. edn. sch. system San Francisco, 1979-84; geol. studies and field trips with local coll. Arbiter Better Bus. Bur., Phoenix, 1987-90; chair UN Children Crusade Drive, Woonsocket, 1948; asst. chair Red Cross Drive, Woonsocket, 1948; pres. Kiwanis Club, Woonsocket, 1948; counselor YMCA, Woonsocket, 1951. 1st lt. USAAF, 1941-46, ETO. Recipient Presdl. citation USAAF, 1945; decorated Air medal with 1 star. Mem. Explorers Club, OXS Aviation Pioneers. Office: PO Box 6519 Yuma AZ 85366-6519

FARLEY, FRANK FREDERIC, retired oil industry executive; b. Perrysburg, Ohio, Oct. 9, 1912; s. Frank Eugene and Mary Teresa (Shiple) Farley; m. Maureen Alice O'Neil, Aug. 28, 1941 (dec. 1988); children: Jeanne Alice, George Francis, Anne Maureen. AB, St. John U., Toledo, Ohio, 1934; MS, U. Detroit, 1936; PhD, Iowa State U., 1941. Chemistry instr. U. Detroit, 1941-42; sr. rsch. chemist Shell Oil Co., Wood River, Ill., 1942-43, rsch. supr., 1943-46; chief rsch. chemist Shell Oil Co., Martinez, Calif., 1946-61, rsch. dir., 1961-64; environ. affairs rep. Shell Oil Co., San Francisco, 1972-77; rsch. mgr. Shell Devel. Co., Emeryville, Calif., 1964-72; cons. Environ. Affairs, Inc., Oakland, Calif., 1977-85, ret., 1985. Contbr. articles to profl. jours.; patentee in rust preventive and chemical manufacture. mem. Am. Chem. Soc., Nat. Soc. Graphology, Serra Club, Rotary. Republican. Roman Catholic.

FARLEY, GEORGE FRANCIS, veterinarian; b. St. Louis, July 15, 1947; s. Francis Frederick and Maureen Alice (O'Neil) F.; m. Georgia Lee Anderson, July 18, 1970; children: Wendy Lynn, Brett Christopher. BS in Animal Sci., U. Calif., Davis, 1969, DVM, 1973. Lic. vet., Calif., Wash. Assoc. vet. Noble Vet. Clinic, Hayward, Calif., 1973-87; hosp. dir. Hayward (Calif.) Vet. Clinic, 1987—; med. dir. Alameda County Animal Control, San Leandro, Calif., 1974-75, Hayward (Calif.) County Animal Control, 1975-76, 80-82; career speaker Moreau High Sch., Hayward, 1984—. Nat. bd. Presbyn. Marriage Encounter, 1985-86. Recipient Cert. USDA, 1973, Calif. State Pers. Bd., 1973. Mem. Am. Vet. Med. Assn., Am. Animal Hosp. Assn., Calif. Vet. Med. Assn., Alameda County Vet. Assn. (dir. 1980-82). Office: Hayward Vet Clinic 605 Greeley Ct Hayward CA 94544

FARLEY, GLENN FRANCIS, software company executive; b. Buffalo, Feb. 21, 1953; s. John and Florence (Freeman) F. BA, Rutgers Coll., 1975, MBA, 1977; MS in Computer Sci., Villanova U., 1982. Cons. Blue Cross, Columbia, S.C., 1988-91; sr. software engr. Bank of Am., Concord, Calif., 1991—; pres. Creative Software, San Francisco, 1990—. Editor Blue Notes mag., 1992. Mem. Assn. for Computing Machinery, Commonwealth Club of Calif. Office: Creative Software Corp 766 Sutter St San Francisco CA 94109

FARLEY, THOMAS T., lawyer; b. Pueblo, Colo., Nov. 10, 1934; s. John Baron and Mary (Tancred) F.; m. Kathleen Maybelle Murphy, May 14, 1960; children: John, Michael, Kelly, Anne. BS, U. Santa Clara, 1956; LLB, U. Colo., 1959. Bar: Colo. 1959, U.S. Dist. Ct. Colo. 1959, U.S. Ct. Appeals (10th cir.) 1988. Dep. dist. atty. City of Pueblo, 1960-62; pvt. practice Pueblo, 1963-69; ptnr. Phelps, Fonda & Hays, Pueblo, 1970-75, Petersen & Fonda, P.C., Pueblo, 1975—; bd. dirs. Pub. Svc. Co. Colo., Denver, Norwest Pueblo, Norwest Sunset, Qual Med Inc. Minority leader Colo. Ho. of Reps., 1967-75; chmn. Colo. Wildlife Commn., 1975-79, Colo. Bd. Agr., 1979-87; bd. regents Santa Clara U., 1987—; commr. Colo. State Fair; trustee Colo. Wildlife Heritage Found., Great Outdoors Colo. Trust Fund. Recipient Disting. Svc. award U. So. Colo., 1987, 93, Bd. of Regents, U. Colo., 1993. Mem. ABA, Colo. Bar Assn., Pueblo C. of C. (bd. dirs. 1991—), Rotary. Democrat. Roman Catholic. Office: Petersen & Fonda PC 650 Thatcher Bldg Pueblo CO 81003

FARMAN, RICHARD DONALD, gas company executive; b. San Francisco, Aug. 20, 1935; s. Carl Edward Jr. and Doris May (Muntz) F.; m. Suzanne Hotchkiss, Sept. 12, 1956; children: Michael H., Charles S. BA in Econs. cum laude, Stanford U., 1957, LLB, 1963. Bar: Calif. 1964. Pvt. practice law Palo Alto, Calif., 1963-69; with Unionamerica, Inc., 1969-78, exec. v.p., sec., gen. counsel, 1969-75, exec. v.p. Unionamerica Ins. Group, 1976-78; v.p. Pacific Enterprises, 1978-82, pres. Pacific Lighting Energy Systems and Cen. Plants, Inc., 1982-86, vice chmn. So. Calif. Gas Co., L.A., 1987-88, chmn. bd., chief exec. officer, 1989—; bd. dirs. Union Bank, Assocs. Electric & Gas Ins. Svcs., The 2000 Regional Partnership; chmn. Pacific Enterprises Corp., Natural Gas Coun. Bd. dirs. L.A. Sports Coun.; vice chmn., bd. dirs. Pub. Svc. Sta. KCET-TV; mem. select panel Project Calif. Lt. USN, 1957-60. Mem. Calif. Bar Assn., Am. Gas Assn. (past chmn., bd. dirs., exec. com. 1988—), Pacific Coast Gas Assn., U.S. C. of C. (energy and natural resources com.), L.A. Area C. of C. (bd. dirs., exec. com.), Project Calif. Select Panel, Calif. Club, L.A. Country Club, Portuguese Bend Club, City Club on Bunker Hill. Republican. Office: So Calif Gas Co 555 W 5th St Los Angeles CA 90013

FARMER, JANENE ELIZABETH, artist, educator; b. Albuquerque, Oct. 16, 1946; d. Charles John Watt and Regina M. (Brown) Kruger; m. Michael Hugh Bolton, Apr. 1965 (div.); m. Frank Urban Farmer, May, 1972 (div.). BA in Art, San Diego State U., 1969. Owner, operator Iron Walrus Pottery, 1972-79; designer ceramic and fabric murals, Coronado, Calif., 1979-82; executed commns. for clients in U.S.A., Can., Japan and Mex., 1972—; pvt. tchr. pottery; instr. U. Calif.-San Diego; designer fabric murals and bldg. interiors; painter rare and endangered animals, Coronado and La Jolla, Calif., 1982—; tchr. Catholic schs., San Diego, 1982-87, Ramona Unified Sch. Dist., 1988—; instr. U. Calif., San Diego, 1979-83, 92—. Mem. Coronado Arts and Humanities Coun., 1979-81; resident artist U. Calif.-San Diego. Grantee Calif. Arts Coun., 1980-81; U. San Diego grad. fellow dept. edn., 1984. Mem. Am. Soc. Interior Designers (affiliate). Roman Catholic. Home: 4435 Nobel Dr Apt 35 San Diego CA 92122-1559

FARMER, JOSEPH COLLIN, chemical engineer, researcher; b. Mt. Airy, N.C., Feb. 12, 1955; s. Collin Edward and Polly (Bowman) F.; m. Janet Laufman. BS in Chem. Engring., Virginia Tech., 1977; PhD in Chem. Engring., U. Calif., Berkeley, 1983. Engr. Union Carbide Tech. Ctr., So. Charleston, W.Va., 1976-79; rsch. asst. Chem. Engring. Dept. U. Calif., Berkeley, 1979-83; mem. tech. staff Sandia Nat. Lab., Livermore, Calif., 1983-87; prin. investigator, dep. group leader Lawrence Livermore Nat. Lab., 1987—. Contbr. numerous articles to profl jours. and proceedings. Vol. Children's Hosp. at Stanford, Palo Alto, Calif., 1988—. NSF fellow Va. Tech., 1975; recipient Joffee award for best paper Interfinish 84, Jerusalem, 1984, Eagle Scout Order of Arrow Boy Scouts Am., 1973. Mem. ASTM, Nat. Assn. Corrosion Engrs., Am. Electroplaters and Surface Finishers Soc. (Gold medal 1985, Silver medal 1990), Electrochem. Soc. (Young Author's award 1986). Roman Catholic. Office: Lawrence Livermore Nat Lab L-352 PO Box 808 Livermore CA 94551-0808

FARMER, WILLIAM MICHAEL, atmospheric research program manager, consultant; b. Nashville, May 10, 1944; s. John Campbell and Hattie Mann (Phillips) F.; m. Jan Miller, Sept. 4, 1966; children: Michael Ryan, Amanda Ford. BS in Engring. Physics, U. Tenn., 1967, MS in Physics, 1968, PhD in Physics, 1973. Physicist ARO, Inc., Tullahoma, Tenn., 1968-73, SAI, Tullahoma, 1973-75; sr. scientist, mgr. Spectron Devel. Labs., Tullahoma, 1975-77; prof. physics Univ. Tenn. Space Inst., Tullahoma, 1977-84; sr. scientist, v.p. Sci. and Tech. Inc., Las Cruces, N.Mex., 1984-89; program mgr. The Bionetics Corp., Las Cruces, 1989—; lectr. in field. Contbr. articles to profl. jours. Mem. Soc. Photographic Instrumentation Engrs., Optical Soc. Am. Methodist. Home: 4309 Mission Bell Las Cruces NM 88001 Office: The Bionetics Corp FNB Ste 900 500 S Main Las Cruces NM 88001

FARMER, WILLIAM ROBERT, comedian, impressionist; b. Pratt, Kans., Nov. 14, 1952; s. Robert Vernon and Mary Frances (Jones) F.; m. Sherry Ann Fanning, Feb. 1, 1980 (div. 1981); m. Jennifer Wynne Shadbolt, June 2, 1984; 1 child, Austin Robert. BS in Journalism, U. Kans., 1975. Ofcl. voice of Goofy and Pluto, Walt Disney Prodns., featured in The Prince and the Pauper, 1990, Goof Troop, 1992; featured actor: America, You're Too Young to Die, Robocop, 1986, Dallas; guest Showtime's Funniest Person in America, PM Mag., Murphy Brown; featured voice artist, Who Framed Roger Rabbit, 1988, Skedaddle; narrator TV and radio commls. (Bronze award Film & TV Festival N.Y. 1984, Gold ADDY award Advt. Club Ft. Worth) 1986; performer comedy routines at various clubs nationwide. Mem. SAG, AFTRA, Acad. TV Arts and Scis., Sigma Chi. Republican. Presbyterian. Home: 4320 Vantage Ave Studio City CA 91604-1754

FARNHAM, MARY GLADE SIEMER, artist; b. Ross, Calif., Nov. 1, 1924; d. Albert Henry and Mabel Meta (Jones) Siemer; children: Thomas Ross, Evan Neil, Gwen Marie, William Blair, Hugh Porter. Student Marin Jr. Coll., 1942-43, Goucher Coll., 1943-44; B.A., U. Calif.-Berkeley, 1947. Profl. athlete, Curry Co., Yosemite, Calif., 1945; advt. prodn. mgr. City of Paris/Hale's, San Francisco, 1947; advt. artist Lipman Wolfe, Portland, Oreg., 1947-48; advt. layout artist Meier & Frank, Portland, 1948; art dir. Olds & King, Portland, 1948-50; free lance comml. artist, Portland, 1950-56; pres. Marin County Devel. Co., San Anselmo, Calif., 1963-78; pres., designer Mary Farnham Designs, Inc., Portland, 1983-89. Exhibited in 13 one woman shows and numerousgroup shows, U.S. & abroad. Mem. pub. art selection panel II, Met. Arts Commn., Portland, 1982-83; bd. dirs. N.W. Artists Workshop, Portland, 1977-78; sec. Artist Membership, Portland Art Assn., 1973-74. Episcopalian. Club: Multnomah Athletic. Avocations: swimming; diving.

FARNWORTH, WARREN MICHAEL, engineer; b. Nampa, Idaho, Dec. 7, 1953; s. Warren J. and Betty Marie (Burkey) F.; m. Susan Dolores Smith, Mar. 31, 1973; children: Robert Warren, Julie Marie, David Michael. Lic. U.S. nuclear regulatory commn. reactor operator. Residential electrician Boise Cascade Homes, Meridian, Idaho, 1973-76; nuclear reactor operator Donald C. Cook, Bridgeman, Mich., 1982-83; engr. Micron Semiconductor, Boise, 1983—. Patentee in field. With USN, 1976-82. Home: 2004 S Banner Nampa ID 83686 Office: Micron Semiconductor 2805 E Columbia Rd Boise ID 83706

FARR, LEE EDWARD, physician; b. Albuquerque, Oct. 13, 1907; s. Edward and Mabel (Heyn) F.; m. Anne Ritter, Dec. 28, 1936 (dec.); children: Charles E., Susan A., Frances A.; m. Miriam Kirk, Jan. 22, 1985. BS, Yale U., 1929, MD, 1933. Asst. pediatrics Sch. Medicine, Yale U., 1933-34; asst. medicine hosp. of Rockefeller Inst. Med. Research, 1934-37, assoc. medicine, 1937-40; dir. research Alfred I. duPont Inst. of Nemours Found., Wilmington, Del., 1940-49; vis. assoc. prof. pediatrics Sch. Medicine, U. Pa., 1940-49; med. dir. Brookhaven Nat. Lab., 1948-62; prof. nuclear medicine U. Tex. Postgrad. Med. Sch., 1962-64, prof. nuclear and environ. medicine Grad. Sch. Bio-Med. Scis., U. Tex. at Houston, 1965-68; chief sect. nuclear medicine U. Tex.-M.D. Anderson Hosp. and Tumor Inst., 1962-67, prof. environ. health U. Tex. Sch. Pub. Health, Houston, 1967-68; head disaster health services Calif. Dept. Health, 1968, chief emergency health services unit, 1968-70, 1st chief bur. emergency med. services, 1970-73; Lippitt lectr. Marquette U., 1941; Sommers Meml. lectr. U. Oreg. Sch. Med., Portland, 1960; Gordon Wilson lectr. Am. Clin. and Climatol. Assn., 1956; Sigma Xi nat. lectr., 1952-53; guest scientist Institut fur Medizinder Kernforschungsanlage, Julich, Germany, 1966; Brookhaven Nat. Lab. lectr., 1990. Mem. NRC adv. com. Naval Med. Res., 1953-68; chmn. NRC adv. com. Atomic Bomb Casualty Commn., 1953-68; mem. adv. com. Naval Res. to Sec. of Navy and CNO, 1969-71; NRC adv. com. on medicine and surgery, 1965-68, exec. com., 1962-65; Naval Research Mission to Formosa, 1953; tech. adviser U.S. delegation to Geneva Internat. Conf. for Peaceful Uses Atomic Energy, 1955; mem. N.Y. Adv. Com. Atomic Energy, 1956-59; mem. AMA Com. Nuclear Medicine, 1963-66; mem. com. med. isotopes NASA Manned Spacecraft Ctr., 1966-68; mem. expert adv. panel radiation WHO, 1957-79; mem. Calif. Gov.'s Ad Hoc Com. Emergency Health Service, 1968-69; mem. sci. adv. bd. Gorgas Meml. Inst., 1967-72; numerous other sci. adv. bds., panels; cons. TRW Systems, Inc., 1966-70, Consol. Petroleum Co., Beverly Hills, Calif., 1946-70. Mem. alumni bd. Yale, 1962-65, mem. alumni fund, 1966-76. With USNR, 1942-46; capt. (M.C.) USNR, ret. Recipient Mead Johnson award for pediatric research, 1940, Gold Cross Order of Phoenix, Greece, 1960, Verdienstkreuz 1st class Fed. Republic Germany, 1963, guest scientist Institut für Medizin der Kerforschungsanlage, Julich, Germany, 1966; named Community Leader in Am., 1969, Disting. Alumni Yale U. Med. Sch., 1989. Diplomate Nat. Bd. Med. Examiners, Am. Bd. Pediatrics. Fellow AAAS, Royal Soc. Arts, Am. Acad. Pediatrics, N.Y. Acad. Scis., Royal Soc. Health, Am. Coll. Nuclear Medicine (disting. fellow); mem. Soc. Pediatric Research, Soc. Exptl. Biology, Harvey Soc., Am. Pediatric Soc., Soc. Exptl. Pathology, Am. Soc. Clin. Investigation, Radiation Research Soc., AMA (mem. council on sci. assembly 1960-70, chmn. 1968-70), Med. Soc. Athens (hon. mem.), Alameda County Med. Assn., Sigma Xi, Alpha Omega Alpha, Phi Sigma Kappa, Nu Sigma Nu, Alpha Chi Sigma. Club: Commonwealth (San Francisco). Author articles on nuclear medicine, protein metabolism, emergency med. services, radioactive and chem. environ. contaminants, environ. noise. Home: 2502 Saklan Indian Dr Apt 2 Walnut Creek CA 94595-3001

FARR, SAM, congressman; b. Calif., July 4, 1941; m. Shary Baldwin; 1 child, Jessica. BSc Biology, Willamette U., 1963; student, Monterey Inst. Internat. Studies, U. Santa Clara. Vol. Peace Corps, 1963-65; budget analyst, cons. Assembly com. Constl. Amendments; bd. suprs. Monterey (Calif.) County; rep. Calif. State Assembly, 1980-93; mem. 103d U.S. Congress from 17th Calif. dist., 1993—. Named Legislator of Yr. Calif. 9 times. Democrat. Office: House of Representatives 1218 Longworth House Office Bldg Washington DC 20515-0517*

FARRAR, B. DALE, software engineer; b. Glendale, Ariz., Nov. 30, 1938; s. Buran and Virgie Lee (Partrige) F.; m. Sue Carolyn Harwell, Aug. 3, 1962; 1 child, Alan Dale. AA, Phoenix Coll., 1960; BS in Physics, Ariz. State U., 1963. Assoc. engr. N.Am. Space and Info., Downey, Calif., 1963-66; performance analyst GE Process Computer, Phoenix, 1966-75; sr. prin. software engr. indsl. automation and ctrl. Honeywell Inc., Phoenix, 1975—. Contbr. articles on software quality and documentation to profl. jours. Chief instr. Ariz. Hunter Edn. Program. Office: Honeywell Inc 16404 N Black Canyon Phoenix AZ 85023

FARRAR, DEBORAH JEAN, pharmacist; b. San Antonio, Sept. 30, 1951; d. Douglas Eugene and Patricia Ann (Dugat) McCarter; children: Jamie Christine, Ryan Douglas. BS in Pharmacy, U. Wash., 1976. Lic. pharmacist, Wash., Calif. Pres., owner Santo Trucking, Kent, Wash., 1981-86; pharmacist Manning's Pharmacy, Seattle, 1986-88; staff pharmacist Pharmacy Corp. Am., Tukwila, Wash., 1989, cons. pharmacist, 1989-90; asst. dir. pharmacy Pharmacy Corp. Am., Kent, 1990, dir. pharmacy, 1990-92; gen. mgr. Pharmacy Corp. Am., L.A., 1992—. Fellow Am. Soc. Cons. Pharmacists; mem. Wash. State Pharm. Assn., Calif. Assn. Healthcare Facilities, U. Wash. Alumni Assn. (life). Office: Pharmacy Corp Am 3370 San Fernando Rd St 107 Los Angeles CA 90065

FARRAR, ELAINE WILLARDSON, artist; b. L.A.; d. Eldon and Gladys Elsie (Larsen) Willardson; BA, Ariz. State U., 1967, MA, 1969, PhD, 1990; children: Steve, Mark, Gregory, JanLeslie, Monty, Susan. Tchr., Camelback Desert Sch., Paradise Valley, Ariz., 1966-69; mem. faculty Yavapai Coll., Prescott, Ariz., 1970-92, chmn. dept. art, 1973-78, instr. art in watercolor and oil and acrylic painting, intaglio, relief and monoprints, 1971-92; faculty advisor Prescott Coll. Master of Arts Program, 1993—. One-man shows include: R.P. Moffat's, Scottsdale, Ariz., 1969, Art Center, Battle Creek, Mich., 1969, The Woodpeddler, Costa Mesa, Calif., 1979; group show Prescott (Ariz.) Fine Arts Assn., 1982, 84, 86, 89, 90, 91, 92, N.Y. Nat. Am. Watercolorists, 1982; Ariz. State U. Women Images Now, 1986, 87, 89, 90, 91, 92; works rep. local and state exhibits; supt. fine arts dept. County Fair; com. mem., hanging chmn. Scholastic Art Awards; owner studio/gallery Willis Street Artists, Prescott. Mem. AAUW, Mountain Artists Guild (past pres.), Ariz. Art Edn. Assn., Nat. Art Edn. Assn., Ariz. Coll. and Univ. Faculty Assn., Ariz. Women's Caucus for Art, Women's Nat. Mus. (charter Washington chpt.), Kappa Delta Pi, Phi Delta Kappa. Republican. Mormon. Home: 535 Copper Basin Rd Prescott AZ 86303-4601

FARRELL, EDWARD JOSEPH, mathematics educator; b. San Francisco, Mar. 28, 1917; s. Christopher Patrick and Ethel Ann (Chesterman) F.; m. Pearl Philomena Rongone, Aug. 21, 1954; children: Paul, Paula. B.Sc., U. San Francisco, 1939; M.A., Stanford U., 1942. Mem. faculty U. San Francisco, 1941—, prof. math., 1968-82, prof. emeritus, lectr., 1982—; Guest lectr. regional and nat. meetings Nat. Council Tchrs. Math., 1966, 67, 69; cons. math. text pubs. Mem. adv. panels NSF, 1966—, dir. summer and in-service insts., 1960-75, dir. confs. geometry, 1967, 68, 70-75; mem. rev. panel Sci. Books. Author math. reports; editor studies teaching contemporary geometry. Served with AUS, 1944-46. NSF faculty fellow, 1956-57. Mem. AAAS, Am. Assn. Physics Tchrs., Nat. Council Tchrs. Math., Sch. Sci. and Math. Assn. Republican. Roman Catholic. Home: 2526 Gough St San Francisco CA 94123-5013

FARRELL, FRANCINE ANNETTE, psychotherapist, educator; b. Long Beach, Calif., Mar. 26, 1948; d. Thomas and Evelyn Marie (Lucente) F.; m. James Thomas Hanley, Dec. 5, 1968 (div. Dec. 1988); children: Melinda Lee Hanley, James Thomas Hanley Jr. BA in Psychology with honors, Calif. State U., Sacramento, 1985, MS in Counseling, 1986. Lic. marriage, family and child counselor, Calif.; nat. cert. addiction counselor. Marriage, family and child counselor intern Fulton Ct. Counseling, Sacramento, 1987-88; pvt. practice psychotherapist Sacramento, 1988—; instr. chem. dependency studies program, Calif. State U., Sacramento, 1985—, acad. coord. chem. dependency studies program, 1988-90; trainee Sobriety Brings a Change, Sacramento, 1986-87; assoc. investigator, curriculum coord. Project S.A.F.E., Sacramento, 1990-91; presenter Sacramento Conf., ACA, 1986, 88, 89, 91, 92, Ann. Symposium on Chem. Dependency, 1993. Presenter (TV series) Trouble in River City: Charting a Course for Change, 1991. Mem. Nat. Coun. on Alcoholism, Calif. Assn. Marriage and Family Therapists, Calif. Assn. Alcoholism and Drug Abuse Counselors (bd. dirs. region 5, 1988-90), Phi Kappa Phi. Roman Catholic. Office: 2740 Fulton Ave # 100 Sacramento CA 95821-5108

FARRELL, JOHN MICHAEL, lawyer; b. Milw., Mar. 9, 1954; s. Daniel Edward and Joan Teresa (Abler) F. AB, Ind. U., 1976; JD, U. Chgo., 1979. Bar: Ind. 1979, Calif. 1981. Law clk. U.S. Dist. Ct., Indpls., 1979-81; litigation assoc. Orrick, Herrington & Sutcliffe, San Francisco, 1981-84, Heller, Ehrman, White & McAuliffe, San Francisco, 1984-87; sr. trial atty. Dist. Atty.'s Office, San Francisco, 1987—; adj. prof. Hastings Coll. Law, San Francisco, 1991—; faculty mem. Nat. Inst. Trial Advocacy, Notre Dame, 1990—. Contbr. articles to profl. jours. Mem. State Bar Calif. (fee arbitrator 1990—), Calif. Dist. Attys. Assn. (lectr. 1990—), Phi Beta Kappa. Democrat. Roman Catholic. Office: Dist Atty's Office 850 Bryant St San Francisco CA 94103

FARRELL, JOHN STANISLAUS, manufacturing company executive; b. County Down, No. Ireland, May 19, 1931; arrived in Can., 1931, naturalized, 1931; s. George Stanislaus and Agnes Anna (McCartney) F.; m. Vyra June white, Aug. 7, 1959; children—John McCartney, Lizanne Jennifer. B.A.Sc. in Elec. Engring., U. Toronto, 1956. Registered profl. engr., Can. With ITT Can., Ltd., Montreal, Que., Can., 1962-69; dir. avionics and transmission ITT Can., Ltd., 1968-69; mktg. dir. Leigh Instruments, Ltd., Carleton Place, Ont., 1969-70; gen. mgr. Leigh Instruments, Ltd., 1970-73; pres., chief exec. officer Gestalt Internat. Ltd., Vancouver, B.C., Can., 1973-76; v.p. Cornat Industries, Ltd., Vancouver, 1976-78; sr. v.p. Versatile Corp., Vancouver, 1978-86; exec. dir. Rimquest Internat., Vancouver, 1986-88; pres. Versatech Trading and Devel. Corp., Vancouver, 1988—, also bd. dirs.; chmn., dir. Auspulp Pty. Ltd., Australia, Jara Mgmt. Inc., U.S.; bd. dirs. Versatech Trading and Devel. Corp., Vancouver, Brigdon Resources, Inc., Calgary, Alta., Can., Napier Internat. Techs. Inc, Vancouver. Served with RCAF, 1950-59. Mem. Profl. Engrs. of Ont. Club: Vancouver Lawn Tennis and Badminton.

FARRELL, KENNETH ROYDEN, economist; b. Ont., Can., Jan. 17, 1927; naturalized, 1958; s. William R. and Velma V. (Wood) F.; m. Mary Souter, Sept. 7, 1951; children: Janet, Betty, Deborah, Robert, Patricia, Lisa. BS, U. Toronto (Can.), 1950, MS, Iowa State U., 1955, PhD, 1958. Economist U. Calif., Berkeley, 1957-71; dep. adminstr. USDA, Washington, 1971-77, adminstr., 1977-81; dir. Nat. Ctr., Resources for the Future, Washington, 1981-87; v.p. U. Calif., Oakland, 1987—; economist Nat. Food Commn., Washington, 1965-66, Nat. Productivity Commn., Washington, 1972-73; mem. Presdl. Task Force, Washington, 1982; cons. Robert Nathan Assocs., 1983-84. Contbr. articles to profl. jours.; author (with others) books. Lt. Royal Can. Navy, 1946-48. Fulbright scholar U. Naples (Italy), 1963-64. Fellow AAAS, Am. Agrl. Econs. Assn. (bd. dirs. 1973-76, pres. 1976-77, named for Disting. Pub. Policy Contbn. 1980, 92); mem. Internat. Assn. Agrl. Econs., Commonwealth Club Calif., Phi Kappa Phi, Gamma Sigma Delta. Office: U Calif Rm 627 300 Lakeside Dr Oakland CA 94612-3560

FARRELL, LARRY DON, microbiology educator; b. Woodward, Okla., Nov. 5, 1942; s. Donal Mervin and Frieda Marie (Rector) F.; m. Julia Ann Robinson, Aug. 8, 1965; children: Denise Eileen, Meghan Kathleen. BS, U. Okla., 1964, MS, 1966; PhD, UCLA, 1970. Postdoctoral and instr. Coll. Medicine U. Ill., Chgo., 1970-72; asst. prof. microbiology Idaho State U., Pocatello, 1972-78, chmn. microbiology dept., 1977-84, assoc. prof., 1978-89, prof., 1989—, asst. chmn. dept. biol. scis., 1988-90. Contbr. articles to profl. jours. Mem. exec. bd. Idaho AIDS Found., former co-dir. edn. task force. Mem. AAAS, Am. Soc. Microbiology, Idaho Acad. Scis., Idaho Com. Correspondence (liaison/pres. 1982-89), Internat. Soc. for AIDS Edn., S.E. Idaho AIDS Coalition, Sigma Xi. Democrat. Home: 843 N 10th Ave Pocatello ID 83201-5249 Office: Idaho State U Dept Biol Scis Pocatello ID 83209

FARRELL, MARK MACAULAY, bank executive; b. Troy, N.Y.; s. John J. and Mary-Elizabeth (O'Brien) F.; m. Cathleen M. Purnell, July 6, 1985; children: Elizabeth L., Helen G. AB, Hamilton Coll., 1974; MA, Tufts U., 1975; PhD, U. N.C., 1982; MBA, Columbia U., 1987; postgrad., U. Tübingen, Fed. Republic Germany, 1974-75, U. Göttingen, Fed. Republic Germany, 1981. Grad. teaching fellow U. (Chapel Hill) N.C., 1976-82; asst. prof. Bowdoin Coll., Brunswick, Maine, 1982-83, East Carolina U., Greenville, N.C., 1983-85; intern Citibank, N.Y.C., 1986; rep. Irving Trust Co., N.Y.C., 1987-89; asst. treas. Bank of N.Y., White Plains, 1989; asst. v.p. Bank of Am. (formerly Security Pacific Bank), Portland, Oreg., 1990—; corp. banking exec. participant Security Pacific Bank Mgmt. Exch., 1991. Contbr. articles to profl. jours. Corp. fundraiser United Way, N.Y.C., 1988, Westchester County, N.Y., 1989, Portland, Oreg., 1992. Kent James Brown fellow, 1981.

FARRELL, PATRICK JOSEPH, lawyer; b. Tucson, Sept. 25, 1951; s. Charles Henry and Mary Agnes (Harrington) F.; m. Catherine Cullen Brophy, Sept. 30, 1978 (div. Mar. 1983); m. Karen Ann Ruby, Oct. 13, 1984; children: Tara Kelly, Kevin Patrick, Kelly Colleen. BS, U. Ariz., 1973, JD, 1976. Bar: Ariz. 1976. Atty. Law Office of Jay S. Kittle, Tucson, 1976-78; atty., shareholder Corey and Farrell, P.C., Tucson, 1978—. Dir. Cerebral Palsy Found., So. Ariz., 1985—, Tucson St. Patrick's Day Parade Com., 1987—; bd. dirs. Downtown Bus. Assn., 1986—, pres., 1991; active Lohse Family br. YMCA, 1993—; officer Exch. Club Downtown Houston, 1978-

84. Mem. ABA (bus. law, real property, probate and trust, law practice mgmt. sects.), Pima County Bar Assn., Assn. Trial Lawyers Am. Republican. Roman Catholic. Home: 2612 E 8th St Tucson AZ 85716-4710 Office: Corey and Farrell PC 1 S Church Ave Ste 830 Tucson AZ 85701-1620

FARRELL, THOMAS JOSEPH, insurance company executive; b. Butte, Mont., June 10, 1926; s. Bartholomew J. and Lavina H. (Collins) F.; m. Evelyn Irene Southam, July 29, 1951; children: Brien J., Susan M., Leslie A., Jerome T. Student U. San Francisco, 1949. CLU. Ptnr. Affiliated-Gen. Ins. Adjusters, Santa Rosa, Calif., 1949-54; agt. Lincoln Nat. Life Ins. Co., Santa Rosa, 1954-57, supr., 1957-59, gen. agt., 1959-74; pres. Thomas J. Farrell & Assos., 1974-76, 7 Flags Ins. Mktg. Corp., 1976-81, Farrell-Dranginis & Assocs., 1981-88; pres., bd. dirs. Lincoln Nat. Bank, Santa Rosa, San Rafael. Pres. Redwood Empire Estate Planning Council, 1981-82, Sonoma County Council for Retarded Children, 1956—, Sonoma County Assn. for Retardard Citizens, City Santa Rosa Traffic and Parking Commn., 1963; del. Calif. State Conf. Small Bus., 1980; mem. Santa Rosa City Schs. Compensatory Edn. Adv. Bd.; bd. dirs. Santa Rosa City Schs. Consumer Edn. Adv. Bd.; pres., nat. dir. United Cerebral Palsy Assn., 1954-55; nat. coord. C. of C.-Rotary Symposia on Employment of People with Disabilities, 1985—; v.p. Vigil Light, Inc.; chmn. bd. dirs. Nat. Barrier Awareness for People with Disabilities Found., Inc.; pres. Commn. on Emoloyment of People with Disabilities, 1986—; mem. Pres.'s Com. on Mental Retardation, 1982-86; chmn. Santa Rosa Community Relations Com., 1973-76; pres. Sonoma County Young Reps., 1953; past bd. dirs. Sonoma County Fair and Expn., Inc.; bd. dirs. Sonoma County Family Service Agy., Eldridge Found., North Bay Regional Ctr. for Developmentally Disabled; trustee Sonoma State Hosp. for Mentally Retarded. Recipient cert. Nat. Assn. Retarded Children, 1962, Region 9 U.S. HHS Community Service award, 1985, Sonoma County Vendor's Human Service award, 1986, Individual Achievement award Community Affirmative Action Forum of Sonoma County, 1986. Mem. Nat. Assn. Life Underwriters, Redwood Empire Assn. CLU's (pres. 1974—), Japanese-Am. Citizens League, Jaycees (Outstanding Young Man of Year 1961, v.p. 1955), Santa Rosa C. of C. (bd. dirs. 1974-75), Calif. PTA (hon. life). Lodge: Rotary. Home: 963 Wyoming Dr Santa Rosa CA 95405-7342 Office: Farrell Dranginis & Assoc 131 Stony Cir Ste 925 Santa Rosa CA 95401-9525

FARRELL, WILLIAM EDGAR, sales executive, infosystems specialist, management consultant; b. Jeanette, Pa., Mar. 13, 1937; s. Arthur Richard and Lelia (Ryder) F.; m. Sara Lynnette Swing, Aug. 20, 1960; children: Wendy J., Tracy L., Rebecca J. BS in Edn., Pa. State U., 1959. Location mgr. IBM Corp., Dover, Del., 1969-72; corp. lobbyist IBM Corp., Washington, 1972-74, planning cons., 1974-78, nat. mktg. mgr., 1978-80, exec. asst., 1980-81; account exec. IBM Corp., Denver, 1981-87, policy exec., 1987-91; pres., CEO Weatherall Co., Inc., Englewood, Colo., 1993—; CFO Wide Horizon, Inc., Denver, 1987-92, chmn. bd. trustees, 1989-92; pres. Exec. Mgmt. Cons., 1987—; sec.-treas., bd. dirs. Electronic Shoe Enterprises Inc., 1991—; bd. dirs. Energaire Corp. Founding mem. River Falls Community Assn., Potomac, Md., 1975; first reader First Ch. of Christ Scientist, Chevy Chase, Md., 1976-80; chmn. Amigo's De Ser; bd. dirs. Rocky Mountain Ser, 1991-92. Recipient Outstanding Contbn. award IBM Corp., 1968. Republican.

FARRER, JOHN, orchestra conductor; b. Detroit, July 1, 1941; s. John and Beulah (Finley) F.; m. Bonnie Bogle, June 3, 1967; children: Matthew, Joanna. B in Music Theory, U. Mich., 1964, M in Music Theory, 1966; diploma, Mozarteum, Salzburg, Austria, 1969. Music dir. Roswell (N.Mex) Symphony Orch., 1972—, Bakersfield (Calif.) Symphony Orch., 1975—; regular cover condr. San Francisco Symphony, 1988—, ASV Records, 1989—, Pickwick Records, 1993—; bd. dirs. N.H. Youth Orch. Condr. (recs.) London Philharmonic Orch., Royal Philharmonic Orch., English Sinfonia. Mem. Am. Symphony Orch. League (mem. standing com. on artistic affairs 1981—, condr. workshops 1986—, condr. continuum 1989—), Assn. Calif. Symphony Orchs. (bd. dirs. 1977-81), Rotary. Office: Bakersfield Symphony Orch 1401 19th St Ste 130 Bakersfield CA 93301

FARRIS, DAVID ALLEN, biology educator; b. Bloomington, Ind., Mar. 26, 1928; s. Willis Paul and Edith Ruth (Shaver) F.; children: David Kemmar, Victoria Margaret. AB, Ind. U., 1950; PhD, Stanford U., 1956. Field asst. Ind. Lake and Stream Svc., Bloomington, Ind., 1942-50; rsch. biologist U.S. Fish and Wildlife Svc., Stanford, Calif., 1954-60; asst. prof. biology San Diego State U., 1960-63, assoc. prof. biology, 1963-66, prof. biology, 1966—; vis. investigator U. Miami, 1966-67. Office: San Diego State U College Ave San Diego CA 92182-0001

FARRIS, DAVID PRESTON, environmental engineer; b. Sacramento, Aug. 1, 1952; s. Prentice Hilman and Lucille Eveline (Preston) F.; m. Michaela Jan Goad, June 9, 1973; 1 child, Ayla J. BS cum laude, Stephen F. Austin State U., 1976; postgrad., Baylor U., 1978; MS, U. Mich., 1981. Environ. chemist Internat. Paper Co., Texarkana, Tex., 1981-86; environ. specialist Kerr-McGee Chem. Corp., Oklahoma City, 1987-88; sr. environ. engr. Weyerhaeuser Paper Co., Longview, Wash., 1988—; cons. Nat. Coun. for Air and Stream Improvement, Corvallis, Oreg., 1989—; presenter confs. in field. Contbr. poetry and short fiction to literary mags. Bd. dirs. Robbins Addition Residents Assn., Longview, 1991—. Recipient Leonard Star award Leonard's Dept. Store, Ft. Worth, Tex., 1970. Mem. Tech. Assn. of Pulp and Paper Industry, Northwest Pulp and Paper Assn. Office: Weyerhaeuser Co 3401 Industrial Way Longview WA 98632-9461

FARRIS, JEROME, federal judge; b. Birmingham, Ala., Mar. 4, 1930; s. William J. and Elizabeth (White) F.; m. Jean Shy, June 27, 1957; children—Juli Elizabeth, Janelle Marie. B.S., Morehouse Coll., 1951, LL.D., 1978; M.S.W., Atlanta U., 1955; J.D., U. Wash., 1958. Bar: Wash. 1958. Mem. firm Weyer, Roderick, Schroeter and Sterne, Seattle, 1958-59; ptnr. Weyer, Schroeter, Sterne & Farris and successor firms, Seattle, 1959-61, Schroeter & Farris, Seattle, 1961-63, Schroeter, Farris, Bangs & Horowitz, Seattle, 1963-65, Farris, Bangs & Horowitz, Seattle, 1965-69; judge Wash. State Ct. of Appeals, Seattle, 1969-79, U.S. Ct. of Appeals (9th cir.), Seattle, 1979—; lectr. U. Wash. Law Sch. and Sch. of Social Work, 1976—; mem. faculty Nat. Coll. State Judiciary, U. Nev., 1973; adv. bd. Nat. Ctr. for State Cts. Appellate Justice Project, 1978-81; founder First Union Nat. Bank, Seattle, 1965, dir., 1965-69. Del. The White House Conf. on Children and Youth, 1970; mem. King County (Wash.) Youth Commn., 1969-70; vis. com. U. Wash. Sch. Social Work, 1977-90; mem. King County Mental Health-Mental Retardation Bd., 1967-69; past bd. dirs. Seattle United Way; mem. Tyee Bd. Advisers, U. Wash., 1984—, bd. regents, 1985—, pres., 1990-91; trustee U. Law Sch. Found., 1978-84. With Signal Corps, U.S. Army, 1952-53. Recipient Disting. Service award Seattle Jaycees, 1965, Clayton Frost award, 1966. Fellow Am. Bar Found.; mem. ABA (exec. com. appellate judges conf. 1978-84, 87—, chmn. conf. 1982-83, del. jud. adminstrn. coun. 1987-88), Wash. Council on Crime and Delinquency (chmn. 1970-72), Am. Bar Found. (bd. dirs. 1987, exec. com. 1989—), State-Fed. Jud. Council of State of Wash. (vice chmn. 1977-78, chmn. 1983-87), Order of Coif (mem. law rev.), U. Wash. Law Sch. Office: US Ct Appeals 9th Cir 1030 US Courthouse 1010 5th Ave Seattle WA 98104-1130

FARRIS, MARTIN THEODORE, economist, educator; b. Spokane, Wash., Nov. 5, 1925; s. Jacob B. and Edith S. (Gunderson) F.; m. Rhoda H. Harrington, Aug. 20, 1948 (dec. 1992); children: Christine A. Farris Zenobi, Diana Lynn, Elizabeth, M. Theodore II. BA, U. Mont., 1949, MA, 1950; PhD, Ohio State U., 1957. Grad. asst. U. Mont., 1949-50; asst. in econs. Ohio State U., Columbus, 1950-51, asst. instr., 1953-55, instr., 1955-57; asst. prof. Ariz. State U., Tempe, 1957-59, assoc. prof., 1959-62, chmn. dept. econs., 1967-69, prof. transp. and pub. utility econs., 1962-72, prof. transp., 1972-88, Regents' prof., 1988-92, prof. emeritus, 1992—; vis. prof. U. Hawaii, 1969-70, vis. scholar, 1979. Author: (with Roy Sampson and David Shrock) Domestic Transportation: Practice, Theory and Policy, 6th edit., 1990; (with Roy Sampson) Public Utilities: Regulation, Management and Ownership, 1973; (with Paul McElhiney) Modern Transportation, 2nd edit., 1973; (with Grant Davis and Jack Holder) Management of Transportation Carriers, 1975; (with Forrest Harding) Passenger Transportation, 1976; (with Dave Bess) U.S. Maritime: History and Prospects, 1981, (with Stephen Happel) Modern Managerial Economics, 1987; contbr. articles to profl. jours. Served with U.S. Army, 1944-46, PTO. Decorated Philippine Liberation medal with bronze star; recipient Outstanding Faculty Achievement award Ariz. State U. Alumni Assn., 1978, Outstanding Faculty Researcher award Coll. Bus. Ariz. State U., 1982, Transp. and Logistics Educator of Yr. award Colo. Transp. Forum, 1991. Mem. Am. Econ. Assn. (Outstanding Contbn. award 1984), Western Econ. Assn. (bd. dirs. 1966-67), Assn. Transp. Practitioners, Transp. Rsch. Forum, Am. Soc. Transp. and Logistics (chief examiner 1961-73, Joseph C. Schleen award 1988), Coun. Logistics Mgmt., Traffic Clubs Internat., Traffic Club Phoenix (pres. 1960, Ariz. Transp. Man of Yr. 1992), Phi Kappa Phi, Omicron Delta Epsilon, Sigma Phi Epsilon, Delta Nu Alpha (Transp. Man of Yr. 1972), Beta Gamma Sigma. Episcopalian. Club: Traffic (Phoenix) (pres. 1960). Home: 6108 E Vernon Ave Scottsdale AZ 85257-1948 Office: Coll Bus Adminstrn Ariz State U Tempe AZ 85287

FARUQUI, G. AHMAD, engineering consultant; b. Jodhpur, Rajasthan, India, June 30, 1932; came to U.S., 1955; s. Ajaz Ahmad and Hameedah (Khatoon) F.; m. Sally A. Furlong, Dec. 26, 1960 (div. 1979); children: Michael A., Tasneem M. BSc, Sind U., Pakistan, 1948; B Engring., Karachi U., Pakistan, 1954; MEE, Colo. State U., 1956. Sr. lectr. elec. engring. U. Peshawar, Pakistan, 1955; instr. elec. engring. Case Inst. Tech., Cleve., 1957-60; project mgr. IBM, Palo Alto, Calif., 1960-67; sect. mgr. Philco Ford, Palo Alto, Calif., 1967-69; cons. Advanced Solutions, San Jose, Calif., 1969-92.

FARWELL, HERMON WALDO, JR., parliamentarian, educator, speech communicator; b. Englewood, N.J., Oct. 24, 1918; s. Hermon Waldo and Elizabeth (Whitcomb) F.; A.B., Columbia, 1940; M.A., Pa. State U., 1964; m. Martha Carey Matthews, Jan. 3, 1942; children—Gardner Whitcomb, Linda Margaret (Mrs. Richard Hammer). Mil. service, 1940-66, advanced through grades to maj. U.S. Air Force; ret., 1966; instr. aerial photography Escola Tecnica de Aviação, Brazil, 1946-48; faculty U. So. Colo., Pueblo, 1966-84, prof. emeritus speech communication; cons., tchr. parliamentary procedure. Mem. Am. Inst. Parliamentarians (nat. dir. 1977-87), Commn. on Am. Parliamentary Practice (chmn. 1976), Ret. Officers Assn., Nat. Assn. Parliamentarians, Am. Legion, VFW. Author: The Majority Rules-A Manual of Procedure for Most Groups; Parliamentary Motions; Majority Motions; editor The Parliamentary Jour., 1981-87, 91-93. Home and Office: 65 Macalester Rd Pueblo CO 81001-2052

FASANELLA, RICHARD S., re-construction/facilities specialist, designer; b. N.Y.C., June 12, 1949; s. Sam Joseph and Rose Teresa (Fillipelli) F.; m. Janie Lynn Owen (dec. 1982); 1 child, Clarissa. Student in Engring., Math, U. Ariz., 1971-73; student in Space Planning, U. Calif., Irvine, 1986-87. Pres. Fasko Constrn., Ariz., 1976-81; CEO Image Builders Inc., Ariz., Calif., 1986—; pres. Eagle Products, Ariz., Calif., 1986—, City Svcs. Corp., Calif., 1987—, Rose Mfg., Ariz., 1986—, Nu-Stone Corp., Ariz., Calif., 1986—; cons. interior design and space planning Internat. Acad. Color Utilization Standards and Space Planning, N.Y.C., L.A., 1986—. Author: Construction Management Systems, 1981. Cons. Nat. Assn. Home Builders, 1979-81. Recipient Space Planning and Interior Use award Internat. Acad. Color Utilization Stds., 1985, 87, 88, 91; named Remodeler of Yr., Nat. Assn. Home Builders, 1979, 81, Residential Remodeler Yr., 1982, 86, 87. Mem. Aircraft Owners and Pilots Assn., Acad. Design and Space Utilization. Office: Image Builders Inc 1058-12 E 1st Santa Ana CA 92701

FASI, FRANK FRANCIS, mayor; b. East Hartford, Conn., Aug. 27, 1920. B.S., Trinity Coll., Hartford, 1942. Mem. Hawaii Senate, 1959—; Dem. mayor City and County of Honolulu, 1969-81, Rep. mayor, 1985—. Mem. Dem. Nat. Com. for Hawaii, 1952-56; del. 2d Constl. Conv., 1968; mem.-at-large Honolulu City Coun., 1965-69. Served to capt. USMCR. Mem. Pacific-Asian Congress Municipalities (founder, past pres., exec. dir.), VFW (former comdr. Hawaii dept.), AFTRA (past v.p.). Office: City Hall Office of Mayor 530 S King St Honolulu HI 96813-3014

FASS, PAULA SHIRLEY, history educator; b. Hannover, Fed. Republic Germany, May 22, 1947; d. Chaim Harry and Bluma Rose (Sieratski) F.; m. John Emmett Lesch, July 13, 1980; children: Bluma Jessica Fass Lesch, Charles Harry Taylor Lesch. AB, Barnard Coll., 1967; MA, Columbia U., 1968, PhD, 1974. Lectr. Rutgers U., New Brunswick, N.J., 1972-73, asst. prof., 1973-74; asst. prof. U. Calif., Berkeley, 1974-78, assoc. prof., 1978-87, prof., 1987—; cons. Aspen Inst. for Humanistic Studies, 1975-76. Author: The Damned and the Beautiful: American Youth in the 1920's, 1977, Outside In: Minorities and the Transformation of American Education, 1989; contbr. articles to profl. jours. Fellow NEH, 1979, 85-86, 91, Rockefeller Found., 1976-77, U. Calif. Regents, 1980-81, Ctr. for Advanced Study in Behavioral Scis. Stanford U., 1991—. Mem. Am. Hist. Assn., Orgn. Am. Historians, History Edn. Soc., Phi Beta Kappa. Jewish. Office: U Calif Dept History Berkeley CA 94720

FASSEL, VELMER ARTHUR, science administrator, physical chemist, educator; b. Frohna, Mo., Apr. 26, 1919; s. Arthur Edward and Alma (Poppitz) F.; m. Mary Alice Katschke, July 25, 1943. B.A., S.E. Mo. State U., 1941; Ph.D., Iowa State U., 1947. Chemist Manhattan Project, Iowa State U., Ames, 1942-47; mem. faculty Manhattan Project, Iowa State U., Ames, 1947—, Disting. prof. sci. and humanities, 1986, prof. chemistry, emeritus sr. scientist, 1986—; sect. chief Ames Lab. U.S. Dept. Energy, 1966-69; dep. dir. Ames Lab., Energy and Mineral Resources Research Inst., 1969-84, prin. scientist Ames Lab., 1984-87; ret.; titular mem., sec., chmn. Commn. Spectrochem.; Methods of Analysis, Internat. Union Pure and Applied Chemistry. Recipient Disting. Alumni award S.E. Mo. State U., 1965, award Spectroscopy Soc. Pitts., 1969, Maurice F. Hasler award, 1971, Anachem award, 1971, IR-100 award Research and Devel. Mag., 1986, Iowa Gov.'s Sci. medal, Iowa State U.'s Disting. Achievement citation, 1987; Ea. Analytical Symposium award, 1987. Fellow AAAS, Optical Soc. Am.; mem. Soc. for Applied Spectroscopy (Ann. medal 1964, Strock medal 1986), Am. Chem. Soc. (Chem. Instrumentation award 1983, Fisher award 1979, Iowa award 1983, Analytic Div. award in Spectrochem. Analysis 1988), Japan Soc. Analytical Chemistry (hon. mem., medal 1981), Assn. Ofcl. Analytical Chemists (Harvey Wiley award 1986), Am. Inst. Physics, Sigma Xi. Home: 17755 Rosedown Pl San Diego CA 92128-2085

FASSETT, WILLIAM EDMOND, pharmacy educator; b. Torrance, Calif., Nov. 8, 1945; s. Minard Webster Fassett and Ruth Georgia (Eyer) Norman; m. Sharon Elaine Johnson, Aug. 6, 1966; children: Mark Edward, David William. BS in Pharm., U. Wash., 1969, PhD, 1992; MBA, U. Puget Sound, 1983. Registered pharmacist, Wash. Pharmacist Ostrom Enterprises, Inc., Kenmore, Wash., 1969-70; sales rep. The Upjohn Co., Kalamazoo, 1970-78, hosp. specialist, 1978-79; mgr. Ostrom's Drugs, Inc., Bothell, Wash., 1979-80; lectr. Sch. Pharmacy U. Wash., Seattle, 1980-84, asst. prof. Sch. Pharmacy, 1984-90, assoc. prof. Sch. Pharmacy, 1990—, mem. speaker's bur., 1981—; prin. Wash. Pharmacy Cons., Woodinville, 1983—; adj. assoc. prof. Coll. Edn. U. Wash., 1993—. Author: (software) CALCWORK, 1986, 92; co-author: (book) Computer Applications in Pharmacy, 1986; editor Computer Medicine/Hosp. Pharmacist, 1990-91; assoc. editor Jour. Pharmacy Teaching, 1990—; contbg. editor Lippincott's Hosp. Pharmacy, 1991—; contbr. articles to profl. jours. Chmn., bd. dirs. EARN, Inc. Youth Employment Svc., Bothell, 1969-70; chmn., mem. adv. bd. INC Spot Family Counseling Ctr., Bothell, 1969-70; vice chmn., bd. dirs. Thurston County chpt. ARC, Olympia, Wash., 1978. NSF fellow, 1968-69. Mem. AAUP, Am. Assn. Colls. Pharmacy (GAPS Excellence award 1987, ho. of dels. 1987-93), Am. Pharm. Assn., Am. Soc. for Pharmacy Law, Wash. State Pharmacists Assn. (bd. mgrs. 1975-78), Kappa Psi, Phi Delta Kappa, Rho Chi. Office: U Wash Sch Pharmacy SC-69 Seattle WA 98195

FASS-HOLMES, BARRY, statistician, researcher; b. Bridgeport, Conn., Jan. 29, 1953; s. Elias Nathan and Rosalind Fass; m. Brenda Fass-Holmes, Dec. 18, 1988. BA in Psychology, Clark U., Worcester, Mass., 1974, MA in Psychology, 1977, PhD in Psychology, 1979. Asst. prof. U. Louisville HSC, 1986-87; asst. rsch. biologist U. Calif. San Diego, LaJolla, 1987-89; customer svc. rep. LaserGo, Inc., San Diego, 1989-90; quality assurance analyst Jostens Learning Corp., San Diego, 1990-92; evaluation analyst San Diego Unified Sch. Dist., 1992—. Contbr. articles to profl. jours. NIH grantee, 1986. Mem. Soc. for Neurosci., Union of Concerned Scientists, Sigma Xi, Phi Beta Kappa. Democrat. Unitarian-Universalist.

FASSIO, VIRGIL, newspaper publishing company executive; b. Pitts., Aug. 10, 1927; s. Domenico and Carolina (Pia) F.; m. Shirley DeVirgilis; children: Richard, David, Michael. BA with honors, U. Pitts., 1949. Founder, editor, pub. Beechview News, Pitts., 1947-51; reporter Valley Daily News, Tarentum, Pa., 1950, circulation mgr., 1951-58; circulation dir. Morning News and Evening Jour., Wilmington, Del., 1958-65; circulation dir. Detroit Free Press, 1965-71, v.p., bus. mgr., 1971; v.p., circulation dir. Chgo. Tribune, 1972-76; v.p., gen. mgr. Seattle Post-Intelligencer, 1976, pub., 1978—; lectr. Am. Press Inst.; cons., lectr. in field. Contbr. articles to profl. jours. Del. White House Conf. on Children, 1960, 70; pres. Seattle-King County Conv. and Visitors Bur., 1982-84; bd. dirs. Mus. Flight, Mus. History and Industry, Pacific Sci. Ctr. Found., Odyssey Maritime Mus., Woodland Park Zool. Soc., Seattle Goodwill Industries, Hope Heart Inst., Medic I Emergency Med. Svcs. Found., Boys and Girls Clubs King County, sports and events coun., Seattle; mem. adv. bd. Seattle Mariners; mem. bd. regents Seattle U., Wash. Coun. Internat. Trade, chmn. 1992-93. Comdr. USNR, 1947-70, ret. Recipient Frank Thayer award U. Wis., 1972, Varsity Letterman of Distinction award U. Pitts., 1974, Bicentennial Medallion of Distinction, 1989, Svc. to Youth award Boys and Girls Clubs King County, 1987, Seattle Goodwill Amb. award, 1991, World Citizen award World Affairs Coun., 1992. Mem. Internat. Circulation Mgrs. Assn. (Man of Yr. award 1964, named to Newspaper Carrier Hall of Fame 1990), Inter-State Circulation Mgrs. Assn. (sec.-treas. 1954-65, Outstanding Achievement award 1967), Seattle C. of C. (bd. dirs.), Downtown Seattle Assn. (chmn. 1990-91), Am. Newspapers Pubs. Assn. (vice chmn. industry affairs com. 1982-86), Rainier Club, Columbia Tower Club, Wash. Athletic Club, Rotary (Community Svc. award 1989). Office: Seattle Post-Intelligencer 101 Elliott Ave W PO Box 1909 Seattle WA 98111

FASSLER, JOSEPH K., food service executive; b. N.Y.C., Jan. 26, 1942; s. Charles and Sallie (Hirshhorn) F. B.S., Okla. State U., 1963. With Restaura, Inc., Phoenix, 1963—, dist. mgr., 1973-75, v.p., 1976-79, exec. v.p., 1980-81, pres., chief operating officer, 1982—; lectr. Sponsor, contbr. Boys Brotherhood Republic, 1963—. With USMC, 1964. Recipient Outstanding Alumni award N.Y.C. Community Coll., 1972, Okla. State U., 1983. Mem. Soc. Foodservice Mgmt., Nat. Restaurant Assn. (bd. dirs.). Office: Restaura Inc Dial Corporate Ctr Dial Tower Phoenix AZ 85077-1005

FATEMAN, RICHARD J., computer science educator, researcher; b. N.Y.C., Nov. 4, 1946; s. Sol C. and Adelaide (Lapidus) F.; m. Martha A. Nelson, June 15, 1968; children: Abigail, Johanna. BS in Physics, Union Coll., 1966; PhD in Applied Math., Harvard U., 1971. Instr., lectr. math. dept. MIT, Cambridge, Mass., 1971-74; scientist Lawrence Livermore/Berkeley (Calif.) Lab., summer 1974, 78; prof. U. Calif., Berkeley, 1974—, chair, prof., 1987-90; bd. dirs. Computing Rsch. Assn. Inc., Washington, Franz. Inc., Berkeley; bd. dirs., treas. Internat. Computer Sci. Inst., Berkeley, 1987-90. Contbr. numerous articles to profl. jours. Bd. dirs. Claremont/Elmwood Neighborhood Assn., Berkeley, 1990—. NSF grantee, and many others. Mem. Assn. for Computing Machinery (chair SIGSAM, 1983-85), Soc. for Indsl. and Applied Math. Home: 2965 Magnolia St Berkeley CA 94705-2329 Office: U Calif Computer Sci Divsn EECS Dept Berkeley CA 94720

FATHAUER, THEODORE FREDERICK, meteorologist; b. Oak Park, Ill., June 5, 1946; s. Arthur Theodore and Helen Ann (Mashek) F.; m. Mary Ann Neesan, Aug. 8, 1981. BA, U. Chgo., 1968. Cert. cons. meteorologist. Rsch. aide USDA No. Dev. Labs., Peoria, Ill., 1966, Cloud Physics Lab., Chgo., 1967; meteorologist Sta. WLW Radio/TV, Cin., 1967-68, Nat. Meteorol. Ctr., Washington, 1968-70, Nat. Weather Svc., Anchorage, 1970-80; meteorologist-in-charge Nat. Weather Svc., Fairbanks, Alaska, 1980—; instr. U. Alaska, Fairbanks, 1975-76, USCG aux., Fairbanks and Anchorage, 1974—. Contbr. articles to weather mags. Bd. dirs. Fairbanks Concert Assn., 1988—, Friends U. Alaska Mus., 1993—. Recipient Outstanding Performance award Nat. Weather Service, 1972, 76, 83, 85, 86, 89, Fed. Employee of Yr. award, Fed. Exec. Assn., Anchorage, 1978. Fellow Am. Meteorol. Soc. (TV and radio seals of approval), Royal Meteorol. Soc.; mem. Am. Geophys. Union, AAAS, Royal Meteorol. Soc., Western Snow Conf., Arctic Inst. N.Am., Oceanography Soc. Republican. Lutheran. Home: 1738 Chena Ridge Rd Fairbanks AK 99709-2612 Office: Nat Weather Svc Forecast Office 101 12th Ave Box 21 Fairbanks AK 99701-6266

FATLAND, JAMES R., mayor. BS in Acctg. and Fin., Calif. State Poly. U.; grad., Greater Ontario (Calif.) Leadership Devel. Program. Former chief adminstrv., fiscal officer Marin County (Calif.) Wastewater Constrn. Program; fin. analyst Adminstrv. Office for Infraestructure San Bernardino County, Calif.; formerly mem. Ontario City Coun., 1988-90; now mayor City of Ontario, 1990—. Officer USCGR. Office: Office of Mayor Civic Ctr 303 E B St Ontario CA 91764

FATTORINI, HECTOR OSVALDO, mathematics educator, mathematician; b. Buenos Aires, Argentina, Oct. 28, 1938; came to U.S., 1962; s. Osvaldo Franco and Concepcion (Marti Ros) F.; m. Natalia Lubow Karanowycz, Nov. 4, 1961; children—Maria Elena, Sonia Isabel, Susana Ines. Licenciado en Matemática, U. Buenos Aires, 1961; Ph.D., NYU, 1965. Research assoc. Brown U., Providence, 1967; prof. U. Buenos Aires, 1971-73; vis. prof. U. Florence, Italy, 1975; asst. prof. UCLA, 1967-70, assoc. prof., 1970-75, prof. math., 1975—; prin. investigator NSF, Washington, 1970—. Author: The Cauchy Problem, 1983; Second Order Differential Equations in Banach Spaces, 1985. Contbr. articles to profl. jours. Mem. Am. Math. Soc., Soc. Indsl. and Applied Math., Union Matemática Argentina, Sociedad Círculo Unidad. Home: 14701 Whitfield Ave Pacific Palisades CA 90272-2647 Office: U Calif Dept Math Los Angeles CA 90024

FAUCHIER, DAN R(AY), construction executive; b. Blackwell, Okla., Sept. 27, 1946; s. Wallace Munroe and Betty Lou F.; m. Sylvia Stephanie Chan Fauchier, Mar. 15, 1969; 1 child, Angele Calista Fauchier. BA cum laude, Southwestern Coll., 1964-68; student, Sch. Theology, Claremont, Calif., 1968-69, Claremont Grad. Sch., 1969-70. Lic. Bldg. Contractor, Calif., Pub. Adminstrn. life credential. Adminstr. Calif. Youth Authority, Paso Robles, Calif., 1969-76; tchr. Chaffey Coll., Rancho Cucamonga, Calif., 1971-74, Pacific Fin. Svcs., Beverly Hills, Calif., 1977-81; pres. Littlefields Corp., Corona del Mar, Calif., 1978-81; systems designer Teltrans Corp., L.A., 1982-85; project mgr. Pacific Sunset Builders, L.A., 1985-87, DW Devel., Fontana, Calif., 1987-90; owner Fauchier Group Builders, Upland, Calif., 1988-93; pres. Empire Bay Devel. Corp., San Bernardino, Calif., 1991-92; project mgr., white systems L.A. Central Library, L.A., 1993—; founding dir. Neighborhood Restoration Project, San Bernardino, Calif., 1991-92. Contbr. cons.: President's Commission on Criminal Justice, 1972; co-author: Consumer Credit, 1984. Deputy Registrar Voters San Bernardino, Calif., 1975; mem. Skid Row Mental Health Adv. Bd., L.A., 1986, Chaffey Coll. Adv. Bd. Rancho Cucamonga, Calif., 1991-93 chmn. Bus. Security Alliance, San Bernardino, Calif., 1992. Named Nat. fellow Woodrow Wilson Fellowship, Princeton, N.J., 1968-69; recipient Full Grad. scholarship State of Calif., Claremont, 1969. Mem. Habitat for Humanity, Self-Realization Fellowship, Inst. for Community Econ., Homeless Coalition, People for Ethical Treatment of Animals, Rainforest Alliance. Home: 814 W 20th St Upland CA 91784 Office: 50 Boright Ave Kenilworth NJ 07033

FAULCONER, KAY ANNE, communications executive; b. Shelbyville, Ind., Aug. 19, 1945; d. Clark Jacks and Charlotte (Tindall) Keenan; BA in English, Calif. State U., Northridge, 1968; MBA, Pepperdine U., 1975, MA in Communications, 1976; children: Kevin Lee, Melissa Lynne. Pres., Kay Faulconer & Assos., Oxnard, Calif., 1977—; instr. Oxnard Coll., U. LaVerne. Dir. bus. adminstrn. of justice programs, Ventura (Calif.) Coll.; former pres., founder Oxnard Friends of Libr.; former exec. bd. Ventura County March of Dimes; mem. PTA; officer, bd. dirs. Oxnard Girls Club. Named Businesswoman of Yr., Ventura Bus. and Profl. Women's Club, 1976; Woman of Achievement, Oxnard Bus. and Profl. Women's Club, 1973, recipient Career Woman award, 1974.Mem. Am. Soc. Tng. and Devel., Am. Assn. Women in Community and Jr. Colls. (Leaders for 80's program), Ventura County Profl. Women's Network. Club: Oxnard Jr. Monday (past pres., hon. life). Home and Office: 601 Janetwood Dr Oxnard CA 93030-3533

FAULHABER, CHARLES BAILEY, Spanish language educator; b. East Cleveland, Ohio, Sept. 18, 1941; s. Kenneth Frederick and Lois Marie (Bailey) F.; m. Jamy Sue O'Banion, June 5, 1971. BA, Yale U., 1963, MPhil, PhD, 1969; MA, U. Wis., 1966. Acting instr. Yale U., 1968-69; asst. prof.

Spanish U. Calif., Berkeley, 1969-75, assoc. prof., 1975-80, prof., 1980—, chmn. dept., 1989—. Author: Latin Rhetorical Theory in Thirteenth and Fourteenth Century Castile, 1972, Medieval Manuscripts in the Library of the Hispanic Society of America, 1983-93, Libros y bibliotecas en la España medieval, 1987; co-author: Bibliography of Old Spanish Texts, 1984, Archivo Digital de Manuscritos y Textos Españoles, 1992. Fulbright fellow, 1967-68, 91; NEH fellow, 1976, grantee, 1978-80, 89-93; Guggenheim fellow, 1982-83. Mem. MLA, Medieval Acad., Am. Assn. for Lit. and Linguistic Computing, Assn. for Computers and Humanities, Asociación Internacional de Hispanistas, Am. Assn. Tchrs. Spanish and Portuguese, Hispanic Soc. Am., Grolier Club. Office: U Calif Dept Spanish Berkeley CA 94720

FAULKNER, DEXTER HAROLD, magazine publishing executive, editor; b. Grand Island, Nebr., Sept. 10, 1937; s. Jack L. and Wanetta May (Howland) F.; student U. Calif.-Fresno, 1956-58, Ambassador Coll., 1958-60; m. Shirley Ann Hume, Jan. 11, 1959; children: Nathan Timothy, Matthew Benjamin. Ordained minister Worldwide Ch. of God. European Bur. chief, 1990-93; exec. editor Plain Truth Mag; editor Good News mag., Youth/90 mag. and Worldwide News-Tabloid. Internat. div. Ambassador Coll., Sydney, Australia, 1960-66, news rsch. asst. dir. Ambassador Coll. Editorial, Pasadena, Calif., 1966-71, regional editor Plain Truth mag., Washington, 1971-75, asst. mng. editor, Pasadena, 1975-78, mng. editor, 1980-82, exec. editor, 1982-90, mng. editor Good News mag., Worldwide News-Tabloid, 1978-85, editor, 1986-90; mng. editor Youth/90 mag., 1981-85, editor, 1986-90; assoc. pastor Kansas City, Topeka, Kans.; instr. mass communications Ambassador Coll., 1980-90; columnist Just One More Thing . . . Mem. Inst. Journalists (London), Profl. Photographers Am. Inc., Bur. Freelance Photographers (London), Nat. Press Club, World Affairs Council (Los Angeles), The Fgn. Press Assn. (London), Internat. Assn. Bus. Communicators, Nat. Press Photographers Assn., Am. Mgmt. Assn., Sigma Delta Chi, Rotary Internat. Mem. Worldwide Ch. God. Contbr. articles, photos on internat. relations, social issues to Plain Truth mag., Good News mag., Worldwide News Publs. Club: Commonwealth of Calif. Home: 7859 Wentworth St Sunland CA 91040-2201 Office: Plain Truth Mag 300 W Green St Pasadena CA 91129-0001

FAULKNER, MAURICE ERVIN, educator, conductor; b. Fort Scott, Kans., Feb. 2, 1912; s. Ervin Phyletus and Minnie Mae (Munday) F.; m. Ellen Stradal, May 24, 1934 (div. 1951); children: Katherine Sydney, Barbara Ellen; m. Suzanne Somerville, Oct. 18, 1958. BS in Music, Fort Hays State U., 1932; postgrad. Interlochen U., 1933; MA in Music, Tchrs. Coll., N.Y.C., 1936; PhD, Stanford U., 1956. Instr. music pub. schs., Kans., 1932-37; assoc. prof. instrumental music Columbia U., summers 1934-40; asst. prof. San Jose (Calif.) State Coll., 1937-40; from asst. prof. to assoc. prof. to prof. emeritus U. Calif., Santa Barbara, 1940—, also chmn. dept.; rsch. papers on Bronze Age musical instruments presented Biennial Archeol. Musicology Symposiums, Congress of Traditional Music of UNESCO, Stockholm, 1984, Hanover, Fed. Republic Germany, 1986, Internat. Trumpet Guild Conf., Rotterdam, The Netherlands, summer 1992; vis. prof. U. Tex., summer 1947; music critic Salzburg (Austria) Festival, 1951—(Reinhardt award 1969, Golden Svc. award 1981), Santa Barbara Star, 1951-56, Santa Barbara News-Press, 1956-82; rsch. musicologist Inst. for Environ. Stress, U. Calif., Santa Barbara, 1979—; participant Vienna (Austria) Philharm. Orch. Symposium, 1990, Internat. Trumpet Guild Conf., Rotterdam, The Netherlands, 1992; condr. Santa Barbara Symphony Orch., 1941-44, All-Calif. High Sch. Symphony Orch., 1941-73, Kern County Honor Band of Calif.; guest condr. Seoul (Korea) Symphony Orch., 1945-46, officer in charge Seoul Nat. U., 1945-46; mus. dir. Santa Barbara Fiesta Bowl Mus. Show, 1951-53. Contbg. editor The Instrumentalist, 1964-86; contbr. articles and criticisms to Mus. Courier, Sat. Rev., Christian Sci. Monitor. Chmn. Santa Barbara Mayor's Adv. Com. on Arts, 1966-69. Lt. (j.g.) to lt. USNR, 1944-46. Fellow Internat. Inst. Arts and Letters (life); mem. Music Acad. West (pres. 1949-85, pres. emeritus 1954—, sustaining dir. 1985—), So. Calif. Sch. Band and Orch. Assn. (hon. life, v.p. 1955), Am. Fedn. Musicians (hon. life), Nat. Music Educators Conf., Internat. Trumpet Guild, U. Calif. Emeriti Assn., Masons, Phi Mu Alpha (life), Phi Delta Kappa. Republican. Presbyterian. Avocation: world traveling. Home and Office: PO Box 572 Goleta CA 93116-0572

FAULKNER, SEWELL FORD, real estate executive; b. Keene, N.H., Sept. 25, 1924; s. John Charles and Hazel Helen (Ford) F.; AB, Harvard, 1949; MBA, 1951; m. June Dayton Finn, Jan. 10, 1951 (div.); children: Patricia Anne, Bradford William, Sandra Ford, Jonathan Dayton, Winthrop Sewell; m. Constance Mae Durvin, Mar. 15, 1969 (div.); children: Sarah Elizabeth, Elizabeth Jane. Product mgr. Congoleum Nairn, Inc., Kearny, N.J., 1951-55; salesman, broker, chmn., pres. Jack White Co. real estate, Anchorage, 1956-86. Mem. Anchorage City Council, 1962-65, Greater Anchorage Area Borough Assembly, 1964-65, Anchorage Area Charter Commn., 1969-70. Pres., Alaska World Affairs Council, 1967-68; treas. Alyeska Property Owners, Inc., 1973-75, pres., 1977-78; pres. Downtown Anchorage Assn., 1974-75; mem. Girdwood Bd. Suprs. Served with USAAF, 1943-45. Mem. Anchorage Area C. of C. (dir. 1973-74), Urban Land Inst., Bldg. Owners and Mgrs. Assn., Nat. Inst. Real Estate Brokers. Clubs: Alaska Notch, Anchorage Petroleum. Office: Faulkner Real Estate 604 K St Anchorage AK 99501-3329

FAUTSKO, TIMOTHY FRANK, mediator; b. Canton, Ohio, Dec. 27, 1945; s. Frank F. and Helen E. (Gozdan) F.; m. Marianne O'Carroll; children: T. Matthew, David F. BA in English, BBA, Walsh Coll., 1967; MA in Human Services Adminstrn., U. Colo., 1972. Trainer Vista Programs, Washington, 1967-70, Nat. Info. Ctr., Boulder, Colo., 1972-76; judicial adminstr. State of Colo., Boulder, 1976—; instr. Colo. Mountain Coll., Regis Univ., Glenwood Springs, Aspen, Colo., 1980—; co-dir. T/SDA & Assocs., Denver, 1975—. Co-author: Volunteer Programs in Prevention/Diversion, 1973, 2d rev. edit., 1978, Solving Problems in Meetings, 1981, QUID-How You Can Make the Best Decisions of Your Life, 1978, Como Tomar las Mejores Deciones de Su Vida, 1985; contbr. articles to profl. jours. Mem. Centennial Com., Glenwood Springs, 1983-85; mem. Mayor's com., Denver, 1977-78. HEW scholar, U. Colo., Boulder, 1971-72; recipient Cert. Appreciation Office of Mayor, Denver, 1978, Colo. Mountain Coll., Glenwood Springs, 1985-86, Outstanding Alumni award Walsh Coll., 1987. Mem. Nat. Assn. Trial Ct. Adminstrs. Home: PO Box 1711 Glenwood Springs CO 81602 Office: Mediation and Arbitration Svcs 1517 Blake PO Box 1711 Glenwood Springs CO 81602

FAVILLE, JAMES DONALD, manufacturing executive; b. Portland, Oreg., Feb. 27, 1934; s. Richard William and Frances Kathryn (Warrens) F.; m. Diana Dewees, Dec. 21, 1955; children: Jeffrey James, Christopher Stephen, David Dewees, Maria. AB, Stanford U., 1955. Pres. Pacific Paper Box & Bindery, Portland, 1957—. Mem. East Portland Rotary. Office: Pacific Paper Box & Bindery 2117 NE Oregon Portland OR 97732

FAW, DUANE LESLIE, retired military officer, law educator, lay worker, author; b. Loraine, Tex., July 7, 1920; s. Alfred Leslie and Noma Leigh (Elliott) F.; m. Lucile Elizabeth Craps, Feb. 20, 1943; children: Cheryl Leigh, Bruce Duane, Debra Leoma, Melanie Loraine. Student, N. Tex. State Coll., 1937-41; J.D., Columbia U., 1947. Bar: Tex. 1948, D.C. 1969, U.S. Supreme Ct. 1969. Commd. 2d lt. USMC, 1942, advanced through grades to brig. gen., 1969, bn. comdr., 1959-61, staff judge adv., 1961-64, policy analyst Marine Hdqrs., 1964-67, dep. chief of staff III Marine Amphibious Force, 1967-68, judge Navy Ct. Mil. Rev., 1968-69; dir. Judge Ad. Div. Marine Hdqrs. USMC, Washington, 1969-71; ret. USMC, 1971; prof. law Pepperdine U. Sch. Law, Malibu, Calif., 1971-85; Bible tchr. So. Presbyn. Ch., Denton, Tex., 1948-50, Camp Pendleton, N.C., 1959-61, Quantico. Va., 1962-63, United Meth. Ch., Arlington, Va., 1963-71; Bible tchr. , elder Presbyn. Ch., Van Horn, Tex., 1950-52; lay speaker, Bible tchr. United Meth. Ch., Tustin and Malibu. Calif., 1972—, mem. ann. conf., 1974-81, 91. Co-author: The Military in American Society, 1978, The Paramony, 1986. Gen. councilor URANTIA Brotherhood, 1979-88, gen. councilor of FELLOWSHIP, 1991—; bd. dirs. Jesusonian Found., Boulder, 1988—, Touch for Health Found., Pasadena, Calif., 1988—. Decorated Air medal with gold star, Navy Commendation medal with gold star, Legion of Merit with combat V with gold star; UN Cross of Gallantry with gold star; VN Honor medal 1st class. Mem. ABA (adv. com. mil. justice 1969-71, adv. com. lawyers in Armed Forces 1969-71), Fed. Bar Assn. (council), Judge Advs. Assn., Am. Acad. Religion, Soc. Bibl. Lit. Club: Masons. Address: 23301 Bocana Malibu CA 90265

FAWCETT, DON WAYNE, anatomist; b. Springdale, Iowa, Mar. 14, 1917; s. Carlos J. and Mabel (Kennedy) F.; m. Dorothy Marie Secrest, 1941; children: Robert S., Mary Elaine, Donna, Joseph. A.B. cum laude, Harvard, 1938, M.D., 1942; D.Sc. (hon.), U. Siena, Italy, 1974, N.Y. Med. Coll., 1975, U. Chgo., 1977, U. Cordoba, Argentina, 1978; M.D. (hon.), U. Heidelberg, Germany, 1977; D.V.M. (hon.), Justus Liebig U., Giessen-Lahn, Germany, 1977; DSc. (hon.), Georgetown U., 1987. Intern surgery Mass. Gen Hosp., Boston, 1942-43; instr. anatomy Harvard Med. Sch., 1946-48, asso. anatomy, 1948-51, asst. prof. anatomy, 1951-55, Hersey prof. anatomy, 1958-80, James Stillman prof. comparative anatomy, 1962-80, sr. asso. dean preclin. affairs, 1975-77; prof. anatomy Cornell Med. Coll., 1955-58; scientist Internat. Lab. Research on Animal Diseases, Nairobi, Kenya, 1980-85. Author: The Cell, 1966, 2d edit., 1981, Textbook of Histology, 1968, 10th edit., 1975, 11th edit., 1986. Served as capt. M.C. AUS, 1943-46; bn. surgeon A.A.A. John and Mary Markle scholar med. sci., 1949-54; recipient Lederle Med. Faculty award, 1954. Fellow Am. Acad. Arts and Sci., Nat. Acad. Sci. U.S., Royal Microscopical Soc. (hon.); mem. AAAS, N.Y. Acad. Sci., Am. Assn. Anatomists (pres. 1964- 65, Henry Gray award 1983, Centennial medal 1987), N.Y. Soc. Electron Microscopists (pres. 1957-58), Histochem. Soc., Tissue Culture Assn. (v.p. 1954-55), Soc. Exptl. Biology and Medicine, Assn. Anatomy Chairmen (pres. 1973-74), Am. Soc. Zoologists, Am. Soc. Mammalogists, Electron Microscope Soc. Am. (Disting. Scientist award in Life Scis. 1989), Soc. Study Devel. and Growth, Harvey Soc., Am. Soc. Cell Biology (pres. 1961-62), Argentine Nat. Acad. Sci., Anat. Soc. So. Africa (hon.), Japanese Anat. Soc. (hon.), Anat. Soc. Australia and N.Z. (hon.), Japanese Electron Microscope Soc., Internat. Fedn. Soc. Electron Microscopy (pres. 1976-78), Am. Soc. Andrology (pres. 1977-78), Soc. Study Reprodn. (Carl Hartman award 1985), Mexican (hon.), Canadian (hon.) Assn. Anatomists. Address: 1224 Lincoln Rd Missoula MT 59802

FAY, ABBOTT EASTMAN, history educator; b. Scottsbluff, Nebr., July 19, 1926; s. Abbott Eastman and Ethel (Lambert) F.; m. Joan D. Richardson, Nov. 26, 1953; children: Rand, Diana, Collin. BA, Colo. State Coll., 1949, MA, 1953; postgrad., U. Denver, 1961-63, Western State U., 1963. Tchr. Leadville (Colo.) Pub. Schs., 1950-52, elem. prin., 1952-54; prin. Leadville Jr. High Sch., 1954-55; pub. info. dir., instr. history Mesa Coll., Grand Junction, Colo., 1955-64; asst. prof. history Western State Coll., Gunnison, Colo., 1964-76, assoc. prof. history, 1976-82, assoc. prof. emeritus, 1982—; adj. faculty Adams State Coll., Alamosa, Colo., Mesa State Coll., Grand Junction, Colo., 1989—; propr. Moutaintop Books, Paonia, Colo.; bd. dirs. Colo. Assoc. Univ. Press; profl. speaker in field; dir. hist. tours. Author: Mountain Academia, 1968, Writing Good History Research Papers, 1980, Ski Tracks in the Rockies, 1984, Famous Coloradans, 1990, I Never Knew That About Colorado, 1993; playwright: Thunder Mountain Lives Tonight!; contbr. articles to profl. jours.; freelance writer popular mags. Founder, coordinator Nat. Energy Conservation Challenge; project reviewer NEH, Colo. Hist. Soc. Served with AUS, 1944-46. Named Top Prof. Western State Coll., 1969, 70, 71; fellow Hamline U. Inst. Asian Studies, 1975, 79. Mem. Western Writers Am., Rocky Mountain Social Sci. Assn. (sec. 1961-63), Am. Hist. Assn., Assn. Asian Studies, Western History Assn., Western State Coll. Alumni Assn. (pres. 1971-73), Internat. Platform Assn. Profl. Guides Assn. Am. (cert.), Colo. Antiquarian Booksellers Assn., Am. Legion (Outstanding Historian award 1981), Phi Alpha Theta, Phi Kappa Delta, Delta Kappa Pi. Home: 1750 Hwy 133 Paonia CO 81428-9709

FAY, RICHARD JAMES, mechanical engineer, executive, educator; b. St. Joseph, Mo., Apr. 26, 1935; s. Frank James and Marie Jewell (Senger) F.; m. Marilyn Louise Kelsey, Dec. 22, 1962; B.S.M.E., U. Denver, 1959, M.S.M.E., 1970; Registered profl. engr., Colo., Nebr. Design engr. Denver Fire Clay Co., 1957-60; design, project engr. Silver Engring. Works, 1960-63; research engr., lectr. mech. engring. U. Denver, 1963-74, asst. prof. Colo. Sch. of Mines, 1974-75, founder, pres. Fay Engring. Corp., 1971—. Served with Colo. N.G., 1962. Mem. Soc. Automotive Engrs. (past chmn. Colo. sect.), ASME (past chmn. Colo. sect., past regional v.p.). Contbr. articles to profl. jours.; patentee in field. Office: 5201 E 48th Ave Denver CO 80216-5316

FAY-SCHMIDT, PATRICIA ANN, paralegal; b. Waukegan, Ill., Dec. 25, 1941; d. John William and Agnes Alice (Semerad) Fay; m. Dennis A. Schmidt, Nov. 3, 1962 (div. Dec. 1987); children: Kristin Fay Schmidt, John Andrew Schmidt. Student, L.A. Pierce Coll., 1959-60, U. San Jose, 1960-62, Western State U. of Law, Fullerton, Calif., 1991-92. Cert. legal asst., Calif. Paralegal Rasner & Rasner, Costa Mesa, Calif., 1979-82; paralegal, adminstr. Law Offices of Manuel Ortega, Santa Ana, Calif., 1982-92; mem. editorial adv. bd. James Pub. Co., Costa Mesa, 1984-88. Contbg. author: Journal of the Citizen Ambassador Paralegal Delegation to the Soviet Union, 1990. Treas., Republican Women, Tustin, Calif., 1990-91; past regent, 1st vice regent, 2nd vice regent NSDAR, Tustin, 1967-92. Mem. Orange County Paralegal Assn. (hospitality chair 1985-87). Roman Catholic. Home: 13571 Hewes Ave Santa Ana CA 92705

FAZIO, VIC, congressman; b. Winchester, Mass., Oct. 11, 1942; m. Judy Kern; children: Dana Fazio, Anne Fazio, Kevin Kern, Kristie Kern. BA, Union Coll., Schenectady, 1965; postgrad., Calif. State U., Sacramento. Journalist, founder Calif. Jour.; congl. and legis. cons., 1966-75; mem. Calif. State Assembly, 1975-78; mem. 96th -103rd Congresses from Calif. 3rd Dist., 1979—, chmn. Dem. Congl. Campaign Com., vice chair Dem. caucus, house steering policy com., chmn. legis. br. appropriations subcom., vice chmn. appropriations subcom. energy and water, appropriations subcom. milt. constrn.; majority whip-at-large 96th-103rd Congress; also co-chmn. Fed. Govt. Svcs. Task Force 96th-101st Congresses, former chmn. bipartisan com. on ethics; former mem. Sacramento County Charter and Planning Commns. Bd. dirs. Asthma Allergy Found., Jr. Statesman, Nat. Italian-Am. Found. Coro Found. fellow; named Solar Congressman of Yr. Mem. Air Force Assn., Navy League, UNICO. Office: House of Representatives Washington DC 20515

FAZZINI, GEORGIA CAROL, corporate executive, business owner; b. Chicago Heights, Ill., Feb. 17, 1946; d. George and Corella A.T. (Roggeveen) Tjemmes; m. Dan Fazzini, Dec. 31, 1964; 1 child, Daniel Edward. Student, Ill. State U., Normal, 1963-64, Nat. Beauty Coll., 1979. Sec. Marshall Erdman & Assocs., Madison, Wis., 1972-73, U. Wis., Madison, 1973-74, Waukegan (Ill.) Devel. Ctr., 1974-75; br. adminstr. Universal Bus. Machines, Boise, Idaho, 1982-83; owner Substitute Sec. Typing Svc., Boise, 1983-87, Revisions Resume Writing Svc., 1987-90; chief exec. officer Diamond Devel. Ctr., Boise, 1988—; cons. Nat. Multiple Sclerosis Soc., Boise, 1983-85; instr. resume writing Dept. Community Edn. Boise Schs., 1986-90, Caldwell Schs., 1989-90; resume cons. Tulsa Psychiat. Ctr., Corp. Assistance Program, 1988, Simplot Aquaculture, Caldwell, Idaho, 1991; lectr. resume writing, Tulsa, 1988, Boise, 1989-91. Pres. New Neighbors' League, Canton, Ohio, 1978-79 (Rose of Month award 1979); vice chmn., bd. dirs., sec., cons. Nat. Multiple Sclerosis Soc., Boise, 1982-86; mem. Idaho Assn. Pvt. Devel. Disability Ctrs., 1989—; guest speaker Miss Teen Pageant, Boise, 1983-84; lobbyist Boise Secretarial Svcs., 1985-86, Idaho Devel. Disability Ctrs., 1989. Mem. Idaho Assn. Pvt. Devel. Disability Ctrs., Nat. Fedn. Ind. Bus. Home: 1519 Aquarius Ct Nampa ID 83651-1422 Office: Diamond Devel Ctr 1119 Caldwell Blvd Nampa ID 83651-1719

FEARN, DEAN HENRY, statistics educator; b. Portland, Oreg., June 8, 1943; s. Clyde Henry Fearn and Sylvia Adele (Dahl) Christensen; m. Gloria June Wilber, Oct. 1, 1966; children: Neal, Justin. BS in Math., U. Wash., 1965; MA in Math., Western Wash. State U., 1967; PhD in Math., U. Calif., Davis, 1971. Teaching asst. U. Calif., Davis, 1967-71; sr. mathematician Aerojet-Gen., Rancho Cordova, Calif., 1969-70; prof. of stats. Calif. State U., Hayward, 1971—. Contbr. articles to profl. jours. Mem. Am. Statis. Assn. (pres. Calif. chpt. 1991-92), Inst. Math. Stats., Am. Math. Soc., Math. Assn. Am., Pi Mu Epsilon. Democrat. Lutheran. Home: 3255 Sunnybrook Ct Hayward CA 94541-3535 Office: Calif State U Dept Stats Hayward CA 94542

FEARON, LEE CHARLES, chemist; b. Tulsa, Nov. 22, 1938; s. Robert Earl and Ruth Belle (Strothers) F.; m. Wanda Sue Williams, Nov. 30, 1971. Student, Rensselaer Polytech. Inst., 1957-59; BS in Physics, Okla. State U., Stillwater, 1961, BA in Chemistry, 1962, MS in Analytical Chemistry, 1969. Rsch. chemist Houston process lab. Shell Oil Co., Deer Park, Tex., 1968-70; chief chemist Pollution Engring. Internat., Inc., Houston, 1970-76; rsch. chemist M-I Drilling Fluids Co., Houston, 1976-83; cons. chemist Profl. Engr. Assocs., Inc., Tulsa, 1983-84; chemist Anacon, Inc., Houston, 1984-85; scientist III Bionetics Corp., Rockville, Md., 1985-86; sr. chemist L.A. County Sanitation Dist., Whittier, Calif., 1986; chemist Enseco-CRL, West Sacramento, Calif., 1986-87; consulting chemist Branham Industries, Inc., Conroe, Tex., 1987-89; adv. laboratorian EILS, QA sect. Wash. State Dept. Ecology, Manchester, 1989—; cons. chemist Terra-Kleen, Okmulgee, Okla., 1988—, Precision Works, Inc., Camarillo, Calif., 1993—. With U.S. Army, 1962-65. Fellow Am. Inst. Chemists; mem. AAAS, Am. Chem. Soc., Am. Inst. Chemists. Home: PO Box 514 Manchester WA 98353-0514 Office: PO Box 488 Manchester WA 98353-0488

FEATHER, LAWRENCE STEVEN, residential care executive, consultant; b. Ridgefield Park, N.J., Jan. 4, 1955; s. Leo and Della Bertha (Shupetsky) F.; m. Barbara Lynn Krone, June 26, 1982. BA cum laude, Boston Coll., 1977, MEd with honors, 1978; postgrad., USIU. Lic. cert. social worker, Mass. Child welfare specialist Brockton (Mass.) Dept. Social Svcs., 1978-79; with sales and purchasing depts. Manor Steel Corp., Park Ridge, Ill., 1979-83; pers. adminstr. Kevan Industries, L.A., 1983-84; cons. Mark Miller & Assocs., Van Nuys, Calif., 1985-87; pers. and tng. supr. Walden Environment, Mission Hills, Calif., 1987-88, dist. dir., 1988-92; exec. dir. Inner Circle FFA, Inc, Van Nuys, 1990—. Mem. Am. Psychol. Assn., Soc. for Indsl. and Organizational Psychology, Pers. and Indsl. Rels. Assn., Calif. State Psychol. Assn. Jewish. Home: 20737 Roscoe Blvd Apt 201 Canoga Park CA 91306-1764 Office: Inner Circle FFA Inc 7120 Hayvenhurst Ave # 204 Van Nuys CA 91406

FEAVER, DOUGLAS DAVID, university dean, classics educator; b. Toronto, Ont., Can., May 14, 1921; came to U.S., 1948; s. Charles John and Margaret Adeline (Brett) F.; m. Margaret Ruth Seaman, June 10, 1950; children: David, John, Paul, Ruth, Peter. B.A., U. Toronto, 1948; M.A., Johns Hopkins U., 1949, Ph.D., 1951; postgrad., Am. Sch. Classical Studies, 1951-52. Instr. Yale U., New Haven, 1952-56; mem. faculty Lehigh U., Bethlehem, Pa., 1956—, prof. classics, 1966-84; internat. dean. Coll. Humanities and Internat. Studies Univ. of the Nations, Kailua, Kona, Hawaii, 1985—; jr. fellow Ctr. Hellenic Studies, 1967-68; ann. research prof. Am. Sch. Classical Studies, 1976-77; dir. Humanities Perspectives on Tech., 1972-75; cons. in field. Author: El mundo en que vivio Jesus, 1972; contbr. articles to profl. jours. Served with RCAF, 1940-45. NEH scholar, 1971-84; cons. NEH, 1975—. Mem. Am. Philol. Assn., Archaeol. Inst. Am., Classical Assn. Atlantic States. Presbyterian. Office: Univ of the Nations 75-5851 KuaKini Hwy Kailua Kona HI 96740

FEAVER, GEORGE A., political science educator; b. Hamilton, Ont., Canada, May 12, 1937; came to U.S., July 4, 1967; s. Harold Lorne and Doris Davies (Senior) F.; m. Nancy Alice Poynter, June 12, 1963 (div. 1978); 1 child, Catherine Fergusson; m. Ruth Helene Tubbesing, Mar. 8, 1986 (div. 1991). B.A. with Honors, U. B.C., 1959; Ph.D., London Sch. of Econs., 1962. Asst. prof. Mt. Holyoke Coll., South Hadley, Mass., 1962-65; lectr., research assoc. London Sch. Econs. and Univ. Coll., London, 1965-67; assoc. prof. Georgetown U., Washington, 1967-68, Emory U., Atlanta, 1968-71; assoc. prof. U.B.C., Vancouver, B.C., Canada, 1971-74, prof., 1974—; vis. fellow Australian Nat. U., Canberra, 1987. Author: From Status to Contract, 1969; editor: Beatrice Webb's Our Partnership, 1975; editor: The Webbs in Asia: The 1911-12 Travel Diary, 1992; co-editor: Lives, Liberties and the Public Good, 1987; contbr. articles to profl. jours., books. Fellow Canada Council, 1970-71, 74-75, Am. Council Learned Socs., 1974-75, Social Scis. and Humanities Research Council of Canada, 1981-82, 86-91. Mem. Can. Polit. Sci. Assn., Am. Polit. Sci. Assn., Am. Soc. for Polit. and Legal Philosophy, Conf. for Study of Polit. Thought, Inst. Internat. de philosophie politique. Club: Travellers' (London). Home: 4776 W 7th Ave, Vancouver, BC Canada V6T 1C6 Office: Univ British Columbia, Dept Polit Sci, Vancouver, BC Canada V6T 1Z1

FEDERICI, TONY, small business owner, state legislator; b. St. Helens, Oreg., Mar. 21, 1937; s. Nickolas and Rose (Albrizio) F.; m. Nancy Alice Weeks, July 10, 1965; children: Nick, Catherine. BA, U. Oreg., 1963. Science instr. Salem Pub. Schs., Oreg., 1963-65; owner Tony's Shoes, St. Helens, 1965—. City councilman City of St. Helens, 1980-88; port commr. Port of St. Helens, 1988-92; state rep. Oreg. State Legislature, Salem, 1993—. With U.S. Army, 1960-62. Mem. Western Ind. Shoe Enterprises (pres. 1979, chmn. 1980), St. Helens Lion Club (pres. 1972—). Democrat. Roman Catholic. Home: 59945 Sunrise Dr Saint Helens OR 97051 Office: Tony's Shoes 1620 Columbia Blvd Saint Helens OR 97051

FEDORCHAK, DIANA RACHELLE, editor, writer; b. Monongahela, Pa., Dec. 5, 1945; d. Michael and Ann Fedorchak. BA, Seton Hill Coll., 1967; MA, Profl. Sch. Psychology, 1986, postgrad., 1989. Editor, tech. writer U. Pitts., 1967-68; dir., asst. v.p., pub. rels. dir. Bank Calif., San Francisco, 1969-79; sr. editor U. Calif., San Francisco, 1979-92; psychology intern Children's Hosp., San Francisco, 1987-88, Sunset Parkside Community Mental Health Agy., San Francisco, 1989-90; freelance editor, writer, 1993—. Hotline counselor Marin (Calif.) Suicide Prevention Ctr., 1975-78, also dep. coroner; vol. San Francisco Gen. Hosp., 1980, trauma ctr.

FEDORKO, CHARLES ANDREW, JR., satellite telecommunications executive; b. Trenton, N.J., May 25, 1947; s. Charles Andrew Sr. and Marian Winifred (Harrison) F.; m. Patricia Elizabeth Riddle, Jan. 1, 1987. AS in Bus. Adminstrn., U. New Haven, 1983; BS in Organizational Behavior, U. San Francisco, 1987, MS in Orgn. Devel., 1989. Lic. gen. class radiotelephone Fed. Communications Commn. Radio personality WGNT Radio, Huntington, W.Va., 1970-71, WICH Radio, Norwich, Conn., 1971-74; ops. mgr. WNLC & WTYD Radio, New London, Conn., 1974-79, WEEX & WQQQ Radio, Easton, Pa., 1979-81; network controller GE Am. Communications, Princeton, N.J., 1981-84; satellite engr. NBC Television Network, N.Y.C., 1984-86; mgr., network ops. Hughes Communications, L.A., 1986—; prof. El Camino Coll., Torrance, Calif., 1989—. Sgt. USAF, 1966-70, Vietnam. Roman Catholic. Home: 25250 B Steinbeck Ave Stevenson Ranch CA 91381-1205 Office: Hughes Communications PO Box 92424 Los Angeles CA 90009-2424

FEDORUK, SYLVIA O., Canadian provincial official, educator; b. Canora, Sask., Can., May 5, 1927; d. Theodore and Annie (Romaniuk) F. BA, U. Sask., 1949, MA, 1951; DSc, U. Windsor, Ont., Can., 1987, U. Western Ont., 1989; LLD, U. Regina, Sask., 1991. Asst. physicist Saskatoon (Sask.) Cancer Clinic, 1951-57, sr. physicist, 1957; asst. prof. U. Sask., Saskatoon, 1956-89, chancellor, 1986-89, prof. emeritus, 1989—; dir. physics svcs. Sask. Cancer Found., 1966-86; lt. gov. Province of Sask., 1988—; cons. in nuclear medicine. Recipient Queen's Jubilee medal, 1977, Century Saskatoon medal, 1982. Fellow Can. Coll. Physicists in Medicine; mem. Can. Ladies Curling Assn. (past pres.), Sports Fedn. Can. (past bd. dirs.). Ukrainian Greek Orthodox. Office: Govt House, 4607 Dewdney Ave, Regina, SK Canada S4P 3V7

FEER, CHARLES LEWIS, lawyer, consultant; b. Bakersfield, Calif., Aug. 3, 1960; s. Kenneth L. and Ruth G. (Gilbreath) F.; m. Teri Lea Thorpe, Sept. 27, 1980 (div. May 1992); 1 child, Candyce Anne. AA, Bakersfield Coll., 1981; BS, Western State U., 1987, JD, 1988; MPA, Calif. State U., Bakersfield, 1992. Asst. mgr. Thrifty Drug Corp., Bakersfield, 1980-82; counselor Kern County Probation Dept., Bakersfield, 1982-83; dep. sheriff Kern County Sheriff's Dept., Bakersfield, 1983-84; pvt. investigator S.W. Investigations, Bakersfield, 1984-88; law clk. Noriega & Alexander, Bakersfield, 1988, Rawson & Tafoya, Bakersfield, 1989; owner Pretrial Svcs., Bakersfield, 1989—; mng. ptnr. Strategic Planning Assocs., Bakersfield, 1990—; instr. Watterson Bus. Coll., Bakersfield, 1988-89. Candidate Kern High Sch. Dist. Trustees, Bakersfield, 1989. Recipient Am. Jurisprudence award, 1986, 87; named Outstanding Young Men of Am., 1988. Mem. Calif. Attys. for Criminal Justice, Nat. Assn. Criminal Def. Lawyers, Wilson INst., U.S. Naval Inst., Fgn. Policy Assn. Republican. Methodist. Home: 4909 Stockdale Hwy #227 Bakersfield CA 93309 Office: Pretrial Svcs 1415 18th St #307 Bakersfield CA 93301

FEES, JOHN T., association executive; b. Phoenix, Apr. 5, 1967; s. O.S. Fees and Nancy (McCallion) Thornhill. BS in History, Ariz. State U., 1985-89; cert., U. London, 1989. Legis. asst. House of Commons, London, 1989; pub. affairs & regional sales mgr. Woodstuff Mfg. Inc., Phoenix, 1990; v.p. alumni assn. Ariz. State U. Student body pres. Ariz. State U., 1988-89; spl. events Kids Voting, Phoenix, 1990; task force Vision Tempe, 1990; precinct committeeman Ariz. Reps., Phoenix, 1988-92; Octoberfest com. Sister City Internat., Tempe, 1984-92. Mem. Ariz. Assn. Industries, Ariz. State U. Bd. Excellence, Ariz. State U. Alumni Assn.(pres., bd. dirs.). Home: 327 E Geneva Dr Tempe AZ 85282-3728

FEES, NANCY FARDELIUS, special education educator; b. Santa Monica, Calif., Mar. 25, 1950; d. Carl August and Dodi Emma (Hedenschau) Fardelius; m. Paul Rodger Fees, June 4, 1971; children: Evelyn Wyoming, Nelson August. BS, Mills Coll., 1971; MA in Edn., Idaho State U., 1975. Cert. tchr., Calif., Idaho, Wyo., R.I. Specialist curriculum mgmt. Barrington (R.I.) High Sch., 1975-81; coordinator learning skills ctr. Northwest Community Coll., Powell, Wyo., 1982-84, instr., 1985—; pres. Children's Resource Ctr., 1985-89, bd. dirs., 1983-89, 91—. Editor (with others) The Great Entertainer, 1984. Vol. Buffalo Bill Hist. Ctr., Cody, Wyo., 1981—; mem. Centennial Com., Cody, 1983; mem. parent's adv. com. Livingston Sch., 1989-92, chmn., 1991-92. Mem. Council Exceptional Children, Assn. Children with Learning Disabilities, Council Adminstrs. of Spl. Edn. Democrat. Episcopalian. Home: 1718 Wyoming Ave Cody WY 82414-3320

FEHR, J. WILL, newspaper editor; b. Long Beach, Calif., Mar. 8, 1926; s. John and Evelyn (James) F.; m. Cynthia Moore, Sept. 4, 1951; children—Michael John, Martha Ann. B.A. in English, U. Utah, 1951. City editor Salt Lake City Tribune, 1964-80, mng. editor, 1980-81, editor, 1981-91. Served to 1st lt. USAF, 1951-53. Mem. Am. Soc. Newspaper Editors, Sigma Chi. Clubs: Hidden Valley, Fort Douglas (Salt Lake City). Home: 468 13th Ave Salt Lake City UT 84103-3229 Office: Salt Lake City Tribune 143 S Main St Salt Lake City UT 84111-1917

FEHR, LARRY MICHAEL, state agency administrator, educator; b. Ellensburg, Wash., Oct. 14, 1952; s. James Thomas and Edna May (Burgess) F.; m. Gina Lynn Ringstad, July 24, 1976; children: Lindsey Brooke, Megan Elizabeth. BA in Sociology and Polit. Sci., Wash. State U., Pullman, 1974; student, U. Wales, Cardiff, Eng., 1972-73; MPA, U. Wash., Seattle, 1983. Teaching asst. Cen. Wash. U., Ellensburg, 1974-75, U. Wash., Seattle, 1975-76; rsch. analyst Inst. for Govtl. Rsch., Seattle, 1975-76; law and justice planner N.W. Regional Coun. of Govts., Bellingham, Wash., 1976-78, planning coord., 1978-81; lectr. in criminal justice & pub. adminstrn. Seattle U., 1987—; exec. dir. Wash. Coun. on Crime & Delinquency, 1981—; founding mem. Wash. Coalition of Crime Victim Advocacy, Seattle, 1986—, N.W. Youth Svcs., Bellingham, 1977-80. Founding mem. Wash. Pub. Interest Rsch. Group, Seattle, 1975-76; pres. Leadership Tomorrow Alumni Assn., Seattle, 1988-89; chmn. youth panel United Way, Bellingham, 1980-81; trustee Internat. Festival of the Arts, Bellingham, 1979-80; mem. vis. com. dept. sociology U. Wash., 1989—; mem. planning com. Seattle Pvt. Industry Coun., 1983-89; mem. Regional Law, Safety and Justice Com., 1990—, Kids Count Adv. Bd., 1992—, State Children's Adminstrn. Adv. Com., 1992—; regional trustee Group Health Coop., 1987-88. Recipient Spl. Achievement award United Way of Whatcom County, 1981, Profl. award Wash. Correctional Assn., 1987, Exceptional Svc. award Cath. Archdiocese, 1987. Mem. Wash. Law and Justice Planning Assn. (pres. 1978-80), Wash. Ctr. for Law Related Edn. (trustee, past pres.), Exec. Dirs. Coalition, Phi Beta Kappa. Home: 4305 212th Ave NE Redmond WA 98053-6019 Office: Wash Coun Crime Delinquency 1305 4th Ave Ste 602 Seattle WA 98101-2401

FEHRER, STEVEN CRAIG, physiology educator, researcher; b. Milw., June 26, 1951; s. Kenneth and LaVerne (Conrad) F. BS with distinction, U. Wis., 1973, MS, 1977; PhD, U. Minn., St. Paul, 1984. Tchr. sci. Wausau (Wis.) East High Sch., 1973-78; rsch. asst. U. Minn., 1979-84, rsch. assoc., 1985-88; rsch. assoc. Tufts U., Medford, Mass., 1984-85; asst. prof. physiology, researcher in avian endocrinology Idaho State U., Pocatello, 1988—. Contbr. articles to profl. jours. Mem. Endocrine Soc., Poultry Sci. Assn., Sigma Xi. Office: Idaho State U Dept Biol Sci Box 8007 Pocatello ID 83209

FEHRIBACH, RONALD STEVEN, investment executive; b. Huntingburg, Ind., Nov. 2, 1949; s. Edwin Joseph and Stella Ann (Edele) F. BS in Polit. Sci., Ind. State U., 1974; postgrad., Rose Hulman Inst. Tech., 1974, Ind. U., 1977; MA, Eastern Ky. U., Richmond, 1980. Crew supr. Ahrens and Son's Nursery, Huntingburg, Ind., 1966-70; constrn. worker Nailer Constrn. Co., Huntingburg, 1971; fin. and program analyst HEW, Chgo., Washington, 1972; investment exec. Moseley, Hallgarten, Estabrook & Weeden Inc., Chgo., 1980-87, LaSalle St. Securities, Inc., Chgo., 1987-93, F.J. Garber & Co., Mesa, Ariz., 1993—; pres. Fehribach Investments Inc., Chgo., 1986—; corp. comdr. Res. Officer Tng. Program, Terre Haute, 1973-74. Capt. U.S. Army, 1975-77, Korea; with Ind. Nat. Guard, 1977-79. Named Rookie of Yr., Moseley Assocs., Boston, 1983; recipient Outstanding Sales award Am. Fin. Group, Boston, 1986.

FEHRMANN, WALTRAUT GERLINDE, logistics analyst; b. Pasadena, Calif., Nov. 20, 1959; d. Klaus Rudolph Arymund and Gerlinde Isolde (Seemayer) F. BA in Math., UCLA, 1983. Logistics engr./system analyst ITT Gilfillan, Van Nuys, Calif., 1984-87; logistics analyst Litton-Data System Divsn., Van Nuys, 1987-90, Rockwell-Space Systems Divsn., Downey, Calif., 1990-92, Rockwell-Rocketdyne Divsn., Canoga Park, Calif., 1992—. Asst. game mgr. Tournament of Roses Rose Bowl Game, 1993. Recipient Exceptional Membership Recruitment Pin, Calif. Jr. C. of C., 1988, Presdl. Medallion of Honor, 1989, Cert. of Appreciation, Pasadena Children's Svcs., 1992, Outstanding Citizen award Rockwell Internat., 1993. Mem. Pasadena Jr. C. of C. (Mem. Adam's Family Outstanding Contbn. 1987, Outstanding New Mem., 1987, Dir. of the Quarter 1988, Outstanding New Bd. Mem., 1988, Presdl. Medallion 1988, Mem. Cathy's Crew-Outstanding Contbn. 1989, Award for Disting. Svc. to Community Devel. v.p. 1989, Project of Quarter 1990, 91, Project of Yr. 1990, Commendation for Exceptional Project Report 1990, Mem. Make It Happen Team-Outstanding Contbn. 1990, Outstanding Chmn. 1991). Home: 8428 Stansbury Ave Panorama City CA 91402 Office: Rocketdyne Canoga Park CA 91304

FEICHTNER, JOHN DAVID, physicist; b. Erie, Pa., July 6, 1930; s. William John and Marie Elizabeth (Sweigard) F.; m. Sheila Harty, June 22, 1957. BS, Stanford U., 1953; MS, N.Mex. State U., 1960; PhD, U. Colo., 1964. Physicist GE, Richland, Wash., 1955-57; sr. scientist Westinghouse R & D, Pitts., 1965-70, fellow scientist, 1970-78, mgr. optical physics, 1978-85; program mgr. SRI Internat., Menlo Park, Calif., 1985-87, Sci. Applications Internat. Corp., Los Altos, Calif., 1987-89; sr. staff scientist Lockheed R & D Div., Palo Alto, Calif., 1989—. Contbr. 22 articles to profl. jours. Mem. Murrysville (Pa.) City Coun., 1977-84, pres., 1982. Lt. USNE, 1957-60. Mem. IEEE (sr.), Am. Phys. Soc., Optical Soc. Am., Optical Soc. No. Calif. (pres. 1988).

FEICK, PAUL ALDEN, computer company executive; b. Sandusky, Ohio, Aug. 6, 1939; s. Adam and Sophia (Laubner) F.; m. Susan A. Class, June 24, 1961; children: Edwin, Douglas, David. BS in Mech. Engring., Case Inst. of Tech., 1961; MBA, Case Western Res. U., 1968. Project engr. Harris Corp., Cleve., 1961-72; project mgr. OMCSA, Milan, 1972-75, Combustion Engring., Cleve., 1975-78; v.p. engring. Baumfolder Corp., Sidney, Ohio, 1978-85; pres. Computer Output Processors and Engring., Tucson, 1985—. Mem. XPLORE Internat., Case Inst. Tech. Alumni Assn., Theta Chi, Phi Kappa Psi. Republican. Methodist. Home: 3121 N Swan # 143 Tucson AZ 85712 Office: Computer Output Processors & Engring Inc 2425 E Medina Rd Tucson AZ 85706

FEIG, STEPHEN ARTHUR, pediatrics educator, hematologist, oncologist; b. N.Y.C., Dec. 24, 1937; s. Irving L. and Janet (Oppenheimer) F.; m. Judith Bergman, Aug. 28, 1960; children: Laura, Daniel, Andrew. AB in Biology, Princeton U., 1959; MD, Columbia U., 1963. Diplomate Am. Bd. Pediatrics, Am. Bd. Hematology-Oncology. Intern Mt. Sinai Hosp., N.Y.C., 1963-64, resident in pediatrics, 1964-66; hematology fellow Children's Hosp. Med. Ctr., Boston, 1968-71, assoc. in medicine, 1971-72; asst. prof. pediatrics UCLA, 1972-77, chief div. hematology and oncology, sch. medicine, 1977—, assoc. prof., 1977-82, prof., 1982—; cons. Olive View Med. Ctr., Van Nuys, Calif., 1973—, Valley Med. Ctr., Fresno, Calif., 1973—, Sunrise Hosp. dept. pediatrics, Las Vegas, Nev., 1980—; med. advisory com. Los Angeles chpt. Leukemia Soc. Am., 1978—; bd. trustees, 1984—; bd. dirs. Camp Ronald McDonald for Good Times; active numerous other pediatric hosp. and med. sch. coms. Reviewer Am. Jour. Pediatric Hematology/Oncology, Blood, Jour. Clin. Investigation, Pediatrics, Pediatric Rsch., Am. Jour. Diseases of Children, Jour. Pediatrics; contbr. articles to profl. jours. Served with USNR, 1966-68. Mem. Am. Soc. Hematology, Soc. Pediatric Research, Am. Pediatric Soc., Internat. Soc. Exptl. Hematology, Am. Assn. Cancer Research. Jewish. Office: UCLA Sch Medicine Dept Pediatrics 10833 Le Conte Ave Los Angeles CA 90024-1602

FEIGENBAUM, CLIFFORD SCOTT, newsletter editor, financial consultant; b. Cin., Nov. 9, 1961; s. Phillip Stanley and Helen Lee (Potts) F.; 1 child, Candice M. Payne-Feigenbaum. BA in Bus. Mgmt., Whitworth Coll., 1986. Retail mgmt. asst. Squire Shop/Kinney Shoes, Spokane, Wash., 1979-82; treas., bookkeeper Discovery Sch., Spokane, 1986-87; bus. and account asst. Sta. KAYU-TV, Spokane, 1987-89; payroll specialist II, Empire Health Svcs., Spokane, 1989-91; creator, pub., co-editor The GreenMoney Jour. Socially Responsible business investing & consumer Resources Newsletter, Spokane, 1992—; guest on socially responsible ethical investing various radio stas., Spokane, also Peace and Justice Action League Seminar, Spokane, 1992. Contbr. articles to profl. jours. Vol. Habitat for Humanity, Spokane Food Bank, also others, 1984—, Oil Smart, alternative transp. programs, Spokane, 1992; vol., bd. dirs. Discovery Sch., 1984-87. Recipient Recycling Leadership award Spokane City and County Solid Waste Disposal Project, 1991. Mem. Whitworth Coll. Alumni Assn., A Spokane Men's Group, various health clubs. Home and Office: W 608 Glass Ave Spokane WA 99205

FEIL, LINDA MAE, tax preparer; b. Dallas, Oreg., Apr. 9, 1948; d. Fred Henry and Ruth Irene (Hoffman) F. AA, West Valley Community Coll., 1975; student, Golden Gate U. Ctr. for Tax Studies, 1975, Menlo Coll. Sch. Bus. Adminstrn., 1978. Enrolled agt. IRS; cert. in fed. taxation. Income tax preparer, office mgr. H & R Block, Inc., Santa Clara, Calif., 1972-74, asst. area mgr., 1974-76; propr. L.M. Feil Tax Service, Santa Clara, 1976-80; ptnr. Tennyson Tax Service, Santa Clara, 1980-81; owner McKeany-Feil Tax Service, San Jose, Calif., 1981-83; owner Feil Tax Service, San Jose, 1983-90, Richmond, Calif., 1990—. Mem. Nat. Soc. Pub. Accts., Nat. Assn. Enrolled Agts. (chpt. sec. 1981-83, chpt. v.p. 1983-84), Mission Soc. Enrolled Agts. (pres. 1984-85, Enrolled Agt. of Yr. 1985), Calif. Soc. Enrolled Agts. (bd. dirs. 1985-86). Home: 4843 Silver Creek Rd Fairfield CA 94533 Office: Feil Tax Svc 3065 Richmond Pky # 106 Richmond CA 94806-1904

FEIN, WILLIAM, ophthalmologist; b. N.Y.C., Nov. 27, 1933; s. Samuel and Beatrice (Lipschitz) F.; m. Bonnie Fern Aaronson, Dec. 15, 1963; children: Stephanie Paula, Adam Irving, Gregory Andrew. BS, CCNY, 1954; MD, U. Calif., Irvine, 1962. Diplomate Am. Bd. Ophthalmology. Intern L.A. County Gen. Hosp., 1962-63, resident in ophthalmology, 1963-66; instr. U. Calif. Med. Sch., Irvine, 1966-69; mem. faculty U. So. Calif. Med. Sch., 1969—, assoc. clin. prof. ophthalmology, 1979—; attending physician Cedars-Sinai Med. Ctr., L.A., 1966—, chief ophthalmology clinic svc., 1979-81, chmn. div. ophthalmology, 1981-85; attending physician Los Angeles County-U. So. Calif. Med. Ctr., 1969—; chmn. dept. ophthalmology Midway Hosp., 1975-78; dir. Ellis Eye Ctr., L.A., 1984—. Contbr. articles to med. publs. Chmn. ophthalmology adv. com. Jewish Home for Aging of Greater L.A., 1993—. Fellow Internat. Coll. Surgeons, Am. Coll. Surgeons; mem. Am. Acad. Ophthalmology, Am. Soc. Ophthalmic Plastic and Reconstructive Surgery, Royal Soc. Medicine, AMA, Calif. Med. Assn., L.A. Med. Assn. Home: 718 N Camden Dr Beverly Hills CA 90210-3205 Office: 415 N Crescent Dr Beverly Hills CA 90210-4860

FEINBERG, RICHARD ALAN, clinical psychologist; b. Oakland, Calif., Aug. 12, 1947; s. Jack and Raechel Sacks (Hoff) F. B.A., Calif. State U.-Hayward, 1969; M.A. in Clin. Psychology, Mich. State U., 1972, Ph.D., 1979; Nat. Register of Health Service Providers in Psychology, 1980. Instr., Merritt Coll., Oakland, 1975-76; clin. psychologist Highland Gen. Hosp., Oakland, 1976-79; asso. Lafayette Center Counseling and Edn., 1978-79; clin. psychologist Tri-City Mental Health Center, Fremont, Calif., 1979-81, dir., 1981-86; pvt. practice clin. psychology, 1976—; participant profl. conf. USPHS fellow, 1969-71. Mem. Am. Psychol. Assn., Calif. Psychol. Assn. Jewish. Office: 38950 Blacow Rd Suite D Fremont CA 94536

FEINHANDLER, EDWARD SANFORD, writer, photographer, art dealer, sports mentor; b. Elko, Nev., Jan. 13, 1948; s. Samuel and Sylvia (Manus) F. BA, U. Nev., Reno, 1972. Supr. underpriveledged Washoe County Extension Program, Reno, 1970-71; sports editor, writer Sagebrush Campus newspaper, Reno, 1971-72; internal salesman, mgr. Trigon Corp., Sparks, Nev., 1975-88; owner, operator Art Internat. Gallery Extraordinaire, Reno, 1981—; tennis dir. City of Sparks, 1991-93; with nat. news Top Ten radio interviews, U.S. and Can., 1978-79; freelance writer and photographer. Contbr. articles to newspapers; extra in various movies; TV interviewee AM Chgo., AM L.A., 1979, Afternoon Exchange, Cleve., 1979, To Tell the Truth, 1975, Reno Tonight TV show, 1989, Fox Across America TV show, 1989. Player, coach Summer Volleyball League, Reno, 1982-85; tennis coach Community Service Ctr., Reno, 1986-88; participant Make-A-Wish Found., Reno, 1985-93, U. Nev. Journalism Dept., 1985-93, UNR Children's Svcs., Reno, 1986-88; coach Cath. Basketball, 1987-89 (2d place); head coach girls Varsity Tennis Bishop Manogue High Sch., 1989-91; spl. olympics, 1989, girls Jr. Varsity Basketball, 1989; active Ptnrs. in Edn., 1988-90, Jr. Achievement, 1989-93, Animal Welfare Inst., Statue of Liberty Found., 1984-91, No. Nev. Cancer Coun., United Blood Svcs., Arthritis Found., Cancer Soc., Sta. KNPB, Ret. Sr. Citizens; Sierra Arts Found. Sgt. U.S. Army, 1968-69, Vietnam. Winner Ugly Man contest U. Reno, 1967, 70-72, No. Nev. Bone Marrow Program, 1991-93; winner ind. category Ugly Bartender contest Multiple Schlerosis, 1989-90; recipient numerous tennis, billiards, volleyball and bowling awards including 1st pl. C div. NNCC Tennis Tournament, 1991, Mixed Doubles Champ., 1992, finalist Sr. Open Singles, Sparks City, 1993, Open Doubles Champ., 1993; world record holder nosedarts and squint, 1972—. Mem. DAV, Orthodox Jewish Union. Democrat. Office: Art Internat Gallery Extraordinaire PO Box 13405 Reno NV 89507-3405

FEINSTEIN, (ALLAN) DAVID, psychologist, author; b. Bklyn., Dec. 22, 1946; s. Sol and Edith (Fuhrman) F.; m. Donna Colleen Eden, Oct. 7, 1984. BA, Whittier (Calif.) Coll., 1968; MA, U.S. Internat. U., 1970; PhD, Union Inst., 1973. Lic. psychologist, Oreg., Calif. Youth dir. San Diego YMCA, 1968-70; instr. Sch. of Medicine Johns Hopkin's U., Balt., 1970-75; sr. clin. psychologist San Diego County Mental Health Svcs., 1975-83; exec. dir. Innersource, Ashland, Oreg., 1983—. Author: Personal Mythology, 1988, Rituals for Living & Dying, 1990; contbr. articles to profl. jours. Mem. APA, Assn. for Humanistic Psychology. Office: Innersource 777 E Main St Ashland OR 97520-2117

FEINSTEIN, DIANNE, U.S. senator; b. San Francisco, June 22, 1933; d. Leon and Betty (Rosenburg) Goldman; m. Bertram Feinstein, Nov. 11, 1962 (dec.); 1 child, Katherine Anne; m. Richard C. Blum, Jan. 20, 1980. BA History, Stanford U., 1955; LLB (hon.), Golden Gate U., 1977; D Pub. Adminstrn. (hon.), U. Manila, 1981; D Pub. Service (hon.), U. Santa Clara, 1981; JD (hon.), Antioch U., 1983, Mills Coll., 1985; LHD (hon.), U. San Francisco, 1988. Fellow Coro Found., San Francisco, 1955-56; with Calif. Women's Bd. Terms and Parole, 1960-66; mem. Mayor's com. on crime, chmn. adv. com. Adult Detention, 1967-69; mem. Bd. of Suprs., San Francisco, 1970-78, pres., 1970-71, 74-75, 78; mayor of San Francisco, 1978-88, U.S. senator from Calif., 1992—; mem. exec. com. U.S. Conf. of Mayors, 1983-88; Dem. nominee for Gov. of Calif., 1990; mem. Nat. Com. on U.S.-China Rels. Mem. Bay Area Conservation and Devel. Commn., 1973-78. Recipient Woman of Achievement award Bus. and Profl. Women's Clubs San Francisco, 1970, Disting. Woman award San Francisco Examiner, 1970, Coro Found. award, 1979, Coro Leadership award, 1988, Pres. medal U. Calif., San Francisco, 1988, Scopus award Am. Friends Hebrew U., 1981, Brotherhood/Sisterhood award NCCJ, 1986, Comdr.'s award U.S. Army, 1986, French Legion of Honor, 1984, Disting. Civilian award USN, 1987; named Number One Mayor All-Pro City Mgmt. Team City and State Mag., 1987. Mem. Trilateral Commn., Japan Soc. of No. Calif. (pres. 1988-89), Inter-Am. Dialogue, Nat. Com. on U.S.-China Rels. Office: US Senate 331 Senate Hart Office Bldg Washington DC 20510-0504

FEIR, SCOTT EUGENE, minister; b. Tacoma, Wash., Sept. 30, 1964; s. Larry E. and Mellodean (Barnes) F.; m. Kimberly Teel, June 23, 1990. AA, Ft. Steilacoom Community Coll., 1985; BA, Seattle Pacific U., 1987; MDiv, Golden Gate Bapt. Sem., 1991, MA, 1992. Ordained to ministry Meth. Ch., 1992. Assoc. min. Richmond Highlands Bapt. Ch., Seattle, 1985-88, Lucas Valley Community Ch., Mill Valley, Calif., 1990-92; sr. min. Fed. Way (Wash.) Free Meth., 1992—; speaker Calif. State Youth Retreat, 1990. Mem. Pacific N.W. Conf. of Free Meths. Home and Office: 32644 49th Pl SW Federal Way WA 98023

FEISS, GEORGE JAMES, III, financial services company executive; b. Cleve., June 24, 1950; s. George James Jr. and Bettie (Kalish) F.; m. Susan Margaret Cassel, May 30, 1981; children: Kalish Ilana Cassel-Feiss, Nika Catherine Cassel-Feiss. BA in Social Studies, Antioch Coll., 1973; MBA in Internat. Fin., Am. Grad. Sch. Internat. Mgmt., Phoenix, 1975. Registered investment advisor; CFP. Ptnr. Healthcare Cons., Seattle, 1976-80; pres. M2 Inc., Seattle, 1980—; cons. Sta. KRAB, Seattle, 1988-89, Zion Christian Acad., Seattle, 1990—. Author: Mind Therapies/Body Therapies, 1979, Hope & Death in Exile - The Economics and Politics of Cancer in the United States, 1981. Bd. dirs. B'nai Brith, Seattle, 1988-91; mem. fin. com. Univ. Child Devel. Sch., Seattle, 1989—; mem. social action com. Am. Jewish Com., Seattle, 1992. Mem. Eastside Estate Planning Coun., Inst. for CFPs, Social Investment Forum, TOES (The Other Econ. Summit). Home: 603 38th Ave Seattle WA 98122 Office: M2 Inc 7811 SE 27th Ste 113 Mercer Island WA 98040

FEIT, MICHAEL DENNIS, physicist; b. Easton, Pa., Nov. 15, 1942; s. Joel E. and Kathryn T. (Bracken) F.; m. Lorraine R. Mauriel, Dec. 30, 1967; children: Sean M., Kathryn R. BA, Lehigh U., 1964; PhD, Rensselaer Poly. Inst., 1970. Rsch. asst. Rensselaer Poly. Inst., Troy, N.Y., 1964-69; rsch. assoc. U. Ill., Urbana, 1969-72; physicist Lawrence Livermore (Calif.) Nat. Lab., 1972—, leader theoretical optical physics group, 1992—; adj. faculty dept. applied sci. U. Calif., Davis, 1985—. Contbr. numerous articles to profl. jours. Fellow Am. Phys. Soc., Optical Soc. Am.; mem. AAAS, Phi Beta Kappa, Sigma Xi. Office: Lawrence Livermore Nat Lab Mail Stop L-296 PO Box 808 Livermore CA 94550

FEITELSON, JERALD STUART, molecular biologist; b. Peekskill, N.Y., Oct. 15, 1953; s. Herbert William and Evelyn Esther (Katz) F.; m. Eva Nagy, Oct. 27, 1985; children: Justine Hannah, Cory David. BS in Life Scis., MIT, 1975; PhD in Genetics, Stanford U., 1981. Rsch. asst. dept. biology MIT, Cambridge, 1974-75; rsch. asst. dept. genetics Stanford (Calif.) U., 1975-81; postdoctoral rsch. fellow dept. genetics John Innes Inst., Norwich, Eng., 1981-84; adj. prof. Waksman Inst. Rutgers U., Piscataway, N.J., 1984-88; sr. rsch. microbiologist Lederle Labs., Am. Cyanamid, Pearl River, N.Y., 1984-88; mgr. molecular biology dept. Mycogen Corp., San Diego, 1988—; grant reviewer NIH, Bethesda, Md., 1986-93, NSF, Washington, 1987-88. Contbr. articles to profl. jours.; patentee in field. NIH Predoctoral Tng. grantee, 1975-81, NIH Postdoctoral Rsch. grantee, 1981-84. Mem. Am. Soc. Microbiology, Fedn. Am. Scientists, Planetary Soc., N.Y. Acad. Scis. Office: Mycogen Corp 4980 Carroll Canyon Rd San Diego CA 92121-1764

FELBERG, DAVID EDWARD, management consultant; b. Pasadena, Calif., May 30, 1957; s. Richard LeRoy and Naniva (McFarlin) F.; m. Laura Marie Bogden, Aug. 31, 1985; children: Julie, Brian. AB, Occidential Coll., 1979; MBA, UCLA, 1983. Cert. cash mgr. Ops. mgr. Crocker Nat. Bank, L.A., 1979-81; intern 1st Interstate Bank, L.A., 1982; cons. KPMG PEat Marwick, L.A., 1983-85; sr. cons. KPMG Peat Marwick, L.A., 1985-87; v.p. CAST Mgmt. Cons., L.A., 1987-88, exec. v.p., 1989—. Mem. Fin. Mgrs. Soc., Acad. Magican Arts. Republican. Office: CAST Mgmt Cons 1620 26th St Ste 2040N Santa Monica CA 90404

FELD, MYRON XANE, urban planner; b. Bklyn., Apr. 29, 1915; s. Abraham Louis and Helen (Taub) F.; m. Sylvia Bayder, Aug. 12, 1938; children: April Marina, Jason Mendy. BS in Engring., CCNY, 1936, MCE, 1937. Registered profl. engr., Calif. Civil engr. U.S. Army Corps of Engrs., N.Y.C., 1937-42; dir. pub. works Boro of Roosevelt, N.J., 1946-49; dir. devel. Israel Inst. Tech., Haifa, Israel, 1949-53; dir. pub. works Twp. of Hamilton, Trenton, N.J., 1953-59; regional engr. air base constrn. U.S. Army, Turkey, Israel, 1959-62; transp. engr. N.J. Motor Vehicle Dept., Trenton, 1962-69; reconstrn. planner, city engr. Jerusalem, 1969-72; regional planner County of Los Angeles, 1974—; asst. prof. gen. engring. Rutgers U., New Brunswick, N.J., 1956-59; guest lectr. Tel Aviv U., Jerusalem, 1970-72. Contbr. articles to profl. jours. Councilman Borough of Roosevelt, 1964-70; mem. planning bd. Twp. of Hamilton, 1953-59. Served as chief warrant officer U.S. Army, 1942-46, PTO. Mem. Assn. Mcpl. Engrs. (sec.-treas. to pres. 1953-59). Office: LA Dept Regional Planning Los Angeles County 320 W Temple St Los Angeles CA 90012-3208

FELDAVERD, NICHOLAS EDWARD, III, educator, musician; b. Sigourney, Iowa, Jan. 3, 1949; s. Nicholas Edward and Nellie Jeanette (Greenlee) F.; m. Joyce Diane Furnas, Dec. 15, 1973; children: Andrea Michelle, Nicholas Edward IV. BS in Edn., S.W. Mo. State U., 1972; M of Music Edn., So. Ill. U., 1978; postgrad., Ariz. State U., 1980—, Phoenix Coll., 1985-87. Band dir. Normandy (Mo.) Pub. Schs., 1973-78, Mesa (Ariz.) Pub. Schs., 1978—; prin. trombonist Mesa Symphony Orch., 1978—; wind coach Met. Youth Orch., Mesa, 1980—; adj./clinician and pvt. instr., 1978—. Mem. Am. Fedn. Musicians, Nat. Assn. Jazz Educators, Ariz. Bd. and Orch. Dirs., Music Educators Nat. Conf. Republican. Office: Taylor Jr High Sch 705 S 32d St Mesa AZ 85204-3943

FELDKAMP, MARCIA LYNN, epidemiologist; b. Wyandotte, Mich., Nov. 5, 1952; d. Alfred Joseph and Phyllis Jean (Hagamen) F.; m. E. Charles Norlin, Oct. 9, 1982; children: Kara Diane Norlin, Alexa Mikel Norlin. AAS, No. Mich. U., 1973; physician asst. cert., U. Utah, 1979, BS, 1982, MSPH, 1986. Cert. physician asst. Radiol. technician Sinai Hosp. Detroit, 1973-74, Denver Gen. Hosp., 1974-76; physician asst. Foothill Family Clinic, Salt Lake City, 1979, Family Health Plan, Salt Lake City, 1980-84; rsch. asst. Rocky Mountain Ctr. Occupational/Environ. Health, Salt Lake City, 1984-86, Genetic Epidemiology, Salt Lake City, 1987-90; reproductive epidemiologist Pregnancy Riskline, Salt Lake City, 1990—; cons. epidemiologist Pediatric Growth Study, Salt Lake City, 1990—, Pregnancy Riskline, Salt Lake City, 1986-90. Contbr. articles to profl. jours. Participant Utah Math./Sci. Network, Salt Lake City, 1989-91. Mem. Utah Acad. Physician Assts. (chairperson com. 1981-84, pres. 1985). Office: Pregnancy Riskline 44 N Medical Dr Salt Lake City UT 84113

FELDMAN, ANNETTE YOUNG, civic worker; b. Hoopeston, Ill., July 23, 1916; d. Reuben and Ida (Horvitz) Yonkelowitz; m. Jerome Feldman, Oct. 19, 1941 (dec. 1986); children: Jill Feldman Crane, Robert. Student, Northwestern U., 1934-36; BS, U. Chgo., 1938, MS, 1940. Nutritionist ARC, Chgo., 1940-41; nutrition cons. Med. Coll. Va., Richmond, 1941-42; specialist food and nutrition U. Ill. Extension Svc., Champaign, 1943-45; tutor East Bay Literacy Coun., 1990—; historian Alameda Contra Costa Med. Aux. Dist. II, 1990—. Editor cookbooks for philanthropic orgns. Chmn. fund drives and disaster food ARC, Hayward, Calif., 1948, bd. dirs., 1954-58; chmn. bldg. fund St. Rose Hosp., Hayward, 1956; chmn. heart fund drive Am. Heart Assn., Hayward, 1958; mem. adult edn. com. Beth Jacob Congregation, Oakland, Calif., 1965; chmn. fund-raising events Scholarships, Inc., Hayward, 1969; pres. Alameda-Contra Costa Med. Aux., 1961-62, condr. nutritional symposium, 1975; charter assoc. Children's Hosp. Found. Circle of Friends, 1985—; life mem. Hayward Sch. Dist. PTA, Hayward Forum Arts; mem. Friends of Hayward Edn. Fund, World Affairs Coun., Women's Am. Orgn. for Rehab. Through Tng., Judah Magnes Mus.; mem. Tamarack br. Children's Med. Ctr. No. Calif.; tutor Inter Bay Literacy Coun., 1990. Recipient Appreciation award Alameda-Contra Costa Med. Aux., 1962. Mem. Am. Dietetic Assn. (life; registered), Bay Area Dietetic Assn., Eden Hosp. Found., AAUW, Chgo. Alumni Assn., Hill and Valley Club, Order of Ea. Star, Hadassah (life mem. Eden chpt., Svc. award 1960). Home: 22119 Prospect St Hayward CA 94541-2627

FELDMAN, FREDRIC JOEL, health products executive; b. N.Y.C., Feb. 9, 1940; s. Morris M. and Minnie (Gesse) F.; m. Claire Judith Gershen, July 8, 1962; children: Eric, Julie. BS in Chemistry, Bklyn. Coll., 1960; MS in Organic Chemistry, U. Md., 1964, PhD in Analytical Chemistry, 1967. Prin.

investigator Walter Reed Inst. Rsch., Washington, 1964-68; dir. atomic absorption R&D Instrumentation Lab., Lexington, Mass., 1968-70, v.p. biomed., 1984-86, pres., 1986-88; program mgr. Beckman Instruments, Fullerton, Calif., 1970-77; dir. European ops. Beckman Instruments, Geneva, Switzerland, 1977-81; div. mgr. Beckman Instruments, Brea, Calif., 1981-84; pres. Microgenics, Concord, Calif., 1988-92; CEO, chmn. Oncogenetics, Phoenix, 1992—; chmn. Blex, Inc., Denver, 1992—. Author: Atomic Absorption Spectroscopy, 1970; contbr. numerous articles to scientific jours. Office: Oncogenetics 1275 Pacific Ave Laguna Beach CA 92651-1958

FELDMAN, LESTER, environmental engineer; b. N.Y.C., Dec. 4, 1948; s. Fred and Celia Feldman; m. Andrea H. Goldstein, Feb. 23, 1980. BS in Engring., U. Mich., 1970, MS in Engring., 1972. Process engr. Bechtel, Inc., San Francisco, 1973-74; sr. environ. specialist Calif. Regional Water Quality Ctrl. Bd., Oakland, 1975—; lectr. Calif. State U.-Sonoma, Rohnert Park, 1978-80. Fellow Fed. Water Pollution Ctrl. Agy., 1971, 72. Office: Calif Regional Water Quality Ctrl Bd 1800 Harrison St Ste 700 Oakland CA 94612

FELDMAN, LOUIS ARNOLD, mathematics educator; b. Bay City, Mich., Nov. 26, 1941; s. Henry and Rebecca Feldman; m. Rosetta Sue Croom, Aug. 3, 1975 (div. Apr. 1981); m. Mary Ellen Rhodes, 0ct. 7, 1988. BS, U. Mich., 1963; MA, U. Calif., Berkeley, 1965, PhD, 1969. Asst. prof. math. Calif. State U. Stanislaus, Turlock, 1968-71, assoc. prof. math., 1971-76, prof. math., 1976—, chair dept. math., 1993—. Contbr. articles to profl. jours. Woodrow Wilson fellow Woodrow Wilson Found., 1963, NSF Grad. fellow, 1963. Mem. Phi Beta Kappa, Phi Kappa Phi. Office: Calif State U Stanislaus 801 W Monte Vista Ave Turlock CA 95380-0299

FELDMAN, STANLEY GEORGE, state supreme court chief justice; b. N.Y.C., N.Y., Mar. 9, 1933; s. Meyer and Esther Betty (Golden) F.; m. Norma Arambula; 1 dau., Elizabeth L. Student, U. Calif., Los Angeles, 1950-51; LL.B., U. Ariz., 1956. Bar: Ariz. 1956. Practiced in Tucson, 1956-81; ptnr. Miller, Pitt & Feldman, 1968-81; justice Ariz. Supreme Ct., Phoenix, 1982, chief justice, 1992—; lectr. Coll. Law, U. Ariz., 1965-76, adj. prof., 1976-81. Bd. dirs. Tucson Jewish Community Council. Mem. Am. Bd. Trial Advocates (past pres. So. Ariz. chpt.), ABA, Ariz. Bar Assn. (pres. 1974-75, bd. govs. 1967-76), Pima County Bar Assn. (past pres.), Am. Trial Lawyers Assn. (dir. chpt. 1967-76). Democrat. Jewish. Office: Ariz Supreme Ct 1501 W Washington St Phoenix AZ 85007-3327

FELDMANN, R. SCOTT, lawyer; b. Stillwater, Okla., May 10, 1961; s. John Earl and Helen Jane (Pharr) F.; m. Catherine Mary Sledge, Mar. 21, 1987; children: Justin Gregory, Spencer Michael. BEE cum laude, Vanderbilt U., Nashville, 1982; MSEE, Air Force Inst. Tech., Dayton, 1984; disting. grad. Portuguese basic course, Def. Lang. Inst., Monterey, Calif., 1986; disting. grad., Squadron Officer's Sch., 1986; MS in Systems Mgmt., U. So. Calif., L.A., 1988; JD, U. Calif., Berkeley, 1993. Assoc. A.T. Kearney, L.A., 1988-90, Kaye, Scholer, Fierman, Hays and Handler, Century City, 1993—; internat. mgmt. cons. in field. Capt. USAF, 1982-88. Decorated Achievement medal with oak leaf cluster; recipient Commendation medal Test Dir. of Yr., 1985, Top Secret clearance. Mem. IEEE, Federalist Soc. (chpt. pres. 1990-93), Toastmasters Internat. (chpt. pres. 1985, 88), Eta Kappa Nu. Republican. Lutheran.

FELICITA, JAMES THOMAS, aerospace company executive; b. Syracuse, N.Y., May 21, 1947; s. Anthony Nicholas and Ada (Beech) F.; AB, Cornell U., 1969; postgrad. Harvard U., 1969, U. So. Calif., 1970, UCLA, 1975-77. Contracting officer U.S. Naval Regional Contracting Office, Long Beach, Calif., 1974-80; sr. contract negotiator space and communications group Hughes Aircraft Co., El Segundo, Calif., 1980-81, head NASA contracts, 1981-84, mgr. maj. program contracts, 1984—. Recipient cost savs. commendation Pres. Gerald R. Ford, 1976. Mem. Cape Canaveral Missile Space Range Pioneer, Nat. Contract Mgmt. Assn., Cornell Alumni Assn. So. Calif., Planetary Soc. Republican. Club: Nat. Space, Hughes Mgmt. Home: 8541 Kelso Dr Huntington Beach CA 92646-4501 Office: 909 N Sepulveda Blvd Los Angeles CA 90245

FELIX, RICHARD JAMES, engineering executive, consultant; b. Sacramento, Apr. 21, 1944; s. Joseph James and Faye Lola (Thornburg) F.; m. Nancy Tucker Thompson, 1970 (div. 1972). Cert., Electronics Tech. A Sch., Treasure Island, Calif., 1963; student, Am. River Coll., 1968-72, Calif. State U., 1972-74. Ptnr. ADRA, Sacramento, 1971-73, Doggie Domes, Sacramento, 1971-72, Fong and Co., Sacramento, 1976-79; project dir. Dynascan Project, Sacramento, 1976-88; dir. research Omni Gen. Corp., Sacramento, 1988—; ptnr. Am. Omnigraph, Sacramento, 1985—; instr. Calif. State U., Sacramento, 1973-74; cons. KDM Design, 1985—. Creator documentary film American River College Rat Decathlon, 1974; editor publicity manual, 1978; contbr. articles to Lasers & Optronics; inventor omnigraph, 1967, Multiplex Video Display System, 1976, Multiplex Video Display System II, 1984. Vol. Leukemia Soc., Sacramento, 1984, Transitional Living and Community Support, 1990-; artist Camellia City Ctr., Sacramento, 1983. With USN, 1962-66. Mem. Mental Health Assn. (bd. dirs. Sacramento-Placer chpt. 1980, 90—, Clifford Beers Award 1983), Mensa. Republican. Episcopalian.

FELIX, ROBIN, defense contractor; b. Wheelus AFB, Tripoli, Libya, Oct. 19, 1954; s. Ernest Robert and Jean Eloise (Goretzka) F.; m. Barbara Ann Fletcher, May 1, 1979; children: Erin Loraine, Ryan Fletcher, Brynn Elyse. BA in Engring. Sci., Dartmouth Coll., 1975; MS in Ops. Rsch., Naval Postgrad. Sch., 1982; postgrad., U. San Diego. Cert. USN reactor (nuclear) elec. operator. Commd. ensign USN, 1978, advanced through grades to lt. comdr., 1986, resigned, 1988; engr., analyst Delfin Systems, Sunnyvale, Calif., 1989-90; San Diego dir. Delfin Systems, 1991—; commdg. officer San Diego Cryptologic Naval Reserve Unit 419, 1992-; electronic telecomm. cons. Civil Air Patrol, Honolulu, 1986-88. Pres. Atsugi (Japan) Players, 1978-79; actor, dir. various community theatre groups, Hawaii, Calif., 1980-88; bd. dirs. various ch. choirs, Japan, Hawaii, Calif., 1978-88. Recipient Best Actor award Aloha Players, 1987, Naval Security Group Pacific, 1988. Mem. SAG, Nat. Security Indsl. Assn. (bd. dirs., newsletter editor San Diego chpt.). Office: Delfin Systems 5055 Viewridge Ave San Diego CA 92123

FELIZ, LUIS RAFAEL, programmer analyst, consultant; b. Mineola, N.Y., June 18, 1967; s. Sergido Bolivar and Maria Martha (Bueno) F. BS in Computer Sci., N.Y. Inst. Tech., 1990. Programmer analyst Good Weather Corp., Syosset, N.Y., 1987-90; mgr. info. systems Agri-Weather Ins. Svcs., Fresno, Calif., 1990—; cons. programmer analyst Fresno YWCA, 1992—. Mem. Assn. for Computing Machinery. Republican. Roman Catholic. Home: 1550 W Ashlan lAve # 212 Fresno CA 93705-1913 Office: Agri-Weather Ins Svcs 2589 N Air Fresno Dr 109 Fresno CA 93727

FELKER, MARTIN ROY, data processing professional; b. N.Y.C., Nov. 3, 1947; s. Seymour and Lillian (Kass) F.; m. Sharon Kessler, Mar. 5, 1979 (div. June 1984). BS, Met. State U., Denver, 1974. Programmer State Compensation Ins. Fund, San Francisco, 1985-87, assoc. programmer/analyst, 1987—. Bd. dirs. Ctr. for Ind. Living, Berkeley, Calif., 1982-84. Mem. Assn. of Computing Machinery. Home: 1626 Dwight Way Apt M Berkeley CA 94703-1800 Office: State Comp Ins Fund 1275 Market St San Francisco CA 94103

FELL, KATHERINE CHRISTINE, artist; b. Tacoma, Wash., Dec. 12, 1948; d. Bobby Gene and Doris Lavonne (Abrahamson) Anderson; m. Charles Dennis Fell, Mar. 10, 1973; children: Christopher Charles, Noah Michael, Peyton Christine. AA in Comml. Art, Chabot Coll., Hayward, Calif., 1968; BA in Art, Calif. State U., Hayward, Calif., 1970. Cert. community coll. instr., Calif. instr. watercolor workshops, Santa Rosa, Calif., 1989-93. Exhibited in one-woman shows at Marin County Civic Ctr., San Rafael, Calif., 1992, Press House Gallery, Buena Vista Winery, Sonoma, 1992, Rochioli Winery, Healdsburg, Calif., 1993; exhibited in group shows at La Petite Gallery, Bozeman, Mont., 1986-89, Eastbay Watercolor Soc. Annual, Oakland, Calif., 1991, 92, El Presidio Gallery, Sonoma, Calif., 1991-92, Ga. Watercolor Soc. Ann., 1993, Rocky Mountain Nat. Exhbn., Golden, Colo., 1992, Nat. Watercolor Okla., Oklahoma City, 1992, La. Watercolor Soc. Internat. Exhbn., New Orleans, 1992. Mem. Santa Rosa Art Guild, 1990-92, Cultural Arts Coun. of Sonoma County, 1992-93, Mont. Inst. of the Arts, 1987-88. Recipient 1st pl. Watercolors award Santa Rosa Art Guild Statewide, 1990, 3d pl. Watercolors award Bodega Bay Allied Arts, 1990, 2d pl. Watercolors awards Cultural Arts Art Show, 1990, Santa Rosa Art Guild Statewide, 1991, 1st pl. Watercolors award Bodega Bay Allied Arts, 1993; featured artist in Am. Artist Watercolor 93 Spring. Mem. Eastbay Watercolor Soc.

FELLER, ROBERT S., SR., consulting company executive; b. N.Y.C.. BS, BA, Calif. State U., L.A., 1965; MBA, UCLA, 1966. Sr. rsch. engr., scientist, sr. project staff engr., cons. Rockwell Internat., Anaheim and Downey, Calif., 1960-66; dir. ops. Gen. Industries, Culver City, Calif., 1966-76; v.p. ops. U.S. Industries Internat., L.A., 1976-83, also bd. dirs.; chief exec. officer, chief exec. cons. Consulting Industries Internat., L.A., 1983—, also bd. dirs. Author: Fortunes from Ideas, 1970 (best seller 1970, 71), Saturn-V Systems & Interfaces, 1966 (White House award), So You Want To Be An Inventor, 1991, A Piece of the Action, 1993, (Fast Profits and Productivity--Free), CLES--Continuing Lifetime Educational Systems, 1993, several others; inventions include Auto-Weld System (now known as Robotics), 1950, Weapons System, 1951, Center-Finder System, 1952, Saf-T Gun Locks, 1958, numerous others. Chmn. fundraising drive ARC, Santa Monica Coll., Calif., 1959; cons. Mayor's Blue Ribbon Adv. Com., West Covina, 1965, L.A. C. of C., 1969-71. Office: Cons Industries Internat Worldway Ctr 91435 Los Angeles CA 90009-1435

FELLIN, OCTAVIA ANTOINETTE, retired librarian; b. Santa Monica, Calif.; d. Otto P. and Librada (Montoya) F.; student U. N.Mex., 1937-39; BA, U. Denver, 1941; BA in L.S., Rosary Coll., 1942. Asst. libr., instr. libr. sci. St. Mary-of-Woods Coll., Terre Haute, Ind., 1942-44; libr. U.S. Army, Bruns Gen. Hosp., Santa Fe, 1944-46, Gallup (N.Mex.) Pub. Libr., 1947-90; post libr. Camp McQuaide, Calif., 1947; freelance writer mags., newspapers, 1950—; libr. cons.; N.Mex. del. White House Pre-Conf. on Librs. & Info. Svcs., 1978; dir. Nat. Libr. Week for N.Mex., 1959. Chmn. Red Mesa Art Ctr., 1984-88; pres. Gallup Area Arts Coun., 1988; mem. Western Health Found. Century Com., 1988, Gallup Multi-Model Cultural Com., 1988—; v.p., publicity dir. Gallup Community Concerts Assn., 1957-78, 85—; organizer Gt. Decision Discussion groups, 1963-85; co-organizer, v.p. chair fund raising com. Gallup Pub. Radio Com., 1989—; mem. McKinley County Recycling Com., 1990—; mem. local art selection com. N.Mex. Art Dirs., 1990; mem. Gallup St. Naming Com., 1958-59, Aging Com., 1964-68; chmn. Gallup Mus. Indian Arts and Crafts, 1964-78; mem. Eccles. Conciliation and Arbitration Bd., Province of Santa Fe, 1974; mem. publicity com. Gallup Inter-Tribal Indian Ceremonial Assn., 1966-68; mem. Gov's. Com. 100 on Aging, 1967-70; mem. U. N.Mex.-Gallup Campus Community Edn. Adv. Coun., 1981-82; N.Mex. organizing chmn. Rehobeth McKinley Christian Hosp. Aux., pres., 1983, aux. scholarship com., 1989—, chmn. scholarship com. 1990—, bd. dirs., corr. sec., 1991—; mem. N.Mex. Libr. Adv. Coun., 1971-75, vice chmn., 1974-75; chmn. adv. com. Gallup Sr. Citizens, 1971-73; mem. steering com. Gallup Diocese Bicentennial, 1975-78, chmn. hist. com., 1975; chmn. Trick or Treat for UNICEF, Gallup, 1972-77; chmn. pledge campaign Rancho del Nino San Huberto, Empalme, Mex.; active Nat. Cath. Social Justice Lobby; bd. dirs. Gallup Opera Guild, 1970-74; bd. dirs., sec., organizer Gallup Area Arts Council, 1970-78; mem. N.Mex. Humanities Council, 1979, Gallup Centennial Com., 1980-81; mem. Cathedral Parish Council, 1980-83, v.p., 1981, century com. Western Health Found., 1988-89. Recipient Dorothy Canfield Fisher $1,000 Libr. award, 1961, Outstanding Community Service award for mus. service Gallup C. of C., 1969, 70, Outstanding Citizen award, 1974, Benemerenti medal Pope Paul VI, 1977, Celebrate Literary award Gallup Internat. Reading 8 Assn., 1983-84, N.Mex. Disting. Pub. Svc. award, 1987, finalist Gov's award Outstanding N.Mex. Women, 1988, Edgar L. Hewett award Hist. Soc. N.Mex., 1992; Octavia Fellin Pub. Libr. named in her honor, 1990. Mem. ALA, N.Mex. Library Assn. (v.p., sec., chmn. hist. materials com. 1964-66, salary and tenure com., nat. coordinator N.Mex. legislative com., chmn. com. to extend library services 1969-73, Librarian of Yr. award 1975, chmn. local and regional history roundtable 1978, Community Achievement award 1983), AAUW (v.p., co-organizer Gallup br., N.Mex. nominating com. 1967-68, chmn. fellowships and centennial fund Gallup br., chmn. com. on women), Plateau Scis. Soc., N.Mex. Folklore Soc. (v.p. 1964-65, pres. 1965-66), N.Mex. Hist. Soc. (dir. 1979-85), Gallup Hist. Soc., Gallup Film Soc. (co-organizer, v.p. 1950-58), LWV (v.p. 1953-56), NAACP, Pax Christi U.S.A., Women's Ordination Conf. Network, Gallup C. of C. (organizing chmn. women's div. 1972, v.p. 1972-73), N.Mex. Women's Polit. Caucus, Pax Christi USA, N.Mex. Mcpl. League (pres. librarian's div. 1979—), Alpha Delta Kappa (hon.). Roman Catholic (Cathedral Guild, Confraternity Christian Doctrine Bd. 1962-64, Cursillo in Christianity Movement, mem. of U.S. Cath. Bishop's Adv. Council 1969-74; corr. sec. Latin Am. Mission Program 1972-75, sec. Diocese of Gallup Pastoral Council 1972-73, corr. sec. liturgical commn. Diocese of Gallup 1977); chmn. Artists Coop., 1985-89; mem. N.Mex. Diamond Jubilee/U.S. Constitution Bicentennial Gallup Com., 1986-87. Author: Yahweh the Voice that Beautifies the Land. Home and Office: 5esa Ave Gallup NM 87301-6021

FELLMAN, JOHN KEEGAN, physiology educator, biochemist; b. St. Louis, Nov. 26, 1952; m. Harriet L. Hughes, Oct. 16, 1976; children: Mary Alice, John Murray. BS, Clemson (S.C.) U., 1974; PhD, U. Idaho, 1982. Postdoctoral fellow U. Idaho, Moscow, 1981-82, 1983; postdoctoral fellow Wash. State U., Pullman, 1983-86; rsch. chemist USDA/ARS, Wenatchee, Wash., 1987-88; asst. prof. U. Idaho, Moscow, 1988-93, assoc. prof., 1993—; pvt. practice post-harvest biochemist cons., pacific n.w., 1988—. Contbr. articles to profl. jours. Mem. AAAS, Am. Soc. Plant Physiologists, Am. Soc.for Horticultural Sci., Internat. Dwarf Fruit Tree Assn., Am. Chem. Soc., Sigma Xi (v.p. 1989-90, pres. 1990-92, U. Idaho chpt.). Office: U Idaho Dept Plant Soil Entomol Moscow ID 83843

FELLMAN, PHILIP VOS, business educator; b. L.A., July 14, 1951; s. Gerald and Muriel (Vos)F. BFA, Calif. Inst. of the Arts, 1974; MA in Edn., MA in Govt., Cornell U., 1979, 88; M.Pub. and Pvt. Mgmt., Yale U., 1986; PhD in Polit. Sci., Cornell U., 1990. Internat. oil traffic specialist Pres.'s Staff, Chevron, San Francisco, 1980-84; vis. asst. prof. Dartmouth Coll., Hanover, N.H., 1990-91; exec. dir. Alaska Inst. Strategic Mgmt., Juneau, 1992—; assoc. prof. mgmt. Sch. Bus. and Pub. Adminstrn., U. Alaska, Juneau, 1992—; vice-chmn. Motion Picture Credit Corp., Beverly Hills, 1990—; dir. Ivy Biotechnology, San Francisco. Editor Alaska Jour. of Pub. Affairs, 1992—; contbr. articles to profl. jours. Mem. Yale Club of No. Calif., Cornell Club of No. Calif. Republican. Office: Univ of Alaska Sch Bus and Pub Adminstrn 11120 Glacier Hwy Juneau AK 99801

FELLOWS, DONALD MATTHEW, university official; b. Palo Alto, Calif., Dec. 7, 1955; s. Wilbur Lombard and Coralie Irene (Hill) F.; m. Jill Anne Fisher, Jan. 19, 1985; children: Lauren Catherine, Ryan Matthew. BA in Pub. Adminstrn., San Diego State U., 1980; postgrad., U. San Diego, 1991—. Asst. v.p. Gt. Am. Bank, San Diego, 1976-82; asst. dir. alumni and devel. San Diego State U., 1982-85; dir. corp. rels. Stanford (Calif.) U., 1985-90; dir. devel. U. San Diego, 1990—; cons. on fundraising. Bd. dirs. Burn Inst., San Diego, 1983-85. Mem. Nat. Soc. Fund Raising Execs., Coun. for Advancement and Support Edn., Rotary. Republican. Roman Catholic. Home: 8896 Calle Tragar San Diego CA 92129 Office: U San Diego Alcala Pk San Diego CA 92110

FELLOWS, LARRY DEAN, geologist; b. Magnolia, Iowa, May 29, 1934; s. John Boyd and Mildred (Herman) F., m. Carolyn Regina Hunter, Aug. 13, 1960; children: Brian David, Graham Boyd, Kyle Raeburn. BS, Iowa State U., 1955; MA, U. Mich., 1957; PhD, U. Wis., 1962. Cert. Am. Inst. Profl. Geologists, Ariz. Bd. Tech. Registration. Geologist Carter Oil Co., Grand Rapids, Mich., 1957-59; asst. prof. Southwest Mo. State Coll., Springfield, Mo., 1962-65; chief stratigraphy sect. Mo. Geol. Survey and Water Res., Rolla, Mo., 1965-71; asst. state geologist Mo. Geol. Survey and Water Res., 1971-74; asst. state geologist, program dir. Mo. Dept. Natural Resources, 1974-79; asst. dir., state geologist Ariz. Bur. Geology Mineral Tech., Tucson, 1979-88; dir., state geologist Ariz. Geol. Survey, Tucson, 1988—. Bd. dirs. Rolla Pub. Libr.; pres. Rolla Community Concert Assn., 1978. Fellowship NSF, U. Mich., 1956-57, U. Wis., 1961-62. Fellow Geol. Soc. Am.; mem. Am. Inst. Profl. Geologists, Assn. Am. State Geologists (pres. 1988-89), Soc. Econ. Paleontologists and Mineralogists, Ariz. Geol. Soc. Office: Ariz Geol Survey 845 N Park Ave # 100 Tucson AZ 85719-4896

FELMLEY, JERRY JOHN, aerospace engineering executive; b. Bloomington, Ill., Feb. 20, 1933; s. John Benjamin and Amy Beatrice (Stephenson) F.; m. Jenrose Pressley Weldon, Apr. 11, 1958 (div. 1989); children: Melissa Felmley Scully, Jennifer Weldon, Amy Felmley Sachs. BS, U. Ill., 1955; MS/MBA, U. Chgo., 1965; Dipl., Indsl. Coll. Armed Forces, Washington, 1975. Owner/prin. Catalyst Assocs., Tucson, 1981—. Contbr. articles to profl. jours. Vol., D.C. Rep. Party, 1981-89. Col. USAF, 1955-81. Decorated Legion of Merit, DFC, Air Medal with 11 oak leaf clusters, others. Mem. AIAA, Air Force Assn., Am. Def. Preparedness Assn., Nat. Def. Transp. Assn., Jolly Green Rescue Pilots Assn., Order of Daedalians, Phi Delta Theta (D.C. alumni pres. 1986-89). Republican. Presbyterian. Home: 5825 N Cerrada Chica Tucson AZ 85718-4115 Office: Catalyst Assocs Cons 5825 N Cerrada Chica Tucson AZ 85718-4115

FELT, JAMES PATTERSON, computer programmer; b. Ogden, Utah, June 13, 1950; s. John Gillingham and Claramay (Patterson) F. BA, Weber State Coll., Ogden, 1974, Weber State Coll., Ogden, 1980; MA, U. Ariz., 1978. Programmer 1st Security Bank, Salt Lake City, 1980-84, sr. programmer, 1984-92; v.p. Felt Auto Parts Co.; newsletter editor Salt Lake City, 1988-90, 92—. Organist, Salt Lake Liberty Stake LDS Ch., 1989—, clk., 1991—. Mem. Am. Guild Organists (Salt Lake chpt. newsletter editor 1988-90, 91—, publicity com. 1991—). Home: 48 W 300 S Apt 801 Salt Lake City UT 84101-2010

FELT, JAMES WRIGHT, philosophy educator, priest; b. Dallas, Jan. 4, 1926; s. Wright Lafayette and Freda Marie (Brown) F. AB, Gonzaga U., 1949, MA, 1950; STL, Alma Coll., 1957; MS in Physics, St. Louis U., 1961, PhD in Philosophy, 1965. Instr. St. Ignatius High Sch., San Francisco, 1950-53; asst. prof. philosophy Santa Clara (Calif.) U., 1965, assoc. prof. philosophy, 1971, prof. philosophy, 1984—. Contbr. articles to profl. jours. Jesuit priest Santa Clara U., 1965—. Mem. Am. Philos. Assn., Am. Cath. Philos. Assn. (exc. coun. 1978-81, 90-92), Metaphys. Soc. Am. (exec. coun. 1994—), Jesuit Philos. Assn. U.S. (pres. 1981-82). Office: Santa Clara U Dept of Philosophy Santa Clara CA 95053

FELTER, JAMES WARREN, painter, curator; b. Bainbridge, N.Y., Aug. 25, 1943. BA, U. South Fla., 1964; student U. Wash. Currently with The Hallo Found., Quito, Ecuador. Studios in West Vancouver, B.C., Can. and Quito. Group shows include: Musee d'Art et d'Histoire, Geneva, Switzerland, 1976, Mus. Modern Art, Sao Paulo, Brazil, 1976; 37th Venice (Italy) Biennale, 1976, Moderna Galerija, Liubljana, 1976, Pratt Graphics Ctr., N.Y.C. Los Angeles Inst. Contemporary Art, 1978, La Post-Avanguardia, Naples, Italy, 1978, Robson Sq., Vancouver, B.C., Can., 1980, Cabo Frio Internat. Print Biennial, Brazil, 1982; represented in permanent collections: City of Vancouver, B.C. Provincial Collection, Manawatu Art Gallery, N.Z., Mildura Arts Centre, Australia, Musee d'Art et d'Histoire, Geneva; commns. include Trademark, OCEPA-Ecuadorian Handcrafts, Quito, 1965, Seattle Opera Assn., 1967, Simon Fraser Univ. Arts Ctr., Burnaby, B.C., 1970, 72; sec.-treas. Internat. Com. on Exhbn. Exchange, 1986—; dir. Galeria de Ocepa, Quito, Ecuador, 1965-66; univ. art curator Simon Fraser U., 1970-85, Simon Fraser Gallery, Burnaby; vis. artist Escuela de Bellas Artes, Univ. Ctr., Ecuador, 1966. Can. Council grantee, 1979. Mem. Western Can. Art Assn. (chmn. 1975-76, 78-80), Can. Mus. Assn., Internat. Council Mus. (internat. com. exhbn. exchange 1980—, sec. 1986-89). Office: Simon Fraser U Ctr for Arts, Simon Fraser Gallery, Burnaby, BC Canada V5A 1S6

FELTNER, WILLIAM CLAYTON, radio station executive; b. Ann Arbor, Mich., Oct. 26, 1958; s. William Roy and Barbara Jo (Hutchinson) F.; m. Maria Rosario Pascual, Feb. 14, 1987; children: William Clayton P., David Joel P. BA in English, U. Nev., Reno, 1981, MA in Journalism, 1988. Teaching asst. Traner Middle Sch., Reno, 1982-83; mktg./pub. rels. staff Sierra Arts Found., Reno, 1983-84; announcer KNIS-Radio, Carson City, Nev., 1983-84, adminstrv. asst., 1984-85, prodn. mgr., 1985-86, news and pub. affairs dir., 1986-90, ops. dir., 1990—. Contbr. articles to profl. jours. Small group leader Carson City Christian Fellowship, 1991-92; mem. adv. bd. Crisis Pregnancy Ctr., Carson City, 1987; counselor Camp Lots-A-Fun for Mentally Retarded, Lake Tahoe, Nev., 1984; vol. Salvation Army Family Emergency Shelter, Reno, 1983; master of ceremonies various pub. events. Mem. Nev. Landmarks Soc. Republican. Home: 808 W Musser Carson City NV 89703 Office: KNIS Radio 6363 Hwy 50 E Carson City NV 89701

FELTON, SAMUEL PAGE, biochemist; b. Petersburg, Va., Sept. 7, 1919; s. Samuel S. and Pearl (Williams) F.; m. Helen Florence Martin, Dec. 31, 1955; 1 child, Samuel Page. Degree in pharmacy, U.S. Army, San Francisco, 1942; BS in Chemistry, U. Wash., 1951, postgrad., 1954. Chief technician U. Wash., Seattle, 1952-59, research assoc., 1959-62, sr. research assoc., 1976—, dir. cen. facilities lab. anesthesiology, 1969-73, dir. water quality lab., 1976-83, dir. biochem. lab. sch. of Fisheries, 1983—; asst. mem., asst. to dir. div. biochemistry Scripps Clinic and Research Found., La Jolla, Calif., 1962-66; asst. biochemist Children's Orthopedic Hosp., Seattle, 1966-68; vis. scientist Va. Inst. Marine Scis. at Coll. William and Mary, Williamsburg, 1985. Mem. bd. of adjustments City of Edmonds, Wash. Served to sgt. MC, U.S. Army 1941-45. Fellow Am. Inst. Chemists; mem. Am. Chem. Soc., Am. Inst. Fishery Research Biologists, N.Y. Acad. of Scis., Soc. Exptl. Biology and Medicine. Office: U Wash Fisheries Rsch & Teaching HF-15 Seattle WA 98195

FENG, JOSEPH SHAO-YING, physicist, electrical engineer; b. Peiping, China, June 21, 1948; came to U.S., 1950; s. Paul Yen Hsiung and Mary (Pai) F. BS in Physics, Calif. Inst. Tech., Pasadena, 1969; MS in Physics, Northwestern U., 1970, MEE, 1971; PhD in Elec. Engring., Calif. Inst. Tech., 1975. Mem. rsch. staff T. J. Watson Rsch. Lab. IBM, Yorktown Heights, N.Y., 1974-77; scientist, engr. IBM Gen. Products Div., San Jose, Calif., 1977—. Inventor in field; contbr. articles to profl. jours. Incorporation chmn. Banner Run, San Jose, 1989. Mem. ASCIT (treas. Pasadena, Calif. chpt. 1968-69), IEEE, Am. Phys. Soc., Mediaeval Acad. of Am., Greenburgh (N.Y.) Karate Club (treas. 1977), Chi Ski (officer 1980-84), Nisei Ski (officer 1986-88).

FENNELL, DIANE MARIE, marketing executive, process engineer; b. Panama, Iowa, Dec. 11, 1944; d. Urban William and Marcella Mae (Leytham) Schechinger; m. Leonard E. Fennell, Aug. 19, 1967; children: David, Denise, Mark. BS, Creighton U., Omaha, 1966. Process engr. Tex. Instruments, Richardson, 1974-79; sr. process engr. Signetics Corp., Santa Clara, Calif., 1979-82; demo lab. mgr. Airco Temescal, Berkeley, Calif., 1982-84; field process engr. Applied Materials, Santa Clara, 1984-87; mgr. product mktg. Lam Rsch., Fremont, Calif., 1987-90; dir. sales and mktg. Ion & Plasma Equipment, Fremont, Calif., 1990-91; pres. Fennell Assocs., Inc., Half Moon Bay, Calif., 1991—; founder, coord. chmn. Plasma Etch User's Group, Santa Clara, 1986-88; tchr. computer course Adult Edn., Half Moon Bay, Calif., 1982-83. Founder, bd. dirs. Birth to Three program Mental Retardation Ctr., Denison, Tex., 1974-75; fund raiser local sch. band, Half Moon Bay, 1981-89; community rep. local sch. bd., Half Moon Bay, 1982-83. Mem. Am. Vacuum Soc., Soc. Photo Instrumentation Engrs., Soc. Women Engrs., Material Rsch. Soc. Home: 441 Alameda Ave Half Moon Bay CA 94019-1365

FENNING, LISA HILL, federal judge; b. Chgo., Feb. 22, 1952; d. Ivan Byron and Joan (Hennigar) Hill; m. Alan Mark Fenning, Apr. 3, 1977; 4 children. BA with honors, Wellesley Coll., 1971; JD, Yale U., 1974. Bar: Ill. 1975, Calif. 1979, U.S. Dist. Ct. (no. dist.) Ill., U.S. Dist. Ct. (no., ea., so., cen. dists.) Calif., U.S. Ct. Appeals (6th, 7th, 9th cir. cts.). Law clk. U.S. Ct. Appeals 7th cir., Chgo., 1974-75; assoc. Jenner and Block, Chgo., 1975-77, O'Melveny and Myers, Los Angeles, 1977-85; judge U.S. Bankruptcy Ct. Cen. Dist. Calif., Los Angeles, 1985—; bd. govs. Nat. Conf. Bankruptcy Judges, 1989-92; pres. Nat. Conf. of Women's Bar Assns., N.C., 1987-88, pres.-elect, 1986-87, v.p., 1985-86, bd. dirs; lectr., program coord. in field; bd. govs. Nat. Conf. Bankruptcy Judges Endowment for Edn., 1992—. Mem., bd. advisors: Lawyer Hiring & Training Report, 1985-87; contbr. articles to profl. jours. Durant scholar Wellesley Coll., 1971; named one of Am's. 100 Most Important Women Ladies Home Jour., 1988. Fellow Am. Bar Found.; mem. ABA (mem. commn. on women in the profession 1987-91, Women's Caucus 1987—, Individual Rights and Responsibilities sect. 1984—, Bus. Law sect. 1986—, Bus. Bankruptcy com.), Nat. Assn. Women Judges (Nat. Task Force Gender Bias in the Cts. 1986-87), Nat. Conf. Bankruptcy Judges (chair ABA liaison com.), Calif. State Bar Assn. (chair com. on women in law 1986-87), Women Lawyers' Assn. of Los Angeles (ex officio mem., bd. dirs., chmn, founder com. on status of women lawyers 1984-85, officer nominating com. 1986, founder, mem. Do-it Yourself Mentor Network 1986—), Phi Beta Kappa. Democrat. Office: US Bankruptcy Ct Rm 1682 255 E Temple St Los Angeles CA 90012

FENSKE, DONNA MARIE, public health nurse; b. Sigourney, Iowa, Dec. 20, 1940; d. Cloyd Herman and Erma Margaret (Vogel) Grimes; m. John Edward Fenske, Dec. 30, 1976; children: Kevin, Craig, Dina Rae, Kristen. BSN, Loretto Heights Coll., Denver, 1962; MA, Fielding Inst., Santa Barbara, Calif., 1978; MPH, Loma Linda U., 1985. RN, Alaska, Mont. Pub. health nurse Denver Vis. Nurses Assn., 1963; staff nurse North Valley Hosp., Whitefish, Mont., 1963-74, insvc. edn. dir., 1972-75; staff nurse Anchorage Alaska Native Med. Ctr., 1975; dir. Continuing Edn. Recognition & Approval program Alaska Nurses Assn., Anchorage, 1975-76; educator Alaska Meth. U. and U. Alaska Sch. Nursing, Anchorage, 1976-78; pub. health nurse State of Alaska, Anchorage and Homer, 1979—; preceptor U. Alaska, Anchorage, 1980—; lectr. Cross Cultural Russian Old Believers, Homer & Anchorage, 1988—; cons., advisor Continuing Edn. Recognition & Approval Alaska Nurses Assn., 1980-87. Mem. Gov.'s Coun. Task Force on Telecomm., Alaska, 1977-78, Gov.'s Coun. on Emergency Med. Svcs., Mont., 1974. Mem. ANA, Alaska Pub. Health Assn., Alaska Nurses Assn. (past pres., dist. chairperson), Ninety Nines Women Pilots, Sigma Theta Tau. Nazarene. Home: PO Box 2112 Homer AK 99603 Office: Homer Health Ctr 195 Bunnell St Ste C Homer AK 99603

FENTON, DONALD MASON, retired oil company executive; b. L.A., May 23, 1929; s. Charles Youdan and Dorothy (Mason) F.; m. Margaret M. Keehler, Apr. 24, 1953; children: James Michael, Douglas Charles. BS, U. Calif., L.A., 1952, PhD, 1958. Chemist Rohm and Haas Co., Phila., 1958-61; sr. rsch. chemist Union Oil Co., Brea, Calif., 1962-67, rsch. assoc., 1967-72, sr. rsch. assoc., 1972-82, mgr. planning and devel., 1982-85; mgr. new tech. devel. Unocal, Brea, 1985-92; cons. AMSCO, 1967-73; co-founder, 1st chmn. Petroleum Environ. Rsch. Forum; chmn. bd. dirs. Calif. Engring. Found., 1991-92. With U.S. Army, 1953-55. With U.S. Army, 1953-55. Fellow Am. Inst. of Chemists, Alpha Chi Sigma; mem. Am. Chem. Soc. Home: 2861 E Alden Pl Anaheim CA 92806-4401

FENTON, JEFFREY HARLAN, telecommunication system engineer; b. L.A., Feb. 17, 1959; s. James Nathan and Cathy Sylvia (Goldblatt) F. BA in Econs., U. Calif. San Diego, La Jolla, 1980; MA in Econs., Stanford U., 1981, MS in Ops. Rsch., 1982; MBA in Telecom., Golden Gate U., 1988. Ops. rsch. analyst Lockheed Missiles & Space Co., Sunnyvale, Calif., 1982-87, sr. ops. rsch. analyst, 1987-92, telecom. system engring. specialist, 1992—. Contbr. articles to profl. jours. Mem. Inst. Mgmt. Scis., Inst. Indsl. Engrs. (Peninsula chpt. treas. 1984-85), U. Calif. San Diego No. Calif. Alumni Assn. (treas. 1991—), Stanford Palo Alto Alumni Club (treas. 1984-87, v.p. 1987-88), Stanford Assocs., Phi Beta Kappa.

FENTON, PARTICK H., lawyer; b. Huntington, Utah, Aug. 16, 1917; s. Robert L. and Melita (McAllister) F.; m. Gloria Butler Gardner, May 15, 1948; children: Tess F. Rawlinson, Ann F. Banks, Patrick Robert. BS in Military Sci., U. Utah, 1947, JDB, 1947. Bar: Utah, 1948. Pvt. practice Cedar City, Utah, 1948—; city atty. Cedar City, 1950-61; dist. atty. 5th Judicial Dist., Utah, 1953-60; magistrate U.S. Dist. Ct., Utah, 1980—. Major U.S. Army 1941-46, ETO, 1950-52, Korea. Mem. Rotary, Franklin Lodge (grand master Utah. 1975). Office: US Courthouse PO Box 337 444 S Main St Cedar City UT 84721

FENTON, TERRY LYNN, author, artist, consultant; b. Regina, Sask., Can., July 1, 1940; s. John Albert and Gertrude (Hirons) F.; m. Sheila Ann Cowie, Dec. 1, 1962; 1 son, Mark. B.A. in English Lit., U. Sask., 1962. Social worker Province of Alta., Edmonton, 1962-65; asst. to dir. Mackenzie Gallery, Regina, 1965-71; dir. Edmonton Art Gallery, 1972-87; artistic dir. Leighton Found., Calgary, 1988—. Author: Anthony Caro, 1986; co-author: Modern Painting in Canada, 1978; author books and catalogues on contemporary art; painter landscapes; co-founder Triangle Artists Workshop, NY, 1982. Office: Edmonton Art Gallery, 2 Sir Winston Churchill Sq, Edmonton, AB Canada T5J2C1

FENTON-BEARD, PRISCILLA JANE, check marketing company executive; b. Vancouver, Wash., Dec. 31, 1947; d. James Hodgins and Florence (Sargent) O'Banion; m. Jon Tobin Beard, Apr. 28, 1990. BA in Edn., Wash. State U., 1970. Tchr., adminstr. Federal Way (Wash.) Pub. Schs., 1970-79; spl. events officer Seattle Symphony, 1979-81; devel. officer Pacific NW Ballet, Seattle, 1981-82; exec. dir. Pacific Arts Ctr., Seattle, 1983-85; pres., chief exec. officer Message! Check Corp., Seattle, 1985—; arts and nutrition cons. State of Wash., Seattle, 1978-79. Author: Nutrition through the Arts, 1978. Bd. dirs. Artists Unltd., Seattle, 1986-87, Pacific Arts Ctr., 1989; mem. Better Bus. Bur., Seattle. Recipient Small Bus. of Yr. award Seattle Mayor's Office, 1989, Entrepreneur of the Yr. award Pacific N.W. Mem. Nat. Fedn. Small Bus., Coop. Am., Greenpeace, Nat. Audubon Soc., NOW. Episcopalian. Office: Message! Check Corp PO Box 3206 Seattle WA 98114-3206

FENWICK, GARY LINDEL, hazardous waste specialist; b. Pocatello, Idaho, Aug 17, 1943; s. James Palmer and Florence (Boren) F.; m. Pennie S. Bray, Aug. 6, 1966 (dec.); children: Anjanette M., Matthew E.; m. Jo Elaine Rohr, May 28, 1993; 1 child, Wendy J. Tundo. BS in Chemistry, Idaho State U., 1966; PhD in Phys. Chemistry, U. Idaho, 1969. Rsch. chemist Pennwalt Chems., King of Prussia, Pa., 1969-70; pvt. practice cons. Pocatello, 1971-76; head chemist Agriculture Exptl. Sta. U. Idaho, Aberdeen, 1976-78; engr. Gould AMI, Pocatello, 1978-91; hazardous waste officer Shoshone-Bannock Tribes, Ft. Hall, Idaho, 1992—; cons. in field. NDEA fellow U. Idaho, 1968. Mem. Sigma Xi. Home: 340 Jefferson St American Falls ID 83211-1133 Office: Shoshone-Bannock Tribes PO Box 306 Fort Hall ID 83203

FERBER, ROBERT RUDOLF, physics researcher, educator; b. New Eagle, Pa., June 11, 1935; s. Rudolf F. and Elizabeth J. (Robertson) F.; m. Eileen Merhaut, July 25, 1964; children: Robert Rudolf, Lynne C. BSEE, U. Pitts., 1958; MSEE, Carnegie-Mellon U., 1966, Ph.D. in Semiconductor Physics, 1967. Registered profl. engr., Pa. Mgr. engring. dept. WRS Motion Picture Labs., Pitts., 1954-58, sec., 1959-76, v.p., 1976-79; sr. engr. Westinghouse Rsch. Labs., Pitts., 1956-67; mgr. nuclear effects group Westinghouse Elec. Corp., Pitts., 1967-71, mgr. adv. engr. energy projects, East Pittsburgh, 1971-77; photovoltaic materials and collector rsch. mgr. Jet Propulsion Lab., Pasadena, Calif. 1977-85, SP100 Project contract tech. mgr., 1985-90, asst. project mgr. shuttle imaging radar, 1990—; v.p. Executaire Inc., Pitts., 1960-64; pres. Tele-Cam Inc., Pitts., 1960-78. Editor: Transactions of the 9th World Energy Conf. 1974, Digest of the 9th World Energy Conf., 1974. Contbr. articles to profl. jours. Patentee in field. Mem. Franklin Regional Sch. Dist. Bd., Murrysville, Pa., 1975-77. Fellow Buhl Found., 1965-66, NDEA, 1976-77. Mem. IEEE (sr.), Am. Solar Energy Soc., ASME (chmn. 1986 Solar Energy Div. Conf.). Republican. Lutheran. Home: 5314 Alta Canyada Rd La Canada Flintridge CA 91011-1606 Office: Jet Propulsion Lab 4800 Oak Grove Dr Pasadena CA 91109-8099

FERDON, EDWIN NELSON, JR., ethnologist; b. St. Paul, June 14, 1913; s. Edwin Nelson and Julie Beatha (O'Meyer) F.; m. Constance Potter Etz, Oct. 14, 1939 (dec. Jan., 1969): children: Richard, Derre, Julie; m. Lola Vearl Baker, June 18, 1972. BA, U. N.Mex., Albuquerque, 1937; MA, U. So. Calif., L.A., 1942. Curator br. mus. Mus. of N.Mex., Santa Fe, 1937-38, curator Mid. Am. archaeology, 1938-40; rsch. assoc. Hispanic studies Mus. N.Mex./Sch. Am. Rsch., Santa Fe, 1940-45, rsch. assoc. in charge Hispanice studies, 1945-57; assoc. dir. in charge Mus. Internat. Folk Art Mus. N.Mex., Santa Fe, 1958-60, coord. interpretation div. dept. anthropology, 1960-61; assoc. dir. Ariz. State Mus. U. Ariz., Tucson, 1961-78, ethnologist Ariz. State Mus., 1978-83, ret., 1983. Author: One Man's Log, 1966, Early Tahiti as the Explorers Saw It, 1981, Early Tonga as the Explorers Saw It, 1987, (monograph) Studies in Ecuadorian Geography, 1950. Fellow AAAS; mem. Sigma Xi. Home: 2141 E Juanita St Tucson AZ 85719-3818

FERDUN, GARETH STANLEY, social service executive; b. Modesto, Calif., Nov. 17, 1937; s. Stanley and Jean (Van Buskirk) F.; m. Georgenne Marie Brann, Feb. 19, 1961; children: Severn, Muir, Destin. Student, UCLA, 1958; BA, U. Calif., Berkeley, 1961; MA, San Francisco State U., 1962. Sr. social research analyst Calif. Youth Authority, Sacramento, 1970-76, project dir. PMES, 1976-83, chief program planning and evaluation, 1983-85, chief mgmt. and policy analysis, 1985-90. Contbr. numerous articles to profl. jours.

FERENCE, HELEN MARIE, nursing consultant; b. Ohio, Sept. 1, 1946; d. Emery and Josephine Leona (Terlecki) F.; m. William Verill Nick. Diploma, Youngstown (Ohio) Hosp. Assn., 1967; BS, Youngstown U., 1970; MS, Ohio State U., 1972; PhD, NYU, N.Y.C., 1979. Cert. advanced cardiac life support; cert. nursing sci. Cons., pres. Nursing Cons. and Rsch., Pebble Beach, Calif., 1972—; dir. rsch. and programs Sigma Theta Tau, Indpls., 1986-88; dir. clin. evaluation, rsch. and nursing standards Mt. Sinai Hosp., N.Y.C., 1986-88; asst. prof. Ohio State U., Columbus, 1972-80; cons. Battelle Meml. Inst., Columbus, 1972-81, VA, Chillicothe, Ohio, 1975-80; asst. prof. NYU, 1979-80; cons. McGraw-Hill, Monterey, Calif., 1981-85; bd. dirs. Mt. Sinai Hosp., N.Y., 1986-88. Editor Notes on Nursing Sci., 1986—. Bd. dirs. Monterey Health Inst. Recipient Laureate: Nightingale Prize, 1991. Fellow Nightingale Soc. (bd. dirs.); mem. Sigma Theta Tau. Home: PO Box 862 Pebble Beach CA 93953-0862

FERGUS, GARY SCOTT, lawyer; b. Racine, Wis., Apr. 20, 1954; s. Russell Malcolm and Phyl Rose (Muratore) F.; m. Isabelle Sabina Beekman, Sept. 28, 1985; children: Mary Marckwald Beekman Fergus, Kirkpatrick Russell Beekman Fergus. SB, Stanford U., 1976; JD, U. Wis., 1979; LLM, NYU, 1981. Bar: Wis. 1979, Calif. 1980. Assoc. Brobeck, Phleger & Harrison, San Francisco, 1980-86, ptnr., 1986—; speaker, instr. Harvard Law Sch. Trial Advocacy Program, 1991; occasional lectr. trial advocacy program Stanford Law Sch., Palo Alto, 1990; trial atty. First Major Consolidated Asbestos Trial in U.S., 1990. Author, inventor (software) Nat. Case Mgmt. for Asbestos Litigation. Mem. ABA. Home: 2855 Jackson St # 302 San Francisco CA 94115-1165 Office: Brobeck Phleger & Harrison 1 Market Plz San Francisco CA 94105-1019

FERGUSON, COREY JOSEPH, airline captain; b. Erie, Pa., Sept. 18, 1953; s. Stanley Joseph and Irene Rosabelle (Blewett) F.; m. Barbara Joan Westerbeck, May 18, 1974; children: Paul Joseph, Stephen John, Kathryn Joan. AAS, Ctrl. Tex. Coll., Killeen, 1975; BS, U. Ctrl. Tex., Killeen, 1976. Lic. airline transport pilot. Airline capt. United Airlines, L.A., 1978—. Instrument flight examiner Army Nat. Guard, Salem, Oreg., 1987-92. With U.S. Army, 1972—. Mem. Airline Pilots Assn. (nat. air traffic control com. 1986-88), Army Aviation Assn. Am. (life), U.S. Army Warrant Officer Assn. (life), Res. Officers Assn. (life). Republican. Roman Catholic. Home: 28382 Ronea Mission Viejo CA 92692-2234

FERGUSON, DAVID JAMES, financial planner; b. Denver, Feb. 23, 1947; s. James Robert and Sylvia N. (Minks) F.; m. Janet M. Webb, June 2, 1970 (div. Dec. 1986); 1 child, Benjamin. BA, Union Coll., Lincoln, Nebr., 1970; MDiv, Andrews U., Berrien Springs, Mich., 1972. Ordained to ministry Seventh-day Adventist Ch., 1987; cert. fin. planner. Pastor Seventh-Day Adventist Ch., Boulder and Gunnison, Colo., Sacramento, 1970-86; fin. cons. Shearson Lehman Hutton, Glendale, Calif., 1986-89; fin. planner TriQuest Fin., Glendale, 1989—; dir. health programming Cen. Seventh-day Adventist Ch., Sacramento, 1980-85. Bd. dirs. Religious Coalition for Cable TV, Sacramento, 1983-85, Christian Edit., Glendale, 1987-90; pres. Glendale Regional Arts Coun., 1988-90, exec. dir., 1990-93. Recipient Svc. to Arts award Glendale Regional Arts Coun., 1990. Mem. Inst. Cert. Fin. Planners (cert.), Internat. Bd. Cert. Fin. Planners. Office: TriQuest Fin 411 N Central Ave Ste 500 Glendale CA 91203-2020

FERGUSON, JACKSON ROBERT, JR., astronautical engineer; b. Neptune, N.J., Aug. 18, 1942; s. Jackson Robert and Charlotte Carter (Rudewick) F.; m. Christina Mary Staley, Aug. 24, 1968; children: Jack Christopher, Joy Heather. BS in Engring. Sci., USAF Acad., 1965; MS in Astronautics, Air Force Inst. Tech., Dayton, Ohio, 1971; PhD in Aerospace Engring., U. Tex., 1983. Registered profl. engr., Tex. Astronautical engr. NORAD, Colorado Springs, Colo., 1972-76; asst. prof. USAF Acad., Colorado Springs, Colo., 1976-80, assoc. prof., 1982-84; chief scientist European Office of Aerospace Rsch. & Devel., London, 1984-86; program mgr. Software Engring. Inst. Air Force Systems Command, Boston, 1986-88; detachment comdr. Air Force Systems Command, Colorado Springs, 1988-91; ind. rev. team mem. USAF Data System Modernization Program, Washington, 1988; vis. prof. USAF Acad., 1991-93; head ind. rev. team USAF System 1 Software devel. program, 1992; sr. mem. tech. staff Carnegie-Mellon U. Software Engring. Inst., 1993—. Contbr. to reference book: Handbook of Engineering Fundamentals, 1984. Parish coun. pres. Our Lady of the Pines Cath. Ch., Black Forest, Colo., 1989. Col. USAF, 1965-91. Recipient USAF Rsch. and Devel. award, 1980. Mem. AIAA, Am. Soc. Engring. Edn. Roman Catholic. Office: Dept Astronautics USAF Acad Colorado Springs CO 80840

FERGUSON, JACQUELINE ANN, resource development consultant, seminar leader; b. Niagara Falls, N.Y., Feb. 1, 1950; d. Joseph T. and Ann A. (Kutlina) Holody; m. Gregory P. Ferguson, Sept. 4, 1971; 1 child, Michael. Student, St. Bonaventure U., 1968-69; BA in History, Ariz. State U., 1972; postgrad., U. Ariz., 1973-74. Analyst City of Tucson, 1975; pers. technician Pima C.C., Tucson, 1975-77, grants specialist, 1977-78, coord. of grants, 1978-81, dir. resource devel., 1981-83; grants devel. mgmt. Tucson Unified Sch. Dist., 1984-91; grants devel. specialist U. Ariz., Tucson, 1991—; seminar dir. Capitol Publs., Inc., Alexandria, Va. Author: Grants for Schools, 1989, Grants for Special Education and Rehabilitative Service, 1990, The Education Grantseeker's Guide to Foundation and Corporate Funding, 1991, Grants for Teachers, 1992, Grants Development and Management Kits, 1992; editor: Grantseeker's Guide to Evaluation. Mem. Nat. Coun. for Resource Devel. Home and Office: 7766 N Red Wing Cir Tucson AZ 85741-1335

FERGUSON, JON PETER, lawyer; b. Richmond, Calif., Oct. 20, 1944; s. James Lavern and Phoebe Elizabeth (Van Dam) F.; children: Peter, Patrick, Aleksander. Cert., Syracuse U., 1963; AA, Green River Coll., Auburn, Wash., 1968; BA, U. Wash., 1970, JD, 1974. Bar: Wash. 1974. Ptnr. firm Ferguson & Skeels, Sumner, Wash., 1974-76; asst. atty. gen., sr. counsel Consumer Protection, Antitrust and Torts div. State of Wash., Seattle, 1976—; instr. Wash. State Patrol Acad., Shelton, Wash., 1984—, Edmonds (Wash.) Community Coll., 1981-83; instr. various legal orgns., Seattle, Spokane and Tacoma, 1977—. Contbr. articles to profl. jours. Scoutmaster, Boy Scouts Am., Auburn and Seattle, 1983-91, explorer advisor, Tacoma and Seattle, 1975-85; chmn. Am. Revolution Bicentennial Com., Sumner, 1976; bd. dirs. Consumer Credit Counseling Svc., Tacoma, 1975-77. Sgt. USAF, 1962-66, Europe. Mem. Wash. State Bar Assn. Home: PO Box 4717 Rollingbay WA 98061 Office: Office of Atty Gen 900 4th Ave Seattle WA 98164

FERGUSON, KEITH MCDOWELL, electrical engineer; b. Corpus Christi, Tex., Oct. 6, 1940; s. Elmer LeRoy and Carol Rushmore F.; m. Margaret Emma-Grace Shank, June 27, 1982. SB, MIT, 1962, SM, 1964, Degree of EE, 1965. Mem. tech. staff Hewlett-Packard Co., Santa Clara, Calif., 1965—; Patentee in field; contbr. articles to profl. jours. Mem. IEEE, Callerlab Internat. Assn. Square Dance Callers, Santa Clara Valley Callers Assn., Tau Beta Pi, Eta Kappa Nu, Sigma Xi (assoc.). Republican. Methodist. Office: Hewlett Packard Co 5301 Stevens Creek Blvd Santa Clara CA 95052

FERGUSON, LARRY EMMETT, educational administrator; b. Coolridge, W.Va., Oct. 19, 1934; s. Clarence Emmett and Marjorie Evelyn (Ransom) F.; m. Lynne Alice Jackson, May 17, 1957 (div. May 1975); children: David (dec.), Karen J. Ramsey; m. Alma Jeanette (Jeanne) Mitchell, Oct. 24, 1975; stepchildren: Dona Williamson, Patti Rae, Terri Musa-Jones, Ron Musa. AAS, Clark Coll., Vancouver, Wash., 1977; BS in Psychology and Elem. Edn., Portland State U., 1979, postgrad., 1979-91. Cert. continuing tchr., Wash. Customer engr. RCA Svc. Co., Portland, Oreg., 1975-77; tchr. Ft. Simcoe Job Corps, White Swan, Wash., 1982-89; mgr. Life Skills Tng. Inst., Vancouver, Wash., 1990—. Bd. dirs. Slocum Theatre Group, Vancouver, Wash., 1982; loaned exec. Consolidated Fed. Campaign, Yakima, Wash., 1988. Master sgt. USAF, 1954-75. Mem. Internat. Order Foresters, Non-Commd. Officers Assn., Am. Legion. Mem. Disciples of Christ. Office: Life Skills Tng Inst 1920 Broadway Vancouver WA 98663

FERGUSON, LESLIE LEE, JR., apiculturist; b. Pomona, Calif., Sept. 12, 1940; s. Leslie Lee Sr. and Wanda Viola (Wells) F.; m. Bonnie B. Bortel, Aug. 20, 1969;1 child, Heather; step-children: Bonnie, Betsey, Peter. BA, Loma Linda U., 1965, MA, 1973. Secondary tchr. Highland View Acad., Hagerstown, Md., 1967-71, Pioneer Valley Acad., New Braintree, Mass., 1971-79; v.p., mgr. Huston-Ferguson Apiaries, Moreno Valley, Calif., 1979—. Editor: (quar. jour.) Calif. Bee Times. Sgt. U.S. Army, 1965-67. Mem. Calif. State Beekeepers Assn. (pres. 1986), Nat. Assn. Tchrs. of Singing, Am. Beekeeping Fedn. Republican. Seventh-day Adventist. Office: Huston-Ferguson Apiaries 27913 Cottonwood Ave Moreno Valley CA 92555-5619

FERGUSON, LLOYD ELBERT, manufacturing engineer; b. Denver, Mar. 5, 1942; s. Lloyd Elbert Ferguson and Ellen Jane (Schneider) Romero; m. Patricia Valine Hughes, May 25, 1963; children: Theresa Renee, Edwin Bateman. BS in Engring., Nova Internat. Coll., 1983. Cert. hypnotherapist, geometric tolerance instr. Crew leader FTS Corp., Denver, 1968-72; program engr. Sundstrand Corp., Denver, 1972-87, sr. assoc. project engr., 1987-90, sr. liaison engr., 1990—; v.p. Valine Corp. Team captain March of Dimes Team Walk, Denver, 1987; mem. AT&T Telephone Pioneer Clowns for Charity. Recipient recognition award AT&T Telephone Pioneers, 1990. Mem. Soc. Mfg. Engrs. (chmn. local chpt. 1988, zone chmn. 1989, achievement award 1984, 86, recognition award 1986, 90, appreciation award 1988), Nat. Mgmt. Assn. (cert., program instr. 1982—, honor award 1987, 90), Am. Indian Sci. and Engring. Soc., Colo. Clowns. Republican. Religious Science. Home: 10983 W 76th Dr Arvada CO 80005-3481 Office: Sundstrand Corp 2480 W 70th Ave Denver CO 80221-2500

FERGUSON, MICHAEL ROGER, newspaper executive; b. Dayton, Ohio, Oct. 15, 1951; s. Earl Roger and Betty Louise (Spahr) F.; m. Kathryn Louise Davis, July 22, 1972; children—Kellie, Stacie, Jacob. A.A., Mt. San Antonio Coll., 1971; B.A. with honors, Calif. State Poly. U., 1973. With Progress Bull. newspaper, Pomona, Calif., 1968-82, bus. mgr. 1973-80, sales mgr., 1980-82; bus. Daily Report newspaper, Ontario, Calif., 1973-78; advt. dir. Vallejo Times-Herald (Calif.), 1982-83; gen. mgr. Woodland Daily Democrat, 1983—. Mem. Calif. Newspapers Pubs. Assn., Woodland C. of C. (dir.). Republican. Methodist. Lodge: Rotary. Home: 1080 Deborah St Upland CA 91786-1206 Office: Inland Valley Daily Bulletin PO Box 4000 2041 E Fourth St Ontario CA 91761

FERGUSON, RANDY KARR, government executive; b. Barksdale AFB, La., Oct. 28, 1951; s. Bruce Russell Karr and Norma Jean (Sanford) F.; m. Marian Louise Hale; 1 child, Heather Louise. BA, Calif. State U., Sacramento, 1975, MA, 1979. Cons. Commn. Econ. Devel., Sacramento, 1974; economist State of Calif., Sacramento, 1974-79; with CIA, Washington, 1979-84; internat. economist Internat. Energy Agy., Paris, 1984-86; govt. exec. State of Calif., Sacramento, 1986—; dir. Northridge Park County Water Dist., Sacramento, 1975-79. Contbr. articles to profl. jours. Bd. dirs., pres. Homeowners Assn., Sterling, Va., 1982-84. Maj. U.S. Army, 1971-74, 91, Desert Storm. Mem. Nat. Assn. Bus. Execs. Republican.

FERGUSON, ROBERT DURRELL, hospital administrator; b. Grand Junction, Colo., Feb. 8, 1934; s. Hollis Durrell and Bernadine (Graves) F. Student, Dominican Ho. of Studies, 1952-69; cert., Xavier Coll. Bus. mgr. St. Pius Priory, Chgo., 1959-69; pub. rels./devel. rep. Vatican, Rome, 1969-74; dir. environ. svcs. St. Mary's Hosp., Grand Junction, Colo., 1975—; chmn. hazardous waste com. St. Mary's Hosp., fire, safety com., infection control com., space com.; cons. environ. svcs. 4 hosps. Mem. Ptnrs., Grand Junction, 1980—; bd. dirs. Rose Hill Fed. Credit Union. Recipient Cert. Appreciation Optimist Internat. Club, 1987, Mesa County Ptnrs., 1985. Mem. Nat. Exec. Housekeeping Assn., Am. Soc. for Healthcare Environ. Svcs., Orgn. of Healthcare Hazard Com. Compliance (cert. 1989). Republican. Roman Catholic. Home: 2496 S Broadway Grand Junction CO 81503

FERGUSON, THOMAS JEFFREY, internist; b. Red Bluff, Calif., Mar. 25, 1955; s. John Thomas and Florence Lovelle (Lassus) F.; m. Sara Kenfield, Aug. 25, 1979; children: James Norman, William John, Amanda Jane. BA in Zoology, Humboldt State U., 1977; MS in Pub. Health, UCLA, 1979, PhD, 1983; MD, U. Calif., Davis, 1987. Diplomate Am. Bd. Internal Medicine, Am. Bd. Preventive Medicine. Postgrad. researcher Jacobs Engring. Co., Pasadena, Calif., 1980-83; intern, resident U. Calif., Davis, 1987-90, resident in occupational medicine, 1990-91, fellow in med. toxicology, 1990-92, assoc. physician in internal medicine, 1991—, asst. clin. prof. occupational and environ. medicine, 1992—; cons. physician poison control ctr. U. Calif., Davis, 1991—. Advisor Calif. Profl. Firefighter Assn., Sacramento, 1991—. Mem. AMA, APHA, ACP, Am. Coll. Occupational/Environ. Medicine, Calif. Med. Assn., Yolo County Med. Soc., Alpha Omega Alpha, Delta Omega, Sigma Xi. Office: Faculty Physicians Group 2055 Anderson Rd Davis CA 95616

FERGUSON, WARREN JOHN, federal judge; b. Eureka, Nev., Oct. 31, 1920; s. Ralph and Marian (Damele) F.; m. E. Laura Keyes, June 5, 1948; children: Faye F., Warren John, Teresa M., Peter J. B.A., U. Nev., 1942; LL.B., U. So. Calif., 1949; LL.D. (hon.), Western State U., San Fernando Valley Coll. Law. Bar: Calif. 1950. Mem. firm Ferguson & Judge, Fullerton, Calif., 1950-59; city atty. for cities of Buena Park, Placentia, La Puente, Baldwin Park, Santa Fe Springs, Walnut and Rosemead, Calif., 1953-59; mcpl. ct. judge Anaheim, Calif., 1959-60; judge Superior Ct., Santa Ana, Calif., 1961-66, Juvenile Ct., 1963-64, Appellate Dept., 1965-66; U.S. dist. judge Los Angeles, 1966-79; judge U.S. Circuit Ct. (9th cir.), Los Angeles, 1979-86; sr. judge U.S. Circuit Ct. (9th cir.), Santa Ana, 1986—; faculty Fed. Jud. Ctr., Practising Law Inst., U. Iowa Coll. Law, N.Y. Law Jour.; assoc. prof. psychiatry (law) Sch. Medicine, U. So. Calif.; assoc. prof. Loyola Law Sch. Served with AUS, 1942-46. Decorated Bronze Star. Mem. Phi Kappa Phi, Theta Chi. Democrat. Roman Catholic. Office: US Ct Appeals 9th Cir 500 Fed Bldg 34 Civic Center Pla Santa Ana CA 92701

FERGUSSON, ROBERT GEORGE, retired army officer; b. Chgo., May 20, 1911; s. Archibald Campbell and Anne (Sheehan) F.; m. Charlotte Lawrence, Nov. 18, 1937; 1 son, Robert Lawrence (dec.). Student, Beloit Coll., 1929-32; B.S., U.S. Mil. Acad., 1936; M.A. in Internat. Relations, Boston U., 1959. Commd. 2d lt. U.S. Army, 1936, advanced through grades to maj. gen., 1962; comdg. officer 14th Inf. Regt., Hawaii, 1955-57; chief army adv. group Naval War Coll., Newport, R.I., 1957-61; asst. div. comdr. 24th Inf. Div., Augsburg, Ger., 1961-62; chief staff Hdqrs. Central Army Group (NATO), Heidelberg, Ger., 1962-65; comdg. gen. U.S. Army Tng. Center, Inf., Ft. Ord, 1965-67; comdr. U.S. Forces, Berlin, 1967-70; ret., 1970; corp. group v.p. manpower planning Dart Industries, Inc., Los Angeles, 1970-78; cons., 1978-82, ret., 1982. Decorated D.S.M., Legion of Merit with oak leaf cluster, Bronze Star with 3 oak leaf clusters, Purple Heart (U.S.); knight comdr. Cross with badge and star Order of Merit (W.Ger.); officer Legion of Honor (France). Mem. Clan Fergusson Soc. (Scotland), Beta Theta Pi. Clubs: Cypress Point (Pebble Beach); Old Capitol (Monterey, Calif.). Home: PO Box 1515 Pebble Beach CA 93953-1515

FERNANDES SALLING, LEHUA, lawyer, state senator; b. Lihue, Hawaii, Dec. 6, 1949; d. William Ernest Fernandes and Evelyn (Ohai) Fernandes; m. Michael Ray Salling, Aug. 14, 1971; 1 child. BS, Colo. State U., 1971; JD, Cleveland Marshall Coll., 1975. Law. Ptnr. Fernandes Salling & Salling, Kapaa Kauai, Hawaii, 1976—; mem. Hawaii Senate, 1982—. Mem. Hawaii State Bar Assn., Maile Bus. and Profl. Women's Club, Kamokila Canoe Club, Zonta. Office: Leipapa A Kamehameha Bldg 235 S Beretania St Honolulu HI 96813

FERNANDEZ, FERDINAND FRANCIS, judge; b. 1937. BS, U. So. Calif., 1958, JD, 1963; LLM, Harvard U., 1963. Bar: Calif. 1963, U.S. Dist. Ct. (cen. dist.) Calif. 1963, U.S. Ct. Appeals (9th cir.) 1963, U.S. Supreme Ct. 1967. Elec. engr. Hughes Aircraft Co., Culver City, Calif., 1958-62; law clk. to dist. judge U.S. Dist. Ct. (cen. dist.) Calif., 1963-64; pvt. practice law Allard, Shelton & O'Connor, Pomona, Calif., 1964-80; judge Calif. Superior Ct. San Bernardino County, Calif., 1980-85, U.S. Dist. Ct. (cen. dist.) Calif., L.A., 1985-89, U.S. Ct. Appeals (9th cir.), L.A., 1989—. Contbr. articles to profl. jours. Vice chmn. City of La Verne Commn. on Environ. Quality, 1971-73; chmn. City of Claremont Environ. Quality Bd., 1972-73; bd. trustees Pomona Coll., 1990—. Fellow Am. Coll. Trust and Estate Counsel; mem. ABA, State Bar of Calif. (fed. cts. com. 1966-69, ad hoc com. on attachments 1971-85, chmn. com. on adminstrn. of justice 1976-77, exec. com. taxation sect. 1977-80, spl. com. on mandatory fee arbitration 1978-79), Calif. Judges Assn. (chmn. juvenile cts. com. 1983-84, faculty mem. Calif. Jud. Coll. 1982-83, faculty mem. jurisprudence and humanities course 1983-85), Hispanic Nat. Bar Assn., L.A. County Bar Assn. (bull. com. 1974-75), San Bernardino County Bar Assn., Pomona Valley Bar Assn. (co-editor Newsletter 1970-72, trustee 1971-78, sec.-treas. 1973-74, 2d v.p. 1974-75, 1st v.p. 1975-76, pres. 1976-77), Estate Planning Coun. Pomona Valley (sec. 1966-76), Order of Coif, Phi Kappa Phi, Tau Beta Pi. Office: US Ct Appeals 9th Cir 125 S Grand Ave Ste 302 Pasadena CA 91105-1652

FERNGREN, GARY BURT, history educator; b. Bellingham, Wash., Apr. 14, 1942; s. Al B. and Wilma E. (Edberg) F.; m. Agnes Loewen, Mar. 26, 1970; children: Suzanne, Anne-Marie, Heather. BA, Western Wash. Coll., 1964; MA, U. B.C., 1967, PhD, 1973. Asst. prof. history Oreg. State U., Corvallis, 1970-78; assoc. prof. history Oreg. State U., 1978-84, prof. history, 1984—. Contbr. articles to profl. jours., chpts. to books. NEH fellow, 1990, Coll. Physicians of Phila. fellow, 1981, Oreg. Com. for Humanities fellow, 1985, 89. Mem. Internat. Soc. of the History of Medicine, Am. Assn. for the History of Medicine, History of Sci. Soc. Republican. Baptist. Home: 2040 NW 23rd St Corvallis OR 97330-1202 Office: Oreg State U Corvallis OR 97331

FERNS, PAT AGNES (PAT YELENOSKY), sales manager; b. Glasgow, Scotland, Mar. 15, 1941; came to U.S., 1958; d. Edward Aloysius Ferns and Margaret Gallagher Hammerton; m. Robert John Yelenosky, Aug. 3, 1963; children: John, Patricia. BS in Chemistry, UCLA, 1964. Rsch. chemist VA Hosp., L.A., 1964-68, Naval Hosp., San Diego, 1968-74; supervisory chemist Scripps-Miles, Inc., La Jolla, Calif., 1979-81, Naval Health Rsch. Ctr., San Diego, 1981-83; biochemical sales specialist Boehringer Mannheim, San Diego, 1983-85, regional mgr., 1985-92, area mgr., 1992—. Mem. steering com. Globeguilders, 1975—, Bahia Guild Cerebral Palsy, 1978-82, Nat. Charity League, 1984—. Roman Catholic. Home: 5365 Pacifica Dr San Diego CA 92109

FERRAGALLO, ROGER JOHN, television art educator; b. Mill Valley, Calif., Dec. 26, 1923; s. Cassiano Ferragallo and Angela (Bellora) Bacci; m. Roshan Nadimi, Aug. 15, 1965 (div. 1986); children: Lygeia, Roia; m. Anna Henny, June 1, 1991. BA in Edn., Art Inst. Chgo., 1950, MA in Edn., 1953. Indsl. designer Chgo., 1953-56; design dir. Roger Ferragallo & Assocs. Inc., San Francisco, 1957-61; art/film prof. Laney Coll., Oakland, Calif., 1961-72; TV prof. Laney Coll., Oakland, 1973-80; dir. of telecomm. Peralta Colls., Oakland, 1981—; gen. mgr. Sta. PCTV Network, Oakland, 1981—; founder, pres. UNESCO Ctr. for Film and Video for Children, Oakland, 1966; telecomm. cons. Wyman Group, Ltd., Sacramento, 1988—; producer Sta. KCSM-TV, San Mateo, Calif., 1990—; computer graphics artist Vision Arts, Walnut Creek, Calif., 1989—. Editor (nat. quar.) Teletrends, 1983; producer (video telecourse) Volcanoes, 1990. Mem. Found. Community Svc. Cable TV, San Francisco, 1985, Bay Cablevision Programming Network, Richmond, 1989, No. Calif. Pub. Access Edn. and Govt. Com., Richmond, 1990, Sta. KTOP-TV Policy Adv. Com., Oakland, 1991. Sgt. maj. USAF, 1942-45. Grantee Peralta Colls. Dist., 1978, Fund for Instl. Improvement, 1980. Mem. Calif. Cable TV Assn., Internat. Stereoscopic Assn., Stereoscopic Soc. Am., Oakland Mus. Assn., No. Calif. Telecomm. Consortium, San Francisco Exploratorium. Home and Office: 5743 San Pablo Dam Rd El Sobrante CA 94803

FERRARI, DOMENICO, computer science educator; b. Gragnano, Piacenza, Italy, Aug. 31, 1940; came to U.S., 1970; s. Giacomo and Erina (Fracchioni) F.; m. Alessandra Ferrari Cella-Malugani, Apr. 16, 1966; children: Giuliarachele, Ludovica. Dr. Ing., Politecnico di Milano, Italy, 1963. Asst. Milano Politecnico di Milano, 1964-67, asst. prof. computer sci., 1967-70, prof., 1976-77; asst. prof. U. Calif., Berkeley, 1970-75, assoc. prof., 1975-79, prof. dept. elec. engring. and computer sci., 1979—, dep. vice chmn. dept. elec. engring. and computer sci., 1977-79, chmn. computer sci., 1983-87; dep. dir. Internat. Computer Sci. Inst., 1988-90; cons. in field. Author: Computer Systems Performance Evaluation, 19787; (with Serazzi and Zeigner) Measurement and Tuning of Computer Systems, 1983; editor: Performance of Computer Installations, 1978, Experimental Computer Performance Evaluation, 1981, Theory and Practice of Software Technology, 1983, Performance Evaluation, 1979-90, Jour. Multimedia Systems, 1993—; contbr. articles to profl. jours. Recipient Libera Docenza, Italian Govt., 1969; O. Bonazzi award Associaz Elettrotecnica Italiana, 1970. Grantee NSF, 1974—, Univ. Calif., 1982—, Def. Advanced Research Projects Agy., 1983—; Commander Order of Merit of the Republic of Italy, 1992. Fellow IEEE (editor Transactions on Software Engring. 1984-87, Trans Parallel and Distributed Systems, 1989-90); mem. Computer Measurement Group (A.A. Michelson award 1987), Assn. Computing Machinery, Univ. Calif. Faculty Club, Kosmos Club (Berkeley). Office: U Calif Computer Sci Div Dept EECS Berkeley CA 94720

FERRARI, DONNA MAE, autobody and mechanical shop owner; b. Grants Pass, Oreg., Oct. 21, 1931; d. Clyde Willis and Lorene Margaret (Hart) Brewer; m. William Dominic Ferrari, June 2, 1956 (div. May 1977), m. Nov. 24, 1977 (div. June 1987); children: Julie Ann Calleja, Jennifer Lynn Tuomi. Student, Humboldt State Coll., 1949-50. Optician Dr. Ferdinand Shaw, San Francisco, 1951-57; co-owner Superb Auto Reconstrn., San Francisco, 1966-77; optician Dr. Donald Schulz, San Francisco, 1977-84; owner Superb Auto Reconstrn., San Francisco, 1987—. Mem. Calif. Autobody Assn., Clement St. West Merchants, Better Bus. Bur. Presbyterian. Office: Superb Auto Reconstrn Co 2535 Clement St San Francisco CA 94121-1817

FERRARI, MARIANNE, publisher; b. Buffalo, Mar. 16, 1946; d. Alfred Julius and Catherine Nureen (Higgens) F. BJ, Northwestern U., 1968. Mem. editorial staff Paper, Film & Foil Converter, Park Ridge, Ill., 1968; taxi driver Northshore Cab, Chgo., 1968; tchr. English The English Sch., Rome, 1970-72; racetrack groom Playfair Raceway, Spokane, Wash., 1973; greenhouse worker Paradise Valley Growers, Phoenix, Ariz., 1974; with publ. and advt. sales Who Do You Know, Phoenix, 1975-78; publisher Ferrari Publs., Phoenix, 1978—, pres., 1985—. Editor: (guides) Ferrari's Places of Interest, 1980—, Ferrari's Places for Women, 1981—, Ferrari's Places for Men, 1985—, Inn Places, 1991—. Mem. Ariz. Book Publs. Assn., Gay and Lesbian Press Assn., Internat. Gay Travel Assn., Australian Gay and Lesbian Travel Assn. Office: Ferrari Publs Inc PO Box 37887 Phoenix AZ 85069

FERRARIO, JOSEPH A., bishop; Educator St. Charles Coll., Catonsville, Md., St. Mary's Sem., Baltimore, Catholic U., Washington, D.C., U. of Scranton, Pa. Ordained Roman Catholic priest, 1951; ord. aux. bishop of Honolulu, titular bishop of Cuse, 1978, bishop of Honolulu, 1982-. Office: Diocese of Honolulu 1184 Bishop St Honolulu HI 96813-2836

FERRARO, ARTHUR KEVIN, broadcasting executive; b. Bronx, Sept. 25, 1934; s. Gaspero and Mary (Unk) F.; m. Jodi J.L. Ferraro, Sept. 1, 1968; children: Guy, Ross, Dena. Student, St. Francis U. Mgr. west coast UPI-Audio div., Los Angeles; news dir. KHJ Radio, Los Angeles; investigative reporter KMPG Radio, Los Angeles; ptnr., mgr. KRRI-FM Radio, Boulder City, Nev., 1982—. Mem. Nev. Broadcasters Assn. (v.p. Las Vegas 1988—), RTV News Assn. (recipient various awards), Calif. State Exposition (Best Radio Newscast award 1974), Golden Miro Found. (Best Radio Comml. award 1985), Sigma Delta Chi (Best Radio Commentary award 1978). Office: Sta KRRI Box 60097 1658 Nevada Hwy Boulder City NV 89006-0097

FERREIRA, JUDITH ANNE, librarian; b. Whittier, Calif., Mar. 14, 1940; d. Emile Roland and Florence Lucile (Binford) Crumly; m. Larry Ferreira, Oct. 14, 1989. BA, Whittier Coll., 1963; MLS, U. So. Calif., 1964. Libr., L.A. County Libr., 1965-69; city libr. Turlock Libr., Calif., 1969-71; libr. Stanislaus County Free Libr., Modesto, Calif., 1971-82, county libr., 1982—. Mem. ALA, AAUW, Calif. Libr. Assn., Calif. County Librs. Assn. Democrat. Mem. Soc. of Friends. Lodge: Soroptimist. Office: Stanislaus County Free Libr 1500 I St Modesto CA 95354-1166

FERREIRA-WORTH, DEIRDRE CHARLYN, corporate executive; b. Salinas, Calif., June 2, 1958; d. Mervyn Malcolm Ferreira and Eva Charlene (Gustaveson) Pascal; m. Kelly Worth, Oct. 27, 1989. BS in Polit. Sci., Calif. State U., 1985. Svc. mgr. Ralphs Grocery Co., Canoga Park, Calif., 1975-85; account mgr. Lever Bros., Santa Ana, Calif., 1985-88, dist. field sales mgr., 1988-89; v.p. retail sales and mktg. Velling Pasarow Corbett, Inc., Monterey Park, Calif., 1989—. Mem. Women's Profl. Racquetball Assn. (pres. 1992-93, ranked 12th nationally, 100 nat. awards, 2d place U.S. Nat. Championships, Sportsmanship award 1992, Calif. State Champion 304, 25-Plus), Calif. Amateur Racquetball Assn. (ranked 2d, Western U.S. champion). Republican. Reorganized Ch. of Jesus Christ of Latter-day Saints.

FERRELL, DANIEL LEE, federal agency administrator; b. Charleston, W.Va., Aug. 12, 1949; s. James Poteet and Shirley (McIntyre) F.; m. Jennifer Park. BA in Internat. Studies, Miami U., Oxford, Ohio, 1971. Claims rep. Social Security Adminstrn., Hamilton, Ohio, 1971-73, Medford, Oreg., 1973-74; field rep. Social Security Adminstrn., Lewiston, Idaho, 1974-75; ops. supr. Social Security Adminstrn., Seattle, 1975-78; br. mgr. Social Security Adminstrn., Aberdeen, Wash., 1978-80; field ops. specialist Social Security Adminstrn., Seattle, 1980-87, reg. pub. affairs dir., 1987—. Founder, coord. Ch. Vols. for SSI Outreach, Seattle, 1990—; bd. dirs. Baseball Benefit for Seattle's Homeless, 1985, 86; mem. pub. affairs com. Seattle Fed. Exec. Bd. Recipient Cert. of Appreciation, Seattle-King County Emergency Housing Coalition, 1985, Cert. of Recognition, Nat. Vets. Svc., Washington, 1990, Award for Patriots, Social Security Adminstrn., Balt., 1990. Mem. Miami U. Alumni Assn. (chpt. pres. 1977-85). Presbyterian. Office: Social Security Adminstrn 2201 6th Ave Seattle WA 98121-1832

FERRELL, JAMES ELLSWORTH, JR., biochemist; b. Gary, Ind., Nov. 3, 1955; s. James Ellsworth and Sara Jane (Crum) F.; m. Britta Lee Erickson, June 20, 1987; 1 child, Peter John. BA, Williams Coll., 1976; PhD, Stanford U., 1984, MD, 1986. Postdoctoral fellow U. Calif., Berkeley, 1986-90; asst. prof. U. Wis., Madison, 1990-92, Stanford (Calif.) U., 1992—; guitarist and vocalist Rooftop Magic, Palo Alto, Calif., 1979-81, The Druids, Palo Alto, 1981-83; bass guitarist Zsa Zsa House, San Francisco, 1987-90. Records and albums include Strange New Birds, 1980, Rock-A-Roni, 1982, Imagination Time, 1989. Recipient Searle Scholars award, 1991, Leukemia Soc. Am. Spl. fellowship, 1989-92, NRSA Postdoctoral fellowship NIH, 1986-89. Mem. Am. Soc. for Cell Biology, AAAS, Am. Soc. for Microbiology. Democrat. Office: Stanford U Dept Pharmacology Stanford CA 94305-5332

FERRELL, NANCY WARREN, writer; b. Appleton, Wis., Aug. 23, 1932; d. Harry and Carolyn (Scheel) Warren; m. C. Ed Ferrell, Mar. 3, 1955; children: Patricia, William. BA, Lawrence Coll., 1954. Tchr. Bur. Indian Affairs, Mt. Edgecumbe, Alaska, 1958-61; statistician Alaska Dept. Labor, Juneau, 1962-66; psychometrist Alaska Dept. Mental Health, Juneau, 1968-72; libr. technician City and Borough of Juneau, 1980—; writer Juneau, 1975—. Author: The Fishing Industry, 1984, Passports to Peace, 1986, Camouflage: Nature's Defense, 1989, New World of Amateur Radio, 1986, U.S. Coast Guard, 1989, U.S. Air Force, 1990; contbr. stories to childrens mags. Mem. Cancer Soc., Juneau, 1975-85. Mem. Soc. Children's Book Writers (judge Golden Kite award 1992), Nat. League Am. Pen Women (1st pl. Nonfiction Nat. Contest 1986), Alaska Libr. Assn. Home: 512 5th St Juneau AK 99801-1014

FERRIS, EVELYN SCOTT, lawyer; b. Detroit, d. Ross Ansel and Irene Mabel (Bowser) Nafus; m. Roy Shorey Ferris, May 21, 1969 (div. Sept. 1982); children: Judith Ilene, Roy Sidney, Lorene Marjorie. J.D., Willamette U., 1961. Bar: Oreg. 1962, U.S. Dist. Ct. Oreg. 1962. Law clk. Oreg. Tax Ct., Salem, 1961-62; dep. dist. atty. Marion County, Salem, 1962-65; judge Mcpl. Ct., Stayton, Oreg., 1965-76; ptnr. Brand, Lee, Ferris & Embick, Salem, 1965-82; chmn. Oreg. Workers' Compensation Bd., Salem, 1982-89. Bd. dirs. Friends of Deepwood, Salem, 1979-82, Salem City Club, 1972-75, Marion County Civil Svc. Commn., 1970-75; com. mem. Polk County Hist. Commn., Dallas, Oreg., 1976-79; mem. Oreg. legis. com. Bus. Climate, 1967-69, Govs. Task Force on Liability, 1986. Recipient Outstanding Hist. Restoration of Comml. Property award Marion County Hist. Soc., 1982. Mem. Oreg. Mcpl. Judges Assn. (pres. 1967-69), Altrusa, Internat., Mary Leonard Law Soc., Western Assn. Workers Compensation Bds. (pres. 1987-89), Capitol Club (pres. 1977-79), Internat. Assn. Indsl. Accident Bds. and Commns. (pres. 1992-93), Phi Delta Delta. Republican. Episcopalian. Home: 747 Church St SE Salem OR 97301-3715 Office: Dept of Ins & Fin Labor & Industries Bldg Salem OR 97310

FERRIS, RONALD CURRY, bishop; b. Toronto, Ont., Can., July 2, 1945; s. Harold Bland and Marjorie May (Curry) F.; m. Janet Agnes Waller, Aug. 14, 1965; children: Elisa, Jill, Matthew, Jenny, Rani, Jonathan. Grad., Toronto Tchrs. Coll., 1965; B.A., U. Western Ont., London, 1970; M.Div., Huron Coll., London, 1973, D.D. hon., 1982. Ordained to ministry Anglican Ch., 1970. Tchr. Pape Ave. Sch., Toronto, 1965-66; prin. Carcross Elem. Sch., Y.T., 1966-68; incumbent St. Luke's Ch., Old Crow, Y.T., 1970-72; rector St. Stephen's Ch., London, Ont., 1973-81; bishop Diocese of Yukon, Whitehorse, 1981—. Author: (poems) A Wing and a Prayer, 1990. Home: 194 Rainbow Rd, Whitehorse, YK Canada Y1A 5E2 Office: Diocese of Yukon, PO Box 4247, Whitehorse, YK Canada Y1A 3T3

FERRIS, RUSSELL JAMES, II, freelance ghostwriter; b. Rochester, N.Y., June 11, 1938; s. Russell James and Phyllis Helen (Breheny) F.; m. Ilma Maria dos Santos, June 29, 1968. Student, St. Bonaventure U., 1956-59; BS, U. Rochester, 1967; MS, Emerson Coll., 1989; PhD, Universal Life Ch., 1983. Cert. social worker. Film inspector City of Rochester, 1962-67; social worker Tulare County, Visalia, Calif., 1967-69, Alameda County, Oakland, Calif., 1969-71; ghostwriter self-employed, San Francisco, 1971—. Author: Crescendo, 1972 and 9 other novels. With USAR, 1956-58. Recipient Botany fellowship Emerson Coll., 1989. Mem. Assn. of U.S. Army, Air Force Assn., Navy League U.S., Ret. Officers Assn. (life), Res. Officers Assn. (life), Am. Mensa Inc. Libertarian. Roman Catholic. Home and Office: 202 Font Blvd San Francisco CA 94132-2404

FERRY, RICHARD MICHAEL, executive search firm executive; b. Ravenna, Ohio, Sept. 26, 1937; s. John D. and Margaret M. (Jeney) F.; m. Maude M. Hillman, Apr. 14, 1956; children: Richard A., Margaret L., Charles Michael, David W., Dianne E., Ann Marie. B.S., Kent State U., 1959. C.P.A. Cons. staff Peat, Marwick, Mitchell, Los Angeles, 1965-69, ptnr., 1969; pres., co-founder Korn/Ferry Internat., Los Angeles, 1969—; bd. dirs. 1st Bus. Bank, L.A., Avery Dennison, Pasadena, Calif., Dole Food Co., Calif., Pacific Mut. Life Ins. Co., Newport Beach, Calif. Trustee Calif. Inst. Tech., L.A.; bd. dirs. Cath. Charities, L.A.; bd. overseers The Music Ctr., L.A. Republican. Roman Catholic. Clubs: Los Angeles Country, Valley Hunt, Vintage, California, Regency (bd. dirs. 1980—) (Los Angeles). Lodge: Knights of Malta. Office: Korn/Ferry Internat 1800 Century Park E Ste 900 Los Angeles CA 90067-1593

FERTIG, TED BRIAN O'DAY, producer, public relations and association executive; b. Miami, May 18, 1937; s. Peter John and Frances Marie (Aswell) F.; A.B., 1960; M.B.A., 1969. Mem. profl. staff Congress U.S., Washington, 1965; dir. mem. relations Nat. Bellas Hess, Inc., Kansas City, 1963-69; mgr. employment/manpower planning Capitol Industries, Inc., 1969-70; pres. Mgmt. Cons. Group, Hollywood, Calif., 1970—, Fertig, Toler & Dumond, Hollywood, 1973; sr. partner Nascency Prodns., Hollywood and Sacramento, 1971—; exec. dir. Soc. Calif. Accts., 1974-83, Ednl. Found., Inc., 1975-80. Pres., Hollywood Community Concert Assn., 1971-72; exec. dir. Hollywood Walk of Fame, 1971-74; sec.-treas. Save the Sign, 1972-73; producer, Santa Claus Lane Parade of Stars, Hollywood, 1971-73; dir. Old Eagle Theatre, Sacramento, Sacramento Film Festival. Trustee, finance chmn. Los Angeles Free Clinics, 1970-71; mem. Calif. Commn. on Personal Privacy. Served with AUS, 1960-62. Cert. assn. exec. Mem. Pub. Relations Soc. Am., Am. C. of C. Execs., Am. Soc. Assn. Execs., Sacramento Soc. Assn. Execs. (pres. 1980). Author: A Family Night to Remember, 1971; Los Ninos Cantores de Mendoza, 1972; (with Paul Yoder) Salute to Milwaukee, 1965. Office: 715 Regatta Dr Sacramento CA 95833-1715

FERY, JOHN BRUCE, forest products company executive; b. Bellingham, Wash., Feb. 16, 1930; s. Carl Salvatore and Margaret Emily (Hauck) F.; m. Delores Lorraine Carlo, Aug. 22, 1953; children: John Brent, Bruce Todd, Michael Nicholas. BA, U. Wash., 1953; MBA, Stanford U., 1955; D of Law (hon.), Gonzaga U., 1982; D of Nat. Resources (hon.), U. Idaho, 1983. Asst. to pres. Western Kraft Corp., 1955-56; prodn. mgr., 1956-57; with Boise Cascade Corp., Idaho, 1957—, pres., chief exec. officer, 1972-78, chmn. bd., chief exec. officer, 1978—; bd. dirs. Albertsons, Inc., Hewlett-Packard Co., West One Bancorp, The Boeing Co.; active mem. Bus. Coun.; mem. exec. com., bd. dirs. Am. Forest and Paper Inst. Chmn. bd. Idaho Community Found.; mem. exec. com., bd. govs. Nat. Coun. Air and Stream Improvement. With USN, 1950-51. Named Most Outstanding Chief Exec. Officer Fin. World, 1977, 78, 79, 80. Mem. NCASI (exec. com., bd. govs.), Arid Club, Hillcrest Country Club, Arlington Club, Links. Office: Boise Cascade Corp PO Box 50 1 Jefferson Sq Boise ID 83728-0202

FERZIGER, JOEL HENRY, mechanical engineering educator, mathematician; b. Bklyn., Mar. 24, 1937; s. Moe L. and Bessie (Steinberg) F.; divorced; children: Ruth, Shoshanna Ferziger Cohen. B in Chem. Engring., Cooper Union, 1957; MS in Nuclear Engring., U. Mich., 1959, PhD in Nuclear Engring., 1962. Prof. dept. mech. engring. Stanford (Calif.) U., 1961—. Recipient Max Planck award, 1991; Fulbright fellow, 1978, Homboldt fellow, 1987. Fellow Am. Phys. Soc.; mem. AIAA, Am. Soc. Mech. Engrs., Soc. Indsl. and Applied Math. Jewish. Office: Stanford U Dept Mech Engring Stanford CA 94305

FESQ, LORRAINE MAE, aerospace and computer engineer; b. Pennsauken, N.J., June 26, 1957; d. John Fred Henry and Natalie Nicola (Nasuti) F.; m. Frank Tai, May 14, 1988. BA in Math., Rutgers U., 1979; MS in Computer Sci., UCLA, 1990, PhD in Coomputer Sci. and Astrophysics, 1993. Sci. programmer Systems and Applied Sci. Corp., Greenbelt, Md., 1979-81; computer engr./mgr. Ball Aerospace Systems Div., Boulder, Colo., 1981-86; systems engr. OAO, El Segundo, Calif., 1986-87; spacecraft systems engr. TRW, Redondo Beach, Calif., 1987—. Contbr. articles to IECEC Proceedings, AAS Proceedings, Diagnostic Workshop (DX-92) Proceedings, NASA Goddard Space Applications of Artificial Intelligence Proceedings. Mem. Playa Del Rey (Calif.) Network, 1988—. MS fellow TRW, 1988-89, PhD fellow, 1990—. Mem. AIAA (sr., tech. com. mem. artificial intelligence tech. com. 1990—), Am. Astronautical Soc., Am. Assn. for Artificial Intelligence, Am. Astronomical Soc. Home: 6738 Esplanade Playa Del Rey CA 90293-7525 Office: TRW MZ/2384 One Space Pk Redondo Beach CA 90278

FETH, FREDERICK CHARLES, human resources administrator, director; b. Tracy, Minn., July 29, 1938; s. Oliver F. and Agnes R. (Starr) F.; m. Lois Ann Johnson, May 26, 1962; children: Shari Lynn, Charles Leonard. BA, De Pauw U., 1960; postgrad., U. Ill., 1960-61. Mktg. rep. Mobil Oil Corp., Worthington, Minn., 1965-67; coll. rels. coord. ADM chem. div. Ashland Oil Co., Mpls., 1967-68; pers. adminstr. Control Data Corp., Mpls., 1968-73; pers. mgr. Control Data Corp., Casper, Wyo., 1973-76; mgr. indsl. rels. Bear Creek Uranium Co., Casper, 1976-77, UNC Mining and Milling, 1977-81; mgr. human resources Silver King Mines, Inc., Casper, 1981-84; dir. human resources Casper Coll., 1984—; freelance cons., Casper, 1985—. Precinct committeeman Rep. Party, Casper, 1986—; mem. exec. coun. Natrona County Reps., Casper, 1991—, chair, 1993—; chair Civil Svc. Commn., Casper, 1988—; mem. exec. coun., pers. com. moderator Wyo. Presbytery, 1991—; bd. dirs. Casper Neighborhood Housing Svcs., pres., 1985. Sgt. U.S. Army, 1961-65. Atlantic Pacific Exch. grantee. Mem. Soc. for Human Resources Mgmt. (pres. Casper chpt. 1985-86, chair legis. affairs com. Wyo. chpt. 1989-91, state coun. dir. Wyo. chpt. 1991—), Wyo. Ministries in Higher Edn. (bd. dirs. 1988-91), Coll. and Univ. Pers. Assn. (chair state membership com. 1989—), Casper Area C. of C. (chair govt. affairs com. 1992—). Home: 2300 Belmont Rd Casper WY 82604-4648 Office: Casper Coll 125 College Dr Casper WY 82601-4699

FETZER, DAVID GUY, small business owner; b. Emory University, Ga., July 19, 1951; s. Rodger Eugene and Helen Margaret (Zimmer) F. Student, Palomar Coll., 1970-72. Owner, operator Writers Cramp Ltd., Escondido, Calif., 1984-89; customer support rep. Beagle Bros. Inc., San Diego, 1989-90; owner, operator AAA Computing, Escondido, 1990—. Mem. North San Diego Apple Users Group (program dir. 1988-90). Democrat. Home and Office: AAA Computing 525-270 W El Norte Pkwy Escondido CA 92026

FEUERSTEIN, GEORG, publishing executive, writer; b. Würzburg, Germany, May 27, 1947; came to U.S., 1981; s. Erwin and Dorothea (Gimperlein) F.; m. Patricia Lamb, Feb. 14, 1985; children: David, Daniel. M Letters, Durham (Eng.) U., 1976; PhD, Greenwich U., Hilo, Hawaii, 1991. Founder, dir. Yoga Rsch. Assn., London, 1969-73, Yoga Rsch. Ctr., Durham, 1978-82; editor Yoga Quar. Rev., Durham, 1978-82; editorial dir. Dawn Horse Press, Clearlake, Calif., 1982-86; co-dir. Integral Pub., Middletown, Calif., 1986—; editor Spectrum Rev., Middletown, 1987-92; co-dir. Cons. for Applied Intuition, Middletown, 1992—; contbg. editor Yoga Jour., San Francisco, 1987—; bd. dirs. Montreaux Meta Resort, Nevada City, Calif., Clearlake Found., Lakeport, Calif. Author: Encyclopedic Dictionary of Yoga, 1990, Holy Madness, 1991, Sacred Sexuality, 1992, over 20 other books. Grantee Leverhulme Trust Fund, 1979, Rockefeller Found., 1990, 91, 92, A New Am. Pl., 1991. Mem. Indian Acad. Yoga, Authors Guild. Office: Integral Pub PO Box 1030 Lower Lake CA 95457

FEUERSTEIN, MARCY BERRY, employee benefits administrator; b. Wellsville, N.Y., June 18, 1950; d. Marshall Newton and Miriam May (Lingle) Jones; m. Ronald Glenn Berry, Aug. 7, 1967 (div.); 1 child, Angelia Lynn; m. Richard Alan Feuerstein, Jan. 8, 1984. Cert. employee benefits specialist, U. Pa. Jr. clk. N.Y. Life Ins., L.A., 1970-73; jr. acct. FMC Corp., Pomona, Calif., 1973-78; sec. Gen. Med. Ctrs., Anaheim, Calif., 1978-79, svc. rep., 1979-80; dir. mktg. svcs. Protective Health Providers, San Diego, 1980-81, Dental Health Svcs., Long Beach, Calif., 1981-87; owner Mar-Rich Enterprises, 1985—; v.p. So. Calif. chpt. Healthdent of Calif., 1987-88; account exec. Oral Health Svcs., Inc., 1988-89; employee benefits adminstr. Imperial Irrigation Dist., El Centro, Calif., 1989—. Mem. NAFE. Republican. Home: 1531 S 19th St El Centro CA 92243-4102 Office: Imperial Irrigation Dist 1284 W Main St El Centro CA 92243-2817

FEVERY, PATRICK EDMOND, financial executive; b. Knokke, Belgium, Dec. 16, 1955; came to U.S., 1980; s. Jacques Bernard and Irene (Berton) F.; m. Lisa Jane Hergenhan, Mar. 31, 1984; children: Alexander, Andrew. BBA, European U., Antwerp, Belgium, 1980; MBA, Claremont (Calif.) Grad. Sch., 1982. Sr. ops. analyst Atlantic Richfield, L.A., 1983-84; mgr. fin. Denny's Restaurant, La Mirada, Calif., 1985-86, Rainbow Techs., Irvine, Calif., 1987-88; contr. Rainbow Technologies, Irvine, Calif., 1988-91, CFO, v.p. fin., 1991—. Office: Rainbow Techs 9292 Jeronimo Irvine CA 92718

FEY, ROBERT MICHAEL, real estate company executive, banker; b. Chgo., Aug. 19, 1942; s. Roy and Ethel Lea (Winograd) F.; m. Cheryl Lynn Newman, July 26, 1964; children: Julie Nicole, Robin Michelle. BA, UCLA, 1964, MBA, 1965. CPA, Calif. Ptnr. Hochman & Fey, CPA's, Beverly Hills, Calif., 1965-68; mgr. internal audits, then mgr. fin. and tax planning Mattel, Inc., Hathorne, Calif., 1968-71; pres. Fey's Canyon Realtors, Palm Springs, Calif., 1969—; v.p. Fey's Canyon Estates Inc., Palm Springs, 1969—; chief fin. officer Bank Palm Springs, 1982-87; sr. real estate advisor Bank Calif., Palm Springs, 1987—; regional v.p. Calif. Assn. Realtors, L.A., 1988-89. Recipient Elijah N. Sells Award Calif. Soc. CPA's, 1965. Mem. Palm Springs Bd. Realtors (bd. dirs., pres. 1984, 87, realtor yr. 1985), Canyon Country Club. Democrat. Jewish. Home: 2000 S Madrona Dr Palm Springs CA 92264-9221 Office: Fey's Canyon Realtors 458 S Palm Canyon Dr Palm Springs CA 92262-7304

FIALER, PHILIP ANTHONY, research scientist, electronics company executive; b. San Francisco, Nov. 6, 1938; s. Harry A. and Elyse E. (Palin) F.; m. Dianne M. Hater, Mar. 4, 1967 (div. 1982); children: Michele S., Melissa L.; m. Sue Eble, Dec. 14, 1985; 1 stepdaughter, Shannon T. Leinbach. BS, Stanford U., 1960, MS, 1964, PhD, 1970. Engr. Lockheed Corp., Sunnyvale, Calif., 1961-67; research assoc. Stanford (Calif.) U., 1967-70; dep. lab. dir., staff scientist SRI Internat., Menlo Park, Calif., 1970-87; chmn., chief tech. officer Mirage Systems, Sunnyvale, Calif., 1984—; research scientist in ionospheric radiosci. and electromagnetic scattering. Contbr. articles to profl. jours. Mem. IEEE, Am. Astronautical Soc., Security Affairs Support Assn. (ann. revs., bus. affairs com.). Democrat. Episcopalian. Home: 742 Torreya

Ct Palo Alto CA 94303-4160 Office: Mirage Systems 537 Lakeside Dr Sunnyvale CA 94086-4055

FIALKOW, PHILIP JACK, medical educator, medical school dean; b. N.Y.C., Aug. 20, 1934; s. Aaron and Sarah (Ratner) F.; m. Helen C. Dimitrakis, June 14, 1960; children: Michael, Deborah. B.A., U. Pa., 1956; M.D., Tufts U., 1960. Diplomate: Am. Bd. Internal Medicine, Am. Bd. Med. Genetics. Intern U. Calif., San Francisco, 1960-61, resident, 1961-62; resident U. Wash., Seattle, 1962-63, instr. medicine, 1965-66, asst. prof., 1966-69, assoc. prof., 1969-73, prof. medicine, 1973—, chmn. dept. medicine, 1980-90, dean Sch. Medicine, 1990—, v.p. for med. affairs, 1992—; chief med. svc. Seattle VA Ctr., 1974-81; physician-in-chief U. Wash. Med. Ctr., Seattle, 1980-90; attending physician Harborview Med. Ctr., Seattle, 1965—; cons. Children's Orthopedic Hosp., Seattle, 1964—. Contbr. articles to profl. jours.; mem. editorial bds. profl. jours. Trustee Fred Hutchinson Cancer Research Ctr., Seattle, 1982-90. NIH fellow, 1963-65; NIH grantee, 1965—. Fellow ACP; mem. Am. Soc. Clin. Investigation, Assn. Am. Physicians, Am. Soc. Human Genetics (bd. dirs. 1974-77), Am. Soc. Hematology, Inst. Medicine, Alpha Omega Alpha. Office: U Wash 1959 NE Pacific St SC-59 Seattle WA 98195-0001

FIBIGER, JOHN ANDREW, life insurance company executive; b. Copenhagen, Apr. 27, 1932; came to U.S., 1934, naturalized, 1953; s. Borge Rottboll and Ruth Elizabeth (Wadmond) F.; m. Barbara Mae Stuart, June 22, 1956; children: Karen Ruth McCarthy, Katherine Louise. B.A., U. Minn., 1953, M.A., 1954; postgrad., U. Wis. With Lincoln Nat. Life Ins. Co., Ft. Wayne, Ind., 1956-57; with Bankers Life Ins. Co. Nebr., Lincoln, 1959-73; sr. v.p. group Bankers Life Ins. Co. Nebr., 1972-73; with New Eng. Mut. Life Ins. Co., Boston, 1973-89; vice chmn., pres., chief operating officer New Eng. Mut. Life Ins. Co., 1981-89; exec. v.p., chief fin. officer Transam. Life Cos., 1991—; vice chmn. Actuarial Bd. for Counseling and Discipline. Trustee, past chmn. Mus. Sci., Boston, 1989-91; trustee New Eng. Med. Ctr., Menninger Found., Shelburne Mus.; bd. dirs. U. So. Calif. Sch. Gerontology. With AUS, 1957-59. Fellow Soc. Actuaries (bd. dirs.); mem. Internat. Actuarial Assn. (coun.), Nat. Acad. Social Ins. (founding mem.), Am. Acad. Actuaries (past pres.).

FIEDLER, JOHN AMBERG, marketing professional; b. Evanston, Ill., Nov. 14, 1941; s. George and Agnes Zoe (Amberg) F.; m. Frances Eudora Murphy, June 18, 1966 (div. 1984); children: Margaret, Neil; m. Lesley A. Bahner, Dec. 28, 1986. BA, U. Wis., 1965; MBA, U. Chgo., 1969. V.p. Leo Burnett Co., Inc., Chgo., 1969-72, 74-79; mgr. decision systems Market Facts, Inc., Chgo., 1972-73; exec. v.p. Ted Bates Co., Inc., N.Y.C., 1980-84; prin., founder, chief exec. officer POPULUS, Inc., Boise, Idaho, 1985—. Coauthor: (book) Psychological Effects of Advertising, 1985; contbr. articles to profl. jours. and confs.; inventor Ballot Box (TM) communication assessment system, 1985. Rsch. dir. Reagan-Bush '84, Wash., 1984; bd. dirs., mem. exec. com. Childreach, U.S.A. Mem. Am. Mktg. Assn., Pla. Club Chgo. Republican. Roman Catholic. Office: POPULUS Inc HC33 Box 3270 Boise ID 83706

FIELD, ALEXANDER JAMES, economics educator, dean; b. Boston, Apr. 17, 1949; s. Mark George and Anne (Murray) F.; m. Valerie Nan Wolk, Aug. 8, 1982; children: James Alexander, Emily Elena. AB, Harvard U., 1970; MS, London Sch. Econs., 1971; PhD, U. Calif., Berkeley, 1974. Asst. prof. econs. Stanford (Calif.) U., 1974-82; assoc. prof. Santa Clara (Calif.) U., 1982-88, acad. v.p., 1986-87, prof., chmn. dept. econs., 1988-93, assoc. dean Leavey Sch. Bus., 1993—; mem. bd. trustees Santa Clara U., 1988-91. Author: Educational Reform and Manufacturing Development in Mid-Nineteenth Century Massachusetts, 1989; author, editor: The Future of Economic History, 1987; assoc. editor Jour. Econ. Lit., 1981—; mem. editorial bd. Explorations in Econ. History, 1983-89. Recipient Nevins prize Columbia U., 1975; NSF rsch. grantee, 1989. Mem. Phi Beta Kappa, Beta Gamma Sigma. Home: 3762 Redwood Cir Palo Alto CA 94306-4255 Office: Santa Clara Univ Dept Econs Santa Clara CA 95053

FIELD, CAROL HART, writer, journalist, foreign correspondent; b. San Francisco, Mar. 27, 1940; d. James D. and Ruth (Arnstein) Hart; m. John L. Field, July 23, 1961; children: Matthew, Alison. BA, Wellesley Coll., 1961. Contbg. editor, assoc. editor, asst. editor City Mag., San Francisco, 1974-76; contbg. editor New West/Calif. Mag., San Francisco, L.A., 1975-80, San Francisco Mag., 1980-82; fgn. corr. La Gola, Milan, Italy, 1990—; cons. The Donatello, San Francisco, 1992. Author: The Hill Towns of Italy, 1983 (Commonwealth Club award 1984), The Italian Baker, 1985 (Internat. Assn. Culinary Profls. award 1986), Celebrating Italy, 1990 (Commonwealth Club award, Internat. Assn. Culinary Profls. award 1991); contbr. articles to profl. jours. Lit. jury Commonwealth Club Calif., San Francisco, 1987, 88, 92; bd. dirs. Women's Forum West, San Francisco, 1990—, The Mechanics' Inst., San Francisco, 1987-92, pres. 1990-92, Bancroft Libr. U. Calif., Berkeley, 1991—, The Headlands Inst., San Francisco, 1992—. Recipient Internat. Journalism prize Maria Luigia Duchessa di City of Parma, Italy, 1987; named Alumna of Yr. Head Royce Sch., Oakland, Calif., 1991. Mem. Accademia Italia della Cucina, Authors Guild, Am. Inst. Wine and Food, Les Dames d'Escoffier. Home and Office: 2561 Washington St San Francisco CA 94115

FIELD, CHARLES WILLIAM, small business owner, consultant; b. Kankakee, Ill., Feb. 4, 1934; s. Euell Charles and Genevieve Thelma (Fletcher) F.; m. Barbara Sue Bird, Sept. 20, 1957; children: Charles Scott, Lynda Lois. BS in Metall. Engring., U. Ariz., 1960. Lic. real estate broker, Ariz. Research metallurgist Titanium Metals Corp. Am., Henderson, Nev., 1960-62; mgr. tech. service Titanium Metals Corp. Am., N.Y.C., 1962-67; with research and mktg. dept. Large Jet Engine div. Gen. Electric Co., Cin., 1967-69; sr. engr. specialist Garrett Corp., Phoenix, 1969-76; realtor Realty Execs., Scottsdale, Ariz., 1976-85; prin. C.W. Field Field & Co., Scottsdale, 1985—; cons. armor titanium specialties U.S. Secret Service. Contbr. articles to profl. jours. Active local Boy Scouts Am., Youth Scottsdale. Recipient commendation U.S. Govt., 1964, Pres's. Round Table award Phoenix Bd. Realtors, 1981, 84. Mem. AIAA, Nat. Assn. Realtors, Scottsdale Rd. Realtors (Million Dollar Club), Rotary (bd. dirs.Scottsdale club), Camelback Country Club. Office: CW Field & Co 6620 E Maverick Rd Paradise Valley AZ 85253-2648

FIELD, CHRISTOPHER ALAN, financial planner; b. Redbank, N.J., May 7, 1965; s. Lester L. and Patricia (Kelleher) F.; m. Michelle Marie Fauque, July 21, 1990. BS in Econs., Mont. State U., 1988, BS in Agrl. Bus., 1988. Cert. fin. planner. Profl. fin. planner Capital Fin. Group, Inc., Helena, Mont., 1989—; tng. mgr. IDS Fin. Svcs., Inc., Helena, Mont., 1991—. Author weekly newspaper column Money Matters, 1991-92. Mem. Mont. Stockgrowers Assn., Mont. Graingrowers Assn., Lions. Office: Capital Fin Group 314 Fuller Ave Helena MT 59601

FIELD, FRED HOWARD, architect; b. San Mateo, Calif., Sept. 15, 1928; s. Fred Howard and Flora Anne (Bagley) F.; m. Delores Elizabeth Manley, Jan. 30, 1951 (dec. June 1991); children: Darci Anne, Rikki Marie, James Russell. Student, Menlo Jr. Coll., 1948, U. So. Calif., 1951; BArch, U. Calif., Berkeley, 1954. Draftsman, designer various architecture firms, San Francisco, 1958-60; specification writer Skidmore, Owings & Merrill, San Francisco, 1960-62; prin. architect Fred H. Field, Sausalito, Calif., 1962-67, San Francisco, 1969-85, San Jose, Calif., 1975-79, San Mateo, 1978-80, Ross, Calif., 1968—; instr. Cogswell Coll., San Francisco, 1968-70. Designer-architect residential, comml., indsl. and institutional bldgs.; contbr. articles to profl. jours. Trustee, dir. Almonte Sanitary Dist., Mill Valley, Calif., 1965; bldg. inspector City of Sausalito, 1964; mem. Am. Legion Marines Meml. Assn. 1st lt. USMCR, 1954-57. Mem. AIA, Nat. Assn. Real Estate Investment Trusts, Nat. Coun. Arch. Registration Bds., Western Constrn. Cons. Assn., Constrn. Specifications Inst., Golden Gate Nat. Park Assn., Sigma Nu. Office: Fred H Field AIA Box 1558 Ross CA 94957

FIELD, JEFFREY FREDERIC, designer; b. Los Angeles, July 6, 1954; s. Norman and Gertrude Clara (Ellman) F.; m. Susan Marie Merrin, Jan. 8, 1978. BA in Art, Calif. State U., Northridge, 1977, MA in Art, 1980. Cert. indsl. plastics tchr., Calif. Designer Fundamental Products Co., N. Hollywood, Calif., 1972-82; designer/model maker The Stansbury Co., Beverly Hills, Calif., 1982-84; mech. engr. Vector Electronic Co., Sylmar, Calif., 1984-87; pres., prin. Jeffrey Field Design Assocs., Sepulveda, Calif., 1987—; cons. MiniMed Techs., Sylmar, 1987—, Best Time Inc., Leander, Tex., 1987—, Spectrum Design, Granada Hills, Calif., 1987—, Raycom Systems Inc., Boulder, Colo., 1988-89, Alfred E. Mann Found. for Sci. Rsch., Sylmar, 1988—, Atomic Elements, L.A., E-O Products, Laguna Hills, Calif., Autogenics, Newbury Park, Calif., 1990—, Pacesetter Systems, Sylmar, 1990—, Baxter Healthcare Corp., Pharmaseal Div., Valencia, Calif., 1990—, Surgidev Corp., Goleta, Calif., 1990—, Indsl. Strength Eyewear/Grafix Mktg. Group, Manhattan Beach & Campbell, Calif., 1991—. Democrat. Jewish. Home and Office: 16715 Vincennes St Sepulveda CA 91343-2711

FIELD, MORTON RICHARD, lawyer; b. Chgo., July 28, 1923; s. Leo and Minnie (Rubin) F.; m. Gloria M. Krause, July 15, 1951; children: Bradley, Cathleen. BA, U. Ill., 1946; LLB, DePaul U., 1948. Bar: Ill. 1948, Calif. 1951, U.S. Ct. Mil. Appeals 1956, D.C. 1957, U.S. Supreme Ct., 1957. Atty.-advisor SEC, Chgo., 1948-50, L.A., 1950-52; ptnr. Wallenstein and Field, L.A., 1952-73, Jackson & Goodstein, L.A., 1973-79, Alschuler Grossman & Pines, L.A., 1979-88, Spensley Horn Jubas & Lubitz, L.A., 1988—; bd. dirs. Frederick's of Hollywood, Inc., L.A. Author: (audiocassette) Going Public, 1991. Capt. U.S. Army, 1942-54. Home: 306 Bronwood Ave Los Angeles CA 90049 Office: Spensley Horn Jubas Lubitz 1880 Century Park E 5th Fl Los Angeles CA 90067

FIELD, RICHARD JEFFREY, chemistry educator; b. Attleboro, Mass., Oct. 26, 1941; s. Jeffrey Hazard and Edna Catherine (Hawkins) F.; m. Judith Lauchaire, Sept. 5, 1966; children: Elijah, Sara. BS, U. Mass., 1963; MS, Holy Cross Coll., 1964; PhD, U. R.I., 1968. Rsch. assoc., vis. asst. prof. U. Oreg., Eugene, 1968-74; sr. rsch. chemist Carnegie-Mellon U., Pitts., 1974-75; asst. prof., then assoc. prof. dept. chemistry U. Mont., Missoula, 1975-83, prof. chemistry, 1984—, chmn. dept. chemistry, 1990—; vis. prof. U. Notre Dame, Ind., 1980, U. Würzburg, Fed. Republic Germany, 1985-86; referee various jours., granting agys., 1970—; mem. NSF panel on grad. fellowships, Washington, 1980-83; asst. dir. EPSCoR program in Mont., NSF, 1990—. Editor: Oscillations and Traveling Waves in Chemical Systems, 1985, Chaos in Chemistry and Biochemistry, 1993; contbr. rsch. articles to profl. publs. Grantee NSF, 1978—; recipient Burlington No. award for scholarship, 1990. Mem. Am. Chem. Soc. (tour speaker 1983, 85, 89, 91, 92, chair Mont. sect. 1979, editorial adv. bd. Jour. Phys. Chemistry 1988—). Roman Catholic. Home: 317 Livingston Ave Missoula MT 59801-8007 Office: U Mont Dept Chemistry Missoula MT 59812

FIELDEN, C. FRANKLIN, III, educator; b. Gulfport, Miss., Aug. 4, 1946; s. C. Franklin and Georgia (Freeman) F.; children: Christopher Michaux (dec.), Robert Michaux, Jonathan Dutton. Student, Claremont Men's Coll., 1964-65; AB, Colo. Coll., 1970; MS, George Peabody Coll. Tchrs., 1976, EdS, 1979. Tutor Proyecto El Guacio, San Sebastian, P.R., 1967-68; asst. tchr. GET-SET Project, Colorado Springs, Colo., 1969-70, co-tchr., 1970-75, asst. dir., 1972-75; tutor Early Childhood Edn. Project, Nashville, 1975-76; pub. policy intern Donner-Belmont Child Care Ctr., Nashville, 1976-77; asst. to urban min. Nashville Presbytery, 1977; intern to prin. Steele Elem. Sch., Colorado Springs, 1977-78, tchr., 1978-86; resource person Office Gifted and Talented Edn. Colorado Springs Pub. Schs., 1986-87; tchr. Columbia Elem. Sch., Colorado Springs, 1987-92; tchr., pre-sch. team coord. Helen Hunt Elem. Sch., Colorado Springs, 1992-93; validator Nat. Acad. Early Childhood Programs, 1992—; cons. Colo. Dept. Edn., Denver, 1993—; lectr. Arapahoe Community Coll., Littleton, Colo., 1981-82; instr. Met. State Coll., Denver, 1981; cons. Jubail Human Resources Devel. Inst., Saudi Arabia, 1982; mem. governing bd. GET-SET Project, 1969-79, 91-93; cons. Colo. Dept. of Edn., Denver, 1993—. Mem. Nashville Children's Issues Task Force, 1976-77, Tenn. United Meth. Task Force on Children and Youth, 1976-77; mem. ad hoc bd. trustees Tenn. United Meth. Agy. on Children and Youth, 1976-77; mem. So. Regional Edn. Bd. Task Force on Parent-Caregiver Relationships, 1976-77; mem. day care com. Colo. Commn. Children and their Families, 1981-82; mem. Citizens' Goals Leadership Tng., 1986-87, Child Abuse Task Force, 4th Judicial Dist., 1986-87; mem. FIRST IMPRESSIONS (Colo. Govs. early childhood initiative) Task Force, 1986-87; mem. El Paso County Placement Alternatives Commn., 1990—; mem. proposal rev. team Colo. Dept. Edn., 1992—, co-chair City/County Child Care Task Force, 1991-92; mem. Colo. State Preschool Adv. Coun., 1993—; charter mem. City/County Early Childhood Care and Edn. Commn., 1993—. Recipient Arts/Bus./Edn. award, 1983; Innovative Teaching award, 1984. Fellow NIMH, 1976; mem. ASCD, Nat. Assn. Edn. Young Children (founding mem., primary caucus 1992—, co-chair Western States Leadership Network 1993), Colo. Assn. Edn. Young Children (legis. com. 1979-84, governing bd. 1980-84, 85-86, 89—, exec. com. 1980-84, 93—, sec. 1980-84, rsch. conf. chmn. 1982, tuitions awards com. 1983-86, chmn. tuition awards com. 1985-86, pub. policy com. 1989—, treas. 1993—), Pikes Peak Assn. Edn. Young Children, Am. Film Inst., Colorado Springs Fine Arts Ctr., Huguenot Soc. Great Britain and Ireland, Nat. Trust Hist. Preservation, Country Club of Colo., Phi Delta Kappa. Presbyterian. Home: PO Box 7766 Colorado Springs CO 80933-7766 Office: 201 E Colfax Ave Denver CO 80203

FIELDER, BARBARA LEE, human resources consultant, management trainer; b. Long Beach, Calif., Dec. 6, 1942; d. Thomas G. Coultrup and Elizabeth L. (Doran) Cox; m. Alford W. Fielder, Apr. 14, 1970; children: Kris, Kimberly, Brian. BSBA, Redlands U., 1979. Cert. tchr., Calif. Sr. compensation analyst The Irvine Co., Newport Beach, Calif., 1973-76; pers. adminstr. Shiley div. Pfizer Co., Irvine, Calif., 1976-78; asst. dir. human resources BASF-Video Corp., Fountain Valley, Calif., 1978-79; pres. Barbara L. Fielder & Assoc., Roseville, Calif., 1979-89, The Felder Group, Ky., 1989—; instr. U. Calif., Davis, 1985-88; workshop leader Nat. Seminars Group, 1989—, Inst. Applied Mgmt. and Law, 1981—. Contbr. articles to profl. jours. Pres. Calif. Employers Coun., 1983-86; mem. Pvt. Industry Coun., Orange County, Calif., 1983-84; past mem. Foothill Adv. Bd., 1987-89; bd. dirs. Industry Edn. Coun. Calif., 1987-89. Recipient Outstanding Svc. award Interstate Conf. Employment Security Agys., Indpls., 1984. Mem. Nat. Speakers Assn., Tenn. Speakers Assn. Presbyterian.

FIELDING, HAROLD PRESTON, bank executive; b. Roaring Springs, Tex., Oct. 18, 1930; s. Rennon Preston and Merle (Woods) F.; m. Ingrid Margarete Eva Ziegler, May 4, 1962; children: Terry Stephen, Harold Preston Jr., Rennon Preston II, Marcel Preston, Noël Preston. AA, Fresno City Coll., 1972; BA, Calif. State U., 1976. Enlisted U.S. Army, 1950, command sgt. major, 1950-72, retired, 1972; br. mgr. Bank of Am., Stockton, Calif., 1972-78; exec. v.p. Bank of Oreg., Woodburn, 1978-84; pres., chief exec. officer Calif. Valley Bank, Fresno, 1984-86; pres., chief exec. officer Am. Samoa Bank, Pago Pago, Am. Samoa, 1986—, bd. dirs. Bd. dirs. Am. Samoa Econ. Devel. Authority, Pago Pago, 1990, C. of C. of Am. Samoa, Pago Pago, 1987, Goodwill Industries of Am. Samoa, Pago Pago, 1988, Tony Solaita Scholarship Trust Fund, Pago Pago, 1990. Mem. Am. Bankers' Assn., Western Ind. Bankers' Assn., Calif. Bankers' Assn., Oreg. Bankers' Assn. Democrat. Roman Catholic.

FIELDS, DARREL REX, engineering consultant; b. Poplar Bluff, Mo., Dec. 14, 1925; s. Roy Dean and Estella Iona (Ball) F.; m. Mary Evelyn Payne, July 2, 1948 (div. Dec. 1979); children: Rhonda Sue, Denise Gay; m. Bette Jane Neuenfeldt, Mar. 24, 1980. BS in Naval Tech., U. Minn., 1946; BSME, U. Ark., 1949; MS in Econs., Baylor U., 1969; MA in Pub. Adminstrn., U. N.Mex., 1987. Registered profl. engr., Calif., N.Mex.; cert. quality engr. Mech. engr. J.C. Lewis Co., Little Rock, 1948; commd. 2d lt. U.S. Army, 1950, advanced through grades to lt. col., 1950; civil engr. U.S. Army Corps Engrs. U.S. Army, Little Rock, 1949-50; nuclear weapons officer U.S. Army, 1950-68; sr. nuclear weapons engr. U.S. Naval Weapons Evaluation Facility, Albuquerque, 1968-87; retired U.S. Army, 1968; cons. engr. Fields Cons. Co., 1987—; quality engr. Sperry-Honeywell, Albuquerque, 1987, EG&G, Albuquerque, 1988, GE Aircraft Engines, Albuquerque, 1988—. Col. N.Mex. State Def. Force, Albuquerque, 1981—; air pollution cons. City of Albuquerque. Lt. (j.g.) USN, 1943-47, PTO. Mem. Am. Soc. Quality Control (vice chmn., chmn. Albuquerque sect. 1971-72), Retired Officers Assn. (life), Res. Officers Assn. (life), Nat. Assn. Uniformed Svcs. (life), Assn. U.S. Army, State Def. Assn. U.S., Nat. Assn. Retired Fed. Employees, Kirtland AFB Officers Club, Pi Alpha Alpha. Democrat. Lutheran. Home and Office: 7501 Scotts Pl NE Albuquerque NM 87109-5323 Office: Fields Cons Co 7501 Scotts Pl NE Albuquerque NM 87109-5323

FIELDS, R. WAYNE, business development executive, consultant; b. Tulsa, Feb. 1, 1941; s. Rance William and Mary Margaret (Bearden) F.; m. Lorraine Eleanor Boucher, Feb. 3, 1967; 1 child, Nicole Marie. BS, Oreg. State U., 1963; PhD, Oreg. Health Scis. U., 1969. Staff scientist NASA, Cambridge, Mass., 1969-70; dir. biophysics lab. Oreg. Health Scis. U., Portland, 1970-78; mgr. advanced devel. B-D Drake Willock, Portland, 1978-84; v.p. Premium Equity Corp., Vancouver, B.C., Can., 1984-87; pres., co-owner Venture Solutions Ltd., Lake Oswego, Oreg., 1987—; cons., Gladstone, Oreg., 1987—; mem. nat. adv. bd. One-Eighty Degrees, Portland, 1989—; bd. dirs. 5 ind. corps., Portland, 1989—. Contbr. articles to profl. jours. Mem. Elks. Home: 6490 Chessington Ln Gladstone OR 97027-1011 Office: Venture Solutions Ltd 4500 Kruse Way Ste 220 Lake Oswego OR 97035-2564

FIENBERG, KAREN DANA, lawyer, computer engineer; b. Harbor City, Calif., Nov. 16, 1966; d. Steven Dale and Arlene Ruth (Feuerstein) F. BA in English, U. Calif., Santa Barbara, 1987; JD, Loyola U., 1990; BS in Computer Engring., Calif. State U., Long Beach, 1992. Clk. Gilbert Kelly Crowley & Jennet, L.A., summer 1988, Fed. Pub. Defender, L.A., summer 1989; sub. tchr. L.A. Unified Schs., 1990; assoc. Poms, Smith, Lande & Rose, L.A., 1993—; vol. staff atty. legal aid Calif. State U., Long Beach, 1991-93. Mem. Computer Law Assn., Orange County Bar Assn., L.A. Bar Assn. Home: 3665 Hughes Ave # 104 Los Angeles CA 90034

FIESTA, LORENZO EDDRADA, insurance executive; b. Dingras, Ilocos, Philippines, Aug. 1, 1950; came to U.S. 1985; s. Sefonias Garo and Ceferina (Eddrada) F.; m. Estefania Tabios Dumlao, Dec. 12, 1981; children: Zonia, Laureen, Lawrence. BS in Commerce, Divine Word Coll., Laoag City, Philippines, 1974. Unit sales mgr. Summit Comml., Vigan, Philippines, 1974-75; mgr./owner El Fiesta Ent., San Nicolas, Philippines, 1976-85; housekeepr Halekulani Hotel, Honolulu, 1985-86; agt. N.Y. Life Ins. Co., Honolulu, 1986-90, sales mgr., 1990—. Bd. dirs. Ilocos Norte Area Mktg. Coop, Philippines, 1980-84, San Nicolas Water Dist., Ilocos, 1982-85. Mem. Hawaii Assn. Life Underwriters. Office: NY Life Ins Co 841 Bishop St # 700 Honolulu HI 96813

FIFE, DENNIS JENSEN, military officer, chemistry educator; b. Brigham City, Utah, Feb. 10, 1945; s. Glen Shumway and June (Jenson) F.; m. Metta Marie Gunther, June 22, 1972; children: Kimball, Kellie, Keith, Kurt, Katie, Kenton. BS in Chemistry, Weber State U., Ogden, Utah, 1969; MBA, Inter-Am. U., San German, P.R., 1973; MS in Chemistry, Utah State U., 1978, PhD in Phsy. Chemistry, 1983. Assoc. chemist Thiokol Chem. Corp., Brigham City, 1969; commd. 2d lt. USAF, 1969, advanced through grades to lt. col.; pilot, instr., flight examiner Hurricane Hunters, Ramey AFB, P.R. and Keesler AFB, Miss., 1971-76; test project pilot 6514th Test Squadron, Ogden, Utah, 1979-81; instr. chemistry USAF Acad., Colorado Springs, Colo., 1977-79, asst. prof., 1983-85, assoc. prof., 1985-90; prof. USAF Acad., 1990; pres. Select Pubs., Inc., Colorado Springs, 1985-90, also chmn. bd. dirs., 1990; mgr. analytical labs. dept. Thiokol Corp., Brigham City, Utah, 1990—. Author: How to Form a Colorado Corporation, 1986; contbr. articles to profl. jours. Active Boy Scouts Am., 1981—, sustaining mem. Rep. Nat. Com., Washington, 1983—. Decorated Air medal with oak leaf cluster; NSF research grantee, 1967-68. Mem. Internat. Union Pure and Applied Chemistry (affiliate), Am. Chem. Soc., Phi Kappa Phi. Republican. Mormon. Office: Thiokol Corp PO Box 707 M/S 245 Brigham City UT 84302-0707

FIFE, JERRY LEO, marketing professional; b. Highmore, S.D., Feb. 24, 1948; s. J. Leo and Leonora (Wright) F.; m. Marva Hotchkiss, Apr. 30, 1978. BS in Engring. Physics, U. Kans., 1971; MBA, U. Phoenix, 1987. Registered profl. engr., Colo. Design engr. David E. Flemming Cons. Engring. Co., Denver, 1971-77; design engr. Auto-Trol, Denver, 1977-79, mgr. internat. tech. supt., 1979-82, mgr. new products, 1982-83; dir. mktg. support Raycom, Boulder, Colo., 1983-84; sr. product planner NBI, Boulder, 1984-88; mgr. product mktg. Topologiz, Denver, 1988-89, Solbourne, Longmont, Colo., 1989-92; with product mktg. Photometrics, Tucson, 1992—. Home: 7231 E Rosslare Dr Tucson AZ 85715 Office: Photometrics 3440 E Britannia Tucson AZ 85706

FIGG, WILLIAM CARL, JR., hotel executive; b. Savannah, Ga., Sept. 12, 1949; s. William Carl Sr. and Virginia (Carroll) F.; m. Susan E. Akins, Feb. 3, 1977; children: Crystal, Lisa, Ashley, William III. BA, The Citadel, Charleston, S.C., 1975; MS, Troy State U., 1978; CHA, Mich. State U., 1981. Area mgr. Howard Johnson Co., Valdosta, Ga., 1974-78; gen. mgr. Key Stone Mgmt., Memphis, 1980-83; v.p. Figg, Inc., Savannah, 1983-84; pres. Energy Inns, Gillette, Wyo., 1984-87; gen. mgr. Holiday Inn, Lubbock, Tex., 1978-80, Florence, S.C., 1987-90; pres. Figg Mgmt. Cons., Florence, 1987-90, Figg Hotel Mgmt., Las Crucas, N.Mex., 1990—. Dir. Gillette Vis. and Conv. Assn., 1986-87; chmn. Florence Accommodation Tax Commn. Served to maj. U.S. Army, 1969-75, Korea, Vietnam, Army N.G., 1975—. Mem. N.E. Wyo. Travel Assn. (pres. 1985-87), Lubbock Hotel Assn. (pres. 1979-80), Florence Hotel Assn. (chmn.), N.Mex. Hotel Assn., N.Mex. Citadel Assn., S.C. Hotel Assn., Las Cruces Hotel-Restaurant Assn. (pres.), N.Mex. Hotel and Motel Assn. (bd. dirs.), Aggie Sports Assn. (bd. dirs.), Rotary. Republican. Office: Holiday Inn 201 E University Ave Las Cruces NM 88005-3392

FIGUEIREDO, CYNTHIA MARSTON, consultant; b. Needham, Mass., Nov. 19, 1954; d. Ernest William and Anna Louise (McElroy) Marston; m. William Arthur Figueiredo, Aug. 14, 1983. BS in Home Econs., Framingham State Coll., 1982; M in Curriculum/Instruction, Chapman Coll., 1991. Cert. tchr. Ariz., Calif., Mass., home economist. Educator home econs. Arlington (Mass.) Pub. Schs., 1982-83, Somerville (Mass.) Pub. Schs., Lowell (Mass.) Pub. Schs., 1985-87, Fontana (Calif.) Unified Sch. Dist., 1989-92; pvt. practice as cons. Mesa, Ariz., 1992—; instr. adult edn. Assabet Valley Vocat. Sch., Marlboro, Mass., 1982-83; GED assessment specialist Project SCALE, Somerville, 1983-87; mem. Family Circle Consumer Bd., 1988. Editor: Chinese Recipes, 1987, Quick and Easy Recipes for Today's Family, 1991. Recipient Tchr. award Lowell Edn. Found., 1987, Cert. Appreciation, Future Homemakers Am., 1992; Greater Nutrition Awareness Plan grantee Mass. State Dept. Edn., 1986, Pride in Lowell grantee Lowell Edn. Found., 1986, ECIA Chpt. 2 grantee Calif. Dept. Edn., 1989, Sex Equity: Life Mgmt. grantee, 1992. Mem. Assn. Supervision and Curriculum Devel., Calif. Home Econs. Assn. (v.p. Citrus dist. 1989-91, pres. 1991-92, Achievement award 1992), Ea. Mass. Hone Econs. Assn. (treas. 1986-87). Home: 1322 N Racine Circle Mesa AZ 85205-4227

FIGUEIREDO, HUBERT FERNANDES, aerospace engineer; b. Elizabeth, N.J., Nov. 21, 1958; s. Fernando and Maria Alexandria F.; m. Donna Maybee, Mar. 26, 1988; children: Jennifer Marie and Christine Alexis. BS in Aerospace Engring., Polytech. Inst. N.Y., 1980; postgrad. in systems mgmt., U. So. Calif., 1986—. Prodn. inspector Amax, Inc., Carteret, N.J., 1978; analytical engr. Pratt and Whitney Aircraft Corp., East Hartford, Conn., 1979; space shuttle mech. systems test engr. Rockwell Internat. Space Div., Palmdale, Calif., 1980-84, pub. rels. speaker, 1981-84; space shuttle mechanisms/structures engr. Lockheed Space Ops. Co., Vandenberg AFB, Calif. and Kennedy Space Ctr., Fla., 1984-87; with B-2 div. Northrop Corp., Palmdale, Calif., 1987-89, engring. specialist, lead structures design engr., 1990-91, group lead engr. B-2 structures design, 1990—; interviewed on progress of space shuttle Challenger on the Spanish Internat. Network, 1983. Mem. rsch. bd. adv. Am. Biog. Inst. Recipient Superior Achievement award Rockwell Internat. Space Div. Mem. AIAA. Republican. Roman Catholic. Office: Northrop B-2 Div D/LW042-4H AF Plant 42 Site 4 Palmdale CA 93550 Address: 2557 Garnet Ln Lancaster CA 93535

FIGUEROA, MICHAEL OTTO, law enforcement official; b. L.A., Dec. 26, 1943; s. Jesse Albert and Elsie (Lea) F.; m. Andrea L. Ashcraft; children: Jeffrey Michael, Noelle Kathryn. AA in Bus. Adminstrn., East Los Angeles Coll., 1965; BA, in Adminstrn., Calif. State Coll.-San Bernardino, 1974; grad. U. So. Calif. Delinquency Control Inst., 1978, Calif. Peace Officers Standards and Tng. Commn. Command Coll., 1985. Cert. peace officer, supr., Calif. Dep. Los Angeles County Sheriff's Dept., 1970-72; patrolman Riverside, Police Dept., Calif., 1972-74, agt., 1974, spl. agt., investigator, 1974-76, sgt., 1976-80, lt. adj. to chief of police, 1980-83, capt., 1983-88, dep. chief, 1988—; cons. on street gangs and graffiti. Bd. dirs. Riverside Area Child Abuse Council, 1980, Riverside Area Rape Crisis, 1977-80; Cub master local Cub Scouts, 1975-77; active local Y-Indian Guides. 1st. lt. AUS, 1966-68. Decorated Bronze Star with oak leaf cluster; named Supr. of Yr., Riverside Police Officers Assn., 1984. . Mem. Internat. Police Assn., Hispanic-Am. Police Command Assn., Latino Peace Officers Assn., Calif. Gang Investigators Assn., Peace Officer Research Assn. Calif., G.I. Forum, Vietnam Vets. of Am., Riverside Athletic Assn., Am. Legion, VFW (Law Enforcement Officer of Yr. 1986, John Edgar Hoover Meml. gold medal for disting. pub. svc.), Command Coll. Alumni Assn. (bd. dirs.), U. Calif.-Riverside Athletic Assn., Athletic Express Track Club (Male Athlete of Yr. 1985, 87) (Riverside), Greater Riverside Hispanic C. of C., Athletic Congress (Masters All-Am. for 5,000- and 10,000-meter run 1988, Masters Nat. Champion 3000 meters indoor track and field 1989). Republican. Roman Catholic. Office: 4102 N Orange St Riverside CA 92501-3671

FIKANI, RICHARD THOMAS, savings and loan association executive; b. Fort Wayne, Ind., Nov. 23, 1964; s. Richard Joseph F. and Barbara Jean (Mauloff) De Aguero; m. Linda Marie Van Wagner, Dec. 3, 1983; children: Carolyn Marie, Jessica Christine. Student, Met. State Coll., Denver, 1981-85. Teller Denver Nat. Bank, 1981-82, teller trainer, 1982, ops. supr., 1983-85; with auto sales dept. Luby Chevrolet, Lakewood, Colo., 1985-86; realtor Moore & Co. Realtors, Arvada, Colo., 1986-89; loan rep. World Savings & Loan, Sacramento, Calif., 1989-90; dist. loan origination mgr. World Savings & Loan, Modesto, Calif., 1990-93; region loan origination mgr. World Savings & Loan, Van Nuys, Calif., 1993—. Mem. Nat. Assn. Realtors, Calif. Assn. Realtors, Modesto Assn. Realtors, Elks. Republican. Home: 717 Twin Peaks St Simi Valley CA 93065 Office: World Savings and Loan 16340 Roscoe Blvd Ste 218 Van Nuys CA 91406

FIKE, EDWARD LAKE, newspaper editor; b. Delmar, Md., Mar. 31, 1920; s. Claudius Edwin and Rosa Lake (Pepper) F.; m. Rosa Amanda Drake, Apr. 1, 1952; children: Rosa, Evelyn, Amy, Melinda. BA, Duke U., 1941; postgrad., U. Cin., 1941-42. Editor, co-pub. Nelsonville (Ohio) Tribune, 1945-48; dir. bur. pub. info. Duke U., Durham, N.C., 1948-52; mem. U.S. del. N. Atlantic Council, Paris, 1952-53; assoc. editor Rocky Mount (N.C.) Evening Telegram, 1953-57; editor, pub. Fike Newspapers, Lewistown and Glendive, Mont., 1957-62; also Fike Newspapers, Wilmington and Tujunga, Calif., 1957-68; assoc. editor Richmond (Va.) News Leader, 1968-70; dir. news and editorial analysis Copley Newspapers, 1970-77; editor editorial pages San Diego Union, 1977-90; lectr. journalism San Diego State U., San Diego Evening Coll. Mem. Pres. Adv. Coun. San Diego State U., 1988-93; bd. dirs. Grossmont Hosp. Found., Armed Svcs. YMCA. Served to lt. USNR, 1942-45. Recipient George Washington award Freedoms Found., 1969-71, 73, 78, Editorial Writing awards N.C. Press Assn., 1954-55, Va. Press Assn., 1969, Calif. Newspaper Pubs. Assn., 1969, 80; Hoover Inst. Media fellow Stanford U., 1990-91. Mem. Scholia Club San Diego, Omicron Delta Kappa. Republican. Methodist. Home: 12244 Fuerte Dr El Cajon CA 92020-8322

FIKE, LARRY LYNN, accountant; b. Woodward, Okla., Oct. 18, 1942; s. Orville William Fike and Ruby Maxine (Jordan) Henderson; m. Tina Yankee, June 27, 1965 (div. Jan. 26, 1986); children: Hilary Greer Fike, Eden Ann. BBA, U. Colo., 1969. CPA, Colo. Mgr., pub. acct. Seidman & Seidman, CPAs, Denver, 1969-74, Fike & Bates, CPAs, Denver, 1974-76, Les Bates & Assocs., CPAs, Denver, 1976-80; corp. sec., treas. Premier Energy Corp., Denver, 1980-81; treas. Cletom Internat. Exploration Co., Inc., Golden, Colo., 1981-83; pub. acct. Larry L. Fike, CPA, Golden, Colo., 1983-86; pub. acct., mgr. Williams, Cohen & Fike, P.C., Wheat Ridge, Colo., 1986-87, Williams, Fike & Mollohan, P.C., Wheat Ridge, Colo., 1987-88, Larry L. Fike, P.C., Wheat Ridge, Colo., 1988—. Author: (monthly columns) Taxation for Realtors, 1988-92. With USN, 1960-63. Mem. AICPA (fellow), Colo. Soc. CPAs (small bus. com. 1987-90, profl. ethics bd. 1990-93). Lutheran. Office: 4465 Kipling St Wheat Ridge CO 80033

FILENER, MILLARD LEE, wholesale, retail distribution company executive; b. Delta, Colo., May 4, 1946; s. Millard Otis and Rosie Everetta F.; m. Connie Sue Einspahr; children: Kimberly, Weslee. BA in Acctg., Western State Coll., Gunnison, Colo., 1972. Mgmt. trainee Am. Parts Systems, Denver, 1972-76; ops. mgr. Am. Parts Systems, Portland, Oreg., 1976; sales mgr. Am. Parts Systems, Portland, 1977; corp. parts mgr. Howard-Cooper Corp., Portland, 1977-79; sales mgr. Mark VII Data Systems, Portland, 1980; dist. mgr. Valley Refuse Removal BFI, Grand Junction, Colo., 1981-82; co-owner, bd. dirs. Superior Trash Co., Montrose, Colo., 1981-84; distrbn. mgr. Meta Systems Inc, Gladstone, Oreg., 1984-87; pres. Meta Systems Inc, Gladstone, 1987-91, The Distribution Group, 1991—; bus. cons., 1991—; bd. dirs. The Distribution Group, 1991—; computer cons. City of Palisade, Colo., 1981. Designed software various bus. applications, 1974—. Mem. West. Colo. Health Facilities Review Bd., Grand Junction, 1982; bd. dirs. Metabolic Health Orgn., Portland, Oreg., 1985-91. With U.S. Army, 1965-67. Office: The Distribution Group Inc PO Box 567 Beavercreek OR 97004

FILES, GORDON LOUIS, lawyer, judge; b. Ft. Dodge, Iowa, Mar. 5, 1912; s. James Ray and Anna (Louis) F.; m. Kathryn Thrift, Nov. 24, 1942; children: Kathryn Lacey, James Gordon. A.B. in Polit. Sci. with honors, UCLA, 1934; LL.B., Yale U., 1937. Bar: Calif. 1937, U.S. Supreme Ct. 1957. Law clk. U.S. Ct. Appeals (8th cir.), 1937-38; enforcement atty. Office Price Adminstrn., 1942; ptnr. Freston & Files, Los Angeles, 1938-59; judge Los Angeles Superior Ct., 1959-62; assoc. justice 2d dist., div. 4 Calif. Ct. Appeal, 1962-64, presiding justice, 1964-82, adminstrv. presiding justice, 1970-82; arbitrator, referee and mediator, 1982-86; mem. Jud. Council Calif., 1964-71, 73-77; mem. governing com. Ctr. for Jud. Edn. and Research, 1981-82; mem. bd. govs. State Bar Calif., 1957-59. Mem. bd. editors Yale Law Jour., 1935-37. Served to lt. USN, 1942-45. Fellow Am. Bar Found.; mem. ABA, Am. Judicature Soc., Inst. Jud. Adminstrn., Los Angeles County Bar Assn. (trustee 1952-56), Calif. Judges Assn. (exec. com. 1971-72), Am. Legion, Order of Coif, Phi Beta Kappa, Phi Delta Phi. Democrat. Clubs: Chancery (pres. 1972-73) (L.A.); Valley Hunt (Pasadena). Home: 154 S Arroyo Blvd Pasadena CA 91105-1535

FILES, L(AWRENCE) BURKE, financial consultant; b. Chgo., Sept. 12, 1961; s. Eben Stuart and Rita (McGoloan) F.; m. Laura Beatrice Ritter, Nov. 17, 1990. Fund mgr. Oppenheimer Rouse, Phoenix, 1982-85; fin. cons. Crystal Resources, Inc., Tempe, Ariz., 1985-87; dir. corp. fin. Am. Nat. Corp., Phoenix, 1987-88; pvt. practice fin. cons. Tempe, 1988—; chmn., pres., bd. dirs. Flexi Lease Ltd., Tempe, 1989—; chmn. Am. Tachyon Internat., Inc.; dir. Tiberia Internat., Ltd. Contbr. articles to profl. jours.; co-host radio show The Am. S.W. Found. Presents, 1988-89. Mem. adv. bd. Gov.'s Solid Waste Mgmt., Phoenix, 1987-88, Gov.'s Bd. Econ. Devel., 1987-88; mem. Mayor's Econ. Devel. Bd., Tempe, 1989; founding mem. Pres.'s Rep. Task Force, Washington, 1987—. Recipient Presdl. medal of merit Pres. of U.S.A. and Rep. Party, 1987. Fellow Am. S.W. Found. (sr.). Roman Catholic. Home and Office: 6815 S McClintock Dr # 1102 Tempe AZ 85283

FILIP, HENRY (HENRY PETRZILKA), physicist; b. Chgo., Mar. 29, 1920; s. Joseph and Aloisie (Filip) Petrzilka; m. Marie Louise Krajcovic, Sept. 17, 1957; children: Henry Jr., Frederick, Marie Louise; 1 stepchild, Jan Janecka. BS, Ill. Wesleyan U., 1944. Tech. asst. Fermi Pile, Manhattan Project U. Chgo., 1944; rsch. asst. atom bomb external trigger system Los Alamos (N.Mex.) Nat. Lab., 1944-49, rsch. asst. internal neutron source for atom bomb, 1949-56, exptl. researcher Rover program Flyable Nuclear Reactor, 1956-72, exptl. researcher isotope separation program, 1972-84, exptl. physicist x-ray analysis of atomic explosions, 1984-85; exptl. physicist Western Rsch. Corp., San Diego, 1985; exptl. physicist Star Wars Laser System Jan Bec Corp., San Diego, 1985-88; cons. x-ray analysis Los Alamos Nat. Lab., 1984-85, Western Rsch. Corp., San Diego, 1984-85. Mem. Pierottis Clowns. Mem. Palisade Lions (bd. mem. 1989-92), Los Alamos Rotary (pres. 1983-87), Los Alamos Kiwanis (hon.). Democrat. Home: 362 W 1st St PO Box 38 Palisade CO 81526

FILIPPUZZI, RICHARD ALAN, engineering executive, marketing professional; b. San Francisco, July 28, 1959; s. Albert Joeseph and Maryldean Elizabeth (Steiner) F.; m. Mary Vizzi. AS in Engring., Coll. San Mateo; postgrad., Cogswell coll.; emergency med. technician, Skyline Coll. Lic. EMT; cert. safety svc. instr. R&D designer Farinon Microwave, San Carlos, 1978-79; R&D designer, mem. emergency relief staff Varian Assocs., 1979-84; sr. R&D designer Medasonics, Mountain View, Calif., 1984-85; R&D design engr. Tri-Data Systems, Sunnyvale, Calif., 1985-88, corp. safety officer, 1985-88; devel. engr. Laser Photonics, Inc., Mountain View, 1988-89; sr. laser product engr. XMR, Inc., Santa Clara, Calif., 1989—; pres. Emeraude Scientific, Menlo Park, Calif., 1989—; mech. engr. Hine Design, Palo Alto, 1991—; instr. computers De Anza Coll., 1982-85. Instr. First-Aid, 1980-89, ARC, Palo Alto, San Mateo County Emergency Med. Scvs., 1980-87; emergency ambulance driver Mobile Life Support, Burlingame, 1981-87., mem. Calif. State Firefighters Assn. Recipient Commendation Millbrae Fire Dept, 1980, 5 Yr. Vol. Svc. ARC, Palo Alto, 1985. Mem. Laser Inst. Am., Internat. Soc. Optical Engring., Am. Mgmt. Assn., Stanford Alumni Assn. (life), Soc. Optical and Quantum Electronics, U.S. Capitol Hist. Soc., Calif. Profl. Engr. Soc. Office: Emeraude Sci 615 8th Ave Menlo Park CA 94025-1852

FILIPSKI, ALAN JAMES, computer scientist, educator; b. Detroit, Oct. 6, 1946; s. Stanley J. and Genevieve Filipski; m. Lois I. Carlson, June 13, 1970; children: Isaac, Anna. BS, Mich. State U., East Lansing, 1970, MS, 1971, PhD, 1976; PhD, Miskatonic U., 1989. Computer programmer Computer Inst. for Social Sci. Rsch., East Lansing, 1969-70; rsch. asst. Mich. State U., 1970-72; systems analyst Mich. State Housing Authority, Lansing, 1972-74; asst. prof. Cen. Mich. U., Mt. Pleasant, 1974-77; vis. asst. prof. Ariz. State U., Tempe, 1977-80; software specialist E-Systems, Garland, Tex., 1980-81; prin. engr. Motorola Corp., Tempe, 1981-86; mem. tech. staff GTX Corp., Phoenix, 1986—. Contbr. articles to profl. jours. Mem. Nat. Coalition Against Censorship, 1989, Phoenix Skeptics, 1989, Great Lakes Light House Keeper's Assn., 1989. NSF Rsch. grantee, 1977-79. Mem. AAAS (pres. Southwest and Rocky Mountain div.), Assn. for Computing Machinery, IEEE, Neural Network Soc., Kesterson Yacht Club, Phi Beta Kappa. Home: 648 W La Donna Dr Tempe AZ 85283-2723 Office: GTX Corp 8836 N 23rd Ave Phoenix AZ 85021

FILLER, GARY B., computer company executive. Chmn. bd., CEO Burke Industries; chmn. bd. Seagate Tech., Inc., 1991—. Office: Seagate Tech Inc 920 Disc Dr Bldg 1 Scotts Valley CA 95066

FILLERUP, MELVIN MCDONALD, artist; b. Lovell, Wyo., Jan. 28, 1924; s. Albert Frederick and Grace Stevenson (McDonald) F.; m. Ruth McNiven, Mar. 11, 1948; children: Selvoy, Melvin, Peter, James, Sharon, Karen, Mary Beth. JD, U. Wyo., 1952. Bar: Wyo. 1952. Lawyer Jones & Fillerup, Cody, Wyo., 1952-72; artist Cody, 1972—. Author: Sidon, 1988; artist: (paintings) Timber Wolves, Autumn on the Southfork, 1981, Crossing the Divide, 1982. Chmn. Am. Red Cross, Wyo., 1956-60, civil rights coms., Wyo., 1962-65. Maj. U.S. Army Res., 1942-60. Recipient Best of Show awards Audubon Soc., 1984, Western States Show, Cody, 1990, Silver medal Buffalo Bill Show, Cody, 1985, Peter Hassrick merit award Rondezvous of Art, Helena, Mont., 1992, Nick Eggenhoffer award CCAL Western States Show, Cody, 1992. Mem. Soc. Animal Artists, Am. Indian and Cowboy Artists (pres. 1982, Gold medal 1981, 82), Wyo. State Bar, Park County Bar Assn. (pres. 1963), Rotary (pres. Cody chpt. 1961). Republican. Mormon. Home: 2007 Kerper Blvd Cody WY 82414-4808 Office: PO Box 938 Cody WY 82414-0938

FILLEY, BETTE ELAINE, publisher, software company executive; b. Phila., June 4, 1933; d. Russell S. and Martha (Spayd) Riley; m. Laurence D. Filley, Oct. 23, 1954; children: Richard David, Barbara Nan Filley Hamilton, Patricia Lynn Filley Messenger, Kathryn Gwyn, Thomas John. Columnist, editor Johnstown (Ohio) Independent, 1957-60; illustrator, columnist Chgo. Sun-Times, 1959-60; publs. editor Sicks Rainier Brewing Co., Seattle, 1962-66; pub. Silent Majority Voice, Seattle, 1971-73; pres. The Name People, Issaquah, Wash., 1985—; freelance writer, editor Seattle, 1966—; caricature artist, various events, 1972—; pub. co. owner Dunamis House. Author: Discovering the Wonders of the Wonderland Trail Encircling Mount Rainier, 1992; assoc. editor Volcano Quar., 1992—, Llama Breeder. Bd. advisors Seattle Area World Relief. Mem. Wash. Press Women, Pacific Northwest Indsl. Editors, Am. Name Soc., Can. Soc. for Study of Names, Wash. Software Assn. Republican. Home and Office: The Name People 19801 SE 123d St Issaquah WA 98027

FILLEY, LAURENCE DUANE, computer programmer, consultant; b. Seattle, Apr. 17, 1932; s. Earnest Edgar and Pearl (Griggs) F.; m. Bette Elaine Riley, Oct. 23, 1954; children: Richard David, Barbara Nan Filley Hamilton, Patricia Lynn Filley Messenger, Kathryn Gwyn, Thomas John. Student, U.S. Naval Acad., 1955, Ohio State U., 1957-58. Template layout worker N.Am. Aviation, 1956-60; indsl. engr. Boeing Aircraft Co., 1960-66; numerical control programmer Boeing Co., Kent, Wash., 1966-84, 87—; pres. Dunamus Corp., Issaquah, Wash., 1984-88; owner Agape Llamas, Issaquah, 1965—; ski instr. Boeing Skibacs, 1980-88, Ullr Ski Sch., 1989—; climb leader Seattle Mountaineers, 1965—. Mem. Profl. Ski Instrs. Am. (cert.). Republican. Home: 19801 SE 123d St Issaquah WA 98027 Office: Boeing Co Kent WA 98031

FILLMORE, WILLIAM L., lawyer; m. Mary Rawson; six children. BA in English Lit. magna cum laude, Brigham Young U., 1972; JD, U. Chgo., 1976. Bar: Colo. 1976, U.S. Ct. Appeals (10th cir.) 1976, U.S. Supreme Ct. 1978, Utah 1980. Assoc. Holland & Hart, Denver, 1976-78; ptnr. Southam & Fillmore P.C., Colorado Springs, 1978-80, Olson & Hoggan, Logan, Utah, 1980-86; assoc. gen. counsel, asst. corp. sec. Brigham Young U., Provo, Utah, 1986-90; of counsel Provo (Utah) office Van Cott, Bagley, Cornwall & McCarthy, Salt Lake City, 1991—; instr. honors program Utah State U., 1982-84. Mem. platform com. Utah Reps., 1984; vice chmn. for Cache County (Utah) Rep. Com., 1983-86; White House intern, 1973. Hinckley scholar Brigham Young U., U. Chgo. Law Sch. scholar. Mem. ABA, Assn. Trial Lawyers Am., Nat. Assn. of Coll. and Univ. Lawyers, Brigham Young U. Alumni Assn. (bd. dirs. 1986-90), C. of C. Provo, Ut. (chmn., bd. dirs.), Mandel Legal Aid Soc., Phi Kappa Phi. Home: 4105 Devonshire Dr Provo UT 84604-5373 Office: Van Cott Bagley Cornwall & McCarthy 3549 N University Ave # 275 Provo UT 84604-4487

FILNER, BOB, congressman; b. 1943; m. Jane Merrill; children: Erin, Adam. BA in Chemistry, Cornell U.; MA in History, U. Del.; PhD in History, Cornell U. Prof. history San Diego State U., 1970—; legis. asst. Senator Hubert Humphrey, 1974, Congressman Don Fraser, 1975; spl. asst. Congressman Jim Bates, 1984; city councilman 8th dist. City of San Diego, 1987-93, dep. mayor, 1991; mem. 103rd Congress from 50th Calif. dist., 1993—. Pres. San Diego Bd. Edn., 1982, mem.-elect 1979-83; chmn. San Diego Schs. of the Future Commn., 1986-87. Democrat. Office: US House of Representatives Office of House Members Washington DC 20515

FILOSA, GARY FAIRMONT RANDOLPH V., II, publishing executive; b. Wilder, Vt., Feb. 22, 1931; s. Gary F.R. de Marco de Viana and Rosaline M. (Falzarano) Filosa; m. Catherine Moray Stewart; children: Marc Christian Bazire de Villadon, III, Gary Fairmont Randolph de Viana, III. Grad., Mt. Hermon Sch., 1950; PhB, U. Chgo., 1954; BA, U. Americas, Mex., 1967; MA, Calif. Western U., 1968; PhD, U.S. Internat. U., 1970. Sports reporter Claremont Daily Eagle, Rutland Herald, Vt. Informer, 1947-52; pub. The Chicagoan, 1952-54; account exec., editor house publs. Robertson, Buckley & Gotsch, Inc., Chgo., 1953-54; account exec. Fuller, Smith & Ross, Inc., N.Y.C., 1955; producer, host Weekend TV series, N.Y.C., 1955-57; editor Apparel Arts mag. (now Gentlemen's Quar.), Esquire, Inc., N.Y.C., 1955-56; prodr./host, Weekend KCET Channel 13, N.Y.C., 1956-57; pres., chmn. bd. Teenarama Records, Inc., N.Y.C., 1956-62; assoc. pub. Laundromatic Age, N.Y.C., 1958-59; pres., chmn. bd. Filosa Publs. Internat., N.Y.C., 1956-61, Los Angeles, 1974-83, Palm Beach, Fla., 1983-88; pres. Montclair Sch., 1958-60, Pacific Registry, Inc., Los Angeles, 1959-61, Banana Chip Corp. Am., N.Y.C., 1964-67; producer Desilu Studios, Inc., Hollywood, 1960-61; exec. asst. to Benjamin A. Javits, 1961-62; dean adminstrn. Postgrad. Ctr. for Mental Health, N.Y.C., 1962-64; chmn. bd., pres. Producciones Mexicanes Internationales (S.A.), Mexico City, 1957-68; chmn. bd., CEO Filosa Films Internat., Beverly Hills, 1962-83, 90-92; chmn. bd., pres. Filosa Films Internat., Palm Beach, Fla., 1984-93; Miami Beach, Fla., 1993—; pres. Casa Filosa Corp., Palm Beach, Fla., 1982-87; dir. tng. Community Savings, North Palm Beach, Fla., 1983-87; chmn. bd., pres. Cinematografica Americana Internationale (S.A.), Mexico City, 1964-74; pub. Teenage, Rustic Rhythm, Teen Life, Talent, Rock & Roll Roundup, Celebrities, Stardust, Personalities, Campus monthly mags., N.Y.C., 1955-61; v.p. acad. affairs World Acad., San Francisco, 1967-68; asst. to provost Calif. Western U., San Diego, 1968-69; assoc. prof. philosophy Art Coll., San Francisco, 1969-70; v.p. acad. affairs, dean of faculty Internat. Inst., Phoenix, 1968-73; chmn. bd., pres. Universite Universelle, 1970-73; bd. dirs., v.p. acad. affairs, dean Summer Sch., Internat. Community Coll., Los Angeles, 1970-72; chmn. bd., pres. Social Directory Calif., 1967-75, Am. Assn. Social Registries, Los Angeles, 1970-76; pres. Social Directory U.S., N.Y.C., 1974-76; chmn. bd. Internat. Assn. Social Registers, Paris, 1974—; surfing coach U. Calif. at Irvine, 1975-77; instr. history Coastline Community Coll., Fountain Valley, Calif., 1976-77; v.p. Xerox-Systemic, 1979-80; chief exec. officer Internat. Surfing League, Palm Beach, 1987—; pres., chief exec. officer Filosa Harrop Internat., Phoenix, 1987-89. Editor: Sci. Digest, 1961-62; author: (stage play) Let Me Call Ethel, 1955, Technology Enters 21st Century, 1966, (mus.) Feather Light, 1966, No Public Funds for Nonpublic Schools, 1968, Creative Function of the College President, 1969, The Surfers Almanac, 1977; (TV series) Surfing USA, 1977, Payne of Florida, 1985, Honolulu, 1991, The Gym, 1992, Sales Pitch, 1992, 810 Ocean Avenue, 1992, One Feather, 1992, The Filosa Newsletter, 1986-92, Conversations with America, 1989—, All American Beach Party, 1989—; contbr. numerous articles to profl. jours. and encys., including Sci. Digest, World Book Ency. Trustee Univ. of the Ams., 1986—; candidate for Los Angeles City Council, 1959; chmn. Educators for Reelection of Ivy Baker Priest, 1970; mem. So. Calif. Com. for Olympic Games, 1977-84. Served with AUS, 1954-55. Recipient DAR Citizenship award, 1959; Silver Conquistador award Am. Assn. Social Registers, 1970; Ambassador's Cup U. Ams., 1967; resolution Calif. State Legislature, 1977; Duke Kahanamoku Classic surfing trophy, 1977; gold pendant Japan Surfing Assn., 1978. Mem. NAACP, NCAA (bd. dels. 1977-82), AAU (gov. 1978-82), Am. Surfing Assn. (founder, pres. 1960-92), Internat. Surfing Counder, pres. 1960—), U.S. Surfing Com. (founder, pres. 1960—), Internat. Surfing League (founder, pres. 1988—), Am. Walking Soc. (founder, pres. 1980-92), Internat. Walking Soc. (founder, pres. 1987-93), Am. Assn. UN, Author's League, Alumni Assn. U. Ams. (pres. 1967-70), Sierra Club, Sigma Omicron Lambda (founder, pres. 1965-92). Episcopalian. Address: PO Box 5921 Miami Beach FL 33154 Office: PO Box 299 Beverly Hills CA 90213

FILZ, CHARLES JOSEPH, engineer, inventor; b. Hood River, Oreg., June 1925; s. William Joseph and Katherine Anna (Fischer) F.; m. Colleen Doughty, 1948 (div. 1973); children: John, Judy, Timothy; m. Norita Clark, 1974. BS in Mfg. Engring., Oreg. State U., 1948. Head of physics shops Oreg. State U., Corvallis, 1950-59; chief of R & D Sorvall, Newtown, Conn., 1959-70; head rsch. Sorvall, Hamilton, Mont., 1970-79; pres. Filz & Assocs., Corvallis, 1974-84, Yachats, Oreg., 1984—; R & D cons. Filz & Assocs., Yachats, 1974—. Contbr. articles to profl. jours. Recipient Master Design award Product Engring. Mag., 1968. Mem. Yachats Lions (bd. dirs. 1992-93). Democrat. Roman Catholic. Home: 95136 Hwy 101 Box 330 Yachats OR 97498

FINAN, ELLEN CRANSTON, English language educator, consultant; b. Worcester, Mass., June 26, 1951; d. Thomas Matthew and Maureen Ann (Moulton) F. BA, U. San Francisco, 1973; MA, U. Calif., Riverside, 1978. ESL specialist U.S. Peace Corps, Finote Selam, Ethiopia, 1974-75; English instr. U. Redlands, Calif., 1977-79; mentor tchr. Jurupa Unified Sch. Dist., Riverside, 1979—; tech. writer Callan Assocs., San Francisco, 1973-74, Wilshire Assocs., Santa Monica, Calif., 1976-77; English instr. U. Pa., Phila., 1979; writing cons. Inland Area Writing Project U. Calif., Riverside, 1980—; tchr., coordinator U. Calif., Riverside, 1982. Author: Prickley Pear, 1981, CAP Attack Handbook, 1987. NEH fellow, 1992; Squaw Valley Community of Writers scholar, 1981, Carnegie Mellon fellow, 1987, NEH Inst. fellow, 1993. Mem. Nat. Council English Tchrs., Assn. Supervision and Curriculum Devel., Alpha Sigma Nu, Phi Delta Kappa. Democrat. Home: 22440 Mountain View Rd Moreno Valley CA 92557-2655 Office: Jurupa Unified Schs 4250 Opal St Riverside CA 92509-7298

FINCH, CALEB ELLICOTT, neurobiologist, educator; b. London, July 4, 1939; came to U.S., 1939; s. Benjamin F. and Faith (Stratton) Campbell; m. Doris Nossamen, Oct. 11, 1975; stepsons: Michael, Alec Tsongas. B.S., Yale U., 1961; Ph.D., Rockefeller U., 1969. Guest investigator Rockefeller U., N.Y.C., 1969-70; asst. prof. Cornell U. Med. Coll., N.Y.C., 1970-72; asst. prof. biology, gerontology U. So. Calif., L.A., 1972-75, assoc. prof., 1975-78, prof., 1978—, ARCO and William Kieschnick prof. neurobiology of aging, 1985—, Univ. prof., 1989—; mem. cell biology study sect. NIH, Bethesda, Md., 1975-78; prin. investigator co-dir. Alzheimer Disease Rsch. Ctr. So. Calif., 1984—; mem. sci. adv. coun. Nat. Inst. Aging, 1987-90; sci. adv. bd. NIH, 1987-90, MacArthur Found. Program on Successful Aging, 1984—; Bennett Cohen lectr. U. Mich., 1993. Author: Longevity, Senescence and the Genome, 1990; editor: Handbook of Biology of Aging, 1977, 85; mem. editorial bd. Jour. Gerontology, 1979-86, Neurobiology of Aging, 1982—, Mech. Aging Devel., 1973—, Synapse, 1992—; contbr. over 250 articles to profl. jours. Recipient Brookdale award 1985, Allied-Signal Inc. award Achievement in Biomed. Aging, 1988, Rsch. award Alzheimer's Assn. L.A., 1989, Cherkin award UCLA, 1991; named Bennet Cohen Meml. Lectr., U. Mich., 1993; postdoctoral fellow, 1969-71; NIH rsch. grantee, 1972—. Fellow AAAS, Gerontol Soc. Am. (chmn. biology sect. 1992-93, Robert W. Kleemeier award 1984); mem. Neurosci. Soc., Endocrine Soc., Neuroendocrine Soc., Psychoneuroendocrine Soc., Iron Mountain STring Band (fiddler 1963—). Home: 2144 Crescent Dr Altadena CA 91001-2112 Office: U So Calif Gerontology Ctr University Park Los Angeles CA 90089-0191

FINCH, FLORA, cosmetologist, educator; b. L.A., Mar. 1, 1947; d. Albert L. and Katie (Salazar) Chavez; m. Jim D. Finch, July 4, 1968; children: Rick, Michael. Cert., Phoenix Acad., 1966; AA, Northland Pioneer Coll., 1985. Hairdresser San Carlos Beuty Salon, Phoenix, 1966-68; hair designer Plaza Three, Phoenix, 1968-69, Good Samaritan Hosp., Phoenix, 1969-70; owner, operator Caravan Beauty, Phoenix, 1971-77, Hair & Nails Naturally, Phoenix, 1974-78; instr. Phoenix Acad., 1979-82, Western Sch. of Beauty, Glendale, Ariz., 1982-83; instr., coord. Northland Pioneer Coll., Showlow and Winslow, Ariz., 1984—; coord. Northland Pioneer Coll. Hair Affair Competition, Showlow and Winslow, 1984-90; ann. speaker Bus. and Profl. Womens of Am., Showlow, 1985-88. Coord. Hands Across Am. Cut-A-Thon, Winslow, 1985. Mem. Nat. Hairdressers Assn., Bus. and Profl. Women, C. of C. (v.p. 1973). Home: PO Box 925 Saint Johns AZ 85936-0925 Office: Northland Pioneer Coll PO Box 610 Holbrook AZ 86025-0610

FINCH, THOMAS WESLEY, corrosion engineer; b. Alhambra, Calif., Dec. 17, 1946; s. Charles Phillip and Marian Louisa (Bushey) F.; m. Jinx L. Heath, Apr. 1979. Student Colo. Sch. Mines, 1964-68. Assayer, prospector Raymond P. Heon, Inc., Idaho Springs, Colo., 1968; corrosion engr. Cathodic Protection Service, Denver, 1973-80, area mgr., Lafayette, La., 1980-81; area mgr. Corrintec/USA, Farmington, N.Mex., 1981-83; dist. mgr. Cathodic Protection Services Co., Farmington, 1983—. Served with C.E., U.S. Army, 1968-72. Mem. Nat. Assn. Corrosion Engrs., Soc. Am. Mil. Engrs., U.S. Ski Assn., Am. Security Council (nat. adv. bd. 1978—), Kappa Sigma. Republican. Lutheran. Home: 1710 E 22nd St Farmington NM 87401 Office: PO Box 388 Farmington NM 87499-0388

FINCH, WARREN IRVIN, geologist; b. Union County, S.D., Oct. 27, 1924; s. Julius Irvin and Dorothy (Hedden) F.; m. Mary Margaret Theisen, Sept. 1, 1951; children: Lawrence, Carolanne, Andrew. BS in Geol. Engring., S.D. Sch. Mines, 1948; MS in Geology, U. Calif.-Berkeley, 1954; postgrad. Colo. Sch. Mines, 1958. Supervisory rsch. geologist U.S. Geol. Survey, Denver, 1972-77; project leader geology working groups Internat. Atomic Energy Agy., Vienna, Austria, 1979-89, mission to Indonesia, 1988, China, 1990; U.S. rep. Nuclear Energy Agy OECD Com., Paris, 1983—. Author: Geology of Epigenetic Uranium Deposits in Sandstone Formations in the United States, 1967, Stratigraphy, Morphology, and Paleontology of Fossil Peccary Herd from Western Kentucky, 1972, others; contbr. articles to profl. jours. Bd. dirs. Mountain Bicyclist Assn., Inc., Denver, 1980-86; scoutmaster Boy Scouts Am., Lakewood, Colo., 1975; geologic advisor William Clark Market House Mus., Paducah, Ky., 1967-69. Served with U.S. Army, 1944-46. Recipient Meritorious Svc. award Dept. Interior, 1981, Unit Excellence of Svc. award Dept. Interior, 1982. Fellow Geol. Soc. Am.(mem. hdqrs. adv. com., 1986-88), Soc. Econ. Geologists (short course com. 1990—); mem. AAAS, Internat. Assn. on Genesis of Ore Deposits,), Colo. Scietific Soc., Denver Regional Exploration Geologists Soc. Roman Catholic. Clubs: Bicycle Racing Assocs Colo. (pres. 1977-79), Denver Field Ornithologists (pres.

1982-83). Lodge: KC (dep. grand knight 1960-61). Home: 455 Dover St Lakewood CO 80226-1147 Office: US Geol Survey MS 939 PO Box 25046 Denver CO 80225-0046

FINCK, KEVIN WILLIAM, lawyer; b. Whittier, Calif., Dec. 14, 1954; s. William Albert and Ester (Gutbub) F.; m. Kathleen A. Miller, Oct. 7, 1989. BA in History, U. Calif., Santa Barbara, 1977; JD, U. Calif., San Francisco, 1980. Bar: Calif. 1980. Assoc. Law Offices of E.O.C. Ord, San Francisco, 1980-85; ptnr. Ord & Finck, San Francisco, 1985-87, Ord and Norman, San Francisco, 1987-88; pvt. practice San Francisco, 1989—; lectr. Internat. Bar Assn., Buenos Aires, 1988, N.Y., 1990, Learning Annex, 1992-93. Author: California Corporation Start Up Package and Minute Book, 1982, 7th edit., 1992; contbr. articles to various profl. jours. Republican Methodist. Office: 601 Montgomery St Ste 1900 San Francisco CA 94111-2668

FINDLAY, DAVID W., financial management consultant; b. Seattle, Mar. 4, 1946; s. Abbot and Dorothy E. (Findlay) Wilcox; m. Linda T. Porter, Feb. 27, 1972; children: Matt, Dawn, Kerry, Ann Marie. BA, U. Wash., 1971. Cert. mgmt. cons.; CPA, Wash. Asst. credit mgr. Fairway Fin., Seattle, 1965-66; credit, data processing, contr. Doces 6th Avenue, Seattle, 1966-71; pub. acct./fin. cons. Arthur Young & Co., Seattle, 1971-81; sr. v.p. URS Cons., Seattle, 1981-88; pres., founder FCS Group, Redmond, Wash., 1988—. Mem. Sewer & Water Assn., Redmond, 1989—; audit com. Greater Seattle YMCA, 1984—. Mem. AICPA, Wash. Soc. CPAs, Inst. Bus. Appraisers, Inst. Mgmt. Cons. (pres. 1988), Wash. Athletic Club. Republican. Lutheran. Office: 15446 Bel Red Rd # 380 Redmond WA 98052-5507

FINDLER, NICHOLAS VICTOR, research computer science educator; b. Budapest, Hungary, Nov. 24, 1930; came to U.S., 1963; s. Otto and Aranka (Hirschkovitz) F.; m. Catherine Ellenbogen, Mar. 5, 1955; children: Marianne N., Michèle C. BE summa cum laude, Budapest U. Tech. Scis., 1953, PhD in Math, Physics, 1956. Research scientist Carnegie Inst. Tech., Pitts., 1963-64; research assoc. U. Pitts., various univs. in U.S.A., Australia and Europe, 1964; assoc. prof. computer sci. U. Ky., Lexington, 1964-66; prof. SUNY, Buffalo, 1966-82; vis. prof., Sr. Fulbright Scholar Tech. U., Vienna, Austria, 1972-73, U. Amsterdam, Free U. of Amsterdam, Holland, 1979-80; vis. scientist Europe Advanced Studies Inst., NATO, Brussels, 1979-80; research prof., dir. artificial intelligence lab. Ariz. State U., Tempe, 1982—; vis. prof., sr. Fulbright scholar Free U., U. Amsterdam, The Netherlands, 1979-80; vis. prof. Inst Computer Sci. U. Zurich; mem. staff applied math. The C.S.R. Co. Ltd., Sydney, Australia, 1959-63; participant summer inst. Rand Corp., Santa Monica, Calif., 1963, cons., 1981; cons. AFHRL, Phoenix, 1985. Author several books; contbr. numerous articles to profl. jours., chpts. to books. Sr. Fulbright scholar Hungarian Acad. Scis.; recipient Centennial award of Merit Office of Pres. Ariz. State U., 1986, medal of Merit Rector U. Helsinki, Finland, 1980. Fellow Brit. Computer Soc.; mem. Assn. Computing Machinery (doctoral dissertation awards com. 1983—, Recognition of Service award 1986), IEEE (sr. mem.), Assn. Computational Linguistics, Cognitive Sci. Soc., others. Democrat. Jewish. Office: Ariz State U Dept Computer Sci Tempe AZ 85258

FINE, RICHARD ISAAC, lawyer; b. Milw., Jan. 22, 1940; s. Jack and Frieda F.; m. Maryellen Olman, Nov. 25, 1982; 1 child, Victoria Elizabeth. B.S., U. Wis., 1961; J.D., U. Chgo., 1964; Ph.D. in Internat. Law, U. London, 1967; cert., Hague (Netherlands) Acad. Internat. Law, 1965, 66; cert. comparative law, Internat. U. Comparative Sci., Luxembourg, 1966; diplome superiere, Faculte Internat. pour l'Enseignment du Droit Compare, Strassbourg, France, 1967. Bar: Ill. 1964, D.C. 1972, Calif. 1973. Trial atty. fgn. commerce sect. antitrust div. U.S. Dept. Justice, 1968-72; chief antitrust div. Los Angeles City Atty.'s Office, also spl. counsel gov. efficiency com., 1973-74; prof. internat., comparative and EEC antitrust law U. Syracuse (N.Y.) Law Sch. (overseas program), summers 1970-72; individual practice Richard I. Fine and Assocs., Los Angeles, 1974; mem. antitrust adv. bd. Bur. Nat. Affairs, 1981—; chmn. L.A. adv. com. London Sch. Econs., 1992—; mem. vis. com. U. Chgo. Law Sch., 1992. Contbr. articles to legal publs. Mem. ABA (chmn. subcom. internat. antitrust and trade regulations, internat. law sect. 1972-77, co-chmn. com. internat. econ. orgn. 1977-79), Am. Soc. Internat. Law (co-chmn. com. corp. membership 1978-83, mem. exec. council 1984-87, budget com. 1992—), Am. Fgn. Law Assn., Fed. Bar Assn., Internat. Law Assn., Brit. Inst. Internat. and Comparative Law, Am. Trial Lawyers Assn., State Bar Calif. (chmn. antitrust and trade regulation law sect. 1981-84, exec. com. 1981-87), Retinitis Pigmentosa Internat. (bd. dirs. 1985-90), Los Angeles County Bar Assn. (chmn. antitrust sect. 1977-78), Ill. Bar Assn., Am. Friends London Sch. Econs. (bd. dirs. 1984—, co-chmn. So. Calif. chpt. 1984—), Phi Delta Phi. Office: 10100 Santa Monica Blvd Los Angeles CA 90067-4015

FINESILVER, SHERMAN GLENN, federal judge; b. Denver, Oct. 1, 1927; s. Harry M. and Rebecca M. (Balaban) F.; m. Annette Warren, July 23, 1954; children: Jay Mark, Steven Brad, Susan Saunders. BA, U. Colo., 1949; LLB, U. Denver, 1952; cert., Northwestern U. Traffic Inst., 1956; LLD (hon.), Gallaudet Coll., Washington, 1970, Met. State Coll., Denver, 1981, N.Y. Law Sch., N.Y.C., 1983, U. Colo., 1988. Bar: Colo. 1952, U.S. Ct. of Appeals (10th cir.) 1952, U.S. Supreme Ct. 1952. Legal asst. Denver City Atty.'s Office, 1949-52; asst. Denver city atty., 1952-55; judge Denver County Ct., 1955-62; judge Denver Dist. Ct., 2d Jud. Dist., 1962-71, presiding judge domestic relations div., 1963, 67, 68; judge U.S. Dist. Ct., Denver, from 1971, elevated to chief judge, 1982; adj. prof. U. Denver Coll. Law and Arts and Sci. Sch., 1955—, Met. State Coll., 1989—; mem. faculty Nat. Coll. Judiciary, Reno, 1967-84, Atty. Gen.'s Advocacy Inst., Washington, 1974—, seminars for new fed. judges, 1974—; elected to Jud. Conf. U.S., 1985-88; mem. Jud. Conf. Com. on Rules for Admission to Practice in Fed. Cts., 1976-79, Com. on Adminstrn. Probation System, 1983-87, Adv. Com. on Criminal Rules, 1984-87, Com. on Bicentennial of Constn., 1985-87, Com. on Criminal Law and Probation Adminstrn., 1988—. Contbr. chpt. to Epilepsy Rehabilitation, 1974, articles and publs. on law, medicine, legal rights of deaf, aging, physically impaired, and many others, 1974-88. Mem. task force White House Conf. on Aging, 1972, presdl. commn., 1980-84; mem. Probation Com., U.S. Cts., 1985-88, Nat. Com. to Study Qualifications to Practice in Fed. Cts., 1976-82, bd. visitors Brigham Young U., 1977-80, Nat. Commn. Against Drunk Driving, 1982-86. Decorated Inspector Gen. 33d degree; recipient numerous awards including medallion for outstanding service by a non-handicapped person to physically disabled Nat. Paraplegia Found., 1972, cert. of commendation Sec. Transp., 1974, Norlin award for outstanding alumni U. Colo., 1988, numerous others. Hon. fellow Am. Coll. Legal Medicine (Chgo.); mem. ABA (nat. chmn. Am. citizenship com. 1968, award of merit Law Day 1968), Colo. Bar Assn. (chmn. Law Day 1964, chmn. Am. citizenship com. 1963, bd. govs. 1982—), Denver Bar Assn. (chmn. Law Day 1964), Am. Judicature Soc., Am. Amateur Radio, B'nai B'rith, Masons, Shriners, Phi Sigma Delta (trustee 1960-66, Nat. Man of Yr. Zeta Beta Tau chpt. 1989). Office: US Dist Ct 1929 Stout St Rm 224C Denver CO 80294-2900*

FINE-THOMAS, WENDY ROBIN, therapist, educator; b. Urbana, Ohio, Dec. 24, 1966; d. James Everett Fine and Julie Orrick (Stewart) Dennison; m. Jeffrey Alan Thomas, Mar. 23, 1991. BS magna cum laude, Santa Clara U., 1989; postgrad., Fuller Grad. Sch. Psychology, 1989—; MA in Theology, Fuller Theol. Sem., 1993. Clin. trainee Inter-Community Alternatives Network, Pasadena, Calif., 1991-92; clinician Rodiger Ctr., Pasadena, 1991-92; teaching asst. Fuller Grad. Sch. Psychology, Pasadena, 1992—; psychol. asst. Life Counseling, Monrovia, Calif., 1992—. Crisis pregnancy counselor Heritage Home, San Jose, Calif., 1988-89; vol. Julian St. Inn, San Jose, 1989. Mem. APA (Div. 35-Psychology of Women), Western Psychol. Assn., Pasadena Area Psychol. Assn., Christian Assn. Psychol. Studies, Assn. for Advancement Psychology, Alpha Sigma Nu, Psi Chi. Presbyterian. Office: 248 E Foothill Blvd Monrovia CA 91016

FINK, HAROLD KENNETH, retired psychotherapist, technical writer; b. East Orange, N.J., Oct. 15, 1916; s. Colin Garfield and Lottie (Muller) F.; m. Sue Evans Carrico Fox, July 2, 1977; 1 stepchild, Burke Fox. A.B., Princeton U., 1938; M.S., Calif. Inst. Tech., 1941; Ph.D., Cornell U., 1943; postgrad. William White Inst. Psychiatry, N.Y.C., 1946-47, Postgrad. Ctr. for Mental Health, N.Y.C., 1948-50. Lic. clin. psychologist. Pvt. practice, N.Y.C., 1946-50, 53-57, La Jolla, Calif., 1951-53, Ft. Lauderdale, Fla., 1957-62; prof., chmn. dept. psychology, guidance dir. Ft. Lauderdale Coll., 1967-71, dean, 1971-73; asst. dir. Phoenix Club Half-way House, Ft. Lauderdale, 1972-73; clin. psychologist forensic service So. Fla. State Hosp. Hollywood, Fla., 1974-75; pvt. practice Plantation, Fla., 1977-82; intake clin. psychologist Hawaii State Hosp., Kaneohe, 1982-84; pvt. practice Honolulu, 1983-84, Kihei, Maui, 1984-89, ret., 1989; intake clin. psychologist Maui Community Mental Health Ctr., Kahului, 1985; instr. psychology adult edn. div. Broward County Sch. Bd., Ft. Lauderdale, Fla., 1960-82; instr. sr. citizens outreach program Broward Community Coll., Ft. Lauderdale, 1979-81; test examiner and evaluator sheltered workshop Mental Health Rehab. Found., Ft. Lauderdale, 1982. Author: Long Journey, 1954, Mind and Performance, 1954. Contbr. over 150 articles to prof. jours. Served to lt. j.g. USNR, 1943-45. Mem. Am. Psychol. Assn. (life), Hawaii Psychol. Assn. (life), N.Y. Acad. Scis. (life mem. psychol. div.), Insts. Religion and Health (charter life mem.), Ft. Lauderdale Acad. of Scis. (charter life mem. and founding mem.), Hawaii Psychol. Assn. (life, sec. pvt. practice com. 1983-84). Democrat. Home and Office: 6025 NW 100th Way Pompano Beach FL 33076

FINK, JAMES BREWSTER, geophysicist, consultant; b. Los Angeles, Jan. 12, 1943; s. Odra J. and Gertrude (Sloot) F. BS in Geophysics and Geochemistry, U. Ariz., 1969; MS in Geophysics cum laude, U. Witwatersrand, Johannesburg, Transvaal, Republic of South Africa, 1980; PhD in Geol. Engring., Geohydrology, U. Ariz, 1989. Registered profl. engr., Ariz., N.Mex.; registered land surveyor, Ariz.; registered profl. geologist, Wyo.; cert. environ. inspector. Geophysicist Geo-Comp Exploration, Inc., Tucson, 1969-70; geophys. cons. IFEX-Geotechnica, S.A., Hermosillo, Sonora, Mex., 1970; chief geophysicist Mining Geophys. Surveys, Tucson, 1971-72; research asst. U. Ariz., Tucson, 1973; cons. geophysics Tucson, 1974-76; sr. minerals geophysicist Esso Minerals Africa, Inc., Johannesburg, 1976-79; sr. research geophysicist Exxon Prodn. Research Co., Houston, 1979-80; pres. Geophynque Internat., Tucson, 1980-90, hydroGeophysics, Tucson, 1990—; cons. on NSF research U. Ariz., 1984-85, adj. lectr. geol. engring., 1985-86, assoc. instr. geophysics, 1986-87, supr. geophysicist, geohydrologist, 1986-88, bd. dirs. Lab. Advanced Subsurface Imaging, 1986—; v.p. R&D Alternative Energy Engring., Inc., Tucson, 1992—; lectr. South African Atomic Energy Bd., Pelindaba, 1979. Contbr. articles to profl. jours. Served as sgt. U.S. Air NG, 1965-70. Named Airman of Yr., U.S. Air NG, 1967. Mem. Soc. Exploration Geophysicists (co-chair internat. meetings 1980, 81, sr. editor monograph 1990, reviewer), Am. Geophys. Union, European Assn. Exploration Geophysicists, South African Geophys. Assn., Assn. Ground Water Scientists, Nat. Water Well Assn. (reviewer), Mineral and Geotech. Explorationists, Ariz. Geol. Soc., Ariz. Computer-Oriented Geol. Soc. (bd. dirs., v.p.), Soc. Engring. and Minerals Exploration Geophysicists. Republican. Home and Office: Hydrogeophysics 5865 S Old Spanish Trl Tucson AZ 85747-9487

FINK, ROBERT MORGAN, biological chemistry educator; b. Greenville, Ill., Sept. 22, 1915; s. William Harvey and Pearl (Smith) F.; m. Kathryn L. Ferguson, Jan. 6, 1941; children—Patricia Kay, Suzanne Joyce. Student, Kans. State Coll., 1933-35; A.B., U. Ill., 1937; postgrad., Lehigh U., 1937-38; Ph.D., U. Rochester, 1942. Mem. faculty UCLA, 1947—, prof. biol. chemistry, 1963-78, prof. emeritus, 1978—; research biochemist VA, 1947-54; Mem. subcom. on internal dose, nat. com. radiation protection Nat. Bur. Standards, 1947-49. Author: Biological Studies with Polonium, Radium and Plutonium, 1950. Mem. Am. Soc. Biol. Chemists. Home: 17774 Tramonto Dr Pacific Palisades CA 90272-3131

FINK, ROBERT RUSSELL, music theorist, university dean; b. Belding, Mich., Jan. 31, 1933; s. Russell Foster and Frances (Thornton) F.; m. Ruth Joan Bauerle, June 19, 1955; children: Denise Lyn, Daniel Robert. B.Mus., Mich. State U., 1955, M.Mus., 1956, Ph.D., 1965. Instr. music SUNY, Fredonia, 1956-57; instr. Western Mich. U., Kalamazoo, 1957-62, asst. prof., 1962-66, assoc. prof., 1966-71, prof., 1971-78, chmn. dept. music, 1972-78; dean Coll. Music U. Colo., Boulder, 1978-93; prin. horn Kalamazoo Symphony Orch., 1957-67; accreditation examiner Nat. Assn. Schs. Music, Reston, Va., 1973-92, grad. commr., 1981-89, chmn. grad. commn., 1987-89, assoc. chmn. accreditation commn., 1990-91, chmn., 1992. Author: Directory of Michigan Composers, 1972, The Language of 20th Century Music, 1975; composer: Modal Suite, 1959, Four Modes for Winds, 1967, Songs for High School Chorus, 1967; contbr. articles to profl. jours. Bd. dirs. Kalamazoo Symnphony Orch., 1974-78, Boulder Bach Festival, 1983-90. Mem. Coll. Music Soc., Soc. Music Theory, Mich. Orch. Assn. (pres.), Phi Mu Alpha Sinfonia (province gov.), Pi Kappa Lambda. Home: 643 Furman Way Boulder CO 80303-5614 Office: U Colo U Colo Boulder CO 80309

FINK, SAMUEL IRA, internist; b. L.A., Nov. 15, 1957; s. Irving Albert and Lois Jean (Goldstein) F.; m. Beloria Brunelle, June 8, 1986; children: Jonathan, Zachary. BA cum laude, Pomona Coll., Claremont, Calif., 1979; MD, U. Tex. Med. Br., Galveston, 1984. Diplomate Am. Bd. Internal. Medicine. Resident in internal medicine Huntington Meml. Hosp.-U. So. Calif. Affiliated Program, Pasadena, 1984-87; fellow in endocrinology, clin. instr. in medicine Los Angeles County/U. So. Calif. Med. Ctr., L.A., 1987-88; practice internal medicine Tarzana, Calif., 1988—; mem. staff AMI Tarzana Regional Med. Ctr., 1988—, Encino (Calif.) Hosp., 1988—; med. cons., AIDS-Link advisor Critical Care Am. Contbr. articles to profl. jours. Achievement Rewards for Coll. Scientists Found. scholar, 1979; Pomona Coll. scholar, 1977-79. Fellow ACP; mem. ACP, AMA, Calif. Med. Assn. (ho. of dels., bd. dirs., mem. ethics and grievancecom.), Los Angeles County Med. Assn. (chmn. task force on quality membership standards, councilor, bd. dirs., pres.-elect), Phi Chi. Office: 5525 Etiwanda Ave Ste 222 Tarzana CA 91356

FINK, STUART HOWARD, accountant; b. N.Y.C., Dec. 13, 1948; s. Arthur Milton and Mollie (Wrubel) F.; m. Robin Heather Heacock, Aug. 25, 1984; children: Laura, Allison. BA, Queens Coll., 1970; MBA, U. Rochester, 1972, Golden Gate U., 1986. CPA. Sr. acct. Brout and Co., N.Y.C., 1972-78; audit rev. mgr. Alexander Grant & Co., San Francisco, 1978-82; acctg. tax mgr. Jones, Schiller & Co., San Francisco, 1982-92; pvt. practice Castro Valley, Calif., 1992—. Pres. Stonegate Terrace Homeowners Assn., San Francisco, 1983-84; com. mem. Jewish Community Fedn. Young Adults, San Francisco, 1980-82; vol. San Francisco Fair, 1983, 85, March of Dimes, San Francisco, 1984. Mem. AICPA, Calif. Soc. CPAs (coop. credit grantors com.), Castro Valley Lions Breakfast Club (bull. editor 1990—, pres. 1991-92). Democrat. Home and Office: 19715 Michaels Ct Castro Valley CA 94546-4012

FINK, TOM, mayor; m. Pat Israelson; 11 children. BS, Bradley U., 1950; JD, U. Ill., 1952. CLU. Pvt. practice ins. brokerage Anchorage, 1958—; mem., speaker Alaska Ho. of Reps., 1966-75; mayor Municipality of Anchorage, 1988—. Office: Office of Mayor 632 W 6th Ave Rm 812 Anchorage AK 99501-2260

FINKBEINER, DEAN ELDEN, real estate appraiser; b. Detroit, Mar. 3, 1936; s. Leonard Howard and Wanda (Tuholke) F.; m. Raquel Gonzales, Apr. 20, 1963; children: Krista Ann, Dean Eric. BS, U. Mich., 1958; BA, U. Ariz., 1959. Lic. sr. real estate appraiser. Ins. adjuster GAB Bus. Svcs., Douglas, Ariz., 1961-62, Las Vegas, Nev., 1962-64; mgr. GAB Bus. Svcs., Kingman, Ariz., 1964-70; supr. GAB Bus. Svcs., Sacramento, Calif., 1970-73; mgr. GAB Bus. Svcs., Kingman, Ariz., 1973-78; real estate appraiser Kingman, 1978—. Bd. mem. Mohave Community Coll., Kingman, Ariz., 1978—; bd. mem., pres. Ariz. Assn. Dist. Gov. Bds., Phoenix, 1991—. Republican. Lutheran. Office: 704 E Beale St Kingman AZ 86401

FINKELSTEIN, JAMES ARTHUR, management consultant; b. N.Y.C., Dec. 6, 1952; s. Harold Nathan and Lilyan (Crystal) F.; m. Lynn Marie Gould, Mar. 24, 1984; children: Matthew, Brett. BA, Trinity Coll., Hartford, Conn., 1974; MBA, U. Pa., 1976. Cons. Towers, Perrin, Forster & Crosby, Boston, 1976-78; mgr. compensation Pepsi-Cola Co., Purchase, N.Y., 1978-80; mgr. employee info. systems Am. Can. Co., Greenwich, Conn., 1980; mgr. bus. analysis Emery Airfreight, Wilton, Conn., 1980-81; v.p. Meidinger, Inc., Balt., 1981-83; prin. The Wyatt Co., San Diego, 1983-88; pres., chief exec. officer W. F. Corroon, San Francisco, 1988—; mem. regional adv. bd. Mchts. and Mfrs. Assn., San Diego, 1986-88; instr. U. Calif., San Diego, 1984-88. Mem. camp com. State YMCA of Mass. and R.I., Framingham, 1982—; pres. Torrey Pines Child Care Consortium, La Jolla, Calif., 1987-88; vice chmn. La Jolla YMCA, 1986-88; bd. dirs. YMCA, San Francisco, 1988—, treas., chmn. fin. and audit com., 1992—; bd. dirs. San Domenico Sch. Found., 1992—. Home: 17 Bracken Ct San Rafael CA 94901-1587 Office: W F Corroon 50 Fremont St Fl 24 San Francisco CA 94105-2230

FINLAYSON-PITTS, BARBARA JEAN, chemistry educator; b. Ottawa, Ont., Can., Apr. 4, 1948; d. James Colin and Jean Burwell (Moore) Finlayson; m. James N. Pitts Jr., May 27, 1976. BSc (Hons.) in Chemistry, Trent U., Ont., Can., 1970; MS in Chemistry, U. Calif., Riverside, 1971, PhD in Chemistry, 1973. Rsch. asst., then postdoctoral rsch. chemist U. Calif., Riverside, 1970-74; asst. prof. chemistry Calif. State U., Fullerton, 1974-77, assoc. prof., 1977-81, prof. chemistry, 1981—; mem. grants rev. panel EPA, 1980-86; mem. adv. bd. series on photochemistry and photophysics CRC Press, 1986—; mem. editorial bd. Revista Internacional de Contaminacion Ambientel; mem. com. on tropospheric ozone NAS, 1989-91, com. atmospheric chemistry, 1989-92; mem. awards program adv. com. Rsch. Corp., 1993—. Author: Atmospheric Chemistry: Fundamentals and Experimental Techniques, 1986; contbr. numerous articles to refereed jours. Mem. AAAS, Am. Chem. Soc., Am. Geophys. Union, Am. Women in Sci., Iota Sigma Pi. Episcopalian. Office: Calif State U Fullerton Dept Chemistry Fullerton CA 92634

FINLEY, JAMES DANIEL, physics educator; b. Louisville, Aug. 2, 1941; s. James Daniel and Lucile (Carter) F.; m. Nancy Carlisle Newton (div. 1982); children: Ian Brendan, Moira Lynn. BA in Math., BS in Physics, U. Tex., 1963; PhD in Physics, U. Calif., Berkeley, 1968. Rsch. scientist Tracor Inc., Austin, Tex., 1962-63; teaching/rsch. asst. U. Calif., Berkeley, 1963-68; asst. prof. physics U. N.Mex., Albuquerque, 1968-73; assoc. prof. physics U. N.Mex., 1973-78, prof. physics, 1978—, chmn. dept. physics, 1985-92; vis. prof. Centro de Inv. y Est. Avanz. del IPN, Mexico City, 1975, 82; vis. prof. U. Canterbury, Christchurch, New Zealand, 1990. Contbr. articles to profl. jours., chpts. to books. Mem. Am. Phys. Soc., Cactus and Succulent Soc. Am., Phi Beta Kappa, Sigma Xi. Office: U NMex Dept Physics and Astronomy Albuquerque NM 87131

FINLEY, JUDITH REID, librarian; b. Colorado Springs, Colo., Mar. 11, 1936; d. James Juan and Margaret (Killian) R.; m. David Dewees Finley, Dec. 28, 1959; children: Bruce B., Karen K., Laura M. BA, Colo. Coll., 1958, MA, 1966. Teaching asst. French Colo. Coll., Colorado Springs, 1959; supr., circulation desk Hoover Libr., Stanford U., 1960-62; rsch. asst. Colo. Coll. Planning Office, 1969-70; coord. photograph collections Tutt Libr. Colo. Coll., Colorado Springs, 1975—, coord. Oral History Project, 1979—; mem. Soc. Colo. Archivists, 1981—. Editor: Growing Up in Colorado Springs, 1981; contbr. articles to profl. jours. Mem. Park and Recreation Bd., Colorado Springs, 1973-78, chmn. 1977-78; mem. City Planning Commn., 1981-87, chmn. 1985-86; bd. Partnership for Community Design, Colorado Springs, 1987—; mem. Colorado Springs Chorale, 1973—. Recipient Grad. fellowship Rotary Found., Grenoble, France, 1958-59. Mem. Woman's Ednl. Soc. (bd. dirs. 1991—). Office: Tutt Library Colorado College 1021 N Cascade Ave Colorado Springs CO 80903

FINLEY, KATHLEEN SUSAN, nursing educator; b. Gilroy, Calif., Nov. 19, 1949; d. Richard Herman and Juanita Dell (Black) Westergard; m. James G. Pullen, Sr., June 21, 1971 (div. June 1983); 1 child, James G. Jr.; m. Glen Finley, Sept. 9, 1989. Assoc. Sci., Pacific Union Coll., 1971; BS, Walla Walla Coll., 1973; MS, U. Portland, 1981. RN; FNP; cert. nursing adminstrn., advanced. Charge nurse Walla Walla Gen. Hosp., Walla Walla, Wash., 1971-72; staff nurse Portland Adv. Med. Ctr., Portland, Oreg., 1972-73; dir. nurses Med. Ctr. Hosp., Portland, 1973-74; edn. instr. Glendale Adv. Med. Ctr., 1974-75; asst. dir. nursing Rogue Valley Meml. Hosp., Medford, Oreg., 1975-83; v.p. nursing Feather River Hosp., Paradise, Calif., 1983-87; v.p. patient care Littleton Hosp./Porter, Littleton, Colo., 1988-90; nursing instr. Rogue Community Coll., Grants Pass, Oreg., 1990-93; pres., gen. mgr. Oreg. Health Profls., Inc., Medford, 1990—; FNP Shady Cove (Oreg.) Clinic, 1993—. Mem. ANA, Am. Coll. Nurse Practitioners, Assn. Seventh-day Adventist Nurses, Oreg. Nurses Assn. Office: PO Box 428 Shady Cove OR 97539

FINN, SARA SHIELS, public relations executive; b. Cin., July 12; d. Paul Vincent and Freda K. Shiels; m. Thomas Finn. BA in English, Maryville Coll., 1950. Reporter La Jolla (Calif.) Jour.; advt. and pub. rels. rep. San Diego Mag., 1964-71; dir. pub. rels. U. San Diego, 1971-87; owner Sara Finn Pub. Rels., San Diego, 1987—; pres. Finn/Hannaford (a divsn. of The Hannaford Co., Washington), San Diego, 1987—; lectr. and cons.; pres. Ptnrs. for Livable Places, 1993—, Internat. Affairs Bd. City of San Diego, 1986—. Pres. Nat. Assn. Alumnae of Sacred Heart, 1979-81. Inducted into Equestrian Order Holy Sepulchre, Rome, 1982; bd. dirs. San Diego Hist. Soc., 1989—; mem. coun. of ministries All Hallows Cath. Ch., La Jolla, Calif., 1983—; active Sister City Assn. San Diego/Tijuana. Mem. Pub. Rels. Soc. Am. (accredited), Inst. Latin Profls., Pub. Rels. Soc. Am. Counselors Acad., San Diego Press Club (charter star), San Diego C. of C. Roman Catholic. Office: 1010 Turquoise St Ste 201 San Diego CA 92109-1266

FINNANE, DANIEL F., professional basketball team executive; m. Carol Finnane; children: Cedric, Kelly, Dan, Ann, David. Grad. Univ. Wis., 1958. CPA. Registered rep. Robert W. Baird and Co., Wis., 1965-68; sr. v.p. Dain Bosworth and Co., Mpls.; pres. First Fin. Group, 1975-82; exec. v.p. TOTAL-TV Inc. cable television system, Janesville, Wis., 1980-85; co-owner, now also pres. Golden State Warriors (Nat. Basketball Assn.), Oakland, Calif.; mem. bd. dirs. Milw. Bucks (Nat. Basketball Assn.), 1978-85. Office: Golden State Warriors Oakland Coliseum Arena Oakland CA 94621*

FINNEMORE, (ERHARDT) JOHN, civil engineer, educator; b. London, Jan. 27, 1937; came to U.S., 1965; s. Hubert John and Gerda Gertrud (Bloemeken) F.; m. Gulshan Gulamani, Aug. 7, 1962; children: (John) Riaz, Priya Jean. BSc in Engring., London U., 1960; MS, Stanford U., 1966, PhD, 1970. Registered profl. engr., Calif. Engr. J.D. and D.M. Watson, London, 1960-62, Found. Can. Engring. Corp. Ltd., Toronto, Ont., 1962-63; mcpl. engr. M.M. Dillon, Ltd., London, Ont., Can., 1963-65; rsch. engr. Metcalf & Eddy Engrs., Palo Alto, Calif., 1969-70; asst. prof. civil engring. Pahlavi U., Shiraz, Iran, 1970-71; sr. engr. Systems Control, Inc., Palo Alto, 1972-76; project mgr. Metcalf & Eddy Engrs., Palo Alto, Calif., 1977-79; assoc. prof. civil engring. Santa Clara (Calif.) U., 1979—; cons. Tyndall & Cahners, Attys. at Law, San Jose, Calif., 1989—, Wahler Assocs. Cons. Engrs., Palo Alto, 1990-91; chmn. tech. rev. com. on treatment plant issues, San Jose, 1981. Co-author: Fluid Mechanics with Engineering Applications, 1985; contbr. articles to profl. publs.; author govt. reports. European Engr. award European Fedn. Nat. Engring. Assns. Fellow ASCE; mem. Inst. Civil Engrs. U.K., Flamenco Soc. No. Calif. in San Jose (adv. bd., bd. dirs. 1985-87, chmn. 1986-87), Nat. Ground Water Assn., Am. Soc. Agrl. Engrs., Calif. Environ. Health Assn., Order of Engr., Sigma Xi, Tau Beta Pi. Home: 22374 Riverside Dr Cupertino CA 95014-3959 Office: Dept Civil Engring Santa Clara U Santa Clara CA 95053

FINNIE, C(LARENCE) HERB(ERT), aerospace company executive; b. San Marcos, Tex., Feb. 22, 1930; s. Clarence Herbert and Robbie Mary (Hinkle) F.; B.S., S.W. Tex. State U., 1951; M.A., U. Calif.-Berkeley, 1955; M.B.A., U. Santa Clara, 1968; m. Bruna Rebecchi, June 28, 1955; children: Elisa Gene, John Herbert, Mary Lea, Ann Catherine. Bur. chief, disk jockey KCNY, 1950; with Lockheed Missiles & Space Co., Inc., Sunnyvale, Calif., 1958—, supr. computer programming, systems analyst, mgr. software design and devel., advanced systems staff engr. sr; free-lance writer, photographer; pres. Creative Imagineering, Sunnyvale, 1984—; cons. in field. Mem. adv. bd. KRON-TV. Served to Capt. USAF, 1951-58. Mem. Assn. Computing Machinery, Nat. Mgmt. Assn., Pentagon Players (charter), Photog. Soc. Am., Air Force Assn., Assn. Old Crows, Marquis Club, Alpha Chi, Beta Gamma Sigma, Phi Mu Alpha Sinfonia. Roman Catholic. Designed and developed first generally used compiler prepared for a digital electronic computer (Univac I), computer game package and a universally used tng. system, 1952; original documentation and reference materials deeded to the Smithsonian Institution. Home: 1582 Lewiston Dr Sunnyvale CA 94087-4148 Office: 1111 Lockheed Way Sunnyvale CA 94089-1212

FINNIE, DORIS G., investment company executive; b. Mpls., Sept. 2, 1919; d. Earl Chester and Marie Ethelee (McGulpin) Gould; m. Donald Johnstone Finnie, May 23, 1939; children: Dianne Elaine Finnie Boggess, Denise Eileen. BA in Journalism, U. Denver, 1941. Adminstrv. asst. Corps. Engrs.,

Ft. Eustis, Va. and Fed. Republic Germany, 1942-52; exec. sec. Nicholson & Co., Lakewood, Colo., 1963-64; office mgr. K&P, Inc., Golden, Colo., 1965-82; exec. sec.-treas. Rocky Mountain Coal Mining Inst., Lakewood, 1982—. Editor Procs. of Rocky Mountain Coal Mining Inst., 1982-92. Vice chair com. to elect Peter Dominick for senator, Jefferson County, Colo., 1960-64; mem. com. Rep. Party, Jefferson County, 1965-68; founder City of Lakewood, 1968; dir. Alzheimer and Kidney Found., Denver, 1970-72. Recipient Ernest Thompson Seton award Camp Fire, Inc., 1963; named Woman of Yr. Denver Area Panhellenic, 1977. Mem. Colo. Soc. Assn. Execs., Rocky Mountain Assn. Meeting Planners (Humanitarian award 1992), Profl. Conv. Mgmt. Assn., Kappa Delta (Outstanding Mem. Alumnae Assn. award 1959, 74, Order of Emerald 1987). Office: Rocky Mountain Coal Mining Inst 3000 Youngfield St Ste 324 Lakewood CO 80215-6553

FINNIGAN, DENNIS MICHAEL, management consultant; b. Buffalo, Aug. 10, 1928; s. Charles Marcellus and Marie Florence (Jacobs) F; m. Barbara Ann Pfeiffer, June 16, 1951; children: Cecilia, Eileen, Dennis Jr., Kathy, Margaret, Teresa, Timothy, Kevin, Marie. BA, Stanford U., 1953, postgrad., 1953-54. With IBM Corp., Buffalo, 1949; dept. mgr. Sunsweet Growers, San Jose, Calif., 1949-51; systems analyst Stanford U., Palo Alto, Calif., 1951-53; v.p. SRI Internat., Menlo Park, Calif., 1953-81; pres. D.M. Finnigan Assocs., Los Altos, Calif., 1981—; chmn. bd. dirs. ABB Flakt, Inc., Atlanta, Blenheim, N.V., Rotterdam, The Netherlands. Bd. dirs. Serene Lakes (Calif.) Property Assn., 1980-84. Staff sgt. USAF, 1946-49. Awarded Royal Order of North Star by His Majesty the King of Sweden, 1983. Mem. Swedish-Am. C. of C. (chmn. San Francisco chpt. 1986-88). Democrat. Roman Catholic.

FIORELLI, JOSEPH STEPHEN, management consultant; b. Phila., Sept. 28, 1950; s. Andrew Joseph and Madeline Mary (Maurelli) F.; m. Margaret Mary Tracy; children: Andrea Lynn, Zachary James. BS, Temple U., 1976, EdM, 1978, PhD, 1983. Asst. dir. adult devel. program United Cerebral Palsy Assn., Phila., 1972-75; asst. dir. interdisciplinary tng. Devel. Disabilities Ctr., Phila., 1977-81; dir. edn. Moss Rehab. Hosp., Phila., 1981-84; orgn. devel. cons. Corning (N.Y.) Glass Works, 1984-86, mgr. planning and adminstrn., 1986-88; mgr. orgn. devel. communications div. Rockwell Internat., Newport Beach, Calif., 1988-90; sr. mgr. Ernst & Young, Costa Mesa, Calif., 1990-91; quality improvement officer Meris Labs, San Jose, Calif., 1992-93; corp. mgr. orgn. excellence Nat. Semicondr., Santa Clara, Calif., 1993—; adj. asst. prof. Temple U., Phila., 1978-80, Cabrini Coll., Radnor, Pa., 1983-84, West Coast U., 1988—; sr. assoc. Star Systems Cons. and Tng., Phila., 1980-84; mem. editorial rev. bd. Jour. Ednl. and Psychol. Cons., Organizational Devel. Jour., 1988—, Jour. Applied Behavioral Sci. Contbr. chpts. to 4 books and articles to profl. jours. Bd. dirs. Pathways Inc., Caton, N.Y., 1987-88; mem. adv. coun. Mayor's Coun. on Handicapped, Phila., 1984, Comml. Agy. Mgmt. program, Cabrinin Coll., 1983. Mem. Orgn. Devel. Network, Orgn. Devel. Inst., Am. Soc. Tng. and Devel., Assn. for Persons with Severe Handicaps, Pa. Assn. Rehab Facilities. Office: Nat Semicondr M/S 16-410 PO Box 58090 2900 Semiconductor Dr Santa Clara CA 95052-8090

FIORINO, JOHN WAYNE, podiatrist; b. Charleroi, Pa., Sept. 30, 1946; s. Anthony Raymond and Mary Louise (Caramela) F.; m. Susan K. Bonnett, May 2, 1984; children—Jennifer, Jessica, Lauren, Michael. Student Nassau Coll., 1969-70; B.A. in Biology, U. Buffalo, 1972; Dr. Podiatric Medicine, Ohio Coll. Podiatric Medicine, 1978. Salesman, E. J. Korvettes, Carle Place, N.Y., 1962-65; orderly Nassau Hosp., Mineola, N.Y., 1965-66; operating room technician-trainee heart-lung machine L.I. Jewish-Hillside Med. Center, New Hyde Park, N.Y., 1967-69; pharmacy technician Feinmel's Pharmacy, Roslyn Heights, N.Y., 1969-70; mgr., asst. buyer Fortunoffs, Westbury, N.Y., 1972-73; bd. certified perfusionist L.I. Jewish-Hillside Med. Center, New Hyde Park, N.Y., 1973-74; clin. instr. cardiopulmonary tech. Stony Brook (N.Y.) Univ., 1973-74; operating room technician Cleve. Met. Hosp., 1975; lab. technician Univ. Hosp., Cleve., 1976-78; surg. resident Mesa Gen. Hosp., 1978-79; staff podiatrist, 1979—; pvt. practice podiatry, Mesa, 1979—; staff podiatrist Sacaton (Ariz.) Hosp., 1979—, Mesa Gen. Hosp., 1979, Valley Luth. Hosp., Mesa, 1985, Chandler Community Hosp., 1985, Desert Samaritan Hosp., Mesa, 1986, podiatrist U.S. Govt. Nat. Inst., Sacaton, 1980-87, Indian Health Services, Sacaton, 1980-87; cons. staff Phoenix Indian Med. Ctr., 1985. Served with USN, 1966-67. Mem. Am. Podiatry Assn., Ariz. Podiatry Assn. (treas. 1984-86), Acad. Ambulatory Foot Surgery, Am. Coll. Foot Surgeons (assoc.), Mut. Assn. Profls., Am. Acad. Pain Mgmt. (cert.), Pi Delta, Alpha Gamma Kappa. Home: 2624 W Upland Dr Chandler AZ 85224-7870 Office: 5520 E Main St Mesa AZ 85205

FIRESTONE, FREDERICK NORTON, surgeon; b. San Francisco, Dec. 6, 1931; s. Fred and Adrienne Henrietta (Norton) F.; children: Julie Sarah, Laurie Lynn, Daniel Norton. AB in Biol. Sci., Stanford U., 1953, MD, 1956. Diplomate Am. Bd. Surgery, Am. Bd. Thoracic Surgery. Intern and resident Boston City Hosp., 1956-59, resident in thoracic surgery, 1964-66; resident pediat. surgery, sr. fellow cardiovascular surgery Childrens Hosp. Med. Ctr., Boston, 1962-63; Asst. clin. prof. surgery Coll. of Medicine U. Calif., Irvine, 1970—; chmn. thoracic surgery Hoag Meml. Hosp. Presbyn., Newport Beach, Calif., 1986-89; chief surgery Coll. Hosp., Costa Mesa, Calif., 1984, vice chief staff, 1985, chief of staff, 1986; cons. vascular lab. Hoag Meml. Hosp., Presbyn., Newport Beach, 1982-90. Contbr. articles to profl. jours. Bd. dirs. Am. Cancer Soc., Orange County, Calif., 1977—, pres., 1983-85; bd. dirs. Newport Found. for the Study of Major Econ. Issues, Newport Beach, 1986—; founder Paramedic Program, Orange County, 1972-76; pres. Am. Heart Assn., Orange County, 1976-77. Capt. Med. Corps, U.S. Army, 1960-66. Fellow ACS; mem. Am. Trauma Soc. (founding), Am. Numismatic Assn. (life), Soc. Thoracic Surgeons, Orange County Surg. Soc. (pres. 1992), Nature Conservancy (life), Nat. Audubon Soc. (life). Republican. Home: 2107 Windward Ln Newport Beach CA 92660-3820

FIRKINS, JAMES THOMPSON, state agency administrator, policy analyst; b. Albuquerque, Aug. 31, 1954; s. E. Bruce and Janice Louise (Thompson) F.; m. Leslie Stone, 1992. BA in Psychology, N.Mex. State U., 1977; MBA in Fin., U. N.Mex., 1990. Trombonist Las Vegas Symphony Orch., 1980-86, New World Brass Quintet, Las Vegas, 1979-86, Legends in Concert, Imperial Palace Hotel, Las Vegas, 1984-86; mem. fin. staff Bruce King for Gov. Campaign, Albuquerque, 1990; spl. projects coord. Energy Minerals and Natural Resources Dept., State of N.Mex., Santa Fe, 1991—; mem. tech. transport working group Western Govs.' Assn., Denver, 1991—. Fund raiser Bill Clinton for Pres. Campaign, Santa Fe, 1992; block capt. Am. Cancer Soc., Albuquerque, 1990. Democrat. Office: Energy Minerals Natural Res 2040 S Pacheco St Santa Fe NM 87505

FIRTH, BRIAN WILLIAM, engineer; b. London, Feb. 7, 1926; came to U.S., 1963; s. Cyril William and Evelyn Marion (Weekes) F. ACGI with honors, City & Guilds Coll., London, Eng., 1946; BSc in Engring. with honors, DIC, Imperial Coll. Sci. & Tech., London, Eng., 1947. Design engr. Continental Aviation & Engring., Detroit, 1963-64; lectr. U. Witwatersrand, Johannesburg, Republic of South Africa, 1965-67; vis. prof. McMaster U., Hamilton, Ontario, Can., 1968; assoc. prof. U. Nev., Reno, 1968-69; test engr. Nev. Auto Test Ctr., Carson City, 1970-71; cons. Carson City, 1971-82; project engr. Mobility Systems & Equipment Co., L.A., 1982-88; cons. Garrett Forensic Engrs., L.A., 1988—. Author: The Constitution of Consensus: Democracy as an Ethical Imperative, 1987. Lt. R.E.M.E., 1951-53, Korea. Mem. Soc. Automotive Engrs., Royal Elec. and Mech. Engrs. Episcopalian. Office: Garrett Forensic Engrs Box 91659 Long Beach CA 90809-1659

FIRTH, DEREK, manufacturing executive; b. Bradford, England, Sept. 9, 1939; came to U.S., 1985; s. Harry and Dorothy Anne (Scholey) F.; m. Susan Rogerson, Feb. 15, 1964 (div.); children: Duncan Richard, Nicholas Daniel; m. Gretchen E. Tester, Jan. 13, 1991. B in Engring., Liverpool (England) U., 1960, M in Engring., 1966. Registered profl. engr., Canada, England. Area mgr. Costain Concrete Co. Ltd., Wishaw, Scotland, 1968-74; plant mgr. Genstar Costain Tie Co. Ltd., Edmonton, Alberta, Canada, 1975-85, v.p., gen. mgr., 1983-85; v.p. mktg. Genstar Costain Tie Co. Ltd., Herndon, Va., 1985-88; v.p., gen. mgr. C.X.T. Inc., Spokane, Wash., 1988—. Mem. Am. Concrete Inst. (pres. Alberta chpt. 1982, chmn. com. 545 1993), Railroad Engring. and Maintenance of Way Suppliers Assn., Am. Railway Engrs. Assn. (assoc.), ASTM. Mem. Soc. of Friends Ch. Home: 2019 Canyon Dr Coeur D Alene ID 83814-9072 Office: CXT Inc PO Box 2420 Spokane WA 99214-4000

FISCH, SANFORD MICHAEL, lawyer; b. Newark, July 27, 1955; s. Theodore W. and Iris Fisch. BA magna cum laude, Boston U., 1977; JD, U. San Diego, 1980; M of Law-Tax, Georgetown U., 1982. Tax specialist Coopers & Lybrand, San Diego, 1982-84; ptnr. Rosenberg and Fisch, San Diego, 1984-88, Armstrong, Fisch & Assocs., San Diego, San Francisco and Santa Clara, Calif., 1988—; tchr. Am. Coll., Bryn Mawr, Pa., 1983. Co-founder San Diego Sr. Olympics, 1988; mem. law review U. San Diego, 1979-80. Recipient Program of Yr. award San Diego Jewish Community Ctr., 1988. Mem. Nat. Mortar Bd. Office: Armstrong Fisch & Assocs 9171 Towne Centre Dr San Diego CA 92122

FISCHER, COLETTE BARBARA, municipal official; b. Chgo., Sept. 22, 1947; d. Aloysius Michael and Ruth Mary (Thomas) Fanning; m. Robert Eugene Fischer, June 5, 1976; 1 child, Nicole Marie. Student, Vassar Coll., 1964-65, U. Calif., Riverside, 1965-67; BA, Golden Coast U., 1987, MBA, 1990. Owner The Bounty Steakhouse, Santa Barbara, Calif., 1976-79; comptr., owner Foremost Dairies, Santa Barbara, 1976-82; bus. office supr. police dept. City of Santa Barbara, 1984-85, supr. payroll and accounts, 1985-87, mgr. waterfront bus., 1987—; owner The Spur Restaurant, Santa Barbara, 1984-87. Republican. Roman Catholic. Home: 2206 Kemper Lakes Ct River Ridge Country Club Oxnard CA 93030 Office: City of Santa Barbara Waterfront Dept 321 E Cabrillo Blvd Santa Barbara CA 93101-1808

FISCHER, EDMOND HENRI, biochemistry educator; b. Shanghai, Republic of China, Apr. 6, 1920; came to U.S., 1953; s. Oscar and Renée (Tapernoux) F.; m. Beverley B. Bullock. Lic. es Sciences Chimiques et Biologiques, U. Geneva, 1943, Diplome d'Ingenieur Chimiste, 1944, PhD, 1947; D (hon.), U. Montpellier, France, 1985, U. Basel, Switzerland, 1988, Med. Coll. of Ohio, 1993. Pvt. docent biochemistry U. Geneva, 1950-53; research assoc. biology Calif. Inst. Tech., Pasadena, 1953; asst. prof. biochemistry U. Wash., Seattle, 1953-56, assoc. prof., 1956-61, prof., 1961-90, prof. emeritus, 1990—; mem. exec. com. Pacific Slope Biochem. Conf., 1958-59, pres. 1975; mem. biochemistry study sect. NIH, 1959-64; symposium co-chmn. Battelle Seattle Research Ctr., 1970, 73, 78; mem. sci. adv. bd. Biozentrum, U. Basel, Switzerland, 1982-86; sci. adv. bd. Friedrich Miescher Inst., Ciba-Geigy, Basel, 1976-84, chmn. 1981-84. Contbr. numerous articles to sci. jours. Mem. sci. council on basic sci. Am. Heart Assn., 1977-80, sci. adv. com. Muscular Dystrophy Assn., 1980-88. Recipient Lederle Med. Faculty award, 1956-59, Guggenheim Found. award, 1963-64, Disting. Lectr. award U. Wash., 1983, Laureate Passano Found. award, 1988, Steven C. Beering award, 1991, Nobel prize in Physiology of Medicine, 1992; NIH spl. fellow, 1963-64. Mem. AAAS, AAUP, Am. Soc. Biol. Chemists (council mem. 1980-83), Am. Chem. Soc. (biochemistry div., mem. adv. bd. 1962, exec. com. div. biology 1969-72, monography adv. bd. 1971-73, editorial adv. bd. Biochemistry Jour., 1961-66, assoc. editor 1966-92), Swiss Chem. Soc. (Werner medal), Brit. Biochem. Soc., Am. Acad. Arts and Scis., Nat. Acad. Scis., Sigma Xi. Office: U Washington Med Sch Dept Biochemistry SJ70 Seattle WA 98195

FISCHER, JOEL, social work educator; b. Chgo., Apr. 22, 1939; s. Sam and Ruth (Feiges) F.; m. Renee H. Furuyama; children: Lisa, Nicole. BS, U. Ill., 1961, MSW, 1964; D in Social Welfare, U. Calif., Berkeley, 1970. Prof. sch. social work U. Hawaii, Honolulu, 1970—; vis. prof. George Warren Brown Sch. Social Work, Washington U., St. Louis, 1977, U. Wis. Sch. Social Welfare, Milw., 1978-79, U. Natal, South Africa, 1982, U. Hong Kong, 1986; cons. various orgns. and univs. Author: (with Harvey L. Gochros) Planned Behavior Change: Behavior Modification in Social Work, 1973, Handbook of Behavior Therapy with Sexual Problems, Vol. I, 1977, Vol. II, 1977, Analyzing Research, 1975, Interpersonal Helping: Emerging Approaches for Social Work Practice, 1973, The Effectiveness of Social Casework, 1976, Fundamentals of Social Work Practice, 1982, Effective Casework Practice: An Eclectic Approach, 1978, (with Martin Bloom) Evaluating Practice: Guidelines for the Helping Professional, 1982, (with Harvey L. Gochros) Treat Yourself to a Better Sex Life, 1980, Helping the Sexually Oppressed, 1986, (with Kevin Corcoran) Measures for Clinical Practice, 1987, (with Daniel Sanders) Visions for the Future: Social Work and Pacific-Asian Perspectives, 1988, (with Martin Bloom and John Orme) Evaluating Practice, 2d edit., 1993, (with Kevin Corcoran) Measures for Clinical Practice, 2d edit., Vol. 1, Covuples, Families, Children, Vol. 2, Adults, 1993, East-West Connections: Social Work Practice Traditions and Change, 1992; mem. editorial bd. 12 profl. jours.; contbr. over 140 articles, revs., chpts. and papers to profl. publs. With U.S. Army, 1958. Mem. Hawaii Com. for Africa, Nat. Assn. Social Workers, Coun. Social Work Edn., Acad. Cert. Social Workers, Nat. Conf. Social Welfare, AAUP, Unity Organizing Com., Hawaii People's Legis. Coalition, Bertha Reynold Soc. Democrat. Home: 1371-4 Hunakai St Honolulu HI 96816-5544 Office: U Hawaii 2500 Campus Rd Honolulu HI 96822-2289

FISCHER, ZOE ANN, real estate and property marketing company executive, real estate consultant; b. L.A., Aug. 26, 1939; d. George and Marguerite (Carrasco) Routsos; m. Douglas Clare Fischer, Aug. 6, 1960 (div. 1970); children: Brent Sean Cecil, Tahlia Georgienne Marguerite Bianca. BFA in Design, UCLA, 1964. Pres. Zoe Antiques, Beverly Hills, Calif., 1973—; v.p. Harleigh Sandler Real Estate Corp. (now Prudential), 1980-81; exec. v.p. Coast to Coast Real Estate & Land Devel. Corp., Century City, Calif., 1981-83; pres. New Market Devel., Inc., Beverly Hills, 1983—; dir. mktg. Mirabella, L.A., 1983, Autumn Pointe, L.A., 1983-84, Desert Hills, Antelope Valley, Calif., 1984-85; cons. Lowe Corp., L.A., 1985. Designer interior and exterior archtl. enhancements and remodelling; designed album cover for Clare Fischer Orch. (Grammy award nomination 1962). Soprano Roger Wagner Choir, UCLA, 1963-64. Mem. UCLA Alumni Assn. Democrat. Roman Catholic. Avocations: skiing, designing jewelry, interior, landscape and new home design, antique collecting.

FISCHL, CHARLES FREDERICK, ballet company executive; b. N.Y.C., Mar. 15, 1950; s. Harry and Theresa (Weidengher) F.; m. Linda Carmella Marrone, Jan. 2, 1971; children: Katrina Theresa, Tanya Ann. Mgr. stage and prodn. Miniola (N.Y.) Theatre, 1965-68, Theatre of the Stars, Atlanta, 1968-73; pres., gen. mgr. Atlanta Ballet, 1974-78; ops. mgr. Dallas Ballet, 1978-79; pres., gen. mgr. Balt. Ballet, 1980-85; gen. mgr. Ballet Ariz., Phoenix, 1985—; Vice-chmn. Am. Assn. Dance Cos., N.Y.C., 1977-79; mem. arts mgmt. bd. Loyola Coll., Balt., 1980-81; dance chmn. Artscape, Balt., 1982-85; coun. mgr. Dance U.S.A., Washington, 1982—. Mem. Phoenix Commn. Arts, Ariz. Arts Commn. Mem. Ind. Assn. Theater Employees, Actors Equity Assn. Office: Southwest Dance 2248 E Charity Dr Phoenix AZ 85028

FISH, JAMES HENRY, library director; b. Leominster, Mass., Feb. 21, 1947; s. Danny Mack and Doris Grace (Harvey) F. BA, U. Mass., 1968; MLS, Ind. U., 1971; MBA, Anna Maria Coll., Paxton, Mass., 1979. Dir. librs. Levi Heywood Meml. Libr., Gardner, Mass., 1971-72; dir. Leominster Public Libr., 1972-77, Robbins Libr., Arlington, Mass., 1977-80; state librarian Mass. State Libr., Boston, 1980-82; dir. Springfield City Libr. (Mass.), 1982-90; city librarian San Jose (Calif.) Pub. Libr., 1990—. Author libr. reports and cons. projects, community analysis, planning and evaluation. Bd. dirs. United Fund Leominster, 1974-76, Vis. Nurses Assn. Leominster, 1974-76, Leominster chpt. ARC, 1975-77; chmn. Leominster Bicentennial Com., 1975-76. With U.S. Army, 1969-71. Decorated Commendation medal; recipient Disting. Service award Arlington C. of C., 1979. Mem. ALA, Pub. Libr. Assn. (New Standards Task Force 1986-87, adv. com. chmn. Pub. Libr. Data Svc., conf. program com., 1988-90), Calif. Libr. Assn., Beta Phi Mu. Office: City Librarian San Jose Pub Library 180 W San Carlos St San Jose CA 95113-2096

FISH, JONATHON KEVIN, publishing company executive; b. Downey, Calif., Mar. 25, 1955; s. Leon Herbert and Mary Ann (McCollum) F. BA, Claremont Men's Coll., 1977. Comml. lines underwriter Royal Ins. Co., Sacramento, 1977-79; cons. Warren, McVeigh & Griffin, Newport Beach, Calif., 1979-82; dir. Nils Pub. Co., Chatsworth, Calif., 1982—; pub. Schwann Publs. subs. Nils Pub. Co., Chatsworth, 1987-91, Musical Am. Mag. subs. Nils Pub. Co., Chatsworth, 1989-91; asst. editor: The Umbrella Book, 1982, (newsletters) NAIC Report, 1982-91, Insight, 1985-91, Ins. & Liability Reporter, 1991-92. Mem. Claremont McKenna Coll. Alumni Assn. (Res Publica), San Fernando Valley Literacy Coun., Laubach Literacy Action. Office: NILS Pub Co 21625 Prairie St Chatsworth CA 91311-5898

FISH, RUBY MAE BERTRAM (MRS. FREDERICK GOODRICH FISH), civic worker; b. Sheridan, Wyo., July 24, 1918; d. Ryan Lawrence and Ruby (Beckwith) Bertram; R.N., St. Luke's Hosp., 1936; postgrad. Washington U., St. Louis, 1941; m. Frederick Goodrich Fish, Apr. 12, 1942; children: Bertram Frederick, Lisbeth Ann Fish Kalstein. Staff nurse Huntington Meml. Hosp., Pasadena, Calif., 1941-42; dr.'s office nurse, Denver, 1943-44; travel cons. Buckingham Travel Agy., Aurora, Colo., 1976—. Bd. dirs. Jefferson County Easter Seal Soc., 1949—, pres., 1952-53, 56-57, 66-67; pres. Colo. Easter Seal Soc., 1960-61; bd. dirs. Nat. Easter Seal Soc., 1968-69, sec. ho. of dels., 1976-77; bd. dirs. Assistance League Denver, 1968-70, 75-76, People to People for Handicapped, 1981— (Vol. of Yr. award 1991); mem. Pres.'s Com. on Employing Handicapped, 1976—; active Rehab. Internat. of U.S.A., 1972—, Rehab. Internat., 1960—. Mem. Dau. Nile-El Mejedel. Home: # 3 6900 W Stetson Pl Littleton CO 80123-1331 Office: 13741 E Mississippi Ave Aurora CO 80012-3628

FISHELMAN, BRUCE C., lawyer; b. Jersey City, Aug. 1, 1949; s. Bernard and Nellie (Greenhaus) F.; m. Bonnie Ellen Fishelman, Apr. 14, 1989; 1 child, Sage Everett; 1 stepchild, Brett Forbes. Student, Duke U., 1967-69; BA, Sarah Lawrence Coll., 1971; JD, U. So. Calif., 1974. Bar: N.J. 1975, N.Y. 1980, Calif. 1985, U.S. Dist. Ct. N.J. 1975, U.S. Ct. Appeals (3d cir.) 1979, U.S. Dist. Ct. (cen. dist.) Calif. 1986, U.S. Ct. Apeals (9th cir.) 1990, U.S. Supreme Ct. 1984. Investigator City of Jersey City, 1975, asst. corp. counsel, mcpl. ct. prosecutor, 1975-80; pvt. practice Jersey City and N.Y.C., 1980-85, L.A., 1985—; atty., pres. Stanbury, Fishelman & Levy, L.A., 1989—; pres. SOB Entertainment Corp., Englishtown, N.J., 1980—, Woodfish Pub. Co., Englishtown, 1980—; v.p. Trade Winds Lake Camp, Englishtown, 1989—. Author: Agents and Managers: California's Split Personality, 1991. Counsel, Jersey City Human Rights Commn., 1976-80; incorporator Jersey City Econ. Devel. Corp., 1980-82; chmn. Joyce Luther Kennard Scholarship fund U. So. Calif. Law Sch., 1989-90. Mem. ABA, Los Angeles County Bar Assn., Beverly Hills Bar Assn., Westwood Bar Assn., Simon Wiesenthal Ctr. Democrat. Jewish. Office: Stanbury Fishelman & Levy 9200 W Sunset Blvd Bldg 1201 West Hollywood CA 90069-3607

FISHER, BARRY ALAN, lawyer; b. L.A., May 15, 1943; s. Harry Benjamin and Fay Doris (Sternfeld) F.; m. Susan E. Landman, June 16, 1968; children: J. Benjamin, Jonathan J., Robert A. A.B., UCLA, 1965, J.D., 1968. Bar: Alaska 1969, R.I. 1969 (spl.), Calif. 1971, U.S. Supreme Ct. 1972. law clk. to chief justice Alaska, 1968-69; Reginald Heber Smith fellow U. Pa., Law Sch., 1969-71; staff counsel Sierra Club Legal Def. Fund, San Francisco, 1972-74; mem. Fleishman, Brown, Weston & Rhode, Beverly Hills, Calif., 1974-77; ptnr. Fleishman, Fisher & Moest, L.A., 1977—; v.p. Human Rights Advs.; justice of peace, R.I., 1971; speaker profl. confs. Bd. dirs. Constitutions Rsch. Ctr., Gypsy Lore Soc., West side Urban Forum. Contbr. articles to profl. jours. Mem. ABA (co-chair first amendment com., co-chair nat. inst. on tort and religion), Calif. Acad. Appellate Lawyers, Calif. Acad. Appellate Lawyers, World Assn. Lawyers, Judges. Contbg. author Government Intervention in Religious Affairs, 1982; mem. adv. bd. Religious Freedom Reporter. Office: Fleishman Fisher & Moest 2049 Century Park E Ste 3160 Los Angeles CA 90067-3275

FISHER, BRUCE DAVID, elementary educator; b. Long Beach, Calif., Dec. 24, 1949; s. Oran Wilfred and Irene (May) F.; m. Mindi Beth Evans, Aug. 15, 1976; 1 child, Jenny Allison Viola. BA, Humboldt State U., 1975, standard elem. credential, 1976, learning handicapped credential, 1977. Instrnl. svcs. specialist Blue Lake (Calif.) Elem. Sch.; resource specialist Fortuna (Calif.) Union Sch. Dist., tchr. 3d grade, tchr. 5th grade, 1988—; curriculum writer. Vice-chmn. Tchr. Edn. and Community Helpers, Arcata, Calif., 1990—; v.p. Sequoia Park Zool. Soc., Eureka, 1989-90, chmn. Whale Fair, 1989—; mem. selection com. Christa McAuliffe Fellowship; bd. dirs. Redwood Environ. Edn. Fair, Eureka, 1990—, Family Wellness Project, 1991; apptd. Calif. Curriculum and Supplemental Materials Commn.; commr. Calif. Curriculum Commn., 1992—. Named Calif. Tchr. of Yr. Dept. Edn., 1991, Favorite Tchr. ABC-TV, 1991; recipient Leadership Excellence award Calif. Assn. Sci. Specialists, 1990, Masonic Meritorious Svc. award for Pub. Edn., 1991, Profl. Best Leadership award Learning Mag., Oldsmobile Corp., and Mich. State U., 1991; Nat. Educator award Miliken Found. Calif. State Dept. Edn., 1991. Mem. Calif. Tchrs. Assn., Calif. Sci. Tchrs. Assn., Calif. Assn. Health, Phys. Edn., Recreation, and Dance. Democrat. Home: 4810 14th St Arcata CA 95521-9778 Office: Fortuna Elem Sch 843 L St Fortuna CA 95540-1997

FISHER, CARL A., bishop; b. Pascagoula, Miss., Nov. 24, 1945. AA, Epiphany Apostolic Coll., Newburgh, N.Y., 1965; BA, St. Joseph's Sem., 1967; MA, Oblate Coll., 1970; MS, Am. U., 1974. Ordained priest Roman Cath. Ch., 1973. Titular bishop of Tlos, aux. bishop of L.A., 1987—. First African-Am. Catholic Bishop in Western U.S. Address: Archdiocese of LA 3555 St Pancratius Pl Lakewood CA 90712

FISHER, DARRELL REED, medical physicist, researcher; b. Salt Lake City, Feb. 12, 1951; s. Wayne Ekman and Zina Vae (Moore) F.; m. Anna Jeanetta Thomas, June 23, 1988; children: Bryan, Jenny, Aaron, Brit, Jake, Kimberly. BA in Biology, U. Utah, 1975; MS, U. Fla., 1976, PhD in Nuclear Engring. Scis., 1978. Rsch. asst. Radiobiology Lab., U. Utah, Salt Lake City, 1973-75; grad. asst. Nuclear Engring, U. Fla., Gainesville, 1975-78; rsch. scientist Battelle, Pacific N.W. Labs., Richland, Wash., 1978-80; sr. rsch. scientist Battelle, Pacific N.W. Labs., Richland, 1980—, tech. group leader, 1991-93, staff scientist, 1993—; affiliate asst. prof. U. Wash. Sch. Medicine, Seattle, 1991—; adj. assoc. prof. Wash. State u., Richland, 1992—; affiliate investigator Fred Hutchinson Cancer Rsch. Ctr., Seattle, 1993—, cons., 1987—, Div. Nuclear Medicine, U. Wash., Seattle, 1986—, NeoRx Corp., Seattle, 1987—. Editor: Current Concepts in Lung Dosimetry, 1983, Inhaled Particles VI, 1988, Population Exposure from the Nuclear Fuel Cycle, 1988; assoc. editor Jour. Health Physics, 1985-91, Antibody Immunoconjugates and Pharmaceuticals, 1991—. Cert. arbitrator Better Bus. Bur. Ea. Wash., Yakima, 1981—. Mem. Am. Assn. Physicists in Medicine, Health Physics Soc. (Elda E. Anderson award 1986, bd. dirs. 1988-93, pres. Columbia chpt. 1983-84), Radiation Rsch. Soc. Republican. Mem. LDS Ch. Home: 229 Saint St Richland WA 99352 Office: Battelle Pacific NW Labs Health Physics Dept Battelle Blvd Richland WA 99352

FISHER, DAVID CLARENCE, optometrist; b. Detroit, Jan. 31, 1960; s. Edward Thomas and Bertha Lynn (Sanders) F. BS in Biol. Sci., U. Calif., Irvine, 1983; MPH in Epidemiolgoy, UCLA, 1985; BS in Visual Sci., So. Calif. Coll. Optometry, Fullerton, 1987, OD, 1989. Lic. optometrist, Calif. Med. researcher U. Calif. Med. Ctr., Orange, 1982-83; epidemiologist Wadsworth VA Hosp., Brentwood, Calif., 1984-85; optometrist U.S. Indian Health Svc., Chinle, Ariz., 1988, Brentwood VA Hosp., 1989, Bellflower (Calif.) Med. Group, 1989-90, Rancho Calif. Vision Ctr., Temecula, Calif., 1990-93; optometrist Norton AFB, 1991-93, George AFB, 1991-93. Dep. sheriff Orange County Sheriff's Dept., Santa Ana, 1986—. Libert U. scholar, 1978-80, USPHS scholar UCLA, 1983-85. Mem. Am. Optometric Assn., Calif. Optometric Assn., Orange County Optometric Assn., Am. Pub. Health Assn., U. Calif.-Irvine Alumni Assn., So. Calif. Coll. of Optometry Alumni Assn., U. Calif.-L.A. Alumni Assn. Office: Whittier Contact Lens Ctr 13127 E Philadelphia Whittier CA 90601

FISHER, DELBERT ARTHUR, physician, educator; b. Placerville, Calif., Aug. 12, 1928; s. Arthur Lloyd and Thelma (Johnson) F.; m. Beverly Carne Fisher, Jan. 28, 1951; children: David Arthur, Thomas Martin, Mary Kathryn. BA, U. Calif., Berkeley, 1950; MD, U. Calif., San Francisco, 1953. Diplomate Am. Bd. Pediatrics. Resident in pediatrics U. Calif. Med. Center, San Francisco, 1953-55, U. Oreg. Hosp., Portland, 1957-58; fellow pediatric endocrinology U. Oreg. Hosp., 1958-60; from asst. prof. to prof. pediatrics Med. Sch., U. Ark., Little Rock, 1960-68; prof. pediatrics Med. Sch., UCLA, 1968-73, prof. pediatrics and medicine, 1973-91, prof. emeritus, 1991–; chief, pediatric endocrinology Harbor-UCLA Med. Ctr., 1968-73, rsch. prof. devel. and perinatal biology, 1975-85, chmn. pediatrics, 1985-89, sr. scientist Rsch. and Edn. Inst., 1991—; dir. Walter Martin Rsch. Ctr., 1986-91; pres. Nichols Inst. Reference Labs, 1991-93; pres., chief sci. officer Nichols Acad. Assocs., 1993—; cons. genetic disease sect. Calif. Dept. Health Svcs., 1978—; mem. organizing com. Internat. Conf. Newborn Thyroid Screening, 1977-88; examiner Am. Bd. Pediatrics, 1971-80, mem. subcom. on pediatric endocrinology, 1976-79. Co-editor: Pediatric Thyroidology, 1985, four other books; editor-in-chief Jour. Clin. Endocrinology and Metabolism, 1978-83, Pediatric Rsch., 1984-89; contbr. chpts. to numerous books; contbr. over 400 articles to profl. jours. Capt. M.C., USAF, 1955-57. Recipient Career Devel. award NIH, 1964-68. Mem. Inst. Medicine NAS, Am. Acad. Pediarics (Borden award 1981), Soc. Pediatric Rsch. (v.p. 1973-74), Am. Pediatric Soc. (pres. 1992-93), Endocrine Soc. (pres. 1983-84), Am. Thyroid Assn. (pres. 1988-89), Am. Soc. Clin. Investigation, Assn. Am. Physicians, Lawson Wilkins Pediatric Endocrine Soc. (pres. 1982-83), Western Soc. Pediatric Rsch. (pres. 1983-84), Phi Beta Kappa, Alpha Omega Alpha. Home: 24582 Santa Clara Ave Dana Point CA 92629 Office: Nichols Inst 33608 Ortega Hwy San Juan Capistrano CA 92690

FISHER, DONALD G., casual apparel chain stores executive; b. 1928; married. B.S., U. Calif., 1950. With M. Fisher & Son, 1950-57; former ptnr. Fisher Property Investment Co.; co-founder, pres. The Gap Stores Inc., San Bruno, Calif., dir., now chmn., chief exec. officer. Office: The Gap Stores Inc 1 Harrison St San Francisco CA 94105

FISHER, EARL MONTY, utilities executive; b. Chgo., June 26, 1938; s. Harry George and Fannie (Feinberg) F.; m. Joyce Leah Bender, Mar. 14, 1959 (div. Dec. 1978); children: Jan Carol, Wendy Robin; m. Teri Jean Janssen, Jan. 27, 1979. Student, La. Trade Tech. Coll., 1961. Apprentice and journeyman Comfort Air Refrigeration Corp., L.A., 1955-64; contractor Bonanza Air Conditioning and Refrigeration Corp., Van Nuys, Calif., 1964—. Bd. dirs. Hidden Hills (Calif.) Homeowners Assn., 1982-84, vice chmn., vp., 1990; chmn. Hidden Hills Rds. Com., 1984-85, Hidden Hills Gate Ops. Commn., 1988—; commr. emergency svcs. City of Hidden Hills, 1986—; pres. Hidden Hills Community Assn., 1991—. Democrat. Office: Bonanza Air Conditioning Heating & Refrigeration Corp 7653 Burnet Ave Van Nuys CA 91405-1081

FISHER, EDITH MAUREEN, human relations/resources development executive; b. Houston, July 29, 1944; d. Freeman and Ruby (Jase) F. AA, L.A. Trade Tech. Coll., 1965; BA, Calif. State U., L.A., 1969; MLS, U. Ill., 1972; PhD, U. Pitts., 1991. Acad. libr. U. Calif., San Diego, 1972-90, adj. lectr. Black Arts program, 1981-90; lectr. sch. libr. and info. science UCLA, 1989; cons., tech. advisor Evaluation and Testing Inst., L.A., 1991; pres. Tenge Enterprises, Encinitas, Calif., 1990—; chair task force Assn. Coll./Rsch. Librs. Recruitment Unrepresented Minorities, Chgo., 1988-90; councilor Calif. Libr. Assn., sacramento, Calif., 1987-90. Contbr. articles to profl. jours. Carnegie fellow, 1971; PhD fellow U.S. Office Edn. Title II B, 1987. Mem. ALA (pres. Black caucus 1988-90), San Diego County Black C. of C., Carlson Learning Co. (Performax assoc.). Office: Tenge Enterprises 204 N El Camino Real Ste E728 Encinitas CA 92024

FISHER, FREDERICK HENDRICK, oceanographer; b. Aberdeen, Wash., Dec. 30, 1926; s. Sam and Astrid (Kristofferson) F.; B.S., U. Wash., 1949, Ph.D., 1957; m. Julie Gay Saund, June 17, 1955 (dec.); children: Bruce Allen, Mark Edward, Keith Russell, Glen Michael. Research fellow acoustics Harvard, 1957-58; research physicist, research oceanographer Marine Phys. Lab., Scripps Instn. Oceanography, La Jolla, Calif., 1958—, assoc. dir., 1975-87, dep. dir., 1987—; dir. research Havens Industries, San Diego, 1963-64; prof., chmn. dept. physics U. R.I., Kingston, 1970-71; mem. governing bd. Am. Inst. Physics, 1984-90. Editor IEEE Jour. Oceanic Engineering, 1988-91. Mem. San Diego County Dem. Cen. Com., 1956-57, 60-62. NCAA nat. tennis doubles champion, 1949; named to U. Wash. Athletic Hall of Fame, 1989; recipient Disting. Svc. award IEEE Oceanic Engring. Soc., 1991. Midshipman U.S. Naval Acad., 1945-47; with USNR, 1945. Fellow Acoustical Soc. Am. (assoc. editor jour. 1969-76, v.p. 1980-81, pres. 1983-84); mem. IEEE (sr.), Marine Tech. Soc., Am. Geophys. Union, Sigma Xi, AAAS, Pi Mu Epsilon. Club: Seattle Tennis. Co-designer research platform FLIP, 1960-62. Home: 3726 Charles St San Diego CA 92106-2843 Office: U Calif Marine Phys Lab Scripps Inst Oceanography La Jolla CA 92093-0701

FISHER, GARY R., utility holding company executive; b. Mar. 25, 1943; m. Susan Fisher. BS in Acctg. and Fin., Northeastern U., Boston, 1966; MS in System Mgmt., U. So. Calif., 1972. Fin. analyst Mobil Chem. Co., Covington, Ga., 1973-75; contr. Mobil Chem. Co., Macedon, N.Y., 1975-76; regional contr. Mobil Oil Corp., Macedon, 1973-78; mgr. capital planning Dart Industries, L.A., 1978-81; dir. fin. planning, analysis and acctg. Pacific Lighting Corp., L.A., 1981-87, dir. investor rels., 1987; v.p., contr. Pacific Enterprises Oil & Gas Co., L.A., 1987-90, Pacific Interstate Co., L.A., 1987-90; asst. to CFO Pacific Enterprises, L.A., 1991—. Capt. USAF, 1967-72. Office: Pacific Enterprises 663 W 5th St Ste 5400 Los Angeles CA 90071

FISHER, JAMES ROBERT, research entomologist; b. Pitts., Nov. 27, 1946; s. Robert Howard and Elizabeth Teresa (Kenyon) F.; m. Linda Lou Henry, June 8, 1968; children: Candace Michelle, Scott James. BS in Biology, Adrian Coll., 1968; MS in Entomology, U. Mo., 1973; PhD in Entomology, U. Idaho, 1977. Rsch. asst. U. Mo., Columbia, 1971-73, U. Idaho, Moscow, 1973-77; extension entomology asst. Wash. State U., Pullman, 1977; rsch. entomologist No. Grain Insects Rsch. Lab. Agrl. Rsch. Svc. USDA, Brookings, S.D., 1977-89; rsch. entomologist Rangeland Insect Lab. Agrl. Rsch. Svc. USDA, Bozeman, Mont., 1989—; asst. prof. plant sci. S.D. State U., Brookings, 1977-89; adj. prof. entomology Mont. State U., Bozeman, 1989—. Contbr. chpts. to books, articles to profl. jours. Bd. dirs. Brookings Swim Club, 1982-89, Brookings Youth Soccer League, 1982-89, U.S. Swimming, S.D., 1983-88; chmn. bd. dirs. U.S. Master's Swimming, S.D., 1982-86, S.D. Swimming, Inc., 1988-89; mem. Pk. and Recreation Bd., Bozeman, Mont., 1991—. Recipient Phillips Petroleum Award for Svc. to Swimming S.D. Swimming, Inc., 1988. Mem. Am. Entomol. Soc., Entomol. Soc. Am., Kans. Entomol. Soc., Mich. Entomol. Soc., Can. Entomol. Soc., Nat. Recreation and Parks Assn., Beta Beta Beta, Gamma Sigma Delta, Sigma Xi, Phi Sigma. Presbyterian. Office: USDA Rangeland Insect Lab Agrl Rsch Svc NPA Mont State U Bozeman MT 59717

FISHER, JOSEPH STEWART, management consultant; b. Athens, Pa., Mar. 3, 1933; s. Samuel Royer and Agnes Corinne (Smith) F.; m. Anita Ann Coyle, May 15, 1954; 1 child, Samuel Royer. BS in Tech. Mgmt., Regis Coll., 1981; postgrad., U. Colo., 1986-87, Iliff Sch. Theology, 1988-89. Field engr. IBM Corp., Syracuse, N.Y., 1956-60; qualtiy analyst, engr. IBM Corp., Endicott, N.Y., 1960-68; systems support adminstr. IBM Corp., Boulder, Colo., 1968-72, field support adminstr., 1972-78, systems assurance adminstr., 1978-79, security adminstr., 1979-87; sec. cons. Fisher Enterprises, Boulder, 1975—; bd. dirs. Vervcraft Inc., Loveland, Colo.; CFO Lexicor Medical Tech., Inc., 1993—. Leadership devel. Boy Scouts Am., Boulder, 1975—, chmn. long range planning, 1982-86; bd. dirs. Longs Peak Coun. 1983-87, Colo. Crime Stoppers, 1983-88, chaplain, 1991—; v.p., chief fin. officer Caring About People, Inc., Colo., 1990—, Helplink, Inc., Boulder, 1991—. With USN, 1952-56, Korea. Recipient Silver Beaver award Boy Scouts Am., Boulder, 1978. Mem. Am. Soc. Indsl. Security (cert. CPP 1984, treas. 1985), Colo. Crime Prevention Assn., Mason (treas. Columbia lodge 1969-85), R.A.M., Optimists. Republican. Methodist. Home and Office: 4645 Bedford Ct Boulder CO 80301-4017

FISHER, KATHLEEN MACPHEE, finance and accounting executive; b. Toyko, Jan. 31, 1955; d. William Mackie Winchester and Sally Ann (Gannon) MacP.; m. John Woodruff Fisher, Dec. 16, 1978. AA, Canada Coll., 1976; BS, U. Redlands, 1980; MBA, U. So. Calif., 1993. Mktg. analyst Raychem Corp., Menlo Park, Calif., 1973-76; staff acct. Addressograph-Multigraph, Santa Ana, Calif., 1979-80; sr. cost acct. Cipher Data Products, Garden Grove, Calif., 1980-83; cost mgr. Hadco Corp., Santa Ana, 1983-85; div. contr. Western Digital Corp., Irvine, Calif., 1985-89; v.p., contr. AST Rsch., Irvine, 1989-92; v.p. finance, CFO Glacier Water Svcs., Inc., Oceanside, Calif., 1992—; pres. Fisher & Assocs., Newport Beach, Calif., 1990—; lectr. in field. Mem. World Trade Orgn.

FISHER, MARVIN MARK, educator, author; b. Detroit, Nov. 19, 1927; s. Julius and Helen (Goldman) F.; m. Jill Ann Jones, Jan. 6, 1956; children: Ann Katherine, Sarah Alice, Laura Ann. AB, Wayne State U., Detroit, 1950, AM, 1952; PhD, U. Minn., 1958. Asst. prof. Ariz. State U., Tempe, 1958-60, assoc. prof., 1960-66, prof., 1966—, chmn. dept. English, 1977-83; vis. prof. Aristotle U., Thessaloniki, Greece, 1961-63, U. Oslo, Norway, 1966-67, U. Calif., Davis, 1969-70, U. Tubingen, Fed. Republic of Germany, 1988-89; cons. Somerset Imports, L.A., 1977-79, NEH, Washington, 1978-80, Hiram Walker, Inc., Windsor, Ont., Can., 1982-84, Morrison Hecker Inc., 1993; mem. nat. screening com. Fulbright-Hays awards Inst. for Internat. Edn., 1977-80. Author: Workshops in the Wilderness, 1967, Going Under, 1977, Continuities, 1986, Herman Melville, 1988; editorial adv. bd. The Centennial Rev., 1990—; contbr. numerous articles to profl. jours. Precinct committeman Ariz. Dems., Tempe, 1986-88; staff mem. Task Force on Excellence, Efficiency and Competitiveness, Phoenix, 1987-88. With U.S. Army, 1946-47. Fulbright grantee Greece, 1961-63, Norway, 1966-67, Fed. Republic Germany, 1988-89. Mem. Nat. Coun. Tchrs. English, Modern Lang. Assn., Western Res. Club, Melville Soc. Am. (pres.-elect 1993), Phi Beta Kappa. Office: Ariz State U Dept English Tempe AZ 85287

FISHER, MONTGOMERY ROSS, general contractor; b. Beverly Hills, Calif., Jan. 17, 1921; s. I. Montgomery and Norma Ann (White) F.; m. Joanne McCormick, Sept. 24, 1949; children: Kathleen McCormick Fisher, Montgomery R., Allison A., Sarah N. BA, BS, U. So. Calif., 1943, LLD (hon.), 1976. Pres., chmn. bd. Montgomery R. Fisher, Inc., L.A., 1945—. Lt. UNS, 1942-45. Home: 424 Robert Ln Beverly Hills CA 90210-2632 Office: 2126 Cotner Ave Los Angeles CA 90025-5799

FISHER, PHILIP ARTHUR, investment manager; b. San Francisco, Sept. 8, 1907; s. Arthur Lawrence and Eugenia (Samuels) F.; m. Dorothy Whyte, Aug. 14, 1943; children: Arthur, Donald, Kenneth. AB, Stanford U., 1927. Founder, investment mgr. Fisher and Co., San Mateo, Calif., 1931—. Author: Common Stocks and Uncommon Profits, 1958, Paths to Wealth Through Common Stocks, 1960, Conservative Investors Sleep Well, 1975. Capt. U.S. Army, 1942-45. Office: Fisher and Co 520 N El Camino Real Ste 422 San Mateo CA 94402-1719

FISHER, PHILIP CONDON, artist; b. Oil City, Pa., Nov. 17, 1930; s. Raleigh Harris and Fredericka Alvina (Faaborg) F.; m. Lois Ann Paddock, Nov. 5, 1955; children: Curtis Condon, Nancy Ann, Denise Marie. Student, Graceland Coll., 1950, U. Nebr., 1955, Famous Artists Schs., Westport, Conn., 1958-61. Advt. illustrator Sioux City (Iowa) Jour., 1967-68; comml. artist Bolstein Creative Printers, Sioux City, 1968-69; comic strip/story strip illustrator "Brenda Starr" Chgo., 1977-78; portrait painter/art dealer Denver, 1979—; art appraiser Fisher's Master Artists, Inc., Golden, Colo., 1984—; copyright registration agt. Fisher's Master Artists, Inc., 1984—; portrait painter Prince Charles Philip, Arthur George Mountbatten, Windsor, 21st Prince of Wales, others. With USAF, 1951-54. Mem. Internat. Platform Assn., Am. Legion, Am. Portrait Soc. Home and Office: 13325 W 15th Dr Golden CO 80401-3507

FISHER, ROBERT AMOS, physical chemist; b. Honey Grove, Pa., Mar. 25, 1934; s. Robert A. and Edna M. (Maus) F.; m. Marianne C. Donadio, Aug. 30, 1958; children: Tracy A. Rice. BS, Juniata Coll., 1956; PhD, Pa. State U., 1960. Rsch. chemist U. Calif., Berkeley, 1960-91, Lawrence Berkeley Lab., 1991--. Contbr. articles to profl. jours. Union Carbide fellow, 1958-60. Mem. Am. Assn. for Advancement Sci., Am. Phys. Soc., Sigma Xi. Home: 1841 Yosemite Rd Berkeley CA 94707 Office: U Calif Low Temperature Lab Berkeley CA 94720

FISHER, ROBERT SCOTT, lawyer; b. Detroit, July 16, 1960; s. Alvin Fisher and Beverly (Raider) Levin. BA, U. Mich., 1982; JD, U. Colo., 1985. Bar: Colo. 1985, U.S. Dist. Ct. Colo. 1985, Mich. 1987, U.S. Ct. Appeals (10th cir.) 1989, U.S. Supreme Ct. 1989. Prin. Law Office of Robert S. Fisher, Colorado Springs, Colo., 1985—. Mem. ABA, Colo. Bar Assn., El Paso County Bar Assn., Phi Delta Phi. Home: 4035 Westmeadow Dr Apt 2227 Colorado Springs CO 80906-6063 Office: 105 E Vermijo Ave Ste 600 Colorado Springs CO 80903-2022

FISHER, SHIRLEY IDA A., photography and humanities educator; b. Cleve., Aug. 7, 1935; d. E. and I. (Morley) F. BFA, Ohio U., 1957, MFA, 1959; postgrad., U. Calif., Berkeley, 1964—, U. Calif., Santa Cruz, 1964—. Instr. Detroit Community Ctr., 1960-63; med. photographer Ford Hosp., Detroit, 1961-63; comml. photographer Detroit, 1960-63; photo producer San Jose State U., 1963-70, prof. photography, 1966-67; prof. photo and humanities, coord. photo dept. De Anza Coll., Cupertino, Calif., 1967—; photojournalist to Mex., Puerto Rican and Costa Rican depts. tourism; photographer in over 50 countries; owner Hispanic and Anglo Publs., San Jose, 1986—, World Images Photography, Cupertino, 1963—; 1st invited Am. photographer to Ecuador. Work represented in internat. mus., embassies, bi-nat. ctrs. and pvt. collections; author, editor: Argentine and Chilean Photo, 1984, Cinco de Mayo en San Jose, 1987; editor: Self Reflections, 1987. Am. participant USIS serving in Ecuador, Uruguay, chile, Bolivia, Venezuela, Brazil, Argentina, 1981-86. Mem. Soc. Photographic Edn., Sister Cities San Jose (Calif.), Friends of Photography, Peninsula Advt. Photographers Assn., Phi Theta Kappa, Kappa Alpha Mu. Home and Office: PO Box 1081 Cupertino CA 95015-1081

FISHER, THOMAS J. (TED), pediatrician; b. Dublin, Ireland, Apr. 27, 1922; came to U.S., 1955; s. Charles and Zelda Jessie (Feldman) F. B of Medicine, B of Surgery, B of Obstetrics, Queens U., Belfast, Ireland, 1949. Diplomate Am. Bd. Pediatrics, Calif. Bd. Med. Examiners. Intern Mt. Zion Hosp., San Francisco, 1955-56; pediatric resident Cedars of Lebanon Hosp., L.A., 1956-58; fellow pediatric cardiology Johns Hopkins Hosp., Balt., 1958-60, Stanford (Calif.) U., 1960-61; pvt. practice pediatrics Daly City, Calif., 1961—; attending pediatrician St. Luke's Hosp., San Francisco, 1962-91. Fellow Am. Acad. Pediatrics; mem. San Francisco Med. Soc., Calif. Med. Assn. Home: 508 Cedar Ave San Bruno CA 94066 Office: 48 Park Plaza Dr Rm 302 Daly City CA 94015

FISHER, THORNTON ROBERTS, physicist; b. Santa Monica, Calif., Feb. 16, 1937; s. Vardis and Margaret (Trusler) F.; m. Yvonne Habib, June 22, 1968. AB, Wesleyan U., 1958; PhD, Calif. Inst. Technology, 1963. Rsch. assoc. Stanford (Calif.) U., 1963-68; rsch., cons. scientist Lockheed Palo Alto (Calif.) Rsch. Lab., 1968-87, program mgr., 1987-89, mgr. space payloads dept., 1989—. Contbr. articles to profl. jours. Recipient NSF fellowship, 1958-62. Mem. Am. Phys. Soc., Soc. Photo-Optical and Instrumentation Engrs., Sigma Xi, Soc. for Indsl. and Applied Math. Republican. Home: 25603 Fernhill Dr Los Altos CA 94024-6335 Office: Lockheed Missiles and Space Dept 91-21/B255 3251 Hanover St Palo Alto CA 94304-1121

FISHER, WESTON JOSEPH, economist; b. Glendale, Calif., Aug. 29; s. Edward Weston and Rosalie Eloise (Bailey) F. BS, U. So. Calif., 1962, MA, 1965, MS, 1971, PhD, 1989. Sr. mgr. Naval Undersea Ctr., Pasadena, Calif., 1964-69; chief exec. officer, prin. Ventura County, Ventura, Calif., 1969-73; So. Calif. dir. County Suprs. Assn., L.A., 1974-75; coord. govtl. rels. So. Calif. Assn. Govts., L.A., 1975-78; devel. dir. Walter H. Leimert Co., L.A., 1979-90; bd. dirs. Gray Energy Corp., L.A., Mission Inn Group, Riverside, Calif. Mem. Medieval Acad. Am., El Dorado Country Club, Univ. Club, South Coast Yacht Club, Cave Creek Club, Scottsdale Athletic Club, Lambda Alpha. Republican. Home: 14624 N 22nd St Phoenix AZ 85022

FISHER, WILLIAM HENRY, education educator; b. York, Pa., July 4, 1912; s. Charles Henry and Mary Naomi (Light) F.; m. Christine Albers, June 25, 1938 (dec. Nov. 1959); 1 child, Charles Albers; m. Ruth Dyer, Dec. 27, 1962. BA in Sociology, Secondary Edn., U. Wash., 1935, MEd, 1943; DEd in Social Studies Edn., Columbia U., 1949. Tchr. social studies Wapato (Wash.) Sr. High Sch., 1936-39, Kirkland (Wash.) Sr. High Sch., 1939-44, Fieldston Sch. of The Ethical Culture Soc., N.Y.C., 1945-47; asst. prof. edn., sociology Eastern Wash. State U., Cheney, 1947-50; asst. prof., supr. student tchrs. U. Ariz., Tucson, 1950-51, Temple U., Phila., 1951-52, Wilkes Coll., Wilkes-Barre, Pa., 1952-53; curriculum dir. Las Vegas (N.Mex.) Pub. Schs., 1953-56, supt. schs., 1956-61; assoc. prof. edn. U. Tex., El Paso, 1961-67, assoc. prof., 1967-71; prof. U. Mont., Missoula, 1971—; vis. prof. (summers) Highlands U., Las Vegas, N.Mex., 1950-55, U. N.Mex., Albuquerque, 1961, Western State Coll., Gunnison, Colo. (summers) 1960, 63, 66, Eastern Ill. U., Charleston, 1967, U. Fla. Gainesville, 1971, U. Tenn., Knoxville, 1976; v.p. student council Tchrs. Coll., Columbia, 1946-47; appointed to commn. to revise the high sch. Phys. Edn. Curriculum, N.Mex., 1954-56; pres. Coop. Program in Ednl. Adminstrn., N.Mex., 1960-61; program chmn. Trans-Pecos Edn. Conf. U. Tex., El Paso, 1963-65; chmn. umbrella com. supporting grad. programs Sch. Edn. U. Mont., 1968-78; chair-discussant numerous nat. and regional meets; instr. in field, Mont. Contbr. numerous articles to profl. jours. Mem. AAUP (pres. U. Tex.-El Paso chpt. 1964-65), NEA, Philosophy of Edn. Soc. (presenter papers ann. meetings), Am. Edn. Studies Assn., Western Social Sci. Assn. (chair, panelist ann. meetings Am. studies sect.), Phi Delta Kappa, Kappa Delta Pi. Home: 604 Plymouth St Missoula MT 59801-4129 Office: U Mont Sch Edn Missoula MT 59812

FISHMAN, LILLIAN, research foundation executive; b. Calgary, Alta., Can., Apr. 28, 1915; d. Charles Simcha Waterman and Ethel (Brandeis) Guttman; m. William Harold Fishman, Aug. 6, 1939; children: Joel Sholom, Nina Esther, Daniel Lewis. BS, U. Alta., 1936; MA in Edn., Boston U., 1967. Cert. dietitian, N.Y.; cert. tchr., Mass. Rsch. asst. dept. biochemistry U. Edinburgh, Scotland, 1939-40; dietitian N.Y. Hosp., N.Y.C., 1940-41; rsch. asst. Bowman Gray Sch. Medicine, Winston-Salem, N.C., 1941-43; rsch. assoc. Sch. Medicine Tufts U., Boston, 1968-76; co-founder, scientist, asst. to pres., mgr. devel. La Jolla (Calif.) Cancer Rsch. Found., 1976-89, fgn. student coord., co-chair adv. bd., 1990—; cons. in field. Pres. Winston-Salem Hadassah, 1943-44; den mother Cub pack Brookline (Mass.) area Boy Scouts Am., 1950-53; edn. chmn. Boston Hadassah, 1960-75; dist. coord. Brookline United Fund, 1952. Mem. Am. Jewish Com., Sigma Xi (treas. Tufts br. 1974-75). Office: La Jolla Cancer Rsch Found 10901 N Torrey Pines Rd La Jolla CA 92037-1005

FISHMAN, NORMAN, engineering consultant; b. Petaluma, Calif., July 18, 1924; s. Max and Tova (Berger) F.; m. Lillian Feinstein, Oct. 29, 1953; children: Devora Ann, David Arden. BS, U. Calif., Berkeley, 1948. Chem. engr. USDA, Albany, Calif., 1949-53; project engr. FMC Corp., San Jose, Calif., 1953-54; chem. engr. SRI Internat., Menlo Park, Calif., 1954-68, dir. polymer tech., 1968-77, cons., 1977-88; freelance cons. Menlo Park, 1988-92; pres., cons. Fishman Assocs., Inc., Menlo Park, 1992—; pres., COO, bd. dirs. Solcas Polymer Inc., San Francisco, 1992—. Contbr. articles to profl. publs., patentee in field. Pres. Jewish Comminty Ctr., Palo Alto, 1976-79; bd. dirs. Consumer Coop. Soc., Palo Alto, 1990-93; chmn. Univ. Students Coop. Assn., Berkeley, 1947-48. Mem. Soc. Advanced Materials and Process Engring., Soc. Plastics Engring., Am. Chem. Soc., Sigma Xi. Democrat. Jewish. Home and Office: 2316 Blueridge Ave Menlo Park CA 94025

FISHMAN, WILLIAM HAROLD, cancer research foundation executive, biochemist; b. Winnipeg, Man., Can., Mar. 2, 1914; s. Abraham and Goldie (Chmelnitsky) F.; m. Lillian Waterman, Aug. 6, 1939; children—Joel, Nina, Daniel. B.S., U. Sask., Can., Saskatoon, 1935; Ph.D., U. Toronto, Ont., Can., 1939; MDhc U. Umea, Sweden, 1983; Dir. cancer rsch. New Eng. Med. Ctr. Hosp., Boston, 1958-72; rsch. prof. pathology Tufts U. Sch. Medicine, 1961-70, prof. pathology, 1970-77, dir. Tufts Cancer Rsch. Ctr., 1972-76; pres. La Jolla Cancer Rsch. Found., Calif., 1976-89, pres. emeritus, 1989—; mem. basic sci. programs merit rev. bd. com. VA, 1971-75; mem. pathobiol. chemistry sect. NIH, Bethesda, Md., 1977-81. Author in field. Rsch. Career award NIH, 1962-77; Royal Soc. Can. rsch. fellow, 1939, 17th Internat. Physiol. Congress-U.K. Fedn. fellow, 1947. Fellow AIC, AAAS; mem. Am. Assn. Cancer Rsch., Am. Soc. Biol. Chemists, Am. Soc. Cell Biology, Am. Soc. Exptl. Pathology, Histochem. Soc. (pres. 1983-84), Internat. Soc. Clin. Enzymology (hon.), Internat. Soc. Oncodevel. Biology and Medicine (hon.). Jewish. Club: University (San Diego). Current work: Basic rsch. on expression of placental genes by cancer cells; monoclonal antibodies; oncodevelopmental markers; immunocytochemistry. Home: 715 Muirlands Vista Way La Jolla CA 92037-6202 Office: La Jolla Cancer Rsch Found 10901 N Torrey Pines Rd La Jolla CA 92037-1005

FISK, CHARLES PALMER, English as Second Language educator; b. Chgo., June 13, 1933; s. Chester Ballou Fisk and Margaret (Palmer) Doane. BA magna cum laude, U. Colo., 1955. Cert. tchr., Calif., Wash., ESL tchr. Tchr. Feather River Prep. Sch., Blairsden, Calif., 1963-86; dist. scout exec. Boy Scouts Am., Spokane, Wash., 1986-88; instr. Adult Edn. Ctr. Spokane City Coll., 1991—. Author: Collecting Scouting Literature, 1990; contbr. articles to profl. jours. Deacon Westminster United Ch. of Christ, 1989-91. With U.S. Army, 1957-59. Mem. Scouts on Stamps Soc. Internat. (bd. dirs. 1963-65), Sierra Club, Spokane Canoe and Kayak Club, Phi Beta Kappa, Alpha Phi Omega. Home: 1854 W Bridge Ave Spokane WA 99201-1815

FISK, EDWARD RAY, civil engineer, author, educator; b. Oshkosh, Wis., July 19, 1924; s. Ray Edward and Grace O. (Meyer) Barnes; student Marquette U., 1945-49, Fresno (Calif.) State Coll., 1954, UCLA, 1957-58; B.S., M.B.A., Calif.-Western U.; m. Oct. 28, 1950; children: Jacqueline Mary, Edward Ray II, William John, Robert Paul. Engr., Calif. Div. Hwys., 1952-55; engr. Bechtel Corp., Vernon, Calif., 1955-59; project mgr. Toups Engring Co., Santa Ana, Calif., 1959-61; dept. head Perliter & Soring, Los Angeles, 1961-64; Western rep. Wire Reinforcement Inst., Washington, 1964-65; cons. engr., Anaheim, Calif., 1965; assoc. engr. Met. Water Dist. So. Calif., 1966-68; chief specification engr. Koebig & Koebig, Inc., Los Angeles, 1968-71; mgr. constrn. services VTN Consol., Inc., Irvine, Calif., 1971-78; pres. E.R. Fisk Constrn., Orange, Calif., 1978-81; corp. dir. constrn. mgmt. James M. Montgomery Cons. Engrs., Inc., Pasadena, Calif., 1981-83; v.p. Lawrance, Fisk & McFarland, Inc., Santa Barbara and Orange, 1983—; pres. E.R. Fisk & Assocs., Orange, 1983—, Gleason, Peacock & Fisk, Inc., 1987-92, v.p. constrn. svcs. Wilsey & Ham, Foster City, Calif.; adj. prof. engring., constrn. Calif. State U., Long Beach, 1987-90, Orange Coast Coll., Costa Mesa, Calif., 1957-78, Calif. Poly. State U., Pomona, 1974; lectr. U. Calif., Berkeley, ITS extension, 1978—, internationally for ASCE Continuing Edn.; former mem. Calif. Bd. Registered Constrn. Insps. Served with USN, 1942-43, USAF, 1951-52. Registered profl. engr., Ariz., Calif., Colo., Fla., Idaho, Ky., La., Mont., Nev., Oreg., Utah, Wash., Wyo.; registered environ. assessor, Calif.; lic. land surveyor, Oreg., Idaho; lic. gen. engring. contractor, Calif.; cert. abritator Calif. Constrn. Contract Arbitration Com. Fellow ASCE (life fellow, past chmn. exec. com. constrn. div., former chmn. nat. com. inspection 1978—), Nat. Acad. Forensic Engrs. (diplomate); mem. Orange County Engring. Council (former pres.), Calif. Soc. Profl. Engrs. (past pres. Orange County), Am. Arbitration Assn. (nat. panel), U.S. Com. Large Dams, Order Founders and Patriots Am. (past gov. Calif.), Soc. Colonial Wars (dep. gov. gen. Calif. chpt.), S.R. (past dir.), Engring. Edn. Found. (trustee), Tau Beta Pi. Republican. Author: Machine Methods of Survey Computing, 1958, Construction Project Administration, 1978, 82, 88, 92, Construction Engineers Complete Handbook of Forms, 1981, 92, Resident Engineers Field Manual, 1992; co-author: Contractor's Project Guide, 1988, Contracts and Specifications for Public Works Projects, 1992. Home: PO Box 4969 Foster City CA 94404 Office: 331 Lakeside Dr Ste B Foster City CA 94404

FISK, LINDA LOREAN, museum registrar; b. San Diego, June 29, 1944; d. Uel Martin and Lillian Madeline (Lichty) F. B.A., San Diego State U., 1967; M.A., U. Wash., 1970. Curatorial asst. San Diego Mus. Man, 1965-68, mus. tech., 1970-74, registrar, 1974—; custodian collections Thomas Burke Meml. Wash. State Mus., Seattle, 1967-70; cons. photographer Chaco Canyon Archeol. Ctr., Albuquerque, 1971-72. Author: (with Judith Strupp Green) A Bibliography of Mexican Ethnographic Fabrics: Textiles and Costume, 1976. Woodrow Wilson Grad. fellowship Hon. mention, 1967. Mem. Am. Assn. Mus. (registrars com.). Democrat. Office: San Diego Mus Man 1350 El Prado San Diego CA 92101-1681

FITCH, JACK, association executive. Grad. high sch., Barry, Ill. Exec. dir. Civilian Congress, San Francisco, 1964—. Editor: (directory) Civilian Congress Annual, 1964—. Mem. Japan Soc. No. Calif., Commonwealth Club of Calif., Internat. Visitors Ctr. of Bay Area. Office: Civilian Congress 2361 Mission St Rm 238 San Francisco CA 94110-1868

FITHIAN, PETER STALKER, retail executive; b. Bridgeport, Conn., July 7, 1928; s. Roswell Curtis and Ada Allerton (Stalker) F.; m. Jean Simons, June 1950 (div. Feb. 1958); children: Peter Jr., Marsha Jean; m. Roberta Bernice Wong, 1970. BS in Hotel Adminstrn., Cornell U., 1951. Asst. mgr. Treadway Inns, Falmouth, Mass., 1954; mgr. Augusta (Ga.) Nat. G.C., 1955, Kona Inn, Kailua-Kona, Hawaii, 1955-56; asst. mgr. Kaiser's Hawaiian Village, Honolulu, 1956-57; pres. Greeters of Hawaii, Ltd., Honolulu, 1957—; participant small co. mgmt. program Harvard U., 1980. Chmn. Hawaii Vis./Conv. Bur., Honolulu, 1970-72, Pacific Ocean Rsch. Assn., Honolulu and Kona, 1976-92; chmn., founder Hawaiian Internat.

Billfish Assn., Honolulu, 1976-92; trustee Internat. Gamefish Assn., Pompano Beach, Fla., 1985-92; bd. dirs. The Billfish Found., Pompano Beach, 1986-92, Nat. Coalition Marine Cons., Savannah, Ga., 1987-92, Aloha Festivals, Honolulu, 1980-82; mem. Western Pacific R.F. Man Coun., Honolulu, 1976-80; vice-chair Visitor Ind. Edn. Com. Lt. (j.g.) USN, 1951-54. Mem. Am. Soc. Travel Agts., Soc. Incentive Travel Execs., Pacific Area Travel Assn., Cornell Soc. Hotelmen (chmn. Hawaii chpt. 1980-85), Waialae Country Club, Balboa Angling Club (life). Office: Greeters of HAwaii 3375 Koapaka St Ste 250 Honolulu HI 96820

FITZGERALD, JAMES MARTIN, federal judge; b. Portland, Oreg., Oct. 7, 1920; s. Thomas and Florence (Linderman) F.; m. Karin Rose Benton, Jan. 19, 1950; children: Dennis James, Denise Lyn, Debra Jo, Kevin Thomas. BA, Willamette U., 1950, LLB, 1951; postgrad., U. Wash., 1952. Bar: Alaska 1953. Asst. U.S. atty. Ketchikan and Anchorage, Alaska, 1952-56; city atty. City of Anchorage, 1956-59; legal counsel to Gov. Alaska, Anchorage, 1959; commr. pub. safety State of Alaska, 1959; judge Alaska Superior Ct., 3d Jud. Dist., 1959-69, presiding judge, 1969-72; assoc. justice Alaska Supreme Ct., Anchorage, 1972-75; judge U.S. Dist. Ct. for Alaska, Anchorage, from 1975, formerly chief judge, now sr. judge. Mem. advisory bd. Salvation Army, Anchorage, 1962—, chmn., 1965-66; mem. Anchorage Parks and Recreation Bd., 1965-77, chmn., 1966. Served with AUS, 1940-41; Served with USMCR, 1942-46. Office: US Dist Ct 222 W 7th Ave Ste 50 Anchorage AK 99513-7579

FITZGERALD, JERRY, security specialist; b. Detroit, Apr. 21, 1936; s. John Middleton and Jessie Lucy (Call); m. Ardra Elizabeth Finney, Dec. 1, 1962. BS, Mich. State U., 1959; MBA, U. Santa Clara, 1964; M Bus. in Econs., Claremont Grad. Sch., 1971, PhD, 1972. CISA, CDP. Indsl. engr. Parke Davis & Co., Detroit, 1959-61; acct. exec. McDonnell & Co., Detroit, 1961-62; assoc. engr. Lockheed Missiles & Space Co., Sunnyvale, Calif., 1962-66; systems analyst Singer/Friden Div., San Leandro, Calif., 1966-68; systems engr. U. Calif., San Francisco, 1968-69; assoc. prof. Calif. State Colls. & Univ., Pomona, Hayward, Calif., 1969-73; sr. mgmt. cons. SRI Internat., Menlo Pk., Calif., 1973-77; pres. Jerry FitzGerald & Assocs., Redwood City, Calif, 1977—. Author: Business Data Communications, 4th ed., 1993, Designing Controls into Computerized Systems, 2nd ed., 1990, Fundamentals of Systems Analysis, 3d ed., 1987, Internal Controls for Computerized Systems, 1981, (software/book) RANK-IT A Risk Assessment Software Tool, CONTROL-IT A Control Spreadsheet Software Tool for PCs and Compatibles; contbr. articles to profl. jours. Recipient Joseph J. Wasserman award, 1980. Mem. EDP Auditors Assn., Inst. Internal Auditors, Info. Systems Security Assn. Office: Jerry FitzGerald & Assocs 506 Barkentine Ln Redwood City CA 94065-1128

FITZGERALD, LORETTA CIEUTAT, lawyer; b. New Orleans, Oct. 17, 1959; d. Roland Ernest and Grace (Nissen) Cieutat; m. John Richard Fitzgerald, May 5, 1990; children: Lylah Sheehan, Myles Christian. BA, Newcomb Coll., New Orleans, 1981; JD, Tulane U., 1985. Bar: La., 1985, Alaska, 1987, Mass., 1992. Law clk. Dept. of Justice, New Orleans, 1981-85; atty. Office of Judges, U.S. Dept. Labor, New Orleans, 1985-87, William Azar Law Firm, Anchorage, 1988—. Contbr. articles to profl. jours. Mem. La. Bar Assn., Mass. Bar Assn., Alaska Bar Assn. (exec. com. on torts 1989—), Am. Acad. Trial Lawyers, Alaska Acad. Trial Lawyers. Democrat. Roman Catholic. Home: 811 W 88th Ave Anchorage AK 99515 Office: 800 E Dimond Blvd Ste 3-440 Anchorage AK 99515

FITZGERALD, RICHARD PATRICK, school administrator; b. Harrisburg, Pa., May 27, 1950; s. Richard Patrick and Virginia Clare (Husic) F.; m. Marilyn G. MacGregor, Nov. 20, 1981; 1 child, Helen. BA, U. Notre Dame, 1972; MA, U. Va., 1973. Tchr. English Collegiate Sch., N.Y.C., 1973-85, dir. ind. studies, 1978-82, dir. devel., 1983-85; master English The Leys Sch., Cambridge, Eng., 1982-83; headmaster Little Red Sch. House, N.Y.C., 1985-88, Branson Sch., Ross, Calif., 1988—; dir. Beginning Tchr. Inst., Nysais, N.Y., 1986-88. Author: The Great Quiet, 1989. Pres., trustee Dan Wagoner Dancers, N.Y.C., 1987-88, Marin Herizon Sch., 1989—, Marin Ballet Co., 1990-93. Mem. Nat. Assn. Ind. Schs., Calif. Assn. Ind. Schs. (trustee 1990—, v.p. 1991-92, 92-93, pres. 1993—), Nat. Assn. Prins. Schs. for Girls, N.Y. State Assn. Ind. Schs., Headmistresses of East, Guild N.Y.C. Headmasters (bd. dirs. 1987-88), Country Day Headmasters Assn. Democrat. Home: PO Box 446 Ross CA 94957-0451 Office: Branson Sch PO Box 877 Ross CA 94957-0888

FITZGERALD, ROBERT LYNN, small business owner; b. Indiana, Pa., Oct. 1, 1939; s. Joseph and Jean (Smith) F.; m. Tomi Higuchi, May 30, 1991; 1 child, Robert Lynn Jr. Student, Orange Coast Coll., 1985-86; BA, U. Redlands, 1990; MA, U.S. Internat. U., 1993. Dist. mgr. Napco Sci., Portland, Oreg., 1981-88; prin., pub. Fitzgerald's Real Estate Yellow Pages, Santa Ana, Calif., 1987—; psychol. sales cons., 1990—. Hospice vol. Orange County (Calif.), Vis. Nurses Assn., 1980; founder Orange County HELP chpt., Santa Ana, 1982. Home: 2700 W Segerstrom Ave # D Santa Ana CA 92704-6547 Home: Fitzgerald's Real Estate Yellow Pages 3941 S Bristol Ste 335 Santa Ana CA 92704

FITZGERALD, TIKHON (LEE R. H. FITZGERALD), bishop; b. Detroit, Nov. 14, 1932; s. LeRoy and Dorothy Kaeding (Higgins) F. AB, Wayne State U., 1958. Ordained deacon, 1971, priest, 1978, bishop Eastern Orthodox, 1987. Enlisted U.S. Army, 1954-57; commd. 2 lt. USAF, 1960, advanced through grades to capt., 1971; air staff, 1966-71, released, 1971; protodeacon Holy Virgin Mary Russian Orthodox Cathedral, L.A., 1972-78, rector, archpriest, 1979-87; bishop of San Francisco Orthodox Ch. in Am., L.A., 1987—. Democrat. Home: 649 Robinson St Los Angeles CA 90026-3612 Office: Orthodox Ch Am Diocese of the West 650 Micheltorena St Los Angeles CA 90026

FITZGERALD, VINCENT JAMES, controller; b. N.Y.C., Nov. 21, 1950; s. Vincent Edward and Joan Mary (Berhman) F. BA, St. John Fisher Coll., Rochester, N.Y., 1972; MBA, Northwestern U., Evanston, Ill., 1974; advanced profl. cert., NYU, 1984. CPA, Ill., N.Y. Staff acct. Deloitte Haskins & Sells, Chgo., 1974-77; sr. internal auditor Am. Hosp. Supply Corp., Evanston, 1977-79; bus. mgr. McGraw-Hill, Inc., N.Y.C., 1979-82; asst. treas. Chem. Bank, N.Y.C., 1982-84; controller Hay Group, Inc., N.Y.C., 1984-88; dir. fin. reporting Reeves Entertainment Group, L.A., 1988—. F.C. Austin scholar, 1972. Mem. AICPA, Calif. State CPAs, Acctg. Rsch. Assn. Republican. Roman Catholic. Home: 8324 Canterbury Ave Sun Valley CA 91352 Office: Reeves Entertainment Group 10877 Wilshire Blvd Los Angeles CA 90024

FITZGERALD, WILLIAM BRENDAN, lawyer; b. Waterbury, Conn., May 4, 1936; s. William Brendan Sr. and Margaret (Cunning) F.; m. Teresa Vannini, Oct. 12, 1963 (div. Oct. 1980); children: W. Brendan III, Nicholas S., Francesca V. BA cum laude, Yale U., 1958; JD, Harvard U., 1961; cert. in higher European Studies, Coll. Europe, Bruges, Belgium, 1962. Bar: Conn. 1961, Calif. 1985. Ptnr. Fitzgerald & Fitzgerald, Waterbury, Conn., 1961-72, Carmody & Torrance, Waterbury, 1972-85, Haight, Dickson, Brown & Bonesteel, Santa Monica, Calif., 1985-88, Dickson, Carlson & Campillo, Santa Monica, 1988—. Rotary Internat. fellow, 1961. Fellow Am. Coll. Trial Lawyers, Roscoe Pound Found; mem. ABA (litigation, torts and ins. sects.), Calif. Bar Assn., Conn. Bar Assn. (acad. continuing profl. devel. 1982, judiciary com. 1982-85, jud. liason com. 1985), Def. Rsch. inst., Assn. So. Calif. Def. Counsel, Am. Arbitrations Assn. (panelist), Conn. Trial Lawyers Assn. (pres. 1985), Am. Bd. Trial Advs., Nat. Bd. Trial Advocacy (diplomate). Democrat. Club: Yale (N.Y.C.). Office: Dickson Carlson & Campillo 120 Broadway Ste 300 Santa Monica CA 90407

FITZPATRICK, DENNIS MICHAEL, information systems executive; b. Jacksonville, Fla., Jan. 10, 1945; s. John J. Fitzpatrick and Roxanne (Cotsakis) Athanassiades; m. Kathleen Irene McDonough, June 10, 1967; children: Michael, Kara. BS, Manhattan Coll., 1967; MBA, CUNY, 1970. Mgr., system engr. Am. Airlines, N.Y.C., 1967-72; v.p. info. systems Western Airlines, L.A., 1972-87; pres. Info. Resources Assn., L.A., 1987-88; v.p. Pacific Info. Mgmt., Culver City, Calif., 1988-92; pres. Pacific Info. Mgmt., Inc., Canada, 1992—. Contbg. author: Information Engineering Management Guide, 1989, Information Strategy Planning, 1991, Business Area Analysis, 1990, Information Resource Assessment, 1990. Named one of Outstanding Young Men Am., 1982. Office: Pacific Info Mgmt 400 Corporate Pointe A755 Culver City CA 90230

FITZSIMMONS, (LOWELL) COTTON, professional basketball executive, former coach; b. Hannibal, Mo., Oct. 7, 1931; s. Clancy and Zelda Curry (Gibbs) F.; m. JoAnn D'Andrea, Sept. 2, 1978 (div.); 1 child, Gary. B.S., Midwestern Univ., Wichita Falls, Tex., M.A. Head coach, athletic dir. Moberly Jr. Coll, Moberly, Mo., 1958-67; head coach Kans. State U., Manhattan, 1967-70; head coach NBA Phoenix Suns, 1970-72, 1988-92, dir. player personnel, 1987-88; head coach NBA Atlanta Hawks, 1972-76; dir. player personnel NBA Golden State Warriors, Oakland, Calif., 1976-77; head coach NBA Buffalo Braves, 1977-78, NBA Kansas City Kings, Mo., 1978-84, NBA San Antonio Spurs, 1984-87; sr. exec. v.p. Phoenix Suns, 1992—. Recipient Coach of the Yr. award Nat. Jr. Coll. Athletic Assn., 1966, 67, Coach of the Yr. award Big 8 Conf., 1970, Coach of the Yr. award NBA, 1979, 89, Coach of the Yr. award Sporting News, St. Louis, 1979, 89; inducted into Mo. Sports Hall of Fame, Jefferson City, 1981, Nat. Jr. Coll. Basketball Hall of Fame, Hutchinson, 1985. Fellow Nat. Assn. Basketball Coaches. Office: Phoenix Suns 2910 N Central Ave Phoenix AZ 85012-2779*

FITZSIMMONS, LISA LYNN, health services administrator; b. Ketchikan, Alaska, June 1, 1964; d. James Calvin and Mary Anne (Murphy) F. BA in Pub. Rels., Speech Communications, U. Nev., 1986. Acct. coord. The Baker Group, Reno, 1986-88; sr. coord. community rels. St. Mary's Regional Med. Ctr., Reno, 1988-89, corp. client rels. rep., 1989-90, supr. health promotion ctr., 1990—. Editor (corp. newsletter) Advantage, 1989-91 (IABC Silver Dollar award 1990); (community newsletter) Lifelines, 1988-89. Intern, vol. Multiple Sclerosis Soc., Reno, 1984-88; com. chmn. Internat. Winter Spl. Olympic Games, Reno, 1988-89, Am. Heart Assn., 1988-90, bd. dirs., 1990—. Recipient Vol. of Yr. award Am. Heart Assn., Nev., 1990-91. Mem. Am. Mktg. Assn., Pub. Rels. Soc. Am. (sec. 1990, treas. 1991), No. Nev. Pers. Assn. (Outstanding Young Woman of Am. 1988), Acad. for Health Svcs. Mktg., Reno Ad Club, Phi Beta Phi (fin. advisor 1991—, Amy Burnham Onken award 1986, Outstanding Alumni award 1992). Office: St Mary's Regional Med Ctr 1155 w 4th St # 104 Reno NV 89503

FITZSIMONS, PATRICK S., police chief; b. N.Y.C., Apr. 16, 1930; s. Patrick Joseph and Mary (Brabazon) F.; m. Olga Parker, Aug. 18, 1959. B.S., Fordham U., 1954; J.D., 1972; J.D. fellow criminal justice, Harvard U. Law Sch., 1972-73. Adj. prof. John Jay Coll. Grad. Sch., N.Y.C.; mem. N.Y.C. Police Dept.; asst. chief programs and policies; now chief of police City of Seattle; chmn. Major City Chiefs Assn.; chmn. FBI Policy Adv. Bd. Bd. dirs. Chief Seattle council Boy Scouts Am. Served to 1st lt. USMC, 1953-56. Recipient award criminal justice Am. Soc. Public Adminstrn. Mem. Fordham U. Law Sch. Alumni Assn., Harvard U. Law Sch. Alumni Assn., Wash. Athletic Club. Office: Police Department 1001 Public Safety Bldg 610 3d Ave Seattle WA 98104

FITZWATER, MARSHA DEAN, financial auditor; b. Salem, Oreg., Feb. 4, 1950; d. Almos Edridge and Laura Buela (Marsh) LeFors; m. Paul Timothy Fitzwater, Dec. 30. 1972. Student, Simpson Coll., 1969-71; BS, Western Oreg. State Coll., 1972; B in Acctg. Sci., U. Puget Sound, 1984, MBA, 1984. Acctg. mgr. Fitzwater & Fitzwater Assocs., Shelton, Wash., 1980-85; ptnr. Old Oreg. Farms, Valley Junction, Oreg., 1988-89; fin. auditor Sr. and Disabled Svcs. Div. State of Oreg., Salem, 1985—; participant Leadership Oreg. Program for Future Leaders in State Govt., 1990-92. Office: 500 Summer St NE 2nd Fl Salem OR 97310-1015

FIX, WILBUR JAMES, department store executive; b. Velva, N.D., Aug. 14, 1927; s. Jack J. and Beatrice D. (Wasson) F.; m. Beverly A. Corcoran, Sept. 20, 1953; children: Kathleen M., Michael B., Jenifer L. BA, U. Wash., 1950. Credit mgr. Bon Marche, Yakima, Wash., 1951-54; controller, ops. mgr. Bon Marche, Boise, Idaho, 1954-58; sr. v.p. Bon Marche, Seattle, 1970-76; exec. v.p. Bon Marche, 1976-77, pres., chief exec. officer, 1978-87; chmn., chief exec. officer, sr. v.p. Allied Stores Corp., 1987-93, chmn. exec. com., 1993—; chmn. Wash. Retail Coun., 1983-84 (sr. exec. adv. bd. 1992); bd. dirs., vice chmn, Wash. Telecommunications Corp., BMC West Corp., Vans, Inc. Mem. pres.'s adv. com. Allied Stores Corp., N.Y., 1968-72; mem. citizens adv. com. Seattle Pub. Schs., 1970-71; v.p. Citizens Council Against Crime; chmn. Seattle King County Conv. & Visitors Bur., 1990. With AUS, 1946-47. Mem. Nat. Retail Mchts. Assn., Controllers Congress, Seattle Retail Controllers Group (past pres.), Fin. Execs. Inst., Western States Regional Controllers Congress (past pres.), Seattle C. of C. (exec. com., bd. dirs.), Assn. Wash. Bus. (fin. adv.), Downtown Seattle Devel. Assn. (exec. com., trustee), Wash. Round Table, Wash. Athletic Club, Columbia Tower Club, Elks, Pi Kappa Alpha, Alpha Kappa Psi, Phi Theta Kappa. Episcopalian. Home: 5403 W Mercer Way Mercer Island WA 98040-4635 Office: The Bon Marché 3d and Pine Seattle WA 98181

FIXMAN, MARSHALL, chemist, educator; b. St. Louis, Sept. 21, 1930; s. Benjamin and Dorothy (Finkel) F.; m. Marian Ruth Beatman, July 5, 1959 (dec. Sept. 1969); children—Laura Beth, Susan Ilene, Andrew Richard; m. Branka Ladanyi, Dec. 7, 1974. A.B., Washington U., St. Louis, 1950; Ph.D., MIT, 1954. Jewett postdoctoral fellow chemistry Yale U., 1953-54; instr. chemistry Harvard U., 1956-59; sr. fellow Mellon Inst., Pitts., 1959-61; prof. chemistry, dir. Inst. Theoretical Sci., U. Oreg., 1961-64, prof. chemistry, research asso. inst., 1964-65; prof. chemistry Yale U., New Haven, 1965-79; prof. chemistry and physics Colo. State U., Ft. Collins, 1979—. Assoc. editor Jour. Chem. Physics, 1962-64, Jour. Phys. Chemistry, 1970-74, Macromolecules, 1970-74, Accounts Chem. Research, 1982-85, Jour. Polymer Sci. B, 1991—. Served with AUS, 1954-56. Fellow Alfred P. Sloan Found., 1961-63; recipient Governor's award Oreg. Mus. Sci. and Industry, 1964. Mem. NAS, Am. Acad. Arts and Scis., Am. Chem. Soc. (award pure chemistry 1964, award polymer chemistry 1991), Am. Phys. Soc. (high polymer physics award 1980), Fedn. Am. Scientists. Office: Colo State U Dept Chemistry Fort Collins CO 80523

FIX-ROMLOW, JEANNE KAY, hair care products company executive; b. Madison, Wis., June 29, 1947; d. Glen H. and Violet M. (Bohnsack) Fix; m. Paul James Romlow, Nov. 7, 1985. Student, Madison Area Tech. Sch., 1966. Mgr. Fashion Fabrics, Madison, 1973-74; promotion dir. Livesey Enterprises, Madison, 1976-77; sales assoc. First Realty Group, Madison, 1977-79; territory mgr. Aerial Beauty and Barber Supply, Madison, 1979-83; regional dir. John Paul Mitchell Systems, Santa Clarita, Calif., 1983-85, v.p., 1986-87, sr. v.p., 1987-91, exec. v.p., 1991—. Home: 11344W Bay Dr Lodi WI 53555-9623 Office: John Paul Mitchell Systems 26455 Golden Valley Rd Santa Clarita CA 91350-2621

FJORDBOTTEN, EDWIN LEROY, Canadian provincial official; b. Claresholm, Alta., Can., Nov. 4, 1938; m. Deanne Marie Perchinsky, Nov. 16, 1962; children: Tracy, Karine. Grad. Camrose Luth. Coll., 1956. Farmer, nr. Granum, Alta., Can., 1960-83; mem. Alta. Legis. Assembly, Edmonton, 1979—, min. of agr., 1982-86, min. of tourism, 1986-87, min. of forestry, Lands and Wildlife, 1987—. Progressive Conservative. Lutheran. Office: Minister of Forestry, Legislature Bldg Rm 408, Edmonton, AB Canada T5K 2B6

FLACH, VICTOR H., designer, educator; b. Portland, Oreg., May 31, 1929; s. Victor H. and Eva (Huget) F. Student of, Jack Wilkinson, R. Buckminster Fuller, W.R. Hovey; B.S., U. Oreg., 1952, M.F.A., 1957; postgrad., U. Pitts., 1959-65. Archtl., elec. engring. and cartographic draftsman with various cos. and U.S. govt. agy., 1948-62; teaching fellow, curator Henry Clay Frick Fine Arts Dept. and Gallery, U. Pitts., 1959-63; docent Frank Lloyd Wright's Fallingwater, Western Pa. Conservancy, 1963-64; prof. art, design, painting, theory and history U. Wyo., Laramie, 1965—; participant R. Buckminster Fuller Geodesic Prototype Projects, 1953, 59; interviewer Heritage series TV program PBS-TV, 1965; cons. Nat. Symposium on Role of Studio Arts in Higher Edn., U. Oreg., 1967. Participant: various TV programs including Arts in Practice series, 1971-77; designer multi-walled murals, U. Oreg., Eugene, 1952, Rainbow Club, 1954, Clear Lake Sch., Eugene, 1956, Sci. Ctr., U. Wyo., Laramie, 1967, one-man and group shows of paintings, photographs, exptl. films and drawings, 1949—; Author and editor: IJHTBIW20 Poems, 1949, 12 New Painters, 1953, IN/SERT Active Anthology for the Creative, 1955-62, Gloss of the Four Universal Forms, 1959, The Anatomy of the Canvas, 1961, The Eye's Mind, 1964, The Stage, 1978, Contextualist Manifesto, 1982, Displacings & Wayfarings, 1986, JW's Orientation Mural, 1990; contbr. poems, articles and photographs to lit. jours., 1949—. Served with U.S. Army, 1953-55. Office: 1618 Custer Sta Laramie WY 82070-4243

FLACHSBART, PETER GEORGE, urban planning educator, consultant; b. St. Louis, Apr. 15, 1944; s. Bernard Ernst and Florence Lillian (Trapp) F.; m. Carol Emiko Minn, July 24, 1976 (div. May 1982); m. Janice Lynne Powell, Aug. 27, 1983. BS in Civil Engring., Washington U., St. Louis, 1966; MS, Northwestern U., 1968, PhD, 1971. Sr. rsch. assoc. U. So. Calif., L.A., 1971-72; lectr. Calif. State U., Dominguez Hills, 1972-73, asst. prof., 1973-76; asst. prof. Stanford (Calif.) U., 1976-80; asst. prof. U. Hawaii at Manoa, Honolulu, 1980-83, assoc. prof., 1983—; cons. U.S. EPA, Washington, 1987, 89, U.S. Agy. Internat. Devel., Washington, 1987, Hawaii Dept. Bus. Econ. Devel. & Tourism, Honolulu, 1988-93, WHO, 1991-92. Contbr. articles to profl. jours. Capt. U.S. Army, 1966-74. Recipient Travel award Nat. Endowmnt Arts, 1969; grantee Stanford U., 1977, U.S. EPA, 1980, 82, Hawaii Office State Planning, 1990-91, Hawaii Dept. Transp., 1990-91. Mem. Am. Planning Assn. (Hawaii chpt., profl. devel. officer 1983—), Air and Waste Mgmt. Assn., Am. Inst. Cert. Planners, Am. Planning Assn., Am. Lung Assn., Sigma Xi. Lutheran. Office: U Hawaii Manoa 2424 Maile Way # 107 Honolulu HI 96822-2281

FLACKS, ERWIN, artist, art broker; b. N.Y.C., Apr. 15, 1926; s. Herman and Theresa (Goldstein) F.; m. Sheryl Silver (div. June 1975); children: Lane Terry Verbeek, Scott Flacks; m. Gail Susan Mantell, Feb. 21, 1981. AA, L.A. City Coll., 1948; BA, Calif. State U., L.A., 1950; MA, Calif. State U., Northridge, 1958. Tchr. L.A. Unified Schs., 1950-75; owner art gallery, Agoura Hills, Calif., 1978-90; art broker Westlake Village, Calif., 1978—; pres. Hollygraf/Fine Art Pub. and Distbr., Hollywood, Calif., 1980—; artist, 1983—; cons. L.A. City Schs., 1958-63; tchr. tchrs. of intellectually gifted students Calif. State U., Northridge, 1960-64. Art commd. for Donald Trump's Taj Mahal, Atlantic City, Disneyworld Corporate Office, Warner Bros. Studios, Harrah's Hotel, Reno, Desert Inn, Las Vegas; works included in numerous pvt. and pub. collections. With USN, 1943-45, PTO. Mem. Westlake Art Guild, United Tchrs. L.A. Office: Fine Art Mktg Co 638 Lindero Canyon Rd # 322 Agoura Hills CA 91301

FLAGG, NORMAN LEE, retired advertising executive; b. Detroit, Jan. 21, 1932; s. Frank and Harriet (Brown) F.; m. Carolanne Flagg; 1 child, James. BFA, U. Miami, Fla., 1958. Advt. supr. Smithkline Beckman, Phila., 1970-75, creative dir., 1975-80; owner Illusions Restaurants, Bryn Mawr, Pa., 1979-87, Illusions Restaurant, Tucson, Ariz., 1984-88. With USMC, 1954-56. Recipient Diana awards Whlse Druggest Assn. 1977, Aesculapius award Modern Medicine 1978. Mem. Acad. Magical Arts.

FLAGLER, WILLIAM LAWRENCE, financial broker; b. Oakland, Calif., June 13, 1922; s. Albert William and Violet Dorthy (Marris) F.; B.A., San Francisco State U., 1951; degree in Library Sci., San Jose State U., 1963; m. Ruth Greiner Gilbert, Aug. 23, 1970; children by previous marriage: Vickie, David, Michael; stepchildren: Denise Gilbert La Hay, Ethan Gilbert. Registered fin. broker. Pres., LaRu Enterprises, San Jose, Calif., 1975—. Active Boy Scouts Am. Served with U.S. Army, World War II, ETO. Republican. Club: Masons. Office: PO Box 10460 San Jose CA 95157-1460

FLAHERTY, LARRY PAUL, electronics manufacturing company executive; b. Salina, Kans., Mar. 10, 1943; s. Paul E. and Bernice Ileen (Pottberg) F.; BEE, U. Kans., 1966; MSE, Ariz. State U., 1969, MBA, 1976; m. Regina Ann Dancho, June 10, 1967; children: Pamela, David, Joseph. Electronics engr. Motorola, Inc., Scottsdale, Ariz., 1966-69, Recognition Equipment, Inc., Dallas, 1969-72; program mgr. Motorola, Inc., 1972-78; prodn. mgr. Hewlett Packard, Greeley, Colo., 1978-86, materials mgr., 1986—. Pres., Homeowners Assn., 1982—; lector St. Elizabeth Ann Seton Cath. Ch., quartermaster com. Troop 97, Boy Scouts of Am. Patentee digital recognition unit for optical character reader. Mem. Assn. Mfg. Excellence. Avocations:camping, skiing, hiking, tennis. Home: 1407 Kenwood Ct Fort Collins CO 80525-1218 Office: 700 71st Ave Greeley CO 80634

FLAIM, STEPHEN FREDERICK, pharmaceutical executive, researcher; b. San Jose, Calif., May 28, 1948; s. Francis Richard and Cecilia Martha (Bihn) F.; m. Kathryn Erskine, Aug. 16, 1975; children: Bryna Kathryn, Celia Elizabeth. BS, U. Santa Clara, 1970; PhD, U. Calif., Davis, 1975. Secondary edn. credential. From spl. faculty appointee to grad. faculty assoc. Pa. State U., Hershey, 1976-82; prin. scientist McNeil Pharm. Corp., Spring House, Pa., 1982-86; rsch. fellow McNeil Pharm. Corp., Spring House, 1986-87; sect. head Squibb Inst. for Med. Rsch., Princeton, N.J., 1987-89; assoc. dir. Bristol-Myers Squibb Corp., Princeton, 1989-90; div. dir. Alliance Pharm. Corp., San Diego, 1990—; vis. assoc. prof. Med. Coll. Pa., Phila., 1985—. Editor: (book) Calcium Blockers, 1982; contbr. over 200 rsch. articles to profl. jours. Pres. Cardiovascular Rsch. Discovery Group, 1990; chmn. bd. dirs. Swim San Diego, 1991. Edwin J. Brown fellow Santa Clara U., 1971; recipient Rsch. Svc. award NHI, 1976-78, Young Investor award NHI, 1980-82. Fellow Am. Heart Assn. (rsch. fellowship 1975-76, British-Am. fellowship 1977), Am. Coll. Clin. Pharmacology; mem. Internat. Soc. for Heart Rsch., Am. Hypertension Soc., Am. Soc. Pharm. and Experimental Theraphy, Am. Physiological Soc., Royal Soc. Medicine. Republican. Roman Catholic. Home: 4455 Foxhollow Ct San Diego CA 92130-2429 Office: Alliance Pharm Corp 3040 Science Park Rd San Diego CA 92121-1102

FLAMING, WADE A, software engineer; b. Goessel, Kans., Aug. 7, 1965; s. Abe Jacob and Velma Bernice (Heibert) F. AA, Hutchinson (Kans.) Community Jr. Coll., 1985; BS, Biola U., 1987. Math, physics tutor Hutchinson (Kans.) Community Jr. Coll., 1984-85; co-op. student engr. divsn. tng. and control systems Honeywell, West Covina, Calif., 1986-87; software engr. Hughes Tng. Inc., West Covina, Calif., 1988—. Republican. Protestant. Home: Apt 1215 2455 Jefferson Court Ln Arlington TX 76006 Office: Hughes Tng Inc PO Box 6171 Arlington TX 76005

FLAMM, DANIEL LAWRENCE, engineer, educator, semiconductor consultant, researcher; b. San Francisco, Sept. 14, 1943; s. Gerald Robert and Esther Lucile (Zwerling) F.; m. Lois Ellen Canter, Oct. 30, 1965; children: Jonathan, Stephen. BS, MIT, 1964, MS, 1966, ScD, 1970. Registered profl. engr., Tex. Asst. prof. Northeastern U., Boston, 1969-70; sr. design programmer Foxboro (Mass.) Co., 1970-72; asst. prof. Tex. A&M U., College Sta., 1972-77; disting. mem. tech. staff AT&T Bell Labs., Murray Hill, N.J., 1977-89; McKay lectr. dept. elec. engring. U. Calif., Berkeley, 1988—; v.p. tech. Mattson Tech., Sunnyvale, Calif., 1991-92; vis. scientist Advanced X-Ray Optics Group Lawrence Livermore Nat. Labs., Livermore, Calif., 1992-93; lectr., cons. in field; chmn. Am. Water Works Assn. Task Force for Standard Methods, Ozone, 1978-85; chmn. Gordon Conf. Plasma Chemistry, 1980; mem. Internat. Union of Pure and Applied Chemistry subcommittee on Plasma Chemistry, 1980-87, adv. bd., rev. bd. NSF, 1981-83, 88. Author, co-author: Plasma Materials Interaction Series; co-editor: Plasma Diagnostics Vol. I, Discharge Parameters and Chemistry, 1989, Plasma Diagnostics Vol. II, Surface Analysis and Interactions, 1989, Plasma-Surface Interactions and Processing of Materials, 1990; mem. editorial bd. profl. jours.; contbg. editor Solid State Tech., 1990—, Microlithography World, 1992—; contbr. numerous articles to profl. jours., chpts. to books; patentee in field. Recipient Cert. Recognition NASA, Moffett Field, Calif., 1978, 79, Thinker award Tegal Corp., Petaluma, Calif., 1985. Mem. Internat. Soc. for Optical Engring., Am. Inst. Chem. Engrs., Am. Vacuum Soc., Am. Radio Relay League, Sigma Xi, Pi Lambda Upsilon. Home: 476 Green View Dr Walnut Creek CA 94596-5459 Office: U Calif Dept Elec Engring Berkeley CA 94720

FLAMM, MELVIN DANIEL, JR., cardiologist; b. L.A., Jan. 29, 1934; s. Melvin Daniel and Mary (Peterek) F.; m. Carla Baker, June 24, 1955; children: Scott Daniel, Bradley John, Jason Andrew, Amanda Paige. BA, UCLA, 1956; MD, Stanford U., 1960. Diplomate Am. Bd. Internal Medicine, Am. Bd. Cardiovascular Disease. Rotating intern Walter Reed Gen. Hosp., Washington, 1960-61; med. resident Stanford U., 1964-66, fellow in cardiology, 1966-68; cardiologist in pvt. practice No. Calif. Cardiology Assocs., Sacramento; clin. prof. medicine U. Calif., Davis; med. dir. Cardiac Catheterization Labs. Sutter Meml. Hosp., Sacramento, 1976-92; chmn. instl. rev. com. Sutter Community Hosps.; examiner Subspeciality Bd. of Cardiovascular Diseases of Am. Bd. Internal Medicine, 1971-75; vis. prof.

cardiology Nat. Def. Med. Sch. and Vets. Gen. Hosp., Taiwan U. Sch. Medicine, 1978, Queen Mary Hosp. of Hong Kong, U. Sch. Medicine and Hong Kong Cardiologic Soc., 1978. Contbr. numerous articles to profl. jours. Trustee Sutter Hosps. Found., 1987-89. Col. M.C., USAF, 1959-74, active res., 1974-84. Fellow ACP, Am. Coll. Cardiology, Coun. on Clin. Cardiology of Am. Heart Assn. (chmn. and mem. rsch. com. and rsch. allocation com. Golden Empire chpt.); mem. AMA, Am. Fedn. Clin. Rsch., Sacramento-El Dorado Med. Assn., Calif. Med. Assn. Office: No Calif Cardiology Assocs 5301 F St # 117 Sacramento CA 95819

FLANAGAN, JAMES HENRY, JR., lawyer; b. San Francisco, Sept. 11, 1934; s. James Henry Sr. and Mary Patricia (Gleason) F.; m. Charlotte Anne Nevins, June 11, 1960; children: Nancy, Christopher, Christina, Alexis, Victoria, Grace. AB in Polit. Sci., Stanford U., 1956, JD, 1961. Bar: Calif. 1962, U.S. Dist. Ct. (no. dist.) Calif. 1962, U.S. Ct. Appeals (9th cir.) 1962, U.S. Dist. Ct. (so. dist.) Calif. 1964, U.S. Dist. Ct. (ea. dist.) 1967, Oreg. 1984. Assoc. Creede, Dawson & McElrath, Fresno, Calif., 1962-64; ptnr. Pettitt, Blumberg & Sherr and successor firms, Fresno, 1964-75; sole practice Clovis, Calif., 1975-92, North Fork, Calif., 1992—; instr. Humprey's Coll. Law, Fresno, 1964-69, bus. Calif. State U., Fresno, 1986—, Coll. of Notre Dame MPA prog., Belmont, 1990-91, Nat. U., 1991—; judge pro tem Fresno County Superior Ct., 1974-77; gen. counsel Kings River Water Assn., 1976-79. Author: California Water District Laws, 1962. Exec. com. parish coun. St. Helen's, 1982-85, chmn., 1985; pres. parish coun. St. John's Cathedral, 1974-82; pres. bd. 3d Fl. Cen. Calif.; bd. dirs. Fresno Facts Found., 1969-70, Fresno Dance Repertory Assn., St. Anthony's Retreat Ctr., Three Rivers, Calif.; v.p. Dispute Resolution Ctr. of Cen. Calif., 1988—. Recipient President award Fresno Jaycees, 1964. Mem. Am. Trial Lawyers Assn., Calif. Bar Assn., Fresno County Bar Assn., Calif. Trial Lawyers Assn. (chpt. pres. 1975, 83, state bd. govs. 1990—), Fresno Trial Lawyers Assn., Stanford Alumni Assn. (life, svc. award), Fresno Reg. Stanford Club (pres. 1979-80), Celtic Cultural Soc. Cen. Calif. (pres. 1977-78), Fresno County and City C. of C. (chmn. natural resources com. 1977-78), Clovis Dist. C. of C., North Fork C. of C. (bd. dirs.), Clovis Big Dry Creek Hist. Soc., Fresno Serra Club (pres. 1980-81, v.p. 1986-87), Rotary, Elks. Republican. Roman Catholic. Home and Office: PO Box 1555 North Fork CA 93643-1555

FLANAGAN, LATHAM, JR., surgeon; b. Pitts., Dec. 2, 1936; s. Latham and Elizabeth Lansing (Bunting) Kimbrough; m. Elizabeth Ruth Losaw, June 26, 1961 (dec. May 1971); 1 child, Jennifer Ruth; m. Mary Jane Flanagan, Mar. 28, 1975; children: Sahale Ann, David Nooroa. MD, Duke U., 1961, student, 1957, MD, 1961. Diplomate Am. Bd. Surgery. Intern U. Calif., San Francisco, 1961-62, resident in surgery, 1962-66, chief resident in surgery, 1965-66; pvt. practice surgery Sacred Heart Hosp., Eugene, Oreg., 1968-84, 85—; clin. sr. instr. in surgery Oreg. Health Scis. U., Portland, 1968-84; assoc. prof. surgery U. Otago, Dunedin (New Zealand) Pub. Hosp., 1984-85; nat. surgeon Cook Islands, 1985. Contbr. articles to profl. jours. Founder White Bird Clinic, Eugene, 1969-71; adv. com. Planned Parenthood of Lane County, 1979-84. With USN, 1966-68, Vietnam. Fellow ACS (pres. Oreg. chpt. 1991-92); mem. AMA, Oreg. Med. Assn., Lane County Med. Soc. (com. chairs 1970's), Am. soc. Bariatric Surgery (chair ins. com.), North Pacific Surg. Soc., Eugene Surg. Soc. (past pres. 1981). Republican. Home: 4495 Pinecrest Dr Eugene OR 97405 Office: 655 E 11th Ave Ste 8 Eugene OR 97401

FLANAGAN, THOMAS JAMES, air force officer, financial consultant; b. Boston. BS, USAF Acad., 1984; MBA, Chapman U., 1993. Commd. 2d lt. USAF, advanced through grades to capt., 1988; chief navigator, flight instr. USAF, Almendorf AFB, Alaska. Robert J. Smith scholar The Falcon Found.

FLANDERS, ALLEN F., architect; b. Paynesville, Minn., Mar. 26, 1945; s. Harold Edward and Beatrice Elizabeth (Schultz) F.; m. Cathleen Ann Pomatto, Sept. 13, 1986; children: Derek C., Lyndsey E. BArch, U. Minn., 1969. Lic. architect., Calif. Project mgr. Carl A. Scholz & Assocs., San Francisco, 1972-73; architect Humberto Bermudez & Assocs., San Francisco, 1973-75, Hellmuth, Obata & Kassabaum, San Francisco, 1975-76; pres. Hope Design Group, San Diego, 1976—. Prin. works include Robert Presley Detention Ctr., Riverside Gen. Hosp., Lindberg Field Upgrade. Member Am. Correctional Assn., 1985, Am. Jail Assn., 1987, Calif. State Sheriffs Assn., 1989. Lt. USN, 1969-72, ETO. Mem. San Diego Taxpayers Assn. (bd. dirs. 1990—), Greater San Diego C. of C. (bd. dirs. 1991—), Scripps Ranch Old Pros, San Diego Kiwanis (bd. dirs. 1992—). Office: Hope Design Group 4520 Executive Dr San Diego CA 92121

FLANDERS, GEORGE JAMES, mechanical engineer, engineering development manager; b. Bunker Hill, Ind., June 3, 1960; s. Melvin S. and Edith J. (Mason) F. BSME, Bradley U., 1982, MBA, 1984. Lab. engr. Materials Testing & Rsch. Lab., Peoria, Ill., 1982; rsch. design engr. Caterpillar Tractor Co., Peoria, 1982-85; staff engr. Bristol Myers Co., Englewood, Colo., 1985-86, sr. engr., bus. unit mgr. arthoscopy and reconstructive surgery products, 1986-87; group engr., Titan project bus. proposal coord. Titan Space Launch Systems, Martin Marietta Astronautics Group, Denver, 1987—; co-founder, chief exec. officer WSG Mgmt. and Holding Group, Denver, 1988—; bd. dirs., sec., chmn., investment com. chmn. Red Rock Fed. Credit Union, 1989—; cons. in field. Area coord. Neighborhood Watch Program, 1988-89; crew leader 10,000 Trees Environ. Project; mem. fin. com. Littleton United Meth. Ch., 1987—. Mem. NSPE, ASME, Soc. Automotive Engrs., Sigma Phi Delta (grand pres. 1988-90, v.p. 1985-87, trustee chmn. 1988-90), Tau Beta Pi, Pi Tau Sigma, Omicron Delta Kappa. Home: 6168 S Lee St Littleton CO 80127-7714 Office: Martin Marietta Astronautics Group PO Box 179 Denver CO 80201-0179

FLANIGAN, DONNA MARIE HERRING, geologist, petroleum company executive; b. Arlington, Va., Jan. 18, 1957; d. Donald Wilson and Bettye Jo (Brake) Herring; m. T. Edward Flanigan III, Apr. 19, 1986. Student, Goddard Coll., 1975; BA in Mus. Studies, Earlham Coll., 1979; MS in Geology, U. Cinn., 1986. Cert. profl. earth scientist. Curator, exhibit designer Joseph Moore Mus., Richmond, Ind., 1977-79; exhibit designer Cinn. Mus. Natural History, 1978-79; curatorial asst., Geology Mus. U. Cinn., 1979-81, grad. asst. dept. geology, 1980-82; geol. asst. Mobil Producing Tex. & N.Mex., Houston, 1981; exploration geologist Marathon Oil Co., Casper, Wyo., 1983-86; prodn. geologist Marathon Oil Co., Midland, Tex., 1986-87; sr. geologist Flanigan & Flanigan, Petroleum Geologists, Midland, 1987-88; dir., officer, geologist Flanigan & Flanigan, Inc., Reno, 1988-93; pvt. practice independent petroleum geologist, 1993—. Chief editor: Oil Fields & Geology of the Pine Valley Eureka County Area, 1990; contbr. numerous articles to profl. jours. Truancy counsellor Cinn. Experience Truancy Guidance, 1982; big sister Big Bros./Big Sisters, Casper, Wyo., 1984-86 (Svc. award 1985). Recipient Poetry award Bain-Swiggett Poetry Prize, 1979, Tex. Poetry Soc. (Odessa chpt.), 1987. Mem. Nev. Petroleum Soc. (pres. 1989-90, dir. 1990-92), Am. Assn. Petroleum Geologists, Geol. Soc. Am., Assn. Women Geoscientists (chpt. sec. 1984-85), Utah geol. Assn., Geol. Soc. Nev., W. Tex. Geol. Soc. (com. chmn. 1987-88, Svc. award 1988). Office: PO Box 13652 Reno NV 89507

FLANIGAN, JAMES J(OSEPH), journalist; b. N.Y.C., June 6, 1936; s. James and Jane (Whyte) F.; m. Anne Fitzmaurice, Jan. 9, 1965 (dec. Oct. 1992); children: Michael, Siobhan Jane. BA, Manhattan Coll., 1961. Fin. writer N.Y. Herald Tribune, N.Y.C. and Paris, 1957-66; bur. chief, asst. mng. editor Forbes Mag., Washington, London, Houston, L.A., N.Y.C., 1966-86; bus. columnist, sr. writer L.A. Times, 1986—, 1980, 83-84, 86—. Cpl. U.S. Army, 1955-57, Germany. Recipient John Hancock award for Fin. Journalism, John Hancock Life Inst., Boston, 1987. Roman Catholic. Office: LA Times Times Mirror Sq Los Angeles CA 90053

FLANNELLY, KEVIN J., psychologist, research analyst; b. Jersey City, Nov. 26, 1949; s. John J. and Mary C. (Walsh) F.; m. Laura T. Adams, Jan. 10, 1981. BA in Psychology, Jersey City State Coll., 1972; MS in Psychology, Rutgers U., 1975; PhD in Psychology, U. Hawaii, 1983. Rsch. asst. dept. psychology U. Ill., Champaign, 1973-75; rsch. intern Alcohol Behavior Rsch. Lab. Rutgers U., New Brunswick, N.J., 1973-75; rsch. scientist Edward R. Johnstone Tng. and Rsch. Ctr., Bordentown, N.J., 1975-78; teaching asst. dept. psychology U. Hawaii, Honolulu, 1980-81, rsch. asst. Pacific Biomed. Rsch. Ctr., 1981-83, asst. prof. Bekesy Lab. Neurobiology, 1983-85; rsch. statistician, statewide transp. planning office Hawaii Dept. Transportation, Honolulu, 1986-89; researcher Office of Lt. Gov., Honolulu, 1989—; statis cons. U. Hawaii Sch. Nursing, Honolulu, 1986, Hawaii Dept. Health, Honolulu, 1986; v.p., rsch. dir. Ctr. Psychosocial Rsch., Honolulu, 1987—; instr. dept. social scis. Honolulu Community Coll., 1981; ptnr. Flannelly Cons., 1991—; rsch. dir. Mktg. Rsch. Inst., 1992—. Editor: Biological Perspective on Aggression, 1984, Introduction to Psychology, 1987; reviewer 8 sci. and profl. jours., 1978—; grant reviewer NSF, 1984—; contbr. numerous articles to profl. jours. Polit. survey cons., Honolulu, 1988—; transp. cons., Honolulu, 1989—; mktg. cons., Honolulu, 1990—. Grantee NIH, 1984, Fed. Hwy. Adminstrn., 1987; N.J. State scholar N.J. Dept. Higher Edn., 1968-72. Fellow Internat. Soc. Rsch. on Aggression; mem. AAAS, Am. Psychol. Soc., Am. Statis. Assn., Internat. Soc. Comparative Psychology, N.Y. Acad. Scis., Pacific and Asian Affairs Coun., Psychonomic Soc., Sigma Xi. Home: 445 Kaiolu St Apt 1207 Honolulu HI 96815-2255 Office: Office of Lt Gov Hawaii State Capitol Honolulu HI 96813

FLANNELLY, LAURA T., mental health nurse, nursing educator, researcher; b. Bklyn., Nov. 7, 1952; d. George A. Adams and Eleanor (Barragry) Mulhearn; m. Kevin J. Flannelly, Jan. 10, 1981. BS in Nursing, Hunter Coll., 1974; MSN, U. Hawaii, 1984, postgrad., 1988—. RN, N.Y., Hawaii. Psychiat. nurse Bellevue Hosp., N.Y.C., 1975, asst. head nurse, 1975-77; psychiat. nurse White Plains (N.Y.) Med. Ctr., 1978-79; community mental health nurse South Beach Psychiat. Ctr., N.Y.C., 1979-81; psychiat. nurse The Queen's Med. Ctr., Honolulu, 1981-83; crisis worker Crisis Response Systems Project, Honolulu, 1983-86; instr. nursing U. Hawaii, Honolulu, 1985-92, asst. prof., 1992—; adj. instr. nursing Hawaii Loa Coll., Honolulu, 1988, Am. Samoa Community Coll., Honolulu, 1987, 89, 90; mem. adv. bd., planning com. Psychiat. Day Hosp. of The Queen's Med. Ctr., Honolulu, 1981-82; program coord. Premenstrual Tension Syndrome Conf., Honolulu, 1984; dir. Ctr. Psychosocial Rsch., Honolulu, 1987—; program moderator 1st U.S-Japan Health Behavioral Conf., Honolulu, 1988; faculty Ctr. for Asia-Pacific Exch., Internat. Conf. on Transcultural Nursing, Honolulu, 1990. Contbr. articles to profl. jours. N.Y. State Bd. Regents scholar, 1970-74; NIH nursing trainee, 1983-84; grantee U. Hawaii, 1986, 91, Hawaii Dept. Health, 1990. Fellow Internat. Soc. Rsch. on Aggression; mem. AAAS, Am. Ednl. Rsch. Assn., Am. Psychol. Soc., Am. Statis. Assn., Nat. League for Nursing, N.Y. Acad. Scis., Pacific and Asian Affairs Coun., Sigma Theta Tau. Home: 445 Kaiolu St Apt 1207 Honolulu HI 96815-2255 Office: U Hawaii Sch Nursing Webster Hall Honolulu HI 96822

FLATEN, MARK DOUGLAS, patient account executive; b. Seattle, Mar. 4, 1959; s. Richard A. and Margaret Geraldine (Mostoller) F.; m. Julie Marie Morford, Mar. 8, 1990; children: Joshua David, Nicole Marie. ABA, Green River C.C., Auburn, Wash., 1980. Dist. mgr. Fournier Newspapers, Kent, Wash., 1980-81; sales rep. Uniway of Cen. Fla., Orlando, 1981-82; br. mgr. Travelers Acceptance, Seattle, 1982-86; account rep. Seattle 1st Nat. Bank, 1986-88; patient account mgr. Orthopedic Phys. Inc., Seattle, 1988—. Mem. Seattle/King County Internat. Credit Assn., Am. Guild Patient Account Mgmt., Soc. Cert. Consumer Credit Execs. (cert. consumer credit exec.). Home: 1301 SW 360th Federal Way WA 98023 Office: Orthopedic Physicians 1229 Madison # 1600 Seattle WA 98104

FLATT, MICHAEL OLIVER, manufacturing company executive; b. Glen Rogers, W.Va., Aug. 14, 1938; s. Reuben Edgar and Margaret Elenor (Gansor) F.; m. Judie Arlene Carroll, Aug. 12, 1961 (div. Oct. 1970); m. Joanie Louise Smith, Nov. 26, 1970; children: Rachel, Joshua. BS in Mech. Engring., U. Ill., 1961. Mfg. engr. Gen. Electric Co., Bloomington, Ill., 1961-63; process engr. Gen. Electric Co., Detroit, 1963-64; quality control mgr. Gen. Electric Co., Daytona Beach, Fla., 1964-65; advance planner Gen. Electric Co., Phoenix, 1965-68; mgr. quality control Computer Memory Devices, Glendale, Ariz., 1968-71; gen. mgr. Continental Cirs. Corp., Phoenix, 1971-75, pres., 1975-83, chmn. bd., 1983-89, pres., CEO, 1993—; prin. Michael O. Flatt, Ltd., Mesa, 1989-93. Author: Printed Circuit Board Basics, 1992; mem. editorial rev. bd. Printed Cir. Fabrication, 1985-89; contbr. articles to tech. mags. Active various state, local and nat. polit. campaigns, Mesa, 1974—; bd. dirs. Prehab Ariz., Mesa, 1981—, pres., 1990-91; bd. dirs. Mesa Ednl. Found., 1990—, v.p., 1992—. Mem. IPC (bd. dirs. 1989—), Inst. for Packaging and Interconnecting Electronic Cirs., Tech. and Mktg. Rsch. Coun., Ariz. Printed Cir. Assn. (founding bd. dirs. 1975), Western Cirs. Assn. (pres. Phoenix chpt. 1972-73), Lions (pres. Phoenix chpt. 1975-76, pres. pres.'s coun. Ariz. chpt. 1975-76), Phi Eta Sigma, Pi Mu Epsilon. Republican. Office: 3502 E Roeser Rd Phoenix AZ 85040

FLATTÉ, MICHAEL EDWARD, physicist, researcher; b. Walnut Creek, Calif., Apr. 14, 1967; s. Stanley Martin and Renelde Marie (Demeure) F.; m. Jennifer Beatrice Kirsch, Aug. 20, 1989; 1 child, Devra Tamar. AB, Harvard U., 1988; PhD, U. Calif., Santa Barbara, 1992. Teaching asst., rsch. asst. dept. physics U. Calif., Santa Barbara, 1989-92, postdoctoral rsch. assoc. Inst. Theoretical Physics, 1992—. NSF fellow, 1988, Russell and Sigurd Varian fellow Am. Vacuum Soc., 1991. Mem. Am. Phys. Soc. Office: U Calif Inst Theoretical Physics Santa Barbara CA 93106

FLAXER, CARL, physician; b. Lynn, Mass., Jan. 9, 1918; s. Moses M. and Rose Rachel (Shriberg) F.; m. Evelyn Esther Sachs, Dec. 3, 1944; children: Michael, Susan, Lisa, Lori. BS, Mass. Coll. Pharmacy, 1938; MD, U. Colo., 1950. Pharmacist Johnson Drug, Waltham, Mass., 1938-40, Lovell Gen. Hosp., Ayer, Mass., 1940-42; intern Fitsimons AMC, Denver, 1950-51; pvt. practice family practice Keenesburg, Colo., 1951-70, Denver, 1980-88; dir. family practice residency Mercy Med. Ctr., Denver, 1970-80; edn. chmn. Colo. Acad. Family Physicians, Denver, 1985-90, pres., 1981-82; mem. Gov.'s Adv. Commn. on Family Medicine, Denver, 1972-80. Contbr. chpts. to books: Family Practice, 1978, Critical Care Issues, 1982. Capt. Med. Corps. U.S. Army, 1951-52. Recipient Recognition award for innovative programs Colo. Hosp. Assn., 1976. Fellow Am. Acad. Family Physicians (founding mem.); mem. Colo. State Med. Soc. Home and Office: 890 Hudson St Denver CO 80220

FLEAGLE, ROBERT GUTHRIE, meteorologist, educator; b. Woodlawn, Md., Aug. 16, 1918; s. Benjamin Edward and Frances Taylor (Guthrie) F.; m. Marianne Diggs, Dec. 19, 1942; children: Robert Guthrie, John B. A.B., Johns Hopkins U., 1940; M.S., N.Y. U., 1944, Ph.D., 1949. Asst. prof. U. Wash., 1948-51, assoc. prof., 1951-56, prof., 1956-87, prof. emeritus, sr. fellow Joint Inst. Study of Atmosphere and Ocean, 1978—, chmn. dept. atmospheric scis., 1967-77; Cons. various bus., instns., govt. agys.; tech. asst. Office Sci. and Tech., Exec. Office of Pres., 1963-64; mem. Nat. Acad. Scis. Com. on Atmospheric Scis., 1962-76, chmn., 1969-73; mem. panel on oceanography Pres.'s Sci. Adv. Com., 1965-66; mem. U.S. com. Global Atmospheric Research Program, 1968-73; mem. NATO adv. panel on meteorology, 1970-73; chmn. BOMAP adv. panel, 1969-73; mem. assembly of math. and phys. scis. Nat. Acad. Scis., 1976-79. Author: (with J.A. Businger) An Introduction to Atmospheric Physics, 1963, 2d edit., 1980; editor: Weather Modification: Science and Public Policy, 1968, Weather Modification in the Public Interest, 1974; contbr. articles to sci. jours. Trustee Univ. Corp. for Atmospheric Research, 1970-78, chmn. bd., 1975-77, chmn. council mems., 1966-67, chmn. membership com., 1987-89. Served from pvt. to capt. AUS, 1942-46. NSF fellow Imperial Coll., London, 1958-59. Fellow AAAS (chmn. sect. atmospheric and hydrological scis. 1977-78), Am. Geophys. Union (pres. meteorol. sect. 1967-70), Am. Meteorol. Soc. (Meisinger award 1959, Cleveland Abbé award 1971, Brooks award 1985, commn. sci. and technol. activities 1965-69, council 1957-60, 73-76, 80-84, pres. 1981); mem. Sigma Xi. Home: 7858 56th Pl NE Seattle WA 98115-6331 Office: U Washington Seattle WA 98195

FLECK, RICHARD FRANCIS, English language educator, writer; b. Phila., Aug. 24, 1937; s. J. Keene and Anne M. (DeLeon) F.; m. Maura B. McMahon, June 29, 1963; children: Richard Sean, Michelle Marie, Ann Maureen. BA, Rutgers U., 1959; MA, Colo. State U., 1962; PhD, U. N.Mex., 1970. Park ranger naturalist Rocky Mountain Nat. Pk., Colo., 1959; instr. English North Adams (Mass.) State Coll., 1963-65; prof. of English U. Wyo., Laramie, 1965-90; prof. intercultural studies, dir. humanities div. Teikyo Loretto Heights U., Denver, 1990—, dir. humanities div., 1991-93; exch. prof. Osaka (Japan) U., 1981-82; vis. prof. SUNY, Cortland, 1988-89; dean arts and humanities C.C. Denver, 1993—. Author: Thoreau and Muir Among the Indians, 1985, Earthen Wayfarer, 1988, Critical Perspectives on Native American Fiction, 1993, (with others) John Muir: His Life and Works, 1993; asst. editor Sage U. Wyo., 1965-67; editor Thoreau Jour. Quar., 1975-77; contbg. editor Paintbrush, 1986—. Dem. precinct committeeman, Laramie, 1968. With USN, 1961-63. Grantee U. Wyo., 1967, 71, Wyo. State Hist. Soc., 1973, Wyo. Humanities Coun., 1979, 80. Mem. N.Y. State Tchrs. Union, Thoreau Soc., Appalachian Mountain Club, Sierra Club. Roman Catholic. Office: CC Denver Office of Dean Arts & Humanities 1111 W Colfax Ave Denver CO 80217

FLECKLES, JOHN ROBERT, academic administrator, history educator; b. Greenfield, Mass., Sept. 22, 1936; s. Elliot Victor and Cheryl Louise (McCabe) F. BA, Blackburn Coll., 1958; PhD, U. Calif., Berkeley, 1981. Instr. Hawaii Loa Coll., Kaneohe, 1971-77, asst. prof., 1977-81, assoc. prof., 1981—, acad. dean, 1984-92; acad. v.p. Hawaii Pacific U., Honolulu, 1992—; dir. Haiku Point Assn., Kaneohe, 1990-92. Mem. Pacific & Asian Affairs Coun., 1991-92. Democrat. Office: Hawaii Pacific U 1188 Fort Street Mall Ste 440 Honolulu HI 96813

FLECKMAN, PHILIP HOWARD, dermatologist, cell biologist; b. Port Arthur, Tex., Apr. 27, 1946; s. Max and Jeanette (Lindenberg) F.; m. Star C. Leonard, Dec. 28, 1977; children: Mahri S. Leonard-Fleckman, Morgen L. Leonard-Fleckman. B.A., U. Tex., 1968; M.D., Washington U., St. Louis, 1973. Diplomate Am. Bd. Dermatology. Intern medicine Barnes Hosp., St. Louis, 1973-74; rsch. assoc. lab. of neurochemistry, NIMH, NIH, Bethesda, Md., 1974-76, med. officer rsch., 1976-78; resident dept. dermatology Yale U., New Haven, 1978-80; instr., 1980-81, asst. prof., 1981-82; asst. prof. med. dermatology U. Wash., Seattle, 1982-88, assoc. prof. dermatology, 1988—; cons. West Haven VA Hosp., Conn., 1980-82; staff physician Yale-New Haven Hosp., 1980-82, Univ. Hosp., Seattle, 1982—. Contbr. articles to profl. jours. Served with USPHS, 1974-78. Recipient Clin. Investigator award NIH, 1980-83; Dermatology Found. fellow, 1980; NIH program project grantee, 1983-91. Fellow Am. Acad. Dermatology; mem. Am. Soc. Cell Biology, Soc. Investigative Dermatology, Am. Fedn. Clin. Research, Fedn. Am. Scientists. Home: 5041 Ivanhoe Pl NE Seattle WA 98105 Office: U Wash Divsn Dermatology RM-14 Seattle WA 98195

FLEER, KEITH GEORGE, lawyer, motion picture executive; b. Bklyn., Feb. 28, 1943; s. Samuel Robert and Sophia M. (Scherer) F.; BA in Govt., Am. U., 1964, JD, 1967. Bar: N.Y. 1968, D.C. 1968, Calif. 1976. Asst. dir. athletics Fordham U., 1967-68; assoc. Gettinger, Gettinger & Manheimer, N.Y.C., 1968-72, Kaye, Scholer, Fierman, Hays & Handler, N.Y.C., 1972-75; sr. counsel Avco-Embassy Pictures, Hollywood, Calif., 1976; assoc. Schiff, Hirsch & Schreiber, Beverly Hills, Calif., 1977; sr. v.p. bus. and legal affairs Melvin Simon Prodn., Inc., Beverly Hills, 1978-81; exec. v.p. Simon, Reeves, Landsburg Prodns., Beverly Hills, 1982-84; v.p. bus. affairs Warner Bros., 1984-88, ptnr. Denton Hall Burgin and Warrens, 1987-88; of counsel Sinclair Tenenbaum & Co., Inc., Beverly Hills, 1989—; guest lectr. U. West Los Angeles Law Sch., 1979-80; legis. counsel N.Y. State Assemblyman, 1969-70. Bus. editor Am. U. Law Rev., 1966-67. Bd. trustees Am. U., 1991—. Recipient Bruce Hughes award Am. U., 1964, Alumni award Am. U. Law Sch., 1967, Stafford H. Cassell award, 1979. Mem. ABA, Beverly Hills Bar Assn., L.A. Copyright Soc. (trustee 1983-90, pres. 1988-89), Acad. of Motion Picture Arts and Scis. Office: 335 N Maple Dr Beverly Hills CA 90210-3857

FLEGAL, A(RTHUR) RUSSELL, JR., toxicologist, geochemist, educator; b. Oakland, Calif., Aug. 30, 1946; s. Arthur Russell Sr. and Barbara (Warren) F.; m. Brenda Dolan, Dec. 18, 1970; children: Heather Dolan, John Arthur. BS, U. Calif., Santa Barbara, 1968; MS, Moss Landing (Calif.) Marine Labs., 1976; PhD, Oreg. State U., 1979. Rsch. assoc. Moss Landing Marine Labs., 1981-85; vis. rsch. assoc. Calif. Inst. Tech., Pasadena, 1981—; assoc. rsch. geochemist U. Calif., Santa Cruz, rsch. geochemist, 1988-92, prof. environ. toxicology, 1992—; vis. scientist Swiss Fed. Inst. Tech., Zurich, Switzerland, 1988; prof. environ. toxicology U. Calif., Santa Cruz, 1992—; vis. scientist Lawrence Livermore (Calif.) Nat. Labs., 1988—; mem. com. Nat. Rsch. Coun., Washington, 1989—, Intergovt. Oceanographic Commn., Paris, 1989—; cons. EPA, Washington, 1989—. Contbr. chpts. to sci. texts, sects. to ency.; contbr. more than 100 articles to profl. jours. Post doctoral fellow Calif. Inst. Tech., 1980, Rsch. fellow, 1980-81. Mem. Am. Chem. Soc., Am. Geophys. Union, Soc. Environ. Toxicology and Chemistry. Office: U Calif Inst Marine Sci Santa Cruz CA 95064

FLEGENHEIMER, DIANA VAUGHN, fundraising executive; b. Denver, Jan. 26, 1945; d. Michael and Virginia Rose (Barnes) Grega; m. Michael Lee, Dec. 1967 (div. Dec. 1973); m. Roy Alan Flegenheimer, July 28, 1974 (div. Jan. 1992); children: Elon Michael, Rachel Anne. AA, Hutchinson (Kans.) Jr. Coll., 1965; BS, Kans. U., 1967; MA, Ariz. State U., 1972. Cert. high sch. tchr., Ariz. Math tchr. various high schs., Ariz. and Mo., 1967-75; devel. officer Ariz. Mus. Sci. and Tech., Phoenix, 1986-88, Desert Botanical Garden, Phoenix, 1988-89, Actors Theatre, Phoenix, 1989-91, TERROS Behavioral Health Svcs., Phoenix, 1991—. Mem. Samaritans, 1987—; women's campaign chmn. United Jewish Appeal, 1984-86; mem. Valley Leadership, 1986-87. Recipient Lee Amada Young Leadership award Jewish Fedn. Greater Phoenix, 1981, Golda Meir award, 1990. Mem. Nat. Soc. Fund Raising Execs. (bd. dirs. Greater Ariz. chpt.), Jewish Bus. and Profl. Women's Nat. Coun., Beta Gamma Sigma, Phi Lambda Theta, Phi Theta Kappa. Democrat. Jewish. Home: 4929 E Laurel Ln Scottsdale AZ 85254 Office: TERROS Behavioral Health Svcs 711 E Missouri Ave Ste 317 Phoenix AZ 85014-2829

FLEISCHER, MARK OWEN, lawyer; b. L.A., Apr. 11, 1948; s. Richard O. and Mary (Dickson) F. BA, U. Exeter, Devon, Eng., 1970; JD, U. So. Calif., 1984. Bar: Calif. 1985, U.S. Dist. Ct. (ctrl. dist.) Calif. 1985. Freelance composer, 1970-74; program dir. Global TV, Sta. KSCI-TV, L.A., 1974-75, pres., gen. mgr., 1975-77; freelance producer, composer, 1977-82; ptnr. Manatt, Phelps & Phillips, L.A., 1985—. Co-author (book) Producing, Financing & Distributing Film, 1992. Res. police officer Santa Monica (Calif.) Police Dept., 1979-87. Office: Manatt Phelps & Phillis 11355 W Olympic Blvd Los Angeles CA 90064

FLEISCHMANN, ERNEST MARTIN, music administrator; b. Frankfurt, Germany, Dec. 7, 1924; came to U.S., 1969; s. Gustav and Antonia (Koch) F.; children: Stephanie, Martin, Jessica. B of Commerce, U. Cape Town, South Africa, 1950, MusB, 1954; postgrad., South African Coll. Music, 1954-56; MusD (hon.), Cleve. Inst. Music, 1987. Gen mgr. London Symphony Orch., 1959-67; dir. Europe CBS Masterworks, 1967-69; exec. dir. L.A. Philharm. Assn. and Hollywood Bowl, 1969-88, exec. v.p., mng. dir., 1988—; bd. dirs. Am. Music Music Ctr., Inc.; mem. French Govt. Commn. Reform of Paris Opera, 1967-68; steering com. U.S. nat. commn. UNESCO Conf. Future of Arts, 1975. Debut as condr. Johannesburg (Republic of South Africa) Symphony Orch., 1942; asst. condr. South African Nat. Opera, 1948-51, Cape Town U. Opera, 1950-54; condr. South African Coll. Music Choir, 1950-52, Labia Grand Opera Co., Cape Town, 1953-55; music organizer Van Riebeeck Festival Cape Town, 1952; dir. music and drama Johannesburg Festival, 1956; contbr. to music publs. Recipient award of merit L.A. Jr. C. of C., John Steinway award, Friends of Music award Disting. Arts Leadership Univ. So. Calif., 1989, L.A. Honors award L.A. Arts Coun., 1989, Live Music award Am. Fedn. Musicians, Local 47, 1991. Mem. Assn. Calif. Symphony Orchs., Major Orch. Mgrs. Conf., Am. Symphony Orch. League, L.A. Philharm. Assn. (bd. dirs. 1984—). Office: Los Angeles Philharm Orch 135 N Grand Ave Los Angeles CA 90012-3013

FLEISHMAN, ALAN MICHAEL, marketing consultant; b. Berwick, Pa., June 28, 1939; s. Benjamin Bennet and Ruth (Sadock) F.; m. Ann Arrasmith, Aug. 3, 1963; children: Elizabeth, Gregory, Keith. BA, Dickinson Coll., 1961; postgrad., Xavier U., 1966-67, Calif. State U., Fullerton, 1968-69. Sales and mktg. planning Procter & Gamble, Cin., 1963-67; sr. product mgr. Baxter Internat., Costa Mesa, Calif., 1967-70; dir. mkgt. Allergan, Inc., Irvine, Calif., 1970-76; exec. v.p. Hudson Vitamins, West Caldwell, N.J., 1976-77; v.p. mktg. and sales Cooper Vision, Inc., Mountain View, Calif., 1977-80; pres. Alan M. Fleishman, Mktg. Cons., San Carlos, Calif., 1980—; instr. U. Calif., Berkeley, 1990—. With U.S. Army, 1961-63. Mem. Am. Mktg. Assn., Med. Mktg. Assn. Democrat. Jewish. Home and Office: 3 Bluebell Ln San Carlos CA 94070

FLEMING, B. JEANNE, psychologist; b. Chattanooga, Apr. 3, 1949; d. Delbert and Gladys Marie (Hicks) Swanson; m. J. Richard Fleming (div.); 1

child, Jason. BSN, U. Fla., 1971; MS in Marriage and Family Counseling, Loma Linda (Calif.) U., 1975; PhD, U.S. Internat. U., San Diego, 1979. Lic. clin. psychologist, Wash., Calif. Nurse various agys; cons. Human Resource Dept. Cowlitz and Wahkiukum Counties (Wash.), 1979; therapist pvt. practice, Vancouver, Wash., 1981-82, Longview, Wash., 1983—; noted pub. speaker, columnist, internat. conf. and workshop presenter; contbr. articles to profl. jours.; mem. family life com. Oreg. conf. Seventh-day Adventists; bd. dirs. Children's Home Soc. Wash.; cons. in field. Friend of the bd. West Coast Chamber Orch., Portland, 85—, bd dirs., 1984, 85, 87, 88, 89; ethics adv. com. dept. ob/gyn. Oreg. Health Sci. U., Portland, 1986-88; steering com. Music Assocs., Portland State U., 1986-89. Mem. Am. Psychol. Assn., Am. Assn. Marriage and Family Therapists, Am. Fertility Soc., Internat. Soc. Study Multiple Personality Dissociation, Soc. Traumatic Stress Disorder, Portland Endometriosis Assn., Western Psychol. Assn., Wash. Psychol. Assn. (exec. bd. 1981-83), S.W. Wash. Assn. Psychologist (sec.-treas. 1981-82). Office: 783 Commerce Ste 200 Longview WA 98632

FLEMING, DALE THOMAS, software executive; b. St. Paul, Minn., Dec. 17, 1951; s. Forrest Charles and Lorraine Lois (Lennartson) F. BA, U. Calif., San Diego, 1973; MBA, Nat. U., 1992. Dist. mgr. Burroughs Corp., San Diego, 1974-78; mgr. computer systems R.J. Software Systems, La Mesa, Calif., 1978-85; mgr. support systems div. Integrated Software Systmes Corp., San Diego, 1985-87; dir. info. systems Trade Svc. Corp., San Diego, 1987—. Chmn. Partnership in Edn., San Diego, 1991-92, mem. bd. govs. Krau Middle Sch., San Diego, 1991-92; bd. dirs. United Way, San Diego, 1992. Mem. Am. Mgmt. Assn., Nat. Constrn. Software Assn. (chmn. com.). Lutheran. Office: Trade Svc Corp 10996 Torreyanna Rd San Diego CA 92121

FLEMING, PEGGY GALE, professional ice skater; b. San Jose, Calif., July 27, 1948; d. Albert Eugene and Doris Elizabeth (Deal) F.; m. Greg Jenkins; 1 son, Andy. Student, Colo. Coll., from 1966. Skating commentator for ABC Wide World of Sports; appears in commls. for Concord Watch. Performer with Ice Capades, from 1968, Ice Follies; performer 7 TV spls.; guest appearance, Fantasy Island; Ambassador of goodwill, UNICEF. Nat. chmn. Easter Seals; trustee Womens Sports Found. Recipient Sports award ABC-TV, 1967; named Woman of Year Reader's Digest, 1969, Female Athlete of Year A.P., 1968; named to Colo. Hall of Fame, 1969. Mem. U.S. Figure Skating Assn. Club: Broadmoor Figure Skating (Colorado Springs, Colo.). Address: care William Morris Agy 151 El Camino Beverly Hills CA 90212

FLEMMING, RONALD RAYMOND, manufacturing company executive; b. Colorado Springs, Colo., June 18, 1944; s. Charles Raymond Flemming and Darlene Bernice (Rollins) DeSylva; m. Vickery Wanty, Sept. 28, 1974; children: Marguerite, Marcus, Lindsay, Samuel. AA, El Camino Coll., L.A., 1972; BA, Columbia (Mo.) Coll., 1978; MA, Webster U., St. Louis, 1982. Test technician Western Electric Co., Denver, 1962-65, Hughes Aircraft Co., El Segundo, Calif., 1965-66; test engr. Northrop Corp., Englewood, Calif., 1968-74; test supr. Fire Alert Co., Denver, 1974-76; mfg. mgr. Monolithic Systems, Denver, 1976-82; dir. mfg. Sigma Design, Denver, 1982-84, Plantronics, Santa Cruz, Calif., 1984-86; mfg. mgr. Atalla-A Tandem Co., San Jose, Calif., 1986—; dir. Ctr. for Employment Tng., Denver, 1976-82. Inventor automatic fireplace damper, toothbrush variation, video kaleidoscope. Lectr. Am. Cancer Soc., Santa Cruz, 1984-88; v.p. Little League Am., Santa Cruz, 1985-86. With U.S. Army, 1966-68. Mem. Am. Prodn. and Inventory Control Soc., Internat. Platform Assn., Green Peace. Office: Atalla-A Tandem Co 2304 Zanker Rd San Jose CA 95131-1196

FLEMMING, STANLEY LALIT KUMAR, family practice physician, state legislator; b. Rosebud, S.D., Mar. 30, 1953; s. Homer W. and Evelyn C. (Misra) F.; m. Marth Susan Light, July 2, 1977; children: Emily Drisana, Drew Anil, Claire Elizabeth Misra. AAS, Ft. Steilacoom Coll., 1973; BS in Zoology, U. Wash., 1976; MA in Social Psychology, Pacific Luth. U., 1979; DO, Coll. Osteopathic Med. Pacific, 1985. Diplomate Am. Coll. Gen. Practice; cert. ATLS. Intern Pacific Hosp. Long Beach (Calif.), 1985-86; resident in family practice Pacific Hosp. Long Beach, 1986-88; fellow in adolescent medicine Children's Hosp. L.A., 1988-90; clin. preceptor Family Practice Residency Program Calif. Med. Ctr., U. So. Calif., L.A., 1989—; clin. instr. Sch. Medicine U. So. Calif., L.A., 1989-90; clin. instr. Coll. Osteopathic Medicine Pacific, Pomona, Calif., 1989-90; clin. asst. prof. Family Medicine Coll. Osteopathic Medicine Pacific, Pomona, 1987—; exam. commr., expert examiner Calif. Osteo. Med. Bd., 1987-89; med. dir. Community Health Care Delivery System Pierce County, Tacoma, Wash., 1990—; clin. instr. U. Wash. Sch. Medicine, 1990—; bd. dirs. Calif. State Bd. Osteo. Physicians Examiners, 1989—, cons., 1989. Lt. col. with med. corps U.S. Army, 1976—. Named Outstanding Young Man of Am. 1983, 1985; recipient Pumerantz-Weiss award 1985. Mem. Fedn. State Bds. Licensing, Am. Osteopathic Assn., Am. Acad. Family Practice, Soc. Adolescent Medicine, Assn. Military Surgeons U.S., Assn. U.S. Army (chpt. pres.), Soc. Am. Military Engrs. (chpt. v.p.), Calif. Med. Assn., Wash. Osteopathic Med. Assn., Calif. Family Practice Soc., Long Beach Med. Assn. (com. mem.), N.Y. Acad. Sci., Calif. Med. Review Inc., Sigma Sigma Phi, Am. Legion. Episcopalian. Home: 7619 Chambers Creek Rd W Tacoma WA 98467-2015 Office: Community Health Care Delivery System of Pierce County J428 J L O'Brien Bldg Olympia WA 98504

FLETCHER, ARCHIE WILLIAM, metallurgical consultant, chemistry educator; b. Allahabad, India, Sept. 5, 1922; came to U.S., 1980; s. William John and Ruth (Ling) F.; m. Florence Louise Lea White, Oct. 20, 1944; children: Hillian Ann, Paul Julian. BSc, Christian Coll., Madras, India, 1941; ARIC, Woolwich Poly., London, 1951. Chartered chemist, engr. Analytical chemist Hopkin & Williams Ltd., London, 1947-51; exptl. officer fuel Rsch. Sta., DSIR, London, 1951-58; sr. prin. scientific officer Warren Spring Lab., Stevenage Herts, U.K., 1958-77; metall. cons. BRGM Orleans, France, 1978-80; sr. rsch. scientist Duval Corp., Tucson, 1980-86; adj. faculty Pima C.C. East, Tucson, 1986—; divisional head Warren Spring Lab., Stevenage Herts, U.K., 1965-77; dep. dir. rsch. Duval Corp., Tucson, 1980-85. Contbr. articles to profl. jours.; patentee in field. Capt. Royal Indian Artillery, 1943-47. Fellow Royal Soc. Chem., Inst. of Mining and Metallurgy. Home: 9422 E Placita Eunice Tucson AZ 85715 Office: Pima CC 8202 E Poinciana Dr Tucson AZ 85730

FLETCHER, BETTY B., federal judge; b. Tacoma, Mar. 29, 1923. B.A., Stanford U., 1943; LL.B., U. Wash., 1956. Bar: Wash. 1956. Mem. firm Preston, Thorgrimson, Ellis, Holman & Fletcher, Seattle, 1956-1979; judge U.S. Ct. Appeals (9th cir.), Seattle., 1979—. Mem. ABA (Margaret Brent award 1992), Wash. State Bar Assn., Am. Law Inst., Fed. Judges Assn. (immediate past pres.), Order of Coif, Phi Beta Kappa. Office: US Ct Appeals 9th Cir 1010 5th Ave Seattle WA 98104-1130

FLETCHER, DONALD WARREN, microbiologist, educator; b. Phoenix, Ariz., June 8, 1929; s. Donald Warren and Ruth Marie Fletcher; children: Lisa, Timothy. BS, Oreg. State U., 1951, MS, 1953; PhD, Wash. State U., 1956. Cert. community coll. tchr., Calif. Instr. Wash. State U., Pullman, 1956-59; asst. prof. San Francisco State U., 1959-62, assoc. prof., 1962-66, prof., 1966-88, prof. emeritus, 1988—; dean coll. liberal arts U. Bridgeport, Conn., 1969-70; assoc. state univ. dean Calif. State U., Long Beach, 1975-88; exec. dir. Ctr. for Advanced Med. Tech., San Francisco, 1966-69, Commn. on Adult Edn. Calif. State U., 1987-88. Author: Microbiology, 1980; contbr. articles to profl. jours. Vice foreman grand jury, 1990-91. Fulbright fellow, 1966, 67; grantee several orgns. Fellow Calif. Acad. Sci., AAAS; mem. Am. Soc. Microbiology, Soc. for Gen. Microbiology, Sigma Xi. Home: 17817 Oriole Ct Penn Valley CA 95946

FLETCHER, HOMER LEE, librarian; b. Salem, Ind., May 11, 1928; s. Floyd M. and Hazel (Barnett) F.; m. Jacquelyn Ann Blanton, Feb. 7, 1950; children—Deborah Lynn, Randall Brian, David Lee. B.A., Ind. U., 1953; M.S. in L.S, U. Ill., 1954. Librarian Milw. Pub. Library, 1954-56; head librarian Ashland (Ohio) Pub. Library, 1956-59; city librarian Arcadia (Cal.) Pub. Library, 1959-65, Vallejo (Calif.) Pub. Library, 1965-70; city librarian San Jose, Calif., 1970-90, ret., 1990. Contbr. articles to profl. jours. Pres. S. Solano chpt. Calif. Assn. Neurol. Handicapped Children, 1968-69. Served with USAF, 1946-49. Mem. ALA (intellectual freedom com. 1967-72), Calif. Library Assn. (pres. pub. libraries sect. 1967), Dem. Century Club, Phi Beta Kappa. Democrat. Mem. Christian Ch. Disciples of Christ (elder, chmn. congregation 1978-79). Home: 7921 Belknap Dr Cupertino CA 95014-4973

FLETCHER, JAMES ALLEN, video company executive; b. Toledo, Sept. 18, 1947; s. Allen Rae and Ruth Helen (Scharf) F.; m. Kathy Jane Barrett, Jan. 25, 1975. AS, West Coast U., 1977, BSEE, 1979. Electronic technician Hughes Aircraft Co., El Segundo, Calif., 1970-72; engring. technician Altec Corp., Anaheim, Calif., 1972-75, Magna Corp., Santa Fe Springs, Calif., 1975-76; engring. technician Odetics Inc., Anaheim, 1976-79, electronic engr., 1979-86; pres., founder Gaslight Video, Orange, Calif., 1986—. Served as sgt. U.S. Army, 1967-69. Mem. Soc. Motion Picture and TV Engrs., Soc. Cable TV Engrs., Mensa, Bikecentennial Club. Libertarian. Office: Gaslight Video 630 N Tustin St Ste 1516 Orange CA 92667-7100

FLETCHER, JERRY LEE, consultant/speaker; b. Cin., Apr. 7, 1942; s. Stanley Eugene and Dolores Mae (Bucheit) F.; m. Suan Katharine Clemens, June 2, 1976; 1 child, Kelly Elizabeth. BS in Design, U. Cin., 1965. Cert. profl. cons. APCA. Account supr. Campbell-Mithun Inc., Mpls., 1969-79; v.p. account svcs. Young & Roehr Inc., Portland, Oreg., 1979-89, CEO, 1989-91; pres. Z-Axis Mktg. Inc., Portland, 1991—. Author: Do-It-Yourself Positioning, 1992, ABC's of Do-It-Yourself Marketing, 1992. 1st lt. U.S. Army, 1966-69. Mem. Assn. of Home Bus., Portland C. of C. (chmn. small bus. programs com. 1992—). Office: Z-Axis Mktg Inc 17387 SW Canyon Dr Lake Oswego OR 97034

FLETCHER, JUDITH ANN, office occupations educator; b. Corvallis, Oreg., Aug. 8, 1943; d. W. Curtis and Dorothy Elizabeth (Stowell) Reid; m. Carlton Eliot Fletcher, Aug. 15, 1964; children: Mary Katherine, Laurel Anne. BA in Secretarial Sci., Oreg. State U., 1965, MS in Bus. Edn./Adult Edn., 1991. Exec. sec. Provident Fed. Savs. & Loans Assn., Boise, Idaho, 1965-66; office occupations educator Treasure Valley Community Coll., Ontario, Oreg., 1968, Treasure Valley Community Coll., Vale Outreach Ctr., Vale, Oreg., 1985—; interim dir. librs. Treasure Valley Community Coll., Ontario, Oreg., 1989-90; libr. dir. Malheur County Penal Libr., Vale, Oreg., 1974-83; libr. asst. Malheur County Libr., Ontario, 1976-81; libr. dir. Vale City Libr., 1979-80. Mem. Vale United Meth. Ch., 1967—. Mem. Vale Garden Club, Pi Delta Psi, Delta Pi Epsilon. Office: TVCC Vale Outreach Ctr 275 Main St N Vale OR 97918-1244

FLETCHER, KIM, savings and loan executive; b. Los Angeles, 1927; married. Grad., Stanford U., 1950. Chmn. bd. dirs. HomeFed Bank, San Diego, 1979—. Office: HomeFed Bank 625 Broadway Ste 1400 San Diego CA 92101*

FLETCHER, LELAND VERNON, artist; b. Cumberland, Md., Sept. 18, 1946; s. Kenneth L. and Marjorie L. (Benecke) F.; m. Janis Traub, July 19, 1978; children: Nathan Fletcher, Joshua Traub. BS, U. Minn., 1972. One man shows include U. Minn. Exptl. Gallery, 1972, La Mamelle Art Ctr., San Francisco, 1976, San Jose State U. Union Gallery, 1978, Place des Nations, Maubeuge, France, 1987, Univ. Art Gallery, Calif. State U., Hayward, 1989, McHenry County Coll. Art Gallery, Crystal Lake, Ill., 1991, Lake County Mus., Calif., 1993; group exhbns. include Mus. Contemporary Art, Sao Paulo, Brazil, 1977, Urbanart '77, Vancouver, Can., 1977, Los Angeles Inst. Contemporary Art, 1978, Inst. Modern Art, Brisbane, 1978, Hansen Gallery, N.Y.C., 1978, Fendrick Gallery, Washington, 1979, 8th Internat. Print Bienale, Cracow, Poland, 1980, Cooper-Hewitt Mus., N.Y.C., 1980, Sch. Art Inst. Chgo., 1981, Metronome Gallery, Barcelona, 1981, 16th Bienal de Sao Paulo, 1981, Neue galerie der Stadt Linz, 1982, Bienal de Pontevedra, Spain, 1983, Lyng by Kunstbibliotek, Denmark, 1984, Otis Art Inst./Parsons Sch. Design, Los Angeles, 1984, 10th Internat. Print Bienale, Cracow, Poland, 1984, Mus. Arte da Univ. Fed. de Mato Grosso, Brazil, 1984, 11th Biennal Internat., Mus. Art Contemporani d'Eivissa, Spain, 1984, Intergrafik '84 Triennale, Berlin, Fiatel Muveszek Klubja Budapest, 1985, Intersection Gallery, San Francisco, 1985, Mus. Petit Format, Couvin, Belgium, 1985, 9th British Internat. Print Biennale, Bradford, Eng., 1986, Victoria and Albert Mus., London, 1986, Sculpt 87/3, Maubeuge, 1987, Fundacio la Caixa, Valencia, Spain, 1987, Acad. Belles Arts Sabadell, Barcelona, 1987, Taliesin Ctr. for Arts, Swansea, Eng., 1987, Worcester (Eng.) City Art Gallery, 1987, Symposium Sculpture en Plein Air, Maubeuge, France, 1987, Richards Gallery, Northeastern U., Boston, 1987, Montserrat Coll. Art, Beverly, Mass., 1987, 11 Internat. Print Biennale, Krakow, 1986, Skulptur Biennale '88 Royal Gardens, Copenhagen, Internat. Biennale Palais des Roi de Majorque, Peripignan, France, 1988, Fine Art Mus., Budapest, Hungary, 1988, Works gallery, San Jose Calif., 1988, Palthehuis Mus., Oldenzaal, The Netherlands, 1989, Budapest Galeria, Hungary, 1989, Stedelijk Hoger Institut, Cultural Ctr., Genk, Belgium, 1989, Inst. Contemporary Art, Clocktower Gallery, N.Y.C., 1989, Corporacion GOG, Pontevedra, Spain, 1989, Ea. Washington U., Spokane Ctr. Gallery, 1989, Munson-Williams-Proctor Inst., Sch. Art Gallery, Utica, N.Y., 1989, 44th Salon des Realities Nouvelles, Grand Palais, Paris, 1990, Buda Castle Palace, Budapest, 1990, Pensacola (Fla.) Mus. Art, 1990, Anchorage (Alaska) Mus. Art, 1990, Fundacao Democrito Rocha, Fortaleza, Brazil, 1991, Miejski Osrodek Kultury, Chelm, Poland, 1991, Bharat Bhavan, Bhopal, India, 1991, Chabot Coll., Hayward, Calif., 1992, Lake County Arts Coun., Lakeport, Calif., 1992, Artisans Gallery, Mill Valley, Calif., 1992, Greenville Mus. Art, N.C., numerous others; represented in permanent collection at Mus. Contemporary Art, Sao Paulo, Mpls. Inst. Arts, Art Mus. of Calif. State U., Long Beach, deSaisset Mus., U. Santa Clara (Calif.), Art Inst. Chgo., Victoria and Albert Mus., London, Museen der Stadt Koln, Ludwig Mus., Cologne, Mus. Plantin-Moretus, Antwerp, Mus. de Arte Moderno, Barcelona, Bradford Mus., Eng., Kunsthalle, Hamburg, Galleria D'Arte Moderna, Trieste, Ecole des Beaux-Arts, Mus. Maubeuge, Musee de la Sculpture en plein Air, Maubeuge, Musee de Maubeuge, FMK Galeria, Budapest, Bur. for Artistic Exhibitions, Cracow, Poland, Kunsthalle Bremen, West Germany, Museu de Arte da Universidad Federal de Mato Grosso, Brazil, others. Address: 3288 Konocti Ln Soda Bay CA 95451-9131

FLETTNER, MARIANNE, cultural organization administrator; b. Frankfurt, Germany, Aug. 9, 1933; d. Bernhard J. and Kaethe E. (Halbritter) F. MBA, Hessel Bus. Coll., 1953. Sec. various cos., 1953-61, Pontiac Motor Div., Burlingame, Calif., 1961-63; sec. Met. Opera, N.Y., 1963-74, asst. co. mgr., 1974-79; artistic adminstr. San Diego Opera, 1979—. Home: 4015 Crown Point Dr San Diego CA 92109-6254 Office: San Diego Opera PO Box 988 San Diego CA 92112-0988

FLICK, LOREN DOUGLAS, structural and investigative engineer; b. Tempe, Ariz., Aug. 19, 1955. BS in Engring., Ariz. State U., 1977; MS in Engring., Okla. State U., 1978. Registered profl. engr., Colo., Okla. Engr. Amoco Corp., Tulsa, 1979-87, CBS Engring., Houston, 1987-88, Wiss, Janney, Elstner Assocs., Denver, 1988—. Contbr. articles to profl. jours. Home: 5903 E Irwin Pl Englewood CO 80112

FLICK, WILLIAM FREDRICK, surgeon; b. Lancaster, Pa., Aug. 18, 1940; s. William Joseph and Anna (Volkl) F.; m. Jacqueline Denise Phaneuf, May 21, 1966; children: William J., Karen E., Christopher R., Derrick W., Brian A. BS, Georgetown U., 1962, MD, 1966; MBA, U. Colo., 1990. Cert. Am. Bd. Surgeons, 1976. Self employed surgeon Cheyenne, Wyo., 1973-84; pres., surgeon Cheyenne Surgical Assocs., 1984—. Trustee Laramie County Sch. Dist. #1, Cheyenne, 1988-92. Maj., chief of surgery USAF, 1971-73. Fellow ACS, Southwestern Surg. Congress; mem. Am. Coll. Physician Execs., Rotary. Republican. Roman Catholic. Office: Cheyenne Surg Assocs 603 E 17th St Cheyenne WY 82001-4709

FLICKINGER, JOE ARDEN, telecommunications educator; b. Cadillac, Mich., Feb. 4, 1949; s. Arden Henry and Stella Frances (Hurst) F.; m. Judith Marie Gardner, Sept. 17, 1971; children: Jan Elsa, Jill Kimberly. BA, Kalamazoo Coll., Mich., 1971; MA, U. So. Calif., 1975; AS, Clatsop Community Coll., 1985; postgrad., U. Oreg. Asst. chief engr. Sta. KUSC-FM, L.A., 1972-74; sta. engr. Sta. KAST-AM-FM, Astoria, Oreg., 1974-75; studio operator, instr. Clatsop Community Coll., Astoria, 1975-88; grad. teaching fellow in telecommunications U. Oreg., Eugene, 1988-90; sr. mktg. cons. RKM Corp., Vancouver, Wash., 1990—; vis. asst. prof. communications Lewis and Clark Coll., Portland, Oreg., 1991-92; asst. prof. communications Radford (Va.) U., Va., 1992—; session organizer on high definition TV, Northcon, 1989, IEEE and ERA Tech. Conf., 1989. Dir. TV muscular dystrophy telethon Astoria Jaycees, 1980, 81; canvasser Friends of Coll., Astoria, 1982; pres. bd. dirs. Sta. KMUN-FM Tillicum Found., Astoria, 1983-84. Mem. IEEE, IEEE Computer Soc., IEEE Communications Soc., Am. Radio Relay League (life), Pacific Telecommunications Coun., Am. Film Inst., Northcom Inner Circle, Nat. Model R.R. Assn., Sunset Empire Amateur Radio Club (sec. 1978-81). Democrat. Presbyterian. Avocations: amateur radio, golf, fishing, astronomy, cooking.

FLINN, ROBERTA JEANNE, management, computer applications consultant; b. Twin Falls, Idaho, Dec. 19, 1947; d. Richard H. and Ruth (Johnson) F. Student Colo. State U., 1966-67. Ptnr., Aqua-Star Pools & Spas, Boise, Idaho, 1978—, mng. ptnr., 1981-83; ops. mgr. Polly Pools, Inc., Canby, Oreg., 1983-84, br. mgr. Polly Pools, Inc., A-One Distributing, 1984-85; comptroller, Beaverton Printing, Inc., 1986-89; mng. ptnr. Invisible Ink, Canby, Oreg., 1989—. Mem. Nat. Assn. Female Execs., Nat. Appaloosa Horse Club, Oreg. Dressage Soc. (pres. North Willamette Valley chpt.) Republican. Mem. Christian Ch. Home: 24687 S Central Point Rd Canby OR 97013-9743

FLINT, JOE (COUNTRY JOE FLINT), radio personality; b. Aug. 6, 1948. Host classical show Sta. KUER-FM, Salt Lake City, 1968; writer, prodr., host rock and roll show Sta. KUTE-AM, Salt Lake City, 1968-69; host easy-listening show Sta. KABI-AM-FM, Abilene, Kans., 1969-70; host country music show Sta. KRGO-AM, Salt Lake City, 1970; host morning drive, comml. copywriter, prodr. Sta. KBBC-AM, Centerville, Utah, 1970-73; prodn. dir., host evening show then morning drive Sta. KSOP-AM-FM, Salt Lake City, 1973; host remote broadcasts, sta. promoter Sta. KOVO-AM, KFMC-FM, Provo, Utah, 1973; dir. music Sta. KSOP-AM-FM, Salt Lake City, 1976-83, promotion dir., 1976-84, program dir., 1979-87, host morning drive, 1973—; promoter, designer, advertiser Country Joe's Records and Tapes, Nashville, 1981—; prodr., dir., host Country Joe's World of Country Music Sta. KOOG-TV, 1987—; master ceremonies concerts/spcl. events Salt Palace Civic Ctr., Capitol Theater, Symphony Hall, Weber State Coll., Weber Sheriff's Ann. Country Jamboree; talent host Utah State Fair, 5 yrs. Recipient Golden Ear award Large Market, 1988; top five finalist Country DJ of Yr. award Acad. Country Music and Country Music Assn., Country Program Dir. of Yr. award Billboard, 1987. Address: 3380 S Redwood Rd Salt Lake City UT 84119

FLINT, LOU JEAN, state education official; b. Ogden, Utah, July 11, 1934; d. Elmer Blood and Ella D. (Adams) F.; children: Dirk Kershaw Brown, Kristie Susan Brown Felix, Flint Kershaw Brown. B.S., Weber State Coll., 1968; M.Ed., U. Utah, 1974, Ed.S, 1981. Cert. early childhood and elem. edn., Utah Bd. Edn., 1968, edn. adminstrn., 1981. Master tchr. Muir Elem., Davis Sch. Dist., Farmington, Utah, 1968-77; edn. specialist Dist. I, Dept. Def., Eng., Scotland, Norway, Denmark, Holland, Belgium, 1977-79; ednl. cons. Office Higher Edn. State of Utah, Utah System Approach to Individualized Learning, Tex., S.C., Fla., Utah, 1979-81; acad. affairs officer Commr. Higher Edn. Office State of Utah, Salt Lake City, 1982—; mem. Equity Vocat. Edn. Bd., Women's Politics Caucus; mem. review com. United Way, 1989—; adv. bd. Women and Bus. Conf.; State bd. dirs. Am. Coun. Edn. Named Exemplary Tchr., Utah State Bd. Edn., 1970-77, Outstanding Educator, London Central High Sch., 1979; recipient Appreciation award, Gov. of Utah, 1983-85, 93, Woman of Achievement award Utah Bus. and Profl. Women, 1985, Pathfinder award C. of C., 1988, Outstanding Educator award YWCA, 1989, Silver Apple award Utah State U., 1992. Mem. AAUW (Edn. Found. award given in her honor, 1986), Nat. Assn. Women's Work/Women's Worth (Disting. Woman award 1987), ACE Nat. Identification Program (Susa Young Gates award 1987), Nat. Assn. Edn. Young Children, Utah Assn. Edn. Young Children (past pres.), Women Concerned About Nuclear War, Utah Jaycee Aux. (past pres. Centerville), Crones Coun., Phi Delta Kappa, Delta Kappa Gamma. Mormon. Author: The Comprehensive Community College, 1980; others. Office: State of Utah Office Commr Higher Edn 355 W North Temple #3 Triad Salt Lake City UT 84180-1205

FLINT, WILLIS WOLFSCHMIDT, artist; b. Kenton, Ohio, Dec. 27, 1936; s. Wilbur Henry and Ilo Edna (Obenour) F. Student, Art Career Sch., N.Y.C., 1957-60, Ins. Allende, San Miguel Allende, Mexico, 1961. Artist trainee Kossack Advt., Tucson, 1961; gen. boardman Mithoff Advt., El Paso, 1962-63; tech. illustrator Volt Tech. Corp., N.Y.C., 1967; gen. illustrator Salesvertising Advt., Denver, 1968; gen. boardman/cons. Burr-Brown Rsch. Corp., Tucson, 1969-71; musician, actor Paul Barons Harmonica Rascals, Bklyn., 1965-85; pvt. practice muralist San Diego, Tucson, N.Y.C., 1976-80; pvt. practice easel painter Tucson, 1985—; originator Fantasy-Expressionism, 1984; pvt. practice art instr., Tucson, 1981-85; cons. muralist Yaqui Indian/Pascua Ctr., Tucson, 1989. Paintings exhibited in group shows at United Way Fund Drive Exhibit, Tucson, United Servicemen's Orgn. Exhibit, Mobile, Ala., Student Union Exhibit U. Ariz., Tucson, La Galeria Instituto, San Miguel de Allende, Margarita De Mena Gallery, N.Y.C.; represented in permanent collections Mr. and Mrs. Charles Hernandez, Queens, N.Y., Mr. and Mrs. Peter Greco, Catskill, N.Y., So. Ariz. Hist. Soc., Tombstone, Ariz. With USN, 1954-57, 1979-81. Recipient scholarship Latham Found., 1958, award of merit Latham Found., 1958, letter commendation U. Ariz. Family Practice, Tucson, 1978, letter commendation Dept. Navy, San Diego, 1979. Mem. The Maverick Artists, Soc. for the Preservation of the Harmonica. Home: 707 W Calle Progreso Tucson AZ 85705

FLOCCHINI, RICHARD JAMES, marketing professional; b. San Francisco, Nov. 30, 1939; s. Armando John and Lena Helen (Tevini) F.; m. Patricia Ann Bisagno, June 18, 1960; children: Richard, Patrick, Bernadette, Michael. BS, U. San Francisco, 1961; postgrad., U. Santa Clara Grad. Sch., 1974. Office mgr. Durham Meat Co., San Francisco, 1955-61; office mgr. Durham Meat Co., San Jose, 1961-65, gen. mgr., 1966-86, procurment, mktg. mgr. wild game products, 1986—; procurment, mktg. mgr. wild game products Sierra Meat, Reno, Nev., 1986—, Durham Night Bird, South San Francisco, 1986—, Kali Meat, South San Francisco, 1986—, Tambellini Meat, San Jose, 1986—, Durham Ranches, Gillette, Wyo., 1986—. With USAR, 1956-62. Republican. Roman Catholic. Office: Durham Meat Co 160 Sunol St San Jose CA 95126

FLOCK, ROBERT ASHBY, retired entomologist; b. Kellogg, Idaho, July 16, 1914; s. Abraham Lincoln and Florence Louise (Ashby) F.; m. Elsie Marie Ronken, Apr. 8, 1950; children: Karen Marie, Anne Louise Checkai. BS, U. Ariz., 1938, MS, 1941; PhD, U. Calif., Berkeley, 1951. Inspector Ariz. Commn. Agriculture and Horticulture, Phoenix, 1938-41, asst. entomologist, 1941-46; lab. tech. U. Calif., Riverside, 1947-52, asst. entomologist, 1952-63; entomologist Imperial County Dept. Agriculture, El Centro, Calif., 1963-85, part-time entomologist, 1985—. Contbr. articles to profl. jours. Mem. Entomol. Soc. Am., Am. Phytopathol. Soc., Pan-Pacific Entomol. Soc., AAAS, Ctr. for Process Studies, Kiwanis (pres. Imperial Valley chpt. 1984-86, Man of Yr. 1986), Sigma Xi. Republican. Methodist. Home: 667 Wensley Ave PO Box 995 El Centro CA 92244 Office: Imperial County Dept Agricu 150 S 9th El Centro CA 92243

FLODINE, LLOYD RANDALL, environmental science specialist, civil engineer; b. Holdrege, Nebr., Apr. 29, 1946; s. Lloyd Albert and Lois Eleanor (Sporing) F.; m. Nancy Louis Swoboda, June 30, 1979; children: Jessica Ann, John Marshall. BSCE, U. Nebr., 1971; postgrad., Ea. N.Mex. U., Clovis, 1980-81, Air Force Inst. Tech., Wright-Paterson AFB, Ohio, 1983, U. Colo., Denver, 1985-88. Supr. inventory and spl. studies Colo. Dept. Hwys., Denver, 1971-78, r.r. crossing specialist, 1978-79, mgr. noise and hazardous waste program, 1984-88, mgr. noise and environ. mitigation program, 1989—; mem. Trust Ter. Planning Commn., Agana, Guam, 1982-83; state rep. noise and vibration subbcom. Transp. Rsch. Bd., Washington, 1986—. Scoutmaster, asst. dist. commr. Boy Scouts Am., Denver, 1971-76, advisor explorer post, 1978-79, mem. pack com., Cannon AFB, N.Mex., 1980-81; del. Rep. County Conv., Denver, 1976; elder St. Andrews Luth. Ch., Arvada, Colo., 1977-78. Capt. USAF, 1979-84. Mem. ASCE (assoc.), Colo. Hazardous Waste Mgmt. Soc., Air Force Assn., Res. Officers Assn., Order of Arrow. Home: 380 S 36th St Boulder CO 80303 Office: Colo Dept Transp Office of Environ Studies 4201 E Arkansas Ave Rm 284 Denver CO 80222

FLOOD, JAMES TYRRELL, broadcasting executive, public relations consultant; b. Los Angeles, Oct. 5, 1934; s. James Joseph and Teresa (Rielly) F.; m. Bonnie Carolyn Lutz, Mar. 25, 1966; children: Hilary C., Sean L. BA in

Liberal Arts, U. Calif., Santa Barbara, 1956; MA in Communications, Calif. State U., Chico, 1981. Publicist Rogers & Cowan, 1959-60, Jim Mahoney & Assocs., 1960-61, ABC-TV, San Francisco and Hollywood, Calif., 1961-64; cons. pub. relations, Beverly Hills, Calif., 1964-72; pub. relations, advt. dir. Jerry Lewis Films, 1964-72; dir. pub. rels. MTM Prodns., 1970-72; pub. relations cons. Medic Alert Found. Internat., 1976-83; owner, mgr. Sta. KRIJ-FM, Paradise, 1983-88; instr. Calif. State U. Sch. Communications, Chico, 1982-89; gen. mgr. KIXE-TV (PBS), Redding-Chico, Calif., 1991—; represented numerous artists including Pearl Bailey, Gary Owens, Ruth Buzzi, Allen Ludden, Betty White, Celeste Holm, Jose Feliciano, Tom Kennedy, Shirley Jones, David Cassidy, others. Pub. rels. dir. Mary Tyler Moore Prodns., 1971. Calif. media cons. Carter/Mondale campaign, 1976; mem. Calif. Dem. Fin. Com., 1982-83. Served with USNR, 1956-58. Mem. Calif. Broadcasters Assn. (bd. dirs. 1986-88).

FLOOD, MICHAEL PATRICK, non-profit organization executive; b. San Fernando, Calif., Dec. 24, 1962; s. Frank and Irene (Birmingham) F.; m. Monicka Guevara, Nov. 21, 1990. BA in Govt., Coll. William and Mary, 1983, MBA, 1988. Profl. soccer player Chgo. Sting Soccer Club, 1984; mgr. transp. USA Today, Springfield, Va., 1985-86; mgmt. intern N.Y. Times Mag. Group, N.Y.C., 1987; mgr., staff profl. First Deposit Corp., San Ramon, Calif., 1988-90; dir. ops. Contra Costa Food Bank, Concord, Calif., 1990—. Co-author: Hunger in The Midst of Affluence, 1993; co-editor William and Mary Bus. Rev., 1988. Bd. dirs. Calif. Brown Bag Adv. Com., Sacramento, 1991—, Loaves and Fishes Soup Kitchen, Pittsburg, Calif., 1992—; chmn. West Contra Costa Emergency Svc. Providers, Richmond, Calif., 1991—. Am. Mktg. Assn. scholar, 1988. Mem. Beta Gamma Sigma. Democrat. Roman Catholic. Home: 5279 Broadway Terr Oakland CA 94618 Office: Contra Costa Food Bank 5121 Port Chicago Hwy Concord CA 94520

FLOR, LOY LORENZ, chemist, corrosion engineer, consultant; b. Luther, Okla., Apr. 25, 1919; s. Alfred Charles and Nellie M. (Wilkinson) F.; BA in Chemistry, San Diego State Coll., 1941; m. Virginia Louise Pace, Oct. 1, 1946; children: Charles R., Scott R., Gerald C., Donna Jeanne, Cynthia Gail. With Helix Water Dist., La Mesa, Calif., 1947-84, chief chemist, 1963—, supr. water quality, 1963—, supr. corrosion control dept., 1956—. 1st. lt. USAAF, 1941-45. Registered profl. engr., Calif. Mem. Am. Chem. Soc. (chmn. San Diego sect. 1965—), Am. Water Works Assn. (chmn. water quality div. Calif. sect. 1965—), Nat. Assn. Corrosion Engrs. (chmn. western region 1970), Masons. Republican. Presbyterian.

FLORA, ERIC S., computer engineer; b. L.A., Nov. 3, 1951; s. LaVere Paul and Ople (Shirley) F.; m. Gayle L. Rollins, May 18, 1985; children: Benjamin J., Amy N. BA cum laude, U. La Verne, 1973; MS in Math. and Computer Sci., Tex. A&M U., 1975. Mem. tech. staff TRW DSG, Redondo Beach, Calif., 1975-78; sr. engr. Northrop Electronics Div., Hawthorne, Calif., 1978-80; project engr. Magnavox Advanced Products and Systems Co., Torrance, Calif., 1980-82; project mgr. TRW SIG, Colorado Springs, 1982—. Mem. IEEE, AIAA, Assn. Computing Machinery, Armed Forces Comms. and Electronics Assn., Pi Mu Epsilon. Office: TRW SIG 1555 N Newport Rd Colorado Springs CO 80916

FLORA, JENNIFER BEACH, financial consultant; b. Cin., Mar. 28, 1955; d. James Gordan and Nancy (Avis) B.; m. Randall Bruce Flora, Oct. 14, 1978; children: Ryan Matthew, Lindsey Rebecca, Whitney Marie. Student, U. Ariz., 1973; BS, No. Ariz. U., 1977; MS in Dietetics and Nutrition, U. Ariz., 1980. Asst. food edn. and svc. tng. program Tucson Unified Sch. Dist., 1978-80; nutritional and behavior edn. counselor Nutrisystem, Tucson, 1980-82; dietitian, office mgr. Office of James G. Beach MD, Tucson, 1984-89; ins. agt. Mass. Mut. Ins. Co., Tucson, 1990-92; ins. and fin. cons. Flora Cos., Tucson, 1992—; devel. specialist United Cerebral Palsy, Tucson, 1992—; dietetic cons. Childbirth Edn. Assn., Tucson, 1982—; pres. Flora Card Co., Tucson, 1991—. Pledge processing chairperson United Cerebral Palsy, Tucson, 1981-92; membership dir. Childbirth Edn. Assn., Tucson, 1981-82; treas. Highland VISTA Neighborhood Assn., Tucson, 1988-90; coach Cactus Little League, Tucson, 1987. Scholar Ariz. State U., 1973; recipient Scholastic Recognition award Ariz. Dietetic Assn., 1977; named Outstanding Young Woman of Am., Outstanding Young Women of Am., 1991. Mem. Highland VISTA Cinco Via (bd. dirs. 1990-92). Democrat. Methodist. Home: 4337 E 14th St Tucson AZ 85711 Office: Flora Cos 4625 E Broadway Tucson AZ 85711

FLORENCE, FRANK EDWARD, protection services official; b. Salt Lake City, Mar. 28, 1943; s. Lloyd and Helen (Shaw) F.; m. Diane Proctor, May 16, 1964; children: Randy Frank, Robert Lloyd, Richard Louis (dec.). Student, U. Utah; cert., Harvard U., 1985; grad., Nat. Fire Acad. Fire fighter Salt Lake City Fire Dept., 1964-72, fire officer, 1972-78, battalion chief, 1978-81, dep. chief, 1981-88, chief dep., 1988-91, fire chief, 1991—. Mem. Nat. Fire Protection Assn. (prin. mem. tech. com. fire reporting systems), Internat. Assn. Fire Chiefs. Mem. LDS Ch. Home: 2964 S 2700 W West Valley City UT 84119 Office: Pub Safety Bldg 315 E 200 S Salt Lake City UT 84111*

FLORENCE, JOSEPH HOWARD, real estate company executive; b. Ogden, Utah, Jan. 16, 1932; s. Leland H. and Goldie (Brian) F.; m. Lurlien Morris, Apr. 18, 1953; children: Nanette, Brad, Julie, Michael. BS, Weber State Coll., Ogden, 1966. Adminstrv. asst. Thiokol Chem. Corp., Brigham City, Utah, 1962-66; broker Merrill Lynch Pierce Fenner Smith, Salt Lake City, 1966-71; pres. Am. Land Fund, Inc., Salt Lake City, 1971-76; v.p. comml. div. Am. Resources Mgmt., Salt Lake City, 1976-90; pres. Arvesco, Salt Lake City, 1976-92; assoc. broker The Haw's Cos., Ogden, Utah, 1992—. Dir., past chmn. Weber State Coll. Devel. Fund, Ogden, 1969—; city councilman City of South Ogden, 1976-83; active Mormon Ch., Ogden. Mem. Weber State Coll. Alumni Assn. (pres. 1979). Office: Arvesco 948 E 7145 S # 102C Midvale UT 84047-1764

FLORENCE, KENNETH JAMES, lawyer; b. Hanford, Calif., July 31, 1943; s. Ivy Owen and Louella (Dobson) F.; m. Verena Magdalena Demuth, Dec. 10, 1967. BA, Whittier Coll., 1965; JD, Hastings Coll. Law, U. Calif.-San Francisco, 1974. Bar: Calif. 1974, U.S. Dist. Ct. (cen. dist.) Calif. 1974, U.S. Dist. Ct. (ea. and so. dists.) Calif., 1976, U.S. Dist. Ct. (no. dist.) Calif. 1980, U.S. Ct. Appeals (9th cir.) 1975, U.S. Supreme Ct. 1984. Dist. mgr. Pacific T&T, Calif., 1969-71; assoc. Parker, Milliken, et al, Los Angeles, 1974-78; ptnr. Dern, Mason, et al, 1978-84, Swerdlow & Florence, A Law Corp., Beverly Hills, 1984—; pres. Westside Legal Services, Inc., Santa Monica, Calif., 1982-83. Served to lt. USNR, 1966-69, Vietnam. Col. J.G. Boswell scholar, 1961. Mem. ABA (co-chmn. state labor law com. 1988-91). Democrat. Home: 1063 Stradella Rd Los Angeles CA 90077-2607 Office: Swerdlow & Florence 9401 Wilshire Blvd Ste 828 Beverly Hills CA 90212-2921

FLORENCE, VERENA MAGDALENA, small business owner; b. Interlaken, Switzerland, Nov. 4, 1946; came to U.S., 1967; d. Paul Robert and Marie (Raess) Demuth; m. Kenneth James Florence, Dec. 10, 1967. BA, U. Calif., Berkeley, 1974; MS, UCLA, 1979, PhD, 1982. Research scientist Procter & Gamble, Cin., 1983; adminstr. Swerdlow & Florence, Beverly Hills, Calif., 1984-89; pres., chief exec. officer, chmn. of bd. Böl Designs, Inc., L.A., 1989—. Contbr. articles to profl. jours. Democrat. Home and Office: 1063 Stradella Rd Los Angeles CA 90077-2607

FLORES, DANNY DICK, school system administrator; b. Clayton, N.Mex., Jan. 6, 1955; s. Daniel and Henrietta Clara Mae (Gonzales) F.; m. Teresa Lynn Tallcott, Nov. 24, 1977; children: Elizabeth Maria, Eric Andrew. MusB in Edn., Ea. N.Mex. U., 1977, M of Music, 1980; cert. in Adminstrn., U. N.Mex., 1984. Band dir. Ruidoso (N.Mex.) Mcpl. Schs., 1978-87; band dir. Portales (N.Mex.) Mcpl. Schs., 1987-89, vice prin., 1989-91; vice prin. Ruidoso Mcpl. Schs., Ruidoso, 1991—. Dir. ch. choir, Ruidoso, 1984-91, youth dir., 1989-91. Mem. Kappa Kappa Psi. Home: PO Box 1261 Ruidoso NM 88345 Office: Ruidoso High Sch 200 Horton Circle Ruidoso NM 88345

FLORES, FILOMENA CANALITA, gerontology educator; b. Cebu City, The Philippines, July 26, 1930; d. Laurencio R. and Magdalen (O'Keefe) Canalita; m. Cesar V. Flores, July 26, 1952; children: Enrico, Andrew. BSN, Philippine Women's U., 1956; MA in Edn. magna cum laude, U. San Carlos, Cebu City, Philippines, 1968; MA in Nursing, U. of the Philippines, 1971; PhD, U. San Carlos, 1985. RN; life teaching credentials. Nurse instr. II Southern Islands Hosp. Sch. Nursing, Cebu City, Philippines, 1951-73; dean Coll. of Nursing Cebu Doctors Coll., Cebu City, 1973-85; accreditor Philippine Assn. Accreditation Schs., Colls. and Univs., Manila, 1984-85; prof. Calif. State U., Fresno, 1985—. Author: (with others) Nursing Research in the Philippines, 1980. Sch. of Health and Social Wk. grantee Calif. State U., Fresno, 1987-88, 1990-93, Affirmative Action Faculty Devel. Prog. grantee, 1988-91. Mem. Calif. Nurses Assn., Asian Pacific Women's Orgn. (chmn. scholarship com.), Sigma Theta Tau (Mu Nu chpt.). Office: Calif State U Cedar and Shaw Fresno CA 93740

FLORES, ROMEO M., geologist, researcher; b. San Fernando, La Union, The Philippines, Apr. 28, 1939; came to U.S., 1960; s. Serapio C. and Gelacia M. Flores; divorced; 1 child, Alejandro N. BS in Geology, U. The Philippines, 1959; Ms in Geology, U. Tulsa, 1962; PhD in Geology, La. State U., 1966. Geologist White Eagle Oil Co., Manila, 1959-60; rsch. petrologist Amoco Rsch. Ctr., Tulsa, 1963; petroleum geologist Amoco Prodn. Co., New Orleans, 1964; asst. prof. to full prof. Sul Ross State U., Alpine, Tex., 1966-75, chmn. dept. geology, 1967-75; rsch. geologist U.S. Geol. Survey, Denver, 1975—; adj. prof. Colo. State U., Fort Collins, 1982—, N.C. State U., Raleigh, 1980—. Contbr. numerous articles to profl. jours. Fellow Geol. Soc. Am.; mem. Soc. Econ. Paleontologists and Mineralogists (Best Paper awards 1984, 90, 91), Am. Assn. Petroleum Geologists. Office: US Geol Survey MS 972 PO Box 25046 Denver CO 80225-0046

FLORES, ROSA ALBA, real estate company executive, lawyer; b. Marysville, Calif., Aug. 14, 1958; d. Antonio Gallardo and Eva (Sierra) F.; m. Manuel Andujo Medrano, Oct. 21, 1989. AB, Harvard U., 1980, JD, 1983; MBA, Stanford (Calif.) U., 1987. Bar: Calif. 1984. Assoc. Brobeck, Phleger & Harrison, L.A., 1983-84; v.p. LaSalle Ptnrs., L.A., 1987—. Mem. State Bar of Calif., L.A. County Bar Assn., Bldg. Owners and Mgrs. Assn., Century City C. of C. Office: LaSalle Ptnrs 355 S Grand Ave Ste # 4280 Los Angeles CA 90071

FLORES, THOMAS R., professional football team executive; b. Fresno, Calif., Mar. 21, 1937; s. Tom C. and Nellie (Padilla) F.; m. Barbara Ann Fridell, Mar. 25, 1961; children: Mark and Scott (twins), Kim. BA, Coll. Pacific, 1959; hon. doctorate, Pepperdine U. Quarterback Oakland Raiders, 1960-66; quarterback Buffalo Bills, 1967-68, Kansas City (Mo.) Chiefs, 1969-70; asst. coach Oakland (now Los Angeles) Raiders, 1972-78, head coach, from 1979; gen. mgr. Seattle Seahawks, 1989-91; pres. Seahawks, 1989—, head coach, 1992—; player rep. AFL, 1966-68. Nat. hon. chmn. Lung Assn. Named Man of Yr. No. Calif. Lung Assn., 1979; Latino of Yr. City of Los Angeles, 1981. Democrat. Roman Catholic. Office: Seattle Seahawks 11220 NE 53rd St Kirkland WA 98033-7595*

FLORES, THOMAS RICHARD, college dean, educator; b. Orofino, Idaho, Feb. 7, 1940; s. Len Benton and Viola Ellen (Roseborough) F.; m. Verla Rae Barney, Sept. 2, 1961; children: Shad Benton, Pilar Louise. BS in Edn., U. Idaho, 1962; MA in Guidance and Counseling, Wash. State U., 1966; PhD in Higher Edn. Adminstrn., U. Tex., 1972. Sch. counselor Lewiston (Idaho) Ind. Sch. Dist., 1962-65, Boise (Idaho) Ind. Sch. Dist., 1965-69; dep. dir. Model IV, Nat. Career Edn., Glasgow, Mont., 1973-77; supt. Bliss (Idaho) Sch. Dist., 1977-83; exec. asst. to pres. Western Wyo. Coll., Rock Springs, 1983-86, dean students, 1986—; mem. adj. faculty U. Wyo.,Laramie, 1984—; bd. dirs. Sweetwater Fed. Credit Union, Rock Springs, 1988—. Contbr. articles to profl. jours. Grantee Nat. Inst. for Edn., 1973-77, U.S. Dept. Edn., 1986-90. Mem. Nat. Assn. Student Pers. Adminstrs., also others. Home: 1337 Uinta St Rock Springs WY 82901-7303 Office: Western Wyo Coll 2500 College Dr Rock Springs WY 82901-5802

FLORES, WILLIAM VINCENT, educator; b. San Diego, Jan. 10, 1948; s. William J. and Velia (Aldrete) F.; m. Carole Mary Dische, July 3, 1973 (div. Jan 1986); children: Antonio Ramon, Diana Maria. BA, UCLA, 1970; MA in Polit. Sci., Stanford U., 1971, PhD in Social Theory/Pub. Policy, 1987. Teaching & rsch. fellow Stanford (Calif.) U., 1971-72; lectr. in polit. sci. Calif. State U., Hayward, 1972-75; program coord. Project Intercept, San Jose, Calif., 1976-78; assoc. dir. Gardner Community Health Ctr., San Jose, 1979-84; lectr. U. Santa Clara, Calif., 1985-87; asst. dir. Inter-Univ. Program for Latino Rsch., Stanford, 1987-88; chair dept. Chicano/Latin Am. studies Calif. State U., Fresno, 1988—. Mem. exec. com. Chicano/Latino Faculty Assn. Calif. State Univ. System, 1992—; chair Com. for Hispanic Ednl. Equity, Fresno, 1990-92; mem. nat. adv. bd. U.S. Students Assn., Washington, 1991—; v.p. Latino Agenda Coalition Calif., L.A., 1984-86. Chicano Fellows Program fellow Stanford U., 1971-72; Ford Found. fellow Stanford U., 1970-74; Compton-Danforth fellow Stanford U., 1984-85.; Rockefeller Humanities fellow, 1993-94; Am. Coun. on Edn. fellow, 1993-94. Mem. Am. Anthropol. Assn., Am. Studies Assn., Nat. Assn. Chicano Studies (co-chair polit. action com. 1986), Am. Polit. Sci. Assn. Democrat. Office: Calif State U Fresno Chicano/Latin Am Studies Fresno CA 03740-0097

FLORIE, TERRY LYNN, naval flight officer; b. NAS Sangley Pt., Philippines, May 18, 1956; s. Julian and Hazel Savannah (Byrd) F.; m. Deborah Louise Murchison, Aug. 31, 1985. BBA, Augusta Coll., 1977. Lt. comdr. USN, 1987—, Augusta, Ga., 1978; lt. comdr. USN, Aviation Schs. Command, Pensacola, Fla., 1978; naval officer USN, Patrol Squadron Five, Jacksonville, Fla., 1979-82, USN, Naval Air Tng. Unit, Sacramento, 1982-85, USN, USS Constellation, San Diego, 1985-88, Fleet Tng. Group, San Diego, 1988-90, Patrol Squadron Nine, Moffett Field, Calif., 1990—. Mem. Civil Air Patrol, Sacramento, 1984-85. Mem. U.S. Naval Inst., Aircraft Owners and Pilots Assn., Cessna Pilots Assn. Republican. Methodist. Home: 1000 Escalon Ave Sunnyvale CA 94086-4125 Office: Patrol Squadron Nine Moffett Field CA 94035

FLOSS, HEINZ G., chemistry educator, scientist; b. Berlin, Aug. 28, 1934; s. Friedrich and Annemarie F.; m. Inge Sauberlich, July 17, 1956; children: Christine, Peter, Helmut, Hanna. B.S. in Chemistry, Technische Universitat, Berlin, 1956, M.S. in Organic Chemistry, 1959; Dr. rer. nat. in Organic Chemistry, Technische Hochschule, Munich, W. Ger., 1961, Dr. habil. in Biochemistry, 1966; D.Sc. (hon.), Purdue U., 1986. Hilfsassistent Technische Universitat, Berlin, 1958-59; hilfsassistent Technische Hochschule, Munich, 1959-61; wissenschaftlicher asst. and dozent Technische Hochschule, 1961-66; on leave of absence at dept. biochemistry and biophysics U. Calif.-Davis, 1964-65; assoc. prof. Purdue U., 1966-69, prof., 1969-77, Lilly Disting. prof., 1977-82, head dept. medicinal chemistry, 1968-69, 74-79; prof. chemistry Ohio State U., Columbus, 1982-87, chmn. dept. chemistry, 1982-86; prof. chemistry U. Wash., Seattle, 1987—, adj. prof. biochemistry medicinal chemistry and microbiology, 1988—; vis. scientist ETH Zurich, 1970; vis. prof. Tech. U. Munich, Fed. Republic Germany, 1980, 86. Mem. editorial bd. Lloydia-Jour. Natural Products, 1971—, BBP-Biochemie und Physiologie der Pflanzen, 1971-84, Applied and Environ. Microbiology, 1974-84, Planta Medica, 1978-83, Jour. Medicinal Chemistry, 1979-83, Applied Microbiology and Biotech., 1984-88, Jour. Basic Microbiology, 1989—. Recipient Lederle Faculty award, 1967, Mead Johnson Undergrad. Rsch. award, 1968, Rsch. Career Devel. award USPHS, 1969-74, Volwiler award, 1979, Humboldt Sr. Scientist award, 1980, McCoy award 1981, award in microbial chemistry Kitasato Inst. and Kitasato U., 1988. Fellow Acad. Pharm. Scis. (Research Achievement award in natural products 1976), AAAS; mem. Am. Chem. Soc., Am. Soc. Biol. Chemists, Am. Soc. Microbiology, Am. Soc. Pharmacognosy (Rsch. award 1988), Phytochem. Soc. N.Am., Sigma Xi (Faculty Research award 1976). Home: 5609 145th Ave SE Bellevue WA 98006-4381 Office: Univ Wash Dept Chemistry BG-10 Seattle WA 98195

FLOURNOY, HOUSTON IRVINE, public administration educator; b. N.Y.C., Oct. 7, 1929; s. William Raymond and Helen (Horner) F.; m. Marjorie Elsie Westerkamp, July 11, 1954 (div. June 1987); children: David Houston, Jean Douglas, Ann Horner; m. Carol Hinse Gates, Oct. 9, 1987. BA, Cornell U., 1950; MA, Princeton U., 1952, PhD, 1956. Research asst. div. law revision and legis. info. N.J. State Legislature, Trenton, 1955; legis. asst. U.S. Senator H. Alexander Smith, 1956-57; asst. prof. govt. Pomona Coll. and Claremont Grad. Sch., Calif., 1957-64, assoc. prof., 1964-67; mem. Calif. State Assembly, Los Angeles, 1961-66; controller State of Calif., Sacramento, 1967-74; prof. U. So. Calif., Sacramento, 1975—, dean Ctr. for Pub. Affairs, 1975-78, chmn. Council of Deans, 1976-77, v.p. govtl. affairs, 1978-81, prof. pub. adminstrn., spl. asst. to pres. for govtl. affairs, 1981—; bd. dirs. Lockheed Corp., Fremont Gen. Corp., Tosco Corp., Fletcher Jones Found., Calif. Council for Environ. and Econ. Balance, 1976-79; mem. Bd. Fgn. Scholarships, U.S. Dept. State, 1976-77; chmn. Gov.'s Adv. Commn. on Tax Reform, 1968-69; pub. gov. Pacific Coast Stock Exchange Bd. Govs., 1975-81; mem. Nat. Commn. on Future of State Colls. and Univs., Am. Assn. State Colls. and Univs., 1971-72. Contbr. articles to profl. jours. Served to 1st lt. USAF, 1952-54, Korea. Fellow Citizenship Clearing House Nat. Conv., Republican Nat. Conv., 1960, Henry P. Duboise Found., 1951. Mem. Nat. Acad. Pub. Adminstrn., Pi Sigma Alpha. Republican. Office: U So Calif 1201 J St Sacramento CA 95814-2906

FLOYD, BRETT ALDEN, mortgage banker, consultant; b. Las Vegas, Nev., Nov. 12, 1963. Branch mgr. Transamerica Fin., West Covina, Calif., 1984-89, Assocs. Fin., San Gabriel, Calif., 1989; area sales mgr. Long Beach Bank, F.S.B., Woodland Hills, Calif., 1989—; cons. Sunwest Cons., L.A., 1990—. Assoc. Ctl. Com., L.A., 1992. Republican. Home: 4342 Gentry Ave Studio City CA 91604 Office: Long Beach Bank 6400 Canoga Ave # 355 Woodland Hills CA 91367

FLUKE, LYLA SCHRAM (MRS. JOHN M. FLUKE), publisher; b. Maddock, N.D.; d. Olaf John and Anne Marie (Rodberg) Schram; m. John M. Fluke, June 5, 1937; children: Virginia Fluke Gabelein, John M. Jr., David Lynd. BS in Zoology and Physiology, U. Wash., Seattle, 1934, diploma teaching, 1935. High sch. tchr., 1935-37; tutor Seattle schs., 1974-75; pub. Portage Quar. mag., Hist. Soc. Seattle and King County, 1980—. Author articles on history. Founder N.W. chpt. Myasthenia Gravis Found., 1953, pres., 60-66; obtained N.W. artifacts for destroyer Tender Puget Sound, 1966; mem. Seattle Mayor's Com. for Seattle Beautiful, 1968-69; sponsor Seattle World's Fair, 1962; charter mem. Seattle Youth Symphony Aux., 1974; bd. dirs. Cascade Symphony, Salvation Army, 1985-87; benefactor U. Wash., 1982-88, nat. chmn. ann. giving campaign, 1983-84; benefactor Sterling Circle Stanford U., MIT, 1984, Wash. State Hist. Soc., Pacific Arts Ctr.; mem. condr.'s club Seattle Symphony, 1978—. Fellow Seattle Pacific U., 1972—; mem. Wash. Trust for Hist. Preservation, Nat. Trust for Hist. Preservation, N.W. Ornamental Hort. Soc. (benefactor, life, hon.), Nat. Assn. Parliamentarians (charter mem., pres. N.W. unit 1961), Wash. Parliamentarians Assn. (charter), IEEE Aux. (chpt. charter mem., pres. 1970-73), Seattle C. of C. (women's div.), Seattle Symphony Women's Assn. (life, sec. 1982-84, pres. 1985-87), Hist. Soc. Seattle and King County (exec. com. 1975-78, pres. women's mus. league 1975-78, pres. Moritz Thomsen Guild of Hist. Soc., 1978-80, 84-87), Highlands Orthopedic Guild (life), Wash. State Hist. Soc., Antiquarian Soc. (v.p. 1986-88, pres. 1988—), Rainier Club, Seattle Golf Club, Seattle Tennis Club, U. Wash. Pres.'s Club. Republican. Lutheran. Address: 1206 NW Culbertson Dr Seattle WA 98177 also: Vendovi Island PO Box 703 Anacortes WA 98221

FLYNN, CHARLES MILTON, JR., research chemist; b. Norwalk, Conn., Feb. 28, 1940; s. Charles Milton and Helen (Miles) F. BS in Chemistry, Calif. Inst. Tech., 1962; PhD in Chemistry, U. Ill., 1967. Postdoctoral researcher dept. chemistry Georgetown U., Washington, 1968-72, U. Va., Charlottesville, 1972-76; rsch. chemist U.S. Bur. Mines Reno (Nev.) Rsch. Ctr., 1976—. Patentee in fields of inorganic chemistry, metallurgy; contbr. articles to profl. jours. Mem. Am. Chem. Soc., Am. Sci. Affiliation, Sigma Xi, Alpha Chi Sigma. Office: US Bur Mines Reno Rsch Ctr 1605 Evans Ave Reno NV 89512-2295

FLYNN, MICHAEL A., copywriter; b. N.Y.C., Aug. 15, 1957; s. Charles Victor and Louise Rose (Locke) F.; m. Elizabeth M.S. Flynn, July 4, 1984. BBA, George Wash. U., 1979. Co-pub. Retail Express, Norwalk, Conn., 1987-88; rsch. adminstrv. asst. N.W. Ayer, N.Y.C., 1980-81, project dir., 1981-82; promotion mgr. DC Comics Inc., N.Y.C., 1982-84, sales and advt. mgr., 1984; sales promotion copywriter Siebel/Mohr, N.Y.C., 1984-89; sales agt. Ron Turner Realtors, Seattle, 1990-91; freelance copywriter Seattle, 1989—. Mem. West Seattle C. of C. Democrat. Episcopalian. Home and Office: 9206 36th Ave SW Seattle WA 98126-3829

FLYNN, RALPH MELVIN, JR., sales executive, marketing consultant; b. Winchester, Mass., May 2, 1944; s. Ralph Melvin and Mary Agnus (Giuliani) F.; m. Rose Marie Petrock (div. 1988); children: John Patrick, Marc Jeffery; m. Carolyn F. Lee. Engr. Bell Tel. Labs., Holmdel, N.J., 1966-68; tech. coord. Expts. in Art and Tech., N.Y.C., 1968-69; exec. v.p. Bestline Products, San Jose, Calif., 1969-73; pres. Internat. Inst. for Personal Achievement, Palo Alto, Calif., 1975-76, Diamite Corp., Milpitas, Calif., 1977-84; dir. mktg. IMMI, Campbell, Calif., 1973-77; v.p. internat. Neo-Life Co., Fremont, Calif., 1984—; pres. Ultra Promotions, Los Gatos, Calif., 1988—, Score Publishing, Saratoga, Calif., 1987—; founder "Coffee Soc.", Cupertino, Calif., 1988—; tech. cons. Robert Rauschenberg, N.Y.C., 1968; cons. Standard Oil Co., San Francisco, 1975, I.B.C., Geneva, 1984—, lst Interstate Bank, L.A., 1985. Author: The Only Variable, 1985, Navigating towards Success, 1986; contbr. articles to profl. publs. Named adm. State of Nebr., 1987; Joseph Kaplan Trust scholar, 196l. Mem. Direct Selling Assn., Rolls Royce Owners Club. Republican. Office: Coffee Soc 21265 Stevens Creek Blvd Cupertino CA 95014-5715

FOCH, NINA, actress, creative consultant, educator; b. Leyden, The Netherlands, Apr. 20, 1924; came to U.S. 1927; d. Dirk and Consuelo (Flowerton) F.; m. James Lipton, June 6, 1954; m. James Lipton, June 6, 1954; m. Dennis de Brito, Nov. 27, 1959; 1 child, Dirk de Brito; m. Michael Dewell, Oct. 31, 1967 (div.). Grad., Lincoln Sch., 1939; studies with Stella Adler. Adj. prof. drama U. So. Calif., 1966-68, 78-80, adj. prof. film, 1987—; creative cons. to dirs., writers, prodrs. of all media; artist-in-residence U. N.C., 1966, Ohio State U., 1967, Calif. Inst. Tech., 1969-70; mem. sr. faculty Am. Film Inst., 1974-77; founder, tchr. Nina Foch Studio, Hollywood, Calif., 1973—; founder, actress Los Angeles Theatre Group, 1960-65; bd. dirs. Nat. Repertory Theatre, 1967-75. Motion picture appearances include Nine Girls, 1944, Return of the Vampire, 1944, Shadows in the Night, 1944, Cry of the Werewolf, 1944, Escape in the Fog, 1945, A Song to Remember, 1945, My Name Is Julia Ross, 1945, I Love a Mystery, 1945, Johnny O'Clock, 1947, The Guilt of Janet Ames, 1947, The Dark Past, 1948, The Undercover Man, 1949, Johnny Allegro, 1949, An American in Paris, 1951, Scaramouche, 1952, Young Man with Ideas, 1952, Sombrero, 1953, Fast Company, 1953, Executive Suite, 1954 (Oscar award nominee), Four Guns to the Border, 1954, You're Never Too Young, 1955, Illegal, 1955, The Ten Commandments, 1956, Three Brave Men, 1957, Cash McCall, 1959, Spartacus, 1960, Such Good Friends, 1971, Salty, 1973, Mahogany, 1976, Jennifer, 1978, Rich and Famous, 1981, Skin Deep, 1988, Sliver, 1993; appeared in Broadway plays including John Loves Mary, 1947, Twelfth Night, 1949, A Phoenix Too Frequent, 1950, King Lear, 1950, Second String, 1960; appeared with Am. Shakespeare Festival in Taming of the Shrew, Measure for Measure, 1956, San Francisco Ballet and Opera in The Seven Deadly Sins, 1966; also many regional theater appearances including Seattle Repertory Theatre (All Over, 1972 and The Seagull, 1973); actress on TV, 1947—, including Playhouse 90, Studio One, Pulitzer Playhouse, Playwrights 56, Producers Showcase, Lou Grant (Emmy nominee 1980), Mike Hammer; series star: Shadow Chasers, 1985, War and Remembrance, 1988, LA Law, 1990, Hunter, 1990, Dear John, 1990, 91, Tales of the City, 1993; many other series, network spls. and TV films; TV panelist and guest on The Dinah Shore Show, Merv Griffin Show, The Today Show, Dick Cavett, The Tonight Show; TV moderator: Let's Take Sides, 1957-59; assoc. dir. (film) The Diary of Anne Frank, 1959; dir. (nat. tour and on-Broadway) Tonight at 8:30, 1966-67; assoc. producer re-opening of Ford's Theatre, Washington, 1968. Hon. chmn. Los Angeles chpt. Am. Cancer Soc., 1970. Recipient Film Daily award, 1949, 53. Mem. AAUP, Acad. Motion Picture Arts and Scis. (co-chair exec. com. fgn. film award, membership com.), Hollywood Acad. TV Arts and Scis. (bd. govs. 1976-77). Office: PO Box 1884 Beverly Hills CA 90213-1884

FOFLYGEN, RONALD WAYNE, manufacturing executive; b. Washington, Pa., Oct. 14, 1944; s. James Wayne and Elma Grace (Dunfee) F.; m. Yvonne Emma Sinnett, Nov. 20, 1965; children: Jeffrey Wayne, Kara Leigh. BSEE, Pa. State U., 1973. Design engr. Midland-Ross Corp., Pitts., 1973-75; chief elec. engr. Crucible Steel, Inc., Midland, Pa., 1975-83; sales mgr. Advanced Tech. Sales, Inc., Pitts., 1983-84; sr. staff BDM Corp., Albuquerque, 1984-87; engring. mgr. Plasmatronics, Inc., Albuquerque, 1987-88; v.p. ops. Indsl. Lasers, Inc., Albuquerque, 1988-90; sr. engr. Martin Marietta Corp., Albuquerque, 1990-93; v.p. prodn. Cell-Robotics Inc., Albuquerque, 1993—; pres. Advanced Tech. Cons., Albuquerque, 1987—. Inventor bar hanger box fastener for elec. constrn. products, patentee in field. Elder Ambridge United Presbyn. Ch., Pa., 1984; deacon Covenant Presbyn. Ch., Albuquerque, 1988, mem. Univ. N.Mex. Hosp. Bio-Med. Engr. Devel. Consortium, Albuquerque, 1992—. With USAF, 1966-70, Viet Nam. Mem. Phi Kappa Phi, Tau Beta Pi, Sigma Tau, Eta Kappa Nu, Phi Eta Sigma, Pa. State Alumni Assn. Republican. Home: 11720 Molly Brown Ave NE Albuquerque NM 87111-5915 Office: Cell-Robotics Inc 2715 Broadbent Pkwy NE Albuquerque NM 87107

FOGEL, ALAN DALE, psychology educator; b. Miami, Fla., Nov. 25, 1945; s. Walter and Sherry (VanKollem) F.; m. Jacqueline Learner, Feb. 3, 1968; children: Dan, Menasheh. BS, U. Miami, 1967; MS, Columbia U., 1968; PhD, U. Chgo., 1976. Asst. prof. U. Javeriana, Bogota, Columbia, 1968-71; instr. Chgo. State U., 1975-76; rsch. assoc. U. Chgo., 1974-76; from asst. prof. to prof. child devel. Purdue U., West Lafayette, Ind., 1976-88; prof. psychology U. Utah, Salt Lake City, 1988—; vis. prof. Free U., Amsterdam, 1990; vis. prof. Nagoya U., Japan, 1983. Author: Infancy, 1991, Developing through Relationships, 1993; editor: The Origins of Nurturance, 1985; editorial bd. Child Devel., 1988-91, Devel. Psychology, 1988-93, Early Devel. and Parenting, 1992—; contbr. articles to profl. jours. Fulbright fellow, 1983-84; grantee March of Dimes Birth Defects, 1983-85, NIH, 1986-90, NSF, 1977-80, 90-91. Fellow APA (div. 7); mem. AAAS, Soc. Rsch. Child Devel. (editorial bd. monographs 1988—), Internat. Soc. Study Behavioral Devel., Internat. Soc. Study Human Ethology, Internat. Soc. Infant Studies. Democrat. Jewish. Office: U Utah Dept Psychology Salt Lake City UT 84112

FOGEL, STEVEN MARC, computer consultant, educator; b. Kansas City, Mo., May 3, 1958; s. Nathan Fogel and Shirley Zoe (Goodman) Shear. BSEE, MS in Computer Sci., Washington U., 1981. Ptnr. Steven Fogel & Assoc., New Orleans, 1981-85; cons. McDonnell Douglas, Oakland, Calif., 1985-86; sr. programmer, analyst McDonnell Douglas, Denver, 1986-89; cons. Intelligent Systems, Inc., Denver, 1989—; adj. prof. Tulane U., New Orleans, 1982-84, Denver (Colo.) U., 1987-90; instr. Colo. U., Boulder, 1990-92, Addison-Wesley, Reading, Mass., 1990—; presenter in field. Mem. IEEE, Assn. for Computing Machinery. Home and Office: 1777 Larimer St #2311 Denver CO 80202

FOGG, BRIAN JEFFREY, writer, editing and design consultant; b. Dallas, Aug. 7, 1963; s. Gary Russell and Cheryl Patricia (Armstrong) F. BA magna cum laude, Brigham Young U., 1990, MA, 1992. Pres. Avatar Writing, Editing & Design, Provo, Utah, 1991—; adj. faculty Brigham Young U., Provo, 1992—; cons. various orgns. Editor: For a Good Time, 1987; editor-in-chief Inscape, 1992—; author numerous essays, poem collection. Bd. dirs., trustee Found. for Student Thought, Provo, 1987—; communications specialist Deseret Internat. Found., Provo, 1992. Mem. Soc. for Tech. Comm., Assn. for Mormon Letters (book rev. editor 1991—), Samuel Hall Soc., Western Lit. Assn., Rocky Mountain MLA, Desert Lang. & Linguistic Soc., Phi Kappa Phi. Mem. LDS Ch. Home: PO Box 7100 Provo UT 84602

FOK, SAMUEL SHIU-MING, engineer, consultant; b. Macau, China, Feb. 15, 1926; came to U.S., 1947.; s. Yan-Nung and Bick-Lan (Cheong) F.; m. Ruth L. Sung, Aug. 16, 1952; children: William David Z.C., John Peter Z.Y., James Andrew Z.M. BChE, Ohio State U., 1949; MS in Chem. Engring., Case Inst. Tech., 1951, PhD in Chem. Engring., 1955. Rsch. engr. Indsl. Rayon Corp., Cleve., 1954-56; sr. staff engr. Shockley Transistor Corp., Mountain View, Calif., 1956-60; mem. tech. staff Fairchild R & D Lab, Palo Alto, Calif., 1960-70; microlithographic cons. Palo Alto, 1970-71; mask tech. mgr. Siliconix, Inc., Santa Clara, Calif., 1971-74; dep. dir. FCT Bros. Co., Ltd., Bangkok, Thailand, 1975-77; prin. engr. Perkin-Elmer Corp., Hayward, Calif., 1977-90; cons. Palo Alto, 1990—; tech. dir. Siliconix Hong Kong, 1973; application specialist Perkin-Elmer EBT Div., Hayward, 1977-90. Contbr. articles to profl. jours. Chartered mem. Stanford Area Chinese Club, 1966; prin. Chinese Lang. Sch., Palo Alto, 1962-66; mem. Pacific Art League of Palo Alto, 1990. Mem. Am. Soc. Testing Materials (F-1 com.), Semiconductor Mfg. Engrs. Inst. (micropatterning com.), Am. Vacuum Soc., Soc. Photographic Instrument Engrs., Chinese Inst. Engrs. Republican. Presbyterian.

FOLEY, DANIEL EDMUND, real estate development executive; b. St. Paul, Mar. 1, 1926; s. Edward and Gerry (Fitzgarld) F.; student U. Minn., 1941-43; m. Paula Evans, Apr. 1, 1946. Chmn. bd. Realty Ptnrs. Ltd., Los Angeles; pres. Alpha Property Mgmt. Served with AUS, 1943-46.

FOLEY, JEFFREY YOUNG, geologist; b. Louisville, Dec. 3, 1951; s. Benjamin Parker and Mary Oleta (Clark) F. BS in Geology, U. Ky., 1977; MSc in Geology, U. Alaska, 1985. Geologist Geol. Survey Ky., Lexington, 1977, City Svcs. Minerals Co., Anchorage, 1977; geologist U.S. Bur. of Mines, Fairbanks, 1979-90, Anchorage, 1990—. Contbr. articles to profl. jours. Disabled ski vol. Challenge Alaska, 1991-92; youth hockey coach Anchorage Youth Hockey, 1991. With U.S. Army, 1970-71, Vietnam. Decorated Silver Star, Bronze Star, Air medal. Mem. Geol. Soc. of Am., Geol. Soc. of Alaska. Office: US Bur of Mines 3301 C St Ste 525 Anchorage AK 99503-3935

FOLEY, PATRICK MICHAEL, insurance company official; b. Cedar Rapids, Iowa, Sept. 7, 1958; s. Ambrose Michael and Ila Justine (Mask) F.; m. Kim Marie Bendel, Sept. 18, 1982; children: Timmothy Patrick, Christopher Michael, Kari Marie and Sarah Grace (twins). BBA in Fin. and Ins., U. Iowa, 1981. CLU; ChFC. Spl. agt. Prudential Ins. Co., Cedar Rapids, 1981-82; devel. mgr. Prudential Ins. Co., Madison, Wis., 1982-85; regional field cons. Prudential Ins. Co., Mpls., 1985-86; gen. mgr. Prudential Ins. Co., Billings, Mont., 1986—. Pres. coun. St. Thomas Cath. Ch., Billings, 1991-92. Mem. Am. Soc. CLU's (pres. Billings 1988-89), S.E. Mont. Life Underwriters (trustee 1987-90), Billings Gen. Agts. and Mgrs. Assn. (pres. 1987-88), Billings Petroleum Club, Yellowstone Country Club. Home: 3318 Ben Hogan Ln Billings MT 59106 Office: Prudential Mont/Wyo Agy 27 N 27th St Ste 2100 Billings MT 59102

FOLEY, ROGER D., judge; b. 1917; s. Roger T. and Helen (Drummond) F. LL.B., U. San Francisco. Bar: Nev. bar 1946. Former atty. gen. Nev.; chief judge U.S. Dist Ct. Nev., Las Vegas, to 1980; judge U.S. Dist Ct. Nev., 1980—. Office: US Dist Ct 300 Las Vegas Blvd S Rm 3035 Las Vegas NV 89101-5812

FOLEY, THOMAS JOSEPH, power planning council official; b. Lawrence, Mass., Nov. 11, 1941; s. John Michael and Josephine Patricia (Hughes) F.; m. Lorraine Leslie O'Connell, Sept. 4, 1965. BS in Math. and Computer Sci., Western Wash. U., 1972, postgrad., 1972-74. Rschr. Gen. Dynamics, Groton, Conn., 1961-68; mgr. econ. analysis Battelle N.W., Richland, Wash., 1974-81; mgr. conservation and generation assessment N.W. Power Planning Coun., Portland, Oreg., 1981—; Mem. com. on energy conservation NAS, through 1991; cons. on nat. energy strategy Dept. Energy; cons. for pub. interest to pub. utility commns., Mass., Vt., Conn., Idaho. Mem. Pi Mu Epsilon. Office: NW Power Planning Coun 851 SW 6th Ave Ste 1100 Portland OR 97204

FOLEY, THOMAS MICHAEL, financial executive; b. Phila., Apr. 21, 1943; s. Thomas Bernard and Alice Mary (Machulsky) F.; m. Jean D. McCrystal, Oct. 1, 1966 (dec. 1973); children: Thomas R., Timothy J., Brian P.; m. Carolyn Jo Forbes, mar. 23, 1974; children: Kathryn A. and Jo A. (twins). BS, LaSalle U., 1965; MBA, Temple U., 1984. CPA, Pa. With Price Waterhouse, Phila., 1965-76; audit mgr. Price Waterhouse, 1970-76; v.p. corp. auditing Mack Trucks, Inc., Allentown, Pa., 1976-80; v.p. info. mgmt. Mack Trucks, Inc., 1980-85; v.p. fin., adminstrn. Albert Nipon, Inc., Phila., 1985-87; sr. v.p., chief fin. officer Phila. Stock Exch., Phila., 1987-90; v.p., chief fin. officer Print Northwest, Inc., Tacoma, 1990—; project leader, Grace Commn., Washington, 1984. Mem. AICPA, Pa. Inst. CPAs, Wash. Inst. CPAs, Fin. Execs. Inst., Printing Industry Fin. Execs. (exec. com.). Republican. Home: 12713 133D Ave SE Rainier WA 98576 Office: Print Northwest Inc PO Box 1418 Tacoma WA 98401-1418

FOLEY, THOMAS STEPHEN, speaker of the U.S. House of Representatives; b. Spokane, Wash., Mar. 6, 1929; s. Ralph E. and Helen Marie (Higgins) F.; m. Heather Strachan, Dec. 1968. B.A., U. Wash., 1951, LL.B., 1957. Bar: Wash. Partner Higgins & Foley, 1957-58; dep. pros. atty. Spokane County, Spokane, 1958-60; asst. atty. gen. State of Wash., Olympia, 1960-61; spl. counsel interior and insular affairs com. U.S. Senate, Washington, 1961-64; mem. 89th-103rd Congresses from 5th Wash. dist., Washington, D.C., 1965—; House majority whip, 1981-86, House majority leader, 1987-89; speaker U.S. Ho. of Reps., 1989—; instr. law Gonzaga U., 1958-60; mem. bd. advisors Ctr. Strategic and Internat. Studies; mem. adv. council Am. Ditchley Found. Bd. overseers Whitman Coll.; bd. advisors Yale U. council; bd. dirs. Council on Fgn. Relations. Mem. Phi Delta Phi. Democrat. Office: 1201 Longworth Bldg Washington DC 20515-4705*

FOLKERTS, MARK ALLEN, software quality engineer; b. Vancouver, Wash., Mar. 24, 1956; s. Alfred George and Edna Laura (Staveland) F.; m. Rosanna Sue Bonney, June 19, 1982; 1 child, Lauren Elizabeth. BSEE, Wash. State U., 1979. Electronic test engr. Data I/O Corp., Issaquah, Wash., 1980-82; quality engr. Data I/O Corp., Redmond, Wash., 1982-87, sr. software quality engr., 1987—. Mem. IEEE, IEEE Computer Soc., Am. Soc. Quality Control (vol. trainer 1987-89, publicity com. chair 1982-92), Assn. Computing Machinery, Astron. Soc. of Pacific, Eastside Astron. Soc. Office: Data I/O Corp 10525 Willows Rd NE Redmond WA 98073-0746

FOLLETT, ROY HUNTER, agronomy educator; b. Cowdrey, Colo., Feb. 27, 1935; s. Roy Lawrence and Frances (Hunter) F.; m. Barbara Ann Delehoy, June 28, 1959; children: Kevin, Karen. BS, Colo. State U., 1957, MS, 1963, PhD, 1969. Soil scientist Soil Conservation Svc., Ft. Collins, Colo., 1963-64; extension agronomist Colo. State U., Ft. Collins, 1964-70; asst. prof. Ohio State U., Columbus, 1970-74; prof. agronomy Kans. State U., Manhattan, 1974-81, Colo. State U., Ft. Collins, 1981—. Author: Our Soils and Their Management, 1990, Fertilizers and Soil Amendments, 1981. Recipient Disting. Educators award, Plant Food Assn., 1989, Meritorious Svc. award, Epsilon Sigma Phi, 1989, Honor Alumni award Colo. State U., 1992. Fellow Am. Soc. Agronomy, Soil Sci. Soc. Am., Soil and Water Conservation Soc.; mem. Alpha Zeta, Sigma Xi, Gamma Sigma Delta (Faculty award 1992). Presbyterian. Home: 1040 Club View Rd Fort Collins CO 80524-1554 Office: Colo State U Dept Agronomy Fort Collins CO 80523

FOLLICK, EDWIN DUANE, chiropractic physician, law educator; b. Glendale, Calif., Feb. 4, 1935; s. Edwin Fulfford and Esther Agnes (Catherwood) F.; m. Marilyn K. Sherk, Mar. 24, 1986. BA, Calif. State U., L.A., 1956, MA, 1961; MA, Pepperdine U., 1957, MPA, 1977; PhD, DTheol., St. Andrews Theol. Coll., Sem. of the Free Protestant Episc. Ch., London, 1958; MS in Libr. Sci., U. So. Calif., 1963, MEd in Instructional Materials, 1964, AdvMEd in Edn. Adminstrn., 1969; student, Calif. Coll. Law, 1965; LLB, Blackstone Law Sch., 1966, JD, 1967; DC, Cleve. Chiropractic Coll., L.A., 1972; PhD, Academia Theatina, Pescara, 1978; MA in Organizational Mgmt., Antioch U., L.A., 1990. Tchr., libr. adminstr. L.A. City Schs., 1957-68; law librarian Glendale U. Coll. Law, 1968-69; coll. librarian Cleve. Chiropractic Coll., L.A., 1969-74, dir. edn. and admissions, 1974-84, prof. jurisprudence, 1975—, dean student affairs, 1976-92, chaplain, 1985—; dean of edn. Cleve. Chiropractic Coll., 1989—; assoc. prof. Newport U., 1982; extern prof. St. Andrews Theol. Coll., London, 1961; dir. West Valley Chiropractic Health Ctr., 1972—. Contbr. articles to profl. jours. Chaplain's asst. U.S. Army, 1958-60. Decorated cavaliere Internat. Order Legion of Honor of Immaculata (Italy); Knight of Malta, Sovereign Order of St. John of Jerusalem; knight Order of Signum Fidei; comdr. chevalier Byzantine Imperial Order of Constantine the Gt.; comdr. ritter Order St. Gereon, numerous others. Mem. ALA, NEA, Am. Assn. Sch. Librarians, L.A. Sch. Library Assn., Calif. Media and Library Educators Assn., Assn. Coll and Rsch. Librarians, Am. Assn. Law Librarians, Am. Chiropractic Assn., Internat. Chiropractors Assn., Nat. Geog. Soc., Internat. Platform Assn., Phi Delta Kappa, Sigma Chi Psi, Delta Tau Alpha. Democrat. Episcopalian. Home: 6435 Jumilla Ave Woodland Hills CA 91367-2833 Office: 590 N Vermont Ave Los Angeles CA 90004-2196 also: 7022 Owensmouth Ave Canoga Park CA 91303

FOLTZ, DONALD JOSEPH, franchise development consultant; b. Chgo., Jan. 23, 1933; s. Joseph M. and Sheldon B. (Morris) F.; m. Carol Elizabeth Seymour, Aug. 29, 1953; children: Kim Foltz Stanton, Joseph Jay. BBA, Western Mich. U., 1955, MBA, 1956. Regional mktg. mgr. Frigidaire Div. Gen. Motors Corp., Denver, 1958-60; co-founder, pres. Mr. Steak, Inc. (Jamco), Denver, 1960-70, The Mktg. Group, Inc., Denver, 1971-78, The Franchise Ctr./DJFA & Assocs., Inc., Denver, 1971—; chmn., dir. Profusion Systems, Inc., Aurora, Colo., 1982-90; pres., dir. Franchise Network U.S.A., Inc., Aurora, 1986-88; bd. dirs. Colo. Industry Tng. Coun., Golden. Author: The College of Franchise Knowledge, 1992. Exec. dir. Runaways, Inc., Denver, 1970-82. 1st lt. U.S. Army, 1956-58. Office: Donald J Foltz & Assocs Inc 5555 Dtc Pky Ste 3210 Englewood CO 80111-3020

FONDOTS, DAVID JOHN, telecommunications company owner, consultant; b. Phila., Jan. 5, 1963; s. David Charles Fondots and Patricia (Sheehi) Cameron. Student, Bard Coll., 1980, U. Md., 1981-82; BS in Mktg., Pacific U., 1992. Intelligence, sgt. U.S. Army, Europe, 1981-84; gen. mgr. 1st Am. Travel Mktg., Atlantic City, N.J., 1984-85; pres. Travel Internat., Phila., 1985-87; dir. mktg. Colo. Prime, Inc., Farmingdale, N.Y., 1987-90; CEO Calif. Suntel, Inc., Newport Beach, Calif., 1992, Product Devel., Inc., Newport Beach, Calif., 1990—; cons. in field. Founding mem. Rep. Small Bus. Assn., Anaheim, Calif., 1991-92; dir. Bush/Quayle '88, N.Y.C., 1988; mem. Orange County Lincoln Club, 1992, 400 Club, Costa Mesa, Calif., 1991-92. Recipient Soldier of Quarter and Yr. award, 1981, 82, 83, 84, Army Achievement award Intelligence Security Comd., 1983. Mem. Lincoln Club. Republican. Roman Catholic. Office: Product Devel 4120 Birch Ste 110 Newport Beach CA 92660

FONG, CARL S., systems and operations analyst; b. Sacramento, June 11, 1959; s. John Ye and Amy Fong m. Denise Lowe, Dec. 12, 1992. AS, Consumnes River Coll., 1979; BS, Calif. Polytech. Inst., 1985; postgrad., U. LaVerne, Calif., 1990-93. Tutor Calif. Polytech. Inst., Pomona, 1983, lab. cons., 1984-85; peripheral operator Security Pacific Automation Corp., Brea, Calif., 1984-85; programmer, analyst I Orange County Dept. of Edn., Costa Mesa, Calif., 1985-86, programmer, analyst II, 1986-87, systems programmer, 1987-89, systems and ops. analyst, 1989—. Mem. Assn. of MBA Execs., Mgmt. Info. System Student Assn., Data Processing Mgmt. Assn. Office: Orange County Dept of Edn 200 Kalmus Dr # 1016C Costa Mesa CA 92626-7932

FONG, HAROLD MICHAEL, federal judge; b. Honolulu, Apr. 28, 1938; m. Judith Tom, 1966; children—Harold Michael, Terrence Matthew. A.B. cum laude, U. So. Calif., 1960; J.D., U. Mich., 1964. Bar: Hawaii 1965. Dep. pros. atty. City and County of Honolulu, 1965-68; assoc. Mizuha and Kim, Honolulu, 1968-69; asst. U.S. atty. Dist. Hawaii, 1969-73; U.S. atty., 1973-78; ptnr. Fong and Miho, Honolulu, 1978-82; judge U.S. Dist. Ct. Hawaii, 1982—, chief judge, 1984-91. Office: US Dist Ct PO Box 50128 Honolulu HI 96850-0001

FONG, HIRAM L., former senator; b. Honolulu, Oct. 15, 1906; s. Lum Fong and Chai Ha Lum; m. Ellyn Lo; children: Hiram, Rodney, Merle-Ellen Fong Gushi, Marvin-Allan (twins). AB with honors, U. Hawaii, 1930, LLD, 1953; JD, Harvard U., 1935; LLD, Tufts U., 1960, Lafayette Coll., 1960, Lynchburg Coll., 1970, Lincoln U., 1971, U. Guam, 1974, St. John's U., 1975, Calif. Western Sch. Law, 1976, Tung Wu (Soochow) U., Taiwan, 1978, China Acad., Taiwan, 1978; LHD, L.I. U., 1968. With supply dept. Pearl Harbor Navy Yard, 1924-27; chief clk. Suburban Water System, 1930-32; dep. atty. City and County of Honolulu, 1935-38; founder, ptnr. law firm Fong, Miho, Choy & Robinson, until 1959; founder, chmn. bd. emeritus Finance Factors, Grand Pacific Life Ins. Co.; founder, chmn bd. Finance Investment Co., Market City, Ltd., Fin. Enterprises Ltd.; pres. Ocean View Cemetery, Ltd.; owner, operator Sen. Fong's Plantation and Gardens, Honolulu; dir. numerous firms, Honolulu; hon. cons. China Airlines. Mem. Hawaii Legislature, 1938-54, speaker, 1948-54; mem. U.S. Senate, 1959-77, Post Office and Civil Service Com., Judiciary Com., Appropriations Com., Spl. Com. on Aging; U.S. del. 150th Anniversary Argentine Independence, Buenos Aires, 1960, 55th Interparliamentary Union (World) Conf., 1966, Ditchley Found. Conf., 1967, U.S.-Can. Inter-Parliamentary Union Conf., 1961, 65, 67, 68, Mex.-U.S. Inter-Parliamentary Conf., 1968, World Interparliamentary Union, Tokyo, 1974; mem. Commn. on Revision Fed. Ct. Appellate System, 1975—; Active in civic and service orgns.; v.p. Territorial Constl. Conv., 1950; del. Rep. Nat. Conv., 1952, 56, 60, 64, 68, 72; founder, chmn. bd. Fin. Factors Found.; founder, pres. Hiram & Ellyn Fong Found.; founder, pres., chmn. bd. Market City Found.; hon. co-chmn. McKinley High Sch. Found., 1989; bd. visitors U.S. Mil. Acad., 1971—, U.S. Naval Acad., 1974—. Served from 1st lt. to maj. USAAF, 1942-44; ret. col. USAF Res. Recipient award NCCJ, 1960, Meritorious Svc. citation Nat. Assn. Ret. Civil Employees, 1963, Horatio Alger award, 1970, citation for outstanding service Japanese Am. Citizens League, 1970, award Am. Acad. Achievement, 1971, oustanding svc. award Orgn. Chinese Ams., 1973, award Nat. Soc. Daus. Founders and Patriots Am., 1974, certificate Pacific Asian World, 1974, Citizen Among Citizens award Boys & Girls Clubs of Hawaii, 1991, Disting. Alumnus award U. Hawaii Alumni Assn., 1991, Kulia I Ka Nu'u award Pub. Schs. Hawaii Found., 1992; decorated Order of Brilliant Star with Grand Cordon Republic of China; Order of Diplomatic Service Merit; Gwanghwan Medal Republic of Korea). Mem. Am. Legion, VFW, Lambda AAlpha Internat. (Aloha chpt.), Phi Beta Kappa. Congregationalist. Home: 1102 Alewa Dr Honolulu HI 96817-1507

FONG, JULITA ANGELA, pathologist; b. Hong Kong, Oct. 11, 1933; d. Eugene F.W. and Thora W. (Wong) Chin; m. Henry S. Fong, June 8, 1959 (dec.); children: Marydaisy, Joseph E. BA, San Francisco Coll. for Women, 1954; MD, Stanford U., 1958. Diplomate Am. Bd. Pathology. Assoc. pathologist Sacramento (Calif.) Med. Ctr., 1964-74; med. dir. Physicians Clin. Lab, Sacramento, 1974-78; lab dir. Fong Diagnostic Lab, Sacramento, 1978—; assoc. clin. prof. pathology U. Calif. Davis Sch. Medicine, 1975—. Mem. AMA, Calif. Med. Assn., Sacramento-El Dorado County Med. Soc., Coll. Am. Pathologists, Am. Soc. Clin. Pathologists, Am. Med. Womens Assn., Soroptimist Internat. of Sacramento. Republican. Office: Meris Labs Inc 7237 E Southgate Dr Sacramento CA 95823-2620

FONS, AUGUST MARION, III, protective services official, educator; b. El Paso, Tex., Jan. 29, 1951; s. August M. Jr. and Nila Anne (Scott) F.; m. Lynn Corbett; children: Trina Anne, Chelsea Marie. AA, N.Mex. Jr. Coll., 1979; BBA, Coll. of S.W., Hobbs, N.Mex., 1987. Police officer, emergency med. technician Alamogordo (N.Mex.) Dept. Police Sta., 1973-76; police officer Hobbs Police Dept., 1976-79, narcotics detective, 1979-81, from police officer to capt., 1982—; fluids engr. IMCO, Houston, 1981-82; instr. N.Mex. Jr. Coll., Hobbs, 1989—; comdr. SWAT team Hobbs Police Dept., 1987-90, instr. in officer survival N.Mex. Law Enforcement Acad., Santa Fe, 1990—. Bd. dirs. Crimestoppers, Hobbs, 1990. With USAF, 1969-73. Mem. Tex. Narcotics Officers Assn., N.Mex. Narcotics Officers Assn., Nat. Drug Enforcement Officers Assn., 5th Jud. Law Enforcement Assn. (pres. 1990—), Nat. Tactical Officers Assn., Hobbs Order of Firefighters, Fraternal Order of Police (treas. 1986-87). Roman Catholic. Home: 1123 E Michigan Dr Hobbs NM 88240-3241 Office: Hobbs Police Dept 300 N Turner St Hobbs NM 88240-8302

FOOTE, BRIAN LYNN, advertising executive, marketing professional; b. Reno, Nov. 28, 1963; s. W. Darrell and Barbara (Brown) F.; m. Leah Jean Wagner. BA in History, Art, U. Nev., 1988. Graphic designer Art Assocs., Reno, 1984-85; animator McCamant Prodns., Reno, 1984-86; instr. Japanese lang. U. Nev., Reno, 1984-91; translator Japanese Inst. Reno, 1984—; pres. C.S.I., Inc., Carson City, Nev., 1987-89, Foote Advt., Inc., Reno, 1987—; editor, dir. art The Corp. Strategist, Inc., Reno, 1989—; pres. Wild West Tours, Ltd., Reno, 1989—; mem. exec. com. Japan Am. Student Conf., Washington, 1986-88; translator Western Discovery, Internat., Reno, 1987—. Illustrator Bus. Today Mag., 1988, The Corp. Strategist, 1989-92; cartoonist Sagebrush Newspaper (Rocky Mountain award 1988-89). Tchr., missionary LDS Ch., Sapporo, Japan, 1982-84. Mem. Phi Beta Kappa. Office: Foote Advt Inc 1280 Terminal Way # 3 Reno NV 89502

FOOTE, DOUGLAS DEAN, natural resources and environmental industry executive; b. Alamosa, Colo., Apr. 17, 1945; s. Colonell Lane and Ruth Marie (Meyer) F.; m. Eleanor Anne Weller, July 27, 1968; children: Hilary Anne, Charles Lane. BSBA, U. Denver, 1965; JD, U. Colo., 1968; LLM, U. London, 1973; postgrad., Harvard U., 1983. Bar: Colo., Conn., U.S. Supreme Ct., U.S. Ct. Internat. Trade. Atty. Rovira, DeMuth & Eiberger, Denver, 1974-75, Climax Molybelenum Co., Golden, Colo., 1975-77; v.p., gen. counsel Copper, Chems. & Asia Pacific Divs. AMAX Inc., Greenwich, Conn., 1977-85; sr. v.p. AMAX Asia/Pacific Group, Hong Kong, 1985-87; spl. counsel Calkins, Kramer, Grimshaw & Harring, Denver, 1987-88; v.p., gen. counsel Bond Internat. Gold Inc., Denver, 1988-90; CEO Pincock, Allen & Holt Inc., Lakewood, Colo., 1990—; pres. Scaltech Inc., Houston, 1993—. Mem. adv. com. State Dept. Law of Sea, Washington, 1979-84, Nat. Fgn. Trade Coun., 1978-83. Lt. comdr. USNR, 1968-74, Vietnam, capt. USNR, 1974-89. Mem. Am. Mining Congress (pub. lands com.), Colo. Supreme Ct. (grievance panel), Colo. Bar Assn. (ethics com.). Episcopalian.

FOOTE, JIM EDWARD, JR., music educator, recording artist; b. Milw., Dec. 5, 1954; s. Jim Edward and Rosetta Olivia (Savage) F.; m. Roberta May Kaminski, Sept. 8, 1978 (div. Oct. 1985); m. Lana René Esias, Aug. 14, 1993. Student, U. Wis., Oshkosh, 1972-77; cert. med. assi., Clayton Career Coll., Santa Clara, Calif., 1987. Musician Sound Spectrum, Manitowac, Wis., 1977-79; courier, mgr. Metpath Labs., Burlingame, Calif., 1980-83; musician, rec. artist Songman Prodns., San Jose, Calif., 1984-87; rec. artist Tritos Prodns., 1985-87; pathology lab. phlebotomist Pathology Labs., Los Gatos, Calif., 1987-88; music tchr. St. Christopher Sch., San Jose, 1987-92; med. asst. Good Health Med. Ctr., San Jose, 1987—; music tchr. Beechwood Sch., Menlo Park, Calif., 1989-93; rec. artist, author 56 Palms Pub. Co., Cathedral City, Calif., 1991—; tchr. Sierra Pacific Bible Coll., San Jose, 1992—; percussionist Jubilee Christian Ctr. Music Dept.; adv. bd. mem. No. Calif. Songwriters Assn., Menlo Park, 1984-85; missionary OC Internat., Colorado Springs, 1988; missionary, group leader Harvest Evangelism, Inc., San Jose, 1991, 92; founder Breaking Free Ministries; music dir. Mighty Women of God and Jubilee Men's Ministry, 1992—. Composer, artist: (album) Footeprints, 1992; author: Footeprints, 1992. Entertainer, musician United Svc. Orgn., Dept. Def., Japan, Korea, Taiwan, Alaska, Germany, 1978-79. Recipient scroll of appreciation, U.S. Army and 7th Army, Europe, 1979, letter of commendation Am. Med. Techs., 1987; named Outstanding Young Man of Am., 1989. Mem. Nat. Cath. Ednl. Assn. (tchr. assoc. 1987-92). Home: 554 Toyon Ave # 6 San Jose CA 95127 Office: 56 Palms Pub Co PO Box 31 Palm Springs CA 92263-0031

FOOTE, PAUL SHELDON, business educator, consultant; b. Lansing, Mich., May 22, 1946; s. Harlon Sheldon and Frances Norene (Rotter) F. BBA, U. Mich., 1967; MBA (Loomis-Sayles fellow), Harvard U., 1971; advanced profl. cert. NYU, 1975; PhD, Mich. State U., 1983; m. Badri Seddigheh Hosseinian, Oct. 25, 1968; children: David, Sheila. Br. mgr., divl. mgr. Citibank, N.Y.C., Bombay, India and Beirut, Lebanon, 1972-74; mgr. planning and devel. Singer Co., Africa/Middle East, 1974-75; instr. U. Mich., Flint, 1978-79; lectr. acctg. Mich. State U., East Lansing, 1977; asst. prof. U. Windsor (Ont., Can.), 1979-81; assoc. prof. Saginaw Valley State Coll., University Center, Mich., 1981-82; asst. prof. Oakland U., Rochester, Mich., 1982-83; asst. prof. NYU, 1983-87; assoc. prof. Pepperdine U., Malibu, Calif., 1987-89; prof. dept. of acctg. Sch. Bus. and Econs. Calif. State U., Fullerton, 1989—; founder, pres. The Computer Coop., Inc., 1981-82. Lt. AUS, 1968-69. Haskins and Sells Doctoral Consortium fellow, 1977. Mem. Am. Acctg. Assn.

FOOTER, SAMUEL JOSEPH, manufacturing company executive; b. West Palm Beach, Fla., Oct. 31, 1930; s. Samuel J. and Selma A. (Widell) F.; m. Patrice Anne Workman, Dec. 21, 1956; 1 child, Nancy Susan. BAChemE, U. Fla., 1954. Prodn. engr. Union Carbide, Charleston, W.Va., 1956-60, Brownsville, Tex., 1960-62; dept. head Union Carbide, Brownsville, 1962-73, prodn. mgr., 1973-79, asst. plant mgr., 1980-83; asst. plant mgr. Union Carbide, Texas City, Tex., 1983-86; plant mgr. Union Carbide, Moses Lake, Wash., 1986-90; pres. Advanced Silicon Materials Inc., Moses Lake, 1990—, CEO, 1992—. Dir. Assn. Wash. Bus., Olympia, 1988—; adv. bd. mem. Sch. Architecture and Engring., Wash. State U., Pullman, 1988—; exec. dir. Grant County Econ. Devel. Coun., Wash., 1991—. Sgt. U.S. Army, 1954-56. Mem. Rotary (dir. 1987—). Republican. Home: 4082 Cove West Dr

Moses Lake WA 98837 Office: Advanced Silicon Materials Inc 3322 Rd N NE Moses Lake WA 98837

FOOTMAN, GORDON ELLIOTT, educational administrator; b. L.A., Oct. 10, 1927; s. Arthur Leland and Meta Fay (Neal) F.; m. Virginia Rose Footman, Aug. 7, 1954; children: Virginia, Patricia, John. BA, Occidental Coll., 1951, MA, 1954; EdD, U. So. Calif., 1972. Tchr., Arcadia, Calif., 1952, Glendale, Calif., 1956; psychologist Burbank (Calif.) Schs., 1956-64, supr., 1964-70, dir. pupil personnel services, 1970-72; dir. div. ednl. support svcs. L.A. County Office Edn., Downey, Calif., 1972—. Lectr. ednl. psychology U. So. Calif., 1972-75, asst. prof. ednl. psychology, 1976—. Pres. Council for Exceptional Children, 1969-70; pres. Burbank Coordinating Council, 1969-70; mem. Burbank Family Service Bd., 1971-72. Served with AUS, 1945-47. Mem. Am. Edn. Research Assn., Am. Assn. for Counseling and Devel. (senator 1983-86, gov. coun., 1989—, exec. com. 1990—, parliamentarian 1991—, western region br. assembly publs. editor 1985-87, chair 1988-89), Calif. Personnel and Guidance Assn. (pres. 1981-82), Calif. Assn. Sch. Psychologists and Psychometrists, Nat., Calif. (monograph editor 1977—), Assns. Pupil Personnel Adminstrs., Calif. Assn. Counselor Educators and Suprs. (trustee), Calif. Assn. Sch. Adminstrs., Calif. Soc. Ednl. Program Auditors and Evaluators (sec. 1975-76, v.p. 1976-77, pres.), Calif. Assn. Measurement and Evaluation in Guidance (sec. 1976, pres. 1979-80), Calif. Inst. Tech. Assocs., Coun. Exceptional Children (pres. Foothill chpt. 1969-70), Phi Beta Kappa, Phi Alpha Theta, Psi Chi. Republican. Presbyn. Home: 1259 Sherwood Rd San Marino CA 91108-1816 Office: 9300 Imperial Hwy Downey CA 90242

FORAKER, DAVID ALAN, lawyer; b. Mpls., Feb. 22, 1956; s. Crawford Jackson and Norma Jane (Settlemoir) F.; m. Nancy Jean Howard, May 9, 1987. MS, St. Cloud State U., 1978; JD, U. Oreg., 1981. Bar: Oreg. 1981. Assoc. McMenamin, Joseph, Babener, Greene & Perris, Portland, Oreg., 1981-83, Greene & Perris, Portland, 1983-84; ptnr. Greene & Markley, P.C., Portland, 1984—; mem. Oreg. Debtor Creditor Bankruptcy Rules Subcom., 1987-93, chair, 1992, Oreg. Debtor Creditor Fast Track Chpt. II Subcom., 1991-93; speaker Oreg. Trial Lawyers Assn., 1987, N.W. Bankruptcy Inst., 1992. Editor: Oreg. Debtor-Creditor News, 1987-93, editor-in-chief, 1988. Mem. ABA, Oreg. Bar Assn., Multnomah County Bar Assn., Am. Bankruptcy Inst. Democrat. Episcopalian. Office: Greene & Markley PC 1515 SW 5th Ave Ste 600 Portland OR 97201-5449

FORBES, DAVID CRAIG, musician; b. Seattle, Feb. 12, 1938; s. Douglas James and Ruby A. (Niles) F.; m. Sylvia Sterling, Aug. 29, 1965 (div. Apr. 1973); 1 child, Angela Rose. Grad., USN Sch. Music, 1957; student, Western Wash. State U., 1960-64. Prin. horn La Jolla (Calif.) Civic Orch., 1958-60, Seattle Worlds Fair Band, 1962, Seattle Opera Co., 1964—, Pacific Northwest Ballet, Seattle, 1964—; asst. prin. horn Seattle Symphony Orch., 1964—; prin. horn Pacific Northwest Wagner Fest., Seattle, 1975—; instr. horn Western Wash. State U., 1969-81, Cornish Inst., Seattle, 1964-78. Served with USN, 1956-60. Mem. NARAS, Internat. Horn Soc. Home: 217 NW Market St Seattle WA 98107-3430

FORBES, KENNETH ALBERT FAUCHER, urological surgeon; b. Waterford, N.Y., Apr. 28, 1922; s. Joseph Frederick and Adelle Frances (Robitaille) F.; m. Eileen Ruth Gibbons, Aug. 4, 1956; children: Michael, Diane, Kenneth E., Thomas, Maureen, Daniel. BS cum laude, U. Notre Dame, 1943; MD, St. Louis U., 1947. Diplomate Am. Bd. Urology. Intern St. Louis U. Hosp., 1947-48; resident in urol. surgery Barnes Hosp., VA Hosp., Washington U., St. Louis U. schs. medicine, St. Louis, 1948-52; asst. chief urology Letterman Army Hosp., San Francisco, 1952-54; fellow West Roxbury (Harvard) VA Hosp., Boston, 1955; asst. chief urology VA Hosp., East Orange, N.J., 1955-58; practice medicine specializing in urology Green Bay, Wis., 1958-78, Long Beach, Calif., 1978-85; mem. cons. staff Fairview State Hosp. U. Calif. Med. Ctr., Irvine, VA Hosp., Long Beach; asst. clin. prof. surgery U. Calif., Irvine, 1978-85; cons. Vols. in Tech. Assistance, 1986—. Contbr. articles to profl. jours. Served with USNR, 1944-46; capt. U.S. Army, 1952-54. Named Outstanding Faculty Mem. by students, 1981. Fellow ACS, Royal Soc. Medicine, Internat. Coll. Surgeons; mem. AMA, AAAS, Calif. Med. Assn., Am. Urol. Assn. (exec. com. North Ctrl. sect. 1972-75, Western sect. 1980—), N.Y. Acad. Scis., Surg. Alumni Assn. U. Calif.-Irvine, Justin J. Cordonnier Soc. Washington U., Confedn. Americana Urologia, Urologists Corr. Club, Notre Dame Club (Man of Yr. award 1965), Union League Club, Phi Beta Pi. Republican. Roman Catholic. Home and Office: 11579 Sutters Mill Cir Gold River CA 95670-7214

FORBES, LEONARD, engineering educator; b. Grande Prairie, Alta., Can., Feb. 21, 1940; came to U.S., 1966; s. Frank and Katie (Tschetter) F.; B.Sc. with distinction in Engring. Physics, U. Alta., 1962; M.S. in E.E., U. Ill., 1963, Ph.D., 1970. Staff engr. IBM, Fishkill, N.Y. and Manassas, Va., 1970-72; IBM vis. prof. Howard U., Washington, 1972; asst. prof. U. Ark., Fayetteville, 1972-75; assoc. prof. U. Calif.-Davis, 1976-82; prof. Oreg. State U., Corvallis, 1983—; with Hewlett-Packard Labs., Palo Alto, Calif., 1978; cons. to Telex Computer Products, D.H. Baldwin, Hewlett-Packard, Fairchild, United Epitaxial Tech., Naval Ocean Systems Ctr.; organizer Portland Internat. Conf. and Exposition on Silicon Materials and Tech., 1985-87. Served with Royal Can. Air Force, 1963-66. Mem. IEEE. Contbr. articles to profl. jours. Home: 965 NW Highland Ter Corvallis OR 97330-9706 Office: Oreg State U Dept Elec Engring Corvallis OR 97331-3211

FORBES, ROSS WILLIAM, network analyst; b. Cleve., Mar. 31, 1949; s. Jack and Esther R. Forbes. Ops. mgr. West Coast Media, Garden Grove, Calif., 1972-75; mgr. corp. ops. Concerned Comms. Corp., Yuba City, Calif., 1975-80; pres. Pacific Majer, Inc., Los Altos, Calif., 1980-90; systems support analyst Ware & Freidenrich, Palo Alto, Calif., 1991—; pres. Project Oscar, Inc., 1985-93. Mem. AMSAT-U.K., AMSAT N.Am. (life), Am. Radio Relay League (life), Quarter Century Wireless Assn. (life), No. Calif. DX Found. Home: PO Box 1 Los Altos CA 94023-0001

FORBIS, RICHARD GEORGE, archaeologist; b. Missoula, Mont., July 30, 1924; s. Clarence Jenks and Josephine Marie (Hunt) F.; m. Marjorie Helen Wilkinson, Nov. 12, 1960; children: Michael, David, Amanda. B.A., U. Mont., 1949, M.A., 1950; Ph.D., Columbia U., 1955. Sr. archeologist Pacific N.W. Pipeline Corp., Western U.S., 1955-56; archeologist Glenbow Found., Calgary, Alta., Can., 1957-63; mem. faculty U. Calgary, 1963—, prof. archaeology, 1968-88, prof. emeritus, 1988—, interim chmn. dept., Killam Meml. fellow, 1977; chmn. Alta. Public Adv. Com. Hist. and Archeol. Resources, 1971-74; mem. Alta. Historic Sites Bd., 1974-78; vis. scientist Can. Nat. Museum Man, 1970. Author: Cluny: An Ancient Fortified Village in Alberta, 1977; co-author: An Introduction to the Archaeology of Alberta, Canada, 1965. Served with AUS, 1943-46. Mem. AAAS, Soc. Am. Archaeology, Can. Archaeol. Assn. (Smith-Wintemberg award 1984), Am. Anthrop. Assn., Plains Anthrop. Conf., Champlain Soc., Sigma Chi. Office: 2500 University Dr NW, Calgary, AB Canada T2N 1N4

FORCIER, JAMES ROBERT, political economist; b. Pasadena, Calif., Nov. 22, 1950; s. Robert Wallace and Laura (Bone) F. BA in Polit. Sci., UCLA, 1973; MPA, U. So. Calif., 1988, PhD in Pub. Affairs, 1991. Mgr. polit. campaign state and local races, San Diego, 1973-75; spl. asst. Calif. State Assembly, San Diego, Sacramento, 1975-77; legis. aide U.S. Senate, Washington, 1975-77; dir. fed. affairs Calif. Energy Commn., Sacramento, 1977-79; mgr. regulatory coordination Pacific Gas and Electric Co., San Francisco, 1979-86, dir. corp. issues, 1986-88; ind. cons. James R. Forcier & Co., Berkeley, Calif., 1988-89; mgr. competition Pacific Bell Directory, San Francisco, 1989-92; mgr. regulatory policy Pacific Bell, San Francisco, 1992—; interviewee Daybreak Sta. KRON-TV, 1989. Author: Judicial Excess, 1993; contbr. articles to periodicals and newspapers. Bd. dirs. San Diego County Dept. Adult Protective Svcs., 1974; treas. Citizens for Kapiloff, San Diego, 1975; candidate Berkeley City Coun., 1988. Mem. Am. Econ. Assn., Nat. Assn. Bus. Econs., Am. Polit. Sci. Assn., Planning Forum (v.p. San Francisco chpt. 1989-90), Issues Mgmt. Assn. (chartered), Pi Sigma Alpha.

FORD, BETTY BLOOMER (ELIZABETH FORD), health facility executive, wife of former President of U.S.; b. Chgo., Apr. 8, 1918; d. William Stephenson and Hortence (Neahr) Bloomer; m. Gerald R. Ford (38th Pres. U.S.), Oct. 15, 1948; children: Michael Gerald, John Gardner, Steven Meigs, Susan Elizabeth. Student, Sch. Dance Bennington Coll., 1936, 37; LL.D. (hon.), U. Mich., 1976. Dancer Martha Graham Concert Group, N.Y.C., 1939-41; model John Powers Agy., N.Y.C., 1939-41; fashion dir. Herpolscheimer's Dept. Store, Grand Rapids, Mich., 1943-48; dance instr. Grand Rapids, 1932-48; pres., bd. dirs. The Betty Ford Ctr., Rancho Mirage, Calif. Author: autobiography The Times of My Life, 1979, Betty: A Glad Awakening, 1987. Bd. dirs. Nat. Arthritis Found. (hon.); trustee Martha Graham Dance Ctr.; mem. theatre mgmt. com. Bob Hope Cultural Ctr.; trustee Eisenhower Med. Ctr., Rancho Mirage; hon. chmn. Palm Springs Desert Mus.; nat. trustee Nat. Symphony Orch.; trustee Nursing Home Adv. and Research Council Inc.; mem. Golden Circle Patrons Ctr. Theatre Performing Arts; bd. dirs. The Lambs, Libertyville, Ill. Episcopalian (tchr. Sunday sch. 1961-64). Home: PO Box 927 Rancho Mirage CA 92270-0927

FORD, FREEMAN ARMS, manufacturing company executive; b. L.A., Feb. 24, 1941; s. Robert Freeman and Janet (Vosberg) F.; m. Diana Vhay, May 28, 1966; children; David, Kimberly, Tod, Erin. AB in Econs., Dartmouth, 1963; MS in Bus., Stanford U., 1980. Aviator USN, Alameda, Calif., 1968; prodn. mgr. Kasper Instruments, Santa Clara, Calif., 1969-71; founder, pres. FAFCO, Inc., Redwood City, Calif., 1971—; past pres. Solar Energy Industries Assn., Washington; dir. H.B. Fuller Co., St. Paul, 1976—. Patentee in field. Office: FAFCO Inc 2690 Middlefield Rd Redwood City CA 94063-3402

FORD, GERALD RUDOLPH, JR., former President of United States; b. Omaha, July 14, 1913; s. Gerald R. and Dorothy (Gardner) F.; m. Elizabeth Bloomer, Oct. 15, 1948; children: Michael, John, Steven, Susan. A.B., U. Mich., 1935; LL.B., Yale U., 1941; LL.D., Mich. State U., Albion Coll., Aquinas Coll., Spring Arbor Coll. Bar: Mich. 1941. Practiced law at Grand Rapids, 1941-49; mem. law firm Buchen and Ford; mem. 81st-93d Congresses from 5th Mich. Dist., 1949-74, elected minority leader, 1965; v.p. U.S., 1973-74, pres., 1974-77; del. Interparliamentary Union, Warsaw, Poland, 1959, Belgium, 1961; del. Bilderberg Group Conf., 1962; dir. Santa Fe Internat., GK Technologies, Shearson Loeb Rhoades, Pebble Beach Corp., Tiger Internat.; mem. internat. adv. coun. Inst. Internat. Studies. Served as lt. comdr. USNR, 1942-46. Recipient Grand Rapids Jr. C. of C. Distinguished Service award, 1948; Distinguished Service Award as one of ten outstanding young men in U.S. by U.S. Jr. C. of C., 1950; Silver Anniversary All-Am. Sports Illustrated, 1959; Distinguished Congressional Service award Am. Polit. Sci. Assn., 1961. Mem. Am., Mich. State, Grand Rapids bar assns., Delta Kappa Epsilon, Phi Delta Phi. Republican. Episcopalian. Clubs: University (Kent County), Peninsular (Kent County). Lodge: Masons. Home: care Judy Risk PO Box 927 Rancho Mirage CA 92262

FORD, HAROLD WARNER, history educator; b. Angola, Ind., Sept. 1, 1915; s. Donald Cameron and Dimple (Sanford) F.; m. Berniece Magnuson, 1942 (dec. Sept. 1962); m. Pamela Sue Ford, June 14, 1963; children: Evelyn Sue Ford Blake, Harold Warner Ford, Jr. BA, Butler U., 1942; BD, Christian Theol. Sem., Indpls., 1949; ThD, Illif Sch. Theology, Denver, 1962. Prof. N.T. and history Lincoln (Ill.) Christian Coll., 1947-58; min. Riverside (Calif.) Christian Ch., 1959-60; prof. N.T. and history, dean Pacific Christian Coll., Long Beach, Calif., 1961-71; prof. N.T. and history Cin. Bible Seminary, 1971-76, Puget Sound Christian Coll., Edmonds, Wash., 1976-91; retired, 1991—. Author: History of the Restoration Plea, 1952, Let Us Think Correctly, 1987, A Second Look at the New Testament, 1988; contbr. articles to profl. jours. Recipient second prize, Christian Rsch. Found., 1962, Christian Svc. Award of Merit, 1993. Republican. Mem. Christian Ch.

FORD, JAMES CARLTON, human resources executive; b. Portland, Mar. 10, 1937; s. John Bernard and Margaret (Reynolds) F.; m. Carolyn Tadina, Aug. 22, 1959; children: Scott, Michele, Mark, Brigitte, Deidre, John. BA in History, U. Portland, 1960; MS in Edn., Troy State U., 1969; MPA, U. Puget Sound, 1976. Cert. sen. profl. in human resources. Commd. 2d lt. USAF, 1960, advanced through grades to lt. col., 1976, adminstr., tng. officer, 1960-70, personnel mgmt. officer, 1971-76; dep. inspector gen. U.S. Air Force Acad., Colorado Springs, Colo., 1977-80; ret. U.S. Air Force Acad., 1980; employment mgr. Western Fed. Savs. (name changed to Bank Western), Denver, 1980-82, v.p. human resources, 1982-88, sr. v.p. mgmt. svcs., 1988-92; dir. career mgmt. AIM Exec., Inc., Cons. Svcs., 1992—; bd. dirs. Rocky Mountain chpt. AM. Inst. of Banking, Denver; adj. prof. U. Colo., Colorado Springs, 1978-79, USAF Acad., Colorado Springs, 1978-80; adv. bd. U. Colo. Contemporary Mgmt. Program, Regis Coll. Career Svcs. Mediator Neighborhood Justice Ctr., Colorado Springs, 1980; vol. allocations com. Pikes Peak United Way, Colorado Springs, 1978-79; vol. campaign exec. Mile Hi United Way, Denver, 1986-89; vol. mgmt. cons. Tech. Assistance Svc., Denver, 1991. Mem. Assn. for Mgmt. of Orgn. Design, Soc. for Human Resource Mgmt., Adminstrv. Mgmt. Soc. Republican. Roman Catholic. Office: AIM Executive Inc 1200 Seventeenth St Ste 1320 Denver CO 80202

FORD, JOHN T., JR., art, film and video educator; b. Rotan, Tex., Feb. 17, 1953; s. John T. and Lala Fern (Shipley) F.; m. Betty Jean Crawford; children: Casey, Craig, Kirk. BA, U. Redlands, 1975. Cert. tchr., Calif. Tchr. art, film, video Yucaipa (Calif.) Joint Unified Sch. Dist., 1976-88; tchr. art and crafts Vacaville (Calif.) Unified Sch. Dist., 1990-92, tchr. video prodn., 1992—; cons. Dist. Fine Arts Insvc., Yucaipa, 1987; co-sponsor Art Club, Will C. Wood High Sch., Vacaville, sponsor Video Club. Creator, coord. (conceptual art) Whole School Environments, Caves, Tubes and Streamers, Forest Edge, 1980-84; creator (comml. art prints) Toy Horse Series, 1982-83. Mem. Yeoman Svc. Orgn., U. Redlands, 1972, Vacaville Sch. Dist. Tech. Com., Dist. Fine Arts Task Force, Yucaipa, 1984-87, Dist. Task Force for Vocat. Edn., 1992; interim dir. Hosanna House, Redlands, Calif., 1975; liaison Sch. Community Svc./San Bernardino County (Calif.) Fire Dept., 1980-81. Recipient Golden Bell award Calif. Sch. Bd. Research Found., 1987, Ednl. Service award Mason's, 1987-88; named one of Outstanding Young Men of Am., 1987, Tchr. of Yr. Calif. Continuation Edn. Assn., 1987-88; grantee Calif. Tchrs. Instructional Improvement Program, 1985; scholar U. Redlands, 1975. Mem. Am. Film Inst. Office: Will C Wood High Sch 998 Marshall Rd Vacaville CA 95687-5799

FORD, LUCY KAREN, social worker; b. Fairbanks, Alaska, Mar. 18, 1954; d. Frederic Earl Ford and Barbara Jean (Suter) Matthews. BA, U. Calif., Berkeley, 1986, MSW, 1988. Lic. clin. social worker. Eligibility worker Napa County (Calif.) Social Svcs., 1975-81; owner Napa Valley Roommate Referral, Napa, Calif., 1981-83; residential counselor Napa County Alcohol Program, 1983-86; mental health worker Napa County Mental Health, 1982-89; rsch. asst. U. Calif., Berkeley, 1985-89, writer, cons. Family Welfare Rsch. Group, 1987-89; rsch. cons. Western Consortium for Pub. Health, Berkeley, 1989; med. social worker Alameda County Health Svcs., Oakland, Calif., 1988-89; psychiat. social worker Ventura (Calif.) County Mental Health, 1990—; pvt. practice, 1991—; adj. prof. Ottowa u., Phoenix, Ariz., 1991—. Co-author: Practical Program Evaluation, 1990; contbr. articles to profl. jours. Mem. NASW, NOW, Am. Orthopsychiat. Assn., Psi Chi, Phi Beta Kappa. Democrat. Home: PO Box 1775 Ojai CA 93023 Office: Ventura County Mental Health 300 Hillmont Ventura CA 93003

FORD, MICHAEL Q., not-for-profit association administrator; b. Washington, Dec. 12, 1949; s. Milton Q. and Jeanne Louise (Goltman) F.; m. Christine Ann Davies, Apr. 24, 1971 (div. June 1980); m. Elizabeth Julia Ginsberg, June 1, 1984; 1 child, Jennifer. BS in Journalism, Ohio U., 1971. Writer, reporter TV Digest, Washington, 1971-72; staff writer Coun. Better Bus. Burs., Washington, 1972-74; staff assoc. Ctr. for Study of Responsive Law, Washington, 1974; exec. dir. Coalition for Health Funding, Washington, 1975-77; dir. Office of Pub. Policy Nat. Coun. on Alcoholism, Washington, 1977-80; pres. Nat. Assn. Addiction Treatment Providers, Irvine, Calif., 1980-93; trustee Commn. on Accreditation of Rehab. Facilities, Tucson, 1985-91. Chmn. legis. com. Nat. Coalition for Adequate Alcoholism Programs, Washington, 1978-80, chmn., 1981. Fellow Am. Coll. of Addiction Treatment Adminstrs. Jewish. Home: 3013 Nestall Rd Laguna Beach CA 92651-2026 Office: Nat Assn Addiction Treatment Providers 25201 Paseo De Alicia # 100 Laguna Hills CA 92653-4612

FORD, PATRICK JOSEPH, university administrator; b. Spokane, Wash., Dec. 5, 1941; s. Edward and Hazel (Anderson) V. BA, Gonzaga U., Spokane, 1966, MA, 1967; PhD, Stanford U., 1972; MDiv., Jesuit Sch. Theology, Berkeley, Calif., 1974. Joined Soc. of Jesus, 1960; ordained priest Roman Cath. Ch., 1974. Asst. to dean Jesuit Sch. Theology, 1971-74; dean Coll. Arts and Scis. Gonzaga U., 1974-79, assoc. prof. higher edn., 1974-79, dean Grad. Sch., 1985-90, prof. higher edn., 1979—, acad. v.p., 1990—; cons.-evaluator Western Assn. Schs. and Colls., Oakland, Calif., 1972—; mem., chair bd. trustees Gonzaga Prep., Spokane, 1974-82; trustee Regis U., Denver, 1982—; commr. N.W. Assn. Schs. and Colls., Seattle, 1976—. Co-author: Changing the Curriculum, 1971, Reform in Graduate and Professional Education, 1974, Quest for Quality, 1990. Mem. Assn. Jesuit Colls. and Univs. Acad. Vice Presidents, Am. Phys. Therapy Asns. (hon.). Office: Gonzaga U Office of Acad VP Spokane WA 99258

FORD, RICHARD CHRISTIAN, mortgage banker; b. San Diego, Dec. 18, 1961; s. R. and Elsa (Schuster) F. BA in Comm., San Diego State U., 1989; AS in Mktg. Mgmt., Mesa Coll., San Diego, 1989, AA in Psychology, 1989, AS in Real Estate, 1991. Lic. real estate agent, Calif. Comml. real estate mgr. John Burnham & Co., San Diego, 1990; govt. rev. auditor Am. Resdl., San Diego, 1991; govt. loan ins. specialist Guild Cos., Inc., San Diego, 1992-93, quality control auditor, 1993—. Editor/pubr. newsletter: Meeting People in San Diego, 1990-92; author: College Survival Guide, 1991. Mem., chair Pacific Reach Planning Com., San Diego, 1988-90; script announcer LaJolla Christmas Parade, 1991, 92. Mem. Speech Comm. Assn. (v.p. 1989), Toastmasters of La Jolla (pres. 1992, Competent Toastmaster 1991, Able Toastmaster 1993, area gov.). Republican. Roman Catholic. Office: Guild Cos Inc 9160 Gramercy Dr San Diego CA 92123

FORD, RUSSELL WILLIAM, newspaper executive; b. Reno, Nev., May 15, 1947; s. Gilbert Leo and Mary Mercedes (Poss) F.; m. Sandra Maria Salmi, July 9, 1971; children: Donna, Diana, Debra, Michael. BS in Bus., U. Nev., 1969. Bundle hauler Reno (Nev.) Newspapers, Inc., 1965-66, mailer, 1966-67, complaint supr., 1967-68, dist. sales mgr., 1968-72, circulation promotion mgr., 1972-73, asst. circulation mgr., 1972-76; circulation dir. Idaho Statesman, Boise, Idaho, 1976-82; west regional dir. Gannett Co., Inc., Washington and Rochester, N.Y., 1982-85; western regional dir. USA Today, Washington, 1985-88, regional v.p., 1988—. Mem. Internat. Circulation Mgr. Assn. (bd. dirs.), Pacific N.W. Circulation Mgr. Assn. (sec.-treas.). Home: 11603 Hidden Valley Rim Rd Boise ID 83709

FORD, VICTORIA, public relations executive; b. Carroll, Iowa, Nov. 1, 1946; d. Victor Sargent and Gertrude Francis (Headlee) F.; m. John K. Frans, July 4, 1965 (div. Aug. 1975); m. David W. Keller, May 2, 1981 (div. Nov. 1985); m. Jerry W. Lambert, Mar. 30, 1991. AA, Iowa Lakes Community Coll., 1973; BA summa cum laude, Buena Vista Coll., 1974; MA in Journalism, U. Nev., Reno, 1988. Juvenile parole officer Iowa Dept. Social Services, Sioux City, 1974-78; staff reporter Feather Pub. Co., Quincy, Calif., 1978-80; tng. counselor CETA, Quincy, 1980; library pub. info. officer U. Nev., Reno, 1982-84; pub. relations exec. Brodeur/Martin Pub. Relations, Reno, 1984-87; pub. relations dir. Internat. Winter Spl. Olympics, Lake Tahoe (Calif.) and Reno, 1987-89; owner Ford Factor Pub. Rels. cons. firm, Reno, 1989—. Contbr. articles to profl. jours. Mem. adv. bd. Reno Philharm., 1985-87, Reno-Sparks Conv. and Visitors Authority, 1985—; bd. dirs Truckee Meadows Habitat for Humanity, 1992-93; mem. Gov.'s Com. on Fire Prevention, 1991-92. Mem. NOW, Pub. Rels. Soc. Am. (charter v.p. Sierra Nev. chpt. 1986-87, pres. 1987-88), Reno Women in Advt., Sigma Delta Chi. Democrat. Home: PO Box 6715 Reno NV 89513-6715 Office: The Ford Factor PO Box 6715 Reno NV 89513-6715

FORD, WALLACE ROY, clergyman, religious organization executive; b. Walnut, Ill., Apr. 7, 1937; s. Roy Wallace and Evelyn Mary (Hand) F.; m. Valerie Laine Brown, Aug. 18, 1961; children: Tara Chantille, Christopher Wallace. BA, Tex. Christian U., 1959; BD, Brite Divinity Sch., Ft. Worth, 1962; Cert. Theologie, U. Geneva, 1963; D of Ministry, Iliff Sch. Theology, Denver, 1978. Ordained to minstry Disciples of Christ, 1962. Pastor La Porte (Tex.) Community Ch., 1964-67, 1st Christian Ch., Boulder, Colo., 1967-83; pres. Colo. Council Chs., Denver, 1981-82; exec. sec. N.Mex. Conf. Chs., Albuquerque, 1983—; chmn. Ch. Fin. Council, Indpls., 1984-86. Author: Wise Up O Men Of God, 1981, Worship and Evangelism, 1981, Snow Melts, 1983. Mem. Nat. Assn. Ecumenical Staff, Theta Phi. Democrat. Office: NMex Conf Chs 124 Hermosa Dr SE Albuquerque NM 87108-2610

FORDEMWALT, JAMES NEWTON, microelectronics educator, consultant, engineer; b. Parsons, Kans., Oct. 18, 1932; s. Fred and Zenia (Chambers) F.; m. Suzan Lynn Hopkins, Aug. 26, 1958 (div. June 1961); m. Elizabeth Anna Hoare, Dec. 29, 1963; children: John William, James Frederick. BS, U. Ariz., 1955, MS, 1956; PhD, U. Iowa, 1960. Sr. engr. GE Co., Evandale, Ohio, 1959-60, U.S. Semcor, Inc., Phoenix, 1960-61; sect. mgr. Motorola Semiconductor Products Div., Phoenix, 1961-66; dept. mgr. Philco-Ford Microelectronics Div., Santa Clara, Calif., 1966-68; assoc. dir. R & D Am. Microsystems Inc., Santa Clara, 1968-71; assoc. rsch. prof. U. Utah, Salt Lake City, 1972-76; dir. microelectronics lab. U. Ariz., Tucson, 1976-87; assoc. prof., lab. mgr. Ariz. State U., Tempe, 1987—, assoc. chair microelectronics, 1992—, asst. chair dept. electronic and computer tech., 1993—; cons. Integrated Cirs. Engring., Scottsdale, Ariz., 1976—, Western Design Ctr., Mesa, Ariz., 1980—; mem. semiconductor com. United Techs. Corp., Hartford, Conn., 1978-87. Author: Silicon Wafer Processing Technology, 1979; editor: Integrated Circuits, 1965; contbr.: MOS Integrated Circuits, 1972. Mem. IEEE, Internat. Soc. for Hybrid Microelectronics (chpt. pres. 1982-83), Electrochem. Soc. Home: 613 W Summit Pl Chandler AZ 85224-1556

FOREMAN, DALE MELVIN, lawyer, state official; b. Los Angeles, May 1, 1948; s. C. Melvin and Sylvia (Ahnlund) F.; m. Gail Burgener, June 24, 1972; children: Mari Elizabeth, Ann Marie, James Sterling. AB cum laude, Harvard U., 1970, JD, 1975. Bar: Wash. 1976, U.S. Dist. Ct. (we. dist.) Wash. 1977, U.S. Ct. Claims 1977, U.S. Dist. Ct. (ea. dist.) Wash. 1981, U.S. Ct. Appeals (9th cir.) 1981, Calif. 1986, U.S. Ct. Appeals (3rd cir.) 1987. Ptnr. Jeffers, Danielson & Foreman, Wenatchee, Wash., 1975-81, Jardine, Foreman & Arch, Wenatchee, 1981-88, Foreman & Arch, Wenatchee, 1988—; mem. 12th legis. dist. Wash. Ho. of Reps., 1993—; mem. Spl. Adv. Commn. on Pub. Opinion, U.S. Dept. of State, 1970-72, com. for deferred compensation State of Wash., 1990—. Author: Whiplash and The Jaw Joint, 1985, Washington Trial Handbook, 1988, Dental Law, 1989, How to Become an Expert Witness, 1989, Crucify Him! A Lawyer Looks at the Trial of Jesus, 1989. Chmn. Chelan County Rep. Cen. Com., Wenatchee, 1977-79, 82-84; bd. dirs. Am. and Fgn. Christian Union, N.Y.C., 1985—, Greater Wenatchee Community Found., 1987—. Mem. ABA, Assn. Trial Lawyers Am., Wash. State Bar Assn., State Bar Calif., Wash. State Trial Lawyers Assn. (bd. govs. 1990—), Harvard Club, Rotary. Presbyterian. Home: 323 Chatham Hill Rd Wenatchee WA 98801-5931 Office: Foreman & Arch 701 N Chelan Ave Wenatchee WA 98801-2026

FORER, LUCILLE KREMITH, clinical psychologist; b. Springfield, Ill.; d. William Frederick and JoAnn Marie (Teubner) Kremith; m. Bertram R. Forer, Sept. 27, 1941; children: Stephen Keith, William Robert. BA, U. Tex., El Paso, 1939; MA, U. So. Calif., 1940, PhD, 1953. Lic. psychologist, Calif. Pers. officer Office Price Adminstrn., Washington, 1941-43, adminstrv. officer, office adminstr., 1943-45; tchr., coord. testing program Psychol. Clinic, UCLA, 1947-49; asst. prof. psychology dept. UCLA, 1953-58; pvt. practice clin. psychology L.A., 1953—; psychol. cons. Welty Ednl. Clinic, L.A., 1969-72. Author: Birth Order and Life Roles, 1970, The Birth Order Factor, 1978, paperback edit., 1979; contbr. articles to profl. jours. Bd. dirs. Friends of Malibu (Calif.) Libr., 1985-89; mem. Malibu Lagoon Soc., 1982—. Fellow Soc. Personality Assessment; mem. APA, Calif. Psychol. Assn. Home and Office: 19854 Pacific Coast Hwy Malibu CA 90265

FOREST, EVA BROWN, nurse, supervisor; b. Ontario, Va., July 7, 1941; d. William Butler and Ruth Pauline (Simpson) Brown; m. Willie J. Forest Jr., Sept. 16, 1961; children: Geraid, Darryl, Angela. AA, Bismarck (N.D.) State Coll., 1981; BSN, U. Mary, Bismarck, 1984. RN, Colo. Charge nurse St. Alexius Med. Ctr., Bismarck, 1984-85, Cedars Health Care Ctr., Lakewood, Colo., 1989-90; staff devel. coord. Park Avenue Bapt. Home, Denver, 1990-91; supr., charge nurse Cedars Health Care Ctr., Lakewood, Colo., 1991—; charge nurse Villa Manor Health Ctr., Lakewood, Colo., 1991—. Vol. for cultural exch. lang., culture and fashions YWCA, Kano, Nigeria; vocalist gospel music workshop, N.D.; pianist adult and children's choir, N.D. Mem. Internat. Platform Assn., DAV Commdrs. Club. Office: Cedars Health Care Ctr Lakewood CO 80214

FORESTIER, DANIELLE, baker, consultant; b. Ray, Ariz., Feb. 28, 1943; d. Earl Francis Ruth and Dorothy Margaret (Steil) Toms; m. Charles H. Schley II, Nov. 11, 1962 (div. 1982); children: Dinah Sara, Charles H. III. BA, Bennington (Vt.) Coll., 1966; Brevet de Maitrise, Baker Boulangerie Candalot, Paris, 1977. Baker Boulangerie Candalot, Paris, 1975-77; owner Les Belles Miches, Santa Barbara, Calif., 1977-82; bakery cons. Dinah Schley, Boulanger, Santa Barbara, 1982-86; tech. cons. Chopin, S.A., Santa Barbara, 1986-89; bakery cons. Danielle Forestier, Boulanger, Oakland, Calif., 1989—; bakery cons. Anheuser Busch, Tampa, Fla., 1984-85, Am. Inst. of Baking, Manhattan, Kans., 1984, 86, Julia Child, Santa Barbara, 1987, Wheat Foods Coun., Washington, 1990—, General Mills, 1991-92, Calif. Apricot Adv. Bd., 1993. Mem. Am. Inst. Wine and Food (founder), Am. Assn. Cereal Chemists, Amicale de Bon Pain, AAUW, San Francisco Profl. Food Soc. Democrat. Home and Office: 470 Weldon Ave Oakland CA 94610

FORGAN, DAVID WALLER, retired air force officer; b. Chgo., Sept. 28, 1933; s. Harold Nye and Ruth Ada (Waller) F.; m. Shirley Dobbins, Oct. 18, 1958; children—Bruce Dobbins, Todd Macmillan. B.S. in Mktg., U. Colo., 1955; M.S. in Mgmt., George Washington U., 1966. Commd. 2d lt. U.S. Air Force, 1956, advanced through grades to maj. gen., 1985, various positions worldwide, 1956-77; dir. programs hdqrs. tactical air command U.S. Air Force, Langley AFB, Va., 1977-79; dir. force devel. U.S. Air Force, Washington, 1979-80; dep. comdr. spl. ops. command U.S. Air Force, Fort Bragg, N.C., 1980-82; asst. chief staff ops. Allied Forces Central Europe, Brunssum, The Netherlands, 1982-85; dep. chief staff ops. U.S. Air Force Europe, Ramstein Air Base, Fed. Republic Germany, 1985-87; comdr. Sheppard Tech. Tng. Ctr. Sheppard AFB, Tex., 1987-89; ret., 1989. Decorated Silver Star, D.F.C. (3), Legion of Merit, Air medal, Def. Disting. Svc. medal, Def. Superior Svc. medal; Aero Cross of Merit (Spain). Mem. Delta Tau Delta. Republican. Home: 4935 Newstead Pl Colorado Springs CO 80906-5978

FORGHANI, BAGHER, research virologist; b. Bandar-Anzali, Guilan, Iran, Mar. 10, 1936; came to U.S., 1969; s. Baba and Jahan (Rahimi) F.; m. Nikoo Alavi, June 12, 1969; children: Niki, Nikta. PhD, Justus Liebig U., Giessen, Fed. Republic Germany, 1965. Postdoctoral fellow Utah State U., Logan, 1965-67; asst. prof. Nat. U. Iran, Tehran, 1967-69; postdoctoral trainee Calif. Dept. Pub. Health, Berkeley, 1970-72; rsch. specialist Calif. Dept. Health Svcs., Berkeley, 1972-81, rsch. scientist, 1981—. Contbr. articles on virology to nat. and internat. sci. jours., also chpts. Mem. Am. Soc. for Microbiology, Nat. Registry Microbiologists. Office: Calif Dept Health Scvs 2151 Berkeley Way Berkeley CA 94704-1011

FORKERT, CLIFFORD ARTHUR, civil engineer; b. Verona, N.D., Oct. 16, 1916; s. Arthur Louis and Bessie (Delamater) F.; grad. N.D. State Coll., 1940; postgrad. M.I.T.; m. Betty Jo Erickson, July 1, 1940; children: Terry Lynn Forkert Williamson, Michael, Debra Edwards. Hwy. engr., N.D., Tex., 1937-40; hydraulic engr. Internat. Boundary Commn. Tex. on Rio Grande and Tributaries, 1940-43; constrn., topographic and cons. engr., Calif. 1946—; now civil engr., prin. Clifford A. Forkert, Civil Engr.; pres. Calif. Poly. Pomona Assos. Capt. USMCR, 1943-46. Registered civil engr. Calif., Oreg., Ariz.; profl. engr., Nev., Ariz.; lic. land surveyor, Nev., Ariz. Mem. Am. Congress and Mapping (life), ASCE (life), Land Surveyors Assn. Calif. (dir.), Alumni Assn. N.D. State Coll. Home: 20821 Skimmer Ln Huntington Beach CA 92646-6548 Office: 22311 Brookhurst St Huntington Beach CA 92646-8450

FORMAN, RICHARD THOMAS, manufacturing executive; b. Newark, July 22, 1935; s. Archibald John and Elise Laurel (Blaufus) F.; m. Margaret Valentine, Mar. 1, 1958; children: Suzanne, Robert, John. Diploma, Indsl. Coll. Armed Forces, 1968; BBA, Bellevue Coll., 1971; MA in Bus. Adminstrn., N.M. - Highlands U., 1976; MA in Procurement Mgmt., Webster Coll., 1981. Commd. 2d lt. USAF, 1956, advanced through grades to lt. col., 1974, ret., 1977; purchasing mgr. Pertec Computer Co., Albuquerque, 1980-81; purchasing, materials mgr. Sparton Techs. Co., Albuquerque, 1981-83; purchasing mgr. ScanOptics, Irvine, Calif., 1983-87; mgr. materials ops. and procurement McDonnell Douglas Computer Systems Co., Santa Ana, Calif., 1987-91; materials mgr. Philips Ultrasound, Inc., Santa Ana, Calif., 1991-92; prin. cons. Supply Mgmt. Svc., Irvine, Calif., 1992—; instr. purchasing and materials mgmt. Fullerton Coll. Mem. VFW (life), Nat. Assn. Purchasing Mgrs. (life, cert., v.p. Orange County affiliate 1989, pres. 1990), Air Force Assn. (life), Ret. Officers Assn. (life), Am. Prodn. and Inventory Control Soc. (cert.). Home: 36 Rocky Knls Irvine CA 92715-3257 Office: Supply Mgmt Svcs 36 Rocky Knoll Irvine CA 92715

FORMBY, BENT CLARK, immunologist; b. Copenhagen, Apr. 3, 1940; naturalized, 1991; s. John K. and Gudrun A. (Dinesen) F.; m. Irene Menck-Thygesen, June 28, 1963 (div. May 1980); children: Rasmus, Mikkel; m. Florence G. Schmid, June 28, 1980. BA in Philosophy summa cum laude, U. Copenhagen, 1959, PhD in Biochemistry, 1968, DSc, 1976. Asst. prof. U. Copenhagen, 1969-73, assoc. prof., 1973-79, prof., 1979-83; vis. prof. U. Calif., San Francisco, 1979-84; sr. scientist, dir. lab. of immunology Sansum Med. Rsch. Found., Santa Barbara, Calif., 1984—; cons. Cell Tech., Inc., Boulder, Colo., 1989—, Immunex Corp., Seattle, 1989—; med. adv. bd. Biocellular Rsch. Orgn., Ltd., London, Childrens Hosp. of Orange County. Editor: Fetal Islet Transplantation, 1988; contbr. articles to profl. jours.; patentee on non-invasive blood glucose measurement. Grantee Juvenile Diabetes Found., 1987, 88, E.L. Wiegand Found., 1993. Mem. N.Y. Acad. Scis., Am. Diabetes Assn. (grantee 1985, 86, 89), Am. Fedn. Clin. Rsch., European Assn. for the Study of Diabetes. Office: Sansum Med Rsch Found 2219 Bath St Santa Barbara CA 93105-4321

FORREST, KENTON HARVEY, science educator, historian; b. Fort Lauderdale, Fla., Oct. 3, 1944; s. Harvey William and Marjorie A. (Boxrud) F. B.A., Colo. State Coll., 1968; M.A., U. No. Colo., 1981. Science tchr. Dunstan Jr. High, Jefferson County Pub. Schs., Lakewood, Colo., 1968—; pres. Tramway Press, Inc., 1983—. Author: Denver's Railroads, 1981; (with William C. Jones) Denver-A Pictorial History, 1973; (with others) The Moffat Tunnel, 1978; Rio Grande Ski Train, 1984, History of the Public Schools of Denver, 1989, Route 3 Englewood, 1990. Trustee Colo. Railroad Hist. Found., Golden, 1975—; mem., 1st pres. Lakewood Hist. Soc. (Colo.), 1976; office Jeffco Credit Union. Mem. NEA (life) Rocky Mountain Assn. Geologists, Colo. Assn. Sci. Tchrs., Nat. Railway Hist. Soc. (Intermountain chpt. pres. 1980-83), Mobile Post Office Soc., Denver Rail Heritage Soc. Home: PO Box 15607 Lakewood CO 80215-0007 Office: Dunstan Jr High Sch 1855 S Wright St Lakewood CO 80228-3963

FORREST, SUZANNE SIMS, research historian; b. Pitts., Nov. 15, 1926; d. Clarence E. and Corinne Tousley (Landgraf) Sims; m. Stephen F. de Borhegyi, July 5, 1949 (dec. 1969); children: Ilona Maria, Stephen Ernest, Carl Robert, Christopher Francis; m. James T. Forrest, Sept. 16, 1978. BA, Ohio State U., 1948; postgrad., U. Okla., 1967; MS, U. Wis., Milw., 1973; PhD, U. Wy., 1987. Asst. to dir. Carnegie Institution Wash., Guatemala City, 1949-50, Inst. Nutrition for Cen. Am., Panama, Guatemala City, 1950-51; tchr. Milw. U. Sch., 1966-1973; coordinator, cont. edn. Alverno Coll., Milw.; dir. Albuquerque (N.M.) Museum, 1974-79; exec. dir. Wy. Council for the Humanities, Wy., 1979-81; curator Bradford Brinton Meml. Mus., Big Horn, Wy., 1988-90; bd. dirs. N.Mex. Endowment for the Humanities, 1993—, Placitas Artists Series, 1989—. Author: Ships, Shoals and Amphoras, 1961, Museums, 1962, Secret of the Sacred Lake, 1967, The Preservation of the Village: New Mexico's Hispanics and the New Deal, 1989. Bd. dirs. N.Mex. Endowment for Humanities, 1993—. Home: 45 Cabezon Rd Placitas NM 87043-9201

FORSBACH, JACK ALAN, lawyer; b. Oklahoma City, Sept. 3, 1932; s. Jacob Allen and Mary Louise (Morton) F. Student, Okla. Bapt. U., 1950-51, U. Tulsa, 1951-52; BA, Okla. State U., 1955; JD, U. Okla., 1957. Bar: Okla. 1959, U.S. Supreme Ct. 1965. Pvt. practice Bartlesville, Okla., 1959-65; claims cons. CIGNA, Toplis & Harding, Inc., L.A., 1965-78; freelance arbitrator L.A., 1978—; fgn. assignments S.E. Asia and Middle East, 1979-83. Judge Mcpl. Ct., Bartlesville, 1959; vol. Traveler's Aid Soc., L.A., 1986—, Braille Inst., L.A., 1991—; appointee Okla. Amb. by Gov. Henry Bellmon, 1989—; county chmn. Nat. Found. March of Dimes, 1959. Mem. Amnesty Internat. (legal support 1986—), Soc. Profls. in Dispute Resolution, ABA (internat. comml. arbitration com., internat. torts and ins. practice com., internat. labor law, internat. security and internat. law, alternative dispute resolution, self insurers and risk mgrs.), Union Internat. des Avocats (entertainment and sports law com.), Okla. Bar Assn., Tulsa County Bar Assn. (exec. dir. 1964), Am. Arbitration Assn. (arbitrator 1978—), Southwestern Legal Found. (rep. 1961-64), Okla. State U. Bar Assn. (life), U. Okla. Coll. Law Assn. (life), Indsl. Rels. Rsch. Assn., State Bar Calif. (internat. law sect.), Delta Theta Phi (tribune). Republican. Home and Office: 8306 Wilshire Blvd Ste 1232 Beverly Hills CA 90211-2382

FORSBERG, CHARLES ALTON, computer, infosystems engineer; b. Willamette, Ill., May 6, 1944; s. Delbert Alton and Margery (McCleary) F. Student, Rensselaer Poly. Inst.; BSEE, U. Wis., 1966, MSEE, 1968; postgrad., various univs. and colls. From design engr. to project leader Tektronix, Portland, Oreg., 1968-74; mgr. R&D Sidereal, Portland, 1974-80; chief engr. Computer Devel. Inc., Portland, 1980-84; pres. Omen Tech. Inc., Portland, 1984—. Developer YMODEM and ZMODEM Protocols for worldwode data transfer. Recognized for outstanding contbn. to field IBM-PC Users Group, Madison, Wis., 1988, Alamo PC Orgn., San Antonio, 1988. Home and Office: 17505V NW Sauvie Island Rd Portland OR 97231-1310

FORSDALE, (CHALMERS) LOUIS, education and communication educator; b. Greeley, Colo., Mar. 8, 1922; s. John Aaron and Wilhelmina (Thorkildsen) F.; m. Elinor Wulfekuhler, Aug. 22, 1947 (dec. 1963); children: Lynn, John; m. Joan Ida Rosengren, May 28, 1964 (div. 1966). B.A., Colo. State Coll., 1942; M.A., Columbia U. Tchrs. Coll., 1947; Ed.D., Columbia U., 1951. Instr. English Tchrs. Coll., Columbia U., N.Y.C., 1947-51; asst. prof. Tchrs. Coll., Columbia U., 1951-55, assoc. prof., 1955-58, prof. communication and edn., 1958-87, prof. emeritus, 1987; vis. assoc. prof. edn. U. So. Calif., Los Angeles, 1957; cons. in communication various businesses, industries and schs., 1965—; vis. scholar Iran Communication and Devel. Inst., Tehran, 1977. Author: Nonverbal Communication, 1974, Perspectives on Communication, 1981; Editor: (with others) Communication in General Education, 1961, 8MM Sound Film and Education, 1962. Served to 1st lt. USAAF, 1943-45. Recipient Tchrs. Coll. Disting. Alumni award Merit, 1989. Democrat. Home: 330 Otero St Santa Fe NM 87501-1906

FORSLUND, THOMAS ODELL, city manager; b. Forest City, Iowa, Aug. 23, 1951; s. Cyrus Odell and Alice Marie (Michelson) F.; m. Barbara Jean Hime, Mar. 1, 1975; children: Eric, Elizabeth. AA, Waldorf Coll., 1971; BA, U. Iowa, 1973; MPA, U. Mo., 1977. Adminstr. City of Richland, Mo., 1977-80, City of Beatrice, Nebr., 1980-86; asst. city mgr. City of Casper, Wyo., 1986-88, city mgr., 1988—. Mem. Am. Soc. Pub. Adminstrn., Am. Mgmt. Assn., Internat. City Mgmt. Assn., Rotary. Lutheran. Office: City of Casper 200 N David St Casper WY 82601-1864

FORSMAN, CHUCK, artist; b. Nampa, Idaho, May 5, 1944; s. Alfred Clyde and Mary Lorraine (DeBoard) F.; m. June 10, 1972; children: Chloe Lewis, Shannon Lewis. Student, Pasadena Coll., 1962-65; BA, U. Calif.-Davis, 1967; postgrad., Skowhegan Sch., 1970; MFA, U. Calif.-Davis, 1971. Teaching asst. U. Calif.-Davis, 1969-70; prof. fin arts U. Colo., Boulder, 1971—; works in permanent collections at Met. Mus. Art, Denver Art Mus., Phoenix Art Mus., Wichita Art Mus., Yellowstone Art Ctr., Billings, Mont., U. Calif.-Davis, Grinnell Coll., Iowa, Ill. State U., Chem. Bank N.Y., United Bank of Denver, Hallmark Cards, West Pub. Co., Mpls., Union League Club of Chgo., Cabot Corp., Boston, others. One man shows at Tibor de Nagy Gallery, 1973, 75, 77, 79, 81, 83, 86, 88, Wichita Art Mus., 1981, Denver Art Mus., 1985, Tucson Art Mus., 1986, Rahr-West Mus., Wis., 1986, Boulder Ctr. Visual Arts, 1988, Nat. Acad. Scis., Washington, 1991, Gallery One, Toronto, Can., 1993, others; group shows include Tibor de Nagy Gallery, 1990, Hubbard Mus., N.Mex., 1990, Rockwell Mus., Corning, N.Y., 1990, Va. Mus. Fine Arts, 1990, Butler Inst. Am. Art, 1989, Denver Art Mus., 1989, Mint Mus., Charlotte, 1991, many others. Adv. bd. Ctr. of the Am. West, 1989—. With U.S. Army, 1968-69. NEA grantee, 1979, 85, Ucross Found. residency, 1986, U. Colo. Faculty fellow, 1979, 88.

FORSSANDER, PAUL RICHARD, inventor, artist, entrepreneur; b. Chgo., Oct. 10, 1944; m. M. Andrea Peake, Dec. 30, 1967. BA in Econs., Marian Coll., Indpls., 1967. Sales and ops. adminstr. ITT Pub., Indpls., 1967-80; v.p., gen. mgr. Kutt Inc., Boulder, Colo., 1982-86; pres., chief exec. officer Skynasaur Inc., Boulder, 1986-89; pres., chief exec. officer, founder Zephyr Co. Inc., Boulder, 1989-91, Quillum Co., 1990—, Notetote Co., Boulder, 1990-91, PRF Designs, 1991—. Inventor flying and wind powered high-tech recreational products and parts, energy generation/conservation products, writing instrument designs, gift and office products; designer glass & metal sculptures, illuminaries & table art; developed forming and finishing process. Bd. dirs. PBS Sta. KGNU, Boulder, 1983-86, EMT Assn. Colo., Boulder, 1985-88; designer of fundraising strategies for non-profit orgns. Mem. Gift Assn. Am., Nat. Sporting Goods Assn., Toy Industry Am., Nat. Soc. Fundraising Execs., Nature Conservancy, Greenpeace, Sierra Club. Home: PO Box 1010 Boulder CO 80306-1010

FORSTE, NORMAN LEE, management consultant; b. Carthage, Mo., Aug. 18, 1935; s. John Edward and Lula Mae (Martin) F.; m. Catherine Jean Culver, July 20, 1958; children: Patricia, Diana, John II, Karl. AA, Am. River Coll., 1961; BA, Calif. State U., 1964, MA, 1971; MBA, Golden Gate U., 1973; PhD in Higher Edn., U. Wash., 1984. Adminstrv. analyst State of Calif., Sacramento, 1962-64, sr. data processing systems analyst, 1966-67, supr. info. systems devel., 1967-68; sr. adminstrv. analyst County of Sacramento (Calif.), 1964-66, dir. systems and data processing dept., 1968-74; dir. adminstrv. data processing div. U. Wash., Seattle, 1974-76; mgr. mgmt. adv. services Deloitte Haskins & Sells, 1976-81, dir. mgmt. adv. services, 1981-85; pvt. practice mgmt. cons., Carmichael, Calif., 1985-90, Kings Beach, Calif., 1990—, Auburn, Calif., 1992—; instr. mgmt. scis. program U. Calif. at Davis, 1968; professorial lectr. mgmt. info. systems Golden Gate U., Sacramento, 1971-74, 79-90; instr. info. systems Calif. State U.-Sacramento, 1982-83; instr. systems analysis and introduction to data processing Am. River Coll., Sacramento, 1968-71. Mem. curriculum adv. com. for data processing Am. River Coll., Sacramento, 1969-74, mem. com. to evaluate vocational and tech. edn. program for accreditation, 1972-73. Served with USAF, 1954-57, 62, maj. USAFR, Ret. Mem. Am. Soc. Pub. Adminstrn. (dir. 1969-71, 84-85), Data Processing Mgmt. Assn. (chpt. pres. 1968-69), Methods and Procedure Assn. (pres. 1969), Calif. Assn. County Data Processors (1st v.p. 1973-74), Air Force Res. Officers Assn. (chpt. v.p. 1971-74, 79-82), Air Force Calif. Dept. Res. Officers Assn. (jr. v.p. 1971). Home and Office: 12140 Elm Ct Auburn CA 95602

FORSTER, BRUCE ALEXANDER, economics educator; b. Toronto, Ont., Can., Sept. 23, 1948; m. Margaret Jane Mackay, Dec. 28, 1968, (div. Dec. 1979); 1 child, Kelli Elissa; m. Valerie Dale Pendock, Dec. 8, 1979; children: Jeremy Bruce, Jessica Dale. BA in Math., Econs., U. Guelph, Ont., 1970; PhD in Econs., Australian Nat. U., Canberra, 1974. Asst. prof. U. Guelph, 1973-77, assoc. prof., 1977-83, prof. econs., 1983-88; vis. assoc. prof. U. B.C., Vancouver, 1979; vis. fellow U. Wyoming, 1979-80, vis. prof., 1983-84, 87; prof. econs., 1987—, dean Coll. Bus., 1991—; vis. prof. Profl. Tng. Ctr., Ministry of Econ. Affairs, Taiwan, 1990, 91, 92, 93; acad. assoc. The Atlantic Coun. of the U.S., cons. in field. Author: The Acid Rain Debate: Science and Special Interest in Policy Formation, 1993; co-author: Economics in Canadian Society, 1986; assoc. editor Jour. Applied Bus. Rsch., 1987, editorial adv. bd., 1987—; editorial coun. Jour. Environ. Econs. and Mgmt., 1989, assoc. editor, 1989-91; contbr. articles to profl. jours. Jayes-Qantas Vis. scholar U. Newcastle, Australia, 1983. Mem. Am. Econ. Assn., Assn. Environ. and Resource Economists, Faculty Club U. Guelph (treas. 1981-82, v.p. 1982-83, 85-86, pres. 1986-87). Avocations: weight lifting, swimming, skiing, scuba diving. Home: 3001 Sage Dr Laramie WY 82070-5751 Office: U Wyo Coll Bus Laramie WY 82071

FORSTER, DANIEL GRANT, sales and marketing executive; b. Hoboken, N.J., Nov. 5, 1960; s. William Harold and Julie Rose (Wigton) F.; m. Konni Jo Selsor, Aug. 15, 1986; children: Tiffany Rae, Jessie Nicole. BS in Bus. Adminstrn., Mgmt., Calif. State U., Long Beach, 1984. Beach lifeguard Long Beach Marine Dept., 1979-84; aquatics dir. Westminster (Calif.) High Sch., 1985-86; sales rep. G.B.T., Inc., Irving, 1985-88, nat. accounts mgr., 1988; dealer, sales mgr. ACOM, Long Beach, 1989-91, dir. sales, 1992—, v.p. sales and mktg., 1992—; speaker seminars, workshops ACOM, Long Beach, 1989-92. Aquatic scholar Loyola U. Chgo., Brown U. Democrat. Home: 24172 McCoy Rd Lake Forest CA 92630 Office: ACOM 2250 Obispo Long Beach CA 90806

FORSTER, ERIC GAD, banker; b. Tel-Aviv, Aug. 19, 1941; s. Karl Samuel and Esther Orna (Kohane) F.; m. Sally Ita Gross, July 12, 1967 (div. 1979); children: Jonathan, Dana, Jill; m. Judith Constance Scott, Oct. 27, 1979; 1 child, Eran. TD, Columbia U./Jewish Theol. Sem., N.Y.C., 1967; MBA, Pepperdine U., 1973. V.p. First State Fed., Pasadena, Calif., 1984-85; banker Home Savs. of Am., L.A., 1986-90, Great Western Bank, L.A., 1990—. Author: The Loan Applicants Bible, 1992; columnist Israel Shelanu, L.A., 1988—; contbr. articles to mags. 1st lt. Calif. NG, 1984-86. Democrat. Jewish. Home: 3255 Midvale Ave Los Angeles CA 90034

FORSTROM, JUNE ROCHELLE, professional society administrator; b. Douglas County, Minn., June 24, 1932; d. George Dewey and Borghild Otillia (Sahl) Nelson; m. Keith William Forstrom, June 23, 1951; children: Mark William, Dawn Rochelle. Grad. high sch., St. Paul. Adminstr. rsch. grants, coord. comm. Geol. Soc. Am., Boulder, Colo., 1973—. Republican. Lutheran. Home: 7705 Baseline Rd Boulder CO 80303-4707 Office: Geol Soc Am 3300 Penrose Pl Boulder CO 80301-9140

FORSYTH, BEN RALPH, academic administrator, retired medical educator; b. N.Y.C., Mar. 8, 1934; s. Martin and Eva (Lazansky) F.; m. Elizabeth Held, Aug. 19, 1962; children: Jennifer, Beverly, Jonathan. Student, Cornell U., 1950-53; MD, NYU, 1957. Diplomate Am. Bd. Internal Medicine. Intern, then resident Yale Hosp., New Haven, 1957-60; postdoctoral fellow Harvard U. Med. Shc., Boston, 1960-61; rsch. assoc. NIH, Bethesda, Md., 1963-66; assoc. prof. med. microbiology, prof. med. coll. U. Vt., Burlington, 1966-90, assoc. dean div. health scis., 1971-85, assoc. v.p. acad. affairs, 1977-78, v.p. adminstrn., 1978-85, sr. v.p., 1985-90; sr. exec. asst. to pres. Ariz. State U., Tempe, 1990—, interim v.p. adminstrv. svcs., 1991-93; interim provost Ariz. State U. West, Phoenix, 1992-93, 1992-93, provost, v.p., 1993—; sr. cons. Univ. Health Ctr., Burlington, 1986-90. Contbr. articles to profl. jours. V.p., chmn. United Way Planning Com., Burlington, 1974-75, Ops. Com., 1975-76, bd. dirs., officer, 1977-89; mem. New England Bd. Higher Edn. Com., Burlington, 1985-89; chmn. U. Vt. China Project Adv. Bd., Burlington, 1989-90. Lt. comdr. USN, 1962-63. Sinsheimer Found. faculty fellow, 1966-71. Fellow ACP, Infectious Diseases Soc. Am.; mem. AMA, Vt. State Med. Soc., Am. Fedn. for Clin. Rsch., Soc. Exptl. Medicine and Biology, Phi Beta Kappa, Alpha Omega Alpha.

FORSYTH, JAMES LORIN, contractor; b. Monterey Park, Calif., May 5, 1942; s. Lorin Bret and Jane (Soots) F.; m. Ingrid, Apr. 2, 1964 (div. 1971); children: Elke, Debi, Sue; m. Daphne R. Bennett, Dec. 28, 1973; 1 child, Benjamin A. AA, Solano Community Coll., 1975. Cert. fire prevention officer, EMT, fire officer; lic. contractor, Calif. Foreman Internat. Mfg. Co., Benicia, Calif., 1967-69; fire lt. Benicia Fire Dept., 1969-91; contractor Winters, Calif., 1990—. Author: Markmanship, 1966. V.p. Benicia Firefighters Assn., 1973, treas., 1985, 86, 87. With U.S. Army, 1961-67. Named Fire Fighter of Yr., Benicia Fire Dept., 1984. Mem. Nat. Fire Protection Assn., Calif. State Fireman's Assn., Solano County Fireman's Assn., Benicia Firefighters Assn., Irwin Meml. Blood Bnak. Home and Office: 20 E Main St Winters CA 95694-1717

FORSYTH, RAYMOND ARTHUR, civil engineer; b. Reno, Mar. 13, 1928; s. Harold Raymond and Fay Exona (Highfill) F.; BS, Calif. State U., San Jose, 1952; M.C.E., Auburn U., 1958; m. Mary Ellen Wagner, July 9, 1950; children: Lynne, Gail, Alison, Ellen. Jr. engr., asst. engr. Calif. Div. Hwys., San Francisco, 1952-54; assoc. engr., sr. supervising, prin. engr. Calif. Dept. Transp., Sacramento, 1961-83, chief geotech. br., 1972-79, chief soil mechanics and pavement br., 1979-83, chief Transp. Lab., 1983-89; cons., lectr. in field. Served with USAF, 1954-56. Fellow ASCE (pres. Sacramento sect., chmn. Calif. council 1980-81); mem. Transp. Research Bd. (chmn. embankments and earth slopes com. 1976-82, chmn. soil mechanics sect. 1982-88, chmn. group 2 council 1988-91), ASTM. Contbr. articles to profl. publs. Home: 5017 Pasadena Ave Sacramento CA 95841-4149

FORT, GERALD MARSHALL, psychologist, consultant; b. Mitchell, S.D., Mar. 16, 1919; s. Lyman Marion and Mildred May (Dunsworth) F.; children: Michael Lyman, Sandra Mae. BA, Grinnell Coll., 1941; MA, U. Minn., 1948, PhD, 1960. Lic. psychologist, Wis., Minn. Assoc. prof. S.D. State U., Brookings, 1949-59; psychol. cons. Humber, Mundie & McClary, Milw., 1959-72; ptnr., mgr. Humber, Mundie & McClary, Mpls., 1972-84; bd. dirs. N. Cen. Career Devel. Ctr. Contbr. articles to profl. jours. Mem. coun. Mt. Zion Luth. Ch., Wauwatosa, Wis., 1966-72, Normandale Luth. Ch., Edina, Minn., 1974-80; mem. coun. Desert Hills Luth. Ch., Green Valley, Ariz., pres., v.p., 1985-90; chmn. Commn. Profl. Leadership, Minn. Synod, Mpls., 1976-82; bd. dirs. Samaritan Counseling Ctr., New Brighton, Minn., 1982-84; pres. Spearfish Canyon Owners Assn., 1988—, bd. dirs. 1986-92; tng. coord., pers. com. Green Valley Recreation Assn., 1985—. Sgt. USAAF, 1941-45. Recipient Disting. Service award Greater Mpls. C. of C., 1984. Mem. Minn. Psychol. Assn. (life). Republican. Club: Edina Country (sec., bd. dirs. 1972-84). Lodge: Kiwanis, Elks. Home and Office: 1865 W Camino Estelar Green Valley AZ 85614

FORTH, KEVIN BERNARD, beverage distributing company executive; b. Adams, Mass., Dec. 4, 1949; s. Michael Charles and Catherine Cecilia (McAndrews) F.; children: Melissa, Brian. AB, Holy Cross Coll., 1971; MBA with distinction, NYU, 1973. Div. rep. Anheuser-Busch, Inc., Boston, 1973-74, dist. sales mgr., L.A., 1974-76, asst. to v.p. mktg. staff, St. Louis, 1976-77; v.p. Straub Distbg. Co., Ltd., Orange, Calif., 1977-81, pres., 1981—, chmn., chief exec. officer, 1986—, also bd. dirs. Commr. Orange County Sheriff's Adv. Coun., 1988—; mem. adv. bd. Rancho Santiago Community Coll. Dist. 1978-80; bd. dirs. Children's Hosp. of Orange County, 1983-85, St. Joseph's Hosp. Found., Orange County Sports Hall of Fame, 1980-89; exec. com., bd. dirs. Nat. Coun. on Alcoholism, 1980-83; mem. pres.' coun. Holy Cross Coll., 1987—; mem. Orange County Trauma Soc.; bd. dirs., pres. Calif. State Fullerton Titan Athletic Found., 1983-85, 89-90 (vol. of yr., 1991); bd. dirs. Freedom Bowl, 1984—, v.p., 1984-85, pres., 1986, chmn., 1986-87, Anaheim Vis. and Conv. Bur., 1989—; bd. dirs. Orangewood Children's Found., 1988—; mem. Calif. Rep. State Cen. Com., Orange County Dept. Edn. Peer Assistance Leadership Coun., Orange County Probation Dept. Community Involvement Bd. Benjamin Levy fellow NYU, 1971-73. Mem. Nat. Beer Wholesalers Assn. (bd. dirs., asst. sec. 1989-90, chmn.'s award for legis. exellence 1990, sec. 1990-91, vice chmn. 1991-92, chmn. 1992—), Calif. Beer and Wine Wholesalers Assn. (bd. dirs., exec. com., pres. 1985), Industry Environ. Coun., Holy Cross Alumni Assn., NYU Alumni Assn., Nat. Assn. Stock Car Auto Racing, Calif. State Fullerton Small Bus. Inst., Sports Car Club Am. (Ariz. state champion 1982), Beta Gamma Sigma. Roman Catholic. Club: Lincoln, Holy Cross (Southern Calif.). Home: 27750 Tamara Dr Yorba Linda CA 92687-5840 Office: Straub Distbg Co Ltd Box 3165 410 W Grove Ave Orange CA 92665

FORTNER, HUESTON GILMORE, lawyer; b. Tacoma, Nov. 1, 1959; s. Hueston Turner Jr. and Deborah Hewes (Berry) F. BS, Tulane U., 1981; JD, U. Miss., 1985. Bar: Miss. 1986, La. 1987, U.S. Dist. Ct. (no. and so. dists.) Miss. 1986, U.S. Dist. Ct. (ea., mid. and we. dists.) La., 1987, U.S. Ct. Appeals (5th cir.) 1986, Calif. 1989, U.S. Dist. Ct. (cen. dist.) Calif. 1989. Clk. Farrer and Co., London, Miss., 1985; assoc. Cliff Finch & Assocs., Batesville, Miss., 1986; pvt. practice New Orleans, 1987-88; atty. Parker, Milliken, Clark, O'Hara & Samuelian, L.A., 1989-90; pvt. prctice L.A., 1990—; participated in Leicester vs. Leicester Rugby Union, 1985; assisted Queen's Counsel in Yussuf Islam (Cat Stevens) vs. Bank of Westminster P.L.C. royalties litigation 1985, Newton vs. NBC, 1988; temporary judge L.A. County Mcpl. Ct., 1991—; ind. film producer. Performing musician; composer numerous mus. works; contbr. editor Rental, 1987-89. Grant NSF, 1976. Mem. ABA (forum com. on entertainment and sports industries), Miss. Bar Assn., La. Bar Assn., State Bar Calif., Assn. Telecommunications Attys., Broadcast Music Itnernat., Nat. Acad. Songwriters, Los Angeles County Bar Assn., Phi Alpha Delta. Presbyterian. Office: Travelers Bldg Ste 1902 3600 Wilshire Blvd Los Angeles CA 90010

FORTUIN, THOMAS MARK, lawyer, television executive; b. Paterson, N.J., Mar. 30, 1946; s. Floyd and Astrid (Sorenson) F. BA, Columbia U., 1967, JD, 1971. Bar: N.Y. 1972, D.C. 1972, Calif. 1978, U.S. Supreme Ct. 1978, U.S. Tax Ct. 1979, U.S. Ct. Claims 1983. Asst. U.S. atty. So. Dist.

N.Y., N.Y.C., 1973-77; counsel Com. on Standards Ofcl. Conduct, Ho. of Reps., Washington, 1977-78; ptnr. Becker and Chameides, Washington, 1978-83; v.p., legal affairs Technicolor, Inc., North Hollywood, Calif., 1983-87; gen. counsel, sec. Four Star Internat., Inc., Hollywood, Calif., 1983-86; v.p. legal and bus. affairs Four star and VidAmerica, Hollywood, 1986-87; pres. Gray and Co. II, Washington, 1987-88; dep. gen. counsel Paramount Pictures Corp, Hollywood, 1988—. Contbg. author: Intruder in Your Home, 1983, Proving Federal Crimes, 1974; contbg. editor: (mag.) Juris Doctor, 1971-73. Mem. ABA, Assn. of Bar of City of N.Y. Republican. Presbyterian.

FORTUNE, JAMES MICHAEL, marketing executive; b. Providence, Sept. 6, 1947; s. Thomas Henry and Olive Elizabeth (Duby) F.; m. G. Suzanne Hein, July 14, 1973. Student, Pikes Peak Community Coll., Colorado Springs, Colo., 1981-83; BSBA in Computer Info. Systems, Regis Coll., 1991. Owner Fortune Fin. Svcs., Colorado Springs, Colo., 1975-79; ptnr. Robert James and Assocs., Colorado Springs, 1979-81; pres. Fortune & Co., Colorado Springs, 1981-88; sr. v.p. mktg. and editorial Phoenix Communications Group, Ltd., Colorado Springs, 1988—, also bd. dirs.; also bd. dirs.; bd. dirs. Colorado Springs Computer Systems, Am. Discount Svcs., Inc., Investor's Bookshelf, Inc., Colorado Network Engring., Inc., Custom Computers of Colo., Corp.; talk show host Sta. KRCC, fin. commentator Wall Street Report, Sta. KKHT, 1983-84. Editor Fortune newsletter, 1981-85, The Can. Market News, 1981-83; editor, pub. Penny Fortune newsletter, 1981—, The Low Priced Investment newsletter, 1986-87, Women's Investment Newsletter, 1987—, Can. Market Confidential, 1988—, Spl. Option Situations, 1988—; pub. Internal Revenue Strategies, 1990, Tax and Investment Planning Strategies for Medical Professionals, 1991; contbr. articles to profl. jours. Cons. Jr. Achievement bus. project, Colorado Springs, 1985. Sgt. U.S. Army, 1968-70, Vietnam. Mem. Direct Mktg. Assn., Elks. Office: 1837 S Nevada Ave Ste 223 Colorado Springs CO 80906-2566

FORTUNER, RENAUD, plant nematologist, researcher; b. Algiers, Algeria, Aug. 20, 1944; came to U.S., 1980; s. Pierre and Paulette (Teisseire) F.; m. Laurel Mariah Whittaker, May 29, 1982; children: Aimery Loyal, Thierry Pierre, Auberry Renaud, Toby Joseph. Ingénieur en Agr., Ecole Superieure Ingenieurs et Techniciens pour L'Agriculture, Paris, 1970; lic. ès Sci., U. Claude Bernard, Lyon, France, 1974, PhD, 1976, doctorate, 1986. Phytopathologist Inst. Tropical Agronomy Rsch., Sefa, Senegal, 1969-71; nematologist Office Recherche Scientifique et Technique Outre Mer, Dakar, Senegal, 1971-75, Abidjan, Ivory Coast, 1975-80; assoc. plant nematologist Calif. Dept. Food and Agr., Sacramento, 1980-87, sr. plant nematologist, 1987—. Author, editor: Nematode Identification and Expert Systems, 1989, Advances in Computer Methods for Systematic Biology, 1993; mem. editorial bd. Revue Nematologie, 1981—; contbr. over 100 articles to profl. jours. With French Nat. Svc., 1969-71. Rsch. grantee NATO, Davis, Calif., 1988, NSF, Davis, 1990, Calif. Dept. Food and Agr., 1991. Mem. European Soc. Nematologists, Soc. Nematologists (chmn. computers in nematology com. 1984-86, mem., chmn. transls. com. 1981-91, mem. systematic resources com. 1981-90), Soc. Systematic Zoology. Office: Calif Dept Food and Agr 1220 N St Rm 340 Sacramento CA 95814

FOSSE, JAMES ALAN, electrical engineer; b. Santa Monica, Calif., Aug. 28, 1955; s. John Benjamin and Carol Josephine (Kuesel) F.; m. Lucretia Ann Myers, Sept. 19, 1987; 1 child, Stuart K. Student, San Diego State U., 1973-76; BSEE, U. Calif., Berkeley, 1978. Sr. engr. MDS Qantel Inc., Hayward, Calif., 1979-81, Osborne Computer Corp., Hayward, 1982-83, Capstone Tech., Inc., Fremont, Calif., 1984—; cons. CCA, Hayward, 1980—. Inventor a method for recovering NRZ info. from MFM data, 1982. Mem. Soc. Info. Display. Office: Capstone Tech 47354 Fremont Blvd Fremont CA 94538

FOSSEEN, NEAL RANDOLPH, business executive, former banker, former mayor; b. Yakima, Wash., Nov. 27, 1908; s. Arthur Benjamin and Florence (Neal) F.; m. Helen Witherspoon, Sept. 26, 1936; children: Neal Randolph Jr., William Roger. AB, U. Wash., 1930; LLD (hon.), Whitworth Coll., 1967. With Wash. Brick, Lime & Sewer Pipe Co., 1923-32, v.p., 1932-38; pres. Wash. Brick & Lime Co., 1938-58; v.p. Old Nat. Bank Wash., 1958-68; v.p. Wash. Bancshares, 1968-71, vice chmn., 1971-72, chmn. bd., pres., 1972-73; dir. Utah-Idaho Sugar Co., 1968-79, 1st Nat. Bank Spokane, 1972-79; chmn. emeritus Old Nat. Bancorp., 1973-77; pres. 420 Investment Co., 1982-84; mem. engring. adv. bd. Washington State U., 1949-79, past chmn., emeritus, 1979—; ptnr. Villa 90 Assocs., West Riverside Investment dir. Day Mines, Inc., 1968-81. Mem. exec. com. Expo '74. Mayor, City of Spokane, 1960-67, mayor emeritus, 1967—; mem. adv. bd. Spokane Intercollegiate Rsch. and Tech. Inst. Past chmn. adv. bd. Wash. State Inst. Tech.; hon. trustee St. Luke's Hosp.; regent emeritus, past chmn. Gonzaga U.; bd. dirs., past pres. council Boy Scouts Am.; bd. dirs. Wash. Rsch. Coun., sec., 1968-74; bd. dirs. YMCA, 1969-80, Pacific Sci. Found., 1970-73, Mountain States Legal Found., 1979-85, Deaconess Hosp. Found.; mem. adv. bd. Grad. Sch. Bus., U. Wash., 1974-81, emeritus, 1981—; mem. adv. bd. dept. History, 1981—; chmn. Regent Gonzaga U., 1948-61; hon. trustee Found. N.W.; trustee Rockwood Found., Gonzaga Dussault Found.; mem. adv. bd. Advanced Tech. Ctr.; Col. USMCR (Ret'd); Recipient Disting. Eagle Scout award Boy Scouts Am., 1976, Silver Beaver, Silver Antelope awards; Non Sibi, Sed Patriae award Marine Corps Res. Officers Assn.; Outstanding Svc. awards Fairchild AFB, Spokane Mcpl. League; Forward Spokane award Spokane County Hotel and Restaurant Coun.; Liberty Bell award Spokane County Bar Assn.; Book of Golden Deeds, Exchange Club; Sister City Outstanding Svc. award Town Affiliation Assn.; Disting. Citizen award Eastern Wash U., 1982; named hon. citizen, Nishinomiya, Japan; Honor Patriot '75, Spokane Percussionauts. Mem. Ret. Officers Assn., Assn. Wash. Bus. (past pres.), Spokane C. of C. (v.p. 1946-51), Spokane-Nishinoniya Sister City Soc. (pres.), Srs. N.W. Golf Assn., Mil. Order World Wars (Perpetual), Order of the Rising Sun (Japan), Balboa de Mazatlan Club (Mex), Spokane Club, Spokane Country Club, Univ. Club, Prosperity Club, Travellers Century Club, Spokane Ski Club, Beta Theta Pi. Home: Rockwood Forest Estates 2609 E Foxwood Ct Spokane WA 99223-3410 Office: US Bank Bldg Spokane WA 99201

FOSSLAND, JOEANN JONES, advertising consultant; b. Balt., Mar. 21, 1948; d. Milton Francis and Clementine (Bowen) Jones; m. Richard E. Yellott III, 1966 (div. 1970); children: Richard E. IV, Dawn Joeann; m. Robert Gerard Fossland Jr., Nov. 25, 1982. Student, Johns Hopkins U., 1966-67; cert. in real estate, Hogan's Sch. Real Estate, 1982. Owner Kobble Shop, Indiatlantic, Fla., 1968-70, Downstairs, Atlanta, 1971; seamstress Aspen (Colo.) Leather, 1972-75; owner Backporch Feather & Leather, Aspen and Tucson, 1975-81; area mgr. Welcome Wagon, Tucson, 1982; realtor assoc. Tucson Realty & Trust, 1983-85; mgr. Home Illustrated mag., Tucson, 1985-87; asst. pub., gen. mgr. Phoenix, Scottsdale, Albuquerque, Tricities Tucson Homes Illustrated, 1990-93; pres. Advantage Solutions Group, Cortaro, Ariz., 1993—; cons. Albuquerque Homes Illustrated, 1987-91. Designer leather goods (Tucson Mus. Art award 1978, Crested Butte Art Fair Best of Show award 1980). Voter registrar Recorder's Office City of Tucson, 1985-91; bd. dirs. Hearth Found., Tucson, 1987—, Ariz. Integrated Residential & Ednl. Svcs., Inc., 1989—; mem. Hunger Project, Holiday Project. Mem. NAFE, Women's Coun. Realtors (treas. Ariz. state chpt. 1993, Tucson Affiliate of Yr. 1991, Leadershp Tng. Grad. designation 1989, treas. state chpt. 1993), Tucson Assn. Realtors (Affilate of Yr. 1988), Rotary. Democrat. Presbyterian. Office: Advantage Solutions Group PO Box 133 Cortaro AZ 85652

FOSTER, BRIAN LEE, dean, educator; b. Princeton, Ill., Dec. 23, 1938; s. Joseph Marion and Vera Mildred (Brenneman) F.; m. Lerke E. Holzwarth, July 7, 1967; children: Catherine Louise, Thomas Brian. BA, No. Ill. U., 1967; AM, U. Mich., 1968, PhD, 1972. Asst. prof. anthropology SUNY, Binghamton, 1972-78, assoc. prof. anthropology, 1978-80; with Ariz. State U., Tempe, 1980—, chair anthropology dept., 1982-86, prof. anthropology, 1983—, dean Grad. Coll., 1986—; pres. Western Assn. Grad. Schs., 1990-91; mem. exec. com. S.E. Asia Studies Summer Inst., 1990—; mem. Grad. Record Exam. Bd., 1991—, chair elect 1993, Test of English as Foreign Language Coun., 1991—, mem. exec. com. Coun. Rsch. Policy and Grad. Edn., 1991—. Author: Social Organization of Four Thai and Mon Villages, 1977, Commerce and Ethnic Differences, 1982; contbr. numerous articles to profl. jours. Woodrow Wilson Found. fellow, 1967-68, Social Science Rsch. Coun./Am. Coun. Learned Socs. fellow, 1970-72, East-West Ctr. fellow, 1978, 80; NSF grantee, 1976-79, 81-83, U.S. Dept. Edn. grantee, 1986-88. Fellow Am. Anthrop. Assn.; mem. Am. Ethnol. Soc., Soc. for Anthropology of Work, Assn. for Asian Studies (southeast Asia coun. 1986-87), Thai-Lao Cambodia Studies Group. Democrat. Office: Ariz State U Grad Coll Tempe AZ 85287-1003

FOSTER, DAVID RAMSEY, soap company executive; b. London, May 24, 1920 (parents Am. citizens); s. Robert Bagley and Josephine (Ramsey) F.; student econs. Gonville and Caius Coll., Cambridge (Eng.) U., 1938; m. Anne Firth, Aug. 2, 1957; children—Sarah, Victoria. With Colgate-Palmolive Co. and affiliates, 1946-79, v.p., gen. mgr. Europe, Colgate-Palmolive Internat., 1961-65, v.p., gen. mgr. household products div. parent co., N.Y.C., 1965-68, exec. v.p., 1968-70, pres., 1970-75, chief exec. officer, 1971-79, chmn., 1975-79. Author: Wings Over the Sea, 1990. Trustee, Woman's Sport Found. Served to lt. comdr. Royal Naval Vol. Res., 1940-46. Decorated Disting. Service Order, D.S.C. with bar, Mentioned in Despatches (2); recipient Victor award City of Hope, 1974, Herbert Hoover Meml. award, 1976, Adam award, 1977, Harriman award Boys Club N.Y., 1977, Charter award St. Francis Coll., 1978, Walter Hagen award, 1978, Patty Berg award, 1986. Mem. Soc. Mayflower Descs. Clubs: Hawks (Cambridge U.); Royal Ancient Golf (St. Andrews, Scotland); Royal St. Georges Golf, Royal Cinque Ports Golf (life), Sunningdale Golf, Swinley Forest Golf (U.K.); Sankaty Head Golf; Racquet and Tennis (N.Y.C.); Baltusrol Golf, Mission Hills Country, Bally Bunion Golf. Home: 540 Desert West Dr Rancho Mirage CA 92270-1310

FOSTER, DAVID SCOTT, lawyer; b. White Plains, N.Y., July 13, 1938; s. William James and Ruth Elizabeth (Seltzer) F.; m. Eleanore Stalker, Dec. 21, 1959; children: David Scott, Robert McEachron. BA, Amherst Coll., 1960; LLB, Harvard U., 1963. Bar: N.Y. 1963, D.C. 1977, Calif. 1978. Jud. law clk. U.S. Dist. Ct. (so. dist.) N.Y., 1963-64; assoc. Debevoise & Plimpton, N.Y.C., 1964-72; internat. tax counsel U.S. Treasury Dept., Washington, 1972-77; ptnr. Brobeck, Phleger & Harrison, San Francisco, 1978-90, Coudert Bros., San Francisco, 1990-91, Thelen, Marrin, Johnson & Bridges, San Francisco, 1991—. Mem. ABA, San Francisco Bar Assn., N.Y. State Bar Assn., Internat. Fiscal Assn., Western Pension and Benefits Confs., Francis Yacht Club (San Francisco). Presbyterian. Office: Thelen Marrin Johnson & Bridges 2 Embarcadero Ctr San Francisco CA 94111

FOSTER, DUDLEY EDWARDS, JR., musician, educator; b. Orange, N.J., Oct. 5, 1935; s. Dudley Edwards and Margaret (DePoy) F. Student Occidental Coll., 1953-56; AB, UCLA, 1957, MA, 1958; postgrad. U. So. Calif., 1961-73. Lectr. music Immaculate Heart Coll., L.A., 1960-63; dir. music Holy Faith Episcopal Ch., Inglewood, Calif., 1964-67; lectr. music Calif. State U., L.A., 1968-71; assoc. prof. music L.A. Mission Coll., 1975-83, prof., 1983—, also chmn. dept. music, 1977—; mem. dist. acad. senate L.A. Community Colls., 1991-92; mem. acad. senate L.A. Mission Coll., 1993—; dir. music 1st Luth. Ch., L.A., 1968-72. Organist, pianist, harpsichordist; numerous recitals; composer O Sacrum Convivium for Trumpet and Organ, 1973, Passacaglia for Brass Instruments, 1969, Introduction, Arioso & Fugue for Cello and Piano, 1974. Fellow Trinity Coll. Music, London, 1960. Recipient Associated Students Faculty award, 1988. Mem. Am. Guild Organists, Am. Musicol. Soc., Nat. Assn. of Scholars, Acad. Senate, Town Hall Calif., L.A. Coll. Tchrs. Assn. (pres. Mission Coll. chpt. 1976-77, v.p., exec. com. 1982-84), Mediaeval Acad. Am. Republican. Anglican. Office: LA Mission Coll Dept Music 13356 Eldridge Ave Sylmar CA 91342-3244

FOSTER, GEORGE MCCLELLAND, JR., anthropologist; b. Sioux Falls, S.D., Oct. 9, 1913; s. George McClelland and Mary (Slutz) F.; m. Mary Fraser LeCron, Jan. 6, 1938; children: Jeremy, Melissa Bowerman. BS, Northwestern U., 1935; PhD, U. Calif. at Berkeley, 1941; DHL (hon.), So. Meth. U., 1990. Instr. Syracuse U., 1941-42; lectr. UCLA, 1942-43; vis. prof. U. Calif.-Berkeley, 1953-55, prof. anthropology, 1955-79, prof. emeritus, 1979—, chmn. dept., 1958-61; acting dir. Mus. Anthropology, 1955-57; lectr. pub. health, 1955-64; anthropologist Inst. Social Anthropology, Smithsonian Instn., 1943-52, dir., 1946-1952; field rsch. Calif. Indians, 1937, Spain, 1949-50, Mexico, 1940—; adviser AID, India-Pakistan, 1955, Afghanistan, 1957, Zambia, 1961, 62, Nepal, 1965, Indonesia, 1973-74, WHO, Sri Lanka, 1975, Malaysia, 1978, India, 1979, 80, 81, Manila, 1983; adviser UNICEF, Geneva, 1976. Author: books including Traditional Cultures and the Impact of Technological Change, 1962, Tzintzuntzan: Mexican Peasants in a Changing World, 1967, Applied Anthropology, 1969, (with B. Anderson) Medical Anthropology, 1978; also monographs, articles. Guggenheim fellow, 1949; fellow Center for Advanced Study in Behavioral Scis., 1969-70. Fellow Am. Anthrop. Assn. (pres. 1970, Disting. Service award 1980); mem. Southwestern Anthrop. Assn. (Disting. Research award 1981), Nat. Acad. Scis., Am. Acad. Arts and Scis., Soc. Applied Anthropology (Malinowski award 1982). Club: Cosmos (Washington). Home: 790 San Luis Rd Berkeley CA 94707-2030

FOSTER, JAMES RONALD, secondary education educator; b. Washington, D.C., July 18, 1938; s. James and Avonelle Larue (Rice) F.; m. Alice Jeanne Young, June 12, 1960; children: Kimberly Jean, Robin Raye, James Leonard. BA in Edn., Ea. Wash. U., Cheney, 1971, BA in Math., 1971; MEd, Wash. State U., Pullman, 1978. Cert. tchr., Wash. Served to staff sgt., electronics supr. USAF, various locations, 1956-68; tchr. Pasco (Wash.) Sch. Dist., 1972—. Mem. Nat. Coun. Tchrs. Math., Wash. Soc. Tchrs. Math., Pasco Assn. Educators (past pres.), Am. Legion. Methodist. Home: 2431 W Klamath Kennewick WA 99336

FOSTER, JOHN ROBERT, lawyer; b. Long Beach, Calif., Feb. 13, 1940; s. Orlon c. and Catherine Rose (Rhind) F.; m. Nancy Crandall, June 17, 1962; children: John Crandall, Christopher Peter, Blayney Robert, Courtland William. BA in History, San Jose State U., 1961; LLB, U. Calif., Berkeley, 1964. Bar: Calif. 1965, U.S. Dist. Ct. (no. dist.) Calif. 1965, U.S. Ct. Appeals (9th cir.) 1965; cert. specialist in probate, estate planning, and trust law. Dep. legis. counsel State of Calif., Sacramento, 1964-65; ptnr. Rusconi, Foster, Thomas & Wilson, APC, Morgan Hill, Calif., 1965—; asst. dist. atty. San Benito County, Hollister, Calif., 1967. Mem. Morgan Hill Unified Sch. Dist. Bd. Edn., 1967-74, 79-83, chmn. bd., 1969-71; councilman City of Morgan Hill, 1984-88, mayor, 1984. Named Citizen of Yr., City of Morgan Hill. Mem. ABA (coms. on partnership and estate planning), Calif. State Bar (state bar exec. com. on estate planning, probate, and trusts), Santa Clara County Bar Assn., Gilroy-Morgan Hill Bar Assn. (past pres.), Morgan Hill C. of C. (past pres.), Lincoln Club of No. Calif., Masons, Rotary (past pres. Morgan Hill). Republican. Methodist. Home: 17630 Black Oak Ct Morgan Hill CA 95037-9442 Office: Rusconi Foster Thomas & Wilson 30 Keystone Ave Morgan Hill CA 95037-4325

FOSTER, KENNITH EARL, life sciences educator; b. Lamesa, Tex., Jan. 20, 1945; s. John Hugh and Mamie (Hyatt) F.; children: Sherry, Kristi. BS, Tex. Tech. U., 1967; MS, U. Ariz., 1969, PhD, 1972. Prof. and dir. Office of Arid Lands Studies, U. Ariz., Tucson, 1983—. Contbr. articles to profl. jours. Grantee NASA, NSF, USDA, 1983—. Home: 651 Avenida Princesa Tucson AZ 85748 Office: Univ of Ariz Office of Arid Lands Studies 845 N Park Ave Tucson AZ 85719

FOSTER, LAWRENCE, concert and opera conductor; b. Los Angeles, 1941. Student, Bayreuth Festival Masterclasses; studied with, Fritz Zweig. Debut as condr., Young Musicians' Found., Debut Orch., 1960; condr., mus. dir., 1960-64, condr., San Francisco Ballet, 1961-65, asst. condr., Los Angeles Philharmonic Orch., 1965-68, chief guest condr., Royal Philharmonic Orch., Eng., 1969-75, guest condr., Houston Symphony, 1970-71, condr. in chief, 1971-72, music dir., 1972-78, Orch. Philharmonique of Monte Carlo, 1979, gen. music dir., Duisburg & Dusseldorf Opera (Ger.), 1982-86, former music dir. Lausanne Chamber Orch., from 1985, now music dir. Aspen (Colo.) Music Festival and Sch.; guest condr. orchs. in U.S. and Europe. (Recipient Koussevitsky Meml. Conducting prize 1966, Eleanor R. Crane Meml. prize Berkshire Festival, Tanglewood, Mass. 1966); condr. Jerusalem Symphony Orch., 1990. Office: care Harrison/Parrott, 12 Penzance, London England W11 also: ICM 8942 Wilshire Blvd Los Angeles CA 90011 also: Aspen Music Festival PO Box AA Aspen CO 81612

FOSTER, MARK EDWARD, lawyer, consultant, international lobbyist; b. Detroit, May 12, 1948; s. Herbert Edward and Joyce Mary (Campbell) F.; m. Miyoko Katabami, Apr. 20, 1974; children: Lorissa Chieko. B.A., Alma Coll., 1970; M.A., U. Calif.-Berkeley, 1972, Japanese lang. cert., 1982, J.D., 1981; postgrad. Stanford Ctr., Tokyo, 1983. Bar: Calif. 1981, Oregon 1989. Grantee, Rockefeller Found. Presbyn. Ch., Geneva and Tokyo, 1972-74; law clk. U.S. Dist. Ct., San Francisco, 1980-81; atty. Hetland & Hansen, Berkeley, Calif., 1981-82; atty. Braun Moriya Hoashi, Tokyo, 1982-84; spl. counsel U.S. Embassy, Tokyo, 1984-85; Japan counsel U.S. Electronic Industries Assn., 1985-86; mng. ptnr. Law Offices Mark E. Foster, Portland, Tokyo, 1988—; lectr., cons. on internat. law and tech. standards, tech. transfer, product compliance, engring. to Internat. Standards Orgn., Geneva, Ministry of Internt. Trade and Industry of Japan, U.S. Dept. Commerce; mem. tech. standards com. for Optoelectronics, Japanese Ministry of Posts and Telecom., 1984-86, tech. standards com. for Intelligent Office Systems, Japanese Ministry of Internat. Trade and Industry, 1984-86. Author articles, books in internat. law and tech. Mem. ABA, Internat. Bar Assn., Calif. Bar Assn., Oreg. Bar Assn., Am. C. of C. in Japan, Portland World Trade (bd. advisors), World Affairs Council. Presbyterian. Office: 1 World Trade Ctr 121 SW Salmon Ste 330 Portland OR 97204

FOSTER, MARY CHRISTINE, motion picture and television executive; b. L.A., Mar. 19, 1943; d. Ernest Albert and Mary Ada (Quilici) F.; m. Paul Hunter, July 24, 1982. BA, Immaculate Heart Coll., Los Angeles, 1967; M of Journalism in TV News Documentary, UCLA, 1968. Dir. research and devel. Metromedia Producers Corp., Los Angeles, 1968-71; dir. devel. and prodn. services Wolper Prodns., Los Angeles, 1971-76; mgr. film programs NBC-TV, Burbank, Calif., 1976-77; v.p. movies and mini series Columbia Pictures TV, Burbank, 1977-81, v.p. series programs, 1981; v.p. program devel. Group W. Prodns., Los Angeles, 1981-87; pres. div. motion pictures and TV Walsh Communications Group, Inc., Los Angeles, 1987-88; ptnr. The Agency, Los Angeles, 1988-90; agt. Shapiro-Lichtman Agy., Los Angeles, 1990—; instr. communications UCLA, 1987; lectr. in field, 1970—. Creator: (TV series) Sullivan, 1985, Auntie Mom, 1986. Bd. dirs. Immaculate Heart High Sch., Los Angeles, 1980—; mem. exec. com. Humanitas Awards, Human Family Inst., 1985—, Los Angeles Roman Cath. Archdiosesan Communications Commn., Los Angeles, 1986—. Mem. Women in Film (bd. dirs. 1974-78), Nat. Acad. TV Arts and Scis. Democrat. Office: Shapiro-Lichtman Agy 8827 Beverly Blvd Los Angeles CA 90048

FOSTER, MARY FRAZER (MARY FRAZER LECRON), anthropologist; b. Des Moines, Feb. 1, 1914; d. James and Helen (Cowles) LeCron; B.A., Northwestern U., 1936; Ph.D., U. Calif., Berkeley, 1965; m. George McClelland Foster, Jan. 6, 1938; children—Jeremy, Melissa Foster Bowerman. Research asso. dept. anthropology U. Calif., Berkeley, 1955-57, 75—; lectr. in anthropology Calif. State U., Hayward, 1966-75; mem. faculty Fromm Inst. Lifelong Learning, U. San Francisco, 1980. Fellow AAAS, Am. Anthropol. Assn.; mem. Linguistic Soc. Am., Internat. Linguistic Assn., Southwestern Anthrop. Assn., Soc. Woman Geographers. Democrat. Author: (with George M. Foster) Sierra Popoluca Speech, 1948; The Tarascan Language, 1969; editor: (with Stanley H. Brandes) Symbol As Sense: New Approaches to the Analysis of Meaning, 1980, (with Robert A. Rubinstein) Peace and War: Cross-Cultural Perspectives, 1986, (with Robert A. Rubinstein) The Social Dynamics of Peace, 1988 (with Lucy J. Botscharow) The Life of Symbols, 1990. Home: 790 San Luis Rd Berkeley CA 94707-2030

FOSTER, MICHAEL WILLIAM, librarian; b. Astoria, Oreg., June 29, 1940; s. William Michael and Margaret Vivian (Carlson) F. BA in History, Willamette U., 1962; MA, U. Oreg., 1965; postgrad., So. Oreg. Coll., 1976. Tchr. Astoria High Sch., 1963-66, librarian, 1970—; tchr. Am. Internat. Sch. of Kabul (Afghanistan), 1966-70; bd. dirs. Astoria High Sch. Scholarships, Inc., AG-BAG Internat. Ltd., Oreg. Pacific Industries, Inc., Astoria Pacific Industries, Inc. Commr. Oreg. Arts Commn., Salem, 1983-91; bd. dirs. Am. Cancer Soc., Clatsop County, Oreg., 1980-87; bd. dirs., treas. Astoria Community Concert Assn., 1964-88, pres., 1989—; bd. dirs., treas. Ed and Eda Ross Scholarship Trust; bd. dirs. Columbia Meml. Hosp. Found., 1992—; bd. dirs. Edward Hall Scholarship Bd. Mem. NEA, Oreg. Edn. Assn., Oreg. Edn. Media Assn., Clatsop County Hist. Soc. (bd. dirs., pres. 1983-87), Ft. Clatsop Hist. Assn. (treas. 1974-91, pres. 1991—, bd. dirs.), Astoria C. of C. (bd. dirs. 1982-88, George award 1985, pres. 1987), Lewis and Clark Trails Heritage Found., Rotary (pres. Astoria club 1986), Beta Theta Pi. Republican. Roman Catholic. Home: 1636 Irving Ave Astoria OR 97103-3621 Office: Astoria High Sch Libr 1001 W Marine Dr Astoria OR 97103-5829

FOSTER, RUTH MARY, business administrator; b. Little Rock, Jan. 11, 1927; d. William Crosby and Frances Louise (Doering) Shaw; m. Luther A. Foster, Sept. 8, 1946 (dec. Dec. 1980); children: William Lee, Robert Lynn. Grad. high sch., Long Beach, Calif. Sr. hostess Mon's Food Host of Coast, Long Beach, 1945-46; dental asst., office mgr. Dr. Wilfred H. Allen, Opportunity, Wash., 1946-47; dental asst., bus. asst. Dr. H. Erdahl, Long Beach, 1948-50; office mgr. Dr. B.B. Blough, Spokane, Wash., 1950-52; bus. mgr. Henry G. Kolsrud, D.D.S., P.S., Spokane, 1958—, Garland Dental Bldg., Spokane, 1958—. Sustaining mem. Spokane Symphony Orch. Mem. Nat. Assn. Dental Assts., Disabled Am. Vets. Aux., Spokane's Lilac City Bus. and Profl. Women (pres.), Nat. Alliance Mentally Ill, Wash. Alliance Mentally Ill, Spokane Alliance Mentally Ill, Internat. Platform Assn., Spokane Club, Credit Women's Breakfast Club. Democrat. Mem. First Christian Ch. Office: Henry G Kolsrud DDS PS 3718 N Monroe St Spokane WA 99205-2895

FOSTER, WANNIE PAUL, lawyer; b. Independence, Mo., Feb. 27, 1938; s. Wannie Perry and Vera Juanita (Kitch) F.; m. Barbara Elizabeth Katzung, Dec. 18, 1965; children: Scott Allan, Laurie Katherine. BA, U. Calif., Berkeley, 1960, JD, 1966. Bar: Calif., U.S. Dist. Ct. (no. , cen. dists.) Calif. Lawyer Burton & Foster, El Cerrito, Calif., 1967-74; sole practice Berkeley, 1974-82; program atty. Continuing Edn. of the Bar, Berkeley, 1982-83; trial lawyer CalFarm Ins. Co., Sacramento, Calif., 1983—. Chmn. Herms dist. Boy Scouts of Am., 1983-84. Capt. USAR, 1960-62. Mem. Berkeley-Albany Bar Assn. (pres. 1980—), Alameda County Bar Assn. (com. mem. 1980), El Cerrito Rotary (pres. 1973), Alpha Kappa Lambda Frat. (pres. bd. dirs. 1977-89). Home: 5500 Ludwig Ave El Cerrito CA 94530 Office: Ginder Foster & Loughman 1995 University Ave # 300 Berkeley CA 94704

FOSTER, WILLIAM JAMES, III, jeweler, gemologist; b. Princeton, N.J., Dec. 9, 1953; s. William James and Frances Alberta (Savidge) F.; m. Lynn Marie McDonald, Sept.6, 1975; children: Trevor James, Tracy Lynn. BA in Geology, Carleton Coll., 1976. Mgr. installations David Beatty Stereo, Kansas City, Mo., 1976-79; programmer U. Mo., Kansas City, 1979-81; staff cons. DST Systems, Inc., Kansas City, 1981-86; owner, mgr. Carats and Crystals, Pismo Beach, Calif., 1986—. Founder, dir., officer Facts About Tomorrow's Energy, Westwood, Kans., 1981-84; councilman City of Westwood, 1980-86, mayor, 1986; councilman City of Pismo Beach, Calif., 1988-92. Mem. Am. Gem Soc., Nat. Assn. Jewelry Appraisers, Gemmological Assn. Great Britain, Pismo Beach C. of C. (bd. dirs. 1986-88, pres. 1988), Cen. Coast Mktg. Coun. (treas., dir. 1988). Republican. Methodist. Home: 2054 Ocean Blvd Pismo Beach CA 93449 Office: Carats and Crystals 580 Cypress St # N4 Pismo Beach CA 93449-2672

FOTSCH, DAN ROBERT, physical education educator; b. St. Louis, May 17, 1947; s. Robert Jarrel and Margaret Louise (Zimmermann) F.; m. Jacquelyn Sue Rotter, June 12, 1971; children: Kyla Michelle, Jeffrey Scott, Michael David. BS in Edn. cum laude, U. Mo., 1970; MS in Edn., Colo. State U., 1973. Cert. K-12 phys. edn. and health tchr. Mo., Colo. Tchr. phys. edn., coach North Callaway Schs., Auxvasse, Mo., 1970-71; grad. teaching asst., asst. track coach Colo. State U., Ft. Collins, 1971-73; tchr. elem. phys. edn., coach Poudre R-1 Sch. Dist., Ft. Collins, 1973—; tchr. on spl. assignment Elem. Phys. Edn. Resource, 1990; adminstrv. asst. Moore Sch., 1992-93; co-dir. Colo. State U. Handicapped Clinic, Ft. Collins, 1973—; dir. Moore Elem. Lab. Sch., Ft. Collins, 1979—, adminstrv. asst., 1992-93; dir. Colo. State U. Super Day Camp, 1979—; presenter for conf. in field. Contbr. articles to profl. jours. State dir. Jump Rope for Heart Project, Denver, 1981. Recipient Scott Key Acad. award, Sigma Phi Epsilon, 1969, Honor Alumni award, Coll. of Profl. Studies of Colo. State U., 1983; grantee Colo. Heart Assn., 1985. Mem. NEA, Poudre Edn. Assn., Colo. Edn. Assn., Colo. Assn. of Health, Phys. Edn., Recreation and Dance (pres. 1979-82, Tchr. award 1977, Honor award 1985), Am. Alliance for Health, Phys. Edn., Recreation and Dance (exec. bd. mem. council on phys.

edn. for children 1983-85, fitness chairperson, convention planner 1986), Internat. Platform Assn., Assn. for Supervision and Curriculum Devel., Cen. Dist. Alliance for Health, Phys. Edn., Recreation and Dance (elem. div. chairperson for phys. edn. 1989—), Phi Delta Kappa (found. rep. 1985), Phi Epsilon Kappa (v.p. 1969, pres. 1970). Republican. Home: 5312 Elderberry Ct Fort Collins CO 80525-5529 Office: Moore Elem Sch 1905 Orchard Pl Fort Collins CO 80521-3210

FOUAD, HUSSEIN YEHYA, electrical engineer; b. Cairo, July 21, 1939; came to U.S., 1963; s. Yehya and Bahga (Abdel Sayed) F.; married, 1971; children: Dalya, Basma, Rafik Daniel. BSc, Cairo U., 1960; MS, Purdue U., 1965, PhD, 1967. Registered profl. engr., Md., Ohio. Sr. engr. Babcock & Wilcox, Lynchburg, Va., 1966-67, Atomic Energy Commn., Cairo, 1967-74, Westinghouse in France, Paris, 1974-80, NUS, Gaithersburg, Md., 1980-83; pres. 3C, Inc., Richland, Wash., 1980—; sr. engr. AEP, Columbus, Ohio, 1983-89; prin. engr. Westinghouse, WHC, Richland, 1990—; adj. prof. Purdue U., West Lafayette, Ind., 1965-66, U. Md., College Park, 1980-83, Ohio State U., Columbus, 1983-89, Wash. State U., Richland, 1990—. Author: Automatic Control, 1965; contbr. articles to profl. jours.; patentee in field. Mem. IEEE, Am. Nuclear Soc., Instrument Soc. Am., Sigma Xi. Home and Office: 2469 Whitworth Richland WA 99352

FOUNTAIN, FREEMAN PERCIVAL, physician; b. Hawley, Minn., Apr. 16, 1921; s. Percival Freeman and Chloie (Ritteman) F.; m. Jerryln Jean McGraw, June 10, 1951; children: Diana, David, Daniel. BA, Stanford U., 1943; BSM, U. N.D., 1949; MD, U. Colo., 1951, MS, 1956. Diplomate Am. Bd. Phys. Medicine and Rehab. Intern Fitzsimmons Army Hosp., Denver, 1951-52; resident Colo. Med. Ctr, Denver, 1953-56; asst. prof. phys. medicine and rehab. U. Louisville, 1956-58, U. Colo., Denver, 1958-60; med. dir. dept. rehab. Lovelace Clinic, Albuquerque, 1960-66; tng. dir. phys. medicien and rehab. Good Samaritan Hosp., Phoenix, 1966-70; pvt. practice Scottsdale, Ariz., 1970—; cons. VA Hosp., Lexington, Ky., 1957-58, Prescott, Ariz., 1957-70, Phoenix, 1957-70. Contbr. articles to profl. jours. Med. examiner USNR Sea Scouts, Phoenix, 1970-75, Boy Scouts Am. Troop 441, Scottsdale, 1970-74. Capt. USNR, 1942-81, PTO, World War II. Fellow Am. Acad. Phys. Medicine and Rehab., Nat. Bd. Med. Examiners; mem. Ariz. Soc. Phys. Medicine and Rehab. (pres. 1984-85), Scottsdale C. of C. Republican. Lutheran. Home: 11618 N Sundown Dr Scottsdale AZ 85260-5542 Office: 7351 E Osborn Rd Ste 106 Scottsdale AZ 85251-6452

FOUQUETTE, MARTIN JOHN, JR., zoology educator; b. Phila., June 14, 1930; s. Martin John and Ruby (Lowry) F.; m. Carol Lynn Legett, 1962 (div. 1972); children: David Brian, Hyla Ann; m. Clemencia Vargas, 1989. BA, U. Tex., 1951, MA, 1953, PhD, 1959. Interim asst. prof. biology U. Fla., Gainesville, 1959-61; asst. prof. U. Southwestern La., Lafayette, 1961-65; assoc. prof. zoology Ariz. State U., Tempe, 1965—, dir. undergrad. studies dept. zoology, 1985-90. Contbr. articles to profl. jours. Capt. USAF, 1953-58. Grantee NSF, 1963-64, 68-69, 72-78, Am. Philosophy Soc., 1960. Fellow Herpetologists League (past gov.); mem. Am. Soc. Ichthyologists and Herpetologists (past gov.), Am. Soc. Zoologists, Am. Soc. Naturalists, Soc. Study of Amphibians and Reptiles, Soc. Systematic Biology, Soc. Study of Evolution, Southwestern Assn. Naturalists, Ariz. Apple Users Group (sec. 1981-82, editor 1982-85, bd. dirs. 1983-92), Sigma Xi, Willi Hennig Soc. Office: Ariz State U Dept Zoology Tempe AZ 85287-1501

FOURNIER, DONALD FREDERICK, dentist; b. Phoenix, Oct. 16, 1934; s. Dudley Thomas and Margaret Mary (Conway) F.; m. Sheila Ann Templeton, Aug. 5, 1957 (div. 1972); children: Julia Marguerite, Donald Frederick, John Robert, Anne Marie Selin, James Alexander; m. Nancy Colleen Hamm, July 10, 1976; children: Catharine Jacinthe, Jacques Edouard. Student, Stanford U., 1952, U. So. Calif., L.A., 1952-54; BSc, U. Nebr., 1958, DDS, 1958. Pvt. practice restorative dentistry Phoenix, 1958—; pres. Hope Mining and Milling Co., Phoenix, 1970—; chief dental staff St. Joseph's Hosp., Phoenix, 1968; vis. prof. periodontology Coll. Dentistry U. Nebr., 1985; faculty Phoenix Coll. Dental Hygiene Sch., 1968-71; investigator Ariz. State Bd. Dental Examiners, 1978-89; mem. Mercy Dental Clinic Staff, 1968-70; dir. Canadian Am. Inst. Cardiology, 1986—. Contbr. articles to profl. jours. Pres. bd. trustees Osborn Sch. Dist., Phoenix, 1976; dir. Lukesmen, Phoenix, 1978-81; patrolman Nat. Ski Patrol, Phoenix, 1974-79; pres. Longview PTa, 1969; mem. adv. bd. Phoenix Crime Commn., 1969-71, Phoenix Coll. Dean's Adv. Bd., 1968-75; mem. The Phoenix House Am. Indian Rehab., 1985-86. Lt. col. Ariz. Army Res. N.G., 1958—. USPHS fellow, 1956-57, 57-58. Fellow Am. Coll. Dentists, Internat. Coll. Dentists; mem. ADA, Ariz. State Dental Assn., Pacific Coast Soc. Prosthodontists, Am. Acad. Orofacial Pain (pres. 1988-89), Am. Acad. Restorative Dentistry (pres. 1991-92), Am. Acad. Gold Foil Operators, Craniomandibular Inst. (dir.), Internat. Assn. Dental Rsch., Acad. Operative Dentistry (charter), U.S. Croquet Assn., Ariz. Croquet Club, Phoenix Country Club, Phi Delta Theta, Xi Psi Phi. Republican. Roman Catholic. Home: 86 E Country Club Dr Phoenix AZ 85014-5435 Office: 199 E Monterey Way Phoenix AZ 85012-2684

FOURNIER, WALTER FRANK, real estate executive; b. Northampton, Mass., Feb. 26, 1912; s. Frank Napoleon and Marie Ann F.; m. Ella Mae Karrey, May 16, 1938; children: Margaret Irene, Walter Karrey. BS in Mktg., Boston U., 1939; postgrad., Anchorage Community Coll., 1963-64, Alaska Pacific U., 1964-65. Coin sales supt. Coca Cola Co., Springfield, Mass., 1939-43; electrician foreman Collins Electric Co., Springfield, 1946-48; sales coord. for pre-fabricated homes Sears Roebuck & Co., Western Mass., 1948-49; wholesale sales rep. Carl Wiseman Steel and Aluminum Co., Great Falls, Mont., 1949-51; supt. City Electric Co., Anchorage, 1951-52; owner, adminstr. Acme Electric Co., Anchorage, 1953-64; appraiser Gebhart & Peterson, Anchorage, 1964-68; broker, owner Walter F. Fournier & Assocs., Anchorage, 1968—; pres. Alaska Mortgage Cons., Anchorage, 1968-69. Pres. Fairview Community Council, Anchorage, 1980-81. Served with U.S. Army, 1928-31, with USN, 1944-45, PTO. Recipient Spl. Recognition award HUD, 1967. Mem. Review Mortgage Underwriters, Inst. Bus. Appraisers, Internat. Soc. Financiers, Soc. Exchange Counselors (rep. 1970), Alaska Creative Real Estate Assn. (pres. 1978, Gold Pan award 1988), Alaska Million Plus Soc. (pres. 1983). Roman Catholic. Lodge: KC. Office: Walter F Fournier & Assocs 613 E 22d Ave Anchorage AK 99503

FOUST, ROSANNE SKIBO, government official; b. Derby, Conn., Feb. 28, 1964; d. John Andrew and Claire Frances (Fallon) S.; m. Joseph V. Foust, Jr., Dec. 30, 1989. BA, Stonehill Coll., N. Easton, Mass., 1986; postgrad., UCLA, 1993. Prog. coord. Internat. Bus. Ctr. of New Eng., Inc., Boston, 1986; dir. spl. events Internat. Bus. Ctr. of New Eng., Inc., 1986-87, dir. mktg., 1987-88; assoc. dir. Alsace (France) Devel. Agy., L.A., 1988-91, regional dir., 1991—, dir. U.S. operations. Editor Palmcrest HOA newsletter, 1990. Mem., Palm Crest Homeowners Assn., Hawthorne, Calif., Pres. 1991, Treas. 1992. Mem. Jr. Achievement Alumni Assn., L.A. County Mus. Art, NAFE, French-Am. C. of C. (bd. dirs. 1990—, v.p. exec. com. 1992—), Am. Mgmt. Assn. Republican. Roman Catholic. Office: Alsace Devel Agy 2029 Century Park E Ste 1115 Los Angeles CA 90067

FOWKES, MARGO SARAH MILLER, city official; b. San Jose, Calif., Sept. 29, 1961; d. Lawrence Jefferson and Martha Elise (Kilgore) Miller; m. Daniel Kirk Fowkes, Sept. 3, 1988. BA in Polit. Sci., Stanford U., 1983; M Pub. Policy, Harvard U., 1988. Budget and policy analyst budget com. U.S. Senate, Washington, 1983-86; cons. Calif. Leadership, Santa Clara, 1987; mktg. support rep. Unisys Corp., Sacramento, 1988-91; cons. Sacramento Housing and Redevel. Agy., 1991-92, coord. enterprise zone, 1992—. Instr. Exploring Your Horizons Program, Sacramento, 1992-93; mem. Jr. League Sacramento, 1990—; bd. dirs. YWCA, Sacramento, 1992—. Recipient state individual devel. speakoff award Calif. Feddn. Bus. and Profl. Women, 1991. Mem. Calif. Assn. Enterprise Zones (treas. 1992—), Calif. Elected Women's Assn. for Edn. and Rsch., Coalition Sacramento Women's Orgns. (chmn. 1991—), Downtown Capitol Bus. and Profl. Women (pres. 1991-92), Moms Club of Folsom (pres. and founder). Republican. Home: 104 Pradera Ct Folsom CA 95630

FOWLER, DON DEE, anthropology and historic preservation educator; b. Torrey, Utah, Apr. 24, 1936; s. Eldon C. Fowler and Ruby (Noyes) Fowler Tippets; m. Janet Ary, May 18, 1960 (div. June 1962); 1 child, Mark Charles; m. Catherine Lousie Sweeney, June 14, 1963. B.A., U. Utah, 1959; Ph.D., U. Pitts., 1965. Asst. prof. U. Nev., Reno, 1964-67, Mamie Kleberg prof. anthropology and historic preservation, 1978—; postdoctoral fellow Smithsonian Inst., Washington, 1967-68, research assoc., 1970—; research prof. Desert Research Inst., Reno, 1968-78. Author: In a Sacred Manner We Live, 1972, Western Photographs of Jack Hillers, 1989, also 30 monographs, over 80 articles; co-editor: American Archaeology, Past and Present, 1986, Anthropology of the Desert West, 1986; editor: Photographed All the Best Scenery, 1972. Grantee various agys., cos., including NSF, 1969-74, Am. Council Learned Socs., 1975. Fellow Am. Anthrop. Assn., Soc. Am. Archaeology (pres.); mem. Explorers Club. Office: U Nev Historic Preservation Program Reno NV 89557

FOWLER, DONA J., biology educator; b. Muncie, Ind., May 8, 1928; d. Cleo E. and Thelma (Broman) Wilson; children: Ann L. Mastenbrook, James Sheldon. BS, Purdue U., 1955, MS, 1962, PhD, 1965. RN Ball Meml. Hosp., Muncie, Ind., 1948-52; research asst. Purdue U., West Lafayette, Ind., 1954-56, teaching asst., 1960-62, research asst., 1962-65; assoc. research analytical chemist Eli Lilly Co., Indpls., 1956-60; asst. prof. Western Mich. U., Kalamazoo, 1965-70, assoc. prof., 1970-78, prof., 1978-88, prof. emeritus, 1988—; rsch. assoc. U. Ariz., Tucson, 1988—; disting. vis. prof. dept. biology U. Ariz., Tuscon, 1980-81, 87-88; vis. scientist Argonne (Ill.) Nat. Lab., 1983, continuing assoc., 1984—; vis. scientist Centre Nationale Recherche Scientifique, Gif-sur-Yvette, France; participant in Gordon Conf. on Chronobiology, 1983; research dir. NSF, 1968-70, NIH, 1977-79; guest scientist Centre Nationale Researche Scientifique, 1973-79. Contbr. articles to profl. jours. Dir. neighborhood program, nat. and state elections Dem. Party, 1974—; swim team meet dir., bd. pres. AAU Masters Swim Program, 1978—. Mem. Am. Soc. Chronobiology, Int. Soc. Chronobiology, Am. Soc. Biometerology, Soc. Photobiology and Photochemistry, Am. Inst. Biol. Scis., Assn. Mondiale Zootechnie., PEO (program dir. Kalamazoo 1970—). Democrat. Unitarian. Home: 8692 N Little Oak Ln Tucson AZ 85704-0966 Office: U Ariz Tucson AZ 85704

FOWLER, JAMES M., artist; b. Indpls., July 30, 1939; s. James M. Fowler III and Royse (Shirk) Barnaby; m. Sui-Hen Fung, Apr. 2, 1970; 1 child, Joseph Royse. BFA, Calif. Coll. Arts and Crafts, Oakland, 1969; MFA, Mills Coll., 1971. Cert. community coll. tchr., Calif. Teaching asst. Calif. Coll. Arts and Crafts, Oakland, 1969, Mills Coll., Oakland, 1970, 71; instr. Dominican Coll., San Rafael, Calif., 1971; pvt. bus. printmaking/photography studio Kentfield, Calif., 1971—; asst. prof. Dominican Coll., San Rafael, 1976—, chmn. art dept., 1982-84. Artist: (photo etching) Lillians Arrival, 1972 (purchase award 1972); photographer: (cibachrome print) South Rim, Grand Canyon, 1976, (San Francisco Art Commn. award 1977). With USAF, 1961-66, Vietnam, Japan. Recipient Hon. Mention award Walnut Creek (Calif.) Art Ctr., 1966, Photography award Marin County Fair Art Show, San Rafael, 1978, Friedman grant Dominican Coll., 1983. Mem. Calif. Soc. Printmakers, Baulines Crafts Guild. Home: 407 Goodhill Rd San Rafael CA 94904-2613 Office: Dominican College Dept Art PO Box 8008 San Rafael CA 94912-8008

FOWLER, NANCY CROWLEY, government economist; b. Newton, Mass., Aug. 8, 1922; d. Ralph Elmer and Margaret Bright (Tinkham) Crowley; m. Gordon Robert Fowler, Sept. 11, 1949; children: Gordon R., Nancy Pualani, Betty Kainani, Diane Kuulei. AB cum laude, Radcliffe Coll., 1943; grad. Bus. Admnstrn. Program, Harvard-Radcliffe U., 1946; postgrad., U. Hawaii, 1971-76. Econ. rsch. analyst Dept. Planning & Econ. Devel., Honolulu, 1963-69; assoc. chief rsch. Regional Med. Program, Honolulu, 1969-70; economist V and VI Dept. Planning and Econ. Devel., Honolulu, 1970-78, chief policy analysis br., 1978-85, tech. info. services officer, 1985-87; staff rep. State Energy Functional Plan Adv. Com., Honolulu, 1983-89, Hawaii Integrated Energy Assessment, 1978-81, Energy Resources Coord.'s Annual Report, 1988-92, Energy Fact Sheets, 1990. Contbr. articles to profl. jours. Recipient Employee of Yr. award Dept. Planning and Econ. Devel., Honolulu, 1977, others. Mem. Hawaii Econs. Assn. (various offices), Travel and Tourism Rsch. Assn., Harvard Bus. Sch. Club, Radcliffe Club of Hawaii, Propeller Club, Port of Honolulu (past pres. and bd. govs.), Navy League Club. Democrat.

FOWLER, NANCY MARY, county government administrator; b. Boston; d. Henry M. and Edna F. (Hanley) F. AB, Creighton U., 1969; M.U.P., San Jose State U., 1976. Planner City of Redwood City (Calif.), 1973; planner planning dept. City of San Jose (Calif), 1973-79, adminstrv. analyst office of mgmt. and budget, 1977-79; budget/oper. analyst City of Palo Alto (Calif.), 1979-81, pub. works adminstr., 1981-86; analyst supr. budget office Santa Clara County, San Jose, 1986-88, dir. justice svcs. Office of County Exec., 1988—. Bd. dirs. Friends Outside, ASPA Santa Clara Valley, San Jose, Shasta/Hanchett Park Neighborhood Assn., San Jose, Evergreen Valley Homeowners Assn., San Jose. Mem. Am. Correctional Assn., Am. Jail Assn. Office: Santa Clara County Office County Exec 70 W Hedding St 11th Fl San Jose CA 95110

FOWLER, NATHANIEL EUGENE, ophthalmologist; b. Rochester, N.Y., Dec. 19, 1922; s. John Denison and Lettie (Oliver) F.; student U. Wis., summers 1940, 41, U. Mich., 1940-43; M.D., U. Rochester, 1946; postgrad. Northwestern U., 1947-48; m. Norma Pammenter, Dec. 27, 1944; children—Leigh Pammenter, James Nathaniel, Richard Edward. Intern Genesee Hosp., Rochester, N.Y., 1946-47; commd. lt. (j.g.), M.C., USN, 1946, advanced through grades to lt. comdr., 1956; chief eye, ear, nose throat dept. U.S. Naval Hosp., Key West, Fla., 1948-51, 54-56; resident in ophthalmology U.S. Naval Hosp., Bethesda, Md., 1951-53; sr. med. officer in U.S.S. Baltimore, 1953-54; practice medicine specializing in ophthalmology, Casper, Wyo., 1956-88; chief of staff Natrona County (Wyo.) Meml. Hosp., 1964-66. Trustee Natrona County Sch. Bd., 1963-70, pres., 1967-68; mem. Natrona County Commn., 1971-82, chmn., 1980; bd. dirs. Natrona County Parks and Pleasure Grounds. Diplomate Am. Bd. Ophthalmology. Fellow ACS, Am. Acad. Ophthalmology; mem. Casper C. of C. (dir. 1962-64), Natrona County Med. Soc. (pres. 1959), AMA, Pan Am. Med. Assn., Pan Am. Assn. Ophthalmology, Wyo. Sch. Bds. Assn., N.Am. Yacht Racing Union. Clubs: Elks, Lions (dir. 1961-64), Masons, Shriners, Casper Mountain Ski, Casper Boat (commodore 1960-62), Nat. Ski Patrol, U.S. Navy League. Home: 2957 Kalakaua Ave Apt 516 Honolulu HI 96815-4615

FOWLER, PETER NILES, lawyer; b. Hamilton, Ohio, Apr. 3, 1951; s. Richard Allen and Blanche (Niles) F. BA, John Carroll U., 1973; MA, U. Ala., Tuscaloosa, 1977, Ball State U., 1979; JD, Golden Gate U., 1984. Bar: Calif. 1984, Nev. 1986, U.S. Dist. Ct. (no. dist.) Calif. 1984, U.S. Ct. Appeals (9th cir.) 1984. Law clk. to assoc. justice Nev. Supreme Ct., Carson City, 1984-85; assoc. Lilienthal and Jacobson, San Francisco, 1985-87; ptnr. Lilienthal & Fowler, San Francisco, 1988--; adj. instr., faculty mem. Golden Gate U. Sch. Law, 1988—, Hastings Coll. of Law, 1989-91, U. San Francisco, 1991—; bd. dirs. Frameline, Project Inform. Contbg. author to books and articles to profl. jours. Co-chair, bd. dirs. Nat. Gay and Lesbian Task Force, Washington, 1983-89; chair, bd. dirs. Nat. Edn. Found. for Individual Rights, San Francisco, 1985—. Recipient Outstanding Leadership award Am. Cancer Soc., 1980. Mem. ABA (hon. mention award 1983), Nat. Lesbian and Gay Law Assn., Calif. Bar Assn., Nev. Bar Assn., San Francisco Bar Assn., Bay Area Lawyers Individual Freedom Assn., Calif. Lawyers for Arts. Democrat. Roman Catholic. Office: Lilienthal & Fowler Mills Tower 220 Montgomery St 15th Fl San Francisco CA 94104-4890

FOWLER, ROLLEN CHARLES, psychologist; b. Glendale, Calif., Mar. 17, 1962; s. Charles William and Virginia Marylyn (English) F.; m. Diane Christine Israel, June 8, 1985; 1 child, Kaelah Doreen. BA, Whitworth Coll., Spokane, Wash., 1986; MS, Ea. Wash. U., Cheney, Wash., 1990; postgrad., U. Oreg., 1992—. Lic. sch. psychologist, Wash. Counselor Cannon Hill Home for Boys, Spokane, 1986-88; residential care trainer Assn. for Retarded Citizens, Spokane, 1988; psychologist II Interlake Sch., Medical Lake, Wash., 1989-92; rsch. asst. U. Oreg., Eugene, 1992—. Graduate teaching fellow U. Oreg., Eugene, 1992—. Mem. Nat. Assn. Sch. Psychologists, Oreg. Sch. Psychologist Assn., Coun. Exceptional Children, Oreg. Coun. Children with Behavioral Disorders, Phi Kappa Phi. Home: 2155 W 16th Ct Eugene OR 97402

FOWLER, RONALD VINCENT, general contractor, owner; b. Oceanside, N.Y., Nov. 24, 1955; s. William Clement and Grace (Dauphaneé) F.; m. Diane Huntington, Nov. 28, 1980; children: Tawna Rochelle, Devon Marie, Amber Rea; m. Delana Maxine Hutchinson, June 6, 1992; children: Randi Maxine, Kevin James. BA, Brigham Young U., 1979. Baker Bageltown, Levittown, N.Y., 1970-73; mechanic Utah Power & Light, Orem, Utah, 1975-76; tchr. asst. Brigham Young U., Provo, Utah, 1976-77; airframe mechanic Grumman Aerospace, Bethpage, N.Y., 1984-85; owner Tri-City Maintenance, Woodland, Calif., 1985—; gen. contractor, owner, operator Tri-City Maintenance, Woodland, Calif., 1980-92. Mem. Woodland Hist. Soc., 1992. Mem. Nat. Assn. Small Bus., Planetary Soc., Nat. Geog. Soc. Reformed Christian. Home: 456 Third St Woodland CA 95695 Office: Tri-City Maintenance 456 Third St Woodland CA 95645

FOWLER, R.S., provincial legislator; b. Edson, Alta., 1932; m. Vera Fowler; children: Cathy, James, Christine, Caroline, Stuart. BA in Polit. Sci., U. Alta., 1973, LLB, 1976. With sales dept. Dunham Bush Canada Ltd.; councillor Town of St. Albert, Alta., 1963-68, mayor, 1965-68, 80-89; with Rowland & Fowler, St. Albert; mem. Alta. Provincial Legis., Edmonton, 1989—; atty. gen. Province of Alta., Edmonton, 1992—; chmn. Capital Region Sewage Commn., 1984-88; dir. Fedn. Canadian Municipalities, 1986-89; solicitor gen., Min. Responsible for Alta. Liquor Control Bd., 1989—; with Profl. Occupations Br. 1989—; Min. Responsible for Native Affairs, 1991—; Min. of Justice, 1992—. Trustee Sturgeon Gen. Hosp.; bd. govs. Athabasca U., 1968-71. Named Citizen of the Decade, Town of St. Albert, 1989. Mem. Progress Club Can., Lions (St. Albert chpt.). Office: Minister of Municipal Affairs, Legislature Bldg Rm 319, Edmonton, AB Canada T5K 2B6

FOWLER, WILLIAM ALFRED, retired physics educator; b. Pittsburgh, Penn., Aug. 9, 1911; s. John McLeod and Jennie Summers (Watson) F.; m. Ardiane Olmsted, Aug. 24, 1940 (dec. May 1988); children: Mary Emily Fowler Galowin, Martha Summers Fowler Schoenemann; m. Mary Dutcher, Dec. 14, 1989. B of Engring. Physics, Ohio State U., 1933, DSc (hon.), 1978; PhD, Calif. Inst. Tech., 1936; DSc (hon.), U. Chgo., 1976, Denison U., 1982, Ariz. State U., 1985, Georgetown U., 1986, U. Mass., 1987, Williams Coll., 1988; Doctorat honoris causa, U. Liège (Belgium), 1981, Observatoire de Paris, 1981. Asst. prof. physics Calif. Inst. Tech., 1939-42, asso. prof., 1942-46, prof. physics, 1946-70, Inst. prof. physics, 1970-82; prof. emeritus, 1982—; conducted rsch. on nuclear forces and reaction rates, nuclear spectroscopy, structure of light nuclei, thermonuclear sources of stellar energy and element synthesis in stars and supernovae and the early universe, including recently proposed inflationary model; study of gen. relativistic effects in quasar and pulsar models, nuclear cosmochronology; Fulbright lectr. Pembroke Coll. and Cavendish lab. U. Cambridge, 1954-55; Guggenheim fellow, 1954-55; Guggenheim fellow St. John's Coll. and dept. applied math. and theoretical physics U. Cambridge, 1961-62; vis. fellow Inst. Theoretical Astronomy, summers 1967-72; vis. scholar program Phi Beta Kappa, 1980-81; asst. dir. rsch. sect. L Nat. Defense Rsch. Com., 1941-45; tech. observer, office of field service OSRD, South Pacific Theatre, 1944; sci. dir., project VISTA, Dept. Def., 1951-52; mem. nat. sci. bd. NSF, 1968-74; mem. space sci. bd. Nat. Acad. Scis., 1970-73, 77-80; chmn. Office of Phys. Scis., 1981-84; mem. space program adv. council NASA, 1971-73; mem. nuclear sci. adv. com. Dept. Energy/Nat. Sci. Found., 1977-80; E.A. Milne Lectr. Milne Soc., 1986; named lectr. univs., colls.; hon. fellow Pembroke Coll., Cambridge U., 1992. Contbr. numerous articles to profl. jours. Bd. dirs. Am. Friends of Cambridge U., 1970-78. Rsch. fellow Calif. Inst. Tech., Pasadena, 1936-39; recipient Naval Ordnance Devel. award USN, 1945, Medal of Merit, 1948; Lammé medal Ohio State U., 1952; Liège medal U. Liège, 1955; Calif. Co-Scientist of Yr. award, 1958; Barnard medal for contbn. to sci. Columbia, 1965; Apollo Achievement award NASA, 1969; Vetlesen prize, 1973; Nat. medal of sci., 1974; Bruce gold medal Astron. Soc. Pacific, 1979; Nobel prize for physics, 1983; Légion d'Honneur, 1989; Benjamin Franklin fellow Royal Soc. Arts; named to Lima Ohio City Schs. Disting. Alumni Hall of Fame, Ohio Sci. and Tech. Hall of Fame; named hon. fellow Pembroke Coll., Cambridge U., 1992. Fellow Am. Phys. Soc. (Tom W. Bonner prize 1970, pres. 1976, 1st recipient William A. Fowler award for excellence in physics So. Ohio sect. 1986), Am. Acad. Arts and Scis., Royal Astron. Soc. (assoc., Eddington medal 1978); mem. NAS (council 1974-77), AAAS, Am. Astron. Soc., Am. Inst. Physics (governing bd. 1974-80), AAUP, Am. Philos. Soc., Soc. Royal Sci. Liège (corr. mem.), Brit. Assn. Advancement Sci., Soc. Am. Baseball Research, Mark Twain Soc. (hon.), Naturvetenskapliga Foreiningen (hon.), Sigma Xi, Tau Beta Pi, Tau Kappa Epsilon. Democrat. Clubs: Athenaeum (Pasadena); Cosmos (Washington). Office: Calif Inst Tech Kellogg 106-38 Pasadena CA 91125

FOX, BARRY JAY, author, speaker; b. Kansas City, Mo., July 31, 1956; s. Arnold and Hannah (Benstog) F.; m. Nadine Taylor. BA, U. Calif., Santa Cruz, 1979; MFA, U. So. Calif., L.A., 1981; PhD, Greenwich U., 1993. Diplomate Am. Acad. Pain Mgmt. Pub., editor The New Health Jour., Beverley Hills, Calif., 1986—; founder, pres. Fox Adminstrv. Med. Svcs. (FoxAms), Beverly Hills., Calif., 1992—; speaker on psychoneuroimmunology, nutrition, health, pub. rels. to various orgns. and convs. Co-author: DLPA, 1985, Wake Up! You're Alive, 1988, Immune for Life, 1989, Making Miracles, 1989, Beyond Positive Thinking, 1991, 14 Day Miracel Plan, 1991, Total Optimisa, 1992, other books; contbg. editor Let's Live, 1989—; feature editor Business Report; contbr. more than 100 articles to profl. jours. Recipient Learned Rsch. award Brandeis U. Nat. Women's Coun., 1990. Mem. Am. Soc. Journalists and Authors, Am. Med. Writers Assn., Toastmasters (ATMS area gov. 1990),l Mensa, Phi Kappa Phi. Office: 9735 Wilshire Blvd 440 Beverly Hills CA 90212

FOX, BRAD, school administrator; b. N.Y.C., Nov. 8, 1947; s. Nathan Daniel and Dorothy Eileen (Bradley) F. BA, San Francisco State U., 1985, recipient teaching credentials; recipient adminstrv. svcs. credential, Calif. State U., Hayward. Cert. tchr., sch. adminstr., Calif. Gen. ptnr. Progressive Video, Berkeley, Calif., 1980-85; sales counselor Whole Earth Electronics, Berkeley, 1985-89; mgr. Whole Earth Electronics, San Mateo, Calif., 1989-90; tchr. Hercules (Calif.) Elem. Sch., 1990, Richmond (Calif.) High Sch., 1990-91; vice-prin. Berkeley High Sch., 1991—; video cons. Far West Lab. Ednl. Rsch., San Francisco, 1991. Contbr. articles to San Francisco Mag. Pres. Grand Illusions Film and Video, San Francisco,l 978-80; founding mem. East Bay Media Ctr., Berkeley, 1979-82; mem. coun. Shattuck Adv. Ctr. Coun., Berkeley, 1979-82; commr. Community Health Adv. Com., Berkeley, 1989-90. Mem. ASCD, ACLU, NAACP, Assn. Calif. Sch. Adminstrs., Tchrs. of English to Speakers of Other Langs., Internat. Educators' Inst., Berkeley Breakfast Club. Home: 512 Neilson St Berkeley CA 94707-1503 Office: Berkeley High Sch 2246 Milvia St Berkeley CA 94704

FOX, BRYAN PATRICK, career officer; b. Great Falls, Mont., Mar. 12, 1958; s. Richard Charles and Nancy Lou (Gannon) F.; m. Laureen Marie Fronsee, June 15, 1991. A in Aircraft Maintenance Tech., Community Coll. of the AF, Great Falls, Mont., 1983; BS, Coll. of Great Falls, 1985. Enlisted Mont. Air NG, Great Falls, 1976, advanced through grades to 1st lt., aircraft mechanic, 1979-88, aircraft foreman, 1989, mgmt. analyst, 1989-90, logistics plans officer, 1990-92, dir. pers., 1992—. Greas., bd. dirs. Great Falls Govt. Employees Credit Union, 1992—; v.p. Great Falls Coin and Currency Club, 1991. Recipient Citizen Soldier award Acad. Mil. Sci., 1987; named Mont. Air NG Airman of Yr. Great Falls C. of C., 1977. Home: 2325 6th Ave S Great Falls MT 59405

FOX, CHRISTOPHER GENE, oceanographer, researcher; b. Phila., Mar. 18, 1952; s. Harry Richard and Jeanne Noyes (Morgan) F.; m. Martha Hill Winsor, Nov. 24, 1979; children: Benjamin Winsor, Emily Winsor. BA with honors, U. Tenn., 1974; MS, Brown U., 1976; PhM, Columbia U., 1982, PhD, 1984. Hydrologist U.S. Geol. Survey, Bay St. Louis, Miss., 1977-78; oceanographer U.S. Naval Oceanographic Office, Bay St. Louis, 1978-85; phys. scientist NOAA, Newport, Oreg., 1985—. Contbr. articles to profl. publs. Commr. Carmel-Foulweather Sanitary Dist., Otter Rock, Oreg., 1987-90. Mem. IEEE, Am. Geophys. Union, Seismological Soc. Am. Home: 6320 SW B Ave Otter Rock OR 97369 Office: NOAA Pacific Marine Environ Lab 2115 SW OSU Dr Newport OR 97365

FOX, FRANCES JUANICE, librarian, educator, retired; b. Vicksburg, Miss., Aug. 17, 1916; d. Willie Amercy Thaxton and Fannye Lou (Spell) Hepfer; m. Leonard John Fox, Feb. 25, 1937; children: Frances Juanice, L. John Jr., Kenneth L., Robert T., William E., Elizabeth Jean. AA, Phoenix Coll., 1959; BS in Edn., Ariz. State U., 1963, MS in Edn., Libr., 1972. Cert. kindergarten, primary, and elem. tchr., cert. libr., cert. religious edn. Diocese of Phoenix. Substitute tchr. Eseambia County Sch. Dist., Pensacola, Fla.,

1936-38; kindergarten tchr. Lollipop Ln. Sch., Phoenix, 1960-61, 1st United Meth. Day Sch., Phoenix, 1961-62; tchr. grade 3 Wilson Elem. Sch., Phoenix, 1962-63; summer libr. R.E. Simpson Elem. Sch., Phoenix, 1964, 65; preschool tchr. Jewish Community Ctr., Phoenix, 1967-68; libr. Audio Visual Ctr. Sts. Simon and Judge Elem. Sch., Phoenix, 1969-82; ret., 1982; cataloger First United Meth. Ch. Libr., Phoenix, 1963, Baker Ctr. Ariz. State Univ. Student Libr., Tempe, 1969. Co-compiler: (libr. manual) Diocese of Phoenix, 1980-81. Organizer, leader Girl Scouts Am., Birmingham, Ala., 1951, 52, Phoenix, 76-83; leader cubs Boy Scouts Am., Birmingham, 1950-52, Phoenix, 52-55; swim instr. ARC, Fla., Ariz., 1933, 34, 53, 54; dance instr. Circle Game and Beginning Dance, Wesley Community Ctr., Phoenix, 1966, 67. Recipient Acad. scholarship Phoenix Coll., Ariz. State Coll., 1959. Mem. ALA, Ariz. State Libr. Assn. (com. on continuing edn. 1979-81), Gold Star Wines of Am., Inc. (past v.p., parlimentarian), DAV Aux. (life), Ariz. PTA (life mem., organizer, v.p.), Phi Theta Kappa, Iota Sigma Alpha Honor Soc. Methodist. Home: 2225 W Montebello Ave Phoenix AZ 85015

FOX, JACK, financial service executive; b. Bklyn., Mar. 8, 1940; s. Benjamin and Rebecca (Shure) F.; m. Carolyn Gleimer, Apr. 16, 1967 (div. Dec. 1975); m. Carole Olafson, July 8, 1987; children: Neal, Stuart. BBA, CCNY, 1961; MBA, CUNY, 1969. Sales specialist Am. Can Corp., N.Y.C., 1962-63; talent agt. Gen. Artists Corp., N.Y.C., 1963-66; bus. specialist N.Y. Times, 1966-70; pres. Ednl. Learning Systems, Inc., Washington, 1971-78; budget dir. Nat. Alliance of Bus., Washington, 1979-80; pres. Computerized Fin. Services, Rockville, Md., 1980-87; regional v.p. Govt. Funding Corp., L.A., 1987-90; owner, mgr. Jack Fox Assocs., San Diego, Calif., 1990—; adj. prof. Am. U., Washington, 1983-85; tchr. fin. Montgomery Coll., Rockville, 1978-86. Author: How to Obtain Your Own SBA Loan, 1983, Starting and Building Your Own Accounting Business, 1984, 2d rev. edit., 1991. Mem. Internat. Platform Assn., Nat. Assn. Accts. Democrat. Jewish. Home and Office: 4149 6th Ave Apt 13 San Diego CA 92103-1450

FOX, JOEL DAVID, political association executive; b. Boston, Apr. 22, 1949; s. Harry L. and Freda (Berry) F.; m. Cydney M. Finkel, May 19, 1974; children: Zachary Daniel, Eric Maxwell. BA, U. Mass., 1971; MA, U. Denver, 1974. Pub. rels. staff L.A. Bicentennial Com., 1976; aide and exec. dir. Howard Jarvis Taxpayers Assn., L.A., 1979-86, pres., 1986—; internat. speaker taxes and initiative process. Contbr. articles to profl. jours. and newspapers; author Calif. ballot initiatives. Gubernatorial appointee Calif. Citizen's Commn. on Ballot Initiatives, 1993; trustee LEARN - L.A. Sch. Reform, 1991—. Office: Howard Jarvis Taxpayers Asn 621 S Westmoreland # 202 Los Angeles CA 90005

FOX, JOSEPH LELAND, fiduciary and business executive; b. Hutchinson, Kans., Aug. 1, 1938; s. George L. and Margaret V. (Crist) F.; m. Barbara Beiser, June 10, 1961 (div. 1964; 1 child, Gary; m. Norma J. Leiker, Dec. 27, 1967; 1 child, Holly. BS in Bus. and Econs., Ft. Hays State Coll., 1967. Ptnr. Fox and Co. CPAs, Denver, 1967-74; chief exec. officer, trustee Energy Resources Tech. Land, Inc. and Tell Ertl Family Trust, Boulder, Colo., 1974—; bd. dirs. Lake Eldora Corp., ERTL, Inc., New Paraho Corp. Comm. officer CAP, 1991-93. Mem. C. of C. Office: New Paraho Corp 3000 Youngfield St Ste 364 Lakewood CO 80215-6553

FOX, KENNETH L., retired newspaper editor, writer; b. Kansas City, Mo., Mar. 18, 1917; s. Henry Hudson and Margaret Patience (Kiely) F.; m. Mary Harbord Manville, June 20, 1975. A.B., Washington U., St. Louis, 1938; student, U. Kansas City, 1939-40. With Kansas City Star, 1938-78, assoc. editor, 1966-78; news analyst Sta. WDAF, Kansas City, 1948-53; war corr., Vietnam and Laos, 1964, corr., No. Ireland, 1973. Served to col. AUS, 1940-46. Recipient 1st place editorial div. nat. aviation writing contest, 1957, 58, 59, 60, 67; named Aviation Man of Year for Kansas City, 1959. Mem. Am. Legion, 40 and 8, Res. Officers Assn., Ret. Officers Assn., Mil. Order World Wars, Phi Beta Kappa, Beta Theta Pi, Pi Sigma Alpha, Sigma Delta Chi. Clubs: Kansas City Press; Ariz. Home: 9796 E Ironwood Dr Scottsdale AZ 85258-4728

FOX, LORRAINE ESTHER, psychologist, human services consultant; b. S.I., N.Y., Aug. 27, 1941; d. Charles Frederick and Dorothy Elizabeth (Clohessy) F. BA, Northeastern Ill. U., 1973, MA, 1976; PhD in Clin. Psychology, Profl. Sch. Psychol. Studies, San Diego, 1989. Cert. in child care; cert. counselor and contract instr. U. Calif., Davis. Exec. dir. The Harbour, Des Plaines, Ill., 1975-81; asst. prof. Coll. St. Francis, Joliet, Ill., 1981-84; dir. clin. services Casa de Amparo, San Luis Rey, Calif., 1984-86; cons. Profl. Growth Facilitators, San Clemente, Calif., 1986—; vis. lectr. U. Ill. Chgo., 1983-84; cons. Arthur D. Little, Washington, 1979-82; contract cons. U. Calif.-Davis; internat. cons. Author tng. tapes on child care info.; various media appearances; pub. speaker; contbr. articles to profl. jours. Bd. dirs. United Ch. Child Care Ctr., Irvine; mem. adv. bd. Bienvenidos Family Svcs., L.A.; community adv. Learning Independence for Emancipation, San Diego. Mem. Calif. Assn. Child Care Workers (com. mem. 1984—, pres. Ill. chpt. 1982-84), ACLU, NOW, Psi Chi, Sierra Club. Home: 1210 Buena Vista San Clemente CA 92672-4932 Office: Profl Growth Facilitators PO Box 5981 San Clemente CA 92674-5981

FOX, RANDEE SUSAN, illustrator, graphic journalist and designer; b. L.A., June 11, 1952; d. Aaron and Irene (Brown) F. Student, Art Ctr., Coll. of Design, Pasadena, Calif., 1969-70. Pub., art dir. Studio Dance Revue, Santa Cruz, Calif., 1983-84; art dir., prodn. mgr., illustrator Community Spirit mag., Carmel, Calif., 1984-86; assoc. art dir., prodn. mgr. The Sun, Santa Cruz, 1986-87; editorial artist The Morning News Tribune, Tacoma, 1987-88; news artist The Seattle Times, 1988—. Poster illustrator Santa Cruz Commn. for Prevention Violence Against Women,, 1983-87, UN Conf. Final Decade for Women, Nairobi, Keyna, 1985, U. Calif., Santa Cruz, 1985-87; judge high sch. art competition Wash. Journalism Edn. Com., Seattle, 1988, 91, 92, tchr., 1990; tchr., speaker Urban Journalism Workshop, Seattle, 1991, 92. Recipient 2d place award for excellence in journalism Soc. Profl. Journalists, 1989, 3d place award, 1991; silver award Soc. Newspaper Design, 1989, 4 awards of excellence, 1990; artist in schs. grantee City of Seattle-Arts Commn., 1991-92. Democrat. Jewish. Office: The Seattle Times Fairview and John Sts Seattle WA 98111

FOX, RICHARD LORAIN, political science educator; b. Toledo, Ohio, Sept. 1, 1946; s. Jack Robert and Pauline Marie (Staschke) F.; m. Sylvia Anna Romero, Dec. 19, 1970; 1 child, Miles C.A. Student, U. Iowa, 1965-66; BA, U. N.Mex., 1975, MA, 1979. Legis. analyst City of Albuquerque City Coun., 1975-77; exec. asst. to pres. Monterey (Calif.) Inst. Internat. Studies, 1977-78; mgmt. analyst State of N.Mex. Fin. Dept., Santa Fe, 1980-88; lectr. U. N.Mex., Albuquerque, 1981—; instr. Albuquerque Tech.-Vocat. Inst., 1987—; free-lance cons. to govts. and mgmt., Albuquerque, 1988—. Contbr. articles to Century Mag., 1980-83, N.Mex. Mag., 1987. Named Young Democrat of Yr. Bernalillo County Young Democrats, Albuquerque, 1972. Mem. Acad. Polit. Sci. Democrat.

FOX, ROBERT AUGUST, food company executive; b. Norristown, Pa., Apr. 24, 1937; s. August Emil and Elizabeth Martha (Deimling) F.; m. Linda Lee Carnesale, Sept. 19, 1964; children: Lee Elizabeth, Christina Carolyn. B.A. with high honors, Colgate U., 1959; M.B.A. cum laude, Harvard U., 1964. Unit sales mgr. Procter & Gamble Co., 1959-62; gen. sales mgr. T.J. Lipton Co., 1964-69; v.p. mktg. Can. Dry Corp., 1969-72; pres., chief exec. officer, dir. Can. Dry Internat., 1972-75; exec. v.p., dir. Hunt-Wesson Foods, Inc., 1975-78; pres., chief exec. officer, dir. R.J. Reynolds Tobacco Internat. S.A., 1978-80; chmn., chief exec. officer, dir. Del Monte Corp., San Francisco, 1980-85; vice chmn. Nabisco Brands, Inc., East Hanover, N.J., 1986-87; pres., chief oper. officer Continental Can Co., Norwalk, Conn., 1988-90; chmn., chief exec. officer Clarke Hooper Am., Irvine, Calif., 1990-92, also bd. dirs.; pres. Revlon Internat., N.Y.C., 1992; pres., CEO Foster Farms, Livingston, Calif., 1993—; bd. dirs. New Perspective Fund, Growth Fund Am., Income Fund Am., Am. Balanced Fund, Clarke Hooper, plc, Crompton & Knowles Corp.; trustee Euro-Pacific Growth Fund. Trustee Colgate U. Mem. San Francisco C. of C. (bd. dir., pres. 1984), Pacific Union Club, The Olympic Club. Office: Foster Farms 1000 Davis St Livingston CA 95334

FOX, SHELLEY ZAPARA, accountant; b. Inglewood, Calif., Aug. 18, 1952; d. Tom M. and Violet J. (Boyko) Zapara; m. Jere Lamont Fox, Nov. 27, 1951; 1 child, Jackie Zapara Fox. BS in Acctg. and Fin., Calif. State U., Fullerton, 1974. CPA, Calif. Staff acct. Friedman, Blumenfeld, Weiser, Minsk and Kraemer, Century City, Calif., 1974-78; tax mgr., acct. Crabtree, Karlen and Arzoo, Riverside, Calif., 1979-86, tax ptnr., 1986—. Mem. AICPA, Am. Soc. Women Accts. (bull. chmn. 1986-90), Calif. Soc. CPAs, Toastmasters Club (treas. 1991-92), Rotary (sec. 1992—). Republican. Home: 2557 Chauncy Pl Riverside CA 92506 Office: Crabtree Karlen and Arzoo 5055 Canyon Crest Dr Riverside CA 92507

FOX, STUART IRA, physiologist; b. Bklyn., June 21, 1945; s. Sam and Bess F.; m. Ellen Diane Berley; 1 child, Laura Elizabeth. BA, UCLA, 1967; MA, Calif. State U., L.A., 1967; postgrad., U. Calif., Santa Barbara, 1969; PhD, U. So. Calif., 1978. Rsch. assoc. Children's Hosp., L.A., 1972; prof. physiology L.A. City Coll., 1972-85, Calif. State U., Northridge, 1979-84, Pierce Coll., 1986—; cons. William C. Brown Co. Pubs., 1976—. Author: Computer-Assisted Instruction in Human Physiology, 1979, Laboratory Guide to Human Physiology, 2d edit., 1980, 3d edit., 1984, 4th edit., 1987, 5th edit., 1990, 6th edit., 1993, Textbook of Human Physiology, 1984, 3d edit., 1990, 4th edit., 1993, Concepts of Human Anatomy and Physiology, 1986, 2d edit., 1989, 3d edit., 1992, Laboratory Guide to Human Anatomy and Physiology, 1986, 2d edit., 1989, 3d edit., 1992, Perspectives on Human Biology, 1991. Mem. AAAS, So. Calif. Acad. Sci., Am. Physiol. Soc., Sigma Xi. Home: 5556 Forest Cove Ln Agoura Hills CA 91301-4047 Office: Pierce Coll 6201 Winnetka Ave Woodland Hills CA 91371-0002

FOX, THOMAS GEORGE, health care educator, university administrator; b. N.Y.C., Sept. 15, 1942; s. Thomas Peter and Alice Cecilia (Ehler) F.; m. Mary Patricia Palmer, Aug. 29, 1980; children: Christopher Adam, Thomas Andrew, Stephen Baron. BA, Trenton State Coll., 1964; MEd, U. Vt., 1966; PhD, U. Mich., 1972. Asst. to dean U. Mass., Amherst, 1966; dir. counseling and student svcs. U. Mich., Ann Arbor, 1966-68, sr. adminstrv. asst. Med. Ctr., 1968-69, adminstrv. assoc., 1969-71; asst. dean Robert Wood Johnson Med. Sch., Piscataway, N.J., 1972-77, assoc. dean, 1977-83; sr. v.p. Robert Wood Johnson Univ. Hosp., New Brunswick, N.J., 1983-86; exec. v.p. U. Health System of N.J., New Brunswick, 1986-90; prof., v.p. devel. and univ. rels. Oreg. Health Scis. U., Portland, 1990—; CEO Univ. Found., 1990—; asst. prof. U. Medicine and Dentistry N.J., 1973-79, assoc. prof., 1979-83, clin. assoc. prof., 1983-90. Co-author Current Planning Projects and Related Studies in United States and Canadian Medical Schools and Teaching Hospitals, 1983; contbr. articles to profl. jours. Mem. Am. Coll. of Healthcare Execs., Assn. of American Med. Colls. (chair planners 1983). Home: 3147 NW 126th Pl Portland OR 97229-3990 Office: Oreg Health Scis U L101 Baird Hall 3181 SW Sam Jackson Park Rd Portland OR 97201-3098

FOXHOVEN, MICHAEL JOHN, retail and wholesale company executive, retail merchant; b. Sterling, Colo., Mar. 2, 1949; s. Mark John and Mary Kathryn (Hagerty) F.; m. Catherine Marie Carricaburu, Feb. 16, 1980; children—Patrick Michael, Rachel Marie. Student U. Colo., 1967-70, U. San Francisco, 1971-72, postgrad. Columbia Pacific U., 1987—. Comml. sales mgr. Goodyear Tire & Rubber Co., Denver, 1978-80, area sales mgr., 1980-81, store mgr., 1981-83, wholesale mgr., 1983-84, appeared in TV commls., 1972; v.p. Foxhovens, Inc., Sterling, 1984-89; cons. Foxhoven Bros., Inc., Sterling, 1984-89; gen. mgr. General Tire, Ventura, Calif., 1989-91; area sales mgr. Bridgestone/Firestone, L.A., 1991; pres. C & M Fin. Svcs., Camarillo, Calif., 1991—; area sales mgr. Bridgestone/Firestone L.A., 1991-92, dist. mgr., 1992—; participant dealer mgmt. seminar, Akron, Ohio, 1973, 85. Mem. mgmt. adv. com. Northeastern Jr. Coll., Sterling, 1976-78; sec. Highland Park Sanitation Dist., Sterling, 1984-89. Mem. Logan County C. of C. Republican. Roman Catholic. Club: Sterling Country. Lodges: Elks, Kiwanis. Office: C & M Fin Svcs 266 Camino Castanada Camarillo CA 93010-1832

FOXLEY, WILLIAM COLEMAN, cattleman; b. St. Paul, Jan. 7, 1935; s. William Joseph and Eileen (Conroy) F. BA, U. Notre Dame, 1957. Pres., chmn. bd. Foxley Cattle Co., Omaha, 1960—. Chmn. bd. Mus. Western Art, Denver. Served with USMCR, 1957-60. Republican. Roman Catholic. Office: Foxley Cattle Co 1727 Tremont Pl Denver CO 80202-4028

FOXX, DANIEL LEROY, JR., history educator; b. Gaffney, S.C., Mar. 19, 1939; s. Daniel LeRoy and Lois Olena (Brown) Fox; m. Mary-Helen Sears, May 30, 1964; children: Wade Patrick, Matthew Paul, Ethan Alexander, Reagan McNeill. BA, Brigham Young U., 1969, MA, 1970; MHL (hon.), Ottawa (Kans.) U., 1989. Instr. East Carolina U., Greenville, N.C., 1970-73; visiting prof. Glendale (Ariz.) Community Coll., 1973—; ops. mgr. Danner Industries, Inc., Phoenix, 1973-74; v.p. MFR Enterprises, Inc., Phoenix, 1974-76; rsch. assoc. Ariz. State Legis. Coun., Phoenix, 1976-77; rsch. coord. Ariz. Med. History Project, Phoenix, 1977-79; assoc. prof. Ottawa U. Phoenix, 1982—. Contbg. author: Applying Adult Development Strategies, 1990; editor Forward, 1990—. Speaker Ariz. State Atty. Gen., 1987. With U.S. Army, 1958-61. Republican. LDS Ch. Office: Ottawa U Phoenix 2340 W Mission Ln Phoenix AZ 85021-2818

FRADKIN, DAVID BARRY, aerospace research executive; b. Washington, Aug. 14, 1941; s. William Stanley and Gertrude (Hoffeld) F.; m. Judith Park, Jan. 2, 1964 (div. June 1976); children: Sheryl Lynn, Jonathan Matthew, Jesse Dor; m. Stacey Ann, Dec. 30, 1979; children: Jennifer Lynn, Benjamin M. BS in Engring., U. Md., 1963; MS in Engring., Princeton U., 1965, MA, 1970, PhD, 1972. Staff mem. Los Alamos (N.Mex.) Nat. Lab., 1965-74, asst. group leader, 1974-77, dep. group leader, 1977-78, group leader, 1978-85, program mgr., 1985-87; participated as program mgr. spl. isotope separation, Los Alamos Lab., 1985-87; sect. leader explosives applications group Los Alamos Lab, 1987—. Patentee isotope separation apparatus and method; contbr. over 20 articles to profl. jours. Religious chmn. Los Alamos Jewish Ctr., 1972-74, bd. dirs., 1972-74, 83-84, pres., 1990-91. Guggenheim fellow Princeton U., 1964. Mem. AAAS, AIAA, Am. Chem. Soc., N.Y. Acad. Scis., Sigma Xi, Tau Beta Pi, Omicron Delta Kappa. Democrat. Jewish. Clubs: Los Alamos Ski, Sports Car del Valle Rio Grand. Home: 24 Pilar St Los Alamos NM 87544-2664 Office: Los Alamos Nat Lab MS J-960 Los Alamos NM 87545

FRAHMANN, DENNIS GEORGE, computer company executive; b. Medford, Wis., June 25, 1953; s. George Henry and Aini (Siikarla) F. BA, Ripon Coll., 1974; MS, Columbia U., 1975; postgrad., U. Minn., 1978-79. Freelance writer Mpls., 1975-77; instnl. designer Control Data Corp., Mpls., 1977-80; mgr. customer edn. Xerox Corp., L.A., 1980-84; product mgr. Xerox Corp., Palo Alto, Calif., 1984-86; nat. mktg. mgr. Xerox Corp., L.A., 1986-87, mgr., cons. rels., 1989—; mgr. Xerox Systems Inst., L.A., 1987-89; bd. advisors Microcomputer Graphics Conf., N.Y.C., 1986-88. Contbg. editor Mpls.-St. Paul Mag., 1977-80; contbr. articles to profl. publs., chpt. to book. Mem. Mcpl. Election Com. L.A., 1985—; mem. SilverLake Improvement Assn., L.A., 1989—; pres. Hyperion Neighborhood Assn., L.A., 1989—. Wingspread fellow Johnson Found., 1971-74. Mem. Phi Beta Kappa. Office: Xerox Corp 101 Continental Blvd El Segundo CA 90245-4530

FRAITAG, LEONARD ALAN, mechanical and design engineer; b. N.Y.C., Dec. 23, 1961; s. David and Lucille Reneé (Jay) F.; m. Dorann Elizabeth Meecham, June 28, 1987; children: Shoshana Elizabeth, Aaron Joseph. BSME, San Diego State U., 1987; AA, Grossmont Coll., 1983. Registered profl. engr., Calif. Design engr. Restaurant Concepts, San Diego, 1987; mech. engr. Vantage Assocs., Inc., San Diego, 1988-89; design engr. Mainstream Engring. Co., Inc., San Diego, 1989, Pilkington Barnes Hind, San Diego, 1989—. Inventor safe product moving device for contact lens. Mem. Masons (officer 1988—), Shriners (noble 1989), Scottish Rite (class pres. 1989), Pi Tau Sigma. Office: Pilkington Barnes Hind 8006 Engineer Rd San Diego CA 92111-1975

FRAKER, MARK ARNOTT, environmental scientist; b. Columbus, Ind., Dec. 13, 1944; s. Ralph Waldo and Carol (Arnott) F.; m. Pamela Norton, May 27, 1967 (div. Feb. 1985); 1 child, Russell; m. Donice Horton, Aug. 23, 1986. BA with honors, Ind. U., 1967, MA, 1969. Biologist, project mgr. F.F. Slaney and Co., Vancouver, Can., 1972-78; biologist, project dir. LGL Ltd., Sidney, B.C., Can., 1978-82; sr. environ. scientist BP Exploration (Alaska) Inc., Anchorage, 1982-91; wildlife, restoration program mgr. divsn. oil spill impact assessment & restoration Alaska Dept. Fish and Game, Anchorage, 1991-93; pvt. practice consulting biologist Sidney, B.C., Can., 1993—; broadcaster CBC, Vancouver, 1970-72; mem. sci. com. Internat. Whaling Com., Cambridge, Eng., 1982-91; adj. prof. U. Alaska, Anchorage, 1985-89; mem. panel NAS, 1987-92; mem. rescue team Barrow Gray Whale Rescue, 1988; mem. adv. com. on polar programs NSF, 1988-90. Author: Balaena mysticetus, 1984; also articles; mem. editorial bd. Biol. Papers of the U. of Alaska. Amb. to Peru, Anchorage Olympic Organizing Com., 1986-89. Woodrow Wilson fellow, Princeton, N.J., 1967. Mem. AAAS, Am. Soc. Mammalogists, Arctic Inst. N.Am., Ottawa Field Naturalists' Club, Can. Soc. Zoologists, Soc. for Marine Mammalogy, The Wildlife Soc., Sigma Xi.

FRAKES, GEORGE EDWARD, history educator; b. L.A., May 12, 1932; s. Samuel Franklin and Frances Mary (Fountaine) F.; m. Catherine Rose Davies, Aug. 7, 1954; children: James B., Laura Lee, Robert M. AB, Stanford U., 1954, AM, 1958; PhD, U. Calif., Santa Barbara, 1966. Cert. tchr. Tchr., counselor Santa Barbara City Schs., 1958-62; from instr. to asst. prof. Santa Barbara City Coll., 1962-65, assoc. prof., 1966-72, prof., dept. chmn., 1972-90; manuscript evaluator fo pub. firms, 1968—; disting. faculty lectr. Santa Barbara City Coll., 1985-86; recipient medal-Nat. Teaching award NISOD, U. Tex., Austin, 1989. Author: Laboratory for Liberty, 1971, From Columbus to Aquarius, 1976; editor: Minorities in California History, 1971, Pollution Papers, 1971; book reviewer varous jours. Mem. adv. com. City Charter Revision Com., Santa Barbara, 1978. Recipient award Nat. Inst. Staff and Orgnl. Devel. U. Tex., Austin, 1989. Mem. Calif. Tchrs. Assn. (local pres. 1978-79), Am. Hist. Assn. (com. on teaching 1976-77), Santa Barbara Hist. Soc., Santa Barbara Trust for Hist. Preservation, The Retired Officers Assn. (local bd. dirs. 1989-90), La Cumbre Golf and Country Club, Sigma Chi. Episcopalian. Home: 735 Willowglen Rd Santa Barbara CA 93105-2439 Office: Santa Barbara City Coll Dept History 721 Cliff Dr Santa Barbara CA 93109-2394

FRAKNOI, ANDREW, astronomical society executive, educator; b. Budapest, Hungary, Aug. 24, 1948; came to U.S., 1959; naturalized; s. Emery I. and Katherine H. (Schmidt) F.; m. Lola Goldstein, Aug. 16, 1992. B.A. in Astronomy, Harvard U., 1970; M.A. in Astrophysics, U. Calif.-Berkeley, 1972. Instr. astronomy and physics Cañada Coll., Redwood City, Calif., 1972-78; exec. dir. Astron. Soc. of Pacific, San Francisco, 1978-92; chmn. dept. astronomy Foothill Coll., Los Altos, Calif., 1992—; part-time prof. San Francisco State U., 1980-92; dir. Project ASTRO Astron. Soc. Pacific, 1992—; fellow Com. for Sci. Investigation of Claims of Paranormal, 1984—; bd. dirs. Search for Extra Terrestrial Intelligence Inst., Palo Alto, Calif., 1984—; host radio program Exploring the Universe Sta. KGO-FM, San Francisco, 1983-84; rev. panelist informal sci. edn. NSF, 1989-93; adv. com. Astrophysics div. NASA, 1992—. Author: Resource Book for the Teaching of Astronomy, 1978, (with others) Effective Astronomy Teaching and Student Reasoning Ability, 1978, Universe in the Classroom, 1985, (with R. Robert Robbins) The Universe at Your Fingertips, 1985, (with T. Robertson) Instructor's Guide to the Universe, 1991, (with Douglas Brown) Instructor's Manual to Discovering the Universe, 1993; editor: The Planets, 1985, Interdisciplinary Approaches to Astronomy, 1985, The Universe, 1987; editor Mercury Mag., 1978-92, The Universe in the Classroom Newsletter, 1985-92; assoc. editor: The Planetarian, 1986-88; columnist monthly column on astronomy San Francisco Examiner, 1986-87 and others. Bd. dirs. Bay Area Skeptics, San Francisco, 1982-91. Recipient award of merit Astron. Assn. No. Calif., 1980; Asteroid 4859 named Asteroid Fraknoi, 1992. Mem. AAAS (astronomy sect. com. 1988-92), Am. Astron. Soc. (astronomy edn. adv. bd. 1988—), Astron. Soc. Pacific (dir. ASTRO project), Am. Assn. Physics Tchrs., Nat. Assn. Sci. Writers, No. Calif. Sci. Writers Assn. (program chmn. 1983-85). Office: Foothill Coll Dept Astronomy 12345 El Monte Rd Los Altos CA 94022

FRAME, JOHN MCELPHATRICK, theology educator, pastor; b. Pitts., Apr. 8, 1939; s. Clark Crawford and Violet Luella (McElphatrick) F.; children by previous marriage: Deborah Rubio, Doreen Kester, David O'Donnell; m. Mary Grace Cummings, June 2, 1984; children: Justin Michael, John Alden. BA, Princeton U., 1961; BD, Westminster Theol. Sem., 1964; MPhil, Yale U., 1968. Ordained to ministry, Orthodox Presbyn. Ch., 1968. Instr. to assoc. prof. apologetics and systematic theology Westminster Theol. Sem., Phila., 1968-80; assoc. prof. apologetics and systematic theology Westminster Theol. Sem., Escondido, Calif., 1987—, prof. apologetics and systematic theology, 1988—; assoc. pastor New Life Presbyn. Ch., Escondido, 1988—, pianist, worship leader, 1980—. Author: Doctrine of Knowledge of God, 1987, Medical Ethics, 1988, Evangelical Reunion, 1991; contbr. many articles to profl. jours. Mem. Evang. Theol. Soc., Soc. Christian Philosophers, Am. Guild Organists, Am. Choir Dirs. Assn. Republican. Home: 3572 Prince St Escondido CA 92025 Office: Westminster Theol Sem 1725 Bear Valley Pkwy Escondido CA 92027

FRAME, LEONARD W., farmer; b. Selma, Calif., Oct. 27, 1917; s. William W. and Olive Fay (Flint) F.; m. Cynthia Claybaugh, Jan. 7, 1942; children: Patricia Rugola, William L. Student, Calif. State Poly., 1935-38. Dairy farmer Fresno, Calif., 1946-72, almond farmer, 1973—; v.p. All West Breeders, Burlington, Wash., 1948-78. Chmn. bd. trustees First Ch. of God, Fresno, 1984-89; dir. Fresno chpt. 110th Air Force Assn., 1948—. Lt. col. USAAF, 1941-45. Decorated D.F.C., Air medal with six oak leaf clusters, Purple Heart. Republican. Ch. of God Anderson, Ind. Home: 3362 N De Wolf Fresno CA 93727

FRAME, TED RONALD, lawyer; b. Milw., June 27, 1929; s. Morris and Jean (Lee) F.; student UCLA, 1946-49; AB, Stanford U., 1950, LLB, 1952; m. Lois Elaine Pilgrim, Aug. 15, 1954; children: Kent, Lori, Nancy, Owen. Bar: Calif. 1953. Gen. agri-bus. practice, Coalinga, Calif., 1953—; sr. ptnr. Frame & Matsumoto, 1965—. Trustee, Baker Mus. Mem. ABA, Calif. Bar Assn., Fresno County Bar Assn., Coalinga C. of C. (past pres.), Masons, Shriners, Elks. Home: 1222 Nevada St Coalinga CA 93210-1239 Office: 201 Washington St Coalinga CA 93210

FRANCE, JOHN LYONS, air force officer; b. Forest City, Mo., Sept. 11, 1933; s. Calvert Glen and Gertrude May (Lyons) F.; B.A. in English, U. Denver, 1963, J.D., 1966; m. Carole Jean Denton, Sept. 16, 1961; children—Allison Lisa, Amy Denton. Commd. 2d lt. USAF, advanced through grades to maj. gen.; now adj. gen., State Colo., Denver; flight leader Colo. Air N.G., later squadron comdr., group comdr., wing comdr. Mem. Air Res. Forces Policy Com.; mem. Tactical Air Command Res. Forces Policy Counil. Decorated D.F.C., Air medal with ten oak leaf clusters. Mem. ABA, Colo. Bar Assn., Air Force Assn. Office: Military Affairs Dept 6848 S Revere Pky Englewood CO 80112-6703

FRANCESCHI, ERNEST JOSEPH, JR., lawyer; b. L.A., Feb. 1, 1957; s. Ernest Joseph and Doris Cecilia (Beluche) F. BS, U. So. Calif., 1978; JD, Southwestern U., L.A., 1980. Bar: Calif. 1984, U.S. Dist. Ct. (cen. dist.) Calif. 1984, U.S. Dist. Ct. (ea. dist.) Calif. 1986, U.S. Dist. Ct. (no. and so. dists.) Calif. 1987, U.S. Ct. Appeals (9th cir.) 1984, U.S. Supreme Ct. 1989. Pvt. practice law L.A., 1984—. Mem. Assn. Trial Lawyers Am., Calif. Trial Lawyers Assn., L.A. Trial Lawyers Assn., Trial Lawyers for Pub. Justice. Office: 12121 Wilshire Blvd Ste 505 Los Angeles CA 90025

FRANCHINI, GENE EDWARD, state supreme court justice; b. Albuquerque, May 19, 1935; s. Mario and Lena (Vaio) F.; m. Glynn Hatchell, Mar. 22, 1969; children: Pamela, Lori (dec.), Gina, Joseph James, Nancy. BBA, Loyola U., 1955; degree in adminstrn., U. N.Mex., 1957; JD, Georgetown U., 1960. Bar: N.Mex. 1960, U.S. Dist. Ct. N.Mex. 1961, U.S. Ct. Appeals (10th cir.) 1970, U.S. Supreme Ct. 1973. Ptnr. Matteucci, Gutierrez & Franchini, Albuquerque, 1960-70, Matteucci, Franchini & Calkins, Albuquerque, 1970-75; judge State of N.Mex. 2d Jud. Dist., Albuquerque, 1975-81; atty.-at-large Franchini, Wagner, Oliver, Franchini & Curtis, Albuquerque, 1982-90; justice N.Mex. Supreme Ct., Santa Fe, 1990—. Chmn. Albuquerque Pers. Bd., 1972, Albuquerque Labor Rels. Bd., 1972, Albuquerque Interim Bd. Ethics, 1972. Capt. USAF, 1960-66. Mem. Am. Bd. Trial Advocates, N.Mex. Trial Lawyers (pres. 1967-68), N.Mex. Bar Assn. (bd. dirs. 1976-78), Albuquerque Bar Assn. (bd. dirs. 1976-78). Democrat. Roman Catholic. Home: PO Box 75327 Albuquerque NM 87194-0327 Office: NMex Supreme Ct PO Box 848 Santa Fe NM 87504-0848

FRANCIS, MARC BARUCH, pediatrician; b. Rochester, N.Y., Mar. 3, 1934; s. Nathan and Beverly (Salsburg) F.; A.B., U. Rochester, 1955; M.D., N.Y. U., 1959; m. Janet Irene Harding, Sept. 21, 1960; children—Josephine, Teresa, Jacqueline, Wallace. Intern, Los Angeles County Harbor Gen. Hosp.,

1959-60; resident in pediatrics Children's Hosp. of Los Angeles, 1960-62; practice medicine specializing in pediatrics, Salt Lake City, 1962-65; clin. instr. pediatrics U. Utah Med. Sch., 1962-70; chief dept. pediatrics Cottonwood Hosp., 1963-65; partner dept. pediatrics Permanente Med. Group Inc., Napa, Calif., 1971—, chief dept., 1982-86. Served to capt. M.C., USAF, 1966-68. Diplomate Am. Bd. Pediatrics. Fellow Am. Acad. Pediatrics; mem. Calif. Med. Assn., Napa County Med. Soc. Clubs: NYU, U. Rochester Alumni. Office: Permanente Med Group Inc 3285 Claremont Way Napa CA 94558-3313

FRANCIS, PETER DAVID, lawyer; b. Seattle, Oct. 28, 1934; s. Jack Albert and Alice Elizabeth (Scudder) F.; m. L. Elva Green, May 30, 1959; children: Thomas Michael, Daniel Green. BA in Polit. Sci., Stanford U., 1956, JD, 1961. Bar: Wash. 1963, D.C. 1963, U.S. Supreme Ct. 1973. Law clk. to justice Wash. Supreme Ct., Olympia, 1961-62; instr. law sch. U. Wash., Seattle, 1962-63; assoc. Garvin, Ashley and Foster, Seattle, 1963-64, Schroeter, Farris, Bangs and Horowitz, Seattle, 1964-65, Offices of Erik Froberg, Seattle, 1965-67; sr. ptnr. Francis and Ackerman, Seattle, 1967-87, Francis & Nichols, Seattle, 1987-92; pvt. practice Seattle, 1992—. Senator Wash. Legislature, Olympia, 1969-78; congl. redistricting commn., Seattle, 1982. With USMC, 1956-59. Named Hon. mem. NOW, Seattle, 1971. Mem. Wash. State Trial Lawyers Assn. (legislator of yr. 1978), Wash. Athletic Club, Met. Dem. Club (bd. dirs., pres. 1987-89), Lions (pres. North cen. chpt. 1976), Green Lake C. of C. (pres. 1970-72, 75-77). Presbyterian. Home: 6026 2d Ave NW Seattle WA 98107 Office: Law Offices Peter D Francis 7310 E Green Lake Dr N Seattle WA 98115-5304

FRANCIS, RICHARD NORMAN, geologist, consultant; b. Fresno, Calif., Feb. 4, 1949; s. Norman Waren and Lois (Mahaffy) F.; m. J.D. Hammers, Nov. 24, 1990. AA, Sierra Coll., 1970; BS, U. Nev., 1972, postgrad., 1985—. Laborer Pacific Gas and Electric Co., Quincy, Calif., 1967-71; technician Soil Conservation Svc., Reno, 1972; geologist Continental Oil Co., Reno, 1973, Internat. Minerals and Chems. Co., Reno, 1974-75, Urania Explorations, Inc., Reno, 1976-78, Corona Gold Co., Reno, 1979-82; cons. geologist Reno, 1982-86, F&M Exploration, Reno, 1986—; geology cons. Denimill Resources, Mont., Corona Gold, Nev., Calif., Atlas Corp., Nev., P.R.C., Inc., Nev. Transwestern Engring Co., Nev., 1982-86, Kleinfelder Engring., Inc., 1991, Nevada Gold, Inc., 1992. Fed. congl. lobyist Amnesty Internat., London, 1980; fed. congl. rep. mineral and petroleum industry, Washington, 1987, Nev. petroleum industry, 1991; state congl. lobbyist rep. mineral industry, Carson City, Nev., 1987. Mem. Am. Soc. Photogrammetry and Remote Sensing (cert., fed. congl. rep. 1988), Nev. Petroleum Soc. (membership com. 1988—), Am. Assn. of Petroleum Geologist. Mem. Bahai Faith. Office: F&M Exploration PO Box 9028 Reno NV 89507-9028

FRANCIS, TIMOTHY DUANE, chiropractor; b. Chgo., Mar. 1, 1956; s. Joseph Duane and Barbara Jane (Sigwalt) F. Student, U. Nev., 1974-80, We. Nev. C.C., 1978; BS, L.A. Coll. Chiropractic, 1982, Dr. of Chiropractic magna cum laude, 1984; postgrad., Clark County Community Coll., 1986—; MS in Bio/Nutrition, U. Bridgeport, 1990. Diplomate Internat. Coll. Applied Kinesiology, Am. Acad. Pain Mgmt.; cert. kinesiologist; lic. chiropractor, Calif., Nev. Instr. dept. recreation and phys. edn. U. Nev., Reno, 1976-80; from tchng. asst. to lead instr. dept. principles & practice L.A. Coll. Chiropractic, 1983-85; pvt. practice Las Vegas, 1985—; asst. instr. Internat. Coll. Applied Kinesiology, 1990. Recipient Key award, 1990, Internat. Cultural Diploma of Hon., 1991. Fellow Internat. Acad. Clin. Acupuncture; mem. Am. Chiropractic Assn. (couns. on sports injuries, nutrition, roentgenology, technic, and mental health), Nev. State Chiropractic Assn., Nat. Strength and Conditioning Assn., Gonsted Clin. Studies Soc., Found. for Chiropractic Edn. and Rsch., Nat. Inst. Chiropractic Rsch., Nat. Acad. Rsch. Biochemists. Republican. Roman Catholic. Home: 3750 S Jones Las Vegas NV 89103

FRANCISCO, WAYNE M(ARKLAND), automotive executive; b. Cin., June 14, 1943; s. George Lewis and Helen M. (Markland) F. Student, Ohio State U., 1962-63; BS in Mktg. and Acctg., U. Cin., 1967; m. Susan Francisco; children: Diana Lynn, W. Michael. Unit sales mgr. Procter & Gamble, Cin., 1967-69; mktg. mgr. Nat. Mktg. Inc., Cin., 1969-70; pres. Retail Petroleum Marketers, Inc., Cin., 1970-72, chmn. bd., chief exec. officer, Phoenix, 1972-85; chmn. bd., chief exec. officer DMC Industries, Inc., 1985—; pres., chief exec. officer Cassia Petroleum Corp., Vancouver, B.C., Can., 1980-84; bd. dirs. P.F.K. Enterprises, F.I.C. Inc., Internat. Investment and Fin. Enterprises, Inc., Alpha Realty, Inc. Class agt. 62G Culver Mil. Acad., 1987-91. Mem. Culver Legion (bd. trustees 1990—), Eugene C. Eppley Club, Phoenix Bd. Appeals, 1978-80; v.p. Cuernavaca Homeowners Assn., 1982, pres., 1983-86. Recipient Image Maker award Shell Oil Co., 1979; Top Performer award Phoenix dist. Shell Oil Co., 1979, 80. Mem. Petroleum Retailers Ariz. (pres. 1977-79), Nat. Congress Petroleum Retailers (adv. bd.), Automotive Svc. Excellence (cert.), Culver Legion (life), Studebaker Drivers Club (zone coord. Pacific S.W. 1983, nat. v.p. 1986, 87, 88, nat. pres. 1989-90, Grand Canyon chpt. pres. 1986), Avanti Owners Assn. (nat. bd. dirs. 1975-91, internat. pres. 1986-89). Republican. Lodge: Optimists (bd. dirs. Paradise Valley club 1984, sec.-treas. 1984). Office: 21824 N 19th Ave Phoenix AZ 85027-2101

FRANCO, JORGE, pathologist; b. Ica, Peru, June 9, 1929; s. Fortunato and Sabina (Cabrera) F.; B.S., San Marcos U., 1947, M.D., 1955; m. Mary Loretta Jones, Sept. 19, 1957; children—Mary Pat, Lori, Ann Marie, Raymond Joseph, Stephen Michael. Came to U.S., 1955. Intern, Bon Secours Hosp., Balt., 1955-56; fellow medicine Stanford Med. Sch., 1956-58, asst. clin. prof. nuclear medicine, 1969-76, assoc. clin. prof., 1976—; resident pathology O'Connor Hosp., San Jose, Calif., 1958-62, assoc. pathologist, 1963—, chief clin. pathology, dir. nuclear medicine, 1968—. Diplomate Am. Bd. Pathology, Am. Bd. Nuclear Medicine. Mem. Am. Fedn. Clin. Research, Am. Soc. Clin. Pathologists, Am. Soc. Hematology, Am. Assn. Blood Banks, Soc. Nuclear Medicine, Am. Inst. Ultrasonics in Medicine, AMA, Calif. Med. Assn., Calif. Soc. Pathologists, Am. Thermographic Soc., Calif. Acad. Medicine, N.Y. Acad. Scis. Contbr. articles to profl. jours.; also clin. and lab. research. Home: 1259 N Central Ave San Jose CA 95128-3105 Office: O'Connor Hosp Tumor Ctr San Jose CA 95128

FRANCO, MADELEINE, communications executive; b. Englewood, N.J., Nov. 10, 1949; d. Manuel Paul and Marthe Margaret (Raymond) F.; m. Richard Edward Bernot, Nov. 20, 1979; children: Richard Alexander, Jordan Edward. BS in Communications summa cum laude, Westminster Coll., Salt Lake City, 1989. Sales staff Nat. Broadcasting Co., N.Y.C., 1968-73; govt. trading staff Goldman, Sachs & Co., N.Y.C., 1974-77, E.F. Hutton, N.Y.C., 1977-78; exec. asst. to dir. Assoc. Western Univs., Salt Lake City, 1979-86; pres. Jordan Richard Assocs./Publicity Ink, Salt Lake City, 1985—. Editor: Teaching Beginning Dance Improvisation, 1990; contbr. articles to profl. jours. Bd. dirs. Ririe-Woodbury Dance Co., chmn., 1989-90; mem. MountainWest Venture Group. The Berkeley Sch. acad. scholar, 1967-68, Westminster Coll. scholar, 1985-89. Mem. Pub. Rels. Soc. Am. (accredited 1992), Utah Assn. Women Bus. Owners (bd. dirs. 1990-91), Alpha Chi. Office: Jordan Richard Assocs 350 S 400 East Ste 206 Salt Lake City UT 84111

FRANCO, MAURICE, physician; b. Lima, Peru, Dec. 6, 1950; came to U.S., 1975; s. Isacco and Esther (Jerusalmi) F.; m. Valerie Remitz; 1 child, Adrian. MD, U. Peruana Cayetano Heredia, Lima, 1974. Diplomate Am. Bd. Internal Medicine, Am. Bd. Pulmonary Disease. Resident internal medicine Baylor Coll. Medicine, Houston, 1975-78, pulmonary fellow, 1978-80; respiratory physiology and biochemistry fellow Stanford (Calif.) U. Sch. Medicine, 1980-82; chief pulmonary diseases, med. dir. respiratory care Kaiser Found. Med. Ctr., Hayward, Calif., 1982—. Fellow Am. Coll. Chest Physicians; mem. Am. Thoracic Soc. Office: 27400 Hesperian Blvd Hayward CA 94545

FRANGOPOL, DAN MIRCEA, civil engineering educator; b. Bucharest, Ilfov, Romania, July 28, 1946; came to U.S., 1983; s. Ioan Mircea and Mariana (Stoenescu) F.; married; children: Andrea D., Radu C. BS, Inst. Civil Engring., Bucharest, 1969; PhD, U. Liege, Belgium, 1976. Asst. prof. Inst. Civil Engring., Bucharest, 1969-74; rsch. engr. U. Liege, 1974-76; assoc. prof. Inst. Civil Engring., Bucharest, 1977-79; project engr. A. Lipski Cons. Engrs., Brussels, 1979-83; assoc. prof. civil engring. U. Colo., Boulder, 1983-88, prof. civil engring., 1988—; lectr. univs. in Europe, N.Am., Japan, 1983—; cons. Transp. Rsch. Bd., Washington, 1989-92; vis. sr. scientist Royal Norwegian Coun. for Sci. and Indsl. Rsch., Trondheim, summers 1990, 92; vis. prof. U. Waterloo, Can., 1991, Nat. Def. Acad., Yokosuka, Japan, 1989, Swiss Fed. Inst. Tech., Lausanne, Switzerland, summer 1989. Author one book; editor two books; mem. editorial bd. internat. jours.; contbr. over 80 articles to profl. jours. Grantee NSF, 1986—, Fed. Hwy. Adminstrn., 1988-91, U.S. Army Corps Engrs., 1989—, Colo. Dept. Hwys., 1992—; rsch. and teaching award civil engring. U. Colo., 1987, 88. Mem. ASCE (chmn. com. on safety of bldgs., 1990—), Am. Concrete Inst., Earthquake Engring. Rsch. Inst., Internat. Assn. for Bridge and Structural Engring., Transp. Rsch. Bd. Office: U Colo Dept Civil Engring CB-428 Boulder CO 80309-0428

FRANK, ALAN, retired psychiatry educator; b. N.Y.C., May 16, 1922; s. Lawrence Kelso and Alice Vermandoir (Bryant) F.; m. Louise Thompson, 1956 (dec. 1964); children: Alexandra, Margaret, Lucia; m. Anita Magnus, May, 1969; 1 child, Loren. BA, Columbia U., 1944, MD, 1949. Diplomate Am. Bd. Med. Examiners; cert. Am. Bd. Psychiatry and Neurology. Head psychiat. div. Student Health Service U. Colo., Boulder, 1956-67; psychiatrist Health Service Pa. State U., State College, 1967-68; asst. prof. psychiatry U. N.Mex., Albuquerque, 1968-92, prof. emeritus, 1992—; cons. in field, 1969—. Fellow Am. Psychiat. Assn. (life), Am. Orthopsychiat. Assn., AAAS, ACP; mem. N.Y. Acad. Scis. Office: 8602 Aztec Rd NE Albuquerque NM 87111-4506

FRANK, DONALD HERBERT, minister; b. Rochester, N.Y., May 12, 1931; s. Oscar Edward and Mary Charlotte (Morgan) F.; m. Anne Sadlon, Aug. 27, 1955; children: Donna Lynn Frank Bertsch, John Edward, James David. BA, Bloomfield (N.J.) Coll., 1954; MDiv, McCormick Theol. Sem., 1957, MA, 1966; DD, Coll. of Idaho, 1980. Ordained to ministry Presbyn. Ch., 1957. Asst. pastor Hamburg (N.Y.) Presbyn. Ch., 1957-60; min. Christian edn. 1st Presbyn. Ch., Pompano Beach, Fla., 1960-63, First Presbyn. Ch., Santa Ana, Calif., 1966-69, Northminister Presbyn. Ch., Evanston, Ill., 1963-66; assoc. pastor Bellflower (Calif.) Presbyn. Ch., 1969-74; pastor Boone Meml. Presbyn. Ch., Caldwell, Idaho, 1974-87; organizing pastor Covenant Presbyn. Ch., Reno, Nev., 1987—; commr. Synod of Pacific, San Anselmo, Calif., 1977-81, 89—. Bd. dirs. Metro Ministry Interfaith Agy., Reno, 1988, Washoe at Risk Task Force on Pub. Edn., Reno, 1988. With USNR, 1948-53. Mem. Rotary. Democrat. Office: Covenant Presbyn Ch 3690 Grant Dr Ste 1A Reno NV 89509-5366

FRANK, DONNA, artist, jewelry designer; b. Crested Butte, Colo., Mar. 25, 1957; d. Robert M. and Pearl (Jorgensen) F.; m. Joe Allen Wilbanks, Aug. 23, 1989. BS in Chemistry, Anthropology, Cornell U., 1972, MA in Motivational Psychology, 1973, PhD in Anthropology, Archaeology, 1976. Anthropologist Africa, 1971; archaeologist Alaskan task force U.S. Dept. of Interior, 1973-74; archaeologist Israel, 1972-73, Mesa Verde (Colo.) Nat. Park, 1982-83; artist, jewelry designer Artists' Loft, Durango, Colo., 1979—; profl. ski instr., Durango, 1980—. Presenter solo exhbns., Denver, Albuquerque, Sacramento, Dallas, Durango; participant in juried shows. Interpretive archaeologist, educator local schs. and youth orgns. Mem. Durango Arts Ctr. and Gallery Assn., Durango Area Chamber, Profl. Ski Instrs. Am. (cert.). Office: Artists' Loft 863 1/2 Main Ave Durango CO 81301

FRANK, GERALD DUANE, postmaster; b. Billings, Mont., Sept. 11, 1948; s. Herman and Elsie (Ostwald) F.; m. Jody Lee Koford, Apr. 28, 1973; children: Jeremy Ryan, Jillian Katherine. Student, Coll. Great Falls, 1970-71, U. Mont., 1984-85. Letter carrier U.S. Postal Svc., Missoula, Mont., 1971-81; PTF clk. U.S. Postal Svc., Kalispell, Mont., 1981-83; postmaster U.S. Postal Svc., Superior, Mont., 1983—; facilitator USPS Rural Employee Involvement, Western Mont., 1989—; inspector USPS 2d Class Codre Team, Western Mont., 1988-91, USPS Audit Team, Western Mont., 1992—; trainer USPS Postmaster Tng., Western Mont., 1988-90. City councilman Superior City Coun., 1987; bd. dirs., treas. Superior C. of C., 1984-90. With USAF, 1967-71, Vietnam. Mem. NAt. Assn. Postmasters (v.p. 1991—, pres. 1993), VFS, Lions (v.p. 1992—). Roman Catholic. Home: 1093 Mullan Rd E Superior MT 59872 Office: US Postal Svc 102 N River St Superior MT 59872

FRANK, LAWRENCE ROBERT, internist; b. N.Y.C., Jan. 4, 1944; s. Ernest and Hilda (Albersheim) F.; m. Nancy Thorner, 1970 (div. 1974). BA, NYU, 1965, MD, 1970. Diplomate Am. Bd. Internal Medicine and Nephrology. Intern straight medicine Lincoln Hosp., Bronx, N.Y., 1970-71; resident first yr. medicine Met. Hosp., N.Y.C., 1971-72; med. dir. hemodialysis San Joaquin Gen. Hosp., Stockton, Calif., 1979—, chmn. infection control com., 1979—; asst. clin. prof. medicine U. Calif., Davis, 1983—; pvt. practice Stockton, 1980—. Editor Sundance Running Club Newsletter, 1990-91. Capt. USAF, 1972-74. Fellow ACP. Office: San Joaquin Gen Hosp PO Box 1020 Stockton CA 95201

FRANK, ROBERT JOSEPH, academic administrator, English educator; b. Dickinson, N.D., July 4, 1939; s. Ralph and Rose (Schoch) F.; m. Arva Marie Utter, Aug. 15, 1964; children: Kirsten, Andrew. BA cum laude, St. John's U., Collegeville, Minn., 1962; MA, U. Minn., 1968, PhD, 1969. Asst. prof. English Oreg. State U., Corvallis, 1969-70, Ea. Mich. U., Ypsilanti, 1970-71; with Oreg. State U., Corvallis, 1971—, chair dept. English, 1978—, prof. English, 1983—; instnl. rep. Nat. Collegiate Athletic Assn., 1987—; interim vice chancellor for acad. affairs Oreg. State System Higher Edn., Eugene, 1990-91; cons. Poet Lore, Washington, 1981-89; gen. editor: N.W. Reprint Series, Oreg. State U., 1988—; institutional rep. NCAA, 1987—; acting provost Portland State U., 1991-92. Author: Don't Call Me Gentle Charles: A Reading of Lamb's Essays, 1976; co-editor: The Pacific Northwest: A Region in Myth and Reality, 1983, The Grains or Passages in the Life of Ruth Rover, 1986, The Line in Postmodern Poetry, 1988. Office: Oreg State U English Dept Moreland Hall Corvallis OR 97331

FRANK, STEPHEN RICHARD, lawyer; b. Portland, Oreg., Dec. 13, 1942; s. Richard Sigmund Frank and Paula Anne (Latz) Lewis; divorced; children: Richard Sigmund II, Theresa Anne; m. Patricia Lynn Graves, Aug. 20, 1988; stepchildren: Brian Kinney, Mathew Kinney. AB in Econs., U. Calif., Berkeley, 1964; JD, Willamette U., 1967. Bar: Oreg., U.S. Ct. Appeals (9th cir.), U.S. Supreme Ct. Assoc. Tooze, Shenker, Duden, Creamer, Frank and Hutchison, Portland, 1967-72, ptnr., 1972—; mem. audit com. Seligman & Latz NYSE, 1981-85, bd. dirs. 1976-85. Editor Willamette Law Jour., 1967. Trustee, sec. Oreg. High Desert Mus., 1977-86; sec., bd. dirs. Palatine Hill Water Dist., 1973-77; bd. dirs. Emanuel Hosp. Found., 1980-83, Portland Ctr. for Visual Arts, 1977-82. Mem. ABA, Assn. Trial Lawyers Am., Oreg. Trial Lawyers Assn., Oreg. State Bar Assn. (dir., sec. minority scholarship program 1981—, sec.-chmn. com. worker's compensation 1974-77), Oreg. Assn. Ins. Def. Counsel, Oreg. Assn. Workers Compensation Def. Counsel. Clubs: Multnomah Athletic; City (Portland). Home: 3103 SW Cascade Dr Portland OR 97201-1813 Office: Tooze Shenker et al 333 SW Taylor St Portland OR 97204-2496

FRANKE, DANIEL DAVID, photographer; b. Seattle, May 18, 1965; s. David August and Patricia Lou (Morrison) F. AA, Art Inst., Seattle, 1988. Head photographer Ackerley Communications Inc., Seattle, 1989-92; owner, operator Dan Franke Photography, Seattle, 1990—; chief exec. officer Pallone Espresso Co., Bellevue, Wash., 1992—; ptnr. SHOTS Inc., Bellevue, 1992—. Office: 2517 42d Ave E Seattle WA 98112

FRANKE, RICHARD HOMER, mathematics educator; b. Herndon, Kans., Apr. 11, 1937; s. Claude E. and Beulah E. (Tannehill) F.; m. J. Amelia Franklin, July 6, 1963; children: Evan, Tanna, Hailey. BS in Math. and Physics, Ft. Hays State U., 1959; MS in Math., U. Utah, 1961, PhD in Math., 1970. Teaching asst. U. Utah, Salt Lake City, 1959-61, teaching assoc., 1966-70, vis. prof., 1977; rsch. engr. Boeing Co., 1961-64; rsch. scientist Kaman Nuclear, Colorado Springs, Colo., 1964-66; from asst. prof. to prof. Naval Postgrad. Sch., Monterey, Calif., 1970-84, prof. math., 1984—, chmn. math., 1992—; vis. prof. Drexel U., Phila., 1980-81; liaison scientist Office Naval Rsch., London, 1988-89. Editor: Information Linkage between Applied Mathematics and Industry, 1980; contbr. articles to profl. jours. Mem., fund raiser Am. Field Svc. chpt. York Sch., Monterey, 1983-86; mem. AFS chpt. Carmel High Sch., 1984-90. Mem. Soc. for Indsl. and Applied Math., Slant 6 Club Am., Sigma Xi (sec. local chpt. 1976-77). Home: 877 Jefferson St Monterey CA 93940-2235 Office: Naval Postgrad Sch Code MA/Fe Monterey CA 93943

FRANKEL, A. STEVEN, clinical psychologist; b. N.Y.C., Aug. 13, 1942; s. Henry Samuel and Lillian (Krasoff) F.; m. Rita Irene Krauss (div. 1991); 1 child, Hali Samantha. BA, U. Vt., 1964; PhD, Ind. U., 1968; postgrad., Loyola U., 1993—. Diplomate in Clin. Psychology/Am. Bd. Profl. Psychology. Asst. prof. psychology U. So. Calif., L.A., 1968-71, assoc. prof. psychology, 1971-79, adj. assoc. prof., 1979-87, clin. prof. psychology, 1987—; exec. dir. adult program Ivylea Manor, Torrance, Calif., 1989—; cons. dissociative disorders Coll. Hosp., Cerritos, Calif., 1991-93; clin. practice Torrance, 1974-92; cons. Nat. Treatment Ctr. for Dissociative Disorders, Torrance, 1993—; cons. in field; lect. in field; active staff Los Altos Hosp., Long Beach., 1989-93; affiliate staff Brotman Meml. Hosp., Culver City, 1982-90, Carter Pacific Hosp., Torrance, 1982-87, active staff, 1987-92; affiliate staff San Pedro Peninsula Hosp., 1979; active staff Del Amo Hosp., Torrance, 1987—. Contbr. numerous articles to profl. jours.; editorial cons. Jour. of Personality and Social Psychology, Psychol. Reports. Active Palos Verdes Unified Sch. Dist., 1985—; bd. trustees Rolling Hills Prep. Sch., Rolling Hills Estates, 1986-89; adv. bd. Community Helpline, Rancho Palos Verdes, 1989—. Grantee U. So. Calif., 1968-69, Ford Found., 1969, U. So. Calif., 1970-71, NSF, 1973-74, NIMH, 1972-77, U. So. Calif., 1977-78. Mem. APA (hosp. practices com. 1987—), Assn. for Advancement of Behavior Therapy, L.A. County Psychol. Assn., So. Calif. Soc. for Clin. and Exptl. Hypnosis, Internat. Soc. for Study of Multiple Personality and Dissociation, Calif. Psychol. Assn. (Div. I bd. dirs. 1981-82), Calif. Assn. Psychology Providers (founding mem., bd. dirs. 1989—). Office: 3134 Pacific Coast Hwy # 389 Torrance CA 90505

FRANKEL, EDWARD IRWIN, financial consultant; b. Aug. 26, 1941. Student, NYU, 1962-68, N.Y. Inst. Fin., 1960-62. Founder, chmn. bd. United Resources, Inc., 1976-84; pres. Syndicates Underwriting Svcs., 1984-87; founder, pres. Edward I. Frankel & Assocs., Rolling Hills Estates, Calif., 1988—; mem. N.Y. Stock Exch., 1966-71. Bd. advisors South Bay Hosp.; past pres. The Wellness Community of South Bay Cities; bd. dirs. South Bay Cancer Found. Mem. Internat. Assn. Fin. Planners, Pres. Assn. Am. Mgmt. Assn., Nat. Assn. Life Underwriters, South Bay Estate Planning Coun., Palos Verdes Breakfast Club. Office: 27520 Hawthorne Blvd Palos Verdes Peninsula CA 90274-3576

FRANKEL, MICHAEL S., telecommunication and automation sciences executive; b. L.A., Sept. 22, 1946; s. Eugene D. and Susana R. (Mutal) F.; m. Shayne M. Larson; children: Jeffrey D. Barrom, Mahriya A. BS in Elec. Engring., Stanford U., 1968, MS in Elec. Engring., 1970, PhD in Elec. Engring., 1973. Instr., rsch. assoc. Stanford U., Palto Alto, Calif., 1968-73, faculty lectr., 1973-74, rsch. engr., 1974-77, sr. rsch. engr., 1978-79; asst. dir. SRI Internat., RPL, Menlo Park, Calif., 1978-80; dept. dir. SRI Internat., AITAD, Menlo Park, 1980-82; ctr. dir. SRI Internat., ITSC, Menlo Park, 1982-87; v.p., divsn. dir. SRI Internat., ITSTD, Menlo Park, 1987—; bd. dirs. Cisco System, Composities Automation Consortium; v.p., dir. ITAD div. SRI Internat., Menlo Park, 1987—; mem. Army Sci. bd. Washington, 1992—. Contbr. articles to profl. jours. adv. bd., corp. affiliate Divsn. Computer Sci., U. Calif., Davis. Recipient Bausch and Lomb Science award. Mem. IEEE, NAS (Radio elec. battle mgmt. panel,Navy 21 study, Naval Studies bd. 1987-88, Radio elec. and acoustic battle mgmt. panel Future Aircraft Carrier study, 1990-91), Am. Defense Preparedness Assn., Armed Forces Communications and Electronics Assn., Cosmo Club, Sigma Xi, Tau Beta Pi.

FRANKISH, BRIAN EDWARD, film producer, director; b. Columbus, Ohio, July 28, 1943; s. John (Jack) Fletcher Frankish and Barbara Aileen (Tondro) Gray; m. Tannis Rae Benedict, Oct. 13, 1985; children: Merlin L. Reed III, Michelle Lynn Reed. AA, Chaffey Coll., 1964; BA, San Francisco State U., 1967. Freelance producer L.A.; prin. Frankish-Benedict Entertainment, L.A. Producer (film) Vice Squad, 1981, (TV series) Max Headroom, 1987; assoc. producer: (films) Elephant Parts, 1981, Strange Brew, 1982, The Boy Who Could Fly, 1985, In the Mood, 1986; exec. producer, unit prodn. mgr. (film) Field of Dreams, 1989, Flight of the Intruder, 1990, American Me, 1991; producer, dir. (theatrical play) Timing is Everything, 1991; 1st asst. dir.: (TV shows) Big Shamus, 1979, Skag, 1979, Why Me?, 1983, Making Out, 1984, Berrengers, 1984, (films) Strange Brew, 1982, Uncle Joe Shannon, 1978, Savage Harvest, 1980, Dead and Buried, 1980, Spring Break, 1982, Brainstorm, 1982-83, The Last Starfighter, 1983, The New Kids, 1983, Aloha Summer, 1984, The Best of Times, 1985, Odd Jobs, 1985, The Fugitive, 1993, Demolition Man, 1993; unit prodn. mgr. Second Serve, 1986; distbr.'s rep. and completion bond rep. Made in Heaven, 1986; other prodn. credits include: Play it Again, Sam, 1971, Everything You Always Wanted to Know About Sex..., 1972, Time to Run, 1972, Haunts, 1975, Mahogany (Montage), 1975, King Kong, 1976, The Betsy, 1977. Mem. Dirs. Guild Am., Calif. Yacht Club.

FRANKLIN, CATHY LOU HINSON, nursing educator; b. Newton, N.C., Nov. 8, 1950; d. Willie A. and Evelyn Irene (Thornton) Hinson; 1 child, John Eric. ADN, Western Piedmont Comm. Coll., 1971; BSN, East Carolina U.; student, Med. U. S.C.; MA, Appalachian State U., 1990. RN, N.C., S.C., Ga., Ala., N.D., Calif. Patient educator Wayne County Meml. Hosp., Goldsboro, N.C.; developer cardiac rehab. & permanent pacemaker implantation programs Wayne County Meml. Hosp.; infection control nurse Charleston (S.C.) Meml. Hosp.; instr. nursing United Health Careers, Inc., San Bernardino, Calif., Caldwell Community Coll., Hudson, N.C.; rsch. coord. weekend/evening nursing program CCC and TI, Boone, N.C. Author: (with others) Fundamentals of Nursing, Nursing the Whole Person; pub. CCC & TI Skillbook; editorial cons. Mosby Nursing Texts; grants writer. Capt. fundraising for Civic Ctr.; speaker for community orgns. Named one of Outstanding Young Women of Am., 1987. Mem. ANA, ADN (coun., membership com.), NCAPNES, Phi Theta Kappa, Phi Kappa Phi, Sigma Theta Tau.

FRANKLIN, JAMES CRAIG, hospital administrator; b. Santa Monica, Calif., Nov. 1, 1958; s. Kenneth Louis and Sheila (Pickard) F.; m. Melinda Ellen Correll, June 25, 1983; children: Hannah Susan, Rebekah Sheila. BS in Fin., Fresno (Calif.) State U., 1980, MBA, 1982. Asst. v.p. market rsch. Guarantee Savs., Fresno, 1982-85, v.p. electronic banking, 1985-89; asst. v.p. planning Valley Children's Hosp., Fresno, 1989-91, v.p. mktg., 1991—; bd. dirs. HQ, Inc., Fresno. Republican. Presbyterian. Office: Valley Childrens Hosp 3151 N Millbrook Fresno CA 93703

FRANKLIN, JANET MARIE, shop owner; b. Spokane, Wash., Oct. 11, 1958; d. James H. and Jean C. (Rupert) W.; m. Jeffery L. Franklin, July 18, 1992. Student in bus. adminstrn., Eastern Wash. U., 1981. Owner tack store Otis Orchards, Wash.; breeder, trainer Reinbeau Ranch, Otis Orchards, Wash., 1976—. Editor: Walkaloosa News, 1985—. Leader, Valley Ridge Riders 4-H Club, Otis Orchards, 1977-82. Mem. Walkaloosa Horse Assn. (founder, registrar 1985—), Am. Quarter Horse Assn., Appaloosa Horse Club, Enland Empire Tenn. Walking Horse Assn., Tenn. Walking Horse Breeders and Exhibitor Assn. (locomotive engr. 1990—). Home and Office: Walkaloosa Horse Assn 3815 N Campbell Rd Otis Orchards WA 99027-9518

FRANKLIN, JIM WILLIAM, secondary education educator; b. Dearing, Kans., June 13, 1935; s. William Herbert and Mary (Raczykowski) F.; m. Myrna Sue Timmons, 1956 (div. 1963); children: Lori Lynn Cole, Kara Dawn Moug; m. Carole Margaret Osgard, Aug. 21, 1965. BA, U. Wyo., 1959. Cert. secondary tchr., Wyo., Wash. Tchr., coach Rawlins (Wyo.) High Sch., 1960-63, Natrona High Sch., Casper, Wyo., 1963-67, Vancouver (Wash.) Sch. Dist., 1967—; cons. Win with Jim, Vancouver, 1978—. With USN, 1953-61. Mem. Am. Legion, Elks. Democrat. Presbyterian. Home: 10816 NW Oxbow Ridge Vancouver WA 98685

FRANKLIN, JOHN PATRICK, electrical engineer. BSEE, La. State U., 1984, MSEE, 1987. Sr. mem. tech. staff Sandia Nat. Labs., Albuquerque, 1987—. Mem. IEEE, Computer Soc. of IEEE, Assn. Computing Machinery. Office: Sandia Nat Labs Dept 5711 PO Box 5800 Albuquerque NM 87185-5800

FRANKLIN, JON DANIEL, journalist, science writer, educator; b. Enid, Okla., Jan. 12, 1942; s. Benjamin Max and Wilma Irene (Winburn) F.; m. Nancy Sue Creevan, Dec. 12, 1959 (div. 1976, dec. 1987); children: Teresa June, Catherine Cay; m. Lynn Irene Scheidhauer, May 20, 1988. B.S. with high honors, U. Md., 1970; LHD (hon.), U. Md., Balt. County, 1981, Coll. Notre Dame, Balt., 1982. With USN, 1959-67; reporter/editor Prince Georges (Md.) Post, 1967-70; sci. writer Balt. Evening Sun, 1970-85; assoc. prof. U. Md. Coll. Journalism, 1985-88, prof., 1988-89; prof., chmn. dept. journalism Oreg. State U., Corvallis, 1989-91; prof. Sch. Journalism U. Oreg., Eugene, 1991—. Author: Shocktrauma, 1980, Not Quite a Miracle, 1983, Guinea Pig Doctors, 1984, Writing for Story, 1986, The Molecules of the Mind, 1987. Recipient James T. Grady medal Am. Chem. Soc., 1975, Pulitzer prize feature writing, 1979, Pulitzer prize explanatory journalism, 1985; Carringer award Nat. Mental Health Assn., 1984; Penney-Missouri Spl. award for health reporting, 1985. Mem. Nat. Assn. Sci. Writers, Soc Profl. Journalists, The Writers Guild, Investigative Reporters and Editors. Office: U Oreg School of Journalism Eugene OR 97403-1299

FRANKLIN, MARSHALL, cardiologist; b. Balt., Nov. 5, 1929; s. Morton and Anna (Rothstein) F.; m. Diana Jean Page; children: M. Gregg, M. Mark, M. Brett. BS, Franklin and Marshall, 1952; MD, U. Md., 1956. Intern Duke Hosp., Durham, N.C., 1956-57; resident Charity Hosp. Tulane Svc., New Orleans, 1957-60; staff cardiac cath. lab. Cleve. Clinic, 1960-64; dir. cardiac lab. Norwalk (Conn.) Hosp., 1964-77; dir. cardiac rehab. Scripps Clinic, La Jolla, Calif., 1984-89; dir. coronary angioplasty Scripps Clinic, La Jolla, 1989-92; dir. clin. cardiology Scripps Clinic, Rancho Bernardo, 1992—. Co-author: The Heart Doctors Heart Book, 1974. Fellow Am. Coll. Physicians, Am. Coll. Cardiology, Am. Heart Assn., Am. Coll. Angiology, Am. Coll. Chest Physicians. Office: Scipps Clinic & Rsch Found 10666 N Torrey Pines Rd La Jolla CA 92037-1027

FRANKLIN, RICHARD ARNOLD, immunologist; b. Cleve., Jan. 19, 1956; s. Robert Elliott and Mildred Delight (Blackburn) F.; m. Cheryl Lynne Charlton, Sept. 24, 1988. BS, U. Ill., 1981, MS, 1986, PhD, 1989. Grad. rsch. asst. U. Ill., Urbana, 1984-89; postdoctoral fellow Inserm U259, Bordeaux, France, 1989-90; rsch. assoc. Nat. Jewish Ctr. for Immunology, Denver, 1990—. Contbr. articles to profl. jours. Recipient Chateaubrian fellowship; George Huff scholar U. Ill., Urbana, 1976, 77. Mem. Am. Assn. Immunologists. Home: 1155 S Milwaukee St Denver CO 80210-2022 Office: National Jewish Ctr Dept Pediatrics K916 1400 Jackson St Denver CO 80206-2761

FRANKLIN, ROBERT BLAIR, cardiologist; b. Buffalo, Dec. 18, 1919; s. Wilson Gale and Frances Eunice (Sullivan) F.; m. Anne W., Jan. 16, 1969; children: Virginia, Richard, Victor, George, Robert, Kathleen. BA, Canisius Coll., Buffalo, 1940; MD, U. St. Louis, 1943. Diplomate Am. Bd. Internal Medicine, Am. Bd. Cardiovascular Diseases. Commd. U.S. Army, advanced through grades to col.; chief med. svc. 130th Sta. Hosp. U.S. Army, Heidelberg, Germany, 1955-58, comdg. officer 5th Surg. Hosp., 1958-59; chief gen. med. svc. Fitzsimons Gen. Hosp. U.S. Army, Denver, 1959-60, chief cardiology svc., 1962-65; comdg. officer 121st Evacuation Hosp. U.S. Army, Seoul, Korea, 1965-66; chief cardiology svc. Letterman Gen. Hosp. U.S. Army, San Francisco, 1966-68; chief cardiology dept. Kaiser Permanente Med. Group, Santa Clara, Calif., 1968-79; dep. comdg. officer 130th Sta. Hosp. U.S. Army, Heidelberg/Seoul/Vicenza, Italy, 1979-89; asst. clin. prof. Med. Coll. Ga., Augusta, 1953-54, U. Colo., Denver, 1963-65, Seoul Nat. U., 1965-66; guest lectr. Phy Yonsei U., Seoul, 1965-66; asst. clin. prof. U. Calif. Med. Sch., San Francisco, 1966-68, 74-79, 89—. Contbr. 35 articles to profl. jours. Decorated Legion of Merit with 3 oak leaf clusters. Roman Catholic. Home: 20 Palomino Circle Novato CA 94947 Office: US Army Silas B Hayes Army Hosp Fort Ord CA 93941

FRANKLIN, SCOTT HARRISON, manufacturing company executive; b. Inglewood, Calif., Oct. 27, 1954; s. Harrison H. and Marjorie June Franklin. Student, Santa Monica (Calif.) Coll., 1974-75. Salesman Sun West Volkswagon, Hollywood, Calif., 1972-75; account exec. Royal Ins. Agys., Encino, Calif., 1976-77; sr. maintenance mechanic Union Plastics Corp., North Hollywood, Calif., 1977-78; prodn. coord. Calif. Gasket and Rubber Corp., Gardena, Calif., 1978-80, quality control mgr., 1980-81, rubber div. mgr., 1981-82, ops. mgr., 1982-83, v.p. ops. mgmt., 1983-84, pres., chief exec. officer, 1984—; cons. various mfg. firms, 1985—. Active Rep. Cen. Com. Mem. Am. Chem. Soc., Am. Soc. Quality Control, Am. Soc. Metals Internat., L.A. Rubber Group Inc., Precision Metalforming Assn., Soc. Mfg. Engrs. (sr.), Calif. Mfrs. Assn., Gardena Valley C. of C., Calif. C. of C., U.S. C. of C. Office: Calif Gasket and Rubber 1601 W 134th St Gardena CA 90249-2013

FRANKO, JOSEPH R., mathematician; b. Bklyn., Sept. 12, 1946; s. Joseph A. and Margaret (Starkie) F.; m. Margery L. Shelton, Feb. 15, 1972; 1 child, Jaemon. BS, Iowa State U., 1970; MS, Calif. Poly. U., 1989. Chemist Foxboro Corp., Foxboro, Mass., 1967-69; therapist Orchard Pl., Des Moines, 1976-80; tchr. Flintridge Acad., LaCanada, Calif., 1981-85; instr. Calif. Poly. U., Pomona, 1985-89; tchr. Flintridge Acad., La Canada, Calif., 1989-90; prof. math. Mt. San Antonio Coll., Walnut, Calif., 1989—; curriculum cons. Calif. Assn. Ind. Schs., 1983-85; ednl. cons. Thresholds, Des Moines, 197-80. Author, performer tv show, Statistics, 1989. With USN, 1964-66. Mem. Calif. Math. Coun., Math. Assn. Am., Nat. Coun. Tchrs. Math., Am. Math. Soc., Calif. Tchrs. Assn., Calif. Faculty Assn. Democrat. Religious Soc. of Friends. Home: 331 May Ave Monrovia CA 91016-2231 Office: Mount San Antonio Coll 1100 N Grand Ave Walnut CA 91789-1341

FRANKOWSKI, CHARLES J., food broker; b. New Brunswick, N.J., Feb. 5, 1945; s. Joseph and Josephine Frankowski; m. Bette Holmes, Mar. 16, 1968; children: Christopher, Nicholas. BA, Calif. State U., 1968. With Kelley-Clarke, Inc., Diamond Bar, Calif., 1972—, retail territory mgr., dist. mgr., retail trainer, schematic mgr., retail sales mgr., account exec., dir. sales, from group dept. mgr. to sr. v.p., pres. Office: Kelley-Clarke Inc 1540 S Bridge Gate Dr Diamond Bar CA 91765

FRANSON, C(ARL) IRVIN, aerospace material and process engineer, educator; b. Hibbing, Minn., Oct. 17, 1934; s. Gunnar Theodore and Ina Selena (Kamb) F.; m. Adele Esther Haselton, June 29, 1968 (div. 1969). BSChemE, Purdue U., 1956; MBA, Santa Clara U., 1963. Cert. secondary tchr., Calif. Process engr. Wyandotte (Mich.) Chem. Corp., 1956-59; materials and process engr. Lockheed Missiles and Space Co., Sunnyvale, Calif., 1959-62, staff engr., 1963-68; devel. engr. Raychem Corp., Menlo Park, Calif., 1962-63; project engr. McCormick Selph, A Teledyne Co., Hollister, Calif., 1968-69; sr. devel. engr. Johnson Controls-Globe Union, Milw., 1969-70; sr. chem. engr. Gen. Telephone-Lenkurt, San Carlos, Calif., 1970-71; sr. materials engr. Ford Aerospace (Loral), Palo Alto, Calif., 1971-91; prin., entrepreneur Sigmaform Corp., Menlo Park, 1963-66; educator Golden Gate U., San Francisco, 1973, Chabot Coll., Hayward, Calif., 1970. Contbg. author: International Encyclopedia of Composites, 1990. Treas. Valley League-San Francisco Symphony, 1987-93. Mem. Soc. for Advancement of Material and Process Engring. (exhibits chmn. 1986 nat. symposium, historian 1974, cofounder No. Calif. chpt. 1960), Internat. Exec. Svc. Corps. (registered), No. Calif. Golf Assn. Home: 8162 Park Villa Cir Cupertino CA 95014-4009

FRANZ, WILLIAM SCOTT, city official; b. Denver, Feb. 25, 1957; s. James Norman and Patricia Alice (Scott) F.; m. Theresa Marie Moore, Mar. 17, 1984; children: Cory David, Nathan Edwin. BA in Bus., Whittier Coll., 1978; MBA in Fin., Golden Gate U., 1982. Asst. contr. Commercial Bank San Francisco, 1978-80, contr., 1980-82; contr. NeoLucid, Inc., Denver, 1982-84; fin. analyst Mellon Fin. Svcs., Denver, 1984-85, sr. fin. analyst, 1985-86, asst. contr., 1986-87, acting contr., 1987-88; fin. officer City and County of Denver, 1988-90, investment officer, 1990—. Unitarian. Home: 790 Washington St # 306 Denver CO 80203-3743 Office: City and County of Denver 144 W Colfax Ave # 350 Denver CO 80202-5307

FRANZIA, JOSEPH STEPHEN, wine company owner; b. Modesto, Calif., Feb. 22, 1942; s. Joseph J. and Helen (Rossini) F.; m. Marilyn L. Conterno, July 25, 1970; children: Damon, Lisa, Gianna, Mia. BA, U. Santa Clara, 1964, MBA, 1965. Nat. sales mgr. Franzia Bros. Winery, Ripon, Calif., 1969-73; co-owner, v.p., sec. Bronco Wine Co., Ceres, Calif., 1973—. Pres. Our Lady of Fatima Sch. Bd., Modesto, 1983, 84. Capt. USMC, 1965-69, Vietnam. Decorated Bronze Star, Purple Heart (3), Service Campaign Ribbons Vietnam. Mem. Wine Inst. (bd. dirs. 1969—), Brotherhood of the Knights of the Vine (supreme knight 1988—). Office: Bronco Wine Co Po Box 789 6342 Bystrum Rd Ceres CA 95307

FRAPPIA, LINDA ANN, management executive; b. St. Paul, May 14, 1946; d. Orville Keith Ferguson and Marilyn Ardis (Morris) Bidwell; 1 child, Jennifer. Grad. high sch., Seattle. Cert. claims adminstr. Claims rep. Fireman's Fund Ins., L.A., 1965-68; adminstrv. asst. to v.p. Employee Benefits Ins., Santa Ana, Calif., 1969-72; claims specialist Indsl. Indemnity Ins., Orange, Calif., 1972-83; claims supr. CNA Ins., Brea, Calif., 1983-85; claims mgr. EBI Ins. Svcs., Tustin, Calif., 1985; v.p. United Med. Specialists, Santa Ana, Calif., 1985-91; chief exec. officer United Ind. Specialists, Santa Ana, 1990—; chief executive officer United Chiropractic Specialists, Santa Ana, 1987—; instr. Ins. Edn. Assn., Brea, 1988—; speaker Western Ins. Info. Svc., Orange, 1976-83. Mem. Calif. Mfrs. Assn., Pub. Agencies Risk Mgmt. Assn., Calif. Self-Insured Assn., Toastmasters Internat. (v.p. Orange chpt. 1978). Republican.

FRARY, DAYNE LEE, geologist; b. Oildale, Calif., Oct. 17, 1949; s. Dana Lee and Alice Nadine (Rose) Kimball; m. Vickie Lynn Bittick, Mar. 7, 1992; stepchildren: Shelly, Kelly. AA, West Valley Coll., 1974; BS, Calif. State U., Bakersfield, 1979. Registered geologist Ariz., Calif., Oreg., Wyo.; registered environ. assessor; cert. property tax appraiser, Calif. Asst. geologist William H. Park & Assocs., Bakersfield, Calif., 1978-82; petroleum geologist U.S. Dept. Energy, Tupman, Calif., 1982-83; sr. oil and gas appraiser Kern County Assessor, Bakersfield, Calif., 1983-88; environ. geologist Active Leak Testing, Inc., San Pedro, Calif., 1989, Uribe and Assocs., Bakersfield, Calif., 1989-91; consulting geologist self-employed, Bakersfield, Calif., 1991—. With USN, 1969-71. Mem. Am. Assn. Petroleum Geologists, San Joaquin Geol. Soc., Internat. Conf. Bldg. Ofcls. Home and Office: 2713 Silver Dr Bakersfield CA 93306

FRARY, RICHARD SPENCER, international consulting company executive; b. Greybull, Wyo., Jan. 29, 1924; s. Frederick Spencer and Margaret Lee Ellen (Chalfant) F.; m. Eros Hunsaker, July 19, 1946; children: Richard Jr., Lorraine, John, James. BSEE, U. Colo., 1949; postgrad., N.Mex. A&M U., 1954-55, So. Meth. U., 1956-57, U. Pa., 1958. Mgr. engring. RCA, Cherry Hill, N.J., 1952-62; v.p. Ultronic Systems Corp., Pennsauken, N.J., 1962-67; v.p. govt. systems Sperry Univac, various locations, 1967-80; v.p. research and engring. A.B. Dick Co., Niles, Ill., 1980-83; with Arthur D. Little Inc., Washington, 1983-90; pvt. practice cons. RSF Assocs., 1990—. With USN, 1943-45, 50-51. Mem. IEEE, Assn. Computing Machinery, Am. Soc. for Info. Sci. Republican. Mormon. Home and Office: RSF Assocs 2898 Juniper Way Salt Lake City UT 84117-7159

FRASER, CATHERINE ANNE, judge; b. Campbellton, N.B., Can., Aug. 4, 1947; d. Antoine Albert and Anne (Slevinski) Elias; m. Richard C. Fraser, Aug. 17, 1968; children: Andrea Claire, Jonathan James. BA, U. Alta., Can., 1969, LLB, 1970; ML, U. London, 1972. Assoc., ptnr. Lucas, Bishop & Fraser, Edmonton, Alta., 1972-89; justice Ct. Queen's Bench Alta., Edmonton, 1989-91; justice Ct. Appeal Alta., Edmonton, 1991-92, chief justice Alta., 1992—; dir. Can. Inst. Adminstrn. Justice, 1991—. Recipient Tribute to Women award YWCA, 1987. Mem. Can. Bar Assn., Edmonton Bar Assn., Law Soc. Alta. Office: Ct Appeal Alta, Law Courts Bldg, Edmonton, AB Canada T5J OR2

FRASER, COSMO LYLE, medical educator, researcher; b. Westmoreland, Jamaica, Jan. 13, 1950; came to U.S., 1970; s. Sydney Arthur and Clara (Dixon) F.; m. Judith Elise Berman, Dec. 5, 1981; children: Adam Jacob, Julian Lyle, Etan Zachary. BSEE, Columbia U., 1975; MD, SUNY, Bklyn., 1979. Diplomate Am. Bd. Internal Medicine. Intern, resident in medicine SUNY Downstate Med. Ctr., Bklyn., 1979-82; fellow in nephrology U. Calif. Sch. Medicine, San Francisco, 1982-84, instr. medicine, 1984-85, asst. prof., 1985-91, assoc. prof., 1991—; chief inpatient dialysis VA Med. Ctr., San Francisco, 1984—; assoc. investigator VA, Washington, 1985, rsch. assoc., 1987. Contbr. articles to med. jours. Rsch. fellow Nat. Kidney Found., 1983. Mem. AAAS, Am. Soc. Nephrology, Internat. Congress Nephrology, Am. Fed. Clin. Rsch., Soc. Neurosci., N.Y. Acad. Scis. Office: VA Med Ctr Nephrology (111J) 4150 Clement St San Francisco CA 94121

FRASER, EARL DONALD, land use planner, consultant; b. Missoula, Mont., Sept. 9, 1912; s. William Issac and Grace Millie (Beeman) F.; m. Elizabeth Argento, May 16, 1942. BArch in City Planning, MIT, 1937; M in Regional Planning, Harvard U., 1939. Town planner Town Planning Bds., Milford and Peterboro, N.H., 1937-38; city planner State Planning Bds., Ala. and Miss., 1939-41; sr. planner Md. Nat. Park and Planning Commn., Silver Spring, 1942-43; planning cons. various cities, Kalamazoo, Mich., 1946-53; exec. dir. Redevel. Agy., San Bernadino, 1954-55; dir. planning Sacramento County, Sacramento, 1955-77; cons. Earl D. Fraser, Sacramento, 1978—; dir. specific plan Am. River Pkwy., 1937; cons. gen. plan Galt, Calif., 1979-54, Jackson, Calif. 1981. Trustee Regional Hosp. Planning Coun. Sacramento, Yolo, and Placer Counties, Calif., 1956-74. Lt. USN, 1943-45. Mem. Am. Planning Assn. (various offices 1946-93), Am. Inst. Cert. Planners (various offices 1946-93), Internat. Torch Club (bd. dirs., sec.-treas. 1947-93). Home and Office: 2237 Ehrborn Way Sacramento CA 95825-4706

FRASER, MARK D., real estate executive; b. Portland, Oreg., Mar. 13, 1951; s. George Edwin and Patricia (Shields) F.; m. Diane Berry, July 27, 1974; 2 children. BBA, U. Oreg., 1974. With sales Norris Beggs & Simpson, Portland, 1974-76; pres. HMS Real Estate, Portland, 1976-83; with sales Grubb & Ellis Co., Portland, 1984-85, sales mgr., 1985-89, sr. v.p., dist. mgr., 1989—; mem. exec. com. Grubb & Ellis Co., San Francisco, 1991-93. Mem. Portland Golf Club, Multnomah Athletic Club. Republican. Office: Grubb & Ellis 1000 SW Broadway # 1000 Portland OR 97205

FRASER, MARK ROBERT, management consultant; b. Mt. Clemens, Mich., Aug. 3, 1953; s. Robert J. and Nancy A. (Wallace) F.; m. Deborah Ann Jenkins, June 9, 1972; 1 child, Stefania Naja. BBA, No. Mich. U., 1975, MPA, 1976. Cert. mgmt. cons., sr. profl. in human resources. Dir. pers. River Dist. Hosp., St. Clair, Mich., 1976-77; mgr. human resources Henry Ford Hosp., Detroit, 1977-80; v.p. ops. Fraser & Co., Ltd., Manitowoc, Wis., 1978-91, Franciscan Health Svcs., Manitowoc, 1984-91; dir. human resources Alexian Bros. Am., Elk Grove Village, Ill., 1980-84; v.p. human resources St. Joseph's Hosp., Denver, 1991—. Bd. dirs. Silver Lake Coll., Manitowoc, 1988-91. Mem. Colo. Alliance of Bus., Colo. Hosp. Assn., Mountain State Employers Coun. (exec. coun.), Inst. Mgmt. Cons., Lakeshore Area Pers. Assn., Lions. Roman Catholic. Office: PO Box 18735 1875 Franklin St Denver CO 80218

FRASIER, GARY W., hydraulic engineer; b. Nebr., July 27, 1937. BS in Agrl. Engring., Colo. State U., 1959; MS in Civil Engring., Ariz. State U., 1966. Agrl. engr. USDA Agrl. Rsch. Svc., Tempe, 1959-67, rsch. hydraulic engr., 1967-78; rsch. hydraulic engr. USDA Agrl. Rsch. Svc., Tucson, 1978-86, rsch. leader, 1986-90; rsch. hydraulic engr. USDA Agrl. Rsch. Svc., Ft. Collins, Colo., 1990—. Editor Jour. Range Mgmt., 1990—, Rangelands, 1984—; contbr. numerous scientific papers to profl. jours. Fellow Soc. Range Mgmt., Soil and Water Conservation Soc. Office: USDA Agrl Rsch Svc 1701 Center Ave Fort Collins CO 80526

FRASIER, GEORGE ERNEST, lawyer; b. Alamosa, Colo., Dec. 15, 1942; s. Ernest L. and Sarah Mae (Siemering) F.; m. Lynn Bergman, Apr. 10, 1964; children: Elise R. and Corrie M. BA in Econs., U. Wash., 1965; LLB, Stanford U. Sch. Law, 1968. Bar: Wash. 1968, U.S. Dist. Ct. (we. dist.) Wash. 1968, U.S. Ct. Appeals (9th cir.) 1970, U.S. Supreme Ct. 1972, U.S. Dist. Ct. (ea. dist.) Wash. 1979. Assoc. Riddell, Williams, Bullitt & Walkinshaw, Seattle, 1968-72, ptnr., 1972—; instr., panelist various continuing legal edn. seminar sponsors, Wash. and Oreg., 1981—. Author in field. Chairperson Home Rule Com., Bainbridge Island, Wash., 1982-84; special dist. counsel Wash. State Bar Assn., Seattle, 1970—. Mem. ABA (bus. law sect.), Wash. Bar Assn. (creditor debtor sect.), Seattle Bar Assn. (creditor deptor sect.), King County Bar Assn., Bus. Bankruptcy Com. Office: Riddell Williams Bullitt 1001 4th Ave Ste 4400 Seattle WA 98154-1065

FRASSINELLI, GUIDO JOSEPH, aerospace engineer; b. Summit Hill, Pa., Dec. 4, 1927; s. Joseph and Maria (Grosso) F.; m. Antoinette Pauline Clemente, Sept. 26, 1953; children: Lisa, Erica, Laura, Joanne, Mark. BS, MS, MIT, 1949; MBA, Harvard U., 1956. Treas. AviDyne Rsch., Inc., Burlington, Mass., 1958-64; asst. gen. mgr. Kaman AviDyne div. Kaman Scis., Burlington, 1964-66; asst. dir. strategic planning N. Am. ACFT OPNS, Rockwell Internat., L.A., 1966-69; mgr. program planning Rockwell Space Systems Div., Downey, Calif., 1970-76; project leader R&D Rockwell Space Systems Div., Downey, 1976-79, chief analyst bus. planning, 1980-85, project mgr. advanced programs, 1986—. Mem. Town Hall of Calif., L.A., 1970—; treas. Ecology Devel. and Implementation Commitment Team Found., Huntington Beach, Calif., 1971-75; founding com. mem. St. John Fisher Parish Coun., Rancho Palos Verdes, Calif., 1978-85. Recipient Tech. Utilization award, NASA, 1971, Astronaut Personal Achievement award, 1985. Fellow AIAA (assoc., tech. com. on econs. 1983-87, exec. com. L.A. sect. 1987-91); mem. Sigma Xi, Tau Beta Pi. Roman Catholic. Home: 29521 Quailwood Dr Palos Verdes Peninsula CA 90274-4930 Office: Rockwell Internat Space Systems Divsn 12214 Lakewood Blvd Downey CA 90241

FRAUCHIGER, FRITZ ARNOLD, museum director; b. Oklahoma City, Sept. 23, 1941; s. Fritz and Lois (Lee) Frauchiger; m. A. Christine Burnett, July 4, 1976; stepdaughter, Jennifer Jane; 1 child, Maximilian. BA, San Jose State Coll., 1969, MA, 1971. Preparer, staff Leland Stanford U. Mus., Palo Alto, Calif., 1970-72; asst. registrar L.A. County Mus. of Art, 1972-73; chief preparer J. Paul Getty Mus., Malibu, Calif., 1973-74; expert Sotheby's, N.Y./L.A., 1974-75; dir. ARCO Ctr for Visual Art, L.A., 1976-84, The Contemporary Mus., Honolulu, 1986-90, Palm Springs (Calif.) Desert Mus., 1990—. With USN, 1960-64, Calif./Pacific. Office: Palm Springs Desert Mus PO Box 2288 Palm Springs CA 92263-2288

FRAUNFELDER, FREDERICK THEODORE, ophthalmologist, educator; b. Pasadena, Calif., Aug. 16, 1934; s. Reinhart and Freida Fraunfelder; m. Yvonne Marie Halliday, June 21, 1959; children—Yvette Marie, Helene, Nina, Frederick, Nicholas. BS, U. Oreg., 1956, MD, 1960, postgrad. (NIH postdoctoral fellow), 1962. Diplomate Am. Bd. Ophthalmology (bd. dirs. 1982-90). Intern U. Chgo., 1961; resident U. Oreg. Med. Sch., 1964-66; NIH postdoctoral fellow Wilmer Eye Inst., Johns Hopkins U., 1967; prof., chmn. dept. ophthalmology U. Ark. Health Scis. Ctr., 1968-78, 1978—; dir. Casey Eye Inst., 1989—, Nat. Registry Drug-Induced Ocular Side Effects, 1976—; vis. prof. ophthalmology Moorfields Eye Hosp., London, 1974. Author: Drug-Induced Ocular Side Effects and Drug Interactions, 1976, 3d edit., 1989, Current Ocular Therapy, 1980, 3d edit., 1990, Recent Advances in Ophthalmology, 8th edit., 1985; assoc. editor Jour. Toxicology: Cutaneous and Ocular, 1984—; mem. editorial bd. Am. Jour. Ophthalmology, 1982-92, Ophthalmic Forum, 1983-90, Ophthalmology, 1984-89; contbr. numerous articles lens and eye toxicity rsch. to profl. jours. Served with U.S. Army, 1962-64. FDA grantee, 1976-86; Nat. Eye Inst. grantee, 1970-87. Mem. AMA, ACS, Am. Acad. Ophthaolmology, Assn. Univ. Profs. in Ophthalmology (pres. 1976), Am. Ophthalmol. Soc., Am. Coll. Cryosurgery (pres. 1977), Assn. Research in Ophthalmology. Lutheran. Clubs: Lions, Elks. Home: 13 Cellini Ct Lake Oswego OR 97035-1307 Office: Casey Eye Inst 3375 SW Terwilliger Blvd Portland OR 97201-4197

FRAUTSCHI, STEVEN CLARK, physicist, educator; b. Madison, Wis., Dec. 6, 1933; s. Lowell Emil and Grace (Clark) F.; m. Mie Okamura, Feb. 16, 1967; children—Laura, Jennifer. B.A., Harvard U., 1954; Ph.D., Stanford U., 1958. Research fellow Kyoto U., Japan, 1958-59, U. Calif.-Berkeley, 1959-61; mem. faculty Cornell U., 1961-62, Calif. Inst. Tech., Pasadena, 1962—; prof. theoretical physics Calif. Inst. Tech., 1966—; vis. prof. U. Paris, Orsay, 1977-78. Author: Regge Poles and S-Matrix Theory, 1963, The Mechanical Universe, 1986. Guggenheim fellow, 1971-72. Mem. Am. Phys. Soc. Home: 1561 Crest Dr Altadena CA 91001-1838 Office: 1201 E California Blvd Pasadena CA 91125-0001

FRAYNE, DAVID PATRICK, senior technologist; b. Inglewood, Calif., Feb. 20, 1965; s. Dennis Kevin and Marilyn Jean (Mount) F.; m. Elizabeth Frances LeBlanc, July 2, 1990; children: Charles Matthew, Sonja Jacqueline. BA in Latin, Loyola Marymount U., 1988; MA in Linguistics, Northwestern U., 1991. Rsch. asst. UCLA, 1986-87; ptnr. Ellipsis Media Software, Santa Clara, Calif., 1987-88; pres. MetaVerbal Tech., Evanston, Ill., 1988—; sr. technologist LifeScan, Inc. div. Johnson & Johnson Co., Milpitas, Calif., 1990-93; pres. FemptoMeme Softics, 1993—. Composer various piano solo and ensemble compositions; contbr. short stories to profl. publs.; author computer program Feature Tester. Roman Catholic.

FRAYSSINET, DANIEL FERNAND, software company executive; b. Rodez, Aveyron, France, June 25, 1956; came to U.S., 1979; s. Leon Privat and Fernande Marie (Foulquier) F.; m. Chantal Luce Hebrard, June 30, 1979 (div. 1988); m. Corinne Yollande Guillaud, Mar. 4, 1989; children: Jennifer, Malorie. BA in Math., Lycee Chaptal, Mende, France, 1974; diploma in Math., Institut Nat. des Scis. Appliquees, Villeurbanne, France, 1976, MSME, 1979. Registered mech. engr. Rsch. asst. Onser, Bron, France, 1977-78; devel. engr. Centech, Glenview, Ill., 1979-82; pres., dir. JMS Inc., Camarillo, Calif., 1985—; CEO, pres., dir. D.P. Tech. Corp., Camarillo, 1982—; dir. Acaso Bus. Ctr., Oxnard, Calif. Author: Adverse Effect of Inertia and Rigidity of Truck Colliding with Lighter Vehicle, 1979; coauthor: (software) Arcade, 1979, Esprit, 1984. Mem. Soc. Mfg. Engrs., Acad. Magical Arts, Inc. Office: D P Tech Corp 1150 Avenida Acaso Camarillo CA 93012

FRAZER, CLOYCE CLEMON, retired educator; b. Warren, Ark., Jan. 2, 1919; s. Charles Columbus and Maude Mae (Jones) F.; m. Beverley Jane Mundorff, Apr. 10, 1942. BA, Calif. State U.-San Jose, 1952, MA, Calif. State U.-Sacramento, 1961. Cert. spl. secondary life diploma in indsl. arts, 1959, gen. secondary life diploma, 1960, standard teaching credentials life, 1971, services, 1971 (all Calif.); FAA comml. pilot lic. with flight instr. cert., 1949, aircraft and power plant lic., 1948. Aircraft mechanic, flight instr., Oakland, Calif., 1946-50; tchr. Folsom (Calif.) Unified Sch. Dist., 1953-54, Sacramento City Unified Sch. Dist., 1954-63; tchr. San Mateo (Calif.) Union High Sch. Dist., 1963-83, dept. head, 1963-73, program evaluator, 1976-77. Pres., Crestmoor High Sch. Faculty Assn., 1965-66; treas. Calif. Aerospace Edn. Assn., 1983—, pres. No. sect., 1978-79, recipient Earl Sams Aerospace Educator of the Yr. award, 1990; mem. advocacy com. San Mateo County Commn. on Aging, 1985-90. Served to major USAF, 1941-79. Recipient honorable mention for sculpture San Mateo County Fair and Floral Fiesta, 1967. Mem. NEA, Calif. Tchrs. Assn., Calif. Ret. Tchrs. Assn. (pres. San Mateo County div. 1986-90), Air Force Assn., Fourteenth Air Force Assn., Western Aerospace Mus., Calif. Indsl. Edn. Assn., Vocat. Edn. Assn., Am. Craft Coun., Aircraft Owners and Pilots Assn., Exptl. Aircraft Assn. (Individual Achievement award 1982), Ret. Officers Assn., Res. Officers Assn. U.S., Epsilon Pi Tau. Democrat. Clubs: Caterpillar, Ret. Officers. Contbr. articles to profl. jours.; co-author curriculum materials. Home: 620 Alameda Belmont CA 94002

FRAZIER, LESLIE BRYN, advertising executive; b. Salt Lake City, Sept. 24, 1965; d. Alton Verness and Donna Roberta (Roberts) F. BA in Comm., U. Utah, 1989. Program coord. Utah Arts Festival, Salt Lake City, 1988-90; acct. coord. Borders, Perrin & Norrander, Salt Lake City, 1988-91; advt. exec. Borders, Perrin & Norrander, Seattle, 1991-92; nat. advt. coord. McCaw Cellular Comm., Seattle, 1992—. mem. The Benefit Gang, 1992—. Mem. Advt. Industry Emergency Fund (bd. dirs. 1993—), Univ. Utah Alumni Assn. (pres. 1992—). Office: McCaw Cellular Comm 5400 Carillon Point Kirkland WA 98033

FREAS, FRANK KELLY, illustrator; b. Hornell, N.Y., Aug. 27, 1922; s. Francis Matthew and Miriam Eudora (Sylvester) K.; m. Pauline H. Bussard, Mar. 26, 1952 (dec. Jan. 1987); children: Jacqueline Deborah, Jeremy Patrick; m. Laura Brodian, June 30, 1988. Grad., Pitts. Art Inst., 1951. Freelance illustrator book and mag., cover artist, 1950—, art dir., cons. pubs., 1952—; cover artist Mad mag., 1955-62, Religious Art Franciscans, 1958-76; designer space posters Smithsonian Instn., 1971; designer space posters insignia Skylab I, 1974; v.p. Environ Assocs., Inc., Virginia Beach, Va., 1974—; artist NASA, 1975; pres. Greenswamp Publs., Virginia Beach, 1984—; illustration dir. Writers of the Future, 1987-92; coordinating judge Illustrators of future, 1987-92; dir. Kelly Freas Studios, 1988—; lectr., cons. colls., art schs. Contbr. Child Welfare League poster, A Voice for Children,

1985-86; pub.: Astounding Fifties, 1971, rev. ltd. edit., 1990, Six-to-go, 1971, Science Fiction Art Print Portfolios, 1972-79, Photoprint Series, 1983—, Ltd. Edit. Prints (6), 1991, Transition, Spl. Limited Edit., 1993; author: Frank Kelly Freas: The Art of Science Fiction, 1977, A Separate Star, 1985; editor, illustrator: Starblaze Editions, 1978-79; designer, promoter research and devel. in microbiologicals, cancer research, nutritional therapies, 1985—, DNA Molecule, Ltd. Edit. Print Pharmacia, 1986; one-man show Chrysler Mus. at Norfolk, 1977, 82, 84, NASA, Langley, Va., 1979, 84, GOH Spacecon 10th anniversary, 1979, GOH SerCon, Louisville, 1980, GOH Baycon, 1983, GOH Moscon, 1983, GOH Maplecon, Ottawa, 1984, GOH World Fantasy Con, Nashville, 1987, GOH Universon Con, Calif., 1988, GOH Chattacon, Chattanooga, 1988, GOH Rivercon, Louisville, 1988, Art GOH Space Conf., Atlanta, 1988, GOH Houston Fantasy Fair, 1988, Art GOH ICON, Stony Brook, N.Y., 1989, Art GOH AmigoCon, El Paso, Tex., 1989, AGOH RustyCon, Seattle, 1989, AGOH Galaxy Fair, Dallas, 1989, GOH Contretemps, Omaha, 1988, GOH Eclecticon, Austin, 1988, Atlanta Fantasy Fair, 1988, Deepsouthcon, Atlanta, 1988, GOH Archon., St. Louis, 1989, GOH Philcon, Phila., 1990, GOH Lunacon, NY, 1991, GOH Context, Edmonton, Alta., Can., 1991, Art GOH Ad Astra, Toronto, Can., 1990, GOH Inconjunction, Indpls., 1990, Art GOH IAFA Conf., Ft. Lauderdale, Fla., 1992, GOH BayCon, San Jose, Calif., 1992, Art GOH GenCon, Milw., 1992, Art GOH SoonerCon, Oklahoma City, 1992, GOH ConDuit, Salt Lake City, 1993; retrospective exhbn. Am. Mus. Natural History, N.Y.C., 1974, Coos Art Mus., Coos Bay, Oreg., 1988, Orlando (Fla.) Sci. Ctr., 1988, Del. Art Mus., Wilmington, 1989—, Park Ave. Atrium, N.Y.C., 1990, OMS Am. Renaissance Gallery, Portland, Oreg., 1990. Bd. govs. Internat. Star Found., Vienna, Va., 1981—. Served with USAAF, 1941-46. Recipient Hugo Achievement award World Sci. Fiction Soc., 1955, 56, 58, 59, 70, 72-76, Frank R. Paul award, 1977, Ink Pot award, 1979, Skylark award New Eng. Sci. Fiction Assn., 1981, ROVA award, 1981, Lensman award, 1982, Phoenix award, 1982, Kelly & Polly Freas Art Scholarship award established, Roanoke, 1982, L.A. Sci. Fantasy Soc. Svc. award, 1983, Neographics award, 1985, Daedalos Life Achievement award, 1987, Art Tchr. Emeritus award, 1988, Chesley award (best mag. cover) Am Sci. Fiction and Fantasy Artists, 1990, Analog Readers' Poll award (best cover), 1991, LA Sci. Fantasy Soc. Art award, 1992; Am. Art Guest of Honor, Eurocon IV, Brussels, 1978, Guest of Honor World Sci. Fiction Conv., Chgo., 1982, Guest of Honor Aggiecon, Tex. A&M U., 1980, 86; named Dean Sci. Fiction Artists, 1972, named to Nat. Hall of Fame, Nat. Assn. Trade and Tech. Schs., 1991. Mem. Soc. Illustrators L.A., Sci. Fiction Writers Assn., So. Fandom Confedn., Assn. Sci. Fiction Writers Am. (pres. 1982, 83), L-5 Soc. (life), Internat. Assn. Astron. Artists, Assn. Sci. Fiction and Fantasy Artists, L.A. Sci. Fiction Assn., Assn. Med. Illustrators, Internat. Assn. for Fantastic in Arts, Dorsai Irregulars Club, Graphic Artist Address: 7713 Nita Ave West Hills CA 91304-5546

FREDERICK, KEITH RICHARD, corporate official; b. Izmir, Turkey, Oct. 18, 1969; s. Ernest John and Gulin Durnev (Imre) F. BA in Econs. with distinction, U. Wash., 1992. Tech. cons. Edmark Corp., Bellevue, Wash., 1988; contract programmer Elfstone Software, Phoenix, 1989; contract programmer and tech. cons. Ednl. Rsch. and Svcs. Ctr., DeKalb, Ill., 1989-90; pres. KRF Internat., Seattle, 1991—; vol. tech. cons. TechAlliance, Kent, Wash., 1988-89; adminstr. USUS, Inc., La Jolla, Calif., 1991—. Designer/programmer: (software) TilEd/PC & TilEd/GS, 1991, StatPro, 1992. Vol. World Affairs Coun., Seattle, 1991. Recipient scholarship U. Wash., Seattle, 1991. Mem. N.Y. Acad. Scis., IEEE Computer Soc., AAAS, Omicron Delta Epsilon. Republican. Home and Office: KRF Internat 525 W Prospect St Seattle WA 98119

FREDERICKS, PATRICIA ANN, real estate broker-executive; b. Durand, Mich., June 5, 1941; d. Willis Edward and Dorothy (Plowman) Sexton; m. Ward Arthur Fredericks, June 12, 1960; children: Corrine Ellen, Lorraine Lee, Ward Arthur II. BA, Mich. State U., 1962. Cert. Grad. Real Estate Inst., Residential Broker, Residential Salesperson. Assoc. Stand Brough, Des Moines, 1976-80; broker Denton, Tuscon, 1980-83; broker-trainer Coldwell Banker, Westlake Village, Calif., 1984-90; broker, br. mgr. Brown, Newbury Park, Calif., 1990—; bd. sec. Mixtec Corp., Thousand Oaks, 1984-92. Contbr. articles to profl. jours. Pres. Inner Wheel, Thousand Oaks, 1991; bd. dirs. Community Leaders Club, Thousand Oaks, 1991, Conejo Future Found., Thousand Oaks, 1989-92. Named Realtor of Yr., Conejo Valley Bd. Realtors, 1991. Mem. Calif. Assn. Realtors (dir. 1988-93), Conejo Valley Assn. Realtors (sec., v.p., pres.-elect 1989-92), President's Club Mich. State U., Conejo Valley Assn. Realtors (pres. 1993), Com. 100, Inner Wheel of Thousand Oaks (pres. 1991), Community Concerts Assn., Alliance for the Arts, Conejo Valley Symphony Guild, Indian Wells Country Club, North Ranch Country Club. Home: 48143 Vista Cielo La Quinta CA 92253 Office: Brown 2321 Michael Dr Thousand Oaks CA 91320

FREDERICKS, WARD ARTHUR, technology executive; b. Tarrytown, N.Y., Dec. 24, 1939; s. Arthur George and Evelyn (Smith) F.; BS cum laude, Mich. State U., 1962, MBA, 1963; m. Patricia A. Sexton, June 12, 1960; children: Corrine E., Lorrine L., Ward A. Assoc. dir. Technics Group, Grand Rapids, Mich., 1964-68; gen. mgr. logistics systems Massey-Ferguson Inc., Toronto, 1968-69, v.p. mgmt. svcs., comptr., 1969-73, sr. v.p. fin., dir. fin. Americas, 1975—; comptr. Massey-Ferguson Ltd., Toronto, Ont., Can., 1973-75; cons. W.B. Saunders & Co., Washington, 1962—; sr. v.p. mktg. Massey/Ferguson, Inc., 1975-80, also sr. v.p., gen. mgr. Tractor div., 1978-80; gen. mgr. Rockwell Graphic Sys., 1980-82; pres. Goss Co.; v.p. ops., Rockwell Internat., Pitts., 1980-84; v.p. Fed. MOG., 1983-84; chmn. MIXTEC Corp., 1984—, also dir., chmn.; dir. Polyfet RF, Inc., Badger Northland Inc., MST, Inc., Calif., Tech-Mark Group Inc., SPECTRA Tech., Inc., MIXTEC Group-Venture Capital, Inc., Unicorn Corp., Mixtec Signal Tech., Harry Ferguson Inc., M.F. Credit Corp., M.F. Credit Co. Can. Ltd. Bd. dirs., mem. exec. com. Des Moines Symphony, 1975-79; exec. com. Conejo Symphony, pres. 1988-90, pres. Westlake Village Cultural Found., 1991; mem. exec. com. Alliance for Arts.; pres. Conejo Valley Indsl. Assn., 1990, 93; mem. Constn. Bicentennial Com., 1987-88, LaQuinta Arts Found.; v.p. Com. Leaders Club, 1988, pres., 1989-90, pres. Westlake Cultural Found, 1991; vice chair Alliance for the Arts; regent Calif. Lutheran U., 1990— (exec. com. 1993—, chmn. acad. affairs 1993—), exec. com. 1992—, chmn. acad. affairs, 1992—. Fellow Am. Transp. Assn., 1962-63, Ramlose, 1962-63. Mem. IEEE, SAR, Am. Mktg. Assn., Nat. Council Phys. Distbn. Mgmt. (exec. com. 1974), Soc. Automotive Engrs., U.S. Strategic Inst., Tech. Execs. Forum (Tech. Corridor 100 award, 1989), Internat. Food Mfg. Assn., Toronto Bd. Trade, Westlake Village C. of C. (chmn. 1990), Cochella Valley Community Concerts Assn. (bd. dirs. 1992—), Old Crows, Assn. for Advanced Tech. Edn., Air Force Assn., Aerospace Soc., Experimental Aircraft Assn., Mil. Order World Wars, Conf. Air Force (col.), Westlake Village C. of C. (chmn. bd. 1990-91), Republican Ctrl. Com., State of Calif., 1993—, Aviation Country Club, Community Leaders Club, Pres.'s Club Mich. State U., North Ranch Country Club, Indian Wells Country Club, Rotary, Flying Rotarians, Beta Gamma Sigma. Author: (with Edward W. Smykay) Physical Distribution Management, 1974, Management Vision, 1988; contbr. articles to profl. jours. Lutheran. also: 48143 Vista Cielo La Quinta CA 92253 Office: Mixtec 327 31255 Cedar Valley Dr Westlake Village CA 91362 also: 41865 Boardwalk Palm Desert CA 92260

FREDERICKSON, CHARLES RICHARD, restaurant executive; b. Coshocton, Ohio, 1938. Grad., Williams Coll., 1960; grad. in laaw, U. Mich., 1963. Chmn. VICORP Restaurants Inc., Denver. Office: VICORP Restaurants Inc 400 W 48th Ave Denver CO 80216-1800

FREDERKING, TRAUGOTT HEINRICH KARL, chemical engineering educator; b. Rhoden, Fed. Republic of Germany, June 21, 1926. MME, Inst. Tech., Hannover, Fed. Republic of Germany, 1954; PhD in Cryogenics, Swiss Fed. Inst., Zurich, 1960. Low temperature work ETH Zurich Helium Lab., 1957-60; prof. chem. engring. UCLA, 1961—; chair Cryogenic Engring. Conf., 1988-89; co-organizer and organizer 1st and 2d Joint Seminar (U.S.-Japan) on Magnet-Stability-Related Heat Transfer, Fukuoka, 1988, L.A., 1991. Recipient R.B. Scott Meml. award, 1971, Disting. Svc. award Cryogenic Engring. Conf., 1991. Fellow Am. Inst. Chem. Engrs.; mem. Am. Phys. Soc., Internat. Inst. Refrigeration, Crogenic Soc. Am., Verein Dt. Ing. Home: 11 314 Homedale St Los Angeles CA 90049

FREDMANN, MARTIN, artistic director ballet, educator, choreographer; b. Balt., Feb. 3, 1943; s. Martin Joseph and Hilda Adele (Miller) F.; m. Kaleriya Fedicheva, Jan. 2, 1973 (div.); m. Patricia Renzetti, June 12, 1980. Student, Nat. Ballet Sch., Washington, 1962-64, Vaganova Sch., Leningrad, 1972. Prin. dancer The Md. Ballet, Balt., 1961-64; dancer The Pa. Ballet, Phila., 1964-65, Ballet of the Met. Opera Co., N.Y.C., 1965-66; prin. dancer Dortmund (Fed. Republic Germany) Ballet, 1973-75, Scapino Ballet, Amsterdam, Holland, 1975-76; tchr. German Opera Ballet, West Berlin, Fed. Republic Germany, 1979, Netherlands Dance Theater, 1979, Royal Swedish Ballet, 1980, San Francisco Ballet, 1981; tchr., coach Australian Ballet, 1982; tchr. Tokyo City Ballet, Hong Kong Ballet, 1985, 86, 87, London Festival Ballet, 1981-83; dir. ballet Teatro Comunale, Florence, Italy, 1984-85; artistic dir. Tampa (Fla.) Ballet, 1984-90; artistic dir. in alliance with The Tampa Ballet Colo. Ballet, Denver, 1987-90; artistic dir. Colo. Ballet, 1987—; tchr. German Opera Ballet, 1982, Ballet Rambert, London, Bat Dor summer course, Israel, 1983, Cullberg Ballet, Sweden, 1983, Hong Kong Acad. For Performing Arts, 1985, 86, 87, 89, 91, Tokyo City Ballet, 1985, 86, 87, 89, 90, Ballet West, 1990, Nat. Ballet Korea, 1991, Dance Divsn. Tsoying High Sch., Kaohsiung, Taiwan, R.O.C., 1992; guest lectr., tchr. Cen. Ballet China, Beijing Dancing Acad., P.L.A. Arts Coll., Beijing, 1990; tchr. Legas Sch., 1978, examiner, 1980; tchr. Eglevsky Sch., N.Y.C., 1980; asst. dir., ballet master Niavaron Cultural ctr., Tehran, Iran, 1978; tchr. Ballet Arts Sch. Carnegie Hall, N.Y.C., 1979-81, choreographer Estonia Nat. Theatre, USSR, 1991; dir. Marin Ballet, Calif., 1981. Choreographer Romeo and Juliet, 1983, A Little Love, 1984, Ricordanza, 1986, Cinderella, 1986, Coppelia, 1987, The Nutcracker, 1987, Beauty and the Beast, 1988, Masquerade Suite, 1989, Silent Woods, 1989, The Last Songs, 1991. Mem. Am. Guild Mus. Artists, Fla. State Dance Assn., Nat. Assn. Regional Ballet. Home: 836 E 17th Ave Apt 3A Denver CO 80218-1449 Office: Colo Ballet 1278 Lincoln St Denver CO 80203

FREDRICKS, ANTHONY THEO, lawyer, retired; b. Georgetown, Idaho, Aug. 10, 1910; s. Charles Henry and Louella Marie (Sorensen) F.; m. Edna Nellie Pershall, Apr. 14, 1934 (dec. July 1945); children: Shirley Fay, Edna Thea, Darylann; m. Epha Jane Sutcliffe, Aug. 12, 1969. Tchr.'s Cert., U. Idaho So. Br., Pocatello, 1931; LLB, George Washington U., 1938, JD, 1968. Bar: U.S. Dist. Ct. D.C. 1938, U.S. Ct. Appeals 1938, U.S. Supreme Ct. 1939, Mont. 1939, Idaho 1945, U.S. Dist. Ct. Idaho 1945. Spl. agt. Div. Investigations, Washington, 1938-41; referee in bankruptcy U.S. Dist. Ct. for Mont., 1941-42; assoc. counsel Reconstruction Fin. Corp., Washington, 1942-44; dir. Fed. Rent Control for Idaho, Boise, 1944-47; Idaho state counsel FNMA, Boise, 1947-51; sr. mem. law firm Boise, 1947-72. Patentee of over-snow vehicle, U.S., 1961, Norway, 1961, Fed. Republic of Germany, 1961, remote control swivelling scaffold, U.S., 1971, 76. Recipient Cert. of Achievement, United Inventors and Scientists of Am., 1976. Mem. ABA, Interamerican Bar Assn. Home: Apt 4222 8700 N La Cholla Blvd Tucson AZ 85741

FREE, WILLIAM ALBERT, retired college president; b. Muskogee, Okla., July 6, 1929; s. Jack and Esther Elizabeth (Eckenrode) F.; m. Mary Lou Skelton, Aug. 25, 1953; children: Janna Dudman, Scott, Joel. BA, Pepperdine U., 1951, MA, 1958. Cert. tchr., counselor, adminstr., Idaho. Tchr., counselor Middleton (Idaho) High Sch., 1958-90; asst. to pres. Columbia Christian Coll., Portland, Oreg., 1990-91, pres., 1991-92. Chmn. Caldwell Planning and Zoning Commn., 1986-90; sec. bd. dirs. Columbia Christian Coll., 1987-91. 1st lt. USAF, 1951-56; brig. gen. Idaho Air N.G., 1979-89. Decorated Legion of Merit, Disting. Svc. Medal, State of Idaho Mil. Div., 1989. Mem. Am. Counseling Assn., Idaho Sch. Counselor Assn. (pres. 1973-74). Ch. of Christ. Home: 710 Chaparro Caldwell ID 83605

FREED, ALVYN MARK, retired psychologist; b. Phila., June 19, 1913; s. Jesse and Amy Esther (Jacobs) F.; m. Margaret May DeHaan, May 22, 1947; children: Lawrence, Jesse Mark. BS, Temple U., 1938, EdM, 1948; PhD, U. Tex., 1955. Lic. psychologist; lic. marriage, family & child therapist, Calif.; cert. sch. psychologist, Calif., Pa.; secondary sch. credential, Calif., Pa. Phys. and health edn. instr. Phila. Schs., 1940-41, 45-47; sch. psychologist Ventura (Calif.) City Schs., 1948-51; field rep. Rand Corp. and Systems Devel. Corp., Santa Monica, Calif., 1955-61; reliability/quality control engr. Aerojet Corp., Sacramento, 1961-64; pvt. practice psychology, 1964-85; sch. psychologist San Juan Unified Sch. Dist., Sacramento, 1965-68; owner, pres., author Jalmar Press Inc., Sacramento, 1970-81; pres. Psychol. Svcs., Inc., Sacramento, 1982-85; founder, 1st pres. Sacramento Acad. for Profl. & Clin. Hypnosis, 1981-82. Author: TA for Kids (and Grown Ups Too), 3d edit., 1977, TA for Tots (and Other Prinzes), 1973, TA for Teens (and Other Important People), 1976, TA for Tots II, 1980, Please Keep On Smoking (We Need the Money), 1980; author, tech. advisor various films and multi-media records; contbr. articles to profl. jours. Cons. Ventura Presch., 1952, Austin (Tex.) Presch., 1954. Sgt. USAF, 1941-45. Mem. Am. Psychol. Assn., Internat. Transactional Analysis Assn. (spl. fields mem.), Am. Soc. Clin. Hypnosis, Calif. State Psychol. Assn., Western Psychol. Assn., Sacramento Psychol. Assn. Home: 1129 Commons Dr Sacramento CA 95825-7054

FREED, ELAINE EILERS, college official; b. Hinton, Iowa, Jan. 14, 1934; d. Frederick E. and Frieda H. (Borchers) E.; m. Douglas W. Freed, June 20, 1953 (div. 1981); children: David, Casey. BA, U. Minn., 1958. Founder, tchr. Colorado Springs (Colo.) Community Sch., 1969-75; owner, mgr. Preservation Svcs., Colorado Springs, 1975-82; exec. dir. Frank Lloyd Wright Home and Studio Found., Oak Park, Ill., 1985-86; v.p. Frank Lloyd Wright Found., Scottsdale, Ariz., 1987-89; fund raiser Colo. Coll., Colorado Springs, 1982-84, dir. corp. and found. support, 1990—. Author: Preserving the Great Plains and Rocky Mountains, 1992. Del., mem. platform com. Dem. Nat. Conv., Chgo., 1968. Writing grantee Graham Found., 1989. Office: Colo Coll 14 E Cache La Poudre St Colorado Springs CO 80903-3243

FREED, ERIC ROBERT, management and financial consultant; b. Cleve., July 8, 1950; s. Axel Robert and Elizabeth (Tushar) F.; m. Patricia Harris (div.); children: Maya Linnea, Kirstin Elizabeth; m. Patricia Ellen Hargrave, Mar. 21, 1981; children: Jaired Robert, Charles Andrew. Student, Williams Coll., 1968-69; BA in Constrn. Mgmt., Columbia Pacific U., 1987, MA in Bus. Adminstrn., 1988; postgrad., Western State U. Registered investment advisor SEC; cert. series 7 24, 63 Nat. Assn. Securities Dealers. Pres. Creative Environments, Escondido, Calif., 1974-81; investment advisor Maison du Phénix, London, 1981-84; cons. investments, mgmt., finance, 1984-88; mng. dir. Corp. Adv. Group, Carefree, Ariz., 1988—. Office: Corp Adv Group PO Box 5708 Carefree AZ 85377-5708

FREED, LINDA RAE, critical care nurse; b. Fond du Lac, Wis., Aug. 27, 1957; d. Donald J. and Patricia R. (Ingalls) Wegener; m. Frank A. Freed, Aug. 22, 1981; children: Stephanie P., Courtney R. AS in Nursing, Weber State Coll., 1981; BS in Nursing, U. Utah, 1985. Cert. critical care registered nurse. Nurse aide Weber Meml. Hosp., Roy, Utah, 1977-79; nurse aide, float pool McKay-Dee Hosp., Ogden, Utah, 1979-80; practical nurse McKay-Dee Hosp., Ogden, 1980-81, staff nurse, charge nurse med. monitoring unit, 1981-86, staff nurse cardiac intensive care unit, charge nurse, 1986—; clin. faculty mem. Salt Lake C.C./Davis Applied Tech. Ctr., Kaysville, Utah, 1992—; preceptor in field. Mem. AACN (No. Utah chpt.), Sigma Theta Tau. Home: 5832 Cedar Ln Ogden UT 84403-5253

FREED, MARCIA, psychiatrist; b. Feb. 18, 1948; d. Herbert and Judith (Sillman) F.; m. Martin L. Schwartz, June 7, 1970. BS in Zoology, Psychology, Duke U., 1970, MD, 1973. Resident gen. psychiatry U. N.C., Chapel Hill, 1973-75, fellow child psychiatry, 1975-77; pvt. practice adult and child psychiatry, 1977—; clin. instr. psychiatry U. Oreg. Sch. Medicine, 1977-87, clin. asst. prof. psychiatry, 1987—; asst. examiner child psychiatry Am. Bd. Psychiatry and Neurology, 1985, asst. examiner adult psychiatry, 1989, 90, 91. Mem. Jr. League Portland, 1985—; pres. Portland Psychiatrists in Pvt. Practice, 1985, Asian Art Coun. of the Oreg. Art Inst., 1989-91. Mem. Am. Psychiat. Assn., Am. Acad. Child and Adolescent Psychiatry, Oreg. Med. Assn. Office: 2250 NW Flanders St Ste 306 Portland OR 97210-3484

FREEDMAN, BARBARA LOUISE, artist, educator; b. Detroit, Nov. 19, 1938; d. Louis and Frances (Wilder) Krakow; m. Richard Russell Fielder, Aug. 21, 1983; children: Debra Jean, Jill Ann. BS in Art Edn., Wayne State U., 1961; MA in Painting, Ea. Mich. U., 1981. Art cons. Grand Rapids (Mich.) Pub. Schs., 1962; substitute tchr. Detroit Pub. Schs., 1963-65; art instr. Birmingham (Mich.) Pub. Schs., 1968-81, head fine arts dept., 1981-91; lectr. in art Sun Cities Mus., Sun City West, Ariz., 1991-92; instr. painting Kuentz Art Ctr., Sun City West, 1991-93; instr. painting and computer graphics Glendale C.C., 1993-94. Author: (computer graphics text) Artist at the Controls, 1991; numerous solo exhbns. includin Rocky Mtn. Nat. Exhibition, Sill Gallery Ea. Mich. U.; contbr. works to profl. mags. Recipient Purchase award Nat. Art. Edn. Assn. Exhibition, 1983, Juror's award Ann. Mich. Watercolor Soc. exhibition, 1984, Juror's award Mich. Fine Arts Competition, 1986, Purchase award Glendale Festival of Arts, 1992; grantee Mich. Coun. for Arts, 1977. Mem. AAUW, Ariz. Watercolor Soc., Mich. Watercolor Soc. (bd. dirs. 1980-86), Phi Kappa Phi. Home: 14408 Yukon Dr Sun City West AZ 85375

FREEDMAN, BART JOSEPH, lawyer; b. New Haven, Sept. 27, 1955; s. Lawrence Zelic and Dorothy (Robinson) F.; m. Esme Detweiler, Sept. 28, 1985; children: Luke Edward, Samuel Meade. BA, Carleton Coll., 1977; JD, U. Pa., 1982. Bar: Wash. 1984, U.S. Dist. Ct. (we. dist.) Wash. 1984, U.S. Ct. Appeals (9th cir.) 1985, U.S. Dist. Ct. (ea. dist.) Wash. 1988. Law clk. to chief justice Samuel Roberts Supreme Ct. Pa., Erie, 1982-83; asst. city solicitor City of Phila., 1984; assoc. Perkins Coie, Seattle, 1984-90, Preston Thorgrimson, Shidler Gates & Ellis, Seattle, 1990—. Chmn. bd. dirs. Seattle Metrocenter YMCA, 1988—; chair Sierra Club Inner City Outings Program, Seattle, 1986-90; chair bd. advisors Earth Svc. Corps/YMCA, Seattle, 1990—. Mem. ABA (com. on corp. counsel 1985—), Wash. State Bar Assn., Seattle-King County Bar Assn. (participant neighborhood legal clinics 1985—). Office: Preston Thorgrimson et al 701 5th Ave Ste 5000 Seattle WA 98104-7078

FREEDMAN, GREGG, real estate appraisal company executive; b. Burbank, Calif., Feb. 1, 1957; s. Morton Ira and Charlotte (Chernick) F.; m. Karol Anne Pierce, Nov. 13, 1985 (div. Nov. 1988); m. Laura Jean Anderson, May 20, 1989; 1 child, Hillary Anne. Student, Pasadena (Calif.) City Coll., U. So. Calif., Citrus Jr. Coll., Azusa, Calif., Calif. State U., L.A. Cert. appraiser; cert. gen. real estate appraiser, cert. rev. appraiser, sr. cert. profl. appraiser. Appraiser, mgr. Freedman and Freedman Cons., Monrovia, Calif., 1984-88; pres. Gregg Freedman and Assocs., Inc., Pasadena, Calif., 1988—. Former commr. City of Duarte Econ. Devel. Coun. Mem. U. So. Calif. Alumni Assn., Kiwanis Club of Monrovia (former bd. dirs.). Home: 195 S Canon Ave Sierra Madre CA 91024 Office: G Freedman & Assocs 468N Rosemead Bl Ste 103 Pasadena CA 91107

FREEDMAN, MICHAEL HARTLEY, mathematician, educator; b. Los Angeles, Apr. 21, 1951; s. Benedict and Nancy (Mars) F.; 1 child by previous marriage, Benedict C.; m. Leslie Blair Howland, Sept. 18, 1983; children: Hartley, Whitney, Jake. Ph.D., Princeton U., 1973. Lectr. U. Calif., 1973-75; mem. Inst. Advanced Study, Princeton, N.J., 1975-76; prof. U. Calif., San Diego, 1976—; Charles Lee Powell chair math. U. Calif., 1985—. Author: Classification of Four Dimensional Spaces, 1982; assoc. editor Jour. Differential Geometry, 1982—, Annals of Math., 1984-91, Jour. Am. Math. Soc., 1987—. MacArthur Found. fellow, 1984-89; named Calif. Scientist of Yr., Calif. Mus. Assn., 1984; recipient Veblen prize Am. Math. Soc., 1986, Fields medal Internat. Congress of Mathematicians, 1986, Nat. Medal of Sci., 1987, Humboldt award, 1988. Mem. Nat. Acad. Scis., Am. Assn. Arts and Scis., N.Y. Acad. Scis. Office: U Calif San Diego Dept Math 9500 Gilman Dr La Jolla CA 92093-0112

FREEDMAN, STANLEY, insurance underwriter; b. Phila., Oct. 1, 1921; s. Benjamin and Mary (Amsterdam) F.; m. Elizabeth Nalls, Aug. 3, 1943; children: Benjamin N., Stanley F. BS in Econs., U. Pa., 1942. CLU. Ins. underwriter N.Y. Life Ins. Co., Lander, Wyo., 1946—; rep. agy. adv. com. N.Y. Life Ins. Co., N.Y.C., 1970, cons. home office product devel., 1977-78; instr. CLU courses, Fremont County, Wyo., 1956-69. Mem., chmn. Fremont County SSS, Lander, 1951-61; bd. dirs., dist. chmn. Boy Scouts Am., Wyo., 1950-56; mem. Lander City Planning Commn., 1955-58; bd. dirs. Lander Little Theatre, 1956-65. Sgt. AUS, 1942-45, PTO. Mem. Nat. Assn. Life Underwriters (nat. quality award 1967—), Million Dollar Round Table (life), Wyo Assn. Life Underwriters (bd. dirs. 1960-70, pres. 1967-68), Top Prodn. Club. N.Y. Life (life), Masons, Rotary (bd. dirs., pres. Lander 1964-78). Home: 567 Cross St Lander WY 82520 Office: NY Life Ins Co 933 Main St Lander WY 82520

FREEDOM, NANCY, neurolinguistic programmer, librarian; b. Washington, Sept. 16, 1932; d. William Heman and Lillian Blanche (Martin) Clements; m. Gerald P. Brierley, Apr. 9, 1954 (div. 1969); children: Glenn Anthony, Lynn Hope. BS, U. Md., 1954; MS, U. Wis., 1961; cert. behavioral sci., U. Mich., 1971; accelerated teaching cert., LIND Inst. Cert. neurolinguistic programming; teaching credential, Calif. Librarian I Madison (Wis.) Pub. Libr., 1961-62; reference and circulation librarian Grandview-Arlington Pub. Libr., Worthington Pub. Libr., Columbus, Ohio, 1964-66; med. librarian Ohio State U. Med. Sch., Columbus, 1966-68; reference librarian Gen. Motors Inst., Flint, Mich., 1969; yoga tchr. adult schs. and librs. Calif., Detroit, 1970—; librarian III Detroit Pub. Libr., 1969-76, Stockton (Calif.)-San Joaquin County Pub. Libr., 1977-79; reference/periodicals librarian Holy Names Coll., Oakland, Calif., 1990; neurolinguistic cons. and trainer Freedom Workshop, Oakland, 1981—; indexer Ronin Press, Berkeley, Calif., 1987—, book indexer Allwon Publishing, Irvine, Calif.; librarian Alameda County Pub. Libr., Berkeley Pub. Libr., Alameda County, Calif., 1988—, City of Alameda Free Libr., 1992. Contbr. book revs. to libr. jours. Bd. dirs. LWV, Prince George's County, Md., 1957, Civic Assn., Colonial Hills, Ohio, 1965; mem. Open Housing Com., Upper Arlington, Ohio, 1967, Pledge of Resistance-San Francisco Bay Area, Calif., 1984-88; mem. NOW, Hemlock Soc. Mem. Internat. Assn. Neurolinguistic Programming (western states rep., bd. dirs.), Am. Soc. Indexers, Calif. Library Assn., Assn. Profls. Treating Eating Disorders (speaker), Last Monday Club Women's Network, Progressive Libr. Workers, Omicron Nu, Beta PHi Mu. Democrat. Mem. Soc. of Friends. Home and Office: Freedom Workshop 540 Alcatraz Ave Ste 205 Oakland CA 94609-1140

FREEHLING, ALLEN ISAAC, rabbi; b. Chgo., Jan. 8, 1932; s. Jerome Edward and Marion Ruth (Wilson) F.; children: Shira Susman, David Matthew, Jonathan Andrew. Student, U. Ala., 1949-51; AB, U. Miami, Fla., 1953; B in Hebrew Lit., Hebrew Union Coll., 1965, MA, 1967; PhD, Kensington U., 1977; DD (hon.), Hebrew Union Coll., 1992. Ordained rabbi, 1967. Asst. to pres. Stylaneze, Inc., 1953-54, Univ. Miami, 1954-56; exec. dir. Temple Israel, Miami, 1956-57; asst. to pres. Stevens Markets, Inc., 1957-59; acct. exec. Hank Meyer Assocs., 1959-60; exec. dir. Temple Emanu-El, Miami Beach, Fla., 1960-62; assoc. rabbi The Temple, Toledo, Ohio, 1967-72; sr. rabbi Univ. Synagogue, L.A., 1972—; adj. prof. Loyola-Marymount U., St. Mary's Coll.; v.p. Westside Ecumenical Coun., 1979-81; v.p. Bd. Rabbis of So. Calif., 1981-85, pres., 1985-87; mem. com. on rabbinic growth Cen. Conf. Am. Rabbis; chair Regional Synagogue Coun., 1984-86; bd. dirs., mem. several coms. and commns. Jewish Fedn. Coun.; cons. social actions Union of Am. Hebrew Congregations, mem. nat. and Pacific-S.W. region coms. on AIDS; mem. Rabbinic Cabinet, United Jewish Appeal; bd. dirs. Israel Bonds Orgn., Nat. Jewish Fund; bd. govs. Synagogue Coun. Am.; bd, dirs., newsletter editor Am. Jewish Com. Guest columnist L.A. Hearld Examiner (Silver Angel award Religion in Media, 1987, 88); guest religion progs. Sta. KCBS, KABC; radio/TV host Nat. Conf. Christians and Jews. Chaplain L.A. Police Dept., 1974-86; bd. dirs., mem. exec. com., chair com. on pub. policy, chair govt. affairs com. AIDS Project L.A.; founding chair, exec. com. chairperson AIDS Interfaith Coun. So. Calif.; mem. adv. bd. L.A. AIDS Hospice Com.; apptd. mem., founding chair L.A. County Commn. on AIDS, 1987-89, chair svcs. com., 1989-91; mem. AIDS-related grants proposal rev. com. Robert Wood Johnson Found., AIDS Task Force of United Way; mem. com. on ethics, medicine and humanity Santa Monica Hosp., L.A. County Commn. on Pub. Social Svcs., 1984-86, City of L.A. Task Force on Diversity of Families, Commn. to Draft Ethics Code for L.A. City Govt.; mem. L.A. County Commn. on Juvenile Delinquency and Adult Crime, 1991—; bd. dirs. Jewish Homes for Aging of Greater L.A., NCCJ, 1989; adv. bd. Westside Children's Mus.; chmn. com. on fed. legislation commn. on law and legislation L.A. Jewish Community Rels. Com. Recipient Bishop Daniel Corrigan commendation Episcopal Diocese, 1987, Humanitarian award NCCJ, 1988, Social Responsibility award L.A. Urban League, 1988, Nat. Friendship award Parents and Friends of Lesbians and Gays, 1989, AIDS Hospice Found. Gene La Pietra Leadership award, 1989, Cath. Archdiocese's Serra Tribute award, 1989, Univ. Synagogue's Avodah award for Community Svc., 1990, Am. Jewish Congress Tzedek award for

Community Leadership and Svc., 1990. Mem. Am. Jewish Congress (pres. 1977-80, 82-84), Physicians Assn. for AIDS Care (nat. adv. bd.), AIDS Nat. Interfaith Network (bd. dirs.), Jr. C. of C. (chair internat. rels. com.), Sigma Alpha Mu, Omnicron Delta Kappa, Phi Mu Alpha. Office: Univ Synagogue 11960 W Sunset Blvd Los Angeles CA 90049-4200

FREELAND, DARRYL CREIGHTON, psychologist, educator; b. Omaha, Feb. 22, 1939; s. Elverson Lafayette and Lauretta Joyce (Coffelt) F.; m. Tina Anne Richmond, July 21, 1979; children—Adam Daniel, Noah Nathan, Sarah Eileen. B.S., U. Nebr., 1961; S.T.B., Fuller Theol. Sem., 1965; M.A., Calif. State U.-Fullerton, 1966; Ph.D., U. So. Calif., 1972. Lic. psychologist, Calif. Tchr. elem. schs., Calif., 1961-66; instr. Glendale Community Coll., Calif., 1966-67, Citrus Community Coll., Glendora, Calif., 1967-79; pvt. practice psychology, Laguna Niguel, Calif., 1969—; field faculty and vis. prof. Calif. State U.-Los Angeles, 1970, San Marino Community Presbyterian Ch., 1972, Calif. Sch. Profl. Psychology, Los Angeles, 1972-73, U. Calif.-Riverside, 1973, Humanistic Psychology Inst., San Francisco, 1976-79, Prof. U. Humanistic Studies, San Diego, 1983—; assoc. prof. psychology U.S. Internat. U., 1986—; asst. dir. clin. tng. Marriage and Family Therapy. 1986-89; mem. pvt. post-secondary com. for qualitative rev. and assessment of licensure Calif. Dept. Edn., 1989—. Finisher, Newport Beach-Irvine Marathon, 1981, San Francisco Marathon, 1982, Long Beach Marathon, 1988. Office: 30131 Town Center Dr Ste 298 Laguna Beach CA 92677-2040

FREELAND, ROBERT FREDERICK, librarian; b. Flint, Mich., Dec. 20, 1919; s. Ralph V. and Susan Barbara (Goetz) F.; m. June Voshel, June 18, 1948; children: Susan Beth Visser, Kent Richard. BS, Eastern Mich. U., 1942; postgrad., Washington & Lee U., 1945; MS, U. So. Calif., 1948, postgrad., 1949; postgrad., U. Mich., 1950-52, Calif. State U., 1956-58, UCLA, 1960; LittD (hon.), Linda Vista Bible Coll., 1973. Music supr. Consol. Schs. Warren, Mich., 1946-47; music dir. Carson City (Mich.) Pub. Schs., 1948-49; librarian, audio-visual coord. Ford Found., Edison Inst., Greenfield Village, Dearborn, Mich., 1950-52, Helix High Sch. Library, 1952-77; librarian, prof. library sci. Linda Vista Bible Coll., 1976—; reference libr. San Diego Pub. Libr. System, 1967—; cons. edn., libr. and multi media. Editor book and audio-visual aids review, Sch. Musician, Dir. and Teacher, 1950-75. Former deacon and elder Christian Reform Ch., libr., 1969-72, Classis archivist, 1991—; pub. affairs officer Calif. wing CAP. With USAAF, 1942-46. Named Scholar Freedoms Found., Valley Forge, Pa., 1976-80. Mem. NEA (life), ALA, Calif. Tchrs. Assn., Music Libr. Assn. So. Calif. (adviser exec. bd.), Calif. Libr. Assn. (pres. Palomar chpt. 1972-73), Sch. Libr. Assn. Calif. (treas. 1956-73), Calif. Media and Libr. Educators (charter mem.), Am. Legion (Americanism chmn. 22d dist. San Diego County, chmn. oratorical contest com. La Mesa post), Ret. Officers Assn., San Diego Aero Space Mus., San Diego Mus. Art. Home: 4800 Williamsburg Ln Apt 223 La Mesa CA 91941-4651 Office: Coll Libr 2075 E Madison Ave El Cajon CA 92019-1109

FREEMAN, DAVID, lawyer, arbitrator, mediator; b. L.A., Oct. 15, 1927; s. David and Viola Eretta (Grubbs) F.; m. Anna Johanne Horton, Aug. 6, 1949. BBA, U. Mich., 1952; JD, Stanford U., 1955. Bar: Calif. 1955. Mem. firm Trippett, Yoakum, Stearns & Ballantine, L.A., 1955-59; asst. dean Sch. Law, assoc. dir. univ. devel. Stanford U., 1959-64; dep. dir. Peace Corps, Washington, 1964; Far East coord. Univ. Rels. and Tng., 1964-66; owner, dir. Edn. Process Innovation Ctr., Washington, 1966-67; chief exec. officer Washington Area Met. Jobs Coun. Inc., Merit Employment & Tng. Coun., Washington, 1966-71; chief hearing and appeals ACTION Agy. U.S. Govt., Washington, 1971-74; pvt. practice Irvine, Calif., 1974-80; vis. prof. Coll. Law Willamette U., Salem, Oreg., 1980-81; asst. dean career devel., vis. prof. McGeorge Sch. Law, Sacramento, 1981-82; ind. arbitrator, mediator labor and employment law, internat. and domestic comml. disputes Nat. Assn. Securities Dealers, 1982—, doing bus. as Pacific Conflict Solutions, Irvine and Sacramento; assoc. urban affairs Nat. Inst. Pub. Affairs, 1967; cons. Fed. Labor Rels. Coun., 1974; roster of arbitrators Fed. Mediation and Conciliation Svc., Calif. Mediation Conciliation Svc., Am. Arbitration Assn., 1982—. Editor: Stanford Lawyers Directory, 1963. Mem. Town Hall, L.A., 1955-61. Petty officer USNR, 1944-46. Mem. ABA (standing com. on econs. law practice), Calif. Bar Assn. (com. on group legal svcs. 1963-64), Palo Alto Bar Assn. (past chmn. constl. rights adv. com.), L.A. Bar Assn. (past chmn., com. def. indigent criminal defendants, Indigent Criminal Def. citation 1957-58), Delta Theta Tau, Phi Alpha Delta. Office: 58 Acacia Tree Ln 2d Fl Irvine CA 92715 also: 209 Country Pl Ste 162 PO Box 22819 Sacramento CA 95822

FREEMAN, DICK, professional baseball executive; m. Judi Freeman; 1 child, Heather. BBA, U. Iowa, 1966. CPA. Acct. Peat, Marwick, Mitchell & Co., San Diego and L.A.; with San Diego Padres, 1981—, chief fin. officer, from 1981, exec. v.p., 1986-89, pres., 1989—; mem. exec. com. Nat. League. Bd. Dirs. San Diego chpt., Imperial County chpt. March of Dimes, nat. trustee; bd. dirs. YMCA. Lt. (j.g.) USN. Mem. Rotary. Office: San Diego Padres PO Box 2000 San Diego CA 92112-2000

FREEMAN, DONALD CARY, educator; b. Boston, Mar. 19, 1938; s. Warren Samuel Freeman and Phyllis Jane (Brown) Ohanian; m. Caroline Ethel Smith, June 30, 1962 (div. Apr. 1970); children: Elizabeth Stone Freeman, Roger Cary Freeman; m. Margaret Helen Rawson, Dec. 19, 1970. AB, Middlebury (Vt.) Coll., 1959; AM, Brown U., 1961; PhD, U. Conn., 1965. Asst. prof. English U. Calif., Santa Barbara, 1965-68; assoc. prof. linguistics U. Mass., Amherst, 1968-70, prof. linguistics, 1970-76; prof. English Temple U., Phila., 1976-81; dir. profl. devel. Shearman & Sterling, N.Y.C., 1981-84; dir. of profl. devel. Baker & McKenzie, London, 1984-87; prof. English and Law U. So. Calif., L.A., 1987—; cons. Clearlines, L.A., 1987—. Editor: Linguistics and Literary Style, 1970, Essays in Modern Stylistics, 1981; contbr. articles to profl. jours. Rsch. fellow NSF, 1967-68. Mem. MLA, Linguistic Soc. Am., Nat. Coun. of Tchrs. of English. Democrat. Home: 1300 Greenleaf Canyon Rd Topanga CA 90290-9515 Office: U So Calif Dept English Los Angeles CA 90089-0354

FREEMAN, HERBERT JAMES, educational administrator; b. Raleigh, N.C., May 14, 1941; s. Hurley Lee and Annie Lee (Upchurch) F.; m. Ollie Faye Mack, Aug. 23, 1965 (div.). BA, Shaw U., 1963; MA, U. Nev., 1978. Cert. elem. tchr., spl. edn. tchr., elem. prin. Elem. tchr., 1963-65, 70-72; spl. edn. tchr. emotionally disturbed, 1965-70; program specialist Clark County Sch. Dist., Las Vegas, Nev., 1972-79, adminstrv. asst., 1979-80, coord. basic adult edn. program, 1984—; prin. Rex Bell Elem. Sch., Las Vegas, 1980-89, Parson Elem. Sch., 1989—; mem. Nev. State Bd. for Child Care, NAACP; choir dir. Zion United Meth. Ch., 1977—, So. Nev. Mass Meth. Chs.; registrar voter registration. Named Boss of Yr., Clark County Assn. Office Personnel, 1982. Mem. Assn. Supervision & Curriculum Devel., Nat. Alliance Black Sch. Educators, Clark County Elem. Prins. Assn., Clark County Assn. Sch. Adminstrs., NAACP, Phi Delta Kappa, Kappa Alpha Psi. Democrat. Home: 1101 Sharon Rd Las Vegas NV 89106-2035 Office: 4100 Thom Blvd Las Vegas NV 89130-2722

FREEMAN, KRISTI TUBBS, medical technologist; b. San Diego, Nov. 6, 1963; d. Duane Gerald and Carol Beth (Sivertsen) Tubbs; m. Vincent Paul Freeman III, Sept. 5, 1992. BA in Biology and Chemistry cum laude, Point Loma Coll., San Diego, 1986. Cert. med. technologist, horseback riding instr. Lab. technician Scantibodies Lab., Santee, Calif., 1985, 86; asst. mgr. lab. Advanced Allergy Mgmt., La Jolla, Calif., 1987-92; med. technologist Grossmont Hosp., La Mesa, Calif., 1992-93, San Diego Blood Bank, 1993—; pvt. instr. horseback riding, La Mesa, Calif., 1978-81; horse breaker and trainer Hartman Thoroughbreds, Alpine, Calif., 1990-93; large animal technician Helen Woodward Equine Hosp., Del Mar, Calif., 1990. Vol. lab. technician Hosp. Vozandes del Oriente, Ecuador, 1985, 87; receptionist Adult Children of Alcoholics, San Diego, 1989-90; vol. Green Oak Ranch (drug and alcohol rehab.), Vista, Calif., 1990. Home: 7255 Charmant Dr # 723 San Diego CA 92122

FREEMAN, MARTIN, computer architect, engineer, educator, researcher; b. Paterson, N.J., Sept. 26, 1944; s. Reubin and Minnie (Kahn) F.; m. Barbara Frutiger Cechmanek, Aug. 17, 1975; children: Robert, Michael. BEE, Rensselaer Polytech. Inst., 1965; MSEE, Columbia U., 1966; PhD in Computer Info. Scis., U. Pa., 1971. Assoc. prof. computer sci. Am. U., Washington, 1971-78; mem. tech. staff Bell Labs., Whippany, N.J., 1978-82; sr. computer architect Signetics Corp., Sunnyvale, Calif., 1982-86; indsl. fellow Stanford (Calif.) U., 1986-87; prin. scientist Philips Rsch. Labs., Palo Alto, Calif., 1988—; vis. assoc. prof. elec. engring. Stanford U., 1977-78; gen. chmn. Second Internat. Symposium on Archtl. Support for Programming Langs. and Operating Systems, Palo Alto, Calif., 1987, First Internat. Workshop on Transaction Machine Architectures, Lake Arrowhead, Calif., 1988; gen. chmn. Hot Chips Symposium, 1991. Inventor pattern matching, memory management units. NSF grantee, 1976-78. Mem. IEEE (Cert. of Appreciation 1988, Computer Soc. of IEEE (chmn. tech. com. on microprocessors 1986-88, P1285 scalable storage interface standards activity 1992—, Cert. of Appreciation 1987, Meritorious Svc. award 1993), AAAS, Assn. for Computing Machinery, Tau Beta Pi, Eta Kappa Nu. Home: 4189 Donald Dr Palo Alto CA 94306-3824 Office: Philips Rsch Palo Alto 4005 Miranda Ave Ste 175 Palo Alto CA 94304-1218

FREEMAN, NANCY LEIGH, microbiologist; b. Seoul, Korea, Feb. 4, 1960; d. Ralph Benson and Elsie Elizabeth (Ferguson) F. BS, U. Wyo., 1982, MS, 1986; PhD, Wash. State U., 1992. Rsch. assoc. Dept. Microbiology U. Wyo., Laramie, 1983-86; teaching asst. Wash. State U., Pullman, 1986-92; postdoctoral rsch. scientist Columbia U., N.Y.C., 1992—; rep. scholastic scholarship Dept. Microbiology, Wash. State U., 1987-92; senator Grad. and Profl. Students Assn., Pullman, 1988; rsch. mentor young scholars NSF, Pullman, 1990. Victor L. Burke scholar Wash. State U., 1987-88. Mem. Am. Soc. Microbiology, Am. Legion (E.L. Blackmore scholar), Sigma Xi. Republican. Roman Catholic.

FREEMAN, NEIL, accounting and computer consulting firm executive; b. Reading, Pa., Dec. 27, 1948; s. Leroy Harold and Audrey Todd (Dornhecker) F.; m. Janice Lum, Nov. 20, 1981. BS, Albright Coll., 1979; MS, Kennedy-Western U., 1987, PhD, 1988. Cert. systems profl., data processing specialist, info. system security profl. Acct. Jack W. Long & Co., Mt. Penn, Pa., 1977-78; comptroller G.P.C., Inc., Bowmansville, Pa., 1978-79; owner Neil Freeman Cons., Bowmansville, 1980-81; program mgr., systems cons. Application Systems, Honolulu, 1981-82; instr. Chaminade U., Honolulu, 1983—; owner Neil Freeman Cons., Kaneohe, Hawaii, 1982—. Author: (computer software) NFC Property Management, 1984, NFC Mailing List, 1984; (book) Learning Dibol, 1984. Served with USN, 1966-68, Vietnam. Mem. Nat. Assn. Accts., Am. Inst. Cert. Computer Profls., Assn. Systems Mgmt. Office: 45-449 Hoene Pl Kaneohe HI 96744

FREEMAN, PATRICIA ELIZABETH, library and education specialist; b. El Dorado, Ark., Nov. 30, 1924; d. Herbert A. and M. Elizabeth (Pryor) Harper; m. Jack Freeman, June 15, 1949; 3 children. BA, Centenary Coll., 1943; postgrad., Fine Arts Ctr., 1942-46, Art Students League, 1944-45; BSLS, La. State U., 1946; postgrad., Calif. State U., 1959-61, U. N.Mex., 1964-74; EdS, Peabody Coll., Vanderbilt U., 1975. Libr. U. Calif., Berkeley, 1946-47; libr. Albuquerque Pub. Schs., 1964-67, ind. sch. libr. media ctr. cons., 1967—. Painter lithographer; one-person show La. State Exhibit Bldg., 1948; author: Pathfinder: An Operational Guide for the School Librarian, 1975, Southeast Heights Neighborhoods of Albuquerque, 1993; compiler, editor: Elizabeth Pryor Harper's Twenty-One Southern Families, 1985; editor: SEHNA Gazette, 1988—. Mem. task force Goals for Dallas-Environ., 1977-82; pres. Friends of Sch. Librs., Dallas, 1979-83; v.p., editor Southeast Heights Neighborhood Assn., 1988—. With USAF, 1948-49. Honoree AAUW Ednl. Found., 1979; vol. award for outstanding service Dallas Ind. Sch. Dist., 1978; AAUW Pub. Service grantee 1980. Mem. ALA, AAUW (dir. Dallas 1976-82, Albuquerque 1983-85), LWV (sec. Dallas 1982-83, editor Albuquerque 1984-88), Nat. Trust Historic Preservation, Friends of Albuquerque Pub. Libr., N.Mex. Symphony Guild, Alpha Xi Delta. Home: 3016 Santa Clara Ave SE Albuquerque NM 87106-2350

FREEMAN, RALPH CARTER, management consultant; b. La Grange, Ga.; s. Ralph Carter and Alice (Cordell) F.; m. Carole Stephens, July 31, 1957 (div. 1977); children: Carter III, Allyson, Stephens, LeAnna; m. Nancy Lynn Brown, May 8, 1977. BBA, Emory U., 1959. Cert. mgmt. cons. From mem. staff to ptnr. Pannell Kerr Forster, Atlanta, Honolulu, 1959-72; mgmt. cons. Touche Ross & Co., Honolulu, 1972-75; pres. FP Industries, Inc., Honolulu, Missoula, Mont., 1975-85, Janas Corp., Huntsville, Ala., 1986-90; prin. The Chestnut Group, San Francisco, 1990—. Contbr. articles to profl. jours. Mem. Inst. Mgmt. Cons. Office: The Chestnut Group One Sansome St Ste 2100 San Francisco CA 94104

FREEMAN, VAL LEROY, geologist; b. Long Beach, Calif., June 25, 1926; s. Cecil LeRoy and Marjorie (Austin) F.; BS, U. Calif., Berkeley, 1949, MS, 1952; m. June Ione Ashlock, Sept. 26, 1959 (div. June 1962); 1 child, Jill Annette Freeman Michener; m. Elizabeth Joann Sabia, Sept. 4, 1964 (div. Oct. 1972); 1 child, Rebecca Sue Freeman Shepard; 1 stepchild, Frank J. Sabia. Geologist, U.S. Geol. Survey, 1949-85, Fairbanks, Alaska, 1955-57, Denver, 1957-70, 74-85, Flagstaff, Ariz., 1970-74, dep. chief coal resources br., until 1985. With USNR, 1943-45. Fellow Geol. Soc. Am. Contbr. articles to profl. jours. Home: 65 Clarkson St Apt 508 Denver CO 80218-3745

FREEMAN, VIVIAN LOIS, state legislator, retired nurse; b. Ashton, Idaho, Aug. 18, 1927; d. Raymond Alvin and Julia Gladys (Sommercorm) Ruff; m. Richard Owen Freeman, Aug. 11, 1951; children: Paul, Mitzi. Nursing degree, U. Utah, 1948. Mem. Nev. State Assembly, 1986-94; mem. adv. bd. Nev. Women's Fund; co-founder pregnancy ctr. Washoe Med. Ctr., 1985. Active Anne Martin Women's Polit. Caucus, chair, 1981, Black Cultural Awareness Soc.; mem. Washoe County Dem. Ctrl. Com., Reno Commn. Status Women, 1979; pres. Elmcrest Elem. and Clayton Mid. Sch. Parent Tchrs. Assns., 1974-76; coord. No. Nevadans ERA, 1978; chair Reno Women's Network, 1981; bd. dirs. Planned Parenthood, 1980-86, Child Care Resource Coun., Food Bank Nev.; trustee Washoe Med. Ctr., 1982-86. Named Woman of Distinction, Soroptomists, 1991, Policy Maker of Yr., Planned Parenthood, 1993. Mem. NAACP, AAUW, Am. Assn. Ret. Persons (Outstanding Contbns. Support Sr. Issues 1990), We. Indsl. Nev. Episcopalian. Office: Nev State Legislature 401 S Carson St Reno NV 89503

FREESTONE, THOMAS LAWRENCE, county government official; b. Mesa, Ariz., July 15, 1938; s. Herbert L. and Margaret (Heywood) F.; m. Phyllis Rogers, Jan. 14, 1961; children: Jeanne Freestone Palmer, Crystal Freestone Davis, Michael, Phillip. Student, Brigham Young U., Ariz. State U., Mesa C.C. Constable East Mesa Justice precinct Maricopa County, 1968-72, chief dep. recorder, 1972-74; mgr. Maricopa County Auto Lic. Bur., Mesa, 1972-74; recorder Maricopa County, 1974-78, mem. bd. suprs., 1978—; pres. Freestone Travels, Inc., Mesa, 1979-83; Mem. Ariz. Jail Assn., Ariz. Jail Standards Adv. Com., various Ariz. Joint Legis. Coms.; past chmn. Rep. State Election Bd.; past precinct committeeman Dist. 29, 21.; del. Conf. on Security and Cooperation in Europe. Mem. Ariz. State Legis. Jt. Study Com. on County Issues, Corp. Commn. Citizens Com.; active Mesa United Way; bd. dirs. Mesa Hist. and Archaeol. Soc., Morrison Found., Mesa, PreHab Found., Mesa, Luth. Healthcare Network, Mesa, Mesa Community Coll. Ho-Chief Found., Cystic Fibrosis Found., March of Dimes, Mesa YMCA; scoutmaster, explorer post advisor Boy Scouts Am. Recipient Outstanding Citizen award Valley Radio, United Way award, 1981, MARC Ctr. award for Outstanding Svc., 1981, Key to City of Mesa, 1992; named Outstanding Citizen of Yr., 1990. Mem. Nat. Assn. Counties (criminal justice and pub. safety steering com. 1884—), Ariz. Assn. Counties, Maricopa Assn. Govts., Nat. Recorders and Clerks Assn., Ariz. Assn. County Recorders (legis. steering com.), Nat. Assn. Election County Officials, Trunk 'N Tusk Club, Mesa C. of C., Chandler C. of C. Republican. Mem. Ch. of Jesus Christ of Latter-Day Saints. Office: Maricopa County Bd Suprs 11 S 3rd Ave 6th Floor Phoenix AZ 85003

FREIBOTT, GEORGE AUGUST, physician, chemist, priest; b. Bridgeport, Conn., Oct. 6, 1954; s. George August and Barbara Mary (Schreiber) F.; m. Jennifer Noble, July 12, 1980 (div.); children: Jessica, Heather, George; m. Arlene Ann Steiner, Aug. 1, 1982. BD, Am. Bible Coll., Pineland, Fla., 1977; BS, Nat. Coll. NHA, International Falls, Minn., 1978; ThM, Clarksville (Tenn.) Sch. Theology, 1979; MD, Western U., Phoenix, 1982; ND, Am. Coll., 1979; MsT, Fla. Sch. Massage, 1977. Diplomate Nat. Bd. Naturopathic Examiners; ordained priest Ea. Orthodox Ch., 1983. Chief mfg. cons. in oxidative chemistry Am. Soc. Med. Missionaries, Priest River, Idaho, 1976-88; mfg. cons. Oxidation Products Internat. div. ASMM, Priest River, 1974—; chemist/oxidative chemistry Internat. Assn. Oxygen Therapy, Priest River, 1985—; oxidative chemist, scientist, priest A.S. Med. Missionaries, Priest River, 1982—; massage therapist Fla. Dept. Profl. Registration, Tallahassee, 1977-91; cons. Benedict Lust Sch. Naturopathy; lectr. in field. Author: Nicola Tesla and the Implementation of His Discoveries in Modern Science, 1988, Warburg, Blass and Koch: Men With A Message, 1990, Free Radicals and Their Relationship to Complex Oxidative Compounds, 1991; contbr. articles to profl. jours. Recipient Tesla medal of Scientific Merit, Benedict Lust Sch. Natural Scis., 1992. Mem. Tesla Meml. Soc., Tesla Coil Builder's Assn., Internat. Bio-Oxidative Med. Found., British Guild Drugless Practitioners, Am. Colon Therapy Assn., Am. Massage Therapy Assn., Am. Naturopathic Med. Assn., Am. Soc. Med Missionaries, Am. Coll. Clinic Adminstrs., Nat. Assn. Naturopathic Physicians, Am. Psychotherapy Asns., Am. Soc. Metals, Am. Naturopathic Assn. (trustee, pres.), Eagles. Home: PO Box 1360 Priest River ID 83856-1360 Office: Am Soc Med Missionary PO Box 1360 Priest River ID 83856-1360

FREIERMUTH, MARK ROBERT, mapper, designer, ESL educator; b. Mpls., Dec. 30, 1958; s. Robert Francis and Constance Alice (Googins) F. AA, Grossmont Coll., 1990; BA in Geography cum laude, Chico State U., 1992. Designer/checker Hauenstein & Burmeister, Mpls., 1981-86; asst. sales mgr. purchasing Amtech-Reliable Elev., El Cajon, Calif., 1986-88; asst. plant mgr. Ascensores del Pacifico, Ensenada BC, Mex., 1988-89; mapper/designer Chambers Cable, Chico, Calif., 1990—; ESL tutor Am. Lang. and Culture Inst., Chico, Calif., 1992—. David W. Lantis scholar Chico State U., 1992. Mem. Golden Key Nat. Hon. Soc., Nat. Dean's List, Gamma Theta Upsilon, Phi Kappa Phi. Republican. Home: 11849 Norway St Coon Rapids MN 55448

FREIHEIT, CLAYTON FREDRIC, zoo director; b. Buffalo, Jan. 29, 1938; s. Clayton John and Ruth (Miller) F. Student, U. Buffalo, 1960. Caretaker Living Mus., Buffalo Mus. Sci., 1955-60; curator Buffalo Zool. Gardens, 1960-70; dir. Denver Zool. Gardens, 1970—. Contbr. articles to profl. jours. Named Outstanding Citizen Buffalo Evening News, 1967. Mem. Internat. Union Dirs. Zool. Gardens, Am. Assn. Zool. Parks and Aquariums (pres. 1967-68 Outstanding Service award). Home: 3855 S Monaco Pky Denver CO 80237-1271 Office: Denver Zool Gardens City Park E 23rd Ave & Steele St Denver CO 80205

FREISE, EARL JEROME, university administrator, materials engineering educator; b. Chgo., Dec. 30, 1935; s. Otto H. and Mary A. (Hoffman) F.; m. Lenore A. Serpico, Dec. 27, 1958; children—Christopher E., Timothy P., Nora A., Lawrence M. B.S. in Metall. Engring., Ill. Inst. Tech., 1958; M.S. in Materials Sci., Northwestern U., 1959; Ph.D. in Metallurgy, U. Cambridge, Eng., 1962. From asst. prof. to assoc. prof. Northwestern U., Evanston, Ill., 1962-77; dir. research office, prof. mech. engring. U. N.D., Grand Forks, 1977-82; asst. vice chancellor research, prof. mech. engring. U. Nebr., Lincoln, 1982-87; dir. rsch. office Inst. Material. Sci., Calif. Inst. Tech., 1987—. Contbr. articles to profl. jours. Fulbright fellow, 1959-61; recipient award for Excellence in Engring. Edn., Western Electric Co., 1971. Mem. Am. Soc. Metals (v.p., pres. Chgo. chpt. 1971-72), AIME, Am. Soc. Engring. Edn. (sec.-treas. Ill.-Ind. sect. 1963-64, 73-74), Soc. Univ. Patent Adminstrs., Nat. Council Univ. Research Adminstrs. (pres. 1984-85), Soc. Research Adminstrs. Office: Calif Inst Tech 1201 E Calif Blvd MS213-6 Pasadena CA 91125

FREITAG, PETER ROY, transportation specialist; b. L.A., Dec. 19, 1943; s. Victor Hugo and Helen Veronica (Burnes) F. Student, U. Fla., 1961-63, George Washington U., 1964-65. Chief supr. Eastern Airlines, L.A., 1965-77; tariff analyst, instr. United Airlines, San Francisco, 1977-84; mng. ptnr. Bentdahl, Freitag & Assoc., San Francisco, 1984-86; v.p. ops. PAD Travel, Inc., Mountain View, Calif., 1985-86; travel mgr. Ford Aerospace, San Jose, Calif., 1986—. Co-editor: (textbook) International Air Tariff and Ticketing, 1983. Vol. San Francisco Bay chpt. Oceanic Soc., 1984-87. Mem. Silicon Valley Bus. Travel Assn., Bay Area Bus. Travel ASsn. Episcopalian.

FREITAS, ROBERT ARCHIBALD, JR., periodical editor and publisher; b. Camden, Maine, Dec. 6, 1952; s. Robert Archibald and Barbara Lee (Smith) G.; m. Nancy Ann Ferrall, Aug. 10, 1974. BS in Physics, Harvey Mudd Coll., 1974, BS in Psychology, 1974; JD, U. Santa Clara, 1979. Dir. Space Initiative Lobbying for Space, Santa Clara, Calif., 1977-82; space automation study editor, Ames Rsch. Ctr. NASA/Am. Soc. Engring. Edn., Moffett Field, Calif., 1980-81; computer sci. study editor, Goddard Space Flight Ctr. NASA/Am. Soc. Engring. Edn., Balt., 1981-82; autonomy and human element in space study editor Ames Rsch. Ctr. NASA/Am. Soc. Engring. Edn., Moffett Field, 1983-84; editor, pub. Value Forecaster, Pilot Hill, Calif., 1988—. Author: Lobbying for Space, 1978; contbr. articles to profl. publs. Recipient Best Fact Article award Analog Sci. Fact/Sci. Fiction, 1981. Mem. AAAS, Internat. Inst. Forecasters, World Future Soc., Nat. Space Soc. (life). Republican. Office: Value Forecaster PO Box 50 Pilot Hill CA 95664-0050

FREITAS, STEPHEN JOSEPH, advertising executive, educator; b. Alameda, Calif., Sept. 16, 1958; s. Richard Joseph Freitas. BA in Geography and Theatre, U. Calif., Berkeley, 1981; MBA in Mktg., Golden Gate U., 1987. Creative dir. Chevron Corp., San Francisco, 1981-88; mktg. mgr. Color 2000, San Francisco, 1988; dir. account planning, sales mgr. Pace Studio, San Francisco, 1989-90; mktg. mgr. Patrick Media Group, Oakland, Calif., 1990—; tchr., educator Barbri Testing, Berkeley, 1990—. Exec. producer (stage mus.) How Do You Keep the Music Playing, 1989, Tune the Grnd Up, 1990. Com. mem. western region coun. Boy Scouts Am., 1990—, local v.p., 1989. Mem. Am. Mktg. Assn. (profl.), Am. Assn. Appraisers (cert.), San Francisco Ad Club. Republican. Roman Catholic.

FRENCH, CLARENCE LEVI, JR., retired shipbuilding company executive; b. New Haven, Oct. 13, 1925; s. Clarence L. Sr. and Eleanor (Curry) F.; m. Jean Sprague, June 29, 1946; children: Craig Thomas, Brian Keith, Alan Scott. BS in Naval Sci., Tufts U., 1945, BSME, 1947; ScD (hon.), Webb Inst., 1992. Registered profl. engr., Calif. Foundry engr. Bethlehem Steel Corp., 1947-56; staff engr., asst. supt. Kaiser Steel Corp., 1956-64; supervisory engr. Bechtel Corp., 1964-67; with Nat. Steel & Shipbldg. Co., San Diego, 1967-86; exec. v.p., gen. mgr. Nat. Steel & Shipbldg. Co., to 1977, pres., chief operating officer, 1977-84, chmn., chief exec. officer, 1984-86, outside dir., 1989—; mem. maritime transp. rsch. bd. NRC. Bd. dirs. United Way, San Diego, YMCA, San Diego; past chmn., bd. dirs. Pres. Roundtable; chmn. emeritus bd. trustees Webb Inst. Lt. USN, 1943-53. Fellow Soc. Naval Architects and Marine Engrs. (hon., past pres.), Shipbuilders Council Am. (past chmn. exec. com.), ASTM, Am. Bur. Shipping; mem. Am. Soc. Naval Engrs., U.S. Naval Inst., Navy League U.S., Propeller Club U.S.

FRENCH, DAVID HEATH, anthropologist, educator; b. Bend, Oreg., May 21, 1918; s. Delbert Ransom and Ellen Evelyn (Fatland) F.; m. Kathrine McCulloch Story, May 15, 1943. Student, Reed Coll., 1935-38; B.A., Pomona Coll., 1939; M.A., Claremont Grad. Sch., 1940; Ph.D., Columbia U., 1949. Jr. profl. asst. United Pueblos Agy., Albuquerque, 1941-42; community analyst War Relocation Authority, Poston, Ariz., 1943-46; Amerindian research Reed Coll., Portland, Oreg., 1947—, from asst. prof. to assoc. prof. anthropology, 1947-59, prof., 1959-88; prof. emeritus Reed Coll., Portland, 1988—, cons. anthropologist, 1988—; reviewer research proposals NSF, Washington, 1961—, NIH, Washington, 1963—; co-investigator pharmacognosy Oreg. State U., Corvallis, 1963-64. Author: Factionalism in Isleta Pueblo, 1948; contbr. chpts. to books, numerous articles to profl. publs. Grantee Wenner-Gren Found., 1951-52, Am. Philos. Soc., 1955, NIH, 1964-67; resident fellow Ctr. for Advanced Study in Behavioral Scis., Stanford, Calif., 1967-68; recipient Cert. Appreciation Confederated Tribes of Warm Springs, Oreg., 1989. Fellow Am. Anthrop. Assn. (exec. bd. 1965-68, Disting. Svc. award 1988), AAAS (coun. 1966-68), Royal Anthrop. Inst.; mem. Soc. Econ. Botany (chmn. membership com. 1964-68), Linguistic Soc. Am., Soc. for Anthropology of Europe, Soc. Ethnobiology, Soc. for Linguistic Anthropology, Sigma Xi. Democrat. Home: 3410 SE Woodstock Blvd Portland OR 97202-8141 Office: Reed Coll Dept Anthropology Portland OR 97202

FRENCH, GEORGINE LOUISE, guidance counselor; b. Lancaster, Pa., May 15, 1934; d. Richard Franklin and Elizabeth Georgine (Driesbach) Beacham; BA, Calif. State U., San Bernardino, 1967; MS, No. Ill. U., 1973; DD, Am. Ministerial Assn., 1978; m. Barrie J. French, Feb. 4, 1956; children: Joel B., John D., James D., Jeffrey D. Ordained minister Am. Ministerial Assn., 1979; cert. counselor NCC bd.. pers. counselor Sages Dept. Store, San Bernardino, 1965-66; asst. bookkeeper Bank Calif., San Bernardino, 1964-65; tchr. Livermore (Calif.) Sch. Dist., 1965-69; guidance counselor Bur. Indian Affairs, Tuba City, Ariz., 1974-80, Sherman Indian High Sch., Riverside, Calif., 1980-82, Ft. Douglas Edn. Ctr., U.S. Army, Salt. Lake City, 1982-86; guidance counselor L.A. Air Force Sta., USAF, 1986-87, edn. svcs. officer, Comiso AFB, Italy, 1987-88; guidance counselor L.A. Air Force Base, 1989-93; extension tchr. Navajo Community Coll., Yavapai Jr. Coll.; personnel counselor USNR, 1976-86. Served with USAF, 1954-56. Cert. guidance counselor, secondary tchr. Mem. Am. Counselor Assn. (cert. counselor), Am. Assn. Retired Persons. Office: LA AFB SNC/DPUE 325 Challenger Way El Segundo CA 90245-4677

FRENCH, STEPHEN WARREN, university administrator, educator, artist; b. Seattle, Sept. 6, 1934; s. George Warren and Madge Evelyn (Marshall) F. m. Hanna Clara Misch, June 10, 1956 (div. May 1971); children: Alexandra, Kenneth, Katharine; m. Toni Virginia Thunen, Aug. 14, 1974 (div. June 1979); 1 child, Elly Kinsell Thunen-French; m. Wanda Waldera, Oct. 19, 1990. BA, U. Wash., 1956, MFA, 1960. Instr. art dept. San Jose (Calif.) State U., 1960-61; from instr. to asst. prof. art dept. U. Wis., Madison, 1961-66; from asst. prof. to prof. San Jose State U., 1966—, assoc. dean Coll. Humanities and Arts, 1990—; vis. artist U. Wash., Seattle, 1972, 73, Mont. State U., Boseman, 1970; mem. collections com. San Jose Mus. of Art, 1990—, mem. arts commn. City of San Jose, 1990-93, chair, 1993—; vice chmn. conv. ctr. art selection com. City of San Jose, 1986—; chmn. Art in Pub. Places Adv. Panel City of San Jose, 1991—. One man show San Jose Mus., 1980; exhibited in group shows at Smithsonian Inst., Washington, 1965, Palace of the Legion of Honor, San Francisco, 1967, British Biennial of Graphic Art, 1969, 71, San Francisco Mus. of Modern Art, 1970. Mem. adv. com. San Jose Inst. of Contemporary Art. Sarah Denny fellow U. Wash., 1958. Mem. Coll. Art Assn., Nat. Assn. Schs. of Art & Design, Nat. Conf. of Art Adminstrs., Phi Beta Kappa, Phi Kappa Phi. Unitarian. Home: 1560 Four Oaks Cir San Jose CA 95131-2653 Office: San Jose State U Dean of Humanities/Arts 1 Washington Sq San Jose CA 95192-0001

FRENSTER, JOHN HENRY, physician; b. Chgo., Oct. 14, 1928; s. Henry and Pauline (Janssen) F.; m. Jeannette A. Hovsepian, June 15, 1958; children: Jeff A., Diane A., Linda A. BS in Chemistry, U. Ill., 1950, MD, 1954. Cert. FACP; diplomate Am. Bd. Internal Medicine and Med. Oncology. Intern Cook County Hosp., Chgo., 1954-55; fellow hematology U. Ill. Hosps., Chgo., 1956-57, resident medicine, 1955-58; postdoctoral fellow Rockefeller U., N.Y.C., 1958-60, asst. prof. biology, 1962-66; asst. prof. medicine Stanford (Calif.) U., 1966-73; chief oncology Santa Clara Valley Med. Ctr., San Jose, Calif., 1972-89; clin. assoc. prof. medicine Stanford U., 1973—; chmn. cancer care Santa Clara Valley Med. Ctr., San Jose, 1972-89, dir. staff corp., 1975-89; cons. medicine Palo Alto (Calif.) VA Med. Ctr., 1966-73, cons. Nat. Cancer Inst., Bethesda, Md., 1973. Contbr. articles to profl. jours. Mem. com. Bicycle Safety, Atherton, Calif., 1970, Beyond War, Palo Alto, 1984. Capt. USAR, 1960-62. Hematology fellow U. Ill., Chgo., 1956, postdoctoral fellow Rockefeller U., 1958. Fellow ACP; mem. IEEE, Am. Assn. Cancer Rsch., Am. Soc. for Hematology, Am. Soc. Cell Biology, Am. Soc. Clin. Oncology, Am. Econ. Assn. Democrat. Mem. Soc. of Friends. Home: 247 Stockbridge Ave Atherton CA 94027-5446

FRENZEL, CHARLES ALFON, physics consultant; b. Port Arthur, Tex., Sept. 24, 1940; s. Alfon and Mary Estelle (Nichols) F.; m. Lydia Ann Melcher, June 2, 1973. BA in Physics, Vanderbilt U., 1969. Sr. rsch. engr. dept. elec. engring. U. Ky., Lexington, 1967-74; pres. Merlin Assocs. Inc., New Orleans, 1974-76, Coastal Sci. Assocs. Inc., Hammond, La., 1976-87; cons. on surface chemistry, Sutter Creek, Calif., 1987—; advisor to U.S. Rep. Dave Treen of La., 1982-83; tech. advisor CCI Svcs. Inc., 1987—; presenter profl. meetings. Contbr. articles to profl. jours. Former mem. Pres. Eisenhower's Sci. Curriculum in Secondary Schs. Com. With USAF, 1966-67. Recipient best sci. paper of yr. award Jour. Can. Spectroscopy, 1970. Mem. AAAS, N.Y. Acad. Scis., Sigma Xi.

FRETER, MARK ALLEN, marketing and public relations executive, consultant; b. Chgo., Oct. 31, 1947; s. John Maher and Christopher Patricia (Allen) F. BA, U. Calif., Santa Barbara, 1969; MBA, U. Calif., Berkeley, 1971. Regional dir. HBO Svcs., Inc., L.A. and Denver, 1979-84; v.p. affiliate rels. X-Press Info. Svcs., Denver, 1984-85; v.p. mktg. Telecrafter Corp., Denver, 1985-86; mktg. dir. Computer Svcs. Corp., Boulder, Colo., 1986-87; prin., v.p. pub. rels. svcs. MultiMedia, Inc., Denver, 1987-88; dir. documentation and corp. comm., product specialist, op. cons. Data Select Systems Inc., Woodland Hills, Calif., 1988-91; also pres. The Aspen Group Ltd., Westlake Village, Calif., 1988—; mgr. mktg. comm. COM Systems Inc., Westlake Village, Calif., 1991—; lectr. Internat. Coun. Shopping Ctrs., N.Y.C., 1977; conf. planner ICSC-West, San Francisco, 1978-79; tng. program devel. HBO, N.Y.C., 1982. Youth coach South Suburban YMCA, Littleton, Colo., 1984-86. Recipient First Pl. cert. for Retail Ad Campaign San Diego Advt. Assn., 1980. Mem. Calif. Cable TV Assn., No. Calif. Promotion Mgrs. Assn. (v.p. 1977-78), So. Calif. Promotion Mgrs. Assn. (sec., treas. 1976-77). Democrat. Mem. Soc. Friends. Office: The Aspen Group Ltd PO Box 4813 Thousand Oaks CA 91359-1813

FRETWELL, LINCOLN DARWIN, career officer, dentist, consultant; b. Moulton, Ala., Sept. 20, 1944; s. Lincoln Coolege and Katherine Alice (Gargis) F.; m. Connie Ruth Comer, Aug. 17, 1974; children: Darbi, Christina, Benjamin. AA, Daytona Beach Jr. Coll., 1969; BA, Fla. State U., 1971; DDS, Med. Coll. Va., 1975. Diplomate Fed. Svcs. Bd. of Gen. Dentistry, Certifying Bd. Gen. Dentistry. Resident in dentistry U. Va., Charlottesville, 1975-77; asst. prof. Sch. Dentistry Med. Coll. Va., Richmond, 1977-81; dental officer U.S. Army, 1981-84; officer in charge Lyster Army Hosp. Dental Clinic, 1984-87; instr. Acad. Health Scis., 1987-91; comdr. Ft. Irwin DENTAC, 1991—. Author: Handbook of Preventive Dentistry, 1978; contbr. articles to profl. jours. Coach U.S. Army Youth Activities, 1986—; leader Boy Scouts Am., Tex. and Calif., 1989—. Recipient Family of Yr. award U.S. Army, 1990-91. Fellow Internat. Coll. Dentists; mem. ADA, Army Aviation Assn. Am. (sec. Alamo chpt. 1989-91), Soc. U.S. Army Flight Surgeons, Acad. Gen. Dentistry (treas. Army 1990—), Pierre Fauchard Acad. (chmn. mil. affairs 1990—), Omicron Kappa Upsilon. Home: 4036 Alvord Dr Fort Irwin CA 92310 Office: Nat Tng Ctr US Army DENTAC Fort Irwin CA 92310

FREVERT, DONALD KENT, hydraulic engineer; b. Des Moines, Mar. 23, 1950; s. Richard Keller and Corine (Twetley) F.; m. Maria Carmen Tarazon, Mar. 16, 1973; children: Richard Paul, Erica Lynn. BS in Hydrology, U. Ariz., 1972; MS in Hydrology and Water Resources, Colo. State U., 1974, PhD in Irrigation and Drainage, 1983. Registered profl. engr., Colo. Engring. aid USDA Agrl. Rsch. Svc., Tucson, 1970-72; grad. rsch. asst. Colo. State U., Fort Collins, 1972-74; hydrologist, water rights engr. Woodward-Clyde Cons., Denver, 1975-76; grad. rsch. asst. Colo. State U., Fort Collins, Colo., 1977-80; hydraulic engr. U.S. Bur. Reclamation, Lakewood, Colo., 1980—; faculty affiliate Colo. State U. civil engring. dept., Ft. Collins, 1986—; trustee Rocky Mountain Hydrologic Rsch. Ctr., 1992—. Co-author: (manuals) Comparison of Equations Used for Estimating Agricultural Crop Evapotranspiration with Field Research, 1983, Applied Stochastic Techniques Users Manual, 1990; contbr. articles to profl. jours. Age group coord. Lakewood Swim Club, 1988—. Recipient of Paul Elliott Ullman scholarship U. Ariz., Tucson, 1969, Pima Mining Co. scholarship, U. Ariz., 1970. Mem. ASCE (chmn. surface water com. 1988-90, mem. exec. com. irrigation and drainage div. 1991—), Phi Kappa Phi, Alpha Epsilon. Home: 2034 S Xenon Ct Lakewood CO 80228-4355 Office: US Bur Reclamation D-5755 PO Box 25007 Denver CO 80225-0007

FREW, HENRY LORIMER, journalist, editor; b. Ralston, Scotland, May 14, 1933; arrived in Can., 1966; s. Henry Lorimer and Margaret McIntyre (Baillie) F.; m. Marjorie-Jean Cripps, Dec. 6, 1957; 1 child, Henry Lorimer. Student, West of Scotland Agrl. Coll., 1951. Writer on renewable resources, 1952—; editor, pub. Maclean Hunter Ltd., Vancouver, B.C., Can., 1972-86; editor Western Wildlife Publs., B.C., 1987—. Editor Western Fisheries, 1972-80, BC Outdoors, 1980-86, The Outdoorsman, 1989—; contbr. numerous articles to newspapers in Europe, Africa, N.Am. Leader Boy Scouts Assn., Scotland, Africa, Can., 1952-77; mem. B.C. Com. for Can. Conservation Strategy, 1985-88. Mem. Outdoor Writers Assn. Am., Outdoor Writers Assn. Can., N.W. Outdoor Writers Assn., Can. Wildlife Fedn., Am. Forestry Assn., Internat. Game Fisheries Assn., Can. Assn. Geographers (editorial bd. 1982-86), B.C. Wildlife Fedn. (cons. 1986—), Ducks Unltd. Home: 34785 McMIllan Ct, Abbotsford, BC Canada V2S 5W4

FREY, BETTY JEAN, retired educator, adult literacy professional; b. Marietta, Ohio, May 12, 1914; d. John Luman and Elsie Louise (Strauss) Gephart; widowed; children: Richard, John, Paul. BA, Marietta Coll., 1937; MEd, U. Ariz., 1966. Tchr. music Washington County Schs., Marietta, 1938-41, Grandview Schs., Columbus, Ohio, 1941-43, Amphitheater Schs., Tucson, 1952-79; vol. trainer of tutors Laubach Literacy, various locations, 1960-92; chmn. Southwest region Laubach Literacy, 1990—; tchr. of English in palaces of royal family, Saudi Arabia, 1991. Inventor tongue-position chart for teaching English to deaf and fgn.-speaking students; author: Basic Helps in Teaching English as a Second Language, 1971, 2d edit., 1976. Mem. Delta Kappa Gamma (pres. 1974-76). Democrat. Methodist. Home: 2806 E Lester St Tucson AZ 85716

FREYMUTH, PETER, education educator, consultant; b. Warmbrunn, Germany, Dec. 4, 1936; came to U.S., 1966; s. Franz and Ilse (Strack) F.; m. Karin Luise Finner, Aug. 18, 1965; children: Malwa, Esther, Florian. DEng, Tech. U., Berlin, 1965. Rsch. assoc. Tech. U., Berlin, 1963-65; rsch. assoc. U. Colo., Boulder, 1966-67, asst. prof., 1967-70, assoc. prof., 1970-80, prof., 1981—; pvt. practice cons., Boulder, 1975—. Mem. Am. Phys. Soc., AIAA, Sigma Xi. Office: U Colo Dept Aerospace Engring Boulder CO 80309-0429

FRIBERG, ARNOLD, artist, illustrator; b. Winnetka, Ill., Dec. 21, 1913; s. Sven Peter and Ingeborg A. (Solberg) F.; m. Hedve Mae Baxter, Dec. 26, 1946 (dec. 1986); children: Patricia, Frank; m. Heidi Hiller Grosskopf, May 29, 1988. Student, Chgo. Acad. Fine Arts, 1934-35. Chief artist/designer Cecil B. DeMille-Paramount Pictures, Hollywood, Calif., 1953-56. Paintings include nearly 300 pictures of Royal Can. Mounted Police, 1937-75, painting for Golden Nugget Casino Hotel, 1977, equestrian portrait of Prince Charles, 1989, Queen Elizabeth, 1991, 15 bibl. paintings for Cecil B. DeMille's "The Ten Commandments", 1956, many historical, western, bibl. pictures; exhibited at Utah Heritage Art Show, 1991; feature artist Red Earth Promotions Rose Festival, Portland, Oreg., 1993. With U.S. Army, 1942-46; ETO. Recipient Freedom Found. award, 1976. Fellow Royal Soc. Arts (London); mem. Chelsea Arts Club (London), Royal Can. Mounated Police (hon. mem.). Home: 4533 Highland Dr Salt Lake City UT 84117-4201

FRICANO, TOM SALVATORE, artist; b. Chgo., Oct. 28, 1930; s. Carmelo and Rose (Aiello) F.; m. Judith Holzheimer, Dec. 17, 1960; children: Fiama Marie, Alesia Marie. BFA, Bradley U., 1953; MFA, U. Ill., 1956; postgrad., U. Italiana per Stranieri, Perugia and Belle Arte, Florence, Italy. Instr. art U. Ill., 1955, Bradley U., 1958-63; faculty Calif. State U., Northridge, 1963—, now prof. art; vis. artist, artist-in-residence Chouinard Art Inst., L.A., 1964, Ohio State U., 1969, U. Utah, Salt Lake City, 1971, Cranbrook Acad. Art, Bloomfield Hills, Mich., 1971, U. Mont., Bozeman, 1972, Sch. Art Inst., Chgo., 1975, Drake U., Des Moines, 1977, U. N.D., Grand Forks, 1980, U. Tex., Austin, 1982, Calif. State Summer Sch. for the Arts, 1987-89; mem. staff for numerous programs San Fernando Valley Arts Coun.; mem. staff programs Bartonville Psychiat. Hosp., Barton, Ill., Bradley U., Peoria, Ill. One-man shows include U. Ill., 1963, 64, Kans. State U., Manhattan, 1964, Ohio State U., 1969, Utah Mus. Fine Art, Salt Lake City, 1971, U. Mont., Tex. Technol. U., Lubbock, 1972, Lakeview Art Ctr., Peoria, Ill., 1973, Comsky Gallery, L.A., 1975, Davidson Galleries, Seattle, 1976, Drake U., 1977, Fresno (Calif.) State U. Gallery, 1978, Pepperdine U., Malibu, Calif., 1979, U. N.D., 1980, Bibo Gallery for Art, Peoria, Ill., 1981, Okla. Art Ctr., Oklahoma City, 1983, Fairweather Hardin Gallery, Chgo., 1988; group shows include Nat Mus., Korea, Oakland Mus. Art, 1970, De Young Mus., San Francisco, Springfield (Mo.) Art Mus., 1976, Laguna Beach (Calif.) Mus. Art, Calif. State U., Library of Congress, Washington, 1977, Mus. Assn. N. Orange County, Fullerton, Calif., Springfield (Ill.) Art Assn., Print Club, Phila., 1980, Lillian Heidenberg Gallery, N.Y.C., 1981, L.A. County Mus. Art, UCLA, 1981, U. Dallas, 1981, 83, Wesleyan Coll., Macon, Ga., 1983, Korean Cultural and Art Found., Seoul, El Camino Coll., Torrance, Calif., 1984, Newport (Oreg.) Ctr. Visual Arts, 1985, Brand Library Galleries, Glendale, Calif., 1985, Portland (Oreg.) Art Mus., 1985, Louis Newman Galleries, Beverly Hills, Calif., 1986, Fairweather Hardin Gallery, 1986, 89, U. Mont., Missoula (traveling), 1987, 89-90, Korean Cultural and Arts Found., 1987, Lancaster (Calif.) Mus., 1987, Calif. Poly. U., Pomona, 1987, Barbican Gallery, London, 1989, U. Tex., Austin, 1990, Calif. State U., Northridge, 1990, Golden West Coll., Huntington Beach, Calif., 1990, The Armory Ctr. for the Arts, 1991; represented in pub. collections at Libr. of Congress, Washington, L.A. County Mus. Art, Art Inst. Chgo., Bklyn. Mus. Art, U. Calgary, Can., Portland (Oreg.) Art Mus., Detroit Inst. Arts, Utah Mus. Fine Art, Salt Lake City, Puskin (USSR) Mus., Phila. Mus. Art, Seattle Art Mus., others; published in The Complete Collagraph, 1980, Watercolor Bold and Free, 1980, Printmaking: A Primary Form of Expression, 1992. Active art therapy programs for handicapped, aged, child guidance groups, others; mem. adv. bd. L.A. Ctr. on Arts and Aging, 1982—. With AUS, 1956-58. Recipient art awards in group shows; Fulbright scholar, Italy, 1960-61; Louis Comfort Tiffany grantee, 1965, Calif. State U. rsch. grantee, 1968, 69, 71, 74, 78, 79, Calif. State U. rsch. grantee, 1988; John S. Guggenheim Meml. fellow, 1969-70. Mem. L.A. Printmaking Soc. (hon. life), Am. Color Print Soc., Boston Printmakers. Democrat. Roman Catholic.

FRICK, MR. See GROEBLI, WERNER FRITZ

FRICKE, MARTIN PAUL, science company executive; b. Franklin, Pa., May 18, 1937; s. Frank Albert and Pauline Jane (Wentz) F.; m. Barbara Ann Blanton, Jan. 3, 1959. BS, Drexel U., Phila., 1961; MS, U. Minn., 1964, PhD, 1967. Prog. mgr., group leader Gen. Atomics, San Diego, 1968-73; prog. mgr., div. mgr. Sci. Applications Internat. Corp., La Jolla, Calif., 1973-77, v.p., 1977-80, corp. v.p., 1980-84; sr. v.p. Systems Group, The Titan Corp., San Diego, Calif., 1984-87, exec. v.p. Techs Group, 1987-89, sr. v.p. corp. ops., 1989-93; mem. cross sect. evaluation working group, Upton, L.I., N.Y., 1970-73, U.S. Nuclear Data Com., Washington, 1970-73. Author publs. in field. Recipient postdoctoral fellowship U. Mich., Ann Arbor, 1967-68, scholarship Pa. Indsl. Chem. Co., 1956-60; grad. fellow Oak Ridge (Tenn.) Assoc. Univs., 1964-67. Fellow Am. Phys. Soc. (panel on pub. affairs 1982-84); mem. Phi Kappa Phi. Roman Catholic. Home: 1606 Via Corona La Jolla CA 92037-7837

FRIDLEY, SAUNDRA LYNN, internal audit executive; b. Columbus, Ohio, June 14, 1948; d. Jerry Dean and Esther Eliza (Bluhm) F. BS, Franklin U., 1976; MBA, Golden Gate U., 1980. Accounts receivable supr. Internat. Harvester, Columbus, Ohio, San Leandro, Calif., 1972-80; sr. internal auditor Western Union, San Francisco, 1980; internal auditor II, County of Santa Clara, San Jose, Calif., 1980-82; sr. internal auditor Tymshare, Inc., Cupertino, Calif., 1982-84, div. contr., 1984; internal audit mgr. VWR Scientific, Brisbane, Calif., 1984-88, audit dir., 1988-89; internal audit mgr. Pacific IBM Employees Fed. Credit Union, San Jose, 1989-90, Western Temporary Svcs., Inc., Walnut Creek, Calif., 1990—; internal audit mgr., 1990-92; dir. quality assurance, 1992—; pres., founder Bay Area chpt. Cert. Fraud Examiners, 1990. Mem. NAFE, Friends of the Vineyards. Mem. Internal Auditors Speakers Bur., Cert. Fraud Examiners (founder, pres. Bay area chpt.), Inst. Internal Auditors (pres., founder Tri-Valley chpt.), Internal Auditor's Internat. Seminar Com., Internal Auditor's Internat. Conf. Com. Avocations: woodworking, gardening, golfing. Home: 19 Windmill Ct Brentwood CA 94513 Office: Western Temporary Svcs 301 Lennon Ln Walnut Creek CA 94598-2418

FRIED, ELAINE JUNE, business executive; b. L.A., Oct. 19, 1943; grad. Pasadena (Calif.) High Sch., 1963; various coll. courses; m. Howard I. Fried, Aug. 7, 1966; children: Donna Marie, Randall Jay. Agt., office mgr. Howard I. Fried Agy., Alhambra, Calif., 1975—; v.p. Sea Hill, Inc., Pasadena, Calif., 1973—. Publicity chmn., unit telephone chmn. San Gabriel Valley unit; past chmn. recipient certificate appreciation, 1987, Am. Diabetes Assn.; past publicity chmn. San Gabriel Valley region Women's Am. Orgn. for Rehab. Tng. (ORT); chmn. spl. events publicity, Temple Beth Torah Sisterhood, Alhambra, membership chmn., 1991-92, v.p. membership, 1991-93; former mem. bd. dirs., pub. relations com., personnel com. Vis. Nurses Assn., Pasadena and San Gabriel Valley, Recipient Vol. award So. Calif. affiliate Am. Diabetes Assn., 1974-77; chmn. outside Sisterhood publicity Congregation Shaarei Torah, 1993—, spl. events publicity, 1993—; co-recipient Ner Tamid award Temple Beth Torah. Contbr. articles to profl. jours. Clubs: B'nai B'rith Women, Hadassah, Temple Beth Torah Sisterhood. Speaker on psycho-social aspects of diabetes, insurance and the diabetic, ins. medicine. Home: 404 N Hidalgo Ave Alhambra CA 91801-2640

FRIED, LOUIS LESTER, information technology and management consultant; b. N.Y.C., Jan. 18, 1930; s. Albert and Tessie (Klein) F.; m. Haya Greenberg, Aug. 15, 1960; children: Ron Chaim, Eliana Ahuva, Gil Ben. BA in Pub. Adminstrn., Calif. State U., Los Angeles, 1962; MS in Mgmt. Theory, Calif. State U., Northridge, 1965. Mgr. br. plant data processing Litton systems, Inc., Woodland Hills, Calif., 1960-65; dir. mgmt. info. systems Bourns, Inc., Riverside, Calif., 1965-68, Weber Aircraft Co., Burbank, Calif., 1968-69; v.p. mgmt. services T.I. Corp. of Calif., Los Angeles, 1969-75; dir. advanced computer systems dept. Stanford Research Inst., Menlo Park, Calif., 1976-85, dir. ctr. for info. tech., 1985-86, dir. worldwide info. tech. practice, 1987-90; v.p. info. tech. cons. Stanford Rsch. Inst., Menlo Park, Calif., 1990—; cons. editor Auerbach Pubs., 1978—, Reston Pubs., 1979—; lectr. U. Calif., Riverside, 1965-69, lectr. mgmt. and EDP. Contbr. numerous articles to profl. jours., textbooks. Mem. Assn. Systems Mgmt. Home: 788 Loma Verde Ave Palo Alto CA 94303-4147 Office: Stanford Rsch Inst Menlo Park CA 94025

FRIEDENBERG, JOAN ELLEN, special needs educator; b. N.Y.C., Dec. 2, 1951; d. Herbert and Faye (Gelman) Friedenberg. Student U. Madrid (Spain), 1970, Inst. Hispanic Culture, Madrid, 1972; BA, Syracuse U.-Utica Coll., 1973; MA, U. Ill., 1975, PhD, 1979. Tchr. elem. sch. Dept. Instrn., Guayama, P.R., 1973-74; curriculum specialist Danville (Ill.) Pub. Schs., 1978-79; lectr. linguistics U. Ill.-Chgo., 1979; instr. English as a 2d lang. Syracuse (N.Y.) U., 1979; asst. prof. bilingual edn. Fla. Internat. U., Miami, 1979-82, assoc. prof., 1982-85; rsch. specialist/project dir. Ctr. on Edn. and Tng. for Empoyment, Ohio State U., Columbus, 1985-91; assoc. prof. bilingual/multicultural edn. Calif. State U. San Marcos, 1991—; cons. U.S. Dept. State, U.S. Dept. Edn., Washington; interpretor U.S. Immigration Svc., Miami, 1980; cons. refugee, state edn. and local edn. agys., Miami, 1980—. Author: (with others) Foundations and Strategies for Bilingual Vocational Education, 1982, Instructional Materials for Bilingual Vocational Education, 1984, The Vocational ESL Handbook, 1984, Finding a Job in the United States, 1986, Teaching Vocational Education to LEP Students, 1988, Recruit LEP Students for Vocational Programs, Conduct Intake Assessment for Limited English Proficient Students, Adapt Instruction for Limited English Proficient Vocational Students, Administer Vocational Programs for Limited English Proficient Students; contbr. articles to profl. jours., chpts. to books. U.S. Dept. Edn. fellow, 1975-78; dissertation research grantee U. Ill., 1978. Mem. Tchrs. English to Speakers of Other Langs., Nat. Assn. Bilingual Edn., Nat. Assn. for Vocat. Edn. Spl. Needs Pers., Nat. Dropout Prevention Network, Nat. Assn. for Indsl. and Tech. Tchr. Educators, Am. Vocat. Assn., Phi Delta Kappa, Phi Kappa Phi, Epsilon Pi Tau, Omicron Tau Theta. Jewish. Office: Cal State U 820 Los Vallecitos Blvd San Marcos CA 92069-1434

FRIEDERICH, JAN, retail grocery executive; b. 1944; married. Grad., U. Hamburg, 1968. With Bund deutscher Konsumgenossenschaften, 1968-71, Coop. Rhein-Main, 1972-76, RHG Leibbrand AHG, 1976-79; with Furr's Inc., Lubbock, Tex., 1979—, pres., chief exec. officer, 1979-90; chief exec. officer Furr's Supermarket, Inc., Albuquerque, 1990—, also chmn. bd. Office: Furr's Supermarkets PO Box 10267 Albuquerque NM 87184

FRIEDERICH, MARY ANNA, gynecology and obstetrics consultant; b. Rochester, N.Y., Nov. 15, 1931; d. Lewis Weniger and Mary Jasper (McGinnis) F.; m. John S. Savage (div. 1987); stepchildren: Steven T. Savage, Scott Allen Savage, Sandra Sue Savage DellaVilla. BA, Cornell U., 1953; MD, U. Rochester, 1957. Diplomate Am. Bd. Ob-Gyn. Intern in ob-gyn. and surgery U. Rochester, N.Y., 1957-58, asst. resident ob-gyn, 1958-59, assoc. resident and fellow ob-gyn and psychiatry, 1959-60, resident and instr. ob-gyn to chief resident, 1960-62, sr. instr. ob-gyn and psychiatry, 1963-66, asst. prof. in ob-gyn and psychiatry, 1966-68, assoc. prof. ob-gyn and psychiatry, 1968-76, clin. assoc. prof. in ob-gyn and psychiatry, 1976-86; med. dir. Planned Parenthood of Cen. and No. Ariz., 1986-89; sr. assoc. cons. in gyn. Mayo Clinc, Scottsdale, Ariz., 1990-91; med. dir. Ariz. Physicians I.P.A., 1989—; assoc. Maricopa County Medicine Assocs., 1991—; sr. assoc. ob-gyn and psychiatry Strong Meml. Hosp. of U. Rochester, 1976-84, attending ob-gyn and assoc. attending psychiatry, 1984-85, attending ob-gyn, 1985-87; staff in gynecology Good Samaritan Hosp., Phoenix; speaker and presenter in field. Editor: Psychosomatic Medicine, Women's Health, Human Sexuality, Jour. of Psychosomatic Ob-Gyn, Social Sci. Medicine, Jour. of Reproductive Medicine, Ob-Gyn, Jour AMA; contbr. numerous articles to profl. jours. Bd. pensions United Meth. Ch. Western N.Y. Conf., 1975-84; bd. dirs. Rochester United Meth. Homes, Goodman Gardens, 1970-82, pres. 1979-82; chairperson personnel com. Alternatives for Battered Women, 1979-81; adminstrv. bd. Asbury First United Meth. Ch., 1984-86; bd. dirs. United Cancer Coun., 1985-86; chairperson program com. Women's Coalition of Health Ann. Health Confs., 1985-86. Mem. AMA, Am. Coll. Ob-Gyn, Am. Med. Women's Assn., Soc. for Sex Therapy and Rsch. (bd. dirs. 1983-85), Am. Soc. Colposcopy and Cervical Pathology, Am. Soc. for Psychosomatic Ob-Gyn (past pres., sec., treas., historian), Soc. for Menstrual Cycle Rsch. (sec., treas. 1981—), Assn. of Reproductive Health Profls., Phoenix Ob-Gyn Soc., Maricopa County Med. Soc., Ariz. State Med. Soc. Republican. Methodist. Home: 10559 N 104th Pl Scottsdale AZ 85258-4941

FRIEDL, RICK, former college president, lawyer; b. Berwyn, Ill., Aug. 31, 1947; s. Raymond J. and Ione L. (Anderson) F.; m. Diane Marie Guillies, Sept. 2, 1977; children: Richard, Angela, Ryan. BA, Calif. State U., Northridge, 1969; MA, UCLA, 1976; postgrad. UCLA, 1984; JD Western State U., 1987. Bar: Calif. 1988, U.S. Dist. Ct. (ctrl. dist.) Calif., 1992. Dept. mgr. Calif. Dept. Indsl. Rels., 1973-78; mem. faculty dept. polit. sci. U. So. Calif., 1978-80; pres. Pacific Coll. Law, 1981-86; staff counsel state fund, Calif., 1988-89; prin. Law Offices of Rick Friedl, 1989—. Author: The Political Economy of Cuban Dependency, 1982; tech. editor Glendale Law Rev., 1984; contbr. articles to profl. jours. Calif. State Grad. fellow, 1970-72. Mem. ABA, Calif. State Bar Assn., Los Angeles County Bar Assn., Am. Polit. Sci. Assn., Latin Am. Studies Assn., Acad. Polit. Sci., Pacific Coast Council Latin Am. Studies, Calif. Trial Lawyers Assn. Home: 13068 Sundown Ct Victorville CA 92392-8875

FRIEDLAND, JACK ARTHUR, plastic surgeon; b. East Chicago, Ind., Feb. 10, 1940; s. Peter and Bettye (Manfield) F.; m. Harriet Anita Simensky, July 1, 1962; children: Margo Lynn, Jonathan Elliott, Julie I. Student, U. Wis., 1958-61; BS, Northwestern U., 1962, MD, 1965. Diplomate Am. Bd. of Surgery, Am. Bd. of Plastic Surgery, Nat. Bd. Med. Examiners. Intern in surgery NYU/Bellevue Med. Ctr., N.Y.C., 1965-66, from surg. resident to chief resident, 1966-70; resident in plastic surgery Inst. Reconstructive Plastic Surgery NYU Med. Ctr., N.Y.C., 1972-74; pvt. practice Phoenix, 1974—; chief of staff children's rehab. svc. State of Ariz., 1984-86; asst. chief of staff Phoenix Plastic Surgery Residency Program, 1974-84; attending physician Phoenix Plastic Surgery Fellowship/Mayo Clinic Residency Programs, 1985—; chief of surgery St. Luke's Hosp. Med. Ctr., Phoenix, 1981-83; chief of plastic surgery Children's Hosp., Phoenix, 1984-86; extra-mural asst. prof. plastic surgery Mayo Med. Sch., 1991—. Bd. dirs. men's arts coun. Phoenix Art Mus., 1975—, Am. Heart Assn., Phoenix, 1985-89, MADD, Phoenix, 1985-86. Maj. USAF, 1970-72. Fellow ACS; mem. AMA, Am. Soc. for Aesthetic Plastic Surgery, Inc. (pres. 1990-91), Am. Soc. Plastic and Reconstructive Surgeons, Am. Assn. Plastic Surgeons, Am. Cleft-Palate-Craniofacial Assn., Ariz. Med. Assn., Maricopa County Med. Assn., Ariz. Soc. Plastic and Reconstructive Surgeons, U. Club of Phoenix (bd. dirs. 1974-84, past pres.), Alpha Omega Alpha. Office: 101 E Coronado Rd Phoenix AZ 85004-1512

FRIEDLANDER, ALAN MARC, fisheries biologist; b. Balt., Nov. 28, 1958; s. Henry Ephraim and Nancy Nessa (Merdler) F. BS in Biology, Roanoke Coll., 1980; MS in Oceanography, Old Dominion U., 1987; postgrad., U. Hawaii, 1991—. Fisheries extension officer U.S. Peace Corps, Kingdom of Tonga, 1982-84; fisheries biologist U. Fla., Gainesville, 1987, Divsn. Fish and Wildlife, St. Thomas, V.I., 1988-90; marine biologist U.S. Nat. Park Svc., St.

John, V.I., 1990-91. Contbr. articles to profl. jours. Mem. Am. Fisheries Soc., Gulf and Caribbean Fisheries Inst., Tropical Fisheries Scientists, Sigma Xi. Democrat. Jewish. Office: Univ Hawaii Dept Zoology 2538 The Mall Honolulu HI 96822

FRIEDLANDER, ARTHUR HENRY, oral and maxillofacial surgeon, researcher; b. Bklyn., Feb. 8, 1942; s. Edward and Nettie (Hardbrod) F.; m. Ida Kreinik, June 17, 1967; 1 child, Mark David. BA, CUNY, Bklyn., 1963; DMD, Temple U., 1967. Diplomate Am. Bd. Oral and Maxillofacial Surgery. Resident in oral and maxillofacial surgery VA Med. Ctr., Bklyn., 1967-71; chief oral and maxillofacial surgery VA Med. Ctr., Northport, N.Y., 1971-82; assoc. prof. surgery SUNY, Stony Brook, 1971-82; chief dental svc. VA Med. Ctr., West Los Angeles, Calif., 1982-89; assoc. prof. surgery Dental Sch. UCLA, 1982—; dir. quality assurance Hosp. Dental Svc. UCLA Med. Ctr., 1986—; chief dental, oral and maxillofacial surgery VA Med. Ctr., Sepulveda, Calif., 1989—; mem. peer review com. UCLA Med. Ctr., 1989—, mem. quality of care assessment com., 1990—; mem. admission com. UCLA Dental Sch., 1989—. Contbr. numerous rsch. articles to profl. jours. Fellow Am. Assn. Oral and Maxillofacial Surgeons (ho. of dels. 1980-88); mem. Am. Coll. Oral and Maxillofacial Surgeons (founder 1977), N.Y. State Soc. Oral and Maxillofacial Surgeons (sec. 1979-82). Home: 12459 Marva Ave Granada Hills CA 91344-1527 Office: VA Med Ctr Chief Dental Svc Sepulveda CA 91343

FRIEDLANDER, CHARLES DOUGLAS, investment company executive, consultant; b. N.Y.C., Oct. 5, 1928; s. Murray L. and Jeane (Sottosanti) F.; m. Diane Mary Hutchins, May 12, 1951; children: Karen Diane, Lauren Patrice, Joan Elyse. BS, U.S. Mil. Acad., 1950; exec. mgmt. program, NASA, 1965; grad., Command and Staff Coll. USAF, 1965, Air War Coll. USAF, 1966. Commd. 2d lt. U.S. Army, 1950, advanced through grades to 1st lt.; officer inf. U.S. Army, Korea, 1950-51; resigned U.S. Army, 1954; mem. staff UN Forces, Trieste, Italy, 1953-54; chief astronaut support office NASA, Cape Canaveral, Fla., 1963-67; space cons. CBS News, N.Y.C., 1967-69; exec. asst. The White House, Washington, 1969-71; pres. Western Ranchlands Inc., Scottsdale, Ariz., 1971-74, Fairland Co. Inc., Scottsdale, 1974—; v.p. bd. dirs. Internat. Aerospace Hall of Fame, San Deigo; space program cons., various cos., Boca Raton, Fla., 1967-69; mem. staff First Postwar Fgn. Ministers Conf., Berlin, 1954; radio/TV cons. space program. Author: Buying & Selling Land for Profit, 1961, Last Man at Hungnam Beach, 1952. V.p. West Point Soc., Cape Canaveral, Fla., 1964. Served to lt. col. USAFR, maj. USAR. Decorated Bronze Star V, Combat Inf. badge; co-recipient Emmy award CBS TV Apollo Moon Landing, 1960. Mem. Nat. Space Club, Explorer's Club, West Point Soc., Chosen Few Survivors Korea, NASA Alumni League.

FRIEDLANDER, SHELDON KAY, chemical engineering educator; b. N.Y.C., Nov. 17, 1927; s. Irving and Rose (Katzewitz) F.; m. Marjorie Ellen Robbins, Apr. 16, 1934; children: Eva Kay, Amelie Elise, Antonia Zoe, Josiah. BS, Columbia U., 1949; SM, MIT, 1951; PhD, U. Ill., 1954. Asst. prof. chem. engring. Columbia U., N.Y.C., 1954-57; asst. prof. chem. engring. Johns Hopkins, Balt., 1957-59, assoc. prof. chem. engring., 1959-62, prof. chem. engring., 1962-64; prof. chem. engring., environ. health engring. Calif. Inst. Tech., Pasadena, 1964-78; prof. chem. engring. UCLA, 1978—, Parsons prof., 1982—, chmn. dept. chem. engring., 1984-88; dir. Engring. Rsch. Ctr. for Hazardous Substances Control. Author: Smoke, Dust, and Haze, 1977. Served with U.S. Army, 1946-47. Recipient Sr. Humboldt prize Fed. Republic of Germany, 1985, Internat. prize Am. Assn. for Aerosol Rsch./Gesellschaft flr Aerosolforschung/Japan Assn. for Aerosol Sci. and Tech., Fuchs Meml. award, 1990; Fulbright scholar, 1960-61; Guggenheim fellow, 1969-70. Mem. NAE, Am. Inst. Chem. Engrs. (Colburn award 1959, Alpha Chi Sigma award 1974, Walker award 1979), Am. Assn. for Aerosol Research (pres. 1984-86). Office: UCLA Dept Chem Engring 5531 Boelter Hall Los Angeles CA 90024

FRIEDMAN, BARRY, financial marketing consultant; b. Bklyn., Apr. 8, 1938; s. Samuel I. and Marion (Meltzer) F.; m. Ellen Barbara Rotkin, Aug. 30, 1958 (div. Nov. 1986); children: Scott Evan, Bradley Howard, Andrea Iris. BSBA, Lafayette Coll., 1959; cert. in fin. planning, Coll. for Fin. Planning, 1982. Cert. fin. planner. Owner Garden State Promotional, South Orange, N.J., 1959-68; v.p. Pa. Securities Co., East Orange, N.J., 1968-73; sr. v.p. McMillen Fin. Svcs., Jacksonville, Fla., 1973-75; pres. Enerdyne Corp., Richardson, Tex., 1975-80; sr. v.p. Murray Fin. Corp., Dallas, 1980-84; owner Barry Friedman Assocs., Dana Point, Calif., 1984—; pres. Conifer Investment Group, Dana Point, 1990—; bd. dirs. Bancon Corp.; pres. North Tex. Fin. Planners, Dallas, 1982-84, chmn., 1984-85; speaker; seminar leader. Contbr. articles to profl. jours. Mem. Internat. Assn. for Fin. Planning (chmn. 1969-72, pres. 1980-85), Mensa. Home and Office: Barry Friedman Assocs 34300 Lantern Bay Dr Apt 24 Dana Point CA 92629-2856

FRIEDMAN, HERBERT JOEL, furniture retail/manufacturing executive; b. N.Y.C., Aug. 16, 1950; s. David and Lillian F.; m. Lois Huntsman, Mar. 22, 1986; children: Sabrina, Gregg, Nicole, Lyndsey. BS, St. Johns U., 1972. Dept. mgr., asst. buyer, buyer Macys-N.Y., N.Y.C., 1972-75; buyer Goldblatt Bros. Stores, Chgo., 1975-78; sr. buyer Emporium-Capwell Dept. Stores, Oakland, Calif., 1978-80; merchandising mgr. Emporium Dept. Stores, San Francisco, 1980-84, divsn. v.p., 1984-89; sr. v.p. Krauses Sofa Factory, Brea, Calif., 1989—; mgmt. sponsor Associated Merchandising Corp., N.Y.C., 1982-86. Fund raiser City of Hope, L.A., 1991—; sponsor Nat. Jr. Basketball Assn., Anaheim, Calif., 1990, 92. Mem. Nat. Club Football Assn. (pres. 1971-73). Home: 7121 E Country Club Ln Anaheim Hills CA 92807 Office: Krauses Sofa Factory Corporate Office 200 N Berry St Brea CA 92623

FRIEDMAN, JULES DANIEL, geologist; b. Poughkeepsie, N.Y., Oct. 24, 1928; s. Jack and Sophie (Seltzer) F.; m. Linda Diane Wheelock, May 2, 1988; children: Susanne K., Jack A., Lisa K. AB, Cornell U., 1950; MS, Yale U., 1952, PhD, 1958. Geologist, br. mil. geology U.S. Geol. Survey, Washington, 1953-64, geologist, br. theoretical and applied geophysics, 1964-72; geologist, br. geophysics U.S. Geol. Survey, Denver, 1973—, chief remote sensing sect., 1982-85; rep. to U.S. Army Corps Engrs. U.S. Geol. Survey, 1959; advisor to Mex. Govt., 1969, NASA, 1969, 70, Brazilian govt., 1970, Nat. Rsch. Coun. Iceland, 1966-71, USN, 1971-72; cons. tech. assistance program UN, 1971; USGS rep. Skylab visual observations team JSC, NASA, 1975. Contbr. numerous articles to profl. jours. Recipient Group Achievement award NASA, 1974, Quality of Scientific Work award, 1979. Fellow Geol. Soc. Am.; mem. Am. Geophys. Union (sec., exec. com., front range br. 1982-83). Home: PO Box 471 Wheat Ridge CO 80034-0471 Office: US Geol Survey MS 964 Denver Fed Ctr Denver CO 80225

FRIEDMAN, KENNETH TODD, investment banker. BSBA, Lewis and Clark Coll., 1979; MBA, Harvard U., 1983. Fin. analyst Dresser Industries, L.A., 1979-80; fin. cons. Am. Appraisal, L.A., 1980-81; mng. dir. Houlihan, Lokey, Howard & Zukin, L.A., 1983-90; pres. Houlihan, Lokey, Howard & Zukin Capital, L.A., 1986-90, Friedman Enterprises, L.A., 1990—; bd. dirs. Hampton Internat., Rivine, Calif.

FRIEDMAN, MICHAEL HOWARD, finance executive; b. Wilkes Barre, Pa., Oct. 7, 1944; s. Samuel and Pauline (Morris) F.; m. Ida M. Iskowitz, June 12, 1966 (div.); children: Tami Beth, Renee Lynn; m. Brenda L. Nightingale, Oct. 28, 1976. Salesman Superior Motors, Kingston, Pa., 1962-72, Sta. WDAU-TV, Seranton, Pa., 1972-73, Delight Form Ind., Easton, Pa., 1973-75, Exquisite Form Ind., Pelham Manor, N.Y., 1975-80; salesman, fin. officer Bronsberg & Hughes Pontiac, Kingston, Pa., 1980-81; fin. mgr. Colo. AMC/Jeep, Aurora, 1981-86, Kumpf Motor Car Co., Englewood, Colo., 1986-93, Mike Naughton Ford, Inc., Aurora, Co., 1993—. With USAF, 1965. Mem. Knights of Pythias. Republican. Jewish. Office: Mike Naughton Ford Inc 150 S Havana St Aurora CO 80012

FRIEDMAN, MILTON, economist, educator emeritus, author; b. Brooklyn, N.Y., July 31, 1912; s. Jeno Saul and Sarah Ethel (Landau) F.; m. Rose Director, June 25, 1938; children: Janet, David. AB, Rutgers U., 1932, LLD (hon.), 1968; AM, U. Chgo., 1933; PhD, Columbia U., 1946; LLD (hon.), St. Paul's (Rikkyo) U., 1963, Loyola U., 1971, U. N.H., 1975, Harvard U., 1979, Brigham Young U., 1980, Dartmouth Coll., 1980, Gonzaga U., 1981; DSc (hon.), Rochester U., 1971; LHD (hon.), Rockford Coll., 1969, Roosevelt U., 1975, Hebrew Union Coll., Los Angeles, 1981, Jacksonville U., 1993; LittD (hon.), Bethany Coll., 1971; PhD (hon.), Hebrew U., Jerusalem, 1977; DCS (hon.), Francisco Marroquin U., Guatemala, 1978. Assoc. economist Nat. Resources Com., Washington, 1935-37; mem. research staff Nat. Bur. Econ. Research, N.Y.C., 1937-45, 1948-81; vis. prof. econs. U. Wis., Madison, 1940-41; prin. economist, tax research div. U.S. Treasury Dept., Washington, 1941-43; assoc. dir. research, statis. research group, War Research div. Columbia U., N.Y.C., 1943-45; assoc. prof. econs. and statistics U. Minn., Mpls., 1945-46; assoc. prof. econs. U. Chgo., 1946-48, prof. econs., 1948-62, Paul Snowden Russell disting. service prof. econs., 1962-82, prof. emeritus, 1983—; Fulbright lectr. Cambridge U., 1953-54; vis. Wesley Clair Mitchell research prof. econs. Columbia U., N.Y.C., 1964-65; fellow Ctr. for Advanced Study in Behavioral Sci., 1957-58; sr. research fellow Stanford U., 1977—; mem. Pres.'s Commn. All-Vol. Army, 1969-70, Pres.'s Commn. on White House Fellows, 1971-74, Pres.'s Econ. Policy Adv. Bd., 1981-88; vis. scholar Fed. Res. Bank, San Francisco, 1977. Author: (with Carl Shoup and Ruth P. Mack) Taxing to Prevent Inflation, 1943, (with Simon S. Kuznets) Income from Independent Professional Practice, 1946, (with Harold A. Freeman, Frederic Mosteller, W. Allen Wallis) Sampling Inspection, 1948, Essays in Positive Economics, 1953, A Theory of the Consumption Function, 1957, A Program for Monetary Stability, 1960, Price Theory: A Provisional Text, 1962, (with Rose D. Friedman) Capitalism and Freedom, 1962, (with R.D. Friedman) Free To Choose, 1980, (with Rose D. Friedman) Tyranny of the Status Quo, 1984, (with Anna J. Schwartz) A Monetary History of the United States, 1867-1960, 1963, (with Schwartz) Monetary Statistics of the United States, 1970, (with Schwartz) Monetary Trends in the U.S. and the United Kingdom, 1982, Inflation: Causes and Consequences, 1963, (with Robert Roosa) The Balance of Payments: Free vs. Fixed Exchange Rates, 1967, Dollars and Deficits, 1968, The Optimum Quantity of Money and Other Essays, 1969, (with Walter W. Heller) Monetary vs. Fiscal Policy, 1969, A Theoretical Framework for Monetary Analysis, 1972, (with Wilbur J. Cohen) Social Security, 1972, An Economist's Protest, 1972, There's No Such Thing As A Free Lunch, 1975, Price Theory, 1976, (with Robert J. Gordon et al.) Milton Friedman's Monetary Framework, 1974, Tax Limitation, Inflation and the Role of Government, 1978, Bright Promises, Dismal Performance, 1983, Money Mischief, 1992; editor: Studies in the Quantity Theory of Money, 1956; bd. editors Am. Econ. Rev, 1951-53, Econometrica, 1957-69; adv. bd. Jour. Money, Credit and Banking, 1968—; columnist Newsweek mag, 1966-84, contbg. editor, 1971-84; contbr. articles to profl. jours. Decorated Grand Cordon of the 1st Class Order of the Sacred Treasure (Japan), 1986; recipient Nobel prize in econs., 1976, Pvt. Enterprise Exemplar medal Freedoms Found., 1978, Presdl. medal of Freedom, 1988, Nat. Medal of Sci., 1988, Prize in Moral-Cultural Affairs, Instn. World Capitalism, 1993; named Chicagoan of Yr., Chgo. Press Club, 1972, Educator of Yr., Cgho. Jewish United Fund, 1973. Fellow Inst. Math. Stats., Am. Statis. Assn., Econometric Soc.; mem. Nat. Acad. Scis., Am. Econ. Assn. (mem. exec. com. 1955-57, pres. 1967; John Bates Clark medal 1951), Am. Enterprise Inst. (adv. bd. 1956-79), Western Econ. Assn. (pres. 1984-85), Royal Economic Soc., Am. Philos. Soc., Mont Pelerin Soc. (bd. dirs. 1958-61, pres. 1970-72). Club: Quadrangle. Office: Stanford U Hoover Instn Stanford CA 94305-6010

FRIEDMAN, PAULA NAOMI, museum public relations director; b. Washington, Feb. 22, 1939; d. Melvin Hillard and Beatrice Patricia (Zisman) F.; children: Carl, Joseph. BA, Cornell U., 1961; MA, San Francisco State U., 1965; MLS, U. Calif., Berkeley, 1975. Asst. libr. Woodward-Clyde Corp., Emeryville, Calif., 1976-77; freelance editor Berkeley, Calif., 1978-82; prodn. editor Ednl. Products Info. Exch. Western Office, Berkeley, 1984-85; libr. Berkeley Pub. Libr., 1984-93; pub. rels. dir. Judah L. Magnes Mus., Berkeley, 1985—; publicist Caring Ctr. Univ. Ave. Coop. Homes, Berkeley, 1979—; coord. Nationwide Rosenberg Poetry Award. Author: (story) Prayer, Merry Christmas, and others, 1969-80, (poem) Inside the Axioms, Minotaur, and others, 1969—; founding and coordinating editor, Open Cell rev., 1969-75; editor: Teamster Rank and File, 1981, Sam Hamburg, 1989, In Their Own Words, 1993, Songs for Our Voices, 1993, and others. Mem. Am. Assn. Mus., Bay Area Mus. Publicists' Roundtable, No. Calif. Book Publicists' Assn.

FRIEDMAN, SHELLY ARNOLD, cosmetic surgeon; b. Providence, Jan. 1, 1949; s. Saul and Estelle (Moverman) F.; m. Andrea Leslie Falchook, Aug. 30, 1975; children: Bethany Erin, Kimberly Rebecca, Brent David, Jennifer Ashley. BA, Providence Coll., 1971; DO, Mich. State U., 1982. Diplomate Nat. Bd. Med. Examiners, Am. Bd. Dermatology. Intern Pontiac (Mich.) Hosp., 1982-83, resident in dermatology, 1983-86; assoc. clin. prof. dept. internal med. Mich. State U., 1984-89, adj. clin. prof., 1989—; med. dir. Inst. Cosmetic Dermatology, Scottsdale, Ariz., 1986—. Contbr. aritcles to profl. jours. Mem. B'nai B'rith Men's Council, 1973, Jewish Welfare Fund, 1973. Am. Physicians fellow for medicine, 1982. Mem. AMA, Am. Osteopathic Assn., Am. Assn. Cosmetic Surgeons, Am. Acad. Cosmetic Surgery, Internat. Soc. Dermatologic Surgery, Internat. Acad. Cosmetic Surgery, Am. Acad. Dermatology, Am. Soc. Dermatol. Surgery, Frat. Order Police, Sigma Sigma Phi. Jewish. Office: Scottsdale Inst Cosmetic Dermatology 5206 N Scottsdale Rd Scottsdale AZ 85253

FRIEDMAN, STANLEY, physician; b. N.Y.C., Mar. 23, 1922; s. Irving and Lena (Schneiderman) F.; m. Lisbeth Moller, Oct. 12, 1972; children: Matt, Wendy. AB, U. Pa., 1942; MD, Chgo. Med. Sch., 1947. Diplomate Am. Bd. Ob./Gyn. Intern Sydenham Hosp., N.Y.C., 1945-47; resident in ob/gyn. Harlem Hosp., N.Y.C., 1953-56; asst. prof. U. Calif., San Francisco, 1968-73; assoc. clin. prof. UCLA Sch. of Medicine, 1974—. Maj. U.S. Army, 1951-53, Korea. Mem. Soc. of Reproductive Surgeons, Am. Soc. Andrology, Am. Fertility Soc., Pacific Coast Fertility Soc., La. Soc. Ob./Gyn. Office: 9675 Brighton Way Ste 420 Beverly Hills CA 90210-5135

FRIEDMAN, WILL JOEL, psychologist; b. L.A., Apr. 28, 1950; s. Martin and Selma F.; m. Dominique Piana, May 26, 1985; 1 child, Gregory Allen. BA, U. Calif.-Irvine, 1971; MS, Calif. State U., L.A., 1979; PhD, Claremont Grad. Sch., Calif., 1986. Lic. clin. psychologist, Calif.; diplomate Am. Soc. Pain Mgmt., Am. Bd. Md. Psychotherapists. Tchr. Sulphur Springs Unified Sch. Dist., Sargus, Calif., 1974-75; psychol. asst. various psychologists, 1977—; pvt. practice psychology Redlands, Calif., 1988-90, Loma Linda, Calif., 1990—; writer OP-ED San Bernardino Sun newspaper; broadcaster, media psychologist Sta. KVCR-FM; assoc. CPC Rancho Lindo Hosp., H.O.P.E., Fontana, Calif.; co-founder Sharp Confidants. cons. in field. Contbr. articles to profl. jours. Recipient Cert. of Appreciation for dedicated vol. svcs., County of L.A. Dept. Health Svcs., 1980, others. Fellow Am. Bd. Med. Psychotherapists; mem. APA, Am. Soc. Med. Psychotherapists, Calif. Psychol. Assn., Assn. Transpersonl Psychology, Am. Soc. Clin. Hypnosis, Am. Acad. Med. Hypnoanalysts, Orange County Soc. Clin. Hypnosis, Pre and Peri Natal Psychology Assn. of N.Am., Christian Assn. for Psychol. Studies, Internat. Soc. for Study Multiple Personality and Dissociation, Psi Chi (Nat. Svc. award 1979). Office: 11354 Mountain View Ave # C Loma Linda CA 92354-3830

FRIEDMANN, PERETZ PETER, aerospace engineer, educator; b. Timisoara, Romania, Nov. 18, 1938; came to U.S., 1969; s. Mauritius and Elisabeth Friedmann; m. Esther Sarfati, Dec. 8, 1964. DSc, MIT, 1972. Engring. officer Israel Def. Force, 1961-65; sr. engr. Israel Aircraft Industries, Ben Gurion Airport, Israel, 1965-69; research asst. dept. aeronautics and astronautics MIT, Cambridge, 1969-72; asst. prof. mech., aerospace and nuclear engring. dept. UCLA, 1972-77, assoc. prof., 1977-80, prof., 1980—; chmn. Dept. Mech Aerospace Nuclear Engring., Los Angeles, 1988-91. Editor in chief Vertica-Internat. Jour. Rotocraft and Powered Lift Aircraft, 1980-90; contbr. numerous articles to profl. jours. Grantee NASA, Air Force Office Sci. Rsch., U.S. Army Rsch. Office, NSF. Fellow AIAA; mem. ASME (structures and materials award 1983), Am. Helicopter Soc., Sigma Xi. Jewish. Office: UCLA Dept Mech Aerospace & Nuclear Engring Rm 46-147N Engring IV Los Angeles CA 90024

FRIEDRICHS, BETTY JOSEPHINE, small business owner; b. Northridge, Calif., Dec. 9, 1960; d. John Joseph and Doris Lilian (Shaw) Williams; m. Wade Leonard Friedrichs, Nov. 11, 1983 (div. 1988); 1 child, Zachary Joseph. BSBA, Calif. State U., Fullerton, 1983. V.p. Copy Masters, Industry, Calif., 1980-82; territory mgr. Xerox, Orange, Calif., 1983; sales mgr. Ameritech Communications, Huntington Beach, Calif., 1983-88, Modern Bus. Automation, Torrance, Calif., 1988-90; pres. Kontek I, Inc., Long Beach, Calif., 1990—. Pres. Boys Club Placentia, Calif., 1991—; mem. allocation com. United Way, Orange, 1988-90; edn. counselor Relief Soc., Huntington Beach, 1991-92. Republican. LDS Ch. Home: Huntington Beach CA 92647 Office: Kontek I Inc 3950 Paramount Blvd # 215 Lakewood CA 90712

FRIEMAN, EDWARD ALLAN, university administrator, educator; b. N.Y.C., Jan. 19, 1926; s. Joseph and Belle (Davidson) F.; m. Ruth Paula Rodman, June 19, 1949 (dec. May 1966); children: Jonathan, Michael, Joshua; m. Joy Fields, Sept. 17, 1967; children: Linda Gatchell, Wendy. BS, Columbia U., 1946, MS in Physics, 1948; PhD in Physics, Poly. Inst. Bklyn., 1951. Prof. astrophys. scis., dep. dir. Plasma Physics Lab. Princeton U., N.J., 1952-79; dir. energy research Dept. Energy, Washington, 1979-81; exec. v.p. Sci. Applications Internat. Corp., La Jolla, Calif., 1981-86; dir. Scripps Instn. Oceanography, La Jolla, 1986—; vice chancellor marine scis. U. Calif., San Diego, 1986—; vice chmn. White House Sci. Coun., 1981-89, Def. Sci. Bd., Washington, 1984-90; mem. Joint Oceanographic Insts., Inc., 1986—, chmn. 1991—; chmn. supercollider site evaluation com. NRC, 1987-88; mem. sci. adv. com. GM, 1987-93, corp. Charles Stark Draper Lab., Inc., 1989—, Sec. Energy Adv. Bd. 1990—, v.p. Space Policy adv. bd., 1992—.; bd. dirs. Sci. Applications Internat. Corp.; chmn. NASA Earth Observing System Engring. Rev., 1991-92, mem. v.p's. space policy adv. bd., 1992—; chmn. President's Com. on Nat. Medal Sci., 1992-93; active Joint Oceanographic Insts., Inc., 1986—, chmn., 1991—. Contbr. articles to profl. jours. Served with USN, 1943-46, PTO. Recipient Disting. Service medal Dept. Energy; Disting. Alumni award Poly. Inst. Bklyn.; NSF sr. postdoctoral fellow; Guggenheim fellow. Fellow Am. Phys. Soc. (Richtmyer award); mem. AAAS, NAS, Am. Philos. Soc., Cosmos Club (Washington). Home: 6425 Muirlands Dr La Jolla CA 92037-6310 Office: Scripps Instn Oceanography Dirs Office 0210 9500 Gilman Dr La Jolla CA 92093-0210

FRIEND, DAVID ROBERT, chemist; b. Vallejo, Calif., Aug. 10, 1956; s. Carl Gilbert and Roberta (Schwarzrock) F.; m. Carol Esther Warren, Dec. 17, 1983; 1 child, Ian, Michael. BS in Food Biochemistry, U. Calif., Davis, 1979; PhD in Agrl. Chemistry, U. Calif., Berkeley, 1983. Polymer chemist SRI Internat., Menlo Park, Calif., 1984-87, sr. polymer chemist controlled release and biomed. polymers dept., 1987-90, assoc. dir. controlled release and biomed. polymers dept., 1990-92, dir. controlled release and biomed. polymers dept., 1992—; leader Biopharms. Rsch. Group, 1990; lectr. U. Calif. Sch. Pharmacy, San Francisco. Assoc. editor Jour. Controlled Release; contbr. articles to scholarly jours.; patentee in field. Mem. Am. Chem. Soc., N.Y. Acad. Scis., Controlled Release Soc., Am. Assn. Pharm. Sci., Sigma Xi. Democrat. Jewish. Home: 454 9th Ave Menlo Park CA 94025 Office: SRI Internat 333 Ravenswood Ave Menlo Park CA 94025-3493

FRIEND, JED, sports association executive; b. Liberty, Tex., Jan. 18, 1958; s. Harlan Dillman and Dorothy Helen (Weil) F. PhD, Tex. A&M U., 1987. Sport mgmt. cons. to profl. teams, 1987—; prof. Rice U., Houston, 1988-90; chief oper. officer/ exec. dir. U.S. Sports Acrobatics Fedn., Colorado Springs, Colo., 1990—. Contbr. articles to profl. jours. Office: PO Box 17043 Colorado Springs CO 80935

FRIES, DAVID SAMUEL, chemist, educator; b. Manassas, Va., June 22, 1945; s. Basil L. and Ruby (Sperau) F.; m. Marjie Ann Strayer, May 1, 1964; children: Susan, Jane, Corey. BA in Chemistry, Bridgewater Coll., 1968; PhD in Medicinal Chemistry, Va. Commonwealth U., 1971. Prof. medicinal chemistry U. of Pacific, Stockton, Calif., 1973—, dean grad. sch., 1993—; vis. rsch. prof. U. Groningen, The Netherlands, 1984-85, German Cancer Rsch. Ctr., Heidelberg, 1989-90; cons. on opioid drug addiction, 1975—. Contbr. articles to profl. jours. and chpts. to books. Rsch. grantee Nat. Inst. on Drug Abuse, NSF. Mem. Am. Chem. Soc., Fedn. Internat. Pharmaceutique, Am. Assn. Colls. Pharmacy, Sigma Xi, Phi Kappa Phi, Rho Chi, Phi Delta Chi. Office: U of Pacific Sch of Pharmacy Stockton CA 95211

FRIES, LITA LINDA, school system administrator; b. Merced, Calif., Feb. 16, 1942; d. Alfred Earl and Juanita Lora (Brown) Griffey; m. George Richard Fries, Feb. 3, 1962; 1 child, Damon Brant. BA, U. Calif., Berkeley, 1966; MS, Calif. State U., 1976. Cert. elem. tchr., secondary tchr., ednl. adminstrator, reading specialist. Tchr. Peace Corps, Mwanza, Tanzania, 1963-65; tchr. Oakland (Calif.) Unified Sch. Dist., 1966-74, tchr. spl. assignment, 1974-84, principal, Burckhalter, 1984-85, program mgr., 1985-90, administr., 1990-92, coord. state and fed. programs, 1992—. Mem. East Bay Reading Assn. (editor 1982-83), Pi Lamda Theta (membership chairperson 1986-88), Delta Kappa Gamma, Phi Delta Kappa. Democrat. Office: Oakland Unified Sch Dist 1025 2d Ave Oakland CA 94606

FRIESE, ROBERT CHARLES, lawyer; b. Chgo., Apr. 29, 1943; s. Earl Matthew and Laura Barbara (Mayer) F.; m. Chandra Ullom; children: Matthew Robert, Mark Earl, Laura Moore. AB in Internat. Rels., Stanford U., 1964; JD, Northwestern U., 1970. Bar: Calif. 1972. Dir. Tutor Applied Linguistics Ctr., Geneva, 1964-66; atty. Bronson, Bronson & McKinnon, San Francisco, 1970-71, SEC, San Francisco, 1971-75; ptnr. Shartsis, Friese & Ginsburg, San Francisco, 1975—; dir., co-founder Internat. Plant Research Inst., Inc., San Carlos, Calif., 1978-86. Chmn. bd. suprs. Task Force on Noise Control, 1972-78; chmn. San Franciscans for Cleaner City, 1977; exec. dir. Nob Hill Neighbors, 1972-81; bd. dirs. Nob Hill Assn., 1976-78, Inst. Range and Am. Mustang, 1988—, Calif. Heritage Coun., 1977-78, Palace Fine Arts, San Francisco Beautiful, 1986—, pres., 1988—; chmn. Citizens Adv. Com. for Embarcadero Project; mem. major gifts com. Stanford U.; bd. dirs. Presidio Heights Neighborhood Assn., 1993—. Mem. ABA, Calif. Bar Assn., Bar Assn. San Francisco (bd. dirs. 1982-85, chmn. bus. litigation com. 1978-79, chmn. state ct. civil litigation com. 1983-90, new courthouse com. 1993—), Lawyers Club of San Francisco, Mensa, Calif. Hist. Soc., Commonwealth Club, Swiss-Am. Friendship League (chmn. 1971-79). Office: Shartsis Friese & Ginsburg 1 Maritime Plz Fl 18 San Francisco CA 94111-3404

FRIESECKE, RAYMOND FRANCIS, management consultant; b. N.Y.C., Mar. 12, 1937; s. Bernhard P. K. and Josephine (De Tomi) F.; BS in Chemistry, Boston Coll., 1959; MS in Civil Engring., MIT, 1961. Product specialist Dewey & Almy Chem. div. W. R. Grace & Co., Inc., Cambridge, Mass., 1963-66; market planning specialist USM Corp., Boston, 1966-71; mgmt. cons., Boston, 1971-74; dir. planning and devel. Schweitzer div. Kimberly-Clark Corp., Lee, Mass., 1974-78; v.p. corp. planning Butler Automatic, Inc., Canton, Mass., 1978-80; pres. Butler-Europe Inc., Greenwich, Conn. and Munich, 1980; v.p. mktg. and planning Butler Greenwich Inc., 1980-81; pres. Strategic Mgmt. Assocs., San Rafael, Calif., 1981—; corp. clk., v.p. Bldg. Research & Devel., Inc., Cambridge, 1966-68. Author: Management by Relative Product Quality; contbr. articles to profl. jours. State chmn. Citizens for Fair Taxation, 1972-73; state co-chmn. Mass. Young Reps., 1967-69; chmn. Ward 7 Rep. Com., Cambridge, 1968-70; vice chmn. Cambridge Rep. City Com., 1966-68; vice-chmn. Kentfield Rehab. Hosp. Found., 1986-88, chmn., 1988-91; Rep. candidate Mass. Ho. of Reps., 1964, 66; pres. Marin Rep. Coun., 1986-91; chmn. Calif. Acad., 1986-88; sec. Navy League Marin Coun., 1984-91. 1st lt. U.S. Army, 1961-63. Mem. NRA, Am. Chem. Soc., Am. Mktg. Assn., Marin Philos. Soc. (v.p. 1991-92), The Planning Forum, The World Affairs Coun. Home and Office: 141 Convent Ct San Rafael CA 94901-1335

FRIESEL, CLAUDE WAYNE, property manager; b. San Jose, Calif., Feb. 9, 1935; s. Claude and Mary Alice (Booth) F.; m. Rachel Joan Zuniga, July 27, 1959; children: Laura Ann, Julie Lynn. Cert., Cabrillo Coll., 1964, Gavilan Coll., 1969. Cert. U.S. Drug Enforcement, WMA Park Mgmt., Calif. Police officer Capitola (Calif.) Police Dept., 1970, Newman (Calif.) Police Dept., 1970; ops. coord. Elenburg Capital, Aptos, Calif., 1985-89, Francis & Freedman, Beverly Hills, Calif., 1989—. Recipient certs. Appreciation Kiwanis, Watsonville, Calif., 1969, Sacramento C. of C., 1991, Rotary, Scotts Valley, Calif., 1983. Mem. Sons in Retirement (cert. 1990). Democrat. Mem. Christian Ch. Home: 92 Falcon Crest Cir Napa CA 94558 Office: Francis & Freedman Property Mgmt 2001 Salvador Ave Napa CA 94558

FRIESEN, ORIS DEWAYNE, software engineer, historian; b. York, Nebr., Jan. 4, 1940; s. Harry H. and Malita Wanda (Ratzlaff) F.; m. Carey Lea Burbank, May 28, 1964; children: Isabelle Anne, Aric Alan. BS, U. Ariz., 1964, MA, 1966; PhD, Ariz. State U., 1982. Computer systems analyst Computer Scis. Corp., Richland, Wash., 1967-69; computer systems designer

GE, Phoenix, 1969-70; database systems designer Honeywell Info. Systems, Phoenix, 1970-84, engring. fellow, database mgmt., 1984-90; engring. fellow, database mgmt. Bull Worldwide Info. Systems, Phoenix, 1990—; adj. prof. engring. Ariz. State U., Tempe, 1984-88; vice chmn. database stds. Am. Nat. Stds. Inst., Washington, 1980-85; gen. chmn. Internat. Conf. on Deductive and Object-Oriented Databases, Scottsdale, Ariz., 1991—. Author: China Reporting: An Oral History of American Journalism in the 1930's-1040's, 1987; editor: Proceedings of Phoenix Conference on Computers and Communications, 1987; contbr. articles to profl. jours. Mem. Phoenix Futures Forum, 1988-91; mem., officer North Tatum Community Homeowners Assn., Phoenix, 1985-88. With USMC, 1958-59. Mem. IEEE (gen. chmn. Phoenix Conf. on Computers and Communications 1990-91), Assn. for Computing Machinery, Assn. Asian Studies, Am. Hist. Assn., Orgn. Am. Historians. Democrat. Home: 5136 E Le Marche Ave Scottsdale AZ 85254 Office: Bull Worldwide Info Systems PO Box 8000 AZ05-H32 Phoenix AZ 85066-8000

FRIESZ, DONALD STUART, marketing professional; b. Cin., Aug. 26, 1929; s. Francis Albert and Ara Ethel (Smith) F.; m. Doris Ann Anderson, Aug. 6, 1955 (dec. Sept. 1983), children: Mark Allan, Carol Ann; m. Mary Lee Dubbell, July 5, 1985; children: Cheryl Dubbell, Paul Dubbell. BBA, U. Cin., 1953. Sales trainee Continental Can Co., Cin., Chgo., 1948-53; sales rep. Virco Mfg. Corp., Kankakee, Ill., 1957-58; regional sales mgr. Virco Mfg. Corp., Columbus, Ohio, 1959-60; div. sales mgr. Virco Mfg. Corp., Conway, Ark., 1961-81; v.p. ednl. sales Virco Mfg. Corp., Conway, 1982; v.p. sales and mktg. Virco Mfg. Corp., L.A., 1983, also bd. dirs.; bd. dirs. Internat. Assn. Sch. Bus. Officials, Reston, Va., 1991—. Pres. Peninsula Camp Gideon's Internat., Palos Verdes, Calif., 1992. Lt. USNR, 1948-49, 53-56. Mem. Univ. Lodge, Beta Omicron Alumni Assn. Theta Chi. Republican. Home: 5717 Sunmist Dr Rancho Palos Verdes CA 90274 Office: Virco Mfg Corp 1331 W Torrance Blvd Torrance CA 90501

FRIEZ, RICK EARL, insurance company manager; b. Forsyth, Mont., Aug. 27, 1945; s. Earl R. and Paula K. Friez; m. Patsy L. Mees, Feb. 12, 1966; children: Todd D., Timothy E., Kami L. BS in Edn., Mont. State U., 1967; grad., State Farm Ins. Career Agt. Sch., Salem, Oreg., 1976, 77, State Farm Ins. Career Agy. Mgrs. Sch., Bloomington, Ill., 1990. Mil. coord. Valley Rural Telephone Coop., Glasgow, Mont., 1974-75; ins. agt. State Farm Ins. Cos., Forsyth, 1976-90; dist. agy. mgr. State Farm Ins. Cos., Billings, Mont., 1990—. Vice chmn. bd. trustees Forsyth Pub. Schs., 1986-92; chmn., pres. Concordia Luth. Ch., Forsyth, 1985-86; Grand Bobcat, Mont. State U. Booster Club, Bozeman, 1976-92. Capt. USAF, 1968—. Mem. Am. Legion, Forsyth Area C. of C., Forsyth Lions Club (1st v.p., program chmn.), Forsyth Country Club (past pres./dir.), Luth. Laymans League (past pres.), Ducks Unlimited, N.Am. Elk Found., Trout Unlimited, Walleye Unlimited, Alpha Gamma Rho (alumni orgn.). Home: 1475 Willow St Forsyth MT 59327 Office: State Farm Ins KIKC Bldg HW 10 W Forsyth MT 59327

FRIGON, JUDITH ANN, electronics executive, office systems consultant; b. Wisconsin Rapids, Wis., Feb. 11, 1945; d. Harold Leslie and Muriel Alice (Berard) Neufeld; m. Gene Roland Frigon, June 17, 1967; children: Shane P., Shannon M., Sean M. Sec., office mgr. George Chapman D.D.S., Fairfax, Va., 1971-75; owner, operator Sunset Motel, Havre, Mont., 1976-78; sec. Wash. State U. Social Research Ctr., Pullman, 1978-80; adminstrv. sec. Wash. State U. Systems and Computing, Pullman, 1980-85, office automation cons., word processing trainer, IBM profl. office system adminstr., 1983-89, microcomputer cons. and trainer, 1989—; systems analyst, programmer Wash. State U. Computing Ctr., Pullman, 1985—; owner Computer Assistance, Tng. and Svcs., Pullman, 1992—. Pres. Pullman Svc. Unit Girl Scouts U.S., 1983-89; v.p. Inland Empire coun. Girl Scouts U.S., Spokane, Wash., 1985-89, pres., 1989—; mem. Pullman Civic Trust, 1986—; mem.-at-large Pullman United Way, 1988-93, mem. admissions and allocations com., 1990-93, mem. communications com., 1990-93; host family for State of Wash. Young Woman of the Yr. candidates (formerly Jr. Miss Program), 1988—, local area judge Young Woman of the Yr., 1985—. Mem. Profl. Secs. Internat., Jaycees (Jayceen of Yr. 1978). Roman Catholic. Home: 1235 NW Davis Way Pullman WA 99163-2815 Office: Wash State U Computing Ctr 2120 Computer Sci Bldg Pullman WA 99164-1220

FRISBEE, DON CALVIN, retired utilities executive; b. San Francisco, Dec. 13, 1923; s. Ira Nobles and Helen (Sheets) F.; m. Emilie Ford, Feb. 5, 1947; children: Ann, Robert, Peter, Dean. BA, Pomona Coll., 1947; MBA, Harvard U., 1949. Sr. investment analyst, asst. cashier investment analysis dept. 1st Interstate Bank Oreg., N.A., Portland, 1949-52, now chmn. bd. dirs.; with PacifiCorp, Portland, 1953—, treas., 1958-60, then v.p., exec. v.p., pres., 1966-73, chief exec. officer, 1973-89, chmn., 1973—; bd. dirs. First Interstate Bancorp, Weyerhaeuser Co., Standard Ins. Co., Portland., Precision Castparts Corp., Portland, First Interstate Bank Northwest Region, Portland. Chmn. bd. trustees Reed Coll.; trustee Safari Game Search Found., High Desert Mus.; trustee Oreg. Ind. Coll. Found.; mem. cabinet Columbia Pacific coun. Boy Scouts Am.; founder Oreg. chpt. Am. Leadership Forum; mem. exec. com. Oreg. Partnership for Internat. Edn.; mem. Internat. Adv. Com. 1st lt. AUS, 1943-46. Mem. Japan-Western U.S. Assn. (exec. coun.), Arlington Club, Univ. Club, Multnomah Athletic Club, City Club (bd. of govs.). Office: PacifiCorp 825 NE Multnomah St Ste 1055 Portland OR 97232-2149

FRISCH, JONATHAN DAVID, epidemiologist; b. Oakland, Calif., Oct. 4, 1963; s. Joseph and Joan Sylvia (Assert) F. BA, U. Calif., Berkeley, 1985, MPH, 1987, PhD, 1990. Tech. asst. Lawrence Berkeley Lab., 1979-83; computer specialist U. Calif., Berkeley, 1983-85, rsch. asst., 1985-88, grad. student instr., 1985-90; rsch. asst. Calif. Birth Defects Monitoring Program, Emeryville, 1986-90; sr. staff epidemiologist Unocal Corp., L.A., 1990—; adj. lectr. UCLA, 1991—. Contbr. articles to profl. jours. Disaster specialist ARC, San Francisco, L.A., 1986—. Mem. Soc. for Epidemiologic Rsch., Am. Pub. Health Assn., Sigma Xi. Office: UNOCAL PO Box 7600 Los Angeles CA 90051

FRISCHKNECHT, LEE CONRAD, broadcasting executive; b. Brigham City, Utah, Jan. 4, 1928; s. Carl Oliver and Geniel (Lund) F.; m. Sara Jean McCulloch, Sept. 3, 1948; children: Diane Frischknecht Etherington, Jill Frischknecht Taylor, Ellen Frischknecht DePola, Amy Frischknecht Blodgett. BS in Speech, Utah State U., 1951; MA in Radio-TV, Mich. State U., 1957. Announcer sta. KID Radio, Idaho Falls, Idaho, 1951-52; producer-director sta. WKAR-TV, East Lansing, Mich., 1953-57, prodn. mgr., 1958-59, program mgr., 1960-61, gen. mgr., 1962-63; dir. sta. rels. Nat. Ednl. TV, N.Y.C., 1964-67; dir. univ. rels. Utah State U., 1969-70; dir. network affairs Nat. Pub. Radio, Washington, 1971, v.p., 1972, pres., 1973-77; communications cons., 1978—; mgr. ed. telecommunications sta. KAET-TV, Phoenix, Ariz., 1980-86; asst. gen. mgr. sta. KAET-TV, Phoenix, 1987—; assoc. prof. radio-TV, Mich. State U., 1962-63; assoc. prof. speech Utah State U., 1968-69; lectr. Ariz. State U., 1981-82. Bd. dirs. Nat. Pub. Radio, 1973-78, Pub. Svc. Satellite Consortium, 1982—, chmn., 1987-90, Ariz. Sch. Svcs. through Ednl. Tech., 1984—. With AUS, 1946-48, Japan. Recipient Outstanding Alumnus in Communications award Mich. State U., 1973, Meritorious Svc. award in Communications, Brigham Young U., 1974, Disting. Svc. award Pacific Mountain Network, 1987. Mem. LDS Ch. Home: 338 E Palmcroft Dr Tempe AZ 85282-2242 Office: Ariz State U Sta KAET-TV Stauffer Hall Tempe AZ 85287

FRISHKOFF, PATRICIA ANN, university director; b. Batavia, N.Y., Jan. 17, 1944; d. Sennette Charles and Marguerite F. (Dorf) Ahl; m. Paul Frishkoff, Oct. 11, 1980; 1 child, Luke Owen. BA in Econs., St. Lawrence U., 1966; DBA, Kent State U., 1974. CPA, CMA. Asst. prof. bus. Old Dominion U., Norfolk, Va., 1970-72; assoc. prof. bus. Slippery Rock (Pa.) State U., 1972-75; assoc. prof. of acctg. U. Toledo, 1975-78; prof. acctg. Oreg. State U., Corvallis, 1978—, dir., family bus. program, 1985—; cons. on family bus., tng. and devel., 1980—. Author: Financial Statement Analysis (1st ed. 1979, 2d ed. 1983, 3d ed. 1986), Cases in Financial Reporting (1st ed. 1981, 2d ed. 1985), Just In Case, 1992; editor: Spouse Survival List, 1988. Adv. bd. SBA, Portland, 1990. SBA Rsch. grant, 1989-90; recipient Leavey Award Freedoms Found., 1989. Mem. AICPA, Am. Acctg. Assn., Family Firm Inst. (bd. dirs.). Office: Oreg State U Family Bus Program Corvallis OR 97331-2603

FRISHKOFF, PAUL, career/life planning consultant, business educator; b. N.Y.C.; s. Louis H. and Hilde Z. (Blum) F.; divorced; children: Rob, Gwen; m. Patricia Ahl, Oct. 11, 1980; 1 child, Luke. BA, Swarthmore U., 1960; MBA, U. Chgo., 1962; PhD, Stanford U., 1970. CPA. Acctg. intern Arthur Andersen & Co., Chgo., 1962; acct. Arthur Young & Co., San Francisco, 1962-64; prof. bus. adminstrn. U. Oreg., Eugene, 1967—; prin., career cons. Eugene, 1983—; ptnr., cons. Leadership in Family Enterprise, Eugene, 1988—; Trustee Oreg. Accts. for Pub. Interest, Portland, 1974-77. Author: Summary Indicators, 1981, Changing Prices, 1982; contbr. articles to profl. jours. Pres. bd. dirs. Looking Glass Youth & Family Svcs., Eugene, 1980—; sec. to bd. dirs. The Common Found., Eugene, 1983—. Recipient Manuscript award Nat. Assn. Accts., 1970; doctoral fellow Ford Found., 1965-66, R.D. Irwin Found., 1967, pub. acctg. fellow U. Chgo., 1960-62. Mem. AICPA, Oreg. Soc. CPAs (bd. dirs. 1986—), Family Firms Inst. Office: U Oreg Sch Bus Eugene OR 97403-1208

FRISHMAN, EILEEN STEINBERG, accountant; b. N.Y.C., Oct. 5, 1946; m. Robert Jules Frishman, June 10, 1967; 2 children. BS in Edn., CCNY, 1967; MA in Edn., U. Conn., 1971; MS in Acctg., Pace U., 1986. CPA. Tchr. Vernon (Conn.) Pub. Schs., 1967-70; ednl. psychologist Granby (Conn.) Pub. Schs., 1971-72; owner, mgr. retail store, East Hartford, Conn., 1972-75; instr. acctg. and fin. Lockyear Coll., Evansville, Ind., 1986-87; field auditor Ind. Dept. Revenue, Evansville, 1987-88; staff acct. Yale & Seffinger, P.C., Denver, 1988-89; taxation analyst Gt.-West Life Assurance Co., Englewood, Colo., 1989—; adj. instr. fin. U. Evansville, 1987. Author: Enjoy Home Winemaking, 1972, rev. 1976. Mem. AICPA, Colo. Soc. CPA's. Home: 5361 S Geneva Way Englewood CO 80111-6222

FRITCHER, EARL EDWIN, civil engineer, consultant; b. St. Ansgar, Iowa, Nov. 24, 1923; s. Lee and Mamie Marie (Ogden) F.; m. Dorsille Ellen Simpson, Aug. 24, 1946; 1 child, Teresa. BS, Iowa State U., 1950. Registered civil engr., Calif. Project devel. engr. dept. transp. State of Calif., Los Angeles, 1950-74, traffic engr. dept. transp., 1974-87; pvt. practice cons. engr. Sunland, Calif., 1987—; consulting prin. traffic engr. Parsons DeLeuw, Inc., 1990—. Co-author: Overhead Signs and Contract Sign Plans, 1989; patentee in field. Served to 2d lt. USAF, 1942-46, 50-51. Mem. Iowa State Alumni Assn. Republican. Methodist. Clubs: Verdugo Hills Numismatic (Sunland), Glendale Numismatic.

FRITSCHE, THOMAS RICHARD, physician, pathologist, educator; b. New Ulm, Minn., Apr. 10, 1951; s. Theodore Roosevelt and Lois (Quast) F.; m. Mary Jo Conway, Sept. 10, 1981. BS in Zoology, U. Minn., 1973, MS in Zoology, 1975, MD, 1981, PhD in Parasitology, 1984. Diplomate Nat. Bd. Med. Examiners, Am. Bd. Pathology in Clin. Pathology; lic. physician and surgeon, Wash. Intern and resident dept. pathology U. Wash., Seattle, 1981-83, chief resident dept. lab. medicine, 1983-84, acting instr. dept. lab. medicine, 1984-86, asst. prof. dept. lab. medicine and microbiology, 1986-92, assoc. prof. dept. lab. medicine and microbiology, 1992—; mem. subcom. on parasitology Nat. Com. for Clin. Lab. Standards, 1988—; cons. Sanofi Diagnostics Pasteur, Chaska, Minn., 1992—. Contbr. chpts. to books and articles to profl. jours. Recipient Young Investigator award Acad. Clin. Lab. Physicians and Scientists. Fellow Coll. Am. Pathologists (microbiology resource com. 1985—), Am. Soc. Clin. Pathologists (microbiology examination com. 1988—), Royal Soc. Tropical Medicine and Hygiene; mem. Am. Soc. Tropical Medicine and Hygiene, Am. Soc. for Microbiology, Wash. State Med. Assn., King County Med. Soc., Sigma Xi. Office: Univ Wash Med Ctr Dept Lab Medicine SB-10 Seattle WA 98195

FRITTS, JON MARK, protective services official; b. Holebrook, Ariz., July 18, 1961; s. Clifford Wolfswinkel and Eleanor (Fritts) Burchell; m. Sherol W. Hayhurst, Feb. 14, 1983; 1 child, Greg A. Police officer Clovis (N.Mex.) Police Dept., 1978-81; narcotics officer, motor officer, field tng. sgt., lt. Hobbs (N.Mex.) Police Dept., 1982—. Bd. dirs. ARC, Hobbs, 1992—. Mem. Hobbs Basketball Officials Assn. (pres. 1986—), Fraternal Order Police, Jaycees (Pub. Safety Officer of Yr. 1990). Republican. Baptist. Home: 1001 Arkansas Hobbs NM 88540 Office: Hobbs Police Dept 300 N Turner Hobbs NM 88240

FRITZLER, GERALD JOHN, artist; b. Chgo., Aug. 27, 1953; s. Alexander and Bernice (Miniar) F.; m. Irene Josephine Jurewicz, Aug. 17, 1974; children: Marena Veronica, Tanya Alexandra. AS in Graphic Arts, Am. Acad. of Art, 1974, AS in Fine Arts, 1976. Art apprentice Graziano, Kraft & Zale Inc., Chgo., 1976; illustrator Picard-Didier Art Studio, Milw., 1976-79; watercolor painter Mesa, Colo., 1979—; exhbn. chmn. Art-USA/Western Colo. Ctr. for the Arts, Grand Junction, 1989; artist-in-residence Rocky Mountain Nat. Park, Estes Park, Colo., 1990, Artists of Am. 10th Anniversary Exhbn., 1990, Nat. Acad. of Western Art, 1991, S.W. Art mag., 1991. Author: Contemporary Western Artists, 1982, Who's Who in American Art, 1984. Bd. dirs. Mesa Area Planning Assn., 1988-90, Western Colo. Ctr. for the Arts, Grand Junction, 1987-89. Am. Acad. of Art scholar, 1975. Mem. Nat. Watercolor Soc., Midwest Watercolor Soc., N.W. Rendezvous Group, Allied Artists Am. (assoc.), Rocky Mountain Nat. Watermedia Soc., Colo. Watercolor Soc., Salmagundi Club of N.Y.C. (non-resident mem.). Roman Catholic. Home: PO Box 253 Mesa CO 81643-0253

FRITZSCHE, DAVID J., marketing, business and society and business strategy educator, administrator; b. Woodstock, Ill., May 6, 1940; s. Melvin L. and Ireta Rae (Goble) F.; m. Nancy J. Olson, Sept. 5, 1965; children: Sonja R., Tanya J. B.S., U. Ill., 1965, M.S., 1968; D.B.A., Ind. U., 1972. Asst. and assoc. prof. mktg. Rochester Inst. Tech., N.Y., 1971-77; assoc. prof. mktg. Ill. State U., Bloomington, 1977-82; prof. mktg., chmn. managerial scis. dept. U. Nev., Reno, 1982-85; prof. bus. adminstrn. U. Portland, 1985-91, vis. prof. dept. mgmt. and orgn. U. Washington, 1991-92; vis. prof. Fla. Internat Univ., Miami, 1992-93. Contbr. articles to profl. jours.; co-authored two mgmt. simulations. Served to capt. U.S. Army, 1969-71. Mem. Acad. Mgmt., Am. Mktg. Assn. (pres. Rochester chpt. 1976-77), Am. Inst. for Decision Scis., Assn. for Bus. Simulation and Experiential Learning (pres. 1988-89), Internat. Assn. Bus. and Soc., Soc. for Bus. Ethics. Home: 12607 SE 41st Pl Apt H 105 Bellevue WA 98006-2323

FRIZZEL, TERESA R., mayor; m. Roger Frizzel. Mem. Riverside (Calif.) City Coun., 1980-83; mayor City of Riverside, 1990—. Office: City of Riverside Office of Mayor 3900 N Main St Riverside CA 92522-0002*

FROEHLICH, ROBERT ELMER, association director, management consultant; b. Milw., Dec. 1, 1942; s. Elmer Alfred and Lucille (Miesler) F.; m. Virginia Owens, Aug. 29, 1965; children: Karen Lynn, Andrew Robert, William Scott. DVM, Iowa State U., 1966; MBA, Keller Sch. Mgmt., 1987. Owner Grafton (Wis.) Vet. Hosp., 1974-89; dir. mgmt. svc. Am. Animal Hosp. Assn., Denver, 1989—. Author: Successful Financial Management for the Veterinary Practice, 1987. Crusade chmn. Am. Cancer Soc., Ozaukee County, Wis., 1987-88. Capt. U.S. Army, 1966-68. Mem. Am. Vet. Med. Assn., Am. Animal Hosp. Assn. (hosp. dir., speaker 1988—, cons. 1989—), Colo. Vet. Med. Assn., Wis. Vet. Med. Assn., Milw. Vet. Med. Assn. (pres. 1975-76). Lutheran. Home: 8875 W Cornell Pl Lakewood CO 80227

FROELICH, JERRY WALTER, radiologist, computer consultant; b. Paterson, N.J., Sept. 11, 1957; s. Frederich and Helen A. (Allen) F.; m Shelley Ann, Jan. 31, 1989; children: Ashley, Courtney, Christopher, Taylor. BA, Birea (Ky.) Coll., 1973; MD, W.Va. U., 1977. Diplomate Am. Bds. Radiology and Nuclear Medicine. Asst. prof. U. Mich., Ann Arbor, 1981-83, clin. asst. prof., 1983-85, clin. assoc. prof., 1985-88; assoc. prof. Harvard Med. Sch., Boston, 1988-89; prof. U. Toronto (Can.), 1989-90; dir. MRI Swedish Med. Ctr. Radiology Imaging Assocs., Englewood, Colo., 1990—. Presenter and patentee in field; author over 60 articles, 70 scientific abstracts, and 15 chapters in books. N.Y. Life Ins. scholar W.Va. U., 1973-77, Appalachian Fund scholar, 1973-77. Mem. AMA, Soc. Nuclear Medicine, Radiol. Soc. N.Am., Am. Coll. Radiology, Colo. Med. Soc. Home: 6600 E Berry Ave Englewood CO 80111

FROHNEN, RICHARD GENE, educator; b. Omaha, Mar. 26, 1930; s. William P. and Florence E. (Rogers) F.; student U. Nebr., Omaha, Mo. Valley Coll., 1948-52; BA, Calif. State U., 1954; MS, UCLA 1961; EdD, Brigham Young U., 1976; grad. Army War Coll., 1982 m. Harlene Grace LeTourneau, July 4, 1958; children: Karl Edward, Eric Eugene. Bus. mgr. athletics and sports publicity dir. U. Nebr., Omaha, 1951-52; pub. rels. dir. First Congl. Ch. Los Angeles, 1953-54, 58-59; writer Los Angeles Mirror News, 1959; gen. assignment reporter, religion editor Los Angeles Times, 1959-61; prof. journalism, dean men Eastern Mont. Coll., Billings, 1961-65; N.W. editor, editorial writer Spokesman-Review, Spokane, 1965-67, also editor Sunday mag.; prof. journalism U. Nev., Reno, 1967-79; exec. dir. devel. Coll. of Desert/Copper Mountain, 1982-85, Ariz. Health Scis. Ctr., Tucson, 1986-90; pub. rels. devel. officer Sch. Med. Scis. U. Nev., 1969-75; adj. prof. mgmt., dir. grad. pros. in Mgmt. U. Redlands (Calif.), 1979-85, 91—; adj. prof. comm. Calif. State Univ., Dominguez Hills, 1991—; cons. Instl. Advancement, Long Beach, Calif., 1990—. Mem. exec. bd. Nev. area coun. Boy Scouts Am., 1968-76, coun. commr., 1973-74, v.p., 1975-76; mem. exec. bd. Yellowstone Valley coun. Boy Scouts Am., 1961-65, coun. pres. 1963-64; v.p. Catalina coun. Boy Scouts Am., 1987-90; mem. exec. bd. Long Beach Area Coun., 1990—; founder, mng. dir. Gt. Western Expdns., 1958-90; adminstrv. asst. to Gov. of Nev., 1985. Served to 1st lt. USMC, 1954-58; now col. Res., ret. Recipient Silver Beaver award Boy Scouts Am., 1974, Pres.' Vol. Action award Coll. Desert/Copper Mountain, 1984, Outstanding Faculty award U. Redlands, 1984; named to Benson High Sch. Hall of Fame, Omaha, 1988. Mem. Assn. Edn. Journalism, Am. Legion, Res. Officers Assn. U.S., Marine Corps Assn., Marine Corps Res. Officers Assn., Am. Humanics Found., Internat. Platform Assn., Nat. Soc. Fund Raising Execs., Planning Execs. Inst., Internat. Communication Assn., Religion Newswriters Assn., Navy League, Semper Fidelis Soc., Am. Mgmt. Assn., Assn. Am. Med. Colls. Group on Pub. Affairs, Counc. for Advancement and Support Edn., Res. Officers Assn. U.S., Assn. for Healthcare Philanthropy, Kiwanis, Lions, Rotary, Kappa Tau Alpha, Alpha Phi Omega, Sigma Delta Chi (sec.-treas. chpt.). Episcopalian. Office: 3737 E 2nd St # 103 Long Beach CA 90803

FROHNMAYER, DAVID BRADEN, law school dean; b. Medford, Oreg., July 9, 1940; s. Otto J. and MarAbel (Fisher) B.; m. Lynn Diane Johnson, Dec. 30, 1970; children: Kirsten, Mark, Kathryn (dec.), Jonathan, Amy. AB magna cum laude, Harvard U., 1962; BA, Oxford (Eng.) U., 1964, MA (Rhodes scholar), 1971; JD, U. Calif., Berkeley, 1967; LLD (hon.), Willamette U., 1988; D Pub. Svc. (hon.), U. Portland, 1989. Bar: Calif. 1967, U.S. Dist. Ct. (no. dist.) Calif. 1967, Oreg. 1971, U.S. Dist. Ct. Oreg. 1971, U.S. Supreme Ct. 1981. Assoc. Pillsbury, Madison & Sutro, San Francisco, 1967-69; asst. to sec. Dept. HEW, 1969-70; prof. law U. Oreg., 1971-81, spl. asst. to univ. pres., 1971-79; atty. gen. State of Oreg., 1981-91; dean Sch. Law U. Oreg., 1991—; chmn. Conf. Western Attys. Gen., 1985-86; pres. Nat. Assn. Attys. Gen., 1987-88. Mem. Oreg. Ho. of Reps, 1975-81. Recipient awards Weaver Constl. Law Essay competition Am. Bar Found., 1972, 74; Rhodes scholar, 1962. Mem. ABA (Ross essay winner 1980), Oreg. Bar Assn., Calif. Bar Assn., Nat. Assn. Attys. Gen. (Wyman award 1987), Round Table Eugene, Order of Coif, Phi Beta Kappa, Rotary. Republican. Presbyterian. Home: 2875 Baker Blvd Eugene OR 97403-1682 Office: U Oreg Office of Dean Sch of Law Eugene OR 97403

FRONEK, JOSEPH E, art conservator; b. Temple, Tex., Apr. 20, 1951; s. Joseph Jerry and Celestine Elizabeth (Barabas) F. BA, U. St. Thomas, 1973; MA, U. Austin, 1977; cert. art cons., NYU, 1981. Intern Bayerische Staatsgemäldesammlungen, Munich, 1980-81; fellow Metropolitan Mus. Art, N.Y.C., 1981-82; chief cons. Huntington Art Gallery U. Tex., Austin, 1982-86; sr. paintings cons., head paintings conservation Los Angeles County Mus. Art, L.A., 1980—; co-organizer Masterpiece in Focus exhbns. Chardin and Rembrandt, Los Angeles County Mus. Art; cons., lectr. in field. Contbr. tech. sects. to catalogues. Mem. Am. Inst. for Conservation (assoc.). Home: 1952 Palmerston Pl Los Angeles CA 90027 Office: LA County Mus Art 5905 Wilshire Blvd Los Angeles CA 90036

FRONTIERE, GEORGIA, professional football team executive; m. Carroll Rosenblum, July 7, 1966 (dec.); children: Dale Carroll, Lucia; m. Dominic Frontiere. Pres., owner L.A. Rams, NFL, 1979—. Bd. dirs. L.A. Boys and Girls Club, L.A. Orphanage Guild, L.A. Blind Youth Found. Named Headliner of Yr., L.A. Press Club, 1981. Office: Los Angeles Rams 2327 W Lincoln Ave Anaheim CA 92801-5102*

FROST, EVERETT L., dean, academic administrator; b. Salt Lake City, Oct. 17, 1942; s. Henry Hoag Jr. and Ruth Salome (Smith) F.; m. Janet Owens, Mar. 26, 1967; children: Noreen Karyn, Joyce Lida. BA in Anthropology, U. Oreg., 1965; PhD in Anthropology, U. Utah, 1970. Field researcher in cultural anthropology Taveuni, Fiji, 1968-69; asst. prof. in anthropology Ea. N.Mex. U., Portales, 1970-74, assoc. prof., 1974-76, asst. dean Coll. Liberal Arts and Scis., 1976-78, dean acad. affairs and grad. studies, 1978-80, v.p. for planning and analysis, dean rsch., 1980—, dean grad. studies, 1983-88; cons., evaluator N. Cen. Assn. Accred. Agy. for Higher Edn., 1989—. Chmn. N.Mex. Humanities Coun., 1980-88; mem. N.Mex. Gov.'s Commn. on Higher Edn., 1983-86; mem. exec. bd. N.Mex. First, 1987—; bd. dirs. Roosevelt Gen. Hosp., Portales, 1989—; pres. bd. dirs. San Juan County Mus. Assn., Farmington, 1979-82; vice chair Portales Pub. Schs. Facilities Com., 1990—. NDEA fellow, 1969-70; grantee NEW, 1979-80, NSF, 1968-69, Fiji Forbes, Ltd., 1975-76, others. Fellow Am. Anthropol. Assn., Am. Assn. Higher Edn., Soc. Coll. and Univ. Planning, Assn. Social Anthropologists Oceania, Anthropol. Soc. Washington, Sch. Am. Rsch., Western Assn. Grad. Deans, Current Anthropology (assoc.) Polynesian Soc., Phi Kappa Phi.

FROST, S. NEWELL, computer company executive; b. Oklahoma City, Dec. 21, 1935; s. Sterling Johnson and Eula Dove (Whitford) F.; m. Patricia Joyce Rose, Aug. 18, 1957; children: Patricia Diane Wiscarson, Richard Sterling, Lindy Layne Harrington. BS Indsl. Engring., U. Okla., Norman, 1957; MS Indsl. Engring., Okla. State U., 1966. Registered profl. engr., Okla. Calif. Asst. mgr. acctg. Western Electric, Balt., 1972-73, mgr. indsl. engring., Chgo., 1973-75, mgr. devel. engring., 1975-76, mgr. acct. mgmt., San Francisco, 1976-78, dir. staff, Morristown, N.J., 1978-79; gen. mgr. distbn. & repair AT&T Techs., Sunnyvale, Calif., 1979-85, area v.p. material mgt. svcs. AT&T Info. Systems, Oakland, Calif., 1985-87, ops. v.p. material mgmt. svcs., San Francisco, 1988-89; dir. configuration ops. Businessland, Inc., San Jose, Calif., 1989-90, dir. svcs. support, 1990-91; exec. v.p. Isotek, Tiburon, Calif., 1991; v.p., gen. mgr. Tree Fresh, San Francisco, 1991-92; CFO Prima Pacific, Inc., San Rafael, Calif., 1992—; bd. dirs. Contract Office Group, San Jose, 1983—, chmn., 1984—. Bd. dirs. Santa Clara County YMCA, San Jose, Calif., 1981-84. Recipient Man of Day citation Sta. WAIT Radio, Chgo. Mem. Nat. Soc. Prof. Engrs. (chmn. edn. com. 1969-70), Am. Inst. Indsl. Engrs. (pres. bd. dirs. 1966-68), Okla. Soc. Profl. Engrs. (v.p. 1968-69). Republican. Baptist. Home: 4144 Paradise Dr Belvedere Tiburon CA 94920-1121 Office: Prima Pacific Inc 1144 4th St San Rafael CA 94901

FROST, STANLEY, judge; b. Clovis, N.Mex., June 1, 1942; m. Bonnie; children: Warren, Wade, Teresa. AB, N.Mex. Highlands U., 1962; JD, George Wahington U., 1967. Bar: N.Mex., 1967. Assoc. Emmett C. Hart, Esq., Tucumcari, N.Mex., 1968-73; chief judge Tenth Judicial Dist., Tucumcari, N.Mex., 1973-91; justice N.Mex. Supreme Ct., Santa Fe, 1991—; part time instr., N.Mex. Magistrate Coll., 1982, 83; faculty advisor Nat. Judicial Coll. Univ. Nev., 1981, del. Nat. Judicial Conf. on the Rights of Victims of Crime, 1983; lectr. various confs.; mem. Standing Com. on Implementation of the State Bar Task Force Report on Women in the Legal Profession, Region IV Criminal Justice Planning Commn., N.Mex. Judicial Standards Commn. Mem. Am. Judicature Soc., Nat. Coun. of Juvenile and Family Ct. Judges, Nat. Conf. of State Trial Judges (com. on judicial immunity), N.Mex. Outdoor Drama Assn. (mem. bd. dirs.), N.Mex. Dist. Judges Assn. (mem. bd. dirs.), N.Mex. Judicial Standards Commn., Kiwanis Internat. Democrat. Methodist. Home: 2414 San Patricio Plz Santa Fe NM 87501 Office: NM Supreme Court 237 Don Gaspar Santa Fe NM 87501*

FRUCHTER, JONATHAN SEWELL, research scientist, geochemist; b. San Antonio, June 5, 1945; s. Benjamin and Dorothy Ann (Sewell) F.; m. Cecelia Ann Smith, Mar. 31, 1973; children: Diane, Daniel. BS in Chemistry, U. Tex., 1966; PhD in Geochemistry, U. Calif., San Diego, 1971. Research assoc. U. Oreg., Eugene, 1971-74; research scientist Battelle Northwest, Richland, Wash., 1974-79, mgr. research and devel., 1979-87, staff scientist, 1987-91, tech. group leader, 1991—. Contbr. numerous articles to profl. jours. Mem. AAAS, Am. Chem. Soc., Phi Beta Kappa, Phi Kappa Phi. Office: Battelle NW PO Box 999 Richland WA 99352-0999

FRUCHTHENDLER, FRED BARRY, insurance executive, consultant, business owner; b. Tucson, July 19, 1951; s. Jacob Carl and Jean (Abend) F. BA, U. Calif., San Diego, 1973. With mgmt. personnel Foodmaker, Inc., San Diego, 1970-73; legal intern Ctr. for Legal & Social Change, San Diego, 1971-73; ins. exec. J.C. Fruchthendler & Co., Tucson, 1973-80, pres., owner, 1980—. Adv. youth group Yonaton AZA-B'nai B'rith Youth, Tucson, 1980—. Recipient Merit award Tucson Fire Dept., 1977; named Outstanding Young Man of Am., 1978, Young Man of Yr., Tucson Jewish Community Coun., 1978. Mem. Ind. Ins. Agts. Am. (bd. dirs. Phoenix chpt. 1987—, 83-86, pres. Tucson chpt. 1987), Profl. Ins. Agts. Am., ISU Internat. (presdl. adv. bd. Hartford, Conn. chpt. 1984-87), Ariz. Acad. Sci. (life), PIA, Kiwanis (chartered). Democrat.

FRUMKIN, GENE, writer, educator; b. N.Y.C., Jan. 29, 1928; s. Samuel and Sarah (Blackman) F.; B.A. in English, UCLA, 1951; m. Lydia Samuels, July 3, 1955 (dec.); children—Celena, Paul. Exec. editor Calif. Apparel News, Los Angeles, 1952-66; asst. prof. English, U. N.Mex., Albuquerque, 1967-71, assoc. prof., 1971-88, prof. 1988—. Mem. Associated Writing Programs, Hawaii Literary Arts Council. Author: The Hawk and the Lizard, 1963; The Orange Tree, 1965; The Rainbow-Walker, 1968; Dostoevsky and Other Nature Poems, 1972; Locust Cry: Poems 1958-65, 1973; The Mystic Writing-Pad, 1977; Loops, 1979; Clouds and Red Earth, 1982, A Sweetness in the Air, 1987, Comma in the Ear, 1990, Saturn Is Mostly Weather: Selected and Uncollected Poems, 1992; mem. editorial bd. Blue Mesa Rev.; co-editor San Marcos Rev., 1976-83; The Indian Rio Grande: Recent Poems from 3 Cultures (anthology), 1977; editor: Coastlines Lit. Mag., 1958-62, N.Mex. Quar., 1969. Home: 3721 Mesa Verde Ave NE Albuquerque NM 87110-7723

FRUSH, JAMES CARROLL, JR., health services consultant; b. San Francisco, Oct. 18, 1930; s. James Carroll and Edna Mae (Perry) F.; m. Patricia Anne Blake, Oct. 29, 1960 (div. 1977); children: Michael, Gloria; m. Carolyn Fetter Bell, Aug. 23, 1978; 1 child, Stephen. BA, Stanford, 1953; postgrad., U. Calif., San Francisco, 1957-58; MA, Saybrook Inst., 1981, PhD, 1985. Ptnr. James C. Frush Co., San Francisco, 1960-70; v.p., bd. dir. Retirement Residence, Inc., San Francisco, 1964-70, pres., 1970—; pres. Nat. Retirement Residence, San Francisco, 1971-89, Casa Dorinda Corp., 1971-89; pres. Marin Shakespeare Festival, 1971-73, James C. Frush Found., 1972-78; adj. prof. gerontology, psychology and theology Spring Hill Coll., Mobile, Ala., 1988—; bd. dirs. Gwynedd Inc., Blue Bell, Pa. Author (with Benson Eschenbach): The Retirement Residence: An Analysis of the Architecture and Management of Life Care Housing, 1968, Self-Esteem in Older Persons Following a Heart Attack: An Exploration of Contributing Factors, 1985; contbr. articles to profl. jours.; producer ednl. films. Bd. dirs. San Francisco Sr. Ctr., 1973-78, Found. to Assist Calif. Tchrs. Devel. Inc., 1987—; mem. adv. bd. Christus Theol. Inst., Mobile, Ala., Westminster Village Spanish Fort, Ala., 1992—. Mem. Gerontol. Soc, Southeastern Psychol. Assn., Assn. for Anthropology and Gerontology, Ala. Humanities Found. (speakers bur. 1993-94), Stanford Alumni Assn., RSVP (adv. bd. Mobile chpt. 1988), C.G. Jung Soc. of Gulf Coast (pres.). Office: care T Pimsleur 2155 Union St San Francisco CA 94123-4003

FRY, GEORGE SINCLAIR, company executive; b. Perry, Iowa, May 19, 1936; s. Everett Claude and Lavina Lillian (Sinclair) F.; m. Claudette Fay Roberts, Sept. 18, 1954 (div. 1973); children: Celeste, George Brian, Duane, Stephanie; m. Christine Irene Powell, Mar. 16, 1974; 1 child, Joel. BS in Aero. Engring., Iowa State U., 1960. Engring. mgr. Collins Radio Co., Cedar Rapids, Iowa, 1960-67; dir. ops. Rockwell Internat., Newport Beach, Calif., 1967-75; module mgr. Am. MicroSystems, Inc., Pocatello, Idaho, 1975-76; dir. ops. GTE Microcircuits, Tempe, Ariz., 1976-91; v.p. Integrated Circuit Engring. Corp., Scottsdale, 1981-91; pres. Aviso Micro Tech., Phoenix, 1991—; dir. Integrated Circuit Engring., Scottsdale. Author: Basics of Clean Room Design, 1989. Mem. IEEE, Inst. Environ. Scis., Masons. Republican. Office: Aviso Micro tech 11219 N 23rd Ave Phoenix AZ 85029

FRY, LINDA SUE, hotel sales director, food products company executive; b. Detroit, May 7, 1961; d. Walter Stephen and Christine Ann (Malinowski) Stevens; m. Daniel Kennth Fry, May 28, 1983; children: Amanda Sue, Travis Michael. BS in Biology, Morningside Coll., 1983. Asst. mgr. Golden Coral Steakhouse, Shawnee, Kans., 1983-84; sales rep. Met. Life Ins. Co., Overland Park, Kans., 1984-85; sales and catering rep. Holiday Inn Downtown, Kansas City, Kans., 1985-87, dir. sales, 1987-88; ops. and adminstrv. mgr. Crissy's Old Fashioned Cheesecake, Inc., Ontario, Calif., 1988—; dir. sales Holiday Inn Ontario Internat. Airport, 1992—; workers compensation cons. The Champ Group. Mem. steering com. City of Festival Assn., Kansas City, 1985-86, pres., 1986-88; ex-officio mem. Kansas City Conv. and Visitors Bur., 1986-88; mem. orgn. com. Statue of Liberty Move to Freedom Tour, Kansas City, 1986; mem. steering com. March of Dimes, Wyandotte County, Kans., 1987, 88, United Way, Wyandotte County, 1987, 88; mem. planning com. Polish Festival Assn., Kansas City, 1986-88; chmn. Centennial Com., 1990-91; mem. com. Christmas on Euclid, 1990, 91,92; state bd. dirs. Kansas City Jaycees, 1987-88; amb. Kansas City C. of C., 1986-88. Mem. NAFE, Nat. Assn. Profl. Saleswoman (chpt. treas. 1985-86), Soc. Govt. Meeting Planners (charter, membership com. 1988-89), Women in Travel (membership chmn. 1987-89), Women in Networking, Bus. Women's Network, Hotel Sales and Mktg. Assn., Nat. Assn. Life Underwriters, Women's Assn. Life Underwriters, Ontario Jaycees (state dir. 1989-90, pres. 1990), Calif. Jaycees (dist. gov. 1991-92, regional dir. 1992-93), Ontario C. of C. (bd. dirs. 1992—, chair community devel. 1992-93, pres.-elect 1993-94, bd. dirs. Ontario Crimestoppers 1989—). Roman Catholic. Home: 1550 N Amador Ontario CA 91764 Office: Holiday Inn Ontario Internat Airport 1801 East G St Ontario CA 91764

FRYE, HELEN JACKSON, federal judge; b. Klamath Falls, Oreg., Dec. 10, 1930; d. Earl and Elizabeth (Kirkpatrick) Jackson; m. William Frye, Sept. 7, 1952; children: Eric, Karen, Heidi; 1 adopted child, Hedy; m. Perry Holloman, July 10, 1980. BA in English with honors, U. Oreg., 1953, MA, 1960, JD, 1966. Bar: Oreg. 1966. Public sch. tchr. Oreg., 1956-63; pvt. practice Eugene, 1966-71; circuit ct. judge State of Oreg., 1971-80; U.S. dist judge Dist. Oreg. Portland, 1980—. Office: US Dist Ct 706 US Courthouse 620 SW Main St Portland OR 97205-3023

FRYE, JUDITH ELEEN MINOR, editor; b. Seattle; d. George Edward and Eleen G. (Hartelius) Minor; student UCLA, 1947-48, U. So. Calif., 1948-53; m. Vernon Lester Frye, Apr. 1, 1954. Acct., office mgr. Colony Wholesale Liquor, Culver City, Calif., 1947-48; credit mgr. Western Distbg. Co., Culver City, 1948-53; ptnr. in restaurants, Palm Springs, L.A., 1948, ptnr. in date ranch, La Quinta, Calif., 1949-53; ptnr., owner Imperial Printing, Huntington Beach, Calif., 1955—; editor, pub. New Era Laundry and Cleaning Lines, Huntington Beach, 1962—; registered lobbyist, Calif., 1975-84. Mem. Textile Care Allied Trade Assn., Laundry & Dry Cleaning Suppliers Assn., Calif. Coin-op Assn. (exec. dir. 1975-84, Cooperation award 1971, Dedicated Svc.award 1976), Nat. Automatic Laundry & Cleaning Coun. (Leadership award 1972), Women Laundry & Drycleaning (past pres., Outstanding Svc. award 1977), Printing Industries Assn., Master Printers Am., Nat. Assn. Printers & Lithographers, Huntington Beach C. of C., Am. Legion Aux. Office: 22031 Bushard St Huntington Beach CA 92646-8490

FRYE, STEVEN WAYNE, publishing consultant, software programmer; b. Rockford, Ill., July 25, 1954; s. Richard Vernon and Colleen Rae (O'Brien) F.; m. Debra Kay Wickliff, May 16, 1981 (div. Nov. 1991); 1 child, Jessalyn Marie. BSBA, Nat. Coll. Bus., 1978. Art dir. The Sat. Evening Post, Indpls., 1978-81; dir. art and prodn. The Country Gentlemen, Indpls., 1978-81; prodn. dir. Denver Mag., 1981-82; dir. art and prodn. Colo. Homes and Lifestyles, Denver, 1981-82; dir. mfg. CommTek Pub., Hailey, Idaho, 1982-86; cons. Frye & Assocs., Hailey, Idaho, 1986—; cons. Inc. Mag., Boston, 1986—, Inside Sports, Chgo., 1987—, Time Venture Publs., San Francisco, N.Y., 1991—, TV Guide, Toronto, 1990—, John Deere, Moline, Ill., 1989—, Nat. Wildlife Fedn., Vienna, Va., 1990—, Walt Disney Publs., Burbank, Calif., 1992—; speaker numerous pub. confs., 1989—. Designer: (software) MFG.PRO, 1986; contbr. articles to profl. jours. Recipient Excellence award Communication Arts Mag., 1985. Mem. Pub. Prodn. Group, Prodn. Club of So. Calif., Denver Prodn. Club. Home: PO Box 967 Hailey ID 83333-0967

FRYER, GLADYS CONSTANCE, nursing home medical director, educator; b. London, Mar. 28, 1923; came to U.S., 1967; d. William John and Florence Annie (Dockett) Mercer; m. Donald Wilfred Fryer, Jan. 20, 1944; children: Peter Vivian, Gerard John, Gillian Celia. MB, BS, U. Melbourne, Victoria, Australia, 1956. Resident Box Hill Hosp., 1956-57; vis. at pediatric cardiac depts. Yale, Stamford U., and U. Calif. San Francisco, 1958; med. registrar Queen Victoria Hosp., Melbourne, Australia, 1959-61; cardiologist Assunta Found., Petaling Jaya, Malaysia, 1961-64; clin. research physician U.S. Army Clin. Research Unit, Malaysia, 1964-66; internist Hawaii Permanente Kaiser Found., Honolulu, 1968-73; practice medicine specializing in internal medicine Honolulu, 1973-88; med. dir. Hale Nani Health Ctr., Honolulu, 1975-89, Beverly Manor Convalescent Ctr., Honolulu, 1975-89; asst. clin. prof. medicine John Burns Sch. Medicine U. Hawaii, 1968-89; med. cons. Salvation Army Alcohol Treatment Facility, Honolulu, 1975-81; physician to skilled nursing patients VA, Honolulu, 1984-88; preceptor to geriatric nurse practitioner program U. Colo., Honolulu, 1984-85; lectr. on geriatrics, Alzheimer's disease, gen. medicine, profl. women's problems, and neurosci., 1961—; mem. ad hoc due process bd. Med. Care Evaluation Com., 1982-88, Hospice Adv. Com., 1982-88; mem. pharmacy com. St. Francis Hosp. Clin. Staff, 1983-89, chmn. 1983-84. Contbr. articles to profl. jours. Mem. adv. com. Honolulu Home Care St. Francis Hosp., 1974-87; mem. adv. bd. Honolulu Gerontology Program, 1983-89, Straub Home Health Program, Honolulu, 1984-87; mem. sci. adv. bd. Alzheimers Disease and Related Disorders Assn., Honolulu, 1984-89; mem. long term care task force Health and Community Svcs. Coun. Hawaii, 1978-84. Special Ops. Exec., War Office, London, 1943-44. Recipient Edgar Rouse Prize in Indsl. Medicine, U. Melbourne, 1955, Outstanding Supporter award Hawaii Assn. Activity Coordinators, 1987. Fellow ACP; mem. AAAS, Hawaii Med. Assn. (councillor 1984-89), Honolulu County Med. Soc. (chmn., mem. utilization rev. com. 1973-89), World Med. Assn., Am. Geriatrics Soc., N.Y. Acad. Sci. Episcopalian.

FRYER, PATRICIA, marine geologist; b. Chester, Pa., June 17, 1948; d. Hubert Randall and Ethel May (Wiley) Wendell; m. Gerard John Fryer, July 24, 1972; 1 child, Katherine Elisabeth. BS, Coll. of William and Mary, 1970; MS, U. Hawaii, 1973, PhD, 1981. Teaching asst. U. Hawaii, Honolulu, 1970-72, rsch. technician, 1973-77, rsch. asst., 1977-80; vis. scientist Princeton (N.J.) U., 1980-81; asst. geologist U. Hawaii, 1981-86, assoc. prof. Geology and Geophysics, 1986-93, prof. Geology and Geophysics, 1993—; cons. U.S. AID, Naples, Italy, 1985, Seafloor Surveys Internat., Hawaii, 1989, U. Hawaii, 1988-91; chief scientist various marine geology rsch. cruises, 1987—; dir. U. Hawaii Young Scholars Program, Honolulu, 1990—. Co-author: Proceedings of the Ocean Drilling Program Initial Reports, 1990; editor: Seamounts Islands and Atolls, 1987, Scientific Results Ocean Drilling Program, 1992; contbr. 41 articles to profl. jours. Judge Hawaii State Sci. and Engring. Fair, Honolulu, 1981—; troop leader Girl Scouts Am., Honolulu, 1985-88. Recipient 22 rsch. awards various fed. agencies, 1982—. Mem. Assn. for Women in Sci., Am. Geophys. Union, Info. Handling Panel of the Ocean Drilling Program, Sigma Xi. Democrat. Office: U Hawaii SOEST/Planetary Geoscis 2525 Correa Rd Honolulu HI 96822

FRYMER, MURRY, columnist, theater critic, critic-at-large; b. Toronto, Ont., Can., Apr. 24, 1934; came to U.S., 1945; s. Dave and Sylvia (Spinrod) F.; m. Barbara Lois Grown, Sept. 4, 1966; children: Paul, Benjamin, Carrie. BA, U. Mich., 1956; student Columbia U., 1958; MA, NYU, 1964. Editor Town Crier, Westport, Conn., 1962-63, Tribune, Levittown, N.Y., 1963-64; viewpoints editor, critic Newsday, L.I., N.Y., 1964-72; asst. mng. editor Rochester Democrat & Chronicle, N.Y., 1972-75; Sunday and feature editor Cleve. Plain Dealer, 1975-77; editor Sunday Mag., Boston Herald Am., 1977-79; film and TV critic San Jose Mercury News, Calif., 1979-83, theater critic, 1983—, columnist, 1983—; instr. San Jose State U., Cleve. State U., judge Emmy awards Nat. Acad. TV Arts and Scis., 1968. Author, dir. musical revue Four by Night, N.Y.C., 1963; author (play) Danse Marriage, 1955 (Hopwood prize 1955). Served with U.S. Army, 1956-58. Mem. Bay Area Theater Critics Assn. Home: 1060 Moongate Pl San Jose CA 95120-2031 Office: San Jose Mercury News 750 Ridder Park Dr San Jose CA 95190-0001

FRYT, MONTE STANISLAUS, petroleum company executive, speaker, advisor; b. Jackson, Mich., Aug. 3, 1949; s. Marion S. and Dorothy A. (Fischman) F.; m. Pollyanna Hayes, May 26, 1990. BS in Aerospace Engring., U. Colo., Boulder, 1971; MBA in Mgmt., U. Colo., Denver, 1988. Field engr. Schlumberger Well Svcs., Bakersfield, Calif., 1971-75; computer R & D engr. Schlumberger Well Svcs., Houston, 1975-77; account devel. engr. Schlumberger Well Svcs., L.A., 1977-78; dist. mgr. Schlumberger Well Svcs., Abilene, Tex., 1978-80, Williston, N.D., 1980-81; v.p. ops. Logmate Svcs. Inc., Calgary, Alta., Can., 1981-84; pres. Fryt Petroleum Inc., Denver, 1984-91; mgr. petrophysics Am. Hunter Exploration, Ltd., Denver, 1991-92; prin. Reservoir Evaluations Group, Denver, 1992—. Mem. Colo. Rep. Com., 1990—, Rep. Nat. Com., Colo. Republican Leadership Program, 1992-93. Mem. Am. Mgmt. Assn., Am. Assn. Petroleum Geologists, Brit. Am. Bus. Assn., German Am. C. of C., Rocky Mountain Assn. Geologists, Greater Denver C. of C., Elks, Rockies Venture Club. Roman Catholic. Home: 24245 Choke Cherry Ln Golden CO 80401-9203 Office: 410 17th St Ste 1220 Denver CO 80202-4425

FRYXELL, KARL JOSEPH, biology educator; b. Las Cruces, N.Mex., June 12, 1953; s. Paul Arnold and Greta (Albrecht) F.; m. Patty P.Y. Pang, July 19, 1987; 1 child, Loren K.S. BA, U. Tex., 1975, BS in Zoology with honors, 1975; PhD in Biology, Calif. Inst. Tech., 1983. Helen Hay Whitney postdoctoral fellow Calif. Inst. Tech., Pasadena, 1983-86, mem. profl. staff, 1986-88; asst. prof. biology U. Calif., Riverside, 1988—. NSF predoctoral fellow Calif. Inst. Tech., 1977-80, NIH predoctoral fellow, 1980-82, Sharp predoctoral fellow, 1982-83. Mem. Genetics Soc. Am., Sierra Club, Phi Beta Kappa, Phi Kappa Phi. Office: U Calif Dept Biology 900 University Ave Riverside CA 92521

FUCALORO, ANTHONY FRANK, academic dean; b. Bklyn., Apr. 17, 1943; s. Gaetano Atillio and Josepina (Noto) F.; m. Liliane Marie-Louise Rigas, June 25, 1967; children: Nicole Antionette, Cristina Veronique. BS, Poly. Inst., Bklyn., 1964; PhD, U. Ariz., 1969. Postdoctoral assoc. N.Mex. State U., Las Cruces, 1969-71; vis. asst. prof. U. New Orleans, 1971-74; prof. chemistry Claremont (Calif.) McKenna Coll., 1974-93, dean of the faculty, 1991—; cons. Occidental Petroleum, Irvine, Calif., Ill. Tool Works, Chgo., Jet Propulsion Lab., Pasadena, Calif. Contbr. many articles to profl. jours.; author many reports. Mem. Am. Chem. Soc. (soc. advisor to Congressman David Dreier). Office: Claremont McKenna Coll Bauer Ctr 500 E 9th St Claremont CA 91711

FUCHS, PETER CORNELIUS, pathologist, medical microbiologist; b. Graz, Styria, Austria, May 16, 1936; came to U.S., 1936; s. Robert Thilo and Martha Leonora (Benndorf) F.; m. Alice M. Shannon, June 4, 1960 (div. 1983); children: Alicia, Mark, Christopher, Theresa; m. Joyce Aileen Parrish, Jan. 28, 1984; children: Kristi, Kevin. BS, Georgetown U., 1957; PhD, U. Md., Balt., 1961, MD, 1963. Diplomate Am. Bd. Pathology (med. microbiology test com. 1980-85), Am. Bd. Med. Microbiology. Fellow in microbiology Mayo Clinic, Rochester, Minn., 1968; intern St. Vincent Hosp. and Med. Ctr., Portland, Oreg., 1963-64, resident in pathology, 1964-68, pathologist, dir. microbiology, hosp. epidemiologist, 1968—. Author: Epidemiology of Hospital Infections, 1979; mem. editorial bd. Am. Jour. Clin. Pathology, 1980-85, Infection Control and Hosp. Epidemiology, 1980—, Diagnostic Microbiology and Infectious Disease, 1983—; contbr. over 100 articles to sci. jours., chpts. to books. Fellow Am. Soc. Clin. Pathologists (chmn. commn. on continuing edn. coun. on microbiology 1977-81), Coll. Am. Pathologists (microbiology resource com. 1978—, vice chmn. 1986—); mem. AAAS, Am. Soc. for Microbiology, Conf. Pub. Health Lab. Dirs., Soc. Hosp. Epidemiologists Am., Hosp. Infection Soc., Pacific NW Soc. Pathologists, Oreg. Pathologists Assn. (pres. 1978), Oreg. Med. Assn., Washington County Med. Soc. Office: St Vincent Hosp and Med Ctr 9205 SW Barnes Rd Portland OR 97225-6622

FUCHS, ROLAND JOHN, geography educator, university administrator; b. Yonkers, N.Y., Jan. 15, 1933; s. Alois L. and Elizabeth (Weigand) F.; m. Gaynell Ruth McAuliffe, June 15, 1957; children: Peter K., Christopher K., Andrew K. BA., Columbia U., 1954, postgrad., 1956-57; postgrad., Moscow State U., 1960-61; MA, Clark U., 1957, PhD, 1959. Asst. prof. to prof. emeritus U. Hawaii, Honolulu, 1958—; chmn. dept. geography U. Hawaii, 1964-86, asst. dean to assoc. dean coll. arts and scis., 1965-67, dir. Asian Studies Lang. and Area Ctr., 1965-67, adj. rsch. assoc. East West Ctr., 1980—, spl. asst. to pres., 1986; vice rector UN U., Tokyo, 1987—; vis. prof. Clark U., 1963-64, Nat. Taiwan U., 1974; mem. bd. internat. orgns. and programs Nat. Acad. Scis., 1976-81, chmn., 1980-81, mem. bd. sci. and tech. in devel., 1980-85; mem. U.S. Nat. Commn. for Pacific Basin Econ. Coop., 1985-87; sr. advisor United Nations U., 1986. Author, editor: Geographical Perspectives on the Soviet Union, 1974, Theoretical Problems of Geography, 1977, Population Distribution Policies in Development Planning, 1981, Urbanization and Urban Policies in the Pacific-Asia Region, 1987; asst. editor Econ. Geography, 1963-64; mem. editorial adv. com. Soviet Geography: Review and Translation, 1966—, Geoforum, 1988—, African Urban Quar., 1987, Global Environmental Change, 1990. Ford Found. fellow, 1956-57; Fulbright Rsch. scholar, 1966-67. Mem. AAAS, Internat. Geog. Union (v.p. 1980-84, 1st v.p. 1984-88, pres. 1988—), Assn. Am. Geographers, (honors award 1982), Am. Assn. Advancement Slavic Studies (bd. dirs. 1976-81), Pacific Sci. Assn. (coun. 1978—, exec. com. 1986—, sec. gen.-treas. 1991—). Home: 5136 Maunalani Cir Honolulu HI 96816-4020

FUCHS, THOMAS, writer; b. Los Angeles, Dec. 2, 1942; s. Daniel and Susan (Chessen) F. BA, U. Calif., Santa Barbara, 1965. Freelance writer, 1966—; dir. research Wolper Prodns., Los Angeles, 1966-69; staff writer You Asked for It, Los Angeles, 1982; staff writer Ripley's Believe It or Not ABC-TV, Los Angeles, 1983-85; mem. Theater West, Los Angeles. Writer: (Tv series pilot) Escape, (TV spls.) What Would You Pay for Yesterday, Henry Fonda: An American Legacy, Crimes of Passion, (one-act plays) Two Old Friends, Yea, Beethoven!, (films) Dinosaur, 1987, Two Old Friends, 1987, A Night of Miracles, 1990, (corp. films) Ralston Purina, Occidental Petroleum, Universal Studios Tour, Mobil Oil, Bank of Am., Simon Wiesenthal Ctr.; author: The Hitler Fact Book, 1990; contbr. articles to L.A. Times, New West, WGA Jour., New Obs., Hollywood Reporter, Travel & Leisure. Mem. acquisitions com. Hollywood Expn., Los Angeles. Mem. Writers Guild Am. Home: 1427 N Hayworth Ave Apt D West Hollywood CA 90046-3818

FUCHS, VICTOR ROBERT, economics educator; b. N.Y.C., Jan. 31, 1924; s. Alfred and Frances Sarah (Scheiber) F.; m. Beverly Beck, Aug. 29, 1948; children: Nancy, Fredric, Paula, Kenneth. BS, NYU, 1947; MA, Columbia U., 1951, PhD, 1955. Internat. fur broker, 1946-50; lectr. Columbia U., N.Y.C., 1953-54, instr., 1954-55, asst. prof. econs., 1955-59; assoc. prof. econs. NYU, 1959-60; program assoc. Ford Found. Program in Econ. Devel. and Adminstrn., 1960-62; prof. econs. Grad. Ctr., CUNY, 1968-74; prof. community medicine Mt. Sinai Sch. Medicine, 1968-74; prof. econs. Stanford U. and Stanford Med. Sch., 1974—, Henry J. Kaiser Jr. prof., 1988—; v.p. research Nat. Bur. Econ. Research, 1968-78, mem. sr. research staff, 1962—. Author: The Economics of the Fur Industry, 1957; (with Aaron Warner) Concepts and Cases in Economic Analysis, 1958, Changes in the Location of Manufacturing in the United States Since 1929, 1962, The Service Economy, 1968, Production and Productivity in the Service Industries, 1969, Policy Issues and Research Opportunities in Industrial Organization, 1972, Essays in the Economics of Health and Medical Care, 1972, Who Shall Live? Health, Economics and Social Choice, 1975; (with Joseph Newhouse) The Economics of Physician and Patient Behavior, 1978, Economic Aspects of Health, 1982, How We Live, 1983, The Health Economy, 1986, Women's Quest for Economic Equality, 1988; contbr. articles to profl. jours. Served with USAAF, 1943-46. Fellow Am. Acad. Arts and Scis., Am. Econ. Assn. (disting.); mem. Inst. Medicine of NAS, Am. Philos. Soc., Sigma Xi, Beta Gamma Sigma. Home: 796 Cedro Way Stanford CA 94305-1032 Office: Stanford U Dept Economics Sncina Hall West Stanford CA 94305-8715

FUENTES, CARMEN A., outreach executive; b. Churinzio, Michuacan, Mexico, Nov. 14, 1965; came to U.S., 1973; d. Pedro Fuentes and Aurora (Aguilar) F.; 1 child, Jessica Alvares. BA in Sociology, Calif. State U. Stanislaus, 1989. Health educator State Migrant Program, Merced, Calif., 1987-89; enumerator U.S. Census, Merced, 1990; outreach exec. Muir Trail Girl Scout Coun., Modesto, Calif., 1990—; radio informant Stas. KLOC, Modesto, KLOQ, Merced, and KNTO, Livingston, Calif., 1990—. Editor Ednl. Opportunity Program newsletter, 1989, Yamato Sch. Site Coun. newsletter, 1990-92. Vice-chair St. Judes Cath. Youth Group, Livingston, 1983; pres. Livingston State Child Devel. Ctr., 1987-89; community liaison Yamato Sch., Livingston, 1992—, treas. site coun., 1992—, pres. site coun., 1993—. Bloss Meml. scholar Calif. State U. Stanislaus, 1984-89. Mem. Mujeres Latinas, Hispanic Leadership Coun., Hispanic C. of C., Red Ribbon Com. Democrat. Home: 1504 Willow Ct Livingston CA 95334 Office: Muir Trail Girl Scout Coun 3621 Forest Glenn Dr Modesto CA 95355

FUERSTENAU, DOUGLAS WINSTON, mineral engineering educator; b. Hazel, S.D., Dec. 6, 1928; s. Erwin Arnold and Hazel Pauline (Karterud) F.; m. Margaret Ann Pellett, Aug. 29, 1953; children: Lucy, Sarah, Stephen. BS, S.D. Sch. Mines and Tech., 1949; MS, Mont. Sch. Mines, 1950; ScD, MIT, 1953; Mineral Engr., Mont. Coll. Mineral Sci. and Tech., 1968; hon. doctorate degree, U. Liege, Belgium, 1989. Asst. prof. mineral engring. MIT, 1953-56; sect. leader, metals research lab. Union Carbide Metals Co., Niagara Falls, N.Y., 1956-58; mgr. mineral engring. lab Kaiser Aluminum & Chem. Corp., Permanente, Calif., 1958-59; asso. prof. metallurgy U. Calif.-Berkeley, 1959-62, prof. metallurgy, 1962-86, P. Malozemoff prof. of mineral engring., 1987—, Miller research prof., 1969-70, chmn. dept. materials sci. and mineral engring., 1970-78; bd. dirs. Homestake Mining Co.; mem. Nat. Mineral Bd., 1975-78; Am. rep. Internat. Mineral Processing Congress Com., 1978—. Editor: Froth Flotation-50th Anniversary Vol., 1962; co-editor-in-chief: Internat. Jour. of Mineral Processing, 1972—; contbr. articles to profl. jours. Recipient Alexander von Humboldt Sr. Am. Scientist award Fed. Republic of Germany, 1984, Frank F. Aplan award The Engring. Found., 1990. Mem. Nat. Acad. Engring., Am. Inst. Mining and Metall. Engrs. (chmn. mineral processing div. 1967, Robert Lansing Hardy Gold medal 1957, Rossiter W. Raymond award 1961, Robert H. Richards award 1975, Antoine M. Gaudin award 1978, Mineral Industry Edn. award 1983, Henry Krumb disting. lectr. 1989, hon. 1989), Soc. Mining Engrs. (dir. 1968-71, Distinguished mem.), Am. Chem. Soc., Am. Inst. Chem. Engrs., Sigma Xi, Theta Tau. Congregationalist. Home: 1440 Le Roy Ave Berkeley CA 94708-1912

FUGAL, JARED WIDDISON, information systems professional; b. Salt Lake City, Mar. 8, 1963; s. John Paul and Elma (Widdison) F.; m. Valene Gurney, Mar. 6, 1992. BS cum laude, Brigham Young U., 1987, postgrad, 1991—. Credit analyst Am. Express, Salt Lake City, 1987-88; acctg., info. systems mgr. Gunthers Comfort Air, American Fork, Utah, 1988—. Mormon missionary, Santiago, Chile, 1982-83, fin. sec. to mission pres., 1983; treas. Brigham Young U. Internat. Folk Dancers, 1986-87. Mem. Phi Kappa Phi. Republican. Home: 205 S 100 E American Fork UT 84003-2329 Office: Gunthers Comfort Air 81 S 700 E American Fork UT 84003-2158

FUHLRODT, NORMAN THEODORE, former insurance executive; b. Wisner, Nebr., Apr. 24, 1910; s. Albert F. and Lena (Schafersman) F.; student Midland Coll., 1926-28; A.B., U. Nebr., 1930; M.A., U. Mich., 1936; m. Clarice W. Livermore, Aug. 23, 1933; 1 son, Douglas B. Tchr., athletic coach high schs., Sargent, Nebr., 1930-32, West Point, Nebr., 1932-35; with Central Life Assurance Co., Des Moines, 1936-74, pres., chief exec. officer, 1964-72, chmn. bd., chief exec. officer, 1972-74, also dir. Named Monroe St. Jour. Alumnus of Month, U. Mich. Grad Sch. Bus. Adminstrn. Gen. chmn. Greater Des Moines United campaign United Community Service, 1969-70. Former bd. dirs. Des Moines Center Sci. and Industry. Fellow Soc. Actuaries. Home: 230 W Laurel St Apt 606 San Diego CA 92101-1466

FUHRIMAN, ROBERT LEE, accountant; b. Nampa, Idaho, June 14, 1940; s. George Moroni and Alta Pearl (Yorgason) F.; m. Ingrid Marie Thomson, June 2, 1965; children: Robert L. Jr., Richard A., Troy C., Kirk E. AD, Ricks Coll., 1960; BS, Brigham Young U., 1965, M. of Accounting, 1966. CPA, CFE. Sr. acct. Ernst & Ernst, Boise, 1966-69; spl. agt. acct. FBI, Sacramento, 1970-71, Seattle, 1971-90; retired FBI, 1990; mgr. fin. adv. svcs. Coopers & Lybrand, Seattle, 1990—; speaker in field. Chmn. troop com. Boy Scouts Am., Bellevue, Wash., 1975-76; numerous leadership positions The CH. of Jesus Christ of Latter Day Saints, Bellevue, 1971—. Mem. AICPA, Nat. Assn. Cert. Fraud Examiners, Wash. Soc. CPA (chmn. litigation svcs. com. 1990-92), Soc. Former Spl. Agts. of FBI. Home: 13910 SE 23d St Bellevue WA 98005 Office: Coopers & Lybrand 1800 First Interstate Ctr 999 3rd Ave Seattle WA 98104-4098

FUHRMAN, BRUCE LIVERMORE, marketing professional; b. Darby, Pa., Apr. 4, 1936; s. Carl Monroe and Rowena (Livermore) F.; m. Janice Marie Schiff, Sept. 6, 1958; children: Steve, Carol, Jim. BS in Aerospace Engring., Northrop Univ., 1961; MBA, Calif. Luth. U., 1985. Design engr. Abex Aerospace, Oxnard, Calif., 1962-65, rsch. and devel. engr., 1965-68, applications engr./mgr., 1968-78, dir. rotating equipment, 1978-82, v.p. mktg., 1982-90, v.p. product support, 1990-91; dir. mktg. Howden Defense Systems, Santa Barbara, Calif., 1991—. Co-developer local structures sch., Camarillo, 1974. Mem. Soc. Automotive Engrs. (chmn. sect. 1985-91). Republican. Presbyterian. Home: 2264 Glenbrook Ave Camarillo CA 93010-1164

FUHRMAN, JED ALAN, biological oceanographer; b. N.Y.C., Oct. 25, 1956; s. Nathan and Fradelle (Gutoff) F.; m. Dorothy Ellen Comeau, Aug. 16, 1981; children: Gabriel Aaron, Rachel Mirabelle. SB, MIT, 1977; PhD, U. Calif., San Diego, 1981. Asst. prof. SUNY, Stony Brook, 1981-86, assoc. prof., 1986-88; assoc. prof. dept. biol. sci. U. So. Calif., L.A., 1988-92, prof., 1992—; vis. prof. U. Copenhagen, 1988. Contbr. articles to sci. jours. NSF fellow, 1977-80; Ritter fellow Bermuda Biol. Sta., 1987. Mem. AAAS, Am. Soc. Limnology and Oceanography (AAAS rep. 1983—), Am. Soc. Microbiology, Oceanography Soc., Am. Geophys. Union. Office: U So Calif Dept Biol Sci Los Angeles CA 90089-0371

FUHRMAN, KENDALL NELSON, software engineer; b. Evansville, Ind., Aug. 1, 1962; s. Ronald Charles and Mildred Elaine (Gulley) F.; m. Susan Ann Bagstad. BS in Computer Sci. and Math., U. Denver, 1984; postgrad., Colo. State U., 1988. Assoc. engr. Am. TV & Communications, Englewood, Colo., 1982-84; mem. tech. staff Hughes Aircraft Corp., Englewood, 1984-85; software engr. Ampex Corp., Golden, Colo., 1985-87, sr. software engr., 1987-88, project leader, 1988-92; project leader Ohmeda, Louisville, Colo., 1992—; cons. in field, Arvada, Colo., 1990—. Contbr. articles to profl. jours.; patentee antialising algorithm, graphics rendering. Mem. Assn. for Computing Machinery, IEEE, Spl. Interest Group Graphics, Spl. Interest Group Computer Human Interaction, Phi Beta Kappa. Home: 8417 Pierson Ct Arvada CO 80005 Office: Ohmeda 1315 Century Dr Louisville CO 80015

FUHRMAN, KEVIN DANIEL, musician, educator; b. Cherokee, Iowa, Dec. 20, 1965; s. Daniel Owen Fuhrman and Sandra Sue Johnson. B in Music Performance magna cum laude, Ariz. State U., 1989. President, owner Fuhrman Music, Phoenix, 1992—; percussion coach various high schs., Phoenix, 1986—; clinician various jr. and sr. high schs., Phoenix, 1986—. Project mgr., creator Valley Big. Bros.-Big Sisters Speakers Bur., Phoenix, 1992. Mem. Percussive Arts Soc. (pres. Ariz. chpt. 1989-90). Lutheran. Home: 2017 N 40th St Phoenix AZ 85008 Office: Fuhrman Music 2017 N 40th St Phoenix AZ 85008

FUHRMAN, ROBERT ALEXANDER, aerospace company executive; b. Detroit, Feb. 23, 1925; s. Alexander A. and Elva (Brown) F. B.S., U. Mich., 1945; M.S., U. Md., 1952; postgrad., U. Calif., San Diego, 1958; Exec. Mgmt. Program, Stanford Bus. Sch., 1964. Project engr. Naval Air Test Ctr., Patuxent River, Md., 1946-53; chief tech. engring. Ryan Aero. Co., San Diego, 1953-58; mgr. Polaris, 1958-64, chief engr. MSD, 1964-66; v.p., asst. gen. mgr. missile systems div. Lockheed Missiles & Space Co., Sunnyvale, Calif., 1966-68; v.p., gen. mgr. Lockheed Missiles & Space Co., 1969, v.p., 1973-76, pres., 1976-83, chmn., 1979-91; v.p. Lockheed Corp., Burbank, Calif., 1969-76; group pres. Missiles, Space & Electronics System Lockheed Corp., 1983-85; pres., chief operating officer Lockheed Corp., Calabasas, Calif., 1986-88; vice chmn. bd., chief operating officer Lockheed Corp., 1980-90; pres. Lockheed Ga. Co., Marietta, 1970-71, Lockheed Calif. Co., Burbank, 1971-73; chmn. bd. dirs. Bank of the West; bd. dirs. Charles Stark Draper Lab., Inc.; mem. Fleet Ballistic Missile Steering Task Group, 1966-70, Def. Sci. Bd. Mem. adv. coun. Sch. Engring., Stanford U.; mem. adv. bd. Coll. Engring., U. Mich. With USNR, 1944-46. Recipient Silver Knight award Nat. Mgmt. Assn., 1969, John J. Montgomery award San Diego Aerospace Mus., 1964, Disting. Citizen award Boy Scouts Am., 1983, Eminent Engr. award Tau Beta Pi, 1983; named to Mich. Aviation Hall of Fame, 1990. Fellow AIAA (hon., pres., Von Karman award 1978), Royal Aero. Soc., Soc. Mfg. Engrs. (award 1973, Donald C. Burnham award 1983, Mich. Aviation Hall of Fame 1991); mem. NAE, Am. Astron. Soc. (sr.), Nat. Aero. Assn., Navy League U.S. (life), Air Force Assn., Assn. U.S. Army, Soc. Am. Value Engrs. (hon.), Santa Clara County Mfrs. Group (past chmn.), Burning Tree Club (Bethesda, Md.), Carmel Valley Country Club (Calif.), Monterey Peninsula Country Club (Pebble Beach, Calif.), Beta Gamma Sigma.

FUJII, KIYO, pharmacist; b. Portland, Oreg., July 1, 1921; s. Kanji and Mitoyo (Kurata) F.; student U. Wash., 1939-42; B.S., St. Louis Coll. Pharmacy, 1943. Pharmacist, C.F. Knight Drug, St. Louis, 1943-48, Sargent Drug, Chgo., 1950-52, Mt. Sinai Hosp., Chgo., 1953-54, Campus Pharmacy, Los Angeles, 1973—; chief pharmacist Evang. Hosp., Chgo., 1948-49, Am. Hosp. Clinic, Los Angeles, 1956-60. Mem. Am., Calif. Pharm. Assns., St. Louis Coll. Pharmacy Alumni Assn., Rho Chi, Sigma Epsilon Sigma. Democrat. Presbyterian. Home: 7913 Kentwood Ave Los Angeles CA 90045-1152

FUJIMOTO, GREGG TAKASHI, underwriter; b. Honolulu, July 24, 1951; s. Tsutomu and Rose (Hakoda) F.; m. Patricia Lea, May 22, 1987; children: Kristyn Mari, Zachary Takashi. BBA, U. Hawaii, 1973. CLU, ChFC. Underwriter Northwestern Mut./Baird Investments, Honolulu, 1973—; exec. dir. Hawaii Estate Planning Coun., Honolulu, 1984. Mem. Honolulu Assn. Life Underwriters, Nat. Assn. Life Underwriters (Nat. Quality award 1976, 78, 79, 81, 82, 84-91, Nat. Sales Achievement 1978-81, Health Ins. Quality 1977-91), Million Dollar Roundtable. Office: Northwestern Mut/Baird Investments 1001 Bishop St Pacific 2600 Honolulu HI 96813

FUJITA, JAMES HIROSHI, history educator; b. Honolulu, July 24, 1958; s. George Hideo and Teruko (Miyano) F. BA, U. Hawaii, 1980, MA, 1983. Grad. asst. U. Hawaii at Manoa, Honolulu, 1980-85, lectr. history, 1986—; lectr. history Kapiolani C.C., Honolulu, 1987—; lectr. Elderhostel Program, Honolulu, 1992. Mem. NEA, Hawaii State Tchrs. Assn., World History Assn., U. Hawaii Profl. Assembly, Phi Alpha Theta. Office: Kapiolani C C 4303 Diamond Head Rd Honolulu HI 96816

FUJITANI, MARTIN TOMIO, software quality engineer; b. Sanger, Calif., May 3, 1968; s. Matsuo and Hasuko Fujitani. BS in Indsl. and Systems Engring., U. So. Calif., 1990. Sec. Kelly Svcs., Inc., Sacramento, 1987; receptionist Coudert Bros., L.A., 1988; rsch. asst. U. So. Calif., L.A., 1988-89; math. aide Navy Pers. Rsch. and Devel. Ctr., San Diego, 1989; quality assurance test technician Retix, Santa Monica, Calif., 1989-90; software engr. Quality Med. Adjudication, Inc., Rancho Cordova, Calif., 1990-92; test engr. Worldtalk Corp., Los Gatos, Calif., 1993—. Assemblyman Am. Legion Calif. Boys State, 1985. Recipient Service Above Self award East Sacramento Rotary, 1986. Mem. Ops. Rsch. Soc. Am. (assoc.), Sacramento Sr. Young Buddhist Assn. (treas. 1990-91), Gen. Alumni Assn. U. So. Calif. (life). Home: 205 Milbrae Ln Apt 2 Los Gatos CA 95030 Office: Worldtalk Corp 475 Alberto Way Los Gatos CA 95032

FUKUDA, NAOMI NOBUKO, medical/surgical nurse; b. Guam, Mar. 10, 1963; d. Reginald Y. and Michiko (Hanzawa) F. AS in Nursing, U. Hawaii, Honolulu, 1983, BSN, 1985, MSN, 1988. Cert. med.-surg. nurse. Staff nurse Kaiser Med. Ctr., Honolulu, 1985-88; clin. staff nurse Kaiser Permanente Hosp., Honolulu, 1988—. Mem. Hawaii Nurse's Assn., Sigma Theta Tau. Home: 94-270 Makapipipi St Mililani HI 96789

FUKUHARA, HENRY, artist, educator; b. L.A., Apr. 25, 1913; s. Ichisuke and Ume (Sakamoto) F.; m. Fujiko Yasutake, Aug. 18, 1938; children: Joyce, Grace, Rackham, Helen. Student with Edgar A. Whitney, Jackson Heights, N.Y., 1972, Rex Brandt, Corona del Mar, Calif., 1974, Robert E. Wood, 1975, Carl Molno, Woodside, N.Y., 1976. Exhibited in group shows at Friends World Coll., Lloyds Neck, N.Y., 1980, Elaine Benson Gallery, Bridgehampton, N.Y., 1979, 83, Nat. Invitational Watercolor, Zaner Gallery, Rochester, N.Y., 1981, Fire House Gallery, 1982, Parrish Art Mus., 1982, Japan-R.I. Exchange Exhibit, Provincetown, R.I., 1986, Kawakami Gallery, Tokyo, 1986, Setagaya Mus. Art, Tokyo, 1988-91, 5th Ann. Rosoh Kai Watercolor Exhbn. Meguro Mus. Art, Tokyo, 1991, 6th Ann. Rosoh Kai Watercolor Exhbn. Meguro Mus. Art, 1992, Stary Sheets Galleries Exhbn., Irvine, Calif., 1992—; represented in permanent collections at Heckscher Mus., Huntington, N.Y., Abilene Mus. Fine Art, Nassau Community Coll., SUNY-Stony Brook, Los Angeles County Mus. Art, Blaine County Mus., Chinook, Mont., Ralston Mus., Sydney, Mont., San Bernardino County Mus., Redlands, Calif., 1984, Riverside Mus. Art, Calif., 1985, Gonzaga U., Spokane, Wash., 1986, Nagano Mus. Art, Japan, 1986, Contemporary Mus. of Art, Hiroshima, 1988, Santa Monica (Calif.) Coll., 1988; instr. Watercolor Venice (Calif.) Adult Sch., 1992-93, tchr. watercolor. Recipient Purchase award Nassau Community Coll., 1976; Best in Show, Hidden Pond, Town of Islip, 1978, Strathmore Paper Co., 1979, Creative Connections Gallery award Foothills Art Ctr., Golden, Colo., 1984, Judges Choice, Mont. Minature Art Soc. 7th Ann International Show, Working with Abandoned Control, 1993, others. Mem. Nat. Watercolor Soc., Ala. Watercolor Soc., Pitts. Watercolor Soc., Nat. Drawing Assn. Address: 1214 Marine St Santa Monica CA 90405

FUKUMOTO, BENJAMIN I., information systems executive; b. Honolulu, Dec. 18, 1938; s. Edward K. and Tsuruko (Kawamoto) F.; m. Elmira E. Kojima, July 27, 1961; children: Reid, Teri Ann, Lori Ann, Eric. BA, U. Hawaii, 1961. Mktg. mgr. IBM Corp., Honolulu, 1967-81; dep. dir. City and County of Honolulu, 1981-83; sales dir. GTE Hawaiian Telephone, Honolulu, 1983-89; gen. mgr. Tandem Computers Hawaii Dist., Honolulu, 1989-92; v.p. SERVCO Pacific, Honolulu, 1992—. Served to capt. AUS, 1961-67, Vietnam. Mem. Armed Forces Communications and Electronics Assn. (pres. 1987-88, meritorious service award 1987), Hawaii C. of C., Honolulu Japanese C. of C. (bd. dirs. 1976-93, officer 1987-91, 1st vice chmn. 1991, chmn. bd. 1992-93), Honolulu Club, Waikiki Athletic Club, Honolulu Rotary, Masons. Democrat. Home: 6852 Niumalu Loop Honolulu HI 96825-1640 Office: SERVCO Pacific 2230-A Alahao Place Honolulu HI 96819

FULBRIGHT, JOHN WILLIAM, real estate executive; b. Beach Grove, Ind., Aug. 7, 1952; s. Richard Stanley and Madonna Sara (Ragan) F.; m. Anne Marie Montpettit, July 30, 1988; children: Katherine Anne, James Richard. BA in History, Ind. U., Bloomington, 1974, MBA in Fin. and Acctg., 1978; JD, U. San Diego, 1988. Lic. contractor, Calif., real estate broker, Calif. Project mgr. The Sickels Group, San Diego, 1984-86; regional v.p. Robert Randall Co., San Diego, 1986-88; v.p. Kaufman & Broad, San Diego, 1989—. Dir. Oceanside Boys & Girls Club. Mem. Bldg. Industry Assn., Am. Arbitration Assn., Ind. State Bar Assn., Delta Upsilon. Home: 3730 Via Las Villas Oceanside CA 92056-7249 Office: Kaufman and Broad 12520 High Bluff Dr Ste 300 San Diego CA 92130-2061

FULCO, ARMAND JOHN, biochemist; b. Los Angeles, Apr. 3, 1932; s. Herman J. and Clelia Marie (DeFeo) F.; m. Virginia Loy Hungerford, June 18, 1955 (div. July 1985); children: William James, Lisa Marie, Linda Susan, Suzanne Yvonne; m. Doris V.N. Goodman, Nov. 29, 1987. B.S. in Chemistry, UCLA, 1957, Ph.D. in Physiol. Chemistry, 1960. NIH postdoctoral fellow Lipid Labs. UCLA, 1960-61; NIH research fellow dept. chemistry Harvard U., Cambridge, Mass., 1961-63; biochemist, prin. investigator Lab. Nuclear Medicine and Radiation Biology, UCLA, 1963-80; asst. prof. dept. biol. chemistry UCLA (Med. Sch.), 1965-70, assoc. prof., 1970-76, prof., 1976—, prin. investigator, lab. biomed. and environ. scis., 1981—; cons. biochemist VA, Los Angeles, 1968-79; mem. UCLA Molecular Biology Inst., 1991—; co-dir. Lipid-Hormone Core Lab., UCLA, 1989—. Author: (with J.F. Mead) The Unsaturated and Polyunsaturated Fatty Acids in Health and Disease, 1976; contbr. over 85 articles to sci. jours. Served with U.S. Army, 1952-54. Mem. Am. Chem. Soc., Am. Soc. Biochem. and Molecular Biology, Am. Oil Chemists Soc., AAAS, Am. Soc. Microbiology, Harvard Chemists Assn., Sigma Xi. Office: U Calif Lab Biomed and Environ Scis 900 Veteran Ave Los Angeles CA 90024-2703

FULDE, WALTER JOHN, aerospace company executive; b. Phila., May 27, 1935; s. Walter Henry and Margarete Johanna (Meyer) F.; m. Catherine Dorothy Pagano, June 27, 1959; children: Walter Anthony, Janette Louise. BS in Econs., U. Pa., 1957; postgrad., San Jose State U., 1964-66. Asst. post engr. quartermaster depot U.S. Army, Phila., 1957-59; personnel supr. Philco Corp., Phila., 1959-63; indsl. rels. mgr. Ford Aerospace Corp., Menlo Park, Calif., 1963-68; indsl. rels. and labor rels. mgr. Ford Aerospace Corp., Palo Alto, Calif., 1968-76; dir. labor rels. Ford Aerospace Corp., Sunnyvale, Calif., 1976-84, program mgr., 1984—; owner Bambi's Card & Gift Stores, Saratoga, Calif., Cupertino, Calif., 1976—; chief exec. officer/owner Ingress Enterprises Cons. Firm, Saratoga, 1989—. Author: Step into your Store, 1988. 1st lt. U.S. Army, 1957. Home: 15164 Montalvo Rd Saratoga CA 95070-6327 Office: Ford Aerospace Corp 1260 Crossman Ave Sunnyvale CA 94089-1116

FULKERSON, WILLIAM MEASEY, JR., college president; b. Moberly, Mo., Oct. 18, 1940; s. William Measey and Edna Frances (Pendleton) F.; m. Grace Carolyn Wisdom, May 26, 1962; children: Carl Franklin, Carolyn Sue. BA, William Jewell Coll., 1962; MA, Temple U., 1964; PhD, Mich. State U., 1969. Asst. to assoc. prof. Calif. State U., Fresno, 1981—; asst. to pres. Calif. State U.-Fresno, 1971-73; assoc. exec. dir. Am. Assn. State Colls., Washington, 1973-77; acad. v.p. Phillips U., Enid, Okla., 1977-81; pres. Adams State Coll., Alamosa, Colo., 1981-87, 88—; interim pres. Met. State Coll., Denver, 1987-88. Author: Planning for Financial Exigency, 1973; contbr. articles to profl. jours. Commr. North Central Assn., Chgo., 1980—; bd. dirs. Acad. Collective Bargaining Info. Service, Washington, 1976, Office for Advancemnet Pub. Negro Colls., Atlanta, 1973-77, Colo. Endowment for Humanities, 1988—. Named Disting. Alumni William Jewell Coll., 1982, Outstanding Alumnus Mich. State U. Coll. Comm., Arts & Scis., 1987. Mem. Am. Assn. State Colls. and Univs. (parliamentarian, bd. dirs. 1992—), Am. Council on Edn. (bd. dirs.), Alamosa C. of C. (dir., pres 1984 Citizen of Yr. award). Lodge: Rotary. Office: Adams State Coll Office of Pres Alamosa CO 81102

FULKS, JAMES ARTHUR, marine corps officer; b. Luling, Tex., Oct. 3, 1946; s. Reaford W. and Betsy B. (Smith) F.; children: Kim Fulks, James Koby, Kip Jay; m. Gayle P. Bartell, Nov. 27, 1985. BS, Utah State U., 1972; MS, Syracuse U., 1987. Commd. 2d lt. USMC, 1968, advanced through grades to col., 1990; commanding officer Marine Barracks, Bermuda, 1981-84; program devel. officer hqrs. USMC, Washington, 1984-87; operation officer III Marine Expeditionary Force, Okinawa, Japan, 1988-89; chief of staff 6-3 Operation Desert Shield 1st Marine Divsn., 1989-90; commanding officer Operation Desert Storm 4th Marine Regiment, 1990-91; commanding officer 5th Marine Regiment, Camp Pendleton, Calif., 1991—. Republican. Office: 5th Marine Regiment 1st Marine Divsn Camp Pendleton CA 92055

FULLER, GARY ALBERT, geography educator; b. Syracuse, N.Y., Oct. 14, 1941; s. Albert Charles and Viola (Whitford) F.; m. Barbara Marie Bruton, Aug. 8, 1964; children: Michael, Teresa, Kathleen, John. BS, SUNY, Oswego, 1964; PhD, Pa. State U., 1972. From asst. prof. to prof. U. Hawaii, Honolulu, 1970—. Mem. Assn. Am. Geographers, Population Assn. Am., Nat. Coun. Geographic Edn. Office: U Hawaii Dept Geography Honolulu HI 96822

FULLER, GLENN R., park ranger; b. Van Nuys, Calif., Sept. 1, 1946; s. Earl D. and Virginia (Allen) F. Masters, Calif. State U., Sacramento, 1972. Park ranger Grand Canyon (Ariz.) Nat. Park, 1975-80, Cape Cod Nat. Park, Wellfleet, Mass., 1980-81, Rocky Mountain Nat. Park, Estes Park, Colo., 1981-82, Golden Gate NRA, San Francisco, 1982-83; park supt. Muia Woods Nat. Monument, Mill Valley, Calif., 1983—. Sgt. U.S. Army, 1970-68. Mem. Friends of the River, Assn. Nat. Park Rangers. Office: Muir Woods Nat Monument Mill Valley CA 94941

FULLER, JAMES WILLIAM, financial director; b. Rochester, Ind., Apr. 3, 1940; m. Raymond S. and Mildred (Osteimeier) F.; m. Mary Falvey, Aug. 22, 1981; childrn: Kristen Anne, Glen William. AA, San Bernardino (Calif.) Valley Coll., 1960; BS, San Jose (Calif.) State U., 1962; MBA, Calif. State U., 1967. V.p. Dean Witter, San Francisco, 1967-71, Shields & Co., San Francisco, 1971-74; fin. mgr. SRI Internat., Menlo Park, Calif., 1974-77; sr. v.p. N.Y. Stock Exch., N.Y.C., 1977-81, Charles Schwab & Co., San Francisco, 1981-85; pres. Bull & Bear Corp., N.Y.C., 1985-87; dir. Bridge Info. Systems, San Fransico, 1987—; bd. dir. Action Trac Inc., L.A., Current Techs. Inc., Vancouver, B.C., Bridge Info. Systems, St. Louis. Bd. dirs. Securities Industry Protection Corp., Washington, 1981-87, Global Econ. Action Inst., N.Y.C., 1989—, Pacific Rsch. Inst., San Francisco, 1991—; bd. trustees U. Calif., Santa Cruz. Lt. USN, 1963-66. Mem. The Family Club (San Francisco), Olympic Club (San Francisco), Jonathon Club (L.A.), Univ. Club (N.Y.C.). Republican. Presbyterian. Home: 2584 Filbert St San Francisco CA 94123 Office: Bridge Info Systems 555 California St San Francisco CA 94104

FULLER, MARY FALVEY, management consultant; b. Detroit, Oct. 28, 1941; d. Lawrence C. and Mathilde G. Falvey; m. James W. Fuller, Aug. 22, 1981. BA in Econs. with honors, Cornell U., 1963; MBA, Harvard U., 1967. Systems engr. IBM Corp., N.Y.C., 1963-65; mgmt. cons. McKinsey & Co., Inc., N.Y.C., 1967-75; v.p. Citibank, N.A., N.Y.C., 1975-78, head asset servicing div., 1977-78; sr. v.p., dir., head adminstrn. div., mem. exec. com., mem. operating com. Blyth Eastman Dillon & Co., Inc., N.Y.C., 1978-80; pres. M.C. Falvey Assocs., Inc., N.Y.C., 1980-81, 82—; v.p. fin. Shaklee Corp., San Francisco, 1981-82; pres. Falvey Autos, Inc., Troy, Mich., 1978-93, also chmn., bd. dirs.; vis. prof. Cornell U. Johnson Grad. Sch. Mgmt., 1992; trustee Fed. Hosp. Ins. Trust Fund, Fed. Old Age and Survivors Ins. Trust Fund, Fed. Disability Ins. Trust Fund, 1984-89, Williamsburg Charter Found. 1988-89; dir. Tech. Funding Inc., 1983-91; mem. regional dealer adv. council Toyota Motor Sales Corp., 1986-88. Mem. Com. for N.Y. Philharmonic, 1975-77; mem. 1979 Adv. Council on Social Security, 1979-80, Pres. Reagan's Transition Task Force on Social Security, 1979-80, Nat. Commn. on Social Security Reform, 1982-83; adminstrv. bd. Cornell U. Council, 1984-86; bd. dirs. St. Francis Hosp. Found., 1992—; trustee Cornell U., 1988—; mem. adminstrn. and legal processes adv. council Mills Coll., 1982-85; chmn. bd. trustees San Francisco Performances, 1981-93. Harvard Bus. Sch. grantee, 1965-67. Republican. Episcopalian. Mem. Global Econ. Action Inst. (internat. steering com. 1990—), Harvard Bus. Sch. Assn. No. Calif. (dir.) Clubs: Commonwealth of Calif. (program com. 1983-85, chmn. Asia-Pacific study sect. 1985-86), Univ. (dir. San Francisco). Home and Office: 2584 Filbert St San Francisco CA 94123-3318

FULLER, NANCY BELLE, social activist; b. Louisville, June 11, 1948; d. James Luther Fuller and Lillian (Abbott) Wells; m. William Earl Grant, June 1984 (div.); 1 child, Austin McWhite; m. James H. Borchardt, Nov. 1, 1986. AA, Stephens Coll., 1969, BFA, 1969. Lic. ins. agt., Calif. Actor, singer, dancer Stratford Festival Theatre Co., film, TV roles, 1970-81; touring mem. Can. Mime Theatre, 1970; ballet demonstrator/tchr. Dance Ctr. West, L.A., 1977; prof. master acting class BGSU, 1980; speaker, activist, writer, 1989—; pres. Calif. chpt. Mothers Alliance for the Rights of Children, 1989—; pub. speaker as activist mother numerous rallies against child sexual abuse, 1987—; rschr., educator. Editor (newsletter) Defend the Children, 1989—; ghostwriter. Mem. SAG, AFTRA, Actors Equity Assn., Can. Actors Equity Assn., Assn. Can. TV and Radio Artists, World Affairs Coun., Nat. Ctr. for Protective Parents, Nat. Ctr. for Redress Incest and Sexual Abuse. Office: Defend the Children PO Box 4241 Walnut Creek CA 94596

FULLER, ROBERT EARL, minister; b. Yuma, Ariz., Oct. 12, 1938; s. George Orville and Treva (Humphrey) F.; m. Aldea Rose Tharp, June 13, 1958; children: Dawn Michelle, David Earl, John Thomas, Steven Andrew. BA, L.A. Bapt. Coll., 1960; BD, Talbot Theol. Sem., La Mirada, Calif., 1964. Pastor, founder Thousand Oaks (Calif.) Bapt. Ch., 1964-79; pastor Berean Bapt. Ch., Fremont, Calif., 1980—; bd. dirs. Regular Bapt. Camp, LaPorte, Calif. Mem. Calif. Assn. of Regular Bapt. Chs. (bd. dirs.). Republican. Office: Berean Bapt Ch 2929 Peralta Blvd Fremont CA 94536-3863

FULLER, ROBERT KENNETH, architect, urban designer; b. Denver, Oct. 6, 1942; s. Kenneth Roller and Gertrude Ailene (Heid) F.; m. Virginia Louise Elkin, Aug. 23, 1969; children: Kimberly Kirsten, Kelsey Christa. BArch, U. Colo., 1967; MArch and Urban Design, Washington U., St. Louis, 1974. Archtl. designer Fuller & Fuller, Denver; architect, planner Urban Research and Design Ctr., St. Louis, 1970-72; pres. Fuller & Fuller Assocs., Denver, 1972—. prin. works include Pattonsburg New Town, Mo., 1972. del. Aspen Design Conf., 1966, bd. dirs. Cherry Creek Improvement Assn., Greater Cherry Creek Steering com., Colo. Arlberg Club, past pres., 1990; bd. dirs. Horizons, Inc.; past pres. Denver East Cen. Civic Assn. Served with USMCR, 1964-70. Mem. AIA (past pres. Denver chpt. 1987, traveling scholar to Gt. Britain, Colo. 1972), Phi Gamma Delta, Delta Phi Delta. Home: 2244 E 4th Ave Denver CO 80206-4107 Office: 3320 E 2d Ave Denver CO 80206

FULLER, WILLIAM DEAN, research executive; b. San Diego, Apr. 6, 1947; s. Gerald Dean and Ilah Onita (Miller) F.; m. Diane Helen Weiss, Apr. 24, 1971; children: Daniel William, Jennifer Ann. BS, Calif. State U., 1969. Rsch. asst. Salk Inst. for Biol. Studies, San Diego, 1969-72; rsch. chemist Terra Marine Biorsch., San Diego, 1972-74; staff rsch. assoc. U. Calif., San Diego, 1974-75; rsch. chemist Calbiochem, San Diego, 1975-78; rsch. dir. BioRsch., Inc., San Diego, 1978—. Inventor high pressure flow peptide syn., 1,1 diaminoalkane sweetners, surgical adhesives, urethane protected NCAs. Mem. AAAS, Am. Chem. Soc., Protein Soc., Peptide Soc., N.Y. Acad. Sci. Office: BioResearch Inc 11189 Sorrento Valley Rd #4 San Diego CA 92121

FULLER, WILLIAM ROGER, mathematics and physics educator; b. North Kingston, R.I., Nov. 4, 1949; s. Roger William and Stefania Theresa (Minta) F. BS, Trinity Coll., Hartford, Conn., 1971; MS, Ind. U., 1972, MA, 1976, PhD, 1979. Tchr. St. Joseph's High Sch., South Bend, Ind., 1976-77, Holy Cross Jr. Coll., Notre Dame, Ind., 1978-80; assoc. prof. U. Portland, Oreg., 1980—; cons. St. Mary's Acad., Portland, 1983. Contbr. articles to profl. jours. 1st lt. USAF, 1973. Mem. Am. Math. Soc., Math. Assn. Am., Soc. for Indsl. and Applied Math., Am. Inst. Physics (referee 1983—), Am. Assn. Physics Tchrs., Internat. Assn. Mathematical Physics, Sigma Pi Sigma. Republican. Roman Catholic. Office: U Portland 5000 N Willamette Blvd Portland OR 97203-5750

FULLERTON, CHARLES MICHAEL, physics educator; b. Oklahoma City, Mar. 10, 1932; s. Joseph Austin and Rose Marsh (Ingraham) F.; m. Jane Jo Wyatt, Dec. 27, 1954; children: Stephanie Malia, Christopher Damien, Amy Juliet. BS in Math., U. Okla., 1954; postgrad., U. N.Mex., 1957-61; MS in Physics, N.Mex. Inst. Mining and Technology, 1964, PhD, 1966. Instr. math, physics Coll. St. Joseph, Albuquerque, 1957-61; from asst. prof. to full prof. U. Hawaii, Hilo, 1966—, dean arts and scis., 1984-91; dir. Cloud Physics Obs., Hilo, 1966-84; dir. mgmt. services State Dept. Health and Social Services, Santa Fe, 1972, dir. personnel services, 1975. Contbr. articles to profl. jours. Served to 1st lt. U.S. Army, 1954-57. Grantee NSF, 1964-66, U.S. Dept. Interior, 1971-77. Mem. Am. Meteorol. Soc., Am. Geophys. Union, Hawaiian Acad. Sci., N.Mex. Acad. Sci., Sigma Xi (local pres. 1975-76). Republican. Roman Catholic. Lodge: Rotary. Office: U Hawaii Coll Arts and Scis Hilo HI 96720-4091

FULLERTON, GAIL JACKSON, university president; b. Lincoln, Nebr., Apr. 29, 1927; d. Earl Warren and Gladys Bernice (Marshall) Jackson; m. Stanley James Fullerton, Mar. 27, 1967; children by previous marriage—Gregory Snell Putney, Cynde Putney Mitchell. B.A., U. Nebr., 1949, M.A., 1950; Ph.D., U. Oreg., 1954. Lectr. sociology Drake U., Des Moines, 1955-57; asst. prof. sociology Fla. State U., Tallahassee, 1957-60; asst. prof. sociology San Jose (Calif.) State U., 1963-67, asso. prof., 1968-71, prof., 1972-91, dean grad. studies and research, 1972-76, exec. v.p. univ., 1976-78, pres., 1978-91; ret., 1991; bd. dirs. Assoc. Western Univs., Inc., 1980-91; mem. sr. accrediting commn. Western Assn. Schs. and Colls., 1982-88, chmn., 1985-86; mem. Pres.'s Commn. Nat. Collegiate Athletic Assn., 1986-91; bd. dirs. Am. Coll. Assn., 1991. Author: Survival in Marriage, 2d edit, 1977, (with Snell Putney) Normal Neurosis: The Adjusted American, 2d edit, 1966. Carnegie fellow, 1950-51, 52-53; Doherty Found. fellow, 1951-52. Mem. Am. Sociol. Assn., Western Coll. Assn. (exec. com., past pres.), San Jose C. of C. (bd. dirs.), Phi Beta Kappa. Home: 1643 Tompkins Hill Rd Fortuna CA 95540

FULLMER, DANIEL WARREN, educator, psychologist; b. Spoon River, Ill., Dec. 12, 1922; s. Daniel Floyd and Sarah Louisa (Essex) F.; m. Janet Satomi Saito, June 1980; children: Daniel William, Mark Warren. B.S., Western Ill. U., 1947, M.S., 1952; Ph.D., U. Denver, 1955. Post-doctoral intern psychiat. div. U. Oreg. Med. Sch., 1958-61; mem. faculty U. Oreg., 1955-66; prof. psychology Oreg. System of Higher Edn., 1958-66; faculty Coll. Edn. U. Hawaii, Honolulu, 1966—, now prof., 1974—; pvt. practice psychol. counseling; cons. psychologist Grambling State U., 1960-81; founder Free-Family Counseling Ctrs., Portland, Oreg., 1959-66, Honolulu, 1966-74; co-founder Child and Family Counseling Ctr., Waianae, Oahu, Hawaii, Kilohana United Meth. Ch., Oahu, 1992; pres. Human Resources Devel. Ctr., Inc., 1974—; chmn. Hawaii State Bd. to License Psychologists, 1973-78. Author: Counseling: Group Theory & System, 2d. edit., 1978, The Family Therapy Dictionary Text, 1991, MANABU, Diagnosis and Treatment of a Japanese Boy with a Visual Anomaly, 1991; co-author: Principles of Guidance, 2d. edit., 1977; author (counselor/cons. training manuals) Counseling: Content and Process, 1964, Family Consultation Therapy, 1968, The School Counselor-Consultant, 1972; editor: Bulletin, Oreg. Coop Testing Service, 1955-57, Hawaii P&G Jour., 1970-76; assoc. editor: Educational Perspectives, U. Hawaii Coll. Edn. Served with USNR, 1944-46. Recipient Francis E. Clark award Hawaii Pers. Guidance Assn., 1972, Thomas Jefferson award for Outstanding Pub. Svc., 1993; named Hall of Fame Grambling State U., 1987. Mem. Am. Psychol. Assn., Am. Counseling Assn. (Nancy C. Wimmer award 1963). Methodist. Office: 1750 Kalakaua Ave Apt 809 Honolulu HI 96826-3725

FULLMER, DONALD KITCHEN, insurance executive; b. Rockyford, Colo., Apr. 11, 1915; s. George Clinton and Florence E. (Kitchen) F.; m. June 5, 1934 (dec. 1987); children: Robert E., Maxine Fullmer Vogt, Phyllis R. Fullmer Danielson. CLU, Am. Coll. Life Underwriting, 1962. Lic. ins. agt., Wash. Life underwriter N.Y. Life, Aberdeen, Wash., 1954-74; ind. gen. agt. Aberdeen, Wash., 1974-81; life underwriter MONY, Bellingham, Wash., 1983-88; ret. County chmn. Rep. Party, Grays Harbor, Wash., 1964-69, mem. state exec. com., 1971-72. With U.S. Army, 1945. Mem. N.W. Wash. Assn. Life Underwriters, Wash. State Assn. Life Underwriters (pres. 1968-69), Twin Harbor Life Underwriters, Masons. LDS. Home: 5464 Bell-West Dr Bellingham WA 98226

FULLMER, JOSEPH ANTHONY, JR., manufacturing company executive; b. Stratford, N.J., May 12, 1943; s. Joseph A. and Mary (Weimer) F.; m. Dolores F. Hering, May 13, 1967; children: Donna L., Cheryl A., Joseph A. III. BS, Drexel U., 1971; postgrad., MIT, 1982. Div. project engr. Manville Corp., Denver, 1973-77, mgr. tech., 1977-78, mgr. project engring., 1978-80, dir. corp. indsl. engring., 1980-85, dir. tech., 1985-86, group ops. mgr., 1986, v.p., gen. mgr., 1986-90; pres. TIMA Inc., Stamford, Conn., 1990-92, Accurate Plastics, Longmont, Colo., 1992—; advisor Project Mgmt. Inst., 1983-85; mem. indsl. adv. bd. Tex. Tech. U., 1985-90. With U.S. Army, 1965-67, Korea. Named Man of Yr. Drexel Evening Coll. Alumni, Phila., 1991. Mem. Am. Inst. Plant Engrs. (pres. 1971-73, Plant Engr. of Yr. 1973), Coun. Indsl. Engring., Am. Inst. Indsl. Engrs., Soc. Sr. Execs. MIT. Roman Catholic. Home: 1777 Larimer St # 1902 Denver CO 80202

FULLMER, STEVEN MARK, banker; b. San Francisco, Mar. 15, 1956; s. Thomas Patrick and Patricia Ann (Carroll-Boyd) F.; m. Rhonda Lynnette Bush, Nov. 8, 1992. BA in Chemistry, Willamette U., 1978, BA in Biology, 1978; MBA, Ariz. State U., 1993. Sr. engr., project leader Honeywell Large Computer Products, Phoenix, 1981-86; bank officer, cons., team leader First Interstate Bank Ariz., Phoenix, 1987—; cons. J.A. Boyd & Assoc., San Francisco, 1985—, ImaginInc. Consulting, Phoenix, 1985—. Contbr. articles to profl. jours. Mem. exec. bd. Grand Canyon coun., Boy Scouts Am., scoutmaster, 1983-88, commr., 1988-92, Dist. com., 1992—; founder, lt. comdr. Maricopa County Sheriff's Adj. Posse, 1982—. Recipient Order of Merit Boy Scouts Am., 1988, Nat. Disting. Commr. award Boy Scouts Am., 1990, Nat. Founder's award Boy Scouts Am., 1991. Mem. Am. Inst. for Certification Computer Profls. (cert. data processor 1985), Mensa, Heard Mus. Coun. Bd., Liberty Wildlife (rehabber), Phi Lambda Upsilon, Phi Eta Sigma, Kappa Sigma (v.p. 1973-74), Alpha Chi Sigma, Sigma Iota Epsilon, Beta Gamma Sigma. Republican. Roman Catholic. Lodge: KC (membership dir. 1988). Office: First Interstate Bank Ariz 114 W Adams St Phoenix AZ 85003-2005

FULLMER, TERRY LLOYD, tax consultant, business consultant; b. Driggs, Idaho, June 23, 1939; s. W. Leigh and Addie B. (Harris) F.; m. Beverly Ann Lowe, July 9, 1970; children: Jody, Wendy, Dana, Christopher, Kelly. AA, Ricks Coll., Rexburg, Idaho, 1959; BA, Brigham Young U., 1963. Enrolled agt.; accredited tax advisor; cert. tax profl. Vol. Peace Corps, Dominican Republic, 1963-65; tchr. Modesto (Calif.) High Sch., 1967, Ganesha High Sch., Pomona, Calif., 1968-69; ins. broker Continental Casualty Ins., L.A., 1969-71; tax cons., owner Fullmer & Assocs., Orange, Calif., 1972—. Trustee Gail Pattison Youth Leadership Trust, Orange, 1986—; chair steering com. Orange Sch Dist., 1988. Mem. Nat. Enrolled Agts. Assn., Calif. Soc. Enrolled Agts., Orange County Soc. Enrolled Agts., Nat. Soc. Tax Profls., Orange C. of C. (pres., bd. dirs.). Mem. LDS Ch. Home: 5251 Pasatiempo Dr Yorba Linda CA 92686 Office: Fullmer & Assocs 2133 W Chapman Ave Ste M Orange CA 92668

FULS-RICHIE, ELVA STOUT, travel consultant; b. Emporia, Kans., Mar. 14, 1924; d. Clyde Carter and Althea Mable (Loomis) Stout; m. Otto P. Fuls, Dec. 22, 1946 (dec. June 1988); children: Sandra Lynn Fuls-Tanahashi, Sharon Kay Fuls; m. J. W. Richie, Aug. 19, 1989. BS, Emporia State U., 1944, MS, 1954. Mgr. credit dept. Montgomery Ward, Emporia, 1945—; tchr. music and drama Waverly, Kans., 1944-45; pvt. tchr. voice Chapman, Kans., 1945-46; vocal instr. glee clubs Clairton (Pa.) Pub. Schs., 1946-50; tchr. English, drama, music, marching band Neosho Rapids, Kans., 1951-56; tchr. Emerson Jr. High, Willow Run, Mich., 1956-57; travel agt. Marlin Travel Inc., Foster City, Calif., 1967-77, 78-79; account corr. Sears Cen. Credit, Mountain View, Calif., 1977-78; travel agt. Austin Travel Agy., Santa Clara, Calif., 1979; travel cons. Cardillo Travel, San Jose, Calif., 1979-82; salesperson Incentive Journeys, San Jose, 1982; travel cons. All Aboard Travel, Los Gatos, Calif., 1982-84, T. Cook Vintage World Travel, Modesto, Calif., 1985—. Pres. PTA, Foster City, Calif., 1978-79, Foster City Newcomers, 1978; leader Girl Scouts, Foster City, 1978; musician Saratoga Light Opera, 1980-82, Sunnyvale Light Opera, Gilbert & Sullivan Soc., San Jose, 1980-82, Opera Assn. San Jose. Mem. Assn. Retail Travel Agts., Pacific Area Travel Assn., Caribbean Tourism Orgn. Home: 4125 McHenry Ave # 117 Modesto CA 95356

FULTON, CHRISTOPHER CUYLER, computer programmer, consultant; b. Burbank, Calif., July 4, 1948; s. Theodore Cuyler Jr. and Thelma Andrea (Pedersen) F. BS in Chemistry, UCLA, 1970, MPH, 1973. Cert. systems programmer. Sr. programmer Calif. Rsch. & Tech., Inc., Chatsworth, 1974-83; sr. programmer/software mgr. Teledyne Controls, Inc., L.A., 1983—; ind. cons. Main Sequence, Canyon Country, Calif., 1991—. Author govt. reports on hypervelocity impact, 1976-79; composer songs and arrangements for piano/voice and other instruments. Advocate for space exploration Space Studies Inst., Princeton, N.J., 1980—, Nat. Space Soc., Washington, 1980—, Planetary Soc., Pasadena, Calif., 1980—. Mem. Alpha Chi Sigma (sec.-treas. 1970). Democrat. Home and Office: 15652 Carrousel Dr Canyon Country CA 91351

FULTON, NORMAN ROBERT, home entertainment company executive; b. Los Angeles, Dec. 16, 1935; s. Robert John and Fritzi Marie (Wacker) F.; A.A., Santa Monica Coll., 1958; B.S., U. So. Calif., 1960; m. Nancy Butler, July 6, 1966; children—Robert B., Patricia M. Asst. v.p. Raphael Glass Co., Los Angeles, 1960-65; credit adminstr. Zellerbach Paper Co., Los Angeles, 1966-68; gen. credit mgr. Carrier Transicold Co., Montebello, Calif., 1968-70, Virco Mfg. Co., Los Angeles, 1970-72, Superscope, Inc., Chatsworth, Calif., 1972-79; asst. v.p. credit and adminstrn. Inkel Corp., Carson, Calif., 1980-82; corp. credit mgr. Gen. Consumer Electronics, Santa Monica, Calif., 1982-83; br. credit mgr. Sharp Electronics Corp., Carson, Calif., 1983—. Served with AUS, 1955-57. Fellow Nat. Inst. Credit (cert. credit exec.); mem. Credit Mgrs. So. Calif., Nat. Notary Assn. Home: 3801 Seamoor Dr Malibu CA 90265-5357

FULTON, RICHARD DELBERT, dean; b. Missoula, Mont., Feb. 5, 1945; s. C. Dulane and E. Benita (Lyon) F.; m. Suzanne Lee Mathews, Nov. 5, 1976; children: David Amil, Effie Lee. BA in English, Ea. Mont. Coll., 1967; MA in English, U. S.D., 1969; PhD in English, Wash. State U., 1975. Instr. U. Md., College Park, 1970-71; asst. dean Wash. State U., Pullman, 1975-82, 83-84; dean in residence Coun. Grad. Schs., Washington, 1982-83; assoc. dean Iona Coll., New Rochelle, N.Y., 1984-86; provost Rocky Mountain Coll., Billings, Mont., 1986-89; dean of faculty Clark Coll., Vancouver, Wash., 1989—; cons. Coun. Grad. Schs., 1983; chair personnel com. Wash. Instrnl. Commn., 1990. Co-editor: Henry Fielding: An Annotated Bibliography, 1980, Union List of Victorian Serials, 1985; editor: Victorian Periodicals Rev., 1993; contbr. numerous articles and revs. on Victorian periodicals and European lit. Bd. dirs. United Way, Pullman, 1976-78. Mem. Rsch. Soc. for Victorian Periodicals (pres. 1989— bd. dirs. 1984—), North Am. Conf. British Studies, Am. Assn. Higher Edn., Nat. Coun. Instrnl. Adminstrs. Democrat. Episcopalian. Office: Clark Coll 1800 E Mcloughlin Blvd Vancouver WA 98663-3509

FULTS, DANIEL WEBSTER, III, neurosurgeon, educator; b. Washington, Aug. 22, 1953; s. Daniel W. Jr. and Helen (Hobbs) F.; m. Carol Gibson, June 16, 1979; 1 child, Erin Marie. BS in Chemistry, U. Tex., 1975; MD, Southwestern Med. Sch., Dallas, 1979. Resident in neurosurgery Wake Forest U., Winston-Salem, N.C., 1979-85; rsch. assoc. dept. biochemistry U. N.C., Chapel Hill, 1985-87; asst. prof. neurosurgery U. Utah, Salt Lake City, 1987-92, assoc. prof. neurosurgery, 1992—. Contbr. numerous articles to profl. jours. Assn. for Brain Tumor Rsch. fellow, 1985-87; recipient Clin. Investigator award NIH Nat. Cancer Inst., 1985-90, First award, 1990—. Mem. Am. Assn. Neurol. Surgeons, Rsch. Soc. Neurol. Surgeons, Utah State Soc. Neurol. Surgeons (pres. 1989—). Office: U Utah Sch Medicine 50 N Medical Dr Salt Lake City UT 84132-0002

FULTZ, PHILIP NATHANIEL, management analyst; b. N.Y.C., Jan. 29, 1943; s. Otis and Sara Love (Gibbs) F.; m. Bessie Learleane McCoy, Mar. 11, 1972. AA in Bus., Coll. of the Desert, 1980; BA in Mgmt., U. Redlands, 1980, MA in Mgmt., 1982. Enlisted USMC, 1967, advanced through grades to capt., 1972, served in various locations, 1964-78, resigned commn., 1978; CETA coord. County of San Bernardino, Yucca Valley, Calif., 1978-85; contract analyst Advanced Technology, Inc., Twentynine Palms, Calif., 1985-88; spl. transit analyst Omintrans, San Bernardino, Calif., 1988-89; tech. analyst Atlantic Rsch. Corp. (formerly Calculon Corp.), Twentynine Palms, Calif., 1988—; mgmt. analyst Marine Corps Base, Twentynine Palms, Calif., 1991—. Founding dir., Unity Home Battered Women's Shelter, Joshua Tree, Calif., 1982, Morongo Basin Adult Literacy; bd. dirs. Twentynine Palms Water Dist., 1991—. Mem. Rotary (sec. Joshua Tree chpt. 1983-85). Republican. Home: 73477 Desert Trail Dr Twentynine Palms CA 92277-2218 Office: Morale Welfare & Recreation Marine Corp Base Twentynine Palms CA 92277-2302

FUNG, SUN-YIU SAMUEL, physics educator; b. Hong Kong, Dec. 27, 1932; came to U.S., 1953; s. Lok-Chi and Lai-Lan (Tong) F.; m. Helen Wu, Feb. 9, 1964; children: Eric, Linette. BS, U. San Francisco, 1957; PhD, U. Calif., 1964. Rsch. physicist Rutgers U., New Brunswick, N.J., 1964-66; asst. prof. physics U. Calif., Riverside, 1966-70, assoc. prof., 1970-76, prof., 1976—, chmn. physics dept., 1980-85, 90-91. Chmn. Chinese Meml. Pavilian Com., Riverside, 1985-88. Mem. AAAS, Am. Phys. Soc., Overseas Chinese Physicist Assn., Chinese Am. Faculty Assn. (pres. 1988-89, 90-92). Office: U Calif Riverside CA 92521

FUNK, MILTON ALBERT, real estate broker; b. Cantonement, Okla., Oct. 12, 1918; s. John Anton and Cornelia Elizabeth (Schwake) F.; m. Earline Myrtle Burkholder, Feb. 15, 1937; children: DeAnne Funk Kiralla, Gary Milton. Cert. in real estate, UCLA, 1960. Owner Realty Sales & Exchange Co., South Gate, Calif., 1961—; sec.-treas. Apt. Investments, Inc., South Gate, 1961—; dir. Apple Valley View Water Assn., cons. to Los Angeles Apartment Assn. Directory, 1987. Served with arty. AUS, 1944-46, PTO. Mem. Calif. Assn. Realtors (regional v.p. 1969, dir.), S.E. Bd. Realtors (pres. 1966, dir. 1980), Los Angeles County Apt. Assn. (dir., sec.), Laguna Shores Owners Assn. (pres.), VFW, Downey and South Gate C. of C's. Home: 11714 Bellflower Blvd Downey CA 90241-5426 Office: 3947 Tweedy Blvd South Gate CA 90280-6193

FUNK, ROBERT NORRIS, college president, lawyer; b. Yakima, Wash., Nov. 10, 1930; s. Edgar Norris and Ione (Anderson) F. BA, U. Oreg., 1952, LLB, 1955; PhD, Stanford U., 1967. Bar: Oreg. 1956. Pvt. practice law Pendleton, Oreg., 1958-62; program coord. Tresidder Union Stanford (Calif.) U., 1962-65, asst. to dean, 1965-66, lectr., asst. dean Sch. Edn., 1966-70; v.p., dean Stephens Coll., Columbia, Mo., 1970-78; faculty mentor Marylhurst (Oreg.) Edn. Ctr., 1979-80; provost Cornish Inst., Seattle, 1980-86; pres. Cornish Coll. Arts, Seattle, 1986—. Contbr. articles on edn. in arts to profl. jours. Capt. U.S. Army, 1955-58. Mem. Am. Assn. for Higher Edn., Oreg. State Bar, Rainier Club. Episcopalian. Office: Cornish Coll Arts 710 E Roy St Seattle WA 98102-4696

FUNK, ROBERT WALTER, education educator; b. Evansville, Ind., July 18, 1926; s. Robert Joseph and Ada Elizabeth (Adams) F.; m. Inabelle McKee, Aug. 20, 1950 (div. 1980); children: Andrea Elizabeth, Stephanie Alyson; m. Charlene Patricia Matejovsky, June 9, 1989. AB, Butler U., 1947, BD, 1950, MA, 1951; PhD, Vanderbilt U., 1953. Asst. prof. Tex. Christian U., Fort Worth, 1953-56; instr. Harvard Divinity Sch., Cambridge, Mass., 1956-57; ann. prof. Am. Sch. Oriental Rsch., Jerusalem, 1957-58; asst. prof. Emory U., Atlanta, 1958-59; assoc. prof. Drew U., Madison, N.J., 1959-66; prof. Vanderbilt Divinity Sch., Nashville, 1966-69, U. Mont., Missoula, 1969-86; pub. Polebridge Press, Sonoma, Calif., 1981—; dir. Westar Inst., Sonoma, Calif., 1985—; chmn. The Jesus Seminar, Sonoma, 1985—; dir. Scholars Press, Atlanta, 1974-80; exec. sec. Soc. Bibl. Lit., 1968-73. Author: Jesus as Precursor, 1975, Language, Hermeneutic, and Word of God, 1966. Adv. com. Flathead Wild & Scenic Rivers Study, Kalispell, Mont., 1970-73. Named Fulbright Sr. scholar U. Tübingen, 1965-66, Guggenheim fellow, 1965-66; recipient fellowship Am. Coun. Learned Socs., 1973-74, Soc. Bibl. Lit., 1980-81. Office: Polebridge Press/Westar 19678 Eighth St E Sonoma CA 95476

FUNKE, CHERYL HUSA, nurse; b. Puyallup, Wash., July 18, 1955; d. Veikko Lennie and Florence Irene Husa; m. James Eric Funke, Mar. 8, 1986; children: Jameson Michael, Andrew Ivar. BSN, Wash. State U., 1977; M of Nursing, U. Wash., 1982. RN. Nurse St. Peter Hosp., Olympia, Wash., 1977-78, Mary Bridge Children's Hosp., Tacoma, 1978, Tacoma Gen. Hosp., 1978-79; pub. health nurse Cowlitz-Wahkiakum Health Dist., Longview, Wash., 1979-80; nurse Group Health Coop. Hosp., Seattle, 1981-84; instr. Everett (Wash.) Community Coll., 1981-84; asst. prof. Intercollegiate Ctr. Nursing Edn., Spokane, 1984-87; nurse Deaconess Med. Ctr., Spokane, 1984-86; pub. health nurse Spokane County Health Dist., 1987—; cons. Spokane Nurse Care, 1985-87. Elder, trustee Woodland Park Presbyn. Ch., Seattle, 1982-84. Spokane Valley United Meth. Ch. Women's Soc. scholar, 1973-76. Mem. ANA (sec. 1986-88), Nurses Assn. Am. Coll. Ob-gyn. (co-chmn. 1984-86), Sigma Theta Tau, Phi Kappa Phi. Democrat. Office: Spokane County Health Dist W 1101 College Spokane WA 99201

FUNSTON, GARY STEPHEN, publishing, advertising executive; b. Phila., July 7, 1951; s. Ralph Gaylord and Adele Rose (DeCintio) F.; m. Nancy Eileen Clark (div. 1974); 1 child, Stephen Blake. Student, DeAnza Coll., 1969-73, San Jose State U., 1973-75. Store mgr. Smith & Foley Shoes Inc., Sunnyvale, Calif., 1970-75; sales rep. The Hoover Co., San Jose, Calif., 1975-78, GTE Directories Corp., Santa Clara, Calif., 1978-81; ptnr., sec., treas. Mailco Advt. Inc., Milpitas, Calif., 1981-83; owner, cons. ADCOM, San Jose, 1983-85; dir. sales mgr. Lomar Trans Western Publs., Ft. Lauderdale, Fla., 1985-87; mgr. sales, mktg. Ameritel, San Deigo, 1987-89; regional sales dir. United Advt. Publs., Union City, Calif., 1989—; sales cons. Republic Telcom, San Jose, 1983-84; mgmt. cons. Norcal Directory Co., San Jose, 1984-85; advt. cons. Yellow Page Programs, San Jose, 1983-85. Contbr. articles to profl. jours. Mem. CAP, Mountain View, Calif., 1983-84, com. mem. Apt. Ind. Forum, San Jose, 1991-93, dinner sponsor, 1991-93, fundraiser, 1991-93. Mem. Calif. Apt. Assn. (suppliers coun. 1990-92, chmn. suppliers com. 1993), Solano-Napa Rental Housing Assn., Tri-County Apt. Assn. (com. mem. 1989-93), Rental Housing Owners Assn. Greater East Bay (bd. dirs. 1990-93), Highland Swingers Golf Club (treas. 1990-93). Republican. Roman Catholic. Home: 22135 Sevilla Rd # 36 Hayward CA 94541 Office: For Rent Mag 32950 Alvarado-Niles Rd # 510 Union City CA 94587

FURAN, RODNEY LUKE LEROY, illustrator, designer, painter, educator; b. Tracy, Minn., Sept. 7, 1927; s. Leo Adolph and Agnes Helen (Bienapfl) F.; m. Barbara Joan Howell, Apr. 2, 1950; children: Eric D., Paul R., Neil W. (dec.), Ruth E., Ronald J. Student, Chouinard Art Inst., L.A., 1949-50, Pasadena (Calif.) City Coll., 1954-56, Famous Artists Sch., Westport, Cin., 1958-62, U. Minn., 1968, Mankato State U., 1971, 74-75. Draftsman Cannon Electric, L.A., 1951-52; design draftsman Fairbanks-Morse, Pomona, 1952-53; artist, illustrator Hycon Mfg. Co., Pasadena, 1953-54; art dir. TRW, L.A. and Denver, 1954-61, Litton Industries, Woodland Hills, Calif., 1961-62, Martin-Marietta, Denver, 1961, 62-64; artist/designer Josten's, Inc., Owatonna, Minn., 1964-68; comml. art instr. Mankato (Minn.) Tech. Coll., 1968-79; art dept. supr. J. Musch & Assocs., Newport Beach, Calif., 1979; concept artist Ford Aeronutronic, Newport Beach, 1979-83; illustrator/designer Los Alamos (N.Mex.) Nat. Labs., 1983—; dept. chairperson Mankato Tech. Coll., 1969-70; LASSP instr. Los Alamos Nat. Lab., 1986—. Artist, designer; prin. works include monument of Sioux Uprising of 62, Cairn of Peace. Del. Rep. Party State Conv., Mpls., 1974; artist, designer Farmfest U.S.A., Lake Crystal, Minn., 1972, 76; mem. troop coms. Boy Scouts Am., scout master, 1964-78. With U.S. Army, 1946-52. Recipient Excellence Merit and Merit award Soc. Tech. Comm., 1984. Mem. Jesus Christ Latter Day Saints. Home: PO Box 116 Yucca AZ 86438 Office: Los Alamos Nat Lab D416 Los Alamos NM 87545

FUREN, WALTER ENOCH, retired government official, consultant; b. Rock Springs, Wyo., Sept. 25, 1930; s. Herman A. and Mildred Ruth (Beckstead) F.; m. Shirley Strickland, Sept. 25, 1976; children: Jerry, Lauren Furen Emery, Mark. BSCE, Utah, 1957. Registered profl. engr., Oreg., N.Mex., D.C. Asst. regional engr. Pacific S.W. region U.S. Forest Svc., San Francisco, 1969-75; dir. engring. U.S. Forest Svc., Albuquerque, 1975-77; asst. dir. engring. U.S. Forest Svc., Washington, 1977-84, dep. dir. engring., 1984-86; intergovtl. liaison officer, sec. Inst. for Solid Wastes, Am. Pub. Works Assn., Washington, 1986-88; prin. investigator rural tech. assistance program Fed. Hwy. Adminstrn., 1986-88. Sgt. U.S. Army, 1950-52. Recipient cert. of merit for exceptional leadership and initiative as acting dir. engring. U.S. Forest Svc., 1986. Mem. ASCE (chmn. urban planning com. Nat. Capital sect. 1984-85), Washington Soc. Engrs. (bd. dirs., pres. 1979-86). Episcopalian. Home: 3370 Emerson Dr Roseville CA 95661

FURER, STANFORD ARTHUR, internist, educator; b. Detroit, July 25, 1916; s. Henry Jay and Lillian Estelle (Goldgleid) F.; m. Jacqueline Therese Wichman, Oct. 23, 1943; children: Judith Lynn, Melissa Ann. AB, U. So. Calif., 1937, MD, 1942. Diplomate Am. Bd. Internal Medicine. Intern L.A. County Hosp., 1941-42, resident in internal medicine, 1945-49; from instr. to assoc. prof. medicine U. So. Calif., L.A., 1949-80; attending physician Cedars-Sinai Med. Ctr., L.A., 1952-92, Midway Hosp., L.A., 1952-92, L.A. County-U. So. Calif. Med. Ctr., 1952-92. Capt. U.S. Army, 1942-46. Mem. Assn. for Breast Cancer Studies (founder, pres. 1989-92), Riviera Country Club, Phi Kappa Phi, Phi Delta Epsilon Grad. Club (past pres.). Home: 1231 Coldwater Canyon Beverly Hills CA 90210

FURIMSKY, STEPHEN, JR., freelance writer; b. Coalton, Ill., Aug. 4, 1924; s. Stephen Sr. and Anna (Petricko) F.; m. Dorothy Conrad, June 8, 1946 (dec. Nov. 1989); children: Stephen III, Karen Ann Segal, Daniel Michael, Melany; m. Janet Fay Green, Dec. 16, 1991; step-children: Bruce Emerson, Peni Emerson, Kara Welliver, Beth Emerson. AB, U. Chgo., 1951; MS in Internat. Affairs, George Washington U., 1967; grad., Air War Coll., 1967. Instr. in polit. sci. Craven Community Coll., New Bern, N.C., 1975-80; owner San Diego Sod, San Marcos, Calif., 1981-84; spl. advocate juvenile ct. Voices for Children, San Diego, 1985-91; sports editor, health and fitness editor Enterprise Newspaper, Fallbrook, Calif., 1989-91; bd. dirs. Marine Corps West Fed. Credit Union, 1991—. Candidate state senate, N.C., 1978. Col. USMC, 1942-73. Decorated Legion of Merit, D.F.C., Bronze Star, Air medal, Cross of Gallantry (Vietman). Mem. VFW (life), Internat. Platform Assn. Republican. Eastern Orthodox. Home: 818 E Alvarado St Apt 29 Fallbrook CA 92028-2322

FURLOW, MARY BEVERLEY, English language educator; b. Shreveport, La., Oct. 14, 1933; d. Prentiss Edward and Mary Thelma (Hasty) F.; divorced, 1973; children: Mary Findley, William Prentiss, Samuel Christopher; m. William Peter Cleary, Aug. 1, 1989. BA, U. Tenn., 1955, MEd, 1972; MA, Governors State U., 1975; cert. advanced study, U. Chgo., 1987. Mem. faculty Chattanooga State Community Coll., 1969-73, Moraine Valley Community Coll., Palos Hills, Ill., 1974-78; English faculty Pima Community Coll., Tucson, 1978—; cons. in field. Contbg. author: Thinking on the Edge; contbr. articles to profl. jours. Named one of Outstanding Educators of Am., 1973. Mem. Internat. Soc. Appraisers, Internat. Soc. Philos. Enquiry, Ariz. Antiquarian Guild, Pi Beta Phi, Cincinatus Soc., Jr. League, Mensa, Holmes Socs., Clan Chattan Soc., DAR, Daughters of the Confederacy, Alpha Phi Omega (Tchr. of Yr. 1973). Democrat. Episcopalian. Home: 1555 N Arcadia Ave Tucson AZ 85712-4010 Office: Pima Community Coll 8202 E Poinciana Dr Tucson AZ 85730-4600

FURMAN, DAVID STEPHEN, art educator, artist; b. Seattle, Aug. 15, 1945; s. Stanley Albert and Lenore (Silverman) F.; m. Luann Lovejoy, Dec. 17, 1983. BA, U. Oreg., 1969; MFA, U. Wash., 1972. Prof. Otis/Parsons, L.A., 1975, Calif. State U., L.A., 1976, Colo. Mt. Coll., Vail, 1976-78, Claremont (Calif.) Grad. Sch., 1973—; prof., studio arts Pitzer Coll., Claremont, 1973—. One-man shows include: Tortue Gallery, Santa Monica, Calif., 1985, 87, 89, 91, Elaine Horwitch Gallery, Santa Fe, 1989, Margulies Taplin Gallery, Miami, Fla., 1990, O.K. Harris Works of Art, N.Y.C., 1990, Judy Youvens Gallery, Houston, 1993. NEA fellow, 1975, 86-87, Fulbright fellow, 1979, sr. artist fellow, 1990. Mem. Nat. Coun. Edn. of Ceramic Arts, Am. Crafts Coun. Home: 4739 N Glen Ivy Rd La Verne CA 91750-2311 Office: Pitzer Coll 1050 N Mills Ave Claremont CA 91711-6101

FURMANSKY, BERT SOL, psychiatrist; b. N.Y.C., Apr. 7, 1945; s. Max and Fay (Katz) F.; children: Leif, Nik, Eliza. BS cum laude, Bklyn. Coll., 1965; MD, NYU, 1969; postgrad., U. Colo., 1989—. Intern Albert Einstein Sch. Medicine, N.Y.C., 1969-70; dir. Laguna (N.Mex.) Indian Health Ctr., 1970-72; resident U. Colo. Health Scis. Ctr., Denver, 1973-76; asst. prof. UCHSC, Denver, 1976—; staff psychiatrist Fitzsimons Army Med. Ctr., Denver, 1976-77; pvt. practice psychiatry Denver, 1976—; psychiat. cons. Denver Dept. Social Svcs., 1977—, Boulder (Colo.) Dept. Social Svcs., 1977-83, Med. Dept. Pub. Svc. Co., Denver, 1980-90, EAP Pub. Svc. Co., Denver, 1984-90, Colo. Juvenile Dist. Ct., Denver, 1989—. Pres. Colo. Interdisciplinary Commn. on Child Custody, 1978; commr. Colo. Gov.'s Commn. on Children & Families, 1980-82, Colo. State Dept. Edn. Task Force, 1990; chmn. Colo. Task Force on Revising Foster Care, 1991. Lt. comdr. USPHS, 1970-72. Fellow APA; mem. Am. Psychiat. Assn., Am. Assn. Social Psychiatry, World Psychiat. Assn., Colo. Psychiat. Soc. (newsletter editor 1990—), Colo. Child and Adolescent Psychiat. Soc. Office: 658 Grant St Denver CO 80203

FURNIVAL, GEORGE MITCHELL, petroleum and mining consultant; b. Winnipeg, Man., Can., July 25, 1908; s. William George and Grace Una (Rothwell) F.; B.Sc., U. Man., 1929; M.A., Queens U., 1933; Ph.D., MIT, 1935; m. Marion Marguerite Fraser, Mar. 8, 1937; children—William George, Sharon (Mrs. John M. Roscoe), Patricia M., Bruce A. Field geologist in Man., Ont., N.W.T., and Que., 1928-36; asst. mine supt. Cline Lake Gold Mines, Ltd., 1936-39; geologist Geol. Survey Can., No. and Southwestern Sask., 1939-42; from 1942-70 employed by the Standard Oil Co. Calif. (Chevron) subs. including following positions: sr. geologist Standard Oil Co. of Calif. (Chevron Standard, Ltd.), Calgary, Alta., 1942-44, asst. to chief geologist, 1944-45, field supt. So. Alta., 1945-46, mgr. land and legal dept., 1948-50, v.p. land and legal, dir., 1950-52, v.p. legal, crude oil sales, govt. relations, dir., 1952-55; pres., dir. Dominion Oil, Ltd., Trinidad and Tobago, 1952-60; v.p. exploration, dir. Calif. Exploration Co. (Chevron Overseas Petroleum, Inc.), San Francisco, 1955-63; staff asst. land to v.p. exploration and land Standard Oil Co. of Calif., 1961-63; chmn. bd., mng. dir. West Australian Petroleum Pty., Ltd. (Chevron operated), Perth, 1963-70; dir. mines Dept. Mines and Natural Resources, Man., 1946-48; v.p., dir. Newport Ventures, Ltd., Calgary, 1971-72; v.p. ops., dir., mem. exec. com. Brascan Resources, Ltd., Calgary, 1973-75, sr. v.p., dir., 1975-77, sr. cons.,

1977-78; pres., chief exec. officer, dir. Western Mines Ltd., 1978-80, exec. v.p., divsn. gen. mgr. Westmin Resources Ltd., also dir., mem. exec. com., 1981-82; dir. Western Mines Inc., 1978-82; pres., acting gen. mgr. Coalition Mining, Ltd.; pres., chief operating officer, dir. Lathwell Resources Ltd., 1983-84; cons. petroleum and mining, 1985—; founder Man. Geol. Survey, 1947; dir. Cretaceous Pipe Line Co., Ltd., Austen & Butta Pty., Ltd., Western Coal Holdings, Inc., Quest Explorations Ltd., San Antonio Resources Inc.; del. Interprovincial Mines Ministers Conf., several years; sec. Winnipeg Conf., 1947. Elected to Order of Can., 1982. Fellow Royal Soc. Can., Geol. Soc. Am., Geol. Soc. Can., Soc. Econ. Geologists; mem. Am. Assn. Petroleum Geologists (hon. life), Engring. Inst. Can., Canadian Inst. Mining and Metallurgy (hon. life mem., past br. chmn., dist. councillor, v.p., chmn. petroleum div., Distinguished Service award 1974, Selwyn G. Blaylock gold medal 1979), Australian Petroleum Exploration Assn. (hon. life mem., chmn. com. West Australian petroleum legislation, councillor, state chmn. for Western Australia), Australian Am. Assn. in Western Australia (councillor), Australian Geol. Soc., Assn. Profl. Engrs., Geologists and Geophysicists of Alta. (hon. life mem., Centennial award 1985), Coal Assn. of Can. (bd.dirs.). Clubs: Calgary Golf and Country, Calgary Petroleum, Ranchmen's. Author numerous govt. and co. papers, reports, reference texts, also sci. articles to profl. jours. Home: 1315 Baldwin Crescent SW, Calgary, AB Canada T2V 2B7

FURSE, ELIZABETH, congresswoman, small business owner; b. Nairobi, Kenya, 1936; came to U.S., 1958, naturalized, 1972; m. John Platt; 2 children (from previous marriage). BA, Evergreen State Coll., 1974; student, U. Wash., Northwestern U. Dir. Western Wash. Indian program Am. Friends Svc. Com, 1975-77; coord. Restoration program for Native Am. Tribes Oreg. Legal Svc., 1980-86; co-owner Helvetia Vineyards, Hillsboro, Oreg.; mem. 103rd Congress from 1st Oreg. dist., Washington, D.C., 1993—. Co-founder Oreg. Peace Inst., 1986. Office: 316 Cannon Washington DC 20515

FURST, ARTHUR, toxicologist, educator; b. Mpls., Dec. 25, 1914; s. Samuel and Doris (Kolochinsky) F.; m. Florence Wolovitch, May 24, 1940; children: Carolyn, Adrianne, David Michael, Timothy Daniel. A.A., Los Angeles City Coll., 1935; A.B., UCLA, 1937, A.M., 1940; Ph.D., Stanford U., 1948; Sc.D., U. San Francisco, 1983. Mem. faculty, dept. chemistry San Francisco City Coll., 1940-47; asst. prof. chemistry U. San Francisco, 1947-49, assoc. prof. chemistry, 1949-52; assoc. prof. medicinal chemistry Stanford Sch. Medicine, 1952-57, prof., 1957-61; with U. Calif. War Tng., 1943-45, San Francisco State Coll., 1945; rsch. assoc. Mt. Zion Hosp., 1952-82; clin. prof. pathology Columbia Coll. Physicians and Surgeons, 1969-70; dir. Inst. Chem. Biology; prof. chemistry U. San Francisco, 1961-80, prof. emeritus, 1980—; dean grad. div., 1976-79; vis. fellow Battelle Seattle Research Center, 1974; Michael vis. prof. Weizmann Inst. Sci., Israel, 1982; cons. toxicology, 1980—; cons. on cancer WHO; mem. com., bd. mineral resources NRC. Contbr. over 250 articles to profl. and ednl. jours. Bd. trustees Pacific Grad. Sch. Psychology. Recipient Klaus Schwartz Commemorative medal Internat. Toxological Congress, Tokyo, 1986, Profl. Achievement award UCLA Alumni Assn., 1992. Fellow Acad. Toxicological Scis. (diplomate), AAAS, Am. Coll. Nutrition, Am. Coll. Toxicology (nat. sec., pres. 1985), N.Y. Acad. Scis., Am. Inst. Chemists; mem. Am. Soc. Pharmacology and Exptl. Therapeutics, Am. Soc. Pharmacology and Exptl. Therapeutics, Am. Chem. Soc., Am. Assn. Cancer Research, Soc. Toxicology, Sigma Xi, Phi Lambda Upsilon. Home: 3736 La Calle Ct Palo Alto CA 94306-2620 Office: U San Francisco Inst Chem Biology San Francisco CA 94117-1080

FURST, RONALD TERRENCE, psychotherapist; b. L.A., Mar. 21, 1949; s. Paul Jack and Evelyn (Brown) F.; m. Cindy Terri Kramer, Sept. 5, 1980; 1 child, Jarrett. BA, Calif. State U., Northridge, 1971, MA, 1972; PhD, Pacific Western U., 1983. Lic. marriage, family and child therapist, Calif. Pres., psychotherapist Furthermore Found., Tarzana, Calif., 1971-84, Personal Devel. Inst., Santa Monica, Calif., 1984—. Mem. Nat. Assn. for Advancement of Psychoanalysis (affiliate), Calif. Assn. Marriage & Family Therapists. Democrat. Jewish. Office: Personal Development Inst 2901 Wilshire Blvd Ste 444 Santa Monica CA 90403

FURUKAWA, JOHN KAZUYA, systems engineer; b. Kobe, Japan, Aug. 8, 1955; came to U.S., 1965; s. Harrison Seiya and Nobu (Tomi) F. BA in Math., UCLA, 1979; BS in Computer Sci., Calif. State U., Dominguez Hills, 1984; MS of Engring. in Systems Engring., West Coast U., 1985; MSEE, Calif. State U., L.A., 1986. Systems engr. Hughes Aircraft Co., Fullerton, Calif., 1984—; cons. South Bay Computers, Gardena, Calif., 1982—. Japanese C. of C. scholar, 1973, Calif. Scholarship Fedn. scholar, 1973. Mem. IEEE, Mensa, Assn. for Computing Machinery, Alpha Beta Kappa, Phi Kappa Phi. Home: 18423 Raymond Ave Gardena CA 90248 Office: Hughes Aircraft Co PO Box 3310 Fullerton CA 92634

FURUTO, DAVID MASARU, mathematics educator; b. Kahuku, Hawaii, Dec. 1, 1945; s. Jitsuo and Miyoko (Edamatsu) F.; m. Marilyn Carmelita Camit, Dec. 26, 1964 (div. 1972); children: Chandra, Brian; m. Sharlene Bernice Choy Lin Maeda, Apr. 1, 1977; children: Linda, Matthew, Michael, Daniel. BS, Ch. Coll. of Hawaii, 1967; MS, U. Ill., 1969; MEd Adminstrn., U. Hawaii, 1977; EdD, Brigham Young U., 1981. Math. teaching asst. U. Ill., Urbana, 1967-69; prof. math. So. Oreg. State Coll., Ashland, 1969-70, Brigham Young U., Laie, Hawaii, 1970-72; prof. math., chmn. dept. U. Hawaii, Windward Community Coll., Kaneohe, 1972-87; prof. and chmn. math., Brigham Young U., Laie, Hawaii, 1987—; pres. Furuto Enterprises; reviewer new books programs Nat. Council Tchrs. of Math., Reston, Va., 1977—; regional coord. Am. High Sch. Math Exam, Am. Jr. High Sch. Math Exam, 1989—. Contbr. articles to profl. jours. Exec. bd. Windward Oahu 4-H, 1972-81; cons., advisor, cubmaster, comsnr. Boy Scouts Am., 1976—; treas. Kahuku Sch. Alumni, 1983—. Named Outstanding Tchr., U. Hawaii, 1976. Mem. Am. Ednl. Research Assn., Am. Math. Assn., Math. Assn. Am. (regional rep.), Hawaii Council Tchrs. Math. (pres. 1976-82, 88-90, v.p. 1992-93, editor 1993—), Hawaii Math. Consortium (pres. 1988—, chmn. Hawaii Math. Championships, 1988—). Democrat. Mormon. Club: Fish Enterprises (pres.). Home: PO Box 84 Laie HI 96762 Office: Brigham Young Univ Divsn Math and Scis PO Box 1967 Laie HI 96762-0960

FUTCH, ARCHER HAMNER, retired physicist; b. Monroe, N.C., Mar. 21, 1925; s. Archer Hamner and Emma Lee (Covington) F.; m. Patricia West, June 13, 1953; children: Lisa Stewart, Jacqueline Lee, Tina Corine. BS, U. N.C., 1949, MS, 1951; PhD, U. Md., 1955. Physicist E.I. Du Pont de Nemours Co., Aiken, S.C., 1955-58, Lawrence Livermore (Calif.) Nat. Lab., 1959-91. Mem. Livermore Planning Commn., 1968-72, Livermore City Coun., 1972-76; mayor City of Livermore, 1976; bd. dirs. Alameda County Water Dist., 1976-80. Mem. Am. Phys. Soc., Phi Beta Kappa, Sigma Xi, Sigma Pi Sigma. Republican. Home: 1252 Westbrook Pl Livermore CA 94550-6430 Office: Lawrence Livermore Nat Lab Livermore CA 94550

FUTTERMAN, DOROTHEA HARDT, electronic information executive; b. Stuttgart, West Germany, Mar. 11, 1955; came to U.S., 1955; d. Paul and Emma (Hacker) Hardt; m. John Arthur Futterman, Aug. 12, 1978. BA in Psychology, Swarthmore Coll., 1976; MA, Cornell U., 1978; PHD in Mgmt., U. Tex., 1983. Asst. prof. mgmt. Wharton Sch. U. Pa., Phila., 1982-85; sr. market analyst AT&T Network Systems, Holmdel, N.J., 1985-87; market analyst Dialog Info. Svcs., Palo Alto, Calif., 1988-90, mgr. product mktg., 1990-92, dir. rsch. and pricing, 1992—. Mem. Silicon Valley Am. Mktg. Assn. Lutheran. Office: Dialog Info Svc 3460 Hillview Ave Palo Alto CA 94304

FYE, RODNEY WAYNE, retired real estate company executive, writer; b. Sutherland, Nebr., Aug. 3, 1928; s. Elmer Theodore and Pearl Gertrude (Combs) F. Grad., Chillicothe Bus. Coll., 1948; BS, Brigham Young U., 1959; secondary teaching cert., U. Utah, 1962; MA, San Francisco State U., 1964. Clk. Union Pacific R.R. Co., Salt Lake City, 1948-57; sec. to pres., sr. staff asst. Hughes Tool Co., L.A., 1958-59; instr. English, Brigham Young U., Provo, Utah, 1959-60; high sch. tchr. Granite Sch. Dist., Salt Lake City, 1960-63; adminstr. Millcreek Terrace Nursing Home, Salt Lake City, 1962-63; instr., dir. instrn. Reading Dynamics No. Calif., 1967-75; owner, mgr. Keycount Properties, San Francisco, 1975-79; pres. Casa Loma Properties, Inc., San Francisco, 1979—, Pan Am. Investments, Inc., San Francisco, 1980—. Author: (musical comedy) Gandy, 1959, (drama) Absinthe and Wormwood, 1964, (non-fiction mystery-adventure) The Trouble With King Michael, 1991. Missionary LDS Ch., Colo., Nebr., 1949-5l; pres. San Francisco Safety Coun., 1980-84. With U.S. Army and USMC, 1953-56, Korea. Republican.

GABELMAN, JOHN WARREN, small business owner, engineer, consultant; b. Manila, May 18, 1921; came to U.S., 1925; s. Charles Grover and Cyprienna Louisa (Turcotte) G.; m. Olive Alexander Thompson, Sept. 22, 1945; children: Barbara Grace, Joan Lynn. Diploma in geol. engring., Colo. Sch. of Mines, 1943, M in Geol. Engr., 1948, DSc, 1949. Registered profl. engr., Colo; registered geologist, Calif. Instr. Colo. Sch. of Mines, Golden, 1946-49; geologist Colo. Fuel & Iron Corp., Pueblo, 1949-52, Am. Smelting & Refining Co., Salt Lake City, 1952-54; dist. geologist AEC, Grand Junction, Colo., 1954-58; geologic advisor AEC, Lima, Peru, 1958-61; chief resource appraisal AEC, Washington, 1961-75; mgr. exploration rsch. Utah Internat., Inc., San Francisco, 1975-83; pres. John W. Gabelman & Assoc., Inc., Danville, Calif., 1983—; cons. in field; mem. Internat. Atomic Energy Working Group, Vienna, Austria, 1970-74. Author: Migration of Uranium & Thorium, 1977; contbr. numerous articles to profl. jours. With USN, 1944-46. Mem. AIME, Assn. Exploration Geochemists, Am. Geophys. Union, Am. Assn. Petroleum Geologists (pres. energy minerals divsn. 1993—), Soc. Mining Engrs., Soc. Econ. Geology, Geol. Soc. Am., No. Calif. Geol. Soc., Computer-Oriented Geol. Soc. Republican. Roman Catholic. Home and Office: 23 Portland Ct Danville CA 94526-4317

GABERSON, HOWARD AXEL, mechanical engineer; b. Detroit, Apr. 11, 1931; s. Axel Rudolph and Lillian (Quatherine) G.; BSME, U. Mich., 1955; MS, MIT, 1957, PhD, 1967; m. Dale Virginia Maitland, Apr. 27, 1969. Stress analysis engr. Raytheon Co., Wayland, Mass., 1957-59; asst. prof. mech. engring. Lowell (Mass.) Tech. Inst., 1959-60; asst. prof. Boston U., 1960-64; assoc. prof. mech. engring. U. Hawaii, 1967-68; shock and vibration rsch. mech. engr. Naval Civil Engring. Lab., Port Hueneme, Calif., 1968-82, div. dir. mech. systems, 1982-87, sr. technologist dynamics, 1987—; bd. dirs. mech. failure prevention group. Contbr. articles to profl. jours.; inventor vibratory locomotion; patentee in field. Mem. ASME, Am. Acad. Mechanics, Soc. Exptl. Mechanics, Soc. Automotive Engrs. (G-5 shock and vibration com.), Inst. Noise Control Engrs. Vibration Inst., Acoustical Soc. Am., Am. Fedn. Aviculture, Alpha Sigma Phi, Sigma Xi, Tau Beta Pi, Pi Tau Sigma. Home: 234 Corsicana Dr Oxnard CA 93030-1303 Office: US Naval Civil Engring Lab Port Hueneme CA 93043

GABLER, ROBERT CLAIR, research chemist; b. Phila., June 6, 1933; s. Robert Clair Sr. and Mary Elizabeth Cecilia (Allen) G.; m. Joan Wyatt, Feb. 1969 (div. July 1975); m. Beatriz Salazar, July 22, 1983. BA, Johns Hopkin's U., 1955; MS, Fla. State U., 1957. Chemist E. I. DuPont de Nemours & Co., Inc., Kinston, N.C., 1959-61; rsch. chemist U.S. Bur. of Mines, College Park and Avondale, Md., 1961-78, 78-87; supervising rsch. chemist U.S. Bur. of Mines, Albany, Oreg., 1987—. Contbr. articles to profl. jours.; patentee in field. Vol. emergency med. technician Kent Island Vol. Fire Dept., Stevensville, Md., 1984-87, Jefferson (Oreg.) Rural Fire Protection Dist., 1987—. With U.S. Army, 1957-59. Mem. Metall. Soc., Am. Inst. Metall. Mining and Petroleum Engrs., Sigma Xi. Democrat. Roman Catholic. Home: 12752 Centerwood Rd SE Jefferson OR 97352-9219 Office: US Bur of Mines 1450 Queen Ave SW Albany OR 97321-2198

GABRIEL, ISRAEL EL, dance educator, choreographer; b. Philippines, Oct. 23, 1944; s. Mariano Pineda and Josefa (Espinoza) G. Studied, Am. Ballet Theatre Sch., Met. Ballet Sch., Ballet Russe de Monte Carlo Sch., Internat. Sch. Dance, Ballet Art Studios, Sch. of Am. Ballet. Lectr. dance Am. Sch. Dance, 1966-68; asst. to the artistic dir., guest artist, ballet master Bat-Dor Dance Co., Tel Aviv, 1968-73; lectr. U. Calif., Irvine, 1973—; artistic dir. Le Ballet Pallas Dance Theatre, Los Alamitos, Calif.; assoc. dir. Calif. Dance Co., L.A.; artistic advisor Montgomery Ballet Co., Silver Spring, Md., Danza Modera, Bogota, Colombia. Danced in the shows Girl Crazy, 1960, Plain & Fancy, 1960; choreographer Dance of the Reed Flutes, Pas de Quatre Imperiale, Valse Blutte, Olympiad I, Caprice, Mystic Side 2, Duetto, Antithesis, Jazz Piece on Ice, Conjugal, Point/Counterpoint, Pure Joy, Nocturne, Fun Time, Eidolon, Le Printemps Eternelle, Concerti for Four, Pas Deux, Lambent, Incipient, Kimberlite, Isla Del Encanto, Memory, Tango, Retrospection, Perjury, Bewegung, Mazurka, Reflection, Petite Concerto, The Good Old Number Eight, Provenance, Solitude, Waltz, Rashomon, Valse, Mirage, Sonata, Condesed ballet Class/Take Four, On the Wing, Tanana Waltz, Waiting..., Pas de Six, Pas de Trois, Harmonic Intoxication, Fire Dance, Celabration, Nostalgic Passion, Longing; danced in broadway show Flower Drum Song; danced at the Hollywood Palace, 1963-66; danced with Yeichi Nimura Danc Co., 1960-62. Mem. Actors Equity Assn. Office: U Calif Sch of Fine Arts Irvine CA 92717

GABRIEL, MICHAEL, hypnotherapist, educator; b. Bklyn., Sept. 27, 1927; s. Benjamin and Martha (Buslow) W.; m. Marie Woltjer, May 27, 1989. BA in English, Bklyn. Coll., 1950; MA in Psychology, Sierra U., 1987; MA in English, Columbia U., 1993. Cert. hypnotherapist. Eligibility worker County of Santa Clara, San Jose, Calif., 1970-72; workshop dir. Wellhouse Seminars, San Jose, 1973—; pvt. practice San Jose, 1973—; instr. West Valley Coll., Saratoga, Calif., 1979—. Author: Voices From The Womb, 1992; contbr. articles to profl. jour. Mem. Assn. for Past Life Rsch. and Therapies (presenter workshops 1989—, bd. dirs.).

GABRIEL, RENNIE, financial planner; b. L.A., July 27, 1948; s. Harry and Milly (Broder) Goldenhar (dec.); m. Judi Robbins, Nov. 24, 1968 (div. Feb. 1989); children: Ryan, Davida; m. Lesli Gilmore, May 5, 1990. BA, Calif. State U., Northridge, 1971; CLU, Am. Coll., 1979, Cert. Fin. Planner, 1988. Ins. agt. Prudential and Provident Mutual, Encino, Calif., 1972-78; pension cons. Shadur LaVine & Assocs., Encino, 1978-81; owner Artist Corner Gallery Inc., Encino, 1977-82; pension and fin. planner Gabriel Tolleson & Stroum, Tarzana, Calif., 1983-87; pension cons., fin. planner Shadur LaVine/Integrated Fin., Encino, 1987-90; dir. pensions U.S. Life of Calif., Pasadena, Calif., 1983; fin. planner Pension Alternatives, Encino, 1990—. Contbr. articles to fin. publs. Mem. Internat. Assn. Fin. Planning (pres. San Fernando Valley chpt. 1992), Nat. Assn. Life Underwriters (Achievement award 1974, Nat. Quality award 1975, Million Dollar Round Table 1990), Internat. Assn. Fin. Planning, CLUs, Inst. Cert. Fin. Planners, Employee Assistance Profls. Assn. (treas. San Fernando Valley chpt. 1992), Apt. Assn. San Fernando Valley-Ventura County (bd. mem. 1992). Office: Fin Svcs 5189 Gaviota Ave Encino CA 91436-1428

GABRIELIAN, ARMEN, computer scientist; b. Tehran, Iran, Aug. 17, 1940; came to U.S. 1959; s. Levon Simon and Eliza Gabrielian; m. Tong Moon, 1974; children: Sonya Emi, Tanya Simone. BS, MIT, Cambridge, Mass., 1963; MS, MIT, 1965, PhD, 1969. Rsch. assoc. U. Waterloo, Ont., Can., 1969-71; postdoctoral fellow U. So. Calif., L.A., 1971-72; ind. cons. L.A., Newport Beach, 1972-77; sr. sys. analyst Fluor Corp., Irvine, Calif., 1977-78; sr. scientist Hughes Aircraft Co., Fullerton, Calif., 1979-87; tech. dir. Thomson-CSF, Inc., Palo Alto, Calif., 1987-91; pres. UniView Systems, Mountain View, Calif., 1991—. Contbr. articles to profl. jours. Mem. IEEE, ACM, Am. Assn. Artificial Intelligence, Sigma Xi, Tau Beta Pi, Eta Kappa Nu.

GABRIELSEN, PAUL THOMAS, clergyman, educational adminstrator; b. Bonners Ferry, Idaho, Aug. 1, 1929; s. Gabriel and Edna Cecelia (Roen) G.; m. Karen Elaine Johnk, July 18, 1954; children: Virginia Kay Gabrielsen Evans, Stephen Paul. BA, Concordia Coll., 1952; MTh, Luther Theol. Sem., 1956; MA, U. Chgo., 1958, U. Minn., 1963; PhD, U.S. Internat. U., 1976. Ordained to ministry, Luth. Ch., 1956. Owner Coll. Contractors, Moorhead, Minn., 1950-58; pastor North Cape Evangelical Luth. Ch., Franksville, Wis., 1958-60; chaplain Augsburg Coll., Mpls., 1960-61; faculty mem., counselor Golden Valley Luth. Coll., Mpls., 1961-70; real estate broker, fin. cons., ptnr. Capital Growth Planning, San Diego, 1970-76; dir. planned giving Luth. Bible Coll., Issaquah, Wash., 1976—; pvt. practice, charitable fin. cons. Kirkland, Wash., 1988—; registered rep. Fin. Network Investment Corp., Bellevue, Wash., 1988—. Author: Why Doesn't God?, 1965; contbr. articles to profl. publs. Mem. Wash. Planned Giving Coun., Kiwanis. Home: 12414 89th Pl NE Kirkland WA 98034-2606 Office: Luth Bible Coll 4221 228th Ave SE Issaquah WA 98027-9264

GABRIELSON, SHIRLEY GAIL, nurse; b. San Francisco, Mar. 17, 1934; d. Arthur Obert and Lois Ruth (Lanterman) Ellison; m. I. Grant Gabrielson, Sept. 11, 1955; children: James Grant, Kari Gay. BS in Nursing, Mont. State U., 1955. RN, Mont. Staff and operating room nurse Bozeman (Mont.) Deaconess Hosp., 1954-55, 55-56; staff nurse Warm Springs State Hosp., 1955; office nurse, operating room asst. Dr. Craft, Bozeman, 1956-57; office nurse Dr. Bush, Beach, N.D., 1957-58; pub. health nurse Wibaux County, 1958-59; staff and charge nurse Teton Meml. Hosp., Choteau, Mont., 1964-65; staff pediatric and float nurse St. Patrick Hosp., Missoula, Mont., 1965-70; nurse, insvc. dir. Trinity Hosp., Wolf Point, Mont., 1970-79; ednl. coord. Community Hosp. and Nursing Home, Poplar, Mont., 1979—; coord. staff devel. Faith Luth. Home, Wolf Point, 1980-81; office nurse Dr. Listerud, 1983—; CPR instr. ARC, Am. Heart Assn., Gt. Falls, Mont., 1979—; program coord. for CNA Poplar Hosp., 1989—; preceptor rural health student nurses Univ. North Dakota, 1993—; condr. workshops and seminars. Author: Independent Study for Nurse Assistants, 1977. Former asst. camp leader Girl Scouts U.S.A.; former mother advisor, bd. dirs. Rainbow Girls; pres. Demolay Mothers Club, 1977; bd. dirs. Mont. div. Am. Cancer Soc., 1984-90, mem. awards com., 1986-89; founder Tri-County Parkinson's Support Group, N.E. Mont. Recipient Lifesaver award Am. Cancer Soc., 1987, Svc. award ARC, 1989, Health and Human Svcs. award Mont. State Dept., 1990, U.S. Dept. Health award, 1990, Outstanding award, U.S. HHS, Mont. Health Promotion award Dept. Health and Environ. Scis. Mem. Am. Nurses Assn., Mont. Nurses Assn. (mem. commn. on continuing edn. 1977-91, chmn. 1984-86), Order Eastern Star, Alpha Tau Delta (alumni pres. 1956). Presbyterian. Home: 428 Hill St Wolf Point MT 59201-1244 Office: Community Hosp-Nursing Home PO Box 38 Poplar MT 59255-0038 also: Listerud Rural Health Clinic 100 Main Wolf Point MT 59201

GABROVSKY, PETER NICOLAEV, computer science educator, consultant; b. Sofia, Bulgaria, Nov. 3, 1944; came to U.S., 1969; s. Nicolai Petrov and Elena (Lalinska) G.; m. Pamela Warrick Kemper, Dec. 21, 1974; children: Vanessa, Alexander, Natasha, Juliana, Isabella. Magister, Warsaw (Poland) U., 1968; PhD, Syracuse U., 1976. Assoc. programmer IBM, Poughkeepsie, N.Y., 1969-71; sr. assoc. programmer IBM, Essex Junction, Vt., 1976-78; v.p. City Nat. Bank, Atchison, Kans., 1978-81; exec. v.p. United Mo. Bank, Kansas City, Mo., 1981-85; assoc. prof. computer sci. U. So. Maine, Portland, 1985-89, Calif. State U., Northridge, 1989—; cons. to various pvt. and pub. instns. Editor Jour. Modern Logic, 1989—; contbr. articles to profl. jours. Mem. Atchison Art Assn. (hon.). Home: 11695 Porter Valley Dr Northridge CA 91326 Office: Calif State U Northridge CA 91330

GAC, FRANK DAVID, materials engineer; b. Granite City, Ill., Mar. 26, 1951; s. Frank John and Betty Marie (Kasprovich) G.; m. Christina Lynn McMullen, Aug. 12, 1973; children: Jessie Lynn, Benjamin Thomas. BS in Ceramic Engring., U. Ill., 1973; MS in Ceramic Engring., U. Mo., Rolla, 1975; postgrad., U. N.Mex., 1982-83; PhD in Materials Sci. and Engring., U. Wash., 1989. Registered profl. engr., N.Mex. Mem. staff Los Alamos (N.Mex) Nat. Lab., 1975-78, sect. leader, 1980-83, staff mem., 1983-84, advanced study candidate, 1984-85; research engr. U. Wash., Seattle, 1979-80; project leader Los Alamos (N.Mex) Nat. Lab., 1986-88, group leader, 1988—; mem. steering com. Advanced Composites Working Group, Cocoa Beach, Fla., 1981—; adj. faculty mem. N.Mex. Inst. Mining and Tech., 1991—. Contbr. articles to profl. jours. Father helper Aspen Elem. Sch., Los Alamos, 1983-84; Sunday sch. supt. Trinity Bible Ch., Los Alamos, 1986, elder, 1987—; deacon, youth leader Sangre de Cristo Covenant Ch., Los Alamos, 1975-79; scoutmaster Boy Scouts Am., Granite City, 1967-69; com. mem. Young Life, Los Alamos, 1988—. Fellow A.P. Green Refractories Co., 1973-74; named Knight of St. Pat 100 Club, U. Ill., Champaign, 1973, one of Outstanding Young Men Am., 1986. Fellow Am. Ceramic Soc. (div. chmn. 1985-86, Cert. 1986, Karl Schwartzwalder Profl. Achievement Ceramic Engring. award 1988, chmn. programs and meetings com. 1987-88, trustee engring. ceramic div. 1991-94); mem. Nat. Inst. Ceramic Engrs. (coord. 1979-80, James I. Mueller Meml. Lecture award 1990), Gideons Internat. (pres. 1976), Young Life (leader 1975-79). Democrat. Home: 1559 41st St Los Alamos NM 87544-1920 Office: Los Alamos Nat Lab MST 4 MS G771 Los Alamos NM 87545

GACONO, CARL B., clinical and forensic psychologist; b. Lebanon, Pa., Jan. 16, 1954; s. V. Carl and Mary Jane (Bowman) G. BA in Psychology, Lebanon Valley Coll., 1976; MA in Guidance and Counseling, Calif. Poly. State U., 1981; PhD in Clin. Psychology, U.S. Internat. U., 1988. Mental health therapist San Luis Obispo (Calif.) County Mental Health, 1979-81, coord. jail counseling program, 1981-83; program cons. San Luis Obispo County Sheriff's Dept., 1983; acad. advisor U.S. Internat. U., San Diego, 1984-85; juvenile intervention specialist San Diego Police Dept.-South Bay Community Svcs., 1985-86; juvenile justice outreach worker Social Advocates for Youth, San Diego, 1985-87; pvt. practice psychotherapy and psychol. evaluations, 1985—; psychologist Atascadero (Calif.) State Forensic Hosp., 1988—; dir. assessment ctr. Atascadero State Hosp., 1988-93; dir. substance abuse treatment program FCI, Ft. Worth; mem. exec. com. Person-Centered Therapy Network, 1982-84; counselor State of Calif. Community Colls. Contbr. articles to profl. jours. Mem. Am. Acad. Forenzic Scis., Am. Orgn. for Correctional Psychology, San Diego Psychology and Law, Soc. for Personality Assessment, Am. Soc. Criminology, Am. Psychol. Assn., Psi Chi. Home: PO Box 200152 Arlington TX 76006

GADAL, LOUIS STEPHEN, artist; b. L.A., Apr. 10, 1936; s. Louis A. and Lois Anna (Northup) G.; m. Lynn M. Gary, May 15, 1966; children: Eric Spencer, Stephanie Jenet. Cert., Chouinard Art Inst., L.A., 1959; postgrad., Otis Art Inst., L.A., 1962-63. Painter Walt Disney, Anaheim, Calif., 1960; freelance illustrator Louis Gadal Illustration, L.A., 1959-62; illustrator QA Archtl. Illustration, L.A., 1962-68, Carlos Diniz Assocs., L.A., 1968-70; drawing instr. Calif. Inst. Arts, Valencia, Calif., 1980-88, Otis Parsons Art Inst., L.A., 1988-90; illustrator Louis Gadal/Archtl. Illustrator, L.A. and Santa Monica, 1970—. 1st sgt. USNG, 1954-62. Recipient Cert. of Excellence San Bernardino Mus., Redlands, Calif., 1980, 2d Prize Sea Heritage Marine Art, Glen Oaks, N.Y., 1990, Liquitex Watercolor award Pa. Watercolor Soc., Mechanicsburg, Pa., 1990, Bronze Maritime Merit award Nat. Park Acad. of Arts, Jackson Hole, Wyo., 1992. Mem. Niagara Frontier Watercolor Soc., Pa. Watercolor Soc., Watercolor West Soc. Republican. Roman Catholic. Home: 3648 Coolidge Ave Los Angeles CA 90066 Office: Louis Gadal Archtl Illus 3107 Pico Blvd Ste H Santa Monica CA 90405

GADBOIS, RICHARD A., JR., federal judge; b. Omaha, June 18, 1932; s. Richard Alphonse Gadbois and Margaret Ann (Donahue) Bartlett; children from previous marriage: Richard, Gregory, Guy, Geoffrey, Thomas; m. Vicki Cresap, May 14, 1993. A.B., St. John's Coll., Camarillo, Calif., 1955; J.D., Loyola U., Los Angeles, 1958; postgrad. in law, U. So. Calif., 1958-60. Bar: Calif. 1959, U.S. Dist. Ct. (cen. dist.) Calif. 1959, U.S. Supreme Ct. 1966. Dep. atty. gen. Calif., 1958-59; ptnr. Musick, Peeler & Garrett, L.A., 1959-68; v.p. Denny's Inc., La Mirada, Calif., 1968-71; judge Mcpl. Ct., L.A., 1971-72, Superior Ct., L.A., 1972-82, U.S. Dist. Ct. (cen. dist.) Calif., L.A., 1982—. Decorated knight Order of Holy Sepulchre (Pope John Paul II). Mem. ABA, Los Angeles County Bar Assn. (trustee 1966-67), State Bar Calif. (profl. ethics com. 1965-70). Republican. Roman Catholic. Home and Office: US Dist Ct 176 Courthouse 312 N Spring St Los Angeles CA 90012-4701

GADOL, NANCY, immunologist, researcher; b. Washington, June 10, 1949; d. Ellis and Selma (Prensky) G. BA, Carnegie-Mellon U., 1971; MS, U. Fla., 1974; PhD, Hahnemann U., 1979. Asst. rsch. immunologist U. Calif., San Francisco, 1979-81, NIH postdoctoral fellow, 1981-83; sr. rsch. assoc. Becton Dickinson, Mountain View, Calif., 1983-85, rsch. scientist, 1985-88, clin. feasibility scientist, 1988-89; rsch. assoc. Irwin Meml. Blood Ctrs., San Francisco, 1990-92; sr. scientist Applied Immune Scis., Santa Clara, Calif., 1993—. Contbr. articles and abstracts to sci. jours. Mem. AAAS, Am. Assn. Immunologists. Office: Applied Immune Scis 5301 Patrick Henry Dr Santa Clara CA 95054-1114

GAETA, FEDERICO CARLOS AREJOLA, chemical, organic and medicinal chemistry researcher; b. Vitoria, Alava, Spain, Nov. 7, 1951; came to U.S., 1965; s. Federico Manuel Gaeta and Teresa Arejola; m. Laura Susan Lehman, Mar. 17, 1989; children: Penelope Thais, Helena Priscilla, Leah Teresa, Julia Raquel. BA in Chemistry, SUNY, Buffalo, 1972; PhD in Chemistry, Rice U., 1977. Post-doctoral assoc. U. Calif., L.A., 1977-79; sr.

scientist Bristol-Myers Squibb Corp., Syracuse, N.Y., 1979-81; sr. scientist Schering-Plough Corp., Bloomfield, N.J., 1981-83, prin. scientist, 1983, sect. leader, 1983-89; dir. rsch. Glytec Corp., San Diego, 1989-90, Cytel Corp., San Diego, 1989—. Contbr. articles to profl. jours.; patentee in field. Recipient Stauffer Chem. Co. fellowship Rice U., 1975-76, Nettie S. Autrey fellowship, 1974-75, Rice Grad. fellowship, 1973-74. Mem. AAAS, Am. Chem. Soc., Am. Peptide Soc., Internat. Union of Pure and Applied Chemistry, N.Y. Acad. Scis. Office: Cytel Corp 3525 John Hopkins Ct San Diego CA 92121

GAGARIN, DENNIS PAUL, advertising agency executive; b. Long Beach, Calif., July 9, 1952. BS in Graphic Design, San Jose State U., 1976. Art dir. Brower, Mitchell, Gum Advt., Los Gatos, Calif., 1976-79, Offield & Brower Advt., Los Gatos, 1979-82; sr. art dir. Tycer, Fultz, Bellack Advt., Palo Alto, Calif., 1982-85; head art dir. TFB/BBDO Advt., Palo Alto, 1985-87; creative dir. Lena Chow Advt., Palo Alto, 1987-90; prin., ptnr. Gagarin/McGeoch Advt. and Design, Redwood City, Calif., 1989—; prof. San Jose (Calif.) State U., 1987-90, now guest lectr.; guest art dir. Western Art Dirs. Club, Palo Alto. Recipient awards for graphic design, art direction. Office: Gagarin/McGeoch Advt-Design 493 Seaport Ct Ste 102 Redwood City CA 94063

GAGE, DELWYN ORIN, state senator, accountant, oil producer; b. Calvin, N.D., Nov. 28, 1930; s. Orin Mann and Beatrice Blanche (Bell) G.; m. Sarah Marlene Brenchley, Jan. 3, 1953; children—Scott, Paul Shelley, Jerri, Mark, Connie. Student Brigham Young U. Acct., R.E. Svare, Shelby, Mont., 1956-59; acctg. ptnr. with Paul W. Wolk, Cut Bank, Mont., 1960-64; pvt. practice acctg., Cut Bank, 1964—; mem. Mont. Senate, 1982—; thoroughbred owner. Served with USMC, 1951-52. Named Jaycee Boss of Yr. Mem. C. of C. Mormon. Club: Elks.

GAGLIANO, GERARD ANTHONY, computer software executive, computer analyst; b. Queens, N.Y., Feb. 17, 1954; s. Gerard and Mathilda (Providenti) G. BSEE in Computer Sci., U. N.Mex., Albuquerque, 1976. Supr. Computer Ctr. U. N.Mex., Albuquerque, 1975-76; software designer EG&G, Albuquerque, 1976-81, chief designer, 1980-81; computer analyst Software Innovations, Albuquerque, 1981-85, v.p., 1985-87, pres., 1987—; corp. liaison Software Innovations/Nat. Semiconductor, Alburqueque, 1984-87, Software Innovations, Bannex Corp., Albuquerque, 1989—. Author computer systems. Roman Catholic. Office: 1465 32d Circle Rio Rancho NM 87124 also: Software Innovations PO Box 44444 Albuquerque NM 87174-4444

GAGNON, MARGARET ANN CALLAHAN, secondary education educator; b. St. Paul, Apr. 8, 1952; d. Leo N. and Ursula A. (Iverson) Callahan; m. Stephen A. Gagnon, July 16, 1977; children: Stephanie, Irlonde, Joseph. BA, U. Minn., 1974; postgrad., Idaho State U., 1979-81. Cert. secondary English, French and German edn. Translator, paralegal computer support Control Data, Bloomington, Minn., 1974-75; home svcs. aide Vis. Home Svcs., Salt Lake City, 1975-76; tchr. Glenwood (Minn.) High Sch., 1976-77; bartender Sunwood Inn., Morris, Minn., 1976-78; waitress Papa John's Pizza, Morris, 1978-79; teaching asst. Idaho State U., Pocatello, 1979-81; tchr. Carden Sch., Pocatello, 1980-81; substitute tchr. Pocatello (Idaho) Sch. Dist., 1981-82; tchr., coach Jackson (Wyo.) Hole High Sch., 1982—. Mem. Wyo. Fgn. Lang. Tchrs. (bd. mem. 1992), Wyo. High Sch. Speech Coaches (sec./treas. 1988-93, v.p. 1993—, Coach of Yr. 1992-93. Home: PO Box 2924 Jackson WY 83001 Office: Teton County Schs # 1 PO Box 568 Jackson WY 83001

GAGNON, WAYNE JOSEPH, graphic designer; b. Alexandria, Minn., May 3, 1949; s. Vergal Joseph and Lilias Christine Ann (Bedman) G. BFA, Mpls. Sch. Art, 1972; postgrad., U. Minn., 1979. Asst. chef Howard's Catering, Mpls., 1971-72; art dir. Diversified Arts Corp., Mpls., 1972-73; exec. art dir. LaBelle and Shallbetter Advt., Mpls., 1973-78; prin. W. Joseph Design Assocs., Seattle, 1978—; instr. Design U. Wash., Seattle, 1985-87, Sch. Visual Concepts, Seattle, 1988-89. Lectr. Monroe (Wash.) Correctional Facility, 1989, Pacific U., Seattle, 1989; speaker Bellingham (Wash.) Art Dirs. and Writers Club, 1989. Recipient awards Comm. Arts, 1986,87, Graphis, 1986, 87. Mem. Seattle Design Assn. (treas. 1983-84, v.p. 1985-86), Am. Inst. Graphic Arts, Soc. Typographic Arts.

GAHAN, KATHLEEN MASON, educational counselor, artist; b. Long Beach, Calif., May 23, 1940; d. Robert Elwyn and Jean Mason (Campbell) Fisher; m. Keith Victor Gahan, Apr. 21, 1961; children: Carrie Jean, Christie Sue. BA, Calif. State U., Long Beach, 1962, MA, 1967; student, Studio Arts Ctrs. Internat., Florence, Italy, 1992. Cert. gen. secondary educator, adminstr., Calif. Tchr. Long Beach Unified Sch. Dist., 1963-70; tchr. Porterville (Calif.) Union High Sch. Dist., 1970-76, counselor, 1976—; coord. gifted and talented edn. Porterville High Sch., 1976-83, coach acad. decathlon team, 1977-82, 85; adminstr. Counseling for Collegeable Hispanic Jrs., Porterville, 1988-90, Counseling for Ptnrship. Acad. in Bus., 1990—; tchr. faculty and staff computer workshop Porterville High Sch., 1992-93; proprietor El Mirador Ranch, Strathmore, Calif., 1978—; salesman real estate, Porterville, 1981-82; income tax return preparer, Lindsay, Calif., 1983-84; organizer SAT preparation workshop, 1981-83. Editor: (cookbook) Mexican Cooking in America, 1974; editor (craft patterns) Glory Bee, 1979-84; group exhibits photography Porterville Coll., 1989, oil paintings, Coll. of Sequoias, 1992. Leader 4-H, Lindsay, 1971-79; mem. exec. com. Math. Sci. Conf. for Girls, Tulare County, 1982-85; adminstr. Advanced Placement Program, Porterville, 1979—; mem. bible study Ch. of Nazarene; charter mem. Tulare County Herb Soc., 1983-85. Recipient 1st pl. Mus. Art, Long Beach, 1961, Orange Blossom Festival Art Show, Lindsay, 1988, 2d pl. Coll. of Sequoias Art Show, Visalia, 1988, Hon. mention Orange Blossom Festival Art Show, Lindsay, 1992, commendation Gov. Bd. and Dist. Adminstrsn., Porterville, Calif., 1975, 82; named Coach of Champion Acad. Decathlon Team, Tulare County, 1982, 85. Mem. AAUW, Calif. Tchrs. Assn., Porterville Educators Assn., Am. Assn. Individual Investors. Republican. Home: 1032 Mountain View Dr Lindsay CA 93247-1626

GAIBER, LAWRENCE JAY, financial company executive; b. Chgo., Mar. 20, 1960; s. Sy Bertrym and Mildred (Dickler) G. BS in Econ., U. Pa., 1982. Mgmt. intern Eisai Co. Ltd, Tokyo, 1980; dept. mgr. Anglo Am. Corp., Johannesburg, Republic of South Africa, 1982-84; pres. Sandton Fin. Group, L.A., 1984—; pres. Swellendam Fin. Group, Studio City, Calif., 1984—, also bd. dirs.; bd. dirs. Lawrand Ltd, Satellite Telecommunication, Inst. Cellular Nutritional Immunology, Introlagater, Gaiber, Introlagater, L.A. Greetings; chmn. Mechanics Express Inc. Contbr. articles to profl. jours and mags. Mem. South Africa Found., Johannesburg, 1984—, Town Hall Calif., 1986; bd. dirs. Brentwood Arts Coun.; vice chmn. western region 1986 Pres.' dinner Rep. Nat. Com., Washington. Recipient Most Active Vol. award S. African Inst. Internat. Affairs, 1983; honoree for contbns. to aspiring entrepreneurial women Mayor Tom Bradley's Office and Nat. Network of Hispanic Women, L.A., 1986. Mem. L.A. Venture Assn., L.A. C. of C., L.A. Jr. C. of C., Van Nuys C. of C., L.A. County Rep. Lincoln Club, L.A. County Young Reps., Brentwood Rep. Club (Pres. 1984—). Clubs: Wharton Bus. Sch., Calif. Yacht.

GAIBER, MAXINE DIANE, public relations director; b. Bklyn., May 6, 1949; d. Sidney and Junia Estelle (Gruberg) Oliansky; m. Stuart Gaiber, May 11, 1971; children: Scott Cory, Samantha Lauren. BA, Bklyn. Coll., 1970; MA, U. Minn., 1972. Tours & curriculum svcs. dir. Mpls. Inst. Arts, 1972-77, assoc. chair edn., 1977-79; cons. mus. edn. Field Mus./Art Inst., Chgo., 1979-82; program coord. Field Mus. of Natural History, Chgo., 1982-83; publs. dir. Art Ctr. Coll. Design, Pasadena, Calif., 1983-85; rsch. dir. Art Ctr. Coll. Design, Pasadena, 1985-86, campaign dir., 1986-88; pub. rels. officer Newport Harbor Art Mus., Newport Beach, Calif., 1988—; instr. L.A. County Mus. Art, 1985—, Art Ctr. Coll. Design, Pasadena, 1986-89, Coll. DuPage, Glen Ellyn, Ill., 1981-83. Editor: Why Design?, 1987; editor/author: Mus. edn. materials, 1972—. Art vol. Mariners Sch., Newport Beach, 1989-93. Fellow Bush Found. 1976. Mem. Pub. Rels. Soc. Am., Am. Assn. Mus. (Edn. Com. rep. 1979-83). Office: Newport Harbor Art Mus 850 San Clemente Dr Newport Beach CA 92660-6399

GAILLARD, MARY KATHARINE, physics educator; b. New Brunswick, N.J., Apr. 1, 1939; d. Philip Lee and Marion Catharine (Wiedemayer) Ralph; children: Alain, Dominique, Bruno. BA, Hollins (Va.) Coll., 1960; MA, Columbia U., 1961; Dr du Troiseme Cycle, U. Paris, Orsay, France, 1964, Dr-es-Sciences d'Etat, 1968. With Centre National de Recherche Scientifique, Orsay and Annecy-le-Vieux, France, 1964-84; maitre de recherches Centre National de Recherche Scientifique, Orsay, 1973-80; maitre de recherches Centre National de Recherche Scientifique, Annecy-le-Vieux, 1979-80, dir. research, 1980-84; prof. physics, sr. faculty staff Lawrence Berkeley lab. U. Calif., Berkeley, 1981—; Morris Loeb lectr. Harvard U., Cambridge, Mass., 1980; Chancellor's Disting. lectr., U. Calif., Berkeley, 1981; Warner-Lambert lectr. U. Mich., Ann Arbor, 1984; vis. scientist Fermi Nat. Accelerator Lab., Batavia, Ill., 1973-74, Inst. for Advanced Studies, Santa Barbara, Calif., 1984, U. Calif., Santa Barbara, 1985; group leader L.A.P.P., Theory Group, France, 1979-81, Theory Physics div. LBL, Berkeley, 1985-87; sci. dir. Les Houches (France) Summer Sch., 1981; cons., mem. adv. panels U.S. Dept. Energy, Washington, and various nat. labs. C0-editor: Weak Interactions, 1977, Gauge Theories in High Energy Physics, 1983; author or co-author 140 articles, papers to profl. jours., books, conf. proceedings. Recipient Thibaux prize U. Lyons (France) Acad. Art & Sci., 1977, E.O. Lawrence award, 1988, J.J. Sakurai prize of APS; Guggenheim fellow, 1989-90. Fellow Am. Acad. Arts and Scis., Am. Physics Soc. (mem. various coms., chairperson com. on women, J.J. Saburai prize 1993); mem. AAAS, NAS. Office: U Calif Dept Physics Berkeley CA 94720

GAINES, HOWARD CLARKE, lawyer; b. Washington, Sept. 6, 1909; s. Howard Wright and Ruth Adeline-Clarke Thomas G.; m. Audrey Allen, July 18, 1936; children: Clarke Allen, Margaret Anne Gaines Munsey. J.D., Cath. U. Am., 1936. Bar: D.C. bar 1936, U.S. Supreme Ct. bar 1946, U.S. Ct. Claims bar 1947, Calif. bar 1948. Individual practice law Washington, 1938-43, 46-47, Santa Barbara, Calif., 1948-51; asso. firm Price, Postel & Parma, Santa Barbara, 1951-54; partner Price, Postel & Parma, 1954-88; of counsel, 1989—; chmn. Santa Barbara Bench and Bar Com., 1972-74. Chmn. Santa Barbara Police and Fire Commn., 1948-52; mem. adv. bd. Santa Barbara Com. on Alcoholism, 1956-67; bd. dirs. Santa Barbara Humane Soc., 1958-69, 85-92; bd. trustees Santa Barbara Botanic Garden, 1960—, v.p., 1967-69; bd. trustees Cancer Found. Santa Barbara, 1960-77; dir. Santa Barbara Mental Health Assn., 1957-59, v.p., 1959; pres. Santa Barbara Found., 1976-79, trustee, 1979—. Fellow Am. Bar Found.; mem. ABA, Bar Assn. D.C., State Bar Calif. (gov. 1969-72, v.p. 1971-72, tres. 1971-72), Santa Barbara County Bar Assn. (pres. 1957-58), Am. Judicature Soc., Santa Barbara Club, Channel City Club. Republican. Episcopalian. Home: 1306 Las Alturas Rd Santa Barbara CA 93103-1600 Office: 200 E Carrillo St Santa Barbara CA 93101-2118

GAINES, JOHN ADRIAN, management consultant; b. Valparaiso, Ind., Dec. 12, 1955; s. Leland Dale and Doris Elinor (Anderson) G.; m. Linda Diane Bilderback, Aug. 22, 1975 (div. Nov. 1985); children: Phillip, Amber; m. Linda Jean West, May 3, 1986; 1 child, Todd. Cert., Dale Carnegie, Lake Havasu, Ariz., 1975; student, Mohave Community Coll., Lake Havasu, 1976, Purdue U., 1979, Rio Salado Community Coll., Tempe, Ariz., 1987. Soil lab. technician Dept. Transp., State of Ariz., Lake Havasu, 1975-78; engrng. technician Ind. State Hwy. Commn., LaPorte, 1978-80; soil conservationist Soil Conservation Svc., USDA, Phoenix, 1980-83; survey party chief Forest Svc., USDA, Phoenix, 1983-85; spl. permits liaison City of Tempe, Ariz., 1985-90; civil mgr. L.A. Cellular Telephone Co., 1990-91; prin., owner J.A. Gaines Assocs., Tempe, 1991—; cons. Cen. Ariz. Coordinating Com., Phoenix, 1988-90. Contbr. articles to profl. jours. Pres. mus. com. United Ch. Christ, Tempe, 1988-89. Recipient Heroism award Am. Legion, Valparaiso, Ind., 1971; music scholar No. Ariz. U., Flagstaff, 1973. Fellow Coyote Club of Ariz. (founder 1989), Phi Theta Kappa; mem. Am. Planners Assn., Am. Pub. Works Assn., Home Builders Assn. Cen. Ariz. Democrat. Office: J A Gaines Assocs 1713 E Broadway Rd # 285 Tempe AZ 85282-1611

GAJDOSIK, RICHARD LEE, physical therapist, educator; b. Balt., Oct. 4, 1949; s. Leo Paul and Hazel Caroline (Ihle) G.; m. Carol Elaine Giller, May 15, 1971; children: Robyn Susanne, Kelly Caroline. BS in Phys. Therapy, U. Ky., 1971; MS in Human Anatomy, U. Cin., 1974; PhD in Cell Biology and Anatomy, U.N.C., Chapel Hill, 1989. Asst. dir. phys. therapy Bethesda North Hosp., Montgomery, Ohio, 1971-72; dir. phys. therapy Barrett Gen. Hosp., Dillon, Mont., 1975-76; instr., clin. supr. U. Mont., Missoula, 1976-79, asst. prof., 1979-80, 82-83, asst. prof., dir. phys. therapy program, 1980-82, assoc. prof., 1983-88, assoc. prof., chmn., 1988-92, prof., chmn., 1992—. Contbr. articles and book revs. to profl. jours.; referee Phys. Therapy Jour., 1985—, Jour. of Orthopaedic and Sports Phys. Therapy, 1989—. Active APTA, Missoula, 1986—. Grantee Found. for Phys. Therapy, 1986-88, U. Mont., 1992—, Murdock Charitable Trust Found., 1992. Mem. Am. Phys. Therapy Assn. (bd. dirs. Mont. chpt. 1986—, chmn. edn. and rsch. com. 1986—, chmn. newsletter com. 1979-83, grantee 1986-87), Sigma Xi. Office: U Mont Missoula MT 59812-1076

GALAMBOS, SUZANNE JULIA, editor, writer, institute administrator; b. St. Paul, May 24, 1927; d. Maxwell Alexander Bolocan-Segell and Ruth Gertrude (Labofsky) Segell; m. Andrew Joseph Galambos, Dec. 16, 1949. BA, U. Minn., 1949. Assoc. dir. The Free Enterprise Inst., L.A., 1961-92, dir., 1992—; v.p. The Universal Scientific Publs. Co., L.A., 1962-92, pres., CEO, 1992—; bd. dirs. The Universal Corp., L.A. Author: The Natives are Friendly-Well Almost, 1968, More Lasting Than Bronze, 1991; editor (essays) Thrust for Freedom, 1991. Office: The Free Enterprise Inst PO Box 4307 Orange CA 92613

GALANE, MORTON ROBERT, lawyer; b. N.Y.C., Mar. 15, 1926; s. Harry J. and Sylvia (Schenkelbach) G.; children: Suzanne Galane Duvall, Jonathan A. B.E.E., CCNY, 1946; LL.B., George Washington U., 1950. Bar: D.C. 1950, Nev. 1955, Calif. 1975. Patent examiner U.S. Patent Office, Washington, 1948-50; spl. partner firm Roberts & McInnis, Washington, 1950-54; practice as Morton R. Galane, P.C., Las Vegas, Nev., 1955—; spl. counsel to Gov. Nev., 1967-70. Contbr. articles to profl. jours. Chmn. Gov.'s Com. on Future of Nev., 1979-80. Fellow Am. Coll. Trial Lawyers; mem. Am. Law Inst., IEEE, Am. Bar Assn. (council litigation sect. 1977-83), State Bar Nev., State Bar Calif., D.C. Bar. Home: 2019 Bannie Ave Las Vegas NV 89102-2208 Office: 302 E Carson Ave Ste 1100 Las Vegas NV 89101

GALARRAGA, ANDRES JOSE, professional baseball player; b. Caracas, Venezuela, June 18, 1961; m. Eneyda G., Feb. 18, 1984; 1 child, Andria. 1st baseman Montreal Expos (Nat. League), 1985-91, St. Louis Cardinals, 1992, Colorado Rockies, 1993—. Mem. Nat. League All-Star Team, 1988, 93; recipient Gold Glove award, 1989-90, Silver Slugger award, 1988. Office: Colorado Rockies 1700 Lincoln St Denver CO 80203

GALAZZO, JORGE LUIS, research scientist; b. San Jose, Santa Fe, Argentina, Apr. 6, 1956; came to U.S., 1984; s. Jorge Juan and Juana Teresa (Boggio) G.; m. Patricia Teresita Bosio, Jan. 3, 1981; children: Paula, Juan Andres. Diploma, U. Nacional Litoral, Santa Fe, Argentina, 1981; MS, Calif. Inst. Tech., 1986, PhD, 1988. Rsch. asst. Intec, Santa Fe, Argentina, 1981-84; rsch. asst. Calif. Inst. Tech., Pasadena, 1984-88, rsch. fellow, 1988-89; sr. scientist Exogene Corp., Monrovia, Calif., 1989—. Contbr. articles to profl. jours. Mem. AICE, Am. Chem. Soc., N.Y. Acad. Sci. Office: Exogene Corp 222 E Huntington Dr Ste 111 Monrovia CA 91016

GALBIS, IGNACIO RICARDO MARIA, foreign languages and literature educator; b. Bilbao, Vizcaya, Spain, May 13, 1931; came to U.S., 1961; s. Ricardo Carlos Maria Galbis de Ajuria and Raquel Aurora Patricia (Rigol) Galbis; m. Sophie Marie Ozores, Nov. 27, 1954; children: Inaki Miguel, Julio Pio, Ricardo Javier, Susana Maria. JD, U. Havana (Cuba), 1952; MA, Miss. State U., 1966; PhD, Syracuse U., 1972. Tchr. Spanish Natchez (Miss.) High Sch., 1962-64; instr. Spanish Miss. State U., Starkville, 1964-65; assoc. prof. U. Maine, Orono, 1966-76; nat. exec. dir. Sigma Delta Pi, Riverside, Calif., 1976—; vis. assoc. prof. U. Calif., Riverside, 1976-78, U. San Francisco, 1978-80; vis. prof. U. Calif., Davis, 1981-82; Del Amo fellow U. So. Calif., L.A., 1982-84; vis. assoc. prof. U. Calif., Irvine, 1984-86, Riverside, 1988-89; exec. dir. Soc. of Basque Studies in Am., 1980—. Author: Unamuno: Tres Personajes Existenciales, 1975, Baroja: El Lirismo de Tono Menor, 1976, Trece Relatos Sombríos, 1978, Perspectivas Críticas, 1980, Como el Eco de un Silencio, 1982. Named to Order of Los Descubridores Sigma Delta Pi, 1978, Order of Don Quijote, 1980; recipient Creative Writing award Cintas Found., 1981. Mem. Am. Assn. Tchrs. Spanish, MLA, Modern Humanities Rsch. Assn., Soc Basque Studies in Am. Republican. Roman Catholic. Home: 600 Central Ave Riverside CA 92507-6503 Office: Sigma Delta Pi PO Box 55125 Riverside CA 92517-0125

GALBRAITH, JOHN ROBERT, insurance company executive; b. Portland, Oreg., Oct. 18, 1938; s. Maurice Kerr and Margaret Ione (Veach) G.; m. Maureen McKovich, Oct. 2, 1971 (div. Mar. 1978); children: Margaret Maureen, Marc Ryan; m. Betty Jean Irelan, Dec. 11, 1987. BA, Willamette U., 1960; MBA, U. Washington, 1962. CPA, Oreg. Staff acct. Ernst & Young, Portland, 1962-65; treas. First Pacific Corp., Portland, 1965-71; v.p., treas. Geo McKovich Cos., Palm Beach, Fla. and L.A., 1971-80; v.p., chief fin. officer SAIF Corp., Salem, Oreg., 1980-82; sr. v.p., chief fin. officer Librerty N.W. Ins. Corp., Portland, 1983—, bd. dir.; bd. dir. Helmsman Mgmt. Svcs. N.W., Inc., Portland, 1987—. With Army N.G., 1957-66. Mem. AICPAs, Fin. Exec. Inst., Fla. Ins. CPAs, Calif. Soc. CPAs, Oreg. Soc. CPAs, Multnomah Athletic Club. Republican. Home: 3025 NE Dunckley St Portland OR 97212-1729 Office: Liberty NW Ins Corp 825 NE Multnomah St Ste 2000 Portland OR 97232-2139

GALBUT, MARTIN RICHARD, lawyer; b. Miami Beach, Fla., June 27, 1946; s. Paul A. and Ethel (Kolnick) G.; m. Cynthia Ann Slaughter, June 4, 1972; children: Keith Richard, Lindsay Anne. BS in Speech, Northwestern U., 1968, JD cum laude, 1971. Bar: Ariz. 1972, U.S. Dist. Ct. Ariz. 1972, U.S. Ct. Appeals (9th cir.) 1972. Assoc. Brown, Vlassis & Bain P.A., Phoenix, 1971-75; founder, ptnr. McLoone, Theobald & Galbut P.C., Phoenix, 1975-86; of counsel Furth, Fahrner, Bluemle & Mason, 1986-89; ptnr. Galbut & Assocs., P.C., Phoenix, 1989—. Contbr. articles to profl. jours. Chmn. Ariz. State Air Pollution Control Hearing Bd., 1984-89; mem. Govs. Task Force on Urban Air Quality, 1986, City Phoenix Environ. Quality Commn., 1987-88; bd. dirs. Men's Art Council Phoenix Art Mus.; bd. dirs. founder Ariz. Asthma Found. Clarion de Witt Hardy scholar, Kosmerl scholar. Mem. ABA, Ariz. State Bar Assn. (lectr., securities law and litigation com. and sect.), Maricopa County Bar Assn., Am. Arbitration Assn. (arbitrator), Nat. Assn. Securities Dealers (arbitrator). Democrat. Jewish. Office: Galbut & Assocs PC 2425 E Camelback Rd Phoenix AZ 85016-4200

GALE, ANDREW GUY, manufacturing executive; b. Encino, Calif., Nov. 22, 1959; s. Dennis Lynn and Joyce (Handrahan) G.; m. JoAnna Ruth Hansen, Feb. 25, 1983; children: Scott, Siara, Shanna, Spencer, Seth. BS in Acctg., Brigham Young U., 1984, BS in Fin., 1984; MBA, Wash. State U., 1988. Cert. mgmt. acct. Ops. acct. Tektronix, Inc., Vancouver, Wash., 1984-86; sr. acct. RCA/Sharp Microelectronics, Vancouver, Wash., 1986-87; acctg. mgr. Tri Quest Plastics Inc., Vancouver, Wash., 1987-88; controller Landa, Inc., Portland, Oreg., 1988-90, v.p. fin., 1990—; speaker in field. Com. chmn. Boy Scouts of Am., Camas, Wash., 1990—; asst. bishop Ch. of Jesus Christ of Latter Day Saints, Camas, 1990—. Named Employee of Yr., Landa, Inc., 1988, Mgr. of Yr., 1991. Mem. Nat. Assn. Accts. Mormon. Office: Landa Inc 13705 NE Airport Way Portland OR 97230

GALE, DANIEL BAILEY, architect; b. St. Louis, Nov. 6, 1933; s. Leone Caryll and Gladys (Wotowa) G.; student Brown U., 1951-53, Ecole Des Beaux Arts, Paris, 1954-55; BArch., Washington U., 1957; m. Nancy Susan Miller, June 15, 1957; children: Caroline Hamilton, Rebecca Fletcher, Daniel Bailey With Gale & Cannon, Architects and Planners, Hellmuth, Obata & Kassabaum, Inc., Architects, St. Louis, and exec. v.p. corp. devel., dir. HOK, Inc., St. Louis, 1961-79; ptnr. Heneghan and Gale, architects and planners, Aspen, Colo., 1967-69; pres., chief exec. officer Gale Kober Assocs., San Francisco, 1979-83; pvt. practice architecture, Belvedere, Calif., 1984—; pres. Program Mgmt. Inc., Belvedere, 1984—. Recipient Henry Adams prize Washington U., 1957. Mem. AIA, Singapore Inst. Architects. Home and Office: 280 Belvedere Ave Belvedere CA 94920

GALE, MARADEL KRUMMEL, educator, consultant; b. Bremerton, Wash., June 13, 1939; d. Bernhard Utz and Florence Claire (Choiniere) Krummel; m. Richard Philip Gale, June 10, 1961 (div. 1976). BA, Wash. State U., Pullman, 1961; MA, Mich. State U., East Lansing, 1967; JD, U. Oreg., 1974. Asst. prof. dept. urban and regional planning U. Oreg., Eugene, 1974-83, lectr. Sch. of Law, 1975-77, asst. prof. community svc. and pub. affairs, 1976-77, spl. asst. Office of the Pres., 1979-80, asst. dean Sch. Architecture, 1980-81, assoc. prof. dept. planning, pub. policy and mgmt., 1983—, dir. Micronesia and South Pacific program, 1988—; vis. asst. prof. Sch. Forestry, Oreg. State U., 1979-80; legis. lobbyist City of Eugene, 1975; mem. faculty U.S. Forest Svc. Land Mgmt. Planning Team, 1979-80; cons. Peace Corps./U.S. AID, Senegal, Kenya, Rwanda, 1986. Mem. adv. com. Bur. of Land Mgmt., Eugene, 1980—, The Micronesia Inst., 1992—; project dir. Peace Corps-Yap (Micronesia), 1988. Named Woman of Yr., Lane County Coun. Orgns., 1986; U.S. Info. Agy. grantee Coll. of Micronesia, 1989, U.S. Dept. Edn. grantee, 1989, U.S. Dept. Interior grantee, 1990—. Mem. Assn. for Women in Devel., Am. Planning Assn. (sec., treas. planning and law divs. 1979-81). Office: U Oreg Dept Planning & Pub Policy Eugene OR 97403

GALEENER, FRANK LEE, physicist; b. Long Beach, Calif., July 31, 1936; s. Floras Frank and Daisy Elizabeth (Lee) G.; m. Janet Louise Trask, June 7, 1959. S.B., MIT, 1958, S.M., 1962; Ph.D. in Physics, Purdue U., 1970. Physicist Lincoln Lab. MIT, Cambridge, 1959-61, physicist Nat. Magnet Lab., 1961-64; scientist Xerox, Palo Alto (Calif.) Research Ctr., 1970-73, mgr. semicondr., research, 1973-77, prin. scientist, 1977-87; prof. dept. physics Colo. State U., Ft. Collins, 1987—; mem. com. on recommendations U.S. Army Basic Sci. Research, 1976-79; co-chmn. adv. panel on amorphous materials div. materials sci. Dept. Energy, 1980; mem. adv. panel solid state physics Office Naval Research, 1980. Editor: (with G. Lucovsky) Structure and Excitations of Amorphous Solids, 1976, (with Lucovsky and S.T. Pantelides) The Physics of MOS Insulators, 1980, (with D.L. Griscom and M.J. Weber) Defects in Glasses, 1986. Recipient George W. Morey award Excellence in Glass Rsch., 1993. Fellow Am. Phys. Soc. (life), Am. Ceramic Soc. (life); mem. Optical Soc. Am., Sigma Xi, Sigma Pi Sigma. Home: 2020 Linden Lake Rd Fort Collins CO 80524-5014 Office: Colo State U Dept Physics Fort Collins CO 80523

GALEF, ANDREW GEOFFREY, investment and manufacturing company executive; b. Yonkers, N.Y., Nov. 3, 1932; s. Gabriel and Anne (Fruchter) G.; m. Suzanne Jane Cohen, June 26, 1954 (div. Feb. 1963); children: Stephanie Anne Galef Streeter, Marjorie Lynn Galef, Michael Lewis; m. Billie Ruth Medlin, Nov. 7, 1964 (div. May 1988); children: Phyllis Anne Galef Bulmer, Catherine Marie Kimmel; m. Bronya Kester. B.A., Amherst Coll., 1954; M.B.A., Harvard U., 1958. Vice pres. Kamkap, Inc., N.Y.C., 1958-60; pres. Kemline Calif., San Jose, 1960-61, Zeigler Harris Corp., San Fernando, Calif., 1961-63; v.p. Fullview Industries, Glendale, Calif., 1963-65; cons. Mordy & Co., Los Angeles, 1965-68; prin. Grisanti & Galef, Inc., Los Angeles, 1968-84; chmn., chief exec. officer Spectrum Group, Inc., Los Angeles, 1978—, pres.; chmn., chief exec. officer MagneTek, Inc., Los Angeles, 1984—; dir. Warnaco Inc., N.Y.C.; bd. dirs. Post Group, Inc., Hollywood, Calif.; chmn. Petco Inc., San Diego. Chmn., bd. advisers Anderson Grad. Sch. Mgmt., UCLA; bd. dirs. Ctr. Theater Group; chmn. The Galef Inst. Served to USAF, 1956-58. Office: Magnetek Inc Ste 1400 11150 Santa Monica Blvd Los Angeles CA 90025-3314*

GALES, SAMUEL JOEL, military logistics specialist; b. Dublin, Miss., June 14, 1930; s. James McNary McNeil and Alice Francis (Smith) Broadus-Gales; m. Martha Ann Jackson (div. Jan. 1978); children: Samuel II (dec.), Martha Diane Gales Bryant, Katherine Roselein, Karlmann Von, Carolyn B., Elizabeth Angelica. BA, Chapman Univ., 1981, MS, 1987. Ordained Eucharist minister, Episcopal Ch., 1985; cert. tchr., Calif. Enlisted U.S. Army, 1948, advanced through grades to master 1st sgt., 1969, ret., 1976; tchr. Monterey (Calif.) Unified Sch. Dist., 1981-82; civilian U.S. Army Directorate of Logistics, Ft. Ord, Calif., 1982—; collateral EEOC counselor Dept. Def., U.S. Army, 1987-93; peer counselor, 1982-84. Active Family Svc. Agy., Monterey, 1979-85; rep. Episc. Soc. for Ministry on Aging, Carmel, Calif., 1980-86, Task Force on Aging, Carmel, 1983-87, vestry man, 1982-85, 91—; ombudsman Monterey County Long-Term Care Program, Calif. Dept. for the Aging, 1993—. Decorated Air medal. Mem. Am. Legion (post comdr. 1973-74), Forty and Eight (chef-de-gare 1979, 80), Monterey Chess Club, Comdr.'s Club Calif. (pres. Outpost 28 1981-82).

Republican. Home: PO Box 919 1617 Lowell St Seaside CA 93955-0919 Office: Self-Svc Supply Ctr 2080 Quartermaster Ave Fort Ord CA 93941

GALINDO, DONALD VERNON, artist; b. Oakland, Calif., Apr. 21, 1925; s. Robert Eli and Josephine G. AB, U. Calif., Berkeley, 1946; BA in Edn., Calif. Coll. Arts and Crafts, 1951, MFA, 1955. Spl. secondary tchr. art credential, Calif. Tchr. art and U.S. history Sequoia Union High Sch., Redwood City, Calif., 1955-56; instr. art Coll. of San Mateo, Calif., 1956-87; freelance artist, Calif., 1954—; judge Walnut Creek (Calif.) Art Festival, 1954, art shows San Francisco Bay area, 1954-80. One-man retrospective show CSM Gallery, 1976; exhibited in group shows, 1954-85. Lt. USNR, 1944-47, 52-54. Recipient 1st prize for painting Sather Gate Art Festival, Berkeley, Calif., 1954, cert. of merit San Francisco Mayor's Hire the Handicapped Com. Mem. Calif. Tchrs. Assn., Los Californianos Genealogy and Hist. Assn., Coll. of San Mateo Ret. Faculty Assn. Republican. Home and Studio: 1268 Rosita Rd Pacifica CA 94044

GALIPEAU, STEVEN ARTHUR, psychotherapist; b. Summit, N.J., Nov. 10, 1948; s. Arthur Harmars and Theresa Louise (Levesque) G.; m. Teresa Louise Shelton, Dec. 28, 1974 (div. 1983); m. Linda Carlotta Holmwood, Apr. 22, 1984; children: Brendan Arthur, Owen William. AB, Boston Coll., 1970; MA, U. Notre Dame, 1972; MDiv, Ch. Divinity Sch. of Pacific, Berkeley, Calif., 1977. Lic. marriage, family and child counselor, Calif. Psychotherapist Family and Children's Ctr. Inc., Mishawaka, Ind., 1972-74; vicar St. Luke's Episc. Ch., Fontana, Calif., 1977-78; assoc. rector St. Edmund's Episc. Ch., San Marino, Calif., 1978-82; dir. Coldwater Counseling Ctr., Studio City, Calif., 1983—; pvt. practice Studio City, 1975—; lectr. C.G. Jung Inst., L.A., 1986—. Author: Transforming Body and Soul: Therapeutic Wisdom in the Gospel Healing Stories, 1990. Mem. Calif. Assn. Marriage and Family Therapists, Nat. Assn. for Advancement of Psychoanalysis. Office: 4419 Coldwater Canyon Ave Ste E Studio City CA 91604-1478

GALL, DONALD ALAN, data processing executive; b. Reddick, Ill., Sept. 13, 1934; s. Clarence Oliver and Evelyn Louise (McCumber) G.; m. Elizabeth Olmstead, June 25, 1960 (div. 1972); children: Christopher, Keith, Elizabeth; m. Kathleen Marie Insognia, Oct. 13, 1973; 1 child, Kelly Marie. BSME, U. Ill., 1956; SM, MIT, 1958, ME, 1960, ScD, 1964. Research engr. Gen. Motors, Detroit, 1956-57; staff engr. Dynatech Corp., Cambridge, Mass., 1959-60; mgr. ctr. systems Dynatech Corp., Cambridge, 1962-63; asst., assoc. prof. Carnegie-Mellon U., Pitts., 1964-69; assoc. prof. surgery and anesthesiology U. Pitts. Sch. Medicine, 1969-73; vis. fellow IBM Research Lab., Rueschlikon, Switzerland, 1970-71; pres. Omega Computer Systems, Inc., Scottsdale, Ariz., 1973—. Contbr. articles to profl. jours.; inventor fuel injection system. Bd. dirs. Scottsdale Boys and Girls Club, 1982—; mem. Scottsdale Head Honchos, 1978-87; mem. Verde Vaqueros, 1987—. Recipient Taylor medal Internat. Conf. on Prodn. Rsch. Mem. AAAS, ASME, Sigma Xi, Pi Tau Sigma, Tau Beta Pi, Phi Kappa Phi. Home: 9833 E Cortez St Scottsdale AZ 85260-6012 Office: Omega Computer Systems Inc 4300 N Miller Rd Ste 136 Scottsdale AZ 85251-3620

GALL, WALTER GEORGE, retired chemist; b. Passaic, N.J., Mar. 11, 1929; s. George and Mary (Lesko) G.; m. Nida Porras, Nov. 26, 1991. BS, Carnegie-Mellon U., 1950, MS, 1950; PhD, U. Rochester, 1953. Rsch. chemist DuPont Exptl. Sta., Wilmington, Del., 1953-62, sr. rsch. chemist, 1963-69, rsch. assoc., 1969-81. Contbr. articles to profl. jours.; patentee in field. Fellow Am. Inst. Chemists; mem. Am. Chem. Soc. (emeritus). Home: 11838 Via Hacienda El Cajon CA 92019

GALLAGHER, DAVID KENT, agricultural vegetation manager, consultant; b. Beech Grove, Ind., Jan. 25, 1931; s. Victor Emerson and Opal Mae (Kinsey) G.; m. Mary Elizabeth Moore, Aug. 25, 1951 (div. June 1982); children: Ann, Kevin, David, Beth, Patrick, Brian, Peter, Robert, Kathryn; m. Paula Joan Weddle, June 2, 1982. Student, Purdue U., 1949-53. Nat. sales mgr. Internat. Minerals & Chems., Skokie, Ill., 1959-68; v.p. mktg. Dairyland Fertilizer, Marshall, Wis., 1969; area mgr. Occidental Corp., Houston, 1970; dist. mgr. Peets Feed, Frankfort, Ind., 1970-73, A.O. Smith Harvestor, Milw., 1973-75, Honnegger, Inc., Fairbury, Ill., 1975; pres. Gallagher & Sons, Inc., Shelbyville, Ind., 1975-82; coord. River Park Inc., Pierre, S.D., 1983-86; vegetation mgmt. Garfield County, Glenwood Springs, Colo., 1986—; cons. Phoenix Corp./Sioux Valley Hosp., Sioux Falls, S.D., 1984-86, Westheffer Co., Inc., Lawrence, Kans., 1991—. Co-author: Northwestern Colorado Poisonous Plants and Noxious Weeds, 1992. Leader 4-H, Shelbyville, Ind., 1954-57, Glenwood Springs, 1987-89; scoutmaster Boy Scouts Am., Shelbyville, 1955-56. Recipient Environ. Awareness award E.I. DuPont., Colo. Outstanding Vegetation Mgr. Yr. award., 1992. Mem. Colo. Weed Mgmt. Assn. (bd. dirs. 1991—), Rocky Mountain Plant Food and Agrl. Chems. Assn., Nat. Roadside Vegetation Mgmt. Assn. Republican. Roman Catholic. Home: 7715 County Rd 331 Silt CO 81652 Office: Garfield Co Vegetation Dept 109 8th St Ste 307 Glenwood Springs CO 81601

GALLAGHER, DENNIS JOSEPH, state senator, educator; b. Denver, July 1, 1939; s. William Joseph and Ellen Philomena (Flaherty) G.; B.A., Regis Coll., 1961; M.A., Cath. U. Am., 1968; postgrad. (Eagleton fellow) Rutgers U., 1972, 86; children: Meaghan Kathleen, Daniel Patrick. With locals of Internat. Assn. Theatrical and Stage Employees, Denver and Washington, 1956-63; tchr. St. John's Coll. High Sch., Washington, 1964-66, Heights Study Center, Washington, 1965-67, Regis Coll., 1967; mem. Colo. Ho. of Reps from 4th Dist., 1970-74; mem. Colo. Senate, 1974—, chmn. Dem. Caucus, 1982-84, Dem. Whip, 1985—. Mem. Platte Area Reclamation Com., 1973—; mem. Denver Anti-Crime Council, 1976-77; trustee Denver Art Mus.; bd. dirs. Cath. Community Services; mem. Colo. Commn. on Aging; mem. Colo. State Adv. Council on Career Edn.; mem. Victim Assistance Law Enforcement Bd., Denver, 1984—; Named Gates Found. fellow Harvard U. Mem. Colo. Fedn. Tchrs. (pres. local 1333, 1972-74), Colo. Calligrapher's Guild, James Joyce Reading Soc. Democrat. Roman Catholic. Home: 2511 W 32nd Ave Denver CO 80211-3323 Office: Regis Coll Dept Communication W 50th Ave & Lowell Blvd Denver CO 80221

GALLAR, JOHN JOSEPH, mechanical engineer, educator; b. Poland, July 3, 1936; came to U.S., 1981; s. Joseph and Sophie (Gallar) Filipecki; m. Christina B. Wilczynski, June 30, 1962; 1 child, Darek A. BSME, State U. Poland, 1957, MSME, 1958; PhD in Tech. Scis., M & M Acad., 1966; professorship, Ahmadu Bello U., Zaria, Nigeria, 1980. Dir., prof. engring. Acad. State U., Poland, 1957-72; dir., prof. engring. Ahmadu Bello U., 1973-81, dir. postgrad. studies, 1976-81; with module design Timex Co., Cupertino, Calif., 1981-82; mgr. mfg. Computer Research Co., Santa Clara, Calif., 1982-84; mgr. hardware devel. Nat. Semiconductor Co., Santa Clara, 1984-85; chief robotics engr. Varian Corp., Palo Alto, Calif., 1986—; dep. vice-chancellor State U., Poland, 1970-71; cons. Enplan Corp., Kaduna, Nigeria, 1980-81, Criticare Tech., Sparks, Nev., 1985-86, also bd. dirs.; mgr. mfg. engring. Retro-Tek Co., Santa Clara, 1986. Contbr. articles to profl. jours.; patentee in field. Trustee, charter charter life mem. Presdl. Task Force, Washington, 1984; mem. Nat. Conservative Polit. Action Com., Washington, 1981. Recipient U.S. Ceremonial Flag Presdl. Task Force; Medal Merit from Pres. Ronald Reagan, Washington, 1985. Mem. NRA. Roman Catholic. Home: 5459 Entrada Cedros San Jose CA 95123-1418 Office: Varian Corp 611 Hansen Way Palo Alto CA 94304-1015

GALLEGLY, ELTON WILLIAM, congressman; b. Huntington Park, Calif., Mar. 7, 1944; married; four children. Attended, Calif. State U., L.A. Businessman, real estate broker Simi Valley, Calif., from 1968; mem. Simi Valley City Coun., 1979; mayor City of Simi Valley, 1980-86; mem. 99th-103rd Congresses from the 21st (now 23rd) dist. of Calif., 1986—; mem. fgn. affairs com., mem. judiciary com., mem. natural resources com.; mem. exec. com. Task Forces on Crime and Strategic Def. Initiative, U.S. Ho. Reps. Rep. Study Com.; mem. Congl. Human Rights Caucus, Congl. Fire Svcs. Caucus; formerly vice-chmn., chmn. Ventura County Assn. govts., Calif. Bd. dirs. Moorpark Coll. Found.

GALLEGOS, JAKE EUGENE, lawyer; b. Tucumcari, N.Mex., Oct. 19, 1935; s. Jacob Vincent and Mary (Letcher) G.; m. Beth Skidmore; children: Jimmie Louise, Jake E. Jr., John Frank, Julie Ione; m. Carole Cooperman; 1 child, Joaquin Andres; m. Felice Gracia Gonzales, Oct. 22, 1982; children: Luis Maximilian, Navona Felice. BA, U. N.Mex., 1956, JD, 1960. Bar: N.Mex, 1961. Asst. U.S. atty. gen. Albuquerque, 1961-62; asst. atty. gen. Santa Fe, N.Mex., 1962-63; dir. Jones, Gallegos, Snead & Wertheim, Santa Fe, 1963-87; dir., pres. Gallegos Law Firm, P.C., Santa Fe, 1987—; mem. bd. advisors Mountain Bell, Albuquerque, 1976-80; mem. policy exam. com. N.W. Mut. Ins., Milw., 1980; trustee Northwestern Mut. Ins. Co., Milw.; dir. Sunwest Bank, Santa Fe. Chmn. bd. trustees St. Vincent Hosp., Santa Fe, 1968-72; dir. Nature Conservancy, Albuquerque, 1981-87, U. N.Mex. Found., Inc., Albuquerque, 1981-90; regent U. N.Mex., Albuquerque, 1991—. Mem. ABA, State Bar (bd. bar examiners 1974-80, judiciary com. 1976-80, antitrust comml. litigation sect. 1984-86), Fed. Bar Com. (chmn. 1980—, specialization com. 1980-90), Am. Law Inst. Democrat. Roman Catholic. Home: 730 Camino Pinones Santa Fe NM 87501 Office: Gallegos Law Firm PC 141 E Palace Ave Santa Fe NM 87501

GALLETTA, JOSEPH LEO, physician; b. Bessemer, Pa., Dec. 21, 1935; s. John and Grace (Galletta) G.; student U. Pitts., 1953-56; MD, U. Santo Tomas, Manila, Philippines, 1962; m. Teresita Suarez Soler, Feb. 19, 1961; children: John II, Angela, Eric, Christopher, Robert Francis, Michael Angelo. Intern, St. Elizabeth Hosp., Youngstown, Ohio, 1963-64; family practice medicine, 29 Palms, Calif., 1967-77, Hemet, Calif., 1977—; chief of staff 29 Palms Community Hosp., 1970-71, 73-76; vice chief of staff Hi-Desert Med. Center, Joshua Tree, Calif., 1976-77; chmn. dept. family practice Hemet Valley Hosp., 1981-83, med. dir. chem. dependency dept., 1985-88; pres. Flexisplint, Inc.; founding mem. Hemet Hospice; former cons. Morongo Basin Mental Health Assn. Hon. mem. 29 Palms Sheriff's Search and Rescue, 1971-77. Bd. dirs. 29 Palms Community Hosp. Dist., Morongo Unified Sch. Dist. Served with M.C. USN, 1964-67. Diplomate Am. Bd. Family Practice. Founding fellow West Coast div. Am. Geriatric Soc.; fellow Am. Acad. Family Practice; mem. AMA, Calif. Med. Assn., Riverside County Med. Assn., Am. Holistic Med. Assn. (charter), Am. Soc. Addiction Medicine, Calif. Soc. Addiction Medicine, Am. Acad. Family Practice, Calif. Acad. Family Practice. Roman Catholic. Established St. Anthonys Charity Clinic, Philippines, 1965; inventor Flexisplint armboards. Home: 27691 Pochea Trl Hemet CA 92544-8161 Office: Westside Medical Pla 37020 Florida Ave Hemet CA 92545-3520

GALLI, DARRELL JOSEPH, management consultant; b. Ft. Bragg, Calif., Nov. 10, 1948; s. Joseph Germain and Esther Edith (Happajoki) G.; B.A. in Transp./Internat. Bus., San Francisco State U., 1975; BS in Computer Info. Systems, 1985; MBA Golden Gate U., 1980; m. Rondus Miller, Apr. 23, 1977 (div. 1981); 1 dau., Troyan Hulda. With Pacific Gas & Electric Co., Santa Cruz, Calif., 1972-73; with Calif. Western R.R., Ft. Bragg, 1975-77, Sheldon Oil Co., Suisun, Calif, 1978-80; mgr. House of Rondus, Suisun, 1974-79; mgmt. cons., Suisun City, 1979—; instr. Solano Coll., 1979-81, Golden Gate U., 1981; mem. faculty U. Md. European div., Heidelberg, W.Ger., 1982-88; owner, mgr. Old Stewart House Bed and Breakfast, Fort Bragg, Calif., 1990—; lectr. Coll. Redwoods, Ft. Bragg, 1989—; coord. Small Bus. Mgmt. Seminar, 1980. Asst. coordinator Sr. Citizens Survey for Solano Coll. and Sr. Citizens Center, 1980. Served with U.S. Army, 1969-71. Lic. Calif. real estate agt. Mem. Am. Assn. M.B.A. Execs., World Trade Assn., Bay Area Elec. R.R. Assn. Republican. Episcopalian. Club: Odd Fellows. Home: 321 Morrow St Fort Bragg CA 95437-3861 Office: 511 Stewart St Fort Bragg CA 95437-3226

GALLIANI, LOWELL ALAN, dental technician, dental laboratory executive; b. San Rafael, Calif., Apr. 27, 1950; s. Julius and Clara Elizabeth (Romani) G.; m. Loretta Marie Pompeii, Sept. 1, 1973 (div. May 1987); m. Maureen Dianne Watkins, Oct. 1, 1989; children: Evan Silletto, Angela Silletto. Student, Coll. Marin, 1968-70. Dental technician De Vreugd Dental Lab., San Rafael, 1970-74, v.p., 1972-74; freelance technician numerous labs. and dentists in numerous states and Can., 1974-75, 86-87; owner, technician Galliani Dental Lab., Bolinas, Calif., 1975-86, San Anselmo, Calif., 1987—. Inventor, developer numerous dental lab. processes and techniques. Mem. Planetary Soc. Democrat. Home: 30 Sierra Ave San Anselmo CA 94960 Office: 761 Sir Francis Drake Blvd Ste 5 San Anselmo CA 94960

GALLIK, JANICE SUSAN, finance executive; b. Akron, Ohio; d. Emil John and Antoinette Mary (Verdi) G.; children: Thomas Butowicz II, Elizabeth Henshaw. BS cum laude, U. Akron, 1965; postgrad., St. Francis Coll., 1978; MS, Ind. U., 1981; EdD, Seattle U., 1988. Mng. ptnr., treas., dir. pub. rels. Buckeye Group, Inc., Orion Inc., 1977-81; contr. D.S. Willett, Inc., 1982-85; mgr. acctg. G. Raden & Sons, Inc., 1986-89; cons. J. Gallik & Assocs., 1985—; controller Merit Steamship Agy., Inc., 1988-91; dir. fin. Seattle Children's Home, 1991—; adj. faculty Seattle Pacific U. Contbr. articles to profl. jours. Trustee, bd. dirs. Columbus 500 Com., 1989—; bd. dirs. Lit. Ctr., 1988-89; bus./community rels. Bellevue Art Mus., 1983-85; bd. dirs., com. mem., dir. pub. rels. Ft. Wayne Philharmonic, 1978-81; treas., pres. Aboite River Women's Club, 1980-81; bd. dirs. Izaak Walton's League, 1980; area rep. Girl Scouts Am.; bd. dirs., pres. Zelienople Jr. Women, 1974-76; med. team search com. Zelienople, Pa., 1976. Scholl scholarship St. Francis, 1978; rsch. grant NYU Ctr. for Entrepreneurship, 1986. Mem. NAFE, Seattle U. Alumni Assn., Seattle C. of C., Acad. Mgmt., Phi Delta Kappa, Alpha Delta Pi. Office: Seattle Children's Home 2142 10th Ave W Seattle WA 98119-2899

GALLIVAN, JOHN WILLIAM, publisher; b. Salt Lake City, June 28, 1915; s. Daniel and Frances (Wilson) G.; m. Grace Mary Ivers, June 30, 1938; children—Gay, John, William, Michael D., Timothy. B.A., U. Notre Dame, 1937. With Salt Lake Tribune, 1937—, promotion mgr., 1942-48, asst. pub., 1948-60, pub., 1960-84; pres. Kearns-Tribune Corp., 1960-86, chmn. bd., 1984—; dir. Tele-Communications, Inc.; pres. Silver King Mining Co., 1960—. Pres. Utah Symphony, 1964-65. Mem. Sigma Delta Chi, Bohemian Club (San Francisco). Clubs: Nat. Press (Washington); Alta (Salt Lake City), Salt Lake Country (Salt Lake City), Rotary (Salt Lake City). Home: 17 S 12th E Salt Lake City UT 84102-1607 Office: Kearns-Tribune Corp 143 S Main St Salt Lake City UT 84111-1917

GALLO, ERNEST, vintner; b. 1909; married. Co-owner, chmn. bd. dirs. E & J Gallo Winery, Modesto, Calif., 1933—. Office: E & J Gallo Winery PO Box 1130 Modesto CA 95353-1130

GALLO, JOSEPH EDWARD, retired electrical engineer, city councilman; b. Bklyn., July 18, 1917; s. Frank and Mary Lucy (Richard) G.; m. Ida Selma Winzinger, Apr. 13, 1941 (dec. 1989); children: Jonathan, David, Jane; m. Mary Jean Nelson, May 3, 1991. BS in Elec. Engring., NYU, 1937; MS in Engring., U. Pa., 1963. Elec. engr. Brewster Aero Corp., N.Y., Pa., 1940-44; chief systems engr. Curtiss-Wright Elecs., Carlstadt, N.J., 1944-58; project engr. RCA Corp., Burlington, Mass., Moorestown, N.J., 1958-83, Camden, N.J., 1958-83; retired, 1983; cons., H.H. Aerospace Co., Lexington, Mass., 1974-76, Esscube Engring. Inc., Marlton, N.J., 1983. Inventor, patentee flight simulator field, 1950's. Mem. Am. Radio Relay League, IEEE, Aircraft Owners Pilots Assn. Republican. Roman Catholic. Home: 219 Chestnut Dr Prescott AZ 86301-1263

GALLOB, JOEL AVROM, lawyer; b. Indpls., Jan. 28, 1951; s. Ben and Ray Eva (Klein) G. BA, CUNY, 1974; JD, Lewis and Clark Coll., 1990. Bar: N.Y., Oreg. Reporter N. Bklyn. News, 1974-79; project dir. Greenpoint Williamsburg Coalition Community Orgn., Bklyn., 1979-81; asst. writer, editor United Jewish Appeal, N.Y.C., 1981-83; computer operator Marine Midland Bank, N.Y.C., 1983-87, mgr., investment libr., 1987; freelance atty., fin. planner Portland, Oreg., 1991—; campaign strategist, pub. rels. operative Steve DiBriengn Campaign for N.Y.C. Coun., 1982. Contbr. articles to profl. jours. Co-founder, co-incorporator Urban Recolonization Project, Queens, 1991; bd. dirs. Ctr. Health and Well Being, Portland, Oreg. Home: 4517 Lakeview Blvd Lake Oswego OR 97035-5451

GALLOWAY, ARNOLD JOHN, aerospace engineer; b. Toledo, Mar. 28, 1939; s. Arnold Carlos and Maggie Ola (Whittaker) G.; m. Beverly Bernice Billups, June 24, 1961; children: Arnold Scott, Pamela Joy. BS in Aero. and Astronautical Engring., U. Mich., 1961, MS in Aerospace Engring., 1963, PhD in Aerospace Engring., 1968. Engr. systems div. Bendix Corp., Ann Arbor, 1961-64; rsch. asst., lectr. U. Mich., Ann Arbor, 1964-68; mem. tech. staff Aerospace Corp., San Bernardino, Calif., 1968-72; sect. mgr. Aerospace Corp., El Segundo, Calif., 1972-79; dept. mgr. def. systems group TRW, San Bernardino, 1979-83; sr. systems engr. mil. space systems div. TRW, Redondo Beach, Calif., 1983-84, asst. project mgr., 1984-91, systems engring. project mgr. space def., 1991—. Contbr. articles to profl. jours. Mem. AIAA. Home: 3825 S Cloverdale Ave Los Angeles CA 90008

GALLOWAY, CLINTON EDMUND, accountant, communications executive; b. Birmingham, Ala., Nov. 30, 1951; s. Thomas Eugene and Mable (Collins) G. BS in Accountancy, No. Ariz. U., 1974. CPA, Calif. Auditor Coopers & Lybrand, San Francisco, 1975-78; stockbroker Smith, Barney, Harris & Upham, Beverly Hills, Calif., 1978-80; pres. 1st St. Securities Corp., L.A., 1981-83; prin. Clinton E. Galloway, CPA, L.A., 1983—; pres. Preferred Communications, Inc., L.A., 1983—; chief oper. officer Can. Internat. Health Svcs., St. Louis, 1988-89. Dir. L.A. Black Media Coalition, 1987-91. Mem. Calif. Soc. CPA's. Office: 10905 Venice Blvd Los Angeles CA

GALLOWAY, KENNETH FRANKLIN, engineering educator; b. Columbia, Tenn., Apr. 11, 1941; s. Benjamin F. and Carrie (Dowell) G.; m. Dorothy Elise Lamar; children: Kenneth Jr., Carole A. BA, Vanderbilt U., 1962; PhD, U. S.C., 1966. Rsch. assoc. Ind. U., Bloomington, 1966-67, asst. prof., 1967-72, assoc. prof., 1972; rsch. physicist Naval Weapons Support Ctr., Crane, Ind., 1972-74; tech. staff Nat. Bur. Standards, Gaithersurg, Md., 1974-77; chief sect. Nat. Bur. Standards, Gaithersurg, 1977-79, chief div., 1980-86; prof. elect. engring. U. Md., 1980-86; prof., dept. head elect. and computer engring. U. Ariz., Tucson, 1986—. Contbr. articles to profl. jours. Sci. and Tech. fellow U.S. Dept. Commerce, 1979-80. Fellow IEEE (gen. chmn. Nuclear and Space Radiation Effects Conf. 1985, v.p. NPSS 1990, chmn. radiation effects com. NPSS 1991—); mem. AAAS, Electrochem. Soc., Am. Phys. Soc., Am. Soc. Engring. Edn., Sigma Xi, Eta Kappa Nu. Office: U Ariz Dept Elec & Computer Eng Tucson AZ 85721

GALLOWAY, PAMELA EILENE, university official; b. Tucson, Dec. 2, 1952; d. David Barnes and Nancy (Harrison) Galloway. BA in Journalism, U. Nev., 1974. Feature writer Reno Gazette Jour., 1973-74; feature writer Reno Newspapers, Inc., 1974-78, lifestyle editor, 1978-80, mem. copy desk/gen. assignment, 1980-81, edn. beat reporter, 1981-84; dir. pub. info. U. Nev. System, Reno, 1984—. Mem. First United Meth. Ch., 1982—; publicity chair Homeowners Assn.; bd. dirs. prison program Kairos, 1984-86; bd. dirs., fund raising chmn. Cursillo Interdenom. Group, 1981-84; no. Nev. publicity chair Gov's. Conf. Women, 1987. Active Citizen's Alert, Friends of the Libr. Recipient Planned Parenthood Pub. Svc. award for no. Nev., 1983. Mem. ACLU, Nev. State Press Assn. (numerous writing awards 1977-78), Nat. Fedn. Press Women (two nat. interview awards), Inc., Internat. Assn. Press Women, Inc., Toastmasters (10 Most Watchable Women No. Nev. 1984). Office: U and CC System Nev Chancellor's Office 2601 Enterprise Rd Reno NV 89512-1608

GALLUP, THOMAS GRANT, insurance agent; b. Idaho Falls, Idaho, Feb. 9, 1953; s. T. Grant and Thelma Elizabeth (Peasley) G.; m. Janet Lorraine Moore, July 29, 1975; children: Deanna, Mike, Wayne, Lloyd, Emily, Jenna. AS, Ricks Coll., Rexburg, Idaho, 1976; BS, Brigham Young U., 1978. CLU, ChFC. Salesman Farm Bur. Ins. Svcs., Pocatello, Idaho, 1980—. Cub scoutmaster Boy Scouts Am., Sugar City, Idaho, 1988-90, varsity scoutmaster, 1990—. Mem. Nat. Assn. Life Underwriters (chmn. multi-line and ethics Idaho Falls 1984-87), Am Soc. CLUs and CHFCs (student devel. chmn. East Idaho chpt. 1987-90, pub. rels. chmn. 1993—, pub. relations chmn. East Idaho Chpt., 1993—). Republican. Mem. LDS Ch. Office: Farm Bur Ins Svcs PO Box 275 303 N 2nd E Rexburg ID 83440

GALM, JOHN ARNOLD, English language educator; b. Moneta, Iowa, Mar. 25, 1934; s. John and Emalie (Schafer) G.; m. Sybil Weir, Oct. 12, 1984; children: Ruth, Paul. BA, St. John's U., 1955; MA, Yale U., 1959, PhD, 1963. Prof. San Jose (Calif.) State U., 1962—, chair English, 1975-84, chair senate, 1990-91. Author: Sidney's Arcadia Poems, 1975; editor, translator: Songs of Bernart de Ventadorn, 1963. Local pres. Am. Fedn. Tchrs., San Jose State U., 1966-68; sec. Coll. Coun., Calif., 1967-68. Fulbright scholar U.S. Fulbright Commn., Fed. Republic Germany, Danforth scholar Danforth Found., Yale U., 1955-62. Mem. MLA, Philol. Assn. Pacific Coast, Phi Kappa Phi. Democrat. Home: 787 E William St San Jose CA 95112-2252 Office: San Jose State U San Jose CA 95192

GALSTER, WILLIAM ALLEN, biochemist, researcher; b. Kenosha, Wis., Apr. 11, 1932; s. Talford DeWillis and Violet (Barnes) G.; m. Rita Pauline Lorenz, Sept. 24, 1955; children: Richard, Christine, David, Marjorie, Patrick. BS, U. Wis., 1957, MS, 1960. Prof. St. Benedict's Coll., Atchison, Kans., 1962-65; asst. prof. Inst. Arctic biology U. Alaska, Fairbanks, 1965-73; rsch. assoc. U. Utah, Salt Lake City, 1973-87; dir. lab. Vets. Hosp., Salt Lake City, 1987—; cons. Am. Acad. Sci., Washington, 1980-83. Author: (chpts.) Fire and Materials, 1982; contbr. articles to profl. jours. President Cath. Diocese of Fairbanks Parish Coun., 1972-78, Wasatch Front Brittany Club, Utah, 1987-91. Sgt. U.S. Army, 1955-57. Grantee Nat. Acad. Sci., 1967-73, Nat. Bur. Standards, 1973-80, U.S. Dept. Transp., 1980-83. Fellow Am. Soc. Cryobiology; mem. AAAS, Am. Chem. Soc.. Home: 4192 Holloway Dr Salt Lake City UT 84124-2650

GALT, JOHN KIRTLAND, physicist, laboratory administrator; b. Portland, Oreg., Sept. 1, 1920; s. Martin Happer and Elsie (Lee) G.; m. Marguerite VanNest, Dec. 30, 1949; children: James Michael (dec.), Lloyd Anthony. A.B., Reed Coll., 1941; Ph.D., MIT, 1947. Mem. tech. staff Bell Labs., Murray Hill, N.J., 1948-57, head solid state and plasma physics dept., 1957-61, dir. solid state electronics lab., 1961-74; dir. solid state scis. research orgn. Sandia Nat. Labs., Albuquerque, 1974-78, v.p., 1978-85; prin. scientist Aerospace Corp., 1985-90; ret., 1990; mem. Air Force Studies Bd., Nat. Acad. Sci., 1971-76, Air Force Sci. Adv. Bd., 1975-82. Cons. editor: McGraw-Hill Ency. Sci. and Tech., 1965-86. NRC fellow, Bristol, Eng., 1947-48. Fellow Am. Phys. Soc., IEEE, AAAS, Nat. Acad. Engring.

GALVAO, LOUIS ALBERTO, import/export corporation executive, consultant; b. Ponta Delgada, Sao Miguel, Portugal, July 5, 1949; came to U.S., 1969; s. Jeremias B. and Margarida M. G.; m. Antonieta A. Galvao, Oct. 26, 1966 (div. 1984); children: Marlene, Vanessa. Degree in Bus. Mgmt., Indsl. & Commerce Sch., Azores, Portugal, 1968; Dr. Universal Life (hon.), Universal Life Ch., 1991. Asst. mgr. sales J.B. Galvao Imports, Azores, 1964-68; asst. supr. Union Carbide Corp., Peabody, Mass., 1969-70, Container Corp. Am., Wakefield, Mass., 1970-73; sales dir. McCulloch Oil Corp., Lake Havash City, Ariz., 1972-74; pres. Sunset Investments Corp., Phoenix, 1974—; v.p. United Universal Enterprises Corp., Phoenix, 1985—; pres. Universal Imports, Inc., Phoenix, 1977—; dir. Global Savings & Loan Ltd., London, 1990—. mem. Nat. Rep. Congl. Com., Washington, 1982— (cert. recognition 1981, 84, 85, Campaign Kickoff award 1984, cert. merit 1992), Rep. Presdl. Task Force, Washington, 1984— (Am. flag dedicated in his honor at Rotunda of U.S. Capital bldg. 1986, life mem., mem. presdl. election registry 1992), Rep. Nat. Com. (cert. recognition 1990, 92), European Movement, U.K., 1990—, Social Dem. Party, Portugal, 1990—, Washington Legal Found.; charter mem. U.S. Def. Com.; del. The Presl. Trust, Washington, 1992. Recipient award U.S. Def. Com., 1984; inducted to Rep. Nat. Hall Honor Rep. Nat. Candidate Trust, 1992. Mem. Am. Mgmt. Assn., Nat. Assn. Export Cos., Profl. Fin. Assts., Heritage Bus. Club, Senatorial Club, Universal Life Ch. Roman Catholic.

GALVEZ, WILLIAM, artist; b. Cali, Colombia, 1945; came to U.S., 1963; Student, Inst. de Bellas Artes/Conservatorio, A.M.V., Cali, 1961-63; studied with Richard Peterson, Calif., 1975-79; studied with Roberto Lupetti, Carmel, Calif., 1980-83. Owner Galvez Pub., Placentia, Calif., 1991—. One-man shows include Galeria Elegante, Palm Desert, Calif., 1980, 83, Klein Art Gallery, Beverly Hills, Calif., 1981, Rainbow Promenade Galleries, Waikiki, Hawaii, 1982, Galeria Maria Luisa, Pasadena, Calif., 1984, San Gabriel (Calif.) Civic Auditorium, 1986, Galeria Figuras, Cali, 1989, 91, Dist. Libr., Placentia, Calif., 1990, Physician's Medicine Group, Long Beach, Calif., 1991, Calif. Colombian C. of C., L.A., 1992; exhibited in group shows at Pomeroy Art Gallery, Cypress, Calif., 1976, 77, 78, Fisher Galleries, Palm Springs, Calif., 1979, Ctr. Art Galleries, Honolulu, 1980, Internat. Art Exch., Anaheim Hills, Calif., 1981, New Masters Gallery, Carmel, 1982, 83, 84, 85, 86, 92, Fine Art Inst., San Bernardino Calif., 1986, Poulsen Galleries, Inc., Pasadena, 1988, 89, Simic Galleries, Inc., Carmel, Beverly Hills, La Jolla, 1988, 1990, 1991, Internat. Art. Galery, N.Y.C., 1990, Galeria Figuras, Cali, 1991, 92, 93, L.A. Art Expo, 1991, Art Fair, Placentia, 1991, Bob Hope

Gala, Corona, Calif., Art Buyers Caraban, Long Beach, Calif., 1992, Laura Larkin Gallery, Del Mar, Claif., 1992, Phyllis Diller Nat. Parkinson found., L.A., 1992, Toronto (Can.) Art Exhbn., 1992, Internat. Colombian Fair, Chgo., 1992, Wayne Newton Gala, Anaheim, Calif., 1992, New England Fine Arts Inst., Boston, 1993, Poulsen Galleries, Inc., Pasadena, Calif., 1992, Internat. Art Gallery, L.A., Paris, 1993. Studio: 1312 E Sao Paulo Ave Placentia CA 92670 also: PO Box 355 Placentia CA 92670

GALVIN, CHARLES EDWARD, JR., legal secretary; b. Atlanta, Jan. 28, 1960; s. Charles Edward and Mary Catherine (Sullivan) G. Student, U. Calif., Berkeley, 1977-80. Sec., word processor Temporaries, Inc., San Francisco, 1981-83; system adminstr. trust dept. Bank of Am. NT&SA, San Francisco, 1983-84; word processing specialist People Connection Inc., San Francisco, 1984-85; legal sec. applications specialist People Connection, San Francisco, 1986-89; legal sec. Jones, Hall, Hill & White, San Francisco, 1985-86, Pettit & Martin, San Francisco, 1989-91, Orrick, Herrington & Sutcliffe, San Francisco, 1991-92; spl. del. Universal Esperanto Assn., 1991—; sr. legal sec./applications specialist People Connection, San Francisco, 1992—. Active Community United Against Violence Lesbian/Gay Speakers Bur., San Francisco, 1990—. Named Eagle Scout Boy Scouts Am., 1976; Princess Beatrix scholar U. Calif., 1979. Mem. League Homosexual Esperantists (pres. 1989-91). Mem. Green Party. Home: 121 Cortland Ave San Francisco CA 94110-5503 Office: People Connection Inc 100 California St Ste 1165 San Francisco CA 94111

GALVIN, ELIAS, bishop. Bishop Desert S.W. Diocese, Phoenix, Ariz. Home: PO Box 467 San Francisco CA 94101 Office: Desert SW Diocese 2933 E Indian School Rd # 402 Phoenix AZ 85016*

GALVIN, GERALD T., police chief; b. San Francisco, May 25, 1942; married; four children. AA in Polit. Sci., Coll. San Mateo, 1963; BA in Sociology, Calif. State U., San Francisco, 1966; MA in Adminstrn. Justice, Calif. Luth. Coll., 1975; grad., advanced and exec. certs., P.O.S.T. Command Coll. Commd. USMC, 1965; dep. sheriff San Mateo Sheriff's Office, Redwood City, Calif., 1964-69; patrolman Berkeley (Calif.) Police Dept., 1969-71; detective Simi Valley (Calif.) Police Dept., 1971-72, lt., 1972-74, commdr., 1974-75; chief police Bishop (Calif.) Police Dept., 1975-76, Marina (Calif.) Police Dept., 1976-80, Clovis (Calif.) Police Dept., 1980-87, Vallejo (Calif.) Police Dept., 1987—. Named Chief of Yr. Nat. Assn. Police Community Rels. Officers, 1989. Mem. Internat. Assn. Chiefs. Police, Police Exec. Rsch. Forum, Calif. Police Chiefs Assn., Solano County Police Chiefs Assn. Office: Vallejo Police Dept 111 Amador St Vallejo CA 94590

GAMBARO, ERNEST UMBERTO, lawyer, consultant; b. Niagara Falls, N.Y., July 6, 1938; s. Ralph and Teresa (Nigro) G.; m. Winifred Sonya Gambaro, June 3, 1961. B.A. in Aero. Engrng. with honors, Purdue U., 1960, M.S. with honors, 1961; Fulbright scholar, Rome U., 1961-62; J.D. with honors, Loyola U., Los Angeles, 1975. Bar: Calif. 1975, U.S. Tax Ct. 1976, U.S. Supreme Ct. 1979, U.S. Ct. Appeals (9th cir.). With Aerospace Corp., El Segundo, Calif., 1962-80, counsel, 1975-80; asst. gen. counsel, asst. sec. Computer Scis. Corp., El Segundo, 1980-88; v.p., gen. counsel, sec. INFONET Svcs. Corp., El Segundo, 1988—; cons. bus. fin. and mgmt., 1968—. Recipient U.S. Air Force Commendation for contbns. to U.S. manned space program, 1969; Purdue U. Pres.'s scholar, 1959-60. Mem. ABA (internat., taxation sects.), Los Angeles Bar Assn. (exec. com. 1976—, founder chmn. sect. law and tech. 1976-78, chmn. bar reorgn. com. 1981-82), Am. Arbitration Assn. Los Angeles Ctr. Internat. Comml. Arbitration (founder, bd. dirs.), Internat. Law Inst. (faculty), St. Thomas More Law Soc., Phi Alpha Delta, Omicron Delta Kappa (past pres.), Tau Beta Pi, Sigma Gamma Tau (past pres.), Phi Eta Sigma. Republican. Newspaper columnist Europe Alfresco; contbr. articles to profl. publs. Home: 6542 Ocean Crest Dr Palos Verdes Peninsula CA 90274-5400 Office: 2100 E Grand Ave El Segundo CA 90245-5098

GAMBINO, JEROME JAMES, nuclear medicine educator; b. N.Y.C., Sept. 13, 1925; m. Jacquelyn Ann Mazzola, Mar. 27, 1948; children: Charles, John, Mary Ellen, Jacquelyn. BA, U. Conn., 1950, MS, 1952; PhD, U. Calif., 1957. Asst. prof. natural scis. SUNY, New Paltz, 1957-59; research radiobiologist UCLA, 1959-61; mem. research staff Northrop Corp., Hawthorne, Calif., 1961-69; dir. edn. nuclear medicine dept. VA Med. Ctr., Los Angeles, 1969—; lectr. anatomy U. So. Calif., L.A., 1963-89, radiol. scis. UCLA, 1978—. Mem. Radiation Research Soc., Soc. Nuclear Medicine (pres. So. Calif. chpt. 1981-82). Office: VA Med Ctr W Los Angeles Wadsworth Divsn Nuclear Med W115 Wilshire and Sawtelle Blvds Los Angeles CA 90073

GAMBLE, LEE ST. CLAIR, architectural and interior designer; b. St. Louis, Aug. 5, 1954; d. James Carr and Dorothy Lee (Wharton) Gamble ; children: Lindsey Elise, Ashley Elizabeth. BS, Skidmore Coll., 1974; degree in Interior Design, N.Y. Sch. Interior Design, 1976. Asst. buyer Abraham & Strauss, Bklyn., 1974-75; mgr. Trevi Co., Pitts., 1975; buyer Saks Fifth Ave., N.Y.C., 1975-77; pres. West Wind Designs, Cody, Wyo., 1977—; owner Southfork Expdns. Ltd., Cody, 1987—; real estate agent Steamboat Springs, Co, Saratoga, Wyo.; cons. design Wyo. Waterfowl Park, Cody, 1984-86, bd. dirs. Bd. dirs. Desarro Wildlife Resources, 1991—. Mem. Zoo Mont. (bd. dirs. 1985—). Republican. Presbyterian. Office: Solitary Ventures Inc PO Box 775287 Steamboat Springs CO 80477

GAMBOA, GEORGE CHARLES, oral surgeon, educator; b. King City, Calif., Dec. 17, 1923; s. George Angel and Martha Ann (Baker) G.; predental certificate Pacific Union Coll., 1943; DDS, U. Pacific, 1946; MS, U. Minn., 1953; AB, U. So. Calif., 1958; EdD, U. So. Calif., 1976; m. Winona Mae Collins, July 16, 1946; children: Cheryl Jan Gamboa Granger, Jon Charles, Judith Merlene Gamboa Hiscox. Fellow oral surgery Mayo Found., 1950-53; assoc. prof. grad. program oral and maxillofacial surgery U. So. Calif., Los Angeles, 1954—; assoc. prof. Loma Linda (Calif.) U., 1958—, chmn. dept. oral surgery, 1960-63; pvt. practice oral and maxillofacial surgery, San Gabriel, Calif., 1955-93. Mem., past chmn. first aid com. West San Gabriel chpt. ARC. Diplomate Am. Bd. Oral and Maxillofacial Surgery. Fellow Am. Coll. Dentists, Am. Coll. Oral and Maxillofacial Surgeons, Am. Assn. Oral and Maxillofacial Surgeons; mem. Internat. Assn. Oral Surgeons, So. Calif. Soc. Oral and Maxillofacial Surgeons, Western Soc. Oral and Maxillofacial Surgeons, Am. Acad. Oral and Maxillofacial Radiology, Marsh Robinson Acad. Oral Surgeons, So. Calif. Acad. Oral Pathology, Profl. Staff Assn. Los Angeles County-U. So. Calif. Med. Ctr. (exec. com. 1976—), Am. Cancer Soc. (Calif. div., profl. edn. subcom. 1977—, pres. San Gabriel-Pomona Valley unit 1989-90), Calif. Dental Soc. Anesthesiology (pres. 1989-93), Calif. Dental Found. (pres. 1991-93), Calif. Dental Assn. (jud. coun. 1990—), San Gabriel Valley Dental Soc. (past pres.), Xi Psi Phi, Omicron Kappa Upsilon, Delta Epsilon. Seventh-day Adventist. Home: 1102 Loganrita Ave Arcadia CA 91006-4535

GAMBON, MARIE ANNE, human resources professional; b. Osmond, Nebr., Jan. 28, 1952; d. Bernard Hugo and Thelma (Moss) Wunderlich; m. R.C. Lloyd Jr., July 24, 1976 (div. 1986); 1 child, Reese Carlton III; m. Kenneth T. Gambon Sr., Nov. 17, 1990. BA in Communications, Wayne State U., 1973. Various positions in human resources communications, edn. IBM, Boulder, Colo., 1974-91; dir. leadership ctr. U.S. West Inc., Englewood, Colo., 1991-92, exec. dir. leadership, 1992—. Home: 5653 Gunbarrel Rd Longmont CO 80503 Office: US West Inc 188 Inverness Dr W Ste 800 Englewood CO 80112

GAMBRELL, THOMAS ROSS, investor; b. Lockhart, Tex., Mar. 17, 1934; s. Sidney Spivey and Nora Katherine (Rheinlander) G.; m. Louise Evans, Feb. 23, 1960. MD, U. Tex., 1957. Company physician Hughes Aircraft, Fullerton, Calif., 1958-65, Chrysler Corp., Anaheim, Calif., 1962-65, L.A. Angels Baseball Team, Fullerton, 1962-64; pvt. practice medicine Fullerton, 1958-91; owner Ranching (Citrus) & Comml. Devel., Ariz., Tex., N.Y. Contbr. articles to profl. jours. Organizer of care for needy elderly, North Orange County, 1962-65. Fellow Am. Acad. Family Physicians; mem. AMA, Calif. Med. Assn., Tex. Med. Assn., Orange County Med. Assn., Mayflower Soc., Sons of Confederacy, Descendants of Royalty Living in Am. Office: PO Box 6067 Beverly Hills CA 90212-1067

GAMBY, LAWRENCE EDWARD, dentist; b. Defiance, Ohio, Feb. 10, 1964; s. Bernard Edward and Emi Frances (Yonekura) G.; m. Lisa Caroline Williams, Aug. 20, 1988; 1 child, Brittany Caroline. Student, U.S. Air Force Acad., 1982-83; BS, Ohio State U., 1987, DDS, 1991. Dental asst. Dr. E. F. Willey, Defiance, 1982-83; dentist U.S. Army Dental Corps., Ft. Lewis, Wash., 1991—. Capt. U.S. Army, 1991—. Mem. ADA, Ohio State U. Coll. of Dentistry Alumni Assn., Howe Milit. Sch. Alumni Assn. (Alumni Achievement award 1992), Alpha Omega. Republican. Episcopalian. Home: 2517-D Barber Dr Fort Lewis WA 98433 Office: Dr Neil Elam & Assocs West Broad St & Wilson Rd Columbus OH 43204

GAMER, NANCY CREWS, director alumni relations, fundraiser; b. Tacoma, Feb. 2, 1937; d. Norman W. and Kathryn (Gibbons) Schaefer; m. J. D. Gamer, June 14, 1960 (div. 1979); children: Jeffrey D., Michael C. BA, Mills Coll., 1959, MA, 1960. Instr. in English Lake Forest (Ill.) Coll., 1960-61, Monterey (Calif.) Peninsula Jr. Coll., 1964-65, Jacksonville (Fla.) U., 1967-69, No. Va. Community Coll., Annandale, 1969-72; tutor Claremont (Calif.) McKenna Coll., fall 1976; alumni sec. Harvey Mudd Coll., Claremont, 1977-78, adminstrv. asst., 1978-79, dir. alumni rels., 1979-91; tutor Claremont (Calif.) McKenna Coll., 1991—. Mem. parents bd. Claremont McKenna Coll., 1982-86; bd. dirs. ARC, Claremont, 1984, 85. Mem. Coun. for Advancement and Support of Edn. Office: Claremont McKenna Coll English Resource Ctr Claremont CA 91711

GAMM, STANFORD RALPH, psychoanalyst; b. Chgo., Aug. 14, 1917; s. Julius and Rae (Green) G.; m. Ethel Anita Thompson, Apr. 24, 1943; children: Michelle Clifton, Annette Godow, Cecile Lindstedt. Student, DePauw U., 1934-37; AB, U. Ill., 1939; MD, U. Ill., Chgo., 1943. Diplomate Am. Bd. Psychiatry and Neurology. Asst. chief & rsch. assoc. chief. Mental Health Clinic Michael Reese Hosp., Chgo., 1949-54, psychiatrist, 1951-73; asst. prof. psychiatry Northwestern U., Evanston, Ill., 1956-73; psychiatrist VA Rsch. Hosp., Chgo., 1956-73; resident assoc. Chgo. Inst. Psychoanalysis, 1957-73; pvt. practice Chgo., 1947-73, San Francisco, 1973—, San Mateo, Calif., 1973—. Lt. USNR, 1943-58. Fellow Am. Psychiat. Assn. (life), Chgo. Psychoanalytic Soc. (life); mem. No. Calif. Psychiat. Soc. Home and Office: 20 Hoods Point Way San Mateo CA 94402-4011 also: 490 Post St San Francisco CA 94102-1408

GAMMELL, GLORIA RUFFNER, sales executive; b. St. Louis, June 19, 1948; d. Robert Nelson and Antonia Ruffner; m. Doyle M. Gammell, Dec. 11, 1973. AA in Art, Harbor Coll., Harbor City, Calif., 1969; BA in Sociology, Calif. State U., Long Beach, 1971. Cert. fin. planner. Bus. analyst Dun & Bradstreet Inc., Los Angeles, 1971-81; rep. sales Van Nuys, Calif., 1981-90; v.p., sec. bd. dirs. Gammell Industries, Paramount, Calif., 1986—. Mem. Anne Banning Assistance League, Hollywood, Calif., 1981-82; counselor YWCA, San Pedro, Calif., 1983-84; fundraiser YMCA, San Pedro, 1984-85; mem. womens adv. com. Calif. State Assembly, 1984-89. Recipient Best in the West Presdl. Citation, 1981-86, 89, 90. Home: 991 W Channel St San Pedro CA 90731-1415

GAMMILL, DARRYL CURTIS, business executive; b. Milw., Jan. 20, 1950; s. Lawrence H. and Eunice B. (Birkett) G. BS, U. Colo., 1973; m. Maureen Mulcahy, Sept. 16, 1972; children: Rebecca, Bridgett, Maureen, Bryann. Lic. gen. and fin. prin.; registered options prin., sr. compliance officer, registered rep., SEC, registered investment advisor, broker dealer, real estate broker, SEC. Stockbroker, Douglas, Stanat, Inc., Denver, 1974; dir. rsch. Pittman Co., Denver, 1975; option specialist B.J. Leonard & Co., Denver, 1976; v.p. rsch., corp. fin. Neidiger, Tucker Bruner, Denver, 1977; chmn., pres., chief exec. officer G.S. Omni Corp., 1979-82; chmn., chief exec. officer Gammill and Co., 1981—; mng. ptnr. GSI Cons., 1988—; mng. ptnr. G.S. Oil, G.S. Leasing; dir. Valudyne, Inc., 1973-79; pres. Chalton Investment Svcs.; chmn., pres. Fusion Mgmt. Corp., 1981-83; chmn. Applied Fusion Rsch. & Tech. Corp., 1982, Pres. Rsch. Mgmt., 1984; gen. partner Fusion Ltd. Trustee Gammill Found.; pres. Platinium Club Inc., 1985-88; founder AudioOptics. Founder Nicholas R. Massaro Ednl. Scholarship, 1985; co-founder Opera Colo. Mem. Fin. Analysts Fedn., Nat. Assn. Security Dealers, Denver Soc. Security Analysts, IEEE, Am. Nuclear Soc., Nat. Energy Assn. (nat. chmn.), Am. Mgmt. Assn., Investment Rsch. Mgmt. Assn., U.S. Ski Assn., Optimists, Elks. Contbr. articles to profl. jours. Home: 28 Red Fox Ln Littleton CO 80127-5713

GANDHI, MIHIR JITENDRA, computer and business management specialist, consultant; b. Bombay, Nov. 13, 1960; s. Jitendra M. and Veena J. Gandhi; m. Minal Kantilal Shah, Sept. 2, 1983; children: Anshul Mihir, Saurin Mihir. BS in Acctg. and Auditing with honors, U. Bombay, 1981; grad. in Systems Analysis and Cobol Programming, Datamatics, 1982; MBA in Bus., Ohio U., 1983. Cert. systems analyst. Programmer, tutor Datamatics, Bombay, 1982; sr. regional applications support specialist Pathfinder Computer Ctr., Woodland Hills and Costa Mesa, Calif., 1984-86; systems engrng. mgr., ctrl. ops. mgr. Connecting Point, Calabasas and L.A., Calif., 1986-90; bus. devel. mgr. Computerland, Northridge and Sherman Oaks, Calif., 1990-91; owner Mihir Gandhi and Assocs. and Compudata Mgmt. Systems, Torrance, Calif., 1991—; grad. assoc. Ohio U., Athens, 1982-83; tutor, cons. Datamatics, Bombay, 1982. Mem. Pegasus (sec., treas. 1992, 93, Trophy Champion 1991), Indian Students Assn., MBA Assn., Planning Forum Indsl. Visits (exec. com. 1979-83). Office: Mihir Gandhi and Assocs 3551 Voyager St Ste 201 Torrance CA 90503

GANDHI, OM PARKASH, electrical engineer; b. Multan, Pakistan, Sept. 23, 1934; came to U.S., 1967, naturalized, 1975; s. Gopal Das and Devi Bai (Patney) G.; m. Santosh Nayar, Oct. 28, 1963; children: Rajesh Timmy, Monica, Lena. BS with honors, Delhi U., India, 1952; MSE, U. Mich., 1957, Sc.D., 1961. Rsch. specialist Philco Corp., Blue Bell, Pa., 1960-62; asst. dir. Cen. Electronics Engring. Rsch. Inst., Pilani, Rajasthan, India, 1962-65, dep. dir., 1965-67; prof. elec. engring., rsch. prof. bioengring. U. Utah, Salt Lake City, 1967—; chmn. elec. engring., 1992—; cons. U.S. Army Med. Rsch. and Devel. Command, Washington, 1973-77; cons. to industry and govtl. orgns.; mem. Internat. URSI Commn. B. and K; mem. study sect. on diagnostic radiology NIH, 1978-81. Author: Microwave Engineering and Applications, 1981; editor: Engineering in Medicine and Biology mag., 1987, Electromagnetic Biointeraction, 1989, Biological Effects and Medical Applications of Electromagnetic Energy, 1990; contbr. over 200 articles to profl. jours. Recipient Disting. Rsch. award U. Utah, 1979-80; grantee NSF, NIH, EPA, USAF, U.S. Army, USN, N.Y. State Dept. Health, others. Fellow IEEE (editor Procs. of IEEE Spl. Issue, 1980, co-chmn. com. on RF safety standards 1988—, Tech. Achievement award Utah sect. 1975); mem. Electromagnetics Acad., Bioelectromagnetics Soc. (bd. dirs. 1979-82, 87-90, v.p., pres. 1991—). Office: U Utah Elec Engring Dept 4516 Merrill Engring Salt Lake City UT 84112

GANDSEY, LOUIS JOHN, petroleum and environmental consultant; b. Greybull, Wyo., May 19, 1921; s. John Wellington and Leonora (McLaughlin) G.; m. Mary Louise Alviso, Nov. 10, 1945; children: Mary M., Catherine K., John P., Michael J., Laurie A. AA, Compton Jr. Coll., 1941; BS, U. Calif. Berkeley, 1943; M in Engring., UCLA, 1958. Registered profl. engr., Calif., environ. assessor. With Richfield Oil Corp., L.A., 1943-65, process engr., processing foreman, sr. foreman, mfg. coord., 1943-61, project leader process computer control, 1961-63, light oil oper. supt., 1963-64, asst. refinery supt., 1964-65; mgr. planning Richfield div. Atlantic Richfield Co., L.A., 1966-68, mgr. evaluation products div., L.A., 1968-69, mgr. supply and transp., Chgo., 1969-71, mgr. planning and mgmt. sci., N.Y.C., 1971, mgr. supply and transp., L.A., 1971-72, mgr. coordination and supply, 1972-75, mgr. domestic crude, 1975-77; v.p. refining Lunday-Thagard Oil Co., South Gate, Calif., 1977-82; petroleum cons. World Oil Corp., L.A., 1982-85; gen. cons., 1986—; instr. chem. and petroleum tech. L.A. Harbor Coll., 1960-65; cons. on oil crops, Austria, 1991; U.S. del. in environ. affairs to Joint Inter-Govtl. Com. for Environ. Protection, USSR, 1991, asphalt tech. to Joint Inter-Govtl. Com. for Highway Design CWS, 1992 . Contbr. articles to profl. jours. Active Boy Scouts of Am. Served with C.E., AUS, 1944-45. Mem. AAAS, AICE, Am. Chem. Soc., Pacific Energy Assn., Environ. Assessment Assn.. Home: 2340 Neal Spring Rd Templeton CA 93465-9610

GANGWERE, HEATHER HENDRY, foreign language educator; b. Orange, Calif., Apr. 11, 1964; d. James Hendry and Phila Margaret (Hurter) Acuff; m. Walter Lewis Gangwere, Nov. 22, 1986. BA, U. Redlands, 1986; postgrad., San Jose State U., 1987-90. Cert. tchr., lang. devel. specialist, Calif. Resident asst. U. Redlands, Calif., 1985-86; substitute tchr. San Jose (Calif.) Sch. Dists., 1986-89; tchr. Spanish and ESL Leland High Sch. San Jose Unified Sch. Dist., 1989—, fgn. lang. dept. chair, 1991—; interpreter Youth Unlimited Gospel Outreach, San Dimas, Calif., 1983—. Youth leader Crossroads Bible Ch., San Jose, 1990; participant Pacific Neighbors, San Jose, 1990—. Mem. Mortar Board, Sigma Delta Pi, Pi Lambda Theta, Omicron Delta Kappa. Home: 16055 Ridgecrest Ave Los Gatos CA 95030-4135

GANNATAL, JOSEPH PAUL, electronics engineer; b. Ventura, Calif., Sept. 9, 1955; s. Paul and Janet Mae (Carpenter) G.; m. Sandy Jean Lincoln, Jan. 14, 1984; children: Leonard Troy Garcia, Jennifer Lynn Garcia, Sarah Jean Gannatal, Samantha Leigh Gannatal. BSME, Calif. Polytech. Inst., San Luis Opisbo, 1979; M in Space Systems Tech., Naval Postgrad. Sch., 1987. Indsl. engr. Nat. Semiconductor, Santa Clara, Calif., 1979-81; spl. projects engr. Pacific Missile Test Ctr., Point Mugu, Calif., 1981—, mgr. devel. program, 1986-89, sr. exec. mgr. devel. program, 1990—. Mem. bldg. com. Camarillo Bapt. Ch., 1984-86. Recipient Spl. Achievement award USN, 1982, 84, Letter of Commendation, USN, 1983, Outstanding Svc. award, 1985, 86, 89, 90, 91, 92. Mem. AIAA, ASME, Nat. Space Soc. (pres. Ventura County chpt. 1990-92). Republican.

GANNON, FRANCES VIRGINIA, marketing and sales professional; b. Washington, May 10, 1929; d. Philip and Ruth Pomona (Garvin) Chaffin; m. Vincent DePaul Gannon, Feb. 4, 1974 (div. 1978). BS in Speech, U. So. Miss., 1951; cert., U.S. Army War Coll., 1969. Commd. 2d lt. U.S. Army, 1951, advanced through grades to col.; WAC recruiting officer Wilkes-Barre, Pa., 1952-55; comdg. officer WAC Co., Ft. MacArthur, Calif., 1955-57, Camp Zama, Japan, 1957-59, Ft. Huachuca, Ariz., 1962-63; personnel officer Ft. Meyers, Va., 1959-61; sec. gen. staff Ft. Huachuca, 1963-64; budget officer Office of Dep. Chief of Staff, Washington, 1964-66; with personnel, dept. of Army Pentagon, Washington, 1964-66; sr. advisor Vietnamese Womens Armed Forces, Saigon, 1967-68; chief WAC Recruiting, Hampton, Va., 1969-72; sr. WAC advisor Hdqrs. U.S. Army, Europe, Heidelberg, Fed. Republic. Germany, 1972-73, dir. Office Equal Opportunity, 1973-74, exec. officer for Dep. Chief of Staff, Intelligence, 1974-75; dir. evaluation U.S. Army Intelligence Ctr. & Sch., Ft. Huachuca, Az., 1975-77; retired U.S. Army, 1977; co-owner, operator Charron House Restaurant, Sierra Vista, Ariz., 1975-79; co-owner Fiesta Fabrics, Sierra Vista, Ariz., 1981-84; dir. mktg. and sales Mountain View Inn, Sierra Vista, Ariz., 1987; resident mgr. InnSuites Hotel, 1988-89, resigned, 1989; chief security div. Sierra Vista ops. Unisys Def. Systems, Inc., Sierra Vista, 1990—. Bd. dirs. Forgash House for Abused Wifes, 1987-91, Ariz. Acad., 1988-90; pres. Huachuca Art Assn., 1986-90; precinct committeewoman Cochise County Rep. Com., 1976-90; leader 4-H Club, 1979; coun. mem. City of Sierra Vista, 1983-87. Decorated Legion of Merit, Bronze Star. Mem. The Ret. Officer Assn. (pres. 1979-80), Ariz. Council of Chpts. (sec. 1980-81), WAC Veterans Assn. Republican. Club: 1200 (pres. 1984-85). Home: 947 S Cardinal Ave Sierra Vista AZ 85635-5419

GANS, ERIC LAWRENCE, French language educator; b. N.Y.C., Aug. 21, 1941; s. Irving and Pearl (Fintell) G.; m. Michele Anne Hausser, Sept. 16, 1969 (div. Feb. 1977); 1 child, Georges; m. Monique Andree Roy, Oct. 15, 1977. BA summa cum laude, Columbia Coll., 1960; MA, Johns Hopkins U., 1961, PhD with distinction, 1966. Instr. SUNY, Fredonia, 1965-67; asst. prof. Ind. U., Bloomington, 1967-69; asst. prof. UCLA, 1969-73, assoc. prof., 1973-76, prof. of French, 1976—; chmn. dept. French UCLA, 1974-77, 81-86; vis. prof. Romance Langs. Dept. Johns Hopkins U., 1978. Author: The Discovery of Illusion: Flaubert's Early Works, 1835-37, 1971, Un Pari contre l'histoire: les premieres nouvelles de Mérimée, 1972, Musset et le drame tragique, 1974, Le Paradoxe de Phédre, 1975, Essais d'esthétique paradoxale, 1977, The Origin of Language: A Formal Theory of Representation, 1981, The End of Culture: Toward a Generative Anthropology, 1985, Madame Bovary: The End of Romance, 1989, Science and Faith: The Anthropology of Revelation, 1990, Originary Thinking: Elements of Generative Anthropology, 1993; contbr. articles to profl. jours. Mem. Modern Lang. Assn. Office: UCLA French Dept Los Angeles CA 90024-1550

GANSINGER, JAMES MICHAEL, lawyer; b. Pitts., Dec. 4, 1945; s. Joseph John and Mary Elizabeth (Grace) G.; m. Kelly LYnn Kennedy, July 7, 1990. BA, Bucknell U., 1967; JD, Stanford U., 1970. Bar: Calif., Colo., U.S. Supreme Ct., U.S. Ct. Appeals (8th, 9th, 10th cirs.). Assoc. Davis Graham & Stubbs, Denver, 1971-75, Stephens, Jones, LaFever & Smith, L.A., 1975-77; ptnr. Jones Bell & Simpson, L.A., 1977-81; sr. ptnr. Gansinger Hinshaw & Buckley, L.A., 1981—; bd. dirs. AmEur Holdings, Inc., L.A., StaffPro, Inc., L.A.; arbitrator N.Y. Stock Exch., 1977—, Nat. Assn. Securities Dealers, L.A., 1977—, Am. Arbitration Assn., L.A., 1980—. Mem. bd. visitors Law Sch., Stanford U., Palo Alto, Calif., 1986—. Mem. L.A. Athletic Club, City Club, Braemar Country Club. Office: Gansinger Hinshaw & Buckley 355 S Grand 29th Fl Los Angeles CA 90017

GANTENBEIN, REX EARL, computer science educator; b. Muscatine, Iowa, Feb. 21, 1950; s. Earl Christopher and E. Louise (Hirschi) G.; m. Judith K. Powers, May 13, 1983. BS in Math., Iowa State U., 1972; MS in Computer Sci., U. Iowa, 1983, PhD in Computer Sci., 1986. Asst. prof. dept. computer sci. U. Wyo., Laramie, 1985-91, assoc. prof., 1991—; proposal referee NSF, 1987—; instr. IBM Corp., Boulder, Colo., 1987—; advisor ACM, U. Wyo., 1986—; lectr. in field. Contbr. articles to profl. jours. Recipient Faculty Growth award U. Wyo., Alumni Assn., 1986, Ellbogen Teaching award U. Wyo., 1991; Motorola computer X equipment grantee, 1988, NSF grantee, 1989, Air Force Office of Sci. Rsch. rsch. assoc., 1991, 92, NASA summer rsch. fellow, 1993. Mem. ACM (bd. dirs. reg. programming contest 1990), IEEE, Computer Profls. for Social Responsibility. Democrat. Office: U Wyo PO Box 3682 Laramie WY 82071-3682

GANTZ, NANCY ROLLINS, nurse; b. Buffalo Center, Iowa, Mar. 7, 1949; d. Troy Gaylord and Mary (Emerson) Rollins. Diploma in Nursing, Good Samaritan Hosp. and Med. Ctr., Portland, Oreg., 1973; BSBA, City Univ., 1986; MBA, Kennedy-Western U., 1987, PhD, 1991. Nurse ICU, Good Samaritan Hosp., 1973-75; charge nurse Crestview Convalescent Hosp., Portland, 1975; dir. nursing svcs. Roderick Enterprises, Inc., Portland, 1976-78, Holgate Ctr., Portland, 1978-80; nursing cons. in field of adminstrn., 1980-84; coord. CCU; mgr. ICU/CCU Tuality Community Hosp., Hillsboro, Oreg., 1984-86; head nurse intensive care unit, cardiac surgery unit, coronary care unit, Good Samaritan Hosp. & Med. Ctr., Portland, 1986-88, mgr. critical care units, 1988-92, asst. v.p. patient care svcs., 1992—, dir. heart ctr. Deaconess Med. Ctr., Spokane, Wash., 1992—; mem. speakers bur. Nurses of Am.; mem. task force Oreg. State Health Div. Rules and Regulations Revision for Long Term Health Facilities and Hosps., 1978-79; numerous internat. and nat. speaking presentations. Mem. Am. Nurses Assn. (cert.), Wash. Nurses Assn., Nat. League Nursing, Am. Assn. Critical Care Nurses (pres. elect greater Portland chpt. 1985-86, pres. 1986-87, bd. dirs. 1985—), Am. Heart Assn., Oreg. Heart Assn., Geriatric Nurses Assn. Oreg. (founder, charter pres.), Clackamus Assn. Retarded Citizens, AACN (chpt. cons. region 18 1987-89, mgmt. SIC region 18, 1990—), AONE Coun. Nurse Mgrs. (bd. dirs. Region 9 1991-92, Sigma Theta Tau. Adventist. Home: 722 E Highland Blvd Spokane WA 99203-3307

GANTZER, JOHN CARROLL, insurance company executive; b. Mpls., Sept. 21, 1947; s. Clarence Louis Gantzer and Ruey Elaine (James) Kimball; m. Barbara Jean Spevacek, Apr. 16, 1967 (div. 1981); m. Patricia Ann Magee, Nov. 26, 1983. BA, Gustavus Adolphus Coll., 1969. Trainee St. Paul Fire & Marine, 1969-71; underwriting mgr. Home Ins. Co., Phoenix, Milw. and Denver, 1971-83; asst. v.p. Mission Ins. Co., L.A., 1983-86; asst. v.p., chief underwriting officer Western Employers Ins., Santa Ana, Calif., 1986-87; cons. Mission Am. Ins., L.A., 1987-88; v.p., corp. sec. Condor Ins. Co., El Segundo, Calif., 1988—. Mem. Nat. Profl. Bus. Fraternity, CPCU (pres. south coast chpt.), Alpha Eta of Alpha Kappa Psi. Republican. Home: 37301 Tampa Ct Palmdale CA 93552 Office: Condor Ins Co 2361 Rosecrans Ave El Segundo CA 90245-4707

GANZ, BARBARA CAROL, dean; b. Pitts., Nov. 7, 1949; d. Irving and Doris (Raden) Levy; m. Martin N. Ganz, Mar. 9, 1969; 1 child, Wayne. BA, Ariz. State U., 1971, MA, 1976. Cert. community coll. tchr., Ariz. Asst. prof. Community Coll. of R.I., Lincoln, 1976-85; dir. of ednl. support Palo Alto Coll., San Antonio, 1985-89; dean of student devel. Pima

Community Coll., Tucson, Ariz., 1989—; co-chair U. Ariz./Pima Community Coll. Transfer Coord. Com., Tucson, 1992; cons.-evaluator North Cen. Assn. Colls. and Schs., 1992. Contbr. articles to profl. jours. Chairperson Am. Heart Assn. Campaign, Lincoln, 1985. Mem. Nat. Coun. Student Devel. Office: 8181 E Irvington Tucson AZ 85709-4000

GAPOSCHKIN, PETER JOHN ARTHUR, programmer analyst, physicist; b. Boston, Apr. 5, 1940; s. Sergei Illarionovich and Cecilia Helena (Payne) G. Student Boston U., 1957-58; B.Sc., MIT, 1961; Ph.D., U. Calif.-Berkeley, 1971. Physicist NAVPRO, Sunnyvale, Calif., 1973-75; computer programmer Fleet Num Ocean Ctr., Monterey, Calif., 1975-79; sr. analyst Informatics, Palo Alto, Calif., 1979-80; instr. Merritt Coll., Oakland, Calif., 1980-81, San Francisco City Community Coll., 1981-82; programmer analyst Bur. Mgmt. Info. Systems, San Francisco Pub. Utilities Commn., 1983—; mem. job acquisition com. Experience Unltd., Oakland, 1982-83. Mem. University Avenue Ctr. Council Consumers Coop. Berkeley, 1978-86, Shattuck Ave. Ctr. Council Consumers Coop. of Berkeley, 1987—. Mem. Am. Astron. Soc., Math. Assn. Am., Assn. Computing Machinery. Unitarian. Club: Toastmasters. Home: 1823-1/2 Delaware St Berkeley CA 94703-1328 Office: 414 Mason St Rm 501 5th Fl San Francisco CA 94102-1718

GARAI, TOMA, manufacturing engineer; b. Arad, Romania, May 27, 1935; came to U.S., 1970; s. Carol and Elizabeth G.; m. Khakshour Parvin, 1983; children: Ellis, Benjamin. MS, Politech U., Brasov, Romania, 1957. R&D staff Anderson Desk Co., Ontario, Calif., 1980—. Home: 5519 Ventura Canyon Ave Van Nuys CA 91401

GARAY, ALON A., orthopedic surgeon; b. Aug. 15, 1957; s. Michael and Alice K. G.; m. Patricia Walsh, Sept. 23, 1990. BA, Brown U., 1979; MD, Georgetown U., 1983. Diplomate Am. Bd. Orthopedic Surgery, Nat. Bd. Med. Examiners. Intern N.Y. Med. Coll., N.Y.C., 1983-84, resident, 1984-88; fellow Hosp. Joint Diseases, N.Y.C., 1988-89; commd. USN, 1979—, advanced through grades to lt. comdr.; staff surgeon U.S. Naval Hosp., Rota, Spain, 1987-90, Naval Hosp., San Diego, 1990—. Mem. Am. Acad. Orthopedic Surgeons, Soc. Mil. Surgeons, San Diego County Med. Soc., Sigma Xi (assoc.). Home: 1615 Ocean Front St San Diego CA 92107 Office: 770 Washington St San Diego CA 72103

GARBARINO, JOSEPH WILLIAM, labor arbitrator, economics and business educator; b. Medina, N.Y., Dec. 7, 1919; s. Joseph Francis and Savina M. (Volpone) G.; m. Mary Jane Godward, Sept. 18, 1948; children: Ann, Joan, Susan, Ellen. B.A., Duquesne U., 1942; M.A., Harvard U., 1947, Ph.D., 1949. Faculty U. Calif., Berkeley, 1949—; prof. U. Calif., 1960-88, dir. Inst. Bus. and Econ. Research, 1962-88, prof. emeritus, 1988—; vis. lectr. Cornell U., 1959-60, UCLA, 1949, SUNY, Buffalo, 1972; Fulbright lectr. U. Glasgow, Scotland, 1969; vis. scholar U. Warwick; mem. staff Brookings Instn., 1959-60; vis. lectr. U. Minn., 1978; labor arbitrator. Author: Health Plans and Collective Bargaining, 1960, Wage Policy and Long Term Contracts, 1962, Faculty Bargaining: Change and Conflict, 1975, Faculty Bargaining in Unions in Transition. Served with U.S. Army, 1942-45, 51-53. Decorated Bronze Star. Democrat. Roman Catholic. Home: 7708 Ricardo Ct El Cerrito CA 94530-3344

GARBER, JEROLD ALLAN, broadcasting executive; b. Peoria, Ill., Aug. 10, 1942; s. Allan Edward and Mary Maxine (King) G.; m. Judith Jane Clause, June 18, 1966 (div. 1977); 1 child, Timothy; m. Susan Annette Colonese, May 21, 1982; stepchildren: Sara, Seth, Jason. BSE, No. Ill. U., 1964; MA, U. Mich., 1969. tchr., mgr. Sta. WHFH-FM, Homewood-Flossmoor High Sch., Flossmoor, Ill., 1964-79; tchr. Prairie State Coll., Chicago Heights, Ill., 1970-79; dir. telecommunications Central Wyo. Coll., Riverton, 1979—; gen. mgr. Sta. KCWC-FM-TV, Riverton, 1979-85; gen. mgr. Idaho Ednl. Pub. Broadcasting System, 1985—; bd. dirs. Rocky Mountain Corp. for Pub. Broadcasting, 1980-88, pres., 1987-88; chmn. bd. dirs. Linknet, Inc., 1990—; cons. in pub. radio and T.V. NDEA fellow, 1969. Writer recreational computer programs, 1985—. Staff officer USCG Aux., 1985—. Mem. Western Ednl. Soc. Telecommunications (bd. dirs. 1979-86, pres. 1986-87), Alpha Psi Omega, Pi Kappa Delta. Democrat. Methodist. Avocations: boating, computer programming, acting and directing. Home: 1515 Shenandoah Dr Boise ID 83712-6667 Office: Sta KAID-TV 1910 University Dr Boise ID 83725-0001

GARBER, MORRIS JOSEPH, statistical consultant, computer programmer; b. N.Y.C., Nov. 6, 1912; s. Isidor and Ethel (Shevack) G.; m. Gloria Ruth Routman, Mar. 7, 1943; children: David I., Diana L. BS in Zoology, Columbia U., 1933; PhD in Genetics, Tex. A&M U., 1951. Asst. prof. genetics Tex. A&M U., College Station, 1947-56; prof. statistics, biometrician U. Calif., Riverside, 1956-80, emeritus, 1980—; statistician, head statis. lab. Internat. Inst. Tropical Agr., 1974-76; cons. research planning and statistics Inter-Am. Inst. Agrl. Scis., Brazilian Enterprise for Agrl. Research, Nat. Ctr. Research in Rice and Beans, 1980-81. Served with Med. Service Corps, AUS, 1941-45. Fellow AAAS, Tex. Acad. Sci.; mem. Am. Genetics Assn., Am. Statis. Assn., Assn. Computing Machinery, Biometric Soc., Sigma Xi. Democrat. Jewish. Club: B'nai B'rith. Home: 3504 Bryce Way Riverside CA 92506-3160 Office: U Calif Riverside Dept Stats 900 University Ave Riverside CA 92521

GARBER, ZEV, Jewish studies educator; b. Mar. 1, 1941; s. Morris Benjamin and Pearl Garber; m. Lois Koppelman, Dec. 26, 1963 (div. Nov. 1975); children: Asher, Dorit; m. Susan Adriana Ehrlich, Oct. 4, 1985. BA, CUNY, Bronx, 1962; MA, U. So. Calif., 1970. Prof. Jewish studies La Valley Coll., Van Nuys, Calif., 1970—. Editor: Methodology in the Academic Teaching of Judaism, 1986, Methodology in the Academic Teaching of the Holocaust, 1988; editor Studies in the Shoah, 1991—. Mem. Nat. Assn. Profs. Hebrew (pres. 1988-90, Recognition award 1990), Am. Acad. Religion, Soc. Bibl. Lit., Am. Oriental Soc., Assn. Jewish Studies. Jewish Orthodox. Office: La Valley Coll 5800 Fulton Ave Van Nuys CA 91401-4062

GARCIA, ALFRED ROBERT, small business owner; b. L.A., Oct. 15, 1957; s. Alfred Daniel and Amelia (Sandoval) G; m. Margaret Rodriguez; children: Nicole Marie, Natalie Michelle. BS, Loyola Marymount U., L.A., 1979. Salesman Roadway Express, Inc., L.A., 1979-83; owner, pres. Alto Systems, Inc., La Mirada, Calif., 1983—; pres. Angel's Bay Trading Co., Inc., 1985—. Sustaining mem. Rep. Nat. Com. Mem. Phi Kappa Theta. Republican. Roman Catholic. Office: 15500 Valley View Ave La Mirada CA 90638-5230

GARCIA, CASIMIRO GILBERT, retired aerospace company technical staff member; b. Salt Lake, N.Mex., Jan. 13, 1930; s. Casimiro and Carolina (Aragón) G.; m. Mary Ellen Coady, Aug. 16, 1978; 1 child: Casimiro Thomas. BBA, Northwestern U., 1968; MBA, Keller Grad. Sch. Mgmt., Chgo., 1980. Sales rep. Consol. Packaging Corp., Chgo., 1963-64; mgr. prodn. control Bemiss-Jason, Inc., Chgo., 1964-67; computer programmer Internat. Harvester Co., Broadview, Ill., 1967-68; computer systems analyst Harris Trust and Savs. Bank, Chgo., 1968-69; sr. computer systems analyst Argonne (Ill.) Nat. Lab., 1969-83; mem. tech. staff The Aerospace Corp., El Segundo, Calif., 1983-90. Counselor Aerospace Corp. Youth Motivation Task Force, San Pedro, Calif., 1989—, Aerospace Corp. Adopt-A-Sch. Program, Carson, Calif., 1990—. Democrat. Roman Catholic. Office: The Aerospace Corp 2350 E El Segundo Blvd El Segundo CA 90245-4691

GARCIA, CURT JONATHAN, company executive; b. Whittier, Calif., Mar. 27, 1960; s. Raymond Arthur and Yvonne Emily (Bailey) G.; m. Cynthia Louise Guerra, Sept. 5, 1981; children: David, Denise, Natalie. BA in Bus. Econs., U. Calif., Santa Barbara, 1983; MS in Procurement and Acquisition Mgmt., Northrop U., L.A., 1991. Cert. profl. contracts mgr. Adminstr. New Life Christian Sch., Santa Barbara, 1983-85; contract acct. Mission Rsch. Corp., Santa Barbara, 1985-88; contr. Pneu Devices, Inc., Santa Barbara, 1988-90; treas., dir. contracts Illgen Simulation Tech., Inc., Santa Barbara, 1990-92; CFO, contracts mgr. Environ. Mgmt. Cons., Inc., Lompoc, Calif., 1992—. Mem. Nat. Contract Mgmt. Assn.

GARCIA, EDWARD J., federal judge; b. 1928. AA, Sacramento City Coll., 1951; LLB, U. Pacific, 1958. Dep. dist. atty. Sacramento County, 1959-64, supervising dep. dist. atty., 1964-69, chief dep. dist. atty., 1969-72; judge Sacramento Mcpl. Ct., 1972-84, U.S. Dist. Ct. (ea. dist.) Calif., Sacramento, 1984—. Served with U.S. Army Air Corps, 1946-49. Office: US Dist Ct 2546 US Courthouse 650 Capitol Mall Sacramento CA 95814-4708*

GARCIA, FLORENCIO OSCAR, library and information specialist, publisher; b. Buenos Aires, Argentina, Mar. 13, 1934; came to U.S., 1970; s. Florencio and Aurora (Santillan) G.; m. Ursula Ruth Noher, Mar. 8, 1962; children: Daniel Oscar, Paul Pared. A in Engrng., U. N.Mex., 1981, BA in Spanish, 1984, MA in Edn., 1988, PhD in Latin Am. Studies, 1993. Ops. engr. King Plz. and Marina, N.Y.C., 1970-71; libr. tech. Geneva Coll., Beaver Falls, Pa., 1971-78; ops. engr. U. N.Mex., Albuquerque, 1979-85, libr. and info. specialist, 1985—; libr. organizer Johnson Ctr. U. N.Mex., Albuquerque, 1985. Author: LIbrarian Puzzle: MARC etc, 1988, L.A. Book Trade Consultant, 1990, Diction.Cosmop.Comput., 1991, Tango: A Bibliography, 1991. Poll worker N.Mex. State, Albuquerque, 1992. Mem. Seminar Acquisition of Latin Am. Libr. Materials (charter). Home: 413 Pennsylvania NE Albuquerque NM 87108 Office: General Libr Univ N Mex Albuquerque NM 87131

GARCIA, JOSE ZEBEDEO, political science educator; b. St. Helena, Calif., Jan. 2, 1945; s. Jose Zebedeo and Marjorie Louise (Lathrop) G.; m. Barbara Hiller, Apr. 1973 (div. Dec. 1976); m. Olivia Nevarez, Apr. 23, 1984; children: Monica Luisa, Cristina. BA, Occidental Coll., 1966; MA, Tufts U., 1968; PhD, U. N.Mex., 1974. Asst. prof. Calif. State U., Chico, 1972-75; asst. to assoc. prof. N.Mex. State U., Las Cruces, 1975—; disting. vis. prof. U.S. Army Sch. of the Americas, Ft. Benning, Ga., 1989-91; speaker U.S. State Dept., various Latin Am. countries, 1984—; cons. various polit. campaigns, 1979—; observer Paraguayan elections, Asuncion, 1989. Contbr. articles to profl. jours. Party chmn. Dona Ana County Dem. Party, Las Cruces, 1979-83; dir. Ctr. for Latin Am. Studies N.Mex. State U., 1991—. Fulbright fellow, Ecuador, 1966-67; Tchr. of Yr. award U.S. Army Sch. of the Ams. Mem. Lat. Am. Studies Assn., Am. Polit. Sci. Assn., Rocky Mountain Latin Am. Studies Coun. Home: 4709 Falcon Dr Las Cruces NM 88001 Office: NMex State U Dept of Govt PO Box 3LAS University Park NM 88003

GARCIA, LLOYD BERT, organizational analyst, educator; b. Greeley, Colo., Oct. 28, 1957; s. Francisco Javier and Ramona Juanita (Flores) G.; m. Carolyn Grace Munyon, Feb. 19, 1977; children: Joseph Anthony, Frances Jean. BBA, U. N.Mex., Albuquerque, 1981. Mgr. Double Chees Corp., Albuquerque, 1981-83; customer svc. rep. Pub. Svc. Co. of N.Mex., Albuquerque, 1983-86; customer acctg. rep. PNM, Albuquerque, 1986-87, supr. EDIT, 1987-90, organizational analyst, 1990—; cons. Albuquerque Bd. of Edn./Pub. Schs., 1988—; facilitator Focus Found., Albququerque, 1990—. PNM key campaign person United Way, Albuquerque, 1990; v.p. Ghetto Boys Vol. Group, Los Alamos, N.Mex., 1973—; pres. Lowell Parent Adv. Coun., Albuquerque, 1986-87, Lowell Parent Faculty Orgn., Albuquerque, 1988-89; chmn. South Region Citizens Adv. Coun., Albuquerque, 1988-89, 90—; mem. Nat. Assessment Gov. Bd. writing achievement levels setting group Dept. Edn., 1992. Home: 1929 Sunshine Ter SE Albuquerque NM 87106-3932 Office: Pub Svc Co NMex Alvarado Sq MS 2516 Albuquerque NM 87158

GARCIA, MARTA IRMA, civilian military official; b. Alamo, Tex., Aug. 17, 1946; d. Modesto and Raquel (Esquivel) Gonzalez; m. Evaristo T. Garcia, June 18, 1965; children: Evaristo T. Jr., David, Reuben. AA, U. Md., Aviano, Italy, 1983; BS, Golden Gate U., Edwards AFB, Calif., 1986, MBA, 1989. Clk. Office of Air Force, Edwards AFB, 1985-87, cost analyst, compt., 1987—; Hispanic program mgr., Edwards AFB, 1988—. Vol. Spl. Olympics, Edwards AFB, 1987; mem. Hispanic coun. United Way, Palmdale, Calif., 1991; mem. intercultural and women's studies com. Antelope Valley Coll., Lancaster, Calif., 1990. Mem. NAFE, Am. Soc. Mil. Compts., Inst. Cost Analysis (cert. profl.), Image (v.p. 1989—), Antelope Valley Latin Profl. Assn. Home: 10740 Crab Apple Ln California City CA 93505-2385 Office: AFFTC/ACC Edwards AFB CA 93523-5000

GARCIA, MARY JANE MADRID, state legislator; b. Dona Ana, N.Mex., Dec. 24, 1936; d. Isaac C. and Victoria M. Garcia. A.A., San Francisco City Coll., 1956; B.S., N.Mex. State U., 1982, B.A. in Anthropology, 1983, M.A. in Anthropology, 1985. Interpretor, translator to USAF Capt., Hotel Balboa, Madrid, Spain, 1962-63; exec. sec. to city mgr. City of Las Cruces, N.Mex., 1964-65; adminstrv. asst. RMK-BRJ, Saigon, Socialist Republic Vietnam, 1966-72; owner Billy the Kid Gift Shop, Mesilla, N.Mex., 1972-81; pres., owner Victoria's Night Club, Las Cruces, 1981—; state senator Dist. 38, N.Mex.; with archaeol. excavations N.Mex. State U. Anthropology Dept., summer 1982, spring 1983. Bd. dirs., sec-treas. Dona Ana Mutual Domestic Water Assn.; mem. Subarea Coun. Health Systems Agy., 1979; bd. dirs. Sun Country Savings Bank, Las Cruces, 1985; treas. Toney Anaya for U.S. Senate, 1978; active Toney Anaya for N.Mex. Gov., 1979-82. Mem. N.Mex. Retail Liquor Assn. Democrat. Roman Catholic. Home: Isaac Garcia St PO Box 22 Dona Ana NM 88032-0022 Office: Senate of N Mex State Capitol Santa Fe NM 87503

GARCIA, RAHN HOWARD, county counsel; b. Alemeda, Calif., Aug. 7, 1953; s. Ralph and Bobbie Lou (Dixon) G.; m. Thelma Marie Lax, June 8, 1991. BA, U. Calif., Riverside, 1974; JD, U. Calif., Davis, 1985. Bar: Calif. 1987. Adminstrv. asst. Santa Cruz (Calif.) Bd. Suprs., 1975-78; health planner Mid-Coast Health Systems, Santa Cruz, 1978-79; asst. dir. Psychol. Field Program, U. Calif., Santa Cruz, 1979-81; state field coord. Calif. Dem. Party, San Francisco, 1985-87; asst. county counsel Santa Cruz County, 1987—. Co-founder Save Soquel (Calif.), 1973; bd. dirs. Eschaton Found., Santa Cruz, 1980, Yes on "O" Com., Santa Cruz, 1979. Calif. State Senate fellow, 1982. Democrat. Office: Office of County Counsel 701 Ocean St Rm 505 Santa Cruz CA 95060

GARCIA, STEPHEN GREGORY, college vice-chancellor; b. Phoenix, Apr. 13, 1947; s. Leo Marquez and Barbara (Saavedra) G.; m. Yolanda Gonzalez, June 23, 1967; children: Leo Anthony, Barbara Christina. BS in Bus. Adminstrn. and Mktg., No. Ariz. U., 1969; MBA in Fin., Nat. U., San Diego, 1977; postgrad., Calif. Community Coll., 1988. Store mgr. W.T. Grant Co., N.Y.C., 1970-75; spl. asst. material control and warehousing San Diego Unified Sch. Dist., 1975-77; dir. fiscal svcs. Newark (Calif.) Unified Sch. Dist., 1977-79; asst. bus. mgr. Covina (Calif.) Unified Sch. Dist., 1979-83; asst. supt. bus. svcs., asst. bus. mgr. Long Beach (Calif.) Unified Sch. Dist., 1983-88, asst. supt. fin. svcs./contr., 1988-89; br. dir. food svcs. L.A. Unified Sch. Dist., 1989-90; vice chancellor, v.p. bus. ops. and fiscal affairs Rancho Santiago C.C. Dist., Santa Ana, Calif., 1990—; mem. liability and property ins., mem. underwriting com. Statewide Assn. Community Colls. Joint Powers Authority, 1990—; chief bus. ofcls. rep. basic skills task force Calif. C.C. Chancellor's Office, 1991—. Ex-officio mem. bd. dirs. Rancho Santiago Coll. Found., 1990—, mem. fin.-investment com., 1990—; mem. project area com. City of Santa Ana Ednl. and Community Facilities Redevel. Plan, 1992—; mem. Commn. on Legislation and Fin. Community Coll. League Calif., 1992—. Recipient Appreciation for Svc. in edn. award Long Beach Unified Sch. Dist., 1989; Commending Svc. in Edn. awards Calif. State Assembly, 1990, Calif. State Senate, 1990, Commending Dedicated Svc. award L.A. Unified Sch. Dist., 1990, Proclamation of Commendation County of Orange, 1990, Commendation for Acad. Excellence, City of Santa Ana, 1990. Mem. Nat. U. Alumni Assn. (life), No. Ariz. U. Alumni Assn., Calif. Assn. Sch. Bus. Ofcls. (past pres. So. sect. 1987-88, mem. fin. com. 1988—, Commending Outstanding Svc. Sch. Bus. 1987), Assn. Calif. C.C. Adminstrs., Assn. Chief Bus. Ofcls. (Calif. C.C. dists.), Nat. Assn. Coll. and Univ. Bus. Ofcls., Nat. Coun. C.C. Bus. Ofcls., Western Assn. Coll. and Univ. Bus. Ofcls., Old Ea. Conf. Bus. Ofcls., Hispanic C. of C. of Orange County, Santiago Philanthropic Club. Democrat. Roman Catholic. Office: Rancho Santiago C C Dist 17th at Bristol St Santa Ana CA 92706

GARCIA-BORRAS, THOMAS, oil company executive; b. Barcelona, Spain, Feb. 2, 1926; came to U.S., 1955, naturalized, 1961; s. Thomas and Teresa (Borras-Jarque) Garcia-Julian; M.S., Nat. U. Mex., 1950; postgrad. Rice U., 1955-56; m. Alia Castellanos Lima, Apr. 30, 1952; children—Erik, Angelica, Laureen, Cliff. Chief chemist Petroleos Mexicanos, Veracruz, Mex., 1950-55; research engr. Monsanto, Texas City, Tex., 1956-60; pilot plant mgr. Cabot and Foster Grant Co., 1960-69; engring. mgr. Signal Chem. Co., Houston, 1969-71; mgmt. and engring. cons., Covina, Calif., 1971-73; project mgr. Occidental Petroleum Co., Irvine, Calif., 1973-79; fleet and indsl. mgr. internat. ops. Wynn Oil Co., Fullerton, Calif., 1979-87; dir. export Sta-Lube, Inc., Rancho Dominguez, Calif., 1987-91; pres. U.S. Products Corp., Las Vegas, Nev. Mem. Internat. Mktg. Assn., Am. Inst. Chem. Engrs., Am. Chem. Soc. Author: Manual for Improving Boiler and Furnace Performance, 1983; contbr. articles to profl. jours. Home: 1430 E Adams Park Dr Covina CA 91724-2925 Office: 516 South Fourth St Las Vegas NV 89101

GARCIA-BUNUEL, LUIS, neurologist; b. Madrid, Spain, Feb. 24, 1931; s. Pedro Garcia and Concepcion Bunuel; came to U.S., 1956, naturalized, 1965; B.A., Universidad de Zaragoza, 1949, B.S., 1949, M.D., 1955; m. Virginia M. Hile, June 30, 1960. Intern, Universidad De Zaragoza Hosp. Clinico, 1955-56 resident in neurology Georgetown U., Washington, 1956-59; NIH fellow in neurochemistry dept. pharmacology, Washington U., St. Louis, 1959-61; practice medicine specializing in neurology St. Louis, 1959-61; instr. neurology Jefferson Med. Coll., Phila., 1961-64, asst. prof. neurology, 1964-67; asst. prof. neurology U. N.Mex., Albuquerque, 1967-72; chief neurology service VA Hosp. Portland, Oreg., 1972; asso. prof. neurology, U. Oreg. Health Center, 1972-84; chief staff Phoenix VA Med. Ctr., 1984—. Diplomate Am. Bd. Neurology and Psychiatry. Fellow Am. Acad. Neurology; mem. AAAS, Am. Soc. Neurochemistry, Oreg. Neuropsychiat. Soc., Portland Myasthenia Gravis Assn. (med. adv. bd.), Sigma Xi, Phi Kappa Phi. Contbr. articles to profl jours. Office: VA Med Ctr 7th Rd Phoenix AZ 85034

GARCIA-WITKOWSKI, PHYLLIS JOSEPHINE, early childhood specialist, headstart consultant; b. Chgo., Aug. 21, 1934; d. Peter Thomas and Louise Phyllis (Smietanski) Witkowski; m. Jesse Garcia, Apr. 14, 1951; children: Kenneth, Thomas, Nancy, Janet, Susan. AA, Daley Coll., Chgo., 1982, AAS, 1983; BA in Edn., Roosevelt U., 1985; MS in Edn., Chgo. State U., 1987. Early childhood tchr., community worker McDowell Settlement, Chgo., 1950-55, youth leader, 1963-67; adminstrv. asst. May D&F, Denver, 1972-77; tchr. U. Chgo. Lab. Sch., 1985-86; tchr. early childhood intervention program Denver Pub. Schs., Chgo., 1988-91; child devel. assoc. Rep. Coun. for Early Childhood Profl. Recognition, Washington, 1986—, Headstart program; ednl. cons. Dept. Health, Edn., Welfare;. Leader Girl Scouts U.S., Chgo., 1963—. Mem. Assn. for Childhood Edn. Internat., Nat. Assn. for Edn. Young Children, Assn. for Supervision and Curriculum Instrn., Assn. for Child Care Cons. Internat. Democrat. Roman Catholic. Home: 709 S Leyden St Denver CO 80224-1439

GARDELLA, DAVID EDWARD, magazine editor; b. Boston, Oct. 13, 1944; s. Joseph Warren and Elena (Shinn) G. BA, Harvard U., 1967; MA, U. Durham, Eng., 1970. Editor Excellence mag. Ross Pub., Novato, Calif. Office: Ross Periodicals 42 Digital Dr Ste 5 Novato CA 94949

GARDENHIRE, DONALD PAUL, application engineer; b. Wichita, Kans., Sept. 16, 1955; s. Donald Lee and Eleanor (McLeod) G.; m. Karen Ladawn Holland, June 20, 1992. AS in Computer Sci., Leeward C.C., 1983. Test engr. Verbatim Corp., Sunnyvale, Calif., 1984-87; sr. application engr. Data Tech. Corp., Santa Clara, Calif., 1987-89; mktg. mgr. Data Tech. Corp., Milpitas, Calif., 1989-90; sales engr. Costar Inc., Cupertino, Calif., 1990-92; sr. application engr. Standard Microsystems Corp., San Jose, Calif., 1992—. With USNR, 1980—.

GARDIN, JOHN GEORGE, II, psychologist; b. Renton, Wash., Jan. 5, 1949; s. John George and Charlotte (Larabee) G.; m. Dana Rothrock, Oct. 22, 1986; children: Greg, Gina, Bret; 1 stepchild, Angie West. BS in Chemistry, Seattle U., 1971; BS in Psychology, U. Wash., 1972; MS in Psychology, Portland State U., 1975; PhD in Psychology, U. Tenn., 1986. Lic. psychologist. Clinician Luth. Family Svcs., Portland, Oreg., 1978-80; mental health specialist Probation Dept. Oreg. State, Roseburg, 1980-81; exec. dir. ADAPT, Roseburg, 1981-85; psychologist, ptnr. South Coast Psychol., Irvine, Calif., 1986-91; assoc. prof. psychiatry U. Calif. Irvine, Dana Point, Calif., 1988-90; med. dir. Chem. Dependency Charter Hosp., Corona, Calif., 1990-91; ptnr. LifeOne, Irvine, 1991-92; pvt. practice psychology Newport Beach, Calif., 1991—; psychologist, founder, clin. dir. Genesis Psychol. Assocs., Newport Beach, 1992—; bd. dirs. Kangaroo Kids Ctr. Medically Fragile Children, 1992—. Pres. Alcohol/Drug Program Dirs. of Oreg., 1984; bd. dirs. Oreg. State Coun. on Alcoholism, 1983; mem. Counselors Credentials Task Force, Oreg., 1984. Mem. APA, Calif. State Psychol. Assn., Am. Athletic Union, Japan Karate-Do Fedn. Office: Genesis Psychol Assocs 200 Newport Center Dr Ste 301 Newport Beach CA 92660

GARDINER, D. BRUCE, lawyer; b. Bremerton, Wash., 1942; s. Arthur P. and Jeanne D. G.; m. K.K. Peterson, 1980; children: Todd, Kevin. BA, U. Wash., 1964; JD, U. Puget Sound, 1976. Bar: Wash., U.S. Dist. Ct. (ea. and we. dists.), Wash., 9th Cir. Ct. Appeals. Ptnr. Gardiner & McKibbin, Bellevue, Wash., 1976-84; prin. The Gardiner Law Firm, Kirkland, Wash., 1984—; systems operator Legal Access in Wash. B.B.S., 1990—. Office: The Gardiner Law Firm 12040-98 Ave NE Ste 101 Kirkland WA 98034

GARDINER, NANCY ELIZABETH, hydrologist and hydrogeologist consultant; b. Boston, June 22, 1964; d. Henry Louis and Elizabeth Mary (Getek) Gorczyca; m. Michael Aaron Gardiner, Aug. 19, 1989. BA in Geology magna cum laude, Smith Coll., 1986; MS in Geology, U. Wis., 1988. Project hydrogeologist Warzyn Engrng., Madison, Wis., 1988-89; sr. project scientist Woodward-Clyde Cons., Oakland, Calif., 1989—. Contbr. articles to profl. jours. Mem. Am. Water Resources Assn., Sigma Xi, Phi Beta Kappa. Democrat. Home: 6518 Gwin Rd Oakland CA 94611 Office: Woodward Clyde Cons 500 12th St Ste 100 Oakland CA 94607

GARDNER, A. BARCLAY, state economic and environmental development executive, consultant and advicate; b. Spanish Fork, Utah, Jan. 25, 1930; s. Archibald Barclay and Virginia (Williams) G.; m. Renee Wilkey, Feb. 16, 1951; children: Kristie Gardner Mikstas, Gregory Barclay, Janeanne Gardner. BS, Brigham Young U., 1954, MS, 1956. Supr., mgr. Utah Dept. Employment Security, Provo, Vernal, and Salt Lake City, 1954-75, dir. adminstr. svcs., Salt Lake City, 1975-78, exec. dir., 1978-86, gov.'s adminstrv. asst., 1986-87, exec. dir. State Dept. Adminstrv. Svcs., 1987; gov's. exec. asst., 1987-88, gov.'s compaign staff, 1988-89; dep., exec. dir. Dept. of Community and Econ. Devel., Salt Lake City, 1989-92. Pres. Interstate Conf. Employment Security Agencies, 1982-83, bd. dirs., 1979-84. Mem. Utah Job Tng. Coordinating Coun., 1983-86, Utah Gov.'s Coun. Econ. Advisers, 1981-84, Nat. Vets. Planning and Coordinating Com., 1984-86, Utah Commn. on Efficiency and Effectiveness in Govt., 1985-86, Practitioners Task Force Nat. Commn. Employment Policy, 1984-86; bd. dirs. Utah br. Nat. Alliance Bus., 1979-80. With U.S. Army, 1950-52, Korea. Mem. Am. Legion. Mormon. Home: 2805 Marcus Rd Salt Lake City UT 84119-4510

GARDNER, AUTREY THADDEUS, JR., industrial technology educator; b. Scottsboro, Ala., Aug. 5, 1939; s. Autrey Thaddeus and Faye Louise (Kennamer) G.; m. Joyce Elva Keel; children: Tracey Anne, Autrey Thaddeus III. BSBA, U. Ala., 1962; postgrad., U. N.D., 1967-70; MA in Communications, U. No. Colo., 1983; postgrad., U. Wy., 1987—. Commd. 2d lt. USAF, Amarillo AFB, Tex., 1962; advanced through grades to major USAF, various locations, 1972; chief of plans 351st Strategic Missile Wing, Whiteman AFB, Mo., 1973-74, supr. maintenance, 1974-76; maintenance staff officer 3901st Strategic Missile Squadron, Vandenberg AFB, Calif., 1976-80; dir. tng. 90th Strategic Missile Wing, F.E. Warren AFB, Wyo., 1980-83; ret. USAF, 1983; asst. prof. So. Ill. U., F.E. Warren AFB, Wyo., 1983—, faculty rep., 1983—. Contbr. articles to profl. jours. Mem. Nat. Assn. Indsl. Technologists, Inst. Indsl. Engrs., Am. Soc. Safety Engrs., Air Force Assn., Ret. Officers Assn. (pres. 1993), Warren AFB Officers Club (bd. dirs. 1982-83), Phi Kappa Phi, Kappa Delta Pi. Republican. Mem. Ch. of Christ. Home: 3300 Carey Ave Cheyenne WY 82001-1269 Office: So Ill U 90 MSSQ/MSE F E Warren AFB WY 82005

GARDNER, CLYDE EDWARD, health care executive, consultant, educator; b. Steubenville, Ohio, Oct. 8, 1931; s. Peter D. and Louella Mary (Gillespie) G.; m. Patricia Jackson, Oct. 4, 1953 (div. Dec. 1977); 1 child, Bruce Stephen. BA, San Francisco State U., 1969, MS, 1971. Adminstr. Gardner Convalescent Hosp., Napa, Calif., 1955-68; exec. dir. Haight Ashbury Free Med. Clinic, San Francisco, 1970-71; lectr. San Francisco State U., 1969-71; dir. planning and rsch. div. N. Country Com. on Area Wide Health Planning, Canton, N.Y., 1971-77; prof. Gov.'s State U., University

Park, Ill., 1977-83; sr. ptnr. Health Care Cons., Park Forest, Ill., 1983-86; exec. dir. Mahoning Shenango Area Health Edn. Network, Youngstown, Ohio, 1986-90; pres., chief exec. officer Mahoney Edn. and Tng. Network, Youngstown, Ohio, 1990-92; pres., CEO Health Sci. Assocs., Tucson, 1992—; bd. dirs. rec. sect. Mahoning Shenango Area Health Edn. Network, Youngstown, 1986-90; adj. prof. SUNY, Canton, 1975-76, Youngstown State U., 1987—. Author: Data Book for Health and Institutional Planning, 1981; author of numerous pub. health planning, health edn. studies and funded pvt., state and fed. health care grants, 1971-90. Pres. Found. I Ctr. for Human Devel., Harvey, Ill., 1978-83, U. Profls. of Ill., Chgo., 1982-83; bd. dirs. Blue Cross/Blue Shield Drug and Alcohol Benefit Study, Chgo., 1980-83. Recipient Recognition award Ill. Dangerous Drugs Commn., 1980, 81, Outstanding Svc. award U. Profls. Ill., 1983-84, Outstanding Svc. award Ill. Fedn. Tchrs., 1983. Democrat.

GARDNER, COLIN RAYMOND, writer, critic; b. Isleworth, Eng., Oct. 15, 1952; came to U.S., 1975; s. Frederick William and Vera Annie (Mappin) G. BA with honors, St. John's Coll., Cambridge, Eng., 1975, MA with honors, 1979; MA, UCLA, 1977, postgrad., 1992—. Mng. editor Synapse Internat. Electronic Music, L.A., 1978-79; music critic L.A. (Calif.) Times, 1982-84; art editor, critic Calif. Mag., L.A., 1985-88; art critic Art Forum Internat., N.Y.C., 1985-92, L.A. (Calif.) Times, 1985-88; art editor, critic The Reader, L.A., 1986-88; grad. advisor Art Ctr. Coll. Design, Pasadena, Calif., 1988-93; lectr. Sch. of the Art Inst. Chgo., 1988, UCLA, L.A., 1988-93. Co-author: (catalog) Hans Burkhart, 1984, Wallace Berman, 1992, Mike Kelley, 1993; editor: (art quarterly) Visions, 1988. Recipient scholarship St. John's Coll., Cambridge, 1972, fellowship UCLA, 1992. Mem. Nat. Writers Union, Coll. Art Assn., Soc. Cinematic Studies. Home: 1015 N Edinburgh Ave # 2 West Hollywood CA 90046

GARDNER, HOMER JAY, electrical engineer; b. El Paso, Tex., Apr. 4, 1942; s. George R. and Faye E. (Folkers) G.; m. Roxy Diane Tolley, Jan. 29, 1966; children: Roger, Shannon, Stefanie. BSEE, Brigham Young U., 1968; MS, Colo. State U., 1973. Devel. engr. IBM Corp., Boulder, Colo., 1968-90; sr. engr. Exabyte Corp., Boulder, 1990—. Patentee in field. Mem. Colo. State Electronics Adv. Com., Denver, 1980-83, chmn., 1982. Mem. IEEE. Republican. Mormon. Home: 8138 Captains Ln Longmont CO 80501-7727 Office: Exabyte 1745 38th St Boulder CO 80301-2630

GARDNER, LEONARD BURTON, II, industrial automation engineer; b. Lansing, Mich., Feb. 16, 1927; s. Leonard Burton and Lillian Marvin (Frost) G.; m. Barbara Jean Zivi, June 23, 1950; children: Karen Sue, Jeffrey Frank. B.Sc. in Physics, UCLA, 1951; M.Sc., Golden State U., 1953, Sc.D. in Engring., 1954; M.Sc. in Computer Sci, Augustana Coll., Rock Island, Ill., 1977. Registered profl. engr.; cert. mfg. engr. Instrumentation engr. govt. and pvt. industry, 1951-89; prof. and dir. Ctr. for Automated Integrated Mfg., 1982—; with computerized systems Naval Electronic Systems Engring. Ctr., San Diego, 1980-82; founder, dir. Automated Integrated Mfg., San Diego; cons. govt. agys. and industry, lectr., adj. prof. vaious univs. and colls., sci. advisor state and nat. legislators, 1980—, speaker in field. Author: Computer Aided Robotics Center; editor: Automated Manufacturing. Contbg. author: Instrumentation Handbook, 1981; contbr. numerous articles to tech. jours. Recipient award U.S. Army. Fellow IEEE; sr. mem. Soc. Mfg. Engrs. (Pres.'s award 1984); mem. ASTM, Nat. Soc. Profl. Engrs., Calif. Soc. Profl. Engrs., Sigma Xi. Home: 10767 Jamacha Blvd # 90 Spring Valley CA 91978-1849

GARDNER, MARSHA LOU STULL, business and organization consultant; b. Joliet, Ill., Sept. 18, 1942; d. Oland Glenn and Lucille (Poates) Stull; m. M. David Gardner, Dec. 31, 1964 (dec. June 1982); children: Brian John, Paul Edmund. Assoc. degree, Joliet (Ill.) Jr. Coll., 1962; cert. mgmt., U. Okla., 1990. Owner Creative Marble Design, Tualatin, Oreg., 1977-82; CEO Tualatin C. of C., 1982-85, Big Bear C. of C., Big Bear Lake, Calif., 1985, Wilsonville (Oreg.) C. of C., 1987-91, Cornerstone Consulting and Assn. Mgmt., Tualatin, Oreg., 1991—. Founder Waverly Children's Home/Guild, Tualatin, 1974; coord. Wilsonville Innovative Transit Assn., 1988, Vision 2020 (Econ. Devel. Workshop), 1989; mem. budget com. City of Tualatin, 1988-91; tour guide chair Canada Days, 1989-90. Recipient Rose City award Wash. County Visitors Assn., 1991. Mem. Oreg. Chamber Execs. (grantee 1988), Oreg. Tourism Alliance (visitor svcs. com.), Small Community Tourism Devel. (coordinating team, grantee 1990), U.S. C. of C. (exec. counselling corps 1990), Portland/Oreg. Visitors Assn., Clackmas Associated C. of C. (v.p. 1990-92, Most Valuable Person 1988), Washington County Visitors Assn. (bd. dirs. 1989-93), Wilsonville Sister City Assn., Oreg. Women in Travel, Women of Wilsonville. Office: PO Box 153 Tualatin OR 97062

GARDNER, NORD ARLING, management consultant; b. Afton, Wyo., Aug. 10, 1923; s. Arling A. and Ruth (Lee) G.; BA, U. Wyo., 1945; MS, Calif. State U., Hayward, 1972, MPA, 1975; postgrad. U. Chgo., U. Mich., U. Calif.-Berkeley; m. Thora Marie Stephen, Mar. 24, 1945; children—Randall Nord, Scott Stephen, Craig Robert, Laurie Lee. With U.S. Army, 1941 Commd. 2d lt., 1945, advanced through grades to lt. col., 1964; ret., 1966; personnel analyst Univ. Hosp., U. Calif.-San Diego, 1966-68; coordinator manpower devel. U. Calif.-Berkeley, 1968-75; univ. tng. officer San Francisco State U., 1975-80, personnel mgr., 1976-80; exec. dir. CRDC Maintenance Tng. Corp., non-profit community effort, San Francisco, 1980-85; pres., dir. Sandor Assocs. Mgmt. Cons., Pleasant Hill, Calif., 1974-86, 91—; gen. mgr. Vericlean Janitorial Service, Inc.; in-charge bus. devel. East Bay Local Devel. Corp., Oakland, Calif., 1980-85; incorporator and pres. Indochinese Community Enterprises, USA, Ltd., Pleasant Hill, Calif., 1985-87; freelance writer, grantsmanship cons., 1987—; ptnr. Oi Kit Bldg. Maint. Svc., 1988-91; dir. univ. rels. Internat. Pacific U., San Ramon, Calif., 1990—; cons. Phimmasone Internat. Import-Export, Richmond, Calif., Lao Lanx-Xang Assn., Oakland Refugee Assn., 1988-90; instr. Japanese, psychology, supervisory courses, 1977-78; bd. dirs. New Ideas New Imports, Inc. Author: To Gather Stones, 1978. Adv. council San Francisco Community Coll. Dist. Decorated Army Commendation medal. Mem. Ret. Officers Assn., Am. Soc. Tng. and Devel., No. Calif. Human Resources Council. Am. Assn. Univ. Adminstrs., Internat. Personnel Mgrs. Assn., Internat. Platform Assn., Coll. and Univ. Personnel Assn., Commonwealth Club of Calif., U. Calif.-Berkeley Faculty Club, San Francisco State U. Faculty Club. Republican. Home: 2995 Bonnie Ln Pleasant Hill CA 94523-4547 Office: Internat Pacific U 2 Annabel Ln Ste 126 San Ramon CA 94583-1343

GARDNER, ROBERT ALEXANDER, counselor; b. Berkeley, Calif., Sept. 16, 1944; s. Robert Sr. and Eleanor Ambrose (Starrett); m. Sandie Gardner, Mar. 22, 1987; 1 stepchild, Heather. BA, U. Calif., Berkeley, 1967; MA, Calif. State U., Chico, 1974; MS, San Francisco State U., 1992. Div. personnel officer Wells Fargo Bank, San Francisco; dir. personnel Transamerica Airlines, Oakland, Calif.; instr. U. Calif., Berkeley; career counselor, outplacement cons. Gardner Assocs., Oakland; bd. dirs. Vocat. Svcs. Author: Achieving Effective Supervision, 1984, rev. edit. 1989, Managing Personnel Administration Effectively, 1986, Career Counseling: Matching Yourself to a Career, 1987. Mem. Am. Counseling Assn., Nat. Career Devel. Assn., Calif. Career Devel. Assn., Calif. Assn. for Counseling and Devel., Rotary. Home: 42 Aronia Ln Novato CA 94945-1805 Office: Gardner Assocs 3873 Piedmont Ave Ste 12 Piedmont CA 94611-5370

GARDNER, WILFORD ROBERT, physicist, educator; b. Logan, Utah, Oct. 19, 1925; s. Robert and Nellie (Barker) G.; m. Marjorie Louise Cole, June 9, 1949; children: Patricia, Robert, Caroline. B.S., Utah State U., 1949; M.S., Iowa State U., 1951, Ph.D., 1953. Physicist U.S. Salinity Lab., Riverside, Calif., 1953-66; prof. U. Wis., Madison, 1966-80; physicist, prof., head dept. soil and water sci. U. Ariz., Tucson, 1980-87; dean coll. natural resources U. Calif., Berkeley, 1987—. Author: Soil Physics, 1972. Served with U.S. Army, 1943-46. NSF sr. fellow, 1959; Fulbright fellow, 1971-72. Fellow AAAS, Am. Soc. Agronomy; mem. Internat. Soil Sci. Soc. (pres. physics commn. 1968-74), Soil Sci. Soc. Am. (pres. 1990, Rsch. award 1962), Nat. Acad. Scis. Office: U Calif Coll Natural Resources Berkeley CA 94720

GARDNER, WILLARD HALE, university administrator; b. Logan, Utah, Dec. 22, 1925; s. Willard and Rebecca Viola (Hale) G.; m. DeAnn Rich, Aug. 28, 1956; children: Julie, Bonnie, Wendy, Scott, Craig, Paul. Student, U. Calif., Berkeley, 1945; BS in Physics, Utah State Agrl. Coll., Logan, 1949; postgrad., U. Utah, 1949-52; MS in Math., Brigham Young U., 1956. Ednl. therapist Ft. Douglas Mil. Hosp., 1952-54; systems analyst Ramo-Wooldridge Corp., 1956-60; sr. systems analyst Informatics, Inc., 1960-63; sr. systems analyst Brigham Young U., Provo, Utah, 1963-72, asst. dir. computer svcs., 1976-80, dir. computer svcs., 1980-84, exec. dir. info. system svcs., 1984-90, assoc. prof. computer sci., 1972-90. spl. cons., 1990—; bd. dirs. Tel Electronics Inc. Bd. dirs. Utah Bd. State Lands and Forestry, 1986—; mem. Nat. Telecommunications Task Force, 1987-90; chmn. Utah State Sci. and Tech. Adv. Coun. Task Force for Networking, 1989-91; mem. Utah State Gov.'s Task Force on Info. Tech., 1989—; mem. Utah Partnership for Ednl. and Econ. Devel., 1990—; mem. Utah Legislature, 1973-85. With USN, 1944-46, Lt. USAR, 1948-53. Mem. Utah Info. Tech. Assn. (founding bd. mem. 1991—).

GAREY, DONALD LEE, pipeline and oil company executive; b. Ft. Worth, Sept. 9, 1931; s. Leo James and Jessie (McNatt) G.; BS in Geol. Engring., Tex. A&M U., 1953; m. Elizabeth Patricia Martin, Aug. 1, 1953; children: Deborah Anne, Elizabeth Laird. Reservoir geologist Gulf Oil Corp., 1953-54, sr. geologist, 1956-65; v.p., mng. dir. Indsl. Devel. Corp. Lea County, Hobbs, N.Mex., 1965-72, dir., 1972-86, pres., 1978-86; v.p., dir. Minerals, Inc., Hobbs, 1966-72, pres., dir., 1972-86, chief exec. officer, 1978-82; mng. dir. Hobbs Indsl. Found. Corp., 1965-72, dir., 1965-76; v.p. Llano, Inc., 1972-74, exec. v.p., chief operating officer, 1974-75, pres., 1975-86, chief exec. officer, 1978-82, also dir.; pres., chief exec. officer, Pollution Control, Inc., 1969-81; pres. NMESCO Fuels, Inc., 1982-86; chmn., pres., chief exec. officer Estacado Inc., 1986—, Natgas Inc., 1987—; pres. Llano Co2, Inc., 1984-86; cons. geologist, geol. engr., Hobbs, 1965-72. Chmn., Hobbs Manpower Devel. Tng. Adv. Com., 1965-72; mem. Hobbs Adv. Com. for Mental Health, 1965-67; chmn. N.Mex. Mapping Adv. Com., 1968-69; mem. Hobbs adv. bd. Salvation Army, 1967-78, chmn., 1970-72; mem. exec. bd. Conquistador coun. Boy Scouts Am., Hobbs, 1965-75; vice chmn. N.Mex. Gov.'s Com. for Econ. Devel., 1968-70; bd. regents Coll. Southwest, 1982-85. Capt. USAF, 1954-56. Registered profl. engr., Tex. Mem. Am. Inst. Profl. Geologists, Am. Assn. Petroleum Geologists, AIME, N.Mex. Geol. Soc., Roswell Geol. Soc., N.Mex. Amigos Club, Rotary. Home: 315 E Alto Dr Hobbs NM 88240-3905 Office: Broadmoor Tower PO Box 5587 Hobbs NM 88241-5587

GAREY, KERRY ANNE, office manager; b. Gallup, N.Mex., Mar. 11, 1957; d. Robert Webb Jr. and Addie Lou (Brown) G. Student, Ariz. State U., 1977-78. Computer mgr. Romney Produce Co., Phoenix, 1978-83; office mgr. Gregory Davis & Co., L.A., 1983—; freelance acct., L.A., 1990—. Vol. UCLA Med. Ctr., 1988; assoc. producer The Paper Courtship Reading, L.A., 1989. Recipient Svc. award UCLA Vol. Aux., 1989. Mem. Nat. Notary Assn. Office: Gregory Davis & Co 1875 Century Park E Bldg 1160 Los Angeles CA 90067-2512

GARFIELD, GENIE MAY, rancher; b. Forsyth, Mont., June 28, 1921; d. Malcolm Kenneth and Edith May (Cox) Philbrick; m. Russell Merritt Garfield, May 11, 1943 (wid. Oct. 1982); 1 child, Debra Garfield Bangs. Student, Mont. State U., 1938-40. Admissions asst. Carleton Coll., Northfield, Minn., 1940-41; sec. 2d Air Force Hdqrs., Spokane, Wash., 1941-45; rancher, 1972—; bd. dirs. 1st INterstate Bank, Colstrip, Mont., 1985 --. Bd. dirs. Hinsdale (N.H.) Sch. Bd., 1958-69, No. Plains Resource Coun., Billings, Mont.; chmn. Bottom Line Rider, 1984—, Hinsdale Nursing Assn., 1968-72; active Rosebud Co. Planning Bd. Forsyth, Mont., 1974-81, Hinsdale Woman's Club, 1953-73. Recipient Conservation Achievement award Soil Conservation Dist. Rosebud Co., Forsyth, Mount., 1990. Home and Office: Diamond Ranch Forsyth MT 59327

GARFIELD, HOWARD MICHAEL, lawyer; b. N.Y.C., Aug. 16, 1942; s. Jack and Pearl (Levine) G.; m. Elizabeth R. Lehmann, Oct. 23, 1978; 1 child, Mackenzie Elizabeth. AB, Stanford U., 1964; postgrad., Harvard U., 1964-65, JD, 1968. Bar: Calif. 1969, U.S. Dist. Ct. (cen. dist.) Calif. 1969, U.S. Dist. Ct. (no. and ea. dists.) Calif. 1972, U.S. Ct. Appeals (9th cir.) 1979, U.S. Supreme Ct. 1981. Assoc. Pacht, Ross, Warne, Bernahrd & Sears, L.A., 1968-70, Ambrose & Malat, Beverly Hills, Calif., 1970-71; ptnr. Garrett, Garfield & Bourdette, San Francisco, 1972-78; of counsel Goldstein & Phillips, San Francisco, 1979; assoc. Long & Levit, San Francisco, 1979-80, ptnr., 1980-83; mem. exec. com. Long & Levit, 1981—; mng. ptnr. Long & Levit, San Francisco, 1983-91; adj. prof. law Golden Gate U., San Francisco, 1979; aide U.S. Ho. Reps., Washington, 1964. Mem. Parks and Recreation Commn., Mill Valley, Calif., 1990—. Mem. ABA, San Francisco Bar Assn., Internat. Assn. Def. Counsel, Def. Rsch. Inst., Scott Valley Club. Democrat. Jewish. Home and Office: Long & Levit Ste 2300 101 California St San Francisco CA 94111-5895

GARGAN, THOMAS JOSEPH, plastic surgeon; b. Denver, Sept. 28, 1952; s. Thomas Joseph and Maria Augusta (Casagranda) G.; m. Nancy Lee Hall, Jan. 20, 1979; children: Daniel Thomas, John William. BA summa cum laude, Colo. Coll., 1974; MD, U. Colo., 1978. Diplomate Am. Bd. Plastic Surgery. Intern Presbyn. Med. Ctr., Denver, 1978-79, resident in surgery, 1978-79; resident in surgery Beth Israel Hosp., Boston, 1979-81, instr. gen. surgery, 1979-82, sr. resident in surgery, 1981-82, chief resident in plastic surgery, 1983-84; sr. resident in plastic surgery Cambridge (Mass.) City Hosp., 1982-83; resident in plastic surgery Children's Hosp. and Brigham and Women's Hosp., Boston, 1983, Newton-Wellesley Hosp., Mass., 1983; clin. fellow in surgery Harvard U. Med. Sch., Boston, 1979-84; clin. instr. plastic surgery U. Colo. Sch. Med., Denver, 1984; chief plastic surgery div. Rose Med. Ctr., 1987—; instr. plastic surgery Cambridge Hosp., Children's Hosp., and Beth Israel Hosp., Boston, 1982-84, Harvard Med. Sch., Boston, 1984. Contbr. articles to profl. jours. Bd. dirs. Rocky Mt. Adoption Exchange. Recipient George B. Packard award for excellence in surgery U. Colo. Med. Ctr., 1978; Eagle Scout; Barnes Chemistry scholar Colo. Coll. Fellow ACS; mem. AMA, Denver Med. Soc. (pres. Gold Star award), Colo. Med. Soc., Am. Soc. Plastic and Reconstructive Surgeons, Rocky Mountain Hand Surgery Soc., Rocky Mountain Soc., Reconstructive Plastic Surgeons, Am. Soc. Aesthetic Plastic Surgeons, Order Hibernians in Am. Home: 10 Blackmer Rd Englewood CO 80110-6109 Office: 601 E Hambden Englewood CO 80110 also: 8400 E Prentice Englewood CO 80111

GARGIULO, FRANCA, marketing and communications consultant; b. N.Y.C., Sept. 11, 1962; d. Theodore Luigi and Gloria (Moschella) G. BS in Fgn. Svc., Georgetown, 1984; postgrad., Coll. of Europe, 1985-86. With internat. mktg. dept. Seagate Tech., Scotts Valley, Calif., 1987-88, LSI Logic, Milpitas, Calif., 1988-89; dir. U.S. Bur. Census, Monterey, Calif., 1989-90; cons. on comm. and mktg., Monterey, 1990—; advisor Washington Workshops Found., 1982-85; regional mgr. Nat. Assn. Mfrs., 1993—. Exec. v.p. Calif. Republican League; active Calif. Rep. Com. Mem. League United L.Am. Citizens, Am. Bus. Women's Assn., Monterey History and Art Assn. Roman Catholic. Home and Office: PO Box 2426 Monterey CA 93942

GARIG, SCOTT ALLEN, emergency management consultant; b. Burbank, Calif., Oct. 28, 1955; s. Rukins Bale and Marion (Lee) G. AA, L.A. Pierce Coll., Woodland Hills, Calif., 1984; student, Valley Coll., Van Nuys, Calif., 1984, Canyons Sch., Valencia, Calif., 1987. Cert EMT, Calif.; cert. life safety instr. Mine Safety and Health Adminstrn. Founder, pres. Terraqua Dynamics, Ltd., Granada Hills, Calif., 1977—; CEO, Calif. Regional Emergency and Disaster Svcs., Van Nuys, 1986—; instr. life safety Comm. Concepts, Lakewood, Calif., 1985-88, Accident Prevention Specialists, Reseda, Calif., 1986; sr. search and rescue cons. Ctr. for Emergency Preparedness and Provisions, Irvine, Calif., 1985-87; life safety cons. LIFEKIT, Inc., Irvine, 1988-91; search and rescue cons. MLC & Assocs., Irvine, 1992—; dir. Resq-Network, L.A., 1992—; mem. BLS affiliate faculty Am. Heart Assn., L.A., 1992—. Amateur radio operator Disaster Comm. Svc., Los Angeles County, 1988; mem. disaster svcs. com. Valley dist. ARC, L.A., 1986—, aux.- comm. USCG; officer Nat. Disaster Med. System/Scottish Am. Emergency Med. Corps. Mem. Mid-San Fernando Valley C. of C. (pub. safety chmn. 1992—), Santa Clarita Valley C. of C., Clan Gregor Soc., Celtic Heritage Soc. (founder, 1st chief Calif. 1983-85), Soc. for Creative Anachronism, Tournament of Roses Radio Assn., Cet Cleidh Soer-Free Sword Legion (founder, chieftain 1989—). Mem. LDS Ch. Home: 9702 Sophia Ave North Hills CA 91343 Office: Calif Regional Emergency Disaster Svcs PO Box 8083 Van Nuys CA 91409

GARINO, TERRY JOSEPH, ceramics scientist; b. Staunton, Ill., Oct. 5, 1960; s. Aldo Charles and Gloria Albina (Brun) G. BS in Ceramics Engring., U. Ill., 1982; PhD in Ceramics Sci., MIT, 1987. Sr. mem. tech. staff Sandia Nat. Labs., Albuquerque, 1987—. Contbr. articles to profl. jours. Mem. Am. Ceramics Soc., Materials Rsch. Soc. Home: 218 Sharon Dr NE Albuquerque NM 87123-2422 Office: Sandia Nat Labs Div 1841 PO Box 5800 Albuquerque NM 87185-5800

GARLAND, CAROLINE MARY, artist, consultant; b. West Allis, Wis., Mar. 13, 1938; d. Peter and Pauline (Pavlovich) Budic; m. Gerard I. Garland, Nov. 22, 1966 (div. Aug. 1991); children: Andrea Jean, Jennifer Ruth. BS, U. Wis., 1959; MS, U. Wash., 1964; postgrad., Alaska Meth. U., 1968-74, U. Alaska S.E., Juneau, 1986—. Tchr. Tudor Hall Sch., Indpls., 1959-60, Seattle Pub. Schs., 1961-64, 65-66, Vicenza (Italy) Am. Schs., 1964-65; tchr. Juneau Sch. Dist., 1978-88, judge gifted and talented program in visual arts, 1987—; instr. U. Wash., Seattle, 1960-61, Alaska Meth. U., Anchorage, 1966-70; auditions judge in visual arts Juneau Arts and Humanities Coun., 1989. Exhibited in Anchorage Fur Rendezvous Art Show, 1976, 77, All Alaska Juried Art Exhbn., 1991, 92, Alaska Watercolor Exhibitions, 1988—, solo shows, 1992-93. Mem. Juneau Lyric Opera, 1987—, bd. dirs., 1989-90, grants officer, 1989—; producer vocal workshops 1989-92; mem. Juneau Bach Soc., 1989-91. Recipient Svc. to Edn. award Acad. for Excellence, Juneau, 1989, also awards for paintings. Mem. Alaska Watercolor Soc., Knickerbocker Artists (assoc.), Fairbanks Arts Assn. Democrat. Home: 117 Behrends Ave Juneau AK 99801

GARLAND, G(ARFIELD) GARRETT, sales executive, golf professional; b. Lakewood, Ohio, Dec. 17, 1945; s. Garfield George and Lois Marie (Calavan) G. BA, U. Colo., 1974. Broker Marcus & Millichap, Newport Beach, Calif., 1982-84; v.p. Pacific Coast Fed., Encino, Calif., 1984-85; dir. of acquisitions Prudential Investment Fund, L.A., 1985-86; v.p. A.S.A.I., L.A. and Tokyo, 1986-89; mgr. Lojack Corp., L.A., 1989-91; pres. Collegiate Scholarship Svcs. of Am., 1991-92; cons. Centinela Hosp. Fitness Inst. Mem. Pres.'s Coun. on Competitiveness, 1992, Childhelp USA. Capt. U.S. Army, 1967-71. Mem. VFW, PGA of Am., L.I.F.E. Found., Am. Legion, World Affairs Coun., Internat. Platform Assn., U.S. Ski Team, Natural Historic Preservation Trust. Home: 6846 Pacific View Dr Los Angeles CA 90068-1832 Office: Lojack Corp 9911 W Pico Blvd Los Angeles CA 90035-2703

GARLETT, MARTI WATSON, educator, consultant; b. Chgo., Sept. 14, 1945; s. James Edward and Phyllis Luree (Northup) Watson; m. Fred Gordon, Aug. 8, 1965; children: Marc Gordon, Kyle Geoffrey. BS in Edn., Emporia (Kans.) State U., 1967; MLS, Peabody/Vanderbilt U., Nashville, 1977; EdS, Wichita (Kans.) State U., 1982. Cert. tchr., reading specialist, ednl. adminstr. Elem. tchr. St. Louis, 1968-70; reading tchr. Hillsboro, Kans., 1973-75; elem. tchr. Nashville, 1975-77; assoc. prof. edn. Friends U., Wichita, Kans., 1977-89; teaching specialist Wichita Pub. Schs., 1989-90; nat. curriculum cons. Econo-Clad Books, Topeka, 1990-92; dir. elem. tchr. edn. Azusa (Calif.) Pacific U., 1992—; Romper Room tchr. KAKE-TV, Wichita, 1978-85; exch. prof. Pusan (South Korea) Women's Coll., 1986; ednl. cons. KAKE-TV News and Info., Wichita, 1985-87; assoc. fellow The Milton Ctr., Wichita, 1983-90. Author: Who Will Be My Teacher?, 1985, Kids with Character, 1989. Mem. Internat. Reading Assn., Nat. Coun. Tchrs. English, Phi Delta Kappa, Chi Omega. Home: 715 Orchard Loop Azusa CA 91702 Office: Azusa Pacific U 901 E Alosta Blvd Azusa CA 91702

GARLOUGH, WILLIAM GLENN, marketing executive; b. Syracuse, N.Y., Mar. 27, 1924; s. Henry James and Gladys (Killam) G.; m. Charlotte M. Tanzer, June 15, 1947; children: Jennifer, William, Robert. BEE, Clarkson U., 1949. With Knowlton Bros., Watertown, N.Y., 1949-67, mgr. mfg. svcs., 1966-67; v.p. planning, equipment systems div. Vare Corp., Englewood Cliffs, N.J., 1967-69; mgr. mktg. Valley Mould div. Microdot Inc., Hubbard, Ohio, 1969-70; dir. corp. devel. Microdot Inc., Greenwich, Conn., 1970-73, v.p. corp. devel., 1973-76, v.p. adminstrn., 1976-77, v.p. corp. devel., 1977-78; v.p. corp. devel. Am. Bldg. Maintenance Industries, San Francisco, 1979-83; pres. The Change Agts., Inc., Walnut Creek, Calif., 1983—; bd. dirs. My Chef Inc.; mem. citizens adv. com. to Watertown Bd. Edn., 1957. Bd. dirs. Watertown Community Chest, 1958-61; ruling elder Presbyn. Ch. With USMCR, 1942-46. Mem. Am. Mgmt. Assn., Inst. Mgmt. Cons. (cert.), Bldg. Svc. Contractors Assn., Internat. Sanitary Supply Assn., Mensa, Am. Mktg. Assn., TAPPI, Assn. Corp. Growth (pres. San Francisco chpt. 1984-85, v.p. chpts. west 1985-88), Lincoln League (pres. 1958), Am. Contract Bridge League (life master), Clarkson Alumni Assn. (Watertown sect. pres. 1955), No. N.Y. Contract Club (pres. 1959), No. N.Y. Transp. Club, Tau Beta Pi. Home: 2557 Via Verde Walnut Creek CA 94598-3451 Office: The Change Agts Inc 1990 N California Blvd Ste 830 Walnut Creek CA 94596-3711

GARMIRE, ELSA MEINTS, electrical engineering educator, consultant; b. Buffalo, Nov. 9, 1939; d. Ralph E. and Nelle (Gubser) Meints; m. Gordon P. Garmire, June 11, 1961 (div. 1975); children: Lisa, Marla; m. Robert Heathcote Russell, Feb. 4, 1979. AB in Physics, Harvard U., 1961; PhD in Physics, MIT, 1965. Rsch. scientist NASA Electronics Rsch. Ctr., Cambridge, Mass., 1965-66; rsch. fellow Calif. Inst. Tech., Pasadena, 1966-73; sr. rsch. scientist U. So. Calif. Ctr. for Laser Studies, L.A., 1974-78, assoc. prof. elec. engring. and physics, 1981-92, assoc. dir. Ctr. for Laser Studies, 1978-83, dir., 1984—, William Hogue prof. of engring., 1992—; vis. fellow Standard Telecommunication Labs., Eng., 1973-74; cons. Aerospace Corp., L.A., 1975-91, sci. adv. bd. Air Force, Washington, 1985-89, TRW, L.A., 1988-89, McDonnell Douglas, St. Louis, 1990—. Contbr. over 160 sci. papers and articles to profl. publs.; patentee in field. Recipient Soroptimist Achievement award Soroptimist Club, L.A., 1970, K. C. Black award N.E. Electronics Rsch. and Engring. Meeting, 1972; named Mademoiselle Woman of Yr. Mademoiselle Mag., 1970. Fellow IEEE (bd. dirs. 1985-89), Optical Soc. Am. (bd. dirs. 1983-86, pres. elect 1992, pres. 1993); mem. NAE, Am. Phys. Soc. (rep. 1962—), Soc. Women Engrs. (sr.), Harvard Radcliffe Club (v.p. 1984-86). Democrat. Office: U So Calif Ctr for Laser Studies DRB17 Los Angeles CA 90089-1112

GARNER, CARLENE ANN, orchestra administrator; b. Dec. 17, 1945; d. Carl A. and Ruth E. (Mathison) Timblin; m. Adelbert L. Garner, Feb. 17, 1964; children: Bruce A., Brent A. BA, U. Puget Sound, 1983. Adminstrv. dir. Balletacoma, 1984-87; exec. dir. Tacoma Symphony, 1987—; cons. Wash. PAVE, Tacoma, 1983-84. Treas. Coalition for the Devel. of the Arts, 1992—; pres. Wilson High Sch. PTA, Tacoma, 1983-85; chmn. Tacoma Sch. Vol. Adv. Bd., 1985-87; pres. Emmanuel Luth. Ch., Tacoma, 1984-86, chmn. future steering com., 1987-93; sec.-treas. Tacoma-Narrows Conf., 1987—; trustee Tacoma Luth. Home. Mem. Northwest Devel. Officers Assn., Am. Symphony Orch. League, Jr. Women's Club Tacoma (pres. 1975-76), Wash. State Fedn. Women's Clubs (pres. Peninsula dist. 1984-86, treas. 1988-90, 3d v.p. 1990-92, 2d v.p. 1992—), Clubwoman of Yr. 1977, Outstanding FREE chmn. Gen. Fedn.), Commencement Bay Woman's Club (pres. 1990-92, trustee). Lutheran. Home: 1115 N Cheyenne St Tacoma WA 98406-3624 Office: Tacoma Symphony PO Box 19 Tacoma WA 98401-0019

GARNER, JOHN CHARLES, employee benefits consultant; b. Alhambra, Calif., Nov. 18, 1949; s. Logan Summers and Ida Louise (Chamness) G.; m. Carolyn Vale Layton, June 26, 1971; 1 child, Caryn Louise. BA, Occidental Coll., 1971. CLU. Jr. adminstrv. asst. Prudential Ins. Co., L.A., 1971-74; bus. mgr. Rocky Mt. (N.C.) Phillies, 1974, Memphis Blues, 1974-75; office mgr. Lincoln Nat. Life Ins., L.A., 1975-77; prin. Olanie, Hurst & Hemrich, L.A., 1977-82, Towers, Perrin, Forster & Crosby, L.A., 1982-87; pres. Garner Cons., Pasadena, Calif., 1987—; publicity chmn. Western Claims Conf., 1993; sports info. dir. Occidental Coll., L.A., 1973-74; chmn. Short Line Enterprises, Inc., Fillmore, Calif., 1988—; treas. Occidental Bus. Assocs., L.A., 1989-90. Editor: Medical/Disability Claims, 1989; contbr. articles to profl. jours. Active March of Dimes, L.A., 1987—, United Way, L.A., 1987-89, Am. Heart Assn., L.A., 1989—. Mem. Am. Soc. CLUs, Orange County Claim Assn., L.A. Claim Assn., L.A. Assn. Health Underwriters, Employee Benefit Planning Assn. Democrat. Presbyterian. Office: Garner Cons 199 S Los Robles Ave Ste 560 Pasadena CA 91101-2458

GARNER, LYNN EVAN, mathematics educator; b. Ontario, Oreg., July 19, 1941; s. Evan Bowen and Sarah Melba (Despain) G.; m. Marjorie Kaye Waite, Sept. 9, 1960; children: Kaylene, Bradley, Kristen, Alisse, Brian. BS,

Brigham Young U., 1962; MA, U. Utah, 1964; PhD, U. Oreg., 1968. Instr. to prof. Brigham Young U., Provo, Utah, 1962—; instr. Waterford Sch., Provo, 1973-89, Meridian Sch., Provo, 1979—; cons. Hewlett Packard Edn. Adv. Com., Corvallis, Oreg., 1992—. Author: Outline of Projective Geometry, 1981, Calculus and Analytic Geometry, 1988, Calculus with H/P Calculators, 1990, Calculus with the HP48, 1992. Mem. Am. Math. Soc., Math. Assn. of Am., Pi Mu Epsilon, Sigma Xi. Mem. Ch. LDS. Office: Brigham Young U 283 TMCB Provo UT 84602

GARON, CLAUDE FRANCIS, laboratory administrator; b. Baton Rouge, Nov. 5, 1942; s. Ivy Joseph and Janith (Latil) G.; m. Sally Sheffield; children: Michele, Anne, Julie. BS, La. State U., 1964, MS, 1966; PhD, Georgetown U., 1970. Predoctoral fellowship La. State U., Baton Rouge, 1964-66; predoctoral traineeship Georgetown U., Washington, 1966-69; postdoctoral fellowship Nat. Inst. Allergy and Inf. Diseases, Bethesda, Md., 1971-73, staff fellowship, 1971-73, sr. staff fellowship, 1973-74, rsch. microbiologist, 1974-81; head electron microscopy Rocky Mountain Labs, Hamilton, Mont., 1981-85, chief, pathobiology, 1985-89, chief, lab of vectors and pathogens, 1989—; bd. govs. Ctr. Excellence in Biotech., Missoula, Mont., 1988—; faculty affiliate U. Mont., 1989—. Mem. editorial bd. Jour. Clin. Microbiology, 1993. Recipient award of merit NIH, Dirs. award, 1988. Mem. Am. Soc. for Microbiology, Am. Soc. Biochemistry and Molecular Biology, Microscopy Soc. Am., Am. Soc. Rickettsiology, Pacific N.W. Electron Microscopy Soc., Lions (pres. Hamilton 1989-90). Office: Rocky Mountain Labs Lab Vectors & Pathogens 903 S 4th St Hamilton MT 59840-2999

GARRAHAN, PAUL JAMISON, insurance executive; b. Altoona, Pa., June 30, 1928; s. Paul J. Sr. and Anna Belle (Figard) G.; m. Peggy Jean Brown, Sept. 10, 1955; children: Melinda Lorraine, Julie Ann. BA in Sociology, Franklin and Marshall Coll., 1951. CLU, ChFC; registered health underwriter. Ins. agt. Paul Revere Life Ins. Co., Albuquerque, 1955-57; dist. mgr. Paul Revere Life Ins. Co., El Paso, Tex., 1958-60; dist. mgr. Paul Revere Life Ins. Co., Phoenix, 1960-66, gen. mgr., 1966—. Mem. Civitan Club, Phoenix, 1962-65. Staff sgt. USAF, 1951-55, Korea. Mem. Nat. Assn. Life Underwriters, Nat. Assn. Health Underwriters, Am. Soc. CLU and ChFC, Gen. Agts. and Mgrs. Assn. (pres. Phoenix chpt. 1978-79, nat. rep. 1979-80, Nat. Mgmt. award 1979, 81, 83, 84, 87, 88, 89, 90, 91, 92, 93). Republican. Methodist. Home: 738 E Gardenia Dr Phoenix AZ 85020 Office: Paul Revere Cos 2800 N Central # 1490 Phoenix AZ 85004

GARRETSON, OWEN LOREN, engineer; b. Salem, Iowa, Feb. 24, 1912; s. Sumner Dilts and Florence (White) G.; m. Erma Mary Smith, Jan. 23, 1932; children: John Albert, Owen Don, Susan Marie, Leon Todd. Student, Iowa Wesleyan Coll., 1930-32; BS, Iowa State U., 1937. Registered profl. engr., Okla., N.Mex., Iowa, Mo. Engr. Bailey Meter Co., Cleve., 1937, St. Louis, 1937-38; engr., dist. mgr. Phillips Petroleum Co., Bartlesville, Okla., 1938-39, Amarillo, Tex., 1939-40, Detroit, 1940-41; mgr. product supply and transp. div. Phillips Petroleum Co., Barlesville, 1942-44, mgr. engring. devel. div., 1944-46, mgr. spl. porducts engring. devel. div., 1946-47; pres. Gen. Tank & Steel Corp., Roswell, N.Mex., United Farm Chem. Co.; pres., dir. Garretson Equipment Co., Mt. Pleasant, Iowa; v.p., dir. Valley Industries, Inc., Mt. Pleasant; pres., dir. Garretson Carburetion of Tex., Inc., Lubbock; v.p., dir. Sacra Gas Co. Roswell, 1957-58; exec. v.p., dir. Arrow Gas. Co. & Affiliated Corps., Roswell, N.Mex., Tex., Utah, 1958-60; asst. to pres. Nat. Propane Corp., Hyde Park, N.Y.; pres., chmn. bd. Plateau, Inc. Oil Refining, Farmington, N.Mex., 1960-82, also bd. dirs.; chmn. bd. S.W. Motels, Inc., Farmington; organizing dir. Farmington Nat. Bank, 1964; cons. Suburban Propane Gas Corp. Whippany, N.J. Contbr. articles to profl. jours.; 42 patents issued in several fields. Mem., past pres. Farmington Indsl. Devel. Svc., N.Mex. Lidquefied Petroleum Gas Commn., 1955-76, chmn., 1956-58; mem. Iowa Gov.'s Trade Commn. to No. Europe, 1970, Iowa Trade Mission to Europe, 1979; mem. com. natural gas/liquefied natural gas Internat. Petroleum Expn. and Congress, 1970-71; mem. Nat. Coun. Crime and Delinquency. Recipient Merit award Iowa Wesleyan Coll. Alumni Assn., 1968, Profl. Achievement Engring. citation Iowa State U., 1986. Mem. ASME, NSPE, Nat. Liquefied Petroleum Gas Assn. (bd. dirs., Disting. Svc. award 1979), Am. Petroleum Inst., Nat. Petroleum Refiner's Assn. (bd. dirs., pres.), Ind. Refiners Assn. Am., Agrl. Ammonia Inst. Memphis (bd. dirs.), N.Mex. Liquefied Petroleum Gas. Assn. (pres., bd. dirs.), Ind. Petroleum Assn. Am., N.Mex. Acad. Sci., Am. Soc. Agrl. Engrs., Am. Soc. Automotive Engrs., N.Mex. Amigos., Am. Inst. Chem. Engrs., Newcomen Soc. N.Am., Soc. Indsl. Archeology, Ancient Gassers (sec., pres.), 25 Yr. Club Petroleum Industry, Masons, Rotary, Phi Delta Theta, Tau Beta Pi. Home: 500 E La Plata St Farmington NM 87401-6940 Office: PO Box 108 Farmington NM 87499-0108

GARRETSON, ROBERT MARK, financial executive; b. Greeley, Colo., Nov. 3, 1951; s. Loren Neville and Marilyn Elizabeth (Ruwaldt) G.; m. Susan Anita Carlson, Apr. 28, 1973; children: Jennifer, Christopher, Courtney, Timothy. BSBA, Colo. State U., 1974, MS in Taxation, 1982. CPA, Colo. Staff acct. Lloyd Spawn & Assocs., Ft. Collins, Colo., 1974-76; controller Pearse Electronics, Inc., Wheatridge, Colo., 1976-78, Environ. Rsch. & Tech., Ft. Collins, 1978-80; v.p. Ctr. St., Inc., Loveland, Colo., 1980-82; chief fin. officer Simons, Li & Assocs., Ft. Collins, 1982-92; owner Robert M Garreston, CPA, 1992—. Chmn. fin. com. Christ United Meth. Ch., Ft. Collins, 1983-86, auditor, 1988; asst. scout master Ft. Collins area Boy Scouts Am., 1985-89. Mem. AICPA, Colo. Soc. CPAs. Republican. Office: 5212 Wisteria Ct Fort Collins CO 80525

GARRETSON, STEVEN MICHAEL, educator; b. L.A., Nov. 2, 1950; s. Fredrick Harmon and Mildred (Mason) G.; m. Candice Kay Clouse, Sept. 23, 1972; children: Joshua Steven, Amanda Jeanine. BA, U. Calif., Irvine, 1972, tchr. credential, 1974; postgrad., U. Calif., Santa Barbara, 1973; MA, U. San Francisco, 1980. Cert. tchr., adminstr., Calif. Tchr. Irvine Unified Sch. Dist., 1974—; energy conservation cons. Irvine Unified Sch. Dist., 1981-85, grant writer, 1983—, archtl. design cons., 1975—, mentor tchr., 1984-86; presenter state social studies conf., 1980. Mem. Irvine Tchrs. Assn. (grievance chmn. 1980-82, treas., 1977-78, v.p., 1978-79, contract negotiator, 1976-84, 89-93, benefits mgmt. bd. 1990—, pres. 1993—), Phi Delta Kappa. Roman Catholic. Office: Northwood Elem Sch 28 Carson Irvine CA 92720-3313

GARRETT, DENNIS ANDREW, police official; b. Phoenix, Feb. 9, 1940; s. Lynn Patrick and Louise A. (Yates) G.; m. Joan Marie Braun, June 12, 1980. AA, Glendale Community Coll., 1975; BS magna cum laude, No. Ariz. U., 1980; MPA, Ariz. State U., 1985. Officer Phoenix Police Dept., 1963-69, sgt., 1969-72, lt., 1972-75, capt., 1975-80, maj., 1980, asst. police chief, 1980-91, police chief, 1991—. Chmn. St. Jerome's Sch. Bd., Phoenix, 1978-79; mem. Valley Leadership, Phoenix, 1985—; bd. dirs. Friendly House; Christian bd. dirs. YMCA; mem. Ariz. Law Enforcement Adv. Coun. Mem. ASPA (pres. Ariz. chpt. 1988-89), Internat. Assn. Chiefs Police, Am. Mgmt. Assn., Ariz. Assn. Chiefs Police, Ariz. Hispanic C. of C., Nat. Orgn. Black Law Enforcement Execs., Fraternal Order Police, Rotary, Phi Kappa Phi. Republican. Roman Catholic. Office: Phoenix Police Dept 620 W Washington St Phoenix AZ 85003-2132

GARRETT, JOAN, marketing professional; b. Boston, Jan. 22, 1953; d. Harry Leigh and Ethel (Clifford) G. BA in Internat. Rels., Boston U., 1974; cert., Emerson Coll., 1978. Export mgr. Orion Rsch., Cambridge, Mass., 1972-75; direct mktg. mgr. Extech Internat., Boston, 1975-79; mgr. pub. rels. and advt. Latin Am. Wang Labs., Lowell, Mass., 1979-80, multi-nat. account rep., 1980-81; account exec. metro N.Y. Wang Labs., N.Y.C., 1981-84; account exec. Wall St. Tandem Computers, N.Y.C., 1985-88; major accounts mgr. Tandem Computers, Cupertino, Calif., 1988-89; br. mgr. telecommunications Tandem Computers, Madrid, Spain, 1989-90; mgr. UNIX solutions mktg. Tandem Computers, Cupertino, 1990-91, mgr. UNIX product sales, 1992-93; founder, prin. V.B.S.I. Bus. Unit Devel., Mountain View, Calif., 1993—. Mem. Uniforum. Home: 1369 Cuernavaca Circle Mountain View CA 94040

GARRETT, ROBERT STEPHENS, public relations executive; b. Bell, Calif., July 12, 1937; s. Sammie Jacob and Martha Ethelwynn (Dench) G.; m. Mary Lynn Harris, Sept. 9, 1955 (div. July 1972); children: Lisa, Julie, Kim; m. Camille Ann Priestley, Feb. 15, 1975; children: Lee Ann, Nikki, Grant. Grad. high sch., Downey, Calif. From machinist to head shipping dept. Axelson Mfg. Co., Vernon, Calif., 1955-60; prodn. control planner, methods analyst autonetics div. Rockwell Internat., Downey, Compton and Anaheim, Calif., 1960-70; pub. relations mgr., property mgr., clinic coordinator, investigator, property researcher and chief adminstr. bd. and care UMEDCO Inc., Long Beach, Calif., 1970-77; dir. ops. Regency Mgmt. Service, Anaheim, 1977-78; cons. med. pub. relations Garden Grove, Calif., 1978—. Bd. dirs. Boys Club of Garden Grove, 1978—, 2d v.p., 1990, 91, 1st v.p., 1992, pres. 1993; bd. dirs. Girls Club of Garden Grove, 1980—, treas., 1983-84, v.p., 1984-86, pres., 1986; traffic commr. City of Garden Grove, 1981—, vice chmn. traffic commn., 1988-89, 92-93, chmn., 1989-90, 93-94. Recipient Garden Grove C. of C. Man of Yr. award, 1992-93; Paul Harris fellow Rotary, 1980. Mem. Rotary (bd. dirs. Paramount Club 1975-76, bd. dirs. Garden Grove Club 1978-79, 92-93), Elks. Republican. Office: PO Box 1221 Garden Grove CA 92642-1221

GARRETT, WILLIAM JERRY, JR., account manager; b. Leaksville, N.C., May 28, 1962; s. William Jerry Sr. and Ellen (Harvey) G.; m. Suzanne Marie Vrh, May 7, 1988. Student, U. de Valencia, 1983; BA in Internat. Bus., Lenoir-Rhyne Coll., 1984. Exhibits supr. Siecor Corp., Hickory, N.C., 1984-86; sales engr. Siecor Corp., Pleasant Hill, Calif., 1986-89; acct. mgr. Siecor Corp., Lodi, Calif., 1989-92; sales mgr. Alcatel, 1992—. Vestryman St. John Bapt. Episcopal. Ch., Lodi, 1990-92, lay eucharistic min., 1990-92, acolyte dir., 1990. Named Eagle Scout, 1977. Republican.

GARRIDO, AUGIE, university athletic coach. Head coach NCAA Divsn. 1A baseball runner-up Calif. State Fullerton Titans, 1992. Office: Calif State Fullerton PO Box 34080 Fullerton CA 92634-9480

GARRIGUES, BEVERLY JEAN, marriage, family and individual counselor; b. L.A., Sept. 15, 1942; d. Wesley Wolf and Yetta (Rosenthal) Landsberg; m. William Charles Garrigues, Aug. 25, 1963; children: Trisha Louise, Jonathan Howard. AA, El Camino Coll., 1962; BS, Calif State. U., Long Beach, 1964; MA, Nat. U., Vista, Calif., 1987. Cert. tchr., lic. marriage and family counselor, Calif. Tchr. Placentia (Calif.) Unified Sch. Dist., 1965-73; trainer San Diego coun. Girl Scouts U.S., 1980-88; educator Women's Resource Ctr., Oceanside, Calif., 1985-86; intern counselor Alpha of San Diego, 1986-88, Casa de Amparo, Oceanside, 1986-87, Oceanside Sch. Dist., 1987-89; intern counselor Mellusi & Wagner Counseling, Carlsbad, Calif., 1988-90, marriage, family and individual counselor, 1990—; marriage, family and individual counselor Temecula Valley Counseling, Temecula, Calif., 1991—; lay minister Episc. Diocese San Diego, 1990—. Author: The Silver Chalice, 1987, The Secret of Love, 1987. Mem. Am. Psychol. Assn., Soc. Mental Health Profls. (treas.), Calif. Assn. Marriage and Family Therapists, San Diego Child Abuse Coalition. Office: Temecula Valley Counseling Svcs Ste 106 28936 Front St Temecula CA 92590

GARRIGUES, GAYLE LYNNE, lawyer; b. Anchorage, Aug. 7, 1955; d. James Martin and Julia Ann (Harris) G. B.A. in Polit.Sci., U. Alaska, 1977; J.D., U. Idaho, 1980. Bar: Alaska 1981, U.S. Dist. Ct. Alaska 1982. Atty. Alaska Legal Services Corp., Kotzebue, 1980-82; assoc. Settles, Kalamarides & Assocs., P.C., Anchorage, 1982; sole practice, Kotzebue, 1982-84; asst. dist. atty. Dept. of Law 2d Jud. Dist., Kotzebue, 1984-87, Fairbanks, 1987—; instr. criminal justice Chuckchi Community Coll., 1985-86. Bd. dirs. Kotzebue Womens Crisis Project, 1982-84; del. Alaska State Dem. Conv., 1974, 84, 88; bd. dirs. Women in Crisis, Counseling and Assistance, 1988—, v.p., 1989-90, 91, pres. 1992—; leader Girl Scouts U.S., 1981-83, 86-87; bd. dirs. Farthest North Girl Scout Coun., 1991—, 1st v.p. 1992—. Mem. Alaska Bar Assn.

GARRIGUS, CHARLES BYFORD, retired literature educator; b. Benton, Ill., June 13, 1914; s. Charles Byford and Ailene Marie (Fowler) G.; m. Ferne Marie Fetters, Dec. 28, 1936 (dec.); children: Marmarie (dec.), Charles, Richmond, Karis, Rose Ann. AB, U. Ill., 1936, MA, 1937. Prof. humanities King's River Coll., Reedley, Calif., 1949-73; Calif. poet laureate for life, 1966—. Author: California Poems, 1955, (poems) Echoes of Being, 1975, (novel) Brief Candel, 1987; editor: Modern Hamlet, 1950. Mem. Calif. Assembly, 1958-86. Democrat. Methodist. Home: 14710 S Dewolf Ave Selma CA 93662-9439

GARRIS, SIDNEY REGINALD, artist management company executive; b. N.Y.C., Dec. 31, 1922; children: Brian, Michael, Ellen, Robin Garris Kaplan. Student, U. So. Calif., Pepperdine U. Jazz disk jockey Symphony Sid, N.Y.C., 1937; violist Artie Shaw Band, 1941; with various radio stas., N.Y.C., Ohio, Mich., Calif.; ptnr. Greif-Garris Mgmt., Palm Springs, Calif.; owner, mgr. New Christy Minstrels, 1962—; guest condr. L.A. Philharm., Royal Philharm. London, Atlanta Pops, Tokyo Symphony, Seattle Symphony, numerous other major orchs. throughout world; co-founder L.A. Neophonic Orch. Former mem. bd. dirs. Young Musicians Found., L.A.; participant New Am. Orch.; former mem. L.A. Philharm. Inst.; mem. Maxine Waters Com. for Ho. of Reps.; candidate for mayor City of Palm Springs, 1992. With USN, World War II. Home and Office: Mesquite Canyon Estates 2112 Casitas Way Palm Springs CA 92264-8214

GARRISON, BETTY BERNHARDT, mathematics educator; b. Danbury, Ohio, July 1, 1932; d. Philip Arthur and Reva Esther (Meter) Bernhardt; m. Robert Edward Kvarda, Sept. 28, 1957 (div. 1964); m. John Dresser Garrison, Jan. 17, 1968; 1 child, John Christopher. BA, BS, Bowling Green State U., 1954; MA, Ohio State U., 1956; PhD, Oreg. State U., 1962. Teaching asst. Ohio State U., Columbus, 1954-56; instr. Ohio U., Athens, 1956-57, San Diego State Coll., 1957-59; teaching asst. Oreg. State U., Corvallis, 1959-62; asst. prof. San Diego State U., 1962-66, assoc. prof., 1966-69, prof., 1969—. Reviewer of articles and books, 1966—; contbr. articles to profl. jours. NSF fellow, 1960-61, 61-62. Mem. Am. Math. Soc., Math. Assn. Am. Home: 5607 Yerba Anita Dr San Diego CA 92115-1027 Office: San Diego State U Math Dept San Diego CA 92182

GARRISON, F. SHERIDAN, transportation executive. CEO Am. Freightways, Harrison, Ark. Office: Am Freightways 2200 Forward Dr Harrison AR 72601-2004

GARRISON, KATHLEEN MARIE, social worker; b. Gt. Falls, Mont., Aug. 18, 1954; d. Harry W. and Frances V. (Gallagher) Keith; m. Robert M. Garrison, Mar. 29, 1980; children: Marie Michelle, Lisa Celeste. BA, U. Mont., 1977, postgrad., 1979-80; postgrad., Western Wyo. Coll., 1986-87. Habilitation aide Boulder River Sch. and Hosp., Boulder, Mont., 1977-78; program implementer Ivy Arts, Missoula, 1978-79; exec. dir. Vol. Info. & Referral Svc., Rock Springs, Wyo., 1980-84; caseworker for S.W. Wyo., Cath. Social Svcs., Rock Springs, 1991—. Founding mem., bd. pres. Children's Discovery Found., Rock Springs, 1992—; bd. dirs. S.W. Counseling Svc., Rock Springs, 1992—. Home: 1017 Ford Circle Rock Springs WY 82901

GARRISON, LESTER BOYD, chemist; b. Eureka, Calif., May 7, 1948; s. Lester Boyd and Marian (Weamer) G.; m. Sandra Marie Ryan, June 21, 1980; children: Jay Patrick, Kaye Camille, Brian Lee. AA in Gen. Edn., Coll. of the Redwoods, 1971-73; BA in Chemistry, Humboldt State U., 1973-76; postgrad. in chemistry, Portland State U., 1978-79; student in sales and mktg., Portland Community Coll., 1983-84; postgrad., City U., 1988—. Rsch. asst. Oreg. Health Scis. U., Portland, 1976-78, sr. rsch. asst., 1978-79; systems engr. Alpkem Corp, Clackamas, Oreg., 1979-81; sr. lab. technician Qatar Gen. Petroleum Corp., Doha, 1981-82; diagnostics prodn. mgr. Alpkem Corp., Clackamas, 1982-85; plant mgr. Alpkem Corp., Orchards, Wash., 1985-86; chief operating officer Intersect, Inc., Longview, Wash., 1987-90; mng. dir. Garrison Lab., Rainier, Oreg., 1990—. Co-author, contbr. articles to profl. jours. With USMC, 1967-71. Decorated Nat. Def. Svc. medal. Mem. AAAS, Am. Chem. Soc., Alexander von Humboldt Marine Scis. Assn. (life) (chmn. marine lab and open house com. 1975), Humboldt State U. Oceanographic Soc. (chmn., co-founder). Office: Garrison Lab 504 E C St Rainier OR 97048-2601

GARRISON, THOMAS S., editorial director; b. Bakersfield, Calif., Jan. 18, 1952; s. Thomas S. and Nell Louise (Chinnis) G.; m. Lorraine D. Irwin, June 24, 1972 (div. 1980); m. Deborah Ann Looker, Mar. 8, 1982. BA in Polit. Sci. magna cum laude, Calif. State U., 1974; MA in Polit. Sci., U. Calif., Davis, 1976; postgrad., U. Calif., Santa Barbara, 1980. Cert. C.C. tchr., Calif. Coord. The Gathering Pl., Santa Barbara, 1981; mng. editor Internat. Acad., Santa Barbara, 1981-89, editorial dir., 1990—. Editorial dir. Current World Leaders, 1981—, Annual Directory of World Leaders 1988-91; author (mag.) The Socialist, 1984, author/editor (mag.) Left Out, 1987—. Chairperson Peace and Freedom Party, Santa Barbara County, 1988—; mem. Socialist Party, USA, 1982—; vice-chmn. Rental Housing Mediation Task Force, Santa Barbara, 1986, sec., 1985. Grantee U. Calif., 1978-79. Mem. ACLU, War Resisters League, Am. Polit. Sci. Assn., U. Calif. at Santa Barbara Alumni Assn. Office: Internat Acad 800 Garden St Ste D Santa Barbara CA 93101

GARRISON, U. EDWIN, military, space and defense products manufacturing company executive; b. 1928. BSME, Miss. State U., 1951. With Thiokol Corp., Ogden, Utah, 1952—, from v.p. to pres. aerospace group, 1983-89, pres., chief exec. officer, 1989—; chmn. bd. Thiokol Corp., Ogden, 1991—. With USN, 1946-48. Office: Thiokol Corp 2475 Washington Blvd Ogden UT 84401-2300*

GARROP, BARBARA ANN, reading specialist; b. Chgo., Sept. 2, 1941; d. Marshall and Esther (Barbakoff) Stickles; widowed; children: Alana Beth, Stacy Lynn. AA with honors, Wright Jr. Coll., Chgo., 1961; BA with honors, Roosevelt U., 1963; MS with honors, Calif. State U., Hayward, 1982. Cert. elem. tchr., reading specialist, Calif. Tchr. Von Humboldt Sch., Chgo., 1963-64, Haugan Sch., Chgo., 1964-67; primary grades reading specialist Mt. Diablo Sch. Dist., Concord, Calif., 1979-80, Mills Elem. Sch., Benicia, Calif., 1980-87, Mary Farmar Sch., Benicia, 1987—; mentor tchr. Benicia Unified Sch. Dist., Benicia, 1989, 92; inst. tchr. leader Calif. Lit. Project, 1991-93; instr. Chapman U. Acad. Ctr., Fairfield, Calif., spring, 1992. Author phonics manual, 1982; featured in article Woman's Day mag., 1982; contbg. author Celebating The National Reading Initiative, 1988. Bd. dirs. Sisterhood of Congregation B'nai Shalom, Walnut Creek, Calif., 1987-88. Grantee Reading Is Fundamental, 1979-80. Mem. NEA, Internat. Reading Assn., Calif. Reading Assn. (Achievement award 1984), Constra Costa Reading Assn., Calif. Tchrs. Assn., AAUW, Pi Lambda Theta. Jewish. Lodge: B'nai Brith Women (v.p. Columbus, Ohio 1971-72, pres. Walnut Creek 1973-74). Office: Mary Farmar Sch 901 Military W Benicia CA 94510-2598

GARRUTO, JOHN ANTHONY, cosmetics executive; b. Johnson City, N.Y., June 18, 1952; s. Paul Anthony and Katherine Helen (DiMartino) G.; m. Denise Kitty Conlon, Feb. 19, 1971 (div. May 1978); 1 child, James Joseph; m. Anita Louise, May 12, 1979 (div. Sept. 1984); 1 child, Christopher Russell; m. Debra Lynn Brady (div. Dec. 1986); m. Michelle Bartok, Apr. 2, 1988. BS in Chemistry, SUNY, Binghamton, 1974; AAS in Bus. Adminstrn., Broome Coll., 1976. Rsch. chemist Lander Co. Inc., Binghamton, 1974-77; rsch. dir. Lander Co. Inc., St. Louis, 1977-79, Olde Worlde Products, High Point, N.C., 1979-81; v.p. rsch. and devel. LaCosta Products Internat., Carlsbad, Calif., 1981-89; chief ops. officer Randall Products Internat., Carlsbad, 1989-91; pres. Dermasearch Internat., 1991-92, Innovative Bioscis. Corp., Oceanside, Calif., 1992—; cons. Trans-Atlantic Mktg., Binghamton, 1975-78; instr. cosmetic sci UCLA, 1991, UCLA Ext. Mem. AAAS, Am. Chem. Soc., Soc. Cosmetic Chemists (newsletter editor 1980-81, publicity chmn. 1984—, edn. chmn. 1987, sec. beauty industry west), Fedn. Am. Scientists, Internat. Platform Assn., N.Y. Acad. Scis. Democrat. Roman Catholic. Office: Innovative Bioscis Corp # 115-116 4168 Avenida de la Plata Oceanside CA 92056

GARRUTO, MICHELLE BARTOK, small business owner; b. Youngstown, Ohio, Feb. 18, 1961; d. Albert James and Judith Ann (Phillips) Bartok; m. John Anthony Garruto, Apr. 2, 1988. BS in Physiol. Psychology, U. Calif., Santa Barbara, 1983. Emergency med. technician, 1984—. Asst. to phys. therapist Santa Barbara Phys. Therapy, 1983-84, Escondido (Calif.) Phys. Therapy, 1984-85; regional sales rep. Ft. Dodge Labs., San Francisco, 1985-87; owner North Coast Therapeutics, Oceanside, Calif., 1987-92; CEO Innovative Bioscis. Corp., 1992—, 1992—. Mem. Nat. Women's Fitness Assn., Women's Enterprise Network, Soc. Cosmetic Chemists, Beauty Industry West (pub. rels. dir. 1991-92, sponsor 1989 Ironman competition). Home: 178 Grandview Levcadia CA 92024 Office: Innovative Bioscis Corp Ste 115 & 116 4168 Avenida de la Plata Oceanside CA 92056

GARRY, STACEY LYNNE, pathologist; b. Bakersfield, Calif., Sept. 20, 1952; d. Stancil Lee Buchanan and Nona Ethel (Pyle) Finn; m. Edward David Garry, Dec. 18, 1982. Student, Bakersfield Coll., 1970-73; BS in Zoology, Idaho State U., 1982; MD, U. Calif., San Francisco, 1986. Diplomate Am. Bd. Med. Examiners, Am. Bd. Pathology-Anatomic and Chem. Pathology. Lab. asst. Kern Med. Ctr., Bakersfield, 1968-72; med. lab. technician Bannock Regional Med. Ctr., Pocatello, Idaho, 1976-77, Pocatello Regional Med. Ctr., 1976-82; resident U. Utah, Salt Lake City, 1986-91; pathologist lab. med. cons. Humana Sunrise Hosp., Las Vegas, Nev., 1991-92; dir. LMC Labs., Las Vegas, Nev., 1992—; cons. U. Utah Cardiovascular Inst., Salt Lake City, 1988-91, Associated & Regional Univ. Pathologists, Salt Lake City, 1989-91, Dermatopathology Inc., Murry, Utah, 1987-91, HGM Laser Inc., Salt Lake City, 1987-89, Symbion Inc., Vancouver, B.C., 1987-91; lectr. Utah State Health Dept., Utah, Oreg., Idaho, Ill. and Wis. State Med. Tech. Soc., Bannock Regional Med. Ctr. Fellow Coll. Am. Pathologists (resident forum chmn. 1990-91, vice-chmn. 1989-90, resident & young physicians sect. 1991—, planning com. 1990-93, com. pathology enhancement); mem. AMA (del. 1983-85, 86-90), Utah State Med. Assn. (del. 1986-90), U. Utah Housestaff Assn. (pres. 1988-90), Soc. for Hematopathology, CAP-HOD (del), Phi Kappa Phi. Home: 1500 Commanche Dr Las Vegas NV 89109-3113 Office: LMC Labs Humana Hosp Sunrise Maryland Pky Las Vegas NV 89109-1627

GARSH, THOMAS BURTON, publisher; b. New Rochelle, N.Y., Dec. 12, 1931; s. Harry and Matilda (Smith) G.; m. Beatrice J. Schmidt; children: Carol Jean, Thomas Burton, Janice Lynn. B.S., U. Md., 1955. Edn. rep. McGraw Hill Book Co., N.Y.C., 1959-68; mktg. mgr. D.C. Heath & Co., Boston, 1969-71; dir. mktg. Economy Co., Oklahoma City, 1971-72; sr. v.p. Macmillan Pub. Co., N.Y.C., 1972-78; pres. Am. Book Co., N.Y.C., 1978-81; founder, pres., dir. Am. Ednl. Computer, Inc., Palo Alto, Calif., 1981-86; founder, chmn., chief exec. officer OmnyEd Corp., Palo Alto, 1987-91; pres. Silver Burdett & Ginn div. of Simon and Schuster, 1991—. Mem. county council Boy Scouts Am., 1963-65; mem. ch. council on Interracial Affairs, 1966-68, pres., 1967; vice-chmn. Madison County Democratic Party, 1967. Mem. Assn. Am. Pubs., Profl. Bookman's Assn., Omicron Delta Kappa, Sigma Alpha Epsilon. Club: Cazenovia Country (founder). Home: 401 Old Spanish Trl Portola Valley CA 94028

GARSHNEK, VICTORIA, physiologist, research educator; b. L.A., July 19, 1957; d. Nicholas and Nadia (Bolotov) G. BS in Biomed. Chemistry, Oral Roberts U., 1979; MS in Physiology, U. Oreg., 1982, PhD in Physiology, 1985. Rsch. technician Sch. Medicine Oral Roberts U., Tulsa, 1979-80; naval aerospace physiologist Naval Aerospace Med. Inst., Pensacola, Fla., 1981-84; space biomed. analyst Gen. Electric/NASA Hdqrs., Washington, 1985-87; sr. rsch. scientist George Washington U./NASA Hdqrs., Washington, 1987-91; asst. rsch. prof. Inst. Space Policy George Washington U., Washington, 1989-91; scientist prin. advanced planning Lockheed Engring. & Scis. Co., Moffett Field, Calif., 1991—; editorial cons. for space physiology and medicine 2d edit. NASA Hdqrs./Lea & Febiger Books, Washington, 1985—; editorial and tech. cons. Time-Life Books: Voyage Through the Universe Series, 1989—; mem. editorial bd. US/USSR Publs., Washington, 1989—. Co-editor: Working in Earth Orbit & Beyond, 1989; contbr. articles to profl. jours. Instr., counselor sch. without walls program NASA Hdqrs., 1988, 89. Lt. (j.g.) USN, 1981-84. Recipient NASA Hdqrs. Cosmos Achievement award 1989, 91. Mem. AIAA, Aerospace Med. Assn. (assoc. fellow, chmn. planning subcom. of edn. and tng. com. 1989-91), Brit. Interplanetary Soc., Medispace Assn. (hon.), Explorers Club (fellow). Republican. Greek Orthodox. Office: Lockhead Engring Co WPO Box 168 Moffett Field CA 94088

GARSIDE, ANTHONY DAVID, credit management; b. Hythe, Kent, Eng., May 2, 1950; came to U.S., 1974; s. David Hobart and Norah Mary (Delafield) G.; m. Rita Kay Martin, Sept. 18, 1977; 1 child, Elizbeth Marie. Higher nat. diploma, West London Coll., Eng., 1971; BS in Bus., Ambassador Coll., 1977; postgrad. Bus. Adminstr., West Coast U., 1978-79. Positions in export sales and management various cos., London, L.A., Pasadena, 1973-80; br. mgr. Ind. Cargo Svcs., L.A., 1980-82; station mgr.

Behring Internat., Seattle, 1982-83; dist. mgr. Robinson Communications, Seattle, 1984; internat. traffic coord. Hapag-Lloyd Agys., Seattle, 1985; sales rep. Telecommunications Cos., Seattle, Tacoma, Bellevue, Wash., 1985-87; asst. credit mgr. Northwestern Drug Co., Auburn, Wash., 1987-90; sr. credit specialist Aldus Corp., Seattle, 1990—. Bd. dirs. Aldus Outreach, 1991-92. Mem. Nat. Assn. Credit Mgrs. (cert. credit exec., credit and fin. devel. div. bd. dirs., legis. awareness dir. 1991, publicity dir. 1992, study group dir. 1993, Nat. Publicity award 1992). Mem. Worldwide Ch. of God. Home: 35829 12th Ave SW Federal Way WA 98023 Office: Aldus Corp 411 1st Ave S Seattle WA 98104

GARSIDE, LARRY JOE, research geologist; b. Omaha, May 2, 1943; s. Edwin Joseph and Ruby Anne (Weaver) G. BS in Geology, Iowa State U., 1965; MS in Geology, U. Nev., 1968. Lab. asst. Iowa State U., Ames, 1965; rsch. asst. U. Nev., Reno, 1965-68; econ. geologist Nev. Bur. Mines & Geology, Reno, 1968-84, chief geologist, dep. dir., 1985-87, acting dir., 1987-88, rsch. geologist, 1988—; exec. sec. Nev. Oil & GAs Conservation Commn., Reno, 1974-75. Contbr. numerous articles to profl. jours. Fellow Geol. Soc. of Am.; mem. Am. Assn. Petroleum Geologists, Soc. Econ. Geologists, Assn. Exploration Geochemists, Geol. Soc. Nev. (pres. 1973-74, sec., treas. 1969-70), Nev. Petroleum Soc. (sec., treas. 1986), Geothermal Resource Coun. (charter). Home: 2670 Margaret Dr Reno NV 89506-8651 Office: Nev Bur of Mines & Geology U Nev 178 Reno NV 89557-0088

GARSIDE, STEVEN L., lawyer, educator; b. Ogden, Utah, June 12, 1957; s. Don Davere G. and Wanda Colleen (Lacey) Maero; m. Colleen Packer, Aug. 7, 1980; children: Jamee D., S. Jace, M. Brandon, Gavin T. BA, Weber State U., 1980; JD, Oklahoma City U., 1983. Bar: Okla. 1983, Utah 1984, Colo. 1990. Legal intern Oklahoma City (Okla.) Attys. Office, 1982-83, asst. city atty., 1983-86; asst. city atty. Layton (Utah) City Attys. Office, 1986—; instr. Weber State Police Acad., Ogden, 1988—. Atty.-coach mock trial team Cen. Davis Jr. High Sch., 1990—. Named Outstanding Young Man of Am., 1988. Mem. ABA, Colo. Bar Assn., Utah Bar Assn., Okla. Bar Assn., Profl. Ski Instrs. Am. Mem. Ch. of Latter Day Saints. Home: 2385 N 2275 E Layton UT 84040-8006 Office: Layton City Attys Office 437 Wasatch Dr Layton UT 84041-3254

GARSKE, JAY TORING, geologist, oil and minerals consultant; b. Fargo, N.D., Jan. 5, 1936; s. Vincent Walter and Margaret Anna (Toring) G.; m. Margo Joan Galloway, Aug. 31, 1957; children: Mara Jayne, Brett Andrew; m. Carol Jean Apker, Apr. 24, 1993. BS in Geology, U. N.D., 1957. Geologist Superior Oil Co., Rocky Mountain Region, 1959-62; pvt. practice cons. geologist Denver, 1962—; pres., bd. dirs. Kudu Oil Corp., Denver, 1982—, Garske Energy Corp., Denver, 1984—, Frontier Gold Resources, Inc., Denver, 1987-92, Omega Oil Corp., Denver, 1992—. 1st lt. U.S. Army, 1958-59. Mem. Am. Assn. Petroleum Geologists, Am. Soc. Photogrammetry and Remote Sensing, Rocky Mountain Assn. Geologists, Colo. Mining Assn., Sigma Gamma Epsilon. Home: 1583 S Spruce St Denver CO 80231-2615 Office: Omega Oil Corp 1616 Glenarm Pl Ste 2970 Denver CO 80202-4304

GARSON, ARNOLD HUGH, newspaper editor; b. Lincoln, Nebr., May 29, 1941; s. Sam B. and Celia (Stine) G.; m. Marilyn Grace Baird, Aug. 15, 1964; children: Scott Arnold, Christopher Baird, Gillian Grace, Megan Jane. BA, U. Nebr., 1964; MS, UCLA, 1965. Reporter Omaha World-Herald, 1965-69; reporter Des Moines Tribune, 1969-72, city editor, 1972-75; reporter Des Moines Register, 1975-83, mng. editor, 1983-88; editor San Bernardino (Calif.) County Sun, 1988—. Recipient Pub. Svc. Reporting award Am. Polit. Sci. Assn., 1969, Prof. Journalism award U. Nebr. at Omaha, 1969, John Hancock award for excellence in bus. and fin. journalism, 1979, Mng. Editors Sweepstakes award Iowa AP, 1976. Mem. Am. Soc. Newspaper Editors, Calif. Soc. Newspaper Editors, Assoc. Press. Mng. Editors. Jewish. Home: 201 Campbell Ave Redlands CA 92373 Office: San Bernardino County Sun 399 N D St San Bernardino CA 92401

GARSTANG, ROY HENRY, astrophysicist, educator; b. Southport, Eng., Sept. 18, 1925; came to U.S., 1964; s. Percy Brocklehurst and Eunice (Gledhill) G.; m. Ann Clemence Hawk, Aug. 11, 1959; children—Jennifer Katherine, Susan Veronica. B.A., U. Cambridge, 1946, M.A., 1950, Ph.D., 1954, Sc.D., 1983. Research assoc. U. Chgo., 1951-52; lectr. astronomy U. Coll., London, 1952-60; reader astronomy U. London, 1960-64, asst. dir. Obs., 1959-64; prof. astrophysics U. Colo., Boulder, 1964—, chair faculty assembly, 1988-89; chmn. Joint Inst. for Lab. Astrophysics, 1966-67; cons. Nat. Bur. Standards, 1964-73; v.p. commn. 14 Internat. Astron. Union, 1970-73, pres., 1973-76; Erskine vis. fellow U. Canterbury, N.Z., 1971; vis. prof. U. Calif., Santa Cruz, 1971. Editor: Observatory, 1953-60; Contbr. numerous articles to tech. jours. Recipient Excellence in Svc. award U. Colo., 1990. Fellow Am. Phys. Soc., AAAS, Optical Soc. Am., Brit. Inst. Physics, Royal Astron. Soc.; mem. Am. Astron. Soc., Royal Soc. Scis. Liege (Belgium). Home: 830 8th St Boulder CO 80302-7409 Office: U Colo Joint Inst Lab Astrophysics Boulder CO 80309

GARTLER, STANLEY MICHAEL, geneticist, educator; b. Los Angeles, June 9, 1923; s. George David and Delvira (Cupferberg) G.; m. Marion Ruth Mitchelson, Nov. 7, 1948. B.S., UCLA, 1948; Ph.D., U. Calif.-Berkeley, 1952. Research assoc. Columbia U., N.Y.C., 1952-57; research asst. prof. U. Wash., Seattle, 1957-60, assoc. prof., 1960-64, prof. genetics, 1964—; dir. NATO meeting on mosaicism, Venice, Italy, 1972. Author: (with R.E. Cole) Inactivation Sexual Differentiation, 1978. Grantee NIH and NSF, 1956—; merit scholar NIH. Mem. NAS, Am. Soc. Human Genetics (dir. 1970, pres.-elect 1986, pres. 1987), Genetics Soc. Am., Soc. Cell Biology, Am. Soc. Naturalists. Home: 9009 42d St NE Seattle WA 98115 Office: U Wash Dept Genetics Seattle WA 98195

GARTNER, HAROLD HENRY, III, lawyer; b. L.A., June 23, 1948; s. Harold Henry Jr. and Frances Mildred (Evans) G.; m. Denise Helene Young, June 7, 1975; children: Patrick Christopher, Matthew Alexander. Student, Pasadena City Coll., 1966-67, George Williams Coll., 1967-68, Calif. State U., Los Angeles, 1969; JD cum laude, Loyola U., Los Angeles, 1972. Bar: Calif. 1972, U.S. Dist. Ct. (cen. dist.) Calif. 1973, U.S. Ct. Appeals (9th cir.) 1973. Assoc. Hitt, Murray & Caffray, Long Beach, Calif., 1972; dep. city atty. City of L.A., 1972-73; assoc. Patterson, Ritner & Lockwood, L.A., 1973-79; mng. ptnr. all offices Patterson, Ritner, Lockwood, Zanghi & Gartner, L.A., Ventura, Bakersfield, and San Bernardino, Calif., 1991—; instr. law Ventura Coll., 1981. Recipient Am. Jurisprudence award Trusts and Equity, 1971. Mem. ABA, Calif. Bar Assn., Ventura County Bar Assn., Nat. Assn. Def. Counsel, Assn. So. Calif. Def. Counsel, Ventura County Trial Lawyers Assn., Direct Relief Internat. (bd. trustees). Republican. Club: Pacific Corinthian Yacht. Home: 6900 Via Alba Camarillo CA 93012-8279 Office: Patterson Ritner Lockwood Zanghi & Gartner 3580 Wilshire Blvd Ste 900 Los Angeles CA 90010-2534

GARTRELL, JOSEPH LEE, business analyst, management consultant; b. Tucson, June 4, 1961; s. Michael Frederick Meyer and Camilla Kay (Boone) G.; m. Erika Jean Larson, July 19, 1989. BA in Mgmt., U. Phoenix, 1991; M in Aeronautical Sci., Embry-Riddle Aeronautical U. Mgr. Cushing Street Restaurant, Tucson, 1986-87; agt. Prin. Fin. Group, Tucson, 1987-88; mgmt. cons. Jeriko Enterprises, Tucson, 1986—; bus. analyst Dun & Bradstreet, Tucson, 1990—; zone mgr. Circle K Corp., 1992—; bd. dirs. Info. & Referral Svcs., Inc. Author: Business Plan Kit for Small Business, 1990, 21st Century Management: The Functional Point, 1991; contbr. articles to profl. jours. Candidate state senate State of Ariz., 1988, city coun. City of Tucson, 1989; vice chmn. Tucson Young Reps., 1988—; bd. dirs. Ariz. Young Reps. League, 1988-90. Methodist. Home: 722 N Tucson Blvd Tucson AZ 85716-4147

GARTZ, PAUL EBNER, systems engineer; b. Chgo., July 17, 1946; s. Friedrich Samuel and Lillian Louise (Koroschetz) G. BSEE, Ill. Inst. Tech., 1969; MSEE, Stanford U., 1970. Engrng. co-op Western Electric, Chgo., 1965-69; mem. tech. staff Bell Telephone Labs., Whippany, N.J., 1969-74; sales mgr. Evelyn Wood Reading Dynamics, N.Y.C., 1975-78; owner Gartz Design, Montclair, N.J., 1976-79; mktg. rep. United Computing Systems, Seattle, 1979; sr. prin. engr. Boeing, Seattle, 1980—; bd. dirs. Walla Walla (Wash.) Coll. of Engring., CASE Outlook, Inc., Portland, Oreg.; chmn. bd., pres. SDF, Inc., L.A.; educator Seattle U., 1987—, Walla Walla Coll., 1989, U. Wash., 1992—. Contbr. articles to profl. publs. Recipient Nat. Hist. Preservation award Nat. Hist. Preservation Soc., N.J., 1980. Mem. Structured Devel. Forum (pres. 1987—), Nat. Coun. Systems Engr., Am. Inst. Aerospace and Astronautics, IEEE (Harry Rowe Mimno award 1987). Home: 9912 Arrowsmith Ave S Seattle WA 98118-5907 Office: Boeing PO Box 3707 MS 7X-MR Seattle WA 98124-2207

GARVER, OLIVER BAILEY, JR., bishop; b. L.A., July 19, 1925. BS, UCLA, 1945; MBA, Harvard U., 1948; STB, Episc. Theol. Sch., Cambridge, Mass., 1962; DD, Ch. Div. Sch. Pacific, 1987. Ordained to ministry Episcopal Ch. as deacon, 1962, as priest, 1963. With Lockheed Aircraft Corp., 1948-59; curate St. Alban's, L.A., 1966-72; urban assoc. Ch. of the Epiphany, L.A., 1966-72; canon to the ordinary Staff Bishop Rusack, 1973-85; consecrated bishop suffragan Diocese of L.A., 1985-89; bishop in residence Harvard Sch., 1989—. With USNR, 1943-46. Mem. Phi Beta Kappa, Beta Gamma Sigma. Office: Harvard Sch 3700 Coldwater Canyon Ave Studio City CA 91604-2399

GARVEY, DORIS BURMESTER, environmental administrator; b. N.Y.C., Oct. 3, 1936; d. William Henry and Florence Elizabeth (Sauerteig) Burmester; m. Gerald Thomas John Garvey, June 6, 1959; children: Deirdre Anne, Gerald Thomas John Jr., Victoria Elizabeth. BA with honors, Wilson Coll., 1958; MA with honors, Yale U., 1959. Rsch. assoc. Princeton U., N.J., 1967-76; environ. scientist Argonne (Ill.) Nat. Lab., 1976-84; staff mem. Los Alamos (N.Mex.) Nat. Lab., 1984-86, regulatory compliance officer, 1986-89, sect. leader environ. protection group, 1989-92, dep. group leader, environ. protection group, 1992—. Contbr. articles to profl. jours. Bd. dirs. N.Mex. Repertory Theater, Santa Fe, 1987-88; mem. Environ. Improvement Bd., Glen Ellyn, Ill., 1980-82. Mem. N.Mex. Hazardous Waste Soc., Women in Sci., Gov.'s Task Force Emergency Response, Nat. Assn. Environ. Profls., Phi Beta Kappa. Democratic. Roman Catholic. Home: 368 Calle Loma Norte Santa Fe NM 87501-1278 Office: Los Alamos Nat Lab PO Box 1663 MS K490 Los Alamos NM 87545

GARVEY, EVELYN JEWEL, mental health nurse; b. Carrizozo, N.Mex., Aug. 23, 1931; d. Everett E. and Jewel A. (Bullard) Bragg; m. Robert J. Garvey, July 10, 1949; children: Nancy, Annie, Catherine, Robert, Michael, Betty. AD, Ea. N.Mex. Coll., 1972. RN, N.Mex.; cert. EMT., N.Mex. Staff nurse N.Mex. Rehab. Ctr., Roswell, 1972; staff nurse Villa Solano State Sch., Roswell, 1972-79, DON, 1979-81; staff nurse Ft. Stanton (N.Mex.) Hosp., 1981—.

GARVEY, JUSTINE SPRING, immunochemistry educator, biology educator; b. Wellsville, Ohio, Mar. 14, 1922; d. John Sherman and Lydia Kathryn (Johnsten) Spring; m. James Emmett Garvey, June 15, 1946; children: Johanna Xandra Kathryn, Michaela Garvey-Hayes. BS, Ohio State U., 1944, MS, 1948, PhD, 1950. Analytical chemist Sun Oil Refinery Lab., Toledo, 1944-46; Office of Naval Rsch. predoctoral fellow in microbiology U. Rochester, N.Y., 1946-47; AEC predoctoral fellow microbiology Ohio State U., Columbus, 1948-50; rsch. faculty chemistry Caltech, Pasadena, Calif., 1951-57, sr. rsch. fellow chemistry, 1957-73, rsch. assoc. chemistry, 1973-74; assoc. prof. biology Syracuse (N.Y.) U., 1974-78, prof. immunochemistry, 1978-89, emeritus, 1990—; vis. assoc. biology Caltech, 1990—; bd. sci. counselors Nat. Inst. Dental Rsch., NIH, Bethesda, Md., 1979-82; ad hoc study sects. NIH, Bethesda, 1979-88. Co-author: (textbook) Methods in Immunology, 1963, 2d edit., 1970, 3d edit., 1977; editorial bd. Immunochemistry Jour., 1964-71, Immunological Methods Jour., 1971-77; contbr. 125 articles to profl. jours. Grantee NIAID, 1951-72, NSF, 1977-79, Nat. Inst. on Aging, 1978-87, Nat. Inst. Environ. Health Scis., 1980-88. Mem. AAAS, Am. Assn. Immunologists, N.Y. Acad. Scis., Sigma Xi.

GASKILL, HERBERT LEO, accountant, engineer; b. Seattle, July 1, 1923; s. Leo Dell and Vesta Rathbone (Dahlen) G.; m. Margaret Helen Jenkins, Mar. 1, 1944 (div.); children—Margaret V., Herbert Leo; m. Opal Jordan, June 13, 1992; 1 child, Ann. B.S. and M.S. in Chem. Engring., U. Wash., 1949, M.B.A., 1976. C.P.A., Wash. Asst. prof. dental materials, exec. officer dept. dental materials Sch. Dentistry, U. Wash., 1950-56; ops. analyst The Boeing Co., Seattle, 1958-71, mktg. cons. govt. programs, 1972-74; pvt. practice acctg., Seattle, 1976-80; hazardous waste mgr. Boeing Co., Seattle, 1980-86, project mgr. western processing remediation, 1986—. Active Seattle Art Mus., Pacific Northwest Aviation Hist. Found. Served to lt. (j.g.) USNR, 1941-46. TAPPI fellow, 1956; U. Wash. Engrng. Expt. Sta. fellow, 1957. Mem. Wash. Soc. C.P.A.s. Contbr. articles to profl. jours. Home: 1236 NE 92d St Seattle WA 98115

GASOWSKI, RONALD EDWARD, artist, educator; b. Hamtramck, Mich., Aug. 22, 1941; s. Edward Stanley and Marcelle E. (Magryta) G.; m. Nancy Lynn Mack, June 11, 1966; children: Timon Ronald, Samuel Edward. BS in Design, U. Mich., 1966; MFA, U. Wash., 1968; hon. degree, U. Sonora, Hermonsillo, Mexico, 1972. Instr. Calif. State U., Hayward, Calif., 1968-71; asst. prof. Arizona State U., Tempe, Ariz., 1971-82, prof. art, 1982-92. Exhibited in musuems and galleries in N. and S. Am., Australia, New Zealand, Europe, Korea, Japan; over 30 solo exhbns. and 100 group shows; prin. works include Phoenix Sky Harbor Internat. Airport, Marivue Park, Phoenix, Ariz. State Hosp., Phoenix, Tempe Performing Arts Ctr., Chandler-Gilbert C.C., Chandler, Ariz. Mem. sub-com. City of Tempe Rio Salado Art Master Plan, 1992, Folk Art Soc. Am., Ariz. State U. Art Mus., Tempe Art Ctr.

GASPAR, ROGELIO G., laboratory technologist; b. Manila, Philippines, Mar. 12, 1965; s. Rodolfo and Leonila (Guevarra) G.; m. Maria Regis, Apr. 6, 1988; children: Ryan Angelo, Anna Giselle. BS in Med. Tech., U. St. Tomas, Manila, 1985. Lab. asst. Inst. Forensic Sci., Oakland, Calif., 1987; lab. tech. Vet. Ref. Lab., San Leandro, Calif., 1987-89, San Francisco AIDS Found., 1988, Fleischmann's Yeast Inc., Oakland, Calif., 1988, Damon Clin. Lab., San Francisco, 1989—; med. technologist Damon Clin. Lab., Pleasanton, Calif., 1988—. Mem. Philippine Assn. of Med. Technologist.

GASPER, LOUIS, sociology educator; b. Lorain, Ohio, Feb. 10, 1911; s. Daniel and Matilda (Cinders) G.; m. Nellie Mabel Kremer, Mar. 27, 1943. DGB, Moody Bible Inst., 1940; BA cum laude, Bowling Green State U., 1947, BS in Edn. cum laude, 1947, MA, 1949; BDiv, Findlay Coll. Grad. Sch. Divinity, 1954; PhD in Am. culture, Case Western Res. U., Cleve., 1958; AMEd, U. So. Calif., 1962; MAc Arts and PhD, Am. Coll. Acupuncture, 1966; MDiv, Winebrenner Theol. Sem., 1968. Ordained to ministry, Bapt. Ch., 1940. With U.S. Steel Corp., 1929-38; minister various chs., Ill., Ohio, 1939-57; tchr. Fostoria (Ohio) High Sch., 1945-47; assoc. prof. history Bluffton Coll., 1949-50; assoc. prof. Florence (Ala.) State U. (name changed to Northern Ala. U.), 1957-58; tchr. L.A. City Schs., 1958-59; assoc. prof. Humboldt State U., Calif., 1959-60; assoc. prof. sociology dir. elem. edn. L.A. Pacific Coll. (name changed to Azusa Pacific Coll.), 1961-63; prof. sociology, chair. dept. sociology L.A. Pierce Coll., 1963-76, emeritus prof., dept. chair, 1976—; prof. sociology, chair dept. philosophy edn. and sociology, 1967-76; pres. faculty assn., 1967-68; chair acad. senate, 1967-68; sr. mem. curriculum com., 1973-76; asst prof. Calif. State U., Northridge, part-time, 1964-67; assoc. prof. Calif. State U., L.A., 1967-71, Long Beach, 1971-73, mem. Emeriti and Retired Family, 1989; mem. rsch. staff U. So. Calif., 1965-68; marriage, family and child counselor, 1963—; intern Am. Inst. Family Rels., Hollywood, Calif., 1963-65, asst. staff assoc., 1965—; coord. Acupuncture Rsch. Inst., sec., dir., 1977—, others; pres. L.A. Internat. U. Samuel Hahnemann Sch. Homoeopathic Medicine. Author: The Fundamentalist Movement, 1963, Introduction to Sociology, 1965, Fundamentals of Sociology, 1966, 2d edit. 1969, Vital Social Problems, 1967; co-author: Harry Elmer Barnes Learned Crusader, 1968, Sociology Syllabus and Readings in Sociology, 1964; contbg. author chpts. to books; contbr. articles to profl. jours. Dual ministerial rel. with United Ch. of Christ, 1962, ARC; com. mem. in formation of the Advanced Med. Aide Corps Cuyahoga County Civil Def. and Cleve. Acad., 1956; Red Cross disaster trainer NASA in Reynoldlite Aluminum Rocket Plant, Tuscumbia, Ala., 1957; appointed by Gov. Wilson Calif. Blue Ribbon Com. for Scope of Practice for acupuncture, 1992. Mem. United Acupuncturists of Calif. (English speaking chmn. bd., 1978—), Am. Sociol. Assn. (emeritus), Acupuncture Rsch. Inst. Alumni Assn. (editor A.R.I. Meridian), Homoepathic Med. Assn. Am. (pres. 1985), Am. Assn. Acupuncture and Oriental Medicine (founder 1981), Calif. Assn. Marriage Counselors (charter, life), Pierce Coll. Faculty Assn. (pres. 1967-68), Group Psychotherapy Assn., So. Calif. Book and Motor Soc. (Bowling Green State U.), Gold Card Peace Officers Assn. (life), Phi Kappa Phi, Alpha Kappa Delta, Kappa Delta Pi. Home: 313 W Andrix St Monterey Park CA 91754-6408

GASPERONI, JOHN LINO, psychologist, educator; b. Detroit, Dec. 6, 1951; s. Lino and Florence (DaPra) G.; m. Lynn Anne Ireland, Aug. 30, 1980 (div. Nov. 1989); m. W. Clayton Goad, June 29, 1991. B in Gen. Studies, U. Mich., 1973; MA in Psychology, West Ga. Coll., 1978; postgrad., Psychol. Studies Inst., 1979-83; PhD in Clin. Psychology, Calif. Inst. Integral Studies, 1986. Lic. psychologist, Calif. Clin. mental health counselor Buena Vista Dr.'s Med. Clinic, San Francisco, 1979-80; night counselor Sunny Hills Children's Ctr., San Anselmo, Calif., 1981; mental health worker Belmont Hills Psychiat. Ctr., Belmont, Calif., 1981-82; assoc. prof. Calif. Inst. Integral Studies, San Francisco, 1982—; from counselor to clin. supr. Conard House, San Francisco, 1982-88; coord. treatment Oak Grove Hosp., Concord, Calif., 1988-89; sr. clinician Tenderloin Outpatient Clinic, San Francisco, 1989-90, dir. tng., 1990—. Mem. APA, San Francisco Soc. for Lacanian Studies. Buddhist. Office: Tenderloin Outpatient Clinic 251 Hyde St San Francisco CA 94102

GASSMAN, VICTOR ALAN, cosmetics executive; b. St. Louis, Nov. 7, 1935; s. Samuel and Hilda (Scalla) G.; m. Betty Cohn, Dec. 24, 1961 (div. 1981); children: Susan L., James C.; m. Lynne Hobbs, Jan. 28, 1984; children: Michael S., Christopher S. BS, BA in Retailing, Washington U., 1957. Divisional sales mgr. Famous Barr, St. Louis, 1957-64; mdse. mgr. May Co., L.A., 1965-77; divisional mdse. mgr. J.W. Robinson, L.A., 1977-83; pres. DEPUTE-div. Dep. Corp., L.A., 1983-85, Liz Claiborne Cosmetics, N.Y.C., 1985-88, Victor Gassman & Assocs., N.Y.C., 1988-90; sr. v.p., gen. mgr. Visage Beaute' Cosmetics, Beverly Hills, Calif., 1990—; pres. Sales, Mktg. and Svcs. Cons., 1993—. Actor Hilton Head Community Playhouse in You Can't Take It With You, 1990, The Boy's Next Door, 1990, Broadway Bound, 1990, Murder Mystery Cruise in Misbegotten Birthday, 1990, Readers Theater in The Madwoman of Chaillot, 1990, Fox TV in Americas Most Wanted, 1990. Dir. YMCA, Boy Scouts, United Fund, Redlands Art Assn., San Bernardino, 1965-71; v.p. Regional Econ. Devel. Coun., San Bernardino, 1970; pres. Arrowhead Allied Arts Coun., San Bernardino, 1969. Capt. U.S. Army, 1957-65. Recipient Buyer of the Yr. award May Co., 1973, Retailer of Yr. award Fragrance Found., 1982, Career Achievement award So. Calif. Cosmetic Assn., 1984, Best New Packaging / TV award Fragrance Found., 1987. Mem. Foragers Cosmetics Assn., Inland Ctr. Mchts. Assn. (pres. 1971), So. Calif. Cosmetics Assn. (bd. dirs. 1990—), Beauty Industry West (bd. dirs. 1990—), Jr. C. of C., Rotary club. Democrat. Jewish.

GAST, NANCY LOU, chemical company executive; b. Appleton, Wis., Aug. 13, 1941; d. Harvey William Gast and June Louella (Mohr) Webster. Med. technologist Palo Alto/Stanford (Calif.) Hosp., 1963-65; med. technologist St. Vincent Hosp., Portland, Oreg., 1965-70, chemistry supr., 1970-81; tech. rep. DuPont-Diagnostic Systems, Claremont, Calif., 1981-83, sales rep., 1983-85, account rep., 1985-87, acct. mgr., 1987—. Vol. med. technologist Health Help Ctr., Portland, 1984-88; bd. dirs. Assocs. of Sisters of Holy Names of Jesus and Mary, Marylhurst, Oreg., 1984-93. Mem. Am. Soc. Med. Technologists, Assn. Oreg. Med. Technologists (treas. 1976-78, chmn. sci. assembly 1992—), Am. Soc. Clin. Pathologists (cert. med. technologist, assoc.). Republican. Roman Catholic. Office: EI DuPont Diagnostic Systems PO Box 51485 Ontario CA 91761-0085

GASTIL, RICHARD WALTER, JR., psychotherapist, educator, consultant; b. Burbank, Calif., June 4, 1953; s. Richard Walter Sr. and Nancy Gastil; m. Kathleen Dolbier, Feb. 6, 1976 (div. July 1985); children: Michael John, Mark Walter. BBA, Calif. State U., Fullerton, 1976; MA, MSW, Calif. Christian Inst., 1982; MA in Psychology, Rosemead Sch. Psychology, La Mirada, Calif.,, 1990. Lic. marriage, family and child counselor. Min. Melodyland Christian Ctr., Anaheim, Calif., 1977-84; bus. adminstr. Melodyland Hotline Ctr., Anaheim, 1976-77; exec. dir. Hotline Help Ctrs., Inc., Anaheim, 1977-88; prof. Calif. Christian Inst., Orange, 1984-88; psychotherapist No. Orange County Psychol. Svc., Orange, 1988—. Vice chmn. City of Anaheim Youth Gang Task Force, 1988-89; chmn. City of Anaheim Community Svcs. Funding Com., 1990; bd. dirs. Anaheim Salvation Army, 1986-90, Vineyard Christian Fellowship, Diamond Bar, Calif., 198-92, Allied Health Exec. Com., Anaheim, 1992; mem. City of Anaheim Community Svcs. Bd., 1987-91. Mem. APA, Calif. Assn. Marriage and Family Therapists, Christian Assn. Psychol. Studies, Cert. Employee Assistance Profls. Office: No Orange County Psychol Svcs 746 E Chapman Ave Orange CA 92666

GASTON, MACK CHARLES, naval officer; b. Dalton, Ga., July 17, 1940; s. John H. and Mildred Felicia (Gillard) G.; m. Lillian Juanita Bonds, Aug. 15, 1965; 1 child, Sonja Marie. BS in Comml. Electronics, Tuskegee U., 1964; diploma, Naval Command and Staff Coll., Newport, R.I., 1977; cert., Indsl. Coll. Armed Forces, Washington, 1983; MBA, Marymount U., 1984. Commd. ensign USN, 1964, advanced through grades to rear adm., 1990; electronic and combat info. officer USS Buck, San Diego, 1965-67; chief engr. USS O'Brien, Long Beach, Calif., 1967-69; engr. nuclear safety Destroyer Squadron 5, San Diego, 1969-71; personal aide to dir. Navy Rsch., Test and Evaluation, Washington, 1971-73; assignment officer Bur. Naval Pers., Washington, 1973-74; exec. officer USS Conyngham, Norfolk, Va., 1974-76; comdg. officer USS Cochrane, Pearl Harbor, Hawaii, 1977-79, USS Cone, Charleston, S.C., 1981-82; dir. navy equal opportunity, spl. asst. to chief Naval Pers. for Equal Opportunity, Washington, 1984-85; comdg. officer USS Josephus Daniels, Norfolk, 1986-88; dir. manpower and pers. readiness for comdr. in chief Atlantic Command, Washington, 1988; mem., fellow Chief of Naval Ops. Strategic Study Group, Washington, 1988-89; dir. surface warfare manpower and tng. Office Chief of Naval Ops., Washington, 1989-90; comdr. field command Def. Nuclear Agy., Albuquerque, 1990-92; comdr. Naval Tng. Ctr., Great Lakes, Ill., 1992—. Speaker, councilor chs., community groups, Navy League, others. Inducted into Dalton Edn. Hall of Fame, 1990. Mem. Nat. Naval Officer Assn. (life), Fed. Exec. Bd. (policy bd. 1990), U.S. Naval Inst., Naval Order of U.S., Surface Warfare Assn., Nat. Mil. Family Assn., Am. Legion, Tin Can Sailors, Inc. Office: Office of Comdr Naval Tng Ctr Great Lakes IL 60088-5000

GATELY, ALEXANDER PATRICK, contractor; b. Cin., July 2, 1949; s. Alexander Francis and Mary (Dewey) G. BBA, Western Mich. U., 1971. Sales trainee Grand Rapids (Mich.) Sash & Door Co., 1971-72; with ter. sales dept. Norco Windows Inc., Grand Rapids, 1972-76, mgr. new accounts, 1976-78; mgr. nat. sales Norco Windows Inc., Hawkins, Wis., 1978-85, v.p. sales and mktg., 1985-88; v.p. ops. Design Master Div. T. J. Internat. Corp., Boise, Idaho, 1988-91; v.p. mfg. Norco Windows Inc., Boise, 1992—. Mem. Nat. Home Builders Assn., Nat. Wood, Window and Door Assn., Nat. Sash and Door Jobbers Assn. Roman Catholic. Office: Norco Windows Inc PO Box 65 380 E Parkcentre Blvd Ste 300 Boise ID 83707

GATES, CHARLES CASSIUS, rubber company executive; b. Morrison, Colo., May 27, 1921; s. Charles Cassius and Hazel LaDora (Rhoads) G.; m. June Scowcroft Swaner, Nov. 26, 1943; children: Diane, John Swaner. Student, MIT, 1939-41; BS, Stanford U., 1943; DEng (hon.), Mich. Tech. U., 1975, Colo. Sch. of Mines, 1985. With Copolymer Corp., Baton Rouge, 1943-46; with Gates Rubber Co., Denver, 1946—, v.p., 1951-58, exec. v.p., 1958-61, chmn. bd., 1961—, now also chief exec. officer; chmn. bd. The Gates Corp., Denver, 1982—, chief exec. officer, from 1982, also bd. dirs.; bd. dirs. Hamilton Oil Corp., Denver, BHP Petroleum-Melbourne, Australia. Trustee Gates Found.; trustee Denver Mus. Natural History, Calif. Inst. Tech., Pasadena. Recipient Community Leadership and Service award Nat. Jewish Hosp., 1974; Mgmt. Man of Year award Nat. Mgmt. Assn., 1965; named March of Dimes Citizen of the West, 1987. Mem. Conf. Bd. (dir.), Conquistadores del Cielo, Denver Club, Outrigger Canoe Club, Waialae Country Club, Boone and Crockett Club, Ltd., Country Club of Colo., Roundup Riders of Rockies, Shikar-Safari Internat., Augusta Nat. Golf Club, Castle Pines Golf Club, Old Baldy Club. Office: Gates Corp 900 S Broadway Denver CO 80209

GATES, DARYL FRANCIS, former police chief; b. Aug. 30, 1926. B.S. in Pub. Adminstrn., U. So. Calif., also postgrad. in Pub. Adminstrn. With Dept. Police City of Los Angeles, 1949—, lt., 1959-63, capt., 1963-65, comdr., 1965-68, dep. chief, 1968-69, asst. chief, 1969-78, chief, 1978-92. Bd. councilors U. So. Calif. Inst. Saftey and Systems Mgmt.; bd. dirs. YMCA,

Los Angeles; mem. Children's Village Adv. Bd. Served with USN, World War II. Mem. Calif. Peace Officers Assn., Internat. police Assn., Calif. Police Chief Assn., Internat. Assn. Chiefs of Police, Women's Peace Officers Assn. Calif., Los Angeles C. of C. Lodge: Rotary. Office: 756 Portola Terr. Los Angeles CA 90042

GATES, JAN ELLEN, packaging engineer; b. Sacramento, Nov. 22, 1953; d. Robert Allan and Margaret Jane (Monday) White; m. Robert Charles Gates, Sept. 6, 1975; children: Evan Robert, Jessica Starr. BS in Food Sci., Mich. State U., 1975, MS in Packaging, 1982. Packaging engr. Mead Johnson & Co., Evansville, Ind., 1977-79, Beatrice/Hunt-Wesson, Fullerton, Calif., 1979-88; sr. packaging engr. Lever Bros., L.A., 1988-91, Syva Co., Cupertino, Calif., 1991—; mem. packaging industry adv. bd. Calif. Poly. Inst., San Luis Obispo, 1990—; editor, coord. Reduce, Recycle, Reuse Task Group for Food and Pharm. Industry, Sunnyvale, Calif., 1992—. Contbg. author: Handbook for Environmentally Responsible, 1992; co-patentee microwave popcorn container. Leader Campfire Boys and Girls, 1991—; treas. Sunnyvale Alliance, Calif. Youth Soccer Assn., 1993. Mem. Inst. Packaging Profls. (bd. dirs. So. Calif. chpt. 1980-91, No. Calif. chpt. 1991—), Sierra Club. Home: 1544 Samedra St Sunnyvale CA 94087

GATES, KARLA DIANE, health services professional; b. Everett, Wash., Apr. 15, 1952; d. Paul Monroe and Winifred June (Meddins) Schutt; m. Thomas J. Gates, Nov. 24, 1984. BA in Psychology, Whitworth Coll., 1974, MA in Applied Behavioral Sci., 1985. Cert. mental health therapist, Wash., cert. marriage and family therapist, Wash. Group life supr. Good Shepard Home, Spokane, Wash., 1974-76; caseworker Toutle (Wash.) River Boys Ranch, 1976-81; coord. youth and young adult ministries 1st Presbyn. Ch., Kelso, Wash., 1981-86; therapist, coord. victims sexual assualt program, sch. cons. program Lower Columbia Mental Health Ctr., Longview, Wash., 1986-92; supr. children's outpatient program Lower Columbia Mental Health Ctr., Longview, 1992; pvt. practice individual, child and family therapist Longview, 1990—; cons. Progress Ctr., Neuromuscular Ctr., Longview, 1991—; parenting classes TIPPS/Cowlitz Co. Human Resources, Kelso, 1992. Youth ministries cons. Presbyn. Ch., Woodland, Wash., 1986, Trinity Luth., Longview, 1987, Bapt. Ch., Ranier, Oreg., 1991; pers. com. 1st Presbyn. Ch., Kelso, 1992—, session/bd. 1993—; bd. dirs. Cowlitz Family Health Ctr., 1993—. Named Outstanding Young Woman of Am., 1983. Mem. Sexual Assault Network. Office: Counseling Assocs 1953 7th Ave Ste 202 Longview WA 98632

GATES, THEODORE ALLAN, JR., software engineer; b. Washington, May 24, 1933; s. Theodore Allan and Margaret (Camp) G.; m. Anne Bissell, Sept. 8, 1955; children: Virginia Anne, Nancy Bissell, Theodore Allan III, Margaret Kenyon. Student, U. Md., 1951-53, 56-57, 68-69. Mem. staff Arthur D. Little Systems, Burlington, Mass., 1976-77, Corp. Tech. Planning, Portsmouth, N.H., 1977-78; project mgr. Honeywell Info. Systems, Phoenix, 1978-81; tech. mgr. Honeywell Info. Systems, Seattle, 1981-83; mgr. data and software engring. ISC Systems Corp., Spokane, Wash., 1983-90; project mgr. Boeing Computer Svcs., Richland, Wash., 1990—. Served with U.S. Army, 1953-56, Korea. Recipient Superior Performance award Census Bur., 1958. Mem. IEEE, AAAS, Assn. for Computing Machinery, Boston Computer Soc., Air Force Assn., U.S. Naval Inst., Berkeley Macintosh Users Group, Gorilla Found., Smithsonian Assocs., Nature Conservancy, Commodores Club (Boston), Masons, Shriners. Lutheran. Home: 4800 Pheasant Ln Richland WA 99352-9563 Office: Boeing Computer Svcs BCS-R LL4-91 PO Box 1970 Richland WA 99352-0539

GATES, WILLIAM HENRY, III, software company executive; b. Seattle, Wash, Oct. 28, 1955; s. William H. and Mary M. (Maxwell) G. Grad. high sch., Seattle, 1973; student, Harvard U., 1975. With MITS, from 1975; founder, chmn. bd. Microsoft Corp., Redmond, Wash., 1976—, now chief exec. officer. Recipient Howard Vollum award, Reed Coll., Portland, Oreg., 1984. Office: Microsoft Corp 1 Microsoft Way Redmond WA 98052-6399*

GATHERS, GEORGE ROGER, physicist; b. Meridian, Okla., Feb. 1, 1936; s. George Walker and Eugenia Midian (Payne) G.; m. Christine Elizabeth Key, Apr. 5, 1969; 1 child, Kevin Michael. AA, Pierce Jr. Coll., 1957; BS, U. So. Calif., 1960; PhD, U. Calif., Berkeley, 1967. Staff physicist Lawrence Livermore (Calif.) Nat. Lab., 1967-68, asst. leader, then leader diagnostics group, 1968-69, staff physicist, 1969-71, sr. physicist isobaric expansion facility, 1972-83, staff physicist H div., 1983-91, staff physicist hazards control, 1991—. Contbr. numerous articles to tech. jours.; author handbook on testing nuclear weapons. Radio operator Radio Amateur Civil Emergency Svcs., Livermore, 1972—; asst. scoutmaster Pleasanton area Boy Scouts Am., 1972-89. Mem. NRA (cert. instr.), Am. Phys. Soc., Christian Businessmen's Com. Republican. Mem. Evangel. Free Ch. Am. Office: Lawrence Livermore Nat Lab PO Box 808 Livermore CA 94550-0808

GATI, FRANK, systems engineer; b. Budapest, Hungary, June 29, 1938; s. Joseph and Ilona (Olah) G.; m. Sally Joann Cytron, Sept. 3, 1972; 1 child, David; children from previous marriage: Zoltan, Lana. BS, Calif. State U., L.A., 1975; MBA, San Francisco State U., 1981. Cons. Bank of Am., Concord, Calif., 1959—. Home: 74 Allston Way San Francisco CA 94127

GATLEY, WILLIAM STUART, SR., mechanical engineer, consultant; b. Pueblo, Colo., Jan. 24, 1932; s. William Perkins and Elizabeth Lenore (Brown) G.; m. Betty Lou Jerome, Dec. 30, 1961 (div. May 1979); children: William Stuart Jr., Gregory J., Christopher E. AB in Pub. Affairs, Princeton (N.J.) U., 1954; BSME, Washington U., St. Louis, 1956, MS in Mech. Engring., 1957; PhD, Purdue U., 1967. Registered profl. engr., Mo. Rsch. engr. Jersey Prodn. Rsch. Co., Tulsa, 1957-64; prof. U. Mo., Rolla, 1966-78; mgr. mech. engring. rsch. Motorola Portable Products, Ft. Lauderdale, Fla., 1978-87; chief mech. engr. Motorola Govt. Electronics, Phoenix, 1987—; prin. Coffeen, Gatley & Assocs., Mission, Kans., 1972-73; pvt. practice cons. 1966—; presenter seminars on noise control, 1969—. Co-author: (textbook) Noise Control for Engineers, 1980; contbr. numerous articles to profl. jours. Instr. Jr. Achievement, Phoenix, 1989. With USAR, 1957-65. Recipient scholarship Princeton U., 1950-54, Washington U., 1957-58; Ford Found. grantee, 1962-66. Mem. ASME, Am. Soc. for Engring. Edn. (chmn.), Inst. Noise Control Engrs., Pi Tau Sigma, Tau Beta Pi, Sigma Xi, Theta Xi. Republican. Episcopalian. Home: 4114 E Sahuaro Dr Phoenix AZ 85028-3543 Office: Motorola Govt Electronics Group PO Box 1417 Scottsdale AZ 85252-1417

GATLIN, DANIEL G., psychotherapist; b. Phoenix, Ariz., Apr. 11, 1957; s. Dan G. and Emma Jean (Walker) G. BA in Anthropology summa cum laude, Chapman Coll., 1979, BA in Art, 1979; MA in Psychology, U.S. Internat. U., San Diego, 1990; postgrad., U.S. Internat. U. Planner Phelps Dodge Corp., Morenci, 1979-80; ceramic sculptor/designer Stoneware Unltd., Inc., Santa Ana, Calif., 1980-86; dir. adminstrn. Alternative Ways Inc., Long Beach, Calif., 1986-87; video editor Belmont Prodns., Long Beach, 1988-90; instr. Loyola Marymount U., L.A., 1990; case mgr. St. John's Hosp., Santa Monica, Calif., 1990—; dir. edn. Fellowship of Pachamama, 1989—. Editor, art dir. (video documentary) For Love and For Life, 1988, A Shaman's World, 1989. Mem. APA, Am. Assn. Marriage & Family Counselors, Calif. Psychological Assn., Calif. Assn. Alcohol & Drug Counselors.

GATLIN, KEN, writer; b. Bellview, Calif., Dec. 11, 1940; s. Jesse Alexander and Hazel Isabel (Bowles) G.; m. Maggie Nystrom, May 22, 1983. Author: (novels) St. Harriet, 1985, The Angelist, 1988, (poetry collection) Felt Mathematics, 1989, (short story collection) Red Dress & Other Stories, 1990. Christian Sufi. Home: 2301 Union St Eureka CA 95501

GATROUSIS, CHRISTOPHER, research insitute administrator, chemist; b. Norwich, Conn., Oct. 8, 1928; s. George John and Irene (Romeliotou) G.; m. Patricia Agnes O'Brien, May 17, 1951 (div. July 1985); 1 child, John F. BA, DePaul U., 1957; MS, U. Chgo., 1960; PhD, Clark U., 1965. Asst. scientist Argonne (Ill.) Nat. Lab., 1956-61; staff scientist Woods Hole (Mass.) Oceanographic Inst., 1964-66; staff scientist Lawrence Livermore (Calif.) Nat. Lab., 1966-70, group leader, 1970-72, asst. div. leader, 1972-73, assoc. div. leader, 1973-75, dep. div. leader, 1975-77, div. leader, 1977-85, assoc. dir., 1985—. Chmn. Livermore Beautification Com., 1969-71. Sgt. USMC, 1948-52. Fellow AEC, 1961-64, Jeppson fellow Clark U., 1963-64. Mem. Am. Chem. Soc. Home: 5179 Diane Ln Livermore CA 94550 Office: Lawrence Livermore Nat Lab PO Box 808 East Ave Livermore CA 94550

GATTI, DANIEL JON, lawyer; b. Racine, Wis., Apr. 22, 1946; s. Daniel John and Rosemary J. (Moore) G.; m. Donna Jeane Wolfe, Mar. 30, 1984; children: Danny, DiAndra, Stephanie, David. BS, Western Oreg. State U., 1968; JD, Willamette U., 1973. Bar: Oreg. 1973, U.S. Dist. Ct. Oreg. 1973, U.S. Ct. Appeals (9th cir.) 1974, U.S. Ct. Appeals (2d cir.) 1985, U.S. Supreme Ct. 1979; cert. trial specialist. Tchr. Lake Oswego (Oreg.) High Sch., 1970; specialist in edn. law Oreg. Dept. Edn., Salem, 1973-75; pres., atty., ptnr. Gatti & Gatti, P.C., Salem, 1975—. Co-author: The Teacher and The Law, 1972, Encyclopedic Dictionary of School Law, 1975, New Encyclopedic Dictionary of School Law, 1983, The Educator's Encyclopedia of School Law, 1990. V.p., bd. trustees Western States Chiropractic Coll., Portland, Oreg., 1976—. Mem. Oreg. Bar Assn., Assn. Trial Lawyers Am., Am. Bd. Trial Advocacy (cert. as trial specialist 1987), Am. Adjudicature Soc., Illahe Club. Office: Gatti Gatti Maier & Assocs 1761 Liberty St SE Salem OR 97302-5198

GAUCH, MATTHEW DONALD, programmer, systems analyst, consultant; b. Eldora, Iowa, Jan. 26, 1963; s. Donald Eugene and Judith Ann (McKay) G.; m. Susan Elizabeth Nelson, Oct. 20, 1990 (div. June 1992). BS in Info. Systems, U. Colo., 1989. Sr. programmer, analyst DI-SYS/SISCOM, Boulder, Colo., 1983-87; tech. cons. Brandon Cons. Group, Denver, 1989-90, 90-91; programmer Comprecare, Aurora, Colo., 1990; programmer, analyst Minicomputer Systems, Inc., Boulder, 1992; pres. Humanized Systems Cons., Ltd., Boulder, 1992—. Mem. Mile High CASE Users' Group (programs dir. 1992—, newsletter contbr.).

GAULKE, MARY FLORENCE, library administrator; b. Johnson City, Tenn., Sept. 24, 1923; d. Gustus Thomas and Mary Belle (Bennett) Erickson; m. James Wymond Crowley, Dec. 1, 1939; 1 son, Grady Gaulke (name legally changed); m. 2d, Bud Gaulke, Sept. 1, 1945 (dec. Jan. 1978); m. 3d, Richard Lewis McNaughton, Mar. 21, 1983. B.S. in Home Econs., Oreg. State U., 1963; M.S. in L.S., U. Oreg., 1968, Ph.D. in Spl. Edn., 1970. Cert. standard pers. supr., standard handicapped learner, Oreg. Head dept. home econs. Riddle Sch. Dist. (Oreg.), 1963-66; library cons. Douglas County Intermediate Edn. Dist., Roseburg, Oreg., 1966-67; head resident, head counselor Prometheus Project, So. Oreg. Coll., Ashland, summers 1966-68; supr. librarians Medford Sch. Dist. (Oreg.), 1970-73; instr. in psychology So. Oreg. Coll., Ashland, 1970-73; library supr. Roseburg Sch. Dist., 1974-91; resident psychologist Black Oaks Boys Sch., Medford, 1970-75; mem. Oreg. Gov.'s Council on Libraries, 1979. Author: Vo-Ed Course for Junior High, 1965; Library Handbook, 1967; Instructions for Preparation of Cards For All Materials Cataloged for Libraries, 1971; Handbook for Training Library Aides, 1972. Coord. Laubach Lit. Workshops for High Sch. Tutors, Medford, 1972. Fellow Internat. Biog. Assn. (life); mem. ALA, So. Oreg. Library Fedn. (sec. 1971-73), Oreg. Library Assn., Pacific N.W. Library Assn., Am. Biog. Inst. (lifetime dep. gov. 1987—), Internat. biog. Ctr. (hon., adv. coun. 1990), Delta Kappa Gamma (pres. 1980-82), Phi Delta Kappa (historian, research rep.). Republican. Methodist. Clubs: Lodge: Order Eastern Star (worthy matron 1956-57). Home: 15140 NE Avenue Rd Salt Springs FL 32134 Office: 2122 Ramona Casa Grande AZ 85222

GAULT, TERRELL WILSON, environmental engineer; b. Chgo., Jan. 29, 1951; s. Clarence W. and Emily (Underwood) G.; m. Mary Anne Braund, May 6, 1978 (div. Dec. 1985); m. Audrey L. Egli, Sept. 16, 1987; 1 child, Patrick. MS in Engring., U. Wash., 1978; BS in Engring., Princeton U., 1973. Project engr. Procter & Gamble Co., Cin., 1973-76; rsch. engr. U. Wash., Seattle, 1976-79; rsch. project leader Pacific Power & Light, Portland, Oreg., 1979-85, sales mgr., 1985-88; account mgr. ONSITE Energy, Portland, 1988-89; environ. dir. engring. Pacific Generation Co., Portland, 1989—. Contbr. articles to profl. jours.; patentee detergent compositions. Pres. Oreg. Repertory Singers, Portland, 1983-85; v.p. Ballet Oreg., Portland, 1988-89; bd. dirs. Oreg. Ballet Theatre, Portland, 1989-92. Recipient Indsl. Mktg. award Edison Electric Inst. Democrat. Office: Pacific Generation Co 500 NE Multnomah St Ste 900 Portland OR 97232-2039

GAULTIERE, KRISTI SOUTHARD, psychotherapist; b. Vancouver, Wash., May 24, 1965; d. Fred William and Lois Elizabeth (Eichenberger) Southard; m. William James Gaultiere, June 13, 1986; children: David William, Jennifer Michelle. BA, Oral Roberts U., 1986; MA in Marriage, Family and Child Counseling, Azusa Pacific U., 1988; D in Psychology, Newport U., 1990. Lic. marriage, family and child counselor, Calif. Exec. asst. Hour of Power, Syndey, Australia, 1985; computer programming asst. Hour of Power, Orange, Calif., 1986-89; dir. coll. youth Crystal Cathedral, Garden Grove, Calif., 1986-88; marriage family trainee South Coast Psychol. Ctr., Irvine, Calif., 1987-89; marriage family intern City Psychol. Group, Garden Grove, 1988-90; psychotherapist New Hope, Tustin, Calif., 1990—. Co-author: Mistaken Identity, 1987. Mem. Calif. Assn. Marriage and Family Therapists. Mem. Christian Ch. Office: New Hope Counseling Ste 12 17501 Irvine Blvd Tustin CA 92680

GAUNT, JANET LOIS, arbitrator, mediator; b. Lawrence, Mass., Aug. 23, 1947; d. Donald Walter and Lois (Neuhart) Bacon; m. Frank Peyton Gaunt, Dec. 21, 1969; children: Cory C., Andrew D. BA, Oberlin Coll., 1969; JD, Wash. U., St. Louis, 1974. Bar: Wash. 1974, U.S. Dist. Ct. (we. dist.) Wash. 1974, U.S. Ct. Appeals (9th cir.) 1978. Assoc. Davis, Wright, Todd, Riese & Jones, Seattle, 1974-80; arbitrator/mediator Seattle, 1981—; dir. Seattle King County Labor Law Sect., 1976-77; mem. Pacific Coast Labor Law Planning Com., 1977-83; com. vice chmn. Wash. State Task Force on Gender and Justice on the Cts., 1987-89; chmn. Wash. Pub. Employment Rels. Commn., Olympia, 1989—. Author, editor: Alternative Dispute Resolution, 1989. Pres. State Bd. of Wash. Women Lawyers, 1986. Mem. Nat. Acad. Arbitrators (dir. rsch. and edn. found. 1991—), Am. Arbitration Assn., Wash. State Bar Assn., Mediation Rsch. Edn. Project (cert. mediator), Wash. Women Lawyers. Office: 19670 Marine View Dr SW Seattle WA 98166-4164

GAUSTAD, RICHARD DALE, financier; b. Anchorage, Oct. 22, 1952; s. Sidney O. and Beulah (Pierce) G.; m. Lynell Dory, May 7, 1982; children: Kelsey, Eric. MusB, Utah State U., 1974; Diploma, LDS Inst. of Religion, Logan, Utah, 1975; postgrad. in law, Newport U. Sch. of Law, 1992—. Pres. Advt. Specialists, Logan, Utah, 1975-77, Cache Card, Logan, Utah, 1976-77, Northridge Enterprises, Inc., Logan, Utah, 1977-81, Nova's Gen. Store, Salt Lake City, 1981-82; chmn. Handicapped Distbrs., Inc., Mesa, Ariz., 1990-91; pres. Phase III Mktg. Corp., Mesa, Ariz., 1982-91, Infocom Capital Corp., Gilbert, Ariz., 1992—, Western Systems, Inc., Carson City, Nev., 1989—; dir. Western Systems, Inc., Gilbert, 1989-92; pres. Factor's Clearing House, Gilbert, 1992; pres. Infocom Capital Corp., Gilbert, 1992. Author: Financial Report Series, Vol. 1, 1990, Vol. II, 1992. Mem. Gilbert C. of C. LDS. Office: Infocom Capital Corp Ste B 102 761 N Monterey Gilbert AZ 85234 also: Factors Clearing House 425 W Guadalupe Ste 103 Gilbert AZ 85234

GAUTHIER, TINA LEE, educator; b. Cut Bank, Mont., Dec. 11, 1953; d. Leo Lawrence and Therese Diane (Kemmer) K.; m. Joseph A. Gauthier, July 2, 1979; 1 child, Joe. BS in Social Scis., Art, Elem. Edn., No. Mont. Coll., 1975. Cert. tchr., Mont., Utah. Substitute tchr. Havre (Mont.) High Sch., 1975, Shelby (Mont.) High Sch., 1976, Cut Bank Pub. Schs., 1984-92; bookkeeper Cut Bank Community Credit Union, 1976-77; bookkeeper, clk. Buttrey Foods, Cut Bank, 1978-79; tutor No. Mont. Coll., Havre, 1979-80; tchr. Glacier Colony Sch., Cut Bank, 1988; at-risk tutor Cut Bank Pub. Schs., 1988-93; pvt. tutor Cut Bank, 1975—. Co-chair and treas. Mental Health Adv. Bd., Cut Bank, 1990-91, chair, 1991-92, pres. 1992-94; pres. Tangled Roots Geneal. Soc., Cut Bank, 1991, 92, Cut Bank PTA, 1992-93; pres. Red Cross 1992-93; adv. Teens in Partnership 1993; mem. Odyssey of Mind, 1991-93. Roman Catholic. Home: 214 4th Ave NW Cut Bank MT 59427-2618

GAVAC, DONNA BRODERICK, writer, educator; b. Portland, Oreg., Sept. 16, 1926; d. W. Morris and Lulu G. (Youngs) Heacock; m. Robert F. Broderick, July 27, 1951 (div. May 1968); children: Bill, Mike; m. Stanley Gavac, June 8, 1979; stepchildren: Tim, Mark, Jan LaValley. BA in History, George Fox Coll., Newberg, Oreg., 1947; MA in History, U. Mich., 1949; PhD In Ednl. Adminstrn., U. Portland (Oreg.), 1960. High sch. tchr. Oreg. and Idaho; asst. prof. history and edn. Portland State U., 1960-65; dir. planning and rsch., assoc. prof. history and edn. Warner Pacific Coll., Portland, 1968-70; dean, assoc. prof. U. Alaska Statewide System, Anchorage, 1971-80; pres., researcher Donley Prodns., Inc., Anchorage, 1980-85; pres., writer Western Wordcraft, Anchorage, 1985—; commr., trustee N.W. Assn. Schs. and Colls., Seattle, 1971-78; abstractor Clio Press, Santa Barbara, 1960-65. Co-author: Teaching of Social Studies, 1963; editor: A.C.C. Plan for the Eighties, 1980; writer, producer weekly TV series Homemakers in History, 1957. Coord. U. Ark. Statewide Planning Group, Fairbanks, 1971-74; loaned exec. United Way Fund Dr., Anchorage, 1975-76; gov., bd. Anchorage Civic Opera Assn., 1978-81; sec.-treas. Community Coll. Coalition Alaska, 1986-88; co-presentor workshops for Counselors and Advisers, Bad Kissingen, Germany, 1983; chmn. com. U. Alaska-Archorage Archives and Records, 1978-82. Recipient U. Alaska rsch. award, Gold Nugget award Alaske Press Women; Named Ford Found. grantee, Dan Forth grantee. Mem. Am. Hist. Assn. (life), Medieval Acad. Am. (life), Renaissance Assn., Nat. Writer's Club, N.W. Assn. Community and Jr. Colls. (trustee, treas., v.p. 1972-77), Nat. Fedn. Press Women, Alaska Press Women. Office: Western Wordcraft PO Box 220707 Anchorage AK 99522-0707

GAY, RICHARD LESLIE, chemical engineer; b. Redlands, Calif., Nov. 17, 1950; s. Philip Leslie and Mary Frances (Finnigan) G. BS in Engring., UCLA, 1973, MS in Engring., 1973, PhD in Engring., 1976. Registered profl. engr. Calif. Rsch. asst. U. Calif., Riverside, 1969-70, UCLA, 1971-76; mem. tech. staff Rockwell Internat., Canoga Park, Calif., 1976-86; mgr. chem. engring. Rockwell Internat., Canoga Park, 1986—; sub-com. mem. for fuel performance Argonne Nat. Lab., Idaho Falls, Idaho, 1987—. Patentee in field; contbr. articles to profl. jours. Mem. Am. Inst. Chem. Engrs., Am. Chem. Soc., Sigma Xi. Republican. Roman Catholic. Home: 10012 Hanna Ave Chatsworth CA 91311-3612 Office: Rockwell Internat 6633 Canoga Ave Canoga Park CA 91303-2703

GAYLAIRD, CHRISTOPHER, architectural firm executive; m. Galye Christopher; children: Katie Marie, Whitney Gayle, Hayley Suzanne. AA, Pasadena City Coll., 1972; BArch, Calif. Poly., 1976. Designer MRC Architects, 1976-77, Barmakian Wolff & Assocs., 1977-81; prin., ednl. coord. Wolff/Lang/Christopher Architects, Inc., Rancho Cucamonga, Calif., 1981—; mem. archtl. tech. adv. com. Mt. San Antonio Coll. Past chmn. City of Upland Archtl. Commn.; mem. legis. implementation com. State Allocation Bd., Cultural League Advocating Support Arts, vestry St. Mark's Episcopal Ch., Diocesan Ctr. Design and Construction Rev. Com., L.A. Recipient Merit award Coalition Adequate Sch. Housing, 1991, Soc. Am. Registered Architects, 1991, Design award Am. Sch. and Univ. Mag., 1991, Coalition Adequate Sch. Housing, 1992, Am. Assn. Sch. Adminstrs., 1993, numerous others. Mem. AIA (com. architecture edn., steering com., Honor award Inland County charter 1990), ASBO, CASBO (so. sect. facility com.), Coun. Ednl. Facility Planners Internat. (pres. southwest region), C. of C. (edn. com.).

GAYLOR, WALTER, writer, military historian; b. Scranton, Pa., Nov. 23, 1913; s. John and Michaelina (Shemis) G.; m. Marjory Stephenson, Nov. 18, 1938; children: W. Thomas, Michael, Peter and Paul (twins). BS, Pa. State U., 1935; MA, Harvard U., 1938, postgrad., 1946-47. Chemist Tidewater Oil Co., Bayonne, N.J., 1935-36; headmaster Annapolis (Md.) Prep. Sch., 1938-41; assoc. prof. Ill. Coll., Jacksonville, 1947-49; editor, pub. Tech. Survey, Elizabeth, N.J., 1949-74; author, mil. historian Mesa, Ariz., 1975—. Maj. USAF, 1941-45, PTO. Mem. 22d Bomb Group Assn. (pres. 1950—, editor newsletter, Hon. Ky. Col. 1949). Republican. Episcopalian. Home and Office: 12/105 1666 S Extension Rd Mesa AZ 85210

GAYLORD, ALBERT STANLEY, court reporter; b. Hollywood, Calif., June 13, 1942; s. Kenneth William and Mary Hill (Gaylord) Brandstater. BS, U. Ams., Mexico City, 1964. Pvt. practice ct. reporter L.A., 1965-70, Portland, Oreg., 1988—; ct. reporter U.S. Dist. Ct., Chgo., 1970-72; verbatim parliamentry reporter Hansard, House of Lords, London, 1972-76. Mem. Nat. Shorthand Reporters Assn. (testing chmn. 1988-91), Oreg. Shorthand Reporters Assn. (testing chmn. 1988-91). Mem. Soc. of Friends. Home: 5425 SW Seymour St Portland OR 97221-1927

GAYNOR, DEAN SCOTT, financial analyst; b. Santa Monica, Calif., Dec. 16, 1964; s. Jerome Bernard and Pauline Fletcher (Cheyney) G. BA in Econs. with minor in Mgmt., U. Calif., Irvine, 1988. Mgr., salesperson GLC Plants & Things, Costa Mesa, Calif., 1980-88; tax analyst Alpha Beta Stores, Inc., Irvine, 1987-88; fin. analyst Douglas Aircraft Co., Long Beach, Calif., 1988-89; credit analyst McDonnel Douglas Fin. Corp., Long Beach, 1989-90, analyst, 1991-92; sr. investment analyst, comml. bond analyst McDonnell Douglas Fin. Corp., Long Beach, 1992—. Author, researcher: (manual) Commercial Loan Fraud Prevention & Detection, 1990 (Co. Recognition award). Advisor Jr. Achievement, Cerritos, Calif., 1989-90; pres. comml. office bldg. condo. owner's assn., 1992. Mem. Douglas Aircraft Mgmt. Club, Toastmasters Internat. (CTM designation ednl. v.p., club mentor 1989—), Order of Omega. Republican. Lutheran. Home: 8163 Prestwick Cir Huntington Beach CA 92646-2020 Office: McDonnell Douglas Fin Corp 340 Golden Shore St Long Beach CA 90802-4249

GAYNOR, JOSEPH, chemical engineering consultant; b. N.Y.C., Nov. 15, 1925; s. Morris and Rebecca (Schnapper) G.; m. Elaine Bauer, Aug. 19, 1951; children—Barbara Lynne, Martin Scott, Paul David, Andrew Douglas. B.Ch.E., Polytechnic Inst. Bklyn., 1950; M.S., Case-Western Res. U., 1952, Ph.D., 1955. Research asst. Case Inst., Cleve., 1952-55; with Gen. Engring. Labs. Gen. Electric Co., Schenectady, N.Y., 1955-66, sect. mgr. research and devel., 1962-66; group v.p. research Bell & Howell Co., 1966-72; mgr. comml. devel. group, mem. pres.' office Horizons Research, Inc., Cleve., 1972-73; pres. Innovative Tech. Assos., Ventura, Calif., 1973—; mem. nat. materials adv. bd. com. NAS; chmn. conf. com. 2d internat. conf. on bus. graphics, 1979, program chmn. 1st internat. congress on advances in non-impact printing techs., 1981, mem. adv. com. 2d internat. congress on advances in non-impact printing techs., 1984, chmn. publs. com. 3rd internat. congress on advances in non-impact printing techs., 1986, chmn. internat. conf. on hard copy media, materials and processes, 1990. Editor: Electronic Imaging, 1991, Procs. Advances in Non-Impact Printing Technologies, Vol. I, 1983, Vol. II, 1988, 3 spl. issues Jour. Imaging Tech., Proc. Hard Copy Materials Media and Processes Internat. Conf., 1990; patentee in field. Served with U.S. Army, 1944-46. Fellow AAAS, AICE, Imaging Sci. and Tech. Soc.; mem. Am Chem. Soc., Soc. PHotographic Scientists and Engrs. (sr., gen. chmn. 2d internat. conf. on electrophotography 1973, chmn. bus. graphics tech. sect. 1976—, chmn. edn. com. L.A. chpt. 1978—), Am. Soc. Photobiology, Sigma Xi, Tau Beta Pi, Phi Lambda Upsilon, Alpha Chi Sigma. Home: 108 La Brea St Oxnard CA 93035-3928 Office: Innovative Tech Assocs 3639 E Harbor Blvd # 203E Ventura CA 93001

GAYNOR, RONALD KEVIN, waste services company executive; b. Owensboro, Ky., Feb. 29, 1952; s. William Broadus and Rosebelle (Adkins) G.; m. Elma Theresa George, Dec. 10, 1977 (div. Feb. 1990); 1 child, Cory Ryan; m. Latricia Bethine Irwin, Aug. 17, 1991. BSCE, U. Ky., 1974, MSCE, 1982. Registered profl. engr., Ky. Engr. ATEC Assocs., Inc., Indpls., 1976-77, project mgr., 1977-78; project mgr. ATEC Assocs., Inc., Saudi Arabia, 1977; ops. mgr. ATEC Assocs., Inc., Louisville, 1978-80; sr. engr. US Ecology, Inc., Louisville, 1980-81, mgr. engring., 1981-82, v.p., 1982-84; pres. US Ecology Cons., Newport Beach, Calif., 1984-85; sr. v.p. US Ecology, Inc., Houston, 1985—; mem. U.S. Coun. on Energy Awareness, 1990—; mem. Am. Nuclear Energy Coun., 1990—. Co-author: Nuclear Waste Management, 1990. Mem. ASME (com. on mixed waste 1990), ASCE, Nat. Soc. Profl. Engrs.

GEARE, JOHN CULLEN, environmental scientist, consultant; b. Pasadena, Calif., Dec. 30, 1949; s. Joseph Paul and Teresa (Cheap) G.; m. Jan Phillips, Oct. 1, 1984; children: Darren, Jody, Laurel, Cary. BA in Environ. Studies and Planning, Calif. State U.-Sonoma, Rohnert Park, 1978. Registered environ. assessor, EMT, Calif. Mgr. health and safety Seagate Tech., Scotts Valley, Calif., 1983-86; mgr. devel. 4 Site Tech., Santa Cruz, Calif., 1987-88; safety specialist Safety Specialists, Santa Cruz, 1988-90; cons. Sierra-Pacific Co., Santa Cruz, 1989-90; owner, mgr. Sierra-Pacific Environ., Santa Cruz, 1989—. With U.S. Army, 1969-71. Mem. Am. Chem. Soc., Air and Waste

Mgmt. Soc., Sierra Club. Mem. Green Party. Office: Sierra-Pacific Environ 221 Dufour St Santa Cruz CA 95060

GEARHART, JANE ANNETTE SIMPSON, retired lawyer; b. Seibert, Colo., Mar. 2, 1918; d. V.L. and Frances Louise (Taylor) Simpson; m. Richard C. Gearhart, July 6, 1946 (div. 1957); 1 child, Suzanne Gearhart Carroll. BA, U. Denver, 1939, LLB, 1942, LLD, 1970. Bar: Colo. 1942, Oreg. 1956. Staff atty. League of Oreg. Cities, Eugene, 1957-60; dep. legis. counsel Oreg. Legis., Salem, 1962-73; adminstrv. law judge Oreg. Employment Div., Eugene, 1977-84; cons. adminstrv. law Corp. Commr., Supt. of Banks, Salem, 1973-86. Trustee Christos Trust, Eugene, 1990. Lt. (j.g.) USNR, 1943-46. Home: 1011 N 14th St Gunnison CO 81230

GEARHART, ROBERT JAMES, JR., secondary educator; b. Phila., Aug. 1, 1961; s. Robert James and Wilma Mae (Wilson) G. BA in History and Polit. Sci., U. Nebr., 1984, cert., 1988. Cert. tchr., N.Mex., Nebr. Tchr. Gallup-McKinley County (N.Mex.) Schs., 1988—. Mem. Found. for Primate Rsch. (bd. dirs. 1987—), McKinley County Fedn. Sch. Employees (chair membership 1990—, comm. dir. 1992). Democrat. Episcopalian. Home: 900 S Boardman D-37 Gallup NM 87301

GEBBIA, KAREN MARIE, lawyer, educator; b. Chgo., July 21, 1958; d. Stephen L. and Doris A. (Melendez) G. BA magna cum laude, Villanova U., 1980; JD cum laude, Georgetown U., 1983. Bar: Ill. 1983, U.S. Dist. Ct. (no. dist.) Ill. 1983, U.S. Ct. Appeals (7th cir.) 1985. Atty. Nachman, Munitz & Sweig, Chgo., 1983-87; assoc. Winston & Strawn, Chgo., 1987-93; asst. prof. law U. Hawaii, Honolulu, 1993—. Contbr. articles to profl. jours. Vol. N.W. Youth Outreach, Chgo., Lakeview Homelss Shelter, La Rabida Children's Hosp.; mem. Chgo. Coun. on Fgn. Rels., People to People Internat. Mem. ABA (bus. law sect., bus. bankruptcy com., commercial fin. svcs. com.), Ill. Bar Assn., Seventh Cir. Bar Assn., Chgo. Bar Assn. Office: U Hawaii W S Richardson Sch Law 2515 Dole St Honolulu HI 96822

GEBBIE, KRISTINE MOORE, health official; b. Sioux City, Iowa, June 26, 1943; d. Thomas Carson and Gladys Irene (Stewart) Moore; divorced; children: Anna, Sharon, Eric. BSN, St. Olaf Coll., 1965; MSN, UCLA, 1968. Project dir. USPHS tng. grant, St. Louis, 1972-77; coord. nursing St. Louis U., 1974-76, asst. dir. nursing, 1976-78, clin. prof., 1977-78; adminstr. Oreg. Health Div., Portland, 1978-89; sec. Wash. State Dept. Health, Olympia, 1989-93; coord. Nat. AIDS Policy, Washington, 1993—; assoc. prof. Oreg. Health Scis. U. Portland, 1980—; chair, U.S. dept. energy secretarial panel on Evaluation of Epidemiologic Rsch. Activities, 1989-90; mem. Presdl. Commn. on Human Imunodeficiency Virus Epidemic, 1987-88. Author: (with Deloughery and Neuman) Consultation and Community Orgn., 1971, (with Deloughery) Political Dynamics: Impact on Nurses, 1975; (with Scheer) Creative Teaching in Clinical Nursing, 1976. Bd. dirs. Luth. Family Svcs. Oreg. and S.W. Wash., 1979-84; bd. dirs. Oreg. Psychoanalytic Found., 1983-87. Recipient Disting. Alumna award St. Olaf Coll., 1979; Disting. scholar Am. Nurses Found., 1989. Fellow Am. Acad. Nursing; mem. Assn. State & Territorial Health Ofcls., 1988 (pres. 1984-85, exec. com. 1980-87, McCormick award 1988), Am. Pub. Health Assn. (exec. bd.), Inst. Medicine, Hastings Ctr., N.Am. Nursing Diagnosis Assn. (treas. 1983-87), Oreg. Pub. Health Assn., Am. Soc. Pub. Adminstrn. (adminstrn. award II 1983), City Club of Portland. Office: 2737 Devonshire Pl NW Ste 315 Washington DC 20008

GEBERT, CARL JUNIOR, engineering executive; b. Columbia City, Ind., Dec. 25, 1937; s. Carl and Goldie Mae (Truman) G.; m. Karen Irene Jones, May 29, 1959; children: Daniel Lee, Ruth Ellen Hendricks. BS in Aero. Engring., Purdue U., 1959; postgrad., UCLA, 1962, U. Calif., Irvine, 1969-70, Calif. State U., Long Beach, 1970-71. Asst. chief criteria div. USAF Western Test Range, Vandenberg AFB, Calif., 1963-65; program mgr. range safety Ford Aerospace, Newport Beach, Calif., 1966-75, program mgr. PAVE TACK/VATS, 1975-78, dep. program mgr. F/A-18 FLIR, 1978-82, program mgr. F/A-18 FLIR Devel., 1982-85; program mgr. Hughes Aircraft, El Segundo, Calif., 1985-86, asst. mgr. systems engring. lab., 1986-88, assoc. mgr., 1988-90, mgr., 1990—. Recipient Cert. of Appreciation for Patriotic Civilian Svc. Safeguard System Command U.S. Army, Huntsville, Ala., 1975. Mem. Am. Def. Preparedness Assn., Internat. Soc. Optical Engring., Nat. Coun. Systems Engring., Sierra Club. Republican. Mem. Evangelical Free Ch. Home: 3601 Flournoy Rd Manhattan Beach CA 90266 Office: Hughes Aircraft Co PO Box 902 El Segundo CA 90245

GEBHARD, BOB, professional sports team executive. Gen. mgr. Colorado Rockies. Office: Colo Rockies 1700 Broadway Ste 2100 Denver CO 80290

GEDDES, BARBARA SHERYL, communications executive, consultant; b. Poughkeepsie, N.Y., May 27, 1944; d. Samuel Pierson and Dorothy Charlotte (Graham) Brush; m. James Morrow Geddes, Feb. 24, 1968 (div. Dec. 1980); 1 child, Elisabeth. BA, Skidmore Coll., 1968. Project leader Four-Phase Systems, Cupertino, Calif., 1976-77, Fairchild Co., San Jose, Calif., 1979-80; mgr. tech. publs. Mohawk Data Scis., Los Gatos, Calif., 1977-79, Sytek Inc., Mountain View, Calif., 1981-83; project mgr. Advanced Micro Computers, Santa Clara, Calif., 1980-81; v.p. communications systems Strategic Inc., Cupertino, 1983-86; pres., mng. ptnr. Computer and Telecommunications Profl. Services, Mountain View, Calif., 1986—; v.p. corp. mktg., sec. First Pacific Networks, Sunnyvale, Calif., 1988—; cons. H-P, Varian, Aydin Energy, Chemelex, also others, 1972—; v.p. Conf. Recorders, Santa Clara, 1975-77; advisor Tele-PC, Morgan Hill, Calif., 1983—. Editor: Mathematics/Science Library, 7 vols., 1971. Contbr. numerous articles to mags. Mem. Santa Clara County Adoptions Adv. Bd., 1971-73, Las Cumbres Archtl. Control Commn., Los Gatos, 1983; advisor Los Altos Hills Planning Commn., Calif., 1978-79. N.Y. State Regents merit scholar, 1962. Mem. Assn. for Computing Machinery (editor 1970-72), Nat. Soc. for Performance and Instrn., Bus. and Profl. Advt. Assn., Women in Communications (pres. San Jose 1983—). Democrat. Home: 910 Mockingbird Ln Palo Alto CA 94306-3719 Office: First Pacific Networks 601 W California Ave Sunnyvale CA 94086-4831

GEDDES, CHARLES LYNN, retired history educator; b. Corvallis, Oreg., Jan. 3, 1928; s. James Edward and Dorothy Marie (Green) G. BS, U. Oreg., 1951; AM, U. Mich., 1954; PhD, U. London, 1959. Asst. prof. Am. U. Cairo, 1956-61, U. Colo., Boulder, 1961-65; Fulbright prof. Tribubhan U., Kathmandu, Nepal, 1965-66; prof. history U. Denver, 1967-92. Author: Guide to Reference Books for Islamic Studies, 1985, A Documentary History of the Arab-Israel Conflict, 1991. Pfc. U.S. Army, 1945-46. Fellow Mid. East Inst.; mem. Am. Oriental Soc., Mid. East Studies Assn., Am. Inst. Yemeni Studies, Am. Inst. Islamic Studies (resident dir. 1965). Home: 3410 W Amherst Ave Denver CO 80236-2504 Office: U Denver Dept History Denver CO 80208

GEE, CHUCK YIM, dean; b. San Francisco, Aug. 28, 1933; s. Don Yow Elsie (Lee) G. AA, City Coll. of San Francisco, 1953; BSBA, U. Denver, 1957; MA, Mich. State U., 1958; PhD (hon.), China Acad. Chin. Cultural U., 1972, U. Denver, 1991. Assoc. dir. Sch. of Hotel and Restaurant Adminstn. U. Denver, 1958-68; cons. East West Ctr., Honolulu, 1968-74; assoc. dean and prof. Sch. of Travel Industry Mgmt. U. Hawaii, 1968-75, dean and prof. Sch. Travel Industry Mgmt., 1976—; vis. prof. Sch. Bus. and Commerce, Oreg. State U., 1975; hon. prof. Nankai U., Tianjin, People's Republic of China, 1987—; cons. Internat. Sci. and Tech. Inst., Washington, 1986—; trustee Pacific Asia Travel Assn. Found., San Francisco; chmn. Govs. Tourism Tng. Coun., Honolulu, 1989-92, chmn. 1992—; acad. coun. Inst. Cert. Travel Agts., Wellesley, Mass., 1989—; mem. Coun. on Hotel, Restaurant and Instnl. Edn., Honolulu Commn. on Fgn. Rels., consultative com. Beijing Inst. Tourism, 1992—; sr. acad. advisor China Tourism Assn. Cons., Inc., 1993—. Author: Resort Development and Management, 1988, 2nd edit.; co-author: The Travel Industry, 1988, 2nd edit., Professional Travel Agency Management, 1990. Bd. dirs. Kuakini Med. Ctr., Honolulu, 1986—, Travel and Tourism Adv. Bd., U.S. Dept. Commerce, Washington, 1982-90, Pacific Rim Found., Honolulu, 1987—; vice-chmn. Tourism Policy Adv. Coun., Dept. Bus. and Econ. Devel., Honolulu, 1978—; chmn. Kuakini Geriatric Care, Inc. (bd. dirs. 1992—); trustee Pata Found., 1984—, Kuakini Health System, 1988—; consulting com. Beijing Inst. Tourism, 1992—; v.p. Hawaii Vision 2020, 1992—; mem. Mayor's Task Force on Waikiki Master Plan, 1992—. With U.S. Army, 1953-55. Recipient NOAH award Acad. Tourism Orgns., 1987, Nat. Excellence in Tourism Edn. award China Tourisn Assn., 1992. Fellow Internat. Acad. Hospitality Rsch.; mem. Pacific Asia Travel Assn. (Grand award for individual edn. 1991, Life award 1990, Presdl. award 1986), Travel Industry Am. (Travel Industry Hall of Leaders award 1988), China Tourism Assn. (award of excellence in tourism edn. 1992), C. of C. of Hawaii, Soc. for Advancement of Food Svc. Rsch. Office: U Hawaii Sch Travel Industry Mgmt 2560 Campus Rd Honolulu HI 96822-2287

GEHRES, ELEANOR AGNEW MOUNT, librarian; b. Riverside, N.J., Feb. 18, 1932; d. Wilton Elbert and Mary Anna (Agnew) Mount; m. E. James Gehres, July 23, 1960. BA in English, U. Va., 1952; MA in Librarianship, U. Denver, 1968, MA in History, 1972, Cert. of Mgmt.-Bus., 1982. Elem. tchr. Norfolk County Schs., Churchland, Va., 1952-59; jr. high tchr. Sch. Dist. #11, Colorado Springs, Colo., 1959-61; librarian Sch. Dist. 1, Denver, 1961-71; asst. prof. U. Denver, 1971-73; grants coord. Colo. State Libr., Denver, 1973-74; mgr. Western History Dept., Denver Pub. Libr., 1974—; instr. Metro. State Coll., Denver, 1975—; bd. dirs. Colo. Hist. Records Adv. Bd., Denver, 1976—, Telecom. Bd., 1992—; hist. cons. videos: Denver: Emergence of a Great City, 1984, Colorado's Black Settlements, 1978. Author printed guide: Denver Urban Environmental Studies, 1971; co-editor: The Colorado Book, 1993; host cable TV show: Conversations, 1985—. Mem. ALA, Western History Assn., Soc. of Rocky Mountain Archivists, Colo. Libr. Assn., Colo. Corral of Westerners (sheriff 1984), Colo. History Group (pres.), Bus. and Profl. Women's Club (v.p. 1987-88), Colo. Women's Hall of Fame (bd. dirs. 1989—), Colo. Preservation Alliance (pres. 1990-93), Colo. Mt. Club, Denver Fortnightly Club, Denver Posse of Westerners, Sierra Club, Colonial Willamsburg. Home: 935 Pennsylvania St Denver CO 80203-3145 Office: Denver Pub Libr 1357 Broadway Denver CO 80203-2165

GEHRES, JAMES, lawyer; b. Akron, Ohio, July 19, 1932; s. Edwin Jacob and Cleora Mary (Yoakam) G.; m. Eleanor Agnew Mount, July 23, 1960. B.S. in Acctg., U. Utah, 1954; M.B.A., U. Calif.-Berkeley, 1959; J.D., U. Denver, 1970, LL.M. in Taxation, 1977. Bar: Colo. 1970, U.S. Dist. Ct. Colo. 1970, U.S. Tax Ct. 1970, U.S. Supreme Ct. 1973, U.S. Ct. Appeals (10th cir.) 1978, U.S. Ct. Claims 1992. Atty. IRS, Denver, 1965-80, atty. chief counsel's office, 1980—. Served with USAF, 1955-58, capt. Res. ret. Mem. ABA, Colo. Bar Assn., Am. Inst. C.P.A.s, Colo. Soc. C.P.A.s, Am. Assn. Atty.-C.P.A.s, Am. Judicature Soc., Am. Acctg. Assn., Order St. Ives, The Explorers Club, Am. Alpine Club, Beta Gamma Sigma, Beta Alpha Psi. Democrat. Contbr. articles to profl. jours. Office: 935 Pennsylvania St Denver CO 80203-3145

GEHRING, GEORGE JOSEPH, JR., dentist; b. Kenosha, Wis., May 24, 1931; s. George J. and Lucille (Martin) G.; m. Ann D. Carrigan, Aug. 2, 1982; children: Michael, Scott. DDS, Marquette U., 1955. Pvt. practice dentistry, Long Beach, Calif., 1958—. Author: The Happy Flosser. Chmn. bd. Long Beach affiliate Calif. Heart Assn.; mem. Long Beach Grand Prix com. of 300; ind. candidate for pres. of the U.S., 1988, 92. Served with USNR, 1955-58. Fellow Internat. Coll. of Denists, Am. Coll. Dentists; mem. Harbor Dental Soc. (dir.), Pierre Fauchard Acad., Delta Sigma Delta. Club: Rotary. Home: 1230E Ocean Blvd # 603 Long Beach CA 90802-6909 Office: 532 E 29th St Long Beach CA 90806-1645

GEHRING, GEORGE MICHAEL, architect; b. Long Beach, Calif., Sept. 23, 1958; s. George Joseph and Joan Marjorie (Dehmlow) G.; m. Andrea Monica Cohen, June 3, 1990. BArch, U. So. Calif., 1981; MBA, UCLA, 1989. Registered architect, Calif. Designer Welton Becket Assocs., Santa Monica, Calif., 1981-84; project designer Dworsky Assocs., L.A., 1984-87; v.p., co-dir. of design The Landau Partnership, Santa Monica, 1987—. Co-designer: (bldgs.) Fluor Corp., Houston, 1982, County of Santa Clara Hall of Justice, 1988; designer: (bldgs.) The Metropolitan, 1989, Westwood Community Ctr., 1989, 811 Wilshire, 1991. Mem. AIA, U. So. Calif. Archtl. Guild, Pres. Club of Vista Del Mar. Office: The Landau Ptnrship Inc 1520 2d St Santa Monica CA 90401-2355

GEHRKE, ROBERT JAMES, physicist; b. Chgo., Nov. 20, 1940; s. Wilhelm August and Gertrude Mary (Kraemer) G.; m. Mary Louise Irwin, Oct. 12, 1963; children: Marie, Therese, Julie, Christine, Karen, Maureen. BS, DePaul U., Chgo., 1962; MS, U. Nev., Reno, 1966. Physicist Phillips Petroleum Co., Idaho Falls, Idaho, 1965-66; sr. physicist Idaho Nuclear Corp., Idaho Falls, 1966-71; assoc. scientist Aerojet Nuclear Corp., Idaho Falls, 1971-76; sci. specialist EG&G Idaho Inc., Idaho Falls, 1976-85, unit mgr., 1985-91, sci. specialist, 1991—; instr. U. Idaho Ext., Idaho Falls, 1977—; project leader Am. Nat. Stds. Inst.; IAEA expert assignment to Korea Rsch. Inst. of Standards and Science Republic of Korea, 1992. Editorial rev. bd. Radioactivity and Radiochemistry Jour., 1990—; reviewer Analytical Chemistry, 1990, Jour. of Applied Radiation and Isotopes, 1988—; contbr. articles to profl. jours. Pres. Bonneville Assn. for Retarded Citizens, Idaho Falls, 1969-70, Idaho Assn. for Retarded Citizens, Boise, 1970-71. Named Disting. Alumnus, U. Nev.-Reno, 1977; recipient UR & D 100 award "Pins Chem. Assay System", 1992. Mem. Am. Nuclear Soc. (sec. environ. scis. div. 1990-93, treas., 1993—, newsletter editor 1990-93, treas. isotope and radiation divsn. 1993—, nuclear data chmn. 1989-92, chmn. Standards Subcommittee on Environ. Remediation of Radioactively Contaminated Sites, 1992—), Am. Chem. Soc., Am. Phys. Soc., Health Physics Soc., Am. Nat. Stds. Inst. Roman Catholic. Office: EG&G Idaho Inc PO Box 1625 Idaho Falls ID 83415-0001

GEIGER, ALLEN RICHARD, research physicist; b. Sayre, Pa., Dec. 31, 1951; s. Richard A. and Francis M. (Aumick) G. BS in Physics, N.Mex. State U., 1975. Research aid N.Mex. State U., Las Cruces, 1975-76; research physicist Deep Space Systems, Las Cruces, 1977-79; chmn. bd. dirs. G.E.I., Las Cruces, 1979-81, PetroLaser, Inc., Las Cruces, N.Mex., 1987—; research physicist Atmospheric Sci. Lab., White Sands Missile Range, N.Mex., 1980-89; pvt. practice cons. to petrochemical industry, 1981—. Patents in non-linear optics and remote sensing. Mem. U.S. Naval Inst. (assoc.), World Space Found. (charter), Planetary Soc. (charter). Republican. Home: PO Box 2425 Las Cruces NM 88004-2425 Office: 300 N Telshor Las Cruces NM 88003-4998

GEIHS, FREDERICK SIEGFRIED, lawyer; b. Omaha, Nebr., Oct. 16, 1935; s. Frederich Siegfried Sr. and Dorothy Pauline (Getzschman) G.; m. Janelle J. Jeffrey, Oct. 22, 1966; children: Jeffrey J., Danielle Desiree. BS in Bus. Adminstrn., U. Nebr., Omaha, 1957; JD, Creighton U., 1962. Bar: Nebr. 1962, U.S. Dist. Ct. Nebr. 1962, U.S. Supreme Ct. 1965, Mich. 1975, Minn. 1978, U.S. Ct. Appeals (9th cir.) 1980, Nev. 1981, U.S. Dist. Ct. Nev. 1981. Atty. City Omaha (Nebr.) Law Dept., 1962-65; pvt. practice law Omaha, 1965-71, Edina, Minn., 1978-80; asst. gen., atty. Upland Industries, Omaha, 1971-75; corp. counsel Detroit and No. Savs. and Loan, Houghton, Mich., 1975-77, Knutson Cos., Inc., Mpls., 1977-78; mng. atty. Legal Assistance N.D., Bismark, 1980; dir. litigation Clark County Legal Svcs., Las Vegas, 1980-82; atty. Bell & Young, Las Vegas, 1982-83, Harding & Dawson, Las Vegas; of counsel Hilbrecht & Assocs., Las Vegas; prin. Law Offices of Frederick Siegfried Geihs, 1991—. Sec. Young Reps., Omaha, 1965-66; treas. Forgotten Ams., Omaha, 1968-70. Mem. ABA, Minn. State Bar Assn., Nebr. State Bar Assn., Nev. Trial Lawyers Assn., Assn. Trial Lawyers Am., Western State Trial Lawyers Assn., Theta Chi, Phi Alpha Delta. Lutheran. Avocations: skiing, jogging, travel. Office: 3376 S Eastern Ave Ste 148 Las Vegas NV 89109

GEIKEN, ALAN RICHARD, contractor; b. Toledo, Aug. 24, 1923; s. Martin Herman and Herta Regina G.; B.S. in Engring., Iowa State U., 1950. Engr., sec. Hot Spot Detector, Inc., Des Moines, 1950-53, sales engr., asst. gen. mgr., 1953-60; pres., owner Alan Geiken Inc., Sacramento, 1960—; cons. on grain storage. Served with USAAF, 1943-45. Mem. Am. Soc. Agrl. Engrs., Council for Agrl. Sci. and Tech., Calif. Warehousemens Assn., Calif. Grain and Feed Assn., Grain Elevator and Processing Soc. Clubs: Sacramento Engrs., Sacramento 50/50 (bd. dirs.). Lutheran. Developed electronic system to maintain healthful condition of stored grain and bulk foods. Address: PO Box 214505 Sacramento CA 95821

GEISLER, PHYLLIS MURIEL, missionary; b. Pasadena, Feb. 28, 1924; d. Bernard Elton and Irma Adriana (Huff) Chamberlain; m. Armin Adolf Geisler, Sept. 28, 1991. BA, Wheaton (Ill.) Coll., 1946; postgrad., Bibl. Sem. N.Y., N.Y.C., 1948-49. Ordained to ministry Congregational Ch., 1950. Missionary The Evang. Alliance Mission, Japan, 1950-90; ret.; assoc. dir. Mataubarako Bible Camp, Matsubarako, Japan, 1963-80; dir. Karuizawa Japanese Lang. Sch., 1980-89. Author lang. course: Religious Language, 1991.

GEIST, JERRY DOUGLAS, electric company executive; b. Raton, N.Mex., May 23, 1934; s. Jacob D. and Jessie Kathleen (Wadley) G.; m. Sharon Ludell Kaemper, June 12, 1956; children: Douglas, Bruce, Robert. Student, U. Mo., 1952-54; BEE, U. Colo., 1956. Registered profl. engr., N.Mex. With Pub. Svc. Co. N.Mex., Albuquerque, 1960-90, v.p. engring. and ops., 1970-71, v.p. corp. affairs, 1971-73, exec. v.p., 1973-76, pres., chmn., CEO, 1976-90, ret., 1990—; chmn. Santa Fe Ctr. Enterprises; bd. dirs. Ch2M Hill, Venture Advisors Investment Funds, Utech Venture Capital Corp. Ltd., Santa Fe Inst.; chmn. bd. RhoMed Inc. Bd. dirs. Nat. Symphony Trusts; mem. adminstrv. bd. 1st United Meth. Albuquerque Econ. Forum. Lt. USN, 1952-59. Mem. Edison Electric Inst. (past chmn.), Albuquerque C. of C. (pres. 1972-73), Bus. Roundtable, Four Hills Country Club, Albuquerque Country Club, Albuquerque Petroleum Club, Links, Tau Beta Pi, Sigma Tau, Eta Kappa Nu, Pi Mu Epsilon. Methodist. Office: 6201 Uptown Blvd NE # 207S Albuquerque NM 87110-9999

GEIST, KARIN RUTH TAMMEUS MCPHAIL, educator, realtor, musician; b. Urbana, Ill., Nov. 23, 1938; d. Wilber Harold and Bertha Amanda Sofia (Helander) Tammeus; m. David Pendleton McPhail, Sept. 7, 1958 (div. 1972); children: Julia Elizabeth, Mark Andrew; m. John Charles Geist, June 4, 1989. BS, Juilliard Sch. Music, 1962; postgrad., Stanford U., 1983-84, L'Academia, Florence and Pistoia, Italy, 1984-85, Calif. State U., 1986-87, U. Calif., Berkeley, 1991, 92. Cert. tchr., Calif.; lic. real estate agt., Calif. Tchr. Woodstock Sch., Musoorie, India, 1957, Canadian, Tex., 1962-66; tchr. Head Royce Sch., Oakland, Calif., 1975-79, 87—, Sleepy Hollow Sch., Orinda, Calif., 1985—; realtor Freeholders, Berkeley, Calif., 1971-85, Northbrae, Berkeley, Calif., 1985-92, Templeton Co., Berkeley, 1992—, 1992—; organist Kellogg Meml., Musoorie, 1956-57, Mills Coll. Chapel, Oakland, 1972—; cashier Trinity U., San Antonio, 1957-58; cen. records sec. Riverside Ch., N.Y.C., 1958-60; sec. Dr. Rollo May, N.Y.C., 1959-62, United Presbyn. Nat. Missions, N.Y.C., 1960, United Presbyn. Ecumenical Mission, N.Y.C., 1961, Nat. Coun. Chs., N.Y.C., 1962; choral dir. First Presbyn. Ch., Canadian, Tex., 1962-66; assoc. in music Montclair Presbyn. Ch., Oakland, 1972-88; site coord., artist, collaborator Calif. Arts Coun. Artist. Artist; produced and performed major choral and orchestral works, 1972-88; prodr. Paradiso, Kronis Quartet, 1985, Magdalena, 1991, 92, Children's Quest, 1993—. Grantee Orinda Union Sch. Dist., 1988. Mem. Berkeley Bd. Realtors, East Bay Regional Multiple Listing Svc., Calif. Tchrs. Assn., Commonwealth Club (San Francisco). Democrat. Home: 7360 Claremont Ave Berkeley CA 94705-1429 Office: Templeton Co 3070 Claremont Berkeley CA 94705

GELBER, DON JEFFREY, lawyer; b. L.A., Mar. 10, 1940; s. Oscar and Betty Sheila (Chernitsky) G.; m. Jessica Jeasun Song, May 15, 1967; children: Victoria, Jonathan, Rebecca, Robert. Student UCLA, 1957-58, Reed Coll., 1958-59; AB, Stanford U., 1961, JD, 1963. Bar: Calif. 1964, Hawaii 1964, U.S. Dist. Ct. (cen. and no. dists. Calif.) 1964, U.S. Dist. Ct. Hawaii 1964, U.S. Ct. Appeals (9th cir.) 1964, U.S. Supreme Ct. 1991. Assoc. Greenstein, Yamane & Cowan, Honolulu, 1964-67; reporter Penal Law Revision Project, Hawaii Jud. Council, Honolulu, 1967-69; assoc. H. William Burgess, Honolulu, 1969-72; ptnr. Burgess & Gelber, Honolulu, 1972-73; prin. Law Offices of Don Jeffrey Gelber, Honolulu, 1974-77; pres. Gelber & Wagner, Honolulu, 1978-83, Gelber & Gelber, Honolulu, 1984-89, Gelber, Gelber, Ingersoll & Klevansky, Honolulu, 1990—; legal counsel Hawaii State Senate Judiciary Com., 1965; adminstrv. asst. to majority floor leader Hawaii State Senate, 1966, legal csl. Edn. Com., 1967, 68; majority counsel Hawaii Ho. of Reps., 1974; spl. counsel Hawaii State Senate, 1983. Contbr. articles to legal publs. Mem. State Bar Calif., ABA (sect. bus. law), Am. Bankruptcy Inst., Hawaii State Bar Assn. (sect. bankruptcy law, bd. dirs. 1991-93, pres. 1993). Clubs: Pacific, Plaza (Honolulu). Office: Gelber Gelber et al 745 Fort Street Mall Ste 1400 Honolulu HI 96813-3877

GELENBERG, ALAN JAY, psychiatrist, educator; b. Phila., May 2, 1944; s. Jacob and Mae R. (Gantman) G.; m. Sherry Ann Mullens, Sept. 17, 1972; children: Sara Ann, David Jesse Mullens, Rebecca Suzann. AB, Columbia Coll., 1965; MD, U. Pa., 1969. Diplomate Am. Bd. Psychiatry and Neurology. Intern in internal medicine Prebyn. U. Pa. Med. Ctr., Phila., 1969-70; fellow, then assoc. prof. Sch. Medicine Harvard U., Boston, 1970-89; resident in psychiatry Mass. Gen. Hosp., Boston, 1970-73, psychiatrist, 1970-89; med. dir. Erich Lindemann Mental Health Ctr., Boston, 1982-83; psychiatrist-in-chief The Arbour, Boston, 1983-89; prof., head dept. psychiatry U. Ariz., Tucson, 1989—. Author: Biological Therapies in Psychiatry; editor: Practitioners Guide to Psychoactive Drugs, 1983, 2d edit., 1990, 3d edit., 1991, Jour. Clin. Psychiatry, 1987—; contbr. to profl. publs. Recipient numerous grants, NIMH, pvt. industry and founds. Fellow AAAS, Am. Psychiat. Assn.; mem. West Coast Coll. Biol. Psychiatrists, Am. Assn. Chairmen Depts. Psychiatry, Pima County Med. Soc., Ariz. Med. Assn., Am. Coll. Psychiatrists, Am. Psychopath. Assn. (fellow), Ariz. Psychiat. Soc., Tucson Psychiat. Soc. Jewish. Office: U Ariz Dept Psychiatry Health Scis Ctr Tucson AZ 85724

GELIN, FRANKLIN CHARLES, college administrator, psychologist; b. Vancouver, B.C., Can., June 14, 1945; s. Philip Aaron and Francine Elizabeth (Vaughan) G.; m. Nancy Lynn Dennett, July 10, 1971; children: Michaela, Byron. BA, San Diego State U., 1967; MA, Stanford U., 1969; PhD, U. Alta., Edmonton, Can., 1972. Instr. psychology Coll. of New Caledonia, Prince George, B.C., 1969-75, dean arts and sci., 1975-79; v.p. acad. studies Capilano Coll., North Vancouver, B.C., 1979—; mem. numerous ednl. orgns., B.C., 1975—; chmn. external rev. com. Camosun Coll., B.C., 1987; co-chmn. Assoc. Credential Provincial Task Force, B.C., 1990—. Contbr. articles to profl. jours. Bd. dirs. Caribou Action Tng. Soc., Prince George, B.C., 1972-79; co-chmn., founder Seymour-Toke Friendship Soc., North Vancouver, 1988-89; mem. adv. bd. Can. Scholarship Trust Found., Toronto, Ont., 1988—; mem. B.C. Coun. Admissions and Transfer, 1993—. Recipient award Can. Coun., 1971. Mem. APA, B.C. Coll. Psychologists (registered), Assn. Can. Community Colls., North Shore Winter Club. Office: Capilano Coll, North Vancouver, BC Canada V7J 3H5

GELLMAN, GLORIA GAE SEEBURGER SCHICK, marketing professional; b. La Grange, Ill., Oct. 5, 1947; d. Robert Fred and Gloria Virginia (McQuiston) Seeburger; m. Peter Slate Schick, Sept. 25, 1978 (dec. 1980); 2 children; m. Irwin Frederick, Gellman, Sept. 9, 1989; 3 children. BA magna cum laude, Purdue U., 1969; student, Lee Strasberg Actors Studio; postgrad., UCLA, U. Calif.-Irvine. Mem. mktg. staff Seemac, Inc. (formerly R.F. Seeburger Co.); v.p. V.I.P. Properties, Inc., Newport Beach, Calif. Profl. actress, singer; television and radio talk show hostess, Indpls., late 1960s; performer radio and television commls., 1960s—. Mem. Orange County Philharm. Soc., bd. dirs. womens com.; mem. Orange County Master Chorale, Orange County Performing Arts Ctr., v.p., treas. Crescendo chpt. OCPAC Ctr. Stars; bd. dirs. Newport Harbor (Calif.) Art Mus., v.p. membership, mem. acquisition coun.; bd. dirs., mem. founders soc. Opera Pacific; patron Big Bros./Big Sisters Starlight Found.; mem. Visionaries Newport Harbor Mus., Designing Women of Art Inst. Soc. Calif.; pres. Opera Pacific Guild Alliance, Spyglass Hill Philharm. Com.; v.p. Pacific Symphony Orch. League; mem. U. Calif. Irvine Found. Bd., mem. devel. com.; chmn. numerous small and large fundraisers. Mem. AAUW, AFTRA, SAG, Internat. Platform Assn., Actors Equity, U. Calif.-Irvine Chancellor's Club, U. Calif.-Irvine Humanities Assocs. (founder, pres., bd. dirs.), Mensa, Orange County Mental Health Assn., Balboa Bay Club, U. Club, Club 39, Islanders, Covergirls, Alpha Lambda Delta, Delta Rho Kappa. Republican. Home: PO Box 1993 Newport Beach CA 92659-0993

GELL-MANN, MURRAY, theoretical physicist; b. N.Y.C., Sept. 15, 1929; s. Arthur and Pauline (Reichstein) Gell-M.; m. J. Margaret Dow, Apr. 19, 1955 (dec. 1981); children: Elizabeth, Nicholas; m. Marcia Southwick, June 20, 1992; 1 stepson, Nicholas Levis. BS, Yale U., 1948; PhD, Mass. Inst. Tech., 1951; ScD (hon.), Yale U., 1959, U. Chgo., 1967, U. Ill., 1968, Wesleyan U., 1968, U. Turin, Italy, 1969, U. Utah, 1970, Columbia U., 1977, Cambridge U., 1980; D (hon.), Oxford (Eng.) U., 1992. Mem. Inst. for Advanced Study, 1951, 55, 67-68; instr. U. Chgo., 1952-53, asst. prof., 1953-54, assoc. prof., 1954; assoc. prof. Calif. Inst. Tech., Pasadena, 1955-56; prof. Calif. Inst. Tech., 1956—, now R.A. Millikan prof. physics; vis. prof. MIT, spring 1963, CERN, Geneva, 1971-72, 79-80; Mem. Pres.'s Sci. Adv. Com., 1969-72; mem. sci. and grants com. Leakey Found., 1977—; chmn. bd. trustees Aspen Ctr. for Physics, 1973-79; founding trustee Santa Fe Inst., 1982, chmn. bd. trustees, 1982-85, co-chmn. sci. bd. 1985—. Author: (with Y. Ne'eman) Eightfold Way. Regent Smithsonian Instn., 1974-88; bd. dirs. J.D. and C.T. MacArthur Found., 1979—. NSF post doctoral fellow, vis. prof. Coll. de France and U. Paris, 1959-60; recipient Dannie Heineman prize Am. Phys. Soc., 1959; E.O. Lawrence Meml. award AEC, 1966; Overseas fellow Churchill Coll., Cambridge, Eng., 1966; Franklin medal, 1967; Carty medal Nat. Acad. Scis., 1968; Research Corp. award, 1969; named to UN Environ. Program Roll of Honor for Environ. Achievement, 1988; Nobel prize in physics, 1969. Fellow Am. Phys. Soc.; mem. NAS, Royal Soc. (fgn.), Am. Acad. Arts and Scis. (v.p., chmn. Western ctr. 1970-76), Council on Fgn. Relations, French Phys. Soc. (hon.). Clubs: Cosmos (Washington); Century Assn., Explorers (N.Y.C.); Athenaeum (Pasadena). Office: Calif Inst Tech Dept Physics Pasadena CA 91125*

GELPI, MICHAEL ANTHONY, entrepreneur; b. Columbus, Ohio, Dec. 28, 1940; s. Andre and Eleanor (Amorose) G. AB, Georgetown U., 1962. Store mgr. Swan Cleaners, Columbus, 1964-65, dist. supr., 1965-68, v.p., 1976-76, exec. v.p., treas., 1976-81, also dir.; v.p. Rainbow Properties, Columbus, 1971-83, pres., 1983-85, chmn. bd., dir. The Neoprobe Corp., Columbus, 1985-89; pres., dir., CEO M.D. Personal Products, Hayward, Calif., 1992—; bd. dirs. Health Options. Trustee Am. Cancer Soc., 1978-92 , crusade chmn., 1979-84, 1st v.p., 1981-84, pres., 1984-85, chmn., 1985-87, trustee Ohio div., 1984-86, state spl. gifts chmn., 1984-86. Mem. City of Columbus AIDS Adv. Coalition, 1987-92, chmn., 1988-92; trustee Players Theatre of Columbus, 1981-88, v.p., 1985-86, pres. 1986-87; trustee German Village Hist. Soc., 1980-81; trustee Cen. Ohio Radio Reading Svc., 1982-88, pres., 1983-85, trustee Town-Franklin Hist. Neighborhood Assn., 1979-85, v.p., 1983-85; chmn. advance gifts Bishops Ann. Appeal, 1981-86; bd. dirs. Human Rights Campaign Fund, 1985-88; trustee Geriatric Svc. Orgn., 1988-92, devel. chair, 1988-92; candidate for Ohio 12th dist. U.S. Congress, 1988, 90. 1st lt. U.S. Army, 1962-64. Roman Catholic. Recipient Vol. of Yr. award Am. Cancer Soc., 1981, Community Svc. award Columbus Dispatch, 1984, Mayor's award for Vol. Svc. to City of Columbus, 1984. Mem. Columbus Club, Athletic Club.

GELTNER, FRANK JOSEPH, JR., university administrator; b. Chgo., Aug. 2, 1941; s. Frank Joseph Sr. and Mary Catherine (Herzig) G.; m. Jo Maitland, Sept. 10, 1977. BA, U. Ill., Chgo., 1967; MA, Memphis State U., 1969; PhD, U. Oreg., 1980. Dir. alumni rels. U. Ill. Alumni Assn., Urbana, 1970-74; assoc. dir. Erb Meml. Union, U. Oreg., Eugene, 1977—. Contbr. articles to profl. jours. Officer Very Little Theatre, Eugene, 1986-90. With U.S. Army, 1960-62. Mem. Assn. of Coll. Unions Internat. (com. on computer applications 1987-89, chair regional rep. region 14 1989-92). Home: PO Box 30171 Eugene OR 97403 Office: U Oreg Erb Meml Union Eugene OR 97403

GELTNER, PETER BENJAMIN, college dean; b. Mwanza, Tanzania, Apr. 1, 1943; came to U.S., 1949; s. Adolf and Elsa (Kohn) G.; m. Sharon Ordman, Apr. 7, 1968. BA in Math., UCLA, 1965, MA in Math., 1968; MS in Computer Sci., U. So. Calif., 1972, PhD in Computer Sci., 1979. Tchr. Dorsey High Sch., L.A., 1965-68; prof. math. Santa Monica (Calif.) Coll., 1968-86, dean bus. and math., 1986-89, adminstrv. dean for computing, 1989—, pres. acad. senate, 1978-79. Author: Geometry for College Students, 1987, 2d edit., 1991; also articles. Mem. Santa Monica Coll. Faculty Assn. (pres. 1982-83), Santa Monica Coll. Mgmt. Assn. (pres. 1988-89), Optimists (pres. Santa Monica 1992-93). Office: Santa Monica Coll 1900 Pico Blvd Santa Monica CA 90405

GENDEL, EUGENE B., museum curator, economics professor; b. Hartford, Conn., Feb. 27, 1948; s. Gil and Esther (Gershman) G.; m. Sandra Denise Bronstein, June 5, 1976; Mara Hope, D. Jacob, Miriam Elise. BA, U. Conn., 1970; MA, Boston U., 1972, PhD, 1979. Asst. prof. Chatham Coll., Pitts., 1977-80, Lafayette Coll., Easton, Pa., 1980-85; curator, adminstr. Calif. Mus. Sci. and Industry, L.A., 1985-93; v.p., sr. fellow Calif. Coun. on Econ. Edn., Long Beach, 1993—; bd. dirs. Quakesafe, Inc., L.A.; part-time instr. Cerritos Coll., Norwalk, Calif., 1990—. Contbr. articles to profl. jours. Mem. Am. Econ. Assn., Omicron Delta Epsilon. Home: 3211 N El Dorado Dr Long Beach CA 90808-3234 Office: Calif Coun Econ Edn 400 Golden Shore Dr # 228 Long Beach CA 90802

GENGOR, VIRGINIA ANDERSON, financial planning executive, educator; b. Lyons, N.Y., May 2, 1927; d. Axel Jennings and Marie Margaret (Mack) Anderson; m. Peter Gengor, Mar. 2, 1952 (dec.); children: Peter Randall, Daniel Neal, Susan Leigh. AB, Wheaton Coll., 1949; MA, U. No. Colo., Greeley, 1975, 77. Chief hosp. intake service County of San Diego, 1966-77, chief Kearny Mesa Dist. Office, 1977-79, chief Dependent Children of Ct., 1979-81, chief child protection services, 1981-82; registered rep. Am. Pacific Securities, San Diego, 1982-85; registered tax preparer State of Calif., 1982—, registered rep. (prin.) Sentra Securities, 1985—; assoc. Pollock & Assocs., San Diego, 1985-86; pres. Gengor Fin. Advisors, 1986—; cons. instr. Nat. Ctr. for Fin. Edn., San Diego, 1986-88; instr. San Diego Community Coll., 1985-88. Mem. allocations panel United Way, San Diego, 1976-79, children's circle Child Abuse Prevention Found., 1989—; chmn. com. Child Abuse Coordinating Council, San Diego, 1979-83; pres. Friends of Casa de la Esperanza, San Diego, 1980-85, bd. dirs., 1980—; 1st v.p. The Big Sister League, San Diego, 1985-86, pres., 1987-89. Mem. Inst. Cert. Fin. Planners, Internat. Assn. Fin. Planning, Inland Soc. Tax Cons., AAUW (bd. dirs.), Nat. Assn. Securities Dealers (registered prin.), Nat. Ctr. Fin. Edn., Am. Bus. Women's Assn., Nat. Assn. Female Execs., Navy League, Freedoms Found. Valley Forge, Internat. Platform Assn. Presbyterian. Avocations: community service, travel, reading. Home: 6462 Spear St San Diego CA 92120-2929 Office: Gengor Fin Advisors 4950 Waring Rd Ste 7 San Diego CA 92120-2700

GENINI, RONALD WALTER, history educator, historian; b. Oakland, Calif., Dec. 5, 1946; s. William Angelo and Irma Lea (Gays) G.; m. Roberta Mae Tucker, Dec. 20, 1969; children: Thomas, Justin, Nicholas. BA, U. San Francisco, 1968, MA, 1969. Cert. secondary edn. tchr., Calif.; adminstrv. svcs. credential. Tchr. Cen. Unified Sch. Dist., Fresno, Calif., 1970—; judge State History Day, Sacramento, 1986—; mem. U.S. History examination devel. team Golden State, San Diego, 1989-93; securer placement of state-registered landmarks. Author: Romualdo Pacheco, 1985; contbr. articles to profl. jours. Bd. dirs. Fresno Area 6 Neighborhood Coun., 1973-74, Fresno City and County Hist. Soc., 1975-78, St. Anthony's sch. bd., Fresno, 1980-84. Named one of Outstanding Young Educators Am., Fresno Jaycees, 1978. Mem. Calif. Hist. Soc. Libertarian. Home: 1486 W Menlo Ave Fresno CA 93711-1305 Office: Cen High Sch 2045 N Dickenson Ave Fresno CA 93722-9643

GENN, NANCY, artist; b. San Francisco; d. Morley P. and Ruth W. Thompson; m. Vernon Chathburton Genn; children: Cynthia, Sarah, Peter. Student, San Francisco Art Inst., U. Calif., Berkeley. lectr. on art and papermaking Am. Centers in, Osaka, Japan, Nagoya, Japan, Kyoto, Japan, 1979-80; guest lectr. various univs. and art museums in U.S., 1975—. One woman shows of sculpture, paintings include, De Young Mus., San Francisco, 1955, 63, Gumps Gallery, San Francisco, 1955, 57, 59, San Francisco Mus. Art, 1961, U. Calif., Santa Cruz, 1966-68, Richmond (Calif.) Art Center, 1970, Oakland (Calif.) Mus., 1971, Linda/Farris Gallery, Seattle, 1974, 76, 78, 81, Los Angeles Inst. Contemporary Art, 1976, Susan Caldwell Gallery, N.Y.C., 1976, 77, 79, 81, Nina Freudenheim Gallery, Buffalo, 1977, 81, Annely Juda Fine Art, London, 1978, Inoue Gallery, Tokyo, 1980, Toni Birckhead Gallery, Cin., 1982, Kala Inst. Gallery, Berkeley, Calif., 1983, Ivory/Kimpton Gallery, San Francisco, 1984, 86, Eve Mannes Gallery, Atlanta, 1985, Richard Iri Gallery, L.A., 1990, Harcourts Modern and Contemporary Art, San Francisco, 1991; group exhbns. include San Francisco Mus. Art, 1971, Aldrich Mus., Ridgefield, Conn., 1972-73, Santa Barbara (Calif.) Mus., 1974, 75, Oakland (Calif.) Mus. Art, 1975, Susan Caldwell, Inc., N.Y.C., 1974, 75, Mus. Modern Art, N.Y.C., 1976, traveling exhbn. Arts Coun. Gt. Britain, 1983-84, Inst. Contemporary Arts, Boston, 1977; represented in permanent collections Mus. Modern Art, N.Y.C., Albright-Knox Art Gallery, Buffalo, Libr. of Congress, Washington, Nat. Mus. for Am. Art, Washington, L.A. County Mus. Art, Art Mus. U. Calif., Berkeley, McCrory Corp., N.Y.C., Mus. Art, Auckland, N.Z., Aldrich Mus., Ridgefield, Conn., (collection) Bklyn. Mus., (collection) U. Tex., El Paso, Internat. Ctr. Aesthetic Rsch., Torino, Italy, Cin. Art Mus., San Francisco Mus. Modern Art, Oakland Art Mus., L.A. County Mus., City of San Francisco Hall of Justice, Harris Bank, Chgo., Chase Manhattan Bank, N.Y.C., Modern Art Gallery of Ascoli Piceno, Italy, various mfg. cos., also numerous pvt. collections; commd. works include, Bronze lectern and 5 bronze sculptures for chancel table, 1st Unitarian Ch., Berkeley, Calif., 1961, 64, bronze fountain, Cowell Coll., U. Calif., Santa Cruz, bronze menorah, Temple Beth Am, Los Altos Hills, Calif., 1981, 17, murals and 2 bronze fountain sculptures, Sterling Vineyards, Calistoga, Calif., 1972, 73, fountain sculpture, Expo 1974, Spokane, Wash; vis. artist Am. Acad., Rome, 1989. U.S./Japan Creative Arts fellow, 1978-79; recipient Ellen Branston award, 1952; Phelan award De Young Mus., 1963; honor award HUD, 1968. Home: 1515 La Loma Ave Berkeley CA 94708-2033

GENNARO, ANTONIO L., biology educator; b. Raton, N.Mex., Mar. 18, 1934; s. Paul and Mary Lou (Gasperetti) G.; m. Virginia Marie Sullivan, May 15, 1955 (div. 1979); children—Theresa Ann, Carrie Marie, Janelle Elizabeth; m. Marjorie Lou Cox, Sept. 27, 1980. B.S., N.Mex. State U., 1957; M.S., U. N.Mex., 1961, Ph.D., 1965. Tchr. biology Las Cruces High Sch., N.Mex., 1957-58; asst. prof. biology St. John's U., Collegeville, Minn., 1964-65; prof. biology Eastern N.Mex. U., Portales, 1965—. Contbr. articles to sci. jours. Served to capt. U.S. Army, 1958-59; mem. Res., 1959-66. Recipient Presdl. Faculty award Eastern N.Mex. U., 1970, Pres.'s Faculty award for excellence in rsch., 1988; Outstanding Sci. award N.Mex. Acad. Sci., 1975. Mem. Southwestern Naturalists (treas. 1974-78), Am. Soc. Mammalogists, Herpetologists League, Sigma Xi, Phi Kappa Phi (pres. 1970-74). Roman Catholic.

GENOVESE, EDGAR NICHOLAS, humanities educator; b. Balt., Sept. 18, 1942; s. E.N. and Elizabeth (Hlobick) G.; m. Janice Kay Hodapp, July 8, 1969; children: Domenica Rose, Charles Anthony. AB, Xavier U., 1964; PhD, Ohio State U., 1970. Instr. Kenwood Sr. High Sch., Essex, Md., 1964-66; prof. classics and humanities San Diego State U., 1970—; dept. classics and humanities chair, San Diego State U.; steering com. mem., Calif. Humanities Project, Davis, 1986-90. Contbr. articles to profl. jours. Mem. Am. Philol. Assn. (sustaining), Golden Key, Phi Kappa Phi. Office: San Diego State U San Diego CA 92182

GENTER, DAVID LEON, zoologist; b. Mar. 11, 1955; s. Donald L. and Arline (Greenizen) G.; m. Joan Ruth Bird, Aug. 8, 1987; 1 child, Amory W.H. BA cum laude, U. Colo., 1981; MS in Zoology, U. Mont., 1985. Cons. Black Hawk (Colo.) Assocs., 1979-81; rsch. assoc. U. Mont., Missoula, 1984-85; dir. Mont. Natural Heritage Program, Helena, 1985—. Co-editor: TES Species of Yellowstone, 1990, Montana Birds, 1992. Trustee Forestvale Cemetery Assn., Helena, 1991—. Recipient Regional Foresters' award USDA Forest Svc., Missoula, 1988, Outstanding Svc. award The Nature Conservancy, Helena, 1989, Spl. Achievement award Kootenai Nat. Forest, Libby, Mont., 1991. Mem. Am. Fisheries Soc. (chmn. endangered fish com. Mont. chpt. 1987—), Sigma Xi. Methodist. Home: 400 Forestvale Rd Helena MT 59601 Office: Mont Natural Heritage Program 1515 E 6th Ave Helena MT 59620

GENTILE, ANTHONY LEO, association executive, consultant; b. N.Y.C., Apr. 23, 1930; s. Leo and Grace (Leone) G.; m. Bettie Lynn, July 3, 1957; children: David Lynn, Michael Leo. BS in Geology, CCNY, 1950; MS Geol. Sci., N.Mex. Tech. U., 1957; PhD in Mineralogy, Ohio State U., 1960. Mem. tech. staff Hughes Rsch. Labs., Malibu, Calif., 1961-68, sect. head, 1968-86, program mgr., 1986-87, sr. scientist, 1987-89, cons., 1990-91; cons., exec. adminstr. Am. Assn. Crystal Growth, Thousand Oaks, Calif., 1990—. Contbr. chpt. to ency., articles to profl. jours.; patentee in field. 1st lt. USAF, 1951-54. Mem. Am. Assn. Crystal Growth (exec. com. 1977-90, pres. western sect. 1977-81, treas. 1981-84, pres., 1984-87, exec. adminstr. 1990—). Office: Am Assn Crystal Growth PO Box 3233 Thousand Oaks CA 91359-0233

GENTRY, JAMES WILLIAM, retired state official; b. Danville, Ill., Aug. 14, 1926; s. Carl Lloyd and Leone (Isham) G.; A.B., Fresno State Coll., 1948; M.J., U. Calif., Berkeley, 1956; m. Dorothie Shirley Hechtlinger, Mar. 18, 1967; 1 stepdau., Susan Mushkin. Field rep. Congressman B.W. Gearhart, Fresno, Calif., 1948, Assemblyman Wm. W. Hansen, Fresno, 1950, sec., 1953-56; exec. asst. Calif. Pharm. Assn., Los Angeles, 1956-69, editor, pub. jour., 1956-69; pub. relations dir. PAID Prescriptions, 1963-64; dir. pub. info. comprehensive Health Planning Council, Los Angeles County, 1969; asst. adminstr., dir. pub. info. So. Calif. Comprehensive Health Planning Council, 1969-71, acting adminstr., 1971-72; exec. sec. Calif. State Health Planning Council, 1972-73, Calif. Adv. Health Council, 1973-85, fed. cons., 1986-88; Calif. Health Care Commn., 1973-75; acting public info. officer Calif. Office Statewide Health Planning and Devel., 1978-79; interim dir. Calif. Office Statewide Health Planning and Devel., 1983; mem. L.A. Civil Svc. Police Interview Bd., 1967-72; asst. sgt.-at-arms Calif. State Assembly, 1950; exec. sec. Calif. Assembly Interim Com. on Livestock and Dairies, 1954-56; mem. adv. bd. Am. Security Council; mem. Calif. Health Planning Law Revision Commn.; former mem. Calif. Bldg. Safety Bd. Mem. Fresno County Republican Central Com., 1950; charter mem. Rep. Presdl. Task Force. Served to col. AUS, 1949-50, 50-53; Korea. Decorated Legion of Merit, Bronze Star medal, Commendation Ribbon with metal pendant ; recipient pub. awards Western Soc. Bus. Publns. Assn., 1964-67. Mem. Am. Assn. Comprehensive Health Planning, Pub. Relations Soc. Am., Ret. Officers Assn. (life), Allied Drug Travelers So. Calif., L.A. Press Club, Mil. Police Assn., Res. Officers Assn. (life), Assn. U.S. Army, U.S. Senatorial Club, The Victory Svcs. Club of London, Pi Gamma Mu, Phi Alpha Delta. Sigma Delta Chi. Editor: Better Health, 1963-67; Orientation Conf. Comprehensive Health Planning, 1969; Commentary, 1969-71. Editorial adv. Pharm. Svcs. for Nursing Homes: A Procedural Manual, 1966. Editor: Program and Funding, 1972; Substance Abuse, 1972. Home: 902 Commons Dr Sacramento CA 95825-6647

GENTRY, MICHAEL LEE, information systems engineer, electronic engineer; b. Durant, Okla., Sept. 20, 1942; s. G. P. and Lucille Elizabeth (Tomlin) G.; m. Lois Jean Jones, June 11, 1968; children: Christopher Michael, Cynthia Lee. BS, Okla. State U., 1964; MS, MIT, 1966; PhD, U. Ariz., 1971; grad., U.S. Army War Coll., 1983. Assoc. engr. Boeing Aircraft Co., Wichita, Kans., 1964-65; electonic engr. Tex. Instruments, Inc., Dallas, 1966-67; electronic engr. CIA, Washington, 1971-73; electonic engr. U.S. Army Info. Systems Command, Ft. Huachuca, Ariz., 1973-89; tech. engr. U.S. Army Info. Systems Engring. Command, Ft. Huachuca, 1989—; instr. Cochise Coll., Sierra Vista, Ariz., 1974-82; mem. indsl. adv. coun. U. Ariz. Coll. of Engring. & Mines, Tucson, 1990—. Contbr. articles to profl. jours. Mem. Planning and Zoning Commn., Sierra Vista, 1977-79; chmn., mem. City Bd. of Adjustments, Sierra Vista, 1975-77. NSF fellow, 1965-66, NDEA fellow, 1967-70. Mem. IEEE (bd. dirs. ann. tech. conf. Phoenix chpt. 1990—), Armed Forces Comm.-Electronics Assn. (bd. dirs. Ft. Huachuca chpt. 1991—). Republican. Home: 1648 Crestwood Dr Sierra Vista AZ 85635-4905 Office: USA Info Systems Engring Command Office Technical Director Fort Huachuca AZ 85613-5300

GEOFFRION, CHARLES ALBERT, university administrator, consultant, research and communications administrator; b. Cambridge, Mass., Apr. 21, 1943; s. Louis Felix and Irene Gertrude (Mercier) G.; m. Moira Marti, July 31, 1965; children: Sabrina, Damien Marcel. BA, Boston U., 1965; MA, Indiana U., 1971. Lectr. So. Ill. U., Edwardsville, Ill., 1972-74, St. Mary's Coll., South Bend, Ind., 1975-78, Ind. U., South Bend, 1975-78; vis. lectr. Inst. on Africa, Notre Dame, Ind., 1979-86; fin. systems mgr. St. Joseph County Govt., South Bend, 1979-82; cons. Resource Mgmt. Assocs., South Bend, 1982-83; cons. faculty rsch. U. Notre Dame, South Bend, 1984-86; dir. found. rels. U. Ariz. Found., Tucson, 1987-90; assoc. v.p. for rsch., dir. rsch. communications U. Ariz., 1990—, Tucson, 1991—; cons. U.S. AID Program in Egypt, 1993—; cons. Festival for Performing Arts, South Bend, 1979-84, Performing Arts Tng. Ctr., East St. Louis, Ill., 1970-75, Tucson Community Found., 1991—, Found. for Internat. Community Assistance, Costa Rica, 1988; mentor Acad. Preparation for Excellence, Tucson, 1987—. Author: Study Guide to Africa, (videotape) Guide to India. Mem. long range planning com. South Bend Art Ctr., 1982-83, Coun. Advancement and Support of Edn.; cons. Jr. Achievement Project Bus., South Bend, 1986; bd. dirs. County Park Found., South Bend, 1984-86; mem. adv. panel WNIT-TV (PBS), Elkhart, Ind., 1983-84; vol. U.S. Peace Corps, Sierra Leone, West Africa, 1965-67. Recipient numerous grants in field. Mem. Assn. Am. Colls. (coun. liberal learning), Nat. Coun. Univ. Rsch. Adminstrs., Intermountain U. Rsch. Adminstrs., Arizonans Cultural Devel., Ariz.-Mex. Commn., Soc. Rsch. Adminstrs., Ventana Canyon Golf and Tennis Club. Roman Catholic. Home: 4460 N Territory Pl Tucson AZ 85715-1807

GEORGE, FRANCIS, bishop. Ordained priest Roman Cath. Ch., 1963. Bishop Diocese of Yakima, Wash., 1990—. Office: Diocese of Yakima 5301-A Tieton Dr Yakima WA 98908

GEORGE, LESLIE EARL, fire chief; b. Eldrado, Okla., July 12, 1930; s. Earl Haskel and Cuba Mae (Huddleston) G.; m. Eleanor Mae Hart, Nov. 20, 1955; children: Leslie Earl Jr., Rickie Dwayne, Jeffery Scott, Gregory Allen. AA, East L.A. Coll., 1966; BA in Mgmt., Redlands U., 1983. Reinforcing iron worker Blue Diamond Corp., L.A., 1949-53; reinforcing ironworker foreman Triangle Steel Co., Vernon, Calif., 1953-54; fire fighter City of El Monte (Calif.) Fire Dept., 1955-56, fire engr., 1956-57, fire capt., 1957-61, adminstrv. capt., 1961-66, fire battalion chief, 1966—. Bd. dirs., pres. Boys' Club El Monte, 1993. With U.S. Army, 1951-53. Mem. Calif. Conf. Arson Investigators (life, pub., editor), Rotary (pres., sec., program chmn.). Home: 2627 Maureen West Covina CA 91792 Office: 3615 Santa Anita Ave El Monte CA 91732

GEORGE, LLOYD D., federal judge; b. Montpelier, Idaho, Feb. 22, 1930; s. William Ross and Myrtle (Nield) G.; m. LaPrele Badouin, Aug. 6, 1956; children: Douglas Ralph, Michele, Cherie Suzanne, Stephen Lloyd. BS, Brigham Young U., 1955; JD, U. Calif., Berkeley, 1961. Ptnr. Albright, George, Johnson & Stephen, 1969-71, George, Steffen & Simmons, 1971-74; judge U.S. Bankruptcy Ct. (Nev. dist.), 1974-84, U.S. Dist. Ct. Nev., 1984—; justice of peace Clark County, Nev., 1962-69. Served with USAF, 1955-58. Office: US Dist Ct 3d Flr 300 Las Vegas Blvd S Las Vegas NV 89101

GEORGE, MARY SHANNON, state senator; b. Seattle, May 27, 1916; d. William Day and Agnes (Lovejoy) Shannon; B.A. cum laude, U. Wash., 1937; postgrad. U. Mich., 1937, Columbia U., 1938; m. Flave Joseph George; children—Flave Joseph, Karen Liebermann, Christy, Shannon Lowrey. Prodn. asst., asst. news editor Pathe News, N.Y.C., 1938-42; mem. fgn. editions staff Readers Digest, Pleasantville, N.Y., 1942-46; columnist Caracas (Venezuela) Daily Jour., 1953-60; councilwoman City and County of Honolulu, 1969-74; senator State of Hawaii, 1974—, asst. minority leader, 1978-80, minority policy leader, 1983-84, minority floor leader, 1987, minority leader, 1987—, chmn. housing com., 1993—, transp. com., 1981-82; mem. Nat. Air Quality Adv. Bd., 1974-75, Intergovtl. Policy Adv. Com. Trade, 1988—, White House Conf. Drug Free Am., 1988—. Vice chmn. 1st Hawaii Ethics Commn., 1968; co-founder Citizens Com. on Constl. Conv., 1968; vice-chmn. platform com. Republican Nat. Conv., 1976, co-chmn., 1980; bd. dirs. State Legis. Leaders Found., 1993—, Hawaii Planned Parenthood, 1970-72, 79-86, Hawaii Med. Services Assn., 1972-86; mem. adv. bd. Hawaii chpt. Mothers Against Drunk Driving, 1984—. Recipient Jewish Men's Club Brotherhood award, 1974, Disting. Svc. award Hawaii Women Layers, 1991, Mahalo award Friends of Libr. Hawaii, 1991; Outstanding Legislator of Yr. award Nat. Rep. Legislators Assn., 1985; named Woman of Yr., Honolulu Press Club, 1969, Hawaii Fedn. Bus. and Profl. Women, 1970; Citizen of Yr., Hawaii Fed. Exec. Bd., 1973, 76. Mem. LWV (pres. Honolulu 1966-68), Mensa, Phi Beta Kappa. Author: A Is for Abrazo, 1961. Home: 782G N Kalaheo Ave Kailua HI 96734-1973 Office: State Office Tower Ste # 501 Honolulu HI 96813

GEORGE, MELVIN RAY, university library director, consultant; b. Grove City, Minn., Feb. 20, 1937; s. Robert Ordean and Irene Helen (Swanson) G.; m. Shirley Jean Hattendorf, June 16, 1962; children: Catherine Margaret, Elizabeth Mary. BS, St. Cloud State U., 1959, MS, 1960; MA, U. Minn., 1965; PhD, U. Chgo., 1979. Asst. instr. St. Cloud (Minn.) State U., 1959-60; English tchr. St. Louis Park (Minn.) Pub. Schs., 1960-63, libr., 1963-65; coll. libr. Elmhurst (Ill.) Coll., 1965-74; dir. learning svcs., univ. libr. Northeastern Ill. U., Chgo., 1974-84; Delpha & Donald Campbell univ. libr. Oreg. State U., Corvallis, 1984—; vis. lectr. Rosary Coll. Grad. Libr. Sch., River Forest, Ill., 1967-74; ind. libr. bldg. cons., 1973—. Contbr. articles to profl. jours. Mem. Am. Libr. Assn., Ill. Libr. Assn. (pres. 1976-77, Libr. of Yr. 1983-84), Oreg. Libr. Assn. Democrat. Episcopalian. Home: 2635 NW Fireweed Pl Corvallis OR 97330-3311 Office: Oreg State U Kerr Libr 121 Corvallis OR 97331-4501

GEORGE, PAULA LOUISE, advertising agency executive; b. Huntington, W.Va., June 16, 1952; d. Emil Ralph and Helen Louise (Hensley) G. BBA in Mktg., Marshall U., 1974. Mktg. mgr. Access Matrix Corp., San Jose, Calif., 1982-83; v.p., dir. mktg. Altus Corp., San Jose, 1983-84; chief exec. officer, founder The SoftAd Group, Sausalito, Calif., 1985—; guest lectr. Stanford U.; participant exec.-in-residence Marshall U., Huntington, W.Va.; keynote speaker Direct Mktg. Assn. Ann. Confs., New Orleans, Atlanta, Advt. Age Creative Workshop, N.Y.C., Montreux Direct Mktg. Symposium, Montreux, Switzerland. Judge Inc. Mags. Entrepreneur of Yr. award; mem. Multimedia Expo, N.Y., Internat. Electronics System, Zurich, Direct Mktg. Bus. Conf., Chgo., Pan-Pacific, Sydney, Australia, Computer Graphics Show , N.Y., European Tech. Roundtable Exhbn., Opio, France. Mem. Internat. Platform Assn., Info. Industry Assn., Direct Mktg. Assn., Assn. Nat. Advertisers, Internat. Direct Mktg. Inst., Direct Mktg. Netherlands. Office: The SoftAd Group Bldg B Ste 300 100 Shoreline Blvd Mill Valley CA 94941

GEORGE, PETER T., orthodontist; b. Akron, Ohio; s. Tony and Paraskeva (Ogrenova) G.; BS Kent State U., 1952; DDS, Ohio State U., 1956; cert. in orthodontics Columbia U., 1962; children: Barton Herrin, Tryan Franklin. Pvt. practice orthodontics, Honolulu, 1962—; cleft palate cons. Hawaii Bur. Crippled Children, 1963—; asst. prof. Med. Sch., U. Hawaii, Honolulu, 1970—; lectr. in field. Mem. Hawaii Gov.'s Phys. Fitness Com., 1962-68; mem. Honolulu Mayor's Health Coun., 1967-72; mem. med. com. Internat. Weightlifting Fedn., 1980-84; chmn. bd. govs. Hall of Fame of Hawaii, 1984; bd. dirs. Honolulu Opera Theatre, 1986-91, chmn. bd. Hawaii Internat. Sports Found., 1988-91. Served to capt. Dental Corps, U.S. Army, 1956-60. Olympic Gold medallist in weightlifting, Helsinki, 1952, Silver medallist, London, 1948, Melbourne, 1956; six times world champion; recipient Disting. Service award Hawaiian AAU, 1968; Gold medal Internat. Weightlifting Fedn., 1976; named to Helms Hall of Fame, 1966. Diplomate Am. Bd. Orthodontics. Fellow Am. Coll. Dentistry, Internat. Coll. Dentistry; mem. Hawaii Amateur Athletic Union (pres. 1964-65), U.S. Olympians (pres. Hawaii chpt. 1963-67, 80—), Am. Assn. Orthodontists, Honolulu Dental Soc. (pres. 1967-68), Hawaii Dental Assn. (pres. 1978), Hawaii Soc. Orthodontists (pres. 1972). Editor Hawaii State Dental Jour., 1965-67. Inventor appliance to prevent sleep apnea. U.S. weightlifting coach USSR, 1979, asst. coach Olympic weightlifting team, 1980. Home and Office: 1441 Kapiolani Blvd Ste 520 Honolulu HI 96814-4474

GEORGE, RONALD M., judge; b. L.A., Mar. 11, 1940. AB, Princeton U., 1961; JD, Stanford U., 1964. Bar: Calif. 1965. Judge L.A. Mcpl. Ct., L.A. County, 1972-77; judge Superior Ct. Calif., L.A. County, 1977-83, supervising judge criminal divsn., 1983-84; dep. atty. gen. Calif. Dept. Justice; assoc. justice 2d dist., divsn. 4 Calif. Ct. Appeal, San Francisco. Mem. Calif. Judges Assn. (pres. 1982-83). Office: Calif Supreme Court 303 2nd St South Tower San Francisco CA 94107*

GEORGE, RUSSELL LLOYD, lawyer, legislator; b. Rifle, Colo., May 28, 1946; s. Walter Mallory and Eleanora (Michel) G.; m. Neal Ellen Moore, Nov. 24, 1972; children: Russell, Charles, Thomas, Andrew. BS in Econs., Colo. State U., 1968; JD, Harvard Law Sch., 1971. Bar: Colo. Shareholder Stuver & George, P.C., Rifle, 1976—. state rep. dist. 57 Colo. Gen. Assembly, 1993—. Fellow Colo. Bar Found.; mem. Colo. Bar Assn., Rotary Internat., Masonic Lodge. Republican. Methodist. Home: 1300 E 7th St Rifle CO 81650 Office: Stuver & George PC PO Box 907 120 W 3d St Rifle CO 81650

GEORGE, THOMAS FREDERICK, chemistry educator; b. Phila., Mar. 18, 1947; s. Emmanuel John and Veronica Mather (Hansel) G.; m. Barbara Carol Harbach, Apr. 25, 1970. B.A. in Chemistry and Math., Gettysburg (Pa.) Coll., 1967; M.S. in Chemistry, Yale U., 1968, Ph.D., 1970. Rsch.

assoc. MIT, 1970; postdoctoral fellow U. Calif., Berkeley, 1971; mem. faculty U. Rochester, N.Y., 1972-85; prof. chemistry U. Rochester, 1977-85; dean Faculty Natural Sci. and Math., prof. chemistry and physics SUNY-Buffalo, 1985-91; provost, acad. v.p., prof. chemistry and physics Wash. State U., Pullman, 1991—, 1991—; Disting. vis. lectr. dept. chemistry U. Tex., Austin, 1978; lectr. NATO Advanced Study Inst., Cambridge, Eng., 1979; Disting. speaker dept. chemistry U. Utah, 1980; Disting. lectr. Air Force Weapons Lab., Kirtland AFB, N.Mex., 1980; mem. com. recommendations U.S. Army Basic Sci. Research, 1978-81; lectr. NATO Summer Sch. on Interfaces under Photon Irradiation, Maratea, Italy, 1986; organizer NSF workshop on theoretical aspects of laser radiation and its interaction with atomic and molecular systems Rochester, N.Y., 1977; vice chmn. 6th Internat. Conf. Molecular Energy Transfer, Rodez, France, 1979; chmn. Gordon Rsch. Conf. Molecular Energy Transfer, Wolfeboro, N.H., 1981; Mem. program com. Internat. Conf. on Lasers, San Francisco, 1981-83, ACS Symposium on Recent Advances in Surface Sci., Rochester sect., 1982, Internat. Laser Sci. Conf., Dallas, 1985, external rev. com. for chemistry Gettysburg Coll., 1984, awards com. ACS Procter and Gamble student prizes in chemistry, 1982-83, Free-electron Laser peer rev. panel Am. Inst. Biol. Sci. Med., alt., bd. trustees Calspan-UB Rsch. Ctr., 1989—; organiser APS Symposium on Laser-Induced Molecular Excitation/Photofragmentation, N.Y., 1987; co-organizer ACS Symposium on Phys. Chemistry High-Temp. Supercondrs., L.A., 1988; co-organizer MRS Symposium on High-Temperature Superconductors, Alfred, N.Y., 1988; chmn. SPIE Symposium on Photochemistry in Thin Films, L.A., 1989; mem. internat. program adv. com. Internat. Sch. Lasers and Applications, Sayanogorsk, East Siberia, USSR, 1989; lectr. on chemistry at cutting edge Smithsonian Instn./Am. Chem. Soc., Washington, 1990; mem. internat. adv. com. Xth Vavilov Conf. Nonlinear Optics, Novosibirsk, USSR, 1990; Am. coord. NSF Info. Exchange Seminar for U.S.-Japan Program of Cooperation in Photoconversion and Photosynthesis, Honolulu, 1990; mem. exec. bd. N.Y. State Inst. on Superconductivity, 1990-91; mem. ONT/ASEE rev. panel for Engring. Edn. postdoctoral fellowship program, 1990; mem. rev panel rsch. experiences for undergrads of sci. and tech. rsch. ctrs., NSF, 1989, mem. rev. panel grad. res. traineeships NSF, 1992; cons., lectr. in field. Co-author: (textbook) Notes in Classical and Quantum Physics, 1990; also over 475 papers in field; mem. editorial bd. Molecular Physics, 1984-90, Jour. Cluster Sci., 1989—; mem. adv. bd. Jour. Phys. Chemistry, 1980-84; mem. adv. editorial bd. Chem. Physics Letters, 1979-81, Chem. Materials, 1989; mem. editorial bd. Jour. Quantum Nonlinear Phenomena (Soviet jour.), 1991—; editor-at-large Marcel Dekker, 1989—; editor: Photochemistry in Thin Films, 1989; co-editor: Chemistry of High-Temperature Superconductors, Vol. I, 1987, Vol. II, 1988, ACS Symposium Series; feature editor Jour. of Optical Soc. of Am., Spectrochimica Acta, Optical Engring. Tchr., scholar Camille and Henry Dreyfus Found., 1975-85; bd. mgrs. Buffalo Mus. Sci., 1986; mem. exec. bd. N.Y. State Inst. on Superconductivity, 1990-91; mem. canvassing com. ACS; mem. external rev. com. for chemistry Gettysburg Coll., 1984; mem. NEASC site visit team Boston U., ten-yr. accreditation, 1989; bd. dirs. Wash. State Inst. for Pub. Policy, 1991—; trustee Wash. State U. Found., 1991—; bd. dirs. Wash. Tech. Ctr., 1992—; mem. exec. com. Northwest Acad. Forum, 1992—; mem. review panel Grad. Rsch. Traineeships, NSF, 1992. Sloan fellow, 1976-80, postdoctoral fellow, 1990, Guggenheim fellow,recipient Disting. Alumni award Gettysburg Coll., 1987, Harrison House award ACS, 1980, Peter Debye award ACS, 1986-88, Pure Chemistry award ACS, 1989—. Fellow Am. Phys. Soc., N.Y. Acad. Scis. (steering com. Inst. Superconductivity 1987—, steering com. Ctr. for Advanced Tech. in Health-Care Instruments and Devices 1988-90); mem. Am. Chem. Soc. (exec. com. phys. div. 1979-82, 85-89, vice chmn. 1985-86, chmn.-elect 1986-87, chmn. 1987-88), Soc. Photo-Optical Instrumentation Engrs., AAAS, European Phys. Soc., Royal Soc. Chemistry (Marlow medal and prize 1979), Coun. Colls. Arts Sci., Phi Beta Kappa, Sigma Xi (exec. com. U. Rochester 1984-85). Democrat. Lutheran. Office: Wash State U Office Provost 422 French Adminstrn Bldg Pullman WA 99164-1046

GEORGE, VANCE, conductor. Formerly assoc. dir. Cleve. Orch. Chorus; now dir. San Francisco Symphony Chorus; bd. dirs. Chorus Am.; formerly chmn. vocal div. Blossom Festival Sch.; dir. choral activities U. Wis., Madison, Kent State U.; assoc. dir., dir. Blossom Festival Chorus, Cleve. Orch. Chorus, Sch. of the Cleve. Orch.; worked with ensembles, toured East Coast; mem. faculty Choral Inst.; vis. assoc. prof. U. Calif. Berkeley. Appeared at Cloisters Mus., N.Y.C., Hadynfest at Kennedy Ctr., Spoleto Festival USA; condr. San Francisco Symphony, San Francisco Symphony Chorus in Handel's Messiah; performed and studied in U.S., Europe, Canada, India. Recipient Grammy award for Best Choral Performance, 1992. Mem. IFCM, ACDA. Office: San Francisco Symphony Chorus 201 Van Ness Ave San Francisco CA 94102-4595

GEORGIADES, GABRIEL GEORGE, aerospace engineering educator; b. Amarousion, Greece, Nov. 23, 1956; came to U.S., 1975; s. George Gabriel Georgiades and Evanthia Spyrou (Ioannou) Georgiadou. BA in Physics cum laude, Jacksonville U., 1979; B. Aerospace Engring., Ga. Inst. Tech., 1979; MS in Aerospace Engring., Pa. State U., 1982. Engr. in tng., Ga. Structural engr. Piper Aircraft Corp., Lock Haven, Pa., 1979-80; prof. aircraft structures Embry-Riddle Aero. U., Prescott, Ariz., 1982-85; prof. aerospace engring. Calif. State Poly. U., Pomona, Calif., 1985—; cons. Naval Weapons Ctr., China Lake, Calif., 1985—, Lockheed Aircraft Svc. Co., Ontario, Calif., 1991—, Field Svc. & Maintenance Co., North Palm Springs, Calif., 1991—, Wyle Labs., El Segundo, Calif., 1992—. Author: Aerospace Structures Lab Manual, 1988. Advisor Minority Engring. Program, Pomona, 1987—, Math. Engring., Sci. Achievement Program, Claremont, Calif., 1988—, Soc. Hispanics in Sci. and Engring., Pomona, 1989—. Recipient Cert. of Achievement, NATO, Belgium, 1974, C.W. Brownfield Meml. award U.S. Jaycees, Lock Haven, 1980. Mem. AIAA (Disting. Svc. award 1985), Aerospace Edn. Assn., Aerial Phenomena Rsch. Orgn., Soc. Automotive Engrs., Sigma Gamma Tau. Orthodox. Office: Calif State Poly U Aerospace Engring 3801 W Temple Ave Pomona CA 91768-2557

GER, SHAW-SHYONG, accountant; b. Kaohsiung, Taiwan, Nov. 19, 1959; s. Jing-Ru and Jui-Mei (Lee) G. BA in econs., Nat. Taiwan U., Taipei, 1981; MBA, Ariz. State U., 1986, M in acctg., 1989. Rsch. asst. Ariz. State U., Tempe, 1988-89; contr. CLH Internat., Inc., Tempe, 1989—. Recipient All Am. Scholar award U.S. Achievement Acad., 1989. Mem. Assn. MBA Exec., Nat. Geog. Soc., Inst. Cert. Mgmt. Accts., Beta Gamma Sigma. Address: PO Box 601 Tempe AZ 85280-0601

GERBA, CHARLES PETER, microbiologist, educator; b. Blue Island, Ill., Sept. 10, 1945; s. Peter and Virginia (Roulo) G.; m. Peggy Louise Scheitlin, June 6, 1970; children: Peter, Phillip. BS in Microbiology, Ariz. State U., 1969; PhD in Microbiology, U. Miami, 1973. Postdoctoral fellow Baylor Coll. Medicine, Houston, 1973-74, asst. prof. microbiology, 1974-81; assoc. prof. U. Ariz., Tucson, 1981-85, prof., 1985—; cons. EPA, Tucson, 1980—, World Health Orgn., Pan Am. Health Orgn., 1989—; advisor CRC Press, Boca Raton, Fla., 1981—. Editor: Methods in Environmental Virology, 1982, Groundwater Pollution Microbiology, 1984, Phage Ecology, 1987; contbr. numerous articles to profl. and sci. jours. Mem. Pima County Bd. Health, 1986-92; mem. sci. adv. bd. EPA, 1987-89. Named Outstanding Research Scientist U. Ariz., 1984, 92; environ. sci. and engring. fellow AAAS, 1984. Mem. Am. Soc. Microbiology (div. chmn. 1982-83, 87-88, pres. Ariz. chpt. 1984-85, councilor 1985-88), Internat. Assn. Water Pollution Rsch. (sr. del. 1985-91), Am. Water Works Assn. Home: 1980 W Paseo Monserrat Tucson AZ 85704-1329 Office: U Ariz Dept Microbiology and Immunology Tucson AZ 85721

GERBER, BARRY ELDON, data processing executive, consultant, writer; b. L.A., May 12, 1942; s. Harry and Elsie (Lubin) G.; m. Jane Bernette Margo, June 7, 1962; children: Margot, Karl, Georg. BA, UCLA, 1964, MA, 1966, CPil, 1972. Prof. Calif. State U., Fullerton, 1968-77; dep. dir. Community Cancer Control, L.A., 1977-82; v.p. info. systems Zenith Ins., Encino, Calif., 1983-85; rsch. assoc. Neuropsychiatric Inst. UCLA, 1982-83, dir. Social Sci. Computing, 1985—; internat. cons. in field. Contbg. editor PC Week Ziff Davis, 1988-90; editor Network Computing, CMP Publs., 1990—; contbr. articles to profl. jours. Office: UCLA Social Sci Computing 2121 Bunche Hall Los Angeles CA 90024

GERBERDING, WILLIAM PASSAVANT, university president; b. Fargo, N.D., Sept. 9, 1929; s. William Passavant and Esther Elizabeth Ann (Habighorst) G.; m. Ruth Alice Albrecht, Mar. 25, 1952; children: David Michael, Steven Henry, Elizabeth Ann, John Martin. B.A., Macalester Coll., 1951; M.A., U. Chgo., 1956, Ph.D., 1959. Congl. fellow Am. Polit. Sci. Assn., Washington, 1958-59; instr. Colgate U., Hamilton, N.Y., 1959-60; research asst. Senator E.J. McCarthy, Washington, 1960-61; staff Rep. Frank Thompson, Jr., Washington, 1961; faculty UCLA, 1961-72, prof., chmn. dept. polit. sci., 1970-72; dean faculty, v.p. for acad. affairs Occidental Coll., Los Angeles, 1972-75; exec. vice chancellor UCLA, 1975-77; chancellor U. Ill., Urbana-Champaign, 1978-79; pres. U. Wash., Seattle, 1979—; bd. dirs. Wash. Mut. Savs. Bank, Safeco Corp., Seattle; cons. Dept. Def., 1962, Calif. Assembly, 1965; mem. Wash. State exec. com. U.S. West Communications. Author: United States Foreign Policy: Perspectives and Analysis, 1966; co-editor, contbg. author: The Radical Left: The Abuse of Discontent, 1970. Trustee Macalester Coll., 1980-83. Served with USN, 1951-55. Recipient Distinguished Teaching award U. Calif., Los Angeles, 1966; Ford Found. grantee, 1967-68. Mem. Am. Polit. Sci. Assn., Assn. Am. Univs. (exec. com. 1985-91), Am. Coun. on Edn. (bd. dirs. 1985-89) , Bus.-Higher Edn. Forum (exec. com. 1992—). Office: U Wash Pres Office 301 Adminstrn Bldg AH-30 Seattle WA 98195

GERBRACHT, (ROBERT THOMAS) (BOB GERBRACHT), painter, educator; b. Erie, Pa., June 23, 1924; s. Earl John and Lula Mary (Chapman) G.; m. Delia Marie Paz, Nov. 27, 1952; children: Mark, Elizabeth, Catherine. BFA, Yale U., 1951; MFA, U. So. Calif., 1952. Cert. tchr., Calif. Art tchr. William S. Hart Jr. and Sr. High Sch., Newhall, Calif., 1954-56; stained glass artist Cummings Studios, San Francisco, 1956-58; art tchr. McKinley Jr. High Sch., Redwood City, Calif., 1958-60, Castro Jr. High Sch., San Jose, Calif., 1960-79; portrait artist, tchr. San Jose, San Francisco, 1979—; instr. art Coll. of Notre Dame, Belmont, Calif., 1958-60, San Jose City Coll., 1967-71, Notre Dame Novitiate, Saratoga, Calif., 1968, West Valley Coll., Saratoga, 1976-79, U. Calif., Santa Cruz, 1980-81; art cons. Moreland Sch. Dist., Campbell, Calif., 1979-80; instr. nationwide workshops, Calif., N.Mex., N.Y., S.C., Vt., Wis., Mex., 1980—. Represented in permanent collection Triton Mus. Art, Santa Clara, Calif.; portraits include Mrs. Bruce Jenner, Austin Warburton, Rev. Cecil Williams; subject of articles in Today's Art and Graphics, Art and Antique Collector, Am. Artist, U.S. ART. Cpl. U.S. Army, 1943-46. Recipient Am. Artist Achievement award Tchr. of Pastels, 1993. Mem. San Jose Art League (Best of Show award 1983, 84), Pastel Soc. Am., Pastel Soc. West Coast (advisor, Best of Show award 1988), Calif. Pastel Painters (advisor), Soc. Western Artists (trustee, Best of Show award 1982, 85, 90, Best Portrait award 1984), Oil Painters Am. Home: 1301 Blue Oak Ct Pinole CA 94564-2145

GERGIANNAKIS, ANTHONY EMMANUEL See ANTHONY

GERICKE, PHILIP OTTO, Spanish language educator; b. Ukiah, Calif., Dec. 24, 1936; s. Otto Luke and Catherine Rose (Levi) G.; m. Patricia Ann Halpern, July 12, 1985; children: Elissa M., Teresa A., Otto L., Thomas N. BA, U. Calif., Riverside, 1958; MA, U. Calif., Berkeley, 1960, PhD, 1965. Assoc. Spanish U. Calif., Riverside, 1962-63, lectr. Spanish, 1963-64, asst. prof. Spanish, 1966-71, assoc. prof. Spanish, 1971-78, prof. Spanish, 1978—; asst. prof. fgn. langs. San Fernando Valley State Coll., Northridge, Calif., 1964-66. Editor, translator: Historical Notes on Lower California (Manuel C. Rojo), 1972; editor: Alfonso de Toledo Invencionario, 1992; contbr. articles to profl. jours. Mem. MLA, Am. Assn. Tchrs. Spanish and Portuguese, Philological Assn. of Pacific Coast, Assn. Internat. de Hispanistas, Phi Beta Kappa. Democrat. Office: U Calif Dept Spanish and Portuguese Riverside CA 92521

GERIG, ROY N(OFZIGER), wildlife biologist, educator; b. Lebanon, Oreg., June 13, 1947; s. Amos B. and Louise Violet (Nofziger) G.; m. Levera Dolores Wilder, Mar. 8, 1975; children: Rhiannon Dawn, Amber Louise. BA in Biology, Calif. State U., L.A., 1974. Teaching cert. secondary biology and gen. sci., Oreg. Sr. gardener L.A. (Calif.) Recreation and Pks., 1975-77; freelance photographer various exhibits, 1979-81; regional reviewer USDA Fed. Crop Ins. Corp., Spokane, Wash., 1981-84; real estate salesman Westcoast Timberlands, Dallas, Oreg., 1985-86; substitute high sch. sci. tchr., instr. various high schs. and community colls., 1988-92; wildlife biologist Bur. of Land Mgmt.-Salem (Oreg.) Dist., 1991—; compiler Dallas Christmas Bird Count, Nat. Audubon Soc., Dallas, 1984-92; field trip leader Salem (Oreg.) Audubon Soc., 1984—. Contbr. articles to profl. jours. Mem. Soc. for Northwestern Vertebrate Biology, Oreg. Field Ornithologists. Home: 18445 Oakdale Rd Dallas OR 97338 Office: Salem Dist BLM 1717 Fabry Rd Salem OR 97306

GERINGER, SUSAN DIANE, educator; b. Madera, Calif., Dec. 23, 1954; d. Gaston D. and Betty L. (Crane) Ownbey; m. Steven A. Geringer, Aug. 30, 1975; children: Steven, Alexandra. BA, Calif. State U., Sacramento, 1978; MA, Calif. State U., 1984; postgrad., NYU, 1987—. Buyer, mgr. Tops N Shirts, Fresno, Calif., 1974-76; retail exec. Macy's Calif., San Francisco, 1978-80; lectr. Am. River Coll., Sacramento, 1981-86; asst. prof. Calif. State U., 1986-92; lectr. Calif. State U., Fresno, 1992—; fashion coord. Calif. State Fair and Exposition, Sacramento, 1981; reader Macmillan Pub. Co., 1989—; legal cons. Tech. Adv. Svc. for Attys., Mass., 1990—. Author: (textbooks) Fashion: Color, Line and Design, 1966, 20th Century Fashion, 1991. Mem. Met. Mus. N.Y., Sacramento Symphony League; bd. dirs. Legal Aux. Sacramento County, 1984-90, Sacramento Children's Receiving Home Guild, 1986. Grad. scholar North Cen. Dist. Cen. Home Econs. Assn., 1989. Mem. AAUW, Am. Collegiate Retail Assn., Fashion Group, Costume Soc. Am., Calif. State U. Sacramento Home Econs. Alumni Assn. (bd. dirs. 1980-92), Home Econs. in Bus., Fashion Group. Democrat. Home and Office: PO Box 207 Madera CA 93639

GERKEN, WALTER BLAND, insurance company executive; b. N.Y.C., Aug. 14, 1922; s. Walter Adam and Virginia (Bl) G.; m. Darlene Stolt, Sept. 6, 1952; children: Walter C., Ellen M., Beth L., Daniel J., Andrew P., David A. BA, Wesleyan U., 1948; MPA, Maxwell Sch. Citizenship and Pub. Affairs, Syracuse, 1958. Supr. budget and adminstrv. analysis Wis., Madison, 1950-54; mgr. investments Northwestern Mut. Life Ins. Co., Milw., 1954-67; v.p. finance Pacific Mut. Life Ins. Co., L.A., 1967-69, exec. v.p., 1969-72, pres., 1972-75, chmn. bd., 1975-87; chmn. exec. com. Pacific Mut. Life Ins. Co., Los Angeles, 1987—, also dir.; sr. advisor Boston Consulting Group; bd. dirs. Whittaker Corp.; co-chair UCI Coll. of Medicine; bd. dirs. So. Calif. Edison Co., Mgmt. Compensation Group, DAC. Bd. dirs. Keck Found., James Irvine Found., Hoag Meml. Presbyn. Hosp.; bd. overseers Rand/UCLA Ctr. for Soviet Studies; trustee Occidental Coll. L.A., Wesleyan U., Middletown, Conn.; chmn. bd. Nature Conservancy Calif., Exec. Svc. Corp. Decorated D.F.C., Air medal. Mem. Calif. Club, Dairymen's Country Club (Boulder Junction, Wis.), Met. Club (Washington), Balboa Bay Club (Newport Beach, Calif., chmn. of bd.), Automobile Club (So. Calif. chpt., chmn. bd. dirs.), Calif. Roundtable (co-chair Calif. Ind. Coll. Network), Pauma Valley Country Club, Calif. Citizens Budget Commn. Office: Pacific Mut Life Ins Co 700 Newport Center Dr Newport Beach CA 92660-6397

GERLICK, HELEN J., tax practitioner, accountant; b. Denver, Dec. 11, 1931; d. JAmes Jeffries and Margaret (Fitzwater) Farrell; m. Jerald James Gerlick, Aug. 25, 1950; children: Michael James, Daniel Lee, Kenneth Dwayne. Grad., Barnes Bus. Sch., 1950, H&R Block Sch., 1974. CPA, Cert. Tax Preparer. Acctg. clerk Colo. Teamsters, Denver, 1956; ins. div. NSLI, Denver, 1956-58; assoc. St. Lukes Acctg., Denver, 1958; acctg. office mgr. Mundix Control Systems, Denver, 1964-83; tax preparer H & R Block, Denver, 1977-79; acct., tax preparer Gerlick's Tax Svc., Wheat Ridge, Colo., 1979—. Mem. NAFE, Am. Bus. Women's Assn. (named Women of Yr. 1977, 81), Nat. Assn. Tax Practitioners, Nat. Pub. Accts. Assn., Pub. Accts. Soc. of Colo. Democrat. Lutheran. Home and Office: 4601 Robb St Wheat Ridge CO 80033

GERMAN, WILLIAM, newspaper editor; b. N.Y.C., Jan. 4, 1919; s. Sam and Celia (Norack) G.; m. Gertrude Pasenkoff, Oct. 12, 1940; children: David, Ellen, Stephen. B.A., Bklyn. Coll., 1939; M.S., Columbia U., 1940; Nieman fellow, Harvard U., 1950. Reporter, asst. fgn. editor, news editor, mng. editor, exec. editor San Francisco Chronicle, 1940—; editor Chronicle Fgn. Service, 1960-77; mng. editor KQED, Newspaper of the Air, 1968; lectr. U. Calif., Berkeley, 1946-47, 68-70. Editor: San Francisco Chronicle Reader, 1962. Served with AUS, 1943-45. Mem. AP Mng. Editors Assn., Am. Soc. Newspaper Editors, Internat. Press Inst., Commonwealth Club (bd. govs. 1991). Home: 150 Lovell Ave Mill Valley CA 94941-1883 Office: San Francisco Chronicle 901 Mission St San Francisco CA 94103-2988

GERMANO, GUIDO, physicist, educator; b. Naples, Italy, Nov. 12, 1959; came to the U.S., 1985; s. Mario and Emma (Vancini) G. BSEE summa cum laude, U. Naples, 1984; MBA, U. Rome, 1985; MS, UCLA, 1987, PhD, 1991. Rsch. assoc. UCLA, 1986-91, asst. prof. radiol. scis., 1992—; dir. nuclear medicine physics Cedars-Sinai Med. Ctr., L.A., 1991—; cons. Nat. Rsch. Coun., Italy, 1986-91, Tower Nuclear Medicine, L.A., 1991. Contbr. articles to profl. jours. and chpts. to books. Fulbright scholar, 1985; recipient J. Weldon Belville award Crump Inst. for Med. Engring., 1987, J.T. Case Rsch. award James T. Case Radiol. Found., 1989, 90. Mem. Soc. Nuclear Medicine, IEEE (grad. scholar 1991), Am. Assn. Physicists in Medicine (N. Baily award 1986), Rotary, Sigma Xi (Outstanding Grad. Sci. award 1990). Office: Cedars Sinai Med Ctr 8700 Beverly Blvd A047 N Los Angeles CA 90048

GERPHEIDE, JOHN HENRY, aerospace engineer; b. Manitowoc, Wis., Sept. 17, 1925; s. Arthur August and Paula Marie (Mahnke) G.; divorced; children: Jane Paula, Sarah Jo. BS, Calif. Inst. Tech., 1945, MS, 1948. Various engring. positions Jet Propulsion Lab., Pasadena, Calif., 1948-62, cons. Apollo support, 1962-64, staff specialist project planning, 1964, sect. mgr. system design and integration, 1964-73, project mgr. devel. Mars landing craft, 1967-68, project mgr. solar electric propulsion, 1973-74, mgr. SEASAT satellite system, 1974-79, chief engr. flight projects office, 1979-81, project mgr. Venus Orbiting Imaging Radar project, 1981, project mgr. Magellan-Venus mission, 1982-89; cons. Rand, Martin Marrieta. Recipient Outstanding Leadership medal NASA, 1990. Mem. Planetary Soc., Sigma Xi. Home: 2165 Queensberry Rd Pasadena CA 91104-3323

GERRODETTE, CHARLES EVERETT, real estate company executive, consultant; b. Alderwood Manor, Wash., June 18, 1934; s. Honoré Everett and Marjorie Violet (Stapley) G.; m. Laurine Carol Manley, Mar. 16, 1956 (div. 1977); children: Stephen Everett, Suzanne Gerrodette Prince; m. Diane Marie Drumm, Dec. 6, 1984. BA in Bus. Adminstrn., U. Wash., 1956, postgrad., 1959; postgrad., NYU, 1956-57. Credit analyst and corr. comml. credit dept. Chase Manhattan Bank, N.Y.C., 1956-57; reviewing appraiser Prudential Ins. Co. Am., Seattle, 1959-67; v.p., sr. loan officer real estate group Seattle 1st Nat. Bank, 1967-90; pres., CEO, Portal Pacific Co., Inc., Seattle, 1990—; real estate advisor, fin. cons. Charles E. Gerrodette, MAI, Seattle, 1990—; instr. appraising Shoreline C.C., Seattle, 1974-76. Contbg. author: Prentice Hall Ency. of Real Estate Appraising, 3d edit., 1978. Mem. blue ribbon com. for planning Shoreline Sch. Dist., Seattle, 1974-75. With U.S. Army, 1957-59. Mem. Am. Arbitration Assn. (panel of arbitrators), Appraisal Inst. (designation 1972, officer, bd. dirs. Wash.-B.C. chpt. 1980-89, pres. 1984, nat. fin. and adminstrn. com. 1982-87, nat. governing counselor 1987-89, nat. fin. com. 1990—), Urban Land Inst., Mortgage Bankers Assn. (income property com.), Columbia Tower Club, Lambda Alpha, N.W. Grad. Assn. Theta Delta Chi (trustee 1960-70, past pres.). Episcopalian. Office: 2125 1st Ave Ste 1204 Seattle WA 98121

GERSON, MICHAEL JOEL, psychologist, educator; b. Chgo., Oct. 9, 1951; s. Emil and Jeannetee (Geftman) G.; m. Barbara Gerson, Aug. 23, 1983 (div. Apr. 1993); 1 child, Daniel Joseph. BA, Calif. State U., Northridge, 1974; MA, Calif. State U., Dominguez Hills, Calif., 1976; PhD, Calif. Grad. Inst., L.A., 1981. Lic. psychologist, Calif.; lic. marriage, family, child psychoanalytic psychotherapist, N.Y.; lic. counselor, Calif. Psychotherapist L.A. County Probation Dept., 1973-76, Friends of the Family, Van Nuys, Calif., 1977-80; systems analyst Hughes Aircraft Co., L.A., 1974-80; pvt. practice psychology Encino, Calif., 1980-92; prof. psychology Calif. Grad. Inst., L.A., 1982-92, Loyola Marymount U., L.A., 1992—; clin. dir. CGI Counseling Ctr., L.A., 1982-86; cons. Valley Free Clinic, Van Nuys, 1986-91, Julia Ann Singer Ctr., L.A., 1989—. Recipient Disting. Prof. award Calif. Grad. Inst., L.A., 1987. Mem. APA, Nat. Assn. for Advancement of Psychoanalysis (cert. bd. mem. 1982—), Calif. Prof. Soc. on Abuse of Children. Jewish. Office: 15720 Ventura Blvd # 602 Encino CA 91436

GERSTENBERGER, DEAN LEE, psychiatrist; b. Lincoln, Nebr., Oct. 17, 1948; s. Howard Walter and Esther Elaine (Thompson) G.; m. Marta Marie Martin, Sept. 6, 1975; children: Blythe, Brett, Blake, Brina. BS, Baker U., 1970; MD, U. Kans., 1974. Diplomate Am. Bd. Psychiatry and Neurology. Intern Allentown (Pa.) Hosp. Assn., 1974; resident Mayo Clinic, Rochester, 1975-78; staff psychiatrist Rochester State Hosp., 1978; med. dir. Coconino Community Guidance Ctr., Flagstaff, Ariz., 1978-82, staff psychiatrist, 1982-88; pvt. practice Flagstaff, 1980-92; med. dir. Community Drug Abuse, Flagstaff, 1988-90; pres. med. staff Aspen Hill Hosp., Flagstaff, 1988-90, med. dir. 1990. Contbr. articles to profl. jours. Deacon Flagstaff Federated Ch., 1980-82, elder, 1984-85. Roman Catholic. Office: PO Box 31206 Flagstaff AZ 86003

GERTH, DONALD ROGERS, university president; b. Chgo., Dec. 4, 1928; s. George C. and Madeleine (Canavan) G.; m. Beverly J. Hollman, Oct. 15, 1955; children: Annette, Deborah. BA, U. Chgo., 1947, AM, 1951, PhD, 1963. Field rep. S.E. Asia World Univ., 1950; asst. to pres. Shimer Coll., 1951; Admissions counselor U. Chgo., 1956-58; assoc. dean students, admissions and records, mem. dept. polit. sci. San Francisco St. U., San Francisco, 1958-63; assoc. dean instnl. relations and student affairs Calif. State Univ., 1963-64; chmn. commn. on extended edn. Calif. State Univs. and Colls., 1977-82; dean of students Calif. State U., Chico, 1964-68, prof. polit. sci., 1964-76, assoc. v.p. for acad. affairs, dir. internat. programs, 1969-70, v.p. acad. affairs, 1970-76; co-dir. Danforth Found. Research Project, 1968-69; coordinator Inst. Local Govt. and Public Service, 1968-70; pres., prof. polit. sci. and public adminstrn. Calif. State U., Dominguez Hills, 1976-84; pres., prof. govt. and adminstrn. Calif. State U., Sacramento, 1984—; chair Accrediting Commn. for Sr. Colls. and Univs. of Western Coll. Assn.; chmn. admissions coun. Calif. State U.; bd. dirs. Ombudsman Found., L.A., 1968-71; com. continuing edn. Calif. Coordinating Coun. for Higher Edn., 1963-64; lectr. U. Philippines, 1953-54, Claremont Grad. Sch. and Univ. Ctr., 1965-69. Co-author: The Learning Society, 1969; author, editor: An Invisible Giant, 1971; contbg. editor Education for the Public Service, 1970, Papers on the Ombudsman in Higher Education, 1979. Mem. pers. commn. Chico Unified Sch. Dist., 1969-76, chmn., 1971-74; adv. com. on justice programs Butte Coll., 1970-76; mem. Varsity Scouting Coun., 1980-84; chmn. United Way campaign Calif. State Univs., Los Angeles Co., 1981-82; bd. dirs. Sacramento Area United Way; mem. bd. dirs., South Bay Hospital Found., 1979-82; mem. The Cultural Commn., Los Angeles, 1981-84; mem. com. govtl. rels. Am. Coun. Edn. Capt. USAF, 1952-56. Mem. Internat. Assn. Univ. Pres. (chmn. N.Am. coun., pres.-elect), Am. Polit. Sci. Assn., Am. Soc. Pub. Adminstrn., Soc. Coll. and Univ. Planning Western Govtl. Rsch. Assn., World Affairs Coun. No. Calif. Assn. Pub. Adminstrn. Edn. (chmn. 1973-74), Western Polit. Sci. Assn., Am. Assn. State Colls. and Univs. (bd. dirs.), Calif. State C. of C. (edn. com.), Sacramento Club (bd. dirs.), Comstock Club. Democrat. Episcopalian. Home: 11463 Forty Niner Cir Gold River CA 95670-7852 Office: Calif State U 6000 J St # 206 Sacramento CA 95819-6022

GERTZ, DAVID LEE, homebuilding company executive; b. Denver, July 30, 1950; s. Ben Harry and Clara (Cohen) G.; m. Bonnie Lee Schulein, June 2, 1973; children: Joshua, Eva. BS, U. Colo., 1972; MBA, U. Colo., Denver, 1993. Real estate broker Crown Realty, Denver, 1972-73; pres. Sunshine Plumbing Co., Lakewood, Colo., 1974-76, Sunshine Diversified, Inc., Lakewood, 1976—, Sunshine Master Builders, Ltd., Lakewood, 1990—; sec.-treas. Wight Lateral Ditch Co., Lakewood, 1987-91. Cub master pack 135 Cub Scouts Am., Lakewood, 1989-91; asst. scout master troop 135 Boy Scouts Am., Lakewood, 1991—; bd. dirs. Hebrew Ednl. Alliance, Denver, 1991—; mem. Anti-Defamation League, Denver, 1989—. Scholar, Evans Scholars, U. Colo., 1968-72. Mem. Home Builders Assn. of Colo. (energy com. 1986—, Lakewood coord. com. 1986—, Jeffco coord. com. 1986—), Jeffco Bd. Realtors. Office: Sunshine Master Builders PO Box 27095 Denver CO 80227

GERVIN, LES STEPHEN, quality engineer; b. San Francisco, Aug. 5, 1948; s. Leon Martin Sr. and June (Haack) G.; m. Shirley Kay Postma, Feb. 5, 1966 (div. 1969); children: Leslie S. Jr., Kelley Rene; m. Stephanie Louise Shoemaker, June 28, 1975; 1 child, Gregory Stephen. BA in Mgmt., U.

Phoenix, 1987. Cert. quality systems auditor. Sr. quality assurance test tech. GenRad, Santa Clara, Calif., 1975-77; staff quality engr. Large Disc Dr. div. Memorex Corp., Santa Clara, Calif., 1977-81; quality assurance project mgr., sr. quality engr. Home Computer div. Atari, San Jose, 1981-82; quality assurance mgr. Distributed Systems div. Convergent Tech., San Jose, 1982-84; corp. quality assurance mgr. Metaphor Computer Systems, Mountain View, Calif., 1984-86; sr. quality engr. U.S. ops. Sun Microsystems Computer Corp., Mountain View, Calif., 1986-93; owner Gervin & Assocs., San Jose, 1993—. V.p. Silicon Valley Rep. Assembly, 1992—, Santa Clara County, 1992—; senate dist. dir. Calif. Rep. Assembly, 1993—; mem. Santa Clara County Rep. Party Ctrl. Com., 3d dist., 1993—. With USAF, 1972-75. Mem. Am. Soc. for Quality Control. Home and Office: Gervin & Assocs 3032 Chippenham Dr San Jose CA 95132-1714

GERWICK-BRODEUR, MADELINE CAROL, marketing and sales professional; b. Kearney, Neb., Aug. 29, 1951; d. Vern Frank and Marian Leila (Bliss) Gerwick; m. David Louis Brodeur; 1 child, Maria Louise. Student, U. Wis., 1970-72, U. Louisville, 1974-75; BA in Econs. magna cum laude, U. N.H., 1979; postgrad., Internat. Trade Inst., Seattle. Indsl. sales rep. United Radio Supply Inc., Seattle, 1980-81; mfrs. rep. Ray Over Sales Inc., Seattle, 1981-82; sales engr. Tektronix, Inc., Kent, Wash., 1982-83; mktg. mgr. Zepher Industries, Inc., Burien, Wash., 1983-85, Microscan Systems Inc., Tukwila, Wash., 1986.; market devel. URS Electronics, Inc., Portland, 1986-88; sr. product specialist John Fluke Mfg. Co. Inc., 1989—; bd. dirs., sec. Starfish Enterprises Inc., Tacoma, 1984-87; com. chmn. Northcon, Seattle and Portland, 1984-86, 88, 90; speaker to Wash. Women's Employment and Edn., Tacoma, 1983—. Recipient Jack E. Chase award for Outstanding Svc. and Contbr. Northcon Founder's Orgn., 1988. Mem. Electronic Mfrs. Assn. (sec. 1982, sec.-treas. 1988, v.p. 1989), Inst. Noetic Scis., Phi Kappa Phi. Office: John Fluke Mfg Co Inc MS270D PO Box 9090 Everett WA 98206-9090

GERWIN, GARY MARK, publisher; b. San Jose, Calif., Sept. 18, 1955; s. Clarence James and Kathleen E. (Richardson) G. BS, Brigham Young U., 1979; MBA, UCLA, 1983, postgrad., 1989—. Product mgr. Atari Internat., Sunnyvale, Calif., 1982-84; regional mgr. ICN Pharm., Costa Mesa, Calif., 1984-86; mgr. mktg. Network Rsch. Corp., Oxnard, Calif., 1986-89; owner, pub. Added Dimensions Pub., L.A. and Oslo, Norway, 1989—; bd. dirs. Oral Care Products, L.A., Platinum Corp., L.A.; spokesman The Ctr. for Men Urological Clinics; host talkshow Men's Private Parts, KIEV Radio, L.A. Author, pub.: The Condom Encyclopedia, 1989, Complete Guied to Potency Restoration, 1990, The World's Top 100 Languages, 1993. Vol. Recordings for the Blind, L.A., 1983-88, Angel View Crippled Children's Ctr., Desert Hot Springs, Calif., 1991—. Mem. Advt. Club L.A. Democrat. Mem. LDS Ch. Home: 69473 Avenida Las Begonias Cathedral City CA 92234 Office: The Ctr for Men/Internat Urological Assoc's Ste 609 9201 Sunset Blvd West Los Angeles CA 90214

GESCHEIDLE, RANDAL ALAN, air force officer; b. Freeport, Tex., Apr. 8, 1956; s. Harrison and Elsie Anita (Blackwell) G.; m. Vickie Jean Woods, June 9, 1979; children: Austin G., Hanna K. BS in Elec. Engring., Tex. A&M U., 1983; MS in Systems Mgmt., Air Force Inst. Tech., Dayton, Ohio, 1989. Cert. in program mgmt., sci. mgmt. Enlisted USAF, 1979, commd. 2d lt., 1984, advanced through grades to capt., 1988; engr. airborne warning and control system USAF, Tinker AFB, Okla., 1984-88; dep. div. chief Phillips Lab., Kirtland AFB, N.Mex., 1989—; assoc. cons. Pacer Group, Dayton, 1988-92. Mem. Assn. for Quality and Participation, Am. Soc. for Quality Control, Am. Mgmt. Assn., Acad. of Mgmt. Home: 3334 49th Loop Albuquerque NM 87116

GESCHEIDLE, ROBERT HEATH, food company manager; b. Ottawa, Ill., May 21, 1959; s. Daniel A. and Mary H. (Heath) G.; m. Susan Taylor, Aug. 28, 1984; children: Shannon, Patrick, Corinne, Rachel. BSBA, Miami of Ohio U., 1981. Mgr. Personnel Pool North Cin. Br., Cin., 1981-82; owner, coal broker co. Cin., 1982-83; ter. sales mgr. Nabisco Foodservice, Syracuse, N.Y., 1984-85; mktg. mgr. Nabisco Foodservice, East Hanover, N.J., 1985-86; regional sales mgr. Nabisco Foods Co.-Foodservice, Atlanta, 1986-89; dir. sales Nabisco Foods Co.-Foodservice, Pleasanton, Calif., 1989—; speaker, cons., Fla., 1987—. Coach numerous soccer teams, N.Y., Ohio; referee S.A.Y. Soccer programs, Ohio, 1982-83. Mem. Nat. Restaurant Assn., Calif. Restaurant Assn. (assoc.), Am. Mgmt. Assn. Home: 7429 Aspen Ct Pleasanton CA 94588 Office: Nabisco Foods Group Foodservice 6140 Stoneridge Mall Rd Pleasanton CA 94588

GESHELL, RICHARD STEVEN, lawyer; b. Colorado Springs, Colo., Aug. 6, 1943; s. Peter Steven and Ann Elizabeth (Irwin) G.; m. Carol Ann Reed, Sept. 6, 1965; 1 child, Carmen Marie. BA in Chemistry, Ariz. State U., 1965; JD, U. Nebr., 1968. Bar: Nebr. 1968, U.S. Dist. Ct. Nebr. 1968, Hawaii 1983, U.S. Dist. Ct. Hawaii 1983, U.S. Ct. Appeals (9th cir.) 1984, U.S. Supreme Ct. 1986. Mem. Robak and Geshell, Columbus, Nebr., 1968-83; ptnr. R. Steven Geshell, Honolulu, 1983—. Bd. dirs. Mariner's Ridge Assn. Served to capt. USAR, 1974-83. Mem. Assn. Trial Lawyers Am., Nebr. Bar Assn., Hawaii Bar Assn., Hawaii Assn. Criminal Def. Lawyers, Hawaii Trial Lawyers Assn., Blue Key (pres. 1964-65), Mid-Pacific C. C., Elks (chief forum 1984, past exalted ruler, trustee), Phi Sigma Kappa (past house mgr, past v.p.). Republican. Home: 1155 Kaluanui Rd Honolulu HI 96825-1357 Office: Ste G225 7192 Kalanianaole Hwy Honolulu HI 96825-1844

GESS, ALBIN HORST, lawyer; b. Lithuania, Apr. 22, 1942; came to U.S. 1956; s. Albin and Emily (Block) G.; m. Brenda Martha Massaroni, Dec. 30, 1966; children: Lisa, Brent. BEE, U. Detroit, 1966; JD, Am. U., 1971. Bar: Calif. 1972, U.S. Dist. Ct. (cen. dist.) Calif. 1972, U.S. Ct. Appeals (9th cir.) 1972, U.S. Supreme Ct. 1977, U.S. Ct. Appeals (1st and 10th cirs.) 1979, U.S. Ct. Appeals (fed. cir.) 1982, U.S. Dist. Ct. (so. and no. dists.) Calif. 1985. Student engr. Detroit Edison Co., 1964-66; patent examiner U.S. Patent Office, Washington, 1966-68; patent agt. Office of Naval Rsch., Washington, 1968-69, Burroughs Corp., Washington, 1969-71; sr. patent atty. Burroughs Corp., Pasadena, Calif., 1971-74; patent atty. Jackson & Jones, Tustin, Calif., 1974-85, Price, Gess & Ubell, Irvine, Calif., 1985—. Fellow Inst. for Advancement of Engring.; mem. ABA (patent, trademark, copyright and litigation sect.), Fed. Bar Assn., Orange County Bar Assn., Orange County Patent Law Assn. (bd. dirs. 1985—, pres. 1990—), IEEE (sec. Orange County sect. 1992, 93), Am. Electronics Assn., Am. Internat. Property Law Assn., L.A. Internat. Property Law Assn., Licensing Execs. Soc., Lions (v.p. 1988, bd. dirs.). Office: Price Gess & Ubell 2100 Main St Ste 250 Irvine CA 92714-6238

GESSEL, DAVID JACOB, computer scientist; b. Phila., Nov. 15, 1966; s. Arnold Hadley and Mary Lou (Sears) G.; m. Michelle Rose, June 20, 1993. B in Physics, MIT, 1991. Scientist MIT Plasma Fusion Ctr., Cambridge, Mass., 1987-88; researcher Ctr. for Systems Automation, Cambridge, 1988-91; scientist Apple Computer Inc., Cupertino, Calif., 1991-93; engr. Interval Rsch. Corp., 1993—. Mem. Soc. for Info. Display.

GESSEL, STANLEY PAUL, emeritus soil science educator; b. Providence, Utah, Oct. 14, 1916; s. Gottlieb and Esther (Heyrend) G.; m. Beverly Ann Pfieffer, June 29, 1974; children—Susan, Paula, Patti, Pamela, Michael. B.S., Utah State Agr. Coll., 1939; Ph.D., U. Calif.-Berkeley, 1950. Instr. Coll. Forest Resources, U. Wash., Seattle, 1948-50, asst. prof., 1950-56, assoc. prof., 1965-60, prof. forest soils, 1960-84, prof. emeritus, 1984—; part-time staff Coll. Forest Resources, U. Wash., Marshall Islands, 1958-64; assoc. dean Coll. Forest Resources, U. Wash., Seattle, 1965-82, dir. spl. programs, 1982-84; bd. dirs. Coniferous Biome Internat. Biol. Program, 1976-84; cons. soil, water and forestry problems, N.S.W. Forestry Commn., 1983-85, rsch. div. N.Z. Forest Svc., 1986—, N.S.W. Forest Commn., 1987, Bikini and Rongelap Island Rehab. Lawrence Livermore Lab., 1986, World Bank Rev. of Forestry in Indonesia, 1990-92. Editor Forest Site Evaluation and Productivity, 1988—, Sustained Productivity of Forest Soils, 1990—; contbr. over 250 articles to sci.l publs., chpts. to books. Mem. Lake City Citizens Adv. Group. Served to capt. USAAF, 1942-45. Recipient citation N.W. Sci. Assn.; named to hon. alumnus Foresters Alumni Assn. U. Wash., 1976. Fellow AAAS, Soil Sci. and Agronomy Soc. Am. (cert.), Soc. Am. Foresters (Forester of Yr. award Wash. state sect. 1985); mem. Internat. Forestry Assn., Tropical Forestry Soc., Internat. Union Forest Rsch. Orgns. (chmn. site group 1970-86, Disting. Svc. award 1988). Home: 8521 Latona Ave NE Seattle WA 98115-2948 Office: U Wash Coll Forest Resources Seattle WA 98195

GESSEL, VAN CRAIG, Japanese literature educator; b. Compton, Calif., Aug. 1, 1950; s. Easton Mathews Gessel and Harrietta Joan (Robinson) Carey; m. Elizabeth Darley, June 28, 1972; children: Peter Darley, Jenny. BA in Polit. Sci., U. Utah, 1973; MA in Japanese, Columbia U., 1975, PhD in Japanese, 1979. Asst. prof. East Asian langs. and culture Columbia U., N.Y.C., 1979-80; asst. prof. modern langs. Notre Dame U., South Bend, Ind., 1980-82; asst. prof. Oriental langs. U. Calif., Berkeley, 1982-89, assoc. prof. Oriental langs., 1989-90; assoc. prof. Asian and N.E. langs. Brigham Young U., Provo, Utah, 1990—, chair dept. Asian and NE langs., 1992—; U. Calif.-Berkeley rep. to exec. com. Inter-Univ. Ctr. for Japanese Studies, Stanford, Calif., 1986-90; dir. East Asia Nat. Resource Ctr., U. Calif., Berkeley, 1986-87. Author: The Sting of Life, 1989; translator: (Endo Shusaku) The Samurai, 1982 (UNESCO translation award), Scandal, 1989. Summer rsch. grantee Global Found., 1992; regents' jr. faculty fellow U. Calif., Berkeley, 1985. Mem. Assn. for Asian Studies, Assn. Tchrs. of Japanese. Republican. Mem. LDS Ch. Office: Brigham Young U Asian and NE Langs Provo UT 84602

GETREU, IAN E(DWIN), electronics engineer; b. Melbourne, Australia, Sept. 14, 1943; s. Leo and Matylda Getreu; m. Beverly S. Salmenson, June 5, 1983. BE with honors, U. Melbourne, 1965, M Engring. Sci., 1967; postgrad., UCLA, 1966-67; PhD, U. Calif., Berkeley, 1972. Sr. engr. Tektronix Inc., Beaverton, Oreg., 1972-79, mgr. integrated cir. computer aided design devel., 1979-83, mgr. advanced products mktg., 1983-85, scientist advanced products, 1985-86; v.p., modeling Analogy Inc., Beaverton, 1986-92, v.p. engring., modeling, 1992—; also bd. dirs. Analogy, Inc., Beaverton, bd. dirs., 1986-90; lectr. U. New South Wales, Sydney, Australia, 1974-75; chmn. Computer Aided Network Design Com., 1980-82. Author: Modeling the Bipolar Transistor, 1976. Bd. dirs. Jewish Fedn. of Portland, 1986-93, v.p. 1989-93. Mem. IEEE (sr.) (cirs. and systems soc. v.p. confs. 1990-91), Internat. Conf. Computer Aided Design (chmn. 1986). Home: PO Box 1356 Beaverton OR 97075-1356

GETREU, SANFORD, city planner; b. Cleve., Mar. 9, 1930; s. Isadore and Tillie (Kuchinsky) G.; B.A. in Architecture, Ohio State U., 1953; M.A. in Regional Planning, Cornell U., 1955; m. Gara Eileen Smith, Dec. 8, 1952 (div. Feb. 1983); children—David Bruce, Gary Benjamin, Allen Dana; m. Kelly Heim, Aug. 8, 1988. Resident planner Mackesey & Reps., consultants, Rome, N.Y., 1955-56; planning dir., Rome, 1956-57; dir. gen. planning, Syracuse, N.Y., 1957-59, dep. commr. planning, 1959-62, commr. planning, 1962-65; planning dir. San Jose, Calif., 1965-74; urban planning cons., 1974—; pres. Sanford Getreu, AICP, Inc., vis. lectr., critic Cornell U., 1960-65, Syracuse U., 1962-65, Stanford, 1965, San Jose State Coll., 1965, Santa Clara U., Calif. State Poly. Coll., DeAnza Coll., San Jose City Coll., U. Calif. at Berkeley; pres. planning dept. League of Calif. Cities, 1973-74; advisor State of Calif. Office of Planning and Research. Past bd. dirs. Theater Guild, San Jose, Triton Mus., San Jose. Mem. Am. Soc. Cons. Planners, Am. Planning Assn., Am. Inst. Cert. Planners, Bay Area Planning Dirs. Assn. (v.p. 1965-74, mem. exec. com. 1973-74), Assn. Bay Area Govts. (regional planning com. 1967-74). Club: Rotary. Home: 105 Coronado Ave Los Altos CA 94022-2222 Office: Ste 101 4966 El Camino Real Los Altos CA 94022

GETREUER, KURT WALTER, optical recording actuator and servo engineer; b. Rijswijk, The Netherlands, Aug. 16, 1954; came to U.S., 1982; s. Manfred and Ferda Jacoba (Broer) G.; m. Dorothea Emma Verdenius; children: Pascal, Peter. BSc, U. Delft, The Netherlands, 1976, MSc, 1978. Engr. Philips, Eidhoven, The Netherlands, 1979-82; engr. Laser Magnetic Storage div. Philips, Colorado Springs, Colo., 1982-88, Applied Magnetics Corp., Monument, Colo., 1988—. Contbr. articles to profl. jours.; patentee in optical disk drive, driving signal, seeking apparatus. Lt. Netherlands Army, 1978-79.

GETTLEMAN, JEFFREY WARREN, marketing executive, lawyer; b. Chgo., Apr. 27, 1946; s. Arthur and Adele Anna (Raudon) G.; m. Elsa Amanda Swenson, June 25, 1972 (div. Feb. 1985); children: Jenna, Tyra; m. Judith Anne Stading, Mar. 30, 1985; children: Benjamin, Rachel. BA, U. Wis., 1968; JD, U. Chgo., 1974. Bar: Ill. 1974, Maine 1984. Band dir. Lake Forest (Ill.) Country Day Sch., 1971; assoc. Keck, Mahin & Cate, Chgo., 1974-78; atty. internat. div. Amoco Corp., Chgo., 1978-84; asst. atty. gen. State of Maine, Augusta, 1984; exec. dir. Elgin (Ill.) Symphony Orch., 1984-85; dir. mktg. and pub. rels. New Orleans Symphony Orch., 1985-86; v.p. mktg. and account svc. Response Media Svcs., Inc., Chgo., 1986-87; account supr. Ogilvy & Mather Direct, Chgo., 1987-89; v.p. mktg. and edn. Western Schs., Inc., San Diego, 1989—. With U.S. Army, 1968-71, Vietnam. Mem. Internat. Mil. Music Soc. Home: 1615 San Altos Pl Lemon Grove CA 91945-3929 Office: Western Schs Inc PO Box 15907 San Diego CA 92175-5907

GEUSS, GARY GEORGE, lawyer; b. Northridge, Calif., Mar. 27, 1958; s. Sanford George and Roberta Jane (Wilson) G.; m. Sara Elizabeth Haarer, Feb. 19, 1983; children: Megan Kathleen, Kaitlin Marie. BA, Calif. State U., Northridge, 1981; JD, Southwestern U., L.A., 1986. Bar: Calif. 1987, U.S. Dist. Ct. (no., cen., so. and ea. dists.) Calif. 1987, U.S. Ct. Appeals (9th cir.) 1987, U.S. Supreme Ct. 1991. Assoc. Lynberg & Watkins, L.A., 1986-89; dep. city. atty. City of L.A., 1989—. Mem. L.A. County Cen. Dem. Com., 1990. Mem. ABA, Calif. Dist. Attys. Assn., L.A. County Bar Assn., Valley Industry and Commerce Assn., Internat. Platform Assn., Common Cause, Sierra Club, Phi Alpha Delta. Office: LA City Attys Office 14410 Sylvan St Van Nuys CA 91401-2615

GEYER, DENNIS LYNN, university registrar; b. Bay City, Mich., Feb. 17, 1950; s. Walter R. and Bettie Jane (Powers) G.; m. Karen Sue Bickel, Sept. 5, 1970; children: Sarah Denise, Zachary Dennis. Student, Northwestern Luth. Coll., 1967-68; BA, Mich. State U., 1971, MA, 1976. Tchr., coach Aurora (Colo.) Jr. High Sch., 1972-74; asst. to the registrar Lansing (Mich.) C.C., 1974-77; counselor Adams County Sch. Dist. # 14, Commerce City, Colo., 1977-78; registrar, asst. dir. student svcs. U. Colo. Health Sci. Ctr., Denver, 1978-88; univ. registrar Humboldt State U., Arcata, Calif., 1988—. Co-author: A Guidebook for Student Services, 1977. Mem. Jaycees, Bay City, 1971-73; mem. Luth. Ch. of Arcata, pres., 1993—, chair edn. com., 1990-93; mem. Lord of Life Luth. Ch., sec., 1983-87, pres., 1987-88. Mem. Am. Assn. Collegiate Registrars and Admissions Officers, Pacific Assn. Collegiate Registrars and Admissions Officers. Home: 1007 Beverly Way Arcata CA 95521-4957 Office: Humboldt State U Admissions and Records Arcata CA 95521-4957

GHAZANFAR, SHAIKH MOHAMMED, economics educator, researcher; b. Jullundar, Brit. India, Apr. 1, 1937; came to U.S., 1958; s. Shaikh Mehboob and Musammat Farhat (Elahi) Bakhsh; m. Rukshsana Sharif, Aug. 16, 1965; children: Farah, Asif, Kashif. BA with honors, Wash. State U., 1962, MA in Econs., 1964, PhD in Econs., 1968. Instr. econs. Wash. State U., Pullman, 1962-64, rsch. economist, 1964, teaching asst., 1965-67, instr., 1967-68; asst. prof. U. Idaho, Moscow, 1968-72, assoc. prof., 1972-77, prof., 1977—, head dept., 1979-81, 93—, coord. internat. studies program, 1990—; vis. prof. U. Punjab, Lahore, Pakistan, fall 1974-75, U. Md., College Park, spring 1974-75, King Abdulaziz U., Jeddah, Saudi Arabia, 1983-86; mem. budget forecast Idaho Ho. of Reps., Boise, 1974-93. Contbr. articles to profl. jours. Mem. Martin Luther King Day Com., Moscow, 1986-90, Latah County Task Force on Human Rights, Moscow, 1988-92; chmn. Malcom Kerr scholarship com. for high sch. students Nat. Coun. on U.S.-Arab Rels., Washington, 1988—. Mem. Am. Assn. Evolutionary Econs., AAUP, Nat. Tax Assn., Mid-Western Econ. Assn., Western Social Scis. Assn., Amnesty Internat., History of Econs. Soc. Office: U Idaho Dept Econs Moscow ID 83843

GHINDIA, GEORGE WILLIAM, sales executive; b. Detroit, July 4, 1958; s. John Vearle and Katherine Sue Ghindia. BBA, Western Mich. U., 1980; MBA, U. Toledo, 1985. Internal auditor McLouth Steel Corp., Detroit, 1979; fin. mgmt. assoc. U.S. Steel Corp., Birmingham, Ala., 1980, div. acctg. analyst, 1981-82; mktg. cons. Inland Steel Industries Corp., Chgo., 1984; pres. Ghindia Mktg. & Advt., Newport Beach, Calif., 1985-89; advt. cons., district sales mgr. Donnelley Info. Pub. (a Dun & Bradstreet Co.), Orange, Calif., 1989—. Founder, dir. Barbara Ann Lipinski Meml. award, Trenton, Mich., 1982—. Mem. Newport Area Profls. (dir. 1986-91, Premier award 1990), Newport Harbor Area C. of C., Irvine C. of C., Costa Mesa C. of C. Roman Catholic. Office: Donnelley Info Pub 681 S Parker St Orange CA 92613-1551

GHISELIN, BREWSTER, author, English language educator emeritus; b. Webster Groves, Mo., June 13, 1903; s. Horace and Eleanor (Weeks) G.; m. Olive F. Franks, June 7, 1929; children: Jon Brewster, Michael Tenant. A.B., UCLA, 1927; M.A., U. Calif.-Berkeley, 1928, student, 1931-33; student, Oxford U., Eng., 1928-29. Asst. in English U. Calif., Berkeley, 1931-33; instr. English U. Utah, 1929-31, 34-38, lectr., 1938-39, asst. prof., 1939-46, assoc. prof., 1946-50, prof., 1950-71, prof. emeritus, 1971, Distinguished Research prof., 1967-68; dir. Writers' Conf., 1947-66; poetry editor Rocky Mt. Rev., 1937-46; assoc. editor Western Rev., 1946-49; lectr. creativity, cons. Inst. Personality Assessment and Research, U. Calif., Berkeley, 1957-58; editorial adv. bd. Concerning Poetry, 1968—. Author: Against the Circle, 1946, The Creative Process, 1952, new paperback edit., 1985, The Nets, 1955, Writing, 1959, Country of the Minotaur, 1970, (with others) The Form Discovered: Essays on the Achievement of Andrew Lytle, 1973, Light, 1978, Windrose: Poems, 1929-1979, 1980, (with others) Contemporary Authors, 1989; (poems) Flame, 1991. Bd. advisors Silver Mountain Found. Ford Found. fellow, 1952-53; recipient award Nat. Inst. Arts and Letters, 1970; Blumenthal-Leviton-Blonder prize Poetry mag., 1973; Levinson prize, 1978; William Carlos Williams award Poetry Soc. Am., 1981; Gov.'s award for arts Utah Arts Council, 1982. Mem. MLA, Utah Acad. Scis., Arts and Letters (Charles Redd award), Phi Beta Kappa, Phi Kappa Phi. Home (winter): 1115 Jefferson Way Laguna Beach CA 92651-3022 Home (summer): 1747 Princeton Ave Salt Lake City UT 84108 Office: U Utah Salt Lake City UT 84112

GIACOPINI, DORENE MARY, hearing officer; b. Torrington, Conn., Apr. 23, 1960; d. Umbert John and Primetta (Fei) G. AB, Harvard Coll., 1982; JD, U. Calif., Berkeley, 1986. Acting dir., legal coord. Found. for Handgun Edn., Washington, 1983; field rep. to Calif. congressman, San Jose, 1987-90; spl. edn. hearing officer McGeorge Sch. of Law, Sacramento, 1990—. Editor-in-chief Berkeley Women's Law Jour., 1985-86. Bd. dirs. Planned Parenthood of Santa Clara County, San Jose, 1990-91, Adult Ind. Devel. Ctr., Santa Clara, 1988-91; coord. adult network Spina Bifida Assn., Stanford, Calif., 1989-91; del. Dem. Nat. Conv., Atlanta, 1988. Kimball scholar, 1982, Inst. of Politics fellow, 1981. Office: McGeorge Sch of Law Spl Edn Hearing Office 3200 Fifth Ave Sacramento CA 95817

GIALANELLA, PHILIP THOMAS, newspaper publisher; b. Binghamton, N.Y., June 6, 1930; s. Felix and Frances (Demuro) G.; 1 son, Thomas Davis. B.A., Harpur Coll., 1952; M.A., State U. N.Y., 1955. Promotion dir. Evening Press and Sta. WINR-TV, Binghamton, 1957-62; v.p., gen. mgr. Daily Advance, Dover, N.J., 1962-66; v.p. Hartford (Conn.) Times, 1966-70; pres., pub. Newburgh (N.Y.) News, 1970-71; exec. v.p. Hawaii Newspaper Agy., Honolulu, 1971-73, pres., 1974-86; pub. Honolulu Star-Bull., 1975-86; pres. USA Today, 1982-83, pub., 1983; exec. v.p., pub. Honolulu Advertiser, 1986—; exec. v.p., chief operating officer Persis Corp., Honolulu, 1986—, pres. Persis Media div., 1986—; v.p., chief operating officer Northwest Media, Inc., Bellevue, Wash., 1986—, Knoxville (Tenn.) Jour., 1988—; chief operating officer Southeast Mags., Inc., Nashville, 1990—; bd. dirs. Capital Investment Co., Hawaii Newspaper Agy. Found., Inc., Hawaii Newspaper Agy., Inc., Waterhouse Properties, Persis Corp., Honolulu Advertiser Inc., N.W. Media, Inc., Knoxville Jour.; v.p., bd. dirs. ASA Properties, Inc., Bay-Area Steuart, Inc., Shiny Rock Mining Corp. Past chmn., memm. exec. com. Nat. Alliaince Businessmen for Hawaii and Micronesia; v.p. Hawaii Newspaper Agy. Found.; mem. Japan-Hawaii Econ. Coun.; bd. govs. East-West Ctr., chmn., 1991; bd. govs. Pacific Asian Affairs Coun.; bd. dirs. Hawaii Theatre Ctr., Honolulu Boy Choir, Honolulu Symphony, Aloha United Way, Aloha coun. Boy Scouts Am., YMCA, Honolulu; mem. adv. group Western Command, U.S. Army. With U.S. Army, 1952-54. Mem. Am. Newspaper Pubs. Assn., Hawaii Pubs. Assn., AP Assn. Calif., AP Assn. Ariz., AP Assn. Hawaii, AP Assn. Nev., Sigma Delta Chi. Roman Catholic. Office: Honolulu Advertiser Inc PO Box 3110 Honolulu HI 96802-3110

GIANNETTI, RONALD ARMAND, psychologist; b. Chgo., May 21, 1946; s. Armando Eugene and Olga (Santarelli) G.; m. Carolyn Jean Openshaw, Nov. 23, 1975; 1 child, Anthony Michael. BA, U. Calif., Berkeley, 1967, PhD, 1973. Chief psychiat. assessment unit VA Med. Ctr., Salt Lake City, 1976-78; asst. prof. dept. psychiatry Ea. Va. Med. Sch., Norfolk, 1978-79; dir. Psychology Internship Tng. Program, Norfolk, 1978-81; assoc. prof. dept. psychiatry Ea. Va. Med. Sch., Norfolk, 1979-85; chair Va. Consortium for Profl. Psychology, Norfolk, 1979-88; prof. dept. psychiatry Ea. Va. Med. Sch., Norfolk, 1985-88; chair psychology programs Fielding Inst., Santa Barbara, Calif., 1988-92, dean of psychology, 1992—; cons. VA Med. Ctr., Hampton, Va., 1982-88, Ea. State Hosp., Williamsburg, Va., 1979-81. Author 35 articles, book chpts., and computer software packages in psychol. assessment and in edn. Mem. adv. bd. Gestalt and Family Inst. of Va., Gloucester, 1979-84, Info. Ctr. of Hampton Roads, Norfolk, 1979-80. Grantee Charles G. Brown Found., 1984, VA, 1977, Found. for Applied Comms. Tech., 1974. Fellow APA, Am. Psychol. Soc. (charter), Soc. for Personality Assessment; mem. Soc. for Computers in Psychology, Assn. for Applied Psychophysiology and Biofeedback. Home: 2224 Chapala St Santa Barbara CA 93105 Office: Fielding Inst 2112 Santa Barbara St Santa Barbara CA 93105

GIARDINA, JAMES MICHAEL, educator; b. San Diego, Apr. 16, 1949; s. James and Madeline (Bianco) G.; m. Leslie Jo Franz, July 21, 1979; children: Lauren B., Anna S. BA, U. Calif., San Diego, 1971; MA, San Diego State U., 1980. Cert. tchr. Tchr. San Diego City Schs., 1977—, San Diego C.C. Dist., 1980—; AP cons. Coll. Bd., Princeton, N.J., 1985—; AP grader Coll. Bd., Princeton, 1989—; AP cons. Coll. Bd., Princeton, 1985—. William Robertson Coe fellowship Stanford (Calif.) U., 1992. Home: 4117 Sherwin Pl La Mesa CA 91941-7031

GIARDINA, RICHARD CONO, university official; b. N.Y.C., Aug. 28, 1944; s. Cono and Nancy (Biondi) G. Cert., Inst. Polit. Studies, Paris, 1964; AB, Fordham U., 1965; PhD, Princeton U., 1969. Asst. prof., then assoc. prof. polit. sci. Bowling Green (Ohio) State U., 1969-76, acting chmn. polit. sci. dept., 1970-71, dir. Little Coll., 1971-72, dir. modular achievement program, 1972-74, dir. univ. div. gen. studies, asst. dean Coll. Arts & Scis., 1974-76; assoc. prof., then prof. internat. rels. San Francisco State U., 1976—, assoc. provost, then assoc. v.p. for acad. programs & planning, 1976—; Edwin S. Corwin teaching fellow Princeton U., 1968; mem. Chancellor's Master Planning Commn., San Francisco Community Coll. Dist., 1982-83; mem. tech. adv. com. on accreditation and pub. policy Calif. Post-Secondary Edn. Commn., Sacramento, 1983-84; mem. vocat. adv. com. San Francisco Unified Sch. Dist., 1985—. Author: The Dynamics of Baccalaureate Reform, 1973; contbr. articles to profl. jours. Bd. dirs. Actors Ark Theatre, San Francisco, 1982-84; trustee Saybrook Inst. and Grad. Sch., San Francisco, 1986-92. Recipient Outstanding Mentor award San Francisco State U., 1986. Mem. Internat. Studies Assn., Am. Assn. for Higher Edn., Assn. for Gen. and Liberal Studies (nat. exec. bd. 1981-84), World Affairs Coun. No. Calif., Phi Beta Kappa. Democrat. Roman Catholic. Office: San Francisco State U Office Acad Programs and Planning 1600 Holloway Ave San Francisco CA 94132-1722

GIAUQUE, GERALD STONE, modern language educator; b. Boise, Idaho, Apr. 10, 1941; s. Raymond Cannon and Margie (Stone) G.; m. Alice Hollist, Nov. 27, 1968; children: Rodney, Eric, Gregory, Stacy, Nicole. BA, Brigham Young U., 1965; MA, U. Oreg., 1967, PhD, 1971. Asst. prof. modern langs. U. Mo., Rolla, 1969-74; assoc. prof., head dept. modern langs. Ga. Inst. Tech., Atlanta, 1974-76; assoc. prof. No. Ariz. U., Flagstaff, 1976-88, prof., 1988—. Author: (with others) The Role of Cognates in the Teaching of the Romance Languages, 1988; contbr. articles to profl. jours. Fulbright scholar U.S. Govt., 1985-86; recipient No. Burlington award No. Ariz. U., 1989. Mem. Am. Assn. Tchrs. French, Am. Coun. Teaching Fgn. Langs., Phi Kappa Phi, Phi Sigma Iota. LDS. Office: No Ariz U Box 6004 Flagstaff AZ 86011

GIBBENS, LINDA IRENE, athletic trainer, educator; b. Boise, Idaho, Apr. 27, 1961; d. Claris Brewer Jr. and Donna Roberta (Clay) Buck; m. Terry Lynn Gibbens, Aug. 12, 1989; 1 child, Patricia Lynn. BA, Linfield Coll.,

1983; MSc, Ind. U., 1985. Registered athletic trainer. Athletic trainer Albertson Coll., Caldwell, Idaho; CPR instr., 1st aid instr. ARC, Caldwell, 1987—. Mem. Nat. Athletic Trainers Assn. (cert.), Nat. Assn. Intercollegiate Athletics-Athletic Trainers Assn., Idaho Assn. Athletic Trainers. Office: Albertson Coll 2112 Cleveland Blvd Caldwell ID 83605

GIBBONS, JAMES ARTHUR, lawyer, pilot; b. Reno, Dec. 16, 1944; s. Leonard A. and Matilda (Hancock) G.; m. T. Dawn Sanders-Snelling, June 21, 1986; children: Christopher, Jennifer, James A. Jr. BS in Geology, U. Nev., Reno, 1967, MS in Mining Geology, 1973; JD, Southwestern U., 1979. Bar: Nev. 1982, U.S. Dist. Ct. Nev. 1982. Hydrologist U.S. Fed. Water Master, Reno, 1963-67; geologist Union Carbide Co., Reno, 1972-75; comml. pilot Western Airlines, Inc., L.A., 1979-88; pilot Delta Airlines, Salt Lake City, 1988—; sr. land mgr., atty. Homestake Mining Co., Reno, 1980-82; pvt. practice Reno, 1982—; environ. atty. Alaskan Wilderness Soc., Anchorage, 1982-83. Contbr. articles to profl. pubs. Mem. Nev. Coun. on Econ. Edn., 1986; mem. Nev. State Assembly, 1988—. Lt. col. Nev. Air Nat. Guard, Persian Gulf, 1990-91; with USAF, 1967-72. Decorated DFC. Mem. Assn. Trial Lawyers of Am., Nev. Trial Lawyers Assn., Rocky Mt. Mineral Law Found., Comml Law League Am., Am. Inst. Mining Engrs., Nev. Landman's Assn. (chmn. 1981-82, cons. atty. 1982-83). Republican. Office: 62 Court St Reno NV 89501-1902

GIBBONS, JAMES MORTIMER, III, business owner; b. N.Y.C., Dec. 13, 1957; s. James M. Jr. and Louise Virginia (Virginia) G. BA in English, Wabash, 1982. CEO, mng. dir. Fitness Unlimited Ltd. Ireland, 1985-89; pres. Fitness Unlimited Inc., Salt Lake City, 1990—. Mem. Salt Lake's Visitor's Bur., Salt Lake City, 1992—. Mem. Internat. Racquet and Sports Assn., Salt Lake City C. of C. Republican. Office: Fitness Unlimited 565 4500 S Salt Lake City UT 84107

GIBBONS, LEROY, developer, fundraiser; b. Holbrook, Ariz., May 3, 1937; s. Lee Roy and Amy (Patterson) G.; m. Lorine Donna Porter, Dec. 18, 1956; children: Donna Lee, Donald LeRoy, Barry Alan, Felicia Anne Sorensen, Joseph Richey, Tricia Dawn Reynolds, Sara Denae. BS in Music, Brigham Young U., 1959, MA in Music, 1965, EdD, 1992. Tchr. pub. schs., Mesa, Phoenix, Ariz., 1969-73; prof. Brigham Young U., Provo, Utah, 1975-77, admissions officer, 1973-75, devel. adminstr., 1977—; del. Exec. Leadership Inst., Ctr. on Philanthropy, Ind. U., Indpls., 1991; mem. Mormon Tabernacle Choir, 1965—. Author: Philanthropy in Utah Higher Education, 1992, Comparative Methods of Teaching Music Reading, 1965; composer/arranger (casette) Sing Unto the Lord Nov., 1988. State del. Rep. Conv., Salt Lake City, 1990; music dir. The Miss Utah Pageant, Salt Lake City; bd. dirs. Acad. Square Sci. Found., Provo, 1989-92. Named Outstanding Band Musician KSL Radio, Salt Lake City, 1959. Mem. Rotary (chpt. Man of the Yr. 1966), Phi Kappa Phi. Republican. LDS. Home: 509 S 590 E Orem UT 84058 Office: Brigham Young Univ 204 B-72 Provo UT 84602

GIBBONS, MICHAEL LAWRENCE, marketing professional; b. New Haven, Conn., May 15, 1969; s. Robert Joseph and Kathryn Antoinette (Sheldon) G.; m. Mary Juanita Dewhirst, Apr. 15, 1992. Student, Villanova U., 1986-88; AS, Ohlone Coll., Fremont, Calif., 1990-92; student, U. Tex., Arlington, 1992—. Systems engr. Tandy Corp., Phila., 1986-87; systems engrng. mgr. Tandy Corp., Orange, Conn., 1988; systems engr. Grid Systems, Stamford, Conn., 1989; mktg. mgr. Grid Systems, Fremont, Calif., 1990-92, Fort Worth, 1992—. Mem. Alpha Gamma Sigma. Home: 1814 Hunters Ridge Dr Grapevine TX 76051

GIBBS, BARBARA KENNEDY, art museum director; b. Newton, Mass., Feb. 15, 1950; d. Frederic Alexander and Jane Jarvis (Ensinger) K. A.B. magna cum laude, Brown U., 1972; M.B.A., UCLA, 1979. Dep. dir. Portland Art Assn., Oreg., 1979-83; dir. Crocker Art Mus., Sacramento, 1983—. Guggenheim intern fellow Solomon R. Guggenheim Mus., 1978. Mem. Assn. Art Mus. Dirs., Am. Assn. Mus. Home: 1036 56th St Sacramento CA 95819-3916 Office: Crocker Art Mus 216 O St Sacramento CA 95814-5399

GIBBS, CHRISTINE GRESHAM, management consulting company executive; b. Portland, Oreg., Nov. 23, 1946; d. Robert Lambert and Barbara (Jones) Gresham; m. Bruce Gibbs (div. 1977); children: Mark Maclean, Gao Ge, Mackay. BA in English, U. Ariz., 1968; MPA, Ariz. State U., 1976; DPA, Ind. U., 1986. Treas. Investors United Life Ins. Co., 1969-70; mgr. Joe Wmeek, CPA, Phoenix, 1971-73; analyst Ariz. League Cities, Phoenix, 1973; planner Gov.'s Office Ariz., Phoenix, 1974-76; dir. state and local govt. rels. Salt River Project, Phoenix, 1976-92; prin. Red Tape, Ltd., Phoenix, 1986—; adj. faculty Ariz. State U. Sch. Pub. Adminstrn., Tempe, 1986—; rsch. analyst Ariz. Legis. Coun.; mem. planning adv. com. Ariz. State U. Sch. Architecture. Bd. dirs. Ctrl. Ariz. Shelter Svcs.; mem. exec. com. Tempe Ctr. for Habilitation; bd. dirs. Ariz. Econ. Forum; mem. adv. bd. Westrends; mem. bus. adv. com. Nat. Ctr. Indian Enterprise; mem. Maricopa Parks Commn. Mem. Am. Soc. Pub. Adminstrn. (pres. elect), Tempe and Chandler C. of C. Home: 2134 E Sanos Dr Tempe AZ 85281 Office: Red Tape Ltd PO Box 60365 Phoenix AZ 85082-0365

GIBBS, ROBERT HARRISON, lawyer; b. Dubuque, Iowa, Mar. 27, 1946; s. Robert Gale and Pauline Elizabeth (Anderson) G.; m. Heather A. Houston, Feb. 28, 1992; children: Camila Melida Duecy Gibbs, Reed Paul Duecy Gibbs. BA, Grinnell (Iowa) Coll., 1964; JD, U. Wash., 1974. Bar: Wash., 1975. Staff atty. Nat. Lawyers Guild, N.Y.C., 1974-75, Seattle, 1975-77; founding ptnr. Gibbs, Douglas Law Firm, Seattle, 1977-90; individual practice Seattle, 1990-92; ptnr. Gibbs & Houston, Seattle, 1993—; mem. lawyers coord. com. AFL-CIO. Mng. editor: Employee and Union Members Guide to Labor Law, 1982-87. Founder, bd. dirs. Joint Legal Task Force on Cen. Am. Refugees, Seattle, 1983; bd. dirs., sec. N.W. Immigrant Rights Project, Seattle, 1992. Recipient Civil Libertarian of Yr. award ACLU of Wash., Ecumenical award Wash. Assn. Chs., 1987. Mem. Am. Immigration Lawyers Assn. (chpt. pres. 1982), Nat. Lawyers Guild (regional v.p. 1978). Democrat. Office: 650 Colman Bldg 811 1st Ave Seattle WA 98104

GIBBS, WILLIAM HAROLD, university administrator; b. Evanston, Ill., Apr. 10, 1950; s. Harold William and Margaret Rose (Heidbreder) G. BS, Ariz. State U., 1973; MBA, U. Ill., 1975. CPA. Mgr. Price Waterhouse, Phoenix, 1975-82; chief fin. officer Apollo Group Inc., Phoenix, 1983-87; pres. U. Phoenix, 1987—. Office: U Phoenix 4615 E Elwood St Phoenix AZ 85040-9999

GIBLETT, PHYLIS LEE WALZ, educator; b. Denver, July 17, 1945; d. Henry and Leah (Pabst) Walz; B.S.B.A. (Estelle Hunter scholar 1963, Denver Classroom Tchr.'s scholar 1963, Outstanding Bus. Edn. Student scholar 1967), U. Denver, 1967, MBA, 1969; m. Thomas Giblett, May 31, 1975; children: Leann Ruth, Douglas Henry, John Peter. Tchr. bus. Aurora (Colo.) South Middle Sch., Aurora Pub. Schs., 1967-80, 82-86, 88—, on leave, 1980-82, 86-88, chmn. bus. dept., 1972-79; evening tchr. S.E. Met. Bd. Coop Services, 1967-68, post secondary/adult classes Aurora Pub. Schs., 1972-75, Community Coll. Denver, North Campus, 1973, Aurora Pub. Schs. Adult Edn., 1983-84; mem. Dist. Tchr. Adv. Com., 1975-79, mem. tech. com. 1991-93, steering com. shared decision making, 1990-93, zero tolerance com., 1992-93; facilitator Mentor com., 1991-92, exploratory tchr. mtg., 1992-93; mem. dist. tech. com. South Middle Sch., Aurora; adviser chpt. Future Bus. Leaders Am., 1976-78; mem. Colo. Curriculum Specialist Com., 1976-77. Treas. Aurora Coun. PTA, 1987-89, Century Elem. Sch. PTA, 1988-89, reflections chmn., 1987-89, 90-93; mem. PTA. Named Miss Future Bus. Tchr., Phi Beta Lambda of Colo., 1965. Mem. Nat., Mountain-Plains (participant leadership conf. 1977), Colo. Bus. Edn. Assns. (pres. 1976-77), Colo. Educators for/About Bus., Am., Colo. vocat. assns., NEA, Colo., Aurora edn. assns., Delta Pi Epsilon (pres.-elect Eta chpt. 1978, pres. 1980-81). Republican. Lutheran.

GIBLEY, CHRISTOPHER PAUL, senior analyst; b. Denver, Aug. 13, 1966; s. Raymond Anthony Gibley and Marian Elizabeth (Roman) Lefkowicz; m. Michelle Marie Sundu. BS, U. Colo., 1991. Shipping clk. Coll. For Fin. Planning, Denver, 1983-86, rsch. asst., 1986-91; staff analyst Denver br. Fed. Res. Bank of Kansas City, 1991-92, sr. analyst, 1992—. Scholar U. Colo., 1987-90. Mem. Am. Prodn. and Inventory Control Soc. (scholar 1990-91), Am. Mgmt. Assn., Beta-Gamma Sigma. Home and Office: 9334 S Cobblecrest Dr Highlands Ranch CO 80126

GIBNEY, FRANK BRAY, publisher, editor, writer, foundation executive; b. Scranton, Pa., Sept. 21, 1924; s. Joseph James and Edna May (Wetter) G.; m. Harriet Harvey, Dec. 10, 1948 (div. 1957); children: Alex, Margot; m. Harriet C. Suydam, Dec. 14, 1957 (div. 1971); children: Frank, James, Thomas; m. Hiroko Doi, Oct. 5, 1972; children: Elise, Josephine. BA, Yale U., 1945; DLitt (hon.), Kyung Hee U., Seoul, Korea, 1974. Corr., assoc. editor Time mag., N.Y.C., Tokyo and London, 1947-54; sr. editor Newsweek, N.Y.C., 1954-57; staff writer, editorial writer Life mag., N.Y.C., 1957-61; pub., pres. SHOW mag., N.Y.C., 1961-64; pres. Ency. Brit. (Japan), Tokyo, 1965-69; pres. TBS-Brit., Tokyo, 1969-75, vice chmn., 1976—; v.p. Ency. Brit., Inc., Chgo., 1975-79; vice chmn., bd. editors Ency. Brit., Chgo., 1978—; pres. Pacific Basin Inst., Santa Barbara, Calif., 1979—; adj. prof. Far Eastern studies U. Calif., Santa Barbara, 1986—; bd. dirs. U.S. Com. for Pacific Econ. Cooperation, 1988—; cons. Com. on Space and Aero. Ho. of Reps., Washington, 1957-59; vice chmn. Japan-U.S. Friendship Commn., 1984-90, U.S.-Japan Com. on Edn. and Cultural Interchange, 1984-90. Author: Five Gentlemen of Japan, 1953, The Frozen Revolution, 1959, (with Peter Deriabin) The Secret World, 1960, The Operators, 1961, The Khrushchev Pattern, 1961, The Reluctant Space Farers, 1965, Japan: The Fragile Super-Power, 1975, Miracle by Design, 1983, The Pacific Century, 1992, Korea's Quiet Revolution, 1993; editor: The Penkovskiy Papers, 1965; Presdl. speech writer, 1964. Served to lt. USNR, 1942-46. Decorated Order of the Rising Sun 3d Class Japan, Order of Sacred Treasure 2d Class Japan. Mem. Council on Fgn. Relations, Tokyo Fgn. Corr. Club, Am. C.of C. (Tokyo), Japan-Am. Soc., Japan Soc. Roman Catholic. Clubs: Century Assn., Yale (N.Y.C.); Tokyo; Tavern, The Arts (Chgo.). Home: 1901 E Las Tunas Rd Santa Barbara CA 93103-1745

GIBSON, ALISON L., producer, director; b. Glen Ridge, N.J., Sept. 8, 1952; s. Howard Gibson II and Murielle (Bruns) Hester. BS cum laude, Syracuse U., 1974. Asst. dir., producer TROS TV Cultural Programming, Hilversum, The Netherlands, 1974-81; producer KQED TV Cultural Programming, San Francisco, 1981-91; ind. video producer dir. self-employed, San Francisco, 1991—; cons. Episcopal Sanctuary Ednl. Programs for the Homeless, San Francisco, 1989—; stage dir. sports TV. Producer, writer: (video documentary) Video and the At-Risk Student, 1992, Turnaround, The Financial Crisis at Bank of America, 1990; assoc. producer: Artwear: The Body Adorned, 1991, (Cine Golden Eagle award 1991), Corridos: Tales of Passion and Revolution, 1987, (George Foster Peabody award 1987), The Sacred Fire (Internat. Emmy award 1977); coordinating producer: (video presentation) San Francisco Symphony Diamond Jubilee (Corp. for Pub. Broadcasting Excellence Emmy 1976), The Stories of Guy de Maupassant (Internat. Emmy 1976). Mem. Internat. Assn. Bus. Communicators, Nat. Assn. TV Arts & Scis. (bd. dirs.). Office: Synthesis Video 3635 Chestnut St Lafayette CA 94549

GIBSON, ARTHUR CHARLES, biologist, educator; b. Bronx, N.Y., Oct. 16, 1947; s. Richard Goodwin and Rosalie (Reinhardt) G.; m. Linda Lee Corey, Aug. 15, 1970; children—Heather Elizabeth, Erin Kathryn. B.A. in Botany, Miami U., 1969; Ph.D. in Botany, Claremont (Calif.) Grad. Sch., 1973. Asst. prof. U. Ariz., Tucson, 1973-79, assoc. prof., 1979-80; assoc. prof. UCLA, 1980-82, prof., 1982—, also dir. Mildred E. Mathias Bot. Garden. Mem. Bot. Soc. Am. Author: (with J.H. Brown) Biogeography, 1983; (with P.S. Nobel) The Cactus Primer, 1986; contbr. articles to profl. jours. Office: UCLA Mildred E Mathias Bot Garden/Botany Bldg Rm 124 Los Angeles CA 90024

GIBSON, DAVID FREDERIC, engineering dean and educator; b. West Newton, Mass., Jan. 10, 1942; s. Lionel C. and Dorothy (McAfee) G.; m. Rebecca Harper, Aug. 24, 1964; children: Karen, Kathleen. BS in Indsl. Engring., Purdue U., 1963, MS in Indsl. Engring., 1964, PhD in Indsl. Engring., 1969. Registered profl. engr., Mont. Indsl. engr. USN, Forest Park, Ill., 1963; rsch. asst. Purdue U., West Lafayette, Ind., 1963-64, instr., 1968; asst. prof. Mont. State U., Bozeman, 1969-72; dean Arkansas Tech., Russellville, 1971-72; from assoc. prof. to prof. Mont. State U., Bozeman, 1972—, asst. dean of engring., 1977-83, dean of engring., 1983—. Contbr. articles to profl. jours. Accreditation visitor Accrediting Bd. for Engring. and Tech., N.Y.C., 1987-90, mem. engring. accreditation com., 1991; mem. Mont. Bd. Profl. Engrs. and Land Surveyors, Helena, 1993—, chmn. Grantee in field. Mem. Am. Soc. for Engring. Edn., Inst. Indsl. Engring., Nat. Soc. Profl. Engrs. (v.p., chmn. profl. engrs. in edn.), Nat. Coun. Engr. Examiners. Lutheran. Home: 2409 Spring Creek Dr Bozeman MT 59715-6191 Office: Mont State U Bozeman MT 59717

GIBSON, DENICE YVONNE, telecommunications and computer executive; b. Grants Pass, Oreg., Apr. 6, 1955; d. Harry Charles Gibson and Bettye Yvonne Bentley Stein. BS in Psychology, U. San Francisco, 1980; MS in Systems Mgmt., U. So. Calif., 1982; postgrad., Stanford U., 1983; PhD in Instl. Mgmt., Pepperdine U., 1990. Documentation coord./systems analyst Argonaut Ins., Menlo Park, Calif., 1977-78; tech. ops. mgr. Amdahl Corp., Sunnyvale, Calif., 1978-85; sr. dir. worldwide mktg. Candle Corp., L.A., 1985-89; v.p. mktg. Panoramic Inc., San Jose, 1989-90; v.p. devel. Tandem Computers, Plano, Tex., 1990-92, v.p. devel. and support, 1992—; adj. prof. info. systems mgmt. U. S.F., 1984-86; guest lectr. Stanford U., U. Calif., Berkeley, U. Calif., Santa Clara; cons. Nat. Sch. Safety Ctr., 1987, Fed. Law Enforcement Tng. Ctr., 1987, Nat. Soc. Secs., 1986, Pacific Bell, 1985, Elxsi Computers, 1983, Trilogy, 1983. Contbr. articles to profl. jours. Mem. IEEE, Engring. Soc., Am. Soc. Tng. and Devel., Am. Mgmt. Assn., Internat. Platform Assn.

GIBSON, ELISABETH JANE, special programs director; b. Salina, Kans., Apr. 28, 1937; d. Cloyce Wesley and Margaret Mae (Yost) Kasson; m. William Douglas Miles, Jr., Aug. 20, 1959 (div.); m. Harry Benton Gibson Jr., July 1, 1970. AB, Colo. State Coll., 1954-57; MA, San Francisco State Coll., 1967-68; EdD, U. No. Colo., 1978; postgrad. U. Denver, 1982. Cert. tchr., prin., Colo. Tchr. elem. schs., Santa Paula, Calif., 1957-58, Salina, Kans., 1958-63, Goose Bay, Labrador, 1963-64, Jefferson County, Colo., 1965-66, Topeka, 1966-67; diagnostic tchr. Cen. Kans. Diagnostic Remedial Edn. Ctr., Salina, 1968-70; instr. Loretto Heights Coll., Denver, 1970-72; co-owner Ednl. Cons. Enterprises, Inc., Greeley, Colo., 1974-77; resource coord. Region VIII Resource Access Project Head Start Mile High Consortium, Denver, 1976-77; exec. dir. Colo. Fedn. Coun. Exceptional Children, Denver, 1976-77; asst. prof. Met. State Coll., Denver, 1979; dir. spl. edn. N.E. Colo. Bd. Coop. Edn. Svcs., Haxtun, Colo., 1979-82; prin. elem. jr. high sch., Elizabeth, Colo., 1982-84; prin., spl. projects coord. Summit County Schs., Frisco, Colo., 1985—; prin. Frisco Elem. Sch., 1985-91; cons. Montana Dept. Edn., 1978-79, Love Pub. Co., 1976-78, Colo. Dept. Inst., 1974-75; cons. Colo. Dept. Edn., 1984-85, mem. proposal reading com., 1987—; pres. Found. Exceptional Children, 1980-81; pres. bd. dirs. N.E. Colo. Svcs. Handicapped, 1981-82; bd. dirs. Dept. Ednl. Specialists, Colo. Assn. Sch. Execs., 1982-84; mem. Colo. Title IV Adv. Coun., 1980-82; mem. Mellon Found. grant steering com. Colo. Dept. Edn., 1984-85; mem. Colo. Dept. Edn. Data Acquisition Reporting and Utilization Com., 1983, Denver City County Commn. for Disabled, 1978-81; chmn. regional edn. com. 1970 White House Conf. Children and Youth; bd. dirs. Advocates for Victims of Assault, 1986-91; mem. adv. bd. Alpine Counseling Ctr., 1986—; mem. placement alternatives commn. Dept. Social Svcs., 1986—; mem. adv. com. Colo. North Cen. Assn., 1988-91; sec. Child Care Resource and Referral Agy., 1992—; mem. Child Care Task Force Summit County, 1989—; mem. tchr. cert. task force Colo. State Bd. Edn., 1990-91; chair Summit County Interagy. Coord. Coun., 1989—. Recipient Vol. award Colo. Child Care Assn., 1992, Ann. Svc. award Colo. Fedn. Coun. Exceptional Children, 1981; San Francisco State Coll. fellow, 1967-68. Mem. Colo. Assn. Retarded Citizens, Assn. Supervision Curriculum Devel., Nat. Assn. Elem. Sch. Prins., North Cen. Assn. (state adv. com. 1988-91), Order Eastern Star, Kappa Delta Pi, Pi Lambda Theta, Phi Delta Kappa. Republican. Methodist. Author: (with H. Padzensky) Goal Guide: A minicourse in writing goals and behavioral objectives for special education, 1975; (with H. Padzensky and S. Sporn) Assaying Student Behavior: A minicourse in student assessment techniques, 1974; contbr. articles to profl. jours. Home: 5736 Greenespointe Way Highlands Ranch CO 80126 Office: Summit County Schs Ctrl Office PO Box 7 Frisco CO 80443-0007

GIBSON, LAURIE ANN, marketing specialist, freelance journalist; b. L.A., Dec. 24, 1962; d. John Alfred and Mary Lorraine (Kinney) G. AA, Pasadena City Coll., 1984, San Diego City Coll., 1992; BA, Calif. State U., Northridge, 1990. Banquet asst., receptionist, sec. The Pasadena Ctr., 1984-90; litigation document analyst Volt Temps., Pasadena, Calif., 1989; registration clk. Pasadena Conv. and Visitors Bur., 1990; proposal writer Community Care Network, San Diego, 1992—; freelance journalist San Diego Community Newspaper Group, 1991-92, Irish Am. Press, L.A., 1991-92; clk. Remedy Temp. Svcs., San Diego, 1991-92; word processing cons. Aristar, San Diego, 1991-92; editor The City Times, 1992. Contbr. over 150 articles to various newspapers. Scholar Copley Newspapers, 1991. Office: Community Care Network 8911 Balboa Ave San Diego CA 92123

GIBSON, MELVIN ROY, pharmacognosy educator; b. St. Paul, Nebr., June 11, 1920; s. John and Jennie Irene (Harvey) G. B.S., U. Nebr., 1942, M.S., 1947, D.Sc. (hon.), 1985; Ph.D., U. Ill., 1949. Asst. prof. pharmacognosy Wash. State U., Pullman, 1949-52; assoc. prof. Wash. State U., 1952-55, prof., 1955-85, prof. emeritus, 1985—. Editor: Am. Jour. Pharm. Edn. 1956-61; editorial bd., co-author: Remington's Pharm. Sci, 1970, 75, 80, 85; editor, co-author: Studies of a Pharm. Curriculum, 1967; author over 100 articles. Served as arty. officer AUS, 1942-46. Decorated Bronze star, Purple Heart; sr. vis. fellow Orgn. for Econ. Cooperation and Devel., Royal Pharm. Inst., Stockholm, Sweden and U. Leiden (Holland), 1962; recipient Rufus A. Lyman award, 1972, Wash. State U. Faculty Library award, 1984; named Wash. State U. Faculty Mem. of Yr., 1985. Founder, charter mem. Am. Diplomates in Pharmacy.; fellow AAAS; assoc. fellow Am. Coll. Apothecaries; mem. N.Y. Acad. Sci., Am. Pharm. Assn., Am. Soc. Pharmacognosy (pres. 1964-65), Am. Assn. Coll. Pharmacy (exec. com. 1961-63, bd. dirs. 1977-79, chmn. coun. of faculties 1975-76, pres. 1979-80, Disting. Educator award 1984), U.S. Pharmacopeia (revision com. 1970-75), Am. Found. Pharm. Edn. (hon. life, bd. dirs. 1980-85, exec. com. 1981-85, vice chmn. 1982-85), AAUP, Acad. Pharm. Sci., Am. Public Health Assn., Fedn. Internat. Pharm., Am. Inst. History of Pharmacy, Am. Acad. Polit. and Social Sci., Sigma Xi, Kappa Psi (Nat. Svc. citation 1961), Rho Chi, Phi Kappa Phi, Omicron Delta Kappa. Democrat. Presbyterian. Club: Spokane. Home: 707 W 6th Ave Apt 41 Spokane WA 99204-2813

GIBSON, RICHARD INGRAM, geophysicist; b. Jonesboro, Ark., Aug. 19, 1948; s. Richard D. and Clena Vee (Ingram) G. Student, Flint (Mich.) Jr. Coll., 1966-68; BS in Geology, Ind. U., Bloomington, 1971; postgrad., U. Calif., Davis, 1972-73. Assoc. instr. geology dept. Ind. U., Bloomington, 1970-72; mineralogist Beck Analytical Svcs., Bloomington and Davis, Calif., 1971-75; geophysicist Aero Svc. Corp., Houston, 1975-76, Gulf Oil Exploration and Prodn. Co., Houston, 1976-84; dir., gravity and magnetics Everest Geotech, Denver and Houston, 1984-89; pres. Everest Geotech, Denver, 1989-91; owner Gibson Consulting, Golden, Colo., 1989—; adj. prof. geophysical field exercise, U. Ark., Dillon, Mont., 1986-88; instr. Geologic Field Sta., Ind. U., Cardwell, Mont., 1989—. Editor, pub.: (newsletter) Life After Gulf, 1984-91; contbr. articles to profl. jours. Recipient 1st prize Ednl. Exhibit, Houston Gem and Mineral Soc., 1977, 1st prize Clin. Investigation, Am. Urol. Assn., 1973, Hon. Mention award in Photography, Houston-Galveston Employees Clubs, 1980; named Outstanding Young Man in Am., 1982. Mem. Tobacco Root Geol. Soc. (co-founder, pres. 1974-77, sec., bd. dirs. 1977-81, Svc. award 1979), Am. Assn. Petroleum Geologists, Geol. Soc. Am., Soc. Exploration Geophysicists, Wyo. Geol. Assn., Mont. Geol. Soc., Rocky Mountain Assn. Geologists, Ind. U. Geology Club (pres. Bloomington chpt. 1969-70). Office: Gibson Consulting PO Box 523 Golden CO 80402-0523

GIBSON, TREVA KAY, university official; b. Harrisburg, Ill., Aug. 12, 1938; d. William Clayton and Margaret Pauletta (Heathman) Humphrey; m. Charles Hurbert Gibson, Sept. 6, 1959; children: Charles H. Jr., Eric Clayton. BS, So. Ill. U., 1960; MEd, U. Mo., St. Louis, 1972; DSc (hon.), Kazakh (USSR) State U., 1990; EdD, Ariz. State U., 1991. Tchr. Perry Cen. Jr. High Sch., Southport, Ind., 1961-64, Granite City (Ill.) High Sch., 1964-65; counselor Kelley High Sch., Benton, Mo., 1967-68, Valley Park (Mo.) High Sch., 1968-69, Hazelwood East High Sch., St. Louis, 1969-76, Bradshaw Mountain High Sch., Prescott Valley, Ariz., 1976-80; dir. placement Grand Canyon U., Phoenix, 1980-82, dean of students, 1982-89, spl. asst. to pres. for internat. rels., 1988—. Mem. World Coun. for Curriculum and Instrn., World Affairs Coun., Cooperative Svcs. Internat. Edn. Consortium, Gov.'s Ariz.-Mexico Commn. Baptist. Home: 2406 W Anderson Ave Phoenix AZ 85023-2210 Office: Grand Canyon U 3300 W Camelback Rd Phoenix AZ 85017-1097

GIBSON, YOLANDA, aviation executive; b. Blackfoot, Idaho, Feb. 12, 1944; d. Verl Deloy and Virginia (Woodland) Goodwin; m. Wayne Dean Stump, Jan. 13, 1962 (div. June 1968); children: Candi Sue, Judy Lynn; m. Max Grant Gibson, May 26, 1972. Grad. high sch., Idaho, 1973. Owner, office mgr. Western Aviation, Inc., Blackfoot, 1973—. Contbr. articles to aviation mags. Mem. Women of Idaho Agriculture Aviation (v.p. 1978-79, pres. 1979-80), Women's Nat. Agrl. Aviation Assn. (sec. 1982, v.p. 1989, pres. 1990, Plaque 1980, 90, 91, Cert. 1980, 89), Women's Pacific Aerial Applicator's Alliance (pres. 1991). Republican.

GIDEON-HAWKE, PAMELA LAWRENCE, fine arts, small business owner; b. N.Y.C., Aug. 23, 1945; d. Lawrence Ian Verry and Lily S. (Stein) Gordon; m. Jarrett Redstone, June 27, 1964; 1 child, Justin Craig Hawke. Grad. high sch., Manhattan. Owner Gideon Gallery Ltd., L.A., 1975—; prin. Pamela L. Gideon-Hawke Pub. Rels., L.A., 1984—. Pres. San Fernando Valley West Point Parents Club, 1990—. Named Friend of Design Industry Designers West Mag., 1987. Mem. Am. Soc. Interior Designers (publicist), Internat. Soc. Interior Designers (trade liaison 1986-88), Network Exec. Women in Hosp. (exec. v.p.), Internat. Furnishings and Design Assn. (pres.). Office: Gideon Gallery Ltd 8121 Lake Hills Dr Las Vegas NV 89128 also: 8748 Melrose Ave Los Angeles CA 90069

GIEDT, WALVIN ROLAND, epidemiologist, educator; b. Eureka, S.D., Aug. 17, 1905; s. Theodore John Peter and Augusta Elizabeth (Pritzkau) G.; m. Lois Della Hosking, Nov. 4, 1932; children: Carol Augusta, Barbara Ellen. BS in Medicine, U. S.D., 1933; MD, U. Chgo., 1937; MPH, Johns Hopkin's U., 1941. Lab. instr. Sch. of Medicine U. S.D., Vermillion, 1933-36, asst. prof. microbiology Sch. of Medicine, 1938-40; chief epidemiologist div. S.D. Dept. Health, Pierre, 1941-43; chief epidemiologist div. Wash. State Dept. Health, Seattle, 1943-71, ret., 1971. Contbr. articles to profl. jours. With USPHS, 1941-66. Mem. Wash. State Pub. Health Assn. (past pres). Democrat. Home: 3201 Pine Rd Bremerton WA 98310-2168

GIEM, ROSS NYE, JR., surgeon; b. Corvallis, Oreg., May 23, 1923; s. Ross Nye and Goldie Marie (Falk) G.; student U. Redlands, Walla Walla Coll.; BA, MD, Loma Linda U.; children: John, David, Paul, James, Ross Nye, Matthew, Julie. Intern, Sacramento Gen. Hosp., 1952-53; resident in ob-gyn, Kern County Gen. Hosp., Bakersfield, Calif., 1956-57, in gen. surgery, 1957-61; practice medicine specializing in gen. surgery, Sullivan, Mo., 1961-70; staff emergency dept. Hollywood Presbyn. Med. Center, 1971-73, Meml. Hosp., Belleville, Ill., 1973-87, St. Elizabeth Hosp., Belleville, Ill., 1973-90; St. Luke Hosp., Pasadena, Calif., 1973-89, Doctors Hosp., Montclair, Calif. 1990—; instr. nurses, physicians, paramedics, emergency med. technicians, 1973-91. Served with AUS, 1943-46. Diplomate Am. Bd. Surgery. Fellow ACS, Am. Coll. Emergency Physicians; mem. AMA, Ill. Med. Assn., Pan Am. Med. Assn., Pan Pacific Surg. Assn., Royal Coll. Physicians (Eng.)

GIER, KARAN HANCOCK, counseling psychologist; b. Sedalia, Mo., Dec. 7, 1947; d. Ioda Clyde and Lorna (Campbell) Hancock; m. Thomas Robert Gier, Sept. 28, 1968. BA in Edn., U. Mo., Kansas City, 1971; MA Teaching in Math/Sci. Edn., Webster U., 1974; MA in Counseling Psychology, Western Colo. U., 1981; MEd Guidance and Counseling, U. Alaska, 1981; PhD in Counseling, Pacific Western U., 1989. Nat. cert. counselor. Instr. grades 5-8 Kansas City-St. Joseph Archdiocese, 1969-73; ednl. cons. Pan-Ednl. Inst., Kansas City, 1973-75; instr., counselor Bethel (Alaska) Regional High Sch., 1975-80; ednl. program coord. Western Regional Resource Ctr., Anchorage, 1980-81; counselor U. Alaska, Anchorage, 1982-83; coll. prep. instr. Alaska Native Found., Anchorage, 1982; counselor USAF, Anchorage, 1985-86; prof. U. Alaska, Anchorage, 1982—; dir. Omni Counseling Svcs., Anchorage, 1984—; prof. Chapman Coll., Anchorage, 1988—; workshop facilitator over 100 workshops on the topics of counseling techs., value clarification, non-traditional teaching approaches, peer-tutor tng. Co-author: Coping with College, 1984, Helping Others Learn, 1985; editor, co-author: A

Student's Guide, 1983; contbg. author developmental Yup'ik lang. program, 1981; contbr. photographs to Wolves and Related Canids, 1990, 91; contbr. articles to profl. jours. Mem. Am. Bus. Women's Assn., Blue Springs, Mo., 1972-75, Ctr. for Environ. Edn., World Wildlife Fund, Beta Sigma Phi, Bethel, Alaska, 1976-81. Recipient 3d place color photo award Yukon-Kuskokwim State Fair, Bethel, 1978, Notable Achievement award USAF, 1986, Meritorious Svc. award Anchorage Community Coll., 1984-88. Mem. Coll. Reading and Learning Assn. (editor, peer tutor sig leader 1988—, Cert. of Appreciation, 1986-93, bd. dirs. Alaska state, coord. internat. tutor program), AACD, Alaska Assn. Counseling and Devel. (pres. 1989-90), Alaska Career Devel. Assn. (pres.-elect 1989-90), Nat. Rehab. Assn., Nat. Rehab. Counselors, Greenpeace, Human Soc. of the U.S. Wolf Haven Am., Wolf Song of Alaska. Home and Office: Omni Counseling Svcs 8102 Harvest Cir Anchorage AK 99502-4682

GIESA, MICHAEL WILLIAM, bank executive; b. Spokane, Wash., Feb. 28, 1943; s. William Maurice and Margaret Lorraine (Gridley) G.; m. Karen Marie Graves, 1966 (div. 1975); 1 child, Kathryn Marie; m. Judith J. Anderson, Nov. 28, 1986. BS, Coll. of Idaho, 1966; MBA, U. Chgo., 1971; grad., Pacific Coast Banking Sch., Seattle, Wash., 1983. Mktg. adminstr. Idaho First Nat. Bank, Boise, 1971-73, trust officer, 1973-81, sr. trust officer, 1981-85; v.p., mgr. West One Bank, Boise, 1985-89; sr. v.p., mgr. West One Trust Co., Salt Lake City, 1989—. Mem. planned giving com. Holy Cross Hosp. Found., Salt Lake City, 1990—. Mem. Rotary. Republican. Roman Catholic. Home: 48 W 300 S American Tower Salt Lake City UT 84101 Office: West One Trust Co 107 S Main St Ste 303 Salt Lake City UT 84111-1919

GIESCHEN, DONALD WERNER, philosophy educator; b. Wausau, Wis., Apr. 23, 1924; s. Gerhard and Lucille Annette (Graber) G.; m. Lorna Jeanne Garon, Dec. 17, 1949; children: Janice L., Donald P., Ruth E., Andrew W. BS, Northwestern U., 1959; MA, U. Minn., 1953, PhD, 1962. Instr. philosophy Gustavus Adolphus Coll., St. Peter, Minn., 1955-58; asst. prof. philosophy Ariz. State U., Tempe, 1959-71, assoc. prof. philosophy, 1971-89, prof. emeritus philosophy, 1989—. Ensign USN, 1943-47, PTO. Mem. Am. Philos. Assn. Home: 1103 E Concorda Dr Tempe AZ Office: Ariz State U Dept Philosophy Tempe AZ 85287-1701

GIESIE, PAMELA DEE, nurse; b. Lynwood, Calif., Apr. 22, 1961; d. Gerald Alan and Anna Mae (Agarth) Bailey; m. William John Giesie, Oct. 25, 1986; children: Austen Tyler, Connor Elliott. BSN, Mt. St. Mary's Coll., Brentwood, Calif., 1986; postgrad. nursing, UCLA, 1992. RN, Calif. Staff nurse UCLA Med. Ctr., 1986-89, clin. instr., 1989-91; coord. staff devel. Saddleback Meml. Med. Ctr., Laguna Hills, Calif., 1991-93; perioperative educator, coord. U.C.I. Med. Ctr., 1993—. Mem. Assn. Oper. Room Nurses, Women's Club (sec. 1992-93). Office: UCI Med Ctr 101 City Dr Orange CA 92668

GIFFIN, WALTER CHARLES, retired industrial engineer, educator, consultant; b. Walhonding, Ohio, Apr. 22, 1936; s. Charles Maurice and Florence Ruth (Davis) G.; m. Beverly Ann Neff, Sept. 1, 1956; children—Steven, Rebecca. B. Indsl. Engring., Ohio State U., 1960, M.S., 1960, Ph.D., 1964. Registered profl. engr., Ohio. Research engr. Gen. Motors Research Labs., Warren, Mich., 1960-61; research assoc. systems research group Ohio State U., Columbus, 1961-62, instr. indsl. and systems engring., 1962-64, asst. prof., 1964-68, assoc. prof., 1968-71, prof., 1971-87, prof. emeritus, 1987—; prof. engring. U. So. Colo., Pueblo, 1987-92; ret., 1992—; cons. in field. Author: Introduction to Operations Engineering, 1971; Transform Techniques for Probability Modeling, 1975; Queueing: Basic Theory and Applications, 1978. NASA Research grantee, 1978-83. Republican. Methodist. Club: Exptl. Aircraft Assn. (Oshkosh, Wis.) (Pueblo, Colo.). Home: 419 S Fairway Dr Pueblo West CO 81007

GIFFORD, ARTHUR ROY, aircraft executive; b. Buffalo, Jan. 27, 1937; s. William Howard and Dorothy Ellen (Logan) G.; m. Anna Marie Boone, July 9, 1960 (div. Feb. 1974); 1 child, Douglas Alan; m. Carolyn Elaine Crowe, Dec. 20, 1974; children: Christine Michelle, Stephen Michael. BA, Butler U., 1964; postgrad., Pacific Luth. U., Tacoma, 1970; MA, U. Wash., 1975. Cert. provisional and standard secondary tchr., Wash. Passenger svc. agt. United Airlines, Seattle, 1966-67; indsl. engr. The Boeing Co., Seattle, 1967-70; prog. mgr. engring. div. Boeing Community Connection, The Boeing Co., Seattle, 1987-91; mgr. assessment reports corp. safety, health and environ. affairs The Boeing Co., 1991—; tchr. Fed. Way (Wash.) Sch. Dist., 1971-87. Bd. dirs. Lyric Theatre and Conservatory, Midway, Wash., 1980-82; treas. Wash. Edn. Theatre Assn., 1973-77, 85-89; treas. ArtsTime '89, Wash. State Centennial All-Arts Conf., 1987-89, long-range planning com., Kent (Wash.) View Christian Sch., 1987—; pres. PTA, Kent View Christian High Sch., 1992—; mem. precinct com. Dem. Orgn. King County, Wash., 1973-75, 93—. Democrat. Methodist. Home: 13904 SE 241st St Kent WA 98042-3315 Office: The Boeing Co PO Box 3707 M/S 7E-HK Seattle WA 98124-2207

GILBERT, DAVID HEGGIE, consultant, retired educational publisher; b. Healdsburg, Calif., Mar. 11, 1932; s. Lindley Dodge and Beatrice (Heggie) G.; m. Margaret Collins, Nov. 8, 1953; children: Stephen, Laura, Jennifer, Michael. Student, U. Calif. at Berkeley, 1949-51; B.A., U. of Pacific, 1956; M.A., U. Colo., 1957. Instr. English Oreg. State U., Corvallis, 1957-60; asst. prof. English Oreg. State U., 1960-64; Oreg. coll. traveler Holt, Rinehart & Winston Inc., N.Y.C., 1964-65; N.Y. acquiring editor in speech, drama and English Holt, Rinehart & Winston Inc., 1965-66; mgr. Holt, Rinehart & Winston Inc. (S.E. div.), Atlanta, 1966-67; assoc. dir. U. Tex. Press, Austin, 1967-74; dir. U. Nebr. Press., Lincoln, 1975-86, Cornell U. Press., Ithaca, N.Y., 1986-89; interim dir. So. Ill. U. Press, 1992-93; cons. in field; Instr. English on TV Oreg. Coll. of Air, 1961-62; moderator Face to Face Ednl. TV, Austin, 1970-72. Mem. Democratic Exec. Com., Benton County (Oreg.), 1959-61. Served with AUS, 1953-55. Mem. Assn. Am. Univ. Presses (dir. 1974-76, 83-84, v.p. 1977-78, pres.-elect 1981-82, pres. 1982-83). Home: 196 SE 130th Dr South Beach OR 97366

GILBERT, GARY LANE, medical products executive; b. Cin., Oct. 5, 1950; s. Hiram Johnson Gilbert and Billie Lois (Frazier) Webb; m. Debra McQuillen, July 19, 1986. Student, U. Ariz., 1970-71; AS in Biol. Sci., San Francisco Coll., 1974; AA in Bus., La Salle Coll., 1976. Cert. auto transfusionist. Owner, pres. Mortuary Assocs., Inc., Tucson, 1976-81; rsch. assoc. VA Hosp., La Jolla, Calif., 1981-83, UCLA Hosp./Med. Ctr., West Los Angeles, Calif., 1983-86; tissue procurement specialist ARC, L.A., 1986-88; zone mgr. Psicor Cardiovascular Asst. Divsn., San Diego, 1988-90; COO/pres. Martin McLane, Inc., San Diego, 1990—. Inventor, patentee Hypotrans 750 and Hypotransit: hypothermic organ transport system. Master councillor Order of De Molay, Old Pueblo chpt., Ariz., 1969. Mem. Orgn. Ind. Bus. Owners, U.S. C. of C., Cousteau Soc., Catalina 36 Yacht Fleet (charter). Office: Martin McLane Inc Ste 1004 7959 Silverton Ave San Diego CA 92126

GILBERT, HEATHER CAMPBELL, manufacturing company executive; b. Mt. Vernon, N.Y., Nov. 20, 1944; d. Ronald Ogston and Mary Lodivia (Campbell) G.; BS in Math. (Nat. Merit scholar), Stanford U., 1967; MS in Computer Sci. (NSF fellow), U. Wis., 1969. With Burroughs Corp., 1969-82, sr. mgmt. systems analyst, Detroit, 1975-77, mgr. mgmt. systems activity, Pasadena, Calif., 1977-82; mgr. software product mgmt. Logical Data Mgmt. Inc., Covina, Calif., 1982-83, dir. mktg., 1983, v.p. bus. devel., 1983-84; v.p. profl. services, 1984-85; mgr. software devel. Unisys Corp., Mission Viejo, Calif., 1985—. Mem. Assn. Computing Machinery, Am. Prodn. and Inventory Control Soc., Stanford U. Alumni Assn. (life), Stanford Profl. Women Los Angeles County (pres. 1982-83), Nat. Assn. Female Execs., Town Hall. Republican. Home: 21113 Calle De Paseo Lake Forest CA 92630-7037 Office: Unisys Corp 25725 Jeronimo Rd Mission Viejo CA 92691-2792

GILBERT, HELEN ODELL, art educator; b. Mare Island, Calif., Apr. 6, 1922; d. Henry Edward Odell and Ruth Stewart Harris; m. Fred Ivan Gilbert Jr., Sept. 18, 1943 (div. 1973); children: Rondi, Kristin, Galen, Gerald, Gil, Lisa, Cara. BA, Mills Coll., 1943; postgrad., Cen. Sch. Art, London, 1960-61, U. Calif., Berkeley, 1966; MFA, U. Hawaii, 1968. Employee Dorothy Wright Liebes Studio, San Francisco, 1944-54; ind. artist Honolulu, 1955—; prof. U. Hawaii, Honolulu, 1968—; v.p. Fine Art Projects, Ltd., Honolulu, 1987-91. Artist (books) Contemporary Women Sculptors (by Watson Jones), 1986, Le Strutture Della Visualita (by Heinz Holz), 1985; one-woman shows include Contemporary Art Ctr., Honolulu, 1983, Seasons Galerie, Deh Haag, The Netherlands, 1984, Galerie Maghi Bettini, Amsterdam, 1984, Galerie Meissner Edition, Hamburg, Fed. Republic Germany, 1984, Sande Webster Gallery, Phila., 1985, 88, Northeastern U., Boston, 1986, Contemporary Art Mus., Honolulu, 1989, Karin Fesel Galerie, Düsseldorf, Germany, 1991, Contemporary Art Mus., Honolulu, 1990; exhibited in group shows 55 Mercer Gallery, NY, 1989, Salon des Artists Graphiques Actuels, Paris Grande Palaise, 1989, Ulrich Mus., Witchita, Kans., 1992. Recipient Purchase award State Foun. on Culture and the Arts, Hawaii, 1972, 73, 76, 78, 81, 83, 86; project grantee Ford Found., 1978, rshc. grantee U. Hawaii, 1969, 70, 81, 90. Mem. Am. Abstract Artists Assn., Soc. Am. Grpahic Artists, The Nat. Arts Club (N.Y.C.), Honolulu Printmakers (Merit awards 1983, 84, 85), Contemporary Art Mus. (Honolulu, founder), Honolulu Acad. Arts (life, Purchase awards 1962, 71, 77). Home: 2081 Keeaumoku Pl Honolulu HI 96822-2553 Office: U Hawaii Dept of Art 2535 The Mall Honolulu HI 96822-2233

GILBERT, JUDITH ARLENE, lawyer; b. L.A., Jan. 9, 1946; d. Beril B. and Dorothy Marilyn (Stern) Gilbert; student U. Calif.-Berkeley, 1963-64; AB in Econs. magna cum laude, UCLA, 1967; JD, Harvard U., 1970; m. Joel Philip Schiff; children: Lauren Michelle, Jared Daniel. Bar: Calif. 1971. Assoc. Rosenfeld, Meyer & Susman, 1970-72, Quittner, Stutman, Treister & Glatt, L.A., 1972-74, Sands, Pachter & Gold, Beverly Hills, Calif., 1974-76; Sr. Counsel legal dept, credit advice, spl. assets-N.Am. Div. Bank of Am. Nat. Trust & Savs Assn., 1977-88, of counsel Denton, Hall, Burgin & Warrens, 1988-90; contract ptnr. Lewis, D'Amato, Brisbois & Bisgaard, 1990-92; spl. counsel Pettit & Martin, 1992—; judge pro tem Mcpl. and Small Claims Ct.; mem. arbitration panel L.A.Superior Ct.; planning com. ann. meeting State Bar Calif., 1986-87, also host com. ann. meeting, 1987; bd. dirs. Pub. Counsel, 1986-89; speaker in field. Mem. L.A. County Com. Human Resources; active Girl Scouts U.S.A., Cystic Fibrosis, City of Hope; bd. govs. Arthritis Found., 1989; co-chair drugs in workplace task force Temple Emanuel, 1989-91; mem. steering com. drugs in workplace program Temple Emanuel-Jewish Fedn. Coun. Mem. ABA (litigation and banking, corp. & comml. sects., comml. transactions litigation com., creditor's rights litigation com., others), Calif. State Bar Conf. (exec. com. 1991—, resolutions com. of state bar, 1986, 1988-90, del. 1972—, vice chair conf. com. living wills and right to die 1977, com. on rights and obligations of unmarried cohabitators 1978-80, and legal separation 1980-81), Los Angeles Bar Assn. (bd. trustees 1984-85, comml. law and bankruptcy, taxation and copyright sects. steering com., co-chair fund raising sub-com. 1986, com. to defeat Prop 61), Beverly Hills Bar Assn. (ex-officio mem. bd. govs., exec. com. 1986-87, pres. 1985-86, 86-87, del. to state bar conf. of dels. 1973-91, vice chair, 1980, chair 1981, atty. fee disputes panel, numerous other positions), L.A. Bankruptcy Forum, Fin. Lawyers Conf., Women in Bus., Calif. Women Lawyers Assn., Women Lawyers Assn. Los Angeles, Fin. Lawyers Conf., Am. Bankruptcy Inst., Comml. Law League Am., Fed. Bar Assn., Thespians, Collegian Singers, Brick Muller Soc., UCLA Alumni Assn. (adv. bd., mem. scholarship bd.), Tower and Flame, Phi Beta Kappa, Gamma Delta Epsilon, Pi Gamma Mu, Omega Delta Epsilon, Phi Chi Theta, Delta Phi Epsilon. Clubs: Merchants, Sutherland (sec.-treas. 1968-69). Office: Pettit & Martin 355 S Grand Ave Ste 3300 Los Angeles CA 90071

GILBERT, RACHEL SHAW, state legislator, real estate broker; b. Ottawa, Kans.; d. Herbert M. and L.C. Ferris (Pile) Shaw; B.A., U. Nebr., 1956; M.A., Coll. of Idaho, 1969; children—Cheryl Allison Gilbert Brady, Kimberly Lynn. Sch. tchr., Nebr., 1952-57; broker Walker & Co. Real Estate, Boise, Idaho, 1969-71; broker-owner Gilbert & Assocs. Realtors, Boise, 1972-82; mem. Idaho Ho. of Reps., 1980-83, Idaho Senate, 1984—. Bd. dirs. United Way, Boise, 1963-68, Boise Philharm. Orch., 1966-68; chmn. Idaho Legis. Dist. 15, 1980, local govt. and taxation com. Mem. Nat. Assn. Realtors (dir. 1980-86), Idaho Assn. Realtors (dir. 1978-80), Idaho Assn. Commerce and Industry (dir.), Boise C. of C. (v.p. 1979). Republican. Home: 1111 Marshall St Boise ID 83706-2537 Office: 1487 N Cole Rd Boise ID 83704-8537

GILBERT, RICHARD JOSEPH, economics educator; b. N.Y.C., Jan. 14, 1945; s. Michael N. and Esther (Dillon) G.; m. Sandra S. Waknitz, Sept. 7, 1974; children: Alison, David. BEE with honors, Cornell U., 1966, MEE, 1967; MA in Econs., Stanford U., 1976, PhD, 1976. Rsch. assoc. Stanford U., Calif., 1975-76; from assist. prof. to assoc. prof. econs. U. Calif., Berkeley, 1976-83; assoc. prof engring-econ. systems Stanford U., 1982-83; prof. econs. U. Calif., Berkeley, 1983—, prof. bus. adminstrn., 1990—; dir. univ. energy rsch. inst. U. Calif., Berkeley, 1983—; prin., treas. Law & econs. Cons. Group, Berkeley, 1989—. Contbr. numerous articles to profl. jours.; editor scholarly jours. Adv. U.S. Dept. Energy, Washington, 1983—, World Bank, Washington, 1980—, NSF, Washington, 1985—, Calif. Inst. Energy Efficiency, Berkeley, 1990—. Fulbright scholar Washington, 1989; vis. scholar Cambridge U., 1979, Oxford U., 1979. Mem. Tau Beta Pi, Eta Kappa Nu, Sigma Xi. Office: Univ Energy Rsch Inst 2539 Channing Way Berkeley CA 94720

GILBERT, ROBERT WOLFE, lawyer; b. N.Y.C., Nov. 12, 1920; s. L. Wolfe and Katherine L. (Oestreicher) Wolfe; m. Beatrice R. Frutman, Dec. 25, 1946; children: Frank Richard, Jack Alfred. BA, UCLA 1941; JD, U. Calif., Berkeley, 1943. Bar: Calif. 1944, U.S. Ct. Appeals. (9th cir.) 1944, U.S. Ct. Appeals. (D.C. cir.) 1976, U.S. Supreme Ct. 1959. Pres. Gilbert & Sackman, P.C. and predecessors, L.A., 1944—; judge pro tem Los Angeles Mcpl. and Superior Ct., Commr. City of L.A. Housing Authority 1953-63; bd. dirs. Calif. Housing Coun. 1955-63; U.S. faculty mem. Moscow Conf. on Law and Econ. Cooperation, 1990. Mem. Internat. Bar Assn., Interam. Bar Assn. (co-chmn. labor law and social security com.), ABA (co-chmn. internat. labor law com.), Fed. Bar Assn., L.A. Bar Assn. (past chmn. labor law sect.), Am. Judicature Soc., Order of Coif, Pi Sigma Alpha. Club: Nat. Lawyers. Contbr. articles to profl. jours. Home: 7981 Hollywood Blvd Los Angeles CA 90046 Office: 6100 Wilshire Blvd Ste 700 Los Angeles CA 90048-5107

GILBERT, STEPHEN L., electrical engineer, chemist; b. Newark, July 26, 1943; s. Edwin O. and Theda (McPerry) G.; m. Lois Virginia Doak, Feb. 11, 1964 (div.); 1 child, Samuel Alexander Paul; m. Nancy Lee Conte, May 23, 1981; children: Nathan Thomas, Noah Charles, Samuel Zachary. BS in Chemistry, St. Joseph's Coll., Phila., 1974; postgrad., U. Pa., 1975. Rsch. assoc. UNIVAC, Blue Bell, Pa., 1965-68, RCA Corp. David Sarnoff Rsch. Ctr., Princeton, N.J., 1968-75; sr. assoc. engr. IBM, Burlington, Vt., 1978; chief engr. Fairbanks Mus. and Planetarium, St. Johnsbury, Vt., 1979; rsch. fellow and mgr. microelectronics U. Minn., Mpls., 1981-89; mgr. microelectronics U. Ariz., Tucson, 1989—; pres. Cons. Svcs., St. Johnsbury, 1975—; cons. UN Indsl. Devel. Orgn., 1984—, TelTech., Mpls., 1984—, Intel, Signetics; expert witness VTC Inc., Honeywell, Linear Tech., Briggs & Morgan, Wilson Sonsini, Goodrich & Rosati; bd. dirs. Minn. Microelectronics Lab Group; mem. fin. mgmt. State Capitol Credit Union. Contbr. articles to profl. jours; patentee in field. David Sarnoff scholar RCA Corp., 1974. Mem. IEEE (sr.), AAAS, Inst. for Environ. Svcs. (sr.), Semiconductor Safety Assn., Minn. Electron Microscopy Assn., Am. Chem. Soc., Materials Rsch. Soc., Atmospheric Pressure Ionization Mass Spectrometry User Group (coord.), Electrochem. Soc. Office: U Ariz Elec & Computer Engring 1230 E Speedway Blvd Tucson AZ 85721-0001

GILBERT, STEVEN EDWARD, music educator, author; b. Bklyn., Apr. 20, 1943; s. Milton and Sylvia Ruth (Meyerson) G.; m. Patricia Jean King, May 28, 1977 (div. Jan. 1994); children: Jonathan King, Matthew Brian. BA, CUNY, Bklyn., 1964; MusM, Yale U., 1967, M. Philosophy, 1969, PhD, 1970. From asst. prof. to prof. dept. music Calif. State U., Fresno, 1970—; ptnr. JAJ Properties, Reno, Nev., 1988—. Co-author: Introduction to Schenkerian Analysis, 1982; music reviewer The Fresno Bee; contbr. articles to profl. jours. and reference books. Mem. Am. Musicological Soc., Soc. for Music Theory, Coll. Music Soc. (life), The Sonneck Soc., Nat. Assn. Scholars, Yale Club of the San Joaquin Valley (pres. 1979-82, treas. 1979—), Porsche Club Am. (region pres. 1986-87). Republican. Jewish. Office: Calif State U Dept Music Fresno CA 93740

GILBERT, SUSAN ANN, nuclear medicine technologist; b. Nampa, Idaho, July 27, 1950; d. Donald E. White and Nancy L. (Clausen) White Melton; m. Joseph William Gilbert, Sept. 15, 1984. BS, U. Wis., LaCrosse, 1973; cert. in nuclear medicine technology, VA Med. Ctr., 1974. Ednl. specialist VA Med. Ctr., St. Louis, 1974-78, nuclear medicine technologist, 1974-82; supr. nuclear medicine technology VA Med. Ctr., Portland, Oreg., 1982—; item writer Nuclear Medicine Tech. Cert. Bd., 1984—. Author: (book) Nuclear medicine Technology Review, 1977, (book chpt.) Curriculum Guide for Nuclear Medicine Technology, 1982; author/editor (book) Quality Assurance, Resource Manual for Nuclear Medicine, 1990; contbr. articles to profl. jours. Mem. Soc. Nuclear Medicine (technologist sect. 1974—, outstanding technologist paper award 1986). Office: VA Medical Ctr Nuclear Medicine PO Box 1034 Portland OR 97207

GILBERTSON, EVA L., radiologist; b. Maddock, N.D., Dec. 23, 1916; d. Henry A. and Anna (Brandrud) G. BA, U. N.D., 1938, BS in Medicine, 1939; MD, Temple U., 1941; MS in Radiology, U. Minn., 1947. Diplomate Am. Bd. Radiology. Fellow in radiology Mayo Clin., Rochester, Minn., 1942-46; radiologist Portland (Oreg.) Clinic, 1946-49; instr. U. Oreg. Med. Sch., Portland, 1946-49; pvt. practice radiology Seattle, 1949-75; staff radiologist U. Wash. Med. Sch., Seattle, 1950-80, Children's Med. Ctr., Seattle, 1955-85, Pacific Med. Ctr., 1981—. Fellow Am. Coll. Radiology; mem. AMA, Am. Roentgen Ray Soc., Radiol. Soc. N.Am., Pacific N.W. Radiol. Soc., Wash. State Radiol. Soc., Mayo Clinic Alumni Assn. Lutheran.

GILBERTSON, OSWALD IRVING, marketing executive; b. Bklyn., Mar. 23, 1927; s. Olaf and Ingeborg (Aase) Gabrielsen; m. Magnhild Hompland, Sept. 11, 1954; children: Jan Ivar, Eric Olaf. Electrotechnician, Sorlandets Tekniske Skole, Norway, 1947; BSEE, Stockholms Tekniska Institut, Stockholm, Sweden, 1956. Planning engr. test equipment design and devel. Western Electric Co., Inc., Kearny, N.J., 1957-61, planning engr. new prodn., 1963-67, engring. supr. test equipment, 1963-67, engring. supr. submarine repeaters and equalizers, 1967-69; engring. mgr. communication cables ITT Corp., Oslo, Norway, 1969-71, mktg. mgr. for ITT's Norwegian co., Standard Telefon og Kabelfabrik A/S (STK), 1971-87, STK Factory rep., 1987-89, Alcatel Kabel Norge AS Factory rep., 1989-92, Alcatel Can. Wire Inc. Factory rep., 1992—; div. mgr. Eswa Heating Systems, Inc., 1980-87, pres., 1987-89. Hon. Norwegian consul, 1981—; apptd. Knight First Class Norwegian Order Merit, 1989. Served with AUS, 1948-52. Registered profl. engr., Vt. Mem. IEEE, Norwegian Soc. Profl. Engrs., Soc. Norwegian Am. Engrs., Sons of Norway. Patentee in field. Home and Office: 6240 Brynwood Ct San Diego CA 92120-3805

GILBERTZ, LARRY E., state legislator, entrepreneur; b. Gillette, Wyo., Feb. 3, 1929; s. Jacob A. and Lena E. (Schlautmann) G.; m. Verna Ann Howell, June 18, 1955; children: Katerine, L.D., Susan, Jay. Mgr. Gilbertz Ranch, Gillette, 1953-62, owner, 1963—; sr. ptnr. Gilbertz Co., Gillette, 1971—; pres. Gilbertz Enterprises, Gillette, 1988—; mem. Wyo. Senate, Cheyenne, 1993—; chmn. U. Wyo. Exptl. Farm, Campbell County, 1970-74. Treas. Sch. Bd. Dist. # 9, Campbell County, 1969-71; active Sch. Dist. Reorgn., Campbell County, 1970, Wyo. Ct. Reform, 1971. With U.S. Army, 1951-53, PTO. Recipient Performance Testing award U. Wyo., 1969-74, Chem. Weed Control award, 1969-74. Mem. Am. Farm Bur., Am. Legis. Exch. Coun., Am. Legion, Wyo. Stockgrowers. Republican. Catholic.

GILES, GERALD LYNN, mathematics, learning enhancement, psychology, computer educator; b. Manti, Utah, Jan. 2, 1943; s. Bert Thorne and Sarah Jenett (Carlen) G.; m. Sharon Ruth Bleak, June 12, 1967; children: Kim, David, Kristie, Becky, Michael, Andrew, Brent, Amber. BA, U. Utah, 1968, MA, 1971. Tchr. Granite Sch. Dist., Salt Lake City, 1968-72; prof. Salt Lake Community Coll., Salt Lake City, 1972—; adj. prof. U. Utah, 1985—; cons. QUE Enterprises, Salt Lake City, 1976—; mem. faculty U. Phoenix, Salt Lake City, 1986—. Author: The Vicious Circle of Life, 1988, The Computer Productivity Planner, 1988. Chmn. Rep. voting dist., Salt Lake City, 1984-86; bishop LDS Ch., 1986-91. Recipient Teaching Excellence award, 1986; named Outstanding Tchr. of Yr., 1986. Mem. Nat. Assn. Devel. Edn., Am. Assn. of Adult and Continuing Edn. Home: 4342 Beechwood Rd Salt Lake City UT 84123-2206 Office: Salt Lake Community Coll PO Box 30808 Salt Lake City UT 84130-0808

GILES, JEAN HALL, retired corporate executive; b. Dallas, Mar. 30, 1908; d. C. D. and Ida (McIntyre) Overton; m. Alonzo Russell Hall, II, Jan. 23, 1923 (dec.); children: Marjorie (Mrs. Kenneth C. Hodges, Jr.), Alonzo Russell III; m. Harry E. Giles, Apr. 24, 1928 (div. 1937); 1 child, Janice Ruth; 1 adopted child, Marjean Giles. Grad. Hamilton State U., PhD (hon.), 1973. comdg. officer S.W. Los Angeles Women's Ambulance and Def. Corps., 1941-43; maj., nat. exec. officer Women's Ambulance and Def. Corps, 1944-45; capt., dir. field ops. Communications Corps of the U.S. Nat. Staff, 1951-52; dir. Recipe of the Month Club. Active Children's Hosp. Benefit, 1946; coord. War Chest Motor Corps, 1943-44; dir. Los Angeles Area War Chest Vol. Corps and Motor Corps, 1945-46; realtor Los Angeles Real Estate Exchange, 1948—, now ret.; also partner Tech. Contractors, Los Angeles. Bd. dirs. Tchr. Remembrance Day Found. Inc. Mem. Los Angeles C. of C. (women's div.), A.I.M., Los Angeles Art Assn., Hist. Soc. So. Calif., Opera Guild So. Calif., Assistance League So. Calif., Needlework Guild Am. (sect. pres. Los Angeles), First Century Families Calif., Internat. Platform Assn. Clubs: Athletic; Town Hall, The Garden (Los Angles); Pacific Coast. Home: 616 Magnolia Ave Long Beach CA 90802-1243

GILES, SUSAN M., medical/surgical nurse; b. Inglewood, Calif., Mar. 28, 1965; d. Michael Paul and JoAnn Patricia (Margan) Stash.; m. Sept. 7, 1991. BSN, Westminster Coll., Salt Lake City, 1987. RN, Calif.; cert. med.-surg. Staff nurse gen. surg. unit St. Joseph Hosp., Orange, Calif., 1987-91; staff nurse gen. med. surg. unit Castle Med. Ctr., Kailua, Hawaii, 1992—. Mem. ANA, Sigma Theta Tau.

GILES, WALTER EDMUND, alcohol and drug treatment executive; b. Omaha, Aug. 9, 1934; s. Walter Edmund and Julia Margaret (Shively) G.; m. Dona LaVonne Foster, Sept. 29, 1970 (dec. 1990); children: Sue, Stephen, Theresa, Marcy, Kim, Tim, Nadine, Charles; m. Yvonne Marie Fink, Nov. 29, 1991; 1 child, Jessica Nicole Farr. BA, U. Nebr., Lincoln, 1972, MA, 1977. Counselor VA Hosp., Lincoln, Nebr., 1969-70; coord. alcohol programs Mcpl. Ct., Lincoln; dir. Orange County Employee Assistance, Santa Ana, Calif., 1977-79; adminstr. Advanced Health Ctr., Newport Beach, Calif., 1979-81; pres. Great West Health Svcs. Inc., Orange, Calif., 1982-86, Pine Ridge Treatment Ctr. Inc., Running Springs, Calif., 1986—. Author (book) The Workbook, 1985, Intervention, 1986; host (radio show) Addictions, 1984. Mem. Nat. Assn. Alcoholism Counselors, Calif. Assn. Alcoholism Counselors. Home: 31361 Easy St Running Springs CA 92382

GILGER, PAUL DOUGLASS, architect; b. Mansfield, Ohio, Oct. 13, 1954; s. Richard Douglass and Marilyn Joan (Hawkins) G. BArch, U. Cin., 1978. Registered architect, Ohio. Architect Soulen & Assocs., Mansfield, Ohio, 1976-81, PGS Architecture/Planning, Los Gatos, Calif., 1981-82, Bottomline Systems, Inc., San Francisco, 1983-85; pvt. practice San Francisco Bay Area, 1985—; set designer Nomad Prodns. Scenic Studios, San Francisco, 1985-87; architect James Gillam, Architect, San Francisco, 1987-90, Hedgpeth Lemmon Architecture, Santa Rosa, Calif., 1990—; booking mgr. 1177 Club, San Francisco, 1985-86, City Cabaret, San Francisco, 1986-87; bd. dirs San Francisco Coun. Entertainment, 1987-90; project architect Lucasfilm Movie Studio Indsl. Light and Magic, San Rafael, Calif., 1991. Author: "Tune the Grand Up", the Jerry Herman Musical revue. Recipient Ohio Community Theatre Assn. award, 1980, Theatrewest Acting award, 1983, Bay Area Critics Cir. award, 1984, 85, Cabaret Gold awards San Francisco Coun. Entertainment, 1985,86, Hollywood Dramalogue award, 1985, San Francisco Focus award, 1985. Home: 631 Spencer Ave # 6 Santa Rosa CA 95404-3315 Office: Hedgpeth Lemmon Architecture 2321 Bethards Dr Santa Rosa CA 95405

GILKEY, GORDON WAVERLY, curator, artist; b. Albany, Oreg., Mar. 10, 1912; s. Leonard Ernest and Edna Isabel (Smith) G.; m. Vivian Malone, Oct. 17, 1938; 1 son, Gordon Spencer. BS, Albany Coll., 1933; MFA, U. Oreg., 1936; ArtsD (hon.), Lewis and Clark Coll., 1957. Mem. art staff Stephens Coll., Mo., 1939-42; prof. art, head dept. Oreg. State U., 1947-64; dean Oreg. State U. (Sch. Humanities and Social Scis.), 1963-73, Oreg. State U. (Coll. Liberal Arts), 1973-77; curator prints and drawings Portland (Oreg.) Art Mus., 1978—; prof. and printmaker-in-resident Pacific N.W. Coll. Art, Portland Art Mus., 1978—; spl. asst. to pres. Portland Art Mus., 1988—; dir. Internat. Exc. Print Exhibits, 1956-78; U.S. adviser IV

Bordighera Biennale, Italy, 1957; chmn. Gov.'s Planning Coun. for Arts and Humanities in, Oreg., 1965-67; mem. Gov.'s Commn. on Fgn. Lang. and Internat. Studies. Ofcl. etcher New York World's Fair, 1939, 1937-39; etcher Nat. Broadcasting Co., Radio City, N.Y.C., 1937-39; artist-author: Etchings: New York World's Fair, 1939; contbr. articles on art; major work in permanent collection, Met. Mus. Art, others. Bd. overseers Lewis and Clark Coll.; trustee Oreg. State U. Found.; chmn. exec. bd. Oreg. French Study Center, Oreg. German Study Center, Oreg. Japan Study Center, Oreg. Latin Am. Study Center, 1966-77. With U.S. Army Air Corps; active duty July 1942, combat intelligence officer, head of War Dept. spl. staff art projects in Europe and chief of Joint-Chiefs-of-Staff Study in Europe of German Psychol. Warfare 1946-47; collected War Dept. Hist. Properties collection of Nazi and German war art; discharged to Res. as maj. USAF, Oct. 1947; col. Res. ret. Decorated officer with decoration Palmes Academiques (France); officer's cross; comdr.'s cross Order of Merit (Fed. Republic Germany); Order Star of Solidarity (Italy); comdr. Order of Merit (Italy); officer Order Acad. Palms (France); chevalier Legion of Honor (France); Grand Cross Order St. Gregory the Illuminator; comdr. Order Polonia Restituta; chevalier Order of Holy Sepulchre; chevalier mil. and hospitaller Order of St. Lazarus; chevalier mil. and hospitaller Order of Our Lady of Mt. Carmel; chevalier St. Dennis of Zante; knight Grand Cross Order of St. Basil the Great; knight Imperial Order of St. Eugene of Trebizond; Order of the Knights of Sinai; comdr. Order Holy Cross of Jerusalem; comdr. Order St. Stephan the Martyr; King Carl XVI Gustaf's Gold Commemorative medal in art Sweden, German Friendship award Soc. Mayflower Descendants, Aubrey R. Watzek award; AIA-Carnegie Corp. fellow, summer 1930, 32. Mem. Portland Art Mus. (founder), Soc. Am. Graphic Artists, Calif. Soc. Printmakers, Coll. Art Assn., UN Assn. Oreg. (past pres.), Oreg. Internat. Coun. (bd. dirs.), Print Coun. of Am., N.W. Print Coun. (trustee), Phi Kappa Phi, Kappa Pi. Home: 1500 SW 5th Ave Portland OR 97201-5458 Office: 1219 SW Park Ave Portland OR 97205

GILL, A(THERTON) L(ESLIE), publishing executive; b. Houston, July 24, 1935; s. Atherton Leslie and Edith (Bobb) G.; m. Joyce M. Mills, NOv. 16, 1956; children: John, Kathy, Cindy. Student, U. Houston, 1954-55, Moody Bible Inst., 1955-56; ThM, Vision Christian U., 1991, PhD, 1992. Ordained min., 1984. Mgr. Mills Bible Store, Houston, 1964-68, Berean Book Store, Whittier, Calif., 1968-70; gen. mgr. Berean Book Stores, South El Monte, Calif., 1970-75; adminstr. Melodyland Christian Ctr., Anaheim, Calif., 1975-78; exec. v.p. Hunter Ministries, Houston, 1978-79; min. Lakewood Ch., Houston, 1979-83; pres. Gill Ministries, Powerhouse Pub., Life Schs. Ministry, Fawnskin, Calif., 1983—; pres. Life Schs. Ministry, 1987—; bd. regents Vision Christian U., Ramona, Calif., 1991—; acad. dean Eagles' Nest Tng. Inst., Irvine, Calif., 1992-93; dir. Faith Network, 1993—. Author: God's Promises for Your Every Need, 1981, Destined For Dominion, 1986-92; Accredited Bible Coll. Curriculum, 1984-92. Mem. Charismatic Bible Ministries, Christian Booksellers Assn. (assoc.). Republican. Office: Gill Ministries PO Box 99 Fawnskin CA 92333

GILL, ELAINE GOLDMAN, publisher; b. Boston, Apr. 28, 1924; d. Lewis and Pauline (Feldbaum) Goldman; m. John Gill, 1950; children: Daniel, Lawrence. BA, U. Calif., Berkeley, 1945; MA, NYU, 1954; postgrad., Columbia U., 1954-56. Instr. Ithaca (N.Y.) Coll., 1960-67; owner Kosmos Restaurant, Trumansburg, N.Y., 1971-79; co-owner The Crossing Press, Freedom, Calif., 1972—.

GILL, GEORGE WILHELM, anthropologist; b. Sterling, Kans., June 28, 1941; s. George Laurance and Florence Louise (Jones) G.; BA in Zoology with honors (NSF grantee), U. Kans., 1963, M.Phil. Anthropology (NDEA fellow, NSF dissertation research grantee), 1970, PhD in Anthropology, 1971; m. Pamela Jo Mills, July 26, 1975 (div. 1988); children: George Scott, John Ashton, Jennifer Florence, Bryce Thomas. Mem. faculty U. Wyo., Laramie, 1971—, prof. anthropology, 1985—; forensic anthropologist law enforcement agys., 1972—; sci. leader Easter Island Anthrop. Expdn., 1981. Served to capt. U.S. Army, 1963-67. Recipient J.P. Ellbogen meritorious classroom teaching award, 1983; research grantee U. Wyo., 1972, 78, 82, Nat. Geog. Soc., 1980, Center for Field Research, 1980, Kon-Tiki Mus., Oslo, 1987, 89, World Monuments Fund, 1989. Diplomate Am. Bd. Forensic Anthropology (bd. dirs. 1985-90). Fellow Am. Acad. Forensic Scis. (sec. phys. anthropology sect. 1985-87, chmn. 1987-88); mem. Am. Assn. Phys. Anthropologists, Current Anthropology (assoc.), Plains Anthrop. Soc., Wyo. Archael. Soc. Republican. Presbyterian. Author articles, monographs, (with others) Skeletal Attribution of Race. Home: 649 Howe Rd Laramie WY 82070-6838 Office: U Wyo Dept Anthropology Laramie WY 82071

GILL, JANE PITTENGER, personnel management consultant; b. Phila., Dec. 16, 1932; d. Nicholas Otto and Cornelia (Chapman) P.; m. Stanley Jensen Gill, June 7, 1952 (dec. June 1991); children: Elizabeth Jensen, Stanley Chapman. BS in Edn., U. Ill., 1954; MA in Counseling, U. Colo., 1975. Staff dir. Boulder (Colo.) County Legal Svcs., 1975-77; legis. and program dir. Colo. Coaliton of Legal Svcs., Denver, 1977-81; dir. legal svcs. Colo. Bar Assn., Denver, 1981-87; cons., pres. Jane P. Gill & Assocs., Boulder, 1987—; commr. Human Rels. Commn., Boulder, 1992—; mem., sec. bd. Colo. Lawyers Trust Account Found., 1983-89; mem. bd. Colo. Jud. Inst., 1989; mem. Nat. Legal Aid and Defender Program, 1975-92. Mem. Boulder Human Rels. Commn., 1992—, chmn., 1993. Recipient Jacob Schaetzle award Colo. Bar Assn., 1989. Home and Office: Jane P Gill & Assocs 495 College Ave Boulder CO 80302

GILL, REBECCA LALOSH, aerospace engineer; b. Brownsboro, Tex., Sept. 17, 1944; d. Milton and Dona Mildred (Magee) La Losh; m. Peter Mohammed Sharma, Sept. 1, 1965 (div.); m. James Fredrick Gill, Mar. 9, 1985; children: Erin, Melissa, Ben. BS in Physics, U. Mich., 1965; MBA, Calif. State U., Northridge, 1980. Tchr., Derby, Kans., 1966; weight analyst Beech Aircraft, Wichita, Kans., 1966; weight engr. Ewing Tech. Design, assigned Boeing-Vertol, Phila., 1966-67, Bell Aerosystems, Buffalo, 1967; design specialist Lockheed-Calif. Co., Burbank, 1968-79; sr. staff engr. Hughes Aircraft Missile Systems, Canoga Park, Calif., 1979-82, project mgr. AMRAAM spl. test and tng. equipment, 1982-85, project mgr. GBU-15 guidance sect., Navy IR Maverick Missile, Tucson, 1985-89, project mgr. Navy IR Maverick Missile, SLAM Seeker Prodn., 1989-92, TOSH program mgr., 1992—; sec. Nat. Cinema Corp. Com. chmn. Orgn. for Rehab. through Tng., 1971-75; speaker ednl. and civic groups. Pres. Briarcliffe East Homeowners Assn. Recipient Lockheed award of achievement, 1977. Mem. NAFE, Soc. Allied Weight Engrs. (dir., sr. v.p., chmn. pub. rels. com.), Aerospace Elec. Soc. (dir.), NOW, Tucson Zool. Soc. (bd. dirs.), Hughes Mgmt. Club (bd. dirs., chmn. spl. events, chmn. programs, parliamentarian, 1st v.p., pres.), Women in Def. (sec., Ariz. chpt.), Las Alturas Homeowners Assn. (v.p.), Tucson Racquet Club. Republican. Office: Hughes Missile Systems Co Bldg 801 MS G25 Tucson AZ 85734

GILL, THOMAS STEFFEN, academic administrator; b. Madison, Wis., Aug. 1, 1944; s. Robert Steffen and Harriet Ann (Krythe) G.; m. Karen Griggs, Feb. 2, 1968; children: Laura, Jacob, Emily, John, Paul. BFA, U. Wis., Milw., 1971; MFA, U. Oreg., 1974; EdD, Brigham Young U., 1993. Rsch. technician rsch. div. Allis Chalmers Mfg. Co., West Allis, Wis., 1964-69; instr. Chemeketa C.C., Salem, Oreg., 1973-75, assoc. dir., 1975-79, dir., 1979-84, dean, 1984-88, asst. to pres., 1988—, adj. instr., 1990—; vis. prof. Willamette U., Salem, 1979-81; vis. artist-design Linfield Coll., McMinnville, Oreg., 1981. C.C. rep. Gov.'s Immigration Coord. Com., Salem, 1988-90. Recipient Outstanding Svc. award Oreg. Commn. on Hispanic Affairs, 1989. Mem. Pacific N.W. Assn. for Instnl. Rsch., Assn. for Instnl. Rsch. Mem. LDS Ch. Home: 4493 46th Ave NE Salem OR 97305 Office: Chemeketa CC PO Box 14007 4000 Lancaster Dr NE Salem OR 97309

GILLAM, ISAAC THOMAS, IV, aerospace corporation executive; b. Little Rock, Feb. 23, 1932; s. Isaac Thomas and Ethel McNeal (Reynolds) G.; m. Norma Jean Hughes, Dec. 21, 1956; children: Michael, Teri, Traci, Kelli. A.B., Howard U., 1952. Joined U.S. Air Force, 1953, advanced through grades to capt., 1963; pilot, 1953-63, comdr. missile launch crew, 1961-63; various positions NASA, 1963-68, mgr. Delta program, 1968-71, program mgr. small launch vehicles, 1971-76, dir. shuttle ops., 1976-77; dep. dir. Dryden Flight Research Center NASA, Edward, Calif., 1977-78; dir. Dryden Flight Research Center NASA, 1978-82; asst. assoc. adminstr. NASA, Washington, 1982-84, asst. adminstr., 1984-87; various positions OAO Corp., 1987-88; v.p. Mission and Computing Support, 1988-89; sr. v.p. Aerospace Systems Group, 1989—. Recipient distinguished service medal NASA, 1976, exceptional service medal NASA, 1981, 82, Presdl. Meritorius Exec. award, 1986. Fellow Am. Astronautical Soc., AIAA (assoc.); mem. Air Force Assn., Am. Mgmt. Assn., Alpha Phi Alpha, Tau Beta Pi. Democrat. Episcopalian. Office: OAO Corp 787 W Woodbury Rd Altadena CA 91001

GILLER, EDWARD BONFOY, retired government official, retired air force officer; b. Jacksonville, Ill., July 8, 1918; s. Edward Bonfoy and Ruth (Davis) G.; m. Mildred Florana Schmidt, July 2, 1943; children—Susan Ann, Carol Elaine, Bruce Carleton, Penny Marie, Paul Benjamin. B.S. in Chem. Engring, U. Ill., 1940, M.S., 1948, Ph.D., 1950. Chem. engr. Sinclair Oil Refining Co., 1940-41; commd. 2d lt. USAAF, 1942; advanced through grades to maj. gen. USAF, 1968; pilot, 1941-46; chief radiation br. (Armed Forces Spl. Weapons Project), Washington, 1950-54; dir. research directorate Air Force Spl. Weapons Center, Albuquerque, 1954-59; spl. asst. to comdr. (Office Aerospace Rsch.), Washington, 1959-64; dir. sci. and tech. Hdqrs. USAF, 1964-67; asst. gen. mgr. for mil. application U.S. AEC, 1967-72; ret. from USAF, 1972; asst. gen. mgr. for nat. security AEC, 1972-75; dep. asst. adminstr. for nat. security U.S. ERDA, 1975-77; rep. of Joint Chiefs of Staff to Comprehensive Test Ban Negotiations, Geneva, Switzerland, 1977-84; sr. scientist Pacific-Sierra Rsch. Corp., Arlington, Va, 1984-92; v.p. Trans Mar Inc., Spokane, Wash., 1992—; cons. in the field. Decorated Silver Star, D.S.M., Legion of Merit with oak leaf cluster, D.F.C., Air medal with 17 oak leaf clusters, Purple Heart; Croix de Guerre France). Fellow Am. Inst. Chemists; mem. AAAS, Am. Inst. Chem. Engrs., Sigma Xi, Alpha Tau Omega. Episcopalian. Home: 216 Wapiti Dr Bayfield CO 81122-9243 Office: Trans Mar Inc E 1936 23d Ave Spokane WA 99203

GILLESPIE, L. KAY, sociology and criminology educator; b. Idaho Falls, Idaho, Apr. 8, 1940; s. Leonard Walter and Ruby (Ricks) G.; m. MariLynn Egbert, May 23, 1970; children: Christopher, Erin, Benjamin, Timothy, Adam. BA, Brigham Young U., 1965, MS, 1969; PhD, U. So. Calif., L.A., 1976. Asst. prof. Ricks Coll., Rexburg, Idaho, 1968-72; instr. sociology U. So. Calif., L.A., 1972-74; mem. Utah State Bd. Pardons, Salt Lake City, 1983; dir. tng. Utah State Dept. Corrections, Salt Lake City, 1983-84; prof. sociology Weber State U., Ogden, Utah, 1974—; dir. girls div. Idaho Youth Tng. Ctr., St. Anthony, Idaho, 1971-72. Author: The Unforgiven: Utah's Executed Men, 1991, Social Problems: Myths & Realities, 1985, Cancer Quackery, 1976; contbr. articles to profl. jours. Hinkley scholar Brigham Young U., 1964-65. Mem. Utah Sociol. Soc. (pres. 1988-89), Western Soc. Criminology, Oreg.-Calif. Trails Assn., Utah Westerners, McConochie Soc. (founder, pres.), Alpha Kappa Delta (coun. mem.). Republican. Mormon. Home: 738 E 5600 S Ogden UT 84405-4806 Office: Weber State U Sociology 1208 Ogden UT 84408

GILLETTE, RICHARD GARETH, physiology educator, researcher; b. Seattle, Feb. 17, 1945; s. Elton George and Hazel I. (Hand) G.; m. Sally A. Reams, Feb. 17, 1978 (div. Nov. 1988); 1 child, Jesse Robert. BS, U. Oreg., 1968; MS, Oreg. Health Sci. U., 1976, PhD, 1993. Rsch. asst. dept. otolaryngology Oreg. Health Sci. U., Portland, 1969-72, grad. rsch. asst., 1973-80; instr. physiology Western State Chiropractic Coll., Portland, 1981-85, asst. prof. physiology, 1985-93, assoc. prof. physiology, 1993—; lectr. neurosci. sch. optometry Pacific U., Forest Grove, Oreg., 1985-86; grad. rsch. asst. R.S. Dow Neurol. Sci. Inst., Portland, 1988-93, vis. scientist, 1993—; co-investigator NIH RO1-NDS Grant, 1990-93. Contbr. articles to profl. jours. NIH Pre-Doctoral Tng. fellow Oreg. Health Sci. U., 1973-76; Tarter Res. fellow Med. Rsch. Found. Oreg., 1989. Mem. AAAS, Soc. for Neurosci., Am. Pain Soc., Internat. Assn. for Study of Pain, N.Y. Acad. Scis. Office: R S Dow Neurol Sci Inst 1120 NW 20th Ave Portland OR 97209

GILLETTE, (PHILIP) ROGER, physicist, systems engineer; b. Mt. Vernon, Iowa, May 12, 1917; s. Clinton Edgar and Celia (Rogers) G.; m. Bettelaine Dunbar, April 26, 1947 (dec. Mar. 1986); children: Kenneth Lee, Sandra Jo. B.A., in Physics, Cornell Coll., 1937; B.S. in Engring. Physics, U. Ill., 1938, M.S. in Physics, 1939, Ph.D. in Physics, 1942. Staff mem. Radiation Lab. MIT, Cambridge, Mass., 1942-45; research engr. Sperry Gyroscope Co., Great Neck, N.Y., 1945-48; physicist Hanford Works Gen. Electric Co., Richland, Wash., 1948-50; sr. research physicist SRI Internat. Menlo Park, Calif., 1950-92. retired, SRI Internat., 1992. Co-author: Pulse Generators, 1948. Bd. dirs. West Bay Opera Assn., Palo Alto, Calif., 1959-64, 1977-79. Mem. AAAS, IEEE (life mem.), Am. Phys. Soc. (life), Sigma Xi, Phi Beta Kappa, Tau Beta Pi, Phi Kappa Phi. Achievements include development of Pulse Transformer Theory, of system design concepts for command, control, communications, and intelligence systems, electronic combat systems, and air combat training systems. Home: 2385 Crestview Dr S Salem OR 97302

GILLETTE, W. MICHAEL, judge; b. Seattle, Dec. 29, 1941; s. Elton George and Hazel Irene (Hand) G.; m. Susan Dandy Marmaduke, 1989; children: Kevin, Saima, Ali. AB cum laude in German, Polit. Sci., Whitman Coll., 1963; LLB, Harvard U., 1966. Bar: Oreg. 1966, U.S. Dist. Ct. Oreg. 1966, U.S. Ct. Appeals (9th cir.) 1966, Samoa 1969, U.S. Supreme Ct. 1970, U.S. Dist. Ct. Vt. 1973. Assoc. Rives & Rogers, Portland, Oreg., 1966-67; dep. dist. atty. Multnomah County, Portland, 1967-69; asst. atty. gen. Govt. of Am. Samoa, 1969-71, State of Oreg., Salem, 1971-77; judge Oreg. Ct. Appeals, Salem, 1977-86; assoc. justice Oreg. Supreme Ct., Salem, 1986—.

GILLHAM, GRANT DAVID, political consultant; b. Alton, Ill., Jan. 7, 1957; s. Richard Clark and Joan Margaret (Long) G.; m. Karen Elizabeth Schulze, Aug. 23, 1987. BA in History, Tulane U., 1979. Sales and mgmt. exec. Kent-Miller, Inc., St. Louis, 1979-81; commd. 2d lt. USAF, 1981, advanced through grades to capt., 1985; pilot 320th bomb wing USAF, Sacramento, Calif., 1982-86; instr. pilot, flight examiner 552d airborne warning control wing USAF, Okla. City, 1986-90; polit. cons. Calif. State Assembly, Sacramento, 1990—; chief exec. officer Gillham Profl. Group, 1991—. Vol. Nat. Coun. Alcoholism, Sacramento, 1984—; mem. alumni admissions com. Tulane U., Santa Clara and Sacramento, Calif., 1988—. Decorated Commendation medal, Air medal and Combat Readiness medal. Republican.

GILLIAM, EARL BEN, federal judge; b. Clovis, N.Mex., Aug. 17, 1931; s. James Earl and Lula Mae G.; m. Barbara Jean Gilliam, Dec. 6, 1956; children—Earl Kenneth, Derrick James. B.A., Calif. State U., San Diego, 1953; J.D., Hastings Coll. Law, 1957. Bar: Calif. 1957. Dep. dist. atty. San Diego, 1957-62; judge San Diego Mcpl. Ct., 1963-74, Superior Ct. Calif., San Diego County, 1975-80, U.S. Dist. Ct. (so. dist.) Calif., San Diego, 1980—; faculty mem. Trial Practice Dept. Western State U., San Diego, 1989—. Bd. dirs. YMCA Salvation Army, Boy's Club. Mem. San Diego County Bar Assn., San Diego County Judges Assn. Office: US Dist Ct 940 Front St San Diego CA 92189-0010

GILLIAM, JACK, insurance agent; b. Pomona, Calif., Apr. 6, 1956; s. Wallace Sailors and Jerri (Coppersmith) Gilliam; m. Freda Joy Bowers, Mar. 18, 1977 (div. Apr. 1979; m. Delma Rodriguez Gilliam, Dec. 28, 1979; children: Benjamin, Jonathan. Student, SW Tex. Jr. Coll., Uvalde, 1980. Dist. agt. Am. Gen., Del Rio, Tex., 1979-83; agt. Prudential, Lancaster, Calif., 1984-86; fin. cons. Gt. Western Bank, L.A., 1987-90; agt. Farmers Ins. Group, Lancaster, 1990—. Mem. Antelope Valley Life Underwriters (bd. dirs. 1992-93, awards com. 1991-92, LUTC com. 1992-93, Cert. award 1992), Exch. Club, Million Dollar Round Table, 1982, Westview Ch., Palmdale, Calif. Home: 44233 Sancroft Lancaster CA 93535 Office: Farmers Ins 1008 W Ave M-4 # G Palmdale CA 93551

GILLIAM, MARY, travel executive; b. Pampa, Tex., Apr. 18, 1928; d. Roy and Hylda O. (Bertrand) Brown; divorced; 1 child, Terry K. AA, Amarillo (Tex.) Bus. Coll., 1949. Flight attendant Braniff Internat. Airways, Dallas, 1950-53; from reservation agt. to mgr. passenger sales Trans-World Airlines, various locations, 1953-81; exec. v.p. Lakewood (Colo.) Travel, 1981; mgmt. cons. Bank One Travel, Columbus, Ohio, 1981-82; pres. Icaria Travel, Inc., Tucson, Ariz., 1986—, Intensive Trainers Inst., Tucson, 1983-92. Mem. Ariz. Rep. Com., 1978—. Recipient Award of Excellence Trans-World Airlines, N.Y.C., 1972, Pres.' Hall of Fame award, 1973. Mem. Am. Soc. Travel Agts. (Industry Svc. award 1980), Inst. Cert. Travel Agts. Republican. Methodist. Office: Icaria Travel Inc 2700 Broadway Blvd Tucson AZ 85745-1700

GILLIE, DENNIS LEE, insurance company executive; b. Cleveland Heights, Ohio, May 2, 1952; s. Melvin L. and Phyllis (Smuin) G.; m. Brenda Bailey, Apr. 17, 1975; children: Lee, Ric, Micahleen, Ben, Dan. BS, Brigham Young U., 1976; teaching cert., Washburn U., 1977. Tchr. Topeka Sch. Dist., 1976-78; agt. N.Y. Life Ins. Co., Provo, Utah, 1978—. Coun. v.p., chmn. varsity scouts Utah Nat. Parks coun. Boy Scouts Am., Provo, 1992—. Recipient Wood Badge Beads award Boy Scouts of Am., 1985, Dist. award of merit Utah Nat. Parks coun. Boy Scouts Am., 1987, Nat. Quality award Nat. Assn. Life Underwriters. Mem. Cen. Utah Assn. Life Underwriters (bd. dirs. 1980-89, pres. 1989-90). Mem. LDS Ch. Office: NY Life Ins Co 3305 N University Ave # 100 Provo UT 84604

GILLIES, JOHN ARTHUR, soil conservationist; b. Jersey City, May 19, 1947; s. John Horace and Mary Adele (Kessler) G.; m. Marie Scherzinger Gillies, June 27, 1970; children: Sarah, Karen, Laura, Mary, Jana. BS, Rutgers U., 1969. Soil conservationist U.S. Dept. Agr. Soil Conservation Svc., Mt. Holy, N.J., 1969-70, Bellingham, Wash., 1976-77; dist. conservationist U.S. Dept. Agr. Soil Conservation Svc., Kelso, Wash., 1977-78, Lynden, Wash., 1978—. Dir. Whatcom County Land Trust, Whatcom County, Wash., 1988—. Lt. USN, 1970-77, Vietnam. Recipient Certs. of Merit U.S. Dept. Agr., 1981-90. Mem. Soil and Water Conservation Soc. Roman Catholic. Office: Soil Conservation Svc 6975 Hannegan Rd Lynden WA 98264-9696

GILLIES, PATRICIA ANN, biologist; b. Berkeley, Calif., Sept. 23, 1929; d. William W. and Barbara (Weddle) Myers; m. Robert W. Gillies, Sept. 17, 1948 (div. 1968); children: Catherine I. Barton, Coila L. McGowan. AB, Calif. State U., Fresno, 1954; MA, Calif. State U., 1961. Tchr. Parlier (Calif.) Unified Sch. Dist., 1955-56; inspector U.S. Dept. Agr., Fresno, 1956-58; teaching asst. Fresno State Coll., 1958-59; pub. health biologist Dept. Health Svcs., State of Calif., Fresno, 1959—; dir. Consolidated Mosquito Abatement Dist., Selma, Calif., 1974—. Contbr. articles to profl. jours. Mem. Soc. Vector Ecologists, Am. Mosquito Control Assn., Calif. Mosquito and Vector Control Assn. Democrat. Episcopalian. Home: 7060 E Butler Ave Fresno CA 93727-9400

GILLIGAN-IVANJACK, CLAUDIA MARLENE, motion picture set artist, writer; b. Indpls., Mar. 21, 1947; d. James Emmitt Gilligan and Pearl Helen (Bodfield) Webster; m. Melvin Chilcoat, Feb. 18, 1966 (div. Sept. 1972); children: Tami Mel0lene, Andy Martin; m. Thomas Robert Ivanjack, Aug. 18, 1988. Forman set artist IATSE Local 729, Hollywood, Calif., 1976—. Author: (poetry) Penelope Noise, 1981, Imagination, 1986, (movie script) Monopoly, 1989, (short stories) The Fish Pond, 1990 (Pen Women award 1990). Rend mediation bd. City Hawthorne, Calif., 1978-79. Mem. MENSA, Am. Nat. Hygiene Soc., N.Am. Fishing Club., Japan Karate Assn. (brown belt 1983). Republican. Home and Office: T&C Set Art 1540 Rosita Dr Simi Valley CA 93065

GILLILAND, HAP, educator, writer; b. Willard, Colo., Aug. 26, 1918; s. Samuel S. and Esther J. (Sandstedt) G.; m. Erma L. Rodreick, Apr. 21, 1946; children: Lori Sargent, Diane Bakun, Dwight. AA, Western State Coll., Gunnison, Colo., 1948, BA, 1949, MA, 1950; EdD, U. No. Colo., 1958. Dir. reading ctr. Ea. Mont. Coll., 1961-78; writer, editor Coun. for Indian Edn., 1970—; coord. bilingual and multicultural edn. and reading Lake and Peninsula Schs., 1980, 81, reading specialist, 1983-84; vis. lectr. Christchurch Tchr.'s Coll., N.Z., 1972, 77, New Eng. U., Australia, 1972; guest prof. U. Alaska, Fairbanks, summer 1976, Mont. State U., summer 1960; dir. No. Cheyenne Campus Experience Project, 1965, Remedial Reading No. Cheyenne Reservation, 1965-68, Crow Indian Reservation Ednl. Survey, 1966-67, Upward Bound Project, 1966-69, NDEA Inst. in Reading, 1967, EPDA Insts. in Remedial Reading, 1969, 70; sch. scholar Mont. com. for Humanities, 1992-93; speaker in field. Author: (textbook) Materials for Remedial Reading and their Use, 1973, Practical Guide to Remedial Reading, 1974, 76, Corrective Reading in the Classroom, 1975, Indian Children's Books, 1979, Teaching the Native American, 1988, 92, (novels) Drums of the Headhunters, 1988, Mystery Tracks in the Snow, 1990; (children's books) The Flood, No One Like a Brother, Broken Ice, Coyote's Pow-wow, How the Dogs Saved the Cheyennes, Legends of Chief Bald Eagle, Bill Red Coyote, We Live on an Indian Reservation, When We Went to the Mountains, The Dark of the Moon; author poetry; contbr. articles to profl. jours. Mem. Mont. State Task Force in Reading, 1974-78; profl. advisor Billings Assn. for Children with Learning Disabilities, 1972-76; v.p. Billings Friendship Force, 1989; pres. No. Cheyenne Scholarship Com., 1966-69, Billings Arts Assn., 1990-92; chmn. bd. Cen. Christian Ch., 1975-77. Mem. Coun. for Internat. Cooperation in Reading Rsch. and Devel. (v.p. N.Am. chpt. 1975-77, pres. 1981-83), Internat. Reading Assn. (Rocky Mont. Regional chmn. 1963-75), Mont. State Reading Coun. (bd. dirs. 1967-77, Kiwanis (bd. dirs. 1986-88), Rocky Mountain Reading Specialists Assn. (exec. dir. 1969-83). Home and Office: 517 Rimrock Rd Billings MT 59102

GILLIS, JOHN SIMON, psychologist, educator; b. Washington, Mar. 21, 1937; s. Simon John and Rita Veronica (Moran) G.; m. Mary Ann Wesolowski, Aug. 29, 1959; children: Holly Ann, Mark, Scott. B.A., Stanford U., 1959; M.S. (fellow), Cornell U., 1961; Ph.D. (NIMH fellow), U. Colo., 1965. Lectr. dept. psychology Australian Nat. U., Canberra, 1968-70; sr. psychologist Mendocino (Calif.) State Hosp., 1971-72; asso. prof. dept. psychology Tex. Tech U., Lubbock, 1972-76; prof. psychology Oreg. State U., Corvallis, 1976—, chmn. dept. psychology, 1976-84; cons. VA, Ciba-Geigy Pharms., USIA, UN High Commn. for Refugees; commentator Oreg. Ednl. and Pub. Broadcasting System, 1978-79; Fulbright lectr., India, 1982-83, Greece, 1992; vis. prof. U. Karachi, 1984, 86, U. Punjab, Pakistan, 1985, Am. U., Cairo, 1984-86. Contbr. articles to profl. jours. Served with USAF, 1968-72. Ciba-Geigy Pharms. grantee, 1971-82. Mem. Am. Psychol. Assn., Western Psychol. Assn., Oreg. Psychol. Assn. Roman Catholic. Home: 7520 NW Mountain View Dr Corvallis OR 97330-9106 Office: Oreg State U Dept Psychology Corvallis OR 97331

GILLIS, PAUL LEONARD, accountant; b. Montevideo, Minn., Nov. 20, 1953; s. Joseph Hans and Verna Ruth (Sjolie) G.; m. Deborah Ann Roller, Sept. 9, 1978. BA, Western State Coll., 1975; MS, Colo. State U., 1976. CPA, Colo. Tax cons. Price Waterhouse, Denver, 1976-78; tax mgr. Price Waterhouse, Singapore, 1978-82; internat. tax mgr. Price Waterhouse, San Francisco, 1982-84; sr. mgr. Price Waterhouse, Denver, 1984-88, mng. tax ptnr., 1988—; mem. adv. coun. Colo. State U.; bd. dirs. World Trade Ctr., Forest Hills Metro Dist.; lectr. World Trade Inst., San Francisco, 1982-84. Author: Accounting for Income Tax, 1988. Treas. Forest Hills Metro Dist., 1992—. Recipient 50 for Colo. award, Colo. Assn. Commerce and Industry. Fellow Colo. Soc. CPAs; mem. AICPAs, Am. Club (Singapore) (treas. 1981-82), Pinehurst Country Club, Denver Athletic Club, Harley Owners Group (Denver chpt.), Chetfield Yacht Club. Home: 22616 Forest Hills Dr Golden CO 80401 Office: Price Waterhouse 950 17th St Denver CO 80202-2828

GILLISPIE, STEVEN BRIAN, systems analyst, researcher; b. Seattle, Oct. 19, 1955; s. Edwin B. and Claudia Mae (Cooper) G. BS in Physics with distinction, U. Wash., 1979, BS in Math., 1979, BS in Psychology, 1983, BA in Gen. Studies, 1983. Software specialist Fla. Computer Graphics, Seattle, 1983-84; data analyst coronary artery surgery study U. Wash., Seattle, 1985-87, sci. programmer dept. radiology, 1987-88, systems analyst dept. radiology, 1988—. Dir. devel. med. imaging software Viewbox, 1992; contbr. articles to profl. jours. Mem. Woodland Park Zool. Soc., Seattle, 1985—; contbg. mem. Nordic Heritage Mus., Seattle, 1991—; patron The High Desert Mus., Bend, Oreg., 1991—; sponsor N.W. Women's Law Ctr., Seattle, 1992—. Mem. MacApp Developers Assn., U. Wash. Alumni Assn. (lifetime). Office: U Wash Dept Radiology RC-05 Seattle WA 98195

GILLMAN, GRETA JOANNE, physician; b. Montreal, Quebec, Can., Aug. 18, 1945; d. Hyman and Fanny (Izenburg) G.; m. Vic Bhoopat, Oct. 17, 1970; children: Lisa, Mitchell. MD, U. Calif., Irvine, 1969. Physician specialist L.A. County Hosp., 1973—; asst. clin. prof. UCLA, 1976—. Home: 13492 Grinnell Cir Westminster CA 92683 Office: LA County Hosp 10005 Flower St Bellflower CA 90706

GILLMAR, STANLEY FRANK, lawyer; b. Honolulu, Aug. 17, 1935; s. Stanley Eric and Ruth (Scudder) G.; m. Constance Joan Sedgwick; children: Sara Tamsin, Amy Katherine. AB cum laude with high honors, Brown U.,

1957; LLB, Harvard U., 1963. Bar: Calif. 1963. Ptnr. Graham & James, San Francisco, 1970-92. Co-author: How To Be An Importer and Pay For Your World Travels, 1979; co-pub.: Travelers Guide to Importing, 1980. Sec. Calif. Council Internat. Trade, 1973-92, hon. counsel, 1980-92, exec. com., 1985-92; mem. Mayor San Francisco Adv. Council Econ. Devel., 1976-82; mem. Title IX Loan Bd., 1982—, sec. 1986-92; dir. The San Francisco Ministry to Nursing Homes, 1992—, treas., 1992—. Served with USNR, 1957-60. Mem. ABA, Calif. State Bar, Bar Assn. San Francisco, Bankers Club (San Francisco); Villa Taverna Club, Inverness Yacht Club. Office: 105 Alta St San Francisco CA 94133

GILMARTIN, MICHAEL RAYMOND, community college administrator; b. National City, Calif., Apr. 19, 1952; s. Raymond Malvern and Barbara Jean (Belt) G.; m. Evangelina Torrez, Oct. 25, 1986 (div. Feb. 1991). BS, San Diego State U., 1974, MS, 1978. Agr. inspector Calif. Dept. Agr., San Diego, 1978-80; biology instr. West Hills C.C., Coalinga, Calif., 1980-86, div. chair, 1986-91, spl. asst. to supt./pres., 1991—; chairperson loss control and safety com. valley ins. program Joint Power Agy., Fresno, Calif., 1988-90. Mem. Am. Inst. Biol. Sci., World Wildlife Fedn., Calif. Campus Environ. Health and Safety Assn., Phi Beta Kappa. Home: 655 Pacific St Coalinga CA 93210 Office: West Hills Community Coll 300 Cherry Ln Coalinga CA 93210

GILMARTIN, PLATT JAY, paint and coating company executive; b. Morris Plains, N.J., Oct. 20, 1952; s. Thomas Joseph and Ethel Louise (Cooper) G.; m. Kathleen Marie Hall, Jan. 25,1 979; children: Courtney Elizabeth, Caitlin Marie. BS, Rutgers U., 1974. Lic. tchr., N.J. Gen. mgr. J.L. Armitage & Co., Newark, 1980-83; ops. mgr. Tnemec Co., Inc., Compton, Calif., 1984-90; sr. sales rep. Unocal Corp., 1990-91; ter. mgr. Ashland Chem. Inc., Orange, Calif., 1991-92; plant superintendent Comlux Coatings, 1993—. Capt. USAF, 1974-79. Mem. L.A. Soc. Coatings Tech. (mfg. com. 1984—), So. Calif. Paint and Coatings Assn. Republican. Roman Catholic. Home: 24158 Royale St Moreno Valley CA 92557-5010

GILMORE, ALLEN DOUGLAS, auto glass executive; b. Kittery, Maine, July 21, 1947; s. Allen Johnston and Margaret Nell (McIntosh) G.; m. Joy Carolyn Gustafson, Aug. 23, 1969; children: Chelsea Jay, Allison Anne. BA, Willamette U., 1969; M Internat. Mgmt., Am. Grad. Internat. Mgmt., 1971. Acct. exec. Levi Strauss & Co., various locations, 1971-75; dist. sales mgr. Levi Strauss & Co., L.A., 1975-76; regional sales mgr. Levi Strauss & Co., San Francisco, 1977-80; dir. sales and mtkg. Levi Strauss & Co., Edmonton, Alta., Can., 1980-82; asst. gen. mgr., mktg. dir. Levi Strauss & Co., Sydney, Australia, 1982-86; v.p. mktg. Winmore Products, Bellevue, Wash., 1986-87; v.p. ops. Trans Am. Glass, Seattle, 1987-93; pres. Mail Movers, Inc., Seattle, 1993—. Mem. Sydney/San Francisco Sister City Com., Sydney, 1982-85; mem. Boys and Girls Club of Mercer Island. Mem. Internat. Mktg. Soc., Am. Mktg. Assn., Sales and Mktg. Execs., Am. Nat. Club (Sydney). Home: 1985 82d Ave SE Mercer Island WA 98040 Office: Mail Movers Inc 1021 6th Ave S Seattle WA 98134

GILMORE, TIMOTHY JONATHAN, physician recruiter; b. Orange, Calif., June 24, 1949; s. James and Margaret (Swanson) G.; m. Blanche Jean Panter, Sept. 3, 1984; children: Erin, Sean and Brian (twins). BA, St. Mary's Coll., Moraga, Calif., 1971. Adminstrv. asst. Gov. Ronald Reagan, Sacramento, Calif., 1971-73; salesman Penn Mutual, Anaheim, Calif., 1973-76; asst. devel. dir. St. Mary's Coll., Moraga, 1976-81; devel. dir. St. Alphonsus Hosp., Boise, Idaho, 1981-83; adminstr. Blaine County Hosp., Hailey, Idaho, 1983-86; exec. dir. Poudre Hosp. Found., Ft. Collins, Colo., 1986-87; nat. recruiting dir. Power Securities Corp., Denver, 1987-89; cons. Horn, Fagan & Lund Exec. Search Cons., Ft. Collins, 1989; v.p. Jackson & Coker Locum Tenens, Inc., Denver, 1990—. Mem. Kiwanis (pres. Moraga club 1980-81, sec. Boise club 1982-83). Republican. Mem. LDS Ch. Home: 2914 Bassick St Fort Collins CO 80526-3738

GILMOUR, CRADDOCK MATTHEW, lawyer; b. Kenilworth, Utah, Nov. 25, 1909; s. Matthew and Caroline Gilmour; m. Jessica Roberts, Aug. 16, 1941; children: C.M. (Sandy) Jr., David R., William C., Duncan M., Ridgely H., Mark A. AB, Stanford (Calif.) U., 1930; LLB, JD, Harvard Coll., 1933; postgrad., Cambridge U., Eng., 1933-34. Lawyer European Legal Dept., Western Electric Co., London, 1934-36, N.Y.C., 1936-37; lawyer Davis Polk & Wardwell, N.Y.C., 1937-41; lawyer, counsel C.F. & I. Steel, Denver, 1946-50, Utah Tax Commn., Salt Lake City, 1950-53; pvt. practice Salt Lake City, 1953-92, ret., 1993; mng. ptnr. Gilmour Lime Co., Salt Lake City, 1969-78. Past sr. warden, mem. vestry St. Marks Episcopal Cathedral, Salt Lake City, 1960-70's. With U.S. Army, 1941-45. Mem. Ft. Douglas Club.

GILPIN, BRUCE WYNDHAM, JR., manufacturing company executive; b. Tacoma, Wash., Sept. 2, 1965; s. Bruce W. and Donna L. (Adams) G. BA in Econs., Occidental Coll., L.A., 1988. Mgmt. trainee Laurence-David, Inc., Eugene, Oreg., 1988-89; tech. sales rep. Plastics div. Laurence-David, Inc., Portland, Oreg., 1989-90; sales mgr. Lilly-Ram Industries, Portland, 1990-91; pres., dir. Rol-Away, Inc., Portland, 1991—. Home: 3484 NW Thurman Portland OR 97210 Office: Rol-Away Inc 1643 SE Foster Rd Portland OR 97206

GILWEE, JON DEVAK, health care executive; b. Long Beach, Calif., Aug. 21, 1952; m. Bernadette Fields, Apr. 4, 1981. BA in Polit. Sci., UCLA, 1976. Campaign coord. Winner/Wagner Assocs., L.A., 1976; account exec. Johnson & Higgins, L.A., 1977-79; asst. exec. dir. Orange County Med. Assn., Orange, Calif., 1979-84; v.p. govt. rels. Hosp. Coun. So. Calif., L.A., 1984—; bd. dirs. Calif. Health Decisions, Inc., Orange; trustee Orange County Poison Prevention Found., 1985—. Bd. dirs. United Way Orange County, Garden Grove, Calif., 1986-90. Recipient Leadership award Orange County Health Planning Coun., 1985. Mem. APHA, Am. Coll. Health Care Execs., Health Care Execs. So. Calif., L.A. Pub. Affairs Officers' Assn., UCLA Alumni Assn., Friends of UCLA Rowing, Delta Sigma Phi. Home: 1318 Frances Ave Fullerton CA 92631 Office: Hosp Coun So Calif 201 N Figueroa St Los Angeles CA 90012

GILYEAT, IAN RHYS, marketing professional; b. Bremerton, Wash., July 23, 1959; s. Glenn Albert Gilyeat and Marjorie Lou (Davis) Dewey; m. Lori Michelle Whitfield, July 18, 1981; children: Brandon, Sean, Adrian, Tialene. Student, Brigham Young U., 1977, 81. Mgr. ops. Stokes Bros., Salt Lake City, 1981-82; asst. mgr. Tropic Copies, Provo, Utah, 1983-85; computer operator, programmer City of Provo, 1984-88; dir. circulation WordPerfect Pub. Corp., Orem, Utah, 1988-92; dir. direct mktg. Word Perfect Pub. Corp., Orem, Utah, 1992—, dir. circulation, 1992-93; database mktg. mgr. Word Perfect Corp., 1993—. Head honcho Youth Devel. Enterprises, Lanai City, Hawaii, 1977-78, Lindy Johnston award, 1977, Old Timers Svcs. award, 1978, 25,000 Club award, 1978; explorer leader Boy Scouts Am., Salt Lake City, 1982, varsity scout leader, Provo, 1984. Mem. Direct Mktg. Assn. Mem. LDS Ch. Office: WordPerfect Pub Corp 270 W Center St Orem UT 84057-4637

GIMBEL, ALFRED ADOLF, employee benefits professional; b. Ladendorf, Austria, Nov. 5, 1944; came to U.S., 1969; s. Adolf and Olga (Hiltz) G.; m. Judy Mae Adams, Mar. 22, 1968; children: Heidi Lynn, Shannon Noel. BSc, U. Man., 1965. Mgmt. trainee GM, Winnipeg, Man., Can., 1965-66; group underwriter, rep. Gt. West Life, Winnipeg, 1966-69, mgr. underwriting, group mgr., 1972-75; group mgr., dir. group sales IDS Life Ins. Co., Detroit and Mpls., 1969-72; cons., exec. v.p., sec.-treas. Byerly & Co., Inc., Denver, 1975—, also bd. dirs. Bd. dirs. Perry Park Met. Dist., Larkspur, Colo., 1986-88. Mem. Denver Rustlers, Optimist Internat., Perry Park Country Club. Republican. Lutheran. Office: Byerly & Co Inc Ste 250 S 7600 E Orchard Rd Englewood CO 80111

GIMMESTAD, MICHAEL JON, academic administrator; b. Mpls., Oct. 23, 1943; s. Walter Anders and Leona Mae (Dorf) G.; m. Effie Louise Gryting, June 19, 1965; children: Chad, Wendy, Cory. BA, St. Olaf Coll., 1965; MS, Ind. U., 1967; PhD, U. Minn., 1970; postgrad., Harvard U., 1986. Tchr. Robbinsdale (Minn.) Pub. Schs., 1965-66; counselor, instr. U. Minn., Mpls., 1967-70; prof. Fla. State U., Tallahassee, 1970-77, chmn. Coun. Edn. Dept., 1972-77; chmn. Psychology Dept. U. No. Colo., Greeley, 1977-83, asst. dean Coll. Edn., 1983-87, interim dean Coll. Edn., 1987-88, assoc. dean Coll. Edn., 1988—. Mem. ASCD, Am. Ednl. Rsch. Assn., Am. Counseling Assn. Home: 5220 27th St Greeley CO 80634-4023 Office: Univ No Colo Coll Education Greeley CO 80639

GINALSKI, MARK, lawyer; b. Fall River, Mass., Aug. 25, 1960; s. William and Kathleen (Collins) G.; m. Diana Maureen Mogerman, June 16, 1984. BS, Ariz. State U., 1983; JD, U. San Francisco, 1986. Bar: Calif., D.C., U.S. Ct. Appeals (9th cir.), U.S. Ct. Appeals (D.C. cir.), U.S. Dist. Ct. (no., ea., so. cen. dists.) Calif., U.S. Tax Ct. Assoc. Fisher & Hurst, San Francisco, 1986-88, Wright, Robinson, McCammon, Osthimer & Tatum, San Francisco, 1988-92, Pandell, Novich & Borsuk, San Francisco, 1992—. Bd. dirs. Design Rev. Bd., Tiburon, Calif., 1988-91; planning commr., Tiburon. Mem. Olympic Club. Home: 2 Lyford Dr Belvedere Tiburon CA 94920-1752 Office: Pandell Novich & Borsuk 525 Market St Ste 3400 San Francisco CA 94105

GINGRICH, JOHN THOMAS, optometrist; b. Boonville, Mo., Nov. 6, 1964; s. John Warren and Jane Margaret (Adams) G.; m. Dabney Keith Prestridge, Feb. 14, 1992. Student, N.E. Mo. State U., 1983-86; OD, U. Mo., St. Louis, 1990. Optician, office mgr. Dr. Eva K. Strube, Golden, Colo., 1990; optometrist Eye Physicians, Billings, Mont., 1990—. Chmn. edn. com. Grace United Meth. Ch., Billings, 1992. Named one of Outstanding Young Men Am., 1989; recipient Paragon Optical Contact Lens Achievement award, 1990. Mem. Am. Optometric Assn., Mont. Optometric Assn., Jaycees, Alpha Phi Sigma. Home: 520 Yellowstone Ave Billings MT 59101 Office: Eye Physicians 1221 N 26th Billings MT 59101

GINN, H. RAND, fish fertilizer company executive; b. Medford, Oreg., Dec. 4, 1942; s. William Shuler and Jean (Rand) G.; m. Judith Whitaker, July 14, 1967; children: William Rand, Andrew Y., Kathryn Jean. BA, Seattle U., 1971. Pres. Brand Maryman Co., Bellevue, Wash., 1971-79, Rand Co., Redmond, Wash., 1975-76; sec., dir. Ski Merchandising Corp., Holyoke, Mass., 1981-82; v.p. O'Day Broadcasting Wash., Seattle, 1978-85, CC Filson Co., Seattle, 1981-86; dir. Omega Photo Co., Bellevue, 1986—; v.p. Image Set, Mercer Island, Wash., 1986—; pres. Alaska Fish Fertilizer Co., Renton, Wash., 1987—. Elder Mercer Island Presbyn. Ch., 1987-90; dir. Cen. Puget Sound Coun. Camp Fire, Seattle, 1987-92, v.p., 1990-92; With U.S. Army, 1968-69, Vietnam. Home: 7376 SE 71st St Mercer Island WA 98040-5345 Office: Alaska Fish Fertilizer Co 865 Lind Ave SW Renton WA 98055-2304

GINN, SAM L., telephone company executive; b. St. Clair, Ala., Apr. 3, 1937; s. James Harold and Myra Ruby (Smith) G.; m. Meriann Lanford Vance, Feb. 2, 1963; children: Matthew, Michael, Samantha. B.S., Auburn U., 1959; postgrad., Stanford U. Grad. Sch. Bus., 1968. Various positions AT&T, 1960-78; with Pacific Tel. & Tel. Co., 1978—; exec. v.p. network Pacific Tel. & Tel. Co., San Francisco, 1979-81, exec. v.p. services, 1981-82, exec. v.p. network services, 1982, exec. v.p., strategic planning and adminstrn., 1983, vice chmn. bd., strategic planning and adminstrn., 1983-84; vice chmn. bd., group v.p. PacTel Cos. Pacific Telesis Group, San Francisco, 1984-86; vice chmn. bd., pres., chief exec. officer PacTel Corp. Pacific Telesis Group, San Francisco, 1986; pres., chief operating officer Pacific Telesis Group, San Francisco, 1987-88, chmn., chief exec. officer, 1988—; mem. adv. bd. Sloan program Stanford U. Grad. Sch. Bus., 1978-85, mem. internat. adv. council Inst. Internat. Studies; bd. dir. 1st Interstate Bank. Trustee Mills Coll., 1982—. Served to capt. U.S. Army, 1959-60. Sloan fellow, 1968. Republican. Clubs: Blackhawk Country (Danville, Calif.); World Trade, Pacific-Union; Rams Hill Country (Borrego Springs, Calif.), Bankers. Office: Pacific Telesis Group 130 Kearny St San Francisco CA 94108-4803*

GINSBURG, SEYMOUR, computer science educator; b. Bklyn., Dec. 12, 1927; s. William and Bessie (Setomer) G.; children—Diane, David. BS, CCNY, 1948; PhD, U. Mich., 1952, M.S., 1949. Asst. prof. math. U. Miami, Coral Gables, Fla., 1951-55; engr. Northrop Corp., Hawthorne, Calif., 1955-56, sr. rsch. engr., 1956-59; sect. head Hughes Aircraft, L.A., 1959-60; sr. mathematician System Devel. Corp., Santa Monica, Calif., 1960-71; Fletcher Jones prof. computer sci. U. So. Calif., L.A., 1966—. Author: An Introduction to Mathematical Machine Theory, 1962, The Mathematical Theory of Context-Free Languages, 1966, Algebraic and Automata-Theoretic Properties of Formal Languages, 1975; Contbr. articles to various publs. Served with U.S. Army, 1946-47. Guggenheim fellow, 1974-75. Fellow IEEE; mem. Am. Math. Soc., Assn. Computing Machinery, Soc. Indsl. and Applied Math., Math. Assn. Am. Jewish. Office: Univ So Calif Computer Sci Dept Los Angeles CA 90089

GIOIA, TED, musician, writer; b. Oct. 21, 1957; m. Tara Munjee, Aug. 17, 1991. AB, Stanford (Calif.) U., 1979, MBA, 1983; BA/MA, Oxford (Eng.) U., 1981. Founder Stanford U. Jazz Studies Program, 1987—. Author: The Imperfect Act, 1988 (Deems Taylor award 1989), West Coast Jazz, 1992; pianist (recording) The End of the Open Road, 1988. Home and Office: 405 El Camino Real # 110 Menlo Park CA 94025

GIORDANO, ANDREW ANTHONY, retired naval officer; b. Passaic, N.J., May 17, 1932; s. Samuel and Sarah (Pollara) G.; m. Felice Rochman, Mar. 3, 1957; children: Andrew Anthony, II, Dean James, Catherine Lisa. B.B.A. cum laude, CCNY, 1953; M.B.A. with distinction, Harvard U., 1962; student, Naval War Coll., 1965; L.H.D. (hon.), Nat. U., San Diego, 1982. Commd. ensign U.S. Navy, 1953, advanced through grades to rear adm., 1978; supply officer U.S.S. Kitty Hawk, Vietnam, 1968-70; ops. officer Aviation Supply Office, Phila., 1970-72; dir. material div. Office of Chief of Naval Ops., Washington, 1977-80; comdr. Naval Supply Systems Command, Chief Supply Corps, 1981-84; sr. v.p. control and ops. Donaldson's of Mpls. unit Allied Stores, 1984-87; exec. v.p., CFO Lamonts Corp., 1987-93; assoc. prof. acctg. George Washington U., 1966-67, Nat. U., 1970-72; prin. The Giordano Group, Alexandria, Va., 1993—; bd. dirs. Cherry, Webb & Touraine; hon. pres. Naval Supply Corps Assn. Decorated Legion of Merit, D.S.M. Roman Catholic. Club: Army-Navy Country (dir.). Office: 1811 S 24th St Arlington VA 22202

GIORDANO, GERARD RAYMOND, educator, author; b. West New York, N.J., July 25, 1946; m. Karen Fritz, July 5, 1975; children: Gabriel, Katherine Ann, Peter. BA, U. Hawaii, 1968; MA, Jersey City (N.J.) State Coll., 1973; PhD, Ohio State U., Columbus, 1975. Prof. W.Va. Coll. Grad. Studies, Charleston, 1975-76, N.Mex. State U., Las Cruces, 1976—; columnist Acad. Therapy, 1984-88. Author: (textbook) Teaching Writing to Students with Learning Disabilities, 1984; mem. editorial bd. Jour. Learning Disabilities, 1984—, Career Devel. in Exceptional Individuals, 1989—. With U.S. Army, 1968-70, Vietnam. Mem. Las Cruces Rotary. Home: 607 Lenox Ave Las Cruces NM 88005-1309 Office: NMex State U Dept Spl Edn PO Box 30001 Las Cruces NM 88003-8001

GIORDANO, PAUL GREGORY, lawyer; b. Indpls., July 6, 1956; s. Albert G. and Marie Jacqueline (Duffey) G. BA summa cum laude, Coll. Notre Dame, Belmont, Calif., 1978; JD, Santa Clara U., 1981. Bar: Nev. 1981, U.S. Dist. Ct. Nev. 1981, Calif. 1982, U.S. Dist. Ct. (no. dist.) Calif. 1982, U.S. Ct. Appeals (9th cir.) 1982. Assoc. Hall & Haveson, Reno, 1981-83; dep. dist. atty. Churchill County, Fallon, Nev., 1983-84; dep. atty. gen. State of Nev., Carson City, 1984-89; chief corp. securities div. Nev. Gaming Control Bd., Carson City, 1989-93; assoc. Lionel, Sawyer & Collins, Las Vegas, 1993—. Treas. Associated Students Coll. of Notre Dame, Belmont, Calif., 1977. Mem. ABA, Nev. Gaming Attys, Internat. Assn. of Gaming Attys. Republican. Roman Catholic. Home: 8455 W Sahara Ave # 173 Las Vegas NV 89117 Office: 1700 Bank of Am Plaza 300 S 4th St Las Vegas NV 89101

GIORDANO-MCCANLESS, ANGELA MARIA, military officer; b. Harvey, Ill., Mar. 14, 1965; d. Ronald Raymond Saunders (stepfather) and Claudia Giovanna (Camilli) Pound; m. Gregory Bryan McCanless, Sept. 7, 1992. BS, U.S. Mil. Acad., 1987. Commd. 2d lt. U.S. Army, 1987, advanced through grades to capt., 1991; terrain analysis platoon leader 63d engr. airborne co. U.S. Army, Ft. Bragg, N.C., 1988-89, co. exec. officer 175th engr. airborne co., 1989, bn. S-1 adjutant 30th engr. airborne bn., 1989-90, co. exec. officer 1st psychol. ops. airborne bn., 1990, team chief Latin Am. 1st psychol. ops. airborne bn., 1991-92; asst. S-3 constrn. officer 555th Combat Engr. Group, Ft. Lewis, Wash., 1992-93, ops. officer, 1993—. Author, editor (Spanish handbook): Psychological Operations, 1991. Decorated Joint Army Achievement medal, Commendation medal, 2 Army Achievement medals. Mem. Am. Mensa, Soc. Am. Mil. Engrs., Assn. Grads. U.S. Mil. Acad., NAFE, Nat. Geographic Soc. Republican. Roman Catholic. Home: 6054 61st Ave SE Lacey WA 98503

GIPSON, GORDON, publishing company executive; b. Caldwell, Idaho, Oct. 26, 1914; s. James Herrick and Esther (Sterling) G.; m. Tryntje Heeling, Dec. 27, 1961; children—Craig, Amy. Student, Coll. Idaho. With The Caxton Printers, Ltd., Caldwell, 1935—; treas. The Caxton Printers, Ltd., 1945—, v.p., 1964—, pub., 1965—, pres., 1991—. Served with USAAF, 1942-45. Club: Elk. Home: 2211 S 10th Ave Caldwell ID 83605-5221 Office: 312 Main St Caldwell ID 83605-3299

GIPSTEIN, MILTON FIVENSON, psychiatrist, lawyer; b. Schenectady, N.Y., Aug. 31, 1951; s. Milton and Evelyn (Mannes) G.; m. Carol Grace Zippin, July 21, 1974; children: Steven Mark, Richard Seth. BA, Columbia U., 1972; MD, SUNY, Syracuse, 1976; JD, U. N.C., 1981. Bar: Mass., 1982; diplomate Am. Bd. Psychiatry and Neurology. Resident psychiat. U. N.C., Chapel Hill, 1976-79; practice medicine specializing in psychiat. Dept. Corrections N.C., Raleigh, 1979-81; med. dir. Brockton (Mass.) Dist. Ct. Clinic, 1981-86, Bridgewater (Mass.) St. Hosp., 1986-87, Charter Hosp. of Aurora, Colo., 1988-91; med. dir. of forensic svcs. Columbine Psychiatric Hosp., Littleton, Colo., 1991—; cons. med.-legal N.C. Legal Aid Soc., Raleigh, 1978-79, forensic Mass. Treatment Ctr. Sexually Dangerous, Bridgewater, 1981-88, psychiat. La. Gov.'s Task Force Mental Health, Baton Rouge, 1982; med.-legal cons. Medical Evaluators, Inc., Denver, 1991—; legal counsel indigent clients mental health Com. Pub. Counsel Services, Boston, 1982-86; lectr. mental health legal advisors com. Law and Mental Health for Mass. Supreme Ct, Boston, 1986. Cons. Pub. Health Adv. Com. Town of Sharon, Mass., 1983-84, Mental Health Legal Advisors Com. Mass. Supreme Ct., Boston, 1985-86; v.p. community affairs Heights Elem. Sch. PTA, Sharon, 1983-84; adv. com. gifted and talented Cherry Creek High Sch., 1992—. Mem. ABA, Mass. Bar Assn., Am. Profl. Practice Assn. Office: Columbine Psychiatric Hosp 8565 S Poplar Way Highlands Ranch CO 80126-3600

GIPSTEIN, ROBERT MALCOLM, physician; b. Springfield, Mass., Mar. 29, 1936; s. Benjamin Louis and Dorothy (Weitzman) G.; 1 child, Jason Harold. BA, Wesleyan U., 1957; MD, Tufts U., 1961. Diplomate Am. Bd. Internal Medicine, Am. Bd. Nephrology. Research assoc. U. N.C., 1965-66; clin. assoc. UCLA Med. Ctr., 1964-65, clin. instr. medicine, 1968-75, asst. clin. prof., 1975-83, assoc. clin. prof., 1983—; dir. hemodial unit St. John's Hosp., Santa Monica, Calif., 1976-78; chief nephrology Santa Monica Hosp., 1975-82, dir. apheresis unit, 1980—, dir. hemodialysis unit, 1978—, chief dept. medicine, 1987—, chief of staff, also mem. exec. bd.; cons. plasmapheresis Wadsworth VA, Los Angeles, 1982. Contbr. articles to med. jours. Served to capt. M.C., U.S. Army, 1966-68. Nat. Kidney Found. grantee, 1980. Fellow ACP; mem. AMA, AAAS, Calif. Med. Assn., Los Angeles County Med. Assn., Am. Soc. Nephrology, Internat. Soc. Nephrology, Am. Soc. Internal Medicine, Internat. Soc. Artificial Organs, Am. Soc. Apheresis. Office: Pacific Med and Nephrology 146 Yacht Harbor Dr Osprey FL 34229

GIRARDEAU, MARVIN DENHAM, physics educator; b. Lakewood, Ohio, Oct. 3, 1930; s. Marvin Denham and Maude Irene (Miller) G.; m. Susan Jessica Brown, June 30, 1956; children—Ellen, Catherine, Laura. B.S., Case Inst. Tech., 1952; M.S., U. Ill., 1954; Ph.D., Syracuse U., 1958. NSF postdoctoral fellow Inst. Advanced Study, Princeton, 1958-59; research assoc. Brandeis U., 1959-60; staff mem. Boeing Sci. Research Labs., 1960-61; research assoc. Enrico Fermi Inst. Nuclear Studies, U. Chgo., 1961-63; assoc. prof. physics, research assoc. Inst. Theoretical Sci., U. Oreg., Eugene, 1963-67; prof. physics, research assoc. Inst. Theoretical Sci., U. Oreg., 1967—, dir., 1967-69, chmn. dept. physics, 1974-76. Contbr. articles to profl. jours. Recipient Humboldt Sr. U.S. Scientist award, 1984-85. NSF research grantee, 1965-79; ONR research grantee, 1981-87. Fellow Am. Phys. Soc.; mem. AAUP. Home: 2398 Douglas Dr Eugene OR 97405-1711 Office: U Oreg Dept Physics Eugene OR 97403

GIRARDIN, DAVID WALTER, chaplain, military officer; b. Detroit, July 9, 1951; s. David Louis and Anna Marie (Didyk) G.; m. Barbara Kimberly White, June 27, 1976; children: David John, Emily Grace. BA in Theology, Andrews U., Berrien Springs, Mich., 1982, MDiv, 1985. RN, Calif. RN Harper Grace Hosp., Detroit, 1973-74, Detroit Indsl. Clinic, 1974-76; physician's asst. thoracic surgery Harper Grace Hosp., Detroit Med. Ctr., 1976-80; commd. ensign USN, 1983, advanced through grades to lt., 1987, chaplain, 1983-87; chaplain naval mobile constrn. bn. THREE USN, Port Hueneume, Calif., 1986-89; chaplain Marine Corps Recruit Depot USN, San Diego, 1989-91, chaplain USS COWPENS (CG-63), 1991—; trainer, cons. Leadership, Edn. and Devel. Cons., Reynoldsburg, Ohio, 1985—; pastor Minn. Conf. Seventh-Day Adventists, Three River Falls, 1984-86. Contbr. articles to newspapers. Decorated Merirariow Svc. medal, Navy Achievement medal. Mem. Naval Res. Assn. (life), NRA (life), Adventist Chaplaincy Ministry, Adventist Mil. and Vets. Orgn.

GIROD, FRANK PAUL, surgeon; b. Orenco, Oreg., Aug. 13, 1908; s. Leon and Anna (Gerig)úG.; m. Nadine Mae Cooper, Aug. 26, 1939; children: Judith Anne, Janet Carol, Franklin Paul, John Cooper. AB, Willamette U., Salem, Oreg., 1929; MD, U. Colo., 1938. Diplomate Am. Bd. Family Practice. Tchr. physics and chemistry, athletic coach Cortez High Sch., Colo., 1929-34; intern U. Colo., Denver, 1938-39; resident surgeon U.S. Marine Hosp., Balt., 1939-41; pvt. practice specializing in family practice and surgery Lebanon, Oreg., 1946—. Trustee, sec. Blue Shield Ops., Oreg., 1950-60; grand marshal Lebanon Strawberry Festival, 1988; mem. bd. of Coun. of Govts. Sr. Svcs., 1991, 92. Decorated Bronze Star; recipient Disting. Svc. First Citizen award Lebanon, Oreg., 1989. Mem. AMA, Oreg. Med. Assn. (trustee), Am. Acad. Family Practice, Kiwanis (pres. 1947-48). Republican. Methodist. Home: 625 E Rose St Lebanon OR 97355-4544 Office: 325 Park St Lebanon OR 97355-3300

GIRTON, LANCE, economics educator; b. Brazil, Ind., July 20, 1942; s. John E. and Barbara (Wollard) G.; m. Kathy Marlock, Apr. 30, 1988; children: Derek, Lance Alan. BA in Econs., So. Ill. U., 1964; MA in Econs., U. Chgo., 1967, PhD in Econs., 1976. Instr. econs. Elmhurst (Ill.) Coll., 1968-69; asst. prof. econs. Mich. Technol. U., Houghton, 1969-71; economist internat. fin. div. Bd. Govs. FRS, Washington, 1971-78; prof. Pa. State U., College Park, 1983-84; vis. prof. U. Utah, Salt Lake City, 1977-78, prof., 1978—; assoc. professorial lectr. George Washington U., Washington, 1975-76; v.p., head rsch. Citicorp Homeowners Inc., St. Louis, 1985-86; cons. Investment Cos. Inst., Washington, 1981-83, World Bank, Washington, 1982—, Congl. Budget Office, Washington, 1980; Murphy Endowment Fund vis. scholar U. Wis., La Crosse, 1979; presenter papers, participant profl. meetings, 1973—; seminar presenter Brown U., U. Chgo., U. Pa., Pa. State U., UCLA, U. Colo., also others; referee profl. jours. Contbr. articles to profl. jours. Univ. scholar So. Ill. U., 1961-64; fellow NIMH, 1966-68. Mem. Am. Econ. Assn. Office: U Utah Dept Econs Salt Lake City UT 84112

GIRVIGIAN, RAYMOND, architect; b. Detroit, Nov. 27, 1926; s. Manoug and Margaret G.; m. Beverly Rae Bennett, Sept. 23, 1967; 1 son, Michael Raymond. AA, UCLA, 1947; BA with honors, U. Calif., Berkeley, 1950; M.A. in Architecture, U. Calif.-Berkeley, 1951. With Hutchason Architects, L.A., 1952-57; owner, prin. Raymond Girvigian, L.A., 1957-68, South Pasadena, Calif., 1968—; co-founder, advisor L.A. Cultural Heritage Bd., 1961—; vice chmn. Hist. Am. Bldgs. Survey, Nat. Park Svc., Washington, 1966-70; co-founder, mem. Calif. Hist. Resources Commn., 1970-78; co-founder, chmn. governing bd. Calif. Hist. Bldgs. Code, 1976-91, chmn. adminstrv. law, 1992-93, chmn. emeritus, 1993—; chmn. Calif. State Capitol Commn., 1985—. Co-editor, producer: film Architecture of Southern California for Los Angeles City Schs, 1965; historical monographs of HABS Landmarks, Los Angeles, 1958-80; historical monographs of Califs. State Capitol, 1974, Pan Pacific Auditorium, 1980, L.A. Meml. Coliseum, 1984, Powell Meml. Libr., UCLA, 1989; designed: city halls for Pico Rivera, 1963, LaPuente, 1966, Rosemead, 1968, Lawndale, 1970 (all Calif.); hist. architect for restoration of Calif. State Capitol, 1975-82, Workman/Temple Hist. Complex, City of Industry, Calif., 1974-81, Robinson Gardens Landmarks, Beverly Hills, Calif., 1983-92, Pasadena (Calif.) Ctrl. Libr., 1982-92, Mt. Pleasant House Mus., Heritage Sq., L.A., 1972—. Mem. St. James Episcopal Ch., South Pasadena, Calif. Served with AUS, 1945-46. Recipient

Archtl. Design medal U. Calif., Berkeley, 1947, Outstanding Achievement in Architecture award City of Pico Rivera, Calif., 1968, Neasham award Calif. Hist. Soc., 1982, Preservationist of Yr. award Calif. Preservation Found., 1987, L.A. Mayor's award for archtl. preservation, 1987, Gold Crown award for advancement of arts Pasadena Arts Coun., 1990, Golden Palm award Hollywood Heritage, 1990. Fellow AIA (Calif. state preservation chmn. 1970-75, state preservation coord. 1970-89, co-recipient nat. honor award for restoration Calif. State Capitol 1983, co-recipient honor award for restoration Pasadena Cen. Libr., Pasadena chpt. 1988); mem. Soc. Archtl. Historians, Nat. Trust for Historic Preservation, Calif. Preservation Found., Calif. Hist. Soc. Independent Democrat. Office: PO Box 220 1401 Fair Oaks Ave South Pasadena CA 91031-0220

GISH, ROBERT FRANKLIN, English language educator, writer; b. Albuquerque, Apr. 1, 1940; s. Jesse Franklin and Lillian J. (Fields) G.; m. Judith Kay Stephenson, June 20, 1961; children: Robin Elaine Butzier, Timothy Stephen, Annabeth. BA, U. N.Mex., Albuquerque, 1962, MA, 1967, PhD, 1972. Tchr. Albuquerque Pub. Schs., 1962-67; prof. U. No. Iowa, Cedar Falls, 1968-91; dir. ethnic studies, prof. English Calif. Poly. State U., San Luis Obispo, 1991—, prof., 1992—. Author: Hamlin Garland: Far West, 1976, Paul Horgan, 1983, Frontier's End: Life of Harvey Fergusson, 1988, William Carlos Williams: The Short Fiction, 1989, Songs of My Hunter Heart: A Western Kinship, 1992; First Horses: Stories of the New West, 1993, North Americn Native American Myths, 1993. Office: Calif Poly State U Ethnic Studies San Luis Obispo CA 93407

GIST, JACK LEE, broadcast executive; b. California, Mo., Aug. 22, 1953; s. Alfred Wade and Pauline (Barbour) G.; m. Pamela June Gabion, June 11, 1989; 1 child, Robert Gabion. Student, Harbor City C.C., 1978-80. Intern Sta. KNAC FM, Long Beach, Calif., 1973-75; program dir., air talent/music dir. Sta. KAOI Radio, Wailuku, Hawaii, 1986—. Mem. adv. com. Am. Lung Assn., Maui County, 1990-92; spokesperson Am. Heart Assn., Maui County, 1988-90, Maui Spl. Olympics, 1987-90. Office: Sta KAOI Radio 1900 Main St Wailuku HI 96793

GITCH, DAVID WILLIAM, healthcare facility administrator; b. Fredericksburg, Iowa, Dec. 25, 1939; s. Carl August and Myra Ann (Laabs) G.; m. Susan Virginia Frykholm, Aug. 24, 1963; children: Mark, Brad, Katie. BA in Bus. and Govt., Valparaiso (Ind.) U., 1962; MBA in Health Care Adminstrn., George Washington U., 1964. Adminstrv. resident Riverside Meth. Hosp., Indpls., 1963-64; adminstrv. asst. Community Hosp., Indpls., 1964-65, asst. dir., 1965-67, assoc. dir., 1967-68; assoc. dir. St. Paul-Ramsey Med. Ctr., St. Paul, 1968-73, chief operating officer, sr. assoc. dir., 1973-80, chief exec. officer, 1980-85; chief exec. officer, adminstr. Harborview Med. Ctr./U. Wash., Seattle, 1985-91; pres., chief exec. officer Harrison Meml. Hosp., Bremerton, Wash., 1991—; mem. clin. faculty U. Wash. Sch. Pub. Health, Seattle, 1985—, U. Minn., Mpls., 1980—. Mem. Com. on Affordable Health Care, Seattle, 1985—; chair Title XIX adv. com. State of Wash., Olympia, 1987-90; bd. dirs. Wash. Hosp. Assocs., 1987—, chmn., 1992-93; mem. exec. com. Nat. Assn. Pub. Hosps., 1988-91. Recipient Recognition award City of St. Paul, 1984. Mem. Am. Hosp. Assn. (ho. dels. 1990—, regional policy bd., chmn. elect metro hosp. governing coun.), Bremerton Area C. of C., Valparaiso U. Alumni Assn. (bd. 1992—). Office: Harrison Meml Hosp 2520 Cherry Ave Bremerton WA 98310-4229

GITLIN, TODD, sociologist, writer; b. N.Y.C., Jan. 6, 1943; s. Max and Dorothy (Siegel) G. BA, Harvard U., 1963; MA, U. Mich., 1966; PhD, U. Calif., Berkeley, 1977. Freelance writer Chgo. and San Francisco, 1965-70; lectr. New Coll. San Jose (Calif.) State U., 1970-76; with U. Calif., Santa Cruz, 1974-77; assoc. prof. sociology, dir. mass communications program U. Calif., Berkeley, 1983-87, prof. sociology, dir. mass communications program, 1987—; mem. editorial bd. Critical Studies in Mass Communication, Phila., 1984—; corr. editor Theory and Soc., St. Louis, 1980—; co-chair Pen-Am. Cen. West, San Francisco, 1987-88, mem. exec. com., 1988—. Author: Busy Being Born, 1974, The Whole World is Watching, 1980, Inside Prime Time, 1983, The Sixties: Years of Hope, Days of Rage, 1987, The Murder of Albert Einstein, 1992; co-author: Uptown: Poor Whites in Chicago, 1970; editor: Watching Television, 1987; contbg. editor: Tikkun mag., 1986-92; mem. editorial bd. Dissent mag., 1989—; columnist N.Y. Observer, 1992—. Bd. dirs. Campaign for Peace and Democracy, N.Y.C., 1986—. Rockefeller Found. fellow, 1980-81; NEH grantee, 1981-82, MacArthur Found. grantee, 1988-89; recipient Nonfiction award Bay Area Book Reviewers Assn., 1984. Mem. Am. Sociol. Assn., Am. Studies Assn. Office: U Calif Dept Sociology 410 Barrows Hall Berkeley CA 94720

GITNICK, GARY LEE, medical educator; b. Omaha, Jan. 13, 1939; s. Nathan Gitnick and Ann Hahn; m. Cherna Lee Gitnick; children: Neil, Kimberly, Jill, Tracy. BS, U. Chgo., 1960, MD, 1963. Prof. medicine UCLA Sch. Medicine, L.A., 1979—; dir. UCLA Health Care Programs, L.A., 1985—; chief of staff UCLA Med. Ctr., L.A., 1990—, chief divsn. digestive diseases, 1993—. Editor: Principles and Practice of Gastroenterolgy and Hepatology, 1989, also numerous others. Trustee Harvard-Westlake Sch., L.A.; pres. Fulfillment Fund. Recipient J. Arnold Bargen award Mayo Clinic, 1969. Fellow Am. Coll. Gastroenterolgy; mem. ACP, Am. Gastroenterological Assn., Rotary (Paul Harris fellow). Home: 17321 Rancho St Encino CA 91316-3946 Office: UCLA Health Plans 924 Westwood Blvd Ste 515 Los Angeles CA 90024-2926

GITTLEMAN, ARTHUR PAUL, computer science and engineering educator; b. Bklyn., Oct. 7, 1941; s. Morris and Clara (Konefsky) G.; m. Charlotte Marie Singleton, June 1, 1986; 1 child, Amanda Eve. BA, UCLA, 1962, MA, 1965, PhD, 1969. Asst. prof. Calif. State U., Long Beach, 1966-70, assoc. prof., 1970-75, chair, math. and computer sci. dept., 1978-83, prof. computer sci. and engring., 1975—. Author: History of Mathematics, 1975. Mem. IEEE Computer Soc., Assn. for Computing Machinery, Math. Assn. of Am., Phi Beta Kappa. Office: Calif State U 1250 N Bellflower Blvd Long Beach CA 90840-0001

GIULIANO, CONCETTO RICHARD, physicist; b. Wakefield, Mass., Mar. 2, 1935; s. Gaetano and Frances (Ferrara) G.; m. Minnie Pearl Doke, Mar. 24, 1952 (div. 1961); children: Richard Allen, Elaine Smith, Diana Toelle; m. Joanne Elizabeth DeForest, June 22, 1985. BS in Chemistry magna cum laude, U. So. Calif., L.A., 1957; PhD in Chem. Physics, Calif. Inst. Tech., 1961. Mgr. optical physics dept. Hughes Rsch. Labs., Malibu, Calif., 1961-89; dep. dir. Textron Def. Systems, Kihei, Hawaii, 1990-92; physicist/cons. Haiku, Hawaii, 1992-93; dir. alliance for photonic tech., rsch. prof. dept. EECE U. N.M., Albuquerque, 1992—; faculty short courses UCLA, U. So. Calif.; tutorial lectr. MIT, Trondheim U., U. Ariz., U. Calif.-San Diego, U.S. Naval Rsch. Lab., Los Alamos Nat. Lab.; lectr. in field. Contbr. 50 articles to profl. jours.; patentee (5) in field. NSF fellow, 1957-61. Fellow IEEE, Optical Soc. Am., Lasers and Electro Optic Soc. of IEEE (pres. 1990, bd. govs. 1987-89); mem. Conf. on Lasers and Electro Optics (chmn. 1985, 87), Sigma Xi, Phi Beta Kappa. Home: 170 Camino Barranca Placitas NM 87043

GIVANT, PHILIP JOACHIM, mathematics educator, real estate investment executive; b. Mannheim, Fed. Republic of Germany, Dec. 5, 1935; s. Paul and Irmy (Dinse) G.; m. Kathleen Joan Porter, Sept. 3, 1960; children: Philip Paul, Julie Kathleen, Laura Grace. BA in Math., San Francisco State U., 1957, MA in Math., 1960. Prof. math. San Francisco State U., 1958-60, Am. River Coll., Sacramento, 1960—; pres. Grove Enterprises, Sacramento, 1961—; pres. Am. River Coll. Acad. Senate, Sacramento, 1966-69; v.p. Acad. Senate for Calif. Community Colls., 1974-77; mem. State Chancellor's Acad. Calendar Com., Sacramento, 1977-79. Founder, producer Annual Sacramento Blues Music Festival, 1976—; producer Sta. KVMR weekly Blues music program, 1978—, music festivals Folsom Prison, 1979-81, Vacaville Prison, 1985. Pres. Sacramento Blues Festival, Inc., 1985—; mem. Lake Tahoe Keys Homeowners Assn., 1983—, Sea Ranch Homeowners Assn., 1977—. Recipient Spl. Service Commendation, Acad. Senate Calif. Community Colls., 1977, Spl. Human Rights award Human Rights-Fair Housing Commn., Sacramento, 1985, W.C. Handy award for Blues Promoter of Yr. Nat. Blues Found., Memphis, 1987, 1st Critical Achievement award Sacramento Area Mus. Awards Commn., 1992. Mem. Faculty Assn. Calif. Community Colls., Am. Soc. Psychical Research, Nat. Blues Found. (adv. com., W.C. Handy Blues Promoter of Yr. 1987). Home and Office: 3809 Garfield Ave Carmichael CA 95608-6631

GIVENS, WILLIAM L., author; b. Cleve., Miss., Apr. 7, 1940; s. Ottis Leon and Rose Jane (Reed) Givens Davis. BA, Delta State U., 1961. Asst. advt. mgr. E. L. Bruce Co., Memphis, 1965-69; account supr. Lake-Spiro-Sherman Advt., Memphis, 1969-75; ptnr. Image Concepts, Memphis, 1975; v.p. Lucky Heart Cosmetics, Memphis, 1975-78; mem. adv. bd. Memphis Mag., 1978-84. Author: Flying With Loran-C, 1985, Film Flubs, 1990, Son of Film Flubs, 1991, Film Flubs: The Sequel, 1992, Best of Film Flubs, 1993, Lost Hollywood: Tales From the Cutting Room Floor, 1994; sr. editor Persona Video Mag., L.A., 1989; editor Animation Mag., L.A., 1989-90. Bd. dirs. L.A. Hist. Theatre Found., 1987—, Opera Memphis, 1983-84; mem. communications adv. com. Episcopal Diocese of L.A., 1985—; pres. Opera Memphis Chorus, 1984; founder L.A. Hist. Theatre Found.; mem. communcations com. All Saints' Episcopal Ch., Beverly Hills, Calif. Recipient 1st place-editorial award So. Lit. Festival, 1961, Aviation-Space Writers Assn., 1985. Mem. Motion Picture Assn. Am. (accredited press corp. 1986—). Democrat. Home and Office: 434 S Maple Dr Beverly Hills CA 90212-4714

GLAD, DAIN STURGIS, aerospace engineer; b. Santa Monica, Calif., Sept. 17, 1932; s. Alma Emanuel and Maude La Verne (Morby) G.; BS in Engring., UCLA, 1954; MS in Elec. Engring., U. So. Calif., 1963. Registered profl. engr., Calif. m. Betty Alexandra Shainoff, Sept. 12, 1954 (dec. 1973); 1 child, Dana Elizabeth; m. Carolyn Elizabeth Giffen, June 8, 1979. Electronic engr. Clary Corp., San Gabriel, Calif., 1957-58; with Aerojet Electro Systems Co., Azusa, Calif., 1958-72; with missile systems div. Rockwell Internat., Anaheim, Calif., 1973-75; with Aerojet Electrosystems, Azusa, 1975-84; with support systems div. Hughes Aircraft Co., 1984-90; with Electro-Optical Ctr. Rockwell Internat. Corp., 1990—. Contbr. articles to profl. jours. Ensign, U.S. Navy, 1954-56; lt. j.g. Res., 1956-57. Mem. IEEE, Calif. Soc. Profl. Engrs., Soc. Info. Display. Home: 1701 Marengo Ave South Pasadena CA 91030-4818 Office: Rockwell Internat Corp Electro-Optical Ctr 3370 E Miraloma Ave Anaheim CA 92803-3105

GLAD, SUZANNE LOCKLEY, museum director; b. Rochester, N.Y., Oct. 2, 1929; d. Alfred Allen and Lucille A. (Watson) Lockley; m. Edward Newman Glad, Nov. 7, 1953; children: Amy, Lisanne Glad Lantz, William E. BA, Sweet Briar Coll., 1951; MA, Columbia U., 1952. Exec. dir. New York State Young Reps., N.Y.C., 1951-57; mem. pub. rels. staff Dolphin Group, L.A., 1974-83; scheduling sec. Gov.'s Office, Sacramento, 1983-87; dep. dir. Calif. Mus. Sci. and Industry, L.A., 1987—. Mem. Calif. Rep. League, Flintridge, 1969—; mem. Assistance League of Flintridge, 1970—, Flintridge Guild Children's Hosp., 1969-89. Mem. Am. Assn. Mus., Sweet Briar Alumnae of So. Calif. (pres. 1972), Phi Beta Kappa, Tau Phi. Episcopalian. Office: Calif Mus Sci and Industry 700 State Dr Los Angeles CA 90037-1210

GLADNER, MARC STEFAN, lawyer; b. Seattle, July 18, 1952; s. Jules A. and Mildred W. (Weller) G.; m. Susanne Tso (div. Feb. 1981); m. Michele Marie Hardin, Sept. 12, 1981; 1 child, Sara Megan. Student, U. Colo., 1970-73; JD, Southwestern U., 1976. Bar: Ariz. 1976, Navajo Tribal Ct. 1978. Law clk. jud. br. Navajo Nation, Window Rock, Ariz., 1976-77, gen. counsel jud. br., 1977-79; pvt. practice law Phoenix, 1979-83; ptnr. Seplow, Rivkind & Gladner, Phoenix, 1983-86, Crosby & Gladner, P.C., Phoenix, 1986—; adj. instr. Coll. Ganado, Ariz., 1978-79. Democrat. Jewish. Office: Crosby & Gladner PC 111 W Monroe St Ste 706 Phoenix AZ 85003-1720

GLADYSZ, JOHN ANDREW, chemistry educator; b. Kalamazoo, Aug. 13, 1952; s. Edward Matthew and Margean Alice (Worst) G. BS in Chemistry, U. Mich., 1971; PhD in Chemistry, Stanford (Calif.) U., 1974. Asst. prof. U. Calif., L.A., 1974-82; assoc. prof. U. Utah, Salt Lake City, 1982-85, prof., 1985—. Assoc. editor Chem. Revs., 1984—; mem. editorial bd. Organometallics, 1990-92, Bull. de la Sociēté Chemique de France, 1992—. Alfred P. Sloan Found. fellow, 1980-84; Camile and Henry Dreyfus scholar and grantee, 1980-85; Arthur C. Cope scholar, 1988; recipient U. Utah Disting. Rsch. award, 1992. Mem. AAAS, Am. Chem. Soc., The Chem. Soc., Alpha Chi Sigma, Sigma Xi. Home: 1149 Charlton Ave Salt Lake City UT 84106-2603 Office: U Utah Dept of Chemistry Salt Lake City UT 84112

GLASER, DONALD A(RTHUR), physicist; b. Cleveland, Ohio, Sept. 21, 1926; s. William Joseph Glaser. B.S., Case Inst. Tech., 1946, Sc.D., 1959; Ph.D., Cal. Inst. Tech., 1949. Prof. physics U. Mich., 1949-59; prof. physics U. Calif., Berkeley, 1959—; prof. physics, molecular and cell biology, and neurobiology U. Calif., 1964—. Recipient Henry Russel award U. Mich., 1955, Charles V. Boys prize Phys. Soc., London, 1958, Nobel prize in physics, 1960, Gold Medal award Case Inst. Tech., 1967, Golden Plate award Am. Acad. of Achievement, 1989; NSF fellow, 1961, Guggenheim fellow, 1961-62, fellow Smith-Kettlewell Inst. for Vision Rsch, 1983-84. Fellow AAAS, Fedn. Am. Scientists, The Exploratorium (bd. dirs.), Royal Soc. Sci., Royal Swedish Acad. Sci., Assn. Rsch. Vision and Ophthalmology, Neurosci. Inst., Am. Physics Soc. (prize 1959); mem. Nat. Acad. Scis., Internat. Acad. Sci., Sigma Xi, Tau Kappa Alpha, Theta Tau. Office: U Calif Dept Molecular & Cell Biology Neurobiology Divsn Stanley Hall Berkeley CA 94720

GLASER, JOHN WILLIAM, health system ethicist; b. Wheeling, W.Va., Apr. 15, 1933; s. Clarence Martin and Margaret Mary (Nordman) G.; m. Mary Ellen Brodhead, Aug. 4, 1972; children: Brian, Meg. BA, Xavier U., 1955; MA in English Lit., Loyola U., 1957; STD, Profl. Sch. Theology, Frankfurt, Germany, 1970; MA in Psychology, U. Detroit, 1976. Asst. prof. moral theology St. Mary of Lake Seminary, Mundelein, Ill., 1969-71; asst. prof. religious studies U. Detroit, 1971-76; therapist Midwest Mental Health Clinic, Dearborn, Mich., 1976-79; dir. program of ethics Sisters of Mery Health Corp., Farmington Hills, Mich., 1979-86; dir. Ctr. for Healthcare Ethics St. Joseph Health System, Orange, Calif., 1986—. Author: Caring for Special Child, 1984; author/editor videos in field, 1982—; photographer: Paulist Press Books, 1972-80; contbr. articles to profl. jours., chpts. to books in field. Bd. dirs., chmn. Share Our Selves, Costa Mesa, Calif., 1990-92; bd. dirs. St. Joseph Ballet Co., Santa Ana, Calif., 1989-92. Mem. Soc. Christian Ethics, Cath. Theol. Soc. of Am., Hastings Ctr., Soc. Health Human Values. Democrat. Roman Catholic. Home: 2106 N Millwood Santa Ana CA 92701

GLASIER, ALICE GENEVA See KLOSS, GENE

GLASRUD, BRUCE ALDEN, university educator; b. Plainview, Minn., Sept. 20, 1940. BA, Luther Coll., Decorah, Iowa, 1962; MA, Ea. N.Mex. U., 1963; PhD, Tex. Tech. U., 1968. Teaching asst. Tex. Tech. U., Lubbock, 1963-64, 65-68; instr. history Tex. Luth. Coll., Seguin, 1964-65; asst. prof. Calif. State U., Hayward, 1968-73; assoc. prof. Calif. State U., 1973-78, prof., 1978—, chair history dept., 1977-81, 84-86, 92-93, prof. history, 1984-86; cons. Panthera Press, Castro Valley, Calif., 1990, Quercus Pub., 1987-90, African Americans in Tex. Conf., 1990-93, Midwest Ctr. for Equal Edn., St. Louis, 1973-78; dir. U. Union Calif. State Univ., 1989-91, CSUH Found., 1991-93; sec. Exec. Com. Acad. Senate, Long Beach, Calif., 1986-87. Coauthor: Promises to Keep, 1972, The Northwest Mosaic, 1977, Race Relations in British North America, 1981; contbr. articles and book reviews to profl. jours. Mem. exec. com. United Profs. Calif., Hayward, 1975-77. Recipient Outstanding Prof. of Yr. award Luther Coll. 1993, Dist. Svc. award, 1992, Meritorious Performance and Profl. Promise award, 1987, 90; NEH summer grantee, 1981; fellow Ea. N.Mex. U., 1962-63. Mem. ACLU, NAACP, Am.-Hist. Assn. (chair local arrangement 1978), Tex. State Hist. Assn., Western History Assn., Calif. Faculty Assn. (pres. 1985-87, del. 1985-88), Calif. History Soc., Immigration History Soc., Amnesty Internat. Democrat. Lutheran. Home: 5030 Seaview Ave Castro Valley CA 94546-2440 Office: Calif State U Dept History Hayward CA 94542

GLASS, JAMES CLIFFORD, college dean, science and mathematics educator; b. L.A., Sept. 26, 1937; s. Chester Edward and Lois Jeanette (Hufford) G.; m. Elizabeth Ann Yager, June 20, 1959 (div. Feb. 1983); children: Becky, Steven, Mary Beth, Sarah; m. Gail Ann Gunner, June 24, 1985. AA, Long Beach Community Coll., 1956; BA in Physics, U. Calif., Berkeley, 1960; MS in Physics, Calif. State U., Northridge, 1965; PhD in Physics, U. Nev., 1968. Assoc. physicist Lawrence Berkeley Lab., 1960-61; physicist Rocketdyne, Canoga Park, Calif., 1961-64; sr. physicist Electro Optical Systems, Inc., Pasadena, Calif., 1964-65; from. asst. prof. to prof. physics N.D. State U., Fargo, 1968-88, chair physics dept., 1974-85, chair engring. sci. dept., 1985-88, prof. engring. physics, 1985-88; dean Coll. Sci., Math. and Tech. Ea. Wash. U., Cherry, 1988—; cons. in field; referee Am. Jour. Physics, 1978—, NSF, NIH, 1978—. Sec. Lake Agassiz Arts Coun., Fargo, N.D., 1986-88; pres. bd. dirs. Spokane Ballet, 1989-90; active F-M Community Theatre, Fargo, 1983-88; vol. Spokane Food Bank, 1988—. Mem. Am. Assn. Physics Tchrs., Am. Phys. Soc., Rotary, Sigma Pi Sigma. Republican. Methodist. Office: Ea Wash U MS 178 Cheney WA 99004

GLASSER, CHARLES EDWARD, academic administrator; b. Chgo., Apr. 3, 1940; s. Julius J. and Hilda (Goldman) G.; m. Hannah Alex, Mar. 8, 1987; children: Gemma Maria, Julian David. BA in History, Denison U., 1961; MA in Polit. Sci., U. Ill., 1967; JD, John F. Kennedy U., 1970. Bar: Calif. 1970, U.S. Ct. Appeals (9th cir.) 1970. Pvt. practice Hineser, Spellberg & Glasser, Pleasant Hill, Calif., 1971-77; dean Sch. Law John F. Kennedy U., Orinda, Calif., 1977-83, pres., 1990—; v.p., gen. counsel Western Hosp. Corp., Emeryville, Calif., 1983-90. Author: The Quest for Peace, 1986. Mem. ABA, Calif. Bar Assn. Office: John F Kennedy U 12 Altarinda Rd Orinda CA 94563-2689

GLASSER, WILLIAM, psychiatrist, educator; b. Cleve., May 11, 1925; children: Joseph, Alice, Martin. BS, Case Western-Reserve U., Cleve., 1945, MA, 1948, MD, 1953; LHD, U. San Francisco, 1990. Pres. Inst. for Reality Therapy, L.A., 1967—. Author: Reality Therapy, 1965, Schools Without Failure, 1969, Control Theory, 1984, The Quality School, 1990. Office: Inst for Reality Therapy 7301 Medical Ctr Dr # 104 Canoga Park CA 91307

GLASSETT, TIM SCOTT, lawyer; b. Salt Lake City, Mar. 29, 1956; s. Joseph M. and Joleen Mildred (Ames) G.; m. Janet Rankin, July 11, 1987. BS cum laude, U. Utah, 1978, MBA, 1981, JD, 1981. Bar: Calif. 1981. Assoc. Adams, Duque & Hazeltine, L.A., 1981-85; corp. counsel H.F. Ahmanson & Co., L.A., 1985—, v.p., 1986, sr. v.p., asst. sec., 1987—, asst. gen. counsel, 1993—; asst. gen. counsel corp. sec. Home Savs. of Am., FSB. Sr. editor Utah Law Rev., 1980-81. William H. Leary scholar U. Utah, 1981. Mem. ABA (fed. regulation securities com. 1983—, Calif. co-chmn. standing com. on membership young lawyers div. 1984-91), State Bar Calif. (resolutions com., conv. dels. 1989), Calif Bus. Roundtable (dep. mem. 1992—), Order of Coif, Sigma Chi. Republican. Office: HF Ahmanson & Co 4900 Rivergrade Rd Baldwin Park CA 91706-1438

GLASSMAN, ARTHUR JOSEPH, software engineer; b. N.Y.C., Apr. 4, 1948; s. Max Samuel and Ruth Rae (Gold) G. SB in Physics, MIT, 1968; MS, Yale U., 1969; PhD, Columbia U., 1977. Sr. programmer Cubic, San Diego, 1978-79; engr. Linkabit, San Diego, 1979-80; sr. scientist Jaycor, San Diego, 1980-91; sr. software engr. SuperSet, San Diego, 1992—. Mem. IEEE, Am. Phys. Soc., Am. Geophys. Union, Am. Stats. Assn.

GLATZER, ROBERT ANTHONY, marketing and sales executive; b. N.Y.C., May 19, 1932; s. Harold and Glenna (Beaber) G.; m. Paula Rosenfeld, Dec. 20, 1964; m. Mary Ann Murphy, Dec. 31, 1977; children: Gabriela, Jessica, Nicholas. BA, Haverford Coll., 1954. Br. store dept. mgr. Bloomingdale's, N.Y.C., 1954-56; media buyer Ben Sackheim Advt., N.Y.C., 1956-59; producer TV commls. Ogilvy, Benson & Mather Advt., N.Y.C., 1959-62; dir. broadcast prodn. Carl Ally Advt., N.Y.C., 1962-63; owner Chronicle Prodns., N.Y.C., 1963-73; dir. Folklife Festival, Smithsonian Inst., Washington, 1973, Expo 74 Corp., Spokane, Wash., 1973-74; pres. Robert Glatzer Assocs., Spokane, 1974—; ptnr. Delany/Glatzer Advt., Spokane, 1979-84; dir. sales/mktg. Pinnacle Prodns., Spokane; adj. faculty Ea. Wash. U., 1987—. Bd. dirs. Riverfront Arts Festival, 1977-78; bd. dirs. Comprehensive Health Planning Council, 1975-78, Spokane Quality of Life Council, 1976-82, Allied Arts of Spokane, 1976-80, Art Alliance Wash. State, 1977-81, Spokane chpt. ACLU, 1979-83, Wash. State Folklife Council, 1983—; commr. Spokane Arts, 1987—; mem. Spokane Community Devel. Bd., 1988—; mem. Shorelines Update Commn., 1988—. Recipient CINE Golden Eagle award (2). Mem. Dirs. Guild Am. Democrat. Jewish. Author: The New Advertising, 1970; co-scenarist Scorpio and other TV prodns. Office: N 10200 Newport Hwy Spokane WA 99218

GLAZEBROOK, CARLA RAE, city official; b. Burbank, Calif., Sept. 12, 1958; d. Raymond A. and Norma J. (Anderson) Colbern; m. Edward L. Glazebrook, June 7, 1980; children: Blake Edward, Grant Michael, Taryn Nicole. BBS, Calif. State U., Fresno, 1980. Real estate agt., mgr., Fresno, 1980-82; dir. western region Assn. for Internat. Practical Tng., Fresno, 1982-91; pres. Group Mgmt. Alternatives, Fresno, 1991-92; dep. city mgr., asst. to mayor City of Fresno, 1992—. Pres. Leadership Fresno Alumni Assn., 1990—; mem. Tree Fresno, 1989—; treas., vol. local elections, Fresno, 1985—; mem. Police Activities League. Mem. Calif. Assn. Leadership Programs (bd. dirs.), Nat. Assn. for Community Leadership (bd. dirs.), Fresno C. of C., World Affairs Coun., Kappa Alpha Theta (v.p. corp. bd. 1979—). Republican.

GLAZER, GUILFORD, real estate developer; b. Knoxville, Tenn., July 17, 1921; s. Aaron Usher and Ida (Bressoff) G.; children: Emerson, Erika Glazer; m. Diane Pregerson, Jan. 29, 1967. Mech. Engr., George Wash. U., 1939; Metallurgy, U. Louisville, 1943. Bd. dirs. The Torrance (Calif.) Co., 1990, Del Amo Fashion Ctr., Torrance, Calif., 1990; owner operator Allegheny Ctr., Pitts; bd. dirs. First Interstate Bank, L.A., Rand-UCLA Ctr. Study Soviet Internat. Behavior, L.A. developer various shopping ctrs. and office bldgs. in U.S. Pres. Reagan Libr. Found., Nixon Libr. Foun.; trustee L.A. Holocaust Meml., Jerusalem Found., Stop Cancer, Bell Shelter for Homeless; founder Ford's Theatre, Washington, Am. Friends of the Israel Def. Force; mem. Wilshire Blvd. Temple, L.A.County Mus. Art, United Jewish Welfare, Unified Fund Music Ctr. With U.S. Armed Forces, 1942-45. Recipient Hon. Fellow U. Tel Aviv. Mem. Nat. Conf. Soviet Jewry, World Affairs Coun., Tamarisk Club, B'nai B'rith, Hillcrest Country Club, Monterey Country Club, Palm Desert Club, Masons. Jewish. Office: Guilford Glazer & Assoc Bldg 1555 1901 Avenue Of The Stars Los Angeles CA 90067-6016

GLAZER, MIRIYAM (MYRA), literature educator; b. N.Y.C., Jan. 15, 1945; d. Harry and Ida (Soroka) Glazer; m. Amiel Schotz, April 16, 1970 (div. 1980); 1child, Avigail. BA, Antioch Coll., 1966; PhD, Brandeis U., 1973. Chmn. Dept. Foreign Lits. and Langs. Ben Gurion U., Beersheba, Israel, 1974-79; v.p. Inst. Advancement Sierra U. Without Walls, Santa Monica, Calif., 1985-87; assoc. prof. lit. and chmn. English Dept. Lee Coll, U. of Judaism, L.A., 1988—, assoc. dean, 1993—; dir. Dovtort Writers' Inst., 1990—; visiting scholar UCLA, 1979-80; corp. sec. STATECRAFT, Boise, Idaho, 1989—; cons. BETA Internat., Santa Monica, 1987—. Editor: Burning Air and Clear Mind: Contemporary Israeli Women Poets, 1981; contbr. articles to profl. jours. Organizer Beersheba Women's Health Collective, 1974-79, Israel Feminist Movement, 1975-79; participant Consultation on Conscience, Washington, 1989. Woodrow Wilson Nat. fellow, 1966; Nat. Inst. Arts and Humanities writing award, 1966; Treasures of Judaica rsch. fellow, U. Judaism, 1989-90, 90-91. Mem. MLA, Assn. Am. Colls., Am. Assn. Religions, Popular Culture Assn., Nat. Women's Studies Assn., Jewish Studies Assn., Bat Kol, Feminist Jewish Retreat. Office: Lee College U Judaism Mulholland Dr Los Angeles CA 90077-1708

GLAZER, REA HELENE See KIRK, REA HELENE

GLEASON, ALFRED M., business executive; b. 1930; married. Student, U. Oreg. With Pacific Power & Light Co. Inc., Portland, Oreg., from 1949, asst. to v.p., 1952-65, mgr. pub. accounts, 1965-68, v.p., 1968-76; pres. Pacific Telecom, Inc. (formerly Telephone Utilities, Inc.), Vancouver, Wash., 1973-82, chmn., from 1982, chief exec. officer, 1973-86, also bd. dirs.; pres. parent co., PacifiCorp, Portland, 1985-92; CEO parent co. PacifiCorp, Portland, 1989-92; bd. dirs. Comdial Corp., Blount Inc., Tektronix, Legacy Health, Fred Meyer, Inc. Office: Pacificorp 700 NE Multnomah Portland OR 97204

GLEASON, DOUGLAS RENWICK, marketing professional; b. Worcestor, Mass., Oct. 27, 1956; s. Sherman M. and Dolores E. (Murad) G. BA, Stanford U., 1978; MBA, UCLA, 1982. Asst. product mgr. Pepsi USA, Purchase, N.Y., 1982-83, assoc. product mgr., 1983-85; product mgr. Carnation Co., Los Angeles, 1985-87; dir. promotion Walt Disney Home Video, Burbank, Calif., 1987-90; dir. film licensing The Walt Disney Co., Burbank, 1990-91; dir. promotion Twentieth Century Fox, Beverly Hills, Calif.,

1991—. Mem. Beta Gamma Sigma. Office: Twentieth Century Fox PO Box 900 Beverly Hills CA 90213

GLEBERMAN, MORTON JEROME, consumer electronics marketing company executive; b. N.Y.C., June 14, 1931; s. Benjamin and Gussie (Geller) G.; divorced; childdren: Lisa, Jodi. Student, NYU, 1950, 51, 54, RCA Insts., N.Y.C., 1956. V.p., gen. mdse. mgr. Lafayette Radio Electronics, Syosset, N.Y., 1957-76; v.p., gen. mgr. Superscope Marantz, Chatsworth, Calif., 1976-81; v.p. mdse. Video Concepts, Denver, 1981-86; v.p. mktg. Ladd Electronics, L.A., 1981-90; sr. v.p. PRS Corp., L.A., 1990—. With U.S. Army, 1952-53. Named Man of Yr. in consumer electronics EIA-United Jewish Appeal, 1975. Office: PRS Corp 10595 Ashton Ave Ste 101 Los Angeles CA 90024

GLEDHILL, BARTON LEVAN, veterinarian; b. Phila., Sept. 29, 1936; s. Albert and Kathryn Barton (LeVan) G.; m. Marianne Palmer, Dec. 19, 1959; children: Christopher, Rebecca. BS, Pa. State U., 1958; VMD, U. Pa., 1961; PhD, Royal Vet. Coll., Stockholm, 1966. Lic. veterinarian, Pa. Asst. prof. U. Pa., Phila., 1966-69; assoc. prof. U. Pa., 1969-72; group leader Lawrence Livermore (Calif.) Nat. Lab., 1973-75, sect. leader, 1975-80, dep. div. leader, 1980-82, div. leader, 1982-91, dep. assoc. dir., 1991—; cons. in field; lectr. in field; Ortho lectr. McMaster U., Ont., 1984; Tap Pharms. lectr. Am. Fertil Soc., Washington, 1990; disting. vis. prof. U. Buenos Aires, Argentina, 1991; Associated We. Univs./U.S. Dept. Energy Disting. lectr., 1992. Contbr. articles to profl. jours.; patentee in field. Active Boy Scouts Am., 1978—. Recipient Alumni Fellows award Pa. State U., 1993. Mem. Am. Coll. Theriogeneologists (pres. 1977), Soc. for Analytical Cytology (pres. 1991—), Am. Soc. Study Breeding Soundness (pres. 1972). Home: 21 Saratoga Ct Alamo CA 94507-2228 Office: Lawrence Livermore Nat Lab PO Box 5507 Livermore CA 94551-5507

GLEESON, JEREMY MICHAEL, physician; b. Napier, Hawkes Bay, N.Z., Nov. 20, 1953; came to U.S., 1984; s. Gerald Lynch and Helen Isobel (Benzeval) G.; m. Susan Jeryl Gladwell, Aug. 31, 1952; children: Catherine, Emily, Nicholas, Timothy. BSc, U. Auckland, N.Z., 1975, MB, ChB, 1978. Diplomate Am. Bd. Internal Medicine, Am. Bd. Endocrinology and Metabolism. Resident in medicine U. Auckland, 1979-84; chief resident in medicine U. Utah, Salt Lake City, 1984-85, fellow in endocrinology, 1985-88; assoc. investigator VA, Salt Lake City, 1988-89; endocrinologist Lovelace Med. Ctr., Albuquerque, 1989—, chmn. endocrinology, 1992—. Fellow Royal Australasian Coll. of Physicians; mem. Am. Coll. Physicians, Am. Diabetes Assn., Assn. Clin. Endocrinologists, Endocrine Soc. Office: 5400 Gibson Blvd SE Albuquerque NM 87108-4763

GLENN, BELINDA, construction engineer; b. Garden City, Kans., June 27, 1963; d. Everett Lee and Karin Kaye (Coerber) G. BS in Constrn. Sci., Kans. State U., 1986. Surveyor Coleman Indsl. Constrn. Co., Wichita, Kans., 1986-87, foreman, 1987; field engr. Herzog Contracting Corp., L.A., 1987-89; project engr. Herzog Contracting Corp., Long Beach, Calif., 1989-90, Sacramento, 1990-92; asst. constrn. engr. Sacramento (Calif.) Regional Transit Dist., 1992—. Mem. Kans. State U. Alumni Assn. Lutheran. Home: PO Box 1038 Gridley CA 95948-1038 Office: Sacramento Regional Transit Dist 2811 O St Sacramento CA 95816

GLENN, CONSTANCE WHITE, art museum director, educator, consultant; b. Topeka, Oct. 4, 1933; d. Henry A. and Madeline (Stewart) White; m. Jack W. Glenn, June 19, 1955; children: Laurie Glenn Buckle, Caroline Glenn Galey, John Christopher. BFA, U. Kans., 1955; postgrad., U. Mo., 1964-69; MA, Calif. State U., 1974. Dir. Univ. Art Mus. & Mus. Studies program, from lectr. to prof. Calif. State U., Long Beach, 1973—; art cons. Archtl. Digest, L.A., 1980-89. Author: Jim Dine Drawings, 1984, Roy Lichtenstein; Landscape Sketches, 1986, Wayne Thiebaud: Private Drawings, 1988, Robert Motherwell: The Dedalus Sketches, 1988, James Rosenquist: Time Dust: The Complete Graphics 1962-92, 1993; contbg. editor: Antiques and Fine Arts, 1991—. Vice-chair Adv. Com. for Pub. Art, Long Beach, 1990—; chair So. Calif. adv. bd. Archives Am. Art, L.A., 1980-90; mem. adv. bd. ART/LA, 1986—, chair, 1992; mem. adv. bd. Decorative Arts Study Ctr., San Juan Capistrano, Calif., 1990—. Recipient Outstanding Contbn. to Profession award Calif. Mus. Photography, 1986. Mem. Am. Assn. Mus., Assn. Art Mus. Dirs., Coll. Art Assn., Art Table, Long Beach Pub. Corp. for the Arts (arts adminstr. of yr. 1989), Long Beach Opera Ring, Kappa Alpha Theta. Office: Univ Art Mus 1250 Bellflower Blvd Long Beach CA 90840

GLENN, DANIEL O., lawyer; b. Elma, Wash., Aug. 1, 1942; m. Carleen Glenn. BA, Cen. Wash. U., 1963; JD, U. Wash., 1972. Bar: Wash., 1972, U.S. Dist. Ct. (W. dist.) Wash., 1972, U.S. Supreme Ct., 1974. Instr. Olympia (Wash.) Schs., 1963-69; ptnr. Buzzard, Brown & Glenn, Olympia, 1972-74, Buzzard & Glenn, Olympia, 1974-76, Buzzard, Glenn & Henderson, Olympia, 1976-77, 85-89, Buzzard, Glenn, Henderson & Morris, Olympia, 1977-85, Glenn, Henderson & Hoffman, Olympia, 1989-92, Glenn & Hoffman, Olympia, 1992—. Mem. ABA, Wash. State Trial Lawyers Assn., Wash. State Bar Assn. Office: Glenn & Hoffman PS 2424 Evergreen Park Dr SW Olympia WA 98502

GLENN, GARY RICHARD, county commissioner; b. Hickory, N.C., June 16, 1958; s. James Richard and Johnnie (Cash) G.; m. Annette Williams, Mar. 4, 1983; children: Heston David, Robert Harrison, Hunter James. BA in Polit. Sci. with honors, Lenoir-Rhyne Coll., 1982. Staff Idaho Freedom to Work Com., Boise, 1978-79, exec. dir., 1980-86; pres. Free Congress PAC, Washington, 1987; exec. v.p. Idaho Cattle Assn., Boise, 1988-90; county commr. ADA County, Idaho, 1991—; congl. lobbyist Nat. Right to Work Com., Springfield, Va., 1983. Editor (mag.) Line Rider, 1988-90. Region chmn. Idaho Rep. Party, 1987-92; alt. Rep. Nat. Conv., New Orleans, 1988; candidate for U.S. Congress 2d Dist. Idaho, 1992. With Army N.G., 1990-93. Freedom Fighter of Yr. Ctr. for Study of Market Alternatives, 1987. Mem. Idaho Cattle Assn., Nat. Cattlemen's Assn., Idaho Assn. Counties, Nat. Conf.Rep. County Ofcls. (chmn. Idaho chpt. 1991-93). Bapt. Home: 1410 Howe St Boise ID 83706 Office: ADA County 650 Main St Boise ID 83702

GLENN, GUY CHARLES, pathologist; b. Parma, Ohio, May 13, 1930; s. Joseph Frank and Helen (Rupple) G.; B.S., Denison U., 1953; M.D., U. Cin., 1957; m. Lucia Ann Howarth, June 13, 1953; children—Kathryn Holly, Carolyn Helen, Cynthia Marie. Intern, Walter Reed Army Med. Center, Washington, 1957-58; resident in pathology Fitzsimons Army Med. Center, Denver, 1959-63; commd. 2d lt. U.S. Army, 1956, advanced through grades to col., 1977; demonstrator pathology Royal Army Med. Coll., London, 1970-72; chief dept. pathology Fitzsimons Army Med. Center, Denver, 1972-77; pres. med. staff St. Vincent Hosp., Billings, Mont.; past mem. governing bd. Mont. Health Systems Agy. Diplomate Am. Bd. Pathology, Am. Bd. Nuclear Medicine. Fellow Coll. Am. Pathologists (chmn. chemistry resources com., chmn. commn. sci. resources, mem. budget program and review com., council on quality assurance, chmn. practice guidelines com., bd. govs.), Am. Soc. Clin. Pathology, Soc. Med. Cons. to Armed Forces, Colo. Assn. Continuing Lab. Edn., Midland Empire Health Assn. (past pres.), Rotary (bd. dirs. local chpt.). Contbr. to profl. jours. Home: 3225 Jack Burke Ln Billings MT 59106-1113 Office: St Vincent Hosp Billings MT 59102

GLENN, JAMES D., JR., lawyer; b. Oakley, Idaho, July 1, 1934; s. Vernal D. and Vilate H. Glenn; student U. Utah, 1952-57, JD, 1960. Bar: Utah 1960, Calif. 1961, Idaho 1978. m. Alice Rexine, Dec. 14, 1956; children: Sheilagh Ann Glenn Thornock, Michelle Glenn Larson, James D. III, Deirdre, David R., Alison. Assoc. counsel Fed. Trade Commn., San Francisco, 1960-61; ptnr. Ferguson & Vohland, 1961-63, Ferguson & Glenn, 1963-65; pvt. practice, Oakland, Hayward and Fremont, Calif., 1965-77, Twin Falls, Idaho, 1987—; ptnr. Webb, Burton, Carlson, Pedersen & Paine, Twin Falls, Idaho, 1977-83; sr. ptnr. Glenn & Henrie, Twin Falls, 1983-87; ; sec. Virger Land Corp., Calif.; counsel Norton Enterprises, Inc., A & B Bean & Grain, Inc., Haney Seed Co., Klein Bros., Ltd., Beta Western, Inc., Loughmiller Farm, Inc. Bd. dirs. So. Alameda County (Calif.) Legal Svcs. Corp., 1969-73. Mem. Phi Kappa Phi. Republican. Mormon. Office: 127 2d St W Twin Falls ID 83301-6019

GLENN, LUCIA HOWARTH, mental health services professional; b. Bklyn., Apr. 21, 1930; d. Arthur Orrel and Kathryn (Wilcox) Howarth; m. Guy Charles Glenn, June 13, 1953; children: Kathryn Holly, Carolyn Helen, Cynthia Marie. BS, Denison U., 1952; MS, Eastern Mont. Coll., 1980. Lic. profl. counselor; nat. cert. counselor; CC mental health counselor. Staff therapist Pastoral Counseling Ctr., Billings, Mont., Christian Psychol. Svcs., Billings; pvt. practice psychotherapist Billings; cons. in field. Contbr. articles to profl. jours. Tng. and Rsch. grantee Am. Assn. Counseling and Devel. Mem. Am. Mental Health Counselors Assn., Gender Issues Spl. Interest Network (nat. chairperson), Mont. Mental Health Counselors Assn. (past pres.). Home: 3225 Jack Burke Ln Billings MT 59106

GLENN, THOMAS MICHAEL, science and technology executive; b. Detroit, July 20, 1940; s. Spencer S. and Mary C. (Snell) G.; m. Patricia Ann Ross, Aug. 25, 1962; children: Thomas M. Jr., Timothy P., Christine D. AB, Rockhurst Coll., 1962; MS, U. Mo., Kansas City, 1965, PhD, 1968. Assoc. prof. pharmacology N.D. State U., Fargo, 1966-68, Fla. A&M U., Tallahassee, 1968-69; postdoctoral fellow dept. pharmacology U. Va., 1969-71; assoc. prof. dept. pharmacology Med. Coll. Pa., 1971-73; prof., chmn. dept. pharmacology U. South Ala., 1973-82, co-dir. clin. pharmacology rsch. unit, 1981-82; exec. dir. biology rsch. pharm. divsn. Ciba-Geigy Corp., 1982-84, sr. v.p., dir. research pharm. div., 1984-88; v.p. pharmacological sci. Genentech Inc., South San Francisco, 1988-89; pres., chief exec. officer BioCryst, Inc., Birmingham, Ala., 1989-91; assoc. vice-chancellor for health affairs Duke U. Med. Ctr., Durham, N.C., 1991; v.p. pharm. devel. Cytel Corp., San Diego, Calif., 1991-93; pres., CEO Phyropharmaceuticals, Inc., San Carlos, Calif., 1993—; vis. assoc. prof. pharmacology U. Miss., Oxford, 1969; mem. cardiovascular and renal ad hoc study sect. NIH, 1978-80, exptl. cardiovascular diseases study sect., 1980-81; mem. Emergency Med. Tng. Adv. Bd., 1979-82; mem. adv. panel cardiovascular drugs U.S. Pharmamcopeial Conv., 1980—; mem. med. staff USA Med. Ctr., 1982; corp. rep. Indsl. Research Inst., 1985-88; cons. Merck, Sharpe and Dohme, 1971-73, Johnson & Johnson Baby Products, Inc., 1981-82. Cons. editor Circulatory Shock, assoc. editor, 1974-80; mem. editorial bd. Internat. Jour. Tissue Reactions, Internat. Jour. Immunotherapy, Drug Devel. Research; manuscript referee Circulation Research, Life Sci., Jour. Pharmacology and Exptl. Therapeutics, Jour. Cardiovascular Pharmacology; contbr. numerous articles to profl. jours. Coach/mgr. Little League Baseball, 1974-78; advisor med. post 410 Boy Scouts Am., 1975-79; mem. Archdjocesan Bd. Cath. Edn., 1979-82, pres.; mem. exec. leadership team Cath. Engaged Encounter, Archdiocese Mobile, 1980-82; trustee N.Y. Hall Sci., 1985-88. NIH fellow, 1965-66, Nat. Heart and Lung Inst. fellow, 1969-71; recipient Alumni Achievement award U. Mo.-Kansas City, 1985. Mem. Am. Soc. Clin. Pharmacology and Therapeutics, Am. Soc. Pharmacology and Exptl. Therapeutics, Am. Physiol. Soc., Indsl. Research Inst., Am. Mgmt. Assn. (research and devel. council 1985—), N.Y. Acad. Sci., Am. Heart Assn. (reserch com. Ala. affiliate 1975-78, chmn. com. for youth 1979-82, bd. dirs. 1980-83, pres. Mobile County div. 1978-79, nominating com. 1980-81, bd. dirs. Northwest N.J. chpt. 1983-85), AAAS, Am. Coll. Clin. Pharmacology, Am. Chem. Soc. (medicinal chemistry div.), Soc. Exptl. Biology and Medicine, Pharm. Mfrs. Assn. (chmn. research and devel. steering com. 1985-88), Shock Soc. (councillor 1978-80, publs. com. 1980-81), Microcirculatory Soc., Am. Soc. Exptl. Pharmacology, Am. Soc. Experimental Pharm. Therapy, Am. Soc. Clin. Pharmacology, Rho Chi, Sigma Xi. Republican. Roman Catholic. Home: 14725 Caminito Porta Delgada Del Mar CA 92014-9613 Office: Phytopharmaceuticals Inc 830 Bransten Rd San Carlos CA 94070

GLENN, VALERIE ROSE, advertising agency executive; b. Enid, Okla., Sept. 12, 1954; d. Phillip George and Merle Lynn (Deuel) Rose; m. John James Glenn, July 17, 1981; children: John Phillip, Kelly Marie. BA in Journalism, U. Nev.-Reno, 1976. Media planner/buyer Dancer Fitzgerald Sample, San Francisco, 1976-78; salesperson Visitor Pubs., Inc., Reno, Nev., 1978-81; v.p. Kelley-Rose, Inc., Reno, 1981—; ptnr. Rose-Glenn Advt., Reno, 1989—. pres. Nev. State Fair, Reno, 1992, 93, Nev. Women's Fund, 1993; bd. dirs. Econ. Devel. Authority of Western Nev., 1991, Western Indsl. Nev., U. Nev. Found.; trustee adv. bd. U. Nev. Bus. Sch. Mem. Reno-Sparks C. of C. (pres. 1991), Reno Women in Advt. (pres. 1985, founding bd. dirs.), Leadership Reno (alumni adv. bd., past sec.), Reno Ad Club (Advt. Person of the Yr. 1986), Am. Mktg. Assn. Republican. Episcopalian. Office: Rose-Glenn Advt 1650 Meadowood Ln Reno NV 89502-6510

GLENNER, GEORGE GEIGER, pathology educator; b. Bklyn., Sept. 17, 1927; s. Francis Richard and Jennie (Geiger) G.; m. Joy Arlene Sharp, Aug. 15, 1979; children: Shelley, Jonathan, Amanda, Sarah. BA, Johns Hopkins U., 1949, MD, 1953. Commd. lt. USPHS, advance through grades to capt., 1961; intern Mt. Sinai Hosp., N.Y.C., 1953-54; resident Mallory Inst. Pathology, Boston, 1954-55; asst. pathologist Harvard U. Sch. Legal Medicine, Boston, 1955; commd. 1st lt. (s.g.) USPHS, 1955, advanced through grades to capt., 1961; rsch. pathologist NIH, Bethesda, Md., 1955-59; chief sect. on histochemistry Nat. Inst. Arthritis, Metabolic and Digestive Diseases, NIH, Bethesda, 1959-71, chief sect. on molecular pathology, 1971-82; vis. scholar U. Calif. Sch. Medicine, La Jolla, 1980-82, prof., 1982—; asst. pathologist Johns Hopkins Hosp., Balt., 1957-58; cons. E.I. Du Pont de Nemours & Co., Willmington, Del., 1985-87, Mayo Clinic, Rochester, Minn., 1989—. Co-author: Tumors of Paraganglion, 1974, Amyloid and Amyloidosis, 1980, Advancing Frontiers in Alzheimers Disease Research, 1987; also over 200 articles. Mem. exec. bd. Nat. Alzheimer's Assn., Chgo., 1981-86; pres. Alzheimer's Family Ctr., Inc., San Diego, 1982—; chmn. Calif. Gov.'s Alzheimer's Disease Task Force, Sacramento, 1985-87. Recipient Meritorious Svc. medal USPHS, 1971, award Deustsche Akadamie Leopoldina, 1973, merit award NIH-Nat. Rsch. Coun. on Aging, 1988, Met. Life Found. award, 1989, Potamkin prize Am. Acad. Neurology, 1989, Glenn Found. award Gerontological Soc. Am., 1991; named Dr. of Yr., San Diego Health Care Assn., 1984, Distinguished Alumnus award John Hopkins Univ. Sch. of Med., 1993, San Diego Citizen of Yr., San Diego Union Newspaper, 1985, Health Citizen of Yr., Nat. Assn. Social Workers, 1990, Vol. of Yr., United Way, J.C. Penney,, 1990. Fellow Coll. Am. Pathologists; mem. Am. Acad. Pathology, Am. Fedn. for Clin. Rsch., Am. Soc. Biol. Chemists, Internat. Acad. Pathology. Home: PO Box 3701 Rancho Santa Fe CA 92067-3701 Office: U Calif Sch Medicine La Jolla CA 92093-0612

GLENNON, THOMAS MANCHESTER, psychologist; b. New Bedford, Mass., July 13, 1954; s. Joseph Raymond and Kathryn (Coffey) G.; m. Jody Elizabeth Kreiman, Nov. 1, 1986; 1 child, Elizabeth Kathryn. BA, Holy Cross Coll., 1976; MA, Pepperdine U., 1978; PhD, Calif. Grad. Inst., 1986. Lic. psychologist, Calif.; lic. marriage, family and child therpist, Calif. Clin. dir. Forte Found, Van Nuys, Calif., 1986-90; pvt. practice Coldwater Clin. Assocs., Studio City, Calif., 1990—; cons. Dubnoff Ctr., North Hollywood, Calif., 1990—, L.A. Child Devel. Ctr., 1986—. Supr. L.A. Free Clinic, 1988-91. Mem. APA (assoc.), Calif. Assn. Marriage and Family Therapists (clin.), L.A. County Psychol. Assn. (clin.), San Fernando Valley Child Abuse Coun. Office: Coldwater Clin Assocs 12456 Ventura Blvd # 3 Studio City CA 91604

GLICK, MILTON DON, chemist, university administrator; b. Memphis, July 30, 1937; s. Lewis S. and Sylvia (Kleinman) G.; m. Peggy M., June 22, 1965; children: David, Sander. AB cum laude, Augustana Coll., 1959; PhD, U. Wis., 1965. Fellow, dept. chemistry Cornell U., Ithaca, N.Y., 1964-66; asst. prof. chemistry Wayne State U., Detroit, 1966-70, assoc. prof., 1970-74, prof., 1974-83, chmn. dept., 1978-83; dean arts and sci. U. Mo.-Columbia, 1983-88; provost Iowa State U., Ames, 1988-91, interim pres., 1990-91; sr. v.p., provost Ariz. State U., Tempe, 1991—. Contbr. articles in structural inorganic chemistry to profl. jours. Trustee EDUCOM, SNOWASS. Office: Ariz State U Office of Provost 203 ADM Bldg Tempe AZ 85287-2803

GLICK, STANLEY, optometrist, photographer; b. N.Y.C., May 27, 1947; s. Samuel Saul and Ida Sonia (Merewitz) G. BA in Chemistry, George Washington U., 1970, MS in Analytical Chemistry, 1973; grad., Armed Forces Inst. Pathology, 1972; OD, New Eng. Coll. Optometry, 1982. Cert. Dr. Optometry. Statistician com. Z AAUP, Washington, 1967-69; forensic pathologist Ga. Bur. Investigation, Atlanta, 1973-78; asst. Office of Gov., Atlanta; pvt. practice L.A.; ofcl. photographer Miss World Pagent, Boston, L.A., 1980—. Photographer (cover) Boston Herald Am., 1980. Pres. Claremont (Calif.) Jaycees, 1984, Merchant Assn., Fontana, Calif., 1983-84; active Fontana Jaycees, 1983-84, North Hills Jaycees, Granada Hills, Calif., 1987-91, Nat. Hist. Trust Preservation, Washington, 1989-91, World Affairs Coun., 1989-91, Northridge Hillel; election ofcl., insp. L.A. County, 1988-93; bd. dirs. Am. Jewish Com., 1987-91, Am. Jewish Congress, 1987-91, optical divsn. United Jewish Fund, Beverly Hills, Calif. Recipient Key to City, City of Miami Beach, 1961; scholar Fla. Sci. Study Found., 1961. Mem. Am. Optometric Assn., Am. Optometric Found., Calif. Optometric Assn. (del. congress 1989-91), San Fernando Valley Optometric Soc., Kiwanis, Calif. Yacht Club, Long Beach Single Sailors. Republican. Jewish.

GLICK, STEVEN MARC, business association executive; b. L.A., June 28, 1947; s. Ben and Shirlee (Sabath) G.; m. Sue Myrle Rudofsky, June 16, 1974; children: Shana Audrey, Andrea Janelle. BA with distinction, U. Calif., Berkeley, 1969; JD, Georgetown U. Law Ctr., 1973. Western co-dir. Law Students Civil Rights Rsch. Coun., San Francisco, 1975-78; cons. San Mateo County Employment and Tng. Div., Redwood City, Calif., 1979-80; exec. dir. Pvt. Industry Coun. San Mateo County, Redwood City, Calif., 1980-84; v.p. edn. and tng. Bay Area Coun., San Francisco, 1984—; instr. Cañada Coll., Redwood City, 1984-85; trustee Burlingame Sch. Dist., 1991—; mem. bus. adv. com. for the chair of Calif. State Assembly Com. on Edn., Sacramento, 1992. Project dir. resource guide An Employer's Guide to Working with Community Colleges in the Bay Area, 1988; assoc. producer TV series Getting the Right Job, 1989. Bd. dirs. San Francisco Sr. Ctr., past pres., 1988-90; v.p. external affairs N. Calif. Human Resources Coun., 1990-92, spl. achievement award, 1988. Mem. Bay Area Human Resource Planners (chair, 1987). Office: Bay Area Coun 200 Pine St Ste 300 San Francisco CA 94104-2702

GLICKMAN, HARRY, professional athletics executive; b. Portland, Oreg., May 13, 1924; s. Sam and Bessie (Karp) G.; m. Joanne Carol Matin, Sept. 28, 1958; children: Lynn Carol, Marshall Jordan, Jennifer Ann. B.A., U. Oreg., 1948. Press agt., 1948-52; pres. Oreg. Sports Attractions, 1952—; mgr. Multnomah (Oreg.) Civic Stadium, 1958-59; pres. Portland Hockey Club, 1960-73; exec. v.p. basketball team Portland Trail Blazers, from 1970, now pres. Trustee B'nai B'rith Jr. Camp, 1965; bd. dirs. U. Oreg. Devel. Fund. Served with AUS, 1943-46. Named to Oreg. Sports Hall of Fame, 1986. Mem. Portland C. of C. (bd. dirs. 1968-72), Sigma Delta Chi, Sigma Alpha Mu. Jewish. Office: Portland Trail Blazers 700 NE Multnomah St Portland OR 97232-2131

GLICKSMAN, JAY, computer scientist; b. Toronto, Ont., Can., May 6, 1953; came to U.S., 1983; s. Murray and Donna (Messinger) G. BSc, U. Toronto, 1975; ME, U. Utah, 1977; PhD, U. B.C., Vancouver, 1983. MTS Tex. Instruments, Dallas, 1983-84; sr. MTS Advanced Decision Systems, Mountain View, Calif., 1985-87; sr. engr. Schlumberger, Palo Alto, Calif., 1988-91; prin. scientist Enterprise Integration Techs., Palo Alto, 1991—, also bd. dirs. Events and tng. coms. Spl. Olympics, Santa Clara County, Calif., 1990—. Mem. IEEE, Am. Assn. for Artificial Intelligence, Assn. for Computing Machinery, Computer Profls. for Social Responsibility. Office: Enterprise Integration Tech Ste 100 459 Hamilton Ave Palo Alto CA 94301

GLISMANN, DIANE DUFFY, health facility administrator; b. Buffalo, Feb. 8, 1935; d. William Howard and Celeste (Strigl) Woodley; m. Richard E. Rahill, Nov. 3, 1956 (div. 1969); children: Kevin, Sharon, Suzanne, Michele; m. James C. Duffy, Nov. 12, 1970 (div. 1983); children: Michael and Julia (twins); m. John D. Glismann, Nov. 28, 1985; children: Linda, Diana, John P., Laura. Diploma in nursing, Sisters of Charity Hosp., 1955; BS, Coll. St. Francis, 1982. Cert. Critical Care Nurse Practitioner, Am. Coll. Surgeons. With emergency dept. Luth. Med. Ctr., 1971-75; dir. nursing Med. Pers. Pool, Denver, 1975-80; exec. dir. Community Health Svcs., Denver, 1982-84; dir. nursing Parkside Health Mgmt., Denver, 1984-85, Western Home Health, Denver, 1985-86; adminstr. Health Care Specialists, Denver, 1986-87; br. mgr. NSI Svcs. Inc., Denver, 1987-91; dir. profl. svcs. HRN Svcs., Inc., Denver, 1991-93; pres., CEO HRN Colo., Denver, 1993—; nurse lobbyist internship program, 1972. Mem. Gov.'s Coun. on Emergency Medicine, Denver, 1975-77; bd. dirs. Colo. Heart Assn., Denver, 1977. Named Colo. Nurse of Yr., 1975. Mem. ANA (state del. 1980), Am. Med. Soc. Aux. (nat. com. on legis. 1992—), Colo. Fedn. Nursing (pres. 1983), Colo. Med. Soc. Aux. (legis chmn. 1989-90, pres.-elect 1989-90, pres. 1990-91), Colo. Med. Soc. Alliance (legis. chmn. 1993—), Colo. Med. Orgn. (polit. action com., bd. dirs. 1990—), Clear Creek County Med. Soc. Aux. (pres. 1988-89). Republican. Roman Catholic. Home: 6864 Wyman Way Westminster CO 80030 Office: HRN Colo 3773 Cherry Creek N Dr # 910 Denver CO 80209

GLOCK, CHARLES YOUNG, sociologist; b. N.Y.C., Oct. 17, 1919; s. Charles and Philippine (Young) G.; m. Margaret Schleef, Sept. 12, 1950; children: Susan Young, James William. B.S., N.Y. U., 1940; M.B.A., Boston U., 1941; Ph.D., Columbia U., 1952. Research asst. Bur. Applied Social Research, Columbia U., 1946-51, dir., 1951-58, lectr., then prof. sociology, 1956-58; prof. sociology U. Calif. at Berkeley, 1958-79, prof. emeritus, 1979—, chmn., 1967-68, 69-71; dir. Survey Research Center, 1958-67; adj. prof. Grad. Theol. Union, 1971-79; Luther Weigle vis. lectr. Yale U., 1968. Co-author: Wayward Shepherds, The Anatomy of Racial Attitudes, Anti-Semitism in America, American Piety; sr. author: Adolescent Prejudice, To Comfort and To Challenge, Religion and Society in Tension, Christian Beliefs and Anti-Semitism, The Apathetic Majority; contbg. editor Rev. Religious Rsch. Sociological Analysis; editor: The New Religious Consciousness, Survey Research in the Social Sciences, Beyond the Classics, Religion in Sociological Perspective, Prejudice U.S.A., Unison-Newsletter of One Voice; contbr. numerous articles on social scis. Active parish edn. Luth. Ch. Am., 1970-72; mem. mgmt. com. Office Rsch. and Planning, 1973-80; bd. dirs. Pacific Luth. Theol. Sem., 1962-74, 80-86,Inst. Rsch. in Social Behavior, 1962-90, Interplayers, 1990-92, One Voice, Inst. Communities and Congregations in Transformation; pres. Cornerhouse Fund, 1982-92; mem. adv. com. Office Rsch. and Evaluation Evangelical Luth. Ch. Am. Capt. USAAF, 1942-46. Decorated Bronze Star, Legion of Merit; recipient Roots of Freedom award Pacific bd. Anti-Defamation League, 1977; Berkeley citation U. Calif., Berkeley, 1979; Rockefeller fellow, 1941-42; fellow Center Advanced Study Behavioral Scis., 1957-58; fellow Soc. for Religion in Higher Edn., 1968-69. Fellow Soc. Sci. Study Religion (Western rep., pres. 1968-69); mem. Am. Assn. Pub. Opinion Research (v.p., pres. 1962-64, pres. Pacific chpt. 1959-60), Am. Sociol. Assn. (v.p. 1978-79), Religious Research Assn., Sociol. Research Assn. Home: 319 S 4th Ave Sandpoint ID 83864-1219

GLOCKNER, WILLIAM DANIEL, JR., business administrator, systems consultant; b. Phila., July 2, 1963; s. William Daniel and Winifred (Manion) G.; m. Susan Mariscal, Dec. 27, 1986. AB, Princeton U., 1985; MBA, UCLA, 1991. V.p. The Distbn. Solution, San Diego, 1985-87; systems cons. Integrated Analysis, San Diego, 1987-89; pres., cons. Infonix Info. Techs., L.A., 1989-91; ops. mgr. Hirsch Pipe & Supply Co., L.A., 1991—. Price Inst. Entrepreneurial Studies fellow, 1990. Mem. Entrepreneur Assn. (pres. 1990-91), Toastmasters (v.p. 1990-91), L.A. Jaycees, Princeton Club So. Calif., UCLA Alumni Assn. Home: 355 Via Montanosa Encinitas CA 92024 Office: Hirsch Pipe & Supply Co 3317 W Jefferson Blvd Los Angeles CA 90018

GLOMB, DIANA, state legislator. BS, Northeast La. U., 1969; MSW, La. State U., 1974. Former social worker; mem. Nev. State Senate, 1991—. Mem. NASW, Nev. Rainbow Coalition. Democrat. Address: 1675 Geary St Reno NV 89503 Office: Nev State Senate State Capitol Carson City NV 89710

GLOVER, CELESTIE JANE, bank officer; b. Roswell, N.Mex., Jan. 21, 1964; d. Walter Frank and Donna Marie (Womack) G. BS, N.Mex. State U., 1986. Real estate appraiser pvt. practice, Las Cruces, N.Mex., 1986; computer oper. Ronny Fouts, Melrose, N.Mex., 1986-87; internal auditor Sunwest Bank Roswell (N.Mex.), 1987-88, regional auditor, 1988-90, compliance officer, 1990-91, compliance officer, loan ops. mgr., 1991—; instr. Am. Inst. Banking, Roswell, 1993. Contbr. articles publ. in Sunwesterner. Bd. dirs. Chaves County Am. Cancer Soc., Roswell, 1992-93, N.Mex. Am. Cancer Soc., Albuquerque, 1992-93; com. mem. SunClasic Charity Open Golf Tournament, Roswell, 1991, 92, 93, Sunwest Christmas Tree Extravaganza, Roswell, 1988-92. Mem. N.Mex. State U. Alumni Assn. Office: Sunwest Bank Roswell PO Box 1858 Roswell NM 88202

GLOWIENKA, EMERINE FRANCES, educator; b. Milw., Mar. 9, 1920; d. Clement Joseph and Sophia Maria (Dettlaff) G. PhD in Sociology, St. Louis U., 1956; PhD in Philosophy, Marquette U., 1973. Prof. philosophy and sociology San Francisco Coll. for Women, 1962-70; prof. philosophy U. San Diego, 1972-74; prof. sociology and philosophy U. N.Mex., Gallup, 1974-88, prof. emeritus, 1988—; prof. philosophy and homiletics Diocesan Sem., Gallup, N.Mex., 1974—. Contbr. articles to profl. jours. Speaker in field. Mem. Am. Cath. Philos. Assn., Am. Philos. Assn. Democrat. Roman Catholic. Home: 110 E Green Ave Gallup NM 87301-6236 Office: U NMex Gallup Br Coll 200 College Rd Gallup NM 87301-5697

GLUCK, DALE RICHARD, public relations consultant; b. Pomona, Calif., Dec. 31, 1952; s. Richard Bellows and Helen (McDowell) G. BS in Communication Arts, Calif. State Poly. U., 1974. Pub. rels. asst. So. Calif. Gas Co., L.A., 1974, Lockheed Aircraft Svc. Co., Ontario, Calif., 1974; editor, asst. v.p. pub. rels., v.p. Security Pacific Nat. Bank, L.A., 1974-84; owner, prin. Gluck & Assocs., Seattle, 1984—; mem. faculty cert. program in pub. rels. U. Wash. Ext., 1992—. Fundraising vol. Interaction/Transition, Seattle, 1989—, vice chair, 1991, chair, 1991—; vice chair Gig Harbor Jazz Soc., Tacoma, 1989, chmn., 1990; asst. venue press chief Goodwill Games, Seattle, 1990. Mem. Internat. Assn. Bus. Communicators (accredited, accreditation bd. San Francisco 1982-88, pres. L.A. chpt. 1978-79, Communicator of Yr., 1980, v.p. svcs. Seattle chpt. 1990, v.p. profl. devel. 1992), Pub. Rels. Soc. Am., Soc. Profl. Journalists. Office: Gluck & Assocs 401 2d Ave S Ste 620 Seattle WA 98104

GLUSHKO, VICTOR, medical products executive, biochemist; b. Kiel, Germany, June 26, 1946; came to U.S., 1951; s. George and Maria Glushko; 1 child, Sarah Rachel Alexandra. AB, Earlham Coll., 1968; PhD, Ind. U., 1972. Rsch. assoc. Meml. Sloan Kettering, N.Y.C., 1973-77; asst. prof. Temple U. Med. Sch., Phila., 1977-83; dir. product devel. Helitrex, Plainsboro, N.J., 1982-85; exec. dir. Am. Biomaterials, Plainsboro, 1985-88; v.p. Vitaphore, Menlo Park, Calif., 1988—. Developer collagen dressings, perio dressing; contbr. articles to profl. jours. Sloan-Kettering fellow, 1972-73; rsch. grantee (9), 1973-82. Mem. Am. Chem. Soc. (chmn. continuing edn. Phila. sect. 1981-82), Am. Assn. Pharm. Sci., N.Y. Acad. Scis., Biophys. Soc., Tissue Culture Assn., Controlled Release Soc., Wound Healing Soc. Home: 2405 Hale Dr Burlingame CA 94010 Office: Vitaphore 1330 O'Brien Dr Menlo Park CA 94025

GNAM, ADRIAN, orchestra director and conductor; b. N.Y.C., Sept. 4, 1940; s. Hugo and Annette (Nussbaum) G.; m. Catharine Dee Morningstar, Aug. 16, 1984; children: Evan Julian, Geneva Nicole. MusB, U. Cin., 1961, BS and MusM, 1962. Asst. condr. N.E. Chamber Orch., Maine, 1966-67; mem. faculty Ohio U., 1969-76; asst. music dir. U. Cin., 1967-76; asst. music dir. Nat. Endowment for the Arts, Washington, 1976-82, music dir., 1982-84; prin. guest condr. Concerto Soloists of Phila., 1980—; music dir., condr. Midland (Mich.) Symphony, 1982-86, Macon (Ga.) Symphony Orch., 1983—, Eugene (Oreg.) Symphony Orch., 1985-89; music dir. Shreveport (La.) Summer Music Festival, 1987—; music dir., condr. Tuscaloosa Symphony Orch., 1993—; prin. oboe Am. Symphony, N.Y.C., 1964-65, Cleve. Orch., 1965-67; guest condr. various locations worldwide; vis. prof. U. Houston Symphony Orch. 1991-92. Rec. artist for Decca, Opus One, Piper and Epic labels; guest condr. (symphony) including, Indpls., Louisville, Anchorage, Santa Fe, Santa Cruz, Vt., Ala., Jacksonville, Trenton, S. Dak., Fla., Columbia, Youngstown, Abilene, Beaumont, Columbus, Amarillo, Grand Rapids, Mich., (music festivals) including, Spoleto, Sewanee, Interlochen, Okla., Chautauqua, Colo., Tex., (orchs.) including, Rumania, Puerto Rico, Venezuela, Mexico City, Italy, Brazil, Yugoslavia (ballet cos.) Cin., Erie, Eugene. Recipient Presdl. citation Nat. Fedn. Music Clubs; Corbett scholar Univ. Cin., 1960-62. Mem. Am. Fedn. Musicians, Am. Symphony Orch. League, Condrs. Guild, Chamber Music Am. Home and Office: 85440 Appletree Ct Eugene OR 97405-9738 also: Macon Symphony Orch PO Box 5700 Macon GA 31208

GNEHM, MAX WILLI, financial consultant; b. Switzerland, July 15, 1943; s. Max Hans and Frieda G.; m. Kimberly A. Smith, Dec. 20, 1992; children from previous marriage: Alexandra Barbara, William Anthony. MBA, Swiss Sch. Bus., 1963; postgrad. Swiss Inst. Mktg. and Fgn. Trade Research. Asst. mgr. Maxwell Sci. Internat. Book Co., 1964-66; mgr. book and periodical div. Internat. Univ. Booksellers, N.Y.C., 1966-69; dir. Internat. div. Richard Abel Co., 1969-74; v.p. mktg. Blackwell of N.Am., Inc., Beaverton, Oreg., 1974-76, pres., 1976-79, also bd. dirs.; pres., chmn. bd. Swiss-Am. Investment Group Inc.; bd. dirs. Swiss Am. Data Net, Swiss Am. Data Exchange, Atlin Investment Group, Inc.; pres., bd. dirs. Transpacific Holding Group Ltd., Malcolm Smith, Inc, Concorde Pacific Exploration, Inc., Interpacific Printing, Inc., Hong Kong Fin. Group Ltd., Pacific Mining, Inc., 1987—; bd. dirs. Macedon Resources Ltd., Lore Corp; mng. dir. JT Racing, 1989-90; pres, chief exec. officer Extreme Sports, Inc. 1991-92; bd. dirs. Captive Air Internat.; dir. sales, mktg. KIK Tire, Inc., 1992—; dir. Ocelot Bicycle Co; pres., chief exec. officer Softouch Mktg. Group, 1992—. Author: New Reference Tools for Librarians, 1965. Mem. ALA, Pres.'s Assn. Home: 3955 Monroe St Carlsbad CA 92008-2737

GO, VAY LIANG WONG, physician, medical educator, editor; b. Ozamis, The Philippines, Aug. 29, 1938; came to U.S., 1963; s. Bee and Shi G.; m. Frisca Yan-Go, Oct. 15, 1963; children: Frances, Lisa, William. AA, U. Santo Tomas, Manila, The Philippines, 1958, MD, 1963. Resident in internal medicine Mayo Clin., Rochester, Minn., 1965-66, resident in gastroenterology, 1967-69; rsch. assoc. Banting & Best Inst. U. Toronto, Can., 1969-71; asst. prof. medicine Mayo Med. Sch., Rochester, 1972-75, assoc. prof. medicine, 1975-78, prof. medicine, 1978-88; dir. divsn. digestive diseases and nutrition NIH, Bethesda, Md., 1985-88; prof., exec. chmn. dept. medicine. Sch. Medicine UCLA, 1988-92; mem. adv. com. gastrointestinal drugs FDA, 1980-83, 1990-93; chmn. nat. pancreatic cancer program Nat. Cancer Inst. Organ Systems Coord. Ctr., 1984-85; chair steering com. Internat. Symposium of Gastroenterology Hormones, 1988-90; mem. adv. com. Internat. Conf. on Brain-Gut Peptides, Beijing, 1988; vis. prof. U. Vt. Med. Ctr., 1991, chmn. planning com. Young Clinician program World Congress of Gastroenterology, 1991—; co-chair organizing com. Interanat. Symposium of Cholecystokinin, Cape Cod, Mass, 1993; mem. internat. adv. com. Internat. Conf. on Gastrointestinal Hormones and Gastrointestinal Motility, Beijing, 1993. Editor-in-chief (peer reviewed journal) Pancreas, 1985—; coeditor (textbook) The Pancreas, 1984, 2d rev. edit., 1993, The Exocrine Pancreas: Biology, Pathobiology, and Diseases, 1985, 2d rev. edit. 1993; assoc. editor Digestive Diseases and Sciences, 1977-82; mem. editorial bd. Regulatory Peptides, 1980-92, Digestive Diseases and Sciences, 1982-90, Gastroenterology International, 1988-90, gastroenterology Japonica, 1989—, contbr. 281 articles and 450 abstracts to profl jours., 100 chpts. to books. Recipient Donald C. Balfour Rsch. award Mayo Found., 1969, Sr. Exec. Svc. award HHS, 1987, Alimurong Lectr. award U. Santo Tomas Alumni Assn., 1988, Apolinaro Mabini award Assn. Philippine Physicians in Am., 1989, Disting. Lectureship, Japan Pancreas Soc., 1991 Allen Meml. Lectureship, SUNY Health Scis. Ctr, 1991, Commemorative Lectureship, 5th Internat. Symposium of Vasoactive Intestinal Polypeptides, 1991. Fellow ACP (exec., mem. gov.'s adv. com. so. Calif. chpt. 1990-92); mem. AAAS, Am. Pancreatic Assn. (pres. 1978-79, 88-89, sec., treas. 1980-85), Am. Assn. Cancer Rsch., Am. Assn. Clin. Rsch., Am. Assn. Clin. Investigation, Am. Gastroenterological Assn. (cancer coun. 1975-78, rsch. com. 1977-80, 83-86, disting. lectr. award 1990), Am. Motility Soc., Am. Soc. Clin. Nutrition, Endocrine Soc., Assn. Profs. Medicine, Internat. Assn. Pancreatology, We. Soc. Clin. Investigation, Mayo Alumni Assn., Sigma Xi (pres. UCLA chpt. 1990). Roman Catholic. Office: Pancreas Editorial Office 1015 Gayley Ave # 587 Los Angeles CA 90024

GOATES, DELBERT TOLTON, child psychiatrist; b. Logan, Utah, Apr. 14, 1932; s. Wallace Albert and Roma (Tolton) G.; m. Claudia Tidwell, Sept. 15, 1960; children: Jeanette, Byron, Rebecca Lynn, Alan, Paul, Jonathan Phillip, Kendra Michelle, George Milton. BS, U. Utah, 1953, MD, 1962; postgrad., U. Nebr., 1965, 67. Intern Rochester (N.Y.) Gen. Hosp., 1962-63; resident Nebr. Psychiat. Inst., Omaha, 1963-67; pvt. practice medicine specializing in child psychiatry Omaha, 1963-67, Albuquerque, 1967-71, Salt Lake City, 1971—; dir. psychiatry Riverdell Psychiat. Ctr., 1986-92, staff psychiatrist, 1992—; asst. prof. child psychiatry U. N.Mex., 1967-71, dir. children's svcs., 1967-71, asst. prof. pediatrics, 1969-71; clin. dir. Children's Psychiat. Ctr., Primary Children's Med. Ctr., Salt Lake City, 1971-77; med. dir. Life Line, 1990—, Tech Help, 1992—; pres. Magic Mini Maker Inc., Salt Lake City, 1972-78; chmn. bd. Intermountain Polytex, Inc. Bishop Ch. Jesus Christ Latter-day Sts., 1968-71; bd. dirs. Utah Cancer Soc., Great Salt Lake Mental Health. Served with MC, AUS, 1953-55. Mem. AMA, Orthopsychiat. Assn. Am., Utah Psychiat. assns., Intermountain Acad. Child Psychiatry (pres. 1974-76), Pi Kappa Alpha, Phi Kappa Phi. Home: 1082 Bonneville Dr Salt Lake City UT 84108 Office: 404 E 45th S Murray UT 84107

GOAY, MICHAEL SONG-CHYE, network manager; b. George Town, Penang, malaysia, Sept. 6, 1964; s. Choon Gaik and Nai Hoey (Ng) G.; m. Monique Kristianty WArdhana, Apr. 28, 1990. BEE, U. Tex., 1987; MS in Health Informatics, U. Minn., 1990. Rsch. asst. Nat. Simulation Resource Ctr., Mpls., 1987-90; database adminstr. Childrens Cancer Study Group, Arcadia, Calif., 1990-92; network mgr. Nat. Childhood Cancer Found., Arcadia, Calif., 1992—; info. system cons. Multi-Fin. Svcs., Montebello, 1990—. Editor SSA newsletter, 1989; contbr. articles to profl. jours. Mem. Assn. Computing Machinery, Inst. Elec. & Electronic Engrs., Alpha Lambda Delta, Tau Beta Pi, Eta Kappa Nu. Home: 19239 E Windrose Dr Rowland Heights CA 91748 Office: Nat Childhood Cancer Found PO Box 60012 Arcadia CA 91066-6012

GOBAR, ALFRED JULIAN, economic consultant, educator; b. Lucerne Valley, Calif., July 12, 1932; s. Julian Smith and Hilda (Millbank) G.; B.A. in Econs., Whittier Coll., 1953, M.A. in History, 1955; postgrad. Claremont Grad. Sch., 1953-54; Ph.D. in Econs., U. So. Calif., 1963; m. Sally Ann Randall, June 17, 1957; children—Wendy Lee, Curtis Julian, Joseph Julian. Asst. pres. Microdot Inc., Pasadena, 1953-57; regional sales mgr. Sutorbilt Corp., Los Angeles, 1957-59; market research assoc. Beckman Instrument Inc., Fullerton, 1959-64; sr. marketing cons. Western Mgmt. Consultants Inc., Phoenix, Los Angeles, 1964-66; ptnr., prin., chmn. bd. Darley/Gobar Assocs., Inc., 1966-73; pres., chmn. bd. Alfred Gobar Assocs., Inc., Placentia, Calif., 1973—; asst. prof. finance U. So. Calif., Los Angeles, 1963-64; assoc. prof. bus. Calif. State U.-Los Angeles, 1963-68, 70-79, assoc. prof. Calif. State U.-Fullerton, 1968-69; mktg., fin. adviser 1957—; bd. dirs. Quaker City Fed. Savs. and Loan Assn.; pub. speaker seminars and convs. Contbr. articles to profl. publs. Trustee Whittier Coll., 1992—. Home: 1100 W Valencia Mesa Dr Fullerton CA 92633-2219 Office: 721 W Kimberly Ave Placentia CA 92670

GOBAR, SALLY RANDALL, educator; b. Santa Maria, Calif., Nov. 27, 1933; d. Vernon Blythe Randall and Leona Margaret (Jackson) Batchman; m. Alfred Julian Gobar, June 17, 1957; children—Wendy Lee, Curtis Julian, Joseph Julian. B.A., Whittier Coll., 1955; M.A., Claremont Grad. Sch., 1967, Ph.D., 1979. Tchr., So. San Francisco High Sch., 1956-57, Santa Ana High Sch., Calif., 1957-61; counselor Sunny Hills High Sch., Fullerton, Calif., 1961-66; head counselor Troy High Sch., Fullerton, 1967-83; asst. prin. Buena Park High Sch., Calif., 1983-84; prin. Fullerton High Sch., 1984-89; adj. prof. Whittier (Calif.) Coll., 1989-91, assoc. prof., 1991—; cons. Coll. Bd., N.Y., 1972-77. Mem. Pres.'s Assocs., Calif. State U.-Fullerton; mem. Pacific Auditorium Found. Bd. Recipient Golden Book award Exchange Club, 1978, Outstanding Service award Calif. Pers. and Guidance Assn., 1980. Mem. Whittier Coll. Alumni Assn., Claremont Grad. Sch. Alumni . Avocations: travel, classical music, piano. Home: 1100 W Valencia Mesa Dr Fullerton CA 92633-2219 Office: Whittier Coll Box 634 Whittier CA 90608

GOBETS, DENNIS RICHARD, computer company executive; b. Tarrytown, N.Y., June 13, 1955; s. Arthur and Ursula (Kuester) G.; m. Linda Ann Parks, June 21, 1980; children: Ember Timothy, Sara Caitlen. BS in Psychology, U. Calif., Santa Barbara, 1977. Printer Fricke-Parks Press, Fremont, Calif., 1978-80; graphics designer Very Graphic Arts, Santa Clara, Calif., 1980; prodn. coord. Intel Corp., Santa Clara, 1980-82; prodn. mgr. Apple Computer, Inc., Cupertino, Calif., 1982—. Prodn. mgr.: So Far - The First Ten Years of a Vision, 1987 (Printing Industry of Am. award 1987). Recipient Merit award N.Y. Art Dirs. Club, N.Y.C., 1984; excellence awards Communications Arts Mag., 1985, 87, Addy Gold award San Francisco Art Dirs. Club, 1988. Mem. Graphic Arts Tech. Found., Nat. Assn. Desktop Pubs., Surfrider Found., Big Stick Surfing Assn., Old Wave Surfing Assn. Office: Apple Computer Inc 10455 Bandley Dr Cupertino CA 95014

GOBLE, ELISE JOAN H., pediatric ophthalmologist; b. Winnipeg, Man., Can., Jan. 23, 1932; d. Michael Samuel and Sarah (Corbin) Hollenberg; m. John Lewis Goble, Oct. 4, 1956; children: John Robert, Michael William. Assoc. in Music, U. Man., 1949, MD, 1956. Resident Columbia Presbyn. Eye Inst., N.Y.C., 1956-59; pvt. practice pediatric ophthalmology San Mateo, Calif., 1959—. Mem. San Mateo Sch. Health Com.; mem. Coordinating Coun. Developmental Disabilities, San Mateo; founder San Mateo chpt. Nat. Assn. Autistic Citizens. Fellow ACS, Am. Bd. Ophthalmology, Am. Bd. Pediatrics; mem. Am. Assn. Pediatric Ophthalmology & Strabismus (charter mem.), San Mateo County Med. Soc., Calif. Med. Assn. Home: 2007 New Brunswick Dr San Mateo CA 94402 Office: 100 S Ellsworth Ste 507 San Mateo CA 94401

GOBLE, PAUL JOHN, software engineer, technical communicator; b. Rapid City, S.D., May 1, 1964; s. Benjamin Leon and Marian Grace (Zeigler) G.; m. Rogene Mae Foster, May 9, 1992. BS in Physics magna cum laude, U. Denver, 1986; MS in Computer Sci., Colo. State U., 1989. Tech. writer Mgmt. Assistance Corp. Am., Ft. Collins, Colo., 1987; systems programmer Colo. State U., Ft. Collins, 1987-89; learning products developer Hewlett-Packard Co., Colorado Springs, Colo., 1989—. Author software manuals. Dir., libr. Rocky Mountain Chamber Orch., Lakewood, Colo., 1980-86; rsch. vol. Belmar Mus., Lakewood, 1982; state del. Dem. party, Denver, 1984, 88; violinist Pikes Peak Civic Orch., Colorado Springs, 1990-91. Mem. IEEE, Soc. Tech. Communication, Assn. Computing Machinery, Toastmasters (sec.-treas. 1991-92), Phi Beta Kappa. Republican. Presbyterian. Office: Hewlett Packard Co 1900 Garden of Gods Rd Colorado Springs CO 80901

GOCHOCO, JOSE LUIS, physician, health facility administrator; b. Balt., Nov. 24, 1952; s. Jacinto Jaramillo and Felicidad (Tantoco) G.; m. Andrea McLaughlin, Aug. 9, 1975 (div. Aug. 1984); m. Catherine Ellen Ralph, Dec. 31, 1991; children: Tamara Allen, Christina, Sean. Student, Boston Coll., 1970-72; BS in Pharmacy, Phila. Coll. Pharmacy and Sci., 1975; DO, Phila. Coll. Osteo. Medicine, 1979. Diplomate Am. Bd. Emergency Medicine, Am. Acad. Osteopathic Emergency Physicians. Intern Phoenix Gen. Hosp., 1979-80, emergency physician, 1983-89, dir. emergency medicine, 1992—; ptnr. Thunderbird Family Medicine, Glendale, Ariz., 1980-83; CEO Mohave Express Care, Lake Havasu, Ariz., 1992—, Western Med. Mgmt., Tempe, Ariz., 1992—, Mohave Emergency Physicians, Tempe, 1992—; dir. emergency medicine Kingman (Ariz.) Regional Med. Ctr., 1989-92. Active Nat. Emergency Med. Polit. Action Com., 1992—. Fellow Am. Coll. Emergency Physicians; mem. Am. Osteo. Assn., Am. Assn. Osteo. Specialists. Republican. Roman Catholic. Office: Mohave Emergency Physicians 1600 W Broadway Ste 113 Tempe AZ 85282

GOCK, TERRY SAI-WAH, psychologist; b. Hong Kong, Aug. 10, 1951; s. Lloyd Gock and Oi-Lin (Chan) Chen. BA in Psychology summa cum laude, Calif. State U., Chico, 1974; PhD in Clin. Psychology, Washington U., 1980; MPA, U. So. Calif., 1990. Lic. psychologist Calif. Postdoctoral fellow Inst. Psychiatry, Law and Behavioral Scis. U. So. Calif. Sch. Medicine, L.A., 1980-81; staff psychologist Pasadena (Calif.) Guidance Clinics, 1981-84; pvt. practice clin. and forensic psychologist South Pasadena and Alhambra, Calif., 1983—; clinic dir., psychologist South Bay Mental Health Svcs. L.A. County Dept. Mental Health, 1984-89, program dir. program HOPE, 1989-90; assoc. dir. Pacific clinics Asian Pacific Family Ctr., Rosemead, Calif., 1990—; mem. panel experts Superior Ct. of the State of Calif., L.A., 1983—; adj. assoc. prof. Calif. Sch. Profl. Psychology, L.A., 1987-90; mem. adv. com. L.A. County Mental Health Assn., L.A., 1987-89. Reviewing editor Haworth Press Jour., 1987-90; contbr. articles to profl. jours. Exec. bd. mem. Nat. Asian Pacific Am. Families Against Substance Abuse, Washington, 1990—; AIDS task force mem. United Way, L.A., 1988—; chmn. HIV/AIDS Com. and Mental Health Com. Asian Pacific Planning Coun., L.A., 1984-91; mem. Family Diversity Task Force L.A. City Coun., 1986-88. Mem. APA (exec. bd. mem. div. 44 1987-91), Calif. Psychol. Assn. (chmn. div. 4 1987-89), L.A. Soc. Clin. Psychologists (bd. dirs. 1987-89), Am. Assn. Suicidology (bd. dirs. 1981-83), Asian Am. Psychol. Assn. Democrat. Office: 2550 W Main St Ste 201 Alhambra CA 91801-1659

GODAGER, JANE ANN, social worker; b. Blue River, Wis., Nov. 29, 1943; d. Roy and Elmyra Marie (Hood) G. BA, U. Wis., 1965; MSW, Fla. State U., 1969. Lic. clin. social worker. Social worker III State of Wis. Dept Corrections, Wales, 1965-71; supervising psychiat. social worker I State of Calif., San Bernardino, 1972-75, La Mesa, 1975-77; psychiat. social worker State of Calif., San Bernardino, 1978-85; supr. mental health services Riverside (Calif.) County Dept. Mental Health, 1985-86; mental health counselor Superior Ct. San Bernardino County, 1986—; mem. adv. bd. Grad. Sch. Social Work Calif. State U., San Bernardino. Mem. Nat. Assn. Social Workers, Acad. Cert. Social Workers (diplomate), Kappa Kappa Gamma Alumnae Assn. Office: Office Mental Health Counselor 700 E Gilbert St Bldg 1 San Bernardino CA 92415-0920

GODARD, DONALD WESLEY, electric utility administrator; b. Portland, Oreg., Apr. 16, 1947; s. Jack Burrell and Muriel Jean (Guyer) G.; children: Wesley, Lindsay, Daniel. BS, Oreg. State U., 1969; MS, U. Ill., 1971; cert., Bettis Atomic Power Lab., Pitts., 1971. Engr. Teledyne Wah Chang Albany, Oreg., 1976; adminstr. Oreg. Energy Facility Sitting Coun., Salem, 1977-83; gubernatorial appointee Northwest Power Planning Coun., Portland, 1984-87; mgr. Canby (Oreg.) Utility Bd., 1987-92, Grant Pub. Utility Dist., 1992—; alt. bd. dirs. Pacific Northwest Utility Conf. Com., Portland, 1989; pres. Oreg. Mcpl. Electric Utilities, Salem, 1989; chmn. Pub. Power Coun., Portland, 1989-92; trustee Northwest Pub. Power Assn., Vancouver, Wash., 1990—. Leader Washington area Boy Scouts Am., 1972-75; chmn. Canby Sch. Bond Com., 1990-91. Lt. USN, 1971-75. Recipient Disting. Svc. award Oreg. Dept. Energy, 1984. Mem. Canby C. of C. (pres. 1990-91), Canby Rotary (bd. dirs. 1988-90), Hazelnut Growers Soc, Sigma Tau, Tau Beta Phi, Phi Kappa Phi, Sigma Chi. Office: Grante Pub Utility Dist PO Box 878 Epimara WA 98823

GODDARD, TERRY, lawyer. BA, Harvard U., 1969; JD, Ariz. State U., 1976. Mayor City of Phoenix, 1983-90; of counsel Bryan Cave, Phoenix, 1990—; trustee Nat. Trust for Historic Preservation. Bd. dirs. Ariz. Theater Co., Ariz. Family and Child Devel. Ctr., Homeward Bound; former pres. Nat. League of Cities, 1989; former chmn. Ariz. Mcpl. Water Users Assn., Maricopa Assn. Govts., govt. and non-profit group Valley of the Sun United Way, Regional Pub. Transp. Authority, Rebuild Am. Coalition; adv. bd. State and Local Legal Ctr. Comdr. USNR 1970—. Mem. State Bar Ariz., Maricopa County Bar Assn., League of Ariz. Cities and Towns. Office: Bryan Cave 2800 N Central Ave Ste 2100 Phoenix AZ 85004-1052

GODDARD, WILLIAM ANDREW, III, chemist, applied physicist, educator; b. El Centro, Calif., Mar. 29, 1937; s. William Andrew and Barbara Worth (Bright) G.; m. Yvonne Amelia Correy, Oct. 27, 1957; children: William Andrew, Susan Yvonne, Cecelia Moniqué, Lisa Sharéll. B.S. in Engring. with highest honors, UCLA, 1960; Ph.D. in Engring. Sci, Calif. Inst. Tech., 1964. Mem. faculty Calif. Inst. Tech., Pasadena, 1964—; asso. prof. theoretical chemistry Calif. Inst. Tech., 1971-75, prof. theoretical chemistry, 1975-78, prof. chemistry and applied physics, 1978-84, Charles and Mary Ferkel prof. chemistry and applied physics, 1984—, dir. Caltech-NSF materials research group, 1985-91; dir. materials/molecular simulation ctr. Beckman Inst., Calif. Inst. Tech., 1990—; co-founder Molecular Simulations, Inc., 1984, Schrodinger Inc., 1990; vis. staff mem. Los Alamos Sci. Lab., 1973-92; cons. GM Rsch. Labs., 1978—, Argonne Nat. Lab., 1978-82, GE Rsch. and Devel. Labs., 1982—, Failure Analysis Assocs., 1988-90; mem. adv. com. for chemistry NSF, 1983-86, chmn., 1985-86; mem. coun. Gordon Rsch. Confs., 1985-87, trustee, 1987-93. Mem. adv. editorial bd. Chem. Physics, 1972-92, Catalysis Letters, 1988—, Computer Methods in Materials Sci. & Engring, 1991—. Mem. bd. on chem. scis. and tech. Nat. Rsch. Coun., 1985-88, mem. nat. materials adv. bd. com. on tribology of ceramics, 1985-88, mem. U.S. nat. com. for internat. union of pure and applied chemistry, commn. on physical scis., math. and resources, 1985-88, mem. nat. materials adv. bd. com. on computer simulation and analysis on complex materials phenomena, 1986-88, mem. bd. on computer sci. and tech., 1988-91, mem. chemistry panel Nat. Sci. Found. Grad. Fellowship program, 1990-93; mem. adv. coun. Dept. Chemistry Princeton U., 1987—; mem. vis. com. for chemistry dept. Weiss Sch. Natural Scis., Rice U., Houston, 1989—. Recipient Buck-Whitney medal for major contbns. in chemistry, 1978; NSF fellow, 1960-61, 62-64; Shell Found. fellow, 1961-62; Alfred P. Sloan Found. fellow, 1967-69. Fellow Am. Phys. Soc., Am. Assn. Advance Sci.; mem. Nat. Acad. Scis., Materials Rsch. Soc., Am. Chem. Soc. (award for computers in chemistry 1988), Am. Vacuum Soc., Calif. Catalysis Soc., Sigma Xi, Tau Beta Pi. Home: 955 Avondale Rd San Marino CA 91108-1133 Office: Calif Inst Tech Beckman Inst Mail Code 139-74 Pasadena CA 91125

GODDEN, JEAN W., columnist; b. Stamford, Conn., Oct. 1, 1933; d. Maurice Albert and Bernice Elizabeth (Warvel) Hecht; m. Robert W. Godden, Nov. 7, 1952 (dec. Dec. 1985); children: Glenn Scott, Jeffrey Wayne. BA, U. Wash., 1974. News editor Univ. Dist. Herald, Seattle, 1951-53; bookkeeper Omniarts Inc., Seattle, 1963-71; writer editorial page Seattle Post-Intelligencer, Seattle, 1974-80, editorial page editor, 1980-81, bus. editor, 1981-83, city columnist, 1983-91; city columnist Seattle Times, 1991—. Author: The Will to Win, 1980, Hasty Put Ins, 1981. Mem. LWV (dir. 1969-71), Wash. Press Assn. (Superior Performance award 1979), Soc. Profl. Journalists, Mortarboard, City Club, Phi Beta Kappa. Office: The Seattle Times PO Box 70 Seattle WA 98111

GODFREY, PAUL BARD, lawyer; b. Denver, Jan. 10, 1927; s. Thurman A. and Florence B. (Bard) G.; children: Brett, Scott. BA, U. Wyo., 1949, JD, 1955. Bar: Wyo. 1955, U.S. Ct. Appeals (10th cir.) 1955, U.S. Dist. Ct. Wyo. 1955, Colo. 1987. Ptnr. Henderson, Thomson & Godfrey, 1955-60, Cheyenne, Wyo., ptnr., Henderson & Godfrey, 1960-67; ptnr. Godfrey & Sundahl, 1975-91, of counsel, 1991—. Chmn. Young Republicans, 1957-58; Rep. committeeman, 1964-66. Served with U.S. Army, 1945-46. Mem. Internat. Acad. Trail Lawyers, Bd. Trial Advs., ABA, Wyo. Bar Assn., Laramie County Bar Assn., Am. Legion, C. of C. (pres. 1961-62). Episcopalian. Lodges: Elks, Shriners, Masons. Home: PO Box 328 Cheyenne WY 82003-0328

GODFREY, RICHARD GEORGE, real estate appraiser; b. Sharon, Pa., Dec. 18, 1927; s. Fay Morris and Elisabeth Maguerite (Stefanak) G.; m. Golda Fay Goss, Oct. 28, 1951; children: Deborah Jayne, Gayle Rogers, Bryan Edward. BA, Ripon Coll., 1949. V.p. 1st Thrift & Loan Assn., Albuquerque, 1959-61; pres. Richard G. Godfrey & Assocs., Inc., Albuquerque, 1961—. Mem. Appraisal Inst. (v.p. 1981-82), Am. Right of Way Assn., Am. Soc. Real Estate Counselors (cert.). Baptist. Home: 1700 Columbia Dr SE Albuquerque NM 87106-3311 Office: 523 Louisiana Blvd SE Albuquerque NM 87108-3842

GODSEY, C. WAYNE, broadcasting executive; b. Lynchburg, Va., Aug. 5, 1946; s. Carl Dodge and Frances Anna (Keesee) G.; m. Anne Marie Ruzicka, Oct., 1979; children: Rebecca Susan, Patricia Anne, Thomas Lawrence. BA in English, Lynchburg Coll., 1968. Reporter Sta. WSOC-TV, Charlotte, N.C., 1969-71, news dir., 1971-74; reporter, producer Newsweek Broadcasting, N.Y.C., 1974-77; news dir. Sta. WTMJ-TV and Radio, Milw., 1977-82; v.p., gen. mgr. Sta. WTMJ-TV, Milw., 1982-84, Sta. WISN-TV, Milw., 1984-87, Sta. KOAT-TV, Albuquerque, 1987—; past state chmn. 1990 Red Ribbon Campaign; past chmn. Albuquerque Bus. Edn. Co., 1988-90; lector Eucharistic Min. Our Lady Annunciation. Bd. dirs. Easter Seal Soc., Milw., 1984-87, Better Bus. Bur., Milw., 1984-87, Big Bros. and Big Sisters, Milw., 1985-87, Centurions of St. Joseph Hosp., Milw., 1985-87, Children's Hosp. Wis., 1987-88, Great Southwest Coun. of Boy Scouts Am., 1991—; mem. N.Mex. Gov.'s Bus. Adv. Com., 1988—; mem. Albuquerque Econ. Forum, 1988—, co-chmn.; mem. Albuquerque Bus. Edn. Compact, 1988-90; mem. N.Mex. Amigos; mem. N.Mex. Open Records Task Force, 1990—, Hon. Commander 551st Flight Tng. Squadron KAFB, 1991-92. Mem. Nat. Assn. Broadcasters (task force on drug and alcohol abuse 1984-86), Wis. Broadcasters Assn. (chmn. legis. liaison com.), Albuquerque Econ. Forum, N.Mex. Broadcasters Assn. (bd. dirs. 1988-91), Albuquerque C. of C. (bd. dirs., Superior Svc. award 1991), Arbitron Adv. Coun., Soc. Profl.

Journalists, U. N.Mex. Lobo Club (bd. dirs.), Four Hills Country Club. Republican. Roman Catholic. Home: 14004 Wind Mountain Rd NE Albuquerque NM 87112-6520 Office: Sta KOAT-TV PO Box 25982 Albuquerque NM 87125-0982

GOEDICKE, JEAN, artist, educator; b. Depass, Wyo., Sept. 24, 1908; s. Ernest Paul and Florence (Walker) G. A.A., Casper Coll., 1960; B.A. with honors, U. Wyo., 1967, M.A., 1971. Rural sch. tchr. Fremont County, Lander, Wyo., 1931-32; social worker WPA, CWA, ERA, Fremont County, 1932-37; program supr. Employment Security Commn. Wyo., Casper, 1938-72; profl. artist Jean Goedicke Watercolors, Casper, 1940—; art instr. and project dir. Mobile Arts Symposium, 1967-78, Friends of Artists, 1978-84; project dir., Casper Artists Guild, 1979—; chmn. Wyo. State Art Gallery Adv. Coun., 1972-79, 50 Yr. Retrospective Art Exhbn., Nicolayson Art Mus., Casper, 1993; Author: This is Wyoming ... Listen, 1977 (poetry), Wyoming Writers Anthology, 1989, 91. Sec. Casper Community Concert Assn., 1966—. Mem. Wyo. Artists Assn. (pres. 1965-66), Scotch and Watercolor Soc. Republican. Episcopalian. Club: Casper Fine Arts. Home: 2125 S Coffman Ave Casper WY 82604-3526

GOEI, BERNARD THWAN-POO (BERT GOEI), supervising architectural designer; b. Semarang, Indonesia, Jan. 27, 1938; came to U.S., 1969; naturalized, 1976; s. Ignatius Ing-Khien Goei and Nicolette Giok-Nio Tjioe; m. Sioe-Tien Liem, May 26, 1966; children: Kimberley Hendrika, Gregory Fitzgerald. BA in Fine Arts, Bandung Inst. Tech. State U. Indonesia, 1961, MA in Archtl. Space Planning, 1964; postgrad., U. Heidelberg, Germany, 1967-68. Co-owner, chief designer Pondok Mungil Interiors Inc., Bandung, 1962-64; dept. mgr., fin. advisor Gumarna Architects, Engrs. and Planners, Inc., Bandung, Jakarta, Indonesia, 1964-67; shop supr., model maker Davan Scale Models, Toronto, Ont., Can., 1968-69; chief archtl. designer George T. Nowak Architects and Assocs., Westchester, Calif., 1969-72; sr. archtl. designer Krisel & Shapiro Architects and Assocs., L.A., 1972-74; sr. supervising archtl. designer The Ralph M. Parsons A/E Co., Pasadena, Calif., 1974—; v.p. United Gruno U.S.A. Corp. Import/Export, Monterey Park, Calif., 1980-89. Mem. Rep. Presdl. Task Force, Washington, 1982—, Nat. Rep. Senatorial Com., Washington, 1983—, Nat. Rep. Congrl. Com., Washington, 1981—, Rep. Nat. Com., 1982—. Recipient Excellent Design Achievement commendation Strategic Def. Initiative "Star Wars" Program, 1988, USAF Space Shuttle Program, West Coast Space-Port, 1984; scholar U. Heidelberg, 1967-68. Mem. NRA, Indonesian Am. Soc., Dutch Am. Soc., Second Amendment Found., The Right to Keep and Bear Arms Com. Roman Catholic. Office: Ralph M Parsons A/E Co 100 W Walnut St Pasadena CA 91124-0001

GOERTZEL, BENJAMIN NATHANIEL, mathematics educator; b. Rio de Janeiro, Dec. 8, 1966; s. Ted George and Carol Sandra (Zwell) G.; m. Gwendolyn Michele Yorgey, June 21, 1988; 1 child, Zarathustra Amadeus. BA in Math., Simon's Rock Coll., Gt. Barrington, Mass., 1985; PhD in Math., Temple U., 1989. Asst. prof. math. U. Nev., Las Vegas, 1989—. Author: The Structure of Intelligence, 1992, The Evolving Mind, 1992; also articles. Mem. Soc. for Chaos Theory in Psychology. Office: U Nev Math Dept 4505 S Maryland Pky Las Vegas NV 89154

GOETZEL, CLAUS GUENTER, metallurgical engineer; b. Berlin, July 14, 1913; came to U.S., 1936; s. Walter and Else (Baum) G.; m. Lilo Kallmann, Nov. 19, 1938; children: Rodney G., Vivian L. Dipl.-Ing., Technische Hochschule, Berlin, 1935; PhD, Columbia U., 1939. Registered profl. engr., Calif. Research chemist, lab. head Hardy Metall. Co., 1936-39; tech. dir., works mgr. Am. Electro Metal Corp., 1939-47; v.p., dir. research Sintercast Corp. Am., 1947-57; adj. prof. NYU, N.Y.C., 1945-57, sr. research scientist, 1957-60; cons. scientist Lockheed Missiles & Space Co., Sunnyvale, Calif., 1960-78; cons. metall. engring. Portola Valley, Calif., 1978—; lectr., vis. scholar Stanford (Calif.) U., 1961-88. Author: Treatise on Powder Metallurgy, 5 vols., 1949-63; contbr. articles to profl. jours. Recipient Alexander von Humboldt Sr. U.S. Scientist award, Fed. Republic Germany, 1978. Fellow Am. Soc. Metals, AIAA (assoc.); mem. AIME (life), Am. Powder Metallurgy Inst. (sr.), Metal Sci. Club N.Y. (life, past pres.), Inst. Metals (life, London). Office: Stanford U Bldg 550 Dept Materials Sci & Engring Stanford CA 94305

GOETZINGER, CAROLYN MARIE, newspaper editor; b. Milw., Oct. 28, 1961; d. Ted S. Goetzinger and Lee C. Alexander-Alley. BA in Journalism, Sociology, Winona State U., 1984. City/county reporter Fairmont (Minn.) Sentinel, 1984-86; copy editor, reporter Yuma (Ariz.) Daily Sun, 1986-87, asst. city editor, 1987-89, city editor, 1989—; Bd. dirs. Kids Voting, Yuma, 1990—; researcher, writer Current Events Challenge, Yuma, 1990—. Mem. LWV (bd. dirs. Yuma chpt. 1990—). Home: 1280 W 24th St Apt 17 Yuma AZ 85364

GOETZKE, GLORIA LOUISE, social worker, income tax specialist; b. Monticello, Minn.; d. Wesley and Marvel (Kreidler) G. BA, U. Minn., 1964; MSW, U. Denver, 1966; MBA, U. St. Thomas, 1977. Cert. enrollment to practice before IRS. Social worker VA Med. Ctr., L.A., 1980—; master tax preparer and instr. H&R Block, Santa Monica, Calif.; clin. instr. UCLA Grad. Sch. of Social Welfare; adj. prof. Calif. State U., Long Beach Grad. Sch. of Social Work. Mem. Nat. Assn. Social Workers (cert.). Lutheran.

GOFF, JOHN SAMUEL, history educator, lawyer; b. L.A., June 20, 1931; s. Samuel J. and Elizabeth (Wilhelm) G.; m. Jean T. Lamb, Aug. 7, 1955 (div. 1964); 1 child, Margaret E.; m. Lyenatte Swafford, Sept. 16, 1967 (div. 1986); 1 child, John S. AB, U. So. Calif., L.A., 1953, AM, 1955, PhD, 1960; JD, Ariz. State U., Tempe, 1974. Bar: Ariz. 1978. From instr. to asst. prof. history West Tex. State U., Canyon, 1957-60; prof. history Phoenix Coll., 1960—, chmn. dept. social scis., 1962-69, dir. legal assistants program, 1975-85. Author books. Mem. Ariz. Hist. Found. (bd. dirs. Tempe 1980-), Ariz. Hist. Soc. (Cen. Ariz. chpt., bd. dirs. Phoenix chpt. 1978—). Presbyterian. Office: Phoenix Coll 1202 W Thomas Rd Phoenix AZ 85013-4234

GOFORTH, CHARLES PRESTON, lawyer; b. Lake Charles, La., Mar. 6, 1950; s. Charles Preston and Mackie V (Miller) G. BA, Tex. Christian U., 1972; JD, U. Va., 1975. Ba: Va., D.C., U.S. Ct. Mil. Appeals. Enlisted U.S. Army, 1975, advanced through grades to capt., 1984; legal advisor U.S. Army Corps Engrs., Tulsa, Okla., 1984; contract negotiator Tex. Instruments, Inc., Dallas, 1984-87; sr. contract adminstr. Murdock Engring. Co., Irving, Tex., 1987-88; mgr. Purchasing Murdock Engring., Dallas, 1988-89; subcontract mgmt. specialist Lockheed Missiles & Space, Sunnyvale, Calif., 1989-91; dir. contracts and adminstrn. Lockheed Integrated Solutions Co., Santa Clara, Calif., 1991—. Author: DSS-W Contract Clause Book, 1979; editor and author mag./jours. The Judge Adv. Legal Svc., 1975-78; editor mag./jour. The Army Lawyer, 1975-78 (Commendation 1978). Decorated various awards and decorations; Nat. Merit scholar, 1968-72. Mem. Nat. Contract Mgmtm. Assn., Nat. Mgmt. Assn. Republican. Presbyterian. Home: 1180 Reed Ave Apt 67 Sunnyvale CA 94086-8445 Office: Lockheed Integrated Solutions Co 881 Martin Ave Santa Clara CA 95050-2903

GOFORTH, NATHAN DAN, police officer; b. Phoenix, Sept. 12, 1951; s. Nathan and Mabel Lettie (Deal) G.; m. Lori Ann Petersen (div. 1984). AA in Bus. Adminstrn., Glendale Community Coll., Ariz., 1974, AA in Adminstrn. Justice, 1976; BS in Pub. Programs, Ariz. State U., 1985. Second asst. mgr. Smittys Big Town, Phoenix, 1967-73, sales rep., 1975-76; sr. inventory auditor Motorola Semiconductor, Phoenix, 1973-74; police officer City Glendale, Ariz., 1976—; Interpretor for deaf Glendale Police Dept., 1976—, peer counselor, 1989—, field tng. officer, 1980—; vol. tchr. Glendale Community Coll. Police Res. Acad., 1989—. Res. hwy. patrolman Ariz. Dept. Pub. Safety, Phoenix, 1975-76; advisor Glendale Explorer Post 469, 1978—, instl. head, 1992. Recipient Dedication to DAV award, 1990-91, Cert. of Appreciation award Independence High Sch., 1990, Outstanding Vol. Svc. award MADD, 1991. Mem. NRA, Ariz. State U. Alumni Assn., Internat. Police Assn., Fraternal Order of Police (treas. 1990—), Ariz. Cts. Assn., Critical Incident Stress Debriefing (S.W. region), Sons of Am. Legion. Office: Glendale Police Dept 6835 N 57th Dr Glendale AZ 85301-3218

GOFORTH, RAYMOND REED, librarian, editor, publisher; b. Fullerton, CA, Feb. 6, 1968; s. Raymond Reed and Eileen Mary (Pitcher) G.; m. Kimberly Anne Richards, Oct. 8, 1988. Grassroots organizer Calif. League Conservation Voters, Santa Ana, 1988; canvasser Greenpeace Action, Seattle, 1989-90; adminstrv. coord. Metroctr. YMCA, Seattle, 1990-91; editor, publisher Bad Haircut Mag., Olympia, Wash., 1987—; libr. The Evergreen State Coll., Olympia, 1991—; mem. hearing bd. The Evergreen State Coll., Olympia, 1991-93. Columnist Cooper Point Jour., Olympia, 1991-92. Vol. campaign staff Dave Elder for State Assembly, 1987, Willard Murray for State Assembly, 1988, Wil Baca for State Assembly, 1990, Calif.; Laura Lake for City Coun., L.A., 1989. Recipient Steven Gibson Meml. award, 1992, 93. Home: PO Box 2827 Olympia WA 98507

GOGARTY, WILLIAM BARNEY, oil company executive, consultant; b. Provo, Utah, Apr. 23, 1930; s. William B. and Zola (Walker) G.; m. Lois Gay Pritchett, Dec. 14, 1951; children: Laura Gay, Colleen, William Shaun, Kathlyn, Michael Barney. BS, U. Utah, 1953, PhD, 1959. Registered profl. engr., Colo. With Marathon Oil Co., Denver and Findlay, Ohio, 1959-86, sr. staff engr., Findlay, 1973-75, assoc. rsch. dir. prodn., Denver, 1975-86, ret. 1986; pvt. practice enhanced oil recovery cons., Littleton, Colo., 1986—; adj. assoc. prof. chem. engring. and metallurgy dept. U. Denver, 1967-73; cons. Ciba-Geigy Corp; mem. Nat. Petroleum Coun. chem. task group Com. on Enhanced Oil Recovery, 1982-84; cons., tchr. Dept. Tech. Cooperation, UN, India, 1986, Rogaland Rsch. Inst., Norsk Hydro and Statoil, Norway, 1987, Petromer Trend Corp., Indonesia, 1988, Petrobras, Brazil, 1989; Muskat lectr. U. Utah, 1985. Contbr. articles to profl. jours.; patentee in field. Mem. Rep. precinct com., Littleton, Colo., 1984. Served to 1st lt. AUS, 1953-55. Mem. NAE, Am. Inst. Chem. Engrs., Soc. Petroleum Engrs. (fluid mechanics and oil recovery process tech. com. 1963-65, monograph com. 1971-73, chmn. monograph com. 1973, textbook com. 1974-76, chmn. textbook com. 1976, program vice chmn. 1977-78, Lester C. Uren award com. 1980-82, chmn. award com. 1982, program com. for Soc. Petroleum Engrs./U.S. Dept. Energy Enhanced Oil Recovery Symposium 1982, Disting. lectr. 1982-83, Lester C. Uren award 1987, region II dir.-elect 1988-89, bd. dirs. 1989-90, Henry Mattson Tech. Svc. award Denver petroleum sect. 1989, Enhanced Oil Recovery Pioneer award Mid-Continent region, 1990), Sigma Xi, Tau Beta Phi, Phi Kappa Phi, Alpha Chi Sigma. Mem. LDS Ch.

GOGOLIN, MARILYN TOMPKINS, educational administrator, language pathologist; b. Pomona, Calif., Feb. 25, 1946; d. Roy Merle and Dorothy (Davidson) Tompkins; m. Robert Elton Gogolin, Mar. 29, 1969. BA, U. LaVerne, Calif., 1967; MA, U. Redlands, Calif., 1968; postgrad., U. Washington, 1968-69; MS, Calif. State U., Fullerton, 1976. Cert. clin. speech pathologist; cert. teaching and sch. adminstrn. Speech and lang. pathologist Rehab. Hosp., Pomona, 1969-71; diagnostic tchr. L.A. County Office of Edn., Downey, Calif., 1971-72, program specialist, 1972-74, cons. lang., 1975-76, cons. orgns. and mgmt., 1976-79, dir. adminstrv. affairs, asst. to supt., 1979—; cons. lang. sch. dists., Calif., 1975-79; cons. orgn. and mgmt. and profl. assns., Calif., 1976—; exec. dir. L.A. County Sch. Trustees Assn., 1979—. Founding patron Desert chpt. Kidney Found., Palm Desert, Calif., 1985. Doctoral fellow U. Washington, 1968; named One of Outstanding Young Women Am., 1977. Mem. Am. Mgmt. Assn., Am. Speech/Hearing Assn., Calif. Speech/Hearing Assn., Am. Edn. Research Assn. Baptist. Office: LA County Office Edn 9300 Imperial Hwy Downey CA 90242-2813

GOHEEN, DAVID WADE, chemical consultant; b. Bellingham, Wash., June 23, 1920; s. Frank B. and Melanie Charlotte (Clement) G.; m. LAura Elizabeth Smith, Nov. 27, 1943; children: Stephen C., Frank W. BS in Chemistry, U. Wash., 1942, PhD in Chemistry, 1951. Weather observer U.S. Weather Bur., Tatoosh Island, Wash., 1940-41; rsch. assoc. U. Mich., Ann Arbor, 1951-52; chief chem. rsch. sect. Crown Zellerbach Corp. Cen. Rsch. Div., Camas, Wash., 1952-55; sr. rsch. chemist Crown Zellerbach Corp. Cen. Rsch. Div., 1955-78; project leader Pioneering Rsch. Crown Zellerbach, 1978-82; v.p. E.M. Seidel Assn., Wed Chem., Gleneden Beach, 1982—; chem. cons. Gaylord Chem. Corp., Slidall, La., 1987—, Scott Paper, Phila., 1987-88; corp. sec., dir. Nana Global Industries, Vancouver, Wash., 1988—; centennial chemist Am. Chem. Soc., Portland, 1976; vis. scientist U. Gronigen (The Netherlands), 1968-69. Contbr. articles to periodicals; patentee in field. 1st lt. U.S. Army, 1942-46. Presbyterian. Home: PO Box 826 2193 NE 3d Ave Camas WA 98607 Office: Eugene M Seidel Assoc Wed Chem PO Box 709 Gleneden Beach OR 97388-0709

GOIN, OLIVE BOWN, biologist; b. Pitts., Dec. 2, 1912; d. Charles Elmer and Anne Louise (Hay) Bown; m. Coleman Goin, June 7, 1940 (dec.); children: Lyndd, Coleman Jr. AB, Wellesley Coll., 1934; MS, U. Pitts., 1936. Asst. lab. mammalogy Carnegie Mus., Pitts., 1934-40; lab. instr. to asst. prof. U. Fla., Gainesville, 1942-46; rsch. assoc. Mus. of No. Ariz., Flagstaff, 1971-80; ret. Author: World Outside My Door, 1953, Introduction to Herpetology, 1962, Comparative Vertebrate Anatomy, Man and the Natural World, 1970, Introduction to Herpetology, 2d edit., 1971, Journey onto Land, 1974, Man and the Natural World, 2d edit. 1975 (all with C. J. Goin); (with C. J. Goin and George Zug) Introduction to Herpetology, 3d edit., 1978; contbr. numerous articles to profl. jours.

GOIN, PETER JACKSON, art educator; b. Madison, Wis., Nov. 26, 1951; m. Chelsea Miller; children: Kari, Dana. BA, Hamline U., 1973; MA, U. Iowa, 1975, MFA, 1976. Assoc. prof. art U. Nev., Reno, 1984—. Author: Tracing the Line: A Photographic Survey of the Mexican-American Border, 1987, Nuclear Landscapes, 1991, Arid Waters: Photographs from the Water in the West Project, 1992, Stopping Time: A Rephotographic Survey of Lake Tahoe, 1992; sole exhbns. include Nora Eccles Harrison Mus. Art, Logan, Utah, 1992, Duke U. Mus. Art, Durham, N.C., 1992, Phoenix Mus. Art, 1992, Indpls. Mus. Art, 1992, Savannah (Ga.) Coll. Art and Design, 1992, Nev. Humanities Com. Travelling Exhibit, 1992 and others. Recipient grant NEA, 1981, 90. Office: Univ Nev Dept Art Reno NV 89557

GOKA, RICHARD SHUNJI, physician, educator; b. Santa Monica, Calif., June 7, 1947; s. Robert Katsutoshi and Miwako (Tanaka) G.; m. Benecia Co Hong, Mar. 31, 1978; children: Kimberly, Kristoffer. BS in Biology, Calif. State U., Hayward, 1972; MD, U. Autonoma de Guadalajara, Mex., 1977. Diplomate Am. Bd. Phys. Medicine and Rehab., Am. Bd. Pain Management. Clin. faculty U. Utah, Salt Lake City, 1981-86; med. dir. Quinney Rehab. Inst., Salt Lake City, 1982-89, Leon S. Peters Rehab. Ctr., Fresno, Calif., 1989-92; med. dir. Villa Serena, Salt Lake City, 1988-89, Western States Adminstrn., Fresno, 1990—; vis. prof. Emory U., Atlanta, 1984-85, U. Autonoma de Guadalajara, Mex., 1984; cons. Learning Svcs. South Valley, Gilroy, Calif., 1990—. Contbr. articles to profl. jours. Cons. State Dept. Rehab., Salt Lake City, 1981-89. Fellow Am. Acad. Phys. Medicine and Rehab.; mem. Am. Congress Rehab. (membership com.), Head Injury, Interdiscipline, Spl. Interest Group (membership com.), Nat. Head Injury Found. Home: PO Box 14089 Fresno CA 93650-4089

GOLD, ANNE MARIE, library director; b. N.Y.C., Feb. 24, 1949; d. James Raymond and Marion Rita (Magner) Scully; m. Steven Louis Gold, Aug. 9, 1974; 1 child, Lauren Z. BA in English, St. Lawrence U., 1971; MS in Libr. Svc., Columbia U., 1972. Libr. N.Y. Pub. Libr., N.Y.C., 1972-74, Oakland (Calif.) Pub. Libr., 1975-80; head reference Solano County Libr., Fairfield, Calif., 1980-82, libr. Vallejo region, 1982-84, coord. libr. brs. and ext. svcs., 1984-86, dir. libr. svcs., 1986-90; county libr. Contra Costa County Libr., Pleasant Hill, Calif., 1990—. Mem. ALA, Pub. Libr. Assn. (Allie Beth Martin award com. 1986-88, chair 1991 nominating com. 1989-91, pub. librs. adv. bd. 1989-93, bd. dirs. 1992-93, chair orgn. and planning com. met. librs. sect. 1988-89, v.p. 1991-92, pres. 1992-93, br. librs. com. small and medium sized librs. sect. 1985-87, 1988 nominating com. 1986-88), Calif. Libr. Assn. (coun. mem. 1985-87, 90-92, exec. bd. 1991-92, co-chair legis. com. 1992-93), Calif. Inst. Librs. (nominating com. 1989, v.p. 1990-91), Calif. Soc. Librs. (com. profl. standards 1986-87), Libr. Adminstrn. and Mgmt. Assn. (program com. 1989-91). Office: Contra Costa County Libr 1750 Oak Park Blvd Pleasant Hill CA 94523

GOLD, MARVIN HAROLD, chemist, consultant; b. Buffalo, June 23, 1915; s. Max and Jennie (Frankel) G.; m. Sophye Mendelson, Aug. 31, 1940; children: Judith May Bloom, Norman Charles. BA, UCLA, 1937; PhD, U. Ill., 1940. Rsch. assoc. Northwestern U., Evanston, Ill., 1940-42; rsch. group leader The Visking Corp., Chgo., 1942-48; sr. scientist Aerojet Gen. Corp., Sacramento and Azusa, Calif., 1948-72; tech. cons./chemist Sacramento, 1972—. Contbr. articles to profl. jours.; inventor/patentee (more than 85) in chems., plastics, coatings, insulations, lubricants. Pres. People to People of Sacramento, 1962-65. Recipient Civilian Meritorious Svc. Citation USN, 1962; Anna Fuller Fund Cancer Rsch. fellow Nat. Cancer Inst., 1940-42. Mem. Am. Chem. Soc. (sec. councilor 1967-68), Sigma Xi (chpt. pres. 1966), Phi Lambda Upsilon. Jewish. Home and Office: 2601 Latham Dr Sacramento CA 95864

GOLD, MICHAEL NATHAN, investment banker, management consultant; b. Chgo., May 3, 1952; s. Julius and Sarah (Blitzblau) G.; m. Cynthia Bilicki, June 19, 1976; children: Aaron Michael, Nathan Matthew. BA, Kalamazoo Coll., 1976; cert. in exec. mgmt., UCLA, 1989. Rsch. fellow Sinai Hosp., Detroit, 1976; rsch. assoc. Molecular Biological Inst., UCLA, L.A., 1976-77; lab mgr., adminstr. Biomed. Engring. Ctr. U. So. Calif., L.A., 1977-80; asst. dir. Crump Inst. for Med. Engring. UCLA, 1980-84, assoc. dir., exec. officer Crump Inst. for Med. Engring., 1984-89; chmn., pres. Therapeutic Environments Inc., Van Nuys, Calif., 1989-91; pres. Michael Gold & Assocs., Van Nuys, 1989—; investment banker Crimson Capital Corp. Ministry of Privatization, Czech Republic, 1991—. Mem. IEEE, Assn. for Advancement of Med. Instrumentation, Clin. Ligand Assay Soc., Am. Assn. for Med. Systems and Informatics, Sea Edn. Assn., Biomed. Engring. Soc., Internat. Soc. for Optical Engring. Office: Michael Gold & Assocs 236 W Mountain St 101 Pasadena CA 91103

GOLD, RICK L., federal government executive; b. Rexburg, Idaho, June 25, 1946; s. Raymond Russell and Thelma (Lee) G.; m. Anamarie Sanone, May 14, 1988; children: Nanette Phillips, Russell. BSCE, Utah State U., 1968, MSCE, 1970. Registered profl. engr., Colo., Mont. Hydraulic engr. U.S. Bur. Reclamation, Provo, Utah, 1969-73; project hydrologist U.S. Bur. Reclamation, Durango, Colo., 1973-75; regional hydrologist U.S. Bur. Reclamation, Billings, Mont., 1975-81; spl. asst. to regional dir. U.S. Bur. Reclamation, Washington, 1981-82; asst. planning officer U.S. Bur. Reclamation, Billings, 1982-83; projects mgr. U.S. Bur. Reclamation, Durango, Colo., 1983-88; regional planning officer U.S. Bur. Reclamation, Salt Lake City, 1988-90, asst. regional dir., 1990—; mem. water quality com. Internat. Joint Commn. Study on Garrison Divsn. Unit, Billings, 1975-77; fed. negotiator Cost Sharing and Indian Water Rights Settlement, Durango, 1986-88; chmn. Cooperating Agy. on Glen Canyon Dam EIS, Salt Lake City, 1990—. Contbr. articles to profl. jours.; author papers. Mem. Rotary Internat., Durango, 1985-87; bd. dirs. United Way of La Plata County, Durango, 1983-88; chmn. Combined Fed. Campaign, La Plata County, 1985. Mem. ASCE, Internat. Com. on Irrigation and Drainage. Office: US Bur Reclamation 125 S State St Salt Lake City UT 84147

GOLD, ROBERT ARTHUR, textile executive; b. N.Y.C., Dec. 25, 1923; s. Herman Gothelf and Rose Alice (Moll) G.; 1 child, Ricci Jaye. BA, UCLA, 1979; MFA, U. So. Calif., 1982. Asst. v.p. Henry Lilling Corp., N.Y.C., 1946-47; regional sales mgr. Storkline Family Corp., N.Y.C., 1947-48; dir. alumni affairs Zeta Beta Tau Fraternity, N.Y.C., 1948-49; v.p. Am. Silk Label Mfg. Co., N.Y.C., 1949-54; merchandising mgr. Fuller Fabrice div. J.P. Stevens Co., N.Y.C., 1954-63; product mgr. Iselin-Jefferson div. Dan River Mills, N.Y.C., 1963-68; ptnr. Rabin Textiles, Inc., L.A., 1968-77; pres. Ragold Corp., L.A., 1977—; vice chmn. Corduroy Coun. Am., N.Y.C., 1967-68. Dist. leader Dem. Party of Queens, N.Y., 1966-67; v.p. Save-A-Life, 1981-82. Lt. USAAF, 1942-46. Mem. Textile Assn. L.A. (bd. dirs. 1976-77). Home and Office: PO Box 491163 Los Angeles CA 90049

GOLD, SHIRLEY JEANNE, state legislator, labor relations specialist; b. N.Y.C., Oct. 2, 1925; d. Louis and Gussie (Lefkowitz) Diamondstein; BA in Music, Hunter Coll., 1945; MA in Behavioral Sci. (Crown-Zellerbach Corp. scholar), Reed Coll., 1962; m. David E. Gold, June 22, 1947; children: Andrew, Dana. Tchr., Portland (Oreg.) Public Schs., 1954-68; pres. Portland Fedn. Tchrs., Am. Fedn. Tchrs./AFL-CIO, 1965-72, pres. Oreg. Fedn. Tchrs., 1972-77; cons. labor relations, 1977-80; mem. Oreg. Ho. of Reps., Salem, 1980-88, majority leader, 1985-88, chmn. legis. rules, ops. and reform, human resources com., 1983-84, revenue com., 1987-88, policy and priorities, com. of edn., commn. of states, from 1987, campaign fin. reform com., from 1987; now state senator Oreg. Senate; senate chair Revenue and Edn. Coms.; mem. Agriculture/Natural Resources Com. and Children's Task Force; mem. Oreg. Tchr. Tenure Rev. Bd., 1965-72; mem. Nat. Multi-State Consortium, 1974; mem. Speak Out Oreg. com. to White House and Congress, 1978; mem. Oreg. Task Force on Tax Reform; mem. Solid Waste Regional Policy Commn., 1989-91; AFL-CIO scholar George Meany Inst., 3 times, 1976-77; commr., nat. vice chmn. Edn. Commn. of States, 1988-90; mem. Oreg. Commn. on Women. Chairperson precinct com., conv. del. Oreg. Democratic Party, 1960-80, dist. leader, chairperson edn. com., 1978-80; charter mem., mem. exec. bd., v.p. Oreg. Council for Cts., 1977-80. Named to Hunter Coll. Hall of Fame, 1985, Citizen of Yr., 1985. Mem. Hunter Coll. Alumni Assn., Reed Coll. Alumni Assn., Pacific N.W. Labor History Assn., Portland Fedn. Tchrs., Oreg. Fedn. Tchrs., Oreg. Fedn. Dem. Women, Oreg. Coalition for Nat. Health Security, Oreg. Women's Polit. Caucus, Com. on Drug Abuse, Northwest Oreg. Health System, ACLU, Coalition Labor Union Women. Jewish. Contbr. articles on labor relations to Willamette Week newspaper, 1977-80; editor Oreg. Tchr. newspaper, 1970-72. Office: S217 State Capitol Salem OR 97310-1347

GOLD, STANLEY P., chemical company executive, manufacturing company executive; b. 1942. AB, U. Calif., 1964; JD, U. So. Calif., 1967. Ptnr. Gang Tyre and Brown, 1967—, Shamrock Holdings Inc., 1985—; pres., chief exec. officer Shamrock Holdings; chmn., CEO, dir. L.A. Gear Inc., L.A., 1992—. Office: Shamrock Holdings 4444 W Lakeside Dr Burbank CA 91505-4054 also: LA Gear Inc 2850 Ocean Park Blvd Santa Monica CA 90405

GOLD, VERA JOHNSON, marketing executive; b. Newcastle, Eng., Aug. 23, 1951; d. Frank and Margaret Mary (Gallagher) Johnson; m. Samuel Gold; children: Margaret, Melanie. Student, Stage Career Ctr., Eng., No. Coll. Commerce, Newcastle; BA in Bus Adminstrn., Gondon U., London; student, European Gemological Inst., Antwerp, Belgium; MS in Fin. Planning, So. States U., 1992. CFP. Dir. sales Cascade Industries, High Wycome, Eng., 1980; radio record promoter Pablo Records, Beverly Hills, Calif., 1981-82; ops. and pub. rels. mgr. Pacific Stock Exchange, L.A., 1982-86; exec. dir. Investors Club of the Air, L.A., 1986-87; co-founder, chief exec. officer Money Radio, L.A., 1986—. Dir. radio program, author mags., tapes, Vera's Voice, 1987; producer musical rev. We're in the Money, L.A. Mem. Asian Bus. Assn., Nat. Assn. Broadcasters, L.A. Press Club, Soroptimists. Office: Money Radio 2300 S Mills Ave Pomona CA 91766

GOLDAPER, GABRIELE GAY, clothing executive, consultant; b. Amsterdam, The Netherlands, May 4, 1937; came to U.S., 1949; d. Richard and Gertrud (Sinzheimer) Mainzer; married, 1957; children: Carolyn, Julie, Nancy. BA in Econs., Barnard Coll., 1959; BS in Edn., U. Cin., 1960; postgrad., Xavier U., 1962. V.p. planning, systems and material control High Tide Swimwear div. Warnaco, Los Angeles, 1974-79; v.p., customer support cons. Silton AMS, Los Angeles, 1979-80; exec. v.p., ptnr. Prisma Corp., Los Angeles, 1980-84; exec. v.p. Mindstar Prods., Los Angeles, 1984-85; gen. mgr. Cherry Lane, Los Angeles, 1985-86; dir. inventory mgmt. Barco Uniforms, Los Angeles, 1986; mgmt. cons. to clothing industry Santa Monica, Calif., 1986—; instr. Calif. State U., 1978-79, UCLA Grad. Bus. Mgmt. Sch., 1979-86, Fashion Inst. Design and Merchandising. 1985—; chmn. data processing com. Calif. Fashion Creators, 1980; mediator Los Angeles County Bar Assn.; cons. Exec. Service Corps; lectr. various colls. Author: A Results Oriented Approach to Manufacturing Planning, 1978, Small Company View of the Computer, 1979; also articles. Elected mem. Commn. on Status Women, 1985-89. Mem. Apparel Mfrs. Assn. (mgmt. systems com. 1978-80), Calif. Apparel Industries Assn. (exec. com., bd. dirs. 1980), Am. Arbitration Assn. Home: 37 Village Pky Santa Monica CA 90405

GOLDBECK, ROBERT ARTHUR, JR., physical chemist; b. Evanston, Ill., July 25, 1950; s. Robert Arthur Sr. and Ruth Marilyn (Nordwall) G.; m. Jennifer Jane Tollkuhn, Aug. 19, 1989; stepchildren: Jessica Kathleen Tollkuhn, Brenna Maurin Tollkuhn. BS, U. Calif., Berkeley, 1974; PhD, U. Calif., Santa Cruz, 1982. Postdoctoral fellow Stanford (Calif.) U., 1983-84, rsch. assoc., 1984-87; rsch. chemist U. Calif., Santa Cruz, 1987—; lectr. in chemistry U. Calif., 1980, 84, 86. Contbr. articles to Biophys. Jour.; contbr. articles to profl. jours. Mem. AAAS, Am. Chem. Soc., Biophys. Soc. Office: U Calif Dept Chemistry/Biochemistry Santa Cruz CA 95064

GOLDBERG, ARTHUR LANCE, accountant, tax consultant; b. L.A., Feb. 17, 1950; s. Murray J. and Harriet (Diamond) G.; m. Susan L. Brierton, June 11, 1972; children: Laura K., Stephanie L. BSBA, U. Ariz., 1972. Adminstrv. asst. S.J. Lind Inc., Tucson, 1976-79; ins. agt. Jacob C. Fruchthendler & Co., Tucson, 1976-79; v.p., acct., tax cons., dir. Murray's Bus. Svc. Inc., Tucson, 1976—. Candidate Tucson City Coun., 1987; mem. steering com. Chuck Ford for Mayor, Tucson, 1991. 1st lt. USAF, 1972-76. Mem. Nat. Soc. Pub. Accts., Nat. Soc. Tax Profls., Pres.'s Club U. Ariz. Office: Murrays Bus Svc Inc 1161 N El Dorado Pl Ste 233 Tucson AZ 85715

GOLDBERG, DAVID BRYAN, biomedical researcher; b. San Bernardino, Calif., Mar. 29, 1954; s. Gus and Rose (Goldrich) G.; m. Dianne Rae, Dec. 19, 1976; children: Jason, Mark, Eric, Ashley. BA, UCLA, 1976, PhD, 1987. Rsch. asst. Calif. State U., L.A., 1976-79; rsch. assoc. UCLA, 1979-82; sci. project mgr. Alpha Therapeutic Corp., L.A., 1989—; adj. prof. Chaffey Coll., Alta Loma, Calif., 1990—. Contbr. articles to N.Y. Acad. Scis., Jour. Clin. Apheresis, Proceedings of ASCO, FASEB Jour., Fedn. Preceedings, Nat. Hemophelia Found. Mem. PTA, Alta Loma, 1991. Basic Rsch. grantee, Cancer Rsch. Ctr., 1987, 88, Cancer Seed grantee 1989; Teaching fellow, UCLA, 1982-87, Rsch. fellow II, City of Hope, Duarte, Calif., 1987-89. Mem. Fedn. Am. Socs. Experimental Biology. Office: Alpha Therapeutic Corp 1213 S John Reed Ct La Puente CA 91745-2455

GOLDBERG, DAVID THEO, justice studies educator, writer; b. Pretoria, South Africa, Jan. 8, 1952; came to U.S., 1978; s. Isidore and Florence (Lief) G.; m. Alena Luter, June 25, 1984; 1 child, Gabriel Dylan. BA in Econs. and Philosophy, U. Cape Town, South Africa, 1973, BA in Philosophy with honors, 1975, MA in Philosophy, 1978; PhD in Philosophy, CUNY, 1985. Adj. asst. prof. NYU, N.Y.C., 1984-87, Hunter Coll., CUNY, 1984-87; co-pres. Metafilms, N.Y.C., 1982-88; asst. prof. Drexel U., Phila., 1987-90; asst. prof. justice studies Ariz. State U., Tempe, 1990-92, assoc. prof., 1992—. Author: Ethical Theory and Social Issues, 1989, Racist Culture: Philosophy and the Politics of Meaning, 1993; editor: Anatomy of Racism, 1990; co-editor: Social Identities: A Journal of Race, Nation and Culture, Jewish Identity, 1993; co-dir. film The Island, 1982. Grantee N.Y. State Coun. on Arts, 1981, NSF, 1991, ACLS, 1988. Mem. Am. Philos. Assn. (mem. com. on Blacks 1992—), Law and Soc. Assn., Greater Phila. Philosophy Consortium (colloquia com. 1989-90), Soc. for Philosophy and Pub. Affairs (exec. com. 1987-88). Office: Ariz State U Sch Justice Studies Tempe AZ 85287

GOLDBERG, EDWARD MORRIS, political science educator; b. N.Y.C., May 18, 1931; s. Harry Abraham and Pauline Goldberg; children: David Powell, Natalie Pauline. BA, Bklyn. Coll., 1953; MA, U. N.Mex., 1956; PhD, U. Pa., 1965. Instr. U. Pa., Phila., 1956-59; asst. dean Calif. State U., L.A., 1968-70, dept. chmn. polit. sci., 1972-77, assoc. dean, 1981-86, asst. prof. polit. sci., 1961-66, assoc. prof. polit. sci., 1966-70, prof. polit. sci., 1970—; vis. prof. U. So. Calif., L.A., 1974; vis. asst. prof. San Diego State U., 1960-61, U. N.Mex., Albuquerque, 1959-60; cons. HUD, Washington, 1971-72, Calif. State Assembly, Sacramento, 1965; rsch. polit. scientist U. Calif., Davis, 1966, 67; rsch. cons. Taxpayers Assn. of N.Mex., Santa Fe, 1957, 60. Author more than 20 pubs. in field; assoc. editor Western Polit. Quarterly jour., 1981-84; contbr. articles to profl. jours. With U.S. Army, 1953-55. Recipient Outstanding Prof. award Calif. State U., L.A., 1985, summer fellowships NEH, 1980, 84, 89. Mem. Western Polit. Sci. Assn. (v.p. 1977-78, pres. 1978-79), So. Calif. Polit. Sci. Assn. (v.p. 1972-73, pres. 1973-74), Am. Polit. Sci. Assn., Internat. Polit. Sci. Assn. Democrat. Office: Calif State Univ Dept Polit Sci Los Angeles CA 90032-8226

GOLDBERG, FRED SELLMANN, advertising executive; b. Chgo., Jan. 22, 1941; s. Sydney Norman and Birdie (Cohen) G.; m. Jerrilyn Toby Tager, Apr. 12, 1964; children—Robin Lynn, Susanne Joy. B.S., U. Vt., 1962; M.B.A., NYU, 1964. Mktg. research mgr. P. Ballantine & Sons, Newark, 1964-67; sr. v.p., mgmt. supr. Young & Rubicam, N.Y.C., 1967-78; sr. v.p., gen. mgr. Young & Rubicam, Los Angeles, 1978-82; exec. v.p., gen. mgr. Chiat-Day, Inc., San Francisco, 1982-85; exec. v.p., chief operation officer Chiat-Day, Advt., L.A., 1985-87; pres., chief exec. officer San Francisco office Chiat-Day, Inc., San Francisco; vice chmn. Chiat/Day Advt., Inc., L.A., 1987-90; founder, pres., chief exec. officer Goldberg Moser O'Neill Advt., San Francisco, 1990—. Republican. Jewish. Office: Goldberg Moser O'Neill 77 Maiden Ln San Francisco CA 94108-5414

GOLDBERG, JUDY HILLER, psychotherapist, educator; b. Milw., July 22, 1933; d. Abraham Benjamin and Sarah (Lucoff) Hiller; m. Alvin Arnold Goldberg, June 9, 1955; children: Jonathan Charles, Benjamin Aaron, Elissa Jean, Adam Michael. BS, U. Wis., 1954; MA, U. Denver, 1969, PhD, 1983, advanced cert. marriage-family therapy, 1985. Instr. Arapahoe Community Coll., Littleton, Colo., 1970-88; psychotherapist Denver, 1985—; adj. prof. U. Denver, 1988—; pres. Com. Coll. div. Speech Comm. Assoc., Washington, 1977-78. Co-author: Comm is Life, 1990; contbr. articles to profl. jours. bd. dirs. Temple Micah, Denver, 1985-88, Comm. Agy. for Jewish Edn., Denver, 1989-92, Denver Inst. for Jewish Studies, 1990-92. Democrat. Office: 167 Adams 3665 Cherry Creek Dr N Denver CO 80209

GOLDBERG, KENNETH YIGAEL, computer science educator, artist; b. Ibadan, Nigeria, Oct. 6, 1961; came to U.S., 1962; m. Melvin Morris and Ann Natalie (Glickman) G. BSEE, U. Pa., 1984, BS in Econs., 1984; MS in Computer Sci., Carnegie Mellon U., 1988, PhD in Computer Sci., 1990. Asst. prof. U. So. Calif., L.A., 1990—; speaker in field. Exhibited Forbes Gallery, Pitts., 1990, Siggraph Art Show, Los Vegas 1991, Computer Graphics State of the Art Show, 9 German Univs., 1992, Siggraph Art Show, Chgo., 1992, Fisher Gallery, L.A., 1992; contbr. articles to profl. jours.; inventor low friction gripper. Co-founder Melvin M. Goldberg fellowship U. Pa. Grantee NSF, 1992. Mem. IEEE, Assn. of Computing Machinery, Sigma Xi. Office: U So Calif Powell Hall 204 Los Angeles CA 90089-0273

GOLDBERG, LEE WINICKI, furniture company executive; b. Laredo, Tex., Nov. 20, 1932; d. Frank and Goldie (Ostrowiak) Winicki; student San Diego State U., 1951-52; m. Frank M. Goldberg, Aug. 17, 1952; children: Susan Arlene, Edward Lewis, Anne Carri. With United Furniture Co., Inc., San Diego, 1953-83, corp. sec., dir., 1963-83, dir. environ. interiors, 1970-83; founder Drexel-Heritage store Edwards Interiors, subs. United Furniture, 1975; founding ptnr., v.p. FLJB Corp., 1976—, founding ptnr., sec. treas., Sea Fin., Inc., 1980, founding ptnr., First Nat. Bank San Diego, 1982. Den mother Boy Scouts Am., San Diego, 1965; vol. Am. Cancer Soc., San Diego, 1964-69; chmn. jr. matrons United Jewish Fedn., San Diego, 1958; del. So. Pacific Coast region Hadassah Conv., 1960, pres. Galilee group San Diego chpt., 1960-61; supporter Marc Chagall Nat. Mus., Nice, France, U. Calif. at San Diego Cancer Ctr. Found., Smithsonian Instn., L.A. County Mus., San Diego Mus. Contemporary Art, San Diego Mus. Art; pres. San Diego Opera, 1992. Recipient Hadassah Service award San Diego chpt., 1958-59; named Woman of Dedication by Salvation Army Women's Aux., 1992. Democrat. Jewish.

GOLDBERG, LESLIE ROBERTA, human resources consultant; b. N.Y.C.; d. William and Margaret (Waterman) G. BA, Hunter Coll., 1969; MS, Lehman Coll., 1974. Cert. in human rels., human resources, tng. Instructional design specialist Yonkers (N.Y.) Bd. Edn., 1969-87; sales and tng. specialist Commerce Clearing House Inc., N.Y.C., 1987-89; human resources cons. Sussman-Automatic Corp., N.Y.C., 1987—; tng. and devel. mgr. Kirk Paper Co., L.A., 1989-91; human resources program mgr. Mchts. & Mfrs. Assn., L.A., 1992—; cons. job search skills for profls. Employment and Devel. Dept., North Hollywood, Calif., 1992; counselor, cons. Worknet, L.A., 1992—; featured in Fortune Mag., TV-KHSC. Mem. ASTD, Pers. and Indsl. Rels. Assn., So. Calif. Women for Understanding.

GOLDBERG, MARK ARTHUR, neurologist; b. N.Y.C., Sept. 4, 1934; s. Jacob and Bertha (Gruslavsky) G.; 1 child, Jonathan. BS, Columbia U., 1955; PhD, U. Chgo., 1959, MD, 1962. Resident neurology N.Y. Neurol. Inst., N.Y.C., 1963-66; asst. prof. neurology Columbia U. Coll. Phys. and Surgs., N.Y.C., 1968-71; assoc. prof. neurology and pharmacology UCLA, 1971-77, prof. neurology and pharmacology, 1977—; chair dept. neurology Harbor UCLA Med. Ctr., Torrance, 1977—. Contbr. articles to profl. jours., chpts. to books. Capt. U.S. Army, 1966-68. Fellow Am. Neurol. Assn., Am. Acad. Neurology; Am. Soc. Neurochemistry, Soc. Neurosci., Assn. Univ. Profs. Neurology. Office: Harbor UCLA Med Ctr 1000 W Carson St Torrance CA 90502-2004

GOLDBERG, MICHAEL ARTHUR, land policy and planning educator; b. Bklyn., Aug. 30, 1941; s. Harold and Ruth (Abelson) G.; m. Rhoda Lynne Zacker, Dec. 22, 1963 (div. 1987); children: Betsy Anne, Jennifer Heli; m. Deborah Nelson, Sept. 7, 1991. B.A. cum laude, Bklyn. Coll., 1962; M.A., U. Calif., Berkeley, 1965, Ph.D., 1968. Acting instr. Sch. Bus. Adminstrn., U. Calif., Berkeley, 1967-68; asst. prof. Faculty of Commerce and Bus. Adminstrn., U. B.C., Vancouver, 1968-71, assoc. prof., 1971-76, prof., 1976—, assoc. dean, 1980-84, dean, 1991—, Herbert R. Fullerton prof. urban land policy, 1981—; mem. Vancouver Econ. Adv. Commn., 1980-82, Can. dept. Finance Deposit Ins. adv. group, 1992—, Can. dept. Internat. Trade, Strategic Adv. Group on Internat. Trade in Financial Svcs., 1991—; vice chmn. B.C. Real Estate Found., 1985-87, chmn. 1987-91; mem. IFC Vancouver, 1985—, vice chmn., 1985-88, chmn., 1988-89, exec. dir. 1989-91; bd. dirs., mem. exec. com. First Corp. Fin. Ltd., 1987-91; commr. B.C. Housing Mgmt. Commn., 1989-92; bd. dirs. Imperial Parking Ltd., VLC Properties Ltd.; vice chmn. Canadian Fedn. Deans of Mgmt. and Adminstrv. Scis., 1991-92, chair, 1992—; adv. com. Fed. Deposit Ins., 1992—; fed. adv. group on trade in fin. svcs., 1991—. Author: (with G. Gau) Zoning: Its Costs and Relevance for 1980's, 1980, The Housing Problem: A Real Crisis?, 1983, (with P. Chinloy) Urban Land Economics, 1984, The Chinese Connection, 1985, (with J. Mercer) The Myth of the North American City, 1985, On Balance, 1989; editor: Recent Perspectives in Urban Land Economics, 1976, (with P. Horwood) North American Housing Markets into the Twenty-first century, 1983, (with E. Feldman) The Rites and Wrongs of Land Use Policy, 1988. Trustee Temple Sholom, 1980-84. Can. Coun. fellow, 1974-75, Social Scis. and Humanities Rsch. Coun. fellow, 1979-80, 84-85, Inst. Land Policy fellow, 1979-80, Urban Land Inst. fellow, 1984—, Homer Hoyt Inst. fellow, 1988—, recipient Can. 125th anniversary medal for service to Can., 1993. Mem. Am. Planning Assn., Western Regional Sci. Assn., Regional Sci. Assn., Canadian Regional Sci. Assn., Canadian Econs. Assn., Am. Real Estate and Urban Econs. Assn. (dir. 1978—, pres. 1984), Urban Land Inst., Vancouver Bd. Trade. Home: # 119 6505 3rd Ave, Delta, BC Canada V4L 2N1 Office: U BC, Dean Commerce & Bus Adminstrn, Vancouver, BC Canada V6T 1Y8

GOLDBERG, MORRIS, internist; b. N.Y.C., Jan. 23, 1928; s. Saul and Lena (Schaunberg) G.; B.S. in Chemistry cum laude, Poly. Inst. Bklyn., 1951; M.D., SUNY, Bklyn., 1956; m. Elaine Shaw, June 24, 1956; children—Alan Neil, Seth David, Nancy Beth. Intern, Jewish Hosp. Bklyn., 1956-57, resident, 1957-58, 61-62, renal fellow, 1958-59; practice medicine, specializing in internal medicine, N.Y.C., 1962-71, Phoenix, 1971—; instr. to asst. clin. prof. internal medicine State U. N.Y. Coll. Medicine, Bklyn., 1962-71; clin. investigator, metabolic research unit Jewish Hosp. Bklyn., 1962-71; cons. in field; mem. staff Phoenix Bapt., Maryvale Samaritan, Good Samaritan, St. Joseph's hosps. Served to capt. M.C., U.S. Army, 1959-61. Diplomate Am. Bd. Internal Medicine. Fellow ACP; mem. Am. Soc. Internal Medicine, AMA, Am. Coll. Nuclear Physicians, Internat. Soc. Internal Medicine, Am. Soc. Nephrology, Am. Soc. Hypertension, Ariz. Med. Assn., 38th Parallel Med. Soc. S. Korea, Ariz., Maricopa County med. assns., Sigma Xi, Phi Lambda Upsilon, Alpha Omega Alpha. Jewish. Contb articles to med. jours. Home: 24 E Wagon Wheel Dr Phoenix AZ 85020-4063

GOLDBERG, ROBERT N., computer scientist; b. Long Branch, N.J., Feb. 16, 1953; s. Isidore L. and Grace Ruth (Reinhardt) G.; m. Charlotte Jane Spritzer, Nov. 30, 1985; 1 child, Max Alexander. BS in Physics, U. Md., 1975; MS in Computer Sci., Rutgers U., 1978, PhD in Computer Sci., 1982. Systems programmer NIH, Bethesda, Md., 1973-76; rsch. fellow Rutgers U., Piscataway, N.J., 1976-81; software specialist Computer Curriculum Corp., Palo Alto, Calif., 1982-85; sr. computer scientist XIDAK, Inc., Palo Alto, 1985—; cons. NIH, Bethesda, 1982-83. Patentee in field. Mem. Assn. for Computing Machinery, Phi Beta Kappa, Phi Kappa Phi, Sigma Pi Sigma. Jewish. Office: XIDAK Inc 3475 Deer Creek Rd Bldg C Palo Alto CA 94304

GOLDBLATT, HAL MICHAEL, photographer, accountant; b. Long Beach, Calif., Feb. 6, 1952; s. Arnold Phillip and Molly (Stearns) G.; m. Shawn Naomi Doherty, Aug. 27, 1974; children: Eliyahu Yonah, Tova Devorah, Raizel, Shoshana, Reuven Lev, Eliezer Noach, Esther Bayla, Rochel Leah, Zalman Ber. BA in Math., Calif. State U., Long Beach, 1975. Owner Star Publs., Las Vegas, 1975—; treas. Goldblatt, Inc., Long Beach, 1980—; pres. SDG Computer Svc., Las Vegas, 1985—; chief fin. officer Martin & Mills Ltd., Las Vegas, 1992-93. Photographer: (photo essays) Mikveh Yisroel, 1978, Chassidic Fabrengen, 1979, A Day at Disneyland, 1985; producer, engr.; (audio cassettes) From the Heart of My Dreams, 1980, Middle Class Dreams, 1981, Uforatzta Trio, 1982. Founder, pres. Jews for Judaism, Long Beach, 1975-82, v.p., 1983—; fundraising chmn. Friends of Lubavitch, Long Beach, 1977; bd. dirs. Congregation Lubavitch, Long Beach, 1987, 91-92. Recipient Gold Press Card award Forty Niner Newspaper, 1973, 74, Floyd Durham Meml. award for Outstanding Community Svc., 1973.

GOLDEN, JULIUS, advertising and public relations executive, lobbyist, investor; b. N.Y.C., Feb. 25, 1929; s. Nathan and Leah (Michlin) G.; m. Constance Lee Carpenter, Dec. 31, 1954 (div. Mar. 1965); children: Andrew Mitchell, Juliet Deborah; m. Diana Zana George, Apr. 30, 1973; 1 child, Jeremy Philip. B.A., U. N.Mex., 1952. Asst. dir. info. U. N.Mex., Albuquerque, 1952-53; writer AP, Albuquerque, part-time 1952-53, staff writer, 1953-55, fgn. corr., S.Am., 1956-59; pres. Group West Advt./Pub. Relations Albuquerque, 1959—; pres., dir. Telemarks, Inc., Albuquerque, Diagnostek, Inc., Albuquerque, Galaxy Broadcasting Co., Albuquerque, Health Care Svcs., Inc., Albuquerque, HPI, Inc., Albuquerque, Hebenstreit Comm., Inc., Albuquerque. Author: A Time to Die, 1975. Active Bernalillo County Lung Assn., 1961-64; mem. Met. Crime Commn., Albuquerque, 1967-71; chmn., 1970-71; mem. Albuquerque Police Commn. Task Force, 1988-89. Served with AUS, 1945-48, PTO, Korea. Recipient Nat. Feature Writing award Sigma Delta Chi, 1952, E.H. Shaffer award N.Mex. Press Assn., 1953. Mem. Pub. Relations Soc. (pres. N.Mex. chpt. 1972), Profl. Journalism Soc. (pres. 1969-70), Pub. Relations Soc. N.Mex. pres. 1972), Am. Advt. Fedn., Sigma Delta Chi. Democrat. Jewish. Clubs: Overseas Press of Am., Albuquerque Press, Petroleum, 4 Hills Country. Home: 1408 Stagecoach Ln SE Albuquerque NM 87123-4429 Office: Group West 7005 Prospect Pl NE Albuquerque NM 87110-4311

GOLDEN, MICHAEL, state supreme court justice; b. 1942. BA in History, U. Wyo., 1964, JD, 1967; LLM, U. Va., 1992. Bar: Wyo. 1967, U.S. Dist. Ct. 1967, U.S. Ct. Appeals (10th cir.) 1967, U.S. Supreme Ct. 1970. Mem. firm Brimmer, MacPherson & Golden, Rawlins, Wyo., 1971-83, Williams, Porter, Day & Neville, Casper, Wyo., 1983-88; justice Wyo. Supreme Ct., Cheyenne, 1988—; mem. Wyo. State Bd. Law Examiners, 1977-82, 86-88. Capt. U.S. Army 1967-71. Office: Wyo Supreme Ct Supreme Ct Bldg PO Box 1737 Cheyenne WY 82002-0001

GOLDENBERG, CHARLES BRUCE, management consultant; b. San Francisco, Mar. 21, 1950; s. Ralph and Edith Ida (Brenner) G.; m. Pamela Catherine Polos, Aug. 25, 1973; children: Alan Charles, Julianne Renee. BSME, U. Calif., Santa Barbara, 1972; MS in Indsl. Engring., Stanford U., 1973. Registered profl. engr., Calif. Project mgr. Kaiser Engrs., Oakland, Calif., 1972-76; mgr. tech. planning Bay Area Rapid Transit Dist., Oakland, 1976-78; dir. materials Peterbilt Motors Co., Newark, Calif., 1978-82; sr. assoc. Booz, Allen & Hamilton, San Francisco, 1982-85; ptnr. KPMG Peat Marwick, San Francisco, 1985—. Contbr. articles to profl. jours. Home: 140 Waldo Ave Piedmont CA 94611 Office: KPMG Peat Marwick 3 Embarcadero Center San Francisco CA 94111

GOLDFARB, I. JAY, accountant; b. N.Y.C., Mar. 8, 1933; s. Joseph and Fay Esther (Hirschhorn) G.; m. Arlene Storch, May 8, 1955; children: Meryl, David. BA, CUNY, 1955. CPA, N.Y., Calif. Staff acct. T.D. Davidson & Co., N.Y.C., 1957-59; ptnr. Rashba & Pokart, N.Y.C., 1959-65; chief fin. officer Fabrics by Joyce Inc., N.Y.C., 1965-66; ptnr. Clarence Rainess & Co., N.Y.C., 1966-71, L.A., 1971-75; sr. ptnr. Joseph J. Herbert & Co., L.A., 1975-78; mng. ptnr. Goldfarb, Whitman & Cohen, L.A., 1978—. Capt. USAF, 1955-57. Recipient Spirit of Life award City of Hope, 1990. Mem. AICPA, N.Y. State Soc. CPAs, Calif. Soc. CPAs, Prof. and Fin. Assoc. City of Hope (pres. 1974-76, dinner chmn. 1977-79), Boys and Girls Club San Fernando Valley (v.p. 1989, treas. 1990-93), Keystone Lodge, Masons. Office: Goldfarb Whitman & Cohen 12233 W Olympic Blvd Los Angeles CA 90064-1034

GOLDIE, RAY ROBERT, lawyer; b. Dayton, Ohio, Apr. 1, 1920; s. Albert S. and Lillian (Hayman) G.; student U. So. Calif., 1943-44, J.D., 1957; student San Bernardino Valley Coll., 1950-51; JD U. So. Calif., 1957; m. Dorothy Roberta Zafman, Dec. 2, 1941; children—Marilyn, Deanne, Dayle, Ron R. Elec. appliance dealer, 1944-54; teaching asst. U. So. Calif. Law Sch., 1956-57; admitted to Calif. bar, 1957; dep. atty. gen. State of Calif., 1957-58; sole practice, San Bernardino, 1958-87. Pres., Trinity Acceptance Corp., 1948-53. Mem. World Peace Through Law Center, 1962—; regional dir. Legion Lex, U. So. Calif. Sch. Law, 1959-75; chmn. San Bernardino United Jewish Appeal, 1963; v.p. United Jewish Welfare Fund San Bernardino, 1964-66, Santa Anita Hosp., Lake Arrowhead, 1966-69. Bd. dirs. San Bernardino Med. Arts Corp. Served with AUS, 1942-43. Fellow Internat. Acad. Law and Sci.; mem. ABA, San Bernardino County Bar Assn., Riverside County Bar Assn., State Bar Calif., Am. Judicature Soc., Am. Soc. Hosp. Attys., Calif. Trial Lawyers Assn. (v.p. chpt. 1965-67, pres. 1967-68), Am. Arbitration Assn. (nat. panel arbitrators), Coachella Valley Desert Bar Assn., Order of Coif, Nu Beta Epsilon (pres. 1956-57). Club: Lake Arrowhead Country (pres. 1972-73, 80-81), Lake Arrowhead Yacht, Club at Morningside (CFO 1992-93, sec. 1993—). Home and Office: 1 Hampton Ct Rancho Mirage CA 92270-2585

GOLDING, GEORGE EARL, journalist; b. Oakdale, Calif., Aug. 26, 1925; s. Herbert Victor and Elva M. (Leydecker) G.; m. Joyce Mary Buttner, July 15, 1948; children: Earlene Golding Bigot, Brad Leslie, Dennis Lee, Frank Edwin, Charlton Kenneth, Daniel Duane. AA, Modesto Jr. Coll., 1950; BA San Francisco State Coll., 1959. Advt. salesman Riverbank News, 1949; galley bank boy, cub reporter San Bernardino Sun, 1951; editor Gustine Standard, 1952; photographer-reporter Humboldt Times, 1952-56; reporter, asst. city editor San Mateo (Calif.) Times, 1956-90; staff writer, corr. UPI; contbg. writer, photographer Nat. Motorist mag.; aviation writer, columnist Flight Log. Pub. relations adviser Powder Puff Derby start. 1972. Served with U.S. Maritime Service, 1943, USAAF, 1944-46, AUS, 1950. Recipient John Swett award Calif. Tchrs. Assn., 1964; nominee McQuaid award Cath. Newsmen, 1965, 68; A.P. and Ency. Brit. photography awards, 1954-55, A.P. newswriting award, 1964. Mem. Am. Newspaper Guild, San Francisco-Oakland News Guild, Aviation/Space Writers Assn. (various awards 1983-84), Peninsula Press Club (founding dir., pres. 1976, co-chmn. awards and installation 1986-87), San Mateo County Arts Council (charter). Home: 1625 Ark St San Mateo CA 94403-1001

GOLDING, WILLIAM GERALD (W. BILL), magazine publisher; b. N.Y.C., Feb. 23, 1924; s. Murray J. and Julia (Roberts) G.; m. Vicky Tuscano, Nov. 5, 1944; 1 child, Jacqueline N. Kaufman. B.A., Cornell U., 1967; HHD (hon.), Ch. of God, Mil. Chaplains Assn., 1960. Editor New York Post, N.Y.C., 1946-51; owner Gold-Gar Pub. Rels., N.Y.C., 1952-60, Jurard of Miami, Inc., Miami, Fla., 1961-70; mgr. Liberty Nat. Ins. Co., Burbank, Calif., 1970-74; editor Herald Examiner News, L.A., 1974-84; pub. L.A. & West Coast Lifestyle Mag., L.A., 1984—; pub. rels. cons. Am. Legion, L.A., pub. Friars Roundtable for Friars Club, Beverly Hills, Calif.; chaplain DAV, Woodland Hills, Calif. Author, Lady Beautiful, 1971. Col. USAF, 1941-77. Named Citizen of the Yr., N.Y.C., 1956. Home: 14148 Burbank Blvd Van Nuys CA 91401

GOLDMAN, DON STEVEN, optical instrumentation executive; b. Davenport, Iowa, May 14, 1950; s. Jerome and Rena (Kovitz) G.; children: Brian M., Stephanie A. BS, U. Wash., 1972, MBA, 1987; PhD, Calif. Inst. Tech., 1977. Rschr. Owens/Corning Fiberglas, Granville, Ohio, 1977-83; bus. devel. mgr., rschr. Battelle, Pacific N.W. Lab., Richland, Wash., 1983-90; product devel. mgr. Guided Wave, El Dorado Hills, Calif., 1990-93; pres. Formed Optical Solutions, 1993—. Contbr. articles to profl. jours.; patentee thin film spectroscopic sensor. Recipient R&D100 award R&D mag., 1991. Mem. Internat. Soc. for Optical Engring.

GOLDSBOROUGH, JAMES OLIVER, journalist; b. N.Y.C., Oct. 1, 1936; s. William West Goldsborough and Caroline Jackson (Crittenden) Adams; m. Marie Noelle Hervé, July 20, 1966 (div. June 1974); children: Alexander Francis, Kelly Adams. BA in Econs., UCLA, 1958. Reporter San Francisco Examiner, 1962, Honolulu Advertiser, 1963, Ariz. Rep., 1964; reporter to city editor to European corr. N.Y. Herald Tribune, Paris, 1965-76; bur. chief Newsweek Mag., Paris, 1977-78; sr. assoc. Carnegie Endowment, N.Y.C., 1979-83; assoc. editor San Jose (Calif.) Mercury News, 1984-89; editorial page editor San Diego Tribune, 1990-91; columnist fgn. affairs San Diego Union Tribune, 1992—. Author: Rebel Europe, 1982; contbr. articles to profl. publs. Founder, v.p. World Forum of Silicon Valley, San Jose, 1987-90; bd. dirs., trustee Am. Sch. of Paris, 1975-79. With U.S. Army, 1958-60. Edward R. Murrow fellow Coun. on Fgn. Rels., 1973-74; recipient Thomas M. Storke award World Affairs Coun. of No. Calif., 1986. Mem. San Diego World Affairs Coun. Republican. Home: 4007-68 Porte de Palmas San Diego CA 92122 Office: San Diego Union Tribune PO Box 191 San Diego CA 92112

GOLDSMITH, DONALD WILLIAM, lawyer, astronomer, writer; b. Washington, Feb. 24, 1943; s. Raymond William and Selma Evelyn (Fine) G.; m. Rose Marien, Apr. 10, 1975 (div. 1978); 1 child, Rachel Evelyn. BA, Harvard U., 1963; PhD, U. Calif., Berkeley, 1969, JD, 1983. Asst. prof. earth and space sci. SUNY, Stony Brook, 1972-74; vis. prof. Niels Bohr Inst., Copenhagen, 1977; vis. instr. physics Stanford (Calif.) U., 1983; vis. lectr. astronomy U. Calif., Berkeley, 1980-88, vis. assoc. prof., 1990-93; assoc. Pillsbury, Madison and Sutro, San Francisco, 1985-87; cons. Cosmos TV program, Los Angeles, 1978-80; pres. Interstellar Media Publs., Berkeley, 1978—. Author: Nemesis, 1985, The Evolving Universe, 1985, Supernova!, 1989, Space Telescope, 1989, The Astronomers, 1991; (with others) The Search for Life in the Universe, 1980, 2d edit. 1992, Cosmic Horizons, 1982, Mysteries of the Milky Way, 1991; co-writer (TV programs) Is Anybody Out There, 1986, The Astronomers, 1991. Recipient 1st prize popular essays in astronomy Griffith Obs./Hughes Aircraft Corp., L.A., 1983, Best Popular Writing by a Scientist award Am. Inst. Physics, 1986, Klumpke-Roberts award for lifetime achievement Astronomy Soc. Pacific, 1990. Home: 2153 Russell St Berkeley CA 94705-1006

GOLDSMITH, MARIANNE See SMITH, MARIANNE

GOLDSMITH, ROBERT HOLLOWAY, manufacturing company executive; b. Buffalo, May 15, 1930; s. Henry Stanhope and Frances Edmere (Shickluna) G.; m. Diane Cecilia Kramer, June 27, 1957 (div. Sept. 1981); children: Janeen, Daena, Maria, Lisa, Joseph; m. Catherine Helen Draper, Oct. 3, 1981; stepchildren: Deborah, Lori. BME, U. Buffalo, 1951; MBA, Xavier U., 1960. Engr. Allied Chem. and Dye Corp., Buffalo, 1951-54; successively engr., mgr., gen. mgr., v.p. and gen. mgr. aircraft engine projects, v.p. strategic planning, v.p. and gen. mgr. gas turbine div. GE, various, 1956-81; sr. v.p. aerospace and indsl. Pneumo Corp., Boston, 1981-82; cons. Robert H. Goldsmith Assocs., Gloucester, Mass., 1982-83; vice chmn., chief ops. officer Precision Forge Co., Oxnard, Calif., 1983-84; sr. v.p. ops. Rohr Industries, Inc., Chula Vista, Calif., 1984-88, sr. v.p. bus. ops., 1988-89, pres., chief oper. officer, 1989-90, chmn., 1989—, also chief exec. officer, 1990—, also bd. dirs. Contbr. articles to profl. jours. Mem. pres.'s council San Diego State U., 1987—; bd. dirs. United Way, San Diego, Calif., 1987—. With U.S. Army, 1954-56. Republican. Roman Catholic. Office: Rohr Industries Inc Foot of H St PO Box 878 Chula Vista CA 91912-0878*

GOLDSMITH, STEVEN ROBERT, newspaper reporter, educator; b. San Francisco, Sept. 6, 1954; s. Lewis Samuel and Lois Joyce (Spencer) G.; m. Kathryn Elva Thompson, June 1, 1986 (dec. June, 1987). BA in English, French, Pitzer Coll., 1976; M in Journalism, U. Calif., Berkeley, 1980. Reporter Richmond (Calif.) Ind. Gazette, 1980-81, Sonora (Calif.) Union-Democrat, 1981-82, Seattle Post Intelligencer, 1988—; adj. instr. Seattle U., 1992. Recipient Atlantic Brucke fellowship, Atlantic Bridge Found., Bonn, Germany, 1990, Robert Bosch fellowship, Robert Bosch Found. Stuttgart, Germany, 1992. Mem. Investigative Reporters and Editors, Soc. Profl Journalists (1st pl. feature writing 1989). Jewish. Office: Seattle Post Intelligencer 101 Elliott Ave W Seattle WA 98119

GOLDSTEIN, BARRY BRUCE, biologist, researcher; b. N.Y.C., Aug. 2, 1947; s. George and Pauline (Kolodner) G.; m. Jacqueline Barbara Aboulafia, Dec. 21, 1968; children: Joshua, Jessica. BA, Queens Coll., 1968; MA, CCNY, N.Y.C., 1974; PhD, CUNY, N.Y.C., 1980. Microbiologist CPC Internat., Yonkers, N.Y., 1968-71; rsch. scientist U. Tex., Austin, 1977-80; v.p. SystemCulture Inc., Honolulu, 1980-83; bioenergy/aquaculture program mgr. N.Mex. Solar Energy Inst., Las Cruces, 1983-89; pres. Ancient Seas Aquaculture Inc., Roswell, N.Mex., 1989-92, Desert Seas Aquaculture Inc., Roswell, 1990—, Hawaii Shellfish Co., Las Cruces, 1991—. Contbr. articles to profl. jours. Recipient Nat. Energy Innovation award Dept. Energy, Washington, 1985; Grad. fellow CUNY, 1971, Jesse Smith Noyes fellow, 1975, Regents scholar SUNY, 1964. Mem. World Aquaculture Soc., Am. Soc. Microbiology, AAAS. Office: Hawaii Shellfish Co PO Box 4209 Albuquerque NM 87196

GOLDSTEIN, DAVID BAIRD, energy program director, physicist; b. Cleve., June 29, 1951; s. Laurence and Gloria Reta (Baumgarten) G.; m. Julia Beth Vetromile, May 17, 1980; children: Elianna Louise, Abraham Micah. AB in Physics, U. Calif., Berkeley, 1973; PhD in Physics, U. Calif., 1978. Rsch. asst. Lawrence Berkeley (Calif.) Lab., 1975-78, staff scientist, 1978-80; sr. scientist Natural Resources Def. Coun., San Francisco, 1980—; sub-com. chair standing standards project com. 90.1 ASHRAE, Atlanta, 1983—; vice-chmn. bd. Consortium for Energy Efficiency, Inc., Sacrmento, 1991—. Contbr. articles to profl. jours. Mem. Am. Phys. Soc., Phi Beta Kappa, Sigma Xi. Jewish. Home: 1240 Washington St San Francisco CA 94108 Office: Natural Resources Def Coun Ste 1825 71 Stevenson St San Francisco CA 94105

GOLDSTEIN, MICHAEL SAUL, sociologist; b. N.Y.C., Aug. 1, 1944; s. Abraham J. and Rose G.; m. Laura Geller, Dec. 23, 1979 (div. May 1992); children: Joshua, Adam, Elana. BA, Queens Coll., Flushing, N.Y., 1965; MA, Brown U., Providence, 1967, PhD, 1971. Lectr. Brown U., Providence, 1970-71; asst. prof. Sch. Pub. Health, UCLA, 1971-78, assoc. prof., 1978-88, prof., 1988—, chair dept. community health, 1988-91. Author: The Health Movement, 1992; author, editor: 50 Simple Things You Can Do to Save Your Life, 1992. Mem. APHA, Am. Sociol. Assn. Soc. for Study Social Problems, Hastings Inst. Soc. Ethics and the Life Scis. Office: UCLA Sch Pub Health Los Angeles CA 90024

GOLDSTEIN, NORMAN, dermatologist; b. Bklyn. July 14, 1934; s. Joseph H. and Bertha (Docteroff) G.; B.A., Columbia Coll., 1955; M.D., SUNY, 1959; m. Ramsay, Feb. 14, 1980; children: Richard, Heidi. Intern, Maimonides Hosp., N.Y.C., 1959-60; resident Skin and Cancer Hosp., 1960-61, Bellevue Hosp., 1961-62, NYU. Postgrad. Center, 1962-63 (all N.Y.C.); ptnr. Honolulu Med. Group, 1967-72; practice medicine specializing in dermatology, Honolulu, 1972—; clin. prof. dermatology U. Hawaii Sch. Medicine, 1973—; bd. dirs. Pacific Laser. Bd. dirs. Skin Cancer Found., 1979—; trustee Dermatol. Found., 1979-82, Hist. Hawaii Found., 1981-87; pres. Hawaii Theater Ctr., 1985-89, Hawaii Med. Libr., 1987-89; mem. Oahu Heritage Council, 1986—. Recipient Henry Silver award Dermatol. Soc. Greater N.Y., 1963; Husik award NYU, 1963; Spl. award Acad. Dermatologia Hawaiiana, 1971. Served with U.S. Army, 1960-67. Fellow ACP, Am. Acad. Dermatology (Silver award 1972), Am. Soc. Lasers Medicine & Surgery, Royal Soc. Medicine; mem. Internat. Soc. Tropical Dermatologists (Hist. and Culture award), Soc. Investigative Dermatologists, Assn. Mil. Dermatologists, AAAS, Am. Soc. Photobiology, Environ. Health and Light Research Inst., Internat. Soc. Cryosurgery, Am. Soc. Micropigmentation Surgery, Small Bus. Council Am. (bus. adv. council), Pacific and Asian Affairs Council, Navy League, Assn. Hawaii Artists, Nat. Stereoscopic Soc., Biol. Photog. Assn., Photog. Soc. Am., Societe Internationale de la Photographie, Friends of Photography, Health Sci. Communication Assn., Internat. Pigment Cell Soc., Am. Med. Writers Assn., Physicians Exchange of Hawaii (bd. dirs.), N.Y. Acad. Sci., Am. Coll. Cryosurgery, Internat. Soc. Dermatol. Surgery, Am. Soc. Preventive Oncology, Soc. for Computer Medicine, Am. Assn. for Med. Systems and Info., computer Security Inst., Japan Am. Soc. Hawaii (bd. dirs.), Pacific Telecom Council, Hawaii State Med. Assn. (mem. public affairs com.), Hawaii Dermatol. Soc. (sec.-pres.), Hawaii Public Health Assn., Pacific Dermatol. Assn., Pacific Health Research Inst., Honolulu County Med. Soc. (gov.), Nat. Wildlife Fedn., Am. Forestry Assn., C. of C., Preservation Action, Pan Pacific Surg. Assn., Am. Coll. Sports Medicine, Rotary, Outrigger Canoe Club, Plaza Club (pres. bd. dirs. 1990-92), Chancellor's Club, Japan-Am. Soc., Oahu Country Club. Contbr. articles to profl. jours. Office: Tan Sing Bldg 1128 Smith St Honolulu HI 96817-5169

GOLDSTEIN, SIMON, credit management executive; b. N.Y.C., Sept. 1, 1935; s. Irving Charles and Tillie (Alpern) G.; m. Roberta Dubowitz, Jan. 4, 1958 (dec. 1968); children: Shari Lynn, David. BA, U. of Redlands, 1986. Ptnr. Parkway Floor Co., Long Branch, N.J., 1958-60; counselor Synanon Found., Santa Monica, Calif., 1961-65; salesman Harry P. Hirsch Carpet Co., Beverly Hills, Calif., 1961-64; owner Distinctive Floor Coverings, Beverly Hills, 1965-67; regional mgr. Nat. Credit Svcs., L.A., 1968-78, v.p., cons., 1990—; asst. contr., nat. credit mgr. Assoc. Internat., L.A., 1979-89; internat. collections project leader Hellmann Internat. Forwarders, Long Beach, Calif., 1989-90. With U.S. Army, 1953-58, Korea. Recipient Cert. of Recognition, Calif. State Assembly, 50th Dist., 1991, Calif. Legislature Assembly Resolution, Calif. Legislature Assembly, 1992. Democrat. Jewish. Home: 13520 Kornblum Ave Hawthorne CA 90250

GOLDSTEIN, STEVEN EDWARD, psychologist; b. Bronx, N.Y., Nov. 25, 1948; s. Maurice and Matilda (Weiss) G.; B.S. in Psychology, CCNY, 1970, M.S. in Sch. Psychology, 1971; Ed.D. in Sch. Psychology, U. No. Colo., 1977. Tchr., N.Y.C. Public Schs., 1970-71, 72-73, tchr., counselor, 1974; extern in sch. psychology N. Shore Child Guidance, 1972; sch. psychologist Denver Pub. Schs., 1975; asst. prof. psychology Northeastern Okla. State U., Tahlequah, 1976-78; coord. inpatient, emergency svcs. Winnemucca (Nev.) Mental Health Center, 1978-80; dir. Desert Devel. Ctr., Las Vegas, Nev., 1980-82; sr. psychologist Las Vegas Mental Health Ctr., 1982-92; pvt. practice psychology, Las Vegas, 1983—; sr. psychologist Desert Regional Ctr., 1992—; participant NSF seminar on biofeedback, 1977. Sec. grad. coun. CUNY, 1971; pres. grad. coun. in edn. CCNY, 1971. Lic. psychologist, Nev.; cert. sch. psychologist, N.Y., Calif. Mem. Am. Psychol. Assn. (Nev. coord. office of profl. practice 1987-88), Biofeedback Soc. Nev. (membership dir. 1982-90), Nev. Soc. Tng. and Devel. (dir. 1982-83), Biofeedback Soc. Am., So. Nev. Soc. Cert. Psychologists (pres. 1984-86). Presenter papers to profl. confs. Office: 1300 S Jones Blvd Las Vegas NV 89158-0001 also: 3180 W Sahara Ste C-25 Las Vegas NV 89102

GOLDSTEIN, STUART WOLF, lawyer; b. Buffalo, N.Y., Sept. 9, 1931; s. Joseph and Esther (Wolf) G.; m. Myra Saft Stuart, June 1960 (dec. Aug. 1981); children: Jeffrey, Jonathan, Meryl. Student, U. Buffalo, 1949-52, JD, 1955; postgrad., U. Va., 1956. Bar: N.Y. 1956, Fla. 1974, Ariz. 1977, U.S. Supreme Ct. 1960, U.S Dist. Ct. (we. dist.) N.Y. 1956, U.S. Ct. Mil. Appeals 1957, U.S. Ct. Appeals (2d cir.) N.Y., 1978, U.S. Dist. Ct. Ariz. 1981. Sole practice Buffalo, 1960-79, 82-85, Phoenix, 1980-82, 85—. Pres., founder Cystic Fibrosis Found., Buffalo, 1960; fund-raiser United Fund, United Jewish Appeal; pres. Boys League; active Erie County Spl. Task Force on Energy, Buffalo, 1978. 1st lt. U.S. Army, 1956-60. Fellow Ariz. Bar Found.; mem. Ariz. State Bar Assn., N.Y. Trial Lawyers Assn., Erie County Trial Lawyers, Ariz. Trial Lawyers Assn. (Ariz. real property sect.), N.Y. State Bar Assn., Fla. Bar Assn., Am. Arbitration Assn., Buffalo Skating Club, Curling Skating Club (legal counsel). Office: 2702 N 3d St Phoenix AZ 85016

GOLDSTEIN, WILLIAM M., composer, producer; b. Newark, Feb. 25, 1942; s. Harry and Sylvia (Hochheiser) G. MusB, Manhattan Sch. Music, 1965, postgrad., 1965-66. Freelance composer, arranger, producer music for TV, film, theater, 1966—; composer-in-residence U.S. Army Band, Ft. Myer, Va., 1966-69. Composer, condr., arranger, producer: (feature films) Hello Again, The Bad Guys, Bingo Long Traveling All Stars, 1976, Eye For an Eye, Force Five, Norman Is That You?, Hello Again, 1987, Shocker, 1989, The Quarrel, 1991, others, (TV films) Connecticut Yankee in King Arthur's Court, 1990, Blood River, 1991, (TV spls.) Omnibus, (Emmy award nomination 1980), Happy Endings (Emmy award nomination 1983), Fame (Emmy award nomination 1983), Hero in the Family, Marilyn: The Untold Story, Mobil Showcase Theatre, others, (documentaries) Television's Greatest Commercials, Parts I-V, The Stars Salute the U.S. Olympic Team, The Mysteries of the Mind, Living Sands of Namib, others, (theater prodns.) Marat Sade, Spread Eagle Four, The Peddler, Total Sweet Success, A Bullet for Billy the Kid 1964, others, (commls.) McDonalds, Buick, Noxema, Duncan Hines, Mitsubishi, others, (records) Switched on Classics, There's No Stopping Us (Sister Sledge), My Touch of Madness (Jermaine Jackson), Old Fashioned Man (Smokey Robinson), Guys and Dolls (Grammy award nomination 1977), Oceanscape, others. Bd. dirs. Calif. State Summer Sch. for the Arts. Recipient Golden Horse award Republic of China, 1981. Mem. Acad. Motion Picture Arts and Scis. (vis. artist 1980).

GOLDSTON, BARBARA M. HARRAL, editor; b. Lubbock, Tex., Jan. 26, 1937; d. Leonard Paul and Olivette (Stuart) Harral; m. John Rowell Toman (div. 1963); 1 child, Stuart Rowell; m. Olan Glen Goldston, 1989. BE, Tex. Christian U., 1959; MLS, U. Hawaii, 1968; postgrad., Golden Gate U., 1980-82. Tchr. pub. elem. schs., various cities, Tex. and Hawaii, 1959-66; contracts abstractor, indexer Champlin Oil Co., Ft. Worth, 1963-64; adminstrv. asst. engring. Litton Industries, Lubbock, Tex., 1964-65; mgr. rsch. library Hawaii Employers' Coun., Honolulu, 1968-72; rsch. cons. Thailand Hotel Study, Touche-Ross Assocs., Honolulu, 1974; dir. med. library U. S.D.-Sacred Heart Hosp., Yankton, 1977-79; editor, adminstrv. coord. book div. ABC-Clio, Inc., Santa Barbara, Calif., 1981-88; free-lance rsch./editorial cons. Albuquerque, 1988-89; instr. Santa Fe Community Coll., 1989—; ptnr. Broome-Harral, Inc., Albuquerque, 1989—. Author, editor with others Hist. Periodical Dir., 5 vols., World Defense Forces compendium. Contbr. Boy's Ranch, Amarillo, Tex., 1987—; mem. Lobero Theater Group, Santa Barbara, 1975-76; mem., treas. Yankton Med. Aux., 1977-79. Mem. ALA, Spl. Libraries Assn., Med. Libraries Assn., Am. Soc. Info. Sci., Albuquerque C. of C., Albuquerque Conv. and Visitors Bur., Better Bus. Bur. Albuquerque, Tex. Christian U. Alumni Assn., Delta Delta Delta. Republican. Episcopalian. Home: 9300 Seabrook Dr NE Albuquerque NM 87111-5863 Office: PO Box 3824 Albuquerque NM 87190-3824

GOLDSTONE, JERRY, surgeon, educator; b. Ontario, Oreg., Nov. 18, 1940; s. Ralph and Annette (Rogoway) G.; m. Linda Francis Kay, July 7, 1962; children: Adam E., Lara E., Stefan G. BS, U. Wash., 1963; MD, U. Oreg., 1965. Intern U. Calif. Hosps., San Francisco, 1965-66, resident, 1966-71, chief resident, 1971-72; asst. prof. U. Calif., San Francisco, 1972-78, assoc. prof., 1978-80, prof., 1984—, acting chmn. dept. surgery, 1986-87, vice chmn. dept. surgery, chief div. vascular surgery, 1987—; prof. surgery U. Ariz., Tucson, 1980-84; Harvey Lozman Meml. lectr. Beth Israel Med. Ctr., 1986; Gore lectr. Royal Australasian Coll. Surgeons, Sydney, Australia, 1985. Editorial bd.: Perspectives in Vascular Surgery, Stroke, Annals of Vascular Surgery, Jour. Surg. Rsch., Jour. Vascular Surgery; contbr. numerous articles to profl. jours. and chpts. to books. Fellow Nat. Heart Inst./NIH, 1968-70. Mem. ACS, Internat. Soc. for Cardiovascular Surgery (sec. 1989-93), Vascular Surgery Biology Club (sec.), Western Vascular Soc., Pacific Coast Surg. Assn., Am. Bd. Surgery, Assn. Acad. Surgery, Soc. Vascular Surgery, Soc. Clin. Surgery. Office: U Calif 505 Parnassus Ave San Francisco CA 94143-0222

GOLDSTRAND, DENNIS JOSEPH, financial planning executive; b. Oakland, Calif., July 12, 1952; s. Joseph Nelson and Frances Marie (Royce) G.; m. Judy A. Goldstrand. BSBA, Calif. State U., 1975; CLU, Am. Coll., 1986, CFC, 1988. Asst. mgr. Household Fin. Corp., San Leandro, Calif., 1975-76; registered rep. Equitable Fin. Svcs., San Francisco, 1976-79; dist. mgr. Equitable Fin. Services, San Francisco, 1979-85; ptnr. Goldstrand & Small Ins. and Fin. Services, Stockton, Calif., 1986-89; owner Goldstrand Fin. & Ins. Svcs., Stockton, 1989—. Speaker Stockton Assn. Life Underwriters, 1986; contbr. articles to Life Ins. Selling mag., 1986, 88. Mem. Stockton Estate Planning Coun. (bd. dirs. 1992-93), Endowment Devel. Com., UOP; v.p. United Way of San Joaquin County Endowment Found., Inc. Mem. Nat. Assn. Life Underwriters (pres. Stockton chpt. 1990-91), Am. Soc. CLU (pres. Stockton chpt. 1989-90), Greater Stockton C. of C., Rotary, Million Dollar Round Table. Home: 9215 Stony Creek Ln Stockton CA 95219-4910 Office: Goldstrand Fin & Ins Svcs 2155 W March Lane Ste 2E Stockton CA 95207

GOLDWATER, BARRY MORRIS, former senator; b. Phoenix, Jan. 1, 1909; s. Baron and Josephine (Williams) G.; m. Margaret Johnson, Sept. 22, 1934 (dec. 1985); children: Joanne, Barry, Michael, Margaret (Mrs. Bob Clay); m. Susan McMurray Wechsler, Feb. 9, 1992. Student, Staunton Mil. Acad., U. Ariz., 1928. With Goldwater's, Inc. (name now Robinson's), from 1929, pres., 1937-53; U.S. senator from Ariz., 1953-65, 69-87; chmn. Armed Services Com.; mem. Commerce Com.; former chmn. Select Com. on Intelligence; mem. Select Com. Indian Affairs; Councilman, Phoenix, 1949-52; mem. adv. com. Indian affairs Dept. Interior, 1948-50. Author: Arizona Portraits (2 vols.), 1940, Journey Down the River of Canyons, 1940, Speeches of Henry Ashurst, The Conscience of a Conservative, 1960, Why Not Victory?, 1962, Where I Stand, 1964, The Face of Arizona, 1964, People and Places, 1967, The Conscience of the Majority, 1970, Delightful Journey, 1971, The Coming Breakpoint, 1976, Barry Goldwater and the Southwest, 1976, With No Apologies, 1979, autobiography (with Jack Casserly) Goldwater, 1988. Rep. candidate for President of the U.S., 1964; bd. dirs. Heard Mus., Mus. No. Ariz., St. Joseph's Hosp. Served as pilot USAAF, 1941-45; col., chief staff Ariz. NG, 1945-52; maj. gen. Res. Recipient award U.S. Jr. C. of C., 1937, Presdl. Medal of Freedom, 1986, Langley Medal, Smithsonian Inst., 1986; named Man of year Phoenix, 1949. Mem. Royal Photog. Soc., Am. Assn. Indian Affairs (dir.), Am. Legion, V.F.W., Municipal League (v.p.), Am. Inst. Fgn. Trade (dir.), Eta Mu Pi, Sigma Chi. Lodges: Masons, Shriner, Elks. Office: PO Box 1601 Scottsdale AZ 85252-1601

GOLITI, MELISSA NAN, governmental affairs professional; b. Fresno, Calif., Apr. 26, 1960; d. Robert Alexander and Margaret (Torosian) G. BA in Polit. Sci., U. Calif., Davis, 1983. Mgr. Found. Resource Ctr., Internat. Assn. Bus. Communicators, San Francisco, 1983-86; title examiner Chgo. Title, Fresno, 1986-87; exec. dir. San Joaquin Valley Rep. Assocs., Fresno, 1987-88; adminstrv. asst. Kings River Conservation Dist., Fresno, 1988-90; govtl. affairs liaison Modesto (Calif.) Irrigation Dist., 1990—. Pres. Fresno County and City Rep. Women, 1988-90; mem. Calif. Rep. Com., 1989-90, Fresno County Rep. Ctrl. Com., 1990.

GOLITZ, LOREN EUGENE, dermatologist, pathologist, clinical administrator, educator; b. Pleasant Hill, Mo., Apr. 7, 1941; s. Ross Winston and Helen Francis (Schupp) G.; MD, U. Mo., Columbia, 1966; m. Deborah Burd Frazier, June 18, 1966; children: Carrie Campbell, Matthew Ross. Intern, USPHS Hosp., San Francisco, 1966-67, med. resident, 1967-69; resident in dermatology USPHS Hosp., Staten Island, N.Y., 1969-71; dep. chief dermatology, 1972-73; vis. fellow dermatology Columbia-Presbyn. Med. Ctr., N.Y.C., 1971-72; asst. in dermatology Coll. Physicians Surgeons, Columbia, N.Y.C., 1972-73; vice-chmn. Residency Rev. Com. for Dermatology, 1983-85. Earl D. Osborne fellow dermal. pathology Armed Forces Inst. Pathology, Washington, 1973-74; assoc. prof. dermatology, pathology Med. Sch. U. Colo., Denver, 1974-88; prof., 88—; chief dermatology Denver Gen. Hosp., 1974—; med. dir. Ambulatory Care Ctr., Denver Gen. Hosp., 1991. Diplomate Am. Bd. Dermatology, Nat. Bd. Med. Examiners. Fellow Royal Soc. Medicine; mem. Am. Soc. Dermatopathology (sec., treas. 1985-89, pres.-elect 1989, pres. 1990), Am. Acad. Dermatology (chmn. coun. on clin. and lab. svcs., coun. sci. assembly 1987-91, bd. dirs. 1987-91, chmn. 1991), Soc. Pediatric Dermatology (pres. 1981), Soc. Investigative Dermatology, Pacific Dermatol. Assn. (exec. com. 1979-89, sec.-treas. 1984-87, pres. 1988), Noah Worcester Dermatol. Soc. (publs. com. 1980, membership com. 1989-90), Colo. Dermatol. Soc. (pres. 1978), Am. Bd. Dermatology Inc. (bd. dirs. 1987—, chmn. part II test com. 1989—), Colo. Med. Soc., Denver Med. Soc., AMA (residency rev. com. for dermatology 1982-89, dermatopathology test com. 1979-85), Denver Soc. Dermatopathology, Am. Dermatol. Assn. Editorial bd. Jour. Cutaneous Pathology, Jour. Am. Acad. Dermatology, Advances in Dermatology (editorial bd. Current Opinion in Dermatology), Women's Dermatologic Soc., So. Med. Assn., Internat. Soc. Pediatric Dermatology, Am. Contact Dermatitis Soc., Am. Soc. Dermatologic Surgery, Physicians Who Care, Am. Bd. Med. Specialties (del.), N.Y. Acad. Scis., AAAS, Brit. Assn. Dermatologists (hon.), Brazilian Soc. Dermatology (hon.), U. Mo. Med. Alumni Orgn. (bd.govs. 1993—); contbr. articles to med. jours. Home: 11466 E Arkansas Ave Aurora CO 80012-4106

GOLLEDGE, REGINALD GEORGE, geography educator; b. Dungog, Australia, Dec. 6, 1937; came to U.S., 1963; s. Lance Golledge; m. Margaret Ruth Mason, 1961 (div. 1974); children: Staphanie, Linda; m. Allison Louise Cahill; children: Bryan, Brittany. BA with honors, U. New Eng., Australia, MA, 1961; PhD, U. Iowa, 1966. Asst. prof. U. B.C., Vancouver, 1965-66; asst. prof. Ohio State U., Columbus, 1966-67, assoc. prof., 1967-71, prof. geography, 1971-77; prof. geography U. Calif., Santa Barbara, 1977—, chmn. dept., 1980-84; dir. Rsch. Unit for Spatial Cognition and Choice, Santa Barbara, 1990—. Co-author: Analytical Behavioral Geography, 1987; co-editor: Behavioral Problems in Geography, 1982, Behavioral Modelling in Geography and Planning, 1988, A Ground for Common Search, 1988, Behavior and Environment, 1993. Fellow Guggenheim Found., 1987. Fellow AAAS; mem. Assn. Am. Geographers (Honors award 1981), N.Y. Acad. Sci., Psychometric Soc., Regional Sci. Assn. N.Am. Classification Soc., Inst. Australian Geographers (hon. life), Gamma Theta Upsilon. Home: 267 Forest Dr Goleta CA 93117-1108 Office: U Calif Dept Geography Santa Barbara CA 93106

GOLODNER, ADAM MARC, lawyer; b. N.Y.C., Aug. 4, 1959; s. Harry and Syril (Kirson) G. BA cum laude, Colo. Coll., 1981; JD, U. Colo., 1985. Bar: Colo. 1985. Ptnr. Moye, Giles, O'Keefe, Vermeire & Gorrell, Denver, 1985—; mem. staff Office Presdl. Pers., Office Polit. Affairs The White House, Washington, 1993—; pro bono lawyer Colo. Lawyers Com., Denver. Mem. nat. staff Clinton/Gore gen. election campaign, 1992; mem. staff Presdl. Inaugural Com., 1993; bd. dirs. Metro Waste Water Reclamation Dist., 1991—, Colo. Children's Campaign, 1990—; adv. bd. to mayor Pope's 1993 visit, Denver, 1992; mem. staff Office Pol. Affairs, Office Presdl. Pers., the White House. Mem. Denver C. of C. (tax & local govt.), Denver Athletic Club. Office: Moye Giles O'Keefe Vermeire & Gorrell 1225 17th St Flr 29 Denver CO 80202-5501

GOLTZ, ROBERT WILLIAM, physician, educator; b. St. Paul, Sept. 21, 1923; s. Edward Victor and Clare (O'Neill) G.; m. Patricia Ann Sweeney, Sept. 27, 1945; children: Leni, Paul Robert. B.S., U. Minn., 1943, M.D., 1945. Diplomate: Am. Bd. Dermatology (pres. 1975-76). Intern Ancker Hosp., St. Paul, 1944-45; resident in dermatology Mpls. Gen. Hosp., 1945-46, 48-49, U. Minn. Hosp., 1949-50; practice medicine specializing in dermatology Mpls., 1950-65; clin. instr. U. Minn. Grad. Sch., 1950-58, clin. asst. prof., 1958-60, clin. assoc. prof., 1960-65, prof., head dept. dermatology, 1971-85; prof. medicine/dermatology U. Calif.-San Diego, 1985—; prof. dermatology, head div. dermatology U. Colo. Med. Sch., Denver, 1965-71. Former editorial bd.: Archives of Dermatology; editor: Dermatology Digest. Served from 1st lt. to capt., M.C. U.S. Army, 1946-48. Mem. Assn. Am. Physicians, Am. Dermatol. Assn. (dir. 1976-79, pres. 1985-86), Am. Soc. Dermatopathology (pres. 1981), Am. Dermatologic Soc. Allergy and Immunology (pres. 1981), AMA (chmn. sect. on dermatology 1973-75), Dermatology Found. (past dir.), Minn. Dermatol. Soc., Soc. Investigative Dermatology (pres. 1972-73, hon. 1988), Histochem. Soc., Am. Acad. Dermatology (pres. 1978-79, past dir.) (hon.), Brit. Assn. Dermatology (hon.), Chilean Dermatology Soc. (hon.), Colombian Dermatol. Soc. (corr. mem.), Can. Dermatol. Soc. (hon. mem.), Pacific Dermatol. Soc. (hon.-mem.), S. African Dermatol. Soc. (hon. mem.), N.Am. Clin. Dermatol. Soc., Assn. Profs. Dermatology (sec.-treas. 1970-72, pres. 1973-74), West Assn. Physicians. Home: 6097 Avenida Chamnez La Jolla CA 92037-7404 Office: U Calif-San Diego Med Ctr Div Dermatology H-8420 200 W Arbor Dr San Diego CA 92103-8420

GOLUBIC, THEODORE ROY, sculptor, designer, inventor; b. Lorain, Ohio, Dec. 9, 1928; s. Ivan and Illonka (Safar) G.; m. Rose Andrina Ieraci-Golubic, Nov. 27, 1958; children: Vincivan, Theodore E., Victor, Georjia. Student Ohio State U., Columbus, 1947-48; BFA in Painting, Miami U., Oxford, Ohio, 1951; student Syracuse U., 1955; MFA in Sculpture, U. Notre Dame, 1957. Asst. to Ivan Mestrovic, 1954-60; guest tchr. U. Notre Dame, 1959; urban planner relevel. dept., South Bend, Ind., 1960-65; sculpture cons., Rock of Ages Corp., 1965-67; instr. Cen. Mo. State U., 1969; instr. San Diego Sculptors' Guild, 1970-71; artist-in-residence Roswell (N.Mex.) Mus. and Art Ctr., 1971-72; sculptor, designer, inventor, 1958—; works include: 4 dimensional sun environ. design, South Bend, Ind., Limestone relief sculpture Cathedral of the Nativity, Dubuque, Iowa, The Crypt Series, ROA Corp., Barre, Vt., bronze St. John Bapt., Lorain, Ohio, 4 pt. surface pick-up, 3 dimensional interconnected integrated cir., multilevel S.I.P. package, isolated heatsink bonding pads (Eureka award Motorola, Inc.), Phoenix, mahogany bas relief U. San Diego. With U.S. Army, 1951-53. Mem. Artists Equity Assn., Coll. Art Assn. Am., Internat. Sculpture Ctr. Contbr. articles to profl. jours.

GOMBOCZ, ERICH ALFRED, biochemist; b. Vienna, Austria, Aug. 29, 1951; came to U.S., 1990; s. Erich and Maria (Mayer) G.; m. Gisela M. Dorner, June 12, 1973 (div. Apr. 1992); children: Manfred Alexander. Cert., T.U., Vienna, 1970-75. With Fed. Inst. for Food Analysis and Rsch., Vienna, 1975-90, head of sect. dept. biochem. analysis, 1980-90, contbr. Cen. Lab. Info. Mgmt. System, 1987-90; chmn. scientific adv. bd. LabIntelligence, Inc., Menlo Park, Calif., 1989—, v.p., dir. rsch., 1979—; speaker and lectr. in field. Editor: Computers in Electrophesis; contbr. articles to profl. jours.; patentee in field. Postdoctoral Rsch. award NIH, Bethesda, Md., 1985-86, 88. Mem. Internat. Assn. for Cereal Chemistry, Internat. Electrophoresis Soc., Am. Electrophoresis Soc. Roman Catholic. Office: LabIntelligence Inc 191 Jefferson Dr Menlo Park CA 94025-1114

GOMEZ, DAVID FREDERICK, lawyer; b. Los Angeles, Nov. 19, 1940; s. Fred and Jennie (Fujier) G.; m. Kathleen Holt, Oct. 18, 1977. BA in Philosophy, St. Paul's Coll., Washington, 1965, MA in Theology, 1968; JD, U. So. Calif., 1974. Bar: Calif. 1975, U.S. Dist. Ct. (cen. dist.) Calif. 1975, U.S. Dist. Ct. (ea. dist.) Calif. 1977, Ariz. 1981, US. Dist. Ct. Ariz. 1981, U.S. Ct. Claims 1981, U.S. Ct. Appeals (9th cir.) 1981, U.S. Supreme Ct. 1981; ordained priest Roman Cath. Ch., 1969. Staff atty. Nat. Labor Relations Bd., Los Angeles, 1974-75; ptnr. Gomez, Paz, Rodriguez & Sanora, Los Angeles, 1975-77, Garrett, Bourdette & Williams, San Francisco, 1977-80, Van O'Steen & Ptnrs., Phoenix, 1981-85; pres. David F. Gomez, PC, Phoenix, 1985—; mem. faculty Practicing Law Inst., 1989. Author: Somos Chicanos: Strangers in Our Own Land, 1973; co-author Advanced Strategies in Employment Law, 1988. Mem. ABA, Maricopa County Bar Assn., Los Abogados Hispanic Bar Assn., Nat. Employment Lawyer's Assn., Calif. State Bar Assn., Ariz. State Bar Asn. (com. on rules of profl. conduct 1991—, civil jury instructions com. 1992—, peer rev. com. 1992—). Democrat.

GOMEZ, LOUIS SALAZAR, college president; b. Santa Ana, Calif., Dec. 7, 1939; s. Louis Reza and Mary (Salazar) G.; m. Patricia Ann Aboytes, June 30, 1962; children: Louis Aboytes, Diana Maria, Ramon Reza. Student, Calif. State Poly. U., 1959-65; BA, Calif. State U., San Bernardino, 1971; MA, Calif. State U., 1975; EdD, U. So. Calif., L.A., 1987. Cert. tchr., counselor, adminstr., Calif. Tchr., counselor San Bernardino City Schs., 1971-76; human rels. coord. San Bernardino Valley Coll., 1976-78, counselor, 1978-82, coord. of counseling, 1982-87; asst. dean student svcs. Crafton Hills Coll., Yucaipa, Calif., 1987-89, dean student svcs., 1989-90, acting pres., 1990-92, pres., 1992—; lectr., Calif. State U., San Bernardino, 1976-81, mem. adv. bd., 1987-91. Mem. San Bernardino Valley Coll. Faculty Assn. (treas. 1980-82), Faculty Assn. Calif. Community Colls., San Bernardino Community Coll. Dist. Mgmt. Assn., Kiwanis (pres. San Bernardino chpt. 1982). Democrat. Roman Catholic. Home: 10682 Berrywood Cir Yucaipa CA 92399-5924 Office: Crafton Hills Coll 11711 Sand Canyon Rd Yucaipa CA 92399-1799

GOMEZ, MARTIN, library director. Dir. Oakland (Calif.) City Pub. Libr. Office: Oakland City Public Library 125 14th St Oakland CA 94612*

GOMI, YASUMASA, bank executive. Pres., CEO, COO Bank Calif. NA Inc., San Francisco, chmn. bd., pres., CEO, 1991—. Office: Bank of Calif NA Inc 400 California St San Francisco CA 94104-1302

GONG, HENRY, JR., physician, educator; b. Tulare, Calif., May 23, 1947; s. Henry and Choy (Low) G.; m. Janice Wong; children: Gregory, Jaimee. BA, U. of the Pacific, 1969; MD, U. Calif., Davis, 1973. Diplomate Am. Bd. Internal Medicine, 1977, Pulmonary Disease subspecialty bd., 1980. Resident in medicine Boston U., 1973-75; fellow in pulmonary medicine

UCLA Med. Ctr., 1975-77; asst. prof., then assoc. prof. Sch. Medicine UCLA, 1977-89, prof. medicine, 1989-93; assoc. chief pulmonary div. UCLA Med. Ctr., 1985-92; chief Environ. Health Svc. Rancho Los Amigos Med. Ctr., 1993—; dir. Environ. Exposure Lab., UCLA, 1988—; mem. pub. health and socio-econs. task force South Coast Air Quality Mgmt. Dist., El Monte, Calif., 1989-90. Contbr. articles to rsch. publs., chpts. to books; editorial bd. Jour. Clin. Pharmacology, 1983—, Heart and Lung jour., 1984—. Elder on session Pacific Palisades Presbyn. Ch., 1984-86, 89-91. Fellow Am. Coll. Chest Physicians (pres. Calif. chpt. 1991-92), Am. Coll. Clin. Pharmacology; mem. Am. Thoracic Soc., Am. Fedn. Clin. Rsch., Western Soc. Clin. Investigation, Air and Waste Mgmt. Assn., Phi Eta Sigma, Phi Kappa Phi. Office: Environ Health Svc Rancho Los Amigos Med Ctr Med Sci Bldg Rm 51 7601 E Imperial Hwy Downey CA 90242

GONG, MAMIE POGGIO, educator; b. San Francisco, June 26, 1951; d. Louis and Mary Lee (Lum) G.; m. Andy Anthony Poggio. BA, U. Calif., Berkeley, 1973, postgrad., 1981-83, MEd, 1982. Tchr. Oakland (Calif.) Unified Sch. Dist., 1974-84, Palo Alto (Calif.) Unified Sch. Dist., 1984—; cons., writer Nat. Clearinghouse for Bilingual Edn., Washington, 1984; cons. ARC Assocs., Oakland, 1983; rsch. asst. dept. edn. Stanford U., 1987-89. Co-author: Promising Practices: A Teacher Resource, 1984. Recipient Kearney Found. award, 1969, others. Mem. Tchrs. English to Speakers Other Langs. (presenter 1990 conf.), Calif. Assn. Tchrs. English to Speakers Other Langs. Democrat. Office: Palo Alto Unified Sch Dist 25 Churchill Ave Palo Alto CA 94306-1099

GONTRUM, PETER BAER, German language educator; b. Balt., Feb. 13, 1932; s. Edwin K. and Mildred B. Gontrum; m. Margaret D. Gontrum, June 12, 1956; children: Catherine, Elsa, David. BA, Haverford Coll., 1954; MA, Princeton U., 1956; PhD, U. Munich, 1958. Teaching asst. Princeton (N.J.) U., 1956-58; instr. U. Chgo., 1958-61; from asst. prof. to assoc. prof. U. Oreg., Eugene, 1961-72, prof., 1972—; dept. head Germanic lang. and lit. U. Oreg., Eugene, 1978-84. Recipient award Am. Phil. Soc. 1960, 65-66, ACLS, 1965-66; Fulbright scholar 1974, Alexander von Humboldt scholar, 1965-66, 71, 79, Ersted award for Disting. Teaching 1969. Home: 1036 Fairmount Blvd Eugene OR 97403-1736

GONZALES, RAFAEL ALFRED, lawyer; b. Toppenish, Wash., July 9, 1951; s. Esteban and Genevieve Alta (Allen) Guzman; m. Jean Carol Hurlburt, Nov. 26, 1971; children: Alexandra Thea, Genevieve Naida. Student, Yakima Valley Community Coll., Wash., 1972-73; BA with honors, Cen. Wash. U., 1976; JD with honors, Gonzaga U., 1986. Bar: Wash. 1986. Reporter Tri-County Tribune, Deer Park, Wash., 1976-77, Omak (Wash.)-Okanogan Chronicle, 1977-79; pub. info. officer Colville Confederated Tribes, Nespelem, Wash., 1979-80; asst. dir. corp. communications Sealaska Corp., Juneau, Alaska, 1980-83; law clk. to presiding judge Wash. Ct. of Appeals, Tacoma, 1986-87; assoc. Cockrill, Weaver & Bjur, P.S., Yakima, Wash., 1987-90; staff atty. Dept. Assigned Counsel, Yakima, Wash., 1990—; adj. prof. Heritage Coll., Toppenish, 1988. Bd. dirs. MUST, Yakima, 1988—, pres. 1922-93; bd. dirs. Cen. Wash. Kidney Found., Yakima, 1988-92; active YMCA. With USMC, 1969-72. Mem. Wash. Bar Assn. (minority and justice task force 1988-91, equality in practice com. 1988—, gov.'s transition criminal justice task force, 1992-93). Unitarian. Home: 907 S 31st Ave Yakima WA 98902-4015 Office: Dept Assigned Counsel 103 N 3d St Ste A Yakima WA 98901-2704

GONZALES, RICHARD DANIEL, manufacturing executive; b. Heidleburg, Germany, July 10, 1959; came to the U.S., 1962; s. Lewis and Josephine (Lucia) G. Student, Cypress Coll., 1976-77, Fullerton Coll., 1976-77, Calif. State U., Fullerton, 1981. Leadman Steel Case, Tustin, Calif., 1981-84; project engr. Allied Signal, Garden Grove, Calif., 1984-87; pres. Advanced Composite Systems, Irvine, Calif., 1987—. Vol. Rep. Cen. Com., Irvine, 1992. Mem. AIA, Irvine C. of C. Office: Advanced Composite Systems 13845-A Alton Pky Irvine CA 92718

GONZALES, RICHARD JOSEPH, lawyer; b. Tucson, Mar. 5, 1950; s. Diego D. and Helen O. (Olivas) G.; m. Julie D. Gonzales; children: Adrianne Dee, Laura Renee, Beau, Barry, Jordan. BA, U. Ariz., 1972, JD, 1975. Bar: Ariz. 1976, U.S. Dist. Ct. Ariz. 1976, U.S. Ct. Appeals 1976. Asst. pub. defender Pima County Pub. Defenders Office, Tucson, 1976-77; dep. atty. criminal div. Pima County Atty.'s Office, Tucson, 1977-80; ptnr. Gonzales & Villarreal, P.C., Tucson, 1980—; assoc. instr. bus. law Pima Community Coll.,Tucson, 1977, criminal law, 1978-80; judge pro tem Pima County Superior Ct., 1983—; magistrate City of South Tucson, 1982-85; spl. magistrate City of Tucson, 1982-85. Mem. Tucson Tomorrow, 1984-87, Citizen's adv. coun. Sunnyside Sch. Dist., 1986-88; chmn. com. Udall for Congress 2d Congl. Dist., United Way Hispanic Leadership Devel. Program, 1984-85, vice-chmn., 1983-84, chmn., 1984-85; bd. dirs. Girls Club of Tucson, Inc., 1980-81, Teatro Carmen, Inc., 1981-85, Sunnyside Devilaides, Inc., 1982-83, Alcoholism Coun. Tucson, 1982-83, Crime Resisters, 1984-85, La Frontera Ctr., Inc., 1985—, Crime Prevention League, 1985; gen. counsel U. Ariz. Hispanic Alumni. Named one of Outstanding Young Men of Am. U.S. Jaycee's, 1980; recipient Vol. of Yr. award United Way Greater Tucson, 1985. Fellow Ariz. Bar Found.; mem. ABA, Ariz. Bar Assn., Pima County Bar Assn., Assn. Trial Lawyers Am., Ariz. Trial Lawyers Assn., Nat. Orgn. on Legal Problems of Edn., Supreme Ct. Hist. Soc., Univ. Ariz. Alumni assn., Phi Delta Phi. Democrat. Roman Catholic. Lodge: Optimists (Optimist of Yr. 1981). Office: Gonzales & Villarreal PC 3501 N Campbell Ave Tucson AZ 85719

GONZALES, RICHARD L., fire department chief. AA in Fire Sci. Tech., Red Rocks C.C., 1988; BS summa cum laude in Bus. Adminstrn., Regis U., 1991; MA, Harvard U., 1991; student, U. Colo. Firefighter Denver Fire Dept., 1972-75, mem. fire prevention bureau, dist. 5 roving officer, 1976-79, mem. training divsn., 1980-81, dist. roving officer firefighter, 1981-82, capt. firefighter pumper 2 and 27, 1982-85, asst. chief, 1985-87, chief fire dept., 1987—; Mem. Nat. Fire Protective Assn. Urban Fire Forum, Internat. Assn. Fire Chiefs, Metro Fire Chiefs Assn., Denver Metro Fire Chiefs Assn., Colo. State Fire Chiefs Assn., Urban Fire Forum, IAFF Local 858 Negotiating Team; bd. trustees Nat. Fire Protection Assn., 1992-95. Mem. adv. bd. U. Colo. Denver Sch. of Pub. Affairs, Red Rocks C.C., Denver Ptnrs., KAZY Denver Marathon; bd. trustees Nat. Multiple Sclerosis Soc.; bd. dirs. Rocky Mountain Poison Drug Found., Chic Chicana, Golden Gloves Charity. Recipient Outstanding Achievement award Hispanics of Colo., 1987; named Young Firefighter of the Yr., 1981. Office: Denver Fire Dept 745 W Colfax Ave Denver CO 80204-2612*

GONZALES, RICHARD ROBERT, academic administrator; b. Palo Alto, Calif., Jan. 12, 1945; s. Pedro and Virginia (Ramos) G.; m. Jennifer Ayres; 1 child, Lisa Dianne. AA, Foothill Coll., 1966; BA, San Jose (Calif.) State U., 1969; MA, Calif. Poly. State U., San Luis Obispo, 1971; grad. Def. Info. Sch., Def. Equal Opportunity Mgmt. Inst. Counselor student activities Calif. Poly. State U., San Luis Obispo, 1969-71, instr. ethnic studies, 1970-71; counselor Ohlone Coll., Fremont, Calif., 1971-72, coord. coll. readiness, 1971; counselor De Anza Coll., Cupertino, Calif., 1972-78, mem. community speakers bur., 1975-78; counselor Foothill Coll., Los Altos Hills, Calif., 1978—, mem. community speakers bur., 1978—; instr. Def. Equal Opportunity Mgmt. Inst., 1984—. Mem. master plan com. Los Altos (Calif.) Sch. Dist., 1975-76; vol. worker, Chicano communities, Calif.; fellow Masters and Johnson Inst. With Calif. Army N.G., now maj. Adj. Gen. Corps, USAR. Recipient Counselor of Yr. award Ohlone Coll., 1971-72; lic. marriage family child counselor, Calif. Mem. Am. Counseling Assn., Am. Coll. Counseling Assn., Calif. Assn. Marriage and Family Therapists, Calif. Community Coll. Counselor Assn., Calif. Assn. Counseling and Devel.- Hispanic Caucus, Calif. Assn. for Humanistic Edn. and Devel., Calif. Assn. for Multi-Cultural Counseling, Res. Officers Assn., La Raza Faculty Assn. Calif. Community Colls., Nat. Career Devel. Assn., Phi Delta Kappa, Chi Sigma Iota. Democrat. Office: Foothill Coll Los Altos Hills CA 94022

GONZALES, STEPHANIE, state official; b. Santa Fe, N. Mex., Aug. 12, 1950; 1 child, Adan Gonzales. Degree, Loretto Acad. for Girls. Office mgr. Jerry Wood & Assocs., 1973-86; dep. sec. of state Santa Fe, N. Mex., 1987-90, sec. of state, 1991; bd. dirs. N.M. Pub. Employees Retirement, N.M. State Canvassing Bd., N.M. Commn. Pub. Records; adv. bd. U.S. Senate Dem. Task Force on Hispanic Issues. Exec. bd. N.M. AIDS Svc. Mem. Nat. Assn. Secs. State, Am. Cancer Soc., Women Execs. in State Govt., United LULAC (Women's coun.), Santa Fe County Dem. Club. Office: Office of the Sec of State State Capitol Rm 420 Santa Fe NM 87503*

GONZALEZ, ALICIA CRISTINA, chemist, educator; b. San Justo, Santa Fe, Argentina, Dec. 28, 1947; came to U.S., 1983; d. Norberto and Sara Gonzalez. M. in Chemistry, U. Litoral, Argentina, 1972; PhD in Chemistry, U. La Plata, Argentina, 1980. Rsch. assoc. SRI Internat., Menlo Park, Calif., 1983-85, Caltech, Pasadena, Calif., 1985-88, Triumf, Vancouver, Can., 1988-90, U. So. Calif., L.A., 1990-92, U. Calif., Irvine, 1992—. Contbr. articles to profl. jours. Mem. Sigma Xi. Home: 2386 E Del Mar # 227 Pasadena CA 91107 Office: U Calif Dept Chemistry Irvine CA 92717

GONZALEZ, ENRICO RAUL, art educator, designer; b. N.Y.C., July 1, 1967; s. Edward John Gonzalez and Barbara Elaine Giné. Student, U. Idaho, 1985-87; BAFA, U. N.Mex., 1990. Instr. art Art Masters Acad., Albuquerque, 1989-92; inter-design sales Sante Fe Pendleton, Albuquerque, 1992-93; owner Erg Fine Art Ltd.; design cons. Delcampio Design Ltd. Furniture Design, Albuquerque, 1989-90, Creative Colaboration, Ltd., Albuquerque, 1990-91, Danzig Distbrs. Inc., Spokane, Wash., 1990-92. Mem. Sigma Phi Epsilon (N.Mex. alpha chpt. bd. dirs. 1988-89). Republican. Roman Catholic. Home: 3501 Indian School Rd NE Albuquerque NM 87106-1142

GONZALEZ, FRED CRAIG, forester; b. San Jose, Calif., Oct. 23, 1955; s. Richard Gonzalez and LaVerne Marilyn (Perry) McDonough; m. Lori Kay Wagner, Feb. 14, 1982; children: Chelsea, Jenna. AA, Chabot C.C., Hayward, Calif., 1975; BS in Forest Resource Mgmt., Humboldt State U., 1979. Cert. silviculturist, USDA. Forester Willamette Nat. Forest, Sweet Home, Oreg., 1976-80; supervisory forester Deschutes Nat. Forest, Bend, Oreg., 1981-84; resource forester Deschutes Nat. Forest, Sisters, Oreg., 1985-88; supervisory resource asst. Wenatchee Nat. Forest, Leavenworth, Wash., 1989—; team leader Wash. Agr. and Forestry Policy Group, Spokane, 1991-93. Contbr. articles to profl. jours. Youth wrestling coach Sweet Home Wrestling Club, 1980-81; Eucharistic min. St. Francis Xavier Ch., Cashmere, Wash., 1991—; participant, mem. Wash. Agr. and Forestry Leadership Program, 1991-92; safety officer Wenatchee Interagy. Fire Team, 1991-92; coord., team mem. Kids' Day for Conservation, 1991—. Humboldt State U. scholar, 1978. Mem. Soc. Am. Foresters (nat. comms. chair 1990-92, nat. cultural diversity com. 1984-88, Oreg. membership chair 1988), North Ctrl. Wash. Resource and Conservation Dist. (forestry com. 1993—), Xi Sigma Pi. Democrat. Roman Catholic. Home: 109 Meadowsweet Pl Cashmere WA 98815 Office: Lake Wenatchee Ranger Dist 22976 Hwy 207 Leavenworth WA 98826

GONZALEZ, IRMA E., federal judge; b. 1948. BA, Stanford U., 1970; JD, U. Ariz., 1973. Law clk. to Hon. William C. Frey U.S. Dist. Ct. (Ariz. dist.), 1973-75; asst. U.S. atty. U.S. Attys. Office Ariz., 1975-79, U.S. Attys. Office (ctrl. dist.) Calif., 1979-81; trial atty. antitrust divsn. U.S. Dept. Justice, 1979; ptnr. Seltzer Caplan Wilkins & McMahon, San Diego, 1981-84; judge U.S. Magistrate Ct. (so. dist.) Calif., 1984-91; ct. judge San Diego County Superior Ct., 1991-92; dist. judge U.S. Dist. Ct. (so. dist.) Calif., San Diego, 1992—; adj. prof. U. San Diego, 1992. Trustee San Diego Mus. Man; pres. Girl Scout Women's Adv. Cabinet. Mem. ABA, Calif. Bar Assn., San Diego County Bar Assn., Ariz. Bar Assn., Pima County Bar Assn., Nat. Assn. Women Judges, Nat. Coun. U.S. Magistrates, Lawyers' Club San Diego, Calif. Judges Assn., Thomas More Soc., La Raza Lawyers, Am. Inns of Ct. Office: US Dist Ct 940 Front St San Diego CA 92189

GONZALEZ, JOAQUIN F., lawyer; b. Bogota, Colombia, Oct. 4, 1938; came to U.S., 1966, naturalized, 1969; s. Jose Joaquin and Leonor (Garcia) G.; m. Susan Barfod, Mar. 30, 1985. PhD in Econs., PhD in Law, Javeriana U., Bogota, 1963; MBA in Fin., Free U. Berlin, 1966. Asst. to pres. Repuestos Automotores S.A., Bogota, 1960-64; adminstrv. asst. Corp. Trust Co., N.Y.C., 1967-69; adminstrv. v.p. Investors Overseas Svcs. Ltd., S.A., Geneva, 1969-71; fin. mgr. Latin Am. Am. Home Products Co., N.Y.C., 1972-74; tax and legal mgr. Europe The Allen Group, Inc., Melville, N.Y., 1975-87; internat. tax counsel Ralston Purina Co., St. Louis, 1987-89; assoc. tax counsel Internat. Guardian Industries Corp., Northville, Mich., 1990-91; tax counsel Apple Computer, Inc., Cupertino, Calif., 1992—; cons., Diriventas, N.Y.C., 1967-69, Eurotrade, Frankfurt, Fed. Republic Germany, 1976-87. Contbr. articles on taxation to various publs. Mem. Internat. Fiscal Assn.

GONZALEZ, LUIS JORGE, educator; b. San Juan, Argentina, Jan. 22, 1936; came to U.S., 1971; s. Juan Francisco and Rita (Gonzalez) Gonzalez-Fernández; m. Ester Gimbernat, Aug. 21, 1968; 1 child, Javier Facundo. MusM, Peabody Conservatory, 1972, D in Mus. Arts, 1977. Prof. Universidad de Cuyo, Argentina, 1962, Collegium Musicum, Buenos Aires, 1964, Universidad Sarmiento, San Juan, 1965-71; part-time prof. Peabody Conservatory, Balt., 1974-75; prof. Universidad Nac de San Juan, 1980-81, U. Colo., Boulder, 1981—. Recipient 3d prize Henrik Wieniawski, 1976, Concorso Internazionale Citta di Trieste, 1978; Guggenheim Found. fellow, 1978-79; grantee Nat. Endowment for Arts of Argentina, 1975-76; recipient award Premio Trinac, 1980, 84, 89, 90, Radio France, 1984, Faculty Arts award U. Colo., 1990. Mem. Am. Music Ctr. Office: U Colo 18th and Euclid Boulder CO 80309

GONZALEZ-DEL-VALLE, LUIS TOMAS, Spanish language educator; b. Nov. 19, 1946. BA in Spanish cum laude, Wilmington Coll.-U. N.C., Wilmington, 1968; MA in Spanish and Spanish-Am. Lits., U. Mass., 1972; Phd in Spanish and Spanish-Am. Lits. five coll. coop. program, Amherst Coll., Hampshire Coll., Mt. Holyoke Coll., Smith Coll., U. Mass., 1972. Asst. prof. modern langs. Kans. State U., 1972-75, assoc. prof. modern langs., 1975-77; assoc. prof. modern langs. and lits. U. Nebr., Lincoln, 1977-79, prof. modern langs. and lits., 1979-86; prof. Spanish and Portuguese U. Colo., Boulder, 1986—, chmn. dept. Spanish and Portuguese, 1986—; reading cons. South-Western Pub. Co., Inc., 1974, Eliseo Torres & Sons, 1974; dir. Ibero-Latin Am. Studies Ctr., 1987—; lectr. in field. Author: La nueva ficción hispanoamericana a traves de M.A. Asturias y G. Garcia Marquez, 1972, La ficción breve de Valle-Inclán, 1990, El Canon: Reflexiones Sobre la Recepción Literaria-Teatral, 1993; co-author: Luis Romero, 1979; gen. editor: Anales de la literatura española contemporánea, 1975—, Siglo xx/20th Century, 1985—; editor: Jour. Spanish Studies: 20th Century, 1972-80, Studies in 20th Century Lit., 1975-79, Annual Bibliography of Post-Civil War Spanish Fiction, 1977-82; contbr. articles, essays, book revs. to profl. jours. Recipient Postdoctoral Rsch. award Coun. for Internat. Exch. Scholars, 1984, 500th Rsch. Award Spanish Fgn. Ministry, 1992; grantee Coun. on Rsch. and Creative Work, U. Colo., 1986-87, Com. for Ednl. & Cultural Affairs, U. Nebr.-Lincoln, Chancellor's Rsch. Initiation Fund, U. Nebr.-Lincoln, 1980-81, Rsch. Coun., U. Nebr.-Lincoln, 1978, 79; Sr. Faculty Summer Rsch. fellow Rsch. Coun., U. Nebr.-Lincoln, 1978, Woodrow Wilson Dissertation fellow, 1971-72, Univ. fellow U. Mass., 1968-69, 70-72, Grad. fellow, 1969-70. Mem. Conf. Editors of Learned Jours. (bd. dirs. 1987—), MLA, Spain's Pen Club (founding 1984), Assn. Colegial de Escritores (spl. rep. to U.S., v.p.), Assn. de Escritores y Artistas Espanoles (U.S. rep.), Fgn. Lang. Adminstrs. of Colo., North Am. Acad. of Spanish Lang. (corrs. mem.), Assn. Europea de Profesores de Espanol, Am. Assn. Tchrs. Spanish and Portuguese, Soc. Spanish and Spanish-Am. Studies (bd. dirs. 1975—), 20th Century Spanish Assn. (exec. sec. 1982—), Circulo de Cultura Panamericano (exec. coun. 1972), Cervantes Soc. Am., Nebr. Fgn. Lang. Assn., Phi Kappa Phi, others. Home: 1875 Del Rosa Ct Boulder CO 80304-1800 Office: U Colo Dept Spanish & Portuguese Boulder CO 80309-0278

GONZÁLEZ-TRUJILLO, CÉSAR AUGUSTO, educator, writer; b. L.A., Jan. 17, 1931; s. José Andalón and Camerina (Trujillo) González; m. Bette L. Beattie, Aug. 30, 1969. BA, Gonzaga U., 1953, MA, Licentiate in Philosophy, 1954; MST, Licentiate in Sacred Theology, U. Santa Clara, 1961; postgrad., UCLA, 1962-65. Tchr. Instituto Regional Mex., Chihuahua, Mex., 1954-57; community devel. specialist Centro Laboral Méx., México D.F., Mex., 1965-68; supr. ABC Headstart East L.A., L.A., 1968-69; employment counselor Op. SER, San Diego, 1969-70; prof., founding chair dept. Chicano studies San Diego Mesa Coll., 1970—; founding chairperson Raza Consortium, San Diego, 1971-72; cons. Chicano Fedn. San Diego, Inc., 1987-89. Author poetry, short fiction and criticism; editor, asst. editor lit. jours., 1976—; contbr. numerous articles to profl. jours. Mem. Ednl. Issues Coordinating Com., L.A., 1968-69; founding bd. dirs. Mex.-Am. Adv. Com. to Bd. of Edn., L.A., 1969-70. Fulbright-Hays fellow, Peru, 1982, NEH fellow, 1984; recipient Svc. award Chicano Fedn. San Diego Inc., 1982, Teaching Excellence award Nat. Inst. Staff and Orgnl. Devel., 1993; named Outstanding Tchr. and Scholar Concilio of Chicano Studies for San Diego, Imperial Valley and Baja Calif., 1990. Mem. Am. Fedn. Tchrs., Nat. Assn. Chicano Studies, La Raza Faculty Assn., Chicano Fedn. San Diego County, Centro Cultural De La Raza (past bd. dirs.), Poets and Writers, Asociación Internacional de Hispanistas. Democrat. Roman Catholic. Office: San Diego Mesa Coll 7250 Mesa College Dr San Diego CA 92111-4902

GOO, DIANTHA MAE, industrial hygienist; b. Honolulu, May 25, 1952. BS, U. Wash., 1974. Indsl. hygienist U.S. Dept. Labor OSHA, Boise, 1976, Carson City, Nev., 1976-78, Augusta, Maine, 1978-82, Honolulu, 1982—. Mem. Am. Conf. Govtl. Indsl. Hygienists. Office: US Dept Labor OSHA 300 Ala Moana Blvd # 5122 Honolulu HI 96850

GOO, DONALD WAH YUNG, architect; b. Honolulu, Jan. 16, 1934; s. Kam Lum and Grace (Ching) G.; m. Laura Ray Luke, July 9, 1960; 1 child, Wayne. B.Arch., U. Ill., 1957. Registered architect, Hawaii, Guam, Calif., Tex., Fla. Staff mem., Skidmore Owings & Merrill, Chgo., 1957; v.p. Wimberly, Whisenand, Allison & Tong, Honolulu, 1969-71, Wimberly, Whisenand, Allison, Tong, and Goo, Inc. Architects and Planners, Honolulu, 1971-80, pres., 1980-89, corp. sec., 1980-85, chief exec. officer, 1985-89; pres., CEO, Wimberly Allison Tong & Goo Inc., Architects and Planners, Honolulu, 1989-92, chmn., 1993—; pres. Arts Council Hawaii, Honolulu, 1978-84; vice chmn. Honolulu City Commn. Culture and Arts, 1985-86, chmn., 1986-90; bd. dirs. Waikiki Improvement Assn. Contbr. articles to profl. jours. Served to 1st lt. USAF, 1957-59. Mem. AIA (pres. Hawaii Soc. 1977, treas. 1973-74, dir. 1984-86, fellow 1988), Constrn. Specifications Inst. (pres. Honolulu chpt. 1975-76), Urban Land Inst. (recreational devel. coun. 1987-90), C. of C. Hawaii (bd. dirs. 1988-91), U. Hawaii Found. (bd. trustees 1991—). Avocations: tennis, travel. Office: Wimberly Allison Tong & Goo Inc Architects & Planners 2222 Kalakaua Ave Honolulu HI 96815-2524

GOOD, MICHAEL ROBERT, mechanical engineer; b. Pitts., Mar. 11, 1961; s. Donald Francis and Betty Ann (Miglio) G.; divorced; 1 child, Kathleen Julia. BSME, U. Notre Dame, 1983. Test engr. Gen. Rsch. Corp., Albuquerque, 1987—. Capt. USAF, 1983-87. Mem. AIAA, Sierra Club. Roman Catholic. Home: 1031 Jefferson SE Albuquerque NM 87108 Office: Gen Rsch Corp 1601 Randolf Rd SE Ste 200S Albuquerque NM 87106

GOOD, THOMAS ARNOLD, pediatrician, consultant; b. Atwater, Minn., Feb. 8, 1925; s. Roy Herbert and Ethel (Whitcomb) G.; m. Roberta Rose Rayeski, June 17, 1968; children: Tara, Sonya, Zachry. BA, BS cum laude, U. Minn., 1948, MB, 1951, MD, 1952. Diplomate Am. Bd. Pediatrics. Intern U. Minn. Hosps., 1951-52, asst. resident in pediatrics, 1952-53; chief resident in pediatrics U. Utah, 1954, post doctorate fellow Arthritis and Rheumatism Found., 1954-57; rsch. instr. U. Utah Sch. Medicine, 1953-56; asst. rsch. prof. in pediatrics U. Utah, 1956-58; asst. prof. in pediatrics U. Md., 1958-63, assoc prof. in pediatrics, 1963-66; assoc. prof. in pediatrics Marquette U., Milw., 1966-71; prof. pediatrics Med. Coll. of Wis., Milw., 1967-76; cons. Churchill County Schs., 1981—, Eagle Valley Childrens Home, 1981—, Western Nev. Community Coll., 1983—. Contbr. numerous articles to profl. jours. Recipient Ross award in rsch. Western Soc. for Pediatric Rsch., 1960. Mem. AMA, Nev. State Med. Assn., Carson-Douglas Med. Soc., AAAS, Western Soc. for Pediatric Rsch., N.Y. Acad. Sci., Intermountain Pediatric Soc., Am. Rheumatism Soc., The Endocrine Soc., Western Soc. for Clin. Rsch., Md. Biological Soc., Soc. Pediatric Rsch., So. Soc. Pediatric Rsch., Mucopolysaccharide Glycoprotein Group, Md. chpt. Nat. Kidney Found., Milw. Pediatric Soc., Am. Soc. Pediatric Nephrology. Office: Carson Childrens Clinic 202 S Minnesota St Carson City NV 89703-4267

GOODALL, FRANCES LOUISE, nurse, production company assistant; b. Gove, Kans., Apr. 30, 1915; d. Francis Mitchell and Ella Aurelia (Brown) Sutcliffe; m. Richard Fred Goodall, Feb. 22, 1946; children: Roy Richard, Gary Frederick. Student, U. Kans., 1932-33, Ft. Hays State Coll., 1933-34; BS in Nursing, U. Wash., 1939. RN, Wash. Nurse King County Hosp. System, Seattle, 1939-41; office nurse Dr. Cassius Hofrictor, Seattle, 1941-42; founder Goodall Prodns., Seattle, 1971—. Pres. Hawthorne Elem. Sch. PTA, Seattle, 1960-61, Caspar Sharples Jr. High Sch. PTA, Seattle, 1967-68; historian Seattle Coun. PTAs, 1964-65, 68-69; den mother Boy Scouts Am., Seattle, 1963-67; active United Good Neighbors, Seattle, 1964-68; treas. Women's Overseas Svc. League, Seattle, 1970-74, treas., 1987-91. 1st lt. Nurses Corps, AUS, 1942-46, PTO. Recipient vol. award King County Hosp. System, 1964, Acorn award Franklin High Sch. PTA, 1965, Woman Achievement Cert. award Past Pres. Assembly, 1992. Mem. U. Wash. Alumni Assn. (v.p. 1966-70), U. Wash. Nursing Alumni Assn., Seattle Mus. Art Soc. (assoc., social com., bd. dirs.), Pres's. Forum, Seattle Fedn. Women's Clubs (chmn. community improvement program 1990—), Seattle Geneal. Soc., Lake City Emblem Club, Order Eastern Star, Seattle Sorosis (pres. 1990—), Sigma Sigma Sigma, Kappa Delta (pres. Seattle alumni 1954-55, sec. alumnae coop. bd. 1963-82), Nat. Assn. Parliamentarians (pres. parliamentary law unit 1989—, treas. 1960-61, 64-66, 75-89), Am. Legion (life mem. Fred Hancock post #19 Renton, Wash.). Republican. Presbyterian. Home: 4111 51st St S Seattle WA 98118

GOODALL, JACKSON WALLACE, JR., restaurant company executive; b. San Diego, Oct. 29, 1938; s. Jackson Wallace and Evelyn Violet (Koski) G.; m. Mary Esther Buckley, June 22, 1958; children: Kathleen, Jeffery, Suzanne, Minette. BS, San Diego State U., 1960. With Foodmaker, Inc., San Diego, 1963—, pres., 1970—, chief exec. officer, 1979—, chmn. bd., 1985—; founder, bd. dir. Grossmont Bank, La Mesa, Calif.; bd. dirs. Thrifty Drug Stores Inc., Van Camp Seafood Inc.; owner, dir., bd. dirs. San Diego Padres Baseball Club. Bd. dirs. Greater San Diego Sports Assn.; mem. Pres.'s Coun. San Diego State U.; chmn. Child Abuse Prevention Found.; dir. San Diego Hall Champions. Recipient Golden Chain award, 1982, Silver Plate award Internat. Foodsvc. Mfg. Assn., 1985; named Disting. Alumni of Yr. San Diego State U., 1974, 89, Golden Chain Operator of Yr. Multi Unit Food Svc. Operators, 1988, State of Israel Man of Yr., 1987, Citizen of Yr. City Club of San Diego, 1992, Marketer of Yr. Acad. Mktg. Sci., 1992; inducted into San Diego Bus. Hall of Fame, 1992. Mem. Am. Restaurant Assn., Fairbanks Ranch Country Club (founder), Univ. Club of San Diego, San Diego Intercollegiate Athletic Coun., Kadoo Club of N. Am. Republican. Office: Foodmaker Inc PO Box 783 San Diego CA 92112-4126

GOOD-BROWN, SUE ANN, nurse, small business owner; b. Webster City, Iowa, Nov. 29, 1960; d. George G. and Faye Joann (Simms) Good; m. Scot Warren Brown, Sept. 24, 1988; 1 child, McKenna; 1 step child, Lindsey. AD in Pol. Sci., Miles Community Coll., Miles City, Mont., 1981, ADN, 1983; cert., Sheffield Sch. of ID, 1990. RN, Mont. Owner, artist Redwater Pearl, Circle, Mont., 1985—; RN McCone County Pub. Health, Circle, 1990—; nurse McCone County Hosp., Circle, 1983-90, McCone County MAF and Nursing Home, Circle, 1992. dir. McCone County Annual Health Fair; active McCone County MSU Ext. Adv. Bd., 1992—, Mont. State Ext. Adv. Bd., 1992-96. Mem. NRA, NOW, NAFE, McCone County Sheepgrowers, Make It Yourself with Wool (dist. dir.), Mont. Woolgrower Women. Methodist. Home: PO Box 138 Circle MT 59215-0138

GOODBY, JEFFREY, advertising agency executive. Grad., Harvard Univ., 1973. Political reporter Boston; began advt. career with J. Walter Thompson; with Hal Riney & Ptnrs. San Francisco; prin., creative dir. Goodby, Berlin & Silverstein, San Francisco, 1983—. Office: Goodby Berlin & Silverstein 921 Front St San Francisco CA 94111-1426*

GOODE, ANDREA HORROCKS, association executive; b. LaGrange, Ill., Feb. 5, 1957; d. Donald Leonard and Margaret Annette (Powell) Horrocks; m. Michael David Goode, July 30, 1983; children: Sean, Michael. BS, Calif. State U., Fullerton, 1980. Tchr. 6th grade Placentia (Calif.) Unified Sch. Dist., 1981-82; dir. prog. svcs. Optometric Ext. Prog. Found., Inc., Santa Ana, Calif., 1982—. Mem. Employment Mgmt. Assn. Democrat. Methodist. Home: 30161 Anamonte Laguna Niguel CA 92677-2354 Office: Optometric Ext Program Found 2912 Daimler St Santa Ana CA 92705-5811

GOODEY, ILA MARIE, psychologist; b. Logan, Utah, Feb. 1, 1948; d. Vernal P. and Leona Marie (Williams) Goodey. BA with honors in English and Sociology, U. Utah, 1976; Grad. Cert. Criminology, U. Utah, 1976, MS in Counseling Psychology, 1984, PhD in Psychology, 1985. Speech writer for dean of students U. Utah, Salt Lake City, 1980-89, psychologist Univ. Counseling Ctr., 1984—; cons. Dept. Social Services, State of Utah, Salt Lake City, 1983—; pvt. practice psychology Consult West, Salt Lake City, 1985-86; pub. relations coordinator Univ. Counseling Ctr., 1985—; cons. Aids Project, U. Utah, 1985—; pvt. practice psychology, Inscapes Inst., Salt Lake City, 1987-88; writer civic news Salt Lake City Corp., 1980—; mem. Senator Orrin Hatch's Adv. Com. on Disability Oriented Legis., 1989—. Author book: Love for All Seasons, 1971; play: Validation, 1979; musical drama: One Step, 1984. Contbr. articles to profl. jours. Chmn. policy bd. Dept. State Social Service, Salt Lake City, 1986—; campaign writer Utah Dem. Party, 1985; appointed to Utah State Legis. Task Force on svcs. for people with disabilities, 1990; chmn. bd. Utah Assistive Tech. Program, 1990—. Recipient Creative Achievement award Utah Poetry Soc., 1974, English SAC, U. Utah, 1978, Leadership award YWCA, 1989, Nat. Golden Rule award J.C. Penny, Washington, 1989, 90, Volunteerism award State of Utah, 1990; Ila Marie Goodey award named in honor. Mem. AAUW, Am. Psychol. Assn., Utah Psychol. Assn., Internat. Platform Assn., Mortar Board, Am. Soc. Clin. Hypnosis, Utah Soc. Clin. Hypnosis, Soc. Psychol. Study Social Issues, League of Women Voters, Phi Beta Kappa, Phi Kappa Phi, Alpha Lambda Delta. Mormon. Clubs: Mormon Theol. Symposium, Utah Poetry Assn. Avocations: theatrical activities, creative writing, travel, political activities. Office: U Utah Counseling Ctr 2450 SSB Salt Lake City UT 84112

GOODMAN, BARBARA JOAN, chemical engineer; b. Mpls., Dec. 17, 1950; d. Clarence Norman and Hortense Susan (Marek) Dufek; m. John Richard Goodman, June 22, 1968 (div. Feb. 1985); children: John Jason, Kris, Jessica; m. Bruce Raymond Field, Aug. 8, 1987; 1 child, Carlie Sara. AS, Front Range C.C., Denver, 1980; BS in Chem.-Petroleum Refining Engring., Colo. Sch. Mines, 1984. Chem. cleanup specialist Colo. Sch. Mines, Golden, 1984; staff engr. Solar Energy Rsch. Inst., Golden, 1984, program mgr. solar energy storage, 1984-86, program mgr. waste mgmt., 1986-91, program mgr. ethanol, 1988-90, ops. mgr., 1989-91, br. mgr. bioprocess & fuels engring. nat. renewable energy lab., 1991-93, br. mgr. analysis & project mgmt., 1993—. Contbr. articles to profl. jours. Vol. United Way, Denver, 1978-80; trustee Leukemia Soc. Am., Denver, 1990. Recipient Presidents awards MRI, 1990, 91; scholar Colo. Scholars, 1980, Coors, 1981, Colo. Sch. Mines Alumni Assn., 1982, Soroptimists Internat., 1983. Mem. AICE. Office: Solar Energy Rsch Inst 1617 Cole Blvd Golden CO 80401

GOODMAN, BEATRICE MAY, real estate professional; b. Rehoboth, Mass., Nov. 12, 1933; s. Manuel Silva and Mercy Elizabeth (Mayers) Bettencourt; m. Sam R. Goodman, Sept. 15, 1957; children: Mark, Stephen, Christopher. BS, Marymount Coll., 1980. Pres. Bettencourt Draperies, Rehoboth, Mass., 1955-56; asst. mgr. Leo H. Spivack Furniture, L.I., N.Y., 1956-57; asst. designer Lillian Decorators, L.I., N.Y., 1957-58; asst. buyer Macy's N.Y., N.Y.C., 1958-59; pres. Beatrice & Beverly, Mt. View, Calif., 1980-82; realtor Coldwell Banker, Menlo Park, Calif., 1984—; pres. The Added Touch, Atherton, Calif., 1984-91; realtor Cornish & Carey Realtors, Menlo Park, Calif., 1991—. Den mother Boy Scouts Am., N.Y.C., 1970-76; active Peninsula Vols., Palo Alto, 1974—, Internat. Friendship Force. Mem. Nat. Bd. Realtors, Orgn. for Rehab. Tng. Home: 60 Shearer Dr Menlo Park CA 94027-3957 Office: Cornish & Carey 1000 El Camino Real Menlo Park CA 94025-4327

GOODMAN, DAVID BRYAN, musician, educator; b. Akron, Ohio, Nov. 24, 1953; s. Jason Jones and Louise (Campbell) G. MusB, Oberlin Coll., 1975; MA in Music, U. Calif., Berkeley, 1977, PhD in Music, 1982. Instr. U. Calif., Berkeley, 1976-82; asst. prof. Pomona Coll., Claremont, Calif., 1982-89; pianist UCLA Extension Film Sch., 1989-91; co-founder, music dir. L.A. Composers Guild, 1991—; affiliate Broadcast Music, Inc., N.Y.C., 1982—; orchestrator film and TV projects, L.A., 1989—. Composer Sinfonia Domestica, 1992, Child's Play, 1991, River's Edge, 1989, Reina de la Selva, 1989, Miroirs, 1987-88, Jody's Ride, 1988, Canto de Esperanza, 1987, A Day in Two Lives, 1984, Village Echoes, 1984, Caged Bird, 1984, Tides of Lemuria, 1982, numerous others. Artist-in-residence Na-Bolom Found., Chiapas, Mex., 1987, 88; Charles Ives scholar Am. Acad. Inst. Arts, Letters, 1978. Mem. L.A. Composers Guild, Broadcast Music Inc., Assn. for Promotion of New Music, Soc. Composers and Lyricists, Am. Fedn. Musicians, Coll. Music Soc., Soc. Composers and Lyricists. Home and Office: 4522 Woodman Ave Apt C 240 Sherman Oaks CA 91423

GOODMAN, GWENDOLYN ANN, nursing educator; b. Davenport, Iowa, Aug. 7, 1955; d. Merle Erwin and Loraine Etta (Mahannah) Langfeldt; m. Mark Nathan Goodman, Oct. 24, 1982; children: Zachary Aaron, Alexander Daniel. BS in Nursing, Ariz. State U., 1977. RN, Ariz. Staff nurse surg. fl. and intensive care unit St. Luke's Hosp. and Med. Ctr., Phoenix, 1977-81; staff nurse intensive care unit Yavapai Regional Med. Ctr., Prescott, Ariz., 1981-82; instr. nursing Yavapai Coll., Prescott, 1982-88, cons., 1986; part-time staff nurse Ariz. Poison Control Ctr., Phoenix, 1980-81; mem. profl. adv. com. Home Health Agy. Yavapai Regional Med. Ctr. Mem. Ariz. Nurses Assn., Sigma Theta Tau (Lambda Omicron chpt.). Democrat. Home: PO Box 450 Prescott AZ 86302-0450

GOODMAN, JOSEPH WILFRED, electrical engineering educator; b. Boston, Feb. 8, 1936; s. Joseph and Doris (Ryan) G.; m. Hon Mai Lam, Dec. 5, 1962; 1 dau., Michele Ann. B.A., Harvard U., 1958; M.S. in E.E., Stanford U., 1960, Ph.D., 1963. Postdoctoral fellow Norwegian Def. Rsch. Establishment, Oslo, 1962-63; rsch. assoc. Stanford U., 1963-67, asst. prof., 1967-69, assoc. prof., 1969-72, prof. elec. engring., 1972—; vis. prof. Univ. Paris XI, Orsay, France, 1973-74; dir. Info. Systems lab., dept. elec. engring. Stanford U., 1981-83, chmn., 1988—; William E. Ayer prof. elec. engring. Stanford U., 1988—; cons. to govt. and industry, 1965—; v.p. Internat. Comm. for Optics, 1985-87, pres., 1988-90, past pres., 1991-93. Author: Introduction to Fourier Optics, 1968, Statistical Optics, 1985; editor: International Trends in Optics, 1991; contbr. articles to profl. jours. Recipient F.E. Terman award Am. Soc. Engring. Edn., 1971. Fellow Optical Soc. Am. (dir. 1977-83, editor jour. 1978-83, Max Born award 1983, Frederick Ives award 1990, v.p. 1990, pres. elect 1991, pres. 1992, past pres. 1993), IEEE (edn. medal 1987), Soc. Photo-optical Instrumentation Engrs. (bd. govs. 1979-82, 88-90, Dennis Gabor award 1987); mem. Nat. Acad. Engring., Electromagnetics Acad. Home: 570 University Ter Los Altos CA 94022-3523 Office: Stanford U Dept Elec Engring McCullogh 152 Stanford CA 94305

GOODMAN, LENN EVAN, philosopher; b. Detroit, Mar. 21, 1944; s. Calvin Jerome and Florence Jeanne (Cohen) G.; m. Madeleine Joyce Goodman, Aug. 29, 1965; children: Allegra Sarah, Paula Tiferet. BA summa cum laude, Harvard U., 1965; PhD, Oxford (Eng.) U., 1968. Vis. asst. prof. philosoph and Near Eastern studies UCLA, 1968-69; from asst. to assoc. prof. philosophy U. Hawaii, Honolulu, 1969-80, prof. philosophy, 1981—; v.p. Inst. for Islamic/Judaic Studies, Denver, 1984-85. Author: Monotheism, 1981, Saadiah's Book of Theodicy, 1988, On Justice, 1991, Avicenna, 1992; editor: Brown Judaic Studies: Studies in Medieval Judaism; contbr. articles to profl. jours. Mem. Am. Philos. Assn., Acad. for Jewish Philosophy, Am. Oriental Soc. Office: U Hawaii Dept Philosophy 2530 Dole St Honolulu HI 96822-2310

GOODMAN, MADELEINE JOYCE, university administrator, human geneticist; b. N.Y.C., Sept. 11, 1945; d. Joseph and Pauline Ida (Applebaum) Schwarzbach; m. Lenn Evan Goodman, Aug. 29, 1965; children: Allegra, Paula. BA, Barnard Coll., 1967; Diploma in Human Biology, Oxford U., 1968; PhD, U. Hawaii, 1973. Asst. prof. U. Hawaii, Honolulu, 1974-79, assoc. prof. 1979-85, prof. 1985—, dir. women's studies, 1978-85, asst. v.p. Acad. Affairs, 1986-92, interim sr. v.p. Acad. Affairs, 1992-93; pres. Pacific Health Research Inst., Honolulu, 1982-86. Author: Sex Differences in the Life Cycle, 1983, The Sexes in the Human Population, 1984 (textbooks). Contbr. articles to profl. jours. Officer Disciplinary Council Hawaii State Supreme Ct., Honolulu, 1983—. Grantee NSF, 1981-84, Am. Cancer Soc., 1982-83, Pub. Health Service, 1987—. Mem. AAAS, Hawaii Assn. Women in Sci. (pres. 1981-83), Human Biology Council, Sigma Xi (nat. lectr. 1987-89, pres. Hawaii chpt., mem. nat. bd. dirs., chair. nat. nominating com.). Office: U Hawaii Office VP Acad Affairs 2444 Dole St Honolulu HI 96822-2330

GOODMAN, MARK N., lawyer; b. Phoenix, Jan. 16, 1952; s. Daniel H. and Joanne G.; m. Gwendolyn A. Langfeldt, Oct. 24, 1982; children: Zachary A., Alexander D. BA, Prescott Coll., 1973; JD summa cum laude, Calif. Western Sch. Law, 1977; LLM, U. Calif.-Berkeley, 1978. Bar: Ariz. 1977, Calif. 1977 U.S. Dist. Ct. (no. dist.) Calif. 1977, U.S. Dist. Ct. Ariz. 1978, U.S. Ct. Appeals (9th cir.) 1978, U.S. Dist. Ct. (so. dist.) Calif. 1981, U.S. Supreme Ct. 1981, U.S. Dist. Ct. (cen. dist.) Calif., 1982, Nebr. 1983, U.S. Dist. Ct. Nebr. 1983. Practice Law Offices Mark N. Goodman, Prescott, Ariz., 1978-79, 81-83, Mark N. Goodman, Ltd., Prescott, 1983-86; ptnr. Alward and Goodman, Ltd., Prescott, 1979-81; ptnr. Perry, Goodman, Drutz & Musgrove, Prescott, 1986-87, Goodman, Drutz & Musgrove, 1987-88; ptnr. Sears & Goodman, P.C., Prescott, 1988-92; ptnr. Goodman Law Firm, P.C., Prescott, 1992—. Author: The Ninth Amendment, 1981. Contbr. articles to profl. jours. Bd. dirs. Yavapai Symphony Assn., Prescott, 1981-84. Notes and comments editor Calif. Western Law Review, 1976. Mem. ABA, Assn. Trial Lawyers Am., Yavapai County Bar Assn. (v.p. 1981-82). Office: Goodman Law Firm PC PO Box 2489 Prescott AZ 86302-2489

GOODMAN, MARY A., photographer; b. Hartford, Conn., July 24, 1934; d. Allan S. and Carlyn Rhoda (Leicher) G. BS in Edn., NYU, 1958; MA in Spl. Edn., Columbia U., N.Y.C., 1961; MSW, Simmons Coll. Social Wk., Boston, 1965. Free lance photographer various locations, 1975—. Photography of notable persons include His Royal Highness Prince of Wales, Her Majesty, Queen Elizabeth, The Queen Mother, Sir Michael Tippett, O.M., Sir Yehudi Menuhin, Dame Morgot Fonteyn, Dame Alicia Markova, many others. Mem. Friends of Photography, Ansel Adams Ctr., San Francisco. Mem. Nat. Soc. Arts and Letters (Tucson br.), N.Y. Acad. Sci., Royal Photographic Soc. G.B. (sec./membership sec. Journalism group 1976-79, pictorial portfolio group 1991—), Photographic Soc. Am., Internat. Ctr. Photography, The Photographers Gallery, Ctr. for Creative Photography, Soc. Southwestern Authors. Home: 6266 N Campbell Ave Tucson AZ 85718-3150

GOODMAN, MICHAEL G., immunological researcher, consultant; b. Denver, July 4, 1946; s. Nelson and Florence (Q.) G.; m. Jacquelyn H. Goodman, Feb. 18, 1978; children: Devin, Brielle. BA, Yale U., 1968; MD, U. Calif., San Francisco, 1972. Diplomate Am. Bd. Internal Medicine. Med. intern U. Miami (Fla.) Sch. Medicine, 1972-73; med. resident I Thomas Jefferson U. Hosp., Phila., 1973-74; med. resident II UCLA/Wadsworth VA Hosp, L.A., 1974-75; rsch. fellow Scripps Clinic & Rsch. Fedn., La Jolla, Calif., 1975-78, asst. mem. I, 1978-80, asst. mem. II, 1980-83, tenured assoc. mem., 1983—; vis. physician U. Calif. Dept. Medicine, San Diego, 1982-84; cons. Ortho Pharm. Corp., Raritan, N.J., 1982—, Cytotech, Inc., Del Mar, Calif., 1983-85; ad hoc mem. med. biochem study sect. NIH, Bethesda, Md., 1987, 88. Contbr. articles to profl. jours.; patentee in field. Recipient USPHS Nat. Rsch. Svc. award NIH, 1975-78, USPHS NIH Rsch. Career Devel. award NIH, 1980-85; grantee NIH, 1978—; Arthritis Found fellow, 1978-80. Fellow Am. Coll. Physicians; mem. Am. Assn. Immunologists, N.Y. Acad. Scis., Am. Assn. Pathologists. Office: Scripps Clinic & Rsch Fedn 10666 N Torrey Pines Rd La Jolla CA 92037-1027

GOODMAN, MURRAY, chemistry educator; b. N.Y.C., July 6, 1928; s. Louis and Frieda (Bercun) G.; m. Zelda Silverman; Aug. 26, 1951; children: Andrew, Joshua, David. BS magna cum laude with honors in Chemistry, Bklyn. Coll., 1949; PhD, U. Calif., Berkeley, 1953. Asst. prof. Polytechnic Inst., Bklyn., 1956-60, assoc. prof., 1960-64, prof. chemistry, 1964-71, dir. polymer rsch. inst., 1967-71; prof. chemistry U. Calif.-San Diego, La Jolla, 1971—, chmn. dept. Chemistry, 1976-81; vis. prof. U. Alta., Can., 1981, Lady Davis Vis. Prof., Hebrew U., Jerusalem, 1982; William H. Rauscher lectr. Rensselaer Poly. Inst., 1982. Editor Biopolymers Jour., 1963—; contbr. numerous articles to profl. jours. Recipient Disting. Alumnus medal Bklyn. Coll., 1964, Scoffone medal U. Padova, 1980, Humboldt award, 1986, Pierce award Peptide Chem. Assn., 1989, Max-Bergmann medal, 1991; NRC fellow Cambridge (Eng.) U., 1955-56. Mem. AAAS, Am. Chem. Soc., Am. Soc. Biol. Chemists, The Chem. Soc. Eng., Biophys. Soc., Council for Chem. Research (sci. adv. bd.), U.S. Nat. Commn., Sigma Xi. Home: 9760 Blackgold Rd La Jolla CA 92037-1115 Office: U Calif San Diego Dept Chemistry 0343 La Jolla CA 92093

GOODMAN, ROBERT CEDRIC, lawyer; b. L.A., Sept. 16, 1956; s. William Arthur and Nancy Jane (Furbush) G. AB, Brown U., 1978; JD, U. Chgo., 1983. Bar: Calif. 1983, U.S. Dist. Ct. (ctrl., ea. and no. dists.) Calif. 1983, U.S. Ct. Appeals (9th cir.) 1983. Chief polit. reporter Sta. KJRH-TV, Tulsa, 1978-80; assoc. Feldman, Waldman & Kline, San Francisco, 1983-89; trial atty. environ. enforcement sect. U.S. Dept. of Justice, Washington, 1989-92; shareholder, chair Environmental Litigation Group Feldman, Waldman & Kline, San Francisco, 1992—; mem. faculty 1991 Nat. Environ. Enforcement Conf., 1991. Mem. editorial bd. Calif. Lawyer mag., 1985-88. Area coord. Mondale for Pres. campaign, San Francisco, 1984. Mem. ABA (vice chair delivery of legal svcs. com. young lawyers div. 1986-88), San Francisco Barristers (chair constnl. law com. 1986-88), Calif. Bar Assn. Democrat. Roman Catholic. Office: Feldman Waldman & Kline PC 235 Montgomery St 27th Flr San Francisco CA 94104

GOODMAN, RUSSELL BRIAN, philosophy educator; b. Pyote, Tex., May 28, 1945; s. Lester Morris and Ruth (Kramer) G.; m. Anne Phinizy Doughty, May 22, 1971; children: Elizabeth Doughty, Jacob Lyon. AB, U. Pa., 1966; MA, Oxford U., Eng., 1970; PhD, Johns Hopkins U., Balt., 1971. Asst. prof. U. N.Mex., Albuquerque, 1971-78; assoc. prof. philosophy U. N.Mex., 1978-91, chair philosophy, 1990—, prof., 1991—; vis. scholar Cambridge (Eng.) U., 1977-78; Fulbright sr. lectr. U. Barcelona, Spain, 1993. Author: American Philosophy and the Romantic Tradition, 1990; contbr. articles to profl. jours. Thouron scholar, U. Pa., 1966-68; William Montgomerie prize, Jesus Coll., Oxford, 1967. Mem. Am. Philos. Assn., MLA, Am. Studies Assn., Soc. for Advancement of Am. Philosophy. Office: Univ NMex Dept Philosophy Albuquerque NM 87131

GOODMAN, SAM RICHARD, electronics company executive; b. N.Y.C., May 23, 1930; s. Morris and Virginia (Gross) G.; m. Beatrice Bettencourt, Sept. 15, 1957; children—Mark Stuart, Stephen Manuel, Christopher Bettencourt. BBA, CCNY, 1951; MBA, NYU, 1957, PhD, 1968. Chief acct. John C. Valentine Co., N.Y.C., 1957-60; mgr. budgets and analysis Gen. Foods. Corp., White Plains, N.Y., 1960-63; budget dir. Crowell Collier Pub. Co., N.Y.C., 1963-64; v.p., chief fin. officer Nestle Co., Inc., White Plains, 1964; chief fin. officer Aileen, Inc., N.Y.C., 1973-74, Ampex Corp., 1974-76; exec. v.p. fin. and adminstrn. Baker & Taylor Co. div. W.R. Grace Co., N.Y.C., 1976-79, Magnuson Computer Systems, Inc., San Jose, Calif., 1979-81; v.p., chief fin. officer Datamac Computer Systems, Sunnyvale, Calif., 1981; pres. Nutritional Foods Inc., San Francisco, 1983-84; chmn., chief exec. officer CMX Corp., Santa Clara, Calif., 1984-88; dir., sr. v.p. Masstor Systems Corp., Santa Clara, 1988—; pvt. cons. Atherton, Calif., 1990—; sr. mgmt. cons. Durkee/Sharlit, 1991—; mng. dir. Quincy Pacific Ptnrs., L.P., 1992—; lectr. NYU Inst. Mgmt., 1965-67; asst. prof. mktg. Iona Coll. Grad. Sch. Adminstrn., 1967-69; prof. Golden Gate U., 1974—; prof. fin. and mktg. Pace U. Grad. Sch. Bus. Adminstrn., 1969-79. Author 7 books, including Controller's Handbook; contbr. articles to jours. Lt. (j.g.) USNR, 1951-55. Mem. Fin. Execs. Inst., Nat. Assn. Accts., Am. Statis. Assn., Am. Econs. Assn., Planning Execs. Inst., Am. Arbitration Assn., Turnaround Mgmt. Assn. Home and Office: 60 Shearer Dr Atherton CA 94027-3957

GOODMAN, STEPHEN KENT, composer, conductor; b. Glendale, Calif., Aug. 12, 1949; m. Kelly Kay Ebinger, Apr. 30, 1984. Student, U. So. Calif., L.A., 1968-69, Calif. Inst. Arts, Valencia, 1971-72, Calif. State U., Northridge, 1974-75, Grove Sch. Music, Studio City, Calif., 1981. Ind. music contr. L.A., 1973-88; ragtime editor West Coast Rag, Fresno, 1990, recording reviewer, 1990; musical commns. from San Diego Symphony Orch., City of Newport, Oreg. Blue Street Jazz Band, Brazil Concert Band. Recipient Cert. of Recognition, State of N.D., 1988. Mem. Am. Soc. Composers, Authors and Publs., Maple Leaf Club, Christian Instrumental Dirs. Assn., Profl. Assn. Diving Instrs. Lutheran. Office: PO Box 5459 Fresno CA 93755-5459

GOODMAN, TERENCE JAMES, actor, writer; b. Fort Dodge, Iowa, Nov. 29, 1950; s. Wayne Alva and Helen Loretta (O'Connor) G. BFA, Ark. State U., 1973; MFA, Utah State U., 1990. Appeared in numerous Broadway prodns., tours, other theater prodns., films, TV, commls., including (film) Ode to Billy Joe, 1976, (TV) Days of Our Lives, 1986, Hill Street Blues, 1987, (stage) Damn Yankees, 1974, Jesus Christ Superstar, 1975; author (screenplay) The Times of Danny Bailey, 1991, (TV episode) Femme Fatales, 1984, (plays) Lost in the Sky, 1989, A Mother's Love, 1991. Recipient Merit Achievement award Am. Coll. Theatre Festival, 1990. Mem. AFTRA, Am. Film Inst., Screen Actor's Guild, Ark. State U. Letterman's Club, Sigma Phi Epsilon. Roman Catholic. Home: 426 S Venice Blvd Venice CA 90291-4644

GOODMAN, WILLIAM LEE, commercial pilot; b. Butte, Mont., May 15, 1946; s. William Lonzo and Phyllis Hilma (White) G.; m. Susan Margaret Thompson, Nov. 29, 1969; children: Kathryn, Margaret, William. BS in Computer Sci., Oreg. State U., 1968; MBA, City U., Seattle, 1982; postgrad., Seattle U.; postgrad. in def. econs., U.S. Naval War Coll., 1986. Cert. airline transport pilot, flight engr., control tower operator, flight instr., FAA. Systems analyst Mohawk Data Scis. Corp., Portland, Oreg., 1974-76; air traffic controller FAA, Pendleton, Oreg., 1976-78; pilot Trans Internat. Airlines, Oakland, Calif., 1978; aerospace engr. Boeing Comml. Airplane Co., Seattle, 1978-86; pilot USAIR, Washington, 1986—. Editor Boeing Tng. Ctr. newsletter Intercom, 1980-82; contbg. editor Boeing Customer Service mag. Advisor, 1982-86. V.p. Homeowners Assn., Auburn, 1982-85. Served to comdr. USNR, 1968-89, Vietnam. Mem. Airline Pilots Assn. Republican. Home: 2912 202d Ct E Sumner WA 98390

GOODNIGHT, SUSAN INA, publisher, speaker; b. Lockport, N.Y., Sept. 28, 1938; d. Frank Andrew and Marion Esther (Woodcock) Freer; m. Edward Raymond, Aug. 13, 1960 (div. July 1987); children: Hannah Beth, Thomas Edward, Sarah Catherine, Laura Elizabeth. BS, SUNY, Buffalo, 1960, MS, 1966. Elem. tchr. Wilson (N.Y.) Cen. Sch., 1960-72, tchr. social studies; tchr. reading Newfane (N.Y.) Cen. Sch., 1972-86; pub. Women's Aglow Fellowship Internat., Lynnwood, Wash., 1987—; area and state retreat speaker Women's Aglow Fellowship Internat., 1985—; regional retreat speaker Women's Aglow Fellowship Internat., Can., 1985—, Australia, 1989; workshop speaker, nat. and internat. confs. Women's Aglow Fellowship Internat., San Antonio, Phoenix, 1989, 90; U.S. bd. mem. Women's Aglow Fellowship Internat., Lynnwood, 1987-90, internat. bd. mem., 1987-80, corp. officer, 1987-90, area bd. pres., 1985-87. Author: Give Me the Mountain, 1984. Republican proxy for Wash. state, 1990. Recipient Community Amb. award Village of Wilson, Turkey, 1961. Mem. Independent Assembly Ch. Office: Women's Aglow Internat Fellowship PO Box 1548 Lynnwood WA 98026

GOODNOW, GORDON JAMES, JR., lawyer; b. Washington, June 7, 1947; s. Gordon James and Wanda (Thomas) G.; m. Diana Arellano, Nov. 19, 1977; children: Gordon James III, Christopher John. AA, Canal Zone Coll., Balboa, 1967; BA, U. Ariz., 1969, MA, 1970; JD, Ariz. State U., 1976. Atty. Ramada Inns, Inc., Phoenix, 1976-77; pvt. practice Phoenix, 1976-77; atty. Ariz. Bd. Med. Examiners, Phoenix, 1976-77; dep. county atty. Maricopa County Atty.'s Office, Phoenix, 1977—; judge pro-tem Superior Ct. Maricopa County, 1991—; mem. ethics com. Maricopa County Atty.'s Office, 1991-92; speaker in field. Mng. editor Ariz. State U. Law Sch. Newspaper, 1974-75. With U.S. Army, 1970-72. Mem. Maricopa County Bar Assn., State Bar Ariz. (pub. law sect.), Phoenix Consumer's Bicycle Club, Phi Kappa Phi. Home: 2544 N 29th St Phoenix AZ 85008 Office: Maricop County Atty's Office 301 W Jefferson St Phoenix AZ 85003

GOODRICH, CRAIG ROBERT, business analyst; b. Lynwood, Calif., Mar. 10, 1949; s. Gordon Llewellyn and Dora Jeannette (Shannon) G. BA in Bus. Adminstrn., Calif. State U., Long Beach, 1972, BA in Psychology, 1986. Salesman Pacific Stereo, Torrance, Calif., 1973; mgr. Radio Shack, Long Beach, 1975-76; inventory contr. L.B. Ball & Co., Long Beach, 1979-84; sales, acctg. and edn. cons. Long Beach, 1984-85; adminstrv. analyst Rockwell Internat., Cypress, Calif., 1986; surcharge tax asst. L.A. County, Calif., 1987; sr. engring. bus. mgmt. analyst McDonnell Douglas, Long Beach, 1987-89, human resources adminstr., 1989-90, budget analyst, 1990—. Mem. Acacia Frat. Home: 1685 Loma Ave Apt 4 Long Beach CA 90804-2751 Office: McDonnell Douglas 5301 Bolsa Ave Huntington Beach CA 92649

GOODRICH, JEFFREY CLAY, sales executive, bank executive; b. Detroit, Apr. 12, 1958; s. Stanley Martin and Freda (Eichen) G.; m. Linda Beth Walker, June 20, 1981; children: Rebecca Ashley, Danielle Elizabeth. BA, Calif. State U., Northridge, 1980; acctg. cert., La Valley Coll., 1984; postgrad, Calif. Luth. U., 1989—. CFP. V.p., mcpl. mktg. rep. Shearson Lehman Bros., Century City, Calif., 1983-88; v.p., fin. cons. Shearson Lehman Bros., Encino, Calif., 1988-89; asst. v.p., regional sales mgr. Griffin Fin. Svcs., Santa Fe Springs, Calif., 1989-90; asst. v.p., nat. mgr. sales adminstrn., mktg. and tng. Griffin Fin. Svc., Santa Fe Springs, 1990-92; v.p. divsn. sales mgr. Wells Fargo Bank, L.A., 1992-93; nat. dir. mktg. and tgn. Fin. Network Investment Corp., Torrance, Calif., 1993—; extension faculty UCLA, 1988, Calif. Luth. U., Thousand Oaks, 1988-89, Coll. for Fin. Planning, Denver, 1988-89, L.A. C.C. Dist., 1988-89. Vol. Youth Motivation Task Force of L.A. County, 1990-91, HSOA Community Outreach Program, L.A., 1990-91. Mem. Internat. Bd. CFP's, Internat. Assn. CFP's, Am. Mgmt. Assn. Home: 51 Coolwater Rd Bell Canyon CA 91307 Office: Fin Network Investment Corp 2780 Skypark Dr # 300 Torrance CA 90505

GOODSELL, DAVID SCOTT, JR., molecular biologist; b. Honolulu, Oct. 25, 1961; s. David Scott and Cheryl Darlene (Dodge) G. BS in Chemistry, BS in Biology, U. Calif., Irvine, 1982; PhD in Biochemistry, U. Calif., L.A., 1987. Rsch. and teaching asst. dept. of Chemistry and Biochemistry U. Calif., L.A., 1982-87; rsch. assoc. dept. of Molecular Biology Rsch. Inst. Scripps Clinic, La Jolla, Calif., 1987—, sci. assoc. dept. moecular biology, 1990-92; asst. rschr. Molecular Biology Inst. U. Calif., L.A., 1992—. Author: The Machinery of Life, 1992; contbr. articles to Am. Scientist, 1992, Sci. Am., 1992, profl. jours. Mem. Assn. for Computing Machinery, Internat. Soc. for the Arts Sci. and Tech., Molecular Graphics Soc. Office: Rsch Inst Scripps Clinic 10666 N Torrey Pines Rd # 5mb La Jolla CA 92037-1027

GOODWIN, ALFRED THEODORE, federal judge; b. Bellingham, Wash., June 29, 1923; s. Alonzo Theodore and Miriam Hazel (Williams) G.; m. Marjorie Elizabeth Major, Dec. 23, 1943 (div. 1948); 1 son, Michael Theodore; m. Mary Ellin Handelin, Dec. 23, 1949; children—Karl Alfred, Margaret Ellen, Sara Jane, James Paul. B.A., U. Oreg., 1947; J.D., 1951. Bar: Oreg. 1951. Newspaper reporter Eugene (Oreg.) Register-Guard, 1947-50; practiced in Eugene until, 1955; circuit judge Oreg. 2d. Jud. Dist., 1955-60; assoc. justice Oreg. Supreme Ct., 1960-69; judge U.S. Dist. Ct. Oreg., 1969-71; judge U.S. Ct. Appeals for (9th cir.), Pasadena, Calif., 1971-88, chief judge, 1988-91, sr. judge, 1991—. Editor Oreg. Law Rev., 1950-51. Bd. dirs. Central Lane YMCA, Eugene, 1956-60, Salem (Oreg.) Art Assn., 1960-69; adv. bd. Eugene Salvation Army, 1956-60, chmn., 1959. Served to capt., inf. AUS, 1942-46, ETO. Mem. Am. Judicature Soc., Am. Law Inst., ABA (ho. of dels. 1986-87), Order of Coif, Phi Delta Phi, Sigma Delta Chi, Alpha Tau Omega. Republican. Presbyn. Club: Multnomah Athletic (Portland, (Oreg.). Home: PO Box 91510 Pasadena CA 91109-1510 Office: US Ct Appeals 9th Cir PO Box 91510 125 S Grand Ave Pasadena CA 91109-1510

GOODWIN, DALE EUGENE, public relation director; b. Spokane, Wash., Dec. 23, 1955; s. V. Eugene and Irene E. (Whyatt) G.; m. Mary Frances O'Neill, Aug. 19, 1989. BA, Wash. State U., 1978; MA, Gonzaga U., 1986. Reporter, copy editor The Spokesman-Rev. Newspaper, Spokane, 1978-81; sports info. dir. Gonzaga U., Spokane, 1981-88, asst. athletic dir., 1985-88, pub. rels. dir., 1989—; mem. strategic planning coun. Gonzaga U., 1990-91. Editor (alumni newspaper) Signum, 1989—, (student recruitment newspaper) Fall Preview, 1989-90. Publicity dir. Inland Empire Sports Awards Banquet, Spokane, 1984-90; tournament dir. Inland N.W. Basketball Classic, Spokane, 1987-89; tech. liaison Goodwill Games-Volleyball, Spokane, 1990; media coord. Pacific 10 Conf. Baseball Tournament, Spokane, 1985-88; results coord. Wash. Centennial Games, Spokane, 1989; program coord. The Muscular Dystrophy Assn., Spokane, 1981; bd. dirs. Spokane Pub. Rels. Coun., 1990—, v.p., 1992-93, pres. bd. dirs., 1993-94; mem. Inland Empire Sports Writers/Broadcasters, sec., 1984; bd. dirs. Goodwill Industries of Inland

NW, sec., 1993. Mem. Internat. Assn. Bus. communicators, Spokane Volleyball Referees Assn. (pres. 1989-94, Contbr. of Yr. 1989, 90, Most Inspirational Referee 1990, Referee of Yr. 1991). Home: 3806 S Morrill St Spokane WA 99223-1255 Office: Gonzaga U 502 E Boone Ave Spokane WA 99258-0001

GOODWIN, JOHN ROBERT, lawyer, educator; b. Morgantown, W.Va., Nov. 3, 1929; s. John Emory and Ruby Iona G.; m. Betty Lou Wilson, June 2, 1952; children: John R., Elizabeth Ann Paugh, Mark Edward, Luke Jackson, Matthew Emory. B.S., W.Va. U., 1952, LLB, J.D., 1964. Bar: W.Va., U.S. Supreme Ct. Formerly city atty., county commr., spl. pros. atty., then mayor City of Morgantown; prof. bus. law W.Va. U.; prof. hotel and casino law U. Nev., Las Vegas; Author: Legal Primer for Artists, Craftspersons, 1987, Hotel Law, Principles and Cases, 1987. Served with U.S. Army, Korea. Recipient Bancroft-Whitney award in Constl. Law'; named Outstanding West Virginian, State of West Virginia. Democrat. Author: Twenty Feet From Glory; Business Law, 3d edit.; High Points of Legal History; Travel and Lodging Law; Desert Adventure; Gaming Control Law; editor Hotel and Casino Letter; past editor Bus. Law Rev., Bus. Law Letter. Home: Casa Linda 48 5250 E Lake Mead Blvd Las Vegas NV 89115

GOODWIN, SANDRA JOAN, management trainer, consultant; b. St. Louis, Sept. 30, 1937; d. Robert Earl and Irma Josephine (Modray) Balencia; m. Earl Victor Goodwin II, July 22, 1980; children: Kathleen Anne, Kristine Annette. Student, Wash. U.; MS in exec. mgmt., U. Calif., Riverside, 1986. Adminstrv. aide Washington U., St. Louis, 1955-65; mgmt. cons. Hughes Heiss & Assocs., San Mateo, Calif., 1975-79; budget analyst San Bernardino (Calif.) County, 1979-80, mgmt. cons., 1980-82, data processing projects mgr., 1982-83, chief edn. and info. services, 1983-87, exec. post dep. county admnstr. officer, 1987-88; owner Mgmt. Assocs. Tng. and Cons. Services, San Bernardino, 1982—. State chairperson Calif. Regional Criminal Justice Planning Bd., San Mateo, 1974-78, regional vice chairperson; exec. asst. San Mateo Bd. Suprs., 1978. Coro Found. scholar, 1976. Mem. Am. Soc. Pub. Adminstrn., Nat. Acad. Polit. Scientists, Am. Soc. Tng. Devel., LWV (chairperson fin., tng. bur. 1973-78), Bus. and Profl. Women, League of Women Voters. Democrat. Lutheran. Home: 648 Palo Alto Dr Redlands CA 92373-7321 Office: Mgmt Assocs PO Box 8505 San Bernardino CA 92412-8505

GOODWINE, JAMES K., JR., aviation consultant, mechanical engineer; b. Evanston, Ill., Mar. 9, 1930; s. James K. Sr. and Janet B. (Dyer) G.; m. Helen L. Murray, June 6, 1959; children: Kathryn J., Robert J. BSME, Purdue U., 1952, MSME, 1958, PhD, 1960. Rsch. engr. Chevron Rsch., Richmond, Calif., 1959-67; mgr. power plant engring. United Airlines, San Francisco, 1970-79, mgr. new aircraft and operational engring., 1979-82, dir. engine tech. svcs., 1982-87, mgr. new tech. engring., 1987-88; sr. assoc. Aviation Mgmt. Systems, Inc., Concord, Mass., 1989—. Bd. dirs. Coordinating Rsch. Coun., Atlanta, 1988-89. Cpl. U.S. Army, 1952-54. Mem. Soc. Automotive Engrs. (chmn. No. Calif. chpt. 1976-77), Commonwealth Club, Sigma Xi. Home: 1423 Enchanted Way San Mateo CA 94402-3621

GOOKIN, THOMAS ALLEN JAUDON, civil engineer; b. Tulsa, Aug. 5, 1951; s. William Scudder and Mildred (Hartman) G.; m. Leigh Anne Johnson, June 13, 1975 (div. Dec. 1977); m. Sandra Jean Andrews, July 23, 1983. BS with distinction, Ariz. State U., 1975. Registered profl. engr., Calif., Ariz., Nev., land surveyor Ariz., hydrologist. Civil engr., treas. W.S. Gookin & Assocs., Scottsdale, Ariz., 1968—. Chmn. adv. com. Ariz. State Bd. Tech. Registration Engring., 1984—. Recipient Spl. Recognition award Ariz. State Bd. Tech. Registration Engring., 1990. Mem. NSPE, Ariz. Soc. Profl. Engrs. (sec. Papago chpt. 1979-81, v.p. 1981-84, pres. 1984-85, named Young Engr. of Yr. 1979, Outstanding Engring. Project award 1988), Order Engr., Ariz. Congress on Surveying and Mapping, Am. Soc. Civil Engrs., Ariz. Water Works Assn., Tau Beta Pi, Delta Chi (Tempe chpt. treas. 1970-71, sec. 1970, v.p. 1971), Phi Kappa Delta (pres. 1971-73). Republican. Episcopalian. Home: 10760 E Becker Ln Scottsdale AZ 85259-3868 Office: W S Gookin & Assocs 4203 N Brown Ave Scottsdale AZ 85251-3946

GOOKIN, WILLIAM SCUDDER, hydrologist, consultant; b. Atlanta, Ga., Sept. 8, 1914; s. William Cleveland and Susie (Jaudon) G.; m. Mildred Hartman, Sept. 4, 1937; children: William Scudder Jr., Thomas Allen Jaudon. BSCE, Pa. State U., 1937. Registered profl. engr. and hydrologist. Engr. U.S. Geol. Survey, Tucson, 1937-38; inspector City of Tucson, 1938-39; steel designer Allison Steel Mfg. Co., Phoenix, 1939-40; engr. Bur. Reclamation, various locations, 1940-53; chief engr. San Carlos Irrigation and Drainage Dist., Coolidge, Ariz., 1953-58; chief engr. Ariz. Interstate Stream Commn., Phoenix, 1956-62, state water engr., 1962-68; adminstr. Ariz. Power Authority, Phoenix, 1958-60; cons. engr. Scottsdale, Ariz., 1968—; mem. exec. com. Cen. Ariz. Project Assn., Phoenix, 1985—. Contbr. articles to profl. jours. Dem. committeeman State of Ariz., 1979-84; Ariz. mem. Com. of 14, Western States Water Coun.; episcopal lay reader. Served to 2d lt. C.E., U.S. Army, 1938-42. Fellow Am. Soc. Civil Engrs.; mem. NSPE (outstanding engr. project 1988), Nat. Water Resources Assn. (small projects com.), Colo. River Water Users' Assn., State Bar Ariz. (assoc.), Assn. Western State Engr. (pres.), Am. Legion, Culver Legion, Order of the Engr., Mason, Chi Epsilon. Home: 9 Casa Blanca Estates Paradise Valley AZ 85253-6919

GOOR, E. PATRICIA, business executive; b. Colo., Aug. 5, 1935; d. Robert and Pauline (Gebhard) Robison; m. Dan Goor, Aug. 28, 1953; children: Ya Dean, Diana, Elizabeth, Jacqueline, Sharon. Diploma, Am. Inst. of Banking, 1976. Real estate rep. Tetrault, Lincoln, Mass., 1965-73; bank officer Bay Bank, Boston, 1973-79, Sun Bank, Orlando, Fla., 1979-81; pres., CEO GA Internat., Inc., Colorado Springs, Colo., 1987—; invited presenter Soc. Automotive Engrs. Patentee in field. Mem. NAFE, Soc. Automotive Engrs. Jewish. Office: GA Internat Inc 4143 Sinton Rd Colorado Springs CO 80907

GORANS, GERALD ELMER, accountant; b. Benson, Minn., Sept. 17, 1922; s. George W. and Gladys (Schneider) G.; m. Mildred Louise Stallard, July 19, 1944; 1 child, Gretchen. BA, U. Wash., Seattle, 1947. CPA, Wash. With Touche, Ross & Co., CPAs and predecessor, Seattle, 1947-88; ptnr. Touche, Ross & Co. (name changed to Deliotte & Touche 1989), 1957-88, in charge Seattle office, 1962-82, mem. policy group, adminstrv. com., 1964-69, dir., 1974-83, sr. ptnr., 1979-88, chmn. mgmt. group, 1982-88, ret., 1988; pres. 600 Park Ter. Condominium Assn., 1993—. V.p. budget and fin. Seattle Worlds Fair, 1962; chmn. budget and fin. com. Century 21 Ctr., Inc., 1963-64; mem. citizens adv. com. Seattle Lic. and Consumer Protection Com., 1965; head profl. div. United Way King County, Seattle, 1963-64, head advanced gifts div., 1965, exec. v.p., 1966, pres., 1967; trustee United Way Endowment Fund, 1984-90; adv. bd. Seattle Salvation Army, 1965-80, treas., 1974-80; fin. com. Bellevue Christian Sch., 1970-77; citizens adv. bd. pub. affairs Sta. KIRO-TV, 1970-71; treas., bd. dirs., exec. com. Scandinavia Today in Seattle, 1981-83; treas., bd. dirs. Seattle Citizens Coun. Against Crime, 1972-80, pres., 1976, 77; bd. dirs. U. Wash Alumni Fund, 1967-71, chmn., 1971; trustee U. Wash. Pres.'s Club, 1980-83; bd. dirs., chmn. devel. com. N.W. Hosp. Found., 1977-83; bd. dirs., treas. N.W. Hosp., 1981-86; chmn. fin. com., vice chmn. bd. Health Resources N.W., 1986-89, bd. dirs., 1986—, chmn. bd., 1989-90; chmn. fin. com. Com. for Balanced Regional Transp., 1981-91; co-chmn. United Cerebal Palsy Seattle Telethon, 1986; chmn. fin. com. fund raising Mus. Flight, 1983-87; mem. assoc. bd. Pacific Scis. Ctr., Seattle, 1986—; active Japanese/Am. Conf. Mayors and C. of C. Pres. vice chmn. U.S. del., 1989-91; chmn. fin. com. Napa Valley Club Homeowners Assn.; bd. dirs., chmn. fin. com. Napa Valley Club Homeowners Assn., 1992—; bd. dirs., 1st pres. 600 Pk. Ter. Condominium Assn., 1993—. Lt. (j.g.) USNR, 1943-45. Recipient Honor award Sr. Svcs. of Seattle and King County, 1990. Mem. AICPA (chmn. nat. def. com. 1969-75, mem. spl. investigation com. 1984-87), Nat. Office Mgmt. Assn. (past pres.), Wash. Soc. CPAs (Outstanding Pub. Svc. award 1988), Seattle C. of C. (chmn. taxation com. 1970-71, bd. dirs. 1971-74, 76-79, 80-81, 85—, exec. com. 1980-83, v.p. 1981-84, 1st vice chmn. 1983-84, chmn. 1984-85, vice chmn. facilities fund dr. 1982-84), Nat. Def. Exec. Res., Nat. Club Assn. (bd. dirs. 1984-93, sec. and mem. exec. com. 1991-93), Assn. Wash. Bus. (bd. dirs. 1983-86). Home: 612 Bellevue Way SE Bellevue WA 98004 also: 122 Valley Club Circle Napa CA 94558 Office: Deloitte & Touche 700 5th Ave Ste 4500 Seattle WA 98104

GORDEN, STEPHEN ARTHUR, optometrist; b. Denver, Mar. 14, 1926; s. Jacob and Charlotte (Kier) G.; m. Celeste Anita Pollock, Aug. 21, 1949; children: Linda Gorden Osatinski, Pamela Gorden Wakefield. BA, U. Colo., 1946; OD, Ill. Coll. Optometry, 1948. Pvt. optometry practice Denver, 1948—. Mem. Am. Optometric Assn. (charter mem. contact lens sect.), Colo. Optometric Assn., Green Gables Country Club (sec. 1971-73), Masons. Republican. Jewish. Home: 240 S Glencoe St Denver CO 80222 Office: 1616 Glenarm Pl Ste 102 Denver CO 80202

GORDER, CHERYL MARIE, book publisher; b. Brookings, S.D., Nov. 7, 1952; d. Shirley William and Arlene Opal (Barenklau) Seas; m. Dale Martin Gorder, Dec. 30, 1972 (June 1, 1992); 1 child, Sarah Lynne. BA, S.D. State U., 1974. Mgr. regional auctions Blue Bird Pub., Tempe, Ariz., 1974-85, pub., 1985—; cons. NIMTEC, Inc., Chandler, Ariz., 1991-92. Author: (book) Home Schools: An Alternative, 1985, Homeless: Without Addresses in America, 1988, Home Business Resource Guide, 1989, Green Earth Resource Guide, 1991; editor: Who's Who in Antiques, 1986, Real Dakota, 1988, Home Education Resource Guide, 1989, Spacedog's Best Friend, 1989, Dr. Christman's Learn to Read Book, 1990, They Reached for the Stars, 1990, The Sixth Sense: Practical Tips for Everyday Safety, 1990, Under Two Heavens, 1991, Survival Guide to Step-Parenting, 1992. Recipient Benjamin Franklin award Pub.'s Mktg. Assn., 1989. Mem. Pub. Mktg. Assn., Am. Bus. Women's Assn., Ariz. Book Pub. Assn. Office: Blue Bird Pub 1739 E Broadway Ste 306 Tempe AZ 85282

GORDON, ANTHONY ROBERT, federal law enforcement official, lawyer; b. Redlands, Calif., Mar. 26, 1959; s. Bruno and Bertha (Jireck) G. AA in Sociology, Crafton Hills Coll., 1979; BA in Polit. Sci., Pub. Adminstrn., Calif. State U., Long Beach, 1981; JD cum laude, Southwestern U., L.A., 1984. Bar: Nev. 1985, U.S. Dist. Ct. Nev. 1985, U.S. Ct. Appeals (9th cir.) 1985, Calif. 1986; Cert. FBI Legal Advisor, 1993. Law clk. U.S. Attys. Office, Las Vegas, Nev., 1985-86; dep. pub. defender Nev. State Pub. Defenders Office, Winnemucca, Nev., 1986-87; chief dep. dist. atty. Lander County Dist. Atty.'s Office, Battle Mountain, Nev., 1987-89; dep. atty. gen. Nev. State Atty. Gen.'s Office, Carson City, Nev., 1989-91; spl. agt. FBI, L.A., 1991—; 1st. ltd. U.S. Army Reserve Judge Advocate Gen. Office, 1992—; dir. Lander County Dept. Emergency Mgmt., Battle Mountain, 1988-89; instr. law No. Nev. C.C., Winnemucca, 1987-89, Western Nev. C.C., Carson City, 1990-91. Contbr. articles to profl. jours. Chmn. Lander County Dem. Cen. Com., Battle Mountain, 1988-91, Lander County Commn. of the U.S. Constitution, Battle Mountain, 1988-91; bd. dirs. Tri-County Devel. Authority, Winnemucca, 1987-89; chmn. Lander County Gen. Improvement Dist. # 1 TV Dist., Battle Mountain, 1989. John Lewis King Meml. scholar San Bernardino (Calif.) County Bar Assn., 1984; recipient Acad. Achievement award FBI Acad., Quantico, Va., 1992; recipient FBI Incentive award Rodney King Civil Rights Investigation, 1993. Mem. ABA, Western Fin. Remedies Enforcement Assn., Nat. Eagle Scout Assn. Roman Catholic. Office: PO Box 262 West Covina CA 91793

GORDON, CHRISTINE CONSTANCE, wildlife biologist, researcher; b. Cambridge, Mass., Feb. 10, 1963; d. Glen Everett and Constance (Herreshoff) G. BS, Colo. State U., 1984; MS, S.D. State U., 1989. Youth conservation enrollee corps Nat. Park Svc., Rock Creek Park, summer 1980, 81; work/learn intern Smithsonian Inst., Edgewater, Md., summer 1983; wildlife technician Dept. Energy/Assoc. Western Univs., Idaho Falls, summer 1984, U.S. Fish and Wildlife Svc., Pinon Canyon Man. Site, Colo., 1985-86; conservation technician Nebr. Game and Parks Commn., North Platte, 1986; rsch. asst. S.D. Coop. Fish and Wildlife Rsch. Unit, Brookings, 1986-89; biologist Directorate Environ. Compliance and Mgmt. Ft. Carson (Colo.) Mil. Reservation, 1989-92; wildlife biologist Bur. Land Mgmt., Fillmore, Utah, 1992—. Contbr. articles to profl. jours. Mem. Wildlife Soc., Nature Conservancy, Nat. Wildlife Fedn., Xi Sigma Pi. Office: Bur Land Mgmt 15 E 500 N Fillmore UT 84631

GORDON, CLAUDE EUGENE, musician; b. Helena, Mont., Apr. 5, 1916; s. James Austin and Nellie G. (Elge) G.; m. Genevieve Alice Pentecost, Apr. 19, 1936 (dec. 1989); children: Gary Anthony, Steven Robert; m. Patricia J. Kasarda, Sept. 22, 1990. Doctorate (hon.), La Sierra U., 1992. Trumpeter NBC, CBS, Motion Pictures, L.A., 1937-69; 1st trumpet big bands, stage shows, hotels, L.A., 1937-44, CBS, Hollywood, 1944-56; orch. leader L.A. and nationwide, 1950-69; condr. TV mus., stage shows for stars, L.A., Reno and Las Vegas, Nev., 1960-69; lectr., instr. clinics Mich. U., No. Ill. U., Fla. State U., North Tex. State U., others, 1970-87; instr. Glaude Gordon Internat. Brass Workshop, La Sierra U., Riverside, Calif.; recorded for all major labels. Author: Brass Playing Is No Harder Than Deep Breathing, The Physical Approach to Elementary Brass Playing, Systematic Approach to Daily Practice, Daily Trumpet Routines, Tongue Level Exercises, 30 Velocity Studies; annotator: Arban Complete Method, 1982; instrument designer: CG Benge trumpet, 1960, Claude Gordon Selmer trumpet, 1977.

GORDON, DONALD HOWARD, podiatrist; b. Ft. Smith, Ark., Nov. 16, 1954; s. Halton Howard and M. Janelle (Carter) G.; m. Carol Ann Miller, Aug. 15, 1975; children: Stephanie, Andrew. BS in Chemistry, Okla. Christian Coll., 1977, BSE in Science, 1977; BS in Basic Medicine, Calif. Coll. Podiatric Medicine, 1981, D in Podiatric Medicine, 1983. Tchr. chemistry, football coach Midwest City (Okla.) High Sch., 1977-79; resident in surgery Calif. Podiatry Hosp., San Francisco, 1983-84, sr. resident in surgery, 1984-85; podiatrist Ambulatory Family Podiatry Group, Daly City, Calif., 1985-87; pvt. practice podiatry Pacifica, Calif., 1987-88; asst. prof. Calif. Coll. Podiatric Medicine, San Francisco, 1987—. Named one of Outstanding Young Men of Am., 1985. Mem. Am. Podiatric Med. Assn., Calif. Podiatric Med. Assn., San Francisco/San Mateo County Podiatry Assn., Am. Coll. Foot Surgeons (assoc.), Pacifica (Calif.) C. of C. (dir. membership com., edn. com. 1985-86, chmn. edn. com. 1986-87), Calif. C. of C. (v.p. 1988). Mem. Ch. of Christ. Office: 1210 Scott St San Francisco CA 94115-4000

GORDON, HELEN HEIGHTSMAN, English language educator, writer; b. Salt Lake City, Sept. 7, 1932; d. Fred C. and Florence Isabel Heightsman; m. Norman C. Winn, Aug. 10, 1950 (div. Sept. 1972); children: Bruce Vernon Winn, Brent Terry Winn, Holly Winn Willner; m. Clifton Beverly Gordon, Feb. 17, 1974. Student, U. Utah, 1959-62; BA in English and Edn., Calif. State U., Sacramento, 1964, MA in English, 1967; EdD, Nova U., 1979. Cert. tchr., Calif.; lic. counselor, Calif. Stenographer, payroll clk. Associated Food Stores, Inc., Salt Lake City, 1951-59; part-time instr. in remedial English U. Utah, Salt Lake City, 1960-61; tchr. high sch. Rio Americano High Sch., Sacramento, 1965-66; assoc. prof., counselor Porterville (Calif.) Coll., 1967-74; prof., counselor Bakersfield (Calif.) Coll., 1974—; chair lang. arts div. Porterville Coll., 1971-74; coord. women's studies Bakersfield Coll., 1977-78, adminstrv. intern, 1982-83; dir. region V, English Coun. of Calif. Two Yr. Colls., 1990-92; articulation coord. Bakersfield Coll., 1992—. Author: (textbook) From Copying to Creating, 2d edit., 1983, Developing College Writing, 1989, Wordforms, Book I & II, 2d edit., 1990, Interplay: Sentence Skills in Context, 1991. Founder, 1st pres. Arts Coun. Writers Club, Bakersfield, 1993; guest mem. editorial bd. Bakersfield Californian Newspaper, 1988; past pres. Unitarian Fellowship of Kern County, Bakersfield, 1976-78. Calif. Fund for Instruction grantee, 1978; U. Utah scholar, 1959-62. Mem. NEA, Am. Assn. Women in Community and Jr. Colls. (founder Bakersfield chpt., pres., program chair 1988-91), Nat. Coun. Tchrs. of English, Faculty Assn. Calif. Community Coll., Calif. Community Coll. Counselors Assn., Textbook Authors Assn. (charter), LWV (pres. Bakersfield chpt. 1981-83, 89-90), Calif. Writers Club, Arts Coun. Wrtiers Club (founder, 1st pres. Bakersfield chpt.). Democrat. Home: 6400 Westlake Dr Bakersfield CA 93308-6519 Office: Bakersfield Coll 1801 Panorama Dr Bakersfield CA 93305-1299

GORDON, HUGH SANGSTER, JR., fire services administrator; b. Winnipeg, Manitoba, Can., July 6, 1949; s. Hugh Sangster Sr. and Margaret Forbes (Johnston) G. BS, U. N.D., 1973, MS, 1975. Cert. arena and pool mgr., fireman. Gen. mgr. recreation commn. City of Flin Flon, Can., 1978-81; supr. field house City of Saskatoon, Can., 1982-84, arena mgr., 1984-85; mgr. facility ops. dept. park and recreation City of Regina, Can., 1985-87, acting. dir. parks and recreation dept., 1986-87, dir. fire svcs., 1987—. Recipient Cert. of Devoted Civil Svc., City of Saskatoon, 1985. Mem. Can. Assn. Fire Chiefs., Saskatchewan Assn. Fire Chiefs (v.p. 1987—). Mem. United Ch. Can. Office: Regina Fire Dept, Box 1790, Regina, SK Canada S4P 3C8

GORDON, JOHN LYNN, environmental chemist, consultant; b. Amarillo, Tex., Dec. 2, 1933; s. Wilson Harold and Ruth (Neptune) G.; m. Janet Elizabeth Willits, May 27, 1955; children: Mark Robert, Carron Alice, Andrew Land. BS in Chemistry, West Tex. State Coll., 1957; postgrad., U. Wis., 1957-59. Chemist U.S. Bur. Mines, Amarillo, 1960-70, Mason & Hanger/Silas Mason, Amarillo, 1970-73; environ. chemist Dames & Moore, Denver, 1973-86, regional mgr. atmospheric svcs., 1984-86, cons., 1978-86; sr. air quality specialist Battelle Project Mgmt. Div., Columbus, Ohio, 1987, Hereford, Tex., 1987-88; v.p. environmental div. N.Am. Weather Cons., Salt Lake City, 1988—. Contbr. articles to profl. jours.; patentee in field. Founder Opportunity Sch., Amarillo, 1969, pres., bd. dirs.; founder Meals-on-Wheels, Amarillo, pres.; pres. Weiland Sch. Parent-Student-Tchr. Assn, Lakewood, Colo., 1982-85. Grad. assistantship U. Wis., Oscar Myer Corp., 1957. Mem. Am. Chem. Soc., Air Pollution Control Assn. (membership chmn. 1983—), Air and Waste Mgmt. Assn. (chmn. Great Basin chpt. 1990-92), Phi Lambda Upsilon. Presbyterian. Office: N Am Weather Cons 1293 W 2200 S Salt Lake City UT 84119-1100

GORDON, JOSEPH HAROLD, lawyer; b. Tacoma, Mar. 31, 1909; s. Joseph H. and Mary (Obermiller) G.; m. Jane Wilson, Sept. 12, 1936 (dec.); children—Joseph H., Nancy Jane; m. Eileen Rylander, Jan. 7, 1967. B.A., Stanford, 1931; LL.B., U. Wash., 1935. Bar: Wash. bar 1935. Since practiced in Tacoma; ptnr. Gordon & Gordon, Tacoma, 1935-50, Henderson, Carnahan, Thompson & Gordon, Tacoma, 1950-57, Carnahan, Gordon & Goodwin, Tacoma, 1957-70, Gordon, Thomas, Honeywell, Malanca, peterson & Daheim, Tacoma, 1970—. Mem. ABA (ho. dels., bd. govs. 1962-72, treas. 1965-72), Wash. State Bar Assn., Tacoma Bar Assn. (past pres.). Presbyn. (elder). Clubs: Rotary, Tacoma, Tacoma Golf and Country. Home: 2819 N Junett St Tacoma WA 98407-6345 Office: Gordon Thomas Honeywell Malanca Peterson & Daheim 2200 One Washington Plz PO Box 1157 Tacoma WA 98401-1157

GORDON, JUDITH, communications consultant, writer; b. Long Beach, Calif.; d. Irwin Ernest and Susan (Perlman) G.; m. Lawrence Banka, May 1, 1977. BA, Oakland U., 1966; MS in Libr. Sci., Wayne State U., 1973. Researcher Detroit Inst. of Arts, 1968-69; libr. Detroit Pub. Libr., 1971-74; caseworker Wayne County Dept. Social Svcs., Detroit, 1974-77; advt. copywriter Hudson's Dept. Store, Detroit, 1979; mgr. The Poster Gallery, Detroit, 1980-81; mktg., corp. communications specialist Bank of Am., San Francisco, 1983-84; mgr., consumer pubs. Bank of Am., 1984-86; prin., specialist consumer info. and edn. Active Voice, San Francisco, 1986—. Author San Francisco Mag., 1990; contbr. edit. The Artist's Mag., 1988—; contbr. to book Flowers: Gary Bukovnik, Watercolors and Monotypes, Abrams, 1990. Vol. From the Heart, San Francisco, 1992, Bay Area Book Festival, San Francisco, 1990, 91, Aid & Comfort, San Francisco, 1987, Save Orch. Hall, Detroit, 1977-81, NOW sponsored abortion clinic project. Recipient Nat. award Merit, Soc. Consumer Affairs Profls. in Bus., 1986, Bay Area Best award, Internat. Assn. Bus. Communicators, 1986, Internat. Galaxy award, 1992. Mem. Nat. Writers Union, Freelance Editorial Assn., Graphic Arts Coun., Women's Nat. Book Assn., Media Alliance, Friends of City Arts and Lectures. Office: 899 Green St San Francisco CA 94133-3788

GORDON, KAREN ELIZABETH, writer; b. Bakersfield, Calif.; d. Paul Aaen Gordon and Camilla Edith (Hall) Collins. BA in English, U. Calif., Berkeley, 1968; MA in English, Calif. State U., Sonoma, 1975. Author, 1983—; assoc. WordSpring, Sacramento, 1992—; assoc., writer Daedalus, Design & Architecture, Paris, 1990—. Author: The Well Tempered Sentence, 1983, The Transitive Vampire, 1984, Intimate Apparel, 1989, The Deluxe Transitive Vampire, 1993, The New Well Tempered Sentence, 1993; reviewer (book) Mirabella, 1990. Recipient New Works award Sacramento Met. Arts Commn., 1988, 89. Mem. NAFE, PEN Internat. Office: WordSpring Ste 7 1021 H St Sacramento CA 95814

GORDON, KATHRYN LEE, sales executive, cattle rancher; b. Portland, Oreg., Oct. 28, 1947; d. Clarence Fay and A. Eileen (Potter) Kyle; m. Richard W. Rippey, Nov. 10, 1967 (div. May 1984); children: Brian W., Janine L. Student, Portland State Coll., 1966-67. Office mgr. Boyer Metal Fabricators Inc., Canby, Oreg., 1977-81; estimator, saleswoman, project mgr. Timsteel Inc., Clackamas, Oreg., 1982-84, Tomlinson Metal Fabricators Inc., Canby, 1984-85; owner, office mgr., estimator, saleswoman, project mgr. Riverside Steel Fabricators Inc., Tualatin, Oreg., 1985-91; dist. sales rep. for Oreg. and Wash., Brown-Strauss Steel, Salt Lake City, 1991—. Mem. Assn. Women in Metal Industries (fund raising com. 1991—, scholarship com. 1991—, projects and planning 1992—), Pacific N.W. Fabricators Assn. Home: 10001 S Kraxberger Rd Canby OR 97013 Office: Brown-Strauss Steel PO Box 501 Pleasant Grove UT 84062

GORDON, LEONARD, sociology educator; b. Detroit, Dec. 6, 1935; s. Abraham and Sarah (Rosen) G.; m. Rena Joyce Feigelman, Dec. 25, 1955; children: Susan Melinda, Matthew Seth, Melissa Gail. B.A., Wayne State U., 1957; M.A., U. Mich., 1958; Ph.D., Wayne State U., 1966. Instr. Wayne State U., Detroit, 1960-62; research dir. Jewish Community Council, Detroit, 1962-64; dir. Mich. area Am. Jewish Com., N.Y.C., 1964-67; asst. prof. Ariz. State U., Tempe, 1967-70, assoc. prof., 1970-77, prof., 1977—, chmn. dept. sociology, 1981-90, assoc. dean for acad. programs Coll. Liberal Arts and Scis., 1990—; cons. OEO, Maricopa County, Ariz., 1968. Author: A City in Racial Crisis, 1978, (with A. Mayer) Urban Life and the Struggle To Be Human, 1979, (with R. Hardert, M. Laner and M. Reader) Confronting Social Problems, 1984, (with J. Hall and R. Melnick) Harmonizing Arizona's Ethnic and Cultural Diversity, 1992. Sec. Conf. on Religion and Race, Detroit, 1962-67; mem. exec. bd. dirs. Am. Jewish Com., Phoenix chpt., 1969-70. Grantee NSF, 1962, Rockefeller found., 1970, 84. Fellow Am. Sociol. Assn.; mem. Pacific Sociol. Assn. (v.p. 1978-79, pres. 1980-81), AAUP, Soc. Study Social Problems (chair C. Wright Mills award com. 1988, treas. 1989—), Ariz. State U. Alumni Assn. (faculty dir. 1981-82). Democrat. Jewish. Home: 5262 N Woodmere Fairway Scottsdale AZ 85250-6456 Office: Ariz State U Office for Acad Programs Coll Liberal Arts and Scis Tempe AZ 85287

GORDON, LOUIS, statistics educator; b. Phila., Dec. 13, 1946; s. Max and Lillian (Glebow) G.; m. Laura Ann Cohen, May 29, 1983; 1 child, Robert. BS, MS, Mich. State U., 1968, Stanford U., 1969; PhD, Stanford U., 1971. Asst. prof. Stanford (Calif.) U., 1971-73; statistician Alza Corp., Palo Alto, Calif., 1973-78, U.S. Dept. Energy, Washington, 1978-83; assoc. prof. math. U. So. Calif., L.A., 1983-88, prof., 1988—; mem. Com. on Nat. Stats., 1987—. Woodrow Wilson hon. fellow, 1968, Fulbright fellow, 1989, Guggenheim fellow, 1989. Fellow Inst. Math. Stats. Office: U So Calif Math Dept DRB-155 Los Angeles CA 90089-1113

GORDON, MARGARET SHAUGHNESSY, economist, educator; b. Wabasha, Minn., Sept. 4, 1910; d. Michael James and Mary (O'Brien) Shaughnessy; m. Robert Aaron Gordon, Aug. 15, 1936 (dec. 1978); children: Robert James, David Michael. B.A., Bryn Mawr Coll., 1931; M.A., Radcliffe Coll., 1933, Ph.D., 1935; student, London Sch. Econs., 1933-34. Instr. Wellesley Coll., 1935-36; research fellow Harvard-Radcliffe Bur. Internat. Research, 1936-39; head research unit Export-Import office OPA, Washington, 1942-43; asst. research economist Inst. Indsl. Relations, U. Calif. at Berkeley, 1950-54, asso. dir., 1954-77, lectr. econs., 1965-77; Mem. Calif. Gov.'s Commn. on Employment and Retirement of Older Workers, 1959-60; mem. Personnel Bd., City of Berkeley, 1961-65, 70-75; asso. dir. Carnegie Commn. on Higher Edn. (name later changed to Carnegie Council on Higher Edn.), 1969-79; mem. Pres.'s Commn. on Income Maintenance Programs, 1968-69; cons. unemployment ins. U.S. Bur. Employment Security, 1962-66; adv. com. research devel. U.S. Social Security Adminstrn., 1965-68, chmn., 1966-67. Author: Employment Expansion and Population Growth, 1954, The Economics of Welfare Policies, 1963, Youth Education and Unemployment Problems: An International Perspective, 1979, Social Security Policies in Industrial Countries: A Comparative Analysis, 1988; editor: Poverty in America, 1965, (with E.F. Cheit) Occupational Disability and Public Policy, 1963, Higher Education and the Labor Market, 1974; mng. editor: Indsl. Relations, 1961-63, 65-66. Mem. council, City of Berkeley, 1965-69; bd. dirs. Consumers Coop. of Berkeley, 1980-87. Mem. Am. Econ. Assn., Indsl. Relations Research Assn.,. Home: 1515 Oxford St Apt 2D Berkeley CA 94709-1504

GORDON, MARILYN, hypnotherapist, author, publisher, teacher; b. Chgo., Dec. 11, 1940; d. Harold David and Gertrude (Goldman) Goldberg; divorced; 1 child, Dana. BA in English, U. Mich., 1962; postgrad., U. Calif., 1963, JFK U., 1983. Cert. clin. therapist. Tchr. Chgo. Pub. Schs., 1964-69; seminar leader Marin County, Calif., 1970—; yoga instr., 1974-83; instr. reading Evelyn Wood Reading Dynamics, 1983-89; pvt. practice hypnotherapist Oakland, Calif., 1987—; author, pub. WiseWord Pub., Oakland, Calif., 1990; speaker, radio and TV personality, 1990—; corporate trainer and cons., 1991; trainer hypnotherapists, 1989—; workshop leader U. Calif., San Francisco, 1986—. Author, pub.: Healing is Remembering Who You Are: A Guide for Healing Your Mind, Your Emotions and Your Life, Manual for Healing with Hypnotherapy; contbr. articles to Jour. Hypnotism. Mem. Nat. Guild of Hypnotists, Pubs. Mktg. Assn., Am. Coun. Hypnotist Examiners, Phi Beta Kappa, Phi Kappa Phi, Pi Lambda Theta. Office: WiseWord Pub PO Box 10795 Oakland CA 94610-0795

GORDON, MARVIN JAY, physician; b. Balt., Jan. 11, 1946; s. Joseph Nathan and Sarah Henrietta (Seidel) G.; m. Linda Susan Merican, Dec. 23, 1968 (div. Oct. 1984); m. Myra Eleanor Sklar, Jan. 27, 1985; children: David, Joseph, Allison, Lisa. BS, U. Md., College Park, 1965; MD, U. Md., Balt., 1969. Diplomate Am. Bd. Internal Medicine, Am. Bd. Gastroenterology, Am. Bd. Quality Assurance and Utilization. Resident in internal medicine U. Md., Balt., 1969-72, Gastroenterology fellowship, 1972-74; pvt. practice Laguna Beach, Calif., 1976—. Contbr. articles to profl. jours. Pres. Temple Beth El, Laguna Niguel, Calif., 1984-85. Major USAF, 1974-76. Fellow Am. Coll. Gastroenterology; mem. Am. Gastroenterol. Assn. Home and Office: 31852 S Coast Hwy Ste 300 Laguna Beach CA 92677-3281

GORDON, MILTON ANDREW, academic administrator; b. Chgo., May 25, 1935; s. Herrmann Andrew Gordon and Ossie Bell; m. Margaret Faulwell, July 18, 1987; children: Patrick Francis, Vincent Michael; 1 stepchild, Michael Faulwell. BS, Xavier U. La., New Orleans, 1957; MA, U. Detroit, 1960; PhD, Ill. Inst. Tech., 1968; postgrad., Harvard U., 1984. Teaching asst. U. Detroit, 1958-59; mathematician Lab. Applied Scis. U. Chgo., 1959-62; part-time tchr. Chgo. Pub. Sch. System, 1962-66; assoc. prof. math. Loyola U., Chgo., 1966-67; dir. Afro-Am. Studies Program Loyla U., Chgo., 1971-77; dean Coll. Arts and Scis., prof. math. Chgo. State U., 1978-86; v.p. acad. affairs, prof. math. Sonoma State U., Rohnert Park, Calif., 1986-90; pres., prof. math. Calif. State U., Fullerton, 1990—; hon. admissions counselor United States Naval Acad., 1979; mem. exec. coun. Calif. State U. Contbr. articles to profl. jours. Chmn. Archdiocese of Chgo. Sch. Bd., 1978-79; bd. govs. Orange County Community Found., Costa Mesa, Calif., 1990—, NCCJ, 1991—; bd. dirs. United Way of Orange County, Irvine, Calif., 1991. Recipient cert. of appreciation Community Ch. Santa Rosa, Calif., 1988; named Adminstr. of Yr., Chgo. State U., 1979. Mem. Am.conf. Acad. Deans (chmn. bd. dirs. 1983-85), Am. Assn. Univ. Adminstrs. (bd. dirs. 1983-86), Calif. Coalition of Math., Sigma Xi, Phi Beta Delta. Roman Catholic. Office: Calif State U Fullerton Office of President PO Box 34080 Fullerton CA 92634-9480

GORDON, MILTON G., real estate counselor, consultant; b. Detroit, June 1, 1922; s. Abe and Anna (Pragg) G.; m. Sandra Louise Driver, Apr. 2, 1966; children: Jonathan, Shoshana Meira. BA, Wayne State U., 1945; MA, UCLA, 1947. Pres. Milton Gordon Co. (Realtors), Los Angeles, 1951-62, Village Realty-Milton Gordon Co., Los Angeles, 1962-63; Calif. real estate commr., 1963; mem. Gov.'s cabinet as sec. bus. and commerce State of Calif., 1964-67; v.p., treas. Hotel del Coronado, Coronado, Calif., 1969—; pres. Milton G. Gordon Corp. (mgmt. cons.'s and real estate counselors), 1967—; Mem. Gov.'s Emergency Resources Planning Commn., 1966, Calif. Council on Criminal Justice, 1979—; mem. adv. com. to Real Estate Commr.; chmn. Senate Commn. on Cost Control in State Govt., Calif.; commr. Los Angeles County Real Estate Mgmt. Commn.; mem. exec. com. Community Rels. Conf. So. Calif.; commr. Los Angeles County Efficiency and Economy Commn.; mem. Calif. Pub. Works Bd., 1963-65; mem. assessment practices adv. com. Los Angeles Assessor; chmn. Calif. Senate Adv. Commn. Cost. Control in Govt., 1986—; commr. Calif. Med. Assistance Commn., 1990—. Chmn. exec. com. U. Judaism, 1972—; bd. dirs. Jewish Theol. Sem. Am., N.Y.C.; chmn. L.A. Police Dept. Permit Appeals Panel, 1993. With AUS, 1942-44. Recipient Outstanding Alumnus award Wayne State U., 1964. Mem. Nat. Assn. Real Estate License Ofcls. (v.p. 1965), Calif. Home Loan Mortgage Assn. (bd. dirs.), D.A.V., Am. Legion. Democrat. Jewish. Address: 10504 Cheviot Dr Los Angeles CA 90064

GORDON, PETER LOWELL, immigration manager; b. Powell, Wyo., Feb. 16, 1953; s. John Eric Gordon and Carol Mae (Peterson) Olson; m. Shigeko Masunaga, Apr. 16, 1983 (div. Feb. 24, 1992). BA in Polit. Sci., Criminal Justice, Calif. State U., L.A., 1975. Asst. cook Country Kitchen, LaCrosse, Wis., 1970-71; asst. mgr. Ky. Fried Chicken, Tujunga, Calif., 1975-76, Parasol Restaurant, Alhambra, Calif., 1976-77; border patrol agt. Immigration and Naturalization Svc., Dept. Justice, San Diego, 1977-80; immigration insp. Immigration and Naturalization Svc., Dept. Justice, Anchorage, 1980-83; immigration examiner Immigration and Naturalization Svc., Dept. Justice, L.A., 1983-87; legalization mgr. Immigration and Naturalization Svc., Dept. Justice, Laguna Niguel, Calif., 1987-90, immigration mgr., 1990—. Co-developer (nat. data base) Legalization Adjustment Processing System, 1987 (Commr.'s award 1987); co-designer Western Svc. Ctr., 1989; co-author Western Svc. Ctr. Guidelines, 1989. Speaker Am. Immigration Lawyers Assn. So. and Northern Calif. Chpts. Mem. ANt. Space soc., Immigration Officer Asns., Fedn. for Am. Immigration Reform, DELTA, Planetary Soc. Republican. Lutheran.

GORDON, PRISCILLA STUART, research institute executive; b. Boston, Nov. 28, 1955; d. Edward Alexander Gordon and Ida Virginia (Raymond) Johnson. BA in Polit. Sci., Tufts U., 1979; MA in Internat. Rels., U. So. Calif., L.A., 1986. Rsch. assoc. Boston U., 1979-80, Tufts U., Medford, Mass., 1981-83; adminstr. Japan Am. Soc., L.A., 1986, Kamar Internat., Torrance, Calif., 1987; v.p. The Claremont (Calif.) Inst., 1988—; adj. faculty Embry-Riddle Aero. U., Daytona Beach, Fla., 1989—, Chaffey Coll., Rancho Cucamonga, 1991—. Adv. bd. mem. White Cane Ctr. for the Blind, Montclair, Calif., 1991—. Mem. Acad. Polit. Sci., Am. Polit. Sci. Assn., Nat. Assn. Scholars, Ctr. for Study of the Presidency, Internat. Trumpet Guild. Republican. Office: The Claremont Inst 250 W 1st St # 330 342 Claremont CA 91711

GORDON, ROBERT EUGENE, lawyer; b. L.A., Sept. 20, 1932; s. Harry Maurice and Minnie (Shafer) G.; m. Gail Annette Yaras, Feb. 18, 1967 (div. 1979); 1 child, Victor Marten. BA, UCLA, 1954; LLB, U. Calif., Berkeley, 1959, JD, 1960; cert., U. Hamburg, Fed. Republic Germany, 1960. Bar: Calif. 1960. Assoc. Lillick, Geary, McHose, Roethke & Myers, Los Angeles, 1960-64, Schoichet & Rifkind, Beverly Hills, Calif., 1964-67; ptnr. Baerwitz & Gordon, Beverly Hills, 1967-69, Ball, Hunt, Hart, Brown & Baerwitz, Beverly Hills, 1970-71; of counsel Jacobs, Sills & Coblentz, San Francisco, 1972-78; ptnr. Gordon & Hodge, San Francisco, 1978-81; sole practice San Francisco, 1981-84, Sausalito, Calif., 1985-89; pvt. practice Corte Madera, Calif., 1989—; adj. prof. entertainment law U. Calif., San Francisco, 1990-91, U. Calif., Berkeley, 1992—. Served to 1st lt. U.S. Army, 1954-56. Mem. ABA (forum com. on entertainment and sports law, exec. com. music sect.), San Francisco Bar Assn., Los Angeles Copyright Soc. (bd. trustees 1970-71), Copyright Soc. of the USA. Home: 35 Elaine Ave Mill Valley CA 94941-1014 Office: 5725 Paradise Dr # 840 Corte Madera CA 94925-1212

GORDON, ROGER L., savings and loan association executive. Formerly sr. exec. v.p., chief oper. officer San Francisco Fed. Savs. & Loan Assn., pres., chief exec. officer, 1990—. Office: San Francisco Fed Savs & Loan 88 Kearny St San Francisco CA 94108-5530

GORDON, RUTH VIDA, structural engineer; b. Seattle, Sept. 19, 1926; s. Solomon Alexander and Leah (Yoffe) G.; m. Michael Herbert Schnapp, Sept. 28, 1949; children—Madeline Ruth, Marcia Lea, Michael Gordon, B.S., Stanford U., 1948, M.S., 1949. Registered structural and civil engr., Calif. Structural designer I. Thompson, Cons., San Francisco, 1950-51; structural designer Bechtel Corp., San Francisco, 1951-53; civil engr. CALTRANS, San Francisco, 1953-54; structural designer Western-Knapp Engring., San Francisco, 1954-55; dist. structural engr. Office of State Architect, San Francisco, 1956-84; cons. structural engr., pres. Pegasus Engring., 1985—; engr. mem. adv. panel of exam. revision project for Bd. Archtl. Examiners, San Francisco, 1979-80; mem. adv. com. for master plan for use of edn. facilities, San Francisco, 1971-72. Bd. dirs. Democratic Women's Forum, San Francisco, 1976-83, 85-87, v.p., 1978-79, 83-85. Wing and Garland scholar, 1948; 1st woman structural engr. State of Calif., 1959. Mem. Structural Engrs. Assn. No. Calif. (1st woman mem., chmn. legis. com. 1978-79, bd. dirs. 1984-86, chmn. profl. policies 1982-83), San Francisco Bay Area Engring. Coun. (del., bd. dirs. 1977-79, treas. 1979-80, sec. 1980-81, v.p. 1981-82, 1st woman pres. 1982-83), Soc. Women Engrs. (sr. mem. v.p. 1976-77, pres. 1978-79, Outstanding Svc. award 1979, 84), ASCE (del. to San Francisco Bay Area Engring. Coun. 1981-85), Calif. Fedn. Bus. and Profl. Women (named to Hall of Fame 1992), Yacht Racing Assn. San Francisco (cert. race officer, co-chmn. race mgmt. com.), U.S. Sailing (judge, sr. race officer, area G race mgr.), Union Sq. Bus and Profl. Women's Club (Woman of Achievement award 1975, 82), Golden Gate Yacht (dir. 1991-92), San Francisco Yacht Aux. Unitarian Home: 726 23d Ave San Francisco CA 94121 Office: Pegasus Engineering PO Box 210425 San Francisco CA 94121

GORDON, STEVEN ERIC, animator, designer; b. Hollywood, Calif., Mar. 23, 1960; s. Wilfred Isadore and Tamara (Bernstein) G.; m. Judith Katherine Ball, June 27, 1981; children: Scott Conrad, Eric Alexander. Grad. high sch., Granada Hills, Calif. Asst. animator Bakshi Prodns., Hollywood, 1977-79, animator, 1979-80; animation dir. Bakshi Prodns., Sun Valley, Calif., 1981-82; layout artist Filmation Studios, Hollywood, 1980-81; animator Disney Pictures, Burbank, Calif., 1982-87; dir. animation Rich Animation, Burbank, Calif., 1987—; story bd. artist Disney TV, Burbank, 1984-91, DIC Enterprises, Burbank, 1986-88; comml. animator Playhouse Pictures, Hollywood, 1986-88, Baer Animation Co., Inc., Hollywood, 1989-90, Cool Prodn., Burbank, 1990-92, Film Roman, North Hollywood, 1991. Democrat. Home: 32449 Scandia Dr Running Springs CA 92382 Mailing: PO Box 2829 Running Springs CA 92382

GORDON, SYDNEY JETER, environmental scientist, consultant; b. Richmond, Va., June 7, 1946; s. Woodrow Wilson and Ashley Brooke (Jeter) G.; m. Judy Ann Monroe, June 8, 1991; children: Thomas Norwood, Katherine Eddins. BS in Physics, Randolph-Macon Coll., 1968; MS in Physics, N.C. State U., 1974; MBA in Mgmt., U. Nev., Las Vegas, 1981. Cert. profl. contracts mgr. Physicist Harry Diamond Labs. U.S. Army, Washington, 1970-72; rsch. physicist EPA, Research Triangle Park, N.C., 1973-74; mgr. project devel. Northrop Svcs., Inc., Research Triangle Park, 1974-84; pvt. practice tech. cons. Las Vegas, 1984-85; bus. mgr. Tetra Tech., Inc. div. Honeywell, San Bernardino, Calif., 1985-88; assoc. Dames & Moore, 1988-92; program devel. Gutierrez-Palmenberg, Inc., Las Vegas, 1992—. Served with U.S. Army, 1968-70. Mem. Nat. Contract Mgmt. Assn., Soc. Am. Mil. Engrs., Phi Beta Kappa. Home: 4295 E Reno Ave Las Vegas NV 89120-1548 Office: Gutierrez-Palmenberg Inc 333 N Rancho Dr Ste 580 Las Vegas NV 89106-7026

GORE, BRYAN FRANK, nuclear scientist, educator; b. Berwyn, Ill., Dec. 3, 1938; s. Greenville D. and Mary Fenley (Bryan) G.; m. Barbara Lucille Boynton, Aug. 3, 1963; children: Marcy Lynn, Russell Bryan, David Bruce. B of Engring. Physics, Cornell U., 1961; MS in Physics, U. Mich., 1964, PhD in Physics, 1967. Asst. prof. physics U. Idaho, Moscow, 1967-68, Cen. Wash. U., Ellensburg, 1969-73; staff scientist, group leader Battelle Pacific N.W. Labs., Richland, Wash., 1973—; rsch. assoc. U. Md., College Park, 1969-70; faculty researcher N.W. Coll. and Univ. Assn. for Sci. (NORCUS), 1972-73; vis. scientist Stanford Linear Accelerator Ctr., Palo Alto, Calif., 1971; mem. faculty Wash. State U., Tri Cities, Richland, 1975-90; reactor operator licensing examiner U.S. Nuclear Regulatory Commn., 1981—; lead instr. probabilistic risk assessment methods and applications U.S. Dept. Energy and U.S. Nuclear Regulatory Commn., 1988-90. Named Tri Cities Engr. of Yr., Tri Cities chpt. NSPE, 1982. Mem. AAUP, ASME (rsch. task force on risk based inspection guidelines 1988—), Am. Nuclear Soc. (chmn. Richland sect. 1980-81), Am. Phys. Soc., Am. Assn. Physics Tchrs. Triangle Fraternity. Office: Battelle NW Labs PO Box 999 Richland WA 99352-0999

GORE, THOMAS GAVIN, insurance and securities broker; b. Pittsburg, Kans., Feb. 8, 1939; s. Harold Gavin and Mary Adele (Brinn) G.; m. Lorraine Elizabeth Riley, Sept. 3, 1960; children: Robert, Gregory. BA, Kans. U., 1962. CLU; ChFC. Agt. Transamerica Life Ins. Co., L.A., 1962-67; br. mgr. Transamerica Life Ins. Co., Newport Beach, Calif., 1968-75; pres. Thomas Gore & Assocs., Inc., Newport Beach, Calif., 1976—. Mem. Million Dollar Round Table, Nat. Assn. Life Underwriters, Assn. Advanced Life Underwriters, Santa Ana Country Club (bd. dirs. 1989—). Republican. Office: Thomas Gore & Assocs Inc 535 Anton Blvd Costa Mesa CA 92626

GORELIK, ALEXANDER, computer engineer; b. St. Petersburg, Russia, Sept. 25, 1964; s. Iza and Regina (Fayenson) G.; m. Irina Glazomitsky. BS in Computer Engring., Columbia U., 1986; MS in Computer Sci., Stanford U., 1991. Computer programmer Booz, Allen & Hamilton, N.Y.C., 1985-86; systems design engr. Amdahl Corp., Sunnyvale, Calif., 1986-91; staff software engr. Sybase Corp., Emeryville, Calif., 1991—. Regents scholar, 1982-86. Mem. Assn. Computing Machinery, Tau Beta Pi. Home: 3131 Grand Lake Dr Fremont CA 94555 Office: Sybase 1650 65th St Emeryville CA 94608

GORENBERG, NORMAN BERNARD, aeronautical engineer, consultant; b. St. Louis, May 18, 1923; s. Isadore and Ethel Gorenberg; m. Lucille Richmond, June 10, 1947; children: Judith Allyn Gorenberg Stein, Carol Ann, Gershom. BSME, Washington U., St. Louis, 1949. Registered profl. engr., Mo. Aero. engr. USAF Wright Air Devel. Ctr., Dayton, Ohio, 1949-51; aerodynamicist McDonnell Aircraft Corp., St. Louis, 1951-59; supervisory engr. Boeing Co., Vertol Div., Phila., 1959-62; R & D engr. Lockheed Corp., Burbank, Calif., 1962-89; vertical takeoff and landing aircraft cons. Dana Point, Calif., 1989—. Contbr. articles to profl. reports. With USAAF, 1943-46. Mem. AIAA, ASME, Am. Helicopter Soc. (chmn. St. Louis sect. 1955-56, nat. aerodyns. com. 1969-70, tech. dir. western region 1969-70), Nat. Mgmt. Assn. (life). Jewish.

GORIN, RALPH EDGAR, software engineer, consultant; b. Boston, Dec. 24, 1948; s. William and Helaine Miriam (Falkson) G. BS, MS, Rensselaer Polytech. Inst., 1970; postgrad., Stanford (Calif.) U., 1970-72. Mem. tech. staff Sanders Assocs., Nashua, N.H., 1970; mem. tech. staff Stanford U., 1972-76, mem. mgmt., 1976-87, dir. acad. computing, 1987-91; tech. staff XKL Systems Corp., Redmond, Wash., 1992—; bd. dirs. Ibuki, Inc., Mountain View, Calif. Author: Introduction to DECsystem-20 Assembly Language, 1981. Treas. Tom Nolan for Congress, 1992. Office: XKL Systems Corp 8420 154th Ave NE Redmond WA 98052

GORMAN, BARBARA ROSE, secretarial service administrator; b. Terre Haute, Ind., Apr. 12, 1945; d. Arthur Clarence and Lena (Laney) Bitts; m. Claude R. Gorman Jr., Apr. 10, 1970. Grad. high sch., Terre Haute. Sec. Levin bros. Wholesale, Terre Haute, 1963-64, Ind. State U., Terre Haute, 1965-70, Firestone Tire and Rubber Co., Salinas, Calif., 1971-73; sales rep. Avon Corp., Aurora, Colo., 1976-79; sec. for regional dir. Jafra Cosmetics, Aurora, 1980-83; prin. B.G. Typing Svc., Lakewood, Colo., 1987-92. Mem. NAFE. Home: 4591 S Buckley Way Aurora CO 80015-1957

GORMAN, MARVIN, science administrator, pharmaceutical industry consultant; b. Detroit, Sept. 24, 1928; s. Meyer and Sara (Evintzky) G.; m. Sue Eisler (div. Nov. 12, 1974); children: David, Judith, Debra; m. Lura Chaney, Oct. 2, 1976. BS in Chemistry, U. Mich., 1950; PhD in Chemistry, Wayne State U., 1955. Sr. scientist Eli Lilly, Indpls., 1956-64, rsch. assoc., 1964-69, advisor, 1969-81, rsch. cons., 1981-82; v.p. infectious disease Bristol-Myers Squibb, Syracuse, N.Y., 1982-86; sr. v.p. rsch. Bristol-Myers Squibb, Wallingford, Conn., 1986-88; exec. v.p., gen. mgr. Bristol-Myers Squibb, Seattle, 1988-91; cons. pharm. industry Key West, Fla., 1991—; v.p. product devel. Pathogenesis Corp., Seattle, 1992—. Editor: (book) Beta-Lactam Antibiotics, 1983; contbr. over 100 articles to profl. jours.; mem. editorial bd. AntiMicrobial Agents & Chemotherapy, 1975-80, Jour. of Antibiotics, 1975-91. Fund raiser Northwood Inst., Indpls., 1980-82; vo. exec. Internat. Exec. Svc. Corps., Stamford, Conn., 1992—. Mem. Am. Chem. Soc. (chmn. 1978), Gordon Rsch. Conf. (chmn. 1974), Am. Soc. for Microbiology, Protein Soc. Home: 421 William St Key West FL 33040-6853

GORMAN, MICHAEL STEPHEN, construction executive; b. Tulsa, Aug. 3, 1951; s. Lawrence Matthew and Mary Alice (Veith) G.; m. Sheryl Lane McGee, Feb. 19, 1972; children: Kelley Lane, Michael Ryan. Student, Colo. State U., 1970, 71. With McGee Constrn. Co., Denver, 1972-74, with sales and estimating dept., 1974-78, gen. mgr., 1978-80, pres., owner, 1980-91; pres. Wisor Group, Boulder, 1990—. Author Sales column Remodeling News Mag., 1993. Mem. Nat. Assn. Remodeling Industry Metro Denver (chmn. membership svcs. com. 1987-91, bd. dirs., pres. 1982-91, regional v.p. 1987-89, nat. sec. 1990-91, Man of Yr. 1982, REgional Contractor of Yr. 1988).

GORMAN, RUSSELL WILLIAM, marketing executive, consultant; b. Glen Ridge, N.J., Aug. 17, 1927; s. William Francis and Emily (Weldon) G.; m. Mieko Deguchi, June 19, 1956. BS, U.S. Merchant Marine Acad., 1949. Lic. merchant marine. Lic. officer Moore McCormack Lines Inc., N.Y., 1949-53; dir. tng. Chevron Shipping Co., San Francisco, 1957-77; mgr. orgn., adminstrn. Utah Internat. Corp., San Francisco, 1977-84; pres. Lumier Inc., San Francisco, 1984-85; v.p. John F. Perry Assocs., Concord, Calif., 1986; pres. Market Devel. Assocs., Danville, Calif., 1986—; bd. dirs. Norlock Tech. Inc., San Mateo, Calif., Internat. Tech. Assocs. Santa Clara, Calif. Mem. Calif. Vets. Coalition for Bush, 1988, Sec. of the Navy Adv. Bd. on Naval History, 1990—; adv. speaker Pete Wilson for Senate Campaign, 1988. Lt. USN, 1954-57, PTO, rear adm. Res. ret. Decorated Legion of Merit (2). Mem. Navy League of the U.S. (v.p. Pacific Ctrl. region 1989—), Res. Officers Assn. of the U.S. (v.p. Navy sect. 1990-92), Naval Res. Assn. (nat. v.p. surface/subsurface 1990—), Oakland C. of C. (vice chmn. mil. affairs com. 1990—). Republican. Methodist. Home: 46 Willowview Ct Danville CA 94526

GORMÉZANO, KEITH STEPHEN, editor, arbitrator; b. Madison, Wis., Nov. 22, 1955; s. Isadore and Miriam (Fox) G.; m. Emma Lee Rogers, Aug. 17, 1986 (div. Nov. 1990). BGS, U. Iowa, 1977, postgrad. in pub. affairs, 1979-80; postgrad. in law, U. Puget Sound, 1984-86. Pub. Le Beacon Presse, Seattle, 1980-89; real estate agt. Jim Stacy Realty, Seattle, 1988-89; arbitrator Better Bus. Bur. Greater Seattle, 1987—; arbitrator Puget Sound Multi Listing Assn., 1988-89, Nat. Assn. Securities Dealers, 1989—, Ford Consumer Appeals Bd., 1991-92, Harborview Med. Ctrs., 1990-91, 92—, Op. Improvement Found., 1980-81; joint labor mgmt. com. Puget Fin. Svcs. U. Wash. Med. Ctr., 1990-91; pub. info. officer; vol. VISTA, 1982-83; dir. ACJS, Inc., 1981-82. Editor M'godolim, 1980-81, Funding Bull. U. Wash. Health Scis. Grantseekers, 1991; pub., editor Beacon Rev., 1980-89. Vice chmn. Resource Conservation Commn., Iowa City, 1979-80; bd. dirs. Seattle Mental Health Inst., 1981-83, Youth Advocates, Seattle, 1984, Atlantic St. Ctr., 1984; mem. City of Seattle Animal Control Commn., 1984-86, vice chmn., 1985-86, chmn., 1986; mem. Selective Svc. System, 1982—, vice chmn. civilian rev. bd. 742, 1985—; mem. Wash. State Local Draft Bd. #18, mem. controlled choice appeals bd. Seattle Sch. Dist., 1989; patient collection rep. U. Wash., 1990-91, Harborview Med. Ctrs., 1990-91, 92-93; mem. Ford Consumer Appeals Bd., 1991-93, Ford Motor Co. Dispute Settlement Bd., 1991-93, Joint Labor-Mgmt. Com., Patient Fin. Svcs., U. Wash. Med. Ctr., 1990-91, Temple B'nai Torah; mem. coordinating com. edn. after dark program Jewish Fedn. Greater Seattle, 1991-92, exec. bd. thirty-something plus Jewish Community Ctr., 1991-92. Named Citizen of the Day Sta. KIXI Radio, 1982. Mem. League United Latin Am. Citizens Amigos (chair 1984-86), U. Iowa Alumni Assn. Jewish. Office: 4226 Fremont Ave N Apt # 5WWW Seattle WA 98103-7282

GORMICAN, STEPHEN PETER, emergency physician; b. Rochester, N.Y., July 28, 1949; s. Maurice J. and Geraldine F. (Iuppa) G.; m. Susan M. Johnson, Sept. 17, 1977; children: Joseph, Laura Betsy. AB in Math., Boston Coll., 1971; MD, U. Toronto, 1975. Diplomate Am. Bd. Emergency Medicine. Intern Mercy Hosp. and Med. Ctr., San Diego, 1975-76; emergency physician Scripps Meml. Hosp., La Jolla, Calif., 1978—; lectr. in field. Contbr. articles to profl. jours. Treas. Coronado (Calif.) Schs. Found., 1992—. Fellow Am. Coll. Emergency Physicians (trauma com. 1984-86); mem. Calif. Med. Assn., San Diego County Med. Soc., San Diego Emergency Physician Soc. Roman Catholic. Home: 15 Catspaw Cape Coronado CA 92118 Office: Scripps Meml Hosp PO Box 28 La Jolla CA 92038

GORMLEY, FRANICS XAVIER, JR., social worker; b. Boston, Apr. 27, 1953; s. Francis Xavier and Catherine Coffee (Ireland) G. Student, Massasoit Community Coll., 1973; BA in Psychology, U. Mass., Boston, 1981; MSW, U. Wash., 1984. Cert. social worker. Coordinator Gerontology Career Program Elder Fest, Chico, Calif., 1981; mgr. Arnold's Restaurant, Cardiff, Wales, 1981-82; med. social worker Harborview Med. Ctr., Seattle, 1983-84; psychotherapist Seattle Counseling Svc., 1982—; clin. social worker Pain Ctr. Swedish Hosp., Seattle, 1984-88, Valley Med. Ctr., Renton, Wash., 1987-88; clin. social worker AIDS program, virology clinic Univ. Hosp., Seattle, 1988—; speaker U. Wash Sch. Social Work Graduation Class, 1984, Social Sensitivity in Health Care U. Wash., 1985—; coord. Coping with AIDS Swedish Hosp. Tumor Inst., 1985; participant Coun. of Internat. Fellowship Italia, Placement Servizi Socio-Sanitari AIDS-Roma, 1991; guest speaker Sta. KIRO-TV, Seattle, 1985, Sta. KPLZ, Seattle, 1985; presentor psychosocial aspects HIV/AIDS Northwest AIDS Edn. & Tng. Ctr. Program, U. Wash. Med. Ctr., 1992, clin. mgmt. of patient with HIV/AIDS El Rio Health Ctr., Cima Colo. Pub. Health Dept., 1992; cons. Assn. Workers Resources, Seattle, 1985—; practicum instr. U. Wash. Seattle Sch. Social Work, 1989—; preceptor, intern Residency Tng. Project Sch. of Medicine/Health Scis., Univ. Wash; HIV/AIDS planning coun. Seattle/King County Pub. Health Dept., 1993; com. for the 25th health scis. open house U. Wash. Editor abstract form Comprehensive Multi-Disciplinary Documentation, Western U.S.A. Pain Soc., 1986. Mem. Seattle Aids Network, 1985—. Mem. NASW (mem. bd. Wash. state chpt. 1988-90), Acad. Cert. Social Workers, Occupational Social Work Orgn. of NASW, Coun. Internat. Fellowship, U. Wash. Alumni Assn., U. Mass. Alumni Assn., Green Key Soc. Democrat. Home: 235 13th Ave E Apt 203 Seattle WA 98102-5861

GORMLY, BARBARA DIESNER, financial consultant; b. Olmutz, Czechoslovakia, Dec. 3, 1943; came to U.S. 1961; d. Robert and Eva (Cooper) Diesner; m. William M. Gormly, Aug. 21, 1965; children: Kirsten Eve, Kellie Blaine. BA in French/Ger. w/hons., U. Tex., El Paso, 1967. Tchr. German/French Hinsdale South High Sch., Hinsdale, Ill., 1967-69, Newark High Sch., San Francisco, 1969-70; tchr. French Community Coll. of Allegheny County, Pitts., 1976-79; v.p. Cons. in Pub. Fin., Scottsdale, Ariz., 1982—, also bd. dirs.; instr. fgn. langs. Maricopa C.C., 1992—; bd. dirs. Women's Adv. Bd. of Great Western Bank, Phoenix, 1985-86, Citibank Adv. Bd., Phoenix, 1986-87. Republican. Methodist.

GORMLY, WILLIAM MOWRY, investment banker; b. Pitts., Mar. 15, 1941; s. Thomas Wilson and Lourene (Blaine) G.; m. Barbara Diesner, Aug. 21, 1965; children: Kirsten Eve, Kellie Blaine. BA in Econs., Dickinson Coll., Carlisle, Pa., 1963; postgrad. Northwestern U., 1967, DePaul U., 1968; grad. banking degree, Rutgers U., 1978. Regional mgr. Harris Bank, Chgo., 1967-69; corp. banking officer Wells Fargo Bank N.A., San Francisco, 1969-73; v.p. 4th Nat. Bank of Wichita, 1973-74, Union Nat. Bank of Pitts., 1974-79; v.p., sr. nat. accts. officer Ariz. Bank, Phoenix, 1979-82; pres. Cons. in Pub. Fin., Ltd., Scottsdale, Ariz., 1982-92; resident advisor Romanian Banking Inst., Bucharest, Romania, 1993—. Mem. Dickinson Coll. Alumni Council, 1975-80; bd. dirs. Ariz. Theatre Co., Phoenix, 1980-83; trustee Northland Pub. Library, Pitts., 1975-79. 1st lt. U.S. Army, 1963-65. Mem. Phi Delta Theta. Republican. Methodist.

GORSUCH, JOHN WILBERT, publisher; b. Bloomingdale, Ohio, Apr. 6, 1930; s. John Simpson and Suzanna Mae (Poe) G.; m. Georgia Anne Batting, Sept. 26, 1953; children—Neil Justin, Greta Jean. B.A., U. N.M., 1956. Field rep., acquisitions editor John Wiley & Sons, N.Y.C., 1957-60; regional sales mgr. coll. dept. Macmillan Co., 1960-64, market mgr., 1965-67; v.p., dir. coll. dept. William C. Brown Co., Dubuque, Iowa, 1967-76; pres. Gorsuch Scarisbrick, pubs., Scottsdale, Ariz., 1976—; Bd. dirs. Dubuque Indsl. Bur., 1971-74. Served with AUS, 1952-54. Home: 7450 E Sage Dr Scottsdale AZ 85250-6440 Office: 8233 N Via Paseo Del Norte Scottsdale AZ 85258-3746

GORTNER, WILLIS ALWAY, II, architect; b. Rochester, N.Y., Oct. 1, 1939; s. Willis Alway and Florence (Pickett) G.; m. Maravillas Blanco, Sept.

6, 1962 (div. 1986); children: Christopher Willis, Eric Tomas; m. Kathleen Nell Lobnow, Apr. 16, 1989. Student, U. Calif., Berkeley, 1957-60; BArch, U. Minn., 1962. Registered architect, Calif. Prin. Gortner & Assocs., Washington, 1969-80; dir. architecture Perkins & Will, San Francisco, 1980-82; architecture studio dir. Whisler-Patri, San Francisco, 1982-88; dir. architecture Arquitectonica, San Francisco, 1988-90, Vickerman-Zachary-Miller, Oakland, Calif., 1990—. Prin. works include St. George's Episcopal Ch. (Guild for Religious Architecture merit award 1970). Dir. Greenbrae (Calif.) Property Owners Assn., 1992—. Mem. AIA (East Bay chpt.), Oakland C. of C. Home: 160 Tioga Ln Greenbrae CA 94904 Office: Vickerman Zachary Miller 101 Broadway Oakland CA 94607

GORTON, JAMES SHELDON, marriage and family counselor; b. Flagler, Colo., July 20, 1949; s. Fosha Sheldon and Marjorie May (Miller) G.; m. Cynthia Ruth Hapip, Aug. 19, 1972; children: Deborah Elizabeth, Victoria Kathryn. MA, Internat. Christian U., 1978; MDiv, Gordon Conwell Theol. Sem., 1981; D in Ministry, Fuller Theol. Sem., 1987; MA, Fielding Inst., 1992, postgrad. Campus dir. Campus Crusade for Christ, Tampa, Fla., 1974-79; pastor young adults Grace Chapel Ch., Lexington, Mass., 1980-85; pastor of marriage and family Bethany Bible Ch., Phoenix, 1985-86; dir. Ctr. for Counseling and Consultation, Paradise Valley, Ariz., 1987—; cons. various bus. and corps., Phoenix, 1987—; bd. dirs. Ctr. for Divorce Recovery, Family Life Corp., Phoenix. Mem. Am. Counselors Assn. Office: Ctr Counseling/Consultation 10565 N Tatum Blvd B-117 Paradise Valley AZ 85253

GORTON, JOHN GREG, metal products executive; b. Kalispell, Mont., May 13, 1947; s. John Frederick and Mary Theresa (Gasperino) G.; m. Feb. 23, 1946; children: J. Greg, Patrick J., Lisa A. BSME, Mont. State U., 1970. Cert. plant engr. Engr. Anaconda Aluminum Co., Columbia Falls, Mont., 1965-71; engring. supr. Anaconda Aluminum Co., Henderson, Ky., 1972-74; prodn. supt. ARCO Metals Co., Henderson, 1974-84; prodn. and maintenance supt. Stauffer Chem. Co., Butte, Mont., 1984-89; plant mgr. Rhone-Poulenc Chems., Butte, 1989-92; engring. mgr. Kaiser Aluminum, Spokane, Wash., 1992—; chpt. pres. Am. Inst. Plant Engrs., Evansville, Ind., 1984. Dir. Butte C. of C., 1990-91. Named Ambassador of Labor Commonwealth of Ky., 1983. Mem. Am. Inst. Plant Engrs., Pioneer St. Rods (treas. 1990-91). Office: Kaiser Aluminum Co E 2111 Hawthorne Mead WA 99021

GORTON, SLADE, senator; b. Chicago, Ill., Jan. 8, 1928; s. Thomas Slade and Ruth (Israel) G.; m. Sally Jean Clark, June 28, 1958; children: Tod, Sarah Jane, Rebecca Lynn. AB, Dartmouth Coll., 1950; LLB with honors, Columbia U., 1953. Bar: Wash. 1953. Assoc. law firm Seattle, 1953-65; ptnr. law firm, 1965-69; atty. gen. State of Wash., Olympia, 1969-81; U.S. Senator from Wash., 1981-87, 89—; ptnr. Davis, Wright & Jones, Seattle, 1987-89; Mem. Wash. Ho. of Reps., 1959-69, majority leader, 1967-69. Trustee Pacific Sci. Center, Seattle, found. mem., 1977-78; mem. Pres.'s Consumer Adv. Council, 1975-77; mem. Wash. State Law and Justice Commn., 1969-80, chmn., 1969-76; mem. State Criminal Justice Tng. Commn., 1969-80, chmn., 1969-76. Served with AUS, 1946-47; to 1st lt. USAF, 1953-56; col. USAFR (ret.). Mem. ABA, Wash. Bar Assn., Nat. Assn. Attys. Gen. (pres. 1976-77, Wyman award 1980), Phi Delta Phi, Phi Beta Kappa. Clubs: Seattle Tennis, Wash. Athletic (Seattle). Office: US Senate 730 Hart Senate Bldg Washington DC 20510-4701*

GOSE, ELLIOTT BICKLEY, English language educator; b. Nogales, Ariz., May 3, 1926; emigrated to Can., 1956, naturalized, 1969; s. Elliott Bickley and Eleanor (Paulding) G.; m. Kathleen Kavanaugh Brittain, Oct. 14, 1950; children: Peter Christoph, Sarah Elliott. BA cum laude, U. Colo., 1949, MA, 1950; PhD, Cornell U., 1954. Instr. English, La. State U., Baton Rouge, 1954-56; mem. faculty U. B.C., Vancouver, 1956-91, prof. English, 1967-91, prof. emeritus, 1991—. Author: Imagination Indulged, 1972, The Transformation Process in Joyce's Ulysses, 1980, The World of the Irish Wonder Tale, 1985, Mere Creatures: A Study of Modern Fantasy Tales for Children, 1988. Pres. The New Sch., Vancouver, 1965-66; trustee Vancouver Sch. Bd., 1973-76. Served with CIC AUS, 1946-47. Can. Council sr. fellow, 1971-72. Mem. Phi Beta Kappa. Home: RR 5 Durrance Rd Box 20, Victoria, BC Canada V8X 4M6

GOSE, RICHARD VERNIE, lawyer; b. Hot Springs, S.D., Aug. 3, 1927. MS in Engring., Northwestern U., 1955; LLB, George Washington U., 1967; JD, George Washington U., 1968. Bar: N.Mex. 1967, U.S. Supreme Ct. 1976, Wyo. 1979; registered prof. engr., N.Mex., Wyo.; children: Beverly Marie, Donald Paul, Celeste Marlene. Exec. asst. to U.S. Senator Hickey, Washington, 1960-62; mgr. E.G. & G., Inc., Washington, 1964-66; asst. atty. gen. State of N.Mex., Santa Fe, 1967-70; pvt. practice law, Santa Fe, 1967-79, Santa Fe/Tucson, 1979—; assoc. prof. engring. U. Wyo., 1957-60; owner, mgr. Gose & Assocs., Santa Fe, 1967-78; pvt. practice law, Casper, Wyo., 1978-83; v.p. Desert Shield Clothing, Inc., 1990—; co-chmn. Henry Jackson for Pres., M.Mex., 1976, Wyo. Johnson for Pres., 1960. With U.S. Army, 1950-52. Mem. N.Mex. Bar Assn., Wyo. Bar Assn., Masons, Phi Delta Theta, Pi Tau Sigma, Sigma Tau. Methodist. Home and Office: PO Box 1169 Tucson AZ 85258-1169

GOSS, JEROME ELDON, cardiologist; b. Dodge City, Kans., Nov. 30, 1935; s. Horton Maurice and Mary Alice (Mountain) G.; m. Lorraine Ann Sanchez, Apr. 20, 1986. BA, U. Kans., 1957; MD, Northwestern U., 1961. Diplomate Am. Bd. Internal Medicine, Am. Bd. Cardiology (fellow, bd. govs. 1981-84). Intern Met. Gen. Hosp., Cleve., 1961-62; resident Northwestern U. Med. Ctr., Chgo., 1962-64; fellow in cardiology U. Colo., Denver, 1964-66; asst. prof. medicine U. N.Mex., Albuquerque, 1968-70; practice medicine specializing in cardiology N.Mex. Heart Clinic, 1970—; mem. bd. alumni counsellors Northwestern U. Med. Sch., 1977-89, mem. nat. alumni bd., 1991—; chief dept. medicine Presbyn. Hosp., Albuquerque, 1978-80, mem. exec. com., 1980-82, bd. dirs. cardiac diagnostic svcs., 1970—. Contbr. articles to profl. jours. Bd. dirs. Presbyn. Heart Inst., Ballet West N.Mex., N.Mex. Symphony Orch., Albuquerque Mus. Found. Lt. comdr. USN, 1966-68. Nat. Heart Inst. research fellow, 1965-66; named one of Outstanding Young Men Am., Jaycees, 1970; recipient Alumni Service award Northwestern U. Med. Sch., 1986. Fellow ACP, ACC, Coun. Clin. Cardiology of Am. Heart Assn., Soc. Cardiac Angiography; mem. Albuquerque-Bernalillo County Med. Soc. (sec. 1972, treas. 1975, v.p. 1980), Alpha Omega Alpha. Republican. Methodist. Office: NMex Heart Clinic 1001 Coal Ave SE Albuquerque NM 87106-5250

GOSS, ROBERT PIKE, JR., professional association administrator; b. N.Y.C., July 29, 1943; s. Robert Pike and Alvor (Frankel) G.; m. Connie Kitchen, Aug. 25, 1966; children: Susan, Robert, Rebecca, Colleen, Aaron, Brendan, Janelle, Jonathan. BA, Brigham Young U., 1967, MS, 1969; JD, Georgetown U., 1977; ABD, U. Colo., 1993. Bar: Va. 1977, Colo. 1988; cert. fin. planner, Colo. Pub. adminstrn. intern N.Y. Dept. Civil Svc., Albany, 1968-69; sr. adminstrv. analyst, then exec. asst. to indsl. com. N.Y. Dept. Labor, Albany, 1969-71, asst. dir. emergency employment program, 1971-73; spl. asst. to dep. sec. Gov. of N.Y., Washington office, 1973-74; dir. employment and vocat. tng. program Nat. Govt. Conf., Washington, 1974-75; spl. asst. to asst. sec., then intergovtl. rels. officer U.S. Dept. Transp., Washington, 1975-78; exec. dir. Ill. Gov.'s Office Manpower and Human Devel., Springfield, 1978-79; Washington counsel, dir. Nat. Conf. State Legislatures, 1979-87; lawyer, pres. Dominion Fin. Planning Svc., Stafford, Va., 1987-88; exec. dir. Inst. Cert. Fin. Planners, Denver, 1988-91; exec. dir., internat. bd. of standards and practices Fin. Planners, Inc., Denver, 1991—; bd. dirs. Fin. Planners Profl. Liability Ins. Co., Vt. 1989-90, Pontiac Fin. Group, Stafford, Va., Acad. for Fin. Svcs., 1991—; mem. fin. and estate planning adv. bd. Commerce Clearing House, Jour. of the Am. Soc. of CLU; chmn. bd. dirs. State Svcs. Orgn., Washington, 1980-86; outside counsel Am. Traffic Safety Svc. Assn., Fredericksburg, Va., 1987-88. Assoc. editor The Tax Lawyer, 1976; columnist Jour. Fin. Planning. Troop chmn. Fredericksburg area Boy Scouts Am., 1982-83. Mem. ABA (task force on legal fin. planning 1989-91, vice chair com. on ethics and malpractice 1992-93), Nat. Assn. Estate Planners, Acad. Fin. Svcs., Colo. bar Assn., Va. Bar Assn., Am. Soc. Pub. Adminstrn., Brigham Young U. Mgmt. Soc. (v.p. Washington chpt. 1987-88, pres. Denver chpt. 1990-92), Phi Kappa Phi, Pi Sigma Alpha. Home: 3611 E Mineral Pl Littleton CO 80122-3634 Office: IBCFP Ste 3050 1660 Lincoln St Denver CO 80264

GOSSAGE, JAMES DEARL, quality department aide; b. Bellingham, Wash., Oct. 16, 1937; s. Dearl Lars and Ilene Loretta (Babcock) G. Test technician final acceptance Martin Marietta Corp., Littleton, Colo., 1959-62; photo asst., photo printer Hagelstein Bros. Studio, N.Y.C., 1963-64; photo printer Gilbert Photo Svc., N.Y.C., 1964-73; with evaluation/AV equipment dept. Ednl. Products Info. Exch. Inst., N.Y.C., 1973-74; troubleshooter audio A Total Electronics Svc., Bellingham, Wash., 1978; quality dept. aide Pioneer Magnetics, Santa Monica, Calif., 1980—; systems operator bull. bd. system the original Off Off Broadway BBS, Santa Monica, 1990—. Photo contbr. to books; photo documentor of Off Off Broadway. With U.S. Army, 1956-59. Home: 1223 Broadway # 322 Santa Monica CA 90404

GOSSARD, EARL EVERETT, physicist; b. Eureka, Calif., Jan. 8, 1923; s. Ralph Dawson and Winifred (Hill) G.; m. Sophia Poignand, Nov. 21, 1948; children: Linda Margaret, Kenneth Earl, Diane Winifred. BA, UCLA, 1948; MS, U. Calif., San Diego, 1951; PhD in Phys. Oceanography, Scripps Instn. Oceanography, 1956. Meteorologist Navy Electronics Lab., San Diego, 1949-55, head radio meteorol. sect., 1955-61; head radio physics div. Navy Electronics Lab. (name now Naval Ocean Systems Ctr.), San Diego, 1961-71; chief geoacoustics program Wave Propagation Lab., NOAA, Boulder, Colo., 1971-73, chief meteorol. radar program, 1973-82; sr. rsch. assoc. Coop. Inst. for Rsch. in Environ. Scis. U. Colo., Boulder, 1982—. Co-author: (with Hooke) Waves in the Atmosphere (Disting. Authorship award Dept. Commerce 1975), 1973; (with Strauch) Radar Observation of Clear Air and Clouds (Disting. Authorship award Dept. Commerce 1985); editor: Radar Observation of the Clear Air, 1980; contbr. over 74 articles to profl. jours. 1st lt. USAAF, 1943-46, CBI. Recipient Silver medal Dept. Commerce, 1976, Citation Am. Geophys. Union, 1986. Fellow Am. Meteorol. Soc.; mem. NAE, Internat. Union Radio Sci. (past chmn. U.S. Commn. F.). Republican. Presbyterian. Home: 1088 Kelly Rd W Sugarloaf Star Rt Boulder CO 80302 Office: U Colo Campus Box 449 Boulder CO 80309

GOSSETT, JEFFREY ALAN, professional football player; b. Charleston, Ill., Jan. 25, 1957. BS in Phys. Edn., Eastern Ill. U. With Kansas City Chiefs, 1981-82, Cleve. Browns, 1983-84, 85-87, Houston Oilers, 1987; punter L.A. Raiders, 1988—. Office: L.A. Raiders 332 Center St El Segundo CA 90245

GOSSETT, NANCY WATKINS, environmental engineer; b. Independence, Mo., Dec. 15, 1955; d. William Benjamin and Ruth Ann (Webb) W.; m. Gary Van Stephenson, Aug. 3, 1991; 1 child from previous marriage, Daniel Alexander Gossett. BSChemE, U. Calif., Davis, 1978. Registered profl. engr., Calif., Wash. Area engr. Bechtel, San Francisco, 1978-86; project engr. IT Corp., Martinez, Calif., 1986-87; project mgr. ECOVA, Redmond, Wash., 1987-88; sr. engr. CH2M Hill, Bellevue, Wash., 1988-90; divsn. mgr. OHM, Redmond, Wash., 1990-91; engring. mgr. SEACOR, Bellevue, Wash., 1991—. Recipient Engring. Excellence award, Wash. Coun. Consulting Engrs., Bellevue, 1989. Mem. AICE, Assn. Women Environ. Profls., Water & Environment Fedn. Office: SEACOR 11040 Main St Bellevue WA 98004

GOTH, JOHN WILLIAM, former mining and metals company executive, consultant; b. Ree Heights, S.D., Apr. 22, 1927; s. Perry E. and Alma L. (Wooley) G.; m. Ree Moulton, Dec. 12, 1952; children: Jay, Patrick, William. B.S. in Metallurgy, S.D. Sch. Mines, 1950, D.B.A. (hon.), 1981; M.Engring. in Metallurgy (Rotary Found. fellow), McGill U., Montreal, Que., Can., 1951; grad., advanced mgmt. program Harvard U., 1973. With AMAX Inc., 1954—; v.p. sales AMAX Inc., Greenwich, Conn., 1972-75; v.p. AMAX Inc., 1975-81, exec. v.p., 1981-82, sr. exec. v.p., 1982-85; pres. Climax Molybdenum Co. div., Greenwich, 1975-78; group exec., molybdenum, nickel, tungsten and specialty metals group Climax Molybdenum Co. div., 1978-85; cons., 1985—; exec. dir. Mineral Info. Inst., Denver, 1987—. Served with USN, 1945-46. Fellow Am. Soc. for Metals (past chmn. govt. and public affairs com.); mem. AIME. Home: 15140 Foothill Rd Golden CO 80401 Office: 1536 Cole Blvd Ste 320 Golden CO 80401-3413 also: Mineral Info Inst 1125 17th St Ste 1800 Denver CO 80202-2033

GOTT, RAYMOND EUGENE, law enforcement officer, consultant; b. Royal Oak, Mich., Sept. 26, 1940; s. Marida and Anna Josephine (Psenicka) G.; m. Sheila Maureen Hopkins, June 21, 1969 (div. 1980); children: Christina Marie, Terri Lynn; m. Linda Ann Butigan, Feb. 14, 1981; 1 stepchild, Karey Lee Gott. AA, El Camino Coll., Torrance, Calif., 1971; B of Pub. Mgmt., Pepperdine U., L.A., 1973; MPA, U. So. Calif., 1975. With Los Angeles County Sheriff's Dept., L.A., 1962—; capt., unit comdr. Pitchess Honor Rancho Los Angeles County Sheriff's Dept., Saugus, Calif., 1985-87; capt., unit comdr. Safe Streets Bur. Los Angeles County Sheriff's Dept., Rancho Dominguez, Calif., 1987-91; capt., unit comdr. Transp. Bur. Los Angeles County Sheriff's Dept., L.A., 1991—; cons. Fed. Law Enforcement Tng. Ctr., Glynco, Ga., 1990—, Office of Juvenile Justice and Delinquency Prevention, Washington, 1989—; bd. dirs. Thomas Jefferson Ctr., Pasadena, Calif., 1989—; chmn. Calif. State Commn. for Revision of Juvenile Ct. Law, 1983; mem. Calif. Task Force to Promote Self Esteem, Personal and Social Responsibility, 1990. Mem. screening com. Big Bros. of Greater L.A., 1976-84. With USN, 1958-62. Mem. Calif. State Juvenile Officers Assn. (pres. 1978, Dan Pursuit award 1983), So. Calif. Juvenile Officers Assn. (pres. 1980). Office: Los Angeles County Sheriff 441 Bauchet St Los Angeles CA 90012

GOTTENBORG, DAVID ANDREW, natural gas executive; b. Portland, Oreg., Apr. 14, 1955; s. Russell Baldwin and Dorothy Marie (Arneson) G.; m. Jean Ellen O'Day, July 29, 1978; children: Erin, Drew. BA, Colo. Coll., 1977; JD, U. Denver, 1981. Bar: U.S. Supreme Ct. 1988. Assoc. Davis, Graham & Stubbs, Denver, 1981-88; mng. ptnr. Fountainhead Resources, Ltd., Denver, 1988—; pres., chmn. Colo. Natural Gas Assistance Corp., Denver, 1988—; chmn. bd. dirs. Colo. Natural Gas Assistance Found., Denver, 1988—, Colo. Equity Fund, Inc., Denver, 1990—. Co-author: American Law Mining, 2d edit., 1985 (6 vols.); editorial cons. (book) Law of Federal Oil & Gas Leases, 2d edit., 1985 (2 vols.); contbr. author Mineral Law Newsletter, 1987-88; contbr. articles to profl. jours. Bd. dirs., chmn. Children's Legal Clinic, Denver, 1984—; pres., chmn. Denver Young Reps., 1987; bd. dirs. Colo. Sci. Ctr., Denver, 1983-85. Named one of 50 for Colo. by Colo. Assn. Commerce & Industry, 1987-88. Mem. Denver Bar Assn., Colo. Bar Assn. Lutheran.

GOTTFRIED, EUGENE LESLIE, physician, educator; b. Passaic, N.J., Feb. 26, 1929; s. David Robert and Rose (Chill) G.; m. Phyllis Doris Swain, Aug. 16, 1957. AB, Columbia U., 1950, MD, 1954. Cert. Nat. Bd. Med. Examiners, Am. Bd. Internal Medicine. Intern Presbyn. Hosp., N.Y.C., 1954-55, asst. resident in medicine, 1957-58; resident Bronx (N.Y.) Mcpl. Hosp. Ctr., 1958-59, fellow in medicine, 1959-60; asst. instr. medicine Albert Einstein Coll. Medicine Yeshiva U., N.Y.C., 1959-60, instr., 1960-61, assoc., 1961-65, asst. prof., 1965-69; assoc. prof. medicine Cornell U. Med. Coll., N.Y.C., 1969-81, assoc. prof. pathology, 1975-81; clin. prof. dept. lab. medicine U. Calif., San Francisco, 1981—, vice chmn. dept. lab. medicine, 1981—; hosp. appointments include asst. vis. physician Bronx Mcpl. Hosp. Ctr., 1960-66, assoc. attending physician, 1966-69; assoc. attending physician N.Y. Hosp., N.Y.C., 1969-81, assoc. attending pathologist, 1975-81, dir. lab. clin. hematology, 1969-81; chief lab. medicine San Francisco Gen. Hosp. Med. Ctr., 1981—, dir. clin. labs., 1981—. Assoc. editor Jour. Lipid Research, 1971-72, 75-77; mem. editorial bd. Jour. Lipid Research, 1972-77. Served to lt. comdr. USNR, 1955-57. Recipient Career Scientist award Health Research Council City of N.Y., 1964-72. Fellow Am. Soc. Hematology, Internat. Soc. Hematology, ACP, Acad. Clin. Lab. Physicians and Scientists; mem. AAAS, Phi Beta Kappa, Alpha Omega Alpha. Office: San Francisco Gen Hosp Clin Labs 1001 Potrero Ave San Francisco CA 94110-3594

GOTTLEIB, FRANZ MICHAEL, communications consultant; b. Balt., Nov. 23, 1948; s. Edward John and Muriel Helen (Faulkner) G. BS, U.S. Naval Acad., 1970; BA in Art, U. Calif., Berkeley, 1977; BFA in Graphic Design, Calif. Coll. Arts and Crafts, Oakland, 1979; MBA in Mktg., Golden Gate U., 1986. Commd. 2d lt. USMC, 1970, advanced through grades to capt., 1974, resigned, 1975; sales mgr. Carnation Co., San Leandro, Calif., 1975; pres. Gottleib Design, San Francisco, 1979-91, Michael Gottleib Lacrosse Graphics, San Francisco, 1988-91, Gottleib Comm./Michael Gottleib Lacrosse Graphics, Helena, Mont., 1992—. Bd. dirs. Siccone Inst., San Francisco, 1985-90. Mem. Helena Advt. Fedn., Helena C. of C. Home: PO Box 1252 Helena MT 59624-1252 Office: Gottleib Comm 25 S Ewing St Helena MT 59601

GOTTLIEB, ALAN MERRIL, association executive; b. L.A., May 2, 1947; s. Seymour and Sherry (Schutz) G.; m. Julie Hoy Versnel, July 27, 1979; children: Amy Jean, Sarah Merril, Alexis Hope, Andrew Michael. Student Georgetown U., 1970; BS in Nuclear Engring., U. Tenn., 1971. Nat. dir. Young Ams. for Freedom, Washington, 1971-72; nat. treas. Am. Conservative Union, Washington, 1971—; pres. Merril Assocs., 1974—; chmn. Citizens Com. for Right to Keep and Bear Arms, Bellevue, Wash., 1974—; pres. Ctr. Def. of Free Enterprise, Bellevue 1976—; pres. Second Amendment Found., Bellevue, 1974—; pub. Gun Week, 1985—; bd. dirs. Nat. Park User Assn., 1988—, Am. Polit. Action Com., 1988—, Chancellor Broadcasting, Inc, Las Vegas, Nev.; pres. Sta. KBNP Radio, Portland, 1990—, Evergreen Radio Network, Bellevue, 1990—. With U.S. Army, 1968-74. Recipient Good Citizenship award Citizens Home Protective Assn., 1978, Cicero award Nat. Assn. Federally Licensed Firearms Dealers, 1982, Second Amendment award Scope, 1983, 91, Roy Rogers award 1987, Golden Eagle award Am. Fedn. Police, 1990. Mem. NRA. Republican. Author: The Gun Owners Political Action Manual, 1976, The Rights of Gun Owners, 1981, Rev. edit., 1991, The Gun Grabbers, 1988, Gun Rights Fact Book, 1989, Guns For Women, 1988, The Wise Use Agenda, 1989, Trashing the Economy, 1993.

GOTTLIEB, LEON HERBERT, business management consultant; b. L.A., Jan. 21, 1927; s. Leonard Jesse and Edna Ida (Zemel) G.; m. Madaline Dorothy Harrison, Mar. 5, 1949 (dec. 1983); children: Mark, Diane; m. Arlene Jean VanGrow, July 13, 1986. Degree in bus. mgmt., Sawyer Bus. Coll., 1948. Advt. salesman L.A. Times, 1948-50; v.p. sales Kermin Frozen Foods, Inc., L.A., 1950-60; v.p. franchise Internat. House of Pancakes div. Internat. Industries, Inc., L.A., 1960-69; pres. Copper Penny Family Restaurants, L.A., 1967-69; bus. mgmt. cons. Leon Gottlieb & Assocs., Tarzana, Calif., 1969—; lectr. various trade assns. and cos. in U.S. and fgn. countries, 1968—; expert witness in restaurant, hotel, retail, and franchising fields. Author: The People Factor, The Best of Gottlieb's Bottom Line, Foodservice/Hospitality Advertising and Promotion; editor/pub. newsletter Gottlieb's Bottom Line; contbr. articles to restaurant business and hotel magazines. Vol. exec. Internat. Exec. Svcs. Corps, Stamford, Conn., 1986—; instr. various minority groups, L.A., 1979—. With USN, 1945-46. Mem. Nat. Restaurant Assn. (mem. action com. 1960—), Am. Arbitration Assn. (arbitrator 1975—), Calif. Restaurant Assn. (mem. edn. com. 1960—), Frozen Food Coun. (pres. Calif. chpt. 1948-50). Home and Office: 4601 Sendero Pl Tarzana CA 91356-4821

GOTTLIEB, SHERRY GERSHON, author, editor; b. L.A., Apr. 6, 1948; d. Harry L. and Evelyn Jellen) Gershon; m. David Neil Gottlieb, Aug. 12, 1971 (div. 1973). BA in Dramatic Arts, U. Calif., Berkeley, 1969. Exec. sec. Budget Films, L.A., 1970-72; script reader United Artists, L.A., 1971-74; owner A Change of Hobbit bookstore, L.A. and Santa Monica, Calif., 1972-91; class coord. UCLA Extension, 1982. Author: Hell No, We Won't Go! Evading the Draft During the Vietnam War, 1991. Named Spl. Guest of Honor, Westercon, 1979. Mem. PEN USA. Democrat.

GOTTLIEB, SHIRLE SHERMAN, writer, copy editor, co-publisher; b. Springfield, Ill., Oct. 30, 1930; d. Abraham Walter and Sara (Sonis) Sherman; m. Arthur Joseph Gottlieb, Jan. 28, 1951; children: Stacey Gottlieb Arthur, Randi Gottlieb Robinson, Gregg, Amy. BA in Comparative Lit., Calif. State U., Long Beach, 1979, MA in Interdisciplinary Creativity/Creative Process, 1981. Art/theatre critic Press-Telegram, Long Beach, 1983-87; free-lance arts writer, 1987—; co-pub., exec. editor Amadeus Press, Long Beach, 1992—; docent U. Art Mus., Long Beach, 1982-85; panel moderator Long Beach Mus. Art, 1992; cons., Long Beach, 1987—. Editor: Stroke: An Owner's Manual, 1992; contbr. theatre review, art reviews and feature stories. Mem. LWV, Long Beach, 1955—; program chmn. Friends of Libr., Long Beach, 1979-90; community rep. Adv. Arts Coun., Coll. of the Arts, Calif. State U., Long Beach, 1987—; planner, presenter Conf. on Aging with Disability, Rancho Los Amigos Hosp., Downey, Calif., 1993. Assn. Internat. des Critiques d'Art, Fine Arts Affiliates (scholarship chmn. 1991-92). Home: 215 Prospect Ave Long Beach CA 90803

GOTTSCHALK, LOUIS AUGUST, psychiatrist, psychoanalyst; b. St. Louis, Aug. 26, 1916; s. Max W. and Kelmie (Mutrux) G.; m. Helen Reller, July 24, 1944; children—Guy H., Claire A., Louise H., Susan E. A.B., Washington U., St. Louis, 1940, M.D., 1943; Ph.D., So. Calif. Psychiat. Inst., 1977. Asst. in neuropsychiatry Washington U. Sch. Medicine, 1944-46; commd. asst. surgeon USPHS, 1946, advanced through grades to med. dir., 1979; instr. psychiatry S.W. Med. Coll., Dallas, 1947-48; research psychiatrist NIMH, Bethesda, Md., 1950-53; coordinator research, research prof. psychiatry U. Cin. Coll. Medicine, 1953-67; attending psychiatrist Cin. Gen. Hosp., 1953-67; faculty Inst. Psychoanalysis, Chgo., 1957-67, So. Calif. Psychiat. Inst., Los Angeles, 1970—; chmn. research com. Hamilton County (Ohio) Diagnostic Center, 1958-67; prof. psychiatry, social sci. and social ecology, dept. psychiatry and human behavior U. Calif. - Irvine Coll. Medicine, 1967—, chmn. dept., 1967-78; also program dir. psychiat. residency tng.; dir. psychiat. services U. Calif. - Irvine Med. Center, 1967-78, dir. cons. and liaison program, 1978-87; sci. co-dir. U. Calif. - Irvine Med. Center (Nat. Alcoholism Research Center), 1978-84; Mem. clin. psychopharmacology study sect. NIMH, 1968-71; mem. research rev. com. Nat. Inst. Drug Abuse, 1973-77, Mental Health Study Center, 1978-84. Author: (with G. C. Gleser) The Measurement of Psychological States through the Content Analysis of Verbal Behavior, 1969, How to Understand and Analyze Your Own Dreams, 1975, Greek edit., 1978, Spanish edit., 1981, 3d rev. edit., 1985; editor: Comparative Psycholinguistic Analysis of Two Psychotherapeutic Interviews, 1961, (with A. H. Auerbach) Methods of Research in Psychotherapy, 1966, (with S. Merlis) Pharmacokinetics of Psychoactive Drugs: Blood Levels and Clinical Responses, 1976, Pharmacokinetics of Psychoactive Drugs: Further Studies, 1979, The Content Analysis of Verbal Behavior: Further Studies, 1979, (with F.L. McGuire and others) Drug Abuse Deaths in Nine Cities: A Survey Report, 1980; (with R. Cravey) Toxicological and Pathological Studies on Psychoactive Drug-Involved Deaths, 1980; (with Winget, Gleser and Lolas) Analisis de la Conducta Verbal, 1984; The Tree of Knowledge, 1985, (with F. Lolas and L.L. Viney) The Content Analysis of Verbal Behavior: Significance in Clinical Medicine and Psychiatry, 1986, (with Lolas) Estudios Sobre Analisis del Comportamiento Verbal, 1987, How to do Self-Analysis and Other Self-Psychotherapies, 1989; editorial bd. Psychosomatic Medicine, 1960-70, Psychiatry, 1967—, Am. Jour. Psychotherapy, 1975—, Methods and Findings in Exptl. and Clin. Pharmacology, 1978—; others; contbr. numerous articles to tech. lit. Recipient Hofheimer Rsch. award, 1955, Franz Alexander Essay prize So. Calif. Psychoanalytic Inst., L.A., 1973; Disting. Rsch. award U. Calif.-Irvine Alumni Assn., 1974; named Disting. Practitioner, Nat. Acad. Med. Practice, 1984; Rockefeller fellow Bellagio Study Ctr., Italy, 1985; NIMH Rsch. Career award, 1960-67; Am. Psychiat. Assn. Found. rsch. prize, 1978. Fellow AAAS, Am. Coll. Neuropsychopharmacology, Am. Coll. Psychiatrists; mem. Assn. for Rsch. Nervous and Mental Diseases, Am. Psychosomatic Soc., Cin. Soc. Neurology and Psychiatry (past pres.), Am. Psychoanalytic Assn., AMA, Orange County Med. Assn., So. Calif. Psychiat. Soc., Am. Assn. Child Psychoanalysts, So. Calif. Psychoanalytic Soc., Phi Beta Kappa, Sigma Xi, Alpha Omega Alpha, Omicron Delta Kappa. Clubs: Cosmos, Balboa Bay. Home: 4607 Perham Rd Corona Del Mar CA 92625-3124 Office: U Calif Coll Medicine Dept Psychiatry & Human Behavior Irvine CA 92717

GOTTSCHALK, MAX JULES, new development specialist, industrial designer; b. St. Louis, Dec. 14, 1909; s. Max William and Kelmie (Mutrux) G.; m. Josephine Pipkin, 1933 (div. 1940); children: Sandra, Jules; m. Cecil Cornsweet, June 8, 1979. BA in Design, Washington U., St. Louis, 1933, postgrad. in psychology and history of art, 1936-38, Sch. Engring., 1942-44. With Knapp Monarch Elec. Co., St. Louis, 1934-36; chief tech. advisor govt. Nfld., Can., 1938-42; chief devel. engr. Hussman Co., St. Louis, 1942-44; sr. engr. devel. Walter Dorwin Teague, N.Y.C., 1942-44; chief engr. Gerald C. Johnson Assocs., N.Y.C., 1946-48; sr. engr. in charge field handling equipment Hughes Aircraft, Tucson, 1952-60; sr. research product design engr. Bell Aerosystems Co., Buffalo, 1962-64; pres. Max's Enterprises, 1986; instr. in design, drafting, perception, electronics, coordinator design and drafting dept., cons. sound recording systems Pima Coll., Tucson, 1967-77; prof., chmn., applied design dept. Pima Jr. Coll., Tucson, 1969-89; cons. Mark A. Simpson Mfg. Co., L.I., N.Y., 1944-52, Plymold Corp., Lawrence, Mass., Wheeldex Corp., White Plains, N.Y., Simpla Research and Mfg. Co., N.Y.C., 1944-52; cons. in interior plantscaping; cons. engr. Burr-Brown Research Corp., Lee Supply, 1964-67; lectr. Coop. Summer Coll., St. John's and Corner Brook, Nfld., 1937-39; cons. art and design Sullivan, Stauffer, Colwell and Bayless, Foote, Cone, and Belding, Gardner Advt., Darcy Advt., 1948-52; indsl. designs and devels. include: new modular chassis systems, electronic test equipment, paper towel holder, rotary card file, 1st open case frozen food refrigeration, 1st self service electronic checkout, use of cellophane for wrapping cheeses and meats, lunar escape vehicle, air cushion vehicle, curtain wall air cooling, intensive care cooling systems, electronics packaging systems; cons. in field, 1985-91; pres. Imagineering, Tucson, 1960—; chief engr. Godesca and Gottschalk Engring., 1970—; owner Max's Enterprises (M.E.), 1980—; work exhibited St. Louis Artist Guild, 1935, St. Louis Art Mus., 1936, St. John's, Can., 1940-42, Mus. Modern Art, N.Y.C., 1948-50, Internat. Canvas Exhibit, Tokyo, 1975, Pima Coll., Rosequist Wohlheim Gallery, Tucson, 1970—, Udinotti Gallery, Scottsdale, Ariz., San Francisco and L.A., Kaibob Art Gallery. Mem. Radio Engring. Soc., Plastic Engring. Soc., Audio Engring Soc. (life). Home: 5620 N Campbell Ave Tucson AZ 85718-4216

GOTTSTEIN, BARNARD JACOB, retail and wholesale food company executive, real estate executive; b. Des Moines, Dec. 30, 1925; s. Jacob B. and Anna (Jacobs) G.; children: Sandra, James, Ruth Anne, David, Robert; m. Rachel Landau, July, 1986. BA in Econs. and Bus., U. Wash., 1949; LLD (hon.), U. Alaska, Fairbanks, 1991. Pres. J.B. Gottstein & Co., Anchorage, 1953-90; chmn. bd. Carr-Gottstein Inc., Anchorage, 1974-90; ret., 1990—; dir. United Bank Alaska, Anchorage, 1975-86. Commr. Alaska State Human Rights Commn., 1963-68; del. Dem. Nat. Conv., 1964, 68, 76, 88, 92; committeeman Dem. Nat. Com., 1976-80; v.p. State Bd. Edn., Alaska, 1983-87, pres., 1987-91. Served with USAF, 1944-45. Jewish. Office: J B Gottstein & Co 6411 A St Anchorage AK 99518-1800

GOUDELOCK, CAROL V., library consultant; b. Milw., Dec. 25, 1938; d. Leo Michael and Regina Mary (Gasper) Schueller; m. Donald Ray Goudelock, July 2, 1971. BA, Marquette U., 1960, MA, 1962; MLS, U. Wis., Milw., 1977. Libr. asst. Milw. Pub. Libr., 1962-65, 74-76; instr. English U. Wis., Oshkosh, 1965-68; asst. prof. Milw. Sch. Engring., 1969-72; libr. Inglewood (Calif.) Pub. Libr., 1977-83, Hughes Aircraft Co., El Segundo, Calif., 1984-88; libr. cons. Inglewood, 1989—; libr. cons. Teradata Corp., El Segundo, 1989-90, Kaiser Permanente, Pasadena, Calif., 1991, Getty Conservation Inst., Marina Del Ray, Calif., 1992; cataloging cons. Iolab Corp., Claremont, Calif., 1991—. Mem. ALA, Spl. Librs. Assn., Calif. Libr. Assn. Office: PO Box 722 Inglewood CA 90307-0722

GOUGE-GERICKE, DORY, human resources executive; b. Victorville, Calif., Oct. 24, 1956; d. Jack Dean Gouge and Mary Ellen (Lewis) McCalley; m. Michael William Gericke, Mar. 30, 1979 (dec. Mar. 1981). AA, DVC, Pleasant Hill, Calif., 1982; BS, U. San Francisco, 1984. Legal sec. Johnson, Pennington & Maines, Hayward, Calif., 1973-77; employment coord. Safeway Stores, Inc., Walnut Creek, Calif., 1977-86; human resources devel. coord. Safeway Stores, Inc., Oakland, Calif., 1986-88; dir. of human resources IFS/Colgate, Inc., Benicia, Calif., 1986—; bd. dirs. Safe Am. Fed. Credit Union, Hayward; mem. adv. bd. Mt. Diablo Rehab., Pleasant Hill, 1982-86. Pers. bd. City of Concord, Calif., 1988-90; bd. dirs. Diablo Valley Employers, Walnut Creek, 1988—. Mem. Soc. of Human Resources Mgmt., No. Calif. Human Resource Coun., Am. Mgmt. Assn. Office: IFS 5100 Park Rd Benicia CA 94510

GOUGH, HARRISON GOULD, psychologist, educator; b. Buffalo, Minn., Feb. 25, 1921; s. Harry B. and Aelfreda (Gould) G.; m. Kathryn H. Whittier, Jan. 23, 1943; 1 child, Jane Kathryn Gough Rhodes. AB summa cum laude, U. Minn., 1942, AM (Social Sci. Research Council fellow 1946-47), 1947, PhD, 1949. Asst. prof. psychology U. Minn., 1948-49; asst. prof. U. Calif.-Berkeley, 1949-54, assoc. prof., 1954-60, prof., 1960-86, prof. emeritus, 1986—, assoc. dir. Inst. Personality Assessment and Research, 1964-67, dir., 1973-83, chmn. dept. psychology, 1967-72; cons. VA, 1951—; dir. cons. Psychologists Press, Inc., 1956—; mem. research adv. com. Calif. Dept. Corrections, 1958-64, Calif. Dept. Mental Hygiene, 1964-69, Gov.'s Calif. Adv. Com. Mental Health, 1968-74, citizens adv. council Calif. Dept. Mental Hygiene, 1968-71; clin. projects research review com. NIMH, 1968-72. Served to 1st lt. AUS, 1942-46, 1986. Recipient U. Calif. the Berkeley citation, 1986, Bruno Klopfer Disting. Contbn. award Soc. Personality Assessment, 1987; Fulbright research scholar, Italy, 1958-59, 65-66; Guggenheim fellow, 1965-66. Mem. Am., Western psychol. assns., Soc. Personality Assessment, Internat. Assn. Cross-Cultural Psychology, Académie National de Psychologie, Soc. Mayflower Desc., Phi Beta Kappa. Clubs: Commonwealth (San Francisco), Capitol Hill (Washington). Author: Adjective Check List, California Psychological Inventory, other psychol. tests; chmn. bd. editors U. Calif. Publs. in Psychology, 1956-58; cons. editor Assessment, 1993—, Jour. Cons. and Clin. Psychology, 1956-74, 77-84, Jour. Abnormal Psychology, 1964-74, Jour. Personality and Social Psychology, 1981-84, Med. Tchr., 1978-84, Cahiers d'Anthropologie, 1978-84, Population and Environment: Behavioral and Social Issues, 1977-80; Current Psychol. Research and Revs., 1985-93, Pakistan Jour. Psychol. Research, 1985—, Jour. Personality Assessment, 1986—, Psychological Assesment, 1991-92, Psychopathology and Behavioral Assessment, 1992—; assoc. editor Jour. Cross-Cultural Psychology, 1969-81. Home: PO Box 909 Pebble Beach CA 93953-0909 Office: U Calif Inst Personality and Social Rsch Berkeley CA 94720

GOUGH, WILLIAM CABOT, engineer; b. Jersey City, Aug. 22, 1930; s. William Lincoln and Lillian May (Mansmann) G.; m. Marion Louise McConnell, Apr. 27, 1959; children: Barbara Louise, William Scott. BS in Engring., Priceton U., 1952, MA in Engring., 1953; postgrad., Harvard U., 1966-67. Registered prof. engr., Calif. Adminstr. engr. Civilian Power Program AEC, Washington, 1953-55, indsl. info. officer, 1958-60, tech. asst. for systems, plans and programs, div. controlled thermonuclear rsch., 1960-74; project engr. nuclear aircraft program USN, Washington, 1955-58; program mgr. fusion power Electric Power Rsch. Inst., Palo Alto, Calif., 1974-77; sr. DOE/EPRI energy program coord., tech. dir. Office Program Assessment and Integration U.S. Dept. of Energy, San Francisco and Palo Alto, 1977-81; dir. DOE Site Office Stanford Linear Accelerator Ctr. Stanford (Calif.) U., 1981-88; ret., 1988; pres. Found. for Mind-Being Rsch., Los Altos, Calif., 1980—; bd. dirs. Sage Seminars, Inc., San Francisco, 1984-88, MERU Found., San Anselmo, Calif., 1988-93; mem. bd. advisors Bonny Found., Salina, Kans., 1990—. Contbr. articles and chpts. to tech. jours. and texts. With USN, 1955-58. Mem. AAAS, Am. Nuclear Soc., N.Y. Acad. Sci., Fedn. Am. Scientists, Soc. for Sci. Exploration, Internat. Soc. Study of Subtle Energies and Energy Medicine (jour. adv. bd. 1990—), Assn. for Humanistic Psychology, World Future Soc., Common Cause, UN Assn. Home and Office: 442 Knoll Dr Los Altos CA 94024-4731

GOULD, CLIO LAVERNE, electric utility and irrigation district exec.; b. Madison, S.D., Feb. 20, 1919; s. Howard Bennett and Moneta Kay (Herrick) G.; student Walla Walla Coll., 1948, U. Wash. Extension, 1954, U. Calif. at San Diego Extension, 1962, Capital Radio Engring. Inst. Corr., 1958-62; diploma elec. engring. Internat. Corr. Schs., 1958; m. Mildred May Newell, Apr. 13, 1942; children: George Marcus, Deanna May (Mrs. Terry L. Paxton). With astronautics div. Gen. Dynamics Corp., San Diego, 1957-66, sr. design engr. research and devel. Atlas and Centaur space vehicles, 1958-66; supt. power and pumping depts. Wellton Mohawk Irrigation & Drainage Dist., Wellton, Ariz., 1966-76, gen. mgr., 1976—. treas. Liga Internat., Inc., San Diego, 1964-65; mem. Colorado River Task Force, 1987-90; mem. exec. bd. ARiz. Agrl. Bus. Coun., 1980-86, v.p.; sec./treas. Irrigation and Electrical Dist. Assoc., 1987—; commr. Ariz. State Water Commn., 1989. Served with AUS, 1941-45; PTO. Recipient Performance award Gen. Dynamics Corp., 1963. Registered profl. engr., Ariz. Mem. IEEE (sr.), AIAA, Nat., Ariz. (pres. chpt. 1977-78) socs. profl. engrs., Photog. Soc. Am., Nat. Water Resources Assn., Ariz. State Reclamation Assn., Colorado River Water Users Assn. (bd. dirs. 1982-92, exec. com. 1984-92), Ariz. Agri-Bus. Council (exec. bd. 1980-87, v.p. 1981). Republican. Seventh-day Adventist (elder 1956-92, chmn. bldg. com. 1970-73). Home: RR 1 Box 4 Wellton AZ 85356-9801 Office: Rt 1 Box 19 Wellton AZ 85356

GOULD, DONALD PAUL, investment mangement company executive; b. L.A., Mar. 13, 1958; s. Mitchell and Eva G.; m. Pamela Lee Achilles, Apr. 15, 1984; 1 child, Daniel Achilles. BA, Pomona Coll., 1979; MBA, Harvard U., 1981. V.p. Bateman Eichler, Hill Richards, L.A., 1981-84, Long Beach Bank, L.A., 1984-85; pres. Huntington Funds, Pasadena, Calif., 1985—. Recipient Richard L. Rosenthal award in investment mgmt. Peter F. Drucker Grad. Mgmt. Ctr. Claremont (Calif.) Grad. Sch., 1988. Mem. Harvard Bus. Sch. Assn. So. Calif., Pomona Coll. Alumni Assn. (pres. 1988-89, various offices). Office: Huntington Funds 251 S Lake Ave # 600 Pasadena CA 91101-3032

GOULD, HERBERT J., electrical engineer; b. Rochester, N.Y., Nov. 6, 1927; s. herman Abraham and Esther Dorothy (Liberman) G.; m. Lisa Gerta Grunwald, June 21, 1981; children: Eliot, Michael, Elizabeth. AA with high hons., Wright Jr. Coll., Chgo., 1959; student, U. So. Calif., L.A., 1961-62. Jr. technician U.S. Gypsum Corp. R & D, Chgo., 1956-58; from jr. engring. aide to engring. aide to sr. engring. aide Hoffman Semiconductor, Evanston, Ill. and El Monte, Calif., 1958-61; jr. engr. Conrac Corp., Duarte, Calif., 1961-66; from jr. engr. R & D to engr. R & D to sr. engr. R & D Internat. Rectifier, 1966—. Patentee in the field of semiconductors. With USN, 1945-47. Recipient Creativity award, Conrac Corp., 1960, 2 Creative Design Incentive awards Internat. Rectifier. Mem. IEEE, Am. Vacuum Soc. Democrat. Jewish. Office: International Rectifier 233 Kansas St El Segundo CA 90245-4382

GOULD, MARTHA B., librarian; b. Claremont, N.H., Oct. 8, 1931. BA in Edn., U. Mich., 1953; MS in Library Sci., Simmons Coll., 1956; cert., U. Denver Library Sch. Community Analysis Research Inst., 1978. Childrens librarian N.Y. Pub. Libr., 1956-58; adminstr. library services act demonstration regional library project Pawhuska, Okla., 1958-59; cons. N.Mex. State Libr., 1959-60; childrens librarian then sr. childrens librarian Los Angeles Pub. Libr., 1960-72; acctg. dir. pub. srvices, reference librarian Nev. State Libr., 1972-74; pub. services librarian Washoe County (Nev.) Libr., 1974-79, asst. county librarian, 1979-84, county librarian, 1984—. Contbr. articles to jours. Treas. United Jewish Appeal, 1981; bd. dirs. Temple Sinai; trustee RSVP, North Nevadans for ERA; No. Nev. chmn. Gov.'s Conf. on Librs., 1990; mem. bd. Campaign for Choice, No. Nev. Food Bank, Nev. Women's Fund (Hall of Fame award 1989); mem. No. Nev. Nat. Conf. Christians and Jews; chair Sierra (Nev.) Community Access TV; mem. Washoe County Quality Life Task Force, 1992—. Recipient Nev. State Libr. Letter of Commendation, 1973, Washoe County Bd. Commrs. Resolution of Appreciation, 1978, Freedom's Sake award AAUW, 1989, Leadership in Literacy award Sierra chpt. Internat. Reading Assn., 1992, Woman of Distinction ward, 1992. Mem. ALA (bd. dirs. intellectual freedom roundtable 1977-79, intellectual freedom com. 1979-83, coun. 1983-86, com. on legis. 1989—), ACLU (bd. dirs., Civil Libertarian of Yr. Nev. chpt. 1988, chair gov.'s conf. for women 1989), Nev. Libr. Assn. (chmn. pub. info. com. 1972-73, intellectual freedom com. 1975-78, govt. rels. com. 1978-79, v.p., pres.-elect 1980, pres. 1981, Spl. Citation 1978, 87). Office: Washoe Country Libr PO Box 2151 301 S Center St Reno NV 89505

GOULD-KARDELL, MAXINE LUBOW, jewelry and collectibles consultant, marketing executive; b. Bridgeton, N.J., Feb. 28, 1942; d. Louis A. and Bernice L. (Goldberg) Lubow; BS, Temple U., 1962, JD, 1968; m. Sam C. Gould, June 17, 1962 (div. Dec. 1984); children: Jack, Herman, David; m. Allen S. Kardell, Mar., 10, 1991. Head resident dept. student personnel Temple U., 1962-66; dir., treas. Hilltop Interest Program, Inc., Los Angeles, 1973-74; law clk. law firms, L.A., 1975-77; with Buffalo Resources Corp., L.A., 1978-82, corp. sec., 1979-82; corp. sec., securities prin. Buffalo Securities Corp., L.A., 1979-82; corp. sec. LaMaur Devel. Corp., L.A., 1979-82; contracts analyst, land dept. Texaco Inc., L.A., 1982-83; exec. dir. Sinai Temple, West Los Angeles, 1983-85; pres. Cutting Edge, L.A., 1986; adminstr. law firm Robinson, Wolas & Diamant, Century City, 1986, acctg. firm Roth, Bookstein & Zaslow, L.A., 1986-87; project coord. Cipher, 1987; mktg. dir. Am. Bus. Capital, Beverly Hills, Calif., 1988—. Mem. Roscomare Valley Assn. Edn. Com., Bel Air, Calif., 1975-76; subcom. chmn. Roscomare Rd. Sch. Citizens Adv. Coun., Bel Air; active various community drives. Recipient Joseph B. Wagner Oratory award B'nai B'rith, 1959, Voice of Democracy award, 1958-59, award Commentator Club, 1959. Mem. ABA (law office econs. sect.), L.A. County Bar Assn. (assoc., law office econs. sect., fee dispute arbitration panel), Nat. Assn. Legal Adminstrs. (Beverly Hills chpt.), NAFE (network dir.), Nat. Assn. Law Firm Mktg. Adminstrs., Calif. Women Lawyers, Women in Bus. (co-chmn. membership com.), Calif. CPA Soc. (adminstr. com.), Nat. Assn. Synagogue Adminstrs., Am. Assn. Petroleum Landmen, Los Angeles Assn. Petroleum Landmen, Textile Profl. Soc., Comml. Fin. Assn., Phi Alpha Theta, Alpha Lambda Delta. Jewish. Home: 2501 Roscomare Rd Los Angeles CA 90077-1814 Office: Am Bus Capital 400 S Beverly Dr Ste 208 Beverly Hills CA 90212-4487

GOULDTHORPE, KENNETH ALFRED PERCIVAL, publisher, state official; b. London, Jan. 7, 1928; came to U.S., 1951, naturalized, 1956; s. Alfred Edward and Frances Elizabeth Finch (Callow) G.; m. Judith Marion Cutts, Aug. 9, 1975; children: Amanda Frances, Timothy Graham Cutts. Student U. Westminster (formerly Regent St. Poly.), 1948-49, Bloomsbury Tech. Inst., 1949-50; diploma City and Guilds of London, 1949; student, Washington U., 1951-53. Staff photographer St. Louis Post-Dispatch, 1951-55, picture editor, 1955-57; nat. and fgn. corr. Life mag., Time, Inc., N.Y.C., 1957-65, regional editor Australia-New Zealand, 1966-68, editorial dir. Latin Am., 1969-70; editor Signature mag., N.Y.C., 1970-73; mng. editor Penthouse mag., N.Y.C., 1973-76, pub. cons., 1976-79; editor, exec. pub. Adventure Travel mag., Seattle, 1979-80; sr. ptnr. Pacific Pub. Assocs., Seattle, 1981-83; editor, pub. Washington mag., 1984-89; vice chmn. Evergreen Pub. Co., 1984-89; dir. tourism, State of Wash., 1989-91; pub./cons., writer, 1991—; tchr. design, editorial techniques Parsons Sch. Design, N.Y.C.; lectr., contbr. elementary schs. lit. progs. Served with Royal Navy, 1946-48. Decorated Naval Medal and bar; recipient awards of excellence Nat. Press Photographers Assn., AP and UP, 1951-57; certs. excellence, Am. Inst. Graphic Arts, 1971, 72, 73, Communication Arts, 1980, 81, 84; spl. award, N.Y. Soc. Publs. Designers, 1980. Mem. Regional Pubs. Assn. (v.p., pres., Best Typography award 1985, Best Spl. Issue 1989), Western Publs. Assn. (Best Consumer Mag. award, Best Travel Mag. awards, 1980, Best Regional and State Mag. award 1985, 86, 88, Best New Publ. award 1985, Best Column award 1985, Best Signed Essay 1986, 87, Best Four-Color Layout 1985, Best Four Color Feature Design), City and Regional Mag. Assn. (William Allen White Bronze awards), Time/Life Alumni Soc., Sigma Delta Chi. Episcopalian. Nominated for Pulitzer Prize for coverage of Andrea Doria disaster, 1956; contbr. articles, photographs to nat. mags., books by Life mag. Home: 3049 NW Esplanade Seattle WA 98117-2624

GOULET, WILLIAM DAWSON, marketing professional; b. Hartford, Conn., Sept. 24, 1941; s. Henry J.K. and Elizabeth Bryne (Dawson) G. BA in English, Marietta Coll., 1963. Field service rep. Conn. Gen. Life Ins. Co., Hartford, 1963-65; sales promotion assoc. Phoenix Mut. Life Ins. Co., Hartford, 1965-69; dir. sales promotion Pacific Nat. Life Ins. Co., San Francisco, 1969-70; v.p. sales and mktg. E.F. Hutton Life Ins. Co., San Francisco, 1970-79; sr. v.p., fin. planning Prudential-Bache, San Francisco, 1979; v.p. GUMP's, San Francisco, 1980-91, mem. exec. com., 1981-91, mktg. cons., 1991-; pres. Campton Advt. Agy., 1980-91; dean ins. faculty Life Ins. Industry Sch., Williamsburg, Va., 1974; mktg. cons. U. of the Pacific, Stockton, Calif., 1972-80. Bd. dirs. Mus. Soc. San Francisco, 1984-90, Friends of Recreation and Parks, 1980—, v.p. bd. dirs., 1986; mem. adv. bd. The McLean Home, Simsbury, Conn., 1985—; mem. hon. bd. govs. The World Corp. Games, San Francisco, 1988; trustee Performing Arts Libr. and Mus., 1990, v.p. bd., 1991, pres. bd., 1992—, Asian Art Mus. Found., 1992. Sgt. USAR, 1963-69. Recipient Lawrence award Life Advertisers Assn., Vancouver, B.C., Can., 1979, Disting. Alumni Lectr. award Marietta Coll., 1985. Mem. San Francisco Grand Prix Assn. (adv. bd. 1986), Western Retail Mktg. Assn. (bd. dirs. 1989—). Democrat. Roman Catholic. Home and Office: PO Box 155 Ross CA 94957

GOVAN, GLADYS VERNITA MOSLEY, retired critical care and medical/surgical nurse; b. Tyler, Tex., July 24, 1918; d. Stacy Thomas and Lucy Victoria (Whitmill) Mosley; m. Osby David Govan, July 20, 1938; children Orbrenett K. (Govan) Carter, Diana Lynn (Govan) Mosley. Student, East Los Angeles Coll., Montebello, Calif., 1951; lic. vocat. nurse, Calif. Hosp. Med. Ctr., L.A., 1953; cert., Western States IV Assn., L.A., 1978. Lic. vocat. nurse, Calif.; cert. in EKG. Intravenous therapist Calif. Hosp. Med. Ctr., cardiac monitor, nurse; ret. Past pres. PTA; charter mem. Nat. Rep. Presdl. Task Force; mem. U.S.. Senatorial Club; active L.A. World Affairs Coun., 1992—. Mem. Am. Legion Aux. (past pres. unit 532), Heritage Found., Am. Acad. Polit. and Social Sci.

GOWDY, PETER DAVID, psychology educator; b. Palo Alto, Calif., Sept. 6, 1963; s. Greig Allen and Catherine (Lutes) G.; m. Adelina Hsu, July 24, 1988. BA, Whitman Coll., 1986; MA, Claremont Grad. Sch., 1988; PhD, U. Calif., Irvine, 1990—. Stats. analyst Claremont, 1984-85; ESL tchr. Pitzer Coll., Claremont, 1987; paralegal C.B. Estrin and Assocs., L.A., 1988-89; coll. instr. Calif. State U., San Bernardino, 1989; tchr. Kumon Ednl. Inst., Irvine, 1991—, U. Calif., Irvine, 1990—; crisis intervention and counseling profl. White Bird Clinic, Eugene, 1984-85. Mem. Optical Soc. Am., Am. Psychol. Assn., Mensa, Sigma Xi, Psi Chi. Office: U Calif Dept Cognitive Scis Irvine CA 92717

GOZANI, TSAHI, nuclear physicist; b. Tel Aviv, Nov. 25, 1934; came to U.S., 1965; s. Arieh and Rivcca (Meiri) G.; m. Adit Soffer, Oct. 14, 1958; children: Mor, Shai N., Or P., Tal. BSc, Technion-IIT, Haifa, Israel, 1956, MSc, 1958; DSc, Swiss Fed. Inst. Tech. (ETH), Zurich, Switzerland, 1962. Registered profl. nuclear engr., Calif.; accredited nuclear material mgr. Rsch. physicist Israel Atomic Energy Commn., Beer-Sheva, 1962-65; rsch. assoc. nuclear engring. dept. Rensselaer Poly. Inst., Troy, N.Y., 1965-66; sr. staff scientist Genera-Atomic & IRT, San Diego, 1966-70, 71-75; prof. applied physics Tel Aviv U., 1971; chief scientist, div. mgr. Sci. Applications Internat. Corp., Palo Alto and Sunnyvale, Calif., 1975-84; v.p., chief scientist Sci. Applications Internat. Corp., Sunnyvale, 1984-87; corp. v.p. Sci. Applications Internat. Corp., Santa Clara, Calif., 1987—. Author: Active Non-Destructive Assay of Nuclear Materials, 1981; co-author: Handbook of Nuclear Safeguards Measurement Methods, 1983; contbr. over 150 articles to profl. jours. Recipient 1989 Laurel award Aviation Week Jour., R&D 100 awd, 1988, Most Innovative New Products, nominee for the Safe Skies award Conway Data Inc., 1991, 92, 93. Fellow Am. Nuclear Soc.; mem. Am. Phys. Soc., Inst. Nuclear Material Mgrs., Indsl. Liaison-Fermi Lab. Office: Sci Applications Internat Corp 2950 Patrick Henry Dr Santa Clara CA 95054-1813

GRABARZ, DONALD FRANCIS, pharmacist; b. Jersey City, Sept. 18, 1941; s. Joseph and Frances (Zotynia) G.; m. Joan Isoldi, Aug. 13, 1966; children: Christine, Robert, Danielle. BPharm, St. Johns U., N.Y.C., 1964. Lic. pharmacist, N.Y., Vt. Dir. qualtiy control and assurance Johnson and Johnson Co., New Brunswick, N.J., 1965-72; dir. quality assurance and regulatory affairs Bard Parker div. Becton Dickinson, Franklin Lakes, N.J., 1972-76; asst. corp. dir. regulatory affairs Becton Dickinson, 1976-80; corp. dir. regulatory affairs C.R. Bard Inc., Murray Hill, N.J., 1980-85; v.p. regulatory affairs, qualtiy assurance Symbion Inc., Salt Lake City, 1985-86; cons. DFG & Assocs., Inc., Salt Lake City, 1986—; mng. ptnr. Internat. Regulatory Consultants, Salt Lake City, N.Y.C., also U.K., 1987-92; lectr. Inst. for Applied Tech., Inst. Internat. Rsch., Ernest & Young, Salt Lake C. C. Author, editor Inspection and Recall Film; co-author: Science, Technology, and Regulation in a Competetive Environment, 1990; contbr. articles to profl. jours. Bd. dirs. v.p., asst. treas. Am. Lung Assn., N.J., 1972-75; chmn. Drug Edn., DuPage County, Ill., 1968. Mem. Health Industry Mfg. Assn. (chmn. Legal and Regulatory commn. 1983), Regulatory Affairs Profl. Soc. (lectr.), Am. Soc. Quality Control, Am. Mfr. Med. Instrumentation Assn., Am. Pharm. Assn., Food and Drug Law Inst. Office: DFG & Assocs PO Box 17801 Salt Lake City UT 84117-0801

GRABER, SUSAN P., judge; b. Oklahoma City, July 5, 1949; d. Julius A. and Bertha (Fenyves) G.; m. William June, May 3, 1981; 1 child, Rachel June-Graber. BA, Wellesley Coll., 1969; JD, Yale U., 1972. Bar: N.Mex. 1972, Ohio 1977, Oreg. 1978. Asst. atty. gen. Bur. of Revenue, Santa Fe, 1972-74; assoc. Jones Gallegos Snead & Wertheim, Santa Fe, 1974-75, Taft Stettinius & Hollister, Cin., 1975-78; assoc., then ptnr. Stoel Rives Boley Jones & Grey, Portland, Oreg., 1978-88; judge, then presiding judge Oreg. Ct. Appeals, Salem, 1988-90; assoc. justice Oreg. Supreme Ct., Salem, 1990—. Mem. Gov.'s Adv. Coun. on Legal Svcs., 1979-88; bd. dirs. U.S. Dist. Ct. of Oreg. Hist. Soc., 1985—, Oreg. Law Found., 1990-91; mem. bd. visitors Sch. Law, U. Oreg., 1986-93. Mem. Oreg. State Bar (jud. adminstrn. com. 1985-87, pro bono com. 1988-90), Ninth Cir. Jud. Conf. (chair exec. com. 1987-88), Oreg. Jud. Conf. (edn. com. 1988-91, program chair 1990), Oreg. Appellate Judges Assn. (sec.-treas. 1990-91, vice chair 1991-92, chair 1992-93), Am. Inns of Ct. (master), Phi Beta Kappa. Office: Oreg Supreme Ct 1163 State St Salem OR 97310

GRACE, JOHN WILLIAM, electrical company executive; b. Swissville, Pa., May 29, 1921; s. Joseph and Ruth Margaret (Bailey) G.; student Am. TV Inst. Tech., 1950; BEE, Drexel U., 1960; m. Ruth Delores Schroeder, Nov. 25, 1950; children: Martha, Joan, Nancy, John William. Technician missiles and surface radar div. RCA, Moorestown, N.J., 1950-56, design engr., 1956-60, project engr., 1960-66; mgr. engring. and sci. exec. EG & G, Inc., Las Vegas, Nev., 1966-73, mgr. bus. devel. operational test and evaluation, Albuquerque, 1973-77; engring. mgr. Instrumentation div., Idaho Falls, Idaho, 1977-79, mgr. systems project office, 1979, mgr. instrumentation program office, 1979-82, mgr. engring. spl. products div., 1982-84, mgr. tech. resources, 1984-91. Active Boy Scouts Am., 1969-71. Served with USNR, 1941-45. Mem. IEEE, Instrument Soc. Am. (dir. sci. instrumentation and research div.), Assn. Old Crows, Am. Legion (post adj. vice comdr. 1950). Episcopalian (pres. couples retreat 1969-70). Patentee contradirectional waveguide coupler. Home: 8311 Loma Del Norte Dr NE Albuquerque NM 87109-4901 Office: EG&G Spl Projects Divsn 2755E E Desert Inn Rd Las Vegas NV 89121-3691

GRACZYKOWSKI, JACEK WOJCIECH, obstetrician-gynecologist, researcher; b. Bydgoszcz, Poland, Aug. 13, 1958; came to U.S., 1987; s. Roman Stanislaw and Ewa (Ratajczak) G.; m. Suzanne Carol Salimbene, June 5, 1988. MD, Acad. Medyczna, Gdansk, Poland, 1983. Diplomate Am. Bd. Ob-Gyn. Resident and intern physician Panstwowy Szpital Kliniczny, Bydgoszcz, 1983-86; asst. prof. Acad. Medyczna, Bydgoszcz, 1986-87; rsch. fellow U. So. Calif., L.A., 1987-90, resident physician, 1990—. Contbr. articles to profl. jours. Mem. Am. Coll. Obstetricians and Gynecologists, Am. Fertility Soc., Am. Soc. Andrology. Home: 4903 W 118th Pl Hawthorne CA 90250

GRADDY, DARRELL WAYNE, postal systems executive; b. Virginia Beach, Va., June 1, 1949; s. Charles R. and Betty S. (Comer) G.; m. Linda Sue Hills, Oct. 10, 1948; children: Carl L., Shari L., Seann C. BSBA, Fla. So. Coll., 1990. Store mgr. Nat. Tea Food Co., Pekin, Ill., 1972-73; shop press operator Caterpillar Tractor Co., Peoria, Ill., 1973-74, accts. payable analyst, 1974-77, systems analyst, 1977-83; systems project mgr. Martin Marietta Data System Co., Orlando, Fla., 1983-84; materials control mgr. Martin Marietta Aerospace, Orlando, Fla., 1984-90, prodn. control mgr., 1990-91; prodn. ops. dir. Martin Marietta Postal Systems Co., Albuquerque, 1991, postal program dir., 1991—; APICS guest speaker in field. Mem. Albuquerque C. of C., 1991—. Recipient Diploma of Completion, Ctr. for Creative Leadership, 1985, Program Mgr. Devel. cert. Martin Marietta Corp., 1989. Mem. Inst. Indsl. Engrs., Am. Prodn. and Inventory Control Soc. Republican. Baptist. Home: 9808 Fostoria NE Albuquerque NM 87111 Office: Martin Marietta Postal Systems Co 7500 Bluewater Rd Albuquerque NM 87121-1976

GRADY, DOLORES ANNE, academic administrator, educator, consultant; b. Wiesbaden, Germany, Apr. 24, 1958. BA, U. No. Colo., Greeley, 1980, MA, 1983; PhD, LaSalle U., L.A., 1993. Cert. tchr., 1987. Instr. Denver Tech. Coll., 1987, Adelphi Bus. Coll., 1984-87; assoc. prof. Colo. Tech. Coll., 1987-91; project mgr. Advanced Skills Edn. Program/Basic Skills Edn. Program Pikes Peak Community Coll., Ft. Carson, Colo., 1991—; adj. prof. Chapman U., Colorado Springs, Colo, 1991—. Bd. dirs. Pikes Peak Mental Health Action League, Jr. League Colorado Springs. Home: 2111 Lockhaven Dr Colorado Springs CO 80909

GRAF, ERICH LOUIS, musician, flutist; b. Ann Arbor, Mich., Apr. 11, 1948; s. Otto Gotthold and Sarah (Weiner) G. Studies with Nelson Hauenstein, U. Mich., 1966-67; studies with Jean-Pierre Rampal, Nice, France Summer Festival, 1968-69; BS, MusM, Juilliard Sch., 1974. 1st flutist and soloist Bklyn. Symphony Orch., 1971-73; mem. S.I. Opera Orch., 1972; 1st flutist Stamford (Conn.) Symphony Orch., 1976; prin. flute N.J. Symphony, 1976; 1st flutist, Symphony Orch. com. chmn. Utah Symphony Orch., Salt Lake City, 1976—; pvt. tchr., 1973—; adj. fac. mem. Bowdoin Coll., 1975-76, U. Utah, 1976-91, Internat. Inst. Music, Taos Ski Valley, 1987; master-classes at numerous colls., festivals, and univs. Performances with Royal Ballet Orch., 1972, N.Y. Philharmonic, 1973-74, Cin. Symphony Orch., 1973, Composer's Showcase Orch., 1975, N.Y.C. Opera Orch., 1974-75, Greenwich Symphony Chamber Series, 1974; solo performances with Beverly Sills, 1976, Julius Baker, 1978, Jean-Pierre Rampal, 1981, 90, Joseph Silverstein, 1985, Roberta Peters, 1986, Ark. Symphony, Ann Arbor Symphony, 1988, Utah Symphony, 1983, 85, 86, 87, 88, 89, 90, 91; chamber music performances include Nat. Flute Conv., Seattle, 1982, Denver, 1985, Mpls., 1990, numerous others; recordings with Columbia, VOX, CRI, Crystal, Desto, RCA, Folkways, Angel, Vanguard, Varese-Sarabande, Pro-Arte; solo recording A Flute Recital; contbr. travel articles to mags. Home: 488 H St Salt Lake City UT 84103-3135 Office: Utah Symphony 123 W South Temple Salt Lake City UT 84101-1496

GRAF, ERVIN DONALD, municipal administrator; b. Crow Rock, Mont., Mar. 9, 1930; s. Emanuel and Lydia (Bitz) G.; m. Carolyn Sue Robinson, Mar. 15, 1956 (div. 1958); m. Eleanor Mahlein, Apr. 13, 1959 (dec. Oct. 1990); children: Debra, Belinda, Corrina, Melanie, Ervin Jr. Enlisted U.S. Army, 1948; served two tours of duty in Vietnam; ret. U.S. Army, 1972; with office and maintenance staff Greenfields Irrigation Dist., Fairfield, Mont., 1972-77, sec. to Bd. Commrs., 1977—. Decorated Bronze star with oak leaf cluster. Mem. Am. Legion (all offices Post #80 and Dist. 8 incl. dist. comdr.). Democrat. Lutheran. Home: 211 6th St N Fairfield MT 59436 Office: Greenfields Irrigation Dist Central Ave W Fairfield MT 59436

GRAF, GARY LYNN, career officer; b. Tucson, Ariz., May 4, 1952; s. Milton Frank and Margret Francis (Prausa) G.; m. Jane Elizabeth Bentley, July 25, 1987. BS, U.S. Naval Acad., 1974. Commd. ensign USN, Annapolis, Md., 1970; advanced through grades to comdr. USN, 1989; div. officer USS Flasher USN, Mare Island, San Diego, Calif., 1975-79; leading engrng. officer, Nuclear Prototype Tng. Unit USN, Idaho Falls, Idaho, 1979-81; ops. officer USS Pollack USN, San Diego, 1982-85, ASW officer Carrier Group Seven, 1985-87; exec. officer USS Mariano G. Vallejo USN, Charleston, S.C., 1987-89; chief staff officer Submarine Squadron Seven USN, Pearl Harbor, Hawaii, 1990-91; commdg. officer USS Pintado USN, 1992—. Decorated 3 Navy Commendation medals, Navy Achievement medal. Home: 92-127 Leipapa Way Makakilo HI 96707 Office: USS Pintado SSN672 FPO AP 96675-2352

GRAF, MITCHEL ALAN, telemarketing company executive; b. Yuma, Ariz., Jan. 23, 1962; s. George Alan Graf and Toni (Tracy) Wright. Student, U. Oreg., 1980-81; B in Biology, Colo. State U., 1984. Dir. mktg. Kootenai Med. Ctr., 1985-86; regional sales mgr. G.E. Mobile Comm., 1986-88; owner CDA Product Mktg., 1987-90; nat. sales mgr. Golden Crown Corp., Coeur d'Alene, Idaho, 1990—; fitness cons. in health club industry. Track and field coach Colo. State U., North Idaho Coll.; mem. Mayor's Com. on Wellness, Coeur d'Alene, 1985-86, Wellness Com. Dist. 271, Coeur d'Alene, 1985-86. Mem. C. of C. Home: 5655 W Highland Dr Coeur d'Alene ID 83814 Office: Golden Crown Corp Box 820 Coeur D Alene ID 83816

GRAFE, WARREN BLAIR, cable television executive; b. N.Y.C., June 22, 1954; s. Warren Edward and Maree Lee (Ahn) G.; m. Pamela Arden Rearick, Mar. 8, 1980 (div. Nov. 1982). Student Kendall Coll., 1974-75, U. Wis.-Platteville, 1975-76; BA, Ind. U., 1979. Sales rep., Sta. WGTC-FM, Bloomington, Ind., 1979-84, account exec., coop. coord., 1980-84; nat. sales rep. Stas. WTTS-WGTC, Bloomington, 1984; sales rep. Sta. KLFF-KMZK, Phoenix, 1985; account exec. Rita Sanders Advt. and Pub. Rels. Agy., Tempe, Ariz., 1985, Am. Cable TV, Phoenix, 1985-86, Dimension Media Svcs., Phoenix, 1986-89, Greater Phoenix Interconnect, 1989—. Recipient Nat. Sales awards, Cable TV Advt. Bur., 1st award, 1986, 2d award, 1987, 3d award, 1991. Mem. Tempe C. of C. (ambassador 1986), Chandler (Ariz.) C. of C., Mesa (Ariz.) C. of C. Home: 5122 E Shea Blvd # 1117 Scottsdale AZ 85254-2413 Office: Greater Phoenix Interconnect 17602 N Black Canyon Hwy # 105 Phoenix AZ 85023-1997

GRAFFIS, JULIE ANNE, interior designer; b. Houston, Jan. 4, 1960; d. Robert B. and Dorothy Gean (Weempe) Hyde; m. William B. Graffis, May 29, 1988; 1 child, Aaron James Hehr. Student, U. St. Thomas, Houston, 1977, Portland C.C., The Dalles, Oreg., 1984-85; AA, North Seattle C.C., 1987. Cert. window fashions profl. assoc., specialist, master Window Fashions Cert. Program. Co-owner Mosier (Oreg.) Shell Svc., 1981-85; quality control mgr. Town & Country Jeep-Eagle, Seattle, 1986-87; cons. Giovi Ford-Mercury, Pullman, Wash., 1988-89; prin., CEO, Interiors by JAG, Vancouver, Wash., 1990—; cons. Habitat for Humanity, Vancouver, 1992—; lectr., presnter interior design workshops. Vol., mem. decorating com. S.W. Wash. Habitat for Humanity, 1992—; mem. Better Bus. Bur. Mem. Window Fashions Edn. and Design Resource Network, Greater Vancouver C. of C. (liaison bus. and edn. partnership 1992—), Inst. Managerial and Profl. Women. Office: Interiors by JAG 1605 F St Vancouver WA 98663-3445

GRAFFT, WILLIAM DAVIS, retired school system administrator; b. Ventura, Calif., Dec. 9, 1929; s. Clark Francis and Aileen (Willard) G.; m. Marilyn Eloise Church, June 16, 1951; children: Katherine, Paul. AB, U. Calif., Berkeley, 1951, MA, 1959, EdD, 1966. Cert. tchr. and adminstr., Calif. Tchr. pub. schs., Oakland, Calif., 1951-52, 55-60, prin., 1960-64; prin. Maxwell Park Sch., Oakland, 1964-65, Ralph J. Bunche Sch., Oakland, 1965-68, Glorietta Sch., Orinda, Calif., 1968-70; asst. supt. Orinda Union Sch. Dist., 1970-78; supr. Mountain View (Calif.) Sch. Dist., 1978-92; chmn. Santa Clara Supts., Santa Clara County, Calif., 1989-91; bd. dirs. Whitney Edn. Found., Los Altos, Calif., 1983-87; speaker, presenter in field. Contbr. articles to profl. jours. Pres., bd. dirs. Life's Garden Sr. Housing, Sunnyvale, Calif., 1985-89; bd. dirs. United Way, Mountain View, 1986-89, YMCA, Mountain View, 1983-87; mem. support com. NASA/Ames Mountain View Space Ctr., 1988-92; sponsor Scaife Scholarship Found.; ednl. activities dir. Friends of Ctr. Performing Arts. Lt. comdr. USNR, 1952-55, Pacific. Recipient Oustanding Adminstr. award Women Leaders in Edn., 1992, Red Triangle award YMCA, 1992, commednation Santa Clara County Suprs., 1992, commendation Calif. Legislature, 1992; Spl. honoree Boy Scouts Am., 1992. Mem. NEA, Individualized Instrn. Assn. (pres. 1978), Assn. Calif. Sch. Adminstrs. (Supt. of Yr. 1992). Democrat. Presbyterian. Home: 313 Lester Ct Santa Clara CA 95051

GRAFMAN, DAYTON FOWLER, musical instrument executive, pianist; b. Chgo., Jan. 25, 1923; m. Laura Ruth Samuels, June 4, 1950; 1 child, Lynn. MusB, Lawrence U., 1944, MusM, 1948. Admissions counselor Lawrence U., Appleton, Wis., 1944-53; dir. admissions Nat. Coll. Edn., Evanston, Ill., 1953-58, asst. to pres., 1958-64, v.p., 1964-76; pres. Friends of Our Little Bros., Phoenix, 1976-78; v.p. devel. Phoenix Symphony Orch., 1978-82; sr. devel. officer Ariz. State U., Tempe, 1983-89; v.p. Steinway div. Allen Piano Co., Scottsdale, Ariz., 1989—; chmn. bd. dirs. Phoenix Symphony Assn., 1990-92, vice chmn., 1992—; Steinway artist, Steinway and Sons, 1989. Performer for recs. Wouldn't It Be Loverly, 1989, Hello Young Lovers, 1989. Home: 4312 N 40th St Phoenix AZ 85018 Office: Allen Piano Co 7077 E Camelback Rd Scottsdale AZ 85251

GRAHAM, BEARDSLEY, management consultant; b. Berkeley, Calif., Apr. 24, 1914; s. Reuben Jacob and Kate Ellen (Beardsley) G.; m. Frances Rose McSherry, June 17, 1951 (div. Mar. 1967); children: McSherry, Heather; m. Lorraine Juliana Shaw, Oct. 22, 1973. BS in Chemistry, Physics and Math., U. Calif., Berkeley, 1935; postgrad. in Electronics, U. Calif., 1938-40, Columbia U., 1941-42; postgrad. in Chemistry, Tufts U., 1942-43. Registered profl. engr., Ariz., Calif., Ky.; lic. real estate broker, Calif. Instr. Edison Elec. Sch., Berkeley; frameman Pacific Tel. & Tel. co., San Francisco, 1937-39; chief engr. Golden Gate Internat. Expn. RCA Mfg. Co., 1939-40; devel. engr. NBC, Hollywood, Calif., N.Y.C., 1940-42; staff mem. radiation lab MIT, Cambridge, 1942-44; chief engr., head dept. spl. products devel. labs. Eclipse-Pioneer div. Bendix Aviation Corp., Teterboro, N.J., and Pacific div., Detroit, 1946-51, chief engr. rsch. labs., tech. cons. to v.p. rsch.; asst. chmn. engrng. dept. Stanford Rsch. Inst., Menlo Park, Calif., 1951-56; pres. Spindletop Rsch., 1961-67; exec. v.p. Sequoia Process Corp., Redwood City, Calif., 1956-57; spl. asst. comml. satellites Lockheed Aircraft Corp., Palo Alto and Sunnyvale, Calif., 1957-61, mgr. satellite systems planning Air Force Satellite Systems Program, mgr. specialty sales dept.; pres. Spindletop Rsch. Inc., Lexington, Ky., 1961-67; cons. Lockheed Aircraft Corp., Palo Alto and Sunnyvale, Calif., 1967—; pvt. practice mgmt. cons. Bend, Oreg., 1967—; pioneer in fields of new techs. and svcs. including econ. devel., air pollution and environ. qualities, nuclear weapons and power, satellite systems; bd. dirs., incorporator (selected by Pres. Kennedy) Communication Satellite Corp., 1962-64; founding chmn. bd. Videorecord Corp. Am.; mem. adv. com. on isotope and radiation devel. AEC, Ky., Atomic Energy and Space Authority, Ky. adv. com. on nuclear energy; rsch. prof. elec. engring. U. Ky., 1965; active in Microwave Communications Inc. (now MCI), Aetna Life Inc., numerous other. Papers on file at Bancroft Libr., U. Calif. at Berkeley. V.p. Bend Urban Area Planning Commn., 1983-87; vice chmn. engrng. tech. adv. com. Cen. Oreg. Community Colls., 1983—, Citizens Com. for Cityhood, Yucca Valley, Calif., 1977; mem. energy adv. com. League Oreg. Cities, 1983-87; active various other civic orgns.; treas., bd. govs. ocm. for art Stanford U., 1956; mem. Bend Traffic-Saftey Com., 1987, Cent. Oreg. Coun. on Higher Edn., 1983—. Named to Hon. Order Ky. Cols. Fellow IEEE (life), AIAA (assoc.); mem. Internat. Solar Energy Soc. (founding sec., bd. dirs. 1953-66), Solar Energy Assn. Oreg. (parliamentarian 1986, exec. bd.), International Club (Washington), Arizona Club, University Club (L.A.). Democrat. Home and Office: 214 Hillcrest Pl Baker City OR 97814-4132

GRAHAM, BONNI JEAN, technical writer; b. San Diego, Dec. 14, 1966; d. Thomas William and Frances Mary (Kirby) G. BA, U. Calif., San Diego, 1990. Tech. writer Data Trek, Inc., Carlsbad, Calif., 1990—. Editor (newsletter) Signature, 1991-92. Mem. Soc. for Tech. Comm. (v.p. 1991-93), Assn. for Computing Machinery (spl. interest group documentation). Home: 4115 Wabash Ave San Diego CA 92104 Office: Data Trek Inc 5838 Edison Pl Carlsbad CA 92008

GRAHAM, BONNIE J., executive secretary; b. Colorado Springs, Colo., Mar. 5, 1943; d. Milton Ernst and Rachel Elsie (Gibbs) Stockman; m. Arthur Graham, June 24, 1961 (div. Apr. 1986); children: Michael, Susan, Curtis. Grad. high sch., Pasadena, Calif. Exec. sec. Glendale (Calif.) Fed. Bank, 1981-90, Walt Disney Imagineering, Burbank, Calif., 1991—. Vol. Bd. of Elections, Temple City, Calif., 1988—, Youth Motivation Task Force; docent Pasadena Civic, 1988—. Mem. NAFE, Profl. Secs. Internat., Meeting Planners Internat., Acad. of Magical Arts, Tournament of Roses Assn. Home: 5326 N Village Circle Dr Temple City CA 91780-3359

GRAHAM, C(LYDE) BENJAMIN, JR., physician; b. Hannibal, Mo., Jan. 15, 1931; s. Clyde Benjamin and Eileen (Legan) G.; m. Pearl Louise Relling, Sept. 7, 1956; 1 dau., Leslie Eileen. Student, Wash. State U., 1948-49; BA with highest honors, U. Ill., 1954; MD, U. Wash., 1958. Diplomate: Am. Bd. Radiology. Intern Children's Hosp. and Med. Ctr., Seattle, 1958-59; resident in radiology U. Wash. Affiliated Hosps., 1959-62; faculty radiology and pediatrics U. Wash. Sch. Medicine, Seattle, 1963—; prof. U. Wash. Sch. Medicine, 1974—; dir. pediatric radiology U. Wash. Hosp., 1964—; dir. radiology Children's Hosp. and Med. Ctr.; cons. pediatric radiology Madigan Gen. Hosp., others; vis. radiologist Pediatric Clinic, Karolinska Inst., Stockholm, 1964. Contbr. articles to profl. publs. Named to Hall of Fame Nat. Wheelchair Basketball Assn., 1979; James Picker Found. fellow, 1962-64; scholar, 1964-66. Fellow Am. Coll. Radiology, Am. Acad. Pediatrics; mem. Soc. Pediatric Radiology (past dir.), Am. Roentgen Ray Soc., Radiological Soc. N.Am., Pacific Coast Pediatric Radiologists Assn. (past pres.), Alpha Omega Alpha. Home: 5116 Kenilworth Pl NE Seattle WA 98105-2841 Office: Childrens Hosp & Med Ctr PO Box 5371C Seattle WA 98105-0371

GRAHAM, DENIS DAVID, curriculum coordinator, marriage and family counselor; b. Santa Rosa, Calif., Oct. 21, 1941; s. Elbert Eldon and Mildred Bethana (Dyson) G.; m. Margaret Katherine Coughlan, Aug. 31, 1968; children: Kathleen Ann, Todd Cameron (dec.). BS in Edn., U. Nev., 1964, MEd, 1973, MA, 1982. Cert. for ednl. personnel; lic. marriage and family therapist, Nev.; nat. cert. counselor Nat. Bd. for Cert. Counselors. Tchr. vocat. bus. edn. Earl Wooster High Sch., Reno, 1964-66, chmn. dept. bus. edn., 1966-67; state supr. bus. and office edn. Nev. Dept. Edn., Carson City, 1967-70, adminstr. vocat. edn. field svcs., 1970-74, asst. dir., 1974-78, vocat. edn. cons., 1978-85; edn. curriculum specialist Washoe County Sch. Dist., Reno, 1985-89, curriculum coord., 1989—; marriage and family counselor Severance & Assocs., Carson City, 1983-85, Mountain Psychiat. Assocs., 1985-87; mem. tng. and youth employment council S.W. Regional Lab. for Ednl. Research and Devel., Los Alamitos, Calif., 1982, mem. career edn. council, 1980-81. Editor Council of Chief State Sch. Officers' Report: Staffing the Nation's Schools: A National Emergency, 1984. Contbr. articles to profl. jours. bd. dirs. U. Nev.-Reno Campus Christian Assn., 1988-90; adv. com. Truckee Meadows Community Coll., Reno, 1988—; mem. Gov.'s Crime Prevention Com., Carson City, 1979-83, Atty. Gen.'s Anti-Shoplifting Com., Carson City, 1974-78, Gov.'s Devel. Disabilities Planning Council, Carson City, 1977-79; bd. dirs. Jr. Achievement No. Nev., 1989-92, sec., mem. exec. com., 1990-91. Recipient award for svc. Bus. Edn. Assn. of No. Nev., 1973; Svc. award YMCA, 1962, 63. Mem. Am. Vocat. Assn., Nat. Assn. Vocat. Edn. Spl. Needs Pers. (Outstanding Svc. award region V 1982), Assn. Suprs. & Curriculum Devel., Am. Assn. Marriage and Family Therapy, Am. Assn. Counseling, Am. Mental Health Counselors Assn., Nev. Vocat. Assn. (Outstanding Svc. award 1991), U. Nev. Reno Alumni Assn. (exec. com. 1971-75), Phi Delta Kappa, Phi Kappa Phi. Democrat. Methodist. Office: 14101 Old Virginia Rd Reno NV 89511-8912

GRAHAM, DOUGLAS JOHN, museum administrator, poet; b. Dunfermline, Scotland, July 6, 1934; came to U.S., 1959, naturalized, 1965; s. Hugh Merton and Ellen Charlotte (Baroness Podmaniczky) G.; children: Robert, Christopher, Anabel, Isis. MBA, N.Y. Inst. Fin., 1961. Ptnr. Mitchell, Hutchins & Co., N.Y.C., William D. Witter Inc., N.Y.C., 1959-72; founder, chmn. bd. trustees The Turner Mus., Denver, 1973—; pres. Internat. Bank Holdings Ltd., 1979—; bd. dirs. Turner Soc. London, patron H.R.H. The Prince of Wales, 1978—. Author: Turner's Cosmic Optimism, 1990, Turner's Angels, 1991, Turner's Rainsbows, 1992. Life mem. St. Andrew's Soc. Colo. Served with M.I., Brit. Army, 1952-59. Mem. Unity Ch. Office: The Turner Mus 773 Downing St Denver CO 80218-3428

GRAHAM, JAMES HERBERT, dermatologist; b. Calexico, Calif., Apr. 25, 1921; s. August K. and Esther (Choudoin) G.; m. Anna Kathryn Luiken, June 30, 1950 (dec. May 1987); children: James Herbert, John A., Angela Joann; m. Gloria Boyd Flippin, July 29, 1989. Student, Brawley Jr. Coll., 1941-42; A.B., Emory U., 1945; M.D., Med. Coll. Ala., 1949. Diplomate: Am. Bd. Dermatology (dir. 1977-87, v.p. 1985-86, pres. 1986-87, Disting. Service medal 1987); diplomate in dermatopathology Am. Bd. Dermatology and Am. Bd. Pathology. Intern Jefferson-Hillman Hosp., Birmingham, Ala., 1949-50; resident in dermatology VA Center and UCLA Med. Center, 1953-56; clin. asst. instr. in medicine UCLA, 1954-56; Osborne fellow and NRC fellow in dermal pathology Armed Forces Inst. Pathology, Washington, 1956-58; vis. scientist Armed Forces Inst. Pathology, 1958-69, chmn. dept. dermatopathology, 1980-88; registrar Registry of Dermatopathology, Armed Forces Inst. Pathology, 1980-88, also program dir. dermatopathology, 1979-88; program dir. dermatopathology Walter Reed Army Med. Center, Washington, 1979-88; asst. prof. dermatology and pathology Temple U., 1958-61, assoc. prof., 1961-65, prof. dermatology, 1965-69, assoc. prof. pathology, 1965-67, prof. pathology, 1967-69; prof. medicine, chief div. dermatology, prof. pathology, dir. sect. dermal pathology and histochemistry U. Calif., Irvine, 1969-78; chief dermatology U. Calif. Med. Ctr., Irvine, 1977-78; prof. emeritus Coll. Medicine, U. Calif., 1978—; head sect. dermatology Orange County (Calif.) Med. Center, 1969-73; cons. dermatology VA Hosp., Long Beach, Calif., 1969-73; chief dermatology sect. VA Hosp., 1973-78, acting chief med. service, 1976; cons. dermatology, dermal pathology Regional Naval Med. Center, San Diego, 1969-82, Long Beach, 1969-78, Camp Pendleton, Calif., 1972-78; cons. dermatology, dermal pathology Meml. Hosp. Med. Center, Long Beach, 1972-86, Fairview State Hosp., Costa Mesa, Calif., 1969-78; cons. for career devel. for rev. clin. investigator applications VA Central Office, Washington, 1973-78; Disting. Eminent physician VA physician and dentist-in-residence program, 1980-88; mem. organizational com. Am. Registry Pathology, Armed Forces Inst. Pathology, Washington, 1976-77; mem. exec. com. Am. Registry Pathology, Armed Forces Inst. Pathology, 1977-78; prof. dermatology, clin. prof. pathology Uniformed Services U. of Health Scis., Bethesda, Md., 1979-88, prof. emeritus, 1989—; program dir. dermatopathology Naval Hosp. and Scripps Clin. and Rsch. Found., San Diego, 1991—. Sr. author: Dermal Pathology, 1972; contbr. articles to profl. publs. Served with M.C. USNR, 1949-53. Mem. AMA and Accreditation Coun. for Grad. Med. Edn. (residency rev. subcom. for dermatopathology 1974-87, mem. residency rev. com. dermatology 1977-87, chmn. 1984-87, cert. of merit 1960), Soc. Investigative Dermatology, U.S. and Can. Acad. Pathology, Am. Soc. Investigative Pathology, Am. Dermatol. Assn. (essay award 1958, v.p. 1986-87), Am. Soc. Dermatopathology (pres. 1975-76, Founder's award 1990, rep. to bd. of mem. Am. Registry Pathology, 1988-92), Dermatopathology Club (pres. 1980-81), Assn. Mil. Dermatologists, Am. Acad. Dermatology (dir. 1974-77, 82, v.p. 1980-81, rep. to bd. mems. Am. Registry Pathology 1977-78), N.Am. Clin. Dermatologic Soc. (hon.), 1973, Pa. Acad. Dermatology, Pacific Dermatol. Assn. (dir. 1972-75, hon. mem. 1981), Dermatology Found., Leader's Soc., Washington Dermatol. Soc. (spl hon.), Phila. Dermatol. Soc. (pres. 1967-68), San Diego Dermatol. Soc., Cutaneous Therapy Soc., Alpha Omega Alpha. Club: Cosmos (Washington).

GRAHAM, JAN, attorney general; b. Salt Lake City. BS in Psychology, Clark U., Worcester, Mass., 1973; MS in Psychology, U. Utah, 1977, JD, 1980. Bar: Utah. Ptnr. Jones, Waldo, Holbrook & McDonough, Salt Lake City, 1979-89; soliciter gen. Utah Atty. Gen.'s Office, Salt Lake City, 1989-93; atty. gen. State of Utah, 1993—; adj. prof. law U. Utah Law Sch.; bar commr. Utah State Bar, 1991; master of bench Utah Inns Ct. VII; mem. Utah Commn. on Justice in 21st Century; bd. dirs. Jones, Waldo, Holbrook & McDonough; bd. trustees Coll. Law U. Utah (pres.). Fin. devel. chair YWCA; chair Ctrl. Bus. Improvement Dist.; mem. Salt Lake City Olympic Bid Com. 1988 Games. Named Woman Lawyer Yr. Utah, 1987. Mem. Am. Arbitration Assn. (nat. panel arbitrators), Women Lawyers Utah (co-founder, mem. exec. com.). Office: 236 State Capitol Salt Lake City UT 84114*

GRAHAM, KIRSTEN R., information service executive; b. Inglewood, Calif., July 20, 1946; d. Ray Selmer and Ella Louise (Carter) Newbury; m. Frank Sellers Graham, July 31, 1981. BS, U. Wis., Oshkosh, 1971; MS, U. Colo., 1980; postgrad., Army War Coll., 1987. Cert. Flight instr. Chief info. svc. Mont. State Dept. Labor and Industry, Helena, Mont.; dir., personal property and bus. lic. div. County of Fairfax, Va.; analyst officer U.S. Army Pentagon, Washington; battalion commdr. U.S. Army, Frankfurt, West Germany; assoc. prof. U.S. Army, West Point, N.Y.; del. People-to-People Women Computer Sci. Profls. program., China. Vice chair, bd. dirs. Helena Industries for Vocationally Disabled; del. to People's Republic of China Citizen's Amb. Program, 1993. LTC U.S. Army, 1964-88. Mem. Data Processing Mgr.'s Assn., Nat. Assn. State Info. Resource Execs.

GRAHAM, LINDA MARIE, museum director, photographer; b. Worcester, Mass., Dec. 16, 1947; d. Henry William Russell and Rose Marie (Magnan) Ohlson; m. Douglas John Merton Graham, Feb. 14, 1984; 1 child, Isis Marina. Freelance photographer, 1969—; co-dir. The Turner Mus., Denver, 1981—, trustee, 1983—. Exhibited in group shows, New East End Gallery, Provincetown, Mass., 1989, Foothills Art Ctr., Golden, Colo., 1990, Photo Mirage Gallery, Denver, 1990, Alternative Arts Alliance, Denver, 1990. Chair music performabce Jr. Symphony Guild, Denver. Mem. Unity Ch. Home and Office: The Turner Mus 773 Downing St Denver CO 80218-3428

GRAHAM, LOIS CHARLOTTE, retired educator; b. Denver, Mar. 20, 1917; d. James Washington Brewster and Martha Wilhemina (Raukohl) Plunkett; m. Milton Clinton Graham, June 30, 1940 (dec.); children: Charlotte, Milton, Charlene, James. Student, Okla. City U., 1935-36; AB, Ouachita Bapt. U., 1939; postgrad., U. Nev., Reno, 1953, 63, 68, Ark. State U., 1954, 59. Cert. tchr., Colo., Nev., Ark. Tchr. Fairmount Sch., Golden, Colo., 1939-40, Melbourne (Ark.) Sch., 1940-41, Blytheville (Ark.) Jr. High Sch., 1944-45, Hawthorne (Nev.) Elem. Sch., 1952-81; substitute tchr. Mineral County Sch. Dist., Hawthorne, 1988—; sr. resource cons. dept. geriatrics U. Nev.-Reno Med. Sch., 1988—, del. to Rural Health Conf., Hawthorne, 1990; officer Mineral County Tchrs. Assn., 1955-65; ad hoc com. Nev. State Tchrs., 1965. Mem. Mineral County Emergency Planning Com., 1991—; asst. to pres. High Sch. PTA, Hawthorne, 1958, Elem. PTA, Hawthorne, 1961; pianist, choir dir., tchr. various chs., 1927—. Recipient Disting. Svc. award. Mem. AAUW (memberhsip v.p. 1988-91, pres. 1991-93), Delta Kappa Gamma (v.p. 1991-92). Republican. Baptist. Home: PO Box 1543 Hawthorne NV 89415-1543

GRAHAM, LOLA AMANDA (MRS. JOHN JACKSON GRAHAM), poet, photographer, writer; b. nr. Bremen, Ga., Nov. 12, 1896; d. John Gainer and Nancy Caroline Idella (Reid) Beall; m. John Jackson Graham, Aug. 3, 1917 (dec.); children: Billy Duane, John Thomas, Helen (Mrs. D. Hall), Donald, Beverly (Mrs. Bob Forson). Student Florence Normal Sch., 1914. Tchr. elem. public sch., Centerdale, Ala., 1914, Eva, Ala., 1915; designed sweaters, 1938-42; free lance photographer and writer, 1950—; editor poetry column Mobile Home News, 1968-69; designer jacket cover for Reader's Digest book Our Amazing World of Nature, designer ski sweaters sold to Catalina Mills and various pattern cos. Recipient numerous nat. prizes, 1950—; Crossroads of Tex. grand nat. in poetry for For Every Monkey Child, 1980; executed prize-winning Sioux Indian and heirloom photog. quilts. Mem. Nat. Poetry Soc. Ina Coolbrith Poetry Soc., Chapparal Poets. Author: How to Print Photos on Cloth for Pillows, Quilts, (poetry) Recycling Center, 1988. Contbr. photographs to Ency. Brit., also numerous mags. and books; designer ski sweaters 1930s. Address: 225-93 Mount Hermon Rd Scotts Valley CA 95066

GRAHAM, MAUREEN ELIZABETH, pastoral counselor; b. Falkirk, Scotland, Dec. 15, 1955; came to U.S., 1983; d. James Robertson and Elizabeth Alston (Graham) G. MA in Psychology with honors, U. St. Andrews, Scotland, 1978, PhD in Psychology, 1983; MMin, Earlham Coll., Richmond, Ind., 1986; DMin, Claremont (Calif.) Coll., 1992. Cert. Am. Assn. Pastoral Counselors. Tutor, rsch. asst. U. St. Andrews, 1979-82, rsch. fellow, 1982-83; residence dir. Earlham Coll., 1985-86; dir. Woolman Hill Quaker Conf. and Retreat Ctr., Deerfield, Mass., 1986-89; pastoral counselor Clinebell Inst., Claremont, 1989-90, Christian Counseling Svc., Redlands, Calif., 1990—; mem. ministry and oversight So. Calif. Quar. Meeting, Religious Soc. of Friends, 1992—. Contbr. articles to profl. jours. Bobby Jones scholar U. St. Andrews, 1978; Lyman Fund grantee, 1989, 90. Mem. Am. Assn. Pastoral Counselors (ethics com. Pacific region 1991—), Quaker Chaplains and Pastoral Counselors. Quaker. Home: 1750 Richard St Pomona CA 91767 Office: Christian Counseling Svc 51 W Olive Ave Redlands CA 92373

GRAHAM, MILTON H., distributing company executive; b. Fairfield, Iowa, Mar. 23, 1919; s. Lonnie D. and Bertha M. (Coffman) G. BA, Parsons Coll., 1941. Prin. Milt Graham Distbg. Co., Phoenix, 1948-60, Milt Graham Assocs., Phoenix, 1960-90, Milt Graham TXTLCARE Systems, Phoenix, 1990—. Mayor City of Phoenix, 1964-70; officer, dir. U.S. Conf. of Mayors, Nat. League of Cities, Nat. Urban Coalition, Internat. Sister Cities, 1964-70, numerous other orgns. 1st lt. USAC, 1942-64, ETO. Republican. Home: 5812 N 12th St Unit 34 Phoenix AZ 85014-2027

GRAHAM, PAMELA SMITH, distributing company executive, artist; b. Winona, Miss., Jan. 18, 1944; d. Douglas LaRue and Dorothy Jean (Hefty) Smith; m. Robert William Graham, Mar. 6, 1965 (div.); children: Jennifer, Eric; m. Thomas Paul Harley, Dec. 4, 1976; stepchildren: Tom, Janice. Student U. Colo., 1962-65, U. Cin., 1974-76. Cert. notary pub., Colo. Profl. artist, craft tchr., art exhibitor Colo., N.J., Ohio, 1968-73; property mgmt. and investor Cin., 1972-77; acct., word processor Borden Chem. Co. div. Borden, Inc., Cin., 1974-78; owner, pres. Hargram Enterprises, Cin., 1977-81; owner, pres. Graham & Harley Enterprises. Morrison, Colo., 1981—; tchr.; cons. County committeewoman Bergen County, N.J., 1972, clk. of session, 1975-79, conv. chmn., 1981; campaign chmn. United Appeal, 1977; lifeline telephone counselor Suicide Hotline, 1985—; victim advisor Abusive Men Exploring New Directions, 1986—. Recipient numerous awards for art exhibits, bus. achievements, 1962—. Mem. NAFE, United Sales Leaders Assn., Nat. Museum of Women in Arts, Colo. Artists Assn., Evergreen Artists Assn. (bd. dirs., pres. 1990, 91), Colo. Calligraphers Guild, Gilpin County Arts Assn., Foothills Art Ctr., Alpha Gamma Chi,

Kappa Kappa Gamma. Republican. Club: Queen City Racquet. Office: Graham & Harley Enterprises 4303 S Taft St Morrison CO 80465-1425

GRAHAM, PRISCILLA MANN, librarian; b. Highland Park, Ill., Jan. 3, 1915; d. William David and Isabel (Browning) Mann; m. Myron J. Graham, Oct. 14, 1939; children: Wendy Stevens, Peter Mann, Robert Allen. Student, Northwestern U., 1936; BS, Calif. Poly. State U., 1970; MLS, San Jose State U., 1972. Ref. libr. Calif. Poly State U. Libr., San Luis Obispo, 1970-80; substitute libr. Cuesta Community Coll., San Luis Obispo, 1988—; staff Historic Preservation Survey, City of San Luis Obispo, 1980-85. Trustee City Libr., San Luis Obispo, 1968-69, mem. cultural heritage com., 1981—. Am. Beautiful grantee, 1972. Mem. AAUW, LWV, Libr. Assn. Calif. Poly. (pres. 1979, Recognition award 1989), Alpha Phi, Beta Phi Mu. Home: 61 Los Palos Dr San Luis Obispo CA 93401

GRAHAM, ROGER JOHN, photography and journalism educator; b. Phila., Feb. 16; s. William K. and Peggy E. (Owens) G.; divorced; children: John Roger, Robb Curt; m. Debbie Kenyon, Dec. 28, 1991. AA, Los Angeles Valley Coll., 1961; BA, Calif. State U., Fresno, 1962, MA, 1967; postgrad, UCLA, 1976. Tchr. Riverdale (Calif.) Sch., 1963, Raisin City (Calif.) Sch., 1964; tchr., counselor Calif. State Prison, Jamestown, 1966; tchr. trainer UCLA's Western Ctr., 1967; chmn. media arts dept. Los Angeles Valley Coll., Van Nuys, Calif., 1968—; vis. prof. Pepperdine U., Malibu, Calif., 1976, Calif. Luth. Coll., Thousand Oaks, 1973. Author: Observations on the Mass Media, 1976, (jour) Jr. Coll. Jour., 1972; photo illustrator: The San Fernando Valley, 1980; contbr. articles to profl. jours.; display advertiser Turlock (Calif.) jour., 1962, Fresno Guide, 1963. Mem. Hayden's Com. for Schs., Santa Monica, Calif., 1984, YMCA, Pacific Palisades, Calif.; pres. Pacific Palisades Dem. Club, 1992; rep. to 41st assembly dist. Calif. Dem. Party State Ctrl. Com., 1993, sec. srs. caucus, 1993—. With USN, 1957. NEH scholar 1981; recipient Mayor's Outstanding Citizen award Los Angeles Mayor's Office, 1974, Extraordinary Service award UCLA, 1971; named one of Outstanding Young Men Am., 1971. Mem. Community coll. Journalism Assn. (nat. pres. 1978—, Nat. Dedication Journalsim award 1972-76), Journalism Assn. Community Colls. (pres. Calif. sect. 1972—), Calif. Srs. Caucus (state sec. 1993—), Los Angeles Prof's. Club, Dem. Club Pacific Pasisades (pres. 1992-93), Am. Legion (sgt. at arms 1986—), Sigma Delta Xi, Phi Delta Kappa, Pi Lambda Theta. Home: 438 E Rustic Rd Santa Monica CA 90402-1114 Office: Los Angeles Valley Coll 5800 Fulton Ave Van Nuys CA 91401-4062

GRAHAM, STEPHAN ALAN, earth sciences educator; b. Evansville, Ind., Apr. 25, 1950. BA, Ind. U., 1972; MS, Stanford U., 1974, PhD, 1976. Rsch. geologist Exxon Prodn. Rsch. Co., Houston, 1976; exploration geologist Chevron USA Inc., San Francisco, 1976-78, prodn. geologist, 1978-80; assoc. prof. Stanford (Calif.) U., 1980-87, prof., 1987—; consulting petroleum geologist, 1980—. Fellow Geol. Soc. Am., Am. Assn. of Petroleum Geologist (assoc. editor AAPG Bull. Sproule award 1985), Soc. Econ. Paleontologists and Mineralogists (councilor, pres. Pacific sect., hon. mem.), Am. Geophys. Union, Sigma Xi. Office: Dept Geol and Environ Scis Stanford U Stanford CA 94305

GRAHAM, STEPHEN MICHAEL, lawyer; b. Houston, May 1, 1951; s. Frederick Mitchell and Lillian Louise (Miller) G.; m. Joanne Marie Sealock, Aug. 24, 1974; children: Aimee Elizabeth, Joseph Sealock, Jessica Anne. BS, Iowa State U., 1973; JD, Yale U., 1976. Bar: Wash. 1977. Assoc. Perkins Coie, Seattle, 1976-83, ptnr., 1983—. Bd. dirs. Wash. Spl. Olympics, Seattle, 1979-83, pres., 1983; mem. Seattle Bd. Ethics, 1982-88, chmn., 1983-88, Seattle Fair Campaign Practices Commn., 1982-88; trustee Cornish Coll. of the Arts, 1986-91, exec. com., 1988; trustee Epiphany Sch., 1987-93, exec. com., 1989-91; mem. exec. com. Sch. Law Yale U., 1988-92, 93—; bd. dirs. Perkins Coie Community Svc. Found., 1988-91; bd. trustees Seattle Reperatory Theatre, 1993—. Mem. ABA, Wash. State Bar Assn., Seattle-King County Bar Assn., Wash. Athletic Club, Columbia Tower Club. Episcopalian. Office: Perkins Coie 1201 3d Ave 40th Flr Seattle WA 98101

GRAHAM, TONI, writer; b. San Francisco, June 24, 1945; d. Joseph Foster and Maxine E. (Johnson) Avila; m. J. Richard Graham, Nov. 23, 1972 (div. 1987); 1 child, Salvatore Z. BA, New Coll. Calif., 1988; MA in English, San Francisco State U., 1992. lectr. Creative Writing Dept. San Francisco State U., 1992; thesis advisor U. San Francisco, 1993. Author short fictions in mags. including Playgirl, Short Story Review, Am. Fiction 88, Five Fingers Review, Mississippi Review, Ascent. Harrold scholar, 1986; story Shadow Boxing cited in Pushcart Prize XIV - Best of the Small Presses, 1989. Mem. Golden Key Honor Soc. Home: 345 Prospect Ave San Francisco CA 94110-5509 Office: C/O Dijkstra Literary Agy 1237 Camino Del Mar Del Mar CA 92014-2505

GRAINDA, JOHN MATTHEW, III, account manager; b. Phillipsburg, N.J., May 2, 1959; s. John M. Jr. and Rose (Mirenna) G.; m. Elizabeth A. Nugent, May 31, 1986; children: John Matthew IV, Michael Joseph. BS in Mktg., Pa. State U., 1981. Sales rep. Alcoa-Closure Systems Internat., Chgo., 1981-85; acct. mgr. Alcoa-Indsl. Products, Chgo., 1985-87, Combibloc, Inc., Columbus, Ohio, 1987-92, Alcoa-Rigid Packaging Divsn., Lakewood, Colo., 1992—. Gov. DCHA, Dublin, Ohio, 1990-92. Mem. Am. Mktg. Assn., Omicron Delta Kappa. Republican. Roman Catholic. Office: ACCOA 143 Union Blvd #900 Denver CO 80228

GRAMM, WARREN STANLEY, economics educator; b. Seattle, Sept. 23, 1920; s. Paul Francis and Genevieve Hazel (Barnecut) G.; m. Marilyn Lorraine Post, June 25, 1949; children: Karen, Christie, Randolph. BA, U. Wash., 1944, MA, 1948; PhD, U. Calif., Berkeley, 1955. Asst. prof. Econs. U. Calif., Davis, 1955-63; assoc. prof. Econs. Alaska Meth. U., Anchorage, 1963-65; prof. Econs. Wash. State U., Pullman, 1965-91, prof. emeritus, 1991—. Contbr. articles profl. jours. Mem. Am. Econs. Assn., Assn. for Evolutionary Econs., History of Econs. Soc. Home: 1455 NW Kenny Dr Pullman WA 99163-3722 Office: Wash State U Dept Econs Pullman WA 99164

GRAMMATER, RUDOLF DIMITRI, retired construction executive; b. Detroit, Nov. 29, 1910; s. D.M. and Amelia (Busse) G.; m. Fredricka W. Cook, Aug. 18, 1943, 1 child, Douglas. Student, Pace Coll., 1928-32; LLB, Lincoln U., 1937. Bar: Calif. 1938; CPA Calif. With Bechtel Corp., San Francisco, 1941-73, treas., v.p., 1955-62, v.p., 1962-71, dir., 1960-73, cons., 1973, v.p., dir. subsidiaries, 1955-71. Mem. ABA, AICPA, Calif. Soc. CPAs, Calif. Bar Assn., Menlo Country Club. Home: 50 Mounds Rd Apt 302 San Mateo CA 94402-1257

GRAMS, THEODORE CARL WILLIAM, librarian, educator; b. Portland, Oreg., Sept. 29, 1918; s. Theodore Albert and Emma Elise (Boehne) G. B.A., U. Wash., 1947; postgrad. Harvard Law Sch., 1947-48; M.S. in L.S., U. So. Calif., 1951. Land title asst. U.S. Bonneville Power Adminstrn., Portland, 1939-45, accountant, 1948-50, librarian, 1951-52; head cataloger, lectr. Portland State U. Library, 1952-59, dir. processing services, 1960-83, prof., 1969-87, prof. emeritus, 1988—. Pres. Portland Area Spl. Librns., 1954-55; panelist on impact new tech. on info. scis. Am. Soc. Info. Sci., 1974, panelist on Libr. Congress svcs., 1976. Author: Allocation of Joint Costs of Multiple-Purpose Projects, 1952, Textbook Classification, 1968; editor: Procs. 4th Am. Soc. Info. Scis. Midyear Meeting, 1975, Special Collections in the Libraries of the Pacific Northwest, 1979, Disaster Preparedness and Recovery, 1983, Technical Services: The Decade Ahead (in Beyond 1984: The Future of Technical Services), 1983. Panelist on community action N.W. Luth. Welfare Assn. Conf., 1969; mem. adv. council Area Agy. on Aging, 1974-75; commr. City-County Commn. Aging, Portland-Multnomah County, 1975-80. Bd. dirs. Hub-Community Action Program, Portland, 1967-70, Project ABLE, 1972-74. HEW Inst. fellow, 1968-69. Mem. Am. Library Assn., AAUP, Multnomah Athletic Club, Beta Phi Mu. Lutheran. Home: 2500 N Rosemont Blvd Tucson AZ 85712-6101

GRAND, RICHARD D., lawyer; b. Danzig, Feb. 20, 1930; came to U.S., 1939, naturalized, 1944; s. Morris and Rena G.; m. Marcia Kosta, Jan. 27, 1952; 1 dau., Cindy. B.A., N.Y. U., 1951; J.D., U. Ariz., 1958. Bar: Ariz. 1958, Calif. 1973, U.S. Supreme Ct. 1973; cert. specialist in injury litigation Ariz. Bd. Legal Specialization. Dep. atty. Pima County, Ariz., 1958-59; pvt. practice trial law Tucson, 1959—; founder, 1st pres. Inner Circle Advocates, 1972-75; founder, 1966; now chmn. Richard Grand Found. Contbr. articles to legal publs. Mem. bd. visitors law sch. Ariz. State U. Recipient citation of honor Lawyers Coop. Pub. Co., 1964. Fellow Am. Acad. Forensic Scis., Internat. Soc. Barristers; assoc. mem. Internat. Med. Soc. Paraplegia, Am. Coll. Legal Medicine; mem. ABA (vice-chmn. com. govtl. liability law, sect. of tort and ins. practice 1986-87), Pima County Bar Assn., N.Y. State Trial Lawyers Assn., Calif. Trial Lawyers Assn., Am. Bd. Trial Advs. (cert. in civil trial advocacy), Brit. Acad. Forensic Scis., President's Club of U. Ariz. Address: 127 W Franklin St Tucson AZ 85701

GRANDIN, TEMPLE, livestock equipment designer, educator; b. Boston, Aug. 29, 1947; d. Richard McCurdy and Eustacia (Cutler) G. BA in Psychology, Franklin Pierce Coll., 1970; MS in Animal Sci., Arizona State U., 1975; PhD in Animal Sci., U. Ill., Urbana, 1989. Livestock editor Ariz. Farmer Ranchman, Phoenix, 1973-78; equipment designer Corral Industries, Phoenix, 1974-75; ind. cons. Grandin Livestock Systems, Urbana, 1975-90, Fort Collins, Colo., 1990—; lectr., asst. prof. animal sci. dept. Colo. State U., Fort Collins, 1990—; chmn. handing com. Livestock Conservation Inst., Madison, Wis., 1976—. Contbg. editor: Meat and Poultry mag., Mill Valley, Calif., 1987—; author: Emergence Labelled Autistic, 1986, Recommended Animal Handling Guidelines for Meat Packers; contbr. articles to profl. publs. Recipient Mertiorious Svc. award Livestock Conservation, Madison, Wis., 1986, Disting. Alumni award Franklin Pierce Coll., 1989; named One of Processing Stars of 1990 Nat. Provisioner, 1990. Mem. Autism Soc. Am. (bd. dirs. 1988—, Trammel Crow award 1989), Am. Soc. Animal Sci., Am. Soc. Agrl. Cons. (bd. dirs. 1981-83), Am. Soc. Agrl. Engrs., Am. Meat Inst. (supplier mem.), Am. Registry of Profl. Animal Scis. Republican. Episcopalian. Home: Grandin Livestock Systems 2918 Silver Plume Dr C-3 Fort Collins CO 80526 Office: Colo State U Animal Sci Dept Fort Collins CO 80523

GRANGER, DAVID WILLIAM, personnel agency executive, educator; b. Reading, Pa., Feb. 22, 1951; s. David Stanley and Gertrude Norma (Zeswitz) G.; m. Lori Burr; children: Amanda Katherine, Kelsey Alexandra. Student, Bapt. Coll., Springfield, Mo., 1969-70. Ins. agt. Nat. Life and Accident Co., Savannah, Ga., 1972-75; line mgr. Kerr S.S. Co., Savannah, 1975-78; gen. line mgr. Kerr S.S. Co., Houston, 1978-8l; dir. pub. affairs Port of Long Beach (Calif.), 198l-85; pres., chief exec. officer Temp. Svcs. Internat., Long Beach, 1985—; guest lectr. Travel and Trade Career Inst., Long Beach, 1985—; mem. adv. bd. Harbor Occupational Ctr., San Pedro, Calif., 1988—. Contbr. editor various mags., 1983. Mem. Internat. Bus. Assn. (com. 1986—), Greater L.A. World Trade Ctr. (com. 1988—), World Trade Svcs. Group (assoc.), Internat. Trade Club L.A. (program dir. 1982-84), Harbor Transp. Club. Republican. Baptist. Office: Temp Svs Internat 6615 E Pacific Coast Hwy # 270 Long Beach CA 90803-4211

GRANLUND, THOMAS ARTHUR, engineering executive, consultant; b. Spokane, Wash., Mar. 1, 1951; s. William Arthur and Louise (Urie) G.; m. Jean MacRae Melvin, May 25, 1974 (div. Feb. 1991). BS, Wash. State U., 1973, BA, 1973; MBA, Gonzaga U., 1982. Engring. adminstr. Lockheed Aeronautical Systems Co., Burbank, Calif., 1978-91; mgmt. cons., 1991—. Co-author: (screenplay) Identities, 1988, Flash, 1989. 1st lt. USAF, 1973-78. Mem. Wash. State U. Alumni Assn. Home: 20924 Ben Ct Santa Clarita CA 91350-1418

GRANT, ART, artist, educator; b. San Francisco, June 22, 1927; s. Mayer and Sarah (Rose) G. AA, San Francisco City Coll., 1945-48; BA, San Francisco State U., 1955; postgrad., San Francisco Art Inst., 1955-56, Coll. of Marin, 1958-62. Instr. art and art edn. San Franciso State U., 1964-69, 66-77, Somona State U., 1968-79, Hayward State U., 1969-71, U. Calif., Davis, 1970-73, St. Mary's Coll., Moraga, Calif., 1976-78, Dominican Coll., San Rafael, Calif., 1977-80; assoc. prof. humanities Lincoln U., San Francisco, 1979—; instr. Golden Gate Theol. Sem., Mill Valley, Calif., 1981; instr. art San Francisco Theol. Sem., San Anselmo, Calif., 1980. Co-author: Sculpture From Junk, 1967. Mem. artist coun. San Francisco Art Inst., 1963-66; charter mem. Artist: Marin, San Rafael, 1962-77. Recipient Sculpture prize Ann. San Francisco Mus. of Modern Art, 1958, Art Festivals, San Francisco, 1960, 77, Sausalito, Calif., 1962, 63, Art prize Food Art Exhibit, Sausalito, 1977; Art Grant Day proclaimed by Mayor Art Agnos of San Francisco, 1988; Marin Arts Coun. grantee, 1990. Home: 154 Ethel Ave Mill Valley CA 94941-2736

GRANT, DAVID MORRIS, chemistry educator; b. Salt Lake City, Mar. 24, 1931; s. David Lewis and Mary Lucille (Greenwood) G.; m. Reva Luella Carlow, Sept. 11, 1953; children: David James, Linda Grant Halling, Heidi Grant Cox, Karen Grant Lindstrom, John Carlow Grant. BS in Chemistry, U. Utah, 1954, PhD in Chemistry, 1957. Du Pont instr. chemistry U. Ill., Champaign-Urbana, 1957-58; asst. prof. U. Utah, Salt Lake City, 1958-62, assoc. prof., 1962-65, prof., 1965-85, disting. prof., 1985—, chmn. dept. chemistry, 1962-73, dean coll. sci., 1976-85; adj. prof. fuels engring., U. Utah, 1985-89, assoc. v.p. acad. and rsch. computing, 1985-92, co-investigator study to improve mgmt. of costly instrumentation trs., 1974-75; lectr. numerous univs., sci. and tech. assns. and confs., 1963—. Mem. editorial bd. Jour Am. Chem. Soc., 1975-76, Jour. Magnetic Resonance, 1969-84; mem. editorial adv. bd. Spectrochimica Acta, 1976-84. Named Sherman Fairchild Disting. Vis. Scholar Calif. Inst. Tech., 1973-74; recipient U. Utah Disting. Rsch. award, 1971-72, Willard Gardner prize Utah Acad. Scis., Arts and Letters, 1971, Gov.'s medal for sci. and tech. State of Utah, 1992. Fellow AAAS; mem. Am. Chem. Soc. (assoc. editor jour. 1975-76, accreditation rev. com. 1985, Gold medal award Calif. sect. 1969, Utah sect. award 1973, award in Petroleum Chem. 1991), Utah Acad. Scis., Arts and Letters (Univ. Disting. Svc. award for Biol. and Phys. Scis. 1989, Univ. Rosenblatt prize for Excellence 1987). Mormon. Office: U Utah Dept Chemistry Salt Lake City UT 84112

GRANT, HOMER HAMILTON, JR., engineering educator; b. Wenatchee, Wash., Feb. 12, 1908; s. Homer Hamilton and Georgia (Sanders) G.; m. Beth Huntley, Jan. 7, 1933; 1 child, Sydney Gail Grant McCauley. BS in Elec. Engring., U. Wash., 1932, MS in Elec. Engring., 1933, EE, 1946; ScD (hon.), Northrop Inst. Tech., 1965. Registered profl. engr., Calif. Rsch. engr., chief rsch. and stats. div. Wash. State Dept. Pub. Svc., 1934-39; statistician Bonneville Power Adminstrn. U.S. Dept. Interior, 1939-40; rsch. engr., transp. economist Calif. Pub. Utilities Commn., 1940-43; asst. to v.p. and gen. mgr., transp. engr. Key System, Oakland, Calif., 1943-46; prof. indsl. engring., acting dean/assoc. dean Sch. Engring. U. So. Calif., 1948-67; pres. Northrop Inst. Tech., Inglewood, Calif., 1967-73; emeritus Northrop U., Inglewood, 1973—; cons. engr. in mgmt. 1946—, indsl. engring, gen. mgmt., feasibility, transp., electric rates, tech. rsch. evaluator U.S. Dept. Transp. 1967, Hanford Atomic Products oper. Gen. Electric Co. 1957, U.S. Army Mgmt. Engring. Tng. Agy. 1962-66; pres. Aquatic Rsch., Inc. and Climax Mfg. Co., 1959-62; trustee Northrup U. 1967-74. Contbr. articles to profl. jours. Dir. Tri County Sanitation Study, Oreg., L.A. Bd. Edn., mem. bd. transp. rate experts, 1950-60; mem. statewide adv. com for pvt. schs. and colls. adv. to State Supt. Pub. Instrn., 1964-67, nat. rsch. adv. com. Am. Transit Assn., 1946, Rapid Transit Action Group, 1948, U. Pres. Transp. Com., 1950, citizens adv. com. Areawide Waste Treatment Area Planning, 1976-78. Fellow Inst. Indsl. Engrs.; mem. IEEE (sr., chmn. mgmt. sessions nat. conf. 1956, mem. Nat. Mgmt. com. 1956-57), NSPE, Inglewood C. of C. (v.p. 1970-73), Long Beach C. of C. (chmn. transp. com. 1952), Am. Soc. Engring. Edn. (chmn. Pacific SW sect. 1959-60), Sunrise Country Club Homeowners Assn. (bd. dirs. 1981-86, pres. 1985-86), Masons (32 deg.), Elks, Sigma Xi, Tau Beta Pi, Alpha Tau Omega, Phi Kappa Phi, Alpha Pi Mu. Republican. Home: 30 Haig Dr Rancho Mirage CA 92270-3807

GRANT, JAMES RUSK, business owner; b. Malvern, Ark., July 22, 1939; s. James Rusk and Maxie (Thompson) G.; m. Ciara Grant, June 30, 1966 (div. 1972); children: Michele Rene, Michael Reed; m. Diane Grant, June 2, 1978. AA in Psychology, Orange Coast U., 1975; BS in Human Svcs., Calif. State U., Fullerton, 1977. V.p. Internat. Recruiting, Van Nuys, Calif., 1978-88; mgr. Snelling & Snelling, Inc., Sunnyvale, Calif., 1988-89; pres. Nugent & Grant, Inc., Santa Clara, Calif., 1989—. Mem. Emergency Ham Radio Santa Clara, Van Nuys Masonic Blue Lodge, San Jose Scottish Rite Masons, Shriners. Republican. Office: Nugent & Grant Inc 5100 Coe Ave 175 Fort Ord CA 93941

GRANT, JOHN CARRINGTON, advertising executive; b. St. Louis, Feb. 2, 1937; s. George Nelson Whitfield and Mary Frances (Tissier) G.; m. Judith Ann Thompson, Oct. 20, 1962; children: Christopher, Susan. Student Westminister Coll., 1960; BS, Washington U., St. Louis, 1969. Account mgr. Darcy, McManus & Masius, St. Louis, N.Y.C. and San Francisco, 1960-68; with Gardner Advt., St. Louis, 1963-66, McCann-Erickson, Seattle, 1974-75; stockbroker Dean Witter, San Francisco, 1968-74; with Tracy-Locke/BBDO, 1975-80; pres. Grant Pollack Advt., Denver, 1980-85; v.p. Brock & Assocs., Denver, 1985-86; dir. Univ. rels. U. Denver, 1987-89; pres. Grant & Assocs., 1989—; exec. v.p., prin. Consortium, 1989—; mem. faculty Met. State Coll., Denver, 1981-82. Mem. Denver Advt. Fedn. Clubs: Denver Athletic, Oxford.

GRANT, KAY, small business owner. BA, San Francisco State U., 1972. Meeting planner Kay Grant & Assocs., San Francisco, 1980—; founder, owner Near Escapes-Adventures Right in Our Own Back Yard, San Francisco, 1985—. Contbr. articles in field to newspaper and mags. Vol. various orgns. including ARC, Broadcast Svcs. for the Blind, others, San Francisco, 1990—. Mem. Meeting Planners Internat., Calif. Writers Club, San Francisco Tour Guide Guild. Office: Near Escapes PO Box 193005 San Francisco CA 94119

GRANT, LAURIE LOUISE, physician assistant, health educator, consultant; b. York, Nebr., Dec. 24, 1953; d. Donald Eugene and Mae Louise (McDill) G.; m. Rory R. Hein, May 26, 1973 (div. Feb. 1993); children: Misty Louise, Miles Jeffrey. AS, Allegheny Coll., 1980; BA in Health & Natural Sci., La Roche Coll., 1981; MS, U. Colo., 1983; postgrad., Loyola U., New Orleans, 1990—. Physician asst. Vista Grande Family Medicine, Colorado Springs, Colo., 1980-84, Erindale Family Medicine, Colorado Springs, 1984-86, Front Range Family Medicine, Colorado Springs, 1986-88, Exec. Park Med. Arts, Colorado Springs, 1988—; health educator, cons. Profl. Health Providers, Colorado Springs, 1984—; tchr., facilitator Nat. Inst. Inner Healing, Colorado Springs, 1991—. Contbr. articles to profl. jours. Mem. pastoral coun. Corpus Christi Ch., Colorado Springs, 1991—, eucharistic min., 1990—; tchr. religious edn. seminars, Colorado Springs, 1986—; inner healing specialist Nat. Inst. Inner Healing, 1988—. Fellow Am. Acad. Physician Assts., Am. Coll. Sports Medicine; mem. Colo. Acad. Physician Assts., Nat. Inst. Inner Healing Specialists. Republican. Roman Catholic. Office: Exec Park Med Arts 2141 N Academy Cir Colorado Springs CO 80907

GRANT, MERWIN DARWIN, lawyer; b. Safford, Ariz., May 7, 1944; s. Darwin Dewey and Erma (Whiting) G.; m. Charlotte Richey, June 27, 1969; children: Brandon, Taggart, Christian, Brittany. BA in Econs., Brigham Young U., 1968; JD, Duke U., 1971. Bar: Ariz. 1971, U.S. Dist. Ct. Ariz., U.S. Dist. Ct. (we. dist.) Tex., U.S. Ct. Appeals (5th, 7th, 8th, 9th and 10th cirs.), U.S. Tax Ct., U.S. Supreme Ct. Pres. Merwin D. Grant, P.C., Phoenix, 1977—; ptnr. Beus, Gilbert & Morrill, Phoenix, 1984—. Guest condr. Phoenix Symphony Orch., 1989. Bd. dirs. Grand Canyon coun. Boy Scouts Am., Phoenix, 1974-76; pres., bd. dirs. Golden Gate Settlement, Phoenix, 1975-80, 84-88; charter mem. Rep. Presl. Task Force, Washington, 1984—. Fellow Ariz. Bar Found.; mem. ABA (litigation sect.), Assn. Trial Lawyers Am., Kiwanis (bd. dirs. Phoenix chpt. 1972-79). Office: Beus Gilbert & Morrill 3200 N Central Ave Ste 1000 Phoenix AZ 85012-2430

GRANT, NANCY MARIE, marketing professional, journalist; b. Tilden, Nebr., Jan. 2, 1941; d. William Gerald and Evelyn Marie (Baughman) Whitford; m. Marvin Ostberg, 1961 (div. 1969); children: Jill Marie Ostberg Bennett, Carolyn Ostberg Chun; m. Richard Grant, 1973 (div. 1975). BA in Journalism, U. Nebr., 1963; postgrad., U. Oreg., 1968, Portland State U., 1978, U. Wash., 1979-83, Seattle Cen. C.C., 1992. Asst. state editor Lexington (Ky.) Leader, 1963; freelance writer Shreveport Times, AP, Natchatoches, La., 1964; info. rep. 1 & 2 Univ. Oreg. News Bur., Old Oreg. Alumni Mag., Faculty Staff Newsletter, Eugene, 1965-70; dir. pub. rels. U. Portland, Oreg., 1971; info. rep. 3 Oreg. Hwy. Div. and Motor Vehicles, 1972-77; dir. Grant Pub. Rels. and Mktg., Seattle, 1979-85; exec. dir., founder Wash. Neurol. Alliance, Seattle, 1985—. Editor U. Oreg. Faculty-Staff Newsletter, 1969, U. Portland Alumni Mag., 1970, Hwy Newsletter and film, 1971-77. Lobbiest Wash. Neurol. Alliance; mem. Gov.'s Com. on Disability Issues and Employment, 1983-86; bd. dirs. Wash. Assembly, 1983-86, Highland Community Ctr., Bellevue, Wash., 1984-86. Recipient Hearst award, 1963. Mem. NAFE. Democrat. Unitarian. Home: 1809 15th Ave # 101 Seattle WA 98102 Office: 1202 E Pike St # 749 Seattle WA 98122

GRANT, RICHARD EARL, nursing administrator; b. Spokane, Wash., Aug. 27, 1935; s. Conrad Morrison and Sylva Celeste (Sims) G.; m. Susan Kimberly Hawkins, Mar. 17, 1979; children: Aaron Sahmie Q., Camber Do'otsie O. BSc cum laude, U. Wash., 1961; MEd, Whitworth Coll., 1974; PhD, Wash. State U., 1980. Cert. ins. rehab. specialist; cert. case mgr. Supr. nursing Providence Hosp., Seattle, 1970-72; asst. prof. nursing Wash. State U., Spokane, 1972-78; dir. nursing Winslow (Ariz.) Meml. Hosp., 1978-79; adminstr. psychiat. nursing Ariz. State Hosp., Phoenix, 1979-80; asst. prof. Ariz. State U., Tempe, 1980-83; assoc. prof. Linfield Coll., Portland, Oreg., 1983-86, Intercollegiate Ctr. for Nursing Edn., Spokane, 1986-88; sr. med. care coord. CorVel Corp., Spokane, 1988-92; med. svcs. cons. Fortis Corp., Spokane, 1992—; cons. Ariz. State Hosp., 1980-82, Pres.'s Commn., Washinton, 1981-83, U. No. Colo., Greely, 1985-86; area med. svcs. cons., 1992—. Author: The God-Man-God Book, 1976, Publications of the Membership (Conaa), 1983, 3d rev. edit., 1985, 4th rev. edit., 1988, Predetermined Careplan Handbook-Nursing, 1988; contbr. articles to profl. jours. Judge Student Space Shuttle Project, Portland, 1983—, Northwest Sci. Expo, Portland, 1983—. Served with U.S. Army, 1953-56. Grantee NIMH, U. Wash., 1961; named one of top Hopi Scholars, Hopi Tribe, Second Mesa, Ariz., 1981. Mem. AAAS, Nat. League for Nursing, Wash. League for Nursing (v.p. 1988-90), Coun. on Nursing and Anthropology (editor 1982-90), N.Y. Acad. Scis., Case Mgmt. Soc. Am., Sigma Theta Tau.

GRANT, WILLIAM WEST, III, banker; b. N.Y.C., May 9, 1932; s. William West and Katherine O'Connor (Neelands) G.; m. Rhondda Lowery, Dec. 3, 1955. BA, Yale U., 1954; postgrad., NYU Grad. Sch. Bus., 1958, Columbia U. Grad. Sch. Bus., 1968, Harvard U. Grad. Sch. Bus., 1971. With Bankers Trust Co., N.Y.C., 1954-58; br. credit adminstr. Bankers Trust Co., 1957-58; with Colo. Nat. Bank, Denver, 1958—; pres. Colo. Nat. Bank, 1975—, chmn. bd., 1986—; chmn. bd. Colo. Capital Advisors; bd. dirs. Plains Petroleum Co., Colo. Nat. Bankshares Inc., Channel 6 Pub. TV. Trustee Denver Mus. Natural History, Gates Found. Denver, Midwest Rsch. Inst., Kansas City; bd. dirs. Sta. KRMA-TV, Inst. Internat. Edn., New World Airport Commn., Samaritan Inst., Mountain State Employers Coun.; vice chmn. Colo. chpt. Nature Conservancy. Mem. Colo. Bankers Assn., Denver C. of C. (dir. Internat. Gateway Com.). Episcopalian. Clubs: Denver Country, Denver. Office: Colo Nat Bank PO Box 5168ta Denver CO 80217-5168

GRASS, GEORGE MITCHELL, IV, pharmaceutical executive; b. Bryn Mawr, Pa., Dec. 31, 1957; s. George Mitchell III and Irma Lucy (Schaffer) G. PharmD, U. Nebr., Omaha, 1980; PhD, U. Wis., 1985. Lic. pharmacist. Staff rschr. Syntex Rsch., Palo Alto, Calif., 1985-91; pres. Precision Instrument Design, Tahoe City, Calif., 1987—; cons. Costar Corp., Cambridge, Mass., 1990—, various pharm. cos., 1991—. Contbr. numerous articles to profl. jours. Recipient Ebert prize, Jour. Pharm. Scis., Washington, 1989. Mem. AAAS, Am. Assn. Pharm. Scientists, Sigma Xi.

GRASSI, JAMES EDWARD, executive director; b. Oakland, Calif., Nov. 19, 1943; s. Dante Carlos and Mae Johanna (Condon) G.; m. Mary Louise Etter, Apr. 10, 1965; children: Daniel James, Thomas William. BS in Recreation Adminstrn., Calif. State U., Hayward, 1966; MPA, Calif. State U., 1971. Ordained to ministry Evangelical Ch.,1992. Recreation supr. Oakland (Calif.) Pks. & Recreation, 1964-66; adminstrv. asst. East Bay Regional Pk. Dist., Oakland, 1966-76; dep. town mgr. Town of Moraga, Calif., 1976-86; exec. dir. Let's Go Fishing & FOCAS Ministries, 1986—; cons. in field; dir. Calif. Recreational Fisheries Counsel, Sacramento, 1968-74; trustee Christian Heritage Coll. Bd., El Cajon, Calif., 1989—. Author: (booklet) Ultimate Fishing Challenge, 1990, (pamphlet) Anchoring Your Lives in Christ, 1990; co-host TV show Fishing Tales, 1988-91; contbr. articles to profl. jours. Bd. dirs. Rotary Internat., 1976-86, YMCA, Hayward, 1977-70. Recipient Legis. Resolution Appreciation and Accomodation, Disting. Employee award Moraga Town Counsel, 1986, Presdl. plaque Calif. Pks. & Recreation Soc., 1980. Mem. U.S. Trout Farmers Aquaculture Assn., Nat. Assn. Evangs. Republican. Evangelical. Home: 22 Del Rio Ct Moraga CA 94556-2031 Office: Let's Go Fishing PO Box 434 Moraga CA 94556-0434

GRASSO, MARY ANN, theatre association administrator; b. Rome, N.Y., Nov. 3, 1952; d. Vincent and Rose Mary (Pupa) Grasso. BA in Art History, U. Calif., Riverside, 1973; MLS, U. Oreg., 1974. Dir. Warner Rsch. Collection, Burbank, Calif., 1975-84; mgr. CBS TV/Docudrama, Hollywood, Calif., 1984-88; exec. dir. Nat. Assn. Theatre Owners, North Hollywood, Calif., 1988—; instr. theatre arts UCLA, 1980-85, Am. Film Inst., L.A., 1985-88. Screen credits: The Scarlet O'Hara Wars, This Year's Blonde, The Silent Lovers, A Bunnies Tale, Embassy. Mem. Nat. Assn. Theatre Owners (exec. dir.), Bus. and Profl. Women's Assn. (Woman of Achievement award 1983), Acad. Motion Pictures Arts and Scis., EARTHSAVE, Nature Conservancy, Phi Beta Kappa. Democrat. Office: Nat Assn Theatre Owners 4605 Lankershim Blvd # 340 North Hollywood CA 91602-1818

GRATTET, PAUL MAURICE, city manager; b. Amsterdam, N.Y., Aug. 16, 1936; s. Paul Albert Grattet and Grace Roseann (Vickary) Hoteling; m. Jean Marilyn Ryken, Aug. 28, 1959; children: Marca Jeanne, Vaun Paul, Kama Lee, Risa Vickary, Timm Ryken. BA in Econs., U. Denver, 1959; student, Syracuse U., 1960-61. Mktg. analyst, fin. analyst Eastman Kodak Co., Rochester, N.Y., 1961-70; asst. dir. budget City of Rochester, 1970-73, dir. fed. program rev., 1973, asst. to city mgr., 1973-76, asst. city mgr., 1976-78, dep. city mgr., 1978-80; city mgr. City of Vancouver, Wash., 1980-90, City of Greeley, Colo., 1991—; bd. dirs. Econ. Devel. Action Partnership. Greeley, 1991—, Conv. and Visitors Bur., Greeley, 1991—; mem. planning com. United Way of Weld County, Greeley, 1992—; mem. adv. bd. Wash. State U., Vancouver, 1986-91. Bd. dirs. Action for A Better Community, Rochester, 1970-75, Rochester Mus. and Sci. Ctr., 1970-80; bd. dirs., pres., chmn. United Cerebral Palsy Assn., Rochester, 1965-78; bd. dirs., pres. Columbia Arts Ctr., Vancouver, 1981-91. With U.S. Army, 1954-56, West Germany. Mem. Internat. City Mgmt. Assn. (corp. mem.), Wash. City Mgmt. Assn. (pres. 1985-86). Democrat. Home: 1725 Glen Meadows Dr Greeley CO 80631 Office: City of Greeley 1000 10th St Greeley CO 80631

GRAUBART, JEFFREY LOWELL, entertainment lawyer; b. Chgo., Aug. 18, 1940; s. John H. and Florence R. G.; m. Mary Linda Carey, June 24, 1973; children: Joshua Gordon, Noah Carey. BS in Fin., U. Ill., 1962; JD, Northwestern U., Chgo., 1965. Bar: Ill. 1965, Calif. 1968, N.Y. 1980. Assoc. Curtis Friedman & Marks, Chgo., 1965-67, Capitol Records, Inc., Los Angeles, 1968-70; prin. Hadfield, Jorgensen, Graubart & Becker, San Francisco, 1970-81; counsel Frankfurt, Garbus, Klein & Selz, P.C., N.Y., 1981-85; prin. Strote, Graubart & Ashley, P.C., Beverly Hills, Calif. and N.Y., 1986-87; counsel Cohen & Luckenbacher, L.A., 1988-90, Engel & Engel, L.A., 1991-92; sec. Paramount Growers, Inc., Delano, Calif., 1968-70; v.p., dir. London Internat. Artists, Ltd., Los Angeles, 1969-70, Jazz Images, Inc., N.Y.C., 1983-86; adj. prof. NYU, 1982-85; lectr. Columbia U. Sch. Law, N.Y.C., 1982-85, UCLA, 1988—, U. So. Calif., 1988—. Contbr. articles to profl. jours. and mags. Dir. Jazzmobile, Inc., N.Y.C., 1982-85; mem. counsel San Francisco Jazz Found., 1980-81. Recipient Deems Taylor award ASCAP, 1981. Mem. NARAS (San Francisco chpt. legal counsel 1973—, gov. 1973-85, gov. and legal counsel N.Y. chpt. 1982-85, gov. L.A. chpt. 1988-92), Internat. Radio and TV Soc., Country Music Assn., Assn. of the Bar of the City of N.Y., Soc. Preservation of Film Music (trustee 1989—, v.p. 1991—). Lodges: B'nai Brith (N.Y. and Los Angeles); Golden Gate (San Francisco) (v.p. 1974-75), Entertainment Industry Unit L.A. (founder, trustee 1988—). Office: 2029 Century Park E # 2700 Los Angeles CA 90067-3041

GRAUE, LOUIS GEOFFREY, data processing executive; b. Sacramento, Apr. 11, 1951; s. Louis Charles and Patricia Joan (Hock) G.; m. Cheryl Arlene Waite, Apr. 14, 1985; children: L. Christopher, Diana Nicole. BS, Bowling Green State U., 1972. Cert. data processor. System programmer Carnegie Mellon U., Pitts., 1972-74; program mgr. Digital Equipment Corp., Culver City, Calif., 1974-88; v.p., mgr. tech. svcs. Security Pacific State Trust Co., Pasadena, Calif., 1988-90, v.p., dir. MIS, 1990-92; dir. MIS Santa Fe Pacific Pipelines, L.A., 1992—. Mem. Data Processing Mgmt. Assn. (v.p. 1992), Soc. Information mgmt. Office: Santa Fe Pacific Pipelines 888 S Figueroa Los Angeles CA 90017

GRAUER, STUART ROBERT, school director; b. N.Y.C., Sept. 28, 1950; s. Herman Robert and Priscilla June (Groat) G.; m. Sally Jo Currie, Mar. 17, 1991. BA, Syracuse U., 1968; MS, L.I. U., 1972; PhD, U. San Diego, 1989. Social studies, English tchr. N.Y. State, 1971-76; elem. tchr. Internat. Sch. of Bern, Switzerland, 1976-80; prin. Internat. Sch. of Basel, Switzerland, 1980-81; asst. dir. Fairbanks Country Day Sch., Rancho Santa Fe, Calif., 1982-90; dir., owner North Coast Ind. Schs., Encinitas, Calif., 1990—; adj. prof. various San Diego Univs., 1989—. Author: (book) Leadership in International Education, 1990. Mem. San Dieguito Lagoon Com., Del Mar, Calif. Home: 3636 Caminito Carmel Landin San Diego CA 92130 Office: N Coast Ind Schs 2210 Encinitas Blvd Ste E Encinitas CA 92024-4359

GRAVES, JOSEPH LEWIS, JR., evolutionary biologist, educator; b. Westfield, N.J., Apr. 27, 1955; s. Joseph L. and Helen (Tucker) G.; m. Suekyung Joe, Mar. 5, 1984; 1 child, Joseph L. III. AB, Oberlin Coll., 1977; PhD, Wayne State U., 1988. Pres.'s postdoctoral fellow U. Calif., Irvine, 1988-90, asst. prof. evolutionary biology, African-Am. studies, 1990—, faculty mentor Howard Hughes biomed. fellowship, 1990—; bd. dirs. Calif. Alliance for Minority Participation Transfer Acad.; mem. panel NSF, Functional & Physiol. Ecology & Nat. Rsch. Coun. Minority Grad. Fellowships. Contr. chpt. to: Genetic Effects on Aging II, 1990, Insect Life Cycles, 1990; contbr. articles to Sci., Genetica, Physiological Zoology, Functional Ecology, Jour. Insect Physiology, Life Sci. Advances: Fundamental Genetics, Jour. Gerontology, Race Relations Abstracts; TV appearance Sta. KCET-TV, 1993. Josiah P. Macy fellow Marine Biol. Lab., Woods Hole, Mass., 1978; NSF fellow, 1979; Thomas Rumble grad. fellow Wayne State U., Detroit, 1985. Mem. Soc. Study Evolution, Genetics Soc. Am., Am. Soc. Naturalists, Gerontol. Soc. Am. Office: U Calif Irvine Dept Evolutionary Biology Irvine CA 92717

GRAVES, KĀ (KATHLEEN R. GRAVES), artist; b. Detroit, Jan. 19, 1938; d. John Joseph and Bertha (Padar) Drake; m. Keith Earl Graves, July 10, 1971. AA, Am. Coll., Paris, 1974; BFA, Ariz. State U., Tempe, 1976; MFA, Ariz. State U., 1979. conductor workshops in field; grad. teaching asst. Ariz. State U., Tempe, 1976-78; artist-in-residence McClintock High Sch., Tempe, 1979-80, Ariz. Commn. on the Arts, Phoenix, 1981-83, S. Mt. High Sch., Phoenix, 1987; adj. faculty painting and dwg. Grand Canyon Coll., Phoenix, 1983-85; faculty assoc. oil painting Ariz. State U., summer 1986; part-time faculty life dwg. Glendale (Ariz.) Community Coll., 1986-87; faculty assoc. Ariz. State U., 1993—. One person shows Elaine Horwitch Gallery, Scottsdale, Ariz., 1986, 90, Winged Horse Gallery, Las Vegas, 1989, John Douglas Cline Gallery, Phoenix, 1981, 83, 84, Fine Arts Ctr. Tempe, 1985, Scottsdale Ctr. Arts, 1982, others; group shows include Hearst Art Gallery, Moraga, Calif., 1990, Internat. Gallery, San Diego, 1989, Navy Pier, Chgo., 1988, 89, Elaine Horwitch Gallery, 1987, 88, 89, Gallery 500, Pa., 1986, Winged Horse Galerie, Las Vegas, 1988, Judaica Mus., Phoenix, 1984, many others. Home and Office: 921 W Lynwood St Phoenix AZ 85007-1914

GRAVES, ROY DANNER, public relations executive; b. Indpls., Mar. 2, 1943; s. Robert Harrison and Ardis Louise (Danner) G.; m. Rebecca Jane Cole, Oct. 30, 1971; children: Gavin Matthew, Aaron Todd. BA, Butler U., Indpls., 1964; MA, U. Wash., 1972. Pub. rels. specialist Cummins Engine Co., Columbus, Ind., 1969-71; pub. rels. rep. Boeing Aerospace-Naval Systems, Seattle, 1972-75; account exec. Communication N.W., Seattle, 1972, 75-77, pres., owner, 1978—; mem. adv. com. pub. rels. cert. course U. Wash., 1989—. Contbr. articles to profl. jours. Chmn. Magnolia Youth Assn., Seattle, 1984-85; bd. dirs. Intiman Theatre, Seattle, 1984-90, v.p. mktg., 1984-88, pres., 1989-90. Lt. USNR, 1961-91, capt. Res. ret. Mem. Pub. Rels. Soc. Am. (accredited, v.p. Puget Sound 1976-77, bd. dirs. Counselors Acad. 1982-85, sec.-treas. 1993), Seattle C. of C. (v.p. Pres.'s Club 1985-87), Wash. Athletic Club, Rainier Club (com. chair 1992), Rotary (com. chair 1992). Office: Communication NW 111 W Harrison St Seattle WA 98119

GRAVES, STEPHEN MATTHEW, executive; b. Potstown, Pa., Apr. 7, 1955; s. John Henry and Marjorie Ann (Kuolt) G.; m. Joann Erb, Mar. 1, 1985; children: Erika, Ian. BA in Criminology, Fla. State U., 1977; BA in Asia Studies, U. Md., Tokyo, 1982; MA in Internat. Bus., Sophia U., Tokyo, 1989. Market analysis GM, Tokyo, 1984-85; mktg. mgr. Bridgestone Corp., Tokyo, 1985-91; territory mgr. Bridgestone Corp., Seattle, 1991—; lectr. Internat. Mgmt. Devel. Studies, Tokyo, 1988-91.

GRAY, ALFRED ORREN, journalism educator, research and communications consultant; b. Sun Prairie, Wis., Sept. 8, 1914; s. Charles Orren and Amelia Katherine (Schadel) G.; m. Nicolin Jane Plank, Sept. 5, 1947; children—Robin, Richard. B.A., U. Wis.-Madison, 1939, M.A., 1941. Reporter-correspondent-intern U. Wis.-Madison and Medford newspapers, 1937-39; free-lance writer, 1938-41, 51-57; intelligence investigator U.S. Ordnance Dept., Ravenna, Ohio, 1941-42; hist. editor, chief writer U.S. Office Chief Ordnance Service, ETO, Paris and Frankfurt, Germany, 1944-46; asst. prof. journalism Whitworth Coll., Spokane, Wash., 1946-48, assoc. prof., 1948-56, head dept. journalism, adviser student publs., 1946-80, prof., 1956-80, prof. emeritus, 1980—, chmn. div. bus. and communications arts, 1958-66, chmn. div. applied arts, 1978-79; cons. research and communications Spokane, 1980—; dir. Whitworth News Bur., 1952-58; prin. researcher, writer 12 hist. and ednl. projects. Author: The History of U.S. Ordnance Service in the European Theater of Operations, 1942-46, Not by Might, 1965, Eight Generations from Gondelsheim: A Genealogical Study, 1980; co-author: Many Lamps, One Light: A Centennial History, 1984; editor: The Synod Story, 1953-55; mem. editorial adv. bd. Whitworth Today mag., 1989-90; contbr. articles to newspapers, mags., jours.; advisor All-Am. coll. newspaper; editorial reader Am. Presbyns.: The Jour. of Presbyn. History, 1992—. Scoutmaster Troop 9, Four Lakes Coun., Boy Scouts Am., Madison, Wis., 1937-41; chmn. Pinewood Addition Archtl. Com., Spokane, 1956—; dir. Inland Empire Publs. Clinic, Spokane, 1959-74; mem. ho. of dels. Greater Spokane Council of Chs., 1968-71; judge Goodwill Worker of Yr. awards Goodwill Industries Spokane County; vice-moderator Synod Wash.-Alaska, Presbyn. Ch. (U.S.A.), 1966-67; bd. dirs. Presbyn. Hist. Soc., 1984—, exec. com., 1986-90, chmn. hist. sites com., 1986-90; mem. Am. Bd. Mission Heritage Commn. for Sesquicentennial of Whitman Mission, 1986; elder Spokane 1st Presbyn. Ch., 1962—, clk. of session, 1984-86, mem. Inland Empire Presbytery Com. for Bicentennial of Gen. Assembly, 1988-89, Inland Empire Presbytery (com. on justice and peacemaking 1988—); Dem. precinct official, Spokane, 1988-92. Served with AUS, 1942-46. Decorated Bronze Star and Army Commendation medals; recipient Printers Ink trophy Advt. Assn. West, 1953, citation Nat. Council Coll. Publ. Advisers, 1967, Outstanding Teaching of Journalism award Whitworth Coll Alumni Assn., 1972; named Disting. Newspaper Adviser, Nat. Council Coll. Publ. Advisers, 1979. Mem. Assn. for Edn. in Journalism, Ea. Wash. Hist. Soc., Coll. Media Advisers (hon.), N.Am. Mycol. Assn., U. Wis. Alumni Assn. Half Century Club, Phi Beta Kappa (pres. profl. chpt. 1949-50, 67-68, 70-71). Democrat. Home: 304 W Hoerner Ave Spokane WA 99218-2124

GRAY, BURL BRADLEY, company executive; b. Mattoon, Ill., June 1, 1938; s. Lawrence Albert Gray and Virginia (Bradley) Cady; m. Sheila Tedrick, 1962 (div. 1980); children: Bradley Kent, Kara Dawne; m. Pamela Wyn Crook, Oct. 19, 1982. BS, So. Ill. U., 1959, MS, 1961, PhD, 1963. Asst. prof. U. Ariz., Tucson, 1963-64; dir. rsch. Behavioral Scis. Inst., Monterey, Calif., 1964-76; disting. scholar in residence Wichita (Kans.) State U., 1976; sr. staff scientist Human Resources Rsch. Orgn., Carmel, Calif., 1976-78; exec. v.p. McFann, Gray & Assocs., Inc., Monterey, 1978-81; pres. McFann, Gray Svcs. Corp., Monterey, 1981-85, McFann Gray & Assocs., Inc., Monterey, 1981-86; gen. mgr. Aeroterra, Inc., Santa Monica, Calif., 1986—; cons. in field; disting. scholar in residence, Wichita, 1976. Author texts: Stuttering and the Conditioning Therapies, 1969, Language Program for Nonlanguage Child, 1973. Fellow Am. Speech and Hearing Assn. (cert. clin. competence/speech), Behavioral Therapy and Rsch. Soc.; mem. APA, AAAS, Assn. for Advancement of Behavior Therapy, N.Y. Acad. Scis. Office: Aeroterra Inc 1637 16th St Santa Monica CA 90404

GRAY, DONALD ALLAN, computer software executive; b. Palo Alto, Calif., Jan. 27, 1964; s. Thomas Leighton and Audrey May (MacGregor) G. BS, U. So. Calif., 1987. Corp. trainer Computer Solutions, Internat., L.A., 1987-89; regional sales mgr. V.I. Corp., Newport Beach, Calif., 1989-91; sales dir. Talarian Corp., Mountain View, Calif., 1991—; bus. plan devel. mgr. Occidental Petroleum, L.A., 1988-89. Home: 1123 20th St San Francisco CA 94107 Office: Talarian Corp 444 Castro St Mountain View CA 94041

GRAY, EDMUND WESLEY, physician; b. Colville, Wash., Nov. 9, 1928; s. Wesley Harold and Helen (Corridan) G.; m. Jane Bloomfield, June 20, 1953; children: Timothy Paul, Sarah Jane, Terrence Wesley. Student, Gonzaga U., 1946-49; MD, U. Wash., 1953. Diplomate Am. Bd. Family Practice. Intern Indpls. Gen. Hosp., 1953-54; pvt. practice Colville, 1956—; health officer N.E. Tri-County Health Dept., Colville, 1973—; med. dir. N.W. Alloys, ALCOA, Addy, Wash., 1975—; cons., mem. Wash. State Physicians Ins. Assn., Seattle. Mem. joint select com. on basic health Wash. Ho. of Reps., Olympia, 1986-87; mem. Wash. Bd. Health, 1986-88, Wash. Basic Health Commn., 1988-89. Capt. M.C., USAF, 1954-56. Recipient Disting. Alumni award Gonzaga U., 1988, Disting. Alumnus award U. Wash., 1992, Achievement in Pub. Health award Wash. Pub. Health Ofcls., 1988. Mem. AMA (del. 1980-87), Am. Occupational Med. Assn., N.W. Occupational Med. Assn. (trustee, sec. 1984-85), Am. Acad. Family Practice, Wash. Acad. Family Practice, Wash. Pub. Health Assn., Wash. Med. Assn. (past sec., v.p., pres. 1985-86), Stevens County Med. Assn. (You Made a Difference award 1987), Spokane County Med. Assn. (hon. life), Colville C. of C. (pres. 1966), Spokane Country Club, Spokane City Club, Elks (exalted ruler Colville 1964, dist. dep. 1968). Democrat. Roman Catholic. Home: 860 E Lst St Colville WA 99114 Office: NE Wash Med Group 1200 E Columbia Ave Colville WA 99114-3397

GRAY, GAVIN CAMPBELL, II, computer information engineer, consultant; b. Levittown, N.Y., Sept. 16, 1948; s. Gavin Campbell Gray and Pauline Louise (Bauerschmidt) Gowen; m. Catherine Ann West, Aug. 23, 1969; children: Jeffrey William, Tamara Pauline. Student, U. Wis., Milw., 1966-71. Programmer, analyst Equitable Variable Life Ins., Farmingdale, N.Y., 1975-77; analyst, programmer Atty.'s Title Svcs., Orlando, Fla., 1977-78; systems analyst Cert. Grocers, Ocala, Fla., 1978-80; supr. R & D, Clay Electric Coop., Keystone Heights, Fla., 1980-86; mgr. info. engring. Coldwell Banker Relocation Svcs., Mission Viejo, Calif., 1986—. Author: IBM GIS Usage for IMS/DLI, 1979; developer software Map-Paint for CICS, methodology Path Evaluation Method (PEM), TRANS-FLOW Programming, Tier Diagramming Method. Mem. Math. Assn. Am., IEEE Computer Soc., N.Y. Acad. Scis. Office: Coldwell Banker Relocation Svcs 27271 Las Ramblas Mission Viejo CA 92691

GRAY, GEORGE, III (SKIP GRAY), lawyer; b. Denver, Sept. 28, 1945; s. George W. Jr. and Juanita (Ross) G.; m. Janice Marianne Gross, June 28, 1969; children: Sean Michael, Aaron Christopher. AA, Mesa Jr. Coll., 1965; BA, Denver U., 1968, MA, 1971, JD, 1985. Bar: Colo. 1986. Jr. high tchr. Denver Pub. Schs., 1970-73; dir. work study fin. aid office Metro State Coll., Denver, 1973-77; staff aide Congl. Dist. 1, Denver, 1977-78; mgr. instl. bldgs. grants program Gov.'s Energy Office, Denver, 1978-81; sr. aide Gov.'s Office, Denver, 1981-82; driver Yellow Cab, Denver, 1983-84; law clk. Manville Corp., Denver, 1984-85; assoc. Holland & Hart, Denver, 1985-88; mng. shareholder Gray & Hahn, P.C., Denver, 1989—; Bd. dirs. Colo. Health Facilities Fin. Authority, Denver. Field staff mem. Lamm for Senate, Colo., 1992, Clinton/Gore Campaign, Colo., 1992. Recipient Vol. Svc. award Denver Pub. Sch., 1980, Excellence Leadership award Colo. Christian Home, 1981; scholar Mesa Jr. Coll., 1963, Denver Pub. Schs., 1963, Colo. Outward Bound, 1967, Sam Carey Bar Assn., 1985. Mem. Colo. Bar. Assn. Democrat. Methodist. Home: 2530 Colorado Blvd Denver CO 80207 Office: Gray & Hahn PC 303 E 17th Ave Ste 700 Denver CO 80203

GRAY, GREGORY EDWARD, physician, educator; b. L.A., Sept. 27, 1954; s. Bruce Everett Gray and Louise (Dillon) Young; m. Lorraine Kulhanek, Feb. 19, 1977; 1 child, Thomas Edward. BS, U. Calif., Davis, 1975, MS, 1976; PhD, U. So. Calif., L.A., 1980, MD, 1983. Diplomate Am. Bd. Psychiatry and Neurology. Nutritionist Cancer Ctr. U. So. Calif., L.A., 1977-79; postgrad. physician L.A. County/U. So. Calif., 1983-87; asst. prof. dept. psychiatry Sch. Medicine, U. So. Calif., 1987-91, assoc. prof., 1991—, chmn. dept. psychiatry, 1993—; chief of psychiatry L.A. County-U. So. Calif. Med. Ctr.; dir. inpatient psychiatry L.A. County-U. So. Calif. Psychiat. Hosp., 1991—; dir. Pacific Geriatric Edn. Ctr., L.A., 1989-92. Contbr. articles to profl. jours. U. Calif. fellow, 1975-76. Mem. AAAS, Assn. Acad. Psychiatrists, Alpha Omega Alpha. Office: LA County U So Calif Psychiat Hosp 1934 Hospital Pl Los Angeles CA 90033-1071

GRAY, HENRY DAVID, minister, religious organization administrator; b. Antrim, No. Ireland, Jan. 18, 1908; came to U.S., 1923; s. Nathaniel and Margaret (Lawther) G.; m. Helen Katharine Lorbeer, Aug. 12, 1930; children—Mildred Ellen, David Lawther, Betsey Charisma. B.A. magna cum laude, Pomona Coll., 1930, D.D. (hon.), 1954; M. Div. summa cum laude, Hartford Theol. Sem., 1933; Ph.D., Edinburgh U., Scotland, 1935; cert. in religious edn., Boston U., 1931; Cert. Theology, Tubingen U., 1935; D. Litt. (hon.), Piedmont Coll., 1976. Ordained minister Congregational Ch., 1935. Numerous positions Congl. Chs., worldwide, 1935—; missionary Congl. Chs., Western Samoa, 1966; dir. 300th anniversary yr. program Old South Ch., Hartford, Conn., 1969-70; minister emeritus Old South Ch., Hartford, 1970—; dir. summer student study Congl. Ch., Europe, Middle East, worldwide, 1948-70; interim minister Hollywood Congl. Ch., Calif., 1971, North Hollywood Congl. Ch., Calif., 1971-72; dean Am. Congl. Ctr., South Pasadena, Calif., 1972—; founding mem. Pasadena Coun. Chs., 1947, Nat. Coun. Chs., 1950; bd. dirs. Greater Hartford Coun. Chs., 1956-60; moderator Hampshire Assn. Congl. Christian Chs., 1938-39, L.A. Assn., 1947-48, Conn. Fellowship, 1957-61, 65, Nat. Assn., 1958-59. Author: Young People In Church Work, 1940, A Theology for Christian Youth, 1941, Words For Today, 1944, Under Orders, 1946, Science and Religion, 1946, Primacy of God, 1947, Christian Doctrine of Grace, 1948 (best full length theol. book Ind. Press, London, 1948), The Christian Marriage Service, 1950, Oneonta Guide Book, 1950, 12 edit., 1985, The Upward Call, 1952, Free Church Polity and Unity Report, 1954, Some Christian Convictions, 1955, A Bible Guide to the Holy Land, 1964, Blue Book of Congregational Usage #1, 1965, #2, 1967, Service Book, 1966, South Church Prayers, 1966, God's Torchbearers, 1970, Heart of Oak, Helm of Destiny, 1970, Hollywood Prayers, 1973, Congregational Usage, 1976, 6th edit., 1990, Congregational Worshipbook, 1978, 3d edit., 1990, Pilgrim Fathers Reach the Pacific, 1981, Soundings, 1980, Waymarks, 1983, Plus Ultra, Vol. 1, 1983, Vol. 2, 1985, The Mediators, 1984, The Souls Working Clothes, 1988, 27th edit. What it Means to be a Member of a Congregational Christian Church, 1993, Congregational Worshipbook, 1991; also 8 vols. of lectures and travelog, 1948-70; editor (monthly mag.) The Congregationalist, 1962-66, (monthly mag.) The Pilgrim Highroad, 1939-42, Congregational Jour., 1975—; contbr. numerous articles to profl. jours., also pamphlets; numerous appearances on TV and radio. Active numerous civic organizations, 1924-70; mem. Hartford City Plan Commn., 1959-70, chmn., 1962-67, 70; mem. Capitol Regional Planning Coun., 1962-67, 70, Conn. Capitol Ctr. Commn., 1966-67, 69-70; organizer Ventura City Environ. Coalition, Calif., 1971; mem. exec. com. Comprehensive Planning Commn., Ventura, Calif., 1973-77; chmn. Cultural Heritage Team, Ventura, 1974-75; pres. South Village, Hartford, 1968-84; mem. Nat. Com. for Scouting, 1939-42; former parliamentarian/vice chmn. Santa Monica Mountains Nat. Commn., Nat. Park Service; founder Congl. World Assembly of Youth, 1949. Recipient numerous awards Boy Scouts Am., Hartford Theol. Sem., Congl. Chs., citation of excellence State of Conn., 1970, Resolution of Profound Appreciation City Council Hartford, 1970, Resolution Commendation award Bd. Suprs. Ventura, 1985, letter of commendation Supt. Nat. Park Service, 1985, citation Conn. Conf. United Ch. Christ, 1985, Spl. Commendation, Internat. Congl. Council, 1987; Gray Hall named in his honor, South Pasadena, Calif., 1955, Hartford, 1960, Alexandroupolis, Greece, 1962, Gray Chapel named for him, Kuzhikode, Kerala, India, 1967, Gray Student Union named for him Lady Doak Coll., Madurai, India, 1967. Fellow Am. Acad. Religion, Royal Anthropol. Inst., Am. Anthropol. Assn.; mem. Soc. Bibl. Lit., Calif. West Congl. Assn. Chs. and Ministers (cons. polity 1984—), Nat. Assn. Congl. Christian Chs. (numerous coms., chmn. coms., offices), Clerics Club, Ventura County Hist. Soc., Calif. Hist. Soc., Nat. Hist. Soc., Am. Congl. Assn. (bd. dirs. 1965-70), United Ref. Ch. History Soc., Brit. Congl. Hist. Circle, Inst. Pacific Studies, Congl. World Assembly Youth (founder, bd. dirs. 1962, chmn. 1985), Congl. Christian Hist. Soc., Congl. Fellowship Conn. (life, exec. com.), Hartford Assn. Congl. Christian Chs. and Ministers (exec. com. 1956-60, citation 1985), Nat. Pilgrim Fellowship (founder, life counselor), Nat. Eagle Scout Assn., Calif. Acad. Scis., West Coast Theol. Club, Conn. Valley Theol. Club, Congl. Mins. Club (Scotland), Pasadena Athletic Club, Wranglers Club, Oneonta Mens Svc. Club (San Gabriel), Nat. World Wildlife Fedn., Sierra Club, Ephebian Soc., Order DeMolay (hon. chevalier), Phi Beta Kappa, Delta Sigma Rho. Republican. Home: 298 Fairfax Ave Ventura CA 93003-2118 Office: Am Congregational Ctr 298 Fairfax Ave Ventura CA 93003

GRAY, JAMES CALDWELL, insurance investigator; b. Powell, Wyo., Aug. 2, 1934; s. William John Gray and Mabel Ruth (Caldwell) Johnson; m. Diana Lynn Schopp, Dec. 27, 1967; children: Kari Lynn, Jennifer Anne, Kevin Caldwell. BA, U. Mont., 1957. CPCU. Trainee to claim mgr. supr. Safeco Ins. Co., various cities, 1965-80; sr. casualty supr. Home Ins. Co., Denver, 1980; pres. Specialized Investigations Inc., Lakewood, Colo., 1980—. Author several tng. and info. bulls. Dir. soccer program Bear Creek Jr. Sports Assn., Denver, 1980-84; pres. Bear Creek Soccer Club, Denver, 1985-87. With U.S. Army, 1957-63. Mem. Soc. CPCU, Am. Mensa Soc., Ins. Inst. Am. Home and Office: 2441 S Garland Ct Lakewood CO 80227-2224

GRAY, JAMES JOSHUA, retail information technology executive; b. Clarence, Mo., Mar. 7, 1942; s. James J. and Mary Ellen (Chinn) G.; m. Phyllis L. Gray, Aug. 19, 1967; children: Stephanie K., Kimberly S. BS in Math., U. Mo., 1970. Systems engr. NCR, Kansas City, Mo., 1970-71; data processing mgr. Dolgin's, Kansas City, Mo., 1971-78; dir. data processing Modern Merchandising, Mpls., 1978-83; v.p. Carr Gottstein, Anchorage, 1983—. Chmn. Hugh O'Brian Youth Found., Anchorage, 1992-93; dir. Jr. Achievement, Anchorage, 1992-93; advisor UAA Sch. of Bus., Anchorage, 1989-92; elections rev. bd. State of Alaska, 1992. Sgt. USMC, 1963-69. Mem. DPMA Edn. Found. (v.p. 1992). Episcopalian. Home: 6700 Spectrum Cir Anchorage AK 99576 Office: Carr Gottstein 6411 A St Anchorage AK 99516

GRAY, JAMES SAMUEL, meetings, conventions, incentive travel executive; b. Lincoln, Nebr., Aug. 15, 1936; s. Horace Woods and Pauline Lucille (Goodale) G.; m. Joan Adele Engdahl, July 31, 1955; children: Jerayne Gray-Reneberg, Jodene Gray Paris, Janell Gray Kluss. Student, U. Nebr., 1954-56, U. Colo., 1966-68. Cert. meeting profl. Regional dir. Mohawk Data Scis. Corp., L.A., 1968-77; sales mgr. Tesdata Systems Corp., L.A., 1977-82; asst. to bishop South Pacific dist. Am. Luth. Ch., Woodland Hills, Calif., 1982-87; chief exec. officer Five Star Meetings & Incentives (formerly Five Star Meeting Mgmt.), Newbury Park, Calif., 1988—. Bd. dirs. Calif. Luth. U. Ednl. Found., Thousand Oaks, Calif., 1988-90. Mem. Meeting Planners Internat. (bd. dirs. So. Calif. chpt. 1990—), Soc. Incentive Travel Execs. Office: Five Star Meeting Mgmt 1207 Knollwood Dr Newbury Park CA 91320-5519

GRAY, JAN CHARLES, lawyer; b. Des Moines, June 15, 1947; s. Charles Donald and Mary C. Gray; m. Anita Marie Ringwald, June 6, 1987; 1 child, Charles Jan. BA in Econs., U. Calif., Berkeley, 1969; MBA, Pepperdine U., 1986; JD, Harvard U., 1972. Bar: Calif. 1972, D.C. 1974, Wyo. 1992. Law clk. Kindel & Anderson, L.A., 1971-72; assoc. Halstead, Baker & Sterling, L.A., 1972-75; sr. v.p., gen. counsel and sec. Ralphs Grocery Co., L.A., 1975—; owner Am. Presidents Resorts, Custer, S.D., Glenrock, Wyo., Lakeside, Calif., Sta. KZMX, Hot Springs, S.D., Sta. KFCR, Custer, S.D.; judge pro tem L.A. Mcpl. Ct., 1977—; instr. bus. UCLA, 1976—, Pepperdine MBA Program, 1985—; arbitrator Am. Arbitration Assn., 1977—; media spokesman So. Calif. Grocers Assn., 1989—, Calif. Grocers Assn.; real estate broker, L.A., 1973—. Contbg. author: Life or Death, Who Controls?, 1976; contbr. articles to profl. jours. Trustee South Bay U. Coll. Law, 1978-79; mem. bd. visitors Southwestern U. Sch. Law, 1983—; mem. L.A. County Pvt. Industry Coun., 1982—, exec. com. 1984-88, chmn. econ. devel. task force, 1986—, chmn. mktg. com. 1991—; mem. L.A. County Martin Luther King, Jr. Gen. Hosp. Authority, 1984—; mem. L.A. County Aviation Commn, 1986-92, chmn., 1990-91; L.A. Police Crime Prevention Adv. Coun., 1986—; Angelus Plaza Adv. Bd., 1983-85; bd. dirs. RecyCAL of So. Calif., 1983-89; trustee Santa Monica Hosp. Found., 1986-91, adv. bd.,

1991—; mem. L.A. County Dem. Cen. Com., 1980-90; del. Dem. Nat. Conv., 1980. Recipient So. Calif. Grocers Assn. award for outstanding contbns. to food industry, 1982; Calif./Nev. Soft Drink Assn. appreciation award for No on 11 Campaign, 1983. Mem. ABA, Calif. Bar Assn., L.A. County Bar Assn. (exec. com. corp. law depts. sect. 1974-76, 79—, chmn. 1989-90, exec. com. barristers sect. 1974-75, 79-81, trustee 1991-93), San Fernando Valley Bar Assn. (chmn. real property sect. 1975-77, L.A. Pub. Affairs Officers Assn., L.A. World Affairs Coun., Calif. Retailers Assn. (supermarket com.), Food Mktg. Inst. (govt. rels. com., govt. affairs coun. lawyers and economists), So. Calif. Businessmen's Assn. (bd. dirs. 1981—, mem. exec. com. 1982—, sec. 1986—, chair 1991—), Town Hall L.A., U. Calif. Alumni Assn., Ephebian Soc. L.A., Harvard Club of So. Calif., Phi Beta Kappa. Home: PO Box 407 Beverly Hills CA 90213-0407 Office: PO Box 54143 Los Angeles CA 90054-0143

GRAY, KARLA MARIE, state supreme court justice. BA, Western Mich. U., MA in African History; JD, U. Calif., San Francisco, 1976. Bar: Mont. 1976, Calif. 1977. Law clk. to Hon. W. D. Murray U.S. Dist. Ct., 1976-77; staff atty. Atlantic Richfield Co., 1977-81; pvt. practice law Butte, Mont., 1981-84; staff atty., legis. lobbyist Mont. Power Co., Butte, 1984-91; judge Supreme Ct. Mont., Helena, 1991—. Mem. Mont. Supreme Ct. Gender Fairness Task Force. Fellow Am. Bar Found., Am. Judicature Soc., Supreme Ct. Hist. Soc.; mem. State Bar Mont., Silver Bow County Bar Assn. (past pres.), Nat. Assn. Women Judges. Office: Supreme Ct Mont 215 N Sanders St Helena MT 59601-4522*

GRAY, MARIE ELISE, artist; b. Bremanger, Norway, Oct. 7, 1914; came to the U.S., 1926; d. Ole Johannes and Ellen (Nielsen) Gjertsen; m. John Maeder, Dec. 22, 1940 (div. 1943); m. Sharod Hale Gray, Apr. 9, 1948. Student, Derbyshire Sch. Fine Art, Seattle, 1963, Cornish Sch. Allied Art, Seattle, 1964-65, Olympic Coll., Bremerton, Wash., 1966. Art instr. YWCA, Seattle, 1968, Univ. Womens Club, Seattle, 1973, Wash. Athletic Club, Seattle, 1975, Sand Point Golf and Country Club, Seattle, 1975-77; juror Art Assn. Co-Arts, 1986, juror selection exhbn., 1988; juror Quad A Art Club Ann. Exhbn., Seattle, 1989. One-woman show at Stillwater Gallery, Seattle, 1988; works exhibited in group shows including Co-Arts Art Assn. Exhbn., 1988 (2d pl. award), Invitational N.W. Watercolor Soc. Signature Mems. 50th Anniversary Exhibit, 1990, Arts Coun. of Snohomish County, Everett, Wash., 1990. Recipinet Edward Monet award Frye Art mus., 1967, Eugene Boudin award, 1968, Award of Excellence, Art Exhbn. of European Born Artists, 1986. Mem. N.W. Watercolor Soc. (juror 1980, 1st pl. award 1979), Nat. League Am. Penwomen (state art chmn. 1980-81, regional art chmn. 1972-73, Grumbacher award 1986), Women Painters Wash. (Honor award 1987, Meml. award 1989), Olympic Art Assn. Republican. Mem. Evangelical Ch. Home: 7723 30th Ave NE Seattle WA 98115-4721

GRAY, PATRICIA JOYCE, court administrator; b. Carlsbad, N.Mex., Feb. 5, 1951; d. Owen Corbett and Bobby Jo (Jones) G.; m. Patrick A. Edwards, Oct. 29, 1981 (div. June 1990). Student, U. Nev., Las Vegas, 1974-77. Receptionist, clk. Nationwide Fin., Las Vegas, 1969-70; dep. clk. U.S. Bankruptcy Ct. for Dist. Nev., Las Vegas, 1970-74, chief dep. clk., 1974-75, chief clk., 1975-79, clk. of ct., 1979—; Mem. bankruptcy work measurement subcom. of adminstrn. bankruptcy system Jud. Conf. U.S., 1989-91; mem. tng. and edn. com. U.S. Bankruptcy Cts. Adminstrv. Office U.S. Cts., 1990-91; mem. Bankruptcy Work Measurement subcom. of Clerk's adv. com. Adminstrv. Office U.S. Cts., 1992—, local rules subcom. Dist. Nev., 1991—. Mem. Nat. Conf. Bankruptcy Clks., Fed. Ct. Clks. Assn. Democrat. Office: US Bankruptcy Ct Foley Fed Bldg 300 Las Vegas Blvd S Las Vegas NV 89101-5812

GRAY, PAUL WESLEY, university dean; b. Cicero, Ill., Jan. 30, 1947; s. Harry B. and Audrey (Tong) G.; m. Rachel E. Boehr, June 3, 1967; children: John M., Janel E., Robert B. BA, Faith Baptist Bible Coll., Ankeny, Tex., 1970; ThM, Dallas Theol. Sem., 1975; MS in Libr. Sci., East Tex. State U., 1977, EdD, 1980; MA, Tex. Woman's U., 1989. Dorm dir. Buckner Baptist Benevolences, Dallas, 1971-75; dir. community living residence IV Dallas County Mental Health/Mental Retardation, Dallas, 1975-78; cataloger W. Walworth Harrison Pub. Libr., Greenville, Tex., 1978-81; v.p. Golden Triangle Christian Acad., Garland, Tex., 1979-83; dir. libr. LeTourneau U., Longview, Tex., 1983-88; dean computer svc. and univ. libr. Azusa (Calif.) Pacific U., 1989—. Mem. ALA, Calif. Libr. Assn., So. Calif. Area Theol. Libr. Assn., Foothill Libr. Consortium. Republican. Baptist. Office: Azusa Pacific U 901 E Alosta Ave Azusa CA 91702

GRAY, PHILIP HOWARD, psychologist, educator; b. Cape Rosier, Maine, July 4, 1926; s. Asa and Bernice (Lawrence) G.; m. Iris McKinney, Dec. 31, 1954; children: Cindelyn Gray Eberts, Howard. M.A., U. Chgo., 1958; Ph.D., U. Wash., 1960. Asst. prof. dept. psychology Mont. State U., Bozeman, 1960-65; assoc. prof. Mont. State U., 1965-75, prof., 1975-92; ret., 1992; vis. prof. U. Man., Winnipeg, Can., 1968-70; chmn. Mont. Bd. Psychologist Examiners, 1972-74; speaker sci. and geneal. meetings on ancestry of U.S. presidents. Organizer folk art exhbns. Mont. and Maine, 1972-79; author: The Comparative Analysis of Behavior, 1966, (with F.L. Ruch and N. Warren) Working with Psychology, 1963, A Directory of Eskimo Artists in Sculpture and Prints, 1974, The Science That Lost Its Mind, 1985, Penobscot Pioneers vol. 1, 1992, vol 2, 1992, vol. 3, 1993; contbr. numerous articles on behavior to psychol. jurs.; contbr. poetry to lit. jours. With U.S. Army, 1944-46. Recipient Am. and Can. research grants. Fellow AAAS, APA, Am. Psychol. Soc., Internat. Soc. Rsch. on Aggression; mem. SAR (v.p. Sourdough chpt. 1990, pres. 1991-93, trustee 1989), Nat. Geneal. Soc., New Eng. His. Geneal. Soc., Gallatin County Geneal. Soc. (charter, pres. 1991-93), Deer Isle-Stonington Hist. Soc., Internat. Soc. Human Ethology, Descs. Illegitimate Sons and Daus. of Kings of Britain, Piscataqua Pioneers, Order Desc. Colonial Psysicians and Chirugiens, Flagon and Trencher. Republican. Home: 1207 S Black Ave Bozeman MT 59715-5633

GRAY, RICHARD ARDEN, wholesale distribution executive; b. Ft. Bragg, Calif., Oct. 29, 1935; s. Arden Howard and Marion Florence (Coolidge) G.; m. Roberta Jeanne Montna, Feb. 5, 1955; children: Mark Alan, Laura Ann, Deborah Marie, Lisa Lynn. AA, Yuba Coll., 1955; BA, Calif. State U., 1957. Cert. coll. instr., Calif. Deputy sheriff Yuba County Sheriffs Dept., Marysville, Calif., 1957; traffic officer Calif. Hwy. Patrol, Ventura, 1958-60, Yuba City, 1961-68; sgt. field ops. officer Calif. Hwy. Patrol, Gardena, 1969-71; lt. exec. officer Calif. Hwy. Patrol, Van Nuys, 1972-76; lt. area comdr. Calif. Hwy. Patrol, Chico, 1977-88; wholesale, retail distbr. Dick Gray Enterprises, Chico, 1989—; instr. Yuba Coll., Marysville, 1965-67, Calif. fish and game hunter safety program, Chico, 1982-86; profl. driver, transporter motor homes, 1989—. Chmn. citizen rev. com. United Way of Butte County, Chico, 1984 (outstanding achievement 1984-86), fundraising campaign chmn. 1986, pres. bd. dirs. 1985; pres., bd. dirs. No. Calif. Counties Exch. Club Child Abuse Prevention Ctr., Chico, 1987-91. With USNR, 1953-61. Mem. Calif. Hwy. Patrolmen Assn., RV Club, Elks (honors 1988, pres. 1988-89), Breakfast Exch. Club (pres., bd. dirs. 1980-81), Exch. Club Greater Chico (sponsor 1983). Republican. Office: Dick Gray Enterprises 236A W East Ave Ste 344 Chico CA 95926

GRAY, RICHARD JEROME, dentist; b. Pomona, Calif., Oct. 25, 1961; s. Oliver Mitchell and Edwina Lou (Ernst) G.; m. Tere Lee Sims, June 25, 1990; 1 child, Alec Mitchell. AA, San Bernardino Valley, 1984; student, U. Calif., Riverside, 1984-86; DDS, U. So. Calif., 1986-90. Missionary LDS Ch., Nauvoo, Ill., 1982-84; resident in gen. practice dentistry USN, Camp Pendleton, Calif., 1990-91, dentist, 1992—; dentist pvt. practice, Fountain Hills, Calif., 1992—. Lt. USN, 1988-92. Mem. ADA, Acad. Gen. Dentistry, Ariz. State Dental Assn., Calif. Dental Assn., San Diego County Dental Soc. Republican. Mem. LDS Ch. Home: 16402 E Ashbrook Dr Fountain Hills AZ 85268 Office: Fountain Hills Family Dentistry 13715 Fountain Hills Blvd Ste 111 Fountain Hills AZ 85268

GRAY, RICHARD MOSS, retired college president; b. Washington, Jan. 25, 1924; s. Wilbur Leslie and Betty Marie (Grey) G.; m. Catherine Claire Hammond, Oct. 17, 1943; children: Janice Lynn Gray Armstrong, Nancy Hammond Gray Schultz. BA, Bucknell U., 1942; MDiv summa cum laude, San Francisco Theol. Sem., 1961; PhD, U. Calif., Berkeley, 1972; doctorate degree (hon.), World Coll. West, 1988. Writer, creative dir. N.W. Ayer & Son, Phila., 1942-58; univ. pastor Portland State U., Oreg., 1961-68; founder, pres. World Coll. West, Petaluma, Calif., 1973-88, pres. emeritus, 1988—; bd. dirs. World Centre, San Francisco, Lifeplan Ctr.; bd. chair Presidio World Coll. Author poetry Advent, 1989. Bd. dirs. Citizens Found. Marin, San Rafael, Calif., 1988—, Marin Ednl. Found., 1989-92; chmn. bd. dirs. Presidio World Coll., 1993—; ruling edler Presbyn. Ch. (U.S.A.). Named Disting. Alumnus of Yr. San Theol. Sem., 1988, Marin Citizen of Yr. Citizens Found., 1988; recipient Svc. to Humanity award Bucknell U., 1992. Mem. Phi Beta Kappa.

GRAY, ROBERT DONALD, electrical engineer; b. Quincy, Ill., May 6, 1924; s. James Arthur and Katherine Elnora (Moore) G.; m. Marie Dolores Albert, July 15, 1951; children: Michael S., Sheilah C. (Gray) Robinson. Student, Washington & Jefferson Coll., 1945-47; BSEE, Okla. State U., 1949; MBA, Northwestern U., Evanston, Ill., 1972. Electrolysis engr. Sinclair Refining Co., 1949-50; North Atlantic field mgr. navigation/communication systems USAF, 1950-51; cons. Lockheed Aircraft Ga. Co., 1951-52; sr. devel. engr. Harris Corp., 1952-54; dir. Gen. Telephone Electronics, Mountain View, Calif., 1954-66; dir. reliability and quality control Gen. Dynamics/Electronics, Rochester, N.Y., 1961-62; v.p. rsch./devel. Lockheed Missiles/Space Co., Sunnyvale, Calif., 1966-79; pres. Gray Assocs., Internat. Air Traffic Control System, Los Altos, Calif., 1980—. With USN, 1941-45; ETO. Mem. IEEE (sr.), Los Altos Golf and Country Clu, Phi Kappa Psi. Republican. Home: 270 Valencia Dr Los Altos CA 94022-2258

GRAY, ROBERT MOLTEN, electrical engineering educator; b. San Diego, Nov. 1, 1943; s. Augustine Heard and Elizabeth DuBois (Jordan) G.; m. Arlene Frances Ericson; children: Timothy M., Lori A. BS, MIT, 1966, MS, 1966; PhD, U. So. Calif., 1969. Elec. engr. U.S. Naval Ordinance Lab., White Oak, Md., 1963-65, Jet Propulsion Lab., Pasadena, Calif., summers 1966, 67; asst. prof. elec. engring. Stanford (Calif.) U., 1969-75, assoc. prof., 1975-80, prof., 1980—, dir. Info. Systems Lab., 1984-87. Author: Probability, Random Processes and Ergodic Properties, 1988, Source Coding Theory, 1990, Entropy and Information Theory, 1990; co-author: Random Processes, 1986, Vector Quantization and Signal Compression, 1992; assoc. editor Math. of Control and System Sci. jour., 1987—; contbr. articles to profl. jours. Fireman La Honda (Calif.) Vol. Fire Brigade, 1970-80, pres., 1971-72; coach Am. Youth Soccer Orgn., La Honda, 1971-78, commr., 1976-78. Japan Soc. for Promotion Sci. fellow, 1981, Guggenheim fellow, 1982, NATO/CNR fellow, 1990. Fellow IEEE (Centennial medal 1984), Inst. Math. Stats.; mem. Info. Theory Soc. IEEE (assoc. editor Trans. 1977-80, editor in chief 1980-83, paper prize 1976), Signal Processing Soc. IEEE (sr. award 1983), Soc. des Ingenieurs et Scientifiques de France. Home: PO Box 160 La Honda CA 94020-0160 Office: Stanford U Dept Elec Engring Stanford CA 94305

GRAY, RONALD D., career officer; b. Dallas, Mar. 31, 1942; s. Jay Olin And Dorothy Josephine (Furlow) G.; m. Patricia Leslie Roberts, June 16, 1964; children: John R., Jennifer N., Jeremy D. BA, Tex. A&M U., 1964; MS, U. So. Calif., L.A., 1973. Commd. 2d lt. USAF, 1964, advanced through grades to brig. gen., 1989; contract maintenance officer 351st Strategic Missile Wing, Whiteman AFB, Mo., 1964-65, missile launch officer, 1966-67; airborne missile launch officer 91st Strategic Missile Wing, Minot AFB, N.D., 1967-70; missile tng. officer 4315th Combat Crew Tng. Squadron, Vandenberg AFB, Calif., 1970-72, Hdqrs. SAC, Offutt AFB, Nebr., 1972-76; missile maintenance officer 381st Strategic Missile Wing, McConnell AFB, Mo., 1976-84; space ops. staff officer Hdqrs. Air Force Space Command, Peterson AFB, Colo., 1985-87, dep. chief of staff, ops., 1989—; wing comdr. 1st Space Wing, Peterson AFB, Colo., 1987-89. Mem. Air Force Assn., Former Students Assn. Tex. A&M U. Republican. Office: AFSPACECOM 21st Space Wing Peterson AFB Colorado Springs CO 80914-1290

GRAY, RONALD FREDERICK, college administrator, engineer; b. Salina, Kans., Feb. 12, 1944; s. Roland Arlington and Dorothy Lavera (Beals) G.; m. Sharon Ann Reich, June 8, 1968; 1 child Darren Scott Gray. BSME, S.D. Sch. of Mones and Tech., Rapid City, 1966. Profl. Engr.- Mech. Sr. engr. The Boeing Co., Seattle, 1966-71; product test engr. Ford Motor Co., Dearborn, Mich., 1972-73; sr. engr. The Boeing Co., Seattle, 1973-74; dir. phys. plant S.D. Sch. of Mines and Tech., Rapid City, S.D., 1974-88, Mesa State Coll., Grand Junction, Colo., 1988—. Me. Assn. of Phys. Plant Adminstrs. Office: Mesa State Coll 1175 Texas Ave Grand Junction CO 81501-7682

GRAY, RONALD LOREN, lawyer; b. Salem, Oreg., June 15, 1964; s. Harley Loren and Lenora (Keopplin) G.; m. Leta Irene Cardiello, July 29, 1978; children: Justin Henry, Brandon Charles. BS, So. Oreg. State U., Ashland, 1976; JD, Willamette U., 1979. Bar: Oreg. 1979, U.S. Dist. Ct. Oreg. 1979. Ptnr. Cotton & Gray, Oregon City, 1979-88; pvt. practice Gladstone, Oreg., 1988—; arbitrator Clackamas & Multnomah County Cts., Portland and Oregon City, 1985—; pro tem dist. ct. judge State of Oreg., Salem, 1987-91; mcpl. judge City of Milwaukee, Oreg., 1988—; judge pro tem City of Oregon, City of Sandy, City of West Linn; bd. dirs., adminstr. Clackamas Indigent Def. Corp., Gladstone,1985—. Mem. Indigent Def. Task Force, Salem, 1989—; pro bono lawyer Oreg. Legal Svcs., Oregon City, 1988—; chmn. bd. Theft Talk Counseling Svc., Portland, 1988-91. Mem. Oreg. Bar Assn. (Pub. Svc. Merit award 1990), Oreg. Trial Lawyers Assn., Oreg. Criminal Def. Lawyers Assn. Office: 15-82d Dr Ste 201 Gladstone OR 97027

GRAY, VERNE ALLEN, real estate investment company executive; b. Denver, Feb. 25, 1943; s. Verne Richard and Aileen Ethel (Cline) G.; m. Nancy Lewis Ebert, June 19, 1982. BA in History, U. Colo., 1965; MLS, U. Wash., 1977. Intelligence analyst Nat. Security Agy., Ft. Meade, Md., 1965-75; ptnr. Pt. Clear Co., Mobile, Ala., 1977-80; gen. mgr. Harvey Canal, Land and Improvement Co., New Orleans, 1980-87; cons. Old Stone Bank, Bellevue, Wash., 1987; trust real estate officer Security Pacific Bank, Seattle, 1988-90; exec. v.p. Lakeshore Investment Corp., Edmonds, Wash., 1990—. Mem. Inst. of Real Estate Mgmt., York Rite Coll., Walter F. Meier Coun. (master 1990-91). Republican. Episcopalian. Home: 480 Mt Olympus Dr Issaquah WA 98027 Office: Lakeshore Investment Corp PO Box 338 Edmonds WA 98020

GRAY, WALTER P., III, museum director, consultant; b. San Francisco, Aug. 8, 1952; s. Walter Patton II and Elsie Josephine (Stroop) G.; m. Mary Amanda Helmich, May 23, 1980. BA in History, Calif. State U., Sacramento, 1976. Rschr. Calif. State R.R. Mus., Sacramento, 1977-80, curator, 1980-81, 85-90, archivist, 1981-85, dir., 1990—; cons. in field, 1976—. Contbr. articles to profl. jours. Democrat. Buddhist. Office: California State Railroad Museum 111 I St Sacramento CA 95814

GRAYBEAL, LYNNE ELIZABETH, lawyer; b. Seattle, May 21, 1956; d. John Olin and Janie Marie (Everly) G.; m. Scott Harron, Oct. 7, 1989. Student, Pomona Coll., 1974-76; BA, Colby Coll., 1979; JD, U. Puget Sound, 1983. Bar: Wash. 1983, U.S. Dist. Ct. (we. dist.) Wash. 1983. Rsch. asst. Charles River Assocs., Boston, 1979-80; assoc. Bogle & Gates, Seattle, summer 1982, 83-85; assoc. Monroe, Stokes, Eitelbach & Lawrence, P.S., Seattle, 1986-89, prin., 1990-92; ptnr. Riddell, Williams, Bullitt & Walkinshaw, 1992—. Sec. Bathhouse Theatre, 1984-86, v.p., 1987; bd. dirs. Wash. Vol. Lawyers for ARts, 1985-89; v.p., bd. dirs. Seattle Found. for Motion Picture ARts, 1988-89. Mem. ABA (chmn. unfair competition trade identity subcom. 1987-88), Wash. State Bar Assn. (chmn. intellectual and indsl. property sect. 1988-89), Wash. State Patent Law Assn., Wash. Women Lawyers (treas. 1989-91, pres. 1992), Greater Seattle C. of C. (curriculum com. 1989-91, Leadership Tomorrow class 1988-89). Home: 2215-2d Ave N 3037 38th W Seattle WA 98199 Office: Riddell Williams et al Ste # 4400 1001 4th Ave Plz Seattle WA 98154

GRAYBILL, DAVID WESLEY, chamber of commerce executive; b. Council Bluffs, Iowa, Apr. 8, 1949; s. John Donald and Dorothy Lorraine (King) G.; m. Kortney Loraine Steinbeck, Aug. 17, 1974; 1 child, Darcy Lorraine. BA in Journalism, U. Iowa, 1971. Cert. econ. developer, Chamber exec. Adminstrv. asst. Iowa City C. of C., 1972-74; exec. v.p. Brighton (Colo.) C. of C., 1974-77; pres. Fremont (Nebr.) C. of C., 1977-83; pres., chief exec. officer Tacoma-Pierce County C. of C., 1983—; pres. Nebr. C. of C. Execs., 1981-82; treas. NE Nebr. Econ. Devel. Dist., 1980-83. Charter mem. Gov.'s Small Bus. Improvement Com., Wash., 1984-86; presiding elder Tacoma (Wash.) Reorganized LDS Ch. Mem. Am. Econ. Devel. Coun. (bd. dirs. 1985-87), Am. C. of C. (bd. dirs. 1990—), Wash. C. of C. Execs. (pres. 1988-89, bd. dirs. 1988-90), Rotary (bd. dirs. Tacoma 1985-87). Office: Tacoma-Pierce County C of C PO Box 1933 Tacoma WA 98401-1933

GRAYSON, ELLISON CAPERS, JR., human resources executive; b. St. Paul, Sept. 7, 1928; s. Ellison Capers and Inez (Santos) G.; m. Jean Mason, Dec. 26, 1953; children: Darby, William. BA, U. Minn., 1950; LHD (hon.), Nat. U., San Diego, 1984. CLU. Gen. agt. Home Life Ins. Co. N.Y., San Francisco, 1955-81; prin. dep., asst. sec. USN, Washington, 1981-84; dir. mktg. and devel. Pvt. Sector Coun., 1985; cons. Washington, 1985-86; sr. v.p. Boyden Internat., San Francisco, 1987-90; dir. Spencer Stuart, San Francisco, 1990—; bd. dirs. StellarNet, Inc., San Francisco; advisory bd. Clark/Bardes, Inc., Dallas. Commr. City and County of San Francisco, 1978-81; pres. bd. dirs. St. Mary's Hosp. and Med. Ctr., San Francisco, 1972-75; co-chmn. nat. finance com. Bush for Pres; bd. regents St. Ignatius Coll. Preparatory, San Francisco. Capt. USN, 1952-55. Named Eagle Scout Boy Scouts Am., 1944; recipient Nat. Brotherhood award Nat. Assn. Christians and Jews, San Diego, 1984. Mem. Sovereign Mil. (knight 1978), Order of St. John of Jerusalem, Knights of Malta, Bohemian Club, Met. Club (Washington), Villa Taverna (San Francisco), St. Francis Yacht Club, Army Navy Club. Republican. Roman Catholic. Home: 95 Sea Cliff Ave San Francisco CA 94121-1122 Office: Spencer Stuart 333 Bush St San Francisco CA 94104-2806

GRAYSON, JOHN WESLEY, business consultant, computer science educator; b. N.Y.C., Sept. 7, 1941; s. Roger Henry and Dorothy Mae (Kenny) G.; children: John Wesley Jr., Carleton Avery. MA, SUNY-Stony Brook, 1974; postgrad. U. West L.A. Sch. Law, 1979. Programmer, Data Stats., Inc., N.Y.C., 1961-62; sr. programmer Computech, Inc., N.Y.C., 1962-65; systems analyst Nat. Shoes, Inc., Bronx, N.Y., 1965-68; sr. systems analyst Acad. Press, Inc., N.Y.C., 1968-69; sr. systems cons. Grumman Aerospace Corp., 1969-71; sr. mgmt. cons. FRB, N.Y.C., 1971-72; coll. lectr., mgr. mgmt. info. systems SUNY-Stony Brook, 1972-76; communications cons. Gen. Telephone Calif., L.A., 1976-79; owner, pres. Bus. Cons. Firm, Glendale, Calif., 1980; lectr. Compton (Calif.) Community Coll., Long Beach City Coll., El Camino Coll., SUNY-Stony Brook; instr. Long Beach City Coll. Treas., Sunset Baseball Little League, Redondo Beach, Calif.; pres. 147th Bd. Election Dist. Insps., N.Y.; trustee Middle Island (N.Y.) Pub. Library; SBA pres. U. West L.A. Sch. Law, 1979; com. examiner Glendale (Calif.) Unified Sch. Dist.; mem. usher bd., lay eucharistic min. St. Luke's Episcopal Ch.; scoutmaster Cub Scouts Am., St. James, N.Y.; mem. West High Sch. Band Assn., Torrance, Calif., West High Sch. PTA. Mem. Data Processing Mgmt. Assn., Assn. Systems Mgmt., ACM (treas.). Republican. Clubs: Suffolk County Republican (Brook Haven, N.Y.); Pioneer Track (N.Y.); Los Verdes Men's Golf; Masons, Shriners. Home and Office: PO Box 4975 Compton CA 90224-4975

GRAZIANO, JOSEPH A., computer company executive; b. 1945. CPA, Merrimack Coll. With Ernst & Whinney, Boston, Rolm Corp., 1976-81; CFO Apple Computer, Inc., Cupertino, Calif., 1981-85, 89—, also exec. v.p.; CFO, v.p. finance Sun Microsystems, Inc., 1987-89. Office: Apple Computer Inc 20525 Mariani Ave Cupertino CA 95014-6201

GRAZIOLI, ALBERT JOHN, JR., real estate developer; b. Honolulu, Jan. 24, 1954; s. Albert John and Kathryn (DeVane) G.; m. Caroline Ann Wilson, Aug. 29, 1981. BA, Rice U., 1976. Sales cons. Coldwell Banker Comml. Real Estate, L.A., 1980-85, sr. sales mgr., 1985-87; v.p. devel. The Koll Co., L.A., 1987-90; project dir. Gentel Corp., Pasadena, Calif., 1990-91; pres. Grazioli Devel. Co., Pasadena, 1991—. Mem. Jonathan Club (chmn. jr. com., community rels. com., entertainment com., membership com., audit & fin. com.). Republican. Office: Grazioli Devel Co 1121 Charles St Pasadena CA 91103

GREANIAS, THOMAS GEORGE, writer, producer; b. Chgo., Feb. 19, 1965; s. George Thomas and Kiki (Koutsoumbis) G.; m. Laura Joan Stonhouse, July 16, 1988. BS in Journalism, Northwestern U., 1987, MS in Journalism, 1987. Mgr. corp. comm. Ameritech Corp., Chgo., 1987-90; pres. Thomas G. Greanias Prodns., West Hollywood, Calif., 1991—.

GREAT, DON CHARLES, music company executive, composer; b. Medford, Oreg., Mar. 11, 1951; s. Donald Charles Sr. and Anna Marie (Huff) G.; m. Andrea Louise Gerber, Oct. 31, 1970. Student, UCLA, 1975-76, 83-86, Dick Grove Sch. Music, 1983-87. Freelance songwriter Metro-Goldwyn-Mayer Records, 20th Century Records, Bell Records, Los Angeles, 1968—; pres. Don Great Music, Inc., Los Angeles, 1972—. Composer music for TV shows including Who's the Boss? (ABC), 227 (NBC), The Jeffersons (CBS), Gimme a Break (NBC), A Different World (NBC), Fact of Life (NBC), Unsolved Mysteries (NBC), Amen (NBC), Freddies Nightmares (Lorimar-Warner Bros. TV), Saved By the Bell (NBC Disney), One Day at a Time (CBS), Married With Children (Fox/Columbia Pictures), Small Wonder (Fox TV), 1978—, Different Strokes (NBC), BJ and the Bear (NBC), Silverspoons (NBC), Sheriff Lobo (NBC), Incredible Hulk (CBS), Sanford (NBC), Real People (NBC), Crimetime After primetime (CBS), Candid Camera, Tales From the Crypt, In Living Color (Fox-TV). Mem. Broadcast Music, Inc. (Best Music Score of Yr. award 1986, named TV Composer of Yr. 1986).

GREAVER, HARRY, artist; b. L.A., Oct. 30, 1929; s. Harry Jones and Lucy Catherine (Coons) G.; m. Hanne Synnestvedt Nielsen, Nov. 30, 1955; children—Peter, Paul, Lotte. BFA, U. Kans., 1951, MFA, 1952. Assoc. prof. art U. Maine, Orono, 1955-66; exec. dir. Kalamazoo Inst. Arts, 1966-78; dir. Greaver Gallery, Cannon Beach, Oreg., 1978—; mem. visual com. Mich. Coun. Arts, 1976-78. One-man exhbns. include Baker U., Baldwin, Kans., 1955, U. Maine, Orono, 1958, 59, Pacific U., 1985; group exhbns. include U. Utah Mus. Fine Arts, 1972-73, Purdue U., 1977, Drawings/U.S.A, St. Paul, 1963, San Diego Mus., 1971, Rathbun Gallery, Portland, Oreg., 1988; 10-yr. print retrospective Cannon Beach Arts Assn., 1989. Mem. adv. bd. Haystack Ctr. for the Arts, Cannon Beach, 1988-91. Recipient Purchase award Nat. Endowment Arts, 1971; grantee U. Maine, 1962-64. Mem. Cannon Beach Arts Assn., 1986-88. Address: PO Box 120 Cannon Beach OR 97110

GREBER, ROBERT MARTIN, entertainment company executive; b. Phila., Mar. 15, 1938; s. Joseph and Golda (Rubin) G.; m. Judith Ann Pearlstein, Dec. 23, 1962; children: Matthew, Jonathan. B.S. in Fin., Temple U., 1962; grad., Sch. Mgmt. and Strategic Studies, 1982-84. Account exec. Merrill Lynch, Phila., 1962-68; portfolio mgr. v.p. Afuture Funds Inc., Lima, Pa., 1968-70; instl. account exec. Merrill Lynch, Phila., 1970-75; officer, mgr.-v.p. Merrill Lynch, Los Angeles, 1975-79; chief fin. officer Lucasfilm Ltd., Los Angeles, 1979-80; pres., chief exec. officer Lucasfilm Ltd., San Rafael, Calif., 1980-84, Diagnostic Networks, Inc., San Francisco, 1984-87; ptnr. Leon A. Farley Assocs., San Francisco, 1988—; co-chmn. Planet Film Co., San Francisco, 1988—. Bd. dirs. KQED Pub. Broadcasting System, San Francisco, 1983, chmn. bd. 1988; bd. dirs. Film Inst. No. Calif., Marin Symphony Orch., 1981-83; trustee Western Behavior Scis. Inst., La Jolla, 1982—. Served with Army N.G., 1959-60.

GRECO, THOMAS HENRY, JR., economics consultant, writer; b. Rochester, N.Y., Oct. 9, 1936; s. Thomas Henry and Mary Pauline (Carr) G.; m. Rosemary Claire Murray, June 20, 1964 (div. 1977); children: Thomas Andrew, Paul Murray. B in Chem. Engring., Villanova U., 1958; MBA, U. Rochester, 1966; postgrad., Syracuse U., 1973-74. Engr. Douglas Aircraft Co., El Segundo, Calif., 1958-60, Bell Aerosystems Co., Buffalo, 1960-63; faculty mem. Rochester Inst. Tech., 1965-79; cons. Rochester, Tucson, 1979—; organizer 4th World Assembly, San Francisco, 1987. Author: Money & Debt, 1989; author, pub.: Free Lance Directory, 1980; inventor, pub. Numerian Population Simulator, 1979; contbr. articles to profl. jours. Mem. Sonoran Bioregion GREENS, Tucson, 1989—; mem. adv. bd. Tucson Coun. on Econ. Conversion, 1990—; dir. Community Info. Resource Ctr., Tucson, 1991—; organizer Bldg. Alternatives for the Local Economy, Tucson, 1992. Mem. NEST, Inc. (treas. 1991—), Sch. Living (pres. 1987-90, editor GREEN REVOLUTION 1988—), Action Linkage. Office: PO Box 42663 Tucson AZ 85733

GREELEY, ROBERT CHARLES, finance consultant; b. Coeur d'Alene, Idaho, July 27, 1948; s. Gerald William and Letha Mae Greeley; m. Celeste Marie Meyer, May 17, 1980. BS in Fin., U. Idaho, 1970; MBA, Golden Gate U., 1983. Comml. lending officer Wells Fargo Bank, San Francisco, 1970-76, asst. v.p., 1976-83; prin. Greeley Cons. Group, Sacramento, 1983—; mem. fin. faculty Calif. State U., Sacramento, 1985; adj. prof. fin. Golden Gate U., Sacramento, 1985—; CFO Calif. Psychol. Health Plan, L.A., 1985-90. Mem. Am. Mktg. Assn. (chpt. pres. 1985-86, Highest Achievement award 1986-87), No. Calif. Comml. Fin. Assn., Sales and Mktg. Execs. (sec.-treas. Sacramento chpt. 1990-91), Sacramento C. of C. (mem. small bus. adv. com. 1991—), Commonwealth Club Calif., Alpha Kappa Psi. Office: Greeley Cons Group 1010 Hurley Way Ste 205 Sacramento CA 95825

GREELEY, RONALD, geology educator; b. Columbus, Ohio, Aug. 25, 1939; s. Edward T. and Elizabeth J. (Graf) G.; m. Cynthia Ray Moody, Aug. 28, 1960; 1 child, Randal Robert. BS in Geology, Miss. State U., 1962, MS in Geology, 1963; PhD in Geology, U. Mo., Rolla, 1966. Instr. geology U. Mo., 1965-66; geologist Chevron Oil Co., Lafayette, La., 1966-67; rsch. scientist NASA-Ames Rsch. Ctr., Moffett Field, Calif., 1967-69, postdoctoral rsch. assoc., 1969-71; rsch. assoc. physics dept. U. Santa Clara, Moffett Field, 1971-77; prof. geology and Ctr. for Meteorite Studies, Ariz. State U., Tempe, 1977—, chmn. dept., 1986-90. Author: (with Iversen) Wind as a Geological Process: Earth, Mars, Venus and Titan, 1986; Planetary Landscapes, 1987; editor: (with Batson) Planetary Mapping, 1990. Capt. U.S. Army, 1967-69. Recipient Pub. Svc. medal NASA, 1977; Grad. Coll. Disting. Rsch. award Ariz. State U., 1982, Outstanding Mentor Grad. Students, 1988. Fellow Geol. Soc. Am. (chmn. planetary geology div.); mem. Am. Geophys. Union, Meteoritical Soc. Office: Ariz State U Dept Geology Tempe AZ 85287-1404

GREEN, ALLAN WRIGHT, winery owner; b. L.A., May 24, 1949; s. Aaron Gus and Jean Carol (Haber) G. BA in Art, UCLA, 1971, MA in Design, 1974. Winery owner/operator Greenwood Ridge Vineyards, Philo, Calif., 1980—. Mem. Anderson Valley Winegrowers Assn. (pres. 1991—). Democrat.

GREEN, BRIAN GERALD, marketing executive; b. Missoula, Mont., Sept. 5, 1954; s. Gerald Jay and Ruth Anne (Althaus) G.; m. Robin Lee McIntyre, May 10, 1980; 1 child, Sean Brian. ASEE, Clark Coll., 1976; BS in Electronics Engring. Tech., Oreg. Inst. Tech., Klamath Falls, 1978; MBA, U. Hartford, 1988. Cert. electronic technician. Field engr. Triad Systems Corp., Hartford, Conn., 1978-79; midwest regional mgr. Triad Systems Corp., Chgo., 1979-81; Northwest regional mgr. Triad Systems Corp., Portland, Oreg., 1981-83; northeast area mgr. Triad Systems Corp., Bristol, Conn., 1983-88, Canadian svc. mgr., 1987-88; western area mgr. Triad Systems Corp., Tracy, Calif., 1988-89; world wide svc. mgr. Sysgen, Inc., Milpitas, Calif., 1989-91; svc. mktg. mgr. Sony Corp. Am., San Jose, 1991-93; self employed cons., 1993—. Mem. Assn. for Svcs. Mgmt. Internat., Masons (Southington, Conn. and Vancouver, Wash. chpts.), Scottish Rite (Hartford), Sphinx Shrine (Hartford). Republican. Methodist. Home: 12140 Carnegie Dr Tracy CA 95376-9149

GREEN, CHARLOTTE KIMBALL, educator; b. Charlotte, N.C., July 28, 1940; d. Stephen Frye and Elizabeth (Chevalier) Kimball; m. John Rogers Green, Oct. 3, 1989. BA, U. Mass., 1962; MS, Calif. Luth. U., 1977. Elem. classroom tchr. L.A. Unified Sch. Dist., 1962-72, curriculum enrichment tchr., 1972-73, regional reading specialist, 1973-76, tchr. adviser-reading & lang. arts, 1976-79, spl. edn. tchr., 1979-92; retired, 1992; grad. instr. reading disabilities Calif. Luth. U., Thousand Oaks, Calif., 1980-85; co-founder, co-dir., instr. Ctr. for Reading & Learning Disabilities, Reseda, Calif., 1977-84; in-svc. class leader L.A. Unified Sch. Dist., 1974-79; panel mem. Instrnl. Materials Evaluation-Reading & Lang. Arts, Calif. State Bd. Edn., 1976-77; observation-participation supervising tchr. Calif. State U.-Northridge, 1991; tech. skills com. mem. L.A. Unified Sch. Dist., 1978; workshop leader L.A. County Literacy Conf., Pasadena, 1979; presenter in field. Religious edn. tchr. various chs., 1964-88; religious instrn. vol. Colston Correctional Instn., Ventura, Calif., 1986-89; mem. ACT adv. com. on tech. edn. Calif. Luth. U., Thousand Oaks, 1987-89; mem. sch. edn. community adv. coun. Calif. State U. L.A., 1987-92. Mem. NEA, Calif. Tchrs. Assn., United Tchrs. L.A. Republican. Home: PO Box 1086 Coeur D Alene ID 83816

GREEN, CYRIL KENNETH, retail company executive; b. Portland, Oreg., June 11, 1931; s. Lionel and Nora Evelyn (Walker) G.; m. Beverly Ann Hutchinson, July 24, 1950; children: Kenneth James, Teri Ann, Tamara Jo Green Easton, Kelly Denise Green Van Horn. Student pub. schs., Portland. Salesperson Fred Meyer Inc., Portland, Oreg., 1947-53, mgr. food dept., 1953-57, supr. food div., 1957-60, buyer food div., 1960-64, head buyer food div., 1964-67; gen. mgr. Roundup Co. subs. Fred Meyer Inc., Spokane, Wash., 1967-70; dir. ops. Fred Meyer Inc., Portland, Oreg., 1970-72, pres., 1972—, chief operating officer, from 1972; vice chmn., bd. dirs. Oreg. Trail chpt. ARC, Portland, 1984-89; bd. dirs. Marylhurst Coll., Portland, 1987—. Office: Fred Meyer Inc 3800 SE 22nd Ave PO Box 42121 Portland OR 97242*

GREEN, DANIEL FRED, forester; b. Seattle, Feb. 28, 1947; s. Fred Davis and Rowena Anne (Pratt) G.; m. Janice Marie Bachman, Sept. 9, 1967 (div. 1979); children: Kelly Colleen, Wendy Alicia; m. Susan Dell Plaisance, Dec. 28, 1984. BS in Forest Mgmt., Oreg. State U., 1969; MS in Forest Sci., U. Idaho, 1976. Forester Oreg. State Forestry Dept., Forest Grove, 1971-73; Millicoma area forester Oreg. State Forestry Dept., Coos Bay, 1973-76; assoc. prof., extension agt. Oreg. State U., Oregon City, 1976-84; owner Green Tree Farm, Oregon City, 1976—; v.p. Woodland Mgmt. Inc., Lake Oswego, Oreg., 1984—; vis. prof. Tech. Inst. of Costa Rica, Cartago, 1984. Vol., host Experiment in Internat. Living, Oregon City, 1986-93; pres. Environ. Learning Ctr., Oregon City, 1978, Environ. Edn. Assn. of Oregn., 1979; chmn. natural resources com. Ptnrs. of the Americas, Oreg. and Costa Rica, 1990-93. Mem. Soc. Am. Foresters (chmn. Portland chpt. 1980), Clackamas County Farm Forestry Assn. (pres. 1986-88). Republican. Office: Woodland Mgmt Inc 5285 Meadows Rd Ste 282 Lake Oswego OR 97035-3228

GREEN, DAVID OLIVER, JR., sculptor, designer; b. Enid, Okla., June 29, 1908; s. David Oliver Green and Ina (Christmas) McBride; m. Jaxine Rhodes Green, Aug. 20, 1929 (dec. Dec. 1983); m. Lilian Stone DeLey, Mar. 15, 1986 (dec. May 1986). Student, Am. Acad. Art, Chgo., 1926, Nat. Acad. Art, 1927. Letterer Nat. Playhouses, Chgo., 1925-30; with lettering/layout Chgo. Herald-Examiner, Chgo., 1931-32; freelance designer London Guarantee Bldg., Chgo., 1932-33; layout artist Charles Daniel Frey Advt., Chgo., 1933-36; package designer Sears Roebuck, Chgo., 1936-37; art dir. advt. Mills Industries, Chgo., 1947-40; prodn. illustrator McDonald Douglas Aircraft, Long Beach, Calif., 1940-42; draftsman Calif. Inst. Tech., Pasadena, Calif., 1943-45; prof. sculpture Otis Art Inst., L.A., 1946-69; Prin. works include Altadena Libr. Bldg., Calif., Lytton Savs. and Loan, Hollywood, Calif.; author: La Partida/The Contest, 1957. Recipient Golden Crown award Pasadena Arts Coun., 1984. Mem. Pasadena Soc. Artists, Soc. for Calligraphy, Pasadena Photochrome Soc. Home and Studio: 176 Jaxine Dr Altadena CA 91001

GREEN, DOROTHY SELMA, environmental volunteer; b. Detroit, Mar. 16, 1929; d. David M. and Helen (Beckwitt) Cohen; m. Jacob (Jack) Isak Green, Aug. 26, 1951; children: Avrom, Hershel, Joshua. BA, U. Calif., Berkeley, 1951. Mem. Environ. Water Leadership Coun.; mem. exec. com., treas. Pub. Ofls. for Water and Environ. Reform, 1991—; commr. L.A. Bd. Water and Power Commrs.; founder, pres. Heal the Bay, L.A., 1985-91; bd. dirs. Planning and Conservation League, 1978—, Westside Urban Forum, 1990—, Calif. League of Conservation Voters, 1975-89, Calif. for Nuclear Safeguards, 1975-76; mem. steering com. Women For, 1972-84; active state and nat. gov. bds. Common Cause, 1973-84, others. Recipient Citation Exceptional Children's Found., 1973, First Annual award Calif. League of Conservation Voters, 1983, Sierra Club L.A. chpt. spl. award, 1987, Superhealer award, Heal the Bay, 1987, Mount Gay Coll. award, 1990; Mayor's Cert. Appreciation, L.A., 1990, Cert. of Tribute, L.A. City Coun., 1991, Citation, County of L.A., 1991, LULU award L.A. Advt. Women, 1992. Democrat. Jewish. Office: Heal The Bay 1640 5th St Ste 112 Santa Monica CA 90401

GREEN, FRANCIS J., retired bishop; b. Corning, N.Y., July 7, 1906. Ordained priest Roman Cath. Ch., 1932; ordained titular bishop of Serra and aux. bishop of Tucson, 1953; named coadjutor Tucson with right of succession, 1960. Bishop Roman Cath. Ch., Tucson, 1960-1981. Address: Ret Bishop of Tucson PO Box 31 192 S Stone Ave Tucson AZ 85702

GREEN, FRANCIS WILLIAM, investment consultant; b. Locust Grove, Okla., Mar. 17, 1920; s. Noel Francis and Mary (Lincoln) G.; B.S., Phoenix U., 1955; M.S. in Elec. Engring., Minerva U., Milan, Italy, 1959; M.S. in Engring., West Coast U., Los Angeles, 1965; m. Alma J. Ellison, Aug. 26, 1950 (dec. Sept. 1970); children—Sharmon, Rhonda; m. Susan G. Mathis, July 14, 1973 (div. July 1979). With USN Guided Missile Program, 1945-49; design and electronic project engr. Falcon missile program Hughes Aircraft Co., Culver City, Calif., 1949-55; sr. electronic engr. Atlas missile program Convair Astronautics, San Diego, 1955-59; sr. engr. Polaris missile program Nortronics div. Northrop, Anaheim, Calif., 1959-60; chief, supr. electronic engr. data systems br. Tech. Support div. Rocket Propulsion Lab., USAF, Edwards AFB, Calif., 1960-67, dep. chief tech. support div., 1967-69; tech. adviser Air Force Missile Devel. Ctr., Holloman AFB, N.Mex., 1969-70, 6585 Test Group, Air Force Spl. Weapons Ctr., Holloman AFB, from 1970; pvt. investment cons., 1978—. Bd. examiners U.S. CSC; mem. Pres.'s Missile Site Labor Relations Com.; cons. advanced computer and data processing tech. and systems engring.; mem. USAF Civilian Policy Bd. and Range Comdrs. Coun; dep. cmdr. State Mil. Forces, 1989—. Served as pilot USAAF, 1941-45. Fellow Am. Inst. Aeros. and Astronautics; mem. IEEE, Nat. Assn. Flight Instrs. Contbr. articles to profl. jours. Home and Office: 2345 Apache Ln Alamogordo NM 88310-4851

GREEN, FRED WILLIAM, lawyer, musician; b. Spokane, Feb. 13, 1952; s. Dale Monte and Peggy Maxine (Spencer) G.; m. Joan P. Willemain, Mar. 17, 1983 (div. Jan. 1991); children: Madeleine Rose, Camille Nichole. BA, Fairhaven Coll., Bellingham, Wash., 1981; JD with honors, U. Wash., 1992. Profl. musician Wash., 1975-91; jud. clk. Wash. State Ct. Appeals, Tacoma, 1991-92; assoc. atty. Preston, Thorgrimson, Shidler, Gates & Ellis, Seattle, 1992—. Organizer, chmn. Walla Walla chpt. ACLU, 1970; mem. Whatcom County Low Income Citizens Com., 1972-74; active in various petition drives; mem. Peoples Orgn. for Wash. Energy Resources, 1979-82; mem. steering com. Whatcom County Nuclear Weapons Freeze Group, 1981-82. Mem. Audubon Soc., Sierra Club, Wash. Trails Assn., Amnesty Internat., Nature Conservancy, Nat. Lawyers Guild, Order of Coif. Home: 6033 45th Ave NE Seattle WA 98115

GREEN, GABRIEL, popular culture educator; b. Whittier, Calif., Nov. 11, 1924; s. Seth Wellington and Alice Mae (Stebbins) G.; m. Helen Isabel Sibert, Nov. 11, 1960 (dec. May 1970). Student, Woodbury Bus. Coll., 1942, Art Ctr. Sch. Photography, L.A., 1943, L.A. City Coll., 1946-48. Owner, operator Studio of Modern Photography, L.A., 1947-50; photographer Reich Photo Studio, San Francisco, 1953-54, L.A. City Bd. Edn., 1955-58; founder-pres. Amalgamated Flying Saucer Clubs Am., Yucca Valley, Calif., 1959—. Author: Prior Choice Economics, 1955, Let's Face the Facts about Flying Saucers, 1967; editor: Flying Saucers Internat., 1957-69. Ind. candidate for Pres. U.S., 1960; Dem. primary candidate for U.S. Senate, 1962; Universal Party candidate Pres. U.S., 1972. With USN, 1943-46, PTO. Democrat. Office: Amalgamated Flying Saucer Clubs PO Box 39 Yucca Valley CA 92286-0039

GREEN, GASTON ALFRED, III, professional football player; b. L.A., Aug. 1, 1966. Student, UCLA. With L.A. Raiders, 1988-90; running back Denver Broncos, 1991—. Office: Denver Broncos 13655 E Dove Valley Pkwy Englewood CO 80112

GREEN, HILARIE CATTELL, financial consultant; b. Meadeville, Pa., Oct. 25, 1959; d. Ronald E. Hicks and Jowaine L. (Cattell) Humphrey; m. John Andersen Green. BS in Biochemistry, SUNY, Plattsburgh, 1981; MBA in Fin., U. Pitts., 1985. ChFA. Rsch. scientist Enzo Biochem., Inc., N.Y.C., 1981-82; researcher Sch. of Medicine U. Pitts., 1983; assoc. scientist Carnegie Mellon U., Pitts., 1983-84; sr. assoc. Wilshire Assocs., Santa Monica, Calif., 1986—. Co-chair LaSalle-Adams Neighborhood Assn., L.A., 1991—. Mem. L.A. Soc. Fin. Analysts, Assn. Investment Mgmt. and Rsch. Office: Wilshire Assocs 1299 Ocean Ave Santa Monica CA 90401

GREEN, HOWARD I., television executive; b. Detroit, Mar. 9, 1936; s. Albert and Fanya (Newman) G. BA, U. Mich., 1957, MA, 1958, JD, 1961. Artistic dir. Counterpoint Theater Co., N.Y.C., 1974-81; v.p. sales, contract & systems adminstrn. domestic/internat. Paramount Pictures Corp., L.A., 1982-92; sr. v.p. sales ops., domestic and internat. TV 20th Century Fox Film Corp., L.A., 1992—. Actor appeared in The Am. Place Theater, The N.Y. Shakespeare Festival, The Repertory Theater of the Lincoln Ctr., The Washington Shakespeare Festival, The Actor's Studio, 1961-81.

GREEN, JACK, geology educator; b. Poughkeepsie, N.Y., June 19, 1925; s. Louis and Marie (Harris) G.; m. Renee Jean Utley, Sept. 21, 1952; children: Kathy, Jeffrey, Nathan, Teresa, Terrence, Ronald. BS, Va. Poly. Inst. and State U., Blacksburg, 1950; PhD, Columbia U., 1954. Registered geologist, Calif. Geologist Std. of Calif., La Habra, 1953-59; rsch. geologist Rockwell Internat., Downey, Calif., 1959-65, McDonnell Douglas Corp., Huntington Beach, Calif., 1965-70; prof. geology Calif. State U., Long Beach, 1970—; cons. in field; mem. adv. com. Idaho Nat. Engring. Lab., 1990—; lectr. in field. Sr. editor: Atlas of Volcanic Landforms, 1971. With U.S. Army, 1943-46. NASA grantee, 1972, fellow, 1981; invitee geothermal rsch. grp. Peoples Rep. of China, Tibet, 1984. Mem. Am. Astron. Soc. Home: 941 Via Nogales Palos Verdes Peninsula CA 90274-1661 Office: Calif State U U Dept Geology Long Beach CA 90840

GREEN, JACK COULSON, utility company manager; b. Salt Lake City, Mar. 3, 1941; s. Jack C. and Matilda (Colby) G.; m. Sharie L. Staples, June 26, 1964; children: Byron, Sharilin Green Miller, Stephenie Green Cooper, Jacquilin. BA, U. Utah, 1965, MBA, 1966; postgrad., Claremont Grad. Sch., 1989—. Fin. analyst Weyerhouser Co., Tacoma, 1966-67, mgr. internat. planning and adminstrn., 1967-73; mgr. gas supply fin. Pacific Enterprises, L.A., 1973-75, mgr. fin. planning and analysis, 1975-77; mgr. gas supply fin. So. Calif. Gas, L.A., 1977-81, mgr. planning and productivity devel., 1981-85, mgr. productivity devel., 1985-86, mgr. productivity devel. and human resource tng., 1986-90, mgr. human resources support, 1990—; asst. prof. Calif. State U., L.A., 1993—; advisor to bd. dirs. San Gabriel Valley Tng. Ctr., La Puente, Calif., 1981—, Valley Fund Corp., Arcadia, Calif., 1981—, San Gabriel Valley Tng. Ctr. Residential Facility, 1983—. Commr. L.A. County Productivity Commn., 1985—, chmn., 1987-90. Recipient Silver Medal award Pacific Coast Gas Assn., 1985. Mem. Am. Quality and Productivity Mgmt. Assn. (chmn. pacific coast coun. 1985-86, bd. dirs. 1986-89, Am. Productivity and Quality Ctr. (adv. coun. 1986-89). Republican. Mem. LDS Ch. Office: So Calif Gas Co 555 W 5th St Los Angeles CA 90013

GREEN, JAMES CRAIG, data systems company executive; b. Gladstone, Mich., Apr. 19, 1933; s. Albert Keene and Margaret Josephine (Craig) G.; student Coll. of Gt. Falls, 1951-53, UCLA, 1962; m. Catherine Maxwell, Nov. 1, 1957; children: Cindi, Shelley, Nancy, James W., Robert. Clk., carrier U.S. Post Office, Gt. Falls, Mont., 1951-57; clk. office and sales Mont. Liquor Control Bd., Gt. Falls, 1957-59; payroll clk. Herald Examiner, Hearst Publs., L.A., 1959-67, data processing mgr., 1967-75, data processing ops. mgr. corp. hdqrs. Hearst Publs., N.Y.C., 1975-78; gen. mgr., v.p. Computer/Data Inc., Billings, Mont., 1978-83; mgr. customer service Big Sky Data Systems, Billings, Mont., 1983-84; pres. FACTS, Inc., 1985—; tax cons., L.A., 1962-75. Cub Scout leader, com. chmn., L.A. coun. Boy Scouts Am., 1973-75; pres. Bus. Office Employees Assn. L.A., 1963-66. Area commr. Black Otter coun. Boy Scouts Am., 1982-84, com. chmn., 1982-84. With USNR, 1951-59. Recipient degree of Chevalier, De Molay Cross of Honor, Legion of Honor degree.; cert. data processing mgr. Mem. Data Processing Mgrs. Assn., L.A. Masonic Press Club, Rainbow Girls Grand Cross of Colors Shrine, Grotto (charter Great Falls). Clubs: Masons, Blue Lodge, York Rite, Scottish Rite, Shrine (Grotto charter mem. Gt. Falls), DeMolay (chpt. advisor 1983—, state advisor 1982—). Writer, negotiator contract Bus. Office Employees Assn., L.A., 1965.

GREEN, JERROLD DAVID, political science educator, academic administrator; b. Boston, Oct. 21, 1948; s. Irwin S. Green and Mildred R. (Lampert) Freedman; m. Madelyne Patick, Mar. 7, 1988; children: Ori, Talia, Jordan Patick. BA, U. Mass., Boston, 1975; MA, U. Chgo., 1977, PhD, 1981. Asst. prof. U. Mich., Ann Arbor, 1980-85; assoc. prof. polit. sci., dir. Ctr. Mid. Eastern Studies U. Ariz., Tucson, 1985—; cons. Rand Corp., 1980-81, U. S. Dept. State, Dept. Def., Agy. Internat. Devel., Washington, 1981—, Mid. East Cons., Inc., 1985-89, Orkand Corp., 1987-89; Fulbright prof. Cairo U., 1982-83. Author: Revolution in Iran: The Politics of Countermobilization, 1982; contbr. articles to profl. jours. Recipient Rsch. award NSF, 1987-90; Rsch. fellow Fulbright Commn., 1983-84, Social Sci. Rsch. Coun., 1983-84; travel grantee Am. Coun. Learned Socs., 1990. Fellow Am. Polit. Sci. Assn., Am. Rsch. Ctr. in Egypt (rsch. fellow 1982-83), Coun. Fgn. Rels., Assn. Israel Studies, Internat. Polit. Sci. Assn., Mid. East Inst., Mid. East Studies Assn., Soc. Iranian Studies, Tucson Com. on Fgn. Rels. Office: Univ Ariz Mid East Ctr Franklin Bldg Rm 204 Tucson AZ 85721

GREEN, JERRY ALAN, lawyer; b. Newark, Jan. 30, 1943; s. Joel Irving and Leona May G.; m. Ellen Sickles, Sept. 10, 1967 (div. 1972). BA, U. Calif., Berkeley, 1964, JD, 1967. Bar: Calif. 1967. Atty. pvt. practice Mill Valley, Calif., 1967—; pres. Med. Decisionmaking Inst., Mill Valley, 1988—; lectr. and presenter in field. Contbr. articles to profl. jours. Mem. Calif. State Bar Assn., San Francisco Bar Assn. Jewish. Office: Med Decisionmaking Inst 20 Sunnyside Ave Ste 200A Mill Valley CA 94941-1928

GREEN, JOEL HENRY, management consultant; b. Colfax, Wash., Oct. 12, 1954; s. Henry Philip and Myrtle E. (Gibson) G.; m. Valerie Jo Norris, Aug. 21, 1981; 1 child, Julia C. BA, Whitman Coll., 1978; MBA, U. Chgo., 1980. Assoc. cons. Theodore Barry & Assoc., Portland, Oreg., 1980-83; sr. mgr. Delitte & Touche, Seattle, 1983-92; prin. Green Consulting Internat., Vancouver, Wash., 1992—; career cons. Whitman Coll., Walla Walla, Wash., 1990—; cert. mgmt. cons. Inst. Mgmt. Consultants, N.Y.C., 1991—. Mem. Royal Oaks Country Club. Home: 4016 Wauna Vista Dr Vancouver WA 98661

GREEN, JOHN WILLIAM, economics educator, consultant; b. Spirit lake, Iowa, Sept. 18, 1942; s. Lowell Joseph and Henrietta (Van Oort) G.; m. Kathleen Sophia Cosgrove, Feb. 17, 1968; children: Kevin Michael, Steven Christopher. BS in Agrl. Econs., S.D. State U., 1965; MS in Agrl. Econs., Okla. State U., 1968; MA in Regional Sci., U. Pa., 1970, PhD in Regional Sci., 1976. Agrl. economist Econ. Rsch. Svc.-USDA, Upper Darby, Pa., 1968-75, Fort Collins, Colo., 1975-85; assoc. prof., chair econs. dept. U. North Colo., Greeley, 1985—; cons., pres. Coal Network Assocs., Fort Collins, 1982-88; pvt. cons., Fort Collins, 1988—. Contbr. articles to profl. jours. 2d lt. USAR, 1966-72. Recipient Econ. Indicators award Econ. Devel. Action Partnership, Greeley, 1988—, Sustainable Agrl. award Ctrl. Colo. Water Conservation Dist., Greeley, 1991-92. Mem. Nat. Assn. Bus. Economists, Am. Econ. Assn., Regional Sci. Assn. Home: 2214 Franklin Rd Fort Collins CO 80524 Office: U No Colo Econs Dept Greeley CO 80631

GREEN, JONATHAN WILLIAM, museum administrator and educator, artist, author; b. Troy, N.Y., Sept. 26, 1939; s. Alan Singer and Frances (Katz) G.; m. Louise Lockshin, Sept. 16, 1962 (div. 1985); children: Raphael, Benjamin; m. Wendy Hughes Brown, Aug. 12, 1988. Student, MIT, 1958-60, Hebrew U., 1960-61; BA, Brandeis U., 1963, postgrad., 1964-67; MA, Harvard U., 1967. Photographer Jonathan Green, Photography, Boston, 1966-76, Ezra Stoller Assocs., Mamaroneck, N.Y., 1967-68; prof. MIT, Cambridge, Mass., 1968-76; dir. Creative Photography Lab MIT, Cambridge, 1974-76; editor Aperture Books and Periodical, N.Y.C., 1972-76; prof. Ohio State U., Columbus, 1976-90, dir. Wexner Ctr. Visual Arts/Univ. Gallery Fine Art, 1981-88, founding project dir., 1981-90; dir. Calif. Mus. Photography, U. Calif., Riverside, 1990—; prof. U. of Calif., Riverside, 1990—; cons. Nat. Endowment for Arts, Washington, 1975-76, 85, 88, Harry N. Abrams, Pubs., N.Y.C., 1982-84, Oxford U. Press, N.Y.C., 1977-82, Polaroid Corp., Cambridge, 1976; co-founder Visible Lang. Workshop, MIT Media Lab., 1973. Author: American Photography, 1984 (Nikon Book of Yr. award 1984, Benjamin Citation 1986), The Snapshot, 1974 (N.Y. Type Dirs. Club award 1974), Camera Work: A Critical Anthology, 1973 (Best Art Book award 1973); editor: Celebrations, 1974; represented in permanent collections Mus. Fine Arts, Boston, Mus. Fine Art, Houston, Cleve. Mus. Art, Va. Mus. Fine Art, Richmond, Princeton U. Art Mus., Bell System Collection, Moderna Museet, Stockholm, Ctr. for Creative Photography, Tucson, De Saisset Art Gallery and Mus., Internat. Ctr. Photography, N.Y.C., MIT, Mpls. Inst. Arts; photographs pub.: American Images: New Work by Twenty Contemporary Photographers, 1979, Aperture: 25 Years of Record Houses, 1981, Architectural Record, Architecture and Urbanism, Progressive Architecture, A Field Guide to Modern American Architecture. Danforth fellow, 1963-67, NEA Photographer fellow, 1978, AT & T fellow, 1979. Office: California Museum Of Photography Downtown Hist Pedestrian Mall 3824 Main St Riverside CA 92501

GREEN, JOSHUA, III, banker; b. Seattle, June 30, 1936; s. Joshua, Jr. and Elaine (Brygger) G.; m. Pamela K. Pemberton, Nov. 1, 1974; children: Joshua IV, Jennifer Elaine, Paige Courtney. B.A. in English, Harvard U., 1958. With Peoples Nat. Bank Wash., Seattle, 1960—; exec. v.p. Peoples Nat. Bank Wash., 1972-75, pres., 1975—, chief exec. officer, 1977—, chmn. bd., 1979-88; chmn. bd., chief exec. officer, vice chmn. U.S. Bank Washington (merger PeoplesBank and Old Nat. Bank), 1988—; chmn. bd., chief exec. officer U.S. Bank Wash. (merger Peoples Bank and Old Nat. Bank), vice chmn. U.S. Bancorp; also bd. dirs.; v.p., dir. Joshua Green Corp.; bd. dirs. U.S. Bancorp. V.p., trustee Joshua Green Found.; trustee Seattle Found., Downtown Seattle Devel. Assn.; chmn. Corp. Coun. for the Arts. Mem. Seattle C. of C. (dir., v.p. 1980—, U. Club, Rainier Club, Seattle Tennis Club, Wash. Athletic Club. Home: 1932 Blenheim Dr E Seattle WA 98112-2308 Office: US Bank of Washington 1415 5th Ave Seattle WA 98171-1001 also: US Bancorp US Bancorp Tower 111 SW 5th Ave PO Box 8837 Portland OR 97208

GREEN, LAWRENCE WINTER, public health educator; b. Bell, Calif., Sept. 16, 1940; s. Clifton Lawrence and Ora Elizabeth (Winter) G.; m. Patricia Mary Fahey, June 11, 1962 (div. Apr. 1981); children: Beth Allison Green Levin, Jennifer Laurie; m. Judith Marilyn Ottoson, May 1, 1982. BS, U. Calif., Berkeley, 1962, MPH, 1966, DrPH, 1968. Project assoc. Ford Found., Dacca, Bangladesh, 1963-65; lectr. U. Calif. Sch. Pub. Health, 1968-70; asst. prof., assoc. prof., prof. Johns Hopkins U. Sch. Pub. Health, Balt., 1970-81, asst. dean, head div. health edn., 1972-79; dir. U.S. Office Health Info. and Health Promotion, Washington, 1979-81; vis. lectr. Harvard U. Ctr. for Health Policy, Boston, 1981-82; prof., dir. Ctr. for Health Promotion Rsch. U. Tex., Houston, 1982-88; v.p. Henry J. Kaiser Family Found., Menlo Park, Calif., 1988-91; prof., dir. Inst. Health Promotion Rsch. U. B.C., Vancouver, Can., 1991—; vis. prof. U. Limburg Sch. Health Sci., Maastricht, The Netherlands, 1987-91; cons. WHO, Geneva, 1974, 82-83, NIH, Bethesda, Md., 1975-88, UN Fund for Population Activities, Beijing, 1984, UNICEF, Beijing, 1991; vis. rsch. social scientist Inst. for Health Policy Studies, U. Calif. Sch. Medicine, San Francisco 1991. Author: Dacca Family Planning Experiment (Beryl Roberts award 1973), Health Education Planning, 1980, Measurement and Evaluation, 1986, Community Health, 1973, 6th edit., 1990, Health Promotion Planning, 1991. Recipient Disting. Svc. citation U.S. Asst. Sec. Health, 1981, commendation Nat. Ctr. for Health Edn., 1986, Jacques Perisot medal Internat. Union Health Edn.; scholar Assn. for Advancement Health Edn., 1986, AAHPERD, 1988-89. Fellow APHA (governing coun. 1974-76, Disting. Career award 1978), Acad. Behavioral Medicine Rsch., Soc. for Pub. Health Edn. (disting., pres. 1984-85), Am. Sch. Health Assn. (hon.), Soc. for Behavioral Medicine (bd. dirs. 1985-88), Am. Acad. Phys. Edn. (assoc.), Eta Sigma Gamma, Delta Omega. Home: 2545 W 2d Ave, Vancouver, BC Canada V6K 1J7 Office: U BC Inst Health Promotion, 6248 Biol Scis Rd, Vancouver, BC Canada V6T 1Z4

GREEN, LESLIE CLAUDE, political science and international law educator; b. London, Nov. 6, 1920; arrived in Can., 1965; s. Israel Willie and Raie (Goldberg) G.; m. Lilian Denise Meyer, Sept. 1, 1945; 1 child, Anne Roslyn. LLB with honors, U. Coll. London, 1941; LLD, U. London, 1971. Lectr. U. Coll. London, 1946-60; prof. internat. law U. Singapore, 1960-65; prof. polit. sci. U. Alta., Edmonton, Can., 1965-69; Univ. prof. U. Alta., Edmonton, 1969-91, Univ. prof. emeritus, 1992—; legal advisor Can. Delegation Conf. on Humanitarian Law, Geneva, 1975-77; acad. in residence to Legal Dept., dept. external affairs, 1974-75, JAG, Nat. Def. Hdqrs., Ottawa, Can., 1979-80; vis. prof. Kyung Hee U., Seoul, Republic of Korea, 1985; hon. prof. of law U. Alta., 1982—; mem. Internat. Com. Experts on Naval Warfare Law, 1989—, Internat. Com. Experts on Environ. Warfare Law, 1991—; cons. war crimes Can. Dept. Justice. Author: International Law Through the Cases, 4th rev. edit., 1978, Law and Society, 1975, Superior Orders in National and International Law, 1976, International Law-A Canadian Perspective, 2d rev. edit., 1988, Essays on the Modern Law of War, 1985; (with O.P. Dickason) The Law of Nations and the New World, 1989, The Contemporary Law of Armed Conflict, 1993. Served to maj. Brit. Army, 1941-46. Recipient Cecil Peace prize U. Bur. Brit. Empire, 1941, Grotius Found. medal, 1954, U. Alta. Research Prize, 1982; fellow Royal Soc. Can., 1980. Mem. Order Can., Athenaeum Club (London), Centre Club (Edmonton). Jewish. Home: 7911 119 St, Edmonton, AB Canada T6G 1W6 Office: U Alta, Dept Polit Sci, Edmonton, AB Canada TGG 2H4

GREEN, MARILYN VIRGINIA, writer; b. Grand Rapids, Mich., Nov. 6, 1948; d. John Robert and Virginia (Tuthill) G.; m. Drew A. McCalley, Apr. 14, 1979. BA, Mich. State U., 1970. Author: Intergenerational Programming in Libraries, 1979, The Button Lover's Book, 1991. Mem. Peninsula Stitchery Guild, San Francisco, 1977-92.

GREEN, MELANIE JANE, speech-language pathology paraprofessional; b. Fremont, Calif., Nov. 23, 1968; d. Robert Lucian and Frances Eileen (Jones) G. BA in Communicative Disorders, Calif. State U., Fullerton, 1992; postgrad., U. Redlands. Child care coord. Calvary Chapel of Fullerton (Calif.), 1986-87; speech pathologist aide Providence Speech and Hearing Ctr., Orange, Calif., 1988-90; activities asst. Western Neuro Care Ctr., Tustin, Calif., 1989-90; speech-lang. pathology paraprofl. Long Beach, Calif., 1990—. Mem. Autism Soc. Am., Nat. Student Speech and Hearing Assn. Home: PO Box 5679 Newport Beach CA 92662

GREEN, MICHAEL I., physicist; b. Suffern, N.Y., Mar. 21, 1930; s. Herman and Sylvia Katherine (Silverman) G.; m. Susan Lea Simon, Feb. 6, 1959; children: Deborah, William Harold. BS, U. Ala., 1953; PhD, Wayne State U., Detroit, 1972. Engr. Westinghouse, Bloomfield, N.J., 1955-57; sr. scientist Lockheed Rsch. Labs., Palo Alto, Calif., 1958-63, Bendix Rsch. Labs., Detroit, 1963-64; cons. Detroit, 1964-74; instr. Wayne State U., 1972-74; accelerator physicist Lawrence Berkeley Lab, Berkeley, Calif., 1974—; dir. Internat. Magnetic Measurement Workshop, 1981—; instr. CERN Acc. Sch., 1992; vis. scientist Superconducting Super Collider Lab., 1992—, European Synchrotron Radiation Facility, Grenbole, France, 1988; cons. in field, 1986—, reviewer jour. articles, 1986—. Contbr. articles to profl. jours. Leader Boy Scouts Explorer Scouts, N.Y., Ala., Calif., 1953—; mem. Dem. Cen. Com., Santa Clara County, Calif., 1961-63. With U.S. Army, 1953-55. Mem. Am. Physical Soc., IEEE, AAAS, Soaring Soc. Am., Pacific Soaring Coun. (v.p. 1984-85), Ames Soaring Club (v.p. 1982-83), Sigma Xi. Jewish. Home: 117 Rheem Blvd Orinda CA 94563-3620 Office: Lawrence Berkeley Lab 1 Cyclotron Rd Berkeley CA 94720

GREEN, MORRIS LEE (MAURY GREEN), writer; b. Raleigh, N.C., May 10, 1916; s. Henry Lee and Ethel May (Emmerson) G.; m. Evelyn Irene Taggart, Aug. 11, 1940 (div. 1978); children: Barbara Sue Green Hager, Lee. BA, U. Ill., 1937. Reporter, editor Chgo. Herald-Examiner, 1937-39, Chgo. Tribune, 1939-56; reporter L.A. Times, 1956-57; writer, producer, reporter KNXT and CBS, L.A., 1957-69; writer, producer, host KNBC and other stas., L.A., 1969-76; freelance writer, cons. L.A., 1976—. Author: Television News: Anatomy and Process, 1969, The Delphi Calculus, 1979; co-author: Sawed-Off Justice, 1976, Evel Knievel on Tour, 1977. Lt. USNR, 1943-45. Recipient Broadcast Media award Calif. State U., San Francisco, 1970, Emmy award Hollywood area TV Acad. Arts and Scis., 1963, 3 Golden Mike awards, RTNA. Mem. SAG, Pacific Pioneer Broadcasters (Diamond Circle award 1992), Writers Guild Am. West, Am. Fedn. TV and Radio Artists, Greater L.A. Press Club (pres. 1970-71).

GREEN, NEAL JEFFREY, organic chemist; b. Bklyn., Oct. 20, 1964; s. Gerald Norman and Reba (Roth) G. BSc in Medicinal Chemistry, SUNY, Buffalo, 1986; PhD, Rensselaer Poly. Inst., 1992. Rsch. assoc. in organic chemistry Oreg. State U., Corvallis, 1992—. Contbr. articles to profl. jours. Mem. NIH (Nat. Rsch. Svc. award 1992—), Am. Chem. Soc. Office: Oreg State U Gilbert Hall 21st and Monroe Sts Corvallis OR 97331

GREEN, NORMAN HARRY, tax lawyer; b. L.A., Nov. 11, 1952; s. Leonard L. and Lily (Merecki) G.; m. Rachel Rubin, Oct. 19, 1980; children: Andrew S., L. Stephen. AB, U. Calif., Irvine, 1974; JD, UCLA, 1979. Bar: Calif. 1979; cert. specialist taxation U.S. Tax Ct. Tax auditor IRS, San Francisco, 1974-76; customs officer U.S. Customs Svc., L.A., 1977; tax acct. Arthur Andersen & Co., L.A., 1979-80; lawyer Barclay & Moskatel, Beverly Hills, Calif., 1980-84; ptnr., lawyer Irsfeld, Irsfeld & Younger, Glendale, Calif., 1984—. Dir., gen. counsel June Ebensteiner Hospice Found., Hospice of the Canyon, Calabasas, Calif., 1990—. Mem. Glendale Bar Assn., L.A. County Bar Assn. (vice chmn. arbitration com. 1985—), Glendale C. of C. (chmn. legis. action com. 1986-89), Kiwanis (Hollywood sec. 1990—). Office: Irsfeld Irsfeld & Younger 100 W Broadway Ste 900 Glendale CA 91210

GREEN, PAUL CECIL, management consultant; b. Oconto, Nebr., Sept. 8, 1919; s. Paul Simpson Green and Ruth Adelaide (Kennedy) Elder; m. Carole Jean Pass, Dec. 21, 1964. BSBA, U. Nebr., 1941; MBA, Harvard U., 1948. CLU. Dir. sales Continental Assurance Co., Chgo., 1948-62, v.p. mktg., 1962-73; v.p. mktg. USLIFE Corp., N.Y.C., 1973-75; sr. v.p. Helmich, Miller and Pasek, Inc., Chgo., 1975-81; pres. Paul C. Green and Assocs., Ltd., Green Valley, Ariz., 1981—; chmn. bd. CLU Jour., Bryn Mar, Pa. Contbr. articles to profl. jours. Precinct capt. Young Repubs., Chgo.; bd. dirs. Green Valley Recreation, Inc.; exec. bd. Green Valley Coordinating Council; pres. Foothills IV Homeowners Assn., Green Valley. Lt. col. USAF, 1942-46. Recipient Achievement award City of Hope, 1977, 78. Mem. Am. Soc. Chartered Life Underwriters, Internat. Assn. Fin. Planners, Life Ins. Mktg. and Research Assn. (chmn. various coms.), Harvard Bus. Sch. Club (Phoenix chpt.), Country Club of Green Valley. Presbyterian. Home: 551 S Paseo Del Cobre Green Valley AZ 85614-2321 Office: PO Box 1448 Green Valley AZ 85622-1448

GREEN, PHILLIP FREEMAN, accountant; b. Albany, Ga., Sept. 23, 1955; s. Phillip Ralph and LaRae (Ellett) G.; m. Vonja Swenson, Aug. 22, 1981; children: Phillip Freeman, Rachel, Matthew Ervin, Angela, Benjamin, Kerry Anne. BS in Acctg. with honors, Brigham Young U., 1980, MS in Acctg., 1981. CPA, Utah, Calif., Oreg. Intern Alexander Grant & Co., CPAs, Kansas City, Mo., 1980; staff acct. Haynie & Co., CPAs, Salt Lake City, 1980-84; tax mgr. Haynie & Co., CPAs, Newport Beach, Calif., 1985, Anderson & Co., CPAs, Temecula, Calif., 1985-88; tax mgr. Kuebler, Thomas & Co., CPAs, Temecula, 1988-90, ptnr., 1990-92; shareholder Burton, Creamer & Co., P.C., Salem, Oreg., 1993—. Bishop Ch. of Jesus Christ of LDS, 1990-92. Named Eagle Scout, Boy Scouts of Am., London, 1981. Mem. AICPA, Calif. Soc. of CPAs (planning com. ann. conf. 1991—, speaker). Republican. Office: Burton Creamer & Co PC 435 Commercial NE Ste 200 Salem OR 97301

GREEN, RICHARD KEVIN, special effect company executive; b. Detroit, Mar. 2, 1957; s. Jack and Dorothy (Clayman) G. BA, Mich. State U., 1979. Field prodr. ABC News, Washington, 1979-81; pres. R. Green Prodns., Seattle, 1982-88, Wildfire Inc., L.A., 1989—. Developer black light spl. effects for film, TV, concert including The Doors, Bill and Ted's Bogus Journey, The Lawnmower Man, Star Trek 6, Singles, Disney parks, Michael Jackson tour and others. Big brother Big Bros., L.A., 1990. Office: Wildfire Inc 10853 Venice Blvd Los Angeles CA 90034

GREEN, ROBERT SCOTT, biotechnology company executive; b. N.Y.C., Aug. 7, 1953; s. Morris and Sophie (Weinstock) G.; m. Jill Susan Bolhack, June 24, 1979; children: Melissa, Meredith. BA, CUNY, 1974; JD, Fordham U., N.Y.C., 1977. Bar: N.Y. 1978, D.C. 1979. Assoc. Paul, Weiss, Rifkind, Wharton & Garrison, N.Y.C., 1979-87; v.p. Kaplan Capital Mgmt. Inc., N.Y.C., 1987-89; pres. Vega Biotechs., Inc., Tucson, 1989-92; pres., bd. dirs. Applitech Inc., Tucson, 1992—; mng. dir. Fusion Assocs., Ltd., Tucson, 1990-91; bd. dirs. Hearing Innovations, Inc., Tucson, Vega Synthecell/Vega Biomolecules Corp., Md., 1992—. Contbr. articles to profl. jours. Mem. N.Y. State Bar Assn. Office: Applitech Inc 6741 N Saint Andrews Dr Tucson AZ 85718

GREEN, SHERYL ANNE, dentist; b. Houston, Mar. 11, 1952; d. Bill J. Green and Barbara L. (Smith) Fathman. BA in Biology, U. Tex., 1976; DDS, U. Tex., San Antonio, 1982; BS in Fin., Metro State Coll., Denver, 1989; MS in Health Adminstrn., U. Colo., 1993. Resident in dentistry VA Hosp., Temple, Tex., 1983; rsch. assoc. dept. neurobiology U. Tex., Austin, 1974-76; dept. reproductive medicine U. Tex. Med. Sch., Houston, 1976-77; dept. periodontics U. Tex. Dental Sch., Houston, 1977-78; dentist Fred Metz, Denver, 1983-84; pvt. practice Denver, 1984-89; resident exec. devel. program Meth. Hosp., 1993. Mem. Junior League of Denver. Mem. Acad. Gen. Dentistry, Am. Soc. Dentistry for Children, Am. Assn. Women in Dentistry, Golden Key, Alpha Epsilon Delta. Republican. Methodist. Home: 3162 S Boston Ct Denver CO 80231-6422 Office: 3955 E Exposition Ave Ste 410 Denver CO 80209-5033

GREEN, TED, professional hockey team coach. Formerly co-coach Edmonton Oilers, NHL; head coach, 1991—. Office: Edmonton Oilers, Northlands Coliseum, Edmonton, AB Canada T5B 4M9*

GREEN, WILLIAM PORTER, lawyer; b. Jacksonville, Ill., Mar. 19, 1920; s. Hugh Parker and Clara Belle (Hopper) G.; m. Rose Marie Hall, Oct. 1, 1944; children: Hugh Michael, Robert Alan, Richard William. BA, Ill. Coll., 1941; JD, Northwestern U., Evanston, Ill., 1947. Bar: Ill. 1947, Calif. 1948, U.S. Dist. Ct. (so. dist.) Tex. 1986, U.S. Ct. Customs and Patent Appeals, U.S. Patent and Trademark Office 1948, U.S. Ct. Appeals (fed. cir.) 1982, U.S. Ct. Appeals (5th and 9th cir.), U.S. Supreme Ct. 1948, U.S. Dist. Ct. (cen. dist.) Calif. 1949, (so. dist.) Tex.1986. Pvt. practice L.A., 1947—; mem. Wills, Green & Mueth, L.A., 1974-83; of counsel Nilsson, Robbins, Dalgarn, Berliner, Carson & Wurst, L.A., 1984-91; of counsel Nilsson, Wurst & Green L.A., 1992—; del. Calif. State Bar Conv., 1982—, chmn., 1986. Bd. editors Ill. Law Rev., 1946; patentee in field. Mem. L.A. world Affairs Coun., 1975—; deacon local Presbyn. Ch., 1961-63. Mem. ABA, Calif. State Bar, Am. Intellectual Property Law Assn., L.A. Patent Law Assn. (past. sec.-treas., mem. bd. govs.), Lawyers Club L.A. (past treas., past sec., mem. bd. govs., pres. 1985-86), Los Angeles County Bar Assn. (trustee 1986-87), Am. Legion (past post comdr.), Northwestern U. Alumni Club So. Calif., Big Ten Club So. Calif., Town Hall Calif. Club, PGA West Golf Club (La Quinta, Calif.), Phi Beta Kappa, Phi Delta Phi, Phi Alpha. Republican. Home: 3570 Lombardy Rd Pasadena CA 91107-5627 Office: Nilsson Wurst & Green 707 Wilshire Blvd # 3200 Los Angeles CA 90017

GREENBERG, ARNOLD ELIHU, water quality specialist; b. Bklyn., Apr. 13, 1926; s. Samuel and Minnie (Gurevitz) G.; m. Shirley E. Singer, Aug. 2, 1952; children: Noah J., Seth M. BS, CCNY, 1947; MS, U. Wis., 1948; SM, MIT, 1950; postgrad., U. Calif., Berkeley, 1970-75. Rsch. engr., biologist U. Calif., Berkeley, 1950-54; asst. chief labs. Calif. Dept. Health Svcs., Berkeley, 1954-82; lab. mgr. East Bay Mcpl. Utility Dist., Oakland, Calif., 1982-91; cons., 1991; instr. in engrng. extension U. Calif., 1963—; instr. Contra Costa Coll., San Pablo, Calif., 1968-82; cons. Lawrence Berkeley Lab., 1973-84; vis. fellow Israel Inst. Tech., Haifa, 1981. Editor: Standard Methods for the Examination of Water & Wastewater, 1971, 75, 81, 85, 89, 92, Laboratory Procedures for the Examination of Seawater & Shellfish, 1985. Col. USPHS, 1955—. Mem. APHA, Am. Acad. Microbiology, Am. Water Works Assn. (hon.).

GREENBERG, BYRON STANLEY, newspaper and business executive, consultant; b. Bklyn., June 17, 1919; s. Albert and Bertha (Getleson) G.; m. Helena Marks, Feb. 10, 1946; children: David, Eric, Randy. Student, Bklyn. Coll., 1936-41. Circulation mgr. N.Y. Post, 1956-62, circulation dir., 1962-63, bus. mgr., 1963-72, gen. mgr., dir., 1973-79; sec., dir. N.Y.. Post Corp., 1966-75, treas., dir., 1975-76, v.p., 1976-81; v.p., dir. Leisure Systems, Inc., 1978-80; pres., chief exec. officer, dir. Games Mgmt. Services, Inc., 1979-80. Bd. dirs. 92d St YMHA, 1970-71, Friars Nat. Found., 1981-82. Served with AUS, 1942-45. Club: Friars. Home and Office: 2560 S Grade Rd Alpine CA 91901-3612

GREENBERG, IRA ARTHUR, psychologist; b. Bklyn., June 26, 1924; s. Philip and Minnie (S.) G.; m. Stella Cantrell, 1949 (div. 1950); m. Judith Rials, 1952 (div. 1954). BA in Journalism, U. Okla., 1949; MA in English, U. So. Calif., 1962; MS in Counseling, Calif. State U. L.A., 1963; PhD in Psychology, Claremont (Calif.) Grad Sch., 1967. Editor, Ft. Riley (Kans.) Guidon, 1950-51; reporter, copy editor Columbus (Ga.) Enquirer, 1951-55; reporter Louisville Courier-Jour., 1955-56, L.A. Times, 1956-62; free-lance writer, L.A., Montclair, Camarillo, Calif., 1960-69, 76—; counselor Claremont Coll. Psychol. Clinic and Counseling Ctr., 1964-65; lectr. psychology Chapman Coll., Orange, Calif., 1965-66; psychologist Camarillo State Hosp., 1967-69, supervising psychologist, 1969-73, part-time clin. psychologist, 1973—; part-time asst. prof. edn. San Fernando Valley State Coll., Northridge, Calif., 1967-69, lectr. psychodrama, social welfare U. Calif. Extension Div., Santa Barbara, 1968-69; vis. prof. edn. U. Nev., Reno, 1977—; vol. psychologist Free Clinic, L.A., 1968-70; staff dir. Calif. Inst. Psychodrama, 1969-71; tng. cons. Topanga Ctr. for Human Devel., 1970-75, bd. dirs., 1971-74, faculty Calif. Sch. Profl. Psychology, 1970—; founder, exec. dir. Behavioral Studies Inst., mgmt. cons., L.A., 1970—; pvt. practice cons. in psychology, psychodrama, hypnosis, 1970—; founder, exec. dir. Psychodrama Ctr. for L.A., Inc., 1971—, Group Hypnosis Ctr., L.A., 1976—; producer, host TV talk show Crime and Pub. Safety, Century Cable, Channel 3, 1983—. Vol. humane officer State of Calif., 1979-89; res. officer L.A. Police Dept., 1980-86; bd. dirs. Human Eucators Coun., 1982-86; capt. Calif. State Mil. Res., 1986-93, maj. 1993—. With AUS, 1943-46; ETO; USAR, 1950-51. Fellow Am. Soc. Clin. Hypnosis; mem. Am. Soc. Group Psychotherapy and Psychodrama, Assn. Rsch. and Enlightenment, L.A. Soc. Clin. Psychologists (dir. 1975), Am. Psychol. Assn., Western Psychol. Assn., Calif. Psychol. Assn., L.A. Psychol. Assns., Am. Soc. for Psychol. Rsch., Group Psychotherapy Assn. So. Calif. (dir. 1974-76, 82-87, pres. 1987-88), Am. Mgmt. Assn., Am. Soc. Bus. and Mgmt. Cons. (nat. adv. coun. 1977—), So. Calif. Soc. Clin. Hypnosis (dir., exec. v.p. 1973-76, pres. 1977-78), So. Calif. Psychotherapy Affiliation (dir. 1976-85), Assn. for Humanistic Psychology, Mensa, Am. Zionist Fedn., Nat. Rifle Assn., Calif. Rifle and Pistol Assn., SW Pistol League, Animal Protection Inst. Am., Airport Psychol. Assocs., Sigma Delta Chi. Clubs: Sierra, Greater L.A. Press; B'nai B'rith; Beverly Hills Gun. Author: Psychodrama and Audience Attitude Change, 1968. Editor, author: Psychodrama: Theory and Therapy, 1974; Group Hypnotherapy and Hypnodrama, 1977. Address: BSI & Group Hypnosis Ctr 11692 Chenault St Ste 206 Los Angeles CA 90049

GREENBERG, MARVIN, music educator; b. N.Y.C., June 24, 1936; s. Samuel and Rae (Sherry) G.; B.S. cum laude, N.Y. U., 1957; M.A., Columbia U., 1958, Ed.D., 1962. Tchr. elem. schs., N.Y.C., 1957-63; prof. music edn. U. Hawaii, Honolulu, 1963—, rsch. cons. Ctr. for Early Childhood Rsch., 1969-71; edn. adminstr. Model Cities project for disadvantaged children Family Svcs. Ctr., Honolulu, 1971-72. Cons. western region Volt Tech. Svcs., Head Start program, 1969-71; Head Start worker, 1972-75; Child Devel. Assoc. Consortium rep., 1975—. Recipient several fed. and state grants for ednl. rsch. and curriculum projects. Mem. Hawaii Music Educators Assn., Music Educators Nat. Conf., Soc. for Rsch. in Music Edn., Coun. for Rsch. in Music Edn. Author: Teaching Music in the Elementary School: Guide for ETV Programs, 1966; Preschool Music Curriculum, 1970; Music Handbook for the Elementary School, 1972; Staff Training in Child Care in Hawaii, 1975; Your Child Needs Music, 1979, Teachers Guides Honolulu Symphony Children's Concerts, 1980—; also articles. Home: 2575 Kuhio Ave # 19-2 Honolulu HI 96815-3971 Office: 2411 Dole St MB 203 Honolulu HI 96822-2398

GREENBERG, MYRON SILVER, lawyer; b. L.A., Oct. 17, 1945; s. Earl W. and Geri (Silver) G.; m. Shlomit Gross; children: David, Amy, Sophie, Benjamin. BSBA, UCLA, 1967, JD, 1970. Bar: Calif. 1971, U.S. Dist. Ct. (cen. dist.) Calif. 1971, U.S. Tax Ct. 1977; CPA, Calif. Staff acct. Touche Ross & Co., L.A., 1970-71; assoc. Kaplan, Livingston, Goodwin, Berkowitz, & Selvin, Beverly Hills, 1971-74; ptnr. Dinkelspiel, Steefel & Levitt, San Francisco, 1975-80; ptnr. Steefel, Levitt & Weiss, San Francisco, 1981-82; pres. Myron S. Greenberg, a Profl. Corp., Larkspur, Calif., 1982—; professorial lectr. tax. Golden Gate U.; instr. U. Calif., Berkeley, 1989—. Author: California Attorney's Guide to Professional Corporations, 1977, 79; bd. editors UCLA Law Rev., 1969-70. Mem. San Anselmo Planning Commn., 1976-77; bd. dirs. Bay Area Lawyers for Arts, 1979-80, Marin County chpt. Am. Heart Assn. (bd. dirs., pres. 1984-90); mem. adv. bd. cert. program in personal fin. planning U. Calif., Berkeley, 1991—. Mem. ABA, AICPA, Marin County (Calif.) Bar Assn., Real Estate Tax Inst. of Calif. Continuing Edn. Bar (planning com.), Larkspur C. of C. (bd. dirs. 1985-87). Democrat. Jewish. Office: 700 Larkspur Landing Cir Larkspur CA 94939-1711

GREENBERGER, ALLEN JAY, history educator; b. Chgo., Mar. 18, 1937; s. Harold and Alice (Ross) G. BA, U. Mich., 1958, MA, 1960, PhD, 1966. Instr. history Smith Coll., Northampton, Mass., 1965-66; from asst. prof. to prof. history Pitzer Coll., Claremont, Calif., 1966—. Author: British Image of India, 1969; editor: Indo-British Rev., 1988, Am. editor, 1987—; contbr. articles to profl. jours.; adv. editorial bd. Victorian Studies, 1980-90. Mem. Assn. Asian Studies, Conf. British Studies, Irish Studies Assn., Phi Beta Kappa, Phi Kappa Phi. Office: Pitzer Coll Claremont CA 91711

GREENE, ALBERT LAWRENCE, hospital administrator; b. N.Y.C., Dec. 10, 1949; s. Leonard and Anne (Birnbaum) G.; m. Jo Linda Anderson, Sept. 3, 1972; children: Stacy, Jeremy. BA, Ithaca Coll., 1971; MHA, U. Mich., 1973. Adminstrv. asst. Harper Hosp., Detroit, 1973-74, asst. adminstr., 1974-77, assoc. adminstr., 1977-80; adminstr. Grace Hosp., Detroit, 1980-84, Harper Hosp., Detroit, 1984-87; pres., chief exec. officer Sinai Samaritan Med. Ctr., Milw., 1988-90, Alta Bates Med. Ctr., Berkeley, Calif., 1990—; bd. dirs. Aetna Health Plans Calif. Trustee Huron Valley Hosp., Milford, Mich., 1984-87. Mem. Am. Coll. Healthcare Execs., Rotary, Blackhawk Country Club, Lakeview Club. Home: 3819 Cottonwood Dr Danville CA 94506-6007 Office: Alta Bates Med Ctr 2450 Ashby Ave Berkeley CA 94705

GREENE, ALVIN, service company executive, management consultant; b. Pitts., Aug. 26, 1932; s. Samuel David and Yetta (Kroff) G.; B.A., Stanford U., 1954, M.B.A., 1959; m. M. Louise Sokol, Nov. 11, 1977; children—Sharon, Ami, Ann, Daniel. Asst. to pres. Narmco Industries, Inc., San Diego, 1959-62; adminstrv. mgr., mgr. mktg. Whittaker Corp., L.A., 1962-67; sr. v.p. Cordura Corp., L.A., 1967-75; chmn. bd. Sharon-Sage, Inc., L.A., 1975-79; exec. v.p., chief operating officer Republic Distbrs., Inc., Carson, Calif., 1979-81, also dir.; chief operating officer Memel, Jacobs & Ellsworth, 1981-87, 87—; pres. SCI Cons., Inc.; dir. Sharon-Sage, Inc., True Data Corp.; vis. prof. Am. Grad. Sch. Bus., Phoenix, 1977-81. Chmn. bd. commrs. Housing Authority City of L.A., 1983-88 . Served to 1st lt., U.S. Army, 1955-57. Mem. Direct Mail Assn., Safety Helmet Mfrs. Assn., Bradley Group. Office: 11990 San Vicente Blvd Ste 300 Los Angeles CA 90049

GREENE, CELENE, association executive. Exec. dir. N.Mex. State Bar, Albuquerque, 1975-79, Minn. State Bar, Mpls., 1979-85, Oreg. State Bar, Portland, 1985—. Mem. Oreg. Soc. Assn. Execs. (treas.), Nat. Assn. Bar Execs. (past pres.), Am. Soc. Assn. Execs. (edn. com., cert. assn. execs. designation 1984, chair western region adv. com.). Office: Oreg State Bar PO Box 1689 5200 SW Meadows Rd Portland OR 97035-0889

GREENE, DAVID SIMEON, accountant; b. Hartwell, Ga., Sept. 11, 1965; s. Samuel Greene and Jeanette (Middleton) Coghlan. BS in Acctg., Clemson U., 1987; postgrad., Fla. Internat., 1990-91. CPA, Calif. Tax mgr. Price Waterhouse, San Francisco, 1990—. Mem. AICPA, Calif. Soc. CPAs, Phi Kappa Phi. Republican. Jewish. Office: Price Waterhouse 555 California St Ste 3800 San Francisco CA 94104

GREENE, FRANK SULLIVAN, JR., business executive; b. Washington, Oct. 19, 1938; s. Frank S. Sr. and Irma O. Greene; m. Phyllis Davison, Jan. 1958 (dec. 1984); children: Angela, Frank, Ronald; m. Carolyn W. Greene, Sept. 1990. BS, Washington U., St. Louis, 1961; MS, Purdue U., 1962; PhD, U. Santa Clara (Calif.), 1970. Part-time lectr. Washington U., Howard U., Am. U., 1959-65; dir. Tech. Devel. Corp., Arlington, Tex., 1985-92; pres. Zero One Systems, Inc. (formerly Tech. Devel. of Calif.) Santa Clara, Calif., 1971-87, Zero One Systems Group subs. Sterling Software Inc., 1987-89; asst. chmn., lectr. Stanford U., 1972-74; bd. dirs. Networked Picture Systems Inc., 1986, pres., 1989-91, chmn., 1991—. Author two indsl. textbooks; also articles; patentee in field. Bd. dirs. NCCJ, Santa Clara, 1980—, NAACP, San Jose chpt., 1986-89; bd. regents Santa Clara U., 1983-90, trustee, 1990—; mem. adv. bd. Urban League, Santa Clara County, 1986-89, East Side Union High Sch., 1985-88. Capt. USAF, 1961-65. Mem. IEEE, IEEE Computer Soc. (governing bd. 1973-75), Assn. Black Mfrs. (bd. dir., 1974-80), Am. Electric Assn. (indsl. adv. bd., 1975-76), Fairchild Rsch. and Devel. (tech. staff, 1965-71), Bay Area Purchasing Coun. (bd. dir. 1978-84), Security Affairs Support Assn. (bd. dir. 1980-83), Sigma Xi, Eta Kappa Nu, Sigma Pi Phi. Office: Network Picture Systems Inc 2041 Mission Coll Blvd Ste 255 Santa Clara CA 95054-1155

GREENE, JAMES FIEDLER, real estate executive; b. Rochester, Minn., Feb. 15, 1958; s. Laurence Francis and Rosalyn Estelle (Ravits) G. BA, Colo. Coll., 1980; MBA, U. Denver, 1987. Lic. real estate broker, Colo. Exec. broker CB Comml. Group, Denver, 1982—. Mem. Alumni awards com. Colo. Coll., Denver, 1986—. Club: Colo. Coll. Gold, Denver Athletic Colo. Office: CB Comml Group 1050 17 St Ste 800 Denver CO 80265-0801

GREENE, JOHN ALAN, lawyer; b. Staten Island, N.Y., Nov. 22, 1947; s. Thomas A. Greene and Kathryn (Breedlove) Kennedy; m. Janice E. Quattrochi, Sept. 1, 1951; children: Richard, Christopher. BA in Polit. Sci., CUNY-Hunter Coll., 1969; JD, St. John's U., Bklyn., 1972; LLM, NYU, 1979. Bar: N.Y. 1973, Ariz. 1979, U.S. Dist. Ct. (ea. and so. dists.) N.Y. 1975, U.S. Ct. Appeals (2d cir.) 1975, U.S. Supreme Ct. 1977. Assoc. counsel The Manhattan Life Ins. Co., N.Y.C., 1972-77; asst. counsel N.Y. Life Ins. Co., N.Y.C., 1977-79; sr. tax counsel The Greyhound Corp., Phoenix, 1979—. Panel mem. Ariz. Community Svc. Legal Assistance Found., 1988—. Republican. Roman Catholic. Office: Arizona State Senate 9429 N 47th St Phoenix AZ 85028-5203 Office: The Greyhound Corp 1701 Greyhound Tower 11 W Clarendon Phoenix AZ 85077

GREENE, JOHN THOMAS, JR., federal judge; b. Salt Lake City, Nov. 28, 1929; s. John Thomas and Mary Agnes (Hindley) G.; m. Kay Buchanan, Mar. 31, 1955; children: Thomas B., John B., Mary Kay. B.A., U. Utah, 1952, J.D., 1955. Bar: Utah 1955. Law clk. Supreme Ct. Utah, Salt Lake City, 1954-55; asst. U.S. atty. Dist. Utah, Salt Lake City, 1957-59; partner firm Marr, Wilkins & Cannon, Salt Lake City, 1959-69, Cannon, Greene & Nebeker, Salt Lake City, 1969-74, Greene, Callister & Nebeker, Salt Lake City, 1974-85; judge U.S. Dist. Ct. Utah, 1985—; spl. asst. atty. gen. State of Utah, 1965-69; spl. grand jury counsel Salt Lake County, 1970; pres. Utah Bar Found., 1971-74, trustee, 1971-88. Author: sect. on mining rights American Law of Mining, 1965; contbr. articles to profl. jours. Pres. Community Svcs. Coun., Salt Lake City area, 1971-73; chmn. Utah Bldg. Authority, 1980-85; mem. Utah State Bd. Regents, 1983-86. Mem. Utah Bar Assn. (pres. 1970-71, chmn. jud. com. 1971-76, chmn. com. post. law sch. tng. 1985-89), ABA (Utah del. to ho. of dels. 1975-81, 82-93, mem. bd. govs. 1988-91, mem. spl. com. delivery legal svc. 1975-81, coun. gen. practice sect. 1974-82, chmn. spl. com. on envrion. law 1971-75, mem. adv. com. Nat. Legal Svc. Corp. 1975-81, chmn. standing com. on jud. selection, tenure and compensation 1985-88), Am. Law Inst. (mem. adv. com. on restatement of law governing lawyers), Order of Coif, other. Mem. LDS Ch. Office: US Courthouse 350 S Main St Salt Lake City UT 84101

GREENE, LAURENCE WHITRIDGE, JR., surgical educator; b. Denver, Jan. 18, 1924; s. Laurence Whitridge Sr. and Freda (Schmitt) G.; m. Frances Steger, Sept. 16, 1950 (dec. Dec. 1977); children: Charlotte Greene Kerr, Mary Whitridge Greene, Laurence Whitridge III; m. Nancy Kay Bennett, Dec. 7, 1984. BA, Colo. Coll., 1945; MD, U. Colo., 1947; postgrad., U. Chgo., 1948-50. Diplomate Am. Bd. of Surgery. Intern St. Lukes Hosp., Denver, 1947-48; sr. intern in ob./gyn. U. Chgo. Lying-In Hosp., 1948-49; surg. resident U. Cin. Gen. Hosp., 1952-55, sr. surg. resident, 1955-57, chief surgery resident, 1957-58; clin. surgery asst. Sch. of Medicine U. Colo., Denver, 1958-61, clin. instr. Sch. of Medicine, 1961-67, asst. clin. prof. Sch. of Medicine, 1967-75, assoc. clin. prof. Sch. of Medicine, 1975-87, clin. prof. Sch. of Medicine, 1987—; adj. prof. zoology and physiology U. Wyo., Laramie, 1970—; mem. staff Ivinson Meml. Hosp., Laramie, Wyo., 1958—; chmn. Wyo. chpt. Com. on Trauma, 1973-89; tchr., mem. adv. staff U. Colo.

Med. Sch., Denver, 1958-83; med. advisor, surgeon U. Wyo. Athletics, Laramie, 1975-80, Wyo. Hwy. Patrol, 1950—. Contbr. numerous articles to profl. jours. Lt. M.C. (s.g.) USN, 1950-52, Korea. Fellow ACS; mem. Am. Assn. for Surgery of Trauma, Southwestern Surgery Congress, Western Surg. Assn., Mont Reed Soc., Masons, Shriners, Sigma Xi. Republican. Episcopalian.

GREENE, MARK EDWARD, consultant, educator; b. Chgo., May 18, 1954; s. Jean Edward Greene and Noreen Eileen (Scanlon) Winter. Diploma in systems renewal consultation, Internat. Inst. Study of Systems Renewal, 1990; BA, Antioch U., 1988, MA in Whole Systems Design, 1990; postgrad., Fielding Inst., Santa Barbara, Calif., 1990—. Prodn. planning supr. Respiratory Care Inc., Arlington Heights, Ill., 1973-79; requirements planning analyst Admiral Home Appliances, Schaumburg, Ill., 1979-81; prodn. control supr. Physio Control Corp., Redmond, Wash., 1981-86; program assoc. Antioch U., Seattle, 1989-92; cons. Seattle, 1986—; adj. faculty Antioch U., Seattle, 1992—; cons. Seattle Police Dept., 1986. Mem. Mayor's Lesbian Gay Task Force, Seattle, 1984-86; bd. dirs. Dorian Group, Seattle, 1986; vol. Seamec, Seattle, 1984. Unitarian. Home and Office: 303 16th Ave E Apt 302 Seattle WA 98112

GREENE, RICHARD MARTIN, artist; b. Utica, N.Y., Oct. 30, 1953; s. Stuart Merwin and Lois Claire (Friedlander) G. BS, MIT, 1974. Exhibit developer The Exploratorium, San Francisco, 1974-76, 80-82; artist San Francisco, 1976-80; programmer Jandel Corp., Sausalito, Calif., 1983-84; artist, inventor San Francisco, 1984—; computer cons., San Francisco, 1984—; artist-in-residence The Exploratorium, San Francisco, 1986-87. Contbr. articles to profl. jours.; inventor, patentee graphic input apparatus; exhibited in group show at IBM Think Pocket, Tokyo, 1984-89. Vol. tutor San Francisco Unified Sch. Dist., 1985-88. Mem. Assn. for Computing Machinery (spl. interest group on graphics). Mem. Green Party. Home and office: 700 31st Ave # 2 San Francisco CA 94121-3541

GREENFIELD-MARCUS, MARGEE ANN, university administrator; b. Louisville, Aug. 26, 1951; d. Gerald and Mildred (Berman) Greenfield; m. Jay Marcus, Nov. 20, 1988; children: Rebekah Mildred, Jennie Faye. BS, Ind. U., 1973, MS, 1979; EdD, No. Ariz. U., 1987. Asst. reg. sales mgr. Garland Corp., N.Y.C., 1974-76; N.Y. rep. and buyer's asst. Gantos Stores of Grand Rapids, N.Y.C., 1977-78; co-op dir. Ind. U., Bloomington, 1978-79; residence hall dir. U. Kans., Lawrence, 1979-81; area coord. residence life No. Ariz. U., Flagstaff, 1981-83; panhellenic advisor No. Ariz. U., 1983-84, asst. dir. Univ. Advisement Ctr., 1984-88, assoc. dir., 1988-91; dir. univ. acad. advising ctr. Ariz. State U., 1991—. Contbr. articles to profl. jours. Mem. AAUW, (v.p. 1988-90), Nat. Acad. Advising Assn. (nat. bd. dirs. 1992-94), Nat. Assn. Student Personnel Adminstrs., No. Ariz. U. Faculty Women's Assn., Ariz. State Univ. Faculty Women's Assn. (bd. dirs., 1993), Beta Sigma Phi. Democrat. Jewish. Office: Ariz State U Univ Acad Advising Ctr Tempe AZ 85287-3002

GREENHALL, CHARLES AUGUST, mathematician; b. N.Y.C., May 5, 1939; s. A. Frank and Miriam (Housman) G. BA, Pomona Coll., 1961; PhD, Calif. Inst. Tech., 1966. Rsch. assoc. Jet Propulsion Lab., Pasadena, Calif., 1966-68; asst. prof. U. So. Calif., L.A., 1968-73; with Jet Propulsion Lab., Pasadena, 1973—, mem. tech. staff, 1981—. Contbr. articles to profl. jours; patentee of frequency stability measurement. Mem. IEEE, Am. Math. Soc., Math. Assn. Am., Soc. Indsl. and Applied Maths. Republican. Home: 1836 Hanscom Dr South Pasadena CA 91030-4008 Office: Jet Propulsion Lab # 298-100 4800 Oak Grove Dr Pasadena CA 91109-8099

GREENLAW, ROGER LEE, interior designer; b. New London, Conn., Oct. 12, 1936; s. Kenneth Nelson and Lyndell Lee (Stinson) G.; children—Carol Jennifer, Roger Lee. B.F.A., Syracuse U., 1958. Interior designer Cannell & Chaffin, 1958-59, William C. Wagner, Architect, Los Angeles, 1959-60, Gen. Fireproofing Co., Los Angeles, 1960-62, K-S Wilshire, Inc., Los Angeles, 1963-64; dir. interior design Calif. Desk Co., Los Angeles, 1964-67; sr. interior designer Bechtel Corp., Los Angeles, 1967-70; sr. interior designer, project mgr. Daniel, Mann, Johnson, & Mendehall, Los Angeles, 1970-72, Morganelli-Heumann & Assos., Los Angeles, 1972-73; owner, prin. Greenlaw Design Assos., Glendale, Calif., 1973—; lectr. UCLA; mem. adv. curriculum com. Mt. San Antonio Coll., Walnut, Calif., Fashion Inst. Design, Los Angeles; bd. dirs. Calif. Legis. Conf. Interior Design. Past scoutmaster Verdugo council Boy Scouts Am.; pres. bd. dirs. Unity Ch., La Crescenta, Calif., 1989-91. Mem. Am. Soc. Interior Designers (treas. Pasadena chpt. 1983-84, 1st v.p. 1985, pres. 1986-87, chmn. So. Calif. regional conf. 1985, nat. dir. 1987—, nat. com. legis., nat. com. jury for catalog award, speaker ho. dels., nat. bd. dirs., medallist award, regional v.p., nat. chair ethics com., nat. exec. com., v.p., treas. 1992 Calif. legislative conf. interior design, chmn. standards task force,), Glendale C. of C. (bd. dirs.), Adm. Farragut Acad. Alumni Assn., Delta Upsilon. Republican. Lodge: Kiwanis (bd. dirs.). Home: 2100F Valderas Dr Glendale CA 91208-1340 Office: 3901 Ocean View Blvd Montrose CA 91020-1514

GREENLEAF, JOHN EDWARD, research physiologist; b. Joliet, Ill., Sept. 18, 1932; s. John Simon and Julia Clara (Flint) G.; m. Carol Lou Johnson, Aug. 28, 1960. MA, N.Mex. Highlands U., 1956; BA in Phys. Edn., U. Ill., 1955, MS, 1962, PhD in Physiol., 1963. Teaching asst. N.Mex. Highlands U., Las Vegas, Nev., 1955-56; engring. draftsman Allis-Chalmers Mfg. Co., Springfield, Ill., 1956-57; teaching asst. in phys. edn. U. Ill., Urbana, 1957-58, rsch. asst. in phys. edn., 1958-59, teaching asst. in human anatomy and physiology, 1959-62; summer fellow NSF, 1962; pre-doctoral fellow NIH, 1962-63; rsch. physiologist Life Scis. Directorate, NASA, Ames Rsch. Ctr., Moffett Field, Calif., 1963-66, 67—; postdoctoral fellowship Royal Gymnastic Inst., Stockholm, 1966-67. Mem. editorial bd. Jour. Applied Physiology, 1989—; contbr. articles to profl. jours. Recipient George Huff award for Scholarship, U. Ill. 1954-55, NASA Spl. Achievement award, 1973. Served with U.S. Army, 1952-53. Exch. fellow Nat. Acad. Scis., 1973-74, 77, 89, NIH, 1980; recipient Disting. Alumni award N.Mex. Highlands U., 1990. Fellow Am. Coll. Sports Medicine (trustee 1984-87), Aerospace Med. Assn. (Harold Ellingson award 1981, 82, Eric Liljencrantz award 1990); mem. Am. Physiol. Soc. (mem. com. on coms. 1984-87), Shooting Sports Rsch. Coun. (internat. shooters devel. fund 1984), Sigma Xi. Home: 12391 Farr Ranch Ct Saratoga CA 95070-6527 Office: NASA Ames Rsch Ctr Life Sci Div MS 239-11 Moffett Field CA 94035-1000

GREENLICK, VICKI RUTH, film producer; b. Detroit, Nov. 15, 1961; d. Merwyn Ronald and Harriet Pauline (Cohen)Greenlick; m. Bernard Joseph Bottomly, Aug. 27, 1988; 1 child, Elizabeth Ann Bottomly. Student, Oberlin (Ohio) Coll., 1979-83. Office mgr. Friends of Les AuCoin, Portland, Oreg., 1985-87; prodn. asst. Signature Prodns., Portland, Oreg., 1987, prodn. coord., 1987-88, producer, 1988-89; exec. producer Signature Films, Portland, Oreg., 1989—. Producer tv comml. (Advt. Age Best 1989, Clio finalist, Emmy finalist). Co-chmn. Cascade Awards Festival, Portland, 1991, 92; mem. Hysterectomy Info. Com., Portland, 1990. Mem. Assn. Ind. Comml. Producers, Oreg. Media Prodn. Assn., Portland Advt. Fedn. Democrat.

GREENSPAN, BERNARD, mathematics educator, consultant; b. N.Y.C., Dec. 17, 1914; s. Harry and Yetta (Siegel) G.; m. Beatrice Meltzer, Aug. 26, 1939; children—Valerie Helen Greenspan Welch, Ellen Freda Greenspan Delaney. B.S., Bklyn. Coll., 1935; M.A., 1936; postgrad. Columbia U., 1936-38; Ph.D., Rutgers U., 1958; postgrad. Rensselaer Poly. Inst., 1960. Instr. math. Bklyn. Coll., 1935-44; instr. Poly. Inst. Bklyn., 1943-44; instr. math. Drew U., Madison, N.J., 1944-47, asst. prof., 1947-58, assoc. prof., 1958-59, prof., 1959-81, prof. emeritus, 1981—, chmn. dept. math., 1959-75; vis. prof. U. Santa Clara, Calif., 1961, Rutgers U., 1971; cons., lectr. math. Bell Telephone Lab., Whippany, N.J., 1953-58; dir. Inservice Math. Inst. NSF, Drew U., Madison, 1961-75, dir. Summer Math. Inst., 1962-74; reader, table leader Advanced Placement Exams Ednl. Testing Service, Princeton, N.J., 1966-72. Contbr. articles in field to profl. jours. NSF fellow, 1958-59. Mem. Am. Math. Soc., Math. Assn. Am. (past chmn. exec. com. N.J. sect.), Sigma Xi, Pi Mu Epsilon, Sigma Phi. Home: 9164 Tangerine St San Ramon CA 94583-3921

GREENSPAN, JOHN S., dentistry educator, educator and administrator; b. London, Jan. 7, 1938; came to U.S., 1976; s. Nathan and Jessie (Dion) G.; m. Deborah, Dec. 1962; children: Nicholas J., Louise C. BSC in Anatomy with 1st class honors, U. London, 1959, B in Dental Surgery, 1962, PhD in Exptl. Pathology, 1967; ScD (hon.), Georgetown U., 1990. Licentiate in dental surgery Royal Coll. of Surgeons of Eng. Asst. house surgeon in conservation and periodontology Royal Dental Hosp. London, 1962; asst. lectr. oral pathology Sch. of Dental Surgery Royal Dental Hosp. of London, U. London, 1963-65, lectr. oral pathology Sch. of Dental Surgery, 1965-68, sr. lectr. oral pathology Sch. of Dental Surgery, 1968-75; prof. oral biology and oral pathology Sch. of Dentisty, U. Calif., San Francisco, 1976—, vice chmn. dept. oral medicine and hosp. dentistry, 1977-82, chmn. div. oral biology, 1981-89, coord. basic scis. Sch. of Dentistry, 1982—; chmn. dept. stomatology U. Calif., San Francisco, 1989—; cons. oral pathology St. John's Hosp. and Inst. of Dermatology, London, 1973-76; cons. dental surgeon St. George's Hosp., 1972-76; prof. dept. pathology Sch. Medicine U. Calif., San Francisco, 1976—; dir. U. Calif. AIDS Specimen Bank, San Francisco, 1982—, U. Calif. Oral AIDS Ctr., San Francisco, 1987—; asso. dir. dental clin. epidemiology program U. Calif., San Francisco, 1987—; dir. U. Calif. AIDS Cin. Rsch. Ctr., San Francisco, 1992—; presenter, lectr. Author: (with others) Opportunistic Infections in Patients with the Acquired Immunodeficiency Syndrome, 1989, Contemporary Periodontics, 1989, Gastroenterology Clinics of North America, 1988, Perspectives on Oral Manifestations of AIDS, 1988, AIDS: Pathogenesis and Treatment, 1988, others; contbr. articles to profl. jours.; editorial cons. Achives of Oral Biology, 1968—, Jour. of Calif. Dental Assn., 1980—; editoral adv. bd. Jour. of Dental Rsch., 1977—; editorial bd. AIDS Alert, 1987-89. Rsch. grantee NIH-Nat. Inst. Dental Rsch., 1978-82, 86-92, U. Calif. Task Force on AIDS, 1983—, rsch. com. Royal Dental Hosp., London, 1964-76, Med. Rsch. Coun. of U.K., 1974-77, chmn. U. Calif. San Francisco Acad. Senate, 1983-85; Nuffield dental scholar, 1958-59; fellow Am. Coll. Dentists, 1982—, AAAS, 1985—; recipient Seymour J. Kreshover Lecture award Nat. Inst. Dental Rsch., NIH, 1989, Rsch. in Oral Biology award Internat. Assn. Dental Rsch., 1992. Mem. Internat. Assn. for Dental Rsch., Royal Soc. Medicine (U.K.), Pathological Soc. (U.K.), Oral Pathology Soc. (U.K.), Royal Coll. Pathologists (U.K.), Am. Acad. Oral Pathology, Am. Assn. for Dental Rsch., Bay Area Tchrs. Oral Pathology, AAAS, Internat. Assn. Oral Pathologists, San Francisco Dental Soc., ADA, Calif. Dental Assn., Calif. Soc. Oral Pathologists Histochem. Soc., Am. Assn. Pathologists. Office: U Calif Sch Dentistry Dept Stomatology Rm 604 HSW San Francisco CA 94143-0512

GREENSTEIN, MERLE EDWARD, import/export company executive; b. Portland, Oreg., June 22, 1937; s. Sol and Tillie Germaine (Schnitzer) G.; m. Patricia Ellen Graves, April 5, 1971; children: Randall Dale, Todd Aaron. BA, Reed Coll., 1959. Pres. Acme Trading and Supply Co., Portland, 1963-82; chmn. MMI Group, Portland, 1982-91, Internat. Devel. Assocs., Portland, 1991—; com. mem. ISRI, Washington, 1987-89; mem. dist. export coun. U.S. Dept. Commerce, 1980—. Chmn. fin. Portland Opera, 1966; bd. dirs. Met. YMCA, 1964-67; del. to China, State of Oreg. Ofcl. Trade Mission, 1979; chmn. Western Internat. Trade Group, 1981-82; mem. State of Oreg. Korea Commn., 1985—; fin. chmn. Anne Frank exhibit, Portland; joint chmn. bldg. campaign Oreg. Mus. Sci. and Industry. Recipient President's E for Export, U.S. Dept. Commerce, 1969; named Citizen of the Week, City of Portland, 1953. Mem. RREC London, City Club, Tualatin Country Club, Masons, Shriners. Office: Internat Devel Assocs 6731 NE 47th Ave Portland OR 97218

GREENWAY, MARLENE LAURA, archaeologist; b. San Diego, Nov. 3, 1940; d. Edward Judd Hill and Erna Lydia (Ehmke) Wells; m. James Carl Greenway, June 22, 1957 (div. 1974); children: James Shean, Terry Lee, Marla Kay. AA in Philosophy with highest honors, Coll. of Redwoods, 1979; postgrad., U. Calif., Irvine, 1981; BA in Anthropology, Humboldt State U., 1984; MA in Cultural Resource Mgmt., Sonoma State U., Rohnert Park, Calif., 1988. Staff archaeologist Arcata (Calif.) Resource Area, 1988-91; dist. lead archaeologist Clear Lake Resource Area, Bur. Land Mgmt., Ukiah, Calif., 1991—; Chairperson Mendocino County Archaeol. Commn., Ukiah, 1988—. Mem. Soc. Am. Archaeology, Soc. Calif. Archaeology, Historic Mining Assn., Lake County Hist. Soc., Pi Gamma Mu. Republican. Home: 144 Fairview Ct Ukiah CA 95482 Office: Bur Land Mgmt 555 Leslie St Ukiah CA 95482

GREENWAY, ROBERT GLEN, psychology educator, land-use planner; b. Seattle, Dec. 13, 1932; s. James Clarence and Helen Louise (Buddenhagen) G.; m. Grace Lou Hutchins, Sept. 11, 1954 (div. July 1968); children: Christine, Mark, Stephan, Erik; m. Donna Marie Dellevecchia, June 30, 1983; 1 child, Aleta. BS, U. Wash., 1955, postgrad., 1955-56; MA, Brandeis U., 1963. Biology rschr. dept. zoology U. Wash., Seattle, 1955-56; writer Sunset mag., Menlo Park, Calif., 1956-59; writer, rschr. Stanford Rsch. Inst., Menlo Park, 1959-60; writer, editor Brandeis U., Waltham, Mass., 1960-63; founding dean, instr. Franconia (N.H.) Coll., 1963-66; dir. inst. rels. U.S. Peace Corps, Washington, 1966-68; dir. planning U. Calif., Santa Cruz, 1968-69; prof. psychology Sonoma State U., Rohnert Park, Calif., 1969—; cons. U. Idaho Sch. Forestry, Moscow, 1990—. Author: Rasberry Exercises, 1970. Mem. Jefferson County Planning Commn., 1991—. Mem. Native American Ch. Home: 1611 Corona St Port Townsend WA 98368 Office: Sonoma State U Dept Psychology Rohnert Park CA 94928

GREENWOOD, HARRY MARSHALL, III, educator; b. Syracuse, N.Y., Dec. 8, 1934; s. Harry Marshall and Thelma Mary (Flack) G.; m. Barbara Hatsume Kasadate; 1 child, Casey. BA, U. Chgo., 1960; MEd, U. Hawaii, 1969. Tchr. Chgo. Pub. Schs., 1962-64; counselor Cook County TB Sanitarium, Chgo., 1960; tchr. Trust Territory of Pacific, 1964-65; tchr. Kauai Pub. Schs., Lihue, Hawaii, 1965-70, psychol. examiner, 1970; diagnostic tchr. Kauai Pub. Schs., Lihue, 1970-84, dist. specialist, 1984-85, diagnostic tchr., 1985—. With USN, 1952-55. Mem. Am. Legion, Hawaii Govt. Employee Assn. Bahai. Home: 241 Waikolia St Kapaa HI 96746 Office: Dept of Edn 3060 Eiwa St Lihue HI 96766

GREENWOOD, RICHARD M., finance company executive, bank executive; b. Fargo, N.D., 1947. Grad., U. Idaho, 1972, Am. Grad. Sch. Internat. Mgmt., 1974. Exec. v.p., CFO Calfed Inc., L.A.; pres., CEO, dir. Citadel Holding Corp., Glendale, Calif. Office: Citadel Holding Corp 600 N Brand Blvd Glendale CA 91203

GREENWOOD, WILBUR ROWE, III, small business owner; b. Albany, N.Y., Apr. 21, 1941; s. Wilbur R. Jr. and Jean (McOrmond) G.; m. Pamela Sheridan Sutton, Nov. 8, 1974; children: Jennifer, Trevor. BA, Yale U., 1963; MBA, Cornell U., 1968. Investment banker Smith Barney, N.Y.C., 1968-75, Foster & Marshall, Seattle, 1976-82, Dain Bosworth, Seattle, 1982-86; pres., CEO Spider Staging Corp., Seattle, 1986—, chmn. bd. dirs.; bd. dirs. Foster & Marshall, Seattle, Advanced Imput Devices. Lt. USNR, 1963-65. Mem. Wash. Athletic Club, Overlake Golf Club, Rainier Club. Home: 4915 84th Ave SE Mercer Island WA 98040 Office: Spider Staging Corp 12720 Gateway Dr Seattle WA 98168

GREEP, LINDA CARYL, speaker, entertainer, school district administrator; b. Chgo., Nov. 8, 1947; d. Vernon Lester and Elaine Dorothy (Brown) George; m. Larry Arthur Greep, Mar. 29, 1969; 1 child, David James. BS in Edn., Ill. State U., 1969. Tchr. Evergreen Sch. Dist., Vancouver, 1978-87, adminstr., 1987—; TV producer, host Columbia Cable of Wash., Vancouver, 1983—; advisor The Columbian newspaper, Vancouver, 1990—; on-air pledge host Oreg. Pub. Broadcasting, Portland, Oreg., 1990—; speaker, cons. in field. Producer, host ednl. video Report Card From Your Schools, 1990 (State Video award 1991); writer, producer PSA/TV programs Kindergarten Reg. PSA, 1988 (Nat. Video award 1989), Bus Safety, 1988 (Nat. Video award 1989); host, producer local children's TV program Columbia Cable, 1983—. Fundraiser chmn. Evergreen Citizens for Schs., Vancouver, 1989—; bd. dirs. Tears of Joy Theatre, Vancouver, 1986-88, Arts Coun. of Clark County, Vancouver, 1986-88; fundraiser Miss Wash. Scholarship Pageant, 1985—. Recipient Best Actress award Lake Oswego Theatre, 1986, Performing Arts award Arts Coun. of Clark County, 1988, Decker Theatre award Columbian newspaper, 1988, Woman of Achievement award Portland/Metro Area, 1989, State Ednl. Advt. award Wash. Sch. Pub. Rels. Assn., 1993, Video award, Wash. Sch. Pub. Rels. Assn., 1993. Mem. Wash. Assn. Sch. Adminstrs. (treas., bd. dirs. 1991-93), S.W. Wash. Hosp. Adv. Coun., Nat. Sch. Pub. Rels. Assn. (Nat. Ednl. Advt. award 1993, Nat. Ednl. Video award 1993), Nat. Speakers' Assn., Oreg. Speakers' Assn, Rotary (Vocat. Svc. award Greater Clark County club 1991, named to Clark County Hall of Fame for arts and entertainment 1993). Methodist. Home: 1908 SE 158th Ave Vancouver WA 98684-9064 Office: Evergreen Sch Dist 13905 NE 28th St Vancouver WA 98682-8099

GREER, DARRELL STEPHEN, finance executive; b. St. Louis, July 4, 1949; s. Roger James and Florence Marie (Kelly) G.; m. Rosemary Fowler, 1973 (div. 1975). BA in Philosophy, Calif. State U., L.A., 1981. Cert. notary pub., Calif. Commd. 2d lt USAF, 1967, advanced through grades to staff sgt.; with ticket dept. L.A. Dodgers, 1982-92; motivational cons. Darrell Greer & Assocs., L.A., 1984-86; ops. asst. Smith-Barney-Shearson, Albuquerque, 1988—. Mem. AFTRA, Screen Actors Guild, Non-Commd. Officers Assn., Mensa(film critic monthly rev. column Lament mag. L.A. chpt. 1987-92), Masons (chaplain). Home: 516 Star Villa Circle Rio Rancho NM 87124-2927 Office: Smith Barney Shearson 1720 Louisiana Blvd # 400 Albuquerque NM 87110

GREER, HOWARD EARL, former naval officer; b. Tyler, Tex., May 1, 1921; s. Earl Abner and Ollie (Lightfoot) G.; m. Dale Price, Nov. 1, 1986; children—Margaret, Darby, David, Briand, Holly, Howard. Student, Tyler Jr. Coll., 1939-40; B.S., U.S. Naval Acad., 1943; M.B.A., George Washington U., 1965. Commd. ensign U.S. Navy, 1943, advanced through grades to vice adm., 1975; comdr. Aircraft Carrier Hancock, 1967-69, Carrier Force, Vietnam, (4 tours), Naval Air Forces, U.S. Atlantic Fleet, Norfolk, Va., 1975-78; dir. CEDAM Internat.; with Hughes Aircraft. Decorated D.S.M. (2), Legion of Merit (4), Knights of Malta Order St. John of Jerusalem. Mem. Assn. Naval Aviation (trustee), Golden Eagles (early pioneer naval aviators, Tailhook Assn., Naval Res. Assn. Republican. Methodist. Clubs: Outrigger Canoe; Oahu Country. Home: 1121 Waieli St Honolulu HI 96821-1244

GREER, RICHARD EWING, SR., language testing company executive; b. Matheson, Colo., Nov. 4, 1935; s. Clarence Alfred and Martha Amelia (Tretter) G.; m. Carolyn Jean Harless, Feb. 1, 1957 (div. July 1983); children: Richard II, Donna, Justin. Student Chinese Mandarin, U.S. Army Lang. Sch., 1957-58; student Korean (honors cert.), Defense Lang. Inst., 1961-62; student Japanese, Sophia U., Tokyo, 1963-64; student Chinese (honors cert.), Yale U., 1964-65. Cert. profl. linguist, Nat. Security Agy. Chief translation sect. Joint Sobe Processing Ctr., Okinawa, 1965-68; army chief instr. U.S. Army Groundforces Tng. Program, Goodfellow AFB, Tex., 1968-70; commdr. U.S. Army Security Agy. Detachment, Goodfellow AFB, Tex., 1970; staff lang. officer Nat. Security Agy. Pacific Rep., Taiwan, 1971; chief linguist B div. Nat. Security Agy., Laurel, Md., 1972-75; army chief instr. USAF Cryptologic Tng. Ctr. and Sch., San Angelo, Tex., 1975-77; pres., CEO Tech. Lan. Systems, Inc., San Angelo, Tex., 1977-88, Englewood, Colo., 1988—. Inventor: Curriculum Devel. System, 1978, ednl. fgn. lang. bd. game, Traipsing Around, 1990; co-author: tests and curricula in 26 foreign lang. and 9 English versions. Decorated Legion of Merit, U.S. Army, 1977. Republican. Office: Tech Lang Systems Inc Southgate IV 6886 S Yosemite Englewood CO 80112

GREERAN, JUDITH RAE, restauranteur; b. Santa Barbara, Calif., Oct. 22, 1939; d. Fred Homer and Iona Minnie (Wallace) Miller; m. Elio R. Giusti, Dec. 21, 1957 (div. June 1962); m. Thomas P. Greeran, June 1, 1980. Student, U. Calif.-Berkeley, 1961-65. Adminstrv. asst. U. Calif., Berkeley, 1961-69; asst. booking agt. Sal Carson Orch., 1969-70; constrn./archtl. analyst Michael Goodman Architect, Berkeley, 1970-74; budget analyst U. Calif., San Francisco, 1974-76; sec.-treas. Berkeley Blue Print, 1976-91, bd. dirs., 1985-91; ptnr. contr. TJ's Bar & Grill Loch Lomond Resort, Cobb, Calif., 1991—; editor Informer. Co-columnist (with Madelyn Martinelli) Middletown Times Star Newspaper, 1992—. Bd. mem. Marina Gardens Assn., San Leandro, Calif., 1988-91; active Earth Island Inst., San Francisco, 1988, U.S. Humane Soc., Washington, 1985—. Mem. 49er Goal Rushers Booster Club (founding mem., v.p.). Democrat. Office: TJ's Bar & Grill Loch Lomond Resort PO Box 1430 Cobb CA 95426-1430

GREEVER, JOHN, mathematics educator; b. Pulaski, Va., Jan. 30, 1934; s. John Jay Greever and Hulah Lily (Loyd) Bentley; m. Margaret LeSueur Quarles, Aug. 29, 1953; children: Catherine Patricia, Richard George, Cynthia Diane. BS in Math., U. Richmond, 1953; MA in Math., U. Va., 1956, PhD in Math., 1958. Asst. prof. math. Fla. State U., Tallahassee, 1958-61; mem. faculty Harvey Mudd Coll., Claremont, Calif., 1961—; prof. math. Harvey Mudd Coll., Claremont, 1970—, chmn. math. dept., 1972-75, founding dir. math. clinic, 1973-75; mem. faculty Claremont Grad. Sch., 1962—; vis. prof. Kyoto (Japan) U. Rsch. Inst. for Math. Sci., 1967-68, U. B.C. Inst. Animal Resource Ecology, Vancouver, 1984-85; rsch. assoc. U. Calif. Dept. Biology, Riverside, 1975-78; vis. rsch. mathematician U. Calif. Dept. Entomology, 1978. Author Theory and Examples of Point Set Topology, 1967; contbr. articles to profl. jours. Mem. AAAS, Am. Math. Soc., Coun. on Undergrad Rsch. (vice chmn. math. and computer scis. sec. 1991-92, chmn. 1992—), Math. Assn. Am. (sec.-treas. So. Calif. sect. 1973-76, pres. 1981-82), Pi Mu Epsilon, Sigma Xi, Kappa Mu Epsilon, Phi Kappa Sigma. Home: 135 W 12th St Claremont CA 91711-3808 Office: Harvey Mudd Coll 277 Olin Claremont CA 91711-5990

GREGERSON, NED OWEN, dentist; b. Gunnison, Utah, Aug. 2, 1940; s. Owen Louis and Edna (Jensen) G.; m. Dixie Ann Christiansen, June 10, 1960; children: Gary Ned, David Lynn, Owen Marc, Ryan N., Kaisa Anne. AA, Snow Coll., 1962; BS, Utah State U., 1963; DDS, U. Wash., 1967. Diplomate Am. Acad. of Pain Mgmt. Dentist Wash. state Health, Seattle, 1967; dentist, pres. Gentle Dental Ctr., Cedar City, Utah, 1971—; dir., pres. Shingle Brook devel. Corp., Cedar City, 1984—, Willow Run Devel. Corp., St. George, Utah, 1984-86; dir., v.p. Cedar Venture Pipeline, Salt Lake City, 1983-87, High Country Drilling Corp., Ogden, Utah, 1981-91; gen. ptnr., dir. Indian Peaks Ent., Salt Lake City, 1980-87. Editorial panel Dental Econs. mag., 1978-80; article reviewer Gen. Dentistry Mag., 1986—. Mem. Thunderbird Booster Club, Cedar City, 1990—. Capt. U.S. Army, 1967-72. Master Acad. Gen. Dentistry; fellow Acad. Dentistry Internat., Pierre Fauchard Acad.; mem. Am. Orthodontic Soc., Utah Acad. Gen. Dentistry (bd. dirs., del. 1987-92, pres. elect, 1990, pres. 1991-92), ADA, Utah Dental Assn. (bd. dirs. 1977-80, ann. conv. bd. 1991-95), So. Utah Dist. Dental Soc. (treas. 1973-74, pres. 1974-75), Am. Acad. Dentistry for Children, Lions. Republican. LDS. Home: 471 S Rosehill Cedar City UT 84720 Office: 747 S Paradise Canyon Cedar City UT 84720

GREGG, LUCIUS PERRY, JR., aerospace executive; b. Henderson, N.C., Jan. 16, 1933; s. Lucius Perry Sr. and Rachel (Jackson) G.; m. Doris Marie Jefferson, May 30, 1959 (dec. Nov. 1980); 1 child, Lucius Perry III. BS in FF, U.S. Naval Acad., 1955; MS in Aero and Astronautics, MIT, 1961; AMP Program, Harvard U., 1975; D of Sci. (hon.), Grinnell Coll., 1973. Pilot, aircraft commdr. mil. air command USAF, 1956-59; project scientist Air Force Office Scientific Rsch., Washington, 1961-65; dir., rsch. coord., assoc. dean sci. Northwestern U., Evanston, Ill., 1965-69; program officer Alfred P. Sloan Found., N.Y.C., 1969-72; pres. First Chgo. U. Finance Corp., Chgo., 1972-79; v.p. First Nat. Bank Chgo., 1972-79; v.p. corp. planning Bristol-Myers Co., N.Y.C., 1979-83; dir. nat. pub. rels., v.p. gov. rels. Citibank/Citicorp, N.Y.C., 1983-87; v.p. pub. affairs N.Y. Daily News, N.Y.C., 1987-89; v.p. corp. communications Hughes Aircraft Co., L.A., 1989—; vis. com. on aero and astronautics MIT, Cambridge, 1971-79; vis. com. on physics Harvard U., Cambridge, 1973-79; mem. commn. on human resources Nat. Acad. Sci., Washington, 1973-78; vice chmn., bd. dirs.Corp. for Pub. Broadcasting, Washington, 1975-81; bd. trustees W Net Pub. TV, N.Y.C., 1981-89; bd. dirs. Chgo. Coun. on Fgn. Rels., Chgo., 1975-79; mem. academic bd. U.S. Naval Acad., Annapolis, Md., 1971-81; mem. NASA U. REls., Washington, 1968-72; chmn. bd. Tulane U., New Orleans, 1972-82; trustee Roosevelt U., Chgo., 1976-79; mem. Ill. Commn. on Urban Gov., Chgo., 1976-79, Chgo. Mayor's Coun. Econ. Advisors, Chgo., 1976-79; intelligence rev. com. Chgo. Police Depart., 1977-79. Maj. USAF, 1965-85. Named Engr. of Yr. Washington Acad. Sci., 1964, One of 10 Outstanding Young Men Chgo. Jr. Assn. Commerce and Industry, 1966. Office: Hughes Aircraft Co 7200 Hughes Terr Los Angeles CA 90045

GREGGS, ELIZABETH MAY BUSHNELL (MRS. RAYMOND JOHN GREGGS), retired librarian; b. Delta, Colo., Nov. 7, 1925; d. Joseph Perkins and Ruby May (Stanford) Bushnell; m. Raymond John Greggs, Aug. 16, 1952; children: David M., Geoffrey B., Timothy C., Daniel R. BA, U. Denver, 1948. Children's librarian Grand Junction (Colo.) Pub. Library,

1944-46, Chelan County Library, 1948, Wenatchee (Wash.) Pub. Library, 1948-52, Seattle Pub. Library, 1952-53; children's librarian Renton (Wash.) Pub. Library, 1957-61, dir., 1962, br. supr. and children's services supr., 1963-67; area children's supr. King County Library, Seattle, 1968-78, asst. coordinator children's services, 1978-86; head librarian Valley View Library of King County Library System, Seattle, 1986-90; cons., organizer Tutor Ctr. Library, Seattle South Community Coll., 1969-72; mem. Puget Sound (Wash.) Council for Reviewing Children's Media, 1974—, chmn., 1974-76; cons. to children's TV programs. Editor: Cayas Newsletter, 1971-74; cons. to Children's Catalog, Children's Index to Poetry. Chmn. dist. advancement com. Kloshee dist. Boy Scouts Am., 1975-78; mem. Bond Issue Citizens Group to build new Renton Library, 1958, 59; mem. exec. bd. Family Edn. and Counseling Ctr. on Deafness, 1991—. Recipient Hon. Service to Youth award Cedar River dist. Boy Scouts Am., 1971, Award of Merit Kloshee dist., 1977, winner King County Block Grant, 1990. Mem. ALA (Newbery-Caldecott medal com. 1978-79, com. chmn. 1983-84; membership com. 1978-80, Boy Scouts com. children's svcs. div. 1973-78, chmn. 1976-78, exec. bd. dirs. Assn. for Libr. Svc. to Children 1979-81, mem. coun. 1985-92, chmn. nominating com. 1986-87, councillor 1989-92, exec. bd. 1989-92, exec. com. 1989-92, coun. orientation com. 1987-89), Wash. Libr. Assn. (exec. bd. children's and young adult svcs. div. 1970-78, chmn. membership com. 1983-90, publs. com. 1988-92, emeritus 1991, mem. elections com.), King County Right to Read Coun. (co-chmn. 1973-77), Pierce-King County Reading Coun., Wash. State Literacy Coun. (exec. bd. 1971-77), Wash. Libr. Media Assn. (jr. high levels com. 1980-84), Pacific N.W. Libr. Assn. (young readers' choice com. 1981-83, chmn. div. 1983-85, exec. bd. 1983-85). Methodist. Home: 800 Lynnwood Ave NE Renton WA 98056-3805

GREGO, PETER, theatre arts educator; b. Pitts., May 29, 1949; s. William Joseph Sr. and Veronica Margaret (Zamulovich) G.; m. Barbara Cavalier, May 24, 1977 (div.). BFA, Carnegie-Mellon U., 1972, MFA, 1973. Instr. Pa. State U., New Kensington, 1973-76; coord. acting program Fla. Sch. of the Arts, Palatka, 1976-78; prof. Calif. State U., Bakersfield, 1978-84, Northridge, 1984—; bd. dirs. Santa Paula (Calif.) Theatre Ctr., Internat. City Theatre, Long Beach, Calif. Grantee NEH, 1984, Calif. State U., 1985-87; recipient Outstanding Dir. Drama-Logue award L.A. Weekly, 1990, Best Ensemble award, 1992; winner Arrow Rock Lyceum Theatre playwriting competition Am. themes, 1991. Office: Calif State U Theatre Dept 18111 Nordhoff St Northridge CA 91330-0001

GREGO-HEINTZ, DONNA MARIE, pediatric physical therapist; b. Phila., July 3, 1956; d. Joseph Francis and Rosemarie (Damico) Grego; m. Stephen Eugene Heintz, Aug. 28, 1982; children: Emily, Lauren, Audrey. BS, U. Del., 1978. Cert. phys. therapist. Staff phys. therapist Nat. Jewish Hosp., Denver, 1978-79, Swedish Med. Ctr., Denver, 1979-80; phys. therapy dept. chief First Creek Sch., Aurora, Colo., 1980-84; pediatric therapy coord. Rose Med. Ctr., Denver, 1984-88; clin. instr. U. Colo., Denver, 1988—; owner, pediatric phys. therapist Theracare, P.C., Englewood, Colo., 1989—. Vol. Alternatives Pregnancy Ctr., Denver, 1986—. Mem. Am. Phys. Therapy Assn. (regional dir. 1986-88), Neurodevel. Treatment Assn., Pediatric Therapist Interest Group (v.p. 1981-83). Republican. Home: 3734 S Ventura Way Aurora CO 80013 Office: Theracare PC Ste 240 6851 S Holly Circle Englewood CO 80112

GREGOIRE, CHRISTINE O., state attorney general; b. Auburn, Wash.; m. Michael Gregoire; 2 children. BA, U. Wash.; JD cum laude, Gonzaga U., 1977. Clerk, typist Wash. State Adult Probation/ Parole Office, Seattle, 1969; caseworker Wash. Dept. Social and Health Scis., Everett, 1974; asst. atty. gen. City of Spokane, Wash., 1977-81, sr. asst. atty. gen., 1981-82; dep. atty. gen. City of Olympia, Wash., 1982-88, atty. gen., 1993—; dir. Wash. State Dept. Ecology, 1988-92. chair Puget Sound Water Quality Authority, 1990-92, Nat. Com. State Environ. Dirs., 1991-92, States/B.C. Oil Spill Task Force, 1989-92. Mem. Nat. Assn. Attys. Gen. (consumer protection and environment com., energy com., children and the law subcom.). Office: PO Box 40100 905 Plum St Bldg 3 Olympia WA 98504-0100

GREGOR, EDUARD, laser physicist; b. Dnepropetrovsk, Ukraine, Jan. 9, 1936; came to U.S., 1955; s. Waldemar and Concordia (Teschke) G.; m. Marie L. Carlin, June 29, 1968; 1 child, Eduard Joseph. BS in Physics, Calif. State U., 1964, MS in Physics, 1966. Instr. Calif. State U., L.A., 1963-66; optical physicist TRW Instruments, El Segundo, Calif., 1966-68; laser physicist Union Carbide (Korad), Santa Monica, Calif., 1968-72; prodn. mgr. holography Quantrad Corp., El Segundo, Calif., 1972-75, ops. mgr., 1975-79; sr. project physicist Hughes Aircraft Co., El Segundo, 1979-82, dept. mgr., 1982—. Contbr. over 20 tech. articles on laser tech., coherent optics and holography to profl. jours. Sgt. U.S. Army, 1959-61. Recipient IR 100 award Indsl. Rsch. Mag., 1975. Mem. Optical Soc. Am., Soc. Photo-optical Instrumentation Engrs. Home: 820 Las Lomas Ave Pacific Palisades CA 90272-2428

GREGORATOS, GABRIEL, medical educator; b. Athens, Greece, Aug. 20, 1929; came to U.S., 1948.; s. Panos M. and Catherine (Monopoli) G.; m. Eva Gallay, Jan. 2, 1953; children: Katherine M., Barbara A., Nicholas S. AB, Hamilton Coll., 1950; MD, N.Y. Med. Coll., 1954. Intern St. Vincent's Hosp., N.Y.C., 1954-55; resident in internal medicine Tripler Army Med. Ctr., Honolulu, 1959-62; resident in cardiology Walter Reed Army Med. Ctr., Washington, 1962-64; commd. 1st lt. U.S. Army, 1956, advanced through grades to col., 1970; chief cardiology Letterman Army Med. Ctr., San Francisco, 1971-76; ret. U.S. Army, 1976; assoc. prof. to prof. of medicine U. Calif., San Diego, 1976-84; chief cardiology Pacific Presbyn. Med. Ctr., San Francisco, 1984-89; prof. medicine, dir. clin. cardiology U. Calif. Davis, Sacramento, 1989—; cons. FDA, Washington, 1973—, VA, San Francisco, 1986-89, Letterman Army Med. Ctr., 1985-92, Naval Hosp., San Diego, 1979-84; chair FDA adv. panel (circulatory system), 1992—. Co-editor: Coronary Care, 1981; contbr. articles to profl. jours. Pres. San Francisco Heart Assn., 1988-89. Decorated Legion of Merit. Fellow ACP, Am. Coll. Cardiology (councillor Calif. chpt. 1989-92, gov. No. Calif. 1993-96), Coun. of Clin. Cardiology, Am. Heart Assn. Democrat. Greek Orthodox. Office: U Calif Davis Med Ctr 4301 X St Rm 2050 Sacramento CA 95817-2214

GREGORY, bishop. Bishop Diocese of Sitka, Alaska. Office: Diocese of Sitka Box 697 Sitka AK 99835*

GREGORY, CALVIN, insurance service executive; b. Bronx, N.Y., Jan. 11, 1942; s. Jacob and Ruth (Cherchian) G.; m. Rachel Anna Carver, Feb. 14, 1970 (div. Apr. 1977); children—Debby Lynn, Trixy Sue; m. 2d, Carla Deane Deaver, June 30, 1979. A.A., Los Angeles City Coll., 1962; B.A., Calif. State U.-Los Angeles, 1964; M.Div., Fuller Theol. Sem., 1968; M.R.E., Southwestern Sem., Ft. Worth, 1969; Ph.D. in Religion, Universal Life Ch., Modesto, Calif., 1982; D.Div. (hon.), Otay Mesa Coll., 1982. Notary pub., real estate lic., casualty lic., Calif.; ordained to ministry Am. Baptist Conv., 1970. Youth minister First Bapt. Ch., Delano, Calif., 1964-65, 69-70; youth dir. St. Luke's United Meth. Ch., Highland Park, Calif., 1969-70; tchr. polit. sci. Maranatha High Sch., Rosemead, Calif., 1969-70; aux. chaplain U.S. Air Force 750th Radar Squadron, Edwards AFB, Calif., 1970-72; pastor First Bapt. Ch., Boron, Calif., 1971-72; ins. agt. Prudential Ins. Co., Ventura, Calif., 1972-73, sales mgr., 1973-74; casualty ins. agt. Allstate Ins. Co., Thousand Oaks, Calif., 1974-75; pres. Ins. Agy. Placement Service, Thousand Oaks, 1975—; head youth minister Emanuel Presbyn. Ch., Los Angeles, 1973-74; owner, investor real estate, U.S., Wales, Eng., Can., Australia. Counselor YMCA, Hollywood, Calif., 1964, Soul Clinic-Universal Life Ch., Inc., Modesto, Calif., 1982. Mem. Apt. Assn. Los Angeles, Life Underwriter Tng. Council. Republican. Clubs: Forensic (Los Angeles); X32 (Ventura). Lodge: Kiwanis (club speaker 1971). Home: 3307 Big Cloud Cir Thousand Oaks CA 91360-1028 Office: Ins Agy Placement Svc PO Box 4407 Thousand Oaks CA 91359-1407

GREGORY, ELEANOR ANNE, artist, educator; b. Seattle, Jan. 20, 1939; d. John Noel and Eleanor Blanche G.; BA, Reed Coll., 1963; MFA, U. Wash., 1966; MEd, Columbia U., 1978, EdD., 1978. Art tchr. Seattle Pub. Schs., 1970-75; instr. N.Y.C. Community Coll., 1977, Manhattan Community Coll., N.Y.C., 1978; asst. prof. N.Mex. State U., Las Cruces, 1978-79; asst. prof. art Purdue U., West Lafayette, Ind., 1979-82, West Tex. State U., Canyon, 1982-84; lectr. Calif. State U., Long Beach, 1985-87, L.A. Unified Sch. Dist., 1988—; one woman shows: Columbia U. Tchrs. Coll., 1976, Watson's Crick Gallery, West Lafayette, 1980, 81, Gallery I, Purdue U., 1980, W. Tex. State U., 1983, Amarillo Art Ctr., 1984, Sch. Visual Concepts, Seattle, 1985; group shows include: El Paso (Tex.) Art Mus., 1979, Ind. State Mus., Indpls., 1980, Lafayette (Ind.) Art Mus., 1982, T. Billman Gallery, Long Beach, 1987; represented in permanent collection: Portland (Oreg.) Art Mus.; mgr. Watson's Crick Gallery, West Lafayette, 1982-83. Mem. Nat. Art Edn. Assn. (pres. women's caucus chpt. 1988-90), N.Y. Soc. Scribes, L.A. Soc. Calligraphy, Internat. Soc. Edn. Through Art, Art Educators of L.A. Episcopalian.

GREGORY, JAMES, actor; b. N.Y.C., Dec. 23, 1911; s. James Gillen and Axemia Theresa (Ekdahl) G.; m. Ann Catherine Miltner, May 25, 1944. Grad. high sch. Actor, 1936—. Actor: (summer stock prodns.) Deer Lake, Pa., 1936-37, 39, Millbrook, N.Y., 1938, Braddock Heights, Md., 1940, Buck's County Playhouse, New Hope, Pa., 1941, Ivy Tower Playhouse, Spring Lake, N.J., 1951, (Broadway shows) Key Largo, 1939, Journey to Jerusalem, 1940, In Time to Come, 1941, Dream Girl, 1945, All My Sons, 1947, Death of a Salesman, 1948-49, Dead Pigeon, 1954, Fragile Fox, 1955, Desperate Hours, 1956-57, (films) The Young Strangers, 1955, Al Capone Story, 1955, Gun Glory, 1956, Nightfall, 1956, The Big Caper, 1956, A Distant Trumpet, 1961, Underwater Warrior, 1962, PT-109, 1965, The Sons of Katie Elder, 1967, The Manchurian Candidate, 1967, Captain Newman, M.D, 1967, Million Dollar Duck, 1968, Clam Bake, Secret War of Harry Frigg, Shoot Out, The Strongest Man in the World, 1974, The Main Event, 1979, Wait Til Your Mother Gets Home, 1982, X-15, Death of a Salesman, also 5 Matt Helm pictures, (TV shows) Big Valley, Bonanza, Gunsmoke, Rawhide, Playhouse 90, Climax, Alfred Hitchcock Presents, Twilight Zone, Quincy, as Inspector Luger in Barney Miller, Mr. Belvedere, 1986. Served with USNR, USMCR, 1942-45, PTO. Mem. Soc. Preservation and Encouragement Barber Shop Quartet Singing Am. Club: Hollywood Hackers, Golf. Home: 55 Cathedral Rock Dr Unit 33 Sedona AZ 86336-8624

GREGORY, JUDITH, research scholar, consultant; b. N.Y.C., Oct. 28, 1951; d. Chon and Dorothy (Evensen) G. BA, Antioch Coll., 1976; MA, U. Calif., San Diego, 1989, postgrad., 1992. Rsch. dir. 9 to 5 Nat. Assn. Working Women, Cleve., 1979-84; rsch. assoc. Dept. for Profl. Employees, AFL-CIO, Washington, 1984-86; rsch. scholar Dept. of Comm., U. Calif. San Diego, La Jolla, Calif., 1990—; adv. bd. mem. Office of Tech. Assessment Panel, Washington, 1983-88; expert testimonies U.S. Congress, Washington, 1981-83; expert witness NLRB, Washington, 1988. Editorial bd. Jour. Office: Tech. and People, 1981-86. Rsch. travel grantee German Marshall Fund of U.S., 1981; rsch. grantee Inst. for Rsch. on Learning. Democrat. Office: U Calif San Diego Dept Comm D 003 La Jolla CA 92093

GREGORY, MICHAEL STRIETMANN, English language educator; b. Oakland, Calif., Oct. 6, 1929; s. Walter and Alexine (Mitchell) G.; m. Ora Thorson, Feb. 2, 1952 (div.); children: Alexa, Tanya; m. Jan. Louise Rosenthal, June 27, 1962 (div.); 1 dau., Erika. A.B., U. Calif., Berkeley, 1952, Ph.D. in Cultural Anthropology, 1969. Instr. in English San Jose (Calif.) State U., 1956-57; mem. faculty dept. English San Francisco State U., 1959—, prof., 1971—, dir. NEXA sci.-humanities convergence program, NEH, 1975—; mem. Nat. Humanities Faculty, 1983-89, Nat. Faculty Arts Humanities Scis., 1989—; founding mem. nat. bd. cons. NEH, 1974—; dir. NEXA Consortium (8 campuses of Calif. State U.); cons. NEH, 12 U.S. Colls. and Univs., 1974—. Author: Sociobiology and Human Nature, 1978, The Recombinant DNA Controversy: Public Policy at the Frontier of Knowledge, 1978; contbr. articles on sci. and humanities, biomedicine, contemporary China, modern lit., history of ideas, photography and painting to profl. jours. Served with USNR, 1951-53. NIMH grantee Hong Kong, 1965-66; Calif. Council for Humanities in Public Policy grantee, 1977, 80, 82-83; Andrew W. Mellon Found. grantee, 1978-81; NEH devel. grantee, 1975-83. Fellow Am. Anthrop. Assn.; mem. MLA, AAAS, AAUP, Nat. Acad. Arts and Scis., Amnesty Internat., Hastings Inst., Inst. Noetic Scis. (mem. causality group), Joseph Conrad Soc. Home: 351 Melrose Ave Mill Valley CA 94941-3461 Office: San Francisco State U Dept English 1600 Holloway Ave San Francisco CA 94132-1722

GREGORY, NELSON BRUCE, motel owner, retired naval officer; b. Syracuse, N.Y., Aug. 4, 1933; s. Nelson Bruce and Josephine (Sully) G.; m. Bonnie K. Bannowsky, May 2, 1961 (div. 1970); children: Elizabeth Jo, Jennifer Kay; m. Patricia Ann Greenhalgh, Oct. 15, 1977; children: Peter Ward, Annette Frances, Michael John, Geoffrey Charles. BS, N.Y. Maritime Coll., 1955; postgrad., USN Pilot Tng., Pensacola, Fla., 1955-57; diploma, NATO Weapons Sch., Oberammergau, Fed. Republic of Germany, 1966, Joint Warfare Sch., Salisbury, Eng., 1967, USN Counter Insurgency, Little Creek, Va., 1968, USAF Space Ops., Montgomery, Ala., 1969. Commd. ens. USN, 1955, advanced through grades to lt. comdr., 1964; operational pilot airborne Early Warning Squadron 2 USN, Patuxent River, Md., 1957-60; flight instr. Airborne Early Warning Tng. Unit USN, Patuxent River, 1960-63; command pilot Air Devel. Squadron 6 USN, McMurdo Sound, Antarctica, 1963-64; airspace control officer NATO, Naples, Italy, 1964-68; chief pilot Naval Support Activity, Danang, Vietnam, 1968-69; space intelligence analyst NORAD, Colorado Springs, Colo., 1969-71; operational pilot Electronic Warfare Squadron 33 USN, Norfolk, Va., 1971-74; ops. officer Nat. Parachute Test Range USN, El Centro, Calif., 1974-75; ret. USN, 1975; owner, gen. mgr. Bonneville Motel, Idaho Falls, Idaho, 1975—. Patron Idaho Falls Symphony/Opera Theater, 1980—; mem. Better Bus. Bur., 1989; POW return sponsor, 1973. Decorated Air medals (3) USN; recipient Vietnamese Gallantry Cross Republic of Vietnam, 1969; Gregory Ridge in Antarctica named for him, 1964. Mem. Ret. Officers Assn. (life), Idaho Falls C. of C., Elks. Republican. Presbyterian. Home: 2000 S Yellowstone Hwy Idaho Falls ID 83402-4325

GREGORY, WILLIAM DAVID (BILL GREGORY), state legislator, marketing executive; b. Grand Rapids, Mich., Mar. 29, 1960; s. William and Shirley (Bagley) G.; m. Teresa Marie Ross, Aug. 17, 1991. BS in Journalism, No. Ariz. U., 1983; MBA, Nat. U., 1992. Mem. mktg. staff Southwest Gas Corp., Las Vegas, Nev., 1986-91; mem. Nev. Assembly, Carson City, 1991-93, asst. minority leader, 1993; v.p. Thomason & Assocs., Las Vegas, 1991-92, Carrara Corp., Las Vegas, 1992—. Bd. dirs. Multiple Sclerosis Soc., Las Vegas, 1990; active Sch.-Bus. Patrnership Program. Recipient Sivler Tongue award Southwest Gas Corp, 1986, Silver medal Pacific Coast Gas Assn., 1988. Mem. Exec. Devel. Assn. (pres. 1989), Quality and Productivity Assn., Citizens for Responsible Govt., Pachyderm Club (pres. 1989). Home and Office: 8916 Coastwalk Circle Las Vegas NV 89117 Office: 401 S Carson St Carson City NV 89710

GREGORY, WILLIAM EDGAR, psychologist; b. Steelville, Mo., Nov. 13, 1910; s. Edward Clark and Rilla Frances (Edgar) G.; m. Ella Virginia Sausser, Mar. 10, 1937 (dec. 1953); 1 child, William Edgar Jr.; m. Muriel Holden Van Gilder, June 10, 1956. BA, Colo. Coll., 1933; postgrad., U. Chgo., 1933-36; BD, Chgo. Theol. Sem., 1936; PhD, U. Calif., Berkeley, 1955. Ordained to ministry United Ch. of Christ, 1937. Asst. min. Jefferson Park Congl. Ch., Chgo., 1934-36; editorial assoc. Advance, Boston, 1936-37; pastor West Congl. Ch., Concord, N.H., 1937-39; acting supt. Ft. Berthold Indian Mission, Elbowoods, N.D., 1939-40; chaplain U.S. Army, 1940-45; dir. ministry svcs. pers. and vets. San Francisco Coun. of Chs., 1945-47; dir. rsch. N. Calif. Coun. of Chs., San Francisco, 1947-48; prof. psychology Coll. of Pacific, Stockton, Calif., 1938—; prof. emeritus U. Pacific, Stockton, 1981—; instr. U. Md. abroad, Verona, Italy, 1965. Mem. APA, Am. Sociol. Assn., Am. Anthropol. Assn., Soc. for Sci. Study Religion, DAV. Democrat. Home: 976 W Mendocino Ave Stockton CA 95204-3024

GREGORYK, MICHAEL DAVID, college administrator; b. Bismarck, N.D., Dec. 11, 1951; s. David P. Gregoryk and Metka H. (Anderson) Hansen; m. Mary L. Shanle; children: Brian, Stefanie, Laryssa, Jason. BA, Minot State U., 1973; postgrad., Chadron State Coll., 1983-85; MS in Bus., U.S. Internat. U., San Diego, 1988. Adj. instr. McCook (Nebr.) C.C., 1975-76; dir. fin. City of McCook, 1975-76; v.p. fin. and adminstrv. svcs. Western Tech. C.C. Area, Scottsbluff, Nebr., 1976-85; v.p. adminstrv. svcs. Palomar C.C., San Marcos, Calif., 1985—; cons. Greater Nebr. Health Systems Agy., Scottsbluff, 1978. Bd. dirs. Vallecitos Water Dist., San Marcos, Calif., 1990—; pres. San Marcos Boys and Girls Club, 1990-91. Mem. Nat. Coun. C.C. Bus. Ofcls. (pres., v.p., treas. 1985-91, Nat. Outstanding Bus. Officer 1991), Assn. Chief Bus. Officers (regional rep. 1991-92, v.p. 1992-93), San Marcos C. of C. (pres. 1989, Man of Yr. 1990). Office: Palomar Coll 1140 W Mission Rd San Marcos CA 92026

GREIFENSTEIN, FREDERICK JOHN, software company executive; b. N.Y.C., Sept. 18, 1946; s. Frederick John and Mar Greifenstein; m. Linda M. Graver, Aug. 23, 1969; children: Amy G., Anne G. BA, Marist Coll., Poughkeepsie, N.Y., 1969; MBA, UCLA, 1992. Pres. Computer Resource Mgmt., Milan, 1974-78, Technos Svc. SRL, Rome, 1978-88, Softsiel Corp., San Diego, 1988-90, Internat. Computer Techs., Reno, 1990-92; exec. v.p., COO, Marathon Systems, San Francisco, 1992—; bd. dirs. Strategic Decisions Ltd., Fetcham Surrey, Eng.; mem. steering com. Corp. for Open Systems, McLean, Va., 1989-90. Author: Metodologia Suiluppo Software, 1992. Rsch. grantee Cen. State Univs. Assn., 1968. Mem. IEEE, IEEE Computer Soc., IEEE Comm. Soc., Info. Tech. Assn. Am. (quality award judge 1991). Home: PO Box 3808 Rancho Santa Fe CA 92067 Office: Marathon Systems 4 Embarcadero Ctr San Francisco CA 94111

GREILS, HOWARD MONROE, psychiatrist; b. N.Y.C., May 1, 1947; s. Willy and Margo (Neuhaus) Greilsheimer. MD, Cornell U., 1973; degree in psychiatry, Harvard U., 1977. Clin. instr. psychiatry Harvard Med. Sch., Boston, 1977-85; clin. assoc. in psychiatry Mass. Gen. Hosp., Boston, 1977-85; pvt. practice Santa Monica, Calif., 1987—. Home and Office: 101 Ocean Ave E 701 Santa Monica CA 90402

GREMBOWSKI, DAVID EMIL, educator, researcher; b. San Diego, May 26, 1951; s. Emil Dem and Delphine Joyce (Kurowski) G.; m. Mary West, June 22, 1974; children: Megan, Leda. BA, Wash. State U., Pullman, 1973, MA, 1975; PhD, U. Wash., Seattle, 1982. Rsch. analyst Stanford Rsch. Inst., Menlo Park, Calif., 1974-76; systems designer flexible intergovtl. grant project City of Tacoma, 1979-80; from rsch. instr. to assoc. prof. U. Wash., Seattle, 1981—; prin. investigator of health svcs. rsch. grants; instr. health program evaluation and health care system. Contbr. articles to profl. jours. Mem. APHA, Internat. Assn. Dental Rsch. (sec., treas. behavioral scis. and health svcs. rsch. group 1988-92), Am. Assn. Dental Rsch., Assn. Health Svc. Rsch., Phi Beta Kappa. Office: U Wash Dept Health Svcs SC 37 Seattle WA 98195

GREMBOWSKI, EUGENE, insurance company executive; b. Bay City, Mich., July 21, 1938; s. Barney Thomas and Mary (Senkowski) G.; m. Teresa Ann Frasik, June 27, 1959; children: Bruce Allen, Debora Ann. AA, Allan Hancock U., 1963; BA, Mich. State U., 1967; MBA, George Washington U., 1972. Cert. profl. contracts mgr.; cert: CLU. Enlisted USAF, 1955, commd. 2d lt., 1968, advanced through grades to capt., 1971; pers. officer USAF, Goldsboro, N.C., 1968-70; chief of procurement USAF, Cheyenne, Wyo., 1971-73; contract analyst USAF, Omaha, 1973-76; chief of contracting USAF, Atwater, Calif., 1976-79; ret. USAF, 1979; office supr. Farmers Ins. Group of Cos., Merced, Calif., 1980-85, office mgr., 1985-86; corp. fleet mgr. L.A., 1986—. Author: Governmental Purchasing: Its Progression Toward Professional Status, 1972. Cubmaster Boy Scouts Am., Goldsboro, 1968; com. chmn. Am. Heart Assn., Merced-Mariposa, Calif., 1985, sec.-treas., 1986. Decorated Commendation medals, 1965, 70, 79; recipient Meritorious Svc. medals Office of the Pres., 1973, 76. Mem. Nat. Contract Mgmt. Assn., Nat. Assn. Fleet Adminstrs., Am. Legion, Air Force Assn. (life mem.), Retired Officers Assn. (life mem.), Toastmasters Internat. Home: 14633 E Mountain Spring St Hacienda Heights CA 91745 Office: Farmers Group Inc 4750 Wilshire Blvd Los Angeles CA 90010-3832

GREN, CONRAD ROGER, auditor; b. Medford, Oreg., Aug. 11, 1955; s. Donald Oswald and Jean Viola (Hoefs) G.; m. Barbara June Kyle, Sept. 5, 1982; children: Eric Conrad Kyle, Kari June Elizabeth, Laura Jean Alyssa. BSBA, Walla Walla Coll., 1978. Acct. bus. office Walla Walla Coll., College Place, Wash., 1974-75, food preparer, cashier for food svc., 1975-77, reader Theology dept., 1975-76; inventory return Northrup, King & Co., Portland, Oreg., 1976-77; audit clk. Corps of Engrs., NPD Audit, Walla Walla, Wash., 1977-78; auditor Corps of Engrs., NPD Audit, Portland, Oreg., 1979-82, 83—; acct. Forest Svc., Deschutes Nat. Forest, Bend, Oreg., 1978-79, Portland Dist., Corps of Engrs., 1982-83. Elder Sunnyside Seventh-day Adventist Ch., Portland, 1988-91, ch./family life coun. mem., 1991-92; constituent del. triennial meeting Oreg. Conf. of Seventh-day Adventists, 1992, spl. edn. session, 1993. Democrat. Home: 21601 SE Edward Dr Clackamas OR 97015-8755 Office: US Army Corps Engrs N Pacific Div 511 NW Broadway Ste 364 Portland OR 97209-3413

GRENARD, JACK, publisher; b. Springfield, Ill., July 15, 1933; s. Edward Merrill and Jane (Ashmore) G.; m. Jane Elizabeth Leverenz, Aug. 16, 1958; children: Mark Edward, Elizabeth Ann. BA, Mich. State U., 1956. Founder, editor Detroit Publ. Cons., Detroit, 1959-80; prin. IntraTech Communications, St. Clair Shores, Mich., 1980-86, Carefree (Ariz.) Communications, 1986—; co-founder Programmable Controls, 1982, VMEbus Systems mags., 1985. Author: Footnotes from the Arid Zone, 1987; publisher PLC Insider's Newsletter, 1981—. Bd. dirs. Care Creek (Ariz.) Mus., 1988-90. With USN, 1956-58. Mem. Computer Press Assn., Indsl. Computing Soc. (founder, columnist Indsl. Computing mag.), Writers of the Purple Sage (founder 1988-92), Kiwanis (chmn. publicity 1987-88). Republican. Unitarian Universalist. Home and Office: PO Box 5268 Carefree AZ 85377-5268

GRENFELL, GEORGE ALBERT, JR., assistant district attorney; b. Modesto, Calif., Mar. 19, 1941; s. George Albert Sr. and Margaret (Armbrust) G.; m. Mary Louise Vieira, May 22, 1971; children: Richelle Louise, Trisha Lynn. BSBA in Econs., Saint Mary's Coll., 1963; JD, Humphrey's Law Sch., 1968. Bar: Calif., 1970. Dep. dist. atty. Tulare County Dist. Atty. Office, Visalia, Calif., 1970-74; asst. dist. atty., adminstr. Fresno (Calif.) Dist. Atty. Office, 1974—; cons. L.A. County Adminstrv. Office, 1980-81; mem. CSNet Workgroup Dept. HHS-Office Child Support Enforcement, Washington, 1988, Calif. rep. time and activity standard com., 1989; mem. Statewide Automated Child Support System Policy Mgmt. Adv. Com. State Dept. Social Svcs., Sacramento, 1989—. Bd. dirs., v.p. Tulare County Legal Aid Soc., Visalia, 1973-77, Fresno County pvt. ind. coun. Parenting Oportunities Program, 1991—; bd. dirs., sec., treas. The Lakes Homeowners Assn., Visalia, 1988-89; mem. child support vision for excellence task force State Dept. Social Svcs., 1992. Recipient Disting. Faculty award, Nat. Dist. Attys. Assn., 1976; named Outstanding Individual Mgr. State Dept. Social Svcs., 1989, Outstanding Individual Achievement (Mgr.) Nat. Child Support Enforcement Assn., 1990. Mem. Calif. Family Support Coun. (bd. dirs., pres. 1975-76, chmn. automation com. 1989-91, Truly B. Knox 1977), Calif. State Bar Assn., Fresno County Bar Assn., Nat. Child Support Enforcement Assn., E Clampus Vitas (chpt. 855), San Joaquin Fine Woodworkers Assn. (pres. 1986-88, newsletter editor, 1989-91). Republican. Roman Catholic. Home: 5536 W Prospect Dr Visalia CA 93721 Office: Dist Atty Family Support 2220 Tulare St Fresno CA 93721-2104

GRENFELL, GLORIA ROSS, freelance journalist; b. Redwood City, Calif., Nov. 14, 1926; d. Edward William and Blanch (Ross) G.; m. June 19, 1948 (div. Nov. 15, 1983); children: Jane, Barbara, Robert, Mary. BS, U. Oreg., 1948, postgrad., 1983-85. Coll. bd., retail sales Meier & Frank Co., Portland, Oreg., 1945; book sales retailer J.K. Gill & Co., Portland, Oreg., 1948-50; advisor Mt. Hood Meadows Women's Ski Program, Oreg., 1968-78; corp. v.p. OK Delivery System, Inc., Oreg., 1977-82; ski instr. Willamette Pass, Oreg., 1983-85, Mt. Shasta, 1986; Campfire girls leader Portland, 1958-72; freelance journalist Marina, Calif., 1986—. Mem. Assn. Jr. League Internat., 1957-87; mem. Rep. Nat. Com., 1991-93. Recipient Golden Poles award Mt. Hood Meadows, 1975. Mem. Soc. Profl. Journalists, Profl. Ski Instrs. Am., U.S. Ski Coaches Assn., Kappa Alpha Theta. Republican. Episcopalian. Home and Office: 3128 Crescent Ave Space 9 Marina CA 93933

GRENIER, JUDSON A., JR., history educator; b. Indpls., Mar. 6, 1930; s. Judson A. Sr. and Beatrice Olivia (Bjeldanes) G.; m. Nancy Hicks, Aug. 9, 1954; children: Karen, Eric, Jonathan, Caddie. BA, U. Minn., 1951; MA, U. Calif., Berkeley, 1952; PhD in History, UCLA, 1965. Teaching asst. U. Calif., Berkeley, 1951-52; analyst IPS U.S. Dept. of State, Washington, 1952; reporter L.A. Mirror-News, 1958, 59; instr. El Camino Coll., Torrance, 1956-65; prof. Calif. State U., Dominguez Hills, 1966—; vis. lectr. UCLA, 1965-66; mem. acad. senate Calif. State U., 1974-83, sec., 1976-78, vice chmn., 1979-80, dir. oral history project, 1986-89; cons. El Pueblo St. Historic Park, L.A., 1980-83, City of Gardena, Calif., 1980-87, City of Torrance, Calif., 1980-82, City of Redondo Beach, Calif., 1985-87, L.A. County Dept. of Edn., 1979-81. Author: California Legacy: Watson-Dominguez Family, 1987; edit. cons. Calif. History; contbr. articles to profl. jours. Recipient Community Disting. Svc. award Calif. State U., 1987; NEH fellow, 1984, Huntington-Haynes fellow, 1985, Newberry Fellow, 1991. Mem. Am. Hist. Assn., Hist. Soc. of So. Calif. (v.p. 1981-83), L.A. 200 (hist. and edn. coms. 1978-81), L.A. Bicentennial Com. (hist. team 1973-76). Home: 587 33d St Manhattan Beach CA 90266 Office: Calif State U 1000 E Victoria St Carson CA 90747-0005

GRENLEY, AARON LEMUEL, insurance sales executive; b. Balt., Nov. 9, 1946; s. Aldred S. and Fredrica (Cohen) G.; m. Ronny Lynn Grenley, Sept. 23, 1966; children: Jennifer R., Michael S. BA in Marine Transp., U.S. Merchant Marine Acad., 1968. CLU. Agt. Lincoln Nat. Life, Balt., 1971-88, Phoenix, 1988—. Contbr. articles to mags. Recipient Nat. Sales Achievement Nat. Quality award Nat. Assn. Life Underwriters, 1971—. Mem. Million Dollar Roundtable (life). Republican.

GRENLEY, PHILIP, urologist; b. N.Y.C., Dec. 21, 1912; s. Robert and Sara (Schrader) G. BS, NYU, 1932, MD, 1936. Diplomate Am. Bd. Urology; m. Dorothy Sarney, Dec. 11, 1938; children: Laurie (Mrs. John Hallen), Neal, Jane (Mrs. Eldridge C. Hanes), Robert. Intern, Kings County Hosp., Bklyn., 1936-38, resident, 1939; resident in urology L.I. Coll. Hosp., Bklyn., 1939-41; pvt. practice medicine specializing in urology, Tacoma, Wash., 1946-90, ret., 1990; urologist Tacoma Gen. Hosp., St. Joseph Hosp., Tacoma, Good Samaritan Hosp., Puyallup, Wash.; pres. med. staff St. Joseph Hosp., Tacoma, 1968-69, mem. exec. bd., 1950-54, 67-68; cons. urologist to Surgeon Gen., Madigan Army Med. Ctr., Tacoma, 1954-87, VA Hosp. at American Lake, 1953-80, USPHS McNeil Island Penitentiary, 1955-82, Good Samaritan Rehab. Ctr., Puyallup, 1960-90; med. cons. State of Wash. Dept. Soc. and Health Svcs., 1990—; chief of urology 210th Gen. Hosp., Ft. Jackson Regional Hosp., Ft. McClellan Regional Hosp., 1941-46; lectr. in sociology U. Puget Sound, Tacoma, 1960—. Trustee Wash. Children's Home Soc., 1951-60, Charles Wright Acad., 1961-69, Wash. State Masonic Home, 1984—; trustee Pierce County Med. Bur., 1949-51, 59-61, 71-73, pres., 1973-74, mem. exec. bd., 1975-77; mem. Lakewood adv. commn. TAE Pierce County Coun., 1992—. With AUS, 1941-46. Fellow ACS; mem. Am. Urol. Assn., AMA, Wash., Pan Am. med. assns., Pierce County Med. Soc., Masons, Shriners (med. dir. 1965-78, imperial coun. 1982-85, potentate 1983), Royal Order Jesters (dir. 1986, 87), Lions, Elks, Red Cross of Constantine (knight). Home: 40 Loch Ln SW Tacoma WA 98499-1432

GRENNAN, CYNTHIA, school superintendent; b. Sterling, Ill., Jan. 4, 1938; d. Francis John and Elza (Pippert) G. B.S., Ill. State U., 1959; M.A., Ariz. State U., 1964. Tchr. Palatine Sch. Dist., Ill., 1959-61, Chandler Sch. Dist., Ariz., 1961-64, Anaheim Union High Sch. Dist., Calif., 1964-67, counselor, 1972-76, psychologist, 1972-76, asst. prin. to asst. supt., 1976-79, supt., 1979—; state supt. com. Assn. Calif. Sch. Adminstrs., Burlingame, Calif., 1984—. Episcopalian. Office: Anaheim Union High Sch Dist PO Box 3520 Anaheim CA 92803-3520

GRESHAM, LOUISE SHANE, epidemiologist, consultant; b. Bklyn., June 20, 1952; d. Harold William and Ethel (Spooner) G. BS, Loma Linda U., 1979; MPH, San Diego State U., 1985; postgrad., U. Calif., San Diego, 1990—. Rsch. assoc. Loma Linda (Calif.) Sch. Medicine, 1979-82; epidemiology analyst Naval Health Rsch., Point Loma, Calif., 1984-85; rsch. assoc. San Diego State U., 1985-87, cons. faculty, 1986—, lectr., 1990-92; staff epidemiologist Ctr. for Neurologic Study, La Jolla, Calif., 1991—; epidemiologist Dept. Health Svcs., San Diego, 1987—; co-dir. San Diego Epidemiology Conf., 1992; cons. Ctr. for Neurologic Study, San Diego, 1985—, Am. Cancer Soc., San Diego, 1984-87. Author: Epidemiology of Neurologic Disorders, 1992; co-editor San Diego State Alumni Newsletter, 1990—; contbr. articles to profl. jours. Recipient Doctoral Incentive award Calif. State U., 1992, Grant-In-Aid Faculty Rsch. award San Diego State U., 1985. Mem. APHA, Grad. Sch. of Pub. Health Alumni Assn. (newsletter coeditor 1990—), San Diego and Imperial County Cancer Control, Phi Kappa Phi. Democrat. Office: Dept of Health Svcs 1700 Pacific Hwy San Diego CA 92101

GRESHAM, ROBERT LAMBERT, JR., insurance company executive; b. Portland, Oreg., Oct. 11, 1943; s. Robert L. and Barbara (Jones) G.; m. Judy L. Norris, Dec. 7, 1974. BS, U. So. Calif., 1965. CPCU. Adjuster Ins. Co. of NoAm., L.A., 1966-68; mgr. R.L. Gresham & Co., Inc., Las Vegas, Nev., 1968-72, pres., 1980—; mem. editorial rev. bd. Adjusters Reference Guide, Omaha, 1980—; dir. Nat. Panel Select Adjusters Cos., Harahan, La., 1985—. Pres. Fraternal Order of Eagles, Las Vegas, 1978, Fraternal Order of Police, Las Vegas, 1973; bd. dirs. Las Vegas Jaycees, 1972. With USNR, 1961-70. Mem. Nev. State Claims Assn. (pres. 1976-77, Nev. Claimsman of Yr. 1973), Calif. Assn. Ind. Ins. Adjusters (pres. 1986-87), Affiliated Ins. Adjusters (pres. 1977-78), So. Nev. Claims Assn. (pres. 1973-74), Nat. Assn. Ind. Ins. Adjusters (pres. 1992), CPCU (pres. So. Nev. chpt. 1983-84). Office: R L Gresham & Co Inc 1200 S 4th St Las Vegas NV 89104-1046

GRETZKY, WAYNE, professional hockey player; b. Brantford, Ont., Can., Jan. 26, 1961; s. Walter and Phyllis G.; m. Janet Jones, July 16, 1988; 3 children: Paulina, Ty Robert, Trevor Douglas. Center Peterborough Petes, Jr. Ont. Hockey Assn., 1977-78, Sault Ste. Marie Greyhounds, 1977-78, Indpls. Racers, World Hockey Assn., 1978-79, Edmonton Oilers (Alta., Can.), NHL, 1979-88, Los Angeles Kings, NHL, 1988—. Player NHL All-Star Game, 1980-92; named Rookie of Yr. World Hockey Assn., 1979, Hart Trophy for Most Valuable Player NHL, 1980-87, 89, Sportsman of Yr. Sports Illus., 1982; recipient Lady Byng Meml. trophy NHL, 1980, 91, 92, Art Ross Meml. trophy NHL, 1981-87, 90, 91, Conn Smythe trophy, 1985, 88; holder NHL career scoring record. Office: care Los Angeles Kings The Forum 3900 W Manchester Blvd Inglewood CA 90306

GREY, HOWARD ALAN, speech-language pathologist; b. Flint, Mich., Aug. 23, 1932; s. Sidney B. and Irene (Wineman) G.; m. Charmaine Lava, Aug. 17, 1957 (div. 1967); m. Marcia Lou Grey, May 7, 1970; children: Adrien MacKenzie, Janet Grey, Karen Kenworthy, Kathy Schwartz, Michael Schwartz, Jill Schiff. BA, U. Calif., L.A., 1957, PhD, 1963; MA, UCLA, 1959. Cert. speech-lang. pathologist, audiologist. Asst. prof. speech San Fernando Valley State Coll., Northridge, Calif., 1961-62; rsch. assoc. St. Johns Hosp. Rsch. Found., Santa Monica, 1963-64; speech-lang. pathologist Hope Guild Clinic/Kennedy Child Study Ctr. St. Johns Hosp., Santa Monica, 1958, 64; cons. Childrens Treatment Ctr. Camarillo (Calif.) State Hosp., 1966-71; clin. dir. Community Speech and Hearing Ctr., Van Nuys, Calif., 1969—; assoc. prof. Calif. State U., L.A., 1970-79. Contbr. articles to profl. jours. With U.S. Army, 1953-55. Scholarship Crippled Children and Adult Soc., 1958, Nat. Grad. scholarship Am. Speech and Hearing Found., 1960; OVR grant Office of Vocat. Rehab., 1962, 63. Fellow Calif. Speech Lang. Hearing Assn., Soc. of Ear, Nose and Throat Advances in Children, Am. Acad. Audiology; mem. Am. Acad. of Otolaryngology Head and Neck Surgery, Am. Speech Lang. Hearing Assn., Am. Psychol. Assn. Office: Community Speech and Hearing Ctr 7140 Balboa Blvd Van Nuys CA 91406

GREY, ROBERT DEAN, biology educator; b. Liberal, Kans., Sept. 5, 1939; s. McHenry Wesley and Kathryn (Brown) G.; m. Alice Kathleen Archer, June 11, 1961; children: Erin Kathleen, Joel Michael. BA, Phillips U., 1961; PhD, Washington U., 1966. Asst. prof. Washington U., St. Louis, 1966-67; from asst. prof. to full prof. zoology U. Calif., Davis, 1967—, chmn. dept., 1979-83, dean biol. scis., 1985—, interim exec. vice chancellor, 1993—. Author: (with others) A Laboratory Text for Developmental Biology, 1980; contbr. articles to profl. jours. Recipient Disting. Teaching award Acad. Senate U. Calif., Davis, 1977, Magnar Ronning award for teaching Associated Students U. Calif., Davis, 1978. Mem. Am. Soc. Cell Biology, Soc. Developmental Biology, Phi Sigma. Lodge: Rotary. Office: U Calif Davis Div of Biol Scis Davis CA 95616

GREYSON, JEROME, chemist, consultant, educator; b. N.Y.C., Nov. 7, 1927; m. Jacqueline Vis, July 27, 1957; children: Clifford, Ann, Paul. BA, Hunter Coll., 1950; PhD in Chemistry, Pa. State U., 1956. Mem. tech. staff Bell Telephone Labs., Murray Hill, N.J., 1956-57, IBM Rsch. Labs., Yorktown Heights, N.Y., 1957-62; phys. chemistry group leader Stauffer Chem. Co., Richmond, Calif., 1962-64; supr. environ. chemistry N.Am. Rockwell, Canoga Park, Calif., 1964-70; dir. blood chem. devel. Miles Labs., Inc., Elkhart, Ind., 1970-82; tech. dir. Precision Sci. Co., Chgo., 1982-86; owner, mgr. J & JG Assocs., Conifer, Colo., 1986—; adj. faculty Metro State Coll., Denver; presented in field to profl. meetings, symposia and confs., 1966-81, including 10th Internat. Congress on Clin. Chemistry, Mexico City, 1978, 3d European Congress Clin. Chemistry, Brighton, Eng., 1979, 1st South East Asian and Pacific Congress Clin. Biochemistry, Singapore, 1979, Analytica 80, Munich, 1980, Mexican Assn. Clin. Biochemistry, Mexico City, 1981, XXXI Italian Congress Clin. Pathology, Sicily, 1981. Author: Carbon, Sulfur, and Nitrogen Pollutants and Their Determination in Air and Water, 1990; contbr. articles to Am. Lab., Biotechniques, Trial, Jour. Auto. Chemistry, Clin. Chemistry, Jour. Immunological Methods, Analytical Chemistry, Jour. Chem. and Engring. Data, Yale. Sci. Mag., Jour. Phys. Chemistry, Desalination, Jour. Polymer Sci., Jour. Electrochem. Soc., also others. With USNR, 1945-46, PTO. Mem. Am. Chem. Soc., Chem. Cons. Colo. (pres. 1989—). Office: J & JG Assocs 10742 S Timothys Rd Conifer CO 80433-8210

GRIBOVICZ, LEE PENN, environmental engineer; b. Tokyo, Feb. 9, 1949; (parents Am. citizens); s. Walter Joseph and Ann (Penn) Gribb; m. Deborah Ann McFadden, Feb. 5, 1971 (div. Dec. 1985); m. Mary Jo Jeffres, Dec. 4, 1987. BS in Environ. Engring. with hons., Mont. Coll. Mineral Sci.-Tech., 1975. Registered profl. engr., Wyo. Environ. engr. Lone Star Cement Co., Houston, 1975-76, Smith Chem. Co., Green River, Wyo., 1976-78; dist. air quality engr. Wyo. Dept. Environ. Quality, Lander, 1978—. Mem. Wyo. Tennis Assn. (bd. dirs. 1986—, pres. 1992), Air Pollution and Waste Mgmt. Assn., Am. Mensa. Office: Wyo Air Quality Div 250 Lincoln St Lander WY 82520

GRIER, CHARLES CROCKER, forestry educator; b. Pasadena, Calif., Sept. 1, 1938; s. Charles Horace and Priscilla Mary (Crocker) G.; m. Jeannie Kathleen Conway, Aug. 20, 1960; 1 child, Charles Christopher. BS in Forestry, U. Wash., 1968, PhD, 1972. Rsch. assoc. in forestry Oreg. State U., Corvallis, 1972-76; rsch. asst. prof. forestry U. Wash., Seattle, 1976-80, assoc. prof., then prof. forestry, 1980-85; prof. forestry No. Ariz. U., Flagstaff, 1985-91; prof., head dept. forest resources Coll. Natural Resources, Utah State U., Logan, 1991-93; prof., dept. head forest scis. Colo. State U., Ft. Collins, 1993—. Contbr. articles to sci. jours. Grantee NSF, 1976, 77, 80, 84, U.S. Dept. Man and Biosphere Consortium, Costa Rica, 1980. Mem. Ecol. Soc. Am., Soil Sci. Soc. Am., Sigma Xi, Xi Sigma Pi. Office: Colo State U Dept Forest Scis Colorado State University CO 80523

GRIER, JAMES EDWARD, lawyer, hotel executive; b. Ottumwa, Iowa, Sept. 7, 1935; s. Edward J. and Corinne (Bailey) G.; m. Virginia Clinker, July 4, 1959; children: Michael, Susan, James, John, Thomas. BSc, U. Iowa, 1956, JD, 1959. Bar: Iowa 1959, Mo. 1959. Mng. ptnr. Hillix, Brewer, Hoffhaus & Grier, Kansas City, Mo., 1964-77, Grier & Swartzman, Kansas City, 1977-89; pres. Doubletree Hotels Corp., Phoenix, 1989—; bd. dirs. Iowa Law Sch. Found., Iowa City, St. Joseph Hosp. and Med. Ctr., Phoenix, Homeward Bound, Phoenix. Home: 3500 E Lincoln Dr Phoenix AZ 85018-1010 Office: Doubletree Hotel Corp 410 N 44th St Phoenix AZ 85008-7605

GRIESCHE, ROBERT PRICE, hospital purchasing executive; b. Berkeley, Calif., July 21, 1953; s. Robert Bowen and Lillian (Price) G.; m. Susan Dawn Albers, June 8, 1985 (div. Apr. 1989); 1 child, Sara Christine. AA, Coll. of the Canyons, Valencia, Calif., 1984. Warehouse supr. John Muir Hosp., Walnut Creek, Calif., 1973-82; purchasing mgr. Henry Mayo Newhall Hosp., Valencia, 1982-85; materials mgr. Foothill Presbyn. Hosp., Glendora, Calif., 1985-87; purchasing dir. Huntington Meml. Hosp., Pasadena, Calif., 1987—; chmn. Huntington Employee Campaign, 1990-92. V.p. Coll. of the Canyons Found., Valencia, 1985-90. Named to Outstanding Young Men of Am., 1988. Mem. Calif. Cen. Svc. Assn. (charter). Republican. Presbyterian. Home: 3651 Cosmos Ct Palmdale CA 93550 Office: Huntington Hosp 100 W California Blvd Pasadena CA 91105

GRIESEMER, ALLAN DAVID, museum director; b. Mayville, Wis., Aug. 13, 1935; s. Raymond John and Leone Emma (Fisher) G.; m. Nancy Jean Sternberg, June 6, 1959; children: David, Paul, Steven. A.B., Augustana Coll., 1959; M.S., U. Wis., 1963; Ph.D., U. Nebr., 1970. Curator; coordinator ednl. services U. Nebr., Lincoln State Museum, 1965-77, assoc. prof., assoc. dir., 1977-79, acting dir., 1980-81, assoc. dir. and coordinator, 1981-82, interim dir., 1982-84; dir. San Bernardino County Mus., Calif., 1984—; mem. faculty dept. geology U. Nebr., Lincoln, 1968-80; lectr. geology U. Nebr., Lincoln State Mus., 1968-80; adj. prof. Calif. State U., San Bernardino, 1986. Contbr. articles to sci. jours., mus. publs., 1965—. Recipient Hon. award Sigma Gamma Epsilon, 1958. Mem. Paleontol. Soc., Nebr. Mus. Conf. (pres. 1976-79), Nebr. Geol. Soc., Nebr. Acad. Scis., Mountain Plains Conf., Mountain Plains Mus. Assn. (pres. 1979), Am. Assn. Museums (v.p. 1983), Am. Assn. State and Local History, Western Museums Conf., Calif. Assn. Masons (bd. dirs.), So. Calif. Acad. Sci.(bd. dirs., treas. 1991-93). Lutheran. Home: 306 La Colina Dr Redlands CA 92374-8247 Office: San Bernardino County Mus 2024 Orange Tree Ln Redlands CA 92374-2850

GRIEVE, HAROLD WALTER, retired interior designer; b. L.A., Feb. 1, 1901; s. Alexander and Maria (Chapman) G.; m. Jetta Goudal, Oct. 11, 1930. Student Los Angeles art schs., 1920-21, Chouinard Sch. Art, 1920-21, Camillo Innocentie, Rome, 1923-24. Art dir. M.P. Studios, 1920-28; art dir. for motion pictures including: Dorothy Vernon of Haden Hall, Lady Windemer's Fan, So This is Paris; interior designer, Los Angeles, now ret.; decorated Colleen Moore Doll House interiors, 1935; interior design work includes homes of George Burns, Jack Benny, Bing Crosby, Erving Thalberg, Norma Schearer, others. Fellow Am. Inst. Interior Designers (life mem., past nat. pres., past local pres.), Acad. of Motion Pictures (founder mem., life mem.), Hist. Soc. So. Calif. Republican. Clubs: Los Angeles Athletic; Beach (Santa Monica, Calif.).

GRIEVE, LEONA LEE, writer; b. Vancouver, B.C., Can., Sept. 7, 1954; d. Harold and Mary (Thiessen) Goodison; m. Gary Allen Grieve, May 31, 1980; children: James Douglas, Meghan Elizabeth. Student, No. Alta. Inst. Tech., 1977. Author novels; author short stories including: An Unopened Letter, Bronte Street, 1989, Threshold of Destiny, Pablo Lennis, 1988, Spite and Malice, Dark Starr, 1988, The Accessory, Lighthouse, 1988, The Shiny Green Beetle, Creative Urge, 1987, A Gift for Loving, Hob-Nob, 1989, A Victimless Crime, Footsteps, 1986. Mem. Willamette Writers. Home: 3700 Marquis Ct Lake Oswego OR 97034

GRIFFEY, KEN, JR. (GEORGE KENNETH GRIFFEY, JR.), baseball player; b. Donora, Pa., Nov. 21, 1969. Grad. high sch., Cin. Outfielder Seattle Mariners, 1989—. Recipient Gold Glove award, 1990-92; named to All-Star team, 1990-93, Silver Slugger team, 1991, Sporting News All-Star team, 1991. Office: Seattle Mariners PO Box 4100 411 1st Ave S Seattle WA 98104

GRIFFIN, DEWITT JAMES, architect, real estate developer; b. Los Angeles, Aug. 26, 1914; s. DeWitt Clinton and Ada Gay (Miller) G.; m. Jeanmarie Donald, Aug. 19, 1940 (dec. Sept. 1985); children: Barbara Jean Griffin Holst, John Donald, Cornelia Caulfield Claudius, James DeWitt; m. Vivienne Dod Kievenaar, May 6, 1989. Student, UCLA, 1936-38; B.A., U. Calif., 1942. Designer Kaiser Engrs., Richmond, Calif., 1941; architect CF Braun & Co., Alhambra, Calif., 1946-48; pvt. practice architecture Pasadena, Calif., 1948-50; prin. Goudie & Griffin Architects, San Jose, Calif., 1959-64, Griffin & Murray, 1964-66, DeWitt J. Griffin & Assocs., 1966-69; pres. Griffin/Joyce Assocs., Architects, 1969-80; chmn. Griffin Balzhiser Affiliates (Architects), 1974-80; founder, pres. Griffin Cos. Internat., 1980—; founder, dir. San Jose Savs. and Loan Assn., 1965-75, Capitol Services Co., 1964-77, Esandel Corp., 1965-77. Pub. Sea Power mag, 1975-77; archtl. works include U.S. Post Office, San Jose, 1966, VA Hosp, Portland, 1976, Bn. Barracks Complex, Ft. Ord, Calif., 1978. bd. dirs. San Jose Symphony Assn., 1973-84, v.p. 1977-79, pres. 1979-81; active San Jose Symphony Found., 1981-86, v.p. 1988-90; bd. dirs. Coast Guard Acad. Found., 1974-87, Coast Guard Found., 1987-90; founder, bd. dirs. U.S. Navy Meml. Found., 1978-80, trustee, 1980—; trustee Montalvo Ctr. for Arts, 1982-88. Served to comdr. USNR, 1942-46, 50-57. Recipient Navy Meritorious Pub. Svc. medal, 1971, Disting. Service medal Navy League of U.S., 1973; Coast Guard Meritorious Pub. Svc. medal, 1975; Navy Disting. Pub. Svc. medal, 1977; Coast Guard Disting. Pub. Svcs. medal, 1977. Fellow Soc. Am. Mil. Engrs.; mem. AIA (emeritus), U.S. Naval Inst., Navy League U.S. (pres. Santa Clara Valley coun. 1963-66, Calif. state pres. 1966-69, nat. dir. 1967—, exec. com. 1968—, pres. 12th region 1969-71, nat. v.p. 1973-75, nat. pres. 1975-77, chmn. 1977-79), U.S. Naval Sailing Assn., Naval Order of U.S., Wash. Athletic Club (Seattle), Marin Yacht Club, St. Francis Yacht Club, Commonwealth of San Francisco Club, Phi Gamma Delta. Republican. Congregationalist. Home and Office: 8005 NE Hunt Club Ln Hansville WA 98340-0124

GRIFFIN, JAMES EDWARD, real estate developer; b. Fall River, Mass., Jan. 27, 1941; s. James Edward and Marion Beatrice (Johnsen) G.; m. Audie Leigh Kilwy, July 21, 1963. AA, Napa (Calif.) Coll., 1965; BS, Calif. State U., Sacramento, 1967. CPA, Calif., Nev. Auditor Authur Young & Co., San Francisco, 1967-69, Providence, 1969-71; v.p. fin. R.I. Land Co., Providence, 1971-79; treas. Moss Land Co., Sacramento, 1979-82; chief fin. officer Equi-Real Devel. Co., Sacramento, 1982-84, Am. Nev. Co., Henderson, Nev., 1984-90; exec. v.p., chief oper. officer Am. Nev. Co., 1990—; sec.-treas. acctg. adv. coun. UNLV, 1991, chmn.-elect, 1992. Recipient Bus. Adminstrn. award Bank Am., 1965. Fellow Nev. Soc. CPAs; mem. AICPA, Inst. Mgmt. Accts. (treas. Las Vegas chpt. 1991, bd. dirs. 1990), Calif. Soc. CPAs, Urban Land Inst. (assoc.), Constrn. Fin. Mgmt. Assn. Home: 192 Camrose St Henderson NV 89014-0620 Office: Am Nev Corp 2501 Green Valley Pky Ste 101 Henderson NV 89014-2158

GRIFFIN, (ALVA) JEAN, entertainer; b. Detroit, June 1, 1931; d. Henry Bethel White and Ruth Madelyn (Gowen) Durham; m. Francis Jay Griffin, July 8, 1958 (dec.); stepchildren: Patra, Rodney; 1 adopted child, Donald; children: Rhonda Jean, Sherree Lee. Student, Anderson Coll., 1952-53; DD (hon.), Ministry of Salvation, Chula Vista, Calif., 1990, Ministry of Salvation, 1990. Ordained minister, 1990. Supr. Woolworth's, Detroit, 1945-46; operator, supr. Atlantic Bell Telephone Co., Detroit, 1947-51, Anderson, Ind., 1952-56; sec. to div. mgr. Food Basket-Lucky Stores, San Diego, 1957-58; owner, mgr. Jay's Country Boy Markets, Riverside, Calif., 1962-87; entertainer, producer, dir., singer Mae West & Co., 1980—; owner The Final Touch, Colorado Springs; tchr. art Grant Sch., Riverside, 1964-65; tchr., adviser Mental Retarded Sch., Riverside, 1976-77; instr. Touch for Health Found., Pasadena, Calif., 1975-79; cons., hypnotist, nutritionist, Riversaide, 1976-79; mem., tchr. Psi field parapsychology. Mem. Rep. Presdl. Task Force, 1983. Recipient svc. award Rep. Presdl. Task Force, 1986. Mem. Parapsychology Assn. Riverside (pres. 1981-82). Mem. Ch. of Religious Science New Thought. Home: 201 Chapel Rd Sedona AZ 86336

GRIFFIN, MERV EDWARD, entertainer, television producer, entrepreneur; b. San Mateo, Calif., July 6, 1925; s. Mervyn Edward and Rita (Robinson) G.; m. Julann Elizabeth Wright, May 18, 1958 (div. June 1976); 1 son, Anthony Patrick. Student, San Mateo Coll., 1942-44; L.H.D., Emerson Coll., 1981. Chmn. bd. MGP (Merv Griffin Prodns.), Beverly Hills, Calif.; owner 6 radio stas. in Hartford, Albany, Providence; owner Teleview Racing Patrol Inc., Miami, Fla., Video Racing Patrol Inc., Seattle, Beverly Hilton Hotel, Beverly Hills, Calif.; chmn. Resorts Internat., Atlantic City and The Bahamas. Performer, Merv Griffin Show radio sta. KFRC, San Francisco, 1945-48, vocalist, Freddy Martin's Orch., 1948-52; contract player, star: So This is Love, Warner Bros., 1953-55; TV master ceremonies, 1958—, Merv Griffin Show, NBC-TV, 1962-63, Westinghouse Broadcasting Co., 1965-69, CBS-TV, 1969-72, syndication, 1972-86; currently producing: Wheel of Fortune, Jeopardy. Trustee Dr. Armand Hammer United World Coll. of Am. S.W. Club: Bohemian (San Francisco). Office: Merv Griffin Enterprises 9860 Wilshire Blvd Beverly Hills CA 90210-3115 also: The Griffin Group 780 Third Ave New York NY 10017

GRIFFIN, RICHARD WELDON, public relations executive, advertising consultant; b. San Diego, Feb. 26, 1954; s. Weldon Wallace and Nadine Janice (Wood) G.; m. Janice Marie DeMuro, Mar. 20, 1981; children: Andrew, Candace. BS in Journalism, San Diego State U., 1977. With pub. rels. and advt. WFC Advt., San Diego, 1983-86, Jansen Assocs., San Diego, 1986-87, Roni Hicks & Assocs., San Diego, 1987-88, Franklin & Assocs., San Diego, 1991-92, Rick Griffin Mktg. Communications, San Diego, 1988—; pub. rels. dir. Gen. Instrument Corp., San Diego, 1989-90; cons. mktg. dept. San Diego Gas & Electric Co., 1990-91. Bd. dirs. San Diego Christian Found., 1986—. Mem. Pub. Rels. Soc. Am. (bd. dirs. 1992—), Pub. Rels. Club San Diego (bd. dirs. 1992—), Internat. Assn. Bus. Communicators (bd. dirs. 1992—), Bldg. Industry Assn. (bd. dirs. 1986—). Republican. Mem. Ch. of Christ. Office: Rick Griffin Mktg Comm 7777 Alvarado Rd # 276 La Mesa CA 91941

GRIFFIN, SYLVIA GAIL, reading specialist; b. Portland, Oreg., Dec. 13, 1935; d. Archie and Marguerite (Johnson) G. AA, Boise Jr. Coll., 1955; BS, Brigham Young U., 1957, MEd, 1967. Cert. advanced teaching, Idaho. Classroom tchr. Boise (Idaho) Pub. Schs., 1957-59, 61-66, 67-69, reading specialist, 1969-90, 91—, early childhood specialist, 1990-91; tchr. evening Spanish classes for adults, 1987-88; lectr. in field; mem. cons. pool U.S. Office Juvenile Justice and Delinquency Prevention, 1991—. Author: Procedures Used by First Grade Teachers for Teaching Experience Readiness for Reading Comprehension, The Short Story of Vowels, A Note Worthy Way to Teach Reading. Advisor in developing a program for dyslexics Scottish Rite Masons of Idaho, Boise. Mem. NEA, AAUW, Internat. Reading Assn., Orton Dyslexia Soc., Horizon Internat. Reading Assn., Idaho Edn. Assn. (pub. rels. dir. 1970-72), Boise Edn. Assn. (pub. rels. dir. 1969-72, bd. dirs. ednl. polit. involvement com. 1983-89), Alpha Delta Kappa. Office: 5007 Franklin Rd Boise ID 83705

GRIFFIN, WILLIAM STANLEY, scientist, researcher; b. St. Joseph, Mo., Apr. 13, 1935; s. William Mellican and Mary Florence (Whitlock) G.; m. Loretta Mae Chanon, July 24, 1965; children: Loretta Lynn, Edward W., Eric J., Evan H., Gene S. Student, U. Mo., 1953-54; BS, MS, MIT, 1958, M in Engring, ScD, 1963. Aerospace engr. NASA, Cleve., 1963-68; aerospace engr., asst. for engring. devel., corp. labs. Northrop Corp., Hawthorne, Calif., 1968-77; chief scientist Hughes Aircraft Co., El Segundo, Calif., 1977—; cons. cardiovascular rsch. St. Vincents Hosp. Cleve., 1964-67. Patentee in field. 1st lt. USAF, 1963-65. Mem. ASME, AIAA, Am. Def. Preparedness Assn. Republican. Methodist. Office: Hughes Aircraft E0-E1/D125 1200 El Segundo Blvd El Segundo CA 90245-0902

GRIFFITH, CARL DAVID, civil engineer; b. Hill City, Kans., Mar. 1, 1937; s. Wilfred Eugene and Veda May (Jackson) G.; m. Mariana Segall, Mar. 26, 1988; stepchildren: Laurie Ann Segall, Allen Segall. BSCE summa cum laude, West Coast U., 1978; MSCE in Water Resources, U. So. Calif., 1980, MS in Engring. Mgmt., 1983. Profl. engr., Calif. Chief draftsman Bear Creek Mining Co., Spokane, Wash., 1959-64; right-of-way technician So. Calif. Edison Co., Los Angeles, 1964-65; engr. treatment plant design of spl. projects br. Metropolitan Water Dist. So. Calif., Los Angeles, 1965—, com. chmn. employees assn.; assoc. prof. Sch. Engring., West Coast U. Sustaining mem. Calif. Republican party. Served with USAF, 1957-58. Mem. ASME, ASCE, NSPE, Am. Water Works Assn., Nat. Mgmt. Assn., Metropolitan Water Dist. Mgmt. Club. Lodge: Masons. Home: PO Box 923122 Sylmar CA 91392-3122 Office: PO Box 54153 Los Angeles CA 90054

GRIFFITH, EVAN JOSEPH, JR., electric power industry executive; b. Little Rock, July 18, 1941; s. Evan Joseph and Altha Irene (Jones) G.; m. Sara Louise McCracken, June 4, 1964; children: Evan J. III, Sheila J., Leah J. BS in Engring., USAF Acad., 1964; MS in Gen. Engring., Okla. State U., 1971. Commd. 2d lt. USAF, 1964, advanced through grades to col., 1984; ret., 1984; budget/program analyst Anchorage Mcpl. Assembly, 1984-89; exec. mgr. fin., planning Chugach Electric Assn., Inc., Anchorage, 1989—; cons. Chambers, Griffith Assocs., Anchorage, 1984-91. Author: Missile Test and Evaluation, 1973; author test plans and final reports, 1971-79; contbr. articles to profl. jours. Bd. dirs. ARC, Anchorage, 1984-85, Commonwealth North, Anchorage, 1985—; bd. dirs., chmn. Armed Svcs. YMCA, Anchorage, 1986-89. Decorated Legion of Merit (2), Disting. Flying Cross (5); recipient Communications and Leadership award Alaska Coun. Toastmasters, 1984, Alaska Disting. Svc. medal Alaska Dept. Vet. and Mil. Affairs, 1984. Mem. Air Force Assn. (Anchorage chpt.). Republican. Presbyterian. Home: 9242 Hiland Rd Eagle River AK 99577 Office: Chugach Electric Assn 5601 Minnesota Dr Anchorage AK 99519-6300

GRIFFITH, J. GORDON, real estate company officer; b. Council Bluffs, Iowa, Dec. 16, 1931; s. Frank L. and Geneva (Seitz) F.; children: Stephen John, Jessica Geneva. BS, Iowa State U., 1953. Chief exec. officer Centurion Investment Corp., Costa Mesa, Calif., 1973—; bd. dirs. Bio-Trends Internat., Sacramento. 2d lt. USAF, 1953-54. Mem. BJA. Office: Centurion Investment Corp 575 Anton Blvd Flr 3D Costa Mesa CA 92626-1910

GRIFFITH, WILLIAM H., academic administrator; b. Sept. 14, 1943; s. William Marion and Mary E. (Foust) G.; m. Judith Ann Barrett, Aug. 17, 1962; children: Mary Ann, Stacey. BS in Acctg., U. Ill., 1967; MS in Mgmt. and Devel. Human Resources, Nat. Coll. Edn., 1982. Acct. U. Ill., Urbana, 1965-69; budget officer Ill. Bd. Regents, Springfield, 1969-74; bus. mgr. Northeastern Ill. U., Chgo., 1974-85; v.p. adminstrn./fin. Montclair State Coll., Upper Montclair, N.J., 1985-89, Calif. State U., Long Beach, 1989—. Mem. Nat. Assn. Coll. and Univ. Bus. Officers, Western Assn. Coll. and Univ. Bus. Officers, Adminstrv. and Bus. Officers Assn., Exch. Club Long Beach. Office: Calif State U Long Beach Adminstrn and Fin SS/A 320 1250 Bellflower Blvd Long Beach CA 90840-0119

GRIFFITH-JOYNER, FLORENCE DELORES, track athlete; b. L.A., Dec. 21, 1959; d. Robert and Florence Griffith; m. Al Joyner; 1 child: Mary Ruth Griffith-Joyner. Student, Calif. State U., Northridge, UCLA. Designed line of sportswear, and uniforms for NBA Ind. Pacers. Actress (prin. role film) The Chaser, (recurring role TV drama) Santa Barbara, guest 227 TV situation comedies; host, commentator various sports events; guest numerous talk shows. Winner Silver medal Summer Olympics, L.A., 1984, 3 Gold medals, 1 Silver medal Summer Olympics, Seoul, Republic of Korea, 1988; U.S. Olympic Com. Sports Woman of the Year 1988, TAC Jesse Owens outstanding track and field athlete, 1988, Internat. Jesse Owens award Most Outstanding amateur athlete, 1988, Tass News Agy. Sports Personality of Yr., 1988, Internat. Fedn. Bodybuilders Most Outstanding Physique 1980s, 1988, UPI and AP Sportswoman of the year, 1988; named Athlete of Yr. Track and Field, 1988, recipient of the Harvard Found. award for outstanding contribution to the field of athletics, 1989, Essence Mag's. Sports award Extraordinary Accomplishments in Athletics, 1989, Golden Camera award from German Advt. Industry, 1989, James E. Sullivan Meml. award as most outstanding athlete in Am., 1989. Office: care US Olympic Commn Media Info 1750 E Boulder St Colorado Springs CO 80909-5746

GRIFFITHS, SIR ELDON WYLIE, international business consultant; b. Wigan, Lancashire, Eng., May 25, 1925; came to U.S. 1992; s. Thomas Herbert Wylie and Edith May (Jones) G.; m. Marie Elizabeth Beatrix den Engelse, 1985. BA, Emmanuel Coll., Cambridge, Eng., 1948, MA, 1957; MA, Yale U., 1949. Corres. Time-Life mags., Denver, L.A., 1949-51; writer Time, N.Y.C., 1951-55; chief European corres. Newsweek, London, 1955-59; fgn. editor Newsweek, N.Y.C., 1959-63; speech writer Prime Minister, London, 1963-64; mem. Parliament Bury St. Edmunds Constituency/Ho. of Commons, Suffolk, Eng., 1964-92; under sec. of state Dept. Environ./Dept. Transport; pres. World Affairs Coun., Orange County, Calif., 1992—; dir. Ctr. for Internat. Bus., Chapman U., 1992—; dir. Stratham/Intervest; cons. numerous cos. in field. Contbr. numerous articles on polit., diplomatic and econ. issues; author 2 books; Columnist Orange County Register. Pres. Spl. Olympics, U.K.; active in numerous other charitable and trade orgns. Mem. Carlton Club (London), Pilgrims Club (London), Royal Overseas League (London), Korea-Am. Friendship Soc. Republican. Anglican Ch. Office: World Affairs Coun PO Box 7587 Laguna Niguel CA 92607

GRIFFITHS, IORWERTH DAVID ACE, psychologist, retired educator; Raised Idaho; s. Iorwerth Vivian and Katherine (Lewis) G.; m. Dorothea Ohs. B.S., U. Idaho; M.S., U. Ariz.; Ed.D., No. Colo. U.; postgrad., Wash. State U., U. Minn. lic. psychologist, Calif. Practice in Calif.; with Sears Roebuck & Co., Dick Graves, Inc., Nev. and Idaho; tchr. public schs. Potlatch, Idaho; counselor public sch. Port Townsend, Wash.; dean of students Eastern Ariz. Coll., Thatcher, Reedley (Calif.) Coll.; prof. edn. Calif. State U., Fresno, 1959-83; dir. U.S. Govt. Counselor Tng. Workshops, 1964. Contbr. articles to profl. jours.; co-author: Principles of Retailing, 1956. Named One of 18 All-Time Outstanding Tchrs., Port Townsend Pub. Schs., 1985. Mem. Am. Personnel and Guidance Assn. (membership chmn. 1961-63), Am. Psychol. Assn., NEA, Calif. Personnel and Guidance Assn. (McDaniel award), Nat. Vocat. Guidance Assn., Assn. Counselor Edn. and Supervision, Calif. State Employees Assn., Kings-Tulare Guidance Assn., San Joaquin Valley Guidance Assn., Fresno Counselors Assn., Kappa Delta Pi, Delta Psi Omega, Phi Delta Kappa. Unitarian. Home: 6462 N Remington Ave Fresno CA 93704-1118

GRIFFITHS, WILLIAM HAROLD, marketing professional; b. Chgo., Apr. 8, 1943; s. G. Findley and Marion Emmeline (Winterrowd) G.; m. Sharon JoAnn Ziebart, Jan. 4, 1944; children: W. Findley, David W. BA in English, Coe Coll., 1966. From fabrication estimator to mgr. inside sales dept. Joseph T. Ryerson & Son, Inc., Chgo. and Mpls., 1969-91; mktg. mgr. Joseph T. Ryerson/West, Seattle, 1991-92, gen. mgr. mktg., 1992—. Bd. dirs. YMCA Trailblazers, Minnetonka, Minn., 1982-83; charter mem. Golden Valley (Minn.) Rotary Club, 1973-75. With U.S. Army, 1967-69. Office: Josehp T Ryerson & Son Inc Ste 200 Bldg 2 16000 Christensen Rd Seattle WA 98188

GRIGGS, GARY BRUCE, earth sciences educator, oceanographer, geologist, consultant; b. Pasadena, Calif., Sept. 25, 1943; s. Dean Brayton and Barbara Jayne (Farmer) G.; m. Venetia Bradfield, Jan. 11, 1980; children: Joel, Amy, Shannon, Callie, Cody. BA in Geology, U. Calif., Santa Barbara, 1965; PhD in Oceanography, Oreg. State U., 1968. Registered geologist, Calif.; cert. engr. geologist. Fulbright fellow Inst. for Ocean & Fishing Rsch., Athens, Greece, 1974-75; oceanographer Joint U.S.A.-N.Z. Rsch. Program, Calif., 1980-81; prof. U. Calif., Santa Cruz, 1968—, chair earth scis., 1981-84; dir. Inst. of Marine Scis., 1991—. Author: (with others) Geologic Hazards, Resources & Environmental Planning, 1983, Living With The California Coast, 1985, Coastal Protection Structures, 1986, California's Coastal Hazards, 1992; editor Jour. of Coastal Rsch. Fellow Geol. Soc. Am.; mem. Am. Geophys. Union, Am. Geol. Inst., Coastal Found. Office: U Calif Div Natural Scis Applied Sciences Rm 272 Santa Cruz CA 95064

GRILLO, LEO, actor, photographer; b. Lawrence, Mass., Feb. 6, 1949; s. Leo F. Sr. and Carmela M. (DeLucia) G.; m. Stacy Grillo; 1 child, Erica. BS in speech, Emerson Coll., Boston, 1970. Actor Glendale, Calif., 1965—; pres., founder Dedication and Everlasting Love to Animals Inc., Glendale, 1979—, Living Earth Prodns., 1990—, Horse Rescue Am., 1991—. Author and editor: (with others) Landscam, 1988; producer, host Safe House, (TV show) Delta Rescue; contbr. articles to mags. Mem. Screen Actors' Guild, AFTRA, Actors Equity Assn. Home: PO Box 11523 Glendale CA 91226-7523 Office: DELTA PO Box 9 Glendale CA 91209-0009

GRILLY, EDWARD ROGERS, physicist; b. Cleve., Dec. 30, 1917; s. Charles B. and Julia (Varady) G.; m. Mary Witholter, Dec. 14, 1942 (dec. 1971); children: David, Janice; m. Juliamarie Andreen Langham, Feb. 1, 1973. BA, Ohio State U., 1940, PhD, 1944. Rsch. scientist Carbide & Carbon Chemicals Corp., Oak Ridge, Tenn., 1944-45; asst. prof. Chemistry U. N.H., Durham, 1946-47; mem. staff U. Calif. Nat. Lab., Los Alamos, N.Mex., 1947-80, cons., 1980—. Contbr. articles to books and profl. jours. Mem. N.Mex. House of Reps., Santa Fe, 1967-70, Los Alamos County Coun., Los Alamos, 1976-78. Mem. Am. Physical Soc., Kiwanis Club, Los Alamos Golf Club (pres. 1974-75). Republican. Home: 705 43d St Los Alamos NM 87544

GRIM, J(OHN) NORMAN, biology educator, electron microscopy consultant; b. Santa Barbara, Calif., Sept. 8, 1933; s. John Charles and Meada Fern (VanNorman) G.; m. Carole Ann Werly, June 20, 1954; children: Stephen Jay, Kristine Louise Grim Weisskopf. BA, U. Calif., Santa Barbara, 1956; MA, UCLA, 1960; PhD, U. Calif., Davis, 1967. Rsch. technician Sch. Medicine UCLA, 1959-60; rsch. technician Zoology Dept. U. Calif., Davis, 1960-67; biology professor No. Ariz. U., Flagstaff, 1967—; pvt. cons., Flagstaff, 1975—; dir. No. Ariz. U. Electron Microscope Facility, Flagstaff, 1968-90. Reviewer books, rsch. articles; contbr. 35 articles to profl. jours. Commr. Boy Scouts Am., Flagstaff, 1989-91, 93—. Col. USAR, ret. Grantee NSF, 1980, 89-90, U.S. Dept. of Army, 1971-74. Mem. Am. Microscopical Soc., Microscopy Soc. Am., Soc. Protozoologists, Ariz. Soc. Electron Microscopy (pres. 1970-71, 78-79), Soaring Soc. Am., Am Aviation Hist. Soc., Sigma Xi. Home: 3610 N Paradise Rd Flagstaff AZ 86004-1611 Office: No Ariz U Biology Dept Box 5640 Flagstaff AZ 86011

GRIMES, CRAIG ALAN, research scientist; b. Ann Arbor, Mich., Nov. 6, 1956; s. Dale Mills and Janet LaVonne (Moore) G.; m. Jean Cardenas, Aug. 18, 1984. BS in Physics, Pa. State U., 1984, BSEE, 1984; MS, U. Tex., 1985, PhD, 1990. Engr. Applied Rsch. Labs., Austin, Tex., 1981-83; chief scientist Crale, Inc., Austin, 1985-90; rsch. scientist Lockeed Rsch. Labs., Palo Alto, Calif., 1990-92; dir. advanced materials lab. Southwall Techs., Palo Alto, Calif., 1992—; rsch. asst. U. Tex., Austin, 1985-88; teaching asst., 1987-90; ; cons. Eastman Kodak, San Diego, 1989, Storage Tech., Boulder, Colo., 1989. Co-author: Essays on the Formal Aspects of E&M Theory, 1992; contbr. articles to profl. jours. Active Nature Conservancy, New Braunfels, Tex., 1988-90, Austin Triathletes, 1987-90. Mem. AAAS, IEEE, Mountain View Masters. Home: 2158 Francis Ave Santa Clara CA 95051-1730

GRIMES, EDWARD CLIFFORD, oil industry executive, consultant; b. Prince Albert, Sask., Can., Oct. 14, 1940; s. Edward Thomas and Ruth (Nyberg) G.; m. Carol K. Lende, June 11, 1960; children: Kelly Edward, Lori Kim. B in Commerce, U. Calgary, Alta., Can., 1970; MBA, U. B.C., Vancouver, Can., 1971. Economist Amoco Petroleum Can., Calgary, 1971-75; gen. mgr. ATCO Industries, Calgary, 1975-83, USS Oilwell Supply, Calgary, 1981-84; pres. CE Natco Ltd., Calgary, 1984-87, Key Oilfield Rentals Ltd., Calgary, 1987—. Mem. Petroleum Svcs. Assn. Can. (pres. 1989-90), Calgary Petroleum Club, The 400 Club, Silver Springs Golf and Country Club. Office: Key Oilfield Rentals Ltd, 950 633 6th Ave SW, Calgary, AB Canada T2P 2Y5

GRIMES, JOSEPH EDWARD, computer science educator; b. Bloomington, Ill., Sept. 28, 1941; s. Edward A. and Mary C. (Kleemann) G.; m. Mary Rae Tures, Aug. 8, 1964; children: Joe, Therese, Christine, Michael, Matthew, Mark. BA, St. Ambrose U., Davenport, Iowa, 1963; MS, Ill. State U., 1968; PhD, Iowa State U., 1973. Tchr., coach Cen. Cath. High Sch., Bloomington, 1963-66; civil engr. McLean County Hwy. Dept., Bloomington, 1966-68; instr. Iowa State U., Ames, 1968-73; prof. computer sci. Calif. Poly. State U., San Luis Obispo, 1973—, mgr. computer svcs., 1986-87; cons. NASA, Moffett Field, Calif., 1974—, Xerox Corp., Santa Clara, Calif., 1989—; mem. Naval Ship Weapons Systems Engring. Sta., Port Hueneme, Calif., 1987-90; expert witness Nat. Cash Register Corp., San Luis Obispo, 1983-85, Ford Motors Corp., 1989. Contbr. articles to profl. jours. Dir. referees San Luis Obispo Youth Soccer, 1982—; chmn. fin. coun., mem. pastoral coun. Old Mission, San Luis Obispo, 1985-89. Mem. Am. Statis. Assn., Assn. for Computing Machinery, Computing Soc. of IEEE, Mu Sigma Rho. Roman Catholic. Home: 650 Evans Rd San Luis Obispo CA 93401-8121 Office: Calif Poly State U Dept Computer Sci San Luis Obispo CA 93407

GRIMES, RUTH ELAINE, city planner; b. Palo Alto, Calif., Mar. 4, 1949; d. Herbert George and Irene (Williams) Baker; m. Charles A. Grimes, July 19, 1969 (div. 1981); 1 child, Michael; m. Roger L. Sharpe, Mar. 20, 1984; 1 child, Teresa. AB summa cum laude, U. Calif.-Berkeley, 1970, M in City Planning, 1972. Research and evaluation coordinator Ctr. Ind. Living, Berkeley, 1972-74; planner City of Berkeley, 1974-76, sr. planner, 1983—, analyst, 1976-83; pres. Vets. Assistance Ctr., Berkeley, 1978—, bd. dirs.; treas. Berkeley Design Advs., 1987—, bd. dirs. Ctr. Ind. Living. Author: Berkeley Downtown Plan, 1988; contbr. numerous articles to profl. jours. and other publs. Honored by Calif. State Assembly Resolution, 1988; Edwin Frank Kraft scholar, 1966. Mem. ASPA, Am. Inst. Cert. Planners, Am. Planning Assn., Mensa, Lade Merrit Joggers and Striders (sec. 1986-89, pres. 1991-93), Lions Internat. (bd. dirs. Berkeley club 1992—), U. Calif. Coll. Environ. Design Alumni Assn. (bd. dirs.). Home: 1330 Bonita Ave Berkeley CA 94709-1925 Office: City of Berkeley 2121 McKinley St Berkeley CA 94703

GRIMM, DANIEL K., state treasurer; b. Aberdeen, Wash., Apr. 5, 1949; s. Rupert T. and Lillian Mae (Brownlee) G.; m. Kathy Raines; 1 child, Whitney K. Student, U. Wash., 1967-69, Uppsala U., Sweden, 1971; BA in English Lit., Columbia U., 1972. State rep. Ho. Reps., Olympia, Wash., 1977-89; state treas., 1989—. Chmn. Ho. Ways & Means Com., Olympia, Wash., 1983-87, State Econ. & Revenue Forecast Coun., 1983-87, Ho. Dem. Caucus, 1981-83, Ho. Dem. Campaign Com., 1981-83, Ho. Higher Edn. Com., 1978-81. Mem. Nat. Assn. State Treasurers. Democrat. Methodist. Office: Treasury Dept Legislature Bldg PO Box 1009 Olympia WA 98507-1009*

GRIMM, LARRY LEON, psychologist; b. Goshen, Ind., Aug. 16, 1950; s. Warren Arden and Elizabeth Ann (Rassi) G.; m. Ann Mae Nelson, July 16, 1977; 1 child, Kirsten Ann. BS in Elem. Edn., No. Ariz. U., 1975, MA in Early Childhood Edn., 1977, EdD in Ednl. Psychology, 1983. Lic. psychologist; cert. sch. psychologist, elem. tchr. Ariz., Nat. Tchr. elem. sch. Page (Ariz.) Unified Dist., 1975-76; grad. asst. Coll. Edn., No. Ariz. U., Flagstaff, 1976; tchr. elem. sch. Litchfield Sch. Dist., Litchfield Park, Ariz., 1976-80; grad. assoc. dept. ednl. psychology No. Ariz. U., Flagstaff, 1980-81; sch. psychologist intern Peoria (Ariz.) Unified Dist., 1981-82; adj. faculty Grand Canyon Coll., Phoenix, 1982; sch. psychologist Child Study Services, Prescott (Ariz.) Unified Sch. Dist., 1982-87; adj. assoc. prof. No. Ariz. U., Flagstaff, 1984—, vis. faculty, 1987-88; postdoctoral fellow in pediatric psychology Child Devel. Ctr. Georgetown U. Med. Ctr., Washington, 1988-89; pvt. practice, 1989—; cons. in field; presenter at convs. Contbr. articles to profl. jours. Chmn. project devel. com. Infant & Toddler Network, 1989-92; mem. family resources adv. bd. first steps program Yavapai Regional Med. Ctr., 1990—. Mem. Am. Psychol. Assn. (publs. com. div. 16), Ariz. Assn. Sch. Psychologists (bd. dirs. No. Ariz., regional dir. 1983-84, pres. 1986-87, newsletter editor, 1986-87, Pres.'s award 1985, 88, 89), Nat. Assn. Sch. Psychologists (Ariz. del. fiscal adv. com. 1987-88, Capitol Network 1988-89), Soc. Pediatric Psychologists, Christian Assn. Psychol. Studies. Republican. Office: PO Box 11255 Prescott AZ 86304-1255

GRIMMICK, HENRY WILLIAM, quality management consultant; b. Troy, N.Y., July 1, 1945; s. Henry and Margaret Jane (Guerineau) G.; m. Dolores Irene Mashuta, June 11, 1966; 1 child, Henry Todd. BSEE, San Diego State U., 1972; MBA, U. San Francisco, 1992. Design engr. Teledyne Ryan Electronics, San Diego, 1972-73; product engring. mgr. Burroughs Corp., San Diego, 1973-80; dir. mfg. Silicon Systems, Inc., Tustin, Calif., 1980-85; cons. H. Grimmick Assocs., Mission Viejo, Calif., 1985-86; div. quality program mgr. Rockwell Internat., Newport Beach, Calif., 1986-87; internat. ops. mgr. Inmac Corp., San Jose, Calif., 1987-89; v.p. Philip Crosby Assocs., Inc., San Jose, 1989-93; pres. Grimmick Cons. Svcs., 1993—; adj. faculty U. San Francisco. Contbr. articles to mags. Mem. adv. bd. Palomar Coll., San Diego, 1979-80. With USN, 1964-68. Mem. Tau Beta Pi, Phi Kappa Phi. Home: 455 Donner Way San Ramon CA 94583-4875 Office: Philip Crosby Assocs Inc 1735 Technology Dr # 850 San Jose CA 95110-1313

GRIMSBO, RAYMOND ALLEN, forensic scientist; b. Portland, Oreg., Apr. 25, 1948; s. LeRoy Allen and Irene Bernice (Surgen) G.; m. Barbara Suzanne Favreau, Apr. 26, 1969 (div. 1979); children: John Allen, Kimberly Suzanne; m. Charlotte Alice Miller, July 25, 1981; children: Sarah Marie, Benjamin Allen. BS, Portland State U., 1972; D of Philosophy, Union for Experimenting Colls. & Univs., Cin., 1987. Cert. of profl. competency in criminalistics DEA Researcher Registration. Med. technician United Med. Labs., Inc., Portland, 1969-74; criminalist Oreg. State Police Crime Lab., Portland, 1975-85; pvt. practice forensic science Portland, 1985-87; pres. Intermountain Forensic Labs., Inc., Portland, 1987—; adj. instr. Oreg. Health Scis. U., Portland, 1987—; adj. prof. Portland State U., 1986-88, adj. asst. prof., 1988—; clin. dir. Intermountain Forensic Labs., Inc., 1988-92, Western Health Lab., Portland; adj. faculty mem. Union Inst.; mem. substance abuse methods panel Oreg. Health Div. Contbr. articles to profl. jours. Fellow Royal Microscopical Soc.; mem. ASTM, Am. Acad. Forensic Scientist, Soc. Forensic Haemogenetics, N.W. Assn. Forensic Scientists, Internat. Assn. Bloodstain Pattern Analysts, Internat. Electrophoresis Soc., Internat. Assn. Identification, Pacific N.W. Forensic Study Club, New Horizons Investment Club. Home: 16936 NE Davis St Portland OR 97230-6239 Office: Intermountain Forensic Labs Inc 11715 NE Glisan St Portland OR 97220-2141

GRINDSTAFF, ELIZABETH ANN, fine artist; b. Phila., June 22, 1955; d. Ernest Yarnall and Evelyn Mildred (Ream) Wurth; m. David Lee Grindstaff, Mar. 20, 1976; children: Benjamin Buck, Jesse Jed, Sheila Rae, Monica Kay. BFA, U. Utah, 1986. Fine artist Salt Lake City, 1986—; judge PTA Reflections, Salt Lake City, 1990. Prin. works include Thawed Weeds with Rock, 1987 (Merit prize 1987), Road Sculpture, 1987 (Hon. mention 1988). Troop leader Girl Scouts USA, Utah Coun., 1991—; art specialist Rosecrest Elem. Sch., Salt Lake City, 1990-92, mem. contest com., 1991-92; music dir. LDS HVII Ward Relief Soc., Salt Lake City, 1990—. Home: 2820 S 2520 E Salt Lake City UT 84109

GRINGAUZ, RAISA, physiatrist; b. Minsk, Belarus, Feb. 16, 1932; came to U.S., 1980; d. Moshe and Luba (Sandler) Gendelev; m. Lazar Gringauz, Jan. 3, 1957; children: Gina Babchin, Dmitry. MD, Minsk State Med. Inst., 1956. Bd. cert. phys. medicine and rehab. Intern internal medicine Minsk Mcpl. Hosp., 1956-57; resident pediatrics Minsk Children's Hosp. # 5, 1958-60; resident phys. medicine and rehab. U. Colo. Scientist Ctr., Denver, 1982-85; fellow PM and R Children's Hosp., Denver, 1985-86; med. dir. rehab. divsn. Wyo. Med. Ctr., Casper, 1986—; counselor Douglas (Wyo.) Meml. Hosp., 1989—. Fellow Am. Acad. Phys. Medicine and Rehab.; mem. AMA (Physician's Recognition award 1990-96), Am. Assn. Electrodiagnostic Medicine, Wyo. Med. Soc., Am. Congress Rehab. Medicine. Republican. Home: 1221 Manor Dr Casper WY 82609

GRISWOLD, MARTHA KERFOOT, social worker; b. Oklahoma City, Mar. 22, 1930; d. John Samuel III and Frances (Mann) Kerfoot; m. George Littlefield Griswold, Jan. 28, 1967. AB, Occidental Coll., 1951; MRE, U. So. Calif., 1956, postgrad., 1962. Cert. social worker. Teen dir. Toberman Settlement, San Pedro, Calif., 1954-56; social worker County of L.A., 1956-62, 1969-72; dir. program to integrate disabled children Internat. Inst., L.A., 1979-80; cons. community orgn. L.A., 1980-84; dir. LIV Disability Resources Ctr., Altadena, Calif., 1984—; instr. Calif. State U., L.A., 1966-68, 1983-84; chair Childrens' Adv. Com. L.A. County Dept. Mental Health, 1985-86; coordinator So. Calif. Conf. on Living Long Term with Disability, 1985-87. Co-host, prodr. radio program on disability Challenge, Sta. KPFK, 1987—, host, prodr. cable TV program on disability issues LIVstyles, 1992—. Mem. Pasadena (Calif.) City Disability Issues Com., 1984-86, Pasadena Strategic Planning Task Force, 1985-86; mem. coun. aging, long term care United Way Region 2, L.A., chair, 1989-90; mem. Pasadena Commn. on Disability Access, 1990-92. Recipient 1986 award So. Calif. Rehab. Assn. Mem. Nat. Assn. Soc. Workers, Calif. Assn. Physically Handicapped, Acad. Cert. Social Workers, Health and Social Service Workers with Disabilities. Congregationalist. Office: LIV Ctr 943 E Altadena Dr Altadena CA 91001-2033

GRIVNA, GORDON MICHAEL, metallurgical and chemical engineer; b. Mpls., Feb. 13, 1959; s. Lawrence and Emma (Tischler) G.; m. LeeAnn Crutcher, Sept. 27, 1986; children: Hannah Dawn, Tanya Nicole. BS in Chem. Engring., U. Minn., 1981, BS in Metall. Engring., 1981. Process engr. Motorola, Phoenix, 1981-86; staff engr. Motorola, Mesa, Ariz., 1986-88, process sect. head, 1988-90, prin. staff scientist, 1990—. Patentee in field. Mem. Am. Vacuum Soc.

GROBER, MATTHEW SCOTT, biologist, educator; b. N.Y.C., Nov. 19, 1959; s. Ronald Leonard and Roberta Lois (Stone) G.; m. Debra LeBlanc, Aug. 17, 1985; children: Aaron Jacob LeBlanc, Mia LeBlanc, Cory LeBlanc. BS, Calif. State U., Long Beach, 1981; PhD, UCLA, 1988. Pres., co-founder Maritech Inc., Long Beach, 1982-84; teaching fellow dept. biology UCLA, 1982-88; NIH postdoctoral fellow sect. neurobiology and behavior Cornell U., Ithaca, N.Y., 1988-92; asst. prof. zoology dept. biol. sci. U. Idaho, Moscow, 1992—; cons. Law Offices of Marc Grober, Nenana, Alaska, 1990-92. Contbr. articles and abstracts to profl. jours. Fellow Smithsonian Tropical Rsch. Inst., 1984; recipient Nat. Rsch. Svc. award NIH, 1988-92. Mem. Internat. Soc. for Neuroethology, Animal Behavior Soc., Am. Soc. Zoologists, Soc. for Neurosci., AAAS, Western Soc. Naturalists, Sigma Xi. Democrat. Jewish. Home: 1628 Hillcrest Dr Moscow ID 83843 Office: U Idaho Dept Biol Scis Moscow ID 83843

GROCH-TOCHMAN, DAVID ANTONÉ, nursing home administrator; b. Toledo, June 7, 1963; s. Anthony John and Rosemarie Helen (Michalak) Groch. BS in Nursing Home Adminstrn., U. Toledo, 1987. With collections/billing Bay Harbor Rehab., Torrance, Calif., 1988; adminstr.-in-tng. Best Care Convalescent Hosp., Torrance, 1988-89; asst. adminstr. Alden Terrace Convalescent Hosp., L.A., 1989, Jewish Homes of L.A., Reseda, Calif., 1989-90; adminstr. Beverly Manor, Santa Barbara, Calif., 1990-91; master program health adminstr. Calif. State U., Northridge, 1991-92; adminstr. Sun Air Convalescent Hosp., Panorama City, Calif., 1991-93; pvt. practice contractor long term care, 1992—; adminstr. health care svcs. Pacific Homes Kingsley Care Ctr., Hollywood, Calif., 1993—. Ombudsman State Ombudsman, L.A., 1989. Mem. Calif. Assn. Health Facilities. Home: 28970 Crags Dr Malibu Lake CA 91301-2906

GRODY, WAYNE WILLIAM, physician; b. Syracuse, N.Y., Feb. 25, 1952; s. Robert Jerome and Florence Beatrice (Kashdan) G.; m. Gaylen Ducker, July 8, 1990. BA, Johns Hopkins U., 1974; MD, Baylor Coll. Medicine, 1977, PhD, 1981. Diplomate Am. Bd. Pathology, Am. Bd. Med. Genetics; lic. physician, Calif. Intern/resident UCLA Sch. Medicine, 1982-85, postdoctoral fellow, 1985-86, asst. prof., 1987—; panelist Calif. Children's Svcs., 1987—, USFDA, Washington, 1989—; mem. DNA tech. com. Pacific Southwest Regional Genetics Network, Berkeley, Calif., 1987—, med., tech. cons. Warner Bros., NBC, Tri-Star, CBS, others, 1987—. Contbg. editor: MD Mag., 1981-91; contbr. articles to profl. jours.; achievements include application of molecular biology to clinical diagnosis, molecular genetics research and AIDS research. Recipient best paper award L.A. Soc. Pathology, 1984, Joseph Kleiner Meml. award Am. Soc. Med. Technologists, 1990; Basil O'Connor scholar March of Dimes Birth Defects Found., 1989. Mem. AAAS, AMA, Am. Soc. Clin. Pathology (DNA workshop dir. 1988—), Am. Soc. Human Genetics, Coll. Am. Pathologists (scholar award 1987), Soc. Inherited Metabolic Disorders, Western Soc. Pediatric Rsch., Am. Coll. Med. Genetics (mem. DNA com.). Democrat. Jewish. Office: UCLA Sch Medicine Divsn Med Genetics & Molecular Pathology Los Angeles CA 90024-1732

GROEBLI, WERNER FRITZ (MR. FRICK), professional ice skater, realtor; b. Basel, Switzerland, Apr. 21, 1915; s. Fritz and Gertrud (Landerer) G.; m. Yvonne Baumgartner, Dec. 30, 1954. Student architecture, Swiss Fed. Inst. Tech., 1934-35. Lic. realtor, Calif. Chmn. pub. relations com. Profl. Skaters Guild Am., 1972—. Performed in ice shows, Patria, Brighton, Eng., 1937; command performance in, Marina, London, 1937, Symphony on Ice, Royal Opera House, 1937; mem. Ice Follies, 1939-81, partner (with Hans Mauch) in comedy team Frick & Frack, 1939-53; solo act as Mr. Frick (assisted by comedy team), 1955-81; numerous TV appearances including Snoopy on Ice, 1973, Snoopy's Musical on Ice, 1978, Sportsworld, NBC-TV, 1978, Donnie and Marie Osmond Show, 1978, Mike Douglas Show, 1978, Dinah Shore Show, 1978; films include Silver Skates, 1942, Lady Let's Dance, 1943, Jinxed, 1981; interviewed by Barbara Walters NBC Today, 1974. Served with Swiss Army, 1934-37. Named Swiss jr. skating champion, 1934; named to Madison Sq. Garden Hall of Fame for 10,000 performances in Ice Follies, 1967, U.S. Figure Skating Assn. World Hall of Fame, 1984; recipient Hall of Fame Ann. award Ice Skating Inst. Am. Mem. SAG, Profl. Skaters Guild Am., Swiss Club of San Francisco (hon.). Office: care US Figure Skating Assn 20 1st St Colorado Springs CO 80906-3697

GROENINGER, EDWARD JOHN, military officer; b. Rockford, Ill., Aug. 19, 1947; s. Edward Vincent and Elizabeth Jane (Mariga) G.; m. Marsha Powell Curran, Dec. 20, 1969; children: Elizabeth Joy, Matthew Lee, Luke William. BS in Edn., Ill. State U., 1969; MS in Edn., No. Ill. U., 1972; MBA, Golden Gate U., 1985; Grad., USAF Squadron Officer Sch., 1979, USAF Fighter Weapons Sch., 1980, RAF Staff Coll., 1987, USAF Air War Coll., 1991. Math tchr. Roosevelt Jr. High Sch., Bellwood, Ill., 1969-70, Fremd High Sch., Palatine, Ill., 1970-72; commd. 2d lt. USAF, 1973, advanced through grades to lt. col., 1989; F-4 pilot Spangdahlem AB, Germany, 1975-77, F-4 instr. pilot, 1977-78; F-4 instr. pilot George AFB, Calif., 1978-80, F-4 weapons and tactics instr. pilot, 1980; Mirage III weapons and tactics instr. pilot RAAF Base Williamtown, Australia, 1980-83; F-4 figher weapons instr. pilot George AFB, Calif., 1983-84; wing weapons officer George AFB, 1984-85, fighter weapons flight comdr., 1985-86, squadron ops. officer, 1985-86; tactical weapons unit staff officer RAF Bentley Priory, Eng., 1988-90; chief current plans br. Hdqrs. NORAD, Peterson AFB, Colo., 1991-92, chief current and counterdrug planning divsn., 1992, chief forces planning divsn., 1993—. Active Boy Scouts Am. Mem. Air Force Assn. Roman Catholic. Home: 3220 Windjammer Dr Colorado Springs CO 80920 Office: HQ NORAD/J5P 250 S Peterson Blvd Ste 116 Peterson AFB CO 80914-3280

GROFF, DAVID HUSTON, academic administrator, director, educator; b. Sacramento, Feb. 15, 1945; s. Philip David and Harriett (Huston) G.; m. Elizabeth Ussher, Sept. 16, 1969; children: Rebecca, Julia. BA, U. Calif., Davis, 1967; MA, Stanford (Calif.) U., 1972, PhD, 1980. Asst. prof. history and humanities Reed Coll., Portland, Oreg., 1976-87, dean of students, 1983-87; asst. dir. div. continuing edn. Linfield Coll., McMinnville, Oreg., 1987-93; dir. Linfield Coll., Portland, 1988—. Author: (chpt. in book) African Bourgeoisie, 1987, Law and Colonialism in Africa, 1987; contbr. articles to profl. jours. Woodrow Wilson Found. fellow, 1967, Ford Found. fellow, 1973, NEH fellow, 1986. Mem. Assn. Concerned Africa Scholars (nat. exec. sec. 1987-90), Am. Hist. Assn., African Studies Assn. Office: Linfield Coll Portland Campus 2255 NW Northrup St Portland OR 97210-2952

GROGAN, STANLEY JOSEPH, JR., consultant; b. N.Y.C., Jan. 14, 1925; s. Stanley Joseph and Marie (Di Giorgio) G.; AA, Am. U., 1949, BS, 1950, MA, 1955; degree, Air War Coll., 1972; MS, Calif. State Coll., Hayward, 1973; EdD, Nat. Christian U., 1974; m. Mary Margaret Skroch, Sept. 20, 1954; 1 child, Mary Maureen. Personnel asst., recruitment asst. CIA, Washington, 1954-56; asst. prof. air sci. U. Calif., Berkeley, 1963-64, Chabot Coll., 1964-70, Oakland Unified Sch. Dist., 1964-83, Hayward Unified Sch. Dist., 1965-68; prof. Nat. Christian U., 1975—, Nat. U. Grad. Studies, Belize, 1975—; pres. SJG Enterprises, Inc., cons., 1967—. Asst. dir. Nat. Ednl. Film Festival, 1971. Pub. rels. cons., 1963—. Bd. dirs. We T.I.P., Inc., 1974. With AUS, 1945; also to lt. col. USAFR, 1948-76; col. Calif. State Mil. Res. Decorated Air medal with oak leaf cluster; recipient citation Korea, 1963. Named to Hon. Order Ky. Cols. Commonwealth of Ky., 1970. Mem. NRA (life), Am. Def. Preparedness Assn. (life), Night Fighter Assn. (nat. publicity chmn. 1967), DAV (life), Air Force Assn., Res. Officers Assn., Phi Delta Kappa, VFW (life), Am. Soc. Indsl. Security, Nat. Def. Exec. Res., Marines Meml., Presidio Officers. Contbr. articles to profl. jours. and newspapers. Home: 2585 Moraga Dr Pinole CA 94564-1236

GROH, RUPERT JAMES, JR., judge; b. Richland Center, Wis., Dec. 5, 1933; s. Rupert James Sr. and Sadie Lenora (Mathews) G.; m. Evelyn Theresa Rausch, June 14, 1958; children: Rupert J. III, Thomas M., Jonathan C., Peter Christian. AB, Ripon Coll., 1955; JD, Marquette U., 1960. Bar: Wis. 1960, Ill. 1965, Calif. 1976, U.S. Dist. Ct. (ea., we. dists.) Wis. 1960, U.S. Dist. Ct. (no. dist.) Ill. 1964, U.S. Dist. Ct. (no. dist.) Ind. 1965, U.S. Ct. Claims 1965, U.S. Tax Ct. 1965. Trial atty. civil rights and tax divs. U.S. Dept. Justice, Washington, 1960-65; v.p. gen. counsel Benefit Trust Life Ins. Co., Chgo., 1965-69; ptnr. Wildman, Harrold, Allen & Dixon, Chgo., 1969-75; prof. law, asst. dean U. Pacific, Sacramento, 1975-84; magistrate judge U.S. Dist. Ct. (we. dist.) Wis., Madison, 1984-91, U.S. Dist. Ct. (ctrl. dist.) Calif., L.A., 1991—. 1st lt. USAR, 1955-63, Mil. Intelligence. Mem. ABA (legal edn. sect.), Ill. State Bar Assn., State Bar Wis., State Bar Calif., Law Club Chgo. Lutheran. Office: US Dist Ct Ctrl Dist Calif 312 N Spring St Los Angeles CA 90012

GROLD, L. JAMES, psychiatrist; b. L.A., May 28, 1932; s. Leo James Grold and Evelyn (Fox) Nichols; m. Janis Jensen, Apr. 4, 1958; children: Eric, Kevin, Katherine. BA, Stanford U., 1953, MD, 1956. Diplomate Am. Bd. Psychiatry and Neurology. Intern Los Angeles County Gen. Hosp., L.A., 1956-57; fellow Menninger Sch. Psychiatry, Topeka, 1957-60; pvt. practice, L.A., 1962—; med. dir. Resthaven Psychiat. Hosp., L.A., 1962-65, Westwood Psychiat. Hosp., L.A., 1965-69; exec. dir. Mental Health Referral Svc. So. Calif. Inc., L.A., 1982-89; dir. profl. edn. Malibu Community Counseling Ctr., 1974-75; mem. staff L.A. PTA Child Guidance Clinic, 1962-63; staff L.A. PTA Child Guidance Clinic, 1962-63; mem. staff Los Angeles County Hosp., 1962-71, Westwood Hosp., 1963-85, St. John's Hosp., 1969-76; asst. clin. prof. U. So. Calif., L.A., 1962-70; also others. Contbr. articles to med. jours. Bd. dirs. Malibu Colony Assn., 1984-88, v.p., 1987-88; chmn. Save Our Beach Legal Fund, 1984-88; mem. vol. med. staff, mem. mental health com., psychiat. cons. Venice Free Clinic, 1990—; advisor to pres. Menninger Found., 1988-89. Capt. M.C., U.S. Army, 1960-62. Recipient cert. of commendation City of L.A., 1987, U.S. Congress, 1988, Venice Family Clinic, 1992. Fellow Am. Psychiat. Assn.; mem. Nat. Assn. Pvt. Psychiat. Hosps. (edn. com. 1962-69), So. Calif. Psychiat. Soc. (chmn. com. on psychiat. hosps. 1064-67, mem. membership com. 1967-68, task force on developing vol. pro bono svcs. 1991—). Office: Ste 414 11665 W Olympic Blvd Los Angeles CA 90064

GROLLMAN, THOMAS BIRD, orthopedist; b. L.A., Nov. 8, 1939. BA magna cum laude, Occidental Coll., 1961; MD, UCLA, 1965. Diplomat Am. Bd. Orthopaedic Surgery. Intern U. Md. Hosp., 1965-66; gen. surgery resident U. Hawaii, Queen's Med. Ctr., 1970; orthopedic resident U. Calif., San Francisco/U. Hawaii, 1970-73; U.S. pub. health svc. officer Peace Corps, Buea, West Cameroon, 1966, Freetown, Sierra Leone, 1967-68, Columbo, Sri Lanka, 1968-69; orthopaedic surgeon Kauai Med. Group, 1973-85; pvt. practice Hawaii, 1985—; chief surgery GN Wilcox Meml. Hosp., Lihue, Kauai, 1979-80, pres. med. staff, 1981-83; apptd. mem. staff Kauai Vets. Mem. Hosp. Waimea, Kauai; apptd. courtesy staff Shriners Hosp. for Crippled Children, Honolulu; apptd. provisional staff St. Francis Hosp., Honolulu. Fellow Aa. Acad. Orthopaedic Surgeons; mem. Hawaii Orthopaedic Assn. (pres. 1979), Western Orthopadic Assn. (sec. Hawaii chpt. 1984-92, pres. Hawaii chpt. 1992—, program chmn. ann. meeting 1988), Kauai County Med. Soc. (pres. 1985-87), Phi Beta Kappa. Address: 3170 B Jerves St Lihue HI 96766

GROMAN, RICHARD PAUL, small business owner; b. Seattle, July 3, 1953; s. Neal Benjamin and Elaine Ruth (Spigle) G.; m. Fern Meryl Rogow, Mar. 27, 1982; children: Rachel, Emily. BA in Bus. Adminstrn., U. Wash., 1976. Buyer Honeywell Inc., Seattle, 1976-79; product mgr. Bruce Franklin Inc., Seattle, 1979-86; owner Summa Mktg., Seattle, 1986-88; pres. West Stock, Inc., Seattle, 1988—. Office: West Stock Inc Ste 400 2013 4th Ave Seattle WA 98121

GRONEMEYER, JEFFREY MICHAEL, studio engineer; b. Badkreutznach, Germany, Nov. 25, 1963; s. Gary Ferdinand and Judith Ellen (Sieferd) G. AA in Gen. Edn., Delta Jr. Coll., Stockton, Calif., 1986; BA in Radio and TV, Calif. State U., Fresno, 1988. Announcer Delta Jr. Coll., Stockton, Calif., 1985-86; assoc. producer pub. affairs Calif. State U., Fresno, 1986-88, announcer news, 1986-88; announcer KBIF, Fresno, 1987-88; engr. KAIL-TV, Fresno, 1987-89, KJEO-Channel 47, Fresno, 1989—. Mem. AFTRA. Home: 4908 N 9th # 220 Fresno CA 93726 Office: Retlaw Broadcasting Po Box 5455 Fresno CA 93755

GRONLI, JOHN VICTOR, college administrator, minister; b. Eshowe, South Africa, Sept. 11, 1932; s. John Einar and Marjorie Gellet (Hawker) G.; came to U.S., 1934, naturalized, 1937; B.A., U. Minn., 1953; M.Div., Luther Theol. Sem., 1958, D.Min., 1978; M.A., Pacific Luth. U., 1975; m. Jeanne Louise Ellertson, Sept. 15, 1952; children—Cheryl Marie Mundt, Deborah Raechel Hokanson, John Timothy, Peter Jonas, Daniel Reuben. Ordained to ministry, 1958; pastor Brocket-Lawton Luth. Parish, Brocket, N.D., 1958-61; Harlowton (Mont.) Luth. Parish, 1961-66; sr. pastor St. Luke's Luth. Ch., Shelby, Mont., 1966-75; missionary Paulinum Sem., Otjimbingwe, Namibia, 1975-76; dean, chmn. dept. philosophy and humanities Golden Valley Luth. Coll., Mpls., 1976-85; dir. Summer Inst. Pastoral Ministry, Mpls., 1980-85, sr. pastor Pella Luth. Ch., Sidney, Mont., 1985—; pres., CEO GEHM Inc., Sidney, Mont., 1991—. Bd. dirs. Mont. Assn. Chs., 1973-75, Richland Homes, Sidney, Mont., 1990—, Ea. Mont. Mental Health Assn., 1993—; sec. bd. for communications and mission support Am. Luth. Ch., 1973-75; mem. dist. council Rocky Mountain Dist., 1963-75, sec., 1963-70; mem. S.African affairs task force SEM Dist., 1978-79; dean S.W. Mont. Conf. Evang. Luth. Ch. in Am.; faculty No. Rockies Inst. Theology, 1986—; trustee Luth. Bible Inst., Seattle, 1986-92. Mem. personnel and guidance assns., Am., Minn. coll. personnel assns. Editor: Rocky Mountain Dist. Yearbook, 1963-70; Rocky Mountain Views, 1973-75; contbr. to Lutheran Standard, 1973-77; contbr. articles to religious jours.

GRONNING, LLOYD JOSEPH, engineering company executive, civil engineer; b. Tacoma, July 12, 1951; s. Neil Roland and Marie Sarafica (Buettner) G.; m. Robyn Mary McAtavey, May 29, 1971; children: John, Jenny, Margaret. BSCE, U. Notre Dame, 1973; MSCE, Colo. State U., 1976; MBA, U. Denver, 1983. Registered profl. engr. Colo., Wyo., N.Mex. Design engr., resident insp. Nelson, Haley, Patterson and Quirk, Greeley, Colo., 1972-76; project engr. M&I Cons. Engrs., Ft. Collins, Colo., 1976-77; mgr. water resources City of Thornton, Colo., 1977-80, utilities dir., 1980-84; pres. Gronning Engring. Co., Denver, 1984—. Mem. ASCE, Cons. Engrs. Council Colo., Am. Waterworks Assn., Colo. Water Congress, Internat. Water Supply Assn. Democrat. Roman Catholic. Home: 9916 Wagner Ln Westminster CO 80030-2527 Office: Gronning Engring Co 12050 Pecos St Ste 100 Denver CO 80234-2711

GROOMS, HENRY RANDALL, civil engineer; b. Cleve., Feb. 10, 1944; s. Leonard Day and Lois (Pickell)ūG.; m. Tonie Marie Joseph; children: Catherine, Zayne, Nina, Ivan, Athesis, Ian, Shaneya, Yaphet Rahsan, Dax, Jevay. BSCE, Howard U., 1965; MSCE, Carnegie-Mellon U., 1967, PhD, 1969. Hwy. engr. D.C. Hwy. Dept., Washington, 1965; structural engr. Peter F. Loftus Corp., Pitts., 1966; structural engr., engring. mgr. Rockwell Internat., Downey, Calif., 1969—. Contbr. articles to profl. jours. Scoutmaster Boy Scouts Am., Granada Hills, Calif., 1982-87; basketball coach Valley Conf., Granada Hills, 1984—; coach Am. Youth Soccer Orgn., Granada Hills, 1985-90; tutor Watts Friendship Sports League, 1989—. Recipient Alumni Merit award Carnegie-Mellon U., 1985; named Honoree Black History Project Western Res. Hist. Soc., 1989. Mem. ASCE, Tau Beta Pi, Sigma Xi. Office: Rockwell Internat Mail Code AD 69 12214 Lakewood Blvd Downey CA 90241

GROSE, GEORGE DENNIS, director college relations; b. Butte, Mont., Apr. 22, 1953; s. George Thomas and Cornelia Alice (Giles) G.; m. Geri Lynn Welsh, Sept. 10, 1983; 1 child, Kyla Denise. BA in English, Carroll Coll., 1975. Communications specialist Helena (Mont.) C. of C., 1976-78, acting exec. dir., 1978; dir. coll. rels. Mont. Coll. Mineral Sci. & Tech., Butte, 1978—; cons. Mont. Tech. Found., Butte, 1988—; pub. address announcer Mont. Tech. Football Program, Butte, 1990—. Vol. Mont. Tech Booster Club, Butte, 1982—, Spl. Olympics, Butte, 1982—; mem. com. Butte C. of C., 1986-88; bd. dirs. ARC, Butte, 1982. Mem. Mont. Press Assn., Mont. Tech. Booster Club, Rocky Mountain Assn. for Retarded Citizens, Butte Men's Bowling Assn., Rotary Internat. Office: Mont Coll Mineral Sci & Tech West Park St Butte MT 59701

GROSECLOSE, WILLIAM BUELL, III, electronic engineer; b. Houston, Mar. 30, 1959; s. William Buell Jr. and Frances (Fertitta) G. BSEE, Lamar U., Beaumont, Tex., 1984; MSEE, Calif. State U., 1989. Electronic engr. Navy Metrology Engring. Ctr., Adv. Tech., Pomona, Calif., 1984-85; electronic engr. Navy Metrology Engring. Ctr. Adv. Metrology, Pomona, 1985-86, Corona, Calif., 1986-91; systems engr. Naval Warfare Assessment Ctr. Systems Engring. Directorate, Corona, 1992—; chmn. DOD Tri-Svc. CCG/ATE Group, 1989-92; tech. rep. U.S. Navy Test Tech. Strategy Team, 1986-92, IEEE 488.2 and IEEE P1174 Com., 1986-92, others. Contbr. articles to profl. jours. Tchr., St. Julianna's CCD prog., Fullerton, 1988-90; dir. Riversierra Charity Tennis Tournament, Riverside, Calif., 1989. Mem. IEEE, MABL, U.S. Tennis Assn., Christian Appalachian Project. Republican. Home: PO Box 1555 Corona CA 91718-1555 Office: Naval Warefare Assess Ctr Corona CA 91720

GROSS, ALLEN, engineer; b. Bklyn., Dec. 28, 1937; s. David and Ann (Green) G.; div.; 1 child: Lisa Rachel. BS in Chem. Engring., CCNY, 1960; MSME, Rensselaer Poly. Inst., 1963. Engr. Pratt & Whitney, East Hartford, Conn., 1960-63; project engr. Rocketdyne, Canoga Park, Calif., 1963-65; tchr. West Coast U., L.A., 1963-68; instr. U. So. Calif., Europe and Asia, 1968-70; project engr. Aerospace Corp., El Segundo, Calif., 1965-68, 70—. Developed, pub. numerous reports, space sensor cost model. Office: Aerospace Corp 2350 E El Segundo Blvd El Segundo CA 90245-4691

GROSS, BARBARA L., industrial hygienist; b. Denver, Aug. 6, 1960; d. Werner M. and Lisbeth C. Gross. BS, Colo. State U., 1982; MS, U San Francisco, 1991. Environ. scientist EPA, San Francisco, 1984-86; coord. health and safety IT Corp., Martinez, Calif., 1986-88; regional indsl. hygienist EPA, San Francisco, 1988-91, chief air inspection sect., 1991—. Mem. Am. Indsl. Hygiene Assn. (scholarship com. No. Calif. sect. 1990, chair scholarship and awards com. 1991-93), Am. Conf. Govtl. Indsl. Hygienists. Office: EPA 75 Hawthorne St San Francisco CA 94105

GROSS, CLARK DAVID, lawyer; b. Glendale, Calif., Nov. 25, 1952; s. Norman Harvey and Lillian (Saks) G. Student, U. Calif., 1971-74; JD summa cum laude valedictorian, Whittier Coll., 1987. Bar: Calif. 1987, U.S. Dist. Ct. (cen., so., no., ea. dists.) Calif. 1988, U.S. Ct. Appeals (9th and fed. cirs.) 1988. Assoc. Robbins, Berliner & Carson, L.A., 1987—. Mem. western regional bd. Anti-Defamation League of B'nai B'rith, L.A., 1990—. Recipient Alumni of Yr. award Whittier Coll., 1992. Mem. ABA (com. on PTO affairs, trademarks 1990—), Calif. State Bar Conf. Dels. (L.A. County Bar Del. 1991—), L.A. County Bar Assn. (com. on legal servers for the poor 1988—, barristers com. on state bar 1988-90), Lawyer's Club L.A. County (treas. 1992—, bd. govs. 1992—, dir. Bridging the Gap program for new attys. 1992—).

GROSS, EMMA ROSALIE, social work educator; b. Aguadilla, P.R., Mar. 7, 1943; d. James Louis and Emma Gross (Alvarez) Ubinas. BA, Reed Coll., Portland, oreg., 1967; MALS, Reed Coll., 1972; MSW, U. Mich., 1978, PhD, 1986. Trainer VESPA, Cayey, P.R., 1965-67; asst. prof. social work Portland State U., 1972-76, Moorhead (Minn.) State U., 1981-82, U. Minn., Duluth, 1982-83; assoc. prof. social work U. Utah, Salt Lake City, 1983—; Peace Corps vol., Colombia, 1963-65. Author: Contemporary American Indian Policy, 1989; editorial bd. Affilia: Jour. of Women in Social Work. Cons., planner Salt Lake County Social Svcs., 1983-87. Mem. Coun. on Social Work Edn., Nat. Women's Studies Assn. Office: Univ of Utah Grad Sch Social Work Salt Lake City UT 84112

GROSS, HERBERT GERALD, space physicist; b. Chgo., Dec. 9, 1916; s. William Theodore and Lucille Eleanor (Powalski) G.; m. Regina Marie Dwyer, Sept. 22, 1951 (div. Dec. 1962); children: Regina Marie, Gerald, Paul, Robert; m. Alice Marie Molway, June 13, 1964; stepchildren: Susan, Margaret, Judith, Joseph. BA in Philosophy, Cath. U. Am., 1940, MS in Physics, 1950; postgrad., Mass. Inst. Tech., 1952-53, Northeastern U., 1954-55, UCLA, 1968, Colo. State U., 1968. Registered profl. engr., Mass. Physicist, project engr. Raytheon Co., Newton, Mass., 1951-58, Edgerton, Germeshausen & Grier Co., Boston, 1958-59; staff scientist Geophysics Corp. Am., Bedford, Mass., 1959-64; prin. scientist McDonnell Douglas Astronautics Co., Huntington Beach, Calif., 1964-75; dir. advanced devel. H Koch & Sons, Anaheim, Calif., 1977-93; pres. Gross Emergency Lighting Co., Santa Ana, Calif., 1993—; cons. Harvard U. Obs., Cambridge, Mass., 1962-63, Sci. and Applications, Inc., La Jolla, Calif., 1975-76, Planning Rsch., Inc., Newport Beach, Calif., 1977-78, Domar, Ltd., 1990-93; mem. task force Nat. Fire Protection Assn.; co-prin. investigator Apollo lunar rocks for luminescence; prin. investigator laser-induced luminescence remote sensing of oil and hazardous materials spills in L.A. Harbor. Inventor in field; contbr. articles to profl. jours. Pres. Cedarwood Assn., Waltham, Mass., 1951-54, Waltham Mus. Club, 1954-55; founder Waltham Community Symphony, 1955; dist. dir. Waltham Hosp. Fund Drive, 1956, Citizens Edn. Adv. Group, Tustin, Calif., 1967; treas. South Coast Homeowners Assn., Santa Ana, Calif., 1974-76, pres., 1976-78; mem. Laguna Beach Arts Festival. Mem. Planetary Soc., Survival and Flight Equipment Assn., Illuminating Engring. Soc., Soc. Automotive Engrs. (exec. com., chmn. A-20C aircraft interior lighting subcom., mem. A-20 aircraft lighting com.), Elks. Roman Catholic. Home and Office: 2011 W Summer Wind Santa Ana CA 92704-7133

GROSS, JAMES IRVAN, JR., health facility manager, quality assurance; b. St. Louis, June 22, 1956; s. James I. Sr. and Barbara (Roth) G. BS in Animal Husbandry, U. Mo., 1978; MS in Animal Sci., U. Calif., Davis, 1981; MBA, U. Miami, 1984. Mgr. U. Miami, Fla., 1981-83, Calif. Primate Rsch. Ctr., Davis, 1983-88, U. Calif. Davis Med. Ctr., Sacramento, 1988—; pvt. practice quality assurance cons., Davis, 1983—. Mem. Am. Assn. Lab. Animal Sci., Am. Coll. Med. Quality, Calif. Assn. Quality Assurance Profls., Northern Calif. chpt. Am. Assn. Lab. Animal Sci. (pres. 1990). Home: 2136 Dinosaur Pl Davis CA 95616-4300 Office: U Calif Davis Med Ctr 2315 Stockton Blvd Sacramento CA 95817-2201

GROSS, JOSEPH FRANCIS, retired bio-engineering educator; b. Plauen, Fed. Republic of Germany, Aug. 22, 1932; s. Joseph and Helen (Doelling) G. BSChemE, Pratt Inst., 1953; PhDChemE, Purdue U., 1956. Research engr., staff mem. Rand Corp., Santa Monica, Calif., 1958-72; prof. chem. engring. U. Ariz., Tucson, 1972-92, emeritus prof. chem. engring. and physiology, 1992—, head chem. engring. dept., 1975-81, dir. Ariz. rsch. labs. microcirculation divsn., 1981—; bd. dirs. Tucson Mus. of Art, 1984. Editor: Mathematics of Microcirculation Phenomena, 1980; co-editor: Finite Elements in Biomechanics, 1982; contbr. articles to profl. jours. Bd. dirs. Tucson Mus. Art, 1984. Recipient Humboldt U.S. Sr. Scientist award Alexander von Humboldt Found., 1979. Fellow AIAA (assoc.), AICE, Am. Inst. Med. and Biol. Engrs. (founding mem.), ASME; mem. Am. Physiol. Soc., Microcirculatory Soc. (pres. 1976-77), Internat. INst. Microcirculation (sec., treas. 1983—), Internat. Soc. Biorheology (treas. 1982-86). Home: PO Box 41445 Tucson AZ 85717-1445 Office: U Ariz Dept Physiology Tucson AZ 85724

GROSS, MICHAEL FRED, sales executive, advertising executive; b. Honolulu, Apr. 14, 1957; s. Ronald James Gross and Wanda Jean (Epps) Harris. BS in Mgmt., U. Nev., 1983. Bus. driver Washoe County Sch. Dist., Sparks, Nev., 1975-79; bar tender Mecca Lounge, Sparks, 1979-82; office mgr. A-1 Electric Co., Sparks, 1982-84; from ops. officer to mgmt. tng. First Interstate Bank, Reno, 1984-86; mktg. and sales assoc. Crystal Bay Group, Incline Village, Nev., 1986-87; tech. support staff AIQ Systems Inc., Incline Village, 1987-88, advt., pub. rels. mgr., 1988-90, dir. sales & support, 1990—; advt. cons. Hoffman Realty, Inc., Incline Village, 1990-91. Pub. rels. adv. Reno Charity Football League, 1989—; v.p. community rels. Am. Mktg. Assn., Reno, 1982-83; youth football coach, Sparks, Reno, Incline Village, 1978—. Democrat. Home: PO Box 5892 866 Northwood Blvd Crystal Bay NV 89450 Office: AIQ Inc PO Box 7530 916 Southwood Blvd Incline Village NV 89450

GROSS, PAUL HANS, chemistry educator; b. Berlin, Apr. 17, 1931; came to U.S., 1962; s. Paul Karl Friedrich and Olga Frieda (Saacks) G.; m. Uta Maria Freudiger, June 8, 1957; children: Thomas, Klaus, Michael, Eva. Diploma, F.U., Berlin, 1958, Dr.rer.nat., 1961. Rsch. chemist Schering A.G., Berlin, 1961-62; postdoctoral fellow U. Pacific, Stockton, Calif., 1962-64; rsch. fellow, instr. Harvard Med. Sch., Boston, 1965-66, Mass. Gen. Hosp., Boston, 1965-66; assoc. prof. U. Pacific, Stockton, Calif., 1966-70, prof., 1970—; vis. prof., vis. scientist Tech. Hochschule, Munich, 1973, Freie U., Berlin, 1978, U. Autonoma, Baja Calif., Mex., 1978, Med. Hochschule Hannover, Germany, 1983, U. de Sevilla, Spain, 1988; cons. Cell Pathways, Inc., Tucson, 1990—, United Pharms., 1984—, Dupont Merck, 1992—. Contbr. numerous articles to profl. jours. Rsch. grantee NSF, 1968, 69-71, Rsch. Corp., 1972-74, Med. Sch. Hann., 1983, NIH, 1987-89. Mem. Gesellschaft Deutscher Chemiker, Am. Chem. Soc., Alpha Chi Sigma, Sigma Xi, Phi Kappa Phi. Office: U of the Pacific Dept Chemistry Stockton CA 95211

GROSS, RICHARD PHILIP, retired business executive; b. San Francisco, Aug. 13, 1903; s. Louis and Ida (Solomon) G.; m. Marion Brownstone, Dec. 7, 1924 (dec. 1981); 1 child, Richard P. Jr. (dec.); m. Lila North, Jan. 8, 1982 (dec. 1982); m. Ruth Heller, Mar. 21, 1987. Student, Stanford U., 1924. Sec. Nat. Smelting Co., San Francisco, 1923-26; salesman Louis Forester, San Francisco, 1926-28; gen. ptnr. Richard P. Gross and Co., San Francisco, 1928-41, Kanter and Gross, San Francisco, 1941-46; gen. ptnr. Stone and Youngberg, San Francisco, 1946-75, ltd. ptnr., 1975—; bd. dir. Berkeley Antibody Co., Inc., David Rabb Real Estate Investment Trust; gov. San Francisco Curb Exch., 1932-38, pres. 1935-38; gov. San Francisco Stock Exch., 1949-50, Pacific Coast Stock Exch., San Francisco, 1957, 58, 68. Mem. Concordia-Argonaut Club (bd. dirs. 1935), City Club. Republican. Jewish. Home: 999 Green St San Francisco CA 94133-3662

GROSS, SOPHIE ANNE, therapist, pre-vocational trainer; b. Denver, Apr. 2, 1957; d. Werner M. and Lisbeth Clare (Kaufman) G. BS in Human Devel., Colo. State U., 1980; cert. emergency med. technician, St. Ive's Presbyn. Hosp., Denver, 1982. Living skills specialist Colo. Mental Health Inst. at Ft. Logan, Denver, 1982-91, psychiat. rehab. practitioner, 1991-92, clin. therapist, pre-vocation trainer, 1992—. Pres. Homeowners' Assn., Littleton, Colo., 1989—. Office: Colo Mental Health Inst Ft Logan 3520 W Oxford Ave Denver CO 80236

GROSS, THOMAS EDWARD, systems analyst; b. Swanton, Ohio, Jan. 20, 1948; s. Edmond John and Ione Yvonne (Hill) G.; m. Cynthia Leigh Lederman, May 12, 1973. BS in Chemistry, Ariz. State U., 1971; MS in Forestry, No. Ariz. U., 1989. Forestry technician U.S. Forest Svc., Payson, Ariz., 1975-87; rsch. asst. No. Ariz. U., Flagstaff, 1987-89, rsch. assoc., 1989-90; systems analyst Environ. Systems Rsch. Inst., Redlands, Calif., 1990—. Contbr. articles to profl. jours. Vol. Save Old Archtl. Redlands, Calif., 1991-92. Kaibah Forest Industries award scholar No. Ariz. U., 1986. Mem. Inst. Mgmt. Sci., Ops. Rsch. Soc. Am., Sigma Xi Sci. Rsch. Soc. (assoc.), Phi Kappa Phi Honor Soc. Democrat. Home: 316 Normandie Ct Redlands CA 92373 Office: Environ Systems Rsch Inst 380 New York St Redlands CA 92373

GROSS, WILLIAM ALLEN, mechanical engineer; b. L.A., Nov. 17, 1924; s. William Allen and Margaret Florence (Hill) G.; m. Shirley Mae Jackson, Aug. 10, 1948 (dec. 1968); children: Constance, Ellen, Mark, David; m. Sharon Carol Philbrick, Aug. 22, 1970. BS, USCG Acad., New London, Conn., 1945; MS, U. Calif.-Berkeley, 1949, PhD, 1951. Lectr. to asst. prof. U. Calif.-Berkeley, 1949-52; asst. prof. Iowa State U., Ames, 1952-55; mem. tech. staff Bell Telephone Labs., Murray Hill, N.J., 1955-56; mem. rsch. staff, mgr. applied mechanics dept. IBM, San Jose, 1956-61; v.p. adv. tech. div., dir. rsch. AMPEX, Redwood City, Calif., 1961-72; vis. lectr. U. Calif.-Berkeley, 1973-74; dean engring. U. N.Mex., Albuquerque, 1974-80, prof. mech. engring, elec. and computer engring., 1974—; vis. prof. Poly. U. Bucharest, 1991,93; dir. Lovelace Inhalation Toxicology Rsch. Inst., Albuquerque, 1976—, U. N.Mex. Tech. Innovative Prog., 1978-87, Renewable Energy Program, Vols. in Tech. Assistance, 1980-81; cons. in field. Editor: Fluid Film Lubrication, 1961; author: Gas Film Lubrication, 1962; editor/author: Fluid Film Lubrication, 1982; patentee in field; contbr. articles to profl. jours. Bd. dirs. Am. Friends Svc. Com., 1970-72, Futures for Children, Albuquerque, 1982-88, Trinity Forum, 1989-92. Recipient Chief Manualito award, Navajo Tribe, 1982; named N.Mex. Engr. of Yr., 1991. Fellow ASME (Centennial award 1978); mem. IEEE (sr. mem.). Democrat. Soc. of Friends. Home: 1401 Las Lomas Rd NE Albuquerque NM 87106-4529 Office: U NMex Dept Mech Engring Albuquerque NM 87131

GROSSBERG, JEFFREY BART, management consultant; b. N.Y.C., May 3, 1946; s. Abraham and Miriam (Silverberg) G.; m. Linda Marcus, Sept. 15, 1976 (div. Feb. 1981). BA, Lehigh U., 1967; postgrad., NYU, 1967-68, New Sch. Social Rsch., N.Y.C., 1968-69. Exec. dir. Inner Game Resources, Malibu, Calif., 1976-78; v.p. devel. DUO Internat., Miami, Fla., 1972-76, 78-82; dir. devel. Children's Home Soc., Miami, 1982-84, Girl Scout Coun. Tropical Fla., Miami, 1984-85; exec. dir. Omega Inst., Rhinebeck, N.Y., 1985-88, Children's Resource Group, Miami, Fla., 1988-90; pres. Nationwide Books, Santa Monica, Calif., 1990-92, Children's Media Resource, Miami, 1992—, Jeff Grossberg and Assocs., Santa Monica, 1984—; cons. JWCH Health Trust, L.A., 1992—, Three Rivers Prodns., L.A., 1992—, Westside Regional Ctr., L.A., 1992—. Home: 1333 Yale St Santa Monica CA 90404

GROSSER, BERNARD IRVING, psychiatry educator; b. Boston, Apr. 19, 1929; s. John and Katherine (Russman) G.; children: Steven, Mark, Minda; m. Karen Grosser. BA, U. Mass., 1950; MS, U. Mich., 1953; MD, Case-Western Res. U., 1959. Diplomate Am. Bd. Psychiatry and Neurology. Intern U. Utah, 1959-60, resident in psychiatry, 1960-65; asst. prof. psychiatry U. Utah Sch. Medicine, Salt Lake City, 1967-71, assoc. prof., 1971-75, prof., 1975—, chmn. dept., 1978—; mem. pre-clin. and clin. psychopharm. rev. com. NIMH, Washington, 1974-79, 80-84, me. sci. adv. bd., 1984-88; mem. merit rev. bd. VA, Washington, 1988-91; sr. sci. advisor Alcohol, Drug Abuse and Mental Health Adminstrn., Washington, 1987-88. Contbr. chpts. to books, articles to profl. jours. Capt. USAF, 1965-67. Grantee NIMH, 1959-84, FDA, 1985-88. Fellow Am. Psychiat. Assn.; mem. Internat. Soc. Psychoneuroendocrinology (treas. 1974-88), Psychiat. Rsch. Soc. (pres. 1986-87), Am. Coll. Neuropsychopharmacology, Soc. Neurosci., N.Y. Acad. Sci. Republican. Jewish. Home: 511 Perry Hollow Rd Salt Lake City UT 84103-4470 Office: U Utah Sch Medicine Dept Psychiatry 50 N Medical Dr Salt Lake City UT 84132-0002

GROSSER, MORTON, management and technology consultant; b. Phila., Dec. 25, 1931; s. Albert Jay and Esther (Mendelstein) G.; m. Janet Dolores Zachs, June 28, 1953; 1 child, Adam. BS, MIT, 1953, MS, 1954; PhD, Stanford U., 1961. Registered securities rep.; securities prin. credential. Rsch. assoc. MIT, Cambridge, 1954-55; engring. designer Raytheon Corp., Waltham, Mass., 1955-56; head of design Clevite Transistor Products, Devel. Div., Waltham, 1956-57; dir. pubis. Boeing Sci. Rsch. Labs., Boeing Corp., Seattle, 1964-66; gen. ptnr., mng. dir. L.H. Alton & Co., San Francisco, 1984-87; pres., mgmt. & technology cons. MG Cons., Palo Alto, Menlo Pk., Calif., 1967-83, 87—; cons. editor 100 Inventions That Shaped World History, 1993. Author: The Discovery of Neptune, 1962, The Hobby Shop, 1967, The Snake Horn, 1973, Diesel: The Man and the Engine, 1978, Gossamer Odyssey: The Triumph of Human-Powered Flight, 1981, On Gossamer Wings, 1982, The Fabulous Fifty, 1990; editor: Boeing Scientific Research Laboratories Review; contbr. articles to profl. jours. and fiction, non-fiction and poetry to lit. mags. Recipient Coats & Clark Grad. fellowship MIT, 1954, Ford Foun. fellowship, 1960, Stanford Teaching fellowship, 1959-60, NIH Postdoctoral fellowship, 1961-62, Stegner Creative Writing fellowship, 1963-64, Commonwealth Club Medal for Literary Excellence, 1991. Mem. AIAA, ASME, Assn. for Computing Machinery, Astron. Soc. of Pacific, Soc. Automotive Engrs., The Authors Guild. Office: MG Consulting 1016 Lemon St Menlo Park CA 94025-6113

GROSSETETE, GINGER LEE, gerontology administrator, consultant; b. Riverside, Calif., Feb. 9, 1936; d. Lee Roy Taylor and Bonita (Beryl) Williams; m. Alec Paul Grossetete, June 8, 1954; children: Elizabeth Gay Blech, Teri Lee Zeni. BA in Recreation cum laude, U. N.Mex., 1974, M in Pub. Adminstrn., 1978. Sr. ctr. supr., Office of Sr. Affairs, City of Albuquerque, 1974-77, asst. dir. Office of Sr. Affairs, 1977—; conf. coord. Nat. Consumers Assn., Albuquerque, 1978-79; region 6 del. Nat. Coun. on Aging, Washington, 1977-84; conf. chmn. Western Gerontol. Soc., Albuquerque, 1983. Contbr. articles to mags. Campaign dir. March of Dimes N.Mex., 1966-67; pres. Albuquerque Symphony Women's Assn., 1972; mem. exec. com. Jr. League Albuquerque, 1976; mem. Gov.'s Coun. on Phys. Fitness, 1987-91, chmn. 1990-91. Recipient N.Mex. Disting. Pub. Service award N.Mex. Gov.'s Office, 1983, Disting. Woman on the Move award YWCA, 1986. Fellow Nat. Recreation and Pk. Assn. (bd. dirs. S.W. regional coun., pres. N.Mex. chpt. 1983-84, Outstanding Profl. award 1982); mem. Am. Soc. Pub. Adminstrn. (pres. N.Mex. coun. 1987-88), S.W. Soc. on Aging (pres. 1984-85, bd. dirs., Outstanding Profl. award 1991), U. N.Mex. Alumni Assn. (bd. dirs. 1978-80, Disting. Alumni award 1985), Las Amapolas Garden Club (pres. 1964), Pi Alpha Alpha, Chi Omega (pres. alumni 1959-60), Pi Lambda Theta. Home: 517 La Veta Dr NE Albuquerque NM 87108-1403 Office: Office of Sr Affairs 714 7th St SW Albuquerque NM 87102-3898

GROSSMAN, ALVIN, publisher; b. Chgo., Sept. 18, 1924; s. Samuel A. and Rose (Brickman) G.; m. Marjorie Lois Epstein, Oct. 1948 (dec. 1972); 1 child, Gary Richard; m. Doris P. Pollak, Aug. 5, 1973; stepchildren: Kenneth Bernard, Robert Paul. BS, U. Ill., 1948; MA, U. Ga., 1950; PhD, U. Wash., 1961. Lic. psychologist Calif., Ga., Wash. Asst. prof. U. Ga., Athens, 1950-51; psychologist Seattle Sch. Dist., 1952-57; guidance cons. Napa County Schs., Napa, Calif., 1957-59; cons. in guidance Calif. State Dept. of Edn., Sacramento, 1959-66, bur. chief info. systems, 1966-71; exec. v.p. Anathon Computer Systems, N.Y.C., 1971-75; adminstr. info. systems San Mateo County Schs./Regional Ctr., Redwood City, Calif., 1975-86; pubr. Doral Pub. Inc., Wilsonville, Portland, Oreg., 1986—. Author: Breeding Better Cocker Spaniels, 1977, The Standard Book of Dog Breeding, 1983, The Great American Dog Show Game, 1986, Data Processing for Educators, 1986 (Best of Yr.), The American Cocker Spaniel, 1988, The Standard Book of Dog Breeding - A New Look, 1992; contbr. articles to profl. jours. 1st lt. USAF, 1943-46, 51-52. NIH grantee, 1950; recipient Hall of Fame award CSC of So. Calif., 1988. Mem. N.W. Assn. Book Pubrs. (pres. 1991—), Calif. Ednl. Data Processing Systems Assn. (pres. 1976, dir. 1963-67), Assn. of Ednl. Data Systems (dir. 1961-63), Wilsonville C. of C. (dir. 1992—). Home: 32025 SW Village Crest Ln Wilsonville OR 97070 Office: Doral Publishing 2619 Industrial St NW Portland OR 97210-0305

GROSSMAN, MAURICE, psychiatrist, educator; b. Phila., Dec. 5, 1907; s. Abraham and Sarah (Bernstein) G.; m. Mollie Froman, Nov. 15, 1938 (div. 1953); children: Paul, Kaye, Carl, Roy. BS, U. N.C., 1927; MD, Jefferson Med. Coll., 1931. Diplomate Am. Bd. Psychiatry and Neurology. Chief rehab. VA Med. Ctr., Palo Alto, Calif., Roseburg, Oreg., Brentwood, Calif., Augusta, Ga., Waco, Tex.; asst. clin. dir. VA Med. Ctr., Roanoke, Va.; pvt. practice, Palo Alto; tng. in psychoanalysis San Francisco Psychoanalytic Inst., 1949-54; asst. clin. prof. psychiatry U. Calif., San Francisco, 1950-59; clin. prof. psychiatry emeritus Stanford (Calif.) U. Sch. Medicine, 1959—; mem. staff psychiat. divsn. Stanford U. Med. Ctr.; mem. U.S. Consultative Com. on Rehab., Calif. Consultative Com. on Rehab., 1950-65. Contbr. chpts. to med. books. Maj. M.C., AUS, 1942-45. Fellow AAAS, Am. Psychiat. Assn. (life, chmn. task force on confidentiality)), Calif. Psychiat. Assn. (co-founder, 1st moderator Calif. dist. 1964-66); mem. No. Calif. Psychiat. Soc. (pres. 1960-61, Outstanding Achievement award 1983), Mid Peninsula Psychiat. Soc. (pres. 1963-64). Office: PO Box 745 Palo Alto CA 94302-0745

GROSSMAN, ROBERT JAMES, architect; b. Spokane, Wash., Feb. 3, 1936; s. George Christian and Corinne (Shelton) G.; m. Shirley Rozelle, Aug. 7, 1956; children: Kevin James, Heidi Rozelle. B Archtl. Engring. with highest honors, Wash. State U., 1959. Lic. architect, Wash. Architect Heylman-Trogdon, Spokane, 1962-64, Trogdon-Smith, Architects, Spokane, 1964-72; prin. architect Trogdon-Smith-Grossman, TSG Architects, Spokane, 1973-83; mng. prin. N.W. Archtl. Co. (A Joint Venture), Spokane, 1979-83; pres., prin. N.W. Archtl. Co., P.S., Seattle, 1983-85, mng. prin., 1986—; coordinating architect for site planning and devel. Expo'74 World's Fair, Spokane, 1971-74; mem. adv. coun. Sch. Architecture, Wash. State U., Pullman, 1986—, mem. adv. bd. Coll. Engring. and Architecture, 1991—. Prin. works include 15 elem. schs., Spokane, sch. projects, pvt. and pub. projects. Bd. dirs., pres. Salvation Army-Booth Care Ctr., Spokane, 1972-85; bd. dirs. Med. Svc. Corp., Spokane, 1984-86; mem. state adv. bd. Lien Law Reform, 1990; founding pres. Downtown Exch. Club of Seattle Found., 1990—; mem. adv. bd. for master planning Children's Hosp., Seattle, 1991—. 1st lt. C.E., U.S. Army, 1960-62. Recipient Disting. Svc. award Govt. State of Wash. and State Commn. for Expo '74, 1974. Mem. AIA (pres. Spokane chpt. 1976), Wash. State Coun. Architects (bd. dirs. 1975-78), Wash. State U. Alumni Assn. (Alumni Achievement award 1990), Exch. Club (bd. dirs. 1988-91). Office: NW Archtl Co 303 Battery St Seattle WA 98121

GROUSSMAN, RAYMOND G., diversified utility and energy company executive; b. Price, Utah, Dec. 15, 1935; s. Raymond K. and Gene E. (Goetzman) G.; m. Marilyn Kaye Jensen, Mar. 16, 1964; children: Katherine Anne Hajeb, Laura Kaye Hunter, Daniel Ray, Adam J. B.S., U. Utah, 1961, J.D., 1966. Bar: Utah 1965, U.S. Supreme Ct. 1978. Police officer Salt Lake City Police Dept., 1962-66; mem. firm Amoss & Groussman, Salt Lake City, 1966-69; staff atty. Utah Legal Services, 1969-70; chief dep. Salt Lake County atty., 1970-71; assoc. Pugsley, Hayes, Watkiss, Campbell & Cowley, Salt Lake City, 1971-74; gen. counsel Mountain Fuel Supply Co., Salt Lake City, 1974-84; v.p. Mountain Fuel Supply Co., 1977-84; v.p., gen. counsel Questar Corp., 1984—; bd. dirs. Wexpro Co., Celsius Energy Co. Bd. dirs. Children's Svc. Soc. Utah, 1976-77; trustee Ft. Douglas Mil. Mus., 1976-84; bd. advisers Energy Law Ctr., U. Utah Coll. Law, 1978—; mem. criminal law revision com. Utah Legis. Coun.; bd. dirs. Utah Legal Svcs., 1970-78; United Way of Salt Lake City, 1982-89; mem. bd. litigation Mountain States Legal Found., 1990—. With U.S. Army, 1957-60, lt. comdr. USCGR, 1967-85, ret. Mem. ABA, Fed. Energy Bar Assn., Am. Gas Assn., Pacific Coast Gas Assn. (chmn. legal adv. coun. 1979-80, 93—), Salt Lake County Bar Assn., Salt Lake Legal Defenders Assn. (dir. 1978—), Am. Corp. Counsel Assn. (bd. dirs. Intermountain chpt. 1990—), Salt Lake City C. of C., Sigma Alpha Epsilon, Delta Theta Phi. Office: Questar Corp 180 E 100 S Salt Lake City UT 84139-0001

GROVE, ANDREW S., electronics company executive; b. Budapest, Hungary, 1936; married; 2 children. B.S., CCNY, 1960, DSc, 1985; Ph.D., U. Calif.-Berkeley, 1963; DEng (hon.), Worcester Poly. Inst., 1989. With Fairchild Camera and Instrument Co., 1963-67; pres., COO, Intel Corp., Santa Clara, Calif., 1967-87, pres., CEO, 1987—, also bd. dirs. Recipient medal Am. Inst. Chemists, 1960, cert. of merit Franklin Inst., 1975, Townsend Harris medal CCNY, 1980, Enterprise award Profl. Advt. Assn., 1987, George Washington award Am. Hungarian Found., 1990, Citizen of Yr. award World Forum Silicon Valley, Exec. of Yr. award U. Ariz., 1993. Fellow IEEE (achievement award 1969, J. J. Ebers award 1974, Engring. Leadership Recognition award 1987); mem. Nat. Acad. Engring. Office: Intel Corp PO Box 58119 2200 Mission College Blvd Santa Clara CA 95052-8119

GROVE, JACK STEIN, naturalist, marine biologist; b. York, Pa., Oct. 29, 1951; s. Samuel Hersner and Myrtle Elenor (Stein) G. AS, Fla. Keys Coll., 1972; BS, U. West Fla., 1976; postgrad., Pacific Western U. Chief naturalist Galapagos Tourist Corp., Guayaquil, Ecuador, 1977-84; rsch. assoc. Sea World Rsch. Inst., San Diego, 1981—, L.A. County Mus. Natural History, L.A., 1982—; expedition leader Soc. Expeditions Cruises, Seattle, 1985-91; marine biologist, underwater photographer Eye on the World, Inc., L.A., 1986-91; assoc. investigator Nat. Fisheries Inst., Guayaquil, 1982-85; park naturalist Galapagosd Nat. Park, Ecuador, 1977-85; founder Zegrahm Expdns., Seattle. Editor: Voyage to Adventure/Antarctica, 1985; sr. editor: Fishes of the Galapagos Islands; photographer film documentaries. NSF grantee, 1986. Mem. Acad. Underwater Scis., Profl. Assn. Diving Instrs. (divemaster), U.S. Nat. Recreation and Parks Assn. (supr.), Am. Soc. Mag. Photographers. Office: Mus Natural History-Fishes 900 Exposition Blvd Los Angeles CA 90007-4000

GROVES, JAMES LEE, hospitality educator, researcher; b. Hutchinson, Kans., June 29, 1950; s. James Arthur and Wanda Lee (Herschberger) G. BA, Kans. State Tchrs. Coll., 1973; MS, Emporia Kans. State Coll., 1976; DPhil, Kans. State U., 1992. Mgr. ops. Vista at Emporia (Kans.), Inc., 1970-79; co-owner Vista at Topeka, Inc., 1979-86; instr. Kans. State U., Manhattan, 1990-92; asst. prof. U. Hawaii at Manoa, Honolulu, 1992—. Mem. Nat. Restaurant Assn., Coun. on Hotel, Restaurant and Educators Instn. Republican. Methodist. Home: 2640 Dole St Apt B-3 Honolulu HI 96822 Office: U Hawaii at Manoa 2560 Campus Rd Honolulu HI 96822

GROVES, SHERIDON HALE, orthopedic surgeon; b. Denver, Mar. 5, 1947; s. Harry Edward Groves and Dolores Ruth (Hale) Finley; m. Deborah Rita Threadgill, Mar. 29, 1970 (div. Apr. 1980); children: Jason, Tiffany; m. Nanely Marie Lamont, July 1, 1980 (div. Dec. 1987); 1 child, Dolores; m. Elaine Robbins, Feb. 7, 1991. BS, U.S. Mil. Acad., 1969; MD, U. Va., Charlottesville, 1976. Commd. 2nd lt. US Army, 1969, advanced through grades to maj.; surg. intern US Army, El Paso, Tex., 1976-77, orthopedic surgery resident, 1977-80; staff orthopedic surgeon US Army, Killeen, Tex., 1980-83; resigned US Army, 1983; staff emergency physician various emergency depts. State of Tex., 1983-84, 87; emergency dept. dir. Victoria (Tex.) Regional Med. Ctr., 1984-86; med. dir. First Walk-In Clinic Victoria, 1986-87; tchr. U. Tex. Med. Br., Galveston, 1986-90; emergency dept. dir. Gulf Coast Med. Ctr., 1988-89; with Amerimed Corp., 1990-92, Primedex Corp., 1992—; lectr. Speakers Bur., Victoria, 1984-86, Cato Inst., Ludwig Von Mises Inst. Contbr. articles to profl. jours. Mem. Victoria Interagy. Council Sexual Abuse, 1984-86; treas. bd. dirs. Youth Home Victoria, 1986-90. Recipient Physician's Recognition award AMA, 1980, 83, 86, 89, 92. Fellow Am. Acad. Neurologic and Orthopedic Surgeons, Internat. Coll. Surgeons (U.S. sect.); mem. Am. Acad. Neurologic and Orthopedic Surgeons, Soc. Mil. Orthopedic Surgeons, Am. Coll. Emergency Physicians, Tex. Med. Found., Assn. Grads. of U.S. Mil. Acad. (life), Am. Assn. Disability Evaluation Physicians, Coalition of Med. Providers, Am. Coll. Sports Medicine, Am. Running and Fitness Assn. (cert. recognition 1987), Internat. Martial Arts Assn., Hurricane Sports Club of Houston, Smithsonian Assocs., So. Calif. Striders Track Club.

GROZA, JOANNA RALUCA, metallurgical engineer; b. Bucharest, Romania, Oct. 14, 1943; came to U.S., 1986; d. Tom and Maria (Negrea) Dimitrescu; m. Horia I. Groza, Aug. 20, 1972; children: George H., Matthew C. MS, Poly. Inst. Bucharest, 1966, PhD, 1972. Registered profl. engr., Calif. Asst. prof. Poly. Inst. Bucharest, 1972-79; assoc. prof. Brasov (Romania) U., 1979-85; product devel. engr. Hudson Internat., Ossining, N.Y., 1986-87; sr. engr. Ceracon, Sacramento, Calif., 1987; lectr. dept. mech., aero., and material sci. engring. U. Calif., Davis, 1987-90, acting assoc. prof., 1990—. Patentee in field; co-author: Plastic Deformation of Non-Ferrous Metals, 1977; contbr. articles to profl. jours. Mem. Am. Soc. Metals. Eastern Orthodox. Office: U Calif Dept Mech Aero & Materials Sci Engring Davis CA 95616

GRUBB, DAVID H., construction company president; b. 1936; married. BSCE, Princeton U.; MSCE, Stanford U. With Swinerton and Walberg Co., San Francisco, 1964—, sr. v.p., then exec. v.p. SF San Structural div., exec. v.p. ops., now pres., also bd. dirs. Office: Swinerton & Walberg Co 580 California St San Francisco CA 94104-1000

GRUBER, ANDRAS, physician, researcher; b. Budapest, Hungary, Jan. 10, 1954; came to U.S., 1986; s. Gyula Foky Gruber and Edit Kardos; m. Anna Szemere, Nov. 1, 1975; 1 child, Nora. BS, Radnòti Sch. of Eötvös L. U., Budapest, 1972; MD, Semmelweis Med. U., Budapest, 1979. Cert. in internal medicine. Resident Postgrad. Med. Sch., Budapest, 1979-84, mem. med. staff, 1984-85; mem. med. staff Szönyi Tibor Hosp., Vác, Hungary, 1985-86; postdoctoral fellow Scripps Clinic and Rsch. Found., La Jolla, Calif., 1986-89, rsch. assoc., 1989-91; sr. rsch. assoc. The Scripps Rsch. Inst., La Jolla, 1991—, asst. mem., 1992—; lectr. in field, 1986—. Contbr. 22 articles to profl. jours., also book chpts., abstracts; patentee in field. Rsch. fellow Immuno Ag. Austria/Scripps Clinic, 1986, Am. Heart Assn./Calif. Affiliate, 1989; rsch. grantee U. Calif. Tobacco-Related Disease Rsch. Program, 1991. Mem. Soc. of Fellows of Scripps Clinic & Rsch. Found., Internat. Soc. Thrombosis & Hemostasis, Am. Heart Assn. Coun. on Thrombosis, N.Y. Acad. Scis. Office: The Scripps Rsch Inst 10666 N Torrey Pines Rd La Jolla CA 92037

GRUBIN, BRIAN LEE, trust administrator; b. Denver, Jan. 1, 1957; s. Eugene Stanley and Shirley Mae (Holmes) G. Student, Colo. State U., 1975-79; BS in Bus., U. Colo., Denver, 1988, postgrad., 1990—. Lab. asst. Natural Resources Lab., Golden, Colo., 1980-81; gen. ledger bookkeeper Fed. Res. Bank, Denver, 1981-85; woodworker Grubin Woodworking, Golden, 1985-87; Datalynx account adminstr. First Trust Corp., Denver, 1989—; notary pub. State of Colo., 1990—. At-large del. Rep. Platform Planning Com., Washington, 1992; empaneled mem. Rep. Presdl. Adv. Com., 1992; mem. presdl. commn. Nat. Rep. Senatorial Com., 1992-93. Episcopalian. Home: 2545 Gray St Edgewater CO 80214 Office: First Trust Corp 717 17th St #2300 Denver CO 80202

GRUCHALLA, MICHAEL EMERIC, electronics engineer; b. Houston, Feb. 2, 1946; s. Emeric Edwin and Myrtle (Priebe) G.; m. Elizabeth Tyson, June 14, 1969; children: Kenny, Katie. BSEE, U. Houston, 1968; MSEE, U. N.Mex., 1980. Registered profl. engr., Tex. Project engr. Tex. Instruments Corp., Houston, 1967-68; group leader EG&G Washington Analytical Services Ctr., Albuquerque, 1974-88; engring. specialist EG&G Energy Measurements Inc., Albuquerque, 1988—; cons. engring., Albuquerque; lectr. in field, 1978—. Contbr. articles to tech. jours.; patentee in field. Judge local sci. fairs, Albuquerque, 1983—. Served to capt. USAF, 1968-74. Mem. IEEE, Instrumentation Soc. Am., Planetary Soc., N.Mex. Tex. Instruments Computer Group (pres. 1984-85), Sigma Xi, Tau Beta Pi, Eta Kappa Nu. Office: EG&G Energy Measurements Inc Kirtland Ops PO Box 4339 Albuquerque NM 87196-4339

GRUEN, CLAUDE, economist, consultant; b. Bonn, Aug. 17, 1931; came to U.S., 1938; s. Walter and Elsbet (Bronne) G.; m. Nina Jaffe Gruen, Sept. 11, 1960; children: Les, Dale, Adam, Joshua, Aaron. BBA, U. Cin., 1954, MA, 1962, PhD, 1964. Instr. Xavier U., Cin., 1963-64; lectr. U. Calif., Berkeley, 1964-70; economist Arthur D. Little Inc., San Francisco, 1964-70; pres., prin. economist Gruen Gruen & Assocs., San Francisco, 1970—. Co-author: Low and Modern Income Housing, 1972; contbr. articles to profl. jours. Capt. USAF, 1954-57. Mem. Urban Land Inst. (mixed use coun.), Western Regional Sci. Assn., Am. Assn. Econs., Lambda Alpha Real Estate. Jewish. Office: Gruen Gruen & Assocs 564 Howard St San Francisco CA 94105-3002

GRUEN, NINA JAFFE, sociologist; b. Cin., Dec. 14, 1933; d. Lester Auer and Rosa (Shor) J.; m. Claude Gruen, Sept. 11, 1960; children: Leslie Walter, Dale Jaffe, Adam Samuel, Aaron Nathaniel, Joshua Claude. BA in Psychology, U. Cin., 1962, MA in Psychology, 1963. Lectr. U. Cin., 1962-63, U. Ky., Covington, 1962-63; cons. Arthur D. Little, Inc., San Francisco, 1966-70; founding ptnr. Gruen Gruen & Assocs., San Francisco, 1970—; bd. trustees The Urban Land Inst., Washington, 1982—; mem. airspace adv. com. Calif. Transp. Commn., Sacramento, 1991—. Co-author: Low-and Moderate-Income Housing in the Suburbs, 1972; contbr. numerous articles to profl. jours. Mem. SECA, San Francisco, 1990, The Christiansen Soc. of San Francisco Ballet Co., 1989. Recipient NSF grant, 1964. Mem. Womens Forum West (bd. dirs.), Internat. Womens Forum, Am. Sociol. Assn., Am. Assn. Pub. Opinion Rsch., Western Regional Sci. Assn., Phi Beta Kappa, Lambda Alpha. Office: Gruen Gruen & Assocs 564 Howard St San Francisco CA 94105-3002

GRUENBERG, MAX F., JR., lawyer; b. San Francisco, Sept. 25, 1943; s. Max Foorman Gruenberg and Dorothy (Lilienthal) Schnier; children: Bruce Leonard, Daniel Suchanan. BA, Stanford, 1965; JD, UCLA, 1970. Bar: Alaska 1970, Calif. 1971, D.C. 1972, U.S. Supreme Ct. 1980. Pvt. practice Anchorage, 1974—; ptnr. Gruenberg & Clover, Anchorage, 1984—; mem. Alaska Ho. of Reps., 1985-92, majority leader, 1987-88, 91-92. Lt. (j.g.) USNR, 1965-67. Fellow Am. Acad. Matrimonial Lawyers. Office: Gruenberg & Clover 2909 Arctic Blvd # 203 Anchorage AK 99503-3810

GRUENFELD, JAY, forest resource and management consultant; b. Ill., Nov. 24, 1924; m. Janet L. Clark, June 9, 1973; 6 children. BSc, Colo. State U., 1948, MF, 1949; diploma in humanities and forestry, Oxford (Eng.) U., 1950. Forest mgr., logging supr., mgr. timber and log sales Weyerhaeuser Co., Wash., 1949-69; resource mgr. Brooks-Scanlon Co., Berid, Oreg., 1969-72; v.p. lands and forests Potlatch Corp., Lewiston, Idaho, 1973-79; pres. Jay Guenfeld Assocs., Seattle, 1980—; bd. dirs. Pope Resources Corp., Makah Forestry Enterprise; pub., editor Pacific Rim Wood Market Report. Contbr. numerous articles to profl. jours. With U.S. Army, PTO. Fulbright scholar. Fellow Soc. Am. Foresters (sect. chmn., mem. coun.); mem. Nat. Forest Products Assn. (chmn. land use com.), Phi Kappa Phi. Office: PO Box 66836 Seattle WA 98166

GRUENWALD, GEORGE HENRY, new products management consultant; b. Chgo., Apr. 23, 1922; s. Arthur Frank and Helen (Duke) G.; m. Corrine Rae Linn, Aug. 16, 1947; children: Helen Marie Gruenwald Orlando, Paul Arthur. BS in Journalism, Northwestern U., 1947; student, Evanston Acad. Fine Arts, 1937-38, Chgo. Acad. Fine Arts, 1938-39, Grinnell Coll., 1940-41. Asst. to pres. Uarco, Inc., Chgo., 1947-49; creative dir., mgr. mdse. Willy-Overland Motors Inc., Toledo, 1949-51; new products, brand and advt. mgr. Toni Co./Gillette, Chgo., 1951-53; v.p., creative dir., account supr. E.H. Weiss Agy., Chgo., 1953-55; exec. v.p., mgmt. supr. North Advt., Chgo., 1955-71; pres., treas., dir. Pilot Products, Chgo., 1963-71; pres., dir. Advance Brands, Inc., Chgo., 1963-71; exec. v.p., dir. Campbell Mithun Inc., Mpls. and Chgo., 1971-72; pres., dir. Campbell Mithun Inc., 1972-79, chmn., dir., 1979-81, chief exec. officer, dir., 1981-83, chief creative officer, dir., 1983-84; vice-chmn., dir. Ted Bates Worldwide, N.Y.C., 1979-80; mgmt. cons. new products, 1984—. Author: New Product Development - What Really Works, 1985, 2d edit. 1992, New Product Development—Responding to Market Demand, 1992, (workbook) New Product Development Checklists: From Mission to Market, 1991; (videos) New Products Seven Steps to Success, 1988, New Product Development, 1989; editor-in-chief Oldsmobile Rocket Cir. mag., 1955-65, Hudson Family mags., 1953-56, expert columnist Mktg. News, 1988—; contbr. articles to profl. jours.; editor., pub. rels. specialist. Trustee Chgo. Pub. TV Assn., 1969-73, Mpls. Soc. Fine Arts, 1975-83, Linus Pauling Inst. Sci. and Medicine, Palo Alto, 1984-92; chmn., v.p., chmn. class reps. Northwestern U. Alumni Fund Council, Chgo., 1965-68; trustee, chmn., pres., chief exec. officer, chmn. exec. com. Twin Cities Pub. TV Corp., 1971-84; trustee Minn. Pub. Radio Inc., 1973-77, vice chmn., 1974-75; bd. dirs., exec. com. Pub. Broadcasting Service, Alexandria, Va., 1978-86, bd. dirs., 1988—, exec. com., 1991-92; vice chmn. Task Force on Funding, 1991-92; delegate Am.'s Pub. TV Stas., Washington; bd. dirs. St. Paul Chamber Orch., 1982-84, San Diego Chamber Orch., 1986-88; mem. adv. bd. San Diego State U. Pub. Broadcasting Community, 1986—. With USAAF, 1943-45, MTO. Recipient Hermes award Chgo. Federated Advt. Clubs, 1963; Ednl. TV awards, 1969, 71, 86. Mem. Am. Assn. Advt. Agys. (mgmt. com. 1976-84), Nat. Soc. Profl. Journalists, Am. Inst. Wine and Food (bd. dirs. 1985-92). Office: PO Box 1696 Rancho Santa Fe CA 92067-1696

GRUENWALD, OSKAR, research institute executive, consultant; b. Yugoslavia, Oct. 5, 1941; came to U.S., 1961; s. Oskar and Vera (Wolf) G. AA, Pasadena City Coll., 1964; BA, U. Calif., Berkeley, 1966; MA, Claremont Grad. Sch., 1967, PhD, 1972. Cert. life standard teaching credential, Calif. Internat. economist U.S. Treasury Dept., Washington, 1967-68; vis. rsch. assoc. U. Erlangen, Nürnberg, Fed. Republic Germany, 1971-72; lectr. Pepperdine U., Malibu, Calif., 1972-73, Santa Monica (Calif.) Coll., 1973-76; ind. researcher and writer, Santa Monica, 1976-83; founder, pres. Inst. for Interdisciplinary Rsch., 1983—; guest lectr. in U.S. and fgn. countries, 1976—; rsch. assoc. Ctr. for Russian and East European Studies, U. Ill., Champaign-Urbana, summers 1976, 79; cons. Inst. for Advanced Philosophic Rsch., Boulder, Colo., 1977—, Com. To Aid Dem. Dissidents in Yugoslavia, Washington, 1980—, Pub. Rsch., Syndicated, Montclair, Calif., 1982—, Freedom House Exch., N.Y.C., 1985—; participant NEH Summer Seminar on Polit. Cultures, U. Calif., 1989. Author: The Yugoslav Search for Man, 1983; co-editor: Human Rights in Yugoslavia, 1986; founder, editor Jour. Interdisciplinary Studies: Internat. Jour. Interdisciplinary and Interfaith Dialogue, 1989—. Grantee Ludwig Vogelstein Found., 1976-77; Recipient Best Pub. Paper in Sci. and Religion award Templeton Found., 1990-92. Mem. Am. Polit. Sci. Assn., Am. Philos. Assn., Am. Assn for Advancement Slavic Studies (cons. Slavic Rev. 1986—), Am. Sci. Affiliation, Inst. for Study Internat. Problems (bd. dirs. 1988—), Internat. Christian Studies Assn. (founder, pres. 1983—, editor newsletter 1983—, Delta Tau Kappa. Office: Inst Interdisciplinary Rsch 2828 3rd St Ste 11 Santa Monica CA 90405

GRUFF, ERIC STEPHEN, inorganic chemist; b. N.Y.C., Oct. 24, 1963; s. Jules and Muriel Ruth (Sobol) G.; m. Kathy Ann McGraw, Aug. 19, 1989. BS in Chemistry, Rensselaer Poly. Inst., Troy, N.Y., 1985; PhD in Chemistry, SUNY, Stony Brook, 1990. Postdoctoral rsch. fellow Salk Inst., La Jolla, Calif., 1990-92; scientist Molecular Biosystems, Inc., San Diego, 1992—. Contbr. articles to profl. jours. Mem. Am. Chem. Soc., Sigma Xi (travel awardee 1990). Home: 2340 Carol View Dr # 310 Cardiff By The Sea CA 92007-2044 Office: MBI 10030 Barnes Canyon Rd San Diego CA 92121

GRUMBLING, HUDSON VIRGIL, JR., internist; b. Indiana, Pa., Aug. 21, 1936; s. Hudson Virgil and Mildred Alice (Seanor) G.; m. Frances Wood Welchans, June 18, 1960; children: Matthew Virgil, Mark David, Daniel Frank, Ruth Maree. BA, U. Mich., 1958; MD, U. Pa., 1962. Bd. cert. internal medicine; med. lic., Ariz., Pa. Intern Akron (Ohio) Gen. Hosp., 1962-63; commd. ensign USNR, 1959; commd. lt. USN, 1963, advanced through grades to capt., 1979; resident internal medicine Phila. Naval Hosp., 1966-69; staff physician Annapolis (Md.) Naval Hosp., 1969-71; resigned USN, 1971; capt. USNR, 1979—; active staff physician Altoona (Pa.) Hosp., 1971-73, W.O. Boswell Meml. Hosp., Sun City, Ariz., 1973—; courtesy staff physician Del E. Webb Meml. Hosp., Sun City West, Ariz., 1987—; chief med. staff W.O. Boswell Meml. Hosp., Sun City, 1990-92; med. dir. Royal Sun West Nursing Ctr., Avondale, Ariz., 1992—; bd. dirs. Sun Health Corp., Sun City, Boswell Meml. Hosp., Sun City. Mem. ACP, AMA, Maricopa

County Med. Assn., Ariz. Med. Assn., Naval Res. Assn., Rotary Internat. (club dir. 1990). Republican. Home: 280 E Campina Dr Litchfield Park AZ 85340 Office: 13640 N Plaza del Rio Blvd Peoria AZ 85381

GRUNDER, ROBERT DOUGLAS, real estate executive; b. Valley Forge, Pa., Aug. 17, 1953; s. Richard Rudolph and Alice Gertrude (Jablow) G.; m. Becky Ann Nelson, May 29, 1982; children: Katherine Victoria, Christopher Nelson. With Grunder Co., 1975—; pres. Grunder Devel., Inc., Fairbank, Alaska, Anchorage and Honolulu, 1983—. Congregationalist. Home: 2914 Crow's Nest Circle Anchorage AK 99515-2704 Office: 615 E 82d Ave Ste 104 Anchorage AK 99518 Mailing Address: PO Box 242523 Anchorage AK 99524-2523

GRUNSTAD, NORMAN LEE, business executive; b. Mankato, Minn., Aug. 5, 1939; s. Neumen Lawrence and Esther Marie (Anderson) G.; m. Holly Anne Hoelz, June 6, 1964. BS, U.S. Mil. Acad., 1964; MA in Bus., Ohio State U., 1972, PhD, 1972. Commd. 2d lt. U.S. Army, 1964, advanced through grades to lt. col., 1980, infantry rifle comdr., 1964-72; prof. U.S. Mil. Acad., West Point, 1972-75, 79-81; chief human resources Berlin Brigade, 1975-76, exec. officer 2d bat., 1976-78; br. chief U.S. Pentagon, Washington, 1981-84; prof. Nat. Def. Univ., Washington, 1984-86, ret., 1987; v.p. Internat. Bus. Ventures Corp., Phoenix, 1987—; exec. dir. Am. Salvage Pool Assn., Phoenix, 1987—. Editor: A Study of Organizational Leadership, 1976; contbr. articles to profl. jours. Decorated Silver star, Bronze star; recipient Gen. McArthur award for Leadership, U.S. Army, 1964; named Top Athlete and scholar C. of C., 1957. Mem. Ohio State Alumni Assn., U.S. Mil. Acad. Alumni Assn., Ariz. Soc. Assn. Mgmt., Am. Soc. Assn. Mgmt., Assn. U.S. Army, The Ret. Officers Assn.

GRUNWALD, BRYAN ELLIOTT, urban planner, architect; b. Richmond, Va., Mar. 21, 1943; s. Fred S. and Clara S. (Silberman) G.; m. Judy Fisher, Oct. 14, 1973; children: Jessica, David. BArch, Va. Poly. Inst. and State U., 1966; MArch, U. Toronto, 1967; M City Planning, U. Pa., 1970. Registered architect, Calif. Architect Marcellus Wright & Ptnrs., Richmond, Va., 1966-67, Geddes Brecher Qualls Cunningham, Phila., 1967-70; urban designer Okamoto Liskamm, San Francisco, 1970-72; planner, architect Tudor Engring. Co., San Francisco, 1972; mng. assoc. architect, planner Wallace McHarg Roberts Todd, San Francisco, 1972-77; prin. HGHB Architects and Planners, San Francisco, 1977-93; pres. Bryan Grunwald Assocs., San Francisco, 1993—; dir. San Francisco Planning and Urban Rsch., 1978—. Mem. AIA (corp.), Urban Land Inst. (mixed use coun.), Am. Inst. Cert. Planners (founding mem.). Office: Bryan Grunwald Assocs 160 Pine St San Francisco CA 94111

GRUSENMEYER, DAVID CLOUSE, dairy science educator, consultant; b. Dayton, Ohio, June 10, 1953; s. Paul Edward and Jean Barbra G.; m. Rebecca Jo Arinson, Apr. 12, 1980. BS, Ohio State U., 1975; MA, MS, Mich. State U., 1978; MBA, Western Wash. U., 1987. Laborer Palean Farms, Dayton, 1965-75; with Montgomery County Fairgrounds, Dayton, 1971-72, Wayne Twp., Dayton, 1973-75; security and life guard Ohio State U., Columbus, 1974-75; with Manpower Inc., Dayton, 1977; coop. extension agt. Wash. State U., Bellingham, 1978—; guest lectr. Sichuan Agrl. U., Yaan, Sichuan, People's Republic of China, 1986, Estonian Acad. Scis., Tartu, Estonia, 1988, Estonian Inst. Agronomy and Land. Reclaimation, Saku, Estonia, 1992; cons. Estonian Agr.-Indsl. Com., Tallinn, Estonia, 1988-91, Cal-Maine Foods Inc., Metter, Ga., 1990-91, Estonian Ministry Agrl.Tallinn, 1991—, U.S. Soviet Exch. Ctr. Project Econ. Devel. in Russia, L.A., 1991—, Brookside AGRA Corp., Highland, Ill., 1992—. Author: (sect.) Evaluation Dairy Reproduction Status, 1989, Maximizing Human Resource Output, 1992; contbr. articles to profl. jours. Active Bellingham Mountain Rescue, 1984—; youth leader Assumption Cath. Ch., Bellingham, 1981-82; bd. dirs. Pub. Employees Credit Union, Bellingham, 1989—, chmn. of bd., 1991-93; mem. devel. team Going Global Project, Wash. State U. Coop. Extension. Recipient numerous awards Nat. Assn. County Agrl. Agts.; named one of Outstanding Young Men Am., Nat. Jaycees, 1983. Mem. Nat. Assn. County Agrl. Agts., Am. Dairy Sci. Assn., Wash. Extension Agts. Assn. (bd. dirs. 1981-84, 90-92), Whatcom (Wash.) C. of C. and Indsutry (agr. com.), Coun. Agrl. Sci. and Tech., Epsilon Sigma Phi (bd. dirs. 1988-90, Team award 1990). Home: 2808 Nevada St Bellingham WA 98226-3535 Office: Wash State U Extension 1000 N Forest St Bellingham WA 98225-5530

GRUSSENDORF, BENJAMIN FRANKLIN, JR., state house speaker; b. Grand Rapids, Minn., Feb. 23, 1942; s. Benjamin F. Sr. and Fern (Ross) G.; m. Karen Solem; children: Timothy, Karla. AA, BA, U. Minn., 1964, MA, 1966; postgrad., Wash. State U., 1970. Tchr. Sitka (Alaska) High Sch., 1967-80, Sitka Community Coll.; state legislator Alaska Ho. Reps., Juneau, 1981—, speaker House, 1985-88, 91—; pres. Alaska Conf. Mayors, Sitka; mem. Alaska Mcpl. League Legis. Com. Assemblyman City and Borough Sitka, 1971, dep. mayor, 1971-75, mayor, 1975-79; chmn. Sitka Charter Commn. Mem. Alaska Jaycees (state chmn. govtl. affairs). Democrat. Club: Alaska Native Brotherhood (Sitka). Lodges: Moose, Elks. Office: Alaska Ho of Reps State Capital # 208 Juneau AK 99811-3100

GRUYE, ERIC KENT, computer graphic artist; b. Los Altos, Calif., Oct. 17, 1964; s. Dale Wayne and Lucia Ann (Sylvester) G. BA, Calif. State U., Chico, 1990. Computer graphics artist Atomic Media Group, San Leandro, Calif., 1989—. Office: Atomic Media Group 1933 Davis St # 213 San Leandro CA 94577

GRYPHON, ROBERT LIPKIND, microcomputer consultant, software developer; b. Missoula, Mont., Sept. 9, 1970; s. Arnold Robert and Linda Louise (Trantham) Lipkind; m. Marie Elizabeth Self, Jan. 11, 1992. AS in Data Processing Tech., Hawaii Pacific U., 1986, BS in Computer Sci., 1987, MBA, 1992, MS in Info. Systems, 1992. Cert. data processor, systems profl., computer programmer, Novell Netware engr., Compaq systems engr., Microsoft profl. for Windows, Microsoft profl. for LAN mgr., Microsoft profl. for Windows for Workgroups, WordPerfect resource. Microcomputer specialist Bays Deaver Hiatt Kawachika & Lezak, Honolulu, 1986-87, Daiei (USA), Inc., Honolulu, 1990-91; network engr., software developer Rational Elegance, Honolulu and Bellevue, Wash., 1987—; network adminstr. Rush, Moore, Craven, Sutton, Morry & Beh, Honolulu, 1988-92; systems engr. SQLSoft, Kirkland, Wash., 1992-93, CNA, Redmond, Wash., 1993—. Contbr. articles to profl. mags.; poems to Hawaii Pacific Rev.; Libertarian Party of Wash. State newsletter, 1992. Mem. IEEE Computer Soc., Assn. for Computing Machinery, Ind. Computer Cons. Assn. Seattle (editor newsletter 1992), Assn. for Systems Mgmt., Data Processing Mgmt. Assn., Assn. of Inst. for Cert. of Computer Profls., Mensa, Alpha Chi, Delta mu Delta, Epsilon Delta Pi. Home: 14636 NE 42d Pl N202 Bellevue WA 98007-3100

GRZANKA, LEONARD GERALD, writer, consultant; b. Ludlow, Mass., Dec. 11, 1947; s. Stanley Simon and Claire Genevive (Rozkuszka) G. BA, U. Mass., 1972; MA, Harvard U., 1974. Asst. prof. Gakushiun U., Tokyo, 1975-78; pub. rels. specialist Pacific Gas and Electric Co., San Francisco, 1978-80; sales promotion writer Tymshare Transaction Svcs., Fremont, Calif., 1980-81; account exec. The Strayton Co., Santa Clara, Calif., 1981-82; mng. editor Portable Computer Mag., San Francisco, 1982-84; prin. Grzanka Assocs., San Francisco, 1984-86; San Francisco bur. chief Digital News, 1986-91; sr. writer Bevilacqua Knight Inc., Oakland, Calif., 1991—; staff asst. Electric Power Rsch. Inst./U.S. Advanced Battery Consortium, Palo Alto, Calif., 1991—; lectr. Golden Gate U., San Francisco, 1985-87. Author: Neither Heaven Nor Hell, 1978; translator, editor: (art catalog) Masterworks of Japanese Crafts, 1977; translator: (book chpt.) Manajo: The Chinese Preface to the Kokinwakshu, 1984 (Literary Transl. award 1984). Sgt. USAF, 1965-69. Fellow Danforth Found., 1974. Mem. United Anglers Calif., Harvard Club of San Francisco (bd. dirs. 1984-88, Cert. Appreciation 1986, 88), Press Club of San Francisco, Phi Beta Kappa, Phi Kappa Phi. Home: 1324 Jackson St # 5 San Francisco CA 94109 Office: BKI 501 14th St # 210 Oakland CA 94612

GUARINO, PATRICIA LAMB, psychotherapist, consultant, social worker; b. Watertown, N.Y., July 24, 1952; d. Martin Murray and Patricia LeClaire (Briggs) Lamb; m. Francis Luis Guarino III, May 18, 1979 (div. Oct. 1983); 1 child, Michael Francis. B in Landscape Architecture, Mich. State U., East Lansing, 1975; MSW, San Diego State U., 1986. Lic. social worker. Mgr. DeCrosta Florist, Billerica, Mass., 1975-76; asst. mgr. F.W. Woolworth, N.Y.C., 1976-78, Saks Fifth Ave., N.Y.C., 1978-79; social svc. worker Lifeline Community Svcs., Vista, Calif., 1984-86; therapist Mission Family Counseling Ctr., San Luis Rey, Calif., 1986-89; asst. dir. Touchstone Family Counseling Ctr., San Luis Rey, 1989-92; pvt. practive Vista, Calif., 1991—; clinician II Ctrl. Peninsula Counseling Svcs., Kenai, Alaska, 1992—; cons. Old Mission Montessori Sch., San Luis Rey, 1988—, Older Adult Counseling Svcs. Mem. NASW, Soc. for Clin. Social Work (assoc., co-chairperson San Diego chpt. 1986-88, student rep. bd. behavioral sci. examiners 1985-86). Roman Catholic. Office: Ctrl Peninsula Counseling Svcs 215 Fidalgo St Ste 102 Kenai AK 99611 also: 400 S Melrose Dr Vista CA 92083 also: Ste 201 456 E Grand Escondido CA 92026

GUAY, GORDON HAY, postal service executive, educator, consultant; b. Hong Kong, Aug. 1, 1948; came to U.S., 1956; s. Daniel Bock and Ping Gin (Ong) G. AA, Sacramento City Coll., 1974; BS, Calif. State U., Sacramento, 1976, MBA, 1977; PhD, U. So. Calif., 1981. Mgmt. assoc. U.S. Postal Svc., Sacramento, 1980-82, br. mgr., 1982-83, fin. mgr., 1983-84, mgr. quality control, 1984-86, mgr. tech. sales and svcs. divsn., 1986-91, dir. mktg. and comm., 1991—; assoc. prof. bus. adminstrn., mktg. and mgmt. Calif. State U., Sacramento, 1981-85; prof. mktg. Nat. U., San Diego, 1984—; pres. Gordon Guay and Assocs., Sacramento, 1979—; cons. Mgmt. Cons. Assocs., Sacramento, 1977-79. Author: Marketing: Issues and Perspectives, 1983; also articles to profl. jours. With U.S. Army, 1968-70. Recipient Patriotic Svc. award U.S. Treasury Dept., San Francisco, 1985. Fellow Acad. Mktg. Sci.; mem. NEA, AAUP, Am. Mgmt. Assn., Am. Mktg. Assn. (Outstanding Mktg. Educator award 1989), Am. Soc. Pub. Adminstrn., Soc. Advancement Mgmt. (Outstanding Mem. 1976), Assn. MBA Execs. Democrat. Office: US Postal Svc 3775 Industrial Blvd West Sacramento CA 95799-0070

GUBAR, BENTLEY, chiropractor; b. Englewood, N.J., Apr. 8, 1960; s. George and Beulah (Weill) G. BS, Seton Hall U., 1981, Nat. Coll. Chiropractic, Lombard, Ill., 1987; D in Chropractic, Nat. Coll. Chiropractic, Lombard, Ill., 1990. Lic. chiropractor, Ariz., Ill.; cert. physiotherapist, Ariz. Rschr. U. Medicine and Dentistry N.J., Newark, 1976-81; pvt. practice Phoenix, 1991—; lectr. in field. Contbr. articles to profl. jours. Physician Ariz. Bikeathon For Multiple Sclerosis, 1991; vol. PBS, Ariz., 1992. Mem. Am. Chiroptactic Assn. (nutrition coun., diagnostic imaging coun., mental health coun.), Ariz. Assn. Chriopractic (pub. rels. com.), N.Y. Acad. Sci., Optimist's Club. Office: 3101 E Shea Blvd Ste 122 Phoenix AZ 85028

GUDMUNDSEN, RICHARD AUSTIN, physicist; b. Salt Lake City, Dec. 27, 1922; s. Austin Gudmundsen and Myrl Goodwin; m. Bernice Sayre, Jan. 1, 1925; children: Joyce, Scott Austin, Mark Richard, Annette, Lee Karl, Eileen. Student, U. Wis., Milw., 1942-43, U. Utah, 1943; B. Engring. in Mech. Engring., U. So. Calif., L.A., 1947, PhD in Physics, 1955. Office of Naval Rsch. fellow U. So. Calif., L.A., 1949-51; mgr. semiconductor labs. Hughes Aircraft Co., Culver City, Calif., 1952-59; pres. Quantum Tech. Labs., Santa Ana, Calif., 1960-63; mgr. lasers and electrooptics Rockwell Internat., Anaheim, Calif., 1963-70, dir. advanced tech., 1970-81; pres. Perceptrix, Inc., Santa Ana, 1982—. Contbr. numerous tech. articles to profl. jours. With U.S. Army, 1943-45, ETO. Decorated Bronze Star. Mem. IEEE (sr.), Am. Phys. Soc., Autonetics Sigma Xi Club (pres. 1975), Sigma Delta Omega, Tau Beta Pi. Republican. Mem. LDS Church. Home: 12052 Larchwood Ln Santa Ana CA 92705

GUDORF, GREG DAVID, marketing and sales executive; b. St. Mary's, Ohio, Mar. 11, 1960; s. David L. and Marion M. (fowler) G.; m. cheryl Ann Brackman, May 12, 1979; children: Eric Michael, Troy Gregory. AS in Bus., Sinclair C.C., Dayton, Ohio, 1986; BA in Mgmt., Antioch U., 1990. V.p. sales Gudorf & Sons, Minster, Ohio, 1978-81; v.p. new bus. MCC, Inc., Dayton, Ohio, 1981-85; gen. mgr. URI, Inc., Cin., 1985-89; dir. sales and mktg. Gen. Instrument, San Diego, 1990—; instr. Small Bus. Mgmt. Kettering (Ohio) Adult Sch., 1989-90. Republican. Roman Catholic. Home: 14263 Barrymore St San Diego CA 92129 Office: Gen Instrument 6262 Lusk Blvd San Diego CA 92121

GUENTHER, ROBERT STANLEY, II, investment and property executive; b. Orange, Calif., Sept. 29, 1950; s. Robert Stanley and Fanny Newman (Shaw) G. BA in Psychology, U. Calif., Santa Barbara, 1975; BA in Sociology, U. Calif., 1975. Pvt. practice Templeton, Calif., 1975—. Home and Office: 7245 El Pomar Dr Templeton CA 93465-9615

GUERBER, STEPHEN CRAIG, community relations executive, mayor; b. Corvallis, Oreg., Oct. 2, 1947; s. Allen Lewis and Thelma Mae (Gilson) G.; m. Donna Kay Panko, Feb. 4, 1968; children: Dani Michelle, Patrick Jason, Suzanne Aleece. BA, Idaho State U., 1969. Publ. editor First Nat. Bank, Portland, Oreg., 1969-70; bus. editor The Idaho Statesman, Boise, 1970-73; info. svcs. dir. Jim Hawkes Advt., Boise, 1973-74; asst. alumni dir. Idaho State U., Pocatello, 1974-76, alumni rels. dir., 1976-78; asst. staff mgr. Mountain Bell, Denver, 1978-80; external info. mgr. U.S. West Communications, Boise, 1980-88; dir. info. U.S. West Found., Boise, 1988-91; mgr. community affairs U.S. West Communications, Boise, 1991—. Councilman City of Eagle, 1984-88, mayor, 1988—; bd. dirs. Assn. Idaho Cities, 1988—, Silver Sage coun. Girl Scouts U.S., 1990—, Am. Festival Ballet, 1984-88, Simplot Vol. Award, 1988; mem. Ada Planning Assn., 1985—, Fourth Idaho Dist. Jud. Coun., 1988—, Ada County Centennial Commn., 1989-90. Recipient Outstanding Pub. Svc. Award Social Svc. Adminstrn., 1983, Profl. Achievement award Idaho State U. Coll. Arts and Scis., 1991; named Idaho Disting. Citizen The Idaho Statesman, 1988. Democrat. Baptist. Home: 699 Ranch Dr Eagle ID 83616-5115 Office: US West Communications 999 Main St Boise ID 83702-9001

GUERRA, FERNANDO JAVIER, political science educator; b. L.A., June 19, 1958; s. Omar Guerra and Marina (Ochoa) Guerra Ulrich; m. Kathleen Marie Greene, May 16, 1982; children: Adam C., Steven J. BA, U. So. Calif., 1980; MA, U. Mich., 1982, PhD, 1990. Asst. prof. Chicano studies and polit. sci. Loyola Marymount U., L.A., 1984-91, assoc. prof. polit. sci., 1991—, chair Chicano studies dept., 1989—, assoc. dean Coll. Liberal Arts, 1992—, asst. to the pres., 1992—. Contbr. articles to profl. jours. Mem. ECACA AQMD, Diamond Bar, Calif., 1992, ECAC, LACTC, L.A., 1992. Mem. Am. Polit. Sci. Asn. (com. on status of Latinos 1991-92), Western Polit. Sci. Assn. (exec. com. 1992—), Nat. Assn. Chicano Studies. Democrat. Roman Catholic. Office: Loyola Marymount U 7101 W 80th St Los Angeles CA 90045

GUERRERO, JOSÉ ALFREDO, software engineer; b. San Francisco, Mar. 18, 1963; s. Vicente (Foncesca) and Maria Isabel (Aceves) G.; m. Alida Mireya Torres, June 24, 1989; 1 child, Kristi Mireya. BS in Computer Sci., Calif. Poly. U., 1989. Day care asst./delivry boy McCoppin Sch./San Francisco Progress, San Francisco, 1976-80; meat packer Armour & Co., South San Francisco, 1980-83; dishwasher, cook El Palenque Restaurant, San Francisco, 1978-83; clock maker Great Am. Trading Co., San Francisco, 1984-85; libr. asst. Calif. Poly. U., San Luis Obispo, 1985-86, application programmer, 1986-87, advanced workstation cons., 1988-89; systems programmer IBM, Boca Raton, Fla., 1988; software engr. Amdahl Corp., Sunnyvale, Calif., 1989—. Mem. Soc. of Hispanic Profl. Engrs. (sec. 1986-87), Assn. of Computer Machinery. Democrat. Roman Catholic. Office: Amdahl 1237 E Argues Ave #214 Sunnyvale CA 92839

GUEST, RICHARD EUGENE, psychologist; b. LaJunta, Colo., Mar. 16, 1944; s. John William and Lorraine Alice (Smith) G.; m. Linda Jeanne Sand, June 5, 1966; children: Elise Michelle, Gregory Douglas. BS, Colo. State U., 1966, postgrad., 1966-67; MDiv, Iliff Sch. Theology, Denver, 1970; PhD, Northwestern U., Evanston, Ill., 1979. Lic. psychologist, Colo. Resident supr. Ft. Logan Mental Health Ctr., Denver, 1968-70; interim Protestant chaplain Denver Gen. Hosp., 1970; dir. Winnetka (Ill.) Youth Orgn., 1973-74; prin. chaplaincy researcher McGaw Med. Ctr., Chgo., 1974-76; adminstr. dir. Des Moines Pastoral Counseling Ctr., 1976-79, co-dir., co-founder grief clinic, 1977-79; dir. Interfaith Ctr. for Edn. in Marriage and Family Living, Ft. Collins, Colo., 1979-81; EAP mgr. EAP Systems, Woburn, Mass., 1987-88; asst. prof. Colo. State U., Ft. Collins, 1988-90, faculty affiliate, 1990—; pvt. practice Ft. Collins, 1981—; dir. Ctr. Human Relationships, Ft. Collins, 1990—; psychol. cons. Iowa Conf. United Meth. Ch., Des Moines, 1977-79; cons. Iowa Children's Family Svcs., Des Moines, 1977-79; v.p., dir. tng. Transitions Mediation Svcs., Ft. Collins, 1982-86; allied health staff Poudre Valley Hosp., 1984-87 and Mountain Crest Hosp., Ft. Collins, 1990—; presenter workshops and presentations; psychologist New Beginnings, Ft. Collins, 1991—. Co-author: Organization and Adminstration of Pastoral Counseling Centers, 1981. Adv. coun. Resource Assistance Ctr. for Non-Profits, Ft. Collins, 1980-82; pres., bd. dirs. Crossroads Safehouse for Battered Women, Ft. Collins, 1981-84; psychol. advisor Hospice of Larimer County, Ft. Collins, 1984-86. Named Outstanding Young Man of Sterling, Jaycees, 1972. Mem. Am. Assn. for Marriage and Family Therapy (clin. mem.), Am. Psychol. Assn., Larimer County Mental Health Profls. Network, Ft. Collins Individual Practice Assn., Beta Beta Beta, Alpha Kappa Delta. Office: Ctr Human Relationships 3000 S College Ave Ste 104 Fort Collins CO 80525-2558

GUETZKOW, HAROLD, international politics educator; b. Milwaukee, Wis., Aug. 16, 1915; s. Albert Charles and Teckla (Prinz) G.; m. Lauris Lynette Steere, Sept. 17, 1944; children: James, Gay, Daniel. BA, U. Chgo., 1936; PhD, U. Mich., 1948. Instr., asst prof. U. Mich., Ann Arbor, 1945-50; assoc. prof., prof. Carnegie Inst. Tech., Pitts., 1950-57; prof., Fulcher chair Northwestern U., Evanston, Ill., 1957-85, Fulcher prof. emeritus, 1985—; sr. intern U.S. Dept. State, Washington, 1969-70, UN Secretariat, N.Y.C., 1970-71; rsch. scholar in Ea. Europe, Latin Am., Asia, Africa, Fulbright, 1981, 83, 84, 87. Co-author, co-editor Simulated International Processes, 1981; co-author, co-inventor: (classroom game) Inter-Nation Simulation Kit, 1966. Mem. Internat. Studies Assn. (pres. 1987), Am. Polit. Sci. Assn., Internat. Soc. Polit. Psychology. Home and Office: 715-B Quetta Ave Sunnyvale CA 94087-1249

GUEVARA, ANNE MARIE, librarian; b. Lynwood, Calif., Dec. 7, 1949; d. Conrad and Philomene (Timko) Goracke; m. Rey Guevara, Jan. 11, 1975; children: Gregory Rey, Angela Marie, Molly Anne. BA, Calif. State U., Long Beach, 1971; MLS, U. So. Calif., 1974. Reference libr. L.A. County Pub. Libr., Norwalk, 1974-76, periodicals libr., 1976-77; info. specialist City of Long BeachPub. Libr., 1977-79; libr. Sacred Heart Sch., Medford, Oreg., 1981—; reference libr. Jackson County Pub. Libr., Medford, 1985-88, children's libr., 1988—. Chmn. arts & crafts Children's Festival, Jacksonville, Oreg., 1981-84. Mem. ALA, Oreg. Libr. Assn., Oreg. Ednl. Media Assn., Medford Storytelling Guild (bd. dirs. 1981-85). Democrat. Roman Catholic. Home: 4460 Dark Hollow Rd Medford OR 97501-9625 Office: Sacred Heart Sch 431 S Ivy St Medford OR 97501-3599

GUGGENHEIM-BOUCARD, ALAN ANDRE ALBERT PAUL EDOUARD, business executive, international consultant; b. Paris, May 12, 1950; came to U.S., 1981, naturalized, 1991; s. Jacques and Micheline (Raffalovich) Guggenheim; m. Suzanne Marton, Mar. 20, 1974; 1 child, Valerie. BS, U. Paris, 1971; MSCE, Ecole Speciale des Travaux Publics, Paris, 1974; MBA in Finance, U. Paris, 1975; grad., French Command-Gen. Staff Res. Coll., 1981. Asst. prof. math. Nat. Sch. Arts and Architecture, Paris, 1972-75; civil engr. Societe Routiere Colas, Paris, 1976-77, French Antilles, 1977-78; chief exec. officer, exec. dir. C.R.P.G., Pointe A Pitre, Guadeloupe, 1978-81; chief exec. officer, chmn. San Joaquin Software Systems, Inc., Stockton, Calif., 1982-86, CalCar Investment Svcs., Inc., Newbury Park, Calif., 1983—; bd. mem. Sucmanu, Paris, 1976-82; bd. of organizers Pacific State Bank, Stockton, Calif., 1985-87. Exec. Editor newsletter L'Action Universitaire, 1970-76. Mem. French Res. Policy Rev. Bd., Paris, 1971-77; mem. Ventura County Rep. Ctrl. Com., Rep. Presdl. Task Force, Rep. Campaign Coun.; candidate Rep. 37th Assembly Dist., Calif. Maj. French Res., 1981. Recipient Gold Medal Omnium Technique Holding, 1975. Fellow Engr. and Scientists france; mem. AAAS, ADPA, Yosemite Club, Rotary. Roman Catholic. Home: 3265 Peppermint St Newbury Park CA 91320-5039 Office: 560 N Moorpark Rd # 121 Thousand Oaks CA 91360-3700

GUGGENHIME, RICHARD JOHNSON, lawyer; b. San Francisco, Mar. 6, 1940; s Richard E. and Charlotte G.; m. Emlen Hall, June 5, 1965 (div.); children: Andrew, Lisa, Molly; m. Judith Perry Swift, Oct. 3, 1992. AB in Polit. Sci. with distinction, Stanford U., 1961; LLB, Harvard U., 1964. Bar: Calif. 1965, U.S. Dist. Ct. (no. dist.) Calif. 1965, U.S. Ct. Appeals (9th cir.) 1965. Assoc. Heller, Ehrman, White & McAuliffe, 1965-71, ptnr., 1972—; spl. asst. to U.S. Senator Hugh Scott, 1964; bd. dirs. Comml. Bank of San Francisco, 1980-81, Global Savs. Bank, San Francisco, 1984-86. Mem. San Francisco Bd. Permit Appeals, 1978-86; bd. dirs. Marine World Africa USA, 1980-86; mem. San Francisco Fire Commn., 1986-88, Recreation and Parks Commn., 1988-92; chmn. bd. trustees San Francisco Univ. High Sch., 1987-90; trustee St. Ignatius Prep. Sch., San Francisco, 1987—. Mem. Am. Coll. Probate Counsel, San Francisco Opera Assn. (bd. dir.), Bohemian Club, Wine and Food Soc. Club, Olympic Club, Chevaliers du Tastevin Club (San Francisco), Silverado Country Club (Napa, Calif.). Home: 2621 Larkin St San Francisco CA 94109 Office: Heller Ehrman White & McAuliffe 333 Bush St San Francisco CA 94104-2806

GUICE, JOHN THOMPSON, retired air force officer; b. Kosciusko, Miss., Nov. 5, 1923; s. Gustave Nathaniel and Anne Mae (McCool) G.; m. Charlotte Webb, Mar. 8, 1949; children—John Thompson, James G., Steven L., Thomas A., Joseph D. B.S. in Engring, U.S. Mil. Acad., 1947; M.S. in Internat. Relations, George Washington U., 1966; disting. grad., Air Command and Staff Coll., 1962, Air War Coll., 1966. Commd. 2d lt. U.S. Army, 1947; advanced through grades to maj. gen. USAF, 1974; tactical and interceptor pilot, 1947-55; officer Air N.G. and N.G., 1956—; dep. dir. Air N.G., 1974-77, dir., 1977-81, ret., 1981. Decorated Legion of Merit, Air Force D.S.M. Mem. Air Force Assn., N.G. Assn., Sigma Chi. Home: 4901 N Calle Luisa Tucson AZ 85718-4925

GUIDERA, JOHN VICTOR, insurance loss prevention consultant, engineer; b. L.A., Feb. 17, 1950; s. George and Shirley Ann (Gottlieb) G. BS in Civil Engring., Calif. Poly. U., 1982. Asst. engr. Indsl. Risk Insurers, Anaheim, Calif., 1973-74, engr., 1974-76; resident engr. Indsl. Risk Insurers, Phoenix, 1976-78; dist. supr. engr. Indsl. Risk Insurers, Anaheim, 1978-85; account cons. Indsl. Risk Insurers, San Francisco, 1985—, sr. account cons., 1991—. Mem. Am. Inst. Avionics & Astronautics (assoc.), Soc. of Fire Protection Engrs. Home: 5480 Louisiana Dr Concord CA 94521-4627 Office: Indsl Risk Insurers 50 California St Ste 3510 San Francisco CA 94111-4783

GUILL, JOHN RUSSELL, architect; b. Hanford, Calif., Jan. 18, 1959; s. George Russell and Julia G.; m. Debra Kay McGuire, Oct. 6, 1984; children: Laura Kay, Alexander Russell. Student, Reedley Coll., 1977-78, Harvard U., 1981; BS cum laude, Calif. State U., Fresno, 1981. Lic. architect, Calif. Draftsman Lew & Patnaude Architects, Fresno, Calif., 1980-83; designer Temple Andersen Moore Architects, Fresno, Calif., 1983-84; project mgr. Edwin S. Darden Architects, Fresno, 1984; sr. architect Stevens Design Group, Mt. Shasta, Calif., 1984—. Planning commn. Mt. Shasta City, 1988—, chmn. planning com., 1990-91; mem., chair bd trustees Meth. Ch., Mt. Shasta, 1990—. Mem. AIA, Phi Kappa Phi, Epsilon Pi Tau. Republican. Methodist. Office: Stevens Design Group 205 N Mt Shasta Blvd Mount Shasta CA 96067

GUILLEMIN, ROGER C. L., physiologist; b. Dijon, France, Jan. 11, 1924; came to U.S., 1953, naturalized, 1963; s. Raymond and Blanche (Rigollot) G.; m. Lucienne Jeanne Billard, Mar. 22, 1951; children—Chantal, Francois, Claire, Helene, Elizabeth, Cecile. B.A., U. Dijon, 1941, B.Sc., 1942; M.D., Faculty of Medicine, Lyons, France, 1949; Ph.D., U. Montreal, 1953; Ph.D. (hon.), U. Rochester, 1976, U. Chgo., 1977, Baylor Coll. Medicine, 1978, U. Ulm, Germany, 1978, U. Dijon, France, 1978, Free U. Brussels, 1979, U. Montreal, 1979, U. Man., Can, 1984, U. Turin, Italy, 1985, Kyung Hee U., Korea, 1986, U. Paris, Paris, 1986, U. Barcelona, Spain, 1988, U. Madrid, 1988, McGill U., Montreal, Can., 1988, U. Claude Bernard, Lyon, France, 1989. Intern, resident univs. hosps. Dijon, 1949-51; asso. dir., asst. prof. Inst. Exptl. Medicine and Surgery, U. Montreal, 1951-53; asso. dir. dept. exptl. endocrinology Coll. de France, Paris, 1960-63; asst. prof. physiology Baylor Coll. Medicine, 1953-57, assoc. prof., 1957-63, prof., dir. labs. neuroendocrinology, 1963-70, adj. prof., 1970—; adj. prof. medicine U. Calif. at San Diego, 1970—; resident fellow, chmn. labs. neuroendocrinology Salk Inst., La Jolla, Calif., 1970-89, adj. rsch. prof., 1989—; Salk Inst.; Disting. Sci. prof. Whittier Inst., 1989—, also bd. dirs. Decorated chevalier Legion d'Honneur (France), 1974, officer, 1984; recipient Gairdner Internat. award, 1974; U.S. Nat. Medal of Sci., 1977; co-recipient Nobel prize for medicine, 1977; recipient Lasker Found. award, 1975; Dickson prize in medicine, 1976;

Passano award sci., 1976; Schmitt medal neurosci., 1977; Barren Gold medal, 1979; Dale medal Soc. for Endocrinology U.K., 1980, Ellen Browning Scripps Soc. medal Scripps Meml. Hosps. Found., 1988. Fellow AAAS; mem. NAS, Am. Physiol. Soc., Am. Peptide Soc. (hon.), Assn. Am.Physicians, Endocrine Soc. (pres. 1986), Soc. Exptl. Biology and Medicine, Internat. Brain Rsch. Orgn., Internat. Soc. Rsch. Biology Reprodn., Soc. Neuro-scis., Am. Acad. Arts and Scis., French Acad. Scis. (fgn. assoc.), Academie Internationale de Medecine (fgn. assoc.), Swedish Soc. Med. Scis. (hon.), Academie des Scis. (fgn. assoc.), Academie Royale de Medecine de Belgique (corr. fgn.), Internat. Soc. Neurosci. (charter), Western Soc. Clin. Rsch., Can. Soc. Endocrinal Metabolism, (hon.), Club of Rome. Office: Whittier Inst 9894 Genesee Ave La Jolla CA 92037-1296

GUILMETTE, RAYMOND ALFRED, radiobiologist, researcher, administrator; b. Laconia, N.H., May 26, 1946; s. Raymond Alfred Sr. and Muriel Dorothy (Fortin) G.; m. Patricia Mary Kerry; children: Todd Michael, Jeremy Matthew. BS in Nuclear Engring., Rensselaer Poly. Inst., 1968; MS in Environ. Health, NYU, 1971, PhD in Radiological Health, 1975; post doctoral, Argonne Nat. Lab., 1975-77. Nuclear engr. Consolidated Edison Power Co., N.Y.C., 1968-69; health physicist N.Y.U., Tuxedo, 1971-74; radiobiologist Inhalation Toxicology Rsch. Inst., Albuquerque, N.M., 1977—; radiochemist Inhalation Toxicology Rsch. Inst., Albuquerque, 1978-81, project coord., 1981—, tech. cons., program mgr., 1989—; adj. prof. Tex. A&M U., 1989—; mem. Sci. Com. on Dosimetry and Metabolism of Radionuclides, Nat. Coun. on Radiation Protection, 1990-91; corr. mem. Task Group on Age-Dependent Dosimetry, Internat. Commn. on Radiological Protection, mem. task group on Internal Dosimetry, DOE task force on Radio Issues; subcom. mem. Radiation Adv. Com., Sci. Adv. Bd., EPA Radio Sci. Assoc. Editor: Health Physics Jour., 1985-90; mem. editorial bd. Internat. Jour. Radiation Biology, 1990—; contbr. articles profl. jours. Com. chmn. Cub Scout Pack 443, Albuquerque, 1982-84, Troop 443 Boy Scouts Am., 1984-87. Mem. Nat. Rsch. Coun. Radon Panel (com. dosimetry/metabolism radionuclides), Am. thoracic Soc., Am. Nuclear Soc., Radiation Rsch. Soc., Health Physics Soc. (pres. Rio Grande chpt. 1983, bd. dirs. 1991-94). Office: Inhalation Toxicology Rsch Inst PO Box 5890 Albuquerque NM 87185-5890

GUIMARY, RAMON CURTIS, transportation, distribution executive, consultant; b. Portland, Oreg., Aug. 31, 1929; s. Adrian Alturas and Ellen Jean (Lund) G.; m. Mary Ellen Hull, July 18, 1959; children: Jeannine H., Jennifer E. Student, U. Wash., 1948-49, Portland State U., 1956-58; BS, U. Oreg., 1960. Traffic mgr. Albers Div. Carnation Co., Portland, 1954-56; traffic supr. Carnation Co., L.A., 1956-58, 60-62; transp. analyst Oreg. Pub. Utility Commn., Salem, 1962-64; traffic mgr., distbr. mgr. Omark Industries, Portland, 1964-85; exec. v.p. Gratron, Inc., Portland, 1987-93; dist. export coun. mem. U.S. Dept. Commerce, Portland, 1976-92; bus. adv. Mt. Hood Community Coll., Gresham, Oreg., 1971—. Sgt. U.S. Army, 1950-52. Named Oreg. Transp. Man of Yr., Delta Nu Alpha, Portland, 1972, 1983. Mem. Am. Soc. Transp. and Logistics (cert. ICC practitioner), Nat. Indsl. Trasnp. League, Assn. Transp. Practitioners. Home: 6707 SE 34th Ave Portland OR 97202

GUINN, STANLEY WILLIS, lawyer; b. Detroit, June 9, 1953; s. Willis Hampton and Virginia Mae (Pierson) G.; m. Patricia Shirley Newgord, June 13, 1981; children: Terri Lanae, Scott Stanley. BBA with high distinction, U. Mich., 1979, MBA with distinction, 1981; MS in Taxation with Distinction, Walsh Coll., 1987; JD cum laude, U. Mich., 1992. CPA, Mich.; cert. mgmt. acct., Mich. Tax mgr. Coopers & Lybrand, Detroit, 1981-87; tax cons. Upjohn Co., Kalamazoo, 1987-89; litigation atty. Brobeck, Phleger & Harrison, 1992—. Served with USN, 1974-77. Mem. AICPA, ABA, Calif. State Bar Assn., San Diego County Bar Assn., No. County Bar Assn., Nat. Assn. Accts., Mich. Assn. CPAs, Inst. Mgmt. Acctg., Phi Kappa Phi, Beta Gamma Sigma, Beta Alpha Psi, Delta Mu Delta. Republican. Presbyterian. Home: 3119 Quiet Hills Pl Escondido CA 92029 Office: Brobeck Phleger & Harrison 550 W C St Ste 1300 San Diego CA 92101

GUINOUARD, DONALD EDGAR, psychologist; b. Bozeman, Mont., Mar. 31, 1929; s. Edgar Arthur and Venabell (Ford) G.; m. Irene M. Egeler, Mar. 30, 1951; children: Grant M., Philip A., Donna I. BS, Mont. State U., Bozeman, 1954; MS, Mont. State U., 1955; EdD, Wash. State U., Pullman, 1960; postdoctoral, Stanford U., 1965; grad., Indsl. Coll. of the Armed Forces, 1964, Air War Coll., 1976. Lic. psychologist, Ariz., counselor, Wash., Mont.; cert. secondary tchr. and sch. adminstr., Wash., Mont. Advanced through grades to col. USAFR, 1946-84, ret., 1984; dir. counseling Consol. Sch. Dist., Pullman, Wash., 1955-60; assoc. prof. Mont. State U., Bozeman, 1960-66; field selection officer Peace Corps, U.S., S.Am., 1962-68; prof. counseling, counseling psychologist Ariz. State U., Tempe, 1966-90; prof. emeritus, 1990; co-owner Forensic Cons. Assocs., Tempe, 1970—; pvt. practice, 1990—; admissions liaison officer USAF Acad., Colo. Springs, 1967-84; assessment officer Fundamental Edn. Ctr. for the Devel. of the Latin American Community, Patzcuaro, Mex., 1963-64; expert witness on vocat. and psychol. disability for fed. and state cts. Contbr. articles to profl. jours. Mem. Ariz. Psychol. Assn., Am. Assn. Counseling & Devel., Reserve Officers Assn. Democrat. Methodist. Home: 112 E Cairo Dr Tempe AZ 85282-3606

GUINOUARD, PHILIP ANDRE, restaurant executive; b. Pullman, Wash., Apr. 9, 1960; s. Donald Edgar and Irene (Egeler) G.; m. Miquela Teresa Padilla, Feb. 16, 1988; childern: Mia, Angela. Student, Mesa (Ariz.) Community Coll. Dir. quality Garcia's, Phoenix, 1978-84; area spr. El Pollo Asado Inc., Phoenix, 1985-89; gen. mgr. Quinto Patio, Evergreen, Colo., 1989-90, Garcia's, Littleton, Colo., 1990—. Mem. Colo. Restaurant Assn. Home: 1714 W Manor St Chandler AZ 85224-2360 Office: Garcias 4725 N Scottsdale Rd Scottsdale AZ 85251-7620

GULATI, AKHILESH, management consultant; b. Lucknow, India, Nov. 14, 1954; parents: Kasturi Lal and Santosh Kumari (Chawla) G. Grad. cert., Directorate Marine Engring. Tng., Calcutta, India, 1975; BS in Naval Architecture, U. Mich., 1984, MS in Marine Engring., 1985; MBA, UCLA, 1989. First engr. IRI Shipping Lines, Tehran, Iran, 1978-83; planning coord. Bay Shipbuilding Corp., Sturgeon Bay, Wis., 1985-87; cons. United Rsch. Co., Morristown, N.J., 1989-91; mktg. dir. Alpha Design and Graphics, Rancho Cucmonga, Calif., 1991—; ptnr. Pivot Mgmt. Cons., Upland, Calif., 1993—; owner, operator Akhil Internat., Rancho Cucamonga, Calif., 1992—. Fellow Inst. for Advancement of Engrs.; mem. Soc. Naval Architects and Marine Engrs. (presenter symposium on ship mgmt., econs. and ops. 1987), , Am. Soc. Quality Control (chmn. 1993—), Rotary. Office: 9540 Center Ave Ste 130 Rancho Cucamonga CA 91730-5840

GULEZIAN, MICHAEL, recording company executive, composer, performer; b. Newark, June 12, 1957; s. Aram and Serpouhie (Maldjian) G. BSBA in Mktg., U. Ariz., 1989, BSBA in Entrepreneurship, 1989. Founder, owner Aardvark Records, Tucson, 1977-81; founder, pres. Now That's Music, BMI, Tucson, 1978—, Timbreline Music, Tucson, 1988—; founder, owner Aardvark Rec. Co., Tucson, 1989—. Producer, composer, performer, artist, arranger (phonograph records, audio cassettes, compact discs) Snow, 1980, Unspoken Intentions, 1981, Distant Memories and Dreams, 1991. Mem. Nat. Assn. Ind. Record Distbrs., Nat. Assn. for Campus Activities (assoc.; Campus Entertainment award 1985, 86), Am. Fedn. Music, Broadcast Music, Inc. (mem., pub.). Office: Timbreline Music PO Box 40493 Tucson AZ 85717

GULL, PAULA MAE, nephrology nurse, medical/surgical nurse; b. L.A., Mar. 7, 1955; d. Gerald Henry and Artemis (Cubillas) Balzer; m. Randell Jay Gull, July 10, 1976. AA, Cypress (Calif.) Coll., 1976; AS with high honors, Rancho Santiago Coll., Santa Ana, Calif., 1985; BSN with high honors, Calif. State U., 1993. Cert. med. surg. nurse. Staff RN U. Calif. Irvine Med. Ctr., Orange, Calif., 1986-87, asst. nurse mgr., 1987-88, nurse mgr., 1988; med.-surg. nurse N000, 1990—. Mem. Am. Nephrology Nurses Assn. Mormon. Home: 24974 Enchanted Way Moreno Valley CA 92557-6410

GUMMIN, BARBARA HALL, entrepreneur; b. Plainfield, N.J., May 10, 1955; d. Calvert and Barbara (Barrows) Hall; m. Glenn Harris Gummin, Nov. 28, 1987; 1 child, Molly. Student, Cath. U. Am., 1973-77, Cornell U., 1982-83. Owner Sandwichboards-ABC Advt., Newport, R.I., 1974-75; owner, pres. Sandwichboard Co., Newport and Washington, 1975-81, Newport Ad-Ventures, 1979-81, Promote It Internat., Inc., Morrison, Colo., 1990—; traffic coord. Young & Rubican Advt. Agy., N.Y.C., 1977-78; mktg. dir. Ridge Athletic Club/Gaiser Corp., Denver, 1983-84; gen. mgr. Ridge Athletic Club/Gaiser Corp., Littleton, Colo., 1984-90; cons. to health club orgns., 1990—; speaker IRSA Assn. of Qualtiy Clubs, Boston; nat. rep. Commit-To-Get-Fit, 1991—. Mem. Ch. of Religious Sci. Home and Office: Promote It Internat Inc 6022 S Willowbrook Dr Morrison CO 80465

GUMPEL, GLENN J., association executive. With Dirs. Guild Am., L.A. Office: Dirs Guild of Am 7920 W Sunset Blvd 6th Fl Los Angeles CA 90046

GUND, GEORGE, III, financier; b. Cleve., May 7, 1937; s. George and Jessica (Roesler) G.; m. Mary Theo Feld, Aug. 13, 1966; children: George, Gregory. Student, Western Res. U., Menlo (Calif.) Sch. Bus. Engaged in personal investments San Francisco, 1967—; cattle ranching Lee, Nev., 1967—; partner Calif. Seals, San Francisco, 1976-77; pres. Ohio Barons, Inc., Richfield, 1977-78; chmn. bd. Northstar Fin. Corp., Bloomington, Minn., from 1978; formerly chmn. bd. Minn. North Stars, Bloomington; chmn., co-owner San Jose Sharks, NHL, San Jose, CA, 1991—; dir. Ameritrust Cleve.; vice-chmn. Gund Investment Corp., Princeton, N.J.; chmn. North Stars Met Center Mgmt. Corp., Bloomington; v.p. hockey Sun Valley Ice Skating, Inc., Idaho. Chmn. San Francisco Internat. Film Festival, 1973—; mem. sponsors council Project for Population Action; adv. council Sierra Club Found.; mem. internat. council Mus. Modern Art, N.Y.C.; collectors com. Nat. Gallery Art; bd. dirs. Calif. Theatre Found., Bay Area Ednl. TV Assn., San Francisco Mus. Art, Cleve. Health Museum, George Gund Found., Cleve. Internat. Film Festival, Sun Valley Center Arts and Humanities, U. Nev. Reno Found., Sundance Inst. Served with USMCR, 1955-58. Clubs: Calif. Tennis (San Francisco), University (San Francisco), Olympic (San Francisco); Union (Cleve.), Cleve. Athletic (Cleve.), Kirkland Country (Cleve.), Rowfant (Cleve.); Ranier (Seattle). Office: 1821 Union St San Francisco CA 94123-4307

GUND, GORDON, management executive; b. Cleve., Oct. 15, 1939; s. George and Jessica (Roesler) G.; m. Llura Liggett; children: Grant Ambler, Gordon Zachary. BA, Harvard U., 1961; DPubSvc (hon.), U. Maryland, 1980; DHL, Whittier Coll., 1993. Pres., chief exec. officer Gund Investment Corp.; gen. ptnr. GUS Enterprises; prin. owner Cleve. Cavaliers, NBA, 1983—; chmn. Nationwide Advt. Svc. Inc.; co-owner San Jose Sharks, NHL, 1990—; mem. bd. govs. NHL, NBA; bd. dirs. Kellogg Co., Corning Inc. Co-founder Nat. Retinitis Pigmentosa Found. Fighting Blindness, 1971, also chmn.; pres., trustee Gund Collection of Western Art; mem. Nat. Adv. Eye Coun., 1980-84. Office: Gund Investment Corp PO box 449 14 Nassau St Princeton NJ 08542-0449

GUNDERSON, CLEON HENRY, management consultant corporation executive; b. Great Falls, Mont., June 5, 1932; s. Leon H. and Mona (Emmett) G.; m. Virginia Ellen Hudson, Aug. 26, 1972; children: Craig H., Robert S., Laura E. BS, Inst. Tech., Dayton, Ohio, 1971, Mont. State U., 1957; MAPA, U. Okla., 1975. Communications engr. Mountain States Tel & Tel, Helena, Mont., 1953-54; aerospace engr. Boeing Co., Seattle, 1957-58; commd. 2nd lt. USAF, 1958, advanced to col., 1974, ret., 1976; pres. Precision Prodn. & Engring., Walla Walla, Wash., 1976-79, Western Skies Energy Systems, Spokane, Wash., 1979-88, Computer Central, Olympia, Wash., 1988-90, C.H. Gunderson & Assocs., Littlerock, Wash., 1990—; Mem. Am. Inst. Elec. Engrs., Seattle, 1957-60, Am. Inst. Indsl. Engrs., Spokane, 1982-85. Inventor heatexchange solar panels, comml. solar panels. Decorated Silver Stars, Disting. Flying Crosses, Purple Heart, Air medals. Mem. Soc. Mfg. Engrs. (sr. mem.), Soc. Mil. Engrs., Nat. Assn. Small Businesses, Toastmasters Internat., Walla Walla C. of C., Canto Blanco Gun Club (Madrid, v.p. 1973-75, Scott Air Force Base Gun Club (v.p. 1975-76), Spokane Gun Club. Republican. Home: 13001 Littlerock Rd Box 246 Littlerock WA 98556 Office: C H Gunderson & Assocs PO Box 246 Littlerock WA 98556-0246

GUNDERSON, ELMER MILLARD, state supreme court justice, law educator; b. Mpls., Aug. 9, 1929; s. Elmer Peter and Carmaleta (Oliver) G.; m. Lupe Gomez, Dec. 29, 1967; 1 son, John Randolph. Student, U. Minn., U. Omaha, 1948-53; LL.B., Creighton U., 1956; LL.M., U. Va., 1982; LL.D., Calif. Western Sch. Law; student appellate judges seminar, N.Y. U., 1971; LL.D., U. Pacific. Bar: Nebr. 1956, Nev. 1958. Atty.-adviser FTC, 1956-57; pvt. practice Las Vegas, 1958-71; justice Nev. Supreme Ct., 1971-89, now sr. justice; instr. bus. law So. regional div. U. Nev.; lectr., author bulls. felony crimes for Clark County Sheriff's Dept.; counsel Sheriff's Protective Assn.; mem. legal staff Clark Council Civil Def. Agy.; legal counsel Nev. Jaycees. Compiler, annotator: Omaha Home Rule Charter; project coordinator: Jud. Orientation Manual, 1974. Chmn. Clark County Child Welfare Bd., Nev. central chpt. Nat. Multiple Sclerosis Soc.; hon. dir. Spring Mountain Youth Camp. Served with U.S. Army. Recipient A.J.S. Herbert Harley award. Mem. Am., Nebr., Nev. bar assns.; Mem. Inst. Jud. Adminstrn., Am. Law Inst., Am. Trial Lawyers Assn., Am. Judicature Soc., Phi Alpha Delta, Alpha Sigma Nu. Office: Nev Supreme Ct 100 N Carson St Carson City NV 89710-0001

GUNDERSON, TED LEE, security consultant; b. Colorado Springs, Colo., Nov. 7, 1928. BBA, U. Nebr. Sales rep. George A. Hormel Co., Austin, Minn., 1950-51; spl. agt. in charge U.S. Dept. Justice FBI, Los Angeles, Dallas, Memphis, Phila., 1951-79; internat. security cons. Ted L. Gunderson & Assocs., Santa Monica, Calif., 1979—; cons. Calif. Narcotic Authority. Author: How to Locate Anyone Anywhere, 1989; appeared on numerous nat. and local TV, radio talk shows; producer: TV documentary on Satanism. Mem. Bel Air U.S. Navy League, Internat. Assn. Chiefs of Police, Internat. Footprinters Assn., Philanthropic Found. (Los Angeles chpt.), Royal Soc. Encouragement of Arts, Mfrs. and Commerce, Sigma Alpha Epsilon.

GÜNER, OSMAN FATIH, physical organic chemist; b. Manisa, Turkey, Feb. 25, 1956; came to U.S., 1982; s. Ahmet Tarik and Ayse Nurcan (Güneysu) G.; m. Nazli Rukiye Erbay, Apr. 23, 1982; children: Kurt Rasim, Sibel Sabahat. BS in Chemistry, Mid. East Tech. U., Ankara, Turkey, 1979, MS in Organic Chemistry, 1981; PhD in Phys. Organic Chemistry, Va. Commonwealth U., 1986. Postdoctoral fellow U. Ala., Birmingham, 1987-89; sr. applications scientist Molecular Design Ltd., San Leandro, Calif., 1989-93, sr. scientist, 1993—. Referee Jour. Organic Chemistry, Jour. Chem. Info. Computational Scis.; contbr. articles to Jour. Am. Chem. Soc., Jour. Organic Chemistry, Inorganic Chemistry, Itnernat. Jour. Quantum Chemistry, Jour. Phys. Chemistry. Fellow Am. Inst. Chemists; mem. Am. Chem. Soc., Calif. Acad. Scis., U.S. Chess Fedn. Office: Molecular Design Ltd 2132 Farallon Dr San Leandro CA 94577-6604

GUNIA, ROBERT E., broadcast industry executive; b. Franklin, Pa., July 30, 1944; s. Paul Frank and Edith (Stout) G. BA in Acctg., Ohio State U., 1968. Br. oper. mgr. E.F. Hutton, Palm Springs, Calif., 1968-73; v.p. oper. Birns Cos., Palm Springs, Calif., 1973-85; pres. Desert Data, Palm Springs, Calif., 1985-89; CFO Vision House, Beverly Hills, Calif., 1989—; bd. dirs. Radio Vision Internat., Beverly Hills, 1989—, Vision Prodns., Beverly Hills, 1991—, Pure Mgmt., Beverly Hills, 1992—; cons. World Concert Network, Beverly Hills, 1991—. Home: 11693 San Vincete # 326 Los Angeles CA 90049 Office: Vision House 9935 Santa Monica Blvd Beverly Hills CA 90212

GUNN, THOMAS M., lawyer. BA, St. Louis U., 1965, JD, 1967. Bar: Mo. 1967. Various fed. govt. positions; with McDonnell Douglas Helicopter Co., Mesa, Ariz., 1975—, now pres., also bd. dirs.; corp. v.p. spl. projects McDonnell Douglas Corp., St. Louis, 1992, v.p. strategic bus. devel., 1992—. Office: McDonnell Douglas Corp PO Box 516 Saint Louis MO 63166

GUNNING, STEVEN RICHARD, telephone communications technician; b. L.A., Jan. 1, 1945; s. Larry and Marion Leah (Schmidt) G.; m. Joyce Canning, Jan. 3, 1969 (div. Jan. 1971); children: Steven, David, Patrick; m. Natalie Amiee, Mar. 10, 1975 (div. Jan. 1987). AA, L.A. Valley Coll., 1981. Piping designer Flour Corp., Commerse, Calif., 1963-64; ground radio repair technician, sgt. USAF, 1964-69; installation technician Sears, Glendale, Calif., 1969-70; electronics test technician Am. Data Systems, Canoga Pk., Calif., 1970; installer, repair technician Pacific Telephone/PAC Bell, Reseda, Calif., 1971—. Active Crippled Children Soc. L.A., Pediatric AIDS Found., United Way. Home: 9764 Natick Ave North Hills CA 91343-2428

GUNSTREAM, ROBBY DEAN, music society executive; b. Pasadena, Calif., Sept. 23, 1951; s. Robby Nelman and Dorothy Jean (Poole) G.; m. Mareth Sinclair, June 6, 1981; children: Corbin Sinclair, Caroline E. Stuart, Colin Saunders Poole. MusB, U. So. Calif., 1974; MusM, Yale U., 1976. Staff assoc. Nat. Assn. Schs. of Music, Reston, Va., 1976-79; asst. dean Conservatory of Music Wheaton (Ill.) Coll., 1979-83; exec. dir. Coll. Music Soc., Missoula, Mont., 1983—. Recipient cert. Ctr. for Black Music Research, Chgo., 1987. Episcopalian. Office: Coll Music Soc 202 W Spruce St Missoula MT 59802-4202

GUNSUL, ALAN L(ANE) W(EBSTER), family physician and surgeon, educator; b. Annette Island, Alaska, Apr. 24, 1926; s. Frank Justice and Phyllis Emmerrette (Webster) G.; m. Barbara Jean Davis, Sept. 12, 1947; children: Magen, Alan, Moira, Maude, Ian. BS in Chemistry and Philosophy, Seattle U., 1960; MD, U. Wash., 1955. Diplomate Am. Bd. Family Practice. Rotating intern Doctors Hosp., Seattle, 1955-56; assoc. Jack R. Morrison, M.D., Seattle, 1956-57; pvt. practice, Seattle, 1957—; mem. staff Highland Community Hosp., Seattle, 1958—, asst. chief staff, 1969, chief staff, 1970, chief family medicine, 1983-92; mem. active and courtesy staff Riverton Gen. Hosp., 1958-84; clin. instr. medicine U. Wash. Sch. Medicine, Seattle, 1988—; team physician Highline High Sch. Staff sgt. USAAF, 1944-46, MTO. Decorated Bronze Star. Fellow Am. Acad. Family Physicians; mem. Wash. State Acad. Family Physicians King County Acad. Family Physicians, Wash. State Med. Soc., King County Med. Soc. Office: 216 SW 156th St Burien WA 98166-2566

GUNTER, WILLIAM DAYLE, JR., physicist; b. Mitchell, S.D., Jan. 10, 1932; s. William Dayle and Lamerta Berniece (Hockensmith) G.; m. Shirley Marie Teshera, Oct. 24, 1955; children—Maria Jo, Robert Paul. B.S. in Physics with distinction, Stanford U., 1957, M.S., 1959. Physicist Ames Research Ctr. NASA, Moffett Field, Calif., 1960-81, asst. br. chief electronic optical engring., 1981-85; pvt. practice cons. Photon Applications, San Jose, Calif., 1985—. Patentee in field. Contbr. articles to profl. jours. Served with U.S. Army, 1953-55. Recipient Westinghouse Sci. Talent Search award, 1950; various awards NASA; Stanford U. scholar, 1950. Mem. Am. Assn. Profl. Cons., Optical Soc. Am., IEEE (sr.), Am. Phys. Soc., Soc. Photo-Optical Instrumentation Engrs., Planetary Soc., Nat. Space Soc., NASA Alumni League. Office: Photon Applications 5290 Dellwood Way San Jose CA 95118-2904

GUNTHER, RICHARD S., business executive; b. Portland, Oreg., May 6, 1925; s. Herman and Bertha (Rosenberg) Cohn; m. Lois Ruth Goldberg, Dec. 28, 1948; children: Mark, Andrew, Daniel. BS in BA summa cum laude, UCLA, 1948; MA, U. So. Calif., 1974. Chmn. Project Renewal, 1979-83; v.p. New Israel Fund, 1985-91; bd. dirs. Strathern Savs. and Loan, Brentwood Savs. and Loan, Dymo Ind.; chmn. bd. United Continental Devel. Corp.; bd. dirs. Boson and Maine Ind. Co-author: Who Needs Mid-Life at Your Age?, 1983. Bd. dirs. KCET Channel 28, KPFK Pub. Radio; mem. various coms. City and County of L.A.; past bd. trustees Esalen Inst.; bd. trustees exec. com. Calif. Sch. Profl. Psychology; chmn. Urban Affairs Task Force, State Calif. Dem. Adv. Com.; past mem. Dem. State Cen. Com. for Calif.; del. 1968 Dem. Nat. Conv., Chgo.; chmn. bldrs. div. United Jewish Welfare Fund, chmn. constrn. sect.; past pres., bd. dirs. Brandeis-Bardin Inst., past. mem. Calif. State Commn. on Wellness and Physical Fitness; mem. Calif.-Israel Econ. Exchange. Home: 2431 Century Hl Los Angeles CA 90067 Office: 2121 Ave of Stars Los Angeles CA 90067

GUPTA, ANIL KUMAR, engineering economist; b. New Delhi, Aug. 7, 1953; came to U.S., 1974; s. Gokal Chand and Chandra (Kanta) G. B. Tech. in Mech. Engring., Indian Inst. Tech., New Delhi, 1974; MS in Indsl. Engring., Kans. State U., 1977; PhD in Bus. Adminstrn., U. So. Calif., 1984. Engring. economist, mgmt. system advisor TRW, Redondo Beach, Calif., 1977—; systems specialist GenCorp AerojetCorp., Azusa, Calif., 1977—; lectr. U. So. Calif., L.A., 1976-77, Calif. State U. Domingus Hills, Carson, Calif., 1977-89. Contbr. articles to profl. jours. Home: PO Box 21 Redondo Beach CA 90277-0021 Office: GenCorp Aerojet Corp 1100 W Hollyvale Ave Azusa CA 91702

GUPTA, BIMLESHWAR PRASAD, mechanical engineer, manager; b. Jaipur, Raj, India, May 17, 1946; s. Hari Prasad and Sarla D. (Agarwal) G.; m. Rajni Garg, Dec. 10, 1974; children: Anjli, Neeraj. BSME, U. Jodhpur, India, 1968; MSME, U. Minn., 1971, MBA, 1974. Registered profl. engr., Colo. Engr. Honeywell Inc., Mpls., 1971-76, sect. mgr., 1976-78; program and div. ops. mgr. Nat. Renewable Energy Lab., Golden, Colo., 1978—; lectr. in field; chairperson nat. and internat. confs. on solar thermal rsch. Guest editor spl. edit. The Energy Jour., 1987; contbr. articles to profl. jours. Mem. ASME (assoc. editor jour. 1983-85, guest editor spl. issue 1984), Internat. Solar Energy Soc., India Assn. Colo. (exec. com. 1983-84, pres. 1991), U. Minn. Alumni Assn., Toastmasters (pres. Lakewood 1985, bd. govs. F-2 area 1988-89). Home: 14373 W Bayaud Pl Golden CO 80401-5339 Office: Nat Renewable Energy Lab 1617 Cole Blvd Golden CO 80401-3305

GUPTA, RAJESH, industrial engineer, quality assurance specialist; b. Calcutta, India, Oct. 27, 1961; came to U.S., 1986; s. Chandra Kumar and Indira (Karnani) G.; m. Amita Negi, Jan. 26, 1989. BSME, Bangalore (India) U., 1984; postgrad. in Indsl. Systems, San Jose State U., 1988. Engr. trainee Incoducts Pvt. Ltd., Bangalore, 1983-84, quality and prodn. control supr., 1984-86; quality assurance engring. supr. Gen. Signals Semiconductor Systems, Fremont, Calif., 1988-89, quality assurance engring. mgr., 1989-90; quality assurance engring. mgr. Semiconductor Systems, Inc., Fremont, 1990—. Mem. NSPE, Soc. Mfg. Engrs., Inst. Indsl. Engrs., Am. Soc. Quality Control. Office: Semiconductor Systems Inc 47003 Mission Falls Ct Fremont CA 94539

GUPTILL, KATHARINE SCHUYLER, nutritional epidemiologist, researcher; b. Riverside, Calif., Dec. 16, 1959; d. Ronald Virgil and Katharine Schuyler (Howard) G.; m. Alex Peter Evans Jr., Aug. 27, 1987; children: Bo, Katie. BA, U. Calif., Berkeley, 1982; DSc, Johns Hopkins U., 1990. Pub. health nutritionist U.S. Peace Corps, Taveuni, Fiji, 1982-84; rsch. asst. Johns Hopkins U., Sch. Pub. Health, Balt., 1985-86; rsch. asst., epidemiologist Nat. Inst. Child Health and Human Devel., Bethesda, Md., 1987-88; nutritionist, field supr. U. Ilorin (Kwara State, Nigeria)/Johns Hopkins U., 1988-89; rsch. asst. Johns Hopkins U., Sch. Pub. Health, Balt., 1989-90; NIH post-doctoral fellow U. Calif., Berkeley, 1990—; cons. Inst. Nutrition of Cen. Am. and Panama, Guatemala City, Guatemala, 1991—. Contbr. articles to profl. jours. Vol. Nelson Mandela's U.S. Tour, Oakland, Calif., 1990, re-election campaign Mayor Lani Hannkock, Berkeley, 1990, Brown for Pres., San Francisco, 1992. Recipient Harry D. Kruse Award in Nutrition, Johns Hopkins U., 1988, Pres.'s Undergrad. fellowship U. Calif., Berkeley, 1980. Mem. APHA. Office: U Calif Dept Nutritional Scis Berkeley CA 94720

GURAK, STANLEY JOSEPH, mathematics and computer science educator; b. Troy, N.Y., June 14, 1949; s. Joseph Steven and Viola Catherine (Trela) G. BS in Math. and Physics, SUNY, Stony Brook, 1971; PhD in Math., UCLA, 1975; MS in Computer Sci., U. Calif., San Diego, 1987. Lectr. math. UCLA, 1975-76; asst. prof. Fla. State U., Tallahassee, 1976-77; asst. prof. U. San Diego, 1977-80, assoc. prof., 1980-83, prof. math. and computer sci., 1983—, head dept. math. and computer sci., 1988-91; vis. rsch. fellow U. New South Wales, Sydney, Australia, 1983, McQuarie U., Sydney, 1992. Contbr. articles to profl. jours. Chancellor's Intern fellow UCLA, 1971. Mem. Am. Math. Soc., Math. Assn. Am., Sigma Pi Sigma. Office: U San Diego Dept Math and Computer Sci Alcala Pk San Diego CA 92110

GURAN, YOLANDA ILEANA, electronics engineering educator; b. Bucharest, Romania, May 18, 1946; came to U.S., 1986; d. Ion and Maia (Lupescu) Grigorescu. MSEE, Poly. Inst. of Bucharest, 1969. Registered profl. engr. elec. engring., Oreg. Rsch. and design engr. Rsch. Inst. for Electronics, Bucharest, 1969-74; prof. engring. Spiru Haret Tech. Ctr. for Electronics, Bucharest, 1974-85; asst. prof. Oreg. Inst. Tech., Klamath Falls, 1986-88; assoc. prof. Oreg. Inst. of Tech.-Met. Campus, Portland, 1989—.

Author: Manual of the Electronics Engineer, 1977, Methods of Teaching Control Systems, 1979; also articles. Camp mgr. Girl Scouts U.S.A., Klamath Falls, 1987-88. Grantee NSF, 1988-90; recipient Tchr. award Portland Met. C. of C., 1990; fellowship DuPont Co., 1990. Mem. IEEE, Am. Soc. Engring. Edn., N.W. Coll. Electronics Educators Assn. (pres.), Women in Engring. Program Advocates Network. Orthodox. Office: Oreg Inst of Tech 7726 SE Harmony Rd Portland OR 97222-1294

GURASH, JOHN THOMAS, insurance company executive; b. Oakland, Calif., Nov. 25, 1910; s. Nicholas and Katherine (Restovic) G.; student Loyola U. Sch. Law, Los Angeles, 1936, 38-39; m. Katherine Mills, Feb. 4, 1934; 1 child, John N. With Am. Surety Co. N.Y., 1930-44; with Pacific Employers Ins. Co., 1944-53; pres., organizer Meritplan Ins. Co., 1953-59; exec. v.p. Pacific Employers Ins. Co., 1959-60, pres., 1960-68, chmn., bd., 1968-76; v.p. Ins. Co. N. Am., 1966-70; exec. v.p., dir. INA Corp., 1968-69, chmn., pres., CEO, 1969-74, chmn., CEO, 1974-75, chmn. bd., 1975, chmn. exec. com., 1975-79; chmn. bd. CertainTeed Corp., 1978-92; chmn. bd. dirs. Horace Mann Educators Corp., Springfield, Ill., 1989—; dir. St. Gobain Corp., chmn.bd. dirs., 1991-92. Trustee emeritus Occidental Coll., L.A.; former trustee Orthopaedic Hosp., Los Angeles; bd. dirs. Weingart Found. Mem. Pa. Soc., Newcomen Soc. N.Am., Am. Soc. French Legion of Honor, Knights of Malta, Calif. Club, Pine Valley (N.J.) Golf Club, L.A. Country Club, Sr. Golf Assn. of So. Calif., Annandale Golf Club, Valley Hunt Club. Office: Ste 610 1000 Wilshire Blvd Los Angeles CA 90017-2463

GURBAXANI, SHYAM H. M., foundation administrator, consultant, educator; b. Karachi, Sind, Pakistan, Dec. 28, 1928; came to U.S., 1949; s. Hassomal Mulchand and Kishni Kundanmal (Mansukhani) G.; m. Shannon Howard, July 18, 1959; children: Andrew Raj, Brian Mohan, Catherine Shannon. BS with honors, Bombay U., 1949; MSEE, Stanford (Calif.) U., 1950; MS in Physics, Rutgers U., 1963, PhD in Solid State, 1965. Br. head Naval Air Devel. CTr., Johnsville, Pa., 1965-66; prof. U. N.Mex., Albuquerque, 1968—; pres. Am. Sci. Found., Inc., Albuquerque, 1978—; mem. rsch. faculty Associated Western Univs., Salt Lake City, 1969-72; guest scientist Lawrence Livermore (Calif.) Nat. Lab., 1973; cons. Gen. Atomics, San Diego, 1989, Air Force Weapons Lab., Kirtland AFB, N.Mex., 1980-84, 89—. Contbr. articles to profl. jours. Mem. IEEE (sr.), Nuclear Electromagnetism (steering com. 1978—), Microwave Theory and Techniques (chair spl. sessions steering com. 1987—). Democrat. Office: U NMex University at Central Ave Albuquerque NM 87131

GURGIN, VONNIE ANN, social scientist; b. Toledo, Nov. 20, 1940. B.A., Ohio State U., 1962; M.A., U. Calif., Berkeley, 1966; D.Criminology, 1969. Research asst. Calif. Dept. Mental Hygiene, San Francisco, 1962-64; research sociologist U. Calif., Berkeley, 1964-66; dir. cons. services Survey Research Center, 1967-68, asst. prof. criminology, 1968-71; research sociologist Social Sci. Research and Devel. Corp., Berkeley, 1966-67; sr. research criminologist Stanford Research Inst. (now SRI Internat.), Menlo Park, Calif., 1971-72; research dir. Inst. Study Social Concerns, Berkeley, 1972—; asst. chief resource for cancer prevention and epidemiology sect. Calif. Tumor Registry, Calif. Dept. Health Services, Emeryville, 1981-86; dir. survey research No. Calif. Cancer Ctr., Belmont, 1982-86; dir. SEER programs No. Calif. Cancer Ctr., 1986; cons.; mgr. dept. family and community health Calif. Med. Assn., San Francisco, 1993—; pres. bd. dirs. Inst. Study Social Concerns, Berkeley; bd. dirs. Elmwood Coll., Berkeley, 1992—. Author reports, monographs, articles. Bd. dirs. Rsch. Guild, Sacramento, 1983-86. Mem. AAAS, Am. Sociol. Assn. Address: 1099 Sterling Ave Berkeley CA 94708

GURNEY, DANIEL SEXTON, race car manufacturing company executive, racing team executive; b. L.I., Apr. 13, 1931; s. John R. and Roma (Sexton) G.; m. Evi B., July 7, 1969; children: Justin B., Alexander R.; children by previous marriage: John, Lyndee, Danny, Jimmy. Grad., Menlo Jr. Coll., 1951. Profl. race car driver, 1955-70; pres., owner Dan Gurney's All Am. Racers, Inc. (doing bus. as); Dan Gurney Eagle Racing Cars, U.S.A., Santa Ana, Calif., 1964—; mgr. Eagle Racing Team (Indpls. 500 winners 1968, 73, 75, U.S. Auto Club Nat. Championship winners 1968, 74), Formula A Championship winners 1968, 69); TV sports commentator; mem. Automobile Competition Com. for U.S.A. Served with U.S. Army, 1952-54, Korea. Recipient numerous racing awards including GTO Driving championship Internat. Motor Sports Assn., 1987 (driver Chris Cord), GTO Mfrs.' championship Internat. Motor Sports Assn., 1987 (mfr. Toyota), Norelco Cup championship, 1987 (driver Willy T. Ribbs), IMSA Camel GTP championship, 1992, IMSA Mfrs. championship for Toyota, 1992. Mem. Screen Actors Guild, AFTRA, U.S. Auto Club, Sports Car Club Am., U.S. C. of C., Championship Auto Racing Teams, Inc., Soc. Automotive Engrs., Fedn. Internationale de L'Automobile, Internat. Motor Sports Assn. Clubs: Balboa Bay, Eagle.

GURNSEY, GARROLD MELVIN, insurance agent; b. Lebanon, Oreg., Feb. 13, 1937; s. Earl Cyrus and Arvella Joy (Honeywell) G.; m. Sally Anne Steers, May 12, 1956; children: Garrold Matthew, Lisa Anne, Tiffany Lynne. CLU, Bryn Mawr, 1980, ChFC, 1985. Mgr. Comml. Credit, Salem, Oreg., 1961-63; asst. mgr. U.S. Nat. Bank, Portland, Oreg., 1963-66; sales and fin. mgr. Frank Chevrolet, Portland, Oreg., 1966-69; owner Gurnsey & Assocs., Portland, Oreg., 1969—; lectr. in field. Contbr. articles to profl. jours. Mem. Oreg. Life Underwriters Assn. (pres. 1988-89), Oreg. Health Underwriters Assn. (pres. 1981-82), Agts. Adv. Com. (pres. 1978-79), Million Dollar Round Table, Nat. Assn. Life Underwriters, Am. Soc. CLU, Am. Soc. ChFC, Internat. Assn. Fin. Planners, Nat. Assn. Health Underwriters, Estate Planning Coun. of Portland. Office: Gurnsey and Assocs 10 SE 102nd Ave Portland OR 97216

GURNSEY, KATHLEEN WALLACE, state legislator; b. Donnelly, Idaho; d. Robert G. and Thelma (Halferty) Wallace; m. Vern L. Gurnsey, May 7, 1950; children: Kristina Johnson, Steve, Scott. BA in Bus. Adminstn., Boise State U., 1976. Mem. Idaho Ho. of Reps., Boise, 1974—. Bd. dirs. YMCA, Boise; elder, pres. Women's Assn. First Presbyn. Ch.; bd. dirs. Fundsy, St. Luke's Aux.; mem. Def. Adv. Com. Women in the Svc., Dept. Def., 1982-84. Named Disting. Citizen Idaho Statesman, Woman of Yr. Soroptimist, Woman Achievment Altrusa Club, Outstanding Alumna Boise State U., 1991. Mem. AAUW (Outstanding Community Svcs. award 1991), Bus. and Profl. Women, Jobs Daus. (Bethel guardian honored quenn). Republican. Presbyterian. Home: 1111 W Highland View Dr Boise ID 83702-1319

GURWITZ-HALL, BARBARA ANN, artist; b. Ayer, Mass., July 7, 1942; d. Jack and Rose (Baritz) Gurwitz; m. James M. Marshall III, Mar. 12, 1966 (div. 1973); m. William D. Hall, May 3, 1991. Student, Boston U., 1960-61, Katherine Gibbs Sch., Boston, 1961-63. Artist-in-residence Desert House of Prayer, Tucson, 1989-91; oblate mem. Benedictine Sisters Perpetual Adoration, 1986—. One-artist shows: Henry Hicks Gallery, Bklyn., 1978, Misty-Mountain Gallery, Tubac, Ariz., 1987, Karin Newby Gallery, Tubac, 1989; exhibited in group shows: Becket (Mass.) Art Ctr., 1978, Winter Gallery, Tucson, 1980, Johnson Gallery, Bisbee, Ariz., Hilltop Gallery, Nogales, Ariz., 1981, Scharf Gallery, Sante Fe, 1982, Data Mus., Ein Hod, Israel, 1985, C.G. Rein Gallery, Tucson, 1986, New West Views, 1985, Mesquite Gallery, Patagonia, Ariz., 1986, Beth O'Donnell Gallery, Tucson, 1989, Karin Newby Gallery, 1989-93, Wilde-Meyer Gallery, Scottsdale, Ariz., 1991-93, ArtWest, 1992; represented in permanent collections: Diocese of Tucson, N.J. Sambul & Co., N.Y.C., Goldman Sachs & Co., N.Y.C., Data Mus., Israel, Desert House of Prayer, Tucson, Ethical Culture Soc., Bklyn., St. Andrews Episcopal Ch., Nogales, Tubac Elem. Sch., numerous private collections U.S., Eur. Mem. Tubac (Ariz.) Village Coun., 1979-86; bd. dirs. Pimeria Alta Hist. Soc., Nogales, Ariz., 1982-84; creator Art Walk, Tubac Sch. System and Village Coun., 1980; set designer, choreographer ann. De Anza Pageant, Tubac Ctr. Arts, 1982—; pastoral asst. St. Ann's Parish, Tubac, 1986-89. Mem. Santa Cruz Valley Art Assn. (hon. mention 1989, 90, 91, Best of Show award 1989, award for excellence 1992), Assn. Contemplative Sisters. Address: PO Box 4007 Tubac AZ 85646

GUSS, HELEN JOANNE FOLEY, personnel manager; b. Mpls., June 20, 1937; d. Bartholomew James and Eileen Agnes (Kenny) Foley; children: Barbara Y., Joanne P., Mary Anne, Gregory. Cert. pers. adminstrn. with distinction, U. Calif., Berkeley, 1986. Cert. profl. in human resources (Human Resources Cert. Inst., sr. cert.). Exec. sec. Ames Taping Tool Systems Co., Belmont, Calif., 1972-80; pers. mgr. Ames Taping Tool Systems Co., Pleasanton, Calif., 1980—. Mem. No. Calif. Human Resource Coun., Soc. Human Resource Mgmt., Tri Valley Human Resource Assn. Democrat. Roman Catholic. Office: Ames Taping Tool System Co 6691 Owens Dr Pleasanton CA 94588

GUSSE, BRIAN RAYMOND, typographer; b. Kingston-on-thames, Eng., May 13, 1948; s. Richard and Marie Patricia (Hickey) G. Grad. high sch. Apprentice printer Daily Advance, Dover, N.J., 1972-74; typesetter L.A. Herald-Examiner, 1974-77; typographer Julie Finger Design Office, L.A., 1977-79, Creative Age Publs., Van Nuys, Calif., 1979-88, Hi-Torque Pub. Co., Mission Hills, Calif., 1988—. Prodn. asst. United Cerebral Palsy Telethon, Van Nuys, 1989—. With USAF, 1968-72. Mem. Internat. Typographical Union, Buick Club of Am. Office: Hi-Torque Pub 10600 Sepulveda Blvd Mission Hills CA 91345-1900

GUSTAFSON, CHERI LYNN, accountant; b. San Jose, Calif., Oct. 23, 1968; d. Elwood Charles and Nancy Ann (Taylor) G. BSBA, San Jose State U., 1992. Coord. Red Hawk, Milpitas, Calif., 1991-92; acct. Dynamic Circuits, Milpitas, 1992—. Mem. Inst. Mgmt. Accts., Beta Alpha Psi (fundraising dir. 1991), Kappa Delta (treas. 1989-91, 92—). Home: 100 Union Ave #20 San Jose CA 95008 Office: Dynamic Circuits 1831 Tarob Ct Milpitas CA 95035

GUSTAFSON, GRANT BERNARD, mathematics educator; b. St. Paul, Mar. 5, 1944; s. Russell Urban and Emma J. (Wabloom) G.; m. Adeline Marie Brist, Dec. 26, 1969; 1 child, Lance A. BA, Ariz. State U., 1965, MS, 1967, PhD, 1968. Prof. U. Utah, Salt Lake City, 1969—. Office: U Utah 113 JWB Math Dept Salt Lake City UT 84112

GUSTAFSON, PAULA, writer, artist; b. B.C., Can., Feb. 25, 1941. co-editor Artichoke mag., Calgary, 1989—; author: Salish Weaving, 1981; contbr. articles to profl. jours. Mem. Can. Coun. Literary Arts (juror), Periodical Writers Assn. of Can. Home: 901 Jervis St # 210, Vancouver, BC Canada V6E 2B6

GUSTAFSON, RANDALL LEE, city manager; b. Sidney, Nebr., Nov. 11, 1947; s. Robert John and Hilda Lydia (Sims) G.; m. Cynthia Ann Taylor, Oct. 18, 1974. Student, U. Kans., 1965-68, Rockhurst Coll., 1968-70; BS in Pub. Adminstrn., Upper Iowa U., 1992. City mgr. City of Bonner Springs, Kans., 1970-77; bus. owner Lambquarters, Dix, Nebr., 1977-83; city mgr. City of Aurora, Mo., 1983-85, City of Sterling, Colo., 1985—; bd. dirs. Logan Area Devel. Co., Sterling. Bd. dirs. Fire and Police Pension Assn. Colo., Denver, 1987—, 13th Jud. Dist. Community Corrections, Brush, Colo., 1988-90; mem. Colo. Mcpl. League Policy Com., Denver, 1987-89. Recipient Disting. Svc. award Jaycees, 1976. Mem. Internat. Assn. City Mgmt. (full mem.), Colo. Assn. City Mgmt., Am. Soc. for Pub. Adminstrn., Govs. Fin. Assn., Rotary, Elks. Republican. Lutheran. Office: Centennial Sq Sterling CO 80751-3365

GUSTAVSON, JOAN ELLEN CARLSON, psychologist; b. Bingham Canyon, Utah, Feb. 26, 1947; d. Leonard Alfred and Melba Ellen (Brown) Carlson; m. Carl Roger Gustavson, June 6, 1964; children: Andrew Roger, Eric Cris. BS, N.D. State U., Fargo, 1982. Interviewer coord. Galveston (Tex.) Family Health Mental Health Survey Project, 1986-87; asst. rsch. dir. Psychiat. Ethology Lab., U. Tex. Med. Br., Galveston, 1985-89; asst. rsch. dir. coyote control project, ctr. environ. studies Ariz. State U., Tempe, 1985—; owner Body Image Distortion and Dissatisfaction Evaluation. Editor: Roses and Catails: A Collection of Readings in Human Sexuality, 1981; contbr. articles to profl. jours. Named One of the Outstanding Young Women of Am., 1982. Mem. Am. Inst. Biol. Sci., Am. Psychol. Soc., Western Psychol. Assn., N.Y. Acad. Sci., Sigma Xi, Phi Kappa Phi. Home: 243 W Calle Monte Vista Tempe AZ 85284-2261 Office: Ariz State U Ctr Environ Studies Tempe AZ 85287-3211

GUSTAVSON, ROBERT A., energy management consulting company executive. Student, U. Calif., Irvine, 1971-73, UCLA, 1978-79. Lic. elec. contractor, Calif. Founder, pres. Energy Design Cons., Costa Mesa, Calif.; auditor Calif. Energy Commn.; condr. tng. seminars and workshops for energy mgmt. systems mfrs., distbrs. and contractors throughout U.S. Coauthor: The Business of Energy Management; contbr. numerous articles to trade jours. Mem. ASHRAE, Assn. Energy Engrs. (sr., Energy Profl. Devel. award 1987), Assn. Profl. Energy Mgrs., Nat. Elec. Contractors Assn. (award for excellence 1983), Builders, Owners and Mgrs. Assn. Office: Energy Design Cons 129 W Wilson St Ste 205 Costa Mesa CA 92627

GUTHRIE, DAVID NEAL, marketing executive; b. Paris, Tex., Feb. 12, 1941; s. Wesley Neal and Marie (Oliver) G.; m. Ramona Jeanne Busch, Feb. 6, 1959; children: David Jr., Scott, Laure. Student, San Antonio Coll., 1959-62, U. Tex., 1962-63, U. Tex., Arlington, 1965-66, U. Mo., 1970-72. From systems analyst to sales mgr. Sperry Univac, St. Louis, 1967-80; sales rep. Computer Sharing Svcs. Inc., St. Louis, 1980-83, Tandem Computers, Inc., St. Louis, 1983-84, Sykes Dataronics, Inc., St. Louis, 1984-85; sales rep. Cray Rsch., Inc., Colorado Springs, 1985-88, mktg. mgr., 1988—. With USMCR, 1957-59. Fellow Mensa. Republican. Home: 42 Jessana Heights Colorado Springs CO 80906 Office: Cray Rsch Inc. 102 S Tejon Ste 1100 Colorado Springs CO 80903

GUTHRIE, EDGAR KING, artist; b. Chenoa, Ill., May 12, 1917; s. David McMurtrie and Emily Henrietta (Streid) G.; m. Eva Ross Harvey, Dec. 8, 1945 (dec. Jan. 1978); children: Melody Bliss Johnson, Mark King Guthrie. BEd, Ill. State U., 1939; MA, Am. U., 1958; graduate, Command and General Staff Coll., Ft. Leavenworth, Kan., 1967. Artist W.L. Stensgaard Co., Chgo., 1939-40, The Diamond Store, Phoenix, 1941-42; presentation artist CIA, Washington, 1955-72; instr. Columbia Tech. Inst., Arlington, Va., 1966-72; owner, later ptnr. Guthrie Art & Sign Co., Winchester, Va., 1976—; instr. U. Hawaii, Lihue, 1980-81; cartoonist The Kauai Times, Lihue, 1981-90; owner Alo-o-oha-ha-ha Caricatures, Lihue, Honolulu, 1980—; cons., artist Shenandoah Apple Blossom Festival, Winchester, 1975-78; cartoonist Internat. Salon of Caricature, Montreal, Can., 1976-77; co-chmn. Kauai Soc. of Artists Art Show, Lihue, 1981. One man shows include 50 Yrs. of Painting-A Retrospective, Lihue, 1984; inventor Artists' Kit; Filmic Artist: (documentary film) The River Nile, 1960 (NBC Emmy Award). Bd. dirs. Civil Def., Virginia Hills, 1954; publicity com. Frederick County Taxpayers Assn., Winchester, 1973, Exch. Club, Winchester, 1977. Lt. col. U.S. Army, 1942-54. Decorated Purple Heart, Bronze star with Oak Leaf cluster; Recipient Special Merit award R.S.A. Aloha Council, Lihue, 1982. Mem. Mus. of Cartoon art, U.S. Naval Combat Artist, Daniel Morgan Mus. (contbr. 1976), Nat. Soc. of Mural Painters (contbr. 1976), Allied Artists of Am. (contbr. 1977), Pastel Soc. Am. (contbr. 1977-78), Am. Watercolor Soc. (contbr. 1982—). Mem. Ch. LDS.

GUTHRIE, JAMES BRYAN, architect; b. Chgo., Jan. 26, 1957; s. Thomas Allan and Marilyn L. (Murphy) G. BS, U. Ill., 1979, MArch, 1982. Architect Krommenhoek, McKeown Architects, San Diego, M.W. Steele, Inc., San Diego; assoc. Gast, Urban Design & Architecture, San Diego; prin. San Diego, 1989—; instr. New Sch. of Architecture, 1987—. Contbr. articles to profl. jours.;. Bd. dirs. Norman Heights Community Devel. Corp, 1988—, Save Our Heritage Orgn., 1988-90; pres. Normal Heights Community Devel. Corp., 1990—. Mem. San Diego Archt. Club (pres. 84-86), AIA, Nat. Trust Hist. Preservation, San Diego Sailing Club, Urban Land Inst., Am. Planning Assn.

GUTHRIE, PATRICIA SUE, newspaper reporter, free-lance writer; b. Buffalo, Sept. 27, 1958; d. Robert and Margaret Ann (Flagstad) G. Student, Buffalo State Coll., 1976-78, U. Buffalo, 1978-79; BS in Journalism, Northern Ariz. State U., 1983. Freelance reporter DesertWest News, Flagstaff, Ariz., 1983-85; reporter The Gallup (N.M.) Independent, 1985-88; freelance writer The Ariz. Republic and other news orgns., 1985-88; reporter The Albuquerque Tribune, 1988—. Recipient Don Bolles award Ariz. Press Club, 1986, George Polk award L.I. U., 1988, Best Investigative Series award N.M. AP Mng. Editors, 1988, Team Reporting award Scripps Howard Newspapers, 1988-89, Nat. Headliner award Atlantic City Press Club, 1989, Unity Awards in Media Lincoln U. of Mo., 1989, Pub. Svc. award N.M. Press Assn., 1989, Pub. Svc. award Mng. Editors AP, 1989, Amicus Honor for Pub. Svc. N.M. Trial Lawyers Amicus Found., 1989, Kiplinger Fellowship award Ohio State U. Journalism Grad. Sch., 1990—; named Disting. Alumnus No. Ariz. U., 1990. Mem. N.M. Press Women (awards for writing, 1987), Edn. Writers Assn., Women in Communications (Clarion award, 1989), Investigative Reporters and Editors, Sigma Delta Chi (v.p. Flagstaff student chpt. 1982-83). Office: Albuquerque Tribune PO Drawer T Albuquerque NM 87103

GUTIERREZ KEETON, REBECCA LISA, student affairs administrator; b. Roswell, N.Mex., Oct. 17, 1963; d. Joe M. Gutierrez and Martha J. Ochoa; m. Arthur Ronald Keeton, Jr., July 18, 1987. MusB, teaching credential, Chapman Coll., 1986; MA in Student Devel., Azusa Pacific U., 1989. Resident dir., leadership coord. U. LaVerne, Calif., 1986-89; coord. student activities Calif. State Poly. U., Pomona, 1989-93; mem. student life staff semester at sea Inst. for Shipboard Edn. U. Pitts., 1993—; cons. Nat. Conf., L.A., 1986—. Recipient Disting. Merit Citation award Nat. Conf., 1991. Mem. Nat. Assn. Campus Activities (commn. multicultural edn. 1991—, chair commn. for multicultural edn. 1993—, leadership fellow 1989-90, Ednl. Found. Commn. award 1991), Nat. Assn. Student Personnel Adminstrs. (new profls. com. 1986-90), Calif. Assn. Coll. Univ. Housing Officers. Home: 2677 A St LaVerne CA 91750 Office: Calif State Poly U Pomona Ste 26 3801 W Temple Ave Pomona CA 91768-4037

GUTIERREZ-MEDINA, HECTOR, Spanish interpreter; b. Mexico City, Mex., Feb. 3, 1951; came to U.S., 1963; s. Benjamin and Emily (Gutierrez) M.; m. Cheryl Ann Creech, June 29, 1985; 1 child, Sabrina. AA, East L.A. Coll., 1975; BA, UCLA, 1978. Spanish ct. interpreter L.A., 1980—. Mem. Am. Translators Assn., Calif. Ct. Interpreters Assn. Democrat. Roman Catholic. Home: 882 Victor Ave # 4 Inglewood CA 90302

GUTIERREZ-RYBURN, BLANCA ROSA, statistician; b. Humacao, P.R., Feb. 9, 1962; d. Victor Antonio Gutierrez and Blanca Rosa Dorna; m. William Christopher Ryburn, Dec. 19, 1992. BS in Math. magna cum laude, U. P.R., Rio Piedras, 1986. Cartographer Def. Mapping Agy., Washington, 1986-87, geodesist, 1987-89; mathematician Naval Weapons Sta.-Seal Beach, Fallbrook, Calif., 1989-90, statistician-engr., 1990—; coll. recruiter Def. Mapping Agy., 1989; chmn. Hispanic Heritage com. Naval Weapons Sta.-Seal Beach, 1989, 92, co-chmn. 1990. Publ. statistical reports on defense systems for U.S. Navy and United Kingdom Royal Navy. Participant Women's Exec. Leadership Program, 1991-92; rep. Occupational Safety and Health Com., 1992—. Mem. Cousteau Soc., San Diego Zool. Soc. Roman Catholic.

GUTMAN, GEORGE ANDRE, molecular biologist, educator; b. Domme, France, Sept. 15, 1945; came to U.S., 1947; s. Peter M. and Frances F. (Reitman) G.; m. Janis Lynn Schonauer, Dec. 30, 1977; children: Pierre Daniel, Marie Elizabeth. AB, Columbia Coll., 1966; PhD, Stanford U., 1973. Postdoctoral fellow Stanford (Calif.) U., 1973-74, Walter and Eliza Hall Inst. Med. Rsch., Melbourne, Australia, 1974-76; asst. prof. U. Calif., Irvine, 1976-82, assoc. prof., 1982-89, prof., 1989—. Fulbright Hays fellow, 1966-67, Arthritis Found. rsch. fellow, 1974-77; USPHS grantee, 1978-90; recipient Rsch. Career Devel. award USPHS, 1978-83. Fellow Am. Assn. for Advancement of Sci.; mem. Am. Assn. Immunology. Office: U Calif Dept Microbiol & Molec Gen Irvine CA 92717

GUTOW, BERNARD SIDNEY, packaging manufacturing company executive; b. Chgo., Nov. 11, 1939; s. Max and Betty (Warshawsky) G.; m. Carol Lerch, June 5, 1960; children: Jeffrey, Bryon. BS in Engring., U. Ill., 1961, MS in Engring., 1962; MBA, U. Santa Clara, 1965. Registered profl. engr., Ill. Sr. engr. Lockheed Missiles, Sunnyvale, Calif., 1962-65; project mgr. U.S. Steel Co., Chgo., 1965-67; engr., prin. A.T. Kearney Co., Chgo., 1967-78; dir. Shaklee, San Francisco, 1978-79; v.p. H.S. Crocker, San Bruno, Calif., 1979-85; v.p., gen. mgr. First Data Resources subs. Am. Express Corp., Tustin, Calif., 1985—, Resource Ptnrs., Redwood Shores, Calif., 1988—. Editor: Plant Engineering Management, 1974; contbr. articles to profl. jours. Pres. Morton Grove Park Dist., Ill., 1973-78; mem. Morton Grove Youth Commn., 1973-78. Recipient Plaque, Morton Grove Park Dist., 1978; cert. Soc. Mfg. Engrs., Chgo., 1975, Bronze award Internat. Film and TV Festival N.Y., N.Y.C., 1984. Mem. ASME (chpt. chmn. 1972-73). Home: 3263 La Mesa Dr San Carlos CA 94070-4244

GUTT, PHILLIP A., management consultant, association executive; b. Austin, Tex.; s. Tadius J. and Barbara J. (Pierson) G.; m. Nancy E. Smith; 1 child, Victoria. BS, U. Ariz., 1977. Founder, co-owner Assn. Mgrs., Inc., Tucson, 1977—, Profl. Property Mgrs., Inc., Tucson, 1979—; pres. Assn. Mgrs., Inc., Tucson and Phoenix, 1987—; cons. Pima County Med. Soc., Tucson, 1990. Campaign mgr. Davis for City Coun., Tucson, 1983, treas., 1984. Mem. Am. Soc. Assn. Execs., Inst. Assn. Mgmt. Cos. (bd. dirs. 1985-86, 90-91, Cert. of Appreciation 1986-91), Rotary. Office: Assn Mgrs Inc 3900 E Timrod St Tucson AZ 85711-4145

GUTTMANN, GEOFFREY DAVID, physicist, researcher; b. London, July 8, 1954; came to U.S., 1966; s. Egon Guttman and Miriam G. (Schmidt) Dean. BS, U. Md., 1981; PhD, U. Calif., Berkeley, 1989. Teaching asst. U. Calif., 1984-86; grad. rsch. asst. Lawrence Berkeley Lab., 1985-89; instr. physics lab. New Coll. of Calif., San Francisco, 1988-89; physicist ARACOR, Sunnyvale, Calif., 1989-90; postdoctoral fellow Los Alamos (N.Mex.) Nat. Lab., 1990—; lectr. Calif. State U., Hayward, 1989-90, Coll. of Santa Fe, 1990—. Contbr. articles to profl. jours. State referee U.S. Soccer Fedn., 1981—; soccer coach Los Alamos Youth Soccer League/Duke City Soccer League, Los Alamos, 1991; referee Nat. Intercollegiate Soccer Ofcls. Assn., 1982—. Mem. Am. Phys. Soc., Am. Assn. Physicists in Medicine, Optical Soc. Am., Soc. Photo Optical Engrs., Sigma Pi Sigma, Sigma Xi. Office: Los Alamos Nat Lab P-4, MS E554 Los Alamos NM 87545

GUY, MILDRED DOROTHY, educator; b. Brunswick, Ga.; d. John and Mamie Paul (Smith) Floyd; BA in Social Sci., Savannah State Coll., 1949; MA in Am. History, Atlanta U., 1952; postgrad. U. So. Calif., U. Colo.; m. Charles H. Guy, Aug. 18, 1956 (div. 1979); 1 child, Rhonda Lynn. Tchr. social studies L.S. Ingraham High Sch., Sparta, Ga.; tchr. English and social studies North Jr. High Sch., Colorado Springs, 1958-84; ret., 1984; cooperating tchr. Tchr. Edn. Program, Col. Coll., 1968-72. Fund raiser for Citizens for Theatre Auditorium, Colorado Springs, 1979; bd. dirs. Urban League, 1971-75; del. to County and State Dem. Conv., 1972, 76, 80, 84; mem. Pike's Peak Community Coll. Council, 1976-83; mem. Colo. Springs Opera Coun. of 500, 1984-88; mem. nominating com. Wagon Wheel council Girl Scouts U.S.A., 1985-87. Recipient Viking award North Jr. High Sch., 1973, Woman of Distinction award Girls Scouts Wagon Wheel Coun., 1989; Outstanding Black Woman of Colorado Springs award, 1975; named Pacesetter, Atlanta U., 1980-81, Outstanding Black Educator of Yr., Black Educators of Dist. II, Colorado Springs, 1984; Outstanding Ednl. Service award Colo. Dept. and State Bd. Edn., 1983, Dedicated Service award Pikes Peak Community Coll., 1983; Outstanding Community Leadership award Alpha Phi Alpha, 1985; award Colo. Black Woman for Polit. Action, 1985, Sphinx award, 1986; named in recognition sect. Salute to Women, Colorado Springs Gazette Telegraph, 1986. Mem. NEA, (life mem.), AAUW, Colo. Coun. of Social Studies, Assn. for Study of Afro-Am. Life and History, Colo. LWV, Friends of Pioneers Mus. (life mem.), NAACP, Negro Hist. Assn. of Colo. Springs (charter, outstanding edl. svc. award 1983, bd. dirs. 1984—), Alpha Delta Kappa, Alpha Kappa Alpha (chpt. pres. 1984-86, award 1986). Baptist. Home: 3132 Constitution Ave Colorado Springs CO 80909-2177

GUY, RICHARD P., state supreme court justice; b. Coeur d'Alene, Idaho, Oct. 24, 1932; s. Richard H. and Charlotte M. Guy; m. Marilyn K. Guy, Nov. 16, 1963; children: Victoria, Heidi, Emily. JD, Gonzaga U., 1959. Bar: Wash. 1959, Hawaii 1988. Former judge Wash. Superior Ct., Spokane, from 1977; now justice Wash. Supreme Ct., Olympia. Capt. USAS. Mem. Wash. State Bar, Spokane County Bar Assn. Roman Catholic. Office: Wash Supreme Ct Temple of Justice PO Box 40929 Olympia WA 98504-0929

GUYTON, SAMUEL PERCY, lawyer; b. Jackson, Miss., Mar. 20, 1937; s. Earl Ellington and Eulalia (Reynolds) G.; m. Jean Preston, Oct. 11, 1959; children: Tamara Reynolds, William Preston, David Sage. BA, Miss. State U., 1959; LLB, U. Va., 1965. Bar: Colo. 1965, U.S. Dist. Ct. Colo. 1965, U.S. Tax Ct. 1977, U.S. Ct. Appeals (10th cir.) 1965, U.S. Ct. Appeals (5th cir.) 1981. Ptnr., Holland & Hart, Denver, 1965—; faculty Am. Law Inst.

ABA, 1976-88; bd. dirs. Genesis Jobs Inc. Sec., trustee Colo. Hist. Found., 1971—, pres., 1983-87; trustee Music Assn. Aspen and Aspen Music Festival, 1980-88; precinct com. chmn. Dem. Party, 1968-70; mem. Gov.'s mansion preservation com., 1989-92, mem. adv. com., 1989-92. Capt. USAF, 1959-62. Fellow Am. Coll. Tax Counsel (bd. regents 1985-92, chmn., pres. 1989-91), Am. Tax Policy Inst. (trustee 1989-92, v.p. 1989-92), Colo. Bar Found.; mem. ABA (sect. taxation 1967—, chmn. sect.'s com. on agr. 1980-82), Colo. Bar Assn. (tax coun. 1983-86, sec. 1983, chmn. 1985-86), Colo. Bar Found., Denver Bar Assn., Rocky Mountain Estate Planning Coun., Greater Denver Tax Csls. Assn. (chmn. 1978), Law Club Denver, Am. Alpine Club (life), Colo. Mountain Club (life), Eleanore Mullen Weckbaugh Found. (trustee), Humphreys Found. (trustee), Colo. Trail Found. (trustee). Mem. United Ch. of Christ. Co-author: Cattle Owners Tax Manual, 1984, Supplement to Federal Taxation of Agriculture, 1983, Colorado Estate Planning Desk Book, 1984, 90; contbr. articles to jours., mags.; bd. advs. Agrl. Law Jour., 1978-82; mem. editorial bd. Jour. Agrl. Tax and Law, 1983-92.

GUZE, BARRY HOBART, psychiatry educator; b. New Haven, June 16, 1956; s. Lucien Barry and Patricia Louise (Hobart) G.; m. Lynne Doughty, June 13, 1982; children: Evan Anthony, Nathan Barry. BA, U. Calif., Berkeley, 1978; MD, Chgo. Med. Coll., 1982. Intern UCLA, 1982-83, resident in psychiatry, 1983-86, fellow in nuclear medicine, 1986-88, asst. prof. psychiatry, 1988—, asst. prof. radiol. scis., 1992—; ward dir. UCLA Neuropsychiat. Hosp., 1988-92; dir. Adult Psychiat. Hosp. Svc., 1992—. Asst. editor Jour. Clin. Brain Imaging, 1989-92. Laughin fellow Am. Coll. Psychiatry, 1986. Mem. Am. Psychiat. Assn., Neuropsychiat. Imaging Assn., West Coast Coll. Biol. Psychiatry, So. Calif. Psychiat. Soc. Office: UCLA Neuropsychiat Hosp 760 Westwood Plz Los Angeles CA 90024-1759

GUZMAN, ALBERT RICHARD, stockbroker; b. Detroit, Dec. 11, 1946; s. Albert A. and Yolanda (DeLuca) G.; m. Ilona M. Willick, Jan. 6, 1980. BS, Calif. State U., L.A., 1970. Mktg. rep. Mobil Oil, L.A., 1971-72; sales rep. Apeco Corp., L.A., 1972-73, Xerox, L.A., 1973-75; dealer Fuller Brush, L.A. and Phoenix, 1975-81; agt. Met. Life, Phoenix, 1981-84, Jackson Nat. Life, Phoenix, 1984-86; office mgr. Marilyn's Restaurant, Phoenix, 1986-91; stockbroker Dean Witter, Phoenix, 1991—. Precinct committeeman Dist. Party, Scottsdale, Ariz., 1991. Office: Western Federal Ste 160 7150 E Camelback Scottsdale AZ 85251

GUZY, MARGUERITA LINNES, educator; b. Santa Monica, Calif., Nov. 19, 1938; d. Paul William Robert and Margarete (Rodowski) Linnes; m. Stephen Paul Guzy, Aug. 25, 1962 (div. 1968); 1 child, David Paul. AA, Santa Monica Coll., 1959; student, U. Mex., 1959-60; BA, UCLA, 1966, MA, 1973; postgrad. in psychology, Pepperdine U., 1988-92. Cert. secondary tchr., quality review team ednl. programs, bilingual, Calif. Tchr. Inglewood (Calif.) Unified Sch. Dist., 1967—, chmn. dept., 1972-82, mentor, tchr., 1985-88; clin. instr. series Clin. Supervision Levels I, II, Ingelwood, 1986-87; clin. intern Chem. Dependency Ctr., St. John's Hosp., Santa Monica, 1988-92; lectr. chem. and codependency St. John's Hosp., Santa Monica, 1992—; tchr. Santa Monica Coll., 1975-76; cons. billingual edn. Inglewood Unified Sch. Dist., 1975—; sch. rep. restructuring edn. for state proposal, 1991—; lead tchr. new hope program at-risk students Inglewood Unified Sch. Dist., 1992; mem. Program Quality Rev. Team Pub. Edn., Calif., 1993. Author: Elementary Education: "Pygmalian in the Classroom", 1975, English Mechanics Workbook, 1986. Recipient Teaching Excellence cert. State of Calif., 1986; named Tchr. of Yr., 1973, 88. Mem. NEA, Calif. Tchrs. Assn., Inglewood Tchrs. Assn. (local rep. 1971-72, tchr edn. and profl. services com. 1972-78), UCLA Alumnae Assn. (life), Prytanean Alumnae Assn. Republican. Club: Westside Alano (Los Angeles)(bd. dirs., treas. 1982-83). Lodge: Masons. Office: Monroe Jr High Sch 10711 S 10th Ave Inglewood CA 90303-2015

GWYNN, ANTHONY KEITH (TONY GWYNN), professional baseball player; b. L.A., May 9, 1960; m. Alicia; children: Anthony, Anisha Nicole. Student, San Diego State U. Player minor league teams Walla Walla and Amarillo, Hawaii, 1981-82; player San Diego Padres, 1982—. Winner Nat. League batting title, 1984, 87, 88, 89; recipient Gold Glove award, 1986-87, 89-91; mem. All-Star team, 1984-87, 89-93. Office: San Diego Padres PO Box 2000 San Diego CA 92112-2000

GWYNNE, GEOFFREY CARRINGTON, priest; b. Burlingame, Calif., June 1, 1960; s. Samuel Carlton Jr. and Nancy Jane (Carrington) G. B. Philosophy, Miami U., Oxford, Ohio, 1982; lay studies diploma, Trinity Episcopal Sch., Ambridge, Pa., 1984; diploma of Anglican studies, Berkeley Divinity Sch., New Haven, 1988; MDiv, Yale U., 1988. Ordained priest, Episcopal Ch., 1989. Youth minister St. Barnabas Episcopal Ch., Bay Village, Ohio, 1982-83, St. Andrews Episcopal Ch., Panama City, Fla., 1983, 84; lay chaplain U. of the South, Sewanee, Tenn., 1984-86; intern in ch. planting Ch. of the Holy Spirit, Lafayette, La., 1985; chaplain intern Nathaniel Witherell Home, Greenwich, Conn., 1986-87; curate Christ Ch. Episcopal, Hudson, Ohio, 1988-89, Christ Episcopal Ch., Denver, 1989—; coll. chaplain U. Denver, 1989—; missionary St. Stephans Soc., Hong Kong, 1992. Coach YMCA, Denver, 1989—; advisor Boy Scouts Am., Denver, 1989—; chpt. advisor Delta Tau Delta, Sewanee, Tenn., 1984-86; bd. dirs. Bridgeway Home for Pregnant Teens, Denver, 1991-92.; co-founder Shepherd's Gate Inner City Mission, 1991. Recipient award Outstanding Young Men Am., 1990; grantee Episcopal Diocese, Coll. and Young Adult Ministries, Denver, 1990, 91, 92.

GYER, MAURICE SANFORD, photogrammetrist; b. Albany, N.Y., Feb. 6, 1933; s. Harry Morris and Rebecca (Fishbein) G.; m. Judith Louise Farley, Feb. 12, 1965 (div. 1979); 1 child, Suzan Victoria. BS, CCNY, 1956. V.p. DBA Systems, Inc., Melbourne, Fla., 1964-67; pres. Gyer & Saliba, Inc., Melbourne, 1979-86; v.p. Sci. Applications Internat. Corp., Tucson, 1986-90; pres. Eclectics, Inc., Tucson, 1990—. Cpl. U.S. Army, 1956-58. Mem. Am. Soc. for Photogrammetry and Remote Sensing (Fairchild award 1989), IEEE, Soc. for Indsl. and Applied Math. Home: 1880 N Frances Blvd Tucson AZ 85712-3561 Office: Eclectics Inc 1880 N Frances Blvd Tucson AZ 85712-3561

GYLSETH, DORIS (LILLIAN) HANSON, librarian; b. Helena, Mont., May 26, 1934; d. Richard E. and Lillie (Paula) Hanson; m. Arlie Albeck, Dec. 26, 1955 (div. Apr. 1964); m. Hermann M. Gylseth, Apr. 29, 1983 (dec. Aug. 1985). BS in Edn., Western Mont. Coll. Edn., 1958; MLS, U. Wash., 1961. Tchr. Helena Sch. Dist., 1955-56, Dillon (Mont.) Elem. Sch., 1957-59, Eltopia (Wash.) Unified Sch. Dist., 1959-60; sch. libr. Shoreline Sch. Dist., Seattle, 1960-64, Dept. of Def., Chateauroux, France, Hanau, Fed. Republic Germany, Tachikawa, Japan, 1964-68, Long Beach (Calif.) Unified Sch. Dist., 1968-70; br. libr. Long Beach Pub. Libr., 1970-74, coord. children's svcs., 1974-85; libr. Long Beach (Calif.) Unified Sch. Dist., 1986—. Bd. dirs. Children's Svcs. Div. Calif. Libr. Assn., 1985; co-chmn. Long Beach Authors Festival, 1978-86; mem. planning coun. Third Pacific Rim Conf. on Children's Lit., UCLA, 1986. Mem. So. Calif. Coun. on Lit. for Children and Young Poeple (bd. dirs. 1974-88, pres. 1982-84), Helen Fuller Cultural Carrousel (bd. dirs. 1985—), Friends of Long Beach Pub. Libr. (bd. dirs. 1988—), Zonta (pres. 1978-80). Home: 5131 Kingscross Rd Westminster CA 92683-4832

HA, CHONG WAN, state government executive; b. Chin-ju, Kyung-Nam, South Korea, Oct. 25, 1938; came to U.S., 1963; s. Kyung-sik and Kyung-Nam (Park) H.; m. Karen Hye-Ja Han, Aug. 19, 1968; children: Jean Frances, Julie Ann. BA in Econs., UCLA, 1970; cert. in exec. mgmt., The Peter F. Drucker Mgmt. Ctr., 1984; MA in Mgmt., Claremont (Calif.) Grad. Sch., 1985. Sr. systems analyst Atlantic Richfield Co., Los Angeles, 1972-78; asst. v.p. 1st Interstate Services Co., Los Angeles, 1978-85; v.p. Ticor Title Ins. Co., Los Angeles, 1985-91; assoc. dir. MCA/Universal Studios, 1991; dir. State of Calif. Stephen P. Teale Data Ctr., Sacramento, 1991—; mem. exec. com. Calif. Forum on Info. Tech.; mem. adv. bd. Govt. Tech. Conf. Res. police officer Monterey Park (Calif.) Police Dept., 1981-82; bd. dirs. Asian Pacific Alumni Assn., UCLA, 1988, Asian Pacific Am. Legal Founnd., L.A., 1988, Korean Youth Ctr., Korean Am. Music Acad. Mem. Soc. of Info. Mgmt., Leadership Edn. for Asian Pacifics, UCLA Chancellers Circle. Home: 5625 Adobe Rd Rocklin CA 95765

HAACK, DAVID WILFORD, biomedical consultant; b. Denver, Nov. 22, 1945; s. Robert Daniel and Jane Evangeline H.; m. Sharon Dee Sollars, June 19, 1987; children: Shelly, Stacey, Alexis. BS, Colo. State U., 1968, MS, 1971, PhD, 1974. Postdoctorate U. Mich., Ann Arbor, 1974-75, asst. prof. dept. anatomy, med. sch., 1975-80; research assoc. dept. physiology, med. ctr. U. Ariz., Tucson, 1980-83; new product devel., product specialist W.L. Gore & Assocs., Inc., Flagstaff, Ariz., 1983-86, coord. worldwide clin. trials, med. products divsn., 1986-88; founder, pres. Life Tech. Internat., Inc., Phoenix, 1988—; vascular specialist Dow Corning Wright Theratex Group, 1990-92; med. info. scientist Cariovascular A/M Group of Merck & Co., Inc., 1992—. Contbr. numerous articles to profl. jours.; speaker in field; patentee in field, 1986. Nat. Research Service award Nat. Inst. Health, 1974, 1980-83. Mem. AAAS, European Vascular Soc. Home and Office: 3018 E Cochise Dr Phoenix AZ 85028-3816

HAAGE, ROBERT MITCHELL, retired history educator, organization leader; b. Garden City, Kans., Mar. 10, 1924; s. William Russell and Mayme Levice (Mitchell) H.; m. Lila Marie Baker, Sept. 7, 1947; children: Lori Deane, Lisa Anne, Melanie Sue. BA, Southwestern Coll., 1947; MDiv, Garrett Bibl. Inst., 1952. Cert. tchr., Kans., Calif. Min. Meth. Ch., Copeland, Kans., 1947-48, Meth. Chs., Ingleside, Spring Grove, Ill., 1948-50; asst. min. First Meth. Ch., Emporia, Kans., 1952-53; tchr. core curriculum Marshall Intermediate Sch., Wichita, Kans., 1953-56; tchr. U.S. history Bellflower (Calif.) High Sch., 1956-57; tchr. math. Chaffey Joint Union High Sch. Dist., Ontario, Calif., 1957-59; tchr. U.S. history Montclair (Calif.) High Sch. Chaffey Joint Union High Sch. Dist., 1959-85; 1st faculty pres. Montclair High Sch., 1959-60; founding pres. Inland Empire Counties Coun. for Social Studies, San Bernardino, Calif., 1961-62; dean student activities Western CUNA Mgmt. Sch., Pomona Coll., Claremont, Calif., 1980-84. Conservation editor Desomount Dustings Newsletter, 1990-92, gen. editor, 1993—. Founding officer Chaffey Dist. Employees Fed. Credit Union, Ontario, 1964-69; pres., bd. dirs. Chaffey Fed. Credit Union, Ontario, 1979-87, dir., 1969—; officer, bd. govs. Mt. Baldy chpt. Calif. Credit Union League, Pomona, 1977-86; bd. dirs., treas. Upper Westwood Homeowners Assn., Pomona, 1982-84, 91-92; conservation chair Desomount Environ. Orgn.; mem. Nat. Wildlife Fedn. Recipient We Honor Ours award Calif. Tchrs. Assn., 1985, Outstanding Svc. award Associated Chaffey Tchrs., 1985. Mem. Univ. Club Claremont (sec.-v.p.-pres. 1986-92, editor newsletters 1986-90, bd. dirs. 1993—, chair fin. com. 1993—, Leadership award 1992), Toastmasters Club 12 (pres. 1964-65, Best Evaluator award 1982, 83, 85), Sierra Club, Phi Delta Kappa (pres. 1977-78, treas. tchrs. adv. group/tchrs. farm and ranch coop. 1984-93, Dist. Svc. award 1978). Democrat. Home: 9541 Tudor Ave Montclair CA 91763

HAALAND, DOUGLAS, controller; b. Detroit, May 3, 1952; s. Lawrence E. Haaland and Evelyn Marie (Marquardt) Vasend; m. Connie Jo Haaland, Feb. 15, 1987 (div. Sept. 1990); children: Troy Douglas, Douglas Arthur, Lawrence E. Student, Mich. Tech. U., Houghton, 1976, No. Mich. U., 1976-80. Asst. resident unit supr. Mich. Dept. Correction, Marquette, 1976-80; gen. mgr. River City Security Svc., Sacramento, Calif., 1980-81; pres., chief exec. officer Regional Corp. Security, Sacramento, 1981-85; gen. edn. instr. Westland Coll., Clovis, Calif., 1985-86; legis. aide Calif. State Assembly, Sacramento, 1986-87; instr. Tng. Ctr., Fresno, Calif., 1987-88; contr. Papagni Vineyards, Madera, Calif., 1988—. Past bd. dirs. No. Calif. March of Dime, Sacramento; mem. founding bd. State Def. Force Assn. Calif., Sacramento, 1988-89; ex officio Fresno Rep. Cen. Com., 1988-90; active Criminal Justice Adv. Com., Sacramento, 1982-83; coord. Gov's. Prop 39 Campaign, Fresno, 1984; campaign coord. Velasco for Assembly, El Monte, Calif., 1986; mem. Calif. Rep. Part Platform Com., 1988-90, Local 7 Selective Svc., 1989; capt. Aide de Camp State Mil. Reserve, 1984. With USAF, 1970-76. Recipient Letter of Appreciation Gov. George Duekmejian, 1984, Citation of Merit, Mich. State Police, 1980, Disting. Svc. award March of Dimes, 1982; named Outstanding Young Man Am, 1987-89. Mem. State Def. Force Assn., United Latino Political Assn. (dir. pub. rels. 1989), Lions (bd. dirs. No. Blackstone chpt. 1990—, sec. Fig Garden 1989-90), Coaches Club. Republican. Lutheran. Home: 4111 N Fruit Ave Apt 205 Fresno CA 93705-2146 Office: Papagni Vineyards 31754 Avenue 9 Madera CA 93638-8404

HAAS, BRADLEY DEAN, clinical pharmacist, consultant; b. Albion, Nebr., Nov. 24, 1957; s. Ernest Duane Jr. and Joy Lou (Fusselman) H. Student, Kearney State Coll., 1976-78; PharmD with distinction, U. Nebr., Omaha, 1981. Registered pharmacist, Nebr., Colo.; cert. hosp. pharmacy residency, basic life support instr. and provider, advanced cardiac life support instr. and provider. Resident hosp. pharmacy U. Nebr. Med. Ctr., Omaha, 1981-82; intensive care clin. pharmacist Mercy Med. Ctr., Denver, 1982-85; home care pharmacist Am. Abbey Homecare, Englewood, Colo., 1985; pharmacy dir. Charter Hosp. of Aurora, Colo., 1989-90; clin pharmacy coord. Porter Meml. Hosp., Denver, 1987-92; asst. dir. clin. pharmacy svcs. Luth. Med. Ctr., Wheat Ridge, Colo., 1992—; cons. Porter Meml. Hosp. Chronic Pain Treatment Ctr., 1987-89, Charter Hosp., 1989-90; adj. asst. prof. pharmacy U. Colo., 1983—; mem. leadership adv. coun. sch. pharmacy U. Colo., 1987-89; mem. adv. bd. Instl. and Managed Healthcare, Ortho Biotech, Inc., 1992—; mem. State Colo./ Medicare D.U.R. Com., 1992—. Author, co-author in field. Vol. Colo. Hosp. Pharmacists Week, Poison Prevention Week, KUSA-TV Health Fair; lectr. Pathfinder's Youth Group- Careers Day; active Colo. Trust. Named Disting. Young Pharmacist of the Year Marion Labs., Colo., 1987, one of Outstanding Young Men of Am., 1987; recipient Acad. Scholarship U. Nebr. Med. Ctr, 1978-81, Excellence in Pharmacy Practice award U. Colo. Sch. Pharmacy, 1988; Marjorie Merwin Simmons Meml. scholar U. Nebr. Found. Fund., 1980; scholar VFW, 1978-81. Mem. Am. Soc. Hosp. Pharmacists (state chpt. grants program selection com. 1989, nominations com. 1990-91, ho. of dels. 1987, 90-92), Colo. Soc. Hosp. Pharmacists (Hosp. Pharmacy Practitioner Excellence award 1988, 89; presdl. officer 1987-89, chair numerous couns. and coms.). Home: 3177 S Halifax St Aurora CO 80013-4313 Office: Luth Med Ctr Pharmacy Dept 8300 W 38th Ave Wheat Ridge CO 80033

HAAS, MICHAEL, political science educator; b. Detroit, Mar. 26, 1938; s. Mark Leo and Isabelle (Helm) H. BA, Stanford U., 1959; MA, Yale U., 1960; PhD, Stanford U., 1964. Lectr. San Jose (Calif.) State Coll., 1963-64; prof. U. Hawaii at Manoa, Honolulu, 1964—; vis. prof. Northwestern U., Evanston, Ill., 1968-69, Purdue U., West Lafayette, Ind., 1969, U. Calif., Riverside, 1969, U. of the Philippines, Quezon City, 1978, San Francisco State U., 1978, Inst. of Southeast Asian Studies, Singapore, 1987, U. London, 1990; adv. bd. Decision Aids, Inc., Urbana, Ill., 1988—; v.p. EKV Fund, 1993—. Author: International Conflict, 1974, The Pacific Way, 1989, The Asian Way to Peace, 1989; editor: Korean Reunification, 1989, Cambodia Pol Pot and The United States, 1991, Genicode by Proxy, 1991, Polity and Society, 1992, Instutional Racism, 1992. Exec. dir. Found. of Hawaiian Aloha, Honolulu, 1978—; dir. Ctr. for Rsch. on Ethic Rels. Social Sci. Rsch. Inst. U. Hawaii, 1991—, chair Cambodia Studies Com., 1991-92. Mem. Peace Sci. Soc. (pres. western br. 1983), Am. Polit. Sci. Assn., Internat. Polit. Sci. Assn., Internat. Studies Assn., Internat. Peace Rsch. Assn., Soc. Advancement of Socio-Econ. Office: U of Hawaii/Manoa 2424 Maile Way Ste 639 Honolulu HI 96822

HAAS, NANCY CAROL, carpenter; b. Ft. Worth, Oct. 26, 1951; d. James Woodrow and Virginia (Croxdale) H.; m. Louis Castagna, Aug. 11, 1980 (div. 1984). Student, Columbia Basin Coll., 1978-79, L.A. Trade Tech., 1988-90. With Girls Rodeo Assn., Ft. Worth, 1974-75; comml. fisherman Bristol Bay Alaska Salmon Fisheries, Dillingham, 1981-84; laborer, union steward Laborers Internat. Union of N.Am. Local 324, Martinez, Calif., 1977-83; journeyman carpenter United Brotherhood of Carpenters Joiners of Am. Local 630, Long Beach, Calif., 1983—. Chairperson fundraiser Diabetes Rsch. Inst., U. Miami Med. Sch., 1990-92; chair pub. rels./polit. edn. com. Carpenters Local Union 630, Long Beach, 1989-91. Mem. Carpenters Local Union 630 (trustee 1990—), So. Calif. Dist. Coun. Carpenters (del. 1990—), L.A. County Bldg. and Constrn. Trades Coun. (del. 1990—) So. Calif. Conf. of Carpenters (del. 1990—), Coalition of Labor Union Women. Democrat. Office: Carpenters Local Union 630 341 E Wardlow Rd Long Beach CA 90807

HAAS, ROBERT DOUGLAS, apparel manufacturing company executive; b. San Francisco, Apr. 3, 1942; s. Walter A. Jr. and Evelyn (Danzig) H.; m. Colleen Gershon, Jan. 27, 1974; 1 child, Elise Kimberly. BA, U. Calif., Berkeley, 1964; MBA, Harvard U., 1968. With Peace Corps, Ivory Coast, 1964-66; with Levi Strauss & Co., San Francisco, 1973—, sr. v.p. corp. planning and policy, 1978-80, pres. new bus. group, 1980, pres. operating groups, 1980-81, exec. v.p., chief operating officer, 1981-84, pres., chief exec. officer, 1984-89, CEO, chmn. bd., 1989—, also bd. dirs.; pres. Levi Strauss Found. Hon. dir San Francisco AIDS Found.; bd. dirs. Bay Area Coun. White House fellow, 1968-69. Mem. Am. Apparel Mfrs. Assn. (bd. dirs.), Brookings Inst. (trustee), Bay Area Com., Conf. Bd., Coun. Fgn. Rels., Trilateral Commn., Meyer Friedman Inst. (bd. dirs.), Phi Beta Kappa. Office: Levi Strauss & Co PO Box 7215 San Francisco CA 94120-7215

HAAS, WALTER A., JR., retired apparel company executive, professional baseball executive; b. San Francisco, Jan. 24, 1916; s. Walter Abraham and Elise (Stern) H.; m. Evelyn Danzig, 1940; children: Robert D., Elizabeth Haas Eisenhardt, Walter J. BA, U. Calif., Berkeley, 1937; MBA, Harvard U., 1939; hon. degree, Wheaton Coll., 1983. Chief exec. officer Levi Strauss & Co., San Francisco, 1958-76, now hon. chmn. exec. com. bd. dirs.; owner, mng. gen. ptnr. Oakland (Calif.) Athletics Baseball Co.; bd. dir. Bank of Am., Bank Am. Corp., UAL, Inc., Mauna Kea Properties, Pacific Tel. Co.; trustee The Bus. Enterprise Trust; former bd. dir. Bank of Am. Bd. dirs. Nat. Park Found.; mem. adv. coun. Reading is Fundamental, Inc.; mem. SRI Internat. Adv. Coun.; mem. Nat. Commn. on Pub. Svc; former mem. Trilateral Commn.; former mem. exec. com., former regional chmn. Nat. Alliance Businessman; former mem. Presdl. Adv. Coun. for Minority Enterprise, Presdl. Task Force on Internat. Devel., 1970, Nat. Ctr. for Voluntary Action, Citizens Commn. on Pvt. Philanthropy and Pub. Needs; former mem. vis. com. Harvard Bus. Sch.; former mem. intercollegiate athletics adv. bd. U. Calif.; former dir. Hunters Point Boys' Club, San Francisco Boys' Club, Bay Area Urban League, Mt. Zion Hosp.; campaign chmn. United Bay Area Crusade, 1956, also bd. dirs.; former chmn. Radio Free Europe, No. Calif.; commr. San Francisco Parking Authority, 1953; former trustee Ford Found., Com. for Econ. Devel.; former co-chmn. bus. steering com. Nat. Cambodia Crisis Com. Named a Leader of Tomorrow Time mag., 1953, Chief Exec. Officer of Yr. Fin. World mag., 1976, Alumnus of Yr., U. Calif. at Berkeley, 1984; recipient Jefferson award Am. Inst. Pub. Service, 1977, Alumni Achievement award Harvard Grad. Sch. Bus., 1979, Chancellor's award U. Calif. at Berkeley Found., 1982, The Alexis De Tocqueville Society award United Way Am., 1985. Mem. Mfrs. and Wholesalers Assn. San Francisco, (pres. 1951), Nat. Urban League (former dir.), Phi Beta Kappa, Alpha Delta Phi. Office: Levi Strauss & Co PO Box 7215 San Francisco CA 94120-7215 also: Oakland Athletics Oakland/Alameda County Coliseum Oakland CA 94621*

HAAS, WALTER J., professional sports team executive; S. Walter A. Jr. and Evelyn (Danzig) H.; m.; 3 children. Former pres. Goldmine Records; exec. v.p. Oakland (Calif.) A's, Am. League, 1980-88, chief oper. officer, 1988-89, pres., chief exec. officer, 1990—. Trustee Evelyn and Walter A. Haas, Jr. Fund, Marin County Day Sch. Office: care Oakland A's Oakland-Alameda County Coliseum Oakland CA 94621*

HAASE, GERALD MARTIN, pediatric surgeon; b. Shanghai, Jan. 29, 1947; s. Warner A. and Jean H.; children: Sean Hale, Ryan Eric., Jessica Ann; m. Peggy Newman. B.A., Johns Hopkins U., 1968; postgrad Wayne State U. Med. Sch., 1968-70; M.D., Tufts U., 1972. Diplomate Am. Bd. Surgery. Resident in surgery U. Colo., Denver, 1972-74, 75-77, resident in pediatric surgery Children's Hosp., Boston, 1974-75; fellow in pediatric surgery Children's Hosp., Columbus, Ohio, 1977-79; practice medicine Denver Pediatric Surgeons, 1979—; chmn. dept. pediatric surgery Childrens Hosp., Denver 1980-91; cons. pediatric surgeon Fitzsimons Army Med. Center, Aurora, Colo., 1982—; clin. asst. prof. surgery U. Colo. Health Sci. Center, Denver, 1979-84, assoc. prof. 1985-91, prof. 1992—; chmn. surg. steering com. Children's Cancer Group, bd. dirs. Am. Cancer Soc. Mem. AMA, Denver Med. Soc., Colo. Med. Soc., Am. Acad. Pediatrics, Am. Pediatric Surg. Assn., A.C.S., Soc. Surg. Oncology, Internat. Soc. Pediatric Oncology, SigmaPhi Epsilon, Delta Phi Alpha. Office: Denver Pediatric Surgeons 1950 Ogden St # 370HC Denver CO 80218

HAASE, ROBERT WILLIAM, executive bottle water company; b. Seattle, June 1, 1950; s. William Delbert and Jeanette Lillian (Lewis) H.; m. Rae Ann Gaedeke (div. Sept., 1979); children: Adam Douglas, Jessica Lynn; m. Constance Elizabeth Jones, July 22, 1989; stepchilden: Stephanie Marie Remus, Samantha Kate Remus. Student, Brevard Coll., 1968-70, St. Andrews Coll., 1970-71. Supr. Fla. Guard Rail Co., Hollywood, Fla., 1971-73; prodn. mgr. Starline Corp., Pompano Beach, Fla., 1973-74; cabinet maker Kramer Woodworking, Washington, Va., 1974-75; ptnr. Country Cupboards, Washington, 1975-77, Nature's Foods, Washington, 1975-77; owner, designer Robert Haase Furniture Design, Washington, 1978-84; gen. mgr., bd. sec. Polar Water Co., Inc., Stockton, Calif., 1984—. Bd. dirs. Better Bus. Bur. Mid Counties, Stockton, Calif., 1990—. Mem. Calif. Bottled Water Assn. (1st v.p.), San Joaquin Employers Coun. (bd. dirs.), Stockton United Soccer Club (bd. pres.). Presbyterian. Office: Polar Water Co Inc PO Box 511 1029 W Fremont St Stockton CA 95201

HAASETH, RONALD CARL, scientist, educator; b. Seattle, Sept. 6, 1952; s. Carl Antone Roosevelt Haaseth and Christine Virginia (Stoll) Coulter. BS in Chemistry, U. Puget Sound, 1974; PhD in Organic Chemistry, U. Wash., 1982. Teaching, research asst. U. Puget Sound, Tacoma, 1972-74; lab. technician U.S. Oil and Refining Co., Tacoma, 1973-74; predoctoral instr., research asst. U. Wash., Seattle, 1974-82, research assoc., 1982-83; asst. prof. U. Minn., Morris, 1984-85; sr. research assoc. U. Mich., Ann Arbor, 1986-89; rsch. assoc. U. Ariz., Tucson, 1989—; instr. organic chemistry and biochemistry Washtenaw Community Coll., 1988-89. Rsch. grantee USPHS, 1978-81. Mem. Am. Chem. Soc., Am. Peptide Soc. (charter), Sigma Nu, Pi Lamda Theta. Home: 3647 E 2d St Apt K Tucson AZ 85716 Office: U Ariz Dept Chemistry Tucson AZ 85721

HABBESTAD, KATHRYN LOUISE, writer; b. Spokane, Wash., Sept. 29, 1949; d. Bernard Malvin and Gertrude Lucille (Westberg) H. BA, U. Wash., 1971; postgrad., Seattle U., 1981-82. Mgr. bus. Seattle Sun, 1974-75; analyst, dep. dir. Research and Planning Office, Seattle, 1975-83; account exec. Southmark Fin. Services, Seattle, 1983-84; stockbroker Interstate Securities, New Bern, N.C., 1985-86; co-founder, assoc. pub. Havelock (N.C.) News, 1986-87; owner ISIS Enterprises, Spokane, 1988—; writer Spokane; sec.-treas. Seattle Sun Pub. Co., 1974-75, Veritas Services, Seattle, 1978-83; chmn. Energy Com. Nat. Congress for Community Econ. Devel., Washington, 1979-82. Treas. Havelock Chili Festival, 1985-87. Mem. Mensa. Home and Office: 3822 131st Ln SE # L-6 Bellevue WA 98006

HABERLIN, WILLIAM EARL, real estate company executive; b. Honolulu, Mar. 26, 1925; s. Earl William Haberlin and Mary Constance (Ferreira) Burroughs; m. Mildred Frances Copley, July 1, 1945; children: James William, Laura Joyce, Judith Ann, Brian Jon. AA, U. Calif., Berkeley, 1944; MBA, Harvard U., 1956. Asst. v.p. United Calif. Bank, L.A., 1963-65; sr. economist Stanford Rsch. Inst., South Pasadena, Calif., 1965-67; sr. v.p. Union Bank, L.A., 1967-81; v.p., corp. sec. Watson Land Co., L.A., 1981—. Contbr. articles to profl. jours. Mem. Pvt. Industry Coun., L.A., 1990—. Comdr. USN, 1943-63. Mem. Rotary Club of L.A., Harvard-Radcliff Club of So. Calif., Harvard Bus. Sch. Alumni Assn., Assn. for Corp. Growth, Assn. for Corp. Economists, Jonathan Club.

HACKBARTH, DOROTHY ALICE, association executive; b. Naperville, Ill., Apr. 21, 1921; d. Walter Dewey and Nellie Louise (Staffeldt) Eichelberger; m. Charles Alfred Hackbarth, Oct. 24, 1942; children: Christofer Lee, Cathleen, Timothy Scott. BA, U. Calif., Berkeley, 1964. Cert. secondard tchr., Calif. Clk. Elgin (Ill.) Watch Factory, 1940-42; sec. Lucien Lelong, Chgo., 1942-43; telephone operator Hinsdale (Ill.) Telephone Co., 1943-44; dress designer Naperville, Ill., 1947-55; tchr. Oakland (Calif.) Unified Sch. Dist., 1965-66, Berkeley Unified Sch. Dist., 1966-78; pres., chief exec. officer Unesco Assn./USA, Inc., Oakland, Calif., 1978—; pres. UN Assn./Alameda City, Oakland, 1968-73; chair Fgn. Lang. Dept. Martin Luther King Sch., Berkeley, 1969-73. Chair Nat. French Contest, Oakland, Calif., 1968-70. Fellowship UNESCO, 1971; recipient Excellence in Teaching award Berkeleyans for Acad. Excellence, 1977; scholarship Calif. PTA, 1977. Mem. Calif. Alumni Assn. Home and Office: 5815 Lawton Ave Oakland CA 94618-1510

HACKER, KENNETH RUSSELL, insurance executive; b. Sharon, Pa., June 28, 1947; s. Russ Edward and Stella (Hibler) H.; children: Tammy, Todd; m. Judy Hacker, Nov. 11, 1990; children: Lisa, Ryan. Student, Penn-Ohio Coll., 1966-68, Youngstown State U., 1968-70. Steel mill worker Westinghouse Electric, Sharon, Pa., 1966-70; ins. agt. N.Y. Life, Youngstown, Ohio, 1970-82, Phoenix, 1982-85; regional dir. First Del. Life, Phoenix, 1985-87; pres. Estate Planning Concepts, Inc., Phoenix, 1987—. Recipient disting. sales award Sales and Mktg. Execs. of Greater Phoenix, 1984. Mem. Ariz. Estate Planning Coun., CLU Soc., Nat. Assn. Life Underwriters (pres. Phoenix chpt. 1987-88), Million Dollar Roundtable (life, state chmn. 1985-92, mem. found., mem. Ct. of Table 1976—). Republican. Office: Estate Planning Concepts 1830 E Thomas Rd Phoenix AZ 85016

HACKER, MARK GREGORY, communications executive; b. N.Y.C., Apr. 17, 1961; s. George L. and Joan L. (Lake) H. BA in Comm., U. Denver, 1984, MA in Comm., 1988. Cable TV dir. Am. Cablevision, Littleton, Colo., 1983-84; gen. mgr. Screenplay Video, Littleton, 1984-86; corp. comm. intern Jones Intercable, Englewood, Colo., 1987-88; mgr. tng. and employee comm. Pace Membership Warehouse, Englewood, 1988—. Mem. Univ. Park Community Coun., Denver, 1991—; mem. alumni mentoring program U. Denver, 1991—. Mem. ASTD, Nat. Trust for Hist. Preservation, Mountain States Employer's Coun., U. Denver Grad. Sch. Alumni Assn., Beta Theta Pi (v.p. alumni assn. 1985-89). Home: 2500 S Monroe Denver CO 80210 Office: Pace Membership Warehouse 5680 Greenwood Plaza Blvd Englewood CO 80111

HACKETT, CAROL ANN HEDDEN, physician; b. Valdese, N.C., Dec. 18, 1939; d. Thomas Barnett and Zada Loray (Pope) Hedden; B.A., Duke, 1961; M.D., U. N.C., 1966; m. John Peter Hackett, July 27, 1968; children: John Hedden, Elizabeth Bentley, Susanne Rochet. Intern. Georgetown U. Hosp., Washington, 1966-67, resident, 1967-69; clinic physician DePaul Hosp., Norfolk, Va., 1969-71; chief spl. health services Arlington County Dept. Human Resources, Arlington, Va., 1971-72; gen. med. officer USPHS Hosp., Balt., 1974-75; pvt. practice family medicine, Seattle, 1975—; mem. staff, chmn. dept. family practice Overlake Hosp. Med. Ctr., 1985-86; clin. instr. U. Wash. Bd. dirs. Mercer Island (Wash.) Preschool Assn., 1977-78; coordinator 13th and 20th Ann. Inter-profl. Women's Dinner, 1978, 86; trustee Northwest Chamber Orch., 1984-85, King County Acad. Family Practice, 1993. Mem. Am. Acad. Family Practice, King County Family Practice, King County Med. Soc. (chmn. com. TV violence), Wash. Med. Soc., DAR, Bellevue C. of C., NW Women Physicians (v.p. 1978), Seattle Symphony League, Eastside Women Physicians (founder, pres.), Sigma Kappa, Wash. Athletic Club, Lakes Club, Seattle Yacht Club. Episcopalian. Home: 4304 E Mercer Way Mercer Island WA 98040-3826 Office: 1414 116th Ave NE Bellevue WA 98004

HACKETT, JOHN PETER, dermatologist; b. N.Y.C., Feb. 10, 1942; s. John Thomas and Helen (Donohue) H.; m. Carol A. Hedden, July 27, 1968; children: John, Elizabeth, Susanne. AB, Holy Cross Coll., 1963; MD, Georgetown U., 1967. Diplomate Am. Bd. Internal Medicine, Am. Bd. Dermatology. Intern Georgetown U. Hosp., 1967-68, resident, 1968-69; fellow Johns Hopkins Hosp., 1972-75, chief resident, 1975; practice medicine specializing in dermatology Seattle, 1975—; chmn. bd. dirs. NW Dental Ins. Co., 1989-92; clin. asst. prof. dermatology U. Wash., 1976-88, clin. assoc. prof., 1988—; active staff Swedish Hosp.; active staff Providence Hosp.; pres. Psoriasis Treatment Ctr., Inc., 1978-80; cons. physician Children's Orthopedic Hosp. Contbr. articles to profl. jours. Bd. dirs. Mercer Island Boys and Girls Club, 1976-81, Seattle Ctr. for Blind, 1979-80, N.W. Chamber Orch., 1983-86. Served to lt. condr. USNR, 1969-71. Mem. Am. Acad. Dermatology, Seattle Dermatol. Soc. (pres. 1981-82), Soc. Investigative Dermatology, Am. Contact Dermatitis Soc., Wash. State Med. Soc., King County Med. Soc. (chmn. media rels. com. 1977-80, grievance com. 1991—), Wash. Physicians Ins. Exch. (chmn. actuarial subcom. 1983-85, chmn. subscribers adv. com. 1986-90, audit com. 1988-92, fin. com. 1990-92), Wash. Athletic Club, Seattle Yacht Club, Lakes Club, Rotary. Office: 1500 Cabrini Tower 901 Boren Ave Seattle WA 98104-3508

HACKETT, RANDALL SCOTT, engineer; b. Grand Rapids, Mich., Oct. 1, 1943; s. Hugh Jerry and Phyllis (Weekes) H.; m. Lyn Susan Swanson, Jan. 11, 1964; children: Katherine Eileen and Elizabeth Evelyn (twins), Kimberly Michele. AA, West Valley Jr. Coll., 1970; BS, Calif. State U., San Jose, 1972. Technician Allen Electronics, Mountain View, Calif., 1963-64, Fairchild Semiconductor, Mountain View, 1964-66, IBM, San Jose, Calif., 1966-68; from assoc. engr. to sr. assoc. engr. IBM, San Jose, 1968-78, staff engr., 1978-89, adv. engr., 1989--. Inventor slave processor, measurement control unit, spelling checking typewriter. Republican. Lutheran. Home: 11048 Alessi Ct Gilroy CA 95020-9123 Office: IBM 5600 Cottle Rd San Jose CA 95193-0001

HACKETT, WILLIAM BOSTOCK, III, sociologist, psychologist, visionary philosopher; b. Columbus, Ohio, Feb. 29, 1928; s. William Bostock Jr. and Elna Bernice (Pearson) H.; (div.); children: Valerie, Roxanne, Jonathan, Rebecca. BA, U. Cin., 1951. Fellow The Ctr. for the Study of Social Structures, Santa Barbara, Calif., 1974—. Columnist, author: The View From A High I.Q., 1993; contbr. Games for the Super Intelligent, 1971. Mayoral candidate City of Santa Barbara, 1989, 93. Mem. Mensa. Office: The Center PO Box 275 Santa Barbara CA 93102-0275

HACKMAN, ROBERT M., nutritional biochemist, educator; b. Pitts., May 29, 1953; s. Arnold and Betty Ann (Edelman) H.; m. Teresa Ann Alvernaz, June 6, 1986; 1 child, Michael R. BA, Johns Hopkins U., 1975; MS, Pa. State U., 1977; PhD, U. Calif., Davis, 1987. Rsch. asst. Nat. Inst. Dental Rsch., Bethesda, Md., 1971-75, Pa. State U., University Park, 1975-77; predoctoral fellow U. Calif., Davis, 1977-81; asst. prof. U. Oreg., Eugene, 1981-87; pres. Robert M. Hackman Internat. Sports Nutrition Consulting Inc., Eugene, 1990—; assoc. prof. of nutrition U. Oreg., Eugene, 1987—. Office: Univ of Oregon Dept Anthropology 304 Gerlinger Hall Eugene OR 97403-1273

HACKNEY, ROBERT WARD, plant pathologist, nematologist, parasitologist, commercial arbitrator; b. Louisville, Dec. 11, 1942; s. Paul Arnold and Ovine (Whallen) H.; m. Cheryl Lynn Hill, June 28, 1969; 1 child, Candice Colleen. B.A., Northwestern U., 1965; M.S., Murray State U., 1969; Ph.D., Kans. State U., 1973.; Postgrad. research nematologist U. Calif., Riverside, 1973-75; plant nematologist Calif. Dept. Food and Agr., Sacramento, 1975-85, sr. plant nematologist, supr. 1985-90, sr. plant nematologist, specialist, 1989—; comml. arbitrator Am. Arbitration Assn., 1980—; chmn. Calif. Nematode Diagnosis Adv. Commn., Sacramento, 1981—. Contbr. articles to profl. jours. Hon. dep. Sheriff, Sacramento, 1982-83. Served with USMC, 1966. NSF grantee, 1974. Mem. Soc. Nematologists, Internat. Council Study of Viruses and Virus Diseases of the Grape, Delta Tau Delta, Sigma Xi. Democrat. Baptist. Home: 2024 Flowers St Sacramento CA 95825-0422 Office: Calif Dept Food & Agriculture Analysis & Identification Br 1220 N St PO Box 942871 Sacramento CA 94271-0001

HACKNEY-SIMMONS, MARY ALICE, nurse; b. Middletown, Ohio, Mar. 7, 1955; d. Byron Allen and Joan Elaine (Meeker) H.; m. Roy Leslie Brown, Sept. 12, 1974 (dec. Nov. 1979); m. Randolph Anthony Hackney-Simmons, July 26, 1980 (div. Nov. 1992). AAS in Nursing, Miami U., 1975; BSN, U. Hawaii, 1991, postgrad., 1993—. CNOR. Staff nurse Shriners' Burn Inst., Cin., 1975-76, Cin. Gen. Hosp., 1976-77, Middletown (Ohio) Hosp., 1977-80; pub. health nurse Middletown Bureau Pub. Health Nursing, 1980-81; staff nurse Ambulatory Care Ctr., Centerville, Ohio, 1981-82, St. Francis Med. Ctr., Honolulu, 1982-84; mgr. Hawaiian Eye Surgictr., Wahaiwa, 1984-85; coord. operating rm. quality assurance and edn. St. Francis Med. Ctr., Honolulu, 1985-87; nurse mgr., patient care coord., surgery The Queen's Med. Ctr., Honolulu, 1987-88, staff nurse, 1988-91; clin. nurse III surgery Queens Med. Ctr., Honolulu, 1991—; negotiator St. Francis Med. Ctr., 1983, 85, Queen's Med. Ctr., 1993; mem. surg. team performing 1st heart transplant in Hawaii St. Francis Med. Ctr., Honolulu, 1987. Recipient Nat. Collegiate Nursing award, U.S. Achievement Acad., Lexington, Ky., 1990. Mem. NOW, ANA, Hawaii Nurses Assn. and Collective Bargaining Orgn. (bd. dirs. 1991—, v. chair Bd. 1992-93, Hawaii rep. ANA Inst. Collective Bargaining 1992-93, HNA, House of Dels., HNA/CBO House of Dels. 1990-92), Assn. Operating Room Nurses (sec. 1987-89, pres. 1989-90, 90-91, unit rep. 1992-93, Profl. Practice Com. 1991-93, nom. com. 1985-87, House of Dels. 1987, 89, 90, 92), Golden Key (charter), Sigma Theta Tau-Gamma Psi (scholar 1990). Buddhist. Home: 3071 Pualei Cir Apt 308 Honolulu HI 96815-4934

HACKWORTH, THEODORE JAMES, JR., city official; b. Denver, Nov. 7, 1926; s. Theodore James and Thelma B. (Hill) H.; m. Doris Evelyn Larson, Dec. 31, 1947; children—James Robert, Joan Evelyn Grady, Linda Jean Hoffman. B.A., U. Denver, 1955. Sales mgr. Continental Baking Co., Denver, 1950-64; mktg. exec. Sigman Meat Co., Denver, 1964-76; v.p. sales Pierce Packing Co., Billings, Mont., 1976-79; city councilman City of Denver, 1979—, pres., 1983-84; cons. EPA. Mem. Denver pub. schs. bd. edn., 1971-77; dir. Urban Drainage and Flood Control Dist., 1981-84; dir. Met. Wastewater Reclamation Dist., 1982—, sec., 1984-85, chmn. elect 1988-89, chmn., 1989—; mem. Denver Regional Council Govts., 1979—, vice chmn., 1981-83, chmn., 1984-86; neighborhood commr. Boy Scouts Am., 1968-69, Western Dist. commr., 1970-71; pres. Harvey Park Improvement Assn., 1969; chmn. Denver Met. Library Task Force, 1982. Served with USAF, 1945-47. Mem. Nat. Assn. Regional Council (bd. dirs. m., chmn. surface trans. task force, pres. 1987-89). Republican. Club: Mt. Vernon Country. Contbr. articles to EPA jours. Home: 3955 W Linvale Pl Denver CO 80236-2212 Office: 3110 S Sheridan Blvd # 304 Denver CO 80227-5507

HADAS, ELIZABETH CHAMBERLAYNE, publisher; b. Washington, May 12, 1946; d. Moses and Elizabeth (Chamberlayne) H.; m. Jeremy W. Heist, Jan. 25, 1970 (div. 1976); m. Peter Eller, Mar. 21, 1984. A.B., Radcliffe Coll., 1967; postgrad. Rutgers U., 1967-68; M.A., Washington U., St. Louis, 1971. Editor U. N.Mex. Press, Albuquerque, 1971-85; dir., 1985—. Mem. Assn. Am. Univ. Presses (pres. 1992-93). Democrat. Home: 2900 10th St NW Albuquerque NM 87107-1111 Office: U NMex Press 1720 Lomas Blvd NE Albuquerque NM 87131-1591

HADBA, CARLOS BENJAMIN, marketing executive; b. Rio de Janeiro, Brazil, May 18, 1960; came to U.S., 1986; s. Benjamin and Celia (Barbosa) H.; m. Luiza Carolina Amoedo, May 15, 1985; children: Anna Gabriela Amoedo, Felipe Amoedo. BSCE, U. Fed. do Rio de Janeiro, 1984; MBA, Stanford U., 1988. Ptnr. Power Construcoes, Rio de Janeiro, 1982-86; mfg. mgr. Raychem Corp., Menlo Park, Calif., 1988—, logistics mgr., 1990-92, mgr. mktg., 1992—; asst. gen. mgr. Raychem-Shanghai Cable Accessories, Ltd., 1988—. Mem. Soc. Mfg. Engrs., Coun. Logistics Mgmt., Stanford Bus. Sch. Alumni Assn. Roman Catholic. Home: 254 Leland Ave Menlo Park CA 94025-6158

HADDAD, EDMONDE ALEX, public affairs executive; b. Los Angeles, July 25, 1931; s. Alexander Saleeba and Madeline Angela (Zail) H.; m. Harriet Ann Lenhart; children: Mark Edmonde, Brent Michael, John Alex. AA, Los Angeles City Coll., 1956; BA, U. Southern Calif., 1958; MA, Columbia U., 1961. Staff writer WCBS Radio News, New York, 1959-61; news commentator, editor KPOL AM/FM Radio, Los Angeles, 1961-67, dir., pub. affairs, 1967-73; exec. dir. Los Angeles World Affairs Council, 1973-84; pres. L.A. World Affairs Coun., 1984-88; deputy asst. sec. of State for Pub. Diplomacy Dept. State, U.S. Govt., Wash., 1987-88; mem. steering com., moderator Conf. Environ., L.A., 1989-90; pres. Nat. Coun. World Affairs Orgns., 1981-83; pres. Radio and TV News Assn. So. Calif., 1965-66; sr. fellow Ctr. Internat. Rels., U. Calif., L.A., 1991—. Contbg. author: How Peace Came to the World, 1985; founder, pub. World Affairs Jour. Quar., 1981; co-host Background Briefing, KPFK Radio, L.A., 1990—. Bd. dirs. Coldwater Counseling Ctr., 1991—. Recipient Am. Polit. Sci. Assn. award for Disting. Reporting of Pub. Affairs, 1967. Mem. Friends of Wilton Pk. (exec. com. So. Calif.). Democrat. Home: 8701 Delgany Ave Unit 314 Playa Del Rey CA 90293

HADDAD, EDWARD RAOUF, civil engineer, consultant; b. Mosul, Iraq, July 1, 1926; came to U.S., 1990; s. Raouf Sulaiman Haddad and Fadhila (Sulaiman) Shaya; m. Balquis Yousef, July 19, 1961; children: Reem, Raid. BSc, U. Baghdad, Iraq, 1949; postgrad., Colo. State U., 1966-67. Project engr., cons. Min. Pub. Works, Baghdad, 1949-63; arbitrator Engring. Soc. & Ct., Kuwait City, Kuwait, 1963-90; tech. advisor Royal Family, Kuwait, 1987-90; cons. pvt. practice Haddad Engring., Albuquerque, 1990—. Organizer Reps. Abroad, Kuwait, 1990. Recipient Hon. medal Pope Paul VI of Rome, 1973. Mem. ASCE, NSPE, KC (chancellor 1992), Am. Arbitration Assn., Sierra Internat. (trustee), Lions (bd. dirs. 1992), Inventors Club (bd. dirs. 1992). Address: 143(A) General Arnold NE Albuquerque NM 87123

HADDEN, EARL FRENCH, consultant, information technology; b. Princeton, W.Va., June 14, 1946; s. Earl French and Doris (Ratliff) H.; m. Frances Elizabeth Schuhsler, Nov. 7, 1970; children: Elizabeth Patricia, Amanda Ratliff. BA, U. N.C., 1968; postgrad., Loyola U., L.A., 1976-79. Programmer analyst IBM Corp., N.Y.C., 1968-69; mgr. to v.p. corp. rsch. Informatics, Inc., Canoga Park, Calif., 1969-81; v.p. sales Candle Corp., L.A., 1981; chmn., chief exec. officer Pacific Info. Mgmt., Culver City, Calif., 1981—. Speaker numerous profl. confs.; contbr. articles to profl. jours. Mem. Can. Info. Processing Soc., Manhattam Country Club. Republican. Presbyterian.

HADDIX, CHARLES E., legislative and regulatory consultant; b. Astoria, Oreg., Nov. 23, 1915; s. Charles H. and Mattie Lee (Wilson) H.; grad. U.S. Maritime Officers Sch., 1943; grad. in traffic mgmt. Golden Gate U., 1951; m. Betty Lee Wylie, Aug. 22, 1948; children—Bruce W., Anne C., C. Brian. Nat. sales mgr. Radio Sta. KLX, Oakland, Calif., 1953-55; West Coast mgr. Forjoe & Co., 1955-60; v.p. Calif. Spot Sales, 1958-60, Radio Calif., KLIP, Fowler, Calif., 1961-63; med. sales rep. Ives Labs., Inc., Sanger, Calif., 1964-73; state govt. rels. cons. Marion Merrill Dow Labs., Inc., 1973-87; Calif. legis. advocate, 1968-85; Ariz., Nev., N.Mex., Oreg., Wash., Idaho, Utah and Mont. legis. advocate, 1975-85. Mem. Central Calif. Forum on Refugee Affairs, 1983—, chmn. 1987-88, state forum chmn., 1988; mem. Calif. State Adv. Council on Refugee Assistance and Svcs., 1988-90; field cons. U.S. Sen. Alan Cranston, 1987-90, Calif. State Sen. Rose Ann Vuich, 1991-92; Refugee coord. Dooley for Congres Campaign, 1990, Bustamente for Assembly Campaign, 1993; commr. Fresno County Econ. Opportunities Commn., 1992—; mem. Clinton Presdl. Transition Planning Found., 1993; mem. U.S. Senate Staff Club, 1987-90. Author: Reminiscenses of an Old Astoria House, 1992, River Travel Memories on the Columbia, 1992, An Adventure in Dredging, 1993. Served with Marina Mercante Nat., Republic of Panama, 1945, U.S. Mcht. Marine, 1939-41, USCG, 1942-45. Mem. U.S. Naval Inst., Internat. Oceanographic Found., Am. Mus. Natural History, Oreg. Hist. Soc., Manuscript Soc., Clatsop County Hist. Soc., Columbia River Maritime Mus., Commonwealth Club of Calif. (San Francisco). Address: 3218 N McCall Sanger CA 93657

HADDIX, ROBERT ALLEN, architect; b. Tucson, Ariz., Mar. 10, 1964; s. David Abner and Geneva Mae (Williams) H.; m. Kimberly Ann Christensen, Aug. 24, 1991. BArch, U. Ariz., 1988. Lic. profl. architect, Utah, Ariz. Civil engring. draftsman S.W. Engrs. & Planners, Tucson, 1983-84; archtl. technician Henningson, Durham, Richardson, Dallas, 1984-85; archtl. draftsman Aros & Goldblatt Architects, Tucson, 1985-86, Burlini/Silberschlag Ltd., Tucson, 1986-87; architect USAF-Hill AFB Utah, Clearfield, 1988-93; hist. preservation officer, architect Barksdale AFB, La., 1993—. Active Nat. Trust for Hist. Preservation. 1st lt., staff officer Utah Air Nat. Guard, Salt Lake City, 1990-93, with Res. Mem. AIA (assoc. dir. western mountain region 1991), Soc. Am. Mil. Engrs. Republican. Presbyterian.

HADDON, TIMOTHY JOHN, mining engineer; b. Harare, Zimbabwe, Nov. 26, 1948; s. Michael Fenton and Eileen Mary (Morton) H.; m. Mary Denise, Feb. 26, 1971; children: Michael Edward, Jennifer Mary. BSc in Mining Engring., Colo. Sch. of Mines, 1970. Registered profl. engr. Australia. Mining engr. Texasgulf Australia, Perth, 1970-75; sr. engr. Texasgulf Inc., N.Y.C., 1976, Amax Iron Ore Corp., Greenwich, Conn., 1977-79; tech. mgr. Amax Australia Ltd., Sydney, Perth, 1979-82; sr. v.p. Amax Iron Ore Corp., Sydney, 1982-85; pres. Amax Pacific Inc., Sydney, 1986; v.p. R&D, CFO Amax Gold Inc., Golden, Colo., 1987; pres., CEO Amax Mineral Investments, Greenwich, 1988; pres., CEO Amax Gold Inc., Golden, 1989—, bd. dirs.; bd. dirs. Amax Gold Inc., Golden. Bd. dirs. Nat. Mining Hall of Fame, Leadville, Colo., 1989—. Geotech. Environ. and Mining, Golden, 1989—; bd. dirs., chmn. pub. affairs com. Gold Inst., Washington, 1989—. Fellow Australasian Inst. Mining and Metallurgy; mem. AIME, Innis Arden Country Club (Conn.), Rolling Hills Country Club (Colo.). Office: Amax Gold Inc 350 Indiana St Golden CO 80401

HADEN, WILLIAM R., academic administrator. Pres. Reed Coll., Portland, Oreg. Office: Reed Coll Office of President 3203 SE Woodstock Blvd Portland OR 97209-8199

HADFIELD, MICHAEL GALE, zoologist, educator; b. Seattle, Feb. 8, 1937; s. Jack I. and Helen M. (Hoxworth) H.; m. Carolyn A. DeJong, Dec. 17, 1977. BA, U. Wash., 1959, MS, 1961; PhD, Stanford U., 1967. Asst. prof. zoology Pomona Coll., Claremont, Calif., 1966-68; asst. prof. U. Hawaii, Honolulu, 1968-75, assoc. prof., 1975-79, prof., 1979—; lectr. in field; panelist USDA Small Bus. Innovative Rsch. Grants in Aquaculture, 1990; vis. prof. Stanford U., 1989, U. Wash., 1984, 86, 88, U. Guam Marine Lab., 1980, 91; rsch. assoc. Bernice P. Bishop Mus., 1983—; mem. natural area res. commn. State of Hawaii, 1983-86, mem. animal species adv. commn., 1988-92; participant NSF Task Group on Invertebrate Teaching, 1991-92; vis. com. dept. organismic and evolutionary biology Harvard U., 1991-93; mem. Nat. Rsch. Coun. Com. Molecular Marine Biology, 1992-93; mem. com. marine biodiversity ocean scis. divsn. NSF, 1993. Bd. editors: Pacific Sci., 1984—; regional editor: Marine Biology, 1988—; assoc. editor: Jour. Exptl. Zoology, 1990—; contbr. articles to profl. jours. Matsuda scholar U. Hawaii, 1989-90; NSF grantee, 1989—; Fulbright fellow, 1961-62, NIH predoctoral fellow, 1962-66. Fellow AAAS; mem. Am. Soc. Zoologists (chmn. div. invertebrate zoology 1991, 92), Western Soc. Naturalists (pres. 1993), Marine Biol. Assn. U.K., Internat. Soc. on Invertebrate Reproduction and Devel., Am. Malacological Union, Unitas Malacologica, Malacological Soc. London, Soc. for Conservation Biology, Sigma Xi (councilor Hawaii chpt. 1991, pres. 1992). Office: Kewalo Marine Lab U Hawaii 41 Ahui St Honolulu HI 96813

HADGES, THOMAS RICHARD, media consultant; b. Brockton, Mass., Mar. 13, 1948; s. Samuel Charels and Ethel Toli (Prifti) H.; m. Beth Evelyn Rastad, Oct. 22, 1988. BA in Biology magna cum laude, Tufts U., 1969; student, Harvard Sch. Dental Med., 1969-71. Announcer Sta. WOKW, Brockton, 1965-67, Sta. WTBS-FM, MIT, Cambridge, 1966-68; announcer, program dir. Sta. WTUR, Medford, Mass., 1967-69; announcer Concert Network, Sta. WBCN-FM, Boston, 1968-78, program dir., 1977-78; program dir. Sta. WCOZ-FM, Blair Broadcasting, Boston, 1978-80, Sta. KLOS-FM, ABC, Los Angeles, 1980-85; sr. programming advisor Pollack Media Group, Pacific Palisades, Calif., 1985-89; pres. Pollack/Hadges Enterprises, Pacific Palisades, 1985-89, Pollack Media Group, 1989—. Named Program Dir. of Yr., Los Angeles Times, 1981. Mem. Phi Beta Kappa. Office: Pollack Media Group 984 Monument St Ste 105 Pacific Palisades CA 90272-3899

HADLEY, HARLAN DWIGHT, retired security officer; b. Belle Plaine, Kans., Mar. 26, 1928; s. Clarnce Harlan Hadley and Geneva-Jane (Gass) Murray; m. Lawanda Marie Byerly, Feb. 3, 1950 (div. Feb. 1975); children: Virlia Jane Hadley-Monroe, Mary Ann Hadley-Vice; m. Mabel Pauline Reich, Dec. 28, 1978; children: Linda Oline Porthen, Alen Dale Hoilien. Cert. painting, Wichita (Kans.) Art Assn., 1946; student, Highline Jr. Coll., Seattle, 1982-83. Art tchrs. asst. Wichita Art Mus. Bellmount, 1944-46; catalog artist asst. Culver Aircraft In North Park, Wichita, 1946-47; security officer N.W. Protective Svcs., 1979-82; security officer Wash. Security, Sea-Tack Airport, 1982-88, Burns Internat., 1988-89. Pres. local chpt. Nat. Safety Coun., Great Bend, Kans., 1970-73; vol. United Fund, 1970-73, ch., charities, 1950-75. With USAF, 1945. Recipient awards Wash. State Ceramic Art Assn., 1990, 91, 92, 93. Home: 4404 S 140th St Tukwila WA 98168-4159

HADLEY, PAUL BURREST, JR. (TABBIT), chef manager, photographer; b. Louisville, Apr. 26, 1955; s. Paul Burrest and Rose Mary (Ruckert) H. Grad. in Computer Ops. and Programming, No. Ky. Vocat. Sch., 1975. Floor mgr. reconciling dept. Cen. Trust Co., Cin., 1974-76; freelance photographer Ky., Ohio, Colo., 1975—; chef mgr. The Floradora, Telluride, Colo., 1978—; pres. Tabbit Enterprises; freelance recipe writer, Telluride, 1978—. Author poetry (Golden Poet award 1989, Silver Poet award 1990); actor: (plays) Of Mice and Men, The Exercise, Crawling Arnold, A Thousand Clowns, The Authentic Life of Billy The Kid, others. Actor The Plunge Players, Telluride; v.p. Telluride Coun. for Arts and Humanities, 1989. Mem. Plan Internat. USA, Christian Children's Fund. Home: PO Box 923 Telluride CO 81435-0923

HADLEY, WILLIAM KEITH, pathologist, microbiologist, educator; b. Eugene, Oreg., Nov. 12, 1928; s. Olin Clair and Elma Ruby (Paulsen) H.; m. Marilyn JoAnn Norville, Nov. 15, 1952; Joan Elizabeth, Ruth Sarah. AB, U. Calif., Berkeley, 1950, PhD, 1967; MD, Yale U., 1959. Diplomate Am. Bd. Pathology. From asst. prof. to prof. lab. medicine U. Calif., San Francisco, 1967-77, prof., 1977—; chief microbiology div. clin. labs. San Francisco Gen. Hosp., 1967—, chair biosafety, infection control coms.; chair biosafety and infection control coms. Contbr. articles to profl. jours. Fellow Am. Soc. Clin. Pathology, Acad. Clin. Lab. Physicians Scientists, Infectious Diseases Soc. Am.; mem. Am. Soc. Microbiology (nat. counselor 1980). Home: 18 Reed Ranch Rd Belvedere Tiburon CA 94920-2071 Office: San Francisco Gen Hosp Microbiology Div 2M35 Clin Labs 1001 Potrero Ave San Francisco CA 94110-3594

HADLEY, WILLIAM MELVIN, college dean; b. San Antonio, June 4, 1942; s. Arthur Roosevelt and Audrey Merle (Barrett) H.; m. Dorothy J. Hadley, Jan. 21, 1967 (div. July 1989); children: Heather Marie, William Arthur; m. Jane F. Walsh, Oct. 13, 1990. BS in Pharmacy, Purdue U., West Lafayette, Ind., 1967, MS in Pharmacology, 1971, PhD in Toxicology, 1972. Registered pharmacist, Ind. Teaching and grad. asst. Purdue U., West Lafayette, 1967-72; asst. prof. U. N.Mex., Albuquerque, 1972-76, assoc. prof., 1976-82, prof., 1982—, asst. dean Coll. Pharmacy, 1984-86, acting dean Coll. Pharmacy, 1985, dean Coll. Pharmacy, 1986—; vis. scientist Lovelace Inhalation Toxicology Inst., Albuquerque, 1981, adj. scientist, 1991—; mem. adv. bd. Waste Edn. Rsch. Consortium, Las Cruces, N.Mex., 1989—; mem. NIH Proposal Rev. Panels, Bethesda, Md., 1983-84; mem. Gov.'s PCB Expert Adv. Panel, Santa Fe, 1985-86; toxicology cons. numerous law firms N.Mex.; mem. sci. adv. bd. Carlsbad Environ. Monitoring Ctr., 1992—; mem. sci. adv. com. S.W. Regional Spaceport, Las Cruces, 1992—. Mem. steering com. United Fund, U.N.Mex., 1987, key person, 1988-93. NIH grantee, 1974-80, 83-87. Mem. AAAS, Am. Assn. Colls. of Pharmacy, Soc. Toxicology (pres. Rocky Mt. chpt. 1990-91), Western Pharmacology Soc., Southwestern Assn. Toxicologists. Office: U NMex Coll Pharmacy Albuquerque NM 87131

HADSELL, VIRGINIA THOMPSON, educational center administrator; b. Oakland, Calif., Nov. 22, 1921; d. William Aird Jr. and Ruth (Parker) Thompson; mem. John Sidney Hadsell, Nov. 30, 1943; children: Sydney Hadsell Farivar, Heidi Hadsell do Nascimento. BA, U. Calif., Berkeley, 1943; MA, Calif. State U., Hayward, 1972. Tchr. geometry and physics Anna Head Sch., Berkeley, 1943-44; tchr. staff sch. U. Ibadan, Nigeria, 1964-65; tchr., reading specialist, coord. secondary reading Berkeley Pub. Schs., 1966-86; founder, exec. dir. N.Am. Coordinating Ctr. for Responsible Tourism, San Anselmo, Calif., 1984—; guest lectr. edn. U. Calif., Berkeley, St. Mary's Coll., Moraga, Calif., 1970-86; conf. speaker Internat. Reading Assn., Calif. Reading Assn., 1970-86; cons. Ecumenical Coalition on Third World Tourism, Bankgok, 1984—, Third World Tourism European Ecumenical Network, Stuttgart, Germany, 1984—. Co-author: On the Go, 1967, Equal Start, 1969; contbr. numerous articles on responsible tourism issues to jours. Mem. San Anselmo Vol. Bd., 1984-87. Travel grantee Skaggs Found., 1985, Presbyn. Ch. U.S.A., 1989, 92, Ch. Women United, 1989, 92. Mem. AAUW, Delta Kappa Gamma (treas. 1980-84, pres. 1984-86). Democrat. Presbyterian. Office: Ctr for Responsible Tourism PO Box 827 San Anselmo CA 94979

HAEBEL, ROBERT EDWARD, retired marine corps officer; b. Marcus Hook, Pa., July 18, 1927; s. William John and Blanche Harriet H.; m. Barbara Louise Shellenberger, Sept. 1, 1951; children: Deborah L., Lisa L., Jeffrey C. B.S. in Edn, West Chester (Pa.) State Tchrs. Coll., 1951; M.A. in Edn, U. N.Mex., 1967; M.A. in Internat. Affairs, George Washington U., 1971. Enlisted in USMC, 1945, commd. 2d lt., 1951, advanced through grades to maj. gen., 1976; service in Korea, Okinawa, Taiwan and Vietnam;

comdg. gen. Force Troops, 1976-78; dir. personnel mgmt. Div. Hdqrs. USMC, 1978-80, asst. dep. chief staff manpower, 1979-80; comdg. gen. Marine Corps Recruit Depot, Parris Island, S.C., 1980-82, 3d Marine Amphibious Force, 1982-84, MCB, Camp Pendleton, Calif., 1984-87; ret. USMC, 1987; with Pub. Health Svcs., County of San Diego, 1988—. Decorated D.S.M., Legion of Merit with Combat V and gold star, Bronze Star with combat V, Purple Heart with gold star. Roman Catholic. Home: 1604 Kings Way Vista CA 92084-3641

HAEN, PETER JOHN, biology educator; b. Udenhout, The Netherlands, Aug. 29, 1938; came to U.S., 1971; s. Johannes Hermanus and Corrie (Boom) H.; m. Annette Marie Devitt, Aug. 19, 1974; children: Scott, David. BEd, Tchr. Tng. Coll., Tilburg, Holland, 1958; MEd, Pedagogical Acad., Tilburg, Holland, 1959; BS in Zoology and Psychology, Nat. U. of Ireland, Cork, 1964, PhD in Biology, 1967. Tchr. St. Aloysius Sch., Tilburg, 1959-61; demonstrator zool. dept. Nat. U. Ireland, 1964-67; head biology dept. Cardinal Otunga Coll., Kisii, Kenya, 1967-71; head sci. dept. Pius X High Sch., Downey, Calif., 1971-72; asst. prof. Loyola Marymount U., L.A., 1972-77, assoc. prof., 1977-83, prof., 1983—; dir., Rosecrans chair conservation Loyola Marymount U., 1973-79. Author: Model Schools Program, 1973; contbr. articles to profl. jours. Govt. of Ireland grantee, 1965-66. Mem. AAAS, Sigma Xi (S.W. regional dir. and bd. dirs. 1989-92), Alpha Sigma Nu.

HAFEN, BRUCE CLARK, academic administrator; b. St. George, Utah, Oct. 30, 1940; s. Orval and Ruth (Clark) H.; m. Marie Kartchner, June 2, 1964; children: Jon, David, Tom, Emily, Sarah, Mark, Rachel. BA, Brigham Young U., 1966; JD, U. Utah, 1967. Atty. Strong, Poelman & Fox, Salt Lake City, 1967-71; assoc. dir. honors program Brigham Young U., Provo, Utah, 1971-73, asst. to pres., 1971-76, asst. dean Law Sch., 1973-74, prof. law, 1973—, dean Law Sch., 1985-89, provost, 1989—; pres. Ricks Coll., Rexburg, Idaho, 1978-85; dir. rsch. and evaluation LDS Ch., Salt Lake City, 1976-78; testifier Congl. and Senate hearings on Civil Rights Act of 1984, U.S. Commn. Civil Rights, 1985. Author: The Believing Heart: Four Essays on Faith, 1986, The Broken Heart: Applying the Atonement to Life's Experiences, 1989, (with others) Brigham Young University--The First 100 Years, 1976, Privacy--Law and Practice, 1987, The Constitution and the Regulation of Society, 1988; contbr. articles to profl. jours. Bd. advisors Ctr. for Religion and Soc., N.Y.C., 1983—; cons. U.S. Office Edn., Washington, 1982; mem. commn. Northwest Assn. Schs. and Colls., 1983-85. Mem. ABA, Utah Bar Assn. (ex officio commr. 1985-89). Mem. LDS Ch. Office: Brigham Young U Office of Provost D-364 ASB Provo UT 84602

HAFEY, EDWARD EARL JOSEPH, precision tool company executive; b. Hartford, Conn., June 7, 1917; s. Joseph Michael and Josephine (Pyne) H.; B.S. in Mech. Engring., Worcester Poly. Inst., 1940; postgrad. Johns Hopkins U., 1943, 44; m. Loyette Lindsey, Oct. 21, 1971; children—Joseph M., Barbara Hafey Beard, Edward F. Instr. dept. mech. enging. Worcester Tech. Inst., 1940-41; mgr. Comfort Air Inc., San Francisco, 1946-47; owner, mgr. Hafey Air Conditioning Co., San Pablo, Calif., 1947—, pres. Hafey Precision Tool, Inc., Laguna Beach, Calif., 1982—; cons. air conditioning U.S. Navy, C.E., Japan, Korea, Okinawa. Served to comdr. USNR, 1941-46. Registered profl. engr., Calif.; named Man of Year, San Pablo, 1962. Mem. Assn. Energy Engrs., Calif. Air Conditioning Service Enging. Soc., Am. Legion, Ret. Officers Assn., Sigma Alpha Epsilon. Republican. Roman Catholic. Clubs: Exchange of Laguna Beach, Marine's Meml. Office: PO Box 417 Laguna Beach CA 92652-0417

HAGA, ENOCH JOHN, computer educator, author; b. L.A., Apr. 25, 1931; s. Enoch and Esther Bouncer (Higginson) H.; student Sacramento Jr. Coll., 1948-49; AA, Grant Tech. Coll., 1950; student U. Colo., Denver, 1950, U. Calif., Berkeley, 1954, Midwestern U., 1950-54; AB, Sacramento State Coll., 1955, MA, 1958; PhD, Calif. Inst. Integral Studies, 1972, diploma tchr. Asian Culture, 1972; m. Elna Jo Wright, Aug. 22, 1957. Tchr. bus. Calif. Med. Facility, Vacaville, 1956-60; asst. prof. bus. Stanislaus State Coll., Turlock, Calif., 1960-61; engring. writer, publs. engr. Hughes Aircraft Co., Fullerton, Calif., 1961-62, Lockheed Missiles & Space Co., Sunnyvale, Calif., 1962, Gen. Precision, Inc., Glendale, Calif., 1962-63; sr. adminstrv. analyst Holmes & Narver, Inc., L.A., 1963-64; tchr., chmn. dept. bus. and math. Pleasanton Unified Dist., Pleasanton, Calif., 1964-92, coordinator computer svcs., adminstrn. and instrn., 1984-85; vis. asst. prof. bus. Sacramento State Coll., 1967-69; instr. bus. and computer sci. Chabot Coll., Hayward, Calif., 1970-89; instr. bus. and philosophy Ohlone Coll., Fremont, Calif., 1972; prof., v.p., mem. bd. govs. Calif. Inst. Asian Studies, 1972-75; pres., prof. Pacific Inst. East-West Studies, San Francisco, 1975-76, also mem. bd. govs.; dir. Certification Councils, Livermore, Calif., 1975-80; mem., chmn. negotiating team Amador Valley Secondary Educators Assn., Pleasanton, Calif., 1976-77, pres., 1984-85. With USAF, 1949-52, with USNR, 1947-49, 53-57. Mem. Internat. Assn. for Computer Information Systems (exec. dir. 1970-74). Coordinating editor: Total Systems, 1962; editor: Automation Educator, 1965-67; Automated Educational Systems, 1967; Data Processing for Education, 1970-71; Computer Techniques in Biomedicine and Medicine, 1973; contbg. editor Jour. Bus. Edn., 1961-69, Data Processing mag., 1967-70. Author and compiler: Understanding Automation, 1965. Author: Simplified Computer Arithmetic, Simplified Computer Logic, Simplified Computer Input, Simplified Computer Flowcharting, 1971-72. Editor: Data Processor, 1960-62, Automedica, 1970-76, FBE Bull., 1967-68. Home: 983 Venus Way Livermore CA 94550-6345

HAGA, TAKEHIKO, steel company executive; b. Nagota, Aichi, Japan, Feb. 24, 1936; came to U.S., 1990; s. Kou and Yasu (Tadakoro) H.; m. Kobayashi Junko, Oct. 17, 1965; children: Yoko, Ichiro, Koji. BS, Tokyo U., 1958. Gen. mgr. Kawasaki Steel Corp., Kobe, Japan, 1982-90; pres. Calif. Steel Inustries, Fontana, Calif., 1990—. Office: Calif Steel Industries 14000 San Bernardino Ave Fontana CA 92335-5258

HAGAN, ALFRED CHRIS, federal bankruptcy judge; b. Moscow, Idaho, Jan. 27, 1932; s. Alfred Elias and Irene Lydia (Wells) H.; m. Doreen M. Auve, July 10, 1953; children: Chris E., Martha Ann, Peter M. BA, U. Idaho, 1953, JD, 1958. Bar: Idaho 1958, U.S. Dist. Ct. Idaho 1958. Asst. atty. gen. State of Idaho, Boise, 1958, dist. judge, 1967-77; dep. pros. atty. Ada County, Boise, 1959; pvt. practice Boise, 1960-67, 77-84; U.S. bankruptcy judge Dist. of Idaho, Boise, 1985—. 1st lt. USAF, 1953-55. Mem. Nat. Conf. Bankruptcy Judges. Office: PO Box 040 550 W Fort St Boise ID 83724

HAGAN, DOROTHY WERMUTH, program director; b. Niagara Falls, N.Y., Aug. 18, 1942; d. Frederick Arthur and Olga Edna (Strasburg) Wermuth; m. William John Hagan, Aug. 28, 1971. Cert., U. Calif. Med. Ctr., San Francisco, 1965; BS, U. Wis., Menomonie, 1964; MS, U. Mich., 1971; PhD, Mich. State U., 1985; postgrad., U. Ariz., 1992. Dietitian U. Mich. Hosps., Ann Arbor, 1965-70; dir. Food and Nutrition Svcs. Children's Hosp. of Mich., Detroit, 1971-84; instr. Wayne State U., Detroit, 1973, 78, Ea. Mich. U., Ypsilanti, Mich., 1984-85; dir., dietetic intern, asst. prof. Oreg. Health Scis. U. and VA Med. Ctr., Portland, 1986—; chmn. Bd. of Licensure of Dietitians, Portland; mem. NIH-Tech. Assessment Conf. Panel on Methods for Vol. Weight Loss and Control, 1992. Author: (coloring book) Carrots, Corn, and Cabbage, 1978; editor (diet manual) Children's Hospital of Michigan, 1972, 78; author, editor hist. booklet The Oregon Dietetic Internship Experience: 60 Years of Success, 1991; contbr. articles to profl. jours. Bd. dirs. Elderway Inc., Portland, 1990-93. Pediatrics Nutrition grantee Am. Dietetic Assn., 1984-85. Mem. Am. Dietetic Assn. (chair pediatric practice group 1983), Ann Arbor Dietetic Assn. (pres. 1972-73), Oreg. Dietetic Assn. (chair edn. and rsch. 1989-90, chair coun. on practice 1991-92), Sigma Xi. Lutheran. Office: Oreg Health Scis U EJH-RM10 3181 SW Sam Jackson Park Rd Portland OR 97201-3011

HAGAR, CHARLES FREDERICK, astronomy educator; b. L.A., Aug. 7, 1930; s. Frederick Charles and Gertrude Edith (Bennett) H. BA in Astronomy, U. Calif., L.A., 1954; MA in Astronomy, U. Calif., Berkeley, 1960. Staff lectr. Griffith Observatory and Planetarium, L.A., 1952-57; asst. mgr. Morrison Planetarium, San Francisco, 1957-60; prof. astronomy San Francisco State U., 1960—, dir. planetarium inst., 1975—; cons. Hong Kong Space Mus. Planetarium, 1978-80, Carl Zeiss, Oberkochien Germany, 1968-80. Author: Planetarium: Window to the Universe, 1980, Planetarium Design and Operation, 1980. Mem. Internat. Planetarium Soc. (disting. svc. award, 1982), Pacific Planetarium Assn. (pres. 1968-69). Republican. Office: San Francisco State U Dept Astronomy 1600 Holloway Ave San Francisco CA 94132-1722

HAGBERG, CHARLES PAUL, compensation executive, human resources manager; b. Cleve., Dec. 24, 1934; s. Paul Leroy and Mary Virginia (Hartzel) H.; m. JoEll Lee McMurray, Apr. 10, 1965; children: Kevin, Kyle, Kelli. BS in Air. Transp. Engring., Purdue U., 1957. Engr. The Boeing Co. Aerospace div., Seattle, 1957-60, pers. supr., 1960-65, pers. mgr., 1965-78, compensation mgr., 1978-82; dir. compensation The Boeing Co. Corp. Hdqs., Seattle, 1982-90, v.p. compensation, 1990—. Mem. Aerospace Industries Assn. (compensation practice com. chair 1986-87). Republican. Office: The Boeing Co PO Box 3707 Seattle WA 98124

HAGE, STEPHEN JOHN, radiology administrator, consultant; b. Chgo., July 22, 1943; s. Steve and Irene (Lewandowski) H.; m. Constance Louise Simonis, June 10, 1967. AAS, YMCA Community Coll., Chgo., 1970. Registered radiol. tech. Staff tech. Highland Park (Ill.) Hosp., 1966-68; chief radiotherapy tech. VA Hines (Ill.) Hosp., 1968-70; chief radiology tech. Gottlieb Meml. Hosp., Melrose Park, Ill., 1970-71; radiology adminstr. S. Chgo. County Hosp., 1971-79; adminstrv. dir. radiology Cedars-Sinai Med. Ctr., Los Angeles, 1979—; cons. Computer Sci. Corp., El Segundo, Calif., 1983—. Contbr. articles to profl. jours. Served with USMC, 1961-64. Recipient 1st pl. Essay award Ill. State Soc. Radiol. Technicians, 1966. Mem. Am. Hosp. Radiology Adminstrs. (charter), Am. Soc. Radiol. Technologists, AAAS, Phi Theta Kappa. Home: 22115 Halsted St Chatsworth CA 91311-4027 Office: Cedars Sinai Med Ctr 8700 Beverly Blvd Los Angeles CA 90048

HAGEDORN, ROBERT, JR., state legislator, educator; b. Elizabeth City, N.C., Feb. 16, 1952; s. Robert L. and Lee M. (Bahlmann) H.; m. Ann Gardiner Stoddart, Nov. 24, 1975 (div. 1990); 1 child, Robert G. BS with honors, U. Colo., 1974; M in Urban Affairs, U. Colo., Denver, 1979; postgrad., U. Colo., 1990—. Reporter Aurora (Colo.) Sun, 1972-75; owner Pub. Rels./Printing, Denver, 1975-79; coll. rels. dir. Peru (Nebr.) State Coll., 1979-80; community rels. dir. Aurora Pub. Schs., 1980-83; account rep. Aspen Graphics, Denver, 1983-87; asst. govtl. rels. dir. Metro Wastewater Reclamation Dist., Denver, 1987-89; instr. Met. State Coll., Denver, 1990—; state rep. Colo.; cons., Aurora, 1989-92. Home: 11633 E 6th Pl Aurora CO 80010

HAGEN, EDNA MAE, medical nurse; b. Jasper, Ark., Nov. 30, 1932; d. Eugene and Dovie (Combs) Keef; m. Harry Hagen, Jan. 4, 1952; children: Catherine, Harry, Jr. ADN, Santa Barbara Coll., 1973. RN, Calif. Staff nurse Cottage Hosp., Santa Barbara, Calif., 1970-74; head nurse to pvt. physician L.A. Price, M.D., Inc., Santa Barbara, 1974—. Mem. U.S. Army Med. Corps, 1951-52. Mem. ANA, CNA.

HAGEN, KIRK DEE, mechanical engineer, educator; b. Ogden, Utah, July 12, 1953; s. Darius and Ellen Virginia (Hicks) H.; m. Jan Rowley, June 9, 1978; children: Kathryn, Jennifer, Alec, Daniel. BS in Physics, Weber State Coll., Ogden, 1977; MSME, Utah State U., 1981; PhD in Mech. Engring., U. Utah, 1989. Sr. engr. Hercules Aerospace, Magna, Utah, 1980-86; prin. engr. Unisys Corp., Salt Lake City, 1986-92; asst. prof. mech. engring. tech. Weber State U., Ogden, 1993—; adj. prof. engring. Salt Lake C.C., Salt Lake City, 1991-93. Contbr. articles to profl. jours. Blazer scoutleader Boy Scouts Am., Centerville, Utah, 1990-91. Mem. ASME, Am. Soc. Engring. Edn., Utah Acad. Scis., Arts and Letters. Mem. LDS Ch. Home: 582 North 220 East Centerville UT 84014 Office: Weber State U Ogden UT 84408

HAGENBUCH, JOHN JACOB, investment banker; b. Park Forest, Ill., May 31, 1951; s. David Brown and Jean Iline (Reeves) H.; children: Henry, Hunter, Hilary. AB magna cum laude, Princeton U., 1974; MBA, Stanford U., 1978. Assoc., Salomon Bros., N.Y.C., 1978-80, v.p., San Francisco, 1980-85; gen. ptnr. Hellman & Friedman, 1985—; bd. dirs. Am. Pres. Cos., Great Am. Investment & Mgmt., Inc., Eagle Industries Inc., Story First Comm. Inc. Bd. govs. San Francisco Symphony, Town Sch. for Boys. Mem. Burlingame Country Club, Pacific-Union Club, Calif. Tennis Club, Villa Taverna Club. Office: Hellman & Friedman 1 Maritime Plz San Francisco CA 94111-3404

HAGENBUCH, RODNEY DALE, stock brokerage house executive; b. Saxville, Wis.; s. Herbert Jenkin and Minnie Leona (Hayward) Hagenbuch; children: Kris, Beth, Patricia; m. LaVerne Julia Scoonover, Sept. 1, 1956. BS, Mich. State U., 1980. Cert. fin. mgr. Designer Olds div. Gen. Motors, Lansing, Mich., 1960-66; institutional account exec. Merrill Lynch, Lansing, 1966-75, institutional mgr., 1975-80; sales mgr. Merrill Lynch, Columbus, Ohio, 1980-82; sr. resident v.p. Merrill Lynch, Tacoma, 1982-93, L.A., 1993—. Bd. dirs. Tacoma Club, 1989-93, treas. 1990, pres. 1993; adv. bd. Charles Wright, 1989-93; mem. econ. devel. bd. City of Tacoma, 1986-93, chmn. 1987-88; pres. Downtown Tacoma Assn., 1986; chmn. Corp. Coun. for the Arts, 1986; pres. Tacoma Symphony, 1988; chmn. Human Resources Commn., Meridian Twp., 1972-74, Meridian Planning Commn., Lansing, 1964-70, Meridian Police and Fire Com., Lansing, 1964-70; pres. adv. bd. U. Wash., Tacoma, chmn., 1992; mem. State Wash. Arts Stabilization Bd., Tacoma Art Mus. Bd., sec. 1992; legis. chmn. N.W. Securities Industry Assn. Mem. Tacoma C. of C. (bd. dirs.), Forward Washington (bd. dirs.). Home: 3627 Dixie Canyon Ave Sherman Oaks CA 91403

HAGENS, WILLIAM JOSEPH, state official, public health educator; b. Bay City, Mich., June 3, 1942; s. Francis Bernard and Lillian May (O'Neill) H.; m. Noel Scantlebury, Apr. 15, 1967; children: Clara O'Neill, Nicholas Barlow. BA, Saginaw Valley Coll., 1969; MA, Wayne State U., 1971; PhD, U. Wash., 1993. Mem. adj. faculty Wayne State U., Detroit, 1971; VISTA vol. Pierce County Legal Assistance, Tacoma, 1971-73; sr. policy analyst Wash. Ho. of Reps., Olympia, 1974—; instr. Pacific Luth. U., Tacoma, 1979-81; clin. prof. Sch. Pub. Health, U. Wash., Seattle, 1984—, mem. vis. com. Sch. Nursing, 1993; mem. health policy project George Washington U., Washington, 1985—; bd. dirs. Area Health Edn. Ctr., Seattle, 1988-90; mem. steering com. Nat. Acad. State Health Policy, 1990—; mem. adv. com. Wash. State Ctr. Health Stats. Contbg. author: Analyzing Poverty Policy, 1975. Participant AIDS symposium Pasteur Inst., Paris, 1987. Recipient Pres. award Wash. State Pub. Health Assn., 1986; NIMH fellow, 1979, WHO internat. travel fellow, 1991. Mem. Am. Pub. Health Assn., Am. Polit. Sci. Assn., Policy Studies Orgn., English Speaking Union, World Affairs Coun., Pi Sigma Alpha. Home: 3214 N 27th St Tacoma WA 98407-6208 Office: Wash Ho of Reps MS AS-33 Olympia WA 98504

HAGENSTEIN, WILLIAM DAVID, consulting forester; b. Seattle, Mar. 8, 1915; s. Charles William and Janet (Finigan) H.; m. Ruth Helen Johnson, Sept. 2, 1940 (dec. 1979); m. Jean Kraemer Edson, June 16, 1980. BS in Forestry, U. Wash., 1938; MForestry, Duke, 1941. Registered profl. engr., Wash., Oreg. Field aid in entomology U.S. Dept. Agr., Hat Creek, Calif., 1938; logging supt. and engr. Eagle Logging Co., Sedro-Woolley, Wash., 1939; tech. foreman U.S. Forest Svc., North Bend, Wash., 1940; forester West Coast Lumbermen's Assn., Seattle and Portland, Oreg., 1941-43, 45-49; sr. forester FEA, South and Central Pacific Theaters of War and Costa Rica, 1943-45; mgr. Indsl. Forestry Assn., Portland, 1949-80; exec. v.p. Indsl. Forestry Assn., 1956-80, hon. dir., 1980-87; pres. W.D. Hagenstein and Assocs., Inc., Portland, 1980—; H.R. MacMillan lectr. forestry U. B.C., 1952, 77; Benson Meml. lectr. U. Mo., 1966; S.J. Hall lectr. indsl. forestry U. Calif. at Berkeley, 1973; cons. forest engr. USN, Philippines, 1952, Coop. Housing Found., Belize, 1986; mem. U.S. Forest Products Trade Mission, Japan, 1968; del. VII World Forestry Congress, Argentina, 1972, VIII Congress, Indonesia, 1978; mem. U.S. Forestry Study Team, West Germany, 1974; mem. sec. Interior's Oreg.-and Calif. Multiple Use Adv. Bd., 1975-76; trustee Wash. State Forestry Conf., 1948-92, Keep Oreg. Green Assn., 1957—, v.p., 1970-71, pres., 1972-73; adv. trustee Keep Wash. Green Assn., 1957—; co-founder, dir. World Forestry Ctr., 1965-89, v.p., 1965-79; hon. Dir. for Life, 1990. Author: (with Wackerman and Michell) Harvesting Timber Crops, 1966; Assoc. editor: Jour. Forestry, 1946-53; columnist Wood Rev., 1978-82; contbr. numerous articles to profl. jours. Trustee Oreg. Mus. Sci. and Industry, 1968-73. Served with USNR, 1933-37. Recipient Hon. Alumnus award U. Wash. Foresters Alumni Assn., 1965, Forest Mgmt. award Nat. Forest Products Assn., 1968, Western Forestry award Western Forestry and Conservation Assn., 1972, 79, Gifford Pinchot medal for 50 yrs. Outstanding Svc. Soc. Am. Foresters, 1987, Charles W. Ralston award Duke Sch. Forestry, 1988. Fellow Soc. Am. Foresters (mem. coun. 1958-63, pres. 1966-69, Golden Membership award 1989); mem. Am. Forestry Assn. (life, hon. v.p. 1966-69, 74-92, William B. Greeley Forestry award 1990), Commonwealth Forestry Assn. (life), Internat. Soc. Tropical Foresters, Portland C. of C. (forestry com. 1949-79, chmn. 1960-62), Nat. Forest Products Assn. (forestry adv. com. 1949-80, chmn. 1972-74, 78-80), West Coast Lumbermen's Assn. (v.p. 1969-79), David Douglas Soc. Western N. Am., Lang Syne Soc., Hoo Hoo Club, Xi Sigma Pi (outstanding alumnus Alpha chpt. 1973). Republican. Home: 3062 SW Fairmount Blvd Portland OR 97201-1439 Office: Ste 803 921 SW Washington St Portland OR 97205

HAGER, EUGENE RANDOLPH, mechanical engineer; b. Omaha, Aug. 3, 1930; s. Eugene Hayes and Annabelle Frances (Kise) H.; m. Pauline Papacalos, Nov. 17, 1956; children: Christopher Randolph, Barry Eugene. BSME, San Diego State U., 1968, MSME, 1971. Registered profl. mech. engr., Calif., S.C. Design engr. Atomics Internal., L.A., 1954-57; prin. engr. Gen. Atomics, San Diego, 1957-89; owner Engring. Connections, La Jolla, Calif., 1989—. Patentee remotely operable vacuum port closure, 1985. Mem. ASME, La Jolla Profl. Men's Soc. (pres. 1985, v.p. 1992), Am. Nuclear Soc. Home and Office: Engring Connections 2322 Bahia Dr La Jolla CA 92037

HAGERTY, KIM LOUISE, lawyer; b. Traverse City, Mich., Dec. 30, 1956; d. Frank Clayton and Louise (Kucera) H.; m. James Randy Bull, May 12, 1978 (div. July 1986). BA magna cum laude, Albion Coll., 1978; JD, U. San Francisco, 1981. Bar: Nev. 1982, Calif. 1982, U.S. Ct. Appeals (9th cir.) Calif. 1988. Law clk. to Hon. Howard D. McKibben Ninth Jud. Dist. Ct. Nev., Minden, Nev., 1981-82; ptnr. Grumer & Hagerty, Inc., Incline Village, Nev., 1982-89; pvt. practice atty. Incline Village, 1989—; dir. Warner Enterprises, Incline Village, 1983—; legal cons., dir. Hagerty Marine Ins., Traverse City, 1984—, Hagerty Classic Auto Ins., Traverse City, 1991—; arbitrator Incline Village Justice Ctr., 1990—. Trustee Sierra Nevada Coll., Incline Village, 1984—, chmn. bd. trustees, 1991—. Mem. Nev. Bar Assn., Calif. Bar Assn. Office: 901 Tahoe Blvd Incline Village NV 89451

HAGERTY, POLLY MARTIEL, banker; b. Joliet, Ill., Aug. 17, 1946; d. George Albert and Gene Alice (Roush) Jerabek; m. Theodore John Hagerty, Feb. 12, 1972. BS in Elem. Edn., Midland Luth. Coll., 1968; MEd in Early Childhood Edn., U. Ill., 1977; MBA in Fin., U. Tex., 1986. Elem. tchr. Madison Heights (Mich.) Sch. Dist., 1968-70, Taft Sch. Dist., Lockport, Ill., 1970-72; systems clerk U.S. Army, The Pentagon, Washington, 1972-74; psychology aide Psychology Clinic U. Ill., Urbana, 1974-75; elem. tchr. Champaign (Ill.) Sch. Dist., 1975-77; with recruitment Standard Oil of Ohio, Cleve., 1977-78; v.p. NCNB Texas-Houston, 1981-88, Citibank, Tucson, 1988-92. Pres. Christus Victor Luth. Ch., League City, Tex., 1985-88, Luth. Ch. of the Foothills, Tuscson, 1990—. Recipient Golden Circle Sales and Svc. award, 1991. Mem. NAFE, U. Ill. Alumni Club, Longhorn Assn. Republican. Lutheran. Home: 439 St Andrews Marble Falls TX 78654

HAGGARD, JOEL EDWARD, lawyer; b. Portland, Oreg., Oct. 10, 1939; s. Henry Edward and Kathryn Shirley (O'Leary) H.; m. Mary Katherine Daley, June 8, 1968; children: Kevin E., Maureen E., Cristin E. BSME, U. Notre Dame, 1961; M in Nuclear Engring., U. Okla., 1963; JD, U. Wash., 1971. Bar: Wash. 1971, U.S. Dist. Ct. (we. dist.) Wash. 1971, U.S. Ct. Appeals (9th cir.) 1971, U.S. Supreme Ct. 1971. Nuclear engr. Westinghouse Corp. Bettis Atomic Power Lab., Pitts., 1963-67; research engr. aerospace div. The Boeing Co., Seattle, 1968; engr., mgmt. cons. King County Dept. Pub. Works, Seattle, 1969-71; assoc. Houghton, Cluck, Coughlin & Riley, Seattle, 1971-74, ptnr., 1975-76; pvt. practice law Seattle, 1977, 85—; ptnr. Haggard, Tousley & Brain, Seattle, 1978-84; judge marriage tribunal, Archdiocese of Seattle, 1975-90; chmn. Columbia River Interstate Compact Commn., 1975—; arbitrator King County Superior Ct., 1986—. Contbr. articles to profl. jours. Bd. trustees, mem. exec. com., past sec. Seattle Symphony. Mem. ABA, Wash. Bar Assn. (past chmn. environ. law sect., mem. fee arbitration com., past mem. rules of profl. conduct com., mem. fee arbitration panel), Seattle-King County Bar Assn., Am. Pub. Works Assn. Clubs: Rainier, Wash. Athletic, Astoria Golf and Country, Magnolia Community (past. pres., bd. dirs.). Office: 1200 5th Ave 1515 IBM Bldg Seattle WA 98101

HAGGERTY, CHARLES A., electronics executive. Student, U. St. Thomas. With IBM, 1964-92; pres., COO Western Digital Corp., Irvine, Calif., 1992—. Office: Western Digital Corp PO Box 19665 Irvine CA 92713*

HAGINO, GERALD TAKAO, state senator; b. Puunene, Maui, Hawaii, July 31, 1949; s. Masao and Lynette (Higashida) H.; m. Cynthia H. Haraguchi, June 30, 1973; children: Steven, Danielle, Sharyse. BS in Biology, U. Hawaii, 1971. Operator Hawaiian Ind. Refinery, 1972-88; researcher Oceanic Inst., 1988—. mem. Hawaii Senate, 1982—. Bd. dirs. West Oahu (Hawaii) YMCA; active Wahiawa Community and Businessmen's Assn. Mem. Lions. Democrat. Office: Office State Senate State Capitol Rm 206 Honolulu HI 96813

HAGLUND, BRUCE THADD, architectural educator; b. Muskegon, Mich., Nov. 8, 1946; s. Jack Andrew and Irene Tres (Lutrey); m. Susan Ellen Weiner, Nov. 19, 1978 (div. 1982); m. Patricia Joy Egashira, Aug. 2, 1987. BS in Math., Ill. Inst. Tech., 1968; MArch, U. Oreg., 1982. Programmer/analyst Planning Rsch. Corp., San Diego, San Jose, Calif., 1972-77, Computervision Corp., Santa Clara, Calif., 1977-78; assoc. prof. U. Idaho, Moscow, 1982—. Author: (with others) Simulating Daylighting with Architectural Models, 1987, Insideout Design Procedures for Passive Environmental Technologies, 2d edit., 1991; contbr. rsch. papers to profl. jours. Advisor Bonneville Power Adminstrn. Energy Smart Tng. Adv. Group, Northwest region, 1989—. Lt. USN, 1968-72. Grantee Washington Water Power Co., Spokane, Wash., 1984-87, Northwest Area Found., 1989, Pend Oreille County, Wash., 1990, Bonneville Power Adminstrn., 1991-92. Mem. Soc. Bldg. Sci. Educators (sec.-treas. 1985, chair 1987, bd. dirs. 1986-88), Daylighting Network N.Am. (bd. dirs. 1987-90), Am. Solar Energy Soc. Office: U Idaho Dept Architecture Moscow ID 83843-6781

HAGSTROM, DAVID ALAN, leadership academy director; b. Oak Park, Ill., Apr. 28, 1935; s. Clarence Edward and Frances (Jackson) H.; m. Nancy Booth (div. 1985); children: Susan Janan, Bruce David; m. Karen Noordhoff, May 11, 1985. BA, Grinnell Coll., 1957; MA Teaching, Harvard U., 1958; EdD, U. Ill., 1966. Cert. tchr., adminstr., Ill., Wis., Alaska. Tchr., sch. adminstr. Evanston (Ill.) Pub. Schs., 1958-75; prof. Nat. Coll. Edn., Evanston, 1975-83, U. Alaska, Juneau, Fairbanks, 1983-91; dir. Alaska Ctr. for Ednl. Leadership, Fairbanks, 1992—; co-owner New Viewpoint Educators, Fairbanks, 1990—. Contbr. articles to profl. ednl. jours. Recipient Next Century Schs. award Nabisco Found., 1990, A+ Educator award U.S. Dept. Edn., 1992. Mem. Alaska Assn. Supervision and Curriculum Devel. (pres. elect 1993—). Democrat. Episcopalian. Home: 1350 Viewpoint Dr Fairbanks AK 99709 Office: Alaska Ctr for Ednl Leadership 3750 Geist Rd Fairbanks AK 99709

HAGUE, ALAN DONALD, broadcasting executive; b. Salt Lake City, Aug. 17, 1951; s. Donald Victor and Lorna (Dangerfield) H.; m. Lynnae June Larsen, Apr. 13, 1969 (div. Dec. 1973); 1 child, Todd; m. Peggy Lee Hoyt, July 10, 1975; children: Mandy, Brad, Emilee, Michael. Student, U. Utah, 1969-70. Disc jockey various radio stas., Salt Lake City, 1966-77; program dir. Sta. KRSP, Salt Lake City, 1969-78, news dir., 1973-74, ops. mgr., 1978-83, exec. v.p., 1978—, gen. mgr., 1983—; exec. v.p. Carlson Communications Internat., 1983—, Sta. KUSW, Salt Lake City, 1987—. Vice chmn. Greater Utah March of Dimes, Salt Lake City, 1980-85, chmn., 1985-88, vol. nat. task force. Mem. Nat. Assn. Broadcasters, Utah Broadcasters Assn. (v.p. 1986-87, pres. 1987-89), Salt Lake Market Broadcasters (pres. 1980-81). Mormon. Home: 8029 Danish Oaks Dr Sandy UT 84093-6583 Office: Sta KRSP-AM-FM 1130 W 5200 S PO Box 57760 Salt Lake City UT 84157-0760

HAGUE, HARLAN HUGH, historian; b. Ft. Worth, Jan. 23, 1932; s. Stanley Wilton and Maggie May (Faires) H.; m. Carol Margaret Jackson,

July 16, 1960; children: Cary Lynn, Leslie Margaret, Merrilee Catherine, Jennifer Michelle. BBA, Baylor U., 1954; MBA, U. Tex., 1960; MA, U. of the Pacific, 1968; PHD, U. Nev., 1974. Contr. Whitehouse Plastics, Ft. Worth, 1960; traffic mgr. Pacific Telephone, San Francisco, 1960-64; market rschr. Kaiser Jeep Internat., Oakland, Calif., 1964; prof. history San Joaquin Delta Coll., Stockton, Calif., 1964-92; cons. NEH, Washington, 1975-79. Author: Road to California, 1978; Contributor: Pioneer Trails West, 1985; co-author: Thomas O. Larkin, 1990 (Caroline Bancroft prize, 1990); contbr. articles to profl. jours.; book rev. editor Pacific Historian, 1985-87; mem. editorial bd. The Californians, 1986-89. Head local orgn. in campaign against nuclear power, 1970's; promoter pro-environ. candidates and initiatives; mem. adv. bd. Holt-Atherton Ctr. for Western Studies, U. of the Pacific, 1985-87, mem. program com. Calif. History Inst., 1991-93. Lt. USNR, 1954-60. Summer grantee NEH, U. Oreg., 1975, 80, rsch. grantee Sourisseau Acad., 1986, Huntington Libr., San Marino, Calif., 1987, Haynes Found., 1990. Mem. Western History Assn. (nominating com. 1991-93, chmn. 1992-93), Calif. Hist. Soc. (trustee 1989—, chair program com. 1992), San Joaquin County Hist. Soc. (publs. com. 1991—), Am. Soc. for Environ. History, Wilderness Soc., Am. Farmland Trust, Planning and Conservation League, Habitat for Humanity, Sierra Club. Democrat. Home: 2462 Sheridan Way Stockton CA 95207

HAHN, BETTY, artist, photographer, educator; b. Chgo., Oct. 11, 1940; d. Eugene Joseph and Esther Josephine (Krueger) H.; widowed. A.B., Ind. U., 1963, M.F.A., 1966. Asst. prof. photography Rochester (N.Y.) Inst. Tech., 1969-75; prof. art U. N.Mex., Albuquerque, 1976—. One-woman shows include Smithsonian Instn., Washington, 1969, Ctr. Photographic Studies, Louisville, 1971, Focus Gallery, San Francisco, 1974, Sandstone Gallery, Rochester, N.Y., 1978, Blue Sky Gallery, Portland, Oreg., 1978, Susan Spiritus Gallery, Newport Beach, Calif., 1977, 82, Witkin Gallery, N.Y.C., 1973, 79, Washington Project for the Arts, 1980, Ctr. Creative Photography, Tucson, 1981, Columbia Coll. Gallery, Chgo., 1982, Port Washington Pub. Library, N.Y., 1984, Mus. Fine Arts, Mus. N.Mex, Santa Fe, 1986, Lehigh U., 1988, U. Mass., Amherst, 1989, Andrew Smith Gallery, Santa Fe, 1991. Named Honored Educator, Soc. for Photog. Edn., 1984; Nat. Endowment Arts grantee, 1977-78, 82-83; N.Y. State Council Arts grantee, 1976. Mem. Soc. Photog. Edn., Coll. Art Assn., Evidence Photographers Internat. Council. Office: Univ N Mex Art Dept Albuquerque NM 87131

HAHN, ELLIOTT JULIUS, lawyer; b. San Francisco, Dec. 9, 1949; s. Leo Wolf and Sherry Marion (Portnoy) H; m. Toby Rose Mallen; children: Kara Rebecca, Brittany Atira Mallen, Michael Mallen. BA cum laude, U. Pa., 1971, JD, 1974; LLM, Columbia U., 1980. Bar: N.J. 1974, Calif. 1976, D.C. 1978, U.S. Dist. Ct. N.J. 1974, U.S. Dist. Ct. (cen. dist.) Calif. 1976, U.S. Supreme Ct. 1980. Assoc. von Maltitz, Derenberg, Kunin & Janssen, N.Y.C., 1974-75; law clk. L.A. County Superior Ct., 1975-76; atty. Atlantic Richfield Co., L.A., 1976-79; prof. Summer in Tokyo program Santa Clara Law Sch., 1981-83; assoc. prof. law Calif. Western Sch. Law, San Diego, 1980-85; atty. Morgan, Lewis & Bockius, L.A., 1985-87; assoc. Whitman & Ransom, L.A., 1987-88, ptnr., 1989—; adj. prof. law Southwestern U. Sch. Law, 1986—, Pepperdine U. Law Sch., 1986—. Author: Japanese Business Law and the Legal System, 1984; contbr. chpt. on Japan to The World Legal Ency.; contbr. articles to Law Rev. Vice-chmn. San Diego Internat. Affairs Bd., 1981-85; bd. dirs. San Diego-Yokohama Sister City Soc., 1982-85, L.A.-Nagoya Sister City Soc., 1986—; mem. master planning com. City of Rancho Palos Verdes, Calif., 1989-91; advisor, exec. com. Calif. Internat. Law Sect., 1990-91, appointee exec. com., 1991—, vice-chmn., 1992—; appointee, trustee Palos Verdes Libr. Dist., 1993—. Vis. scholar Nihon U., Tokyo, 1982; vis. lectr. Internat. Christian U., Tokyo, 1982. Mem. ABA, State Bar of Calif., L.A. County Bar Assn. (bd. dirs. internat. sect., exec. com. Internat. Legal Sec. 1987—, appointee pacific rim com. 1990—, chmn. 1991-92), Assn. Asian Studies, U. Pa. Alumni Club (pres. San Diego chpt. 1982, pres. coun. Phila., 1983), Anti-Defamation League, State Bar Calif. (advisor exec. com., internat. sec. 1990-91, mem. exec. com., internat. sec. 1991—, vice-chmn. 1992—), Japanese-Am. Soc. Legal Studies (book rev. editor Seattle 1983-85). Jewish. Office: Whitman & Ransom 633 W 5th St Los Angeles CA 90071-2005

HAHN, ERWIN LOUIS, physicist, educator; b. Sharon, Pa., June 9, 1921; s. Israel and Mary (Weiss) H.; m. Marian Ethel Failing, Apr. 8, 1944 (dec. Sept. 1978); children: David L., Deborah A., Katherine L.; m. Natalie Woodford Hodgson, Apr. 12, 1980. B.S., Juniata Coll., 1943, D.Sc., 1966; M.S., U. Ill., 1947, Ph.D., 1949; D.Sc., Purdue U., 1975. Asst. Purdue U., 1943-44; research assoc. U. Ill., 1950; NRC fellow Stanford, 1950-51, instr., 1951-52; research physicist Watson IBM Lab., N.Y.C., 1952-55; assoc. Columbia U., 1952-55; faculty U. Calif., Berkeley, 1955—, faculty rsch. lectr., 1959, prof. physics, 1961—, assoc. prof., then prof. Miller Inst. for Basic Research, 1958-59, 66-67, 85-86; vis. fellow Brasenose Coll., Oxford (Eng.) U., 1981-82, Eastman vis. prof., 1988-89; cons. Office Naval Rsch., Stanford, 1950-52, AEC, 1955—; spl. cons. USN, 1959; adv. panel mem. Nat. Bur. Standards, Radio Standards div., 1961-64; mem. NAS/NRC com. on basic rsch.; advisor to U.S. Army Rsch. Office, 1967-69; faculty rsch. lectr. U. Calif., Berkeley, 1979. Author: (with T.P. Das) Nuclear Quadrupole Resonance Spectroscopy, 1958. Served with USNR, 1944-46. Recipient prize Internat. Soc. Magnetic Resonance, 1971, award Humboldt Found., Germany, 1977, Alumni Achievement award Juniata Coll., 1986, citation U. Calif., Berkeley, 1991; co-winner prize in physics Wolf Found., 1984; named to Calif. Inventor Hall of Fame, 1984; Guggenheim fellow, 1961-62, 69-70, fellow NSF, 1961-62; vis. fellow Brasenose Coll., Oxford U., 1969-70, life hon. fellow, 1984—. Fellow AAAS, Am. Phys. Soc. (past mem. exec. com. div. solid state physics, Oliver E. Buckley prize 1971); mem. NAS (co-recipient Comstock prize in electricity, magnetism and radiation 1993), Slovenian Acad. Scis. and Arts (fgn.), French Acad. Scis. (fgn. assoc.). Home: 69 Stevenson Ave Berkeley CA 94708-1732 Office: U Calif Dept Physics 367 Birge Hall Berkeley CA 94720

HAHN, HAROLD THOMAS, physical chemist, chemical engineer; b. N.Y.C., May 31, 1924; s. Gustave Hahn and Lillie Martha (Thomas) H.; m. Bennie Joyce Turney, Sept. 5, 1948; children: Anita Karen, Beverly Sharon, Carol Linda, Harold Thomas Jr. Student, Hofstra U., 1941-43; BSChemE, Columbia U., 1943-44; PhD in Chemistry, U. Tex., 1950-53. Chem. engr. Manhattan Dist. U.S. Army, Los Alamos, N.Mex., 1945-47; chem. engr. U. Calif., Los Alamos, 1947-50; sr. scientist Gen. Electric Co., Hanford, Wash., 1953-58; sect. chief, chem. research dept. Phillips Petroleum Co., Idaho Falls, Idaho, 1958-64; sr. staff scientist Lockheed Missiles & Space Co., Palo Alto, Calif., 1964-92; private cons., 1992—. Contbr. articles to profl. jours.; patentee in field. Pres. Edgemont Gardens PTA, Idaho Falls, 1963-64; commr. cub scout div. Stanford area council Boy Scouts Am., Palo Alto, 1973-76, also cubmaster pack 36, 1973-80, chmn. troops 36 and 37, 1975-77; mem. adminstrv. bd. Los Altos Meth. Ch. Served to col. U.S. Army, 1944-46, with res., 1946-84, col. res. ret. Humble Oil Co. fellow, 1952, Naval Bur. Ordnance fellow, 1953. Fellow Am. Inst. Chemists; mem. Magnetics Soc. IEEE (elected sen. mem.), Calif. Acad. Scis., Internat. Platform Assn., Am. Chem. Soc., AIAA, Sigma Xi, Phi Lambda Upsilon, Kappa Rho. Republican. Home and Office: 661 Teresi Ln Los Altos CA 94024-4162

HAHN, HELENE B., motion picture company executive; b. N.Y.C.. BA, Hofstra U.; JD, Loyola U., Calif., 1975. Bar: Calif. 1975. V.p. bus. affairs Paramount Pictures Corp., L.A., sr. v.p. bus. affairs, 1983-84; sr. v.p. bus. and legal Walt Disney Studios, Burbank, Calif., 1984-87, exec. v.p., 1987—. Recipient Frontrunner award in bus. Sara Lee Corp., 1991, Big Sisters Achievement award, 1992, Clairol Mentor award, 1993.

HAHN, JOAN CHRISTENSEN, drama educator, travel agent; b. Kemmerer, Wyo., May 9, 1933; d. Roy and Bernice (Pringle) Wainwright; m. Milton Angus Christensen, Dec. 29, 1952 (div. Oct. 1, 1971); children: Randall M., Carla J. Christensen Tesadale; m. Charles Henry Hahn, Nov. 15, 1972. BS, Brigham Young U., 1965. Profl. ballroom dancer, 1951-59; travel dir. E.T. World Travel, Salt Lake City, 1969—; tchr. drama Payson High Sch., Utah, 1965-71, Cottonwood High Sch., Salt Lake City, 1971—; dir. Performing European Tours, Salt Lake City, 1969-76; dir. Broadway theater tours, 1976—. Bd. dirs. Salem City Salem Days, Utah, 1965-75; regional dir. dance Latter-day Saints Ch., 1954-72. Named Best Dir. High Sch. Musicals, Green Sheet Newspapers, 1977, 82, 84, 90, Utah's Speech Educator of Yr., 1990, 91, named to Nat. Hall of Fame Ednl. Theatre Assn., 1991; recipient 1st place award Utah State Drama Tournament, 1974, 77, 78, 89, 90, 91, Tchr. of Yr. award Cottonwood High Sch., 1989-90, Limelight award, 1982, Exemplary Performance in teaching theater arts Granite Sch. Dist., Salt Lake City, 1982; named to the Nat. Hall of Fame, Ednl. Theatre Assn., 1991. Mem. Internat. Thespian Soc. (sponsor 1968—, internat. dir. 1982-84, trustee 1978-84), Utah Speech Arts Assn. (pres. 1976-78, 88-90), NEA, Utah Edn. Assn., Granite Edn. Assn., Profl. Travel Agts. Assn., Utah High Sch. Activities Assn. (drama rep. 1972-76), AAUW (pres. 1972-74). Republican. Mormon. Avocations: reading; travel; dancing. Home: 685 S 1st E PO Box 36 Salem UT 84653-0036 Office: Cottonwood High Sch 5715 S 1300 E Salt Lake City UT 84121-1099

HAHN, JULIE MAYA, college counselor; b. Pitts., July 21, 1943; d. Saul and Louise (Ritterskamp) Rosenzweig; m. Robert Edward Hahn, Oct. 12, 1968; children: Eric Russell, Daniel Roland. BA, Washington U., St. Louis, 1965; MEd, U. Rochester, 1970. Counselor Santa Rosa (Calif.) Jr. Coll., 1978—; owner Countdown to Coll. Author: Have You Done Your Homework?, 1985. Mem. steering com. Friends of Kagoshima, Santa Rosa, 1990, Sonoma County Forum Bd. Mem. AAUW (v.p. Santa Rosa chpt. 1990), Sonoma County Forum (program chair 1992). Home: 1657 El Camino Way Santa Rosa CA 95404-3046 Office: 1501 Mendocino Ave Santa Rosa CA 95401-4332

HAHN, MARK STEPHEN, computer security specialist, educator; b. L.A., June 13, 1953; s. Lester Curtis and Sandra Donelen (Bailey) H. BS in Computer Sci., Calif. Polytech. State U., 1976. Programmer Gesco Corp., Fresno, Calif., 1976-80; security analyst Northrop, El Segundo, Calif., 1980, SKK, Inc., Rosemont, Ill., 1980-82; security specialist Gesco Corp., Fresno, 1982-83, mktg. support specialist, 1983-84; computer security specialist Candle Corp., L.A., 1984-88, 91-92, instr., 1988-91; security cons. Coles Myer, Ltd., Melbourne, Australia, 1986; sr. cons. Vanguard Integrity Profls., Orange, Calif., 1992—. Contbr. articles to profl. jours. Mem. EDP Auditors Assn., Computer Sci. Inst., Alpha Epsilon Pi (chpt. pres. 1975, bd. govs. 1975, Outstanding Scribe 1974). Home: 11684 Ventura Blvd # 895 Studio City CA 91604-2652

HAHN, ROBERT GREGORY, communications systems executive, filmmaker; b. Omaha, July 10, 1948; s. Norman Louis and Diana Zelma (Lagman) H. BA in Communications, U. Pa., 1970, Cert. in Microbiol. Engring., 1972. Prin. Biologia Lab., Santa Fe, N.Mex., 1971-78; pres. Travel Svc. Everywhere, Santa Fe, Ft. Worth, 1978-85; pres., chmn. Tropic Seas Rsch. Inc., 1983—; rsch. assoc. Space Biospheres Ventures, Oracle, Ariz., 1986-88, dir. communications systems, 1989—, dir. mktg., 1988-91; bd. dirs. Decisions Team Ltd., Travel Svc. Everywhere, Oceans Expdns. Inc., Inst. of Ecotechnics, co-founder; pres. Inst. of Ecotechnics, London, 1980-84 (scientific chief Amazon Expdn., 1980-82); expdn. chief Around the Tropic World Expdn., 1983-86. Co-dir. (film series) Journeys to Other Worlds, 1989; inventor, co-inventor Microbial Plant Root Treatment, 1974, Explorers Plant Lab., 1991; freelance photgrapher, 1962—; photographer UPI, AP 1967-70; contbr. articles to profl. jours. Mem. ecotourism com. Ariz. Office of Tourism, Phoenix, 1990-91. Am. Chem. Soc./Nat. Sci. Found. grantee, 1965; named High Chief Royal Family of Western Samoa, 1984. Fellow Royal Geographical Soc. (founding mem. rainforest club), Explorers Club; mem. Sci. Exploration Soc. (founding mem.), Internat. Soc. of Ethnopharmacology. Home: PO Box 689 Oracle AZ 85623-0689 Office: Space Biospheres Ventures PO Box 689 Oracle AZ 85623

HAIG, DAVID M., property and investment management specialist; b. New Rochelle, N.Y., May 20, 1951; s. Alexander Salusbury and Joan (Damon) H.; m. Myrna B. Murdoch, Oct. 1, 1983. Student, Marlboro Coll., 1974. Trustee Estate of S.M. Damon, Honolulu, 1982—; bd. dirs. First Hawaiian, Inc., First Hawaiian Bank, Honolulu. Trustee Hawaii Pacific Coll., Honolulu, 1988; bd. dirs. YMCA Met. Honolulu, 1985—, YMCA USA, Chgo., 1990—, Hawaii Foodbank Inc., Honolulu, 1987—, Aloha United Way, 1990—. Mem. Oahu Country Club, Waialae Country Club, Rotary. Office: 165 S King St Ste 1215 Honolulu HI 96813-3526

HAIG, PIERRE VAHE, radiation oncologist, educator; b. Beirut, Lebanon, Sept. 24, 1917; came to U.S., 1922; s. Bahadrian B. and Helen (Kaloustian) H.; m. Alice Jernazian, Jan. 1, 1948; children: Helen, Mari, Theodore. AB, Occidental Coll., 1938; MD, U. So. Calif., 1943. Diplomate Am. Bd. Radiology. Intern Los Angeles (Calif.) County Hosp., 1942-43, resident radiology, 1946-49, chief physician radiation oncology and nuclear medicine, 1950-67; radiation oncologist Kaiser Permanente Med. Group, L.A., 1967-70; dir. radiation oncology St. Jude Med. Ctr., Fullerton, Calif., 1970-90; chmn. med. quality rev. com. Med. Bd. Calif., Orange County, 1984—; instr. to clin. prof. U. So. Calif., L.A., 1950-92; asst. clin. prof. to assoc. clin. prof. Loma Linda (Calif.) U., 1952-68; cons. in radiology Long Beach (Calif.) VA Hosp., 1952-79. Contbr. articles to profl. jours. Major AUS, 1943-46, ETO. Fellow Am. Coll. Radiology, L.A. Acad. Medicine; mem. AMA, Radiol. Soc. N.Am., Soc. Nuclear Medicine (emeritus), Monarch Bay Club, Phi Beta Kappa, Alpha Omega Alpha. Office: 220 Monarch Bay Dana Point CA 92629

HAIGH, STEPHEN GARY, software engineer; b. Leeds, Yorkshire, Eng., July 16, 1959; came to U.S., 1985; s. Douglas and Evelyn Alice (Crampton) H.; m. Ann Ruth Willcox, May 28, 1983; children: Megan, Jacob. BSc in Computer Engring., Teesside Poly., Eng., 1981; MBS, San Francisco State U., 1991. Contractor Phillips Internat. B.V., Eindhoven, The Netherlands, 1982-85, AT&T Bell Labs., Holmdel, N.J., 1985-89; software R & D mgr. Hitachi Am. Ltd., Brisbane, Calif., 1989-91, Cypress Semicondr., San Jose, Calif., 1991—. Patentee in field. Office: Cypress Semicondr 3901 N 1st St San Jose CA 95134

HAIGHT, TIMOTHY ROBINSON, editor; b. Hollywood, Calif., June 11, 1945; s. George and Thelma (Robinson) H.; m. Dara Gail Thornton, Aug. 4, 1984; children: Michael, Heather. BA, Stanford U., 1966, PhD, 1978. Asst. prof. U. Wis., Madison, 1978-83; new tech. mgr. Sta. WHA-TV, Madison, 1983-84; assoc. prof. Calif. State U., L.A., 1984-87; West coast bur. chief Communications Week, San Jose, Calif., 1987-90; editor at large Network Computing, San Jose, 1990-93, exec. editor features and opinion, 1993—. Co-author: The Mass Media, 1978; editor: Telecommunications Policy and the Citizen, 1979; contbr. articles to profl. jours. Office: Network Computing 1054 Saratoga-Sunnyvale Rd San Jose CA 95129

HAIGHT, WAYNE RICHARD, fisheries biologist, consultant; b. Kirkland, Wash., Mar. 14, 1960; s. Eugene Russell and Verona Olive (Garvie) H.; m. Cheryl Yvonne Cloutier, Apr. 28, 1991. BS, Western Wash. U., Bellingham, 1983; MS, U. Hawaii, 1989, postgrad., 1993—. Fisheries coord. Profish Internat., Seattle, 1984-86; rsch. asst. U. Hawaii, Honolulu, 1986-89; fisheries mgmt. biologist Point No Point Treaty Coun., Kingston, Wash., 1989-91; rsch. fishery biologist Nat. Marine Fisheries Svc., Honolulu, 1991—; marine biologist U.S. AID/RDA Internat., 1991—. Contbr. articles to profl. jours. Project officer Combined Fed. Campaign, Honolulu, 1992. Recipient Commendable Performance award NOAA, 1991, 92; grantee Nat. Undersea Rsch. Ctr., 1989, Nat. Seagrant Coll. Program, 1987. Mem. Am. Fisheries Soc., Western Soc. Naturalists, Soaring Soc. Am., Sigma Xi. Democrat. Episcopalian. Office: Nat Marine Fisheries Svc 2570 Dole St Honolulu HI 96822

HAILE, DAVID LEWIS, educator; b. Greensburg, Pa., Dec. 7, 1955; s. Walter Frank Sr. and Harriet Maygreen (Quarles) H. B. Music, St. Vincent Coll., 1978; M. Music, Duquesne U., 1987. Bass trombonist, artist in residence Foothills Brass Quintet, Blessed Sacrament Cathedral, Greensburg, 1982-83; freelance musician Greensburg, 1975-87; band instr. Immaculate Conception Sch., Irwin, Pa., 1980-87; prin. bass trombonist Am. Wind Symphony Orch., Pitts., 1984-87; band instr., gen. music tchr. St. Benedict the Moor Sch., Pitts., 1985, 87; freelance musician Las Vegas, Nev., 1987—; band instr. Cashman Mid. Sch., Clark County Sch. Dist., Las Vegas, 1987—. Named one of Outstanding Young Men of Am., 1987. Home: 1217 Norma Joyce Ln Las Vegas NV 89128 Office: Cashman Mid Sch 4622 W Desert Inn Rd Las Vegas NV 89102

HAILE, LAWRENCE BARCLAY, lawyer; b. Atlanta, Feb. 19, 1938; m. Ann Springer McCauley, March 28, 1984; children: Gretchen Vanderhoef, Eric McKenzie, Scott McAllister. B.A. in Econs, U. Tex., 1958, LL.B., 1961. Bar: Tex. 1961, Calif. 1962. Law clk. to U.S. Judge Joseph M. Ingraham, Houston, 1961-62; pvt. practice law San Francisco, 1962-67, L.A., 1967—; mem. firm Federman, Gridley, Gradwohl, Flaherty & Haile, L.A., 1991—; instr. UCLA Civil Trial Clinics, 1974, 76; lectr. law Calif. Continuing Edn. of Bar, 1973-74, 80-89; mem. nat. panel arbitrators Am. Arbitration Assn., 1965—. Assoc. editor: Tex. Law Rev, 1960-61; Contbr. articles profl. publs. Mem. State Bar Calif., Tex., U.S. Supreme Ct. Bar Assn., Internat. Assn. Property Ins. Counsel (founding mem., pres. 1980), Phi Delta Phi, Delta Sigma Rho. Club: Vintage Auto Racing Assn. (bd. dirs.). Office: Bldg 3110 2029 Century Park E Los Angeles CA 90067-3017

HAILE, MARCUS ALFRED, chemistry educator; b. Haviland, Kans., Oct. 14, 1930; s. William Oral and Myrna May (Stotts) H.; m. Lynne Helene Hunsucker, Mar. 20, 1964; children: Marta Helene, Cavan William. BS, Pepperdine U., 1955; Master, U. No. Iowa, 1968. Cert. secondary tchr., Calif. Tchr. chemistry Hamilton High Sch., L.A., 1957-67; prof. chemistry L.A. City Coll., 1969—, also pres. acad. senate, 1972-73. Author: Experimental General Chemistry, 1973, 76, Gen. Analytical Chemistry, 1987; contbr. articles to profl. jours. Chmn. Amateur Athletic Union So. Calif. Swimming U.S. Swim, Los Angeles, Ventura and Santa Barbara Counties, Calif., 1980-81. Served with U.S. Army, 1950-52. NSF grantee, 1967-68. Mem. Am. Chem. Soc., Am. Fedn. Tchrs., Calif. Thoroughbred Breeders Assn. Democrat. Home: 22404 Kearny St Calabasas CA 91302-5861 Office: Los Angeles City Coll 855 N Vermont Ave Los Angeles CA 90029-3500

HAILEY, FRANK WILLIAM, architect, urban planner, restorationist; b. Nevada City, Calif., Aug. 21, 1941; s. Cordell Steven and Onieonta (Von Arnim) H. AA, Pasadena (Calif.) Community Coll., 1966; BFA, U. So. Calif., L.A., 1968. Registered architect, Calif. Planner, urban designer William L. Pereira Assocs., L.A., 1968-72; project planner, urban designer Environ. Systems Internat., L.A., 1972-73; project architect, planner Keehan & Assocs., Yountville, Calif., 1973-74, Bechtel Corp., San Francisco, 1974-85; project mgr. Leo A. Daly, San Francisco, 1986-87; sr. project mgr. The Architects Collaborative, San Francisco, 1988-91, Gordon H. Chong & Assocs., San Francisco, 1991-92; pvt. practice cons. hist. preservation Mill Valley, Calif., 1991—. Chairman Ecumenical Housing Design Rev. Bd., San Rafale, Calif., 1982. With U.S. Army, 1960-62, ETO. Mem. AIA, Am. Planning Assn. Home and Office: 58 Alta Vista Ave Mill Valley CA 94941-1316

HAINES, DAVID WAYNE, commercial printing executive; b. Everett, Wash., Jan. 28, 1956; s. Vernon Pringle and Norma Zee (Robinson) H.; m. Yvonne Alice Watts, Apr. 21, 1979; children: Kenneth David, Corry Daniel. BA in Vicoed, Western Wash. U., 1978. System mgr. K & H Printers, Everett, 1979-81, sales rep., 1981-84, sales mgr., 1984-87, gen. mgr., 1987-91, pres., 1991-92; v.p. Pacific Printing Industries, Seattle, 1992—; treas. Pacific Printing Industries, Seattle, 1991-92. Bd. dirs. ARC, Everett, 1985-89, Boy Scouts Am., Everett, 1991—; chmn. Cub Scouts Pack 16, Mukilteo, Wash., 1991-92; chair 24 hour challenge Am. Cancer Soc., Everett, 1991-92. Recipient Gold Eagle, Boy Scouts Am., 1992. Mem. Rotary Club. Office: K & H Printers Inc 1611 Broadway Everett WA 98201

HAINES, GAIL KAY, freelance science writer; b. Mt. Vernon, Ill., Mar. 15, 1943; d. Samuel Glenn and Audrey Claire (Goin) Beekman; m. Michael Philip Haines, May 8, 1964; children: David Michael, Cindy Lynn. AB in Chemistry, Washington U., St. Louis, 1965. Chemist Mallinckrodt, St. Louis, 1965-66; sci. writer Olympia, Wash., 1969—. Author: 15 books including: Test Tube Mysteries, 1987, Micro Mysteries, 1988, Sugar is Sweet, 1992. Mem. Nat. Bd. Dirs. Girl Scouts of the U.S., N.Y.C., 1990—. Recipient Sci. Writing award, Am. Inst. Physics, N.Y.C., 1990—, Writer's award. Gov. Washington State, 1989. Mem. Am. Chem. Soc., Internat. Union of Pure and Applied Chemistry, Seattle FreeLance Writers (pres. 1991), Pacific N.W. Writers' Conf. (v.p., bd. dirs. 1987—). Home: 4145 Lorna Ct SE Olympia WA 98503

HAINSWORTH, BRAD E., communications executive; b. Salt Lake City, Oct. 27, 1935; s. Norman Eric and Hattie (Hendrickson) H.; m. Jacquelin Webster, July 18, 1958; children: Todd Brad, Traci Webster, Julie Webster. BA, U. Utah, 1963, MA, 1966, PhD, 1968. Asst. prof. U. Montana, Missoula, 1968-71; adminstrv. asst. U.S. Congress, Washington, 1971-72; staff asst. to pres. The White House, Washington, 1972-73; dep. asst. sec. Dept. of Interior, Washington, 1973; prof., chmn. dept. pub. affairs Pepperdine U., L.A., 1974-76; fed. affairs coordinator Getty Oil Co., 1977-81; dep. lt. gov. State Utah, Salt Lake City, 1981-84; assoc. prof. Brigham Young U., Provo, Utah, 1984-91, prof., 1991—; lectr. U. So. Calif., 1975-76; adj. prof. Calif. State U., 1977-81, Peppervine U., L.A., 1977-81; adj. instr. U. Utah, 1983-84. Author: One Wagon West, 1986; contbr. articles to profl. jours. Mem. Rep. cen. com., Provo, 1988, asst. mgr. No-on 14 Campaign, 1976; mgr. Shoup For Congress, Missoula, 1970. With U.S. Army, 1958-60. Mem. Pub. Rels. Soc. Am. Office: Brigham Young U Provo UT 84602

HAIR, KITTIE ELLEN, secondary educator; b. Denver, June 12, 1948; d. William Edward and Jacqueline Jean (Holt) H. BA, Brigham Young U., 1971; MA in Social History, U. Nev., Las Vegas, 1987. cert. tchr., Nev. Health educator Peace Corps, Totota, Liberia, 1971-72; tchr. Clark County Sch. Dist., Las Vegas, Nev., 1972-77, 1979—; missionary Ch. Jesus Christ Latter-Day Saints, Alta., Can., 1977-79. Recipient Outstanding Faculty award U. Nev./Southland Corp., Las Vegas, 1991. Mem. NEA, Nat. Coun. for Social Scis., Clark County Tchrs. Assn., ACLU, Phi Kappa Phi, Phi Alpha Theta, Delta Kappa Gamma. Democrat. Office: Eldorado High Sch 1139 Linn Ln Las Vegas NV 89110-2628

HAIRE, JAMES, production director; b. Phoenix, Oct. 21, 1938; s. James Clifford and Dorothy (Crum) H. B.F.A., U. Ariz., 1958; M.A., Northwestern U., 1960. Cons. in field. Producer: Little Eyolf, Actors Playhouse, 1964, Arms and the Man, East End Theater, N.Y.C., 1964; stage mgr.: Nat. Repertory Theater, 1965-67, A Touch of the Poet, 1967; opening season Ford's Theater, Washington, 1968-69; Woody Allen's Don't Drink the Water nat. tour, 1969-70; new musical Georgy, Wintergarden Theater, N.Y.C., 1969, Slow Dance on the Killing Ground, 1970, And Miss Reardon Drinks a Little, 1971; prodn. stage mgr. Am. Conservatory Theater, San Francisco, 1971-85, prodn. dir., 1985—. Recipient Hon. MFA, A.C.T. Conservatory, 1980, Theatrecrafts Internat. award for Distinction in Am. Theater, 1991, Lifetime Achievement award Bay Area Theatre Critics Awards, 1993. Address: 694 28th St San Francisco CA 94131

HAISCH, BERNHARD MICHAEL, astronomer; b. Stuttgart-Bad Canstatt, Fed. Republic Germany, Aug. 23, 1949; s. Friedrich Wilhelm and Gertrud Paula (Dammbacher) H.; m. Pamela S. Eakins, July 29, 1977 (div. 1986); children: Katherine Stuart, Christopher Taylor; m. Marsha A. Sims, Aug. 23, 1986. Student, St. Meinrad (Ind.) Coll., 1967-68; BS in Astrophysics, Ind. U., 1971; PhD in Astronomy, U. Wis., 1975. Rsch. assoc. Joint Inst. Lab. Astrophysics, U. Colo., 1975-77, 78-79; vis. scientist space rsch. lab. U. Utrecht, The Netherlands, 1977-78; rsch. scientist Lockheed Rsch. Lab., Palo Alto, Calif., 1979-83, staff scientist, 1983—; dep. dir. Ctr. for EUV Astrophysics U. Calif., Berkeley, 1992—; guest investigator Internat. Ultraviolet Explorer, Einstein Obs., Exosat, ROSAT Obs., ELIVE Obs., 1980—; vis. fellow Max Planck Inst. Extraterr. Physik, Garching, Germany, 1991-93. Mng. editor: Jour. Sci. Exploration, Solar and Stellar Flares, 1989; assoc. editor: The Astrophys. Jour., 1993—; mem. editorial bd. Solar Physics, 1992—; assoc. editor: Astrophys. Jour., 1993—; contbr. numerous articles to profl. jours. Fellow Royal Astron. Soc.; mem. AIAA (space sci. and astronomy tech. com.), Internat. Astron. Union, Am. Astron. Soc., Astron. Soc. of Pacific, European Astron. Soc., Phi Beta Kappa, Sigma Xi, Phi Kappa Phi, Commonwealth Club Calif. Office: Lockheed Palo Alto Rsch Lab Div 91-30 3251 Hanover St Bldg 252 Palo Alto CA 94304-1121

HAKEEM, MUHAMMAD ABDUL, artist, educator; b. N.Y.C., Oct. 15, 1945; s. Cheveland and Ruby (Rountrea) Marshall; m. Sheron Fatima, Nov. 27, 1987. Student of sculpture and painting, Pratt Inst., Pietrasanta, Italy, 1972; BFA, Pratt Inst., 1974; MA, Tchr. Coll., 1976; MEd, Columbia U., 1980. Artist N.Y. Daily News, 1976-78; asst. technician Bklyn. Mus., 1980-81, instr. African Art, 1981; tchr. Holy Rosary Sch., Bklyn., 1982-89; arts and crafts specialist Fresh Air Fund Camp, Fishkill, N.Y., 1983 summer, Camp Merrimac, Contoo Cook, N.H., 1986-88 summer; art tchr. Yonkers (N.Y.) Pub. Sch., 1989-90; adj. prof. Naropa Inst., Boulder, 1991—. Exhibited in group shows at Bklyn Mus., 1973, Lynn Kottler Galleries, 1974, Hansen Galleries, 1974, Galleries Internat., 1975, Community Gallery, 1977, Waverly Gallery, Inc., 1977, Allan S. Park Gallery, 1978, Greenwich Bar and Restaurant, 1979, Macy Gallery, 1980, West Side Story, 1981, Lynn Kottler Galleries, 1981, World Trade Expo-Keane Mason Gallery, 1981, Tabor Gallery, 1982, Gallery II, St. George, Utah, 1984, Beulahland, 1986, Morin-Miller Galleries, 1987, 89, Ednl. Alliance, 1988, Steamboat Springs (Colo.) Art Coun./Eleanor Bliss Ctr. for the Arts of the Depot (hon. mention), 1992, Boulder (Colo.) Art Ctr., 1993, Louisville (Colo.) Arts Ctr., 1993; contbr. articles to profl. jours. Art tchr. Lower East Side Community Sch., N.Y.C., 1976-77, Urban League, Bkyn., 1969 summer; counselor Office of Cath. Edn., Bklyn., 1987-88. Mem. Colo. Artists Register, Kappa Delta Pi (Kappa chpt.). Home: 2900 E Aurora Ave #312 Boulder CO 80303

HAKKILA, EERO ARNOLD, nuclear safeguards technology chemist; b. Canterbury, Conn., Aug. 4, 1931; s. Jack and Ida Maria (Lillquist) H.; m. Margaret W. Hakkila; children: Jon Eric, Mark Douglas, Gregg Arnold. BS in Chemistry, Cen. Conn. State U., 1953; PhD in Analytical Chemistry, Ohio State U., 1957. Staff mem. Los Alamos (N.Mex.) Nat. Lab., 1957-78, assoc. group leader safeguard systems, 1978-80, dep. group leader, 1980-82, group leader, 1982-83, project mgr. internat. safeguards, 1983-87, program coord., 1987—. Editor: Nuclear Safeguards Analysis, 1978; contbr. numerous articles to profl. jours. Fellow Am. Inst. Chemists; mem. N.Mex. Inst. Chemists (pres. 1971-73), Am. Chem. Soc., Am. Nuclear Soc. (exec. com. fuel cycle and waste mgmt. div. 1984-86), Inst. Nuclear Materials Mgmt. Office: Los Alamos Nat Lab PO Box 1663 Los Alamos NM 87545-0001

HALBEDEL, ELAINE MARIE, astronomer; b. Auburn, N.Y., Sept. 8, 1951; d. Walter John and Loretta Teresa (Wilczek) Gugula; m. Allan A. Hendry, June 23, 1973 (div. 1981); m. William N. Halbedel, Oct. 24, 1983. BS, U. Mich., 1972; MS, Northwestern U., 1973, PhD, 1977. Vis. lectr. U. Wis.-Parkside, Kenosha, 1978; post-doctoral assoc Ga. State U., Atlanta, 1979-81; dir. Corralitos Observatory, Las Cruces, N.Mex., 1981—. Contbr. over 50 rsch. articles to profl. jours. Mme. Am. Astronomical Soc., Sigma Xi. Office: Corralitos Observatory PO Box 16314 Las Cruces NM 88004

HALBERG, CHARLES JOHN AUGUST, JR., mathematics educator; b. Pasadena, Calif., Sept. 24, 1921; s. Charles John August and Anne Louise (Hansen) H.; m. Ariel Arfon Oliver, Nov. 1, 1941 (div. July 1969); children—Ariel (Mrs. William Walters), Charles Thomas, Niels Frederick; m. Barbro Linnea Samuelsson, Aug. 18, 1970 (dec. Jan. 1978); 1 stepchild, Ulf Erik Hjelm; m. Betty Reese Zimprich, July 27, 1985. B.A. summa cum laude, Pomona Coll., 1949; M.A. (William Lincoln Honnold fellow), UCLA, 1953, Ph.D., 1955. Instr. math. Pomona Coll., Claremont, Calif., 1949-50; assoc. math. UCLA, 1954-55; instr. math. U. Calif.-Riverside, 1955-56, asst. prof. math., 1956-61, assoc. prof. math., 1961-68, prof. math., 1968—, vice chancellor student affairs, 1964-65; dir. Scandinavian Study Center at Lund (Sweden) U., 1976-78; docent U. Goteborg, Sweden, 1969-70; bd. dirs. Fulbright Commn. for Ednl. Exchange between U.S. and Sweden, 1976-79. Author: (with John F. Devlin) Elementary Functions, 1967, (with Angus E. Taylor) Calculus with Analytic Geometry, 1969. Served with USAAF, 1945-46. NSF fellow U. Copenhagen, 1961-62. Mem. Math. Assn. Am. (chmn. So. Calif. sect. 1964-65, gov. 1968), Am. Math. Soc., Swedish Math. Soc., Sigma Xi, Phi Beta Kappa. Home: PO Box 2724 Carlsbad CA 92018-2724

HALBHERR, JOSEF ANTON, hotel chain executive; b. Ulm, Germany, Mar. 19, 1947; came to U.S., 1990; s. Alois and Maria (Glaser) H.; m. Marie Paule Schmidt, Sept. 7, 1977; children: Patricius Alexander, Lucia Fiona. Grad., Sch. Hotel Adminstrn., Heidelberg, Germany, 1976; student, Mewes EKS, Frankfurt, Germany, 1984. Various positions to gen. mgr. various hotels, Manila, Seoul, Bali, Indonesia, 1967-80; resident mgr. Sheraton Hotel, Abu Dhabi, United Arab Emirates, 1980-81; gen. mgr. Sheraton Hotel, Sana'a, Yemen, 1981-82; regional mgr. Sodexho, Jeddah, Saudi Arabia, 1983-84; resident mgr. Peninsula Group, Singapore, 1984-85; gen. mgr. Peninsula Group, Beijing, 1985-86, Regal Hotels Internat., Hong Kong, 1987-89; v.p. planning Regal-Aircoa Cos. Inc., Denver, 1990, sr. v.p. planning, 1990-91, sr. v.p. internat. devel., 1991—. Scholar Cornell Soc., Germany, 1973. Mem. Chaine des Rotisseurs, Disciples d'Escoffier, Cornell Soc. Hotelman, Mewes Strategic Mgmt., Activitas Heidelberg, U.S.-German C. of C. Office: Regal-Aircoa Cos Inc 4600 S Ulster St Denver CO 80237

HALDEMAN, MICHAEL DAVIS, publisher, writer, editor; b. Phila., Feb. 19, 1947; s. William Charles and Aileen (Davis) H.; m. Roberta Helen Maddox, July 10, 1976 (div. 1985); children: Norah Kate, Lucas Merwan. Student, Stanford U., 1965-66, U. Colo., 1967-68, 71-72. Ptnr. The Mediaworks, Boulder, Colo., 1975-81, The Mediaworks, Ltd., Boulder and Denver, 1977-85; owner Michael Haldeman Info. & Media Svcs., Boulder and Denver, 1982-88, Whitehorse Prodns., Denver and Boulder, 1988—; founding editor New Periodicals Index, Boulder/Denver, 1977-85; editor Broken-Down Furniture News, Denver, 1981-86, WhiteHorse Mag., Denver/Boulder, 1988—. Contbr. over 40 articles to jours.; composer over 175 songs, 5 rock operas. Mem. Rocky Mountain Book Pubs. Assn. Office: Whitehorse Prodns 805 W Moorhead Cir Ste E Boulder CO 80303

HALE, ARCHIE DOUGLAS, career officer; b. Mobile, Ala., Dec. 29, 1949; s. Weaman and Annie Lue (Hudson) H.; m. Emma Marie James, Sept. 10, 1973; children: Vanderlyn Smith, Brian. Assoc. of Applied Aerospace, C.C. Air Force, 1985, C.C. Air Force, 1986; BA, Columbia Coll., 1987. Commd. officer USAF; bd. dirs. Oahu Community Credit Union, Wahiawa, Hawaii. Speakers bur. Lowry AFB, Denver, 1986, handicapped rights, 1986; high sch. mentor Community Resources, Denver, 1988; meal-on-wheels Vols. Am., Denver, 1986; scout leader Denver Area Scouting Post 2760, com. chmn., 1986-88. Mem. Masons. Baptist. Home: 2318-A Apollo Ave Honolulu HI 96818 Office: 6924th Elec Security Group Wheeler AFB HI 96854

HALE, BRUCE DONALD, marketing professional; b. Oak Park, Ill., Dec. 21, 1933; s. Edward Garden and Mildred Lillian (Pelc) H.; m. Nancy Ann Novotny, July 2, 1955 (div. 1976); children: Jeffrey Bruce, Karen Jill Hale; m. Connie Luella Green Gunderson, Apr. 21, 1979. BA in Econs., Wesleyan U., Middletown, Conn., 1955. Trainee Caterpillar Tractor Co., Peoria, Ill., 1955-56, dealer tng. rep., 1956-59; dist. rep. Caterpillar Tractor Co., Albuquerque, 1959-62; asst. sales mgr. Rust Tractor Co., Albuquerque, 1962-65; gen. sales mgr. Rust Tractor Co., Albuqerque, 1965-71, v.p. sales, 1971-81, v.p. mktg., 1981—; bd. dirs. Mega Corp., Albuquerque. Mem. Am. Mining Congress, Soc. Mining Engrs., Associated Contractors N.Mex., Associated Equipment Distbrs., Rocky Mountain Coal Mining Inst., N.Mex. Mining Assn., Albuquerque Country Club. Home: 9508 Layton Pl NE Albuquerque NM 87111 Office: Rust Tractor Co 4000 Osuna Rd NE Albuquerque NM 87109

HALE, CARL DENNIS, electronics company executive; b. Oakland, Calif., July 12, 1949; s. William Francis and Irene Helegard (Knoth) H.; children: Telissa, Desiree, Michael. BS, San Jose State U., 1974; mfg. studies program, Gen. Electric Co., San Jose, 1976. Prodn. planner Gen. Electric, San Jose, Calif., 1974-77; mfg. engr. Gen. Electric, Paterson, N.J., 1977-78; advisor, prodn. mgr. Gen. Electric Co., San Jose, 1978-79; materials mgr. Spectra Physics, Mountain View, Calif., 1979-81; factory parts mgr. Hewlett-Packard, Mountain View, 1981-82; materials mgr. Hewlett-Packard, Santa Clara, 1982-86; mgr. prodn. sect. Hewlett-Packard, San Jose, 1986-88, materials mgr. rsch. and devel., 1988-89; logistics mgr. Hewlett-Packard, Santa Clara, 1989—; part time instr. San Jose State U., 1985—. Author: (manuals) Material Requirements Planning, 1981, Conceptual Manufacturing, 1983, How to Professionally Qualify Suppliers, Apics Internat. Conf., 1987, Building World Class Service in Suppliers, Inst. for Internat. Rsch. Conf., 1990. Mem. Am. Prodn. and Inventory Control Soc. (cert. prodn. and inventory mgmt.), Club Sport. Republican. Roman Catholic. Home: 3102 3 Lakemont Dr San Ramon CA 94583 Office: Hewlett-Packard 370 W Trimble Rd San Jose CA 95131-1008

HALE, CECIL, communications educator; b. St. Louis, Aug. 3, 1945; s. Cecil and Allean (Cunningham) H.; m. Patricia Thomas (div. 1979); children: Juanita, Tasha, Cecil-Jamil. Student, So. Ill. U., 1963-66; MA, Internat. U. of Comm., Washington, 1975; PhD, Union Inst., Cin., 1978. Lic. by FCC. Announcer, asst. gen. mgr. WMPP Radio, 1964-68; announcer XPRS Radio, L.A., 1972-74; announcer, asst. program/music dir. WNOV Radio, Milw., 1968-70, WVON Radio, Chgo., 1970-77; nat. dir., mgr. Phonogram/Mercury Records, Chgo., 1977-78; v.p. Capitol Records, Inc., Hollywood, Calif., 1978-81; prof. San Francisco State U., 1984—, City Coll. San Francisco, 1986—; prof. Mass Media Inst. Stanford U., 1987—; cons. N.T.A., Lagos, Nigeria, 1982-83, Gallo Winery, Inc., Modesto, Calif., 1977, Capitol Records, Inc., Hollywood, 1981-82, Congl. Caucus, Washington, 1975. Author: The Music Industry, 1990; exec. producer phono records. Recipient Key to City and City Coun. Resolution, L.A., 1980, Outstanding Tchr. award Acad. Senate, City Coll. San Francisco, 1990, San Francisco State U. Faculty award, 1986. Mem. NAACP, AAUP, NEA, Nat. Acad. Recording ARts and Scis., Am. Fedn. Musicians, Am. Fedn. TV and Radio Artists, Am. Fedn. Tchrs., Masons, Alpha Phi Alpha. Avocations: flying, computers. Home: 2517 Lake St San Francisco CA 94121 Office: City Coll San Francisco 50 Phelan Ave San Francisco CA 94112

HALE, CLAUDIA JOAN, real estate broker; b. Nampa, Idaho, Jan. 19, 1937; d. Clarence Stephen Pilcher and Palma Mae (Bowman) Wilson; m. Robert Irving Hale, Aug. 2, 1935; children: Russell, Robert, Richard, Rhonda. Grad. high sch., Hillsboro, Oreg. Lic. broker, residential specialist. Piano tchr. Hillsboro, 1955-86; owner, operator Don's Plumbing, Hillsboro, 1977-84; realtor Century 21 Hearthside, Hillsboro, 1984-89, Century 21 Foster & Clark, Hillsboro, 1989-91, Century 21 Campbell & Assoc., Hillsboro, 1991-92; owner, sec. Bob's Design Engring. Inc., Hillsboro, 1986—. Mem. C. of C. (Outstanding Woman 1976), Epsilon Sigma Alpha Internat. (state pres. Alpha Upsilon chpt. 1982-83).

HALE, DEAN EDWARD, social services administrator; b. Balt., Aug. 4, 1950; s. James Russell and Marjorie Elinor (Hoerman) H.; BASW, U. Pa., 1975; postgrad. U. Oreg., 1976, U. London, 1974, U. Mont., 1968-71; m. Lucinda Hoyt Muniz, 1979; children: Christopher Deane, Lydia Alice JeeSoo. Dir. recreation Hoffman Homes for Children, Gettysburg, Pa., 1970; social worker Holt Adoption Program, Inc., Eugene, Oreg., 1975-78; supr. social svcs. Holt Internat. Children's Svcs., Eugene, 1978-84, Asia rep., 1984-90, program mgr., 1990—; guest lectr. U. Oreg.; cons. internat. child welfare, 1982—; co-founder Family Opportunities Unltd. Inc., 1981—. Author: Adoption, A Family Affair, 1981, When Your Child Comes Home, 1986. Pres. Woodtique Heights Homeowners Assn., 1980-91, bd. dirs.; pres. Our Saviour's Luth. Ch., 1981-85; bd. dirs. Greenpeace of Oreg., 1979-84; cons., campaign worker Defazio for Congress 1988, 1987-90; mem. Westside Neighborhood Quality Project, 1988—. Named Outstanding New Jaycee, Gettysburg Jaycees, 1971. Mem. Nat. Assn. Social Workers (bd. dirs. 1978-80, sec. 1979-80), Nat. Assn. Christian Social Workers, Acad. Cert. Baccalaureate Social Workers. Home: 931 Taylor St Eugene OR 97402-4451 Office: PO Box 2880 1195 City View St Eugene OR 97402

HALE, DIANA, sales executive, artist; b. Chgo., Nov. 30, 1933; d. Bessie Marie Spinner Schultz; children: Dionne, Denise, Danielle, Darlene. AA, Ohio U., Athens, 1954. With KNUU Radio, Las Vegas, Nev., 1977—; gen. sales mgr. KNUU Radio, 1987—; profl. actress/entertainer including live radio, tv, major movies, stage, recordings, tv commls., tv progs., USO tours, night clubs, Las Vegas prodns. Appeared in (movies) Always in My Heart, My Friend Flicka, Thunderhead; mem. (recording and performing trio) The Vogues, 1955-58; performed at Riviera and Sands hotels, Las Vegas, Adolphus Hotel, Dallas, Tonight Show, Am. Bandstand, others; worked as singer-actress throughout Hawaiian Islands, 1960. Mem. Internat. Assn. Bus. Communicators (bd. dirs., sec. 1984-86), Greater Las Vegas Advt. Fedn. (charter mem. 1980—, bd. dirs. 1988—, pres. 1991-92), Am. Advt. Fedn. (pub. svc. com. 1992—). Democrat. Office: KNUU (KNEWS) Radio 2001 E Flamingo Rd Las Vegas NV 89119-5117

HALE, RONALD F., consultant; b. Mexico City, June 9, 1943; came to U.S., 1946; s. Robert Fraser and Rena Muriel (Stonehouse) H.; m. Wendy Lynn Speight, Aug. 8, 1968 (div. Mar. 1977); m. Ellen Becker, June 10, 1977; children: Jesse David, Luke Benjamin. Student, U. Catolica, Lima, Peru, 1964; BA, Swarthmore (Pa.) Coll., 1965; postgrad., U. Calif., 1965-66; MS in Edn., U. So. Calif., 1976. Tchr., intern Tchr. Corps/Tulare Co. Schs., Visalia, Calif., 1968-69; dir. youth edn. program Am. Friends Svc. Com., Balt., 1970-73; dir. coop. edn. Community Coll. Vt., Montpelier, 1973-76; evaluation dir. Cen. Coast Counties Devel. Corp., Aptos, Calif., 1976-77; mem. core faculty Antioch U./West, Monterey, Calif., 1977-78; sr. planner Cen. Coast Counties Devel. Corp., Aptos, 1977-79; planner, resource developer Siete Del Norte Community Devel. Corp., Estanola, N.Mex., 1979-81; dir. advising and retention Coll. Santa Fe, 1981-82; dir. fac., career planning St. John's Coll., Sante Fe, 1983-91; pres. R. Hale & Assocs., Santa Fe, 1991—; cons. various orgns., Santa Fe, 1979—; bd. dirs. Ctr. For Creative Community, Santa Fe; trainer, cons. Human Svcs. Inst., Greensboro, N.C., 1990—. Contbr. articles to profl. jours. Bd. pres. S.W. Pickers, Sante Fe, 1983-88; mem. coll. placement coun. Liberal Arts Task Force, 1983-91; active Coun. for Liberal Learning, 1984-87. Mem. S.W. Traditional and Bluegrass Music Assn., N.Mex. Career Devel. Assn., Rocky Mountain Coll. Placement Assn. (presenter), Nat. Soc. For Internships and Experiential Edn. (conf. host), Santa Fe C. of C. (edn coun. 1984, 1989-90). Democrat. Home and Office: PO Box 6816 Santa Fe NM 87502-6816

HALE, VIOLET ELAINE, director food service, graphoanalyst; b. Atwood, Kans.; d. Frank and Lola Mae (Threlkel) Wederski; m. Everett David Hale, June 25, 1948; children: Diana Elaine, Chester Duane, Ray Don. Student, IGAS, 1980. Asst. food svc. dir. Manitou Springs (Colo.) Sch., 1967-84, ret., 1984. Author poems, songwriter; inventor cap shaper dryer, sliced bread stacker. Mem. Manitou Springs Hist. Soc. (v.p. 1989-92). Methodist. Office: Manitou Springs Hist Soc 9 Capitol Hill Ave Manitou Springs CO 80829-1618

HALER, LAWRENCE EUGENE, technology educator, councilman; b. Iowa City, Iowa, Jan. 24, 1951; s. Eugene Hilbert and Mary Elizabeth (Hans) H.; m. Jenifer Lea Leitz, June 1, 1974. BA, Pacific Luth. U., 1974. Reactor operator UNC Nuclear Industires, Richland, Wash., 1974-80, lead cert. instr., 1980-81, mgr. tng. adminstrn., 1981-82, sr. ops. analyst, 1982-85; sr. specialist Gen. Physics Corp., Columbia, Md., 1985-86; sr. instr. Rockwell Hanford Ops., Richland, 1986-88; tech. instr. Westinghouse Hanford Co., Richland, 1988-89, sr. specialist instr., 1989—; bd. dirs. Benton-Franklin County Bd. Health, Richland, Sci. and Tech. Park, Richland. Chmn. Benton County Reps., Richland, 1976-78, state committeeman, 1988-90; councilman City of Richland, 1990—; active community econ. devel. com., Nat. league Cities. Mem. Richland C. of C. (chmn. legis. affairs com. 1988-93), Kiwanis (bd. dirs. Richland chpt. 1988—). Lutheran. Home: PO Box 1319 Richland WA 99352-1319 Office: Richland City Coun 505 Swift Blvd Richland WA 99352-3553

HALES, ROBERT LYNN, airport executive; b. Payson, Utah, May 12, 1927; s. Robert Elmo and Zelma Fay (Elmer) H.; m. Jean E. Lutz, Aug. 17, 1951; children: Wendy, Susan, Janice, Jeffrey. BSBA, U. Phoenix, San Jose, Calif., 1984. Floatation operator Kennecott Copper Corp., Magna, Utah, 1946-51; with flight crew schedule dept. United Airlines Inc., L.A., 1951-54; aircraft router United Airlines Inc., Denver, 1954-69; maintenance planner United Airlines Inc., Chgo., 1969-71; div. rep. ramp and customer svcs. United Airlines Inc., San Francisco, 1971-80, ops. shift mgr., 1980-82; site mgr. Tech. Mgmt. Corp., Alameda, Calif., 1983-84; airport duty mgr. San Francisco Internat. Airport, 1985—; travel cons., Pleasanton, Calif., 1971—. Poll watcher Reps., Crystal Lake, Ill., 1970; precinct vol., Pleasnton, Calif.; counselor, fundraiser Boy Scouts Am. With USN, 1945-46, PTO. Republican. Mormon. Home: 2033 Foxswallow Rd Pleasanton CA 94566-5537 Office: San Francisco Internat PO Box 8097 San Francisco CA 94128-8097

HALEY, JOHN DAVID, petroleum consulting company executive; b. Denver, Mar. 16, 1924; s. Peter Daniel and Margaret Dorothy (O'Haire) H.; m. Annie Loretta Breeden, June 20, 1951; children—Laura, Patricia, Brian, Sharon, Norine, Kathleen. Profl. engr. Colo. Sch. Mines, 1948. Registered profl. engr., Colo., Okla. Petroleum engr. Creole Petroleum, Venezuela, 1948-50, field engr. Texaco Inc., La., 1950-52; staff engr. Carter Oil (Exxon), Tulsa, 1954-56; petroleum cons. Earlougher Engring., Tulsa, 1956-61, resident mgr., Denver, 1961-62; v.p. prodn. Anschutz Corp., Denver, 1962-86; v.p. Circle A Drilling, Denver, 1967-78; dir. Circle A Mud, Denver, 1983-86; pres. Greylock Pipeline, Denver, 1983-86, Anschutz Pipeline, Denver, 1984-86; pres. Haley Engring. Inc., 1987—; mem. pres.'s council Colo. Sch. Mines, 1985—; bd. dirs. Alumni Assn., 1992—. Rep. committeeman, Littleton. Lt. comdr. USNR, 1943-46, 52-54. Mem. Soc. Petroleum Engrs. (bd. dirs. Denver chpt. 1965), Soc. Petroleum Evaluation Engrs. (bd. dirs. 1992—), Ind. Petroleum Assn. Am., Ind. Petroleum Assn. Mountain States, Am. Petroleum Inst. (citation for service), Internat. Assn. Drilling Contractors, Rocky Mountain Oil & Gas Assn. (bd. dirs. 1988—), Soc. Profl. Well Log Analysts, Petroleum Club (Denver chpt.). Roman Catholic. Home: 561 E Caley Dr Littleton CO 80121-2212

HALEY, SALLY FULTON, artist; b. Bridgeport, Conn., June 29, 1908; d. John Poole and Elizabeth (Akers) H.; m. Michele Russo, June 29, 1935; children: Michael Haley, Gian Donato. BFA, Yale U., 1931. One-woman shows include Marylhurst Coll., 1965, Maryhill Mus. Fine Arts, Washington, 1975, Portland Art Mus., 1960, 75, Woodside Gallery, Seattle, 1971, 76, 79, Gov's. Office, Oreg. State Capitol, 1976, Wentz Gallery, Pacific N.W. Coll. Art, 1984, Fountain Gallery Art, Portland, 1962, 72, 77, 80, 81, 84, 86; exhibited in group shows Stewart Gallery, Boston, 1947, San Francisco Mus. Art, 1949, Walker Art Ctr., Mpls., 1954, Denver Art Mus., 1956, 57, 3d Pacific Coast Biennial Exhbn., 1960, Francis J. Newton's Collection, Bush House, 1964, Seattle Ctr. Art Pavilion, 1976, Womans Bldg., L.A., 1977, Laura Russo Gallery, 1993, Oreg. Group Show, Expn. '86 World's Fair, Vancouver, B.C.; represented in permanent collections Fred Myer Trust, Wash. State U., State Capitol Bldg., Salem, Portland Art Mus., The Laura Russo Gallery, Portland, Lynn McAllister Gallery, Seattle, Barby Investment Co., AT&T, Kaiser Found., numerous others; retrospective, Marylhurst Coll., 1993. Named Artist of Yr. Neighbor Newspaper Community, Portland, 1984; recipient Woman of Achievement award YWCA, 1988, Govs. Award for the Arts, 1982, 89, Hubbard award Hubbard Mus., Ruidoso Downs, N.Mex., 1990-91.

HALEY, THOMAS JOHN, retired pharmacologist; b. Crosby, Minn., Nov. 4, 1913; s. Thomas Edward and Ida May (Young) H.; m. Edna Baker, June 1, 1944 (div. Sept. 1963); m. Jeanne Wall, Sept. 24, 1964; children: Kathyleen, Barbara. BS, U. So. Calif., 1938, MS, 1942; PhD, U. Fla., 1945. Lic. pharmacist, Calif., Nev. Grad. asst. instr. U. Fla., Gainesville, 1942-45; med. dir. E.S. Miller Labs Inc., L.A., 1945-47; chief pharmacology toxicologist Lab. Nuclear Medicine UCLA, 1947-66; prof. pharmacology U. Hawaii Med. Sch., Honolulu, 1966-69; leader pharmacology & toxicology Rsch. Triangle Inst., Research Triangle Park, N.C., 1969-71; adj. prof. pharmacology & toxicology U. N.C. Med. Sch., Chapel Hill, 1969-71; pharmacologist Food & Drug Adminstrn. Nat. Ctr. Toxicology Rsch., Pine Bluff, Ark., 1971-82; adj. prof. pharmacology U. Ark. Med. Ctr., Little Rock, 1971-82. Author: Clinical Toxicology, 1948, 1972, Respiratory Nervous System Ion Radiology, 1962, 1964, Manual of Toxicology, 1987. Sci. com. air pollution L.A. County, 1948-66. Mem. Inst. Strahlenhemat & Biol. (internat. mem.), L.A. C. of C. (clean air com. 1954-56), Oceanside City Coun. (hazard waste com. 1986-91). Democrat. Roman Catholic. Home: 774 Rivertree Dr Oceanside CA 92054-7456

HALFANT, GARY D., small business owner; b. Washington, Aug. 1, 1953; s. Manny and Jean Frances (Eddinger) H.; m. Gwyn Reneé Jones, Dec. 24, 1987 (div. Apr. 1992); 1 child, Garic David. Grad. high sch., Sacramento. Pres. G's Herbs, Sacramento, 1974-78, G's Herbs Internat., Ltd. (now G's Seasonings Co.), Portland, Oreg., 1978-92.

HALFF, ROBERT HART, retired advertising executive; b. San Antonio, Dec. 1, 1908; s. Alexander Hart and Alma (Oppenheimer) H. BS, U. Pa., 1929; postgrad., Columbia U., NYU, UCLA. Buyer-furs Joske Bros. Co., San Antonio; asst. creative dir. Compton Advt., L.A.; screenwriter Metro Goldwyn Mayer Studios, Culver City, Calif. Bd. dirs., trustee, hon. chairperson, bd. dirs. acquisitions com., mem. modern & contemporary art coun. L.A. County Mus. of Art. With USN, 1934-37.

HALFORD, SHARON LEE, crime victim services administrator, educator; b. Clifton, Colo., July 22, 1946; d. Robert Lee and Florence V. (Kubly) Eighmy; m. Allen A. Dreher, Jan. 29, 1967 (div. Jan. 1979); children: Heidi Ann, Gretchen Christine, Kirsten Beth; m. Donald Gary Halford, May 23, 1986. BS in Edn., U. Colo., 1969; postgrad., U. Denver, 1981-83; M in Criminal Justice, U. Colo., 1987. Legal asst. 1st Jud. Dist. Atty., Golden, Colo., 1979-81; victim witness coord. 18th Jud. Dist. Atty., Englewood, Colo., 1983-92; mem. faculty Aurora (Colo.) Community Coll. Criminal Justice Dept., 1989—; bd. dirs. Mem. Domestic Violence Task Force, Douglas County, Colo., 1985-92, Arapahoe County, Colo., 1985—; trainer Rape Assistance and Awareness Program, Denver, 1985-91, MADD, 1990-92, Colo. Victim Witness Copords. Coalition, 1991; mem. 18th Judicial Dist. Child Advocacy Ctr. Com., 1990—, Gov.'s Victims' Compensation and Assistance Coord. Com., 1991—, Criminal Justice Educators Task Force, 1992—, Colo. Corrections Consortium, 1992—, Colo. Crime Victim Rights Constl. Ammendment Com., 1990—. Fellow Nat. Orgn. for Victim Assistance, Nat. Victim Ctr.; mem. Colo. Orgn. for Victim Assistance (pres.), S.W. Criminal Justice Educators Assn., Am. Criminal Justice Assn. Democrat. Methodist. Office: CC Aurora 16000 E Centretech Pkwy Aurora CO 80011

HALFPENNY, JAMES CARSON, scientist, educator, author; b. Shreveport, La., Jan. 23, 1947; s. Donald Frazier and Dorothy (Carson) H. BS, U. Wyo., 1969, MS, 1970; PhD, U. Colo., 1980. Various positions with govt. conservation agys., parks and univ conservation programs, 1966—; coord. long-term ecol. rsch. program U. Colo., Boulder, 1980-91; rsch. assoc. Inst. Arctic and Alpine Rsch., U. Colo., 1980-87, 92, fellow, 1987-91, affiliate, 1991—; instr. Teton Sci. Sch., Kelly, Wyo., 1980—, affiliate, 1992—, Aspen (Colo.) Ctr. for Environ. Studies, 1984—, Yellowstone (Wyo.) Inst., 1984—, Rocky Mountain Nature Assn., 1987, 90, 92; pres. A Naturalist's World, Boulder, 1985—; staff trainer Colo. Div. Wildlife, 1979, 83, 91, sci. advisor 1982-85; staff trainer Yellowstone Nat. Park, 1985-86, 88, Grand Teton Nat. Park, 1990, Rocky Mountain Nat. Park, 1992; grant proposal rev. bd. NSF, 1984—, Nat. Geog. Sci., 1984—; trustee Thorne Ecol. Inst., Boulder, 1982-84; mem. Indian Peaks Wilderness Area Adv. Panel, Boulder, 1982-86, others; speaker mammal tracking, alpine and winter ecology, Republic of China's endangered wildlife. Author: A Field Guide to Mammal Tracking, 1986, Winter: An Ecological Handbook, 1989; editor (booklets) Mountain Rsch. Sta.: its environment and rsch., 1982, Long Term Ecol. Rsch. in the U.S.: a network of rsch. sites, 1982, 83, 84; contbr. articles to profl. jours. and mags. on nat. history. Mem. sci. adv. panel EOP program U. Colo., 1982-84; mem. sci. coun. Greater Yellowstone Coalition; bd. advisors Teton Sci. Sch., Moran, 1985-89; bd. dirs. Nat. Outdoor Leadership Sch., Lander, Wyo., 1975-80, chmn., 1978-79. With USNR, 1969-71, Vietnam. Decorated Navy Achievement medal with combat "v", Vietnamese Gallantry Cross with palm (Republic Vietnam); recipient Roosevelt Meml. grant Am. Mus. Natural History, 1979, Walker Van Riper grant U.Colo., 1979, Kathy Lichty Fund grant U. Colo., 1979, Book Plate award Denver Pub. Libr. Friends Found. Fellow The Explorer Club; mem. AAAS, Ecol. Soc. Am., Am. Inst. Biol. Scis., Am. Soc. Mammalogists, Internat. Soc. Cryptozoology, Southwestern Assn. Naturalists, N.W. Sci. Assn., Colo.-Wyo. Acad. Sci., Orgn. Biol. Field Stas., Sci. Coun. Greater Yellowstone Coalition, Sigma Xi. Office: A Naturalist's World PO Box 989 300 Scott Gardiner MT 59030

HALKO, JOSEPH ANTHONY, artist; b. Great Falls, Mont., Aug. 11, 1940; s. Martin Emory and Helen Maxine (Swartz) H.; m. Margaret Ann Smith, June 14, 1969; children: Michelle Ann, Stephanie Jo. Student, Fisk Studios, 1964; BS, Coll. of Great Falls, 1970. Environ. chemist Anaconda Co., Great Falls, 1970-71; taxidermist Great Falls Sporting Goods, 1959-76; freelance artist Cascade, Mont., 1976—; juror various art shows, Mont., 1976—; tchr. sculpture workshops YWCA, Great Falls, 1985—. Illustrator: Century in the Foothills, 1975. Mem. bd. trustees Sch. Dist. 3, Cascade, 1990-93; mem. Sacred Heart Pastoral Coun., Cascade, 1987—; mem. C.M. Russell Mus., Great Falls, 1975—, High Desert Mus., Bend, Oreg., 1989—. Mem. Allied Artists of Am., Soc. Animal Artists of N.Y., N.W. Rendezous Group (pres. Helena, Mont. chpt. 1987, Merit award 1979, 81, 91), Lions (1st, 2d and 3d v.p. Cascade chpt. 1983—). Home: 2573 Old US Hwy # 91 Cascade MT 59421

HALL, ANTHONY ELMITT, plant physiologist; b. Tickhill, Yorkshire, Eng., May 6, 1940; came to U.S., 1964; s. Elmitt and Mary Lisca (Schofield) H.; m. Bretta Reed, June 20, 1965; children: Kerry, Gina. Student, Harper Adams Agrl. Coll., Eng., 1958-60; student in agrl. engring., Essex Inst. Agrl. Engring., Eng., 1960-61; BS in Irrigation Sci., U. Calif., Davis, 1966, PhD in

Plant Physiology, 1970. Farmer Dyon House, Austerfield, Eng., 1955-58; extension officer Ministry of Agr., Tanzania, 1961-63; research asst. U. Calif., Davis, 1964-70, asst. research scientist, 1971; research fellow Carnegie Inst., Stanford, Calif., 1970; prof. U. Calif., Riverside, 1971—, cons. on African agrl. devel., 1974—. Editor: Agriculture in Semi-Arid Environments, 1979; adv. editor (jour.) Irrigation Sci.; tech. editor (jour.) Crop Sci.; mem. editorial adv. bd. Field Crops Research, Vigna Crop Adv. Com. USDA; contbr. articles to profl. jours. Mem. Am. Soc. Plant Physiologists, Am. Soc. Agronomy, Crop Sci. Soc. Am., Scandinavian Soc. Plant Physiology, Alpha Zeta, Gamma Sigma Delta, Phi Beta Kappa, Phi Kappa Phi. Office: U Calif Dept Botany and Plant Scis Riverside CA 92521

HALL, BRONWYN HUGHES, economics educator; b. West Point, N.Y., Mar. 1, 1945; d. Richard Roberts and Elizabeth (Flandreau) Hughes; m. Robert Ernest Hall, June 25, 1966 (div. Apr. 1983); children: Christopher Ernest, Anne Elizabeth. BA, Wellesley Coll., 1966; PhD, Stanford U., 1988. Programming analyst Lawrence Berkeley (Calif.) Lab., 1963-70; sr. programmer econometric programming Harvard U., Cambridge, Mass., 1971-77; owner, opr. Time Series Processor, Palo Alto, Calif., 1976—; from rsch. economist to faculty rsch. fellow Nat. Bur. Econ. Rsch., Stanford, Calif., 1977—; from asst. prof. to assoc. prof. U. Calif., Berkeley, 1987—; mem. data base rev. com. U.S. SBA, Washington, 1983-84; ind. econometric programming cons. ednl. instns., Cambridge, 1970-77. Mem. editorial bd. Econ. of Innovation and New Tech., Uxbridge, Eng., 1989—; contbr. articles on econs. to profl. publs. Sloan Found. dissertation fellow, 1986-87, Nat. fellow Hoover Inst. on War, Revolution, and Peace, Stanford U., 1992-93; NSF rsch. grantee, 1989—. Mem. Am. Econ. Assn. (mem. census adv. com. 1990—), Am. Fin. Assn., Am. Statis. Assn., Econometric Soc., Assn. for Computing Machinery. Home: 123 Tamalpais Rd Berkeley CA 94708-1948 Office: U Calif Dept Econs 611 Evans Hall Berkeley CA 94720

HALL, CECILIA VASQUEZ, counselor, coach; b. Tucson, Jan. 18, 1947; d. Ramon Aguirre and Hortencia (Riesgo) Vasquez; m. Larry K. Hall, Sept. 23, 1971; 1 child, Frederick. BS in Phys. Edn., U. Ariz., 1968, MEd in Guidance and Counseling, 1972. Tchr. phys. edn. Tucson Unified Sch. Dist., 1968-72, guidance counselor, 1972-81, mem. profl. internship program, 1981—, head counseling dept., 1976-78, head softball coach, 1976-87, athletic dir., 1981-83; mem. admissions & guidance com., chmn. program planning com. The Coll. Bd.-Western Region; head softball coach Pima Community Coll., Tucson, 1988—. Mem. Hispanic Sports Enrichment Program, Tucson, 1985—; vol. Arthritis Found., Tucson. Named Coach of Yr., Tucson Citizen/Ariz. Star, 1981, 83; recipient Community Svc. award Nosotros, 1987, 88, 89, 90, 91. Mem. Nat. Softball Coaches Assn., Ariz. C.C. Athletic Conf. Softball Coaches Assn. (softball coach of yr. 1992), U. Ariz. Hispanic Alumni Assn., Alpha Delta Kappa (state pres. 1988-90, S.W. regional grand v.p. 1991-93). Home: 9236 E Palm Tree Dr Tucson AZ 85710-8629 Office: United Sch Dist 1302 S Avenida Vega Tucson AZ 85710-5196

HALL, CHARLES FREDERICK, space scientist, government administrator; b. San Francisco, Apr. 7, 1920; s. Charles Rogers and Edna Mary (Gibson) H.; m. Constance Vivienne Andrews, Sept. 18, 1942; children—Steven R., Charles Frederick, Frank A. B.S., U. Calif., Berkeley, 1942. Aero. research scientist NACA (later NASA), Moffett Field, Calif., 1942-60; mem. staff space projects NACA (later NASA), 1960-63; mgr. Pioneer Project, NASA, 1963-80. Recipient Disting. Service medal NASA, 1974, Achievement award Am. Astronautical Soc., 1974, Spl. Achievement award Nat. Civil Service League, 1976, Astronautics Engr. award Nat. Space Club, 1979. Home: 817 Berry Ave Los Altos CA 94024-5416

HALL, CHRISTOPHER ERIC, academic administrator, human resources consultant; b. Lynwood, Calif., Jan. 10, 1951; s. John William and Marjorie Jeane (Von Schriltz) H.; m. Monika Bachmann, May 7, 1980 (dec. June 1987); children: Rebekka Trini, David John Friedrich. Student, Calif. State U., Fullerton, 1969-74, BA, 1978; EdM, Boston U., 1986; postgrad., U. So. Calif., 1986—. Announcer Sta. KMMT-FM, Mamoth Lakes, Calif., 1974; broadcaster U.S. Army Ordnance Ctr. and Sch., Aberdeen Proving Grounds, Md., 1975; U.S. Army broadcaster Am. Forces Network, Germany, Ramstein, 1975-76; U.S. Army broadcaster Am. Forces Network, Europe, Frankfurt, Germany, 1976-78, mgr. TV studio ops., 1979-87; supr. pers. mgmt. Frankfurt area exch. Army and Air Force Exch. Svc., Offenbach, Germany, 1978-79; faculty lectr. Azusa (Calif.)-Pacific U., 1987-88; mgr. pers. svcs. Calif. State U., Long Beach, 1988—; cons. human resources Corp. Stationers, L.A., 1990—, Calif. State U., Fullerton, 1990, Calif. State U. Dominguez Hills, Carson, 1992. Mem. police sgt. interview exam. bd., City of L.A., 1991. Mem. Phi Delta Kappa, Phi Delta Gamma. Home: 15226 Fernview St Whittier CA 90604 Office: Calif State U 1250 Bellflower Blvd Long Beach CA 90840-0121

HALL, CYNTHIA HOLCOMB, federal judge; b. Los Angeles, Feb. 19, 1929; d. Harold Romeyn and Mildred Gould (Kuck) Holcomb; m. John Harris Hall, June 6, 1970 (dec. Oct. 1980); A.B., Stanford U., 1951, J.D., 1954; LL.M., NYU, 1960. Bar: Ariz. 1954, Calif. 1956. Law clk. to judge U.S. Ct. Appeals 9th Circuit, 1954-55; trial atty. tax div. Dept. Justice, 1960-64; atty.-adviser Office Tax Legis. Counsel, Treasury Dept., 1964-66; mem. firm Brawerman & Holcomb, Beverly Hills, Calif., 1966-72; judge U.S. Tax Ct., Washington, 1972-81, U.S. Dist. Ct. for central dist. Calif., Los Angeles, 1981-84; cir. judge U.S. Ct. Appeals (9th cir.), Pasadena, Calif., 1984—. Served to lt. (j.g.) USNR, 1951-53. Office: US Ct Appeals 9th Cir 125 S Grand Ave Pasadena CA 91105

HALL, DAVID CHARLES, communications director; b. Council Bluffs, Iowa, Apr. 22, 1955; s. Charles Gustave and Mary Michela (Zaccone) H.; m. Kathleen Denise Kissel, June 25, 1977 (div. June 1984); children: Heather Leigh, Christopher David; m. Mary Beth Montgomery, June 1, 1985; children: Patrick Montgomery, Mary Jennifer. BS in Communication, U. Wyo., 1977. Gen. mgr. KUWR-FM, Laramie, Wyo., 1976-77; news dir. KFBC-AM-FM, Cheyenne, Wyo., 1977-78; pub. info. specialist Wyo. Hwy. Dept., Cheyenne, 1978-79; dir. Nat. First Day Cover Mus. Unicover Corp., Cheyenne, 1979-81; dir. China Stamp Agy. Unicover Corp., Cheyenne, 1981; ALUMNEWS Editor U. Wyo. Alumni Assn., Laramie, 1981-83; dir. pub. affairs Meml. Hosp., Cheyenne, 1983-90, dir. communication, 1990—; pres. Wyo. Soc. Hosp. Mktg. and Pub. Rels., Cheyenne, 1985-86, 88-89, sec./treas. 1989-91. Com. mem. Am. Cancer Soc., Cheyenne, 1985-86, United Blood Svcs., Cheyenne, 1985-86, Southeast Wyo. Tourism Coun., Cheyenne, 1980-81; vol. Cheyenne Symphony Orch., 1991—; bd. dirs. Cheyenne Little Theatre Players, 1992—. Office: Meml Hosp Laramie County 300 E 23rd St Cheyenne WY 82001-3790

HALL, DAVID STANLEY, aerospace transportation executive; b. Oak Park, Ill., Jan. 12, 1935; s. Clifford Francis and Alice Elizabeth (Brandenburger) H.; m. Arlene Carole Denzler, June 7, 1957 (div. 1984); children: Sheridan, D. Michael, Tina; m. LaNette Vinson, July 21, 1984 (div. 1991); m. Roseann Hannon, July 31, 1992. BEE, Ill. Inst. Tech., 1957; MS, U. So. Calif., 1972. Cert. air transport pilot; registered profl. safety engr., Calif. Flight test engr. Lockheed Advanced Devel., Burbank, Calif., 1962-66; sr. flight test engr. Garrett AiResearch, Phoenix, Ariz., 1967-69, sr. product safety specialist, 1973-78; lectr. U. So. Calif., L.A., 1969-72; pres. Hall Rsch. Assocs., Phoenix, 1979-90; lectr. Ariz. State U., Tempe, 1973-86, Internat. Ctr. for Aviation Safety, Lisbon, 1986-89; cons. NASA/Goddard, Greenbelt, Md., 1979-84, Nat. Taiwan U., 1971. Contbr. numerous articles to profl. jours. Founding bd. chmn. Scottsdale (Ariz.) Christian Acad., 1968. Lt. USN, 1957-62. Mem. AIAA, SAE, Internat. Soc. Air Safety Investigators, Mensa. Home: 2111 Lido Cir Stockton CA 95207-6014

HALL, DONALD NORMAN BLAKE, astronomer; b. Sydney, New South Wales, Australia, June 26, 1944; came to U.S., 1967; s. Norman F.B. and Joan B. Hall. B.Sc. with honors, U. Sydney, 1966; Ph.D. in Astronomy, Harvard U., 1970. Research assoc. Kitt Peak Nat. Obs., Tucson, 1970-72, assoc. astronomer, 1972-76, astronomer, 1976-81; dep. dir. Space Telescope Sci. Inst., Balt., 1982-84; dir. Inst. Astronomy U. Hawaii, Honolulu, 1984—; mem. space sci. bd. Nat. Acad. Sci., 1984-88, mem. astronomy adv. com. NSF, 1984-87; mem. astrophysics council NASA, 1984-88. Mem. Am. Astron. Soc. (Newton Lacey Pierce prize 1978), Internat. Astron. Union. Office: U Hawaii Inst Astronomy 2680 Woodlawn Dr Honolulu HI 96822-1897

HALL, FREDDIE LEE, JR., army chaplain; b. Richmond, Va., May 26, 1943; s. Freddie Lee and Thelma Lorrain (Henry) H.; m. Abna Reid Hall, Oct. 30, 1980;children: Michael Anthony, Derrick LaMont. BTh., Washington Bapt. Sem., 1972; BS, Luther Rice Coll., 1976; MDiv., Howard U., 1981; grad., Combined Arms Svc. Sch., Ft. Leavenworth, Kans., 1986. Commd. 2d lt. U.S. Army, 1976, advanced through grades to maj., 1989; chaplain 3/68th ADA Bn. U.S. Army, Ft. Bragg, N.C., 1981-83; chaplain 530th S&S Bn. U.S. Army, Ft. Bragg, 1983-84; asst. DISCOM chaplain 2nd Inf. Div. SUP COM U.S. Army, Camp Casey, Korea, 1984-85; group chaplain 46th Support Group U.S. Army, Ft. Bragg, 1985-86; INSTL troops support chaplain U.S. Army, 1986-88; dep. COSCOM chaplain U.S. Army, Ft. Bragg, 1988-89; with Command and Gen. Staff Coll., Ft. Leavenworth, 1987—; chaplain 160th Signal Brigade, Germany, 1989-91; dep. post chaplain Presidio, San Francisco, Calif., 1992—; voting mem. Funds Coun., Ft. Bragg, 1986-89, Presidio, San Francisco, 1992—. Decorated Meritorious Svc. medal, Army Commendation medal with two oak leaf clusters. Mem. Assn. U.S., Am. Legion, Am. Mgmt. Assn., Assn. of U.S. Army and Mil. Chaplains Assocs. Democrat. Disciple of Christ. Home: 416A Washington Blvd San Francisco CA 94129 Office: Post Chapel Presidio of San Francisco San Francisco CA 94129

HALL, GORDON R., state supreme court chief justice; b. Vernal, Utah, Dec. 14, 1926; s. Roscoe Jefferson and Clara Maud (Freestone) H.; m. Doris Gillespie, Sept. 6, 1947; children: Rick Jefferson, Craig Edwin. B.S., U. Utah, 1949, LL.B., 1951. Bar: Utah 1952. Solo practice Tooele, Utah, 1952-69; county atty. Tooele County, 1958-69; judge 3d Jud. Dist. Utah, 1969-77; assoc. justice Supreme Ct. Utah, 1977-81, chief justice, 1981—; chmn. Utah Jud. Coun., 1983—, pres. Conf. Chief Justices, 1988-89; chmn. Nat. Ctr. State Cts., 1988-89; pres. Utah Assn. Counties, 1965; mem. Pres.'s Adv. Com. OEO, 1965-66. Served with U.S. Maritime Svc., 1944-46. Mem. ABA, Utah Bar Assn. Office: Utah Supreme Ct 332 State Capitol Salt Lake City UT 84114-1181

HALL, GREGORY CLARK, architect; b. Clark AFB, Luzon, Phillippines, Jan. 22, 1950; s. Arthur Iassic and Janet (Baker) H. AA, Seminole Jr. Coll., Sanford, Fla., 1972; BArch, U. Hawaii, 1987. Lic. architect, 1992. Carpenter Constrn. Tech., Honolulu, 1972-75; filmaker Niteworks, Sunset Beach, Hawaii, 1974-80; ocean recreation specialist City of Honolulu Parks and Recreation, Haleiwa, Hawaii, 1975-80; surfboard builder Summerfield Rd./Lightning Bolt, Haleiwa, 1968-82; designer Hawaiian Hydroseed Irrigation, Lahina, Maui, 1982; systems analyst Alpha Data Systems, Honolulu, 1982-86; prin., designer Moonlight Ink Archtl., Honolulu, 1984—; pvt. airplane pilot Honolulu, 1990; archtl. designer Moonlight Ink, Honolulu, 1988-92; race car owner/driver Grom Porsche, Honolulu, 1990-92. Author: Surfboard Building in Hawaii, 1980; artist paintings and sculpture, 1982. Graphic designer MADD, Honolulu, 1991; water safety instr. ARC, 1976. Recipient Cert. of Appreciation for meritorious svc. City and County of Honolulu, 1976. Mem. AIA (assoc. Hawaii chpt., honorable mention design award 1986, design excellence award 1987), Porsche Club Am. (driver), Sports Car Club Am. (driver), Smithsonian Air and Space. Republican.

HALL, HAROLD ROBERT, computer engineer; b. Bakersfield, Calif., Feb. 7, 1935; s. Edward Earl and Ethel Mae (Butner) H.; m. Tenniebee May Hall, Feb. 20, 1965. BS, U. Calif., Berkeley, 1956, MS, 1957, PhD, 1966. Chief engr. wave-filter div. Transonic, Inc., Bakersfield, 1957-60; chief design engr. Circuit Dyne Corp., Pasadena and Laguna Beach, Calif., 1960-61; sr. devel. engr. Robertshaw Controls Co., Anaheim, Calif., 1961-63; research engr. Naval Command, Control and Ocean Surveillance Ctr., rsch. and devel. divsn. Navy Research Lab., San Diego, 1966—; bd. dirs. Circuit Dyne Corp., Pacific Coil Co. Recipient Thomas Clair McFarland award U. Calif., Berkeley, 1956, NSF fellow, 1957. Mem. IEEE, Acoustical Soc. Am., Phi Beta Kappa. Home: 5284 Dawes St San Diego CA 92109-1231 Office: Naval Command Control & Ocean Surveillance Ctr Rsch & Devel Divsn San Diego CA 92152-5352

HALL, HOWARD PICKERING, mathematics educator; b. Boston, July 8, 1915; s. George Henry and Elizabeth Isabel (McCallum) H.; m. Ellen Marguerite Ide, June 25, 1945 (dec. 1984); children: Charlotte McCallum, Stephanie Wilson, Lindsey Louise, Gretchen Elizabeth. AB, Harvard U., 1936, MS, 1937, DSc, 1951. Registered structural engr., Ill., 1953. Instr., civil engring. Brown U., Providence, 1937-38; structural analyst Mark Linenthal, Engr., Boston, 1938-39; instr., asst. prof., assoc. prof. civil engring. Northwestern U., Evanston, Ill., 1939-56; design engr. field engr. Porter, Urquart, Skidmore, Owings, Merrill, Casablanca, Fr. Morocco, 1951-53; dean, sch. engring., acad. v.p. Robert Coll., Istanbul, Turkey, 1956-68; dir. of studies, acting headmaster St. Stephen's Sch., Rome, 1968-72; prof. math. Iranzamin Internat., Tehran, Iran, 1973-80; math. tchr. Vienna Internat. Sch., 1980-83, Copenhagen Internat. Sch., 1983-86; cons. S.J. Buchanan, Bryan, Tex., Eng., 1955. Contbr. articles to profl. jours. Served to Capt. U.S. Army, 1942-46, ETO. Recipient Clemens Herschel award Boston Soc. Civil Engrs., 1954. Mem. AAAS, Sigma Xi. Home: 301 SW Lincoln St Apt 1101 Portland OR 97201-5031

HALL, JAMES CARTER, engineering manager; b. Syracuse, N.Y., Jan. 2, 1958; s. James Albert and Mae Belle (Hooks) H.; m. Evelyn Sue Cooper, Dec. 30, 1982; 1 child, Nicole Dawn; m. Christy Ann Martin, Oct. 19, 19911 1 child, Courtney Elizabeth. BSET, U. Houston, 1982. Process engr. Texas Instruments, Houston, 1978-81; process/equipment engr. Advanced Micro Devices, Austin, Tex., 1981-84, facilities engr., 1984-89; engring. mgr. Systems Chemistry, Milpitas, Calif., 1989—. Mem. NFPA, SEMI. Office: Systems Chemistry Inc 370 Montague Expwy Milpitas CA 95035

HALL, JAMES MARCELL, water resources planning engineer; b. Sacramento, Jan. 5, 1951; s. Claude Newton and Annie Mai (Cobitt) H.; m. Sandra Jones Davis, Nov. 12, 1978 (div. Dec. 1987); m. Kathleen Marie Gadway, Jan 31, 1989. AA in Math Sci, Am. River Coll., Sacramento, 1971; BSCE, U. Pacific, 1974; MSCE, Stanford U., 1978. Registered profl. engr., Calif. Civil, structural and hydraulic engr. U.S. Army Corps of Engrs., Sacramento, 1974-81; sr. civil engr. Resource Mgmt. Internat., Sacramento, 1981-88; assoc. civil engr. East Bay Mcpl. Utility Dist., Oakland, Calif., 1988—; v.p. Davis and Hall, Inc., Fair Oaks, Calif., 1977-78; pres. AFSCME Local 2019 Union, Oakland, 1992-93. Sec. United Neighborhood Watch Assn., Berkeley, Calif., 1991-93. Mem. ASCE (AMF pres. 1976-77), Synthesis Inst. Home: 2905 Newbury St Berkeley CA 94703 Office: East Bay Mcpl Utility Dist 375 11th St Oakland CA 94607

HALL, JOHN ROBERT, physicist; b. Omaha, Nov. 20, 1948; s. Ivan Francis and Opal Maude (Church) H.; m. Gloria Alexandria Velcoff, June 15, 1975 (div. 1989). BS in Physics, Calif. State U., Northridge, 1977, MS in Physics, 1983. Engr. Litton Guidance & Control, Woodland Hills, Calif., 1974-83, engr. specialist, 1983-87, prin. investigator, 1987—. Author computer programs: RememDir, 1988, Typwtr., 1985, HDIS, 1983. With USAF, 1968-72. Me. Litton Mgmt. Club. Democrat.

HALL, LARRY D., energy company executive, lawyer; b. Hastings, Nebr., Nov. 8, 1942; s. Willis E. and Stella W. (Eckoff) H.; m. Jeffe D. Bryant, July 5, 1985; children: Scott, Jeff, Mike, Bryan. BA in Bus., U. Nebr., Kearney; JD, U. Nebr. Bar: Nebr., Colo. Ptnr. Wright, Simmons, Hancock & Hall, Scottsbluff, Nebr., 1967-71; atty., asst. treas. KN Energy Inc., Hastings, 1971-73, dir. regulatory affairs, 1973-76; v.p. law divsn. KN Energy Inc., Lakewood, Colo., 1976-82, sr. v.p., 1982-85, exec. v.p., 1985-88, pres., COO, 1988—, also bd. dirs.; bd. dirs. Colo. Assn. Commerce and Industry, Gas Rsch. Inst., Colo. Alliance for Bus., MLA, Rocky Mountain Oil and Gas Assn. Mem. ABA, Fed. Energy Bar Assn., Nebr. Bar Assn., Colo. Bar Assn., Pres. Assn., Midwest Gas Assn. (chmn.), INGAA, MGA, CAB (bd. dirs.), Hiwan Country Club, Elks, Masons, Club 30. Democrat. Presbyterian. Home: 1892 Sugarbush Dr Evergreen CO 80439-9415 Office: KN Energy Inc PO Box 15265 Lakewood CO 80215-0007

HALL, LOIS RIGGS, symphony orchestra administrator, state senator; b. Beeville, Tex., May 22, 1930; d. Ira Franklin and Pearl Ophelia (McCoy) Riggs; student Tex. Women's U., 1947-49, U. Tex., Austin, 1949-50; m. Walter William Hall, Dec. 28, 1950 (dec.); children—Robert Macfarlane, Elaine Denise, Judith Lea. Exec. sec. N.Mex. Symphony Orch., Albuquerque, 1975—; mem. N.Mex. Senate, 1980-85. Active Boy Scouts Am., Girl Scouts U.S.A., Officers Wives Clubs; 2d v.p. Albuquerque Symphony Women's Assn.; bd. dirs. Friends of Music, 1986-88; treas., publicity dir. N.Mex. Aviation Assn. Republican. Home: 620 Datiz NE Albuquerque NM 87108 Office: PO Box 769 Albuquerque NM 87103-0769

HALL, MARIAN ELLA See **ROBERTSON, MARIAN ELLA**

HALL, MARK RONALD, microbiology educator; b. Detroit, Apr. 15, 1941; s. Mark W. and Anne (Crockett) H.; m. Nancy J. Renick, Apr. 11, 1969; children: Matthew Brian, Erin Marie. BS, Western Mich. U., 1964; MS, Wayne State U., 1968, PhD, 1971. Postdoctoral Scripps Clinic and Rsch. Found., La Jolla, Calif., 1971-73; asst. prof. Med. Coll. Ga., Augusta, 1973-77; assoc. prof. microbiology U. Nev. Sch. Medicine, Reno, 1977-92, prof. microbiology, 1992—. Contbr. articles to profl. jours.; patentee parasite vaccine. Grantee NIH, 1976-81, Am. Cancer Soc., 1977-80, Ft. Dodge Lab., 1986-91, VA, 1991—, USDA, 1990—. Mem. AAAS, Am. Soc. for Microbiology, Am. Soc. for Virology, Tissue Culture Assn., Sigma Xi. Office: U Nev Sch Medicine Reno NV 89557

HALL, RAYMOND G., physiologist, researcher; b. Sherman, Tex., Mar. 11, 1937; s. Ramon and Wynne Hall; m. Janice Hall, Sept. 8, 1959; children: Jon, Julie Nelson, Jacklyn Moon. BA, Union Coll., Lincoln, Nebr., 1959; MA, Walla Walla Coll., 1961; PhD, Loma Linda U., 1968. Postdoctoral fellow U. Colo., Boulder, 1969-70; physiologist Sch. Medicine, Loma Linda (Calif.) U., 1970—. Mem. Am. Soc. for Cell Biology, Sigma Xi (pres. chpt. 1992). Office: Loma Linda U Loma Linda CA 92354

HALL, RICHARD DENNIS, agribusiness and international trade writer; b. Troy, N.Y., Apr. 12, 1935; s. Dennis John and Clara Eleanor (Hanson) H.; m. Joyce Ann Huntington, June 7, 1957; children: Brian Huntington, Roger Hanson. BS, Boston U., 1957. Gen. assignment reporter Worcester (Mass.) Telegram and the Evening Gazette, 1957-60; city hall reporter, columnist Springfield (Mass.) Union, 1960-65; reporter Fresno (Calif.) Bee, 1965-77, agr. water reporter, 1977-79; Washington corr. McClatchy Newspapers, 1979-83; agribus. writer Fresno (Calif.) Bee, 1983-91, ret., 1991; mem. 9th Ann. Conf. European and Am. Journalists, Maastricht, The Netherlands, 1985. Author: Fresno County in the 20th Century, 1987, Hanford Hometown America, 1990; contbg. editor Calif. Farmer mag., 1986—. Docent local history tours, Hanford, Calif., 1987. Recipient Agribus. Invitation award, Taiwan, 1983. Mem. Garden of the Sun Corral Western History Club. Home and Office: 1978 Mulberry Dr Hanford CA 93230-2046

HALL, RICHARD EDWARD, amusement park executive; b. L.A., Feb. 1, 1951; s. David Harwood and Betty Jane (Mowers) H.; m. Francine Marie Berns, Apr. 19, 1975; children: Mathew, Jeffery, David. BS, Portland State U., 1975. Founder, v.p. Athletic Tng. Equipment Co., Clackamas, Oreg., 1976-85; founder, pres. Grand Slam USA, Inc., Salem, Oreg., 1982—; founder, v.p. Automated Batting Cages, Inc., Salem, Oreg., 1985—; founder, pres. Smith-Hall Industries, Salem, Oreg., 1986—, Oregon Batting Cage, Corp., Salem, Oreg., 1989—; pres. J&J Amusements, Inc., San Juan Capistrano, Calif., 1990—. Mem. Internat. Assns. of Amusement Pks. and Attractions, World Waterpark Assn., Miniature Golf Assn. Am. (bd. dirs.), City of Salem C. of C. Office: Automated Batting Cages Inc 8811 Huff Ave NE Salem OR 97303

HALL, RICHARD EUGENE, psychologist; b. Indpls., Feb. 15, 1936; s. Leon Arthur and Maude Lee (Rorher) H.; m. Shirley Tomkins, June, 1958 (div. 19620; 1 child, Laura J.; m. Patricia A. King, Feb. 28, 1964; children: Kelly A., Diana L., Michael R. AB in Chemistry, Ind. U., 1958; PhD in Neurosci., U. Calif., San Diego, 1973; PhD in Clin. Psychology, Internat. Coll., 1983. Lic. psychologist, Calif. Asst. prof. Bowman Gray Sch. of Medicine, Winston-Salem, N.C., 1973-76; med. researcher UCLA, 1976-85; pvt. practice clin. psychologist L.A. and Riverside, Calif., 1985—. Lt. USN, 1959-68. Mem. Am. Coll. Forensic Psychologists, Calif. Attys. for Criminal Justice (assoc.). Republican. Methodist. Office: 3638 University Ave Ste 243 Riverside CA 92501-3334

HALL, ROBERT EMMETT, JR., investment banker, realtor; b. Sioux City, Iowa, Apr. 28, 1936; s. Robert Emmett and Alvina (Faden) H.; m. Marna Thiel, 1969. BA, U. S.D., 1958, MA, 1959; MBA, U. Santa Clara, 1976; grad. Am. Inst. Banking, Realtors Inst. Grad. asst. U. S.D., Vermillion, 1958-59; mgr. ins. dept., asst. mgr. installment loan dept. Northwestern Nat. Bank of Sioux Falls, S.D., 1959-61, asst. cashier, 1961-65; asst. mgr. Crocker Nat. Bank, San Francisco, 1965-67, loan officer, 1967-69, asst. v.p., asst. mgr. San Mateo br., 1969-72; v.p., Western regional mgr. Internat. Investments & Realty, Inc., Washington, 1972—; owner Hall Investment Co., 1976—; pres. Almaden Oaks Realtors, Inc., 1976—; instr. West Valley Coll., Saratoga, Calif., 1972-82, Grad. Sch. Bus., U. Santa Clara (Calif.), 1981—. Treas., Minnehaha Leukemia Soc., 1963, Lake County Heart Fund Assn., 1962, Minnehaha Young Republican Club, 1963. Mem. Am. Inst. Banking, San Mateo C. of C., Calif. Assn. Realtors (vice chmn.), Beta Theta Pi. Republican. Roman Catholic. Clubs: Elks, Rotary (past pres.), K.C., Almaden Country, Mercedes Benz Calif. Home: 6951 Castlerock Dr San Jose CA 95120-4705 also: 8864 Rubicon Dr Homewood CA 96142 Office: Hall Enterprises 6501 Crown Blvd Ste 106 San Jose CA 95120-2992

HALL, SUSAN JEAN, educator; b. Long Beach, Calif., Jan. 12, 1951; d. Owen Parson and Goldie Marie (Lutz) H. BA in Music, U. of the Pacific, 1973, MA in Polit. Sci., 1981; postgrad., U. So. Calif., 1981-83. Tchr. Lincoln Unified Sch. Dist., Stockton, Calif., 1973-80; writer Teledyne Inet, Torrance, Calif., 1981-82; data mgmt. coordinator Northrop Corp., Hawthorne, Calif., 1982-83; proposal adminstr. Rockwell Internat. Corp., El Segundo, Calif., 1983; tchr. Lodi (Calif.) Unified Sch. Dist., 1983—, fine arts dir., 1984—; chairperson Lodi PTA, 1985—. Author: National Socialism: The German Tragedy, 1981; composer: Sonata in C, 1975. Dem. campaigner, Lodi, 1976-80; donator, drive chmn. Lodi Life Mission, 1986; 1st violinist Stockton Symphony. Mem. Nat. Tchrs. Assn., Calif. Tchrs. Assn., Music Educators Assn. Home: 1753 Cape Cod Cir Lodi CA 95242-4204 Office: Nichols Sch 1301 S Crescent Lodi CA 95242

HALL, TENNIEBEE M., editor; b. Bakersfield, Calif., May 21, 1940; d. William Elmer and Lillian May (Otis) Hall; m. Harold Robert Hall, Feb. 20, 1965. BA in Edn., Fresno State Coll., 1962; AA, Bakersfield Coll., 1960. Cert. tchr., Calif. Tchr. Edison (Calif.) Sch. Dist., 1963-65; substitute tchr. Marin and Oakland Counties (Calif.), Berkeley, 1965-66; engring. asst. Pacific Coil Co., Inc., Bakersfield, 1974-81; editor United Ostomy Assn., Inc., Irvine, Calif., 1986-91. Co-author: Treating IBD, 1989, Current Therapy in Gastroenterology, 1989; author, designer: Volunteer Leadership Training Manuals, 1982-84; contbr. articles to Ostomy Quar., 1973—. Mem. Pacific Beach Town Coun., San Diego, 1977—; campaign worker Maureen O'Connor (1st woman mayor of city), San Diego, 1986; mem. Nat. Digestive Diseases Adv. Bd. NIH, Washington, 1986-91; various vol. activities, 1966-74, 81-86. Recipient Outstanding Svc. award VA Vol. Svc., Bur. of Vets. Affairs, Washington, 1990. Mem. Nat. Assn. Parliamentarians (unit v.p. 1988-90), United Ostomy Assn. Inc. (regional program dir. 1980-84, pres. 1984-86, Sam Dubin award 1983, Industry Adv. award 1987, local commendation San Diego chpt. 1978), Crohn's and Colitis Found. Am. (nat. trustee 1986—, nat. v.p. 1987-92, local commendation San Diego chpt. 1988). Home and Office: 5284 Dawes St San Diego CA 92109-1231

HALL, TERESA YVONNE, elementary educator; b. Kingman, Kans., Aug. 12, 1963; d. William Leon and Mary Ann (Galant) Garrison; m. John Haley Hall, June 24, 1989. BA in Liberal Arts, Fresno Pacific Coll., 1985. Cert. bilingual, multiple subject tchr., Calif. Asst. diving coach Madera (Calif.) Marlins, 1979-88, head coach, 1989—; head coach Hoover High Sch., Fresno, Calif., 1986-89, Madera High Sch., 1990-92; bilingual tchr. Washington Elem. Sch., Madera, 1986-88, Sierra Vista Elem. Sch., Madera, 1989—; head coach Clovis (Calif.) West High Sch., 1992—. Author ednl. materials in field. Lay leader Madera United Meth. Ch., 1989—. One Meter Nat. Champion, U.S. Masters Diving, 1989. Mem. PEO Sisterhood (chaplain 1989-91, corr. sec. 1991—), U.S. Diving Assn., Madera Unified Tchrs. Assn. Methodist. Home: 2512 Grapewood Way Madera CA 93637

HALLAM, ROBERT J., performing company executive, consultant; b. Edmonton, Alta., Can., Oct. 24, 1952; s. Donald Robert and Mary (Dutton)

H.; m. Sydney Ann Scott, Oct. 5, 1984; 1 child, Robert Ian. MusB, U. Alta., 1976, MBA, 1983. Adminstrv. mgr. Edmonton Opera, 1983-85, gen. mgr., 1985-89, gen. dir., 1989-91; gen. dir. Vancouver (B.C.) Opera, Can., 1991—; chmn. Can. com., dir. Opera Am., Washington, 1987—, treas., 1990—; cons. Opera Sask., Regina, 1989-90. Office: Vancouver Opera, 845 Cambie St Ste 500, Vancouver, BC Canada V6B 4Z9

HALLBAUER, ROBERT EDWARD, mining company executive; b. Nakusp, B.C., Can., May 19, 1930; s. Edward F. and Lillian Anna (Kendrick) H.; m. Mary Joan Hunter, Sept. 6, 1952; children: Russell, Catherine, Thomas. BS in Mining Engring., U. B.C., 1954. Registered profl. engr., B.C. Various engring. and supervisory positions Placer Devel., Salmo, B.C., 1954-60; mine supr. Craigmont Mines Ltd., Merritt, B.C., 1960-64, mine mgr., 1964-68; v.p. mining Teck Corp., Vancouver, B.C., 1968-79, sr. v.p., 1979—; pres., chief exec. officer Cominco Ltd., Vancouver, 1986—, also bd. dirs. Recipient Edgar A. Scholz medal B.C. and Yukon Chamber of Mines, 1984. Mem. Assn. Profl. Engrs., Can. Inst. Mining, Metallurgy and Petroleum (Inco medal 1992). Home: 6026 Glenwynd Pl, West Vancouver, BC Canada V7W 2W5 Office: Cominco Ltd, 200 Burrard St #500, Vancouver, BC Canada V6C 3L7

HALLECK, CHARLES WHITE, lawyer, former judge; b. Rensselaer, Ind., July 6, 1929; s. Charles Abraham and Blanche (White) H.; m. Carolyn L. Wood, Dec. 23, 1950 (div. Oct. 1969); children: Holly Louise, Charles White, Todd Alexander, Heather Leigh, Heidi Lynne, William Hemsley, Hope Leslie; m. Jeanne Wahl, May 16, 1970. A.B., Williams Coll., 1951; J.D., George Washington U., 1957; LL.D. (hon.), St. Joseph's Coll., 1971. Asst. U.S. atty. for D.C., 1957-59; assoc. Hogan and Hartson, Washington, 1959-65; judge Superior Ct. D.C., 1965-77; mem. firm Lamb, Halleck & Keats, Washington, 1977-80; sole practice, 1980-86, photojounalist, 1986—. Served with USNR, 1951-55; to lt. Res. (ret.). Mem. Beta Theta Pi, Phi Delta Phi.

HALLENBECK, POMONA JUANITA, artist; b. Roswell, N.Mex., Nov. 12, 1938; d. Cleve and Juanita Henriette (Williams) H.; children: Cheryl Ellis, Cynthia Ellis-Ralph, Catherine Ellis-Timmons. AA, Ea. N.Mex. U., 1965; BFA, Art Student's League, 1976; postgrad., Pan Am. Art Sch., 1976-77. Mgr. Paul Anderson Photography, San Antonio, Tex., 1951-54; tchr. Roswell (N.Mex.) Ind. Sch. Dist., 1960-64; dir., instr. Sketchbox Sch. Art, Galveston, Tex., 1965-71; monitor etching class Art Student's League, N.Y.C., 1975-77; dir., instr. Alleyworks Atlier, Austin, Tex., 1978-81; dir., proprietor, artist Sketchbox Studio, Roswell, 1982-92; instr. Elderhostel program Ghost Ranch, Abiquiu, N.Mex, 1984-93; coord. Calender project Ghost Ranch, Abiquiu, N.Mex., 1992—; owner, proprietor Pomona's Accent Line, Roswell, 1986-92; cons. Pomona's Accent Line, Roswell, 1988-92; artist, demonstrator Roswell (N.Mex.) Mus. and Art Ctr., 1981-90, Roswell (N.Mex.) Ind. Sch., 1982-90. Illustrator: (book covers) Julian of Norwich, Nachman, Pseudo Dionysius, Classics of Western Spirituality, Naming the Powers, Unmasking the Powers, Engaging the Powers; exhibited in Southwest Expressions Gallery, Chgo, 1990, 91, Claire's Mountain Village, Ruidoso, N.Mex., 1990-93. Mem. Rosewell (N.Mex.) Humane Soc., 1990—, Ghost Ranch Compadres, Sant Fe, 1990-93, People for the Ethical Treatment of Animals, 1993, Roswell Assurance Home for Children, 1990; arts program coord. Ghost Ranch. Recipient scholarship Altrusa Club, 1973, Purchase award Am. Artist, N.Y.C., 1975; named best of show Ghost Ranch Compadre show, N.Mex., 1990, Altusa Fashion Show, N.Mex., 1990; grantee Whitney Enterprises, San Diego, 1990, artist-in-residence grantee Ghost Ranch, Santa Fe, 1992. Mem. Soc. Illustrators, Taos Fine Arts Assn., N.Mex. Watercolor Soc., Supts. Salon of Paris (bronze medal 1988), Ghost Ranch Found. Ctr., Roswell Mus. and Art Ctr., U.S. Humane Soc. Democrat. Presbyterian. Office: Sketchbox Studio of Art HC77 Box 11 Abiquiu NM 87510

HALLETT, DEAN CHARLES, entertainment company executive; b. Encino, Calif., June 9, 1958; s. William Charles and Sally (Lane) H.; m. Kelli Lynn Frisinger, July 2, 1983; children: Drew Charles, Makenzie Rae. BBA cum laude, U. So. Calif., L.A., 1980. CPA. From staff acct. to sr. audit mgr. Ernst & Whinney, L.A., 1981-88; contr. Anthony Industries, Inc., L.A., 1988-90; mgr., corp. mgmt. audit The Walt Disney Co., Burbank, Calif., 1990-91; dir. fin. Buena Vista Pictures Mktg. subs. Walt Disney Studios, Burbank, 1991—; campus recruiting coord. U. So. Calif., L.A., 1985-88; exchange visitor Ernst & Whinney, London, 1986-87. Mem. AICPA, Calif. Soc. CPA, U. So. Calif. Acctg. Circle. Republican. Office: The Walt Disney Co 500 S Buena Vista St Burbank CA 91521-1427

HALLETT, JOHN, physics educator; b. Bristol, Eng., Dec. 2, 1929; m. Joan Terry Collar, July 12, 1960; children: Jennifer, Joyce, Elaine, Rosemary. BS, U. Bristol, 1953; Diploma, Imperial Coll., London, 1954; PhD, U. London, 1958. From asst. lectr. to lectr. Imperial Coll., London, 1959, 1962-66; asst. prof. UCLA, 1960-62; rsch. prof., Desert Rsch. Inst. chmn. atmospheric sci. program U. Nev., Reno, 1966—. Contbr. articles to profl. jours. Fellow Royal Meteorol. Soc.; mem. Internat. Glaciological Soc., Am. Meteorol. Soc.

HALLIDAY, JOHN MEECH, investment company executive; b. St. Louis, Oct. 16, 1936; s. William Norman and Vivian Viola (Meech) H.; m. Martha Layne Griggs, June 30, 1962; children: Richard M., Elizabeth. BS, U.S. Naval Acad., 1958; MBA, Harvard U., 1964. Dir. budgeting and planning Automatic Tape Control, Bloomington, Ill., 1964-66; dir. planning Ralston-Purina, St. Louis, 1966-67, v.p. subsidiary, 1967-68, dir. internat. banking, 1967-68; v.p. Servicetime Corp., St. Louis, 1968-70; assoc. R.W. Halliday Assocs., Boise, Idaho, 1970-87; v.p. Sawtooth Comm. Corp., Boise, 1970-73, Comdr. Corp., 1979-81; pres., CEO, bd. dirs. ML Ltd., San Francisco, H.W.L. Inc., San Francisco, 1985-93; pres. Halliday Labs., Inc., 1980-91; exec. v.p., bd. dirs. Franchise Fin. Corp. Am., Phoenix, 1980-85; bd. dirs., v.p. Harvard Bus. Sch. Assn. No. Calif., 1980-87; bd. dirs. FFAC, Irvine, Calif., 1989-92; pres., CEO, bd. dirs. Cycletrol Diversified Industries, Inc., 1992—. Pres. Big Bros. San Francisco, 1978-81; trustee, pres. U. Calif.-Santa Cruz Found., 1988—. Lt. comdr. USNR, 1958-66. Mem. ACLU, Restaurant Assn. (v.p. 1969-70). Republican. Episcopalian. Clubs: Family, Olympic (San Francisco), Scott Valley Tennis (Mill Valley, Calif.). Home: 351 Corte Madera Ave Mill Valley CA 94941-1013 Office: 625 Market St Ste 602 San Francisco CA 94105-3308

HALLIDAY, ROY ARTHUR, research psychologist, educator; b. San Francisco, Sept. 30, 1934; s. Harold A. and Frieda E. (Dolan) H.; m. Margaret D. Tennison, Feb. 4, 1941; children: Eric A., Karl O., Jacom R., Aija R. AB, Calif. State U., Hayward, 1963; MA, U. Nebr., 1967; PhD, U. Calif., San Francisco, 1980. Asst. prof. psychology U. Calif., San Francisco, 1980-84, assoc. prof., 1984-88, prof., 1988-91, prof. emeritus, 1991—; rsch. scientist No. Calif. Inst. for Rsch. and Edn., San Francisco, 1991—; cons. editor Psychophysiology, 1974—, Biol. Psychology, 1974—, Biol. Psychiatry, 1974—, Electroencephalography and Clin. Neurophysiology, 1974—. Contbr. chpt. to books, articles to profl. jours. Bd. dirs. Tri City Health Inc., Fremont, Calif., 1976-80. Recipient Chancellor award for pub. svc. U. Calif., San Francisco, 1980. Mem. Soc. for Psychophysiol. Rsch. Home: 37859 3d St Fremont CA 94536 Office: VAMC (116T) 4150 Clement St San Francisco CA 94536

HALLIDAY, WILLIAM ROSS, retired physician, speleologist, writer; b. Atlanta, May 9, 1926; s. William Ross and Jane (Wakefield) H.; m. Eleanore Hartvedt, July 2, 1951 (dec. 1983); children: Marcia Lynn, Patricia Anne, William Ross III; m. Louise Baird Kinnard, May 7, 1988. BA, Swarthmore Coll., 1946; MD, George Washington U., 1948. Diplomate Am. Bd. Vocat. Experts. Intern Huntington Meml. Hosp., Pasadena, Calif., 1948-49; resident King County Hosp., Seattle, Denver Children's Hosp., L.D.S. Hosp., Salt Lake City, 1950-57; pvt. practice Seattle, 1957-65; with Wash. State Dept. Labor and Industries, Olympia, 1965-76; med. dir. Wash. State Div. Vocat. Rehab., 1976-82; staff physican N.W. Occupational Health Ctr., Seattle, 1983-84; med. dir. N.W. Vocat. Rehab. Group, Seattle, 1984, Comprehensive Med. Rehab. Ctr., Brentwood, Tenn., 1984-87; dep. coroner, King County, Wash., 1964-66. Author: Adventure Is Underground, 1959, Depths of the Earth, 1966, 76, American Caves and Caving, 1974, 82; co-author: (with Robert Nymeyer) Carlsbad Cavern: The Early Years, 1991; editor Jour. Spelean History, 1968-73; contbr. articles to profl. jours. Mem. Gov.'s North Cascades Study Com., 1967-76; mem. North Cascades Conservation Coun., v.p., 1962-63; pres. Internat. Speleological Found., 1981-87; asst. dir. Internat. Glaciospeleological Survey, 1972-76. Served to lt. comdr. USNR, 1949-50, 55-57. Fellow Am. Coll. Chest Physicians, Am. Acad. Compensation Medicine, Nat. Speleological Soc. (bd. govs. 1988—, chmn. Hawaii Speleological Survey 1989—, chmn. 1st, 3d, 6th Internat. Symposia on Vulcanospeleology, chmn. Internat. Union Speleology Working Group on Volcanic Caves 1990—), Western Speleological Survey (dir. 1957-83, dir. rsch. 1983—), Explorers Club; mem. Soc. Thoracic Surgeons, AMA, Am. Congress Rehab. Medicine, Am. Coll. Legal Medicine, Wash. State Med. Assn., Tenn. State Med. Assn, King County Med. Soc., Am. Fedn. Clin. Rsch., Am. Spelean History Assn. (pres. 1968), Brit. Cave Rsch. Assn., Nat. Trust (Scotland). Clubs: Mountaineers (past trustee), Seattle Tennis.

HALLIGAN, JAMES EDMUND, university administrator, chemical engineer; b. Moorland, Iowa, June 23, 1936; s. Raymond Anthony and Margaret Ann (Crawford) H.; m. Ann Elizabeth Sorenson, June 29, 1957; children: Michael, Patrick, Christopher. M.S. in Chem. Engring, Iowa State U., 1962, M.S., 1965, Ph.D., 1968. Registered profl. engr., Tex., N.Mex. Process engr. Humble Oil Co., 1962-64; mem. faculty Tex. Tech U., 1968-77; dean engring. U. Mo., Rolla, 1977-79; dean engring. U. Ark., Fayetteville, 1979-82, vice chancellor for acad. affairs, 1982-83, interim chancellor, 1983-84; pres. N.Mex. State U., Las Cruces, 1984—; v.p. engring. Kandahar Cons. Ltd.; mem. Gov. Tex. Energy Adv. Council, 1972-74. Served with USAF, 1954-58. Recipient Disting. Teaching award Tex. Tech U., 1972, Disting. Research award, 1975, 76; Disting. Teaching award U. Mo., Rolla, 1978. Mem. Am. Chem. Soc., Nat. Soc. Profl. Engrs., Am. Inst. Chem. Engrs., Am. Soc. Engring. Edn., Tau Beta Pi, Phi Kappa Phi, Pi Mu Epsilon. Roman Catholic. Club: Rotary. Home: PO Box 5074 Las Cruces NM 88003-5074 Office: NMex State U Box 3Z 208 Hadley Hall Las Cruces NM 88003

HALLMARK, R. ELAINE, lawyer, mediator, consultant; b. Pasadena, Calif., Dec. 9, 1942; d. James Steele Temple and Ruth Evelyn (Cordill) Raabe; m. William Lewis Hallmark, Apr. 2, 1961; children: William Royce, Kimberly Anne Bates. Student, Stanford U., 1960-61; BA in Polit. Sci., George Washington U., 1965; JD, Lewis and Clark U., 1976. Bar: Oreg. Caseworker State of Oreg. Welfare and Children's Svcs., Eugene, Salem, Portland, 1966-73; sole practitioner of law Portland, 1976-78, 86-88; educator, adminstr. Creative Initiative Found., Portland, 1977-81; trainer, adminstr. Beyond War Found., Palo Alto and Portland, 1981-83; atty. Bonneville Power Adminstrn., Portland, 1984-85; mediator Confluence N.W., Portland, 1988—; chair Oreg. Dispute Resolution Com., Salem, 1989-92. Author legal articles. Mem. Oreg. State Bar (exec. com. ADR sect. 1989—), Multnomah Bar Assn. (chair ADR com. 1988-91, award of merit 1989), Soc. Profls. in Dispute Resolution (co-chair environ. and pub. disputes sector). Office: Confluence NW PO Box 8182 Portland OR 97207

HALLOCK, C. WILES, JR., athletic official; b. Denver, Feb. 17, 1918; s. Claude Wiles and Mary (Bassler) H.; m. Marjorie Louise Eldred, Mar. 23, 1944; children: Lucinda Eldred Hallock Rinne, Michael Eldred. A.B., U. Denver, 1939. Sports info. dir. U. Wyo., 1949-60, track coach, 1952-56; sports info. dir. U. Calif., Berkeley, 1960-63; dir. pub. relations Nat. Collegiate Athletic Assn., 1963-68; dir. Nat. Collegiate Sports Services, 1967-68; commr. Western Athletic Conf., 1968-71; exec. dir. Pacific-8 Conf., San Francisco, 1971-83; historian Pacific 10 Conf., 1983. Mem. Laramie (Wyo.) City Council, 1958-60. Served to lt. comdr. USNR, World War II. Decorated Air medal; mem. Nat. Football Found. and Hall of Fame Honors Ct. Mem. Nat. Collegiate Athletic Assn., Nat. Assn. Collegiate Dirs. Athletics (Corbett award 1983), Collegiate Commrs. Assn., Coll. Sports Info. Dirs. Am. (Arch Ward award 1963), Football Writers Assn. Am. (past dir.), U.S. Basketball Writers Assn., Lambda Chi Alpha. Presbyn. Home: 235 Western Hills Dr Pleasant Hill CA 94523-3167 Office: 800 S Broadway Walnut Creek CA 94596-5218

HALLOCK, JOSEPH THEODORE (TED), electric conservation-planning council official; b. L.A., Oct. 26, 1921; s. Joseph Homer and Mary Elizabeth (Peninger) H.; m. Phyllis Natwick, Jan. 1946 (div. Mar. 1968); children: Stephanie, Christopher, Leslie; m. Jacklyn Louise Goldsmith, Sept. 12, 1969. BS in Journalism, U. Oreg., 1948. Assoc. editor Down Beat mag., Chgo., 1947-48; program dir. Sta. KPOJ, Portland, Oreg., 1948-53; dir. pub. affairs J. Henry Helser & Co., Portland, 1953-58; state coord. Oreg. Centennial Commn., Portland, 1958-59; pres. Ted Hallock Inc., Portland, 1959-63; pres. The Hallock Agy. Inc., Portland, 1981-88, corp. sec., 1988—; mem. Oreg. Senate, Salem, 1963-83; Oreg. mem. Pacific N.W. Power Coun., Portland, 1988—. Trustee Portland Art Mus., 1987-88. Capt. USAAF, 1943-45, ETO. Decorated DFC, Air medal with three oak leaf clusters, Purple Heart with oak leaf cluster. Mem. AFTRA, Soc. Profl. Journalists. Democrat. Presbyterian. Office: 2445 NW Irving St Portland OR 97210

HALLORAN, JAMES VINCENT, III, marketing consultant; b. Greenwich, Conn., May 12, 1942; s. James Vincent and Rita Lucy (Keator) H.; m. Barbara Sharon Case, Sept. 7, 1974. BME, Cath. U. Am., 1964; MBA, U. Chgo., 1973. Mktg. rep. Rockwell Internat., El Segundo, Calif., 1973-76, bus. area mgr., 1976-80, bus. analysis mgr., 1980-84; asst. dir. market analysis H. Silver & Assocs. Inc., Torrance, Calif., 1984-87, dir. mktg., 1987-90; program mgr. Tech. Tng. Corp., Torrance, 1990-91; prin. Bus. Info. & Analysis, Redondo Beach, Calif., 1991—. Commr. Redondo Beach Housing Adv. and Appeals Bd., 1985-89; mem. citizens adv. bd. South Bay Union High Sch. Dist., Redondo Beach, 1983. Capt. USAF, 1964-68. Libertarian. Home and Office: 612 S Gertruda Ave Redondo Beach CA 90277-4245

HALLORAN, MICHAEL JAMES, lawyer; b. Berkeley, Calif., May 20, 1941; s. James Joseph and Fern (Ogden) H.; m. Virginia Smedberg, Sept. 6, 1964; children: Pamela, Peter, Shelley. BS, U. Calif., Berkeley, 1962, LLB, 1965. Bar: Calif. 1966, D.C. 1979. Assoc. Keatinge & Sterling, L.A., 1965-67; assoc. Pillsbury, Madison & Sutro, San Francisco, 1967-72, ptnr., 1973-90; mng. ptnr. Pillsbury, Madison & Sutro, Washington, 1979-82; exec. v.p., gen. counsel BankAm. Corp. and Bank of Am., San Francisco, 1990—. Editor: Venture Capital and Public Offering Negotiation, 1982. Chmn. planning com. Orinda (Calif.) Assn., 1976-78, City of Orinda, 1987-88; mem. corp. governance, shareholder rights and securities transactions com. Calif. Senate Commn., 1986—; dir. Am. Arbitration Assn. Found. Health Corp. Mem. ABA (chmn. state regulation of securities com. 1981-84, mem. coun. of sect. of bus. law 1986-90, chmn. banking law com. 1992—), Bar Assn. San Francisco, Bankers Club San Francisco, Orinda Country Club, Univ. Club (Washington). Office: BankAm Corp 555 California St San Francisco CA 94104

HALLORAN, RICHARD COLBY, research executive, former news correspondent; b. Washington, Mar. 2, 1930; s. Paul James and Catherine (Lenihan) H.; m. Carol Prins, June 21, 1958; children: Christopher Paul, Laura Colby, Catherine Anne; m. Fumiko Mori, Nov. 11, 1978. AB with distinction, Dartmouth Coll., 1951; MA, U. Mich., 1957. Staff writer, then asst. fgn. editor Business Week mag., 1957-61; Tokyo bur. chief McGraw-Hill World News, 1962-64; Asia specialist Washington Post, 1965-66; bur. chief Washington Post, Tokyo, 1966-68; Washington corr. Washington Post, 1968-69; Washington corr. N.Y. Times, 1969-72, Tokyo bur. chief, 1972-76, investigative reporter Washington Bur., 1976-78, energy corr., 1978-79, def. corr., 1979-84, mil. corr., 1984-89; dir. comm. and journalism East-West Ctr., Honolulu, 1990—; adj. fellow Pacific Forum/Ctr. Strategic and Internat. Studies. Author: Japan: Images and Realities, 1969, Conflict and Compromise: The Dynamics of American Foreign Policy, 1973, To Arm a Nation: Rebuilding America's Endangered Defenses, 1986, Serving America: Prospects for the Volunteer Force, 1988. Mem. Honolulu Com. Fgn. Rels., Pacific and Asian Affairs Coun. 1st lt. AUS, 1952-55. Recipient citation for interpretation fgn. affairs Overseas Press Club, 1969, George Polk award for nat. reporting L.I. U., 1982, Gerald R. Ford prize for disting. reporting on nat. def. Gerald R. Ford Found., 1988, Outstanding Civilian Svc. medal U.S. Army, 1989; Ford Found. fellow Columbia U., 1964-65, Woodrow Wilson nat. fellow Furman U., S.C., Luther Coll., Iowa, Union Coll., N.Y., U. Redlands, Calif., Linfield Coll., Oreg., Goucher Coll., Md., adjunct fellow, Pacific Forum Ctr. for Strategic and Internat. Studies, Honolulu. Mem. Fgn. Corrs. Club (Tokyo). Roman Catholic. Home: 1065 Kao'opulu Pl Honolulu HI 96825 Office: East-West Ctr 1777 East-West Rd Honolulu HI 96848

HALOPOFF, WILLIAM EVON, industrial designer, consultant; b. Los Angeles, May 31, 1934; s. William John Halopoff and Dorothy E. (Foote) Lawrence; m. Nancy J. Ragsdale, July 12, 1960; children: Guy William and Carolee Nichole. BS, Art Ctr. Coll. Design, 1968. Internat. indsl. design cons. FMC Corp. Cen. Engring. Lab., Santa Clara, Calif., 1969-81; mgr. indsl. design Tandem Computers, Cupertino, Calif., 1981-93; design cons. Halopoff Assocs., San Jose, Calif., 1984—. Patentee in field. Served with U.S. Army, 1957-59. Mem. Indsl. Designers Soc. Am., Soc. Automotive Engrs. (chmn. subcom. 29 1979-85). Home: 17544 Holiday Dr Morgan Hill CA 95037-6303

HALPENNY, LEONARD CAMERON, water resources consultant, hydrologist; b. Winnipeg, Manitoba, Can., June 21, 1915; came to U.S., 1926, naturalized, 1939; s. Jasper and Lillian Hartley (Brown) H.; m. Cora Elizabeth Jett, Jan. 25, 1941; children: Carol Jean, Philip Cameron. BS in Petroleum Engring., U. Tex., 1938; postgrad., U. Ariz., 1958. Registered profl. engr., Ariz., N.Mex., Utah; registered geologist, Ariz., Calif. Hydrologist U.S. Geol. Survey, Austin, Tex., 1937-39, Tucson, 1939-41; field engr. Marathon Oil, Hobbs, N.Mex., 1941-43; hydrologist U.S. Geol. Survey, Tucson, 1945-51, dist. chief, 1951-55; cons. hydrologist World Mining Consultants, Angola, 1955-57; cons. water resources Water Devel. Corp., Tucson, 1957—; spl. master Cappaert v. U.S., U.S. Dist. Ct., Las Vegas, 1973-78; expert witness for many water lawsuits. Co-inventor water stage recorder (Nash Conservation award); contbr. articles to several mags. With U.S. Army, 1943-45, ETO. Mem. ASCE, Am. Assn. Petroleum Geologists, Am. Geophys. Union, Am. Water Resources Assn., Am. Water Works Assn., Ariz. Geol. Soc., Ariz. Water and Pollution Control Assn., Internat. Assn. Sci. Hydrology, Internat. Soc. Sugar Cane Technologists, Nat. Water Well Assn., U.S. Com. on Irrigation Drainage and Flood Control. Home and Office: Water Devel Corp 3938 E Santa Barbara Ave Tucson AZ 85711-4744

HALPERIN, MARK WARREN, English language educator; b. N.Y.C., Feb. 19, 1940; s. George Waldo and Minna (Scharzer) H.; m. Barbara Scott, July 15, 1966; 1 child, Noah Corey. BA, Bard Coll., 1960; MFA in Poetry, U. Iowa, 1966. Jr. physicist Maclet Labs., Inc., Stamford, Conn., 1960-62; electron microscope tech. Rockefeller Inst., N.Y.C., 1963-64; instr. English Cen. Wash. U., Ellensburg, 1966—; prof. English Cen. Wash. U., 1990—; vis. prof. English, U. Ariz., 1976-77; exch. prof. English, Schimane U., Matsue, Japan, 1986-87; lectr. English, Estonian Inst. Human Lit. Moscow State Linguistic U., Russia, 1991. Author: Backroads, 1977 (US Award 1976), A Place Made Fast, 1982, The Measure of Islands, 1990. Recipient Glasscock Poetry award Mt. Holyoke Coll., 1960; Fulbright lectureship USIS, Soviet Union, 1991. Home: RR 4 Box 279A Ellensburg WA 98926 Office: Central Washington Univ Dept of English Ellensburg WA 98926

HALPERN, GEORGES MAURICE, physician, consultant; b. Warsaw, Poland, Sept. 7, 1935; came to France, 1935, came to U.S., 1981; s. Bernard Neftali and Renee Rachel (Nysenholc) Halpern Gelbard; m. Marie Catherine Guillard, 1958 (div. 1963); m. Genevieve Bourineau, 1965 (div. 1969); m. Emiko Oguiss, May 14, 1971; children: Emmanuelle Miyoko, Emilie Hideko. Baccalaureate summa cum laude, Lycee Henri IV, Paris, 1953; BS in physics, chemistry, biology, Faculty of Scis., Paris, 1954; degree in nuclear medicine, Institut National des Science et Techniques Nucleaires, Saclay, France, 1965; MD silver medal, Faculty of Medicine, Paris, 1964; med. diplomate, U. Paris, 1964, PhD, DSc with highest honors, 1992. Practicing internist, allergist Allergy and Clinical Immunology Clinic, Paris, 1964-83; dir. program research Inst. ImmunoBiologie, Paris, 1966-78; chief sci. advisor 3M Diagnostic Systems, Santa Clara, Calif., 1983-88; pres. BioDelta, Frame, Medintern, Portola Valley, Calif., 1985—; adj. prof. medicine U. Calif. Sch. Medicine, Davis, 1986—; chmn. Framtec Inc., 1987-90; med. dir. French Pharmacy Hong Kong, Kowloon, 1970-77; cons. Lab. Cassenne, Paris, 1970-78, Pharmacia, Bois d'Arcy, France, 1971-83, Vittel U.S.A., Newport Beach, 1983-89; vis. research scholar Stanford U., Palo Alto, Calif., 1981-83. Author: L'Allergie et la Peau, 1976 (gold medal 1977), Allergies, 1985; editor in chief (med. jour.) Allergie et Immunologie, 1969-84; contbr. recipes to cooking mag., 1969-71 (merite agricole 1974); inventor IgG4 FAST. Recipient Prix Auguste Becard, Soc. de Gastronomie Medicale, Paris, 1969, Medal of Honor, Czech. Soc. J.E. Purkynje, Prague, 1977, Medal of Vermeil, City of Paris, 1985. Fellow European Acad. of Allergy, The Royal Soc. Medicine, Am. Acad. Allergy; mem. Colombian Acad. Medicine (corresponding mem.), GAILL (gen. sec.), Internat. Congress Food and Health (co-pres.). Lodge: Pacifica GODF (past master). Home: 9 Hillbrook Dr Portola Valley CA 94028-7933

HALPERN, JOSEPH YEHUDA, mathematics and computer science researcher, educator; b. Tel Aviv, May 29, 1953; came to U.S., 1977; s. Israel and Eva (Grosz) H.; m. Gale Evelyn Jacobs, Aug. 31, 1980. BS, U. Toronto, Can., 1975; AM, Harvard U., 1979, PhD, 1981. Head math. dept. Bawku (Ghana) Secondary Sch., 1975-77; postdoctoral fellow MIT and Harvard U., Cambridge, Mass., 1981-82; mem. rsch. staff Almaden Rsch. Ctr. IBM, San Jose, Calif., 1982—, mgr. math. and related computer sci. dept., 1987-89; vis. indsl. prof. Stanford U., Palo Alto, Calif., 1984-85, cons. prof. computer sci. dept., 1985—; program chmn. Conf. Theoretical Aspects Reasoning About Knowledge, 1986, Assn. Computing Machinery Symposium Principles Distributed Computing, 1986, Assn. Computing Machinery Symposium Theory Computing, 1991. Author: Reasoning About Knowledge; editor: Theoretical Aspects of Reasoning About Knowledge, Procs. of 1st Conf., 1986; editor Infor. and Computation, 1984—, Logic and Computation, 1990—, Jour. of the Assn. Computing Machinery, 1992—; contbr. over 100 articles to profl. jours., conf. procs., and books. Recipient MIT Press Award for Best Paper Internat. Joint Conf. on Artificial Intelligence, 1985, Publisher's Prize, 1989. Office: IBM Almaden Rsch Ctr K53/802 650 Harry Rd San Jose CA 95120-6099

HALPIN, CHARLES AIME, archbishop; b. St. Eustache, Man., Can., Aug. 30, 1930; s. John S. and Marie Anne (Gervais) H. BA, U. Man., 1950; BTh, U. Montreal, 1956; Licentiate Canon Law, Gregorian U., Rome, 1960. Ordained priest Roman Catholic Ch., 1956; named monsignor Roman Cath. Ch., 1969, consecrated bishop, 1973; asst. St. Mary's Cathedral, Winnipeg, Man., 1956-58; vice chancellor, sec. to archbishop Archdiocese Winnipeg, 1960; officialis Archdiocesan Matrimonial Tribunal, 1962; vice-officialis Regional Matrimonial Tribunal, Regina, Sask.; archbishop of Regina, 1973—. Mem. Western Cath. Conf. Bishops (past pres.), Can. Conf. Cath. Bishops (bd. dirs.).

HALPIN, TIMOTHY PATRICK, air force officer; b. Worcester, Mass., Mar. 13, 1960; s. Daniel Joseph Halpin and Angelina (Ferranti) Wilkes; m. Rachel Esther Hanneman, Aug. 3, 1991; children: Alyssa Kristin, Patrick Stephan. BBA in Mgmt., U. Mass., 1982. Commd. 2d lt. U.S. Air Force, 1982, advanced through grades to capt., 1986; instr. electronic warfare various locations, 1984-91, 93d Bomb Wing, Castle AFB, Calif., 1991—. Decorated DFC, Air medal (3). Republican. Christian. Home: 850 Olivewood Dr # 4 Merced CA 95348-1222

HALSEY-BRANDT, GREG, mayor. BA in Geography, U. B.C., MA in Geography. Town planner, alderman, 1981-90; mayor City of Richmond, B.C., 1990—; chmn. Mandate and Communications Com.; mem. Vancouver Regional Transit Commn., vice chmn bd., dir., Greater Vancouver Regional Dist.; bd. dirs. Tourism Vancouver, Fraser Basin Mgmt. Program; mem. Richmond Chamber of Commerce, Planning Inst. of British Columbia. Mem. Planning Inst. B.C., Richmond C. of C. Office: Office of the Mayor, 6911 No 3 Rd, Richmond, BC Canada V6Y 2C1*

HALSTEAD, LESTER MARK, psychologist; b. San Pedro, Calif., June 15, 1927; s. Lee and Luti June (Newcomer) H.; m. Eleanor Grace Bradford, Sept. 25, 1949; children: Lester Mark Jr., Michael, Edward, Richard, Alexander. BS, Brigham Young U., 1960; MS, U. Utah, 1963; PhD, U. So. Calif., L.A., 1976. Cert. ednl. psychologist. Psychologist Clark County Juvenile Ct., Las Vegas, Nev., 1963-70; sch. psychologist Baldwin Park (Calif.) Sch. Dist., 1970—; pvt. practice Huntington Beach, Calif., 1975—; counselor North Park High Sch., Baldwin Park, 1975—. Author: Effective Intervention for Dealing With High Risk Youth. Bd. dirs. Parent Support Group, Baldwin Park, 1975-88, Huntington Beach, 1977-88. With U.S. Merchant Marines, WWII. Mem. ACSA (svc. award 1988), IPSA (recognition award 1987). Republican. Mem. LDS Ch. Home: 5642 Kern Dr Huntington Beach CA 92649-4533 Office: Baldwin Park Sch Dist 4600 Bogart Ave Baldwin Park CA 91706-2798

HALTERMAN, HAROLD LELAND, lawyer; b. Vallejo, Calif., Oct. 11, 1950; s. Harold Prescott and Lorraine Edna (Lowery) H.; m. Margaret M. Russell, June 23, 1991; 1 child, Alexander Cheff; 1 stepchild, Joshua L. Brooks. AB, U. Calif., Berkeley, 1974, JD, 1979. Bar: Calif. 1979, U.S. Dist. Ct. (no. dist.) Calif. 1979. Precinct coord. Com. to Elect Ronald V. Dellums, Oakland, Calif., 1970; adminstrv. aide U.S. Rep. Ronald V. Dellums, Oakland, 1971-80, dist. counsel, 1980-92, dist. dir., gen. coun., 1993—; precinct coord. Com. to Re-elect Ronald V. Dellums, Oakland, 1972, mgr. campaign, 1974; pres., dir. Surviving in the '80s, Oakland, 1979-92. Author: Defense Sense, 1983; writer, critic San Francisco Bay Guardian, 1981-85. Mem. com. Dems. United, Oakland, 1972-76; chair Mayor's Adv. Com., Berkeley, 1974-76, 79-81; mem. steering com. Berkeley Citizens Action, 1974-76, 81; mem. Human Rights Advs., 1979-92; mem. ctrl. com. Exec. Award Calif. Dem. Party, 1986-92; bassist, vocalist Third Pary (rythym and blues band), 1989-92. Recipient Svc. award Lions Club, 1966. Mem. ACLU (bd. dirs. 1983-92, pres. 1988-91), Ctrl. Com. for Conscientious Objectors, State Bar Assn. Calif., Alameda Dem. Lawyers Com., Nat. Lawyers Guild, Boalt Hall Alumni Assn. Office: US Rep Ronald V Dellums 201 13th St Ste 105 Oakland CA 94612

HALVERSON, STEVEN THOMAS, lawyer; b. Enid, Okla., Aug. 29, 1954; s. Robert James Halverson and Ramona Mae (Ludke) Selenski; m. Diane Mary Schueller, Aug. 21, 1976; children: John Thomas, Anne Kirsten. BA cum laude, St. John's U., 1976; JD, Am. U., 1979. Bar: Va. 1979. Asst. project dir. ABA, Washington, 1977-79; with Briggs & Morgan, St Paul., 1980-83; v.p. M.A. Mortenson Cos., Mpls., Denver, Seattle, 1984—; bd. dirs. Associated Gen. Contractors Colo., Ctr. for New West, Greater Denver Corp, Denver Partnership. Co-author: Federal Grant Law, 1982; contbr. articles to profl. jours. Bd. dirs. Regis U., Central City Opera. Republican. Roman Catholic. Home: 2013 Montane Dr E Golden CO 80401-9123 Office: MA Mortenson Cos 1875 Lawrence St Ste 600 Denver CO 80202-1870

HALVERSTADT, JONATHAN SCOTT, personal growth systems developer, consultant, lecturer; b. Fresno, Calif., Oct. 21, 1952; s. Lee W. and Dorothy W. (Weller) Halverstadt. BA in Contemporary Christian Ministries, Fresno Pacific Coll., 1977; MS in Counseling, Calif. State U., Fresno, 1993. Disk jockey, promotions dir. Sta. KFIG, Fresno, 1979-80; news anchor, talk show host Sta. KMJ, Fresno, 1980-82; freelance actor, announcer ABC, CBS, NBC, radio & TV commls., 1982—; owner Jonathan Scott Prodns., Fresno, 1978—, Dreikus Relationship Ctr., Fresno, 1987-91; co-owner O-Togarden Concepts, Fresno, 1988-92, Jonathan M. Scott & Assocs., Fresno, 1991—; editor AM Mag., Fresno, 1989; facilitator Family Communications Ctr., Fresno, 1987-89; guest artist Christian Camping Internat., Calif. and Oreg., 1975-78. Author: Today, 1974; TV appearances include ABC's General Hospital, 1982-91; writer, producer, performer (album) Mush, 1977. Media cons. Armstrong for Mayor campaign, Clovis, Calif., 1980, John Burns for Supt. of Schs., Fresno County, 1990; guest speaker numerous Career Day programs, Fresno and Clovis, 1981-90; v.p. Easter Seal Soc. of Cen. Calif., Fresno, 1983-87. Recipient Golden Oak award Fresno Advtg. Fedn., 1984, 88, Silver Microphone award, Waco, Tex., 1987. Mem. ACA, AFTRA (nat. bd. dirs. 1987-92, v.p. Fresno chpt. 1982-92), Assn. for Counselor Edn. (v.p. 1992-93), Calif. Assn. Marriage and Family Therapists. Office: Jonathan M Scott & Assocs PO Box 16172 Fresno CA 93755

HALVORSON, ALFRED RUBIN, mayor, consultant, education educator; b. Milan, Minn., Jan. 22, 1921; s. Chris and Alice (Kleven) H.; m. Dorothy F. Boxrud, Apr. 23, 1944; children: Gary A., Joan D. Halvorson Felice. BS, U. Minn., 1944, PhD, 1949. County extension agt. Agr. Extension Svc. of Minn., St. Paul, 1945; soil fertility researcher Oreg. State U., Klamath Falls, 1949-54; extension agronomist Purdue U., Lafayette, Ind., 1954-57; extension soil scientist Wash. State U., Pullman, 1957-86, prof. emeritus, 1986—; cons. ACF & Shirley Fetilizer Ltd., Brisbane, Australia, 1964, Saudi Arabia Farming Ops., Riyadh, 1984, U.S. AID, Sanaa, North Yemen, 1987. City councilman, City of Pullman, 1987-91, mayor, 1991—. With M.C. U.S. Army, 1945. Mem. Kiwanis (chair com. Pullman chpt.). Republican. Lutheran. Home and Office: 325 SE Nebraska St Pullman WA 99163-2239

HALVORSON, ARDELL DAVID, research leader, soil scientist; b. Rugby, N.D., May 31, 1945; s. Albert F. and Karen (Mygland) H.; m. Linda Kay Johnston, Apr. 11, 1966; children: Renae, Rhonda. BS, N.D. State U., 1967; MS, Colo. State U., 1969, PhD, 1971. Soil scientist Agr. Rsch. Svc., USDA, Sidney, Mont., 1971-83; soil scientist Agr. Rsch. Svc., USDA, Akron, Colo., 1983-88, rsch. leader, 1988—. Contbr. over 100 articles to profl. jours., chpts. to books. Fellow Am. Soc. Agronomy (assoc. editor 1983-87), Soil Sci. Soc. Am. (chmn. div. S-8, 1989), Soil and Water Conservation Soc. (chpt. pres. 1991); mem. Crop Sci. Soc. Am., Lions (treas. Akron club 1987-92), Masons, Elks. Office: USDA Agrl Rsch Svc PO Box 400 Akron CO 80720

HAM, GARY MARTIN, psychologist; b. Lincoln, Nebr., Feb. 6, 1940; s. Wendell E. and Sally Bertha (Lind) H. BS in Psychology, Wash. State U., 1963, MS in Psychology, 1965; PsyD, Newport U., 1988. Lic. psychologist, Calif.; cert. tchr., Calif, counselor. Clin. psychologist Riverside (Calif.) County Dept. Mental Health, 1967—; tchr., cons., pub. speaker, researcher Riverside County Dept. Mental Health, 1967—. Clin. psychologist Riverside County SP Disaster Response Team, 1985—, ARC Distaster Team. 1st lt. USAF, 1964-67. Mem. APA, ASCD, Am. Mental Health Counselors Assn., Am. Critical Incident Stress Found., Calif. Psychol. Assn., Air Force Soc. Psychologists, Psi Chi, Sigma Phi Epsilon. Office: Riverside County Dept Mental Health 9990 County Farm Rd Riverside CA 92503-3518

HAMACHEK, TOD RUSSELL, manufacturing executive; b. Jan. 3, 1946; m. Barbara Callister, 1969; children: Mark, Elizabeth. BA, Williams Coll., 1968; MBA, Harvard U., 1970. Nat. sales mgr. Harris Corp., Westerly, R.I., 1970-74; asst. to pres. Gt. Western Malting Co., Vancouver, Wash., 1974-76; v.p. sales Gt. Western Malting Co., Vancouver, Oreg., 1976-79, pres., chief exec. officer, 1979-84; pres., chief ops. officer Penwest, Ltd., Bellevue, Wash., 1984-85, pres., chief exec. officer, 1985—; sr. v.p. Univar Corp., Seattle, 1982-84; bd. dirs. N.W. Natural Gas Co., Dekalb Genetics Corp., Blethen Corp. Bd. dirs., pres. 100 Club Wash.; bd. dirs. Pacific Sci. Ctr., Va. Mason Hosp.; trustee Lakeside Sch., Seattle Found., Wash. Roundtable, Lewis & Clark Coll.; v.p. Wash. Pulp and Paper Found. Mem. PNW, Young Pres.' Orgn., U. Wash. Grad. Sch. Bus. Adminstrn. (chmn. adv. bd.). Office: Penwest Ltd 777 108th Ave NE Ste 2390 Bellevue WA 98004-5193

HAMAI, JAMES YUTAKA, business executive; b. L.A., Oct. 14, 1926; s. Seizo and May (Sata) H.; B.S., U. So. Calif., 1952, M.S., 1955; postgrad. bus. mgmt. program industry exec., UCLA, 1963-64; m. Dorothy K. Fukuda, Sept. 10, 1954; 1 child, Wendy A. Lectr. chem. engring. dept. U. So. Calif., Los Angeles, 1963-64; process engr., sr. process engr. Fluor Corp., Los Angeles, 1954-64; sr. project mgr. central research dept. Monsanto Co., St. Louis, 1964-67, mgr. research, devel. and engring. graphic systems dept., 1967-68, mgr. comml. devel. New Enterprise div., 1968-69; exec. v.p., dir. Concrete Cutting Industries, Inc., Los Angeles, 1969-72; pres., dir. Concrete Cutting Internat., Inc., Los Angeles, 1972-78, chmn. bd., 1978—; cons. Fluor Corp., Los Angeles, 1970-72; dir. Intech Systems Co., Ltd., Tokyo, Cutting Industries Co., Ltd., Tokyo, Techno Trading Co., Ltd., Tokyo; internat. bus. cons. Served with AUS, 1946-48. Mem. Am. Inst. Chem. Engrs., Am. Mgmt. Assn., Tau Beta Pi, Phi Lambda Upsilon. Club: Rotary (gov. dist. 1982-83). Home: 6600 Via La Paloma Palos Verdes Peninsula CA 90274-6449 Office: 20963 S Lamberton Ave Long Beach CA 90810-1078

HAMAN, SARAH ARMSTRONG, librarian; b. Atlanta, Dec. 25, 1949; d. James Blanding and Margaret Ann (Hill) H.; m. Benjamin M. McKelway III, Mar. 20, 1971 (div. 1974); m. Thomas Harry Clegg, June 24, 1992; children: Sage Mirrim Clegg-Haman, Heather Anne Clegg-Haman. Student, William & Mary Coll., 1968-70, City Coll. San Francisco, 1974-75; AA, Mendocino Coll., 1990; student, Sonoma State U., 1990-91. Libr. clk. Mendocino County Libr., Willits, Calif., 1979-84; instrnl. asst. Sherwood Sch., Willits, 1985-87; elem. libr. Brookside Sch./Baechtel Grove Middle Sch., Willits, 1987—; Calif. Sch. Employee's Assn. rep. Willits (Calif.) Unified Sch. Dist. Adv./Budget Com., 1991—. Bd. mem. Willits (Calif.) Young Actors Theater, 1992—, sec., 1993—. Democrat. Home: 27081 Oriole Dr Willits CA 95490 Office: Brookside Sch Libr Spruce & Lincoln Willits CA 95490

HAMAR, H. JEFFREY, hardwood company executive; b. Calumet, Mich., Apr. 21, 1958; s. Edward Kenneth and Marilynn (Postma) H. BA, Carthage Coll., Kenosha, Wis., 1980. Gen. mgr. Denver Hardwood, 1984-86; sales mgr. Galleher Hardwood Co., L.A., 1980-84, pres., 1986—. Recipient Outstanding Young Alumni award Carthage Coll., 1989; named Young Exec. of Yr. Nat. Assn. Floor Covering Distbrs., 1991. Republican. Office: Galleher Hardwood Co 12906 Telegraph Rd Santa Fe Springs CA 90670-4041

HAMBIDGE, DOUGLAS WALTER, archbishop; b. London, Mar. 6, 1927; emigrated to Can., 1956; s. Douglas and Florence (Driscoll) H.; m. Denise Colvill Lown, June 9, 1956; children—Caryl Denise, Stephen Douglas, Graham Andrew. A.L.C.D., London U., 1953, B.D., 1958, D.D., 1969. Ordained deacon Church of England, 1953, priest, 1954, consecrated bishop, 1969; asst. curate St. Mark's Ch., Dalston, London, 1953-55; priest-in-charge St. Mark's Ch., 1955-56; incumbent All Saints Ch., Cassiar, B.C., Can., 1956-58; rector St. James Parish, Smithers, B.C., 1958-64, North Peace Parish, Ft. St. John, B.C., 1964-69; canon St. Andrew's Cathedral, 1965; lord bishop of Caledonia, 1969-80, New Westminster, B.C., 1980-81; lord archbishop of New Westminster and metropolitan of B.C., 1981-93; prin. St. Mark's Theol. Coll., Dar es Salaam, Tanzania, 1993—; mem. Anglican Consultative Coun., 1985-93. Mem. Vancouver Club, Arbutus Club.

HAMBURG, DANIEL (DAN), congressman; b. St. Louis, 1948; m. Carrie Hamburg, 1972; 4 children. Ba with honors in History, Stanford U., 1970; MA in Philosophy and Religion, Calif. Inst. Integral Studies, 1992. Founder, tchr. Mariposa Sch., 1970-80; dir. Ukiah Valley Child Devel. Ctr., 1970-80; exec. dir. North Coast Opportunities Inc., 1986-93; bd. suprs. Mendocino County, Calif., 1981-85; dir. cultural studies program People's Republic of China, 1984-90; mem. 103d Congress from 1st Calif. Dist., 1993—. Mem. Rotary. Democrat. Office: Ho of Reps 114 Cannon Bldg Washington DC 20515

HAMBY, JEANNETTE, state legislator; b. Virginia, Minn., Mar. 15, 1933; d. John W. and Lydia M. (Soderholm) Johnson; m. Eugene Hamby, 1957; children—Taryn Rene, Tenya Ramine. BS, U. Minn., 1956; MS, U. Oreg., 1968, PhD, 1976. Vice chmn. Hillsboro High Sch. Dist. Bd., 1973-81; mem. Washington County Juvenile Services Com., 1980—; mem. suggested legis. com. Council State Govts., 1981—, Oreg. state rep., 1981-83; mem. Oreg. State Senate from 5th dist., 1983—. Mem. Oreg. Mental Health Assn., Am. Nurses Assn., Oreg. Nurses Assn., Am. Vocat. Assn., Oreg. Vocat. Assn., Oreg. Vocat./Career Adminstrs., Phi Kappa Phi, Phi Delta Kappa. Lutheran. Republican. Office: Oreg State Senate State Capitol Salem OR 97310 Home: 952 NE Jackson School Rd Hillsboro OR 97124-2314

HAMERSLOUGH, WALTER SCOTT, health and physical education educator; b. Needles, CA, Dec. 15, 1935; s. Walter Kenneth and Frances (Brown) H.; m. V. Darlene Berdan, Dec. 17, 1961; children: Kenneth Scott, Rhonda Darlene. BA, La Sierra Coll., 1958; MA, U. Redlands, 1964; EdD, U. Oreg., 1971. Tchr. Fairview Elem. Sch., San Bernardino, Calif., 1958-59, Loma Linda (Calif.) Elem. Sch., 1959-60; hist., phys. edn. tchr. Loma Linda Acad., 1960-63; prof. health and phys. edn. La Sierra U., Riverside, Calif., 1963—; cons. YMCA, Intercommunity Home for Exceptional Children. Coach Alvord Pony League, 1978-80 (v.p., 1980), Alvord Little League, 1975-78. Mem. Am. Coll. Sports Medicine, Am. Alliance for Health, Phys. Edn., Nat. Intramural Sports Assn., SDA Health, Phys. Edn. Recreation Assn. (exec. dir. 1983—), Western Coll. Phys. Edn. Soc. (So. Calif. Rep. 1981-87), Phi Epsilon Kappa. Republican. Adventist. Office: La Sierra U Health Phys Edn Dept Riverside CA 92515

HAMERTON-KELLY, ROBERT GERALD, religion educator; b. Capetown, Republic of South Africa, Dec. 26, 1938; came to U.S., 1962; s. Robert Hamerton-Kelly and Johanna (Loubser) Hobbs; m. Rosemary Ann Daly, Jan. 13, 1962; children: Ruth Miriam, Paul Robert, Christopher Nguyen. BA, Cambridge (U.K.) U., 1961, MA, 1966; PhD, Union Theol. Sem., N.Y.C., 1966. Asst. prof. Scripps Coll., Claremont, Calif., 1965-70; assoc. prof. McCormick Theol. Sem., Chgo., 1970-72; dean of chapel, prof. religious studies Stanford (Calif) U., 1972-86, sr. rsch. scholar Inst. for Internat. Studies, 1986—. Author: Sacred Violence, 1992, God the Father, 1979, Divine Passion, 1987; editor: Violent Origins, 1987. Mem. Am. Acad. of Religion, Soc. of Bibl. Lit., Colloquium on Violence and Religion. Democrat. United Methodist. Home: 365 Forest Ave # 2F Palo Alto CA 94301 Office: CISAC Stanford U 320 Galvez St Stanford CA 94305

HAMIDJAJA, WIRIADI WILLY, banking executive; b. Jakarta, Indonesia, Dec. 1, 1962; came to U.S., 1981; s. Hady and Suryatin (Chandra) H. BS in Applied Math., Fla. Inst. Tech., 1984; MBA, U. Notre Dame, 1986. Sr. acct. 1st Source Bank, South Bend, Ind., 1986-87, dir. systems and planning, 1987-90; asst. v.p. 1st Source Bank, South Bend, Ind., 1990-92; v.p. Republic Internat. Bank of N.Y., Beverly Hills, Calif., 1992—. Outreach chmn. Christian Businessmen's Com., South Bend, 1988-89, membership chmn., 1990; chmn. program sales Blue and Gold Game, U. Notre Dame, 1990-92; mem. UN Assn. of U.S.A. Mem. Assn. MBA Execs., Partnership for Better Air Travel, Notre Dame Club L.A., Indonesian Bus. Soc. Overseas: Kesehatan 7/31, Jakarta 10160, Indonesia

HAMILL, CAROL, biologist, writing instructor; b. San Diego, July 15, 1953; d. William David Sr. and Katharine Louise (Garlock) H.; m. Apr. 1, 1978 (div. Feb. 1980); 1 child, Jason John Voutas. Student, San Diego State U., 1972-73, Worcester State Coll., 1975-78; BS in Natural Scis., U. Calif., Riverside, 1980; postgrad., Calif. State U., San Bernardino, 1986-92. Lab. asst. Worcester State Coll., 1976-78; ind. biologist Calif., 1983-86; lab. asst. Calif. State U., San Bernardino, 1987-88; mem. adj. faculty Riverside C.C., 1990-93; lab. asst. dept. biochemistry U. Calif., Riverside, 1979-80, instr., 1992—; freelance writer, 1988—; speaker in field. Contbr. articles to Off Duty, Natural Food and Farming, Country Rev., Sr. Highlights, Our Town, Palm and Pine, and others, over 50 articles to nat. and local mags. Mem. publicity com. Orange Empire Rwy. Mus., Perris, Calif., 1989—. Mem. AAAS, N.Y. Acad. Scis., Ecol. Soc. Am. Democrat. Episcopalian. Home: 11681 Dalehurst Rd Moreno Valley CA 92555 Office: PO Box 7960 Moreno Valley CA 92552-7960

HAMILL, MARK, actor; b. Oakland, Calif., Sept. 25, 1951; m. Marilou York, 1978; children: Nathan, Griffin, Chelsea. Student, L.A. City Coll., 1969-70. Performed at Renaissance Faire, Agoura, Calif., 3 seasons; appeared in TV series Texas Wheelers, 1974; played in TV movies Eric, 5, Sarah T.: Portrait of a Teen-age Alcoholic, 1975, Delancey Street: The Crisis Within, 1975, Mallory, Circumstantial Evidence, 1976, The City, 1977, 1983, Earth Angel, 1991; other TV roles in Bill Cosby Show, 1970, Gen. Hospital, 1972-73, Partridge Family, 1971, Owen Marshall Counselor At Law, 1972, Night Gallery, 1972, The FBI, 1972, Room 222, 1973, The Magician, 1973, Manhunter, 1974, Cannon, 1974, Bronk, 1975, Lucas Tanner, 1975, Sreets of San Francisco, 1975, Petrocilli, 1975, Med. Ctr., 1976, Marcus Welby, M.D., 1976, One Day At a Time, 1976, (pilot) Eight is Enough, 1977, The Muppet Show, 1980, Amazing Stories, 1986, Alfred Hitchcock Presents, 1987, Hooperman, 1989, The Flash, 1991; appeared in motion pictures Star Wars, 1977, Corvette Summer, 1978, The Big Red One, 1980, The Empire Strikes Back, 1980, Night the Lights Went Out in Georgia, 1981, Return of the Jedi, 1983, Britannia Hospital, 1983, Slipstream, 1988, Black Magic Woman, 1991, Picture Perfect, 1991, Sleepwalkers, 1992, The Guyver, 1992, Time Runner, 1993, Midnight Ride, 1993; Broadway debut in Elephant Man, 1981; appeared in Amadeus, 1982, Harrigan 'N Hart, 1985, The Nerd, 1987; off-Broadway appearance in Room Service, 1986; on- and off-Broadway in Harrigan 'N Hart, 1984; voice work in Wizards, 1977, Jeannie cartoon, 1973-75, Batman: The Animated Series, 1992; radio work in Empire Strikes Back, Star Wars, 1989. Address: The Hamill Exch care Nacolle Parsons PO Box 526177 Salt Lake City UT 84152-6177 also: Agy for the Performing Arts 9000 Sunset Blvd Los Angeles CA 90069

HAMILTON, ALLEN EMERSON, JR., electrical contractor; b. Eugene, Oreg., June 1, 1935; s. Allen Emerson and Lillian Theresa (Dippert) H.; m. Barbara Lee Killian, Sept. 17, 1960; children: James A., Karen L., Kurt M. BS, U. Oreg., 1957; MS, NYU, 1958. Gen. mgr. Hamilton Electric, Inc., Eugene, 1960-89; mktg. mgr. Cherry City Electric, Inc., Eugene, 1989-92; chpt. mgr. Oreg. Pacific-Cascade Chpt. Nat. Elec. Contractors Assn., Eugene, 1992—; owner Neal & Hamilton, Eugene, 1980-90. Campaign chair Larry Campbell for State Rep., Eugene, 1977-93; pres. Eugene/Springfield Conv. Bur., 1980-81, Lane County Fair Bd., Eugene, 1991. 1st lt. USAF, 1958-60. Recipient Leadership award Jr. Achievement, 1975; named No. Calif. Constrn. Man of Yr. San Francisco Elec. Contractors, 1988. Mem. Nat. Elec. Contractors Assn. (v.p. 1981-85, dir. Oreg. Pacific Cascade chpt. 1976-91, nat. pres. 1986-89, James H. McGraw award 1978, L.K. Comstock award 1989), Coun. Indsl. Rels. (co-chair 1986-89), Eugene Execs. Assn. (pres. 1969), Acad. Elec. Contractors (chair 1990-93), Eugene Area C. of C. (pres. 1977-78), Eugene Elks, Masons. Republican. Home: 2159 Escalante St Eugene OR 97404-2288 Office: Nat Elec Contractors Assn PO Box 11528 Eugene OR 97440

HAMILTON, ALLEN PHILIP, financial advisor; b. Albany, Calif., Oct. 17, 1937; s. Allen Philip Sr. and Barbara Louise (Martin) H.; m. Mary Williams, July 18, 1981 (div. Mar. 1987). BA in Bus. Mgmt., St. Mary's U., San Jose, Calif., 1961; AA, Contra Costa State Coll., 1957; Bus. Assoc. degree, NW Mo. State U., 1969; postgrad., San Jose State U., 1959-61. Cert. fin. planner. Fin. advisor Consolidated Investment Svcs., Kansas City, Mo., 1968-70; pres., chief exec. officer Balanced Mgmt. Assn., Mission, Kans., 1969-72, Advanced Svc. Assn., Overland Park, Kans., 1971-78; divisional mgr. Waddell & Reed, Inc., Kansas City, 1978-81; sr. v.p., regional dir. WZW Fin. Svcs., Kansas City, 1981-86; exec.v.p. Skaife & Co., Orinda, Calif., 1986-88; v.p., mktg. dir. Consolidated Securities Corp., Walnut Creek, Calif., 1988; sr. dir. and cert. trainer Club Am., Inc., L.A., 1990—; CFP, prin. Hamilton Fin. Adv., Am. Investment Svcs., Pleasant Hill., Calif., 1989—; silver mktg. distbr., corp. trainer, Can. mktg. distbr. and trainer Nikken, Inc. Internat., numerous fgn. countries, 1991—; sales mgr., ind. distributor, sales trainer Alpine Industries, 1992—; sr. dir. Club Am. OTC Pink Shts., L.A., 1990-92; presdl. dir. FundAmerica, Irvine, Calif., 1988—; guest speaker in field. Author: (with others) The Financial Planner A New Profession, 1986. Asst. dist. commr. Boy Scouts Am., Kansas City, Kans., 1970-79; corp. dir. United Campaign, Overland Park, Kans., 1965-73; active TV show Kidney Found., Kansas City, Mo., 1969-70; sr. arbitrator San Francisco Bay Area Better Bus. Bur., 1986—. Lt. U.S. Army, 1963-65. Recipient Citation Nat. Campaign Re-election 1992, 1992m Senatorial Commn. Rep. Senatorial Inner Circle, 1991. Mem. Inst. Cert. Fin. Planners, Internat. Assn. for Fin. Planning (v.p., bd. dirs. 1982-87, practitioner div.), Registry of Fin. Planning Practitioners, Mt. Diablo Distbrs. Assn. Republican. Home: 14 Donegal Ct Ste 5 Pleasant Hill CA 94523

HAMILTON, CHARLES EDWARD, JR., communication consultant; b. Balt., Dec. 22, 1957; s. Charles Edward and Dorothy Isabel (Gettel) H. BA in Internat. Studies, Johns Hopkins U., 1978; MA in Journalism, U. Minn., 1979; PhD in Pub. Comm., U. Md., 1992. Contract specialist U.S. Dept. Energy, Washington, 1979-81; mgr. human devel. programs Corp. for Pub. Broadcasting, Washington, 1981-85; instr. U. Md., College Park, 1985-88, 90; interim gen. mgr. WWOZ-FM, New Orleans, 1988; asst. gen. mgr. WBJC-FM, Balt., 1988-89; vis. asst. prof. George Washington U., Washington, 1989-90; mgr. Jack Straw Prodns., Seattle, 1990-92; pres. Charles Hamilton Comm. Svcs., Seattle, 1985—; tng. cons. KCMU-FM, Seattle, 1992; bd. dirs., tng. cons. Earth on the Air, Seattle, 1991-92; trainer Pyramid Comm. Internat., Washington, 1988; rsch. cons. Ctr. for TV Rsch., U. Leeds, Eng., 1987. Editor: Analysis of the Skills Used in Public Broadcasting's Key Jobs, 1985; contbr. articles to profl. jours. Mem. Nat. Fedn. Community Broadcasters (judge Golden Reel awards 1991), Nat. Assn. Broadcasters (judge Crystal Radio awards 1990). Home and Office: Charles Hamilton Comm Svcs 400 Harvard Ave E #306 Seattle WA 98102

HAMILTON, CHARLES HOWARD, metallurgist; b. Pueblo, Colo., Mar. 17, 1935; s. George Edwin and Eva Eleanor (Watson) H.; m. Joy Edith Richmond, Sept. 7, 1968; children: Krista Kathleen, Brady Glenn. BS, Colo. Sch. Mines, 1959; MS, U. So. Calif., 1965; PhD, Case Western Res. U., 1968. Research engr. Space div. Rockwell Internat., Downey, Calif., 1959-65; mem. tech. staff Los Angeles div. Rockwell Internat., 1968-75; tech. staff, phys. metallurgy Sci. Ctr., Thousand Oaks, Calif., 1975-77, group mgr. metals processing, 1977-79, prin. scientist, 1979-81, dir. materials synthesis and processing dept., 1982-84; assoc. prof. Washington State U., Pullman, 1984-87, prof., 1987—; chmn. Rockwell Corp. tech. panel, materials research and engring; co-organizer 1st Internat. Symposium Superplastic Forming, 1982, Internat. Conf. on Superplasticity and Superplastic Forming, 1988. Sr. editor Jour. Materials Shaping Tech.; dep. editor Scripta Metallurgica et Materialia, 1989—; contbr. tech. articles to profl. publs.; patentee advanced metalworking and tech. Named Rockwell Engr. of Yr., 1979; recipient IR 100 award Indsl. Research mag., 1976, 80. Fellow Am. Soc. Metals; mem. AIME (shaping and forming com.), Sigma Xi. Home: 410 SE Crestview St Pullman WA 99163-2211

HAMILTON, DARDEN COLE, flight test engineer; b. Pitts., Nov. 28, 1956; s. Isaac Herman Hamilton and Grace osborne (Fish) thorp; m. Linda Susanne Moser, Aug. 7, 1976; children: Christopher Moser Hamilton, Elijah Cole Hamilton. BS in Aeronautics, St. Louis U., Cahokia, Ill., 1977; postgrad. in aeronautical tech., Ariz. State U. Licensed pilot; licensed airframe and power mechanic. Engr. McDonnell Douglas Aircraft Co., St. Louis, Mo., 1977-80; group leader, engring. Cessna Aircraft Co., Wichita, Kans., 1980-83, sr. flight test engr., 1983-85; sr. flight test engr. Allied-Signal Aerospace Co., Phoenix, 1986-92; flight test engr. specialist Allied-Signal Aerospace Co., 1992—. North cen. sect. comdr. Royal Rangers Boys Ministry; charter mem. Lifeline Community Ch. Mem. Soc. Flight Test Engrs., Ariz. State Rifle and Pistol Assn. (life). Republican. Lodge: Masons. Home: 4501 W Paradise Ln Glendale AZ 85306-2729 Office: Allied-Signal Aerospace Co Propulsion Engine Div 111 S 34th St Phoenix AZ 85034-2892

HAMILTON, DAVID MIKE, publishing company executive; b. Little Rock, Feb. 25, 1951; s. Ralph Franklin and Mickey Garnette (Chappell) H.; m. Carol Nancy McKenna, Oct. 25, 1975; children: Elisabeth Michelle, Caroline Ellen. BA, Pitzer Coll., 1973; MLS, UCLA, 1976. Cert. tchr. library sci., Calif. Editor Sullivan Assocs., Palo Alto, Calif., 1973-75; curator Henry E. Huntington Library, San Marino, Calif., 1976-80; mgr. prodn., mktg. William Kaufmann Pubs., Los Altos, Calif., 1980-84; pres. The Live Oak Press, Palo Alto, 1984—; cons. editor, gen. ptnr. Sensitive Expressions Pub. Co., Palo Alto, 1985—. Author: To the Yukon with Jack London, 1980, The Tools of My Trade, 1986; contbg. author (jour.) Small Press, 1986; (books) Book Club of California Quarterly, 1985, Research Guide to Biography and Criticism, 1986. Sec. vestry Trinity Parish, Menlo Park, 1986, bd. dirs., 1985-87; trustee Jack London Ednl. Found., San Francisco; bd. dirs. ISYS Forum, Palo Alto, 1987—; pres. site coun., mem. supt.'s adv. com. Palo Alto Unified Sch. Dist. Mem. ALA, Coun. on Scholarly, Med. and Ednl. Publs., Am. Assn. Artificial Intelligence (bd. dirs. 1984—, dir. publs.), Bookbuilders West (book show com. 1983), Author's Guild, Soc. Tech. Communication (judge 1984), Assn. Computing Machinery (chmn. pub. com. 1984), Soc. Scholarly Pubs., Sierra Club, Book Club Calif. Democrat. Episcopalian. Home: 2620 Emerson St Palo Alto CA 94306-2310 Office: The Live Oak Press PO Box 60036 Palo Alto CA 94306-0036

HAMILTON, DONALD BENGTSSON, author; b. Uppsala, Sweden, Mar. 24, 1916; s. Bengt L.K. and Elise (Neovius) H.; m. Kathleen Stick, 1941 (dec. Oct. 28, 1989); children: Hugo, Elise, Gordon, Victoria. B.S., U. Chgo., 1938. Writer and photographer, 1946—. Creator Matt Helm series; author books including Death of a Citizen, 1960, The Wrecking Crew, 1960, The Removers, 1961, The Silencers, 1962, Murderer's Row, 1962, The Ambushers, 1963, The Ravagers, 1963, The Shadowers, 1964, The Devastators, 1965, The Betrayers, 1966, The Menacers, 1968, The Interlopers, 1969, The Intriguers, 1972, The Intimidators, 1974, The Terminators, 1975, The Terrorizers, 1977, The Retaliators, 1976, The Poisoners, 1971, Cruises with Kathleen, 1980, The Mona Intercept, 1980, The Revengers, 1982, The Annihilators, 1983, The Infiltrators, 1984, The Detonators, 1985, The Vanishers, 1986, The Demolishers, 1987, The Frighteners, 1989, The Threateners, 1992; contbr. articles on hunting, yachting, and photography to mags. Mem. Mystery Writers Am., Western Writers Am., Outdoor Writers Assn. Am. Office: PO Box 1045 Santa Fe NM 87504-1045

HAMILTON, EDWARD SYLVESTER, minister; b. The Dalles, Oreg., July 10, 1939; s. Lester Sharp and Dorothy Ann (Jurgensmeier) H.; m.

Myrlene Louise Jacobson, Nov. 15, 1981; children: Kim Michelle, Tami Leigh. BS in Psychology, Lewis & Clark Coll., Portland, Oreg., 1962; MDiv, Fuller Sem., 1985, postgrad., 1991—. Ordained Presbyn. Ch., 1986. Purchasing mgr. various cos., Portland, Oreg., 1966-71; owner, ptnr. United Pub. Co., Boise, Idaho, 1971-80; owner Peninsula Dry Cleaners, Gig Harbor, Wash., 1981-82; intrn Fircrest (Wash.) Presbyn. Ch., 1983; staff intern Associated Ministries, Tacoma, Wash., 1984; co-pastor Eagle River (Alaska) Presbyn. Ch., 1986-88; co-pastor (interim) Community Presbyn. Ch., Redmond, Oreg., 1988-90; co-pastor First Presbyn. Ch., Marysville, Calif., 1990—; bd. dirs. Alaska Housing Ministries, Anchorage, 1986-88; organizing bd. chmn. Eagle River Food Bank, 1986-88, founding pres. Eagle River Clergy Assn., 1986-88; chmn. Congregational Renewal Com., Sacramento (Calif.) Presbytery, 1990-92. Chaplain Yuba County Sheriff's Dept., Marysville, Calif., 1990—; chmn. Yuba County Substance Abuse Com. Home: 928 E 22nd Marysville CA 95901-3404 Office: First Presbyn Ch 1940 Freeman Marysville CA 95901

HAMILTON, GAVIN FRANCIS, retired college dean; b. Nokomis, Sask., Can., Aug. 6, 1930; s. William and Elizabeth Ross (Illingworth Cunningham) H.; m. Jean Elizabeth Haight, July 6, 1956; children: Lyle Murray, Heather Anne, William Bruce, Nancy Jean, Gavin Robert, Brent Alexander. DVM, Ont. Vet. Coll., Guelph, Can., 1952; PhD, Colo. State U., 1970; D. of Divinity, St. Andrews Coll., Saskatoon, Can., 1982. Diplomate Am. Coll. Vet. Surgeons. Pvt. practice Saskatoon, Sask., Can., 1952-66; asst. clin. prof. Western Coll. Vet. Medicine, U. Sask., Saskatoon, 1966-67, assoc. prof., 1970-73, prof., 1973-93, head dept. clin. studies, 1980-82, dean, 1982-92, dean emeritus, 1993—; cons., team leader Canadian Internat. Devel. Agy., Indonesia, 1987-88; cons. Commonwealth Vet. Assn. Animal Health Asst. Tng., 1984-92. Pres. Sask. Livestock Assn., 1987-88. Mem. Sask. Vet. Med. Assn. (pres. 1962-63), Canadian Vet. Med. Assn. (pres. 1966-67), Am. Vet. Med. Assn. (Ho. of Dels. 1958), Am. Coll. Vet. Surgeons. Home: 304-230 Saskatchewan Cres E, Saskatoon, SK Canada S7N 0K6 Office: U Sask, Dept Vet Madicine, Saskatoon, SK Canada S7N 0W0

HAMILTON, HARRY LEMUEL, JR., academic administrator; b. Charleston, S.C., May 26, 1938; s. Harry Lemuel and Velma Fern (Bell) H.; m. LaVerne McDaniel, June 26, 1965 (div. 1978); children: David M., Lisa L. BA in Physics, Beloit Coll., 1960; MS in Meteorology, U. Wis., 1962, Phd in Meteorology, 1965. Asst. prof. atmospheric sci. SUNY, Albany, 1965-71, assoc. prof., 1971-90, dir. ednl. opportunity program, 1968-71; chairperson atmospheric sci. SUNY, 1976-83, dean undergrad. studies, 1983-88; rsch. scientist GE, Schenectady, N.Y., 1973-75; sr. v.p., provost Chapman U., Orange, Calif., 1990—. Trustee Beloit (Wis.) Coll., 1972—; bd. dirs. Albany Med. Ctr., 1988-90, Mohawk Hudson Community Found., 1988-90; pres. Empire State Inst. for Performing Arts, Albany, 1986-90. Mem. Am. Meteorol. Soc., Am. Assn. for Higher Edn., Sigma Xi. Office: Chapman U 333 N Glassell St Orange CA 92666-1099

HAMILTON, JAMES WILLIAM, psychiatrist, writer, artist; b. Hamilton, Ont., Can., May 12, 1933; came to U.S., 1961; s. Fraser Burnett and Dorothy May (Henry) H.; m. Marion Irene Black, June 21, 1958 (div. 1983); children: Kathleen, Susan, Jennifer, Allison. MD, U. Toronto, 1957. Diplomate Am. Bd. Psychiatry and Neurology. Psychiatry resident U. Hosp., Ann Arbor, Mich., 1961-62, Northville (Mich.) State Hosp., 1962-64; pvt. practice Ann Arbor, 1964-66; full-time faculty, Dept. of Psychiatry U. Cin., 1966-69, Yale U., New Haven, Conn., 1969-71; pvt. practice Cin., 1971-76; full-time faculty, Dept. of Psychiatry Med. Coll. of Wis., Milw., 1976-84; sabbatical Calif., 1984-85, painter, sculptor, 1985-88; pvt. practice Santa Fe, N.Mex., 1988-93, Albuquerque, 1993—; painter, sculptor, photographer, writer. Author 46 sci. papers; paintings and sculptures exhibited at Tucson Art Inst., 1986, La Pileta Gallery, Tucson, 1987, Rep Gallery, Santa Fe, 1990, 93, St. John's Coll. Gallery, Santa Fe, 1990, Raw Space Gallery, Albuquerque, 1991, Salt of the Earth Gallery, Albuquerque, 1992, Cloud Cliff Gallery, Santa Fe, 1992; photographics exhibited at Tybie Satin Gallery, Santa Fe Pub. Libr., 1990, Hour Color Space, Santa Fe, 1991, 92 (twice), Salt of the Earth Gallery, 1991. Mem. Wis. Psychoanalytic Soc., Ariz. Psychoanalytic Study Group. Home and Office: 700 Roehl Rd NW Albuquerque NM

HAMILTON, JERALD, musician; b. Wichita, Kans., Mar. 19, 1927; s. Robert James and Lillie May (Rishel) H.; m. Phyllis Jean Searle, Sept. 8, 1954; children: Barbara Helen, Elizabeth Sarah, Catharine Sandra. MusB, U. Kans., Lawrence, 1948, MusM, 1950; postgrad., Royal Sch. Ch. Music, Croydon, Eng., summer 1955, Union Theol. Sem. Sch. Sacred Music, N.Y.C., summer 1960; studies with, Laurel Everette Anderson, Andre Marchal, Catharine Crozier, Gustav Leonhardt. From instr. to asst. prof. organ and theory Washburn U., Topeka, 1949-59; dir. Washburn Singers and Choir, 1955-59; asst. prof. organ, dir. univ. singers and chorus Ohio U., Athens, 1959-60; asst. prof. organ and ch. music U. Tex., Austin, 1960-63; lectr. ch. music Episcopal Theol. Sem. S.W., Austin, 1961-63; mem. faculty U. Ill., Urbana-Champaign, 1963-88, prof. music, 1967-88, prof. emeritus, 1988—; organist, choirmaster chs. in Kans. and Tex., 1942-63; organist, choirmaster Episcopal Ch. St. John the Divine, Champaign, 1963-88, St. John's Cathedral, Albuquerque, 1988—; mem., chmn. commn. ch. music Episc. Diocese Kans., 1951-59; mem. bishop's commn. ch. music Episc. Diocese of Springfield, 1978-80, 82-88; concert organist, 1955—; with Phyllis Stringham Concert Mgmt. Author (with Marilou Kratzenstein) Four Centuries of Organ Music, Detroit Studies in Music Bibliography No. 51, 1984. Fulbright scholar, 1954-55. Mem. Assn. Anglican Musicians, Am. Guild Organists, Omicron Delta Kappa, Pi Kappa Lambda, Phi Mu Alpha. Episcopalian. Home: 724 Ranchitos Rd Corrales NM 87048-9586 Office: St John's Cathedral PO Box 1246 Albuquerque NM 87103-1246

HAMILTON, JOEL RAYMOND, state government administrator; b. Kansas City, Mo., Oct. 16, 1948; s. Raymond Rosenbond and Florence Venetta (Butler) H.; m. Diana Lynne Gronewold. AA, N.Mex. State U., Alamogordo, 1973; BA, N.Mex. State U., 1974; MA, U. No. Colo., 1981. Adult probation-parole officer N.Mex. Correction Dept., Alamogordo, 1974-79, 83-90, dist. supr., 1979-81; dep. dir. field svcs. divsn. N.Mex. Correction Dept., Santa Fe, 1981-83; assoc. warden programs So. N.Mex. Correctional Facility, N.Mex. Corrections Dept., Las Cruces, 1983; region adminstr. Children, Youth and Families Dept., Roswell, N.Mex., 1990—; adj. instr. Park Coll. Resident Ctr., Holloman AFB, N.Mex., 1986-89; instr. N.Mex. State U., Alamogordo, 1988-89. Precinct vice-chair Otero County Democrat Party, Alamogordo, 1991; bd. mem. Otero County Coun. on Alcohol and Alcohol Abuse, Alamogordo, 1988-90; bd. dirs. Otero County United Way, Alamogordo, 1989-90; com. co-chairperson Reach 2000, Roswell, N.Mex., 1990—. With U.S. Army, 1968-71, Vietnam. Named Outstanding Centennial Alumnus, N.Mex. State U., 1987; recipient over 100 % award Otero County United Way, 1990. Mem. N.Mex. Correctional Assn. (pres. 1978-79), Am. Correctional Assn., 12th Jud. Dist. Law Enforcement Assn. Presbyterian. Office: NMex Children Youth & Families Dept Ste 1010 400 N Pennsylvania Ave Roswell NM 88201

HAMILTON, KRIS PAUL, structural engineer, consultant; b. Ephrata, Wash., June 9, 1947; s. Paul B. and Jeanne R. (Newell) H.; m. Jean C. Elwood, Dec. 28, 1968; children: Ellen, Andrew. BA, Whitman Coll., 1970; BS in Engring., Columbia U., 1970; MS in Engring., Stanford U., 1973. Registered profl. engr. in 10 states. Staff engr. I. Thompson Assocs., San Francisco, 1971-74, Earl and Wright, San Francisco, 1974-76; structural engr. Northwest Cons., Bellingham, Wash., 1976-78; pvt. practice Bellingham, 1978-81; assoc. Geiger Assocs., Bellingham, 1981-88; ptnr. Geiger Gossen Hamilton Liao Engrs., Bellingham, 1988—. Patentee floating modular structural system; contbr. tech. articles to profl. publs. Session mem. 1st Presbyn. Ch., Bellingham, 1990—. Cited in Those Who Made Marks in Constrn., Engring. News-Record, 1990. Mem. ASCE (standards devel. com. for air-supported structures 1989—), Structural Engrs. Assn. Wash. Office: Geiger Gossen Hamilton Liao 1215 Cornwall Ave Bellingham WA 98225

HAMILTON, MARTIN ALVA, statistician, consultant; b. Lander, Wyo., June 18, 1939; s. Alva Wester and Ruth Margaret (King) H.; m. Mary Talovich, Dec. 2, 1967; children: Wade, Katrina, Gordon. BS, U. Wyo., 1961, MS, 1962; PhD, Stanford U., 1968. Statistician Nat. Cancer Inst., Bethesda, Md., 1968-70, Mont. State U., Bozeman, 1970—; prof. Mont. State U., Bozeman, 1980; dir. Mont. State U. Cons. Svcs., Bozeman, 1988-90; acting dir. Ctr. for Interfacial Microbial Process Engring., Bozeman, 1991-92. Contbr. chpts. to books and articles to profl. jours. Scientist USPHS, 1968-70. Recipient Fulbright scholarship Fulbright Commn., U. Aberdeen, Scotland, 1962-63, Rsch. Career Devel. award Nat. Inst. Environ. Health Sci., Research Triangle Park, N.C., 1979, Wiley Faculty award for meritorious rsch. Mont. State U., Bozeman, 1984. Mem. AAAS, Am. Statis. Assn. (editorial bd. 1981-82), The Biometric Soc. (regional com. mem. 1983-85), Inst. Math. Stats., Soc. for Epidemiologic Rsch., Com. of Pres.' of Statis. Socs. (treas. 1986-88). Office: Dept Math Scis Mont State Univ Bozeman MT 59717-0240

HAMILTON, NANCY JEANNE, structural engineer; b. Rochester, Minn., Jan. 1, 1959; d. Michael Joseph and Joanne Marguerite (Brunger) H.; m. Robert Scott Edwards; 1 child, Sarah Marie Hamilton Edwards. BS in Archtl. Engring., Calif. Poly. State U., San Luis Obispo, 1981; MSCE, MIT, 1984. Registered civil and structural engr., Calif. Project engr. KPFF Cons. Engrs., Los Angeles, 1984-85, project mgr., 1986-88; project mgr. Ove Arup amd Ptnrs. Internat., Los Angeles, 1988-89; assoc. Ove Arup and Ptnrs. Internat., Los Angeles, 1989—; theatre design specialist Ove Arup amd Ptnrs. Internat.; vis. critic architecture Calif. Poly State U., 1986; vis. lectr., critic UCLA Sch. Architecture, 1991, 92. Recipient scholarships Rotary Club Redding, Calif. chpt., 1977, Women's Archtl. League So. Calif., 1980. Mem. Earthquake Engring. Research Inst., Am. Concrete Inst., ASCE, Sigma Xi, Tau Beta Pi. Republican. Roman Catholic. Home: 9523 Lucerne Ave Culver City CA 90232-2905 Office: Ove Arup & Ptnrs Calif 2440 S Sepulveda Blvd # 180 Los Angeles CA 90064

HAMILTON, PENNY RAFFERTY, writer, educator; b. Altoona, Pa., Feb. 18, 1948; d. William E. and Lois B. (Noel) Rafferty; m. William A. Hamilton, Dec. 21, 1971. AA, Columbia (Mo.) Coll., 1968; BA, Columbia (Md.) Coll., 1976; MA, U. Nebr., 1978, PhD, 1981; postdoctoral studies, Menninger Found., Topeka, 1984. Community educator U.S. Forces in Europe, Fulda, Fed. Republic of Germany, 1972-74; health educator Nebr. State Govt., Lincoln, 1974-84; v.p. Advanced Rsch. Inst., Winter Park, Colo., 1984—; spl. features editor, newspaper columnist Sun Newspapers/Capital Times, Lincoln, 1982-91; dir. pub. affairs Sta. KHAT-KMXA, Lincoln, 1986-92. Bd. dirs. Cornhusker Boy Scouts Am. coun., Lincoln, 1986. Set world and nat. aviation speed record, 1991. Mem. Lincoln Ind. Bus. Assn. (bd. dirs. 1989-92, v.p. 1989-90). Home: PO Box 2001 Granby CO 80446 Office: Advanced Rsch Inst PO Box 3499 Winter Park CO 80482

HAMILTON, ROBERT LEE, clergyman; b. Denver, Mar. 14, 1935; s. Clyde Melvin and Elsie Lenora (Esterling) H. BA summa cum laude, Cornell Coll., Mt. Vernon, Iowa, 1957; MDiv summa cum laude, Iliff Sch. Theology, Denver, 1960. Ordained minister Methodist Ch., 1960. Pastor Hanna (Wyo.) and Medicine Bow Meth. Ch., 1959-60, Erie (Colo.) United Meth. Ch., 1961-63; assoc. pastor Warren United Meth. Ch., Denver, 1963-64, First United Meth. Ch., Salt Lake City, 1964-66; sr. pastor United Meth. Ch., Lovell-Deaver, Wyo., 1966-69; chaplain intern St. Elisabeth's Hosp., Washington, 1969-70; assoc. pastor Washington Park United Meth. Ch., Denver, 1970-75, sr. pastor, 1975-81; sr. pastor First United Meth. Ch., Ft. Collins, Colo., 1981—; chair conf. progam and arrangements Colo. com. Rocky Mountain ann. conf. United Meth. Ch., 1983-91. Pastor in prison ministry Kairos Prison Ministry, Colo. State Penitentiary, 1987-92. Elizabeth Iliff Warren fellow Iliff Sch. Theology, 1961. Mem. Phi Beta Kappa. Office: First United Meth Ch 1005 Stover St Fort Collins CO 80524

HAMILTON, SCOTT SCOVELL, professional figure skater, former Olympic athlete; b. Toledo, Aug. 28, 1958; adopted s. Ernest Scovell and Dorothy (McIntosh) H. Grad. high sch., Bowling Green, Ohio, 1976; student, Metro State Coll., 1979. Amateur competitive career includes Nat. Figure Skating Championships: jr. men's 1st pl., 1976, sr. men's 9th pl., 1977, 3d pl., 1978, 4th pl., 1979, 3d pl., 1980, 1st pl., 1981, 82, 83, 84, Mid-Western Figure Skating Championships: sr. men's 3d pl., 1977, 78, 79, Norton Skate Championships (now Skate Am.): men's div. 1st pl., 1979, 80, 81, 82, South Atlantic Figure Skating Championships: sr. men's div. 1st pl., 1980, Eastern Figure Skating Championships: sr. men's 1st pl., 1980, 81, 82, 83, 84, World Figure Skating Championships: men's div. 5th pl., 1980, , 1st pl. 81, 82, 83, 84, Nat. Sports Festival Championships: 1st pl. men's div., 1981; Winter Olympics: men's div. 5th pl., Lake Placid, N.Y., 1980, 1st pl., Sarajevo, Yugoslavia, 1984, Nippon Hoso Kykai Figure Skating Championships, men's div. 1st pl., 1982, Golden Spin of Zagreb Championships, men's div. 1st pl., 1983; Profl. competitive career includes Nutrasweet/NBC TV World Profl. Figure Skating Championships mens. div., 1st pl., 1984, 86, 2d pl., 85, 87, 88, 89, 91; World Challenge Champions/ABC TV men's div., 2d pl., 1985, 1st pl., 1986; U.S. Open men's div. 1st pl., 1990, 2d pl., 1991, Diet Coke Profl. Skaters Championship men's div. 1st pl., 1992, Hershey's Kisses Pro-Am. Figure Skating Championships 2d Place Men's divsn. 1993; profl. performances include Nat. Arena Tour Ice Capades, 1984-85, 85-86, star Scott Hamilton's Am. Tour, 1986-87, 1990-91, co-star Concert On Ice, Harrah's Hotel, Lake Tahoe, Nev., 1987, spl. guest star Festival On Ice, Nat. Theatre Tour, 1987, star Discover Card Stars On Ice Nat. Arena Tour, 1987-88, 88-89, star Festival On Ice, Harrah's Hotel, 1988, guest star ABC/TV spl. Ice Capades With Kirk Cameron, 1988, A Very Special Christmas, ABC/TV, 1988, An Olympic, Calgary Christmas, ABC/TV, 1988, star and mus. comedy and acting debut Broadway On Ice, Harrah's Hotel and Nat. Theatre Tour, 1989; CBS/TV Sports Figure Skating Commentator 1984-91 various skating competitions and CBS/TV coverage Winter Olympics, Albertville, France, 1992; star, dir., producer Scott Hamilton's Celebration On Ice, Sea World of Calif., 1988, Scott Hamilton's Time Traveler: An Odyssey On Ice, Sea World of Calif., 1989; host, guest star TV spl. A Salute To Dorothy Hamill, 1988; star, co-producer Discover Card Stars On Ice, Nat. Arena Tour, 1989-91; guest star CBS/TV spl. Disney's Christmas on Ice, 1990; co-producer, star Discover Card Stars on Ice Nat. Arena Tour, 1991-92; co-host, star HBO TV spl. Vail Skting Festival, 1992; co-producer Star Discover Card Stars on Ice Nat. Arena Tour, 1992-93; guest TV spl. A Disney Christmas on Ice, 1992; creator original concepts in arena figure skating. Cons. Friends of Scott Hamilton Found. named in his honor to fundraise and benefit youth oriented causes throughout U.S., 1988, Scott Hamilton's Friends and Legends 1st Annual Celebrity Charity Golf Tournament, Ford's Colony, Williamsburg, Va., 1991; participant fundraising Athletes for Reagan, March of Dimes, Am. Cancer Soc., Spl. Olympics, Starlight Found., United Way Adoption Home Socs., Make A Wish Found, Big Bros., 1984—, Athletes For Bush, Adult and Ped. AIDS Rsch., Edn. and Funding, 1988—, Homeless, 1989—, Great Am. Workout for Pres.'s Coun. Phys. Fitness & Sports, 1990, 92. Winner Olympic Gold medal, Sarajevo, 1984; U.S. Olympic Com. awards and honors include carrier Am. Flag in opening ceremonies Lake Placid, 1980, Figure Skating Athlete of Yr., 1981, 82, 83, 84, Athlete of Yr., 1981, Olympic Spirit award, 1987; recipient Olympia award Southland Corp., 1984, Achievement award March of Dimes, 1984, Colo. Athlete of Yr. award Denver Athletic Club, 1984, Most Courageous Athlete award Phila. Sportswriters Assn., 1985, Profl. Skater of Yr. award Am. Skating World mag., 6, Jacques Favart award Internat. Skating Union, 1988, The Crown Royal Achievement award from House of Seagrams and Jimmy Heuga Ctr., 1991, Clairol's Personal Best award, 1991, Spirit of Giving award U.S. Figure Skating Assn., 1993; inducted U.S. Olympic Hall of Fame, 1990, World Figure Skating Hall of Fame, 1990; honoree nat. com. for adoption, 1992. Hon. mem. Phila. Skating Club, Humane Soc. Republican. Office: care Michael Sterling & Assocs 4242 Van Nuys Blvd Sherman Oaks CA 91403-3710

HAMILTON, WILLIAM FREDERICK, III, programmer, analyst; b. Youngstown, Ohio, Mar. 1, 1943; s. William Frederick and Carol (Zito) H.; m. Joan C. Filmer, Apr. 25, 1975 (div. 1989). AA, Pierce Coll., Woodland Hills, Calif., 1987. Programmer Occidental Life, L.A., 1968-71; programmer/analyst Oroweat, L.A., 1977-78, Mercury Ins., L.A., 1978-80; sr. programmer/analyst Valley Nat. Bank, Phoenix, 1981-83, Union Bank, L.A., 1983-84, Great Western Bank, Northridge, Calif., 1984-89; cons. sr. programmer/analyst Tentek, Inc., Glendale, Calif., 1989—; info. engr. Tentek, Inc., 1990—; programmer, analyst GTE, 1991-93; sr. programmer, analyst Glendale Fed. Bank, 1993—. Author: Center of the Vortex, 1986, Alien Magic, 1989, Cosmic Top Secret, 1991; contbr. articles to profl. jours. With USAF, 1961-65. Libertarian. Office: 249 N Brand Blvd # 651 Glendale CA 91203

HAMLETT, DALE EDWARD, retired art educator; b. Memphis, Mo., Aug. 15, 1921; s. John Emerson and Gladys Kathryn (Reese) H.; m. Mozelle Elizabeth Lowe, Aug. 11, 1946; children: Sharon Mullen, Brenda Kilmer, Gena Renee. BS, N.E. Mo. State U., 1944; student, Am. Acad. Art, Chgo., 1941-42, 44-47; MA, U. N.Mex., 1963; MFA, Eastern N.Mex. U., 1984. Package designer Montgomery Ward & Co., Chgo., 1947-51; comml. artist Ward Hicks Advt. Agy., Albuquerque, 1951-64; artist in residence N.Mex. Inst. of Mining and Tech., Socorro, 1964-69; prof. art Eastern N.Mex. U., Portales, 1969-87, prof. emeritus, 1987—; art cons., advisor Golden Libr. Eastern N.Mex. U., 1987-89; judge Llano Escalero Art Assn., Hobbs, N.Mex., 1989; art lectr. Amarillo, Tex., 1990; art lectr. Clovis Pub. Libr., 1993. Exhibited in one-man shows including N.Mex. Art League Gallery, Albuquerque, 1975, Pines Gallery, Ruidoso, N.Mex., 1976, Geranimo Mus. Gallery, Truth of Consequences, N.Mex., 1978. Springville (Utah) Mus. Art, 1979, Martin Spears Meml. Libr. Gallery, Socorro, 1980, Coll. S.W. Gallery, Hobbs, N.Mex., 1980, Garrett Studio Gallery, Boise, Idaho, 1981, Pub. Libr. Gallery, Emmett, Idaho, 1981, Macey Gallery, Sorocco, 1986, Sheldon Jackson Coll., Sitka, Alaska, 1990, Eastern N.Mex. U. Gallery, Portales, 1991, Clovis (N.Mex.) Community Coll. Gallery, 1992, Clovis-Carver Pub. Libr., Clovis, 1992. Elder, Presbyn. Ch., Portales, 1990; painting demonstrator pub. schs., Portales, 1990. Named Disting. Prof. Art by Friends of Eastern N.Mex. U. and Bd. Regents, 1989. Mem. LaEscelero Art Guild, Pintores Art Assn., N.Mex. Art League, N.Mex. Watercolor Soc. Home: 2104 S Avenue H Portales NM 88130-7114

HAMLIN, DONALD WALTER, county official; b. July 20, 1936; s. Oliver Alfred and Genevieve June (Jankiewicz) H. AA in Psychology, Compton Coll., 1956; BS in Police Adminstrn., Calif. State U., L.A., 1967, BA in Sociology, 1971, BSBA, 1974; AS in Logistics Mgmt., Community Coll. Air Force, 1992. With Bethlehem Steel Corp., Calif., 1956-59; dep. sheriff L.A. County Sheriff Dept., 1959-69; security officer Deluxe Gen., L.A., 1970-72; plant protection officer Hughes Aircraft and Summa Corp., L.A., 1975-77; police officer L.A. Community Coll. Dist., 1977-88; dep. marshal Los Angeles County Marshal's Office, Van Nuys, Calif., 1988-93. With USN, 1953-58, USAFR, 1978—. Mem. Internat. Police Assn., Am. Legion, Al Malaikah Shrine Temple, L.A. Scottish Rite, Southeast Masonic Lodge, Calif. State U., L.A. Alumni Assn., Peace Officers Shrine Club, Alpha Kappa Psi, Pi Sigma Epsilon. Home: 333 N Lincoln St Burbank CA 91506-2111

HAMLIN, EDMUND MARTIN, JR., engineering manager; b. Utica, N.Y., June 9, 1949; s. Edmund Martin and Catherine Mary (Humphreys) H.; m. Nancy Ann Christensen, June 26, 1971; 1 child, Benjamin John (dec.). BSEE, Clarkson U., 1971; postgrad., U. So. Calif., 1972-73, RPI Hartford Grad. Ctr., 1980-82, UCLA, 1987-8; 1987-88, 91—. Engr. NASA Flight Rsch. Ctr., Edwards, Calif., 1971-75; sr. engr. NASA Flight Rsch. Ctr., Edwards, 1976-79; project engr. Sundstrand Energy Systems Div., Belvidere, Ill., 1975-76; sr. engr. Teleco Oilfield Svcs., Meriden, Conn., 1979-80, mgr. electronic systems, 1980-83, the sr. staff engr., 1984; sr. engr. NASA Ames-Dryden, Edwards, Calif., 1984-85; asst. chief flight systems NASA Ames-Dryden, Edwards, 1985-90, chief flight instrumentation, 1990—. Inventor: position measurement system, 1976, method for determining and correcting magnetic interference in boreholes, 1988, method for computing borehold azimuth while rotating, 1989. Vice-pres. bd. trustees Tehachapi (Calif.) Unified Sch. Dist., 1989—. Capt. U.S. Army, 1971-75. Mem. Instrument Soc. of Am., AIAA, Aircraft Owners and Pilots Assn. Home: 22220 Valley Vista Dr Tehachapi CA 93561-9549 Office: NASA Ames-Dryden Flight Rsch Facility PO Box 273 Edwards CA 93523-0273

HAMLIN, SUSAN ELIZABETH, lawyer, educator; b. Boise, Idaho, Nov. 15, 1966. BA, U. Idaho, 1989, JD, 1992. Bar: Idaho 1992. Lectr. U. Idaho, Moscow, 1990-92; legal extern U.S. Atty.'s Office, Boise, 1991; law clk. Atty. Gen., Boise, 1992, Idaho Dist. Judge and Snake River Adjudication, 1992-93. Assoc. mem. Idaho Law Rev., 1990-91. Mem. ABA, Idaho Trial Lawyers Assn., Idaho Vol. Lawyers for the Arts, Idaho Water User Assn., Phi Alpha Theta (pres. 1987-88), Alpha Gamma Delta (pres. 1987-88). Office: Twin Falls Courthouse PO Box 126 Twin Falls ID 83303

HAMM, GEORGE ARDEIL, educator, hypnotherapist, consultant; b. San Diego, Aug. 13, 1934; s. Charles Ardeil and Vada Lillian (Sharrah) H.; m. Marilyn Kay Nichols, July 1, 1972; children—Robert Barry, Charles Ardeil II, Patricia Ann. B.S. in Music, No. Ariz. U., 1958, M.A. in Music Edn., 1961; M.A. in Ednl. Adminstrn., Calif. Lutheran Coll., 1978, M.S. in Guidance and Counseling, 1981. Cert. secondary sch. tchr., adminstr. pupil personnel services, Calif., clinical hyprotherapist. Tchr. music Needles (Calif.) High Sch., 1958-61; sociology, psychology tchr, counselor Hueneme High Sch., Oxnard, Calif., 1961—; founder Nat. Judo Inst., Colorado Springs, Colo., Coll. Sport Sci., Nat. Judo Inst.; cons. applied sport hypnotherapy; creator teaching program. Served with USMC, 1953-55; Korea. Mem. Am. Fedn. Tchrs., Am. Council Hypnotist Examiners, U.S. Judo Assn. Inc. (6th Degree Black Belt; named sr. level coach of Judo, 1980, cert. rank examiner), Phi Delta Kappa, Kappa Delta Pi. Republican. Mormon. Contbr. numerous articles to nat. and internat. Judo jours. Pioneer ednl. hypnosis. Home: 2560 Ruby Dr Oxnard CA 93030-8607 Office: Hueneme High Sch 500 W Bard Rd Oxnard CA 93033-6399

HAMM, PATRICIA ANN, principal; b. Rapid City, S.D., May 22, 1943; d. Jesse Jerald and Gladys Pearl (Felton) Bauer; m. Joseph Nicholas Hamm, June 11, 1966 (div. 1983); children: Michele, Christopher. BS, U. S.D., 1965; MEd, S.D. State U., 1985; adminstrv. endorsement, Ellsworth AFB, 1988. 3rd grade tchr. St. Vrain Valley Dist., Longmont, Colo., 1965-66; 2d grade tchr. Yankton (S.D.) Schs., 1966-68, Rapid City Schs., 1968-73; 5th grade tchr. Douglas Schs., Ellsworth AFB, S.D., 1980-85; counselor Douglas Schs., Ellsworth AFB, 1985-90; instr. grad. sch. S.D. State U., Ellsworth AFB, 1988-92; elem. sch. prin., rural schs. community edn. dir. Meade Schs. 56-1, Sturgis, S.D., 1990-92; elem. sch. prin. Sunrise Drive Sch., Catalina Foothills Sch. Dist., Tucson, 1992—; instr. staff devel. S.D. State U., Gillette and Douglas, Wyo., 1990-92; presenter S.D. Sch. Counselors Assn., 1990, various sch. dists., 1985-92. Bd. dirs. Rapid City Child Protection Coun., 1989-92; trainer Improvisation Theater, 1987-88; mem. Family Advocacy Com., Ellsworth AFB, 1989-90. Recipient S.D. Curriculum Devel. award, 1985. Mem. ASCD, Am. Assn. Counseling and Devel., Nat. Assn. Elem. Prins., s.D. Assn. Counseling and Devel., S.D. Assn. Elem. Prins., Black Hills Reading Coun., Phi Kappa Phi. Office: Catalina Foothills Sch Dist 5301 E Sunrise Dr Tucson AZ 85718

HAMM, ROBERT M., principal; b. Midland, Tex., July 24, 1944; s. Lee William Thelma (Ford) H.; m. Mary Catherine Champine, Apr. 1, 1967; 1 child, Elizabeth LeClair. BS in Edn., Tex. Tech U., 1970, MEd, 1971. Cert. tchr., Calif. Vol. VISTA, Redding, Calif., 1966-68; tchr. Waco (Tex.) Ind. Sch. System, 1972-80; prin. St. Louis Cath. Sch., Waco, 1980-89, Sacred Heart Acad., San Diego, 1989—; bd. dirs. Heart of Tex. Study of Am. Heritage, Waco, 1971-88; mem. edn. commn. Sacred Heart Cath. Ch., San Diego, 1989—. Writer curriculum in field. Bd. dirs. Downtown Waco, Inc., 1973-78, Tex. State Hist. Com., Austin, 1973-78. With U.S. Army, 1968-70. Republican. Roman Catholic. Home: 4267 Loma Riviera Ln San Diego CA 92110 Office: Sacred Heart Acad 4875 Saratoga Ave San Diego CA 92110

HAMM, WILLIAM GILES, banking executive; b. Washington, Dec. 29, 1942; s. John Edwin and Letty Belle (Wills) H.; m. Kathleen Kelley, Sept. 5, 1970; 1 child, Giles Alexander. AB, Dartmouth Coll., 1964; MA, U. Mich., 1966, PhD, 1969. Budget examiner Bur. of the Budget, Washington, 1969-72; chief HUD br. Office of Mgmt. & Budget, Washington, 1972-76; dep. assoc. dir. Office of Mgmt. & Budget, 1976-77; legis. analyst Calif. Legis., Sacramento, 1977-86; v.p. World Savs. & Loan, Oakland, Calif., 1986-91; sr. v.p. Fed. Home Loan Bank of San Francisco, 1991-92, exec. v.p., COO, 1992—. Bd. visitors Duke U., Durham, 1986-89, U. Calif., Davis, 1986—. Recipient William A. Jump award, Civil Svc. Commn., 1975, Presdl. commendation, 1973, 74. Fellow Nat. Acad. Pub. Adminstrn., Coun. for Excellence in Govt.; mem. Commonwealth Club, Phi Beta Kappa, Phi Kappa Phi. Office: Fed Home Loan Bank San Francisco 600 California St San Francisco CA 94108-2704

HAMMAN, STEVEN ROGER, vocational rehabilitation specialist; b. Santa Monica, Calif., Nov. 2, 1946; s. Roy Ernest H. and Joan Barbara (Werner) Scott; m. Christine Frances Solomon, May 29, 1976; children: Zachary

Charles, Tamara Edith, Bryan Joseph. AA, Northeastern Colo. U., 1967; BA, Colo. State Coll., 1970; MA, U. No. Colo., 1972; MS, Drake U., 1981. Cert. vocat. expert, rehab. counselor, ins. rehab. specialist. Social worker Poudre-Thompson Transp. Corps, Ft. Collins, Colo., 1974-78; placement specialist Missoula (Mont.) Rehab. Ctr., 1978-80; rehab. counselor Adolph Coors Co., Golden, Colo., 1981; rehab. counselor, br. mgr. Nat. Rehab. Cons., Duluth, Minn., 1981-82; Mont. case svcs. dir. Nat. Rehab. Cons., Missoula, 1982-83; case svcs. dir. Northwest U.S. Nat. Rehab. Cons., Spokane, Wash., 1983-86; rehab. cons., pres., chief exec. officer Vocability, Inc., Post Falls, Idaho, 1986—; counselor, trainer Community Corrections Program, Ft. Collins, 1976. Community organizer VISTA, Clay, W.Va., 1973-74; pres., bd. dirs. Mountain Van Spl. Transp., Missoula, 1980; bd. dirs. Heritage Place I and II, Coeur d'Alene Homes Inc.; mem. coun. Calvary Luth. Ch., Post Falls. Mem. Nat. Assn. Rehab. Practitioners in the Private Sector., Vocat. Evaluation and Work Adjustment Assn. (registered cons. Americans with Disabilities Act). Office: Vocability Inc PO Box 772 Post Falls ID 83854-0772

HAMMELL, GRANDIN GAUNT, forms management business consultant; b. Rumson, N.J., Aug. 10, 1945; s. Grandin Kenneth and Catherine Elizabeth (Conklin) H.; m. Darlene Faye Settje, Nov. 21, 1972; children: Grandin Jeffrey, Heidi Grechen. B of Bus. Sci., Calif. State U., Los Angeles, 1979. V.p. Security Pacific Bank, N.A., Los Angeles, 1973-87; exec. v.p. The Wellington Group, Rolling Hills Estate, Calif., 1987-89; bus. cons. Cambridge Bus. Forms, Burbank, Calif., 1991—; speaker seminars on estate planning, so. Calif., 1983-90. Exec. producer radio program The World of Money. Mem. planned giving com. of So. Calif. chpt. Arthritis Found., 1987—; v.p. Burbank Ednl. Found., 1984—; vol. Polit. Service. Glendale, 1988—; chmn. fund raising com. L.A. County Natural History Mus. Mem. Glendale Estate Planning Commn., Burbank C. of C. (ednl. com. 1989—). Office: Cambridge Bus Forms 1725 W Burbank Blvd Burbank CA 91506-1734

HAMMER, JAN HAROLD, television station manager; b. Boise, Idaho, May 28, 1939; s. Frederick Allen Hammer and Violet (Gardner) Goicoechea; m. Jane M. Hammer, June 15, 1957 (div. 1972); children: Julie, Christopher, Angela, Gregory. Student, Ea. Mont. Coll., 1963-64, Boise State Coll., 1965-66. Nat. sales mgr. KIVI/KPVI TV, Boise, 1972-77; campaign mgr. Gov. John V. Evans, Idaho, Boise, 1978, spl. asst., 1977-79; congl. candidate Idaho's First Congl. Dist., Boise, 1980; nat. sales mgr. KOKI-TV, Tulsa, 1981-85; gen. sales mgr. KTTY-TV, San Diego, 1985-86; gen. mgr. KJCT-TV, Grand Junction, Colo., 1986—; head govt. rels. we. dist. ABC-TV Affiliates Assn., 1986—. Creator TV awareness campaign on environ. Colo. Cares, 1990. Advisor Mesa County Econ. Devel. Coun., Grand Junction, 1986—; dir. Mus. of Western Colo., Grand Junction, 1987-91; dir. Rural Colo. Pvt. Industry Coun., Denver. Staff sgt. U.S. Army, 1956-64. Recipient Best TV News Story award Colo. Broadcasters Assn., Denver, 1988. Mem. Nat. Assn. Broadcasters, The Jefferson Awards, Grand Junction Lion's Club (dir. community betterment com. 1986—). Democrat. Roman Catholic. Home: 2673 Catalina Dr Grand Junction CO 81506 Office: KJCT-TV 8 Foresight Circle Grand Junction CO 81506

HAMMER, KEARNEY LEE, business adviser, lawyer; b. Everett, Wash., Mar. 26, 1947; s. Alton Andrew and Inga (Langland) H.; m. Gail Charleen McPherson, Mar. 15, 1968; children: Kirsten, Erik, Janne. BA in Acctg., U. Wash., 1969, JD, 1972; LLM in Taxation, NYU, 1973. Bar: Wash., 1972, Commonwealth of No. Marianas, 1974; lic. real estate broker, Calif. Asst. prof. bus. U. Guam, Barrigada, 1974-75; instr. law NYU, N.Y.C., 1972-73; ptnr. Trapp, Gayle, Teker, Hammer & Lacy, Agana, Guam, 1973-77; prin. Kearney Lee Hammer, P.C., Arlington, Wash., 1977-83; spl. asst. to exec. com. Allright Auto Parks, Inc., Houston, 1983-87; pres. Trident Capital Mgmt., Inc., Novato, Calif., 1987—; adviser to Harter/Smith, Inc., Belvedere, Calif., 1990—, Total Network Telecommunications, Inc., Las Vegas, Nev., 1992, Fish Art, Inc., Santa Cruz, Calif., 1992; ann. lectr. Fed. Res. Bank San Francisco, 1986. Treas., bd. dirs. Am. Cancer Soc., Agana, 1977; adult leader cub pack Houston area Boy Scouts Am., 1986. Mem. Eagle Scout Assn. Republican. Lutheran.

HAMMER, SUSAN W., mayor; b. Monrovia, Calif., Dec. 21, 1938; d. James Nathan and Katrine (Krutzsch) Walker; m. Philip Hammer, Sept. 4, 1960; children: Philip, Hali, Matthew. BA in History, U. Calif., Berkeley, 1960. Svc. rep. Pacific Telephone Co., Berkeley, 1960-61; staff asst. Peace Corps, Washington, 1962-63; councilwoman City of San Jose, Calif., 1980-81, 83-90, spl. asst. to mayor, 1981-82, vice mayor, 1985-87, mayor, 1991—. Bd. dirs. San Jose Mus. Art, 1971-90,, pres., 1978-80; mem. governing bd. NCCJ, 1978—; mem. adv. bd. Community Found. Santa Clara County, 1978—; mem. Santa Clara County Transp. Com., 1976-77, Santa Clara County Juvenile Justice Commn., 1974-80, San Jose Fine Arts Comm., 1980, Victim-Witness Adv. Bd., 1977—, Children's Health Coun. San Jose, 1981-89, Santa Clara Valley Leadership Program, 1986—, Childrens Shelter Project, 1991—, Am. Leadership Forum, 1992—; past chmn. parents adv. com. Trace Sch. Recipient Rosalie M. Stern Community Svc. award U. Calif., 1975, Disting. Citizen of San Jose award Exch. Club, 1979, Investment in Leadership award Coro Found., 1985, Tzedek award for honor, compassion and community svc. Temple Emanu-El, 1987, recognition award YWCA, Santa Clara County, 1989, resolution of commendation Assn. for Responsible Alcohol Control, 1990, Woman of Achievement award The Women's Fund, 1990, Dox Quixote award Nat. Hispanic U., 1991, Friends of Bay Area Mcpl. Elections Com. award, 1991. Democrat. Office: Office of Mayor 801 N 1st St San Jose CA 95110

HAMMERBACK, JOHN CLARK, communications educator; b. San Francisco, Oct. 6, 1938; s. William Joseph and Susan (Ridzik) H.; m. Jean Melton, Aug. 29, 1965; children: Kristen, Karen. BA, San Francisco State Coll., 1962; MA, U. Okla., 1965; PhD, Ind. U., 1970. Teaching asst. dept. speech communication U. Okla., Norman, 1963-65, Ind. U., Bloomington, 1965-68; prof. speech communication Calif. State U., Hayward, 1968—, chmn. dept. speech and drama, 1972-79, affirmative action liason officer, 1986-88, asst. v.p. rsch. faculty affairs, 1988-91; lectr. U. N.Mex., Albuquerque, 1977, Oreg. State Coll., 1989; lectr. Rotary, Kiwanis and Lions clubs; speech writer for local polit. candidates, Fremont, Calif., 1978—; dir. Conf. in Rhetorical Criticism, 1987—. Author: A War of Words: Chicano Rhetoric of the 1960s and 1970s, 1985, In Search of Justice: Studies in Speech Communication in the Indiana Tradition, 1987; contbr. articles, papers, and book reviews to profl. publs. Bd. dirs. Community Counseling and Edn. Ctr., Fremont; v.p. Greater Kimber Area Homeowners Assn., 1984. Faculty Research grantee Calif. State U., Hayward, 1975; Meritorious Service award, 1985. Mem. Western Speech Communication Assn. (2d v.p. 1979-80, mem. legis. assembly 1974-77, chmn. 1980, 1st v.p. 1981-82, chief conv. planner 1982-83, pres. 1983-84, assoc. editor jour. 1979-81, 84-87, 90—, disting. svc. award com. 1985, nominating com. 1984, chmn. membership com. 1980, mem. search com. 1989), Rhetoric Soc., Speech Communication Assn. (com. on intercultural 1976, chair elect Public Address Divsn., 1993), Execs. Club (pres., 1991). Home: 203 Fisalia Ct Fremont CA 94539-3028 Office: Calif State U Hayward CA 94539

HAMMERMAN, KENNETH JAY, internist, gastroenterologist, educator; b. Bklyn., Mar. 27, 1945; s. May and Gertrude (Strauss) H.; m. Robin Cheryl Baker, June 9, 1968; children: Peter Seth, Elizabeth Emily. BS in Chemistry, Bklyn. Coll., 1965; MD, NYU, 1969. Intern Yale New Haven (Conn.) Hosp., 1969-70, jr. resident, 1970-71; sr. resident U. Calif., San Francisco, 1973-74, fellow in gastroenterology, 1974-76, asst. prof. medicine, 1976-78; assoc. clin. prof. medicine San Francisco, 1986—, pvt. practice, 1978—; chief med. staff St. Francis Meml. Hosp., San Francisco, 1987-89, trustee, 1987—. Contbr. articles to profl. jours. Lt. comdr. USPHS, 1971-73. Fellow ACP; mem. No. Calif. Soc. Clin. Gastroenterology (pres. 1987), Sigma Xi, Alpha Omega Alpha. Office: San Francisco Internal Med 1199 Bush St San Francisco CA 94109

HAMMETT, BENJAMIN COWLES, psychologist; b. Los Angeles, Nov. 18, 1931; s. Buell Hammett and Harriet (Cowles) Graham; m. Ruth Finstrom, June 18, 1957; children: Susan Hood, Sarah, Carol Bress, John. BS, Stanford U., 1957; PhD, U. N.C., 1969. Lic. psychologist, Calif. Staff psychologist Children's Psychiat. Ctr., Butner, N.C., 1965-67; sr. psychologist VA Treatment Ctr. for Children, Richmond, Va., 1968-71; asst. prof. child psychiatry Va. Commonwealth U., Richmond, 1968-71; instr. psychology Western Grad. Sch. Psychology, 1980—; pvt. practice clin. psychology Palo Alto, Calif., 1972-92; rsch. psychologist, 1992—; affiliate staff mem. O'Connor Hosp., San Jose, Calif., 1980—; v.p. bd. dirs. Mental Rsch. Inst., Palo Alto, 1982-83, pres. bd. dirs., 1983-85, treas. 1990-92, mem. staff 1992—. Co-author chpts. to two books. Vol., scoutmaster Boy Scouts Am., 1952-54; vol. Peninsula Conservation Ctr., Palo Alto, 1983—, Calif. Acad. Scis., San Francisco, 1987—; treas. John B. Cary Sch. PTA, Richmond, Va. 1969-70. Named Eagle Scout, 1947; grantee NIMH, 1970. Mem. Am. Psychol. Assn., Am. Psychol. Soc., Am. Group Psychotherapy Assn., Internat. Transactional Analysis Assn. (cert. clin. mem.), Assoc. Applied Psychophysiol. & Biofeedback (cert. Biofeedback Cert. Inst. Am.), Biofeedback Soc. Calif., Calif. State Psychol. Assn., Assn. for the Advancement of Gestalt Therapy, El Tigre Club (sec. 1954). Democrat. Unitarian. Home: 301 Lowell Ave Palo Alto CA 94301-3812

HAMMING, RICHARD WESLEY, computer scientist; b. Chgo., Feb. 11, 1915; s. Richard J. and Mabel G. (Redfield) H.; m. Wanda Little, Sept. 5, 1942. B.S., U. Chgo., 1937; M.A., U. Nebr., 1939, Ph.D. in Math, 1942. With Manhattan Project, 1945-46; with Bell Telephone Labs., 1946-76; mem. faculty Naval Postgrad. Sch., Monterey, Calif., 1976—; adj. prof. computer sci. Naval Postgrad. Sch., 1976—. Author books, papers in field. Fellow IEEE (Piore award 1979, $10,000 prize medal named in his honor 1986, 1st recipient of same 1988); mem. Assn. Computing Machinery (Turing prize 1968), Nat. Acad. Engring., Am. Math. Assn., AAAS. Office: Naval Postgrad Sch Code CS Hg Monterey CA 93943

HAMMOND, JUDY MCLAIN, business services executive; b. Downey, Calif., June 24, 1956; d. Ernest Richard and Bernice Elaine (Thompson) McLain; m. Dennis Francis Hammond, Aug. 15, 1981. BS in Mgmt., Pepperdine U., 1982; MBA, U. So. Calif., 1986. Br. mgr. Kelly Svcs., Encino, Calif., 1978-81; mktg. mgr. Payco Am. Corp., Encino, 1981-83, GC Svcs. Corp., Santa Ana, Calif., 1983-86; pres. Resource Mgmt. Svcs., Norwalk, Calif., 1986—. Author: Collect More From Collection Agencies. Mem. adv. com. Cerritos Coll. Mem. Toastmasters. Office: 9915 Pioneer Blvd Santa Fe Springs CA

HAMMOND, LEWIS MAYNARD, horticulturist; b. Bellingham, Wash., July 22, 1918; s. Frank Lewis and Bertha Louise (St. John) H.; m. Elizabeth Annette Whiting, July 16, 1944; children: Louise Grace, Ruth Anne, Daniel Bruce, James Allen; m. Joyce S. Whiteing, June 13, 1993. Student, Wash. State Coll., 1938-39, U. Calif. Santa Barbara, 1940-41; Cert. in Tropical Agriculture, U. Fla., 1972-73. Intelligence clk. U.S. Army Air Corps, Australia, 1942-44; nursery man, owner Ingelwood (Calif.) Nursery, 1945-61; landscape contractor self-employed, Santa Barbara, Calif., 1966-72; agrl. tchr. Agy. for Internat. Devel., Sandoa, Zaire, 1961-65; agrl. missionary Nat. Coun. Chs., Juba, Sudan, 1974-77, United Meth. Ch., Gbarnga, Liberia, 1977-83; ret., 1984—. Artist, author: (cartoon strip) Plant Talk, 1974. Mem. City Beautiful C. of C., Inglewood, 1946-60, Channel City Club, Santa Barbara, 1965-72, United Meth. Ch., 1926—; pres. Meth. Men, Inglewood, 1948-60. Recipient St. Mark Peace prize, 1983. Mem. Calif. Assn. Nurserymen, Calif. Assn. Landscape Contractors, Toastmasters Internat. Republican. Methodist. Home: 635 Sheehy Rd Nipomo CA 93444

HAMNER, HOMER HOWELL, economist, educator; b. Lamont, Okla., Oct. 22, 1915; s. Homer Hill and Myrtle Susan (Edwards) H.; m. Winnie Elvyn Heafner, May 8, 1943 (dec. Aug. 23, 1946); 1 dau., Jean Lee (Mrs. Richard L. Nicholson); m. Marjorie Lucille Dittus, Nov. 24, 1947; 1 dau., Elaine (Mrs. Alan M. Yard). A.A., Glendale Coll., 1936; A.B., U. So. Calif.; A.B. (Gen. Achievement scholarship 1936-37), 1938, J.D., 1941, A.M., 1947, Ph.D., 1949. Fellow and teaching asst., dept. econs. U. So. Calif., 1945-49; prof. and chmn. dept. econs. Baylor U., 1949-55; editor research com. Baylor Bus. Studies, 1949-55, lectr. summer workshop, 1954; prof., chmn. dept. bus. adminstrn. and cons. U. Puget Sound, Tacoma, Wash., 1955-58; dir. sch. bus. adminstr. and econs. U. Puget Sound, 1959-63, Edward L. Blaine chair econ. history, 1963—; also occasional lectr. Roman Forums, Ltd., Los Angeles, 1936-40; lectr. Am. Inst. Banking, 1949-50; lectr. Southwest Wholesale Credit Assn., 1949, James Connally AFB, 1950; cons. State of Wash. tax adv. council, 1957-58, State of Wash. Expenditures Adv. Council, 1960. Author: Population Change in Metropolitan Waco, 1950; reviewer, contbr. to Jour. of Finance. Served with U.S. Army, 1941-44. Fellow Found. Econ. Edn., Chgo., Inst. on Freedom, Claremont Men's Coll.; mem. AAUP, Am. Econ. Assn., Southwest Social Sci. Assn. (Tex. chmn. membership com.), Nat. Tax Assn., Am. Finance Assn., Am. Acad. Polit. and Soc. Sci., Order of Artus, Waco McLennan County Bar Assn. (hon.), Phi Beta Kappa, Phi Kappa Phi, Omicron Delta Gamma, Delta Theta Phi, Phi Rho Pi (degree highest achievement 1936). Methodist. Home: 4404 N 44th St Tacoma WA 98407-6604

HAMOS, ROBERT EUSTACE, engineering executive; b. Cedar Rapids, Iowa, Sept. 24, 1941; s. Eustace Steve and Lucille (Andes) H.; m. Diane Margaret Pillard, Sept. 5, 1966; children: Leslie S., Kerri A. BS in Indsl. Tech., Iowa State U., 1967; MA in Bus., U. No. Iowa, 1975. Indsl. engr. Lennox Industries Inc., Marshalltown, Iowa, 1967-68, process control engr., 1969-71, chief engr., 1972-76; mgr. products Lennox Industries Inc., Dallas, 1977-85; mgr. engring. Lennox Industries Inc., Murfreesboro, Tenn., 1986-87; v.p. engring. Teledyne Laars, Moorpark, Calif., 1987—. Advisor Big Bros./Big Sisters, Dallas, 1984-85, Marshalltown, 1975-77. With U.S. Navy, 1960-64. Named Outstanding Young Religious Leader, Marshalltown C. of C., 1973. Fellow Am. Soc. Heating Refrigeration Engrs.; mem. Am. Soc. Gas Engrs., Soc. Mfg. Engrs. (cert. mfg. engr.). Democrat. Presbyn. Home: 560 Fairfield Rd Simi Valley CA 93065 Office: Teledyne Laars 6000 Condor Dr Moorpark CA 93021

HAMPTON, WILLIAM C., environmental engineer, consultant; b. Pendleton, Oreg., May 23, 1956; s. Richard Westgate and Jeanne Virginia (Littleton) H.; m. Felicity Kathryn Adamson, Apr. 11, 1981; children: Kathryn Opal, Caleb Adamson. BSME, MIT, 1979; MBA in Internat. Bus., U. Oreg., 1989, MA in Asian Studies, 1989. Registered profl. engr., Oreg. Engr. Arabian Am. Oil Co., Ras Tanura, Saudi Arabia, 1979-80; petroleum engr. Royal Dutch Shell, The Hague, The Netherlands, 1981, Shell (Oman), Muscat, 1982-85; environ. engr. Dept. Environ. Quality, Pendleton, 1989-90; project mgr. Riedel Environ., Taiwan and, Portland, Oreg., 1990—; instr. Blue Mountain C.C., Pendleton, 1990. Mem. budget com. Pendleton Sch. Bd., 1990; asst. coord. Frohmeyer for Gov. Campaign, Morrow County, Oreg., 1990; mem. N.W. Regional China Coun. Chiles scholar and Todd-Wengert scholar U. Oreg., 1988. Mem. ASME, Soc. Petroleum Engrs. Republican. Office: Riedel Environ 4555 N Channel Ave Portland OR 97208-3320

HAMREN, NANCY VAN BRASCH, bookkeeper; b. L.A., Feb. 2, 1947; d. Milton Carl and Winifred (Taylor) Van Brasch; m. Jerome Arthur Hamren, Feb. 14, 1981; children: Emily Allison, Meredith Ann. Student, Pasadena City Coll., 1964-65, San Francisco State Coll., 1966-67, U. Oreg., 1975-79. Bookkeeper Springfield Creamery, Eugene, Oreg., 1969—, also bd. dirs.; originator Nancy's Yogurt, Nancy's Cultured Dairy Products. Active mem. Oreg. Shakespearean Festival, Ashland, 1986, Oreg. Nat. Abortion Rights Action League, Sta. KLCC-PBS Radio. Mem. LWV, Audubon Soc., N.Am. Truffling Soc., The Wilderness Soc., Oreg. Pub. Broadcasting, Buhl (Idaho) Arts Coun., Conservation Internat. Democrat. Unitarian. Home: 1315 Ravenswood Dr Eugene OR 97401-1912 Office: Springfield Creamery 29440 Airport Rd Eugene OR 97402-9537

HAMRICK, JOSEPH EUGENE, JR., information services specialist; b. Chapel Hill, N.C., Feb. 4, 1954; s. Joseph Eugene Sr. and Emily Southerland (Cole) H.; m. Elaine Kay Metcalf, Oct. 2, 1982; children: Aubrie Nicole, Allison Laurel, Wendy-Anne Alisa, Claire Elise. BS in Computer and Mmt. Sci, Met. State Coll., Denver, 1989. Cert. system profl. Inst. for Cert. Computer Profls. Programmer, analyst Aviation Mgmt. Systems, Denver, 1980-83; mgr., AVsoft devel. PHH Aviation Systems, Golden, Colo., 1983-86; programmer, analyst Columbine Systems, Inc., Golden, 1986-88; dir., info. svcs. Property Asset Mgmt., Denver, 1988—; cons., pres. Bridgeware, Denver, 1985—. Cons. Terry Considine U.S. Senate Campaign, Denver, 1985-86. Sgt. USAF, 1975-79. Presbyterian. Home: 2272 S Grape St Denver CO 80222-6263 Office: Property Asset Mgmt 1873 S Bellaire St Denver CO 80222-4341

HAN, ITTAH, lawyer, political economist, high technology, computer engineering and financial strategist; b. Java, Indonesia, Jan. 29, 1939; came to U.S., 1956, naturalized, 1972; s. Hongtjioe and Tsuiying (Chow) H. BS in Mech. Engring. and Elec. Engring., Walla Walla Coll., 1960; MA in Math., U. Calif., Berkeley, 1962; BA in French, U. Colo., 1965, MS in Elec. Engring., 1961; MSE in Computer Engring., U. Mich., 1970; MS in Computer Sci., U. Wis., 1971; MBA in Mgmt., U. Miami, Fla., 1973; BA in Econs., U. Nev., 1977; MBA in Tax, Golden Gate U., 1979, MBA in Real Estate, 1979, MBA in Fin., 1980, MBA in Banking, 1980, MPA in Adminstrv. Orgn. and Mgmt., 1984, ME in Computer Engring. U. Idaho, 1991, JD, Whittier Coll., 1991. Bar: Calif. 1992; cert. fin. planner. Salesman, Watkins Products, Walla Walla, Wash., 1956-60; instr. Sch. Engring. U. Colo., Denver, 1964-66; systems engr. IBM Corp., Oakland, Calif., 1967-69, Scidata Inc., Miami, Fla., 1971-72; chief of data processing Golden Gate Bridge, Hwy. and Transp. Dist., San Francisco, 1973-74; mgr. info. systems tech. and advanced systems devel. Summa Corp., Las Vegas, Nev., 1975-78; mgr. systems devel. Fred Harvey Inc., Brisbane, Calif., 1978-80; chmn. corp. systems steering com., mgr. systems planning Amfac Hotel & Resorts, Inc., 1978-80; tax strategy planner, innovative turnaround fin. strategy planner, chief exec. Ittahhan Corp., 1980—; exec. v.p. Developers Unltd. Group, Las Vegas, 1982-84; v.p. Fidelity Fin. Co., Las Vegas, 1984-85; exec. v.p. John H. Midby and Assocs., Las Vegas, 1982-84, 1986—; sec., treas., dir. River Resorts Inc., Las Vegas, 1983-84; sec., treas. Goldriver Ltd., Las Vegas, 1983-84; pres. Weststar Gen. Ptnr. Co., 1984-85, Developers Group Service Co., 1984-86; chief exec. officer, pres. Very High Tech. Polit. Economy Turnaround Management Strategist, Inc., 1986—; chief exec. officer, pres. Artificial Intelligence Computer Engring. and Expert Systems Engring., Inc., 1986—; pres. Orion Land Devel. Co., Las Vegas, 1987-89, Very High Tech. Computer Engring., Inc., Las Vegas, 1988—; instr. U. Nev. Sch. Elec. Engring., Reno, 1981; systems designer, cons. in field. Mem. IEEE, Internat. Bd. of Stds. and Practices for CFP, Inc., Calif. Bar Assn., Assn. Computing Machinery, Am. Assn. Artificial Intelligence, Am. Math. Assn., Inst. Cert. Fin. Planners, Am. Contract Bridge League. Republican. Home and Office: 2501 W Fulano Way Las Vegas NV 89102

HAN, JIAWEI, computer scientist, educator; b. Shanghai, China, Aug. 10, 1949; came to U.S., 1979; arrived in Can., 1987; s. Yu-chang Han and Jia-zhi Wang; m. Yandong Cai, July 3, 1979; 1 child, Lawrence. BSc, USTC, Beijing, China, 1979; MSc, U. Wis., 1981, PhD, 1985. Asst. prof. Northwestern U., Evanston, Ill., 1986-87, Simon Fraser U., Burnaby, B.C., Can., 1987-91; assoc. prof. Simon Fraser U., Burnaby, 1991—. Contbr. articles to profl. jours. Grantee NSF, 1986-88, NSERC, 1988—. Mem. IEEE (conf. program com. 1990-92), ACM, Assn. Logic Programming. Office: Simon Fraser Univ, Sch Computing Sci, Burnaby, BC Canada V5A 1S6

HAN, LI-MING, financial educator; b. Lotung, Taiwan, June 4, 1953; came to U.S., 1981; d. Hsi-Mou and Wen-Shu (Chen) H.; m. Jonathan C. Wu, Mar. 25, 1979. BS, Fu Jen U., Taiwan, 1975; MS, Nat. Taiwan U., 1977; PhD, U. Tex., 1987. Rsch. specialist Food and Drug Bur., Taiwan, 1978-81; asst. prof. U. Tex., San Antonio, 1987-88, Wash. State U., Pullman, 1988—. Contbr. articles to profl. jours. Univ. fellow U. Tex., 1985, 87; Summer Rsch. Stipend grantee Wash. State U., 1990, 91; recipient best feature article award Jour. Risk and Ins., 1991. Mem. Am. Risk and Ins. Assn., Fin. Mgmt. Assn. Office: Wash State U Pullman WA 99164-4746

HANABLE, WILLIAM SHANNON, historian; b. Pitts., Dec. 16, 1938; s. William Thomas Shannon and Jean Wilson (Morrison) H.; m. Eloise Wasson, July 22, 1967; 1 child, Amy Shannon. BA in History, Alaska Meth. U., 1970, MAT in History, 1975; PhD in Edn., Social Change, Walden U., 1981; postgrad., Air War Coll., 1990. State historian Alaska Div. Parks, Anchorage, 1970-73, chief, History and Archeology, 1973-80; exec. dir. Alaska Hist. Commn., Anchorage, 1980-87; historian Nat. Park Svc. Alaska region, Anchorage, 1987-89; dep. command historian Alaskan Air Command, Anchorage, 1989-92; dep. dir. Joint Fed. State Commn. on Policies and Programs Affecting Alaska Natives, Anchorage, 1992—; history instr. U. Alaska Anchorage, 1990; chair State Historic Sites Adv. Com., 1977-80; co-chair State Hist. Records Adv. Bd., 1980-87; Pacific N.W. Awards chair Am. Assn. State and Local History, Nashville, 1980-84; adj. asst. prof. history, Embry-Riddle Aeronautical U. Anchorage, 1992—. Author: Alaska's Copper River, 1982; Military Support for Exxon Valdez Oil Spill Cleanup, 1990, The Exxon Valdez Oil Spill and the National Park Service, 1991; (with Joan M. Antonson) Sitka National Park, 1987, Alaska's Heritage, 1985, The Environmental Obstacle Course, 1991, ALCOM's Navy, 1992; editor: The Alaska Jour., 1976-78; editor, pub.: The Aleutian Times, 1986-87; contbr. articles to profl. jours. With USAF, 1956-69, USNR, 1969—. Recipient Excellence in History award Pacific Air Forces, 1990, 91, Excellence in Spl. Studies award USAF, 1992. Mem. Alaska Hist. Soc. (pres. 1987-90, President's award 1973, Historian of the Yr. 1983, Trail Blazer award 1987).

HANAUER, JOE FRANKLIN, real estate executive; b. Stuttgart, Fed. Republic Germany, July 8, 1937; came to U.S., 1938; s. Otto and Betty (Zurndorfer) H.; m. Jane Boyle, Oct. 20, 1972; children: Jill, Wendy, Jason, Elizabeth. BS, Roosevelt U., 1963; postgrad., U. Chgo. Pres. Thorsen Realty, Oak Brook, Ill., 1974-80; sr. v.p. Coldwell Banker, Newport Beach, Calif., 1980-83, pres., 1984, chmn. bd., CEO, 1984-88; prin. Combined Investments LP, Laguna Beach, Calif., 1989—; chmn. Grubb & Ellis Co., San Francisco, 1993; bd. dirs. MAF Bancorp, Chgo.; chmn. policy adv. bd. Joint Ctr. for Housing Studies Harvard U.; chmn. bd. dirs. Grubb & Ellis Co., San Francisco, 1993—. Bd. dirs. Chgo. Chamber Orch., 1976-82; trustee Roosevelt U. Mem. Nat. Assn. Realtors (exec. com.). Home: 105 S La Senda Dr Laguna Beach CA 92677-3311 Office: Combined Investments LP 361 Forest Ave Ste 200 Laguna Beach CA 92651-2410

HANAWALT, PHILIP COURTLAND, biology educator, researcher; b. Akron, Ohio, Aug. 25, 1931; s. Joseph Donald and Lenore (Smith) H.; m. Joanna Thomas, Nov. 2, 1957 (div. Oct. 1977); children: David, Steven; m. Graciela Spivak, Sept. 10, 1978; children: Alex, Lisa. Student, Deep Springs Coll., 1949-50; BA, Oberlin Coll., 1954; MS, Yale U., 1955, PhD, 1959. Postdoctoral fellow U. Copenhagen, Denmark, 1958-60, Calif. Inst. Tech., Pasadena, 1960-61; rsch. biophysicist, lectr. Stanford U., Calif., 1961-65, assoc. prof., 1965-70, prof., 1970—, chmn. dept. biol. scis., 1982-89; mem. physiol. chemistry study sect. NIH, Bethesda, Md., 1966-70, chem. pathology study sect., 1981-84; adv. com. Am. Cancer Soc., N.Y.C., 1972-76; chmn. 2nd ad hoc Senate Com. on Professoriate Stanford U., 1988-90; NSF Fellowship review panel, 1985. Author: Molecular Photobiology, 1969; author, editor: DNA Repair: Techniques, 1988; contbr. over 300 papers to profl. publs.; mng. editor DNA Repair jour., 1982-92; assoc. editor jour. Cancer Rsch., Molecular Carinogenesis, Gene Expression, Biotechniques. Recipient Outstanding Investigator award Nat. Cancer Inst., 1987, Excellence in Teaching award No. Calif. Phi Beta Kappa, 1991, Environ. Mutagen Soc. Annual Rsch. award, 1992, Peter and Helen Bing award for Disting. Teaching, 1992; Hans Falk lectr. Nat. Inst. Environ. Health Scis., 1990; Fogarty Sr. Rsch. fellow, 1993. Fellow AAAS, Am. Acad. Microbiology; mem. NAS, Am. Assn. Cancer Rsch., Genetics Soc., Biophys. Soc., Am. Soc. Biochemistry and Molecular Biology, Environ. Mutagen Soc. (pres. 1993—), Radiation Rsch. Soc., Phi Beta Kappa. Home: 317 Shasta Dr Palo Alto CA 94306-4542 Office: Stanford U Herrin Biology Labs Stanford CA 94305-5020

HANCE, ANTHONY JAMES, pharmacologist, educator; b. Bournemouth, Eng., Aug. 19, 1932; came to U.S., 1958; s. Walter Edwin and Jessie Irene (Finch) H.; m. Ruth Anne Martin, July 17, 1954; children: David, Peter, John. BSc, Birmingham U., 1953, PhD, 1956. Rsch.fellow in electrophysiology Birmingham U., Eng., 1957-58; rsch. pharmacologist UCLA, 1959-62; rsch. assoc. pharmacology Stanford U., Palo Alto, Calif., 1962-65, asst. prof., 1965-68; assoc. prof. U. Calif., Davis, 1968—. Contbr. articles to profl. jours. Mem. AAAS, Am. Soc. for Pharmacology and Exptl. Therapeutics, Biomed. Engring. Soc., Assn. for Computing Machinery. Home: 1103 Radcliffe Dr Davis CA 95616-0944 Office: U Calif Med Sch Dept Med Pharmacology & Toxicology Davis CA 95616-8654

HANCOCK, DON RAY, researcher; b. Muncie, Ind., Apr. 9, 1948; s. Charles David and June Lamoine (Krey) H. B.A., DePauw U., 1970. Community worker Fla. Meth. Spanish Ministry, Miami, 1970-73; seminar designer United Meth. Seminars, Washington, 1973-75; info. coord. SW Rsch. and Info. Ctr., Albuquerque, 1975—; cons. State Planning Coun. on

Radioactive Waste Mgmt., Washington, 1980-81; task force mem. Gov.'s Socioecon. Com., Santa Fe, 1983; pub. adv. bd. WIPP Socioecon. Study, Albuquerque, 1979-81. Writer mag. articles. Bd. chmn. Roadrunner Food Bank, Albuquerque, 1981-92, N.Mex. Coalition Against Hunger, 1978-85; bd. dirs. Univ. Heights Assn., Albuquerque, 1977-82, 85, 88-89, 90-93, United Meth. Bd. of Ch. and Society, Washington, 1976-80. Democrat. Office: SW Rsch and Info Ctr PO Box 4524 Albuquerque NM 87196-4524

HANCOCK, EMILY STONE, psychologist; b. Syracuse, N.Y., Nov. 18, 1945; d. Theodore McLennan and Eleanor Sackett (Stone) H.; m. Philip Yenawine, Aug. 28, 1965 (div. 1970); 1 child, Tad. BA, Syracuse U., 1971; MSW, Boston U., 1974; EdD, Harvard U., 1981. Lic. clin. social worker, Mass., Calif.; ACSW. Clin. social worker Children's Hosp., Boston, 1974-77; pvt. practice Mass., Calif., 1976—; co-founder, therapist Divorce Resource Ctr., Cambridge, 1976-78; teaching fellow Harvard U., 1978-79; counselor Alameda County Superior Ct., Oakland, 1982—; screening coord. U. Calif., San Francisco Dept. Pediatrics, 1982-85; faculty Ctr. for Psychol. Studies, Albany, Calif., 1982—; chairwoman Askwith Symposium and Colloquia, Cambridge, 1979. Author: The Girl Within, 1989; editor: Harvard Ednl. Rev., 1979-81; contbr. articles to numerous profl. jours. fellow HEW, 1972-74, Danforth Found., 1978-80, NIMH, 1981-82; grantee Radcliffe Coll., 1978, 80, Woodrow Wilson Found., 1980. Mem. APA, Acad. Cert. Social Workers, Phi Beta Kappa, Phi Kappa Phi. Home and Office: 1230 Glen Ave Berkeley CA 94708-1841

HANCOCK, LONI, mayor; b. N.Y.C., 1940; children: Leita, Mara. BA, Ithaca Coll.; MA, Wright Inst. Mem. Berkeley City Council, 1971-79, Berkeley's Waterfront Adv. Commn., 1984-86; mayor City of Berkeley, 1986—; mem. Bay Area Air Quality Mgmt. Dist., 1990—, Alameda County Congestion Mgmt. Agy., 1991—. Mem. Berkeley Parent Nursery Schs., 1964-68, Berkeley Citizens Action Com., 1975-93; mem., past pres. New Dem. Forum, 1982—; v.p. Berkeley Office of Econ. Opportunity, 1969-71, Local Gov. Commn., Literacy Vols. of Am., Youth Project; past regional dir. of ACTION, 1977-80; exec. dir. Shalan Found., San Francisco, 1981-86; mem., co-founder LeConte Neighborhood Assn,. 1969-71. Mem. Sierra Club, Nat. Women's Polit. Caucus. Office: City of Berkeley Office of Mayor 2180 Milvia St Fl 5 Berkeley CA 94704-1100

HANCOCK, N(EWELL) LES(LIE), accountant; b. Pitts., Apr. 13, 1943; s. Newell Francis and Mildred Helen (Bouveroux) H.; m. Margaret Ann Kendrick, Nov. 30, 1968; children: Michelle Lynn, Jennifer Ann, Marie Noelle. BSBA, U. Denver, 1966; postgrad., various schs., 1969—. CPA, Colo. Supr. Pannell, Kerr, Forster, Denver and Atlanta, 1969-78; mgr. Wolf & Co. of Colo., Inc., Denver, 1978-79, 83-84; supr. Kafoury, Armstrong & Co., Reno, 1979-82; pvt. practice acctg. Arvada, Colo. and Reno, 1982—; mgr. Ashby, Armstrong & Co., Denver, 1984-87; asst. contr. 1st Resorts Inc. and Great Am. Mgmt. Group Inc., Lakewood, Colo., 1987-89; group leader subcontract auditing sect. Nat. Renewable Energy Lab., Golden, Colo., 1989—. Served to 1st lt. U.S. Army, 1966-69. Mem. AICPA, Colo. Soc. CPA's (report rev. com. 1984-90, pvt. co. practice com. 1990-93, accountancy regulation com. 1993—), Nev. Soc. CPA's (bd. dirs. Reno chpt. 1982-83, auditing standards com. 1981-82, vice chmn. acctg. principles com. 1981-83), Hospitality Accts. Assn. (sec. 1976-77). Republican. Baptist. Office: PO Box 740535 Arvada CO 80006-0535

HANCOCK, SUSAN HUNTER, educational administrator; b. Fresno, Calif., Apr. 3, 1944; d. Bertram Harry Jr. and Virginia Hawes (MacCracken) Hunter; m. Jack Edward Hancock, Sept. 15, 1979; 1 child, Craig. BA, Calif. State U., Fresno, 1966; MS, Oreg. State U., 1971. Dean women Boise State U., Idaho, 1971-72; asst. to dean students Humboldt State U., Arcata, Calif., 1972; asst. dean students, Calif. State U., Northridge, 1972-76; asst. statewide dean Chancellor's Office Calif. State U. System, 1976-80; v.p. student life Chapman Coll., Orange, Calif., 1982-91; cons., 1985—; dean of students Pacific Oaks Coll., 1991—. Bd. dirs. ARC, San Fernando Valley, Calif., 1973-76; vol. guide Greater Los Angeles Zoo Assn., 1983-85; bd. dirs. Orange County Sexual Assault Network. Recipient Service to Los Angeles City award Los Angeles City Planning Commn., 1968; named Bicentennial Woman of Yr., Los Angeles Human Relations Commn. 1976. Mem. Nat. Assn. Student Personnel Adminstrs. (bd. dirs. 1976-78, 1984-89, 1988-89, chair nat. conf. 1989, v.p. 1984-86, chmn. research div. 1976-78, editorial bd. jour. 1978-81), Calif. Coll. Personnel Assn., Nat. Assn. Women in Edn. and Counselors, Phi Mu, Delta Kappa Gamma. Democrat. Lodge: Soroptimists. Home: 481 Cedar Crest Claremont CA 91711 Office: Pacific Oaks Coll 5 Westmoreland Pl Pasadena CA 91103

HANCOCKS, DAVID MORGAN, museum director, architect; b. Kinver, Worcestershire, Eng., May 5, 1941; came to U.S., 1972; s. Cecil and Eva Alice (Morgan) H.; m. Anthea Page Cook, Feb. 16, 1982; children: Samuel Morgan, Thomas David, Morgan Page. BSc with honors, U. Bath, Eng., 1966, BArch with honors, 1968. Registered architect, U.K. Architect Zool. Soc. London, 1968-69, West of Eng. Zool. Soc., Bristol, 1970-72; coord. design Woodland Pk. Zool. Gardens, Seattle, 1973-74, dir., 1975-84; pvt. practice design Melbourne, Australia, 1985-89; exec. dir. Ariz.-Sonora Desert Mus., Tucson, 1990—; cons. Singapore Zool. Gardens, 1979-89, Zool. Soc. Victoria, Australia, 1986-89. Author: Animals and Architecture, 1971, Master Builders of the Animal World, 1973 (writing award State of Wash. Govs. 1974), 75 Years: A History of Woodland Park Zoological Gardens, 1979. Bd. dirs. Allied Arts, Seattle, 1976-85, Chamber Music Soc., Seattle, 1984-85. Fellow Discovery Inst., Seattle; recipient Disting. Svc. award Am. Soc. Landscape Architects, 1975, Outstanding Pub. Employee of Yr. award Seattle Mcpl. League, 1983, WPZS medal Woodland Pk. Zool. Soc., 1991. Mem. Am. Assn. Mus., Am. Assn. Zool. Pks. and Aquariums, Am. Assn. Bot. Gardens and Arboreta, Royal Inst. Brit. Architects (assoc.). Home: 6760 N Placita Manzanita Tucson AZ 85718-1226 Office: Ariz-Sonora Desert Mus 2021 N Kinney Rd Tucson AZ 85743-8918

HANDEL, WILLIAM KEATING, advertising and sales executive; b. N.Y.C., Mar. 23, 1935; s. Irving Nathaniel and Marguerite Mary (Keating) H.; m. Margaret Inez Sitton; children: William Keating II, David Roger. BA in Journalism, U. S.C., 1959, MA in English Lit. 1960. Account supr. Ketchum, MacLeod & Grove, Pitts., 1960-67; mgr. advt. and pub. rels. ITT Gen. Controls, Glendale, Calif., 1967-80; mgr. corp. comm. Fairchild Camera and Instrument Corp., 1980-84; dist. mgr. Cahners Pub. Co., 1984-90; founder, chief exec. officer Tri-Dimensional Mktg. Communications Agy., 1990-91, Penton Pub. Co., 1991—; pub. rels. counsel Calif. Pvt. Edn. Schs., 1978-87; chmn. exhibits Mini/Micro Computer Conf., 1977-78. Bd. dirs. West Valley Athletic League; bd. dir. L.A. chpt. USMC Scholarship Found.; pub. rels. cons. Ensenada, Mexico Tourist Commn., 1978; chmn., master of ceremonies USMC Birthday Ball, L.A., 1979-82. With USMC, 1950-53. Decorated Silver Star, Bronze Star, Purple Heart (4), Navy Commendation medal with combat V; recipient Pub. Svc. award L.A. Heart Assn., 1971-73. Mem. Bus. and Profl. Advt. Assn. (cert. bus. communicator, past pres.), 1st Marine Div. Assn., Navy League (bd. dir.), AdLinx Golf Club of So. Calif., Torrey Pines Golf Club, Griffith Pk. Golf Club, Nueva España Boat Club, Bajamar Country Club, Ensenada Country Club, Ensenada Fish and Game Club (Baja, Mex.), U. S.C. Alumni Club (pres. L.A. chpt.), Sigma Chi (chpt. adv.). Republican. Roman Catholic. Home: 2428 Badajoz Pl Carlsbad CA 92009-8006

HANDFORD, JACK, fashion education consultant; b. Piedmont, Mo., Aug. 4, 1917; s. Jack and Ethel Collins (Bunyard) H.; m. Virginia Lee Snigg, Sept. 19, 1942 (dec. 1983). BFA, Chouinard Art Inst., L.A., 1946; MFA, Kensington U., Glendale, Calif., 1977; EdD, Kensington U., 1978. Apparel designer Chic Lingerie, L.A., 1946-50; instr. Chouinard Art Inst., L.A., 1946-61; apparel designer Calif. Girl, L.A., 1952-56; designer/owner Handford Ent., Inc., L.A., 1956-72; dir./owner Calif. Fashion Inst., L.A., 1961-72; instr. UCLA Ext., 1972-83; assoc. chmn. fashion dept. Otis/Parsons, L.A., 1981-89; guest lectr. Calif. Dept. Edn., Sacramento, 1964-69, Calif. State U., L.A., 1969-79; part-time instr. Fullerton Coll., 1975-83; conductor/planner in field; mem. various fashion adv. bds. Author: Professional Patternmaking, 1974, 2d edit. 1984, Professional Pattern Grading, 1980; contbr. articles to profl. jours. With USNR, 1942-45. Fellow Costume Soc. Am. (nat. bd. dirs. 1977-86, reg. pres. 1977-79); mem. Calif. Fashion Designers (pres. 1950-52), Costume Coun. (bd. dirs. 1978-80). Episcopalian. Home: 2500 Honolulu Ave Apt 105 Montrose CA 91020-1876

HANDRON, DEANNE WESTFALL, management consulting executive; b. Hollywood, Calif., Jan. 6, 1955; d. Winfield Sidney Westfall and Joy Elaine (Hobbs) Friedman; m. Michael ANthony Handron, Dec. 3, 1983; children: Matthew, Jonathan, Caitlin. BA, U. So. Calif., 1977; MBA, Cornell U., 1979. Cert. mgmt. cons. Inst. Mgmt. Cons. Cons. Arthur Young & Co., San Jose, Calif., 1979-82; mgr. Arthur Young & Co., San Jose, 1982-85; prin. Arthur Young & Co., L.A., 1986-88; ptnr. Arthur Young & Co., Seattle, 1988-90; dir. n.w. cons. group Ernst & Young, Seattle, 1990—. Office: 22518 SE 46th Pl Issaquah WA 98027-9999

HANDSCHUMACHER, ALBERT GUSTAVE, corporate executive; b. Phila., Oct. 20, 1918; s. Gustave H. and Emma (Streck) H.; children: Albert, David W., Megan, Karin, Melissa. B.S., Drexel Inst. Tech., 1940; diploma, U. Pitts., 1941, Alexander Hamilton Inst., 1948. Prodn. mgr. Jr. Motors Corp., Phila., 1938-40; sales engr. Westinghouse Electric Co., Pitts., 1941; with Lear, Inc., Grand Rapids, Mich., 1945-57; beginning as sales mgr. central dist., successively asst. to pres., asst. gen. mgr., v.p. and gen. mgr., sr. v.p., dir. sales, pres., dir. Lear, Inc., 1959-62; v.p., gen. mgr. Rheem Mfg. Co., 1957-59; pres., dir. Lear Siegler, Inc., 1962-65; underwriting mem. Lloyd's of London. Trustee Drexel U., City of Hope; nat. advisor Am. Heart Assn.; mem. coun. UCLA Internat. Student Ctr. Maj. USAAF, 1942-45. Recipient 60th Anniversary Alumni award for outstanding achievements and services field of indsl. mgmt. Drexel U., 1951, Outstanding Alumni award, 1971; Man of Year award City of Hope, 1970; Man of Year award Nat. Asthma Assn., 1978; named to Abington High Sch. Hall of Fame, 1989. Clubs: Jonathan, Bel Air (Calif.) Country; Wings (N.Y.C.), Metropolitan (N.Y.C.); Confrerie de la Chaine des Rotisseurs, Beverly Hills; Le Mirador Country (Switzerland); Astro (Phila.). Home and Office: 1100 Stone Canyon Rd Los Angeles CA 90077-2918

HANDZLIK, JAN LAWRENCE, lawyer; b. N.Y.C., Sept. 21, 1945; s. Felix Munso and Anna Jean Handzlik; m. Barbara Jean Hartzell, Aug. 6, 1967; children: Grant, Craig, Anna. BA, U. So. Calif., 1967; JD, UCLA, 1970. Bar: Calif. 1971, U.S. Dist. Ct. (cen. dist.) Calif. 1971, U.S. Ct. Appeals (9th cir.) 1971, U.S. Supreme Ct. 1975, U.S. Tax Ct. 1979, U.S. Dist. Ct. (no. dist.) Calif. 1979, U.S. Dist. Ct. (ea. dist.) Calif. 1981, U.S. Dist. Ct. (so. dist.) Calif. 1982, U.S. Ct. Appeals (2d cir.) 1984, U.S. Ct. Internat. Trade 1984. Law clk. to Hon. Francis C. Whelan, U.S. Dist. Ct. (cen. dist.) Calif., L.A., 1970-71; asst. U.S. atty. fraud and spl. prosecutions unit criminal div. U.S. Dept. Justice, L.A., 1971-76; assoc. Greenberg & Glusker, L.A., 1976-78; ptnr., prin. Stilz, Boyd, Levine & Handzlik, P.C., L.A., 1978-84; prin. Jan Lawrence Handzlik, P.C., L.A., 1984-91; ptnr. Kirkland & Ellis, L.A., 1991—; del. U.S. Ct. Appeals (9th cir.) Jud. Conf., L.A., 1983-85; counsel to ind. commn. on the L.A. Police Dept., 1991; dep. gen. counsel to Hon. William H. Webster office of Spl. Adv. to L.A. Police Commn., 1992. Bd. dirs. The Friends of Child Advs., L.A., 1987—; bd. judges Nat. and Calif. State Moot Ct. Competition Teams, UCLA Moot Ct. honors program. Mem. ABA (sects. criminal justice, com. white collar crime 1991—, Calif. white collar crime com. mem. exec. com. 1993—, litigation, com. complex crimes 1989—), Fed. Bar Assn., State Bar Calif. (sects. on criminal law and litigation), L.A. County Bar Assn. (coms. on fed. cts. 1988—, chair criminal practice subcom. 1989-90, fed. appts. evaluation 1989—, white collar crime def. 1991—, mem. exec. com. 1991—), Nat. Assn. Criminal Def. Lawyers. Office: Kirkland & Ellis 300 S Grand Ave Ste 3000 Los Angeles CA 90071-3140

HANEMAN, VINCENT SIERING, JR., consulting engineer, educator, university dean; b. Orange, N.J., Feb. 19, 1924; s. Vincent Siering and Helen (Harris) H.; m. Adelaide Russell, Oct. 3, 1961; children: Vincent Siering III, Charles Frederick, Rosalyn Tullos, Kaye Kavisic. S.B., MIT, 1947; M.S. in Aero. Engring, U. Mich., 1950, Ph.D., 1956. Registered profl. engr., Ohio, Okla., Tex., Ala., Alaska. Asst. head flight research Project Meteor, Mass. Inst. Tech., 1947-49; project head automatic wind tunnel data reduction U. Mich., 1949-51; project officer analogue computer research Wright Air Devel. Center, Ohio, 1951-52; asso. prof., asst. dept. head aero. engring. Air Force Inst. Tech., Wright Patterson AFB, Ohio, 1955-59; chief spl. projects div. guidance and control directorate Air Force Ballistic Missile Div., 1959-60; pres., sr. asso. Haneman Assos., Richardson, Tex., 1960-66, Stillwater, Okla., 1967-72, Auburn, Ala., 1972-73; chmn. bd. Haneman Assos., Inc., Richardson, Stillwater and Auburn, 1961-73; exec. v.p. Haneman Assos., Inc., Stillwater, 1966-67; prof. mech. engring., dir. engring. research, asso. dean Coll. Engring., Okla. State U., 1966-72; prof. aeros. engring., dean Sch. Engring., Auburn U., 1972-80; prof. mech. engring., dean sch. engring. U. Alaska, Fairbanks, 1980-91, prof. emeritus, dean emeritus sch. engring., 1991—; cons. flight simulator project U. Mich., 1952-55, Gen. Electric Co., Gen. Dynamics, Space Tech. Labs., Chance Vought Corp., Ling Temco-Vought, Nat. Acad. Scis., Union Carbide, Auburn U., State of Ark., U. Tex. Pan-Am., Brownsville, others. Contbr. articles on instrumentation, control and guidance, aircraft performance, engring. edn. to tech. jours. Mem. Army Sci. Adv. Panel, 1967-77; chmn. night low level com. Project Master, Point of Contact Airmobile. Served to 1st lt. USAAF, 1943-45, MTO; to maj. USAF, 1951-60; to maj. gen. Res., moblzn. asst. to dep. chief staff for research and devel. Decorated D.S.M., Legion of Merit with oak leaf cluster, D.F.C. with oak leaf cluster, Air medal with 7 oak leaf clusters, Air Force Commendation medal. Assoc. fellow Am. Inst. Aeros. and Astronautics; fellow Am. Soc. Engring. Edn. (past sec. mech. and aero. divs., past nat. chmn. aero. div., past mem. gen. council, past mem. exec. com., past chmn. engring. research council, past 1st v.p., chmn. dean's inst. 1978, chmn. planning factors com. Engring. Coll. Council 1976-80, pres. 1980-81), Am. Astronautical Soc. (sr.), Am. Helicopter Soc., IEEE, Nat. Soc. Profl. Engrs. (ethics com. 1974-75, nat. chmn. Engring. Week 1977, 78, chmn. cost of engring. edn. com., nat. dir. 1979-80), Ala. Soc. Profl. Engrs. (state chmn. Engring. Week 1973-76), Alaska Soc. Profl. Engrs. (pres. 1985-86, pres. Fairbanks chpt. 1982-83, gov. 1974—, exec. com. Sustaining U. Program com.), Nat. Conf. Advancement Research (ad hoc mem. exec. com. 1977-79), Sigma Xi, Tau Beta Pi, Sigma Tau, Phi Kappa Phi, Pi Epsilon Gamma, Sigma Nu. Address: 1258 Viewpointe Dr Fairbanks AK 99709

HANES, JOHN G., lawyer, state legislator; b. Cheyenne, Wyo., 1936; s. Harold H. and Mary Elizabeth (Grier) H.; m. Liv Hanes; children: Greg, Clint. BS in Bus. Adminstrn., U. Wyo., 1958, JD, 1960. Dep. Sec. of State State of Wyo.; pvt. practice Cheyenne, 1965—; atty. Wyo. Senate, 1967-71; mcpl. judge City of Cheyenne, 1970-73; mem. Wyo. Ho. of Reps. Vol. Cheyenne Frontier Days; mem. Heels; Rep. precinct committeeman, 1976—. With U.S. Army JAGC. Mem. C. of C., Rotary (pres. 1982-83, dist. gov. 1990-91), Sigma Nu. Home: 848 Creighton St Cheyenne WY 82009 Office: 600 Boyd Bldg 1720 Carey Ave Cheyenne WY 82001

HANEY, HAROLD LEVON, public relations executive; b. Clearfield, Pa., May 23, 1929; s. Ferdinand Nevling and Esther Ulu (Watson) H. Asst. to pres. Louis E. Shecter Advt., Balt.; set designer Alexander Film Co.; prodn. mgr. Glenn Brill Advt. Agy.; copy dir. H.W. Clark Advt. Agy.; pres. Haney Advt.; asst. dir. State of Colo. Office of Tourism, 1952-72, dir., 1972-84; pres. Hal Haney Assocs., 1984—; founder, pres. Internat. Cloning Inst.; founder Gov.'s Colo. Tourism Conf.; instr. internat. and domestic tourism devel. Arapahoe Coll.; founder Four Corners Regional Tourism Orgn.; chmn. recreational and travel steering com. Denver Pub. Schs.; developer, presenter tourism seminars. Contbr. travel articles to local, regional, nat. and internat. publs.; writer and dir. 12 motion picture and TV films; contbr. to Books of the Yr. for Ency. Brit. Founder, past pres. and chmn. bd. Historic Denver, Inc.; trustee Temple Events Ctr.; pres. Bellevue-Hale Neighborhood Assn.; founder Rocky Mountain Baroque Flute Ensemble; bd. dirs. Inter-neighborhood Cooperation. Named U.S. Travel Dir. of Yr., U.S. Travel Industry Assn.; recipient 4 Gold Brahm awards for excellence in advt. design and art, 2 Cris awards for film prodn., 3 awards Internat. Film Festival, 3 awards for best travel films Am. Film Festival, Gold Medal award Art Dirs. Club Denver, Spl. award Gov.'s Tourism Bd., numerous others. Mem. Nat. Writers Club, Soc. Am. Travel Writers (co-chmn. conf.), Colo. Hist. Soc., Denver Bot. Gardens, Denver Mus. Natural History, Denver Art Mus., Denver Zool. Found., Colo. Mining Museum, Masons (32 deg.), Scottish Rite. Home: 1440 Ash St Denver CO 80220

HANEY, ROBERT LOCKE, insurance company executive; b. Morgantown, W.Va., June 14, 1928; s. John Ward and Katherine Eugenia (Locke) H. BA, U. Calif., Berkeley, 1949. Sr. engr. Pacific Telephone Co., San Francisco, 1952-58; mgmt. analyst Lockheed Missiles & Space Co., Sunnyvale, Calif., 1958-64; sr. cons. John Diebold, N.Y.C., 1964-65; sr. indsl. economist Mgmt. & Econs. Research, Inc., Palo Alto, Calif., 1965-67; prin. economist Midwest Research Inst., Kansas City, Mo., 1967-69; dir. mktg. coordination Transam. Corp., San Francisco, 1969-73; staff exec. Transam. Ins. Corp., L.A., 1974-82; 2d v.p. Transam. Life Cos., L.A., 1982—; cons. in field. Co-author: Creating the Human Environment, 1970. Lt. (j.g.) USN, 1949-52. Mem. Scabbard & Blade. Republican. Episcopalian. Home: 2743 Tiburon Ave Carlsbad CA 92008-7908 Office: Transamerica Life Cos 1150 S Olive St Los Angeles CA 90015-2211

HANF, JAMES ALPHONSO, poet, government official; b. Chehalis, Wash., Feb. 3, 1923; s. William G. and Willa DeForest (Davis) H.; m. Ruth G. Eyler, Aug. 16, 1947; 1 child, Maureen Ruth. Grad. Centralia Jr. Coll., 1943, DLitt (hon.) World U. Ariz., 1980 Naval architect technician P.F. Spaulding, naval architects, Seattle, 1955-56, Puget Sound Bridge & Dredge Co. (Wash.), 1953-55, Puget Sound Naval Shipyard, 1951-53, 56-93; cons. Anderson & Assocs., ship bldg.; cons. The Rsch. Bd. Advs., Am. Biographical Inst., Inc.; guest lectr. on poetry and geneal. rsch. methods to various lit. socs., 1969—; contbr. hundreds of poems to lit. jours., anthologies and popular mags.; poetry editor Coffee Break, 1977-82. Recipient Poet Laureate Recognition award Internat. Biog. Centre of Cambridge, Eng., grand prize World Poetry Soc. Conv., 1985, 86, , 90, Golden Poet award World of Poetry in Calif., 1985-90, Silver Poet award Calif. sponsored nat. contest, 1989, numerous other awards. Judge poetry contest, Australia and India, 1985; named Man of Yr. Abaas, 1989—; named Internat. Eminent Poet Internat. Poet Acad. of Madras, India, 1987. Mem Internat. Poetry Soc. (Poet Laureate Wash. State award 1981), World of Poetry Soc. (Golden Poet award 1985-88, Poet Laureate award 1979), Kitsap County Writers Club (pres. 1977-78), Internat. Fedn. Tech. Engrs., Nat. Hist. Locomotive Soc., Kitsap County Hist. Soc., Puget Sound Geneal. Soc., Western World Haiku Soc., Olympic Geneal. Soc. (pres. 1974-75), N.Y. Poetry Forum, World Poets Resource Ctr., Literarische Union, Académie Européenne des Scis., Des Arts Et Des Letters (corr.), Internat. Soc. Poets Md. (hon. charter), Internat. Platform Assn., Calif. Fedn. Chaparral Poets, Internat. Biog. Assn., Am. Biog. Inst. (Silvermedal 1985, Gold medals of honor 1987), World Sadhak Soc. (hon.). Baptist. Home: PO Box 374 Bremerton WA 98310-0075

HANIFEN, RICHARD CHARLES, bishop; b. Denver, June 15, 1931; s. Edward Anselm and Dorothy Elizabeth (Ranous) H. BS, Regis Coll., 1953; S.T.B., Cath. U., 1959, M.A., 1966; J.C.L., Pontifical Lateran U., Italy, 1968. Ordained priest Roman Catholic Ch., 1959; asst. pastor Cathedral Parish, Denver, 1959-66; sec. to archbishop Archdiocese Denver, 1968-69, chancellor, 1969-76; aux. bishop of Denver, 1974-83; 1st bishop of Colorado Springs, Colo., 1984—. Office: Bishop of Colo Springs 29 W Kiowa St Colorado Springs CO 80903-1403

HANKAMER, JORGE, linguistics educator; b. Alvin, Tex., Sept. 12, 1940. BA, Rice U., 1962, MA, 1966; PhD, Yale U., 1971. Asst. prof. Harvard U., Cambridge, Mass., 1973-78, assoc. prof., 1978-80; assoc. prof. U. Calif., Santa Cruz, 1980-82, prof., 1982—; assoc. acad. vice chancellor, 1990—. Series editor Garland Pub. Co., N.Y.C., 1975—; contbr. articles to profl. jours. Mem. Linguistic Soc. Am. (dir. summer inst. 1991), N.Y. Acad. Scis., Acoustical Soc. Am., Assn. for Computational Linguistics, Assn. for Computing Machinery. Home: 321 High St Santa Cruz CA 95060-2611 Office: U Calif Office of Acad Vice Chancellor 299 McHenry Libr Santa Cruz CA 95064

HANKINS, HESTERLY G., III, computer systems analyst; b. Sallisaw, Okla., Sept. 5, 1950; s. Hesterly G. and Ruth Faye (Jackson) H. BA in Sociology, U. Calif., Santa Barbara, 1972; MBA in Info. Systems, UCLA, 1974; postgrad., Golden Gate U., 1985-86, Ventura Coll., 1970, Antelope Valley Coll., 1977, La Verne U., 1987. Cert. community coll. tchr., Calif. Applications programmer Xerox Corp., Marina Del Rey, Calif., 1979-80; computer programmer Naval Ship Weapon Systems Engring. Sta. of Port Hueneme, Oxnard, Calif., 1980-84; spl. asst. to chief exec. officer Naval Air Sta. of Moffett Field, Mountain View, Calif., 1984-85; mgr. computer systems project Pacific Missile Test Ctr., Oxnard, 1985-88, MIS Def. Contract Adminstrn. Svcs. Region, Oxnard, 1988—; instr. bus. West Coast U., Camarillo, Calif., 1987-88, De Anza Coll., Sunnyvale, Calif., 1985, Nat. U., Los Angeles, 1988—; lectr. bus. Golden Gate U., Los Altos, Calif., 1984; instr. computer sci. Chapman Coll., Sunnyvale, 1984, Ventura (Calif.) Coll., 1983-84; cons. City of Los Angeles Police Dept., Allison Mortgage Trust Investment Co.; minority small bus. assn. cons. UCLA. Author: Campus Computing's Accounting I.S. As a Measurement of Computer Performance, 1973, Campus Computer, 1986, Network Planning, 1986, Satellites and Teleconferencing, 1986, Quotations, 1992, Quotable Expressions and Memorable Quotations of Notables, 1993. Mem. St. Paul United Meth. Ch., Oxnard, Calif., 1986-87; fundraiser YMCA Jr. Rodeo, Lake Casitos, Calif.; key person to combine fed. campaign United Way. Named one of Outstanding Young Men in Am. U.S. Jaycees, 1980, Internat. Leader of Achievement and Man of Achievement, Internat. Biog. Centre, Cambridge, Eng., 1988. Mem. Nat. Assn. Accts., Calif. Assn. Accts., Intergovtl. Council on Tech. Info. Processing, Assn. Computing Machinery (recipient Smart Beneficial Suggestion award 1984), IEEE, Fed. Mgrs. Assn., Alpha Kappa Psi (sec. 1972-73). Office: National Univ 9920 S La Cienega Blvd Inglewood CA 90301-4423

HANKS, EUGENE RALPH, land developer, cattle rancher, retired naval officer; b. Corning, Calif., Dec. 11, 1918; s. Eugene and Lorena B. Hanks; m. Frances Elliot Herrick, Mar. 4, 1945; children: Herrick, Russell, Stephen, Nina. Student, Calif. Poly. Coll., 1939-41, U. So. Calif., 1949-50, Am. U., 1958-59; grad., Command and Staff Coll., Norfolk, Va., 1960. With Naval Aviation Flight Tng.,V-5 Program USN, 1941-42, commd. ensign, 1942, advanced through grades to capt., 1963; carrier fighter pilot, Am. Ace, six victories, 1942-45; test pilot Naval Air Test Ctr., 1946-48; mem. Navy Flight Exhbn. Team Blue Angels, 1950; comdg. officer fighter squadrons, 1952-61; 1st ops. officer U.S.S. Constellation, 1961-62; dir. ops. Naval Missile Test Ctr., 1963-66; test dir. Joint Task Force Two, Albuquerque, 1966-69; ret., 1969; owner, developer Christmas Tree Canyon, Cebolla Springs and Mountain River subdivs., Mora, N.Mex., 1969—. Decorated Navy Cross, D.F.C. with star (2), Air medal (7), Legion of Merit; named Citizen of Yr. Citizen's Com. for the Right to Keep and Bear Arms, 1987, 93. Mem. Ret. Officers Assn., Am. Fighter Aces Assn., Combat Pilots Assn., Assn. Naval Aviation, Am. Forestry Assn., NRA, Blue Angels Assn., Naval Aviation Museum Found., Legion of Valor. Republican. Home and Office: Christmas Tree Canyon PO Box 239 Mora NM 87732-0239

HANKS, GARY ARLIN, psychology educator; b. Salt Lake City, July 2, 1944; s. John D. and Erva (Wright) H.; m. Diana Twelves, 1968 (div. 1978); m. Suzanne Warnock Ostler, Dec. 20, 1984 (div. 1985); stepchildren: Shannon, Shawn, Ryan, Leslie. BS, U. Utah, 1968, MSW, 1972; clin. cert. dept. psychiatry Washingtonian, Harvard U., 1973; PhD in Psychology, Calif. U., L.A., 1977. Cert. social worker. Asst. prof. U. South Fla., Tampa, 1973-74; clinician LDS Ch. Social Svcs., L.A., 1975-77; chief psychiat. social worker William Beaumont Army Med. Ctr., El Paso, Tex., 1977-78; chmn. dept. psychology Internat. Relative Psychology Inst., Salt Lake City, 1984—. Author: Maturity Analysis Test, 1985, Spirituality Analysis Test, 1986, Relative Psychology, 1991, Relative Religion, 1991, Relative Analysis, 1991. Missionary LDS Ch., Fed. Republic Germany, 1963; polit. activist. Capt. U.S. Army, 1968-78. Rsch. grantee NIMH, 1973. Mem. Am. Fedn. Clin. Social Workers. Office: Internat Relative Psychology Inst 1898 E 3300 S Salt Lake City UT 84106-3974

HANLEY, FRED WILLIAM, librarian, educator; b. Booneville, Miss., May 13, 1939; s. John Martin and Ethel May (Robertson) H.; m. Bethany Nell Holt, June 21, 1971; children: Seth Patrick, Cassandra May. BS, Lambuth Coll., Jackson, Tenn., 1961; BD, Meth. Theol. Sch., Delaware, Ohio, 1964; MA in History, Ariz. State U., 1966, MA in Counseling, 1968. Cert. secondary tchr., Ariz. Assoc. pastor Prospect Street Meth. Ch., Marion, Ohio, 1961-64; tchr. history Phoenix Union High Sch. Dist., 1965-74, curriculum coord., 1974-78, chmn. English dept., 1978-89, chmn. libr. dept., 1989—. Editor Ariz. Health Svcs. jour., 1965. Bd. dirs. Wesley Found., Tempe, Ariz., 1964-69; vol. Am. Cancer Soc., Phoenix, 1985-91. Recipient Tchr. of Yr. award West High Sch., Phoenix, 1969, Disting. Alumnae award Lambuth Coll., 1979. Mem. ALA, NEA, Ariz. Edn. Assn. Democrat.

Home: 10411 W Flower Avondale AZ 85323 Office: Alhambra High Sch 3839 W Camelback Rd Phoenix AZ 85019

HANLEY, KEVIN LANCE, maintenance manager; b. Oil City, Pa., Nov. 25, 1961; s. Harold Edward and Helen Louise (Banta) H.; m. Patricia Yolanda DeLeon, Sept. 29, 1984; children: Jennifer Jessica, Kevin Lance Jr. Grad. high sch., Titusville, Pa.; diploma, McDonald's Regional Hdqs., L.A., 1986. Maintenance supr. Paschen Mgmt. Corp. McDonald's, Camarillo, Calif., 1980-86, asst. mgr., 1986-88, maintenance cons., 1988-89; mgr. phys. plant Westmont Coll., Santa Barbara, Calif., 1988—; gen. cons. "R" Cleaning Maintenance, Santa Paula, Calif., 1989-91. Sec.-treas. Ch. of God of Prophecy, Ventura, Calif., 1987—, co-pastor, 1988—. Republican. Office: Westmont Coll 955 La Paz Rd Santa Barbara CA 93108

HANNA, DONALD EUGENE, academic administrator; b. Garden City, Kans., Aug. 20, 1947; s. Joseph Walkup and Iris Anzina (Brown) H.; m. Karna Ostrum; children: Jason Dean, Elizabeth Courtnry. BA in Anthropology and History, U. Kans., 1969; MS in Edn., SUNY, Buffalo, 1974; PhD in Adult and Continuing Edn., Mich. State U., 1978. With Tchr. Corps, Lackawanna, N.Y., 1971-72, Peace Corps, Afghanistan, 1972-74; acad. advisor, instr. Mich. State U., East Lansing, 1974-77; asst. prof. adult, higher and continuing edn. U. Ill., Urbana-Champaign, 1979-83, asst. head div. extramural courses, 1977-79, head div. extramural courses, 1979-83; prof. adult and continuing edn. Wash. State U., Pullman, 1983—, dir. continuing edn. and pub. svc., 1983-85, acting vice provost extended univ. svcs., 1985-87, assoc. vice provost extended univ. svcs., 1987—; cons. in field; co-organizer Internat. Telecomm. Symposium, 1990; bd. dirs. S.W. Wash. Joint Ctr. for Edn., 1985-87; founding mem. Ea. Wash. Area Health Edn. Ctr., 1986; sec. Nat. Univs. Degree Consortium, 1989-92. Contbr. articles to profl. publs., chpts. to books. Kellogg Found. fellow, 1987-90; recipient numerous grants. Mem. Western Ednl. Telecom. Coop. (steering com. 1988-91), Nat. U. Continuing Edn. Assn. (bd. dirs. 1984-86), Wash. Higher Edn. Telecom. System (sec. bd. dirs. 1985-89). Home: 700 NE Michigan Pullman WA 99163 Office: Wash State U 106 Van Doren Hall Pullman WA 99164-5220

HANNA, STANLEY SWEET, physicist, educator; b. Sagaing, Burma, May 17, 1920; s. Alexander Carson and Hazel (Ames) H.; m. Jane Reeves Martin, Dec. 27, 1942; children: David Stanley, Peter Alexander, Susan Lee. A.B., Denison U., 1941, D.Sc., 1970; Ph.D., Johns Hopkins U., 1947. Mem. faculty Johns Hopkins U., 1943-55, asst. prof. physics, 1948-55; asso. physicist Argonne Nat. Lab., 1955-60, sr. physicist, 1960-63, cons., 1963-68; prof. physics Stanford U., 1963—; researcher on nuclear structure, giant resonances, polarizations of nuclear radiations, positron polarization, lifetimes of nuclear states, resonance absorption, analogue states, electron scattering, nuclear moments, intermediate energy physics, weak and hyperfine interactions; cons. Los Alamos Sci. Lab., 1967-74. Chmn. nuclear physics panel, com. on physics Nat. Acad. Scis., 1964-65. Served with AUS, 1945-46. Guggenheim fellow, 1958-59; Humboldt awardee, 1977; fellow Inst. for Advanced Study, Ind. U., 1983. Fellow Am. Phys. Soc. (organizing com. nuclear physics div. 1966-67, exec. com. 1967-68, 75-82, vice chmn. 1975-76, chmn. 1976-77, nuclear physics councillor 1978-82, publ. com. 1980-83, chmn. com. 1981-83, mem. exec. com. 1979-82); mem. Phi Beta Kappa, Sigma Xi, Omicron Delta Kappa. Home: 784 Mayfield Ave Palo Alto CA 94305-1044 Office: Stanford U Dept Physics Varian Bldg Stanford CA 94305

HANNA, WILLIAM JOHNSON, electrical engineering educator; b. Longmont, Colo., Feb. 7, 1922; s. William Grant and Anna Christina (Johnson) H.; m. Katherine Fagan, Apr. 25, 1944; children: Daniel August, Paul William. BSEE, U. Colo., 1943, MS, 1948, D in Elec. Engring., 1951. Registered profl. engr., Colo., Kans. Mem. faculty U. Colo., 1946-91, prof. elec. engring., 1962-91, prof. emeritus, 1991—; cons. in field; mem. Colo. Bd. Engring. Examiners, 1973-85. Author articles, reports. Served to 1st lt. AUS, 1943-46. Recipient Faculty Recognition award Students Assn. U. Colo., 1956, 61, Alfred J. Ryan award, 1978, Archimedes award Calif. Soc. Profl. Engrs., 1978, Outstanding Engring. Alumnus award U. Colo., 1983, Faculty Service award, 1983; named Colo. Engr. of Yr. Profl. Engrs. Colo., 1968; named to Hon. Order of Ky. Cols. Mem. IEEE, Am. Soc. Engring. Edn., Nat. Soc. Profl. Engrs. (pres. Colo. 1967-68), Nat. Coun. Engring. Examiners (pres. 1977-78, Disting. Svc. award with spl. commendation 1990), AIEE (chmn. Denver 1961-62). Republican. Presbyterian. Club: Masons. Home and Office: 27 Silver Spruce Nederland Star Route Boulder CO 80302

HANNIGAN, MAURICE J., protective services official; b. San Francisco, Jan. 20, 1941; s. John M. and Evelyn M. (Fitzgerald) H.; m. Sue A. Goforth, May 4, 1963; children: Patrick, Maureen, Colleen, Kristine. Student, FBI Nat. Acad., 1977; BA, Golden State U., 1978; postgrad., U. Calif., Davis, 1987, FBI Exec. Inst., 1985. Traffic officer Calif. Hwy. Patrol, L.A. and Redwood City, 1965-70; sgt. Calif. Hwy. Patrol, San Jose, 1970-73; lt. Calif. Hwy. Patrol, Sacramento, 1973-79, capt., 1979-83, asst. chief, 1983-84, dep. commr., 1984-89, commr., 1989—. Contbr. articles to profl. publs. Chair com. on law enforcement Gov. Policy Coun. on Drugs and Alcohol, 1989—; chmn. Gov.s' Auto Theft Adversary Com., 1989, Gov.'s Task of Heavy Comml. Vehicle and Dirver Safety, 1989—. Mem. Calif. Peace Officers Assn. (4th v.p. 1990—, Mickie Raineyh Meml. award 1989), Internat. Assn. Chief of Police (mem. exec. com. state and provincial police 19889), Am. Mgmt. Assn. Republican. Roman Catholic.

HANNUM, GERALD LUTHER (LOU), retired tire manufacturing company official; b. Syracuse, N.Y., May 31, 1915; s. Ralph Charles and Coral (Snyder) H.; m. Carolyn Russell Osgood, Nov. 29, 1941; children: Nancy, Susan, Jean. AB, Syracuse U., 1937; MA, Kent State U., 1971. Supr. forecasting and inventory control B.F. Goodrich, Arkon, Ohio, 1961-67; econ. planning specialist, staff for v.p. planning B.F. Goodrich Co., 1967-75, econ. planner, 1946-75; ret., 1975. Councilman City of Medford, Oreg., 1977-82, 89—, mayor, 1983-86; bd. dirs. United Way, Medford, 1986—; pres. Crater Lake coun. Boy Scouts Am., 1987-90. Lt. USNR, 1943-52, PTO. Recipient Silver Beaver award Boy Scouts Am., 1987. Mem. League Oreg. Cities (pres. 1983, Richards award 1989), Rotary. Home: 2900 Seckel St Medford OR 97504

HANOWELL, ERNEST GODDIN, physician; b. Newport News, Va., Jan. 31, 1920; a. George Frederick and Ruby Augustine (Goddin) H.; m. Para Jean Hall, June 10, 1945; children: Ernest D., Deborah J. Hanowell Orick, Leland H., Dee P. Hanowell Martinmaas, Robert G. Diplomate Am. Bd. Internal Medicine. Intern USPHS Hosp., Norfolk, Va., 1948-49; resident in internal medicine USPHS Hosp., Seattle, 1952-55; chief medicine USPHS Hosp., Ft. Worth, 1955-57; dept. chief medicine USPHS Hosp., Boston, 1957-59; chief medicine USPHS Hosp., Memphis, 1964-65, Monterey County Gen. Hosp., 1969-70; mem. IM and Cardiology staff Kaiser Permanente Med. Group, Sacramento, 1971-87; writer Auburn, Calif., 1987--; clin. asst. Tufts Med. Sch., 1960-61; cons. chest disease Phila. Gen. Hosp., 1960-61; asst. prof. U. Md. Med. Sch., 1961-64; instr. U. Tenn. Med. Sch., 1964-65; asst. clin. prof. Sch. Medicine, U. Calif., Davis, 1973-81; mem. attending staff Cardiac Clinic Stanford U. Med. Sch. 1967-69. Mem. sch. bd. Salinas, Calif., 1968-69; bd. dirs. Am. Heart Assn., Tb and Health Assn. Served with AUS, 1943-46. Fellow ACP, Am. Coll. Chest Diseases; mem. AWA, Crocker Art Mus. Assn., Comstock Club (Sacramento), Phi Chi. Home and Office: 1158 Racquet Club Dr Auburn CA 95603-3042

HANRETTA, ALLAN GENE, psychiatrist, pharmacist; b. Galveston, Tex., June 24, 1930; s. Aloysius Thomas and Genevieve M. (Feeney) H.; m. Carolyn Jean Jacobs, Sept. 4, 1954; children: Allan Thomas, Patrice M., Mark D. BS in Pharamcy, U. Tex., Austin, 1952, BA in Arts and Sci., 1957; MD, U. Tex., Galveston, 1959. Diplomate Am. Bd. Psychiatry and Neurology. Gen. rotating intern USPHS Hosp., San Francisco, 1959-60; resident in psychiatry U. Tex. Med. Br., Galveston, Tex., 1960-63; fellow in clin. electroencephalography Meth. Hosp.-Tex. Med. Ctr., Houston, 1963-64; pvt. practice, Santa Barbara, 1964-83; chief staff Dani's Psychiat. Hosp., Santa Barbara, 1971-79; mem. med. staff Cottage Hosp., St. Francis Hosp., Goleta Valley Community Hosp., Camarillo State Hosp., 1964—. Lectr. Santa Barbara Pharm. Assn., 1975. Lt. (j.g.) USN, 1952-54. Recipient contbn. to pharmacy award Santa Barbara Pharm. Assn., 1975. Mem. AMA, Am. Psychiat. Assn., So. Calif. Psychiat. Assn., Santa Barbara Psychiat. Soc. (pres. 1977-79). Home: 3728 Calle Cita Santa Barbara CA 93105

HANSCH, JOACHIM HORST, music director; b. Bad Grund, Hartz, Germany, Oct. 5, 1946; came to U.S., 1976; s. Frank and Johanna (Klimke) H. Intermediate Cert., Blacktown, Australia, 1959; Leaving Cert., Parramatta, Australia, 1961. Broadcast Operators Cert. Proficiency, Marconi Sch. Wireless, "B.O.C.P.", 1964. Audio tech. A.W.A., Sydney, Australia, 1964-65, mastering engr., 1965-70; mastering engr. Festival Records, Sydney, Australia, 1970-76; mastering engr. Kendun Recorders, L.A., 1976-77, studio mgr., mastering engr., 1977-79; studio mgr., mastering engr. Artisan Sound Recorders, Hollywood, Caif., 1979-81; owner, engr. Dinkum Recording Svc., Hollywood, Calif., 1981-88; dir. music Cannon Films, Beverly Hills, Calif., 1988-91, MGM Pathe Comm. Co., Beverly Hills, Calif., 1991-92; pres. edel Am. Records, Inc., North Hollywood, Calif., 1992—. Mem. NARAS, Audio Engring. Soc. Office: edel Am Records Inc 4640 Lankershim Blvd Ste 511 North Hollywood CA 91602

HANSEN, ARLEN JAY, English language educator; b. Rolfe, Iowa, Oct. 24, 1936; s. Carl E. and Lorene L. (Kipfer) H.; m. D. Lynn Hansen, Aug. 15, 1959; children: Laura, Kip, James. BS in Math., Iowa State U., 1958; MA in English, U. Iowa, 1962, PhD in English, 1969. Lectr. Bradley U., Peoria, Ill., 1962-66; teaching, rsch. fellow U. Iowa, Iowa City, 1966-69; prof. English, chmn. dept. U. Pacific, Stockton, Calif., 1969-91, prof. emeritus, 1993—; sr. Fulbright prof. Technische U., Aachen, Germany, 1985-86, U. Vienna, Austria, 1980-81; mem. screening and selection com. Coun. for Internat. Exch. Scholars, Washington, 1989-91. Author: Expatriate Paris: A Cultural and Literary Guiide to Paris of the 1920s, 1990; editorial bd. The Californians: A Mag. of Calif. History, Sebastapol, 1979—. Mem. bd. Calif. Coun. for Humanities, San Francisco. Decorated Order of the Pacific; grantee NEH, 1988, Rockefeller Found., 1975, Am. Coun. Learned Socs., 1976. Mem. MLA, Nat. Coun. Tchrs. English. Democrat. Home: 7819 Rosewood Dr Stockton CA 95207-1402 Office: Dept English U of the Pacific Stockton CA 95211

HANSEN, CARYL JEAN, fundraiser; b. Berkeley, Calif., Nov. 3, 1929; d. Edward Harrison and Winifred (MacNally) Harms; m. Jordan DeBard Hall, Apr. 24, 1955 (div. June 1968); children: Jennifer Ann Tefaaora, Rebecca Jean Humphrey; m. Robert Frazar Hansen, Mar. 15, 1975. AB in Journalism, Stanford (Calif.) U., 1951. Mng. editor The Piedmonter, Oakland, Calif., 1954-62; ednl. asst. Oakland Pub. Libr., 1962-64; press dir. United Way, San Francisco, 1964-67; dist. pub. rels. dir. Children's Home Soc. of Calif., San Francisco, 1967-76, asst. dir. of devel., 1987-91, dir. of devel., 1991—; freelance writer San Francisco, 1976-88. Author: Your Choice, 1980, I Think I'm Having A Baby, 1982, One for the Road, 1984, Small Wonder, 1986; contbr. articles to nat. publs. Bd. dirs., pres. Calif. Crafts Mus., San Francisco, 1980-87. Capt. USMC, 1951-54. Recipient ARC Gold award Mercom, 1991, Bronze award for brochure Nat. Media Conf., 1989, Astrid award, 1991. Mem. Nat. Soc. of Fund Raising Execs., U.S. Marine Corps. Combat Corr. Assn., Calif. Writers Club (pres. 1972-74), Glass Art Soc. (bd. dirs., sec.). Office: Childrens Home Soc of Calif 3200 Telegraph Ave Oakland CA 94609

HANSEN, CLIFFORD PETER, rancher; b. Zenith, Wyo., Oct. 16, 1912; s. Peter Christoffersen and Sylvia Irene (Wood) H.; m. Martha Elizabeth Close, Sept. 24, 1934; children: Mary Elizabeth, Peter Arthur. BS, U. Wyo., 1934, LLD (Hon.), 1965. Chmn. Teton County Bd. of Commissioners, Jackson, Wyo., 1943-51; pres. U. Wyo. Bd. of Trustees, Laramie, Wyo., 1955-63; commissioner Snake River, Idaho, Wyo., Columbia Interstate, 1943-50; pres. Wyo. Stock Growers Assn., Cheyenne, Wyo., 1953-55; chmn. Sec. of Agr. Adv. com., Washington, 1956-62; v.p. Jackson State Bank, Jackson, 1953-69; gov. State of Wyo., Cheyenne, 1963-66; U.S. Senator State of Wyo., Washington, 1967-78; owner Hansen Ranch, Jackson Hole; mem. (Pres. appt.) Com. on Federalism Washington 1981, Bd. of Dirs. Pacific Power & Light Portland, 1979-83, Bd. Dir. 1st Wyo. Bank Corp. Cheyenne 1979-83. Mem. U. Wyo. Found.; chmn. steering com. Jefferson Energy Found.; bd. dirs. emeritus Mountain States Legal Found., Gottsche Found. Rehab. Ctr.; trustees Buffalo Bill Hist. Ctr., Political Economy Rsch. Ctr. Recipient Medallion Svc. Award U. Wyo. Laramie 1965, Stockman of the Century Wyo. Stock Growers Assn. Cheyenne 1972, Disting. Alumnus award U. Wyo. Mem. 33 degree Masonic Frat., Buffalo Bill Hist. Assn. Republican. Episcopalean. Office: Peter A Hansen Bldg PO Box 1887 Jackson WY 83001-1887

HANSEN, CURTIS LEROY, federal judge; b. 1933. BS, U. Iowa, 1956; JD, U. N.Mex., 1961. Bar: N.Mex. Law clk. to Hon. Irwin S. Moise N.Mex. Supreme Ct., 1961-62; ptnr. Snead & Hansen, Albuquerque, 1962-64, Richard C. Civerolo, Albuquerque, 1964-71, Civerolo, Hansen & Wolf, P.A., 1971-92; dist. judge U.S. Dist. Ct., N.Mex., 1992—. Mem. ABA, State Bar N.Mex., Albuquerque Bar Assn., Am. Coll. Trial Lawyers, Am. Bd. Trial Advocates, Albuquerque Country Club, Albuquerque Petroleum Club. Office: 500 Gold Ave Sw 11th Fl PO Box 689 Albuquerque NM 87102

HANSEN, DONALD CURTIS, manufacturing executive; b. Marinette, Wis., Mar. 13, 1929; s. Curtis Albert and Dagmar Anne (Johnson) H.; m. Joan Mary Crant, Nov. 9, 1973. BBA, Carroll Coll., 1952. Purchasing agt. Prescott/Sterling Co., Menominee, Mich., 1954-62; mfrs. rep. Don C. Hansen Assocs., Phoenix, 1962-63; sales mgr. Karolton Envelope Co., San Francisco, 1964-72; owner, pres. San Francisco Envelope Co., 1972-79; owner Curtis Swann Cards, San Francisco, 1977-79; pres., owner Don C. Hansen, Inc. (doing bus. as The Envelope Co.), Oakland, Calif., 1979—. Mgr., organizer Twin City Civic Chorus, Menominee, 1959; bd. dirs. Menominee C. of C., 1958. Served with U.S. Army, 1952-54. Mem. Envelope Printing Specialists Assn. (bd. dirs. 1983—, pres. 1983-84), Envelope Mfrs. Assn. Am., San Francisco Lithograph and Craftsmans Club, Printing Industries of No. Calif. (bd. dirs. 1980—), Harbor Point Tennis Club (Mill Valley, Calif.), San Francisco Tennis Club (bd. govs. 1989-92), Wing Point Country Club (Bainbridge, Wash.), Masons, Shriners. Republican. Office: The Envelope Co PO Box 23853 Oakland CA 94623-0853

HANSEN, FLORENCE MARIE CONGIOLOSI (MRS. JAMES S. HANSEN), social worker; b. Middletown, N.Y., Jan. 7, 1934; d. Joseph James and Florence (Harrigan) Congiolosi; m. James S. Hansen, June 16, 1959 (dec. Nov. 1989); 1 child, Florence M. BA, Coll. New Rochelle, 1955; MSW, Fla. State U., 1960; PhD, Union Inst., 1992. Caseworker, Orange County Dept. Pub. Welfare, N.Y., 1955-57, Cath. Welfare Bur., Miami, Fla., 1957-58; supr. Cath. Family Service, Spokane, Wash., 1960, Cuban Children's Program, Spokane, 1962-66; founder, dir. social service dept. Sacred Heart Med. Ctr., 1968-85, dir. Kidney Ctr., 1967-91. Asst. in program devel. St. Margaret's Hall, Spokane, 1961-62; trustee Family Counseling Svc. Spokane County, 1981—, also bd. dirs.; mem. budget allocation panel United Way, 1964-76, mem. planning com., 1968-77, mem. admissions com., 1969-70, chmn. projects com. 1972-73, active work with Cuban refugees; mem. kidney disease adv. com. Wash.-Alaska Regional Med. Program, 1970-73. Mem. Spokane Quality of Life Commn., 1974-75. Mem. Nat. Assn. Social Workers (Wash. chpt. pres. 1972-74, Wash. State Social Worker of Yr. 1991, Nat. Social Worker of Yr. 1991), Acad. Cert. Social Workers (charter). Roman Catholic. Home: 5609 W Northwest Blvd Spokane WA 99205-2039 Office: Nangoma Health Ctr, Box 830022, Mumbwa Zambia

HANSEN, FREDERIC J., state environmental agency director; b. Portland, Oreg., Mar. 22, 1946; s. Vernon Edward and Ella Freda (Schacher) H. BA in Math. and History, U. Oreg., 1968; MA in History, McMaster U., 1969; postgrad., Johns Hopkins U., 1970. Asst. historian U.S. Nat. Park Service, Washington, 1970; office mgr. U.S. Senate, Washington, 1970-71; exec. asst. U.S. Ho. of Reps., Washington, 1971-75; spl. asst. to pres. Clemency Bd. for Vietnam Era Veterans, Washington, 1975; exec. officer Peace Corps., Washington, 1975-77; dep. dir. office of the pres. Fed. Cash Mgmt. Project, Washington, 1977-78; chief dep. state treas. State of Oreg., Salem, 1978-84; dir. Oreg. Dept. of Environ. Quality, Portland, 1984—; Co-chair hazardous waste identification rule com., EPA; task force air implementation, EPA; mem. groundwater adv. com. Urban Inst. 1989-90, relative risk reduction com. Sci Adv. bd. to EPA, 1989-90, Gov.'s State Agy. Growth Coun., 1990—, State EPA com. 1987—. Mem. groundwater adv. com. Urban Inst. 1989-90, State EPA com. 1987—, relative risk reduction com. Sci adv. bd. to EPA, 1989-90; mem. Gov.'s State Agy. Growth Coun., 1990—. Woodrow Wilson Nat. Found. vis. fellow, 1987—. Mem. Phi Eta Sigma, Phi Beta Kappa. Office: Environmental Quality Dept 811 SW 6th Ave Portland OR 97204-1305

HANSEN, JAMES DOUGLAS, retail executive; b. Mpls., Dec. 16, 1954; s. Gordon A. and Margaret L. (Larson) H.; m. Laura D. Wagner, Feb. 9, 1985. BSBA, U. Minn., 1976. Supr. salesperson Daytons, Mpls., 1970-76; salesperson Nordstrom, Seattle, 1976-77; dept. mgr. Powers Dept. Store, Mpls., 1977; sales rep. Famolare Inc., N.Y.C., 1978-81; sales exec. Burnett Realty, Minnetonka, Minn., 1981; mng. ptnr. Anders' Footwear, Richland, Wash., 1981—. Chmn. adv. coun. Salvation Army, Richland, 1989—; mayor pro tem City of Richland, 1990—; pres. Richland Mainstreet Assn. Mem. Richland C. of C. (chmn. parade 1988—, petition chair 1989), Uptown Merchant Assn. (pres. 1989-90). Republican. Baptist. Home: 127 Canyon Ct Richland WA 99352-9409

HANSEN, JAMES LEE, sculptor; b. Tacoma, Wash., June 13, 1925; s. Hildreth Justine and Mary Elizabeth H.; m. Annabelle Hair, Aug. 31, 1946; children—Valinda Jean, Yauna Marie. Grad., Portland Art Mus. Sch. mem. faculty Oreg. State U., Corvallis, 1957-58, U. Calif., Berkeley, 1958, Portland State U., 1964—, U. Oreg., 1967. One-man shows include Fountain Gallery, Portland, Oreg., 1966, 69, 77-81, U. Oreg. Art Mus., Eugene, 1970, Seligman (Seders Gallery), Seattle, 1970, Portland Art Mus., 1971, Cheney Cowles Meml. Mus., Spokane, Wash., 1972, Polly Freidlander Gallery, Seattle, 1973, 75, 76, Smithsonian Instn., Washington, 1974, Hodges/Banks Gallery (now Linda Hodges Gallery), Seattle, 1983, Abanté Gallery, Portland, 1986, 88; group exhbns. include N.W. Ann. Painters and Sculptors, Seattle, 1952-73, Oreg. Ann. Painters and Sculptors, Portland Art Mus., 1952-75, Whitney Mus. Am. Art, N.Y.C., 1953, Santa Barbara (Calif.) Mus. Art, 1959-60, Denver Art Mus., 1960, San Francisco Art Mus., 1960, Smithsonian Instn., Washington, 1974, Wash. State U., Pullman, 1975; represented in permanent collections Graphic Arts Center, Portland, State Capitol, Olympia, Wash., U. Oreg., Eugene, Salem (Oreg.) Civic Center, Clark Coll., Vancouver, Wash., Portland Art Mus., Transit Mall, Portland, Fresno (Calif.) Mall, Seattle Art Mus., Gresham Town Fair (Oreg.), Oreg. Health Scis. U., Portland, various banks and schs., numerous commns.; represented by Abanté Gallery, Portland, Wilkey Gallery, Seattle, Arneson Fine Art, Vale, Colo. Address: 28219 NE 63d Ct Battle Ground WA 98604

HANSEN, JAMES V., congressman; b. Salt Lake City, Utah, Aug. 14, 1932; s. J. Vear and Sena C. H.; m. Ann Burgoyne H., 1958; children—Susan, Joseph James, David Burgoyne, Paul William, Jennifer. B.S., U. Utah, 1960. Mem. Utah Ho. of Reps., 1973-80, speaker of house, 1979-80; mem. 97th-103rd Congresses from 1st Utah dist., Washington, D.C., 1981—; pres. James V. Hansen Ins. Agy., Woodland Springs Devel. Co.

HANSEN, JOHN LESLIE, management consultant; b. Ealing, Eng., Oct. 15, 1958; came to U.S., 1963; s. Arthur Edward and Angeline Rose (Lombardo) H. BA in Econs., New Coll., Sarasota, Fla., 1982; MBA, U. Calif., Berkeley, 1984. Corp. banking officer Crocker Bank, San Francisco, 1984-86; asst. v.p. Wells Fargo Bank, San Francisco, 1986-87; sr. assoc. Booz, Allen & Hamilton, Singapore, 1988-91; cons. Edgar, Dunn & Co., San Francisco, 1991—. Counsellor twin star youth group Newman Hall, Berkeley, 1984-87; trustee New Coll. Found., 1992—. Scholar S.W. Fla. br. English Speakiing Union U.S., 1980, San Francisco br. French-Am. C. of C., 1983. Roman Catholic. Office: Edgar Dunn & Co 847 Sansome St San Francisco CA 94111

HANSEN, KENNETH RUSSELL, artist; b. Jan. 20, 1926; s. Bendix and Elsie Marie (Rytter) H.; m. Leonore Adell Wolf, Nov. 22, 1950; children: Kirk Russell, Kristn Rae. PhB, U. N.D., 1950; DDS, Northwestern U., 1953. Cert. Dentist. Trainee J.C. Penney Co., Miles City, Mont., 1950-52; pvt. practice dentist Missoula, Mont., 1957-78; artist Polson, Mont., 1978—; pres. 2nd Dist. Dental Soc., Missoula, 1961, Mont. Watercolor Soc., Polson, 1986. Artist: A Time of Life, 1980 (1st watercolor award), Oranges with Bag, 1987 (1st Mont. award); author: American Artist Magazine, 1986. Mem. Nat. Watercolor Soc. (signature), Midwest Watercolor Soc. (signature), Mont. Watercolor Soc. (signature). Home and Office: 2989 Kings Point Rd Polson MT 59860

HANSEN, LEONARD JOSEPH, author, journalist; b. San Francisco, Aug. 4, 1932; s. Einar L. and Margie A. (Wilder) H.; m. Marcia Ann Rasmussen, Mar. 18, 1966 (div.); children: Barron Richard, Trevor Wilder. AB in Radio-TV Prodn. and Mgmt., San Francisco State Coll., 1956, postgrad. 1956-57; cert. IBM Mgmt. Sch., 1967. Jr. writer Sta. KCBS, San Francisco, 1952-54; assoc. producer and dir. Ford Found. TV Rsch. Project, San Francisco State Coll., 1955-57; crew chief on live and remote broadcasts Sta. KPIX-TV, San Francisco, 1957-59, air promotion dir. and writer Sta. KPIX-TV, San Francisco, 1959-60; pub. rels. mgr. Sta. KNTV-TV, San Jose, Calif., 1961; radio and TV promotion mgr. Seattle World's Fair, 1962; pub. relations and promotion mgr. Century 21 Ctr., Inc., Seattle, 1963-64; pub. rels. dir. Dan Evans for Gov. Com., Seattle, 1964; propr., mgr. Leonard J. Hansen Pub. Rels., Seattle, 1965-67; campaign mgr. Walter J. Hickel for Gov. Com., Anchorage, 1966; exec. cons. to Gov. of Alaska, Juneau, 1967; gen. mgr. No. TV, Inc., Anchorage, 1967-69; v.p. mktg. Sea World, Inc., San Diego, 1969-71; editor, pub. Sr. World Publs., Inc., San Diego, 1973-84; chmn. Sr. Pubs. Group, 1977-89; speaker and mktg. cons. to sr. citizens, 1984-92; panelist, pub. affairs radio programs, 1971-92; lectr. journalism San Diego State U., 1975-76. Writer weekly syndicated column Mainly for Seniors, 1984—, syndicated column Travel for Mature Adults, 1984—; writer, journalist The Mature Market; contbg. editor Mature Life Features, news/feature syndicate, 1987-90; chmn. Mature Mkt. Seminars, 1987-90; author Life Begins at 50-The Handbook for Creative Retirement Planning, 1989; pres., pub. Mature Market Editorial Svcs., 1991—. Founding mem. Housing for Elderly and Low Income Persons, San Diego, 1977-78; mem. Mayor's Ad Hoc Adv. Com. on Aging, San Diego, 1976-79; vice chmn. Housing Task Force, San Diego, 1977-78; bd. dirs. Crime Control Commn., San Diego, 1980, San Diego Coalition, 1980-83; del. White House Conf. on Aging, 1981. Served with U.S. Army, 1953-55. Recipient numerous service and citizenship awards from clubs and community orgns. Mem. Pub. Rels.Soc. Am. (accredited), Soc. Profl. Journalists (Best Investigative Reporting award 1979), Internat. Platform Assn., San Diego Press Club (Best Newswriting award 1976-77, Headliner of Yr. award 1980), Am. Assn. Travel Editors (profl. mem.).

HANSEN, MATILDA, state legislator; b. Paullina, Iowa, Sept. 4, 1929; d. Arthur J. and Sada G. (Thompson) Henderson; m. Robert B. Michener, 1950 (div. 1963); children: Eric J., Douglas E.; m. Hugh G. Hansen. BA, U. Colo., 1963; MA, U. Wyo., 1970. Tchr. history Englewood (Colo.) Sr. High Sch., 1963-65; dir. Albany County Adult Learning Ctr., Laramie, Wyo., 1966-78, Laramie Plains Civic Ctr., 1979-83; treas. Wyo. Territorial Prison Corp., Laramie, 1988—, also bd. dirs. Author: (textbooks) To Help Adults Learn, 1975, Let's Play Together, 1978. Legislator Wyo. Ho. of Reps., Cheyenne, 1975—, minority whip, 1987-88, asst. minority leader, 1991-92; mem. mgmt. coun. Wyo. State Legislature, Cheyenne, 1983-84; chair Com. for Dem. Legislature, Cheyenne, 1990-92. GE fellow in econs. for high sch. tchrs., 1963; named Pub. Citizen of Yr., Wyo. Assn. Social Workers, 1980-81. Mem. LWV Wyo. (v.p. 1966-68), LWV Laramie (bd. dirs. 1966—), Nat. Conf. State Legislators (vice chair human recources 1983, nat. exec. com. 1990—), Laramie Area C. of C., Laramie Women's Club, Faculty Women's Club. Mem. Soc. of Friends. Home: 1306 E Kearney St Laramie WY 82070-4142 Office: Wyo House of Reps State Capitol Cheyenne WY 82002

HANSEN, MICHAEL ROY, chemist; b. Bremerton, Wash., July 27, 1953; s. Roy Vernon and Bonnie Jean (St. Cyr) H.; m. Valerie Jean Paulson, Feb. 14, 1984 (div. Aug. 14, 1987); 1 child, Ryan Ernest. BS in Chemistry, BS in Molecular Biology, U. Wash., 1978. Rsch. scientist Weyerhaeuser, Federal Way, Wash., 1987—; chemistry instr. Highline Community Coll., Des Moines, Wash., 1991—. Patentee in field. With U.S. Army, 1972-75. Mem. AAAS, Am. Chem. Soc., Soc. Plastics Engrs., N.Y. Acad. Soc. Office: Weyerhaeuser Technology Ctr 32901 Weyerhaeuser Way S Federal Way WA 98003

HANSEN, NANCY C. URDAHL, special education educator; b. Tacoma, May 17, 1940; d. Arthur Selmer and Doris Lavina (Perry) Urdahl; m. John Raymond Hansen, Apr. 2, 1966 (div.); children: John Raymond, Julia

Amy. BA, U. Puget Sound, 1969; postgrad., Gov.'s State U., 1972-73; AA, Seattle C.C., 1978; MEd, U. Wash., 1979. Cert. spl. edn. tchr., Wash. Tchr. Grace Migrant Sch., Park Forest, Ill., 1970-71, Rainbow Valley Child Care Ctr., Seattle, 1977-78; tchr. aide Highline Pub. Schs., Seattle, 1978, Experimental Edn. Unit U. Wash., Seattle, 1978; vol. coord. Camp Fire Inc., Seattle, 1979-80; researcher Mott Rehab. Svcs., Mountlake Terrace, Wash., 1980-82; tchr. South Kitsap Sch. Dist., Port Orchard, Wash., 1980-82, resource rm. tchr., 1982—; interviewer King County Interagy. Project U. Wash., Seattle, 1978-80; sec. Queen Anne Juvenile Ct. Conf. Com., Seattle, 1976-78. Contbr. articles to profl. jours. Mem. citizen adv. group Piecre County Comprehensive Plan, Tacoma, 1992; co-coord. Keep Wash. Liveable, Tacoma, 1990; sec., co-founder Peninsula Neighborhood Assn., Gig Harbor, Wash., 1988-91, bd. dirs., 1992; coord. & co-founder Peninsula Stream Monitors, Gig Harbor, 1992—. Mem. Wash. Edn. Assn., South Kitsap Edn. Assn., Learning Disabilities Assn. Wash., Alpha Phi Sorority.

HANSEN, PARTICK STEVEN, disaster and emergency services coordinator; b. L.A., Sept. 12, 1953; s. Robert Fred and Kathleen Joyce (Woolsey) H. BA in Govt., Mont. State U., 1974, MS in Earth Scis., 1976. Asst. city and county planner Sweet Grass County, Big Timber, Mont., 1977-78, 90; justice of the peace Sweet Grass County, Big Timber, 1978-83, dep. coord. of disaster and emergency svcs., 1978—, asst. drug and alcohol counsellor, 1984-85, sheriffs' dispatcher, 1984-90. Commencement speaker Big Timber Grade Sch./Sweet Grass County Rural Schs., 1986, 88, Sweet Grass High Sch., 1987; mem. Hyalite Challenge Steering Com., Bozeman, 1987-89; mem., bd. dirs. I Can Do Ranch, Big Timber, 1990—; mem. Big Timber Christian Men's Fellowship, 1980—, pres. 1982-83, 91-92. Recipient Americanism award and scholarship Am. Legion, 1970, Babe Ruth Sportsmanship award, 1970; Starr Ford scholar, 1970; Jane Buttrey Meml. Fund scholar, 1973. Home: Box 979 208 Bramble Big Timber MT 59011 Office: Sweet Grass County Disaster & Emergency Svcs Box 345 Big Timber MT 59011

HANSEN, RANDALL GLENN, school psychologist, consultant; b. Fayetteville, N.C., Dec. 9, 1946; s. Glenn Sidney and Ramona Mary (Blocker) H.; m. Wanda Kay Moller (div. Dec. 1990); 1 child, Nicholas Glenn. BS in Secondary Edn., Black Hills State U., Spearfish, S.D., 1971; BA in Social Work, Chadron (Nebr.) State Coll., 1978; MEd in Counseling-Guidance-Pers. Svcs., S.D. State U., 1982; cert. sch. psychology licensing program, Moorhead (Minn.) State U., 1986; PhD in Clin. Sch. Psychology, Walden U., Mpls., 1991. Nat. cert. sch. psychologist; cert. social worker, counselor; lic. ednl. psychologist, Calif. Tchr., counselor Sky Ranch for Boys, Camp Crook, S.D., 1971-72; social worker I, S.D. Dept. Social Svvcs., Rapid City, 1972-73; multi-county svc. area supr. S.D. Dept. Social Svvcs., Mitchell and Sioux Falls, 1979-85; asst. mgr. Pioneer Market, North Platte, Nebr., 1973-74; county dir. Frontier County Div. Pub. Welfare, Curtis, Nebr., 1974-75; quality control reviewer Nebr. Dept. Pub. Welfare, Scottsbluff, 1975-77, asst. income maintenance rep., 1977-79; sch. psychologist Tracy (Minn.), Milroy, Balaton and Walnut Grove Schs., 1985-88, Palo Verde Unified Sch. Dist., Blythe, Calif., 1988—; sch. psychol. cons. Desert Ctr. Unified Sch. Dist., Eagle Mountain, Calif., 1988—; pub. speaker on learning disabilities and how mind processes info., 1986—. Author: (psychol. test) Children's Attention-Deficit Hyperactivity Inventory, 1991. Bd. dirs. Food Svcs. Ctr., Sioux Falls, 1980-85, Educators Interested in Spl. Edn., Marshall, Minn., 1985-88; counselor Crisis Line, Sioux Falls, 1981-85; softball coach Project Awareness, Sioux Falls, 1984. Named Vol. of Month, Crisis Line, 1984. Mem. NASP, AACD, Menninger Found., Doctorate Assn. N.Y. Educators. Democrat. Home: 8401 E Hobsonway Space 34 Blythe CA 92225 Office: Counseling Ctr 689 N Lovekin Blvd Blythe CA 92225-1136

HANSEN, ROBERT DENNIS, educational administrator; b. San Francisco, July 17, 1945; s. Eiler Cunnard and Muriel Lenore (Morrison) H.; BA, U. San Francisco, 1967, MA in Counseling and Guidance, 1971, MA in Supervision and Adminstrn., 1973; EdD, U. La Verne, 1988; m. Karen Calder, Apr. 21, 1990; children from a previous marriage: April Michelle, Alison Nicole, Andrew Warren. Tchr., dept. chmn., counselor, dir. student affairs, attendance officer South San Francisco Unified Sch. Dist., 1968-74, coordinator, asst. prin. Jurupa Unified Sch. Dist., Riverside, Calif., 1974-78; prin., asst. supt. San Gabriel (Calif.) Sch. Dist., 1978-91; supt. Rosemead (Calif.) Sch. Dist., 1991—; adj. prof. U. La Verne, Calif., 1988—. Exec. bd. South San Francisco PTA, 1968-74. Named hon. chpt. farmer Future Farmers Am.; recipient Hon. Service award Calif. State PTA. Mem. U. San Francisco Edn. Alumni Soc. (pres. 1972-73), Nat. Assn. Year-Round Edn., U. San Francisco Alumni Assn., Am. Assn. Sch. Adminstrs., Assn. Calif. Sch. Adminstrs., Assn. for Supervision and Curriculum Devel., Phi Delta Kappa. Republican. Episcopalian. Mason (32 deg.). Home: 172 S Country Club Rd Glendora CA 91740-3923 Office: Rosemead Sch Dist 3640 N Rio Hondo Ave West Covina CA 91790

HANSEN, ROBERT GUNNARD, philatelist, entrepreneur; b. Chgo., Aug. 16, 1939; s. Earl F. and Mildred E. (Hargrave) H.; A.A., Lincoln Coll., 1960; B.A., Culver Stockton Coll., 1962; M.B.A., U. So. Calif., 1966; postgrad. UCLA Extension, 1962-67; m. Bertha Golds, Aug. 10, 1960; children—Karin Lee, Lisa Marie. With Litton Industries, 1962-63, Sterer Engring., 1963-69; mktg. and contracts ofcl. Santa Barbara Research Ctr., 1969-73; pres., chief exec. officer, R.G. Hansen & Assocs., Santa Barbara, 1974—; pres., owner The Silver Penny and Santa Barbara Stamp & Coin, 1969—; owner, CEO, pres. Univ. Travel Bureau, 1990—; guest lectr. Santa Barbara City Coll. Mem. Am. Vacuum Soc., Am. Philatelic Soc. (life), Am. Numismatic Assn., Hawaii Numismatic Assn., Sci. and Engring. Coun. Santa Barbara (pres. 1989), Token and Medal Soc., Masons, York Rite. Scottish Rite, Shriners, Royal Order of Scotland, Channel City, Royal Arch Masons, Rotary Internat. (Paul Harris fellow 1990). Research and publs. on cryogenics, electro-optics, infrared radiation; patentee in field. Republican. Presbyterian. Office: 631 Chapala St Santa Barbara CA 93101-3311

HANSEN, RONALD GREGORY, civil engineer; b. Waipahu, Hawaii, Aug. 22, 1929; s. Erling M. and Geraldine J. (Nettleton) H.; m. Theresa J. Cunningham, Feb. 5, 1955; children: Eric L., Karen A., Maureen A., Timothy E. BCE, U. Santa Clara, 1952; MSCE, U. So. Calif., 1958, postgrad., 1958-66; M in Pub. Adminstrn., U. Alaska, 1981. Registered civil engr., Alaska, Wash., Oreg., Calif. Engr. Calif. Dept. Water Resources, Los Angeles, 1957-67; sr. engr. Water Quality Control Bd., Los Angeles, 1967-71; chief water pollution control State of Alaska, Juneau, 1971-79; sr. engr. KCM Inc. and EMPS Engring, Juneau, 1980-85; pres. Hansen Engring., Juneau, 1985—. Former scoutmaster, mem. bldg. com. S.E. Alaska, Boy Scouts Am.; mem., chmn. Juneau Parks and Recreation Adv. Com., 1983-91. Served to lt. col., C.E., USAR. Mem. Am. Water Works Assn., ASCE, Water Environ. Fedn., Am. Acad. Environ. Engrs., Am. Water Resources Assn., Internat. Water Resources Assn., NSPE. Republican. Roman Catholic. Home and Office: Hansen Engring 4117 Birch Ln Juneau AK 99801-8909

HANSEN, SIGVARD THEODORE, JR., orthopaedic surgeon, educator; b. Spokane, Wash., Nov. 30, 1935; s. Sigvard Theodore and Beverly Esther (Means) H.; m. Mary Jane Weinmann, Aug. 20, 1960; children: Christopher Michael, Eric Theodore; m. Dalia Maria Nalis, Sept. 19, 1987. BA cum laude, Whitman Coll., 1957; MD, U. Wash., 1961. Diplomate Am. Bd. Orthopaedic Surgery. Intern, King County Hosp., Seattle, 1961-62; resident in surgery U. Wash., Seattle, 1965-69, asst. prof. orthopaedic surgery 1971-75, assoc. prof., 1975-79, prof., 1979—, chmn. dept., 1981-85; cons. Madigan Army Hosp., 1975—; bd. overseers Whitman Coll., 1985—. Served with USN, 1962-65. NIH summer research fellow, 1957, 58. Mem. Am. Acad. Orthopaedic Surgery, Am. Orthopaedic Assn., Assn. Bone and Joint Surgeons, Western Orthopaedic Assn., Am. Orthopaedic Foot and Ankle Soc., AO-N. Am. Found. (pres. 1986-92), Assn. for Study Internal Fixation (bd. dirs. 1984—), M.E. Mueller Found. (bd. dirs. 1986—), Phi Beta Kappa. Editor, co-editor med. texts; contbr. articles to med. jours., chpts. to books. Home: 2563 Magnolia Blvd W Seattle WA 98199-3631 Office: 325 9th Ave Seattle WA 98104-2499

HANSEN, WALTER EUGENE, insurance executive; b. Woodland, Wash., May 15, 1929; s. August Hans and Esther Johanna (Johnson) H.; m. Barbara Inez Cowart, Oct. 1950; m. Donna Carol Phillips, Aug. 1, 1953; children: Larry, Monty, Gena, Martin, Lori, Bradley, Walter Eugene Jr. Grad. high sch. Farmer, logger, 1943-51; svc. mgr. Sears Roebuck & Co., L.A. and Portland, Oreg., 1951-57; agt. various ins. cos., 1957-63; dist. mgr. Bankers Life & Casualty Co., 1960-61; state mgr. Protective Security Life Ins. Co., 1963-65; regional mgr. Amn. Pacific Life Ins. Co., 1963-72; owner Pacific N.W. Ins. Svc., Portland, 1963—, Am. Pacific Agys., Portland, 1970—; owner N. Fork Motors, Woodland, Wash., 1987—, Vancouver, Wash., 1989—; owner Nat. Rsch. Assocs., Seattle, 1968—, N. Fork Ranch, 1962—. Active Boy Scouts Am.; chmn. Community USA Bicentennial Commn., 1976; mem. Wash. State Centennial Com., 1989. Mem. Internat. Platform Assn., Nat. Assn. Life Underwriters, Accident and Health Underwriters Assn., Smithsonian Assocs., Navy League of U.S. Home: PO Box A Woodland WA 98674-1124 Office: PO Box 12225 Portland OR 97212-0225

HANSEN, WAYNE RICHARD, radioecologist; b. Oakgrove, Wis., Aug. 6, 1939; s. Richard Lyman and Helen Ann (Nethig) H.; m. Nancy Jane Rohde, Sept. 10, 1960; children: Richard W., William R. BS, U. Wis., Eau Claire, 1961; MS, U. Kans., 1963; PhD, Colo. State U., 1970. Diplomate Am. Bd. Health Physics (bd. dirs. 1990—). Health physicist U. Colo., Boulder, 1963-67, Bur. Radiol. Health, Rockville, Md., 1970-71, EPA, Washington, 1971-75; sr. radiobiologist NRC, Washington, 1975-77; group leader environ. surveillance Los Alamos Nat. Lab., 1977-84, dep. div. leader health, safety and environ., 1984-87, chief scientist environ. rsch., 1987-90, group leader environ. scis., 1990—; sr. scientist accident response group Dept. Energy, Albuquerque, 1986—. Contbr. articles to profl. jours., chpt. to book. Vice chmn. N.Mex. Gov.'s Radiation Tech. Adv. Coun., Sante Fe, 1983—, NCRP Sci. Com. 64. Fellow AAAS; mem. Health Physics Soc. (coun. Rio Grande chpt. 1988-90), N.Mex. Acad. Sci. Lutheran. Home: 557 Bryce Ave Los Alamos NM 87544-3607 Office: Los Alamos Nat Lab MS J495 PO Box 1663 Los Alamos NM 87545

HANSLER, JEFFREY KURT, executive; b. Newport Beach, Calif., June 26, 1957; s. Kurt and Joyce Hansler; m. Kimberley Gibbs. BA in Psychology, U. Calif., Irvine, 1979. Sales rep. Apple Computer, Newport Beach, Calif., 1980-82; v.p. mktg. Holland Automation, Santa Ana, Calif., 1982-86; regional mgr. Talaris Systems, San Diego, 1986-87; broker Multinest Options, Newport Beach, 1987-88; v.p. mktg./sales Nat. Advancement, Santa Ana, Calif., 1988-92; pres. Oxford Co., Huntington Beach, Calif., 1992—. Author: OC Metropolitan, 1992, Sales and Marketing Strategies and News, 1992. Vol. Chris Cox Congl. Mktg. Court, Newport Beach, 1992. Mem. Am. Mktg. Assn. (dir. mktg.). Republican. Office: Oxford Co 523 18th St Huntington Beach CA 92648

HANSON, DALE, pension fund administrator; b. Madison, Wis., Nov. 5, 1942; 4 children by previous marriage; m. Lynn Hanson; 2 children. BA in Bus. Adminstrn., U. Wis., 1967. From analyst to divsn. head Wis. Wage and Salary Adminstrn., 1967-74; various positions, COO Wis. Dept. Employee Trust Funds, 1974-87; CEO Calif. Pub. Employee's Retirement System, 1987—. Office: Calif Pub Employee's Retirement System PO Box 942701 Sacramento CA 94229-2701

HANSON, DENNIS WAYNE, human resources manager; b. Madison, Wis., Aug. 19, 1948; s. Harry DuWayne and Irene Edith (Busse) H.; m. Vickie Lynne Wray, Apr. 4, 1980; children: Edward, Brittanie, Madison. BA in Polit. Sci., U. Wis., 1971, MS in Bus., 1977. V.p. adminstrn. Am. Furniture Products, Madison, 1976-78; personnel rep. Varian Assocs., Salt Lake City, 1978-82; human resources mgr. Memorex Corp., Santa Clara, Calif., 1982-84, IOMEGA Corp., Roy, Utah, 1984-93; employee rels. mgr. Morton Internat., Ogden, Utah, 1993—; chmn. Ogden (Utah) Job Svc. Employers Com., 1988-93, Utah State Job Svc. Employers Com., 1993—; mem. Ptnrs. in Edn., Weber County, Utah, 1988—, chmn. Student Devel. Adv. Com., Applied Tech. Ctr., Ogden, 1988—. Chmn. employers' com. Utah State Job Svc. Recipient Partners Recognition award Weber County Schs., Ogden, 1990. Mem. Soc. for Human Resources Mgmt. Office: Morton Internat Auto Safety Products Divsn 3350 Airport Rd Ogden UT 84405

HANSON, DUANE ALLEN, psychologist; b. Princeton, Minn., July 19, 1950; s. Lawrence Edward and Liela Christine (Brynteson) H. BA in Psychology, U. Minn., 1973; MDiv, MA in Psychology, Trinity Sem., Deerfield, Ill., 1985. Chpt. dir. and trainer Campus Crusade for Christ, L.A., Manila, 1973-81; ter. mgr. Perry County Pizza Co., La Mirada, Calif., 1986-88; mktg. dir. Buena Park (Calif.) Community Hosp., 1987-88, intake counselor, 1988-90; psychol. tester Orange County Community Hosp., Buena Park, 1990—; outplacement cons. Campus Crusade for Christ, San Bernardino, Calif., 1990, 91, recruiting cons., Springfield, Mass., 1991, Campus Crusade Hdqs., Orlando, Fla., 1993. Mem. focal point leadership com., leader 37 Plus, 1st Evang. Free Ch., Fullerton, Calif., 1992. Republican.

HANSON, GEORGE PETER, retired research botanist, real estate investor; b. Conde, S.D., July 20, 1933; s. George Henry and Rosa Wilhelmina (Peterson) H.; m. Barbara Jean Graves, Aug. 20, 1958; children: David, Carole, Heather, Peter; m. Gloria Ann Gauntt, June 1, 1969. BS in Agronomy, S.D. State U., 1956, MS in Plant Breeding, 1958; PhD in Genetics, Ind. U., 1965. Asst. prof. biology Thiel Coll. Greenville, Pa., 1962-65; asst. prof. botany Butler U., Indpls., 1965-67; sr. biologist L.A. State and County Arboretum, Arcadia, Calif., 1968-82; real estate investor, 1971—. Mem. Apt. Assn. of Greater L.A. Methodist. Contbr. numerous articles in field to profl. jours. Home: 1345 W Haven Rd San Marino CA 91108-2018

HANSON, GERALD WARNER, county official; b. Alexandria, Minn., Dec. 25, 1938; s. Lewis Lincoln and Dorothy Hazel (Warner) H.; m. Sandra June Wheeler, July 9, 1960. AA, San Bernardino Valley (Calif.) Coll., 1959; BA, U. Redlands (Calif.), 1979; MA, U. Redlands, 1981; postgrad., Pepperdine U., 1992—. Cert. advanced metrication specialist. Dep. sealer San Bernardino (Calif.) County, 1964-80, div. chief, 1980-85, dir. weights and measures, 1985—. Mem. Redlands Rent Rev. Bd., 1985—; bd. dirs. House Neighborly Svc., Redlands, 1972-73, Boys Club, Redlands, 1985-86; mem. Redlands Planning commn., 1991—. With USN. Fellow U.S. Metric Assn. (treas. 1986-88, 92—); mem. NRA (life), Nat. Conf. on Weights and Measures (asst. treas. 1986—), Western Weights and Measures Assn. (pres. 1987-88), Calif. Assn. Weights and Measures Ofcls. (1st v.p. 1987—), Calif. Rifle and Pistol Assn. (life), Masons, Shriners, Kiwanis (treas. Redlands club 1983—). Home: 225 E Palm Ave Redlands CA 92373-6131 Office: San Bernardino County Dept Weights and Measures 777 E Rialto Ave San Bernardino CA 92415-0001

HANSON, HILARY RUTH, public relations executive; b. San Rafael, Calif., Sept. 14, 1963; d. Allan Morris and Naomi Hanson. BS in Journalism, U. Oreg., 1985. Pub. rels. mgr. Manning & Assocs., San Diego, 1985-86; pub. rels. account exec. Palmer, Sharit & Co., San Diego, 1986-87; pub. rels. v.p./account supr. Ketchum Pub. Rels., San Francisco, 1987—. Recipient Golden Quill Internat. Assn. Bus. Communicators, 1990; scholarship U. Oreg. Sch. Journalism, 1981-84. Mem. Pub. Rels. Soc. Am. (Silver Anvil award 1989), Phi Beta Kappa. Office: Ketchum Pub Rels 55 Union St San Francisco CA 94111-1217

HANSON, HOWARD PAUL, environmental research scientist; b. Peoria, Ill., Jan. 1, 1950; s. Edwin Eugene and Marilyn (Sedgwick) H.; m. Claire Marie Smith, Mar. 26, 1983. BS in Aero. and Astro. Engring., U. Ill., 1972; PhD in Atmospheric Sci., U. Miami, Fla., 1979. Rsch. assoc. NRC, Washington, 1979-81; rsch. assoc. Coop. Inst. for Rsch. in Environ. Scis., U. Colo., Boulder, 1981-85, fellow and assoc. dir., 1985—, sr. rsch. assoc., 1991—; vis. scientist Nat. Ctr. Atmospheric Rsch., Boulder, 1985; mission scientist NASA, NOAA, 1981-87; cons. Jason Group, LaJolla, Calif., 1991. Contbr. articles to profl. jours.; editor, guest editor: Modelling and Prediction of the Upper Layers of the Ocean, 1977, Deep-Sea Research, GATE Supplement II, 1979, Progress in Oceanography, 1981. NRC fellow, 1979-81; rsch. grantee NSF, NASA, Office Naval Rsch., NOAA, DOE, 1981—; recipient NASA Group Achievement award, 1991. Mem. Am. Meteorol. Soc., Am. Geophys. Union, The Oceanography Soc., Sigma Xi, Tau Beta Pi. Office: CIRES/Univ of Colo Campus Box 216 Boulder CO 80309-0216

HANSON, JOHN J., lawyer; b. Aurora, Nebr., Oct. 22, 1922; s. Peter E. and Hazel Marion (Lounsbury) H.; m. Elizabeth Anne Moss, July 1, 1973; children from their previous marriages—Mark, Eric, Gregory. A.B., U. Denver, 1948; LL.B. cum laude, Harvard U., 1951. Bar: N.Y. bar 1952, Calif. bar 1955. Asso. firm Dewey, Ballantine, Bushby, Palmer & Wood, N.Y.C., 1951-54; ptnr. firm Gibson, Dunn & Crutcher, L.A, 1954—; mem. exec. com. Gibson, Dunn & Crutcher, 1978-87, adv. ptnr, 1991—. Contbr. articles to profl. jours. Trustee Palos Verdes (Calif.) Sch. Dist., 1969-73. Served with U.S. Navy, 1942-45. Fellow Am. Coll. Trial Lawyers; mem. Am. Bar Assn., Los Angeles County Bar Assn. (chmn. antitrust sect. 1979-80), Bel Air Country Club. Home: 953 Linda Flora Dr Los Angeles CA 90049-1630 Office: Gibson Dunn & Crutcher 333 S Grand Ave Los Angeles CA 90071-1504

HANSON, KENNETH MERRILL, physicist; b. Mt. Vernon, N.Y., Apr. 17, 1940; s. Orville Glen and Marion (Chamberlain) H.; m. Earle Marie Low, June 1964 (div. July 1989); children: Jennifer Anne, Keith Merrill. BE in Physics, Cornell U., 1963; MS in Physics, Harvard U., 1967, PhD in Physics, 1970. Rsch. assoc. Lab. of Nuclear Studies, Ithaca, N.Y., 1970-75; mem. staff Los Alamos (N.Mex.) Nat. Lab., 1975—. Author: (with others) Radiology of Skull and Brain, 1979, Image Recovery, 1987; contbr. articles to profl. jours. Recipient Award Excellence, Dept. Energy, 1986. Mem IEEE (sr.), Am. Phys. Soc., Soc. Photo Optical Instrumentation Engrs. (program com. imaging conf. 1984—). Office: Los Alamos Nat Lab MSP 940 Los Alamos NM 87545

HANSON, LAMONT DIX, credit union executive; b. Shelley, Idaho, June 30, 1954; s. Keith B. and Reva (Patterson) H.; m. Diane Searle, June 12, 1976; children: Gregory LaMont, Paul Wendell, Scott Keith, Marc Dix, Todd Searle. BS, Brigham Young U., 1978. loan officer East Idaho Fed. Credit Union, Idaho Falls, 1978-80, ops. mgr., 1980-84, v.p., 1984-87, pres., 1987—; dir. Ea. Idaho Chpt. of Credit Unions, Idaho Falls, 1979-83, Idaho Credit Union League, Boise, Idaho, 1987-89. Scout Leader Boy Scouts of Am., Idaho Falls, 1990. Mem. Credit Union Exec. Soc. Mem. LDS Ch. Office: East Idaho Fed Credit Union PO Box 1865 540 3d St Idaho Falls ID 83403

HANSON, LARRY KEITH, plastics company executive; b. Hawkins, Wis., Aug. 14, 1932; s. Harold and Clara Pauline (Lund) H.; m. Patricia Rosalie Sammarco, Aug. 6, 1955; children: Lawrence Keith, John Steven, James Paul. BS, U.S. Mcht. Marine Acad., 1955. Engr. Curtis-Wright Corp., Woodridge, N.J., 1955-58; sales engr. Gits Bros. Mfg. Co., Chgo., 1958-66, Aeroquip Corp., Burbank, Calif., 1966-70; exec. v.p. Furon Co., Laguna Niguel, Calif., 1970—; mng. dir. Furon SA/NV subs. Furon Co., Kontich, Belgium, 1983-90; exec. v.p. Furon Co., Laguna Niguel, Calif., 1990—. Patentee in field. Mem. ASME, Soc. Automotive Engrs. Office: Furon Co. 29982 Ivy Glenn Dr Laguna Niguel CA 92677-9999

HANSON, RICHARD EDWIN, civil engineer; b. Sioux City, Iowa, July 22, 1931; s. Gustav Edwin and Delia Thelma (Horton) H.; m. Joann Gager Terhune, Nov. 6, 1954 (div. Jan. 1971); children: Richard Edwin Jr., John William, Tamara Terhune; m. Lillie Gwenette Capitanio, Feb. 21, 1987. BSCE, Iowa State U., 1953; postgrad., U.S. Army Gen. Staff Coll. Registered profl. engr., Iowa. Engr.-in-tng. U.S. Army Corps Engrs., Washington, 1957-58; sr. co. engr. Dickinson Constrn. Co., Chgo., 1959-62; asst. chief constrn. mgmt. Goddard Space Flight Ctr., NASA, Greenbelt, Md., 1963-69; chief project mgmt. U.S. Postal Svc., Washington, 1969-70; chief Air Force project mgmt. U.S. Army Corps Engrs., Washington, 1971-77; chief of constrn. U.S. Army Corps Engrs., Balt., 1977-81; chief of constrn. South Atlantic div. U.S. Army Corps Engrs., Atlanta, 1982-85; chief of constrn. U.S. Army Corps Engrs., Washington, 1986-91; dir. constrn. ops. Pacific Ocean div. U.S. Army Corps Engrs., Honolulu, 1991—. Editor: Corps Engrs. Constrn. Newsletter, 1988-91. Pres. Walbrooke Manor Citizens Assn., Lanham, Md., 1963-64. 1st lt. C.E., U.S. Army, 1953-57. Mem. ASCE, NSPE, Soc. Am. Mil. Engrs. (bd. dirs. Washington chpt. 1988-91), Beta Theta Pi. Republican. Home: 44-125 Kahinani Way Kaneohe HI 96744

HANSVICK, CHRISTINE L., psychology educator; b. Vesta, Minn., Nov. 10, 1949; married; two children. BBA, S.W. State U., Marshall, Minn., 1971; MA in Psychology, U. Windsor, Ont., 1975, PhD in Psychology, 1977. Asst. prof. U. Man., Winnipeg, 1977-79; asst. prof. Pacific Luth. U., Tacoma, Wash., 1979-84, assoc. prof., 1985—; cons. Tacoma Arts Commn., 1989, Good Samaritan Hosp., Puyallup, Wash., 1990, Focus Groups Office Pub. Info., PLU, 1992, Tacoma/Pierce Co. C. of C., 1991; earthquake preparedness adv. bd. U. Wash., Seattle, 1990-91. Contbr. articles to profl. jours. Co-chair Dome Dist. Devel. Com., Tacoma, 1989-90; group leader family support Maple Valley Presbyn. Ch., 1990-91, Little Ch. on the Prairie, Tacoma, 1988-89, coord. small groups program, 1985-87; active global citizenship Kent First Presbyn. Ch., 1992, session, 1993—. Recipient Disting. Alumni award S.W. State U., 1992. Mem. AAUW, Parkland Revitalization Opportunities through Urban Devel., Environ. Design Rsch. Assn., Tacoma/Pierce County C. of C. (phys. image task force 1988-90, cons. 1987-90), City Club of Tacoma. Presbyterian. Home: 22931 130th Pl SE Kent WA 98031-3729 Office: Pacific Luth U Tacoma WA 98447

HAO, WEI MIN, chemistry educator; b. Chiayi, Taiwan, Apr. 7, 1953; came to U.S., 1976; s. Paul L.C. and Icie (Hsieh) H.; m. Mei-Huey Liu, Sept. 3, 1954; 1 child, Daphne Der-Shuen Hao. BS, Fu Jen Cath. U., Taipei, Taiwan, 1976; SM, MIT, 1979, MIT, 1981; PhD, Harvard U., 1986. Rsch. scientist Max-Planck-Institut für Chemie, Mainz, Germany, 1986-90; faculty U. Mont., Missoula, 1991—; cons. EPA, Taipei, 1989-90. Author: (with others) Fire in the Tropical Biota, 1990, Proceedings of the 28th Liege International Astrophysical Colloquium, Cointe-Ougree, Belgium, 1989; contbr. articles to profl. jours. Mem. Air Pollution Adv. Coun., Missoula, 1991. Mem. Am. Geophys. Union. Home: 1909 36th St Missoula MT 59801 Office: USDA Forest Svc Intermountain Fire Scis Lab PO Box 8089 Missoula MT 59807

HAPPEL, KENNETH MALCOLM, computer scientist; b. N.Y.C., June 8, 1949; s. Carl Frederick and Katherine King (Kehlor) H.; m. Riemke Rip, 1974 (div. 1977); m. Marie-Jose Kaasenbrood, Feb. 14, 1990; 1 child, Lieneke. Student, U. Calif., Santa Barbara. Quality engr. EMI Holland Prodns., Haarlem, Netherlands, 1975-77; tech. dir. Technovation, Arnhem, Netherlands, 1978-82, Synterials Plc., London, 1982-83, Devtech Bv., Heerlen, 1984-89; sr. staff engr. Gen. Dynamics Electronics, San Diego, 1989-91; CEO, chmn. Omnigon, San Diego, 1991—. Inventor Hyperknowledge. Mem. IEEE, Assn. for Computing Machinery, Computer Simulation Soc. Republican.

HARAD, GEORGE JAY, manufacturing company executive; b. Newark, Apr. 24, 1944; s. Sidney Solomon and Irma Miriam (Feigenblatt) H.; m. Beverly Marcia Silverman, June 12, 1966; children—Alyssa Dawn, Matthew Corde. B.A., Franklin and Marshall Coll., 1965; M.B.A. with high distinction, Harvard Bus. Sch., 1971. Staff cons. Boston Cons. Group, 1970-71; asst. to sr. v.p. housing Boise (Idaho) Cascade Corp., 1971; asst. to v.p. Boise Cascade Corp., Palo Alto, Calif., 1971; mgr. corp. devel. Boise Cascade Corp., 1976-80, dir. retirement funds, risk mgmt., 1980-82, v.p., contr., 1982-84, sr. v.p., chief fin. officer, 1984-89, exec. v.p., chief fin. officer, 1989-90, exec. v.p. paper, 1990-91, pres., COO, 1991—, also bd. dirs.; bd. dirs. Allendale Ins. Co., Inst. Paper Sci. and Tech.; mem. internat. bus. com. Am. Paper Inst., 1984—. Founder, pres. Boise Coun. for Gifted and Talented Students, 1977-79; bd. dirs. Boise Philharm. Assn., 1983-84; dir. bd. trustees Coll. Idaho, 1986-91. Grad. Prize fellow Harvard Grad. Sch. Arts and Scis., 1965-69, Frederick Roe fellow Harvard U. Sch. Bus., 1971; George F. Baker scholar, 1970-71. Mem. Nat. Assn. Mfrs. (bd. dirs.), Phi Beta Kappa, Century Club (Boston), Arid Club, Crane Creek Country Club. Home: 224 E Braemere Rd Boise ID 83702-1710 Office: Boise Cascade Corp PO Box 50 1 Jefferson Sq Boise ID 83728-0202

HARBAUGH, DANIEL PAUL, lawyer; b. Wendell, Idaho, May 18, 1948; s. Myron and Manuelita (Garcia) H. BA, Gonzaga U., 1970, JD, 1974. Bar: Washington 1974. Asst. atty. gen. State of Wash., Spokane, 1974-77; ptnr. Richter, Wimberley & Ericson, Spokane, 1977-83, Harbaugh & Bloom, P.S., Spokane, 1983—; bd. dirs. Spokane Legal Svcs., 1982-86; bd. govs. LAWPAC, Seattle, 1982-92. Bd. dirs. Spokane Ballet, 1983-88; chpt. dir. Les Amis du Vin, Spokane, 1985-88; mem. Spokane County Civil Svc. Commn., 1991—, Gonzaga U. Pres'. Coun., 1991—. Mem. ABA, Wash. State Bar Assn. (spl. dist. counsel 1982—, mem. com. rules for profl. conduct 1989-92), Spokane County Bar Assn., Wash. State Trial Lawyers Assn. (v.p. 1988-89, co-chair worker's compensation sect. 1992—), Am. Trial Lawyers Assn., Nat. Orgn. Social Security Claimants Reps., Internat. Wine & Food

Soc. (pres. local chpt. 1989-91), Alpha Sigma Nu, Phi Alpha Delta. Democrat. Roman Catholic. Clubs: Spokane, Spokane Country. Office: Harbaugh & Bloom PS N 9 Post Ste 210 Spokane WA 99201

HARBAUGH, JOHN WARVELLE, applied earth sciences educator; b. Madison, Wis., Aug. 6, 1926; s. Marion Dwight and Marjorie (Warvelle) H.; m. Josephine Taylor, Nov. 24, 1951 (dec. Dec. 25, 1985); children: Robert, Dwight, Richard. B.S., U. Kans.-Lawrence, 1948, M.S., 1950; Ph.D., U. Wis., 1955. Prodn. geologist Carter Oil Co., Tulsa, 1951-53; prof. applied earth sci. Stanford U., 1955—. Author: (with J.H. Doveton and J.C. Davis) Probability Methods in Oil Exploration, 1977, (with G. Bonham-Carter) Computer Simulation in Geology, 1981, (with D.M. Tetzlaff) Simulating Clastic Sedimentation, 1989. Recipient Haworth Disting. Alumni award U. Kans., 1968, Krumbein medal Internat. Assn. Math. Geologists, 1986. Fellow Geol. Soc. Am.; mem. Am. Assn. Petroleum Geologists (Levorsen award 1970, Disting. Svc. award 1987). Republican. Home: 683 Salvatierra St Stanford CA 94305-8539 Office: Stanford U Dept Applied Earth Scis 307 Mitchell Stanford CA 94305

HARBER, M(ICHAEL) ERIC, industrial engineer; b. Tulsa, Okla., Nov. 14, 1965; s. Charles C. and Joyce F. (Allen) H.; m. Alyson Kelley, Sept. 1, 1990. Student, Oxford U., 1987; BS in Indsl. Engring. and Mgmt., Stanford U., 1988. Cert. in systems integration. Rsch. asst. Amoco Rsch. Ctr., Tulsa, 1985; quality control and design asst. Nutter engring. divsn. Patterson-Kelly, Tulsa, 1986; indsl. engring. coop. intern space systems divsn. Gen. Dynamics, San Diego, 1987; indsl. engring. cons. Hewlett-Packard, Cupertino, Calif., 1988; mgmt. assoc., asst. mgr. backcards divsn. Citicorp, San Mateo, Calif., 1988-90; sr. mgmt. analyst El Camino Healthcare System, Mountain View, Calif., 1990—; co-chairperson, mentor program adv. bd. Silicon Valley Indsl. Engring., Sunnyvale, Calif., 1993—; mem. adv. task force Ergonomic-Repetive Strain Injury, Mountain View, 1993—; speaker in field. Recipient Engr.'s ring Order of Engr., 1993. Sr. mem. Inst. Indsl. Engrs. (chpt. pres. 1992-93); mem. NSPE, Am. Soc. Quality Control, Soc. Health Systems, Healthcare Info. Mgmt. Systems Soc., Soc. Engring. Mgmt. Systems, Calif. Soc. Profl. Engrs. Presbyterian. Home: 20800 Homestead Rd Cupertino CA 95014 Office: El Camino Healthcare System 2500 Grant Rd Mountain View CA 94039

HARBISON, JOHN ROBERT, management consultant; b. Phila., Mar. 1, 1953; s. Robert James III and Elizabeth (Thompson) H.; m. Renata Kawczynski, May 25, 1980; children: Peter, Robert. AB, Harvard U., 1975, MBA, 1980; MS, NYU, 1976. CPA, N.Y. Sr. acct. KPMG Peat Marwick, N.Y.C., 1975-78; v.p. Booz, Allen & Hamilton, L.A., 1980—; leader aerospace practice Booz, Allen & Hamilton, Bethesda, Md., 1990—, also bd. dirs. Contbr. articles to various publs. Home: 916 Via Panorama Palos Verdes Estates CA 90274 Office: Booz Allen & Hamilton 5220 Pacific Concourse Dr Los Angeles CA 90045

HARBORD, ANNE MARIE, consulting dietetics company executive; b. Detroit, Nov. 9, 1954; d. Lionel Joseph and Mary Ellen (Beaushaw) H.; m. Scott H. Reed, May 27, 1978 (div. Apr. 1980); m. Charles Bloom, June 18, 1988; children: Erica, Mark Alexander. BS in Dietetics, Mich. State U., 1976; MS Nutrition, Food Mgmt., Calif. Poly. U., 1985. Registered dietition, Calif. Clin. dietitian Saga Foods Co., Kalamazoo, 1976-78; cardiac dietition Anaheim (Calif.) Meml. Hosp., 1978; dir. dietary svcs. Care Enterprises, Orange, Calif., 1978-88; owner, mgr. Geriatric Nutrition Mgmt., Encinitas, Calif., 1988—; speaker in field; quality assurance cons. Health Care div. ARA Living Ctrs. and Retirement Homes, Verduga Hills, Calif., 1979. Pub. (continuing edn. prog.) Nutritional Problems in the Elderly; editor: Dietary Policy and Procedure Manual for Long-Term Care, 1984, Recipes Standardized for Long-Term Care, 1986. Calif. Dietetic Assn. grad. scholar, 1984. Mem. Am. Dietetic Assn., Calif. Assn. Health Facilities (chmn. cons. dietitian practice group 1981-85, treas. 1990-91), Am. Soc. Enteral and Parenteral Nutrition, San Diego Dietetic Assn. (edn. chmn. 1988-89, dist. rep. 1989-91). Roman Catholic. Home and Office: Geriatric Nutrition Mgmt 5027 Nighthawk Way Oceanside CA 92056

HARBOUR, JERRY LEE, human factors engineering manager, geologist; b. Everett, Wash., Mar. 31, 1949; s. Joe and Ione Marie (Nelson) H.; m. Pamela L. Weekley, May 28, 1988; children: Chris L., Megan M. BS, Western Wash. U., 1972; MS, Ea. Wash. U., 1976; PhD, Okla. State U., 1988. Cert. geologist. Mgr. Phillips Petroleum Co., Bartlesville, Okla., 1980-86; sr. scientist Idaho Nat. Engring. Lab., Idaho Falls, Idaho, 1988-90; mgr. EG&G Rocky Flats, Golden, Colo., 1990—. Contbr. articles to profl. jours. Named Outstanding Trainer, Royal Geol. Soc. of London, 1984; recipient NSPI Best Article of the Year award. Mem. Human Factors Soc., Nat. Soc. Performance and Instrn., Orgnl. Design and Mgmt., Phi Kappa Phi. Home: # 508 3100 Cherry Creek Dr S Denver CO 80209 Office: EG&G Rocky Flats PO Box 464 Golden CO 80402

HARCOURT, MICHAEL FRANKLIN, premier of Province of British Columbia; b. Edmonton, Alta., Can., Jan. 6, 1943; s. Frank Norman and Stella Louise (Good) H.; m. Mai-Gret Wibecke Salo, June 26, 1971; 1 son, Justen Michael. B.A., U. B.C., 1965, LL.B., 1968. Bar: B.C. 1969. Founder dir. Vancouver Community Legal Assistance Soc., 1969-71; partner firm Lew, Fraser & Harcourt, 1971-79; pres. Housing & Econ. Devel. Consulting Firm, Vancouver, from 1977; alderman City of Vancouver, 1972-80; mayor, 1980-86, mem. Legis. Assembly, 1986—, leader, New Dem. Party of British Columbia, 1987—, former leader of opposition, leader of govt.; asst. dir. Justice Devel. Commn., Vancouver; dir. Housing Corp. B.C. Mem. Law Soc. B.C. New Democrat. Mem. United Ch. Can. Office: Legislative Assembly, Parliament Bldgs, Victoria, BC Canada V8V 1X4

HARCOURT, ROBERT NEFF, educational administrator, journalist; b. East Orange, N.J., Oct. 19, 1932; s. Stanton Hinde and Mary Elizabeth (Neff) H. BA, Gettysburg Coll., 1958; MA, Columbia U., 1961. Cert. guidance, secondary edn., career and vocat. guidance, N.Mex. Social case worker N.J. State Bd. Child Welfare, Newark and Morristown, 1958-61; asst. registrar Hofstra U. and asst. to evening dean of students CCNY, 1961-62; housing staff U. Denver, 1962-64; fin. aid and placement dir. Inst. Am. Indian Arts, Santa Fe, 1965—; appointed by corp. pres. to adv. bd. Genre Ltd. Art Pubs., L.A., 1986—; nat. color ad participant The Bradford Exchange, Chgo., 1986—. Donor Am. Indian Library collection Gettysburg (Pa.) Coll. With U.S. Army, 1954-56; Ger. Named hon. Okie, Gov. Okla., 1970; decorated Nat. Def. medal; postmasters fellow U. Denver, 1962-64; col. a.d.c. to N.Mex. Gov. David F. Cargo, 1970. Mem. Am. Contract Bridge League (exec. bd. Santa Fe unit; life master), SAR, Santa Fe Council Internat. Relations, Am. Assn. Counseling and Devel., Internat. Platform Assn., Assn. Specialists in Group Work (charter), Adult Student Personnel Assn. (charter), Southwestern Assn. Indian Affairs, Phi Delta Kappa (past mem. exec. bd. local chpt.), Alpha Tau Omega, Alpha Phi Omega, Safari Club Internat. Home: 2980 Viaje Pavo Real Santa Fe NM 87505-5344 Office: Inst Am Indian Arts CSF Campus Santa Fe NM 87504

HARDAWAY, FRANCINE OLMAN, communications executive; b. N.Y.C., May 14, 1941; d. Chauncey Samuel and Sybil (Rosen) O.; m. John M. Hardaway (div. 1981); children: Samantha, Chelsea. BA, Cornell U., 1962; MA, Columbia U., 1963; PhD, Syracuse U., 1968. Prof. Maricopa Community Coll., Phoenix, 1968-79, Ariz. State U., Tempe, 1973-79; founder, chief exec. officer Hardaway Connections, Phoenix, 1980—; bd. dirs. Ctrl. Ariz. Shelter Svcs., Phoenix, Ariz. Small Bus. United, Phoenix, Ariz. Econ. Coun., Phoenix, Phoenix Pride Commn., 1991—, Ariz. Software Assn., 1991—, Phoenix Community Alliance, 1992—, Phoenix Local Devel. Corp., 1990—. Author: Thinking Into Writing, 1975, Creative Rhetoric, 1976, Writing Through Reading, 1976. Commr. Phoenix Sister Cities Commn., 1989—. Mem. Assn. Corp. Growth, Pub. Rels. Soc. Am., Valley Forward Assn. (exec. com. 1990—), Rotary Internat. Office: Hardaway Connections 40 N Central Ave Ste 410 Phoenix AZ 85004-4424

HARDAWAY, TIM (TIMOTHY DUANE HARDAWAY), basketball player; b. Chgo., Sept. 12, 1966. Student, U. Tex. at El Paso. With Golden State Warriors, 1989—. Named to NBA All-Rookie team, 1990, All-Star team, 1991, 92, 93. Office: care Golden State Warriors Oakland Coliseum Arena Oakland CA 94621

HARDEN, MARVIN, artist, educator; b. Austin, Tex.; s. Theodore R. and Ethel (Sneed) H. BA in Fine Arts, UCLA, 1959, MA in Creative Painting, 1963. Tchr. art Calif. State U., Northridge, 1968—, Santa Monica (Calif.) City Coll., 1968; mem. art faculty UCLA Extension, 1964-68; mem. visual arts fellowship/painting panel Nat. Endowment Arts, 1985. One-man shows include Ceeje Galleries, L.A., 1964, 66, 67, Occidental Coll., L.A., 1969, Whitney Mus. Am. Art, N.Y.C., 1971, Eugenia Butler Gallery, L.A., 1971, Irving Blum Gallery, L.A., 1972, Los Angeles Harbor Coll., 1972, David Stuart Galleries, L.A., 1975, Coll. Creative Studies, U. Calif., Santa Barbara, 1976, James Corcoran Gallery, L.A., 1978, Newport Harbor Art Mus., 1979, L.A. Mcpl. Art Gallery, 1982, Conejo Valley Art Mus., 1983, Simard Gallery, L.A., 1985; group shows include U.S. State Dept. Touring Exhbn., USSR, 1966, Oakland (Calif.) Mus. Art, 1966, UCLA, 1966, Mpls. Inst. Art, 1968, San Francisco Mus. Art, 1969, Phila. Civic Ctr. Mus., 1969, Mus. Art, R.I. Sch. Design, 1969, N.S. State Mus., 1969, Everson Mus. Art, Syracuse, 1969, La Jolla (Calif.) Mus., 1969, 70, High Mus. Art, Atlanta, 1969, Flint (Mich.) Inst. Arts, 1969, Ft. Worth Art Center Mus., 1969, Contemporary Arts Assn., Houston, 1970, U. N.Mex., 1974, U. So. Calif., 1975, Bklyn. Mus., 1976, Los Angeles County Mus. Art, 1977, Newport Harbor Art Mus., 1977, Frederick S. Wight Gallery, UCLA, 1978, Cirrus Editions, Ltd., L.A., 1979, Franklin Furnace, N.Y.C., 1980, Art Ctr. Coll. Design, L.A., 1981, Alternative Mus., N.Y.C., 1981, Laguna Beach Mus. (Calif.), 1982, L.A. Inst. Contemporary Art, 1982, Mus. Contemporary Art, Chgo., 1983, Mint Mus., Charlotte, N.C., 1983, DeCordova and Dana Mus. and Park, Lincoln, Mass., 1983, Equitable Gallery, N.Y.C., 1984, L.A. Municipal Art Gallery, 1984, 1985, Cirrus, L.A., 1986, 1990, Heal the Bay, Surfboard Art Invitational, 1990, Pasadena Armory Ctr. for the Arts, 1992, Claremont Coll. West Gallery, L.A., 1992; represented in permanent collections include Whitney Mus. Am. Art, N.Y.C., Mus. Modern Art, N.Y.C., N.Y. Pub. Libr. Spence Collection, Getty Ctr. for Arts and Humanities, Los Angeles County Mus. Art, Atlantic Richfield Co. Corp. Art Coll., Grunwald Ctr. Graphic Arts UCLA, City of Los Angeles, Metromedia, Inc., L.A., San Diego Jewish Community Center, Berkeley (Calif.) U. Mus., Home Savs. & Loan Assn., L.A., also pvt. collections. Bd. dirs. Images & Issues, 1980-86; mem. artists adv. bd. L.A. Mcpl. Art Gallery Assn., 1983-86. Recipient UCLA Art Council award, 1963, Disting. Prof. award Calif. State U. Northridge, 1984, Exceptional Merit Service award Calif. State U. Northridge, 1984; Nat. Endowment Arts fellow, 1972; awards in Visual Arts, 1983; Guggenheim fellow, 1983. Mem. L.A. Inst. Contemporary Art (co-founder 1972). Home: PO Box 1793 Cambria CA 93428-1793 Office: Calif State U Northridge 18111 Nordhoff St Northridge CA 91330-0001

HARDEN, PATRICK ALAN, journalist, news executive; b. Twickenham, Eng., Aug. 13, 1936; s. Ernest William and Annie Ceridwen (Jones) H.; m. Connie Marie Graham, Nov. 2, 1963; children: Marc Graham, Ceri Marie. Cert. in journalism, Ealing (Eng.) Tech. Coll., 1957. With UPI, 1960-78; regional exec. UPI, London, 1968-69; European picture mgr. UPI, London and Brussels, 1969-72; regional exec. UPI, Detroit, 1973-75; gen. mgr. UPI Can. Ltd., Montreal, 1976-78, UP Can., Toronto, 1979-82; dir., sec. UP Can., 1979-82; treas. UPI Can. Ltd.; gen. mgr. Edmonton (Alta.) Sun, 1982-84, pub., 1984-92; v.p. Toronto Sun Pub. Corp., 1989—; v.p., bur. chief Washington, 1992—. Mem. senate U. Alta. Recipient Merit award City of Edmonton, 1992. Mem. Can. Daily Newspapers Assn. (bd. dirs.), Edmonton C. of C. (bd. dirs.), , Edmonton Club (pres. 1991-92). Office: Ste 1271 National Press Bldg Washington DC 20045

HARDER, KELSIE T., artist, educator; b. Trenton, Tenn., Mar. 8, 1942; s. Kelsie Brown Harder and Geneva Lee (Tomlin) Carlson; m. Kumiko Tanaka, Oct. 2, 1991; children: Tsunami Tomlin and Tanaka Solomon (twins). Student, Claremont (Calif.) Men's Coll., 1960-61, Ventura (Calif.) Coll., 1961-62; BA, U. Nev., 1973-75. Artist self-employed, 1957-93; prof. Truckee Meadows C.C., Reno, 1978-93; chmn. art dept. Truckee Meadows C.C., 1982-91. Contbr. articles to profl. jours., mags., textbooks; numerous one-man shows; represented in over 100 collections. Recipient numerous regional and national awards. Office: Truckee Meadows CC 7000 Dandini Blvd Reno NV 89512-3999

HARDER, MICHAEL UPHAM, airline executive, pilot; b. Mt. Kisco, N.Y., Jan. 21, 1953; s. John Worthington and Joan Lewis (Hopkinson) H.; m. Nora Mary Kochanik, Sept. 20, 1981. Student, U. Wash., 1971-75, Seattle Community Coll., 1976-77. Pilot All Alaskan Seafoods, Inc., Kodiak, 1979, Yute Air Alaska, Inc., Dillingham, 1980-81, S.W. Airways, Inc., Dillingham, 1981-83, Armstrong Air Svc., Inc., Dillingham, 1983-84, Hermens Air, Inc., St. Marys and Bethel, Alaska, 1985; pilot, chief pilot MarkAir, Inc., Dillingham, 1985-87; pres., chief pilot, dir. ops. Starflite, Inc., Dillingham, 1987-. Mem. Dillingham City Planning Commn., 1985-87. Recipient Flight Safety award FAA, Dept. Transp., 1983. Mem. Alaska Air Carriers Assn. (safety award 1987), Alaska Aviation Safety Found. Democrat. Episcopalian. Home: PO Box 824 Dillingham AK 99576-0824 Office: Starflite Inc PO Box 824 Dillingham AK 99576-0824

HARDESTY, DONALD LYNN, anthropology educator; b. Terra Alta, W.Va., Sept. 2, 1941; s. Ezra J. and Mary A. (Jenkins) H.; m. Susan A. Bennett, Aug. 29, 1969. AB in Anthropology, U. Ky., 1964; MA in Anthropology, U. Oreg., Eugene, 1967, PhD in Anthropology, 1972. Prof. U. Nev., Reno, 1968—; pres. Soc. for Hist. Archaeology, 1987. Author: Ecological Anthropology, 1977, Archaeology of Mining, 1988; co-editor: Environment and Society, 1974. Home: 5000 Lakeridge Ter E Reno NV 89509

HARDGRAVE, PHIL, writer; b. Longview, Tex., July 14, 1950; s. E.J. Jr. and Mary C. (Roberts) H.; m. Stephanie Hardgrave, July 25, 1985; 1 child, Gregory. BS in Comm., U. Tex., 1972. Author: Landscape Gardens, 1990, Garden Soil, 1990, Landscape New Homes, 1991, Garden Fresh Tomatoes, 1992. Democrat. Home: PO Box 145 Forest Knolls CA 94933

HARDIE, GEORGE GRAHAM, casino executive; b. Cleve., Aug. 19, 1933; s. William M. and Helen (Graham) H.; children: George Graham Jr., Jennifer. With sales dept. Hardie Bros., Pitts., later various mgmt. positions, operator dist. sales agys.; owner, driver, trainer, racer standardbred horses, 1963—; owner, mgr. Profile, Inc., Bell Gardens, Calif., 1973—; mng. ptnr., gen. mgr. Bell Gardens Bicycle Club Casino, 1981—; mayor City of Cathedral City, Calif., 1988-90, mayor pro tem, 1990-92; owner, mgr. Profile Comm. Inc., 1990—, Nut Kettle Inc., 1990—; owner, mgr. investment and acquisitions co. Hardie Group, 1990—; owner Emerald Meadows Ranch, 1989—. Active community and civic affairs. Recipient Congl. award, 1987; commendation L.A. County Suprs., 1987, L.A. County Office Dist. Atty., 1987; resolution Calif. Senate, 1987, cert. of recognition City of Bell Gardens, 1987. Mem. Calif. Harness Drivers Guild (past pres.), Western Standardbred Assn. (past bd. dirs.), Golden State Greyhound Assn. (organizer, pres. 1973), Bell Gardens C. of C. (pres. 1986). Office: Bell Gardens Bicycle Club 7301 Eastern Ave Bell Gardens CA 90201

HARDING, ETHEL M., state legislator; b. Fishtail, Mont., Oct. 19, 1927; m. Warren Harding; 2 children. Student, Heald's Bus. Coll. Clk., recorder Lake County, Mont., 1967-84; owner, operator Mission Valley Concrete, 1967-84; rep. State of Mont., 1985-86, senator, 1987—. Republican. Mem. Ch. of Nazarene. Office: PO Box 251 Polson MT 59860-0251 also: Mt State Senate State Capitol Helena MT 59620

HARDING, KAREN ELAINE, chemistry educator and department chair; b. Atlanta, Sept. 5, 1949; d. Howard Everett and Ruth Evangeline (Lund) H.; m. Bruce Roy McDowell, Aug. 30, 1975. BS in Chemistry, U. Puget Sound, Tacoma, 1971; MS in Environ. Chemistry, U. Mich., 1972; postgrad., Evergreen State Coll., 1972, 84, Yale U., 1986, Columbia U., 1991. Chemist Environ. Health Lab., Inc., Farmington, Mich., 1972-73, U. Mich. Med. Sch., Ann Arbor, 1973-75; instr. chemistry Schoolcraft Coll., Livonia, Mich., 1975-77; chair chemistry dept. Pierce Coll., Tacoma, 1977—; adj. prof. U. Mich., Dearborn, 1974-77; instr. S.H. Alternative Learning Ctr., Tacoma, 1980-83, Elderhostel, Tacoma, 1985-89. Mem. County Solid Waste Adv. Com., Tacoma, 1989—, Superfund Adv. Com., Tacoma, 1985-89, Sierra Club, Wash., 1989—; mem., past pres. Adv. Com. Nature Ctr., Tacoma, 1981-87. Faculty Enhancement grantee Pierce Coll., 1990; recipient Nat. Teaching Excellence award, 1991. Mem. NW Assn. for Environ. Studies (treas. 1985—), Am. Chem. Soc., Ft. Steilacoom Running Club (race dir. 1986—). Office: Pierce Coll 9401 Farwest Dr SW Tacoma WA 98498-1999

HARDING, ROBERT EDWARD, JR., lawyer, arbitrator; b. Danville, Ky., May 31, 1927; s. Robert E. Sr. and Olivia (Napier) H.; m. Iola Willhite; children: Roberta, Olivia. BA, Ky. State U., 1954; JD, U. Ky., 1957. Bar: Ky. 1950, N.Mex. 1971, U.S. Supreme Ct. 1963. Corr. officer USPHS, Lexington, Ky., 1952-58; atty. NLRB, Washington, N.Y.C., 1958-74; adj. prof. U. N.Mex., Albuquerque, 1975-87; EEO cons. R.E. Harding, Jr., Atty.-at-Law, Albuquerque, 1980-86, arbitrator, 1981—. Pres. Albuquerque br. NAACP, 1971; pres. bd. dirs. Albuquerque Child Care Ctrs., 1980; vol. arbitrator Better Bus. Bur., Albuquerque, 1991; mem. N.Mex. Adv. Com., U.S. Commn. on Civil Rights, Washington, 1981. Cpl. U.S. Army, 1946-47. Recipient Cert. of Recognition The N.Mex. Regional Med. Program, 1976; named Arbitrator of the Yr. Better Bus. Bur., 1987; Cert. of Appreciation Toney Anaya, Gov. N.Mex., 1984, Sickle Cell Coun. of N.Mex., Inc., 1990, Women United for Youth, Inc., 1989. Mem. Nat. Bar Assn. (life), State Bar of N.Mex. (fellow 1988), Ky. Bar Assn., Albuquerque Bar Assn., N.Mex. Black Lawyers Assn., Soc. of Profls. in Dispute Resolution. Office: R E Harding Jr PO Box 14277 Albuquerque NM 87191

HARDING, WAYNE EDWARD, III, accountant; b. Topeka, Sept. 29, 1954; s. Wayne Edward and Nancy M. (Gean) H.; BS with honors in Bus. Adminstrn., U. Denver, 1976, MBA, 1983; m. Janet Mary O'Shaughnessy, Sept. 5, 1979 (div. Mar. 1985); m. Karen Ruttan, Oct. 10, 1987. Partner, HKG Assocs., Denver, 1976-77; staff auditor Peat, Marwick, Mitchell & Co., Denver, 1976-78; auditor Marshall Hornstein, P.C., Wheat Ridge, Colo., 1978-79; sr. auditor Touche Ross & Co., Denver, 1979-80; controller Mortgage Plus Inc., 1980-81; sec.-treas. Sunlight Systems Energy Corp., 1980-81; ptnr. Harding, Newman, Sobule & Thrush, Ltd., Denver, 1981-82; pvt. practice specializing in microcomputer applications and litigation support, 1982-89; acct., v.p. Great Plains Software, Fargo, N.D., also dir. CPA ptnr. rels.; founder Discount Computer Rentals, Inc., 1985; dir. Harding Transp., Harding Tech. Leasing, Crown Parking Products; lectr. to various profl. groups on computer tech. Class agt., mem. alumni council Phillips Exeter Acad., Exeter, N.H., 1973-83; bd. dirs., treas. Legal Center for Handicapped Citizens, Denver, 1979-80; vol. Denver Bridge, 1984-85. Mem. AICPA (instr.), Colo. Soc. CPAs (chmn. CPE com. 1987-89, instr.), Beta Alpha Psi, Pi Gamma Mu, Beta Gamma Sigma. Republican. Mem. editorial bd. Practical Acct. Mag.; contbr. articles in field of microcomputers to profl. jours. including Jour. Acctg. on Micro Computers. Home: 6029 S Kenton Way Englewood CO 80111-5727 Office: 6000 E Evans Ave Denver CO 80222-5406

HARDING, WILLIAM HARRY, writer; b. Paterson, N.J., Sept. 26, 1945. Student, Bucknell U., 1966; BS, Upsala Coll., 1968. Regular contbr. L.A. Times Book Rev., 1978-80; pres., chmn. Harding Enterprises, Inc., Fallbrook, Calif., 1978—; book critic Westways Mag., L.A., 1980-88; sports editor The Californian Newspaper, Temecula, Calif., 1986-90; cons. Rancho Damacitas Child Care Agy., Temecula, 1990—. Author: (novels) Rainbow, 1979, Young Hart, 1983 (N.J. Inst. Tech. award 1984), Mill Song, 1985, (children's novel) Alvin's Famous No-Horse, 1992, (screenplay) The Shadow Hills, 1992. Founder Temecula Valley Little League, 1980; v.p. Rainbow (Calif.) Property Owners Assn., 1990-92, pres., 1992—; assoc. baseball coach Linfield High Sch., Temecula, 1991—; mem. sch. bd. Vallecitos, 1992—. Lt. USN, 1968-74, Vietnam. Decorated Air medal (21), Navy medal of commendation for valor. Mem. Authors Guild Am., Writers Guild Am. West. Office: Harding Enterprises Inc 1953 Huffstatler St Fallbrook CA 92028

HARDISON, ROY LEWIS, marketing professional; b. Brea, Calif., Sept. 5, 1929; s. Arthur Abbott and Norma Doris (Lovering) H.; m. Frances Lucille Jacobsen, Aug. 21, 1949; children: Martin Arthur, Bradley Lewis, Steven Dean. BS in Econ. Entom., U. Calif., Berkeley, 1951. With sales Calif. Spray Chem., Modesto, 1951-59; asst. br. mgr. Chevron Chem. Co. (formerly Calif. Spray Chem.), Lindsay, Calif., 1960-61; br. mgr. Chevron Chem. Co. (formerly Calif. Spray Chem.), Yuba City, Calif., 1962-67; asst. dist. mgr. Chevron Chem. Co. (formerly Calif. Spray Chem.), Woodland, Calif., 1968-70; dist. mktg. specialist Chevron Chem. Co. (formerly Calif. Spray Chem.), Modesto, Calif., 1970-73; cen. coast dist. rep. Chevron Chem. Co. (formerly Calif. Spray Chem.), Salinas, Calif., 1973-75; mgr. East Asia Chevron Chem. Internat., Inc., Tokyo, 1976-84; prod. prom. specialist Chev. Chem. Co., Fresno, Calif., 1984-86; with regulatory affairs Moyer Products, Inc., Fresno, 1987-92; tech./market devel. profl. Best Sulfur Products Inc., Fresno, Calif., 1992—. Mem. Lions (sec., pres. 1954—). Republican. Presbyterian. Home: 7332 N Pacific Ave Fresno CA 93711-0571 Office: Best Sulfur Products Inc 5427 E Central Ave Fresno CA 93725

HARDISTY, DONALD MERTZ, music educator; b. Butte, Mont., Feb. 24, 1932; m. Barbara B. Hardisty; 2 children. BME with honors, U. Mont., MusM in Edn., 1956; DMA, U. Rochester, N.Y., 1969. Instr. in bassoon and theory U. Ariz., Tucson; assoc. dir. choral activities, prin. bassoonist Tucson Symphony; dir. bands Calif. State U., Chico; assoc. prof. N.Mex. State U., Las Cruces, 1969-79, prof., chmn. theory and grad. music edn., 1979—; owner Don's Collectibles, Las Cruces; guest condr. and clinician, author, composer in music. Prin. bassoonist Las Cruces Symphony; restoration artist for Bossons (Congleton, Eng.) and Hummel artware; owner Don's Collectibles. Mem. Assn. of Composers and Pubs. of Am., Nat. Alliance for Arts in Edn., Nat. Assn. Col. Wind and Percussion Instrs., Music Tchrs. Nat. Assn., Music Educators Nat. Conf., Internat. Double Reed Soc., Assn. Concert Bands of Am. and Abroad Inc. (past pres., exec. sec., treas. 1987-92). Home: 3020 Majestic Ridge Las Cruces NM 88001-4639

HARDISTY, HUNTINGTON, naval commander. Comdr. in chief U.S. Pacific Command Camp H.M. Smith Hi. Office: Comdr in Chief US Pacific Command Camp Smith HI 96861

HARDISTY, TERESA KARNITSCHNIG, physician; b. Cambridge, Eng., May 29, 1960; came to U.S., 1960; d. Heinz Helmut and Ann Russell (Gaddum) Karnitschnig; m. John Thomas Hardisty, Jan. 17, 1980; children: Huntington, John Nicholas, Sarah Ann. BA in Biochemistry and Biology summa cum laude, U. Calif., San Diego, 1982, MD, 1986. Cert. in pediatric advanced life support. Resident in pediatrics U. Calif. San Diego, La Jolla, 1986-89, chief resident in pediatrics, 1989-90; pediatric cons. Patient Care Med. Group Balboa Naval Hosp., San Diego, 1990-91; pediatrician Sharp Rees Stealy Med. Group, San Diego, 1991—. Republican. Episcopalian. Office: Sharp Rees-Stealy Pediatrics 7808 El Cajon Blvd Ste J La Mesa CA 91941

HARDWAY, JAMES EDWARD, rehabilitation management facilty administrator; b. Pueblo, Colo., Nov. 26, 1944; s. William Jeremiah and Margaret Ann (Rinker) H.; m. Mary Frances Walker, Sept. 9, 1967; children: Tina Marie, Catherine Ann, William James. BA, U. So. Colo., 1969; MS, U. Wis.-Stout, Menomonie, 1971; postgrad., U. Toledo, 1972—. Cert. vocat. evaluator, work adjustment specialist; lic. nursing home adminstr., Wyo. Counselor Pueblo (Colo.) Diversified Industries, 1969-70; vocat. evaluator Penta County Vocat. Schs., Perrysburg, Ohio, 1971-82; dept. mgr. Magic City Enterprises, Cheyenne, Wyo., 1982-88; case mgr. Profl. Rehab. Mgmt., Cheyenne, 1989-91, regional mgr., 1992—; speaker State of Ohio Spl. Needs Conf., Ohio, 1972-80; cons. Wyo. State Tng. Sch., Lander, 1977. Pres. bd. dirs. Laramie County Community Action, Cheyenne; bd. dirs. Handicapped Employment Agy., Cheyenne, Wyo. Alzheimer's Assn. With U.S. Army, 1964-65. Mem. Kiwanis (bd. dirs.). Home: 12309 White Eagle Rd Cheyenne WY 82009

HARDWICK, GARY CLIFFORD, lawyer; b. Detroit, May 4, 1960; s. Willie Steve and Mary Louise (Dixon) H.; m. Susan Annette Hall, July 2, 1988; 1 child, Bailey Alexander. BA, U. Mich., 1982; JD, Wayne State U., 1985. Bar: Mich. 1985, U.S. Dist. Ct. (ea. dist.) Mich. 1985. Law clk. to presiding justice U.S. Bankruptcy Ct. for Ea. Dist. Mich., Detroit, 1985-87; atty. Mich. Consol. Gas Co., Detroit, 1988-90; asst. U.S. trustee U.S. Dept. Justice, L.A., 1990—. Author poetry. Mich. competition scholar, 1978-82, Antoz scholar, 1982. Mem. ABA, Mich. Bar Assn., Calif. Bar Assn., Wolverine County Bar Assn., Assn. Corp. Counsel. Baptist. Office: 221 S Figueroa Ste 800 Los Angeles CA 90012

HARDWICK, WILLIAM ROBERT, mining engineer; b. Phoenix, Mar. 30, 1907; s. William and Exilda May (Hocken) H.; m. Adda Jane Giroux, Dec. 23, 1939. Student, U. Ariz., 1928-35. Asst. mining engr., chemist, mine engr. Phelps Dodge Corp., 1935-42, 47; devel. engr. Kennecott Copper

Corp., Ray, Ariz., 1948-50, cons. engr., 1950-51; field engr. Sterns-Roger Mfg. Co., Silver Bell, Ariz., 1951-52; mineral exam. and devel. engr. U.S. Bur. Mines, Tucson, 1953-57, mining methods research engr., 1957-60, project leader div. mineral resources, 1961-62, project leader application of nuclear explosives to mining, 1963-72. Contbr. numerous articles on mining methods, costs. Capt. ordnance U.S. Army, 1942-46. Mem. Ariz. Geol. Soc., N.Mex. Geol. Soc., Ariz. Pioneer Hist. Soc., Am. Legion, Theta Tau, Elks. Democrat. Episcopalian. Home: 1802 E Spring St Tucson AZ 85719-3335 Office: 1722 E Copper St Tucson AZ 85719-3118

HARDY, BEN(SON B.), orchid nursery executive; b. Oakland, Calif., Nov. 22, 1920; s. Lester William and Irene Isabell (Bliss) H.; student pub. schs., Oakland, Calif., Concord, Calif.; grad. photo Intelligence Sch., Denver, 1949. Served as enlisted man U.S. Navy, 1942-48; joined USAF, 1948, advanced through grades to capt., 1957; with 67th Reconnaisance Squadron, Korea, 1951-52, Hdqrs. Squadron, Thule AFB, 1956, resigned, 1957; material requirements analyst-coord. Teledyne Ryan Aero. Co., San Diego, 1958-73, 83—; dispatcher-coord. Cubic Western Data Co., San Diego, 1977-80; owner-ptnr. orchid nursery. Pres. Exotic Plant Soc., 1976-78, 81-84, San Diego Gesneriad Soc., 1978; dir. 23d Western Orchid Congress, 1979. Decorated Bronze Star; recipient Letter of Commendation NASA, also others. Mem. Am. Orchid Soc. (life), N.Z. Orchid Soc., San Diego County Orchid Soc. (life, pres. 1972-73, 75-76), Pacific Orchid Soc. Hawaii, Hoya Soc. Internat. (pres. 1981-83), Cymbidium Soc. Am., Orchid Digest Corp., Auckland Orchid Club, Orchid Badge Club Internat. (found. 1988, pres. 1991—). Home: 9443 E Heaney Cir Santee CA 92071-2919

HARDY, CHARLES EXTER, III, minister; b. Atlanta, Dec. 22, 1960; s. Charles Exter Jr. and Loretta (Westmoreland) H.; m. Claudia Gail Barton, Jan. 11, 1986; children: Lauren Nicole, Charles Exter IV. BS in Agr., U. Tenn., 1982; MDiv, Golden Gate Sem., 1987. Youth minister Stock Creek Bapt. Ch., Knoxville, Tenn., 1981-82, Cen. Bapt. Ch., Waycross, Ga., 1982-83, Rollingwood Bapt. Ch., San Pablo, Calif., 1983-84; minister to deaf El Camino Bapt. Ch., Sacramento, 1984; youth min. Narwee (N.S.W. Australia) Bapt. Ch., 1985; asst. pastor First Bapt. Ch., El Sobrante, Calif., 1986-87; pastor First Bapt. Ch., Winters, Calif., 1987-90, First So. Bapt. Ch., Davis, Calif., 1991—; participator mission trips to Indonesia, 1986, Jamaica, 1988, Ecuador, 1990, Argentina, 1992. Author: (play) Cheap Show, 1990. Mem. Winters (Calif.) Ministerial Assn. (pres. 1989-90). Home: 2650 Belmont Dr Davis CA 95616-1539

HARDY, CHARLES LEACH, federal judge; b. L.A., Jan. 24, 1919; s. Charles Little and Dorothy (Leach) H.; m. Jean McRae, Jan. 26, 1947; children: Charles M., Caroline, Catherine, John L. Julianne, Eileen, Sterling A., Steven W., Janette. BS, U. Ariz., 1947, LLB, 1950. Bar: Ariz. 1949. Pvt. practice Phoenix, 1949-66; dep. county atty. Maricopa County, Ariz., 1952-55; asst. atty. gen. State of Ariz., 1956-59; judge Ariz. Superior Ct., 1966-80; U.S. dist. judge Ariz. Dist., Phoenix, 1980—. Pres. Young Democratic Clubs Ariz., 1956-57, nat. committeeman, 1957-58; chmn. Maricopa County Dem. Cen. Com., 1958-59; mem. Ariz. Bd. Crippled Children's Services, 1965. Served with F.A. AUS, 1941-45. Decorated Bronze Star. Mem. ABA, Am. Judicature Soc., State Bar Ariz., Maricopa County Bar Assn. Mem. LDS Ch. Office: US Dist Ct US Courthouse & Fed Bldg 230 N 1st Ave Ste 6031 Phoenix AZ 85025-0005

HARDY, DONALD MCCOY, JR., utility development company executive; b. Baton Rouge, Apr. 14, 1944; s. Donald McCoy and Effie Hardy; m. Marilyn Jones, May 29, 1965; children: Christopher, Jennifer, Leah. BS, La. State U., 1966; MS, Rice U., 1970, PhD, 1970. Rsch. physicist Lawrence Livermore (Calif.) Lab., 1972-77, Solar Engery Rsch. Inst., Golden, Colo., 1977-78; exec. v.p. PanAero Corp., Lakewood, Colo., 1979-81; chmn., pres. PanAero Corp., Lakewood, 1981—. Contbr. articles to profl. jours. Postdoctoral fellowship Nat. Ctr. Atmospheric Rsch., 1971. Mem. Am. Wind Energy Assn., Am. Phys. Soc., N.Y. Acad. Scis., Sigma Xi, Sigma Pi Sigma, Pi Mu Epsilon. Office: PanAero Corp 200 Union Blvd Ste 317 Lakewood CO 80228-1831

HARDY, DUANE HORACE, federal agency administrator, educator; b. Ogden, Utah, June 8, 1931; s. Willis and Julia Mary (Garder) H.; m. Janet Myrnel Slater, Aug. 3, 1951; children: Rochelle Anne Leishman, Leslie Kaye Woolston, Kathy Korinne Davis. AA, Weber State Coll., 1951. Cert. EEO investigator/counselor. Ordained Mormon bishop, 1987. Enlisted U.S. Army, 1951, advanced through grades to lt. col., 1967, ret., 1971; EEO investigator U.S. Postal Svc., San Bruno, Calif., 1978—, EEO instr., 1982—. Mem. EEO civic council, Salt Lake City, 1978—. Republican. Mormon. Lodge: Kiwanis. Home: 120 W 5200 S Ogden UT 84405-6627 Office: US Postal Svc 3680 Pacific Ave Ogden UT 84401-9998

HARDY, ERWIN, entrepreneur, inventor; b. Winter Garden, Fla., Nov. 21, 1964; s. James and Ethel (Brown) H.; 1 child, Erwin II. BS in Bus. Administrn., Bethune-Cookman Coll., Daytona Beach, Fla., 1988; MBA, Nat. U., San Diego, 1992. Computer lab. asst. Bethune-Cookman Coll., 1984-88; mgr. trainee Family Bargain Ctr., San Diego, 1990-91; chief exec. officer Creid, Inc., San Diego, 1991—. Inventor high-tech. products. With USN, 1988-90. Home: 1329 3rd Ave # 171 Chula Vista CA 91911

HARDY, GORDON ALFRED, music educator, music school president; b. Hudson, Ind., Aug. 18, 1918; s. Carl Alfred and Gayle (Pike) H.; m. Lillian Studebaker, May 19, 1945; children—John Studebaker, Christopher Bartlett, Susan, Jeffrey Pike. B.A., B.Mus., U. Mich., 1941, M.Mus., 1946; B.S., Juilliard Sch. Music, 1952. Teaching fellow Juilliard Sch. Music, 1952-53, teaching asst., 1953-54, mem. faculty lit. and materials of music dept., 1954—, asso. dean, 1963-69, dean students, 1970-76; dean Aspen (Colo.) Music Sch., 1963-66, exec. v.p., 1966-75, pres., 1976-89, pres. emeritus, 1990—. Author: (with Arnold Fish) Music Literature-A Workbook for Analysis, vol. I, Homophony, 1963, vol. II, Polyphony, 1966. Bd. dirs. Juilliard Repertory Project, 1968, Juilliard Inst. Spl. Studies, 1969. Served to lt. USNR, 1942-45. Mem. Theta Chi. Home: 149 E 73rd St New York NY 10021-3555

HARDY, LEROY CLYDE, political science educator, consultant; b. Welch, Okla., Mar. 29, 1927; s. Howard Lee and Pearl Irene (Headley) H. BA, U. Calif., Santa Barbara, 1946-49; PhD, UCLA, 1955. Lectr. polit. sci. Calif. State U., Long Beach, 1953-55, asst. prof., 1955-58, assoc. prof., 1958-63, prof., 1963—; sr. rsch. assoc. Claremont (Calif.) McKenna Coll., 1980, 87—, vis. prof., 1991; cons. Calif. Assembly on Redistricting, 1960-61, Calif. Gov. re: Senate Reapportionment, 1964-65, Calif. Congrl. Del., 1965, 67, 69-73, 80-81; vis. prof. U. Calif., Santa Barbara, 1962, UCLA, 1964-65. Author: California Government, 1964, 4th edit., 1973; co-author: Politics in California, 1965; author, co-author (monographs) Redistricting Series, 1989-91; editor: Reapportionment Politics in 50 States, 1980, Redistricting Politics in 50 States, 1992, Bibliography on Representation and Redistricting, 1992. With USN, 1945-46. Rsch. grantee Haynes Found., 1952-53, 89-90, 91-92. Mem. Am. Polit. Sci. Assn., Western Polit. Sci. Assn., So. Polit. Sci. Assn., Midwestern Polit. Sci. Dept. Democrat. Methodist. Home: 1800 Fanwood Ave Long Beach CA 90815-4511 Office: Calif State U 1250 Bellflower Blvd Long Beach CA 90840

HARDY, LOIS LYNN, educational seminar training company executive; b. Seattle, Aug. 20, 1928; d. Stanley Milton and Helen Berniece (Conner) Croonquist; m. John Weston Hardy, July 29, 1951 (div. 1974); children: Sarah Lynn, Laura Lynn; m. Joseph Freeman Smith, Jr., Apr. 18, 1981; stepchildren: Nancy Smith Willis, Martha Smith Dahlquist. BA, Stanford U., 1950, MA, 1952; postgrad., U. Calif., Berkeley, 1957-78, U. San Francisco, 1978-81. Cert. life secondary tchr., life counselor, adminstr., Calif.; lic. career and ednl. counselor, Calif. Tchr., counselor Eastside Union High Sch. Dist., San Jose, Calif., 1951-55; dir. Lois Lynn Hardy Music Studio, Danville, Calif., 1955-69; high sch. tchr. San Ramon Unified Sch. Dist., Danville, 1969-71, counselor, 1971-83; dir. Growth Dynamics Inst., Alamo, Calif., 1976—; instr. Fresno (Calif.) Pacific Coll., 1976-79, Dominican Coll., San Rafael, Calif., 1979—; cons., trainer Personal Dynamics Inst., Mpls., 1976—, Performax Internat., Mpls., 1979—, San Jose Unified Sch. Dist., 1986-86, Novato (Calif.) Unified Sch. Dist., 1985-86, IBM, San Francisco, 1984, corp. and ednl. cons., 1951—. Author: How To Study in High School, 1952, 3d edit., 1973; (with B. Santa) How To Use the Library, 1954; How To Learn Faster and Succeed: A How to Study Workbook For Grades 1-14, 1982, rev., 1985; author various seminars; contbr. numerous articles to profl. jours. Choir dir., organist Community Presbyn. Ch., Danville, 1966-68, elder, 1974-75; speaker to numerous orgns., 1955—. Named Musician of Yr., Contra Costa County, 1978, Counselor of Yr., No. Calif. Personnel and Guidance Assn., 1980; Olive S. Lathrop scholar, 1948, AAUW scholar, 1950; recipient Colonial Dames prize in Am. History, 1950. Mem. Am. Assn. Counseling and Devel., Calif. Assn. Counseling and Devel., Calif. Tchrs. Assn., Calif. Career Guidance Assn., Nat. Speakers Assn., Am. Guild Organists, Stanford U. Alumni Assn., Calif. Assn. for the Gifted, Delta Zeta. Democrat. Presbyterian. Office: Growth Dynamics Inst PO Box 1053 Alamo CA 94507-7053

HARDY, MARK RICHARD, college official, marriage counselor, clergyman; b. McCloud, Calif., Sept. 5, 1957; s. Richard Earl and Joann (Hall) H.; m. Julie Dee Smith, Aug. 29, 1982; children: Jessica, John. BS in Youth Ministry, Liberty U., Lynchburg, Va., 1981; MA in Counseling, Grace Theol. Sem., Winona Lake, Ind., 1987; postgrad., The Master's Sem., L.A., 1988-92. Commd. minister Community-Bible Ch., 1981. Assoc. pastor Coeur d'Alene (Idaho) Bible Ch., 1981-86; dean ministry The Master's Coll., L.A., 1988-89, dean pastoral care, 1989, dir. off-campus ministries, 1989-92; dir. Ctr. Biblical Counseling, Coeur d'Alene, Idaho, 1992—; marriage and family counselor Ctr. Bibl. Counseling, Simi Valley, Calif., 1989-92; interim pastor Carlin Bay (Idaho) Community Ch., 1983-84. Author: The Life and Time Management System, 1984. Bd. dirs. Spokane (Wash.) Bible Coll. (now Moody Northwest), 1984-86, 93—. Republican. Home: 3015 N 4th Apt # 39 Coeur d'Alene ID 83814 Office: Ctr Biblical Counseling 901 Best Ave Coeur D Alene ID 83814

HARDY, MAX LEE, professional society administrator; b. Alva, Okla., Sept. 30, 1932; s. Lee and Belva Marie (Marsh) H.; m. Dorothy Rausler Alger, 1961 (div.); m. Mary Elizabeth Arp Senti, Dec. 21, 1981; 1 child, Bennett Lee. BM, Roosevelt U., 1953, M in Music, 1959. Fgn. circulation mgr. Playboy Mag., Chgo., 1956-60; mem. faculty L.A. Conservatory Music, 1960-69, Calif. Inst. Arts, L.A., 1960-69; assoc. nat. tournament dir. Am. Contract Bridge League, Las Vegas, 1973—. Author: Five Card Majors-Western Style, 1974, Two Over One Game Force, 1981, rev. edit., 1990, Splinters and Other Shortness Bids, 1987; assoc. editor Popular Bridge Mag., 1964—; founding editor L.A. County Bridge News, 1964-69. With U.S. Army, 1954-56. Republican. Home and Office: Box 28219 Las Vegas NV 89126-2219

HARDY, ROBERT EUGENE, broadcast educator; b. Monroe County, Ind., Oct. 17, 1926; s. Alfred McMean and Nota Montana (Stanger) H.; m. Mary Margaret Wise (div. 1954); children: Steven Van, Timothy Dow; m. Betty Joan Hodgin, May 6, 1954; children: Cheri Lynn, Melodi Jo. AAS, Ariz. Western Coll., 1972; BS, No. Ariz. U., 1976. Cert. Meth. lay speaker. Announcer various radio stas. Ind., 1945-51; announcer, projectionist, audio control, producer-dir. Sta. WTTV-TV, Bloomington, Ind., 1951-57; performer Profl. Entertainment Br. U.S. Army, Honolulu, Japan, Korea, Germany, 1957-59; producer, dir., ops. dir., booth announcer, performer Sta. WTVP-TV, Decatur, Ill., 1959-60; gen. mgr., program dir, copywriter, disc jockey Sta. WITE, Brazil, Ind., 1960-61; program dir., staff announcer, copywriter Sta. KATO, Safford, Ariz., 1962-63; gen. mgr. Sta. KAKA, Wickenburg, Ariz., 1963-64; ops. dir. Sta. KIVA-TV, Yuma, Ariz., 1964-70; dir. broadcasting radio Ariz. Western Coll., Yuma, 1970—; creator music show Hayloft Frolic, toured with Grand Ole' Opry, 1953; presenter Country Boy Concerts, 1967—; apptd. Ariz. Gov.'s Motion Picture Adv. Bd., 1978. Recorded 5 albums; actor (plays) Ah Wilderness, 1968, Look Homeward Angel, 1969, Odd Couple, 1970; (films) Zavala, 1970, The Animal, 1971, Night of the Lepus, 1972; (TV films) Bearcats, 1971, Petrocelli, 1974. Mem. SAG, Am. Fedn. Musicians. Home: 1321 W 8th Ave Yuma AZ 85364-4571 Office: Ariz Western Coll PO Box 929 Yuma AZ 85366-0929

HARDY, STEPHEN FRANCIS, dentist; b. Buffalo, Feb. 18, 1955; s. Ralph Ronald and Kathrine Marie (Minahan) H.; m. Vicki Lynn Nelson, Aug. 5, 1977; 1 child, Patrick Stephen. AS, Grossmont Coll., El Cajon, Calif., 1979; BS in Biology, San Diego State U., 1982; DMD, Temple U., 1986. Lic. dentist Ariz., Pa. Assoc. David Tagge, D.D.S., Escondido, Calif., 1986-87, Craig Myrmel D.D.S., Phoenix, 1988-89; pvt. practice Phoenix, 1989—; cons. Sion Tech., Denver, 1989—, Cottrel Dental, London, 1990, Ash-Temple Dental Supply, Toronto, Ont., 1990-91. With USN, 1972-75. Mem. Am. Dental Assn. Office: 13650 N 19th Ave Phoenix AZ 85029

HARDY, WAYNE RUSSELL, insurance broker; b. Denver, Sept. 5, 1931; s. Russell Hinton and Victoria Katherine (Anderson) H.; m. Carolyn Lucille Carvell, Aug. 1, 1958 (July 1977); children: James Russell Hardy, Jann Miller Hardy. BSCE, U. Colo., 1954; MS in Fin. Svcs., Am. Coll., 1989. CLU; ChFC. Western dist. mgr. Fenestra, Inc., San Francisco, 1956-63; ins. and investment broker John Hancock Fin. Svs., Denver, 1963—; Wayne R. Hardy Assocs., Denver, 1963—; speaker convs. and sales seminar, 1977, 81, 84, 85, 89; chmn. John Hancock Agt.'s Adv. Com., 1983-84. Chmn. Colo. Coun. Camera Clubs, Denver, 1962; bd. dirs. Porter Charitable Found., Denver, 1983-85; deacon, class pres. South Broadway Christian Ch., 1961-65; mem. Denver Art Mus., Denver Botanic Gardens, Rocky Mountain Estate Planning Coun., Alliance Francaise. Capt. U.S. Army, 1954-56. Mem. Am. Soc. CLU and ChFC (pres. Rocky Mountain chpt. 1990-91), Nat. Assn. Life Underwriters (pres. Denver chpt. 1983-84, Nat. Quality award 1968), Nat. Football Found. (bd. dirs. Denver chpt. 1992—), Million Dollar Round Table (life), U. Colo. Alumni (bd. dirs. 1990-92), U. Colo. Alumni C Club (bd. dirs. 1972-74), Univ. Club, Greenwood Athletic Club, Village Tennis Club, Rocky Mountain Optimist Club (pres. 1984-85). Republican. Home: 6178 E Hinsdale Ct Englewood CO 80112 Office: Ste 935 621 17th St Denver CO 80293

HARELSON, HUGH, magazine publisher; b. Phoenix, Oct. 25, 1930; s. C. L. and Frances (Gilbert) H.; m. Dorothy Jan Dedman, Aug. 24, 1957; children—Matthew, Scott. B.A., U. Ariz., 1952. News editor Bisbee Daily Rev., Ariz., 1955-56; writer, editor Ariz. Republic, Phoenix, 1956-70; news editor Scottsdale Daily Progress, Ariz., 1961-62; news. dir. Sta. KTAR-TV subs. NBC, Phoenix, 1970-73; dir. info. services U. Ariz., 1973-81, exec. dir. univ. relations, 1981-82; pub. Ariz. Hwys. Mag., Ariz. Dept. Transp., Phoenix, 1982—; v.p., bd. dirs. Ariz. Nature Conservancy; bd. dirs. Walter Cronkite Ctr. for Telecommunications and Journalism. Past pres. Vol. Bur Maricopa County. Served to 1st lt. U.S. Army, 1952-54. Mem. Ariz. Acad., U. Ariz. Alumni Assn. (past pres.). Republican. Methodist. Home: 1011 W Coronado Rd Phoenix AZ 85007-1760 Office: Ariz Hwys Mag 2039 W Lewis Ave Phoenix AZ 85009-2893

HARGIS, JOSEPH PAUL, retired police detective, systems analyst; b. Chgo., Jan. 10, 1948; s. Ira Clair and Geraldine Marie (Kelley) H.; m. Maria Luisa Morales, Apr. 3, 1981; adopted children: Gena Marie Ursua, James Paul Ursua. BS in Computer Info. Systems, Calif. State U., L.A., 1991, postgrad., 1991—. Officer L.A. Police Dept., 1969-78, detective, 1979-87, detective supr., 1987-91, supr., info systems unit, gang info. sect., 1988-91, retired, 1991; mem. Gang Reporting Evaluation and Tracking System com., Calif. Dept. Justice, L.A., 1989-91. Sgt. U.S. Army, 1966-69, Vietnam. Mem. Math. Assn. Am., LAPALS (Paradox Users Group), ABACUS Computer Soc., Beta Gamma Sigma, Phi Kappa Phi, Golden Key Honor Soc. Office: PO Box 4036 Diamond Bar CA 91765-0036

HARGISS, JAMES LEONARD, ophthalmologist; b. Manhattan, Kans., June 15, 1921; s. Meade Thomas and Julia Baldwin (Wayland) H.; m. Helen Natalie Berglund, July 19, 1947; children: Phillip M., Craig T., D. Reid. BS, U. Wash., 1942; MD, St. Louis U., 1945; MSc in Medicine, U. Pa., 1952. Diplomate Nat. Bd. Med. Examiners, Am. Bd. Ophthalmology. Intern U.S. Naval Hosp., PSNS Bremerton, Washington, 1945-46; resident physician G.E. Geisinger Meml. Hosp. and Foss Clinic, Danville, Pa., 1949-51; practice medicine specializing in ophthalmic surgery Seattle, 1951-58; ophthalmic surgeon Eye Clinic of Seattle, 1958—, pres., 1962-91, chief exec. officer, 1985-91; asst. clin. instr. U. Wash. Sch. Medicine, 1958—. Contbr. chapter to book, 1987, articles to Ophthalmology, 1964-80. Dist. chmn. King County Rep. Cen. Com., 1962-70. Served as physician/surgeon with USNR, 1945-48. Recipient Citation of Merit Washington State Med. Assn., 1959, Cert. of Award Am. Acad. Ophthalmology and Otolaryngology, 1975; Wendell F. Hughes fellow, 1960. Fellow AMA (Cert. of award 1960), Am. Coll. Surgeons, Am. Acad. Ophthalmology (honor award), Am. Soc. Ophthalmic Plastic and Reconstructive Surgery (charter) (Lester T. Jones award 1979), De Bourg Soc. of St. Louis U., Lions (Lake City pres. 1960-61), Alpha Omega Alpha. Office: Eye Clinic of Seattle 1601 16th Ave Seattle WA 98122-4098

HARGRAVE, ROBERT, family counselor, mayor; b. L.A., Mar. 1, 1938; s. Thomas Kenneth and Julia (Becker) H.; m. Gloria Eileen Smith, June 16, 1962; children: Margaret, Thomas, James. BA in English, Loyola U., L.A., 1960; postgrad., U. Chgo., 1960-61; MS, Calif. State U., Carson, 1988. Lic. marriage, family and child counselor, Calif. Tchr. St. John Vianney High Sch., L.A., 1961-63; mgr. Pacific Tel., L.A., 1963-85; counselor Family Svc. Long Beach, Calif., 1987-91, program dir., 1991—; mayor City of Lomita, Calif., 1987-88, 91-92; drug educator Calif. State U., Carson, 1988-90. Mem. traffic commn. City of Lomita, Calif., 1970-73, planning com., 1973-83, mem. coun., 1983—, mayor, 1987, 91. Republican. Roman Catholic. Home: 25925 Cypress St Lomita CA 90717-2903 Office: Bob Hargrave PO Box 1505 Lomita CA 90717-5505

HARGREAVES-FITZSIMMONS, KAREN ANN, painter, illustrator; b. Highland Park, Mich., July 19, 1945; d. Richard Hollowell and Belle Helen (Edson) Hargreaves; m. Thomas Fitzsimmons, Mar. 20, 1978. BA, Oakland U., 1967; MA, U. Mich., 1971. Counselor Mich. State Employment Commn., Detroit, 1969-73; art dir. Katydid Prodns., Santa Fe, 1973—; instr. Ann. Sumi-e Lecture/demonstrations, Oakland U., Mich., 1984-88, Corpus Christi Coll., Oxford U., Eng., 1985, Ctr. for Creative Studies, Detroit, 1986. Two-woman show includes Hakumon Internat. Festival of Arts, Toyko, 1974; one-woman shows include Am. Cultural Ctr., Tokyo, 1974, Tokyodo Bunka Salon, 1983, Genkan Gallery, Toyko, 1984, USIS Am. Cultural Ctr. Gallery, Tokyo, 1985, Komaba Garden Gallery, Tokyo, 1985, William Pelletier Gallery, Ann Arbor, Mich., 1986, Aura Gallery, Santa Fe, 1993; open studio shows include West Bloomfield, Mich., 1987, 88, Kamakura, Japan, 1989, Peymeinade (Cannes), France, 1990, 91, Santa Fe, 1992, 93; group exhbns. include 18th Ann. Oakland County Art Show, 1980, 8th Mich. Ann. Juried Show, 1980, Southfield Civic Ctr., 1980, Ann Arbor Art Assn. Show, 1980, Birmingham-Bloomfield Art Assn. Gallery, 1980-82, Ann Arbor Art Assn. Gallery, 1980-82, Detroit Inst. Arts Rental Gallery, 1980-88, Laurel Seth Gallery, Santa Fe, 1993. Home: 1 Balsa Rd Santa Fe NM 87505

HARGROVE, DAVID LAWRENCE, civil engineer, consultant; b. El Paso, Tex., July 11, 1953; s. Luther C. and Lillian A. (McNamara) H.; m. Bonnie J. Taylor, Jan. 4, 1975; children: Taylor, Alysen, Robyn. Student, U. Tex., El Paso, 1971-73; BSCE, U. Colo., Denver, 1977. Registered profl. engr., Colo. Dispatcher El Paso (Tex.) Natural Gas Co., 1971-72; student engr. Southwestern Indsl., El Paso, 1972-73; steel detailer Midwest Steel & Iron Works, Denver, 1973-77; engr. McCall, Ellingson & Morrill, Inc., Denver, 1978-84; design mgr. EHMG Engrs., Aurora, Colo., 1984-87; assoc. Richard Weingardt Cons., Inc., Denver, 1987—; mem. Cons. Engrs. Coun. Colo., 1991—, adv. bd. engrng. coun. State of Colo., 1992—. Editor Roundup, 1971; contbr. articles to profl. jours. Coach Skyline Soccer Assn., 1985-90, Club Denver Soccer, 1991—; league dir. S.E. Denver Baseball League, 1988—. Named Young El Pasoan of the Yr. Optimist Club, El Paso, 1971, Young Texan of Month Optimist CLub, Tex., Mar. 1971, one of Outstanding Young Men Am. U.S. Jaycees, Denver, 1981; recipient Dean's Leadership award U. Colo., Denver, 1977, Outstanding Engrng. Project award, Colo. and Nat., 1991. Mem. Profl. Svcs. Mgmt. Assn. (Great Works award, 1987; chpt. pres. 1987-91), Order of the Engr., Assoc. Engrng. Students, Bandid Softball Assn. (Outstanding Leader 1989), Am. Soc. Civil Engrs., U. Colo. Engrng. Alumni and Friends (chmn. 1985). Presbyterian. Office: Richard Weingardt Cons Inc 9725 E Hampden Ave Ste 200 Denver CO 80231-4917

HARGROVE, JOHN JAMES, federal judge; b. Bay Shore, N.Y., May 4, 1942; s. John A. and Cecelia L. Hargrove; m. Jane A Nagle, Oct. 21, 1967; children: David, Kristin, Kelly, Kathryn. BAin Polit. Sci., U. Notre Dame, 1964, JD, 1967. Bar: N.Y. 1968, Calif. 1971. Atty. Gant & Asaro, San Diego, 1972-76; ptnr. Weeks, Willis, Hoffman & Hargrove, San Diego, 1976-79, Strauss, Kissane, Davis & Hargrove, San Diego, 1979-83, Britton & Hargrove, San Diego, 1983-84; prin. John J. Hargrove & Assocs., San Diego, 1984-85; judge Bankruptcy Ct., City of San Diego., 1985—; adj. prof. Calif. Western Sch. Law, 1986. Coach University City Bobby Sox Softball Team; lector Our Mother of Confidence Roman Cath. Ch.; trustee U. Notre Dame, 1987-89. Lt. col. USMCR, 1968-90. Mem. U. Notre Dame Alumni Assn. (bd. dirs. 1985-89, pres. 1988-89). Republican. Office: US Bankruptcy Ct 940 Front St Rm 522N San Diego CA 92189-0010

HARKER, BRADLEY KENT, psychologist; b. Calgary, Alta., Can., Nov. 3, 1959; s. Robert Greene and Anita June (Wood) H.; m. Shelly Marie Turner, Dec. 10, 1988; children: Erin Marie, Daniel Kent. BA, U. Calgary, 1985; MEd, Brigham Young U., 1987, PhD, 1991. Behavioral analyst Alta. Children's Hosp., Calgary, 1986; counselor Brigham Young U., Provo, Utah, 1986-89, counseling clk., 1990-91; psychol. intern Timanogos Mental Health, Provo, 1989-90; postdoctoral intern U. Calgary Counseling Svcs., 1991—; pvt. practice Calgary, 1991—. Mem. Am. Assn. Applied and Preventative Psychology. Mem. LDS Ch. Home: 180 Scenic Cove Circle NW, Calgary, AB Canada T3L 1N2

HARKER, ROGER GEORGE, manufacturing company executive; b. Silver City, N.Mex., Jan. 28, 1945; s. Robert Asa Geraldine (Smiley) H.; m. Sheryl Martin, Oct., 1973; children: Matthew, Bradley, Amanda. BSEE, U. Calif., Berkeley, 1966. V.p. engring. Bently Nev. Corp., Minden, 1971-76, exec. v.p., gen. mgr., 1976-86, pres., 1986—, also bd. dirs.; bd. dirs. Bently Nev. Corp. Trustee St. Mary's Found. Mem. ASME, Am. Petroleum Inst., Instrument Soc. Am. Office: Bently Nev Corp PO Box 157 Minden NV 89423-0157

HARKINS, CRAIG, management consultant; b. Boston, May 1, 1936; s. Edwin Craig and Shirley Nadine (Pike) H.; m. Betty Letitia Hester, June 17, 1961 (div. 1985); children: Daniel, Sean, Lance; m. Donna Marie Hamlin, Sept. 1, 1990. BA, Colby Coll., Waterville, Maine, 1958; MA, NYU, 1959; Profl. Dipl., Columbia U., N.Y.C., 1963; PhD, Rensselaer Poly. Inst., Troy, N.Y., 1978. Computer operator Pacific Mutual, L.A., 1957; reporter Evening Independent, St. Petersburg, Fla., 1960-61; pub. rels. mgr. IBM, N.Y./Calif, 1961-82; mgmt. cons. Hamlin Harkins Ltd., San Jose, 1982—. Co-editor: Guide to Writing Better Technical Papers, 1982; contbr. numerous articles to profl. jours. Sec. Hudson River Sloop Restoration, Poughkeepsie, N.Y., 1972-76; communications/mktg. com. United Way, Santa Clara, Calif., 1981—; mem. mktg. com. San Jose Cleve. Ballet, 1991—. With USMCR, 1961-66. Mem. Internat. Communication Assn., Peninsula Mktg. Assn., Soc. for Tech. Communication (bd. dirs. 1980-81), IEEE Profl. Communications Soc. (sec. 1977-80). Democrat. Roman Catholic. Home: 1301 Mariposa Ave San Jose CA 95126-2624 Office: Hamlin Harkins Ltd 1611 The Alameda San Jose CA 95126-2202

HARLAN, JOHN MARSHALL, medicine educator; b. Chgo., July 18, 1947; s. Robert O. and Norine (Grumley) H.; m. Joanne Harlan, Dec. 22, 1973; children: Jeremy, Jason. BS, Loyola U., 1969; MD, U. Chgo., 1973. Diplomate Am. Bd. Internal Medicine Hematology and Oncology. Resident in medicine U. Calif., San Francisco, 1973-76; fellow in hematology U. Wash., Seattle, 1976-78, instr., 1979, asst. prof., 1979-84, assoc. prof., 1984-88, prof., 1989—; chief sect. hematology Harborview Med. Ctr., U. Wash., 1984—, head div. hematology, 1990—. Contbr. book chpts. and articles to profl. jours. Vol. Am. Heart Assn., Seattle. Recipient Clinical Scientist and Established Investigation awards Am. Heart Assn., 1979-84. Mem. Am. Soc. Hematology, Am. Soc. for Cell Biology, Am. Soc. for Clin. Investigation, Am. Assn. of Physicians. Office: U Wash Div of Hematology Rm 10 Seattle WA 98195

HARLAN, KATHLEEN T. (KAY HARLAN), business consultant, professional speaker and seminar leader; b. Bremerton, Wash., June 9, 1934; d. Floyd K. and Rosemary (Parkhurst) Troy; m. John L. Harlan, Feb. 16, 1952 (div. 1975); children: Pamela Kay, Kenneth Lynwood, Lianna Sue; m. Stuart Friedman, Nov. 10, 1991. Chair Kitsap-North Mason United Way, 1968-70; owner, operator Safeguard N.W. Systems, Tacoma, 1969-79; devel., mgr. Poulsbo (Wash.) Profl. Bldg., 1969-75; pres. Greenapple Graphics, Inc., Tacoma, 1976-79; owner, mgr. Iskrem Hus Restaurant, Poulsbo, 1972-75; pres. Bus. Seminars, Tacoma, 1977-82; owner, mgr. Safeguard Computer Ctr., Tacoma, 1982-91; owner Total Systems Ctr., Tacoma, 1983-88; mem.

Orgnl. Renewal, Inc., Tacoma, 1983-88; assoc. mem. Effectiveness Resource Group, Inc., Tacoma, 1979-80; pres. New Image Confs., Tacoma, 1979-82; speaker on mgmt. and survival in small bus.; CEO Manage Ability, Inc., profl. mgmt. firm, 1991—. Contbg. author: Here is Genius!, 1980; author small bus. manuals. Mem. Wash. State Bd. Boundary Rev. for Kitsap County, 1970-76, Selective Svc. Bd. 19, 1969-76; co-chair Wash. State Small Bus. Improvement Coun., 1986; del. White House Conf. on Small Bus., 1986; chair Wash. State Conf. on Small Bus., 1987; mem. exec. bd. Better Bus. Bur., 1983-88; mem. exec. bd. Am. Leadership Forum, 1988—; dir. Bus. Leadership Week, Wash. State, 1990—; co-chair Pro-Tech. Pierce County, 1993-94. Recipient Nellie Cashman award; named Woman Entrepreneur of Yr. for Wash. State, 1986, 87. Mem. Tacoma-Pierce County C. of C. (lifetime exec. bd. 1985—, chair spl. task force on small bus. for Pierce County 1986-87, treas. 1987-88, chair-elect 1988-90, chair 1990-91). Office: Manage Ability Inc One Pacific Bldg 621 Pacific Ave Ste 14 Tacoma WA 98402

HARLAN, RAYMOND CARTER, communication executive; b. Shreveport, La., Nov. 13, 1943; s. Ross E. and Margaret (Burns) H.; m. Nancy K. Munson, Sept. 3, 1966 (div. 1978); children: Kathleen Marie, Patrick Raymond; m. Sarah J. Kinzel, Sept. 1, 1979 (div. 1982); m. Linda Frances Gerdes, Mar. 30, 1985; stepchildren: Kimberly Jo Gerdes, Kellie Leigh Raffa, Ryan William Gerdes. BA in Speech and Drama cum laude, Southwestern U., 1966; MA in English, U. Tex., 1968; MA in Speech & Theatre Arts, Bradley U., 1976. Commd. 2d lt. USAF, 1968, advanced through grades to maj., 1980, ret., 1988; pres. ComSkills Tng., Aurora, Colo., 1988—; asst. prof. Bradley U., Peoria, Ill., 1972-76; instr., asst. prof., course dir. Air Force Acad., Colorado Springs, 1976-81; asst. prof. Air Force Inst. Tech., Dayton, Ohio, 1987-88; internat. trainer Inst. for Internat. Rsch., London, 1990-92. Author: The Confident Speaker, 1993; co-author: Telemarketing That Works, 1991; contbr. articles and revs. to profl. jours. Decorated Air Force Commendation medal with three oak leaf clusters, Air Force Meritorious Svc. medal with one oak leaf cluster; recipient George Washington Honor Medal Freedom Found., 1983, Leo A. Codd award Am. Def. Preparedness Assn., 1st Prize ann. poetry contest Ariz. State Poetry Soc., 1979. Mem. ASTD, Nat. Speakers Assn. (chpt. dir. 1989-91), Speech Comm. Assn., Nat. Writers Club, Air Force Assn., Ret. Officers Assn., Assn. for Bus. Comm. Lutheran. Office: ComSkills Tng 17544 E Wesley Pl Aurora CO 80013-4174

HARLEY, NED RICHARD, psychiatrist; b. Detroit, Mar. 29, 1942; s. Louis Maurice and Dorothy Mildred (Gershenson) H.; children: Ben, Alicia. AB, Dartmouth U., 1963, B in Med. Sci., 1964; MD, Harvard U., 1966; MArch, U. Colo., 1983. Bd. cert. in psychiatry, 1975. Intern Mt. Zion Hosp., San Francisco, 1966-67; residency Mass. Mental Health Ctr. Harvard Tech. Hosp., 1967-70; psychiatrist U. Colo., Boulder, 1970-77, Boulder (Colo.) Psychiat. Inst., 1976-83; med. dir. eating disorders program Boulder (Colo.) Meml. Hosp., 1984-87; dir. psychiatry Mercy Med. Ctr., Denver, 1987-89; pvt. practice psychiatry Vail, Colo., 1990—. Author: Exciting Vail and Beaver Creek Guide Book, 1992; co-author: Let's Go Skiing: Your learning Guide to Sensational Skiing; principal works include Grand Traverse development, Lions Ridge Loop. Home and Office: PO Box 4577 Vail CO 81698-4577

HARLEY, ROBERT WALLACE, insurance agency official; b. Buffalo, Sept. 15, 1941; s. Alexander William and Marie Eleanor (Stott) H.; m. Shirley Ann Harley, 1969 (div. Dec. 1977); m. Molly Kesler; children: Dawn Marie, Bradley Robert, Elizabeth June. AA, Chaffey Coll., Alta Loma, Calif., 1959; MS in Fin. Svcs., Am. Coll., Bryn Mawr, Pa., 1984. CLU. Aerospace engr. N.Am. S&ID/Rockwell Internat., Downey, Calif., 1959-66, Convair Corp., San Diego, 1966-67; agt., supr. Mut. Benefit Life, Santa Ana, 1967-73; career supr. Aetna Life & Casualty, San Francisco, 1973-75; brokerage mgr. Aetna Life & Casualty, Spokane, Wash., 1975-83; pres., owner Fidelity Assocs. Fin. Svcs. Inc., Spokane, 1983—. Pres. Spokane Youth Symphony, 1987-88; bishop, clk. LDS Ch., 1987—. Mem. Million Dollar Round Table, Spokane CLU Assn. (pres. 1988-89), Wash. State Estate Planning Coun., Spokane Life Underwriters Assn., Inland Empire Fly Fishing Club. Republican. Office: Fidelity Assocs Fin Svcs 501 S Bernard St 3d Fl Spokane WA 99204

HARLOW, CHARLES VENDALE, JR., finance educator, consultant; b. Long Beach, Calif., May 18, 1931; s. Charles Vendale and Lucille (Morris) H.; m. Luann Jones, July 6, 1956; children: Jeffrey, Pamela, John. BA, Stanford U., 1953; MBA, U. So. Calif., 1960, DBA, 1968. Ptnr. Harlow & Harlow Investments, Long Beach, 1955-68; pres. Cambistics, Inc., Long Beach, 1968-88; asst. prof. Calif. State U., Long Beach, 1968-71, assoc. prof., 1971-75, prof. fin., 1975—; mng. dir. Cambistics Securities Corp., Long Beach, 1990—. Co-author: The Commodity Futures Trading Guide, 1969 (100 Best Books in Bus. award), The Futures Game, 1974, How to Shoot From the Hip Without Getting Shot in the Foot: Making Smart Strategic Choices Every Day, 1990. 1st lt. USMC, 1953-55. NSF grantee, 1968. Mem. Va. Country Club. Republican. Office: Cambistics PO Box 15596 Long Beach CA 90815-0596

HARLOW, RICHARD LANTZ, retail executive; b. Bell, Calif., July 5, 1944; s. Charles V. and Margery (Horton) H.; m. Colleen S. Kenney, Apr. 9, 1965; children: Robert, William, Mendy. BS in Natural Resource Mgmt., Humboldt State U., 1968, MS in Natural Resource Policy, 1969. Cert. adminstrv. mgr. Am. Mgmt. Assn. Range conservationist U.S. Bur. Land Mgmt., Susanville, Calif., 1968-71; pub. affairs officer U.S. Bur. Land Mgmt., Folsom, Calif., 1972-74; resource area mgr. U.S. Bur. Land Mgmt., Bakersfield, Calif., 1974-76, Ridgecrest, Calif., 1976-79; congl. affairs staff U.S. Bur. Land Mgmt., Washington, 1980-82; dist. mgr. U.S. Bur. Land Mgmt., Lakeview, Oreg., 1982-89; tng. ctr. mgr. U.S. Bur. Land Mgmt., Phoenix, 1989-92; owner/mgr. Dicks Ent./C&D Collectibles, Phoenix, 1992—; prof. Lassen Community Coll., Susanville, 1970-71, founding dir. SAge Community Coll., Lakeview, 1986-89. Chmn. Lake County Sch. Dist. #7 Bd., Lakeview, 1987-88. Mem. Lakeview C. of C. (mng. dir. 1988), Paradise Village Lions (pres. 1989-90), Lakeview Lions (pres. 1987). Office: C&D Collectibles PO Box 11895 Phoenix AZ 85061-1895

HARMAN, JANE LAKES, congresswoman, lawyer; b. N.Y.C., June 28, 1945; d. A. N. and Lucille (Geier) Lakes; m. Sidney Harman, Aug. 30, 1980; children: Brian Lakes, Hilary Lakes, Daniel Geier, Justine Leigh. BA, Smith Coll., 1966; JD, Harvard U., 1969. Bar: D.C. 1969, U.S. Ct. Appeals (D.C. cir.) 1972, U.S. Supreme Ct. 1975. Spl. asst. Commn. of Chs. on Internat. Affairs, Geneva, Switzerland, 1969-70; assoc. Surrey & Morse, Washington, 1970-72; chief legis. asst. Senator John V. Tunney, Washington, 1972-73; chief counsel, staff dir. Subcom. on Rep. Citizen Interests, Com. on Judiciary, Washington, 1973-75; adj. prof. Georgetown Law Ctr., Washington, 1974-75; chief counsel, staff dir. Subcom. on Constl. Rights, Com. on Judiciary, Washington, 1975-77; dep. sec. to cabinet The White House, Washington, 1977-78; spl. counsel Dept. Def., Washington, 1979; ptnr. Manatt, Phelps, Rothenberg & Tunney, Washington, 1979-82, Surrey & Morse, Washington, 1982-86; of counsel Jones, Day, Reavis & Pogue, Washington, 1987-92; mem. 103rd Congress from 36th Calif. dist., 1992—; mem. vis. coms. Harvard Law Sch., 1976-82, Kennedy Sch. Govt., 1990—. Counsel Dem. Platform Com., Washington, 1984; vice-chmn. Ctr. for Nat. Policy, Washington, 1981-90; chmn. Dem. Nat. Com. Nat. Lawyers' Coun., Washington, 1986-90. Mem. Phi Beta Kappa. Democrat. Office: 325 Cannon House Office Bldg. Washington DC 20515 also: Ste 960 5200 W Century Blvd Los Angeles CA 90045 also: 3031 Torrance Blvd Torrance CA 90503

HARMAN, ROBERT CHARLES, anthropology educator; b. L.A., July 24, 1936; s. Louis and Charlotte (Silver) H.; m. Melinda David, June 10, 1967 (div. 1973); 1 child, Reverdy Gale Harman Burgess. BA, U. Calif., Santa Barbara, 1962; MA, U. Ariz., 1964, PhD, 1969. Asst. prof. anthropology Calif. State U., Long Beach, 1969-74; assoc. prof. anthropology Calif. State U., 1974-80, prof. anthropology, 1980—, acting chmn. dept. anthropology, 1988-89. Author: Cambios medicos y sociales en una comunidad Maya Tzeltal, 1974; contbr. articles to profl. jours. NIH fellow, 1967-69; Wenner-Gren grantee, 1970; NIH grantee, 1971. Fellow NIH, 1967-69; Wenner-Gren grantee, 1970, grantee NIH, 1971. Fellow Am. Anthrop. Assn., Soc. for Applied Anthropology; mem. Southwestern Anthrop. Assn. (pres. 1989-90), So. Calif. Applied Anthropology Network (pres. 1991-93), Assn. for Anthropology and Gerontology, Soc. for Med. Anthropology, Soc. for L.Am. Anthropology, Guatemala Scholars Network. Unitarian. Office: Calif State U Dept Anthropology Long Beach CA 90840

HARMEL, HILDA HERTA See **PIERCE, HILDA**

HARMON, RICHARD LINCOLN, public relations executive; b. Seattle, Aug. 13, 1923; s. Merle Simpson and Alice Mathilda (Nielsen) H.; m. Anne Lipsky, Apr. 8, 1944 (div. 1967); children: Susan G., Sherry Lynn; m. Mary Ann Horner, July 9, 1967. BA, San Diego State U., 1949. Reporter San Diego Daily Jour., 1949-50; assoc. editor Whittier (Calif.) Star-Reporter, 1950-52; reporter L.A. Examiner, 1952-56; with pub. rels. dept. Gen. Dynamics Corp., San Diego, 1956-60; mgr. communications Cohu Electronics, San Diego, 1960-71; dir. pub. rels./advt. ITT Cable Hydrospace Div., National City, Calif., 1971-78; dir pub. rels. ITT Cannon Electric, Santa Ana, Calif., 1972-81; product press rels. mgr. Hewlett-Packard Co., Palo Alto, Calif., 1981-88, pub. rels. cons., 1988-92; pub. rels. cons San Juan Capistrano, Calif., 1992—; lectr. in pub. rels. San Diego State U., 1968-72, Calif. State U., Fullerton, 1972-80, 1992-93, San Jose State U., 1985-91. Contbr. articles to profl. jours. Pub. rels. chmn. Am. Cancer Soc., San Diego, 1976-80, Smoking Rsch. Inc., San Diego, 1965-67; pub. rels. dir. Balboa dist. Boy Scouts Am., San Diego, 1964-66; bd. dirs. Family Svc. Assn., San Diego, 1964-65. Mem. APR, Pub. Rels. Soc. of Am. (Silicon Valley chpt. pres. 1987, Orange County chpt. bd. dirs. 1981, 92, San Diego County chpt. pres. 1966, bd. dirs.), Pub. Rels. Club of San Diego (pres. 1966, Profl. of Yr. 1967). Democrat. Methodist. Home: 27232B Via Capote San Juan Capistrano CA 92675

HARMON, ROBERT HENRY, insurance agent; b. Ames, Iowa, Dec. 23, 1930; s. Laurence Barnes and Minnie Barbara (Oberhansley) H.; m. Carolee Larsen, Aug. 18, 1955; children: David, Christine, Pamela, Jill, Holly. BS, U. Utah, 1954; MBA, UCLA, 1956. CLU; ChFC. Field underwriter Home Life N.Y., L.A., 1956-57, asst. mgr., 1958-61; mgr. Home Life N.Y., Salt Lake City, 1961-81; owner, mgr., ind. agt. Confidential Planning Cons., Salt Lake City, 1981—; chmn. agt. adv. coun. Banner Life Ins. Co., 1992. Com. chmn. Utah Cancer Soc., Salt Lake City, 1971; pres. Pine Canyon Ranch for Boys, Salt Lake City, 1974-77; bd. dirs. Salt Lake coun. Boy Scouts Am.-Handicapped, 1987—; bd. dirs., mem. planned giving com. Utah Symphony, Salt Lake City, 1990—. Mem. Nat. Assn. Life Underwriters (com. chmn. 1976-79, nat. quality award 1967—, nat. sales achievement award 1980—), Am. Soc. CLU's (pres. Salt Lake City 1965-66), Utah Assn. Life Underwriters (chpt. pres. 1977-78), Salt Lake Assn. Life Underwriters (pres. 1971-72, Agt. of Yr. award 1980), Salt Lake Estate Planning Coun. (v.p. 1974-75), Million Dollar Round Table. Republican. Mem. LDS Ch. Office: Confidential Planning Cons 420 E South Temple Ste 303 Salt Lake City UT 84111

HARMON, WARREN WAYNE, educator; b. Colton, Calif., Feb. 13, 1936; s. Renick Elkin and Henrietta Frances (Stûwich) H.; m Margaret Ann Schonberger, Nov. 21, 1959; children: Andrea Jane, Fritz Warren. AA, San Bernardino Valley Coll., 1958; BA, San Diego State Coll., 1961, MA, 1964. Lic. secondary tchr., Calif. Chmn. social sci. Roosevelt Jr. High Sch., San Diego, 1962-66; geography instr. Mesa Coll., San Diego, 1966; geography instr. Grossmont Coll., El Cajon, Calif., 1967-84, div. coord., 1984, prof. geography, dept. chmn. of earth scis., 1984-89, dean humanities & social scis., 1989-90, dean math., phys. and behavioral scis. div., 1990-92, prof. geography, 1992—; geog. cons. UCLA, 1986-88. Author: Geography of California, 1976; co-author Geographic Perspectives on American Westward Expansion, 1986; contbr. articles to profl. jours. Co-founder So. Calif. Tourette Syndrome Assn., Mission Viejo, Calif, 1974; chief Indian Guides, La Jolla, Calif., 1978. Named Outstanding Educator of Am., Fuller and Dees, 1974, Disting. Chair of Sci. Grossmont Coll., 1988-89. Mem. San Diego County Social Sci Adv. Coun., Nat. Coun. for Geog. Edn., Calif Geography Soc. (exec. bd. mem. 1978), Calif. Geog. Alliance (charter mem.), Fulbright Alumni Assn. (Fulbright scholar 1970-71), La Jolla Play Readers Club, Gamma Theta Upsilon. Democrat. Methodist. Office: Grossmont Coll 8800 Grossmont College Dr El Cajon CA 92020-1765

HARMS, GLENN EDWARD, minister, pastor; b. Newton, Kans., Jan. 8, 1939; s. Ed and Minnie (Rutschman) H.; m. Helen L. Janzen, Feb. 20, 1959; children: David Edward, Debbie Kaye. Grad. in pastoral theology, Western Bible Coll., Denver, 1969. Ordained to ministry Bapt. Ch., 1969. Pastor Calvary Bapt. Ch., Chadron, Nebr., 1969-71; pastor, founder Foothills Bapt. Ch., Loveland, Colo., 1971—. Mem. High Plains Bapt. Fellowship (founding mem.), Internat. Fellowship of Bapts. Republican. Office: Foothills Bapt Ch 4000 W 22nd Loveland CO 80538

HARNDEN, JEFFREY NEILL, human factors system engineer and executive, management consultant; b. Denver, Nov. 28, 1955; s. Willard Joe Sr. and Ethel Alice (McNeil) H. AA, Thomas Edison State Coll., 1987; cert. in Pub. Adminstrn., Metro. State Coll., Denver, 1989; MSC D, U. Colo., Boulder, 1973-91. Pres., owner T.S. Rsch. Assocs., Denver, 1986—; bd. dirs. United Bus. Assocs., Denver, Future-Tech Internat. Inc., Denver, Portos Mgmt. and Mktg. Internat. Inc., Denver, Cen. City Yellow Taxicab and Livery, Denver. Author: The Romance of the Hollow Ring, 1992; inventor hold-up alarm switcher, oil additive, transmission fluid additive. Local organizer, head del., head of mission Model U.N., N.Y.C., 1989-91; local organizer, team mem. Nat. Mock Trial, Drake Law Sch., Des Moines, 1989-91; precinct com., election judge Denver County and Boulder County, Colo., 1974—; del. state and county polit. convs., Denver, 1974—. With USMCR and USAR, 1974-77. Mem. ASPA, Am. Soc. for Personnel Adminstrs., Soc. for Human Resource Mgmt., Nat. Assn. Accts., Inst. Mgmt. Accts., Am. Mktg. Assn., Western Govtl. Rsch. Assn., Colo. Water Congress, Mensa, Sigma Delta Phi (internat. pres. and policy bd. chmn. 1989—), Phi Chi Theta (asst. regional dir. 1988-91). Office: TS Rsch Assocs PO Box 8916 Denver CO 80201

HARNICHER, DAVID JOHN, insurance company executive; b. Warren, Ohio, Sept. 3, 1950; s. John Paul and Irene Louise (Metro) H.; married, 1983. BS in Bus. Adminstrn., Ohio State U., 1973, MBA, 1979. LUTCF. Mem. sales staff Burroughs Corp., Columbus, Ohio, 1973-74; cost coord. Rockwell Internat. Corp., Columbus, Ohio, 1974-79; mgmt. cons. Vredenberg & Assocs., McLean, Va., 1979-82; developer The Harnicher Co., Houston, 1982-89; broker rep. The Paul Revere Ins. Co., Houston, 1989-91; gen. mgr. The Paul Revere Ins. Co., Salt Lake City, 1991—. Fellow Life Underwriters Tng. Coun.; mem. Nat. Assn. Health Underwriters, Nat. Assn. Life Underwriters. Office: Paul Revere Ins Co 10 N State St Salt Lake City UT 84103

HARNSBERGER, THERESE COSCARELLI, librarian; b. Muskegon, Mich.; d. Charles and Julia (Borrell) Coscarelli; B.A. cum laude, Marymount Coll., 1952; M.L.S., U. So. Calif., 1953; postgrad. Rosary Coll., River Forest, Ill., 1955-56, U. Calif., Los Angeles Extension, 1960-61; m. Frederick Owen Harnsberger, Dec. 24, 1962; 1 son, Lindsey Carleton. Free-lance writer, 1950—; librarian San Marino (Calif.) High Sch., 1953-56; cataloger, cons. San Marino Hall, South Pasadena, Calif., 1956-61; librarian Los Angeles State Coll., 1956-59; librarian dist. library Covina-Valley Unified Sch. Dist., Covina, Calif., 1959-67; librarian Los Angeles Trade Tech. Coll., 1972—; med. librarian, tumor registrar Alhambra (Calif.) Community Hosp., 1975-79; tumor registrar Huntington Meml. Hosp., 1979—; pres., dir. Research Unltd., 1980—; free lance reporter Los Angeles' Best Bargains, 1981—; med. library cons., 1979—; reviewer various cookbooks, 1991—. Author numerous poems. Chmn. spiritual values com. Covina Coordinating Council, 1964-66; chmn. Neighborhood Watch, 1976—. Mem. ALA, Internat. Women's Writing Guild, Calif. Assn. Sch. Librarians (chmn. legis. com.), Covina Tchrs. Assn., AAUW (historian 1972-73), U. So. Calif. Grad. Sch. Libr. Sci. (life), Am. Nutrition Soc. (chpt. Newsletter chmn.), Nat. Tumor Registrars Assn., So. Calif. Tumor Registrars Assn., Med. Libr. Assn., So. Calif. Libr. Assn., So. Calif. Assn. Law Libr., Book Publicists So. Calif., Am. Fedn. Tchrs. Coll. Guild, Calif. Libr. Assn., Assn. Poetry Bibliographers, Faculty Assn. Calif. Community Colls., Immaculate Heart Coll. Alumnae Assn., Loyola, Marymount Alumnae Assn. (coord., Pi Lambda Theta. Author: (poetry) The Journal, 1982, To Julia: in Memoriam; contbr. articles to profl. jours. Office: 2809 W Hellman Ave Alhambra CA 91803-2737

HARO See **KAGEMOTO, HARO**

HARP, ROBERT GEORGE, JR., hospitality corporation executive; b. Balt., May 28, 1959; s. Robert George and Delores (Creutzer) H.; m. Jill Stephenson, June 4, 1983; children: Preston Robert, Natalie Joy. BA in Econs., Wheaton Coll., 1980, MA in Communications with high honors, 1981; ThM, Dallas Theol. Sem., 1985. Lic. real estate broker. Real estate broker The Swearingen Co., Dallas, 1986-87; dir. of devel., v.p. of real estate Global Hospitality Corp., San Diego, 1987—. Contbr. articles to profl. jours. Precinct capt. San Diego Count Rep. Com.; edn. chmn., dir. San Diego CCIM chpt. Named one of Outstanding Young Men of Am., 1985. Mem. Nat. Assn. Realtors, Realtors Nat. Mktg. Inst., Calif. Assn. Realtors, San Diego Bd. of Realtors, Cert. Comml. Investment Mem. (San Diego chpt.). Republican.

HARP, RUFUS WILLIAM, set decorator; b. Bastrop, La., Nov. 28, 1923; s. Robert Edward and Anna Lee (Kirkpatrick) H. BA, La. State U., 1947, MA, 1951. Asst. prof. U. Ga., Atlanta, 1952-54; set decorator Ford Found. Radio & TV, N.Y.C., 1954-55, CBS-TV, N.Y.C., 1955-69, Carol Burnett Show, Hollywood, Calif., 1969-78; pvt. practice set decorator Hollywood, 1978-85; set decorator ABC Circle Film "Moonlighting", Hollywood, 1985-89, Joe Hamilton Prodn. "Mama's Family", Hollywood, 1985-89, 20th Century Fox "L.A. Law", 1991; pres., chief exec. officer Prop Services West, Los Angeles, 1978—; pres. Billy Wolf Inc., Los Angeles, 1980—; dir. Marbil Prodn., Los Angeles, 1986—. Served to 1st. lt., USAF, 1943-46, ETO. Mem. NATAS (Emmy award 1965, 77, 79, 89, with 23 nominations 1964-90). Democrat. Baptist. Office: Prop Svcs West 915 N Citrus Ave Los Angeles CA 90038-2401

HARPER, DONALD CALVIN, dean; b. Claresholm, Alta., Can., Oct. 31, 1942; s. William James and Effie Mabel (Slonaker) H.; m. Kathleen Ann Paton, May 18, 1968; children: Christopher Bradley, Angela Dawn. BA, U. Alta., Edmonton, 1963, MA, 1970. Rsch. asst. exec. coun. Province of Alta., 1966-67, rsch. asst. dept. of youth, 1967-69; instr. sociology Grande Prairie Regional Coll., Alta., 1969-71, registrar, 1971-74, registrar, dir. student svcs., 1974-79, dir. student and community svcs., 1979-80, instr. humanities and social scis., 1980-81, chairperson acad. devel., 1981-84, dean acad. and applied studies, 1984-93; mem. task force Worth Royal Com. Ednl. Planning, 1970-71; chairperson acad. coun. Gran Prairie Regional Coll., 1969-70, 78-80; mem. Alta Coun. Admissions & Transfer, 1974-77, 79-82, 89-92; chairperson com. Sr. Acad. Officers, Alta, 1990-92. Pres. Grande Prairie Little Theatre, 1978-80; bd. dirs. Prairie Gallery, 1980-81, 84-86, other community bds.; regional dir. Alta. Fedn. Home and Sch. Assns., 1990-92; mem. Can. Program adv. com. Assn. Can. C.C., 1991—. Home: 8517 100A St, Grande Prairie, AB Canada T8V 3C4

HARPER, GLORIA JANET, artist, educator; children: Dan Conyers, Jan Shriver. Student, Famous Artists Sch., 1967-69, 69-71; BA in Comml. Art, Portland C.c., 1981; postgrad., Valley View Art Sch., 1982-89, Carrizzo Art Sch., 1983-88, Holdens Portrait Sch., 1989; studied with Daniel Greene, 1989. Cert. art educator. Artist, art instr. Art By Gloria, Pendleton, Oreg., 1980—; owner Art By Gloria Art Sch. and Gallery, Pendleton, 1991—; lectr., workshop presenter in field, 1980—. Paintings and prints included in various mags. Mem. NAFE, Water Color Soc. Am., Nat. Mus. Women in Arts, So. Career Inst. Profl. Legal Assts. (area rep.), Profl. Legal Assts., C. of C. Home: PO Box 1734 Pendleton OR 97801 Office: Art By Gloria 133 S Main Pendleton OR 97801

HARPER, JUDSON MORSE, university administrator, consultant, educator; b. Lincoln, Nebr., Aug. 25, 1936; s. Floyd Sprague and Eda Elizabeth (Kelley) H.; m. Patricia Ann Kennedy, June 15, 1958; children: Jayson K., Stuart H., Neal K. B.S., Iowa State U., 1958, M.S., 1960, Ph.D., 1963. Registered profl. engr., Minn. Instr. Iowa State U., Ames, 1958-63; dept. head Gen. Mills, Inc., Mpls., 1964-69, venture mgr., 1969-70; prof., dept. head agrl. and chem. engring. Colo. State U., Ft. Collins, 1970-82, v.p. for rsch., 1982—, interim pres., 1989-90; cons. USAID, Washington, 1972-74, various comml. firms., 1975—. Author: Extrusion of Foods, 1982, Extrusion Cooking, 1989; editor newsletter Food, Pharm. & Bioengring. News, 1979-83, LEC Newsletter, 1976-89; contbr. articles to profl. publs.; patentee. Mem. sch. bd. St. Louis Park, Minn., 1968-70. Recipient Food Engring. award Dairy and Food Industry Supply Assn. and Am. Soc. Agrl. Engrs., 1983, Cert. of Merit, U.S. Dept. Agr.-Office Internat. Coop. and Devel., 1983, Svc. award CIATECH, Chihuahua, Mex., 1980, Disting. Svc. award Colo. State U., 1977, Charles Lory Pub. Svc. award, 1993, Prof. Achievement citation Iowa State U., 1986. Fellow Inst. Food Technologists (Internat. award 1990); mem. AAAS, Am. Inst. Chem. Engring. (dir. 1981-84), Am. Soc. Agrl. Engrs. (com. chmn. 1973-78, hon. engr. Rocky Mountain region), Am. Chem. Soc., Am. Soc. Engring. Edn. (com. chmn. 1976-77). Mem. Ind. United Methodist Ch. Home: 1818 Westview Rd Fort Collins CO 80524-1891 Office: Colo State U Office VP Rsch Fort Collins CO 80523

HARPER, KENNETH CHARLES, clergyman; b. Detroit, Aug. 31, 1946; s. Charles Burdett and Marion Anna (Pankau) H.; m. Sharon Kay Royse, June 14, 1969; children: Charles William, David Peter, Andrew Scott. BS in Edn., Ill. State U., 1969; MDiv, Trinity Evang. Div. Sch., Deerfield, Ill., 1973; ThM, Princeton (N.J.) Theol. Sem., 1976; D of Ministry, San Francisco Theol. Sem., San Anselmo, Calif., 1986; postgrad., Pepperdine U., 1989—. Ordained to ministry Presbyn. Ch., 1974. Edn. advisor Amwell Valley Commn., Reaville, N.J., 1973-74; asst. pastor 1st Presbyn. Ch., Mt. Holly, N.J., 1974-77; pastor 1st Presbyn. Ch., Herrin, Ill., 1977-82; sr. pastor 1st Presbyn. Ch., Westminster, Calif., 1982—. Contbr. book revs. and articles to religious jours. Mem. Evang. Theol. Soc., Presbyns. for Renewal, Assn. Psychol. Type. Democrat. Office: 1st Presbyn Ch 7702 Westminster Blvd Westminster CA 92683-4092

HARPER, KIMBALL TAYLOR, ecologist, educator; b. Oakley, Idaho, Feb. 15, 1931; s. John Mayo and Mary Ella (Overson) H.; m. Caroline Frances Stepp, June 7, 1958; children: Ruth L., James K., Gay A., Denise C., Karla D., Steven S.. BS, Brigham Young U., 1958, MS, 1960; PhD, U. Wis., 1963. Range technician U.S. Forest Svc., Moab and Moticello, Utah, 1957-58; range scientist U.S. Forest Svc., Ogden, Utah, 1958-59; rsch. asst. U. Wis., Madison, 1959-63; asst. prof., then assoc. prof. U. Utah, Salt Lake City, 1963-73; prof. Brigham Young U., Provo, Utah, 1973—, chmn. dept. botany and range sci., 1973-76; vis. scholar U. Calif., Berkeley, 1984-85; mem. Mono Lake com. NRC, Washington, 1986-87. Editor, co-author: Intermountain Biogeography, 1978, Ecological Impacts of Weather Modification, 1981; mem. editorial bd. Great Basin Naturalist, 1977-87; contbr. numerous articles to profl. jours. Ward bishop LDS Ch., Spanish Fork, Utah, 1978-83. Served as cpl. U.S. Army, 1953-55, Korea. Grantee NSF, U.S. Forest Svc., U.S. Bur. Land Mgmt., U.S. Army., 1965—. Fellow AAAS; mem. Am. Bot. Soc., Ecol. Soc. Am. (editor, mem. editorial bd. jour. 1965-67, 1975-79), Soc. for Range Mgmt., Am. Inst. For Biol. Scis., Soc. for Study Evolution, Brit. Ecol. Soc., Phi Kappa Phi. Republican. Home: 410 S 300 E Spanish Fork UT 84660-2422 Office: Brigham Young U Dept Botany and Range Sci Provo UT 84602

HARPER, RICHARD HENRY, film producer, director; b. San Jose, Calif., Sept. 15, 1950; s. Walter Henry and Priscilla Alden (Browne) H.; m. Ann Marie Morgan, June 19, 1976; children: Christine Ann, Paul Richard, James Richard. Show designer Walt Disney Imagineering, Glendale, Calif., 1971-76; motion picture producer, dir. Harper Films, Inc., La Canada, Calif., 1976—. Producer, dir. (films) Impressions de France, Disney World, Fla., 1982, Magic Carpet Round the World, Disneyland, Tokyo, 1983, American Journeys, Disneyland, Calif., 1985, Collecting America, Nat. Gallery Art, Washington, 1988, Hillwood Mus., Washington, 1989, Journey Into the 4th Dimension for Sanrio World, Journey Into Nature for Sanrio World, Japan, 1990, Masters of Illusion, Nat. Gallery of Art, Washington, 1992. Recipient more than 150 awards world-wide for outstanding motion picture prodn. including Silver trophy Cannes, France Internat. Film Festival, 2 Gold awards Internat. Festival of the Ams., 1981, 82, 14 Golden Eagle C.I.N.E. awards, 1977-92, Emmy award Nat. Acad. TV Arts and Scis., 1993.

HARPER, ROBERT LEVELL, pharmaceutical company executive; b. Wichita, Kans., Nov. 11, 1942; s. Cleo Levell and Mary Florence (Weaver) H.; m. Margaret Lucille Madden, Jan. 20, 1961 (div. 1980); children: Douglas Warren, Susan Denise; m. Maria Elain Davis, June 20, 1981;

stepchildren: Laura Elaine Emery, Melissa MacAlpin Emery. Cert. med. rep., Sterling Mgmt. Inst. Sales rep. Dorsey Labs. div. Sandoz Pharms., Tulsa, 1967-70; mgr. key accounts Sandoz Pharms., Houston, 1970-72; div. mgr. Dorsey Pharms. div. Sandoz Pharms., Kansas City, Mo., 1972-85; mgr. govt. affairs Sandoz Pharms., Sacramento, 1985—; rotating mgr. Sandoz Pharms., East Hanover, N.J., 1985. Donor Kansas City Coll. Osteo. Medicine, 1973; co-founder first aid program state CAP, Oklahoma City, 1973; leader youth program YMCA, Johnson County, Mo., 1977-79; leader youth baseball Johnson County, 1976-79; del. Nat. Baseball Congress, Houston, 1971, 72, 73; mem. med. edn. for srs. SRx Regional Program, 1985—. With USAFR, 1960-64. Recipient appreciation award Calif. State Firemen's Assn., Sacramento, 1987. Mem. Nat. Assn. Legis. Svcs., Calif. Medication Edn. Coalition, Calif. Mfrs. Assn., Pharm. Mfrs. Assn., Calif. Derby. Home: 11370 Tunnel Hill Way Gold River CA 95670-7240

HARPER, VERA JEAN, convalescent home activity director, music therapist; b. Spokane, Wash., Apr. 20, 1925; d. James Young Wellington and Lucia Annie (Bisbee) Wilson; m. Glenn F. Harper, June 26, 1946 (div. 1982); children: David, Ruth Ann. Student, Wash. State U., 1944-46. Storekeeper Naval Supply Depot, Spokane, 1943-45; libr. attendant Wash. State U., Pullman, 1945-52; sec. Pullman (Wash.) Pub. Schs., 1952-57; piano tchr. Pullman, 1960-62, Des Moines, Wash., 1965—; activity coord. Midway Manor Convalescent, Des Moines, 1971—. Mem. com. Annexation King County to Des Moines, 1986. Recipient Appreciation award Friend to Friend Greater Seattle, Des Moines, 1985; named to Hall of Fame, Wash. Health Care Assn., 1993. Mem. Nat. Cert. Coun. Activity Profls. (cert. activity dir., bd. dirs. 1991—), Nat. Assn. Activity Profls. (regional state contact 1989-90, conv. co-chmn. 1987-90), Wash. State Assn. Activity Profls. (pres. 1987-89, Activity Dir. of Yr. 1991), Kiwanis (sec., treas. Kiwanian of Yr. 1991-92). Presbyterian. Home: 23449 25th Ave S Des Moines WA 98198-8717

HARRELL, LYNN MORRIS, cellist; b. N.Y.C., Jan. 30, 1944; s. Mack and Marjorie (Fulton) H.; m. Linda Blandford, Sept. 7, 1976. Student, Juilliard Sch. Music, Curtis Inst. Music. Piatigorsky prof. cello U. So. Calif., L.A., 1987-93; prof. internat. cello studies Royal Acad. Music, London, 1988-93; artistic dir. L.A. Philharm. Inst., 1988-91; prin. Royal Acad. Music, London, 1993—. Prin. cellist, Cleve. Orch., 1963-71; debut Carnegie Hall, N.Y.C., 1963 ; soloist with maj. orchs. U.S. and Europe: rec. artist London/Decca Records, EMI/Angel, RCA, CBS, Deutsche Gramaphon. Recipient 1st Piatigorsky award, Grammy award, 1981, 87, 88; co-recipient 1st Avery Fisher award, 1975. Office: care IMG 22 E 71st St New York NY 10021-4911

HARRICK, JIM, university athletic coach. Head coach NCAA Divsn. 1A basketball, ranked #4 UCLA Bruins, 1992. Office: UCLA 405 Hilgard Ave Los Angeles CA 90024

HARRIGAN, JOHN FREDERICK, banker; b. Eau Claire, Wis., June 22, 1925; s. Frederick H. and Marion F. (Farr) H.; m. Barbara Heald, July 1, 1950; children—Sarah H. Gruber, Peter Christopher. Student, U. Wis., 1946-49; grad., Rutgers U. Stonier Grad. Sch. Banking, 1965. With First Nat. Bank Oreg., Portland, 1949-71, exec. v.p., 1971; chmn. bd., chief exec. officer Pacific Nat. Bank Wash., Seattle, 1971-74, dir., 1971-80; vice chmn. bd. dirs. United Calif. Bank, Los Angeles, 1974-75; pres., dir. Western Bancorp., Los Angeles, 1975-80; chmn., chief exec. officer Union Bank, Los Angeles, 1980-88, dir., 1980-90, cons., 1990-; bd. dirs. Nordstrom, Inc. Bd. dirs. Los Angeles Civic Light Opera Assn., Peregrine Fund. Mem. L.A. Country Club, Eldorado Country Club, Valley Club, Montecito. Office: Union Bank Bldg 210 1900 Avenue Of The Stars Los Angeles CA 90067-4303

HARRIMAN, JOHN HOWLAND, lawyer; b. Buffalo, Apr. 14, 1920; s. Lewis Gildersleeve and Grace (Bastine) H.; m. Barbara Ann Brunmark, June 12, 1943; children—Walter Brunmark, Constance Bastine, John Howland. A.B. summa cum laude, Dartmouth, 1942; J.D., Stanford U., 1949. Bar: Calif. 1949. Assoc. firm Lawler, Felix & Hall, Los Angeles, 1949-55; asst. v.p., then v.p. Security Pacific Nat. Bank, Los Angeles, 1955-72; sr. v.p. Security Pacific Nat. Bank, 1972-85; of counsel Argue Freston Pearson Harbison & Myers, 1985-86; sec. Security Pacific Corp., 1971-85; dir. Master Metal Works. Mem. L.A. adv. coun. Episcopal Ch. Found., 1977-79; mem. Republican Assocs., 1951—, trustee, 1962-72; mem. Calif. Rep. Central Com., 1956-69, 81—, exec. com., 1960-62, 81-84; mem. L.A. County Rep. Central Com., 1958-70, exec. com., 1960-62, vice chmn., 1962; chmn. Calif. 15th Congl. Dist. Rep. Central Com., 1960-62, Calif. 30th Congl. Dist. Rep. Central Com., 1962; treas. United Rep. Fin. Com. L.A. County, 1969-70; chmn. L.A. County Reagan-Bush campaign, 1980, co-chmn., 1984; exec. dir. Calif. Rep. Party, 1985-86. With USAAF, 1943-46. Mem. Am. Bar Assn., Am. Soc. Corp. Secs. (pres. Los Angeles region 1970-71), State Bar Calif., Los Angeles Bar Assn., Town Hall Los Angeles, Phi Beta Kappa, Theta Delta Chi, Phi Alpha Delta. Clubs: Beach (Santa Monica, Calif.); California (Los Angeles); Lincoln, Breakfast Panel (pres. 1970-71).

HARRINGTON, GLENN LEWIS, insurance company executive; b. Fitchburg, Mass., Dec. 18, 1942; s. Lewis Lowe and Eleanor Frances (Mansfield) H.; m. Marcia Anne Browning, Sept. 3, 1971. Ed., Gordon Coll., 1960-63, Suffolk U., 1963-64. Underwriter Hartford Life Ins. Co., Boston, 1964-66; mktg. mgr. Dentsply Internat., York, Pa., 1966-70; asst. v.p. mktg. Family Life Ins. Co., Seattle, 1971-88; v.p. mktg. Family Life and Merrill Lynch Life Ins. Cos., Seattle, 1988—. V.p., trustee Seattle Opera. Mem. Royal Philatelic Soc. (London), Rainier Club, Coll. Club. Home: PO Box 99689 Seattle WA 98199-0689 Office: Merrill Lynch Life Ins Co Seattle WA 98101

HARRINGTON, MARK GARLAND, oil company executive, venture capitalist; b. San Antonio, Mar. 5, 1953; s. Lloyd Hampton and Gray (Dugger) H.; divorced; 1 child, Alexandra Beall. BBA in Fin., U. Tex., 1976, MBA, 1977. Assoc. U.S. Trust Co. N.Y., N.Y.C., 1977-78, Carl H. Pfozheimer & Co., N.Y.C., 1978-81; ptnr. Carl H. Pfozheimer & Co., 1981-85; pres., CEO Harrington & Co. Internat., N.Y.C., 1986—, HCO Can. Ltd., Calgary, 1987—; chmn., CEO HarCor Energy, Inc., L.A., 1987—; bd. dirs. Jefferson Gas Systems, Washington. Dir. Third St. Music Sch., N.Y.C., 1978-89, Found. for New Am. Music, L.A., 1986—. Mem. Ind. Petrol Assn., Petroleum Exploration Soc. N.Y., Brook Club N.Y., Racquet and Tennis Club (N.Y.), Coronado Club (Houston). Republican. Episcopalian. Office: HarCor Energy Inc 11766 Wilshire Blvd # 720 Los Angeles CA 90025-6538

HARRINGTON, MAURA JAYE, management researcher, consultant; b. Boston, Oct. 8, 1964; d. John Francis and Kathleen Frances (Santry) H. BS, Georgetown U., 1986; MBA, Claremont Grad. Sch., 1991, MA, 1992. Resident dir. Georgetown U., Washington, 1986-87; rsch. asst. Tomas Rivera Ctr., Claremont, Calif., 1987-89; intern in market rsch. Kaiser Permanente, Pasadena, Calif., 1988-88, mgmt. rschr. orgn. effectiveness, 1988-92; assoc. dir. for rsch. Achieving Styles Inst., Pasadena, 1991—; computer cons. Claremont Grad. Sch., 1988—; coord. Inst. for Applied Social & Policy Rsch., Claremont, 1992. Mem. ASTD, APA, ODN, Acad. Mgmt., Western Psychol. Assn., Sigma Xi, Alpha Phi Omega. Roman Catholic. Home: Apt 98 1238 W Arrow Hwy Upland CA 91786 Office: Claremont Grad Sch 130 E 9th St Claremont CA 91711

HARRINGTON, NORMAN WILLIAM, pharmacist; b. Tucson, Ariz., Dec. 21, 1948; s. William Houston and Ruth Elizabeth (Sullivan) H.; m. Catherine Lynn Lacenski, June 5, 1976; children: April Elizabeth, Colleen Marie. BS in Pharmacy, U. Ariz., 1972. Registered pharmacist, Ariz. Pharmacist Ft. Belknap Indian Hosp., Harlem, Mont., 1973-78, Colville Indian Health Ctr., Nespelem, Wash., 1978-84, Gallup (N.M.) Indian Med. Ctr., 1984-86, Apothecary Shops, Inc., Flagstaff, Ariz., 1987-91, Goodwin St. Pharmacy, Prescott, Ariz., 1991-92, Rx Plus subs. Osco Drug, Flagstaff, 1992—. With Indian Health Svc., 1972-86. Mem. Ariz. Pharm. Assn., Soc. No. Ariz. Pharmacists (pres. 1989-90). Republican. Roman Catholic. Home: 3325 S Andrea Dr Flagstaff AZ 86001-9013 Office: Osco Drug # 2330 3506 E Route 66 Flagstaff AZ 86004

HARRINGTON, WALTER HOWARD, JR., state judge; b. San Francisco, Aug. 14, 1926; s. Walter Howard and Doris Ellen (Daniels) H.; B.S., Stanford, 1947; J.D., Hastings Coll., U. Calif., 1952; m. Barbara Bryant, June 1952 (div. 1973); children—Stacey Doreen, Sara Duval; m. 2d, Hertha Bahrs, Sept. 1974. Admitted to Calif. bar, 1953; dep. legislative counsel State of Calif., Sacramento, 1953-54, 55; mem. firm Walner & Harrington, Sacramento, 1954; dep. dist. atty. San Mateo County, Redwood City, Calif., 1955-62; practiced in Redwood City, 1962-84; judge San Mateo County Mcpl. Ct., 1984-90, Superior Ct., 1990—. Chmn., San Mateo County Criminal Justice Council, 1971-76, San Mateo County Adult Correctional Facilities Com., 1969-71; pro tem referee San Mateo County Juvenile Ct., 1967-72. Served as ensign USNR, 1944-46. Mem. San Mateo County Bar Assn. (pres. 1969, editor publs. 1964-74), State Bar Calif. (editorial bd. 1968-81, vice chmn. 1969, 74-75, chmn., editor 1975-76), San Mateo County Legal Aid Soc. (pres. 1971-72), Order of Coif, Delta Theta Phi. Republican. Episcopalian. Office: Hall of Justice 401 Marshall St Redwood City CA 94063-1655

HARRINGTON-LLOYD, JEANNE LEIGH, interior designer; b. L.A.; d. Peter Valentine and Avis Lorraine (Brown) Harrington; m. James Wilkinson, Dec. 17, 1966 (div. Mar. 1976); m. David Lloyd, Nov. 27, 1985. BS in Psychology, U. Utah, 1984; cert., Salt Lake Sch. Interior Design, 1985; MS in Mgmt., Marylhurst Coll., 1990. With Mary Webb-Davis Agy., L.A., 1970; model, actress McCarty Agy., Salt Lake City, 1983-85; contract designer Innerspace Design, Salt Lake City, 1985-89; space planning and utilization mgr. U.S. Bancorp, Portland, Oreg., 1991—. Mem. Internat. Facilities Mgmt. Assn. Democrat. Home: 4580 SW Natchez Ct Tualatin OR 97062-8769

HARRIS, BARBARA HULL (MRS. F. CHANDLER HARRIS), social agency administrator; b. L.A., Nov. 1, 1921; d. Hamilton and Marion (Eimers) Baird; student UCLA, 1939-41, 45-47; m. F. Chandler Harris, Aug. 10, 1946; children—Victoria, Randolph Boyd. Pres., Victoria Originals, 1955-62; partner J.B. Assos., cons., 1971-73; statewide dir. vols. Children's Home Soc. Calif., 1971-75. Los Angeles County Heart Sunday chmn. Los Angeles County Heart Assn. (recipient Outstanding Service award 1965), 1965, bd. dirs., 1966-69; mem. exec. com. Hollywood Bowl Vols., 1966-84, chmn. vols., 1971, 75; chmn. Coll. Alumni of Assistance League, 1962; mem. exec. com. Assistance League So. Calif., 1964-71, 72-80, 83-89, pres., 1976-80; bd. dirs. Nat. Charity League, Los Angeles, 1965-69, 75, sec., 1967, 3d v.p., 1968; ways and means chmn., dir. Los Angeles Am. Horse Show, 1969; dir. Coronet Debutante Ball, 1968, ball bd. chmn., 1969-70, 75, 84, mem. ball bd., 1969—; pres. Hollywood Bowl Patroness com., 1976; v.p. Irving Walker aux. Travelers Aid, 1976, 79, pres., 1988-89; pres. So. Calif. alumni council Alpha Phi, 1961, fin. adviser to chpts. U. So. Calif., 1961-72, UCLA, 1965-72; benefit chmn. Gold Shield, 1969, 1st v.p., 1970-72; chmn. Golden Thimble III Needlework Exhbn., Hosp. of Good Samaritan, 1975; bd. dirs. UCLA Affiliates, 1976-78, KCET Women's Council, 1979-83, Region V United Way, 1980-83; pres. Jr. Philharmonic Com., 1981-82; bd. dirs. Los Angeles Founder chpt. Achievement Rewards for Coll. Scientists, 1980-91, pres., 1984-85. Recipient Ivy award as outstanding Alpha Phi alumna So. Calif., 1969; outstanding alumni award for community service UCLA, 1978; Mannequin's Eve award, 1980. Mem. Hollywood C. of C. (dir. 1980-81). Home: 7774 Skyhill Dr Los Angeles CA 90068-1232

HARRIS, CHARLES SOMERVILLE, athletics coach, educator; b. Richmond, Va., Aug. 22, 1950; s. Robert O. and Dorothy J. H.; m. Lenora Billings, Aug. 10, 1973. BA, Hampton (Va.) Inst., 1972; MA, U. Mich., 1973. Info. asst. U. Mich., Ann Arbor, 1973, asst. dir. athletics, 1973-79; dir. recreational and intramural athletics U. Pa., Phila., 1979-85; dir. athletics Ariz. State U., Tempe, 1985—; cons. athletics Hampton U., 1990-91, SUNY, Buffalo, 1990-91; chmn. Pac-10 com. NCAA. Editorial cons. Coll. Athletics Rev.; contbr. articles to profl. jours. Mem. exec. com. Valley of the Sun YMCA, Phoenix; active mens basketball com. NCAA, fin. aid com. Named Outstanding Young Philadelphian, Phildelphia mag., 1980. Mem. Nat. Assn. Dirs. Collegiate Athletics (exec. com.), Sigma Pi Phi, Kappa Alpha Psi (regional citation 1978). Home: PO Box 1002 Tempe AZ 85224 Office: Ariz State U Dept Athletics Tempe AZ 85287-2505

HARRIS, CHRISTIE LUCY, author; b. Newark, Nov. 21, 1907; d. Edward and Matilda (Christie) Irwin; m. Thomas A. Harris, Feb. 13, 1932; children: Michael, Moira, Sheilagh, Brian, Gerald. Tchrs. cert., Provincial Normal Sch., Vancouver, B.C., Can., 1925. Tchr. B.C., 1925-32; free-lance scriptwriter Canadian Broadcasting Corp. radio, 1936-63; women's editor B.C. News Weekly, Abbotsford, 1951-57. Author: Raven's Cry, 1966, Mouse Woman books (3), 1976, 77, 79, The Trouble With Princesses, 1980, others. Decorated Order of Can., 1981; recipient Can. Book of Yr. medal for Children's book, 1967, 77; Can. Council Children's Lit. prize, 1981. Mem. Writers' Union Can. (life). Address: 430 Arnold Ave, Victoria, BC Canada V8S 3M2

HARRIS, CLARK EVERETT, sales executive; b. San Pedro, Calif., Apr. 4, 1966; s. Robert Everett and Mary (Bourquin) H. BA, U. Calif., Santa Barbara, 1988; MBA, San Francisco State U., 1992. West Coast sales mgr. The Wine Spectator, San Francisco, 1989—; vineyard mgr. Blue Ridge Vineyards, Napa, Calif., 1988—. Republican. Home: 1345 Chestnut # 1 San Francisco CA 94123 Office: The Wine Spectator 601 Van Ness Ave Ste 2014 San Francisco CA 94102

HARRIS, CLAUDE, fire department chief. Fire chief Seattle Fire Dept. Office: Seattle Fire Dept Office of the Chief 301 2nd Ave S Seattle WA 98104-2680*

HARRIS, DALE RAY, lawyer; b. Crab Orchard, Ill., May 11, 1937; s. Ray B. and Aurelia M. (Davis) H.; m. Toni K. Shapkoff, June 26, 1960; children: Kristen Dee, Julie Diane. BA in Math., U. Colo., 1959; LLB, Harvard U., 1962. Bar: Colo. 1962, U.S. Dist. Ct. Colo. 1962, U.S. Ct. Appeals (10th cir.) 1962, U.S. Supreme Ct. 1981. Assoc. Davis, Graham & Stubbs, Denver, 1962-67, ptnr., 1967—, chmn. mgmt. com., 1982-85; speaker, instr. various antitrust seminars; bd. dirs. Lend-A-Lawyer, Inc., 1989—. Mem. campaign cabinet Mile High United Way, 1986-87, chmn., atty. adv. com., 1988, sec., legal counsel, trustee, mem. exec. com. 1989—; trustee The Spaceship Earth Fund, 1986-89, Legal Aid Found. Colo., 1989—; mem. devel. coun. U. Colo. Arts & Scis. dept., 1985—; area chmn. law sch. fund Harvard U., 1978-81. With USAR, 1962-68. Fellow ABA, Am. Bar Found., Colo. Bar Found., Colo. Bar Assn. (chmn. antitrust com. 1980-84; coun. corp. banking and bus. law sect. 1978-83, bd. govs. 1991—, exec. com. 1993—), Denver Bar Assn. (chmn. Centennial Com. 1990-91, pres.-elect 1992-93, pres. 1993—, bd. trustees 1992—), Colo. Assn. Corp. Counsel (pres. 1973-74), Denver Law Club (pres. 1976-77), Phi Beta Kappa, Univ. Club, Union League Club (Chgo.), Rotary (Denver). Home: 2032 Bellaire St Denver CO 80207-3722 Office: Davis Graham & Stubbs 370 17th St PO Box 185 Denver CO 80201

HARRIS, DARRYL WAYNE, publishing executive; b. Emmett, Idaho, July 29, 1941; s. Reed Ingval and Evelyn Faye (Wengreen) H.; m. Christine Sorenson, Sept. 10, 1965; children: Charles Reed, Michael Wayne, Jason Darryl, Stephanie, Ryan Joseph. B.A., Brigham Young U., 1966. Staff writer Deseret News, Salt Lake City, 1965, Post-Register, Idaho Falls, 1966-67; tech. editor Idaho Nuclear Corp., Idaho Falls, 1967-68; account exec. David W. Evans & Assos. Advt., Salt Lake City, 1968-71; pres. Harris Pub., Inc., Idaho Falls, 1971—; pub. Potato Grower of Idaho mag., 1972—, Snowmobile West mag., 1974—, Sugar Producer mag., 1974—, Blue Ribbon mag., 1987-90, ShowAction mag., 1987—, Western Guide to Snowmobiling, 1988—, Houseboat Mag., 1990—. Campaign mgr. George Hansen for Congress Com., 1974, 76; campaign chmn. Mel Richardson for Congress Com., 1986; 1st counselor to pres. Korean Mission, Ch. Jesus Christ of Latter-day Saints, Seoul, Korea, 1963, area public communications dir., Eastern Idaho, 1976-86; High Priest, Ch. Jesus Christ of Latter-Day Saints, 1987-91, high coun. Idaho Falls Ammon Stake, 1987-91; founder Blue Ribbon Coalition, 1987; v.p. Teton Peaks Council Boy Scouts Am., 1987-92; publicity chmn. Upper Snake River Scout Encampment, 1988; founder , pres. Our Land Soc., 1989-92. Mem. Agr. Editors Assn., Internat. Snowmobile Industry Assn. (Best Overall Reporting journalism award 1979, 80), Western Publs. Assn., World Champion Cutter and Chariot Racing Assn. (historian 1966-80), Nat. Snowmobile Found. (founder 1988), Kappa Tau Alpha. Lodge: Idaho Falls Kiwanis (pres. 1978, Disting. Club Pres. award 1978). Office: Harris Pub Inc 520 Park Ave Idaho Falls ID 83402-3516

HARRIS, DAVID JACK, artist, painter, educator; b. San Mateo, Calif., Jan. 6, 1948; s. Jack McAllister and Audrey Ellen (Vogt) H. BA, San Francisco State U., 1971, MA, 1975. Dir. Galerie de Tours, San Francisco, 1971-72; lectr. Chabot Coll., Hayward, Calif., 1975-80; interior designer David Harris Assocs., San Mateo, 1975-85; freelance artist, painter San Mateo, 1975—; art cons. David Harris Assocs., Belmont, Calif., 1980—; v.p. Coastal Arts League Mus., Half Moon Bay, Calif., 1988—; ptnr., art dir. Fine Art Pub., Palo Alto, Calif., 1989—; bd. dirs. 1870 Gallery and Studios, Belmont, 1978—, gallery dir., 1989—, owner, partner HSW Gallery, San Francisco. Painter murals Chartered Bank of London, 1979, Caesar's Hotel, Las Vegas, 1984, Pacific Telephone, San Francisco; author mus. catalog California Concepts, 1988; rep. in permanent collections: Ask Computer, Palo Alto, Shared Fin., Harris Corp, Bain and Co., San Francisco, Verilink, Litton Industries, Foothill Bank, Los Altos, Chartered Bank of London, San Francisco, Stanford U., Palo Alto, Golden Nugget Hotel, Atlantic City, Nat. Bank of Detroit, Crisafi, Sciabica, Woodward, D.J. Crisafi and Co., Sheraton Grande, L.A., others. Recipient Purchase award North Cen. Washington Mus., 1988. Mem. Internat. Soc. Interior Designers, Coastal Arts League Mus. (v.p. 1988—, Zoe Tierny award 1988). Home and Office: 1870 Ralston Ave Belmont CA 94002-1859

HARRIS, DAVID JOEL, foundation executive; b. Miller, S.D., Sept. 22, 1950; s. Joel Chips and Amy Ruth (Rietz) H.; m. Susan Claire Hagius, June 30, 1979; children: John, Jennifer. BA, Earlham Coll., Richmond, Ind., 1972; MS, Purdue U., 1975; PhD, U. Hawaii, 1983. Vis. rsch. asst. Internat. Ctr. Tropical Agr., Cali, Colombia, 1975-76; rsch. assoc. U. Hawaii, Honolulu, 1976-83; sr. rsch. fellow Internat. Ctr. Tropical Agr., 1984-87; mgr. Calif.-Nev. United Meth. Found., San Francisco, 1988-92, exec. v.p., 1992—. Contbr. articles to profl. jours. Pres. Mothers Against Drunk Driving, Sonoma County, Calif., 1989-91. Recipient Lubrizol award, 1971; Purdue grad. fellow, 1972; NSF fellow, 1973. Mem. Commonwealth Club of Calif., Phi Beta Kappa. Methodist. Home: 355 Gemma Cir Santa Rosa CA 95404-2733 Office: Calif Nev United Meth Found 1579 Farmers Ln Ste 283 Santa Rosa CA 95405-7535

HARRIS, DAVID THOMAS, immunologist; b. Jonesboro, Ark., May 9, 1956; s. Marm Melton and Lucille Luretha (Buck) H.; m. Francoise Jacqueline Besencon, June 24, 1989. BS in Biology, Math. and Psychology, Wake Forest U., 1978, MS, 1980, PhD in Microbiology and Immunology, 1982. Fellow Ludwig Inst. Cancer Rsch., Lausanne, Switzerland, 1982-85; rsch. asst. prof. U. N.C., Chapel Hill, 1985-89; assoc. prof. U. Ariz., Tuscon, 1989—; cons. Teltech, Inc., Mpls., 1990—; bd. sci. advisors Cryo-Cell Internat., 1992—; bd. dirs. Ageria, Inc., Tucson, 1992—. Co-author chpts. to sci. books, articles to profls. jours.; reviewer sci. jours.; co-holder 2 scientific patents. Grantee local and fed. rsch. grants, 1988—. Mem. AAAS, Am. Assn. Immunologists, Reticuloendothelial Soc., Internat. Soc. Devel. and Comparative Immunology, Scandanavian Soc. Immunology. Democrat. Mem. Ch. of Christ. Office: U Ariz Dept Microbiology Bldg 90 Tucson AZ 85721

HARRIS, DEBRA CORAL, physical education educator; b. Portland, Oreg., Feb. 4, 1953; d. Raymond Dale and Kathleen Caroline (Himpel) H. AA, Cen. Oreg. Community Coll., 1974; BS in Health and Phys. Edn., So. Oreg. State Coll., 1976, MST in Health Edn., 1982. Tchr. phys. edn., coach Franklin High Sch., Portland, 1976-79; instr. health, phys. edn., tennis coach Mt. Hood Community Coll., Gresham, Oreg., 1979-80; health and phys. edn. specialist, coach Inza R. Wood Middle Sch., Wilsonville, Oreg., 1980-86; tchr. health and phys. edn. West Linn (Oreg.)High Sch., 1986—; mem. planning com. Seaside Health Conf., Oreg. Dept. Edn., 1985-87; writer AIDS curriculum, 1987-88; cons. health edn. textbooks Glenco Pub. Co., 1987-88. Mem. AIDS subcom. ARC, Portland, 1988-89, safety svcs. com. 1988—, sex edn. coalition com. Planned Parenthood, Portland, 1988-90, com. women's sport leadership network U. Oreg., Eugene, 1988—. Recipient Vol. of Month award ARC, 1984, Profl. Leadership award Oreg. Gov's. Coun. for Health Phys. Edn. Fitness & Sport, 1986, Outstanding Health/Phy. Edn. award Portland State U., 1988, Nat. High Sch. Physical Educator of the Year award, 1993. Mem. Am. Alliance Health, Phys. Edn., Recreation & Dance (nat. pub. affairs & legis. com. 1987—), Oreg. Alliance Health, Phys. Edn., Recreation & Dance (pres. 1984-85), Oreg. Assn. Advanced Health Edn. (pres. 1987-89), AAUW, Oreg. Edn. Assn. (uniserv treas. 1985-86), Kappa Delta Pi. Home: 8315 SE Mill St Portland OR 97216-1434 Office: West Linn High Sch 5464 W A St West Linn OR 97068

HARRIS, EDWARD A., producer, writer, director; b. Elizabeth, N.J., Dec. 14, 1946; s. Howard E. and Bernice W. Harris; m. Chris Garrison, May 16, 1987. Student music composition and theory, U. Okla., 1964-67, Los Angeles Community Coll., 1977, UCLA, 1978. Singer, songwriter, 1962—; pres., exec. producer Myriad Prodns., Los Angeles, 1965—; creative dir. Myriad Graphics, Los Angeles, 1976—; producer, assoc. dir. Columbia Music Hall, Hartford, Conn., 1972-75; film and TV producer, 1971—; multi-media entertainment cons., Los Angeles, 1977—; field producer Good Morning Am., also Good Night Am., ABC-TV, 1975-77; exec. producer, dir. The Act Factory, Los Angeles, 1977-83; sr. ptnr. Myriad-Fritz Prodns., Los Angeles, 1977-83; v.p. Sports Prodns., Am. Videogram, Inc., Los Angeles, 1986-87; ptnr. Myriad/Knox Prodns., Los Angeles, 1987-92, H-two-O Prodns., L.A., 1987-92; exec. producer Gateway Group, San Francisco, 1974-75; dir. Performance Evaluation Workshop, Los Angeles Songwriter's Expo, 1978-83; co-dir. SPVA Performing Arts Workshop, Los Angeles, 1980; exec. dir. Nat. Sports Found., L.A., 1993—. Composer over 30 songs; exec. producer: (TV show) The National Sports Tributes, 1991—; producer: (TV sports mag.) The Clubhouse, 1982—, (TV series) Boating World, ESPN, 1987-92. Pres. Wintonbury Mall Mchts. Assn., Bloomfield, Conn., 1971-72. Mem. Am. Fedn. Musicians, AGVA, Soc. for Preservation of Variety Arts, Alpha Epsilon Pi, Kappa Kappa Psi.

HARRIS, ELIHU MASON, mayor; b. L.A., Aug. 15, 1947; m. Kathy Neal, Aug. 14, 1982. BS in Polit. Sci. with honors, Calif. State U., 1968; M in Pub. Adminstrn., U. Calif., Berkeley, 1969; JD, U. Calif., Davis, 1972. Bar: Calif., D.C. Pvt. practice Calif., 1977-78; formerly mem. Calif. Legis. Assembly, from 1978; now mayor City of Oakland, Calif.; prof. pol. sci. and adminstrn. of justice Calif. State U., Hayward and Sacramento campuses. Former chmn. Joint Legis. Audit Com., Assembly Com. on Fair Employment Practices and the Select Com. on Judicial Eficiency and Improvement, also former mem. Ways and Means, Judiciary, and Health and Transp. coms.; mem. Niagara Movement Dem. Club. Dr. Martin Luther King Rsch. fellow U. Calif. Davis Sch. Law; finalist White House Fellowships competition, 1977-78. Mem. ABA (exec. dir. 1975-77), NAACP, Charles Houston Bar Assn., Calif. Assn. Black Lawyers, Black Am. Polit. Assn. Calif. (former chmn.), Kappa Alpha Psi. Office: Office of Mayor 1 City Hall Plz Oakland CA 94612-1901

HARRIS, EMMA EARL, nursing home executive; b. Viper, Ky., Nov. 6, 1936; d. Andrew Jackson and Zola (Hall) S.; m. Ret Haney Marten Henis Harris, June 5, 1981; children: Debra, Joseph, Wynona, Robert Walsh. Grad. St. Joseph Sch. Practical Nursing. Staff nurse St. Joseph Hosp., Bangor, Maine, 1973-75; office nurse Dr. Eugene Brown, Bangor, 1975-77; dir. nurses Fairborn Nursing Home, Ohio, 1977-78; staff nurse Hillhaven Hospice, Tucson, 1979-80; asst. head nurse, 1980; co-owner Nu-Life Elderly Guest Home, Tucson, 1980—. Author: Thoughts on Life, 1988. Vol. Heart Assn., Bangor, 1965-70, Cancer Assn., Bangor, 1965-70. Mem. NAFE. Democrat. Avocations: theatre, opera. Home: 1082 E Seneca St Tucson AZ 85719-3567

HARRIS, ERIC ALBERT, hardware engineer; b. Budapest, Hungary, Apr. 3, 1920; s. Victor Michael V. and Rela (Ettinger) Loewe H.; m. Nelly Chender, June 28, 1946 (div. 1961); 1 child, David Alan; m. Beatrix Sybil Berger, Sept. 29, 1967. BEE, UCLA, 1948; PhD in Nuclear Physics, U. Innsbruck, 1949. Engr. KMTR Corp., Hollywood, Calif., 1948-50; engr. TV CBS, Inc., N.Y.C., 1950-61; recording cons. CBS-TV, Munich, 1960-61; video mktg. mgr. AMPEX Corp., Fribourg, Switzerland, 1961-72; sr. engr. AMPEX Corp., Redwood City, Calif., 1980-83; cons. Mayo Clinic, Rochester, Minn., 1972-80; sr. software writer Gould Inc., Santa Clara, Calif., 1983-84; sr. software engr. CAE/Tektronix, Santa Clara, Calif., 1984-87; cons. Eribea Assocs., Half Moon Bay, Calif., 1984—. Capt. OSS, 1943-46. Mem. IEEE, Computer Soc., Soc. Motion Picture and TV Engrs. Democrat. Jewish. Home and Office: 132 Ocean Blvd Half Moon Bay CA 94019

HARRIS, ERIC NATHAN, bank executive; b. Phoenix, Mar. 9, 1959; s. Edward Nathan and Barbara Lee (Kohler) H.; m. Janet Marie Houle, Apr. 26, 1986; children: Elliot Nathan, Carter Mathew. BA cum laude in Econs., Whitman Coll., Walla Walla, Wash., 1981. Rsch. asst. John D. Herbert & Assocs., Phoenix, 1980, rsch. assoc., 1981-82; product devel. officer, corp. officer Valley Nat. Bank, Phoenix, 1982-84, product mgr., asst. v.p., 1984-87, sr. market mgr., asst. v.p., 1987-90, v.p., bus. mgr., 1991—; mem. Ariz. Educational Loan Program Adv. Coun. Mem. Am. Inst. Banking (chmn. mktg. com. Ariz. 1987-88), Wiharu Toastmasters (pres. 1988-89), Valley Tennis Assn. (rules com. 1987-88), Valley Bowling League, Phoenix Direct Mktg. Club, Phi Beta Kappa. Republican. Episcopalian. Office: Valley Nat Bank A248 PO Box 71 Phoenix AZ 85001-0071

HARRIS, F. CHANDLER, emeritus university administrator; b. Neligh, Nebr., Nov. 5, 1914; s. James Carlton and Helen Ayres (Boyd) H.; m. Barbara Ann Hull, Aug. 10, 1946; children: Victoria, Randolph Boyd. AB, UCLA, 1936. Assoc. editor Telegraph Delivery Spirit, Los Angeles, 1937-39; writer, pub. service network radio programs University Explorer, Sci. Editor, U. Calif., 1939-61; pub. information mgr. UCLA, 1961-75, dir., 1975-82, dir. emeritus, 1982—. Mem. pub. relations com., western region United Way, 1972-75; bd. dirs. Am. Youth Symphony, Los Angeles, 1978—, v.p., 1983—; bd. dirs. Hathaway Home for Children, 1982-88. Recipient 1st prize NBC Radio Inst., 1944; Harvey Hebert medal Delta Sigma Phi, 1947, Mr. Delta Sig award, 1972; Adam award Assistance League Mannequins, 1980, Univ. Service award UCLA Alumni Assn., 1986. Mem. Western Los Angeles Regional C. of C. (dir. 1976-80), U. Calif. Retirees Assn. Los Angeles (pres. 1985-87), Sigma Delta Chi, Delta Sigma Phi (nat. pres. 1959-63). Club: UCLA Faculty (sec. bd. govs. 1968-72). Editor Interfraternity Research Adv. Council Bull., 1949-50, Carnation, 1969-80, Royce Hall, 1985. Home: 7774 Skyhill Dr Los Angeles CA 90068-1232

HARRIS, FREDERICK ALLAN, physicist, educator; b. Bay City, Mich., Dec. 27, 1941; s. John and Margaret Wilhelmina (Large) H.; m. Joan Page Williamson, May 1, 1965; children—Frederick Allan, Robert Daniel. B.S.E., U. Mich., 1963, M.S., 1965, Ph.D., 1970. Asst. physicist U. Hawaii, Honolulu, 1970-76, assoc. physicist, 1976-78, assoc. prof. dept. physics and astronomy, 1978-86, prof., 1986—; proceedings editor Workshop on Physics and Experiments at Linear e e- Colliders. Contbr. articles to profl. jours.; proceedings editor Tenth Hawaii Conf. in High Energy Physics. Mem. Am. Phys. Soc., Hawaiian Acad. Sci., Hawaii Bonsai Assn. (treas.), Pacific Bonsai Club , Sigma Xi. Office: U Hawaii Dept Physics and Astronomy Honolulu HI 96822

HARRIS, GARY M., physicist, consultant; b. Wadsworth, Ohio, Feb. 26, 1943; s. Charles F. and Geraldine M. (Barnett) H.; m. Marsha L. Longsdorf (div. 1978); children: Vega Harris Tabata, Nik, Dianthe. BS in Physics, U. Akron, 1968, MS in Physics, 1971. Mgr. Babcock & Wilcox Co., Barberton, Ohio, 1962-66, Goodyear Aerospace Corp., Akron, Ohio, 1966-72, Xerox Data Systems, El Segundo, Calif., 1972-75, Computer Automation, Irvine, Calif., 1975-77; bus. area mgr. Elec. Memories & Magnetics, Encino, Calif., 1977-80; sr. mgr. Xerox Corp., Sunnyvale, Calif., 1980-90; v.p. Frox Inc., Sunnyvale, 1990-92; pres. Global 2000, Belmont, Calif., 1992-93; dir. Sharp Corp., Japan, 1993—; v.p. mktg. The Planning Forum, South Bay Chpt., 1988-90; bd. dirs. Ahead Tech., Inc., 1989-90. Vice chmn. Planning Commn., Belmont, Calif., 1990-92, chmn, 1993—. Mem. Am. Mensa, Intertel, Sigma Pi Sigma. Republican. Home: 2007 Forest Ave Belmont CA 94002

HARRIS, GEORGE E., JR., lawyer; b. June 10, 1955; s. George E. and Marilyn Harris; m. Suzi Harris; children: Alicia, Adam, Tiffany, Jacob. BA in Econs., Brigham Young U., 1978; JD, Washington U., St. Louis, 1981. Bar: Mo. 1981, Utah 1986. Assoc. Bryan, Cave, McPheeters & McRoberts, St. Louis, 1981-85, Jones, Waldo, Holbrook & McD., Salt Lake City, 1985-86; assoc. Callister, Duncan & Nebeker, Salt Lake City, 1986-87, shareholder, dir., 1987—. Athletic scholar Brigham Young U., 1973-77, scholar Washington U., 1978-81. Mem. ABA, Utah State Bar, Mo. State Bar, Nat. Assn. Bond Lawyers. Home: 1987 E Gunderson Ln Holladay UT 84124 Office: Callister Duncan & Nebeker Kennecott Bldg Ste 800 10 East South Temple Salt Lake City UT 84133

HARRIS, HOWARD JEFFREY, marketing and printing company executive; b. Denver, June 9, 1949; s. Gerald Victor and Leona Lee (Tepper) H.; m. Michele Whealen, Feb. 6, 1975; children: Kimberly, Valerie. BFA with honors, Kansas City Art Inst., 1973; M. of Indsl. Design with honors, Pratt Inst., 1975; postgrad. Graphic Arts Research Center, Rochester Inst. Tech., 1977; cert. mktg. exec., U. Utah, 1987. Indsl. designer Kivett & Myers, Architects, 1970-71; indsl. designer United Research Corp., Denver, 1971-72; indsl. designer, asst. to v.p., pres. JFN Assos., N.Y.C., 1972-73; dir. facility planning Abt & Assos., Cambridge, Mass., 1973-74; v.p. design, prodn., and research Eagle Direct, Denver, 1974—; pres. HSR Corp., Denver. Mem. Indsl. Designers Soc. Am., Graphic Arts Tech. Found., Design Methods Group, The Color Group, Nat. Assn. Counsel for Children, Am. Advt. Fedn. Democrat. Jewish. Office: 5105 E 41st Ave Denver CO 80216-4420

HARRIS, JERILYN ROLINSON, educator, consultant; b. Shaker Heights, Ohio, Oct. 28, 1942; d. Myron Arthur and Bertha Kathryn (Lamneck) Rolinson; m. Michael Ford Harris, June 25, 1966; children: Kelli Michelle, Ryan Rolinson. BS, UCLA, 1964, MS, 1966. Life gen. secondary, life standard secondary, clear biol. scis. credentials, Calif. Tchr. Beverly Hills (Calif.) Unified Sch. Dist., 1965-70; sci. tchr. Ukial (Calif.) Unified Sch. Dist., 1978—; cons. Calif. Dept. Edn., Sacramento, 1986-89, Ednl. Testing Svc., Trenton, N.J., 1992—; chmn. Commn. on Tchr. Credentialing, 1992—; tchr. rep. to Calif. Presdl. Inaugural, 1989. Chmn. bd. dirs. Mendocino Community Hosp., Ukiah, 1985-87; chmn. Sunset Rev. Com., Sacramento, 1986-87. Named Educator of Yr., Mendocino County C. of C., 1991. Mem. AAUW, AAAS, NSTA, NEA, Nat. Assn. Biology Tchrs., Calif. Sci. Tchrs. Assn. (policy com. 1984—), Calif. Biology Educators Assn. (sec. 1991—), Phi Delta Kappa. Office: Ukiah High Sch 1000 Low Gap Rd Ukiah CA 95482

HARRIS, JOE NEWTON, naval officer; b. Konawa, Okla., June 7, 1946; s. George William and Oberia Mae (Sanders) H.; m. Tacy Lynn Cook, Nov. 21, 1983; 1 child, Cassandra Simone. BA, Duke U., 1968; MBA, Nat. U., 1975; MS, Naval Postgrad. Sch., Monterey, Calif., 1979. Commd. ensign USN, 1968, advanced through grades to comdr., 1983; avionics officer E-2 Aircraft Squadron, San Diego, 1970-73, head ops. dept., 1980-82; contract monitoring officer Fleet Combat Direction Systems, San Diego, 1973-76; tactical data systems officer USS Enterprise, Alameda, Calif., 1976-78; mem. staff Naval Postgrad. Sch., 1978-80, 82-84, mem. faculty, 1982-84; program mgr. Security Assistance Acctg., Denver, 1984-88; fin. compt. Naval Air Sta. Miramar, San Diego, 1988—. Treas. Navy Relief Aux., 1988—. Decorated Air medal with six oak leaf clusters. Mem. Am. Soc. Mil. Compts. (pres. San Diego chpt. 1989—), Delta Sigma Phi. Home: 933 Tarento Dr San Diego CA 92106-2827 Office: Naval Air Sta Miramar Code l00 San Diego CA 92145

HARRIS, KEITH STELL, psychologist; b. Morrilton, Ark., Oct. 19, 1952; s. Earle Gaines and Katie Lee (Stell) H. PhD in Clin. Psychology, U.S. Internat. U., San Diego, 1988. Lic. psychologist, Calif., Ariz. Served to E-6 USAF, 1975-87, separated, 1987; clinic supr., psychologist San Bernardino County Dept. Mental Health, San Bernardino, Calif., 1988—. Mem. APA, Calif. Psychol. Assn., Nat. Register Health Svc. Providers in Psychology. Home: 1832 E Newgrove St Lancaster CA 93535-3483 Office: Dept Mental Health 700 E Gilbert St San Bernardino CA 92415-0001

HARRIS, KIP KING, architect; b. Sheridan, Wyoming, May 22, 1945; s. Donald Corwin and Florence Alline (King) Harris; m. Marina Littig, Sept. 7, 1969. AB in English, Dartmouth Coll., 1967; AM in Gen. Studies in Humanities, U. Chgo., 1971; MArch, U. Utah, 1978. Lic. architect, Utah, Alaska, Calif., Ariz. Draftsman Inoway & Matsubayashi Architects, Salt Lake City, 1977-78; intern architect Wallace N. Cooper 2, Architect, Salt Lake City, 1978-79, Fowler/Ferguson/Kingston/Ruben Architects, Salt Lake City, 1979-83; prin. FFKR Architects/Planners II, Salt Lake City, 1983—. Author: Confronting the Older House, 1979. Mem. Salt Lake City Art Design Bd., 1986-92; bd. dirs. Utah Media Arts Ctr., 1985-89. Dartmouth Gen. fellowship, 1969, U. Chgo. fellowship, 1969; recipient Lorenzo Young award U. Utah, 1978, Utah Arts Coun. Photo Purchase award, 1992. Mem. AIA (Student Gold medal 1978). Office: FFKR Architecture/Planning/Interior Design 132 Pierpont Ave Ste 200 Salt Lake City UT 84101-1901

HARRIS, LARA, actress; b. Oak Park, Ill., Aug. 22, 1962; d. Donald Paul and Sharon Lee (Walsh) H. Student, U. Ill., 1980-82. Translator St. James Press, Chgo., 1980-82; model Elite Models, Paris, 1982, Wilhelmina Models, N.Y.C. and L.A., 1983—; actress Met. Talent Agy., N.Y.C., L.A., 1986—; 1972. Appeared in movies No Man's Land, 1987, Blood Red, 1988, The Fourth War, 1989, Too Much Sun, 1990, The Fisher King, 1990, Singles, 1991, All Tied Up, 1992, Demolition Man, 1993. Mem. SAG, Actors Equity Assn., Phi Eta Sigma, Alpha Lambda Delta.

HARRIS, LAWRENCE KENNETH, entertainment industry consultant; b. Bklyn., June 10, 1935; s. Harry and Frieda (Pavlow) H.; m. Freyda Schultz, June 1961 (div. 1972); m. Mary Ellen Miranda, Aug. 1975 (div. Feb. 1980); m. Carole Ann Lotterman, Sept. 20, 1986; children: Owen, Julie. BA in Govt., U. Mich., 1956; JD, Harvard U., 1959. Instr. of law U. Mich. Law Sch., Ann Arbor, 1959-60; assoc. Wickes, Riddell, Bloomer, Jacobi & McGuire, N.Y.C., 1960-63; atty. CBS Records, N.Y.C., 1963-66; sr. v.p. Elektra Records, N.Y.C., 1966-69; pres. Ampex Record Corp., N.Y.C., 1969-71; sr. v.p. bus. and adminstrn. CBS Records, N.Y.C., 1971-76; sr. v.p., gen. mgr. Portrait Records, L.A., 1976-80; sr. v.p. Twentieth Century Fox, L.A., 1980-86; pvt. practice cons. L.A., 1986—. Dist. leader Campaigns for Jack Kennedy, Kenneth Keating, and John Lindsey, N.Y.C. Home: 3081 E Hillcrest Dr Thousand Oaks CA 91362-3157

HARRIS, MARILYN RITTENHOUSE, writer; b. Gary, Ind., Feb. 25, 1935; d. Melvin Andrew and Edith (Sherwood) R.; m. Carlyle Smith Harris, Dec. 27, 1968. BA with distinction, Purdue U., 1957; MA, N.Mex. State U., 1958; MS, U. So. Calif., 1966, U. Hawaii, 1977; cuisine régionale, Le Cordon Bleu, Paris, 1993. Cert. tchr., libr. Tchr. of English The Kamehameha Schs., Honolulu, 1964-65; libr. U. Calif., Santa Barbara, 1966-69; lectr. food seminars Kapiolani Community Coll., Honolulu, 1989, 90, Lyon's Arboretum, Honolulu, 1990; cons. U. Hawaii Press, Honolulu, 1990. Author: Mangos, Mangos, Mangos, 1989, Tropical Fruit Cookbook, 1993. Mem. Delta Gamma Alumnae Assn. (Cable award 1980). Home: 966 Koae St Honolulu HI 96816-5005 Office: U Hawaii Press c/o Wiley 2840 Kolowalu St Honolulu HI 96822

HARRIS, MARTIN STEPHEN, aerospace executive; b. Greenville, S.C., Nov. 23, 1939; s. Vitruvius Aiken and Clara Margaret (Thackston) H.; m. Helen C. Dean, Sept. 7, 1963 (div. May 1980); children: Dean, Susan, James; m. Prudence Cooper Bolstad, Jan. 20, 1990 (dec. Mar. 10, 1993). BS in Physics, Furman U., 1962; MS in Physics, Fla. State U., 1967; ret., USAF, 1982. Commd. 2d lt. USAF, 1962, advanced through grades to maj., 1973, ret., 1982; sr. project engr. Hughes Aircraft Co., El Segundo, Calif., 1982-84, section head, 1984-86, space vehicle mgr., 1986-89, asst. program mgr., 1989—. Mem. Sigma Alpha Epsilon.

HARRIS, MARY BIERMAN, psychology educator; b. St. Louis, Feb. 9, 1943; d. Norman and Margaret (Loeb) Bierman; m. Richard Jerome Harris, June 14, 1965; children: Jennifer, Christopher, Alexander. BA, Radcliffe U., 1964; MA, Stanford U., 1965, PhD, 1968. From asst. prof. to full prof. U. N.Mex., Albuquerque, 1968—; vis. assoc. prof. Ohio State U., Columbus, 1974-75; vis. prof. U. NSW, Australia, 1981-82, U. Ga., 1988-89; mem. adv. bd. Nat. Inst. Edn.-N.Mex. State U. Project, Las Cruces, 1978-80; cons. NIH, Washington, 1980-81. Editor: Classroom Uses of Behavior Modification, 1972; contbr. articles to profl. jours. Bd. dirs. Rio Grande Planned Parenthood, Albuquerque, 1984—, pres., 1992-93. Rsch. grantee NIH Heart, Lung and Blood Inst., 1985-87. Mem. Am. Psychol. Soc., Am. Ednl. Rsch. Assn., Phi Beta Kappa, Sigma Xi. Democrat. Home: 1719 Rita Dr NE Albuquerque NM 87106-1129 Office: U NMex Coll Edn Albuquerque NM 87131

HARRIS, MICHAEL DAVID, journalist; b. Phila., Feb. 11, 1950; s. Morton Louis and Jane (Kirby) H. BA, Temple U., 1973; postgrad., Calif. State U., L.A., 1976-79. Reporter Progress Newspapers, Alhambra, Calif., 1977-78, City News Svc., L.A., 1978-81, United Press Internat., L.A., 1981-90; editor Sta. KFWB-AM/All News, L.A., 1985—; reporter The Daily Jour., L.A., 1991—. Contbr. articles to major newspapers. Office: The Daily Jour 915 1st Ave Los Angeles CA 90033-2625

HARRIS, MICHAEL GENE, optometrist, educator, lawyer; b. San Francisco, Sept. 20, 1942; s. Morry and Gertrude Alice (Epstein) H.; BS, U. Calif., 1964, M. Optometry, 1965, D. Optometry, 1966, MS, 1968; JD, John F. Kennedy U., 1985; children: Matthew Benjamin, Daniel Evan. Bar: Calif., U.S. Dist. Ct. (no. dist.) Calif. Assoc. practice optometry, Oakland, Calif., 1965-66, San Francisco, 1966-68; instr., coord. contact lens clinic Ohio State U., 1968-69; asst. clin. prof. optometry U. Calif., Berkeley, 1969-73, dir. contact lens extended care clinic, 1969-83, chief contact lens clinic, 1983—, assoc. clin. prof., 1973-76, asst. chief contact lens svc., 1970-76, assoc. chief contact lens svc., 1976—, lectr., 1978-80, sr. lectr., 1980—, vice chmn. faculty Sch. Optometry, 1983-85, prof. clin. optometry, 1984-86; clin. prof. optometry, 1986—, dir. residency program, 1993—; John de Carle vis. prof. City U., London, 1984; vis. rsch. fellow U. New South Wales, Sydney, Australia, 1989; sr. vis. rsch. scholar U. Melbourne, Australia, 1989, 92; pvt. practice optometry, Oakland, Calif., 1973-76; mem. ophthalmic devices panel, med. device adv. com. FDA, 1990—; lectr., cons. in field; mem. regulation rev. com. Calif. State Bd. Optometry; cons. hypnosis Calif. Optometric Assn., Am. Optometric Assn.; cons. Nat. Bd. Examiners in Optometry, Soflens div. Bausch & Lomb, 1973—, Barnes-Hind Hydrocurve Soft Lenses, Inc., 1974-87, Sola-Barnes Hind, 1987—, Contact Lens Rsch. Lab., 1976—, Wesley-Jessen Contact Lens Co., 1977—, Palo Alto VA, 1980—, Primarius Corp., Cooper Vision Optics Alcon, 1980—; co-founder Morton D. Sarver Rsch. Lab., 1986; Planning commr. Town of Moraga, Calif., 1986, vice-chmn., 1987-88, chmn. 1988-90; mem. Town Coun., Moraga, Calif., 1992—; founding mem. Young Adults div. Jewish Welfare Fedn., 1965—, chmn. 1967-68; commr. Sunday Football League, Contra Costa County, Calif., 1974-78. Charter Mem. Jewish Community Ctr. Contra Costa County; founding mem. Jewish Community Mus. San Francisco, 1984; Para-Rabbinic, Temple Isaiah, Lafayette, Calif., 1987, bd. dirs., 1990; life mem. Bay Area Coun. for Soviet Jews, 1976; bd. dirs. Jewish Community Rels. Coun. of Greater East Bay, 1979—, Campolindo Homeowners Assn., 1981—; pres. student coun. John F. Kennedy U. Sch. Law, 1984-85. Fellow U. Calif., 1971; Calif. Optometric Assn. Scholar 1965, George Schneider Meml. scholar, 1964. Fellow Am. Acad. Optometry (diplomate cornea and contact lens sect.; chmn. contact lens papers; mem. contact lens com. 1974—, vice chmn. contact lens sect. 1980-82, chmn. 1982-84, immediate past chmn. 84-86, chmn. jud. com. 1989—, chmn. by-laws com. 1989—), Assn. Schs. and Colls. Optometry (coun. on acad. affairs), AAAS, Prentice Soc.; mem. Assn. for Rsch. in Vision and Ophthalmology, Am. Optometric Assn. (proctor 1969—, cons. on hypnosis, mem. contact lens sect., mem. position papers com., com. on ophthalmic standards, subcom. on testing and certification), Calif. Optometric Assn., Assn. Optometric Contact Lens Educators, Am. Optometric Found., Mexican Soc. Contactology (hon.), Nat. Coun. on Contact Lens Compliance, Internat. Soc. Contact Lens Rsch., Calif. State Bd. Optometry (regulation rev. com.), Calif. Acad. Scis., U. Calif. Optometry Alumni Assn. (life), ABA, Assn. Trial Lawyers Am., Calif. Trial Lawyers Assn., Calif. Young Lawyers Assn., Contra Costa Bar Assn., Mus. Soc., JFK U. Sch. Law Alumni Assn., Benjamin Ide Wheeler Soc. U. Calif., Mensa. Democrat. Lodge: B'nai B'rith. Editor current comments sect. Am. Jour. Optometry, 1974-77; editor Eye Contact, 1984-86, assoc. editor The Video Jour. Clin. Optometry, 1988—, consulting editor Contact Lens Spectrum, 1988—; editor: Problems in Optometry, Special Contact Lens Procedures; Contact Lenses and Ocular Disease, 1990; contbr. chpts. to books; author various syllabuses; contbr. articles to profl. pubs. Home: 43 Corte Royal Moraga CA 94556-1624 Office: U Calif Sch Optometry Berkeley CA 94720

HARRIS, MICHAEL HATHERLY, educational administrator; b. Indpls., Sept. 8, 1940; s. John Edward and Bessie (Hatherly) H.; m. Diane Harris; children: Christopher, Erik, Megan. BA, Macalester Coll., 1966; MA, U. Denver, 1970. Account exec. Benson Optical Co., Mpls., 1966-70; tchr. Adams County Sch. Dist. 14, Commerce City, Colo., 1970-75, dir. student svcs., 1975-80; prin. Portland (Oreg.) Pub. Schs., 1980—. Mem. Met. Youth Commn., Portland. Mem. Oreg. Assn. for Alternative Edn. (pres. 1988, lobbyist, Spl. Svc. award 1993). Home: 4340 SW Vacuna St Portland OR 97219 Office: Portland Pub Schs 501 N Dixon Portland OR 97201

HARRIS, MICHAEL RICHARD, financial and tax advisor; b. Boise, Idaho, Aug. 23, 1936; s. Sydney and Merle (Meadows) H. BA, Stanford U., 1958, MA, 1962, PhD, 1966; JD, UCLA, 1981. Bar: Calif. 1981, U.S. Dist. Ct. (cen. dist.) Calif. 1981, U.S. Ct. Appeals (9th dist.) 1982. Adminstr., mem. history dept. Pomona Coll., Claremont, Calif., 1964-69; dir. inst. in higher edn. Claremont U. Ctr., 1969-72, asst. dean, asst. prof. history, edn., 1970-72; chair, instr. Marlborough Sch., L.A., 1972-78; assoc. Paul N. Crane Assocs., L.A., 1981-82; owner Michael R. Harris & Assocs., L.A., 1983-86; v.p., mgr. Security Pacific Exec. Fin. Svcs., L.A., 1986-91; prin. EFP Assocs., L.A., 1991—; analyst Calif. State Scholarship Com., Sacramento, 1965-68; bd. dirs. L.A. Clearinghouse for Minorities, 1966-68; bd. editors Dialogue, A. Jour. of Mormon Thought, Palo Alto, Calif., 1966-76; mem. adv. coun. UCLA Law Sch., 1982-93; arbitrator Beverly Hills Bar Assn., 1983-92; mem. adv. bd. sch. nursing program minorities UCLA, 1993—. Author: Five Counterrevolutionists in Higher Education, 1970; contbr. articles to profl. jours. Bd. dirs. Mormon History Assn., 1969-72. Mem. State Bar Calif., Malibu Bar Assn., Federalist Soc. Republican. Episcopalian. Home: 20725 Seaboard Rd Malibu CA 90265 Office: EFP Assocs 12424 Wilshire Blvd Bldg 630 Los Angeles CA 90025-1040

HARRIS, NANCY HOWARD, paper conservator, writer; b. Utica, N.Y., Nov. 5, 1949; d. William Page Harris and Gertrude (Howard) Owens; div. 1980. BA with honors, U. Mich., 1972; MA in Art History, NYU, 1975, diploma in Conservation, 1977. Grad. fellow NYU, 1977-78; paper conservator Detroit Inst. Arts, 1978-80; sr. paper conservator Harry Ranson Humanities Rsch. Ctr., U. Tex., Austin, 1980-82; paper conservator Gen. Libr., U. Calif., Berkeley, 1983—; cons. Cartoon Art Mus., San Francisco, 1986—, JFK U. Ctr. for Mus. Studies, San Francisco, 1987-88, State Archives, Sacramento, 1992; sec. Bay Area Art Conservation Guild, San Francisco, 1982-85. Contbr. articles to profl. jours. Recipient grant NEA, 1979, 80, NEH, 1985, Dept. of Edn., 1988, 91, 92. Episcopalian. Office: Libr Univ Calif Rm 416 Doe Berkeley CA 94720

HARRIS, RICHARD EUGENE VASSAU, lawyer; b. Detroit, Mar. 16, 1945; s. Joseph S. and Helen Harris; m. Milagros A. Brito; children: Catherine, Byron. AB, Albion Coll., 1967; JD, Harvard U., 1970; postdoctoral, Inst. Advanced Legal Studies, London, 1970-71. Bar: Calif. 1972. Assoc. Orrick, Herrington, Rowley & Sutcliffe, San Francisco, 1972-77; ptnr. Orrick, Herrington & Sutcliffe, San Francisco, 1978—; faculty Calif. Tax Policy Conf., 1987; speaker univ, govtl. and profl. groups. Mem. Christian Edn. Bd., Piedmont (Calif.) Community Ch., 1983-86. Knox fellow Harvard U., 1970-71. Mem. ABA (coun. urban state and local govt. sect. 1983-88, vice chmn. govt. liability com. 1982-84, antitrust law sect. franchising com. 1978-81, state action subcom. 1981—, BOULDER task force 1983-84, litigation sect. corp. counsel com., subcom. chmn. 1980-82, 83—, vice chmn. 1982-83, co-chmn. Nat. Insts. Antitrust Liability 1983, 85, bus. law sect., SEC investigation atty.-client privilege waiver task force 1988, pub. interest issues com. 1985—, tax sect., state and local taxes com. 1989—, tax litigation com. 1992—), Bar Assn. San Francisco (fed. cts. com. 1977—, appellate cts. com. 1987—, ethics com. 1987—, antitrust com. 1980—), Calif. Bar Assn. (bus. law sect., antitrust sect., intellectual property sect., tax sect.), Assn. Bus. Trial Lawyers No. Calif., Assn. Profl. Responsibility Lawyers, Am. Law Inst. (coms. for Restatement Law Unfair Competition, 1991—, Restatement Law Governing Lawyers, 1991—, Restatement Tort: Products Liability, 1993—), Phi Beta Kappa. Office: Orrick Herrington & Sutcliffe 400 Sansome St San Francisco CA 94111-3143

HARRIS, RICHARD JEROME, psychology educator; b. Vicksburg, Miss., May 17, 1940; s. Frederick Arthur and Mary Elizabeth (Gieselbreath) H.; m. Mary Margaret Bierman, June 14, 1965; children: Jennifer Mary, Christopher Richard, Alexander Norman. Student, Calif. Inst. Tech., 1958-61; BS, U. Wis., 1963; MA, Stanford U., 1966, PhD, 1968. Instr., acting co-chmn. psychology & sociology dept. Talladega (Ala.) Coll., 1965-66; psychology rsch. assoc. Palo Alto VA Hosp., Mountain View, Calif., 1967-68; lectr. Stanford (Calif.) U., 1968; asst. prof. U. N.Mex., Albuquerque, 1968-72; assoc. prof. psychology U. N.Mex., 1972-83, prof. psychology, 1983—; vis. assoc. prof. Ohio State U., Columbus, 1974-75, vis. prof. U. Ga., Athens, 1988-89; action editor Jour. Personality Social Psychology, 1979; mem. edit. bd. Jour. Experimental Social Psychology, 1977-90. Author: A Primer of Multivariate Statistics, 1975, 2d rev. edit., 1985, An Analysis of Variance Primer, 1993; contbr. articles to profl. jours. Vis. fellow, U. New South Wales, Kensington, Australia, 1981-82. Fellow Am. Psychol. Soc., Soc. Personality and Social Psychology; mem. Soc. Multivariate Experimental Psychology, Soc. Experimental Social Psychology, Psychonomic Soc., Soc. Applied Multivariate Rsch. (pres. 1977-79), Soc. Advancement Social Psychology. Democrat. Home: 1719 Rita Dr NE Albuquerque NM 87106-1129 Office: U NMex Dept Psychology Albuquerque NM 87131

HARRIS, ROBERT GEORGE, illustrator; b. Kansas City, Mo., Sept. 9, 1911; s. Harry George and Lena Mary (Stevens) H.; m. Marjorie Elnora King, Dec. 26, 1935; children: Craig, Marcia. Student, Kansas City Art Inst., 1928-30, Art Students League, N.Y.C., 1931-32, Grand Cen. Art Sch., N.Y.C., 1931-32. illustrator Sat. Evening Post, Ladies Home Jour., McCall's, Cosmopolitan, RedBook, Good Housekeeping, 1939-65; portrait painter Justice Dept., Washington, Union Pacific R.R., N.Y.C., Ariz. State U., Beta Sigma Phi Hdqrs., Seabury Western Theol. Sem., many corp. and family portraits, 1965—. Mem. Soc. Illustrators (life). Home: PO Box 1124 Carefree AZ 85377-1124

HARRIS, ROGER J., entrepreneur; b. Chgo., Nov. 20, 1930; s. Stanley and Mary (Koba) Pokwinski; married, 1948 (div. Jan. 1970); 1 child, Linda; m. Betty J. Henry, Nov. 21, 1971. BS in Commerce, Roosevelt U., Chgo., 1956; postgrad., Loyola U. Law Sch., Chgo., 1959-62. Systems sales rep. Univac, Chgo., 1953-55; merchandising systems analyst Montgomery Ward, Chgo., 1956-62; cons. Haskins & Sells, Chgo., 1962-65; prin. A.T. Kearney, L.A., 1965-70; bus. cons. Roger J. Harris and Assocs., Inc., Calif. and Alaska, 1970—; conf. leader Am. Mgmt. Assn., L.A., 1970-82. Mem. Am. Soc. of Accts., Small Bus. Adminstrn. (chmn. score/ACE program 1990-91). Office: 207 E Northern Lights Blvd Anchorage AK 99503

HARRIS, SIDNEY EUGENE, dean, management educator; b. Atlanta, Ga., July 21, 1949; s. Nathaniel and Marian (Johnson) H.; m. Mary A. Styles, July 24, 1971; 1 child, Savaria Brandy Harris. BA, Morehouse Coll., 1971; MS, Cornell U., 1975, PhD, 1976. Mem. tech. staff Bell Telephone Labs., Holmdel, N.J., 1973-78; asst. prof. Ga. State U., Atlanta, 1978-82, assoc. prof., 1982-87; prof. mgmt. Claremont (Calif.) Grad. Sch., 1987—, dean, 1991—; bd. dirs. Family Savs. and Loan, L.A., chair audit com., 1991—; cons. Coca-Cola Co., Atlanta, 1991—. Editor MIS Quar., 1991. Bd. dirs. Peter F. Drucker Non-Profit Found., N.Y.C., 1991—; vice chmn. L.A. County Productivity Commn., L.A., 1991; mem. Family Support Adv. Bd., 1990. Recipient Vol. Svc. award Nat. Computer Com. Bd., 1986. Mem. Assn. of Computing Machinery, Inst. of Mgmt. Sci., Lincoln Club, Sigma Xi. Office: Claremont Grad Sch Peter F Drucker Grad Mgmt Ctr Claremont CA 91711

HARRIS, SIGMUND PAUL, physicist; b. Buffalo, Oct. 12, 1921; s. Nathan N. and Ida (Lebovitz) H.; m. Florence Katcoff, Sept. 19, 1948; 1 child, Roslyn. BA cum laude, SUNY, Buffalo, 1941, MA, 1943; postgrad., Yale U., 1943; PhD, Ill. Inst. Tech., 1954. Physicist Metall. Lab. U. Chgo., 1943-44; jr. scientist Los Alamos (N.Mex.) Nat. Lab., 1944-46; assoc. physicist Argonne Nat. Lab., Chgo., 1946-53; sr. physicist Tracer Lab., Inc., Boston, 1954-56; sr. research engr. Atomics Internat., Canoga Park, Calif., 1956-64; head physics sect. research div. Maremont Corp., Pasadena, Calif., 1964-66; from asst. prof. to full prof. L.A. Pierce Coll., Woodland Hills, Calif., 1966-86, prof. physics emeritus, 1986—; cons. Space Scis. Inc., Monrovia, Calif., 1968—. Author: Introduction to Air Pollution, 1973. Patentee method for measuring power level of nuclear reactor, apparatus for producing neutrons. Mem. Am. Nuclear Soc., Am. Assn. Physics Tchrs., Am. Phys. Soc., Phi Beta Kappa, Sigma Xi. Home: 5831 Saloma Ave Van Nuys CA 91411-3018 Office: 6201 Winnetka Ave Woodland Hills CA 91371-0002

HARRIS, STEPHEN JAMES, psychologist, educator, counselor, consultant; b. Tacoma, Aug. 31, 1955; s. Jack Lewis and Jean Hyslop (Aitken) H.; m. Deanna Sharon Goff, July 15, 1979; children: Melody Renee, Christina Joy. BA, Pacific Luth. U., 1976; MA, Fuller Theol. Sem., 1980; PhD, Fuller Sem. Grad. Sch. Psychology, 1981. Lic. psychologist, Calif., marriage, family and child counselor. Clin. psychologist Our Self Counseling Assn., Santa Ana, Calif., 1982-87, Lighthouse Counseling Ctr., San Juan Capistrano, Calif., 1987—; adj. prof. Azusa (Calif.) Pacific U., 1986-90, Fuller Sem. Grad. Sch. of Psychology, Pasadena, Calif., 1990—; cons. Parents of Children Who Learn Differently, San Juan Capistrano, 1987-90, Kids Unltd., San Juan Capistrano, 1989-90. Pacific Luth. U. scholar, 1973. Mem. APA, Calif. Psychol. Assn., Toastmasters Internat. (2d Pl. 1987). Home: 67 Calle Sol San Clemente CA 92672-9302 Office: Lighthouse Counseling Ctr 27124 Paseo Espada Ste 805 San Juan Capistrano CA 92675-2741

HARRIS, STEPHEN LEROY, humanities educator; b. Aberdeen, Wash., Feb. 5, 1937; s. Glenn Edwin and Ruby O. (Bell) H.; divorced 1985; children: Geoffrey Edwin, Jason Marc. BA, U. Puget Sound, 1959; MA, Cornell U., 1961, PhD, 1964. Asst. prof. Wash. State U., Pullman, 1964-65; prof. humanities Calif. State U., Sacramento, 1965—, chmn. Humanities dept., 1972-76, 92—; lectr. and talk show participant local and national TV. Author: Fire Mountains of the West, 1988, The New Testament: A Student's Introduction, 1988, Agents of Chaos, 1990, Touchstones: Classic Texts in the Humanities, 1990, Understanding the Bible, 3d edit., 1992. Woodrow Wilson fellow, Woodrow Wilson Fellowship Assn., Princeton, N.J., 1960-61. Mem. Westar Inst. Biblical Scholars. Democrat. Office: Calif State U Dept Humanites 6000 Jay St Sacramento CA 95819-6083

HARRIS, WARREN LYNN, software research and development director; b. Albequerque, May 8, 1966; s. Jerry Dale and Viola Guadalupe (Gutierrez) H. BS, Ariz. State U., 1988. Programming mgr. I.P.C. Computer Svcs., Inc., Tempe, Ariz., 1985-89; software systems engr. Intel Corp., Chandler, Ariz., 1990; dir. software R&D Pics, Inc., Tempe, 1990-91, Parics, Div. of Ansoft Corp., Tempe, 1991—. Mem. IEEE, Assn. for Computing Machinery, Golden Key Nat. Honor Soc., Mortar Bd., Upsilon Pi Epsilon. Home: 6210 W Minnezona Phoenix AZ 85033 Office: Parics Div Ansoft Corp 6210 West Minnezona Phoenix AZ 85033

HARRISON, ALENE, nursing educator. BS, Idaho State U., 1965; MS, U. Mich., 1969; EdD, Temple U., 1988. Charge nurse Hillside Hosp., Glen Oaks, N.Y., 1965-66; staff nurse Roosevelt Hosp., N.Y., 1966-78; clin. specialist Gracie Square Hosp., N.Y., 1969-70; instr. Lenox Hill Hosp. Sch. Nursing, N.Y., 1970-72, Skidmore Coll. Dept. Nursing, N.Y., 1972-77; asst. prof. College Misericordia Dept. Nursing, N.Y., 1977-80; nursing bds. reviewer Am. Jour. Nursing Co., N.Y., 1981—; asst. to assoc. prof. Wilkes Coll. Dept. Nursing, Wilkes Barre, Pa., 1980-87; assoc. prof. Idaho State U. Dept. Nursing, Pocatello, Idaho, 1987-89, chairperson, 1989—. Contbr. articles to profl. jours. Bd. dirs. Am. Cancer Soc., sec. Bannock County chpt. 1989—; v.p. bd. dirs. S.E. Idaho In-Home Svcs. Mem. ANA, AAUP, Am. Assn. Coll. Nursing, Am. Orthopsychiatric Assn., Idaho Nursing Assn., Idaho Orgn. Nurse Execs., Nat. League Nursing, N.Y. Acad. Scientists, Sigma Theta Tau. Home: 1518 Bench Rd Apt 6C Pocatello ID 83201-2415

HARRISON, CAROLE ALBERTA, museum curator, restaurateur, civic worker; b. Dayton, Ohio, Jan. 16, 1942; d. Chester Arthur and Mildred Irene (Focke) Shaw; student U. Dayton, 1959-60, U. Colo., 1960-61; children: Amelia Holmes, Ann Elizabeth, Abigail Shaw. With Council for Pub. TV, Channel 6, Inc., Denver, 1972-78, Hist. Denver, Inc., 1973-88; owner Old Number One Fire House Restaurant, Two Forks Restaurant, The Third Oasis, Fourth Estate at the Denver Press Club; general mgr The Denver Petroleum Club; dir. devel. Sewall Rehab. Center, Denver, 1979-80; exec. v.p. Marilyn Van Derbur Motivational Inst., Inc., 1980-82. Bd. dirs. Center for Public Issues, Denver, 1979-82, Passages, 1982-88, Hall of Life, 1981-83, Historic Denver, 1982-84, Denver Firefighters Mus., 1979—; bd. dirs. KRMA-TV Vols., 1970—, pres., 1973-74; founder Com. for Support of Arts, Denver, 1978-79; chmn. Graland Country Day Sch. Auction, 1979, 80, Channel 6 Auction, 1971, 72, Colo. Acad. Auction, 1980, The Hundred Most Interesting Women in Denver, 1988; mem. Denver Mayor's Task Force on Infrastructure Fin., 1988-90; bd. dirs. Met. Denver and Colo. Conv. and Visitors Bur. Mem. Leadership Denver Alumni Assn. (dir. 1980-82), Colo. Restaurant Assn., Denver C. of C. (govt. relations com. 1983-87, state local affairs council 1987-88, urban affairs). Home: 2450 E 5th Ave Denver CO 80206-4245 Office: 1326 Tremont Pl Denver CO 80204-2120

HARRISON, CHARLES WAGNER, JR., applied physicist; b. Farmville, Va., Sept. 15, 1913; s. Charles Wagner and Etta Earl (Smith) H.; m. Fern F. Perry, Dec. 28, 1940; children—Martha R., Charlotte J. Student, U.S. Naval Acad. Prep. Sch., 1933-34, U.S. Coast Guard Acad., 1934-36; BS in Engring., U. Va., 1939, EE, 1940; SM, Harvard U., 1942, M in Engring., 1952, PhD in Applied Physics, 1954; postgrad., MIT, 1942, 52. Registered profl. engr., Va., Mass. Engr. Sta. WCHV, Charlottesville, Va., 1937-40; commd. ensign U.S. Navy, 1939, advanced through grades to comdr., 1948; research staff Bur. Ships, 1939-41, asst. dir. electronics design and devel. div., 1948-50; research staff U.S. Naval Research Lab., 1944-45, dir.'s staff, 1950-51; liaison officer Evans Signal Lab., 1945-46; electronics officer Phila. Naval Shipyard, 1946-48; mem. USN Operational Devel. Force Staff, 1953-55; staff Comdg. Gen. Armed Forces Spl. Weapons project, 1955-57; ret. U.S. Navy, 1957; cons. electromagnetics Sandia Nat. Labs., Albuquerque, 1957-73; instr. U. Va., 1939-40; lectr. Harvard U., 1942-43, Princeton U., 1943-44; vis. prof. Christian Heritage Coll., El Cajon, Calif., 1976. Author: (with R.W.P. King) Antennas and Waves: A Modern Approach, 1969; contbr. numerous articles to profl. jours. Fellow IEEE (Electronics Achievement award 1966, best paper award electromagnetic compatibility group 1972); mem. Internat. Union Radio Sci. (commn. B. and H), Electromagnetics Acad., Famous Families Va., Sigma Xi. Home: 2808 Alcazar St NE Albuquerque NM 87110-3516

HARRISON, CRAIG ROYSTON, philosophy educator; b. London, England, Mar. 6, 1933; came to U.S., 1949; s. Nathaniel Kay and Marian Belle (Pond) H.; m. Marion Moses, Feb. 10, 1974 (dec. Jan. 1992); children: Russell, Jennifer. BA, Stanford U., 1959, PhD, 1967. Asst. prof. Idaho State U., Pocatello, 1962-63; instr. Iowa State U., Ames, 1963-66; asst. prof. San Jose (Calif.) State U., 1966-69; asst. prof., assoc. prof. San Francisco State U., 1969—. Contbr. articles to profl. jours. Served to sgt. USMC, 1953-56. Mem. San Francisco Amateur Astronomers, Phi Beta Kappa. Democrat. Espicopalian. Home: 1699 Fulton St San Francisco CA 94117 Office: San Francisco State U Philosophy Dept 1600 Holloway Ave San Francisco CA 94132-1722

HARRISON, DON EDMUNDS, oceanographer; b. New Haven, Conn., Aug. 22, 1950; s. Don Edward Jr. and India Boozer Harrison. BA, Reed Coll., 1972; MS, Harvard U., 1973, PhD, 1977. Affiliate prof. U. Wash., Seattle, 1984—; oceanographer Pacific Marine Environ. Lab./Ocean Climate Rsch. Div., Seattle, 1984—; lectr. Harvard U., Cambridge, Mass., 1977-78; vis. prof. MIT, Cambridge, 1978-84. Mem. Am. Meterol. Soc., Oceanography Soc., Phi Beta Kappa. Office: NOAA/PMEL/OCRD 7600 Sand Point Way NE Seattle WA 98115-6349

HARRISON, EARLE, former county official; b. Rainsville, Ala., May 20, 1903; s. Robert Lee and Sarepta Ophelia (Hansard) H.; m. Joan Mary Jackson, Jan. 24, 1942. AB, Northwestern U., 1929, postgrad. in bus. adminstrn., 1942; LLB, Chgo.-Kent Coll. Law, 1935. With Marshall Field & Co., Chgo., 1929-68; div. operating mgr. Marshall Field & Co., 1958-60, v.p. operations, 1960-64, v.p., treas., 1964-68; bd. dirs. Credit Bur. Cook County, 1949-69, pres., 1958-69; mem. bd. suprs., chmn. planning and zoning com. Lake County, Ill., 1970—; cons. finance and adminstrn. to hosps. and health care instns. Commr. Northeastern Ill. Planning Commn., 1970—; pres. Northeastern Ill. Plan Commn., 1973, now mem. exec. com.; ret. pres., bd. dirs. Family Fin. Counseling Svc. Greater Chgo.; bd. dirs. Condell Meml. Hosp., Libertyville, Ill., 1971—, adminstr., 1973—, pres., 1975-78, bus. cons., 1978—. Mem. Phi Delta Phi. Episcopalian. Home: 2801 N Kentucky Ave Apt 121 Roswell NM 88201-5877

HARRISON, ETHEL MAE, financial executive; b. Ft. Dodge, Iowa, June 11, 1931; d. Arthur Melvin and Grace Gwendolyn (Hall) Cochran; m. Cleo Arden Goss, June 17, 1951 (div. 1962); m. Clarence Hobert Harrison, Dec. 23, 1965 (dec. Feb. 1993). Dipl., Internat. Corres. Schs., Riverside, Calif., 1986. Tax preparer Goss Tax Svc., Riverside, 1953-61; tax preparer H & R Block, Inc., Riverside, 1972-84, supr./bookkeeper, 1974-79; owner, pres. Ethel Harrison's Tax Svc., Riverside, 1984—. Mem. NAFE, Riverside Tax Cons. Assn. (sec. 1988—), Am. Soc. Profl. and Exec. Women, Am. Inst. Profl. Bookkeepers, Soc. of Calif. Tax Profls., Nat. Assn. Tax Cons., Nat. Soc. Tax Profls., Nat. Assn. Tax Preparers, Inland Soc. Tax Cons., Nat. Taxpayers Union. Home and Office: 10460 Gramercy Pl Riverside CA 92505-1300

HARRISON, JOHN CONWAY, state supreme court justice; b. Grand Rapids, Minn., Apr. 28, 1913; s. Francis Randall and Ethlyn (Conway) H.; m. Ethel M. Strict; children—Nina Lyn, Robert Charles, Molly M., Frank R., Virginia Lee. LLD, George Washington U., 1940. Bar: Mont. 1947, U.S. Dist. Ct. 1947. County atty. Lewis and Clark County, Helena, Mont., 1934-60; justice Mont. Supreme Ct., Helena, 1961—. Pres. Mont. TB Assn., Helena, 1951-54, Am. Lung Assn., N.Y.C., 1972-73, Mont. coun. Boy Scouts Am., Great Falls, Mont., 1976-78. Col. U.S. Army. Mem. ABA, Mont. Bar Assn., Kiwanis (pres. 1953), Sigma Chi. Home: 215 S Cooke St Helena MT 59601-5143 Office: Mont Supreme Ct 215 N Sanders St Helena MT 59601-4522

HARRISON, KEITH MICHAELE, law educator; b. Washington, Nov. 6, 1956; s. Charles Thomas Harrison Sr. and June Earlene (Bell) Harrison-Russ; m. Karen Marie Anderson, Aug. 21, 1982; children: Michaele Marie, David Tyler. BA, St. John's Coll., Santa Fe, N.Mex., 1977; JD, U. Chgo., 1981. Bar: Ill. 1981, D.C. 1982, N.Y. 1985. Clin. teaching fellow Antioch Sch. Law, Washington, 1985-86; asst. prof. law No. Ill. U., DeKalb, 1986-89, U. Denver, 1989—; vis. prof. Syracuse Univ. Coll. Law, 1993. V.p. Sam Cary (Colo.) Scholarship Endowment Fund, 1991. Served to lt. USCG, 1981-85. Mem. D.C. Bar Assn., Sam Cary Bar Assn. (treas. 1991), Multiplikatoren Group (Germany). Office: U Denver Coll of Law 1900 Olive St Denver CO 80220-1879

HARRISON, KEN L., holding company and electric utility executive; b. Bakersfield, Calif., Oct. 14, 1942. BS, Oreg. State U., 1964, MA, 1966. Cert. fin. analyst. V.p. 1st Interstate Bank, Portland, Oreg., 1966-75; asst. to pres. Portland Gen. Electric Co., 1975-78, v.p., 1978, chief fin. officer, 1978-80, sr. v.p., 1980-87, pres., 1987-88, also bd. dirs., chmn. bd., pres., chief exec. officer; chmn. bd., chief exec. officer Portland Gen. Corp., also bd. dirs.; chmn., chief exec. officer Portland Gen. Electric Co. Office: Portland Gen Corp 121 SW Salmon St Portland OR 97204-2901

HARRISON, MICHAEL ALEXANDER, computer scientist, educator, entrepreneur; b. Phila., Apr. 11, 1936; s. Milton Harrison and Mamie May (Gross) Barron; m. Evalee Solomon, Aug. 23, 1959 (div. July 1971); 1 child, Craig; m. Susan Lois Graham, Oct. 16, 1971. BS, Case Inst., 1958, MS, 1959; PhD, U. Mich., 1963. From asst. to assoc. prof. U. Calif., Berkeley, 1963-71, prof., 1971—; founder Gain Tech., Palo Alto, Calif., 1989-92, also chmn. bd. dirs.; cons. inf field, 1965—; vis. prof. MIT, Cambridge, 1969-70, Hebrew U., Jerusalem, 1969-70, Stanford U., Palo Alto, 1981. Author: Introduction to Switching and Automation Theory, 1965, Introduction to Linear Automata, 1971, Introduction to Formal Length, 1978, The Technology War, 1987; contbr. articles to profl. jours. Ford Found. fellow, 1960, Guggenheim fellow, 1969-70; recipient Univ. medal U. Helsinki, 1980. Fellow AAAS, IEEE; mem. Assn. for Computing Machinery (v.p. 1982-84, numerous awards). Republican. Office: U Calif Div Computer Sci Berkeley CA 92720

HARRISON, PATRICK GEORGE, publisher, small business owner; b. San Franciso, Sept. 7, 1943; s. Wesley Newton Sr. and Gladys Marie (Butler) H. AA in English, Foothill Jr. Coll., Los Altos Hills, Calif., 1964; cert. clin. hypnotherapy, Wash. Sch. Profl. Hypnotherapy, Federal Way, Wash., 1973. V.p., br. mgr. Am. Savs. and Loan Assn., San Francisco, 1967-69, Fidelity Savs. and Loan Assn., Palo Alto, Calif., 1971-72; customer rels. dir. Sunset Book Co., Menlo Park, Calif., 1969-71; freelance writer, 1972-84; clk. U.S. Postal Svc., Eugene, Oreg., 1984—; pub. For Kids' Sake Pubs., Eugene, 1987—; new product developer Pat's Pending Co., Eugene, 1989—; corp. pres. Mayan God., Inc., Eugene, 1990—; founder Joy of Gardening, Eugene, 1982-84; developer chocolate truffles Mayan God Hot 'n' Sassy, 1988. Author: (poster-poem) For Kids' Sake, 1978. Home and Office: Mayan Gold Inc For Kids' Sake Pubs PO Box 70182 Eugene OR 97401-0111

HARRISON, WALTER ASHLEY, physicist, educator; b. Flushing, N.Y., Apr. 26, 1930; s. Charles Allison and Gertrude (Ashley) H.; m. Lucille Prince Carley, July 17, 1954; children: Richard Knight, John Carley, William Ashley, Robert Walter. B Engring. Physics, Cornell U., 1953; M.S., U. Ill., 1954, Ph.D., 1956. Physicist Gen. Elec. Research Labs., Schenectady, 1956-65; prof. applied physics Stanford(Calif.) U., 1965—, chmn. applied physics dept., 1989-93. Author: Pseudopotentials in the Theory of Metals, 1966, Solid State Theory, 1970, Electronic Structure and the Properties of Solids, 1980; editor: The Fermi Surface, 1960. Guggenheim fellow, 1970-71; recipient von Humboldt Sr. U.S. Scientist award, 1981; vis. fellow Clare Hall, Cambridge U., 1970-71. Fellow Am. Phys. Soc. Home: 817 San Francisco Ct Stanford CA 94305 Office: Stanford U Dept Applied Physics Stanford CA 94305

HARRISON, WILLIAM HARDIN, retired career officer; b. Pembroke, KY., July 2, 1933; s. Benjamin Wallis Harrison and Mona Lee (Sandbach) Frisco; m. Josie Steele Patton, Oct. 21, 1967; children: William Patton, Charles Hardin. BA with distinction, William Jewell Coll., 1954; grad., Officer Candidate Sch., 1955, Airborne Sch., 1955, Inf. Officer Sch. Advanced Course, 1962, U.S. Army Command and Gen. Staff Coll., 1968, U.S. Army War Coll., 1974; MS, Shippensberg State Coll., 1974, Air Assault Sch., 1981. Enlisted U.S. Army, 1954, commd. 2d lt., 1955, advanced through grades to lt. gen.; with B Battery 65th Field Arty., 3d Armor div., Ft. Knox, Ky., 1954; A Co., 506th Inf. Bn. (Airborne) 101st Inf. Div. (Airborne), Ft. Jackson, S.C., 1955; student 10th Officer Candidate Co., Student Brigade U.S. Army Inf. Sch., Ft. Benning, Ga., 1955; comdr. C Co. 506th Airborne Battle Group 101st Airborne Div., Ft. Campbell, Ky., 1959-61; comdr. Battle Group S3 34th Inf., 7th Inf. Div., Republic of Korea, 1962-63; aide-de-camp Comdg. Gen. XIV Corps, Mpls., 1963-65, Chief of Staff, AFSE, Naples, Italy, 1963-69; sector, regimental adviser, spl. asst. to dep. sr. adviser II Corps, Vietnam, 1966-67; staff officer J3 (NMCC) Office of the Joint chiefs of Staff, Washington, 1968-70; comdr. 2d Bn., 48th Inf. 3d Armored Div., Fed. Republic Germany, 1970-72, asst. chief of staff, G1, 1972-73; chief tng. programs, Doctrine and Tng. Devel. U.S. Army Tng. Sch., Ft. Benning, Ga., 1974-75; asst. chief of staff, G3, Army Sect. Armish-MAAG, Teheran, Iran, 1975-77; comdr. 4th (Phoenix) Brigade 2d Armored Div., Ft. Hood, Tex., 1978-79; asst. chief of staff, G3/Dir. Plans and Tng. XVIII Airborne Corps and Ft. Bragg, Ft. Bragg, N.C., 1979-81; chief of staff 101st Airborne Div. (Air Assault) and Ft. Campbell, 1981-82; exercise dir., Eagle Strike III 101st Airborne Div. (Air Assault), Ft. Campbell, 1982; asst. div. comdr. (Support) 2d Inf. Div., Republic of Korea, 1983-84; comdg. gen. 7th Inf. Div. (Light) and Ft. Ord., Calif., 1985-87, I Corps and Ft. Lewis, Ft. Lewis, Wash., 1987-89, 6th U.S. Army and Presidio of San Francisco, 1989-91; ret., 1991. Deacon Bapt. Ch., 1977. Decorated D.S.M. with one oak leaf cluster, Bronze Star, Meritorious Svc. medal with one oak leaf cluster, Joint Svc. Commendation medal with two oak leaf clusters, Combat Infantryman badge, Expert Infantryman badge, Joint Chiefs of Staff Identification badge, Master Parachutist badge, Good Conduct medal, Air Assault badge. Mem. Rotary, Sigma Nu (pres. 1952-54), Phi Alpha Theta. Republican. Home: 7302 Amber Ln SW Tacoma WA 98498

HARRISON, WILLIAM RIDGEWAY, medical anthropologist; b. Chgo., Nov. 1, 1961; s. William John and Margherita Mary (Cimino) H.; m. Dianne Karen Patterson, Mar. 13, 1981; 1 child, Joshua John. BA, Ariz. State U., 1989; MA, U. Ariz., 1991, PhD, 1991—. Rsch. asst. Andrus Gerontology Ctr., L.A., 1979-80; pathologist aide Damon Clin. Labs., Phoenix, 1981-82; lab. assoc. Nat. Health Labs., Phoenix, 1983-85; libr. specialist Ariz. State U., Tempe, 1985-86, curational asst., 1986-87, edn. specialist, 1987-89; rsch. assoc. infectious disease VA Hosp., Tucson, 1990-91; teaching asst. anthropology U. Ariz., Tucson, 1990-91, rsch. specialist pediatrics, 1991—. Author: (presentations) Oldest Case of Cocci, 1990 (outstanding case 1990), Valley Fever: Paleopathology and explanatory Models of Modern Severity, 1992; (with others) Merck Manual, 16th edit., 1992, Evidence of Coccioidomycosis in the Skeleton of an Ancient Arizona Indian, 1991, Scanning Electron Microscopy and Paleopathology, 1991. Mem. Am. Anthropol. Assn., Soc. Med. Anthropology. Home: 1939 S Calle Media Casa Grande AZ 85222 Office: U Ariz Dept Anthropology Haury Bldg Tucson AZ 85721

HARROD, CHARLES SCOTT, internist; b. Delaware, Ohio, Oct. 4, 1953; s. John Paul and Darlene L. (Panknin) H.; m. Linda Charette, July 3, 1976 (div. July 1979); m. Jennifer Jean Eaglin, Oct. 25, 1980; children: Clark Scott, Christina Sue, Curtis Stuart. BS, Miami U., 1975; MD, Ohio State U., 1978. Diplomate Am. Bd. Internal Medicine. Resident internal medicine Ind. U., Indpls., 1981—; staff internist San Luis Valley Med. PC, Alamosa, Colo., 1981—. Mem. Med. Soc. (pres. 1985). Republican. Lutheran. Home: 7 Mountain View Pl Alamosa CO 81101-2544 Office: 1847 2nd St Alamosa CO 81101-2398

HARROP, DIANE GLASER, shop owner, mayor; b. Lafayette, Ind., June 2, 1953; d. Donald Anthony and Mary Ophelia (Rohner) G.; m. Randolph Allen Harrop, Aug. 7, 1976; children: William Donald, Steven Randolph. BE, U. Kans., 1975. Researcher U. Kans. Speech Dept., Lawrence, 1973-75; clk., book designer Pruett Pub. Co., Boulder, Colo., 1975; debate coach, English tchr. Olathe (Kans.) High Sch., 1975-76; cash items teller Converse County Bank, Douglas, Wyo., 1976-79; owner, mgr. R-D Pharmacy & Books, Douglas, 1979—; mayor City of Douglas, 1989-91, councilmember, 1991—; appt. Wyo. Econ. Devel. and Stabilization Bd., 1991—. Creator original jewelry (silverwork 1st prize winner Wyo. State Fair 1978). First woman councilmember City of Douglas, 1987-89, mayor 1989—; gov's. appointee, 1st chmn. State Adv. Coun. on Innovative Edn., Wyo., 1991; charter pres. Converse County Hosp. Aux., 1985; sec.-treas. Converse County Joint Powers Bd., 1987; bd. dirs. Nicolaysen Art Mus., 1987; mem. Wyo. Mcpl. League Legis. Com. (chmn. 1988—); mem., exhibitor Firearms Engravers Guild of Am., 1988, 89; moderator Congl. Ch.; Douglas chpt. pres. Wyo. Jaycee Women, 1984-85; mem. P.E.O. Sisterhood Chpt. N, 1983-84, Zonta Internat. (treas. 1982-83); pres. Friends of Wyoming State Fair, 1990—; bd. dirs. Ea. Wyoming Mental Health, 1991; Wyo. adv. com. Dwight D. Eisenhower Math. and Sci. Grant, 1992. Recipient Celebrate Literacy award Internat. Reading Assn. Wyo., 1988, Outstanding Community Svc. award Douglas C. of C., 1991, Apple for Edn. award Gov. Mike Sullivan, 1992; named one of Outstanding Young Women in Am., 1983-86. Mem. Mountains and Plains Booksellers (bd. dirs. 1992—), Douglas C. of C., Am. Booksellers Assn., Nat. Fedn. Ind. Businesses. Republican. Office: R-D Pharmacy & Books 206 Center St Douglas WY 82633-2543

HARROP, DONALD BRUCE, film company executive. Student, U. Utah, 1948-51. With mktg. and sales Nehi Beverage Co., Salt Lake City, 1951-53, Dixie Cup Co., Eaton, Pa., 1953-55; mktg. and sales mgmt. exec. Am. Greetings Corp., Cleve., 1955-68; v.p., regional sales dir. The World Acad., Inc., Cin., 1968-70; pres. Don Harrop & Assocs., 1975-82; gen. mgr. The Best Western Chieftain Inn, Chambers, Ariz., 1982-85; exec. dir. in mktg. and sales The Journey Assocs., Inc., Phoenix, 1985-89; exec. v.p., chief operating officer Filosa Films Internat., Inc., Beverly Hills, Calif., 1990—; ind. contractor Simmons Market Rsch. Bur., N.Y.C. With U.S. Army, 1945-47. Home: 7202 E Ed Rice Ave Mesa AZ 85208-2713

HARSEN, EDWARD CHARLES, dioristics analyst; b. N.Y.C., Dec. 30, 1958; s. Edward James and Joan Marie (Collins) H. AAS, Suffolk C.C., 1978. Entertainer St. John the Bapt. High Sch., West Islip, N.Y., 1972-76; factotum Black Hole Sch. of Poethnics, Smithtown, N.Y., 1977-83; bus. mgr. St. Press & Mag., Port Jefferson, N.Y., 1981-82; pres., CEO Com. to End All Coms., Smithtown, 1980-83, phenomenologist, 1980-83; expeditor Com. to End All Coms., Portland, Oreg., 1991—; counselor Cave Lake Industries, Ronkonkoma, N.Y., 1983-87; gastromantic County Seats, Inc., Riverhead, N.Y., 1987-90; polymertor Key Foods, Hampton Bays, N.Y., 1990-91; cons. Good Ground Press, Hampton Bays, 1979-82, diviner Inlet Dredging Inc., Shinnecock, N.Y., 1986-91; harpist Sylvan Ct., Portland, 1992. Author: Rent, 1978, Surf Club, 1982; inventor Torus Model of Monad. Named Poet of Yr., World of Poetry, 1984. Mem. Poetry Club by Mail. Taosim.

HARSHA, PHILIP THOMAS, aerospace engineer; b. N.Y.C., Feb. 22, 1942; s. Palmer and Catherine (Redinger) H.; m. Jean Ann Quinn, Oct. 23, 1965; children: Peter Charles, Evan Michael. BS in Engring. Sci., SUNY, Stony Brook, 1962, MS in Engring. Sci., 1964; PhD in Aerospace Engring., U. Tenn., 1970. Combustion rsch. engr. Gen. Electric Co., Cin., 1964-67; lead rsch. engr. Aro, Inc., Arnold Engring. Devel. Ctr., Tenn., 1969-74; rsch. specialist R&D Assoc., Marina Del Rey, Calif., 1974-76; div. mgr. Sci. Applications Internat. Corp., Chatsworth, Calif., 1976-85; chief aero. scientist Lockheed Aero. Systems Group, Burbank, Calif., 1985-88; chief project engr. Rocketdyne div. Rockwell Internat., Canoga Park, Calif., 1988-90; dep. program dir. Nat. Aero-Space Plane Program, 1990—. Contbr. articles to profl. jours. Recipient Disting. Alumnus award U. Tenn. Space Inst., 1984. Mem. AIAA, ASME, N.Y. Acad. Sci., Sigma Xi. Republican. Methodist. Home: 7235 Cirrus Way West Hills CA 91307 Office: Rockwell Internat Rocketdyne Div 6633 Canoga Ave Canoga Park CA 91303-2703

HARSTAD, KENNETH GUNDER, mechanical engineer, researcher; b. Hillsboro, N.D., Mar. 8, 1939; s. Henry J. and Ruth J. Harstad. BSME, U. N.D., 1961; MS, MIT, 1962; PhD, Calif. Inst. Tech., 1967. Mem. tech. staff Jet Propulsion Lab., Pasadena, Calif., 1967—. Contbr. articles to profl. jours. Office: Jet Propulsion Lab 4800 Oak Grove Dr Pasadena CA 91109-8099

HART, DAVID PAUL, safety and occupational health administrator; b. Little Rock, Ark., Nov. 29, 1933; s. F.M. and Hanna M. (Taylor) H.; m. Ollie M. Hart, Aug. 24, 1960; children: Rosalyn R. Harris, Chris. B equivalency, USAF, 1971; AA in Mid-Mgmt., Altus Jr. Coll., 1975; AA in Bus. Adminstrn., Western Okla. State Coll., 1976. Cert. safety exec., mgr. and specialist. Commd. 2d lt. USAF, 1954, advanced through grades to MSGT, ret., 1975; safety and occupational health mgr. Corps. of Engrs., San Francisco, 1989—. Contbr. articles to profl. jours. Am. Soc. of Safety Engrs. (San Francisco chpt., Solano County Econ. Devel. Task Force, Marina Lions Club, Bus. Profl. Women Club. Office: 211 Main St CESPN-SO San Francisco CA 94105

HART, DONALD PURPLE, bishop; b. N.Y.C., Apr. 22, 1937; s. Donald Buell Hart and Ann Wentworth (Ayres) Herrick; m. Elizabeth Ann Howard, Sept. 8, 1962; children: Sarah, Thomas. BA, Williams Coll., 1959; B of Divinity, Episc. Div. Sch., Cambridge, Mass., 1962. Curate Ch. of the Redeemer, Chestnut Hill, Mass., 1962-64; priest-in-charge Good Shepherd Mission, Huslia, Alaska, 1964-69; diocesan staff Native Ministry, Anchorage, Alaska, 1969-73; rector St. Matthew's Ch., Fairbanks, Alaska, 1973-83, St. James Ch., Keene, N.H., 1983-86; bishop Diocese of Hawaii, Honolulu, 1986—. Chmn. St. Andrew's Priory Sch., Honolulu, 1986—, Seabury Hall Sch., Makawao, Hawaii, 1986—, St. John's Sch., Tumon Bay, Guam, 1986—; bd. govs. Iolani Sch., Honolulu, 1986—. Home: 3337 Niolopua Dr Honolulu HI 96817-1052 Office: Episcopal Ch in Hawaii 229 Queen Emma Sq Honolulu HI 96813-2304

HART, EDWARD LEROY, poet, educator; b. Bloomington, Idaho, Dec. 28, 1916; s. Alfred Augustus and Sarah Cecilia (Patterson) H.; m. Eleanor May Coleman, Dec. 15, 1944 (dec. Dec. 1990); children: Edward Richard, Paul LeRoy, Barbara, Patricia; m. Leah Yates Bryson, Apr. 30, 1993. BS, U. Utah, 1939; MA, U. Mich., 1941; DPhil (Rhodes scholar), Oxford (Eng.) U., 1950. Instr. U. Utah, Salt Lake City, 1946; asst. prof. U. Wash., Seattle, 1949-52; asst. prof. Brigham Young U., Provo, Utah, 1952-55, assoc. prof., 1955-59, prof., 1959-82, prof. emeritus, 1982—; vis. prof. U. Calif., Berkeley, 1959-60, Ariz. State U., summer 1968. Author: Minor Lives, 1971, Instruction and Delight, 1976, Mormom in Motion, 1978; (poems) To Utah, 1979, Poems of Praise, 1980; More Than Nature Needs, 1982, God's Spies, 1983; contbr. articles to profl. jours. Lt. USNR, 1942-46. Am. Philos. Soc. grantee, 1964; First prize in poetry and biography Utah State Inst. Fine Arts, 1973,75; Fulbright-Hays sr. lectr. Pakistan, 1973-74; recipient Charles Redd award Utah Acad., 1976, Coll. Humanities Disting. Faculty award Brigham Young U., 1977. Fellow Am. Coun. Learned Socs., Found. Econ. Edn.; mem. MLA, Rocky Mountain MLA, Am. Soc. 18th Century Studies, Utah Acad. Sci., Arts and Letters, Phi Beta Kappa, Phi Kappa Phi. Democrat.

Mormon. Home: 1401 Cherry Ln Provo UT 84604-2848 Office: Brigham Young U Dept English Provo UT 84602

HART, E(DWARD) RICHARD, historian, cultural association administrator; b. Salt Lake City, Dec. 27, 1945; s. Edward L. and Eleanor (Coleman) H.; m. Mary Lou Cook, 1967 (div. 1973); 1 child, Jeffery L.; m. Lynette Westendorf, July 27, 1974; 1 child, Reuben C. BA, U. Utah, 1969, MA, 1971. Rsch. assoc. Am. West Ctr., Salt Lake City, 1969-75; writer Salt Lake City, 1975-77; dir. Inst. Am. West, Sun Valley, Idaho, 1977-84; exec. dir. Inst. N.Am. West, Seattle, 1984—; expert witness Zuni (N.Mex.) Indian Tribe, 1979—, US. Dept. Justice, N.Mex and Washington, 1985—. Author: (with T. J. Ferguson) A Zuni Atlas, 1985; editor: I Will Die an Indian, 1979, FARM, 1980, That Awesome Space, 1981. Dir. No. Rockies Folk Festival, Hailey, Idaho, 1979-80, 82-83; panelist, chmn. Idaho State Govs. Poet Laureate Panel, Boise, 1983-84, NEA Folk Arts Panel, Washington, 1985-88; panelist Idaho State Traditional Arts Panel, Boise, 1985-88, N.Mex. Traditional Arts Panel, Albuquerque, 1986-88. Humanities fellow Nat. Endowment for Humanities, 1979; many grants NEH, NEA, and state based arts and humanities couns. Mem. Western History Assn., Am. Soc. Ethnohistory, Am. Folklore Soc., Am. Soc. Environ. History, N.Mex. Hist. Soc. Office: Inst N Am West 110 Cherry St Ste 202 Seattle WA 98104-2215

HART, ELDON CHARLES, educator; b. Plain City, Utah, Mar. 1, 1915; s. Charles Walter and Mildred (England) H.; m. Julina Smith, June 8, 1938; children: Eldon, Julina, Mildred, Lewis. BA, Brigham Young U., 1938; BS, U. Ill., 1939, MA, 1940, PhD, 1963. Coll. adminstr. Ricks Coll., Rexburg, Idaho, 1940-80; physics libr. U. Ill., Urbana, 1961-64; pres., instr. Aero Technicians, Inc., Rexburg, 1972—. Mem. Rotary Internat. Republican. Mem. LDS. Home: 151 N First East Rexburg ID 83440 Office: Aero Technicians Inc 318 Airport Rd Rexburg ID 83440

HART, ELIZABETH KAYE, athletic administrator; b. Ogden, Utah, Mar. 20, 1943; d. William Maurice and Elizabeth Marie (Keseling) H. BS, Utah State U., 1965, MS, 1970; PhD, U. Utah, 1974. Instr. phys. edn., coach, adminstr. So. Utah State Coll., Cedar City, 1965-68, U. Utah, Salt Lake City, 1968-69, Midwestern Coll., Denison, Iowa, 1969-70, N.Mex. State U., Las Cruces, 1970-73; asst. prof. phys. edn., coach U. Tenn., Knoxville, 1973-75; assoc. prof. phys. edn., adminstr. Temple U., Phila., 1975-82; assoc. dir. athletics Utah State U., Logan, 1982—; guest speaker ednl. instns., Logan and surrounding areas, 1982-92; coun. chairperson High Country Athletic Conf., Laramie, Wyo., 1986-87; mem. exec. com. Big West Conf., Calif., 1990-92. Mem. NCAA (fin. conditions in intercollegiate athletics com., study of rules fedn., 1992—), Nat. Assn. Collegiate Women Athletic Adminstrs. (bd. dirs. 1987-89, pres. 1989-91, past pres. 1991-92), mem. Utah State U. Profl. Employees Assn. (pres. 1985-88). Office: Utah State U Spectrum Logan UT 84322-7400

HART, FRANK JAMES, systems engineer; b. San Francisco, May 8, 1947; s. Frank Hjalmer and Naomi June (Hockett) H.; m. June Ellen Peters, Apr. 28, 1973; children: Bret Allen, Katy Rose. AS, Mission Coll., Santa Clara, Calif., 1980; BSE, San Jose State U., 1985. Field svc. rep. Wang Labs., San Mateo, Calif., 1972-74; tech. specialist Signetics, Sunnyvale, Calif., 1974-80; test engr. Signetics, 1980-83, applications engr., 1983-86; sr. hardware applications engr. Fairchild/Intergraph, Palo Alto, 1986—. Inventor patents issued and pending; contbr. articles to profl. jours. Mem. Soc. Tech. Communication. Home: 2811 Mark Ave Santa Clara CA 95051-2329

HART, GARY W., former senator, lawyer; b. Ottawa, Kans., Nov. 28, 1936; m. Lee Ludwig, 1958; children: Andrea, John. Grad., Bethany Nazarene Coll., Okla.; LLB, Yale U., 1964. Bar: Colo. 1964. Began career as atty. U.S. Dept. Justice, Washington; then spl. asst. to sec. U.S. Dept. Interior; practiced in Denver, 1967-70, 72-74; nat. campaign dir. Senator George McGovern Democratic Presdl. Campaign, 1970-72; U.S. senator from Colo., 1976-84; of counsel Davis, Graham & Stubbs, Denver, 1985—; founder, 1st chmn. Environ. Study Conf., 1975; congl. adviser Salt II Talks, 1977; adviser UN Spl. Session on Disarmament, 1978; chmn. Nat. Commn. on Air Quality, 1978-81; founder Congl. Mil. Reform Caucus, 1981. Author: Right From the Start, 1973, A New Democracy, 1983, America Can Win, 1986, The Strategies of Zeus, 1987, Russia Shakes the World, 1991; co-author: The Double Man, 1985. Student vol. John F. Kennedy Presdl. Campaign, 1960; vol. organizer Robert F. Kennedy Presdl. Campaign, 1968; bd. visitors U.S. Air Force Acad., 1975—, chmn., 1978-80; nat. co-chmn. Share Our Strength, 1985; candidate for Democratic presdl. nomination, 1983-84, 87-88. Office: Davis Graham & Stubbs 370 17th St Ste 4700 Denver CO 80202-5682

HART, HOWARD FRANKLIN, lawyer; b. Syracuse, N.Y., Sept. 5, 1947; s. Earl E. and Leona (Altman) H.; m. Helene Hayat, May 23, 1985; 1 child, Sarah. AB, Cornell U., 1969; JD, Harvard U., 1972. Bar: N.Y. 1973, Calif. 1982. Assoc. Hughes Hubbard & Reed, N.Y.C., 1972-80; ptnr. Hughes Hubbard & Reed, N.Y.C., L.A., 1980-86, Rodi, Pollock, Pettker, Galbraith, & Phillips, L.A., 1986-89; v.p., gen. counsel Carlsberg Mgmt. Co., Santa Monica, Calif., 1989—.

HART, IRL LESTER, protective services professional; b. Ericson, Nebr.; s. Clement Irl and Ethel Jane (Kizer) H.; m. Florence Dorothy Robinson, Apr. 9, 1943 (div. Nov. 1981); children: Milford, Cletia, Rebecca, Thomas. BA, Nebr. Cen. Coll., 1950; grad., Cen. Luth. Sem., 1955; postgrad., Aims C.C., 1988. Cert. dep. sheriff. Pastor Nebr. Ann. Conf., 1941-63; franchise holder King's Food Host, Greeley, Colo., 1963-76; restaurant owner Greeley, 1976-82; corrections officer Weld County Sheriff Dept., Greeley, 1983-85, 86—. Mem. Fraternal Order of Police. Republican. Methodist. Office: Weld County Sheriff Dept 910 10th Ave Greeley CO 80631

HART, IRVING HARLOW, III, mathematics educator; b. San Antonio, Nov. 10, 1938; s. Irving Harlow Jr. and Caroline (Williams) H.; m. Deborah Nichols, July 1, 1962; children: Maryelizabeth, John, Alexis, Emily. BS, U. N.Mex., 1960; MS, San Diego State U., 1969. Tchr. Sonoma (Calif.) Valley High Sch., 1964-66, San Diego City Schs., 1966-67; asst. prof. U. San Diego, 1969-72; prof. math. Oreg. Inst. Tech., Klamath Falls, 1972—. Info. officer USN Acad., Klamath Falls, 1972—; planning commr. City of Klamath Falls, 1978-81; City councilman, 1989—; dir. Citizens Responsible Geothermal, Klamath Falls, 1981-88. Capt. USNR, 1960-90. Mem. Math. Assn. Am., Am. Math. Assn., Oreg. Math. Assn. 2 Yr. Colls. (sec. 1990-92). Republican. Episcopalian. Home: 2052 Lavey St Klamath Falls OR 97601-4106 Office: Oreg Inst Tech 3201 Campus Dr Klamath Falls OR 97601-8801

HART, JEAN MACAULAY, clinical social worker; b. Bellingham, Wash.; d. Murry Donald and Pearl N. (McLeod) Macaulay; m. Richard D. Hart, Feb. 3, 1940 (dec. Mar. 1973); children: Margaret Hart Morrison, Pamela Hart Horton, Patricia L.; m. Lawrence Duling, Jan. 20, 1979 (dec. May 1992); children: Lenora Daniel, Larry, Jane. BA, Wash. State U., 1938; MSW, U. So. Calif., 1961. Lic. clin. social worker, Calif.; accredited counselor, Wash. Social worker Los Angeles County, 1957-58; children's service worker Dept. Children's Services, Los Angeles, 1958-59; program developer homemakers services project Calif. Dept. Children's Services, Los Angeles, 1962-64, developer homemaker cons. position, 1964-66; supr. protective services Dept. Children's Services, Los Angeles, 1966-67; dep. regional service adminstrn. Dept. Los Angeles County Children's Services, 1967-76; adminstr. Melgon Home for Developmental Disability, 1985-86. Mem. Portals Com., Los Angeles, 1974, Travelers Aid Bd., Long Beach, Calif. 1969. Recipient Nat. award work in community, spl. award for work with emotionally disturbed Com. for Los Angeles, 1974. Mem. AAUW, Nat. Assn. Social Workers (former delegate), Acad. Cert. Social Workers. Republican. Congregationalist. Club: Wing Point Golf and Country (Bainbridge Island, Wash.). Address: 7300 Quill Dr Downey CA 90242

HART, JOHN, artistic director; b. London, 1924. Student, Sch. Sadler's Wells Ballet. Dancer Sadler's Wells Royal Ballet, London, 1938-42, from 1946; created roles in ballets of Ninette de Valois, appeared in premieres of works by Frederick Ashton, including The Wanderer, 1941, Sylvia, 1952 Sadler's Wells Royal Ballet, later asst. dir., then adminstr., from 1975; artistic dir. Ballet West, Salt Lake City, 1985—; formerly artistic dir. PACT Ballet Co., S. Africa; formerly chmn. dance div. U.S. Internat. U., San Diego; formerly dance dir. San Diego Opera. Author: Ballet and Camera, The Royal Ballet. Recipient 1st Adeline Genee Gold Medal Royal Acad. Dancing, Queen Elizabeth award outstanding achievement in ballet, 1970; decorated comdr. Order Brit. Empire, 1971. Office: Ballet West 50 W 200 S Salt Lake City UT 84101-1642

HART, JOHN LEWIS (JOHNNY HART), cartoonist; b. Endicott, N.Y., Feb. 18, 1931; s. Irwin James and Grace Ann (Brown) H.; m. Bobby Jane Hatcher, Apr. 26, 1952; children: Patti Sue, Perri Ann. Ed. pub. schs. Comic strip, B.C., nationally syndicated, 1958—, (with Brant Parker) The Wizard of Id, 1964—. Served with USAF, 1950-53, Korea. Recipient award for best humor strip Nat. Cartoonists Soc., 1967; named Outstanding Cartoonist of Year, 1968; Yellow Kid award Internat. Congress Comics for best cartoonist, Lucca, Italy; France's highest award for best cartoonist of year, 1971. Mem. Nat. Comics Council, Nat. Cartoonists Soc. Office: care Creators Syndicate 5777 W Century Blvd Ste 700 Los Angeles CA 90045-5677

HART, JOSEPH H., bishop; b. Kansas City, Mo., Sept. 26, 1931. Ed., St. John Sem., Kansas City, St. Meinrad Sem., Indpls. Ordained priest Roman Catholic Ch., 1956; consecrated titular bishop of Thimida Regia and aux. bishop Cheyenne Wyo., 1976; apptd. bishop of Cheyenne, 1978. Office: Bishop's Residence PO Box 468 Cheyenne WY 82003-0468

HART, MARIAN GRIFFITH, retired educator; b. Bates City, Mo., Feb. 5, 1929; d. George Thomas Leon and Beulah Winiferd (Hackley) Griffith; m. Ashley Bruce Hart, Dec. 23, 1951; children: Ashley Bruce Hart II, Pamela Cherie Hart Gates. BS, Cen. Mo. State Coll., 1951; MA, No. Ariz. U., 1976. Title I-Chpt. I reading dir. Page (Ariz.) Sch. Dist.; Title I dir. Johnson O'Malley Preschool, Page Sch. Dist.; dist. reading dir. Page Sch. Dist. Contbr. articles to profl. jours. and children's mags. Vol., organizer, mgr., instr. Page Community Adult Lit. Program; lifetime mem. Friends of Page Pub. Libr., sec. bd., 1990-91; sec. bd. dirs. Lake Powell Inst., 1993. Mem. Lake Powell Inst. (bd. dirs. 1992, Page Main St. Vol. of Yr. 1992), Delta Kappa Gamma (pres. chpt. 1986-90, historian 1990-92, Omicron state coms., scholarship 1988-89, nominations 1991), Beta Sigma Phi (pres. chpt., v.p. chpt.). Home and Office: 66 S Navajo Dr PO Box 763 Page AZ 86040

HART, MICHAEL JOHN, environmental management; b. Manchester, N.H., July 7, 1946; s. Wilfred Norman and Agnes Hedvega (Filipowitz) H.; m. G. Mary Falvey, Aug. 15, 1976; children: Jocelyn Elizabeth, Catherine Mary. BA, Colo. U., 1968; MBA, Denver U., 1989. Radio announcer Sta. KRNW, Boulder, Colo., 1971-73; resource mgr. Flatiron Cos., Boulder, Colo., 1973-79; v.p. Flatiron Sand & Gravel, Boulder, Colo., 1979-89; pres. Hart & Assocs., Boulder, Colo., 1989—; chmn. of bd. Thorne Ecol. Inst., Boulder, 1991-93; pres. Colo. Rock Products Assoc., Denver, 1989; bd. dirs. Nat. Aggregates Assoc., Silver Springs, Md., 1992, Nat. Sand and Gravel Assoc., Silver Spring, 1983-86. Contbr. articles to profl. jours. Mem. LWV, BOulder, 1992, Pvt. Industry Coun., Boulder, 1989, Sch. Dist./Capital Needs Com., Boulder, 1990-92. Named Man of Yr., Colo. Sand & Gravel Assoc., 1979. Mem. Soc. for Ecol. Restoration, Assn. State Wetland Mgrs., Environ. Law Inst., Colo. Water Congress, Nat. Stone Assn., Nat. Aggregates Assn., Beta Gamma Sigma. Office: Hart and Assocs 2255 Meadow Ave Boulder CO 80304

HART, N. BERNE, retired banker; b. Denver, Jan. 6, 1930; s. Horace H. and Eva (Saville) H.; m. Wilma Jean Shadley, Sept. 17, 1952; children: Linda Lea Hart Frederick, Patricia Sue Hart Sweeney, David Bruce. BA, Colo. Coll., 1951; postgrad., Colo. Sch. Banking, 1958-60. Sales trainee U.S. Rubber Co., 1953; exec. trainee United Bank of Denver N.A., 1954-56, asst. operations mgr., 1956-58, asst. cashier, 1958-61, asst. v.p., 1961, cashier, 1961-65, v.p. ops., 1965-69, sr. v.p. personal banking div., 1969, sr. v.p., trust officer, 1969-73; v.p. United Banks Colo. Inc., 1974, exec. v.p., 1975-77, pres., 1977-78, chmn., 1979-92; mem. fed. adv. council Fed. Res. Bd., 1983-85; bd. dirs. Great-West Life Assurance Co., Norwest Corp., Norwest Colo., Great-West Lige and Annuity Ins. Co. Past chmn. bd. dirs. St. Joseph Hosp., Denver; past chmn. bd. trustees Colo. Sch. Banking. Served to capt. USMCR, 1951-53. Named Denver Met. Exec. of Year Denver chpt. Nat. Secs. Assn., 1968; recipient Torch of Liberty award Anti-Defamation League, 1986, Colo. Bus. Leader of 1988 award, 1988. Mem. Colo. Bankers Assn. (past pres.), Adminstrv. Mgmt. Soc. (past pres. Denver chpt.), Colo. Assn. Commerce and Industry (chmn. 1985-86), Bank Adminstrn. Inst. (chmn. 1980-81), Beta Theta Pi. Republican. Clubs: Rotary (Denver) (pres. 1982-83), University (Denver); Denver Country, Thunderbird Country, Rancho Mirage Country. Home: 2552 E Alameda Ave Apt 99 Denver CO 80209-3325

HART, RICHARD LAVERNE, retired college dean; b. Cozad, Nebr., Dec. 10, 1929; s. David Lane and Carrie Belle (Queale) H.; m. Ramona Jean Fecht, July 28, 1956; children: Jay Huston, David Lane. BA, Nebr. Wesleyan U., 1950; EdM, U. Nebr, 1955, EdD, 1960. Tchr. Wakefield (Nebr.) High Sch., 1950-51, Cozad (Nebr.) High Sch., 1954-57; supr. social studies U. High Sch. U. Nebr., Lincoln, 1957-60; asst. prof. edn. U. Maine, Orono, 1960-62; from asst. prof. to assoc. prof., chmn. dept. curriculum and instrn. U. Wis., Milw., 1962-69; prof., chmn. dept. sec. edn. Kent (Ohio) State U., 1969-73, assoc. dean Coll. Edn., 1973-78; dean Coll. Edn. Boise (Idaho) State U., 1978-91; bd. dirs. N.W. Regional Ednl. Lab., Portland, Oreg., 1984-90; mem. profl. standards commn. State of Idaho, Boise, 1981-84, 87-90—. Co-editor: Student Unrest: Threat or Promise, 1970. Bd. dirs. Boise Sch. Vols., 1979-91, Ada County United Way, Boise, 1983-87. Cpl. U.S. Army, 1951-53, Korea. Named Ednl. Adminstr. of Yr., Nat. Assn. Ednl. Office Pers., 1986. Mem. Tchr. Edn. Coun. State Colls. and Univs. (pres. 1988-90), Idaho Assn. Supervision and Curriculum Devel. (pres. 1978-80), Idaho Assn. Colls. of Tchr. Edn. (pres. 1982-84), Rotary (chmn. Boise chpt. scholarship com. 1987-90, pres.-elect 1993—), AARP (VOTE com. Idaho 1st congl. dist.). Democrat. Lutheran. Home: 1517 Oriole Way Boise ID 83709-1326

HART, RONALD LEON, minister; b. Lodi, Calif., Feb. 6, 1937; s. John Henry Leon and Dorothy Harriet (Solkema) H.; m. Patricia Anne Pattison, Aug. 6, 1965; children: Tricia Raelyn Hart Brooks, Ryan Leon Hart. Diploma, Eugene Bible Coll., 1957; studnet, Clark Coll., 1959-61; BA, Cascade Coll., 1964, cert. tchr., 1968; MEd, U. Portland, 1971; HHD (hon.), Fla. Beacon Bible Coll., 1988. Ordained to ministry Christian Ch., 1966. Exec. dir. HiVenture Youth Outreach, Vancouver, Wash., 1966-87; pastor Walnut Grove Ch., Vancouver, 1975-91. city councilman Vancouver, 1980-91; bd. dirs. C-Tran, Vancouver, 1984-91, Intergovernmental Resource Ctr., 1981-91, Nat. Assn. Regional Couns., Washington, 1987-91. Mem. Rotary (pres. 1972-73, dist. gov. 1987-88). Mem. Open Bible Standard Chs. Home: 918 NW 50th St Vancouver WA 98663-1602 Office: PO Box 1525 6004 NE 72d Ave Vancouver WA 98661

HART, RUSS ALLEN, telecommunications educator; b. Seguin, Tex., June 30, 1946; s. Bevelly D. and Hattie V. (Reeh) H.; m. Judith Harwood, 1984 (div. 1986); m. Patricia Barrios, Mar. 22, 1987. BA, Tex. Tech. U., 1968; MA, U. Ariz., 1976; PhD, U. Wyo., 1984. Chief cinematographer, producer-dir. dept. med-TV-film, health sci. ctr. U. Ariz., Tuscon, 1973-77; instr., coord. ednl. TV and cinematography U. Wyo., Laramie, 1977-81; assoc. prof., dir. biomed. communication Mercer U., Macon, Ga., 1981-84; prof., dir. instructional telecommunications Calif. State U., Fresno, 1984—; condr. ednl. confs.; tech. cons. for distance edn. Contbr. articles to profl. jours. Served to capt. USAF, 1968-73. Recipient Cert. Merit, Chgo. Internat. Film Festival, 1975, 1st place INDY Indsl. Photography award, 1976, 2d place INDY Indsl. Photography award, 1975, Silver plaque Chgo. Internat. Film Festival, 1978, Winner of case study competition Internat. Radio and TV Soc., 1989. Mem. Assn. for Ednl. Communications and Tech. (rsch. session chmn. 1983), Am. Assn. Adult and Continuing Educators (mem. eval. task force 1986), Broadcast Edn. Assn., Health Sci. Communications Assn. (mem. continuing edn. subcom. 1983), Biol. Photog. Assn. (film judge 1975), Alliance for Distance Edn. in Calif. (founding mem. 1991), Phi Delta Kappa, Phi Kappa Phi. Office: Calif State U Dept Instructional Telecom Fresno CA 93740-0050

HART, STEPHEN JOHN, optical engineer; b. London, July 18, 1960; came to U.S., 1988; s. Herbert Stephen Arnold and Elizabeth Kathleen (Millner) H. BSc, U. London, 1981. Cons. Icon Holographics, Ltd., London, 1983-84; rsch. asst. Imperial Coll. of Sci. Tech. and Medicine, London, 1984-88; dir. Satori Ltd., Holoplex Systems, Ltd., London, 1985—; dir. of R&D Voxel, Laguna Hills, Calif., 1988—, 1988—; sec. Voxel, Laguna Hills, 1989—; chmn. Holoplex Systems, Ltd., London, 1988—. Co-inventor improvements in/or relating to holography. Founder, Grand Wizard in Perpetuity Ancient Illuminated Seers of Bavaria, Queen Mary Coll. Chapel, London, 1979. Recipient Award for Bravery High Sheriff of Greater London, 1986. Mem. IEEE, Optical Soc. of Am., Soc. of Photo-Optical Instrumentation Engrs., Soc. for Info. Display, Assn. for Computing Machinery, Burger King Kids Club. Democrat. Office: Voxel 26081 Merit Circle # 117 Laguna Hills CA 92653

HART, THOMAS ARTHUR, education educator; b. Buenos Aires, Aug. 18, 1905; came to U.S., 1915; s. Joseph Lancaster and Tennessee Ann (Hamilton) H.; m. Catherine Royer, Sept. 26, 1976 (dec. July 1985); m. Dorothy Elvira Carlstrom, Mar. 9, 1986; children: Roger Carlstrom, R. William Carlstrom. BS, William and Mary Coll., 1930; MS, Emory U., 1933, MA, 1937; PhD, U. Chgo., 1941. Prof. biology West Ga. Coll., Carrollton, 1933-42; fgn. service officer U.S. State Dept., various nations in Latin Am., 1945-63; prof. edn. U. Pitts., 1963-76; program asst. R. William Carlstrom and Assocs., Seattle, 1987—; cons. ministries of edn., Bolivia, Ecuador, Paraguay, Venezuela, Brazil, 1963-77. Author: Compendium de Biologia (2 vols.), 1962; contbr. articles to profl. jours. Served to lt. col. U.S. Army, 1943-45, PTO. Mem. Sigma Xi. Democrat. Unitarian. Home: 900 University St Apt 5Q Seattle WA 98101-2728

HART, THOMAS WHEELER, real estate executive; b. Oakland, Calif., Dec. 5, 1945; s. Melvin Greenhalgh and Annabell (Wheeler) H.; m. Cherlyn Olson, Jan. 31, 1969; children: Justin Thomas, Daria Ann, Christopher Andrew, Lauren Alexandra. BS in Bus. Mgmt., Brigham Young U., 1970; MBA, Harvard U., 1972. Lic. real estate broker, Calif. Spl. asst. to Pres. of U.S. The White House, Washington, 1972-73; v.p. devel. Marriott Corp., Washington, 1974-82; v.p. The Shorenstein Co., San Francisco, 1982—. Mem. exec. com. Yes on Propositions 111 & 108, Sacramento, 1990; mem. Brigham Young U. Alumni Bd., 1990—. Office: The Shorenstein Co 555 California St Ste 4900 San Francisco CA 94104

HART, TIMOTHY RAY, college official, lawyer; b. Portland, Jan. 5, 1942; s. Eldon V. and Wanda J. (Hillyer) H.; m. Mary F. Barlow, Aug. 31, 1964 (div. Dec. 1975); children: Mark, Matthew, Marisa, Martin; m. Annette Bryant, Aug. 8, 1981. AA, San Jose City Coll., 1968; BA, San Jose State U., 1970; MA, Wash. State U., 1973; JD, San Joaquin Coll. Law, Fresno, Calif., 1983. Bar: Calif. 1983, U.S. Dist. Ct. (ea. dist.) Calif. 1983. Police officer City of Santa Clara, Calif., 1965-71; chief of police U. Idaho, Moscow, 1971-73; crime prevention officer City of Albany, Oreg., 1973-75; instr. criminal justice Coll. of Sequoias, Visalia, Calif., 1975-81, dir. paralegal dept., 1981-83, chmn., dir. adminstrn. justice div., 1983-88; assoc. dean instruction, 1988—; sole practice, Visalia, 1983—. Bd. dirs. Sprout Ranch for Deaf Children, Tulare County Humane Soc. With USAF, 1960-63. Mem. ABA, Calif. Bar Assn., Assn. Trial Lawyers Am., Assn. Criminal Justice Educators, Am. Criminal Justice Assn., Delta Phi. Mennonite. Home: 3039 W Packwood Ct Visalia CA 93277-7197 Office: Coll of Sequoias 915 S Mooney Blvd Visalia CA 93277-2234

HART, WILLY, university director; b. Nov. 8, 1951; m. Elke Robbins, Sept. 9, 1988. BA with honors, Webster Coll., 1974; MS in Human Svcs., So. Ill. Univ., Edwardsville, 1976. Resident mgr. Housing Office So. Ill. Univ., Edwardsville, 1974-76; family housing area dir. Univ. Housing U. Oreg., Eugene, 1977-81, dir. facilities maintenance, 1981-82, dir. support svcs., 1982-85; adminstrv. svcs. mgr. Human Resources U. Oreg., Eugene, 1985-90, training mgr., 1990-91; assoc. dir. facilities Univ. Residences Western Wash. U., Bellingham, 1991—; cert. adminstr. PREP Inc., Bend, Oreg., 1988; mem. State Oreg. Personal Rules Review, Salem, 1989-91. Loaned exec. United Way Lane County, Eugene, 1986, bus. campaign sect. leader, 1988, pub. divsn. chair, 1989. Mem. Northwest Assocs. of College and Univ. Housing Officers. Office: We Wash U Office Univ Residencies Bellingham WA 98226

HARTER, LAFAYETTE GEORGE, JR., emeritus economics educator; b. Des Moines, May 28, 1918; s. Lafayette George and Helen Elizabeth (Ives) H.; m. Charlotte Mary Toshach, Aug. 23, 1950; children—Lafayette George III, James Toshach, Charlotte Helen. B.A. in Bus. Adminstrn, Antioch Coll., 1941; M.A. in Econs, Stanford, 1948, Ph.D., 1960. Instr. Menlo Coll., Menlo Park, Cal., 1948-50; instr. Coll. of Marin, Kentfield, Calif., 1950-60; prof. econs. dept. Oreg. State U., 1960-85, prof. emeritus, 1985—, chmn. dept., 1967-71; mem. panel arbitrators Fed. Mediation and Conciliation Service, 1965—, Oreg. Conciliation Service, 1967—; mem. Univ. Centers for Rational Alternatives. Author: John R. Commons: His Assault on Laissez-faire, 1962, Labor in America, 1957, Economic Responses to a Changing World, 1972; editorial bd. Jour. Econ. Issues, 1981-84. Assoc. campaign chmn. Benton United Good Neighbor Fund, 1970-72, campaign chmn., v.p., 1972-73, pres., 1973-74, vice chmn.; pub. mem. Adv. Commn. on Unemployment Compensation, 1972, 73, chmn., 1974-78; Bd. dirs. Oreg. Coun. Econ. Edn., 1971-89; pub. mem. local profl. responsibilities Oreg. State Bar Assn., 1980-83; pub. mem. Oreg. Coun. on Ct. Procedures, 1985—, bd. mem. Community Econs. of Corp., Community Econ. Stabilization Corp. Lt. comdr. USNR, 1941-46. Mem. AAUP, Am. Arbitration Assn. (pub. employment disputes panel 1970—), Am. Western econ. assns., Indsl. Rels. Rsch. Assn., Am. Assn. for Evolutionary Econs., Oreg. State Employees Assn. (v.p. faculty chpt. 1972, pres. 1973), Am. Assn. Ret. Persons (pres. local chpt.). Democrat. Mem. United Ch. of Christ (moderator 1972, 73; mem. fin. com. Oreg. conf. 1974-82, dir. 1978-81, mem. personnel com. 1983-85). Home: 3755 NW Van Buren Ave Corvallis OR 97330-4952

HARTFORD, MARGARET ELIZABETH, social work educator, gerontologist; b. Cleve., Dec. 12, 1917; d. William A. and Inez (Logan) H. BA, Ohio U., 1940; MS, U. Pitts., 1944; PhD, U. Chgo., 1962. Dir. youth svc. YWCA, Canton, Ohio, 1940-42; program cons. Intercultural Rels. Am. Svc. Inst., Pitts., 1943-48, exec. dir., 1948-50; prof. social work Case Western Res. U., Cleve., 1950-75; founding dir. Sch. Gerontology U. So. Calif., L.A., 1975-77, prof. gerontology, social work, 1977-83, prof. emeritus, 1983—; instr. Claremont (Calif.) Adult Sch. Dist., 1983—, mentor/tchr. adult edn., 1990—; instr. retirement Pasadena (Calif.) City Coll., 1983-84, Mt. San Antonio Coll., 1988-90; cons. pre-retirement, retirement planning to corps. and ednl. systems, various cities, 1980—; freelance writer, cons., lectr. 1970—. Author: Groups in Social Work, 1973, (workbook) Making the Best of the Rest of Your Life, 1982, Leaders Guide to Making the Best of the Rest of Your Life, 1986, monthly column on succesful aging Pomona Valley Community Svcs. on Aging Newsletter, also numerous articles. Commr. human svcs., City of Claremont, 1986-89; trustee Mt. San Antonio Gardens Retirement Com., 1985-92, sec. 1988-91; v.p. Mt. San Antonio Gardens Club Coun. Residents Orgn., 1991—; trustee Corp. Pilgrim Pl. Ret. Community, chmn. health and svcs. com., 1987—; bd. dirs., trustee Vol. Assn. Rancho Santa Ana Botanic Gardens, 1991-92; chmn. vol. pers. com. St. Ambrose Episcopal Ch., Claremont, 1988—. Named Outstanding Contbn. to Social Work, Alumni Assn. Schs. Social Work U. So. Calif., 1984, Outstanding Contbr. Social Group Work, Com. Advancement of Group Work, Toronto, Ont., Can., 1985, Woman of Yr., Trojan Women U. So. Calif., 1976, Woman of Yr. YWCA of Pomona Valley, 1989, Vol. of Yr. L.A. County Coun. on Aging, 1990; recipient Dart award for Inovative Teaching, U. So. Calif., 1974, 1st pl. award at juried show Am. Assn. Chinese Brush Painting, 1987, 2nd pl. short story Sedona Writers Contest, Hon. Mention non fiction, 1989, County Commnr. Citation State of Calif. Ho. of Reps. Fellow Gerontol. Soc. Am.; mem. AAUW, Nat. Assn. Social Workers (cert., nat. chmn. 1962-64, group work sect., chmn. Cleve. chpt. 1969-72), Am. Soc. Aging (chmn. program com. 1983-85, City of Claremont com. on aging, chmn. 1991, program chair 1985—), Delta Kappa Gamma, Alpha Xi Delta. Episcopalian. Home: 900 E Harrison Ave Apt A30-31 Pomona CA 91767-2050

HARTH, ROBERT JAMES, music festival executive; b. Louisville, June 13, 1956; s. Sidney and Teresa O. H.; m. Melanie Lynn Pope; 1 child, Jeffrey David Harth Curtis. B.A. in English, Northwestern U., 1977. Assoc. mgr. Ravinia (Ill.) Festival Assn., 1977-79; v.p., gen. mgr. Los Angeles Philharm. Assn., 1979-89, Hollywood Bowl, 1979-89; pres., chief exec. officer Aspen (Colo.) Music Festival and Sch., Music Assocs. of Aspen, Inc., 1989—. Office: Aspen Music Festival & Sch PO Box Aa Aspen CO 81612-7428 also: 250 W 54th St 10th Fl E New York NY 10019

HARTIG, MARY SWIATECK, association executive; b. Buffalo, Aug. 8, 1951; d. Charles E. and Leocadia (Banaszkiewicz) Swiateck; m. Norman

Francis Hartig, Aug. 19, 1972; 1 child, Andrew Michael. Student, Oakland C.C., 1978-79, Brigham Young U., 1990-92. Founder, exec. officer Polish Surname Network, Newbury Park, Calif. Author: Polish Roots-American Branches, 1992, Polish Surname Directory - An Inventory of Those Researching Polish Ancestry, 1992. Mem. Polish Geneal. Soc., Polish Am. Hist. Assn., Western N.Y. Geneal. Soc., Conejo Valley Geneal. Soc. (periodical libr. 1990—). Roman Catholic. Home and Office: 158 S Walter Ave Newbury Park CA 91320

HARTIN, WILLIAM JOHN, software engineer; b. Eureka, Calif., Feb. 17, 1962; s. William James and Arlene Adele (McRae) H. BA in Math., Humboldt State U., 1985. Pvt. practice computer cons., programmer Eureka, 1985-86; grad. programming asst. Calif. Poly. U., San Louis Obispo, 1986-87; software engr. Sierra On-Line, Oakhurst, Calif., 1987-91; instr. Calif. Poly. State U., San Luis Obispo, 1993—; pres. Goat Mountain Software, North Fork, Calif., 1988-90. Chief programmer computer game Helicopter Simulator, 1989, Macintosh Game Interpreter for Space Quest, Hoyle, 1990. Mem. Assn. Computing Machinery, Math. Assn. Am., Soc. Indsl. Applied Maths. Republican.

HARTL, JOHN GEORGE, film critic; b. Wenatchee, Wash., June 28, 1945; s. David and Georgiann (MacLean) H. BA in Journalism, U. Wash., 1967. Film critic Seattle Times, 1966—. Office: Seattle Times PO Box 70 Fairview Ave N & John St Seattle WA 98111-0070

HARTLEY, ALBERT EDWARD, insurance agent; b. Seattle, Mar. 17, 1924; s. Edward Albert and Gertrude (Lachance) H.; m. Eileen Barnawell, Mar. 8, 1945 (div. May 1973); 1 child, Kevin B.; m. Marny W. Woodsmall, May 17, 1974. BA in Econs., Berea Coll., 1947. CLU, chartered fin. con. Am. Coll. Ins. agt. Prudential Ins. Co., Trenton, Mich., 1957-84, Sun Plan Fin. Svcs., Tucson, 1984—. Bd. dirs., treas. Cooperative Svcs., Detroit, 1967-80. Democrat. Office: Sun Plan Fin Svcs 3208 E Ft Lowell Rd Ste 105 Tucson AZ 85716-1625

HARTLEY, GRACE VAN TINE, foundation administrator; b. San Francisco, Aug. 24, 1916; d. Ellis Charles and Nadine (Allen) Van Tine; m. Frank Brooke Hartley (div. 1974); children: Shirley Hartley Hill, Linda Hartley Sims, Brooke Hartley Hudson, Jessie Hartley Brady, Frank. Student, De Anza Coll., 1975-77, Coll. of Marin, 1985-86. V.p. Barron & Hartley Builders, Alameda, Calif., 1946-72; pres. Aurley Apt. Houses, Sunnyvale, Calif., 1974-86; exec. dir. George Demont Otis Found., San Francisco, 1974—; pres. Western Arts Acad. Found., San Rafael, Calif. Author, producer: (audio visual) American Artists National Parks, 1976 (Bicentennial award 1976); exhibited in group shows at Golden Gate Collection, 1974 (Soc. Western Artists award 1974), Otis Centennial, 1980 (Calif. History Ctr. award 1980). Pres. Rep. Women's Club, Alameda, 1960-62; active Rep. State Cen. Com., Alameda, 1964, Ronald Reagan Presdl. Task Force, Corte Madera, 1978-80. Recipient cert. Achievement Internat. Platform Assn., Washington, 1982, Presdl. Achievement award Rep. Party, Corte Madera, 1987. Presbyterian.

HARTLINE, JANE A., marketing manager, journalist; b. Cape Girardeau, Mo., Dec. 2, 1950; d. Earl Tiffin and Wanda (Raby) H.; m. Leonard L. Yoon, Feb. 29, 1975. BJ, U. Mo., 1972; MPA, Portland State U., 1981. Reporter Bulletin-Journ. Newspaper, Cape Girardeau, 1972-74; pub. info. coord. Mo. Dept. Social Svcs., Jefferson City, 1974-76; pub. info. specialist Portland (Oreg.) State U., 1976-78; pub. info. dir. Oreg. Dept. of Labor and Industries, Portland, 1978-80; mktg. mgr. Metro Washington Park Zoo, Portland, 1980—; cons. City of Yachats, Oreg., 1983-84, YWCA, Portland, 1982-83. Co-author: Cross Country Ski Lodges, OR, WA, ID, 1981, Cross Country Ski Lodges, MT, WY, UT, 1983; contbr. articles to profl. jours. Vice chmn. Oreg. Nature Conservancy, Portland, 1986—; bd. dirs., edn. com. chmn. Portland Audubon Soc., 1986—; dir. Mult. Co. Soil and Water Conservation Dist., 1985—; pres. Friends of Mult. Co. Libr., 1986. Mem. Fellow Am. Assn. Zoolo. Pks. and Aquriums (pub. rels. com.), West Multnomab Soil and Water Conservation Dist. (bd. dirs.). Office: Metro Washington Park Zoo 4001 SW Canyon Rd Portland OR 97221-2705

HARTMAN, BRADY CHAMBERS, JR., computer systems firm executive; b. West Palm Beach, Fla., Dec. 7, 1961; s. Brady Chambers H. and Catherine (Stevens) Earhart. BSEE, Boston U., 1983. Software engr. General Dynamics, San Diego, 1983-85, Teledyne Electronics, Newbury Park, Calif., 1985-86; cons. Minisystems Assn., San Diego, 1986-88; lead engr. NSR Co., Oceanside, Calif., 1991-93; pres., chief exec. officer BCH Systems, San Diego, 1988—. Recipient Outstanding Achievement award Nat. Systems and Rsch., Oceanside, 1992. Mem. IEEE (officer 1982-83).

HARTMAN, HOWARD LEVI, mining engineering educator, consultant; b. Indpls., Aug. 7, 1924; s. Howard Levi and Catherine Gladys (Miller) H.; m. Bonnie Lee Sherrill, June 8, 1947; children: Sherilyn Hartman Knoll, Greg Alan. Student, Colo. Sch. Mines, 1942-44; BS, Pa. State U., 1946, MS, 1947; PhD, U. Minn., 1953. Registered profl. engr., Colo., Pa. Instr. Pa. State U., University Park, 1947-48, prof., dept. head and assoc. dean, 1957-67; mining engr. Phelps Dodge Corp., Bisbee, Ariz., 1948-49; state mine dust engr. Mine Inspector's Office, Phoenix, 1949-50; instr. U. Minn., Mpls., 1950-54; from asst. prof. to assoc. prof. Colo. Sch. Mines, Golden, 1954-57; prof., dean Calif. State U., Sacramento, 1967-71, Vanderbilt U., Nashville, 1971-80; Drummond endowed chair mining engrng. U. Ala., Tuscaloosa, 1980-89; adj. prof. engrng. Calif. State U., Sacramento, 1989—; chmn. Fed. Metal and Nonmetallic Mine Safety Bd. Rev., Washington, 1971-75; Warren lectr. U. Minn., 1965; Disting. lectr. Can. Inst. Mining and Metallurgy, 1966; cons. engr. Standard Oil N.J., Tulsa, 1961-64, Ingersoll-Rand Co., Bedminster, N.J., 1964-66, Inst. for Technol. Research, São Paulo, Brazil, 1977, 85, Bechtel Corp., San Francisco, 1982—. Author, editor various books including: Mine Ventilation and Air Conditioning, 1971, 82, Introductory Mining Engineering, 1987; contbr. articles to profl. jours. Mem. Human Rights Commn., Nashville, 1975-79. Served to lt. (j.g.) USNR, 1942-44. Recipient Faculty Service award Nat. Univ. Continuing Edn. Assn., 1985. Disting. mem. Soc. Mining Engrs. (chmn. com., Mineral Industries Edn. award 1965, Book Pub. award 1982, Hartman Mine Ventilation award 1989); mem. Am. Soc. for Engring. Edn., Met. Opera Guild, Sigma Xi, Kappa Sigma. Democrat. Presbyterian (elder). Club: Yosemite Assn. (El Portal, Calif.). Home: 4052 Alex Ln Carmichael CA 95608-6728 Office: Calif State Univ Sch Engring & Computer Sci 6000 J St Sacramento CA 95819-2605

HARTMAN, PETER ARNOLD, school district superintendent; b. Elgin, Ill., May 27, 1937; s. Arnold Wayne and Mildred Louella (VanHorn) H.; m. Sundra Sue Reppert, June 11, 1960; children: Beth, Bonnie, Julie, Peter. BA, MS, Calif. State U., Fullerton; PhD, Stanford U. Asst. to supt. Fremont Union High Sch. Dist., Sunnyvale, Calif., 1968-69; asst. supt. adminstrv. svcs. Newark (Del.) Sch. Dist., 1970-73; supt. Hamilton Township Sch. Dist., Hamilton Square, N.J., 1973-78, South Bay Union Sch. Dist., Imperial Beach, Calif., 1978-83, Saddleback Valley Unified Sch. Dist., Mission Viejo, Calif., 1983—; instr. Calif. State U., Fullerton, 1989—; corp. mem. Blue Shield. Mem. Am. Assn. Sch. Adminstrs., Am. Edn. Rsch. Adminstrn., Assn. Calif. Sch. Adminstrs., Suburban Sch. Supts., Rotary. Office: 25631 Diseno Dr Mission Viejo CA 92691-3199

HARTMAN, PHIL EDWARD, actor; b. Brantford, Ont., Can., Sept. 24, 1948; came to U.S., 1957; Appeared in films Cheech and Chong's Next Movie, 1980, Weekend Pass, 1984, Pee-Wee's Big Adventure (also co-writer), The Last Resort, 1985, Blind Date, Three Amigos, 1986, The Brave Little Toaster (voices), Amazon Women on the Moon, 1987, Fletch Lives, Quick Change, 1989, CB4, 1993; mem. cast TV program Saturday Night Live, 1986—. Recipient Emmy award for best writing in a musical or variety program, 1990.

HARTMAN, ROBERT LEROY, artist, educator; b. Sharon, Pa., Dec. 17, 1926; s. George Otto and Grace Arvada (Radabaugh) H.; m. Charlotte Ann Johnson, Dec. 30, 1951; children: Mark Allen, James Robert. B.F.A., U. Ariz., 1951, M.A., 1952; postgrad., Colo. Springs Fine Arts Center, 1947, 51, Bklyn. Mus. Art Sch., 1953-54. Instr. architecture, allied arts Tex. Tech. Coll., 1955-58; asst. prof. art U. Nev., Reno, 1958-61; mem. faculty dept. art U. Calif., Berkeley, 1961—, prof., 1972-91, prof. emeritus, 1991—, chmn. dept., 1974-76; mem. Inst. for Creative Arts, U. Calif., 1967-68. One man exhbns. include, Bertha Schafer Gallery, N.Y.C., 1966, 69, 74, Santa Barbara Mus. Art, 1973, Cin. Art Acad., 1975, Hank Baum Gallery, San Francisco, 1973, 75, 78, San Jose Mus. Art, 1983, Bluxome Gallery, San Francisco, 1984, 86, U. Art Mus., Berkeley, 1986, Instituto D'Arte Dosso Dossi, Ferrara, Italy, 1989, Victor Fischer Galleries, San Francisco, 1991, Triangle Gallery, San Francisco, 1992; group exhbns. include Richmond Mus., 1966, Whitney Mus. Biennial, 1973, Oakland Mus., 1976, San Francisco Arts Commn. Gallery, 1985 (award), Earthscape Expo '90 Photo Mus., Osaka, Japan, 1990; represented in permanent collections, Nat. Collections Fine Arts, Colorado Springs Fine Arts Center, Corcoran Gallery, San Francisco Art Inst., Roswell Mus., Princeton Art Mus. U. Calif. humanities research fellow, 1980. Office: U Calif Dept Art Berkeley CA 94720

HARTMAN, ROSALIND ANN, nursing educator, administrator; b. Waterbury, Conn., Jan. 13, 1950; d. Anthony Joseph and Dolores (Galgota) Stankus; m. William Richard Hartman, Feb. 28, 1981; children: Hanns William, Hannah Ruth. BSN, Georgetown U., 1971; MSN, U. Calif., San Francisco, 1974. RN, Calif. Staff nurse Georgetown U., Washington, 1971-73, U. Calif., San Francisco, 1973-74; instr. Kauai (Hawaii) C.C., 1974-76; instr. Coll. of Marin, Kentfield, Calif., 1976—, dir. nursing, 1991-92, dir. nursing and allied health, 1992—. Co-author: Work Manual for Reeder's Maternity Nursing Textbook, 1987. Mem. ADN Dirs. Orgn., Regional Health Com. Office: Coll of Marin College Ave Kentfield CA 94904

HARTMAN-IRWIN, MARY FRANCES, retired language professional; b. Portland, Oreg., Oct. 18, 1925; d. Curtiss Henry Sabisch and Gladys Frances (Giles) Strand; m. Harry Elmer Hartman, Sept. 6, 1946 (div. June 1970); children: Evelyn Frances, Laura Elyce, Andrea Candace; m. Thomas Floyd Irwin, Apr. 11, 1971. BA, U. Wash., 1964-68; postgrad., Seattle Pacific, 1977-79, Antioch U., Seattle, Wash., 1987, Heritage Inst., Seattle, Wash., 1987. Educator language Kennewick (Wash.) Dist. #17, 1970-88; guide Summer Study Tours of Europe, 1971-88. Sec. Bahai Faith, 1971—, libr., Pasco, Wash., 1985-88; bd. trustees Mid Columbia Coun. Girl Scouts U.S.; exec. bd. trustees; mem. Literacy Coun. Fulbright summer scholar, 1968. Mem. NEA, Wash. Edn. Assn., Kennewick Edn. Assn., Nat. Fgn. Lang. Assn., Wash. Fgn. Lang. Assn., Literacy Coun. Home: 1119 W Margaret St Pasco WA 99301-4134

HARTMANN, DENNIS LEE, atmospheric science educator; b. Salem, Oreg., Apr. 23, 1949; s. Alfred R. and Angeline K. (Van Handel) H.; m. Lorraine E. Obuchowski, July 28, 1973; children—Alan C., Jennifer M. B.S., U. Portland, 1971; Ph.D., Princeton U., 1975. Research assoc. McGill U., Montreal, Que., Can., 1975-76; vis. scientist Nat. Ctr. Atmospheric Research, Boulder, Colo., 1976-77; asst. prof. U. Wash. Seattle, 1977-83, assoc. prof. atmospheric sci., 1983-88, prof. atmos sci., 1988—; mem. MAP panel NRC, 1981-87. Assoc. editor Jour. Atmospheric Scis., 1983—, Jour. Geophys. Research, 1985-88; mem. editorial bd. Contbr. to Atmospheric Physics.; contbr. articles to sci. jours. Fellow Joint Inst. for Study of Atmosphere and Ocean (sr.), Am. Meteorol. Soc. (Fellow, com. upper atmosphere 1978-83, chmn. com. 1980-82, com. undergrad. awards 1983-85, com. climate variations, 1993—); Fellow AAAS, Nat. Acad. Scis. (space sci. bd. com. on earth scis. 1987-90, U.S. Toga panel 1990—), Internat. Commn. Dynamic Meterology. Office: U Wash Dept Atmospheric Scis AK-40 Seattle WA 98125

HARTSOUGH, GAYLA A. KRAETSCH, management consultant; b. Lakewood, Ohio, Sept. 16, 1949; d. Vernon W. and Mildred E. (Austin) Kraetsch; m. James N. Heller, Aug. 20, 1972 (div. 1977); m. Jeffrey W. Hartsough, Mar. 12, 1983; 1 child, Jeffrey Hunter Kraetsch Hartsough. BS, Northwestern U., 1970; EdM, Tufts U., 1973; MEd, U. Va., 1978, PhD, 1978. Vol. VISTA, Tenn., 1970-71; asst. tchr. Perkins Sch. for the Blind, Watertown, Mass., 1971-72; resource tchr. Fairfax (Va.) County Pub. Schs., 1972-76; asst. dir. ctr. U. Va., Charlottesville, 1976-79; sr. program officer Acad. for Edn. Devel., Wahsington, 1978-80; mng. cons. Cresap/TPF&C, Washington, 1980-86; pres. KH Consulting Group, L.A., 1986—; pres. Orgn. Women Execs., L.A., 1986—; adv. coun. No. Trust of Calif., L.A., 1991—, Sch. of Speech at Northwestern U., Evanston, Ill., 1992—. Contbr. more than 20 articles to profl. jours. Co-founder L.A. Higher Edn. Roundtable, L.A., 1987—. Recipient Outstanding Woman of Achievement award Century City C. of C., 1991. Home: 15624 Royal Ridge Rd Sherman Oaks CA 91403 Office: KH Consulting Group 1901 Ave of the Stars #1774 Los Angeles CA 90067

HARTUNG, DOROTHY ALLEN, educator; b. Luana, Iowa, Nov. 23, 1903; d. Burr and Edythe (Russell) Allen; m. Conrad Theodore Hartung, June 25, 1933; children: Allen John, Charles Edward. BA in Edn., State Coll. of Wash., 1929, life diploma, 1934. Tchr. Fairview and Plaza, Wash., Plaza, 1922-23; elem. tchr. Greenacres schs., 1924-25; tchr. Clarkston (Wash.) Jr. High Sch., 1927-28; reading and speech tchr. James Madison Jr. High Sch., Seattle, 1929-33; tchr. R.F.D. # 2 Small Sch., Pullman, Wash., 1933-34; tchr. rural schs. R.F.D. # 1, Pullman, 1934-35; substitute tchr. Spokane Dist. 81 West Valley High Sch., 1935; English and history tchr. Lindberg High Sch., Spokane County, 1935-37, Odessa High Sch., Lincoln County, 1959-61, 67-69; mgr., owner Hartung Gardens, Veradale, Wash., 1985—. Active newsletter Spokane Valley Republican Women, Spokane Valley, circa 1955, Spokane Valley Ch. Women United, circa 1975; past pres. Ch. Women United, Spokane Valley; pres. Cen. Valley PTA, Spokane Valley, 1957-58, Valley Mission Park Assn., Spokane Valley, 1952; area dir. Congl. Christian Women, Wash. and Idaho dist., 1962; bd. mem. YMCA-Spokane Valley, 1956-57; bd. mem. Spokane chpt. and Wash. chpt. UN Assn. Named Valiant Woman, Ch. Women United, Spokane, Wash., 1989. Mem. Wash. Edn. Assn. (pres. Spokane County H.8 unit 1936-37, state adv. com. on social issues 1937-38), Pi Lambda Theta. Home: 12912 E 12th Spokane WA 99216

HARTUNG, MARY, state legislator; m. Morris Hartung; children: Elizabeth, Susan, David. Retailer; former rep. from dist. 10 Idaho Ho. of Reps.; state senator Idaho Senate, 1990—. Bd. dirs. Payette Libr. Named Outstanding County Chmn., Idaho Rep. Party, 1982-83; named to Idaho Rep. Hall of Fame. Mem. Payette C. of C. Home: PO Box 147 Payette ID 83661

HARTWICK, THOMAS STANLEY, aerospace company executive; b. Vandalia, Ill., Mar. 19, 1934; s. William Arthur and Bernice Elizabeth (Daniels) H.; m. Alberta Elaine Lind, June 10, 1961; children: Glynis Anne, Jeffrey Andrew, Thomas Arthur. BS, U. Ill., 1956; MS, UCLA, 1958; PhD, U. So. Calif., 1969. Mgr. quantum electronics dept. Aerospace Corp., El Segundo, Calif., 1973-75, asst. dir. electronics research lab., 1975-79; mgr. electro-optical devel. lab. Hughes Aircraft Co. subs. Gen. Motors Corp., El Segundo, 1979-82, chief sci. advanced tactical programs, 1982-83; mgr. electro-optics research ctr. TRW Corp., Redondo Beach, Calif., 1983-86, mgr. microelectrics ctr., 1986-90, program mgr., 1990—; chmn., bd. dirs. Laser Tech. Inc., Hollywood, Calif.; cons. mem. U.S. Dept. Def. Adv. Group on Electronic Devices, Washington, 1977—, group C chmn., 1988—; mem. Japan/U.S. Tech. Assessment Team, Washington, 1984; mem. Army Rsch. Labs. Adv. Bd., 1993—. Contbr. articles to profl. jours.; inventor FAR Infrared Laser, 1975. Mem. Am. Phys. Soc., Optical Soc. Am., (com. mem. 1976-79), Am. Def. Preparedness Assn. (dep. chmn. West Coast seminar 1987-88). Office: TRW Inc One Space Park 1 Space Park Blvd Rm 2830 Redondo Beach CA 90278-1071

HARTWIG, ROBERT ALLEN, JR., municipal government official; b. Mason City, Iowa, June 9, 1958; s. Robert Allen and Shirley June (Orvis) H.; m. Glenda Gayle Grubbs, Aug. 18, 1979; children: David Christian, Amanda Gayle. BBA in Acctg. and Fin., U. Iowa, 1980. CPA, Colo. Auditor Alexander Grant & Co., Denver, 1980-84; acct. III, systems analyst City of Aurora, Colo., 1984; chief acct. City of Westminster, Colo., 1984-89; fin. dir. City of Greenwood Village, Colo., 1989-91; prin. Hartwig & Assocs., 1991—; bd. dirs. North Metro Fire Consortium, Westminster, 1989—, chmn., 1991—; bd. dirs. Westminster Housing Authority, 1989—; lectr. profl. tng. course on audit workpaper techniques, 1985. City councilman City of Westminster, 1989—; precinct capt. Rep. Cen. Com., Jefferson County, 1989—, Nat. League Cities, 1989—. Mem. Govt. Fin. Officers Assn. (spl. rev. com. 1985-86, cert. achievement for excellence in fin. reporting 1984-87), Govtl. Acctg. Standards Bd. (com. on acctg., auditing, and fin. reporting 1986-87), Colo. Soc. CPAs (CPAs in industry, govt. and edn. com. 1989-90), Colo. Assn. Mcpl. Tax Auditors. Lutheran. Home: 6612 W 113th Ave Broomfield CO 80020-3032 Office: Hartwig and Assocs # 2 Garden Ctr Ste 303 Broomfield CO 80020

HARTZ, BRIAN D., radio production executive; b. El Paso, Tex., Jan. 27, 1965; s. Michael C. and Doris J. (Anders) H. BA in English, BA in Radio Broadcasting, U. Tex., El Paso, 1988. Personality, engr. Sta. KTEP, El Paso, 1986-87, Sta. KHEY, El Paso, 1987-88; morning drive personality, program dir., ops. mgr., prodn. dir. Sta. KGRT, Las Cruces, N.Mex., 1988-92. Recipient Nat. Stephen King Writing award Doublday Book Co., N.Y.C., 1983. Office: Sta KGRT PO Box 968 Las Cruces NM 88004

HARUDA, FRED DAVID, neurologist; b. N.Y.C., Mar. 16, 1950; s. Joseph Stanley and Iva Fern (Lindstrom) H.; m. Alexandria Stephanie Francis, May 28, 1983; 1 child, Ashleigh Francis. BA cum laude, Whitman Coll., 1972; MD, U. Chgo., 1976, MS, 1977; diploma in pediatrics, Johns Hopkins U., 1978; diploma in child and adult neurology, Neuro Inst. Columbia U., 1981; diploma in pediatrics, Johns Hopkins U., 1978. Attending physician Salinas (Calif.) Valley Meml. Hosp., 1981—; prin. Fred D. Haruda, M.D., Salinas, 1981-89; mng. ptnr. Ctrl. Coast Neurol. Assocs., Salinas, 1989—; cons. Natavad Med. Ctr., Salinas, 1981—, Mee Meml. Hosp., King City, Calif., 1988—; clin. instr. U. Calif., San Francisco, 1981-86, clin. asst. prof., 1986—; cons. child neurology San Andreas Regional Ctr., Salinas, 1981—; mem. quality coordinating coun. Salinas Valley Meml. Hosp., 1984-86, 90— (bd. cert. neuro., child neuro, Peds, EEG). Contbr. articles to profl. jours. and textbooks. Dist. chmn. Boy Scouts Am., 1993—. Fellow Am. Acad. Pediatrics; mem. Am. Acad. Neurology, AMA, Calif. Med. Assn., Child Neurology Soc., Am. Epilepsy Soc., Am. EEG Soc., Am. Med. EEG Soc. Office: Cen Coast Neurol Assocs 535 E Romie Ln Salinas CA 93901-4026

HARVEY, DONALD, artist, educator; b. Walthamston, Eng., June 14, 1930; s. Henry and Annie Dorothy (Sawell) H.; m. Elizabeth Clark, Aug. 9, 1952; children—Shan Mary, David Jonathan. Art tchrs. diploma, Brighton Coll. Art, 1951. Art master Ardwyn Grammar Sch., Wales, 1952-56; mem. faculty dept. art U. Victoria, B.C., Can., 1961—; now prof. painting U. Victoria. One man exhbns. include, Albert White Gallery, Toronto, 1968, retrospective, Art Gallery of Victoria, 1968; represented in permanent collections, Nat. Gallery Can., Montreal Mus., Albright-Knox Mus., Seattle Art Mus. Mem. accessions com. Art Gallery of Victoria, 1969-72. Can. Council fellow, 1966. Mem. Royal Can. Acad. of Arts (full academician), Can. Group Painters, Can. Painters and Etchers. Home: 1025 Joan Crescent, Victoria, BC Canada V8S 3L3 Office: Univ of Victoria, Victoria, BC Canada

HARVEY, ELAINE LOUISE, artist, educator; b. Riverside, Calif., Mar. 1, 1936; d. Edgar Arthur and Emma Louise (Shull) Siervogel; m. Stuart Herbert Harvey, June 16, 1957; children: Kathleen Robin, Laurel Lynn, Mark Stuart. BA with highest honors, with distinction, San Diego State U., 1957. Cert. gen. elem. tchr., Calif. Tchr. Cajon Valley Schs., El Cajon, Calif., 1957, 58; free-lance artist El Cajon, 1975—; tchr. Athenaeum Sch. Music & Art, 1990—; juror various art exhbns., Calif., 1983—; lectr., 1984—; tchr. painting seminars, 1987—. Editor: Palette to Palate, 1986; contbr. The Artists Mag., 1987, The New Spirit of Watercolor, 1989, California Art Review, 1989, The Artists of Southern California, 1989, Splash, 1990, Splash II, 1992, Watercolor Techniques for Releasing the Creative Spirit, 1992. Trustee San Diego Mus. Art, 1985, 86; leader El Cajon Coun. Girl Scouts of U.S., 1968; vol. art tchr., San Diego area pub. schs., 1973-76; choral dir. Chapel of Valley United Meth., 1991—. Recipient Merit award La. Watercolor Soc., 1984, Arches Canson Rives award Midwest Watercolor Soc./Tweed Mus., Greenbay, Wis., 1984, Winsor Newton award Midwest Watercolor Soc./Neville Mus., Duluth, Minn., 1985, McKinnon award Am. Watercolor Soc. 1985, Creative Connection award Rocky Mountain Nat. Exhbn., 1986, 1st Juror's award San Diego Internat. Watercolor Exhbn., 1986, Dassler Mochs award Adirondacks Exhbn. of Am. Art, 1988, Arjomari/Arches/Rives award Watercolor West, Brea Cultural Ctr., 1990. Mem. Nat. Watercolor Soc. (bd. dirs. 1987, 88, elected juror 1989), Watercolor West (bd. dirs. 1986, 87, 88), West Coast Watercolor Soc. (pres. 1993—), San Diego Watercolor Soc. (pres. 1979, 80, chmn, internat. exhbn. 1980, 81, Silver Recognition award 1986), San Diego Mus. Art Artist's Guild (pres. 1985, 86, bd. dirs. 1986-87, 90—), Western Fedn. Watercolor Socs. (del. 1983-91), Rocky Mountain Nat. Watermedia Soc., Allied Artists of Am., Grossmont Garden Club (Elson Creativity Trophy 1977, 79). Home and Studio: 1602 Sunburst Dr El Cajon CA 92021

HARVEY, GREGORY ALAN, microcomputer technology educator, consultant; b. Harvey, Ill., Feb. 15, 1949; s. Kenneth Herman and Mildred Faye (Pounds) H. BA, U. Ill., 1970; teaching credential, San Francisco State U., 1982. Mem. drafting and design staff Bechtel Engring., San Francisco, 1973-81; computer cons., prin. Harvey & Assocs., San Francisco, 1981—; profl. lectr., Golden Gate U., San Francisco, 1987-; computer cons., PCTeach, Inverness, Calif., 1984-. Author (computer books) Communication in Writing, 1984, Mastering SuperCalc 3, 1985, Mastering Q&A, 1986, Lotus 1-2-3 Desktop Companion, 1987, WordPerfect Desktop Companion, 1987, Mastering WordStar, 1987, Lotus 1-2-3 Instant Reference, 1988, WordPerfect Instant Reference, 1988, DOS Instant Reference, 1988, Understanding HyperCard, 1988, HyperTalk Instant Reference, 1988, The Complete Lotus 1-2-3 Handbook, 1989, Mastering PageMaker on the MacIntosh, 1990, Encyclopedia Wordperfect, 1990, Que's Wordperfect Windows Quick-Start, 1991, Que's Lotus 1-2-3 Windows QuickStart, 1991, PCWorld's Wordperfect Windows, 1991, Greg Harvey's Excel 4 Handbook Windows, 1992, Greg Harvey's Excel 4 Handbook Macintosh, 1992, IGD's Excel for Dummies, 1992, IDG's 1-2-3 for Dummies, 1992, IDG's DOS for Dummies Command Reference, 1993. Mem. Macs of Marin, Berkeley Macintosh Users Group. Democrat. Zen Buddhist. Home: 60 Kyleswood Pl Inverness CA 94937-9717 Office: Harvey & Assocs PO Box 1175 Point Reyes Station CA 94956-1175

HARVEY, JAMES GERALD, educational consultant, counselor, researcher; b. California, Mo., July 15, 1934; s. William Walter and Exie Marie (Lindley) H. BA Amherst Coll., 1956; MAT (fellow), Harvard U., 1958, MEd, 1962. Asst. to dean grad. sch. edn. Harvard U., Cambridge, Mass., 1962-66, dir. admissions, fin. aid, 1966-69; dir. counseling service U. Calif., Irvine, 1970-72; edni. cons., Los Angeles, 1972—. Author: (ednl. materials) HARVOCAB Vocabulary Program, 1985—. 1st lt. USAF, 1958-61. Amherst Mayo-Smith grantee, 1956-57; UCLA Adminstrv. fellow, 1969-70. Mem. Am. Ednl. Research Assn., Nat. Council Measurement in Edn., Am. Counseling Assn. Address: 1845 Glendon Ave Los Angeles CA 90025

HARVEY, JAMES ROSS, finance company executive; b. Los Angeles, Aug. 20, 1934; s. James Ernest and Loretta Berniece (Ross) H.; m. Charlene Coakley, July 22, 1971; children: Kjersten Ann, Kristina Ross. B.S. in Engring., Princeton U., 1956; M.B.A., U. Calif., Berkeley, 1963. Engr. Chevron Corp., San Francisco, 1956-61; acct. Touche, Ross, San Francisco, 1963-64; chmn. bd. Transamerica Corp., San Francisco, 1965—; bd. dirs. Sedgwick Group, Pacific Telesis Group, McKesson Corp., Charles Schwab Corp. Trustee St. Mary's Coll., Walter A. Haas Sch. Bus., U. Calif., Bay Area Coun., The Nature Conservancy, Mt. Land Reliance, Nat. Park Found.; vice chmn. Presidio Coun. With AUS, 1958-59. Mem. Bohemian Club, Pacific-Union Club, The Fly Fishers Club, London. Office: Transam Corp 600 Montgomery St San Francisco CA 94111-2702

HARVEY, JOSEPH PAUL, JR., orthopedist, educator; b. Youngstown, Ohio, Feb. 28, 1922; s. Joseph Paul and Mary Justinian (Collins) H.; m. Martha Elizabeth Toole, Apr. 12, 1958; children: Maryalice, Martha Jane, Frances Susan, Helen Lucy, Laura Andre. Student, Dartmouth, 1939-42; M.D., Harvard, 1945. Diplomate: Nat. Bd. Med. Examiners. Intern Peter Bent Brigham Hosp., Boston, 1945-46; resident Univ. Hosp., Cleve., 1951-53, Hosp. Spl. Surgery, N.Y.C., 1953-54; instr. orthopedics Cornell Med. Coll., N.Y.C., 1954-62; mem. faculty Sch. Medicine, U. So. Calif., Los Angeles, 1962-92; prof. orthopedic surgery U. So. Calif., 1966-92, prof. emeritus, 1992—; chmn. sect. orthopedics Sch. Medicine, U. So. Calif., 1964-78; dir. dept. orthopedics U. So. Calif.-Los Angeles County Med. Center, 1964-79, mem. staff, 1979—. Editor-in-chief: Contemporary Orthopedics. Served to capt. AUS, 1946-48. Exchange orthopedic fellow Royal Acad. Hosp., Upsala, Sweden, 1957. Fellow Western Orthopedic Assn., Am. Acad. Orthopedic Surgery, A.C.S., Am. Soc. Testing Materials; mem. AMA, Calif.

Med. Assn., Los Angeles County Med. Assn., Am. Rheumatism Assn., Am. Orthopedic Assn., Internat. Soc. Orthopedics and Truamatology. Club: Boston Harvard. Home: 2050 Lorain Rd San Marino CA 91108-2548 Office: 39 Congress St Pasadena CA 91105

HARVEY, KAREN LYNNE GARCIA, product development artist; b. San Diego, Nov. 27, 1953; d. Manuel and Basilisa Marta (Oquita) Garcia; m. William John Morgan Harvey, Mar. 17, 1979 (div. May 1985); 1 child, William John Morgan. BA, U. Calif., San Diego, 1975; postgrad., San Diego State U., 1975-76. Purchasing agt. The Fine Art Store, San Diego, 1976-84; product devel. artist, airbrusher Livingstone Inc., San Diego, 1987-91; product devel. artist Wild Things/Artfactory, San Diego, 1991—. Mem. U. Calif. San Diego Alumni Assn. Office: Wild Things/Artfactory 10463 Austin Dr Spring Valley CA 92179

HARVEY, KENNETH RICARDO, city official; b. Little Rock, Jan. 19, 1956; s. Boss Esau and Ella Jean (Thompson) H.; m. Kathi Ann Harvey, Mar. 24, 1979; 1 child, Kenneth Jared. AA, Spokane Falls Community Coll., 1976; BFA in Radio/TV, Ea. Wash. U., 1981. Pub. rels. dir. House of Solomon, Spokane, 1975-76; TV engr. KREM-TV, Spokane, 1978-90; dir. promotions KGA/KDRK-FM Radio, Spokane, 1981-83; community rels. dir. Tacoma (Wash.) Pub. Libr., 1983-86; pubr./owner Write Pubs., Tacoma, 1986-87; desktop pub. sales cons. Quantum Computers, Tacoma, 1987-88; pub. info. officer, cable adminstr. City of Reno, Nev., 1989—; bd. dirs. KUNR-FM Ethnic Prog. Advisory, Reno, 1989— (Community adv. bd. 1992); bd. dirs., minority advisory Reno Gazette Jour., 1989-91. Editor newsletter, Renoscape, 1989-90 (Silver Scroll 1989), Working Together, 1989-90, The Winner's Edge, 1986-88, The Eye of Tomorrow, 1976. With USCG, 1974-75. Mem. Nat. Fedn. Local Cable Programmers, Nat. Assn. Telecommunications Officers & Advisors, Pub. Rels. Soc. Am., Internat. Assn. Bus. Communicators, No. Nev. Black Cultural Awareness Soc. (bd. dirs. 1990—), Habitat for Humanity. Office: City of Reno 490 S Center St Reno NV 89501-2191

HARVEY, MARC SEAN, lawyer, consultant; b. N.Y.C., May 4, 1960; s. M. Eugene and Coleen (Jones) H. BA with honors, So. Ill. U., 1980; JD, Southwestern U., 1983; postgrad., Loyola Marymount U., L.A., 1984-86. lectr. Loyola Marymount U., 1986; judge pro tem Culver (Calif.) Mcpl. Ct., 1991—. Counsel U.S. SBA, L.A., 1982-83; counsel enforcement div. U.S. SEC, L.A., 1983-84; counsel State Farm Ins. Co., L.A., 1984-85, 20th Century Ins. Co., Woodland Hills, Calif., 1985-86; pvt. practice Encino, Calif., 1986—; lectr. Loyola Marymount U., 1986; judge pro tem Culver (Calif.) Mcpl. Ct., 1991. Charter mem., trustee Rep. Presdl. Task Force, Washington, 1981—; mem. Nat. Rep. Senatorial Com., Washington, 1983—, Rep. Congl. Leadership Coun., Washington, 1987—, Rep. Senatorial Inner Cir., Washington, 1988—; victory fund sponsor Nat. Rep. Congl. Com., Washington, 1984—; judge pro tem Culver Mcpl. Ct., 1991— (Judge Pro Tem of Yr. award 1991). Recipient 1st Pl. Essay award VFW, 1976, So. Ill. U. scholarship, 1979-81. Mem. ABA, ATFA, SAG, Am. Trial Lawyers Assn., Calif. Trial Lawyers Assn., L.A. Bar Assn., L.A. Trial Laywers Assn., Themis Soc., Nat. Honor Soc. Home and Office: Law Offices Marc S Harvey 16530 Ventura Blvd Encino CA 91436-2006

HARVEY, PAUL W., electronics engineer, consultant; b. Aug. 12, 1957. BSEE, MIT, 1979. Integrated circuit design engr. Harris Semiconductor, Melbourne, Fla., 1979-81; sr. integrated circuit design engr. Advanced Micro Devices, Sunnyvale, Calif., 1981-85; sr. cons. Logical Cons. Corp., Palo Alto, Calif., 1985-86; owner Integrated Circuit Design Cons., Santa Clara, Calif., 1986—. Co-inventor, patentee 22V10 PAL output. Mem. IEEE, Prof. and Tech. Cons. Assn. Office: Integrated Circuit Design Cons Ste 310 1556 Halford Ave Santa Clara CA 95051-2694

HARVEY, RICHARD BLAKE, political science educator; b. Los Angeles, Nov. 28, 1930; s. George Blackstone and Clara Ethel (Conway) H.; m. Patricia Jean Clougher, Aug. 29, 1965; 1 child: Timothy Harvey. BA, Occidental Coll., 1952; MA, UCLA, 1954, PhD, 1959. Prof. polit. sci. Whittier (Calif.) Coll., 1960—, acad. dean, 1970-80, chmn. polit. sci. dept., 1984-87. Author: Earl Warren, Governor of California, 1970, Dynamics-California Government and Politics, 1991; contbr. articles and book revs. to profl. jours. Grantee Haynes Found., 1961, 68. Mem. Am. Polit. Sci. Assn., Western Polit. Sci. Assn., So. Calif. Polit. Sci. Assn., Newcomen Soc., Pi Sigma Alpha. Democrat. Presbyterian. Club: University. Home: 424 E Avocado Crest Rd La Habra Heights CA 90631-8128 Office: Whittier Coll Whittier CA 90608

HARVEY, RICHARD DUDLEY, marketing consultant; b. Atlanta, Sept. 24, 1923; s. Robert Emmett and June (Dudley) H.; BA, U. Denver, 1947; postgrad. various bus. seminars Harvard U., Stanford U.; m. Donna Helen Smith, Oct. 12, 1944 (dec. Mar. 1990); 1 child, Louise Dudley. Various positions in sales, sales promotion and mktg. The Coca-Cola Co., St. Louis, Denver and Atlanta, 1948-60, v.p., brand mgr., mktg. mgr., mktg. dir., Atlanta, 1965-70, v.p. orgn. and mktg. devel., 1970-75; sr. v.p. mktg. Olympia Brewing Co., Olympia, Wash., 1975-78; pres. Sound Mktg. Svcs. Inc., Seattle, 1978—; dir. Lone Star Brewing Co., San Antonio. Mem. mayor's housing resources com., Atlanta, 1968-70; program chmn. United Way, Atlanta, 1969; trustee Episcopal Radio-TV Found., Atlanta, 1961-88, vice chmn. 1975-84, emeritus trustee, 1988—; bd. dirs. Oreg. Shakespearean Festival Assn., 1982-86; chmn. mktg. com., trustee Seattle Symphony, 1983-88; mem. assistance com. Albers Sch. Bus. Seattle U., 1988-92; gov.'s adv. com. bus. devel. and job retention, State of Wash., 1988-92. Served with USAAF, 1942-45. Mem. Am. Mktg. Assn. (pres. 1983-84), Mktg. Communications Execs. Internat. (pres. 1984-85), Inst. Mgmt. Cons., Phi Beta Kappa, Omicron Delta Kappa. Democrat. Episcopalian. Clubs: Seattle Tennis. Home: 3837 E Crockett St Seattle WA 98112-2422 Office: Sound Mktg Svcs Inc PO Box 22443 Seattle WA 98122-0443

HARVEY, STEWART CLYDE, pharmacologist, retired educator; b. Denver, Feb. 16, 1921; s. John Alden and Marie Bronson (Barfoot) H.; m. Joyce Contance Payne, Dec. 27, 1947 (dec. June 1964); children: Janet Ann Harding, Stephen John; m. Eunice Marie Munk, July 2, 1965. BA, U. Colo., 1943, postgrad., 1946; PhD, U. Chgo., 1948. Instr. U. Colo., Boulder, 1943-46; instr., chmn. pharmacology Dental Coll. U. Tex., Houston, 1948-49; instr. pharmacology U. Utah, Salt Lake City, 1949-51, asst. prof. pharmacology, 1951-53, assoc. prof. pharmacology, 1953-74, prof. pharmacology, 1974-88, prof. emeritus, 1988—; vis. prof. U. Southampton, Eng., 1972-73; mem. rev. panel on pharmacology and toxicology NIH, Bethesda, Med., 1965-66; mem. Utah Heart Rsch. Com., Salt Lake City, 1955-66; cons. com. on drugs AMA, Chgo.; mem. panel on rev. antacids FDA, Bethesda, 1972-74; ad hoc cons. Med. Letter, NSF; cons., expert witness on alcohol and drugs to various cts., 1952-90. Author chpts. in books; assoc. editor Remington's Pharm. Scis., 1963-90, Circulation Rsch., 1958-63. Chmn. 1st senatorial dist. Utah Dem. Party, Salt Lake City, 1953-62; scoutmaster Boy Scouts of Am., Salt Lake City, 1957-65; charter mem. Utah Environ. Ctr., Salt Lake City, 1970-72; mem. Citizens Adv. Panel to U.S. Army Engrs., Ogden, Utah, 1970-72. Rsch. grantee NIH, Am. Heart Assn., Utah Heart Assn., Gividan-Delawana. Democrat. Home: 1652 Yale Ave Salt Lake City UT 84105-1720 Office: U Utah Dept of Pharmacology 2C 219 University Medical Ctr Salt Lake City UT 84132

HARVEY, WILLIAM DUBEE, publishing company executive; b. Washington, Feb. 18, 1937; s. William DuBee Harvey and Erna Ann (Grishkot) Barrere; m. Ann McDowell, Apr. 10, 1980. AA, Orange Coast Coll., Costa Mesa, Calif., 1976; BA, Long Beach State Coll., 1978; MA, Newport U., Newport Beach, Calif., 1979, PhD, 1980. Pres. Drapemobile, Costa Mesa, 1976-86; pres., CEO, Ike & DuDatt Pubs., Huntington Beach, Calif., 1986—. Author, editor: Then, the Toaster Said... With USAF, 1955-58. Recipient all awards for journalism. Mem. Am. Mensa (5 awards), Pacific Press Club, Orange County Press Club. Home and Office: 9361 La Jolla Cir Huntington Beach CA 92646

HARVEY, WILLIAM GEORGE, artist, architect; b. Amityville, N.Y., May 12, 1932; s. William George and Pauline Frances (Belrose) H.; m. Sondra Elaine Burns, Oct. 18, 1951 (div. 1987); children: Robin Lee, Matthew Darrell, Gavin William, Mavis Ann. Student, The Cooper Union, N.Y., 1950-53, Art Students League, 1952-56. Registered Architect, N.Y., Ariz. Designer Architects Associated, N.Y.C., 1953-60, E. L. Varney Assocs., Phoenix, 1961-64, Katz, Waisman, Blumenkranz, Stein, Webber, N.Y.C., 1965-69; architect Russell McCaleb, Architect, Phoenix, 1971-75; self employed architect Phoenix, 1975-85, self employed artist, 1985—; instr. Scottsdale (Ariz.) Community Coll., 1991—. Artist: Haydens Mill, 1992 (Philip Isenberg award 1993), The Lavender Pit, 1990 (Ralph Fabri Medal of Honor, Gold medal 1991), The Race, 1990 (Silver medal 1991), In The Days Before Ice, 1989 (Ciba Geigy award 1989). Mem. Tex. Watercolor Soc. (signature mem.), Miss. Watercolor Soc., Nev. Watercolor Soc., Western Colo. Watercolor Soc. (Spl. award 1992), Coatamundi Soc., Ariz. Watercolor Assn. (juried). Home: # 1017 5800 W Charleston Blvd Las Vegas NV 89102 Office: Harvey/LaJeunesse 6811 E Presidio Rd Scottsdale AZ 85254

HARVILL, DORIS HOLVE, educator; b. Santa Ana, Calif., Oct. 15, 1936; d. Alfred Adelbert and Susanna (Winkler) Holve; div. 1985; children: Sharon Harvill McAuliffe, Julie Ann, Thomas Lawrence. BS in Phys. Edn., UCLA, 1962; MEd in Adminstrn., Azusa Pacific U., 1991. Cert. tchr., Calif. Tchr. phys. edn., English Aquinas High Sch., San Bernardino, Calif., 1978-86; tchr. English, lang. arts Perris (Calif.) Union High Sch., 1986—, dept. chairperson, 1992-93; tchr., cons. Inland Area Writing Project, Riverside, Calif., 1988-93; cons., writer, trainer School Research and Service Corp., Mission Viejo, Calif., 1990-93; presenter at profl. confs. Columnist ednl. newsletters. Troop leader Redlands coun. Girl Scouts U.S., 1968-78. Mem. Calif. Assn. Tchrs. English, So. Calif. Tchrs. English. Home: 628 Fountain Ave Redlands CA 92373 also: 312 Doris Ave Aptos CA 95003 Office: Perris Union Sch Dist 1151 North A St Perris CA 92370-1909 also: Perris Union High Sch 175 E Nuevo Rd Perris CA 92370

HARWARD, NAOMI MARKEE, retired social worker and educator, volunteer; b. Neponset, Ill., Feb. 25, 1907; d. Joshua Waite and Josephine (Eldridge) Markee; m. Albert Harward, Dec. 25, 1936 (dec. Dec. 1979); children: Alfred, Phyllis Ann, Paulina. BA in History and Polit. Sci., Northwestern U., 1929; BD, Garrett Bibl. Inst., Evanston, Ill., 1931; MA in Religious Edn., U. Chgo., 1934, MA in Social Svc. Adminstrn., 1941. Group worker, dir. primary children South Chgo. Communityy Ctr., 1931-33; caseworker, chmn. placing Joint Svc. Bur., Chgo., 1934-36; supr. field work Sch. Soc. Svc. Adminstrn., U. Chgo., 1936-40; dir. rsch. project Works Progress Adminstrn., Chgo., 1940-41; from caseworker to dist. asst. dir. ARC, Chgo., 1941-44; from lectr. to prof., dir. undergrad. social welfare Ariz. State U., Temple, 1955-76; prof. emeritus Ariz. State U., Tempe, 1976—; frequent lectr. Ariz. State U., at nat. confs. and pub. meetings; mem. adv. bd. Ariz. Area 1 Agy. on Aging, Phoenix, 1980-86; dir. health care forum County Bd. Suprs., Phoenix, 1988—. Officer numerous local action and vol. groups; co-founder Ariz. chpt. Gray Panthers, former mem. nat. bd. dirs., vice chmn., founder, chmn. nat. task force on disability, 1986—; state chmn. Mecham Recall, 1987-88; mem. exec. com. Ariz. Health Care Campaign; participant Ariz. Town Hall, 1985—, Ariz. Women's Town Hall, 1988—; mem. nursing home aids consortium bd. Ariz. Dept. Edn., 1985—; chmn. Coalition for Improved Long Term Care, 1976-85; mem. Tempe Ad Hoc Com. on Mobile Homes, 1985-86, regional conf. Fed. Highway Adminstrn., Calif. facilitator section on sr. drivers, 1993. Recipient Adv. of Yr. award Ctr. for Law in Pub. Interest, 1986, "Women Helping Women" award Soroptomists of Mesa, 1989, Lifetime Achievement award Ariz. Dist. 27 Dem. Party; grantee Vocat. Rehab. Adminstrn., 1966-67, NIMH, 1969-76. Mem. NASW (past officer, chmn. nursing home com. Ariz. chpt. 1976-82, award 1980, 87, 89), Acad. Cert. Social Workers, Am. Pub. Welfare Assn., Ariz. Civil Liberties Union (Disting. Citizen of Yr. award 1987), AFSCME (ret. mem.), Ch. Women United. Methodist. Home and Office: 1027 E Concorda Dr Tempe AZ 85282-2419

HARWICK, BETTY CORINNE BURNS, sociology educator; b. L.A., Jan. 22, 1926; d. Henry Wayne Burns and Dorothy Elizabeth (Menzies) Routhier; m. Burton Thomas Harwick, June 20, 1947; children: Wayne Thomas, Burton Terence, Bonnie Christine Foster, Beverly Anne Carroll. Student, Biola, 1942-45, Summer Inst. Linguistics, 1945, U. Calif., Berkeley, 1945-52; BA, Calif. State U., Northridge, 1961, MA, 1965; postgrad., MIT, 1991. Prof. sociology Pierce Coll., Woodland Hills, Calif., 1966—, pres. acad. senate, 1976-77, pres. faculty assn., 1990-91, chair dept. for philosophy and sociology, 1990—; co-founder, faculty advisor interdisciplinary religious studies program Pierce Coll., Woodland Hills, 1988—, creator courses in religious studies in philosophy and sociology depts., Pierce Coll. Author: (with others) Introducing Sociology, 1977; author: Workbook for Introducing Sociology, 1978. faculty rep. Calif. Community Coll. Assn., 1977-80. Alt. fellow NEH, 1978. Mem. Am. Acad. Religion, Soc. Bibl. Lit., Am. Sociol. Assn. Presbyterian. Home: 19044 Superior St Northridge CA 91324-1845 Office: LA Pierce Coll 6201 Winnetka Ave Woodland Hills CA 91371-0002

HARWICK, MAURICE, lawyer; b. L.A., Feb. 6, 1933; m. Saowapa Butranon, July 4, 1970; children: Manasnati, Manasnapa. AA, L.A. City Coll., 1954; JD, Southwestern U., 1957. Bar: Calif., 1958; U.S. Supreme Ct., 1962. Dep. dist. atty. County of Los Angeles, 1958-60; pvt. practice law, Santa Monica, Calif., 1960—; judge pro tem Municipal Ct., 1966-67, 80-81, 85-92; past advisor to dist. atty. Los Angeles County. Chmn. bd. rev. Los Angeles Community Colls. and City Schs.; mem. Project Safer Calif. gov.'s com., 1974-75. Mem. ABA, Calif. Bar Assn., Los Angeles County Bar Assn., Dist. Attys. Assn. L.A., Criminal Cts. Bar Assn. (pres. 1972, bd. govs.), Assn. Trial Lawyers Am., Los Angeles County Dist. Attys. Assn., Vikings. Office: 2001 Wilshire Blvd Ste 600 Santa Monica CA 90403-5690

HARZ, G. MICHAEL, lawyer; b. N.Y.C., Apr. 18, 1951; s. Victor and Arlene (Nadohl) H. BSCE, Cornell U., 1973; JD, U. Denver, 1989. Bar: Colo. 1989. Pres. Zibeq Enterprises, N.Y.C., 1975—. Regent scholar N.Y. State Edn. Dept., 1969-73; recipient Nat. Collegiate Legal Studies award U.S. Achievement Acad., 1988,. Home: 1156 Aspen Dr Evergreen CO 80439-4804

HASAN, WAQAR, computer scientist, researcher; b. Jalaun, India, Apr. 1, 1963; came to U.S., 1984; BS in Computer Sci., Indian Inst. Tech., 1984; postgrad., Stanford U., 1984—. Asst. engr. USDL, Lucknow, India, 1984; research asst. Stanford U., Palo Alto, Calif., 1984-88; research intern DEC, Hudson, Mass., 1985, Intellicorp, Mountain View, Calif., 1986, IBM, Almaden, Calif., 1987; with tech. staff Hewlett Packard Labs., Palo Alto, 1988—. Contbr. articles to profl. jours.; patentee method to intergrate knowledge-based system with arbitrary rel-bd system. Office: Hewlett Packard Labs Bldg 3 Upper 1501 Page Mill Rd Palo Alto CA 94303-0969

HASELMIRE, MICHAEL JOSEPH, financial planner; b. Union City, Ind., Nov. 10, 1940; s. Joseph Maurice and Anna (Johnson) H.; m. Julia May Ruscitti, June 29, 1971 (div. Feb. 1978); 1 child, Christian G.; m. Carol Ann Dewberry, July 30, 1978; children: Ian M., Laurel B. AD, Southwestern Coll., 1961; BS, San Diego State U., 1963. Cert. fin. planner, ChFC, CLU. Asst. mgr. Pacific Mut. Life, Portland, Oreg., 1974-78; mgr. Pacific Mut. Life, Seattle, 1978-84; asst. gen. agt. Conn. Mut. Life, Seattle, 1984-86; owner Omega Fin. Group, Seattle, 1986—. Active Life Underwriters Polit. Action, Seattle, 1984—; past v.p. Seattle Gen. Agts. and Mgrs., 1983-84, sec.-treas., 1982-83. With USNR, 1958-59. Mem. Am. Soc. CLUs, Alpha Gamma Sigma. Republican. Home: 436 SW 185th Pl Normandy Park WA 98166 Office: Omega Fin Group PO Box 66522 Seattle WA 98166-0522

HASENOEHRL, DANIEL NORBERT FRANCIS, priest; b. Portland, July 12, 1929; s. Norbert Frank and Anna Teresa (Feucht) H. Student, U. Portland, 1947-49; BA, Mt. Angel Sem., St. Benedict, Oreg., 1951; MEd, U. Portland, 1958. Ordained priest Roman Cath. Ch., 1960. Counselor/registrar Mt. Angel Prep. Sch., Oreg., 1960-64; counselor Mt. Angel Sem., St. Benedict, Oreg., 1962-71; acad. dean/registrar Mt. Angel Sem., 1964-71, acting pres., 1969-70, instr., 1963-71; assoc. pastor Our Lady of Sorrows Parish, Portland, 1972-75; chaplain Marylhurst Coll., Lake Oswego, Oreg., 1975-81, Dammasch State Hosp., Wilsonville, Oreg., 1975—. With U.S. Army, 1952-54. Mem. Nat. Cath. Chaplains Assn., Assn. for Religious Values in Counseling, Am. Mental Health Counselors Assn., Am. Assn. for Higher Edn. Democrat. Roman Catholic. Home: PO Box 19113 Portland OR 97280-0113 Office: Dammasch State Hosp Pastoral Services Wilsonville OR 97070

HASH, JOE KEVIN, writer; b. Columbus, Ohio, Oct. 25, 1957. BA, Ohio State U., 1979, MA, 1981. Ptnr. The Concord Agy., Columbus, Ohio, 1981-83; sr. copywriter Shelly Berman Communicators, Columbus, Ohio, 1983-85; lectr. Ohio State U. Dept. English, Columbus, Ohio, 1983-85; advt. coord. CompuServe Inc., Columbus, Ohio, 1985-87; mktg. specialist U. Calif.-Davis Med. Ctr., Sacramento, 1990—; freelance writer, Sacramento (Calif.), L.A., San Francisco, Cleve., 1987—, Am. Greetings Corp., Cleve., 1992—. Head writer (TV spl.) Modern Medical Breakthroughs, 1988, (TV pilot) Manhunt International, 1992.

HASHIMOTO, LLOYD KEN, communications executive; b. Cheyenne, Wyo., Sept. 21, 1944; s. Harry H. and Bettie M. (Kadota) H. Student in chemistry, 1963-65, student in elec. engring., 1969-72, student in edn., 1979; BSin Vocat. Edn., U. Wyo., 1992. Prin. Teltron Electronics, Laramie, Wyo., 1972—; audio visual technician U. Wyo., Laramie, 1972—; mem. internat. panel Electonics Mag., 1974, 1976; instr. workshops and seminars High Tech to a Lay Person, 1978; instr. workshop radio direction finding, 1988—. Contbr. articles to profl. jours. Program chmn., unit and dist. commr. Snowy Range Dist. Boy Scouts Am., Laramie, 1985—, eagle scout, 1961, active, Wood Badge, N.C., 1987, award of merit, 1991, instr. Longs Peak Coun. With U.S. Army, 1965-69. Mem. IEEE, Assn. Ednl. Communications Tech. (assoc. audio visual technician S.E. Wyo. chp.), Soc. Internat. Devel. (Wyo. chpt.), Assn. for Field Svc. Mgrs. Internat., Am. Legion, Masons, Laramie Shrine Club. Home: 504 S 26th St Laramie WY 82070-9999 Office: Teltron Electronics PO Box 1049 Laramie WY 82070-1049

HASHIRO, BRIAN SATORU, county administrator; b. Wailuku, Hawaii, Aug. 1, 1953; s. Itsuo and Rose K. Hashiro. BSCE, U. Hawaii, 1976, MBA, 1984. Registered profl. engr., Hawaii. Civil engr. I Hwys. div. State of Hawaii, Kahului, 1977; civil engr. ARC Engrs., Lahaina, Hawaii, 1977-78, E. T. Ige Constrn. Co., Wailuku, Hawaii, 1978-79; civil engr. III waste mgmt. div. County of Maui, Wailuku, 1979-82, civil engr. IV waste mgmt. div., 1982-85, dep. dir. pub. works dept., 1985-89, chief staff engr. dept. pub. works, 1989-90, chief solid waste div., 1990-92, chief field ops. and maintenance hwys. div., 1992—; chmn. Solid Waste Adv. Com., Wailuku, 1990-92. Lodge advisor Order of Arrow, Boy Scouts Am., Wailuku, 1985—; mem. U. Hawaii Found., Honolulu, 1984—; mem. Wailuku Hongwajni Mission, Wailuku, 1953—; bd. dirs. Maui Econ. Opportunity, Kahului, 1985-86; 2d v.p. Hawaii Soc. Profl. Engrs., Honolulu, 1989-90. Recipient Silver Beaver award Boy Scouts Am., 1989, State Young Engr. of Yr. award Hawaii Soc. Profl. Engrs., 1985. Mem. Nat. Recycling Coalition, Nat. Solid Waste Mgmt. Assn., Solid Waste Assn. N.Am., Am. Pub. Works Assn., Water Environ. Fedn., Nat. Soc. Profl. Engrs. Buddhist. Office: County of Maui Hwys Div 1827 Kaohu St Wailuku HI 96793

HASKAYNE, RICHARD FRANCIS, petroleum company executive; b. Calgary, Alta., Can., Dec. 18, 1934; s. Robert Stanley and Bertha (Hesketh) H.; m. Lee Mary Murray, June 25, 1958. B.Comm., U. Alta., 1956; postgrad., U. Western Ont., 1968. Chartered acct., Alta. With Riddell, Stead & Co., chartered accts., Calgary, 1956-60; corp. acctg. supr. to v.p. fin. Hudson's Bay Oil & Gas Co., Ltd., Calgary, 1960-73; compt. Canadian Arctic Gas Study Ltd., 1973-75; sr. v.p. to pres. Hudson's Bay Oil & Gas Co. Ltd., Calgary, 1975-81; pres., chief exec. officer Home Oil Co., Ltd., Calgary, 1981-91, also bd. dirs.; chmn. bd. Nova Corp. of Alta., Calgary, 1992—; pres., CEO, bd. dirs. Interprovincial Pipe Line Co., 1987-91; chmn., CEO, bd. dirs. Interhome Energy Inc., 1989-91; bd. dirs. ManuLife Fin., Fording Coal Ltd., Can. Imperial Bank of Commerce, TransAlta. Utilities Corp., Alta. Energy Co. Ltd., Home Oil Co. Ltd., Crestar Energy Inc. Chmn. bd. govs. U. Calgary. Fellow Fin. Execs. Inst.; mem. Calgary Petroleum Club (past pres.), Calgary Golf and Country Club, Earl Grey Golf Club, Ranchmen's Club, U. Calgary Chancellor's Club, Libr. Club, Commerce Club, Alta. Inst. Chartered Accts., Kappa Sigma. Office: Nova Corp of Alta, 2030 Bankers Hall 855 2d St SW, Calgary, AB Canada T2P 4J8

HASKELL, ERIC TODD, humanities and French literature educator; b. Marysville, Calif., Oct. 2, 1950; s. Coburn Haskell and Joanne (Taverner) Olson; m. Danielle Floquet, July 7, 1973; children: Olivia Hanna, Jean-Christophe. French Lettres, U. Paris, 1971; BA cum laude, Pomona Coll., 1973; MA, U. Calif., Irvine, 1975, PhD, 1979. Teaching asst. French U. Calif., Irvine, 1974-77, teaching assoc. humanities, 1977-78; lectr. French Scripps Coll., Claremont, Calif., 1978, asst. prof., 1979-85, assoc. French and humanities, chairperson French dept., 1985-90, mem. faculty exec. com., 1992—; dir. Clark Humanities Mus., Scripps Coll., 1984—; lectr. numerous ednl. and cultural instns.; curator several mus. exhbns. including Personal Edens: The Gardens and Film Sets of Florence Yoch, Huntington Gallery, San Marino, Calif., 1992. Contbr. articles to various publs.; guest editor Word and Image: A Jour. of Verbal/Visual Inquiry, 1987. Bd. dirs. Claremont Heritage 1988-90, Banning Residence Mus., 1992—, Rancho Los Alamitos Found., 1992—; mem. adv. bd. Decorative Arts Study Ctr., 1987—. Mellon Found. rsch. and exhbn. grantee, 1981. Mem. MLA, Internat. Comparative Lit. Assn., Internat. Assn. Word and Image Studies, Interdisciplinary 19th Century Studies Assn. (treas. 1986-88), 19th Century French Studies Assn., Philol. Assn. Pacific Coast (presiding officer lit. and other arts 1983, 87) Soc. Internat. Poïétique, Friends of French Art, Assn. Amis Vieilles Maisons Françaises. Office: Scripps Coll 1030 N Columbia Ave Claremont CA 91711-3948

HASKETT, JAMES ALBERT, university official; b. Franklin, Ind., Mar. 2, 1942; s. John Wendell and Helen Elizabeth (Buscher) H.; m. Martha Brooks Vandivort, Apr. 4, 1970. BS, Ind. U., 1964, PhD, 1970. Systems programmer Ind. U., Bloomington, 1970-82, mgr. distributor processing systems, 1982-84, mgr. performance analysis and capacity planning, 1984-88; dir. computer svcs. Ctrl. Wash. U., Ellensburg, 1988-91, dir. higher edn. info. resources, 1991—; mem. adj. faculty Ind. U., 1980-81. Creator hist. exhibit Acad. Computing in Retrospect: From CSB to BACS, 1986; contbr. articles to profl. jours. Vol. programmer Monroe County Libr., Bloomington, 1977. Mem. Assn. Computing Machinery (presenter, track chmn. 1989-90), Geographic Info. Coun. (higher edn. rep. 1990—, vice chair/chair elect 1991-92, chair 1993—). Office: Dept Info Resources Ctrl Wash U Ellensburg WA 98926

HASKINS, MARIAN MCKEEN, nursing administrator; b. N.Y.C., Jan. 27, 1954; d. Sean and Margaret (Hegarty) McKeen; m. Thomas Creed Haskins, Sept. 27, 1981. BS in Nursing, Hunter Coll., N.Y.C.; MA in Marriage, Family and Child Counseling, Calif. Family Study Ctr., Burbank. Lic. marriage, family and child counselor. Critical care registry nurse Critical Care Svcs., Inc., L.A., 1978-79; staff devel. cons.-instr. Profl. Med. Educators, Northridge, Calif., 1979; clin. nurse III respiratory intensive care unit UCLA, 1979-81; counselor marriage, family and child svcs. Encino, Calif., 1981-89; critical care edn. coord. Daniel Freeman Meml. Hosp., Inglewood, Calif., 1981-89, profl. nurse, case mgr., 1990—. Recipient Outstanding Nurse award UCLA, 1980; Named one of Top Ten Nurses in State of Calif., 1993. Mem. Am. Assn. Critical Care Nurses (charter mem., program com. chair L.A. chpt), Case Mgmt. Soc. Am., Calif. Assn. Marriage and Family Therapists, Am. Assn. Marriage and Family Therapists, Am. Assn. Psychiat. Nurses. Home: 22566 Cardiff Dr Santa Clarita CA 91350-3028 Office: Daniel Freeman Meml Hosp Nursing Adminstrn 333 N Prairie Ave Inglewood CA 90301-4514

HASLUND, SHANNON LEE, accountant; b. Mercer Island, Wash., Sept. 5, 1966; d. William Baxter and Diana L. (Fanning) H. Bachelor degree, U. Ariz., 1989. Inventory control Holmes Tuttle Ford, Tucson, 1987-89; project acct. Capital Growth Properties, La Jolla, Calif., 1989-90; sr. project acct. Koll Mgmt. Svcs., Newport Beach, Calif., 1990-93; cons. Kenneth, Leventhal & Co., Newport Beach, 1993—; bd. dirs. 223 Co., Seattle, 1989—. Vol. Red Cross, Orange County, Calif., 1992, Young Profls. Against Cancer. Mem. Daughters of Pioneers, Jaycees. Office: Kenneth Leventhal & Co 660 Newport Ctr Dr Newport Beach CA 92625

HASPER, KURT T., JR., clinical engineer; b. Evergreen Park, Ill., Aug. 12, 1946; s. Kurt T. and Eleanor F. (Marshall) H.; m. Carol Anne Bolding, Aug. 12, 1966; children: Kurt III, Eric, Craig. AS in Biomed. Tech., Phoenix Coll., 1978; BS in Health Svcs. Adminstrn., U. Phoenix, 1983. Self employed electronics technician Phoenix, 1974-75; mem. faculty Phoenix Coll., 1978; biomed. engring. mgr. St. Joseph's Hosp. and Med. Ctr., Phoenix, 1975-92; v.p. ops. I.C. Med., Inc., Phoenix, 1992—; mem. biomed. adv. com. Phoenix Coll. 1975-79, Glendale (Ariz.) C.C., 1990-91; mem. tech. adv. com. end stage renal disease region IV, U.S. Govt. Albuquerque, 1982. Mem. editorial rev. bd. Jour. Clin. Engring., 1992—; contbr. articles to profl. jours. Chmn. Deer Valley planning com. City of Phoenix, 1987; mem. Phoenix Futures Forum, 1989; scoutmaster Boy Scouts Am., Phoenix, 1974-84. With USN, 1966-74. Mem. Internat. Soc. Optical Engrs., N.Y. Acad. Scis., Assn. Advancement Med. Instrumentation, Am. Coll. Clin. Engrs. Home: 4118 W Michigan Ave Glendale AZ 85308-1707 Office: IC Med Inc Ste 202 2340 W Shangri La Phoenix AZ 85029

HASS, DAVID WAYNE, business owner; b. Antioch, Calif., Sept. 23, 1960; s. Calvin Wayne and Virginia Lee (Mathers) Stone; m. Sandra Dee Deppe, Aug. 31, 1991; children: Timothy, Samantha, Tiffani. Grad. high sch., Antioch, Calif. Gen. mgr. Delta Canvas Inc., Antioch, Calif., 1980-85, West Coast Canvas, Lodi, Calif., 1985-86, Tops By Tony, Portland, Oreg., 1986-87; owner Creative Canvas Prodn., Rainer, Oreg., 1987-89, S and D Top Shop, Longview, Wash., 1989—. Patentee in field. With USN, 1978-80, Japan. Republican. Roman Catholic. Office: S and D Top Shop 1220 Ocean Beach Hwy #B Longview WA 98632

HASSELL, DENNIS EDWARD, data processing executive; b. Yakima, Wash., July 11, 1945; s. William Henry and Iris Barbara (Miller) H.; m. Sandra R. McCune, Jan. 29, 1966 (div. Apr. 1977); children: Christopher, Douglas; m. Ana Maria Vergara, Nov. 2, 1980 (div. Nov. 1985); m. Sharon Ann Boudreaux, Sept. 4, 1988. BSEE, Wash. State U., 1968. Profl. engr. Colo.; cert. data processing. Electronics engr. IBM, San Jose, Calif., 1967-68; tech. dir. Monitor Gen., Inc., Denver, 1972-74; cons., pvt. practice Denver, 1974-78; sr. test engr. Amdahl Corp., Sunnyvale, Calif., 1978-82; v.p. mfg. systems Trans-Micro Systems, San Jose, Calif., 1982-83; producer Werner Erhard & Assocs., San Francisco, 1983-85; cons. Hassell & Assocs., Palo Alto, Calif., 1985—. Capt. USAF, 1968-72. Mem. Interex HP Users Group. Office: Hassell & Assocs 1327 Alma St Palo Alto CA 94301-3502

HASSELL, H(UGH) ROBERT, manufacturing company executive; b. Portland, Oreg., Mar. 6, 1945; s. Albert Errol and Margaret Mary (Thon) H.; m. Judy Terjeson, June 13, 1970; children: Molly Anne, Tiah Marie, Wolf. BS in Econs., Portland State U., 1972. Computer ops. supr. Consol. Freightways, Portland, 1968-72; mgr. systems and programming divs. Multnomah County, Portland, 1972-75; gen. mgr. Mgmt. Info. Systems Freightliner Corp., Portland, 1975—. With U.S. Army, 1966-68. Mem. Oreg. Club of Portland (bd. dirs.), Phi Gamma Delta. Home: 11275 SW Viewmount Ct Tigard OR 97223-3731 Office: Freightliner Corp 4747 N Channel Ave Portland OR 97217

HASSELL, JOHN DAVID, public relations manager; b. Newport News, Va., Feb. 3, 1958; s. James Lafayette Jr. and Carolyn (Phalen) H. BA, Coll. of William and Mary, 1980. News reporter Gloucester (Va.) Mathews Gazette Jour., 1978-80; intern Caterpillar Inc., Washington, 1980; pub. affairs trainee Caterpillar Inc., Peoria, Ill., 1981-83; govtl. affairs rep. Caterpillar Inc., San Leandro, Calif., 1983-84, Sacramento, 1984-85; pub. affairs mgr. FMC Corp., Santa Clara, Calif., 1985-89, project mgr., 1989-91; mem., working coun. Santa Clara County Mfg. Group, 1985—. Trustee Mission City Community Fund, Santa Clara, 1988—, Triton Mus. of Art, Santa Clara, 1987—; chmn. Santa Clara C. of C. and Conv. Visitors Bur., 1990-91. Mem. Peninsula chpt. Pub. Rels. Soc. Am., Calif. Taxpayers Assn. (bd. dirs. 1985—), Rotary. Democrat. Roman Catholic. Home: 976C Kiely Blvd Santa Clara CA 95051-5097 Office: FMC Corp 2830 De La Cruz Blvd Santa Clara CA 95050-2619

HASSOUNA, FRED, architect, educator; b. Cairo, Mar. 26, 1918; s. Amin Sami and Dawlat (Mansour) H.; came to U.S., 1948, naturalized, 1953; diploma in architecture with honors Higher Sch. Fine Arts, Cairo, 1940; diploma in Egyptology with 1st class honors U. Cairo, 1944; diploma in civic design U. Liverpool (Eng.), 1946; M.Arch., M.S. in Pub. Adminstrn., U. So. Calif., 1950; m. Verna Arlene Dotter, Mar. 9, 1950. Architect, curator Cairo Mus., Egypt, 1940-44; lectr. archaeology and architecture Alexandria U., Egypt, 1944-45, 47-48; dir. planning Huyton-with-Roby Urban Dist. Council, Huyton, Eng., 1946-47; lectr. city planning U. So. Calif., 1950-55; architect Kistner, Wright and Wright, architects and engrs., Los Angeles, 1952-53; project architect Welton Becket and Assocs., architects and engrs., Los Angeles, 1954-56, Albert C. Martin and Assocs., architects and engrs., 1956-58; faculty architecture East Los Angeles Coll., 1958-75, prof. architecture, head dept. architecture; prof., head dept. architecture Saddleback Coll., 1975-83; pvt. planning cons., architect, Los Angeles, 1950-75, Laguna Niguel, 1975—. Mem. indsl. tech. adv. bd. Calif. State U. at Long Beach, 1963-83; mem. adv. bd. on environ. and interior design U. Calif., Irvine, 1976-83; pres. Calif. Council Archtl. Edn., 1977; mem. liaison com. architecture, landscape architecture, urban and regional planning in Calif. higher edn., 1976-83. Registered architect, Calif.; recipient hon. cultural doctorate World U. Roundtable, Tucson, 1983. Fellow Internat. Inst. Arts and Letters (life); mem. emeritus AIA, Am. Planning Assn. Home and Office: 31242 Flying Cloud Dr Laguna Niguel CA 92677

HASSRICK, PETER HEYL, museum director; b. Phila., Apr. 27, 1941; s. Royal Brown and E. Barbara (Morgan) H.; m. Elizabeth Drake, June 14, 1963; children: Philip Heyl, Charles Royal. Student, Harvard U., 1962; BA, U. Colo., 1963; MA, U. Denver, 1969. Tchr. Whiteman Sch., Steamboat Springs, Colo., 1963-67; also bd. dirs. Whiteman Sch., Steamboat Springs; curator of collections Amon Carter Mus., Ft. Worth, 1969-75; dir. Buffalo Bill Hist. Ctr., Cody, Wyo., 1976—. Author: Frederic Remington, 1973, The Way West, 1977, (with others) The Rocky Mountains, 1983, Treasures of the Old West, 1984, (with others) Frederic Remington, The Masterworks, 1988, (with others) Frontier America, 1988, Charles M. Russell, 1989. Office: Buffalo Bill Hist Ctr PO Box 1000 Cody WY 82414-1000

HASTINGS, EDWARD WALTON, theater director; b. New Haven, Apr. 14, 1931; s. Edward Walton and Madeline (Cassidy) H. B.A., Yale, 1952; postgrad., Royal Acad. Dramatic Art, London, 1953, Columbia U., 1955-56. bd. dirs. Asian/Am. Theater Co., 1986, Arts Internat., 1987, Eugene O'Neill Found., 1993; guest instr. Shanghai Drama Inst., 1984. Dir. Australian premiere Hot L Baltimore, 1975, Shakespeare's People, nat. tour, 1977; Yugoslavian premiere Buried Child, 1980; Macbeth, Guthrie Theatre, Mpls., 1981, 84 Charing Cross Road, nat. tour, 1983, others; exec. dir., Am. Conservatory Theatre, San Francisco, 1965-80, free-lance dir., 1980-86; artistic dir. Am. Conservatory Theatre, San Francisco, 1986-92. Served with U.S. Army, 1953-55. Mem. Coll. of Fellows of the Am. Theatre. Club: Elizabethan (New Haven). Office: Am Conservatory Theatre 450 Geary St San Francisco CA 94102-1243

HASTINGS, MERRILL GEORGE, JR., publisher, marketing consultant; b. Dedham, Mass., May 12, 1922; s. Merrill G. and Emita E. (Zeil) H.; m. Priscilla G. Brayton, July 31, 1948; children: William, Deborah. Educ., Bowdoin Coll., 1946. Chmn. bd., pres. Skiing Pub. Co., Denver, 1950-64, Colorado Mag., Inc., Denver, 1964-77, Mountain Bus. Pubs., Denver, 1972-77, Hastings, Johnsus & White, Vail, Colo., 1977-79, Energy Pub. Co., Denver, 1980-82, Pulse Pubs., Denver, 1985-87, Living Will Ctr., Denver, 1990—. Founder Nat. Cancer Survivors Day, 1988. Served with Brit. Army, 1944-45. Recipient Austrian IXth Winter Olympic medal, Innsbruck, 1964. Mem. Colo. Press Assn. Home: Sunnyvail Ranch McCoy CO 80463 Office: 1064 Poppycreek Rd McCoy CO 80463

HASTRICH, JEROME JOSEPH, bishop; b. Milw., Nov. 13, 1914; s. George Philip and Clara (Dettlaff) H. Student, Marquette U., 1933-35; BA, St. Francis Sem., Milw., 1940, MA, 1941; student, Cath. U. Am., 1941. Ordained priest Roman Cath. Ch., 1941; assigned to Milw. Chancery, 1941; curate St. Ann's Ch., Milw., St. Bernard's Ch., Madison, Wis.; asst. chaplain St. Paul U. Chapel, then U. Wis.; sec. to bishop of Diocese U. Wis., Madison, Wis., 1946-52; chancellor Diocese Madison, Wis., 1952-53; apptd. vicar gen. Diocese Madison, 1953, domestic prelate, 1954, protonotary apos., 1960; aux. bishop, 1963-67, titular bishop of Gurza and aux. of Madison, 1963; pastor St. Raphael Cathedral, Madison, 1967-69; bishop Gallup, N.Mex., 1969-90, ret.; diocesan dir. Confraternity Christian Doctrine, 1946—, St. Martin Guild, 1946-69; aux. chaplain U.S. Air Force, 1947-67; pres. Latin Am. Mission Program; sec. Am. Bd. Cath. Missions; vice chmn. Bishop's Com. for Spanish Speaking; mem. subcom. on allocations U.S. Bishops Com. for Latin Am.; founder, episcopal moderator Queen of Americas Guild, 1979—; pres. Nat. Blue Army of Our Lady of Fatima, 1980—. Mem. Gov. Wis. Commn. Migratory Labor, 1964—. Club: K.C. (hon. life mem.). Home: PO Box 1777 Gallup NM 87305-1777

HATAI, THOMAS HENRY, international marketing professional; b. Tokyo, Dec. 27, 1937; came to U.S., 1951; s. Isamu Herbert and Kiyoko (Kume) H.; m. Geraldine Hatai, Jan. 19, 1970 (div. 1978); children: Dickson Y., Keio Gijuku Yochisha. BS, Woodbury Coll., 1965. Supr. internat. dept. Union Bank, L.A., 1964-66; with mgmt. United Airlines, L.A., 1966-69; v.p. far east Travel Systems Internat., Oakbrook, Ill., 1969-75; pres. Hatai Internat., L.A., 1975-78; pres., chief exec. officer Pace Mktg., Inc., La Habra, Calif., 1983-91; founder, vice chmn. bd. dirs., CEO Yamamo Cosmetics Inc.; pres., CEO Yamamo Products Inc. (dba AVEC); chmn. Pace Products, Inc., La Habra, 1983—; bd. dris. Taiyo Estate Devel., Inc., Del., Taiyo Leasing U.S.A., Inc., La Habra, Taiyo Holding U.S.A. Inc., Del.; pres. D.B.H. Global, Ltd., La Habra, 1983—. Illustrators: The Marty Story, 1954, The St. Meinrad Story, 1954. Mem. United Internat. Club (bd. dirs. 1969 Japan), U.S. C. of C. Republican. Home: 8544 Buena Tierra Pl Buena Park CA 90621-1002 Office: Pace Mktg Inc 1251C S Beach Blvd La Habra CA 90631-6301

HATCH, GEORGE CLINTON, television executive; b. Erie, Pa., Dec. 16, 1919; s. Charles Milton and Blanche (Beecher) H.; m. Wilda Gene Glasmann, Dec. 24, 1940; children: Michael Gene Zbar Arnow, Diane Glasmann Orr, Jeffrey Beecher, Randall Clinton, Deepika Hatch Avanti. AB, Occidental Coll., 1940; MA in Econs., Claremont Coll., 1941; HHD (hon.), So. Utah State U., 1988. Pres. Communications Investment Corp., Salt Lake City, 1945—; chmn. Sta. KUTV, Inc., Salt Lake City, 1956—; dir. Republic Pictures Corp., Los Angeles, 1971—; pres. Sta. KVEL, Inc., 1978—; treas. Standard Corp., Ogden, 1984—; past mem. Salt Lake adv. bd. First Security Bank Utah; past chmn. Rocky Mountain Pub. Broadcasting Corp.; past chmn. bd. govs. Am. Info. Radio Network; past bd. govs. NBC-TV Affiliates. Past pres. Salt Lake Com. on Fgn. Relations; past mem. Utah Symphony Bd., Salt Lake City; past chmn. Utah State Bd. Regents, 1964-85. Recipient Svc. to Journalism award U. Utah, 1966, silver medal Salt Lake Advt. Club, 1969, Disting. Svc. award Utah Tech. U., 1984. Mem. Nat. Assn. Broadcasters (past pres., radio bd. dirs., Ambassador to Inter-Am. Meetings in Latin Am. 1962), Utah Broadcasters Assn. (past pres.; Mgmt. award 1964, Hall of Fame award 1981), Phi Beta Kappa, Phi Rho Pi (life). Democrat. Club: Salt Lake City Advt. (Silver medal award 1969). Lodge: Rotary. Office: Sta KUTV Inc 2185 S 3600 W Salt Lake City UT 84119-1151

HATCH, JOHN DAVIS, design consultant, art historian; b. Oakland, Calif., June 14, 1907; s. John Davis and Gethel (Gregg) H.; m. Olivia Phelps Stokes, Oct. 14, 1939; children: John Davis VI, Daniel Lindley, James Stokes, Sarah Stokes Saeger. Student, U. Calif., 1926-28; student Far Eastern Studies, Harvard U., 1931; student Near East Studies, Princeton U., summer 1938; student Am. Studies, Yale U., 1940. Landscape architect Santa Barbara, Calif., 1925, Seattle, 1928; exec. sec. Seattle Art Inst., 1928-29, dir., 1929-31; v.p. Western Assn. Art Museums, 1929-30; surveyed facilities and materials for Far Eastern studies in U.S. and Can., 1931-32, Am. studies in U.S. colls. and univs. for Am. Council Learned Socs., 1938-39; dir. U.S. art projects in New Eng., 1933-34; mem. McDowell Colony, 1938; asst. dir. Isabella Stewart Gardner Mus., Boston, 1932-35, Carnegie Corp., N.Y., 1935-37; founder, adviser So. Negro Colls. Coop. Exhibits Group, 1936-41; founder Am. Artist Depository, 19378, Am. Drawing Ann., 1940, Commn. on Art Studies, 1938; Dir. Albany Inst. History and Art, 1940-48; chmn. Albany-Nijmegen Holland Com., 1948; vis. prof. U. Oreg., 1948-49, U. Calif., summer 1949, U. Mass., summer 1971; dir. Norfolk Mus. Arts and Scis., 1950-59; pres. Phelps Stokes Corp., 1959-62; coordinating adviser, acting chmn. fine arts div. Spelman Coll., Ga., 1964-70; v.p. Nevada Co.; Chmn., founder Old Curtisville, 1965, pres. emeritus, 1981—; former trustee Lenox Sch., Hoosac Sch.; hon. keeper Cape Henry Light House, Assn. for Preservation Va. Antiquities, 1948—. Author: American sect. Great Drawings of All Times, 1962, Historic Survey of Painting in Canada, 1946, Historic Church Silver in the Southern Diocese of Virginia, 1952; Editor: Parnassus, 1937-39, Albany County Hist. Assn. Record, 1941-48, Early Am. Industries Chronicle, 1942-49; 100 Am. drawings, Dublin, London, Paris, 1976-77; had pioneer exhibit The Negro Artist Comes of Age, 1943, Painting in Canada, 1944, Thomas Cole, 1942, Outdoor Sculptors of Berkshires, 1978. Donated (with others) Anson Phelps Stokes Ref. Libr. to U. Liberia, 1980. Fellow Morgan Library, Met. Mus. N.Y., Nat. Gallery, Washington. Mem. Master Drawing Assn. (trustee, founder 1962), Am. Drawing Soc. (adv. bd.), Am. Assn. Mus. (founder N. Eastern conf. 1941, S.E. conf. 1951); founding mem. Internat. Mus. Assn. Episcopalian. Clubs: Rotary, Grolier (N.Y.C.), Cosmos (Washington), Quail Run (Santa Fe), Harvard Musical (Boston). Home: 640 Camino Lejo Santa Fe NM 87501-4836

HATCH, KENNETH L., television executive; b. Vernal, Utah, Aug. 4, 1935; s. Lois and Alva Le Roy Hatch; m. Marsha Kay Rich, Dec. 7, 1974; children: Sean, Ryan, James, Michael, Elizabeth-Ann. BS in Banking and Fin., U. Utah, 1957; postgrad. Stanford U., Harvard Grad. Sch. Bus. Gen. sales mgr. KSL, Salt Lake City, 1963-64; gen. sales mgr. KIRO-TV, Seattle, 1964-66, asst. gen. mgr., 1965-67, gen. mgr., 1967-71, sr. v.p., 1971-80, pres., chief exec. officer, 1980-87; chmn. bd., mem. exec. com., KIRO, Inc.; sr. v.p. Bonneville Internat. Corp.; bd. dirs. Bear Creek, Inc., Wash., Olympic Bank. Bd. dirs. United Way King County, 1984-86, chmn. mktg. com., 1987, co-chmn. communications com., 1988; assoc. chmn. Boy Scouts Annual Fundraising Event, 1985; bd. dirs. Seattle Opportunities Industrialization Ctr., Seattle Conv. & Bus. Bur.; mem. adv. bd. Providence Hosp. Found.; amb. Children's Found. Assocs., 1986. Mem. Nat. Assn. Broadcasters Television & Radio Polit. Action Com., Torbet Radio Reps., Inc. (bd. dirs. N.Y.C. chpt. 1982-84), Sales & Mktg. Execs. Internat. (pres. 1969), Seattle C. of C. (bd. trustees 1986-88). Recipient Spl. Svc. award United Way, 1986, Bus. Man of Yr. award BYU, 1986, Keynote Speaker award Eastside Ins. Women's Pub. Rels. Banquet, 1986. Mem. Ch. of Christ. Clubs: Seattle Advt. Club (bd. dirs. 1967), Rainier of Seattle, Bellevue Athletic, Wash. Athletic, Overlake Golf and Country.

HATCH, ORRIN GRANT, senator; b. Homestead Park, Pa., Mar. 22, 1934; s. Jesse and Helen (Kamm) H.; m. Elaine Hansen, Aug. 28, 1957; children: Brent, Marcia, Scott, Kimberly, Alysa, Jess. B.S., Brigham Young U., 1959; J.D., U. Pitts., 1962; LLD (hon.), U. Md., 1981; MS (hon.), Def. Intelligence Coll., 1982; LLD (hon.), Pepperdine U., 1990, So. Utah State U., 1990. Bar: Pa. 1962, Utah 1962. Ptnr. firm Thomson, Rhodes & Grigsby, Pitts., 1962-69, Hatch & Plumb, Salt Lake City, 1976; mem. U.S. Senate from Utah, 1977—, past chmn. labor and human resources com., mem. Senate Labor and Human Resources Com., Senate Fin. Com., ranking minority mem. Senate Judiciary Com. Author ERA Myths and Realities, 1983; contbr. articles to newspapers and profl. jours. Recipient Outstanding Legislator award Nat. Assn. Rehab. Facilities, Legislator of Yr. award Am. Assn. Univ. Affiliated Programs, Legis. Leadership award Health Profl. Assn., many others. Mem. Am., Nat., Utah, Pa. bar assns., Am. Judicature Soc. Republican. Mormon. *

HATCH, PAMELA POST, software research and development specialist; b. Oak Park, Ill., Mar. 13, 1942; d. Edgar A. and Elisabeth (Esten) Post; m. Robert E. Hatch, May 23, 1964; children: Gretchen Denise, Jessica Lea. BSBA, City Univ., Bellevue, Wash., 1983; M of Software Engring., Seattle U., 1988. Cert. in data processing. Electronic technician Granger Assn., Palo Alto, Calif., 1960-62; sr. programmer analyst GTE Sylvania, Mt. View, Calif., 1963-71; sr. programmer Info. Sci., Inc., Menlo Park, Calif., 1974-77; programmer-analyst Scott Paper Co., Everett, Wash., 1977-79, mgmt. analyst, 1979-82, systems mgr., 1983-85; dir. R&D The System Works, Inc., Redmond, Wash., 1985-92; mgr. corp. info. & control systems Oreg. Steel Mills, Portland, 1992—; Spl. Interest Group chairperson PRIME Computer User Group, Seattle, 1983-85. Pres. of corp. Cottage Lake Presbyn. Ch., Woodinville, Wash., 1990-91, fin. chairperson, elder, 1975—; policy/procedures chairperson Com. on Ministry, Presbytery, Everett, 1987-91; chair personnel com. North Puget Sound Presbytery, Everett, 1979-81; bd. mem., chair computer com. Synod of Ala. N.W., Seattle, 1988-90. Mem. IEEE, Assn. for Computing Machinery, Wash. Software Assn. Home: 637B SE Linn St Portland OR 97202 Office: Oreg Steel Mills 14400 N Rivergate Portland OR 97208

HATCH, ROBERT FREDERICK, oil industry executive; b. Chgo., Aug. 27, 1934; s. Lester Warren and Mabel Dorothy Christina (Fulton) H.; m. Sandra Karen Thunander, Dec. 23, 1964; children: Hilary Joy, Holly Christina, Heather Daisy. BA, Valparaiso U., 1958; JD, Northwestern U., Chgo., 1960. Atty. Tenney Sherman Bentley & Guthrie, Chgo., 1960-66; stockbroker White Weld & Co., Inc., Chgo., L.A., 1966-70; real estate broker, developer George Elkins Co., Beverly Hills, Calif., 1970-72; v.p. George Elkins Co., Beverly Hills, 1978-79; v.p. devel. Donald Bren Co., Sherman Oaks, Calif., 1973; fin. cons. Robert F. Hatch Co., L.A., 1974-78; pres. Filtration Systems Inc., Hawthorne, Calif., 1979-80; ptnr. Cambrian Energy Systems, Santa Monica, Calif., 1980—. State Senator 19th Dist. Ill., 1962-66; ward committeeman Cook County (Ill.) Rep. Cen. Com., 1964-66; del. Rep. Nat. Conv. 1976; mem. Pres. Reagan Commn. on Housing, Washington, 1982, L.A. County Integrated Waste Mgmt. Com. With U.S. Army, 1953-55. Mem. Solid Waste Assn. N.Am. (landfill gas com.), Riviera Tennis Club. Presbyterian. Home: 125 N Layton Dr Los Angeles CA 90049-2019 Office: Cambrian Energy Systems 3420 Ocean Park Blvd Ste 2020 Santa Monica CA 90405-3304

HATCH, RONALD RAY, engineer; b. Freedom, Okla., Dec. 28, 1938; s. Richard Verni and Elma Lottie (Carberry) H.; m. Nancy Elene Bates, Dec. 30, 1960; children: Richard, Rebecca, Sondra, Wendy, Randall, Ronald, Jeffrey, Nathan, Abigail, Peter, Robert, Marcy, Melanie. BS in Physics and Math., Seattle Pacific Coll., 1962. Physicist Johns Hopkins Applied Physics Lab., Silver Spring, Md., 1963-65; engr. Boeing Co., Seattle, 1965-70, Magnavox, Torrance, Calif., 1970—. Author: Escape from Einstein, 1992; Patentee method and apparatus for automatic calibration of magnetic compasses, 1986, method for precision dynamic differential positioning, 1989, method and apparatus for precision attitude determination,1990; contbr. numerous articles to profl. jours. Mem. Inst. Navigation (marine rep. 1991-93, we. region v.p. 1992-93). Republican. Baptist. Home: 1142 Lakme Ave Wilmington CA 90744 Office: Magnavox 2829 Maricopa St Torrance CA 90503

HATCH, STEVEN GRAHAM, publishing company executive; b. Idaho Falls, Idaho, Mar. 27, 1951; s. Charles Steven and Margery Jane (Doxey) H.; BA, Brigham Young U., 1976; postgrad. mgmt. devel. program U. Utah, 1981; m. Rhonda Kay Frasier, Feb. 13, 1982; children: Steven Graham, Kristen Leone, Cameron Michael. Founder, pres. Graham Maughan Enterprises, Provo, Utah, 1975—, Internat. Mktg. Co., 1980—; dir. Goldbrickers Internat., Inc. Sec., treas. Zions Estates, Inc., Salt Lake City, Kansas City, Mo. Eagle Scout Boy Scouts Am., 1970; trustee Villages of Quail Valley, 1984-88. Recipient Duty to God award, 1970. Mem. Provo Jaycees, Internat. Entrepreneurs Assn., Mormon Booksellers Assn., Samuel Hall Soc. (exec. v.p. 1979), U.S. C. of C., Provo C. of C. (chmn. legis. action com. 1981-82, mem. job svc. employer com.). Republican. Mormon (missionary France Mission, Paris 1970-72, pub. rels. dir. 1972). Club: Rotary (Provo bd. dirs. 1992-93). Office: Graham Maughan Pub Co 50 E 500 S Provo UT 84606-4809

HATCHER, DAVID ALTON, JR., social worker; b. Houston, Aug. 20, 1946; s. David Alton and Ruth Anette (Popoff) H.; m. Alminda Presto, Aug. 19, 1969 (div. 1976); children: Arnel, Helen, David, James; m. Paz B. Hatcher, Dec. 14, 1979. BA in Behavioral Sci., Nat. U., San Diego, 1983; MA in Psychology, Nat. U., 1985. Cert. drug and alcohol counselor, Calif. Commd. USN, 1963-85, advanced through grades, ret. 1985; counselor Betty Ford Ctr., Rancho Mirage, Calif., 1985-89; social worker Riverside County, Indio, Calif., 1989—. Recipient Leadership award, Nat. U., 1983, 84. Mem. Calif. Assn. Drug and Alcohol Counselors (reg. v.p. 1981-85, reg. dir. 1985-87, sec. 1989—), K.C. (fin. sec. 1988—, faithful navigator 1990—). Republican. Roman Catholic. Home: 66624 Mission Lakes Blvd Desert Hot Springs CA 92240-1904 Office: 44-700 Palm Suite A Indio CA 92201

HATCHER, HERBERT JOHN, biochemist, microbiologist; b. Mpls., Dec. 18, 1926; s. Herbert Edmond and Florence Elizabeth (Larson) H.; m. Beverly J. Johnson, Mar. 28, 1953 (dec. July 1985); children: Dennis Michael, Steven Craig, Roger Dean, Mark Alan, Susan Diane, Laura Jean; m. Louise Fritsche Nelson, May 24, 1986; children: Carlos Howard Nelson, Kent Robert Nelson, Carolyn Louise Tyler. BA, U. Minn., 1953, MS, 1964, PhD, 1965. Bacteriologist VA Hosp., Wilmington, Del., 1956-57; microbiologist Smith, Kline, French, Phila., 1957-60, Clinton (Iowa) Corn Processing, 1966-67; microbiologist, biochemist Econs. Lab. Inc., St. Paul, 1967-84; biochemist EG&G Idaho Inc., Idaho Falls, 1984-90; co-owner B/CG Cons. Svcs., Idaho Falls, 1990—; affiliate prof. U. Idaho; adj. prof. Mont. State U., Bozeman; cons. EG&G Idaho, Inc., Idaho Falls, Henkel Corp. N.J., 1986. Chmn. bd. edn. Cross of Christ Luth. Ch., Coon Rapids, Minn., 1974-76; pres. chpt. Aid Assn. Luths., Idaho Falls, 1986; pres.-elect St. Johns Luth. Ch., 1988, pres., 1989. With USNR, 1945-46. Mem. Am. Soc. Microbiologists, N.Y. Acad. Scis., Idaho Acad. Scis., Am. Chem. Soc. (fuel div., microbial tech. and biochem. div.).

HATCHER, JOHN CHRISTOPHER, psychologist; b. Atlanta, Sept. 18, 1946; s. John William and Kay (Carney) H.; BA, U. Ga., 1968, MS, 1970, PhD, 1972. Psychologist, Clayton Mental Health Ctr., Atlanta, 1971-72; dir. intern tng. psychology svc. Beaumont Med. Center, El Paso, Tex., 1972-74; dir. family therapy program Langley Porter Inst., U. Calif., San Francisco, 1974-88, dir. ctr. for study of trauma, San Francisco, 1989—; adj. prof. dept. psychology U. Tex., 1972-74, dept. ednl. psychology and guidance, 1972-74; asst. clin. prof. psychology U. Calif., San Francisco, 1974-80, assoc. clin. prof., 1980-86, clin. prof., 1986—; cons. city and state govts. in U.S., Europe, Mexico, Asia, Far East; internat. cons. in hostage negotiation, kidnapping and terrorism chmn., Mayors Commn. on Family Violence, San Francisco, 1974-77; advisor arson task force San Francisco Fire Dept., 1977-81; advisor U.S. State Dept., 1985-90; advisor U.S. Congress Task Force on Tech. and Terrorism, 1990-91; adv. bd. Nat. Firehawk Found., 1980-86; advisor CBS-TV, 1975-80; spl. asst. to Mayor of San Francisco in charge of People's Temple Jonestown Case, 1978-80; mem. Calif. State Legis. Task Force on Missing Children, 1987-89; adv. bd. Nat. Minority Vietnam Vet. PTSD Study, 1991; prin. investigator U.S. Dept. Justice Families of Missing Children Project, Reunification of Missing Children Project, Obstacles to Recovery in Parental Abduction Project; assoc. investigator NIMH Adult and Adolescent Response to Distaster Project, U.S. Dept. Justice Models Treatment for Families of Missing Children Project. Fellow Am. Psychol. Assn. (chmn. com. hostage families); mem. Calif. Psychol. Assn. (chmn. task force on terrorism, disting. humanitarian award, 1991), Soc. Police and Criminal Psychology, Assn. Advancement Psychology, Am. Family Therapy Assn., Internat. Council Psychologists, Phi Kappa Phi. Author: (with Himelstein) Handbook of Gestalt Therapy, 1976; (with Brooks) Innovations in Counseling Psychology, 1977, (with Gaynor) Psychology of Child Firesetting, 1987; assoc. editor Am. Jour. Family Therapy; sr. editor Family Therapy Jour., mem. editorial bd. Family Psychology Jour., Jour. Traumatic Stress. Office: U Calif Dept Psychiatry 401 Parnassus Ave San Francisco CA 94143-0001

HATFIELD, CHARLES DONALD, newspaper executive; b. Huntington, W.Va., June 15, 1935; s. Howard Donald and LaUna (Wilson) H.; m. Sandra Gail Soto, June 11, 1955; children: John Christopher, Lisa, Joel Thomas. BA, Marshall Coll., 1977. Mem. sports staff Huntington Advertiser, 1953-60, asst. news editor, 1960-67, mng. editor, 1972-79; news editor Herald-Advertiser, Huntington, 1967-69, mng. editor, 1969-72; exec. editor Herald-Dispatch, Huntington, 1979-82, pub., editor, 1982-85; regional v.p. Gannett Co., Inc. E., Huntington, 1985-86; pub., editor and regional v.p. Tucson Citizen and Gannett West, 1986—. Author: Don Hatfield Cleans Out His Attic, 1986. Bd. dirs. United Way, Tucson, 1987—, Pima County Econ. Devel., Tucson, 1988—, Tucson Mus. Art, 1989—. Mem. AP Mng. Editors Assn. (treas 1986-88), Am. Soc. Newspaper Editors, Am. Newspapers Pubs., Ariz. Newspaper Assn., La Paloma Club, Tucson Country Club. Office: Tucson Citizen PO Box 26767 Tucson AZ 85726

HATFIELD, JOEL THANE, music educator, minister; b. Kansas City, Mo., Apr. 15, 1964; s. Jimmie LeRoy and Martha Marie (Lunn) H.; m. Dianna Virginia Phillips, Apr. 21, 1990. BS, William Jewell Coll., 1988; M in Ch. Mus. cum laude, Midwestern Bapt. Theol. Sem., 1992. Lic. gospel ministry, 1988. Bus. mgr. Liberty (Mo.) Symphony Orch., 1984-85; minister of mus. & youth Providence Bapt. Ch., Kansas City, Mo., 1986-89; minister of music First Bapt. Ch., Oak Grove, Mo., 1989-90; mus. asst. First Bapt.

Ch., N. Kansas City, Mo., 1990-91; prof. voice & ch. music Prairie Bible Coll., Three Hills, Alta., Can., 1991-93; exec. bd. Blue River-Kans. City Bapt. Assn., 1989-90; mem. subcom. governance, adminstrn. Am Assn. Bible Colls., coll. acad. com. Prairie Bible Coll., 1992-93; messenger Clay-Platte Bapt. Assn., Kans. City, 1985-89, music minister's coun., 1988-89; treas. Northwest Mo. Regional Symphony Orch. Conf., 1984-85; chmn. religious affairs com. Midwestern Bapt. Theol. Sem., 1989-90, com. chapel/spiritual devel., 1989-90, com. missions and special lectrs., 1990-91; worship leader Prairie Tabernacle Congregation, 1991-92, mem. worship com. 1992; seminar leader worship, ch. music; vocal soloist for recitals, concerts. Asst. scoutmaster, other offices Boy Scouts of Am. Troop 320, Liberty, Mo., 1981-85. Recipient resolution recognizing svc. City Coun. Liberty, Mo. 1982. Mem. The Hymn Soc. of the U.S. and Can., Alberta Choral Fedn., So. Bapt. Ch. Music Conf., Nat. Eagle Scout Assn., Phi Mu Alpha Sinfonia (pres. Kappa Mu chpt. 1984-85, treas. Kappa Mu chpt. 1983-84). Baptist.

HATFIELD, MARK O., senator; b. Dallas, Oreg., July 12, 1922; s. Charles Dolen and Dovie (Odom) H.; m. Antoinette Kuzmanich, July 8, 1958; children: Mark, Elizabeth, Theresa, Charles. A.B., Willamette U., 1943; A.M., Stanford U., 1948. Instr. Willamette U., 1949, dean students, asso. prof. polit. sci., 1950-56; mem. Oreg. Ho. of Reps., 1951-55, Oreg. Senate, 1955-57; sec. State of Oreg., 1957-59, gov., 1959-67; U.S. senator from Oreg., 1967—, ranking minority mem. appropriations com.; mem. energy and natural resources com., rules and adminstrn. com., joint printing com., joint libr. com.; mem. select com. Indian Affairs. Author: Not Quite So Simple, 1967, Conflict and Conscience, 1971, Between A Rock and A Hard Place, 1976; co-author: Amnesty: The Unsettled Question of Vietnam, 1976, Freeze! How You Can Help Prevent Nuclear War, 1982, The Causes of World Hunger, 1982; co-author: What About the Russians, 1984. Served to lt. j.g. USN, 1943-45, PTO. Recipient numerous hon. degrees. Republican. Baptist. Office: US Senate 711 Hart Senate Bldg Washington DC 20510

HATFIELD, PAUL GERHART, federal judge, lawyer; b. Great Falls, Mont., Apr. 29, 1928; s. Trueman LeRoy and Grace Lenore (Gerhart) H.; m. Dorothy Ann Allen, Feb. 1, 1958; children—Kathleen Helen, Susan Ann, Paul Allen. Student, Coll. of Great Falls, 1947-50; LL.B., U. Mont., 1955. Bar: Mont. bar 1955. Asso. firm Hoffman & Cure, Gt. Falls, Mont., 1955-56, Jardine, Stephenson, Blewett & Weaver, Gt. Falls, 1956-58, Hatfield & Hatfield, Gt. Falls, 1959-60; chief dep. county atty. Cascade County, Mont., 1959-60; dist. ct. judge 8th Jud. Dist., Mont., 1961-76; chief justice Supreme Ct. Mont., Helena, 1977-78; U.S. Senator from Mont., 1978-79; U.S. dist. judge for Dist. of Mont., Gt. Falls, 1979—; Vice chmn. Pres.'s Council Coll. of Great Falls. Author standards for criminal justice, Mont. cts. Served with U.S. Army, 1951-53. Korea. Mem. Am., Mont. bar assns., Am. Judicature Soc. Roman Catholic. Office: US Dist Ct PO Box 1529 Great Falls MT 59403-1529

HATHAWAY, LOLINE, zoo and botanic park curator; b. Whitter, Calif., June 27, 1937; d. Richard Franklin and F. Nadine (Applegate) H.; 1 child, Patrick Paul Kundtz. BA, Reed Coll., Portland, Oreg., 1959; PhD, Washington U., St. Louis, 1969. Instr. St. Louis U., 1966-68; curator of edn. Chgo. Zool. Soc., Brookfield, Ill., 1968-71; cons. on terrestrial biology Ryckman, Edgerly, Tomlinson & Assocs., St. Louis, 1972-75; marina mgr. Lake Piru (Calif.) Recreation Area, 1976-77; curator, dir. Navajo Nation Zool. and Botanical Park, Window Rock, Ariz., 1983—. Vice chmn., chmn. City of Santa Fe Springs (Calif.) Traffic Commn., 1979-83; mem. Navajo Estates Vol. Fire Dept., Yah-ta-hey, N.Mex., 1984-85; bd. dirs. Hathaway Ranch Mus., Santa Fe Springs, 1986—; leader 4-H Club, 1989—. Mem. AAAS (vice chmn. Southwest-Rocky Mountain div. sci. edn. sect. 1983-84, chmn. 1984-85), Am. Assn. Zool. Parks and Aquariums, Am. Assn. Bot. Gardens and Arboretums, Assn. Living Hist. Farms and Agr. Mus., Am. Inst. Biol. Scis., Sierra Club (Ozarks chpt. founder, bd. dirs., sec. Great Lakes chpt. 1963-72). Democrat. Lodge: Kiwanis. Home: 27 S LaChee PO Box 4172 Yatahey NM 87375 Office: Navajo Nat Zool and Bot Park PO Box 308 Window Rock AZ 86515-0308

HATHAWAY, PAUL L., JR., natural gas company executive; b. Coronado, Calif., Sept. 12, 1934; s. Paul L. Hathaway; m. Rita M., Oct. 17, 1959; children: Paul III, Richard, David, Brian. Student, Stanford U., 1952-53; BS in Gen. Engring., U.S. Naval Acad., 1957. Registered profl. engr., mech. div., Calif. Jr. engr. San Diego Gas & Electric, 1962-70, v.p. gas div., 1970-75; v.p. gas ops. div. Consol. Edison Co. of N.Y.C., 1975-77; v.p. govt. and pub. relations N.W. Natural Gas Co., Portland, Oreg., 1978-81, sr. v.p. ops., 1981-84, sr. v.p. corp. devel. and human resources, 1984-87, sr. v.p. market services and human resources, 1987-90, sr. v.p. mktg. dists. & adminstrv. svcs., 1990-92, sr. v.p. dists. and adminstrv. svcs., 1992—; v.p. N.W. Geothermal (subs. N.W. Natural Gas), Portland, 1981-85; pres. Oreg. Nat. Gas Devel. (subs. N.W. Natural Gas), Portland, 1983-87, Pacific Sq. Corp. (subs. N.W. Natural Gas), Portland, 1987—. Contbr. papers to profl. publs. Active St. Vincent Hosp. and Med. Ctr., 1992-93; trustee St. Vincent Med. Found., 1992—. Served to capt. USNR. Fellow Am. Leadership Forum (sr.); mem. Am. Gas Assn. (sponsor operating sect. gas control com. 1981-84, mem. operating sect. mng. com. 1981-84), Pacific Coast Gas Assn. (exec. com. operating sect., 1984-85, chmn. adminstrv. svcs. exec. com. 1987—), Assn. N.W. Gas Utilities (trustee 1982—), Portland C. of C. (energy com. 1982-85), Task Force on Bus. Devel. and Social Issues (chmn. 1987-91), Assoc. Oreg. Industries (bd. dirs. 1980-88), Assoc. Oreg. Industries Found. (bd. dirs. 1989-91), Rotary (Portland chpt. pres.). Republican. Clubs: Arlington (Portland); Oswego Lake Country (Lake Oswego, Oreg.). Office: NW Natural Gas Co 220 NW 2nd Ave Portland OR 97209-3943

HATHORN, CLAY GATES, journalist; b. Lafayette, La., Mar. 8, 1962; s. Everett Martin and JoAnn (Gates) H. BA, U. Ark., 1983. Editor Childress (Tex.) Index, 1983-84; reporter Log Cabin Democrat, Conway, Ark., 1985-86; bur. chief, writer The Comml. Appeal, Memphis, 1986-89; ptnr. Metro. Comms., Seattle, 1992—; freelance journalist, 1989—; article screener Pacific N.W. Writers Conf., Seattle, 1992—. Contbr. articles to profl. jours. Tutor S.T.A.R.S. Tutoring, Cen. Area Youth Assn., Seattle, 1991-92; leader Utne Reader Neighborhood Salon, Seattle, 1991-92. Mem. Pacific N.W. Basketball Ofcls. Assn., Elliott Bay Writers Club. Democrat. Home and Office: 906 E John St # 410 Seattle WA 98102-5762

HATICO, ELLIOT JOSE, savings and loan executive; b. Kailua, Hawaii, Sept. 8, 1955; s. Jose and Lillian Reiko (Nakashima) H. BEd, U. Hawaii, 1978, MBA, 1991. Tchr. Cathedral Sch., Honolulu, 1979-81, Dept. of Edn., Hawaii, Honolulu, 1981-84; counselor Keolu Elem. Sch., Kailua, 1984-85; tchr. King Intermediate Sch., Kaneohe, Hawaii, 1985-86; br. mgr. Territorial Savs. and Loan, Kaneohe, 1986-89; tng. coord. Territorial Savs. and Loan, Honolulu, 1989-91, v.p. ops., 1991—. Pres. Kailua Youth Athletic Club, 1977; dir. Kaneohe Bus. Group, 1989; mem. Windward Drug Coalition, Kaneohe, 1989. Named Outstanding Counselor, Hawaii Sch. Counselor Assn., 1985. Mem. Beta Gamma Sigma. Democrat. Roman Catholic. Office: Territorial Savs and Loan 925 Bethel St Honolulu HI 96813-4307

HATTENHAUER, DARRYL CLYDE, educator of American Literature; b. Sacramento, Calif., Oct. 29, 1948; s. Clyde Edward and Clara Marie (Collins) H. BA, Calif. State U., Sacramento, 1971, MA, 1977; PhD, U. Minn., 1984. Instr. Winona (Minn.) State U., 1982-83; asst. prof. Bemidji (Minn.) State U., 1983-86; vis. prof. LaVerne U., Athens, Greece, 1986; Fulbright tchr. Svendborg (Denmark) Tchrs. Coll., 1986-87; Fulbright lectr. Vasteras (Sweden) U., 1987-88; asst. prof. Ariz. State U. West, Phoenix, 1988—; book reviewer Studies in Am. Indian Lit., L.A., 1990—; reader Popular Culture Rev., Las Vegas, 1989—; course designer Inst. for Curriculum Design, Phoenix, 1988-89. Contbr. articles to profl. jours. Mem. MLA, Am. Studies Assn., Am. Lib. Assn., Coll. English Assn., Coll. Lang. Assn., Steinbeck Soc., Fulbright Alumni Assn. Office: Ariz State U West 4701 E Thunderbird Rd Phoenix AZ 85032-5540

HATTER, TERRY JULIUS, JR., federal judge; b. Chgo., Mar. 11, 1933. A.B., Wesleyan U., 1954; J.D., U. Chgo., 1960. Bar: Ill. 1960, Calif. 1965, U.S. Dist. Ct. 1960, U.S. Ct. Appeals 1960. Adjudicator Chgo., 1960-61; assoc. Harold M. Calhoun, Chgo., 1961-62; asst. pub. defender Cook County Chgo., 1961-62; asst. U.S. atty. No. Dist. Calif., San Francisco, 1962-66; chief counsel San Francisco Neighborhood Legal Assistance Found., 1966-67; regional legal svcs. dir. Exec. Office Pres. OEO, San Francisco, 1967-70; exec. dir. Western Ctr. Law and Poverty, L.A., 1970-73; exec. asst. to mayor, dir. criminal justice planning L.A., 1974-75; spl. asst. to mayor, dir. urban devel., 1975-77; judge Superior Ct. Calif., L.A., 1977-80, U.S. Dist. Ct. (cen. dist.) Calif., L.A., 1980—; assoc. clin. prof. law U. So. Calif. Law Ctr., L.A., 1970-74; prof. law Loyola U. Sch. Law, L.A., 1973-75; mem. faculty Nat. Coll. State Judiciary, Reno, 1974; lectr. Police Acad., San Francisco Police Dept., 1963-66, U. Calif., San Diego, 1970-71, Colo. Jud. Conf., 1973; mem. bd. councilors U. So. Calif. Law Ctr. V.p. Northbay Halfway House, 1964-65; vice chmn. Los Angeles Regional Criminal Justice Planning Bd., 1975-76; mem. Los Angeles Mayor's Cabinet Com. Econ. Devel., 1976-77, Mayor's Policy Com., 1973-77, chmn. housing econ. and community devel. com., City Los Angeles, 1975-77, chmn. housing and community devel. tech. com., 1975-77; vice chmn. Young Dems. Cook County, 1961-62; chmn. bd. Real Estate Coop; bd. dirs. Bay Area Social Planning Coun., Contra Costa, Black Law Center L.A., Nat. Fedn. Settlements & Neighborhood Ctrs., Edn. Fin. & Governance Reform Project, Mexican Am. Legal Def. & Ednl. Fund, Nat. Health Law Program, Nat. Sr. Citizens Law Ctr., Calif. Law Ctr., L.A. Regional Criminal Justice Planning Bd.; mem. exec. com. bd. dirs. Constl. Rights Found; trustee Wesleyan Univ. Meth. Ch.; mem. bd. visitors U. Chgo. Law Sch. Mem. NAACP (exec. com., bd. dirs. Richmond chpt.), Nat. Legal Aid & Defender Assn. (dir., vice chmn.), L.A. County Bar Assn. (exec. com.), Am. Judicature Soc., Charles Houston Law Club, Phi Delta Phi, Order Coif. Office: US Dist Ct 312 N Spring St Los Angeles CA 90012-4701

HATTERY, DAVID RUSSELL, systems analyst; b. Phoenix, June 17, 1955; s. Russell David and Lucy (Webb) H.; m. Karen Kakuschka, Feb. 28, 1987. AA, Glendale C.C., 1978; BS, Linfield Coll., 1989; MBA, Marylhurst Coll., 1992. Acad. systems programmer Am. Grad. Sch. Internat. Mgmt., Glendale, Ariz., 1976-80; staff analyst DASD/Cap Gemini N.Am., Portland, Oreg., 1980-81; instr. Western Bus. Coll., Portland, 1981-84; systems engr. Electronic Data Systems Govt. Svcs. Group, Portland, 1984-88; project analyst First Farwest Ins., Portland, 1988-89; profl. staff mem. Computer People, Inc., Portland, 1989-90; programmer/analyst IV First Interstate Bank, Portland, 1990—. Vol. speech coach, judge Phoenix Union High Sch. System, 1974-78; vol. judge Nat. Forensic League, Portland, 1981. Mem. Am. Mgmt. Assn., Assn. Computing Machinery, Toastmasters (club pres. 1987-88, v.p. edn. 1988-89, area gov. 1989-90, div. gov. 1990-91, Dist. Champion 1992, Area Gov. of Yr. 1990, Competent Toastmaster 1988, Able Toastmaster 1989, Able Toastmaster Bronze award 1990, Able Toastmaster Silver award 1991). Republican. Office: 1st Interstate Bank 1300 SW 5th Ave Portland OR 97208

HATTORI, TODD TOSHIHARU, public relations specialist; b. Ogden, Utah, Dec. 29, 1962; s. Tommy Toshiyuki and Kimiko (Adachi) H. BA in Speech Communication, U. Utah, 1987, substance abuse counseling cert., 1991. Lic. counselor, Utah. With sales and display depts. Nordstrom, Ogden, 1987-88; graphic designer Bailey's Printing, Ogden, 1988-89; word processor Salt Lake County Alcohol & Drug Div., Salt Lake City, 1989-90, pub. rels. specialist, 1990—. Vol. boutique Ballet West, Salt Lake City, 1989—; Salt Lake County Disaster Pub. Info. 2d Dir., 1991—; vol. bd. dirs. no. Utah chpt. Alzheimer's Assn., 1991—; vol. Salt Lake Men's Choir Pub. Rels. Advisor, 1991—. Buddhist. Home: 390 W 2200 N Clearfield UT 84015-3542 Office: Salt Lake County Divsn Alcohol & Drugs 2001 S State St Ste 2300S Salt Lake City UT 84190-0001

HAUCK, DENNIS WILLIAM, author, technical writer; b. Hammond, Ind., Apr. 8, 1945; s. Floyd William and Wilma (Frey) H. BS in Math., Ind. U., 1964-67; MS in Math., U. Vienna, Austria, 1972. Editor IUFOR Svcs. Inc., Munster, Ind., 1973-76; mng. editor Countrywide Publs., N.Y.C., 1976-80; tech. writer EPCO Inc., Reno, 1980-83, Odenberg Inc., Sacramento, Calif., 1984-91; freelance writer Sacramento, 1991—; cons. in field. Editor Jour. of Ufology, 1973-76; author: William Shatner: A Biography, 1992, The Alchemical Works of Gottlieb Latz, 1992, Haunted Places Guidebook, 1993, First Matter, 1993. Active mem. Greenpeace, San Francisco. Mem. Authors Guild, Soc. for Tech. Comm., Nat. Writers Club, Calif. Writers Club, Nat. Writers Union. Office: Hauck Editorial Svcs 5550 Franklin Blvd Ste 101 Sacramento CA 95820

HAUENSTEIN, DONALD HERBERT, JR., consultant; b. Canton, Ohio, Dec. 29, 1942; s. Donald Herbert and Mary Alice (Andrichs) H.; m. Maria Del Socorro Moreno, June 5, 1965 (div. Apr. 1979); children: Carlos Ian, Marissa Renee; m. Carol King, May 28, 1988. B in Indsl. Engring., Ohio State U., 1970, MS in Indsl. Engring., 1970; MBA, U. Houston, 1977; exec. mgmt. program, UCLA, L.A., 1986. Indsl. engr. Schlumberger Well Svcs., Houston, 1970-72, supr. of methods, 1972-75; mgr. engring. svcs. Dresser Atlas, Houston, 1975-80; mgr. mfg. engring. VETCO Offshore, Ventura, Calif., 1980-83; dir. mfg. engring. HR Textron, Valencia, Calif., 1983-88; dir. spl. projects HR Textron, Valencia, 1988-90; owner, retail Abacus Cons. Svcs., Saugus, 1990—. Pres. St. Christopher's Sch. Bd., Houston, 1976-79, bd. dirs. Orchard Ln. Condominium Assn., Oxnard, Calif., 1986, Arbor Park Condominium Assn., 1987. With USAF, 1961-65. Mem. Tau Beta Pi, Alpha Pi Mu. Republican. Roman Catholic. Home: 28025 Tupelo Ridge Dr Santa Clarita CA 91354-1326 Office: Abacus Cons Svcs 23001 Soledad Canyon Rd Saugus CA 91350

HAUGE, LAWRENCE JESSEN, management consultant; b. Tacoma, Wash., Feb. 10, 1928; s. Philip Enoch and Margrethe H.; m. Helen Jensen, June 22, 1952 (div. 1975); children: Jan DiConti, Steven Philip, David Lawrence; m. Beverly Jean Milligan, Oct. 17, 1975. BA, Pacific Luth. U., Tacoma, 1950, BEd, 1951, MA, 1962; EdD, Wash. State U., 1980. Tchr. Clover Park Sch. Dist., Tacoma, 1953-57, vice prin., 1957-63, asst. to supt., 1967-75; dir. alumni rels. Pacific Luth. U., Tacoma, 1963-67; coord. curriculum and instrn. Ednl. Svc. Dist. 167, Wenatchee, Wash., 1975-77; asst. to supt. Wanatchee Sch. Dist., 1977-83; exec. dir. United Way of Chelan & Douglas Counties, Wenatchee, 1985-90; pres. L/B Cons., Wenatchee, 1990—. Vice chair State Coun. on Vol. and Citizen Svc., Olympia, 1988—. Lt. col. USAR, 1953-75. Mem. Kiwanis (pres. 1969-70, lt. gov. 1970-71, dist. chair 1971-72). Lutheran. Home: 1608 Washington St Wenatchee WA 98801

HAUGEN, MARY MARGARET, state legislator; b. Camano Island, Wash., Jan. 14, 1941; d. Melvin Harry and Alma Cora (Huntington) Olsen; m. Basil Badley; children: Mary Beth Fisher, Katherine Heitt, Richard, James. Mem. Wash. Ho. Reps., Olympia, 1982-1992, past mem. natural resources com., transp. com., mem. joint legis. com. on criminal justice system; mem. Wash. Senate, Olympia, 1993—; chmn. govt. ops. com., transp. com., natural resource com. Wash. State Senate. Mem. Camano Homeowners Assn.; mem. United Meth. Ch. Mem. LWV, Nat. Order Women Legislators, Wash. State Sch. Dirs. (resolution com.), Elected Wash. Women, Greater Marysville Bus. and Profl. Women. Democrat. Lodge: Order Ea. Star. Home: 1268 N Olsen Rd Camano Island WA 98292-8708 Office: Wash State Legislature JAC WAC 414 Olympia WA 98504

HAUK, A. ANDREW, federal judge; b. Denver, Dec. 29, 1912; s. A.A. and Pearl (Woods) H.; m. Jean Nicolay, Aug. 30, 1941; 1 dau., Susan. AB magna cum laude, Regis Coll., 1935; LLB, Cath. U. Am., 1938; JSD (Sterling fellow), Yale U., 1942. Bar: Calif. 1942, Colo. 1939, D.C. 1938, U.S. Supreme Ct. 1953. Spl. asst. to atty. gen., counsel for govt. antitrust div. U.S. Dept Justice, Los Angeles, Pacific Coast, Denver, 1939-41; asst. U.S. atty., Los Angeles, 1941-42; with firm Adams, Duque & Hazeltine, Los Angeles, 1946-52; individual practice law Los Angeles, 1952-64; asst. counsel Union Oil Co., Los Angeles, 1952-64; judge Superior Ct., Los Angeles County, 1964-66; U.S. dist. judge Central Dist. Calif., 1966—, chief judge, 1980-82, now sr. judge, chief judge emeritus; instr. Southwestern U. Law Sch., 1939-41; lectr. U. So. Calif. Law Sch., 1947-56; vice chmn. Calif. Olympic Com., 1954-61; ofcl. VIII Olympic Winter Games, Squaw Valley, 1960; Gov. Calif.'s del. IX Olympic Games, Innsbruck, Austria, 1964. Bd. dirs. So. Calif. Com. for Olympic Games. Served from lt. to lt. comdr., Naval Intelligence USNR, 1942-46. Recipient scroll Los Angeles County Bd. Suprs., 1965, 66, 75; Alumnus of Yr. Regis Coll., 1967; named to Nat. Ski Hall of Fame, 1975. Mem. Los Angeles County Bar Assn. (chmn. pleading and practice com. 1963-64, chmn. Law Day com. 1965-66), State Bar Calif. (corps. com., war work com. past vice-chmn.), ABA (com. criminal law sect.), Fed. Bar Assn., Lawyers Club Los Angeles, Am. Judicature Soc., Am. Legion, Navy League, U.S. Lawn Tennis Assn., Far West Ski Assn. (Nat. Sr. Giant Slalom champion 1954), Yale Law Sch. Assn. So. Calif. (dir., past pres.), Town Hall. Clubs: Yale of So. Calif. (dir. 1964-67), Newman; Valley Hunt (Pasadena); Jonathan (Los Angeles). Office: US Dist Ct 312 N Spring St Los Angeles CA 90012-4701

HAULENBEEK, ROBERT BOGLE, JR., government official; b. Cleve., Feb. 24, 1941; s. Robert Bogle and Priscilla Valerie (Burch) H.; BS, Okla. State U., 1970; m. Rebecca Marie Talley, Mar. 1, 1965; children—Kimberly Kaye, Robert Bogle, III. Micro paleon. photographer Pan Am. Rsch. Co., Tulsa, 1966-67; flight instr. Okla. State U., 1970; air traffic control specialist FAA, Albuquerque, 1970-73, Farmington, N.Mex., 1973-78, flight svc. specialist, Dalhart, Tex., 1978-80, Albuquerque, 1980—; staff officer CAP, Albuquerque, 1970-73, Farmington, 1974-78, advanced through grades to col., 1988, dir. ops. for hdqrs., 1981-86, N.Mex. Wing dep. commdr., 1986-88, N.Mex. Wing comdr., 1988-91; mem. faculty Nat. Staff Coll., Gunter Air Force Sta., Montgomery, Ala., 1981-82; dir. South West Region Staff Coll., Albuquerque, 1986. With U.S. Army, 1964-65. Recipient Meritorious Svc. award CAP, 1978, 81, 82, Lifesaving award, 1982, distng. svc. award, 1991. Mem. Exptl. Aircraft Assn., Nat. Assn. Air Traffic Specialists (facility rep. 1978-86), Aircraft Owners and Pilots Assn. Republican. Presbyterian. Home: 5229 Carlsbad Ct NW Albuquerque NM 87120-2322

HAUNOLD, ALFRED, geneticist; b. Hollabrunn, Austria, Oct. 7, 1929; came to U.S., 1953; naturalized 1964.; s. Karl L. and Maria (Schleyer) H.; m. Mary F. Bacchi, Aug. 18, 1959; children: Christopher, Monica, Michelle, Julie, Karl, Erik, Jennifer. Diploma in Engring., U. Vienna, Austria, 1951, D in Agr. Sci., 1952; PhD, U. Nebr., 1960. Fulbright fellow U. Nebr., Lincoln, 1953-54, asst. in agronomy, 1955-60, asst. prof., 1960-64; with agr. extension svc. Austrian Govt., Vienna, 1954-55; profl. analyst Smithsonian Inst., Washington, 1964-65; rsch. geneticist, prof. agronomy U.S. Dept. Agr., Oreg. State U., Corvallis, 1965—; cons. UNO-Unido, Nairobi, 1981, Govt. Mex., U. Monterrey, 1968, 71, 76. Assoc. editor Crop Sci. Jour., 1978-81; contbr. chpts. to books. Mem. Am. Soc. Brewing Chemists (mem. editorial bd. 1987-93, chmn. publ. com. 1989-93, bd. dirs. 1989-93), Crop Sci. Soc. Am., Hop Rsch. Coun. Republican. Roman Catholic. Home: 1325 NW Forest Dr Corvallis OR 97330-1703 Office: Oreg State U Crop & Soil Sci Dept Corvallis OR 97331-3002

HAUPTLY, PAUL DAVID, marketing professional; b. Jersey City, June 3, 1944; s. John James and Genevieve Elaine (Dunt) H.; m. Cathy Bennet, Dec. 19, 1992; 1 child, Michael David. BS, Rutgers U., 1975. Mil. sales mgr. Hoke Inc., Cresskill, N.J., 1974-77; mktg. mgr. Raychem Corp., Menlo Park, Calif., 1977-87; pres., chief exec. officer Polytrace Systems Inc., Fremont, Calif., 1987—. Inventor patents issued and pending. With USN, 1968-70. Mem. U.S. Navy Cryptographic Vets. Office: Polytrace Systems Inc 44948 Osgood Rd Fremont CA 94539-6101

HAUSAM, NEAL ALLEN, civil engineer, real estate developer; b. Peoria, Ill., Oct. 17, 1939; s. George Melville and Elizabeth (Miklas) H.; m. Beverly Jo Beyer, Apr. 1962 (div. 1967); children: Kelly Kathleen, Neal Curtis. BSCE, Bradley U., 1962. Registered profl. civil engr., Alaska, Oreg., Nev., Wash., Calif.; registered surveyor, Alaska, Oreg.; registered contractor, Calif. Owner Constrn. Testing Lab., Anchorage, 1973-81, Alaska Engring. Svcs., Anchorage, 1973-81, Neal Hausam Realty, Anchorage, 1978-82; developer Hamack, Vista View, Bay View, Holiday Park, Alaska, 1974-80; owner Crystal Water Lodge, Iliamna Lake, Alaska, 1976-79; assoc. broker Century 21 Heritage Homes and Investments, Inc., Anchorage, 1979-81; mgr. Oil Field Contractors of Alaska, Anchorage, 1979-81; owner Residential Housing Devel. Co., Salem, Oreg., 1981-85; constrn. and projects mgr. Fleming Foods, Inc., Pleasanton, Calif., 1982-86; mgr. Contractor's Quality Control, Taywood, Berg and Riedel, Alaska, 1988-89; construction, projects mgr. Scocaries Warehouse Markets, Nev., 1989-90; dist. mgr. testing lab. divsn. Profl. Svc. Industries, Seattle, 1992—; mem. Municipality of Anchorage Constrn. Adv. Com., 1979-81; surveying trainer, Alaska Laborers Union, Anchorage, 1979-81. Inventor inflation device, 1963. Mem. Joe Hayes Mayorial Campaign, Anchorage, 1982. Mem. Porsche Club of Am. Republican. Office: 7400 3d Ave S Seattle WA 98108

HAUSDORFER, GARY LEE, mortgage banker; b. Indpls., Mar. 26, 1946; s. Walter Edward and Virginia Lee (Bender) H.; AA, Glendale Coll., 1966; BS, Calif. State U.-L.A., 1968; m. Debora Ann French, Dec. 17, 1966; children: Lisa Ann, Janet Lee. Rsch. officer Security Pacific Bank, L.A., 1968-73; v.p., mgr. W. Ross Campbell Co., Irvine, Calif., 1973-81; sr. v.p. Weyerhaeuser Mortgage Co., Irvine, 1982-87; exec. v.p., ptnr. L.J. Melody & Co. of Calif., 1987-89; pres. Hausdorfer Co., 1989—. Councilman, City of San Juan Capistrano, 1978—, mayor, 1980-81, 84-85, 88-90; chmn. Capistrano Valley Water Dist., 1980-81, San Juan Capistrano Redevel. Agy., 1983-84, 85—, South Orange County Leadership Conf.; bd. dirs. Orange County Trans. Corridor Agy., Orange County Transit Dist.; chmn. Orange County Transp. Authority. Recipient cert. of commendation Orange County Bd. Suprs., 1981, congl. commendation, 1985, Theodore Roosevelt Conservation award Pres. Bush, 1990. Mem. Mortgage Bankers Assn. Am., Calif. Mortgage Bankers Assn., Orange County Mortgage Bankers Assn. (dir. 1979-80), Calif. League of Cities. Republican.

HAUSE, NORMAN LAURANCE, retired manufacturing company executive; b. Fort Lupton, Colo., July 26, 1922; s. Laurance Edward and Daisy Theresa (Schieck) H.; m. Marjorie Beryl Clinton, Mar. 10, 1946; children: Penny, Robin, Pamela. BA, U. Colo., 1947, PhD, 1950. Asst. U. Colo., Boulder, 1947; rsch. chemist Electrochems. dept. DuPont Co., Niagara Falls, N.Y., 1950-56; rsch. supr. Exptl. Sta. DuPont Co., Wilmington, Del., 1956-60, lab. mgr. Exptl. Sta., 1960-65, lab. dir. Chestnut Run Lab., 1965-70, rsch. mgr. Polymer Products div., Plastic Products Dept., 1970-79, tech. mgr. Ethylene Polymers div. Polymer Products Dept., 1979-82, ret., 1982. Contbr. articles to profl. jours.; patentee in field. Active various civic assns. Lt. (j.g.) USN, 1942-46. Mem. Am. Chem. Soc., Sigma Xi, Phi Beta Kappa, Phi Lambda Upsilon. Republican. Home: 35 Hy-View Ln Sedona AZ 86336

HAUSEL, WILLIAM DAN, economic geologist; b. Salt Lake City, July 24, 1949; s. Maynard Romain and Dorthy (Clark) H.; m. Patricia Kemp, Aug. 14, 1970; children: Jessica Siddhartha, Eric Jason. BS in Geology, U. Utah, 1972, MS in Geology, 1974. Astronomy lectr., Hansen Planetarium, Salt Lake City, 1968-72; rsch. asst. U. Utah, 1972-74; teaching asst. U. N.Mex., Albuquerque, 1974-75; project geologist Warnock Cons., Albuquerque, 1975; geologist U.S. Geol. Survey, Casper, Wyo., 1976-77; staff geologist Geol. Survey of Wyo., Laramie, 1977-81, dep. dir., 1981-91, sr. econ. geologist, 1991—; cons. Western Gold Exploration and Mining, Anchorage, 1988, 89, Chevron Resources, Georgetown, Mont., 1990, Fowler Resources, Phillipsburg, Mont., 1992, A and E Diamond Exploration, Calif., 1993; assoc. curator mineralogy Wyo. State Mus., Cheyenne, 1983-90. Author: Partial Pressures of Some Lunar Lavas, 1972, Petrogenesis of Some Representative Lavas, Southwestern Utah, 1975, Exploration for Diamondiferous Kimberlite, 1979, Gold Districts of Wyoming, 1980, Ore Deposits of Wyoming, 1982, Geology of Southeastern Wyoming, 1984, Minerals and Rocks of Wyoming, 1986, The Geology of Wyoming's Precious Metal Lode and Placer Deposits, 1989, Economic Geology of the South Pass Greenstone Belt, 1991, Economic Geology of the Cooper Hill Mining District, 1992, Mining History and Geology of Wyoming's Metal and Gemstone Districts, 1993; contbr. over 150 articles to profl. jours. and 2 books. Grantee NASA, 1981, Office of Surface Mining, 1979, U. Wyo., 1981-92, U.S. Geol. Survey Coop. Geologic Mapping Initiative, 1985-88, Union Pacific Resources, 1991, 92. Mem. Wyo. Geol. Assn., Am. Inst. Mining Engrs., Wyo. Profl. Geologists, Soc. Econ. Geologists, U. Utah Geology Club (pres. 1969-71), U. Utah Karate Club, Laramie Bushido Dojo Karate (pres. 1985-88), U. Wyo. Campus Shotokan Karate Club (instr. 1988—). Avocations: karate, sketching, astronomy. Home: 4238 Grays Gable Rd Laramie WY 82070-6911 Office: Geol Survey of Wyo PO Box 3008 Laramie WY 82071-3008

HAUSSMANN, NORMAN JOSEPH, printing account executive; b. Cleve., Oct. 30, 1940; s. Karl Fredrick and Rose Hilda Josephine (Buchholz) H.; m. Virginia Lee Dow, Dec. 29, 1962; children: Deborah, Patricia, Kathleen. AA, L.A. City Coll., 1960; BS, Calif. State U., L.A., 1962. Aviation officers tng. USN, Pensacola, Fla., 1962-63; naval flight officer USN, 1963-66; printing acct. exec. Anderson Lithograph, L.A., 1966-73, Triangle Lithograph, L.A., 1973-83, Overland Printers, Hawthorne, Calif., 1983-92, So. Calif. Graphics, Culver City, 1992—; naval air reservist Naval Air Sta.

Pt. Mugu, Oxnard, Calif., 1963-84; commanding officer Patrol Squadron 65, USN Pt. Mugu, Oxnard, Calif., 1981-83. Recipient Vietnam War Decorations, USN, 1966, Letters of Commendation, USN, 1983. Mem. Ret. Officers Assn., Naval Res. Assn. Republican. Roman Catholic. Office: So Calif Graphics 8432 Steller Dr Culver City CA 90232

HAUTALUOMA, JACOB EDWARD, psychology educator, college associate dean; b. Chatham, Mich., June 28, 1933; s. Toivo Jack and Irja Aurora (Nikkinen) H.; m. Betty Lou Johnson, Mar. 24, 1956; children: Jodi, Grey. BA, U. Minn., Duluth, 1955; MS, PhD, U. Colo., 1967; postgrad., Yale U., 1971-72. Indsl. engr. Am. Steel & Wire, Duluth, Minn., 1955-60; assoc. dean Coll. Natural Scis. and prof. psychology Colo. State U., Ft. Collins, 1965—; vis. prof. U. Minn., Duluth, 1972, U. Hawaii, 1973, Oreg. State U., 1977; lectr. Helsinki Sch. Econs., Finland, 1980, U. Iceland, Reykjavik, 1977, 81; prog. assoc. NSF, Washington, 1986-87; cons. in field. Contbr. articles to profl. jours. Mem. com. Indian Hills Community Assn., Ft. Collins, 1988—; ch. councilman Trinity Luth. Ch., Ft. Collins, 1981-83, 89-90. With USAFR, 1957. Fulbright fellow, 1977, 80, NIMH fellow, 1960-61, 63-64, others. Mem. Am. Psychol. Assn., Soc. for Psychol. Study of Social Issues, Acad. Mgmt., Rocky Mt. Psychology Assn., Colo. Wyo. Assn. Indsl./Orgnl. Psychology. Democrat. Lutheran. Home: 701 Dartmouth Trl Fort Collins CO 80525-1522 Office: Colo State U Dept Psychology Fort Collins CO 80523

HAVARD, JOHN FRANCIS, mining consultant; b. Helena, Mont., Mar. 15, 1909; s. Francis Thompson and Margaret (Raleigh) H.; m. Faith Hartley, Aug. 19, 1943 (dec. 1991); children: David, Edith Ann Havard Britts, John, Patrick. Student Mont. Sch. Mines, 1929-32; BPhil in Geology, U. Wis., 1934, BS, MPhil, 1935; cert. Engr. Mines, 1943; postgrad. Harvard U., 1957. Registered geologist, profl. engr. Engr., works mgr., chief engr. mines, U.S. Gypsum Co., Chgo., 1935-52; asst. resident mgr. Potash Co. Am., Carlsbad, N.Mex., 1952-53; v.p. Fibreboard Corp., San Francisco, 1953-62; v.p., sr. v.p. Kaiser Engrs., Oakland, Calif., 1962-77; sr. cons. Kaiser Engrs., Oakland, 1977-81; pvt. practice mining cons., Nevada City, Calif., 1977-85. Contbr. articles to tech. pubs. Recipient Disting. Service citation Coll. Engring., U. Wis., 1986. Mem. U.S. Nat. Com. on Geology, Washington, 1975-79. Fellow AAAS; mem. Soc. Mining Engrs. (pres. 1976, Disting. Mem. 1977, Pres.' Citation 1979), AIME (hon. mem. 1984, dir. 1975-78, Krumb lectr. 1979, Hardinge award 1982), Soc. Econ. Geologists (sr.). Republican. Episcopalian. Home: 18552 Augustine Rd Nevada City CA 95959-9709

HAVENS, CANDACE JEAN, planning consultant; b. Rochester, Minn., Sept. 13, 1952; d. Fred Z. and Barbara Jean (Stephenson) H.; m. Bruce Curtis Mercier, Feb. 22, 1975 (div. Apr. 1982); 1 child, Rachel; m. James Arthur Renning, Oct. 26, 1986; children: Kelsey, Sarah. Student, U. Calif., San Diego, Darmouth Coll., Am. U., Beirut, 1973-74; BA in Sociology, U. Calif., Riverside, 1977. Project coord. social svc. orgn. Grass Roots II, San Luis Obispo, Calif., 1976-77; planning enforcement technician City San Luis Obispo, 1977-81, asst. planner, 1981-83; assoc. planner City of San Luis Obispo, 1983-86, coord. parking program, 1986-88, spl. asst. to city adminstr., mgr. constr. libr. and parking structures, 1989, planning cons., 1991—. Past pres. Nat. Charity League, Riverside; mem. San Luis Obispo Med. Aux., 1986—, San Luis Obispo Arts coun., 1986—; pres. bd. dirs. San Luis Obispo Children's Mus., 1990-91, pres. 1990-91, CFO, 1993. Mem. AAUW, San Luis Obispo Med. Aux., Toastmasters (sec. 1986-87, v.p. 1987-88, pres. 1989-90, treas. 1991-92). Office: PO Box 1395 San Luis Obispo CA 93406-1395

HAVENS, CARL BRADFORD, retired research scientist; b. Hope, Mich., May 30, 1918; s. Boyd L. and Mary Ada (Gransden) H.; m. Grace Jeannette Cummins, Oct. 1, 1936 (div. Apr. 1990); children: David Carl, Sandra Jeanette, Paul Lewis. BS, U. Mich., 1944. Chem. engr. Dow Chem. Co., Midland, Mich., 1944-47, group leader, 1948-58; plant supt. Dow Chem. Co., Bay City, Mich., 1959-61; rsch. mgr. Dow Chem. Co., Cleve., 1961-65, Fresno, Calif., 1966-76; rsch. scientist Dow Chem. Co., Granville, Ohio, 1976-86. 55 U.S. patents and 100 fgn. patents in field; contbr. articles to profl. jours. Republican. Presbyterian.

HAVENS, KENNETH HAROLD, SR., general contrator; b. Squankum, N.J., Oct. 20, 1930; s. Byron Ellsworth and Minnie (Matthews) H.; m. Shirley Ann Gurba, Jan. 19, 1952; children: Kenneth Harold Jr., Karen Ann Havens Roberts, Andrew William. AA, Phoenix Coll., 1961. Carpenter apprentice Lakewood, N.J., 1949-51, Phoenix, 1955-57; carpenter foreman Leonard-Doremus-Day, Phoenix, 1957-62, E. Hargrave Co. (Constrn. Co.), Phoenix, 1963; constrn. supt. F & F Constrn. Co., Phoenix, 1964-66; gen. foreman Van Dyke Dail Constrn., Phoenix, 1966-68; owner Havens Constrn. Co., Tyrone, N.Mex., 1968—. Mayor Town of Silver City, N.Mex., 1989-92; com. mem. City Charter Silver City, 1988—; elder Presbyn. Ch. Staff Sgt. USAF, 1951-55. Kenneth H. Havens, Sr. Day proclaimed July 31, 1992 in his honor Dan Dunnagan, Mayor and Silver City Town Coun., 1992. Mem. Assn. of Commerce and Industry (Albuquerque, bd. dirs. 1979—), Silver City Prospectors (pres. 1987-88), Copper Crest Country Club, Elks, Lions (pres. 1979-80, dist. gov. 1983-84), Masons. Republican. Home: PO Box 2159 Silver City NM 88062-2159 Office: Havens Constrn Co PO Box 2159 811 Market Silver City NM 88061

HAVENS, THOMAS R.H., history educator; b. Chambersburg, Pa., Nov. 21, 1939; s. Paul Swain and Lorraine (Hamilton) H.; children: William H., Carolyn S., Katherine E. AB in History, Princeton U., 1961; AM in History, U. Calif., Berkeley, 1962, PhD in History, 1965. Asst. prof. history U. Toronto, Can., 1965-66; prof. history Conn. Coll., 1966-91; prof. history U. Ill., Urbana, 1991-93, head dept. East Asian Langs. and Cultures, 1991-93; prof. history and E. Asian languages U. Calif., Berkeley, 1993—; vis. prof. history Wesleyan U., 1979-80. Author: Nishi Amane and Modern Japanese Thought, 1970, Farm and Nation in Modern Japan, 1974, Valley of Darkness: The Japanese People and World War II, 1978, Artist and Patron in Postwar Japan, 1982, Fire Across the Sea: The Vietnam War and Japan 1965-75, 1987. Fulbright Rsch. scholar Waseda U., Tokyo, 1972-73, 90-91, NEH fellow, 1968, 90, John Simon Guggenheim Meml. Foudn. fellow, Waseda U., 1976-77, Japan Found. Profl. fellow, 1980-81. Office: E Asian Libr Durant Hall U Calif Berkeley CA 94720

HAVER, CHRISTOPHER STERLING, real estate developer; b. Phoenix, Feb. 6, 1966; s. Ralph Burgess and Joyce Ann (Watkins) H. BS in Fin., San Diego State U., 1990. Lic. real estate broker, ins. agt., Ariz., Calif. Dir. syndicate ops. 1992 Am.'s Cup Knight & Carver Yachtctr., San Diego, 1990-92; pres. C. Sterling Haver, Real Estate Developer, San Diego, 1992—; pres. 1995 Am.s Cup Mission Bay Organizing Com. Vol. Boys and Girls Clubs of Am., Phoenix, 1985-89. U. So. Calif. Alumni scholar, 1984. Mem. Japan Am. Soc., Future Forty, Sigma Chi. Republican. Roman Catholic. Home: 3940 Gresham #321 San Diego CA 92109

HAVRAN, WENDY LYNN, immunologist; b. Houston, Sept. 1, 1955; d. George Anton and Myra Laverne (Faulkner) H. BS, Duke U., 1977; PhD, U. Chgo., 1986. Sr. rsch. technician Med. Ctr. Duke U., Durham, N.C., 1977-79, rsch. analyst Med. Ctr., 1980-82; postdoctoral fellow U. Calif., Berkeley, 1987-91; asst. prof. Scripps Rsch. Inst., La Jolla, Calif., 1991—; speaker, Greece, 1989—. Contbr. articles to profl. jours. Vol. Hyde Park Food Pantry, Chgo., 1984-86; Sunday Sch. tchr., Chgo. and N.C., 1978-86. Lucille P. Markey Scholar, Miami, Fla., 1989—, Mary Gibbs Jones Scholar Jones Found., Houston, 1973-77. Mem. Am. Assn. Immunologists (Travel award 1989). Office: Scripps Rsch Inst Dept Immunology Imm 8 10666 N Torrey Pines Rd La Jolla CA 92037-1027

HAWES, GRACE MAXCY, archival specialist, writer; b. Cumberland, Wis., Feb. 4, 1926; d. Clarence David and Mabel Hannah (Erickson) Maxcy; student U. Wis., 1944-46; BA, San Jose State U., 1963, MA, 1971: m. John G. Hawes, Aug. 28, 1948 (dec.); children: Elizabeth, John D., Mark, Amy. Library asst. NASA, Langley, Va., 1948-49; archival specialist Hoover Archives, Stanford U., 1976-80, adminstrv. asst., 1980-89; rsch. asst. Hoover Inst., 1989—. Mem. Soc. Am. Archivists, Western Assn. Women Historians, Women in Hist. Research, Calif. Archivists Assn., Inst. Hist. Study. Author: The Marshall Plan for China: Economic Cooperation Administration, 1948-1949, 1977. Home: 410 Sheridan Ave Apt 220 Palo Alto CA 94306-2021 Office: Stanford U Hoover Inst Stanford CA 94304

HAWK, DOUGLAS JAMES, architect; b. Charlotte, N.C., May 15, 1959; s. James Vaugh and Connie (Smail) H. BArch, Calif. Polytech. State U., San Luis Obispo, 1982. Lic. architect Calif. Draftsman Murphy & Bunch Architects, Auburn, Calif., 1982-88; owner, prin. architect Douglas Hawk, Architect, Auburn, 1988—. Office: 414 Auburn-Folsom Rd Auburn CA 95603-3931

HAWKE, RONALD SAMUEL, electrical engineer; b. Oakland, Calif., Mar. 4, 1940; s. Samuel Henry and Marian (Howland) H.; m. Nancy Lee Wirth, May 23, 1975; children: Laura, Gusty, Veronica, Theresa, Monisa. AA, Coll. of San Mateo, 1959; BSEE, U. Calif., Berkeley, 1961. Elec. engr. U. Calif., Livermore, 1961—, program leader; guest scientist Max Planck Inst., Stuttgart, Fed. Republic Germany, 1973-74; cons. Orbex Enterprises, Livermore, 1984—. Contbr. over 50 articles to tech. jours.; patentee in field. Recipient Peter Mark award, 1992. Mem. Am. Phys. Soc., Electromagnetic Launcher Assn. (pres. 1989-91), Internat. Order of Old Fellows. Home: 2369 Westminster Way Livermore CA 94550-1747 Office: U Calif L-153 PO Box 808 Livermore CA 94551-0808

HAWKEN, JANET GRACE, business owner; b. Fairbanks, Nov. 15, 1952; d. Thomas A. Williams and Gloria J. (Carter) Morris; m. Harvey H. Hawken, Oct. 30, 1984; children: Jason J., Daniel W.; stepchildren: Matt, David, Andy, Tom. BBA, U. Wash., 1974. Cert. profl. model. Fitness instr. GiGi's Figure Studio, Burien, Wash., 1967-70; typist, receptionist Kelly Girls, Seattle, 1970-76; sr. supr., beauty cons. Shaklee U.S.A., Inc., Maple Valley, Wash., 1971—; pub. rels. mgr. Olympic Racquet/Health Club, Ballard, 1981-85; owner, mgr. Crystal Creek Garden Weddings, Maple Valley, 1987—; nutritional and fitness cons. various corp. and pvt. clubs, 1985-88. Co-founder, sec. Wash. State Crime Edn. Task Force, Seattle, 1988—. Mem. Toastmasters Internat. (pres. 1984-85, Able Toastmaster 1983, 1st Pl. Speech Contest, 1985), Alpha Delta Epsilon. Republican. Mem. LDS.

HAWKER, VANESSA KAYE, fiscal analyst; b. Albuquerque, June 2, 1967; d. Fred Walter and Gloria Ann (Fox) H. BA, U. N.Mex., 1989, postgrad., 1989—. Financial analyst Albuquerque T-VI, 1987—. Del. Albuquerque Met. Alumnae Panhellenic, v.p., 1991-92, pres., 1992-93; vol. mediator N.M. Center for Dispute Resolution. Mem. Soc. Human Resource Mgrs. Roman Catholic. Office: Albuquerque T-VI 525 Buena Vista SE Albuquerque NM 87106

HAWKES, GLENN ROGERS, psychology educator; b. Preston, Idaho, Apr. 29, 1919; s. William and Rae (Rogers) H.; m. Yvonne Merrill, Dec. 18, 1941; children—Kristen, William Ray, Gregory Merrill, Laura. B.S. in Psychology, Utah State U., 1946, M.S. in Psychology, 1947; Ph.D. in Psychology, Cornell U., 1950. From asst. prof. to prof. child devel. and psychology Iowa State U., Ames, 1950-66, chmn. dept. child devel., 1954-66; prof. human devel., rsch. psychologist U. Calif., Davis, 1966-89, prof. emeritus, 1990—, acad. coord. Hubert Humphrey fellowship program, 1990—, assoc. dean applied econs. and behavioral scis., 1966-83, chmn. dept. applied behavioral scis., 1982-86, chmn. teaching div., 1970-72, prof. behavioral scis. dept. family practice, Sch. Medicine; vis. scholar U. Hawaii, 1972-73, U. London, 1970, 80, 86; bd. dirs. Creative Playthings Inc., 1962-66. Author: (with Pease) Behavior and Development from 5 to 12, 1962; (with Frost) The Disadvantaged Child: Issues and Innovations, 1966, 2d edit., 1970; (with Schultz and Baird) Lifestyles and Consumer Behavior of Older Americans, 1979; (with Nicola and Fish) Young Marrieds: The Dual Career Approach, 1984. Contbr. numerous articles to profl. and sci. jours. Served with AUS, 1941-45. Recipient numerous research grants from pvt. founds. and govtl. bodies; recipient Iowa State U. faculty citation, 1965, Outstanding Service citation Iowa Soc. Crippled Children and adults, 1965, citation Dept. Child Devel., 1980, Coll. Agrl. and Environ. Scis., 1983; named hon. lt. gov. Okla., 1966. Home: 1114 Purdue Dr Davis CA 95616-1736 Office: U Calif Dept Applied Behavioral Scis Internat House 10 College Park Davis CA 95616

HAWKEY, PHILIP A., city manager; b. Lima, Ohio, Sept. 26, 1946; s. George D. and Beatrice A. (Coon) H.; m. Dena Spanos, Oct. 18, 1969; children: George, Aaron, Ann. BA, Baldwin-Wallace Coll., 1968; MA, Ohio State U., 1972; JD, Cleve. State U., 1975. Bar: Ohio, 1976. Adminstrv. asst. City of Cleve., 1972-76; city adminstr. City of Wooster, Ohio, 1976-79; city mgr. City of Kettering, Ohio, 1979-82; dep. city mgr. City of Cin., 1982-86; city mgr. City of Toledo, 1986-90, City of Pasadena, Calif., 1990—. Mem. adv. coun. State and Local Legal Ctr., Washington. Mem. Internat. City Mgmt. Assn. (v.p.). Home: 1136 Wotkyns Dr Pasadena CA 91103-2838 Office: City Hall 100 N Garfield Ave Pasadena CA 91109-7215

HAWKINS, ALMA MAE, dance educator; b. Rolla, Mo., Sept. 11, 1904; d. Alton N. and Lola (Grey) H. BS, U. Mo., 1927; MA, Columbia U., 1932, EdD, 1952. Tchr. high sch. Rolla, 1927-31; tchr. Emporia (Kans.) Stae Tchrs. Coll., 1933-34; tchr. phys. edn. and dance YWCA, Mpls., 1934-38; prof. UCLA, 1953-77, prof. emeritus, 1977—. Author: Modern Dance in Higher Education, 1954, Creating Through Dance, 1964, Dance A Projection for the Future, 1968, Moving from Within A New Method for Dance Making, 1991.

HAWKINS, DANIEL BALLOU, geology, chemistry educator emeritus; b. Dillon, Mont., Jan. 24, 1934; s. William Watson and Catherine Marion (Jones) H.; m. Mildred J. Schmitt, June 20, 1954 (div. July 1973); children: Michael, William, Elizabeth; m. Joan Helm, Nov. 8, 1973; stepchildren: Patricia Dalley, Carol Dalley, James Dalley. BS in Chemistry, Mont. State Coll., 1956, MS in Chemistry, 1957; PhD in Geochemistry, Pa. State U., 1961. Analytical chemist U.S. Geol. Survey, Denver, 1957-58; geochemist U.S. Atomic Energy Commn., Idaho Falls, 1961-67; assoc. prof. geology U. Alaska, Fairbanks, 1967-71, prof. geology and chemistry, 1985-90, prof. geology and chemistry emeritus, 1990—; head. dept. geology U. Alaska, Fairbanks, 1972-76, acting dir. grad. studies, 1985; head minerals lab. Alaska div. Geol. Surveys, Fairbanks, 1979. Contbr. articles to profl. jours. Mem. Internat. Com. on Nat. Zeolites (bd. dirs. 1976—), Internat. Zeolite Assn. (bd. dirs. 1977-83), Phi Kappa Phi, Sigma Xi. Home: PO Box 80167 Fairbanks AK 99708-0167 Office: U Alaska Dept Geology and Geophysics Fairbanks AK 99775

HAWKINS, DAVID RAMON, psychiatrist, writer, researcher; b. Milw., June 3, 1927; s. Ramon Nelson and Alice-Mary (McCutcheon) H.; children: Lynn Ashley, Barbara Catherine. BS, Marquette U., 1950; MD, Med. Coll. Wis., Milw., 1953; PhD, Columbia Pacific U., 1993. Med. dir. North Nassau Mental Health Ctr., Manhasset, N.Y., 1956-80; dir. rsch. Brunswick Hosp., L.I., N.Y., 1968-79; pres. Acad. Orthomolecular Psychiatry, N.Y.C., 1970-80; dir. Inst. Spiritual Rsch., Sedona, Ariz., 1979-88, The Rsch. Inst., Sedona, 1988—; pres. Attractor Rsch., Sedona, 1989—; bd. dirs. Huxley Inst. Biosocial Rsch., N.Y.C., 1970-80; pres. Seorp-Gard Co., Sedona, 1989—; guest lectr. U. Notre Dame, Harvard U., U. W.Va., U. Mich., 1970-88; guest on TV news and interview shows including McNeal-Lehrer, Barbara Walters, Today, 1972-76; cons. U.S. Navy, Dept. Health Edn. Welfare, Congress. Author: Force vs. Power, 1993, (with Linus Pauling) Orthomolecular Psychiatry, 1973; contbr. articles to profl. jours. With U.S. Navy, 1945-46, PTO. Rsch. grantee N.Y. State Dept. Mental Hygiene, annually, N.Y. State Legis., 1967-87; recipient Mosby Book award, 1953. Mem. AMA, APA, Ariz. Med. Soc., Ariz. Psychiat. Soc., Country Western Dance Club of Sedona (pres.), Elks, Alpha Omega Alpha. Office: Rsch Inst SR2 Box 817 Sedona AZ 86336

HAWKINS, DEBRA LYNN, software development administrator; b. L.A., Dec. 29, 1949; d. Sam and Justine (Mlynar) Wysowski; m. Robert James Hawkins, Oct. 19, 1979 (div. Dec. 1988); children: Ian W., Jeffrey S. Grad., high sch., Whittier, Calif., 1968. Cert. masonry contractor, Calif. Sr. customer svc. rep. Delta Airlines, Santa Ana, Calif., 1982-88; owner R.J. Constrn., Walnut, Calif., 1988-91; v.p. Unique Devels., Pahrump, Nev., 1991—. Roman Catholic. Home: 2300 N Jason Pahrump NV 89041 Office: Unique Developments PO Box 6000 # 140 Pahrump NV 89041

HAWKINS, JAMES VICTOR, state official; b. Coeur d'Alene, Idaho, Sept. 28, 1936; s. William Stark and Agnes M. (Ramstedt) H.; m. Gail Ruth Guernsey, June 19, 1959; children—John William, Nancy Clare. B.S., U. Idaho, 1959; postgrad., Am. Savs. and Loan Inst., 1960-67, Pacific Coast Banking Sch., 1970—. Mgmt. trainee Gen. Telephone Co. of N.W., Coeur d'Alene, 1959-60; asst. mgr. First Fed. Savs. & Loan Assn., Coeur d'Alene, 1960-67; v.p., gen. mgr. Idaho S.W. Devel. Co., Boise, 1967-68; v.p., trust officer First Security Bank of Idaho, N.A., Boise, 1968-72; pres. Statewide Stores Inc., Boise, 1972-82; spl. projects adminstr. Lucky Stores Inc., 1982-84; pvt. practice fin. cons. Boise, 1984-87; dir. dept. commerce State of Idaho, Boise, 1987—. Bd. dirs., chmn. adv. bd. Coll. Bus. and Econs. U. Idaho; bd. dirs. Idaho Coun. Econ. Edn., Boise United Fund, Boise Art Assn.; pres., mem. U. Idaho Found.; exec. bd. Coun. State Community Affairs Agys.; bd. dirs., pres. Nat. Assn. State Devel. Agys.; mem. Indsl. Devel. Rsch. Coun.; mem. exec. com. Coun. State and Community Devel. Agys.; bd. dirs. Idaho Total Quality Inst.; chmn. Idaho R.R. Adv. Coun. Named Outstanding Young Idahoan Idaho Jr. C. of C., 1967; Eagle Scout. Mem. Am. Inst. Banking, Boise C. of C., U. Idaho Alumni Assn. (mem. exec. bd.), Elks, Coeur d'Aleue, Rotary, Crane Creek Country Club, Arid Club (Boise), Phi Gamma Delta. Episcopalian. Home: 4937 N Hollow Ln Boise ID 83702-1739

HAWKINS, KEVIN FRANCE, public relations executive; b. Detroit, July 21, 1959; s. Harold Edward and Mary Eva (Lewis) H. BA, U. Miami, 1981; M of Pub. Rels., U. So. Calif., 1985. Pub. rels. coord. Multi-Entertainment, Inc., North Miami Beach, Fla., 1980-81; account exec. Dorr Pub. Rels., Toluca Lake, Calif., 1982-83; account supr. James Agy. Pub. Rels. and Advt., L.A., 1983-85; v.p. pub. rels. Great Western Fin. Corp., Beverly Hills, Calif., 1985—. Co-author: ARM White Paper: A Guide to ARMS, 1990; contbr. chpt. to book, numerous articles to newspapers and mags.; creator consumer videos on real estate. Pub. rels. cons. L.I.F.E. Hunger Relief Orgn., L.A., 1986-91; vol. pub. rels. D.A.R.E., Seattle and Miami, 1991—; pub. rels. advisor A.R.C.S., L.A., 1990. Named to Outstanding Young Men of Am., 1989. Mem. Nat. Assn. Real Estate Editors (2d v.p. 1991—, 1st place award 1988, 89), Publicity Club L.A., Pub. Rels. Soc. Am. (Prism award 1988, 89). Republican. Methodist. Home: 8533 Forsythe St Sunland CA 91040 Office: Great Western Fin Corp 8484 Wilshire Blvd Beverly Hills CA 90211

HAWKINS, LONNY W., software engineer; b. Pocatello, Idaho, Apr. 2, 1956; s. Talmadge Porter and Virginia Ruth (Kazmierski) H.; m. Linda Fay Larson, June 16, 1990; 1 child, Linnia Rose. BS, U. Idaho, 1983. Quality engr. Varian Assocs., Palo Alto, Calif., 1982-83; software engr. Encoder Products Co., Sandpoint, Idaho, 1983-89, product mgr., 1989—. Contbr. articles to profl. jours. Office: Encoder Products Co 1601B Dover Rd Sandpoint ID 83864

HAWKINS, ROBERT LEE, health facility administrator; b. Denver, Feb. 18, 1938; s. Isom and Bessie M. (Hugley) H.; A.A., Pueblo Jr. Coll., 1958; B.S., So. Colo. State Coll., 1965; M.S.W., U. Denver, 1967; m. Ann Sharon Hoy, Apr. 28, 1973; children—Robert, Jeanne, Julia, Rose. Psychiat. technician Colo. State Hosp., Pueblo, 1956-58, 1962-63, occupational therapist asst., 1964-65, clin. adminstr. psychiat. team, 1969-75, dir. community services, 1975-92, asst. supt. clin. svcs., 1992—, supr. vol. services, 1975—, mem. budget com., 1975—; asst. supt. clin. svcs., 1992—; counselor (part-time) Family Service Agy., Pueblo, 1968-69, exec. dir., 1969-70; mem. faculty U. So. Colo., 1968-75; partner Human Resource Devel., Inc., 1970-75. Mem. Pueblo Positive Action Com., 1970; chmn. adv. bd. Pueblo Sangre de Cristo Day Care Center, 1969-72; chmn. Gov.'s So. Area Adv. Council of Employment Service, 1975-76, chmn. Pueblo's City CSC, 1976-77, Pueblo Community Corrections, 1985-87, Pueblo Civil Service Commn., 1988—; commr. Pueblo Housing Authority, 1986—, Colo. Commn. Higher Edn., 1987—; mem. gov's. adv. com. Mental Health Standards, 1981—; mem. Colo. Juvenile Parole Bd., 1977; bd. dirs. Pueblo United Fund, 1969-74, pres., 1973; bd. dirs. Pueblo Community Orgn., 1974-76, Spanish Peaks Mental Health Center, 1976—, Neighborhood Health Center, 1977-79, Pueblo Community Corrections, 1983—, Pueblo Legal Svcs., 1983—. Bd. dirs. Posada Shelter for Homeless, 1990—, Boys Girls club, 1991—. With U.S. Army 1958-62. Mem. Nat. Assn. Social Workers (nominating com. 1973-76), ACLU (dir. Pueblo chpt. 1980—), NAACP, Broadway Theatre Guild. Democrat. Methodist. Club: Kiwanis. Home: 520 Gaylord Ave Pueblo CO 81004-1312 Office: Colo State Hosp 1600 W 24th St Pueblo CO 81003-1499

HAWKS, KATHERINE A., special education educator; b. Vancouver, Wash., May 25, 1943; d. Kenneth Charles and Mary Elizabeth (Rumbaugh) H. BS in Edn., U. Idaho, 1965; MA, Mich. State U., 1970. Cert. in spl. edn. and phys. edn., Wash., Tex., South Africa. Phys. edn. tchr. Schoenbar Jr. High Sch., Ketchikan, Alaska, 1965-66, Wapato (Wash.) Jr. High Sch., 1966-68, Port Wheel Jr. High Sch. (with Dept. Def.), Okinawa, Japan, 1968-69, Queenstown (South Africa) Girls' High Sch., 1971, Roosevelt Elem. Sch., Granger, Wash., 1972-73; adapted phys. edn. Browns for Cerebral Palsied, Pinetown, South Africa, 1971-74, Bill Buchanan/Aged, Durban, South Africa, 1985; lectr. phys. edn., adapted phys. edn. U. Durban, Westville, South Africa, 1975-76; adapted phys. edn. tchr., supr. Denton (Tex.) State Sch., 1977-80; spl. edn. tchr. Congress Jr. High Sch., Denton, Tex., 1980-81, Fulton Sch. Deaf, Durban, South Africa, 1986-87, Evergreen Elem. Sch., Tacoma, Wash., 1988—; adapted phys. edn. cons. Child Guidance Clinic, U. Durban, 1975-76, Tex. Women's U., Denton, Tex., 1977; speaker Nat. Conf. on Perceptual Motor Phys. Edn. for Cerebral Palsied Children, South Africa. 1974, Nat. Conf. for Health, Phys. Edn. and Recreation, Phys. Edn. for Cerebral Palsied Children, South Africa, 1975. Coached Spl. Olympics, Denton, Tex., 1977-81; mem. Amnesty Internat., 1973-76; treas. Rainbow Landowners Cooperative, Denton, 1983. Mem. NEA, Wash. Edn. Assn. Democrat. Office: Clover Park Sch Dist 10020 Gravelly Lake Dr SW Tacoma WA 98499

HAWLEY, JOHN WILLIAM, environmental geologist; b. Evansville, Ind., Oct. 7, 1932; s. William McKinley and Evelyn (Caldwell) H.; m. Diane Rose Bandyk, Aug. 30, 1961; children: Glynis Jo Hawley Albrecht, Charles Philip, George Michael. BA, Hanover Coll., Ind., 1954; PhD, U. Ill., 1962. Lic. geologist. Project leader U.S. Soil Conservation Svc., Las Cruces, N.Mex., 1962-71, Lubbock, Tex., 1971-74; rsch. geologist U.S. Soil Conservation Svc., USDA Regional Ctr., Portland, Oreg., 1975-77; sr. geologist N.Mex. Bur. Mines & Mineral Resources, N.Mex. Tech., Socorro, 1977—; adj. grad. faculty mem. N.Mex. Tech., 1981—; collaborator Earth and Environ Sci. div. Los Alamos Nat. Lab., 1985—; office mgr. N.Mex. Tech., Office of State Geologist, N.Mex. Bur. Mines & Mineral Resources, Albuquerque, 1991—. Editor: Guidebook to the Rio Grande Rift, 1978; co-author: Guidebook to the Desert Soil - Geomorphology Project, 1981, Geology and Ground Water Resources, Dona Ana County, New Mexico, 1971. Troop com. chair Boy Scouts Am., Socorro, 1978-79, cubmaster, 1979-80. With DE, U.S. Army, 1954-56. NSF fellow, 1960-62; N.Mex. Eminent scholar N.Mex. Commn. on Higher Edn., 1989. Fellow AAAS (nominating com. Geol.-Geog. sect. 1993-95, Cert. of Merit 1987), Geol. Soc. Am. (Kirk Bryan award 1983), N.Mex. Geol. Soc. (pres. 1969, hon. mem. 1982). Republican. Unitarian-Universalist. Home: 1000 Vassar Dr NE Albuquerque NM 87106 Office: N Mex Bur of Mines 2808 Central Ave SE Albuquerque NM 87106

HAWLEY, NANCI ELIZABETH, public relations and communications professional; b. Detroit, Mar. 18, 1942; d. Arthur Theodore and Elizabeth Agnes (Fylling) Smisek; m. Joseph Michael Hawley, Aug. 28, 1958; children: Michael, Ronald, Patrick (dec.), Julie Anne. Pres. Tempo 21 Nursing Svcs., Inc., Covina, Calif., 1973-75; v.p. Profl. Nurses Bur., Inc., L.A., 1975-83; cons. Hawley & Assocs., Covina, 1983-87; exec. v.p. Glendora (Calif.) C. of C., 1984-85; dir. membership West Covina (Calif.) C. of C., 1985-87; exec. dir. San Dimas (Calif.) C. of C., 1987-88; mgr. pub. rels. Soc. for Advancement of Material and Process Engrs., Covina, 1988-92; small bus. rep. South Coast Air Quality Mgmt. Dist., 1992—. V.p. Sangabriel valley chpt. Women in Mgmt. Recipient Youth Motivation award Foothill Edn. Com., Glendora, 1987. Mem. NAFE, Pub. Rels. Soc. Am., Soc. Nat. Assn. Publs., Am. Soc. Assn. Execs., Nat. Assn. Membership Dirs., Profl. Communicators Assn. So. Calif., Kiwanis Internat. (sec. 1989-90, pres. West Covina 1990-91, Kiwanian of Yr. 1989). Office: South Coast Air Quality Mgmt Dist 21865 E Copley Dr Diamond Bar CA 91765

HAWLEY, PHILIP METSCHAN, retail executive, consultant; b. Portland, Oreg., July 29, 1925; s. Willard P. and Dorothy (Metschan) H.; m. Mary Catherine Follen, May 31, 1947; children: Diane (Mrs. Robert Bruce Johnson), Willard, Philip M. Jr., John, Victor, Edward, Erin, George. BS, U. Calif., Berkeley, 1946; grad. advanced mgmt. program, Harvard U., 1967.

With Carter Hawley Hale Stores, Inc., L.A., 1958-93, pres., 1972-83, chief exec. officer, 1977-93, chmn., 1983-93; bd. dirs. Atlantic Richfield Co., BankAm. Corp., AT&T, Johnson & Johnson, Weyerhaeuser Co. Trustee Calif. Inst. Tech., U. Notre Dame; mem. vis. com. UCLA Grad. Sch. Mgmt., Bus. Coun., Bus. Roundtable, Conf. Bd.; chmn. L.A. Energy Conservation Com. 1973-74. Decorated hon. comdr. Order Brit. Empire, knight comdr. Star Solidarity Republic Italy; recipient Award of Merit L.A. Jr. C. of C., 1974, Coro Pub. Affairs award, 1978, Medallion award Coll. William and Mary, 1983, Award of Excellence Sch. Bus. Adminstrn. U. So. Calif., 1987, Bus. Statesman of Yr. award Harvard Bus. Sch., 1989, 15th ann. Whitney M. Young Jr. award L.S. Urban League, 1988; named Calif. Industrialist of Yr. Calif. Mus. Sci. and Industry, 1975. Mem. Calif. Retailers Assn. (chmn. 1993—), Phi Beta Kappa, Beta Alpha Psi, Beta Gamma Sigma. Clubs: Calif., L.A. Country; Bohemian Pacific-Union (San Francisco); Newport Harbor Yacht (Newport Beach, Calif.); Multnomah (Portland); Links (N.Y.C.). Office: 444 S Flower St Ste 2280 Los Angeles CA 90071-2901

HAWLEY, ROBERT CROSS, lawyer; b. Douglas, Wyo., Aug. 7, 1920; s. Robert Daniel and Elsie Corienne (Cross) H.; m. Mary Elizabeth Hawley McClellan, Mar. 3, 1944; children—Robert Cross, Mary Virginia, Laurie McClellan. BA with honors, U. Colo., 1943; LLB, Harvard U., 1949, JD, 1989. Bar: Wyo. 1950, Colo. 1950, U.S. Dist. Ct. Colo. 1950, U.S. Dist. Ct. Wyo. 1954, U.S. Ct. Appeals (10th cir.) 1955, Tex. 1960, U.S. Ct. Appeals (5th cir.) 1960, U.S. Supreme Ct. 1960, U.S. Dist. Ct. (so. dist.) Tex. 1961, U.S. Ct. Appeals (D.C. cir.) 1961, U.S. Ct. Appeals (8th cir.) 1979, U.S. Ct. Appeals (11th cir.) 1981, U.S. Dist. Ct. (we. dist.) Tex. 1987. Assoc. Bannister Weller & Friedrich, Denver, 1949-50; sr. atty. Continental Oil Co., Denver, 1952-58, counsel, Houston, 1959-62; ptnr., v.p. Ireland, Stapleton & Pryor, Denver, 1962-81; ptnr. Dechert Price & Rhoads, Denver, 1981-83, Hawley & VanderWerf, Denver, 1983—; pres. Highland Minerals, Denver; bd. dirs. Bank of Denver; speaker oil and gas insts. Contbr. articles to Oil & Gas Bd. dirs. Am. Cancer Soc., Denver, 1967-87, treas., 1981-82; chmn. U. Colo. Devel. Found., 1960-61; bd. dirs. Rocky Mountain Arthritis Found., 1987—; mem. adv. bd. ARC, 1988—; chmn. Retarded Children Campaign, 1963; dir. 1st annual East Seal Clinic, 1966-68; bd. dirs. Craig Hosp., 1964-68. Lt. col. U.S. Army, Korean War. Recipient Alumni Recognition award U. Colo., Boulder, 1958, Meritorious Service award Monticello Coll., Godfrey, Ill., 1967, Humanitarian award Arthritis Fedn., 1992, Honored Lawyer award Law Club, 1993; Sigma Alpha Epsilon scholar, 1941-43. Mem. Denver Assn. Oil and Gas Title Lawyers (pres. 1983-84), Denver Petroleum Club (pres. 1978-79), Harvard Law Sch. Assn. Colo. (pres. 1980-81), Associated Alumni U. Colo. (pres. and bd. dirs. 1956-57), Law Club, Denver (pres. 1958-59), ABA, Colo. Bar Assn., Denver Bar Assn., Tex. Bar Assn., Wyo. Bar Assn., Fed. Energy Bar Assn. (legal and lands com.), Interstate Oil Compact Comn., Harvard Alumni Assn., Rocky Mountain Oil and Gas Assn., Rocky Mountain Petroleum Pioneers (pres. 1991-92), Wyo. Pioneer Assn., Chevaliers du Tastevin, Denver Country Club, Petroleum Club, Gyro Club, Univ. Club Denver, Colo. Arlberg Club, Mile High Club, U. Colo. Alumni Club (pres. 1993, Living Legend award "C" Club). Republican. Episcopalian. Author, co-author: Landman's Handbook, Law of Federal Oil and Gas Leases, Problems of Surface Damages, Federal Oil and Gas Leases—The Sole Party in Interest Debacle. Office: Hawley & VanderWerf 730 17th St Ste 730 Denver CO 80202-3516 Home: 4401 E 3d Ave Denver CO 80220

HAWN MYERS, PATRICIA LYNN, school nurse; b. Montreal, Que., Can., June 9, 1968; d. Norman William and LaVaughn Eileen (Wise) Hawn; m. Brian J. Myers, May 27, 1989; 1 child, Nathanael Gregory. BSN magna cum laude, Grand Canyon U., 1990. RN, Ariz. Staff nurse Cactus Children's Clinic, Glendale, Ariz., 1989-91; sch. nurse Peoria (Ariz.) Unified Sch. Dist., 1991—. Mem. Classroom Tchrs. Assn., Sch. Nurse Orgn. Ariz., Peoria Edn. Assn., Alpha Chi, Sigma Theta Tau. Republican. Home: 6844 W Caron Dr Peoria AZ 85345 Office: Pioneer Elem Sch 6315 W Port Au Prince St Glendale AZ 85306

HAWORTH, LARRY EUGENE, software company executive; b. Noblesville, Ind., Oct. 10, 1946; s. Marvin Eugene and Martha Ellen (Lawrence) H. MS in Indsl. Mgmt., Purdue U., 1970; B of Indsl. Engring., GM Inst., 1971. Indsl. engr. Sears Roebuck and Co., Chgo., 1971-73; asst. treas., various positions Wickes Cos., San Diego, 1973-82; pres. Wind Power Systems Corp., San Diego, 1982-85; gen. mgr. Metrocast (British Telecom Co.), San Diego, 1985-89; pres., owner SalePoint Systems Corp., San Diego, 1989—; bd. dirs. Madrid Condominium Assn., San Diego; part-time lectr. San Diego State U., 1974-76. Recipient Superior Performance award IBM, 1988-91; named # 19 on Inc. 500 for 1991, Inc. Mag., 1992. Mem. Owosso C. of C. (chmn. indsl. div. 1978), United Way of Shenandoah, Iowa (pres. 1980-81), Alpha Tau Iota. Office: SalePoint Systems Corp 6197 Cornerstone Ct E # 103 San Diego CA 92121

HAWS, ROBERT DUNN, airline executive; b. Stamford, Conn., Oct. 30, 1932; s. Henry Ernst and Gabriella (Dunn) H.; m. Frances Bailey Pryor, Mar. 12, 1955; children: Robin Haws Kaimikaua, George Allderdice, Cynthia Haws Hart. BA, Yale U., 1954. Acct. exec. Hill and Knowlton, Inc., N.Y.C., 1958-62; v.p. Sea Life, Inc., Honolulu, 1962-69; pres., CEO Royal Hawaiian Airways, Inc., Honolulu, 1969-86; v.p. Hawaiian Airlines, Inc., Honolulu, 1987-90; v.p. ops. Scenic Airlines Inc., Las Vegas, 1990-92. Lt. (j.g.) USNR, 1954-58. Mem. Kaneohe Yacht Club (commodore 1983-84), Storm Trysail Club. Home: 8161 Round Hills Cir Las Vegas NV 89113

HAWTHORNE, DOUGLAS BRUCE, journalist, author; b. Mineola, N.Y., Aug. 12, 1948; s. Frank Douglas and Jean Rae (Spencer) H.; m. Marjorie Jo Rheinscheld, Dec. 21, 1979. AA in Journalism, Pima Community Coll., 1981; BA in Broadcast Communications, U. Ariz., 1983, MA in Journalism, 1985. City editor, reporter The Tombstone (Ariz.) Epitaph, 1985; copy editor, reporter Territorial Pubs., Inc., Tucson, 1986—; freelance writer Tucson, 1987—. Author: Men and Women of Space, 1992. With USNR, 1965-69. Fellow Brit. Interplanetary Soc.; mem. Nat. Space Soc., Aerospace Ambs., Aviation Space Edn. Assn., U. Ariz. Alumni Assn., Golden Key Nat. Hon. Soc., Phi Theta Kappa, Phi Kappa Phi. Republican. Home and Office: 5946 N Camino Del Conde Tucson AZ 85718-4312

HAWTHORNE, MARION FREDERICK, chemistry educator; b. Ft. Scott, Kans., Aug. 24, 1928; s. Fred Elmer and Colleen (Webb) H.; m. Beverly Dawn Rempe, Oct. 30, 1951 (div. 1976); children: Cynthia Lee, Candace Lee; m. Diana Baker Razzaia, Aug. 14, 1977. B.A., Pomona Coll., 1949; Ph.D. (AEC fellow), U. Calif. at Los Angeles, 1953; D.Sc. (hon.), Pomona Coll., 1974; PhD (hon.), Uppsala U., 1992. Research asso. Iowa State Coll., 1953-54; research chemist Rohm & Haas Co., Huntsville, Ala., 1954-56; group leader Rohm & Haas Co., 1956-60; lab. head Rohm & Haas Co., Phila., 1961; vis. lectr. Harvard, 1960, Queen Mary Coll., U. London, 1963; vis. prof. Harvard U., 1968; prof. chemistry U. Calif. at Riverside, 1962-68, U. Calif. at Los Angeles, 1968—; vis. prof. U. Tex., Austin, 1974; mem. sci. adv. bd. USAF, 1980-86, NRC Bd. Army Sci. and Tech., 1986-90; disting. vis. prof. Ohio State U., 1990; mem. dir.'s external adv. bd. div. M, Los Alamos (N.Mex.) Nat. Lab., 1991—. Editor: Inorganic Chemistry, 1969—; Editorial bd.: Progress in Solid State Chemistry, 1971—, Inorganic Syntheses, 1966—, Organometallics in Chemical Synthesis, 1969—, Synthesis in Inorganic and Metalorganic Chemistry, 1970—. Recipient Chancelors Research award, 1968, Herbert Newby McCoy award, 1972, Am. Chem. Soc. award in Inorganic Chemistry, 1973, Tolman Medal award, 1986, Nebr. sect. Am. Chem. Soc. award, 1979, Disting. Service in the Advancement of Inorganic Chemistry award Am. Chem. Soc., 1988, Disting. Achievements in Boron Sci. award, 1988, Bailar medal, 1991; sr. scientist Alexander von Humboldt Found., Inst. Inorganic Chemistry U. Munich, 1990—; Sloan Found. fellow, 1963-65, Japan Soc. Promotion Sci. fellow, 1986; named Col. Confederate Air Force, 1984. Fellow AAAS; mem. U.S. Nat. Acad. Scis., Am. Acad. Arts and Scis., Aircraft Owners and Pilots Assn., Sigma Xi, Alpha Chi Sigma, Sigma Nu. Club: Cosmos. Home: 3415 Green Vista Dr Encino CA 91436-4011

HAWTHORNE, NAN LOUISE, writer, editor, community services agency official; b. Hawthorne, Nev., Jan. 3, 1952; d. Louis Frederick Haas and Merle Forrest (Ohlhausen) Ritter; m. James Denver Tedford, Dec. 20, 1981. BS, No. Mich. U., 1981. Freelance writer, editor, indexer, Seattle, 1974—; coord. Circles of Exch., Seattle, 1984—; mgr. vols. Community Svcs. for Blind and Partially Sighted, Seattle, 1989—; host, co-host talk show Evergreen Radio Reading Svc., Seattle, 1989—. author: Loving the Goddess Within, 1991; co-indexer: Women's Book of Healing, 1988; indexer, editor: WomanSpirit Index, 1989; editor Information Guide for Blind Persons in Washington, 1990; contbg. writer Hestia Mag., 1993—. Mem. Sagewoman Adv. coun., 1988-90, Wash. State Coun. on Volunteerism and Citizen Svcs., 1992—; trainer United Way of King County Vol. Ctr., 1992—; bd. dirs., dir. vols. Ageras of King County, 1992—. Mem. Assn. Vol. Adminstrn. Office: Circles of Exch 9594 1st Ave NE Ste 333 Seattle WA 98115-2012

HAY, ANDREW MACKENZIE, merchant banking and commodities company executive; b. London, Apr. 9, 1928; came to U.S., 1954, naturalized, 1959; s. Ewen Mackenzie and Bertine (Buxton) H.; MA in Econs., St. John's Coll., Cambridge U., 1950; m. Catherine Newman, July 30, 1977. Commodities trader, London and Ceylon, 1950-53; v.p. Calvert Vavasseur & Co. Inc., N.Y.C., 1954-61, pres., 1962-78, pres. Calvert-Peat Inc., N.Y.C., 1978—, Andrew M. Hay, Inc.; chmn. Barretto Peat Inc., N.Y.C., 1974-88; Pacific NW cons. Am. Assn. Exporters and Importers, 1982—; radio and TV appearances. Mem. adv. com. on tech. innovation Nat. Acad. Scis., 1978; bd. dirs. Winston Churchill Found.; treas., trustee World Affairs Coun. Oreg., 1986—; apptd. Her Majesty's hon. Brit. consul., 1987; dean Oreg. Counsular Corps, 1991. Capt. Brit. Army. Decorated comdr. Order Brit. Empire. Mem. Am. Importer Assn. (pres. 1977-79), Pacific N.W. Internat. Trade Assn. (exec. dir. 1986—), Brit. Am. C. of C. (pres. 1966-68), Philippine Am. C. of C. (pres. 1977-79), St. George's Soc. (bd. dir.), St. Andrew's Soc. (bd. dir.), Recess Club, Downtown Assn. (N.Y.C.), U. Club, Arlington Club. Episcopalian. Author: A Century of Coconuts, 1972. Home and Office: 3515 SW Council Crest Dr Portland OR 97201-1403

HAY, JOEL W., health economist, educator; b. Boston, Nov. 22, 1952. BA, Amherst Coll., 1974; MPhil, Yale U., 1976, PhD, 1980. Asst. rsch. prof. U. So. Calif., 1978-80; asst. prof. U. Conn., Farmington, 1980-84, Storrs, 1981-84; sr. rsch. fellow Hoover Inst. Stanford U., Calif., 1985-92; assoc. prof. and chmn. U. So. Calif., 1992—; sr. policy analyst, Project HOPE, Millwood, Va., 1983-85; vis. scholar, Chinese U., Hong Kong, 1990-91; health care advisor, Hungarian Parliament, Budapest, 1991-92; tech. cons., Health Care Financing Adminstrn., Balt., 1992; health care task force mem., Am. Heart Assn., Washington, 1992. Author: (book) Health Care in Hong Kong, 1992; contbr. numerous articles to profl. jours. Office: U So Calif Dept Pharm Econs 1985 Zonal Ave Los Angeles CA 90033

HAY, JOHN LEONARD, lawyer; b. Lawrence, Mass., Oct. 6, 1940; s. Charles Cable and Henrietta Dudley (Wise) H.; 1 child, Ian. AB with distinction, Stanford U., 1961; JD, U. Colo., 1964. Bar: Colo. 1964, Ariz. 1965, D.C. 1971. Assoc. Lewis and Roca, Phoenix, 1964-69, ptnr., 1969-82; ptnr. Fannin, Terry & Hay, Phoenix, 1982-87, Allen, Kimerer & LaVelle, Phoenix, 1987—; bd. dirs. Ariz. Life and Disability Ins. Guaranty Fund. Mem. Dem. Precinct Com., 1966-78, Ariz. State Dem. Com., 1968-78; chmn. Dem. Legis. Dist., 1971-74; mem. Maricopa County Dem. Cen. Com., 1971-74; bd. dirs. ACLU, 1973-78; bd. dirs. Community Legal Svcs., 1983-89, pres., 1987-88. Mem. ABA, Maricopa County Bar Assn. (bd. dirs. 1972-85), Ariz. State Bar Assn., Assn. Life Ins. Counsel, Ariz. Licensors and Franchisors Assn. (bd. dirs. 1985—, pres. 1988-89), Ariz. Civil Liberties Union (bd. dirs. 1967-84, pres. 1973-77, Disting. Citizen award 1979). Home: 201 E Hayward Ave Phoenix AZ 85020-4037 Office: Allen Kimerer LaVelle 2715 N 3d St Phoenix AZ 85004

HAY, JOHN WOODS, JR., banker; b. Rock Springs, Wyo., Apr. 23, 1905; s. John Woods and Mary Ann (Blair) H.; A.B., U. Mich., 1927; m. Frances B. Smith, Dec. 28, 1948; children—Helen Mary, John Woods III, Keith Norbert, Joseph Garrett. Pres., dir. Rock Springs Nat. Bank, 1947—, Rock Springs Grazing Assn., 1939—, Blair & Hay Land & Livestock Co., Rock Springs, 1949—. Trustee, v.p. William H. and Carrie Gottsche Found. Mem. Sigma Alpha Epsilon. Republican. Episcopalian. Clubs: Masons, Shriners, Jesters, Rotary. Home: 502 B St Rock Springs WY 82901-6213 Office: 333 Broadway St Rock Springs WY 82901-6242

HAY, RICHARD LAURENCE, theater scenic designer; b. Wichita, Kans., May 28, 1929; s. Laurence Charles and Ruth Mary (Rhoades) H. BA, Stanford U., 1952, MA, 1955. Tech. dir., designer Oreg. Shakespeare Festival, Ashland, 1953-55, prin. scenic designer, 1970—; instr. drama Stanford U., Palo Alto, Calif., 1957-62, assoc. prof., 1965-69; assoc. artistic dir. for design Denver Ctr. Theater Co., 1984-91; freelance scenic designer Guthrie Theater, Mpls., Am. Conservatory Theater, San Francisco, Mo. Repertory Theater, Kansas City, Mark Taper Forum, Los Angeles, Old Globe Theater, San Diego, Berkekey (Calif.) Repertory Theater, others; theatre designer: Source and Space Theatres, Denver Ctr. Theatre Co., New Old Globe Theatre and Festival Stage, Old Globe Theatre, San Diego, Intiman Theatre, Seattle, Black Swan, Angus Bowmer Theatre, Elizabethan Stage, Oreg. Shakespeare Festival. Author: (with others) A Space for Magic: Stage Settings by Richard L. Hay, 1979; exhibitor Prague Quadriennial, 1987, U.S. Inst. Theatre Tech. Biennial Scenography Expn., 1984, 88, 90. Recipient Critics award Hollywood (Calif.) Drama-Logue, 1982, 85, 86, 89, Gov's. award for the Arts State of Oreg., 1989; Fulbright grantee, 1955. Mem. United Scenic Artists, U.S. Inst. Theatre Tech., League Hist. Am. Theaters. Democrat. Congregationalist. Home: 707 Liberty St Ashland OR 97520 Office: Oreg Shakespeare Festival PO Box 158 Ashland OR 97520-0158

HAY, WILLIAM CHARLES, professional hockey team executive; b. Saskatoon, Sask., Can., Dec. 9, 1935; s. Charles and Florence (Miller) H.; m. Nancy Ann Woodman, Aug. 24, 1957; children: Pam, Penny, Donald. B.S. in Geology, Colo. Coll., 1958. Profl. hockey player Chgo. Black Hawks, 1958-67; mgr. Sedco Drilling Co., Calgary, Alta., 1967-70, gen. mgr., from 1970; gen. mgr. Hi-Tower Drilling Co., Calgary, Alta., from 1970; formerly pres., chief operating officer Hockey Can.; pres. Calgary Flames Hockey Club, NHL, 1991—. Office: Calgary Flames, PO Box 1540 Sta M, Calgary, AB Canada T2P 3B9*

HAY, WILLIAM WINN, natural history and geology educator; b. Dallas, Oct. 12, 1934; s. Stephen J. and Avella (Winn) H. B.S., So. Meth. U., 1955; postgrad. U. Zurich, Switzerland, 1955-56; M.S., U. Ill., 1958; Ph.D., Stanford U., 1960. Mem. faculty dept. geology U. Ill., Urbana, 1960-73; mem. faculty Rosenstiel Sch. Marine and Atmospheric Sci., U. Miami., Fla., 1968-82; chmn. div. marine geology, 1974-76, interim dean, 1976-77, dean, 1977-80; pres. Joint Oceanographic Instns., Inc., Washington, 1979-82; dir. U. Colo. Mus., Boulder, 1982-87; prof. geol. scis., fellow Coop. Inst. for Rsch. in Environ. Sci., U. Colo., Boulder, 1983—; prof. GEOMAR, Christian-Albrechts U., Kiel, Germany, 1990—; mem. adv. panel sedimentary and geochem. processes Joint Oceanographic Instns. for Deep Earth Sampling, 1989-92; mem. sci. adv. com. Ocean Drilling Program, 1979-83; mem. exec. com. div. ocean sci. NSF, 1982-85. Editor: Studies in Paleo-Oceanography, 1974. Univ. Coll. London fellow, 1972—; recipient Francis P. Shepard medal Soc. Econ. Paleontologists and Mineralogists, 1981, Best Paper award Gulf Coast sect., 1970; Alexander von Humboldt prize, 1991-92. Fellow Geol. Soc. Am., Geol. Soc. (London), Coop. Inst. Rsch. in Environ. Scis.; mem. Am. Assn. Petroleum Geologists. Office: U Colorado Dept Geological Scis Campus Box 250 Boulder CO 80309 also: Geomar, Wischhofstr 1-3, D24148 Kiel Germany

HAYASHI, ALAN T., community college educator; b. Honolulu, Mar. 10, 1954; s. Harold T. and Sally J. (Nakamoto) H. BSc, AB, U. Calif., Riverside, 1975; postgrad., Ohio State U., 1983-84. Cert. secondary tchr., single subject teaching and community coll. instr.'s credentials, Calif. Tchr., coach boys track and girls basektball Jurupa Jr. High Sch., Jurupa Unified Sch. Dist., Riverside, Calif., 1976-79; tchr. math., coach acad. decathlon and knowledge bowl Channel Islands High Sch., Oxnard (Calif.) Union High Sch. Dist., 1979-91; instr. Oxnard Coll., Ventura County C.C. Dist., 1989—; casino dealer Harrah's Hotel & Casino, Stateline, Nev., 1980-81; teaching asst., instr. Ohio State U., Columbus, 1983-84; mathematician Pacific Missile Test Ctr., U.S. Dept. Def., Point Mugu, Calif., 1990; textbook reviewer Calif. Dept. Edn., 1981, 89; statistician Channel Islands High Sch. football team, 1980—. Mem. choir 1st Presbyn. Ch., Oxnard, 1979-83; newsletter editor Internat. Rels. Coun. Riverside, 1975-77. Recipient Chpt. Outstanding Tchr. award Calif. Mini-Corp., 1991-92, Tandy Tech. scholar nat. semi-finalist, 1990-91; named Tchr. of Yr., Calif. Scholastic Fedn. Chpt., 1989, Channel Islands High Sch. Tchr. of Yr., 1983; NSF fellow, 1981, 82. Mem. NEA, Math. Assn. Am., Nat. Coun. Tchrs. Math., U. Calif.-Riverside Alumni Assn., Calif. Fedn. Tchrs., Ventura County Math. Coun. Office: Oxnard Coll 4000 S Rose Ave Oxnard CA 93033-6699

HAYASHI, GRANT SHIUICHI, computer scientist, consultant; b. Honolulu, Mar. 8, 1957; s. Shizuya and Tomeno (Imamura) H.; m. Sharon Merri Zane, Nov. 19, 1982. BS, U. Hawaii, 1981. Programmer Trident Data Systems, L.A., 1981-85, chief scientist, 1987—; cons. Hayashi and Assoc.s, L.A., 1985-87. Mem. Assn. Computing Machinery. Office: Trident Data Systems 5933 Century Blvd # 700 Los Angeles CA 90045

HAYDEN, HENRY THOMAS, military officer, foreign service officer, writer, educator; b. Louisville, July 14, 1941; s. Quentin Joseph and Anna Evelyn (Buckner) H.; m. Sheila Cockayne, Nov. 4, 1982; 1 child, Alessandra Jayne. MBA, Pepperdine U., 1975; MA in Internat. Rels., U. So. Calif., London, U.K., 1983. Lic. pilot, parachutist, scuba diver. With fgn. svc., 1965-67, Vietnam, 1967-69; enlisted USMC, 1975, served in Saudi Arabia/Kuwait, 1990-91, advanced through grades to lt. col., 1992; adj. prof. U. Md., Iwakuni, Japan, 1985-86, Webster U., Camp Pendleton, Calif., 1988-89, Nat. U., San Diego, 1989-90, USAF Spl. Ops. Sch., Hurlburt Field, Fla., 1992—. Author: Shadow War: Special Operations and Low Intensity Conflict, 1992; contbr. articles to profl. jours. Mem. Am. Def. Preparations Assn., U.S. Naval Inst., Marine Corps Assn. Republican. Roman Catholic. Home: PO Box 432 Pahrump NV 89041

HAYDEN, RON L., library director; b. San Pedro, Calif., Dec. 24, 1948; s. Larnie Alphonsis and Myrtie Louise (Pilcher) H.; m. Marilee Ann Brubaker, May 30, 1971 (dec. June 1978); m. Susan Ann Huffman, Jan. 1, 1982. AA, Golden West Coll., 1969; BA, Long Beach State U., 1972; MLS, Fullerton U., 1974. Reference sr. libr. Huntington Beach (Calif.) Libr., 1975-79, pub. svc. libr., 1979-86, libr. dir., 1986—; liason Libr. Patrons Assn., Huntington Beach, 1986—. Author: Collection Development Library Journal, 1979. Recipient Award of Excellence Calif. S.W. Recreation Park Conf., 1990. Mem. ALA (Libr. in Media award, Best of Show award 1990), Calif. Libr. Assn., Friends Libr., So. Calif. Tennis Assn., Rotary (bd. dirs., vocat. chmn. 1988—). Home: 215 Elmira Ave Huntington Beach CA 92648-4920 Office: Huntington Beach Libr 7111 Talbert Ave Huntington Beach CA 92648-1296*

HAYDEN, TOM, state legislator, author; b. Royal Oak, Mich., Dec. 11, 1939; children: Troy, Vanessa. Grad., U. Mich. Co-founder Students for a Democratic Soc., 1961, pres., 1962, 63; staff Student Non-violent Coordinating Com., 1963; co-founder Econ. Research and Action Project, 1964; leader Newark Community Union Project, 1964-67; founder Indochina Peace Campaign; candidate for U.S. Senate in Calif. Democratic Primary, 1976; founder, chmn. Calif. Campaign for Econ. Democracy, 1977—; chmn. SolarCal Council, State of Calif., 1978-82; mem. Calif. State Assembly, 1982-92, Calif. State Senate, 1992—. Author: Port Huron Statement, 1962, Rebellion in Newark, 1967, Rebellion and Repression, 1969, Trial, 1970, The Love of Possession is a Disease with Them, 1972, The American Future, 1980, Reunion: A Memoir, 1988; co-author: The Other Side, 1967, Reunion, 1988; contbr.: articles to periodicals including Washington Post, Los Angeles Times, N.Y. Times. Office: California State Senate 10951 W Pico Blvd 202 Los Angeles CA 90064

HAYDEN, TONY MARTIN, protective services official; b. Compton, Calif., Jan. 4, 1957; s. Joseph Edward and Winifred Louise Hayden; m. Michelle Mercier, Feb. 6, 1988; children: Tawanna, Tony Jr. AA, Compton Community Coll., 1978, cert. of achievement, 1984; cert. of completion, South Bay Police Res. Acad., 1990. Sch. police officer Compton Unified Sch. Dist. Police Dept., 1978-84; sch. police officer Pomona (Calif.) Unified Sch. Dist. Police Dept., 1984-86, sch. police sgt., 1986-89, acting chief, 1989-90, chief of police, 1990—; cons. Stevenson Security Svcs., Chino Hills, Calif., 1989—. Mem. Calif. Community Coll. Police Chiefs, Peace Officer Assn. L.A. County, Am. Fedn. Police, Calif. Gang Investigators Assn., Calif. Narcotic Officers Assn., Calif. Sch. Peace Officers Assn., Peace Officer Rsch. Assn. Calif., Nat. Assn. Chiefs of Police, Nat. Orgn. Black Law Enforcement Execs. Home: 159 S Wilmington Ave Ste H Compton CA 90220 Office: Pomona Sch Dist Police Dept 800 S Garey Ave Pomona CA 91766

HAYDU, CLAIRE R., medical-legal, quality assurance and mental health consultant; b. N.J., May 13, 1954; d. Thomas and Dorothy (Balucha) H.; m. Cruz D. Maturino, Apr. 17, 1982; children: Joaquin, Julian, Natalya. BSN, Trenton State Coll., 1976. RN, Calif., N.J. Nurse cons., educator, and recruiter in quality assurance State of Calif.; ind. med. legal cons. Haydu & Assocs., Brea, Calif. Home: 443 S Walnut Ave Brea CA 92621-5346

HAYES, BRENT CHARLES, artist; b. Toledo, May 13, 1971; s. Arthur Ray and C. Irene (Smith) Owen. Student, U. Hawaii, 1989. Nat. sports artist Hayes Artistic Impressions, Kahului, Hawaii, 1987—. Exhibited in group shows at Ctr. Art Galleries, Westin Hotel, Maui, Hawaii, 1989, Sunset Art Galleries, Maui, 1990, Royal Art Galleries, Maui, 1991, Mamone Gallery, Union Square, 1992, Fisherman's Wharf, San Francisco, 1992, Addi Galleries, Harrah's, Lake Tahoe, Pebble Beach Lodge, 1992, Hyatt Regency, Maui, 1992, Interncontinental Hotel, Maui, Royal Art Gallery, Maui, 1992, Thomas Charles Gallery, Caesar's Forum, Las Vegas, 1993. Mem. Lahaina Art Soc. Office: Hayes Artistic Impressions 1736 E Charleston # 303 Las Vegas NV 89104

HAYES, BYRON JACKSON, JR., lawyer; b. L.A., July 9, 1934; s. Byron Jackson and Caroline Violet (Scott) H.; m. DeAnne Saliba, June 30, 1962; children: Kenneth Byron, Patricia DeAnne. Student, Pomona Coll., 1952-56; B.A. magna cum laude, Harvard U., LL.B. cum laude, 1959. Bar: Calif. 1960, U.S. Supreme Ct. 1963. Assoc., McCutchen, Black, Verleger & Shea, L.A., 1960-68, ptnr., 1968-89; ptnr. Baker & Hostetler, 1990—. Trustee L.A. Ch. Extension Soc. United Meth. Ch., 1967-77, pres., 1974-77, chancellor ann. conf. Pacific and S.W., 1979-86; Dir., pres. Pacific and S.W. United Meth. Found., 1978-84. Named layperson of yr. Pacific and S.W. Ann. Conf., United Meth. Ch., 1981; recipient Bishop's award United Meth. Ch., 1992. Mem. ABA, Am. Coll. Mortgage Attys. (regent 1984-90, 91—, pres. elect 1992-93), Calif. Bar Assn., Assn. Real Estate Attys., L.A. County Bar Assn. (chmn. real property sect. 1982-83), Toluca Lake Property Owners Assn. (sec. 1990—), Pomona Coll. Alumni Assn. (pres. 1984-85), Lakeside Golf Club (Toluca Lake, Calif.), Univ. Club (L.A.). Office: Baker & Hostetler 600 Wilshire Blvd Fl 9 Los Angeles CA 90017-3212

HAYES, CLAUDE QUINTEN CHRISTOPHER, research scientist; b. N.Y.C., Nov. 15, 1945; s. Claude and Celestine (Stanley) H. BA in Chemistry and Geol. Sci., Columbia U., 1971, postgrad., 1972-73; postgrad., N.Y. Law Sch., 1973-75; JD, Western State Law Sch., 1978. Cert. community coll. tchr. earth scis., phys. sci., law, Calif. Tech. writer Burroughs Corp., San Diego, 1978-79; instr. phys. scis. Nat. U., San Diego, 1980-81; instr. bus. law, earth scis. Miramar Coll., 1978-82; sr. systems analyst Gen. Dynamics Convair, 1979-80, advanced mfg. technologist, sr. engr., 1980-81; pvt. practice sci. and tech. cons. Calif., 1979—; instr. phys. sci., geography, bus. law San Diego Community Coll. Dist., 1976-82, 85-90; U.S. Dept. Def. contractor Def. Nuclear Agy., Strategic Def. Initiative Agy., USAF, Def. Advance Rsch. Projects Agy., 1986—, U.S. Army, 1991—; adj. prof. phys. chemistry San Diego State U., 1986-87; adj. prof. internat. bus. and computer sci. U. Redlands (Calif.) Grad. Sch., 1986-88; def. research contractor to Maxwell Labs., Naval Oceans Systems Ctr.; tech. cons. Pizza Hut Inc., Carts of Colo. Contbr. articles to profl. jours.; patentee in field. Mem. Am. Chem. Soc., N.Y. Acad. Sci., Am. Inst. Aero. and Astronautics. Home and office: 3737 3d Ave #308 San Diego CA 92103

HAYES, ERNEST M., podiatrist; b. New Orleans, Jan. 21, 1946; s. Ernest M. and Emma Hayes; m. Bonnie Ruth Beigle, Oct. 16, 1970. B.A., Calif. State U., Sacramento, 1969; B.S., Calif. Coll. Podiatric Medicine, San Francisco, 1971, D.P.M., 1973. Resident in surg. podiatry Beach Community Hosp., Buena Park, Calif., 1973-74, dir. residency program, 1974-75; practice podiatry, Anaheim, Calif., 1974-80, Yreka, Calif., 1980—; sr. clin. instr. So. Calif. Podiatric Med. Center, Los Angeles, 1975-78; vice chmn. podiatry dept. Good Samaritain Hosp., Anaheim, Calif., 1978-79; mem. med. staff Mercey Med. Ctr., Mt. Shasta, Calif. Bd. dirs. Little Bogus Ranches Home Owners Assn., 1981-83, pres., 1983-84. Fellow Nat. Coll. Foot Surgeons; mem. Am. Assn. Podiatric Physicians and Surgeons, Am. Coun. Cert. Podiatric Physicians and Surgeons (cert.), Kiwanis. Baptist. Home: PO Box 958 Yreka CA 96097-0958 Office: 1009 S Main St Yreka CA 96097-3324

HAYES, GORDON GLENN, civil engineer; b. Galveston, Tex., Jan. 2, 1936; s. Jack Lewis and Eunice Karen (Victery) H. BS in Physics, Tex. A&M U., 1969. Registered profl. engr., Alaska, Tex. Rsch. technician Shell Devel. Co., Houston, 1962-68; rsch. assoc. Tex. Trans. Inst., College Station, 1969-71, asst. rsch. physicist, 1971-74, assoc. rsch. physicist, 1974-80; traffic safety specialist Alaska Dept. Transp. & Pub. Facilities, Juneau, 1981-83, state traffic engr., 1983-85, traffic safety standards engr., 1985-90; owner Alaska Roadsafe Cons., Juneau, 1990-92, Hayes Highway Consulting, Carson City, Nev., 1992—. Author of numerous pubs. in the hwy. safety field; producer of numerous documentary films in the hwy. safety field. Petty officer USN, 1953-57. Mem. ASCE, Nat. Com. on Uniform Traffic Control Devices (signs tech. com.) Inst. Transp. Engrs., Mensa. Home: 665 Bluerock Rd Gardnerville NV 89410

HAYES, GREGORY MICHAEL, secondary education educator, coach; b. Queens, N.Y., Dec. 28, 1954; s. John Aloysius and Patricia Marie (Kennedy) H.; m. Jan MArie McGlothlin, Aug. 4, 1990; 1 child, Megan Kimberly. BA, UCLA, 1977, MEd, 1980. Asst. basketball coach UCLA, 1977-81; basketball coach Athletes In Action U.S.A., 1977-85; substitute tchr. Placentia (Calif.) Unified Sch. Dist., 1981-82; nat. shooting instr. Shot Doctor, Inc., various locations, 1986—; tchr., coach Canyon High Sch., Canyon Country, Calif., 1982—; coach boys varsity basketball, girls varsity softball, Canyon High Sch., Canyon Country, Calif., coach Bernie Milligan All Star Game, 1991—. Advisor Staying Alive, Canyon Country, 1988—; mem. adv. bd. Macker Tournament, Santa Clarita, 1990—; vol. worker L.A. Olympic Sports Festival, 1991; mem. Grace Bapt. Ch. Orch. Named Coach of Yr. Golden League, 1987. Mem. Calif. Tchrs. Assn., Fellowship Christian Athletes, So. Calif. Interscholastic Basketball Coaches Assn. (immediate past pres.), Canyon Theatre Guild (actor, worker 1988—), UCLA Alumni Assn. Office: Canyon High Sch 19300 Nadal St Santa Clarita CA 91351-1298

HAYES, JEANNE, information services executive; b. Chgo., Oct. 22, 1942; d. Raymond John and Margaret (Burke) H.; m. Thomas T. Olkowski, Aug. 5, 1967; 1 child, Colin F. Hayes. BA, Marquette U., 1965; postgrad., U. Mich., 1965-67. Tchr. Southfield (Mich.) Pub. Schs., 1965-67, Clarksville (Ind.) Pub. Schs., 1967-69, Jefferson County Schs., Lakewood, Colo., 1969-70; v.p. product devel. Curriculum Info. Ctr., Denver, 1972-78; gen. mgr. Denver office Market Data Retrieval, Shelton, Conn., 1979-80; pres. Quality Education Data, Inc., Denver, 1981—. Mem. Denver Athletic Club, Jr. Symphony Guild. Democrat. Home: 9 Albion St Denver CO 80220 Office: Quality Edn Data Inc 1600 Broadway Denver CO 80202

HAYES, MARILYN JO, communications educator, writer; b. El Paso, Aug. 11, 1934; d. Herbert and Glenn Francis (Aaron) Evans; m. William Lamar Hayes, Mar. 1, 1979; children: Terri Jo Rucker, Kim Laraine Cameron. BA in Communs. and Bus., Loretto Hts. Coll., Denver, 1982; MA in Human Rels., Webster U., St. Louis, 1983; PhD Edn., U. Tex., 1993. Asst. pers. mgr. Ranger Ins., Houston, 1965-68; social worker Harrison County Headstart, Biloxi, Miss., 1968-70; liaison officer Community Rels. Svc., USDJ, Atlanta, 1969-70; dir. info svcs. Marine Mil. Acad., Harlingen, Tex., 1980; tech. writer Craig Hosp., Englewood, Colo., 1981-82; asst. dir. admissions Loretto Hts. Coll., Univ. Without Walls, Denver, 1982-83; grad. program coord. Webster U., Ft. Jackson, Columbia, S.C., 1983-84; asst. prof. St. Edward's U., New Coll., Austin, Tex., 1984-91; assoc. rep. Taylor Pub. Co., Las Vegas, 1991—; co-owner, writer Lamar Hayes Advt. and Design, Las Vegas, 1980—; instr. Park Coll., Austin, 1985-90; staff writer Ireland Mktg., Denver, 1980-81. Contbr. articles to profl. jours. Mem. Mental Health-Mental Retardation Bd., Austin, 1975-78; mem. Citizens' Adv. Coun. to Mayor, Jackson, Miss., 1970, others. Named Outstanding Tchr. of Yr., St. Edward's U., 1990, other awards. Mem. World Communs. Assn., Phi Kappa Phi, Kappa Delta Pi.

HAYES, SHIRLEY ANN, special education educator; b. Lindsay, Calif., June 15, 1955; d. Clarence Berwin and Betty Francis (Matthews) Fox; m. Darren Wayne Hayes, Feb. 11, 1990; children: Norman Tony Whited Jr., Samuel Hayes, James Hayes. AA, Porterville Jr. Coll., Calif., 1982; BA, Calif. State U., Bakersfield, 1984; specialist cert., Fresno (Calif.) Pacific Coll., 1985. Teaching asst. Porterville Developmental Ctr., 1977-84, tchr. of severly handicapped, 1984—. Sec. PTA, West Pubnam Sch., Porterville, 1992—. Mem. Ednl. Svc. Profl. Orgn. (chairperson 1990), Calif. State Employees Assn. (sec., job steward 1990—). Home: PO Box 8624 Porterville CA 93258 Office: Porterville Devel Ctr PO Box 2000 Porterville CA 93258

HAYES, WILLIAM LAMAR, graphic designer; b. Albuquerque, May 9, 1935; s. Jack Guernsey and Betty (Gentry) H.; m. Marilyn Jo Evans, Mar. 1, 1979; 1 child, Sean Thomas. AB, San Jose (Calif.) Coll., 1957; MFA, U. Tex., 1989. Art asst. dir. BBDO Advt., Dallas, 1962-65; assoc. art dir. Henderson Advt., Greenville, S.C., 1965-68; art dir. Howard Swink Advt., Marion, Ohio, 1969-75; photographer Marine Mil. Acad., Harlingen, Tex., 1976-79; graphic designer Lamar Hayes Graphic Design, Austin, Columbia, Denver, 1980-89; assoc. prof. art No. Ariz. U., Flagstaff, 1990-91; pub. rep. Taylor Pub. Co., Las Vegas, 1991—; instr. Community Coll. So. Nev., Las Vegas, 1993—. Capt. USAR, 1957-71.

HAYMOND, J. BRENT, chemical company executive, state legislator; b. Provo, Utah, Sept. 18, 1936; s. Edwin James and Helen (Harmer) H.; m. Marilyn Woodward, June 20,1959 (div. 1971); children: Michael, Diane, David, Mary Ann; m. Janis S. Haymond, Dec. 20, 1975; 1 child, Eric James; stepchildren: Cathy, Pam, David; foster children: Debbie, Dawnette. BS, Brigham Young U., 1960; MBA, Northwestern U., 1962. Mgr. mktg. IBM, Seattle, 1962-70; mgr. data ctr. EDP, Vancouver, B.C., 1971-72; v.p. McKesson Drug Co., San Francisco, 1973-75; v.p., gen. mgr. Martin Wolfe, San Diego, 1976-78; pres. Weidmar Comm., Provo, 1979-82, Intex Corp., Springville, Utah, 1983-89, Cantex Corp., Salt Lake City, 1990—; mem. Utah State Ho. Reps., 1991—. Mayor City of Springville, Utah, 1982-86; bd. dirs. Utah Mcpl. Assn. Power, Sandy, 1984-93, Springville World Folkfest, 1985-93; pres. bd. dirs. Springville Mus. Art, 1988-93. Mem. C. of C., Kiwanis. Republican. Mem. LDS Ch. Home: 164 W 200 S Springville UT 84663

HAYNE, HARRIET ANN, state legislator, rancher; b. Puget Island, Washington, Sept. 11, 1922; d. Albert Greger and Angeline Marie (Benjaminsen) Danielsen; m. Jack McVicar Hayne, Apr. 3, 1946; children: Mary Joan, John David, Alice Sue, Nancy Ann. Student, Heads Bus. Coll., San Francisco, 1941-42, Wash. State U., 1946-47. Rep. Mont. Legis. Assembly, 1979-80, 84—. Precinct, then state committeewoman, vice-chmn., active various campaigns Mont. Reps., Pondera County, 1964. Served as staff sgt. USMC, 1943-45. Mem. Am. Nat. Cattlewomen, Nat. Order Women Legislators, Am. Farm Bur., Am. Legion (aux.), Women Marines Assn., Nat. Fedn. Rep. Women. Lutheran.

HAYNER, HERMAN HENRY, lawyer; b. Fairfield, Wash., Sept. 25, 1916; s. Charles H. and Lillie (Reifenberger) H.; m. Jeannette Hafner, Oct. 24, 1942; children: Stephen, James K., Judith A. BA, Wash. State U., 1938; JD with honors, U. Oreg., 1946. Bar: Wash. 1946, Oreg. 1946, U.S. Dist. Ct. Wash. 1947, U.S. Ct. Appeals (9th cir.) 1947. Asst. U.S. atty. U.S. Dept. Justice, Portland, Oreg., 1946-47; atty. City of Walla Walla, Wash., 1949-53; ptnr. Minnick-Hayner, Walla Walla, 1949-93; mem. Wash. State exec. bd. U.S. West, Seattle, 1988—. Regent Wash. State U., Pullman, 1965-78; dir. YMCA, Walla Walla, 1956-67. Lt. col. Infantry, 1942-46. Decorated Bronze Star medal and four Battle Stars; recipient Disting. Svc. award Jr. C. of C., 1951, Wash. State U. Alumni award, 1988. Fellow ABA, Am. Coll. Trust & Estate Counsel; mem. Wash. State Bar Assn., Walla Walla County Bar Assn. (pres. 1954-55), Walla Walla C. of C. (merit award 1977, dir. 1973-88), Rotary (pres. 1956-57), Walla Walla Country Club (pres. 1956-57). Republican. Lutheran. Home: 1508 Ironwood Dr Walla Walla WA 99362-9254 Office: Minnick-Hayner PO Box 1757 Walla Walla WA 99362-0348

HAYNER, JEANNETTE CLARE, state legislator; b. Jan. 22, 1919; m. Herman H. Hayner, 1942; children: Stephen A., James K., Judith A. BA, U. Oreg., 1940, JD, 1942, PhD (hon), Whitman Coll., 1992. Atty. Bonneville Power Co., Portland, Oreg., 1943-47; mem. Wash. Ho. of Reps., 1972-76, Wash. Senate from Dist. 16, 1977-92, minority leader, 1979-80, 83-86, majority leader, 1981-82, 87-92; dist. chmn. White House Conf. on Children and Youth, 1970; dir. Standard Ins. Co. Portland, 1974-90. Mem. Walla Walla Dist. 140 Sch. Bd., 1956-63, chmn. bd., 1959-61; mem. adv. bd. Walla Walla Youth and Family Svc. Assn., 1968-72; active YWCA, 1968-72; chmn. Walla Walla County Mental Health Bd., 1970-72; former mem. Wash. Coun. on Crime and Delinquency, Nuclear Energy Coun., Bonneville Power Regional Adv. Coun., State Wash. Organized Crime Intelligence Adv. Bd.; mem. Coun. State Govts. Governing Bd.; former asst. whip Republican Caucus. Mem. Wash. State Centennial Commn. Recipient Merit award Walla Walla C. of C., Pres's. award Pacific Luth. Univ., 1982, Pioneer award U. Oreg., 1988, Lifetime Achievement award Wash. State Ind. Colls., 1991, Washington Inst. Columbia, 1991; named Legislator of Yr. Nat. Rep. Legislators' Assn., 1986, Chairman's award, 1989, Wash. Young Rep. Citizen of Yr., 1987, Legislator of Yr. Nat. Rep. Legislators Assn., 1989. Mem. Oreg. Bar Assn., Delta Kappa Gamma (hon.), Kappa Kappa Gamma. Lutheran. Home: PO Box 454 Walla Walla WA 99362

HAYNES, CALEB VANCE, JR., geology and archaeology educator; b. Spokane, Wash., Feb. 29, 1928; m. Elizabeth Hamilton, Jan. 11, 1954; 1 child, Elizabeth Anne.. Student, Johns Hopkins U., 1947-49; degree in geol. engring., Colo. Sch. Mines, 1956; PhD, U. Ariz., 1965. Mining geology cons., 1958-60; sr. project engr. Am. Inst. Research, Golden, Colo., 1956-60; sr. engr. Martin Co., Denver, 1960-62; geologist Nev. State Mus. Tule Springs Expedition, 1962-63; research asst. U. Ariz., Tucson, 1963-64, asst. prof. geology, 1965-68, prof. geoscis., anthropology, 1974—, Regents prof., 1991—; assoc. prof. So. Meth. U., Dallas, 1968-73, prof., 1973-74. Served with USAF, 1951-54. Guggenheim fellow 1980-81, Smithsonian sr. post doctoral fellow, 1987 ; grantee NSF, Nat. Geographic Soc., others. Fellow AAAS, Geol. Soc. Am. (Archeol. Geology award 1984); mem. NAS, Am. Quaternary Assn. (pres. 1976-78), Soc. Am. Archaeology (Fryxell award 1978), Sigma Xi. Office: U Ariz Dept Anthropology Tucson AZ 85721

HAYNES, WILLIAM ARTHUR, computer software engineer; b. Peoria, Ill., Mar. 5, 1947; s. William Clarence and Dorothy Louise (Starr) H.; m. Marcia Ellen McShane, June 20, 1976 (div. 1981); 1 child, Benjamin; m. Gloria Marie Sonnier, June 4, 1988. Student, U. Ill., 1965-67. Cert. electronic technician, Oreg. Engring. aide City of Peoria, 1968; supervising technician Good Vibes Sound Co., Champaign, Ill., 1972-74; engr. Vetter Fairing Co., Rantoul, Ill., 1975; owner W.A. Haynes Enterprises, Eugene, Oreg., 1976-78; tech. asst. Lane County Head Start, Eugene, 1979-80; svc. mgr. Ace Electronics, Eugene, 1981-84; electronic technician U. Oreg., Eugene, 1985-87; programmer Paul Mace Software Inc., Ashland, Oreg., 1987-90; sr. software engr. Momentum Devel. Inc., Ashland, 1990—. Author computer programs. Mem. Internat. Assn. Computer Investigative Specialists (mem. DOS processing cert. com. 1992—). Office: Momentum Devel Inc 240 E Hersey St # 11 Ashland OR 97520

HAYS, HOWARD H. (TIM HAYS), editor, publisher; b. Chgo., June 2, 1917; s. Howard H. and Margaret (Mauger) H.; m. Helen Cunningham, May 27, 1947 (div. Dec. 1988); children: William, Thomas; m. Susie Gudermuth, Sept. 1992. B.A., Stanford U., 1939; LL.B., Harvard U., 1942. Bar: Calif. 1946. Spl. agt. FBI, 1942-45; reporter San Bernardino (Calif.) Sun, 1945-46; asst. editor Riverside (Calif.) Daily Press, 1946-49, editor, 1949-65, editor, co-pub., 1965-83, editor, pub., chief exec. officer, 1983-88, editor, chmn., chief exec. officer, 1989-92, chmn. bd., 1992—; Mem. Pulitzer Prize Bd., 1976-86; mem. AP Bd., 1980-89, vice chmn. 1988-89. Bd. visitors John S. Knight Fellowhsips for Profl. Journalists at STanford U., 1986—, Sch. Journalism U. So. Calif., 1991-93. Recipient Dist. award Calif. Jr. C. of C., 1951; named Pub. of Year Calif. Press Assn., 1968. Mem. Calif. Bar Assn., Am. Soc. Newspaper Editors (dir. 1969-76, pres. 1974-75), Stanford Alumni Assn. (dir. 1970-74), Internat. Press Inst. (chmn. Am. com. 1971-72, mem. exec. bd. 1977-83), Am. Press Inst. (bd. dirs. 1973—, chmn. 1978-83), New Directions for News (bd. dirs. 1987-92), Nature Conservancy Calif. (bd. dirs. 1982-86), Kappa Tau Alpha. Office: Press-Enterprise 3512 14th St Riverside CA 92501-3878

HAYS, JOHN BRUCE, molecular biologist, biotechnology educator; b. Springfield, Ill., June 21, 1937; s. Loren Eastman and Mary Elizabeth (Russell) H.; m. Judith Gail Gumm, Sept. 1, 1961; children: Elinor, Stephen, Laura. Student, Deep Springs Coll., 1954-56; BS, U. N.Mex., 1960; PhD, U. Calif. San Diego, La Jolla, 1968. Postdoctoral rsch. fellow dept. biology Johns Hopkins U., Balt., 1969-72; from asst. prof. chemistry to prof. U. Md., Balt., 1972-87; prof. agrl. chemistry Oreg. State U., Corvallis, 1987—, dept. head, 1987-90; ad hoc mem. various study sects. NIH, Bethesda, Md., 1979-85; co-dir. Bioresource Rsch. undergrad. program; rsch. in resistance of plants, frogs, bacteria to UV light. Contbr. articles to profl. jours. Mem. Ch. Good Samaritan, Corvallis, 1987—. Lt. (jg) USN, 1963-66. Recipient faculty rsch. fellowship Am. Cancer Soc., 1981-85; grantee NIH, Am. Cancer Soc., USDA. Mem. Am. Soc. Biochemists and Molecular Biologists, Am. Soc. for Microbiology, Genetics Soc. Am. Episcopalian. Home: 6920 NW Cardinal Dr Corvallis OR 97330-9527 Office: Oreg State U Dept Agrl Chemistry Corvallis OR 97331

HAYS, PATRICK GREGORY, health care executive; b. Kansas City, Kans., Sept. 9, 1942; s. Vance Samuel and Mary Ellen (Crabbe) H.; m. Penelope Ann Hall, July 3, 1976; children: Julia L., Jennifer M. Meyer, Emily J. Meyer, Drew D. Meyer. B.S. in Bus. Adminstrn, U. Tulsa, 1964; M.H.A., U. Minn., 1971; postgrad., U. Mich. Grad. Sch. Bus. Adminstrn., 1977. Mfg. analyst N.Am. Rockwell Corp., Tulsa, 1964-66; asst. adminstr., adminstr. for ops. Henry Ford Hosp., Detroit, 1971-75; exec. v.p. Meth. Med. Ctr. of Ill., Peoria, 1975-77; adminstr. Kaiser Found. Hosp., Los Angeles, 1977-80; pres. Sutter Community Hosps. and Sutter Health, Sacramento, 1980—; trustee Cen. Area Teaching Hosps., Inc., L.A., 1977-79; clin. preceptor U. Minn.; clin. prof. grad. program in health svcs. adminstrn. U. So. Calif.; mem. exec. com. St. Jude Children's Rsch. Hosp. Midwest Affilate, Peoria, 1975-77; past chmn. adv. bd. grad. program in health svcs. adminstrn. U. So. Calif., Sacramento; bd.dirs. Hosp.Coun. No.Calif., 1986, The Healthcare Forum, 1987-89; bd. dirs., exec. com. Found. Health Inc., HMO, 1987-90, U.S. Bank Calif.; chmn. bd. Option Care Inc., 1986-90, Calif. Assn. Hosp. and Health Systems, 1991, Regent, Am. Coll. Healthcare Exec.; mem. adv. bd. the Governance Inst.; exec. Legent Am. Coll. Healthcare, 1989-95, founding pres. Sacramento Regional Purchasing Coun.; bd. dir. U.S. Bank of Calif., mem. civil justice reform act com., U.S. Dist. Ct., Ea. Calif. Contbr. articles on health services to publs. Mem. Pvt. Industry Coun., Sacramento Employment and Tng. Agy., 1984-85; bd. dirs. Consumer Credit Counselors Sacramento, 1984-87, Sacramento Area United Way, campaign chair, 1992-93; bd. dirs. Comstock Club, 1986-89; pres. Sacramento Camellia Festival Assn., 1987-88; chmn. Whitney M. Young Jr. Award, 1987; pres. Sacramento Regional Purchasing Coun., 1989-90. With U.S. Army, 1966-69. Decorated Army Commendation medal, cert. of appreciation Dept. Army; recipient Commendation resolution Calif. Senate, 1979, Whitney M. Young award Sacramento Urban League, 1983; named Chief Exec. Officer of Yr., Soc. for Healthcare Planning and Mktg. of Am. Hosp. Assn., 1991; USPHS fellow, 1969-71, Calif. Assn. Hosps. and Health Systems Walker fellow, 1989. Fellow Am. Coll. Healthcare Execs. (Calif. regent); mem. Calif. Assn. Hosps. and Health Systems (chmn. bd. dirs. 1991), Sacramento-Sierra Hosp. Assn. (exec. com., bd. dirs., pres. 1984), Royal Soc. Health (U.K.), Am. Mgmt. Assn. (President's Club), Hollywood C. of C. (revitalization com. 1979), Sacramento C. of C. (bd. dirs. 1982-85, 87-88), Vol. Hosps. Pacific (bd. dirs.), Rotary (bd. dirs. Sacramento 1987-89), Kappa Sigma, chmn. Calif. Assn. of Hosp. & Health Systems, 1991—. Presbyterian. Office: Sutter Health 2800 L St PO Box 160727 Sacramento CA 95816

HAYS, RICK F., public relations executive; b. St. Joseph, Mo., Oct. 27, 1952; s. William Andy and Alma LaVonne (Temple) H.; m. Jane Reid, Aug. 16, 1975; children: Matthew Patrick, Benjamin Reid, Lara Elizabeth. BS in Journalism, U. No. Colo., 1973. Editor Town & Country News, Greeley, Colo., 1973-74; pub. relations rep. Mountain Bell, Greeley, 1974-77; pub. relations supr. Mountain Bell, Tucson, 1977-79; pub. relations mgr. Mountain Bell, Denver, 1979-83; dir. regional pub. rels. U S WEST Communications, Boise, Idaho, 1984—; chair Idaho Bus. Week, 1991; mem. mktg. com. Boise Area Econ. Devel. Coun., 1987—; chair edn. com. IACI, 1993—. Coach Capital Youth Soccer, 1986-93; mem. troop com. Boy Scuts Am., 1989—; mem. strategic com. Idaho Edn. Project, 1990-91; mem. exec. bd. Ada County United Way, Boise, 1991—; mem. adv. bd. Boise Sch. Ptnrs. in Edn., 1991—; active Schs. 2000, 1992—; mem. ecumenical commn. Cath. Ch., 1990—. Recipient award Idaho Assn. Supervision and Curriculum Devel., 1990. Mem. Pub. Rels. Soc. Am. (bd. dirs. 1988—), Jaycees (bd. dirs. Greeley, Colo. 1976-77). Roman Catholic. Office: US WEST Comm 999 Main 11th Fl Boise ID 83702

HAYS, RONALD JACKSON, naval officer; b. Urania, La., Aug. 19, 1928; s. George Henry and Fannie Elizabeth (McCartney) H.; m. Jane M. Hughes, Jan. 29, 1951; children: Dennis, Michael, Jacquelyn. Student, Northwestern U., 1945-46; B.S., U.S. Naval Acad., 1950. Commd. ensign U.S. Navy, 1950, advanced through grades to adm., 1983; destroyer officer Atlantic Fleet, 1950-51; attack pilot Pacific Fleet, 1953-56; exptl. test pilot Patuxent River, Md., 1956-59; exec. officer Attack Squadron 106, 1961-63; tng. officer Carrier Air Wing 4, 1963-65; comdr. All Weather Attack Squadron, Atlantic Fleet, 1965-67; air warfare officer 7th Fleet Staff, 1967-68; tactical aircraft plans officer Office Chief Naval Ops., 1969-71; comdg. officer Naval Sta., Roosevelt Roads, P.R., 1971-72; dir. Navy Planning and Programming, 1973-74; comdr. Carrier Group 4, Norfolk, Va., 1974-75; dir. Office of Program Appraisal, Sec. of Navy, Washington, 1975-78; dep. and chief staff, comdr. in chief U.S. Atlantic Fleet, Norfolk, Va., 1978-80; comdr. in chief U.S. Naval Force Europe, London, 1980-83; vice chief naval ops. Dept. Navy, Washington, 1983-85; comdr. in chief U.S. Pacific Command, Camp H.M. Smith, Hawaii, 1985-88; pres., chief exec. officer Pacific Internat. Ctr. for High Tech. Rsch., Honolulu, Hawaii, 1988-92. Decorated D.S.M. with 3 gold stars, Silver Star with 2 gold stars, D.F.C. with silver star and gold star, Legion of Merit, Bronze Star with combat V, Air Medal with numeral 14 and gold numeral 3, Navy Commendation medal with gold star and combat V. Baptist. Home: 869 Kamoi Pl Honolulu HI 96825-1318 Office: Pacific International Ctr 711 Kapiolani Blvd Ste 200 Honolulu HI 96813-5249

HAYS, TODD ALAN, marketing, public relations executive; b. Milw., Apr. 30, 1961; s. Elbert and Pearl (Kemnitz) H. Student, Pasadena City Coll., 1979-80, Art Ctr. Coll. of Design, Pasadena, 1980-82; BA, U. So. Calif., 1984. Writer, publicist, art dir. Lorne Green Prodns., L.A., 1982-83; prodn. coord. McCall/Coppola, L.A., 1983-84; art dir./prodn. supr. Light Fx/ Richard Taylor, L.A., 1983-85; casting asst. Marsha Kleinman & Assocs., L.A., 1985-87; dir. mktg. and pub. rels. April Greiman, Inc., L.A., 1987-91; pres. Todd Hays Group, Pasadena, 1991—; prodn. designer Blanc Comm., L.A., 1984; publicist CCPI, L.A., 1983-85. Contbr. articles to profl. jours.; writer TV spl.: Urban Wilderness, 1984. Mem. Pasadena Arts Coun., Am. Inst. Graphic Arts (v.p. 1988—), MOCA Contemporaries. Office: Todd Hays Group 1679 Monte Vista St Pasadena CA 91103-1309

HAYSOM, IAN RICHARD, newspaper editor; b. Hull, Yorkshire, England, Dec. 17, 1949; arrived in Can., 1973; s. John and Cathleen Haysom; m. Wendy Elizabeth Sheppard, Oct. 30, 1971; children: Amy, Janice, Timothy, Paul. Grad., Nat. Coun. Tng. Journalists, 1972. Reporter, sub-editor Ilford Recorder, 1969-72; sub-editor Evening Standard, London, 1972-73; reporter Hamilton Spectator, Ont., Can., 1973-75; reporter Ottawa Jour., Ont., Can., 1975-77, film critic, 1977-78, entertainment editor, 1978-79; editor lifestyles-features Ottawa Citizen, 1979-81; editor lifestyles-features Vancouver Sun, B.C., Can., 1981, city editor, 1982-85, asst. mng. editor, 1985-89; editor in chief The Province, Vancouver, 1989-91, The Vancouver Sun, 1991—. Home: 1405 Jefferson, West Vancouver, BC Canada V7T 2B3 Office: The Vancouver Sun, 2250 Granville St, Vancouver, BC Canada V6H 3G2

HAYWARD, ARTHUR D'ALANSON, physician; b. Mo., Md., Mar. 19, 1946; s. Joseph Hunter and Rosemary (Barber) H.; m. Christine Victoria Talarico, Feb. 16, 1973; children: Lisa Shelby, Gregory Philip. BA, Yale Coll., 1968; MD, Columbia Coll., 1972. Diplomate Am. Bd. Internal Medicine. Resident Harlem Hosp., N.Y.C., 1972-74; lt. comdr. Indian Health Svc. USPHS, Tahlequah, Okla., 1974-77; resident Oreg. Health Scis. U., Portland, 1977-78; chief dept. of medicine Sunnyside Med. Ctr., Clackamas, Oreg., 1989—; asst. clin. prof. Oreg. Health Scis. U., Portland, 1990—. USPHS grantee, 1969, 72, 88. Fellow ACP; mem. City Club Portland, Sierra Club, Oreg. Health Scis. U. Alumni (coun.). Home: 3830 SW Ridgewood Ave Portland OR 97225-2666 Office: Sunnyside Med Ctr 10180 SE Sunnyside Rd Clackamas OR 97015

HAYWARD, FREDRIC MARK, social reformer; b. N.Y.C., July 10, 1946; s. Irving Michael and Mildred (Feingold) H.; m. Ingeborg Beck, Aug. 18, 1971 (div. 1974). BA, Brandeis U., Waltham, Mass., 1967; MA, Fletcher Sch. Law & Diplomacy, Medford, Mass., 1968, MALD, 1969. Exec. dir. Men's Rights, Inc., Boston, 1977—; vis. lectr. Tufts U., Medford, Mass., 1979; lectr. in field; conductor workshops in field; adv. bd. Ctr. for Men's Studies, 1988—. Author 3 published anthologies; contbg. editor: The Liberator, Forest Lake, Minn., 1988-89; contbg. writer Spectator, Berkeley, Calif., 1988—; contbr. articles to profl. jours. Farrell Fellowship on Men, 1989; Fletcher Sch. Law and Diplomacy fellow, 1967-69. Mem. Nat. Congress for-Men (bd. dirs. 1981-90), Am. Fedn. TV and Radio Artists, Men's Internat. (bd. dirs. 1982-86), Sacramento Valley Men's Coun., Children's Rights Coun. Office: Mr Inc PO Box 163180 Sacramento CA 95816-9180

HAYWARD, STEVEN FREDRIC, editor; b. Pasadena, Calif., Oct. 16, 1958; s. James Francis and Jean (Schulz) H.; m. Allison Rittenhouse, May 20, 1989. BS in Bus., Lewis & Clark Coll., 1980; MA in Govt., Claremont Grad. Sch., 1983. Dir. Golden State Ctr. Claremont (Calif.) Inst., 1985-92; exec. editor Inland Bus. Mag., Claremont, 1985-92; rsch. and editorial dir. Pacific Rsch. Inst., San Francisco, 1992—; contbg. editor Reason Mag., L.A., 1990—. Contbg. author Ency. of the American Right, 1993; contbr. articles to profl. jours. Commr. Calif. Citizens Compensation Commn., Sacramento, 1990—. Olive Garvey fellow Mont Pelerin Soc., 1990, 92, Earhart Found. fellow, 1986-87, Weaver fellow Intercollegiate Studies Inst., 1985-86. Republican. Episcopalian. Home: 811 18th St Sacramento CA 95814 Office: Pacific Rsch Inst 755 Sansome St Ste 450 San Francisco CA 94111

HAYWORTH, JOHN DAVID, JR., sportscaster, commentator, broadcaster; b. High Point, N.C., July 12, 1958; s. John David and Gladys Ethel (Hall) H.; m. Mary Denise Yancey, Feb. 25, 1989; children: Nicole Irene, Hannah Lynne. BA in Speech and Polit. Sci., N.C. State U., 1980. Sports anchor, reporter Sta. WPTF-TV, Raleigh, N.C., 1980-81, Sta. WLWT-TV, Cin., 1986-87; sports anchor Sta. WYFF-TV (formerly Sta. WFBC-TV), Greenville, S.C., 1981-86, Sta. KTSP-TV, Phoenix, 1987—; radio commentator; play-by-play broadcaster. Dist. committeeman Ariz. Rep. Com., Scottsdale, 1988-89; bd. dirs. Am. Humanics Found., Ariz. State U., Tempe, 1991-92; chmn. Scout-A-Rama, Theodore Roosevelt coun. Boy Scouts Am., 1991-92. Recipient honor roll award Atlantic Coast Conf., 1977, Young Am. award Unharrie coun. Boy Scouts Am., 1979, Friend of Edn. award Sch. Dist. Greenville County, 1985, Sch. Bell/Friend of Edn. award S.C. Dept. Edn., 1985. Mem. Rotary (bd. dirs. Phoenix 1989-90). Baptist. Office: Sta KTSP-TV 511 W Adams St Phoenix AZ 85003

HAZEL, JOANIE BEVERLY, elementary educator; b. Medford, Oreg., Jan. 20, 1946; d. Ralph Ray Lenderman and Vivian Thelma (Holtane) Spencer; m. Larry Aydon Hazel, Dec. 28, 1969. BS in Edn., So. Oreg. Coll., Ashland, 1969; MS in Edn., Portland State U., 1972; postgrad., U. Va., 1985. Elem. tchr. Beaverton (Oreg.) Schs., 1972-76, Internat. Sch. Svcs., Isfahan, Iran, 1976-78; ESL instr. Lang. Svcs., Tucker, Ga., 1983-84; tchr. Fairfax (Va.) Schs., 1985-86; elem. tchr. Beaverton (Oreg.) Schs., 1990—. Mem. U.S. Hist. Soc., Platform Soc., Smithsonian Instn., Am. Mus. Natural Hist., Nat. Mus. Women in Arts, U.S. Hist. Soc., The United Nations, The Colonial Williamsburg Found., Wilson Ctr., N.Y. Acad. Scis., Beta Sigma Phi. Home: 9247 SW Martha St Portland OR 97224-5577

HAZELBAUER, GERALD LEE, molecular biologist; b. Chgo., Sept. 27, 1944; s. Carl Frederick and Margaret Jane (Ort) H.; m. Linda Lea Randall, Aug. 29, 1970. BA, Williams Coll., 1966; MS, Case Western Res. U., 1968; PhD, U. Wis., 1971. Postdoctoral fellow U. Wis.-Madison, 1971, Inst. Pasteur, Paris, 1971-73; research fellow U. Uppsala, Sweden, 1973-75, asst. prof., 1975-80; assoc. scientist Wash. State U., Pullman, 1981-82, assoc. prof., 1982-85, prof., 1985—, dir. biotech. tng. program, 1989—. Editor: Taxis and Behavior, 1978; editorial bd. Jour. of Bacteriology, 1976—. Contbr. articles to profl. jours. Postdoctoral fellow Muscular Dystrophy Assn. 1972-73,

NSF, 1971-72; Alfred P. Sloan Found. Research fellow in Neurosci., 1973-75; Neurosci. Devel. award McKnight Found., 1982-84, Faculty research award Am. Cancer Soc., 1985-90; NIH grantee, 1975-78, 82—, NSF grantee, 1985-91. Mem. Am. Soc. Microbiology, Am. Soc. Biol. Chemists, European Chemoreception Research Orgn. Home: 920 NE D St Pullman WA 99163-3904 Office: Wash State U Dept Biochemistry/Biophysics Pullman WA 99163

HAZEN, PAUL MANDEVILLE, banker; b. Lansing, Mich., 1941; married. BA, U. Ariz., 1963; MBA, U. Calif., Berkeley, 1964. Asst. mgr Security Pacific Bank, 1964-66; v.p. Union Bank, 1966-70; chmn. Wells Fargo Realty Advisors, 1970-76; with Wells Fargo Realty Advisors, San Francisco, 1979—, exec. v.p., mgr. Real Estate Industries Group, 1979-80, mem. exec. office Real Estate Industry Group, 1980, vice-chmn. Real Estate Industries Group, 1980-84, pres., chief oper. officer Real Estate Industries Group, 1984—, also dir. Real Estate Industries Group, 1984—; pres., treas. Wells Fargo Mortgage & Equity Trust, San Francisco, 1977-84; with Wells Fargo & Co. (parent) San Francisco, 1978—, exec. v.p., then vice-chmn., now pres., chief operating officer, dir., 1978—; trustee Wells Fargo Mortgage & Equity Trust; bd. dirs. Pacific Telesis Group. Office: Wells Fargo & Co 420 Montgomery St San Francisco CA 94163-0001*

HAZEWINKEL, VAN, manufacturing executive; b. L.A., Oct. 2, 1943; s. Ben J. and Betty J. (Bishop) H.; m. Linda Bennett, Sept. 11, 1965; children: Van, Karey. BS, Calif. State U., Long Beach, 1967. With Daily Indsl. Tools Inc., Costa Mesa, Calif., 1959—, v.p., 1966-78, pres., 1978—. Founding mem. bd. dirs. Greater Irvine (Calif.) Indsl. League, 1970-73. Mem. Soc. Mfg. Engrs. Office: 3197D Airport Loop Dr Costa Mesa CA 92626-3412

HE, XING-FEI, physicist; b. Chenghai, Guangdong, People's Republic of China, Mar. 1, 1958; arrived in Can., 1991; s. Pei-Yao He and Shan-Shan Du; m. Chun Peng, Dec. 17, 1986. BS, Zhongshan U., Guangzhou, 1982, MS, 1985; PhD, Australian Nat. U., Canberra, 1992. Rsch. fellow Inst. Microelectronics Zhongshan U., 1985-88; PhD scholar Australian Nat. U., Canberra, 1988-91; NSERC Internat. fellow dept. physics U. B.C., Vancouver, Can., 1992—. Contbr. 30 rsch. articles to profl. jours. Izaak W. Killam Meml. fellow (hon.), 1992—. Mem. Am. Phys. Soc.

HEAD, IVAN LEIGH, law educator; b. Calgary, Alta., Can., July 28, 1930; s. Arthur Cecil and Birdie Hazel (Crockett) H.; m. Barbara Spence Eagle, June 23, 1952; children: Laurence Allan, Bryan Cameron, Catherine Spence, Cynthia Leigh; m. Ann Marie Price, Dec. 1, 1979. B.A., U. Alta., 1951, LL.B., 1952; LLM, Harvard U., 1960; LLD (hon.), U. Alta., 1987, U. West Indies, 1987, U. Western Ont., 1988, U. Ottawa, 1988, U. Calgary, 1989, Beijing U., 1990, St. Francis Xavier U., 1990, U. Man., 1991, U. Notre Dame, 1991. Bar: Alta. 1953; Queen's Counsel, Can. Practiced in Calgary, 1953-59; partner firm Helman, Barron & Head, 1955-59; fgn. service officer Dept. External Affairs, Ottawa, Kuala Lumpur, 1960-63; prof. law U. Alta., 1963-67; asso. counsel to Minister of Justice, Govt. of Can., 1967-68; spl. asst. to prime minister of Can., 1968-78; pres. Internat. Devel. Research Centre, Ottawa, 1978-91; prof. law U. B.C., Vancouver, Can., 1991—; bd. dirs. Salzburg Seminar, Can. Inst. Internat. Affairs, Inter Am. Diologue, Soc. Internat. Devel. Author: International Law, National Tribunals and the Rights of Aliens, 1971, On a Hinge of History, 1991; editor: This Fire Proof House, 1967, Conversation with Canadians, 1972; contbr. articles to profl. jours. Trustee Internat. Food Policy Rsch. Inst., 1979-88; mem. Ind. Commn. on Internat. Humanitarian Issues, 1983-87. Decorated officer Order of Can.; officer Grand Cross, Order of The Sun (Peru); Chief Justice's medallist U. Alta. Law Sch.; Frank Knox Meml. fellow Harvard Law Sch., 1959-60. Mem. Internat. Law Assn., Can. Council Internat. Law, Can. Inst. Internat. Affairs, Am. Soc. Internat. Law, Law Soc. Alta., Inter-Am. Dialogue. Anglican. Home: 2343 Bellevue Ave, West Vancouver, BC Canada V7V 1C9 Office: U BC, Faculty Law, Vancouver, BC Canada V6T 1Z1

HEADDING, LILLIAN SUSAN (SALLY HEADDING), writer; b. Milw., Jan. 1, 1944; d. David Morton and Mary Davis (Berry) Coleman; m. James K. Hill (div. 1976); children: Amy Denise; m. John Murray Headding (div. 1987). BA, U. Nev., 1975; MA, U. Pacific, 1976. With Gimbels, Milw., 1963-65; retail mgr. Frandisco Corp., N.Y.C., 1965-66; store mgr. Anita Shops, Los Angeles, 1966-68, Clothes Closet, Sunnyvale, Calif., 1969-70; owner Lillian Headding Interiors & Comml. Design, Pittsburg, Calif., 1976-88; mfrs. rep. and assoc. J.G. West, San Francisco, 1989—; karate instr. Sch. of the Tiger, Pleasant Hill, Calif., 1988—, 1st degree black belt, 1973—. Author: (as Sally Davis): When Gods Fall; author short stories, poetry. Bd. dirs. and co-founder Community Action Against Rape, Las Vegas, 1972-75; self-def. expert Las Vegas Met. Police Dept., 1972-75, North Las Vegas (Nev.) Police Dept.; co. supr. Family & Children's Svcs., Contra Costa County, Calif., 1985-86. Mem. Walnut Creek Writers Group (pres.), Berkeley Women's Writers Group, Philippine Hawaiian Black Belters Assn. Democrat. Jewish. Office: # 33 5333 Park Highlands Blvd Concord CA 94521-3718

HEADLEE, ROLLAND DOCKERAY, association executive; b. Los Angeles, Aug. 27, 1916; s. Jesse W. and Cleora (Dockeray) H.; m. Alzora D. Burgett, May 13, 1939; 1 dau., Linda Ann (Mrs. Walter Pohl). Student, UCLA, 1939. Asst. mgr. Par Assocs., Los Angeles, 1935-43, Finance Assocs., 1946-58; financial cons., lectr., 1958-63; account exec. Walter E. Heller & Co., Los Angeles, 1963-66; exec. dir. emeritus Town Hall Calif., Los Angeles, 1966—; dir. Am. Internat. Bank, Mfrs. Assocs., R.H. Investment Corp. Mem. adv. bd., bd. dirs., Los Angeles council Boy Scouts Am. Served to 1st lt. AUS, 1943-46. Mem. Mensa, Los Angeles World Affairs Council, Newcomen Soc. Methodist. Clubs: Commonwealth of Calif, Economic of Detroit, Los Angeles Stock Exchange. Home: 8064 El Manor Ave Los Angeles CA 90045-1434

HEADLEY, JUDY ANNE, educational technology staff developer; b. Dallas, Feb. 11, 1942; d. Jerry P. and Mary Helen (Wheeler) Scoggins; m. Jerry E. Headley, Oct. 21, 1961; children: Garrett Headley, Kevin Headley. BS, Calif. State U., 1965, MA in Edn. Adminstrn., 1989. Tchr. Andasol Sch., L.A., 1965-66, Kellogg Sch., Goleta, Calif., 1966-67; coord. gifted edn. Hope Sch. Dist., Santa Barbara, Calif., 1977-83; tech. dir. Tchr. Edn. and Computer Ctr., Santa Barbara, Calif., 1983-87; edn. cons. Jostens Learning Corp., San Diego, 1987-90, staff devel. spec., 1990—; prof. ext. U. Calif. Santa Barbara, 1984-87; edn. cons. Calif. State Social Studies Project, 1986, Santa Barbara City Schs., 1987-88; planning bd., presenter Calif. State Elem. Tech. Inst., San Bernardino, 1987. Author: Training for Josten Learning Research Writing Product, 1991-92. Mem. Starr King Parent Child Workshop, Santa Barbara, 1970-72, Las Aletas, 1979-83, AAUW, 1979-82; presenter Calif. Computer Using Edn., San Mateo, Calif., 1983-87. Mem. ACSD, Nat. Coun. Tchrs. English, Internat. Reading Assn. Home: 815 Willowglen Rd Santa Barbara CA 93105

HEADLEY, NATHAN LEROY, laboratory executive; b. Phila., Jan. 1, 1936; s. Russell A. and Mary Ellen (Miller) H.; m. Barbara Pinkney, Dec. 28, 1957 (div. Feb. 1986); children: Kimberly, Robert; m. Dolly Day Lopshire, Dec. 18, 1987. AB, MS in Econs., Bucknell U., 1958. Exptl. test pilot Boeing Co., Phila., 1962-70; pres. Med. Diagnostic Ctrs. Inc., Norristown, Pa., 1971-75; various exec. positions to exec. v.p. Nat. Health Labs., Inc., La Jolla, Calif., 1976-85; COO Merris Lab., San Jose, Calif., 1986-89; pres., CEO, bd. dirs. Physicians Clin. Lab. Inc., Sacramento, 1989—. Capt. USMCR, 1958-62. Republican. Methodist. Office: Physicians Clin Lab Inc 3301 C St Ste 100E Sacramento CA 95618

HEADY, FERREL, political science educator emeritus; b. Ferrelview, Mo., Feb. 14, 1916; s. Chester Ferrel and Loren (Wightman) H.; m. Charlotte Audrey McDougall, Feb. 12, 1942; children—Judith Lillian, Richard Ferrel, Margaret Loren, Thomas McDougall. A.B., Washington U., St. Louis, 1937, A.M., 1938, Ph.D., 1940; hon. degrees, Park Coll., 1973, John F. Kennedy U., 1974, U. N.Mex., 1993. Jr. adminstrv. technician, also adminstrv. asst. Office Dir. Personnel, Dept. Agr., 1941-42; vis. lectr. polit. sci. U. Kansas City, 1946; faculty U. Mich., 1946-67, prof. polit. sci., 1957-67; dir. Inst. Pub. Adminstrn., 1960-67; acad. v.p. U. N.Mex., Albuquerque, 1967-68; pres. U. N.Mex., 1968-75, prof. pub. adminstrn. and polit. sci., 1975-81, prof. emeritus, 1981—; Asst. to commr. Com. Orgn. Exec. Br. of Govt., 1947-49; dir., chief adviser Inst. Pub. Adminstrn., U. Philippines, 1953-54; mem. U.S. del. Internat. Congress Adminstrn. Scis., Spain, 1956, 80, Germany, 1959, Austria, 1962, Poland, 1964, Mexico, 1974; exec. bd. Inter-Univ. Case Program, 1956-67; sr. specialist in residence East-West Center, U. Hawaii, 1965; mem. Conf. on Pub. Service, 1965-70; chmn. bd. Assoc. Western Univs., 1970-71; commr. Western Interstate Commn. Higher Edn., 1972-77; mem. commns. on bus. professions and water resources, mem. exec. com. Nat. Assn. State Univs. and Land Grant Colls., 1968-75. Author: Administrative Procedure Legislation in the States, 1952, (with Robert H. Pealy) The Michigan Department of Administration, 1956, (with Sybil L. Stokes) Comparative Public Administration: A Selective Annotated Bibliography, 1960, Papers in Comparative Public Administration, 1962, State Constitutions: The Structure of Administration, 1961, Public Administration: A Comparative Perspective, 1966, rev. edit., 1979, 4th edit., 1991; contbr. profl. jours. Chmn. state affairs com. Ann Arbor Citizens Council, Mich., 1949-52; mem. exec. com. Mich. Meml.-Phoenix Project and Inst. Social Research, 1960-66; mem. Gov. Mich. Constl. Revision Study Commn., 1960-62; schs. and univs. adv. bd. Citizens Com. for Hoover Report, 1949-52, 54-58; cons. to Ford Found., 1962; chmn. Council on Grad. Edn. in Pub. Adminstrn., 1966; mem., vice chmn. N.Mex. Gov.'s Com. on Reorgn. of State Govt., 1967-70; mem. N.Mex. Am. Revolution Bicentennial Commn., 1970-73, N.Mex. Gov.'s Com on Tech. Excellence, 1969-75, Nat. Acad. Pub. Adminstrn. Served to lt. USNR, 1942-46. Recipient Faculty Disting. Achievement award U. Mich., 1964, N.Mex. Disting. Pub. service award, 1973, award of distinction U. N.Mex. Alumni Assn., 1975, Outstanding Grad. Tchr. award U. N.Mex., 1981-82, Fulbright sr. lectureship, Colombia, 1992. Mem. Am. Polit. Sci. Assn., Am. Soc. Pub. Adminstrn. (pres. 1969-70), AAUP (chmn. com. T 1957-61), Am. Council Edn. (mem. commn. on fed. relations 1969-72), Phi Beta Kappa, Phi Kappa Phi. Presbyterian. Home: 2901 Cutler Ave NE Albuquerque NM 87106-1714

HEALD, JACK WENDELL, retired educator; b. Phoenix, Sept. 3, 1925; s. Judson Thomas and Margaret A. (Peart) H.; m. Mary Ann Higuera, July 28, 1950; children: Blaine Carter, Mark Charles, Eugenie Carmen. BA, Calif. State, Turlock, 1962; MA, U. Pacific, 1968. Farm dir. KAYL, Storm Lake, Iowa, 1950-56; program dir. KWIN, Ashland, Oreg., 1955-57; mgr. Radio Sta. KURY, Brookings, Oreg., 1958-59; broadcast engr. Radio Sta. KTUR, Turlock, Calif., 1959-61; speech instr. Merced (Calif.) and Modesto (Calif.) Jr. Coll., 1962-64, THS, Turlock, 1964-73; dir. of forensics Calif. State Univ., Stan., Turlock, 1974-75, THS, Turlock, 1975-80; nat. dir. Fordson Tractor Club, Cave Junction, Oreg., 1980-93; owner, operator Fordson Home Hostel, Cave Junction, 1990-93. Author: How to Teach Speech and Debate, Highschool, 1985, The REAL Fordson, 1988; editor, pub. Fordson Tractor Club Newsletter, 1976-93. Historian BR9, EDGETA, Merlin, Oreg., 1982-93. Cpl. U.S. Cavalry, 1945-47. Fellow Early Day Gas Engine & Tractor Assn., Pi Kappa Delta. Democrat. Home: 250 Robinson Rd Cave Junction OR 97523-9719

HEALEY, LAURETTE ANN, direct response licensing and merchandising executive; b. Massapequa, N.Y., July 30, 1954; d. Phillip Bernard and Geneva Laurette (Musalo) H. BA in Dramatic Arts, U. Calif., Santa Barbara, 1977; MBA, Pepperdine U. Pres., CEO True North Entertainment, Inc., L.A., 1988-90; founder Pacific Media Ventures, Inc., L.A., 1990-93. Mem. NAFE, Dirs. Guild Am., Women in Film. Office: 15149 Weddington St Sherman Oaks CA 91411

HEALY, BARBARA ANNE, insurance company executive, financial planner; b. Chgo., May 21, 1951; d. William James Healy and Eileen Mary (Dooley) Dashiell; m. Gerald Lally Angst, June 9, 1973 (div. Sept. 1977). BA, No. Ill. U., 1973; MBA, DePaul U., 1976. Cert. fin. planner. Dept. head, instr. St. Benedict High Sch., Chgo., 1973-76; account rep. Xerox Corp., Chgo., 1976-78, mktg. specialist, 1978-79, high volume sr. sales exec., 1979-81; western dist. mgr. McGraw Hill, N.Y.C., 1981-82; fin. planner United Resources Ins. Service, Torrance, Calif., 1982-83, sales mgr., 1983-85, exec. v.p., 1985-86; regional v.p. United Resources Ins. Service, Foster City, Calif., 1986-89; v.p., nat. mktg. dir. Met. Life Resources (formerly United Resources Ins. Svcs.), Phoenix, 1990—; Tempe, Ariz.; instr. Trenton City Coll., Riverside, Ill., City Coll. Chgo., Northeastern Ill. U., Chgo., Prairie State Coll., Chicago Heights, 1976-81. Author: Financial Planning for Educators, 1987; contbr. articles to prof. jours.; speaker in field. Mem. Internat. Assn. Fin. Planners, Inst. Cert. Fin. Planners, Registry Fin. Planning Practitioners, Nat. Council Fin. Edn. Republican. Roman Catholic. Home: 10301 N 48th Pl Paradise Vly AZ 85253-1033 Office: Met Life Resources 1501 W Fountainhead Ste 650 Tempe AZ 85282-1846

HEALY, BARBARA MARY, public health nurse; b. Sydney, Australia; came to U.S., 1965; d. Leo Joseph and Doreen Elizabeth (Maunsel) H. BSN in Pub. Health Nursing, Calif. State U., Carson, 1988; grad., U.S. Army Command and Staff Gen. Coll., 1987; postgrad., Calif. State U., San Jose, 1988—; M in Mil. and Polit. Sci., Command & Staff Gen. Coll., Leavenworth, Kans., 1989. RN; cert. critical care infection control practitioner, advanced cardiac life support instr., advanced life support burn instr. Critical care and pediatric staff nurse Toronto (Can.) Gen. Hosp. and Hosp. Sick Children, 1961-65; asst. head nurse ICU Stanford (Calif.) U. Med. Ctr., 1965-68; nurse CCU U.S. Army, Tacoma, 1968-70; nurse ICU and M.U.S.T. unit Lai Khi U.S. Army, Vietnam, 1968-70; clin. instr. CCU Sydney Hosp., U. Sydney, 1971-74; nurse spl. procedure lab. Kaiser Hosp., Santa Clara, Calif., 1974-89; primary care case mgr. HomeMed of Am. Inc., 1989—; chief nursing edn. and devel. USAR Gen. Hosp., Sunny Vale, Calif., 1974—; instr. tng. course Assn. for Practitioners in Infection Control Inc., 1989. Basic life support instr. ARC, 1989; advanced burn life support provider/instr. Am. Burn Assn., 1988; advanced trauma life support tng. Am. Coll. Surgeons, 1988; advanced cardiac life support, mem. Am. Heart Assn., 1988. Lt. col. USAR, 1974—. Decorated Army Commendation medal with oak leaf cluster. Mem. Am. Nurses Assn., Diagnostic Med. Sonographers Assn., Gastroenterologist Assns., C.P.R., Infection Control Practitioner. Home: 85 Baringa Rd, 2063 Northbridge New South Wales, Australia

HEALY, JAMES BRUCE, cooking school administrator, writer; b. Paterson, N.J., Apr. 15, 1947; s. James Burn and Margaret Mercy (Patterson) H.; m. Alice Fenvessy, May 9, 1970; 1 child, Charlotte Alexandra. BA, Williams Coll., 1968; PhD, The Rockefeller U., 1973. Mem. faculty Inst. Advanced Study, Princeton, N.J., 1973-75; J.W. Gibbs instr. physics Yale U., New Haven, Conn., 1975-77, research affiliate, 1977-80; dir. Healy-Lucullus Sch. French Cooking, New Haven, 1978-80, Boulder, Colo., 1980—; cons. Claudine's, Denver, 1985-86; vis. instr. Salem (Mass.) State Coll., 1984, and various culinary schs. Author: Mastering the Art of French Pastry, 1984; contbr. articles and revs. on restaurants and cooking to mags. and profl. jours. Mem. Internat. Assn. Cooking Profls. (cert.), Confederation Nationale des Patissiers, Glaciers, et Confiseurs de France. Presbyterian. Home and Office: Healy-Lucullus Sch French Cooking 840 Cypress Dr Boulder CO 80303-2820

HEALY, KIERAN JOHN PATRICK, lighting designer, consultant; b. London, June 6, 1957; came to U.S., 1980; citizen of Ireland.; s. Denis Finbarr and Dawn Josephine (O'Hannigan) H.; m. Debra Leslie Liebling, Jan. 6, 1990. Student, Isleworth Polytechnic, Middlesex, Eng., 1975-76. Lighting designer Music, The Who, 1976-80, The Rolling Stones, U.S.A., 1980; v.p. Showlites, L.A., 1980-81; freelance in TV, lighting designer, 1982-89; dir. photography Klages Group Inc, Hollywood, Calif., 1989—. Lighting designer for TV programs, including Live Aid, Liberty Weekend Opening Ceremonies, Gracelands in Africa, Arsenio Hall Show, other spls. Mem. Nat. Acad. Cable Programming (ACE Nomination 1988), Acad. TV Arts and Scis. (Emmy Nominations 1984, 87, 89, 92), Assn. Cinemotograph Techs. and Allied Trades, Internat. Photographers Guild. Roman Catholic. Office: The Klages Group Inc 1438 N Gower St Los Angeles CA 90028-8318

HEALY, WINSTON, JR., educational administrator; b. Evanston, Ill., Oct. 20, 1937; s. Winston and Margaret (Lee) H.; m. Judith Becker, June 24, 1976; children—Nathaniel, Sarah, Jason, Elisabeth. B.A., Williams Coll., 1960; M.A., U. Hawaii, 1968; Ed.D., U. Mass., 1982. Tchr. English, Punahou Sch., Honolulu, 1960-67, chmn. dept. English, 1966-67, dean adminstrn., 1967-69, secondary sch. prin., 1969—. Chmn. bd. Early Sch.; v.p., Hawaii Pub. Radio, 1978-88; mem. Joint Econ. Council; mem. exec. bd. Honolulu Community Scholarship Program. Served with Hawaii Air N.G., 1960-71. Coe fellow; Nat. Assn. Ind. Schs. fellow, 1972-73. Mem. Nat. Assn. Secondary Sch. Prins., Assn. Supervision and Curriculum Devel., Nat. Council Tchrs. English (nat. adv. bd. achievement awards), Hawaii Council Tchrs. English (past pres.). Congregationalist. Home: 45 Piper's Pali Honolulu HI 96822 Office: 1601 Punahou St Honolulu HI 96822-3399

HEALY-FRENCH, FLORENCE MARGARET, actress, writer; b. Mineral Point, Wis., Dec. 15, 1921; d. George Ulmont and Florence Elizabeth (Reynolds) Healy; m. Burt Henry French, May 1, 1945; children: Christofer, Melania, Stephanie, Lachlan. BFA in Speech and Drama, U. Iowa, 1943; MA in English, Tex. Tech. U., 1967, postgrad., 1967-68; postgrad., U. So. Calif., 1976-78. Repertory actress Cleve. Playhouse, 1942-46; instr. speech U. Iowa, Iowa City, 1948-49; instr. English Imperial High Sch., Pasadena, Calif., 1968-74, Ambassador Coll., Pasadena, 1974-78; actress summer repertory Chautauqua (N.Y.) Repertory, 1943-45, Grist Mill Playhouse, Andover, N.J., 1952; guest artist, spl. lectr. Brigham Young U., Provo, Utah, 1953-58; spl. lectr. Kalamazoo Coll., 1955-60; with Sta. KBAC, Pasadena, 1973-75; bd. dirs. Aquarian Films, Park City, Utah; pub. Helois Press, 1993. Author: Lively Proverbs of the Folk, 1967, The Grammar Gang, 1973, The Children's Word Book, 1983; contbr. articles to profl. jours.; appeared in films Sweepstakes, 1978, Wait 'Till Spring, Bandini, 1989, The Secret of Lost Creek, 1989. Rockefeller Found. acting scholar Cleve. Playhouse, 1942-43; Danforth Found. fellow Pacific Sch. Religion, Berkeley, Calif., 1960; travel grantee Kalamazoo Coll., 1960. Mem. Desk and Derrick (sec. 1984), Purple Mask, Zeta Phi Eta (pres. 1942), Pi Omicron Delta, Pi Delta Phi. Home: 1388 Garrison St # G104 Lakewood CO 80215

HEAPHY, JAMES CULLEN, III, plastics company executive; b. Detroit, Mar. 28, 1952; s. James Cullen Jr. and Elizabeth Jane (Davidson) H.; m. Debra Sue Klebanoff, Sept. 6, 1981; children: James Cullen IV, David Alexander. BS, U. San Francisco, 1982. Asst. supr. communications Kaiser Found. Hosps., San Francisco, 1977-78, supr. communications, 1978-82; project mgr. J. Di Cristina & Son, San Francisco, 1982-84; gen. mgr. Western Plastics, San Francisco, 1984—; freelance writer In These Times, 1986-89; seminar leader Butler-Johnson Corp., San Jose, Calif., 1988—, KBC Publs., Hackensack, N.J., 1989—. Editor Space for All People newsletter, 1980-86; columnist Cabinet Mfg. and Fabricating Jour., 1990—. Pres. Marin Dem. Club, 1987-92; mem. Calif. Dem. Cen. Com., 1989-92, Dem. Cen. Com. Marin, 1991-92; bd. dirs. Marin Sane Freeze, 1990-91. Mem. Decorative Laminate Products Assn. (sect. chmn. 1989—, vol. award 1990). Home: 33 Larkspur St American Canyon CA 94589 Office: Western Plastics 1440 Bancroft Ave San Francisco CA 94124-3603

HEARD, RONALD ROY, motion picture producer; b. Denver, Oct. 3, 1947; s. John Arthur and Louise Marie (Smith) H.; m. Kim Widing Aug. 12, 1967 (div. 1969). BS, Colo. State U., 1969; postgrad., U. Colo., 1969-72, U. Paris/Sorbonne, 1964-65. Prodn. design/stage mgr. The Rolling Stones, London, 1969-86; property/set dresser Universal Studios, Universal City, Calif., 1978-79, Warner Bros. Studios, Burbank, Calif., 1979-80; producer stage plays Hollywood, 1980-85; music video cons. L.A., 1984—; corres. CBS Network News, Chgo., 1971-72; writer/photographer UPI/Nat. Geographic/Denver Post, 1969-73; ptnr. Silver Screen Ptnrs. II and III, L.A., 1986—; chief exec. officer, pres. Radio Safari, 1991—; owner Yankee Pride Ent., North Hollywood, Calif., 1986—. Exec. com. Dem. Party, Larimer County, Colo., 1972-79; Dem. candidate for Ho. of Rep., 1972, 76. Named honorary citizen of S.D. by Gov. Richard Kneip, 1972. Mem. Am. Film Inst., Smithsonian Instn., Statue of Liberty/Ellis Island Cen. Commn. Democrat.

HEARN, ANTHONY CLEM, computer scientist; b. Adelaide, Australia, Apr. 13, 1937; came to the U.S., 1962; s. Clem and Elma Frances (Almond) H.; m. Jo Elaine Johnson, May 16, 1970; children: Alison Margaret, David John. Degree, U. Adelaide, 1958, degree in math. with honors, 1959; PhD in Theoretical Physics, U. Cambridge, 1962. Prof. physics U. Utah, Salt Lake City, 1971-78, prof. computer sci., 1973-81, dir. computer sci. div., 1973-74, chmn. dept. computer sci., 1974-80; head info. scis. dept. RAND Corp., Santa Monica, Calif., 1980-84, corp. rsch. staff mem., 1984-90, resident scholar, 1990—; cons. USRA Sci. Coun., 1980, Lawrence Livermore Nat. Labs., 1980, Hewlett Packard Corp., Palo Alto, Calif., 1983, NSF Adv. Com. for Advanced Scientific Computing, 1984. Shell Commonwealth scholar, 1958; Alfred P. Sloan Found. fellow, 1967-69. Fellow Cambridge Philos. Soc.; mem. Am. Phys. Soc., Spl. Interest Group on Symbolic and Algebraic Manipulation (chmn. 1981-83). Office: Rand 1700 Main St Santa Monica CA 90407-2138

HEARN, CHARLES VIRGIL, minister; b. Westport, Ind., Sept. 4, 1930; s. Forrest V. and Emma Florence (Marsh) H.; Ph.D., Thomas A. Edison U., 1972; D.D., Trinity Hall Coll. and Sem., 1977; diploma Palm Beach Psychotherapy Tng. Center, 1976; m. Linda Elmendorf; children by previous marriage—Debra Lynn, Charles Gregory, Martin Curtis. Ordained to ministry Methodist Ch., 1958; pastor various Meth. chs., Ind., Tex., Wyo., Calif., 1958-70; interpersonal minister St. Alban's Ch. of the Way, San Francisco, 1974—; clergyman and counselor Green Oak Ranch Boys Camp, Calif., 1969-70; dir. rehab. Mary-Lind Found., Los Angeles, 1970-71; med. asst. Fireside Hosp., Santa Monica, Calif., 1971-72; dir. alcoholism program Patrician Hosp., Santa Monica, 1972-74; propr., exec. dir. Consultation & Referral, Santa Monica, 1974—. Vice chmn. Western Los Angeles Alcoholism Coalition, 1974-78; pres. bd. dirs. Trinity Hall Coll. and Sem. Served with U.S. Army, 1951-53; Korea. Decorated Bronze Star; diplomate Am. Bd. Examiners in Psychotherapy, Bd. Examiners in Pastoral Counseling. Fellow Am. Acad. Behavioral Sci., Internat. Council Sex Edn. and Parenthood of Am. U.; mem. Am. Ministerial Assn. (pres. 1981—), Nat. Assn. Alcoholism Counselors, Calif. Assn. Alcoholism Counselors, Cons. on Alcoholism for Communities, Nat. Council Family Relations, Am. Coll. Clinic Adminstrs., Assn. Labor-Mgmt. Adminstrs. Democrat. Contbr. numerous articles on psychotherapy to profl. publs. Office: 1244 11th St Apt D Santa Monica CA 90401-2018

HEARNE, STANA DRESHER, non-profit organization administrator; b. Globe, Ariz., Aug. 30, 1926; d. Oscar Stanley and Lucy (Jones) Dresher; m. Benjamin Foreman Hearne, July 10, 1946 (June, 1981); children: Linda Sue, Benjamin Stanley, John Thomas. BA in Social Scis., U. Calif, Riverside, 1963. Paralegal Elizabeth Anderson Law Firm, Oakland, Calif., 1978-85; exec. dir. Citizens for the Eastshore State Park, Berkeley, Calif., 1986—; mem. East Bay Regional Park Dist. Adv. Com., Oakland, 1987-92; dir. Bay Trail Project, Oakland, 1989—. Mem. Regional Planning Com. ABAG, Oakland, 1975—; mem. Air Quality Mgmt. Dist Adv. Coun., San Francisco, 1979-92, pres. 1989; chair local task force, Integrated Waste Mgmt. Program, San Leandro, Calif., 1989—. Office: PO Box 6087 Albany CA 94706

HEARON, WILLIAM MONTGOMERY, retired chemist; b. Kankakee, Ill., Feb. 20, 1914; s. William Edward and Dora (Wilson) H.; m. Barbara Olsen, Dec. 16, 1944; children: Steven E., Leigh, Holly. BS in Chemistry, U. Denver, 1935, MS in Chemistry, 1937; PhD, MIT, 1940. Rsch. chemist Eastman Kodak, Rochester, N.Y., 1940-43; asst. prof. MIT, Cambridge, Mass., 1946-47; chief fundamental rsch. sect. ctrl. rsch. div. Crown Zellerbach Corp., Cames, Wash., 1947-49, asst. dir. rsch. ctrl. rsch. div., 1949-55; gen. mgr. chem. products div. Crown Zellerbach Corp., Cames, 1955-60; v.p. R & D Crown Zellerbach Corp., San Francisco, 1960-67; pvt. practice mgmt. cons. Portland, Oreg., 1967-69; asst. to v.p. Boise Cascade Corp., Portland, 1969-77, dir. chem. ops., 1977-79; pvt. practice cons. Portland, 1979-90. Patentee in field; contbr. articles to profl. jours. Maj. Corp. of Engrs., U.S. Army, 1943-46. Recipient Honor award Comml. Chem. Devel. Assn., N.Y.C., 1965, R & D award Tech. Assn. Pulp & Paper Industry., Syracuse, N.Y., 1975, fellowship, Washington, 1975. Mem. Irvington Club. Presbyterian. Home: 5337 SW 34th Pl Portland OR 97201

HEARST, WILLIAM RANDOLPH, III, newspaper publisher; b. Washington, June 18, 1949; s. William Randolph and Austine (McDonnell) H.; m. Margaret Kerr Crawford, Sept. 23, 1990; children: William, Adelaide, Caroline. A.B., Harvard U., 1972. Reporter, asst. city editor San Francisco Examiner, 1972-76, publisher, 1984—; editor Outside Mag., 1976-78; asst. mng. editor Los Angeles Herald Examiner, 1978-80; mgr. devel. Hearst Corp., 1980-82; v.p. Hearst Cable Communications Div., 1982-84. Bd. dirs. Sun Microsystems; trustee Carnegie Inst. Washington. Office: San Francisco Examiner 110 5th St San Francisco CA 94103-2972

HEATH, GARY BRIAN, manufacturing firm executive, engineer; b. Pueblo, Colo., Nov. 5, 1954; s. William Sidney Heath and Eleanor Aileen (Mortimer)

Svedman, (stepfather) Donald Svedman; m. Francine Marie Tamburelli, Apr. 28, 1990. BSME, U. So. Colo., 1979; MBA, U. Phoenix, 1984. Engr. ADR Ultrasound Corp., Tempe, Ariz., 1979-81; sr. engr. Technicare Ultrasound, Englewood, Colo., 1981-83; engring. mgr. COBE Labs., Inc., Lakewood, Colo., 1983-89; dir. mfg. COBE BCT, Inc., Lakewood, 1989—; Patentee fluid flow transfer device, pressure diaphragm for fluid flow device. Mem. Soc. Mfg. Engrs., Soc. Plastics Engrs. Home: 2436 S Dover Ct Lakewood CO 80227-3109 Office: COBE BCT INC 1201 Oak St Lakewood CO 80215-4498

HEATH, GEORGE ROSS, oceanographer, university dean; b. Adelaide, Australia, Mar. 10, 1939; s. Frederick John and Eleanora (Blackmore) H.; m. Lorna Margaret Sommerville, Oct. 5, 1972; children: Amanda Jo, Alisa Jeanne. B.Sc., Adelaide U., 1960, B.Sc. with honors, 1961; Ph.D., Scripps Instn. Oceanography, U. Calif., San Diego, 1968. Geologist S. Australian Geol. Survey, Adelaide, 1961-63; asst. prof. oceanography Oreg. State U., Corvallis, 1969-72, assoc. prof., 1972-75, prof., dean, 1978-84; assoc. prof. oceanography U. R.I., Narragansett, 1974-77, prof., 1977-78; dean, prof. U. Wash., Seattle, 1984—; co-chmn. exec. com., mem. bd. oceans and atmosphere Nat. Assn. State Univs. and Land Grant Colls., 1992-93; chmn. bd. ocean sci. and policy NRC, 1984-85, mem. bd. radioactive waste mgmt., 1982-90; chmn. bd. govs. Joint Oceanographic Instns., Inc., 1982-84; v.p. SCOR, 1984-90; chmn. performance assessment peer rev. panel Waste Isolation Pilot Plant, 1987—; bd. dirs. Monterey Bay Aquarium Rsch. Inst., 1987—, Long Live the Kings; environ. analyst Sta. KIRO-TV, Seattle, 1993—. Contbr. articles to profl. jours. Recipient Fulbright award, 1963. Fellow AAAS, Geol. Soc. Am., Am. Geophys. Union; mem. Clay Mineral Soc., Oceanography Soc., The Maritime Mus. (panel advisor). Home: 3857 50th Ave NE Seattle WA 98105 Office: U Wash COFS HN-15 Seattle WA 98195

HEATH, HUNTER, III, endocrinology researcher, educator; b. Dallas, June 8, 1942; s. Hunter Jr. and Velma M. (Brandon) H.; m. Glenna A. Witt, July 25, 1965; 1 child, Ethan Ford. BA in Chemistry, Tex. Tech Coll., 1964; MD, Washington U., St. Louis, 1968. Intern, then resident in medicine U. Wis. Hosps., Madison, 1968-70; fellow in endocrinology and metabolism Walter Reed Army Med. Ctr., Washington, 1970-72; chief endocrinology sect. Letterman Army Med. Ctr., San Francisco, 1972-74; rsch. fellow in biochemistry and metabolism Grad. Sch. Medicine Mayo Clinic, Rochester, Minn., 1974-76, from asst. prof. to prof. medicine, cons. and researcher in endocrinology, 1976—, head endocrine rsch. unit, 1984-88, assoc. dir., dir. clin. rsch. ctr., 1986-88; dir. for rsch. Mayo Clinic, Scottsdale, Ariz., 1988-90; prof. medicine, chief divsn. endocrinology, metabolism and diabetes U. Utah, Salt Lake City, 1991—; me. adv. com. NIH, Bethesda, Md., 1985-88; pres., bd. dirs. Advances in Mineral Metabolism, Inc., Rochester, 1986-89; mem. select panel of physicians FAA, Washington, 1986-87. Mem. Sch. Dist. Task Force on Lang. Arts Edn., Rochester, 1984. Maj. U.S. Army, 1970-74. Fellow ACP (editorial bd. 1985-88); mem. Am. Soc. for Clin. Investigation, Am. Soc. for Bone Mineral Rsch. (councillor 1985-88), Endocrine Soc. (publs. com. 1985-88), Western Assn. Physicians, Exptl. Aircraft Assn. (chmn. aeromed. adv. coun. Oshkosh, Wis. 1987-89). Office: U Utah Sch Medicine 50 N Medical Dr Rm 4C116 Salt Lake City UT 84132

HEATH, LARMAN JEFFERSON, JR., computer information systems educator, consultant; b. Walters, Okla., July 24, 1950; s. Larman Jefferson and Mary Ruth (Culbert) H.; m. Maria Teresa Buitrago, Dec. 27, 1983 (div. Nov. 1989). BA in History, U. Okla., 1972; MA in Latin Am. History, U. de las Am., Puebla, Mexico, 1979; postgrad., Oklahoma City U., 1976, Cen. State U., Edmond, Okla., 1978-90; MS in Info. Systems, Western Internat. U., 1993. Cert. systems profl., computer programmer, data processor. Computer programmer Okla. Water Resources Bd., Oklahoma City, 1981; customer svc. rep. Tandy Computers, Oklahoma City, 1982-84; programmer/analyst Okla. Employment Security Commn., Oklahoma City, 1984-85; adj. instr. Oklahoma City Community Coll., 1983-85; instr. computer sci. data processing, assoc. instr. history Northland Pioneer Coll., Holbrook, Ariz., 1985-92; cons. bus. info. systems, Show Low, Ariz., 1986-92, Phoenix, 1992—. Mem. Assn. Inst. for Cert. Computer Profls. (Ariz. Network dir. 1990—), Ind. Computer Cons. Assn. (Phoenix assoc. mem.), Phoenix PC User Groups. Home: 2529 W Cactus Rd Apt 1008 Phoenix AZ 85029

HEATHCOCK, CLAYTON HOWELL, chemistry educator, researcher; b. San Antonio, Tex., July 21, 1936; s. Clayton H. and Frances E. (Lay) H.; m. Mabel Ruth Sims, Sept. 6, 1957 (div. 1972); children: Cheryl Lynn, Barbara Sue, Steven Wayne, Rebecca Ann; m. Cheri R. Hadley, Nov. 28, 1980. BSc, Abilene Christian Coll., Tex., 1958; PhD, U. Colo., 1963. Supr. chem. analysis group Champion Paper and Fiber Co., Pasadena, Tex., 1958-60; asst. prof. chemistry U. Calif.-Berkeley, 1964-70, assoc. prof., 1970-75, prof., 1975—, chmn., 1986-89; chmn. Medicinal Chemistry Study Sect., NIH, Washington, 1981-83; mem. sci. adv. coun. Abbott Labs., 1986—. Author: Introduction to Organic Chemistry, 1976; editor-in chief Organic Syntheses, 1985-86, Jour. Organic Chemistry, 1989—; contbr. numerous articles to profl. jours. Recipient Alexander von Humboldt U.S. Scientist, 1978, Allan R. Day award, 1989, Prelog medal, 1991. Mem. AAAS, Am. Acad. Arts and Scis., Am. Chem. Soc. (chmn. div. organic chemistry 1985, Ernest Guenther award 1986, award for creative work in synthetic organic chemistry 1990, A.C. Cope scholar 1990), Chem. Soc. London, Am. Soc. Pharmacognosy. Home: 20 Highgate Ct Kensington CA 94707-1115 Office: U Calif Dept Chemistry Berkeley CA 94720

HEBNER, PAUL CHESTER, retired oil company executive, consultant; b. Dec. 29, 1919; s. Henry G. and Mabel (Gross) H.; m. Dorothy Farrell, Feb. 16, 1943; children—Richard P., Kathleen D., Susan M., Christine L., Elizabeth A., Jeannie M. Acct., adminstrv. asst. Altman-Coady Co., Columbus, Ohio, 1940-41; mgr. acctg., exec. adminstr. T&T Oil Co. (and assoc. cos.), L.A., 1954-57; with Occidental Petroleum Corp., L.A., 1957-91, cons., 1991—. L.S.B. Leakey Found. fellow.

HEBSON, ROBERT TADD, engineering executive; b. San Francisco, Feb. 6, 1938; s. Thomas Gutchaw Hebson and Martha Alice (Smith) Houlihan; m. Opal Barnett, July 12, 1959; children: Shauna Louise, Cathy Alice, Dawn Elizabeth. AA in Elect Tech., San Francisco City Coll., 1958; BS in Elec. Engring., San Jose State U., 1964; MS in Systems Engring., West Coast U., 1969. Engr. Gen. Dynamics, Pomona, Calif., 1964-69; engring. dir. Kaiser Electronics, San Jose, Calif., 1969—. Office: Kaiser Electronics 2701 Orchard Pky San Jose CA 95134-2083

HECHT, CHIC, ambassador, former senator; b. Cape Giradeau, Mo., Nov. 30, 1928; m. Gail Hecht; children: Lori, Leslie. B.S., Washington U., St. Louis, 1949; postgrad., Mil. Intelligence Sch., Ft. Holibird, Mo., 1951. Mem. Nev. State Senate, 1966-74, Rep. minority leader, 1968-72; mem. U.S. Senate from Nev., 1982-89, mem. Banking, Housing and Urban Affairs Com., chmn. housing and urban affairs subcom., mem. Energy and Natural Resources Com., mem. Senate Select Com. on Intelligence; amb. to The Bahamas, 1989-93. Served with U.S. Army, 1951-53. Mem. Nat. Counter Intelligence Corps. (past pres.), Nat. Mil. Intelligence Assn.

HECHT, KARL EUGENE, banker; b. Clovis, N.Mex., Aug. 5, 1956; s. Harold and Mary (Byerly) H.; m. Candace Dawn Downey, Aug. 18, 1978; children: Jonathan David, Joshua Caleb. Student, N.Mex. State U., 1974-76, So. Meth. U., 1988. Compliance officer Citizens Bank, Clovis, N.Mex., 1979—; trust officer Citizens Bank, Clovis, 1985—; instr. Clovis C.C., 1982—. Mem. Am. Bankers Assn. (corp. trust assocs. 1989-90), Ind. Bankers Assn. N.Mex., N.Mex. Am. Inst. Banking (bd. dirs.), Lions (pres. 1988), Bright Hopes Found. (bd. dirs. 1989-90). Republican. Home: PO Box 1274 Clovis NM 88102-1274 Office: Citizens Bank 421 Pile St Clovis NM 88101-7540

HECK, CATHY LAURA, insurance professional; b. Chgo., Jan. 6, 1966; d. Neal Roy and Alma Marie (Hornbeck) H. BA in Communication Arts and Sci., Rosary Coll., River Forest, Ill., 1988. Supr. Telemktg. Co., Chgo., 1985-88, Direct Response Corp., Glenview, Ill., 1988-90; claim adjustor Viking Ins. Co., Irvine, Calif., 1990—. Roman Catholic. Home: 27801 Espinoza Mission Viejo CA 92692-2104

HECK, STEPHEN JOHN, information technology services executive; b. Chgo., Oct. 15, 1946; s. Kenneth Eugene and Helen Lucille (Dyer) H.; m. Julie Elizabeth Johnson, Jan. 10, 1969; children: Erika, Gretchen. BA in Social Scis., Portland (Oreg.) State u., 1968, MPA, 1982; MSW, U. Wash., 1973. Social work intern VA, Seattle, 1972-73; family cons. Boys & Girls Aid Soc., Portland, 1973-74; clin. social worker Childrens Svcs. div. State of Oreg., Portland, 1974-79, Edgefield Lodge, Inc., Portland, 1979-82; contracts specialist Jet Propulsion Lab., Pasadena, Calif., 1982-84; systems analyst Bonneville Power Adminstrn., Portland, 1984-90; program dir. Advanced Data Concepts, Inc., Portland, 1990—; instr., cons. Marylhurst (Oreg.) Coll., 1988—; adj. assoc. prof. Portland State U., 1984—; field instr. Sch. of Social Work, Portland State U., 1975-81. Illustrator (book) Somewhere After 29, 1976; monthly columnist (newsletter) Heck of a Column, 1990—; author (screenplay) Remembrance, 1992. V.p. Foster Parents Assn., Portland, 1979-82, Burnside Projects, Inc., Portland, 1988-90; com. chmn. City Club of Portland, 1985-88. With U.S. Army, 1969-71. Recipient Achievement award Presdl. Mgmt. Intern Program, 1984. Mem. Nat. Contract Mgmt. Assn. (treas. 1991-92), Quality Assurance Inst., Assn. Quality 7 Participation, Portland State U. Faculty Assn., Phi Kappa Phi. Democrat. Home: 2817 NE Mason Portland OR 97211 Office: Advanced Data Concepts Inc 700 NE Multnomah Portland OR 97232

HECKER, DAVID ALAN, English, humanities and American Studies educator; b. Mandan, N.D., Nov. 20, 1939; s. Adam George and Lily Aster (Peterson) H.; m. Helen J. Black Hecker; children: Jeffrey, Michelle. BA, Minot State. U., 1961; MA, U. Minn., 1964; PhD, Wash. State U., 1983. Instr. English, humanities and Am. studies Olympic Coll., Bremerton, Wash., 1964—; coord. Am. Culture Program, Olympic Coll., 1977—, coord. ann. writers' conf., 1992, 93; speaker Wash. State Community Coll. Bd. Trustees Ann. Conv., Silverdale, 1989. Book reviewer Western Am. Lit. Jour., 1987—; co-editor Signals Lit. Jour., 1992, 93; contbr. articles to profl. jours. Grantee NEH, 1977, 80, 90, Wash. Com. for Humanities, 1985. Mem. Am. Studies Assn. (program chair), Community Coll. Humanities Assn., Wash. State Historic Soc., Smithsonian, Audubon. Office: Olympic Coll HS&S Div 16th & Chester Bremerton WA 98310

HECKLER, GERARD VINCENT, lawyer; b. Utica, N.Y., Feb. 18, 1941; s. Gerard Vincent and Mary Jane (Finocan) H. BA, Union Coll., Schenectady, 1962; JD, Syracuse U., 1970. Bar: Ill. 1971, Calif. 1980, Mass. 1986, N.Y. 1986, U.S. Supreme Ct. 1985. Assoc. Martin, Craig, Chester & Sonnenschein, Chgo., 1970-73, Goldstein, Goldberg & Fishman, Chgo., 1973-76; ptnr. Heckler & Enstrom, Chgo., 1976-80; pvt. practice law L.A., Irvine, 1980-85; sr. trial atty. Law Office of Harden Bennion, L.A., 1985-87, Rafferty & Polich, Cambridge, Mass., 1987-8; trial atty. Acret, Gropman & Turner, L.A., 1989-92; instr. trial skills and evidence Calif. State Bar, 1987—; judge pro tem L.A. Mcpl. Ct., 1991—. Lt. USCG, 1964-67, Vietnam. Mem. Calif. State Bar (Bd. Govs. commendation 1986), L.A. County Bar Assn., Acad. Family Mediators, Ill. Bar Assn., Mass. Bar Assn., N.Y. Bar Assn. Office: 4 Hutton Ctr Ste 300 Santa Ana CA 92707

HECKMAN, RICHARD AINSWORTH, chemical engineer; b. Phoenix, July 15, 1929; s. Hiram and Anne (Sells) H.; m. Olive Ann Biddle, Dec. 17, 1950; children: Mark, Bruce. BS, U. Calif., Berkeley, 1950, cert. hazardous mgmt. U. Calif., Davis, 1985. Registered profl. engr., Calif. With radiation lab. U. Calif., Berkeley, 1950-51; chem. engr. Calif. Rsch. & Devel. Co., Livermore, 1951-53; assoc. div. leader Lawrence Livermore Nat. Lab., 1953-77, project leader, 1977-78, program leader, 1978-79, energy policy analyst, 1979-83, toxic waste group staff engr., 1984-86, waste minimization project leader, 1986-90; div. dir. hazardous waste mgmt. Nationwide Technologies, Inc., Oakland, 1990-91; mng. dir. Heckman & Assocs., 1991-92; v.p. environ. scis. Pan Am. Resources Inc., Pleasanton, Calif., 1992—, also bd. dirs.. Mem. Calif. Radioactive Materials Forum. Co-author: Nuclear Waste Management Abstracts, 1983; patentee in field. Bd. dirs. Calif. Industries for Blind, 1977-80, Here and Now Disabled Svcs. for Tri-Valley, Inc., 1980. Calif. Fellow Am. Inst. Chemists, Acad. Hazardous Materials Mgmt.; mem. AAAS, Am. Acad. Environ. Engrs. (diplomate), Am. Chemistry Soc., Am. Inst. Chem. Engrs., Am. Nuclear Soc., Soc. Profl. Engrs., Water Environ. Fedn., Air and Waste Mgmt. Assn., Internat. Union Pure and Applied Chemistry (assoc.), Nat. Hist. Soc., N.Y. Acad. Scis., Internat. Oceanographic Soc., Environ. Assessment Assn. (registered environ. assessor Calif.), Engrs. Club San Francisco, Commonwealth Club San Francisco, Richmond Yacht Club, Island Yacht Club (commodore 1971), Midget Ocean Racing Club (sta. 3 commodore 1982-83), U.S. Yacht Racing Union, Midget Ocean Racing Assn. No. Calif. (commodore 1972). Home and Office: Pan Am Resources Environ Scis Dept 5683 Greenridge Rd Castro Valley CA 94552-2625

HECKSCHER, ERIC, media organization executive, writer; b. Brussels, Apr. 3, 1923; came to U.S., 1948; s. Kay and Germaine (Scaron) H; m. K. Donovan, 1959 (dec. 1961); children: Daniela, Gail, Shari-Lynn, Ingrid. Cert. naval scis., U. Southampton, Eng., 1942; PhD in Psychology, Inst. des Etudes Superieures en Sciences Humaines, Montreal, Can., 1974; cert., Learning Systems Inst., Paris. Cert. in clin. child psychology. Asst. dir. Marsden Found. for Gifted Youth, Santa Barbara, Calif., 1952-55; mgr. video sonics Hughes Aircraft Co., Culver City, Calif., 1955-58; exec. producer Auca Films Inc, Hollywood, Calif., 1958-63; producer Plan Alto Produções, São Paulo, Brazil, 1963-65; dir. devel. Playboy Enterprises, Chgo., 1965-67; dir. manpower Booz Allen Hamilton, London and Paris, 1967-71; chief mgmt. communication UN, Geneva, 1971-80; pres. Media and Talent Orgn. Inc., Beverly Hills, Calif., 1980—; dir. edn. Valley Coll., Los Angeles, 1986—; prof. psychology Cath. U., São Paulo, 1960-63; exec. producer Eric Heckscher Prodn. Internat., Beverly Hills, 1958—. Author: Sleep with the Angels, My Love..., 1963; scriptwriter (TV film) 'Twas the Night After Christmas, 1985; producer, dir., writer numerous films; contbr. articles to profl. jours. Served to capt. Brit. Naval Intelligence, 1941-46. Fellow Am. Orthopsychiat. Assn., Internat. Council Psychologists; mem. Internat. Communications Inst., Soc. of Motion Picture and TV Engrs., Am. Mgmt. Assn., Am. Film Inst., Soc. Internat. Applied Psychology. Home and Office: Media & Talent Orgn Inc PO Box 16897 Beverly Hills CA 90209-2897

HEDAHL, GORDEN ORLIN, actor, director, drama educator; b. Minot, N.D., Jan. 2, 1946; s. Chester Owen and Delores May (Johnson) H.; m. Kathleen Josephine Sawin, Sept. 2, 1967 (div.); children: Marc Oscar, Melissa Ann; m. Jean Louise Loudon, Dec. 31, 1983. BS, U. N.D., 1968, MA in Theater and Media, 1972; PhD, U. Minn., 1980. Postdoctoral fellow Purdue U., West Lafayette, Ind., 1981-82; chmn. dept. theater and dance U. Wis., Whitewater, 1970-89, assoc. dean Coll. Arts, 1990-91, acting assoc. vice chancellor, 1991-92; dean Coll. Liberal Arts U. Alaska, Fairbanks, 1993—; acad. planner U. Wis. System, 1990-91; drama and film cons. Summer Migrant Program, Burlington, Wis., 1972-73; actor Ind. Repertory Theatre, Indpls., 1981-82; freelance dir., actor, child drama and filmmaking cons. Author: (plays) Tall Tales and True, 1976, The Brothers Grimm, 1977, Land of the Rising Sun, 1979, Trolls and Other Fjord Folk, 1983, Andersen's Storybook, 1986, The Magic of Oz, 1987, African Folk Tales, 1989, Tell Me a Story, 1992; editor: Technical Theatre Course Guide-K to 12, 1983, The Making of a Musical-Videotape, 1983, Guide to Curriculum Planning in Classroom Drama and Theatre, 1989, Agriculture and Natural Resource Education for 2020, 1991. Gov. Gt. Lakes Region Children's Theatre Assn., 1977-78, 80-81; bd. govs. Wis. Alliance for Arts Edn., 1985-88. Recipient Outstanding New Dir. award Children's Theatre Assn. Am., 1977, Outstanding Educator award Whitewater Regional Jaycees, 1980, Roseman Excellence in Teaching award u. Wis. System, Whitewater, U. Wis. Faculty Devel. grantee, 1981-82, Undergrad. Teaching Improvement grantee, 1982-83, Wis. Inst. Race and Ethnicity, 1990—. Mem. Am. Alliance for Theatre and Edn. (chair multi-cultural com. 1990-92, editor newsletter 1991—), Theatre in Higher Edn., Wis. Theatre Assn. (bd. govs. 1977-81, 82-86), Internat. Assn. Theatre for Children and Youth. Lutheran. Office: U Alaska Fairbanks Coll of Liberal Arts 405 Gruening Fairbanks AK 99775-0980

HEDDERLY-SMITH, DAVID ARTHUR, consulting economic geologist; b. Seattle, Jan. 24, 1948; s. Arthur Hedderly-Smith and Prudence (Lambuth) Trudgian. BS in Geology, Western Wash. State Coll., 1971; MS in Geol. Scis., U. Wash., 1975; postgrad., U. Utah, 1987—. Project geologist Bren Mac Mines, Ltd., Vancouver, B.C., Can., 1972-74; exploration geologist Cities Svc. Minerals Corp., Anchorage, 1975-77; geologist Bear Creek Mining Co. (Kennecott Corp.), Spokane, Wash., 1977; sr. geologist, v.p. Greatland Exploration, Ltd., Anchorage, 1977-80; dep. dir. div. minerals and energy Alaska Dept. Natural Resources, Anchorage, 1981-84; assoc. instr., rsch. asst. U. Utah, Salt Lake City, 1988-91; cons. econ. geologist D.A. Hedderly-Smith & Assocs., Anchorage and Park City, Utah, 1984—; cons. Sealaska Corp., Juneau, Alaska, 1988—; bd. dirs. Mt. Andrew Mining Co., Park City. Contbr. articles to profl. jours. Dem. candidate for Alaska Ho. of Reps., 1984; dep. campaign mgr. Glen Olds for U.S. Senator, 1986. Fellow Soc. Econ. Geologists; mem. Assn. Exploration Geochemists, Soc. Mining Engrs., Alaska Miners Assn., N.W. Mining Assn., Utah Geol. Assn., Profl. Ski Instrs. Assn. (cert. level II). Episcopalian. Office: PO Box 443 Park City UT 84060

HEDGPETH, JOEL, soil and water chemist, researcher, consultant; b. Dinuba, Calif., Oct. 31, 1911; s. George Pierce and Sarah (Blair) H.; m. Allee Boyd Smith, Mar. 31, 1939; children: Joel, Charles Boyd, George Pierce, Sara. BS in Agr., Oreg. State Coll., Corvallis, 1934. Lab. technician, dairy products salesman, plant supt. Golden State Co. Ltd., El Centro, Calif., 1934-38; sales mgr. Golden State Co. Ltd., Fresno, Calif., 1938-43; owner, operator dairy farm, Clovis, Calif., 1943-50; cotton and cattle operator Calif., 1950-59; developer methods of treating waters and soil overcoming both alkali and acid conditions, 1959—; chmn. bd. Bio-Ag Industries Corp., Fresno, 1959—. Author in-house manuals for edn. of sales pers. and customers; patentee in field. Home: 723 Almond Dr Clovis CA 93612 Office: Bio-Ag Indsl Corp 2820 E Church Ave Fresno CA 93706

HEDLUND, ELLEN KATHERINE, university administrator; b. Evanston, Ill., Feb. 26, 1963; d. William Francis and JoAnn (King) Sheehan; m. Martin Robert Hedlund, Oct. 22, 1988. BA, Denison U., 1985; MEd, Ariz. State U., 1992. Asst. to the dean of student life Denison U., Granville, Ohio, 1985-87; residence hall dir. Ariz. State U., Tempe, 1987-88; sr. acad. advisor Ariz. State U. West, Phoenix, 1989—. Vol. Schoolhouse, Phoenix, 1989—, Christmas in April, Phoenix, 1992—. Mem. Nat. Assn. of Acad. (conf. presenter 1989, 90, 91, 93), Ariz. Coll. Pers. Assn. (conf. presenter 1990), Univ. Career Women, Nat. Assn. of Women in Edn. Home: 2121 W Myrtle Phoenix AZ 85021 Office: Ariz State U West 4701 W Thunderbird Phoenix AZ 85069-7100

HEDLUND, RICHARD THOMAS, life insurance administrative officer; b. Pasedena, Calif., 1948. Pepperdine Coll., 1970, U. So. Calif., 1971. Sr. v.p. administrn. Transam. Life Ins. (subs. Transam. Ins. Corp. Calif.), L.A. Home: 2019 Elluns Pl Arcadia CA 91006 Office: Transamerica Occidental Life Ins Co 1150 S Olive St Los Angeles CA 90051-0101*

HEDMAN, GEORGE WILLIAM, lawyer; b. Chgo., Sept. 29, 1923; s. George Edward and Susan Welde (Dent) H.; m. Louisa Wetherbee, Apr. 26, 1947 (div. 1973); children: Mark, C. William, Jason; m. Evelyn L. Ramey, Jan. 1, 1987; children: David, Rebecca, Richard. JD, Ill. Tech., 1950; PhD in Psychology, Fla. Inst. Tech., 1981. Bar: Hawaii 1950, Am. Samoa 1953, Fla. 1956. Pvt. practice Honolulu, 1950-53, Melbourne, Fla. and Port Angeles, Wash., 1962—; attorney gen. Govt. Am. Samoa, Pago Pago, 1953-55; exec. Edison Electric Inst., N.Y.C., 1956-62. Author: Florida's New No-Fault Divorce Law, 1973, Divorce Without (Much) Agony, 1978. Mem. Brevard County Sch. Bd., Titusville, Fla., 1968-72. Sgt. U.S. Army, 1943-46. Mem. Fla. Bar Assn. Home: 112 W Highway # 101 Port Angeles WA 98362

HEDRICK, JOSEPH WATSON, JR., judge; b. Fresno, Calif., Nov. 29, 1924; s. Joseph Watson and Kathryn (Watson) H.; m. Coleena Alice Wade, June 17, 1949; children—Joseph Wade, Robert S. B.S., U. Calif.-Berkeley, 1950; LL.B., U. Calif.-San Francisco, 1952. Bar: Calif. 1953. Assoc. Rowell Lamberson & Thomas, Fresno, 1953; mcht., Fresno, 1954; atty. Fresno County Legal Services, Inc., 1967; ptnr. Lerrigo, Thuesen & Thompson, Fresno, 1971, Lerrigo, Thuesen, Walters, Nibler & Hedrick, Fresno, from 1972; judge Modesto div. Ea. Dist. Calif., U.S. Bankruptcy Ct., 1980—. Served with AUS, 1943-46. Office: US Bankruptcy Ct PO Box 5276 Modesto CA 95352-5276

HEDRICK, WALLACE EDWARD, director state lottery; b. Malad, Idaho, Nov. 11, 1947; s. Clarence Franklin and Beth S. Hedrick; BS, U. Nev., Reno, 1970; MA, U. No. Colo., Greeley, 1974; m. Jerrie S. Deffenbaugh, Nov. 20, 1980; children: Ann Elizabeth, Ryan Wallace, Hallie Sue. Regional dir. No. Idaho, Idaho Planning and Community Affairs Agy., Moscow, 1970-73, assoc. chief, Boise, 1973-75; project dir. Pacific N.W. Regional Commn., Boise, 1975-76; pres. Resources N.W., Inc., Boise, 1976-88; dir. Idaho State Lottery, 1988—. Sec.-treas. Idaho Citizens for Responsible Govt., 1978-80; trustee, chmn. Joint Sch. Dist. 2, 1985—; trustee Meridian Sch. Bd.; bd. dirs. Nat. Vandal Boosters, Inc. Served with USAR, 1971. Democrat. Home: 9413 Knottingham Dr Boise ID 83704-2234 Office: Idaho State Lottery 1199 Shoreline Ln Ste 100 Boise ID 83702-9101

HEDRICKS, CYNTHIA ANN, educator; b. Lancaster, Pa., June 23, 1949; 1 child, Charles Meade. BA in Psychology, Franklin & Marshall Coll., 1974; MA in Exptl. Psychol., U. Hartford, 1981; MA in Biopsychology, U. Chgo., 1981, PhD in Biopsychology, 1985. Postdoctoral fellow Carolina Population Ctr., U. N.C., Chapel Hill, 1985-87; project dir. U. Ill., Chgo., 1987-90; asst. prof. U. So. Calif., L.A., 1991—; rsch. cons. Givaudan-Roure, Inc., Teaneck, N.J.; faculty in residence U. So. Calif., 1992—. Mem. N.Y. Acad. Scis., Conf. on Reproductive Behavior, Soc. for Menstrual Cycle Rsch. (2d v.p. 1991—, newsletter editor 1991—), U. So. Calif. Med. Faculty Women's Assn., U. So. Calif. Feminist Coun., World Rsch. Network on the Sexuality of Women and Girls, Sigma Xi. Office: U So Calif CSA-203 2250 Alcazar St Los Angeles CA 90033

HEDSTROM, KENNETH GERALD, insurance company executive; b. Spokane, Wash., Oct. 27, 1939; s. Elof Gerald Hedstrom and Audrey Ellen (Cox) Crawford; m. Sandra Elaine Vandersluys, Oct. 17, 1964; children: Kelli Anne, Kristina Suzanne. Grad. high sch., Spokane, 1957. Collection mgr. Pacific Fin., Spokane, 1960-63; credit mgr. Sears, Medford, Oreg., 1963-76; field underwriter Mony Fin. Services, Medford, Oreg., 1976—. Bd. dirs. Consumer Credit Counseling Service, Medford, 1967-1984, 1st Ch. of the Nazarene, Medford, 1981-90, Blossom Hill Child Devel. Ctr., Medford, 1981-1986. Served with USCG, 1958-60. Recipient Mony Top Club award Mony Fin. Svcs., 1986, 79—. Mem. Rogue Valley Life Underwriters (pres. 1984-86), Jackson County C. of C., Oreg. Life Underwriters (bd. dirs. 1984-86), Nat. Assn. Life Underwriters (Nat. Sales Achievement award 1978-90, Nat. Quality award 1978-90, Million Dollar Round Table 1984-92). Republican. Home: 1445 N Keeneway Dr Medford OR 97504-5583 Office: Oreg Pacific Fin Group Inc 1032 E Jackson St Medford OR 97504-7000

HEDSTROM, SUSAN LYNNE, maternal/women's health nurse; b. Dowagiac, Mich., Jan. 17, 1958; d. Clinton J. and Gloria Anna (Hyink) Moore. ADN, Southwestern Mich. Coll., 1978. RN, Mich., Ind., S.C., Calif. Staff nurse obstetrics unit Lee Meml. Hosp., Dowagiac, Mich., 1979-81, Meml. Hosp., South Bend, Ind., 1981-90; with MRA Staffing Systems, Inc., Ft. Lauderdale, Fla., 1990—; staff nurse traveler MUSC, Charleston, S.C., 1990-91; nurse Desert Hosp., Palm Springs, Calif., 1991, Ind. U. Hosp., Indpls., 1992, Valley Med Ctr., Fresno, Calif., 1992—. Mem. NAACOG. Office: MRA Staffing Systems 7771 W Oakland Park Blvd Fort Lauderdale FL 33351-6796

HEDWALL, JEANETTE NICKEL, area manager; b. Madison, Wis., Mar. 21, 1937; d. George Julius and Sophie Marie (Lorenzen) Nickel; children: Tamra Haldeman, Thomas Klevgaard. Student, U. Wis., 1956-57. Keyboard sales person Forbes Meagher Music, Madison, Wis., 1970-77; mgr. Sherman Clay, Seattle, 1977-91; area mgr. Sherman Clay, Las Vegas, 1991—. Recipient Spl. Achievement award Sherman Clay. Mem. Nat. Assn. Music Merchants. Home: #297 2245 N Green Valley Pky Henderson NV 89014

HEEBNER, CHARLES FREDERICK, retired botanist; b. Norwich, Conn., Apr. 30, 1938; s. Raymond Harold and Stella Rose (Dudek) H.; m. Beverly Cora Banks, Oct. 17, 1959; 1 child, Kelli Arden. BA, U. Conn., 1960, MS, 1963; PhD, Wash. State U., 1970. Plant physiologist U.S. Fish & Wildlife Svc., Olympia, Wash., 1968-74; rsch. assoc. Western Wash. Rsch. & Exptl.

Sta., Puyullup, Wash., 1974-76; forest geneticist Wash. Dept. Natural Resources, Olympia, 1977-83.

HEEKIN, VALERIE ANNE, telecommunications technician; b. Santa Monica, Calif., Nov. 7, 1953; d. Edward Raphael and Jane Eileen (Potter) H. AA, L.A. Valley Coll., 1980; BS magna cum laude, Calif. Baptist Coll., 1987. Telecommunications technician Pacific Bell Co., Canoga Park, Calif., 1971—; pres. Odyssey Adventures, Inc., Sylmar, Calif., 1987—. Pres. Parkwood Sylmar Homeowners Assn., 1981-89; activist civil rights. Republican. Roman Catholic. Office: Odyssey Adventures PO Box 923094 Sylmar CA 91392-3094

HEER, DONALD GARY, mortuary science practitioner; b. Igloo, S.D., June 29, 1948; s. Edgar and Rita Jean (Knight) H.; m. Carol J. Matson, June 10, 1968; children: Jill, Gary. Diploma, Dallas Inst. Mortuary Sci., 1969. Cert. funeral svc. practitioner. Trainee Behrens Mortuary, Rapid City, S.D., 1966-68; funeral dir. Gale Funeral Home, Brush, Colo., 1969-79; funeral dir., CEO Heer Mortuary, Brush, 1979—; bd. dirs. First Security Bank, Ft. Lupton, Brush and Yuma, Colo. Bd. dirs. East Morgan County Hosp. Dist., Brush, 1985—, Hospes of Morgan County, Inc. Mem. Nat. Funeral Dirs. Assn. (disaster mgmt. task force 1990-92), Colo. Funeral Dirs. Assn. (pres. 1987-88, funeral dir. of the yr. 1988), Nat. Found. for Mortuary Care (bd. dirs. 1992—), Brush Rotary Club (treas. 1989—), Bunker Hill Country Club. Home: 512 Edmunds St Brush CO 80723 Office: Heer Mortuary 222 Cameron Brush CO 80723

HEER, EWALD, engineer; b. Friedensfeld, Germany, July 28, 1930; s. Johannes and Lilli Friedericke (Jauch) H.; came to U.S., 1956. Diploma Archtl. Engring., Sch. Hamburg, 1953; B.S., CUNY, 1959; M.S., Columbia U., 1960, C.E., 1962; Dr Engring. Sc. magna cum laude, Tech. U., Hannover, Fed. Republic Germany., 1964; m. Hannelore M. Oehlers, Jan. 26, 1952; children: Thomas Ewald, Eric Martin. Engr. Hinz Architects, Hamburg, Fed. Republic Germany, 1952-55; design engr. Hewitt Robins Co., N.Y.C., 1956-59; rsch. engr. Weidlinger Cons., N.Y.C., 1959-62, McDonnell Douglas, St. Louis, 1964-65; rsch. mgr. GE, Phila., 1965-66; rsch. mgr. Jet Propulsion Lab., Pasadena, Calif., 1966-70, program mgr. advanced studies, 1971-76, dir. rsch. program autonomous systems and space mechanics, 1976-84, pres. Heer Assocs., Inc., 1984—; program mgr. Lunar exploration office NASA, Washington, 1970-71; adj. prof. U. So. Calif., 1973-84, dir. Inst. Technoecon. Studies, 1978-84. Fellow ASME; assoc. fellow AIAA; mem. ASCE, IEEE, Am. Mgmt. Assn., Internat. Fedn. Theory Machines and Mechanisms, Sigma Xi. Editor: Remotely Manned Systems, 1973, Robots and Manipulator Systems I & II, 1977, Machine Intelligence and Autonomy for Aerospace Systems, 1988; contbr. articles to profl. jours. Home: 5329 Crown Ave La Canada Flintridge CA 91011-2807 Office: 4800 Oak Grove Dr Pasadena CA 91109-8099

HEERMANS, JOHN MICHAEL, electrical, chemical engineer; b. The Dalles, Oreg., Nov. 24, 1958; s. Donald Jerome and Motrona A. H.; m. Karen Marie Hudson, Nov. 8, 1987. BS in Chem. Engring., U. Calif., Santa Barbara, 1983; MSEE, U. So. Calif., L.A., 1989. Engr. Grumman Aerospace Corp., Nas Pt. Mugu, Calif., 1983-86; project engr. Hughes Aircraft Co., El Segundo, Calif., 1986—. Republican. Seventh-Day Adventist. Office: Hughes Aircraft Co PO Box 92426 RE/R31/G517 Los Angeles CA 90009

HEERS, ARTHUR FRANK, electrical engineer; b. Dragerton, Utah, June 20, 1944; s. Robert G. and Margaret (Babcock) H.; m. Mary Margaret Snyder, June 15, 1967; children:L Jennifer Lin, Jesse Frank. BS, Stanford U., 1966, MSEE, 1968. Application engr. Hewlett Packard, Sunnyvale, Calif., 1968-70; design engr. Campbell Sci., Inc., Logan, Utah, 1981-87, v.p. engring., 1987—, also bd. dirs.; tchr. San Francisco State Coll., 1968-70. Co-inventor ultrasonic level detection patent. Mem. Phi Beta Kappa. Home: 590 N 100 W Mendon UT 84325 Office: Campbell Sci Inc 815 W 1800 N Logan UT 84321-1784

HEFFELFINGER, DAVID MARK, optical engineer; b. Ft. Worth, Jan. 10, 1951; s. Hugo Wagner and Betty Lu (Graf) H.; m. Barbara Lynne Putnam, May 1, 1980; children: Jakob, Leon, Stacy. MS in Physics, Wayne State U., 1984. Project scientist GM Rsch. Lab., Warren, Mich., 1978-90; grad. rsch. asst. Wayne State U., Detroit, 1982-84; optical group leader Bio-Rad Labs., Richmond, Calif., 1990—. Contbr. articles to Jour. Applied Physics, Bull. Am. Phys. Soc. Recipient Vaden Miles award Wayne State U., 1982. Mem. AAAS, Internat. Soc. Optical Engring., Optical Soc. Am. Office: Bio Rad Labs 2000 Alfred Nobel Dr Hercules CA 94547

HEFFERN, RICHARD ARNOLD, author; b. Orange, Calif., July 24, 1950; s. Frank Schnepp Heffern and Mary Claire (Dominguez) Elliott; m. Matilde Lopez, Aug. 21, 1971; children: Christina Marie, Richard Arnold Jr. Student, Fullerton Coll., 1968-71, Calif. State U., Fullerton, 1971-75. Lab. technician Natural Products Devel. Corp., Orange, 1971-76; sr. editor Trinity Ctr. Press., Beaumont, Calif., 1974-77; freelance Santa Ana, Calif., 1971—. Author: The Herb Buyers Guide, 1973, The Complete Book of Ginseng, 1976, Secrets of the Mind-Altering Plants of Mexico, 1974, The Use of Herbs in Weight Reduction, 1975, Time Travel: Myth or Reality, 1977; cons.: (book) New Age Nutrition, 1974, Elementary Treatise in Herbology, 1974, Dictionary of Health and Nutrition, 1976, Advanced Treatise in Herbology, 1978.

HEFFLINGER, LEROY ARTHUR, agricultural manager; b. Omaha, Feb. 14, 1935; s. Leroy William and Myrtle Irene (Lampe) H.; m. Carole June Wickman, Dec. 23, 1956; children: Dean Alan, Andrew Karl, Roger Glenn, Dale Gorden. BS in Fin., U. Colo., 1957. Mgr. Hefflinger Ranches, Inc., Toppenish, Wash., 1963-73; pres. Hefflinger Ranches, Inc., 1973—; bd. dirs. Hop Adminstrv. Com., Portland, Oreg., 1980-86; trustee Agr. and Forestry Edn. Found., Spokane, Wash., 1988—, vice chmn., 1993. Vestryman, bd. dirs. St. Michael's Ch., Yakima, Wash., 1969-74; mem. capital campaign com. Heritage Coll., Toppenish, 1990-91. Capt. USAF, 1958-63. Mem. Hop Growers Am. (bd. dirs., past pres.), Hop Growers Wash. (bd. dirs., past treas.), Beta Theta Pi. Republican. Episcopalian. Office: Hefflinger Ranches Inc PO Box 47 Toppenish WA 98948-0047

HEFFNER, CAROLYN DEE, English language educator, theater director; b. Columbus, Ohio, Apr. 20, 1947; d. Delbert Russell and Carol Mae (Rhodeback) Krumm; m. Dennis Dean Heffner, Mar. 21, 1970; children: Todd Dean, Heidi Dawn, Andrew Del. BA, Otterbein Coll., 1969; MLS, U. Mich., 1969; MA, St. John's Coll., 1988. Cert. tchr., N.Mex. Govt. documents clk. Otterbein Coll. Libr., Westerville, Ohio, summer 1968; sub. tchr. Columbus Pub. Schs., spring 1970; libr. United Theol. Sem., Dayton, Ohio, 1970-71; English tchr. McCurdy Sch., Espanola, N.Mex., 1971-72, English tchr., drama tchr., 1975—. Chairperson Espanola Valley Community Activities, 1975-80; bd. dirs. City Beautiful Com., Espanola, 1988-90; adult vol. 4-H, Rio Arriba County, N.Mex., 1984-88. Recipient AP summer inst. award N.Mex. Ednl. Assistance Found., 1991. Mem. Nat. Assn. Deaconesses/Home Missionaries (communication facilitator, newsletter editor 1988—), N.Mex. Coun. Tchrs. English (judge awards 1984-90), Tau Delta, Phi Kappa Phi, Beta Phi Mu. Methodist. Home: 605 Camino Santa Cruz Espanola NM 87532 Office: McCurdy Sch PO Box 127 Espanola NM 87532

HEFFNER, HERBERT FLOYD, public relations executive, consultant; b. Bklyn., Aug. 23, 1936; s. William Winfield II and Doris Rosemary (Miller) H.; m. Suzanne Elizabeth Bogert, Dec. 27, 1959; children: Grace, William Winfield III, John Andrew. BS, Pa. State U., 1958; MBA with distinction, NYU, 1966. Mktg. writer We. Electric, AT&T, N.Y.C., 1961-65; dir. comm. Sealtest Foods div. Nat. Dairy Prodrs. Corp., N.Y.C., 1966-72; pres. Bert Heffner Comm. Inc., Leonia, N.J., 1973-78; dir. pub. info. Detroit Edison, 1979-89; mgr. pub. info. Sacramento Mcpl. Utility Dist., 1990-91; mgr. area rels. Lawrence Livermore (Calif.) Nat. Lab., 1991—. Prodr. Higher Horizons, 1965-68 (Peabody award 1966); contbr. articles to profl. jours. Chmn. Conservative Ednl. Inst., Leonia, 1964-66; mem. Clarksburg (Calif.) Adv. Coun., 1992—; trustee Leonia Sch. Bd., 1966-74, Clarksburg Libr. Bd., 1992—. Home: PO Box 448 Clarksburg CA 95612 Office: U Calif Lawrence Livermore Nat Lab PO Box 808 L790 Livermore CA 94550

HEFLEY, JOEL M., congressman; b. Ardmore, Okla., Apr. 18, 1935; s. J. Maurice and Etta A. (Anderson) H.; m. Lynn Christian, Aug. 25, 1962; children: Janna, Lori, Juli. B.A., Okla. Baptist U., 1957; M.S., Okla. State U., 1963. Exec. dir. Community Planning and Research, Colorado Springs, Colo., 1966-86; mem. Colo. Ho. of Reps., 1977-78, Colo. Senate, 1979-87, 100th-103rd Congresses from 5th Colo. dist., 1987—; mem. armed svcs. com., mem. natural resources com., mem. small bus.-SBA com. Republican. Baptist. Clubs: Rotary, Colorado Springs Country. Office: House of Representatives 2442 Rayburn Washington DC 20515-0605

HEFNER, CASSANDRA JEWELL, mortgage banker, investment banker, marketing executive; b. Dubuque, Iowa, Aug. 7, 1956; d. Milton Dudley and Aderine Lorraine (Lang) Ebner; 1 child, Andrew Jackson. Student, Glendale Community Coll., 1975, 83-85, Ariz. State U., 1984. Loan officer Sutter Trust Co., Phoenix, 1977-78; asst. v.p. Saguaro Savs. & Loan, Phoenix, 1978-81; account exec. Verex Assurance Co., Phoenix, 1981-84; v.p. Citicorp, Phoenix, 1984—. Mem. Ariz. Mortgage Bankers Assn. (bd. dirs. 1986–), Assn. Profl. Mortgage Women (pres. 1983). Methodist. Office: Citibank 3300 N Central Ave Ste 800 Phoenix AZ 85012-2504

HEGARTY, GEORGE JOHN, academic administrator, English educator; b. Cape May, N.J., July 20, 1948; s. John Joseph and Gloria Anna (Bonelli) H.; m. Joy Elizabeth Schiller, June 9, 1979. Student, U. Fribourg, Switzerland, 1968-69; BA in English, LaSalle U., Phila., 1970; Cert., Coll. de la Pocatiere, Que., Can., 1970; postgrad., U. Dakar, Senegal, 1970, Case Western Res. U., 1973-74, U. N.H., 1976; MA in English, Drake U., 1977; postgrad., U. Iowa, 1977; DA, Drake U., 1978; Cert., UCLA, 1979, U. Pa., 1981. Tchr. English, Peace Corps vol. College d'Enseignment General de Sedhiou, Senegal, 1970-71; tchr. English Belmore Boys' and Westfields High Schs., Sydney, Australia, 1972-73; teaching fellow in English Drake U., Des Moines, 1974-76; mem. faculty English Des Moines Area Community Coll., 1976-80; assoc. prof. Am. lit. U. Yaounde, Cameroon, 1980-83; prof. Am. lit. and civilization Nat. U. Cote D'Ivoire, Abidjan, 1986-88; dir. ctr. for internat. programs and svcs. Drake U., Des Moines, 1983-91; prof. grad. program intercultural mgmt. Sch. for Internat. Tng., The Experiment in Internat. Living, Brattleboro, Vt., 1991-93; provost, prof. English Teikyo Loretto Heights U., Denver, 1992—; acad. specialist USIA, 1983-84; workshop organizer/speaker Am. Field Svcs., 1986; cons. Coun. Internat. Ednl. Exch., 1986; evaluator Assn. des Univ. Partiellment Entierèment de Langue Francais, 1987, Iowa Humanities Bd., 1990-91, USIA's Ctr. for Univ. Cooperation and Devel., 1991; cons. in field. Book reviewer African Book Pub. Record, Oxford, Eng., 1981—, African Studies Rev., 1990—; host, creator TV show Global Perspectives, 1989-91; exhibitor of African art, 1989—; contbr. articles to profl. jours. Commr. Des Moines Sister City Commn., 1984-87, 91; bd. dirs. Iowa Sister State Com., 1988-91. Drake U. fellow, 1971-72, 74-76; Nat. Endowment for Humanities grantee, 1981; Fulbright grantee, USIA, 1980-83, 86-88. Mem. NAFSA, Assn. Internat. Educators (sectional chmn. Region IV 1986-87, Vt. rep. 1992), Assn. Internat. Edn. Adminstrs., Internat. Soc. for Intercultural Edn., Tng. and Rsch. Inst. Internat. Edn., Chautauqua Park Nat. Hist. Dist. Neighborhood Assn. (pres. 1991). Home: PO Box 1111 3001 S Federal Blvd Denver CO 80236-2711 Office: Teikyo Loretto Heights U 3001 S Federal Blvd Denver CO 80236-2711

HEGRENES, JACK RICHARD, educator; b. Fargo, N.D., Feb. 27, 1929; s. John and Ivy Anna (Jacobson) H.; B.S., U. Oreg., 1952, M.S., 1955; M.A., U. Chgo., 1960, Ph.D., 1970. Caseworker, Clackamas County Public Welfare Commn., Oregon City, Oreg., 1956-59, casework supr., 1960-62; instr. dept. psychiatry U. Oreg. Med. Sch., Portland, 1962-64, instr. Crippled Children's div., 1966-68, asst. prof., 1969-73, asso. prof. dept. public health and preventive medicine, and Crippled Children's div. Oreg. Health Scis. U., 1973—; adj. assoc. prof. social work Sch. Social Work, Portland State U., 1973-92 . La Verne Noyes scholar, U. Chgo., 1958-60; NIMH fellow, U. Chgo., 1964-66. Mem. Nat. Assn. Social Workers, Am. Public Health Assn. Lutheran. Contbr. articles to profl. jours. Home: 187 Oswego Summit Lake Oswego OR 97035

HEGSTAD, MICHAEL JAMES, electronics manufacturing company executive; b. Slayton, Minn., Dec. 15, 1953; s. Minver Oswald and Delrose Gertrude (Heydlauff) H.; m. Jan Marie Herzig; children: Thomas Michael, Ryan James. BSME, U. Minn., 1977, MBA, 1978. Software engr. Hewlett-Packard, Loveland, Colo., 1979-81; mgr. prodn. control Hewlett-Packard, Lake Stevens, Wash., 1981-83, mgr. materials sect., 1983-86, mgr. materials and CIM sect., 1986-87; mgr. mfg. engring. Hewlett-Packard, San Diego, 1988-89, mgr. site svcs. and CIM, 1989-91, mgr. mfg., 1992—; adviser U. Calif. Ext. Sch., San Diego, 1989—. Contbg. author: Manufacturing Excellence, 1988. Hewlett-Packard campaign co-chmn. United Way, San Diego, 1991. Fellow Am. Prodn. and Inventory Control Assn. Home: 14209 Sand Hill Rd Poway CA 92064

HEIDT, RAYMOND JOSEPH, insurance company executive; b. Bismarck, N.D., Feb. 28, 1933; s. Stephen Ralph and Elizabeth Ann (Hirschkorn) H.; BA, Calif. State U., San Jose, 1963, MA, 1968; PhD, U. Utah, 1977; m. Joyce Ann Aston, Jan. 14, 1956; children: Ruth Marie, Elizabeth Ann, Stephen Christian, Joseph Aston. Claims supr. Allstate Ins. Co., San Jose, Calif., 1963-65; claims mgr. Gen. Accident Group, San Francisco, 1965-69; owner, mgr. Ray Heidt & Assocs., Logan, Utah, 1969-76; v.p. claims Utah Home Fire Ins. Co., Salt Lake City, 1976—; with Utah State U., 1970-76; dir. Inst. for Study of Pacifism and Militarism; vice-chmn. Benton County Parks and Recreation Bd., 1987-90. Active, Republican Party; mem. Kennewick Historic Preservation Commn., 1989-90, 1st chmn., 1989-90, Magna Area Coun., 1992, pres. 1993. With U.S. Army, 1952-57. Decorated Bronze Star. Mem. Southeastern Wash. Adjusters' Assn. (pres. 1988-90), Utah Claims Assn. (pres. 1977-78), Lions, Am. Legion. Mormon. Home: 8138 Danbury Dr Magna UT 84044-2225

HEILMAN, MARLIN GRANT, photographer; b. Tarentum, Pa., Sept. 29, 1919; s. Marlin Webster and Martha (Grant) H.; widowed; 1 child, Hans. BA in Econs., Swarthmore Coll., 1941. Prin. Grant Heilman Photography, Inc., Lititz, Pa., 1948—. Author and photographer: Farm Town, 1974, Wheat Country, 1977, FARM, 1988; photographer: Psalms Around us, 1970. Capt. U.S. Army, 1941-45. Decorated Bronze Star, Croix de Guerre, French Army, 1945, Hon Legionaire Firs Clas, French Fgn. Legion, 1943.

HEILMAN, WAYNE JOHN, newspaper reporter; b. Chgo., May 21, 1957; s. John Edward and Virginia Lois (Anderson) H.; m. Donna Jean Emmerich, June 26, 1982; children: Katherine, Christopher, Carrie. B of Journalism, U. Mo., 1979. Reporter Columbus (Nebr.) Telegram, 1980-82; bus. writer Gazette Telegraph, Colorado Springs, Colo., 1982—. Treas. Ecumenical Social Ministries, Colorado Springs, 1991-92, Pinon Valley Neighborhood Assn., Colorado Springs, 1992; vice chmn. St. Mary's Cathedral Pastoral Coun., Colorado Springs, 1986. Mem. Colorado Springs Press Assn. (v.p. 1990-92, treas. 1986-90). Democrat. Roman Catholic. Office: Gazette Telegraph 30 S Prospect St Colorado Springs CO 80903

HEILMEIER, LORI A., public health investigator; b. Denville, N.J., Oct. 11, 1969; d. Edmund J. and Ella R. (Sueper) H. BA, U. Colo., 1992. Pub. health investigator Boulder (Colo.) Community Hosp., 1989—; rsch. asst. Colo. State Dept. Health, Denver, 1992. Vol. nat. and internat. svc. tng., Boulder, 1991-93. Mem. Golden Key. Mem. Christian Ch. Home: 2227 Canyon Blvd #162 Boulder CO 80302

HEIMANN, JANET BARBARA, trail consultant; b. Santa Cruz, Calif., Dec. 18, 1931; d. John Louis and Charlotte Lucina (Burns) Grinnell; m. Richard Frank Gustav, July 10, 1953; children: David Robert, Gary Alan, Kathleen Janet. BS, U. Calif., Berkeley, 1954. vol. trail researcher Monterey County Parks Dept. Pres. Folsom Freedom Trails, Placer County, Calif., 1980-83; chmn. Adopt-a-Trail, Folsom Lake Trail Patrol, Placer County, 1986-88; bd. dirs. Loomis Basin Horseman Assn., Placer County, 1986-87. Mem. AAUW. Republican. Home and Office: 11565 McCarthy Rd Carmel Valley CA 93924-9207

HEIMBUCH, BABETTE E., bank executive; b. 1948. Student, U. Calif., 1972. Audit mgr. Peat Marwick Mitchell & Co., 1973-81; corp. contr. Zoetrope Studios, 1981-82; CFO, exec. v.p., treas. First Fed. Bank Calif. (subs. First Fed. Fin. Corp.), Santa Monica, CFO, sr. exec. v.p., treas., pres. Office: First Fed Bank Calif 401 Wilshire Blvd Santa Monica CA 90401-1416*

HEIN, JAMES RODNEY, research geologist, oceanographer; b. Santa Barbara, Calif., Mar. 15, 1947; s. Warren C. and Beatrice E. (Gale) H.; children: Lanée T., Tasha R. BA, Oreg. State U., 1969; PhD, U. Calif., Santa Cruz, 1973. Lectr. in earth scis. U. Calif., Santa Cruz, 1972-73, 80; rsch. geologist, oceanographer U.S. Geol. Survey, Menlo Park, Calif., 1973—; internat. group leader Internat. Geol. Correlations Projects, Paris, 1976-86, 91—; program leader USA-Russia Geochemistry of Marine Sediments, Palo Alto, Calif., 1988—, USA-Korea Marine Mineral Deposits, Palo Alto, 1988—. Editor, contbg. author: Siliceous Deposits in the Pacific Region, 1983, Siliceous Sedimentary Rock-Hosted Ores and Petroleum, 1987, Siliceous Deposits of the Tethys and Pacific Regions, 1989; assoc. editor (jour.) Geo-Marine Letters, 1990—; contbr. 160 articles to publs. Careers councilor Palo Alto & Gunn High Schs., Palo Alto, 1984—. Nat. Rsch. Coun. postdocotral associateship, 1974. Fellow Geol. Soc. Am.; mem. AAAS, Am. Geophys. Union, Geochem. Soc., Oceanography Soc., Internat. Assn. Sedimentologists, Calif. Acad. Scis. Office: US Geol Survey MS 999 345 Middlefield Rd Menlo Park CA 94025-3591

HEIN, KENNETH CHARLES LAWRENCE, priest, educator; b. Longmont, Colo., June 2, 1938; s. Peter Joseph and Lena Josephine (Keller) H. BA in Latin, St. Benedict's Coll., Atchison, Kans., 1964; STB, Coll. di Sant'Anselmo, Rome, Italy, 1967; ThD, U. Tübingen, Fed. Republic Germany, 1973. Benedictine monk Holy Cross Abbey, Canon City, Colo., 1960—, bus. mgr. 1985-88, treas., 1988-92; priest Roman Cath. Ch., 1969—; sem. tchr. St. Thomas Theol. Sem., Denver, 1972-74; tchr. high sch.modern langs. The Abbey Sch. Theology, Canon City, 1974-83, acad. dean, 1981-83; tchr. St. Anselm's Coll., Manchester, N.H., 1983-85; chaplain Fitzsimon's Army Med. Ctr., Aurora, Colo., 1989-92; adminstr. Holy Cross Abbey, Canon City, Colo., 1992—; bd. dirs. Theol. Inst. Holy Cross Abbey, 1974-78; mem. Med.-Moral Bd. St. Thomas More Hosp., 1980—; presenter in Anglican Roman Cath. dialog, 1975-76, med.-moral issues, 1979—. Contbr. numerous articles to profl. jours.; translater Psalms of Bible, 1989. Founder Abbey Students Aid to Poor, 1974-83; mem. Birthright, Woodbury, N.J., 1985—. Office: Holy Cross Abbey 2951 E Us Hwy 50 Canon City CO 81215-1510

HEIN, SIMEON, statistical educator; b. N.Y.C., Mar. 20, 1963; s. John and Jane (Harmon) H. BA, Hampshire Coll., 1985; MA, U. Ariz., 1987; PhD, Wash. State U., 1992. Rsch. asst. U. Ariz., Tucson, 1985-87, teaching asst., 1986-87; computer cons. Social Data Processing Ctr., Pullman, Wash., 1987; data analyst Social Econ. Scis. Rsch. Ctr., Pullman, 1988; statis. cons. Wash. State U., Pullman, 1989, tchr., 1989-93, asst. prof., 1993—; rsch. assoc. Internat. Inst. for Applied Systems Analysis, Laxenburg, Austria, 1989. Recipient Ann Depew Madison award Wash. State U., 1989, Goethe Inst. fellowship Deutsche Academishe Dienst, 1986, grad. fellowship U. Ariz., 1985. Mem. AAAS, Am. Sociol. Assn., Pacific Sociol. Assn. Home: 405 Ponderosa Ct # 201 Moscow ID 83843

HEINDL, CLIFFORD JOSEPH, physicist; b. Chgo., Feb. 4, 1926; s. Anton Thomas and Louise (Fiala) H. B.S., Northwestern U., 1947, M.S., 1948; A.M., Columbia U., 1950, Ph.D., 1959. Sr. physicist Bendix Aviation Corp., Detroit, 1953-54; orsort student Oak Ridge Nat. Lab., 1954-55; asst. sect. chief Babcock & Wilcox Co., Lynchburg, Va., 1956-58; research group supr. Jet Propulsion Lab., Pasadena, Calif., 1959-65, mgr. research and space sci., 1965—. Served with AUS, 1944-46. Mem. AIAA, Am. Nuclear Soc., Health Physics Soc., Planetary Soc., Am. Phys. Soc. Home: 179 Mockingbird Ln South Pasadena CA 91030-2047 Office: 4800 Oak Grove Dr Pasadena CA 91109-8099

HEINEMAN, ADAM JOHN, engineer; b. Portland, Oreg., Oct. 5, 1924; s. Adam and Bertha (Schacht) H.; m. Elsie Barbara Tschida, Apr. 6, 1947 (div. 1974); m. Violet Blanchard Richardson, Sept. 30, 1975; children: Connie Jean, Neal John, Gail Margaret. BS in Engring., Oregon State U., 1949. Registered profl. engr., Oreg. Various field positions C.E., Portland, 1949-56, chief, navigation div., 1972-85, chief, ops. div., 1985-87, chief, planning div., 1987-88; materials engr. R. J. Tipton Assoc. Engrs., Caracas, Venezuela, 1956-58; resident engr. Junction Dam Bechtel Corp., Placerville, Calif., 1958-59; marine mgr. Port of Portland, 1959-67, 70-72, asst. gen. mgr., 1967-70; cons. Oreg. and Wash., 1988—. Chmn. St. Mary's Home for Boys, Beaverton, Oreg. 1990—. With USN, 1943-46, PTO. Named Hon. Disting. Citizen State of Wash., 1982; recipient Outstanding Svc. award Portland Community Coll., 1976-77, C.E. Meritorious Civilian Svc. award, 1980, Pres.' award Pacific N.W. Waterways Assn., 1988. Fellow: ASCE.

HEINER, DOUGLAS CRAGUN, pediatrician, educator; b. Salt Lake City, July 27, 1925; s. Spencer and Eva Lillian (Cragun) H.; m. Joy Luana Wiest, Jan. 8, 1946; children: Susan, Craig, Joseph, Marianne, James, David, Andrew, Carolee, Pauli. BS, Idaho State Coll., 1946; MD, U. Pa., 1950; PhD, McGill U., 1969. Intern Hosp. U. Pa., Phila., 1950-51; resident, fellow Children's Med. Ctr., Boston, 1953-56; asst. prof. pediatrics U. Ark. Med. Ctr., Little Rock, 1956-60; assoc. prof. pediatrics U. Utah Med. Ctr., Salt Lake City, 1960-66; fellow in immunology McGill U., Montreal, 1966-69; prof. of pediatrics Harbor-UCLA Med. Ctr., Torrance, 1969—. Author: Allergies to Milk, 1980; contbr. over 150 original articles to profl. jours. and chpts. to books; editorial bd.: Journal of Allergy and Clinical Immunology, 1975-79, Allergy, 1981—, Journal of Clinical Immunology, 1981—. Scoutmaster Boy Scouts Am., Salt Lake City, Rancho Palos Verdes, Calif., 1963-66, com. chmn. Rancho Palos Verdes, 1979-81; high coun. mem. Mormon Ch., Rancho Palos Verdes, 1983-86. 1st lt. U.S. Army, 1951-53. Recipient Disting. Alumni award Idaho State U., 1987. Fellow Am. Pediatric Soc., Am. Acad. Allergy and Clin. Immunology (food allergy com. 1981—), Am. Coll. Allergy and Immunology; mem. Soc. for Pediatric Rsch., Western Soc. for Pediatric Soc. (Ross award 1961), Am. Assn. Immunologists, Clin. Immunology Soc., Am. Acad. Pediatrics. Republican. Office: Harbor UCLA Med Ctr 1000 W Carson St # 4J Torrance CA 90502-2004

HEINEY, JERI JOELLE, family educator; b. Klamath Falls, Oreg., Sept. 14, 1966; d. Gearold Orvil Herman and Micki (Wolff) Dwelley; m. Allen Lambert Heiney, Nov. 1, 1988; 1 child, Chad Allen. AS, Oreg. Inst. Tech. Cert. emergency med. technician. Fine jewelry asst. mgr. Fred Meyer, Klamath Falls, 1988-90; family educator Sierra Cascade Family Opportunities Head Start, Tulelake, Calif., 1990—. Emergency med. technician, Tulelake, 1992—; activist Allegiance of Am., Tulelake, 1992; camp counselor Girl Scouts Am., 1990. Mem. Delta Kappa Gamma (corr. sec. 1992). Democrat. Home and Office: PO Box 916 Tulelake CA 96134

HEINLEIN, KENNETH BRUCE, state agency administrator, sociology educator; b. Lombard, Ill., June 25, 1949; s. Albert George and Katherine Mary (Kunz) H.; m. Gayle Anne May, Aug. 11, 1973. BS, U. Wyo., 1975; MA, Colo. State U., 1979. Rehab. counselor, rehab. dir. Magic City Enterprises, Cheyenne, Wyo., 1977-80; devel. disabilities cons., program mgr. div. commun. program Dept. Health and Social Svcs., Cheyenne, 1980-88, dep. dir., 1988-89, dir., 1989-91; dir. Dept. Health, Cheyenne, 1990-91, liaison officer, 1991—; instr. sociology Chapman U., Cheyenne, 1979—. Contbr. articles to profl. jours. Del., Republican Party County Conv., Laramie, 1984. Sgt. USAF, 1968-72, Viet Nam. Named Counselor of Yr., Nat. Assn. for Retarded Citizens, 1977; name to Outstanding Young Men in Am., 1981. Christian. Office: Div Devel Disabilities Herschler 1 West Cheyenne WY 82002

HEINLEIN, OSCAR ALLEN, former air force officer; b. Butler, Mo., Nov. 17, 1911; s. Oscar A. and Katherine (Canterbury) H.; B.S., U.S. Naval Acad., 1932; M.S., Calif. Inst. Tech., 1942; M.S. in Mech. Engring., Stanford, 1949; certificate in mining U. Alaska, 1953; grad. Air War Coll., 1953; student spl. studies U. Ariz., 1956-57, Eastern Wash. U., Clark County Community Coll., Las Vegas, Nev., 1988, U. Nice, France; D.D., Universal Sem., 1970; AA Clark County Community Cm. Catharine Anna Bangert, May 1, 1933 (div. Apr. 1937); 1 dau., Catharine Anna; m. 2d, Mary Josephine Fisher, Aug. 25, 1939 (dec. Dec. 1977); 1 son, Oscar Allen III; m. 3d, Suzanne Birke, Feb. 23, 1980; 1 son, Michael Andre Bertin. Marine engr. Atlantic Refining Co., Phila., 1934; civil engr. Annapolis Mineral Devel. Co., Calif., 1935-37; enlisted as pvt. U.S. Army, 1937, advanced through grades to col., 1944; comdr. Ladd AFB, Alaska, 1953-54, 11th Air Div., Fairbanks,

Alaska, 1954, Air Force Logistics Command Support Group, Vandenberg AFB, Calif., 1960-65, prof. air sci. U. Ariz., Tucson, 1955-58; insp. Gen. Mobile Air Material Area, Ala., 1958-60; ret. 1965; now cons.; pres. O.A. Heinlein Merc. Co., Butler, Mo., 1934—; vis. prof. U. Nev., Reno; dep. dir. civil def. Boulder City, Nev., 1967; dir., sec. Boulder Dam Fed. Credit Union, 1973-79; mem. Boulder City Police Adv. Com., 1976; ordained minister Bapt. Ch., 1976. Active Boy Scouts Am. Mem. Clark County (Nev.) Republican Central Com., 1966, Exec. com., 1970; mem. Rep. Central Com., 1966; Rep. candidate Nev. Assembly, 1972; mem. Boulder City Charter Commn. Mem. community coll. adv. bd. U. Nev., 1970. Served with USN, 1928-32; to 2d lt. USMC, 1932-34. Decorated Legion of Merit, Air medal, Army, Navy and Air Force commendation medals. Mem. Inst. Aero. Scis., Am. Meteorol. Soc., Nat. Research Assn., Am. Radio Relay League, SAR, Am. Polar Soc., VFW, Daedalians, Mensa, So. Nev. Amateur Radio Club, Inst. Amateur Radio, Quarter Century Wireless Assn., Ret. Officers Assn., Air Force Assn., Nat. Rifle Assn. (life), Armed Forces Communications and Electronics Assn., USS Nevada Assn., CAP, Am. Legion, Am. Assn. Ret. Persons, West Coast Amateur Radio Service, Soc. Wireless Pioneers. Mason, Nev. Rifle and Pistol Assn. (bd. dirs.), Vet. Wireless Operator's Assn. Clubs: MM (San Diego); Intertel (Ft. Wayne, Indiana); Missile Amateur Radio (pres. 1961-65 Vandenberg AFB); Explorers (N.Y.C.); Arctic Circle Prospectors', High Jumpers (Fairbanks, Alaska); Boulder City Gem and Mineral; Stearman Alumnus; Marines Memorial (San Francisco). Author: Big Bend County, 1953. Inventor. Home: 107 Wyoming St Boulder City NV 89005-2818

HEINRICH, MILTON ROLLIN, biologist; b. Linton, N.D., Nov. 25, 1919; s. Fred and Emma A. (Becker) H.; m. Ramona G. Cavanagh, May 31, 1966. AB magna cum laude, U. S.D., 1941; MS, U. Iowa, 1942, PhD, 1944. Physiologist Naval Med. Rsch. Inst., Bethesda, Md., 1946; postdoctoral fellow U. Pa., Phila., 1947-49; rsch. assoc. Amherst (Mass.) Coll., 1949-58; sr. postdoctoral fellow U. Calif., Berkeley, 1958-60; asst. prof. biochemistry U. So. Calif., L.A., 1960-63; scientist, adminstr. NASA,, Ames Rsch. Ctr., Moffett Field, Calif., 1963-84; pres., cons. Zerog Corp., Los Altos Hills, Calif., 1985-91; cons. space sta. biology, 1985—. Editor: Extreme Environments...Microbial Adaptation, 1976, Reports U.S. Experiments on Soviet Cosmos 1129, 1981; contbr. articles to profl. jours. Lt. (j.g.) USNR, 1944-47. Recipient Cosmos Group award, NASA, Ames Rsch. Ctr., 1981, 84, Space Sta. Achievement award, 1984. Fellow Explorers Club; mem. AIAA, Am. Chem. Soc., Am. Soc. Biochemistry and Molecular Biology,. Sigma Xi, Phi Beta Kappa, Phi Lambda Upsilon, Phi Eta Sigma. Home: 27200 Deer Springs Way Los Altos CA 94022-4325

HEINS, MARILYN, college dean, pediatrics educator, author; b. Boston, Sept. 7, 1930; d. Harold and Esther (Berow) H.; m. Milton P. Lipson, 1958; children: Rachel, Jonathan. A.B., Radcliffe Coll., 1951; M.D., Columbia U., 1955. Diplomate Am. Bd. Pediatrics. Intern, N.Y. Hosp., N.Y.C., 1955-56; resident in pediatrics Babies Hosp., N.Y.C., 1956-58; asst. pediatrician Children's Hosp. Mich., Detroit, 1959-78; dir. pediatrics Detroit Receiving Hosp., 1965-71; asst., assoc. dean student affairs Wayne State U. Med. Sch., Detroit, 1971-79; assoc. dean acad. affairs U. Ariz. Med. Coll., Tucson, 1979-83, vice dean, 1983-88, prof. pediatrics, 1985-88. Author: (with Anne M. Seiden) Child Care/Parent Care, 1987; mem. editorial bd. Jour. AMA, 1981-91; contbr. articles to profl. jours. Bd. dirs. Planned Parenthood So. Ariz., 1983, pres., 1988-89, Ariz. Ctr. for Clin. Mgmt.,1991—, Nat. Bd. Med. Examiners, 1983-88; mem. adv. bd. So. Ariz. Women's Fund, 1992—, Ariz. State Hosp., 1985-88. Recipient Alumni Faculty Service award Wayne State U., 1972, Recognition award, 1977, Women on the Move Achievement award YWCA Tucson, 1983; mem. Ariz. Ctr. Clin. Mgmt. 1990—. Fellow Am. Orthopsychiat. Assn., Am. Acad. Pediatrics; mem. Assn. Am. Med. Colls. (chair group on student affairs 1976-79), Am. Hosp. Assn. (chmn. com. med. edn. 1985), Soc. Health and Human Values, Women in Sci. and Engrng. U. Ariz. (bd. dirs. 1979-88), Exec. Women's Council Tucson, Ariz. Med. Assn. (com. on med. svc. 1985-87), Pima County Med. Soc., Pima County Pediatric Soc., Ambulatory Pediatric Assn., AAAS, Am. Pub. Health Assn. Home: 6530 N Longfellow Dr Tucson AZ 85718-2416

HEINZ, DON J., agronomist; b. Rexburg, Idaho, Oct. 29, 1931; s. William and Berniece (Steiner) H.; m. Marsha B. Hegsted, Apr. 19, 1956; children: Jacqueline, Grant, Stephanie, Karen, Ramona, Amy. BS, Utah State U., 1958, MS, 1959; PhD, Mich State U., 1961; grad., Stanford U. Exec. Program, 1982. Assoc. plant breeder Experiment Sta. Hawaiian Sugar Planters' Assn., Aiea, 1961-66, head dept. genetics and pathology, 1966-78, asst. dir., 1977-78, v.p. and dir., 1979-85, pres., dir. experiment sta., 1986—; cons. Philippines, Egypt, Colombia, Reunion; mem. adv. com. plants Hawaii Dept. Agr., 1970—, Pres. Nat. Commn. Agriculture and Rural Devel. Policy, 1988. Contbr. articles to sci. jours. on sugarcane breeding, cytogenetics, cell and tissue culture techniques. Served with USAF, 1951-54. Mem. AAAS, Internat. Soc. Sugar Cane Technologists (chmn. com. germplasm and breeding 1975-86), Sigma Xi. Mem. LDS Ch. Home: 224 Ilihau St Kailua HI 96734-1654 Office: Hawaiian Sugar Planters PO Box 1057 99-193 Aiea Heights Dr Aiea HI 96701

HEINZ, THOMAS JOSEPH, engineering sales executive; b. Chgo., Apr. 19, 1955; s. Lawrence Joseph and Mary Ellan (Flad) H.; m. Carole Thomas, Apr. 16, 1988; 1 child, Ian Robert. BS in Chemistry, U. Wis., Stevens Point, 1977. Sales and svc. rep. IMCO Svcs., Houston, 1978-79, field svc. engr., group supr., 1979-81, internat. sales and svc. rep., 1981-85; sales engr. M-I Drilling Fluids, Ventura, Calif., 1985-90; sr. sales engr. M-I Drilling Fluids, Bakersfield, Calif., 1991—; cons. H & D Cons., Balik papin, Indonesia, 1990-91. Republican. Roman Catholic. Home: 1952 Laurelwood Ct Thousand Oaks CA 91362-1207 Office: M-I Drilling Fluids 6301 Seven Seas Ave Bakersfield CA 93302

HEINZE, RUTH-INGE, educator, researcher; b. Berlin, Nov. 4, 1919; came to U.S., 1955; d. Otto and Louise (Preschel) H. Gr. Latinum, Interpreter Coll., Berlin, 1967; BA, U. Calif., Berkeley, 1969, MA, 1971, PhD, 1974. Producer, writer Ednl. Broadcast, Berlin, 1963-73; lectr. U. of Chiang Mai, Thailand, 1971-72; staff rsch. asst. human devel. dept. U. Calif., San Francisco, 1974, rsch. assoc. Ctr. for S.E. Asian Studies, 1974—; lectr. Mills Coll., Oakland, Calif., 1974; adj. faculty Saybrook Inst., San Francisco, 1984—, Calif. Inst. for Integral Studies, 1984—. Author: The Role of the Sangha in Modern Thailand, 1977, Tham Khwan - How To Contain The Essence of Life, 1982, Trance and Healing in Southeast Asia Today, 1988, Shamans of the 20th Century, 1991. Prodr. Universal Dialogue Series, Berkeley, 1979—; nat. dir. Ind. Scholars of Asia, 1981—; bd. dirs. Oakland Asian Cultural Ctr., 1987—. Recipient grant Am. Inst. for Indian Studies, 1975,78, Fulbright-Hays Rsch. grant, 1978-79. Mem. Internat. Assn. for the Study of Traditional Asian Medicine, Nat. Pictographic Soc., Ind. Scholars of Asia, Assn. for Asian Studies. Home and Office: 2321 Russell St Apt 3A Berkeley CA 94705-1959

HEISING, RALPH ALLEN, physician; b. Bismarck, N.D., Dec. 20, 1929; s. Earl Jerome and Ethel Smythe (McGuigan) H.; m. Nancy Ann Peterson, June 19, 1954; children: Karen, Scott, Stuart, Douglas. PhB, U. N.D., 1951, BS, 1953; MD, Harvard U., 1955; grad. sch. medicine, U. Pa., 1959. Intern U.S. Naval Hosp., Bethesda, Md., 1955-56; resident U.S. Naval Hosp., Phila., 1956-58; dermatologist LaMesa (Calif.) Dermatology Med. Group, Inc., 1963—; prof. clin. medicine U. Calif., San Diego, 1983—. Lt. comdr. USN, 1955-63. Fellow Am. Acad. Dermatology, Am. Soc. Dermatopathology, Am. Coll. Physicians; mem. AMA, N.Am. Clin. Dermatol. Soc., Am. Bd. Dermatology, Calif. Med. Assn., San Diego Med. Soc. Home: 5760 Daffodil Ln San Diego CA 92120 Office: LaMesa Derm Med Group Inc 8881 Fletcher Pkwy #325 La Mesa CA 91942

HEIST, PAULUS A., psychologist, educator; b. Waverly, Iowa, Aug. 2, 1917; s. Ernst G. and Emma K. (Goppelt) H.; children—Martin, Lauren, Jerome. BA, Luther Coll., Decorah, Iowa, 1939; MA, U. Ill., 1948; Ph.D., U. Minn., 1956; D.Hum. (hon.), Wartburg Coll., 1972. Lic. psychologist, Calif. Counselor U. Minn., 1948-50; assoc. prof. psychology Oreg. State U., 1950-56; research dir. Ctr. for Study Higher Edn. U. Calif., Berkeley, 1956-68, dir. Ctr. for Study Undergrad. Edn., 1968-73, prof. higher edn. Grad. Sch. Edn., 1968—; cons. to numerous instns. of higher edn.; staff clinician Holistic Health Assocs.; trustee 5 acad. bds. Contbr. articles to profl. jours., chpts. to 7 books; editor, cons. 2 jours. With U.S. Army, 1942-46, WWII. Fellow Am. Psychol. Assn., AAAS; mem. Am. Ednl. Research Assn., Am. Assn. Higher Edn., AAUP, Western Psychol. Assn. Office: U Calif Grad Sch Higher Edn Tolman Hall Berkeley CA 94720

HEISTAND, JOSEPH THOMAS, retired bishop; b. Danville, Pa., Mar. 3, 1924; s. John Thomas and Alta (Hertzler) H.; B.A. in Econs., Trinity Coll., Hartford, Conn., 1948, D.D. (hon.), 1978; M.Div., Va. Theol. Sem., 1952, D.D. (hon.), 1977; m. Roberta Crieger Lush, June 1, 1951; children—Hillary Heistand Long, Andrea Deferrier, Virginia Redmon. With Internat. Harvester Co., 1948-49; ordained to ministry Episcopal Ch., 1952; rector Trinity Ch., Tyrone, Pa., 1952-55; chaplain Grier Sch., Birmingham, Pa., 1952-55; asso. rector St. Paul's Ch., Richmond, Va., 1955, rector, 1955-69; rector St. Philip's in the Hill Ch., Tucson, 1969-76; bishop coadjutor Episcopal Diocese Ariz., Phoenix, 1976-79; bishop of Ariz., 1979-92; retired 1992 . Served with AUS, 1943-45. Decorated Bronze Star with oak leaf cluster, Purple Heart; Croix de Guerre (France). Office: PO Box 13647 Phoenix AZ 85002-3647*

HEITLER, BRUCE F., entrepreneur; b. Denver, June 12, 1945; s. Emmett H. and Dorothy (Shwayder) H.; m. Susan Kaye McCrensky, June 6, 1971; children: Abigail, Sara, Jesse, Jacob. BA, Yale U., 1967, JD, 1972; MCP, U. Calif., Berkeley, 1969. Bar: Colo. 1973. Assoc. Holme Roberts & Owen, Denver, 1972-74; project mgr. Cen. Devel. Group, Denver, 1974-76; pres. Heitler Devel., Inc., Denver, 1976—; vice chmn., bd. dirs. Nexus Greenhouse Corp., Northglenn, Colo.; pres., bd. dirs. Colo. Biogenix, Inc., Denver; owner, operator Discovery Door Children's Ctr., Denver, 1990—. Trustee E. Roosevelt Inst. for Cancer Rsch., Denver, 1975—, Social Sci. Found. U. Denver, 1989—; active Yale Devel. Bd., New Haven, Conn., 1986-90. Mem. Colo. Yale Assn. (pres. 1991—), Cactus Club (pres. 1986-88). Jewish. Office: Heitler Devel Inc 1410 Grant St Ste 303 Denver CO 80203-1846

HEITMAN, GREGORY ERWIN, state official; b. Lewiston, Idaho, June 7, 1947; s. Elmer William and Carmelita Rose Ann (Kinzer) H.; m. Phyllis Ann Pryor, Sept. 25, 1982. BS in Math., U. Idaho, 1969, MBA, 1971; student, Wash. State U., 1965-67. Student communications dir. Assoc. Students U. Idaho, Moscow, 1970-72, advisor, apt. mgr. dept. housing, 1971-72; traffic fatality analyst Idaho Dept. Transp., Boise, 1973-74; ops. mgr. Region IV Health & Welfare State of Idaho, Boise, 1974-78, supr. computer svcs., div. environ. in health and welfare, 1978-85; supr. field svcs., program dir. Idaho Vital Statistics, Boise, 1985—; acting dir. Idaho Ctr. for Health Statistics, Boise, 1988-89, spl. asst. program and policy devel., 1989—; mem. med. records adv. com. Boise State U., 1987—, cons., lectr. 1987—. Active various charitable orgns.; precinct committeeman Dem. of Latah County, 1972; election day coord. Ada County, 1986; vol. Am. Cancer Soc., 1990, Easter Seals, 1992. Mem. Idaho Pub. Health Assn., Assn. Vital Records and Health Statistics, Idaho Pub. Employees Assn., Assn. Govt. Employees. Roman Catholic. Home: 5103 Shalecrest Ct Boise ID 83703-3442 Office: Idaho Vital Statis 450 W State St Boise ID 83702-6005

HEITMAN, HUBERT, JR., animal science educator; b. Berkeley, Calif., June 2, 1917; s. Hubert and Blanche (Peart) H.; m. Helen Margaret McCaughna, Aug. 7, 1941; children: James Hubert (dec.), William Robert. B.S., U. Calif.-Davis, 1939; A.M., U. Mo., 1940, Ph.D., 1943. Asst. instr. animal husbandry U. Mo., 1939-43; mem. faculty U. Calif., Davis, 1946—, prof. animal sci., 1961-87, prof. emeritus, 1987—, chmn. dept., 1963-68, 81-82, acad. asst. to vice chancellor acad. affairs, 1971-78; livestock supt. Calif. State Fair, 1948-59; v.p. at large Nat. Collegiate Athletic Assn., 1975-77; pres. Far Western Intercollegiate Athletic Conf., 1971-72, 77-78, Golden State Conf., 1979-80, Cal Aggie Athlete Hall of Fame, 1989—. Pres. Yolo County Soc. Crippled Children, 1954-56; Bd. dirs. Calif. Soc. Crippled Children and Adults, 1954-56. Served to capt., San. Corps AUS, 1943-46. Mem. AAAS, Am. Soc. Animal Sci. (pres. Western sect. 1953), Animal Behavior Soc., Internat. Soc. Biometeorologists, Calif., N.Y. acads. scis., Nutrition Soc. (Gt. Britain), Brit. Soc. Animal Prodn., Sigma Xi, Alpha Zeta, Gamma Sigma Delta, Gamma Alpha, Sigma Chi. Home: 518 Miller Dr Davis CA 95616-3617

HEITSMITH, WILLIAM RICHARD, educational consultant; b. Colo. Springs, Colo., May 26, 1939; s. Richard Howe and Faye (Knox) H.; m. Marjorie Kay Wilkinson June 9, 1963; children: Richard David, Jonathan Howe; m. Janet Ruth Hilton, June 20, 1981. BA in Social Sci., U. No. Colo., 1963, MA in Social Sci., 1965; EdD in Adminstrn., Curriculum, U. Colo., 1984. Cert. adminstr., ctrl. admistr., elem., secondary prin. Pres. and cons. edn., bus., govt. Orgnl. Systems Consulting, Inc., 1976-92; high sch. tchr. Englewood (Colo.) Schools, 1966-72, coord. of curriculum, 1973-76, staff devel., 1980-82, high sch. tchr., 1977-91, program coord., 1987-91; bd. dirs. Englewood Sch's. Accountability Com., 1968-71; legis. commn. Englewood educators., 1968-72; bus. cons. several sch. dists. State of Colo., 1980-92; v.p. Englewood Edn. Found., 1992—. Author, editor: The OSC Letter & Foundation Happenings, 1992, Fastrack, 1993. legis. liaison Colo. Edn. Assn., 1971-73; elder Presbyn. Ch., chair Edn. Commn., Commn. Stewardship, and Fin., Green Mt. Presbyn., 1990—. Grantee Leadership Inst. Stanford Univ. Wyo., 1974. Mem. ASTD, Soc. of Human Performance Tech., Assn. Supervision & Curriculum Devel., Phi Delta Kappa, Phi Delta Theta. Home: 9203 West Kentucky Pl Lakewood CO 80226

HEJHALL, ROY CHARLES, electrical engineer; b. Duluth, Minn., Aug. 11, 1932; s. Charles Joseph Hejhall and Florence Mary (Patwell) Wales; m. Virginia Lee Hoke, June 9, 1956 (div. 1968); children: Jeffrey, Jody, Julie; m. Audrey Ruth Bailey, June 28, 1970. BS in Engrng., U.S. Naval Acad., 1956.; Commd. ensign USN, 1956, advanced through grades to lt., 1961; tech. staff Motorola, Phoenix, 1961—; tech. advisor Am. Radio Relay League, Newington, Conn., 1977—. Contbr. articles to profl. jours. Mem. Elks. Republican. Office: Motorola 5005 E Mcdowell Rd Phoenix AZ 85008-4295

HELD, JAY ALLEN, missionary; b. Canton, Ohio, Dec. 15, 1961; s. Earl E. and E. Jean (Robinson) H.; m. Laureen Elizabeth Allen, Mar. 19, 1988. BS in Theology, Bapt. U. Am., 1985, postgrad.; MA in Counseling, Western Sem., 1990; MA in Missions, Grace Theol. Sem., 1990. Ordained to ministry Canton Baptist Temple, 1990. Inner-city missionary Forest Hills Bapt. Ch., Decatur, Ga., 1980-84; asst. to pastor Allgood Rd. Bapt. Ch., Marietta, Ga., 1984-85, Eastland Bapt. Ch., Orlando, Fla., 1985; tchr. high sch. Eastland Christian Sch., Orlando, 1985; inner-city missionary North Portland Bible Fellowship, Portland, 1989-91, Mt. Sinai Community Bapt. Ch., Portland, 1991—; camp counselor Camp C.H.O.F., Dalton, Ohio, summer, 1981, 82; adolescent counselor Youth Guidance Assn., Portland, 1986-88; program dir. Youth Outreach, Vancouver, Wash., 1988-89; tchr. North Portland Bible Clubs, 1989; instr. North Portland Bible Coll., 1991—. Mem. Oreg. Gang Task Force, Portland, 1989; tchr., counselor Bidge Bible Club, Mt. Sinai Community Bapt. Ch., 1990—. Mem. Oreg. Mediation Assn., Portland Urban League. Home: 517 NE Morris St Portland OR 97212-3160

HELFERT, ERICH ANTON, management consultant, author, educator; b. Aussig/Elbe, Sudetenland, May 29, 1931; came to U.S., 1950; s. Julius and Anna Maria (Wilde) H.; m. Anne Langley, Jan. 1, 1983; children: Claire L., Amanda L. BS, U. Nev., 1954; MBA with high distinction, Harvard U., 1956, DBA, 1958. Newspaper reporter, corr., Neuburg, Fed. Republic of Germany, 1948-52; rsch. asst. Harvard U., 1956-57; asst. prof. bus. policy San Francisco State U., 1958-59; asst. prof. fin. and control Grad. Sch. Bus. Adminstrn., Harvard U., 1959-65; internal cons., then asst. to pres., dir. corp. planning Crown Zellerbach Corp., San Francisco, 1965-78, asst. to chmn., dir. corp. planning, 1978-82, v.p. corp. planning, 1982-85; mgmt. cons., San Francisco, 1985—; co-founding dir. Modern Soft, Inc.; mem. Dean's adv. coun. San Francisco State Bus. Sch., sch. fin. Golden Gate U.; bd. dirs., past chmn. and pres. Harvard U. Bus. Sch. No. Calif.; trustee Saybrook Inst. Author: Techniques of Financial Analysis, 1963, 7th edit., 1991, Valuation, 1966, (with others) Case Book on Finance, 1963, Controllership, 1965; contbr. articles to profl. jours. Exch. student fellow U.S. Inst. Internat. Edn., 1950; Ford Found. doctoral fellow, 1956. Mem. Assn. Corp. Growth (past pres., bd. dirs. San Francisco chpt.), Inst. Mgmt. Cons., Commonwealth Club, Phi Kappa Phi. Roman Catholic. Home: 111 W 3rd Ave # 401 San Mateo CA 94402-1521 Office: 1777 Borel Pl Ste 508 San Mateo CA 94402-3514

HELFFERICH, MERRITT RANDOLPH, geophysical research administrator; b. Hartford, Conn., Aug. 10, 1935; s. Reginald Humphrey and Virginia (Merritt) H.; m. Carla Anne Ostergren, July 11, 1959 (div. 1977); children: Deirdre Alida Helfferich Heath, Tryntje Bronwyn; m. April Evalyn Crosby, Aug. 24, 1985. BA, U. Alaska, 1966; MPA, Harvard U., 1990. Surveyor Golden Valley Electric Assn., Fairbanks, Alaska, 1965-66; engrng. technician Geophys. Inst., U. Alaska, Fairbanks, 1966-69, field technician, meteorologist Poker Flat Rsch. Range, 1969-76, head tech. svcs., 1976-83, asst. dir., 1986-88, assoc. dir., 1988—; ice technician S.S. Manhattan Humble Oil Co./U. Alaska, Northwest Passage Voyage, 1969; assoc. v.p. human resources U. Alaska, Fairbanks, 1983, asst. to chancellor, 1983-86; legis. liaison U. Alaska, Fairbanks, 1983-86; adv. bd. Polar Ice Coring Office, Fairbanks, 1989—; bd. dirs. Internat. Small Sattelite Orgn., Washington. Editorial bd. U. Alaska Press, Fairbanks, 1986—. Commr. Alaska Women's Commn., Juneau, 1988-89; mem., co-chair Main St. Fairbanks, 1990—; mem. Fairbanks Native Cultural Ctr. Com., 1991—; chair Fairbanks North Star Borough Riverfront Commn., 1992—. Helfferich Glacier named in his honor U.S. Bd. Geographic Names, 1971; recipient Antarctic Svc. medal NSF, 1971, Nick Begich Scholarship Fund award, 1989. Fellow Explorers Club (program chair Alaska Yukon chpt. 1991—); mem. AIAA, AAAS, U.S. Space Found., Am. Geophys. Union. Democrat. Home: PO Box 80769 Fairbanks AK 99708-0769 Office: Geophys Inst Univ Alaska Fairbanks Fairbanks AK 99775-0800

HELFOND, WENDY WORRALL, graphic designer, feature writer; b. Davenport, Iowa, Sept. 11, 1963; d. Gerald Charles and Joan Margaret (Kraus) Worrall; m. Randy George Helfond, July 11, 1987 (div.); 1 child, Katharine Joanne. BA in Broadcast Journalism, U. So. Calif., L.A., 1985; student, Inst. of Children's Lit., 1990—. Sr. employee communications rep. Walt Disney Co., Burbank, Calif., 1985-89. Editor: (newsletter) The Disney Newsreel, 1985-89, Town & Gown Jrs. of L.A., 1991—, newsletter chair 1992-93, corr. sec.; v.p. RB Chorale, 1992—. Vol. Athletes & Entertainers for Kids, L.A., 1987-90; mem., editor, scholarship chair, Trojan Jr. Aux., L.A., 1986-88, '88-89, '89-90, pres. 1990-91, parliamentarian, 1991-92; mem. 10th reunion com. Mt. Carmel High Sch., San Diego, 1990-91. Mem. U. So. Calif. Alumni Assn., Disneyland Alumni Assn. Home: 11456 Palito Ct San Diego CA 92127-1443

HELFORD, PAUL QUINN, media manager, lecturer; b. Chgo., June 27, 1947; s. Norman and Eleanor (Kwin) H.; m. Leslie Gale Weinstein, July 11, 1971; children: Ross Michael, Benjamin Keith. BA, U. Ill., 1969; MA, Northeastern Ill. U., 1977. Cert. tchr., Ill., Oreg. Tchr. John Hersey High Sch., Arlington Heights, Ill., 1969-73; freelance writer Mill Valley, Calif., 1973-75; mgr., program dir. Sta. KOZY-TV, Eugene, Oreg., 1976-88, mktg., sales, and program dir. Group W Cable, 1984-88; producer, with mktg. Northland Broadcasting, Flagstaff, Ariz., 1989-91; lectr. cinema and broadcasting No. Ariz. U., 1989—; dir. Native Am. Video Workshops, 1991—, Flagstaff Festival of the Arts Film Festival, 1992; writer New Times, Phoenix, 1992—. Writer, producer Paul Helford's Hollywood Oldies, 1976-81, In Review, 1981, Live from the Fair, 1981-85, Group W Cable Minutes, 1984-85, Bad Horror and Sci. Fiction, 1985 (Award for Cable Excellence 1986), KOZY movie promotional spots 1976-88 (Award for Cable Excellence 1984, 88, CLIO award nomination 1988, 1989); contbr. articles to profl. jours. Recipient CLIO award 1984, 86, Cable Mktg. Grand award, 1981, 85. Mem. Nat. Assn. Cable Programmers. Home: 5145 Hickory Dr Flagstaff AZ 86004-7391 Office: Northland Broadcasting PO Box 3421 Flagstaff AZ 86003-3421

HELGASON, DEAN EUGENE, technical writer, educator; b. Chgo., May 21, 1940; s. Kristvin S. Helgason and Alice (Joscelyne) Shultz; m. Carole Anne Schwocher, Feb. 10, 1967; children: Carlie, Kerstin, Branden. Student, U. N.Mex., 1969-72; BSBA, U. Phoenix, 1987. Tech. writer Sun Electric Corp., Chgo., 1965-68; instr. Albuquerque Tech.-Vocat. Inst., Albuquerque, 1970-71; dept. head Ariz. Automotive Inst., Glendale, Ariz., 1972-75; mgr. Hamilton Test Systems, Tucson, 1976-90; mgr. tech. support and tng. Techlink Control Systems, Inc., Tucson, 1990-91; ednl. technologist McDonnell Douglas Corp., Tucson, 1992—; instr. Pima Community Coll., Tucson, 1987—; cons. Automotive Tech. Data, Phoenix, 1976-80; automotive adv. com. Pima Coll., 1981—. Contbr. articles to profl. jours. With USMC, 1961-64. Mem. Soc. Automotive Engrs. Home: 751 N Banff Ave Tucson AZ 85748-2716 Office: Techlink Control Systems Inc 2700 E Bilby Rd Tucson AZ 85706-4506

HELGERSON, RICHARD, English language educator; b. Pasadena, Calif., Aug. 22, 1940; s. Donald Theodore and Viola Dolores (Huss) H.; m. Marie-Christine David, June 8, 1967; 1 child, Jessica. BA, U. Calif., Riverside, 1963; MA, Johns Hopkins U., 1964, PhD, 1970. Prof. English Coll. Notre-Dame d'Afrique, Atakpamé, Togo, 1964-66; asst. prof. English U. Calif., Santa Barbara, 1970-76, assoc. prof., 1976-82, chair dept. English, 1989-93, prof. English, 1982—; vis. prof. Calif. Inst. Tech., Pasadena, 1987-88; chair Huntington (Calif.) Libr. Rsch. Rev., 1986-87. Author: The Elizabethan Prodigals, 1976, Self-Crowned Laureates, 1983, Forms of Nationhood, 1992; contbr. numerous articles to profl. jours. Fellow Woodrow Wilson Found., 1963-64, NEH, 1979-80, Huntington Libr., 1984-85, Guggenheim Found., 1985-86, Folger-NEH, 1993—. Mem. MLA (exec. com. English renaissance div. 1988-92), N.Am. Conf. on Brit. Studies, Renaissance Soc. Am., Spenser Soc. Am. (pres. 1988), Shakespeare Assn. Am., Western Humanities Conf. (exec. com. 1988-91). Democrat. Home: 334 E Arrellaga St Santa Barbara CA 93101-1106 Office: U Calif Dept English Santa Barbara CA 93106

HELGESON, DUANE MARCELLUS, librarian; b. Rothsay, Minn., July 2, 1930; s. Oscar Herbert and Selma Olivia (Sateren) H.; B.S., U. Minn., 1952. Librarian, Chance-Vought Co., Dallas, 1956-59, System Devel. Corp., Santa Monica, Calif., 1959-62, Lockheed Aircraft, Burbank, Calif., 1962-63, C.F. Braun Co., Alhambra, Calif., 1963-74; chief librarian Ralph M. Parsons Co., Pasadena, Calif., 1974-79; pres. Mark-Allen/Brokers-in-Info., Los Angeles, 1976-80; phys. scis. librarian Calif. Inst. Tech., Pasadena, 1980-84; corp. librarian Montgomery Watson, Pasadena, 1985—; mem. adv. bd. Los Angeles Trade Tech. Coll., 1974-79, U. So. Calif. Library Sch., 1974-79. Served with USAF, 1952-54. Mem. Spl. Libraries Assn. (chmn. nominating com. 1974). Co-editor: (with Joe Ann Clifton) Computers in Library and Information Centers, 1973. Home: 2706 Ivan Hill Ter Los Angeles CA 90039-2717 Office: Montgomery Watson 250 N Madison Ave Pasadena CA 91101-1684

HELKER, KEITH PHILIP, accountant; b. Waukesha, Wis., Sept. 6, 1952; s. Philip Lewis and Elizabeth (Miller) H.; m. Ruth Ann Papke, Jan. 11, 1975; children: Michelle Ann, Michael Keith. BBA, U. Wis., Whitewater, 1974. Cost acct. AMF-Harley Davidson, Milw., 1974-76, plant acct., 1976-78, supr. cost acctg., 1978-80; cost systems analyst AMPCO-Pittsburg, Milw., 1980-82; mgr. cost and budgeting McQuay Perfex, Grenada, Miss., 1982-85; mgr. cost acctg. Republic Airlines, Mpls., 1985-86; dir. acctg. svcs. NW Airlines, Mpls., 1986-91; dir. maint., fin. and adminstrn. Evergreen Internat. Airlines, McMinnville, Oreg., 1991—; cons. Hawaiian Airlines, 1991. Lutheran. Home: 1617 Trestle View Ct Newberg OR 97132-1116 Office: Evergreen Internat Airlines 3850 Three Mile Ln Mcminnville OR 97128

HELLE, JOHN HAROLD (JACK HELLE), fishery research biologist; b. Williston, N.D., Apr. 26, 1935; s. Harold Cliford and Alice (Linquist) H.; m. Marilyn D. Matthews, Dec. 27, 1959; children: Jeanmarie Helle Davis, Joanna. BS, U. Idaho, 1958, MS, 1961; PhD in Fishery Sci., Oreg. State U., 1979. Fishery rsch. biologist U.S. Fish and Wildlife Svc., Auke Bay, Alaska, 1960-70, Nat. Marine Fisheries Svc., Auke Bay, 1971—; hon. rsch. fellow Marischal Coll., U. of Aberdeen, Scotland, 1964-65. Fellow Am. Inst. Fishery Rsch. Biologists (pres. 1990-92); mem. Am. Fisheries Soc. (cert. fisheries scientist), Pacific Fishery Biologists. Office: Auke Bay Fisheries Lab 11305 Glacier Hwy Juneau AK 99801

HELLENTHAL, JOAN ELIZABETH, artist; b. Phila., Apr. 25, 1945; d. William Edward and Elizabeth Anna (Roddy) Gardner; m. Cort Hellenthal, Sept. 1, 1973 (div. July 1991); 1 child, Gareth Gardner. BA in Fine Art, Brown U., 1967; MA in Fine Art, San Jose State U., 1981. Artist San Francisco Mus. Modern Art Rental Gallery, 1982—, Art Mus. Santa Cruz (Calif.) Rental Gallery, 1989—. Exhbns. include Montalvo Ctr. for Arts, Saratoga, Calif., 1983, U. Calif. Santa Cruz, 1989, Grimes Gallery, Carmel, Calif., 1989, Internat. Juried Show, Buffalo, 1991, Chaminade Conf. Ctr., Santa Cruz, 1991; represented in permanent collections Paine Webber, Chevron. Inst. Santa Cruz Art League; mem. exhbn. com. Art Mus. Santa

Cruz, 1987-88; mem. staff San Jose State Art Gallery, 1980; mem. adv. com. Open Studios, Santa Cruz, 1986; mem. site coun. Bonny Doon Sch., Santa Cruz, 1986-87. Mem. Art Mus. Santa Cruz, Santa Cruz Art League, Cultural Coun. Santa Cruz. Home and Studio: 854 Martin Rd Santa Cruz CA 95060

HELLENTHAL, S. RONALD, finance company executive; b. Santa Cruz, Calif., Oct. 26, 1949. BA in Bus., Baylor U., 1969, MBA, 1975; BA in Bus., U. Air Force, Colorado Springs, Colo., 1973; postgrad., Portland State U., 1980—. Investigator, dept. def. fed. govt., 1970-73; with law enforcement county govt., 1973-75; transp. cons., 1975-78; owner Rohn Mgmt. Co., Portland, 1978-80; pres. Rohn Mgmt. Corp., Portland, 1980—, Northwest Tours, Inc., Portland, Seattle, 1984—; pres., treas. Monty D. Moore & Co., Portland, 1984—; pres. Rohn Marine Svcs., Seattle, 1986—; chmn. bd. dirs. Rohn Mgmt. Corp., Portland, Northwest Tours, Inc., Seattle; pres. N.W. Tours, Inc. Executours, Rohn Mgmt. Corp., Rohn Marine Svcs., Bar H Ranches & Cattle Co., Hellenthal & Assocs. Staff sgt., U.S. Army, 1966-70, Vietnam, USAFR ret. Mem. Nat. Tour Assn., Portland/Oreg. Visitors Assn., Seattle/King County Visitors Assn., Griffith Park Club. Democrat. Roman Catholic. Office: Rohn Mgmt Corp PO Box 8637 Portland OR 97207-8637 also: 3025 SW 1st Ave Portland OR 97201

HELLER, ANTHONY FERDINAND, electronics engineer; b. N.Y.C., Oct. 6, 1944; s. Louis Richard and Alma Gunda (Shauer) H. BA in Psychology, Hofstra U., 1967; MS in Indsl. Psychology, San Diego State U., 1971. Rsch. analyst Navy Med. Neuropsychiat. Rsch. Unit, San Diego, 1967-71; prin. Montessori Internat. Youth U., Stonybrook, N.Y., 1971-72; mgr. Pacific Stereo, L.A., 1972-80; owner, operator Heller Automotive Security Systems, Lawndale, Calif., 1981-85; nat. dir. tng. Anes Electronics, Marina del Rey, Calif., 1985-90, Directed Electronics, San Marcos, Calif., 1990-91; engr. AudiovoxWest Corp., Cerritos, Calif., 1991—; instr. Fred Kennedy Assocs., San Pedro, Calif., 1991—; owner, operator Tng. Cons. Internat., Redondo Beach, Calif., 1990—. Assoc. editor: Autosound and Communications, 1987-89, C.A.R.S. Mag., 1989—. Active Am. Brotherhood Aimed Toward Edn., Torrance, Calif., 1992. Recipient Cert. of Recognition Calif. Crime Prevention Officers Assn., 1989, City of Newport Beach, 1990. Mem. 5th Chpt. Motorcycle Club (road capt. 1981-83, v.p. 1983-84), Port Royal Yacht Club (charter), Chosen Few Motorcycle Club, Hermosa Beach Alano Club (bd. dirs., sp. events coord. 1992—). Home: Vessel Gypsy Boy Port Royal Marina 555 Harbor Dr # 5 Redondo Beach CA 90277

HELLER, DONALD HERBERT, lawyer; b. N.Y.C., June 1, 1943; s. Nathan and Sylvia (Wexler) H.; m. Lesley Siskin, July 24, 1976; children: Michael, Joshua, Alexandra. BA in Econs., Queens Coll., 1966; JD, Bklyn. Law Sch., 1969. Bar: N.Y. 1969, Calif. 1973, U.S. Dist. Ct. (cen., no. and ea. dists.) Calif. 1974, U.S. Ct. Appeals (9th cir.) 1974. Asst. dist. atty. N.Y. County, N.Y.C., 1969-73; asst. U.S. atty. Calif. Dist. Ct. (ea. dist.), Sacramento, 1973-77; sole practice Sacramento, 1977—; judge pro tempore Sacramento County Superior Ct., 1986—. Mem. ABA, Sacramento County Bar Assn., Assn. Trial Lawyers Am., Calif. Trial Lawyers Assn. Republican. Home: 5160 Keane Dr Carmichael CA 95608-6043 Office: 701 University Ave Apt 150 Sacramento CA 95825-6700

HELLER, JULES, writer; b. N.Y.C., Nov. 16, 1919; s. Jacob Kenneth and Goldie (Lassar) H.; m. Gloria Spiegel, June 11, 1947; children: Nancy Gale, Jill Kay. AB, Ariz. State Coll., 1939; AM, Columbia U., 1940; PhD, U. So. Calif., 1948; DLitt, York U., 1985. Spl. art instr. 8th St. Sch., Tempe, Ariz., 1938-39; dir. art and music Union Neighborhood House, Auburn, N.Y., 1940-41; prof. fine arts, head dept. U. So. Calif., 1946-61; vis. asso. prof. fine arts Pa. State U., summers 1955, 57; dir. Pa. State U. (Sch. Arts), 1961-63; founding dean Pa. State U. (Coll. Arts and Architecture), 1963-68; founding dean Faculty Fine Arts York U., Toronto, 1968-73; prof. fine arts Faculty of Fine Arts, York U., 1973-76; dean Coll. Fine Arts, Ariz. State U., Tempe, 1976-85; prof. art Coll. Fine Arts, Ariz. State U., 1985-89; prof. emeritus, dean emeritus, 1990—; vis. prof. Silpakorn U., Bangkok, Thailand, 1974, Coll. Fine Arts, Colombo, Sri Lanka, 1974, U. Nacional de Tucumán, Argentina, 1990, U. Nacional de Cuyo, Mendoza, Argentina, 1990; lectr., art juror; Cons. Open Studio, 1975-76; mem. vis. com. on fine arts Fisk U., Nashville, 1974. Printmaker; exhibited one man shows, Gallery Pascal, Toronto, U. Alaska, Fairbanks, Alaskaland Bear Gallery, Visual Arts Center, Anchorage, Ariz. State U., Lisa Sette Gallery, 1990, Centro Cultural de Tucumán, San Miguel de Tucumán, 1990; exhibited numerous group shows including Canadian Printmaker's Showcase, Pollack Gallery, Toronto, Mazelow Gallery, Toronto, Santa Monica Art Gallery, L.A. County Mus., Phila. Print Club, Seattle Art Mus., Landau Gallery, Kennedy & Co. Gallery, Bklyn. Mus., Cin. Art Mus., Dallas Mus. Fine Arts, Butler Art Inst., Oakland Art Mus., Pa. Acad. Fine Arts, Santa Barbara Mus. Art, San Diego Gallery Fine Arts, Martha Jackson Gallery, N.Y.C., Yuma Fine Arts Assn., Ariz., Toronto Dominion Centre, Amerika Haus, Hannover, Fed. Rep. Germany, U. Md., Smith-Andersen Galleries, Palo Alto, Calif., Grunewald Ctr. Graphic Arts, L.A., Univ. So. Fla., Tampa, Sheldon Meml. Gallery, Lincoln, Nebr., Santa Cruz (Calif.) Mus., Drake U., Iowa, Bradley U., Ill., Del Bello Gallery, Toronto, Honolulu Acad. Fine Arts; represented in permanent collections, Long Beach Mus. Art, Library of Congress, York U., Allan R. Hite Inst. of U. Louisville, Ariz. State U., Tamarind Inst., U. N.Mex., Zimmerli Mus. Rutgers U., N.J., Can. Council Visual Arts Bank, also pvt. collections; author: Problems in Art Judgment, 1946, Printmaking Today, 1958, revised, 1972, Papermaking, 1978, 79; contbg. artist: Prints by California Artists, 1954, Estampas de la Revolucion Mexicana, 1948; illustrator: Canciones de Mexico, 1948; author numerous articles. Adv. bd. Continental affairs com. Americas Soc., 1983-86. With USAAF, 1941-45. Can. Coun. grantee; Landsdowne scholar U. Victoria; Fulbright scholar, Argentina, 1990. Mem. Coll. Art Assn., Authors Guild, Internat. Assn. Hand Papermakers (steering com. 1986—), Nat. Found. Advancement in the Arts (visual arts panelist 1986-90, panel chmn. 1989, 90), Internat. Assn. Paper Historians, Internat. Coun. Fine Arts Deans (pres. 1968-69). Home: 6838 E Cheney Rd Paradise Valley AZ 85253-3525

HELLER, RONALD IAN, lawyer; b. Cleve., Sept. 4, 1956; s. Grant L. and Audrey P. (Lecht) H.; m. Shirley Ann Stringer, Mar. 23, 1986. AB with high honors, Univ Mich., 1976, MBA, 1979, JD, 1980. Bar: Hawaii 1980, U.S. Ct. Claims 1982, U.S. Tax Ct. 1981, U.S. Ct. Appeals (9th cir.) 1981; Trust Territory of Pacific Islands 1982, Republic of Marshall Islands 1982; CPA, Hawaii. Assoc. Hoddick, Reinwald, O'Connor & Marrack, Honolulu, 1980-84; ptnr. Reinwald, O'Connor & Marrack, 1984-87; stockholder, bd. dirs. Torkildson, Katz, Jossem, Fonseca, Jaffe & Moore, Honolulu, 1988—; adj. prof. U. Hawaii Sch. Law, 1981; author, instr. Hawaii Taxes. Bd. dirs. Hawaii Women Lawyers Found., Honolulu, 1984-86, Hawaii Performing Arts Co., Honolulu, 1984—. Actor, stage mgr. Honolulu Community Theatre, 1983-87, Hawaii Performing Arts Co., Honolulu, 1982-87. Mem. AICPA, ABA, Hawaii State Bar Assn., Hawaii Soc. CPAs (chmn tax com. 1985-86, legis. com. 1987-88, bd. dirs. 1988—), Hawaii Women Lawyers. Office: Torkildson Katz Jossem 700 Bishop St Honolulu HI 96813-4124

HELLICKSON, KAZUKO SATO, contract administrator; b. Tokyo, Apr. 9, 1947; d. Jun and Misao (Kobayashi) Sato; m. Howard Adrian Hellickson, Apr. 4, 1970 (dec. Oct. 1974). BA in English Lit., Macalester Coll., 1969; BS in Consumer Sci., U. Wis., 1978. Sr. engr. in contract tech. requirements, sr. contract specialist Martin Marietta Corp., Denver, 1979-82, sr. contract specialist, 1984-86, contract adminstr., 1986-90, chief contract adminstr., 1991—; configuration engr. Gen. Telephone and Elec., Westborough, Mass., 1982-84. Bd. dirs. Congress Park Neighbors, Denver, 1979; vol. pub. TV, Nat. Contract Mgmt. Assn. Mem. Nat. Def. Preparedness Assn., Smithsonian, Omicron Nu. Office: Martin Marietta Corp PO Box 179 Denver CO 80201-0179

HELLMAN, F(REDERICK) WARREN, investment advisor; b. N.Y.C., July 25, 1934; s. Marco F. and Ruth (Koshl) H.; m. Patricia Christina Sander, Oct. 5, 1955; children: Frances, Patricia H., Marco Warren, Judith. BA, U. Calif., Berkeley, 1955; MBA, Harvard U., 1959. With Lehman Bros., N.Y.C., 1959-84, ptnr., 1963-84; exec. mng. dir. Lehman Bros., Inc., N.Y.C., 1970-73; pres. Lehman Bros., Inc., 1973-75; ptnr. Hellman Ferri Investment Assocs., 1981-89, Matrix Ptnrs., 1981—; gen. ptnr. Hellman & Friedman, San Francisco; bd. dirs. DN & E Walter, Am. Pres. Cos., Lt., Levi Strauss & Co., Williams-Sonoma, Inc., Il Fornaio (Am.) Corp., Gt. Am. Mgmt. & Investment, Inc., Franklin Resources, Inc., Basic Am., Inc., Eagle Industries, Inc.; trustee The Brookings Inst. Bd. dirs. Children Now, U. Calif. San Francisco Found. Mem. Bond Club, Piping Rock Club, Century Country Club, Pacific Union Club. Office: Hellman & Friedman One Maritime Plz 12th Fl San Francisco CA 94111

HELLREICH, PHILIP DAVID, dermatologist; b. Bklyn., Sept. 19, 1941; s. Emanuel and Sophie (Kopplemann) H.; m. Carolyn Hellreich, Nov. 3, 1965 (div. 1972); 1 child, Jennifer Bliss; m. Janice Mirian Wills, Sept. 28, 1974. BA, Hamilton Coll., 1962; MD, SUNY, Syracuse, 1966. Resident in dermatology USPHS, S.I., N.Y., 1967-69; fellow in dermatology Columbia U./Presbyn. Hosp., N.Y.C., 1969-70; dep. chief dept. dermatology USPHS, S.I., 1970-71; asso. clin. prof. medicine U. Hawaii, Honolulu, 1984—; clin. dermatologist Honolulu Med. Group, 1971-72, Windward Med. Group, 1972-73; clin. dermatologist in pvt. practice Kailua Dermatology Assocs. Ltd., Hawaii, 1973—; cons. VA Outpatient Clinic, Honolulu, 1972-79. County chair Honolulu County Rep. Party, 1988-91; 3d vice chair Rep. Party State of Hawaii, Honolulu, 1992. Recipient 1st prize Fred Wise Meml. Lectureship, N.Y. Acad. Medicine, 1969. Fellow Am. Acad. Dermatology; mem. AMA, Internat. Soc. Dermatologists, Hawaii Med. Assn., Hawaii Fed. Physicians and Dentists (pres. 1984-88, chmn. legis. com. 1988—). Office: Kailua Dermatology Assocs 40 Aulike St # 311 Kailua HI 95734

HELLWARTH, ROBERT WILLIS, physicist, educator; b. Ann Arbor, Mich., Dec. 10, 1930; s. Arlen Roosevelt and Sarah Matilda (Townsend) H.; m. Abigail Gurfein, Sept. 20, 1957 (div. 1979); children: Benjamin John, Margaret Eve, Thomas Abraham; m. Theresia deVroom, Dec. 20, 1985; 1 child, William Albert Detroit. B.S., Princeton U., 1952; D.Phil. (Rhodes scholar), St. John's Coll., Oxford (Eng.) U., 1955. Sr. scientist, mgr. Hughes Research Labs., Malibu, Calif., 1956-70; vis. assoc. prof. elec. engring. and physics U. Ill., Urbana, 1964-65; research assoc., sr. research fellow Calif. Inst. Tech., Pasadena, 1966-70; NSF sr. postdoctoral fellow Clarendon Lab.-St. Peter's Coll., Oxford (Eng.) U., 1970-71; George Pfleger prof. elec. engring., prof. physics U. So. Calif., Los Angeles, 1970—. Author monograph, articles in field; asso. editor: IEEE Jour. Quantum Electronics, 1964-76. Grantee NSF; Grantee Dept. Energy; Grantee Air Force Office Sci. Research; Grantee U.S. Army Research Office. Fellow IEEE (Quantum Electronics award), Am. Phys. Soc., AAAS, Optical Soc. Am. (Charles Hard Townes award); mem. Nat. Acad. Engring., Nat. Acad. Scis., AAUP, Phi Beta Kappa, Sigma Xi, Eta Kappa Nu. Home: 711 16th St Santa Monica CA 90402-3005 Office: U So Calif Physics Dept SSC 303 Los Angeles CA 90089-0484

HELLYER, CONSTANCE ANNE, writer, communications executive; b. Puyallup, Wash., Apr. 22, 1937; d. David Tirrell and Constance (Hopkins) H.; m. Peter A. Corning, Dec. 30, 1963 (div. 1977); children: Anne Arundel, Stephanie Deak; m. Don W. Conway, Oct. 12, 1980. BA with honors, Mills Coll., 1959. Grader, researcher Harvard U., Cambridge, Mass., 1959-60; researcher Newsweek mag., N.Y.C., 1960-63; author's asst. Theodore H. White and others, N.Y.C., 1964-69; freelance writer, editor Colo., Calif., 1969-75; writer, editor Stanford (Calif.) U. Med. Ctr., 1975-79; communications dir. No. Calif. Cancer Program, Palo Alto, 1979-82; comm. dir. Stanford Law Sch., Palo Alto, 1982—. Founding editor (newsletter) Insight, 1978-80, Synergy, 1980-82; editor (mag.) Stanford Lawyer, 1982—; contbr. articles to profl. jours. and mags. Recipient Silver Medal award Council Advancement and Support of Edn., 1985, 89. Mem. No. Calif. Sci. Writers Assn. (co-founder, bd. dirs. 1979-93), Phi Beta Kappa. Democrat. Home: 2080 Louis Rd Palo Alto CA 94303-3451 Office: Stanford Law Sch Stanford CA 94305-8610

HELMBOLD, RICHARD, writer, scholar; b. Whittier, Calif., June 29, 1950; s. John Lloyd and Dorothy Ruby (Grooms) H. Student, Mt. San Antonio Coll., 1968-73, San Francisco State U., 1973-76. Founder, coord. ABSURD, Pomona, Calif., 1970, Covina, Calif., 1971-73, San Francisco, 1973-79, Rosemead, Calif., 1980-81; writer, scholar San Francisco, 1976-79, Rosemead, 1980-81, Versailles, France, 1988-89, Palo Alto, 1982—; artist, cons. Author: (novel) Woman in the Rain, 1989, (poetry) Grief of Love, 1986, Forefather's Blood, 1992, (short stories) Simon's Neurosis, 1992, Protocol For Judgment Day, 1993. Organizer Vietnam Moritorium Com., L.A., 1969; activist YIPPIE!, So. Calif., 1969-71.

HELMER, DAVID ALAN, lawyer; b. Colorado Springs, May 19, 1946; s. Horton James and Alice Ruth (Cooley) H.; m. Jean Marie Lamping, May 23, 1987. BA, U. Colo., 1968, JD, 1973. Bar: Colo. 1973, U.S. Dist. Ct. Colo. 1973, U.S. Ct. Claims, 1990, U.S. Ct. Appeals (10th cir.) 1993, U.S. Supreme Ct. 1991. Assoc., Neil C. King, Boulder, Colo., 1973-76; mgr. labor rels., mine regulations Climax Molybdenum Co., Inc. div. AMAX, Inc., Climax, Colo., 1976-83; prin. Law Offices David A. Helmer, Frisco, Colo., 1983—; sec., bd. dirs. Z Comm. Corp., Frisco, 1983-90. Editor U. Colo. Law Rev., 1972-73; contbr. articles to legal jours. Bd. dirs. Summit County Council Arts and Humanities, Dillon, Colo., 1980-85, Advisor for Victims Assault, Frisco, 1984—; legal counsel Summit County United Way, 1983—, v.p., bd. dirs., 1983-88; bd. dirs., legal counsel Summit County Alcohol and Drug Task Force, Inc., 1984—, Pumpkin Bowl Inc./Children's Hosp. Burn Ctr., 1989—. Chmn. Summit County Reps., 1982-89; chmn. 5th Jud. Dist. (Colo.) Rep. Com., 1982-89; chmn. resolutions com. Colo. Rep. Conv., 1984, del. Rep. Nat. Com., 1984; chmn. reaccreditation com. Colo. Mountain Coll., Breckenridge, 1983; founder, bd. dirs. Dillon Bus. Assn., 1983-87, Frisco Arts Coun., 1989—; atty. N.W. Colo. Legal Svcs. Project, Summit County, 1983—; mcpl. judge Town of Dillon, Colo., 1982—, Town of Silverthorne, Colo., 1982—. Master sgt. USAR, 1968-74. Mem. ABA, Colo. Bar Assn. (bd. govs. 1991—), Continental Divide Bar Assn. (pres. 1991—), Summit County Bar Assn. (pres. 1990—), Dillon Corinthian Yacht Club (commodore local club 1987-88, club champion 1989-91, Colo. Cup Colo. State Sailing Championships 1991), Phi Gamma Delta. Lutheran. Home: 0352 Snake River Dr Dillon CO 80435-0300 Office: 619 Main St PO Box 868 Frisco CO 80443

HELMUTH, PHILIP ALAN, tax consultant; b. Alhambra, Calif., Dec. 29, 1965; s. Melvin I. and Elsie (Borkholder) H. Student, MiraCosta Coll., 1985-89, Palomar Coll., 1989-90. Data entry operator Melco Bus. Svc., Vista, Calif., 1980-83, bookkeeper, 1983-91; ptnr., tax cons. Melco Bus. Svc., Vista, Underwater Schs. of Am., Oceanside, 1985-86; owner, notary pub. Vista, 1987—. Mem. Nat. Notary Assn. (com. mem. editorial adv. com. 1990—, pub. image com. 1990—), Inland Soc. of Tax Cons., Escondido Grad. Spokesman Club (sec. 1991-92, pres. 1992-93). Office: Melco Bus Svc 410 S Santa Fe Ave Ste 102 Vista CA 92084

HELPRIN, BENSON RAIMON, fine arts educator; b. Bklyn., July 11, 1933; s. Benjamin Edel and Shirley (Levine) H.; m. Mary Lovejoy Pierce, 1958 (dec. 1987); children: Cathryn Eldridge, Pamela, Heather Sydney; m. Tekla Coleman Valley, July 6, 1991. BPA, BFA, Art Ctr. Coll. Design, Pasadena, Calif., 1963, MFA, 1965. Asst. prof. Calif. State U., L.A., 1969-72; advt. photographer L.A., 1972-79; co-dir. The Rolles Internat. Seminar on Photography, London, 1977-79; contbg. editor Petersen's Photographic Mag., L.A., 1975-86; prof. fine art San Jose (Calif.) State U., 1980—. Author: Photo Lighting Techniques, Self-Assignments in Photography; contbr. articles on photography to profl. jours. Named Outstanding Prof. San Jose State U., 1984, award L.A. Art Dirs., 1975, 76, 77. Mem. Mensa. Home: 16135 Loretta Ln Los Gatos CA 95032 Office: San Jose State U 1 Washington Square San Jose CA 95192

HELPRIN, MARK, author; b. N.Y.C., June 28, 1947; s. Morris A. and Eleanor (Lynn) H.; m. Lisa Kennedy, June 28, 1980; children: Alexandra Morris, Olivia Kennedy. A.B., Harvard U., 1969, A.M., 1972; postgrad., Magdalen Coll., Oxford (Eng.) U., 1976-77. Author: A Dove of the East and Other Stories, 1975, Refiner's Fire, 1977, Ellis Island and Other Stories, 1981, Winter's Tale, 1983, Swan Lake, 1989, A Soldier of the Great War, 1991; contbg. editor The Wall St. Jour. Served with Israeli Army and Air Force, 1972-73. Recipient Prix de Rome, Am. Acad. and Inst. Arts and Letters, 1982, Nat. Jewish Book award, 1982; sr. fellow Hudson Inst. Fellow Am. Acad. in Rome.

HELSLEY, EDWARD FRANCIS, elevator company executive; b. Evansville, Ind., Jan. 25, 1943; s. Edward Rufus Helsley and Marguerite (Raney) Schmidt; m. Harriett Ann Hanna, Dec. 30, 1966; children: John Paul, Elizabeth Jane. BS, USC, 1965. Contractor lic. Calif., Nev., N.Mex., La. Chief oper. officer Elevator div. Dover Corp., Memphis, 1972-82, U.S. Elevator Corp., San Diego, 1982—; bd. dirs. Kimball Elevator Co., Salt Lake City, 1985—, Ctrl. Elevator Co., N.Y.C., 1988—. Capt. USAF, 1967-72. Decorated Air medals, DFC. Mem. Nat. Assn. Elevator Contractors, Nat. Assn. Elevator Safety Authorities, Bldg. Owners and Mgrs. Assn., NRA, Sigma Chi. Republican. Home: 10350 Rue Finisterre San Diego CA 92131 Office: US Elevator Co 10728 US Elevator Rd Spring Valley CA 91978

HELSLEY, MARVIN EDWARD, accountant, small business owner; b. Essex, Mo., Aug. 20, 1922; s. Sherman E. and Iva I. (Miles) H.; m. Paula M. Helsley, Apr. 30, 1959; children: William R., Judith M., Carla L., Patrick D., Marci L. BBA, Woodbury Coll., 1948. CPA, Calif. Founding ptnr. Helsley, Mulcahy & Fesler, Tustin, Calif., 1950—; chief fin. officer Orco Block Found., Tustin, 1990—, Rick J. and Nancy M. Muth Found., Tustin, 1990—, Peter and Mary Muth Found., Tustin, 1990—; bd. dirs. Metalclad Corp., Anaheim, Calif. Sgt. U.S. Army, 1940-45, ETO. Mem. AICPAs, Calif. Soc. CPAs, Soc. Calif. Accts. (dist. gov. 1977-78), U.S. Nat. Sr. Open Golf Assn. (bd. dirs. 1990—), Big Canyon Country Club. Republican. Office: Helsley Mulcahy & Fesler 335 Centennial Way Tustin CA 92680-3794

HELTON, THOMAS JOE, computer scientist, writer; b. Ft. Wayne, Ind., Aug. 15, 1944; s. Vernon L. and Isabelle E. (Price) H.; m. Karen Sue Andersen, Dec. 21, 1965 (div. Apr. 1978); children: Thomas Vernon, Heather Lea; m. Mary Elizabeth Martin, Feb. 12, 1979; children: Amity Rae, Sara May, Duane Thomas, Thomas Joe, Benjamin Samuel. AB, Ind. U., 1968, MBA, 1970; postgrad., U. Chgo., 1972. CPA Ill., 1973, Mo., 1977. Supr. Touche Ross & Co., Chgo., 1970-74; asst. controller Federated Dept. Stores, Dallas, 1975-76; dir., fin. pub. rels. May Dept. Stores Co., St. Louis, 1977-79; contr. Cole Nat. Corp., Richmond Hts., Ohio, 1980-83; pres. Thinc, Bremerton, Wash., 1983-84; lectr. Grays Harbor Coll., Aberdeen, Wash., 1984-85; systems mgr. Southwestern Bell Telephone Co., St. Louis, 1985-92; sr. systems analyst Group Health Coop. of Puget Sound, Seattle, Wash., 1993—; columnist John Wiley & Sons, N.Y.C., 1990—. Contbr. articles to profl. jours. Mem. Borland Internat. Exec. Adv. Bd., Scotts Valley, Calif., 1987-90; v.p. Protect Our Pets, Bridgeton, Mo., 1989-92. Walter E. Heller fellow, 1969. Mem. ACM, AAAI, Internat. Neural Network Soc., Level 5 Users Group (exec. v.p. 1988-92), Beta Gamma Sigma. Home: 9040 Anderson Hill Rd Silverdale WA 98383 Office: Group Health Cooperative Puget Sound 521 Wall St Seattle WA 98121

HELZER, JAMES DENNIS, hospital executive; b. Fresno, Calif., Apr. 27, 1938; s. Alexander and Katherine (Scheidt) H.; m. Joan Elaine Alinder, Feb. 25, 1967; children: Amy, Rebecca. B.S., Fresno State Coll., 1960; M.Hosp. Adminstrn., U. Iowa, 1965. Adminstrv. asst. Twilight Haven, Fresno, Calif., 1960-61; asst. adminstr. U. Calif. Hosps. and Clinics, San Francisco, 1965-68; asst. adminstr. Fresno Community Hosp., 1968-71, exec. adminstr., 1971-82, pres., chief exec. officer, 1982-91; pres., chief exec. officer Community Hosps. Cen. Calif., 1983-91. Served with U.S. Army, 1961-63. Fellow Am. Coll. Hosp. Adminstrs.; mem. Am., Calif. hosp. assns. Presbyterian. Club: Rotary. Home: 5909 E Hamilton Ave Fresno CA 93727-6226

HEM, JOHN DAVID, research chemist; b. Starkweather, N.D., May 14, 1916; s. Hans Neilius and Josephine Augusta (Larsen) H.; m. Ruth Evans, Mar. 11, 1945; children: John David Jr., Michael Edward. Student, Minot State Coll., 1932-36, N.D. State U., 1937-38, Iowa State U., 1938; BS, George Washington U., 1940. Analytical chemist U.S. Geol. Survey, Safford, Ariz., 1940-42, 43-45, Roswell, N.Mex., 1942-43; dist. chemist U.S. Geol. Survey, Albuquerque, 1945-53; rsch. chemist U.S. Geol. Survey, Denver, 1953-63, Menlo Park, Calif., 1963—; rsch. advisor U.S. Geol. Survey, 1974-79, mem. water rsch. adv. com., 1984—. Author: Study and Interpretation Chemistry of Natural Water, 3d rev. edit., 1985; contbr. articles to profl. publs., chpts. to books. Recipient Meritorious Svc. award U.S. Dept. Interior, 1976, Disting. Svc. award U.S. Dept. Interior, 1980, Sci. award Nat. Water Well Assn., 1986, O.E. Meinzer award Geol. Soc. Am., 1990, Special award Internat. Assn. Geochemistry and Cosmochemistry, 1992. Mem. Am. Chem. Soc., Am. Geophys. Union, Am. Water Works Assn., Geochem. Soc., Soc. Geochemistry and Health. Democrat. Lutheran. Home: 3349 St Michael Ct Palo Alto CA 94306-3056 Office: US Geol Survey MS 427 345 Middlefield Rd Menlo Park CA 94025-3591

HEMANN, RAYMOND GLENN, aerospace company executive; b. Cleve., Jan 24, 1933; s. Walter Harold Marsha Mae (Colbert) H.; BS, Fla. State U., 1957; postgrad. U.S. Naval Postgrad. Sch., 1963-64, U. Calif. at Los Angeles, 1960-62; MS in Systems Engring., Calif. State U., Fullerton, 1970, MA in Econs., 1972, cert. in tech. mgmt. Calif. Inst. Tech., 1990; m. Lucile Tinnin Turnage, Feb. 1, 1958; children: James Edward, Carolyn Frances; m. Pamela Lehr, Dec. 18, 1987. Aero. engring. aide U.S. Navy, David Taylor Model Basin, Carderock, Md., 1956; analyst Fairchild Aerial Surveys, Tallahassee, 1957; research analyst Fla. Rd. Dept., Tallahassee, 1957-59; chief Autonetics div. N.Am. Rockwell Corp., Anaheim, Calif., 1959-69; v.p., dir. R. E. Manns Co., Wilmington, Calif., 1969-70; mgr. Avionics Design and Analysis Dept. Lockheed-Calif. Co., Burbank, 1970-72, mgr. Advanced Concepts div., 1976-82; gen. mgr. Western div. Arinc Research Corp., Santa Ana, 1972-76; dir. Future Requirements Rockwell Internat., 1982-85; dir. Threat Analysis, Corp. Offices, Rockwell Internat., 1985-89; pres., chief exec. officer Advanced Systems Rsch., Inc., 1989—; adj. sr. fellow Ctr. Strategic and Internat. Studies, Washington, 1987—; cons. various corps. U.S. govt. agys.; sec., bd. dirs. Calif. State U., Fullerton, Econs. Found., 1989—; mem. naval studies bd. panels Nat. Acad. Scis., 1985—, Arms Control Working Group; asst. prof. ops. analysis dept. U.S. Naval Postgrad. Sch., Monterey, Calif., 1963-64, Monterey Peninsula Coll., 1963; instr. ops. analysis Calif. State U., Fullerton, 1963, instr. quantitative methods, 1969-72; program developer, instr. systems engring. indsl. rels. ctr. Calif. Inst. Tech., 1992—; lectr. Brazilian Navy, 1980, U. Calif., Santa Barbara, 1980, Yale U., 1985, Princeton U., 1986, U.S. Naval Postgrad. Sch., 1986, Ministry of Def., Taiwan, Republic of China, 1990; Calif. Inst. Tech., 1992; mem. exec. forum Calif. Inst. Tech., 1991—. Chmn. comdr.'s adv. bd. CAP, Calif. Wing, 1990—; reader Recording for the Blind, 1989—. With AUS, 1950-53. Syde P. Deeb scholar, 1956; recipient honor awards Nat. Assn. Remotely Piloted Vehicles, 1975, 76; named to Hon. Order Ky. Cols., 1985. Comml., glider and pvt. pilot. Fellow AAAS; assoc. fellow AIAA; mem. IEEE, Ops. Rsch. Soc. Am., Air Force Assn., Nat. Coalition for Advanced Mfg. (adv. bd. 1990—), N.Y. Acad. Scis., Assn. Old Crows, Phi Kappa Tau (past pres.). Episcopalian. Contbr. articles to profl. jours. and news media.

HEMENWAY, STEPHEN JAMES, record producer; b. San Gabriel, Calif., Aug. 26, 1955; s. Glenn Stephen and Patricia Ann (Reese) H.; m. Pamela Ann Caulkins, June 15, 1974 (div. Sept. 1983); children: April Lynn, Stacie Michelle, Ashley Renee. AS, Chaffey Coll., Alta Loma, Calif., 1981. Rec. artist Phil Good Records, Ontario, Calif., 1978-80; songwriter Airing Music, Ontario, Calif., 1979-84; prod. Brass Star Records, Chino Hills, Calif., 1984—; publisher Brass Star Music, Chino Hills, Calif., 1988—; music arranger Brass Star Records, Chino Hills, 1984—; promoter Games and Entertainment Unlimited, Chino Hills, 1985-89; cons. Sound Prodns., Westminister, Calif., 1987—; songwriter/publisher Broadcast Music, Inc., 1975—; pres., music arranger Brass Star Records. Actor, artist, prod. Plays, Music, 1968—; music arranger A Chino Hills Christmas, Regina. Dep. sheriff, L.A. County, 1978. Republican. Roman Catholic. Office: Brass Star Records 14852 Pipe Line Ave Chino CA 91709-1942

HEMMINGS, PETER WILLIAM, orchestra and opera administrator; b. London, Apr. 10, 1934; s. William and Rosalind (Jones) H.; m. Jane Frances Kearnes, May 19, 1962; children—William, Lucy, Emma, Rupert, Sophie. Grad. Gonville and Caius Coll., Cambridge, 1957; LL.D. (hon.), Strathclyde U., Glasgow, 1978. Clk., Harold Holt Ltd., London, 1958-59; planning mgr. Sadlers Wells Opera, London, 1959-65; gen. adminstr. Scottish Opera, Glasgow, 1962-77; gen. mgr. Australian Opera, Sydney, 1977-79; mng. dir. London Symphony Orch., 1980-84; gen. dir. Los Angeles Music Ctr. Opera Assn., 1984—; gen. mgr. New Opera Co., London, 1956-65, dir. Royal Acad. Music; gen cons. Compton Verney Opera Project. Served to lt. Brit. Signal Corps, 1952-54; Fed. Republic Germany. Fellow Royal Scottish Acad. Music, Royal Acad. Music (hon.); mem. Internat. Assn. Opera Dirs., 1977-79, Opera Am. (v.p.). Anglican. Club: Garrick (London). Home: 775 S

Madison Ave Pasadena CA 91106-3831 Office: LA Music Ctr Opera 135 N Grand Ave Los Angeles CA 90012-3013

HEMMY, MARY LOUISE, social work administrator; b. Mpls., Nov. 14, 1914; d. Albert H. and Mary (Scott) H. BS, U. Minn., 1936, MA in Social Wk., 1941. Caseworker Washington U. Med. Ctr., St. Louis, 1937-40, Ill. Svcs. for Crippled Children, Springfield, 1941-42; instr., asst. prof. Sch. Social Wk., Washington U., 1942-45; dir. social wk. dept. Washington U. Med. Ctr., 1945-52; assoc. prof., dir. social wk. Coll. Medicine, U. Ill., Chgo., 1952-53; exec. dir. Am. Assn. Med. Social Workers, Washington, 1953-55; prof. sch. medicine sch. social work U. Pitts., 1956-59; exec. dir. Benjamin Rose Inst., Cleve., 1959-77; mem. spl. med. adv. group VA, 1963-68; mem. Ohio Bd. Examiners Nursing Home Adminstrs., 1973-77. Mem. Nat. Assn. Social Workers (bd. dirs. 1961-63), Am. Assn. Homes for Aging (bd. dirs. 1963-70). Home: 13505 SE River Rd Portland OR 97222-8097

HEMPHILL, ALAN POLK, management consultant; b. Montgomery, Ala., Aug. 22, 1933; s. Alan Polk and Elizabeth Evans (Orr) H.; m. Jean Tilden Baker, June 8, 1957; children: Elizabeth, Alan, Laurie. BSEE, U.S. Naval Acad., 1957; MA in Mgmt., Nat. U., 1987. Commd. ensign U.S. Navy, 1957, advanced through grades to lt. comdr., 1977; various assignments, San Diego, 1957-77; mgr. Prestige Properties, Poway Calif., 1977-80; founder Orion Bus. Systems, San Diego, 1980-82; pres., chief exec. officer Sta. KBSC-TV, Glendale, Calif. (sta. received 12 Emmy awards), 1982-83; chmn., bd. dirs. Oak Broadcasting Systems, Glendale, 1983-84; pres. Community Bus. Cons., San Diego, 1984-85; prof. computer sci. Nat. U., Vista, Calif., 1984—; trustee Sta. KBSC-TV Stock of Oak Industries, San Diego, 1982-84; panelist TV series On Edge, 1986-88; cons. Oak Industries, San Diego, 1984; bd. dirs. Community Bus. Cons., San Diego, 1984; sr. v.p. Orion Network Solutions, 1990-91. Contbr. articles and columns to profl. jours. and Commnunity News Network, Inc., chpts. to books. Gen. mgr. Remember the Pueblo, San Diego, 1968; pres., chmn. bd. Green Valley Civic Assn., Poway, 1974-75; pres., bd. dirs. North County Bd. of Jr. Achievement, 1979. Mem. Nat. U. Alumni Assn. (pres. 1991—), Kiwanis (pres. Rancho Bernardo chpt. 1980-81), Nat. U. Alumni Assn. (pres. 1991—).

HEMPHILL, ANDREA RENEA, magazine editor; b. Sioux Falls, S.D., Sept. 6, 1967; d. Danny C. and Vera M. (Beach) R. BA in Journalism, Adams State Coll., 1988. Asst. editor Style Mag., Ft. Collins, Colo., 1988-89; communications dir. Scuba Schs. Internat., Ft. Collins, 1989-91; assoc. editor Mus. Store Mag., Denver, 1991-92, managing editor, 1992—. Author: (tech. manual) Instructor's Guide to Learning and Instruction Methodology, 1991; contbr. articles to mag. Office: Mus Store Assn 501 S Cherry St Ste 460 Denver CO 80222-1327

HEMPHILL, DALLAS CAMPBELL, logging engineer, consultant; b. Whangarel, New Zealand, May 24, 1945; came to U.S., 1976; s. Desmond Campbell and Thelma Audrey (Swinbourn) H.; m. Leonora Jane Wesson, May 30, 1970; children: Kjersten, Marguerette. BSc, Auckland (New Zealand) U., 1967; MSc, U. B.C., Vancouver, Can., 1970. Registered profl. engr., Oreg. Logging planner New Zealand Forest Svc., Kaingaroa Forest, 1965-73; logging engr. Fletcher Timber Co., Taupo, New Zealand, 1973-76; project mgr., engr. Weyerhaeuser Co., Springfield, Oreg., 1977-81; pres. Logging Engring. Internat., Inc., Eugene, Oreg., 1981—. Mem. Assn. Cons. Foresters (chmn. Oreg. chpt. 1987-88, bd. dirs. West 1988-91), Soc. Am. Foresters (del-at-large Emerald chpt. 1986-87). Office: Logging Engring Internat Inc 3621 Vine Maple St Eugene OR 97405

HEMPHILL, NORMA JO, special event planning and tour company executive; b. Enid, Okla., Nov. 25, 1930; d. Wyatt Warren and Wanda Markes (Parker) Stout; m. Benjamin Robert Hemphill, June 21, 1952; children: Susan Colleen, Robert Gary. Student, Okla. State U.; BA, U. Calif., Berkeley, 1955. Former acct. Better Bus. Bookkeeping, Lafayette, Calif.; tchr., Head Start tchr. Chino (Calif.) Elem. Sch., 1966-68; pres., founder Calif. Carousel and Carousel Tours, Lafayette, 1972—; speaker Founders Day Univ. Calif., Berkeley, 1993; speaker in field; cons., dir. various orgns. Former mem. bd. dirs. PTA, Moraga, Calif., Lafayette; bd. dirs. Children's Home Soc., Upland, Calif., 1965-69; past demonstration tchr. Presbytery of Bay Area, San Francisco; past supt. 1st Presbyn. Ch., Oakland, Calif., elder, 1977—, trustee, 1980; mem. hon. bd. adv. com. Festival of Lake, Oakland, 1982; bd. govs. Goodwill Industries, 1978-79; founder, chmn. Joint Svc. Clubs Foster Children's Ann. Christmas Party. Named Person of Yr. award Advt.-Mktg. Assn. East Bay, 1978; co-recipient Event of Yr. award, Am. Pub. Rels. Assn., 1984. Mem. Lake Merritt Breakfast Club (Oakland, spl. events com., bd. govs., named Citizen of Community 1992), Lake Merritt Inst. (hon.), Soroptomist (very important women honor roll Diablo Valley 1990, keynote speaker 1991), Pi Beta Phi (bd. dirs., spl. events com. Contra Costa County chpt., Founder's Day speaker U. Calif.-Berkeley 1993). Office: Calif Carousel & Carousel Tours PO Box 537 Lafayette CA 94549-0537

HEMPHILL, THOMAS JOHN, sales engineer; b. Havre, Mont., Nov. 8, 1945; s. Robert Madison and Rita L. (Bohlig) H.; m. Merle E. McKeeman, Oct. 9, 1969; children: Michael Madison King, John Thomas Ward. BA, Ctrl. Wash. U., 1970. Asst. loan officer U.S. Bank, Gresham, Oreg., 1971-72; sales rep. Barwick Pacific, Honolulu, 1972-74; contracts, purchasing Boeing, Seattle, 1974-76; sales, contract adminstr. G.E. Thermal Systems, Tacoma, 1976-79; regional sales rep. Western Plastics Corp., Tacoma, 1979-82; northwest region sales engr. Advanced Drainage Systems, Tacoma, 1982—. Author, editor of product brochures. Mem. Jaycees, Gresham, 1972; bd. dirs. St. Lukes Episcopal Ch., Tacoma, 1974—. With USN, 1967-69, Hawaii. Mem. Assn. Gen. Contractors, Utility Contractor Assn., Turf Grass Assn., Pierce Landscape Contractor Assn. Episcopalian. Home: 2306 Vista View Dr Tacoma WA 98406-1619

HEMRY, LARRY HAROLD, immigration inspector; b. Seattle, Jan. 4, 1941; s. Harold Bernard and Florence Usborne (Achilles) H.; m. Nancy Kay Ballantyne, July 10, 1964 (div. Apr. 1976); children: Rachel Dalayne, Aaron Harold, Andrew LeRoy. BA, Seattle Pacific Coll., 1963; postgrad., Western Evang. Sem., Portland, Oreg., 1969, 70. Ordained to ministry Free Meth. Ch., 1968. Clergyman Free Meth. Ch., Vancouver, B.C., Can., 1963-64, Mt. Vernon, Wash., 1968-69; clergyman Colton (Oreg.) Community Ch., 1969-71; edit clk. Moody Bible Inst., Chgo., 1964-66; pres., founder Bethel Enterprises, Colton, 1969-71; immigration insp. U.S. Immigration and Naturalization Svc., Sumas, Wash., 1972—. Author, historian: Some Northwest Pioneer Families, 1969, The Hemry Family History Book, 1985; author: An Earnest Plea to Earnest Christians, 1969. chmn. com. to establish and endow the James A. Hemry meml. scholarship fund Seattle Pacific U., 1975. Fellow Seattle Pacific U. (Centurians Club); mem. The Nature Conservancy, The Sierra Club. Office: US Immigration and Naturalization Svc PO Box 99 Sumas WA 98295-0099

HENAGER, CHARLES HENRY, civil engineer; b. Spokane, Wash., July 11, 1927; s. William Franklin and Mary Agnes (Henry) H.; m. Dorothy Ruth Parker, May 6, 1950; children: Charles Henry, Jr., Donald E., Roberta R. BS in Civil Engring., Wash. State U., 1950. Registered profl. engr., Wash. Instrumentman Wash. State Dept. Hwys., Yakima, 1950-52; engr. Gen. Electric Co., Richland, Wash., 1952-62; shift supr., reactor GE, Richland, Wash., 1962-63, sr. engr., 1963-65; sr. devel. engr. Battelle Pacific N.W. Labs., Richland, 1965-68, sr. rsch. engr., 1968—. Contbr. articles to profl. jours.; patentee in field. With USN, 1945-46. Fellow Am. Concert Inst. (tech. activities com. 1987-89, Del Bloem award 1986), ASTM (subcom. 1980-92), ASCE (pres. Columbia sect. 1961-62); mem. Kennewick Swim Club (pres. 1962-63), Sigma Tau, Tau Beta Pi, Phi Kappa Phi. Republican. Methodist. Home: 1306 N Arthur Pl Kennewick WA 99336-1545 Office: Battelle Pacific NW Labs Battelle Blvd Richland WA 99352

HENCH, PHILIP KAHLER, physician; b. Rochester, Minn., Sept. 19, 1930; s. Philip Showalter and Mary Genevieve (Kahler) H.; m. Barbara Joan Kent, July 10, 1954; children: Philip Gordon, John Kahler, Amanda Kent. BA, Lafayette Coll., 1952; MD, U. Pitts., 1958; MSc in Medicine, U. Minn., 1965. Intern U. Colo. Med. Ctr., 1958-59; fellow in medicine and rheumatology Mayo Graduate Sch., Rochester, Minn., 1959-63; with Inst. for Arthritis and Metabolic Diseases, NIH, Bethesda, Md., 1963-64; asst. div. rheumatology Scripps Clinic and Rsch. Found., La Jolla, Calif., 1965-66, assoc., 1966-70, assoc. mem., 1970-74, mem., head, 1974-82, sr. cons., 1982—; adj. asst. mem. Dept. Molecular and Exptl. Medicine; mem. dept. acad. affairs Scripps Clinic and Rsch. Found.; asst. clin. prof. U. Calif. Sch. Medicine, San Diego, 1973—; cons. to pharm. cos.; mem. People to People Mission to China on Study of Aging, 1982. Contbr. articles on rheumatic diseases, pain and sleep disorders to profl. jours.; mem. editorial com. Rheumatism Revs., 1974-84; editorial reviewer Arthritis and Rheumatism, Jour. Rheumatology, 1985—; bd. spl. cons. Patient Care mag., 1987—. Recipient Arthritis Found. award (6), San Diego chpt., 1971-80; Philip S. Hench scholar Mayo Grad. Sch. Medicine, 1965. Fellow ACP, Am. Coll. Rheumatology (chmn. nonarticular rheumatism study group 1975-82, com. on preventive and rehab. medicine 1984-85, com. on rheumatologic practice 1975-77); mem. AMA, Am. Coll. Rheumatology, Nat. Soc. Clin. Rheumatologists, Am. Pain Soc., Calif. Med. Assn., Internat. Assn. for Study Pain, La Jolla Acad. Medicine, Arthritis Found. (bd. govs. San Diego chpt. 1965—, Best Doctors in Am. award 1992-93), San Diego Hist. Soc., San Diego Mus. Fine Arts (bd. advisors), San Diego Opera (bd. advisors). Republican. Home: 7856 La Jolla Vista Dr La Jolla CA 92037-3530 Office: Scripps Clinic & Rsch Found 10666 N Torrey Pines Rd La Jolla CA 92037-1027

HENDERSON, B. SCOTT, computer programmer; b. San Jose, Calif., Nov. 7, 1966; s. Jerry B. and P. Diane (Melsness) H. BS in Computer Sci. and Math., U. Puget Sound, 1988; MS in Computer Sci., Oreg. State U., 1990. Systems programmer Weyerhaeuser Co., Federal Way, Wash., 1988-90, 90—. Mem. IEEE Computer Soc., Assn. for Computing Machinery. Home: 29112 77th Ave S Roy WA 98580 Office: Weyerhaeuser Co 33405 8th Ave S Federal Way WA 98003

HENDERSON, DONALD WAYNE, salon owner; b. Havre, Mont., May 24, 1951; s. Robert Charles and Octa Beverly (Francois) H. Cert., Dahls Beauty Coll., Great Falls, Mont., 1975. Pres. Penthouse Salon Profls. Inc., Great Falls, 1979—; presenter workshops, seminars, tng. sessions. Sgt. U.S. Army, 1968-72, Vietnam. Decorated Silver Star; named Entrepreneur of the Yr., 1991. Mem. Paris Gibson Sq. (bd. dirs. 1988—), Mont. Cosmetologists Assn. (bd. dirs.), Great Falls Leadership Program, Great Falls Ad Club. Office: Penthouse Salon Profls Inc 313 Central Ave Great Falls MT 59401-3113

HENDERSON, DOUGLAS JAMES, physicist; b. Calgary, Alta., Can., July 28, 1934; came to U.S., 1956; s. Donald Ross and Evelyn Louise (Scott) H.; m. Rose-Marie Steen-Nielssen, Jan. 21, 1960; children: Barbara, Dianne, Sharon. BA in Math., U. B.C., Vancouver, 1956; PhD in Physics, U. Utah, 1961. Asst. prof. physics U. Idaho, Moscow, 1961-63; assoc. prof. Ariz. State U., Tempe, 1963-64; prof. physics and math. U. Waterloo, Ont., Can., 1964-69; research scientist IBM Research Div. IBM Corp., San Jose, Calif., 1969-90, IBM Corp., Salt Lake City, 1990-92, Utah Supercomputing Inst./IBM Partnership, U. Utah, Salt Lake City, 1990—; adj. prof. chemistry and math. U. Utah, 1990—; adj. prof. physics Utah State U., 1990—. Author: Statistical Mechanics and Dynamics, 1964, 2d rev. edit., 1982; editor: Physical Chemistry-An Advanced Treatise, Vols. 1-15, 1966-75, Theoretical Chemistry-Advances and Perspectives, Vols. 1-5, 1975-81, Fundamentals of Inhomogeneous Fluids; assoc. editor: Jour. Chem. Physics, 1974-76; mem. editorial bd. Ultitas Mathematica, 1971-87, Jour. Phys. Chemistry, 1984-90, Jour. Chem. Phys., 1990-92, Electrochimica Acta, 1991—; mem. adv. bd. Chem. Abstracts, 1981-83; also articles. Missionary Ch. Jesus Christ Latter Day Saints, Africa, 1957-59; vol. Loma Prieta Vol. Fire Dept., Los Gatos, Calif., 1983-89. Recipient Johnathan Rodgers award, 1954, Ariz. State U. Faculty award, 1963, IBM Outstanding Research Contbrn. award, 1973, 87; Univ. Gt. War scholar, 1953, Daniel Buchanan scholar, 1955; Fellow Corning Glass Found., 1959, Alfred P. Sloan Found., 1964, 66, Ian Potter Found., 1966, Commonwealth Sci. and Indsl. Research Orgn., 1966; named Manuel Sandoval Vallarta Physics lectr., Mex., 1985, 88. Fellow Inst. Physics, Am. Phys. Soc., Am. Inst. Chemists; mem. Can. Assn. Physicists, Am. Chem. Soc., Mexican Nat. Acad. Sci. (corr. mem.), Mathematical Assoc. Am. Democrat. Office: Utah Supercomputing Inst 85 SSB U Utah Salt Lake City UT 84112

HENDERSON, FRANK, illustrator, graphic artist; b. St. Louis, Feb. 8, 1948; s. Ronald Evert and Lou Ella (Shyrock) H.; m. Denice Joy Abraham, Oct. 31, 1992. A in Fine Arts, Florissant Valley Com. Coll., Mo., 1971; BS, Lindenwood Coll. II, 1971; cert. comml. art, U. Mo., 1973. Cert. tchr., Mo. Tech. illustrator, draftsman McDonnell Douglas Aircraft Corp., St. Louis, 1966-67; art tchr. Reorganized Sch. Dist. No. 4, Winfield, Mo., 1971-72; asst. art dir. Unicom Advt. Agy., Albuquerque, 1973-75; art dir. Boretsky & Assocs., Inc., Albuquerque, 1975-76; comml. artist Bus. Graphics, Inc., Albuquerque, 1976-77; illustrator Am. Furniture Co., Albuquerque, 1977-81; S.W. regional advt. mgr. Smith's Mgmt. Corp., Albuquerque, 1981-89; printer newspaper composition Albuquerque Pub. Co., 1989-92; graphic artist, illustrator Universal Printing & Pub., Inc., Albuquerque, 1992—; art cons. Your Host N.Mex. Mag., Albuquerque, 1974-75; art judge N.Mex. State Fair, Albuquerque, 1978-80. Illustrator The Oregon Trail, 1992, Cats Mag., 1992, German Religion Comes to America, 1978; graphic designer Campbell Soup Nat. Advt., 1982. Mem. N.Mex. Art League, Albuquerque, 1978. Recipient 3d pl. Mixed Media award N.Mex. State Fair Commn., 1989, 2d pl. Specialty Advt. award N.Mex. Advt. Fedn., 1974, Cert. Art award Mo. Coun. on the Arts, 1970, Mo. Coll. Art Assn., 1970. Mem. NEA, Mo. State Tchrs. Assn., Classroom Tchrs. Assn. Home: 7224 Gatling NE Albuquerque NM 87109-5308 Office: Universal Printing & Pub 1224 Bellamah NW Albuquerque NM 87104

HENDERSON, HOLLIS ALLEN, transportation consultant, railway engineer; b. Decatur, Ala., Nov. 11; s. Roy C. and Alice M. (Johnson) H.; m. Gean, Aug. 2, 1945 (dec. 1965); m. JoAnn Wessel, Feb. 25, 1967; children: Hollis, Mike, Candice, Richard, Kathy. AAME, U. Ga. Tech., 1942; BSEE, U. Utah, 1959; Degree in Transp. Mgmt., Stanford U., 1962. Cert. Railway Engr. Advanced to chief mechanical officer So. Pacific Transp. Co., San Francisco, 1946-72, chief mechanical officer, 1972-77; v.p. equipment Consolidated Rail Corp., Phila., 1977-83; v.p. ops. CSX Corp., Alexandria, Va., 1983-87; prin. Henderson Cons., San Diego, 1987—. Author in field. With USN, 1942-45. Mem. Assn. Am. Railroads, N.Y. Railway Assn. (pres. 1980), Pacific Railway Assn. (v.p. 1959). Republican. Protestant. Home and Office: 18575 Lancashire Way San Diego CA 92128

HENDERSON, LAVELL MERL, retired biochemistry educator; b. Swan Lake, Idaho, Sept. 9, 1917; s. George Merl and Nellie Marie (Gambles) H.; m. Maurine Criddle, Aug. 16, 1939; children: Janet Louise, Jeanne, Linda Marie. BS, Utah State U., 1939; MS, U. Wis., 1941, PhD, 1947. Instr. U. Wis., Madison, 1947-48; asst. prof. U. Ill., Urbana, 1948-57; prof., head Okla. State U., Stillwater, 1957-63; prof., head U. Minn., St. Paul, 1963-74, prof, assoc. dean, 1974-84, prof. emeritus, 1984—; mem. food and nutrition bd. NAS, Washington, 1965-71; mem. nutrition study sect. NIH, Washington, 1973-77, nutrition sci. tng. com. Nat. Inst. Gen. Med. Sci., Washington, 1965-69. Editor: Advances in Nutrition Research, 1976-84; editorial bd. Jour. Nutrition, 1965-68, 83-86; contbr. articles to profl. jours. Bd. dirs. Hormel Inst., Austin, Minn., North Star Rsch. & Devel., Mpls.; site visitor U.S. Office Edn., Title II, Washington, 1964-65. Grantee NIH, 1951-84; recipient Borden award Am. Inst. Nutrition, 1970. Mem. Am. Chem. Soc., Am. Soc. Biochemistry & Molecular Biology, Am Inst. Nutritin (pres. 1977, fellow 1986). Home: 8612 Mt Majestic Rd Sandy UT 84093-1833

HENDERSON, MICHAEL DOUGLAS, freelance journalist; b. London, Mar. 15, 1932; s. Arthur Douglas and Erina Doreen (Tilly) H.; m. Erica Mildred Hallowes, Apr. 16, 1966; 1 child, Juliet. Freelance journalist newspapers, mags., 1952—; columnist (For A Change) Union Jack; TV moderator Oreg. Pub. Broadcasting, Portland, 1978-79; radio commentator Sta. KBOO Radio, Portland, 1980—, Oreg. Pub. Broadcasting, 1985-86, 90-93, Sta. KMUN Radio, Astoria, 1988—, Jefferson Pub. Radio, 1992—; cable TV host Liberty/TCI, Portland, 1980-90. Author: From India with Hope, 1970, Experiment with Untruth, 1978, A Different Accent, 1985, On History's Coattails, 1988, Hope for a Change, 1991. Vol. Moral Re-Armament, 1950—, coun. mgmt. U.K., 1968—, N.W. rep., 1978—, bd. dirs. U.S., 1986—; mem. Episc. Peace Commn., West Oreg.; mem. edn. commn. Ecumenical Ministries Oreg. Recipient George Washington Honor medal Freedoms Found., 1986, 89, World Peace award Bahai's, Portland, 1989, award of excellence Acad. Religious Broadcasting, Seattle, 1987. Mem. Inst. Journalists U.K., Soc. Profl. Journalists, N.W. Writers, Inc., N.W. Assn. Book Pubs., Willamette Writers (past pres.), Oreg. Assn. Christian Writers, World Affairs Coun. Oreg. (past pres.), English-Speaking Union (past pres.). Home: 10605 SW Terwilliger Pl Portland OR 97219

HENDERSON, PATRICIA MCGOVERN, state human rights agency executive; b. Mobile, Ala., Aug. 6, 1940; d. Thomas Joseph and Babe Hope (Lowery) McGovern; children—Thomas Bain III, Patrick Sean. Student, Loretto Coll., Nerinx, Ky., 1958-61; B.A. in Psychology, Hawaii Pacific Coll., 1976; M.A., in Psychology, Antioch U., Honolulu, 1981. Cert. mgmt. Queen's Med. Ctr., 1977; cert. U. Ala. Sch. Medicine, 1979; cert. Neuropsychiat. Inst., UCLA, 1980. Dir., exec. sec. Mission and Youth Office for Catholic Diocese and Charities, Mobile, 1961-64; spl. edn. tchr. Ala. State Dept. Pub. Edn., Mobile, 1966-69; spl. edn. tchr., adminstr., social worker St. Peter Claver Sch. and Ctr., Tampa, Fla., 1970-72; chief adminstr., dir., prin., ednl. dir., social worker Salvation Army Kauluwela Corps, Kula Kokua Therapeutic Sch., The Self Ctr., Malama Makua Rehab. Ctr., 1973-77; exec. dir., chief exec. officer Protection and Advocacy Agy. of Hawaii and State Client Assistance Agy. of Hawaii, Honolulu, 1977-91, pres., 1988-91; cons. in field. Author, editor: A Self Advocate-You Have the Right to Speak for Yourself, 1978. Co-author, co-editor The Answer Book for Parents on the Right to Education for the Handicapped Child, 1983. Bd. dirs. State Dept. Health Adv. Com., Honolulu, 1979—, Gov.'s State Planning Council on Developmental Disabilities, 1986—; chmn. human rights com. State Dept. Health, 1982—; co-chmn. Mayor's City and County Transp. for Handicapped/Elderly Task Force, 1984—. Recipient Disting. Service award Salvation Army, 1977; Keen, Dedicated, Outstanding Profl., Highest Calibre award Salvation Army, 1977; Spl. Contbns. Internat. Yr. of Disabled Persons award State Hawaii and Internat. Yr. Disabled Persons Council, 1981; Promotion and Advancement of Women award Hawaiian Telephone Co., 1984; Disting. American award Am. Biog. Inst., 1985; Quality Advocacy Service award Nat. Assn. Protection and Advocacy Systems, 1987. Mem. Nat. Tourette Syndrome Assn. (NW regional dir. 1984—), Nat. Assn. Protection and Advocacy Systems (exec. bd. dirs., officer 1987—), Nat. Client Assistance Orgn. (exec. bd. dirs., officer 1987—). Avocations: travel; theater; music; art collecting; photography.

HENDERSON, RICKEY HENLEY, professional baseball player; b. Chgo., Dec. 25, 1958. With minor league baseball clubs, 1976-79; profl. baseball player Oakland A's, 1979-84, 89-93, N.Y. Yankees, 1985-89, Toronto Blue Jays, 1993—. Winner Am. League Gold Glove, 1981; named Most Valuable Player, American League, 1990, Am. League All-Star team, 1980, 82-88, 90-91. Office: Toronto Blue Jays, 1 Blue Jay Way / Ste 3200, Toronto, ON Canada M5V 1J1

HENDERSON, SAMMY WAYNE, physicist; b. Breckenridge, Tex., Feb. 21, 1957; s. Clovis Wendell and Joyce Marie (Stockton) H.; m. Paula Banister, Apr. 30, 1983; children: Mary Elizabeth, Jonathan Austin. BS in Physics/Math., Henderson State U., Arkadelpia, Ark., 1979; PhD in Physics, Tex. A&M U., 1986. Laser physicist Coherent Tech., Inc., Boulder, Colo., 1986—. Contbr. articles to profl. jours. Henderson State U. Ben Thaxton Meml. scholar, 1978. Mem. Optical Soc. Am., APS, Sigma Pi Sigma. Republican. Home: 7770 Durham Way Boulder CO 80301-4119 Office: Coherent Techs Inc 3300 Mitchell Ln Boulder CO 80301-2272

HENDERSON, TERRY LYNN MORELAND, English language and humanities educator; b. Steubenville, Ohio, July 21, 1953; d. Homer Guy and Hazel M. (Conard) Moreland; m. Timothy Henderson, Aug. 4, 1985; children: Jessica Neptune, Caitlin Leda. BA, Oberlin Coll., 1975; MA, Calif. State U., L.A., 1989; student, Met. State Coll., Denver, 1976-78; postgrad., U. Nebr., 1975. Tchr. Allen Art Mus., Oberlin, Ohio, 1974-75; tchr. intern Tchr. Corps, Emporia, Kans., 1975; in quality control Mathematica, Inc., Denver, 1976-78; tchr. Jefferson County Schs., Denver, 1978-79; dir. H-C Community Ctr., Cadiz, Ohio, 1981-82; tchr. L.A. Unified Schs., 1982—; coord. humanities Univ. High Sch., L.A., 1991—. Author: Moreau and Yeats: Symbols of Divinity, 1989. Am. Coun. Learned Socs. fellow UCLA, 1992—; Barnes and Noble scholar Calif. State U., 1988, Irwin-Swerdlow scholar, 1986, 89, Potter-Raskin scholar, 1988; recipient Calif. State Rsch. award, 1989. Mem. NEA, Calif. Tchrs. Assn., United Tchrs. of L.A., English Coun. of L.A., Calif. Tchrs. of English, Nat. Coun. Tchrs. English. Home: 233 N Ridgewood Pl Los Angeles CA 90004

HENDERSON, THELTON EUGENE, federal judge; b. Shreveport, La., Nov. 28, 1933; s. Eugene M. and Wanzie (Roberts) H.; 1 son, Geoffrey A. B.A., U. Calif.-, Berkeley, 1956, J.D., 1962. Bar: Calif. 1962. Atty. U.S. Dept. Justice, 1962-63; assoc. firm FitzSimmons & Petris, 1964, assoc., 1964-66; directing atty. San Mateo County (Calif.) Legal Aid Soc., 1966-69; asst. dean Stanford (Calif.) U. Law Sch., 1968-76; ptnr. firm Rosen, Remcho & Henderson, San Francisco, 1977-80; judge U.S. Dist. Ct. (no. dist.) Calif., San Francisco, 1980—; asso. prof. Sch. Law, Golden Gate U., San Francisco, 1978-80. Served with U.S. Army, 1956-58. Mem. ABA, Nat. Bar Assn., Charles Houston Law Assn. Office: US Dist Ct PO Box 36060 450 Golden Gate Ave San Francisco CA 94102

HENDERSON, VICTOR WARREN, behavioral neurologist, educator, researcher; b. Little Rock, Aug. 20, 1951; s. Philip S. and N. Jean (Edsel) H.; m. Barbara Ann Curtiss, May 24, 1975; children: Gregory, Geoffrey, Stephanie, Nicole. B.S., U. Ga., 1972; M.D., Johns Hopkins U., 1976; Diplomate Am. Bd. Psychiatry and Neurology. Intern in internal medicine Duke U., Durham, N.C., 1976-77; resident in neurology Washington U., St. Louis, 1977-80; fellow in behavioral neurology Boston U., 1980-81; asst. prof. neurology U. So. Calif., Los Angeles, 1981-86, assoc. prof. neurology, gerontology, and psychology, 1986-93, prof. neurology, gerontology and psychology, 1993—, chief div. cognitive neurosci. and neurogerontology, 1989—, dir. Alzheimer's Disease Rsch. Ctr. Consortium So. Calif. Clin. Core, 1985—, dir. Neurobehavior Clinic/Bowles Ctr. for Alzheimer's and Related Diseases, 1988—; chief neurology svc. L.A. County, U. So. Calif. Med. Ctr., 1992—; vis. scientist MIT, 1988-89. Author: (with others) Principles of Neurologic Diagnosis, 1985. Contbr. articles to profl. jours. Nat. Merit scholar, 1968; grantee Hurd Found., Mather Found., Doheny Found., NIH, French Found., 1984—. Fellow Am. Acad. Neurology; mem. Am. Neurological Assn., Soc. for Neurosci., Acad. of Aphasia, Gerontol. Soc. Am., Behavioral Neurology Soc., Internat. Neuropsychol. Soc., World Fedn. Neurology (rsch. groups on the dementias, on aphasia and cognitive disorders, and history of neuroscis.), L.A. Soc. Neurol. Scis. (sec.-treas. 1987-88, pres. 1990-91), Nat. Aphasia Assn. (adv. bd. 1990—).

HENDERSON, WILLIAM DARRYL, career officer, journalist; b. Trail, B.C., Can., Aug. 26, 1938; came to U.S., 1953; s. Willima Roland and Flora (McCallum) H.; m. Marilyn Jean Rapp, Nov. 1964 (div. 1981); children: Gregory, Timothy; m. Mary Ann Gutman, Dec. 6, 1985. Student, U. Vienna, Austria, 1959-60; BA in Polit. Sci., Stanford U., 1961; PhD in Internat. Rels. and Comparative Politics, U. Pitts., 1970; honor grad., Comd. and Gen. Staff Coll., 1974; postgrad., Nat. War Coll., 1982. Commd. 2d lt. U.S. Army, 1961, advanced through grades to col., 1988; writer San Francisco Examiner, 1990; writer, cons. Can. Govt., Ottawa, 1991-92; appointed presdl. commr. Women in the Armed Forces, Washington, 1992—; asst. prof. U.S. Mil. Acad., West Point, N.Y., 1972; mil. corr. San Francisco Examiner, 1991. testified Senate and House Annual Svcs. Com., 1993. Author: Why the Viet Cong Fought, 1980, Cohesion, The Human Element in Combat, 1985, The Hollow Army, 1990; included in book of Best Newspaper Editorials for 1990-91; contbr. articles to profl. jours. Decorated Legion of Merit, Bronze Star, Purple Heart, Combat Infantryman's Badge. Home and Office: 19880 Lark Way Saratoga CA 95070

HENDERSON-DIXON, KAREN SUE, psychologist; b. Bloomington, Ill., Mar. 25, 1946; d. Charles Lewis and Faye Lanore (Wantland) Henderson; m. David Thomas Biggs, Dec. 2, 1967 (div. 1972); m. Dean Eugene Dixon Jr., Jan. 13, 1973; children: Christopher, Matthew. BA, U. Calif., Berkeley, 1966; MS, San Jose (Calif.) State Coll., 1971; PhD, Union Inst., 1991. Lic. clin. psychol., Alaska; cert. community coll. tchr. Pvt. practice, Anchorage, 1980—; cons. Alaska Youth and Parent Found., Anchorage, 1989—, Parents United, Anchorage, 1989; mental health cons. Rural Alaska Community Action Program, Anchorage, 1988; cons., mem. adolescent treatment team Charter North Hosp., Anchorage, 1985-88; cons. Infant Impaired Hearing Program, Anchorage, 1984-85, Parent Tng. Ctr., Anchorage, 1980-82; psychiat. social worker Langdon Psychiat. Clinic, Anchorage, 1976-80; instr. in psychology U. Alaska Community Coll., Anchorage, 1974-81; parole agt.

narcotic outpatient program State Dept. Corrections, Oakland, Calif., 1972-74; group counselor II, caseworker Alameda County Probation Dept., Oakland, Calif., 1971-72; cons. psychologist Alviso (Calif.) Econ. Devel. Program, 1971-72; instr. psychology Coll. of Alameda, 1973; faculty advisor for coop. edn. U. Alaska Community Coll., 1975-76. Sec., liaison to bd. Susitna Sch. PTA, Anchorage, 1983-84; co-chmn. optional bd. Susitna Sch., 1984-85, chmn., 1985-86, vol. coord., 1988-89. Mem. APA, Alaska Psychol. Assn. Democrat. Office: 2550 Denali Ste 1608 Anchorage AK 99503-2000

HENDLER, LAWRENCE, physicist; b. N.Y.C., Nov. 24, 1953; s. Harold and Adele (Gross) H.; m. Smadar Livneh, July 26, 1976; children: Shanni, Omer, Adi. BS, Haifa U., Tivon, Israel, 1978; MSc, Tel Aviv U., Israel, 1985. Rsch. physicist Optrotech, Nes Ziona, Israel, 1985-87, Opal Techs., Nes Ziona, Israel, 1987-89; project leader G.S. Semiconductor Systems, Fremont, Calif., 1989-90; mgr. G. S. Electroglas, Santa Clara, Calif., 1980-90; mem. com. Internat. Semiconductor Mfg. Sci. Symposium, Mountain View, Calif., 1990—; cons. Chip Express, Santa Clara, 1990—. Contbr. articles to profl. jours. Mem. Am. Soc. Quality Control, Soc. Optical Engrs. Jewish. Home: 10330 Colby Ave Cupertino CA 95014 Office: G S Electroglas 3001 Coronado Dr Santa Clara CA 95054-3204

HENDLEY, ASHLEY PRESTON, JR., clinical social worker; b. Tyler, Tex., Sept. 15, 1938; s. Ashley Preston Sr. and Theresa Marie (Parenti) H.; m. Vivian Janis Rodriguez, June 24, 1960 (div. Jan. 1977); children: Gerald Michael, Ashley Preston III, William Loy, Brian Matthew; m. Ann Louise Cherry, Dec. 29, 1984. BA in Comparative Sociology, U. Puget Sound, 1979; MSW, U. Wash., 1983. Cert. social worker, Wash. Clin. instr. U. Wash., Seattle, 1985—; cons., bd. dirs. Pierce County AIDS/HIV Adv. Bd., Tacoma, Wash., 1989—. Contbr. articles to profl. jours. Cons., bd. dirs. Children's Indsl. Home, Tacoma, 1989—; cons. City of Tacoma Sr. Svcs., 1983—; guardian ad liten Superior Ct. State of Wash., County of Pierce, Tacoma, 1990-92. With U.S. Army, 1956-76, Vietnam. Mem. Am. Assn. Spinal Cord Injury Psychologists and Social Workers (assoc. editor 1988—). Roman Catholic. Home: 10501 Idlewild Rd SW Tacoma WA 98498 Office: VA Med Ctr American Lake Tacoma WA 98493

HENDREN, ROBERT LEE, JR., college president; b. Reno, Oct. 10, 1925; s. Robert Lee and Aleen (Hill) H.; m. Merlyn Churchill, June 14, 1947; children: Robert Lee IV, Anne Aleen. BA magna cum laude, Coll. Idaho, LLD (hon.); postgrad., Army Univ. Ctr., Oahu, Hawaii. Owner, pres. Hendren's Inc., 1947—; pres. Albertson Coll. Idaho, Caldwell, 1988—; bd. dirs. 1st Interstate Bank Idaho. Trustee Boise (Idaho) Ind. Sch. Dist., chmn. bd. trustees, 1966; chmn. bd. trustees Coll. Idaho, 1980-84; bd. dirs. Mountain View coun. Boy Scouts Am., Boise Retail Merchants, Boise Valley Indsl. Found., Boise Redevel. Agy., Ada County Marriage Counseling, Ada County Planning & Zoning Com., Blue Cross Idaho. Recipient Silver and Gold award U. Idaho. Mem. Boise C. of C. (pres., bd. dirs.), Idaho Sch. Trustees Assn., Masons, KT, Shriners, Rotary (Paul Harris fellow). Home: 3504 Hillcrest Dr Boise ID 83705 Office: Albertson Coll Idaho 2112 Cleveland Blvd Caldwell ID 83605-9990

HENDRICK, HAL WILMANS, human factors educator; b. Dallas, Mar. 11, 1933; s. Harold Eugene and Audrey Sarah (Wilmans) H.; m. Mary Francis Boyle; children: Hal L., David A., John A. (dec.), Jennifer G. BA, Ohio Wesleyan U., 1955; MS, Purdue U., 1961, PhD, 1966. Cert. profl. ergonomist; registered psychologist, Tex. Asst. prof. U. So. Calif., L.A., assoc. prof., 1979-86; exec. dir., dean Inst. of Safety and Systems Mgmt., U. So. Calif., L.A., 1986-87; prof., dean Coll. of System Sci., U. Denver, 1987-90; prof. U. So. Calif., 1986—; pres. Bd. Cert. of Profl. Ergonomists, 1992—. Author: Behavioral Research and Analysis, 1980, 2d edit., 1989, 3rd edit., 1990.; editor six books; contbr. articles to profl. jours. Lt. col. USAF, 1956-76. Fellow Human Factors Soc. (pres. L.A. chpt. 1986-87, pres. Rocky Mountain chpt. 1989-90), Am. Psychol. Soc., Am. Psychol. Assn.; mem. Internat. Ergonomics Assn. (pres. Geneva, 1990—, sec. gen. 1987-89, exec. com. 1984-87, U.S. rep.), Ergonomics Soc. (U.K.), Soc. for Indsl. and Orgnl. Psychol. Democrat. Home: 7100 E Crestline Ave Englewood CO 80111 Office: Inst Safety & System Mgmt U So Calif Los Angeles CA 90089-0021

HENDRICKS, BRIAN JAMES, insurance company executive, consultant; b. Idaho Falls, ID, Aug. 18, 1948; James Andrew and Zelta (Walker) H.; m. Cora Lee Jones, June 5, 1990; children: Brian J. II, Todd J., Berkley J. BA, ID State U., 1973; CLU, Am. Coll., 1981, ChFC, 1983. Chartered Fin. Cons. Tchr. Ch. Jesus Christ Latter Day Saints, Veracruz, Mex., 1968-70; shipping Roger Bros. Seed Co., Pocatello, Idaho, 1970-73; field underwriter Mut. N.Y., Boise, Idaho, 1973-77; agt., owner State Farm Mut. Ins. Co., Soda Springs, Idaho, 1977—; ptnr. South Main Partnership, Soda Springs, 1989—; fin. cons. Hendricks Ins. Agy., Soda Springs, Idaho, 1985—; owner Chile-Mex.-U.S.A. Cons. and Fin., 1990—; pres. Caribou Internat. Cons. Assn., 1991—. Scout master Boy Scouts Am., Pocatello, Idaho, 1983-90, asst. sect. advisor Order of the Arrow, 1992—; planning and zoning commr. City of Soda Springs, 1992—. Mem. Soda Springs Bishopric, 1993; asst. lodge advisor Order of Arrow, 1984-91. Recipient Merit award Boy Scouts Am., Pocatello, Idaho, 1989, Founders award Boy Scouts Am., 1992. Mem. C. of C., Kiwanis Club. Mem. LDS Ch. Office: Hendricks Ins Agy 240 S Main St Soda Springs ID 83276-1657

HENDRICKS, FANNY-DELL See **FANNY-DELL**

HENDRICKS, KYLE JAMES, physicist; b. Newton, Iowa, May 9, 1958; s. Bryce Martin and Sara Carmen (Bush) H.; m. Carla Kaye Lehman, July 28, 1979; children: Jenna Erin, Morgan Marie. BS, U. Iowa, 1980, MS, 1982; PhD, U. N.Mex., 1989. Undergrad. asst. U. Iowa, Iowa City, 1978-80; grad. rsch. asst. U. Iowa, 1980-82; physicist Air Force Weapons Lab., Albuquerque, 1982-84, Air Force Inst. Tech., Dayton, Ohio, 1984-86, Phillips Lab., Kirtland AFB, Albuquerque, 1987-91; rsch. prof. U. N.Mex., Albuquerque, 1991; sr. physicist USAF Phillips Lab., Kirtland AFB, Albuquerque, 1991—; advisor postdoctoral program Nat. Rsch. Coun., Washington, 1991—. Contbr. articles to profl. jours. Capt. USAF, 1982-91. Recipient USAF Rsch. and Devel. award Dept. of Air Force, 1988. Mem. Am. Phys. Soc., Sigma Xi. Office: Phillips Lab PL/WSR High Energy & Rsch Tech Facility 3550 Aberdeen Ave SE Facility Kirtland AFB NM 87117-6008

HENDRICKSON, ELIZABETH ANN, educator; b. Bismarck, S.D., Oct. 21, 1936; d. William Earl and Hilda E. (Sauter) Hinkel; m. Roger G. Hendrickson, Apr. 18, 1960; 1 child, Wade William. BA, Jamestown Coll., 1958; postgrad., U. Calif., Davis, 1962, Calif. State U., Sacramento, 1964, U. San Diego, 1985-88, Ottawa U., 1986-88. Cert. tchr., Calif. Tchr. Napoleon (N.D.) High Sch., 1958-59, Kulm (N.D.) High Sch., 1959-61, Del Paso Jr. High Sch., Sacramento, 1961, Mills Jr. High Sch., Rancho Cordova, Calif., 1961—. Mem. NEA, AAUW, Calif. Assn. for Gifted, Calif. Edn. Assn., Sacramento Area Gifted Assn., Soroptimists (news editor Rancho Cordova club 1985, sec. 1986). Democrat. Lutheran. Home: 2032 Kellogg Way Rancho Cordova CA 95670-2435

HENDRICKX, LEONARD HENRY, non-profit agency executive, consultant; b. Kellogg, Idaho, July 10, 1953; s. Leonard H. and Martha (Larsen) H. BA, SUNY, Albany, 1980. Program mgr. City of Redondo Beach, Calif., 1977-80; exec. dir. Am. Indian Community Ctr., Spokane, Wash., 1982-88, Ea. Wash. Regional Health Coun., Spokane, 1989; dir. Cheney (Wash.) Ecumenical Outreach, 1990-91; adminstr. Spokane Urban Indian Health, 1990—; officer East Plateau Indian Co-op, Spokane, 1985-90; pres. Clearwater Communications, Spokane, 1988-91; cons. Coeur d'Alene Tribe of Idaho, Plummer, 1984-86, Sacheen Lake (Wash.) Water Dist., 1987; mag. pub. HERBS!/Jour., 1988-90. Recipient Mayoral Proclamation City Coun., Spokane, 1985, Model Program award Nat. League of Cities, 1979. Mem. Mensa (treas. Ea. Wash./No. Idaho chpt. 1985-87). Democrat. Office: SUIHS/CHS 905 E 3rd Ave Spokane WA 99202-2246

HENDRIX, LOUISE BUTTS, retired educator, author; b. Portland, Tenn., June 16, 1911; d. Luther Edward and Johnny Henrietta (McNeill) B.; m. Edwin Alonzo Hendrix, Aug. 1, 1934 (dec. May 1991); childern: Lynette Louise, Edwin Alonzo Jr. AB, Chico (Calif.) State Coll., 1932; postgrad., Sacramento State U., 1934-62, Coll. Pacific, 1934-62; Diploma of merit, U Delle Arti, Parma, Italy, 1982. Tchr. jr. high sch. Rio Vista, Calif., 1932-34; newspaper worker Chico Enterprise, 1930-32; tchr. jr. high sch. Alpaugh, Calif., 1944-45; newspaper corr. Sacramento Bee, Marysville Appeal Dem., Live Oak, Calif., 1945-52, Oroville Mercury Register Marysville Appeal Dem., Biggs, Calif., 1935-40; tchr. jr. high sch. Live Oak, 1952-69; ret., 1969. Author: Better Reading and Writing with Journalism, 1974, Sutter Buttes--Land of Histum Yani, 1980, 5th rev. edit., 1989, Petals and Blossoms, 1983, Squaw Man, 1987; contbr. poetry to profl. jours. Mem. Sutter County Parks and Recreation Commn., Yuba City, 1977-80; founder Save Sutter Buttes Assn., Inc., Yuba City, 1978, sec., treas., 1978-90. Recipient Poet of Yr. award World Congress Poets, Orlando, Fla., 1986, Gold Poet award World of Poetry Conv., Anaheim, Calif., 1988. Fellow Internat. Poetry Soc.; mem. AAUW, Calif. Retired Tchrs. Assn., Sierra Club (Conservationist of Yr. 1974), Woman's Club (pres. Yuba City chpt. 1978-79). Democrat. Roman Catholic. Home: 1354 Geneva Ave Yuba City CA 95991-6711

HENDRY, LINDA MAY, chef, food service administrator; b. Batavia, N.Y., Apr. 27, 1957; d. Marion McPherson and Ida Mae (Burr) Harmon; m. John Bernard Hendry, Apr. 12, 1986; children: Jacob, Bernard, Benjamin Raymond. AA, Johnson & Wales Coll., Providence, 1977. With Marriott Inn, Providence, 1976; prep cook Vincents on the Hill, Providence, 1976-77; lead cook The Cranberry Goose, Hyannis, Mass., summer 1977; kitchen supr. Marriott, Denver, 1977-80; prodn. mgr. Marriott, Portland, 1980-83; sous chef Marriott, Denver, 1983-85; exec. chef Marriott, 1985-87, dir. restaurants, 1988-89; chef Carte d'Or Catering, Denver, 1989-91; dir. food and beverage Embassy Suites, Denver, 1991—; food and beverage dir. Ansco Investment Corp., Denver. Mem. Chef de Cusine Soc. Home: 8925 W 78th Ave Arvada CO 80005-4308

HENDY, SCOTT GARY, veterinarian; b. Upland, Calif., Mar. 16, 1951; s. Stanley Bert and Gertrude Mary (Van Dorin) H.; m. Sandra Gayle Hartman, June 17, 1973; children: Lara Katherine, Chad Alan. BS with high honors, U. Calif., Davis, 1973, DVM, 1975. Pvt. practitioner vet. medicine Bailey Vet. Clinic, Roseburg, Oreg., 1975-78; pvt. practitioner, owner Parkway Animal Hosp., Roseburg, 1978—; trustee Wildlife Safari Found., Winston, Oreg., 1987—. Bd. dirs. United Way, Roseburg, 1985-91, YMCA, Roseburg, 1984-88. Regent scholar U. Calif., Davis, 1971-75. Mem. AVMA, Am. Animal Hosp. Assn., Oreg. Vet. Med. Assn. (chair continuing edn. com. 1983-87, 2d v.p. 1987, pres. 1988), Southwestern Oreg. Vet. Med. Assn. (pres. 1978, sec.-treas. 1981—), Phi Kappa Phi, Alpha Zeta, Phi Zeta. Republican. Home: 9800 Buckhorn Rd Roseburg OR 97470 Office: Parkway Animal Hosp 2655 NW Broad St Roseburg OR 97470

HENG, STANLEY MARK, military officer; b. Nebraska City, Nebr., Nov. 4, 1937; s. Robert Joseph Sr. and Margaret Ann (Volkmer) H.; m. Sharon E. Barrett, Oct. 10, 1959; children: Mark, Nick, Lisa. Student, Command and Gen. Staff Coll., 1969, Nat. Def. U., 1979; BA, Doane Coll., 1987. Commd. adj. Nebr. N.G., 1966, advanced through grade to major gen., 1966-87; adj. Nebr. Mil. Dept., Lincoln, 1966-77, adminstrv. asst., 1978-86; adj. gen., civil def. dir. State of Nebr., Lincoln, 1987—. Mem. N.G. Assn. U.S., N.G. Assn. Nebr. (exec. sec. 1967-71, Svc. award 1970), Adj. Gens. Assn., Am. Legion. Democrat. Mem. United Ch. of Christ. Office: Mil Dept 1300 Military Rd Lincoln NE 68508-1090

HENKE, SHAUNA NICOLE, public safety dispatcher; b. San Bernardino, Calif., Oct. 25, 1966; d. Gary Duane and Pamela Denyne (Duke) H. BA, U. San Francisco, 1988. Cert. P.O.S.T. dispatcher, Calif. Pub. rels. dir. Sta. KUSF Radio, San Francisco, 1986; theater and recreational asst. Hamilton Field Recreation, Novato, Calif., 1986-89; morning asst., newswriter Sta. KTID Radio, San Rafael, Calif., 1987-88; dispatcher Warren Security, San Rafael, Calif., 1988-89; pub. safety dispatcher Twin Cities Police Dept., Larkspur/Corte Madera, Calif., 1989—. Named Outstanding Young Woman, Outstanding Young Women of Am., 1987. Mem. Marin Emergency Dispatchers Assn. (bd. dirs.), Twin Cities Police Officers Assn. Office: Twin Cities Police Dept 250 Doherty Ave Larkspur CA 94939

HENKELS, MARK, social science educator; b. Phila.; s. John Bernard and Jean (Merkl) H.; m. Marcella Dupler, May 16, 1989; 1 child, Max. BA, Whitman Coll., 1980; MA, U. Va., 1984; PhD, U. Utah, 1988. Prof. Western Oreg. State Coll., Monmouth, 1988—; co-chair polit. sci. sect. Oreg. Acad. of Sci., 1990—; chair polit. sci. sect. Western Oreg. State U., 1990—. Teaching fellow U. Utah, 1982-86, Mariners, Eccles fellow, 1986-88. Mem. Am. Soc. Pub. Adminstrn., Western Social Sci. Assn., Assn. Oreg. Faculty, AFL-CIO. Home: 7540 NE Pettibone Dr Corvallis OR 97330-9641 Office: Western Oreg State U Polit Sci Dept Monmouth OR 97361

HENLEY, ERNEST MARK, physics educator, university dean emeritus; b. Frankfurt, Germany, June 10, 1924; came to U.S., 1939, naturalized, 1944; s. Fred S. and Josy (Dreyfuss) H.; m. Elaine Dimitman, Aug. 21, 1948; children: M. Bradford, Karen M. B.E.E., CCNY, 1944; Ph.D., U. Calif. at Berkeley, 1952. Physicist Lawrence Radiation Lab., 1950-51; research assoc. physics dept. Stanford U., 1951-52; lectr. physics Columbia U., 1952-54; mem. faculty U. Wash., Seattle, 1954—; prof. physics U. Wash., 1961—, chmn. dept., 1973-76, dean Coll. Arts and Scis., 1979-87, dir. Inst. for Nuclear Theory, 1990-91; researcher and author numerous publs. on symmetries, nuclear reactions, weak interactions and high energy particle interactions; chmn. Nuclear Sci. Adv. Com., 1986-89. Author: (with W. Thirring) Elementary Quantum Field Theory, 1962, (with H. Frauenfelder) Subatomic Physics, 1974, 2nd edit. 1991, Nuclear and Particle Physics, 1975. Bd. dirs. Pacific Sci. Ctr., 1984-87, Wash. Tech. Ctr., 1983-87; trustee Associated Univs., Inc., 1989—. Recipient sr. Alexander von Humboldt award, 1984, T.W. Bonner prize Am. Physics Soc., 1989, Townsend Harris medal CCNY, 1989; F.B. Jewett fellow, 1952-53, NSF sr. fellow, 1958-59, Guggenheim fellow, 1967-68, NATO sr. fellow, 1976-77. Fellow Am. Phys. Soc. (chmn. div. nuclear physics 1979-80, pres. elect. 1991, pres. 1992), AAAS (chmn. physics sect. 1989-90); mem. Nat. Acad. Scis., Sigma Xi. Office: U Wash Physics Dept FM 15 Seattle WA 98195

HENLEY, KENNETH JAMES, restaurant owner; b. Worthing, Sussex, Eng., Sept. 23, 1939; came to U.S., 1976; s. Joseph James and Alice May (Cozens) H.; m. Sonia Judith Kendall, Oct. 6, 1963 (div. 1987); children: Nigel, Karen, Katrina; m. Barbara Carr Glover, Dec. 19, 1989. BS in Oil Tech., London U., 1961. Sales engr. Shell Oil Co., London, 1962-64; petroleum engr. Texaco, Inc., Trinidad, W.I., 1964-72; v.p. Baker Hughes Inc., Houston, 1972-82, Resco Inc., Houston, 1982; mktg. mgr. U.S. Enertek Inc., Houston, 1983-91; owner Log Inn Supper Club, Rock Springs, Wyo., 1991—. Mem. Soc. Petroleum Engrs. (br. chmn. 1972-74), Rotary. Home and Office: 529 B St Rock Springs WY 82901

HENNER, WILLIAM DAVID, oncologist; b. Cin., Apr. 5, 1949; s. William George and Julia Margaret (Ryan) H.; m. Paulette Mary Brensinger, Jan. 7, 1978; 1 child, Claire Juliette. BS, U. Va., 1971; MD, U. Pa., 1977, PhD, 1977. Diplomate Am. Bd. Internal Medicine; cert. Nat. Bd. Med. Examiners, Med. Oncology. Med. intern U. Chgo., 1977-78, med. resident, 1978-80; fellow med. oncology Dana Farber Cancer Inst., Boston, 1980-82; asst. prof. medicine Harvard U., Boston, 1982-88; assoc. prof. medicine Oreg. Health Sci. U., Portland, 1988—; mem. radiation study sect. NIH, 1989—. Contbr. articles to profl. jours. Mem. Am. Soc. Clin. Oncology, Am. Assn. Cancer Rsch. Democrat. Office: 3181 SW Sam Jackson Park Rd Portland OR 97201-3011

HENNESSY, THOMAS ANTHONY, columnist; b. Redbank, N.J., Feb. 5, 1936; s. William and Etta (Cariccioli) H.; m. Jeanne Kresge (div.); children: Daniel, Diana, Patricia; m. Deborah Wong, Sept. 24, 1971; stepchildren: Jacqueline, John Tien. Diploma, U.S. Army Lang. Sch., Monterey, Calif., 1954; student, U. Pitts., 1968-70. Reporter Bergen Record, Hackensack, N.J., 1960-62, Pitts. Post-Gazette, 1962-64; press sec. Mayor J. Barr/City of Pitts., 1965-70; pub., editor The Pitts. Forum, 1970-75; editor and reporter Detroit Free Press (subs. Knight Ridder)ú, Detroit, 1975-80; columnist Press-Telegram (subs. Knight Ridder), Long Beach, Calif., 1980—; TV talk show host, Hennessy and Friends, Long Beach, 1981-83; speaker, lectr. numerous community orgns., So. Calif., 1981—; part-time writing instr. Calif. State U., Long Beach, 1982-84. Author: (newspaper series) Pacific Notebook, 1985 (Mark Twain AP award 1985), Cerritos Air Disaster, 1986 (Headliners award 1986). Co-chmn. Operation Desert Salute, Long Beach, 1991; exec. producer Simmons Cable and Press Telegram "Let's Fight Back", Long Beach, 1990; co-chmn. (with USMC), constrn. Tarawa Monument, Long Beach, 1988. Sgt. U.S. Army, 1954-58, Germany. Recipient Disting. Reporting award Sigma Delta Chi, Rochester, N.Y., 1978, Silver Gavel award ABA, Detroit, 1978, Genesis award Fund for Animals, L.A., 1986, Excellence in Community Svc. award Knight-Ridder Newspaper Group, Miami, Fla., 1991, Celebrate Reading award, Long Beach. 1992, others. Office: Press-Telegram 604 Pine Ave Long Beach CA 90844

HENNEY, CHRISTOPHER SCOT, immunologist; b. Sutton-Coldfield, Eng., Feb. 4, 1941; s. William Scot and Rhoda Agnes (Bateman) Henney; m. Janet Barnsley, June 20, 1964; children: James Scot, Samantha Jane. BS with honors, U. Birmingham, Eng., 1962, PhD in Exptl. Pathology, 1965, DSc. in Research Immunology (hon.), 1973. Immunologist WHO, Lausanne, Switzerland; assoc. prof. medicine and microbiology med. sch. Johns Hopkins U., Balt., 1978; prof. microbiology and immunology U. Wash., Seattle, 1978-81; head. basic immunology Fred Hutchinson Cancer Research Ctr., Seattle, 1978-81; co-founder, sci. dir., vice chmn. Immunex Corp., Seattle, 1981-89; co-founder, sci. dir., exec. v.p. ICOS Corp., Seattle, 1989—. Mem. Am. Assn. Immunology (sect. editor 1972-73), Reticuloendothelial Soc. (sect. editor 1978-79), Am. Cancer Soc. (chmn. immunology rev. com. 1982-83), NIH (mem. pathology study sect. 1978-82). Office: ICOS Corp 22021 20th Ave SE Bothell WA 98021

HENNIGAN, JAMES MICHAEL, lawyer; b. Tucson, Nov. 2, 1943; s. James Edward and Alice Elizabeth (Boehm) H.; m. Phyllis Lynn Rothkopf, Aug. 26, 1973; children: Amanda Michelle, Cassandra Asch. BA, U. Ariz., 1966, JD with distinction, 1970. Bar: Ariz. 1970, Calif. 1974. Trial atty. U.S. Dept. of Justice, Washington, 1970-72; assoc. Snell & Wilmer, Phoenix, 1972-73; ptnr. Lovitt, Hannan & Hennigan, San Francisco, 1973-75, Martori, Meyer, Hendricks & Victor, Phoenix, 1975-77, Howrey & Simon (formerly Hennigan & Mercer), 1983—; lectr. U. Ariz., 1973—, The Am. Law Inst., 1993—; law rep. 9th Cir. Judicial Conf., 1993—. Author law rev. article The Essence of Standing: The Basis of a Constitutional Right to be Heard, 1969. Founder, chmn., Dir.'s Roundtable, L.A. County Mus. of Art, 1982—; bd. of visitors U. Ariz., Coll. of Law. Mem. Am. Bd. Trial Advs., Am. Law Inst., L.A Bar Assn. (bd. dirs. litigation sect.), State Bar of Ariz., State Bar of Calif., Order of Coif. Office: Howrey & Simon 444 S Flower St Ste 3100 Los Angeles CA 90071

HENNIGAN, THOMAS ANTHONY, video producer; b. Cleve., Jan. 24, 1954; s. Thomas Anthony Scully and Shirlee (Gotliffe) Hennigan. BS, Lewis-Clark State Coll., 1976, teaching cert., 1989; MA, Wash. State U., 1984. Cert. secondary sch. tchr., Idaho, Wash. Designer Lewiston (Idaho) Civic Theatre, 1984-86; tchr. Valley Christian Sch., Lewiston, 1986-88; producder, writer Lewis Clark State Coll. Ednl. Technical Ctr., Lewiston, 1988—; instr. video Lewis and Clark State Coll., Lewiston, 1992. Author, lyricist: (musicals) Beran and Luthien, 1984, Cuchulainn, 1986. Grantee: State of Idaho, 1990, Project Learning Tree, 1992. Republican. Advent Christian. Home: 612 9th Ave Lewiston ID 83501 Office: Lewis-Clark State Coll Ednl Tech Ctr 500 8th Ave Lewiston ID 83501

HENNING, LISBETH LEE, historic preservationist; b. CLinton, Okla., Dec. 18, 1955; d. Lorenz Ellsworth and LaVelle Orene (Swinney) Boyd; m. John Henning, May 30, 1981. BA, Tenn. Tech. U., 1978; MS, Ball State U., 1982. Assoc. dir. Mountain T.O.P., Nashville, 1978-80; survey & info. ctr. coord. Hist. Landmarks Found. Ind., Indpls., 1982-84, dir. community svcs., 1984-87; program assoc. Western Regional Office Nat. Trust Hist. Preservation, San Francisco, 1987-89, asst. dir., 1989—; instr. Ind. U./Purdue U., Indpls., 1983-87; lectr. Coll. Architecture & Planning Ball State U., Muncie, Ind., 1986-87; cons. in field. Mem. Am. Soc. Tng. & Devel., Calif. Preservation Found. Office: Nat Trust Hist Preservation 1 Sutter St #707 San Francisco CA 94104

HENRICH, JUDY REA, real estate syndicate executive; b. San Pedro, Calif., Mar. 21, 1945; d. Thomas Harold and G. Daphne (Clements) Wilson; m. Thomas Michael Henrich, Feb. 6, 1965; children: Kimberli Ann, Jeffrey Thomas. Grad., high sch., 1962. Registered rep., prin. NASD. Mgr. pub. rels. and community rels. Kaiser Aetna's Rancho Calif., Temecula, 1972-80; pres., CEO Rancon Securities Corp., Temecula, 1980—; mem. adv. bd. Temecula Br. Bank of Commerce, 1992—. Mem. citizens adv. bd. Rancho Water Dist., Temecula, 1991—; mem. adv. coun. U. Calif. Riverside Sch. Mgmt. Republican. Roman Catholic. Home: 30410 Del Rey Rd Temecula CA 92591 Office: Rancon Securities Corp 27720 Jefferson Ave Temecula CA 92590

HENRICKSON, EILER LEONARD, geologist, educator; b. Crosby, Minn., Apr. 23, 1920; s. Eiler Clarence and Mabel (Bacon) H.; m. Kristine L. Kuntzman; children: Eiler Warren, Kristin, Kurt Eric, Ann Elizabeth. BA, Carleton Coll., 1943; PhD, U. Minn., 1956. Geologist U.S. Geol. Survey, Calif., 1943-44; instr. Carleton Coll., 1946-47, 48-51, asst. prof., 1951-53, 54-56, assoc. prof., 1956-62, prof., 1962-70, Charles L. Denison prof. geology, 1970-87, chmn. dept., 1970-78, wrestling coach, 1946-58, 83-87; prof. geology, chmn. dept. Colo. Coll., 1987—; instr. U. Minn., 1947-48, 53-54; vis. lectr. numerous univs., Europe, 1962; cons. Jones & Laughlin Steel Corp., 1946-58, Fremont Mining Co., Alaska, 1958-61, G.T. Schieldahl Co., Minn., 1961-62, Bear Creek Mining Co., Mich., 1965-66, U. Minn. Messenia Expdn., 1966-75, Exxon Co., 1977-78, Cargill Corp., Mpls., 1983-84, Leslie Salt Co., San Francisco, 1985-86, various other cos.; research scientist, cons. Oak Ridge (Tenn.) Nat. Lab., 1985-86; cons. Argonne Nat. Lab., 1966-78, research scientist, summers, 1966-67; field studies metamorphic areas, Norway and Scotland; dir. young scholars program NSF, 1988-90. Author: Zones of Regional Metamorphism, 1957. Dir. Northfield Bd. Edn., 1960-63; steering com. Northfield Community Devel. Program, 1966-67. Served as 1st lt. USMCR, 1943, AUS, 1944-46. Fulbright research scholar archeol. geology, Greece, 1966-87. Mem. AAAS, Mineral Soc. Am., Nat. Assn. Geology Tchrs., Minn. Acad. Sci (vis. lectr.), Am. Geol. Inst., Geol. Soc. Am., Soc. Econ. Geologists, Rocky Mountain Assn. Geologists, Nat. Wrestling Coaches and Ofcls. Assn., Archaeol. Inst. Am. (vis. lectr.), Sigma Xi. Home: 19560 Four Winds Way Monument CO 80132-9309 Office: Colo Coll Dept Geology Colorado Springs CO 80903

HENRIE, KIM BARTON, marketing professional; b. Ely, Nev., Aug. 17, 1951; s. Keith Larsen and Faye (Barton) H.; m. Linda Maree Casper, Aug. 2, 1974; children: Justin, Seth, Asher, Blake, Taylor. BS, Brigham Young U., 1975, MBA, 1977. Mgr. Y-Tex Corp., Cody, Wyo., 1977-80; mktg. mgr. Reliance Co., Walnut Creek, Calif., 1980-81; pres., owner K.B. Henrie & Assocs., Inc., San Ramon, Calif., 1981—; chmn., owner Brit. Am., San Ramon, 1983—. Author: The Insiders Guide to Greater Wealth and Bargains, 1985, Small Business Savvy, 1988. Club: Blackhawk (Calif.). Office: 7 Crow Canyon Ct Ste 250 San Ramon CA 94583-1698

HENRIKSEN, MELVIN, educator, mathematician; b. N.Y.C., N.Y., Feb. 23, 1927; s. Kaj and Helen (Kahn) H.; m. Lillian Viola Hill, July 23, 1946 (div. 1964); children—Susan, Richard, Thomas; m. Louise Levitas, June 12, 1964. B.S., Coll. City N.Y., 1948; M.S., U. Wis., 1949, Ph.D. in Math, 1951. Asst. math., then instr. extension div. U. Wis., 1948-51; asst. prof. U. Ala., 1951-52; from instr. to prof. math. Purdue U., 1952-65; prof. math., head dept. Case Inst. Tech., 1965-68; research assoc. U. Calif. at Berkeley, 1968-69; prof., chmn. math. dept. Harvey Mudd Coll., 1969-72, prof., 1972—; mem. Inst. Advanced Study, Princeton, 1956-57, 63-64; vis. prof. Wayne State U., 1960-61; rsch. assoc. U. Manitoba, Winnipeg, Can., 1975-76; vis. prof. Wesleyan U., Middletown, Conn., 1978-79, 82-83, 86-87, 93-94. Author: (with Milton Lees) Single Variable Calculus, 1970; assoc. editor: Algebra Universalis, 1993—; contbr. articles to profl. jours. on algebra, rings of functions, gen. topology. Sloan fellow, 1956-58. Mem. Am. Math. Soc., Math. Assn. Am. (assoc. editor Am. Math. monthly 1988-91). Home: 504 W Bowling Green Dr Claremont CA 91711-2716

HENRIKSSON, THOMAS MARTIN, chemist, researcher; b. Kristofta, Sweden, Dec. 13, 1951; came to U.S., 1980; s. Hjalmar Valfrid and Hildur Linnea (Almer) H.; m. Diana Marie Lander, Mar. 15, 1980; children: Sarah, Kristofer. BS, U. Lund, Sweden, 1973; PhD, U. Lund, 1982. Postdoctoral fellow U. Calif., Berkeley, 1982-85; rsch. chemist Sclavo, Inc., Sunnyvale, Calif., 1985-88; scientist Athena Neuroscis. Inc., South San Francisco, 1988-89, Cetus Corp., Emeryville, Calif., 1989-91; prin. scientist Chiron Corp., Emeryville, Calif., 1991—. Contbr. articles to sci. jours. Pvt. Army, 1973-74, Sweden. Mem. Am. Chem. Soc., Am. Assn. for Clin. Chemistry, AAAS.

Roman Catholic. Office: Chiron Corp 4560 Horton St Emeryville CA 94608

HENRY, BRIAN JAMES, radio broadcasting; b. Fresno, Calif., June 29, 1961; s. James Bennett and Nancy Lane (Schedler) H. AA, Napa Coll., 1982; BA, U. Calif., Berkeley, 1984. Chief engr. KVON/KVYN-FM radio stas., Napa, Calif., 1979-81; transmitter supr. KFTY TV sta., Santa Rosa, Calif., 1981-82; engr. KABL AM/FM radio sta., San Francisco, 1982-83, KSFO-KYA-FM radio sta., San Francisco, 1982-84; gen. ptnr. KLLK-AM/KLLK-FM radio sta., Willits/Ft. Bragg, Calif., 1984—. Mem. Willits C. of C. (bd. dirs. 1990-92). Office: KLLK AM-FM Radio 12 W Valley St Willits CA 95490

HENRY, CHARLES PATRICK, political science educator; b. Newark, Ohio, Aug. 17, 1947; s. Charles Patrick and Ruth (Holbert) H.; m. Loretta Jean Crenshaw, Aug. 23, 1968; children: Adia Jean, Charles Wesley, Laura Anne. BA, Denison U., 1969; MA, U. Chgo., 1971, PhD, 1974. Asst. prof. Howard U., Washington, 1973-76; asst. prof., asst. dean, dir. Denison U., Granville, Ohio, 1976-80; assoc. prof. Afro-Am. studies dept. U. Calif., Berkeley, 1981—. Co-author: The Chitl'n Controversy, 1978; author: Culture and African-American Politics, 1990, Jesse Jackson, 1991. Mem. Nat. Coun. for Black Studies (sec. 1982-84), Nat. Conf. Black Polit. Scientists, Am. Polit. Sci. Assn. (congl. fellow 1971-72), Amnesty Internat. (chmn. bd. dirs. 1986-88, mem. internat. exec. com. 1989—). Office: U Calif Afro-Am Studies Dept Berkeley CA 94720

HENRY, DAVID ALLEN, advertising executive; b. Cedar Rapids, Iowa, Apr. 16, 1950; s. Don Albert and Anna Mae (Manwiller) H.; m. Elise Marie Cohen, June 7, 1981 (div. Apr. 1988); children: Lauren, Erica, Sylvia. BBA, U. Iowa, 1972. V.p. mktg. Movie Systems, Inc., Denver, 1975-77; chmn., chief exec. officer Henry Gill Silverman Advt., Denver, 1977—; mem. bd. advisors Entrepreneurial Inst. Denver, 1989. Bd. dirs. Direction 2,000 Found., Littleton, Colo., 1990; nat. advisor White House Conf. for Drug-Free Am., Washington, 1988. Recipient Award of Merit, United Way Mile High Child Care, Denver, 1988, Cert. of Appreciation, Communities for Drug-Free Colo., 1989, Sch. Restructuring Program, Gov. of Colo., 1990, Cert. of Merit, Keep Denver Beautiful, 1990. Mem. Am. Mktg. Assn., Am. Assn. Advt. Agys. (mem. western bd. govs. 1988—, chmn. bd. dirs. Rocky Mountain Coun. 1988), Denver Advt. Fedn. (bd. dirs. 1987—), Denver Press Club, Greater Denver C. of C. (mem. bd. advisors 1990, Cert. of Appreciation 1989). Office: Henry Gill Silverman Advt 1225 17th St Ste 2500 Denver CO 80202-5525

HENRY, HOWARD WARD, court reporter; b. Dodge City, Kans., Jan. 5, 1927; s. Edwin Ruthvan and Grace Louisa (Meeks) H.; m. Zona Gail Ehret, Sept. 11, 1955; children: Sharon Kay, Daniel Kent. AA, Dodge City (Kans.) Jr. Coll., 1948; student, Cain-Powell Bus. Coll., Dodge City, 1948, Profl. Sec. Sch., San Francisco, 1949; BA, U. N.Mex., 1960. Cert. shorthand reporter. Ct. reporter 6th Jud. Dist. Ct., Deming, N.Mex., 1951-57, Howard W. Henry & Co., Albuquerque, 1957-92, U.S. Dist. Ct., Albuquerque, 1965-82. With USN, 1944-46, 50-51, PTO. Mem. VFW, Am. Legion, Nat. Shorthand Reporters, N.Mex. Shorthand Reporters. Democrat. Home: 1500 Cliffside NW Albuquerque NM 87105

HENRY, JOSEPH R., marketing executive, healthcare consultant; b. Salem, Mass., Apr. 17, 1945; s. Joseph P. and Rita A. (Welch) H.; m. Carla J. Redemann, Jan. 5, 1972; children: Kelly M., Scott A. BS in Engring., U.S. Mil. Acad., West Point, 1968; MA in Edn., U. Md., 1977; MS in Hosp. Adminstrn., Baylor U., 1983. Commd. 2d lt. U.S. Army, 1968, advanced through grades to lt. col., ret., 1989; assoc. adminstr. AFIP, Washington, 1974-76; regional dir. Army Med. Dept. Recruitment, Washington, 1976-79; adminstr. Army Inst. Dental Rsch., Washington, 1979-81; pers. dir. Ft. Campbell Hosp., Ky., 1982-84; HRD dir. Army Med. Command, Europe, 1984-86; hosp. inspector European army hosps., 1986-88; hosp. adminstr. Fitzsimons Army Med. Ctr., Aurora, Colo., 1988-89; v.p. mktg. DAKKRO Corp., Denver, 1989—; COO Med. Evaluators, Colorado Springs, 1990—. Decorated Legion of Merit. Mem. Acad. for Health Svcs. Mktg. (treas. 1991—), West Point Soc. Denver (bd. dirs. 1991—). Home: 2602 S Kingston Ct Aurora CO 80014-1723 Office: DAKKRO Corp 950 S Cherry St Ste 914 Denver CO 80222-2666

HENRY, KAREN HAWLEY, lawyer; b. Whittier, Calif., Nov. 5, 1943; d. Ralph Hawley and Dorothy Ellen (Carr) Hawley; m. John Dunlap, 1968; m. Charles Gibbons Henry, Mar. 15, 1975; children: Scott, Alexander, Joshua; m. Don H. Phemister, June 21, 1991; children: Justin Phemister, Jonathan Phemister, Keith Phemister. BS in Social Scis., So. Oreg. Coll., 1965; MS in Labor Econs., Iowa State U., 1967; JD, U. Calif., 1976. Instr., Medford (Oreg.) Sch. Dist., 1965-66; rsch. asst. dept. econs. Iowa State U., Ames, 1966-67; dir. rsch. program Calif. Nurses Assn., San Francisco, 1967-72; labor rels. coord. Affiliated Hosps. of San Francisco, 1972-79; ptnr. Littler, Mendelson, Fastiff & Tichy, San Francisco, 1979-86; mng. ptnr. labor and employment law Weissburg and Aronson, Inc., San Francisco, 1986-90; prin. Karen H. Henry, Inc., Sacramento, 1991—. Author: Health Care Supervisor's Legal Guide, 1984, Nursing Administration Law Manual, 1986, ADA: Ten Steps to Compliance, 1992; edit. bd. Health Care Supervisor; contbr. articles on employment law issues to profl. jours. Mem. Calif. Soc. Healthcare Attys. (bd. dirs. 1986-87, pres. 1987-88), Am. Hosp. Assn. (ad hoc labor atty. com.), State Bar of Calif., Sacramento Bar Assn., Thurston Soc., Order of Coif. (law jour.). Office: Karen H Henry Inc Senator Hotel Office Bldg 1121 L St Ste 1000 Sacramento CA 95814-3500

HENRY, PHILIP LAWRENCE, marketing professional; b. Los Angeles, Dec. 1, 1940; s. Lawrence Langworthy and Ella Hanna (Martens) H.; m. Claudia Antonia Huff, Aug. 9, 1965 (div. 1980); children: Carolyn Marie, Susan Michelle; m. Carrie Katherine Hoover, Aug. 23, 1985. BS in Marine Engring., Calif. Maritime Acad., 1961. Design engr. Pacific Telephone Co., San Diego, 1963-73; service engr. Worthington Service Corp., San Diego, 1973-78; pres. Realmart Corp., San Diego, 1978-81; dir. mktg. Orbit Inn Hotel and Casino, Las Vegas, 1981-84; pres. Comml. Consultants, Las Vegas, 1984—, Gray Electronics Co., Las Vegas, 1986—; chmn. bd. Gray Mktg., Henderson, Nev., 1993—. Inventor electronic detection device, 1986. Served to lt. (j.g.) USNR, 1961-67. Republican. Mem. Christian Sci. Ch. Home: 1843 Somersby Way Henderson NV 89014-3876

HENRY, RICHARD ANTHONY, organization administrator; b. N.Y.C., Jan. 25, 1951; s. Junius Stergus Henry and Nancy (Venters) Mitchell; m. Genée Dylene Jackson, Aug. 15, 1986. Cert. mgmt. and orgn. devel., L.I. U., Bklyn., 1984, cert. human rels., 1984; BA in Adminstrn. and Mgmt., Columbia Pacific U., San Rafael, Calif., 1986, MA in Adminstrn. and Mgmt., 1987. Cert. mediator; cert. agrl. mediator. Program dir. Bd. Edn. City of N.Y., 1973-74; sr. bus. cons. Murtha, Gainza & Assocs., N.Y.C., 1976-81; human resource dir. Tower Isle's Frozen Foods, Bklyn., 1981-84; pres., founder Creative Think Tank, N.Y.C., San Francisco, 1984—; dir. Payne County Dispute Resolution Ctr., Stillwater, Okla., 1987-90; drug edn. coord. Coyle, Perkins, Perry, Glencoe, Stillwater Bds. Edn., 1989-90; exec. dir. YouthBuild San Francisco, 1990—; cons. human rels. com. City of Stillwater, 1985-90, Community Housing Resources Bd., Stillwater, 1985-90, Stillwater, Perry, Coyle, Clencoe Bds. Edn., 1989-90. Author: Beyond the Skull, 1975, Of Days Gone By, 1990, Short-Timer, 1992. Mem. Stillwater and Okla. Womans Polit. Caucus, 1986-90. Named Good Guy of Yr. Okla. and Stillwater Womans Polit. Caucus, 1989. Mem. World Affairs Coun. No. Calif. Home: PO Box 9996 Berkeley CA 94709

HENRY, RICHARD JOSEPH, nursing home management executive; b. Melrose, Mass., Sept. 1, 1954; s. Richard Joseph and Janet Louise (Behrle) H.; m. Diane Marrianne Rael, June 20, 1987. ABA, Chattanooga Community Coll., 1976; ThB, So. Coll., Collegedale, Tenn., 1980; postgrad., George Washington U., 1980-81. Asst. adminstr. Care More, Inc., Chattanooga, 1980-81; dir. devel./adminstrn. Macon (Ga.) Health Care Ctr., 1981-82; adminstr. Sierra Health Care Ctr., Truth or Consequence, N.Mex., 1982-84, Belen (N.Mex.) Health Care Ctr., 1984-85; asst. dir. ops./adminstrn. West Mesa Health Care Ctr., Albuquerque, 1985-86; adminstr. Hobbs (N.Mex.) Health Care Ctr., 1986-87; dir. adminstrv. svcs. Care More, Inc., Macon, 1987-88; adminstr., exec. dir. Aloha Health Care Ctr., Kaneohe, Hawaii, 1988—; COO Aloha Mgmt. Co., Kaneohe, Hawaii, 1990—; registered preceptor Hawaii Adminstr.-in-Tng. Program, 1989—. Mem. Hawaii Joint Tech. Adv. Com., Honolulu, 1989—; v.p., bd. dirs. Po'Ailani Mental Health Ctrs., Honolulu, 1989—; pub. rels. com. Kaneohe Bus. Group, 1988—. With USAF, 1972-74, USNG, 1974-78. Named Adminstr. of the Yr. Care More, Inc., 1985. Mem. Rotary (pres.-elect Windward Oahu chpt., dir. community svcs. 1988—, Rotarian of Yr. 1990), Am. Coll. Health Care Adminstrs. (pres., sec. 1989—), Hawaii Long Term Care Assn. (pres. 1992-94), N.Mex. Health Care Assn. (v.p. 1985-87). Republican. Home: 1344 C Kamahele St Kailua HI 96734 Office: Aloha Mgmt Co Ste 309 46-001 Kamehameha Hwy Kaneohe HI 96744

HENRY, SHIRLEY ANN, press executive; b. L.A., Apr. 23, 1937; d. Austin Perry Shaver and Ann (Pitrucka) Wilhelm; m. Walter Sigman Henry, July 1, 1955 (dec. Oct. 1985); children: Debbie Henry Johnson, Shelly Henry Dozier, Derek Sigman; m. Charles J. Vitale, Feb. 11, 1989. AA with honors, Contra Costa Coll., San Pablo, Calif., 1969. Lic. R.N., Calif. Nurse, VA Hosp., Martinez, Calif., 1970-73; chief exec. officer Lamorinda Press, Lafayette, Calif., 1976—, v.p. Lafayette C. of C., 1992-93. Mem. Nat. Assn. Quick Printers, Printing Industries No. Calif. Baptist. Avocations: skiing, scuba diving, travel. Office: Lamorinda Press 3409 Mt Diablo Blvd # C Lafayette CA 94549-3914

HENRY, WALTER L., cardiologist, educator; b. Cumberland, Md., Feb. 20, 1941; s. Walter and Virginia Mae (Keller) H.; BSEE cum laude, U. Pitts., 1963; MD, Stanford U., 1969. Intern, Bronx Mcpl. Hosp., N.Y.C. and Albert Einstein Coll. Medicine, 1969-70, resident in internal medicine, 1970-71; clin. asso. Nat. Heart, Lung and Blood Inst., Bethesda, Md., 1971-73, sr. investigator, 1973-78; prof. medicine, chief div. cardiology U. Calif., Irvine, 1978—, vice chancellor health scis., dean Coll. Medicine. With USPHS, 1971-78. Diplomate Am. Bd. Internal Medicine. Recipient Disting. Alumnus award U. Pitts. Engring. Alumni Assn, 1985, Profl. Achievement award U. Calif., Irvine, 1986. Bd. dirs. Opera Pacific, pres. 1990-91. Mem. Am. Soc. Echocardiography (pres. 1981-83), N. Am. Soc. Cardiac Radiology, Am. Heart Assn., Am. Coll. Cardiography (area gov. So. Calif. 1985-88), Am. Fedn. Clin. Rsch., Pres.'s Circle of NAS (co-founder), Eta Kappa Nu, Alpha Omega Alpha, Omicron Delta Kappa. Editorial bd. Am. Heart Jour. Contbr. articles to profl. jours. Office: U Calif Irvine Med Surg I Rm 118 Irvine CA 92717

HENRY-THIEL, LOIS HOLLENDER, human resources executive; b. Phila., Jan. 19, 1941; d. Edward Hubert and Frances Lois (Nesler) Hollender; m. Charles L. Henry, Oct. 24, 1964 (div. 1971); children: Deborah Lee, Randell Huitt, Andrew Edward; m. Brian L. Thiel, Jan. 1, 1989. BA, Thomas A. Edison Coll., 1979; MSW, Fordham U., 1981; PhD in Psychology, City U. L.A., 1992. Cert. social worker, Ariz., N.Y., N.J.; lic. svc. profl., career counselor, Ariz. Personnel asst., sec. IBM, Paterson, N.J. and St. Louis, 1964-66; minister's asst. Grace Luth. Ch., St. Cloud, Fla., 1966-68; adminstr./tchr. Fla. Finishing Acad., St. Cloud, 1968-70; adminstrv. asst. Newark Book Ctr., 1972-77; intern, med. social worker Jersey City Med. Ctr., 1979-80; intern, psychiatric/med. social worker VA Med. Ctr., Lyons, N.J., 1980-81; sch. social worker Lakeview Learning Ctr., Budd Lake, N.J., 1981-82; mgr. human resources Terak Corp., Scottsdale, Ariz., 1982-85; v.p. counseling and bus. devel. Murro & Assocs., Phoenix, 1985-88, exec. v.p. cons., 1988-91; prin. career cons. Henry & Assocs., Scottsdale, 1982—; career cons., individual/family counselor/psychotherapist, speaker, Henry & Assocs., Scottsdale, 1982—; mem. employers com. Ariz. Dept. Econ. Security; cons. in field. Coordinator-vol. Job-A-Thon, Phoenix, 1983. Fellow Am. Orthopsychiat. Assn.; mem. Internat. Assn. Outplacement Profls. (treas. Ariz. region 1992—), Am. Electronics Assn. (human resources coun. 1982-84), Nat. Assn. Social Workers, Soc. Human Resource Mgmt., Am. Compensation Assn., Ariz. Affirmative Action Assn. Office: Henry and Assocs 6900 E Camelback Rd Scottsdale AZ 85251-2431

HENSCHEN, CARMELISA THERESA, art educator; b. Alton, Ill., June 5, 1949; d. Dino and Carmen Bernice (Balster) Castelli; children: Andrew, Sarah Lauren. BA cum laude, Ariz. State U., 1972, MA, 1982. Artist Del E. Webb Corp., 1969-70; instr. art Jefferson Co., Colo., 1972-73; instr. art Scottsdale (Ariz.) Unified Schs., 1973-77, tchr. coord., 1976-77; instr. art & photography, yearbook advisor Tempe (Ariz.) Union High Sch. Dist., 1977—; instr. fitness Fitness First, Tempe, 1984—; artist, designer, photographer Creative Connection, Tempe, 1985—; sales agt. Am. West Airlines, Phoenix, 1990—; art cons. Essential News, Tempe, 1990—; art masterpiece chmn. Mesa Unified Dist., 1989-90; chmn. Ariz. Youth Art Month, Phoenix, 1976-78; adminstrv. asst. Ariz. Art Edn. Assn., Phoenix, 1976-77. Citizen advocate Univ. Royal Home Owners Assn., Tempe, 1986; precinct chmn. Ariz. Dem. Party, Tempe, 1985; rec. sec. Roosevelt Parent-Tchr. Orgn., Mesa, 1989; leader Girl Scouts Am., Mesa, 1989, Boy Scouts Am., Mesa, 1988. Named Ariz. Art Edn. Assn. Outstanding Art Educator, 1979, one of Outstanding Young Women of Am., 1980. Mem. Am. Coun. Exercise, Soc. for the Arts, Tempe Secondary Edn. Assn. Office: McClintock High Sch Tempe AZ

HENSEL, JEFFREY, geologist, consultant; b. Detroit, Nov. 15, 1962; s. Manfred Karl and Liane Bertha (Freuck) H.; m. Kimberly Ann Habel, Sept. 6, 1986; 1 child, Rachael Anna. BS in Geology, Wayne State U., 1984; MS in Environ. Studies, Calif. State U., Fullerton, 1992. Registered geologist, Wyo., Calif.; registered environ. assessor, Calif. Geologist GMC Assocs. Inc., Northville, Mich., 1985-86, BCL Assocs. Inc., Long Beach, Calif., 1986-89; environ. geologist Radian Corp., Irvine, Calif., 1989—; advisor environ. affairs dept. and environ. studies bd. Calif. State U., Fullerton, 1990-92. Mich. Indsl. Soc. grantee, 1984. Mem. Nat. Water Well Assn., Ducks Unltd. Republican. Roman Catholic. Office: Radian Corp 7 Corporate Park Ste 240 Irvine CA 92714-5107

HENSLEY, PAUL WAYNE, insurance company executive; b. Fornfelt, Mo., Nov. 3, 1939; s. Eskew and Jesse (Burton) H.; m. Sandra J. Oliver; children: Stephanie, Todd, Stacia, Timothy. BSBA, S.E. Mo. State U., 1967. CLU, ChFC; cert. ins. counselor. Sales mgr. Allstate Ins. Co., Denver, 1967-81, Met. Life, Denver and Olympia, Wash., 1981-86; asst. v.p. Sunset Life Ins. Co., Olympia, 1986—. Staff sgt. U.S. Army, 1960-66. Mem. Ins. Inst. Am. (assoc. mgmt.), Soc. CLU & ChFC, S.W. Wash. Assn. Life Underwriters (bd. dirs. 1992), S.W. Wash. Estate Planning Assn., Kiwanis (bd. dirs., sec. 1983-90). Republican. Office: Sunset Life Ins Co 3200 Capitol Blvd S Olympia WA 98501-3304

HENSON, HOWARD KEITH, computer consultant; b. Ft. Monmouth, N.J., July 12, 1942; s. Howard William and Pauline (Hudgens) H.; m. Carolyn P. Meinel, Dec. 25, 1967 (div. 1982); children: Gale, Windy, Valerie, Virginia; m. Arel Lucas, Aug. 22, 1982; 1 child, Amber Lucas Henson. BSEE, U. Ariz., 1969. Chief engr. Sta. KTKT, Tucson, 1960-62; engr. Sta. KVOA-TV, Tucson, 1962-63; field engr. Heinrichs Geoexploration Co., Tucson, 1963-69; design engr. Burr-Brown Rsch. Corp., Tucson, 1970-72; pres. Analog Precision, Inc., Tucson, 1972-82, 84-85; ind. cons. Tucson, 1982-84, San Jose, Calif., 1985—. Patentee in field; contbr. articles to profl. jours. Pres. L-5 Soc., Tucson, 1975-77; bd. dirs. Alcor Life Ext. Found., Riverside, Calif., 1992—. Recipient Founder award L-5 Soc., 1980. Mem. IEEE (sr. mem.), Nat. Space Soc. (bd. dirs. 1991—). Home and Office: 1794 Cardel Way San Jose CA 95124

HENSON, PETER MITCHELL, immunology and respiratory medicine executive; b. Moreton in Marsh, England, Aug. 25, 1940; came to U.S., 1967; S. Edwin Roland Witham and Irene May (Whitmee) H.; m. Janet Elizabeth Neilan, Dec. 22, 1962; children: Neil, Ruth. BVM&S with William Dick medal for best graduate, Edinburg (Scotland) U., 1963, BS in Bacteriology with first class honors, 1964; PhD, U. Cambridge, England, 1967. Rsch. fellow dept. exptl. pathology Scripps Clinic and Rsch. Found., La Jolla, Calif., 1967-69, assoc. dept. exptl. pathology, 1969-72, assoc. mem. dept. immunopathology, 1972-77; dir. rsch. dept. pediatrics Nat. Jewish Hosp. and Rsch. Ctr., Nat. Asthma Ctr., Denver, 1977-80, vice-chmn. dept. pediatrics, 1980-82, asst. v.p. profl. svcs., 1981-82, v.p. biomedical svcs., 1982-84; prof. pathology sch. medicine U. Colo., Denver, 1977—, prof. dept. medicine, sch. medicine, 1980—, co-head pulmonary dvsn. dept. medicine, health scis. ctr., 1986-87, assoc. dean hosp. affairs health scis. ctr., 1985—; exec. v.p. biomedical affairs Nat. Jewish Ctr. Immunology and Respiratory Medicine, Denver, 1985-92; exec. v.p. acad. affairs U. Colo., Nat. Jewish Ctr. Immunology and Respiratory Medicine, Denver, 1992—. Mem. editorial bd. Am. Jour. Pathology, 1982-88, Am. Review for Respiratory Disease, Pulmonary Pharmacology, 1988-92 and other profl. jours. Recipient Am. Heart Assn. Established investigatorship, 1969-70, Research Career Devel. award NIH, 1970-75, Parke Davis award Am. Assn. Pathologists, 1980; named Margaret A. Regan prof. Pulmonary Inflammation, 1991. Mem. Royal Coll. Vet. Surgeons, Brit. Soc. Immunology, Am. Assn. Pathology, Am. Assn. Immunologists, Am. Thoracic Soc., Am. Soc. Cell Biology, Am. Acad. Allergy and Immunology, Reticuloendothelial Soc. (Marie T. Bonazinga award 1991). Office: Nat Jewish Ctr Immunology and Respiratory Medicine 1400 Jackson St Denver CO 80206

HEPLER, KENNETH RUSSEL, manufacturing executive; b. Canton, Ohio, Mar. 31, 1926; s. Clifton R. and Mary A. (Sample) H.; m. Beverly Best, June 9, 1945; 1 child, Bradford R. Student, Cleve. Art Inst., 1946-47, Case Western Res. U., 1948-50. V.p., adminstr. A. Carlisle and Co., San Francisco, 1954-67; pres. K.R. Hepler and Co., Menlo Park, Calif., 1968-73, Paramount Press., Jacksonville, Fla., 1974-75; pvt. practice printing broker, 1976-80; chmn. Hickey and Hepler Graphics Inc., San Francisco, 1981—; instr. printing prodn., San Francisco City Coll. With USAAC, 1943-45. Mem. San Francisco Litho Club (pres. 1972), Phila. Litho Club (sec. 1975-76), Newtown Exchange Club (pres. 1976), Elks. Republican. Presbyterian. Office: Hickey & Hepler Graphics Inc 1485 Bay Shore Blvd San Francisco CA 94124-3002

HEPLER, MERLIN JUDSON, JR., real estate broker; b. Hot Springs, Va., May 13, 1929; s. Merlin Judson and Margaret Belle (Vines) H.; m. Lanova Helen Roberts, July 25, 1952; children: Nancy Andora, Douglas Stanley. BS in Bus., U. Idaho, 1977; grad., Realtors Inst., 1979. Cert. residential specialist. Enlisted USAF, 1947, advanced through grades to sgt., 1960, ret., 1967; service mgr. Lanier Bus. Products, Gulfport, Miss., 1967-74; sales assoc. Century 21 Singler and Assn., Troy, Idaho, 1977-79; broker B&M Realty, Troy, 1979—. Mem. Nat. Assn. Realtors, Am. Legion, U. Idaho Alumni Assn., Air Force Sgts. Assn. Republican. Lodge: Lions. Home: 1081 Driscoll Ridge Troy ID 83871-9605 Office: B&M Realty W 102 A St PO Box 187 Troy ID 83871-0187

HEPNER, ABE, chemical engineer; b. Mexico City, Mexico, May 23, 1931; came to U.S. 1963; s. Wolff and Itka (Prenski) H.; m. Martha Remba, Sept. 30, 1956; children: Mireya, Diana. MS chem. engr., U. Autonoma de Mexico, Mexico City, 1955. Tech. dir. Pinturas el Aguila S.A., Mexico City, 1956-58; chief executive officer Solventes y Barnices SRL, Mexico City, 1958-63; gen. mgr. B & A Processing, Bklyn., 1963-74; pres. E.J.A. Imports Inc., Palos Verdes, Calif., 1970-90, Cal-Chrome Div. Allen Group, Wilmington, Calif., 1974-83; chief executive officer Hepner Cons., Torrance, Calif., 1983—; cons. Amana Metals/Industrias Medrano, L.A./Mexico City, 1985-90, Grosh Studios, Hollywood, Calif., 1985-87, Allen Group, Inc., Melville, N.Y., 1983-85, Bleiweis Belshaw & Wall, Torrance, Calif., 1985-89. Bd. dirs. U.S. Senatorial adv. bd., Washington. Mem. South Bay Jewish Community Ctr. (exec. v.p. 1985-89), Jewish Fedn., Pot Lock Investment Club (pres. 1985-86). Democrat. Office: Hepner Consulting 3848 W Carson St Ste 200 Torrance CA 90503-6704

HEPTINSTALL, TERRY CASH, computer sales account manager; b. Selma, Ala., May 31, 1954; s. Fred Bernard and June Isabella (Carter) H.; m. Debra Thurman, Feb. 23, 1973 (div. Aug. 1979); m. Carola Ellen Ballenthin, Aug. 8, 1980; children: Ian Cash, Jana Ellen. Degree in Liberal Arts, Long Beach City Coll., 1981; BSBA, Calif. State U., Long Beach, 1983. Electronic technician McDonell Douglas, Long Beach, 1979-82; computer salesman A-Vidd Electronics, Long Beach, 1982-84; sales acct. mgr. Hewlett-Packard, Long Beach, 1984—; owner Computer Systems/Consulting, Long Beach, 1988—. Mem. VFW, Long Beach, 1990—. Sgt. USAF, 1973-78, Vietnam. Office: Hewlett Packard Ste 100 Bldg 3 5245 Pacific Concourse Dr Los Angeles CA 90045

HERB, EDMUND MICHAEL, optometrist, educator; b. Zanesville, Ohio, Oct. 9, 1942; s. Edmund G. and Barbara R. (Michael) H.; divorced; children—Sara, Andrew; m. Jeri Herb. O.D., Ohio State U., 1966. Pvt. practice optometry, Buena Vista, Colo., 1966—; past prof. Timberline campus Colo. Mountain Coll. Mem. Am. Optometric Assn., Colo. Optometric Assn. Home: Lost Creek Ranch Buena Vista CO 81211 Office: 115 N Tabor St Buena Vista CO 81211 also: Leadville Colorado Med Ctr Leadville CO 80461

HERBAUGH, ROGER DUANE, computer and software company executive; b. Mt. Vernon, Wash., May 20, 1957; s. Donald Lloyd and Kathleen Joyce (Anderson) H.; m. Anne Louise Finlayson, May 8, 1993; children: Andrew David, Celeste Jane, Trevor Allan, Vanessa Anne, Deirdre Rose. AA, Skagit Valley Coll., 1984; BA, Western Wash. U., 1986. Computer programmer Stockmar Northwestern, Mt. Vernon, 1986-87; chief exec. officer, computer cons. Herbaugh & Assocs., Inc., Mt. Vernon, 1987—, also pres. bd. dirs.; cons. Shell Oil co., Anacortes, Wash., 1986—, BP Oil Co., Ferndale, Wash., 1989—, ARCO, Blaine, Wash., 1989—; bd. dirs., pres. Software Plus, Inc., Mt. Vernon, 1991—. Sgt. U.S. Army, 1975-81. Mem. Microsoft Cons. Rels., Burlington C. of C., Anacortes C. of C., Kiwanis (asst. sec., bd. dirs. Mt. Vernon chpt.). Republican. Mem. LDS Ch. Office: Herbaugh & Assocs Inc Ste 201 1686 S Burlington Blvd Burlington WA 98233

HERBERGER, ROY A., JR., academic administrator. B in Bus. and Mktg., U. Tex., 1966, MA in Comm., 1968; D in Bus., Mktg. Mgmt. Sci., Econs., U. Colo., 1971. Mem. bank tng. program First Nat. Bank, Midland, Tex., 1961-64; oil field svcs. Sun Oil Co., 1965-66; assoc. dean acad. affairs Grad. Sch. Bus. U. So. Calif., L.A., 1973-82, dir. internat. bus. edn. and rsch. program, 1976-82; dean Edwin L. Cox. Sch. Bus. So. Meth. U., Dallas, 1982-89; pres. Thunderbird-Am. Grad. Sch. Internat. Mgmt., Glendale, Ariz., 1989—; mem. FSLIC adv. bd. Mercury & Ben Milam Savs., 1986-89; chmn. Joint Legis. Study Com. on Internat. Trade, State of Ariz.; bd. dirs., chmn. internat. com. Greater Phoenix Econ. Coun.; mem. adv. bd. Japan-Am. Soc. Phoenix; bd. dirs. Sta. KCCN/KCCN Broadcasting Co, Inc., Honolulu, Compas, Inc., Inroads, Samaritan Health System, Ariz., WeSave Mortgage, Pinnacle West Capital Corp., Ban. Am. Ariz.; appt. Internat. Trade and Tourism Adv. Bd.; cons. Getty Oil Co., A & M Record Co., L.A., Yamaha Internat., L.A., Honda U.S.A., Torrance, Calif., Toyota Motor Sales, Torrance, P. T. Astra Internat., Jakarta, Indonesia, Mexicana Airlines, Nihon Keizai Shimbun, Inc., Tokyo, Warner Comm., Recreational Vehicles, Inc., Doyle, Dane & Bernback, Inc., Superior Music L.A., O. Y. Mercantile, Helsinki, Finland, GE. Editor: Management in a World Perspective, 1974; bus. editor Colo. Bus., 1969-70; mem. editorial bd. European Bus. Jour.; contbr. articles to profl. jours. Trustee Lee Optical Pension & Profit Trust, 1983-92; active Dimension Cable Svcs. Community Adv. Bd., Greater Phoenix Leadership. Recipient Award for Ednl. Program Devel., Columbia Broadcasting Corp., 1972, Spl. Svcs. award Japan-Am. Soc., 1982, Outstanding Alumni award U. Tex., 1984; grantee Toyota Ednl. Found. for Internat. Bus. Simulation. Mem. Am. Mgmt. Assn. (internat. coun.), Am. Assembly Collegiate Sch. Bus. (chair internat. affairs com., mem. accredation and implementation com., intermat. edn. trust fund task force), Ariz. C. of C. (bd. dirs.), Coun. on Fgn. Rels., Sigma Iota Epsilon, Beta Gamma Sigma. Office: Am Graduate Sch Internat Mgmt Thunderbird Campus Office of President Glendale AZ 85306*

HERBERT, GAVIN SHEARER, JR., health care products company executive; b. Los Angeles, Mar. 26, 1932; s. Gavin and Josephine (D'Vitha) H.; children by previous marriage Cynthia, Lauri, Gavin, Pam; 2d. m. Ninetta Flanagan, Sept. 6, 1986. B.S., U. So. Calif., 1954. With Allergan, Inc., Irvine, Calif., 1950—; v.p. Allergan, Inc., 1956-61, exec. v.p., pres., 1961-77, chmn. bd., chief exec. officer, 1977-91, chmn. bd., 1992—; pres. Eye and Skin Care Products Group Smith Kline Beckman Corp., 1981-89; exec. v.p. Smith Kline Beckman Corp., 1986-89; bd. dirs. Beckman Instruments, Inc., Cytel Corp. Trustee U. So. Calif.; bd. dirs. Richard Nixon Presdl. Found., Estelle Doheny Eye Found. With USN, 1954-56. Mem. Pharm. Mfrs. Assn. (bd. dirs.), Rsch. to Prevent Blindness (bd. dirs.), Big Canyon Country Club, Newport Harbor Yacht Club, Pacific Club, Beta Theta Pi. Republican. Office: Allergan Inc PO Box 19534 2525 Dupont Dr Irvine CA 92715-1599

HERBERT, LAWRENCE FISK, investment management company executive; b. Denver, May 2, 1953; s. Wilbur Fisk and Dorthy Ann (Spafford) H. BS, U. Colo., 1975. Registered investment advisor. Rep. Bio Feedback

Systems, Inc., Boulder, Colo., 1975-77; account exec. Merrill Lynch, Denver, 1977-79; pres. 21st Century Video Corp., Cherry Creek, Colo., 1980-82; account exec. Boettcher & Co., Lakewood, Colo., 1983-88; pres. Fisk Investment, Denver, 1989—. Author materials in field. Pro se intervenor Pub. Utilities Commn., Denver, 1989-92; amicus curiae Colo. Supreme Ct., Denver, 1992. Named to Outstanding Young Men of Am., 1989. Presbyterian. Home and Office: 2110 Garland St Lakewood CO 80215

HERBERT, VICTOR, school system administrator. Supt. Phoenix public schs. Office: Phoenix UNHSD 210 4502 N Central Ave Phoenix AZ 85012-1852

HERBISON, JOHN (STEVE), wholesale and retail company executive; b. Spokane, Wash., June 10, 1939; s. Ralph Neil and Ernestine Elizabeth (Vawter) H.; m. Bettie Esther Walker, Aug. 16, 1969; children: Gretchen Lynn, Kelly Anne, John Stephen. BBA, U. Wash., 1961; postgrad., Gonzaga U., 1964. Store services contact man URM Stores, Inc., Spokane, 1963-64, mem. store devel. dept., 1964-66, buyer, 1966-71, dir. purchasing, 1971-74, v.p. sales, 1974-83, exec. v.p., 1983-85, chief oper. officer, 1985-89, pres., chief exec. officer, from 1989; bd. dirs. Grocers Equipment and Fixtures Co., Washington, Rosauers Supermarkets, Spokane, chmn. bd., 1989-90, Peirone Produce Co., Spokane, chmn. bd., 1989—, Western Family Foods, URM Devel. Corp., Spokane, Mchts. Ins. Agy., Spokane. Bd. dirs. St. John's Cathedral, Spokane, 1980-90, Inland Empire coun. Boy Scouts Am., Spokane, 1984-92, Spokane Community Colls. Found., 1986-87, Mus. Native Am. Indian Cultures, 1990-92. Mem. Nat. Grocers Assn. (bd. dirs.), Nat. Wholesale Grocers Assn. (bd. govs. 1989-92), Assn. Wash. Bus. (bd. dirs. 1987—), Spokane C. of C. (chmn. bd. 1993—), Spokane Country Club, Rotary. Republican. Episcopalian. Home: 14011 N Rivilla Ln Spokane WA 99208-9767 Office: U R M Stores Inc PO Box 3365 Spokane WA 99220-3365

HERDEG, HOWARD BRIAN, physician; b. Buffalo, Oct. 14, 1929; s. Howard Bryan and Martha Jean (Williams) H.; m. Beryl Ann Fredricks, July 21, 1955; children: Howard Brian III, Erin Ann Kociela. Student Paul Smith's Coll., 1947-48, U. Buffalo, 1948-50, Canisius Coll., 1949; DO, Phila. Coll. Osteopathic Medicine, 1954; MD, U. Calif.-Irvine Coll. Medicine, 1962. Diplomate Am. Acad. Pain Mgmt. Intern, Burbank (Calif.) Hosp., 1954-55; practice medicine specializing in gen. medicine, surgery and pain mgmt., Woodland Hills, Calif., 1956—; chief med. staff West Park Hosp., Canoga Park, Calif., 1971-72, trustee, 1971-73; chief family practice dept. West Hills Regional Med. Center (formerly Humaua Hosp. West Hills, 1982-83, 84-85, 88-89), mem. exec. com., 1984-85, 88-89, Mem. Hidden Hills (Calif.) Pub. Safety Commn., 1978-82; bd. dirs. Hidden Hills Community Assn., 1971-73, pres., 1972; bd. dirs. Hidden Hills Homeowners Assn., 1973-75, pres., 1976-77; bd. dirs. Woodland Hills Freedom Season, 1961-67, pres., 1962; mem. Hidden Hills City Council, 1984—, mayor pro tem, 1987-90, mayor, 1990-92. Recipient disting. service award Woodland Hills Jr C. of C., 1966. Mem. Woodland Hills C. of C. (dir. 1959-68, pres. 1967), Theta Chi, Gamma Pi. Republican. Home: 24530 Deep Well Rd Hidden Hills CA 91302-1210 Office: 22600 Ventura Blvd Woodland Hills CA 91364-1415

HERDRICH, NORMAN WESLEY, magazine editor; b. Spokane, Wash., July 17, 1942; s. Fred N. and Florice J. (Birchill) H.; m. Mary Susan Webb, Aug. 16, 1975; children: Megan Marie, Heidi Susan, Kristin Ruth. B.S., Wash. State U., 1969. Field editor Northwest Unit Farm Mags., Spokane, 1969-78; prodn. editor Western Farmer-Stockman Mags., Spokane, 1978—. Served with USNR, 1963-65. Mem. Wash. State Grange, Soc. Profl. Journalists, Nat. Rifle Assn., Spokane Editorial Soc. (sec.-treas. 1974-77, 1st v.p. 1977-78, pres. 1978-79), Wash. Wool Growers Assn., Soc. Profl. Journalists. Methodist. Club: Spokane Press (dir. 1978, treas. 1979). Home: 12711 E Saltese Ave Spokane WA 99216-0373 Office: Rev Tower W 999 Riverside Spokane WA 99210-1615

HEREMAN, WILLY ALOIS MARIA, mathematics educator; b. Lokeren, Belgium, Sept. 17, 1954; came to U.S. 1983; s. Achiel Emma and Mariette Irma (Tijdgat) H. BS in Math., U. Ghent, Belgium, 1974, MS in Math., 1976, PhD in Math., 1982. Rsch. asst. State U. Ghent, 1976-82; NATO rsch. fellow U. Iowa, Iowa City, 1983-84, 85-86; rsch. assoc. State U. Ghent, 1984-85; asst. prof. math. U. Wis., Madison, 1986-89; assoc. prof. math. Colo. Sch. Mines, Golden, 1989—. Contbr. numerous articles to profl. jours. Laureate, Royal Acad. Scis., Lit. and Fine Arts of Belgium, 1985. Mem. Am. Math. Soc., Soc. Indsl. and Applied Math. Home: 2225 Bluff St Boulder CO 80304-3715 Office: Col Sch Mines Dept of Math Golden CO 80401

HERGER, WALLY W., JR., congressman; b. Yuba City, Calif., May 20, 1945. Formerly mem. Calif. State Assembly; mem. 100th-102d Congresses from 2d Calif. dist., 1987—; mem. agr., mcht. marine and fisheries coms. 100th-103rd Congresses from 2d Calif. dist.; mem. budget com., mem. ways and means com.; owner Herger Gas, Inc. Office: US House of Representatives 2433 Rayburn Washington DC 20510*

HERGERT, RICHARD GARY, government official, property tax assessment executive; b. Seattle, Aug. 9, 1949; s. Wilfred Adam and Beatrice Stella (Bergseth) H.; m. Patricia Jaclyn McDougall, Sept. 11, 1971; children: Elizabeth Anne, Thomas Scott, Gary James. BA, U. Wash., 1972. Cert. assessor, Wash. Alcoholism worker Seattle/King County Dept. Health, 1972-74; systems analyst King County Dept. Assessments, Seattle, 1974-83, sect. supr., 1983-91, supr. comml. appraisal sect., 1991—; data processing sect. chief, Wash. Army NG, Seattle, 1976-82; data processing instr. USAR, Tacoma, 1982-85; data processing technician USAR, Seattle, 1985—; cons. for proposed city incorporations Renton, Wash., Fed. Way, Wash., 1987-88. Bd. dirs., v.p. Northshore Youth Basketball Assn., Woodinville, 1986-89; founder Northshore Spirit Girls Basketball Assn.; basketball coach Bothell High Sch., 1989—; bd. dirs. City of Woodinville Inc. Yes! Com., 1986-89. Mem. Internat. Assn. of Assessing Officers (King County chpt.). Home: 16231 194th Ave NE Woodinville WA 98072-9265 Office: King County Dept Assessment King County Adminstrn Rm 853 Seattle WA 98104

HERING, WILLIAM MARSHALL, human resource development executive; b. Indpls., Dec. 26, 1940; s. William Marshall and Mary Agnes (Clark) H.; m. Suzanne Wolfe, Aug. 10, 1963. BS, Ind. U., 1961, MS, 1962; PhD, U. Ill., Urbana, 1973. Tchr. Indpls. pub. schs., 1962-66; asst. dir. sociol. resources project Am. Sociol. Assn., 1966-70; dir. social sci. curriculum Biomed. Interdisciplinary Project, Berkeley, Calif., 1973-76; staff assoc. Tchrs. Ctrs. Exchange, San Francisco, 1976-82; dir. research Far West Lab. Ednl. Research and Devel., San Francisco, 1979-82, sr. research assoc., 1982-85; mgr. human resource devel. Bank Am., San Francisco, 1985—; mem. Nat. Adv. Bd. Educ. Resource Info. Ctr.; cons. U.S. Dept. Edn.; pres. Social Sci. Educ. Consortium, 1981-82, bd. dirs., 1979-81; bd. dirs. San Francisco Chamber Orch., 1986—. Nat. Inst. Educ. grantee, 1979-82, 82—. Mem. Am. Soc. Tng. and Devel. (v.p. 1986), Golden Gate Soc., Nat. Audubon Soc., Phi Delta Kappa. Republican. Episcopalian. Contbr. over 100 articles on social studies edn., staff devel., ednl. research and evaluation to profl. jours. Home: 731 Duboce Ave San Francisco CA 94117-3214 Office: PO Box 37000 Dept # 8531 San Francisco CA 94137-0001

HERLINGER, DANIEL ROBERT, hospital administrator; b. Boskovice, Czechoslovakia, Oct. 27, 1946; came to U.S., 1950, naturalized, 1956; s. Rudolf and Ingeborg (Gessler) H.; m. Susanne Reiter, June 1, 1969; children—Lisa, Rebecca, Joanna. B.S., Loyola U., Chgo., 1968; M.B.A., George Washington U., 1971. Asst. adminstr. Michael Reese Hosp., Chgo., 1971-73; v.p. Mercy Hosp., Chgo., 1973-84; pres. St. John's Regional Med. Ctr., Oxnard, Calif., 1984—. Fellow Am. Coll. Hosp. Adminstrs.; mem. Am. Hosp. Assn. Jewish. Lodge: Rotary. Home: 1648 Aspenwall Rd Westlake Vlg CA 91361-1704 Office: St John's Regional Med Ctr 1600 N Rose Ave Oxnard CA 93030-4598

HERLOCKER, JOHN ROBERT, priest; b. Greenville, Tex., Feb. 11, 1935; s. James Harry and Doyle Douglas (Williams) H.; m. Peggy Ann Felmet, Feb. 28, 1959; children: John Robert, James Madison, Dorsey Elizabeth, Katherine Susannah, Douglas Reed-Bryant. BBA, U. Tex., 1956; MDiv, U. of South, 1967. Vicar St. Mary's Episcopal Ch., Winnemucca, Nev., 1969-72; rector Holy Trinity Episcopal Ch., Ukiah, Calif., 1972-74; fiscal officer Episc. Diocese of Eastern Oreg., Redmond, 1974-79; diocesan adminstr. Episc. Diocese of Idaho, Boise, 1979-82, archdeacon, 1982-90, canon to ordinary for adminstrn., 1990—. Mem., bd. dir., treas. Hogar Infantil, Inc., Chiapas, Mexico. With USN, 1956-58. Mem. Kiwanis Club. Home: 3262 Scenic Dr Boise ID 83703-4719

HERMAN, ANDREA MAXINE, newspaper editor; b. Chgo., Oct. 22, 1938; d. Maurice H. and Mae (Baron) H.; m. Joseph Schmidt, Oct. 28, 1962. BJ, U. Mo., 1960. Feature writer Chgo.'s Am., 1960-63; daily columnist News Am., Balt., 1963-67; feature writer Mainichi Daily News, Tokyo, 1967-69; columnist Iowa City Press-Citizen, 1969-76; music and dance critic San Diego Tribune, 1976-84; asst. mng. editor features UPI, Washington, 1984-86, asst. mng. editor news devel., 1986-87; mng. editor features L.A. Herald Examiner, 1987-91; editor/culture We/Mbl Newspaper, Washington, 1991—. Recipient 1st and 2d prizes for features in arts James S. Copley Ring of Truth Awards, 1982, 1st prize for journalism Press Club San Diego, 1983. Mem. Soc. Profl. Journalists, Am. Soc. Newspaper Editors, AP Mng. Editors, Women in Communications. Office: We/Mbl Newspaper Ste 1020 1350 Connecticut Ave NW Washington DC 20036

HERMAN, GEORGE ADAM, writer; b. Norfolk, Va., Apr. 12, 1928; s. George Adam and Minerva Nevada (Thompson) H.; m. Patrici Lee Glazer, May 26, 1955 (div. 1989); children: Kurt, Erik, Karl, Lisa, Katherine, Christopher, Jena, Amanda; m. Patricia Jane Piper Dubay, Aug. 25, 1989; children: Lizette, Paul, Kirk, Victoria. PhB, Loyola Coll., 1950; MFA, Cath. U., 1954; cert. fine arts, Boston Coll., 1951,52,53. Asst. prof. Clarke Coll., Dubuque, Iowa, 1955-60, Villanova (Pa.) U., 1960-63; asst. prof., playwright in residence Coll. St. Benedict, St. Joseph, Minn., 1963-65; chmn. theatre dept. Coll. Great Falls, Mont., 1965-67; media specialist Hawaii State Dept. Edn., Honolulu, 1967-75, staff specialist, 1975-83; sr. drama critic Honolulu Advertiser, 1975-80; artistic dir. Commedia Repertory Theatre, Honolulu, 1978-80; freelance writer, lectr. Portland, Oreg., 1983—; lectr. Portland State U., 1985—; film actor SAG, L.A., 1975—. Author: (plays) Company of Wayward Spirits, 1963 (McKnight Humanities award 1964), Mr. Highpockets, 1968, A Stone for Either Hand, 1969, Tenebrae, 1984, (novel) Carnival of Saints, 1993. Pres. local chpt. Nat. Sch. Pub. Rels. Assn., Honolulu, 1981-83; bd. dirs. Honolulu Community Theatre, 1981-82, Hawaii State Theatre Coun., Honolulu, 1981. With U.S. Army, 1950-52. Named Genesian Jewel Nat. Cath. Theatre Conf., 1949; recipient Hartke Playwrighting award Cath. U., 1954, Excellence award Am. Security Coun., 1967. Mem. Am. Legion, Amnesty Internat., Ednl. Theatre Assn. (bd. dirs. 1990—).

HERMAN, HARRY MARTIN, III, music composition educator, composer; b. York, Pa., Mar. 7, 1953; s. Harry Martin Herman Jr. and Patricia Ann (Wetzel) Hansen; m. Christen Kay Smith, May 11, 1985; children: Paul Alexander, Kaija Rose. BA, Duke U., 1976; MA, U. Pa., 1979; PhD, U. Calif., Berkeley, 1990. Dir. Scholar Cantorum, Atlanta, 1979-81; pres., artistic dir. Music Alliance Inc., Atlanta, 1980-84; asst. to the dir. San Francisco Contemporary Music Players, 1984-85; ind. rschr. I'nstitut de recherche et coordination d'acoustique et musique, Paris, 1985-87; exch. scholar Stanford U., Palo Alto, Calif., 1987-89; instr. U. Calif., Berkeley, 1988-89; assoc. prof. Calif. State U., Long Beach, 1989—; vis. asst. prof. Hamilton Coll., Clinton, N.Y., 1981; composer-in-residence Ga. Coun. for the Arts, Atlanta, 1981, 82, Camargo Found., Cassis, France, 1983, 87; affiliate artist Headlands Ctr. for the Arts, Sausalito, Calif., 1989. Composer: Hawthorne Symphony, 1989, (piano solo) Arena, 1990, (opera in 2 acts) The Scarlet Letter, 1992, (for 2 pianos) Parallel City, 1992, The Fractal Bow, 1993; condr.: Atlanta New Music Ensemble, 1979-83; co-condr.: Berkeley Contemporary Chamber Players, 1985, 88; contbr. article to Sci. Am., 1993. Composer and panelist Internat. Computer Music Conf., Tokyo, 1993. Fulbright grantee U. Paris, 1985-86; Boulez fellow L.A. Philharm., 1989, Orchestra Libr. Info. Svc. New Music Reading fellow Am. Symphony Orch. League, 1988, Polish Sect. fellow Internat. Soc. Contemporary Music, 1986, composer fellow Cabrillo Music Festival, Santa Cruz, Calif., 1990; recipient Dramalogue award, L.A., 1992. Mem. Broadcast Music Inc. (affiliate composer), Soc. for Electro-Acoustic Music in the U.S., Am. Music Ctr., Coll. Music Soc., Smithsonian Instn., U.S. Lighthouse Soc. Office: Calif State U UMC-306 1250 Bellflower Blvd Long Beach CA 90840

HERMAN, JAMES WILEY, accountant; b. Andrews, Tex., Oct. 8, 1946; s. Wiley Grandville and Beulah Fay (Ray) H.; m. Lucille Marlaine Harthun, Dec. 27, 1969; children: Nathan Wiley, Brad Alan, Jason Robert. BS, Western Oreg. U., 1969. CPA, Wa. Tchr. Merritt Davis Bus. Coll., Salem, Oreg., 1973-76; acct. Anderson & Deaton CPAs, Osburn, Idaho, 1976-78; pres. James W. Herman CPA, P.C., White Salmon, Wash., 1978—; bd. dirs. Skyline Found., White Salmon. Councilman City of White Salmon, 1986—; treas. Lions, Osburn, 1977; sponsor White Salmon Little League. With USMC, 1969-75, Vietnam. Mem. AICPA, Oreg. Soc. CPAs, Washington Soc. CPAs, Mt. Adams C. of C., Elks (chmn. trustees 1989). Office: James W Herman CPA PC 1000 E Jewett Blvd White Salmon WA 98672

HERMAN, MICHAEL ALAN, music educator, musician; b. Davenport, Iowa, Jan. 11, 1945; s. William Watt and Leona Lillian (Markovitch) H.; m. Willitte Hisami Ishii, Nov. 23, 1980. Student, U. Iowa, 1967. Host Sta. WSUI Radio/TV, U. Iowa, Iowa City, 1964-65; internat. freelance folk and blues musician, 1965—; pvt. practice guitar tchr. nationwide, 1973—; owner, coord. entertainment Topaz Prodns., Oakland, Calif., 1992—; owner, entertainment coord. Redwood Music, Oakland, Calif., 1973—; entertainment chmn. Mill Valley (Calif.) Fall Arts Festival, 1980—; entertainment coord. San Francisco Folk Music Club, 1980-85; entertainment cons. Miss. Valley Blues Soc., Davenport, 1989—; freelance writer, journalist, 1990—. Songwriter Rock Island, 1975; musician, songwriter, arranger and producer (cassette, CD) Everyday Living, 1989; performer, arranger (mus. score) Smokin, 1990; performer Bread & Roses, 1992—. Volunteer Project Helping Hands, San Francisco, 1990; musician, organizer, arranger Freedom Song Network, San Francisco, 1986—; educator Blues in the Schs. program, 1986—. Am. Conservatory Theatre scholar, 1970; recipient Cert. of Merit, Nat. Traditional Country Music Found., 1986-88. Mem. Miss. Valley Blues Soc., Quad Cities Friends of the Heritage Arts. Democrat. Office: Topaz Productions PO Box 2725 Oakland CA 94602-3202

HERMAN, MICHAEL HARRY, physicist, researcher; b. Hartford, Conn., June 8, 1954; s. Richard Allen and Barbara Jane (Weinstein) H.; m. Susan Barbara Blum, Apr. 5, 1981; children: Edward, Beth, Andrea. BA in Physics, Grinnell Coll., 1976; PhD in Physics, Pa. State U., 1982. Sr. engr., materials tech. Intel Corp., Santa Clara, Calif., 1982-84; sr. device physicist, tech. devel. Intel Corp., Santa Clara, 1984-87; staff scientist Charles Evans & Assocs., Redwood City, Calif., 1987-89; sr. scientist Charles Evans & Assocs., Redwood City, 1989-91; head of characterization Power Spectra, Inc., Sunnyvale, Calif., 1991—. Contbr. chpt. to Analysis of Microelectronic Materials and Devices, 1991; contbr. articles to Jour. Electronic Materials, Jour. Applied Physics. Mem. IEEE, Am. Phys. Soc., Materials Rsch. Soc., Soc. Photometric Instrumentation Engrs., Phi Beta Kappa, Phi Kappa Phi. Home: 10401 N Blaney Ave Cupertino CA 95014-2333 Office: Power Spectra 919 Hermosa Ct Sunnyvale CA 94086-4103

HERMAN, RONALD CHARLES, molecular biologist; b. N.Y.C., Apr. 5, 1948; s. Harry and Charlotte (Sussman) H. BA, Queens Coll., 1969; MPhil, Columbia U., 1973, PhD, 1974. Post-doctoral fellow MIT, Cambridge, 1974-77; sr. staff fellow NIH, Bethesda, Md., 1977-80; rsch. scientist N.Y. State Dept. Health, Albany, 1980-86; sr. staff researcher Syntex Rsch., 1986—; lectr. Albany Med. Coll., N.Y., 1982-84, adj. asst. prof., 1984-86. Contbr. articles in molecular biology and biochemistry to profl. jours. Scholar, N.Y. State Regents, 1965; fellow Columbia U., 1969, NIH, 1974; rsch. grantee NIH, 1981, 86. Mem. Am. Chem. Soc., Am. Soc. Microbiology, Am. Soc. Virology. Democrat. Jewish. Home: 467D Costa Mesa Ter Sunnyvale CA 94086-4173 Office: Syntex Rsch 3401 Hillview Ave Palo Alto CA 94304-1397

HERMANN, JAMES RAY, management executive; b. Richmond, Calif., Dec. 25, 1946; s. R. Ray and Jimmie (Ball) H.;m. Jacqueline Ferrari Feusier, Dec. 22, 1970; children: Nicole Alison, Ivette Alison. BA, San Francisco State U., 1968; JD, U. Calif., San Francisco, 1972. Bar: Calif. 1972, U.S. Dist. Ct. (no. dist.) Calif. 1972, U.S. Ct. Appeals (9th cir.) 1972, U.S. Tax Ct. 1973, U.S. Supreme Ct. 1978; CPA, Calif.; cert. fin. planner, real estate appraiser, real estate broker, life and disability ins. broker; lic. series 7 and 22 Nat. Assn. Securities Dealers. Dean Sch. of Acctg. Armstrong Coll., Berkeley, Calif., 1975-77; mng. atty. Yanello & Flippen Law Offices, Oakland, Calif., 1977-79; chief operating officer Bus. Fin. Group, Walnut Creek, Calif., 1979-81; prin. Antonini Profl. Corp., San Francisco, 1981-86; CEO Rolex Mgmt. Group, Orinda, Calif., 1985—; dir. Heald Bus. Coll., Oakland, Calif., 1992—; chmn. Wall St. Capital Mgmt., Orinda, 1987-91, J.R. Hermann Prodns., Inc., Orinda, 1985-91; arbitrator Am. Arbitration Assn., San Francisco, 1987—; pres. Nova Images, Inc., Orinda, 1992—; cons. Geneva Corp., Irvine, Calif., 1987-89, Strategic M/A Internat. Inc., Reading, Pa., 1989-90, GVA Fin. Group, Inc., Phoenix, 1990-91; lectr. Fund Raising Sch., Ind. U., 1992—; lectr. fin. seminars numerous orgns., 1984—. Author: Adding Financial Planning to Your Practice, 1984, Case Studies in Financial Planning, 1985, Accountant's Guide to Financial and Estate Planning for Business Owners, 1990; columnist Outlook Mag., 1986-88; contbr. articles to profl. jorus. Capt. spl. forces U.S. Army, 1970-72. Mem. ABA, AICPA, Internat. Biog. Ctr. (adv. coun. 1988—), Calif. Soc. CPA's (chmn. fin. planning com. 1985-87), Univ. Club (co.n. mem. 1987-89). Office: Rolex Mgmt Group 50 El Castillo Orinda CA 94563-1935

HERMES, SUZANNE ELIZABETH, health facility manager; b. Tucson, Mar. 2, 1947; d. Howard and Helene (Quass) Schatteles; m. Sept. 22, 1967 (div. Dec. 31, 1991); children: Daniel Mark, Brian Lee, Laurel. BA in Elem. Edn., U. Ariz., 1972; M of Counseling, U. Del., 1985. Cert. rehab. counselor. Tchr. Tucson Unified Sch. Dist., 1972-73, Clear Creek Ind. Sch. Dist., League City, Tex., 1976-78; instr., mentor Widener U. Brandywine, Wilmington, Del., 1979-85; vocat. counselor Intercorp, Wilmington, Del., 1975-86, Washington, 1986-88; vocat. supr. Crawford Health and Rehab., Washington, 1988-89; mgr. Crawford Health and Rehab., Tucson, 1989-92; pvt. practice vocat. rehab. counselor Tucson, 1992—. Mem. AACD, Nat. Rehab. Assn., Ariz. Rehab. Assn., Ariz. Assn. Workers Compensatiion, Ariz. Vocat. Rehab. Profls., Soc. Human Resource Mgrs. Home: 1773 N Wrightstown Pl Tucson AZ 85715

HERNÁNDEZ, FERNANDO VARGAS, lawyer; b. Irapuato, México Sept. 8, 1939; came to U.S., 1942, naturalized, 1957; s. José Espinosa and Ana María (Vargas) H.; m. Bonnie Corrie, Jan. 8, 1966 (div. Feb. 1991); children: Michael David, Alexandra Rae, Marcel Paul. B.S., U. Santa Clara, 1961, M.B.A., 1962; J.D., U. Calif.-Berkeley, 1966. Bar: Calif. 1967, U.S. Dist. Ct. (no. dist.) Calif. 1967. Sole practice law, San Jose, Calif., 1967—; lectr. law Lincoln U.; lectr. bus. U. Santa Clara. Mem. San Jose Housing Bd., 1970-73; arbitrator, judge protem Santa Clara County Superior Cts., 1979-93. Chmn. bd. trustees Calif. Rural Legal Assistance, 1973-75; bd. dirs. San Jose Civic Light Opera, 1981-83. Served with AUS, 1962-63. Mem. Calif. State Bar Assn., Santa Clara County Bar Assn. (chmn. torts sect. 1977-78, features editor In Brief mag. 1990-93), Calif. Trial Lawyers Assn., (bd. govs. 1979-82), Santa Clara County Trial Lawyers Assn. (pres. elect 1981), Assn. Trial Lawyers Am., ABA, U. Santa Clara Alumni Assn. (pres. San Jose chpt. 1977-78), La Raza Lawyers Assn. Democrat. Roman Catholic. Club: Democratic Century, N. San Jose Optomist. Contbg. editor to legal pleadings books. Office: 40 S Market St Ste 410 San Jose CA 95113

HERNANDEZ, JO FARB, museum director; b. Chgo., Nov. 20, 1952. BA in Polit. Sci. & French with honors, U. Wis., 1974; MA in Folklore and mythology, UCLA, 1975; postgrad., U. Calif., Davis, 1978, U. Calif., Berkeley, 1978-79, 81. Registration UCLA, 1974-75, 1975; Rockefeller fellow Dallas Mus. Fine Arts, 1976-77; asst. to dir. Triton Mus. Art, Santa Clara, Calif., 1977-78, dir., 1978-85; adj. prof. mus. studies John F. Kennedy U., San Francisco, 1978; grad. advisor arts adminstrn. San Jose (Calif.) State U., 1979-80; dir. Monterey (Calif.) Peninsula Mus. Art, 1985—; lectr., panelist, juror, panelist in field; vis. lectr. Am. Cultural Ctr., Jerusalem, 1989, Binational Ctr., Lima, Peru, 1988, Daytona Beach Mus. Art, 1983, Israel Mus., 1989, U. Chgo., 1981, others. Contbr. articles to profl. publs.; guest on various TV and radio programs. Bd. dirs. Bobbie Wynn and Co. of San Jose, 1981-85, Santa Clara Arts and Hist. Consortium, 1985; bd. dirs. Non-Profit Gallery Assn., 1979-83, v.p., 1979-80. Mem. Am. Assn. Mus. (mus. assessment program surveyor 1990, lectr. 1986, nat. program com. 1992-93), Calif. Assn. Mus. (chair annual meeting 1990, chair nominating com. 1988, 90, 93, bd. dirs. 1985—, v.p. 1987-91, pres. 1991-92), Artable, Am. Assn. Mus., Am. Folklore Soc., Western Mus. Conf. (bd. dirs., exec. com. 1989-91, program chair 1990), Nat. Coun. for Edn. in Ceramic Arts, Phi Beta Kappa. Office: Monterey Peninsula Mus Art Assn 559 Pacific St Monterey CA 93940-2880

HERNANDEZ, LILLIAN A., small business owner; b. Inglewood, Calif., May 12, 1959; d. John Erling and Lillian Alice (Hastings) Johnson; m. David Robert Hernandez, Aug. 11, 1979; children: Linda Marie, Amber Michelle, Christine Lee. AA, Cerritos Jr. Coll., 1981; BS in Bus., Calif. State U., Long Beach, 1986. Cert. quality circle facilitator. Note teller Bank of Am., Bellflower, Calif., 1978-79; computer operator Piping Products West, Vernon, Calif., 1981; counselor/asst. mgr. Zoe Employment Agy., Los Alamitos, Calif., 1981-82; pers. asst./quality circle facilitator Hazel of Calif. Inc., Santa Fe Springs, 1982-86; employment coord. PARTNERS Nat. Health Plans, San Bernardino, Calif., 1987-89; owner Cream Whippeeze, Riverside, Calif., 1989-91; Riverside County media coord. William Dannemeyer for U.S. Senate, 1991-92; Interview panalist City of Riverside, Calif., 1990. Chmn. Citizens' Adv. Affirmative Action Com., Riverside, Calif., 1990; founding mem. Riverside Citizens for Responsible Behavior, 1990; mem. Christian Voters League, Riverside, 1990; bd. dirs. Greater Riverside Hispanic Chamber, 1989-91; mem. Community Rels. Commn., chmn. recreation and culture, 1989-90, parliamentarian, 1988-90; assoc. mem. Calif. Rep. State Cen. Com.; mem. community rels. com., law enforcement policy com., Calif. Rep. State Com., Riverside County Ctrl. Com.; vice-chair 2dsupervisoral dist. Mem. Personnel and Indsl. Rels. Assn. Republican. Office: Cream Whippeeze 2139 Macbeth Pl Riverside CA 92507-5816

HERNANDEZ, RICK MARK, protective services official; b. Carlsbad, N.Mex., Jan. 13, 1966; s. Richard Cerda and Niuma Maria (Franco) H.; 1 child, Raquel Andrea. BS, U. N.Mex., 1989. Tchr.'s asst. daycare U. N.Mex., Albuquerque, 1985-87; office asst. II Inst. Pub. Law, Albuquerque, 1987-89; sales assoc. May D&F Co., Albuquerque, 1989-91; youth program supr. Bernalillo County Juvenile Detention Ctr., Albuquerque, 1991—. Vol. probation officer Juvenile Justice Ctr., 1987. Mem. Sigma Phi Epsilon. Democrat. Roman Catholic. Home: PO Box 35441 Albuquerque NM 87176-5441

HERNANDEZ, TONY J., computer company executive, state representative; b. Denver, Nov. 18, 1951; s. Amos A. and Estella C. (Vigil) H. BS in Social Work, Colo. State U., 1973; MSW, U. Denver, 1975; MS in Mgmt. and Pub. Policy, Carnegie-Mellon U., 1981. Exec. cons. IBM, 1981—; state rep. House Dist. 2 Colo. Gen. Assembly, 1984—; co-chmn. pub. policy com. Gov.'s Initiative Teen Pregnancy; mem. House Fin. Com., House Appropriation Com., Gov.'s Job Tng. Coordinating Coun., Superconducting Super Collider Steering and Adv. Com., Inner City Parish Bd., Hispanic Agenda Steering Com., Am.-Israeli Friendship League, Hispanic League, Family Focus; chmn. Hispanic Inst. Ednl. Opportunity and Econ. Devel.; past pres. Brothers Redevel. Recipient Commitment to Ednl. Opportunity award Colo. State U. Upward Bound, 1986, Outstanding Contribution and Work for Hispanic Community award Hispanic Agenda, 1986, Community Svc. award C.C. Denver, 1989, Pub. Svc. award Carnegie-Mellon U. Alumni, 1989, Legistator of Yr. award Econ. Developers Coun. Colo., 1989, Recognition award Hispanic Leadership Opportunity Program, 1990, Achiever award Regional and Nat. Trio, 1990, Outstanding Support Ednl. Opportunity award Colo. State U., 1991, Good Guys award Colo. Women's Political Caucus, 1992. Democrat. Home: 1285 S Clay St Denver CO 80219

HERNANDEZ-STEPHENS, RACQUEL COREEN, science educator, elementary school educator; b. Fontana, Calif., June 25, 1970; d. William George and Constance (Dominguez) Stephens; m. Joseph Hernandez, June 29, 1991. AA in Liberal Studies with honors, Mt. San Antonio Coll., 1987; BSBA, Calif. State Poly., 1990, postgrad., 1992—. Owner Advance Tutoring, Ontario, Calif., 1985—; tchr. Carden Arbor View Sch., Upland, Calif., 1987-88; tchr. 3rd grade St. Louise Cath. Sch., Covina, Calif., 1990—; prof. sci. Calif. State U., Fullerton, 1991—; pvt. tchr. ESL, Ontario, 1985—. Mem. Pi Sigma Epsilon (v.p. 1989-90). Republican. Home and Office: 2249 Greenwood Pl # C Ontario CA 91761

HEROLD, RALPH ELLIOTT, motion picture arts educator; b. L.A., Dec. 5, 1919; s. Henry Danelle and Isabelle (Baker) H. BS, St. Andrews Coll., 1951; PhD in Mgmt. Sci., Clayton U., 1978. Instr. media sci. L.A. City Schs., 1949-56; staff asst. flight ops. Hughes Aircraft Co., Culver City, Calif., 1955-57; mgr. logistics & program control N.Am. Aviation, L.A., Canoga Park, Downey, Calif., 1957-67; mgr. quality assurance McDonnell Douglas Astronautics, Huntington Beach, Calif., 1967-70; dir. motivational sci. Systematix, Fullerton, Calif., 1970-74; pers. dir. Chapman U., Orange, Calif., 1974-75; instr. Am. film heritage Rancho Santiago C.C., Santa Ana, Calif., 1976—. Contbr. numerous articles to profl. jours.; prodr. film-to-video Objective Kobe, own color footage of Kobe, Japan in WWII. Lt. col. U.S. Army Signal Corps, 1940-63, PTO. Mem. Theater Hist. Soc. Am., Ret. Officers Assn., Cinecon, Hollywood Stuntman's Assn. Home: 161 Avenida Majorca Apt N Laguna Hills CA 92653

HERR, RICHARD, history educator; b. Guanajuato, Mexico, Apr. 7, 1922; s. Irving and Luella (Winship) H.; m. Elena Fernandez Mel, Mar. 2, 1946 (div. 1967); children: Charles Fernandez, Winship Richard; m. Valerie J. Jackson, Aug. 29, 1968; children: Sarah, Jane. A.B., Harvard U., 1943; Ph.D., U. Chgo., 1954. Instr. Yale U., 1952-57, asst. prof., 1957-59; assoc. prof. U. Calif., Berkeley, 1960-63, prof. history, 1963-91, prof. emeritus, 1991—, chancellor's fellow, 1987-90; directeur d'études associé, sixième sect. Ecole Pratique des Hautes Etudes, Paris, 1973; dir. Madrid Study Center, U. Calif., 1975-77; vis. fellow Clare Hall, Cambridge U., Eng., 1984-85; vis. prof. U. Alcalá. Henares, Spain, 1991; bd. dirs. Inst. Hist. Study, San Francisco, 1983-84. Author: The Eighteenth Century Revolution in Spain, 1958, Tocqueville and the Old Regime, 1962, Spain, 1971, Rural Change and Royal Finances in Spain at the End of the Old Regime, 1989 (Leo Gershoy award Am. Hist. Assn. 1990); co-editor, contbr.: Ideas in History, 1965, Iberian Identity, 1989; editor, contbr.: The New Portugal, Democracy and Europe, 1993; asst. editor: Jour. Modern History, 1949-50; mem. editorial bd.: French Historical Studies, 1966-69, Revista de Historia Económica, Spain, 1983—; editor Memorias del cura liberal don Juan Antonio Posse, 1984. With AUS, 1943-45. Decorated Comendador of the Orden de Isabel la Católica (Spain); recipient Bronze medal Collège de France, Paris, The Berkeley citation U. Calif., 1991; Social Sci. Rsch. Coun. grantee, 1963-64; Guggenheim fellow, 1959-60, 84-85; NEH sr. fellow, 1968-69. Fellow Am. Acad. Arts and Scis.; mem. Am. Hist. Assn., Am. Philos. Soc., Soc. for French Hist. Studies, Soc. for Spanish and Portuguese Hist. Studies, Real Academia de la Historia Madrid (corr.). Office: U Calif Dept History Berkeley CA 94720

HERRERA, FRANCISCO RAFAEL, political advisor; b. Salvatierra, Mex., Nov. 11, 1943; came to U.S., 1944; s. Jess and Josephine (Rodriguez) H. BA, St. John's Coll., Camarillo, Calif., 1965; MS, San Diego State U., 1975; MPA, Harvard U., 1986. City coun. rep. City Mgr.'s Office, San Diego, 1978-80; sr. com. cons. Office of Mayor, San Diego, 1980-83; dir. intergovtl. rels. U.S. Senator Pete Wilson, Washington, 1983-85; dir. Dept. Binational Affairs City of San Diego, 1986-88; cons. San Diego, 1988-89; sr. policy advisor U.S. Senator Pete Wilson, San Diego, 1989-91; asst. to gov. for internat. affairs Gov. of Calif., Sacramento, 1991-93; internat. rels. dir. San Diego Gas & Electric, 1993—. Bd. govs. Arthritis Found., San Deigo, 1987-90; founding mem. Border Trade Alliance, 1986; bd. dirs. San Diego Arthritis Found. Recipient Outstanding Pub. Svcs. award Oxnard Harbor Dist., 1985, Outstanding Appointed Official award Calif. Hispanic C. of C., 1992. Mem. San Diego County Internat. Trade Commn. (commr. 1986-90), Harvard U. Alumni Assn. (exec. coun. Kennedy Sch. Govt., past pres. 1989-92). Roman Catholic. Office: San Diego Gas & Electric 101 Ash St Ste EB-1612 San Diego CA 92112

HERRERA, JOHN, professional football team executive; married; 7 children. BA in History, U. Calif., Davis. Tng. camp asst. L.A. Raiders, 1963-68, pub. rels. asst., 1968, pub. rels. dir., 1978-80, sr. exec., 1985—; formerly dir. player pers. B.C. Lions, 2 seasons; gen. mgr. Sask. Roughriders, 1983-84; with scouting depts. Tampa Bay Buccaneers, 1975-76, Washington Redskins, 1977. Office: Los Angeles Raiders 332 Center St El Segundo CA 90245-4098

HERRERA, ROBERT BENNETT, retired educator; b. L.A., July 24, 1913; s. Royal Robert and Rachel (Mix) H.; AA, L.A. City Coll., 1934; AB, UCLA, 1937, MA, 1939; m. Agnes Mary MacDougall, May 18, 1941; children: Leonard B., Mary Margaret, William R. Tchr. high sch., Long Beach, Calif., 1939-41; statistician U.S. Forest Survey, Berkeley, Calif., 1941-45; faculty L.A. City Coll., 1946-79, prof. math., 1966-79, chmn. math. dept., 1975-79, ret., 1979; lectr. math. UCLA, 1952-75; cons. Ednl. Testing Svc., Princeton, 1965-68, Addison Wesley Pub. Co., 1966-68, Goodyear Pub. Co., 1970-76. Mem. Math. Assn. Am. (past sec. So. Calif. sect., past gov.), Am. Math. Soc., AAAS, Internat. Oceanic Soc., Phi Beta Kappa, Pi Mu Epsilon. Democrat. Author: (with C. Bell, C. Hammond) Fundamentals of Arithmetic for Teachers, 1962. Home: 2737 S Kihei Rd # 159 Kihei HI 96753-9699 Office: PO Box 134 Kihei HI 96753-0134

HERRERA, SHIRLEY MAE, personnel and security executive; b. Lynn, Mass., Apr. 5, 1942; d. John Baptiste and Edith Mae Lagasse; m. Christian Yanez Herrera, Apr. 30, 1975; children: Karen, Gary, Ivan, Iwonne. AS in Bus., Burdette Bus. Coll., Lynn, 1960; student, Wright State U., 1975-78. Cert. facility security officer, med. asst. in pediatrics. Med. asst. Christian Y. Herrera, M.D., Stoneham, Mass., 1972-74; human resource adminstr. MTL Systems, Inc., Dayton, Ohio, 1976-79; dir. pers. and security Tracor GIE, Inc., Provo, Utah, 1979—; cons. on family dynamics family enrichment program Hill AFB, Utah, 1980-82; cons. on health care memt. Guam 7th Day Adventist Clinic, 1983; cons. on basic life support and CPR, Projecto Corazon, Monterrey, Mex., 1987—; mem. adv. com. Utah Valley Community Coll. Sch. Nursing, 1991—; faculty mem. Inst. for Reality Therapy, 1991—. Contbg. editor Inside Tractor, 1991—. Chmn. women's aux. YMCA Counselling Svcs., Woburn, Mass., 1970; chmn. youth vols. ARC, Wright-Patterson AFB, Dayton, 1974-76; trustee Quail Valley Homeowner's Assn., Provo, 1988-89; rep. A Spl. Wish Found., Provo, 1989. Recipient James S. Cogswell award Def. Investigative Svc., Dept. Def., 1987. Mem. NAFE, Soc. for Human Resource Mgmt., Inst. for Reality Therapy (cert.), Pers. Assn. Cen. Utah, Internat. Platform Assn., Women in Mgmt. (coun. mem. 1991—), Nat. Classification Mgmt. Soc. (chairperson Intermountain chpt. 1992—). Republican. Home: 3824 Little Rock Dr Provo UT 84604-5234

HERRERIAS, PAUL KEVIN, organization development consultant; b. Sebastopol, Calif., Oct. 2, 1955; s. Robert Ernest and Carrol Jane (Clark) H.; m. Danielle Ann Simon, July 17, 1988; children: Michelle Paige, Kathryn Clark. BS in Bus. Adminstrn., U. San Francisco, 1977, MA in Human Resources and Orgn. Devel., 1992. CPA, Calif. Auditor Deloitte & Touche, San Francisco, 1977-79; search cons. The Chester Group, San Francisco, 1979-81; v.p., founder Montgomery Profls., Inc., San Francisco, 1981-85; prin. Paul K.Herrerias Fin. Exec. Search, San Francisco, 1985-86; mgr. search cons. KPMG Peat Marwick, San Francisco, 1986-87; prin., founder Lear, Herrerias & Lee, San Francisco, 1987-91; exec. dir. Herrerias & Assocs., San Francisco, 1991—; exec. dir. LIBRA Group, San Francisco, 1990—. Bd. dirs. Telegraph Hill Dwellers, San Francisco, 1986-87. Bank Am. scholar, 1973. Mem. Calif. Soc. CPAs (bd. dirs., officer San Francisco chpt. 1989—, mem. long-range planning task force 1991, state bd. dirs. 1990-92, nominations com. 1991), Nat. Assn. Accts. (bd. dirs., officer San Francisco chpt. 1977-85, pres. 1983-85), U. San Francisco Alumni Acctg. Assn. (pres. 1983-85). Home: 272 Forrest Ave Fairfax CA 94930 Office: Herrerias & Assocs PO Box 537 Fairfax CA 94978

HERRICK, EARL GEORGE, accountant, financial planner; b. Inglewood, Calif., July 22, 1938; s. Charles E. Herrick and Elsie C. (Van Leeuwen) Hipsher; m. Karin RosepLesch, July 31, 1961; children: Danny, Kirk. BS in Acctg., Calif. State U., Pomona, 1968. CPA, Calif.; CFP. Plant mgr. Jer Mari Lingerie, La Puente, Calif., 1961-62; internal auditor Day & Night Mfg., La Puente, 1962-67; pers. adminstr., sr. auditor Arthur Andersen & Co., L.A., 1967-74; asst. controller Beverly Enterprises, Pasadena, Calif., 1975-79; v.p., controller Casa Blanca Convalescent Homes, San Marino, Calif., 1979-83; v.p. fin. CQ Enterprises, San Diego, 1983-89, Pacific Sun Realty, La Mesa, Calif., 1989-90; prin. Earl G. Herrick, CPA, Encinitas, Calif., 1975—. With U.S. Army, 1957-60. Mem. AICPAs, Calif. Soc. CPAs, Nat. Assn. Accts. (v.p. 1978). Office: 1991 Village Park Way Ste 155 Encinitas CA 92024-1966

HERRICK, ROBERT WALLACE, electrical engineer; b. Santiago, Chile, Aug. 7, 1963; came to U.S., 1964; s. Bruce Hale and Dianne Herrick. BS in Electronics Engring. Tech., DeVry Inst. Tech., Atlanta, 1984; MSEE, U. Ill., 1987. Sr. engr. McDonnell Douglas Electronic Systems Co., Berkeley, Mo., 1987-92; rsch. asst. dept. electrical engring. U. Calif., Santa Barbara, 1992—. Contbr. articles to Jour. Vacuum Sci. and Tech., Photonic Tech. Letters. Bell and Howell Ednl. grantee Bell and Howell Inc., 1984. Mem. IEEE, Laser and Electro-Optics Soc., Tau Alpha Pi. Republican. Presbyterian. Home: 40 S Patterson Ave Apt 202 Santa Barbara CA 93111-2012 Office: U Calif Dept Electrical Engring Santa Barbara CA 93106-9560

HERRICK, TRACY GRANT, fiduciary; b. Cleve., Dec. 30, 1933; s. Stanford Avery and Elizabeth Grant (Smith) H.; B.A., Columbia U., 1956, M.A., 1958; postgrad. Yale U., 1956-57; M.A., Oxford U. (Eng.), 1960; m. Maie Kaarsoo, Oct. 12, 1963; children—Sylvi Anne, Alan Kalev. Economist, Fed. Res. Bank, Cleve., 1960-70; sr. economist Stanford Research Inst., Menlo Park, Calif., 1970-73; v.p., sr. analyst Shuman, Agnew & Co., Inc., San Francisco, 1973-75; v.p. Bank of Am., San Francisco, 1975-81; pres. Tracy G. Herrick, Inc., 1981—; lectr. Stonier Grad. Sch. Banking, Am. Bankers Assn., 1967-76; commencement speaker Memphis Banking Sch., 1974; bd. dirs. Jefferies Group, Inc., Jefferies & Co., Inc., Anderson Capital Mgmt., Inc. Fellow Fin. Analysts Fedn.; mem. Assn. Investment Mgmt. Rsch., Sacramento Security Analysts Soc., San Francisco Soc. Security Analysts. Republican. Congregationalist. Author: Bank Analyst's Handbook, 1978; Timing, 1981; Power and Wealth, 1988; contbr. articles to profl. jours. Home: 1150 University Ave Palo Alto CA 94301-2238

HERRING, JENNY LORNA, public relations executive; b. Longmont, Colo., May 8, 1960; d. William Malcolm and Jean Ann (Smith) H.; m. Patrick Lee Brophy, May 17, 1986. BS in News Editorial Journalism, U. Colo., 1982. Freelance writer Longmont Daily Times-Call, Longmont, 1980-86; assoc. Michael Vickers Assocs. Inc., Boulder, Colo., 1983-87; acct. exec. Vickers and Knaus, Boulder, 1987—; cons. Boulder Creek Festival, Boulder, 1990-91. Chair Young Career Woman Competition Boulder Bus. & Profl. Women, Boulder, 1988-89. Nat. Fed. of Piano Guild Tchrs. scholar, 1978, Edith Welker scholar, 1978, Gene Cervi Journalism scholar, 1981. Mem. Pub. Rels. Soc. Am. (accredited, Colo. chpt.). Baptist. Home: 2888 Bluff St #137 Boulder CO 80301 Office: Vickers & Knaus 4909 Pearl E Circle Ste 203 Boulder CO 80301

HERRING, MICHAEL EARL, environmental health specialist; b. Warsaw, N.C., June 30, 1958; s. Alfred Earl and Virginia (Kennedy) H.; m. Sharolyn Marie Lynts, Sept. 20, 1986; children: Jaron Lynts, Callie Marie. BS in Environ. Health, East Carolina U., 1980; MPH, U. Tex., 1993. Registered sanitarian, N.C. Sanitarian Durham County Health Dept., Durham, N.C., 1980-83, environ. health supr., 1983-88; commd. lt. comdr. USPHS, 1988; field environ. health specialist USPHS, Fairbanks, Alaska, 1988-89, sr. environ. health specialist, 1989-91, dist. environ. health specialist, 1992—; speaker, presenter in field; mem. numerous state and local profl. environ. health coms.; former chmn. Ad Hoc Com. To Study Job Title Sanitarian. Editor, author: Environmental Health Field Reference Guide for Public Health Sanitarians, 1985. Recipient Sanitarian of Yr. award North Cen. Environ. Health Dist., 1986, cert. of merit N.C. Environ. Health Sect., 1988, Outstanding Svc. award N.C. Environ. Health Suprs. Assn., 1988, Alaska Environ. Health Assn., 1992 ; named Environ. Health Specialist of Yr. award Alaska Area Native Health Svc., 1989. Mem. Nat. Environ. Health Assn. (bd. dirs. 1991-92), Alaska Environ. Health Assn. (pres. 1991-92), N.C. Environ. Health Suprs. Assn. (exec. com. 1985-88, sec./treas. 1987, pres.-elect 1988), Ctrl. N.C. Environ. Health Suprs. Assn. (sec./treas. 1986, pres. 1987), N.C. Environ. Health Section (exec. com. 1985), N. Ctrl. Environ. Health Dist. (sec./treas. 1984, pres. 1985), Commd. Officers Assn. USPHS, Res. Officers Assn. U.S. Democrat. Methodist. Home: 10402 Country Breeze San Antonio TX 78240

HERRINGER, FRANK CASPER, diversified financial services company executive; b. N.Y.C., Nov. 12, 1942; s. Casper Frank and Alice Virginia (McMullen) H.; m. Maryellen B. Cattani; children: William Laurence, Sarah Cattani, Julia Ellen Cattani. A.B. magna cum laude, Dartmouth, 1964, M.B.A. with highest distinction, 1965. Prin. Cresap, McCormick & Paget, Inc. (mgmt. cons.), N.Y.C., 1965-71; staff asst. to Pres., Washington, 1971-73; adminstr. U.S. Urban Mass Transp. Adminstrn., Washington, 1973-75; gen. mgr., chief exec. officer San Francisco Bay Area Rapid Transit Dist., 1975-78; exec. v.p., dir. Transamerica Corp., San Francisco, 1979-86, pres., 1986—, chief exec. officer, 1991—; bd. dirs. Sedgwick Group plc (London), Unocal Corp., Occidental Life Ins. Co., TIG Holdings, Inc., Transam. Fin. Group, Transam. Leasing. Trustee Calif. Pacific Med. Ctr. Mem. Phi Beta Kappa. Clubs: San Francisco Golf, Olympic, Pacific Union, Villa Taverna. Office: Transam Corp 600 Montgomery St San Francisco CA 94111-2702

HERRITY, ANDREW CHARLES, financial executive; b. Birmingham, Eng., July 10, 1948; came to U.S., 1967; s. Charles Stephen and Bridget (Farrell) H.; m. Terry Lynn Call, Sept. 19, 1970; children: Tabitha Lynn, Elizabeth Anne. BA in Econs., U. So. Calif., 1971; MBA, Calif. Poly. Inst., 1981. Cert. community coll. tchr., Calif. Ops. officer Bank of Am., L.A., 1971-74; exec. v.p. Southwest Savs. and Loan Assn., L.A., 1974-84; chief exec. officer Mission Savs. and Loan Assn., Riverside, Calif., 1984-89; chief fin. officer Life Bible Coll., San Dimas, Calif., 1989—; lectr. in bus. and mgmt. Azusa Pacific U., 1991—; pres. Andrew Herrity Co., 1992—. Fundraising chmn. Riverside County unit ARC, 1976-79; mem. econ. devel. com. Riverside C. of C., 1976-79; ch. coun. Christian Life Ctr., Riverside, 1976—; bd. dirs. C.S. Lewis Found., 1992—. Mem. Toastmasters Internat. (Speaker of Yr. 1977, 89). Office: Calif Baptist Coll 84-32 Magnolia Ave Riverside CA 92504

HERRMAN, MARCIA KUTZ, child development specialist; b. Boston, June 16, 1927; d. Cecil and Sonia (Schneider) Kutz; m. Bayard F. Berman, July 23, 1949 (div. 1960); m. William H. Herrman, June 23, 1961; 1 child, Fred. BA, Smith Coll., 1949; MA, Pacific Oaks Coll., 1974. Cert. tchr., Calif. NIMH intern Cedars-Sinai Med. Ctr., L.A., 1966-67; ednl. therpist L.A. Child Guidance Clinic, 1967-69, Child and Family Study Ctr., Cedars-Sinai Med. Ctr., 1969-71; dir. tng., asst. project dir. handicapped early edn. program Dubnoff Ctr., North Hollywood, Calif., 1972-76; child devel. cons. various schs., agys. and families, Studio City, Calif., 1969—; cons. L.A. Child Guidance Clinic, Head Start, Child Care and Devel. Svcs., 1969-73; profl. expert L.A. Unified Sch. Dist., 1976-80; vis. faculty mem. Pacific Oaks Coll., Pasadena, Calif., 1970-76. Vol. Alliance for Children's Rights, 1992—, Child Advocate's Office, Superior Ct. L.A., 19983—; active polit. campaigns, 1950's and 1960's' mem. dependency ct. com. Children's Commn., L.A. County, 1988—; mem. L.A. Foster Care Network, 1987—; mem. L.A. County MacLaren Children's Ctr. Task Force, 1990-92; mem. community adv. com. St. Josephs Ctr., 1992—. Recipient Vol. of Yr. award L.A. County Bd. Suprs., 1986, Commendation for Dedicated Svc. to Community, 1991, Recognition award for Outstanding Svc. to Children L.A. County Inter-Agy. Coun. on Child Abuse, 1991; Sophia Smith scholar, 1949. Fellow Am. Orthopsychiat. Assn.; mem. N.Y. Acad. Scis., Assn. Child Devel. Specialists, Nat. Ct. Appointed Spl. Advocate Assn. Democrat. Jewish. Home and Office: 3919 Ethel Ave Studio City CA 91604-2204

HERRMANN, CAL C., scientist; b. East Chicago, Ill., Oct. 9, 1930; s. Cedric Carl and Rebecca (Firebaugh) H.; m. Jean Lani Kwon, June 16, 1961; children: Alix Kamakaokalani, Eric Manaolana, Conrad Kamahao. AB, U. Chgo., 1951, MS, 1956; ScD, U. Paris, France, 1974. Scientist Melpar, Inc., Falls Church, Va., 1963-65; asst. prof. Am. U., Washington, 1965-66; chemist U.S. Army Electronics Command, Ft. Monmouth, N.J., 1966-70; sr. scientist ESB Rsch. Ctr., Yardley, Pa., 1970-72; charge de rsch. Nat. Ctr. Sci. Rsch., Paris, 1972-75; dir. rsch. Synthatron Corp., Edgewater, N.J., 1975-77; project mgr. U. Calif., Berkeley, 1977-88; mgr. analytical lab. Matrecon, Inc., Alameda, Calif., 1988-89; sr. scientist Bionetics NASA Ames Rsch. Ctr.–Moffett Field, Calif., 1989-93; v.p. Water and Environment Techs., Inc., Richmond, Calif., 1993—; cons. Gen. Hydroponics, San Rafael, 1988—. Contbr. articles to profl. jours.; patentee in field. Mem. Internat. Desalination Assn., Am. Phys. Soc., N.Y. Acad. Sci., Ill. State Acad. Sci., Am. Water Works Assn., Hydroponic Soc. Am. Home: 5621 Sierra Ave Richmond CA 94805-1905 Office: Water and Environment Techs Inc 15-J Koch Svc Rd Corte Madera CA 94925

HERRMANN, CONRAD BEADLE, portfolio manager; b. Plainfield, N.J., Aug. 4, 1960; s. Lacy Bunnell and Elizabeth Occumpaugh (Beadle) H.; m. Dianna Marie Jones, Aug. 25, 1990. BA, Brown U., 1982; MBA, Harvard U., 1989. CFA. Asst. v.p. Aquila Mgmt., N.Y.C., 1983-85, v.p., 1985-87; asst. portfolio mgr. Franklin Group of Funds, San Mateo, Calif., 1989-91; portfolio mgr. Franklin Group of Funds, San Mateo, 1991—. Mem. Assn. for Investment Mgmt. and Rsch., Security Analysts of San Francisco. Office: Franklin Resources Inc 777 Mariners Island Blvd San Mateo CA 94404

HERRMANN, GEORGE, mechanical engineering educator; b. USSR, Apr. 19, 1921. Diploma in Civil Engring., Swiss Fed. Inst. Tech., 1945, PhD in Mechanics, 1949. Asst., then asso. prof. civil engring. Columbia, 1950-62; prof. civil engring. Northwestern U., 1962-69; prof. applied mechanics Stanford, 1969—; cons. SRI Internat., 1970-80. Contbr. 230 articles to profl. jours; editorial bd. numerous jours. Fellow ASME (hon. mem., Centennial medal 1980); mem. ASCE (Th. v. Karman medal 1981), Nat. Acad. Engring., AIAA (emeritus). Office: Stanford U Div Applied Mechanics Durand Bldg 281 Stanford CA 94305-4040

HERRON, ELLEN PATRICIA, retired judge; b. Auburn, N.Y., July 30, 1927; d. David Martin and Grace Josephine (Berner) Herron; A.B. Trinity Coll., 1949; M.A., Cath. U. Am., 1954; J.D., U. Calif.-Berkeley, 1964. Asst. dean Cath. U. Am., 1952-54; instr. East High Sch., Auburn, 1955-57; asst. dean Wells Coll., Aurora, N.Y., 1957-58; instr. psychology and history Contra Costa Coll., 1958-60; dir. row Stanford, 1960-61; assoc. Knox & Kretzmer, Richmond, Calif., 1964-65. Bar: Calif., 1965. Ptnr. Knox & Herron, 1965-74, Knox, Herron and Masterson, 1974-77 (both Richmond, Calif.); judge Superior Ct. State of Calif., 1977-87; pvt. judge, 1987-90; pvt. judge Jud. Arbitration and Mediation Svc., Inc., 1990—; ptnr. Real Estate Syndicates, Calif., 1967-77; owner, mgr. The Barricia Vineyards, 1978—. Active numerous civic orgns. Democrat. Home: 51 Western Dr Richmond CA 94801-4011

HERSCHER, URI DAVID, academic administrator, history educator, rabbi; b. Tel Aviv, Mar. 14, 1941; s. Joseph and Lucy (Strauss) H.; m. Eleanor Grant, June 15, 1969 (div. 1983); children: Joshua, Gideon; m. Myna Meshul, Oct. 14, 1990. BA, U. Calif., Berkeley, 1964; MA in Hebrew Lit., Hebrew Union Coll., Cin., 1970; DHL, Hebrew Union Coll., L.A., 1973. Dir. admissions Hebrew Union Coll., Cin., 1970-72, asst. to pres., 1972-75; exec. v.p., prof. Am. Jewish history Hebrew Union Coll., Cin., N.Y.C., L.A. and Jerusalem, 1975—. Author: Jewish Agricultural Utopias in America, 1981; co-author: On Jews, America and Immigration, 1980; editor: A Century of Memories, 1983; co-editor: Queen City Refuge, 1989; contbr. articles to profl. jours. Mem. Cen. Conf. Am. Rabbis, Am. Jewish Com., Assn. Reform Zionists Am., L.A. Jewish Fedn. (bd. dirs). Office: Hebrew Union Coll 3077 University Ave Los Angeles CA 90007-3796

HERSCHLER, ELIJAH DAVID, artist; b. Bklyn., Mar. 1, 1940. BArch, Cornell U., 1962; MFA, Claremont (Calif.) Grad. Sch., 1967. One man exhbn. includes Santa Barbara Mus., La Jolla Mus., Palm Springs Mus., The Kennedy Space Mus., The Aspel Inst.; represented in permanent collections Denver Mus. Art, Mus. Modern Art, Seoul, San Diego Mus. Art, U. Iowa Mus. Art, Phoenix Mus. Art, La Jolla (Calif.) Mus. Contemporary Art, Hirshhorn Mus., Phoenix Mus., San Diego Mus., Palm Springs Mus., also in numerous corp. and pvt. collections; prin. works include kinetic sculptures. Home: PO Box 5859 Santa Barbara CA 93150-5859

HERSCHLER, LESLIE NORMAN, elementary school educator; b. Hollywood, Calif., Dec. 22, 1958; s. Melvin H. and Ruth Celia (Pianko) H.; m. Jill Belman Gottfried, June 26, 1988. BA in Psychology, U. Calif., Irvine, 1979; cert. teaching, Calif. State U., Long Beach, 1985; MS, Nat. U., 1988. Educator Lynwood (Calif.) Unified Sch. Dist., 1985—; leadership team Will Rogers Elem. Sch., Lynwood, 1990-91. Crisis listener Hotline So. Calif., 1978—. Democrat. Jewish. Home: 6762 Acacia Ave Garden Grove CA 92645-3020 Office: Lynwood Unified Sch Dist 11321 Bullis Rd Lynwood CA 90262

HERSHBERGER, ROBERT GLEN, dean of architecture; b. Pocatello, Idaho, Apr. 4, 1936; s. Vernon Elver and Edna Syvilla (Kinsley) H.; m. Deanna Marlene Van Dyke, Mar. 25, 1961; children: Vernon, Andrew. AB, Stanford U., 1958; BArch, U. Utah, 1959; MArch, U. Pa., 1961, PhD, 1969. Registered architect, Idaho, Ariz. Project architect Spencer & Lee, Architects, San Francisco, 1961-63; project designer GBQC Architects, Phila., 1967-69; asst. prof. Idaho State U., Pocatello, 1963-65; adj. asst. prof. Drexel U., Phila., 1967-69; practicing architect Archtl. & Planning Cons., Tempe, Ariz., 1969-87; prof. Sch. of Architecture Ariz. State U., Tempe, 1969-87, acting dir. Sch. Architecture, 1986-87, assoc. dean. Coll. of Architecture and Environ. Design, 1987; dean, prof. Coll. Architecture U. Ariz., Tucson, 1988—; chair Environ. Design Rsch. Assoc., Washington, 1976-79, chair Architects in Edn. Com. AIA, Washington, 1983-85; pres. Rio Salado Chpt. AIA, Tempe, 1981, 74-88; bd. dirs. So. Ariz. Chpt. AIA, Tucson, 1988—, pres. 1993. Prin. works include Covenant Bapt. Ch. (AIA Merit award), Urban Renewal Plan Downtown Tempe (AIA Citation), Hershberger residence (AIA honor 1990). Bd. dirs. Rio Salado Found.; mem. Tempe Design Rev. Com., 1985-87, Tempe Elec. Adv. Com., 1982-85, Pocatello Planning Commn., 1962-65; mem. Pub. Arts Com., U. Ariz., 1988—, chair campus design rev. adv. com. Recipient Crescordia Environ. Excellence award Valley Forward Assn., 1986, Hon. Mention award Ariz. Hist. Mus. competition, 1985. Mem. Rotary Internat., Catalina Day Care Ctr. (bd. dirs.). Democrat. Methodist. Home: 4001 E Elmwood St Tucson AZ 85711-2817 Office: U Ariz Coll of Architecture Tucson AZ 85711

HERSHISER, OREL LEONARD, IV, professional baseball player; b. Buffalo, Sept. 16, 1958; s. Orel Leonard H. III and Millie H.; m. Jaimie (Byars) Hershiser, Feb. 7, 1981; 2 sons, Orel Leonard V, Jordan Douglass. Student, Bowling Green State U. Pitcher minor league teams Clinton, Ia., 1979, San Antonio, 1980-81, Albuquerque, 1982-83; with Los Angeles Dodgers, 1983—; mem. Nat. League All-Star Team, 1987, 88. Named Nat. League Cy Young award winner, 1988, Most Valuable Player 1988 World Series. Office: Los Angeles Dodgers Dodger Stadium 1000 Elysian Park Ave Los Angeles CA 90012-1112

HERSHMAN, LYNN LESTER, artist; 1 dau., Dawn. B.S., Case-Western Res. U., 1963; M.A., San Francisco State U., 1972. Prof. U. Calif., Davis, 1984—; Vis. prof. art U. Calif., Berkeley, Calif. Coll. Arts and Crafts, San Jose State U., 1974-78; asso. project dir. Christo's Running Fence, 1973-76; founder, dir. Floating Mus., 1975-79; ind. film/video producer and cons., 1979—. Author works in field; one-man shows include Santa Barbara Mus. Art, 1970, Univ. Art Mus., Berkeley, Calif., 1972, Mills Coll., Oakland, Calif., 1973, William Sawyer Gallery, 1974, Nat. Galleries, Melbourne, Australia, 1976, Mandeville Art Gallery, U. Calif., San Diego, 1976, M.H. de Young Art Mus., 1978, Pallazo dei Diamonte, Ferrara, Italy, 1978, San Francisco Art Acad., 1980, Portland Center Visual Arts, 1980, New Mus., New Sch., N.Y.C., 1981, Inst. Contemporary Art, Phila., 1981, Anina Nosai Gallery, N.Y.C., 1981, Contemporary Art Center, Cin., 1982, Toronto, Los Angeles Contemporary Exhibits, 1986, Univ. Art Mus. Berkeley, 1987, Madison (Wis.) Art Ctr., 1987, Intersesction for the Arts, San Francisco, Pacific Film Archive, A. Space, "Guerilla Tactics" Toronto, Can., Venice Bienalle Global Village; group exhbns. include Cleve. Art Mus., 1968, St. Paul Art Ctr., 1969, Richmond (Calif.) Art Ctr., 1970, 73, Galeria del Sol, Santa Barbara, Calif., 1971, San Francisco Art Inst., 1972, Richard Demarco Art Gallery, Edinburgh, Scotland, 1973, Laguna Beach (Calif.) Art Mus., 1973, Univ. Art Mus., Berkeley, Calif., 1974, Bronx (N.Y.) Mus., 1975, Linda Ferris Gallery, Seattle, 1975, Madenville Art Gallery, San Diego, Contemporary Arts Mus., Houston, 1977, New Orleans, 1977, Ga. Mus. Art, Athens, 1977, New Mus., N.Y., 1981, Calif. Coll. Arts and Crafts, 1981, San Francisco Mus. Modern Art, 1979, 80, 90, Art-Beaubourg, Paris, 1980, Ars Electronica, 1989, Am. Film Inst., 1989, Mus. Moving Image Internat. Ctr. for Photography, 1989, Kitchen Ctr. for Video-Music, N.Y., 1990, Robert Koch Gallery, San Francsico, 1990, Inst. Contemporary Art, London, 1990, Frankfurt (Germany) Art Fair, 1990, Inst. Contemporary Art, Boston, 1991, Oakland (Calif.) Mus., 1991, La Cite des Arts et des Nouvelles Technologies, Montreal, 1991, Richard F. Brush Art Gallery, Canton, N.Y., 1992, Jack Tilton Gallery, N.Y., 1992, Southeastern Ctr. for Contemporary Art, Winston-Salem, N.C., 1992, Bonner Kunstverein, Bonn, Germany, 1992, Chgo. Ave. Armory, 1992. Bd. dirs. San Francisco Art Acad., Spectrum Found., Motion a Performance Collective. Western States Regional fellow (film/video), 1990; grantee Nat. Endowment for the Arts, (2) Art Matters Inc., San Francisco Found., NY State Council for the Arts, Zellerbach Family Fund, Inter Arts of Marin, Gerbode Found., The Women's Project; recipient Director's Choice award San Francisco Internat. Film Festival, 1987, tribute 1987 Mill Valley Video Festival, Exptl. Video award 1988, 1st prize Montbelliard, France, 1990, 2d prize, Vigo, Spain, 1992, 1993 Ars Electronica, Austria, WRO Poland, Nat. Film Theater, London. Mem. Assn. Art Pubs. (dir.). Office: 1935 Filbert St San Francisco CA 94123

HERTLEIN, FRED, III, industrial hygiene laboratory executive; b. San Francisco, Oct. 17, 1933; s. Fred and Herta (Komning) H.; m. Clara Kam Fung Tse, Apr. 1958 (div. Apr. 1982); children: Fritz, Hans Wernher, Lisa Marie, Gretel Marga. BS in Chemistry, U. Nev., 1956; postgrad., U. Hawaii, Manoa, 1956-58. Cert. profl. chemist, indsl. hygienist, safety profl., hazard control mgr., bldg. insp. and mgmt. planner, biol. safety profl. Grad. teaching ast. in chemistry U. Hawaii, Honolulu, 1956-58; air pollution sampling sta. operator Truesdail Labs., Honolulu, 1957; chemist oceanographical research vessels Dept. Interior, 1957-59; with Bechtel-Hawaiian Dredging, 1959; co-owner marine survey co. Honolulu, 1959-60; radiochemist Pearl Harbor (Hawaii) Naval Shipyard, 1959-62, indsl. hygienist med. dept., 1962-69, head indsl.hygiene br., 1969-72; indsl. hygiene program mgr. Naval Regional Med. Clinic, Pearl Harbor Naval Sta., 1972-78; pres., dir. lab. and indsl. hygiene, co-owner Indsl. Analytical Lab., Inc., Honolulu, 1978--; pres. F. Hertlein & Assocs., 1970-78; asst. clin. prof. U. Hawaii Sch. Pub. Health, 1973—. Contbr. articles to profl. jours. Named Outstanding Male Fed. Employee, Honolulu Fed. Exec. Council, 1967, Citizen of Day citation Sta. KGU76, Honolulu, 1972, cert. of achievement Toastmasters Internat., 1974, expression of appreciation U. Hawaii Sch. Pub. Health, 1985. Fellow Am. Inst. Chemists (life); mem. AAAS, Am. Acad. Indsl. Hygiene, Am. Chem. Soc., Am. Indsl. Hygiene Assn., Gesellschaft fü Aerosolforschung, Gesellschaft Deutscher Chemiker, Profl. Assn. Diving Instrs. (instr. emeritus), Tubists Universal Brotherhood Assn. (life). Home: 1493 Kaweloka St Pearl City HI 96782-1513 Office: Indsl Analytical Lab Inc 3615 Harding Ave Ste 304 Honolulu HI 96816-3735

HERTNEKY, RANDY LEE, optometrist; b. Burlington, Colo., Jan. 9, 1955; s. Harry Francis and Darleen Mae (Walters) H.; m. Laura Ann Ciaccio, Nov. 28, 1981; children: Lisa Kay, Erin Elizabeth. BA, U. Colo., 1977; OD, So. Calif. Coll. Optometry, Fullerton, 1981. Pvt. practice optometry Yuma, Colo., 1982—. Precinct committeeman Yuma County Reps., 1986—; mem. bd. rev. Boy Scouts Am., Yuma, 1982—; chmn. Yuma High Sch. Bldg. Com., 1987-89; bd. dirs. Yuma Hosp. Found., 1990—; chmn. Yuma Sch. Curriculum Com., 1993. Mem. APHA, Colo. Optometric Assn. (trustee 1989-90), Lions (treas. 1987-88, pres. 1991-92, Lion of Yr. 1991-92), Coll. of Optometrists in Vision Devel. (assoc.), KC (sec. 1990—). Roman Catholic. Office: 107 S Main St Yuma CO 80759-1913

HERTWECK, E. ROMAYNE, psychology educator; b. Springfield, Mo., July 24, 1928; s. Garnett Perry and Nova Gladys (Chowning) H.; m. Alma Louise Street, Dec. 16, 1955; 1 child, William Scott. BA, Augustana Coll., 1962; MA, Pepperdine U., 1963; EdD, Ariz. State U., 1966; PhD, U.S. Internat. U., 1978. Cert. sch. psychologist, Calif. Night editor Rock Island (Ill.) Argus Newspaper, 1961; grad. asst. psychology dept. Pepperdine Coll., L.A., 1962; counselor VA, Ariz. State U., Tempe, 1963; assoc. dir. Conciliation Ct., Phoenix, 1964; instr. Phoenix Coll., Phoenix, 1965; prof. Mira Costa Coll., Oceanside, Calif., 1966—, mem. senate coun., 1968-70, 85-87, 89-91, chmn. psychology-counseling dept., 1973-75, chmn. dept. behavioral sci., 1976-82, 87-88, 90-91; part-time lectr. dept. bus. adminstrn. San Diego State U., 1980-84, Sch. Human Behavior U.S. Internat. U., 1984-89; prof. psychology Chapman Coll. World Campus Afloat, 1970; pres. El Camino Preschs., Inc., Oceanside, Calif., 1985—. Bd. dirs. Lifeline, 1969, Christian Counseling Center, Oceanside, 1970-82; mem. City of Oceanside Childcare Task Force, 1991—, City of Oceanside Community Rels. Commn., 1991—, mem. steering com. Healthy Cities Project City of Oceanside, Calif., 1993—. Mem. Am., Western, North San Diego County (v.p. 1974-75) psychol. assns., Am. Assn. for Counseling and Devel., Nat. Educators Fellowship (v.p. El Camino chpt. 1976-77), Am. Coll. Personnel Assn., Phi Delta Kappa, Kappa Delta Pi, Psi Chi, Kiwanis (charter mem. Carlsbad club, dir. 1975-77). Home: 2024 Oceanview Rd Oceanside CA 92056-3104 Office: Mira Costa Coll PO Box 586312 Oceanside CA 92058-6312 Office: El Camino Preschs Inc 2002 California St Oceanside CA 92054-5693

HERTZBERG, ABRAHAM, aeronautical engineering educator, university research scientist; b. N.Y.C., July 8, 1922; s. Rubin and Paulien (Kalif) H.; m. Ruth Cohen, Sept. 3, 1950; children: Eleanor Ruth, Paul Elliot, Jean R. BS in Aero. Engring., Va. Poly. Inst., 1943; MS in Aero. Engring., Cornell U., 1949; postgrad., U. Buffalo, 1949-53. Engr. Cornell Aero. Lab., 1949-57, asst. head aerodynamics research, 1957-59, head aerodynamics research, 1959-65; dir. aerospace & energetics rsch. program U. Wash., 1966-93, prof. astronautics emeritus, 1966—; prin. investigator numerous fed. rsch. grants; cons. Aerospace Corp., past mem. sci. adv. bd. USAF, Olin-Rocket Rsch., STI Optronics; past mem. electro-optics panel SAB, mem. various ad hoc coms.; mem. space systems & tech. adv. com., research and tech. subcom., past mem. research and tech. adv. council NASA; mem. plasma dynamics rev. panel NSF, U.S. Army.; honored speaker Laser Inst. Am., 1975, Citizens of Sendai, 1991; mem. theory adv. com. Los Alamos Nat. Lab.; vis. lectr. Chinese Acad. Scis., Beijing, 1983, 88; Paul Vieille lectr. 7th Internat. Shock Tube Symposium, 1969, 89, 17th Internat. Symposium on Shock Waves and Shock Tubes, 1989. Editor Physics of Fluids, 1968-70; contbr. numerous articles on modern gas dynamics, high powered lasers, controlled thermonuclear fusions processes, space laser solar energy concepts, space energy concepts and new ultra velocity propulsion concepts to profl. jours. Served with AUS, 1944-46. Honored speaker Laser Inst. Am. Fellow AIAA (Dryden lectr. 1977, Agard lectr. 1978, Plasmadynamics and Lasers award 1992); mem. NAE, Am. Phys. Soc., Internat. Acad. Astronautics, Sigma Xi. Office: U Washington Aerospace & Engring Rsch Bldg FL-10 Seattle WA 98195

HERTZBERG, ALANSON LEE, data processing executive; b. Berkeley, Calif., July 21, 1945; s. Lee Brown and Viola May (Knowlton) H.; m. Avril Yvette Klapper, July 30, 1966 (div. 1973); 1 child, Sean Colin; m. Jane Louclare Hansjergen, Oct. 11, 1985. BA, Calif. State U., Sacramento, 1966, MA, 1972. Cert. secondary edn., community coll. teaching, community coll. adminstrn., Calif. Tchr. Elk Grove (Calif.) Unified Sch. Dist., 1967-72, 74-85; instr. Calif. State U., Sacramento, 1972-74; coord. computer svcs. Los Rios Community Coll. Dist., Sacramento, 1983—; owner, pres. Complete Computer Solutions, Elk Grove, 1985—. Contbg. editor: Electronic Learning Mag., 1983—; contbr. articles to profl. jours.; author various computer programs. Active Elk Grove Planning Adv. Bd. to Sacramento County Suprs., 1992—. Named one of Top 10 Ednl. Computer Cons. in U.S. Scholastic Pub., 1988; recipient Great Tchr. award Cosumnes River Coll., 1989. Mem. No. Calif. Community Coll. Computer Consortium (pres. 1991-92, v.p. 1990-91), Cosumnes River Coll. Acad. Senate (sec. 1987-89, senator 1985-87), Amnesty Internat., Greenpeace, Nature Conservancy. Democrat. Home: 9635 Webb St Elk Grove CA 95624 Office: Cosumnes River Coll 8401 Center Pkwy Sacramento CA 95823

HERTZBERG, HAROLD JOEL, lawyer; b. Los Angeles, July 29, 1922; s. Irving J. and Clara (Goldinger) H.; m. Leona Garber, July 28, 1946; 1 child, Rita Campbell. BS, UCLA, 1943, LLB, 1958. Bar: Calif. 1959, U.S. Dist. Ct. (cen. dist.) Calif. 1959. Sole practice Beverly Hills, Calif., 1959-62; ptnr. Hertzberg, Childs & Miller and predecessor firms, Beverly Hills, 1962-85; ptnr. Rosenfeld, Meyer, & Susman, Beverly Hills, 1985-91, of counsel, 1992—. Author: Accounting for Fiduciaries. Mem. Pres. Beverly Hills Estate Planning Council, 1972. Served to lt. (j.g.) USN, 1943-46, PTO. Home: 1333 S Beverly Glen Blvd Los Angeles CA 90024-5239 Office: Rosenfeld Meyer & Susman 9601 Wilshire Blvd Fl 4 Beverly Hills CA 90210-5288

HERTZMAN, PHILLIP ALAN, family physician, educator; b. St. Louis, Mar. 25, 1946; s. Melvin Lester and Zelda Louise (Sherman) H.; m. Jeri Beth Berger, Sept. 1, 1971; children: Rachel, Marc. AB in Econs. cum laude, Washington U., St. Louis, 1967, MD, 1971. Diplomate Am. Bd. Family Practice. Intern in internal medicine George Washington U., Washington, 1971-72; resident in family medicine, chief resident St. John's Mercy Med. Ctr., St. Louis, 1975-77; pvt. practice, Los Alamos, N.Mex., 1977—; clin. asst. prof. dept. family, community and emergency medicine U. N.Mex. Sch. Medicine, Albuqerque, 1982—; chief family practice svc. Los Alamos Med. Ctr. Hosp., 1978-82, sec., 1981, vice chief staff, 1983; manuscript reviewer Jour. AMA, Physician and Sports Medicine, Mayo Clin. Proc., Jour. Musculoskeletal Medicine, 1990, Nature, Am. Jour. Medicine; moderator Conf. on Eosinophilia Myalgia Syndrome, 1990; mem. vis. faculty St. John's Hosp., Santa Monica, Calif., 1990, St. Louis, also others; temp. advisor WHO; coord. Toxic Oil Syndrome/Eosinophilia Myalgia Syndrome Project. Contbr. articles to med. jours. Mem. Oppenheimer Com., Los Alamos, chmn., 1985. With USPHS, 1972-74. Fellow Am. Acad. Family Physicians; mem. ACP, Am. Coll. Rheumatology, N.Mex. Med. Assn. Los Alamos County Med. Soc. (pres. 1985, legis. com., liaison com. health and environ. dept.). Home: 227 El Conejo St Los Alamos NM 87544-2428 Office: Los Alamos Family Practice West Rd Los Alamos NM 87544

HERZ, MICHAEL JOSEPH, marine environmental scientist; b. St. Paul, Aug. 12, 1936; s. Malvin E. and Josephine (Daneman) H.; m. Joan Klein Levy, Feb. 3, 1962 (div. 1982); children: David M., Daniel J., Ann K.; m. Naomi Brodie Schalit, Aug. 21, 1984; children: Nathaniel B., Hallie R. BA, Reed Coll., 1958; MA, San Francisco State U., 1962; PhD, U. So. Calif., 1966. Program coord. postdoctoral tng. program U. Calif., San Francisco, 1969-73, asst. prof., 1969-73, assoc. prof. in residence, 1973-74; exec. dir., dir. water quality tng. program San Francisco Bay. chpt. Oceanic Soc., 1974-77; nat. exec. v.p., nat. co-dir. rsch. and policy Oceanic Soc., San Francisco, 1977-84; sr. rsch. scientist San Francisco State U., 1984-88; exec. dir. and baykeeper San Francisco Bay-Delta Preservation Assn., 1989—; chmn. bd. govs. Tiburon Ctr. Environ. Studies, San Francisco State U., 1985-86; NRC com. mem. Effectiveness of Oil Spill Disperants, Washington, 1985-87; mem. com. on ocean disposal of radwaste Calif. Dept. Health, Sacramento, 1985—; mem. tech. adv. com. Calif. Office of Oil Spill Prevention and Response, 1992—; bd. dirs. Citizens for a Better Environment, 1986—, Friends of the Earth, Washington, 1989—, Aquatic Habitat Inst., 1986-89; mem. Alaska Oil Spill Commn., 1989-90, tech. adv. com. Calif. Office Oil Spill Prevention and Response, 1986—. Author, co-editor: (books) Memory Consolidation, 1972, Habituation I & II, 1973; contbr. reports to profl. publs. Chmn. community adv. bd. Sta. KQED (Pub. Broadcast System affiliate), 1979-85, San Francisco, citizens adv. com. San Francisco Bay Conservation and Devel. Commn., 1979—, chmn. 1984; mem. tech. adv. com. San Francisco Bay Regional Water Quality Control Bd., Oakland, Calif., 1979-82, Assn. Bay Area Govts., Oakland, 1983-84; mem. bay area adv. com. Sea Grant Marine Adv. Program, San Francisco, 1983-89; mem. com. Bur. Land Mgmt., Pacific States Regional Tech. Working Group, 1979-83. Served with U.S. Army, 1958-59. Predoctoral fellow NIMH, U. So. Calif., 1963-64; postdoctoral fellow NIMH, UCLA Brain Research Inst, 1966-68. Mem. AAAS, Calif. Acad. Scis., San Francisco Bay and Estuarine Assn., San Francisco Oceanic Soc., Oceanic Soc. (bd. dirs. 1984-89, 86—), Sigma Xi.

HERZBERG, DOROTHY CREWS, educator; b. N.Y.C., July 8, 1935; d. Floyd Houston and Julia (Lesser) Crews; m. Hershel Zelig Herzberg, May 22, 1962 (div. Apr. 1988); children: Samuel Floyd, Laura Jill, Daniel Crews. AB, Brown U., 1957; MA, Stanford U., 1964; JD, San Francisco Law Sch., 1976. Legal sec. various law firms, San Francisco, 1976-78; tchr. Mission Adult Sch., San Francisco, 1965-66; tchr. secondary and univ. levels Peace Corps, Nigeria, 1961-63; investigator Office of Dist. Atty., San Francisco, 1978-80; sr. adminstr. Dean Witter Reynolds Co., San Francisco, 1980-83; registered rep. Waddell and Reed, Oakland, Calif., 1983-84; fin. services rep. United Resources, Hayward, Calif., 1984-85, Ind. Planning Corp., San Francisco, 1985-86; tax preparer H&R Block, 1987; revenue officer IRS, 1987-89; now tchr. ESL, Richmond Sch. Dist. Editor: (newsletters) Coop. Nursery Sch. Council, 1969-71, Miraloma Life, 1976-82, Dem. Women's Forum, 1980-81, Stanford Luncheon Club, 1984-85. Bd. dirs. LWV, San Francisco, 1967-69, mem. speakers bur., 1967-80; pres. Council Coop. Nursery Schs., San Francisco, 1969-71; bd. dirs. Miraloma (Calif.) Improvement Club, 1977-88, pres., 1980-81; alt. for supr. San Francisco Mayor's Commn. on Criminal Justice, 1978. Democrat. Unitarian. Club: West Portal Toastmistress. Home: 2237 Haste St Apt 4 Berkeley CA 94704-2134

HERZBERG, GERHARD, physicist; b. Hamburg, Germany, Dec. 25, 1904; emigrated to Can., 1935, naturalized, 1945; s. Albin and Ella (Biber) H.; m. Luise H. Oettinger, Dec. 29, 1929 (dec.); children: Paul Albin, Agnes Margaret; m. Monika Tenthoff, Mar. 21, 1972. Dr. Ing., Darmstadt Inst. Tech., 1928; postgrad., U. Goettingen, U. Bristol, 1928-30; D.Sc. hon causa, Oxford U., 1960; D.Sc., U. Chgo., 1967, Drexel U., 1972, U. Montreal, 1972, U. Sherbrooke, 1972, McGill U., 1972, Cambridge U., 1972, U. Man., 1973, Andhra U., 1975, Osmania U., 1976, U. Delhi, 1976, U. Bristol, 1975, U. Western Ont., 1976; Fil. Hed. Dr., U. Stockholm, 1966; Ph.D. (hon.), Weizmann Inst. Sci., 1976, U. Toledo, 1984; LL.D., St. Francis Xavier U., 1972, Simon Fraser U., 1972; Dr. phil. nat., U. Frankfurt, 1983, others. Lectr., chief asst. physics Darmstadt Inst. Tech., 1930-35; research prof. physics U. Sask., Saskatoon, 1935-45; prof. spectroscopy Yerkes Obs., U. Chgo., 1945-48; prin. research officer NRC Can., Ottawa, 1948; dir. div. pure physics NRC Can., 1949-69, disting. research scientist, 1969—; Bakerian lectr. Royal Soc. London, 1960; holder Francqui chair U. Liege, 1960. Author books including: Spectra of Diatomic Molecules, 1950; Electronic Spectra and Electronic Structure of Polyatomic Molecules, 1966, The Spectra and Structures of Simple Free Radicals, 1971, (with K.P. Huber) Constants of Diatomic Molecules, 1979. Appt. to Queen's Privy Coun. for Can., 1992. Recipient Faraday medal Chem. Soc. London, 1970, Nobel prize in Chemistry, 1971; named companion Order of Can., 1968, academician Pontifical Acad. Scis., 1964. Fellow Royal Soc. London (Royal medal 1971), Royal Soc. Can. (pres. 1966, Henry Marshall Tory medal 1953), Hungarian Acad. Sci. (hon.), Indian Acad. Scis. (hon.), Am. Phys. Soc. (Earle K. Plyler prize 1985), Chem. Inst. Can.; mem. Internat. Union Pure and Applied Physics (past v.p.), Am. Acad. Arts and Scis. (hon. fgn. mem.), Am. Chem. Soc. (Willard Gibbs medal 1969, Centennial fgn. fellow 1976), Nat. Acad. Sci. India, Indian Phys. Soc. (hon.), Japan Acad. (hon.), Chem. Soc. Japan (hon.), Royal Swedish Acad. Scis. (fgn., physics sect.), Nat. Acad. Sci. (fgn. assoc.), Faraday Soc., Am. Astron. Soc., Can. Assn. Physicists (past pres., Achievement award 1957), Optical Soc. Am. (hon., Frederic Ives medal 1964). Home: 190 Lakeway Dr, Rockcliffe Pk, Ottawa, ON Canada K1L 5B3 Office: Nat Rsch Coun, Ottawa, ON Canada K1A 0R6

HERZER, RICHARD KIMBALL, franchising company executive; b. Ogden, Utah, June 2, 1931; s. Arthur Vernon and Dorothy (Cortez) H.; m. Phyllis Ann McCullough, Mar. 29, 1958; children: Diane E., Mark V., Craig K. BS, UCLA, 1958. Vice-pres., contr. United Rent All, Inc., L.A., 1967-71; dir. fin. planning Internat. Industries Inc., North Hollywood, Calif., 1971-73, v.p., controller, 1973-75, v.p. fin., 1975-79, pres., 1979—, chmn. bd., chief exec. officer, 1983—; pres. IHOP Corp., 1979—, also bd. dir. Trustee So. Calif. chpt. Multiple Sclerosis, 1984—. 1st lt. U.S. Army, 1953-56. Mem. Calif. Restaurant Assn. (bd. dirs. 1985—), Phi Delta Theta. Republican. Home: 4411 Woodleigh Ln La Canada Flintridge CA 91011-3542 Office: IHOP Corp 525 N Brand Blvd Glendale CA 91203-1903

HERZING, ALFRED ROY, computer executive; b. Kitchener, Ont., Can., June 23, 1958; naturalized, 1982; s. Alfred Georg and Kaethe (Binder) H.; m. Marjorie, Aug. 20, 1983; 1 child, Adam. BSEE, Calif. Poly. Inst., 1981. Telecom. engr. Union Oil Co., L.A., 1982-84; computer planning analyst Union Oil-UNOCAL, 1984-86; supr. facilities mgmt. UNOCAL Corp. Info. Svcs., Anaheim, Calif., 1986-89, bus analyst, 1989, mgr. planning and analysis, 1989-91, mgr. tech. & bus. assessment, 1991—; speaker ENTELEC, Dallas, San Antonio, 1983, 85. Host athletic tournament Alfred Roy Herzing Invitational Frisbee Golf Tournament, 1980—. Mem. IEEE, Toastmasters (L.A. chpt. pres. 1986-87, gov. Area 12 1987-88, adminstrv. lt. gov. Dist. 52 1988-89, ednl. lt. gov. Dist. 52 1989-90, dist. gov. 1990-91, Toastmaster of Yr. 1986, 87, 88, 89, Disting. Toastmaster 1990). Republican. Home: 20365 Via La Vieja Yorba Linda CA 92687 Office: UNOCAL 5460 E La Palma Ave Anaheim CA 92807

HERZOG, RAYMOND EDWARD, retired oil company official; b. Elizabeth, N.J., Aug. 24, 1923; s. William F. and Edna M. (Specht) H.; m. Marjorie Lucille Haisch, Nov. 19, 1944; children: Mark Lee, Peter Alan. BSChemE, Worcester Poly. Inst., 1944, MSChemE, 1947. Registered profl. engr., Pa. Devel. engr., various other positions Atlantic Richfield Co., Phila., 1947-72; various positions Atlantic Richfield Co., L.A., 1972-84, sr. policy cons., 1975-84; ret., 1984. Cons., project mgr. Exec. Svc. Corps, L.A., 1984—; co-founder, bd. dirs. Calif. Handicapped Skiers, Arcadia, 1989—; chmn. St. Barnabas Sr. Ctr., L.A., 1990—. Lt. comdr. USNR, 1944, mem. Res. ret. Mem. Ret. Officers Assn. (treas. San Pedro chpt. 1986—), Palos Verdes Golf Club, Sigma Xi. Home: 1517 Granvia Altamira Palos Verdes Estates CA 90274

HERZOG, WHITEY (DORREL NORMAN ELVERT HERZOG), professional baseball team executive; b. New Athens, Ill., Nov. 9, 1931. Infielder, outfielder Washington Senators, 1956-58, Kansas City Athletics, 1958-60, Balt. Orioles, 1961-62, Detroit Tigers, 1963; scout Kansas City Athletics, 1964, coach, 1965; coach N.Y. Mets, 1966, dir. player devel., 1967-72; mgr. Tex. Rangers, 1973; coach Calif. Angels, 1974-75, interim mgr., 1974; mgr. Kansas City Royals, 1975-79; mgr. St. Louis Cardinals, 1980-90, v.p., 1990; sr. v.p., dir. player pers. Calif. Angels, 1991—. Named Sporting News Man of Year, 1982, Nat. League Mgr. of Year, 1985. Office: care Calif Angels PO Box 2000 Anaheim CA 92803-2000

HESH, JOSEPH MCLEAN, minister, author; b. Macomb, Ill., July 7, 1954; s. William Leonard and Charlotte (McLean) H.; m. Claudia Sue Wallies, Aug. 9, 1975; 1 child, Corrie Elizabeth. BS, Ill. State U., 1976; RMT, Ellisville State Sch., 1976; ThM, Dallas Theol. Sem., 1981. Ordained to ministry Christian Ch., 1981. Chaplain's asst. Ellisville (Miss.) State Sch., 1977; youth worker and pastor Scofield Meml. Ch., Dallas, 1978-81, 81-86; youth pastor Pulpit Rock Ch., Colorado Springs, Colo., 1986—; recording artist Aspen Breeze Prodns. Author: Crossroads Series, 1990; composer, songwriter. Presenter Next Exit Tour, 1992; musician, speaker camps, confs., concerts. Home: 3826 Manchester St Colorado Springs CO 80907-4829 Office: Pulpit Rock Ch 301 Austin Bluff Pky Colorado Springs CO 80918-3922

HESKES, SCOTT EARLE, construction manager; b. San Francisco, Jan. 21, 1952; s. James and Ida Ellen (Shainsky) H.; m. Rebecca Angela Petrulli, July 3, 1983. BA, San Francisco State U., 1976. Engring. aide BP Alaska, San Francisco, 1976-80; project mgr. Scopus Constrn., San Francisco, 1980-82; ops. mgr. Swinerton & Walberg, San Francisco, 1982-86; constrn. mgr. Koll Constrn., Pleasanton, Calif., 1986—. Mem. No. Calif. Constrn. Inst. Home: 14 Holiday Dr Alamo CA 94507 Office: Koll Constrn 7031 Koll Center Pky # 150 Pleasanton CA 94566-3101

HESS, CHARLES EDWARD, environmental horticulture educator; b. Paterson, N.J., Dec. 20, 1931; s. Cornelius W. M. and Alice (Debruyn) H.; children: Mary, Carol, Nancy, John, Peter; m. Eva G. Carroad, Feb. 14, 1981. BS, Rutgers U., 1953; MS, Cornell U., 1954, PhD, 1957; DAgr (hon.), Purdue U., 1983; DSc (hon.), Delaware Valley Coll., Doylestown, Pa., 1992. Asst. prof. Purdue U., West Lafayette, Ind., 1958-61, assoc. prof., 1962-64, prof., 1965; research prof., dept. chmn. Rutgers U., New Brunswick, N.J., 1966, assoc. dean, dir. N.J. Agrl. Exptl. Sta., 1970, acting dean Coll. Agrl. and Environ. Sci., 1971, dean Cook Coll., 1972-75; dean Coll. Agr. and Environ. Scis., U. Calif.-Davis, 1975-89; assoc. dir. Calif. Agrl. Exptl. Sta., 1975-89; asst. sec. sci. and edn. USDA, Washington, 1989-91; prof. dept. environ. horticulture U. Calif., Davis, 1991—, dir. internat. programs Coll. Agrl. and Environ. Scis., 1992—; cons. AID, 1965, Office Tech. Assessment, U.S. Congress, 1976-77; chmn. study team world food and nutrition study Nat. Acad. Scis., 1976; mem. Calif. State Bd. Food and Agr., 1984-89; mem. Nat. Sci. Bd., 1982-88, 92—, vice chmn., 1984-88; co-chmn. Joint Coun. USDA, 1987-91. Mem. West Lafayette Sch. Bd., Ind., 1963-65, sec., 1963, pres., 1964; mem. Gov.'s Commn. Blueprint for Agr., 1971-73; bd. dirs. Davis Sci. Ctr., 1992—; trustee Internat. Svc. for Nat. Agrl. Rsch., The Hague, Netherlands, 1992—. Served with AUS, 1956-58. Mem. U.S. EPA (biotechnology sci. adv. com. 1992—), AAAAS (chmn. agriculture sect. 1989-90), Am. Soc. Hort. Sci. (pres. 1973), Internat. Plant Propagators Soc. (pres. 1973), Agrl. Research Inst., Phi Beta Kappa, Sigma Xi, Alpha Zeta, Phi Kappa Phi. Office: U Calif Coll Agrl & Environ Scis Dept Environ Horticulture Davis CA 95616

HESS, DOROTHY HALDEMAN, college official; b. Bareville, Pa., July 2, 1941; d. Titus Myer and Anna Mae (Haldeman) H. BA, Elizabethtown Coll., 1965. Tchr. French and German, Millville (N.J.) Jr. High Sch., 1965-67; tchr., dir. Full Day Head Start, Lancaster, Pa., 1967-72; ednl. cons. and trainer Day Care Ctrs. Inc., Harrisburg, Pa., 1972-74; supr. database Architectron Ltd., Newport Beach, Calif., 1980-83; info. specialist Woodbury U., L.A., 1983-85; asst. dir. adminstrv. computing Scripps Coll., Claremont, Calif., 1985-87, dir. info. systems and computing, 1987—. Contbg. author: CWIS and Networks, 1992, Administrative Systems, 1993. Mem. Internat. POISE Users Group Inc. (founding, bd. dirs. 1987-91, pres.-elect 1992-93, pres. 1993-94), Assn. for Mgmt. of Info. in Higher Edn. (speaker 1991), Inst. for Ednl. Computing. Office: Scripps Coll 1030 Columbia Ave Claremont CA 91711

HESS, HENRY LEROY, JR., bankruptcy judge; b. LaGrande, Oreg., Mar. 29, 1924; s. Henry Leroy and Estrid (Johanson) H.; m. Betty Lou Stone, Oct. 15, 1949; children: David Leroy, Steven Lee. BS, U. Oreg., 1947, JD, 1949. Bar: Oreg. 1949. Ptnr. Conklin & Hess, Pendleton, Oreg., 1949-52; sole practice Pendleton, 1952-73; bankruptcy judge U.S. Dist. Ct. Oreg., Pendleton, 1958-73, Portland, 1973—. Chmn. Pendleton United Fund, 1956, Umatilla County Dec. Cen. Com., Pendleton, 1952-54. Ensign USN, 1943-46, PTO. Mem. Oreg. State Bar Assn., Comml. Law League, Nat. Conf. of Bankruptcy Judges, Tualitin Country Club, Elks. Home: 7790 SW Miner Way Portland OR 97225-3028 Office: US Dist Ct 900 Orbanco Bldg 1001 SW 5th Ave Portland OR 97204-1118

HESS, RICHARD ALFRED, insurance executive, educator; b. N.Y.C., Nov. 19, 1926; s. Bernard Hess and Rhea (Abrahams) Newman; m. Mary Ellen Andrews, Apr. 3, 1953 (div. June 1981); children: Robert A., Pamela A., John A.; m. Alice A. March, Nov. 21, 1992. BA, Columbia U., N.Y.C., 1950, cert. CLU, 1959. CLU. V.p. John C. Paige & Co., N.Y.C., 1955-65, Fred S. James, N.Y.C., 1965-68, Schiff Terhune & Co., N.Y.C., 1968-78; exec. v.p. Schiff Terhune & Co., L.A., 1978-84, GNW Ins., L.A., 1984—; chmn. ins. com. Cedars Sinai Hosp., L.A., 1985-90, mem. exec. com., bd. govs., 1988—; adj. prof. ins. NYU, 1976-80; guest lectr. U. So. Calif. Extension, U. Calif., Berkeley. Capt. Larchmont (N.Y.) Fire Dept., 1976-78. With USN, 1945-47. Home: 245 S Carmelina Ave Los Angeles CA 90049-3903 Office: GNW Ins 11500 W Olympic Blvd Los Angeles CA 90064-1524

HESS, RICHARD LOWELL, broadcast executive; b. Forest Hills, N.Y., Oct. 19, 1951; s. Richard Farmer and Barbara Evelyn (McCann) H.; m. Mary Elizabeth McIntyre, Sept. 17, 1983. BS, St. Johns U., 1973. Sr. project dir. Nat. Tele Cons., Glendale, Calif., 1983—; audio/video sys. engr. ABC-TV, N.Y.C., 1973-81; dir. engring. McCurdy Radio Ind., Toronto, Ont., 1981-83. Patentee in field. Mem. Audio Engring. Soc., Soc. Motion Picture and TV Engrs., Nat. Fire Protection Assn., Constrn. Specifications Inst., Sons of the Revolution. Episcopalian. Office: Nat Tele Cons 1651 Gardena Ave Glendale CA 91204-2713

HESS, TED HAROLD, corporate company executive; b. Harrisburg, Pa., Feb. 7, 1932; s. Harold Leroy and Ferol Avalon (Stickel) H.; m. Joy Garber, May 21, 1955; children: Dianne Marie, Lorilee Evelyn, Ted Douglas. BA in Fine Arts, Pa. State U., State College, 1953; MBA, Ohio State U., 1967. Logistics mgr. Can. Air Def. Command, North Bay, Ont., 1967-70; mgmt. cons. Air Force Inspector Gen., Norton AFB, Calif., 1970-72; logistics dir. Mil. Equipment Delvery Group, Phnom Penh, Kampuchea, 1972-73; asst. dir. Tactical Air Command, Langely AFB, Va., 1973-76; material mgmt. dir. Davis-Monthan AFB, Tucson, 1976-80; mgr. prodn. control IBM, Tucson, 1980-84, mgr. product transfer, 1984-86, coord. strategic planning, 1986-87; pres. Ted Hess Cons., Tucson, 1987—; instr. in field; assoc. area chmn. strategic mgmt. U. Phoenix, 1985-89. Author: Meeting the Leadership Challenge, 1988, Strategic Planning, 1988, Managing Your Most Precious Resource--Time, 1988, Building and Maintaining the Success Team, 1991. Recipient Men of Achievement award Internat. Biog. Centre, 1987. Leadership award Biog. Inst., 1987. Mem. ASTD (pres. 1991), Nat. Speakers Assn., Am. Soc. Prodn. and Inventory Control, Toastmasters Internat. (pres. 1985-86). Republican. Methodist. Home and Office: Ted Hess Cons 7500 E Boulders Pkwy # 55 Scottsdale AZ 85262

HESS, WILFORD MOSER, botany educator, electron optics director; b. Clifton, Idaho, Feb. 18, 1934; s. Lewis William and Arvilla (Moser) H.; m. Carlene Falkenburg, July 2, 1954; children: Carl Zane, Carla Ann. BS, Brigham Young U., 1957; MS, Oreg. State U., 1960, PhD, 1962. Asst. prof. Brigham Young U., Provo, Utah, 1962-66, assoc. prof., 1966-71, prof., 1971—, dir. electron optics lab., 1975—, chmn. botany and range sci. depts., 1987—. Contbr. articles to profl. jours. Purdue U. fellow, 1963, Oakridge Inst. Nuclear Studies fellow, 1964, U. Tex. fellow, 1964-65, Swiss Fed. Inst. of Tech. fellow, 1966-67; NIH grantee 1969-74, Karl G. Maeser Rsch. grantee Brigham Young U., 1972. Mem. AAAS, Am. Phytopath. Soc., Bot. Soc. Am., Mycological Soc. Am., Microscopy Soc. Am., Phi Kappa Phi. LDS. Office: Brigham Young U 129 WIDB Provo UT 84602

HESSE, BRADFORD WILLIAM, psychologist, educator; b. Boise, Idaho, July 9, 1957; s. Richard William and Norma Lydia (Hovik) H.; m. Nicola Kay Rudd, Dec. 19, 1980; 1 child, Brenton Richard. BS, Brigham Young U., 1982; MS, U. Utah, 1986, PhD, 1989. Instr. Brigham Young U., Provo, Utah, 1980-82; teaching fellow U. Utah, Salt Lake City, 1982-86; rsch. asst. U. Utah Med. Ctr., Salt Lake City, 1986-88; postdoctoral fellow Carnegie Mellon U., Pitts., 1988-90; rsch. scientist Am. Insts. for Rsch., Palo Alto, Calif., 1989—; adj. instr. U. San Francisco, 1991—; co-dir. Ctr. for Rsch. on Tech., Palo Alto, 1991—. Contbr. articles to profl. jours. Recipient Presidential scholarship Brigham Young U., Provo, 1975. Mem. Am. Psych. Assn., Assn. for Computing Machinery. Democrat. Office: Am Insts for Rsch PO Box 1113 1791 Arastradero Rd Palo Alto CA 94302

HESSE, CHRISTIAN AUGUST, mining industry consultant; b. Chemnitz, Germany, June 20, 1925; s. William Albert and Anna Gunhilda (Baumann) H.; B. Applied Sci. with honors, U. Toronto (Ont., Can.), 1948; m. Brenda Nora Rigby, Nov. 4, 1964; children: Rob Christian, Bruce William. In various mining and constrn. positions, Can., 1944-61; jr. shift boss N.J. Zinc Co., Gilman, Colo., 1949; asst. layout engr. Internat. Nickel Co., Sudbury, Ont., 1949-52; shaft and tunnel engr. Perini-Walsh Joint Venture, Niagara Falls, Ont., 1952-54; constrn. project engr. B. Perini & Sons (Can.) Ltd., Toronto, Ottawa, and New Brunswick, 1954-55; field engr. Aries Copper Mines Ltd., No. Ont., 1955-56; instr. in mining engring. U. Toronto, 1956-57; planning engr. Stanleigh Uranium Mining Corp. Ltd., Elliot Lake, Ont., 1957-58, chief engr., 1959-60; subway field engr. Johnson-Perini-Kiewit Joint Venture, Toronto, 1960-61; del. Commonwealth Mining Congress, Africa, 1961; with U.S. Borax & Chem. Corp., 1961-90; mng. dir. Yorkshire Potash, Ltd., London, 1970-71, gen. mgr., pres. Allan Potash Mines Ltd., Allan, Sask., Can., 1974, chief engr. U.S. Borax & Chem. Corp., L.A., 1974-77, v.p. engring., 1978-81, 87-90, v.p. and project mgr. Quartz Hill molybdenum project, 1981-90; v.p. Pacific Coast Molybdenum Co., 1981-90, v.p. mining devel., 1984-90. Sault Daily Star scholar, Sault Sainte Marie, Ont., Can., 1944. Fellow Inst. Mining and Metallurgy; mem. SME/AIME, Can. Inst. Mining and Metallurgy (life), Assn. Profl. Engrs. Ont., Prospectors and Developers Assn., N.W. Mining Assn., Alaska Miners Assn., L.A. Tennis Club. Lutheran. Office: 2701 Lake Hollywood Dr Los Angeles CA 90068-1629

HESSER, JAMES EDWARD, astronomical researcher; b. Wichita, Kans., June 23, 1941; arrived in Can., 1977; s. J. Edward and Ina (Lowe) H.; m. Betty Hinsdale, Aug. 24, 1963; children: Nadja Lynn, Rebecca Ximena, Diana Gillian. BA, U. Kans., 1963; MA, Princeton U., 1965, PhD, 1966. Rsch. assoc. Princeton (N.J.) U. Obs., 1966-68; from jr. astronomer to assoc. astronomer Cerro Tololo Inter-Am. Obs., La Serena, Chile, 1968-77; sr. rsch. officer Dominion Astrophys. Obs., NRC, Victoria, B.C., Can., 1977—; assoc. dir. Cerro Tololo Inter-Am. Obs., La Serena, Chile, 1974-76; assoc. dir. Dominion Astrophys. Obs., NRC, Victoria, B.C., Can., 1984-86, dir., 1986—. Editor: CTIO Facilities Manual, 1973, 2d rev. edit., 1978, Star Clusters, 1980; co-editor: Late Stages of Stellar Evolution, 1974; contbr. more than 175 articles to profl. and sci. jours. Mem. Am. Astron. Soc. (councilor 1985-88, v.p. 1991-94), Astron. Soc. Pacific (bd. dirs. 1981-84, v.p. 1985-86, pres. 1987-88), Can. Astron. Soc., Internat. Astron. Union, Royal Astron. Soc. Can. Home: 1874 Ventura Way, Victoria, BC Canada V8N 1R3 Office: Dominion Astrophys Obs NRC, 5071 W Saanich Rd, Victoria, BC Canada V8X 4M6

HESSON, JOHN EDWARD, psychology educator; b. Phila., Aug. 25, 1938; s. John Harry and Helen Virginia (McDonough) H. BS in Social Sci., Am. U., 1964; MA in Psychology, Temple U., 1966, PhD in Psychology, 1972. Asst. prof. St. Joseph's U., Phila., 1972-76; assoc. prof. Met. State Coll., Denver, 1976-81, prof., 1981—; vis. asst. prof. Temple, Phila., 1971-72. Contbr. articles to profl. jours. Mem. exec. com. Colo. Dem. Party, 1979. With U.S. Army, 1961-63. Recipient Cert. of Recognition, Denver Dem. Party, 1983, Nat. Alliance of Businessmen, 1977, 78, Phila. Dem. Party, 1974; NSF fellow Temple U., 1969-70. Mem. Am. Psychol. Assn., Southern Soc. for Philosophy and Psychology, Soc. for Indsl. and Organizational Psychology. Roman Catholic. Office: Met State Coll 1006 11th St # 54 Denver CO 80204-2025

HESTER, GERALD LEROY, retired superintendent schools; b. Seattle, Aug. 6, 1928; s. Ernest Orien and Louise (Drange) H.; m. Carol Joyce Johnston, Aug. 2, 1953; children—Mark Wyn, Sue Ann. B.S., Wash. State U., 1950, B.Ed., 1953; M.Ed., Western Wash. State Coll., 1957; Ed.D., Columbia U., 1964. Prin. jr. high sch. Bellevue Sch. Dist., Wash., 1959-64, dir. guidance, 1964-65; supt. Vashon Sch. Dist., Wash., 1965-69, Auburn Sch. Dist., Wash., 1969-73, Vancouver Sch. Dist., Wash., 1973-80, Spokane Sch. Dist., Wash., 1980—; exec. com. People to People, 1985—; Gov.'s High Tech Com., 1988—; mem. Provost Commn. on Tchr. Edn., Wash. State U., Pullman, 1983-84; mem. adv. bd. U. Wash. Sch. Edn., Seattle, 1974; mem. Citizens Adv. Com. Higher Edn. Consortium, Spokane, Wash., 1984; bd. mem. Wash. Council for Econ. Edn., Seattle, 1984. Bd. dirs. Inland Empire coun. Boy Scouts Am., 1981-89 , YMCA, 1982—; chmn. edn. div. United Way, Spokane, 1981-82. Served to 1st lt. U.S. Army, 1951-52. Recipient Civic Fame award Rotary Club 21, Spokane, 1982; listed among Top 100 Educators, Exec. Educator Mag., 1984, 87, 89, 90; recipient Alumni Achievement award Wash. State U., 1985, 88, 93; named Edn!. Adminstr. of Yr. Nat. Assn. Edn. Office Pers., 1989. Mem. Am. Assn. Sch. Adminstrs. (adv. com. , finalist nat. supt. of yr. 1990, leadership for learning award 1992), Suburban Sch. Supts. (pres. 1982-83), Wash. Assn. Sch. Adminstrs. (exec. bd. 1971-74), 1st Class Sch. Dist. Supts. (pres. 1984), Spokane C. of C. (bd. trustees 1983-87, exec. com. 1985-88), Phi Delta Kappa. Clubs: Royal Oaks Country (Vancouver, Wash.) (pres. 1972-73); Spokane Country, Spokane, Prosperity (Spokane, Wash., pres. 1993). Lodge: Rotary. Home: S 5203 St Andrews Ln Spokane WA 99223

HETHERINGTON, CHERYL KEIKO, lawyer; b. Honolulu, July 24, 1952; d. Sidney Ichiro and Nancy (Murakami) Hashimoto; m. J. George Hetherington, Nov. 25, 1978. Student Whitman Coll., 1970-72; BA U. Wash.-Seattle, 1974; JD, Hastings Coll. Law, San Francisco. Bar: Hawaii 1979, U.S. Dist. Ct. Hawaii 1979. Counselor Planned Parenthood of Seattle-King County, 1974-76; atty. Law Offices Sidney I Hashimoto, Honolulu, 1979-82; sole practice, Honolulu, 1982—. Contbr. articles to profl. publs. Mem. Hawaii State Bar Assn., Hawaii Women Lawyers, ABA, Hastings Alumni Assn., U. Wash. Alumni Assn., Mortar Board, Honolulu Club, Alpha Chi Omega Found., Alpha Kappa Delta. Democrat. Home: PO Box 10633 Honolulu HI 96816-0633

HETHERINGTON, JOHN, ophthalmologist, educator; b. East Orange, N.J., Oct. 9, 1930; s. John and Marjorie Adele (Brown) H. BS, Springfield (Mass.) Coll., 1953; MD, Jefferson Med. Sch., Phila., 1960; ophthalmology residency, U. Calif., San Francisco, 1966. Diplomate Am. Bd. Ophthalmology. Clin. instr. U. Calif. Sch. Medicine, San Francisco, 1966-68; asst. clin. prof. U. Calif. Sch. Medicine, 1968-73, assoc. clin. prof., 1973-79, clin. prof., 1979—; Bd. Dirs. Found. Glaucoma Rsch. (sec. 1978—). Co-author: Diagnosis and Therapy of the Glaucomas, Edition 5; assoc. editor: Archives of Ophthalmology; contbr. articles to profl. jours. Hon. mem. New Zealand Ophthalmology Soc.; hon. fellow Philippine Acad. of Ophthalmology and Otolaryngology. Mem. AMA, Internat. Perimetric Soc., Glaucoma Soc. of Internat. Congress of Ophthalmology (pres. 1990—), Calif. Med. Soc., Pan Am. Glaucoma Soc., San Francisco Med. Soc. Office: 490 Post St San Francisco CA 94102-1401

HETLAND, JOHN ROBERT, lawyer, educator; b. Mpls., Mar. 12, 1930; s. James L. and Evelyn (Lundgren) H.; m. Mildred Woodruff, Dec. 1951 (div.); children: Lynda Lee Catlin, Robert John, Debra Ann Allen; m. Anne Kneeland, Dec. 1972; children: Robin T. Kneeland Willcox, Elizabeth J. Kneeland. B.S.L., U. Minn., 1952, J.D., 1956. Bar: Minn. 1956, Calif. 1962, U.S. Supreme Ct, 1981. Practice law Mpls., 1956-59; assoc. prof. law U. Calif., Berkeley, 1959-60, prof., 1960—; prin. Hetland & Kneeland, PC, Berkeley, 1959—; vis. prof. law Stanford U., 1971, 80, U. Singapore, 1972, U. Cologne, Fed. Republic Germany, 1988. Author: California Real Property Secured Transactions, 1970, Commercial Real Estate Transactions, 1972, Secured Real Estate Transactions, 1974, 1977; co-author: California Cases on Security Transactions in Land, 2d edit., 1975, 3d edit., 1984, 4th edit., 1992; contbr. articles to legal, real estate and fin. jours. Served to lt. comdr. USNR, 1953-55. Fellow Am. Coll. Real Estate Lawyers, Am. Coll. Mortgage Attys., Am. Bar Found.; mem. ABA, State Bar Calif., State Bar Minn., Order of Coif, Phi Delta Phi. Home: 20 Red Coach Ln Orinda CA 94563-1112 Office: 2600 Warring St Berkeley CA 94704

HETT, JOAN MARGARET, civic administrator; b. Trail, B.C., Can., Sept. 8, 1936; s. Gordon Stanley and Violet Thora (Thors) Hett; B.Sc., U. Victoria (B.C., Can.), 1964; M.S., U. Wis., Madison, 1967, Ph.D., 1969. Ecologist, Eastern Deciduous Forest Biome, Oak Ridge Nat. Lab., 1969-72; coor. sites dir. Coniferous Forest Biome, Oreg. State U., Corvallis and U. Wash., Seattle, 1972-77; ecol. cons., Seattle, 1978-84; plant ecologist Seattle City Light, 1984-86; supr. Rights-of-Way, Seattle City Light, 1986-91, vegetation mgmt. mgr., Seattle City Light, 1991—. Mem. Ecol. Soc. Am., Brit. Ecol. Soc., Am. Inst. Biol. Scis., Am. Forestry Assn., Sigma Xi. Contbr. articles to profl. jours.; research in plant population dynamics, land use planning, forest sucession.

HETTINGER, MARY ELIZABETH, marketing administrator; b. Winchendon, Mass., Dec. 27, 1960; d. Melvin Alonzo and Helen (Lis) Metzger; m. Kenneth John Hettinger, June 11, 1983; children: Allison Catherine, Matthew Ryan. BS in Journalism, Ohio U., 1982, MFA in Arts Adminstrn., 1984. Asst. pub. rels. dir. Berkman & Daniels Mktg. Communications, San Diego, 1984; pub. rels. asst. Larrick Mktg. Communications, San Diego, 1984; pub. rels. mgr. Reuben H. Fleet Space Theater and Sci. Ctr., San Diego, 1984-90, dir. mktg., 1990—. Recipient Merit award for ann. report Pub. Rels. Club San Diego, 1988; named to Outstanding Young Women of Am., 1991. Mem. Pub. Rels. Soc. Am., Inter-Mus. Promotion Coun., Balboa Park Communicators. Office: Reuben H Fleet Space Theater & Sci Ctr 1875 El Prado San Diego CA 92101

HETTINGER, TODD ROBERT, company executive; b. Greeley, Colo., Feb. 14, 1969; s. Lowell Duane and Jennie Lee (Trimble) H. Sr. acct. exec. Stuart-James Investment Bankers, Irvine, Calif., 1989-90; pres., CEO T.R.H. Enterprises, Littleton, Colo., 1990—; chmn. Hettinger Corp., Littleton, 1990—; pres. T.R.H. Engring. Corp., Littleton, 1990—, Hettinger Pub. Co., Littleton, 1991—; v.p. Hettinger Mech. Systems, Inc., Littleton, 1990—. Author: Deepest State of Delirium, 1988, The Oblation, 1989, Auriferous Reflections, 1990, Contemplating Evil, 1993; editor newsletter The Republic, 1987—.

HETZEL, FREDRICK WILLIAM, biophysicist, educator; b. Toronto, June 28, 1946; came to U.S., 1974; BS, U. Waterloo, Ontario, Canada, 1970, MS, 1971, PhD, 1974. Sr. CA rsch. scientist Radiation Med. Dept. Div. Radiology, Buffalo, N.Y., 1976-78; asst. prof. Biophysics Dept. SUNY, Buffalo, N.Y., 1977-78; rsch. prof. Grad. Div. Niagra (N.Y.) U., 1978; sr. radiation biologist Therapeutic Radiology, Henry Ford Hosp., Detroit, 1978-82; adjunct asst. prof. Biology Dept. Wayne State U., Detroit, 1979-85; clin. assoc. prof. Physics Dept. Oakland U., Rochester, Mich., 1982-85; assoc. prof. Physics Dept. Oakland U., Rochester, 1985-87; dir. radiobiology Neurology Dept. Henry Ford Hosp., Detroit, 1982-90; prof. Physics Oakland U., Rochester, Mich., 1987-93, dir. radiation oncology rsch., 1991-93; dir. R & D Presbyn./St. Luke's Med. Ctr., Denver, 1993—; co-organizer, guest faculty Hyperthermia and Cancer Therapy, Seattle, 1984, Madison, Wis., 1985, Durham, N.C., 1987; profl. cons. hyperthermia FDA Regulations, Protocol Design, 1986; mem. med. staff bylaws com. Henry Ford Hosp., 1989; mem. radiation study sect. DHHS/NIH/DRG, 1989-93. Assoc. editor: Radiation Rsch., 1987-91. Grantee NIH, 1979-88, 86-90 (2), 87-90, 92—. Mem. N.Am. Hyperthermia Group (memberhsip com. 1987-88, sec.-treas. 1989-91), Am. Assn. Physicians in Medicine (chmn. task group), Am. Soc. Clin. Oncology, Am. Coll. Med. Physics. Home: 1969 Monaco Pky Denver CO 80220 Office: Presbyn/St Luke's Med Ctr Denver CO 80218

HETZLER, LISA LEANNE, clinical social worker; b. Altadena, Calif., Apr. 19, 1949; d. Kenneth Paddleford and Ruth Magdalene (Adams) Knipe; m. Timothy Clair Hetzler, Aug. 15, 1970. BS in Gerontology with highest honors, U. So. Calif., L.A., 1987, MSW, 1990. Owner Wind Rose Travel Agy., Hermosa Beach and Fountain Valley, Calif., 1980-83; clin. social worker intern Jewish Family Svc., Long Beach, Calif., 1988-89, Airport Marina Counseling Svc., Westchester, Calif., 1989-90; clin. social worker Robert F. Kennedy Med. Ctr., Hawthorne, Calif., 1991-93; supr. social. svc. Rehab. Care at Brotman Med. Ctr., Culver City, Calif., 1993—. Mem. NASW, Soc. Clin. Social Work, Am. Soc. Aging, U. So. Calif. Alumni Assn., Bichon Frise Club Greater L.A. (bd. dirs., treas. 1990-91, v.p. 1993—), Los Amigos de la Humanidad. Home: 540 Marine Ave Manhattan Beach CA 90266

HEUMAN, DONNA RENA, lawyer; b. Seattle, May 27, 1949; d. Russell George and Edna Inez (Armstrong) H. BA in Psychology, UCLA, 1972; JD, U. Calif., San Francisco, 1985. Cert. shorthand reporter, 1978—; owner, Heuman & Assocs., San Francisco, 1978-86; real estate broker, Calif., 1990—. Mem. Hastings Internat. and Comparative Law Rev., 1984-85; bd. dirs. Saddleback, 1987-89. Jessup Internat. Moot Ct. Competition, 1985, N. Fair Oaks Mcpl. Adv. Coun., 1993—, vice chair, 1992—. Mem. ABA, NAFE, Nat. Shorthand Reporters Assn., Women Entrepreneurs, Calif. Shorthand Reporters Assn., Calif. State Bar Assn., Nat. Mus. of Women in the Arts, Calif. Lawyers for the Arts, San Francisco Bar Assn., Assn. Trial Lawyers Am., Commonwealth Club, World Affairs Council, Zonta (bd. dirs.). Home: 750 18th Ave Menlo Park CA 94025-2018 Office: Superior Ct Calif Hall of Justice Redwood City CA 94063

HEUSCHELE, WERNER PAUL, veterinary researcher; b. Ludwigsburg, Federal Republic of Germany, Aug. 28, 1929; came to U.S., 1932, naturalized, 1951; s. Karl August and Margarete Anna (Wagner) H.; m. Carolyn René Bredeson, Jan. 1, 1983; children: Eric W.K., Mark R., Jennifer M. Student, San Diego State Coll., 1947-50; BA in Zoology, U. Calif., Davis, 1952, DVM, 1956; student, NIH, Bethesda, Md., 1966; PhD in Med. Microbiology, Virology, Immunology, U. Wis., 1969. Diplomate Am. Coll. Vet. Microbiologists, Am. Coll. Zoological Medicine. Mgr. veterinary hosp. Zool. Soc. San Diego, 1956-61, head, microbiology/virology, 1981-86, dir. research, 1986—; research veterinarian Plum Island Animal Disease Lab., Orient Point, N.Y., 1961-70; tng. resident in vet. pathology Armed Forces Inst. Pathology, Washington, 1965-66; assoc. prof. infectious disease Kansas State U., Manhattan, 1970-71; head, virology, research and devel. Jensen-Salsbery Labs., Kansas City, Kans., 1971-76; prof. vet. preventive medicine Ohio State U., Columbus, 1976-81; cons. Syntro Corp., San Diego, 1985-88, SIBIA, San Diego, 1983-90, UN-FAO-UNDP, Maracay, Venezuela, 1979, 80; grant rev. panelist USDA, Washington; mem. com. on bovine tuberculosis eradication, com. on animal health and vet. medicine, bd. on agrl. NRC, 1992—. Contbr. articles to profl. jours. Mem. USDA (VS adv. blue-ribbon panel 1987-91), Am. Assn. Zool. Pks. and Aquariums (profl. fellow), Am. Assn. Zoo Veterinarians (pres. 1958-59, sec., treas. 1959-61), Am. Vet. Med. Assn., Wildlife Disease Assn. (v.p. 1985-87), Internat. Union for Conservation of Nature and Natural Resources Vet. Specialist Group (species survival com.), Columbus Zoo Assn. (bd. dirs. 1977-81), Am. Coll. Vet. Microbiologists (bd. govs. 1984-87), U.S. Animal Health Assn., Sigma Xi, Phi Zeta. Home: 4690 59th St San Diego CA 92115-3830 Office: Zool Soc San Diego PO Box 551 San Diego CA 92112-0551

HEVIA, MARTHA, principal, educational and counseling consultant; b. Camagüey, Cuba, July 29, 1941; came to U.S., 1960; s. Victor and Claudina (Gomez) H.; m. Suarez, June 28, 1962 (div. 1980); children: Marthe Suarez-Hevia, Dionisio Suarez-Hevia. Student, Habana U.; BS, Mercy Coll., 1971; MA in Counseling, Montclair State U., 1974; MA in Edn. Adminstrn., U.S. Internat. U., 1990. Jr. high sch. tchr. Camagüey (Cuba) Dept. Edn., 1959-60; adminstr. Head Start, Office of OEO, San Juan, P.R., 1963-67; prin., counselor Adult Learning Ctr., Dept. Edn., Newark, 1969-74; dir. Community Resource Ctr., Union Coll., Cranford, N.J., 1974-77; counselor, tchr. Ctl. High Sch., Morgan Hill (Calif.) Unified, 1977-90; prin. Cen. High Sch., 1990—; exec. bd. mem. Nat. Health Coun. St. Elizabeth (N.J.) Hosp., 1974-77, State Civil Svcs. Commn., Trenton, 1975-77, Ednl. Opportunity Program, Union Coll., Crawford, N.C., 1974-77, Bridge Counseling Ctr., Morgan Hill, 1984-87; mem., v.p. Calif. Continuation Edn. Assn., 1985—; mem. Assn. Calif. Sch. Adminstr., 1990—, Self Esteem Nat. Orgn., 1989—, Delta Kappa Gamma Soc., Morgan Hill, Calif, 1983-86. Author: Student Personnel Services and Guidance Program, 1978, Senior Information Handbook, 1986. Mem. Rotacare Adv. Com., St. Louise Hosp., Morgan Hill, Calif., 1991, The Challenge Adv. Com., City of Morgan Hill, Calif., 1991, U.S. Internat. U. Adv. Com., San Diego, 1992. Named Adminstr. of Yr. Head Start Program Dept. Labor, San Juan, 1965, Outstanding Tchr. of Yr., Ctl. High Sch., 1980-91. Mem. Morgan Hill Unified Leadership Team, Morgan Hill Unified Curriculum Coun., Morgan Hill Unified Secondary Cabinet. Roman Catholic. Office: Ctrl High Sch PO Box 927 Morgan Hill CA 95037

HEWES, DOROTHY WALKER, history educator; b. Milan, Ill., Apr. 15, 1922; d. Raymond Forrest and Maude Gertrude (Hull) Walker; m. David Danforth Hewes, June 11, 1949; children: Andrew, Christopher, Rosemary, John. BS, Iowa State U., Ames, 1943; MA, Calif. State U., Northridge, 1969; PhD, Union Inst., 1974. Various postions in cons., 1943—; prof. family studies San Diego State U., 1974-92, prof. emeritus, 1992—; chair history and archives com. Nat. Assn. for the Edn. of Young Children, Washington, 1974—; U.S. mem. rsch. com. History of Early Childhood Edn., Paris, 1987—. Author: (with B. Hartman) Early Childhood Education Administration, 1979, 4th edit., 1988; editor: Administration: Making Programs Work, 1979; producer (video tape) Linkages-Preschools & Third World Parents, 1989. Staff sgt. USMC, 1942-46. Mem. Nat. Assn. Early Childhood Tchr. Educators, Internat. Standing Conf. for the History of Edn., Orgn. Mondiale pour l'Education Prescholaire, Phi Beta Delta (charter), Delta Phi Upsilon (hon.). Office: San Diego State U 5300 Campanile Dr San Diego CA 92182-0282

HEWITT, EDWIN, mathematician, educator; b. Everett, Wash., Jan. 20, 1920; s. Irenaeus Prime and Margaret (Guthrie) H.; m. Carol Blanchard, Mar. 4, 1944 (div. Apr. 1962); children: Margaret, Elizabeth; m. Pamela Jones Meyer, May 28, 1964 (div. Oct. 1973). A.B., Harvard, 1940, M.A., 1941, Ph.D., 1942. Ops. analyst USAAF, 1943-45; Guggenheim fellow, mem. Inst. Advanced Study, 1945-46, 55-56; asst. prof. math. Bryn Mawr Coll., 1946-47; lectr. U. Chgo., 1947-48; mem. faculty U. Wash., Seattle, 1948—, prof. math., 1954-86, prof. math. emeritus, 1986—; vis. prof. U. Uppsala, Sweden, 1951-52, Australian Nat. U., Canberra, 1963, 70, 76, U. Tex., 1972-73, Math. Inst. of Acad. Scis., USSR, 1969-70, 73, 76, U. New S. Wales, 1976, 78, 82, U. Erlangen-Nürnberg, 1975-76, 86, U. Hokkaido (Japan), 1982, U. Passau, (Fed. Republic Germany), 1986, U. Fairbanks, Ala., 1983; Mem. div. math. NRC, 1957-69, exec. com, 1960-62, 67-69; mem. U.S. Nat. Com. for Math., 1973-77, chmn., 1975-77. Author: Theory of Functions of a Real Variable, 1961, (with Kenneth A. Ross) Abstract Harmonic Analysis I, 1963, Vol. II, 1970, (with Karl R. Stromberg) Real and Abstract Analysis, 1965; also research papers. Recipient Alexander von Humboldt Found. prize, 1975, 86. Mem. Am. Math. Soc. (council 1955-65), Math. Assn. Am., Phi Beta Kappa, Sigma Xi. Home: 5624 56th Ave NE Seattle WA 98105-2163 Office: U of Wash Dept Mathematics GN 50 Seattle WA 98195

HEWITT, JERENE CLINE, educator; b. Chinook, Mont., Dec. 25, 1917; d. Charles G. and Dorothy Elizabeth (Strother) Grobee; m. Ronald A. Cline, 1938 (dec.); children: Alan, Scott, Mike; m. William F. Hewitt, June 25, 1977 (dec.). BA, Calif., Irvine, 1966, MFA, 1968, PhD, 1981. Mgr. dept. correspondence Dun & Bradstreet, L.A., 1939-41; statistician Lockheed, 1941-44; freelance writer, editor, 1948—; teaching asst. U. Calif., Irvine, 1966-67, teaching assoc., 1967-68; asst. prof. English Calif. State U., L.A., 1968-71; assoc. prof. Pasadena (Calif.) City Coll., 1971-80, prof., 1980-83, dir. creative writing program dept. English, 1973-83, prof. emerita, 1983—; owner Words, Inc., Whittier, Calif. Author: Selected Poems, 1968, Essentials, 1972, The Epigram in English, 1981; contbr. poetry, articles and short stories to publs. Mem. AAUP, MLA, Acad. Am. Poets, Writers' Club Whittier (pres. 1962-64, bd. dirs.), PCC Retirees Assn. (bd. dirs.), UCLA Alumni Scholarships. Home: 13713 Philadelphia St Whittier CA 90601-4423

HEWITT, WILLIAM JAMES, municipal official; b. Apr. 29, 1944; m. Sharon Hewitt; 3 children. BS, Brandon (Can.) U.; cert. in adult edn., Red River C.C., Winnipeg, Can.; cert. in pub. adminstrn., Assiniboine Coll., Brandon; cert. in fire svc. mgmt., Internat. City Mgmt. Assn. cert. fire fighter, fire prevention officer, fire svc. instr., Can. Vol. fire fighter Virden Vol. Fire Dept., 1964-68; fire fighter City of Brandon Fire Dept., 1968-73; asst. fire commr. Office Manitoba Fire Commr., 1973-78, mgr. field svcs. sect., 1978-86; fire chief City of Saskatoon, Can., 1986—; developer Manitoba Fire Coll., apptd. prin., 1978; past chair Manitoba Fire Svcs. Mobile Radio Comm. Com., Manitoba Fire Coll. Protection Tech. Adv. Com., Manitoba Pub. Fire Safety Edn. Com. Contbr. articles to profl. jours.; presenter confs. in Boston, Memphis, Cin., Toronto, Regina, Yellowknife, Winnipeg, Ottawa, others; speaker in field. Mem. Internat. Soc. Fire Svc. Instrs. (bd. dirs. 1976-92), Internat. City Mgmt. Assn. (instr. firesvc. adminstrn. program), Internat. Fire Svcs. Tng. Assn. (fire svc. instr. textbook and fire dept. ops. textbook coms. 1976-81), Internat, Assn. Fire Chiefs (1st v.p. Can. divsn.), Nat. Fire Protection Assn., Can. Fire Chief's Assn. (bd. dirs.), Sask. Fire Chief's Assn. (pres.), Sask. Profl. Qualifications and Standards Bd. (chmn.), Sask. C. of C., N.D. State Fireman's Assn. (hon. life). Office: Fire Depart, City Hall, Saskatoon, SK Canada S7K 0J5*

HEWLETT, WILLIAM (REDINGTON), manufacturing company executive, electrical engineer; b. Ann Arbor, Mich., May 20, 1913; s. Albion Walter and Louise (Redington) H.; m. Flora Lamson, Aug. 10, 1939 (dec. 1977); children: Eleanor Hewlett Gimon, Walter B., James S., William A., Mary Hewlett Jaffe; m. Rosemary Bradford, May 24, 1978. BA, Stanford U., 1934, EE, 1939; MS, MIT, 1936; LLD (hon.), U. Calif., Berkeley, 1966, Yale U., 1976, Mills Coll., 1983; DSc (hon.), Kenyon Coll., 1978, Poly. Inst. N.Y., 1978; LHD (hon.), Johns Hopkins U., 1985; EngD (hon.), U. Notre Dame, 1980, Utah State U., 1980, Dartmouth Coll., 1983; PhD, Rand Grad. Inst.; D Electronic Sci. (hon.), U. Bologna, Italy, 1989; HHD(hon.), Santa Clara U., 1991. Electromedical researcher, 1936-39; co-founder Hewlett-Packard Co., Palo Alto, Calif., 1939, ptnr., 1939-46, exec. v.p., dir., 1947-64, pres., 1964-77, chief exec. officer, 1969-78, chmn. exec. com., 1977-83, vice chmn. bd. dirs., 1983-87, emeritus dir., 1987—; mem. internat. adv. council Wells Fargo Bank, 1986-92; trustee Rand Corp., 1962-72; trustee Carnegie Inst., Washington, 1971-90, trustee emeritus, 1990—, chmn. bd. 1980-86; dir. Overseas Devel. Council, 1969-77; bd. dirs. Inst. Radio Engrs. (now IEEE), 1950-57, pres. 1954; coord. chpt. on rsch. in industry for 5-Yr. Outlook Report, NAS, 1980-81; mem. adv. coun. on edn. and new techs. The Tech. Ctr. of Silicon Valley, 1987-88; past bd. dirs. Chrysler Corp., FMC Corp., Chase Manhattan Bank, Utah Internat. Inc. Contbr. articles to profl. jours.; patentee in field. Trustee Stanford U., 1963-74, Mills Coll., Oakland, Calif., 1958-68; mem. Pres.'s Gen. Adv. Com. on Fgn. Assistance Programs, Washington, 1965-68, Pres.'s Sci. Adv. Com., 1966-69; San Francisco regional panel Commn. on White House Fellows, 1969-70, chmn., 1970; pres. bd. dirs. Palo Alto Stanford Hosp. Ctr., 1956-58, bd. dirs., 1958-62; dir. Drug Abuse Council, Washington, 1972-74, Kaiser Found. Hosp. & Health Plan Bd., 1972-78; chmn. The William and Flora Hewlett Found., 1966—; bd. dirs. San Francisco Bay Area Council, 1969-81, Inst. Medicine, Washington, 1971-72, The Nat. Acads. Corp., 1986—, Monterey Bay Aquarium Rsch. Inst., 1987—, Univ. Corp. for Atmospheric Rsch. Found., 1986-88. Lt. col. AUS, 1942-45. Recipient Calif. Mfr. of Yr. Calif. Mfrs. Assn., 1969, Bus. Statesman of Yr. Harvard Bus. Sch. No. Calif., 1970, Medal of Achievement Western Electronic Mfrs. Assn., 1971, Industrialist of Yr. (with David Packard) Calif. Mus. Sci. and Industry and Calif. Mus. Found., 1973, Award with David Packard presented by Scientific Apparatus Makers Assn., 1975, Corp. Leadership award MIT, 1976, Medal of Honor City of Boeblingen, Germany, 1977, Herbert Hoover medal for disting. service Stanford U. Alumni Assn., 1977, Henry Heald award Ill. Inst. Tech., 1984, Nat. Medal of Sci. U.S. Nat. Sci. Com., 1985, Laureate award Santa Clara County BUs. Hall of Fame Jr. Achievement, 1987, World Affairs Coun. No. Calif. award, 1987, Degree of Uncommon Man award Stanford U., 1987, Laureate award

Nat. Bus. Hall of Fame Jr. Acievement, 1988; Decorated Comdr.'s Cross Order of Merit Fed. Republic Germany, 1987, John M. Fluke Sen. Meml. Pioneer award, Electronics Test Mag., 1990, Silicon Valley Engring. Hall of Fame award Silicon Valley Engring. Coun., 1991, Exemplary Leader award Am. Leadership Forum, 1992, Alexis de Tocqueville Soc. award United Way, Santa Clara County, 1991, Nat. Inventors Hall of Fame award Nat. Inventors Hall of Fame Found. Akron, 1992, NAE Founders' award, 1993. Fellow NAE, IEEE (life fellow, Founders medal with David Packard 1973), Franklin Inst. (life, Vermilye medal with David Packard 1976), Am. Acad. Arts and Scis.; mem. NAS (panel on advanced tech. competition 1982-83, president's circle 1989—), Instrument Soc. Am. (hon. life), Am. Philos. Soc., Calif. Acad. Sci. (trustee 1963-68), Assn. Quadrato della Radio, Century Assn. N.Y.C. Office: Hewlett-Packard Co 1501 Page Mill Rd Palo Alto CA 94304-1100

HEXT, KATHLEEN FLORENCE, regulatory compliance officer; b. Bellingham, Wash., Oct. 7, 1941; d. Benjamin Byron and Sarah Debell (Youngquist) Gross.; m. George Ronald Hext, June 13, 1964 (div. 1972); m. William H. Lewis, Nov. 14, 1992. BA magna cum laude, Lewis & Clark Coll., Portland, Oreg., 1963; MA, Stanford U., 1964; MBA, UCLA, 1979. CPA; chartered bank auditor; cert. info. systems auditor. Chief exec. officer Internat. Lang. Ctr., Rome, 1970-77; sr. auditor Peat, Marwick, Mitchell & Co., L.A., 1979-81; mgr. fin. audit Lloyds Bank, L.A., 1981-83, mgr. EDP audit, 1983-85; dir. corp. audit First Interstate Bancorp, L.A., 1985-89, sr. v.p., gen. auditor, 1989-91, sr. v.p., chief compliance officer, 1991—; treas., Arcadia H.O. Assoc., El Monte, Calif., 1982-84, 86-88, pres., 1985. Recipient Edward W. Carter award UCLA, 1979. Mem. AICPA, Inst. Internal Auditors, Calif. Soc. CPA. Republican. Episcopalian. Avocations: photography, microcomputers, reading. Home: 1226 Upland Hills Dr S Upland CA 91786-9173 Office: First Interstate Bancorp 633 W 5th St Ste 7-11 Los Angeles CA 90071-2005

HEY, NIGEL STEWART, communications executive; b. Morecambe, Eng., June 23, 1936; came to U.S., 1947, naturalized, 1955; s. Aaron and Margery (Kershaw) H.; m. Miriam L. Lamb, Oct. 13, 1960 (div. 1975); children—Brian Douglas, Jocelyn Anne, Jonathan Aaron; m. Sue Ann Gunn, July 21, 1978. B.A., U. Utah, 1958; Ph.D., Internat. Coll., London, 1980. Communications dir. Weltech Coll., Salt Lake City, 1961-64; exec. editor Newspaper Printing Corp., Albuquerque, 1964-67; head media relations Sandia Nat. Labs., Albuquerque, 1967-72, supr. pub. info., 1982-92; mgr. mgmt.info., 1992—; editorial dir. IMSworld Publs., London, 1972-82. Author: The Mysterious Sun, 1971; How Will We Feed the Hungry Billions?, 1972; How Will We Explore the Outer Planets, 1973; assoc. editor Bermuda Mid-Ocean News, 1958-61; exec. editor Albuquerque News, 1964-67; assoc. pub. World Drug Market Manual, 1972-82; editor Eurosci. Intelligence Report, 1972-76; pub. ILAC Directory, 1981-82; assoc. editor Manufacturing Technology, Energy and Environment, Testing Technology, 1990—. Mem. AAAS, Pub. Rels. Soc. Am., Nat. Assn. Sci. Writers, Assn. Brit. Sci. Writers. Home: 701 Alondra Ln NW Albuquerque NM 87114-1101 Office: Sandia Nat Labs MS 4524 Albuquerque NM 87185-5800

HEYCK, THEODORE DALY, lawyer; b. Houston, Apr. 17, 1941; s. Theodore Richard and Gertrude Paine (Daly) H. BA, Brown U., 1963; postgrad. Georgetown. U., 1963-65, 71-72; JD, N.Y. Law Sch., 1979. Bar: N.Y. 1980, Calif. 1984, U.S. Ct. Appeals (2nd cir.) 1984, U.S. Supreme Ct. 1984, U.S. Dist. Ct. (so. and ea. dists.) N.Y. 1980, U.S. Dist. Ct. (we. and no. dists.) N.Y. 1984, U.S. Dist. Ct. (cen. and so. dists.) Calif. 1984, U.S. Ct. Appeals (9th cir.) 1986. Paralegal dist. atty. Bklyn., 1975-79; asst. dist. atty. Bklyn. dist., Kings County, N.Y., 1979-85; dep. city atty., L.A., 1985—; bd. dirs. Screen Actors Guild, N.Y.C., 1977-78. Mem. ABA, AFTRA, Bklyn. Bar Assn., Assn. Trial Lawyers Am., N.Y. Trial Lawyers Assn., N.Y. State Bar Assn., Calif. Bar Assn., Fed. Bar Council, L.A. County Bar Assn., Screen Actors Guild, Actors Equity Assn., Nat. Acad. TV Arts and Scis., Screen Actors Guild, Home: 2106 E Live Oak Dr Los Angeles CA 90068-3639 Office: Office City Atty City Hall E 200 N Main St Los Angeles CA 90012-4110

HEYDMAN, ABBY MARIA, academic dean; b. Des Moines, June 1, 1943; d. Frederick Edward and Zeta Margaret (Harrington) Hitchcock; m. Frank J. Heydman, Dec. 20, 1967; 1 child, Amy Lee. BS, Duchesne Coll., 1967; MN, U. Wash., 1969; PhD, U. Calif., Berkeley, 1987. Registered nurse, Calif. Staff nurse Bergan Mercy Hosp., Omaha, 1964-65; student health nurse St. Joseph's Hosp., Omaha, 1965-66, instr. sch. nursing, 1966-68; staff nurse Ballard Community Hosp., Seattle, 1968-69; instr. Creighton U., Omaha, 1969-70, asst. prof., 1970-74, acting dean, 1971-72; chairperson nursing dept. St. Mary's Coll., Moraga, Calif., 1978-85; dean nursing program Samuel Merritt-Saint Mary's Coll., Oakland and Moraga, Calif., 1985—; acad. dean Samuel Merritt Coll., Oakland, 1989—; lectr. U. Calif., San Francisco, 1974-75. Contbr. articles to profl. jours. Chmn. Newman Hall Community Council, Berkeley, 1985-87; bd. dirs. Oakland YMCA, 1981-83. Mem. ANA, Calif. Assn. Colls. of Nursing (sec. 1984-86, pres. 1986-88), Am. Assn. Colls. of Nursing (program com. 1991—), Calif. Nurses Found. (bd. dirs. 1986-88), Nat. League for Nursing, Sigma Theta Tau, Phi Kappa Delta. Roman Catholic. Home: 244 Lakeside Dr Oakland CA 94612 Office: Samuel Merritt Coll 370 Hawthorne Ave Oakland CA 94609

HEYER, CAROL ANN, illustrator; b. Cuero, Tex., Feb. 2, 1950; d. William Jerome and Merlyn Mary (Hutson) H. BA, Calif. Lutheran U., 1974. Freelance artist various cos., Thousand Oaks, Calif., 1974-79; computer artist Image Resource, Westlake Village, Calif., 1979-81; staff writer, artist Lynn-Davis Prodns., Westlake Village, Calif., 1981-87; art dir. Northwind Studios Internat., Camarillo, Calif., 1988-89; illustrator Touchmark, Thousand Oaks, 1989—; represented by Bush Galleries; cons. art dir., writer Lynn-Wenger Prodns., 1987-89; guest speaker Thousand Oaks Libr., Authors' Faire, Calif. Luth. U.; judge Mag. Merit award Soc. Children's Book Writers, 1990. Illustrator (children's books) A Star in the Pasture, 1988, The Dream Stealer, 1989, The Golden Easter Egg, 1989, All Things Brigt and Beautiful, 1992, Rapunzel, 1992, Prancer, The Artist Market, also cover art for Dragon mag., Dungeon mag., Aboriginal Science Fiction mag. and various novels, books and games including (books) Bugs Bunny Coloring Book, Candyland Work Book, The Dragon Sleeps Step Ahead Workbook; interior art for various publs. including (mags.) Amazing Stories two covers, Interzone, Aboriginal Science Fiction Mag., Alfred Hitchcocks Mystery Magazine,(book) Tome of Magic (also art for game cards); writer (screenplay) Thunder Run, 1986; illustrator, writer (children's books) Beauty and the Beast, 1989, The Easter Story, 1989, The Christmast Story, Excalibur, Robin Hood, 1993; paintings for line of Fantasy Art Prints, Scafa/Tornabene, religious art prints. Recipient Lit. award City of Oxnard Cultural Arts Commn. and Carnegie Art Inst., 1992, Best Cover Art Boomerang award, 1989, Cert. of Merit Soc. Illustrators, 1990-92, Cert. Excellence Alumni Career Achievement award Calif. Luth. U., 1993, Print's Regional Design Annual award, 1992. Mem. Soc. Children's Book Writers (Magazine Merit award 1988, judge 1990), Assn. Sci. Fiction and Fantasy Artists (nominated 3 Chesley awards, 1991), Soc. of Illustrators (cert. Merit 1990), Westlake Village Art Guild. Home and Office: Touchmark 925 Ave Arboles Thousand Oaks CA 91360

HEYL, ALLEN VAN, JR., geologist; b. Allentown, Pa., Apr. 10, 1918; s. Allen Van and Emma (Kleppinger) H.; student Muhlenberg Coll., 1936-37; BS in Geology, Pa. State U., 1941; PhD in Geology, Princeton U., 1950; m. Maxine LaVon Hawke, July 12, 1945; children: Nancy Caroline, Allen David Van. Field asst., govt. geologist Nfld. Geol. Survey, summers 1937-40, 42; jr. geologist U.S. Geol. Survey, Wis., 1943-45, asst. geologist, 1945-47, assoc. geologist, 1947-50, geologist, Washington and Beltsville, Md., 1950-67; staff geologist, Denver, 1968-90; cons. geologist 1990—; disting. lectr. grad. coll. Beijing, China and Nat. Acad. Sci., 1988; chmn. Internat. Commn. Tectonics of Ore Deposits. Fellow Instn. Mining and Metallurgy (Gt. Brit.), Geol. Soc. Am., Am. Mineral. Soc., Soc. Econ. Geologists; mem. Inst. Genesis of Ore Deposits, Geol. Soc. Wash., Colo. Sci. Soc., Rocky Mountain Geol. Soc., Friends of Mineralogy (hon. life), Evergreen Naturalist Audubon Soc., Sigma Xi, Alpha Chi Sigma. Lutheran. Contbr. numerous articles to profl. jours., chpts. to books. Home: PO Box 1052 Evergreen CO 80439-1052

HEYMAN, IRA MICHAEL, university chancellor, law educator; b. N.Y.C., May 30, 1930; s. Harold Albert and Judith (Sobel) H.; m. Therese Helene Thau, Dec. 17, 1950; children: Stephen Thomas (dec.), James Nathaniel. AB in Govt., Dartmouth Coll., 1951; JD, Yale U., 1956; LLD (hon.), U. Pacific, 1981, Hebrew Union Coll., 1984, U. Md., 1986, SUNY, Buffalo, 1990. Bar: N.Y. 1956, Calif. 1961. Legis. asst. to U.S. Senator Ives, 1950-51; assoc. Carter, Ledyard & Milburn, N.Y.C., 1956-57; law clk. to presiding justice U.S. Ct. Appeals (2d cir.), New Haven, 1957-58; chief law clk. to Supreme Ct. Justice Earl Warren, 1958-59; acting assoc. prof. law U. Calif., Berkeley, 1959-61, prof. law, 1961—, prof. city and regional planning, 1966—, vice chancellor, 1974-80, chancellor, 1980-90; vis. prof. Yale Law Sch., 1963-64, Stanford Law Sch., 1971-72; bd. dirs. Pacific Gas & Electric Co., 1985—. Editor Yale Law Jour.; contbr. articles to profl. jours. Sec. Calif. adv. com. U.S. Commn. Civil Rights, 1962-67; trustee Dartmouth Coll., 1982—, chmn., 1991—; mem. Lawyers' Com. for Civil Rights under Law, 1977—; chmn. exec. com. Nat. Assn. State Univs. and Land Grant Colls., 1986; bd. regents Smithsonian Instn., 1990—. 1st lt. USMC, 1951-53, capt. Res. ret. Decorated chevalier Legion of Honor (France). Democrat. Office: U Calif Sch Law Berkeley CA 94720

HEYNSSENS, JULIE B., electrical engineer; b. Augusta, Ga., May 31, 1965; d. Vernon Broadus and Dorothy May (Sheffield) Bodenheimer; m. Paul B. Heynssens, June 27, 1987; children: Gwendolyn May, Ian Paul. BSEE, Auburn U., 1987; MSEE, Ariz. State U., 1991. Elec. engr. Motorola, Cellular, Arlington Heights, Ill., 1990-92; engr. Nat. Optical Astron. Observatories, Tucson, 1992—. Mem. exec. com. Lamar County Republican Party, Hattiesburg, Miss., 1982-84; pres. Dunwoody Young Republicans, Atlanta, 1981-82. Mem. IEEE, Women in Astronomy, Eta Kappa Nu. Home: PO Box 40067 Tucson AZ 85717 Office: NOAO PO Box 26732 Tucson AZ 85726-6732

HEYWOOD, THOMAS KAY, academic athletic coordinator, coach; b. Salt Lake City, Mar. 19, 1959; s. Joseph Fred and Rita (Heywood) H.; m. Sherri Lynnette Garbett, May 9, 1981; children: Joseph Jack, Alisha Ann, Kirt Thomas, Spencer Allen. AAS, Ricks Coll., Rexburg, Idaho, 1981; BA, Weber U., 1984; MS, Brigham Young U., 1987. Sales mgr. Utah Jazz, 1980-81; transformer mgr. Utah Power and Light, 1981-83; profl. basketball player (drafted) Golden State Warriors, 1983; profl. basketball player Francana Brazil Basketball, 1983-84, C.B.A. Basketball, Casper, Wyo., 1984-85; tchr., coach Morgan High Sch. Sem. (LDS Ch.), Utah, 1985-86; admissions coord., asst. coach Ricks Coll., Rexburg, Idaho, 1986-92; dir. assistantships Ricks Coll., Rexburg, 1987-92, dir. selective recruitment, 1989-92; athletic acad. coord., head women's basketball coach, asst. men's basketball coach Colo. Northwestern Community Coll., 1992—. Asst. scoutmaster Boy Scouts Am., Rexburg, 1987, scout explorer basketball coach, 1987; mem. Make-a-Wish Found., 1991. Recipient Best Basketball Game Ever Played award Ricks Coll., 1978, Basketball award Big Sky Athletic All Conf., 1983, West Valley City First Athlete of Yr. award West Valley C. of C., 1985. Mem. LDS Ch. Home: 227 Ridge Rd Rangely CO 81648 Office: Colo Northwestern Coll 500 Kennedy Dr Rangely CO 81648-3598

HEYWOOD, TOM TURNER, mining engineer; b. Rochdale, Lancashire, Eng., Aug. 1, 1925; came to U.S., 1975; s. Thomas Taylor and Gladys (Turner) H.; m. Betty Dunlop, May 9, 1952 (dec. June 1974); children: Sally Anne, Ian Gordon. BSc in Engring. and Mining, Royal Sch. of Mines, London, 1945; A.R.S.M., Assoc. Royal Sch. Mines, London, 1945. Chartered engr., U.K. Jr. mining engr. C.P. Manganese Ore Co. Ltd., Nagpur, India, 1945-47; shift boss Geita (Tanzania) Gold Mining Co., Ltd., 1948-50; mining engr. Sierra Leone Devel. Co. Ltd., Marampa, West Africa, 1951-52; mine supt. Emmco, Bukit Besi, Malaysia, 1953-57, Sematan Bauxite Ltd., Sarawak, Malaysia, 1958-59; gen. mgr. Curacao Mining Co. N.V., Netherlands Antilles, 1960-69; mining cons. Robertson Rsch. Pty. Ltd., Sydney, N.S.W., Australia, 1970-72; prin. mining engr. Ralph M. Parsons Co., Pasadena, Calif., 1975-82; self-employed mining cons. Studio City, Calif., 1983—; mining cons., Sydney, 1973-74. Fellow Inst. Mining and Metallurgy; mem. Soc. Mining Engrs. AIME (chmn. So. Calif. sect. 1989-90). Home and Office: 4230 Tujunga Ave Studio City CA 91604

HIATT, PETER, library educator; b. N.Y.C., Oct. 19, 1930; s. Amos and Elizabeth Hope (Derry) H.; m. Linda Rae Smith, Aug. 16, 1968; 1 child, Holly Virginia. B.A., Colgate U., 1952; M.L.S., Rutgers U., 1957, Ph.D., 1963. Head Elmora Br. Library, Elizabeth, N.J., 1957-59; instr. Grad. Sch. Library Service Sci. Rutgers U., 1960-62; library cons. Ind. State Library, Indpls., 1963-70; asst. prof. Grad. Library Sch., Ind. U., 1963-66, assoc. prof., 1966-70; dir. Ind. Library Studies, Bloomington, 1967-70; dir. continuing edn. program for library personnel Western Interstate Commn. for Higher Edn., Boulder, Colo., 1970-74; dir. Grad. Sch. Library and Info. Sci., U. Wash., Seattle, 1974-81, prof., 1974—; prin. investigator Career Devel. and Assessment Center for Librarians, 1979-83, 90-93; dir. library insts. at various colls. and univs.; adv. project U.S. Office Edn.-ALA, 1977-80; bd. dirs. King County Libr. System, 1989—, pres., 1991, sec., 1993; prin investigator Career Devel. and Assessment Ctrs. for Libzs.: Phase II, 1990-93. Author: (with Donald Thompson) Monroe County Public Library: Planning for the Future, 1966, The Public Library Needs of Delaware County, 1967, (with Henry Drennan) Public Library Services for the Functionally Illiterate, 1967, (with Robert E. Lee and Lawrence A. Allen) A Plan for Developing a Regional Program of Continuing Education for Library Personnel, 1969, Public Library Branch Services for Adults of Low Education, 1964; dir., gen. editor: The Indiana Library Studies, 1970; author: Assessment Centers for Professional Library Leadership, 1993; mem. editorial bd. Coll. and Rsch. Librs., 1969-73; co-editor Leads: A Continuing Education Newsletter for Library Trustees, 1973-75, Octavio Noda; author chpts., articles on library continuing edn. and staff devel. Mem. ALA (officer), Pacific N.W. Library Assn., Spl. Libraries Assn., Assn. Library and Info. Sci. Educators (officer, Outstanding Service award 1979), Am. Soc. Info. Sci., Adult Edn. Assn., ACLU. Home: 19324 8th Ave NW Seattle WA 98177-3023 Office: U Wash Grad Sch Libr and Info Sci Seattle WA 98195

HIATT, STEVEN LEE, restaurant consultant; b. Corvallis, Oreg., Oct. 8, 1958; s. Bobby Lee and Joyce Ella (Skutely) H.; m. Jenifer Ann Vennes, June 20, 1981; children: Candice, Andrew, Erik. BBA, Oreg. State U., 1980; M in Mgmt., G.E.O. Atkinson Willamette U., 1984. Cons. H&H Cons., Portland, Oreg., 1985-88; restaurant gen. mgr., team managed unit Taco Bell, Inc., Fairfield, Calif., 1988—. Republican. Roman Catholic. Home: 1072 Valley Oak Way Fairfield CA 94533

HIBBARD, JUDITH HOFFMAN, public health educator, researcher; b. L.A., Nov. 30, 1948; d. Arnold Mandel and Marian (Carob) Hoffman; m. Michael John Hibbard, Aug. 1, 1968; 1 child, Johanna. BS, Calif. State U., Northridge, 1974; MPH, UCLA, 1975; DrPH, U. Calif., Berkeley, 1982. Clin. dir. Family Planning, San Jose, Calif., 1978; lectr. San Jose State U., 1978-79; rsch. assoc. Ctr. Health Rsch., Portland, Oreg., 1980-82; asst. prof. U. Oreg., Eugene, 1982-88, assoc. prof., 1988—; adj. investigator Ctr. Health Rsch., Portland, 1982—; mem. Com. on Fed. Stats., 1984—; bd. dirs. Oreg. Pub. Health Assn., 1984-88, Oreg. Rsch. Inst., 1991-92; mem. exec. bd. Gerontology Ctr., Eugene, 1987-90; mem. exec. com. Ctr. for Study of Women, Eugene, 1988-89. Contbr. articles to profl. jours. Recipient New Investigator Rsch. award Nat. Inst. Aging, 1983-86, Dissertation Rch. award Nat. Ctr. Health Svcs. Rsch., 1981-82; grantee NIA, 1988-91, Nat. Ctr. Health Svcs. Rsch., 1985-88, Office of Substance Abuse Prevention, 1990—. Fellow Soc. Pub. Health Edn.; mem. Am. Pub. Health Assn., Am. Sociol. Assn. Office: U Oregon 119 Hendricks Hall Eugene OR 97403

HIBBARD, RICHARD PAUL, industrial ventilation consultant, lecturer; b. Defiance, Ohio, Nov. 1, 1923; s. Richard T. and Doris E. (Walkup) H.; BS in Mech. Indsl. Engring., U. Toledo, 1949; m. Phyllis Ann Kirchoffer, Sept. 7, 1948; children: Barbara Rae, Marcia Kae, Rebecca Ann, Patricia Jan, John Ross. Mech. engr. Oldsmobile div. Gen. Motors Corp., Lansing, Mich., 1950-56; design and sales engr. McConnell Sheet Metal, Inc., Lansing, 1956-60; chief heat and ventilation engr. Fansteel Metall. Corp., North Chicago, Ill., 1960-62; sr. facilities and ventilation engr. The Boeing Co., Seattle, 1962-63; ventilation engr. environ. health div. dept. preventive medicine U. Wash., 1964-70, lectr. dept. environ. health, 1970-82, lectr. emeritus, 1983—; prin. Indsl. Ventilation Cons. Svcs., 1983—; chmn. Western Indsl. Ventilation Conf., 1962; mem. com. indsl. ventilation Am. Conf. Govtl. Indsl. Hygienists, 1966—; mem. staff Indsl. Ventilation Conf., Mich. State U., 1955—. With USAAF, 1943-45, USAR, 1946-72. Recipient Disting. Svc. award Indsl. Ventilation Conf., Mich. State U., 1975, 93. Mem. Am. Soc. Safety Engrs. (R.M. Gillmore Meml. award Puget Sound chpt.), ASHRAE, Am. Inst. Plant Engrs., Am. Indsl. Hygiene Assn. (J.M. Dallevalle award 1977), Am. Foundryman's Soc. Lodges: Elks, Masons. Contbr. articles on indsl. hygiene and ventilation to profl. jours. Home: 41 165th Ave SE Bellevue WA 98008-4721

HIBBERT, JULIA HEGSTED, artist; b. Idaho Falls, Idaho, Mar. 29, 1938; d. Victor Orville and Julia Genivieve (Howe) H.; m. Roger Jacob Contor, Sept. 8, 1956 (div. Aug. 1971); children: Bryce Adam, Patrick Victor, Craig Roger; m. Delvan Dee Hibbert, Apr. 2, 1976; 1 child, David Dee. Student, Stephens Coll., Columbia, Mo., 1955-56, Skagit Valley Community Coll., Mount Vernon, Wash., 1970, Sergei Bongart Sch., Santa Monica, Calif., 1972, Ricks Coll., Rexburg, Idaho, 1973-75. Animal portrait painter Wolf Track Studio, 1963-80; freelance artist Wolf Track Studios, 1966—; owner, operator Wolf Track Studio & Art Gallery, Sedro Woolley, Wash., 1969-70; owner, prin. Wolf Track Studio, Rexburg, Idaho, 1971-76; paste up artist Rexburg Standard & Jour., 1972-75; art tchr. Idaho Primitive Arts & Crafts, Victor, 1982, 83, Valley Art Guild, Rigby, Idaho, 1986; cons. Teton Valley Arts & Humanities Assn., Driggs, Idaho, 1989—, Nat. Pk. Svc., 1956-70; back drop painter Pierre's Playhouse, Victor, 1987—. Logo designer Wood Hosp., Salt Lake City, 1988, Am. Buffalo Assn., 1978, Blizzard Oil Field Svcs., Mont., 1982; illustrator Book of Mormon Poems, 1975, BLizzard Lumber Co., Mont., 1972, Hubair, Moab, Utah, 1967; columnist Tetonia Ward Newsletter, 1981-82, 85; contbr. articles to profl. jours. Active Econ. Devel. Coun. Teton Valley, Driggs, 1984-90; mem. The Heritage Found., Washington, 1986-89; city clk. City of Tetonia, 1986-87; merit badge counselor Boy Scouts Am., Driggs, 1989—; pres. Relief Soc. Tetonia 1st LDS Ch., 1989—, counselor Primary, 1988-89, geneology tchr., 1987, sec. Relief Soc., 1984-86, counselor Stake Relief Soc., 1977-80, bd. dirs. Stake Singles LDS Ch., 1973-76; notary public, 1989-93. Mem. Wildlife of Am. West Art Mus.; founding mem. Teton Valley Community Arts Assn. (sec. 1992-93, news reporter 1993—). Republican. Office: Wolf Track Studio 260 W Hwy 33 Tetonia ID 83452-5358

HIBBS, JOHN DAVID, software executive, engineer, business owner; b. Del Norte, Colo., Jan. 26, 1948; s. Alva Bernard and Frances Ava (Cathcart) H.; m. Ruthanne Johnson, Feb. 28, 1976. BSEE, Denver U., 1970. Elec. engr. Merrick and Co., Denver, 1972-73; lighting engr. Holophane div. Johns Manville, Denver, 1973-79; lighting products mgr. Computer Sharing Svcs., Inc., Denver, 1979-83; pres., owner Computer Aided Lighting Analysis, Boulder, Colo., 1983-86, Hibbs Sci. Software, Boulder, 1986—. Author CALA, CALA/Pro and PreCALA lighting programs. With USNR, 1970-72. Recipient 1st prize San Luise Valley Sci. Fair, 1963. Mem. IEEE, Illuminating Engring. Soc. North Am. (chmn. computer com. 1988-91), Computer Soc. IEEE (chmn. computer problem set com. 1991—). Home: 5105 Independence Rd Boulder CO 80301 Office: 2888 Bluff St Ste 515 Boulder CO 80301

HICK, KENNETH WILLIAM, business executive; b. New Westminster, B.C., Can., Oct. 17, 1946; s. Les Walter and Mary Isabelle (Warner) H. BA in Bus., Eastern Wash. State Coll., 1971; MBA (fellow), U. Wash., 1973, PhD, 1975. Regional sales mgr. Hilti, Inc., San Leandro, Calif., 1976-79; gen. sales mgr. Moore Internat., Inc., Portland, 1979-80; v.p. sales and mktg. Phillips Corp., Anaheim, Calif., 1980-81; owner, pres., chief exec. officer K.C. Metals, San Jose, Calif., 1981-87; owner, pres., chief exec. officer Losli Internat. Inc., Portland, Oreg., 1987-89; pres. Resources N.W. Inc., 1989—; communications cons. Asso. Pub. Safety Communication Officers, Inc., State of Oreg., 1975-93; numerous cons. assignments, also seminars, 1976—. Contbr. to numerous publs., 1976—. Mem. Oreg. Gov.'s Tax Bd., 1975-76; pres. Portland chpt. Oreg. Jaycees, 1976; bd. fellows U. Santa Clara, 1983—. Served with USAF, 1966-69. Decorated Commendation medal. Mem. Am. Mgmt. Assn., Am. Mktg. Assn., Assn. M.B.A. Execs., Assn. Gen. Contractors, Soc. Advancement Mgmt., Home Builders Assn. Roman Catholic. Home: 17627 Kelok Rd Lake Oswego OR 97034-6655 Office: Resources N/W Inc PO Box 1909 Lake Oswego OR 97035-0209

HICKEL, WALTER JOSEPH, state governor, investment firm executive; b. nr. Claflin, Kans., Aug. 18, 1919; s. Robert A. and Emma (Zecha) H.; m. Janice Cannon, Sept. 22, 1941 (dec. Aug. 1943); 1 son, Theodore; m. Ermalee Strutz, Nov. 22, 1945; children: Robert, Walter, Jack, Joseph, Karl. Student pub. schs., Claflin; D.Eng. (hon.), Stevens Inst. Tech., 1970, Mich. Tech. U., 1973; LL.D. (hon.), St. Mary of Plains Coll., St. Martin's Coll., U. Md., Adelphi U., U. San Diego, Rensselaer Poly. Inst., 1973, U. Alaska, 1976, Alaska Pacific U., 1991; D.Pub. Adminstrn. (hon.), Willamette U. Builder, owner Traveler's Inn, Anchorage, 1953-82, Fairbanks, Alaska, 1955-82, Hickel Investment Co., Anchorage, 1947—, Hotel Captain Cook, Anchorage, No. Lights Shopping Ctr., Univ. Shopping Ctr., Anchorage, Valley River Shopping Ctr.; gov. State of Alaska, 1966-69, 90—; sec. U.S. Dept. Interior, 1969-70; former mem. world adv. council Internat. Design Sci. Inst.; former mem. com. on sci. freedom and responsibility AAAS. Mem. Republican Nat. Com., 1954-64; bd. regents Gonzaga U.; bd. dirs. Salk Inst., 1972-79, NASA Adv. Coun. Exploration Task Force. Named Alaskan of Year, 1969, Man of Yr. Ripon Soc., 1970; recipient DeSmet medal Gonzaga U., 1969, Horatio Alger award, 1972, Grand Cordon of the Order of Sacred Treasure award His Imperial Majesty the Emperor of Japan, 1988. Mem. Pioneers of Alaska, Alaska C. of C. (former chmn. econ. devel. com.), Equestrian Order Holy Sepulchre, Knights Malta. Clubs: KC, Capitol Hill, Washington Athletic (Washington). Home: Gov's House 716 Calhoun Ave Juneau AK 99801 Office: Office of the Gov PO Box 110001 Juneau AK 99811-0001

HICKERNELL, FREDERICK SLOCUM, research physicist, educator; b. Phoenix, Jan. 16, 1932; s. Frederick Azeriah and Alice Vernece (Slocum) H.; m. Thresa Elizabeth Kerr, June 25, 1954; children: Frederick John, Diana Elizabeth, Robert Kerr, Thomas Slocum. BA in Edn., Ariz. State U., 1953; cert. in meteorology, UCLA, 1954; MS in Physics, Ariz. State U., 1959, PhD in Physics, 1966. Instr. Ariz. State U., Tempe, 1957-58, faculty assoc., 1981-83; engr. Goodyear Aerospace Co., Litchfield Park, Ariz., 1958-60; tech. staff Motorola, Inc., Phoenix and Scottsdale, Ariz., 1960—, Dan Noble fellow, 1987; vis. prof. U. Ariz., Tucson, 1985-87, adj. prof., 1987—; speaker at confs. and ednl. meetings. Patentee in field; contbr. to profl. pubs. Scout leader Phoenix area Boy Scouts Am., 1971-77; chair bd. dirs. Valley Christian Ctrs., Phoenix, 1971-74; vice chair, treas. Orangewood Estates, Phoenix, 1976-92; trustee Am. Bapt. Homes of West, Oakland, Calif., 1988-92. Maj. USAF, 1953-57, ret., 1992. Recipient cert. of recognition NASA, 1974; named Layman of Yr. Am. Bapt. Men. Ariz., 1979. Fellow IEEE (adminstrv. com. 1975—, chair ultrasonics symposium 1977, 92, newsletter editor 1977—), Am. Sci. Affiliation (v.p. 1993); mem. Am. Phys. Soc., Am. Meterol. Soc., Am. Vacuum Soc., Sigma Xi. Home: 5012 E Weldon Ave Phoenix AZ 85018-6141 Office: Motorola Inc 8201 E McDowell Rd Scottsdale AZ 85257-3893

HICKERSON, GLENN LINDSEY, leasing company executive; b. Burbank, Calif., Aug. 22, 1937; s. Ralph M. and Sarah Lawson (Lindsey) H.; m. Jane Fortune Arthur, Feb. 24, 1973. B.A. in Bus. Adminstrn, Claremont Men's Coll., 1959; M.B.A., N.Y. U., 1960. Exec. asst. Douglas Aircraft Co., Santa Monica, Calif., 1963; sec., treas. Douglas Fin. Corp., Long Beach, Calif., 1964-67, regional mgr. customer financing, 1967; exec. asst. to pres. Universal Airlines, Inc., Detroit, 1967-68, v.p., treas., asst. sec., 1968-69, pres., 1969-72; v.p., treas., asst. sec. Universal Aircraft Service, Inc., Detroit, 1968-69, chmn. bd., 1969-72; v.p., treas. Universal Airlines Co., Detroit, 1968-69, pres., 1969-72; group v.p. Marriott Hotels, Inc., Washington, 1972-76; dir. sales Far East and Australia Lockheed Calif. Co., 1976-78, dir. mktg. Americas, 1978-79, dir. mktg. Internat., 1979-81, v.p., internat. sales, 1981-83; v.p. comml. mktg. internat. Douglas Aircraft Co., McDonnell Douglas Corp., 1983-89; mng. dir. GPA Asia Pacific, El Segundo, Calif., 1989-90; exec. v.p. GATX Air, San Francisco, 1990—. Bd. govs. Keck Ctr. for Internat. Strategic Studies; mem. Calif. Export Adv. Council. Served to lt. (j.g.) USCGR, 1960-62. H.B. Earhart Found. fellow, 1962. Mem. Internat. Assn. Charter Airlines (exec. com. 1971). Home: 2562 Green St San Francisco CA 94123-4629 Office: GATX Air 4 Embarcadero Ctr San Francisco CA 94111-4106

HICKEY, HARRISON R., JR., sanitary engineer, mathematics educator, jazz musician; b. Kiefer, Okla., June 6, 1925; s. Harrison R. and Bessie Mabel (Kratzer) H.; m. Gloria D'Angelo, Mar. 27, 1957 (div. Dec. 1978); children: Brian Martin, Vincent Russell. BSChemE, Okla. State U., 1954; M in San. Engring., U. Fla., 1962, PhD in San. Engring., 1963. Registered profl. engr., Okla.; cert. Am. Bd. Indsl. Hygiene, 1964. Sr. engr. Kaiser Aluminum and Chem. Co., Ravenswood, W.Va., 1955-63; prof. med. sch. U. Okla., Oklahoma City, 1963-64; pres. Environ. Rsch., Inc., Lakeland, Fla., 1965-67; mgr. system svcs. TRW, Inc., Reston, Va., 1967; mem. tech. staff Mitre Corp., McLean, Va., 1969-71; chief applied rsch. staff Tenn. Valley Authority, Chattanooga, 1971-81; program dir. pub. bathing pl. Okla. State Health Dept., Oklahoma City, 1981-87; instr. math. and statistics Napa Valley Coll., Calif., 1988-91, Butte Coll., Oroville, Calif., 1990—. Music arranger, musician jazz tenor sax with Al Donahue and Ralph Flanagan Bands U.S. tours, 1950-53; contbr. articles to profl. jours. Leader Feather River Big Dam Dance Band, 1991—. U.S. Pub. Health Svc. grad. sch. traineeship, 1961-62. Mem. Masons, Shriners, Moose, Eagles. Home and Office: 375 Hillcrest Ave Oroville CA 95966-9435

HICKEY, WINIFRED E(SPY), state senator, social worker; b. Rawlins, Wyo.; d. David P. and Eugenia (Blake) Espy; children—John David, Paul Joseph. B.A., Loretto Heights Coll., 1933; postgrad. U. Utah, 1934, Sch. Social Service, U. Chgo., 1936; LLD (hon.) U. Wyo., 1991. Dir. Carbon County Welfare Dept., 1935-36; field rep. Wyo. Dept. Welfare, 1937-38; dir. Red Cross Club, Europe, 1942-45; commr. Laramie County, Wyo., 1973-80; mem. Wyo. Senate, 1980-90; dir. United Savs. & Loan, Cheyenne. Pres., bd. dirs. U. Wyo. Found., 1986-87; pres. Meml. Hosp. of Laramie County, 1986-88; chmn. adv. council div. community programs Wyo. Dept. Health and Social Services; pres. county and state mental health assn., 1959-63; trustee, U. Wyo., 1967-71; active Nat. Council Cath. Women. Named Outstanding Alumna, Loretto Heights Coll., 1959, Woman of Yr. Commn. for Women, 1988, Legislator of Yr. Wyo. Psychologists Assn., 1988. Democrat. Club: Altrusa (Cheyenne). Pub. Where the Deer and the Antelope Play, 1967.

HICKLIN, RONALD LEE, music production company executive; b. Burlington, Wash., Dec. 4, 1937; s. Wendell C. and Theodora (Van Voorhis) H.; m. Marlene Paige Folk, July 10, 1959; children: Jennifer Lynn, Mark Allan. Student, U. Wash., 1956-57. Pres. S.A.T.B. Inc., L.A., 1979—, HLC/Killer Music, Hollywood, Calif., 1982—; pres. T.T. B.B., Inc. Hollywood, 1989—; ptnr. Killer Tracks, Primat Am., Hollywood, 1990—. Lead tenor The Eligibles, 1958-62; vocal dir., singer Piece of Cake Inc., 1968-81; arranger, producer Calif. Raisin Adv. Bd., 1982 (recipient 2 Clios 1983); producer/co-writer Wheaties, 1983 (Clio award); producer/composer Gatorade, 1983; producer/performer Levi's 501 Blues, 1984. With USAF, 1959-65. Mem. NARAS (MVP award 1973, 75), AFTRA (nat. bd. dirs. 1970-85, local bd. dirs. 1968-85), Screen Actors Guild (nat. bd. dirs. 1975), Am. Fedn. Musicians, Hollywood C. of C. Home: 30 Kewen Pl San Marino CA 91108-1104 Office: HLC/Killer Music 6532 W Sunset Blvd Los Angeles CA 90028-7213

HICKMAN, BERT GEORGE, JR., economist, educator; b. Los Angeles, Oct. 6, 1924; s. Bert George and Caroline E. (Douglass) H.; m. Edythe Anne Warshauer, Feb. 9, 1947; children: Wendy Elizabeth, Paul Lawrence, Alison Diane. B.S., U. Calif.-Berkeley, 1947, Ph.D., 1951. Instr. Stanford U., 1949-51; research asso. Nat. Bur. Econ. Research, 1951-52; asst. prof. Northwestern, 1952-54; mem. sr. staff Council Econ. Advisers, 1954-56; research assoc. Brookings Instn., 1956-58, mem. sr. staff, 1958-66; prof. Stanford U., 1966—; vis. prof. U. Calif. at Berkeley, 1960, London Grad. Sch. Bus Studies, 1972-73, , Inst. Advanced Studies, Vienna, Austria, 1974, 1975, Kyoto U., 1977; NSF fellow Netherlands Econometric Inst., Rotterdam, 1964-65; Ford Found. Faculty research fellow, 1968-69; mem. com. econ. stability Social Sci. Research Council, 1959-61, chmn., 1962—; hon. prof. U. Vienna, 1985—; chmn. Energy Modeling Forum working group on macroecon. impacts of global modeling Stanford U., 1982-83; Am. coord. US-USSR program on econ.-math. macromodeling Am. Coun. Learned Socs., 1988-90. Author: Growth and Stability of the Postwar Economy, 1960, Investment Demand and U.S. Economic Growth, 1965, (with Robert M. Coen) An Annual Growth Model of the U.S. Economy, 1976; Editor: Quantitative Planning of Economic Policy, 1965, Econometric Models of Cyclical Behavior, 1972, Global International Economic Models, 1983, International Monetary Stabilization and the Foreign Debt Problem, 1984, International Productivity and Competitiveness, 1992; co-editor: Global Econometrics, 1983, Macroeconomic Impact of Energy Shocks, 1987; contbr. articles to profl. jours. Served with USNR, 1943-46. Vis. fellow Internat. Inst. Applied Systems Analysis, 1979, 80; resident fellow Rockefeller Found., 1989; named Hon. Prof. U. Vienna, Austria. Fellow Econometric Soc.; mem. Am. Econ. Assn. (chmn. census adv. com. 1968-71, tech. subcom. to rev. bus. cycle devels. 1962-68, nominating com. 1978-79, chmn. seminar on global modeling, conf. on econometrics and math. econs. 1975-83), Phi Beta Kappa, Phi Eta Sigma. Home: 904 Lathrop Dr Palo Alto CA 94305-1060 Office: Stanford U Dept Econs Stanford CA 94305

HICKMAN, CRAIG RONALD, author; b. Borger, Tex., Dec. 5, 1949; s. Winston Whitehead and Verla (Bingham) H.; m. Pamela Lewis, Nov. 17, 1972; children: Jared Winston, Kimberly Michelle, Leigh Megan. BA in Econs. cum laude, Brigham Young U., 1974; MBA with honors, Harvard U., 1976. Cons. Ernst & Ernst (now Ernst & Young), L.A., 1976-77; sr. planning analyst Dart Industries, L.A., 1977-79; campaign mgr. Wright for Gov., Salt Lake City, 1980; mgr. cons. svcs. Arthur Young & Co. (now Ernst & Young), 1980-83; pres. Bennett Info. Group, Salt Lake City, 1983-85; chmn., pres. Mgmt. Perspectives Group, Provo, Utah, 1985-91; author, cons. Provo, 1985—; cons. Frito-Lay, Dallas, 1985, Procter & Gamble, Cin., 1986, AT&T, ea. U.S., 1986, Fla. Power & Light, 1987, Systematic Mgmt. Svcs., Phila., 1988, Geneva Steel, Vineyard, Utah, 1989, Found. Health Corp., Sacramento, 1990; keynote speaker numerous corp. confs., U. Md., Notre Dame, Head Start Program, Dalhousie U., numerous assns. and USIA, India, Israel, 1985-92. Co-author: Creating Excellence, 1984 (nat. bestseller paperback 1986), The Future 500, 1987; author: Mind of a Manager, Soul of a Leader, 1990 (internat. bestseller paperback 1992), Practical Business Genius, 1991, The Strategy Game, 1993; contbr. articles and commentaries to profl. jours. Mem. ASTD. Republican. Mem. LDS Ch. Home: 3751 N Littlerock Dr Provo UT 84604

HICKMAN, DAVID FRANCIS, marketing professional; b. Flint, Mich., July 26, 1947; s. Clarence Joseph and Rejeania Emeline (Nickerson) H.; m. Laura Elizabeth Agness, Jan. 27, 1971. BS, Purdue U., 1970; MBA, Ind. No. U., 1978. Dept. head Armour Food Co., Balt., 1970-71; dist. sales mgr. Armour Food Co., Nashua, N.H., 1971-73; regional sales mgr. Armour Food Co., Pitts., 1973-75; nat. sales mgr. La Choy Food Products, Archbold, Ohio, 1975-85; mktg. mgr. Beatrice/Hunt-Wesson, Inc., Fullerton, Calif., 1985—. Republican. Home: 2970 Malaga Cir Diamond Bar CA 91765-3840 Office: Hunt Wesson Inc 1645 W Valencia Dr # 653 Fullerton CA 92633-3899

HICKMAN, GRACE MARGUERITE, artist; b. Reno, Nev., Nov. 7, 1921; d. Charles Franklin and Jeannie (McPhee) Wolcott; m. Robert Frederick Hickman, Apr. 10, 1943; children—John Charles, Carol Ann Hickman Harp, David Paul. Student Emily Griffiths Opportunity Sch., Denver, 1968-71, Red Rocks Community Coll., Golden, Colo., 1974-75, Loretto Heights Coll., Denver, 1983-85. Tchr. art Aurora Parks & Recreation, Colo., 1979-81; instr. paint workshop Marine Resource Ctr., Atlantic Beach, N.C., 1981, 82; lectr. color theory Aurora Artists Club, 1985; instr. creative color Acapulco Art Workshops, 1987, 88; tchr. color theory and art fundamentals Colo. Free U., 1991-92. One woman shows include Internat. House, Denver, 1974, Foothills Art Ctr., Golden, Colo., 1975, Greek Market Place, Denver, 1976, Marine Resource Ctr., Atlantic Beach, N.C., 1983, Depot Art Ctr., Littleton, Colo., 1984, Sheraton DTC, Women's Bank Denver, 1986, NYU Sch. Environmental Medicine, Tuxedo, 1987, Studio Paul Kontny, Denver, 1988. group shows include: Wellshire Presbyn. Ch., Denver, 1975, Brass Cheque Gallery, Denver, 1978, Colo. Women in Arts, Denver, 1979, Garelick's Gallery, Scottsdale, Ariz., 1982; Bold Expressions, Littleton, Colo., 1983. represented in permanent collections: Augustana Luth. Ch., Denver, South Shores Ins. Agy., Huntington Beach, Calif., Texon Gen. Partnership, Englewood, Colo., others. Coordinator figure study Bicentennial Art Ctr., Aurora, 1986; pres. Depot Art Ctr., Littleton, Colo., 1980-82. Mem. Nat. Mus. for Women in the Arts, Artists Equity Assn., Colo. Artists Equity Assn. (chmn. publicity Colo. 1% for Art 1976-77), Pastel Soc. Am., Littleton Fine Arts Guild (pres. 1976-77), Art Students League, Colo. Speakers Bur. (coordinator), Nat. Mus. Women in Arts. Democrat. Lutheran. Club: Aurora Athletic. Avocations: swimming; reading; art history. Home: 12361 E Bates Cir Aurora CO 80014-3311

HICKMAN, MAXINE VIOLA, social services administrator; b. Louisville, Miss., Dec. 24, 1943; d. Everett and Ozella (Eichelberger) H.; m. William L. Malone, Sept. 5, 1965 (div. 1969); 1 child, Gwendolyn. BA, San Francisco State U., 1966; MS, Nova U., 1991; postgrad., Calif. Coast U., 1991—. Lic. State of Calif. Dept. Social Svcs. IBM profl. mechanic operator Wells Fargo Bank, San Francisco, 1961-65; dept. mgr. Sears Roebuck & Co., San Bruno, Calif., 1966-77; adminstr. Pine St. Guest House, San Francisco, 1969-88; fin. planner John Hancock Fin. Svcs., San Mateo, Calif., 1977-81; chief exec. officer Hickman Homes, Inc., San Francisco, 1981—; cons. BeeBe Meml. Endowment Found., Oakland, Calif., 1990—, Calif. Assn. Children's Home-Mems., Sacramento, 1989—. Mem. NAACP, San Francisco. Named Foster Mother of Yr., Children's Home Soc. Calif., 1985, Woman of Yr., Gamma Nu chpt. Iota Phi Lambda, 1991. Mem. Foster Parents United, Calif. Assn. Children's Homes, Nat. Bus. League, Order of Ea. Star, Masons (worthy matron), Alpha Kappa Alpha. Democrat. Baptist. Office: Hickman Homes Inc 67 Harold Ave San Francisco CA 94112-2331

HICKOK, ROBERT BLAIR, musician, educator, dean; b. Slaton, Tex., Feb. 2, 1927; s. George B. and Wilhemina (Paul) H.; m. Roanne Newman; children: Paul, Laura. BMusic, Yale U., 1949. Prof., dean Bklyn. Coll. of the City, 1952-77; dean of music N.C. Sch. of the Arts, Winston, 1977-85; dean of fine arts U. Wis., Milw., 1986-88, U. Calif., Irvine, 1988—; bd. dirs. Irvine (Calif.) Barclay Theatre, 1988—; mem. bd. advisors Orange County Philharm. Soc., Irvine, 1992—. Author: Exploring Music, 5th edit., 1993; editor various choral music. Mem. bd. advisors Orange County Arts Coun., 1989; mem. strategic planning coun. Art Inst. So. Calif., 1989-90; mem. commn. on arts Nat. Assn. State Univs. and Land-Grant Colls., 1990-92. Sgt. U.S. Army, 1950-52. Recipient cert. of merit for disting. svc. as condr. and adminstr. Yale U. Sch. Music Alumni Assn., 1984. Home: 12 Young Ct Irvine CA 92715 Office: U Calif Irvine Sch Fine Arts (FAT 300) Irvine CA 92717

HICKS, BETHANY GRIBBEN, lawyer; b. N.Y., Sept. 8, 1951; d. Robert and DeSales Gribben; m. William A. Hicks III, May 21, 1982; children: Alexandra Elizabeth, Samantha Katherine. AB, Vassar Coll., 1973; MEd, Boston U., 1975; JD, Ariz. State U., 1984. Bar: Ariz. 1984. Pvt. practice, Scottsdale and Paradise Valley, Ariz., 1984-91; law clk. to Hon. Kenneth L. Fields Maricopa County Superior Ct. (s.e. dist.), Mesa, 1991-93, judge pro tem, 1993—; magistrate Town of Paradise Valley, Ariz., 1993—. Mem. Jr. League of Phoenix, 1984-91; bd. dirs. Phoenix Children's Theatre, 1988-90; parliamentarian Girls Club of Scottsdale, Ariz., 1985-87, 89-90, bd. dirs., 1988-91; mem. exec. bd., sec. All Saints' Episcopal Day Sch. Parents Assn., 1991-92, pres., 1993—. Mem. ABA, State Bar Ariz., Maricopa County Bar Assn. Republican. Episcopalian. Club: Paradise Valley Country.

HICKS, CLINTON ROBERT, author; b. Austin, Tex., Mar. 16, 1960; sRobert Glendon and Sandra Gail (Land) H.; m. Rosanna Dill, Oct. 11, 1987; 1 child, Angelina. BA in Anthropology, Rice U., 1982. Editorial asst. Social Studies Sch. Svc., Culver City, Calif., 1985-86; tech. writer JM Montgomery Cons. Engrs., Pasadena, Calif., 1986-87, Phoenix Software, L.A., 1987-88; sr. editor, mgr. tech. publs. Peter Norton Computing, Santa Monica, Calif., 1988-90; author CRH Publs., Santa Fe, 1990—; editor OnWord Press, 1992—. Author: Cool Mac Animation, 1992; co-author: Guide to Norton Utilities/MAC, 1990, DOS 5 Handbook, 1991 (Best-Seller 1992), Outside the Macintosh, 1992. Cert. of Merit Soc. for Tech. Communication, 1990. Democrat. Roman Catholic. Office: CRH Publs 1106 Calle de los Suenos Santa Fe NM 87505-5111

HICKS, DAVID EARL, author, inventor; b. Indpls., Jan. 1, 1931; s. John Arthur and Marguerite (Barnes) H.; m. Shirlene Lavan Barlow, Jan. 22, 1958 (div. June 1973); children: Sharon Lynn, Brenda Kay; m. Margaret Leigh Payne, Feb. 17, 1977; children: David Bradley, Leslie Ann, Brian Patrick. Grad., Nat. Radio Inst., 1953; student, Purdue U., 1959-60, Miami-Dade Community Coll., 1971-72. Cert. advanced paramedic. Tech. writer, editor Howard W. Sams, Inc., Indpls., 1958-64; tech. writer Systems Engring. Labs, Inc., Ft. Lauderdale, Fla., 1964-67; publs. mgr. Novatronics, Inc., Pompano Beach, Fla., 1967-69; pres. Datatek, Inc., Ft. Lauderdale, 1969-71; tech. writer Systems Devel. Corp., Colorado Springs, Colo., 1973-74, Ford Aerospace Corp., Colorado Springs, 1974-76; pres. Nutronics Corp., Colorado Springs, 1982-87; tech. writer Digital Equipment Corp., Colorado Springs, 1978-88; pres. Innovation USA Mag., Colorado Springs, 1989; pvt. practice tech. con., inventor Colorado Springs, 1964-65, 75-78, 87—; tech. cons. Japan Electronics, Tokyo, 1962-63, Nutronics Corp., Longmont, Colo., 1987. Author of eight tech. books (two made best seller list) including: Citizens Band Radio Handbook, 1961, Amateur Radio-VHF and Above, 1965, CB Radio Operating Procedures, 1976; contbr. articles to electronics jours.; inventor of new electric charging system, 1978, awarded U.S. patent, 1981; lectr. numerous sci. and invention seminars, 1978—. Communications officer CD, Indpls., 1962-63; judge sci. fair Pub. Sch. System, Colorado Springs, 1986-87. Served with USN, 1948. Recipient Red Cross Hall of Fame, Indpls., 1963; grantee U.S. Dept. of Energy, 1984; recipient Nat. Energy Resources Tech. Innovation award, 1989, Disting. Leadership award Am. Biog. Inst. 1990, cert. of merit Internat. Biog. Ctr., 1990. Mem. Soc. of Am. Inventors (bd. dirs., Pres. award 1989), Am. Radio Relay League, Author's Guild, Author's League of Am. Republican. Office: PO Box 25053 Colorado Springs CO 80936-5053

HICKS, JIMMIE LEE, physiologist, medical educator; b. Laramie, Wyo., Dec. 17, 1936; s. Elmer L. Hicks and Juanita Mary (Beggs) Komenich; m. Shirley Roll, Apr. 5, 1959; children: Lori Lee, James John. BS, U. Wyo., 1959, MS, 1963; PhD, Colo. State U., 1971. Instr. biology Coll. St. Thomas, St. Paul, 1963-67; asst. prof., then assoc. prof. physiology U. Health Sci./Coll. Osteo. Medicine, Kansas City, Mo., 1971-83; prof. physiology, dir. rotations Coll. Osteo. Medicine of Pacific, Pomona, Calif., 1983-86, asst. dean, prof. physiology, 1986-89, assoc. dean, prof. physiology, 1989-92, assoc. dean basic scis., 1992—. Scout leader Heart of Am. coun. Boy Scouts Am., Kansas City, 1974-83, Old Baldy coun., Ontario, Calif., 1983—; vol. Mt. Baldy Region United Way, 1987—. With U.S. Army, 1959-61. Served to capt. USAR. Recipient Silver Beaver award Boy Scouts Am., 1990. Home: 1315 Greenvale Cir Upland CA 91786-1755 Office: Coll Osteo Medicine Pacific College Pla Pomona CA 91766-1889

HICKS, JOHN VICTOR, author; b. London, Feb. 24, 1907; s. James and Harriet Hicks. DLitt, U. Sask., Saskatoon, 1987. Acct. Govt. Province Sask., Prince Albert, 1950-72. Author: Now is a Far Country, 1978, Winter Your Sleep, 1980, Silence Like the Sun, 1983, Rootless Tree, 1985, Five and Sixes, 1986, Side Glances: Notes on the Writer's Craft, 1987, Sticks and Strings, 1988, Month's Mind, 1992. Recipient lifetime award Sask. Arts Bd., Regina, 1990, Order of Merit, Sask, 1992, Can. 125 Commemorative medal, 1993; named Hon. fellow U. Emmanuel Coll., Saskatoon, 1979. Mem. Sask. Writers' Guild. Anglican. Home: 222 21st St E, Prince Albert, SK Canada

HICKS, KERRY DOUGLAS, military officer, educator; b. Cordell, Okla., Oct. 6, 1962; s. Pershing and Sandra Lee (Weltmer) H.; m. Juanita Carol Burk, July 1, 1989. BS in Aeronautics and Astronautics, U. Ill., 1985; MS Astronautical Engring., Air Force Inst. Tech., 1986, PhD, 1989. Commd. 2d lt. USAF, 1985, advanced to capt.; engr. Astronautics Lab., USAF, Edwards AFB, Calif., 1989-91; engr. Phillips Lab. USAF, Edwards AFB, Calif., 1991—; adj. prof. Chapman Coll., 1991—. Author software, 1986—. Mem. AIAA (chpt. chmn. 1986-87), Air Force Assn., Planetary Soc., U. Ill. Alumni Assn.

HICKS, LESLIE, guide, outfitter, horse breeder and trainer; b. Waco, Tex., Sept. 22, 1952; d. Herbert Leon and Mary Dees (McDermott) H.; m. Harry William Mott, Apr. 30, 1977 (div. 1982). BA in Anthropology, Tex. Tech U., 1975. Lic. outfitter; lic. guide; cert. emergency med. technician, alpine and nordic profl. ski instr. Pvt. governess Tucson, 1977-78; guide Bi-State Outfitters, Raton, N.Mex., 1978-79; CEO bldg. destruction co., La Veta, Colo., 1984—; profl. ski patrol Cuchara (Colo.) Valley Resort, 1981-88, profl. ski instr., 1988-89; CEO Dark Horse Outfitters, purveyors rare and unusual adventure, La Veta, 1980—; horsemanship dir. Boy Scouts Am., Walsenburg, Colo., 1986-89; guide, outfitter Echo Canyon Guest Ranch, La Veta, 1991-92; CEO wholesale greenhouse Herb's Herbs, La Veta, 1991—; trail builder Echo Canyon Guest Ranch, 1991-92. Mem. Colo. Outfitters Assn., Am. Quarter Horse Assn., Nature Conservancy, Colo. Farm Bur., Friends of the Arts Guild, Nat. Arbor Day Found. Home: PO Box 393 La Veta CO 81055

HICKS, MORRIS ALVIN, dentist; b. Scottville, Ill., Aug. 31, 1936; s. Charles Alvin and LaFern (Watkins) H.; m. Marlene Elizabeth Henerhoff, June 3, 1956 (div. 1983); children: Melinda, Murray, Myron; m. Linda Lee Giller, Mar. 26, 1983; children: Teri, Joe, Traci, Curt. BS, Western Ill. U., 1958, U. Ill., 1963; DDS, U. Ill., Chgo., 1965; MEd, U. Tex., 1966. Sci. tchr. Roodhouse (Ill.) High Sch., 1958-60; commd. officer dentist U.S. Pub. Health Svc., 1965-69; pvt. practice dentist Tucson, 1969—. Pres. Sertoma, 1974; gov. Sertoma Ariz. dist., 1975. Major USPHS, 1965-69. Fellow Acad. Gen. Dentistry; mem. So. Ariz. Dental Assn. (pres. 1981-82), Ariz. Dental Assn. (pres. 1989-90), ADA (alt. del. 1987—), Am. Coll. Dentists, Pierre Fauchard Acad., Am. Equilibratim Soc., Masons, Scottish Rite, Shriners. Republican. Home: 9392 N Calle Buena Vis Tucson AZ 85737-4904 Office: 7040 N Oracle Rd Tucson AZ 85704-4388

HICKS, ROBERT ALVIN, psychology educator; b. San Francisco, July 25, 1932; s. James B. and Vera L. (Brand) H.; m. Maralee Jeffries, June 15, 1957; 1 child, Gregory J. BA, U. Calif., Santa Barbara, 1955; MA, San Jose State U., 1960; PhD, U. Denver, 1964. Psychometrist San State (Calif.) U., 1957-61, prof., 1966—, NIH-MBRS program dir., 1980—; lectr., asst. prof. U. Denver, 1961-66; exec. officer Western Psychol. Assn., San Jose, 1985—. Contbr. articles to profl. jours. Fellow APS; mem. Psychonomic Soc., Sleep Rsch. Soc., Sigma Xi. Office: San Jose State U Dept Psychology San Jose CA 95192-0189

HICKSON, ERNEST CHARLES, financial executive; b. L.A., July 14, 1931; s. Russell Arthur and Marilyn Louise (Mambert) H.; m. Janice Beleal, Sept. 5, 1959; children: Arthur, Jennifer, Barton. BS, U. So. Calif., 1961; postgrad., UCLA Grad. Sch. of Bus. Admin., 1961-63. Lic. real estate broker, Calif., 1986. Credit supr. ARCO (Richfield Oil), L.A., 1955-60; asst. v.p. Union Bank L.A., 1960-64; v.p. County Nat. Bank (now Wells Fargo), Orange, Calif., 1964-67; v.p., sr. loan ofcr. City Bank, Honolulu, 1967-70; exec. v.p., dir. U.S. Fin., Inc., San Diego, 1970-73; exec. v.p. Sonnenblick Goldman, L.A., 1973-76; pres. First Hawaiian Devel., Honolulu, 1976-82; pres., CEO TMH Fin. Corp., Santa Ana, Calif., 1982—. Author: (novel) The Developers, 1978; editor: (monthly newsletter) Financial Marketing, 1978-83. Staff sgt. USAF, 1950-53. Recipient Exec. award Grad. Sch. of Credit and Fin. Mgmt., Stanford U., 1964, Assocs. award The Nat. Inst. of Credit, UCLA, 1959. Mem. U. So. Calif. Assocs., U. So. Calif. Pres.'s Circle, Urban Land Inst., Town Hall, Center Club (Costa Mesa), Pacific Club (Honolulu), Outrigger Canoe Club (Honolulu), Phi Gamma Delta. Democrat. Episcopalian. Office: TMH Fin Corp Griffin Towers 6 Hutton Centre Dr Santa Ana CA 92707

HIDALGO, JESSE ELILIO, computer operations analyst; b. Manila, July 8, 1950; came to U.S, 1973; s. Augusto Mina and Trinidad (Elilio) H.; m. Edna Jose Hidalgo, June 27, 1976; children: Derrek Jose, Jenalynne Jose, Jesse Jerome. BS in Biology, Philippine Union Coll., Baesa, 1973. Cert. income tax preparer. Clk., chauffeur Calif. Pellet Mill, San Francisco, 1973-74, computer operator, 1974-78; sr. computer operator San Jose (Calif.) Hosp., 1979-88; lead/sr. computer operator Joint Data Concepts, San Jose, 1988-92; ops. analyst, help desk IBM, Boulder, Colo., 1992—. Staff sgt. USAFR, 1984. Disting. Desert Storm Hero. Seventh-Day Adventist. Home: 820 Mt Evans Ct Louisville CO 80027 Office: IBM Diagonal Hwy Boulder CO 80301

HIDALGO, MIGUEL, transportation company executive; b. Detroit, Nov. 10, 1958; s. Manuel and Ann (Molina) H.; m. Rausdha Nelly Cachoa, Nov. 14, 1992; children: Jesahel, Monica Natasha. BA in Communications, Pepperdine U., 1981; MBA in Internat. Bus., Nat. U., 1991, MS Aero. Mgmt., 1991, postgrad. in law, 1992—. Owner Pacific Trans Service, Los Angeles, 1981-83; legal adminstr. Hidalgo & Assocs., Los Angeles, 1985-90; ops. and customs Aero Calif. Airlines, San Diego, 1990-91; ops. mgr. AeroCargo, San Diego, 1992—. Contbr. articles to profl. jours. Active S.W. Rep. Project; advisor Polit. Edn. Project. With USN, mem. Res. ret., 1985-91. Mem. Am. Legal Adminstrs., Pepperdine Assocs., Huntington Library, Sigma Epsilon Frat. (mem. bd. dirs. 1992—). Republican. Roman Catholic. Office: AeroCargo Brown Field Airport 1424 Continental St San Diego CA 92173

HIDDLESTON, RONAL EUGENE, drilling and pump company executive; b. Bristow, Okla., Mar. 21, 1939; s. C.L. and Iona D. (Martin) H.; m. Marvelene L. Hammond, Apr. 26, 1959; children: Michael Scott, Mark Shawn, Matthew Shane. Student, Idaho State U., 1957-58. With Roper's Clothing and Bishop Redi-Mix, Rupert, Idaho, 1960-61; pres., chmn. bd., gen. mgr. Hiddleston Drilling, Rupert, 1961-66, Mountain Home, Idaho, 1966—. Mem. Mountain Home Airport Adv. Bd., 1968—; hon. mem. Idaho Search and Rescue. Mem. Nat. Water Well Assn. (dir., past pres.), Idaho Water Well Assn. (dir., past pres.), Pacific N.W. Water Well Assn. (dir.), N.W. Mining Assn., Nat. Fedn. Ind. Businessmen, Ground Water Inst. (bd. dirs.), Aircraft Owners and Pilots Assn., Ducks Unltd., Nat. 210 Owners Club, Optimists, Masons, Shriners. Home: 645 E 17th N Mountain Home ID 83647-1726 Office: RR 3 Box 610D Mountain Home ID 83647-9806

HIEL, CLEM, aerospace engineer, educator; b. Beveren, Belgium, Sept. 20, 1952; came to U.S., 1981; s. Louis and Maria (Suy) H.; m. Hilde Van Dun, Dec. 16, 1983; children: Lynn, Tom. BSME, Antwerp (Belgium) Inst. Tech., 1974; MSME, U. Brussels, 1978, PhD, 1983. Asst. prof. U. Brussels, 1978-84, assoc. prof., 1984-87; aerospace engr. NASA, Moffett Field, Calif., 1987—; cons. Glasforms, San Jose, Calif., 1988-92; adj. prof. San Jose State U., 1988—; vis. prof. U. Brussels, 1988—; student advisor, mentor NASA, Moffett Field, 1992. Editor: Design with Composites, 1985, 2d rev. edit., 1986; mem. editorial bd. European Jour. Mech. Engring., 1989—; patentee for interleaving of composites, 1991; contbr. 75 articles to profl. jours. NRC fellow 1983; NATO fellow 1985. Home: 6080 Elmbridge Dr San Jose CA 95129 Office: NASA Ames Rsch Ctr MS 213-3 Moffett Field CA 94035

HIGDON, BERNICE COWAN, retired educator; b. Sylva, N.C., Feb. 26, 1918; d. Royston Duffield and Margaret Cordelia (Hall) Cowan; m. Roscoe John Higdon, Aug. 12, 1945; children: Ronald Keith, Rodrick Knox, Krista Dean. BS, Western Carolina U., 1941; cert. tchr., So. Oreg. Coll., 1967; student, Chapman Coll., 1971. Cert. tchr., Calif. Prin., tchr. Dorsey Sch., Bryson City, N.C., 1941-42; expeditor Glenn L. Martin Aircraft Co., Balt., 1942-45; tchr. elem. sch. Seneca, S.C., 1945-46, Piedmont, S.C., 1946-47; tchr. elem. sch. Columbia, S.C., 1950-51, Manteca, Calif., 1967-68; kindergarten tchr. 1st Bapt. Ch., Medford, Oreg., 1965-67; tchr. elem. sch. Marysville (Calif.) Unified Sch. Dist., 1968-83; tchr. Headstart, Manteca, 1968. Past counselor Youth Svc. Bur., Yuba City, Calif.; troop leader Girl Scouts U.S.A., Medford, 1962-63; past Sunday sch. tchr. 1st Bapt. Ch., Medford; bd. dirs. Christian Assistance Network, Yuba City, 1984-85; aux. vol. Fremont Med. Ctr., Yuba City, 1984—; deaconess Evang. Free Ch., Yuba City, 1991-93. Recipient cert. of appreciation Marysville Unified Sch. Dist., 1983, Christian Assistance Network, 1985; cert. of recognition Ella Elem. Sch., Marysville, 1983. Mem. Calif. Ret. Tchrs. Assn., Nat. Ret. Tchrs. Assn., Sutter Hist. Soc., AAUW, Am. Assn. Ret. Persons. Home: 1264 Charlotte Ave Yuba City CA 95991-2804

HIGDON, POLLY SUSANNE, judge; b. Goodland, Kans., May 1, 1942; d. William and Pauline Higdon; m. John P. Wilhardt (div. May 1988); 1 child, Liesl. BA, Vassar Coll., 1964; postgrad., Cornell U., 1967; JD, Washburn U., 1975; LLM, NYU, 1980. Bar: Kans. 1975, Oreg. 1980. Assoc. Corley & Assocs., Garden City, Kans., 1975-79, Kendrick M. Mercer Law Offices, Eugene, Oreg., 1980-82; pvt. practice law Eugene, 1983; judge U.S. Bankruptcy Ct., Eugene, 1983—. Active U.S. Peace Corps, Tanzania, East Africa, 1965-66. Mem. Am. Bankruptcy Inst., Nat. Conf. Bankruptcy Judges, Nat. Assn. Women Judges. Office: US Bankruptcy Ct PO Box 1335 211 E 7th Rm 404 Eugene OR 97440-1335

HIGGINBOTHAM, LLOYD WILLIAM, mechanical engineer; b. Haydentown, Pa., Nov. 24, 1934; s. Clarence John and Nannie Mae (Piper) H.; m. Genevieve Law, Oct. 17, 1953 (div.); 1 child, Mark William; m. Mary Bannaian, July 23, 1966; 1 child, Samuel Lloyd. With rsch. and devel. TRW Inc., Cleve., 1953-57; pres. Higginbotham Rsch., Cleve., 1957-64; pres., chief exec. officer Lloyd Higginbotham Assocs., Woodland Hills, Calif., 1964—;

cons. grad. engring. programs UCLA, Calif. State U., L.A., U. So. Calif.; pres. adv. com. Pierce Coll., L.A.; adv. com. So. Calif. Productivity Ctr.; cons. various Calif. legislators. Mem. Town Hall Calif.; pres. San Fernando Valley Joint Com. Engrs., 1992-93. Recipient Community Svc. award City of Downey, Calif, 1974, Archimedes award NSPE, Outstanding Contbr. Recognition, 1986, Outstanding Leadership Recognition, 1987, William B. Johnson Meml. Internat. Interprofl. award, 1992. Fellow Inst. Advancement of Engring. (exec. dir. 1984—); mem. Soc. Carbide and Tool Engrs. (chmn. 1974-76), Soc. Mfg. Engrs. (chmn. San Fernando Valley chpt. 1977-79, numerous awards), San Fernando Valley Joint Coun. Engrs. (advisor, pres. 1981-82, 92-94), Profl. Salesmen's Assn., Am. Soc. Assn. Execs., L.A. Coun. Engrs. and Scientists (exec. mgr. 1984—), L.A. Area C. of C., Toastmasters, Masons. Republican. Office: Higginbotham Assocs 24300 Calvert St Woodland Hills CA 91367-1113

HIGGINS, BILL EDWARD, chemist; b. Woodland, Calif., Dec. 31, 1961; s. Thomas Engel and Lynn (Williams) H.; m. Linda Grace Slanec, June 22, 1984. BA, Augustana Coll., Rock Island, Ill., 1984; MS, U. Calif., San Diego, 1986, PhD, 1989. Process engr. Censtor Corp., San Jose, Calif., 1989, sr. engr., 1989-92; engr. Quantum Corp., Milpitas, Calif., 1992—. Contbr. articles on magnetic rec. tech. to profl. jours. Regents fellow U. Calif., 1984-89. Mem. IEEE, Sigma Pi Sigma. Home: 3610 Louis Rd Palo Alto CA 94303 Office: Quantum Corp 500 McCarthy Milpitas CA 95135

HIGGINS, JAMES BRADLEY, dentist; b. Richmond, Ind., July 3, 1941; s. James Randall and Mildred Ethel (White) H.; m. Dorothy Campbell, Dec. 29, 1964; children: Kimberly, Amy, Michaelle Ann, James. DDS, Ind. U., Bloomington, 1966. Resident dentist Ind. State Mental Hosp., Richmond, 1966; pvt. practice dentistry San Jose, Calif., 1968—; lectr. hypnosis Calif. Dental Assts. Assn., 1974-88; cons. Calif. State Bd. Dental Examiners, 1978-80; co-chmn. Santa Clara County Dentist Peer Rev. Com., 1982-84; dental lectr. San Jose Unified Sch. Dist. Bd. dir. Santa Clara County Health Dept., San Jose, 1986-90, Noble Sch. Parent Tchr. Adv. Bd., San Jose; life mem. NAACP. Capt. Dental Corp, USAF, 1966-68. Mem. ADA, Santa Clara County Dental Soc., Calif. Dental Assn., Nat. Dental Assn. Democrat. Office: 4600 Alum Rock Ave San Jose CA 95127-2463

HIGGINS, JON STANLEY, investment company executive; b. Chgo., Sept. 4, 1941; s. Stanley John and Helen Francis (House) H.; m. Janet Kathryne Moore, June 17, 1967; children: Jon Samuel, Rebecca Jane. Student, Whitman Coll., 1959-60; AA, Menlo Coll., 1961; BS cum laude, UCLA, 1968, MBA, 1969. Br. mgr. Freed Fin. Co., Las Vegas, Nev., 1963-66; mgmt. cons. Cresap, McCormick & Paget, San Francisco, 1969-74; planning mgr. Bechtel Group, San Francisco, 1974-77, chief auditor, 1979-80, mgr. mgmt. info., 1983-86; sr. regional rep. Bechtel Group, Seoul, Republic of Korea, 1980-83; exec. asst. to pres. Bechtel Investments, San Francisco, 1986-88, CFO, 1988—; chmn. bd. Petro Source Corp., Houston; bd. dirs. Fremont Investment Advisors, San Francisco, BecField Drilling Svcs., Houston, J. P. Morgan S.E. Asia, Ltd., Singapore. Pres. Las Vegas Lenders Exch., 1964, Westminster Assn. Retail Bus., Westminster, Calif., 1966; dir. Am. C. of C., Seoul, 1982-83. Mem. World Trade Club, World Affairs Coun., Commonwealth Club, Fin. Execs. Inst. Office: Bechtel Investments Inc 50 Fremont St Ste 3600 San Francisco CA 94105

HIGGINS, MICHAEL WILLIAM, computer scientist; b. Batavia, N.Y., Jan. 12, 1957; s. Gibson Ambrose and Gertrude Mary (Coe) H. BS in Computer Sci., San Diego State U., 1978. Programmer Blue Ribbon Sports, Portland, Oreg., 1979-80; cons. U.S. Dept. State, 1981-82; mgr. tech. support Byer Calif., San Francisco, 1983—. Author computer programs DBA Tools, 1991. Recipient medal of svc. Govt. of Indonesia, 1982. Mem. Internat. Oracle Users Group, Sequent Users Resource Forum. Republican. Roman Catholic. Office: Byer Calif 66 Potrero Ave San Francisco CA 94103

HIGGINS, PAUL ANTHONY, industrial engineer; b. Brisbane, Queensland, Australia, Nov. 7, 1964; came to U.S. 1987.; s. Daniel Leo and Patricia Margret (Creedon) H.; m. Bernadette Burnell, May 25, 1989. BS in Engring., U. Queensland, 1986; MS in Engring. Mgmt., U. Mo., Rolla, 1989. Project engr. Lindsay Ekert & Assocs., Brisbane, 1986-88; plant engr. Clorox Co., St. Louis, 1988-91; sr. engr. Clorox Co., Oakland, Calif., 1991—. Mem. Inst. Indsl. Engrs., Am. Soc. Engring. Mgmt., Rolla Jaycees (pres. 1990). Office: Clorox Co 1221 Broadway Oakland CA 94588-8005

HIGGINS, RUTH ANN, social worker, family therapist; b. Rock Valley, Iowa, Sept. 23, 1944; d. Neal and Tillie (Feekes) Vonk; m. 1972 (div. Sept. 1986); children: Ashlie Kay, Steven Grant. BA, Northwestern Coll., 1966; MA, U. Colo., 1978; LCSW, U. Denver, 1983. Cert. profl. tchr., Colo., social worker, Colo. Tchr. Adams County Dist. 12, Northglenn, Colo., 1967-69, Dept. Def., Clark AFB, The Philippines, 1969-70, Jefferson County Schs., Lakewood, Colo., 1970-75; social worker Boulder (Colo.) County Mental Health Ctr., 1977, Boulder Community Counseling Ctr., 1979-81, Columbine Counseling Ctr., Broomfield, Colo., 1981—; sch. social worker Adams County Sch. Dist. 12, Northglenn, Colo., 1985—; part time social worker Hospice of Metro Denver, 1984-85, Boulder Valley Pub. Schs., 1985, Lutheran Hospice Care, Wheatridge, Colo., 1985. Author, editor: Nothing Could Stop the Rain, 1976. Mem. Nat. Assn. Social Workers. Democrat.

HIGGINSON, JOHN, retired military officer; b. St. Louis, Oct. 24, 1932; s. John and Clara Elizabeth (Lindemann) H.; married; children: Robert, Mark, Patrick, Paul. BA, St. Mary's U., 1954; BS, Naval Postgrad. Sch., 1966; MS, George Washington U., 1968. Ensign USN, advanced through grades to rear adm., ret.; comdr. Helicopter Anti-submarine Squadron 2, 1973-74, Helicopter Anti-submarine Squadron 10, 1976-78, Amphibious Squadron 7, 1981-83, Amphibious Group 3, 1985; comdr. Naval Surface Group, Long Beach, 1986, ret., 1990-92; pres. Long Beach C. of C.; prof. mgmt. Naval War Coll., Newport, R.I. Co-author: Sea and Air, The Marine Environment, 1962, 2nd. edit., 1973. Bd. dirs. United Way, L.A., Long Beach Symphony, Long Beach Youth Activities, DARE, Inc., USO, Leadership Long Beach, St. Mary's Med. Ctr., Meml. Med. Ctr. of Long Beach; trustee Long Beach City Coll. Found., Long Beach Civic Light Opera; mem. exec. bd. of Long Beach Boy Scouts of Am.; mem. exec. coun. Industry-Edn. Coun. of Calif.; former chmn. L.A. Combined Fed. Campaign. Mem. Navy Helicopter Assn. (former pres.), Fed. Exec. Bd. (former chmn.), Rotary. Home: 5341 Las Lomas Park Estates Long Beach CA 90815

HIGH, THOMAS W., utilities company executive; b. Oakland, Calif., Dec. 7, 1947; s. William A. and Vera D. (Blumann) H.; m. Nancy J. Hughes, June 8, 1969. B.A., U. Calif., Berkeley, 1968; student advanced mgmt. program, Harvard, 1992. Dir. legis. services Pacific Gas and Electric Co., San Francisco, 1982-84, asst. sec., 1984-85, corp. sec., 1985-86, v.p., corp. sec., 1986-91, v.p., asst. to chmn., 1991—. Trustee Am. Conservatory Theatre, 1991—; mem. coun. Friends of the Bancroft Libr. Office: Pacific Gas and Electric Co 77 Beale St B 32 San Francisco CA 94177

HIGHLAND, MARILYN RAE SCHNELL, business owner; b. Cleve., Dec. 2, 1956; d. Burton and Sandra Ileen (Greenwald) Schnell; m. Kenneth James Highland, Oct. 20, 1985. BSCE, Carnegie Mellon U., 1979. EIT Pa., Calif. Engr. McDonnel Douglas, Long Beach, Calif., 1979-81; program mgr. Printronix, Irvine, Calif., 1983-88; test engring. mgr. Rugged Digital Systems, Mountain View, Calif., 1988-90; mgr. Advanced Process Engring. Adaptec Inc., Milpitas, Calif., 1990-92; v.p. Highland Metals Inc., San Jose, Calif., 1990-92. Vol. Furry Friends, Morgan Hill, Calif., 1990—, 2d Harvest Food Bank, San Jose, 1990—. Mem. Soc. Women Engrs. Office: Highland Metals Inc PO Box 23216 San Jose CA 95153

HIGHLANDER, RICHARD WILLIAM, communications executive; b. Beckley, W.Va., Feb. 17, 1940; s. Ronald William and Lucille Bernice (Bland) H.; m. Ida Mae Canterbury, June 26, 1965; one child, Alison Renee. BA, Rutgers U., 1963; MA, U. Ga., 1972. Commd. 2d lt. U.S. Army, 1963, advanced through grades to lt. col., 1979, ret., 1984; dir. communications, def. systems group FMC Corp., Santa Clara, Calif., 1984—. Contbr. articles to profl. jours., Freedom Found. award 1966, 81. Trustee San Jose Repertory Co., 1985. Decorated Legion of Merit with bronze oak leaf cluster, Bronze Star with two bronze oak leaf clusters, Purple Heart. Mem. PRSA (accredited), Assn. U.S. Army, Internat. Assn. Bus. Communicators, Calif. Mfrs. Assn. (bd. dirs. 1985, chmn. bd. 1993), Aerospace Industries Assn. (comm. coun.), Rotary, San Jose Met. C. of C. (bd. dirs.). Republican. Methodist. Home: 1486 Oak Canyon Dr San Jose CA 95120-5711

HIGHT, HAROLD PHILIP, retired security company executive; b. Crescent City, Calif., Apr. 17, 1924; s. Vernon Austin and Mary Jane (Gontau) H.; m. Margaret Rose Edelman, Nov. 19, 1945 (div. 1949); children: Linda Marie, Beverly Sue; m. Doris Louise Dunn, June 20, 1982. Student police sci., Coll. of Redwoods, 1969. With Pan Am. World Airways, South San Francisco, Calif., 1945-51, 52; officer Richmond (Calif.) Police Dept., 1952-54; aircraft electrician Internat. Atlas Svc., Oakland, Calif., 1954-56; security officer radiation lab. AEC, Livermore, Calif., 1956-58; chief police Port Orford (Oreg.) Police Dept., 1958-61; dep. sheriff, sgt., evidence technician Del Notre County Sheriff's Dept., Crescent City, 1961-85; security officer, sgt. Del Notre Security Svc., Crescent City, 1985. With USN, 1941-45, 51-52. Mem. Internat. Footprint Assn. (sec., treas. bd. dirs. Crescent City 1985—), Navy League U.S. (2d v.p. Crescent City 1984—), Tin Can Sailors, Masons, Scottish Rite (32d degree), Elks, Grange. Republican. Roman Catholic. Home: 110 Lafayette Way Crescent City CA 95531

HIGHTOWER, LEN, dean of student affairs; b. Louisville, Ky., Mar. 8, 1955; s. Guy Thomas and Betty Lee (Jaggers) Barker; m. Mary JAn Brazo, Dec. 20, 1980; 1 child, Luke Aaron. BB in Psychology, Westmont Coll., 1978; MA in Social Sci. with honors, Azusa (Calif.) Pacific U., 1980; PhD in Edn., Claremont (Calif.) Grad. Sch., 1992. Dir. counseling & student life, assoc. dean res. life John Brown U., Siloam Springs, Ark., 1980-83; adj. prof. Azusa Pacific U., 1983-84; assoc. dean sch.-based student svcs. Calif. State U., Long Beach, 1985-86; dean student affairs U. La Verne (Calif.), 1986—; cons. R. Rood and Assocs., Azusa, 1983-84; chair task force on diversity U. La Verne, 1992—; chair sm. coll. and u. netowrk, 1992; created office minority student affairs, U. La Verne, 1990. Presenter in field. Exec. com. mem. Pomona Valley Mental Health Adv. Bd., 1988-92. Mem. Am. Assn. Higher Edn. (assessment forum), Nat. Assn. Student Pers. Adminstrs., Assn. Instnl. Rsch., Soc. Coll. and U. Planners. Presbyterian. Office: U La Verne 1950 3rd St La Verne CA 91750

HIGUCHI, WESLEY KENJI, loan officer; b. Honolulu, Nov. 4, 1964; s. Leslie and Jane Kiyono (Nishioka) H.; m. Joyce Y. Shiroma, July 4, 1987; children: Paula, Warren. BBA, U. Hawaii, 1987. Actuarial analyst Hawaii Med. Assn., Honolulu, 1987-89; fin. cons. John Hancock Fin. Svcs., Honolulu, 1989-90; loan officer, br. mgr. Fin. Factors, Ltd., Kahului, Hawaii, 1990—. Treas. Pukalani (Hawaii) Bapt. Ch., 1990-92; tutor Makawao (Hawaii) Dept. Edn., 1990-92. Home: RR 2 Box 95 Kula HI 96790 Office: Fin Factors Ltd Ste 160 33 Lono Ave Kahului HI 96732

HILBE, JOSEPH MICHAEL, statistics educator, statistician, consultant, editor; b. L.A., Dec. 30, 1944; s. Rader John and Nadyne (Anderson) H.; m. Cheryl Lynn Swisher; children: Matthew, Heather, Michael, Mitchell. BA, Calif. State U., Chico, 1968; JD, LaSalle U., 1973; MA, U. Hawaii, 1974; PhD, UCLA, 1988. Lic. arbitrator. Instr. philosophy, law & quantitative reasoning, dept. chair U. Hawaii, Pearl City, 1970-86; head coach, track and field U. Hawaii, Manoa, 1979-85; dir. biostatistics N.W. Hosp., Seattle, 1986-89; chief exec. officer Accusoft Inc., Lynnwood, Wash., 1989-90; sr. biostatistician, epidemiologist Health Svcs. Adv. Group Inc., Phoenix, 1990-91; statis. subcontractor Health Care Financing Adminstrn. (Medicare), 1991—; prof. Ariz. State U., 1992—; editor Stata Tech. Bull., 1991-93; speaker Internat. Congress on Methods Sci., Bucharest, Romania, 1971, Royal Statistical Soc., London, 1993; cons. Puget Sound Spine Inst., Seattle, 1988-90, Profl. Rev. Orgn. Wash., Seattle, 1989—; vis. prof. U. Mex., 1992; v.p. rsch., dir. biostatistics Helath Scis. Inst., Pa., 1993—. Author: (books) Experiencing Philosophy, 1970, Fundamentals of Conceptual Analysis, 1977, Sentential Logic, 1986; (computer software) Quick Statistics, 1989, generalized linear models module, sample size module stata, 1993. Nat. chmn. AAU Jr. Olympic Girls Track and Field, Indpls., 1979-82, TAC Girls Track and Field, Indpls., 1980-83, TAC Sports Medicine, Sci. Edn., Indpls., 1984-88; pres. Hawaii TAC, 1980-84; lead competition ofcl. Olympic Games, L.A., 1984; broadcast coord. Goodwill Games, Seattle, 1990. Nat. Pentathlon Champion, AAU, 1968, 78, 79; World List 400 Track and Field News, 1965, World List 100, 1967; vis. scholar U. Louvain, Belgium. Mem. Am. Statis. Assn. (columnist statis. computing & graphics news 1991—). Home: 10952 N 128th Pl Scottsdale AZ 85259-4464

HILBRECHT, NORMAN TY, state legislator, lawyer; b. San Diego, Feb. 11, 1933; s. Norman Titus and Elizabeth (Lair) H.; m. Mercedes L. Sharratt, Oct. 24, 1980. B.A., Northwestern U., 1956; J.D., Yale U., 1959. Bar: Nev. 1959, U.S. Supreme Ct. 1963. Assoc. counsel Union Pacific R.R., Las Vegas, 1962; partner firm Hilbrecht & Jones, Las Vegas, 1962-69; pres. Hilbrecht, Jones, Schreck & Bernhard, 1969-83, Hilbrecht & Assocs, 1983—, Mobil Transport Corp., 1970-72; gen. counsel Bell United Ins. Co., 1986—; assemblyman Nev. Legislature, 1966-72, minority leader, 1971-72; mem. Nev. Senate, 1974-78; asst. lectr. bus. law U. Nev., Las Vegas.; chmn. adminstrv. law com. Nev. State Bar, 1991—. Author: Nevada Motor Carrier Compendium, 1990. Mem. labor mgmt. com. NCCJ, 1963; mem. Clark County (Nev.) Democratic Central Com., 1959-80, 1st vice chmn., 1965-66; del. Western Regional Assembly on Ombudsman; chmn. Clark County Dem. Conv., 1966, Nev. Dem. Conv., 1966; pres. Clark County Legal Aid Soc., 1964, Nev. Legal Aid and Defender Assn., 1965-83. Served to capt. AUS, 1952-67. Named Outstanding State Legislator Eagleton Inst. Politics, Rutgers U., 1969. Mem. ABA, Am. Judicature Soc., Am. Acad. Polit. and Social Sci., Assn. Trial Lawyers Am., State Bar Nev. (chmn. adminstrv. law com.), Nev. Trial Lawyers (state v.p. 1966), Am. Assn. Ret. Persons (mem. state legis. com. 1991—), Clark County Bar Assn., Elks, Phi Beta Kappa, Delta Phi Epsilon, Theta Chi, Phi Delta Phi. Lutheran. Office: 723 S Casino Center Blvd Las Vegas NV 89101-6716

HILDEBRAND, CAROL ILENE, librarian; b. Presho, S.D., Feb. 15, 1943; d. Arnum Vance and Ethel Grace (Cole) Stoops; m. Duane D. Hildebrand, Mar. 21, 1970. BA, Dakota Wesleyan U., Mitchell, S.D., 1965; M.Librarianship, U. Wash., 1968. Tchr. Watertown (S.D.) High Sch., 1965-67; library dir. Chippewa County Library, Montevideo, Minn., 1968-70, The Dalles-Wasco County Library, The Dalles, Oreg., 1970-72; librarian Salem (Oreg.) Pub. Library, 1972-73; library dir. Lake Oswego (Oreg.) Pub. Library, 1973-82; asst. city librarian Eugene (Oreg.) Pub. Libr., 1982-91, acting city libr., 1991-92, library dir., 1993—; cons. in field; conductor workshops in field. Vice chmn. League Women Voters, Lane County, 1987; bd. dirs. Oreg. Libr. PAC, 1986—; sec. Citizens for Lane County Library, 1985-88. Mem. ALA (chpt. councilor 1990—), AAUW (bd. dirs. 1986), Pacific N.W. Libr. Assn. (pres. 1989-98), Oreg. Libr. Assn. (pres. 1976-77), Rotary (sec. 1992—), Phi Kappa Phi. Methodist. Office: Eugene Public Library 100 W 13th Ave Eugene OR 97401-3484

HILDEBRAND, DON CECIL, helicopter company executive; b. Camp Cooke, Calif., Dec. 1, 1943; s. Cecil and Gladys Helen (Buschmeier) H.; m. Rita Ann Wojdyla, July 25, 1964 (div. 1991); children: Jeffrey James, Denise Lynn; m. Kathy Glaspie, June 13, 1992. BA, U. Ariz., 1978. Chief pilot Tucson Police Dept., 1970-80; pres. S.W. Helicopters, Inc., Tucson, 1981—; Dir. Airborne Law Enforcement Assn., Los Angeles, 1976-78; pilot examiner FAA, Phoenix, 1979—; counselor accident prevention FAA, Phoenix, 1988. Pres. Vietnam Helicopter Pilot Assn., Phoenix, 1982. With U.S. Army, 1966-69, Vietnam. Mem. SAG, Am. Helicopter Soc., Vietnam Veterans Assn., Veterans of Fgn. Wars, Aircraft Owners & Pilots Assn., The Planetary Soc. Republican. Catholic. Home: 2530 S Kevin Tucson AZ 85748 Office: SW Helicopters Inc 6666 S Plumer Ave Tucson AZ 85706-7006

HILDEBRANDT, PETER WARREN, computer engineer, executive; b. Columbus, Ohio, Aug. 28, 1963; s. Theodore Ware and Mary Kathryn (Babcock) H. BSEE summa cum laude, N.C. State U., 1985. Hardware engr. U. N.C., Greensboro, 1979-81; sr. student programmer Precision Visuals, Inc., Boulder, Colo., 1981-82; contract programmer Geo-Based Systems, Raleigh, N.C., 1982-83; software engr. Vectrix Corp., Greensboro, 1982-85; sr. software architect Tektronix, Inc., Beaverton, Oreg., 1985-90; v.p. engring. Micro Forecasts, Inc., Portland, Oreg., 1990—; ind. cons., Beaverton, 1985-90. Patentee for Cursor for Use in 3-D Imaging Systems, Stereoscopic Graphics Display Terminal with Image Data Processing. Recipient Rensselaer medal Rensselaer Poly. Inst., 1981. Mem. IEEE, Assn. Computing Machinery, Tau Beta Pi, Eta Kappa Nu. Home: 2338 NE 32nd Ave Portland OR 97212 Office: Micro Forecasts Inc 319 SW Washington St Ste 420 Portland OR 97204

HILDEBRANT, ANDY MCCLELLAN, electrical engineer; b. Nescopeck, Pa., May 12, 1929; s. Andrew Harmon and Margaret C. (Knorr) H.; m. Rita Mae Yarnold, June 20, 1959; children: James Matthew, David Michael, Andrea Marie. Student, State Tchrs. Coll., Bloomsburg, Pa., 1947-48, Bucknell U., 1952-54, UCLA, 1955-57, Utica Coll., 1965-70. Rsch. analyst Douglas Aircraft Co., Santa Monica, Calif., 1954-57; specialist engring. GE, Johnson City, N.Y., 1957-58, Ithaca, N.Y., 1958-64; elec. engr. GE, Utica, N.Y., 1964-70, Sylvania Electro Systems, Mountain View, Calif., 1970-71, Dalmo-Victor Co., Belmont, Calif., 1971-72, Odetics/Infodetics, Anaheim, Calif., 1972-75, Lear Siegler, Inc., Anaheim, 1975-78, Ford Aerospace, Newport Beach, Calif., 1978-79, THUMS Long Beach Co., Long Beach, Calif., 1979—; elec. engring. cons. Perkin-Elmer, Auto Info. Retrieval, Pi-Gem Assn., Pasadena, Calif., Palo Alto, Calif., 1971-73. Patentee AC power modulator for a non-linear load. Juror West Orange County Mpcl. Ct., Westminster, Calif., 1979, U.S. Dist. Ct., L.A., 1991-92. With USN, 1948-52. Recipient Cert. Award in Indsl. Controls Tech., Calif. State U., Fullerton, 1991-92. Mem. Orange County Chpt. Charities (sec. 1988), KC (past grand knight 1987-88). Republican. Roman Catholic. Home: 20392 Bluffwater Cir Huntington Beach CA 92646-4723 Office: THUMS Long Beach Co 300 Oceangate Long Beach CA 90802-6801

HILDNER, ERNEST GOTTHOLD, III, solar physicist, science administrator; b. Jacksonville, Ill., Jan. 23, 1940; s. Ernest Gotthold Hildner Jr. and Jean (Johnston) Duffield; m. Sandra Whitney Shellworth, June 29, 1968; children: Cynthia Whitney, Andrew Duffield. BA in Physics and Astronomy, Wesleyan U., 1961; MA in Physics and Astronomy, U. Colo., 1964, PhD in Physics and Astronomy, 1971. Experiment scientist High Altitude Obs., Nat. Ctr. Atmospheric Rsch., Boulder, Colo., 1972-80, vis. scientist, 1985-86; chief solar physics br. NASA Marshall Space Flight Ctr., Huntsville, Ala., 1980-85; dir. space environment lab. NOAA Environ. Rsch. Labs., Boulder, 1986—; mem. com. on solar and space physics NRC, Washington, 1986-90; chmn. Com. on Space Environment Forecasting, fed. coord. for meteorology, Washington, 1988—. Contbr. rsch. papers in solar and interplanetary physics, 1971—; co-inventor spectral slicing X-ray telescope with variable magnification. Mem. AAAS, Am. Geophys. Union (assoc. editor Geophys. Rsch. Letters 1983-85), Am. Astron. Soc. (councillor solar physics div. 1979-80), Internat. Astron. Union, Sigma Xi. Office: NOAA Space Environment Lab 325 Broadway (R/E/SE) Boulder CO 80303-3328

HILDRETH, CHARLES STEVEN, military career officer; b. Ontario, Oreg., May 6, 1949; s. Daniel Clifford and Lowanda Mae (Lewis) H.; m. Mary Inis Coltrera, Aug. 20, 1969 (div. Jan. 1972); 1 child, Karla Marie; m. Pamela Jane Gowin, July 20, 1977;children: Zachary Samuel. BS in Edn., Idaho State U., 1973; MA in Edn., Chapman Coll., 1979. Cert. elem. edn. tchr., Idaho, Calif., Mont., Alaska, Wash.; cert. comml. pilot. Enlisted U.S. Army, 1968, advanced through grades to maj., 1987; chief logistic div. U.S. Army Med. Activity, Ft. Wainwright, Alaska, 1989-92; dep. dir. logistics Brooke Army Med. Ctr., Ft. Sam Houston, Tex., 1992—; founding project officer Army Med. Dept. Rgt., Ft. Sam Houston, Tex., 1985-87. Author: (with others) Army Housekeeping Manual, 1982; editor: Army Cadre Manual, 1987. Mil. coord. March of Dimes, San Antonio, 1989. Mem. NEA, Army Aviation Assn., Assn. U.S. Army, Dust Off Assn., Nat. Exec. Housekeeping Assn. (registered exec. housekeeper). Republican. Baptist.

HILEMAN, LINDA CAROL, elementary education educator; b. Aliquippa, Pa., Mar. 29, 1947; d. Charles Allen and Aurelia (Oprean) Cunningham; m. Hazen E. Hileman, June 11, 1971. BS, Clarion (Pa.) U., 1969, MEd, 1970; EdS, U. Wyo., 1977. Sci. tchr. Center Area Schs., Monaca, Pa., 1970-71; intermediate tchr. Purchase Line Schs., Commodore, Pa., 1971-72; tchr. 5th grade Carbon County #2 Schs., Medicine Bow, Wyo., 1972-73; team tchr. Carbon County #2 Schs., Saratoga, Wyo., 1973-80, prin. middle sch., 1980-83, tchr. math. and sci., 1983—; adj. instr. U. Wyo., Laramie, 1988—; participant Marine Resource Inst., Key Largo, Fla., 1990, Nat. Radio Astronomy Obs., Green Bank, W.Va., 1992.; presenter in field. Co-author: First Women of Wyoming, 1990, Trek of the Mammoth II: 1890-1990, 1993. Dir. Bible Sch. First Presbyn. Ch., Saratoga, 1985-87; moderator Presbyn. Women, Saratoga, 1988-92, vice moderator, 1992—; mem. Wyo. Commn. for Women, 1975-92. Named Tchr. of Yr. Saratoga Edn. Assn., 1977, Educator of Yr. Vets. Orgn., Saratoga, 1990, Wyo. Elem. Sci. Tchr. of Yr. Wyo. Sci. Tchrs. Assn., 1991; recipient Presdl. Award for Elem. Sci. Teaching, 1992. Mem. Delta Kappa Gamma (pres. chpt. 1984-86). Republican. Home: PO Box 1322 Saratoga WY 82331 Office: Saratoga Elem Sch 221 Spring St Saratoga WY 82331

HILES, JOHN CLIFFORD, III, marine investigator, employment agency executive; b. Biloxi, Miss., June 29, 1959; s. John C. Jr. and Vanessa D. (Adams) H.; m. Kimberly A. Freshour, June 10, 1984; 1 child, Colton John. BA in Criminal Justice, Wash. State U., 1982. Fisherman Alaska, 1973-83; detective Police Dept., Wash., 1983-90; owner, pres. Alaska Fisheries Employment Network, Tacoma, 1990—, John C. Hiles & Assocs., Tacoma, 1990—; marine investigator LeGros, Buchanan, Paul & Whitehead, Seattle, 1992—. Bd. dirs. Homeless Employment Partnership, Tacoma, 1992; vol. Tacoma Rescue Mission, 1992. Mem. Fishing Industry Pers. Assn. Wash., Wash. State Marine Adjusters Assn., Internat. Propeller Club. Office: LeGros Buchanan Paul & Whtiehead 701 5th Ave Ste 2500 Seattle WA 98104

HILGARD, ERNEST ROPIEQUET, psychologist; b. Belleville, Ill., July 25, 1904; s. George Engelmann and Laura (Ropiequet) H.; m. Josephine Rohrs, Sept. 19, 1931; children—Henry Rohrs, Elizabeth Ann Jecker. B.S., U. Ill., 1924; Ph.D., Yale, 1930; D.Sc., Kenyon Coll., 1964; LL.D., Centre Coll., 1974; D.Sc., Northwestern U., 1987, Colgate U., 1987. Asst. instr. in psychology Yale U., 1928-29, instr., 1929-33; successively asst. prof., asso. prof., prof. psychology Stanford, 1933-69, emeritus prof., 1969—, exec. head dept., 1942-50, dean grad. div., 1951-55; Bd. dirs., pres. Ann. Reviews, Inc., 1948-73; With USDA, Washington, 1942, OWI, 1942-43, Office Civilian Requirements, WPB, 1943-44; Collaborator, div. child devel. and tchr. personnel Am. Council Edn., 1940-41; nat. adv. mental health council USPHS, 1952-56; fellow (Center Advanced Study Behavioral Scis.), 1956-57; Mem. U.S. Edn. Mission to Japan, 1946. Author: Theories of Learning, 1948, rev. deit., 1981, Introduction to Psychology, 1953, rev. edit., 1987, Hypnotic Susceptibility, 1965, Hypnosis in the Relief of Pain, 1975, rev. edit., 1983, Divided Consciousness, 1977, rev. edit., 1986, American Psychology in Historical Perspective, 1978, Psychology in America: A Historical Survey, 1987; editor: Fifty Years of Psychology, 1988. Bd. curators Stephens Coll., Mo., 1953-68. Recipient Warren medal in exptl. psychology, 1940; Wilbur Cross medal Yale U., 1971; Gold medal Am. Psychol. Found., 1978. Hon. fellow Brit. Psychol. Assn.; mem. Am. Psychol. Assn. (pres. 1948-49), Am. Acad. Arts and Scis., Nat. Acad. Edn., Soc. Psychol. Study Social Issues (chmn. 1944-45), AAAS, Nat. Acad. Scis. (sci. reviewing award 1984), Am. Philos. Soc., Internat. Soc. Hypnosis (pres. 1973-76, Benjamin Franklin gold medal 1979), Sigma Xi. Home: Apt 518 850 Webster St Palo Alto CA 94301-2837 Office: Stanford U Psychology Dept Bldg 420 Rm 206 Stanford CA 94305-2130

HILGEMAN, GEORGIA KAY, organization executive; b. Chgo., Sept. 9, 1950; d. James Thomas and Georgia (Kambiss) Trembois; m. Juan F. Rios, Aug. 27, 1971 (div. 1976); m. Robin Dale Hilgeman, Dec. 2, 1977; children: Monica, Ryan. BA in Social Svc., San Jose State U., 1972, MA in Counselor Edn., 1975. Sch. counselor Evergreen Sch. Dist., San Jose, Calif., 1971-83; founder, exec. dir. Vanished Children's Alliance, San Jose, 1981—; resource person to numerous local, state, fed. and internat. agys., 1981—; condr. tng. for worldwide groups on missing children, 1981—; expert witness in ct. cases involving missing children, 1985—; v.p. bd. dirs. Child Net, 1987-89; chmn. nonprofit orgn. liaison com. Nat. Ctr. for Missing and Exploited Children, Washington, 1986-89; advisor, trainer victim offender reconciliation group Calif. Dept. Corrections, 1988—; mem. adv. bd. Missing and Exploited Children Comprehensive Action Program. Speaker on missing children issues, 1976—; founder, mem. Victim Support Network for Santa Clara County, San Jose, 1985—; mem. Nat. Orgn. Victim Assistance, Washington, 1987—; cons. Office Juvenile Justice and Delinquency Prevention, U.S. Dept. Justice, Washington, 1989—. Recipient For Those Who Care award Sta. KRON-TV, San Francisco, 1985, Woman of Achievement award Soroptimist Internat., 1988, Gov.'s Victim Svc. award Calif. Office Criminal Justice Planning, 1988, award Calif. Dept. Corrections, 1990, numerous others. Home: PO Box 2052 Los Gatos CA 95031-2052 Office: Vanished Childrens Alliance 1407 Parkmoor Ave Ste 200 San Jose CA 95126-3430

HILGERT, RONALD FRANCIS, engineering educator; b. Willmar, Minn., June 19, 1947; s. LeRoy H. and Norma H. (Hatlen) H.; m. Deborah Rose Depue, July 1, 1978; 1 child, Noah Shane. BA in Polit. Sci., U. Minn., 1970; AA in Structural Engrng., San Juan Coll., 1983. Instr. San Juan Coll., Farmington, N.Mex., 1980-86; instr., dept. head Constrn. Sch., Albuquerque, 1986-89; dir. edn. Career One, Tucson, Ariz., 1989-93; dir. edn. engrng. Westin La Paloma, Tucson, 1991—. Editor: (newsletter) Construction School News, 1986-89, Career News, 1990-91. Cons. Albuquerque Homeless Shelter, 1989, Albuquerque Assn. Retarded Citizens, 1989; active Ariz. Desert Mus., Tucson, 1991, Tucson Environ. Coalition, 1992. Mem. Nat. Assn. Trade Sch. Tchrs. Democrat. Roman Catholic. Home: 6974 N Asterion Tucson AZ 85741 Office: Westin La Paloma Resort 3800 Sunset Tucson AZ 85741

HILKER, WALTER ROBERT, JR., lawyer; b. Los Angeles, Apr. 18, 1921; s. Walter Robert and Alice (Cox) H.; children: Anne Katherine, Walter Robert III. BS, U. So. Calif., 1942, LLB, 1948. Bar: Calif. 1949. Sole practice Los Angeles, 1949-55; ptnr. Parker, Milliken, Kohlmeier, Clark & O'Hara, 1955-75; of counsel Pacht, Ross, Warne, Bernhard & Sears, Newport Beach, Calif., 1980-84. Trustee Bella Mabury Trust; bd. dirs. Houchin Found. Served to lt. USNR, 1942-45. Decorated Bronze Star. Mem. ABA, Calif. Bar Assn., Orange County Bar Assn. Republican. Clubs: Spring Valley Lake Country (Apple Valley, Calif.); Balboa Bay (Newport Beach, Calif.). Home and Office: 7 Mill Creek Irvine CA 92715

HILL, ALETTE OLIN, technical communications educator; b. Bronxville, N.Y., Jan. 25, 1933; d. Oscar Charles and Florence (Thompson) Olin; m. Boyd Howard Hill, Jr., Jan. 26, 1956; children: Boyd Buchanan, Michael Howard. Student, U. Paris, 1952-53; AB, Duke U., 1954; MA, U. Va., 1959; PhD, U. N.C., 1967. Adminstrv. asst. UN, N.Y.C., 1954; editor The Rand Corp., Santa Monica, Calif., 1957-58, La. State U., Baton Rouge, 1962-64; asst. prof. U. So. Calif., L.A., 1966-67, U. Colo., Boulder, 1967-69; dir. Office of Innovative Edn., U. Colo., Boulder, 1975-80; assoc. prof. Met. State Coll., Denver, 1981—. Author: Mother Tongue, Father Time, 1986; contbr. articles to profl. jours. Dupont fellow U. Va., Charlottesville, 1954-55, fellow So. Fellowship Fund, 1960-61, fellow AAUW, 1965-66; scholar German Govt. Exch., 1961-62. Mem. Internat. Assn. for Semiotic Studies, Soc. for Tech. Communication, Soc. for Internat. Edn. Tng. and Rsch., Ozark Ctr. for Lang. Studies, Colo. Women's Studies Assn., Colo. Assn. for Internat. Edn., Denver-Metro Teaching and Rsch. Colloquium on Women, Phi Beta Kappa. Office: Met State Coll Denver Campus Box 35 PO Box 173362 Denver CO 80217-3362

HILL, ANDREW WILLIAM, jazz musician, composer; b. Chgo., June 30, 1937; s. William Robert and Hattie (Mathews) H.; m. La Verne Bradford, Jan. 8, 1963 (dec. Jan. 1989). MusB, New Coll. Calif., San Francisco, 1980. Performer with Charlie Parker Detroit; accompanist with Dinah Washington, Johnny Hartman, others, 1954-60, performer Roland Kirk Band, 1954-60, rec. artist with Roland Kirk, 1960-62; rec. artist Blue Note Records, 1961-63, 63-70; composer in residence Colgate U., Hamilton, N.Y., 1963-70; Heritage touring fellow Smithsonian Instn., 1970-72; mus. dir. New Coll. Calif., San Francisco, 1971-76; mus. panelist Calif. Arts Coun., 1984-89. Compositions include Bobby's Tune, 1989, Golden Sunset, 1989, Spiritual Lover, 1989, Pinnacle, Tail Feathers, Monk's Glimpse, Tripping, Chilly Mac, Ball Square, Domani, La Verne, Verona Rag, Tinkering, Retrospect, Refuge, New Monastery, Flight 19, Spectrum, Dedication, Point of Departure, 1965. Home and Office: JAZZFUND 606 NW Front Ave Portland OR 97209-3756

HILL, ANNA MARIE, manufacturing executive; b. Great Falls, Mont., Nov. 6, 1938; d. Paul Joseph and Alexina Rose (Doyon) Ghekiere. AA, Oakland Jr. Coll., 1959; student, U. Calif., Berkeley, 1960-62. Mgr. ops. OSM, Soquel, Calif., 1963-81; purchasing agt. Arrow Huss, Scotts Valley, Calif., 1981-82; sr. buyer Fairchild Test Systems, San Jose, Calif., 1982-83; materials mgr. Basic Test Systems, San Jose, 1983-86; purchasing mgr. Beta Tech., Santa Cruz, Calif., 1986-87; mgr. purchasing ICON Rev., Carmel, Calif., 1987-88; materials mgr. Integrated Components Test System, Sunnyvale, Calif., 1988-89; mfg. mgr. Forte Communications, Sunnyvale, 1989—; cons., No. Calif., 1976—. Counselor Teens Against Drugs, San Jose, 1970, 1/2 Orgn., Santa Cruz, 1975-76. Mem. Am. Prodn. Invention Control, Nat. Assn. Female Execs., Nat. Assn. Purchasing Mgmt., Porsche Club Am., Am. Radio Relay League. Democrat. Club: Young Ladies Radio League. Home: 733 Rosedale Ave # 4 Capitola CA 95010-2248 Office: Forte Communications 1050 E Duane Ave Ste J Sunnyvale CA 94086-2626

HILL, ANTHONY WHITING, electronic sales engineer; b. Boston, Aug. 5, 1930; s. Philip Cushing and Marie Teresa (Whiting) H.; m. Sandra Shepherd, Aug. 17, 1952; children: Darcelle Sisley Hill Cooper, Donald Coby. BSEE, U. Calif., Berkeley, 1958. Owner Hill's Sch. of Danse, Hayward, Calif., 1958-74; electronic sales engr. Anthem Electronics, San Jose, Calif., 1974—. With USNR, 1952-54. Home: 18938 Walnut Rd Castro Valley CA 94546-2006 Office: Anthem Electronics 1160 Ridder Park Dr San Jose CA 95131

HILL, CARL REUBEN, healthcare consulting firm executive; b. Redlands, Calif., Mar. 17, 1957; s. W. Harold and Doris E. (Ley) H.; m. Marguerite M. Coyne, Oct. 17, 1992. BA, Chapman U., Orange, Calif., 1978; MA, U. So. Calif., 1984. Owner Pizza Chalet Restaurant, Riverside, Calif., 1978-79, Palo Alto, Calif., 1979-81; mgr. Sandy's Ski & Sport, West Los Angeles, Calif., 1981-83, GTA Cons., Pasadena, Calif., 1984-86, HCM Cons., Torrance, Calif., 1986-87; sr. mgr. Price Waterhouse, Denver, 1987-89; owner Peak Cons., La Mirada, Calif., 1989—. Bd. mem. T.H. Pickens Respiratory Therapy Sch., Denver, 1987-89; Gala bd. mem. White Meml. Hosp., L.A., 1991; mem. alumni bd. Chapman U., Orange, Calif., 1992-93. Mem. Am. Hosp. Assn., Healthcare Fin. Mgmt. Assn., Healthcare Info. Mgmt. Systems Soc. Home and Office: Peak Cons 13311 S Sandown Ste 234 La Mirada CA 90638

HILL, DALE RICHARD, military officer; b. Charleston, W.Va., Dec. 20, 1939; s. Cecil Thomas Jr. and Frances Eileen (Gillespie) H.; m. Linda Lee Ergeson, Apr. 20, 1962 (dec. 1971); m. Debbie Kay Hildebrant, Feb. 19, 1972; children: Mark, Bret, Lara, Dale, Adam. BS, W.Va. State Coll., 1967; MA, Cen. Mich. U., 1977; grad., USA Command and Gen. Staff Coll., 1982. Commd. 2d lt. U.S. Army, Ft. Benning, Ga., 1968; advanced through grades to lt. col. U.S. Army, 1984; aide-de-camp USA Operational Test and Evaluation Agy., Falls Church, Va., 1976-80; ops. officer Hdqrs. 3 Bde, 2 Infantry div., Camp Howze, Republic of Korea, 1980-81; emergency action officer Hdqr. Readiness Command, MacDill AFB, Fla., 1981-82; plans tng. officer Hdqrs. Multinat. Force & Observers Sinai, El Gorah, 1982-83; chief current ops. Hdqr. I Corps., Ft. Lewis, Wash., 1983-86; commdr. Yakima (Wash.) Firing Ctr., 1986-89; dep. project mgr. Global Assocs. Yakima div. MPRC Yakima Tng. Ctr., 1991—. Democrat. Home: 100 N 56th Ave #17 Yakima WA 98908 Office: MPRC Yakima Tng Ctr Global Assocs Yakima Div Yakima WA 98901

HILL, DANIEL MILTON, architect; b. Watsonville, Calif., Sept. 15, 1956; s. Harold Dean and Blossom Gloria (Barr) H.; m. Marcia Kay Whisler, July 18, 1981. Student, Northwest Christian Coll., 1974-76; AS, Lane Community Coll., Eugene, Oreg., 1977; BArch, U. Oreg., 1980. Registered profl. architect, Oreg.; cert. Nat. Coun. Archtl. Registration Bds. Carpenter, job capt. G.F. Martin Investments & Constrn., Eugene, 1975-80; designer, constrn. mgr. Solar Concepts Inc., Eugene, 1981-83; architect, prin. Arbor South Architecture, Eugene, 1983—; part-time tchr. archtl. design/drawing Lane Community Coll., Eugene, 1986—, mem. adv. bd., 1987-92. Contbr. articles to profl. jours. Bd. dirs. Jasper (Oreg.) Mountain Ctr. Home for Abused Children, 1985—. Recipient Energy Efficient Design award State of Oreg./Bonneville Power Adminstrn., 1982, Design award Eugene Water 7 Elec. Bd., 1983, 86, 89. Mem. AIA (southwestern Oreg. chpt. 1985, assoc. dir. 1985, treas. 1990). Republican. Mem. Christian Ch. Office: Arbor South Architecture PC 1600 Executive Pkwy Ste 200 Eugene OR 97401

HILL, DAVID ALLAN, electrical engineer; b. Cleve., Apr. 21, 1942; s. Martin D. and Geraldine S. (Yoder) H.; m. Elaine C. Dempsey, July 9, 1971. BSEE, Ohio U., 1964, MSEE, 1966; PhD in Elect. Engrng., Ohio State U., 1970. Vis. fellow Coop. Inst. for Rsch. Environ. Sci., Boulder, Colo., 1970-71; rsch engr. Inst. for Telecommunication Scis., Boulder, 1971-82; sr. scientist Nat. Inst. Standards and Tech., Boulder, 1982—; adj. prof. U. Colo., Boulder, 1980—. Editor Geosci. and Remote Sensing Jour., 1980-84, Antennas and Propagation Jour., 1986-89; contbr. over 100 articles to profl. jours., chpt. to book. Recipient award for best paper Electromagnetic Compatability Jour., 1987. Fellow IEEE (chpt. chmn. 1975-76, editor 1986-89); mem. Electromagnetic Soc. (bd. dirs. 1980-86), Internat. Union Radio Sci. (nat. com. 1986-89), Colo. Mountain Club (Boulder), Sierra Club. Office: Nat Inst Standards & Tech 813-07 325 Broadway St Boulder CO 80303-3328

HILL, EARL MCCOLL, lawyer; b. Bisbee, Ariz., June 12, 1926; s. Earl George and Jeanette (McColl) H.; m. Bea Dolan, Nov. 22, 1968; children: Arthur Charles, John Earl, Darlene Stern, Tamara Fegert. BA, U. Wash., 1960, JD, 1961. Bar: Nev. 1962, U.S. Ct. Clms. 1978, U.S. Ct. Apls. (9th cir.) 1971, U.S. Sup. Ct. 1978. Law clk. Nev. sup. ct., Carson City, 1962; assoc. Gray, Horton & Hill, Reno, 1962-65, ptnr. 1965-73; ptnr. Hill Cassas & de Lipkau, Reno, 1974—, Sherman & Howard, Denver, 1982-91; judge pro tem Reno mcpl. ct., 1964-70; lectr. continuing legal edn.; mem. Nev. Commn. on Jud. Selection 1977-84; trustee Rocky Mountain Mineral Law Found. 1976—, sec. 1987-88. Mem. ABA, State Bar Nev. (chmn. Com. on Jud. Adminstrn. 1971-77), Washoe County Bar Assn., Nev. Trial Lawyers Assn., Am. Judicature Soc., Lawyer Pilots Bar Assn., Soc. Mining Law Antiquarians (sec./treas. 1975—). Club: Prospectors. Contbr. articles to profl. publs. Office: Holcomb Profl Ctr 333 Holcomb Ave Ste 2790 Reno NV 89502-1648

HILL, EDWARD JEFFREY, personnel specialist, researcher; b. Santa Cruz, Calif., Apr. 7, 1953; s. Edward Eyring and LaDean (Jones) H.; m. Juanita Ray, May 5, 1976; children: Sarah, Jeffrey, Aaron, Abigail, Hannah, Heidi, Emily, Amanda. BA, Brigham Young U., 1977, M in Organizational Behavior, 1984. Customer support rep. IBM, Tacoma, 1977-79; systems mktg. support rep. IBM, Olympia, Wash., 1979-80; mktg. support industry specialist IBM, Seattle, 1980-81, mktg. support program specialist, 1981; employment and resource planning asst. IBM, Atlanta, 1984-86, pers. rsch. assoc., 1986; systems engr. IBM, Phoenix, 1986-90; pers. applications advisor IBM, Tarrytown, N.Y., 1990—; intern IBM Americas/Far East, Mt. Pleasant, N.Y., 1983; cons. Ejido Magdaleno Aguilar, Tamaulipas, Mex., 1983-84. Author: Comprehensive Concordance to the Pearl of Great Price, 1972; editor: (newsletter) Dad/s, 1988—. Missionary LDS Ch., Cordoba, Argentina, 1972-74, high councilor, Puyallup, Wash., 1979-80, bishophric, Tacoma, 1981-82; scouting coord. Boy Scouts Am., Mesa, Ariz., 1988-90. Mem. Assn. for Couples in Marriage Enrichment, Marriage and Family Enrichment of Ariz. (bd. dirs. 1988—), Nat. Coun. of Family Rels. Home: 1085 N 400 E Logan UT 84321

HILL, EUGENE DUBOSE, JR., consulting engineer; b. Louisville, Aug. 22, 1926; s. Eugene DuBose and Lila Perrin (Robinson) H.; m. Margaret Preston Hodges, Feb. 18, 1950; children: Eugene DuBose III, Margaret Hill Hilton, Virginia Hill Martinson. BS in Engrng., Princeton U., 1948. Asst. chemist Devoe & Raynolds Co., Louisville, 1948-50; rschr., salesman, asst. sec. Louisville Cement Co., 1950-59; sales rep., spl. masonry rep., asst. v.p. sales tech. svcs., dir. product quality and devel. Ideal Cement Co. (later divsn. of Ideal Basic Industries), 1959-85; assoc. Openaka Corp., Inc., Denver, 1985—. Lt. (j.g.) USNR, 1944-46. Fellow Am. Concrete Inst. (bd. dirs. 1981-84, tech. activities com. 1987-93); mem. ASTM. Episcopalian. Home and Office: 3910 S Hillcrest Dr Denver CO 80237

HILL, GORDON R., purchasing executive; b. Burbank, Calif., Apr. 7, 1950; s. Frank H. and Leah S. Hill; m. Chaluay K. Hill, May 14, 1976; children: Brenda, David, Michael. BS, U. So. Calif., 1972; MBA, Ariz. State U., 1983. Cert. Purchasing Mgr. Assoc. buyer Procter and Gamble, Cinn., 1977-79; sr. buyer Armour-Dial, Inc., Phoenix, 1979-84; sr. buyer Sperry Corp., Phoenix, 1984-86, subcontract adminstrn., 1986-87; purchasing mgr. Honeywell, Inc., Phoenix, 1987-92; dir. purchasing Anacomp, Inc., San Diego, 1992—. Commdr. USNR, 1972—. Decorated Joint Svc. Commendation medal; Trustee scholar U. So. Calif., 1969, Calif. State scholar, 1969. Office: Anacomp Inc PO Box 85125 San Diego CA 92138

HILL, GORDON TUSQUELLAS, career consultant; b. L.A., Nov. 27, 1948; s. Gordon William and Mercedes Florence (Tusquellas) H.; m. Anna Priscilla Bonilla, July 7, 1973; children: David Anthony, Michael Louis. BA, Loyola U., L.A., 1971; MS in Edn., U. So. Calif., 1973, MPA, 1978. Assoc. dir. alumni rels. Loyola Marymount U., L.A., 1975-76; recruitment officer L.A. Dept. Water and Power, 1976-80; coll. recruitment mgr. 1st Interstate Bank, L.A., 1980-84; employment mgr. Calif. 1st Bank, San Diego, 1984-87; mng. ptnr. Kennedy-Hill Co., Newport Beach, Calif., 1987-88; v.p. Drake, Beam, Morin, Inc., Riverside, Calif., 1988-92; mng. dir. Right Assocs., Irvine, Calif., 1992—; membership chair Pers. Mgmt. Assn., San Diego, 1985-87; bd. dirs. Orange County Employers Adv. Coun., Tustin, Calif., 1988-92, Occupational Tng. Svcs., San Diego, 1985-87, Inland Empire Employers Adv. Coun., Riverside, Calif., 1990-92. Leader Webelos, 1988-93; leader higher edn. com. Indsl. League, 1993—; asst. cubmaster Huntington Beach (Calif.) area Boy Scouts Am., 1988-92, asst. scoutmaster, 1990-92, cubmaster, 1990-92, scoutmaster, 1993—. 1st lt. USAF, 1971-75. Recipient Award of Merit Boy Scouts Am., 1992. Mem. Pers. Indsl. Rels. Assn. Republican. Roman Catholic. Home: 8821 Dorsett Dr Huntington Beach CA 92646 Office: Right Assocs 18400 Von Karman Ave # 250 Irvine CA 92715

HILL, HAROLD EUGENE, communications educator; b. Keokuk, Iowa, Sept. 7, 1918; s. Grover Clevel and Letha Agnes (McKinney) H.; m. Dorothy May Crays, July 4, 1941; children: Sandra Lu, Wade Crays, Kathy Lynn. B.S., U. Ill., Urbana, 1940, M.S., 1954. Writer, announcer, dir., producer, program dir. Sta.-WILL-AM-FM-TV, Urbana, 1946-54; mem. faculty U. Ill., Urbana, 1946-56; sportscaster Sta. WDWS, Champaign, Ill., 1950-55; exec. v.p., treas. Nat. Assn. Ednl. Broadcasters, Washington, 1954-66; assoc. dir. Edn. Media Ctr., U. Colo., Boulder, 1967-72; assoc. prof. speech and drama Edn. Media Ctr., U. Colo., 1967-72; prof. communication Edn. Media Center, U. Colo., 1972-80, chmn. dept. communication, 1976-80, prof. broadcast journalism, 1980-84, prof. emeritus, 1984—; bd. dirs. Nat. Center Communication Arts and Scis., Sta. KRMA-TV (pub. TV), 1967-84, Sta. KGNU (pub. radio), 1977-79, Sta. KCPT (pub. TV), 1984—; subchmn. new tech. Colo. Commn. on Higher Edn., 1979-82; trustee Ednl. Communication Found. TV editor: AV Guide, 1968-74; editorial bd.: Audiovisual Communications Rev, 1974, Audiovisual Instrn, 1975. Chmn. ednl. adv. com. Champaign Schs., 1950-52. Served to maj. U.S. Army, 1940-46. Named Hon. Citizen Tex., Hon. Citizen Louisville, Hon. Citizen New Orleans, hon. Ky. Col., hon. La. Col. Mem. Assn. Ednl. Communication and Tech. (Disting. Service award 1978, dir., pres., book rev. editor, editorial bd. assn. jour. 1977-87), Ednl. Media Council (exec. dir.), Western Ednl. Soc. Telecommunications (dir.), Speech Communication Assn., Nat. Assn. Ednl. Broadcasters (dir.), Colo. Ednl. Media Assn. (dir., pres.), Broadcast Edn. Assn., Colo. Broadcasters Assn., Colo. Drama and Speech Assn. (dir.), Colo. Media Dirs., Sigma Delta Chi, Alpha Kappa Psi, Kappa Tau Alpha. Democrat. Episcopalian. Club: Exchange (pres. Ill. State Exchange Clubs 1956). Office: U Colo Sch Journalism PO Box 287 Boulder CO 80309-0001

HILL, HARRY DAVID, human resources executive; b. Whittier, Calif., Oct. 29, 1944; s. Harry Boreman and Winifred Nell (Purvis) Hill; m. Linda Mae Price, Nov. 8, 1969; 1 child, Jon Ryan. AA, Los Angeles Harbor Coll., Wilmington, Calif., 1964; BA in Polit. Sci., UCLA, 1966; M of Pub. Adminstrn. in Human Resources, U. So. Calif., 1972. Personnel aide City of Anaheim, Calif., 1966-67, personnel analyst, 1967-71, sr. personnel analyst, 1971-75, personnel services mgr., 1975-83, asst. human resources dir., 1983-88, asst. labor rels. dir., 1988—; supervisory com. chmn. Anaheim Area Credit Union, 1981-89, bd. dirs., 1989—. Mem. So. Calif. Pub. Labor Council (treas. 1986-87, pres. 1988), Internat. Personnel Mgmt. Assn. (western region pres. 1983-84), So. Calif. Personnel Mgmt. Assn. (pres. 1978-79), Coop. Personnel Services (bd. dirs. 1987). Democrat. Office: City of Anaheim 200 S Anaheim Blvd 4th Flr Anaheim CA 92805-3859

HILL, JIM, state official; 1 child, Jennifer. BA in Econs., Mich. State U., 1969; MBA, Indiana U., 1971, JD, 1974. Asst. atty. gen. Oreg. Dept. of Justice, 1974-77; hearing referee Oreg. Dept. of Revenue, 1977-81; personal specialist and cons. State Farm Ins., 1984-86; elected mem. Oreg. House of Reps., 1983-87, Oreg. State Sen., 1987-93; dor. mktg. PEN-NOR, Inc., Portland Gen. Contractors, 1986-88; corp. accts. mgr. for Latin Am. Mentor Graphics, 1988-93. Office: State of Oregon 159 State Capital Bldg Salem OR 97310*

HILL, JOHN EARL, mechanical engineer; b. Ely, Nev., July 18, 1953; s. Earl M. and Florence (Lagos) H.; m. Terry Lynn Biederman, Oct. 3, 1981; 1 child, Felicia Biederman. BA in Social Psychology, U. Nev., 1974, BSME, 1981. Cert. engr. in tng. Machinist B&J Machine and Tool, Sparks, Nev., 1977-78; designer, machinist Screen Printing Systems, Sparks, Nev., 1978, Machine Svcs., Sparks, 1978-81; computer programmer U. Nev., Reno, 1980-81; design engr. Ford Aerospace and Communications Corp., Palo Alto, Calif., 1981-82, 86-88; contract design engr. Westinghouse Electric Corp., Sunnyvale, Calif., 1982-83; contract project engr. Adcotech Corp., Milpitas, Calif., 1983-84; sr. engr. Domain Tech., Milpitas, 1984-85; project engr. Exclusive Design Co., San Mateo, Calif., 1985-86; automation mgr. Akashic Memories Corp., San Jose, Calif., 1988—; ptnr. Automated Bus. Svcs., San Jose. Mem. Robotics Internat. of Soc. Mfg. Engrs., Tau Beta Pi, Pi Mu Epsilon, Phi Kappa Phi. Home: 147 Wildwood Ave San Carlos CA 94070-4516 Office: Akashic Memories Corp 305 W Tasman Dr San Jose CA 95134-1704

HILL, JUDITH DEEGAN, lawyer; b. Chgo., Dec. 13, 1940; d. William James and Ida May (Scott) Deegan; m. Dennis M. Havens, June 28, 1986; children by previous marriage: Colette M., Cristina M. BA, Western Mich. U., 1960; postgrad. Harvard Law Sch., 1983; cert. U. Paris, Sorbonne, 1962; JD, Marquette U., 1971; postgrad. Harvard U., 1984. Bar: Wis. 1971, Ill. 1973, Nev. 1976, D.C. 1979. Tchr., Kalamazoo (Mich.) Bd. Edn., 1960-62, Maple Heights (Ohio), 1963-64, Shorewood (Wis.) Bd. Edn., 1964-68; corp. atty. Fort Howard Paper Co., Green Bay, Wis., 1971-72; sr. trust adminstr. Continental Ill. Nat. Bank & Trust, Chgo., 1972-76; atty. Morse, Foley & Wadsworth Law Firm, Las Vegas, 1976-77; dep. dist. atty., criminal prosecutor Clark County Atty., Las Vegas, 1977-83; atty. civil and criminal law Edward S. Coleman Profl. Law Corp., Las Vegas, 1983-84; pvt. practice law, 1984-85; atty. criminal div. Office of City Atty., City of Las Vegas, 1985-89, pvt. practice law, 1989—. Bd. dirs. Nev. Legal Services, Carson City, 1980-87, state chmn., 1984-87; bd. dirs. Clark County Legal Services, Las Vegas, 1980-87, Nev. Hist. Preservation Assn.; mem. Star Aux. for Handicapped Children, Las Vegas, 1986—, Nev. Symphony Guild; Greater Las Vegas Women's League, 1987-88; jud. candidate Las Vegas Mcpl. Ct, 1987, Nev. Symphony Guild, Variety Club Internat., Las Vegas Preservation Group. Recipient Scholarship, Auto Specialties, St. Joseph, Mich., 1957-60, St. Thomas More Scholarship, Marquette U. Law Sch., Milw., 1968-69; juvenile law internship grantee Marquette U. Law Sch., 1970. Mem. ABA, Nev. Bar Assn., So. Nev. Assn. Women Attys., Ill. Bar Assn., Washington Bar Assn., Children's Village Club (pres. 1980) (Las Vegas, Nev.). Home: 521 Sweeney Ave Las Vegas NV 89104-1436 Office: 726 S Casino Center Blvd Ste 211 Las Vegas NV 89101-6700

HILL, KEITH ROLAND, financial planner, insurance broker; b. Tyler, Tex., June 14, 1951; s. Emmett Hill and Willie Mae (Campbell) Hill-Wilson; m. Augusta Louise Barfield, Dec. 26, 1980; children: Kellus R. Kerrun R. Student, U. Abilene, Tex., 1970-72, U. of Sam Houston, 1972-74; BS in Biology, U. Tex., 1977. Cert. tchr. Sr. program dir. C.E.T.A. Govt. Agy., Tyler, 1977-78; entrepreneur exec. Oxford Group, Ltd., Aurora, Colo., 1978—. chief judge City of Aurora Mcpl. Elections, 1985—; basketball ofcl. YMCA, Aurora, 1990—. Recipient award Rotary, 1966, Optimist, 1966, Pacesetter award Merril-Dow Corp., 1979; named Colo. Outstanding Leader Western Image Publs., 1989. Mem. Am. Mgmt. Assn., Nat. Life Underwriters Tng. Coun., Colo. Cert. Life & Health Underwriters Assn. (cert. life underwriter). Home: PO Box 441410 Aurora CO 80044 Office: Oxford Group Ltd PO Box 441410 Aurora CO 80044

HILL, MARK COLLINS, state government official; b. Madison, Wis., Aug. 19, 1951; s. Richard William and Lois Ruth (Eliezer) H.; m. Shirley Bernece Becher, Aug. 25, 1991. BA, U. of Pacific, 1973; MPA, U. So. Calif., 1975. Budget analyst State of Calif. Dept. Fin., Sacramento, 1975-85, prin. budget analyst, 1985-87, asst. program budget mgr., 1987—. Home: 4381 Virgusell Cir Carmichael CA 95608 Office: State of Calif Dept Fin 915 L St Sacramento CA 95814

HILL, NATHAN SCOTT, educator, art administrator and critic; b. Fremont, Calif., Jan. 6, 1962; s. N. Eugene and Patricia (Yeager) H.; m. Laura S. Weir, Aug. 19, 1984. BA in Polit. Sci., George Washington U., 1985; MA in Govt., U. Va., 1988; postgrad., U. Calif.-Davis. Rsch. asst. Inst. Govtl. Affairs U. Calif., Davis, 1988—; co-dir. Calif. Art Rsch., Davis, 1991—. Art critic The Davis Enterprise, 1993—; author, co-author, editor, presenter articles, chpts., papers on art history, cultural instns., polit. sci. Commr. City of Davis Peace & Justice Commn., 1990-92, chmn., 1991-92; commr. City of Davis Civic Arts Commn., 1992—. World Affairs Coun. scholar U. Calif.-Davis, 1983; du Pont fellow U. Va., 1985-86; adminstrn. fellow Nat. Endowment for Arts, Washington, 1991; rsch. fellow U. Calif. Washington Ctr., 1992—. Mem. Am. Polit. Sci. Assn., Am. Culture Assn., Pi Sigma Alpha. Home: 1136 Stonybrook Dr Napa CA 94558 Office: U Calif Dept Polit Sci Davis CA 95616

HILL, PATRICK RAY, power quality consultant; b. Bad Constatt, Germany, Sept. 5, 1950; s. Basil Clayton and Gladys Marie (Burdin) H.; m. Patricia Ann Rath, Dec. 18, 1981; children: Danielle K. Irvin, Michael E. Irvin, Chandra K., John T.C. AAS, North Idaho Coll., 1981, AS in Liberal Arts, 1986. Applications engr. Transtector Systems, Inc., Hayden Lake, Idaho, 1981-84; dir. engrng. No. Techs., Inc., Spokane, Wash., 1985-89; co-founder RayAnn Corp., Bothell, Wash., 1989—. Sgt. U.S. Army, 1969-79, Vietnam. Mem. IEEE (assoc.), Nat. Fire Protection Assn. Republican. Baptist.

HILL, ROBERT COLGROVE, JR., data processing marketing representative; b. Waterbury, Conn., Apr. 6, 1963; s. Robert Colgrove and Mary Catherine (McGrath) H. BSBA, The Citadel, 1985; supply officer credential, Navy Supply Corps Sch., 1986. Commd. ensign USN, 1985, advanced through grades to lt., 1988; asst. supply officer, ships' disbursing officer USN, Long Beach, Calif., 1986-87, asst. supply officer, ships' food svcs. officer, 1987-89; naval acquisition and contracting officer Naval Regional Contracting Ctr., Long Beach, 1989-90; resigned USN, 1990; bank mktg. rep. Ceridian Corp., L.A., 1990—. Lt. USNR, 1990—. Mem. Assn. Citadel Men, Navy Supply Corps Assn. Episcopalian. Home: 102 Pomona Ave Long Beach CA 90803-3489

HILL, ROBERT LARRY, magazine editor; b. Portland, Oreg., Dec. 10, 1946; s. Lawrence Palmer and Alta Ella (Phillips) H.; m. Luana Hellmann, Apr. 1, 1978; children: Julia Elizabeth, Lawrence Norman. BA, U. Oreg., 1969; MA, Tufts U., 1972, U. Oreg., 1974. Reporter Easton (Md.) Star-Democrat, 1975; assoc. editor Pub. Utilities Fortnightly, Washington, 1975-77; staff writer The Guide, Harrisburg, Pa., 1978-79; writer Fairchild Publs., San Francisco, 1980-81; editor Oreg. Bus. mag., Portland, 1981—. Contbr. articles to prof. mags. Sgt. U.S. Army, 1969-71. Mem. Oreg. Hist. Soc., Sons and Daus. of Oreg. Pioneers, Japan-Am. Soc. of Oreg., Soc. of Bus. Editors and Writers, World Affairs Coun. of Oreg. Office: Oreg Bus Mag 921 SW Morrison St Ste 407 Portland OR 97205-2722

HILL, ROBERT MARTIN, police detective, consultant, lecturer; b. Hammond, Ind., Dec. 10, 1949; s. Donald Edwin and Norma Jeanne (Beal) H.; m. Connie Carolina Nordquist, Dec. 19, 1970. BA, U. Minn., 1974; postgrad., U. Phoenix; cert. in fin. fraud, IRS, Glynco, Ga., 1984; cert. in questioned documents, U.S. Secret Service, Glynco, Ga., 1986. Cert. police officer, Ill., Minn., Ariz. Police officer Rolling Meadows (Ill.) Police Dept., 1970-72, St. Paul Police Dept., 1972-79; police officer Scottsdale (Ariz.) Police Dept., 1980-81, police fraud detective, 1981—; com. mem. Fraud Ariz. Banker's Assn., 1985-86; lectr. various colls. and orgns. Recipient Dirs. Commendation U.S. Secret Svc., Washington, 1986; named Investigator of Yr. Econ. Crime Investigators, 1991. Mem. Internat. Assn. Credit Card Investigators (v.p. 1985-86, pres., bd. dirs. 1986-88, Nat. Law Enforcement

Officer of the Yr. award 1986, Ariz. chpt. Police Officer of the Yr. 1984, 86), Internat. Assn. Auto Theft Investigators. Republican. Baptist. Office: 9065 E Via Linda Scottsdale AZ 85258

HILL, ROGER EUGENE, physicist; b. San Bernardino, Calif., Feb. 12, 1936; s. George Eugene and Alice Marie (Greek) H.; m. Bette Cerf Ross, Aug. 14, 1955 (div. Dec. 1974); children: Catherine Marie, Teresa Jean, Diana Louise; m. Louise Mary Jackson, May 8, 1993. BS, St. Mary's Coll., Moraga, Calif., 1957; PhD, U. Calif., Berkeley, 1964. Rsch. assoc. U. Chgo., 1963-66; prin. sci. officer Rutherford High Energy Lab., Chilton, Didcot, Berks, U.K., 1966-68; vis. scientist CERN, Geneva, 1968; tech. mgr. Geonuclear Nobel Paso, S.A., Paris, 1969-78; sr. rsch. scientist U. N.Mex., Albuquerque, 1982-86; sect. leader Los Alamos (N.Mex.) Nat. Lab., 1986—; sci. liaison officer Joint Verification Experiment, USSR, 1988; tech. advisor U.S. Delegation Nuclear Testing Talks, Geneva, 1988-89. Contbr. articles and papers to profl. jours. Recipient Excellence award Dept. Energy, 1990. Mem. Am. Phys. Soc., Am. Assn. Physics Tchrs. Office: Los Alamos Nat Lab Ms D406 Los Alamos NM 87545

HILL, WALTER EDWARD, JR., geochemist, extractive metallurgist; b. Moberly, Mo., June 4, 1931; s. Walter Edward and Louise Katherine (Sours) H.; m. Beverly Gwendolyn Kinkade, Sept. 8, 1951; children: Walter III, Michele, Janet, Sean, Christopher. BA in Chemistry, U. Kans., 1955, MA in Geology, 1964. Cert. safety instr., Mine Safety and Health Adminstrn. Mgr. standards div. Hazen Rsch. Inc., Golden, Co., 1974-79; lab dir. Earth Scis. Inc., Golden, Colo., 1979-80; tech. svcs. supr. Texasgulf Inc., Cripple Creek, Colo., 1980-82; gen. mgr. Calmet, Fountain, Colo., 1983; tech. svs. mgr. Marathon Gold, Craig, Colo., 1984-85; cons., 1985-86; chief chemist Nev. Gold Mining, Winnemucca, 1987-88; ops. mgr. Apache Energy & Minerals, Golden, Colo., 1989-91; cons., 1991—; speaker in field. Contbr. 28 articles to profl. jours. Sgt. U.S. Army, 1950-52. Fellow Am. Inst. Chemists (life); mem. Assn. Exploration Geochemists, Kans. Geol. Soc., Denver Mining Club. Republican. Roman Catholic. Home and Office: 1486 S Wright St Lakewood CO 80228-3857

HILLER, STANLEY, JR., financial company executive; b. San Francisco, Nov. 15, 1924; s. Stanley and Opal (Perkins) H.; student Atuzed Prep. Sch., U. Calif., 1943; m. Carolyn Balsdon, May 25, 1946; children: Jeffrey, Stephen. Pres. Hiller Aircraft div. Kaiser Cargo, Inc., Berkeley, Calif., 1944-45; organized Hiller Aircraft Corp. (formerly United Helicopters, Inc.), Palo Alto, Calif., 1945, became pres. and chief exec. officer, 1950-64 (co. bought by Fairchild Stratos 1964), mem. exec. com. Fairchild Hiller Corp., 1965; chmn. bd., chief exec. officer Reed Tool Co., Houston, Bekins, 1980, York Internat., 1985, Baker Internat. Corp., 1975; chmn. bd. Levolor Corp., 1988-93; ptnr. Hiller Investment Co.; dir. Boeing Co. Recipient Fawcett award, 1944; Distinguished Svc. award Nat. Def. Transp. Soc., 1958; named 1 of 10 Outstanding Young Men U.S., 1952. Hon. fellow Am. Helicopter Soc.; mem. Am. Inst. Aeros. and Astronautics, Am. Soc. of Pioneers, Phi Kappa Sigma. Office: Hiller Investment Co 3000 Sandhill Rd Ste 260 Menlo Park CA 94025-7116

HILLERMAN, TONY, writer, former journalism educator; b. Sacred Heart, Okla., May 27, 1925; s. August Alfred and Lucy Mary (Grove) H.; m. Marie Elizabeth Unzner, Aug. 16, 1948; children: Anne, Janet Hillerman Grado, Anthony Jr., Monica Hillerman Atwell, Steven, Daniel. Student, Okla. State U., 1942-43; BA, U. Okla., 1948; MA in English, U. N.Mex., 1965, LittD (hon.), 1990; LittD (hon.), Ariz. State U., 1991. Police reporter Borger (Tex.) News-Herald, 1948; reporter, city editor constn. Morning Press, Lawton, Okla., 1949-50; polit. reporter UP, Oklahoma City, 1950-52; bur. mgr. UP, Santa Fe, 1952-54; reporter, then city editor and editor The New Mexican, Santa Fe, 1954-62; prof. journalism U. N.Mex., Albuquerque, 1965-87, asst. to pres., 1963-65, 81-84. Author: (novels) The Blessing Way, 1970, The Fly on the Wall, 1971, The Boy Who Made Dragonfly, 1972, Dance Hall of the Dead, 1973 (Edgar Allan Poe award 1973), Listening Woman, People of Darkness, The Dark Wind, The Ghostway, Skinwalkers, 1986 (Anthony award 1987), A Thief of Time, 1988 (Macavity award Mystery Readers Internat. 1988, Dept. Interior award 1990), Talking God, 1988 (Media award Am. Anthrop. Assn. 1990), The Joe Leaphorn Mysteries, Coyote Waits, 1990, Sacred Clowns, 1993; (non-fiction) The Great Taos Bank Robbery, New Mexico, Rio Grande, The Spell of New Mexico, Indian Country, The Best of the West; also articles, audio recs. With inf. U.S. Army, 1943-45; ETO. Decorated Bronze Star, Silver Star, Purple Heart; recipient Golden Spur award Western WRiters Am., 1987, Spl. Friend of Dineh award Navajo Tribal Coun., 1987, Grand Prix de Littérature Policière award, France, Ambassador award Ctr. for the Indian, 1992. Mem. Mystery Writers Am. (Edgar Allen Poe award 1974, pres. 1988, Grand Master award 1991), Internat. Crime Writers Assn. Democrat. Roman Catholic.

HILLERS, VIRGINIA NERLIN, food science educator; b. Joliet, Mont.. BS, Mont. State U., 1961; MS, Iowa State U., 1963; PhD, Wash. State U., 1984. Ext. food specialist Wash. State U., Pullman, 1984—; chair food safety task force Wash. State U., Pullman, 1991—; mem. adv. com. Wash. Food Safety Enhancement, Olympia, 1991—. Speaker to community orgns.; contbr. 15 articles to profl. jours. Mem. Soc. Nutrition Edn. (div. chair 1989-90), Am. Dietitics Assn., Inst. of Food Technologists (regional communicator 1985—), Internat. Assn. Milk and Environ. Sanitations. Office: Food Sci Human Nutrition Wash State U Pullman WA 99164-6376

HILLES, SHARON LEE, applied linguist; b. Eugene, Oreg., July 21, 1944; d. Theodore Dwight and Lila Lucille (Hughes) Hilles; m. George Bernard Wilber, Sept. 1, 1984. BA in German summa cum laude, UCLA, 1975, MA in TESL, 1983, PhD in Applied Linguistics, 1989. Teaching asst., teaching assoc. UCLA, 1982-88, lectr. English, 1988-90; asst. prof. dept. English and fgn. langs. Calif. State Poly. U., Pomona, 1990-92, assoc. prof., 1992—; tchr. adult edn. Centinella Valley Unified Sch. Dist., 1978-80; tchr. ESL Cambria English Inst., 1979-82; ESL coord. Belmont Community Adult Sch., 1986-87, chair dept. ESL, 1987-89; mem. bd. advisors ORT Tech. Insts., 1992—; cons. and presenter in field. Co-author: International Communication Course, Books I-III, Business Communication Course, Books I-III; contbr. articles to profl. jours. Mem. TESOL, Calif. Assn. TESOL, Phi Beta Kappa. Libertarian. Episcopalian. Office: Calif State Poly U 3801 W Temple Pomona CA 91768-4010

HILLIAR, CHARLES, artist; b. Coldwater, Mich., Aug. 17, 1949; s. Harvey Raymond and Leona Mae (Lindsey) H. Student, BCC Coll., Mich., Inst. Graphic Arts, Chgo.; studied with Michel-Henry; studied with Pierre Ramel, Ecole d'MAC'AVOY. Exhibited in group shows at Palm Springs (Calif.) Gallery, 1986, 87, 88, 89, Salon de la Societe Nationale d'Horticulture de France, 1989, 90, 91, 92, Salon d'Automne, Gran Palais, Paris, 1990, 91, 92, Jeannette C. McIntyre Gallery, Palm Springs, 1990, 91, Stan 90, France, 1990, Salon France Am., La Maison Francaise, French Embassy, Washington, 1991, Galerie Jean Lammelin, Paris, 1991, L' Art Contemporain, Neuilly Sur Seine, France, 1991, French Art Now, Oklahoma City, 1991, Galerie De L'Isle, Montreal, Can., Dimensions, Paris. Active LaQuinta Arts Found., Dorton Dyslexia Soc., Barbara Sinatra Childrens' Found., Northwoods Found. Mem. Internat. Assn. Contemporary Art and Vice (pres.), Assn. Pour La Promotion Du Patrimoine Artistique Francais. Home: 7515 N Winchester Chicago IL 60626

HILLIS, RICHARD K., painter, art educator; b. Cin., Oct. 3, 1936; s. Walter and Irene (Allen) H.; m. Sharon DiGiacinto, Aug. 5, 1983; children: Tiffany DiGiacinto-Hillis, Nikos DiGiacinto-Hillis. BFA, Ohio U., 1960, MFA, 1962; DA, Carnegie Mellon U., Pitts., 1973. Instr. Foothill Coll., Los Altos, Calif., 1963-64, Bradley U., Peoria, Ill., 1964-65, Ill. State U., Normal, 1966-67; asst. prof. art Ea. N.Mex. U., Portales, 1967-69, Kent (Ohio) State U., 1969-73; assoc. prof. art Tex. Tech. U., Lubbock, 1973-74, Stephen F. Austin U., Nacogdoches, Tex., 1974-82; prof. art Glendale (Ariz.) Coll., 1982—; works in permanent collections at Ark. Art Ctr., Little Rock, Hoyt Inst. Fine Arts, New Castle, Pa., Glendale Arts Commn., Muscarelle Mus. Art, Coll. William and Mary, many pvt. collections; contbr. articles to profl. jours. One man shows at Ohio U., 1962, Midwestern U. Art Gallery, Wichita Falls, Tex., 1965, W. Liberty State Coll. Art Gallery, W.Va., 1971, Phoenix Coll. Performing Arts Ctr., 1984, Scottsdale Coll. Performing Arts Ctr., 1985, Sun City Mus. Art, 1988; exhibited in group shows at Tubac Ctr. for the Arts, 1989, Artspace, Phoenix, 1989, Braithwaite Gallery, Utah, 1989, Matrix Gallery, Sacramento, 1989, Sun City Mus. Art, 1989, Minot (N.D.) Art Gallery, 1989, The Little Gallery, Ariz., 1989, many others. With USN, 1954-57. Recipient numerous art awards various exhbns, Combined Donors award L.A. Watercolor Sco., 1991, Award of Excellence Two Flags Internat. Art Exhbn., 1992, Don Ruffin Meml. Art Exhbn., 1991, Hooked on Colored Pencils award Sch. Arts Mag., 1991. Mem. Coll. Art Assn. Am., AAUP, Phoenix Mus., Found. in Art Theory and Edn., Higher Edn. in Art, Peoria Arts Commn. (chmn.). Home: 6741 W Cholla St Peoria AZ 85345-5818

HILL-JONES, KATHLEEN LOIS, executive director; b. Denver, Sept. 11, 1955; d. James Jenkins and Elaine (Marcella) Hill; m. Clinton Daniel Jones, Feb. 14, 1982; 1 child, Terrence Drake. BA, Colo. Women's Coll., 1977. Choreographer Fashion Bar TV Comml., Denver, 1981-84, Pure Gold Cheerleaders USFL, Denver, 1985-89, Kenny Rodgers Western Wear, Denver, 1990; exec., art dir. Hill Acad. of Dance and Dramatics, Denver, 1976—; bd. dirs. Colo. Dance Alliance, Denver, 1986-89; guest judge I Love Dance, Portland, Oreg., 1991—. Performer MEt. Troupers Charity Entertainers, Colo., 1970-76. Named Young Careerist, Bus. and Profl. Women of Am., 1978; recipient Scholastic scholarships Colo. Women's Coll., 1973-77. Mem. Colo. Dance Alliance, Colo. Dance Festival. Democrat. Roman Catholic. Office: Hill Acad Dance/Dramatics 1338 S Valentia St #110 Denver CO 80231

HILLMAN, MILTON HENRY, ophthalmologist, lawyer; b. Bklyn., Dec. 10, 1929; s. Nathan William Hillman and Esther (Deutsch) Waller; m. Mia Muriel Larsgaard, July 4, 1969; 1 child, Joseph Dana (dec.). BS, U. Miami, Fla., 1951, MD, 1956; JD, Glendale U., 1990. Bar: Calif. 1990; diplomate Am. Bd. Ophthalmology, Nat. Bd. Med. Examiners. Intern L.A. County Gen. Hosp., 1956-57; staff physician Rancho Los Angeles Hosp., Downey, Calif., 1958; flight surgeon USAF, U.S and Japan, 1958-61; pvt. practice medicine Santa Cruz, Calif., 1962-66; resident in ophthalmology Hollywood Presbyn. Hosp., L.A., 1966-69; pvt. practice ophthalmology Hollywood, Calif., 1970-91; pvt. practice law Pasadena, Calif., 1991—; sr. instr. ophthalmology Hollywood Presbyn. Hosp., L.A., 1970—. Capt. USAF, 1958-61. Fellow ACS, Am. Soc. Cataract & Refractive Surgery, Am. Bd. Ophthalmology, Am. Coll. Legal Medicine; mem. ABA, AMA, L.A. Soc. Ophthalmology, Calif. Med. Assn., L.A. County Med. Assn., Calif. Bar Assn., L.A. County Bar Assn. Home and Office: 1200 S Oak Knoll Ave Pasadena CA 91106

HILLS, ALAN LEE, investment and commercial banker; b. Corning, N.Y., May 3, 1954; s. Donald M. and Velma J. (Weir) H.; m. Stephanie L. Miller, Dec. 15, 1984. BA in Acctg., U. South Fla., 1974; MBA in Fin., U. Pa., 1977. C.P.A., Fla. Asst. v.p. The Bank of N.Y., N.Y.C., 1977-79; v.p. E.F. Hutton & Co., N.Y.C., 1979-81, Prudential-Bache Securities, N.Y.C., 1981-84; mng. dir. First Interstate Cogeneration Capital Assocs., San Francisco, 1984-87; sr. mng. dir. Cogeneration Capital Assocs., Larkspur, Calif., 1987-89, also bd. dirs.; managing dir. Cogeneration Fin. Inc., Mill Valley, Calif., 1990-91. Contbr. (book) Creative Financing for Energy Conservation & Cogeneration, 1984. Scholar Shell Oil Found., 1975-76. Mem. No. Calif. Cogeneration Assn. (bd. dirs. 1985-92), L.A. Power Producers Assn. (bd. dirs. 1992—). Office: Sumitomo Bank Ltd Ste 3700 611 W 6th St Los Angeles CA 90017

HILLS, LINDA LAUNEY, advisory systems engineer; b. New Orleans, June 21, 1947; d. Edgar Sebastien and Isabel (James) Launey; m. Marvin Allen Hills Sr. Jan. 29, 1977 (div. July 1982); 8 stepchildren. Student, Navy Avionics Schs., Memphis and San Diego, 1979-89; certs. in IBM Tech. Tng., System Mgmt. Schs., Chgo. and Dallas. Cert. disaster recovery planner. Sec. Calhoun and Barnes Inc. Co., New Orleans, 1965; clk. typist Social Security Adminstrn., New Orleans, 1965-67, U.S. Marshal's Office, New Orleans, 1967-69; supr. U.S. Atty.'s Office, New Orleans, 1969; with clk.'s office U.S. Dist. Ct. (ea. dist.) La., New Orleans, 1969-73; steno, sr. sec. Kelly Girl and Norrell Temp Services, New Orleans, 1974; aviation electronic technician, PO2 USN, Memphis and San Diego, 1974-78; customer engr. trainee IBM, Dallas, 1979; customer engr., systems mgmt. specialist IBM, San Diego, 1979-84; system ctr. rep. NSD Washington System Ctr. IBM, Gaithersburg, Md., 1984-87; ops. specialist mktg. dept. IBM, San Diego, 1987—, adv. systems engr., 1988-91; lectr., cons. in field. Author 5 books. Vol. Touro Infirmary, Dialysis Unit, New Orleans, 1965-67, New Orleans Recreation Dept. 1964-68, PALS-Montgomery County Mental Health Orgn., Bethesda, Md., 1984-87, various polit. candidates, 1963—; mem. Calif. Gov.'s Subcom. on Disaster Preparedness. Mem. NAFE, ACP, DAV, Info. System Security Assn., Women Computer Profls. San Diego, Data Processing Mgmt. Assn., San Diego Zoolog. Soc., Assn. System Mgmt., Smithsonian Instn. (resident assoc.), Nat. Trust Hist. Preservation. Office: PO Box 261806 San Diego CA 92196-1806

HILLS, REGINA J., journalist; b. Sault Sainte Marie, Mich., Dec. 24, 1953; d. Marvin Dan and Ardithanne (Tilly) H.; m. Vincent C. Stricherz, Feb. 25, 1984. B.A., U. Nebr., 1976. Reporter UPI, Lincoln, Nebr., 1976-80, state editor, bur. mgr., 1981-82; state editor, bur. mgr. UPI, New Orleans, 1982-84, Indpls., 1985-87; asst. city editor Seattle Post-Intelligencer, 1987—; panelist TV interview show Face Nebr., 1978-81; vis. lectr. U. Nebr., Lincoln, 1978, 79, 80; columnist weekly feature Capitol News, Nebr. Press Assn., 1981-82. Recipient Outstanding Coverage awards UPI, 1980, 82. Mem. U. Nebr. Alumni Assn., Zeta Tau Alpha. Office: Seattle Post-Intelligencer 101 Elliott Ave W Seattle WA 98119-4220

HILLS, SANDRA LONGMAN, naturopathic physician, nutritionist; b. St. Petersburg, Fla., Apr. 15, 1934; d. John Eldridge and Phoebe (Longman) Hills; divorced. AA, St. Petersburg Jr. Coll., 1954; BS, John F. Kennedy U., Orinda, Caif., 1975; MS in Nutrition, Naturopathic Dr., Anglo Am. Inst. Drugless Ther., Renfrew, Scotland, 1982. Tennis profl., club mgr. various Calif. locations, 1964-72; mgr., nutritionist Lafayette (Calif.) Natural Food Store, 1972-75; mgr., founder Moraga (Calif.) Nutrition Ctr. Health Store, 1975-79; nutritionist in pvt. practice Moraga, 1975-88; sales rep. Seroyal Vitamin Co., 1979-81; dist. sales mgr. several dietary aids cos., 1981-83, Basic Organics Co., 1977-88; phys. therapist, chiropractic asst., nutritionist Hills Well Body Chiropractic Ctr., Santa Rosa, Calif., 1988—. Author 3 books, children's stories; contbr. poems to anthologies. Mem. Internat. Acad. Applied Nutrition, Internat. Coll. Applied Nutrition, Internat. Acad. Preventive Medicine, Internat. Naturopathic Assn., Internat. Found. for Promotion of Homeopathy, Nat. Health Fedn., Am. Nutrition Soc. So. Calif., Am. Nutrition Soc. No. Calif. (founder, pres.), Calif. Assn. Nuerologically Handicapped, Nutrition Rsch. Am. (founder, pres.), others. Home and Office: 6689 Montecito Blvd Santa Rosa CA 95409

HILLYARD, LYLE WILLIAM, lawyer; b. Logan, Utah, Sept. 25, 1940; s. Alma Lowell and Lucille (Rosenbaum) H.; m. Alice Thorpe, June 24, 1964; children: Carrie, Lisa, Holly, Todd, Matthew. BS, Utah State U., 1965; JD, U. Utah, 1967. Bar: Utah 1967. Pres. Hillyard, Anderson & Olsen, Logan, 1967—; senator State of Utah, Salt Lake City, 1985—. Rep. chmn. Cache County, Logan, 1970-76; Utah State Rep., 1981-84; pres. Cache County C. of C., 1977. Named one of Outstanding Young Men of Am., Utah Jaycees, 1972; recipient Disting. Svc. award, Logan Jaycees, 1972, Merit award Cache Valley coun. Boy Scouts Am., 1981. Mem. ABA, Utah State Bar Assn., Cache County Bar Assn., Assn. Trial Lawyers Am., Am. Bd. Trial Advocates. Mormon. Club: Big Blue (Logan). Lodge: Kiwanis. Office: Hillyard Anderson & Olsen 175 E 1st N Logan UT 84321-4688

HILMAS, DUANE EUGENE, toxicologist; b. Virginia, Minn., Jan. 6, 1938; s. Eugene A. and Hilma M. (Luoma) H.; m. Barbara Louise Heldman, Dec. 30, 1961; children: Natalie L., Gregory E., Kenneth D., Aric T., Corey J. AS, Virginia Jr. Coll., 1956; BS, U. Minn., 1959, DVM, 1961; MSPH, U. N.C., 1964; PhD, Colo. State U., 1972. Diplomate Am. Coll. Vet. Preventive Medicine. Veterinarian in pvt. practice Cloquet, Minn., 1961; commd. 1st lt. U.S. Army, 1962, advanced through grades to col., 1985, retired, 1985; sr. program mgr. Battelle, Columbus, Ohio, 1985; health effects dir. EG&G Rocky Flats, Golden, Colo., 1991. Patentee in field; contbr. articles to profl. jours. Mem. Am. Vet. Med. Assn., Am. Coll. Vet. Preventive Medicine (continuing edn. chair 1988-89), Soc. Exptl. Biology and Medicine, Health Physics Soc., Radiation Rsch. Soc., Soc. Risk Analysis. Home: 7523 Estate Cir Longmont CO 80503-7260

HILPERT, BRUCE EMIL, museum curator; b. Ft. Campbell, Ky., Aug. 18, 1950; s. Joseph and Alberta Mayton (Krausse) H.; m. Barbara Lynne Wherry, June 8, 1974; 1 child, Morgan Claire. BA, U. Ariz., 1972, MA, 1977. Exhibits specialist Ariz. Hist. Soc., Tucson, 1976-78, asst. curator exhibits, 1978; curator John C. Fremont House, Tucson, 1978-83; exhibit designer Varineau, Hilpert & Assocs., Tucson, 1980-83; registrar of collections Ariz. Hist. Soc., Tucson, 1983-85; assoc. curator exhibits Ariz. State Museum, Tucson, 1985-87, curator pub. programs, 1987—; cons. Sonoran Heritage Project, Tucson, 1981, Tribal Mus. Tech. Assistance Prog., Ariz., 1990—; faculty Collections Care Tng. Prog., Am. Assn. Mus., 1986-88. Contbr. articles to profl. jours. Grantee NEH, 1987, 90, Rockefeller Found., 1991. Mem. Tucson Assn. Museums (pres. 1984-85, sec. 1987-88), Museum Assn. Ariz., Am. Assn. State & Local History, Nat. Assn. Museum Exhibitors. Democrat. Office: Ariz State Mus U Ariz Tucson AZ 85721

HILPERT, EDWARD THEODORE, JR., lawyer; b. Frazee, Minn., Apr. 29, 1928; s. Edward Theodore Sr. and Hulda Gertrude (Wilder) H.; m. Susan Hazelton, May 5, 1973. AB, U. Wash., 1954, JD, 1956. Bar: Wash. 1956, U.S. Dist. Ct. (we. dist.) Wash. 1956, U.S. Tax Ct. 1959, U.S. Ct. Appeals (9th cir.) 1959, U.S. Supreme Ct. 1970. Law clk. to Hon. George H. Boldt U.S. Dist. Ct. (we. dist.) Wash., Tacoma, 1956-58; assoc. Ferguson & Burdell, Seattle, 1958-63, ptnr., 1963-91; sr. ptnr. Schwabe, Williamson, Ferguson & Burdell, Seattle, 1992—; mem. exec. com. 9th cir. Jud. Conf., San Francisco, 1987-90. Judge pro tem Seattle Mcpl. Ct., 1971-80. Capt. USAR, 1946-49, 50-52, Korea. Mem. ABA, Rainier Club (chmn. art com. 1990-92), Seattle Tennis Club, Broadmoor Golf Club. Republican. Lutheran. Home: 1434 Broadmoor Dr E Seattle WA 98112-3744 Office: Schwabe Williamson et al Pacific First Centre 1420 5th Ave # 3400 Seattle WA 98101-2339

HILTON, BARRON, hotel executive; b. Dallas, 1927; s. Conrad Hilton. Founder, pres. San Diego Chargers, Am. Football League, until 1966; v.p. Hilton Hotels Corp., Beverly Hills, Calif., 1954; pres., chief exec. officer Hilton Hotels Corp., Beverly Hills, 1966—, chmn., 1979—, also dir.; chmn., pres., dir. Hilton Equipment Corp, Beverly Hills, Calif; mem. gen. adminstrv. bd. Mfrs. Hanover Trust Co., N.Y.C. Office: Hilton Hotels Corp 9336 Civic Center Dr Beverly Hills CA 90210-3964

HILYARD, DAVID FRANKLIN, optician; b. Hartland, Maine, Mar. 16, 1949; s. Clarence Emery and Glenda Irene (Doughty) H.; m. Darrie Jean Young, Sept. 28, 1984; children: Lisa, Chad, Wyatt. Student, Norwalk Tech. Inst., 1968-69. Optical technician Laser Optics, Inc., Danbury, Conn., 1966-69, 71-76; radio team chief, sgt. U.S. Army, 1969-71; master optician, supr. Zygo Corp., Middlefield, Conn., 1976-85; specialist, chief optician UCO/Lick Observatory, U. Calif., Santa Cruz, 1985—. Author: (manual) Conventional Optical Polishing Procedures, 1982, Keck Telescope High Resolution Spectograph Optical Components, 1993; co-author: (technical report) University of California Tech. Report #49 Mosaic Project, 1988, Keck Telescope High Resolution Spectograph Design Review, 1990. Mem. Am. Inst. of Physics, Optical Soc. of Am., Soc. of Photo-Optical Instrumrntation Engrs. Home: 255 Cottini Way Santa Cruz CA 95060 Office: Univ of California Lick Observatory 1156 High St Santa Cruz CA 95064

HIMONAS, JAMES DEMOSTHENES, JR., business executive; b. N.Y.C., Nov. 26, 1932; s. James D. and Rose Marie (Giglio) H.; m. Jill Saxon, May 9, 1969. BA in Polit. Sci., Rutgers U., 1954; MBA in Mktg., Columbia U., 1960. Merchandising dir. Seagram Distillers, 1960-62; sales mgr. Blue Crest Wine & Spirits, Inc., 1962-65; mktg. dir. Lehn & Fink div. Sterling Drug Co., 1965-67; sr. v.p. Ogilvy & Mather, Inc., N.Y.C., 1968-71; exec. v.p. Ogilvy & Mather, Inc., L.A., 1971-74; pres., dir. Rosenfeld, Sirowitz & Lawson/ West, Inc., L.A., 1974-76; pres. Novitas, Inc., L.A., 1977—. With USAF, 1955-58. Upson Meml. scholar, 1950-54; Samuel Bronfman Found. fellow, 1958-60. Mem. Flintridge Riding Club. Office: 1657 Euclid St Santa Monica CA 90404-3723

HIMSL, MATHIAS ALFRED, state senator; b. Bethune, Sask., Can., Sept. 17, 1912; s. Victor S. and Clara C. (Engels) H.; came to U.S., 1913; B.A., St. John's U., Collegeville, Minn., 1934; M.A., U. Mont., 1940; m. Lois Louise Wohlwend, July 18, 1940; children—Allen, Marilyn Himsl Olson, Louise Himsl Robinson, Kathleen, Judith Himsl Choury. Tchr., supt. schs., Broadus, Mont., 1934-45; sec. Himsl Wohlwend Motors, Inc., Kalispell, Mont., 1945-68; pres. Skyline Broadcasters, Inc., radio sta. KGEZ, Kalispell, 1958—; part-time instr. Flathead Valley Community Coll., 1969-72; mem. Mont. Ho. of Reps. from Flathead County, 1966-72, Mont. Senate from 3d dist., 1972-91; Senate pres. pro tempore, 1989. Chmn. Flathead County Republican Com., 1952-64; del. Rep. Nat. Conv., 1964; bd. govs. ARC, 1956-59. Roman Catholic. Club: Elks.

HINCH, STEPHEN WALTER, manufacturing engineer; b. Seattle, July 13, 1951; s. Harlan Delmer and Ivy Roslyn (Thrush) h.; m. Nicolette Constance Obritsch, Sept. 11, 1976; children: Gregory P., Juliana G. BS, MS in Engring., Harvey Mudd Coll., 1974. Mfg. engr. Hewlett-Packard Co., Santa Rosa, Calif., 1974-78; mfg. engring. mgr. Hewlett-Packard Co., Rohnert Park, Calif., 1978-84; corp. SMT program mgr. Hewlett-Packard Co., Palo Alto, Calif., 1984-88, Santa Rosa, Calif., 1988—; rsch. and devel. mgr. Hewlett-Packard Co., Santa Rosa, 1988—; instr. Inst. Interconnection and Packaging of Electronic Circuits, Lincolnwood, Ill., 1985—. Author: Handbook of Surface Mount Technology, 1988; contbr. chpts. to books, tech. articles to profl. jours. Mem. Surface Mount Tech. Assn. (bd. dirs.), Electronics Industry Assn. (IPC surface mount council), Internat. Soc. Hybrid Electronics. Republican. Office: Hewlett-Packard Co 1412 Fountain Grove Pky Santa Rosa CA 95403-1788

HINCH, WILLIAM HARRY, retired consulting engineer; b. Amity, Colo., June 16, 1919; s. William Harry and Eleanor H. (Hargreaves) H.; m. Josephine Ann Benedeck, June 26, 1940: 1 child, William Harry Jr. BSEE, U. Denver, 1940; postgrad., U. Chgo., U. Denver, Los Alamos U., 1941-47. Registered profl. engr., Colo. V.p., gen. mgr., co-founder Engring. Cons., Inc., Denver, 1958-71; projects include Yanhee Multipurpose Project, Thailand, Kremasta Hydroelectric Project, Greece, Brahmaputra Multipurpose Project, East Pakistan, Uda Walawe Irrigation and Power Project, Ceylon, Power System Study, Yugoslavia; indsl. fellow Cen. Sci. Co., Chgo., 1940-41; jr. engr. Pub. Svc. Co. Colo., 1941; rsch. asst. U. Chgo.; inst. engr. Hanford (Wash.) Engring. Works; head health physics, manhattan project U. Calif., Los Alamos, N.Mex., 1942-46; design and supervisory engr. U.S. Bur. Reclamation, 1941-42, 46-57; instr. engring. physics U. Denver, 1946-47; lectr. on nuclear radiation numerous schs., socs., med. and mil. groups, 1955-65; investor since 1971. Editor Feasibility Studies, 1953-70; contbr. articles to profl. jours. Mem. Mayor's Commn. on Civil Def., 1948-50; bd. dirs. U. Denver Alumni Bds., 1950-59; trustee Colo. Acad., Denver, 1973-79. Recipient Engring. Innovation awards U.S. Bur. Reclamation, Denver, 1953-57, Bronze medal Am. Nuclear Soc., Washington, 1962, Outstanding Alumnus award U. Denver, 1969, Cert. Recognition, Soc. Nuclear Medicine, Chgo., 1977. Mem. IEEE, NSPE, Internat. Conf. on Large Electric High Tension Systems, Cons. Engrs. Coun., U.S. Com. on Large Dams, Colo. Soc. Engrs., Colo. Engring Coun., Reclamation Tech. Club, Sigma Pi Sigma. Club: Pinehurst Country. Home: 3922 S Chase Way Denver CO 80235-3133

HINCHEY, BRUCE ALAN, environmental engineering company executive; b. Kansas City, Mo., Jan. 24, 1949; s. Charles Emmet and Eddie lee (Scott) H.; m. Karen Adele McLaughlin, Nov. 27, 1969 (div. Nov. 1983); children: Scott Alan, Traci Denise. Student, U. Mo., Rolla, 1967-71. Source testing crew chief Ecology Audits, Inc., Dallas, 1971-76; lab. mgr. Ecology Audits, Inc., Casper, Wyo., 1976-78; mgr. ops. Ecology Audits, Inc., Dallas, 1978-79; v.p. Kumpe & Assoc. Engrs., Casper, 1979-81; pres. Western Environ. Svcs. and Testing, Inc., Casper, 1981—; pres. Mining Assocs. Wyo., Cheyenne, 1986-87. Mem. Wyo State Ho. of Reps., Cheyenne, 1989—, chmn. mines, minerals bus. and econ. devel. com.; active Natrona County Rep. precinct, Casper, 1986—, Am. Legis. Exch. Coun., 1989—; chair Natrona County Rep. Party, 1988-89. 1st lt. C.E., U.S. Army NG, 1971-79. Mem. Am. Inst. Mining Engrs., Nat. Fedn. Ind. Bus. (Guardian award), Air Pollution Control Assn., Casper C. of C., Rotary, Shriners, Masons. Baptist. Office: Western Environ Svcs and Testing Inc 6756 W Uranium Rd Casper WY 82604-1513

HINCHEY, DEBORAH MARIE, horticulturist, landscape designer; b. Madisonville, Ky., Aug. 19, 1954; d. Charles Edward and Carolyn Jean (Ford) Brown; m. Ken M. Hinchey, Jan. 25, 1992; 1 child, Casey Carruth-

Hinchey. BS, Murray State U., 1976; MS, U. Alaska, 1985. Head gardener Anchorage Internat. Airport, 1974-76; chemist, horticulturist Kenai (Alaska) Native Assn., 1977; mgmt. trainee Bell's Nursery, Anchorage, 1978; asst. mgr. Kenai Nursery, 1978; gardener Municpality of Anchorage, 1978-80; gardener Experimental Farm U. Alaska, Fairbanks, 1980-85; owner, mgr. Debbie's Horticulture Svc., Anchorage, Alaska, 1985—; bd. dirs. Alaska Revolving Rsch. Acct., 1989-90. Author: Survey of Horticulture Industry in Alaska, 1986. Mem. of founding group, pres. bd. dirs. Alaska Botanical Gardens, Anchorage, 1986, 88, 89, 92—,. Recipient Beautifications awards (3) Anchorage C. of C., 1987. Mem. Anchorage Garden Club (exec. bd. pres., v.p., sec.-treas 1987-91, Outstanding Member award 1989), Alaska Horticulture Assn. (bd. dirs. 1985-89, pres. 1989), Alaska State Fedn. of Garden Clubs (sec. 1991—, Mann Leiser Meml. Community Svc. award 1992). Home and Office: Debbies Horticulture Svc 1353 W 16th Ave Anchorage AK 99501

HINCK, FRANKLIN NEIL, horse breeder, rancher; b. Circle, Mont., Jan. 27, 1930; s. M. L. and Zella May (Perkins) H.; m. Norma Louise Wheeler, Oct. 17, 1952; children: Troy Neil, Linda Louise, Debra Sue, Brenda May, Tammy Lynn, Teresa Dawn, Sherry Kay, Rusty Lee. Sheep hearder Preston Bros. Sheep Co., Bedford, Wyo., 1943-45; jockie Ind. Fair Cir., Idaho, Wyo., 1945-47; profl. cowboy Ind. Rodeo Cir., Idaho, Wyo., 1945-50; pvt. practice logger Wyo., 1952-58; pvt. practice rancher Star, Idaho, 1958—; mink rancher Moyle Mink Ranch, Star, 1960-64; pvt. practice dairyman Star, 1958-73; grain mill supr. Star (Idaho) Milling Co. and Feed, 1958-61; pvt. practice horse breeder Idaho, Wyo., 1941—; founder, pres. Neil Horse Hinck Tng. and Breaking Sch., Star, 1984—. Sgt. U.S. Army, 1950-52, Korea. Mem. Blazer Horse Assn., Inc. (founder, chmn. bd. 1967—), Blazer Horse Riding Club (dir. 1968—). Home and Office: Blazer Horse Assn Inc 820 N Can-Ada Rd Star ID 83669

HINCKLEY, GORDON B., church official; s. Bryant S. and Ada (Bitner) H.; m. Marjorie Pay, Apr. 29, 1937; children: Kathleen Hinckley Barnes, Richard G., Virginia Hinckley Pearce, Clark B., Jane Hinckley Dudley. Asst. to Council of Twelve Apostles, Church of Jesus Christ Latter Day Saints, 1958-61, mem. council, 1961-81, now mem. First Presidency. Office: First Presidency LDS Ch 47 E South Temple Salt Lake City UT 84150-0001 also: Bonneville Internat Corp Broadcast House 55 N 3d W Salt Lake City UT 84110

HINCKLEY, GREGORY KEITH, financial executive; b. San Francisco, Oct. 3, 1946; s. Homer Clair and Josephine F. (Gerrick) H. B.S. in Math. and Physics, Claremont Men's Coll., 1968; M.S. in Applied Physics, U. Calif.-San Diego, 1970; M.B.A., Harvard U., 1972. C.P.A., Ill. Second v.p. Continental Bank, Chgo., 1972-78; dir. fin. ITEL Corp., San Francisco, 1978-79; group controller Raychem Corp., Menlo Park, Calif., 1979-83; v.p. fin., chief fin. officer Bio-Rad Labs., Richmond, Calif., 1983-89; sr. v.p. fin., chief fin. officer Crowley Maritime Corp., San Francisco, 1989-91; v.p. finance, CFO VLSI Tech. Inc., San Jose, 1992—; bd. dirs. Advanced Molecular Systems, Vallejo, Calif. Fulbright fellow, Eng., 1968. Mem. Am. Inst. CPA's. Home: 4 Walsh Dr Mill Valley CA 94941-2600

HIND, GREG WILLIAM, apparel executive; b. San Francisco, Sept. 18, 1946; s. Harry William and Diana Vernon (Miesse) H.; m. Jane Ellen Hruby, Apr. 19, 1980; children: Meegan Elizabeth, Kirsten Anne. BA in Phys. Edn., San Jose State U., 1970; MS in Phys. Edn., Calif. Poly. State U., San Luis Obispo, Calif., 1976. Grand assistantship dept. phys. edn. Calif. Poly. State U., San Luis Obispo, 1970-71, 74; founder, pres., chmn. bd. Hind, Inc., San Luis Obispo, 1972—; mem., chmn. home econs. adv. com. on textile Calif. Poly. State U., 1988—. Sec. Found. for Performing Arts Ctr., San Luis Obispo, 1986—, chair campaign cabinet, 1991—; mem. adv. com. San Luis Obispo County Coun. on Arts, 1989—; chmn. Music and the Arts for Youth, San Luis Obispo, 1986-88; v.p. bd. dirs. San Luis Obispo County chpt. Friday Night Live; dist. chair Econ. Adv. Com. for County of San Luis Obispo, 1992—; bd. dirs. San Luis Obispo County Econ. Project, 1992—; mem. Mayor's Econ. Strategy Task Force, 1993. Recipient Calif. Sm. Bus. of Yr. award, U.S. Sml. Bus. Adminstrn., 1988, Nat. Reg. 9 Sml. Bus. of Yr. award, 1988. Mem. San Luis Obispo Golf and Country Club. Office: Hind Inc 3765 S Higuera St San Luis Obispo CA 93401-7437

HIND, HARRY WILLIAM, pharmaceutical company executive; b. Berkeley, Calif., June 2, 1915; s. Harry Winham and B.J. (O'Connor) H.; m. Diana Vernon Miesse, Dec. 12, 1940; children—Leslie Vernon Hind Daniels, Gregory William. B.S., U. Calif., Berkeley, 1939; LL.D., U. Calif.-Berkeley, 1968; D.Sc. (hon.), Phila. Coll. Pharmacy, 1982. Founder Barnes-Hind Pharms., Inc., Sunnyvale, Calif., 1939—; now chmn. emeritus Pilkington/Barnes-Hind, Inc. Contbr. articles to profl. jours.; designer ph meter and developer of ophthamic solutions. Mem. chancellor's assocs. U. Calif.; trustee emirtus U. Calif.-San Francisco Found. Recipient Ebert award for pharm. research, 1948, Eye Research Found. award, 1958, Helmholtz Ophthalmology award for research, 1968, Carbert award for sight conservation, 1973, Alumnus of Yr. award U. Calif. Sch. Pharmacy, 1965, Disting. Service award U. Calif. Proctor Found., 1985, Commendation by Resolution State of Calif., 1987, Pharmaceutical Achievements commendation State of Calif. Assembly, Hon. Recognition award Contact Lens Mfrs. Assn., 1990. Fellow AAAS; mem. Am. Pharm. Assn. (Man of Yr. Pharmacist's Planning Svc. 1987), Am. Optometric Assn. (Man of Yr. award, 1987), Contact Lens Soc. Am. (Hall of Fame 1989), Am. Assn. Pharm. Scientists, Am. Chem. Soc., Calif. Pharm. Assn., N.Y. Acad. Scis., Los Altos Country Club, Sigma Xi, Rho Chi, Phi Delta Chi. Office: 810 Kifer Rd Sunnyvale CA 94086-5203

HINDS, DAVID STEWART, biology educator; b. La Jolla, Calif., Dec. 3, 1939; s. Joseph J. and Enid (Fleay) H.; m. Janet Miller, June 1961 (div.); children: Michael Shaun, Jeffrey Wayne; m. E. Annette Halpern, June 8, 1974; 1 child, Patrick Halpern. BA, Pomona Coll., 1962; MS, U. Ariz., 1964, PhD, 1970. From asst. prof. to assoc. prof. Calif. State U., Bakersfield, 1970-76, prof., 1976—; chmn. biol. dept., Calif. State U., Bakersfield, 1986-88, assoc. dean arts & scis., 1990; vis. prof. Flinders U., Adelaide, Australia, 1985-86, 87, 90. Named rsch. scholar, Fulbright, Australia, 1985-86; rschr. NSF, 1990, Flinders U., Australia, 1985, 1987, 1990, Calif. State U., Bakersfield, 1990, Australia Sci. Dept. Mem. AAAS, Am. Physiol. Soc., Am. Soc. Mammalogists, Ecol. Soc. Am., Am. Inst. Biol. Sci. Home: 10900 Enger St Bakersfield CA 93312-3231

HINERFELD, SUSAN HOPE SLOCUM, writer, editor; b. N.Y.C., Aug. 6, 1936; d. Milton Jonathan and Belle Esther (Gibralter) Slocum; m. Robert Elliot Hinerfeld, June 27, 1957; children: Daniel Slocum, Matthew Ben. BA, Wellesley Coll., 1957. Co-author: Manhattan Country Doctor, 1986; editor: Wellesley After-Images, 1974; contbr. articles, book revs. to various publs. Mem. Authors Guild, Nat. Book Critics Cir. Democrat. Home: 131 S Cliffwood Ave Los Angeles CA 90049

HINES, NORMAN MILES, software engineer; b. Portage, Wis., Jan. 6, 1958; s. Jacob Albert and Genevieve Harriet (Mantz) H. BS, U. Wis., 1980; MBA, U. Mich., 1985; postgrad., Calif. State U., Chico. Cert. tchr. C.C., Calif. Software engr. ADP, Ann Arbor, 1980-81, Omicron, Inc., Novi, Mich., 1981-83, Charles S. Davis and Assocs., Detroit, 1983-84, Danlaw, Inc., Farmington Hills, Mich., 1984-87, Martin Marietta TSI, Ridgecrest, Calif., 1987—; tchr. Cerro Coso C.C., Ridgecrest, 1989—. Mem. SME, Soc. for Creative Anachronism (A.O.A. 1991), Mensa, Assn. for Computing Machinery, Math. Assn. of Am., IEEE Computer Soc., China Lake ACM SIGAda. Presbyterian. Home: 1035 Sherri St Ridgecrest CA 93555

HINES, ROBERT STEPHAN, academic dean; b. Kingston, N.Y., Sept. 30, 1926; s. Harry Jacob and Gertrude (Paine) H.; m. Germaine Lahiff, Dec. 9, 1950. BS, Juilliard Sch., 1952; MusM, U. Mich., 1956. Dir. choral activities Gen. Motors Corp., Detroit, 1952-57; asst. prof. So. Ill. U., Carbondale, 1957-61; prof. Wichita State U., 1961-71; vis. prof. U. Miami, Coral Gables, Fla., 1972; prof. U Hawaii Manoa, Honolulu, 1972-80, chmn. music dept., 1980-84, dean, coll. arts and humanities, 1984—. Author, editor: Composers Point of View: Choral Music, 1963, The Composers Point of View: Orchestral Music, 1970, Singer's Manual of Latin Diction and Phonetics, 1975, Ear Training and Sight-Singing: An Integrated Approach, Vol. I, II, 1979; prin. works include over 200 choral editions and arrangements. Mem. Honolulu Chamber Music Bd., 1980-84, Hawaii Pub. TV Bd., 1981. Mem. Coll. Music Soc., Am. Choral Dir. Assn., Am. Assn. Higher Edn., Goldey Key. Democrat. Home: 555 University Ave Apt 3500 Honolulu HI 96826-5046 Office: U Hawaii Coll Arts and Humanities 2500 Campus Rd Honolulu HI 96822-2289

HINES, WES RAY, art educator, artist; b. Eugene, Oreg., June 9, 1953; s. Raymond Lee and Mickey (Johnson) H.; m. Kane Marie Brodie, Aug. 1, 1980; children: Erika Kane, Luke Wesley. BS in Fine Arts & Art Edn., U. Oreg., 1977. Art tchr., chair art dept. Sch. Dist. # 5, Kalispell, Mont., 1977—, curriculum coord., 1985—. Mem. Nat. Art Edn. Assn. (Mont. Art Educator of Yr. 1988), Mont. Art Edn. Assn. (pres. 1987-89), NEA, Mont. Edn. Assn., KC. Democrat. Roman Catholic. Office: Flathead High Sch 644 4th Ave W Kalispell MT 59901

HINES, WILLIAM CLIFFORD, investment advisor, financial planner; b. Peoria, Ill., Oct. 21, 1936; s. Donald Murray and Bernadine Elmira (McKeel) H.; m. Jacqueline Jane Jackson, Aug. 22, 1959 (div. July 1972); children: Jeffrey Alan, Judith Lynn, Jeanne Marie, Jennifer Lea; m. Sherrill Ann Jenkins, Dec. 28, 1974. Student, Purdue U., 1954-55; BSME, Bradley U., 1960. Registered investment advisor. Mech. engr. Richards-Wilcox, Aurora, Ill., 1960-61, The Vendo Co., Aurora, 1961-64, Univac Co., St. Paul, 1964-65, Control Data Corp., St. Paul, 1965-73; fin. planner Investors Diversified Svcs., Mpls., 1974-78; investment advisor Hines Fin. Svcs., Tucson, 1978—; support mgr. Control Data Corp., Geneva, Switzerland, 1970-72. Mem. Assn. Fin. Planning. Home: 7787 E Entrada de Ventana Tucson AZ 85715-6421 Office: Hines Fin Svcs 6601 E Grant Rd Ste 212 Tucson AZ 85715

HINES, WILLIAM EVERETT, publisher, producer, cinematographer, writer; b. San Bernardino, Calif., Apr. 2, 1923; s. Everett Ellsworth and Etta Elvira (Gillard) H. Student, UCLA, 1941-43, 46; BA, U. So. Calif., L.A., 1950, MA, 1951. Cameraman, film editor N.Am. Aviation, Inc., L.A. and Downey, Calif., 1951-53; founder, pres. Ed-Venture Films, L.A., 1954—; sec., treas. Sampson Prodns., S.A., Panama, 1956-60; v.p. Intro-Media Prodns., Inc., L.A., 1971-75; pres., pub. Ed-Venture Films/Books, L.A., 1985—; cons., expert witness, L.A., 1965—; lectr., instr., L.A., 1958—. Author: Job Descriptions...For Film & Video, 4 edits., 1961-84, Operating Tips for Film and Video, 1993; writer Operating Tips column for Internat. Photographer mag., 1987—; contbr. numerous features to profl. jours.; producer: (ednl. film) Running For Sheriff, 1954 (Merit award 1955, 56); producer films., commls. Mem. profl. adv. bd. Calif. State U., Long Beach, 1973—, Northridge, 1974—; chmn. bd. trustees Producers and Film Craftsmen Pension and Health Plans, L.A., 1965-79. Sgt. USAAF, 1943-46. Recipient Spl. citation City of L.A., 1966. Mem. Nat. Assn. Broadcast Employees and Technicians, Internat. Photographers Guild, Internat. Alliance Theatrical Stage Employees (exec. bd. dirs. 1989—, dir. tng. 1992—), Soc. Oper. Cameramen (charter, sec. 1984—, corp. liaison 1991—), Am. Film Inst., Publishers Mktg. Assn., Nat. Geog. Soc., Assn. Film Craftsmen (pres., mem. exec. bd. 1957-79), Masons, Shriners, Ephebian Soc., Sigma Nu (Epsilon Pi chpt.). Office: Ed-Venture Films/Books 1122 Calada St Los Angeles CA 90023-3115

HINGER, CHARLES FREDERICK, banker, small business owner; b. Springfield, Ohio, Dec. 18, 1954; s. Robert Frederick and Suzanne Jane (Culp) H.; life ptnr. Jay A. Beatty, Sept. 4, 1988. BA, U. Tex., 1981; MDiv, Pacific Luth. Theol. Sem., 1985. Develop. asst. Pacific Luth. Theol. Sem., Berkeley, Calif., 1985-86, dir. ann. fund, 1986-88; dir. devel. Encampment for Citizenship, Berkeley, 1989; analyst global securities Bank of Am., San Francisco, 1990-92, sr. adminstr. comml. bank group, 1992—; ptnr. Jay Beatty Interior Design, San Francisco, 1992—. Vol. Am. Cancer Soc., San Francisco, 1991, Luth. Lesbian and Gay Ministries, San Francisco, 1991—. Democrat.

HINRICHS, EDGAR NEAL, retired geologist; b. New York, N.Y., Dec. 14, 1922; s. Edgar Gerhard and Lucile (Cazier) H.; m. Gertrude Elaine Verstegen, Sept. 30, 1950; children: Daniel Karl, Richard Neal, Jeffrey Andrew. BA, Oberlin Coll., 1947; MS, Cornell U., 1950. Geologist U.S. Geol. Survey, Denver, Colo., 1948-86; vol. geologist U.S. Geol. Survey, 1987—. Vol. driver ARC, 1990—; lt. USNR, 1941. Fellow Geol. Soc. of Am.; mem. Colo. Sci. Soc. (sec. 1953-55).

HINRICHS, MARK CHRISTIAN, electrical engineer; b. Decatur, Ill., May 30, 1953; s. Edmund Carl and Dorothy Clara (Keller) H.; m. Marlene Elaine Krommenhoek, Apr. 24, 1976; children: Jeffrey Mark, Peter Eugene, Benjamin Paul. AA, Bethany Luth. Coll., 1973; BSEE, U. Minn., 1975; MSEE, Ga. Inst. Tech., 1991. Registered profl. engr., Iowa, N.Mex. Engring. mgr. N.W. Iowa Power Coop., LeMars, 1975-84; staff mem. Los Alamos (N.Mex.) Nat. Lab., 1984—; frequency coord. Utilities Telecommunications Coun., LeMars, 1976-78; cons. in field. Mem. POW/MIA League of Families, Washington, 1984—, Am. Radio Relay League, Newington, Conn., 1970—. Mem. IEEE (local bd. dirs. 1982-84), IEEE Power Engring. Soc., IEEE Power Electronics Soc. Republican. Lutheran. Home: 406 Catherine Ave Los Alamos NM 87544-3565 Office: Los Alamos Nat Lab PO Box 1663 Los Alamos NM 87545-0001

HINSHAW, DAVID B., JR., radiologist; b. L.A., Dec. 28, 1945; s. David B. Sr. and Mildred H. (Benjamin) H.; m. Marcia M. Johns, Aug. 7, 1966; children: Amy, John. BA in German and Pre Medicine, Loma Linda U., Riverside, Calif., 1967; MD, Loma Linda U., 1971. Diplomate Am. Bd. Radiology. Intern Loma Linda U. Med. Ctr., 1971-72, resident diagnostic radiology, 1972-74; neuroradiologist 2d Gen. Army Hosp., Landstuhl, Fed. Republic Germany, 1975-77; asst. prof. Loma Linda U. Sch. Medicine, 1975-80, assoc. prof., 1981-85, prof., 1986—, vice chmn. dept. radiation scis., 1988-90, chmn. dept. radiology, 1990—; dir. sect. magnetic resonance imaging, Loma Linda, 1983—; cons. U.S. Army Med. command, Europe, 1976-77, Jerry L . Pettis Meml. VA Hosp., 1980—. Contbr. numerous articles to profl. jours., book chpts. in field of radiology. Maj. U.S. Army, 1975-77. Recipient Pres's. award Loma Linda U., 1971, Donald E. Grggs award Internal Med. Fellow Am. Coll. Radiology, Walter E. McPherson Soc. (Outstanding Faculty Research award 1987); mem. AMA (Physicians Recognition award 1980-83, 84—), Am. Soc. Neuroradiology (sr., program com. 1989, chmn. pub. rels. com. 1989-90), Western Neuroradiol. Soc., Radiol. Soc. N.Am., Calif. Med. Assn., San Bernardino County Med. Assn., Inland Radiol. Soc. (pres. 1989-90), Calif. Radiol. Soc., Assn. Univ. Radiologists, Soc. Magnetic Resonance Imaging, Soc. Magnetic Resonance in Medicine, Fedn. Western Socs. Neurol. Scis., Am. Roentgen Ray Soc., Am. Soc. Head and Neck Radiology, L.A. Radiol. Soc., Soc. Chmn. Acad. Radiology Depts., Alpha Omega Alpha (pres. Epsilon chpt. 1987). Republican. Seventh-day Adventist. Office: Loma Linda U Med Ctr Dept Radiology 11234 Anderson St Loma Linda CA 92354-2870

HINSHAW, ERNEST THEODORE, JR., private investor, former Olympics executive, former financial executive; b. San Rafael, Calif., Aug. 26, 1928; s. Ernest Theodore and Ina (Johnson) H.; m. Nell Marie Schildmeyer, June 24, 1952; children: Marc Christopher, Lisa Anne, Jennifer, Amy Lynn. A.B., Stanford U., 1951, M.B.A., 1957. Staff asst. to pres. Capital Research and Mgmt. Co., Los Angeles, 1957-58; dir. planning Capital Research and Mgmt. Co., 1967-68; fin. analyst Capital Research Co., Los Angeles, N.Y.C., 1958-68; v.p. Capital Research Co., 1962-71, mgr. N.Y.C. office, 1962-66; dir., exec. v.p. Am. Funds Service Co., Los Angeles, 1968-69; pres. Am. Funds Service Co., 1969-72, chmn. bd., 1972-82; dir. pres. Capital Data Systems, Inc., Los Angeles, 1971-73; chmn. Capital Data Systems, Inc., 1973-79; v.p. Capital Group, Inc., Los Angeles, 1973-83; sr. v.p. Growth Fund Am., 1973-74, pres., 1974-76, chmn. bd., 1976-82, now dir.; sr. v.p. Income Fund Am., 1973-74, pres., dir., 1974-76, chmn. bd., 1976-82, now dir.; commr. yachting 1984 Olympic games Los Angeles Olympic Organizing Com., 1980-84; dir. Capital Research & Mgmt. Co., 1972-83; mem. guest faculty Northwestern U. Transp. Center, 1965-66; mem. ops. com. Investment Co. Inst., 1970-74. Bd. dirs. Newport Harbor Nautical Mus., 1989-92, Girl Scout Coun. Orange County, 1993—; mem. investment com. Hoag Hosp. Found., 1992—. Served to 1st lt. USMC, 1951-53. Mem. Soc. Airline Analysts (sec. 1965-66), Los Angeles Soc. Fin. Analysts, N.Y. Soc. Security Analysts, Am. Statis. Assn., Town Hall Calif., Nat. Kite Class (pres. 1968-69), Lido 14 Internat. Class Assn. (pres. 1978-79), Assn. Orange Coast Yacht Clubs (commodore 1976), So. Calif. Yachting Assn. (commodore 1979), B.O.A.T., Inc. (dir. 1977-81), Pacific Coast Yachting Assn. (dir. 1979-80), U.S. Yacht Racing Union (dir. 1980-81). Democrat. Clubs: Wall Street (N.Y.C.); University (Los Angeles); Lido Isle Yacht (Newport Beach, Calif.) (commodore 1973); Stanford U. Sailing (trustee 1984—); St. Francis Yacht (San Francisco); Ft. Worth Boat. Home: 729 Via Lido Soud Newport Beach CA 92663-5530

HINSHAW, HORTON CORWIN, physician; b. Iowa Falls, Iowa, 1902; s. Milas Clark and Ida (Bushong) H.; m. Dorothy Youmans, Aug. 6, 1924; children—Horton Corwin, Barbara (Mrs. Barbara Baird), Dorothy (Mrs. Gregory Patent). A.B., Coll. Idaho, 1923, D.Sc., 1947; A.M., U. Calif., 1926, Ph.D., 1927; M.D., U. Pa., 1933. Diplomate Am. Bd. Internal Medicine, Nat. Bd. Med. Examiners. Asst. prof. zoology U. Calif., 1927-28; adj. prof. parasitology and bacteriology Am. U., Beirut, Lebanon, 1928-31; instr. bacteriology U. Pa. Sch. Medicine, 1931-33; fellow, 1st asst. medicine. Mayo Found., U. Minn., 1933-35, asst. prof., 1937-46, assoc. prof., 1946-49; cons. medicine Mayo clinic, 1935- 49, head sec. medicine, 1947-49; clin. prof. medicine, head div. chest diseases Stanford Med. Sch., 1949-59; clin. prof. medicine U. Calif. Med. Sch., 1959-79, emeritus prof., 1979—; chief thoracic disease svc. So. Pacific Meml. Hosp., 1958-69; dir. med. svcs.and chief staff Harkness Community Hosp. and Med. Ctr., San Francisco, 1968-75; Dir. med. ops. Health Maintenance No. Calif., Inc.; mem. Calif. Com. Regional Med. Programs, 1969-75. Author: Diseases of the Chest, rev. edit., 1980; co-author: Streptomycin in Tuberculosis, 1949; contbr. over 215 articles to med. publs.; co-discoverer antiTB chemotherapy, exptl. and clin., with several drugs. Del. various internat. confs., 1928-59. Recipient Disting. Alumnus award Mayo Found., 1990. Fellow A.C.P., Am. Coll. Chest Physicians; hon. mem. Miss. Valley Med. Assn.; mem. AMA, Nat. Tb Assn. (bd. dirs., chmn. com. therapy, v.p. 1946- 47, 67-68, rsch. com.), Am. Thoracic Soc. (pres. 1948-49, hon. life 1979), Am. Clin. and Climatol. Soc., Minn. Med. Assn., Am. Bronchoesophalogical Assn., Am. Soc. Clin. Investigation, Cen. Soc. Clin. Rsch., Soc. Exptl. Biology and Medicine, Aero-Med. Assn., Am. Lung Assn. (hon., Hall of Fame 1980), Minn. Soc. Internal Medicine, Sigma Xi, Phi Sigma, Gamma Alpha. Mem. Soc. of Friends. Home: Box 546 512 San Rafael Ave Belvedere Tiburon CA 94920

HINTZ, JOHN ARNOLD, college official; b. Chgo., Jan. 21, 1945; s. Arnold and Henrietta (Boerman) H.; m. Arnette Jean Valis, Sept. 3, 1966; children: Patrick, Alissa. BS in Edn., No. Ill. U., 1967, MS in Edn., 1969; PhD, Mich. State U., 1974. Head resident advisor No. Ill. U., De Kalb, 1969-70; residence hall advisor Mich. State U., East Lansing, 1970-73; coord. residential life and student activities SW State U. U., Marshall, Minn., 1974-83, acting dean students, 1983-85, asst. to pres., 1985-86; dean students Mont. Coll. Mineral Sci. and Tech., Butte, 1986-88, v.p. for adminstrn. and student affairs, 1988—; mem. Univ. System Funding Study Com., Helena, Mont., 1988-89, Mont. Tracks Project.-Am. Indians in Edn. Task Force, Helena, 1989-90. Contbr. articles to profl. jours. Trustee St. Mark Luth. Ch., Butte. Ill. State Tchrs. scholar State of Ill., 1963-67; rsch. fellow NDEA, 1973-74. Mem. Am. Coll. Pers. Assn., Nat. Assn. Coll. and Univ. Bus. Officers, Am. Assn. Collegiate Registrars and Admissions Officers, Coll. and Univ. Pers. Assn., Butte C. of C. (edn. com. 1989—), No. Ill. U. Cavaliers. Democrat. Office: Mont Coll Mineral Sci-Tech West Park St Butte MT 59701-8997

HIRAI, KIHEI, bank executive; b. Tokyo, June 18, 1930; came to U.S., 1985; s. Heiji and Masashi (Katayama) H.; m. Aiko, Nov. 22, 1959; children: Kazuo, Eiji. BA, Tokyo U. Edn., 1954. Dept. mgr. Mitsui Bank, N.Y.C., 1967-71; chief rep. Mitsui Bank, Toronto, 1973-75; exec. v.p. Mitsui Mfg. Bank, L.A., 1976-80; gen. mgr. Mitsui Bank, Singapore, 1980-83; sr. v.p. City Bank, Honolulu, 1985-91, exec. v.p., 1991—; dir. K&H Pacific, Inc., Honolulu, 1990—. Chair Aloha United Way, Internat. Div., Honolulu, 1991. Office: City Bank 201 Merchant St Honolulu HI 96813

HIRAMINE, KAY KIZO, sales executive; b. Upland, Calif., July 24, 1964; s. Kay Kizo and Hiroko May (Ueno) H.; m. Julie Menick, May 20, 1989. BA, Occidental Coll., 1986. Sales rep. Procter & Gamble Dist. Co. Inc., Orange, Calif., 1986-88; indsl. assoc. CB Comml. Real Estate, Glendale, Calif., 1988-90; legal asst. Sidley & Austin, L.A., 1991-92; nat, internat. sales mgr. Charles E. Fuller Inst., Pasadena, Calif., 1992—. Co-founder, church-planter Vision Christian Fellowship, South Pasadena, Calif., 1989—. Republican. Home: 313 Raymondale Dr South Pasadena CA 91030-2115

HIRAMOTO, JUDY MITSUE, artist; b. Tokyo, July 28, 1951; came to U.S., 1952; m. Richard T. and Lily Y. (Hirayanagi) H. BA, Antioch U., 1973; MFA, San Francisco State U., 1992. Ceramic instr. U.S. Embassy, Tokyo, 1979-81; asst. dir. Japanese Cultural Ctr., Los Altos Hills, Calif., 1988; artist in residence Creative Growth Art Ctr., Oakland, Calif., 1988-91; ceramic instr. Acad. of Art Coll., San Francisco, 1991—. One-woman show include Himovitz/Salomon Gallery, 1988, Purdue U., 1986, Am. Club, Tokyo, 1980, Seibu Dept. Store, Fujisawa, Japan, 1980. Fellow Sigma Omnicron Pi, 1989; Kuwahara Creative Art grant Japanese Am. Citizens League, 1986, Visual Arts grant Barbara Deming Meml. Fund, 1989. Mem. AAUW (fellowship 1990), Asian Am. Women Artists Assn., Coll. Art Assn. Home: 315 Granada Ave San Francisco CA 94112

HIRANO-NAKANISHI, MARSHA JOYCE, university administrator; b. Chgo., Oct. 10, 1949; d. Ben Bin and Alice Chiyeko (Korenaga) Hirano; m. Don Toshiaki Nakanishi, Dec. 28, 1974; 1 child, Thomas. BS in Math., Stanford U., 1971; EdD in Policy Analysis, Harvard U., 1981. Tchr. Salinas (Calif.) Unified Sch. Dist., 1972; rsch. assoc. Edn. Devel. Ctr., Newton, Mass., 1973-74; co-editor-in-chief Harvard Ednl. Rev., Cambridge, 1974-75; site coord. CUNY Grad. Ctr. and Inst. for Responsive Edn. Internat. Proj, L.A., 1977-79; rsch. mgr. Nat. Ctr. Bilingual Rsch., Los Alamitos, Calif., 1981-84; assoc. dir. Calif. State U., L.A., 1984-86; dir. instl. rsch. Calif. State U., Northridge, 1986-89; dir. analytic studies Calif. State U., 1989—; bar examiner Calif. State Bar, System Office Commn. of Bar Examiners, San Francisco, 1988-91; commr. Calif. State Bar, Commn. on Jud. Nominees' Evaluation, San Francisco, 1991—; commr. L.A. City Commn. on the Status of Women, 1991—; survey cons. Nat. Opinion Rsch. Ctr., Chgo., 1985—; policy analysis cons. Childhood and Govt. Project, Boalt Hall, U. Calif., Berkeley, 1976-77, Edn. Reform Project, L.A., 1976. Co-editor: The Education of Asian and Pacific Americans, 1983; contbr. articles to profl. jours. Cen. L.A. chair Harvard-Radcliffe Alumni Sch. Com., 1990—; bd. dirs. YWCA of L.A., 1985-89; mem. corp. rsch. com. United Way, L.A., 1986—. Danfort-Kent fellow, 1974-81; So. fellow, 1974-75; Harvard U. fellow, 1973-75. Mem. Asian Pacific Women's Network (scholarship com. chair 1989-90), Coll. Bd. Rsch. and Devel. Coun., Harvard Grad. Sch. Ednl. Alumni Assn. (bd. dirs. 1989—), Am. Ednl. Rsch. Assn. (div. program chair 1991). Home: 4501 Berkshire Ave Los Angeles CA 90032-1317 Office: Calif State U 400 Golden Shore St Ste 116 Long Beach CA 90802-4209

HIRAYAMA, PATRICK SHIN, systems administrator; b. Seattle, Aug. 30, 1967; s. Yutaka Joseph and Etsuko Nancy (Tamaki) H. BS in Computer Sci., Seattle U., 1988. Microcomputer support specialist Fred Hutchinson Cancer Rsch. Ctr., Seattle, 1989-91, systems adminstr., 1991—. Mem. IEEE, Assn. for Computing Machinery. Office: Fred Hutchinson Cancer Rsch Ctr 1124 Columbia St LV 101 Seattle WA 98104

HIROHATA, DEREK KAZUYOSHI, air force officer; b. Dos Palos, Calif., June 26, 1963; s. Vincent Yoshinobu and Gertrude Sumiko (Kimura) H. BA in Polit. Sci., Calif. State U., Fresno, 1987; MA in Aerospace Sci., Embry Riddle U., 1992; postgrad., So. Ill. U. Commd. 2d lt. U.S. Air Force, advanced through grades to capt., 1991; ground launched cruise missile launch control officer Italy and U.K., 1988-90; emergency actions officer 501 Tactical Missile Wing, RAF Greenham Common, U.K., 1989-90; chief force mgmt. 513 Svcs. Squadron, RAF Mildenhall, U.K., 1990-92. Mem. Air and Space Smithsonian, Officers' Christian Fellowship, Air Force Assn., Air Force Edn. Soc., U.S. Capitol Hist. Soc., Calif. State U. Fresno Alumni Orgn., West Coast Karate Assn., Sigma Nu. Republican. Methodist. Home: PO Box 243 Russell Rd South Dos Palos CA 93665

HIROHATA, LAURIE ANN, state agency official; b. Merced, Calif., Sept. 29, 1958; d. Lawrence T. and Carolyn (Yamamoto) H. BA in Psychology, BS in Human Devel., U. Hawaii, 1980; MSW, U. Kans., 1983; EdM, U. Ill., 1988. Adminstrv. asst. Cath. Social Svcs. Individualized Svcs. to the Elderly, Honolulu, 1983-84; family and community svcs. specialist Easter Seal Soc. Hawaii, Honolulu, 1984-85; rural groups coord. Honolulu Gerontology Program, 1986; program specialist Hawaii State Coun. on Vocat. Edn., Honolulu, 1986-87; rsch. asst. U. Ill. Transition Inst., Champaign, 1987-88;

planner Hawaii Dept. Human Svcs., Honolulu, 1988-90, Office of State Planning, Honolulu, 1990—; part time lectr. Honolulu Community Coll. Human Svcs. Dept., 1990—; project dir. Hawaii Assistive Tech. Svcs. Project, Honolulu; part time pvt. practice cons./trainer vocat. counseling spl. needs, 1990—; part time lectr. Human Svcs. Dept. Honolulu Community Coll., 1990—. Editor reference guide Kans. Bds. and Commns., 1988. Vol. Community Svc. Sentencing Program, Honolulu, 1985; advocate Palolo Residents to Stop Hillside Devel., 1987. Mem. Am. Assn. for Counseling Devel., Nat. Assn. Social Workers, Health and Community Svcs. Coun. of Hawaii, Young Dems., Phi Delta Kappa, Kappa Delta Pi, Phi Upsilon Omicron (Beta Alpha chpt.). Home: 1760 Nanea St Apt 403 Honolulu HI 96826-3659 Office: Office State Planning Pvt Practice PO Box 62302 Honolulu HI 96839-2302 also: Hawaii Assistive Tech Svcs Project 677 Ala Moana Blvd Ste 403 Honolulu HI 96813

HIROMOTO, ROBERT ETSUO, physicist; b. L.A., Aug. 6, 1946; s. Charles Haruji and Yaeko (Fujiyoka) H.; 1 child, Scott Charles. BS, Calif. State U., Long Beach, 1969; PhD, U. Tex., 1978. Dir. for tech. programs No. N.Mex. Community Coll., Espanola, 1978-79; rsch. staff mem. Los Alamos (N.Mex.) Nat. Lab., 1980—. Regional editor Parallel Computing jour., 1989—; contbr. articles to profl. jours. With U.S. Army, 1970-72, Italy. Home: 4256 Urban St Los Alamos NM 87544-1736 Office: Los Alamos Nat Lab MS B-265 Los Alamos NM 87545

HIRONO, MAZIE KEIKO, state legislator; b. Fukushima, Japan, Nov. 3, 1947; came to U.S., 1955, naturalized, 1957; d. Laura Chie (Sato) H. B.A., U. Hawaii, 1970; J.D., Georgetown U., 1978. Dep. atty. gen., Honolulu, 1978-80; house counsel INDEVCO, Honolulu, 1982-83; sole practice, Honolulu, 1983-84, Shim, Tam, Kirimitsu & Naito, 1984-88; mem. Hawaii Ho. of Reps., Honolulu, 1980—. Del., State Democratic Party Conv., Honolulu, 1972-82; bd. dirs. Nuuanu YMCA, Honolulu, 1982-84, Moiliili Community Ctr., Honolulu, 1984. Mem. U.S. Supreme Ct. Bar, Hawaii Bar Assn., Phi Beta Kappa. Democrat. Office: Ho of Reps State Capitol Rm 331 Honolulu HI 96813

HIROTA, DENNIS ISAO, engineering executive, civil engineer; b. Honolulu, Apr. 4, 1940; s. Sam O. and Yukino (Yamane) H.; m. Kathryn Ennis, Jan. 6, 1968; children: Maile Marie, Dan. H. BSCE, U. Mich., 1963, MS, 1964, PhD, 1970. Profl. engr., Hawaii. Exec. v.p. Sam O. Hirota, Inc., Honolulu, 1971-86, pres., 1986—; bd. dirs. Ctrl. Pacific Bank, Honolulu, CPB, Inc., Honolulu. Capt. USAF, 1968-71. Mem. Pacific Club, Mid-Pacific Country Club. Home: 706 Puuikena Dr Honolulu HI 96821 Office: Sam O Hirota Inc 864 S Beretania St Honolulu HI 96813

HIROZAWA, SHUREI, retired banker; b. Eleele, Hawaii, May 12, 1919; s. Masaichi and Sada (Uyeda) H.; m. Betty Fumiko Fujii, Oct. 5, 1957; children: Gail Reiko, Joan Emiko, Robert Kenji. BA, U. Iowa, 1950. With McBryde Sugar Co., Eleele, 1937-46; reporter Honolulu Star-Bull., 1950-62, bus. editor, 1962-70; asst. v.p. First Hawaiian, Honolulu, 1970-72, v.p., 1972-91; ret., 1991; bd. dirs. Oceanic Cablevision, Honolulu, Freedom Forum Fellowship Com., Honolulu. Mem. vestry St. John's Episcopal Ch., Eleele, 1943-46, St. Mary's Episcopal Ch., Honolulu, 1980-82; bd. dirs. St. Andrews Priory Sch., Honolulu, 1978-84. Mem. Soc. Profl. Journalists (pres. HOnolulu chpt. 1962, treas. 1976-84), Am. Statis. Assn. (Hawaii chpt.), Hawaii Econ. Assn., Japanese Cultural Ctr. of Hawaii, Hawaii C. of C., Honolulu Japanese C. of C., Honolulu Press Club (treas. 1970-84). Home: 3577 Woodlawn Dr Honolulu HI 96822-1451

HIRSCH, ANTHONY T., physician; b. N.Y.C., Jan. 29, 1940; s. Robert S. and Minna Hirsch; m. Barbara Hershan, July 8, 1961; children: Deborah, Kenneth, Steven. BS cum laude, Tufts U., 1961, MD, 1965. Diplomate Am. Bd. Pediatrics, Am. Bd. Allergy-Immunology. Pvt. practice pediatrics Children's Med. Group, L.A., 1973-84; chair dept. pediatrics, dir. residency tng. program in pediatrics White Meml. Med. Ctr., L.A., 1984—. Capt. USAF, 1969-71. Fellow Am. Acad. Pediatrics (chair access task force Calif. br., mem. nat. access task force, chair com. on child health financing, mem. coun. on pediatric practice), Am. Acad. Allergy-Immunology. Office: White Meml Med Ctr Dept Pediatrics 414 N Boyle Ave Los Angeles CA 90033

HIRSCH, PAUL FREDERICK, film editor; b. N.Y.C., Nov. 14, 1945; s. Joseph Hirsch and Ruth Lenore (Schindler) Bocour); m. Jane Dickinson Brown, June 9, 1974; children: Gina Katharine, Eric Michael. BA, Columbia U., 1966. Editor: (feature films) Hi, Mom, 1970, Sisters, 1972, Phantom of the Paradise, 1974, Obsession, 1975, Carrie, 1976, Starwars, 1977, The Fury, 1978, King of the Gypsies, 1978, Home Movies, 1980, The Empire Strikes Back, 1980, Blowout, 1981, The Black Stallion Returns, 1982, Footloose, 1983, Protocol, 1984, Ferris Bueller's Day Off, 1986, The Secret of My Success, 1987, Planes, Trains and Automobiles, 1987, Steel Magnolias, 1989, Coupe De Ville, 1990, Dutch, 1991, Raising Cain, 1992, Falling Down, 1993, Wrestling Ernest Hemingway, 1993. Mem. Acad. Motion Picture Arts & Scis. (exec. bd. film editors' br., Acad. award for film editing 1978), Am. Cinema Editors. Home: 1127 Las Pulgas Pl Pacific Palisades CA 90272

HIRSCH, WALTER, economist, researcher; b. Phila., Apr. 21, 1917; s. Arnold Harry and Ann Belle (Feldstein) H.; m. Leanore Brod, Feb. 12, 1939 (dec. 1985); stepchild, Stephen M. Gold; children: Jeffrey A., Robert A.; m. June Freedman Gold Clark, Dec. 16, 1986. BS in Econs., U. Pa., 1938; LLD (hons.), Chapman Coll., 1968. Economist U.S. Bur. Stats., Washington and N.Y.C, 1946-50, Dept. USAF, Washington, 1950-51, Nat. Prodn. Auth., Washington, 1952-53; dir. indsl. mobilization Bur. Ordnance Dept. USN, Mechanicsburg, Pa., 1954-56; ops. rsch. analyst Bur. Supplies and Accts. Dept. USN, Arlington, Va., 1956-58; economist, ops. rsch. analyst Internat. Security Affairs Office Sec. of Def., Arlington, 1958-61; chief ops., rsch. analyst Gen. Svcs. Adminstrn., Washington, 1961-63; ops. rsch. analyst Spl. Projects Office Sec. of Def., Arlington, 1963-67; dir. ednl. rsch. U.S. Office Edn., San Francisco, 1967-72; cons. on loan to Office of Dean Acad. Planning San Jose (Calif.) State U., 1972-74. Author: Unit Man-Hour Dynamics for Peace or War, 1957, Internal Study for Office Secretary of Defense: Sharing the Cost of International Security, 1961. Vol. De Young Mus., San Francisco, 1981-84, Calif. Palce of Legion of Honor, Phila. Mus. Art, 1984-86; pres. Met. Area Reform Temples, Washington, Nat. Fedn. Temple Brotherhoods; supporter Phila. Orch., San Francisco Symphony, San Francisco Conservatory Music, Curtis Inst. With USAAF, 1942-46. Recipient Meritorious Civilian Svc. award Navy Dept., 1956. Mem. Pa. Athletic Club, Commonwealth Club of Calif., World Affairs Council, Press Club of San Francisco, Phi Delta Kappa.

HIRSCHBERG, MICHAEL ERIC, restaurateur; b. Mineola, N.Y., Jan. 22, 1952; s. Dimitri Robeert and Jean (Sullivan) H.; m. Darlene Ruth Pullen, Oct. 3, 1981; children: Paris Samuel Pullen, Brittany Ruth Selby. BA in English Lit., SUNY, Albany, 1973. Owner, chef Mandala Cafe, Santa Rosa, Calif., 1974-80, Restaurant Matisse, Santa Rosa, 1982-91; pres., CEO, Medici Corp. (doing bus. as Ristorante Siena), Santa Rosa, 1985—, Mezzaluna Bakery, Santa Rosa, 1990—; bd. dirs. SCAMP, Santa Rosa. Bd. dirs. Sonoma County Conv. and Visitors Bur., Santa Rosa, 1987—, also past pres. Office: Ristorante Siena 1229 N Dutton Ave Santa Rosa CA 95404

HIRSCHFELD, GERALD JOSEPH, cinematographer; b. N.Y.C., Apr. 25, 1921; s. Ralph and Kate (Zirker) H.; m. Sarnell Ogus, June 5, 1945 (div. June 1972); children—Alec, Marc, Eric, Burt; m. Julia Warren Tucker, July 28, 1981. Student, Columbia U., 1938-40. Dir. photography Signal Corps Photog. Ctr. U.S. Army, 1945-47; cinematic instr. New Inst. for Film, Bklyn., 1947-49; freelance dir. photography for TV and Film N.Y.C., 1949-54; dir. photography, v.p. MPO Videotronics, Inc., N.Y.C., 1954-72; freelance dir., cameraman, cinematographer N.Y.C., Hollywood (Calif.), 1972—; cinema instr. Am. Film Inst., Los Angeles, 1980, Tahoe Film and Video Workshop, Lake Tahoe, Nev., 1984, Washington Film and Video Assn., 1987. Cinematographer for films including: Young Frankenstein, My Favorite Year, Diary of a Mad Housewife, The Neon Empire (ACE award nomination 1990); author: Image Control, 1992. With Signal Corps U.S. Army, 1941-45. Mem. Internat. Photographer's Union, Am. Soc. Cinematographers. Home and Office: 361 Scenic Dr Ashland OR 97520-2623

HIRSCHFIELD, ALAN J., entrepreneur. B.S., U. Okla.; M.B.A., Harvard U. V.p. Allen & Co., Inc., 1959-67; v.p. fin., dir. Warner Bros. Seven Arts, Inc., 1967-68; with Am. Diversified Enterprises, Inc., 1968-73; pres., chief exec. officer Columbia Pictures Industries, N.Y.C., 1973-78; vice chmn., chief operating officer 20th Century-Fox Film Corp., L.A., 1979-81; chmn. bd., chief exec. officer 20th Century-Fox Film Corp., 1981-85; cons., investor entertainment industries, L.A., 1985-89; mng. dir. Wertheim Schroder & Co., L.A., 1990—; co-CEO, Data Broadcasting Corp., 1990—; bd. dirs. Texana Internat., Cantel Internat., CPP/Belwin Inc., Americscribe Internat. Bd. dirs. Conservation Internat. Office: PO Box 7443 Jackson WY 83001-7443

HIRSCHHORN, ELIZABETH ANN, environmental engineer, consultant; b. Phila., June 12, 1962; d. Arthur J. and Rita (Fein) H. BSCE, Johns Hopkins U., 1984. Registered profl. engr., Md. Project mgr. Buchart-Horn, Inc., Balt., 1984-91, Metcalf & Eddy, Inc., Redwood City, Calif., 1991—. Mem. ASCE, NSPE, Am. Water Works Assn., Md. Soc. Profl. Engrs. Office: Metcalf & Eddy Inc 555 Twin Dolphin Dr Ste 400 Redwood City CA 94065

HIRSCHMAN, CHARLES, JR., sociologist, educator; b. Atlanta, Nov. 29, 1943; s. Charles Sr. and Mary Gertrude (Mullee) H.; m. Josephine Knight, Jan. 29, 1968; children: Andrew Charles, Sarah Lynn. BA, Miami U., Oxford, Ohio, 1965; MS, U. Wis., 1969, PhD, 1972. Vol. Peace Corps, Malaysia, 1965-67; prof. Duke U., Durham, N.C., 1972-81, Cornell U., Ithaca, N.Y., 1981-87, U. Wash., Seattle, 1987—; Cons. Ford Found., Malaysia, 1974-75; chair social scis. and population study sect. NIH, Washington, 1987-91. Author: Ethnic and Social Stratification in Peninsula Malaysia, 1975; contbr. articles to profl. jours. fellow Ctr. Advanced Study in the Behiavioral Scis., Stanford, Calif., 1993—. Mem. Assn. for Asian Studies (bd. dirs. 1987-90), Population Assn. Am. (bd. dirs. 1992—). Office: U Wash Dept Sociology DK-40 Ctr Studies Demography Seattle WA 98195

HIRSCHMANN, FRANZ GOTTFRIED, aerospace executive; b. Kempten, Germany, Oct. 4, 1945; came to U.S., 1973; s. Kurt Rudolf G. and Linda (Krieger) H.; m. Cindy Villarica, Nov. 27, 1992. BS, FWG Coll., Cologne, Fed. Republic Germany, 1965; MA, U. Bonn, Fed. Republic Germany, 1973; MBA, Pepperdine U., 1981. Mktg. mgr. Western U.S. and S. Am. regions United Techs./Ambac, L.A., 1978-80; mktg. mgr. Western U.S. and Pacific regions Buehler Inc., L.A. and N.C., 1981-83; mgr. internat. mktg. Gen. Dynamics, Pomona, Calif., 1983-84, mgr. info. svcs., 1984-88, mgr. spl. projects, 1988-89; mgr. competitor analyses Hughes Aircraft Co., Canoga Park, Calif., 1989-91; mgr. bus. devel. and market rsch. Hughes Aircraft Co., Canoga park, Calif., 1991-93, mgr. strategic planning, 1993—; owner cons. bus., 1992—. Author: Mandaic Inscription, 1970; inventor deciphering lang. computer. Vol. Lincoln Club, L.A., 1981; co-founder Retinitis Pigmentosa Found. Mem. Nat. Mgmt. Assn., Pepperdine U. Alumni Assn., Sierra Club (leader, vice chmn. coun. 1990-93). Democrat. Lutheran. Home: 20544 Gresham St West Hills CA 91306-1044 Office: Hughes Aircraft Co 8433 Fallbrook Ave # 26146N Canoga Park CA 91304-3226

HIRSEN, JAMES L., real estate executive, lawyer; b. Chgo., Aug. 18, 1950; m. Margaret A., Mar. 15, 1976. JD, 1980. Bar: Calif. 1980. Lawyer Gregg & Osborne, Beverly Hills, Calif., 1980-83; atty., real estate exec. SBD Group, Inc., Santa Ana, Calif., 1985—; officer Real Estate Investment Adv. Coun., L.A., 1987—. Vol. Rep. Nat. Com., Newport Beach, Calif., 1992. Mem. Orange County Bar Assn. Republican. Roman Catholic. Home: 1701 Port Margate Pl Newport Beach CA 92660-5323

HIRSH, NORMAN BARRY, management consultant; b. N.Y.C., Apr. 20, 1935; s. Samuel Albert and Lillian Rose (Minkow) H.; m. Christina M. Poole, Sept. 21, 1957 (div. 1967); children: Richard Scott, Lisa Robin; m. Sharon Kay Girot, Dec. 29, 1973; 1 child, Sharon Margaret. BSME, Purdue U., 1956; cert. in mgmt., UCLA, 1980. Mech. engr. Ford Motor Co., Dearborn, Mich., 1956-58; design engr. Gen. Dynamics, San Diego, 1958-62; mech. engr. aircraft div. Hughes Tool Co., Culver City, Calif., 1962-65, project engr. aircraft div., 1965-69, engr. mgr. aircraft div., 1969-72; dep. program dir. Hughes Helicopters, Culver City, 1972-79, v.p., 1979-84; v.p., gen. mgr. Hughes Helicopters, Mesa, Ariz., 1984-85; exec. v.p. McDonnell Douglas Helicopter Co., Mesa, 1986-90; pres. Rogerson Hiller Corp., Port Angeles, Wash., 1990-93, Rogerson Aircraft Corp. Flight Structures Group, Port Angeles, 1990-93; cons. in field. Served with U.S. Army. Recipient Disting. Engring. Alumnus award Purdue U., 1990, Outstanding Mech. Engring. Alumnus award, 1991. Hon. fellow Am. Helicopter Soc. (chmn. 1986-87); mem. Assn. U.S. Army, Army Aviation Assn. Am., Am. Def. Preparedness Assn., Nat. Aeronautic Assn., Helicopter Assn. Internat.

HIRSHLEIFER, DAVID ADAM, economist, educator; b. L.A., Sept. 4, 1958; s. Jack and Phyllis Hirshleifer; m. Siew Hong Teoh. BS, UCLA, 1980; PhD, U. Chgo., 1985. Asst. prof. Anderson Grad. Sch. Mgmt., UCLA, 1984-90, assoc. prof. fin. econs., 1990—. Contbr. articles to profl. jours. Office: UCLA 405 Hilgard Ave Los Angeles CA 90024-1301

HIRSON, ESTELLE, retired educator; b. Bayonne, N.J.; d. Morris and Bertha (Rubinstein) Hirson; student UCLA, U. So. Calif., summers 1949-59, San Francisco, summer 1955, U. Hawaii, 1955; B.E., San Francisco State U., 1965. Tchr. High St. Homes Sch., Oakland, Calif., 1949-54, Prescott Sch., 1955-60, Ralph Bunche Sch., 1960-72; owner Puzzle-Gram Co., Los Angeles, 1946-49; pres. Major Automobile Co., 1948-60. Chpt. v.p. City of Hope, San Francisco, 1962-63; bd. dirs. Sinai-Duarte Nat. Med. Center, 1946-50, also parliamentarian, life mem. Mem. NEA, Calif., Oakland, Los Angeles tchrs. assns., Sigma Delta Tau. Democrat. Mem. Order Eastern Star; Scottish Rite Women's Assn. (v.p. L.A. 1982, fin. sec. 1989). Rights to ednl. arithmetic game Find the Answer 1948, 51. Home: 8670 Burton Way Apt 328 Los Angeles CA 90048

HIRST, WILMA ELIZABETH, psychologist; b. Shenandoah, Iowa; d. James H. and Lena (Donahue) Ellis; m. Clyde Henry Hirst (dec. Nov. 1969); 1 child, Donna Jean (Mrs. Alan Robert Goss). AB in Elementary Edn., Colo. State Coll., 1948, EdD in Ednl. Psychology, 1954; MA in Psychology, U. Wyo., 1951. Lic. psychologist, Wyo. Elem. tchr., Cheyenne, Wyo., 1945-49, remedial reading instr., 1949-54; assoc. prof. edn., dir. campus sch. Nebr. State Tchrs. Coll., Kearney, 1954-56; sch. psychologist, head dept. spl. edn. Cheyenne (Wyo.) pub. schs., 1956-57, sch. psychologist, guidance coordinator, 1957-66, dir. rsch. and spl. projects, 1966-76, also pupil personnel, 1973-84; pvt. cons., 1984—; vis. asst. prof. U. So. Calif., summer 1957, Omaha U., summer 1958, U. Okla., summers 1959, 60; vis. assoc. prof. U. Nebr., 1961, U. Wyo., summer 1962, 64, extension div., Kabul, Afghanistan, 1970, Cath. U., Goias, Brazil, 1974; investigator HEW, 1965-69; prin. investigator effectiveness of spl. edn., 1983-84; participant seminar Russian Press Women and Am. Fedn. Press Women, Moscow and Leningrad, 1973. Sec.-treas. Laramie County Coun. Community Svcs., 1962; mem. speakers bur., mental health orgn.; active Little Theatre, 1936-60, Girl Scout Leaders Assn., 1943-50; mem. Adv. Coun. on Retardation to Gov.'s Commn.; mem., sec. Wyo. Bd. Psychologist Examiners, 1965-71 vice chmn., 1971-74; chmn. Mayor's Model Cities Program, 1969; mem. Gov.'s Com. Jud. Reform, 1972; adv. council Div. Exceptional Children, Wyo. Dept. Edn., 1974; mem. transit adv. group City of Cheyenne, 1974; bd. dirs. Wyo. Children's Home Soc., 1968, treas., 1978-84; rsch. on women's prisons State of Wyo., 1989; bd. dirs. Goodwill Industries Wyo., chmn., 1981-83; mem. Wyo. exec. com. Partners of Americas, 1970-86; del. Internat. Conv. Ptnrs. of Ams., Jamaica, 1987; del., moderator pers. com. Presbytery of Wyo., 1987-90, mem. mission program com., 1991—, Work Opportunities Adv. com. to Bd. Trustees AARP, 1992—; Friendship Force ambassador to Honduras, 1979; chmn. bd. SE Wyo. Mental Health Center, 1969; elder 1st Presbyn. Ch., Cheyenne, 1978—, also bd. deacons; chmn. adv. assessment com. Wyo. State Office Handicapped Children, 1980, 81; mem. allocations com. United Way of Laramie County, active People to People Internat., Citizen Amb. Program, Child Welfare Project, 1992; participant People to People Internat. Citizen Amb. Program, child welfare project assist Lithuania, Latvia, Estonia, 1992. Named Woman of Year, Cheyenne Bus. and Profl. Women, 1974. Diplomate Am. Bd. Profl. Psychology. Mem. APA, ASCD, Internat. Council Psychologists (chmn. Wyo. div. 1980-85), AAUP, Am. Assn. State Psychology Bds. (sec.-treas. 1970-73), Wyo. Psychol. Assn. (pres. 1962-63), Laramie County Mental Health Assn. (bd. mem., corr. sec. 1963-69, pres.), Wyo. Mental Health Assn. (bd. mem.), Internat. Platform Assn., Am. Ednl. Research Assn., Assn. for Gifted (Wyo. pres. 1964-65), Am. Personnel and Guidance Assn., Am. Assn. Sch. Adminstrs., NEA (life, participant seminar to China 1978), AAUW, Cheyenne Assn. Spl. Personnel and Prins. (pres. 1964-65, mem. exec. bd. 1972-76), Nat. Fedn. Press Women (dir. 1979-85), DAR (vice regent Cheyenne chpt. 1975-77), AARP (state coordinator 1988-92, preretirement planning specialist 1986-88, state coord. worker force program, 1992, leadership coun., state del. nat. conv. 1990, pilot project Wyo. state delivery for retirement planning 1990—, AARP Works, mem. work opportunities adv. com. bd. trustees, 1992—, coop. project state govt. edn. assn. and AARP work force vols. video for retirement planning statewide 1993), Psi Chi, Kappa Delta Pi, Pi Lambda Theta, Alpha Delta Kappa (pres. Wyo. Alpha 1965-66). Presbyn. Lodge Soc. Colonial Dames XVII Century, Order Eastern Star, Daus. of Nile. Clubs: Wyo. Press Women, Zonta (pres. Cheyenne 1965-66, treas. dist. 12 1974). Author: Know Your School Psychologist, 1963; Effective School Psychology for School Administrators, 1980. Home and Office: 3458 Green Valley Renne WY 82001-6124

HIRTH, RUSSELL JULIUS, aerospace engineer; b. Chgo., Nov. 11, 1924; s. Julius and Elsa Margaret (Pfeiffer) H.; m. Helen Lois Keller, Sept. 7, 1947; (div. Jan. 1973);children: Christine Elise Hirth Corbett, Mark David, Andrew Russell; m. Barbara Winifred Kiefer, Feb. 24, 1973; stepchildren: Gregory, Douglas, James, Suzanne. Student, U. Oreg., 1944; BSEE, Purdue U., 1949; BS in Computer Sci., Metro State, 1981. Test engr. Gen. Electric Co., Schenectady, N.Y., 1949-53; systems project engr. Bendix Corp., South Bend, Ind., 1953-61; systems test engr. Martin Marietta Co., Orlando, Fla., 1961-69, systems engr., 1970-91; pres./dir. Hirth Cons., Denver, 1990—. Author automated sequences for Viking Landers, currently intact landed on Mars. Mem. Presbyterian Players, South Bend, Ind. 1954-60 (various roles), Orange Blossom Playhouse, Orlando, Fla., 1961-69, Robinson Chapel and Chorus, Ft. Wayne, Ind. (dir.), Lakewood Players, Denver/Lakewood, Colo. (pres., dir.), 1962-88. Named Best Supporting Actor, 1979, Best Tech. Set Designer, 1978, Lakewood (Colo.) Players. Mem. BOE. Mem. Disciples of Christ Ch. Address: 9611 Allison Way Broomfield CO 80021

HISCOCKS, PATRICK DENNIS, lawyer; b. Burbank, Calif., Mar. 12, 1956; s. Dale Richard and Mary Ellen (Melody) H. BA, Calif. State U., Northridge, 1987; JD, Southwestern U., 1990. Bar: Calif., 1990. Prodn. mgr. The Drapery House, North Hollywood, Calif., 1978-87; atty. L.A. City Atty.'s Office, 1990-91; law clk. to judge U.S. Bankruptcy Ct., L.A., 1991—. Democrat. Roman Catholic. Office: US Bankruptcy Ct Ste 1482 255 Temple St Los Angeles CA 90012

HISE, MARK ALLEN, dentist; b. Chgo., Jan. 17, 1950; s. Clyde and Rose T. (Partipilo) H. AA, Mt. San Antonio Coll., Walnut, Calif., 1972; BA with highest honors, U. Calif., Riverside, 1974; MS, U. Utah, 1978; DDS, UCLA, 1983. Instr. sci. NW Acad., Houston, 1978-79; chmn. curriculum med. coll. prep program UCLA, 1980-85; instr. dentistry Coll. of Redwoods, Eureka, Calif., 1983; practice dentistry Arcata, Calif., 1983—; participant numerous radio and TV appearances. Editor: Preparing for the MCAT, 1983-85; contbr. articles to profl. jours.; speaker in field. Henry Carter scholar U. Calif., 1973, Calif. State scholar 1973, 74, Rgents scholar U. Calif., 1973; Calif. State fellow, 1975, NIH fellow, 1975-79. Mem. AAAS, ADA, Calif. Dental Assn., Acad. Gen. Dentistry, Nat. Soc. for Med. Research, Norht Coast Scuba Club (Eureka, Calif.). Roman Catholic. Home and Office: 1225 B St Arcata CA 95521-5936

HITCHCOCK, HAROLD RALPH, property manager; b. Chgo., July 5, 1950; s. Hadley Robert and Helen Marie (Luongo) H.; m. Bernadette Pabilonia Nazal, July 5, 1982. Student, Black Hawk C.C., 1968-70. Lic. real estate agt. Stock clk. Jewel Food Stores, Moline, Ill., 1966-70; front end mgr. Travelodge Hotel, Honolulu, 1973-76; asst. mgr. Marine Surf Hotel, Honolulu, 1976-79; gen. mgr. Seaside Lanai Hotel, Honolulu, 1979-80; resident mgr. Four Paddle Condominium, Honolulu, 1980—. With U.S. Army, 1970-73. Mem. Inst. of Real Estate Mgmt. Roman Catholic. Home and Office: Four Paddle AOAO 2140 Kuhio Ave Honolulu HI 96815-2308

HITCHCOCK, JOHN DAVID, apiculturist; b. Jaffna, Ceylon, Apr. 7, 1909; came to U.S., 1919; s. William Edwin and Harriet Abbey (Houston) H.; m. Marion Alice Prahl, June 8, 1946; children: Penny Louise, Nancy Kay. BSc, U. Mass., 1932; MSc, U. Minn., 1935. Entomologist Bee Rsch. Lab. USDA, Laramie, Wyo., 1936-59; apiculturist Bee Disease Investigations Lab., Laramie, 1959-73; ret., 1973; apiculturist honey bee population studies, studies on arsenic poisoning of honey bees, Wyo., Colo., Utah; pioneer in study of gregarine parasite in U.S. honey bees, 1947, chalk brood disease in U.S. honey bees, 1972. Mem. Laramie Parks and Recreation Bd., 1975-81. 2d lt. U.S. Army, 1942-46, CBI. Mem. Entomol. Soc. Am., Nat. Assn. Ret. Fed. Employees (pres. Wyo. Fedn. chpts. 1975), Soc. for Preservation and Encouragement Barber Shop Quartet Singing in Am. (pres. Laramie chpt. 1959-60, 81-82), Sigma Xi (pres. Wyo. chpt. 1962). Home: 1873 N 15th St Laramie WY 82070-1935

HITCHCOCK, VERNON THOMAS, farmer, retired lawyer; b. Selma, Ind., Feb. 21, 1919; s. Lucian Elmer and Loda Alice (King) H.; m. Betty Kathryn Orr, May 24, 1949; children: Brenda, Linda, Nancy, Debra, Randolph. BS in Agr., Purdue U., 1940; JD, Stanford U., 1953. Bar: Calif. 1954, U.S. Supreme Ct. 1961. Pilot Southwest Airways, San Francisco, 1946, TWA, Kansas City, Mo., 1947-51; pvt. practice Healdsburg, Calif., 1954-55; dep. atty. gen. State of Calif., Sacramento, 1956; dep. county counsel Sonoma County, Santa Rosa, Calif., 1957-65; exec. dir. Libyan Aviation Co., Tripoli, 1966-67; legal counsel Sonoma County Schs., 1967-82; farm mgr. Selma, Ind., 1975--; originator Freedom Under Law program. Author: The Airline to Infinity. Active Am. Security Council, 1965--. Served to comdr. USNR, 1941-79. Mem. Res. Officers Assn., U.S. naval Inst., Naval Order U.S., Commonwealth Club San Francisco, Quiet Birdmen, Odd Fellows. Republican. Episcopalian.

HITCHENS, DAVID WILLIAM, health facility administrator; b. Evanston, Ill., Oct. 16, 1955; s. Matthew Eugene and Annamae (De Caluwe) H.; m. Barbara Steiner, Apr. 26, 1980; children: Sharon, Collette. BA, Marquette U., 1977. Dir. materials mgmt. The Children's Hosp., Denver, 1983-88; materials mgr. Nat. Jewish Ctr. Immunology and Respiratory Medicine, Denver, 1988—. Roman Catholic. Home: 6800 S Sherman St Littleton CO 80122-1024 Office: Nat Jewish Ctr 1400 Jackson St Denver CO 80206-2761

HITE, ROBERT WESLEY, wastewater reclamation executive; b. Ft. Scott, Kans., Mar. 18, 1936; s. Woodward Vannoy and Corinne Winifred (Wright) H.; m. Sarah Catherine Hoper, Aug. 20, 1960; children: Katherine, John, Laura, Martha, Amy. Student, Netherlands Coll., Breukelen, The Netherlands, 1956-57; BA, Colo. Coll., 1958; JD, NYU, 1961. Bar: Colo. 1961, U.S. Dist. Ct. Colo. 1961, U.S. Ct. Mil. Appeals 1965, U.S. Supreme Ct. 1965, U.S. Ct. Appeals (10th cir.) 1973. Judge advocate USN, Newport, R.I., 1962-65; sole practice Denver, 1965-69; sr. v.p., gen. counsel Mr. Steak Inc., Denver, 1969-88; mgr. Met. Denver Wastewater Reclamation Dist., 1988—, also bd. dirs. Pres. 7th Ave. Homeowners Assn., Denver, 1975—. Mem. ABA, Colo. Bar Assn., Denver Bar Assn., Colo. Assn. Corp. Counsel (pres. 1974-76), Colo. Wyoming Restaurant Assn. (bd. dirs. 1987-88), Assn. Met. Sewerage Agys. (bd. dirs. 1992—), Colo. Coll. Alumni Assn. (bd. dirs. 1984-88). Republican. Presbyterian. Club: Law. Lodge: Rotary. Office: Met Denver Wastewater Reclamation 6450 York St Denver CO 80229-7499

HITLIN, DAVID GEORGE, physicist, educator; b. Bklyn., Apr. 15, 1942; s. Maxwell and Martha (Lipetz) H.; m. Joan R. Abramowitz, 1966 (div. 1981); m. Abigail R. Gumbiner, Jan. 2, 1982. BA, Columbia U., 1963, MA, 1965, PhD, 1968. Instr. Columbia U., N.Y.C., 1967-69; research assoc. Stanford (Calif.) Linear Accelerator Ctr., 1969-72, asst. prof., 1975-79, mem. program com., 1980-82; asst. prof. Stanford U., 1972-75; assoc. prof. Calif. Inst. Tech., Pasadena, 1979-85, prof. physics, 1985—; mem. adv. panel U.S. Dept. Energy Univ. Programs, 1983; mem. program com. Fermi Nat. Accelerator Lab., Batavia, Ill., 1983-87, Newman Lab., Cornell U., Ithaca, N.Y., 1986-88; mem. rev. com. U. Chgo. Argonne Nat. Lab., 1985-87; chmn. Stanford Linear Accelerator Ctr. Users Orgn., 1990—; mem. program com. Brookhaven Nat. Lab., Upton, N.Y., 1992—. Contbr. numerous articles to profl. jours. Fellow Am. Phys. Soc. Home: 1704 Skyview Dr Altadena CA 91001-2143 Office: Calif Inst of Tech Dept Physics 356-48 Lauritsen Pasadena CA 91125

HIX, LARRY JAMES, nurse anesthetist, educator; b. Batesville, Ark., Nov. 17, 1947; s. James Donel and Carmel Lucille (Hon) H.; m. Andriana Moungrides, Sept. 10, 1971; children: Christopher Lawrence, Reneé Andriana, Phillip Alexander. BSN, U. Okla., 1976. RN. Enlisted man U.S. Army,, 1967, advanced through grades to capt.; PAR supr. Bapt. Med. Ctr., Oklahoma City, 1976-78; with U.S. Army Med. Dept., Washington, 1978-86; ret., 1986; dir. anesthesia svcs. Breckinridge Meml. Hosp., Hardinsburg, Ky., 1986-87, St. Mary's Hosp., Reno, 1987-90, Churchill Regional Med. Ctr., Fallon, Nev., 1987-90; propr., mgr. Anchor Anesthesia Svcs., San Diego, 1990—; cons. anesthesia for plastic surgery So. Calif. Assn. for Plastic Surgery, Laguna Nigel, Calif., 1990-92; instr. neonatal recusitation Woodland (Calif.) Meml. Hosp., 1992-93. Campaign organizer Com. To Elect Perot for Pres., Fresno, Calif., 1992. Mem. Am. Assn. Nurse Anesthetists (cert.). Democrat. Home and Office: 13970 Mennonite Pt San Diego CA 92129

HIXON, ROBIN RAY, food service executive, writer; b. Vancouver, Wash., May 4, 1954; s. Charles Donovan and Leona Margaret (Teske) Hixson. Exec. chef, Am. Culinary Fedn., 1972-77. Cert. Am. Restaurant Assn., 1992. Apprentice Redlion Inns, Vancouver, 1972-77, exec. chef, 1977-80; exec. chef Hilton Hotel, Baton Rouge, 1981; chief steward Delta Queen Steamboat Co., New Orleans, 1981-86, gen. mgr., 1986-88; exec. chef Icicle Seafoods Inc., Seattle, 1989-92, Sea Spirit Cruise Lines, Inc., 1992—. Author: American Regional Cuisines, 1987; contbr. articles to profl. jours. Mem. Nat. Trust for Hist. Preservation, 1982-92, Wash. Hist. Preservation, 1990-92, Oreg. Pub. Broadcasting, 1990-92, N.Y. Met. Opera, 1973-80; performer Peruvian Singers, 1972-74. Mem. Am. Culinary Fedn. (writer 1985-91), Chefs De Cuisine Soc. Oreg. (sgt. at arms 1974-80). Democrat. Home: 311 NE 85th St # G Vancouver WA 98665 Office: 1701 Broadway # 262 Vancouver WA 98663

HJELMSTAD, WILLIAM DAVID, lawyer; b. Casper, Wyo., Apr. 4, 1954; s. Alvin Gordon and A. Thecla (Walz) H.; children: Jennifer Ashley, Allison Caitlin. AA in Social Sci., Casper Coll., 1974; BS in Psychology, U. Wyo., 1976, JD, 1979. Bar: Wyo. 1979, U.S. Dist. Ct. Wyo. 1979. Dept. county pros. atty. Hot Springs County, Thermopolis, Wyo., 1979-80; asst. pub. defender Natrona County, Casper, Wyo., 1980-82; sole practice, Casper, 1981—. Mem. ABA (mem. family law com. 1983-84, adoption com. 1983-84), Wyo. State Bar Assn. (mem. alcohol and substance abuse com., lawyers assistance com. 1988—), Natrona County Bar Assn., Wyo. Trial Lawyers Assn., Assn. Trial Lawyers Am., Am. Judicature Soc., Acad. Family Mediators, Wyo. Cowboy Shootout Com. Lodges: Elks, Kiwanis. Home: PO Box 90001 Casper WY 82609-1001

HJORTSBERG, WILLIAM REINHOLD, author; b. N.Y.C., Feb. 23, 1941; s. Helge Reinhold and Anna Ida (Welti) H.; m. Marian Souidee Renken, June 2, 1962 (div. 1982); children—Lorca Isabel, Max William.; m. Sharon Leroy, July 21, 1982 (div. 1985). BA, Dartmouth Coll., 1962; postgrad., Yale U., 1962-63, Stanford U., 1967-68. Ind. author, screenwriter, 1969—; adj. prof. media and theatre arts Mont. State U., 1991—. Author: Alp, 1969, Gray Matters, 1971, Symbiography, 1973, Toro! Toro! Toro!, 1974, Falling Angel, 1978, Tales & Fables, 1985, films: Thunder and Lightning, 1977, Legend, 1986; co-author TV film: Georgia Peaches, 1980; contbg. editor Rocky Mountain mag, 1979; contbr. fiction to Realist, Playboy, Cornell Rev., Penthouse, Oui, Sports Illustrated; contbr. criticism to N.Y. Times Book Rev. Recipient Playboy Editorial award, 1971, 78; Wallace Stegner fellow, 1967-68; Nat. Endowment Arts grantee, 1976. Mem. Authors Guild, Writers Guild Am. Home and Office: Main Boulder RT Mc Leod MT 59052

HLUBEK, JEFFRY JOSEPH, communications executive; b. Amboy, Ill., Jan. 31, 1946; s. Adolph Joseph and Regina Marie (Kuhn) H.; m. Sheila Anne Webb, Feb. 15, 1969. BA, U. Iowa, 1968, MA, 1972. Vice pres., sr. counselor Young & Rubicam, Cedar Rapids, Iowa, 1978-87; prin. Communication Specialties, Arcata, Calif., 1987—. With U.S. Army, 1968-70. Mem. Pub. Rels. Soc. Am. (counselors acad.), Ingomar Club. Home: 225 Shirley Blvd Arcata CA 95521-6527

HO, DONALD TAI LOY, entertainer, singer; b. Honolulu, Aug. 13, 1930; s. James A. Y. and Emily L. (Silva) H.; m. Melvamay Kolokea Wong, Nov. 22, 1951; children: Donald Jr., Donalei, Dayna, Dondi, Dori, Dwight. Student, Springfield Coll., 1950; BS, U. Hawaii, 1954. Entertainer Honey's, Kaneohe, Hawaii, 1959-61, Flamingo Hotel, Las Vegas, Nev., 1964-72, Duke Kahanamoku's, Honolulu, 1964-70, Polynesian Palace, Honolulu, 1970-81, Don Ho's, Waikiki, 1981-82, Hilton Hawaiian Village, Honolulu, 1982-90, Hula Hut, Honolulu, 1991-92, Outrigger's Polynesian Palace, Honolulu, 1992—; with Alii's, Midway Island, 1964, Barabosa Club, San Francisco, 1965, Coconut Grove, Ambassador Hotel, L.A., 1965-68, 1967 Tour U.S./Can., Royal Box, Americana Hotel, N.Y.C., 1968, Empire Rm., Chgo., 1968; with Variety Club, Ambassador of Variety Club, Honolulu, 1978-87. Rec. with Reprise Co., Los Angeles, 1963-65 (Mainland, Can. tour Sept.-Dec. 1980). Served to 1st lt. USAF, 1954-59. Office: Don Ho Enterprises Ltd 3954 Gail St Honolulu HI 96815

HO, IWAN, research plant pathologist; b. Souzhou, Jiangsu, China, Apr. 15, 1925; came to U.S., 1956; m. Mei-Chun Chang, Nov. 29, 1975; 1 child, Tomur M. BS, Nat. Shanghai U., 1946; MS, La. State U., 1958; PhD, Oreg. State U., 1984. Microbiologist Seattle Pub. Health Dept., 1962-66; research plant physiologist Forestry Scis. Lab., Corvallis, Oreg., 1970—; courtesy asst. prof. Coll. Forestry, Oreg. State U. Mem. Mycol. Soc. Am., Am. Soc. Plant Physiologists, Internat. Soc. Plant Molecular Biology, Sigma Xi. Democrat. Episcopalian. Home: 1686 SW Bullevard St Philomath OR 97370-9538 Office: Forestry Sci Lab Pacific NW Rsch Sta 3200 Jefferson Corvallis OR 97333

HO, PAUL LEUNG, pediatrician; b. Taipei, Taiwan, Republic of China, Dec. 2, 1961; came to U.S. 1971; s. Andrew Pei-Chi and Esther (Ku) H.; m. Lydia Faith Ng Ho, July 1, 1989. BS, Biola U., LaMirada, Calif., 1983; MD, Oral Roberts U., 1987. Diplomate Am. Bd. Pediatrics. Physician U. So. Calif. Med. Ctr., L.A., 1987-90; pediatrician Kaiser Med. Ctr., Harbor City, Calif., 1990—; coord. Child Abuse Clinic, Kaiser Med. Ctr., 1990—. Chmn. workshop com. adult fellowship Bread of Life Ch., 1991—. Fellow Am. Acad. Pediatrics; mem. L.A. Pediatric Soc., Christian Med. Soc. Republican. Baptist. Office: Kaiser Med Ctr 25825 S Vermont Ave Harbor City CA 90710-3599

HO, RODNEY JIN YONG, educator, medical researcher; b. Rangoon, Burma, May 21, 1959; came to U.S., 1977; s. David Shoon-Khat and Po-Kin (Paw) H.; m. Lily S. Hwang, July 10, 1988; 1 child, Beatrice Eirene. BS, U. Calif., Davis, 1983; MS, U. Tenn., 1985, PhD, 1987. Teaching asst. U. Tenn., Knoxville, 1984-85, rsch. asst., 1985-87; post-doctoral fellow, assoc. investigator Stanford (Calif.) U. Sch. Medicine, 1987-90; asst. prof. pharmaceutics Sch. Pharmacy U. Wash., Seattle, 1990—; affiliate investigator of pharmacology Fred Hutchinson Cancer Rsch. Ctr., Seattle, 1991—. Author: Liposomes as Drug Carriers, 1988, Topics in Vaccine Adjuvant Research, 1991; patentee immunoliposome assays, composition and treatment for herpes simplex; contbr. numberous articles on infectious diseases, pharmaceutical sciences, virology, immunology and biochemistry to sci. jours. Mem. AAAS, Am. Assn. Coll. Pharmacy, Am. Assn. Pharm. Scientists, Am. Chem. Soc., Biophys. Soc., Internat. Soc. Antiviral Rsch., N.Y. Acad. Sci. Office: U Wash Sch Pharmacy Dept Pharmaceutics Seattle WA 98195

HO, STUART TSE KONG, investment company executive; b. Manila, Nov. 18, 1935; came to U.S., 1936; s. Chinn and Betty (Ching) H.; m. Mary Lois Lee, June 17, 1961; children: Peter, Cecily, Heather. BA, Claremont (Calif.) McKenna, 1957; JD, U. Mich., 1963. Bar: Hawaii. Asst. sec. to chmn. bd. Capital Investment of Hawaii, Honolulu, 1965—; trustee Coll. Retirement Equities Fund, N.Y.C.; bd. dirs. Bancorp Hawaii, Inc., Honolulu, Gannett Co., Inc., Rosslyn, Va., Aloha Airgroup, Inc., Honolulu. Representative Hawaii Ho. of Reps., Honolulu, 1966-70, majority fl. leader, 1968-70; del. Constnl. Conv. of 1968, Honolulu, 1968; regent U. Hawaii, Honolulu, 1971-74. 1st lt. U.S. Army, 1958-60, ETO. Democrat. Office: Capital Investment Hawaii Ste 1700 733 Bishop St Honolulu HI 96813-4019

HOADLEY, WALTER EVANS, economist, financial executive, lay worker; b. San Francisco, Aug. 16, 1916; s. Walter Evans and Marie Howland (Preece) H.; m. Virginia Alm, May 20, 1939; children: Richard Alm, Jean Elizabeth (Mrs. Donald A. Peterson). A.B., U. Calif., 1938, M.A., 1940, Ph.D., 1946; Dr.C.S., Franklin and Marshall Coll., 1963; LL.D. (hon.), Golden Gate U., 1968, U. Pacific, 1979; hon. degree, El Instituto Technologico Autonomo de Mexico, 1974. Collaborator U.S. Bur. Agrl. Econs., 1938-39; rsch. economist Calif. Gov.'s Reemployment Commn., 1939, Calif. Gov.'s State Planning Bd., 1941; rsch. economist, teaching fellow U. Calif., 1938-41, supr. indsl. mgmt. war tng. office, 1941-42; econ. adviser U. Chgo. Civil Affairs Tng. Sch., 1945; sr. economist Fed. Res. Bank Chgo., 1942-49; economist Armstrong World Industries, Lancaster, Pa., 1949-54, treas., 1954-60, v.p., treas., 1960-66, dir., 1962-87; sr. v.p., chief economist, mem. mng. com. Bank of Am. NT & SA, San Francisco, 1966-68, exec. v.p., chief economist, mem. mng. com., mem. mgmt. adv. council, chmn. subs., 1968-81; ret., 1981; sr. research fellow Hoover Inst., Stanford U., 1981—; dir. PLM Internat., Transcisco Industries, Inc., Selected/Venture Advisers; dep. chmn. Fed. Res. Bank, Phila., 1960-61, chmn., 1962-66; chmn. Conf. Fed. Res. Chairmen, 1966; faculty Sch. Banking U. Wis., 1945-49, 55, 58-66; adviser various U.S. Govt. agys.; Wright Internat. Bd. Econ. and Investment Advisors, 1987—; spl. adviser U.S. Congl. Budget Office, 1975-87; mem. pub. adv. bd. U.S. Dept. Commerce, 1970-74; mem. White House Rev. Com. for Balance Payments Statistics, 1963-65, Presdl. Task Force on Growth, 1969-70, Presdl. Task Force on Land Utilization, Presdl. Conf. on Inflation, 1974; gov. Com. on Developing Am. Capitalism, 1977—, chmn. 1987-88. Mem. Meth. Ch. Commn. on World Service and Fin. Phila. Conf., 1957-64, chmn. investment com., 1964-66; bd. dirs., exec. com. Internat. Mgmt. and Devel. Inst., 1976—; trustee Pacific Sch. Religion, 1968-89; adviser Nat. Commn. to Study Nursing and Nursing Edn., 1968-73; trustee Duke U., 1968-73, pres.'s assoc., 1973-80; trustee Golden Gate U., 1974—, chmn. investment com., 1977—; trustee World Wildlife U.S.Fund The Conservation Found., 1987-90; mem. periodic chmn. adminstrv. bd. Trinity United Meth. Ch., Berkeley, Calif., 1966-84; mem. adminstrv. bd., advisor Lafayette (Calif.) United Meth. Ch., 1984—; mem. bd. overseers vis. com. Harvard Coll. Econs., 1969-74; chmn. investment com. Calif.-Nev. Meth. Found., 1968-75, mem., 1976-91; mem. Calif. Gov.'s Council Econ. and Bus. Devel., 1978-82, chmn., 1980-82; trustee Hudson Inst., 1979-84; co-chmn. San Francisco Mayor's Fiscal Adv. Com., 1978-81, mem. 1981—; chmn. Bay Area Econ. Advisers, 1982—; spl. adviser Presdl. Cabinet Com. Innovation, 1978-79; mem. Calif. State Internat. Adv. Com., 1986—; regent U. Calif., 1990-91; mem. adv. coun. Calif. Environ. Technology Partnership, 1993—. Fellow Am. Statis. Assn. (v.p. dir. 1952-54, pres. 1958), Nat. Assn. of Bus. Economists, Internat. Acad. Mgmt.; mem. Am. Fin. Assn. (dir. 1955-56, pres. 1969), Conf. Bus. Economists (chmn. 1962), Atlantic Coun. of U.S. (dir. 1985—), U.S. Coun. for Internat. Bus. (sr. trustee 1992—), Commonwealth Club of Calif. (pres. 1987), Internat. Conf. Comml. Bank Economists (chmn. 1978-81), Am., Western Econ. Assns., Am. Marketing Assn., Am. Bankers Assn. (chmn. urban and community affairs com. 1972-73, mem. econ. adv. council 1976-78), Nat. Bur. Econ. Rsch. (dir. 1965-81), Western Fin. Assn., dir., mem. steering com., U. Calif. Alumni Assn. (pres. 1989-91, chmn. investment com. 1983-89), U.S. Nat. Com. on Pacific Econ. Cooperation (vice chmn. 1984-89, mem. exec. com. 1989—), Wright Internat. Bd. Econ. and Investment Advisors, Caux Internat. Roundtable, St. Francis Yacht Club, Commonwealth Club, Pacific Union Club, Bankers Club, Silverado Country Club, Phi Beta Kappa (dir. 1986—), Kappa Alpha. Office: Bank of Am Dept 3001-B PO Box 37000o CA 94137-0001

HOAG, JOHN ARTHUR, bank executive; b. Freeport, N.Y., Sept. 29, 1932; s. John Hoag and Viola (Babcock) Hobson; m. Jeanette Makaio, Dec. 5, 1959; children: Steve, Vanessa, Kanani. BS, U. Mo., 1955; grad., Pacific Coast Banking Sch., Wash., 1970; MBA, U. Hawaii, 1977. Account exec. Walston & Co., N.Y.C., 1960; mgmt. trainee 1st Hawaiian Bank, Honolulu, 1960, br. mgr., Hilo, 1968, Island v.p., 1970-76, sr. v.p., mgr., 1976, exec. v.p. loan group, 1979, pres., 1989—, also bd. dirs.; pres. 1st Hawaiian Inc., Honolulu, 1991—, also bd. dirs.; vice chm. 1st Interstate Bank Hawaii, Honolulu, 1991—; Mem. bd. regents Tokai Internat. Coll., 1992. Bd. dirs. Hawaii Med. Svc. Assn., 1981-93, Honolulu, Polynesian Cultural Ctr., 1990—, Honolulu, Kapiolani Med. Ctr. for Women and Children, Honolulu, 1989—. Capt. USMC, 1955-60. Mem. Pres.'s Club U. Hawaii, Hawai Bankers Assn., C. of C. of Hawaii (chmn. bd. 1992-93). Mem. LDS Ch. Office: 1st Hawaiian Bank 1132 Bishop St Penthouse Honolulu HI 96813 also: First Hawaiian Bank PO Box 3200 Honolulu HI 96847

HOAGLAND, ALBERT JOSEPH, JR., psychotherapist, hypnotherapist, minister; b. Clayton, N.J., July 2, 1939. Cert. psychiat. tech., Ancora State Hosp., 1958; RN, Monmouth Med. Ctr., 1961; BS, Monmouth Coll., 1964; MSW, Rutgers U., 1966; M.Div., Fuller Theol. Sem., 1978; D in Ministry, Boston U., 1981; PhD, Am. Inst. Hypnotherapy, 1989, D.C.H., 1991; postgrad., Samra U. of Oriental Medicine. Ordained to ministry Disciples of Christ, 1978; lic. clin. social worker, Calif., marriage, family and child counselor, Calif.; cert. sch. counselor, anger therapist, eating disorders therapist. Pvt. practice counseling, 1959—; psychiat. technician, RN N.J. State Hosp., 1958-66; instr., cons. Los Angeles County Dept. Probation, 1972-75; instr. psychology Calif. Grad. Inst., 1973; instr. Chapman Coll., 1972-74; instr. psychology Calif. State U., Dominguez Hills, 1974; instr. Torrance (Calif.) Adult Sch., 1977-79, 81-85; pastor Ariz., 1984-85, Calif., 1978-79, 81-84, Mass., 1979-81; subs. tchr. Marana (Ariz.) Sch. Dist., 1985; instr. Beverly Hills Adult Sch., 1984—; exec. dir. Personal Counseling Svcs. and Hypnotherapy Ctr., San Pedro, 1986—; religious educator various retreats, programs, summer camps, etc., 1975—. Author: Anger to Intimacy, 1988; editor Jonestown Collection, 1978, Professional Papers from the Desert, 1970, What's Your Problem?, 1989; producer (film) Gestalt Art Therapy, 1974. Mem. Congress of Disciples Clergy, Disciples of Christ Hist. Soc., Disciples Peace Fellowship; trainer, cons. L.A. Coun. Exploring div. Boy Scouts Am., 1971-74, 88—, explorer post advisor, 1988—; coach Palos Verdes (Calif.) Soccer Program, basketball and soccer Torrance City Sports Program; dir. YWCA Delinquency Prevention Program, San Pedro, 1986-89; chair community adv. coun. San Pedro High Sch.; campaigned for mayor. Recipient Adult God and Svc award, 1989. Mem. Nat. Tchrs. Assn., Nat. Assn. Social Workers, Am. Assn. Marriage and Family Therapists, Am. Osteo. Assn., Nat. Assn. Christians in Social Work, Harbor Area Police Clergy Coun. (pres.), Am. Bd. Hypnotherapists, Nat. Assn. Clergy Hypnotherapists, World Fedn. Mental Health, Clowns of Am., San Pedro Rotary (sec.), Phi Delta Kappa. Democrat. Home: 3318 Torrance Blvd Torrance CA 90503-5011 Office: Personal Counseling Svcs and Hypnotherapy Ctr PO Box 367 San Pedro CA 90733-0367

HOAGLAND, DENNIS ROY, trust banker, financial consultant; b. Bell, Calif., Oct. 12, 1942; s. Clyde Roy and Dorothy Ann (Redford-Thomas) H.; m. Mary Ellen Hales, Sept. 20, 1968; children: Jason Roy, Jonathan Hales, David Wayne. BS, Brigham Young U., 1968; JD, Western States U., San Diego, 1973; grad. cert. in bus., U. Wash., 1980. Cert. trust and fin. advisor. Asst. to CEO, Redway Truck & Warehouse Corp., L.A., 1968-70; sr. trust officer Bank Am., San Diego, La Jolla, Calif., 1970-72; v.p., truste officer So. Calif. 1st Nat. Bank, La Jolla, 1972-75; v.p., mgr. Crocker Nat. Bank, San Diego, 1975-80; v.p., mktg. mgr. Crocker Nat. Bank, Newport Beach, Calif., 1980-81; v.p., regional mgr. Crocker Nat. Bank, Fresno, Calif., 1981-85; exec. dir. St. Agnes Med. Ctr. Found., Fresno, 1985-87; v.p., gen. mgr. 1st Interstate Bank Calif., Beverley Hills, Calif., 1987-91, Sacramento, 1991—; pres., CEO, Marden Enterprises, Fresno, 1981—; chmn. bd. Green & Barter Arabian Horse Ranches, Scottdale, Ariz. and Lehi, Utah, 1990—. Vice chmn. bd. dirs. Calif. Sch. Profl. Psychology, fresno, 1982-87; dist. chmn. Boy Scouts Am., 1983-85. Mem. Sacramento Estate Planning Coun., Brigham Young U. Cougar Club, Rotary. Republican. Mem. LDS Ch. Office: 1st Interstate Bank Calif 930 K St Ste 200 Sacramento CA 93711

HOAGLAND, SAMUEL ALBERT, lawyer, pharmacist; b. Mt. Home, Idaho, Aug. 19, 1953; s. Charles Leroy and Glenna Lorraine (Gridley) H.; m. Karen Ann Mengel, Nov. 20, 1976; children: Hiliary Anne, Heidi Lynne, Holly Kaye. BS in Pharmacy, Idaho State U., 1976; JD, U. Idaho, 1982. Bar: Idaho 1982, U.S. Dist. Ct. Idaho 1982, U.S. CT. Appeals (9th cir.) 1984. Lectr. clin. pharmacy Idaho State U., Pocatello, 1976-78, lectr. pharmacy law, 1985-86, dean's adv. council Coll. Pharmacy, 1987-92; hosp. pharmacist Mercy Med. Ctr., Nampa, Idaho, 1978-79; retail pharmacist Thrifty Corp., Moscow, Idaho, 1980-82; assoc. Dial, Looze & May, Pocatello, 1982-89, Prescott & Foster, Boise, Idaho, 1989-90; pvt. practice, 1990—; gen. counsel Design Innovations and Rsch. Corp., 1991—; chmn. malpractice panel Idaho Bd. Medicine, Boise, 1983—, adminstrv. hearing officer, 1986—. Contbr. to law publs. Bd. dirs. Cathedral Pines Camp, Ketchum, Idaho. Mem. ABA, Idaho State Bar Assn., Idaho Pharm. Assn., Idaho Trial Lawyers Assn., Boise Bar Assn., Capital Pharm. Assn., Am. Pharm. Assn., Idaho Soc. Hosp. Pharmacists (bd. dirs.), Am. Soc. Pharmacy Law, Flying Doctors Am. (Atlanta) (bd. dirs.). Home: 11901 W Mesquite Dr Boise ID 83706-0813 Office: 2309 Mountain View Dr Ste 205 Boise ID 83706-1065

HOANG, DUC VAN, theoretical pathologist, educator; b. Hanoi, Vietnam, Feb. 17, 1926; came to U.S. 1975, naturalized 1981; s. Duoc Van and Nguyen Thi (Tham) H.; m. Mau-Ngo Thi Vu, Dec. 1, 1952; 1 child, Duc-An Hoang-Vu. M.D., Hanoi U. Sch. Medicine, Vietnam, 1953; DSc, Open Internat. U., Sri Lanka, 1989. Dean Sch. Medicine Army of the Republic of Vietnam, Saigon, 1959-63; dean Minh-Duc U. Sch. Medicine, Saigon, 1970-71; clin. prof. theoretical pathology U. So. Calif. Sch. Medicine, L.A., 1978-92; adj. prof. Emperor's Coll. Traditional Oriental Medicine, Santa Monica, Calif., 1988—; sci. and med. dir. Quantum Internat. Ltd., 1992—. Author: Towards an Integrated Humanization of Medicine, 1957; The Man Who Weights the Soul, 1959; Eastern Medicine, A New Direction?, 1970; also short stories; translator: Pestis, introduction to the work of Albert Camus, Vietnamese translation of La Peste; editor: The East (co-founder); jour. Les Cahiers de l'Asie du Sud-Est. Founder, past pres. Movement for Fedn. Countries S.E. Asia; co-founder, past v.p. Movement for Restoration Cultures and Religions of Orient; active Vo-Vi Meditation Assn. Am.; mem. The Noetic Inst., 1988—, Internat. Found. for Homeopathy, 1987; founder, pres. Intercontinental Found. for Electro-Magnetic Resonance Rsch., 1989—; coord. Unity and Diversity World Health Coun., 1992—. Named hon. dean The Open Internat. U. of Complementary Medicines, Sri Lanka, 1989; Unity-and-Diversity World Coun. fellow, 1990—. Mem. AAUP, Assn. Clin. Scientists, Am. Com. for Integration Eastern and Western Medicine (founder), Assn. Unitive Medicine (founder, pres.). Republican. Roman Catholic. Clubs: U. So. Calif. Staff, U. So. Calif. Faculty Members (Los Angeles). Home: 3630 Barry Ave Los Angeles CA 90066-3202 Office: LAC-USC Med Ctr Los Angeles CA 90033-1084

HOARE, TYLER JAMES, sculptor; b. Joplin, Mo., June 5, 1940; s. Melvin James and Dorotha Maude (Beadle) H.; m. Kathy Joyce Quinn, Mar. 9, 1963; 1 dau., Janet Elaine. Student, U. Colo., 1959-60, Sculpture Center, N.Y.C., 1960-61; BFA, U. Kan., 1963; postgrad., Calif. Coll. Arts and Crafts, 1965-67. instr. extension U. Calif. at Berkeley, 1973—; guest lectr. San Francisco Art Inst., San Francisco State Coll. Exhibited one man shows, New Center U.S. Art Gallery, Kansas City, Mo., 1964, Jewish Community Center Gallery, Kansas City, Studio C, Berkeley, Calif., 1965, Derby Gallery, Berkeley, Lucien Labaudt Gallery, San Francisco, 1966, U. Calif.-Berkeley, 1966, 67, Free U. Berkeley Gallery, Fredric Hobb's San Francisco Art Center, 1967, Green Gallery, San Francisco, 1968, St. Mary's Coll., 1969, John Bolles Gallery, San Francisco, 1969, 71, San Francisco State Coll., 1970, Camberwell Sch. Art, London, Eng., 1971, State U. N.Y. at Albany, Atherton Gallery, Menlo Park, Calif., 1972, Stanford, 1973, Richmond (Calif.) Art Ctrs., 1983, Calif. State U. Hayward, Keokuk (Iowa) Art Ctr., Olive Hyde Art Ctr., Fremont, Calif., John Bolles Gallery, San Francisco, Cen. Sch. Art & Design, London, 1974, Daly City (Calif.) Civic Ctr., San Mateo (Calif.) Arts Coun./Sunshine Gallery, County of San Mateo Hall of Justice, 1975, Purdue U. Gallery 1, 1976, Spiva Art Ctr., Mo. So. State Coll., 1977, Manner of Speaking, San Franciso, Stuart Gallery, Berkeley, 1978, Studio 718, San Francisco, 1980, Geotrope Gallery, Berkeley, 1981, Studio Nine, Benicia, Calif., Marin County Civic Ctr., San Rafael, 1982, Solano Community Coll., Suison City, Calif., 1983, Oakland Art Assn. Gallery, 1986, Coastal Art League Mus., Half Moon Bay, Calif., 1989; exhibited in numerous group shows 1963, The Trading Co. II, U. Calif., Berkeley, 1989, Western Wash. U. Bellingham, 1989, Calif. Mus. of Photography, 1989, U. Calif., Riverside, 1989, Eye Tahoe, Venice, Calif., 1989, Holsum Roc Gallery, Chgo., 1989, Cleve. Inst. of Art, 1989, Sonoma State U. Art Gallery, 1989, Rohnert Park, Calif., 1989, Gallery 25, Fresno, Calif., 1989, The Art Store Gallery, L.A., 1989, Art-Pool, Buda-Ray U. Budapest, Hungary, 1989, Jr. Coll. Albany, N.Y., 1989, Ohlone Coll. Art Gallery, Fremont, Calif., 1990, Alcorcon Culture Office, Madrid, N.Y., 1990, Corr. Sch., N.Y.C., Balley Art Gallery, Walnut Creek, Calif., 1990, Mercer Gallery, 1990, Monroe Community Coll. Rochester, N.Y., 1990, Acad. of Art Coll. Gallery, San Francisco, 1990, Sonama State U., 1990, Can. Union, Scarborough, Ont., Can., 1990, Sangamon State U., Springfield, Ill., 1990, Jr. Coll. of Albany, 1990, Adirondack Community Coll., Glen Falls, N.Y., 1990, Contemporary Tech. Art, Museo Internat. De Electrografia, 1990, Monroe Community Coll., Mercer Gallery, Rochester, N.Y., 1991, Wilder Gallery, Los Gatos, Calif., 1991, Buda-Ray U., 1991, Guy Bleus Archives, Belgium, 1991, Art Electro-Images, Paris, 1991, Action Art Internat., Chgo., 1991, Goodwill, Kent, Wash., 1991, Electrografia Museo Internat., Spain, 1991, Contemporary Art Gallery, Aono, Japan, 1991, Shadow Archive, Kenosha, Wis., 1991, Oakland Mus., Calif., Pasadena Mus., Calif., Calif. Palace of Legion of Honor, San Francisco, San Francisco Mus., Library of Congress, Pratt Graphics Center, Los Angeles County Mus., Cin. Mus.; represented in permanent collections, USIA, Washington, SUNY-Albany, Oakland Mus., Calif. Coll. Arts and Crafts, others. Address: 30 Menlo Pl Berkeley CA 94707

HOBBS, GUY STEPHEN, financial executive; b. Lynwood, Calif., Feb. 23, 1955; s. Franklin Dean and Bette Jane (Little) H.; m. Laura Elena Lopez, Jan. 6, 1984; 1 child, Mariah Amanda. BA, U. Calif., Santa Barbara, 1976; MBA, U. Nev., 1978. Sr. rsch. assoc. Ctr. for Bus. and Econ. Rsch., Las Vegas, Nev., 1978-80; pvt. practice mgmt. cons. Las Vegas, 1979-82; mgmt. analyst Clark County, Las Vegas, 1980-81, sr. mgmt. analyst, 1981-82, dir. budget and fin. planning, 1982-84, comptroller, dir. fin., chief fin. officer, 1984—; lectr. in mgmt. Coll. Bus. and Econs., U. Nev., Las Vegas, 1977-88; pres. Pacific Blue Ent., 1991—. Author publs. in field. Chmn. com. Panasonic/Las Vegas Invitational Golf Tournament, 1983, 84, 85; mem. exec. bd. Community Action for Lake Mead, Las Vegas, 1990. Mem. Am. Assn. Budget and Program Analysts, Am. Soc. Pub. Adminstrn. (Pub. Adminstr. of Yr. 1987), Govt. Fin. Officers Assn. (Fin. Reporting Achievement award 1984-92, Disting. Budget Presentation award 1993), Math. Assn. Am., Internat. City Mgmt. Assn., So. Nev. Over-the-Line Players Assn. (bd. dirs., treas. 1985-90, Mem. of Yr. 1988), Ops. Mgmt. Assn. Republican. Office: Clark County 225 Bridger Ave Las Vegas NV 89155-0001

HOBBS, KENNETH BURKETT, foundation administrator, consultant; b. Appalachia, Va., Dec. 18, 1930; s. Earl Kaylor and Mary Katherine (Horner) H.; m. Faye Rollins, Oct. 28, 1950; 1 child, George Bradford. BS in Pharmacy, Auburn U., 1956, MS in Ednl. Adminstrn., 1959; postgrad., Ohio State U., U. Wash., 1960, 69; D Comml. Sci. (hon.), London Inst. Applied Rsch., Eng., 1973. Exec. dir. Ohio Acad. Sci., Columbus, 1959-61; chief, TV and Radio NASA, Washington, 1961-63; adminstrv. asst. Battelle Columbus Labs., Ohio, 1963-66; exec. officer Battelle Seattle Rsch. Ctr., 1966-73; exec. v.p. John Young Sci. Cen., Orlando, Fla., 1973-80; pres. Rollins-Hobbs Assocs., Inc., Winter Park, Fla., 1980-89, Kadlec Med. Ctr. Found., Richland, Wash., 1990—; pres. bd. dirs. Neurological Ctr., Richland, 1990—; instr. Auburn U., 1956-59. Producer-dir. TV programs, exec. producer (motion picture) The John Glenn Story, 1963; art editor Literary Mag., U. N.C. Pres. bd. dirs. Friends of the (Richland) Libr.; mem. bd. visitors Winthrop Coll., rock Hill, S.C., 1981-82; fund devel. worker Citizens for a Progressive Richland, 1990; rschr. John H. Glenn senatorial campaign, 1965. Comdr. USN, 1956-59. Disting. Wash. State Citizen, one of 10 Outstanding Young Men of Columbus. Fellow Ohio Acad. Sci., AAAS; mem. Soc. Rsch. Adminstrs. (pres. 1968), Seattle Salvation Army Adv. Bd. (chmn. 1967), Assn. Healthcare Philanthropy, Explorers Club, Tri-City Country Club, Rotary, Phi Kappa Tau, Alpha Phi Omega, Phi Delta Kappa. Republican. Home: 27 Galaxy Ln Richland WA 99352-1713

HOBSON, MARK STEPHAN, writer; b. Des Moines, Aug. 17, 1950; s. Bernard Hobson and Barbara Jean (Parrott) Jauch; m. Marilyn Marie Schutte, June 3, 1973 (div. June 1983); m. Diane M. Burroughs. BS, U. Iowa, 1976. Freelance writer L.A., 1981—; editor, writer Roderunner Travel Guide, Jackson, Wyo., 1983; writer, prodr. Third Coast Prodns., L.A., 1983-85; tech. writer Bell Labs., N.J., 1985-87; tchr. Jackson Hole Arts Coun., Jackson, 1983-85. Author: Honor Clean, 1978, Roderunner Travel Guide to Big Wyoming, 1983; author feature film scripts (CINE Golden Eagle awards 1984-85), documentary films, shorts films, play. With USMC, 1969-70.

HOBUSS, JIM J., small business owner; b. Harvey, Ill., Oct. 30, 1955; s. Orville Hugo Robert and Yvonne Arlene (Cullen) H.; m. Robin Gayle Sokol, Apr. 9, 1984; children: Heidi Monique, Jill Leighlia, Andrew James Robert. AS, Portland Community Coll., 1976; BS, Portland State, 1988. Programmer Assoc. Computer Svcs., Tigard, Oreg., 1978-80, Blue Cross of Oreg., Portland, 1980-81; devel. ctr. mgr. U.S. Nat. Bank of Oreg., Portland, 1981-91; pres. HCS Inc., Portland, 1988—. Author: Application Development Center, 1991, (jour.) CASE/CASM Industry Survey Report, 1991. Campaign mgr. Com. to Elect Richard Scariano, Gresham, Oreg., 1990-91. With USAR, 1975-78. Mem. Assn. for Systems Mgmt., Rotary Club, Nat. Speakers Assn. Home: 18004 SE Marie St Portland OR 97236-1338 Office: Hobuss Computer Solutions 18004 SE Marie St Portland OR 97236-1338

HOCH, ALAN RANDALL, credit union executive; b. Montrose, Colo., May 16, 1948; s. Richard and Ethel Elizabeth (Weber) H.; m. Judy Lina Staby, Aug. 6, 1990. BS in Edn., U. Colo., 1970, MBA, 1976. Loan officer Mcpl. Credit Union, Denver, 1978-80; mgr., pres. Boulder (Colo.) Standards Fed. Credit Union, 1980-84; pres. Denver Fire Dept. Fed. Credit Union, 1985—; chmn. Members Mortgage Corp., Englewood, Colo., 1986-91; bd. dirs. Colo. Credit Union League, Arvada. With U.S. Army, 1971-74, Vietnam. Mem. Denver Round Table, Porsche Club Am. Home: 1701 S Ames St Denver CO 80232-7213 Office: Denver Fire Dept Fed Cred U 2201 Federal Blvd Denver CO 80211-4641

HOCH, ORION LINDEL, corporate executive; b. Canonsburg, Pa., Dec. 21, 1928; s. Orion L.F. and Ann Marie (McNulty) H.; m. Jane Lee Ogan, June 12, 1952 (dec. 1978); children: Andrea, Brenda, John; m. Catherine Nan Richardson, Sept. 12, 1980; 1 child, Joe. B.S., Carnegie Mellon U., 1952; M.S., UCLA, 1954; Ph.D., Stanford U., 1957. With Hughes Aircraft Co., Culver City, Calif., 1952-54; with Stanford Electronics Labs., 1954-57; sr. engr., dept. mgr., div. v.p., div. pres. Litton Electron Devices div., San Carlos, Calif., 1957-68; group exec. Litton Components div., 1968-70; v.p. Litton Industries, Inc., Beverly Hills, Calif., 1970, sr. v.p., 1971-74, pres., 1982-88, chief exec. officer, 1986—, chmn., 1988—, also dir.; pres. Intersil, Inc., Cupertino, Calif., 1974-82; bd. dirs. Measurex Corp., Coun. Internat. Advisers Swiss Bank Corp. Trustee Carnegie-Mellon U. Served with AUS, 1946-48. Mem. IEEE, Sigma Xi, Tau Beta Pi, Phi Kappa Phi. Office: Litton Industries Inc 360 N Crescent Dr Beverly Hills CA 90210-4867*

HOCH, WILLIAM HENRY, surgeon, urologist; b. N.Y.C., Feb. 22, 1944; s. Saul and Dorothy Louise (Edelson) H.; m. Susan Jo Solomon, Sept. 20, 1943; children: Jeffrey Stewart, Laura Elizabeth. AB, Ohio State U., 1965; MD, Johns Hopkin's U., 1969. Diplomate Am. Bd. Urology. Intern, then resident Case Western Res. U., Cleve., 1969-74; urologist Woodland (Calif.) Clinic Med. Group, 1976-90; pvt. practice urologist Davis, Calif., 1991—; sec., treas. Sutter Davis Hosp., chief of staff, 1993—. Author: (chpt.) Campbell's Urology, Lewis Textbook of Surgery; contbr. articles to profl. jours. With USAF, 1974-76. Fellow ACS; mem. Am. Urologic Assn. Office: 1105 Kennedy Pl Ste 2 Davis CA 95616-1272

HOCHBERG, FREDERICK GEORGE, accountant; b. L.A., July 4, 1913; s. Frederick Joseph and Lottie (LeGendre) H.; 1 child, Ann C. May. BA, UCLA, 1937. Chief acct., auditor Swinerton, McClure & Vinnell, Managua, Nicaragua, 1942-44; pvt. acctg. practice, Avalon, Calif., 1946-66; designer, operator Descanso Beach Club, Avalon, 1966; v.p. Air Catalina, 1967; treas. Catalina Airlines, 1967; pres. Aero Commuter, 1967; v.p., treas., dir. bus. affairs William L. Pereira & Assocs., Planners, Architects, Engrs., L.A., 1967-72; v.p., gen. mgr. Mo. Hickory Corp., 1972-74; prin. Fred G. Hochberg Assocs., Mgmt. Cons., 1974—; v.p. Vicalton S.A. Mexico, 1976—; v.p., gen. mgr. Solar Engring. Co., Inc., 1977-79; pres. Solar Assocs. Internat., 1979-83. Chmn. Avalon Transp. Com., 1952, Avalon Harbor Commn., 1960, Avalon Airport Com., 1964-66, Harbor Devel. Commn., 1965-66; sec. Santa Catalina Festival of Arts, 1960, Avalon City Planning Commn., 1956-58; pres. Avalon Music Bowl Assn., 1961, Catalina Mariachi Assn., 1961-66; treas. City of Avalon, 1954-62, Catalina Island Mus. Soc., 1964, councilman, 1962-66, mayor, 1964-66; bd. dirs. L.A. Child Guidance Clinic, 1975-86, advisor to bd., 1986—, treas., 1978-79, pres., 1979-81; bd. dirs. Los Aficionados de L.A., 1977—, pres., 1980-83, 87-88; pres. Nat Assn. Taurine Clubs, 1982-85. With USNR, 1944-45. Named Catalina Island Man of Yr., 1956. Mem. Avalon Catalina Island C. of C. (past pres., bd. dirs. 1948-62), Soc. Calif. Accts., Mensa, Am. Arbitration Assn. (panel), El Monte C. of C., Town Hall-West (vice-chmn.), Internacional Tertulias, Internacional Peregrinación Mex. Lodge: Rotary (Avalon pres. 1956).

HOCHBERGER, JOHN RICHARD, bank officer; b. Blue Island, Ill., Oct. 18, 1960; s. John Richard and Ruth Bessie (Stevo) H.; m. Marissa Lina Planta, Jan. 11, 1986, children: Jaryd James, Ryan Daniel. BS MetE, U. Wis., 1983. Rsch. engr. Gen. Dynamics Corp., Pomona, Calif., 1983-88, sr. rsch. engr., 1988-91; sr. loan rep., asst. mgr. Borrower's Funding, Diamond Bar, Calif., 1991—; loan officer CenFed Bank, Glendora, Calif., 1992-93; mortgage banker Sycamore Fin. Group, Inc., Diamond Bar, Calif., 1993—. Co-inventor chip holding device, 1984. Mem. Mensa. Office: Sycamore Fin Group Inc Ste 100 1400 Montefino Ave Diamond Bar CA 91765

HOCHSCHILD, CARROLL SHEPHERD, company administrator, educator; b. Whittier, Calif., Mar. 31, 1935; d. Vernon Vero and Effie Corinne (Hollingsworth) Shepherd; m. Richard Hochschild, July 25, 1959; children: Christopher Paul, Stephen Shepherd. BA in Internat. Rels., Pomona Coll., 1956; Teaching credential U. Calif., Berkeley, 1957; MBA, Pepperdine U., 1985; cert. in fitness instrn., U. Calif., Irvine, 1988. Cert. elem. tchr., Calif. elem. tchr. Oakland Pub. Schs. (Calif.), 1957-58, San Lorenzo Pub. Schs. (Calif.), 1958-59, Pasadena Pub. Schs. (Calif.), 1959-60, Huntington Beach Pub. Schs. (Calif.), 1961-63, 67-68; adminstrv. asst. Microwave Instruments, Corona del Mar, Calif., 1968-74; co-owner Hoch Co., Corona del Mar, 1978—. Rep. Calif. Tchrs. Assn., Huntington Beach, 1962-63. Mem. AAUW, P.E.O. (projects chmn. 1990-92, corr. sec. 1992—), Internat. Dance-Exercise Found., NAFE, Am. Soc. for Tng. and Devel. (Orange County chpt.), Assistance League Newport-Mesa. Republican. Presbyterian. Clubs: Toastmistress (corr. sec. 1983), Jr. Ebell (fine arts chmn. Newport Beach 1966-67).

HOCHSCHILD, RICHARD, medical instruments executive, researcher; b. Berlin, Germany, Aug. 28, 1928; came to U.S., 1939; s. Paul and Ann Ida (Schosstag) H.; m. Carroll Corinne Shepherd, July 25, 1959; children: Christopher Paul, Stephen Shepherd. BA in Physics, Johns Hopkins U., 1950; MA in Physics, U. Calif., Berkeley, 1957. Tech. adv. U.S. Atomic Energy Commn., N.Y.C., 1951-53; chief 300 area U.S. Atomic Energy Commn., Hanford, Wash., 1953-54; pres. Metrol, Inc., Pasadena, Calif., 1957-60; asst. to v.p. Budd Co., Phoenixville, Pa., 1960-61; pres. Microwave Instruments Co., Corona del Mar, Calif., 1962-74; chief exec. officer Hoch Co., Corona del Mar, 1975—; cons. in field. Patentee and author in field. Office: Hoch Co 2915 Pebble Dr Corona Del Mar CA 92625-1518

HOCKENSMITH, SCOTT FRANKLIN, telecommunications company executive; b. Greensburg, Pa., Dec. 23, 1949; s. Scott Franklin Jr. and Margaret May (Hager) H.; m. Clare Ann Connor, Aug. 22, 1970; children: Christy Ann, Scott Franklin IV. BS in Bus. Logistics, Pa. State U., 1971; MBA, So. Ill. U., Edwardsville, 1976. Cert. airline transport pilot rating FAA; registered rep. series 7 SEC. Commd. 2d lt. USAF, 1971, advanced through grades to major, 1983; pilot Continental Airlines, Denver, 1977-84; mktg. rep. ROLM, Denver, 1984-86; mktg. instr. ROLM, An IBM Co., Santa Clara, Calif., 1986-87; mktg. edn. mgr. ROLM, An IBM and Siemens Co., Santa Clara, 1987-88, svc. mktg. mgr., 1988-90; svc. br. mgr. ROLM, An IBM and Siemens Co., Denver, 1990-91; ret. USAF Res., 1991; sales and svc. br. mgr. ROLM, A Siemens Co., Denver, 1991—. Nat. coord. World Marriage Day, Denver, Santa Clara, 1986-87; presenter World Wide Marriage Encounter, Denver, Santa Clara, 1980-92. Served in Vietnam, Persian Gulf. Decorated Vietnam Svc. medal, SW Asia Svc. medal. Republican. Roman Catholic.

HOCKFELD, MARLA GAIL GERECHT, advertising and public relations executive; b. St. Louis, Aug. 22, 1965; d. Harold and Susan Kay (Krashine) Gerecht; m. Randy Allen Hockfeld, Jan. 16, 1993. BA in Communication, U. Ala., Tuscaloosa, 1986. Pub. rels. intern U. Ala. U. Rels., Tuscaloosa, 1985-86; credit hostess Bullock's Dept. Store, Las Vegas, Nev., 1985-88; publicity dir., editor The Jewish Reporter newspaper Jewish Fedn. of Las Vegas, 1987-93, leadership coord., 1989-92; owner So. Nev. Advt. and Pub. Rels.; newsletter editor Bryce Hosp., Tuscaloosa, spring 1986; pub. rels. intern R & R Advt. Ltd. of Las Vegas, summer 1986. Clarinetist Community Concert Band. Mem. Jewish Bus. and Profls., Connections, Women in Comms.

HOCKNEY, DAVID, artist; b. Bradford, Yorkshire, Eng., July 9, 1937; s. Kenneth and Laura H. Attended, Bradford Coll. Art, 1953-57, Royal Coll. Art, London, 1959-62; D (hon.), Royal Coll. Art, London, 1992; hon. degree, U. Aberdeen, 1988, Royal Coll. Art, London, 1992. Lectr. U. Iowa, 1964, U. Colo., 1965, U. Calif. Berkeley, 1967; lectr. UCLA, 1966, hon. chair of drawing, 1980. One-man shows include Kasmin Gallery, 1963-89, Mus. Modern Art, N.Y.C., 1964, 68, Stedelijk Mus., Amsterdam, Netherlands, 1966, Whitechapel Gallery, London, 1970, Andre Emmerich Gallery, N.Y.C., 1972—, Musee des Arts Decoratifs, Paris, 1974, Museo Tamayo, Mexico City, 1984, L.A. Louver, Calif., 1986, 89-90, Nishimura Gallery, Tokyo, 1986, 89, Met. Mus. Art, 1988, L.A. County Mus. Art, 1988, Tate Gallery, London, 1988, 92, others; designer: Rake's Progress, Glyndebourne, Eng., 1975; sets for Magic Flute, Glyndebourne, 1978, Parade Triple Bill, Stravinsky Triple Bill, Met. Opera House, 1980-81, Tristan und Isolde, Los Angeles Music Ctr. Opera, 1987; Turandot Lyric Opera, Chgo., 1992—, San Francisco Opera, 1993, Die Frau Ohne Schatten, Covent Garden, London, 1992, L.A. Music Ctr.Opera, 1993; author: David Hockney by David Hockney, 1976, David Hockney: Travels with Pen, Pencil and Ink, 1978, Paper Pools, 1980, David Hockney Photographs, 1982, Cameraworks, 1983, David Hockney: A Retrospective, 1988, Hockney Paints the Stage, 1983, Hockney's Alphabet, 1991; illustrator: Six Fairy Tales of the Brothers Grimm, 1969, The Blue Guitar, 1977, Hockney's Alphabet, 1991. Recipient Guinness award and 1st prize for etching, 1961, Gold medal Royal Coll. Art, 1962, Graphic prize Paris Biennale, 1963, 1st prize 8th Internat. Exhbn. Drawings Lugano, Italy, 1964, 1st prize John Moores Exhbn. Liverpool, Eng., 1967, German award of Excellence 1983, 1st prize Internat. Ctr. of Photography, N.Y., 1985, Kodak photography book award for Cameraworks, 1984, Praemium Imperiale Japan Art Assn., 1989. Office: 7508 Santa Monica Blvd West Hollywood CA 90046-6407

HODES, ABRAM, pediatrician; b. Jeannette, Pa., Mar. 2, 1922; s. Samuel and Rachel (Gross) H.; m. Mildred Rose Hodes, June 22, 1947; children: Alan Eliot, Jay Michael. BS, Pa. State U., 1942; BM, Northwestern U., 1945, MD, 1946. Sch. pub. health physician San Bernardino (Calif.) County Health Dept., 1950-51; pvt. practice San Bernadino, 1950—. Chmn. San Bernardino Israel Bond Assn., 1967, United Jewish Appeal, 1981, 90-93. Fellow Am. Acad. Pediatrics; mem. Am. Med. Soc., Calif. Med. Soc., San Bernardino County Med. Soc., Optimists (life), B'nai B'rith (pres. 1991-94), Jewish War Vets, Phi Beta Kappa, Phi Delta Epsilon. Republican. Home: 604 Avery St San Bernardino CA 92404-1708

HODGES, JOSEPH GILLULY, JR., lawyer; b. Denver, Dec. 7, 1942; s. Joseph Gilluly Sr. and Elaine (Chanute) H.; m. Jean Todd Creamer, Aug. 7, 1971; children: Ashley E., Wendy C., Elaine V. BA, Lake Forest Coll., 1965; JD, U. Colo., 1968. Bar: Colo. 1968, U.S. Dist. Ct. (dist. Colo.) 1969, U.S. Ct. Mil. Appeals 1969. Assoc. Hodges, Kerwin, Otten & Weeks, Denver, 1969-73; assoc. Davis, Graham & Stubbs, Denver, 1973-76, ptnr., 1976-86; pvt. practice lawyer Denver, 1986—. Bd. dirs. Arapahoe Colo. Nat. Bank, Littleton, Colo., 1971-90, Cherry Creek Improvement Assn., Denver, 1979-91; bd. trustees Lake Forest (Ill.) Coll., 1977-87; pres. Colo. Arlberg Club, Winter Park, Colo., 1984-85; treas. St. Johns Episcopal Cathedral, Denver, 1981—. Capt. USAR, 1969-74. Named Best Lawyers in Am., Woodward/White, N.Y.C., 1991-92. Fellow Am. Coll. Trust and Estate Counsel (state chmn. 1991—); mem. ABA (chmn. probate sec. G-2 tech. 1990—), Am. Judicature Soc., Colo. Bar Assn. (chair probate coun. 1981-82), Denver Bar Assn., Denver Estate Planning Coun., Colo. Planned Giving Roundtable (bd. 1991—), Rotary Club Denver, Kappa Sigma, Phi Alpha Delta. Republican. Office: 3300 E 1st Ave #600 Denver CO 80206

HODGES, RICHARD EDWIN, educator; b. L.A., Nov. 21, 1928; s. Charles Edward and Helen Florence (Barnes) H.; m. Lois Marie Sorensen, Sept. 1, 1962; children: Susan Margaret, Charles Richard. BE, Oreg. State U., 1953; BS in Edn., Oreg. Coll. of Edn., 1953, MS, 1958; EdD, Stanford U., 1964. With editorial dept. L.A. Examiner, L.A., 1948-50; elem. sch. tchr., prin. Salem (Oreg.) Pub. Schs., 1953-61; research assoc. Stanford U., Palo Alto, Calif., 1962-64; asst., assoc. prof. U. Chgo., 1964-75; dir., sch. edn. U. Puget Sound, Tacoma, Wash., 1975-85; prof. U. Puget Sound, Tacoma, 1985—; editor The Elem. Sch. Jour., U. Chgo., 1971-75; cons. Nat. Inst. Edn. and USOE, Washington, 1971-75, various textbook publs. and ednl. film producers, 1964; manuscript reviewer, various ednl. publs., 1964—. Co-author: Spelling: Structure and Strategies, 1972; author: (booklets) Learning to Spell, 1981, Improving Spelling and Vocabulary Development in Secondary Schools, 1982; co-editor: Language and Learning to Read, 1972, A Dictionary of Reading and Related Terms, 1981; contbr. articles, chpts. to profl. books and jours. Cpl. U.S. Army, 1946-47, Japan. Fellow Nat. Conf. on Research in English (pres. 1973-74); mem. Internat. Reading Assn., Hist. of Reading Special Interest Group, IRA (pres. 1984-85), Nat. Council Tchrs. of English, Nat. Soc. Study of Edn., Phi Delta Kappa. Home: 1030 Claremont Ct Tacoma WA 98466-6517 Office: Univ Puget Sound Tacoma WA 98416

HODGINS, JACK STANLEY, author; b. Comox Valley, Vancouver Island, B.C., Can., Oct. 3, 1938; s. Stanley H. and Reta A. (Blakely) H.; m. Dianne Child, Dec. 17, 1960; children: Shannon, Gavin, Tyler. B.Ed., U. B.C., 1961. Tchr. high sch. English and creative writing Nanaimo, B.C., 1961-79; tchr. workshops, cons. and speaker in field, 1976—; writer-in-residence Simon Fraser U., Vancouver, 1977, U. Ottawa (Ont.), 1979; prof. U. Victoria. Author: fiction Spit Delaney's Island, 1976 (B.C. Eaton's Book award 1977), The Invention of the World, 1977 (Gibson's First Novel award 1978), The Resurrection of Joseph Bourne, 1979 (Gov. Gen. Can. award fiction 1980), The Honorary Patron, 1987, The Barclay Family Theatre, 1981, Innocent Cities, 1990; (travel book) Over Forty in Broken Hill, 1992; (children's novel) Left Behind in Squabble Bay, 1988; textbook Teaching Short Fiction, 1978; editor: textbook The Frontier Experience, 1976, The West Coast Experience, 1976; co-editor: textbook Voice and Vision, 1971; contbr. articles mags., newspapers. Recipient President's medal U. Western Ont., 1973, Periodical Distbrs. award, 1979, Can.-Australia award, 1986; grantee Can. Council, 1973, 80. Mem. Writers Union Can., PEN. Address: care agent Bella Pomer, 22 Shallmon Blvd, Toronto, BC Canada V8W 2Y2

HODGSON, GREGORY BERNARD, software systems engineer; b. Chgo., July 17, 1946; s. John George and Lucille (Nass) H.; m. Kathleen Patricia, Aug. 11, 1972 (div. July 1974); m. Kathryn Marie Maytum, Feb. 14, 1976. BS in Computer Engring., U. Ill., 1972. Computer programmer specialist Lockheed Missiles and Space Co., Sunnyvale, Calif., 1972-81, software systems engr., 1981-89; software systems cons. Lockheed Missiles and Space Co., Sunnyvale, 1989—; cons. in field. Served with U.S. Army, 1966-69. State of Ill. VA scholar, 1970-72. Mem. Nat. Mgmt. Assn., Ill. VA Assn. (coord. fed. and state affairs 1970-72). Republican. Roman Catholic. Home: 469 1/2 Curie Dr San Jose CA 95123-4925

HODGSON, KENNETH P., mining executive, real estate investor; b. Canon City, Colo., Sept. 20, 1945; s. Cecil L. and Jaunita J. (Murrie) H.; m. Rebecca K. Thompson, Feb. 15, 1967; 1 child, Amber K.; m. 2d, Rita J. Lewis, Apr. 22, 1979. Student Metro Coll., 1966-68. With Golden Mining Corp., Utah, 1973-79, Windfall Group Inc., Utah, 1976-77; pres. Houston Mining, Ariz., 1979-82; v.p. Silver Ridge Mining, Inc., Gold Ridge Mining Inc., Ariz., 1979-82; pres. Ken Hodgson & Co., Inc., Canon City, 1983-91; Riken Resources Ltd., 1985—. Recipient numerous safety awards. Mem. AIME. Republican. Presbyterian. Lodges: Moose, Elks.

HODNETT, RICHARD MCINNIS, plastic surgeon; b. Shreveport, La., Jan. 25, 1956; s. Charles and Lois (McInnis) H. BS, La. State U., 1978, MD, 1983. Physician Richard M. Hodnett, M.D., West Valley, Utah, 1990—. Office: 4052 W Pioneer Pky #208 West Valley City UT 84120

HODSON, CHRISTINE ANN, psychologist; b. Chgo., Oct. 19, 1951; d. Roger Mithoff and Patricia Ann (Hill) H.; m. Gerard Fischer Jr., May 10, 1986; 1 child, Nathan David. BA, U. Calif., Santa Cruz, 1974; MS, Calif. State U., 1976; PhD, U. Md., 1982. Lic. psychologist, Calif. Therapist U. Md. Parent/Child Svc., College Park, 1978-80; psychometrist Prince George's Sch. Dist., Prince George's County, Md., 1979-80; trainee Alameda County Mental Health, Oakland and Fremont, Calif., 1980-82; pvt. practice Oakland and Fremont, 1983—; family ct. counselor Alameda County Family Ct. Svcs., 1982—; cons. schs., shelters, 1980-83; presenter at profl. confs. Contbr. to profl. publs. NIMH fellow, 1976. Mem. Am. Psychol. Assn., No. Calif. Soc. Cln. Hypnosis. Office: Alameda County Family Ct Svcs 1221 Oak St Oakland CA 94612

HODSON, NANCY PERRY, real estate agent; b. Kansas City, Mo., Nov. 19, 1932; d. Ralph Edward Perry and Juanita (Youmans) Jackman; m. William K. Hodson, Oct. 4, 1974 (div. Jan. 1985); children: Frank Tyler, Lisa Thompson, Suzanne Desforges, Robert Hodson. Student, Pine Manor Jr. Coll., 1950-51, Finch Coll., 1951-53. Cert. real estate agt., Calif.; cert. interior designer. Owner Nancy Perry Hodson Interior Design, L.A. and Newport Beach, Calif., 1974-82; agt. Grubb and Ellis, Newport Beach, 1990, Turner Assocs., Laguna Beach, Calif., 1990-92. Founder U. of Calif. Arboretum, Irvine, 1987, Opera Pacific, Costa Mesa, Calif., 1987; mem. U. of Calif. Rsch. Assocs., Irvine, 1986; pres. Big Canyon Philharm., Newport Beach, 1990; bd. dirs. Jr. Philharm., L.A., 1975-78. Mem. Big Canyon Country Club, L.A. Blue Ribbon 400 (1975-78), Jr. League Garden Club (pres. 1990-91), Big Canyon Garden Club (pres. 1989-91), Inst. of Logopedics (chmn. 30th Anniversary 1965), Guilds of Performing Arts Ctr. Presbyterian.

HOEFT, ARTHUR PETER, analytical laboratory official, coal sampling consultant; b. Sheboygan, Wis., May 25, 1945; s. Arthur A. and Marjorie A. (Trimberger) H.; m. Patricia A. Slesar, July 10, 1970; children: Alexis, Erika. BS in Chemistry, St. Norbert Coll., West DePere, Wis., 1967; MS in Chemistry, Colo. State U., Ft. Collins, 1971, MS in Bus. (scholar), 1973. R&D chemist Am. Can. Co., Neenah, Wis., 1967-68; analytical chemist Core Lab., Inc., Casper, Wyo., 1973-74, lab. supr., 1974-76, coal svcs. coord., 1976-79; coal ops. mgr. Core Lab., Inc., Denver, 1980-85; pres., chief exec. officer The A.P. Hoeft Co., Denver, 1985—; cons. coal sampling and testing, analyses, lab. design; condr. coal analysis seminar. Contbr. articles to profl.; patentee in field. Decorated Army Commendation medal. Mem. ASTM, AIME, Am. Chem., Colo. Mining Engrs. Home: The A P Hoeft Co 8754 E Eastman Ave Denver CO 80231

HOEFT, CYNTHIA ANN, computer specialist; b. Phoenix, July 20, 1955; d. Willard Wendal and JoAnn (Skubitz) Tolman; m. David Randall Hoeft, July 6, 1974; children: Danny, Richie, Casey. Student, No. Ariz. U., Flagstaff, 1973-76, No. Ariz. U., Yuma, 1990-93. Computer operator, reports supr. Planning Rsch. Corp., Yuma, 1976-82; supervisory computer specialist U.S. Bur. of Reclamation, Yuma, 1983—. Bd. dirs. Yuma Pop Warner, publicity dir., 1985-92. Named to Outstanding Young Women of Am. Republican. Roman Catholic. Home: 2660 10th Pl Yuma AZ 85364

HOEN, LINDA LEE, private investigator, sentencing consultant; b. Auburn, Calif., Oct. 15, 1952; d. Harry Hutchinson Snelling and Darlene (Nelson) Wakefield; m. David Phillip Hoen, Feb. 10, 1981; children: Christopher Robert, Judith Lawson. Student, Coll. of Marin, San Rafael, Calif., 1982, Napa Valley Coll., 1982-87, U. Calif., Davis, 1989-90. Correctional peace officer Calif. Dept. Corrections, Sacramento, 1979-85, parole agt., 1985-90; owner, mgr. Voir Dire Investigative Svcs., Vacaville, Calif., 1991—. Cons. Parents Murdered Children, Concord, Calif., 1991—; vol. Pete Wilson for Gov., L.A., 1990; mgr. Mike Nail for Judge, Benicia, Calif., 1992; Bd. dirs. Coalition on Victims Equal Rights, 1990-91; founder, mem. Com. Against Sexual Harrassment, 1985-86. Mem. Calif. Assn. Lic. Investigators, Calif. Correctional Peace Officers Assn. (bd. dirs. 1991—), Parole Agts. Assn. Calif. (bd. dirs. 1987-89, recognition award 1987), MADD. Republican. Roman Catholic. Home: 125 Breakwater Way Vacaville CA 95688 Office: Voir Dire Investigative Svc Box 6531 Vacaville CA 95696

HOERNI, JEAN AMÉDÉE, electronics consultant; b. Geneva, Sept. 26, 1924; came to U.S., 1953, naturalized, 1959; s. Robert and Jeanne (Berthoud) H.; children—Michael, Anne, Susan. B.S., U. Geneva, 1947, Ph.D., 1950; Ph.D., Cambridge U., 1952. Founder, research physicist Fairchild Semiconductor Corp., 1957-61; v.p. Teledyne, Inc., Mountain View, Calif., 1961-63; cons. Los Altos, Calif., 1963-67; founder, pres. Intersil, Inc., Cupertino, Calif., 1967-75; electronics cons. Seattle, Hailey, Idaho, 1975—; bd. dirs. DEEPA Textiles, Inc. Patentee in semiconductor planar process field. Recipient John Scott medal City of Phila., 1966; Longstreth medal Franklin Inst., 1969; Semmy award, 1985. Fellow IEEE. Address: Apt 302 302 Lakeside Ave S Seattle WA 98144

HOEVEL, MICHAEL JAMES, management consultant; b. Pasadena, Sept. 16, 1944; s. Richard Anthony and Caroline Josephine (Cristilli) H.; m. Sandra Kay Baird, June 18, 1966; children: Kristina Anne, Steven Michael. BS, Calif. State U., Long Beach, 1967. Mgmt. trainee Shell Oil Co., Long Beach, 1967; jr. adminstrv. asst. City of L.A., 1967-69, personnel analyst, 1969-72; cons. Peat, Marwick Main & Co., L.A., 1972-73, sr. cons., 1973-75; ptnr. Poirier, Hoevel & Co., L.A., 1975—. Bd. dirs. Maga-Link/Communications Bridge, L.A., 1986-87, chmn. fin. com. and exec. com., 1988—. Mem. Calif. River Expdns. (pres.), Coun. on Logistics Mgmt., Assn. of Human Resource Profls., Soc. for Human Resources Mgmt., Acad. TV Arts and Scis., Calif. Exec. Recruiters Assn. (sec.-treas. 1984-87), Harvard Olde Boys Rugby Club, Alpha Kappa Psi (life mem., pres. 1964-65). Republican. Roman Catholic. Office: Poirier Hoevel & Co 12400 Wilshire Blvd Los Angeles CA 90025-1019

HOEVELER, SARAH E., television news anchor; b. Madison, Wis., Sept. 16, 1961; d. David and Sally Sonja (Schee) H.; m. Jonathan Mark Ralston, Apr. 4, 1992. BS in Agrl. Journalism, U. Wis., 1984. Reporter Sta. WMTU-TV, Madison, 1984-86; reporter, anchor Sta. KTNV-TV, Las Vegas, Nev., 1986-89, Sta. KVBC-TV, Las Vegas, Nev., 1989—. Recipient Best Over-All Reporting award United Press Internat., 1989, Best News Story award, 1991, Best Investigative Reporter award AP, L.A., 1989, Emmy award Best Reporting Emmy Soc. San Diego chpt., 1991. Mem. Soc. Profl. Journalists, Women in Comm. Office: Sta KUBC-TV 1500 Foremaster Ln Las Vegas NV 89108

HOFERT, JACK, consulting company executive, lawyer; b. Phila., Apr. 6, 1930; s. David and Beatrice (Schatz) H.; m. Marilyn Tukeman, Sept. 4, 1960; children: Dina, Bruce. BS, UCLA, 1952, MBA, 1954, JD, 1957. Bar: Calif. 1957; CPA, Calif. Tax supr. Peat, Marwick Mitchell & Co., L.A., 1959-62, tax mgr., 1974-77; v.p. fin. Pacific Theaters Corp., L.A., 1962-68; freelance cons. L.A., 1969-74; tax mgr. Lewis Homes, Upland, Calif., 1977-80; pres. Di-Bru, Inc., L.A., 1981-87, Scolyn, Inc., L.A., 1988—; dir. Valley Fed. Savs. and Loan Assn., 1989-92. Mem. UCLA Law Rev., 1956-57; contbr. articles to tax, fin. mags. Served with USN, 1948-49. Home and Office: 2479 Roscomare Rd Los Angeles CA 90077-1812

HOFF, RENAE, lawyer; b. Caldwell, Idaho, Feb. 23, 1951; d. Edwin Herbert Hoff and Agnes Mary (Stoltz) Feiling; m. Craig L. Gibson. BA, Coll. of Idaho, 1979; JD, Southwestern U., 1981. Bar: Idaho 1981, U.S. Dist. Ct. Idaho 1981, U.S. Ct. Appeals (9th cir.) 1986. Assoc. Gunn & Hoff, Caldwell, 1981-90; magistrate judge Third Jud. Dist. of Idaho, 1990—; referral atty. pro bono panel Idaho State Bar, 1983-90 (Equal Access to Justice award 1988, 93, mem. Vol. Lawyers Policy Coun. 1989—, coun. chair 1992); bd. dirs. Idaho Legal Aid Svcs., Inc., 1986-90; staff atty. Indsl. Spl. Indemnity Fund, 1986-90; city atty. Marsing ID, 1987-90; Homedale City prosecutor, 1987-90; bd. dirs. Mercy House. Mem. ABA, Nat. Assn. Women Judges, 3d Jud. Bar Assn., Assn. Trial Lawyers Am., Idaho Trial Lawyers Assn. , Idaho Women Lawyers, Canyon County Lawyers Club (pres. 1990). Democrat. Office: Canyon County Ct Annex 120 9th Ave S Nampa ID 83651-3898

HOFFBERG, JUDITH A., editor, publisher, consultant; b. Hartford, Conn., May 19, 1934; d. George and Miriam (Goldenberg) H. BA cum laude, UCLA, 1956, MA, 1960, MLS, 1964. Cataloger Johns Hopkins U., Bologna Ctr., Italy, 1964-65; intern, cataloger Library of Congress, Washington, 1965-67; fine art librarian U. Pa., Phila., 1967-69; bibliographer art lit. and langs. U. Calif., San Diego, 1969-71; Brand art ctr. librarian Glendale Pub. Library, Calif., 1971-73; exec. sec. Art Libraries Soc. N. Am.,

1973-78; editor, pub. Umbrella, 1978—; free-lance archivist, Pasadena, Calif., 1978—. Italian Govt. grantee, 1960-61; Kress Found. grantee, Eng., 1972; Nat. Endowment for Arts grantee, 1979, 80; Fulbright grantee, N.Z., 1984. Mem. ALA, Art Libraries Soc. N.Am. (lifetime mem., chmn., exec. sec.), Soc. Arch. Historians (dir. 1977-80), Coll. Art Assn. (bd. dirs. 1975-79), Internat. Assn. Art Critics (Am. sect.). Home and Office: PO Box 40100 Pasadena CA 91114-7100

HOFFENBLUM, ALLAN ERNEST, political consultant; b. Vallejo, Calif., Aug. 10, 1940; s. Albert A. and Pearl Estelle (Clarke) H. BA, U. So. Calif., 1962. Mem. staff L.A. County Rep. Com., 1967-71; staff dir. Rep. Assembly Caucus Calif. legislature, Sacramento, 1973-75; polit. dir. Calif. Rep. Com., L.A., 1977-78; owner Allan Hoffenblum & Assocs., L.A., 1979—. Capt. USAF, 1962-67, Vietnam. Decorated Bronze Star medal. Mem. Internat. Assn. Polit. Cons., Am. Assn. Polit. Cons. Jewish. Office: 9000 W Sunset Blvd Ste 406 West Hollywood CA 90069-5804

HOFFLUND, PAUL, lawyer; b. San Diego, Mar. 27, 1928; s. John Leslie and Ethel Frances (Cline) H.; m. Anne Marie Thalman, Feb. 15, 1958; children: Mark, Sylvia. BA, Princeton (N.J.) U., 1950; JD, George Washington U., 1956. Bar: D.C. 1957, Calif. 1957, U.S. Dist. Ct. D.C. 1957, U.S. Dist. Ct. (so. dist.) Calif. 1957, U.S. Ct. Mil. Appeals 1957, U.S. Ct. Appeals (D.C. cir.) 1957, U.S. Ct. Claims 1958, U.S. Ct. Appeals (9th cir.) 1960, U.S. Supreme Ct. 1964, U.S. Tax Ct. 1989. Assoc. Wencke, Carlson & Kuykendall, San Diego, 1962-63; ptnr. Carlson, Kuykendall & Hofflund, San Diego, 1963-65, Carlson & Hofflund, San Diego, 1965-72; Christian Sci. practitioner San Diego, 1972-84; adj. prof. law Nat. U. Sch. Law, San Diego, 1985—; arbitrator Mcpl. Cts. and Superior Ct. of Calif., San Diego, 1984—; pvt. practice San Diego, 1985—; judge pro tem Mcpl. Ct. South Bay Jud. Dist., 1990—; disciplinary cousel to U.S. Tax Ct., 1989—; asst. U.S. atty. U.S. Dept. of Justice, L.A., 1959-60, asst. U.S. atty. in charge, San Diego, 1960-62, spl. hearing officer, San Diego, 1962-68; asst. corporation counsel Govt. of D.C., 1957-59. Author: (chpt. in book) Handbook on Criminal Procedure in the U.S. District Court, 1967; contbr. articles to profl. jours. Treas. Princeton Club of San Diego; v.p. Community Concert Assn., San Diego; pres. Sunland Home Found., San Diego, Trust for Christian Sci. Orgn., San Diego; chmn. bd. 8th Ch. of Christ, Scientist, San Diego. With USN, 1950-53, comdr. JAGC, USNR, 1953-72, ret. Mem. ABA, San Diego County Bar Assn., Inst. Global Ethics, World Affairs Counsel, Phi Delta Phi. Democrat. Home and Office: 6146 Syracuse Ln San Diego CA 92122-3301

HOFFMAN, ALLAN SACHS, chemical engineer, educator; b. Chgo., Oct. 27, 1932; s. Saul A. and Frances E. (Sachs) H.; m. Susan Carol Freeman, July 29, 1962; children: David, Lisa. B.S. in Chem. Engring, MIT, 1953, M.S. in Chem. Engring, 1955, Sc.D. in Chem. Engring, 1957. Instr. chem. engring. MIT, Cambridge, 1954-56; asst. prof. MIT, 1958-60, asso. prof., 1965-70; research engr. Calif. Research Corp., Richmond, 1960-63; asso. dir. research Amicon Corp., Cambridge, 1963-65; prof. bioengring. and chem. engring. U. Wash., Seattle, 1970—; asst. dir. Center for Bioengring., 1973-83; cons. to various govtl., indsl. and acad. orgns., 1958—; UN adviser to Mexican govt., 1973-74. Author: (with W. Burlant) Block and Graft Copolymers, 1960; Contbr. numerous articles on chem. engring. to profl. jours.; Patentee in field. Kimberly Clark fellow, 1954-55, Visking fellow, 1955-56, Fulbright fellow, 1957-58, Battelle fellow, 1970-72. Mem. Am. Chem. Soc., Am. Inst. Chem. Engrs., Am. Soc. for Artificial Internal Organs, Internat. Soc. Artificial Internal Organs (trustee, bd. dirs. 1987-1990), Soc. for Biomaterials (pres. 1983-84, Clemson award for biomaterial sci. lit., 1985), Controlled Release Soc. (Excellence in Guiding Grad. Rsch. award 1989), Japan Biomaterials Soc. (Biomaterials Sci. prize 1990). Home: 4528 W Laurel Dr NE Seattle WA 98105-3841 Office: U Wash Bioengring Ctr FL 20 Seattle WA 98195

HOFFMAN, CHARLES FENNO, III, architect; b. Greenwich, Conn., May 28, 1958; s. Harrison Baldwin Wright and Louise Elkins (Sinkler) H.; m. Pia Christina Ossorio, Dec. 27, 1980; children: Wilhelmina C. L., Frederic W. S., Henry F. BA in Environ. Design, U. Pa., 1983; MArch, U. Colo., 1986. Designer Fenno Hoffman & Assocs., Boulder, Colo., 1983—; pvt. practice designer Boulder, 1985; assoc. William Zmistowski Assoc. Architects, 1987—, Pellecchia-Olson Architects, Boulder, 1989—; prin. Fenno Hoffman Architects PC, Boulder, Colo., 1991—; cons. Summit Habitats, Inc., 1984—; design cons. The Denver Ptnrship, 1985, Downtown Denver, Inc., 1985; guest critic U. Colo., 1990-91, guest lectr., 1991-92. Prin. works include Ca' Venier Mus. for Venice Bienalle, 1985, Cleveland Place Connection, Denver, 1985 (1st prize 1985), hist. renovated house, Boulder, 1986, 3 Gates 3 Squares, Denver, 1986, Geneva Ave. House, 1992; author: Urban Transit Facility, A Monorail for Downtown Denver, 1985. Mem. Am. Planning Assn., Architects & Planners ofBoulder. Democrat. Episcopalian. Clubs: Rallysport Racquet (Boulder). Office: 505 Geneva Ave Boulder CO 80302

HOFFMAN, DARLEANE CHRISTIAN, chemistry educator; b. Terril, Iowa, Nov. 8, 1926; d. Carl Benjamin and Elverna (Kuhlman) Christian; m. Marvin Morrison Hoffman, Dec. 26, 1951; children: Maureane R., Daryl K. BS in Chemistry, Iowa State U., 1948, PhD in Nuclear Chemistry, 1951. Chemist Oak Ridge (Tenn.) Nat. Lab., 1952-53; mem. staff radiochemistry group Los Alamos (N.Mex.) Sci. Lab., 1953-71, assoc. leader chemistry-nuclear group, 1971-79, div. leader chem.-nuclear chem. div., 1979-82, div. leader isotope and nuclear chem. div., 1982-84; prof. chemistry U. Calif., Berkeley, 1984—; faculty sr. scientist Lawrence Berkeley (Calif.) Lab., 1984—; dir. G.T. Seaborg Inst. for Transactinium Sci., 1991—; panel leader, speaker Los Alamos Women in Sci., 1975, 79, 82; mem. subcom. on nuclear and radiochemistry NAS-NRC, 1978-81, chmn. subcom. on nuclear and radiochemistry, 1982-84; (hon.) mem. commn. on radiochem. and nuclear techniques Internat. Union of Pure and Applied Chem., 1983-87, chmn., 1987-91, assoc. mem. 1992—; mem. com. 2d Internat. Symposium on Nuclear and Radiochemistry, 1988; planning panel Workshop on Tng. Requirements for Chemists in Nuclear Medicine, Nuclear Industry, and Related Fields, 1988, radionuclide migration peer rev. com., Las Vegas, 1986-87, steering com. Advanced Steady State Neutron Source, 1986-90, steering com., panelist Workshop on Opportunities and Challenges in Research with Transplutonium Elements, Washington, 1983; mem. energy rsch. adv. bd. cold fusion panel, Dept. Edn., 1989-90; mem. NAS separations subpanel of separations tech. and transmutation systems panel, 1992-93. Contbr. numerous articles in field to profl. jours. Recipient Alumni Citation of Merit Coll. Scis. and Humanities, Iowa State U., 1978, Disting. Achievement award Iowa State U., 1986; fellow NSF, 1964-65, Guggenheim Found., 1978-79. Fellow Am. Inst. Chemists (pres. N.Mex. chpt. 1976-78), Am. Phys. Soc., AAAS; mem: Am. Chem. Soc. (chmn. nuclear chemistry and technology div. 1978-79, com. in sci. 1986-88, exec. com. div. nuclear chem. and tech. 1987-90, John Dustin Clark award Cen. N.Mex. sect. 1976, Nuclear Chemistry award 1983, Garvan medal 1990), Am. Nuclear Soc. (co-chmn. internat. conf. Methods and Applications of Radioanalytical Chemistry 1987), Norwegian Acad. Arts and Scis, Sigma Xi, Phi Kappa Phi, Iota Sigma Pi, Pi Mu Epsilon, Sigma Delta Epsilon, Alpha Chi Sigma. Methodist. Home: 2277 Manzanita Dr Oakland CA 94611 Office: Lawrence Berkeley Lab MS70A-3307 NSD Berkeley CA 94720

HOFFMAN, DONALD DAVID, cognitive and computer science educator; b. San Antonio, Dec. 29, 1955; s. David Pollock and Loretta Virginia (Shoemaker) H.; m. Geralyn Mary Souza, Dec. 13, 1986; 1 child from previous marriage, Melissa Louise. BA, UCLA, 1978; PhD, MIT, 1983. MTS and project engr. Hughes Aircraft Co., El Segundo, Calif., 1978-83; rsch. scientist MIT Artificial Intelligence Lab, Cambridge, Mass., 1983; asst. prof. U. Calif., Irvine, 1983-86, assoc. prof., 1986-90, full prof., 1990—; cons. Fairchild Lab. for Artificial Intelligence, Palo Alto, Calif., 1984; panelist MIT Corp. vis. com., Cambridge, 1985, NSF, Washington, 1988; conf. host IEEE Conf. on Visual Motion, Irvine, 1989; conf. host Office of Naval Rsch. Conf. on Vision, Laguna Beach, Calif., 1992. Co-author: Observer Mechanics, 1989; contbr. articles to profl. jours. Vol. tchr. Turtle Rock Elem. Sch., Irvine, 1988-90. Recipient Distinguished Scientific award, Am. Psychol. Assn., 1989; grantee NSF, 1984, 87. Mem. AAAS. Office: U Calif Dept Cognitive Sci Irvine CA 92717

HOFFMAN, ELAINE JANET, artist; b. Oak Park, Ill., Aug. 19, 1925; d. Dewitt Alexander and Magda Catherine (Christensen) Patterson; m. Carl Rudolph Hoffman; children: Clayton, Lynda Hoffman Snodgrass, Byron. Degree, Averett Coll., Danville, Va., 1945; BA, Marylhurst Coll., Lake Oswego, Oreg., 1978; grad., Northwest Watercolor Sch., Chgo., 1965, North Light Art Sch., Oreg., 1990. Active Lake Oswego Arts Devel. Com., 1989—, Lake Oswego Adult Ctr., 1989—; deacon Lake Grove Presbyn. Ch., Lake Oswego, 1982—. Mem. Art Inst. Oreg., Portland Critique Group, Portland Watercolor Group, Watercolor Soc. Oreg. Home: 16695 Glenwood Ct Lake Oswego OR 97034-5033

HOFFMAN, FRANKLIN THOMAS, army officer, artist, metalsmith; b. El Paso, Sept. 10, 1953; s. Franklin A. and Evelyn M. (Parker) H. BA in Art cum laude, U. Alaska, 1982. Enlisted U.S. Army, 1972, commd. 2d lt., 1982, advanced through grades to capt., 1985; comdr. HHB 1st Cavalry, Ft. Hood, Tex., 1988-90; asst. prof. mil. sci. Mont. State U., Bozeman, 1990—. designer-craftsman U.S. Army Europe, Germany, 1984. Decorated Meritorious Svc. medal. Mem. Soc. N.Am. Goldsmiths, Am. Legion, Mont. Orienteering (founder), 1CD Assn. (sec.-treas. Big Sky chpt. 1991-92). Office: Mont State U Dept Mil Sci Bozeman MT 59717-0216

HOFFMAN, GEORGE ALAN, consulting company executive; b. Albany, N.Y., May 16, 1937; s. Irving Marshall and Margaret (Coyne) H.; m. Kim Thi Nguyen, Oct. 10, 1971; children: Caroline, Christine. AB, U. Calif., Berkeley, 1980, MBA, 1982. Mgmt. analyst Am. Can Co., N.Y.C., 1966-69; cons. Vietnamese Air Force, Bien Hoa, Vietnam, 1970-74, Puslitbang, Jakarta, Indonesia, 1974-75; v.p. Union Bank, Oakland, Calif., 1987—. Author: Indonesian Production-sharing Oil Contracts, 1982. Mem. Mensa. Club: Commonwealth (San Francisco). Office: 460 Hegenberger Rd Oakland CA 94621-1496

HOFFMAN, JAMES IRVIE, III, educational administrator; b. Trenton, N.J., Dec. 23, 1941; s. James Irvie Jr. and Sarah (Smith) H.; m. Ellen Payne, June 14, 1968; 1 child, Donald James. BS, Allegheny Coll., 1963; MS, Mich. State U., 1965, PhD, 1969. Instr. Mich. State U., East Lansing, 1967-69; asst. prof., then assoc. prof. U. Wis., Oshkosh, 1969-79, chmn. dept. geology, 1975-78, prof., 1979, assoc. dean Coll. Letters and Sci., 1979-84, dean Coll. Letters and Sci., 1984-90; sr. v.p., provost Eastern Washington U., 1990—; tech. mem. Wis. Metallic Mining Coun., Madison, 1978—; mem. Hazardous Waste Mgmt. com., Madison, 1981, Legis. Coun. Groundwater Coun., Madison, 1982-84. Author field guide to Fox River Valley, 1980; contbr. articles to sci. publs. Mem. Am. Inst. Profl. Geologists (pres. 1982-84), Nat. Assn. Geology Tchrs. (pres. 1980), Coun. Colls. Arts and Scis., Internat. Coun. Fine Arts Deans, Am. Water Resources Assn., Geochem. Soc., Sigma Xi, Sigma Gamma Epsilon. Office: Coll Letters and Sci Univ Wis Oshkosh Eastern Washington U Cheney WA 99004-2496

HOFFMAN, JASON PAUL, internal auditor, network and database administrator; b. San Francisco, Dec. 5, 1968; s. David Edward and Cheryl Ann (Moreiss) H. BA in Bus. Econs. and Legal Studies with honors, U. Calif., Santa Cruz, 1990. Cert. internal auditor, info. systems auditor. Database/application info. specialist IBM Corp., Palo Alto, Calif., 1989; asst. computer lab mgr. U. Calif., Santa Cruz, 1988-89, teaching asst., 1988-90; sr. internal auditor U. Calif., San Francisco, 1990—. Mem. Inst. Internal Auditors, EDP Auditors Assn., U. Calif. Santa Cruz Alumni Assn., Internat. Networking Assn. Office: U Calif San Francisco Box 0818 1855 Folsom St Ste 107 San Francisco CA 94143

HOFFMAN, JOHN WAYNE, biochemist; b. Hartford, Conn., May 6, 1947; s. Eael and Mae Lois (Shackelford) H.; m. Elvira Marquez Monzon, June 22, 1990. Student, Hartford Sem., 1969; BS in Biochemistry, U. Tex., 1978; MBA in Mktg., U. Calif., 1985. Health svcs. specialist Hoffman La Roche Labs., Nutley, N.J., 1972-74; pharm. sales person Averest Labs., N.Y.C., 1978-80; staff sci. Lawrence Livermore Lab., Livermore, Calif., 1980-84; cons. Biogenex Lab., Dublin, Calif., 1984; staff sci. Naval Bioscis. Lab., Berkeley, Calif., 1984-86; mgr. product devel. Xytronyx, Inc., San Diego, 1986—; pres., CEO Texerv, 1991—. Contbg. author: Rapid Diagnosis of Infectious Disease, 1985; patentee in field. With A.I.D.S. adv. task force Urban League, San Diego, 1989—. Recipient Silver Star award U.S. Army, 1967, Combat Infantry award, 1966; recipient Community Svc. award Hartford Health Svcs., 1973. Mem. Am. Chem. Soc. Republican. Episcopalian. Office: Xytronyx Inc 6555 Nancy Ridge Dr San Diego CA 92121-3221

HOFFMAN, MARY CLAIRE, systems analyst; b. Cambridge, Mass., Sept. 24, 1947; d. Clarence Cowles and Helen Claire (Sullivan) Davis; m. Dan William Hoffman, Feb. 23, 1974; children: Anne Maritza, Michael Ben. BA magna cum laude, Occidental Coll., 1969, MA, 1970. Tech. proofreader Jet Propulsion Lab., Pasadena, Calif., 1970; tchr. Rosamond (Calif.) High Sch., 1970-71; supr. Equitable Life Assurance, Santa Ana, Calif., 1971-74; mgr. credit/collections Coast Leasing Co., Santa Fe Springs, Calif., 1980-82; systems analyst Y-K Assocs., Glendale, Calif., 1982—. Mem. The Towne Singers, La Canada, Calif., 1986—, pres., 1991-93; exec. team Temple Sinai Sisterhood, Glendale, Calif., 1991-93. Named Women Who Make a Difference, Women's Conf. Jewish Fedn. Coun., West Covina, Calif., 1992. Mem. Women's Am. Ort (exec. team Angeles Crest chpt. 1991-93). Office: Y Knot Assocs 2076 Valderas Dr # F Glendale CA 91208-1339

HOFFMAN, MICHAEL JEROME, humanities educator; b. Phila., Mar. 13, 1939; s. Nathan P. and Sara (Perlman) H.; m. Margaret Boegeman, Dec. 27, 1988; children from previous marriages: Cynthia, Matthew. BA, U. Pa., 1959, MA, 1960, PhD, 1963. Instr. Washington Coll., Chestertown, Md., 1962-64; asst. prof. U. Pa., Phila., 1964-67; from asst. prof. to prof. U. Calif., Davis, 1967—, asst. vice chancellor acad. affairs, 1976-83, chmn. English dept., 1984-89; dir. Humanities Inst., Davis, 1987-91; chmn. joint projects steering com. U. Calif./Calif. State U., 1976-87; chmn. adv. bd. Calif. Acad. Partnership Program, 1985-87; dir. Calif. Humanities Project, 1985-91; coord. writing programs U. Calif. at Davis, 1991—. Author: The Development of Abstractionism in the Writings of Gertrude Stein, 1965, The Buddy System, 1971, The Subversive Vision, 1972, Gertrude Stein, 1976, Critical Essays on Gertrude Stein, 1986, Essentials of the Theory of Fiction, 1988, Critical Essays on American Modernism, 1992. With USAR, 1957-61. Nat. Def. Edn. Act fellow U.S. Govt., 1959-62. Mem. Modern Lang. Assn. (Am. lit. group). Democrat. Jewish. Home: 4417 San Marino Dr Davis CA 95616-5012 Office: U Calif Dept English Davis CA 95616

HOFFMAN, NEIL JAMES, art school administrator; b. Buffalo, Sept. 2, 1938; s. Frederick Charles and Isabella Dias (Murchie) H.; m. Sue Ellen Jeffery, Dec. 30, 1960; children: Kim, Amy, Lisa. B.S., SUNY-Buffalo, 1960, M.S., 1967. Chmn. unified arts dept. Grand Island Pub. Schs. (N.Y.), 1968-69; assoc. dean, assoc. prof. Coll. Fine and Applied Art Rochester Inst. Tech. (N.Y.), 1969-74; dir. program in artisanry Boston U., 1974-79; dean, chief adminstrv. officer Otis Art Inst., Parsons Sch. Design, Los Angeles, 1979-83; pres. Sch. Art Inst. Chgo., 1983-85, Calif. Coll. Arts and Crafts, Oakland, 1985—; prof. photographer; mem. local arts couns. local arts orgns., state arts orgns., nat. arts orgns. Mem. evaluation team Western Assn. Schs. and Colls., 1982—; chmn. cultural planning process City of Oakland, 1986-91. Mem. Phi Delta Kappa. Office: Calif Coll Art & Crafts Office of President 5212 Broadway Oakland CA 94618-1487

HOFFMAN, PAUL FELIX, geologist, educator; b. Toronto, Ont., Can., Mar. 21, 1941; s. Samuel and Dorothy Grace (Medhurst) H.; m. Erica Jean Westbrook, Dec. 4, 1976; 1 child, Guy Samson. BS, McMaster U., 1964; MA, Johns Hopkins U., 1965, PhD, 1970. Lectr. Franklin & Marshall Coll., Lancaster, Pa., 1968-69; rsch. scientist Geol. Survey Can., Ottawa, Ont., 1969-92; lectr. U. Calif., Santa Barbara, 1971-72; prof. U. Victoria, B.C., Can., 1992—; lectr. U. Calif., Santa Barbara, 1971-72; dist. lectr. Am. Assn. Petroleum Geologists, 1979-80; vis. prof. U. Tex., Dallas, 1978, Columbia U., 1990; adj. prof. Carleton U., 1989-92; mem. Internat. Union Geol. Scis. Commn. on Precambrian Stratigraphy, 1976, Internat. Commn. Lithosphere Working Group on Mobile Belts, 1986-90. Fairchild Found. vis. scholar Calif. Inst. Tech., 1974-75; recipient Bowncoker medal Ohio State U., 1989. Fellow Royal Soc. Can., Geol. Assn. Can. (past pres.' medal 1976, Logan medal 1992), Geol. Soc. Am.; mem. Am. Geophys. Union, Can. Soc. Petroleum Geologists (Douglas medal 1992), Nat. Acad. Sci. U.S. (fgn. assoc.). Home: 3018 Blackwood St, Victoria, BC Canada V8T 3X4 Office: U Victoria, Sch Earth and Ocean Scis, PO Box 1700, Victoria, BC Canada V8W 2Y2

HOFFMAN, RODNEY JOSEPH, computer scientist; b. San Antonio, Oct. 10, 1950; s. Herbert Irving and Jewel (Greenberg) H. BA, Rice U., 1972; MS, U. So. Calif., L.A., 1974. Rsch. asst., teaching asst. U. So. Calif., L.A., 1972-78; tech. staff mem. Xerox Corp., El Segundo, Calif., 1979-92, Jet Propulsion Lab., Pasadena, Calif., 1992—; instr. Occidental Coll., L.A., 1978—; reader Ednl. Testing Svc., Princeton, N.J., 1987—. Contbr. articles to profl. jours. Bd. dirs. Nat. Orgn. Gay & Lesbian Scientists and Tech. Profls., Pasadena, Calif., KCET-TV Community Adv. Bd., L.A. Mem. IEEE, Computer Profls. for Social Responsibility (nat. treas. 1988-92), Assn. for Computing Machinery. Office: PO Box 77076 Los Angeles CA 90007-0076

HOFFMAN, ROLLAND EDWARD, social services administrator; b. South Bend, Ind., Jan. 20, 1931; s. Edward William and Elsie Martha (Schultz) H.; m. Marilyn Jo McClure, Apr. 22, 1960; children: Chriss, Pamela. BS in Speech, Northwestern U., 1954, postgrad., 1954. Prodn. worker Studebaker Corp., South Bend, Ind., 1949-50; assoc. producer Mr. Wizard Show, Sta. WNBQ, Chgo., 1952-54; announcer, writer, producer WKZO Radio and TV, Kalamazoo, Mich., 1954; dir. employee and pub. relations Ball-Band Plant, U.S. Rubber Co., Mishawaka, Ind., 1956-58; assoc. exec. dir. campaign United Fund St. Joseph County Inc., South Bend, Ind., 1958-62; assoc. exec. dir. campaign and adminstrn. United Fund and Community Services Tarrant County Inc., Ft. Worth, 1962-65, exec. dir., 1965-70; pres., chief exec. officer Mile High United Way, Denver, 1970-89; prin. Found. Group, 1989—; chmn. bd. adv. com. Mut. Am., N.Y.C., 1976—; vice chmn. nat. profl. adv. com. United Way Am. Active Nat. Com. for Adoption, Washington, 1980—; trustee pres.'s leadership class U. Colo., 1985—. Sgt. AUS, 1954-56. Lodge: Rotary. Office: 384 Inverness Dr S Ste 207 Englewood CO 80112-5803

HOFFMAN, WAYNE MELVIN, retired airline official; b. Chgo., Mar. 9, 1923; s. Carl A. and Martha (Tamillo) H.; m. Laura Majewski, Jan. 26, 1946; children—Philip, Karen, Kristin. B.A. summa cum laude, U. Ill., 1943, J.D. with high honors, 1947. Bar: Ill. bar 1947, N.Y. bar 1958. Atty. I.C. R.R., 1948-52; with N.Y.C. R.R. Co., 1952-67, exec. asst. to pres., 1958-60, v.p. freight sales, 1960-61, v.p. sales, 1961-62, exec. v.p., 1962-67; chmn. bd. N.Y. Central Trans. Co., 1960-67, Flying Tiger Line, Inc. and Tiger Internat., Inc., 1967-85; trustee Aerospace Corp., 1975-86, 87—; dir. Rohr Industries; bd. dirs. Rohr Industries, Sun America, Inc. Trustee McCallum Theatre, Palm Desert, Calif., Eisenhower Med. Ctr., Rancho Mirage, Calif. Served to capt. inf. AUS, World War II. Decorated Silver Star, Bronze Star with oak leaf cluster, Purple Heart with oak leaf cluster; Fourragere (Belgium). Mem. ABA, Phi Beta Kappa, Bohemian Club (San Francisco), Vintage Country Club (Indian Wells). Home: 74-435 Palo Verde Dr Indian Wells CA 92210 Office: 2450 Montecito Rd Ramona CA 92065-1698

HOFFMAN, WENDY MAUREEN, marketing, public relations executive; b. Montrose, Colo., July 18, 1950; d. Harold Thomas and Mary Eileen (McEachern) Rawson; m. Gordon Joseph Hoffman, Mar. 4, 1972; children: Nicholas Joseph, Angela Eileen. AA, Mesa Coll., 1969; BA, Adams State Coll., 1971; postgrad., U. Minn., 1991—. Editor family living The New Mexican, Santa Fe, 1973-75; freelance editorial cons. Los Alamos, N.Mex., 1975-81; editor lifestyles Los Alamos Monitor, 1981-89; dir. mktg., pub. rels. Los Alamos Med. Ctr., 1989—. Contbr. numerous articles to newspapers. Bd. dirs. Los Alamos Family Coun., 1989—; mktg. dir. Polit. Campaign State House, Los Alamos, 1991—, pub. rels. dir., 1976, 78; numerous vol. activities in youth projects, Los Alamos, 1981—. Mem. Nat. Fed. Press Women, N.Mex. Press Women (dir. high sch. communications contest 1989-91), Am. Mktg. Assn. Acad. Health Svcs. Mktg. (Flash Brilliance Gold award 1991). Independent. Roman Catholic. Office: Los Alamoa Med Ctr 3917 West Rd Los Alamos NM 87544

HOFFMAN, WILLIAM CHARLES, mathematician; b. Portland, Oreg., Aug. 11, 1919; s. William Charles and Myra (Mayo) H.; m. Ruth Ann Ketler, 1950 (div. 1975); children: Nancy Lindsley, Robert; m. Dorothea Maree Hanlon, May 15, 1975; 1 child, Brian. BS, U. Calif., Berkeley, 1943; MA, UCLA, 1947, PhD, 1953; postgrad., Cornell U., 1949-50. Head analysis staff USN Electronics Lab., San Diego, 1947-49, 52-55; res. physicist Hughes Res. Labs., Culver City, Calif., 1951-2, 59; cons., mathematician Rand Corp., Santa Monica, Calif., 1955-58; sr. lectr. of radiophysics U. Queensland, St. Lucia, Australia, 1960; mem. math. lab. Boeing Scientific Res. Labs., Seattle, 1961-66; prof. math. sci. Oreg. State U., Corvallis, 1966-69, Oakland U., Rochester, Mich., 1969-85; vis. prof. N.Mex. State U., Las Cruces, 1985-87; cons. Sierra Vista, Ariz., 1987—; mem. CUPM Panel on Math. in Life Scis., Berkeley, 1968-71, USA commns. Internat. Scientific Radio Union, 1947-55; bd. dirs. Acad. for Gifted and Talented of Mich., 1982-85; chmn. Internat. Conf. on Geometric Psychology, Marseilles, France, 1976. Editor: Statistical Methods in Radio Propagation, 1960; discovered psychol. theory of geometric psychology, 1964-88; contbr. papers to profl. jours. Bd. dirs. CD, Mercer Island, Wash., 1964-65; active planning and zoning commn. City of Sierra Vista, 1988-90. Mem. Am. Math. Soc., Am. Statistical Assn., Soc. for Indsl. and Applied Math., Psychometric Soc., Am. Ednl. Res. Assn., Delta Upsilon. Republican. Office: PO Box 2005 Sierra Vista AZ 85636-2005

HOFFMANN, JON ARNOLD, aeronautical engineer, educator; b. Wausau, Wis., Jan. 13, 1942; s. Arnold D. and Rita J. (Haas) H.; m. Carol R. Frye. BSME, U. Wis., 1964, MSME, 1966. Register profl. engr., Calif. Research engr. Trane Co., 1966-68; prof. aeronautical engring. Calif. Poly. State U., San Luis Obispo, 1968—; research engr. Stanford U. NSF Program, 1970; research fellow Ames Research Ctr. NASA/ASEE, 1974-75; tech. cons. NASA/AMES Research Ctr., 1977; design engr. Cal/ Poly ERDA contract, 1976-77; prin. investigator NASA-ARC Cooperative Agreement, 1983. Contbr. articles to profl. jours. Grantee NASA, NSF. Mem. ASME. Home: 1044 Via Chula Robles Arroyo Grande CA 93420 Office: Calif Poly State U Dept Aero Engring San Luis Obispo CA 93407

HOFFMANN, KATHRYN ANN, humanities educator; b. Rockville Centre, N.Y., Oct. 26, 1954; d. Manfred and Catherine (Nanko) H.; m. Brook Ellis, Nov. 25, 1987. BA summa cum laude, SUNY Buffalo, 1975; MA, The Johns Hopkins U., 1979, PhD, 1982. Cert. French lit. & language tchr. Asst. prof. U. Wis.-Madison, 1981-88, U. Hawaii-Manoa, Honolulu, 1992—; mng. ptnr. Yuval Design Partnership, Chgo., 1988-92. Assoc. editor Substance, 1982-87; contbr. articles to profl. jours.; designer clothing accessories. Grantee NEH, 1993; fellow Inst. Rsch. in Humanities, 1984-85, Am. Coun. Learned Socs., 1984-85. Mem. MLA, Hawaii Assn. Language Tchrs., Phi Beta Kappa. Home: 2640 Dole St # C-6 Honolulu HI 96822 Office: U Hawaii Manoa Dept European Languages & Lit 1890 East-West Rd Moore 483 Honolulu HI 96822

HOFFMANN, TONY DALE, certified water specialist; b. Salt Lake City, May 16, 1960; s. Fritz Otto Ernst and Ursula Erna (Shoenrock) H.; m. Lenore Carolyn Desoto, May 25, 1984; children: Anthony Michael, Morgan James. Student, Truckee Meadow C.C., 1982-83, Brigham Young U., 1983-84. Plumber, owner Root-O-Matic, Sparks, Nev., 1984-90; regional v.p. Primerica Fin. Svcs., Reno, Nev., 1986-92; cert. water specialist Water Systems of Western Nev., Sparks, 1990—. Precinct chmn. Republican Party, Washoe County, Nev., 1988, county del., Washoe County, 1988, state del., Reno, 1988; state assembly candidate Ind. Am., Sparks, 1992. Named one of Outstanding Young Men of Am., OYMA Com., 1985, for honorable 2 yr. mission svc. LDS Ch. Mem. Water Quality Orgn. (cert. water specialist 1992-95), Nat. Ctr. for Constl. Studies, Nat. Rife Assn., John Birch Soc. (pub. rels. chmn. 1990-92), Eagle Forum (photographer 1987-92). Home: 2380 18th St Sparks NV 89431

HOFFMANN, WILLIAM FREDERICK, astronomer; b. Manchester, N.H., Feb. 26, 1933; s. Maurice and Charlotte (Hibbs) H.; m. Silke Elisabeth Margaretha Schneider, June 5, 1965; children: Andrea Charlotte, Christopher James. AB in Physics, Bowdoin Coll., 1954; PhD in Physics, Princeton U., 1962. Instr. physics Princeton (N.J.) U., 1958-61; rsch. assoc. NASA-GISS, N.Y.C., 1962, staff astronomer, 1965-73; instr. physics Yale U., New Haven, 1963-64; adj. assoc. prof. Columbia U., N.Y.C., 1970-73; prof. astronomy U. Ariz., Tucson, 1973—. Editor: (with H.Y. Chiu) Gravitation & Relativity, 1964. Pres. Spuyten Duyvil Assn., N.Y.C., 1971. NSF fellow, 1954; Danforth fellow, 1954-58. Fellow AAAS, mem. Am. Physics Soc., Am.

Astron. Soc., Sigma Chi, Phi Beta Kappa. Home: 4225 E Kilmer St Tucson AZ 85711-2825 Office: U Ariz Steward Obs Tucson AZ 85721

HOFFMEISTER, GERHART, German language educator; b. Giessen, Germany, Dec. 17, 1936; came to U.S., 1966, naturalized citizen, 1993; s. Johannes and Inge Caecilie (Johannsen) H.; m. Margaret von Poletika, May 28, 1966 (div. Dec. 1988); 1 child, George A. Degree, U. Bonn, Fed. Republic Germany, 1963, U. Cologne, Fed. Republic Germany, 1966; PhD, U. Md., 1970. Student tchr. U. Cologne, 1964-66; instr. U. Md., 1966-70; asst. prof. U. Wis., Milw., 1970-74; assoc. prof. Wayne State U., Detroit, 1974-75; assoc. prof. U. Calif., Santa Barbara, 1975-79, prof., 1979—, bd. dirs. Comparative Lit. program, 1991—. Author: (with others) Germany 2, 000 Years III, 1986; editor: Goethe in Italy, 1988, French Revolution, 1989, European Romanticism, 1989. Recipient award Am. Philos. Assn., 1974, Max Kade Found., 1986, 88. Mem. MLA, Am. Assn. Tchrs. German, Goethe Soc. N.Am. Home: 117 Calle Alamo Santa Barbara CA 93105-2818 Office: U Calif Dept German Santa Barbara CA 93106

HOFMAN, ELAINE D., state legislator; b. Sacramento, Sept. 20, 1937; d. Willard Davis and Venna (Gray) Smart; m. Cornelius Adrianus Hofman, Dec. 14, 1956; children: Catharina, John, Casie, Cornelius. BA, Idaho State U., 1974. Tchr. music edn. Sch. Dist. 25, Pocatello, Idaho, 1977-84; spl. asst. to Gov. Evans State of Idaho, Pocatello, 1984-87; field rep. to Congressman Stallings 2d Dist. Congressional Office, Pocatello, 1987-89; mem. Idaho Ho. of Reps., Pocatello, 1990—. Recipient Elect Lady award Lambda Delta Sigma, 1991; named Idaho Mother of Yr., Am. Mother's Assn., 1992, S.E. Idaho Family of the Yr., 1980. Democrat. Mem. Ch. of Jesus Christ of Latter-day Saints. Home: 216 S 16th Ave Pocatello ID 83201

HOFMANN, ALAN FREDERICK, biomedical educator, researcher; b. Balt., May 17, 1931; s. Joseph Enoch and Nelda Rosina (Durr) H.; m. Marta Gertrud Pettersson, Aug. 15, 1969 (div. 1976); children: Anthea Karin, Cecilia Rae; m. Helga Katharina Aicher, Nov. 3, 1978. BA with honors, Johns Hopkins U., 1951, MD with honors, 1955; PhD, U. Lund, Sweden, 1965; MD honoris causis, U. Bologna, Italy, 1988. Intern, then resident dept. medicine Columbia Presbyn. Med. Ctr., N.Y.C., 1955-57; clin. assoc. clin. ctr. Nat. Heart Inst., NIH, Bethesda, Md., 1957-59; postdoctoral fellow, dept. physiol. chemistry U. Lund, Sweden, 1959-62; asst. physician Hosp. of the Rockefeller U., N.Y.C., 1962-64; outpatient physician N.Y. Hosp., N.Y.C., 1963-64; assoc. physician Hosp. of the Rockefeller U., N.Y.C., 1964-66; cons. in medicine, assoc. dir. gastroenterology unit Mayo Clinic, Rochester, Minn., 1966-77; attending physician Med. Ctr. U. Calif.-San Diego, 1977—; asst. prof. dept. medicine Rockefeller U., N.Y.C., 1964-66; assoc. prof. medicine and biochemistry U. Minn. Mayo Grad. Sch., 1966-69, assoc. prof. medicine and physiology, 1969-70, prof. medicine and physiology, 1970-73; prof. medicine and physiology Mayo Med. Sch., 1973-77; cons. physiology Mayo Clinic, Rochester, 1975-77; prof. medicine U. Calif., San Diego, 1977—, adj. prof. pharmacy, U. Calif., San Francisco, 1986—; vis. prof. pharmacy U. Mich., Ann Arbor, 1980-85. Patentee solvent for direct dissolution of cholesterol gallstones, breath test for pancreatic exocrine function, bile acid replacement therapy; contbr. numerous articles to profl. jours., books, films. Recipient Travel award Wellcome Trust, 1961-63, Travel award NSF, 1964, Sr. Scientist award Humboldt Found., Fed. Republic of Germany, 1976, 91 (shared prize) Eppinger Prize, Falk Found., 1976, Disting. Achievement award Modern Medicine mag., 1978 Chancellor's Rsch. Excellence award U. Calif., 1986; Nat. Fedn. fellow, 1959-61, USPHS fellow, 1962-63, Fogarty Internat. Sr. fellow NIH, 1986; Rockefeller Found. scholar, Bellagio, Italy, 1980. Fellow AAAS; mem. Am. Assn. Study of Liver Disease (numerous coms., pres. 1984), Swedish Soc. for Gastroenterology (hon.), Soc. Gastrointestinal Radiology (hon.), Gastroent. Soc. Australia (hon.), Chilean Soc. Gastroent. (hon.), Brit. Soc. Gastroent. (hon.), Royal Flemish Acad. for Medicine Belgium (hon., fgn. corr. mem.), German Soc. for Gastroenterology (hon.), Am. Soc. Clin. Investigation, Am. Assn. Physicians, Am. Liver Found. (chmn. sci. adv. bd. 1986-91), Am. Physiol. Soc., Am. Gastroent. Assn. (chmn. biliary diseases coun. 1991—, Disting. Achievement award 1970, co-winner Beaumont prize 1979), Am. Physiol. Soc., Phi Beta Kappa, Sigma Xi, Alpha Omega Alpha, Omicron Delta Kappa. Home: 5870 Cactus Way La Jolla CA 92037-7069 Office: U Calif San Diego Dept Medicine PO Box 0813 La Jolla CA 92093-0813

HOFMANN, DAN J., education educator, small business owner; b. Limon, Colo., July 28, 1945; s. Stephen Christian and Esther Elma (Miller) H.; m. Nancy Carol McVehil, Jan. 15, 1945; children: H. Phillips, Melinda Celeste. BA in Hotel Mgmt., Food Svc., Tourism, Alaska Pacific, Anchorage, 1986, MBA, 1987, cert. element teaching, 1989. Mgr. McDonalds Corp., Boulder, Colo., 1964-71, Anchorage, Alaska, 1971-76. Author poetry, stories, 1986, 87. Mem. Am. Edn. Assn., Nat. Edn. Assn. Methodist. Home: 3706 Tree Cir Anchorage AK 99502

HOFMANN, FRIEDER KARL, biotechnologist, consultant; b. Eppstein, Hessen, Fed. Republic of Germany, June 15, 1949; came to U.S., 1984; s. Friedrich Karl and Anna Johannette (Heist) H.; m. Sigrid Marianne Thomae, Sept. 5, 1975. MS, J.W. Goethe U., Frankfurt, Fed. Republic of Germany, 1977, PhD, 1981. Staff scientist, asst. prof. J.W. Goethe U., Frankfurt, 1977-81; sci. mgr. Brunswick Corp., Eschborn, Fed. Republic of Germany, 1982-84; tech. dir. Biotechnetics, San Diego, 1984-90; pres. Hofmann & Co., Oceanside, Calif., 1990—. Author: (with others) Scale-Up and Downstream Processing of rDNA Products, 1991, GMP Production of Monoclonal Antibodies, 1991; contbr. over 40 articles to profl. jours. Recipient Senckenberg prize Senckenberg Rsch. Soc., Frankfurt, Fed. Republic of Germany, 1977; Kirkpatrick Chem. Engring. Achievement Honor award, Chem. Engring., 1989, Parenteral Drug Assn. Jour. award, Parenteral Drug Assn., Pa., 1985. Mem. Am. Chem. Soc., Am. Inst. Chem. Engrs., Tissue Culture Assn., European Soc. for Animal Cell Tech. Office: Hofmann & Co 2360 Autumn Dr Ste C Oceanside CA 92056-3528

HOGAN, CLARENCE LESTER, retired electronics executive; b. Great Falls, Mont., Feb. 8, 1920; s. Clarence Lester and Bessie (Young) H.; m. Audrey Biery Peters, Oct. 13, 1946; 1 child, Cheryl Lea. BSChemE, Mont. State U., 1942, Dr. Engring. (hon.), 1967; MS in Physics, Lehigh U., 1947, PhD in Physics, 1950, D in Engring. (hon.), 1971; AM (hon.), Harvard U., 1954; D in Sci. (hon.), Worcester Poly. U., 1969. Rsch. chem. engr. Anaconda Copper Mining Co., 1942-43; instr. physics Lehigh U., 1946-50; mem. tech. staff Bell Labs., Murray Hill, N.J., 1950-51, sub-dept. head, 1951-53; assoc. prof. Harvard U., Cambridge, Mass., 1953-57, Gordon McKay prof., 1957-58; gen. mgr. semi-conductor products div. Motorola, Inc., Phoenix, 1958-60, v.p., 1960-66, exec. v.p., dir., 1966-68; pres., chief exec. officer Fairchild Inst., Mt. View, Calif., 1968-74, vice chmn. bd. dirs., 1974-85; bd. dirs. MEMC HUELS; gen. chmn. Internat. Conf. on Magnetism and Magnetic Materials, 1959, 60; mem. materials adv. bd. Dept. Def., 1957-59; mem. adv. coun. dept. electrical engring. Princeton U.; mem. adv. bd. sch. engring. U. Calif., Berkeley, 1974—, adv. bd. dept. chem. engring. Mont. State U., 1988—; mem. nat. adv. bd. Desert Rsch. Inst., 1976-80; mem. vis. com. dept. electric engring. and computer sci. MIT, 1975-85; mem. adv. coun. div. electrical engring. Stanford U., 1976-86; mem. sci. and ednl. adv. com. Lawrence Berkeley Lab., 1978-84; mem. Pres.'s Export Coun., 1976-80; mem. adv. panel to tech. adv. bd. U.S. Congress, 1976-80. Patentee in field; inventor microwave gyrator, circulator, isolator. Chmn. Commn. Found. Santa Clara County, Calif., 1983-85; mem. vis. com. Lehigh U., 1966-71, trustee, 1971-80; trustee Western Electronic Edn. Fund; mem. governing bd. Maricopa County Jr. Coll.; bd. regents U. Santa Clara. Lt. (j.g.) USNR, 1942-46. Recipient Community Svc. award NCCJ, 1978, Medal of Merit Am. Electronics Assn., 1978, Berkeley Citation U. Calif., 1980; named Bay Area Bus. Man of Yr. San Jose State U., 1978, One of 10 Greatest Innovators in Past 50 Yrs. Electronics Mag., 1980. Fellow AAAS, IEEE (Frederick Philips gold medal 1976, Edison silver medal Cleve. Soc. 19078, Pioneering medal for microwave theory and tech. 1993), Inst. Elec. Engrs. (hon.); mem. NAE, Am. Phys. Soc., Menlo Country Club, Masons, Sigma Xi, Tau Beta Pi, Phi Kappa Phi, Kappa Sigma. Democrat. Baptist. Home: 36 Barry Ln Menlo Park CA 94027-4023

HOGAN, CURTIS JULE, union executive, industrial relations consultant; b. Greeley, Kans., July 25, 1926; s. Charles Leo and Anna Malene (Rousello) H.; m. Lois Jean Ecord, Apr. 23, 1955; children: Christopher James, Michael Sean, Patrick Marshall, Kathleen Marie, Kerry Joseph. BS in Indsl. Rels., Rockhurst Coll., 1950; postgrad., Georgetown U., 1955, U. Tehran, Iran, 1955-57. With Gt. Lakes Pipeline Co., Kansas City, Mo., 1950-55; with Internat. Fedn. Petroleum and Chem. Workers, Denver, 1955-85; gen. sec. Internat. Fedn. Petroleum and Chem. Workers, 1973-85; pres. Internat. Labor Rels. Svcs., Inc., 1976—; cons. in field; lectr. Rockhurst Coll., Kansas City, 1951-52. Contbr. articles to profl. publs. Served with U.S. Army, 1945-46. Mem. Internat. Indsl. Rels. Assn., Indsl. Rels. Rsch. Assn., Oil Chem. and Atomic Workers Internat. Union. Home: 435 S Newport Way Denver CO 80224-1321

HOGAN, MERVIN BOOTH, mechanical engineer, educator; b. Bountiful, Utah, July 21, 1906; s. Charles Ira and Sarah Ann (Booth) H.; m. Helen Emily Reese, Dec. 27, 1928; 1 son, Edward Reese. B.S., U. Utah, 1927, M.E., 1930; M.S., U. Pitts., 1929; Ph.D., U. Mich., 1936, postgrad.; Sterling fellow, Yale U., 1937-38. Registered profl. engr., Conn., Mich., N.Y., Utah, Va. chartered engr., U.K. Design engr. Westinghouse Electric Corp., East Pittsburgh, Pa., 1927-31; asst. prof. mech. engring. U. Utah, Salt Lake City, 1931-36, asso. prof., 1936-39, prof., 1939-56, chmn. dept. mech. engring., 1951-56, prof., 1971-76, prof. emeritus, 1976—; mgr. product design engring. GE, Syracuse, N.Y., 1956-65; mgr. design assurance engring. GE, Phoenix, 1965-70; cons. engr. GE, Waynesboro, Va., 1970-71; cons. Chgo. Bridge & Iron, 1950-56. Author: Mormonism and Freemasonry: The Illinois Episode, 1977, The Origin and Growth of Utah Masonry and Its Conflict with Mormonism, 1978, Mormonism and Freemasonry under Covert Masonic Influences, 1979, Freemasonry and the Lynching at Carthage Jail, 1981, Freemasonry and Civil Confrontation on the Illinois Frontier, 1981, The Involvement of Freemasonry with Mormonism on the American Midwestern Frontier, 1982; contbr. articles to engr. jours., numerous articles to Masonic publs. Recipient Merit of Honor award U. Utah, 1981. Fellow ASME, Inst. Mech. Engrs. (London), Yale Sci., Engring. Assn.; mem. IEEE (sr.), Nat. Eagle Scout Assn., DeMolay Legion of Honor, S.R. in State N.Y., Utah Soc. SAR (pres. 1983-84), Aztec Club, Timpanogos Club, Elfun Soc., Rotary, Masons (33 deg.), Shriners, Prophets, KT, DeMolay, Quatuor Coronati Lodge 2076, Sigma Xi, Phi Kappa Phi, Tau Beta Pi, Pi Tau Sigma, Sigma Nu, Theta Tau, Alpha Phi Omega, Phi Lambda Epsilon. Home: 921 Greenwood Terr Douglas Park Salt Lake City UT 84105 Office: U Utah 3008 Merrill Engring Bldg Salt Lake City UT 84112

HOGAN, MICHAEL R(OBERT), federal judge; b. Oregon City, Oreg., Sept. 24, 1946; s. Robert G. and Ervy Maxine (Barklow) H.; m. Christine Campbell, June 21, 1971; children: Matthew R., Joshua D., Michelle C. A.B., U. Oreg. Honors Coll., 1968; J.D., Georgetown U., 1971. Bar: Oreg. 1971, U.S. Ct. Appeals (9th cir.) 1971. Law clk. to chief judge U.S. Dist. Ct. Oreg., Portland, 1971-72; assoc. Miller, Anderson, Nash, Yerke and Wiener, Portland, 1972-73; magistrate judge U.S. Dist. Ct. Oreg., Eugene, 1973-91, dist. judge, 1991—; bankruptcy judge U.S. Dist. Oreg., Eugene, 1973-80. Mem. ABA, Oreg. State Bar Assn. Baptist. Office: US Courthouse 211 E 7th Ave Eugene OR 97401-2722

HOGAN, VELVIN REEVES, test engineer; b. Greenville, Tex., Nov. 6, 1944; s. Reeves and Evelyn Marie (Webb) H.; m. Carol Kathleen Whitcomb, Dec. 30, 1967; children: Thomas Reeves, Melissa Kathleen. AA, San Jose (Calif.) C.C., 1971; postgrad., San Jose State U., 1971-77. Assoc. elec. engr. Caelus Memories, Inc., San Jose, 1969-75; sr. devel. engr. Memorex Corp., Santa Clara, Calif., 1975-78; sr. engring. mgr. Storage Tech. Corp., Louisville, Colo., 1978-84; prin. test engr. Digital Equipment Corp., Colorado Springs, Colo., 1984-87; sr. engring. mgr. Seagate Tech., Scotts Valley, Calif., 1987-91; prin. test engr. Micropolis Corp., Chatsworth, Calif., 1992—. With USN, 1966-69, Vietnam. Mem. ANSI (X3B7.1 com. test methodology com. 1984-87). Republican. Mem. Ch. of Christ. Home: 306 Colville Dr San Jose CA 95123 Office: Micropolis Corp 21211 Nordhoff St Chatsworth CA 91311

HOGARTH, BURNE, cartoonist, illustrator; b. Chgo., Dec. 25, 1911; s. Max and Pauline H.; m. Constance Holubar, June 27, 1953; children: Michael, Richard, Ross. Student Art Inst. Chgo., 1925-27, Chgo. Acad. Fine Arts, 1926-29, Crane Coll., 1928-30, U. Chgo., 1930-32, Northwestern U., 1931-32, Columbia U., 1956-57. Asst. cartoonist to Lyman Young, Tim Tyler's Luck, N.Y.C., 1934; cartoonist Pieces of Eight, McNaught Syndication, N.Y.C., 1935; free lance artist King Features, N.Y.C., 1935-36; staff artist Johnstone Agy., N.Y.C., 1936-37; cartoonist Sunday Color Page, Tarzan, United Feature Syndication, N.Y.C., 1937-50, Sunday page Drago, Post-Hall Syndication, N.Y.C., 1946, Miracle Jones, United Features, N.Y.C., 1948; founder Sch. Visual Arts, N.Y.C., 1947-70, v.p., coord. curriculum, instr., 1947-70; author Watson-Guptill, N.Y.C., 1958-89; instr. Parsons Sch., N.Y.C., 1976-79; pres. Pendragon Press Ltd., N.Y.C., 1975-79; with Art Ctr. Coll. Design, Pasadena, Calif., 1982—, Otis Art Inst., Parsons Sch. Design, L.A., 1981—; seminar presenter U. Colo., Boulder; spl. guest German Comics Fair, Cologne, Berlin, 1990; participant traveling exhbn. Sites 1990-92, U.S.; numerous exhbns. worldwide including Musee des arts decoratives, Louvre, Paris, 1968, 69, Smithsonian Inst., 1990—, Gallery Karikatury, Warsaw, 1990; one man show Paris, 1967, Bibliotheque Municipale, 1985, Palais de Longchamps, Marseille, France, 1985; group show Gallery Karikatury, Warsaw, Poland, 1990; represented in permanent collections: Smithsonian Instn., Mus. Cartoon Art, U. Colo., U. Wyo., Mus. Art, Gijon, Spain, others. Author: Dynamic Anatomy, 1958, Drawing the Human Head, 1965, Dynamic Figure Drawing, 1970, Drawing Dynamic Hands, 1977, Dynamic Light and Shade, 1981, Dynamic Wrinkles and Drapery, 1991, The Arcane Eye of Hogarth, 1992; creator graphic novels Tarzan of the Apes, 1972, Jungle Tales of Tarzan, 1976, Golden Age of Tarzan, 1979, Life of King Arthur, 1984, The Arcane Eye of Hogarth, 1992; author (videocassette) Draw THe Human Head, 1989. Trustee NCS Milt Gross Fund., 1980; active 43d Ann. Conf. on World Affairs, Boulder, 1990. Named Best Illustration Cartoonist, Nat. Cartoonists Soc., 1974, 75, 76, Artist of Yr., Pavilion of Humour, 1975; recipient Premio Emilio Freixas Silver plaque V-Muestra Internat. Conv., 1978, Pulcinella award V-Mostra Internat. del Fumetto, 1983, Caran D'Ache Silver plaque Internat. Comics Conv., 1984, Adamson Silent Sam award Comics '85 Internat. Conv., 1985, Golden Palms award Cesar Illustration Group, Paris, 1988, Premio Especial award 7th Internat. Salon of Humor, Barcelona, Spain, 1989, Golden Lion award Burroughs Bibliophiles, U. Louisville, 1990, Bronze trophy German Comics Fair, Cologne, Fed. Republic Germany, 1990, L'Age D'Or award Cesar Illustration Group, 1992, Lifetime Achievement award Kansas City Comic Conv., 1992. Mem. Nat. Cartoonists Soc. (pres. 1977-79, Reuben Silver plaque 1993), Mus. of Cartoon Art, Am. Soc. Aesthetics, Nat. Art Edn. Assn., WHO, Graphic Arts Soc., Internat. Assn. Authors of Comics and Cartoons. Address: 6026 W Lindenhurst Ave Los Angeles CA 90036

HOGGATT, CLELA ALLPHIN, English language educator; b. Des Moines, Sept. 9, 1932; d. Addison Edgar and Frances (Buckallew) Philleo; m. Charles Allphin; children: Beverly, Valerie, Clark, Arthur, Frances; m. John Hoggatt. AA, Grand View Jr. Coll., 1952; BA summa cum laude, U. No. Iowa, 1954; MA, Tex A&I U., 1961. Cert. life tchr. Iowa, Tex.; permanent life community coll. credential, Calif. Tchr. social studies Los Fresnos (Tex.) Jr. High Sch., 1954-55; tchr. English Cummings Jr. High Sch., Brownsville, Tex., 1956-59, Fickett Jr. High Sch., Tucson, 1963-66, Portola Jr. High Sch., L.A., 1956-59; instr. speech Tex. Southmost Jr. Coll., Bronsville, 1959; tchr. history and English Ysleta High Sch., El Paso, Tex., 1963-66; prof. English L.A. Trade-Tech. Coll., 1969-75, L.A. Mission Coll., 1975—. Author: Women in the Plays of Henrik Ibsen, 1975, The Writing Cycle, 1986, Good News for Writers, 1990; contbr. to Words, Words, Words, 1981, Emily Dickinson: A Centennial Celebration, 1890-1990, In the West of Ireland, John Trumball: An Anthology in Memoriam. Grand View Jr. Coll. scholar, 1951-52, U. No. Iowa scholar, 1953-54. Mem. Nat. Coun. Tchrs. English, Am. Mensa, Pi Gamma Mu. Democrat. Office: LA Mission Coll 13356 Eldridge Ave Sylmar CA 91342-3244

HOGNER, DON LA RUE, probation officer; b. Claremore, Okla., July 28, 1937; s. Ned Edward and Zelma Iris (Richardson) H.; m. Ramona Leila Gee, May 29, 1959; children: Sonja, Tatia. BA in Philosophy, Calif. State U., Fresno, 1964. Social worker Fresno (Calif.) County Dept. Social Svcs., 1964-68; dep. probation officer Fresno County Probation Dept., 1968-73, unit supr., 1973-74, supt. of juvenile camp, 1974-75, asst. chief probation officer, 1975-83, chief probation officer, 1983-88; chief probation officer Alameda County Probation Dept., Oakland, Calif., 1988—; peer reviewer Nat. Inst. Justice, Washington, 1991—; bd dirs. Calif. Probation, Parole and Corrections Assn., 1992—, chmn. Alameda County Children's Issues Policy Bd., Oakland, 1992—. Contbr. articles to profl. jours. Bd. dirs. Spl. Advocates for Youth, Fresno, 1982; chmn. adv. bd. Fresno Pre-Release Ctr., 1984; mem. adv. bd. Nat. Intermediate Sanctions Project, Washington, 1991; chmn. chaplains coordinating com. Calif. Dept. Corrections, Sacramento, 1991. Recipient Commendation resolution Calif. Assembly, Sacramento, 1988. Mem. Chief Probation Officers of Calif. (pres. 1990—, Chief Probation Officer of Yr. 1992), Nat. Assn. of Probation Execs., Am. Probation and Parole Asssn., Calif. Probation, Parole and Corrections Assn. Democrat. Home: 3119 E Kerckhoff Fresno CA 93702

HOGUE, JOHN HAROLD, author; b. L.A., Oct. 29, 1955; s. Harold Austin and Irene Lillian (Hall) H. Profl. singer various theatres, 1972-77. Author: Nostradamus and the Millennium, 1986, Endless Tomorrow: 777 Predictions for the New Millennium, 1993. Mem. World Acad. Creative Sci., Art and Consciousness, Assn. Rsch. and Enlightenment. Office: 433 13th Ave E #301 Seattle WA 98102-5176

HOHLMAYER, EARL J., service company executive; b. Springfield, Ohio, June 8, 1921; s. Carl Elton and Margaret (Waggaman) H.; m. Yvonne Hohlmayer, Aug. 15, 1971 (div. 1975); m. Nikki Vramis, Feb. 14, 1976. Student, Solano Coll., 1967. V.p. Hohlmayer's Laundry Inc., Springfield, 1953-55; pres. Hohlmayer's Chevron Cleaner, Fairborn, Ohio, 1955-62; sales mgr. German Auto Parts, Long Beach, Calif., 1962-64; sales rep. Fgn. Auto Supply, Anaheim, Calif., 1964-66; sales mgr. Vern Gardner Fgn. Auto, Oakland, Calif., 1966-67; foreman Aero Mechanics, Fairfield, Calif., 1967-72; mgr., ptnr. Commodore Valet Svc., Pittsburg, Calif., 1979-80; pres. Modern Commodore Cleaner, Antioch, Calif., 1981—. Contbr. articles to Rivertown Express, 1988, Antioch Currents, 1988, Daily Ledger, 1989; producer hist. videotapes. Active Antioch Civic Arts Commn., 1988; pres. Antioch Hist. Soc., 1982-87; bd. dirs. Antioch Rivertown Dist., 1988. Tech. sgt. USAAF, 1941-46, USAF, 1948-53. Mem. Sports Car Club Am. (regional exec. 1956), Solano Yacht Club (commodore 1974), Elks, Masons, Moose. Home: 19 W 7th St Antioch CA 94509-1741

HOHN, EDWARD LEWIS, lawyer, real estate developer; b. Winslow, Ariz., Aug. 11, 1933; s. Lewis Murle and Nora (Day) H.; children: Edward, Ilsa, Kirsten, Isolda, Kristopher, Ursla. BS, Ariz. State U., 1955; JD, Cumberland Law Sch., 1965. Bar: Ariz. 1965, U.S. Ct. Appeals (9th cir.), U.S. Supreme Ct. 1971. Owner, mgr. Winslow Dry Cleaners, 1961-63; pvt. practice Phoenix, 1965—; developer Arcadia Plaza, Phoenix, 1970-72, RV Resort, 1975—, U.S. Adventure Vacation Club, Inc., 1985—. Capt. USAF, 1955-60. Mem. Am. Bd. Trial Advocates, Fed. Ct. 9th Cir. Bar Assn., Ala. State Bar Assn., Ariz. State Bar Assn., Ariz. State Trial Attys. (pres. 1974-75), Internat. Combat Pilot Assn. (nat. dir. 1970—), Ariz. Antique Airplane Assn. (dir. 1970-75), Aircraft Owner's and Pilot Assn. (legal counselor 1988), Lions, Elks. Democrat. Baptist. Home: 4915 N 45 Pl Phoenix AZ 85018-9999 Office: 4344 E Indian School Rd Phoenix AZ 85018-5331

HOHNER, KENNETH DWAYNE, fodder company executive; b. St. John, Kans., June 24, 1934; s. Courtney Clinton and Mildred Lucile (Forrester) H.; m. Sherry Eloi Anice Edens, Feb. 14, 1961; children: Katrina, Melissa, Steven, Michael. BS in Geol. Engring., U. Kans., 1957. Geophysicist Mobil Oil Corp., New Orleans, Anchorage, Denver, 1957-72; sr. geophysicist Amerada Hess Corp., Houston, 1972-75, ARAMCO, London, 1975-79; far east area geophysicist Hamilton Bros., Denver, 1979-83; owner Hohner Poultry Farm, Erie, Colo., 1979—; pres. Hohner Custom Feed, Inc., Erie, Colo., 1982—. Mem. Soc. Exploration Geophysicists. Home and Office: 3398 Weld County Rd 4 Erie CO 80516

HOIVIK, THOMAS HARRY, educator; b. Mpls., June 6, 1941; s. Tony Horace and Helen Lenea (Carlsen) H.; m. Judith Lisa Kohn; children: Todd, Gregory. BA, U. Minn., 1963; grad. with distinction, Naval Test Pilot Sch., 1969; MS with distinction, Naval Postgrad. Sch., 1973; grad. with distinction, Naval War Coll., 1976; MA, Salve Regina U., 1988. Cert. exptl. test pilot, air transport pilot, jet aircraft, helicopter, glider single and multi-engine. Commd. ensign USN, 1963, advanced through grades to capt., 1963-91; test pilot Naval Air Test Ctr., Patuxent River, Md., 1968-71; program mgr. H-53 aircraft Naval Air Systems Command, Washington, 1976-78; comdg. officer Helicopter Mine Countermeasure Squadron 14, Norfolk, Va., 1978-80; dir. U.S. Naval Test Pilot Sch., Patuxent River, 1980-82; fed. exec. fellow Ctr. for Strategic and Internat. Studies, Washington, 1982-83; chair tactical analysis Naval Postgrad. Sch., Monterey, Calif., 1983-85; comdg. officer Naval Air Sta., Willow Grove, Pa., 1985-87; chair applied systems analysis Naval Postgrad. Sch., Monterey, 1987-91, prof. acquisition mgmt., 1991—; mem. U.S. Congrl. Study Group on Nat. Strategy, Washington, 1982-83, World Economy, 1982-83; cons. U.S., Internat. Govt. Orgns., 1990—; founder, pres. Lysonics Rsch. Internat., 1993; flight demonstration pilot Paris Internat. Air Show, 1967. Contbr. articles to profl. jours. Bd. dirs. Vocat. Edn. Bd., Montgomery County, Pa., 1985-87, Congrl. Svc. Acad. Appointment Bd., Phila., 1985-87; youth leader, counselor YMCA, St. Paul, 1955-61. Recipient Legion of Merit Pres. of U.S., 1987, Outstanding Youth Leadership award YMCA, 1960; established U.S. Helicopter Speed Record, 1966. Mem. AIAA, Soc. of Exptl. Test Pilots, Internat. Test and Evaluation Assn., Nat. Contract Mgmt. Assn., Ops. Rsch. Soc. Am., Mil. Ops. Rsch. Soc., U. Minn. "M" Club, Disable Am. Vets (life), Sigma Alpha Epsilon. Office: Naval Postgrad Sch Monterey CA 93943

HOKAMA, YOSHITSUGI, immunologist; b. Kohala, Hawaii, Oct. 25, 1926; s. Royei and Kamado (Matsudo) H.; m. Haruko Yoshimoto, Feb. 3, 1951; children: Jon Keith Yoshimoto, Julie Lynn Rosemary Yoshimoto. BA, UCLA, 1951, MA, 1953, PhD, 1957. Asst. researcher UCLA, 1958-66; assoc. prof. Calif. State U., L.A., 1964-66, U. Hawaii, Honolulu, 1966-68; lab. dir. prof., Honolulu, 1968—, Accupath Labs., Honolulu, 1974—; cons. Courtland Lab., Los Angeles, 1964-66; cons. immunologist SKCL-Accupath Lab., Honolulu, 1974—. Co-author: Immunology and Immunopathology, 1982; assoc. editor Jour. Clin. Lab. Analysis, 1986—; mem. editorial bd. Jour. of Natural Toxins, 1991—; contbr. articles to profl. jours. Com. mem. Hawaii Cancer Commn., 1983—. Mem. Assn. Am. Immunologists (reticuloendothelial soc.), Am. Soc. Investigative Pathology, Am. Soc. Microbiologists, Am. Assn. Cancer Rsch. (div. medicinal chemistry), Am. Chem. Soc., Japanese-Am. Citizens League Club. Democrat. Episcopalian. Office: U Hawaii Dept Pathology 1960 EW Rd Honolulu HI 96822

HOKANA, GREGORY HOWARD, engineering executive; b. Burbank, Calif., Nov. 24, 1944; s. Howard Leslie and Helen Lorraine (Walker) H.; m. Eileen Marie Youell, Apr. 29, 1967; children: Kristen Marie, Kenneth Gregory. BS in Physics, UCLA, 1966. Design engr. Raytheon Co., Oxnard, Calif., 1967-74; staff engr. Bunker Ramo Corp., Westlake Village, Calif., 1974-84; mgr. analog engring. AIL Systems, Inc., Westlake Village, 1984-91; mgr. product devel. Am. Nucleonics Corp., Westlake Village, 1991—. Mem. Assn. Old Crows. Democrat. Methodist. Office: Am Nucleonics Corp 696 Hampshire Rd Westlake Village CA 91361-2512

HOKE, DEAN EDWARD, television station executive; b. Springfield, Ohio, Aug. 1, 1950; s. Joseph Dean and Dawn (Clifford) H.; 1 child from previous marriage, Andrew; m. Nancy Baer, Feb. 4, 1989. BA, Urbana (Ohio) U., 1975; MS, U. Louisville, 1979; cert. in mgmt., U. Pa., 1984. Asst. dir. admissions and records Bellarmine Coll., Louisville, 1975-79, dir. alumni affairs, 1979-83; dir. external affairs Sta. WKPC-TV, Louisville, 1983-86, asst. gen. mgr., 1986-89; gen. mgr. Sta. WEDW-TV, Stamford, Conn., 1989-90, Sta. KOCV-TV/FM, Odessa, Tex., 1990-91; exec. dir. Alaska Pub. Television - Sta. KAKM, Anchorage, 1991—. Trustee Urbana U., 1984—; dir. Young Leaders Inst., Louisville, 1987; mem. Leadership Louisville; pres. Anchorage Community Cultural Consortium. Named to Hon. Order Ky. Cols., 1983, Outstanding Young Citizen Jaycees, Louisville, 1985. Mem. Pacific Mountain Network Assn., Nat. Soc. of Fund Raising Execs., Pub. Broadcast Svc., Rotary. Office: Sta KAKM-TV 3877 University Dr Anchorage AK 99508

HOLBERT, JOSEF PAUL, journalist; b. Manhattan, Kans., Nov. 3, 1936; s. Bernard Paul and Selma Fern (York) H.; m. Carolyn Lee Peck, Feb. 27, 1960; children: Christopher Gene, Gretchen Ann. Student, Kans. State U., 1953-57. Mng. ptnr. Kilby Assocs. Advt., Omaha, 1958-61; mng. editor Glenwood Springs (Colo.) Sage Newspaper, 1961-65; polit. editor Anchorage Times Newspaper, 1965-67; press sec. to gov. State of Alaska, Juneau, 1967-

68; press sec. Sec. of Interior, Washington, 1968-70; press advanceman Pres., Washington, 1970-74; v.p., advisor, pub. rels. The Hilton Head Co., Head Island, S.C., 1970-74; pres. Profl. Media Group, Inc., Head Island, 1974-78; sr. v.p. Lusky Assocs./Hill & Knowlton, Inc., Denver, 1979-84; pres. Holbert Heismann Roman Adv., Inc., Denver, 1984-89; profl. tv producer/dir. Alaska, Colo., 1979—; profl. videographer Colo., Mex., Carribean, 1979—; outdoor writer Alaska, Colo., Utah, Wyo., 1989—; motorsports pub., editor, writer Colo., 1979—. Ghost writer: Who Owns America?, 1970; author: tv commls., films (1 Emmy award). Mem. NATAS, NRA, Profl. Assn. Diving Instrs., Porsche Club Am. (Heinmiller award, 1985). Republican. Roman Catholic. Home: 1237 Pearl St Denver CO 80203-2516

HOLBO, PAUL SOTHE, academic administrator; b. Wildrose, N.D., July 10, 1929; s. John and Dagny Christine (Sothe) H.; m. Kay Ann Neilson, Mar. 10, 1962; children: John Christian, Christine Louise. BA with high honors, Yale U., 1951; MA, U. Chgo., 1955, PhD, 1961. Lectr. U. Chgo., 1956-58; instr., asst. prof., assoc. prof., then prof. history U. Oreg., Eugene, 1959—, assoc. dean, then acting dean Coll. Liberal Arts, 1970-74, vice provost, 1982—; chief reader Am. history Ednl. Testing Svc., Princeton, N.J., 1969-72; chair test devel. com. Coll. Bd., N.Y.C., 1981-85, chair Western regional acad. adv. panel, San Jose, 1986-88; chair Oreg. State System/Community Coll. Coord. Com., 1984-85. Author: United States Policies Toward China, 1969, Tarnished Expansion, 1983; co-editor: The Eisenhower Era, 1974; founding editor jour. Diplomatic History, 1977. Rep. candidate for Oreg. State Senate, 1990. Cpl. U.S. Army, 1951-53. Mem. Am. Hist. Assn. (Pacific br. coun. 1984-87), Orgn. Am. Historians (Binkley-Stephenson award 1969), Soc. Historians Am. Fgn. Rels., Phi Beta Kappa. Home: 2090 Broadview St Eugene OR 97405-5536 Office: U Oreg 103 Johnson Hall Eugene OR 97403

HOLBROOK, JAMES RUSSELL, lawyer; b. Kansas City, Mo., Sept. 24, 1944; s. Newell James and Martha Inez (Russell) H.; m. Meghan Zanolli, Feb. 12, 1983. Student, MIT, 1962-63; BA, Grinnell (Iowa) Coll., 1966; MA, Ind. U., 1968; JD, U. Utah, 1974. Bar: Utah 1974, U.S. Ct. Appeals (10th cir.) 1977, U.S. Supreme Ct. 1980. Law clk. to chief judge U.S. Dist. Ct. Utah, Salt Lake City, 1973-75; pvt. practice Salt Lake City, 1975-78, asst. U.S. Atty. of Utah, 1978-80; ptnr. Giauque & Williams, Salt Lake City, 1980-82; gen. counsel Intermountain Power Agy., Murray, Utah, 1982-83; ptnr. Callister, Duncan & Nebeker, Salt Lake City, 1983—; mem. adv. com. on revisions to local rules of practice U.S. Dist. Ct. Utah, 1989—; adj. prof. U. Utah Coll. Law, Salt Lake City, 1984-88, 90—. Articles editor Jour. Contemporary Law, 1973-74; contbr. articles to profl. jours. Mem. bd. Internat. Visitors Utah Coun., Salt Lake City, 1984—; mem. exhbns. coun. Utah Mus. Fine Arts, Salt Lake City, 1986-92; bd. govs. Salt Lake Found., Salt Lake City, 1987-92. With U.S. Army, 1968-70, Vietnam. Decorated Bronze Star; NSF fellow, 1966-68, Woodrow Wilson Found. fellow, 1966. Mem. ABA, Utah Bar Assn. (commr. 1988-90), Fed. Bar Assn. (pres. Utah chpt. 1984-85), Sutherland Inn of Ct. (master of the bench 1984—), Alta Club, Phi Beta Kappa, Sigma Phi Epsilon. Democrat. Home: 775 Hilltop Rd Salt Lake City UT 84103-3311 Office: Callister Duncan & Nebeker 800 Kennecott Bldg Salt Lake City UT 84133

HOLDCROFT, LESLIE THOMAS, clergyman, educator; b. Man., Can., Sept. 28, 1922; s. Oswald Thomas and Florence (Waterfield) H.; student Western Bible Coll., 1941-44; BA, San Francisco State Coll., 1950; MA, San Jose State Coll., 1955; postgrad. Stanford, 1960, 63, U. Cal., 1965-67; DDiv., Bethany Bible Coll., 1968; m. Ruth Sorensen, July 2, 1948; children: Cynthia Ruth, Althea Lois, Sylvia Bernice. Instr. Western Bible Coll., 1944-47; instr. Bethany Bible Coll., 1947-55, dean edn., 1955-68, v.p., 1967-68; pres. Western Pentecostal Bible Coll., 1968-87; acad. cons., researcher, Clayburn, B.C., 1991—; pastor Craig Chapel, 1959-68; dir. Can. Pentecostal Corr. Coll., Clayburn, 1985-90. Pres., Assn. Canadian Bible Colls., 1972-76. Author: The Historical Books, 1960, The Synoptic Gospels, 1962, The Holy Spirit, 1962, The Pentateuch, 1951, Divine Healing, 1967, The Doctrine of God, 1978, The Four Gospels, 1988, Anthropology: A Biblical View, 1990, Soteriology: Good News in Review, 1990, Ecclesiology: Christ's Treasure on Earth, 1992. Home: 34623 Ascott Ave, Abbotsford, BC Canada V2S 5A3 Office: Box 123, Clayburn, BC Canada V0X 1E0

HOLDEN, ERNEST LLOYD, automotive company owner, association executive; b. Erie, Pa., May 2, 1941; s. Edmund Hudson and Ruth Marie (Mallory) H.; m. Sharon Glee Smith, Mar. 14, 1964 (div. July 1971); children: Vanessa Rene, James George; m. Carol Lee Christensen, July 9, 1985. BS, Edinboro State Coll., 1965. Cert. tchr., Pa., Ariz. Speedway mgr. U.S. Auto Raceways, Cleve., 1977-79; dir. automotive racing programs PPG Industries, Cleve., 1980-81; owner Holden Motor Co., Inc., Phoenix, 1986—; founder, pres. Solar and Electric Racing Assn., Phoenix, 1990—; cons. motorsports history BBC, Birmingham, Eng., motorsports sales White Way Sign Co., Chgo., 1985—; bd. dirs., co-founder Nat. Auto Racing Hist. Soc., Cleve., 1979—; lectr. arthritis symposium Boswell Hosp./Sun Found., Phoenix, 1983; founder APS Solar & Electric 500 Auto Race, 1990—. Author: The Arthritis Survival Book, 1983; producer, dir. (video prodn.) The Racing Cars and Craft of Myron Stevens, 1981; inventor, patentee auto tire design; contbr. articles to profl. jours. Adv. bd. Harrington Arthritis Research Ctr., Phoenix, 1984; mem. New England Hist. Genealogical Soc. Mem. Vet. Motor Car Club Am. (nat. bd. govs. 1980—), Automotive Svc. Assn., Optimistic Arthritics Club (v.p. 1984-85). Republican. Office: Solar & Electric Racing Assn 11811 N Tatum Blvd Ste 3031 Phoenix AZ 85028-1630

HOLDEN, GEORGE FREDRIC, brewing company executive, public policy specialist, consultant; b. Lander, Wyo., Aug. 29, 1937; s. George Thiel Holden and Rita (Meyer) Zulpo; m. Dorothy Carol Capper, July 5, 1959; children: Lorilyn, Sherilyn, Tamilyn. BSChemE, U. Colo., 1959, MBA in Mktg., 1974. Adminstr. plastics lab. EDP, indsl chems. plant, prodn. process engring., tool control supervision, aerospace (Minuteman, Polaris, Sparrow), Parlin, N.J., Salt Lake City, Cumberland, Md., 1959-70; by-product sales, new market and new product devel., resource planning and devel. and pub. rels. Adolph Coors Co., Golden, Colo., 1971-76; dir. econ. affairs corp. pub. affairs dept., 1979-84, dir. pub. affairs rsch., 1984-86; owner Phoenix Enterprises, Arvada, 1986—; mgr. facilities engring. Coors Container Co., 1976-79; instr. brewing, by-products utilization and waste mgmt. U. Wis.; cons., speaker in field. Mem. bd. economists Rocky Mountain News, 1990—; mem. Heritage Found. Ann. Guide to Pub. Policy Expert, 1987—, Speakers Bur., Commn. on the Bicentennial U.S. Constitution, 1991-93; del. Colo. Rep. Conv., 1976—; bd. dirs. Colo. Pub. Expenditures Coun., 1983-86, Nat. Speakers Assn., Colo. Speakers Assn. (bd. dirs. 1987-90, 91-93), Nat. Assn. Bus. Economists, Colo. Assn. Commerce and Industry Ednl. Found. Sr. fellow budget policy Independence Inst. Colo. "ThinkTank". Mem. U.S. Brewers Assn. (chmn. by-products com., Hon. Gavel, 1975), Am. Inst. Indsl. Engrs. (dir. 1974-78). Co-author: Secrets of Job Hunting, 1972; The Phoenix Phenomenon, 1984, TOTAL Power of ONE in America, 1991; contbr. articles to Chem. Engring. mag., 1968-76, over 350 published articles, white papers in field; over 900 speeches, 250 appearances on radio talk shows nationwide. Home: 6463 Owens St Arvada CO 80004-2732 Office: Phoenix Enterprises PO Box 1900 Arvada CO 80001-1900

HOLDEN, JEFFREY DONALD, radio executive; b. Chgo., Aug. 5, 1956; s. Donald Marelli and Eileen Joan (Rancour) H.; m. Deborah Marie Lehner, June 30, 1979; children: Derrick Robert, Bennett Thomas. BA, No. Ill. U., 1978. Account exec. Sta. WIFR-TV, Rockford, Ill., 1978-79; media buyer Avalanche Advt., Chgo., 1979-80; account exec. Sta. WLAK-FM, Chgo., 1980-81, John Blair & Co., Chgo., 1981-82, RKO Radio Sales, Chgo., 1982-83; office mgr. RKO Radio Sales, Dallas, 1983-85; gen. sales mgr. Stas. KSFM & KSMJ-Duffy Broadcasting, Sacramento, 1985-88, Sta. KQPT-FM-Duchossois Comm., Sacramento, 1988-92; gen. mgr. Stas. KRFD-FM & KMYC-AM, Sacramento, 1992—; mem. steering com. Radio Advt. Bur. Mng. Sales Conf., Dallas, 1989. Mem. Sacramento Advt. Club (pres. 1989-90). Roman Catholic. Office: Stas KRFD-FM & KMYC-AM 1605 Simpson Ln Marysville CA 95901

HOLDEN, RONALD MICHAEL, writer; b. Portland, Oreg., July 27, 1942; s. Max Michael and Gertrude Julie (Isaac) H.; m. Glenda Mary McPherson, Dec. 18, 1965; children: Michael, David, Dominic. BA, Yale U., 1963. Newsman KGW Radio & TV, Portland, 1967-71; news mgr. King TV, Seattle, Wash., 1971-74; news dir. WJZ TV, Balt., 1974-76; exec. editor The Weekly, Seattle, 1977-79; cons. Weyerhaeuser Co., Tacoma, Wash., 1979-81, Stimson Lane Wine & Spirits, Woodinville, Wash., 1989-90; pres. Holden Pacific, Inc., Seattle, 1981—; designed/escorted various nationally marketed tours of French wine country, 1985—. Author: Northwest Wine Country, 1989, Touring Wine Country/Washington, 1987, Touring Wine County/Oregon, 1984; contbr. articles, columns to regional tour publs. and newspapers. With U.S. Army, 1964-67, Fed. Republic Germany. Recipient Gov.'s award Internat. Brotherhood of Knights of the Vine, Oreg., 1985. Mem. French-Am. C. of C. (founding bd. dirs.), Wash. Wine Writers (founder, Wine of Yr. award), Wash. Wine Inst., Oreg. Winegrowers Assn., Soc. Wine Educators, Seattle Enol. Soc., Les Amis du Vin (bd. dirs. Seattle chpt.). Home and Office: 814 35th Ave Seattle WA 98122-5206

HOLDEN, WILLIAM WILLARD, insurance executive; b. Akron, Ohio, Oct. 5, 1958; s. Joseph McCullem and Lettitia (Roderick) H.; m. Kim Homan, Aug. 31, 1985; 1 child, Jennifer Catharine. BA, Colgate U., 1981. Crime ins. trainee Chubb & Son, Inc., N.Y.C., 1981-82; exec. protection dept. mgr. Chubb & Son, Inc., San Jose, Calif., 1982-85, Woodland Hills, Calif., 1986-91; v.p., mgr. Fin. Svcs. Group, Inc., Rollins, Hudig, Hall, L.A., 1991—; tng. analyst Chubb & Son, Inc., Warren, N.J., 1985-86. Co-author manual: Chubb Claims Made Training, 1985; contbr. articles to Colgate alumni mag. Mgr., coach Campbell (Calif.) Little League, 1983-85; pres. Le Parc Homeowners Assn., Simi Valley, Calif., 1987-89; mem. Community Assn. Inst., L.A., 1986—. Mem. Profl. Liability Underwriting Soc. (L.A. steering com.). Republican. Office: Rollins Hudig Hall of So Calif Universal City CA 91608

HOLDER, JENNIFER LYNN, ecologist, toxicologist; b. San Francisco, Oct. 21, 1961; d. Alder James Holder and Martha (Sanborn) Hassenplug; m. Marco Antonio Rigonati, June 3, 1989; 1 child, Alessandra. BA, U. Calif., Santa Cruz, 1983; PhD, U. Calif., Berkeley, 1991. Rsch. asst., teaching asst. U. Calif., Berkeley, 1984-90, lectr., 1990; lectr. Holy Names Coll., Oakland, Calif., 1991; ecologist, toxicologist Jacobs Engring., Pasadena, Calif., 1991—; cons. in field, 1991—. Recipient Geraldine K. Lindsay award AAAS, 1989. Mem. Soc. Environ. Toxicology and Chemistry, Animal Behavior Soc., Soc. Am. Naturalists, Soc. for the Study of Evolution, Sigma Xi. Office: Jacobs Engring 2530 Arnold Dr Martinez CA 94553

HOLDERMAN, JOHN LORAN, financial broker; b. Dixon, Ill., Mar. 5, 1944; s. Donald Kenneth and E.J. (Huggins) H.; divorced; 1 child, Angela Dyan. Student, East Moline (Ill.) Jr. Coll., 1983. Gen. mgr. Progressive Graphics, Oreg., Ill., 1972-76; with Storm Printing, Dallas, 1976-81; owner resale shop Rockford, Ill., 1981-90; pres. JLH Enterprises, Chula Vista, Calif., 1992—. With USN, 1969-72, Vietnam. Democrat. Roman Catholic. Home: 1329 3d Ave # 437 Chula Vista CA 91911-4396

HOLDSWORTH, JANET NOTT, women's health nurse; b. Evanston, Ill., Dec. 25, 1941; d. William Alfred and Elizabeth Inez (Kelly) Nott; children: James William, Kelly Elizabeth, John David. BSN with high distinction, U. Iowa, 1963; M of Nursing, U. Wash., 1966. RN, Colo. Staff nurse U. Colo. Hosp., Denver, 1963-64, Presbyn. Hosp., Denver, 1964-65, Grand Canyon Hosp., Ariz., 1965; asst. prof. U. Colo. Sch. Nursing, Denver, 1966-71; counseling nurse Boulder PolyDrug Treatment Ctr., Boulder, 1971-77; pvt. duty nurse Nurses' Official Registry, Denver, 1973-82; cons. nurse, tchr. parenting and child devel. Teenage Parent Program, Boulder Valley Schs., Boulder, 1980-88; bd. dirs., treas. Nott's Travel, Aurora, Colo., 1980—; instr., nursing coord. ARC, Boulder, 1979-90, instr., nursing tng. specialist, 1980-82. Mem. adv. bd. Boulder County Lamaze Inc., 1980-88 ; mem. adv. com. Child Find and Parent-Family, Boulder, 1981-89; del. Rep. County State Congl. Convs., 1972-92, sec. 17th Dist. Senatorial Com., Boulder, 1982-92; vol. Mile High ARC, 1980; vol. chmn. Mesa Sch. PTO, Boulder, 1982-92, bd. dirs., 1982—, v.p., 1983—; elder Presbyn. ch. Mem. ANA, Colo. Nurses Assn. (bd. dirs. 1975-76, human rights com. 1981-83, dist. pres. 1974-76), Coun. Intracultural Nurses, Sigma Theta Tau, Alpha Lambda Delta. Republican. Home: 1550 Findlay Way Boulder CO 80303-6922 Office: Teenage Parent Program 3740 Martin Dr Boulder CO 80303-5499

HOLE, ROBERT BRUCE, computer consultant and programmer; b. Ann Arbor, Mich., Jan. 3, 1943; s. R. Duncan and Elizabeth A. (Reed) H.; m. Ellen K. Ridenour, Jan. 26, 1962 (div. Aug. 1988); children: Robert B. Jr., Michael E. AA, DeAnza Coll., Cupertino, Calif., 1969; student, U. Calif., Berkeley, 1969-71. Real estate broker, Calif., 1964-74, Assoc. Nat. Brokers, Walnut Creek, Calif., 1974-80, Marcus Co., Walnut Creek, 1980-82, Damé Co., San Ramon, Calif., 1982-83; computer cons. and programmer Specialized Computing, Pleasant Hill, Calif., 1983—. Author computer programs The Closer, Ad Traker. Office: Specialized Computing 3333 Vincent Rd Ste 207 Pleasant Hill CA 94523

HOLL, MARY KATHERINE, education educator; b. Chgo., Aug. 20, 1958; d. Richard Fredrick and Ann Marie (Schiller) H. BA, Concordia U., River Forest, Ill., 1980; MA, Adelphi U., Garden City, N.Y., 1985. Tchr. Martin Luther High Sch., Maspeth, N.Y., 1980-84; coach St. Francis Coll., Brooklyn Heights, N.Y., 1984-85; assoc. prof. edn., dir. athletics Concordia U., Irvine, Calif., 1985—. Mem. AAHPERD, U.S. Volleyball Assn. (coaching accreditation program level 2), NAIA (exec. com., sec.), Golden State Athletic Conf. (exec. com., sec.). Lutheran. Office: Concordia Univ 1530 Concordia Irvine CA 92715-3299

HOLLAND, H. RUSSEL, federal judge; b. 1936; m. Diane Holland; 3 children. BBA, U. Mich., 1958, LLB, 1961. With Alaska Ct. System, Anchorage, 1961, U.S. Atty.'s Office, Dept. Justice, Anchorage, 1963-65; assoc. Stevens & Savage, Anchorage, 1965-66; ptnr. Stevens, Savage, Holland, Erwin & Edwards, Anchorage, 1967-68; sole practice Anchorage, 1968-70; ptnr. Holland & Thornton, Anchorage, 1970-78, Holland, Thornton & Trefry, Anchorage, 1978, Holland & Trefry, Anchorage, 1978-84, Trefry & Brecht, Anchorage, 1984; judge U.S. Dist. Ct. Alaska, Anchorage, 1984—. Mem. ABA, Alaska Bar Assn., Anchorage Bar Assn. Office: US Dist Ct 222 E 7th Ave # 54 Anchorage AK 99513-7545*

HOLLAND, HENRY NORMAN, marketing consultant; b. Norfolk, Va., Oct. 13, 1947; s. Henry Norman and Edith Leigh (O'Bryan) H.; m. Linda Diane Eggerking, June 1, 1968 (div. 1983); 1 child, Steven Frederick; m. Jane Elizabeth Bond, Dec. 27, 1983. BA, Chaminade Coll., 1972; MBA, U. Hawaii, 1977. Lic. ins. broker, Calif. Mgr. Chevron USA, Honolulu, 1965-75; dealer Dillingham Chevron, Honolulu, 1975-82; gen. mgr. Barcat Enterprises, San Francisco, 1982-85; counselor E.K. Williams of San Francisco, 1985; gen. mgr. Woodside (Calif.) Oil Co., 1985-88; cons. Holland Bus. Mgmt., San Francisco, 1989—; dir. Chevron Fed. Credit Union, Honolulu, 1971-75. Contbr. articles to profl. jours.; author tng. seminars, newsletter, safety programs. Loaned mgr. United Way, Honolulu, 1972; nation chief YMCA Indian Guides, Kailua, Hawaii, 1976-79. With U.S. Army, 1967-69, Vietnam. Mem. English Speaking Union, Met. League San Francisco Symphony, Golden Gate Nat. Parks Assn., San Francisco Mus. Soc., Chevron Adv. Coun., Nat. Assn. Enrolled Agts., Calif. Assn. Enrolled Agts., VFW. Republican. Presbyterian. Office: 1700 Broadway # 506 San Francisco CA 94109

HOLLAND, JOHN RAY, minister; b. Fisher County, Tex., June 3, 1933; s. John Ramsey and Josephine Pearce (Cooper) H.; m. Doris Jean Hines, Jan. 1, 1953; children: Bradley Ray, Johnnea Lee, John Barton, Joanna Joy. Grad., L.I.F.E. Bible Coll., 1953; DD, Oral Roberts Coll., 1981; LLD (hon.), Oral Roberts U., 1989. Ordained to ministry Internat. Ch. of Foursquare Gospel, 1980. Pastor Internat. Ch. of Foursquare Gospel, 1954-77; pres. L.I.F.E. Bible Coll., Can., 1969-75; supr. S.W. dist. Internat. Ch. of Foursquare Gospel, 1977-89; pres. Internat. Ch. of Foursquare Gospel, L.A., 1989—; supr. Western Can. region Internat. Ch. of Foursquare Gospel, 1969-75, mem. internat. bd., L.A., 1975-77, pres. L.I.F.E. Inc., 1989—, chief exec. officer internat. bd., 1989—; pastor Angelus Temple, 1975-77. Editor Advance, 1988—. Bd. dirs. Madge Meadwell Founds., 1970-75. Mem. Am. Bible Soc. (bd. dirs. 1989—), World Pentecostal Fellowship (bd. dirs. 1989—), Nat. Assn. Evangs. (bd. dirs. 1989—). Office: Internat Ch of the Foursquare Gospel 1910 W Sunset Blvd Los Angeles CA 90026-3247

HOLLAND, KENNETH JOHN, retired editor; b. Mpls., July 19, 1918; s. John Olaf and Olga Marie (Dahlberg) H.; m. Maurine M. Strom, Aug. 15, 1948; children: Laurence, Wesley. B.A. in Religion, Union Coll., Lincoln, Nebr., 1949; postgrad., Vanderbilt U. Div. Sch., 1964-69. Chemist Capitol Flour Mills, St. Paul, 1937-40; copy editor So. Pub. Assn., Nashville, 1949-51; asso. editor These Times, 1952-56, editor, from 1957; editor These Times (merged with Rev. and Herald Pub. Assn.), Washington, 1981—, Signs of the Times (merged with These Times), Boise, Idaho, 1984-93; ordained to ministry Seventh-day Adventist Ch., 1958; condr. editorial councils overseas, writers workshops, U.S. Author: books, the most recent being The Choice, 1977. Served with U.S. Army, 1941-43; with USAAF, 1943-45. Recipient Am. In God We Trust Family medal Family Found. Am., 1980, Disting. Service award Union Coll., Lincoln, 1984, Silver Angel award Religion in Media, 1986, 87, 88, 1990. Mem. Assoc. Ch. Press (award of merit 1976, 77, 78, 80, 85, 87, 89, Citation of Honor 1990), Ams. United for Separation Ch. and State, Religious Public Relations Council, Internat. Platform Assn. Republican. Club: Wexford Country, Hilton Head Island, S.C. Office: Signs of the Times Pacific Press Pub Assn PO Box 7000 Boise ID 83707-1000

HOLLAND, MICHAEL JAMES, computer services administrator; b. N.Y.C., Nov. 20, 1950; s. Robert Frederick and Virginia June (Wilcox) H.; Anita Garay, Jan. 5, 1981 (Aug. 1989); 1 child, Melanie. BA in Comparative Lit., Bklyn. Coll., 1972. Field med. technician 3rd Marine Div., Okinawa, Japan, 1976-77, 1st Marine Div., Camp Pendleton, Calif., 1978-79; clin. supr. Naval Hosp. Subic Day, Philippines, 1979-81; dept. head Tng. Ctr. USMCR, Johnson City, Tenn., 1981-84; clin. supr. No. Tng. Area, Okinawa, 1984-85, 3rd Marine Air Wing, Camp Pendleton, 1985-88; cons. Naval Regional Med. Command, San Diego, 1988-90; system analyst Naval Med. Info. Mgmt. Ctr. Detachment, San Diego, 1990-92; computer svcs. adminstr. U.S. Naval Hosp., Guam, 1993—. Mem. Fleet Res. Assn., Nat. City C. of C. (com. 1989-91), Assn. for Computing Machinery.

HOLLAND, ROBIN JEAN, personnel company executive; b. Chgo., June 22, 1942; d. Robert Benjamin and Dolores (Levy) Shaeffer; 1 child, Robert Gene. BA in Pub. Rels. magna cum laude, U. So. Calif., 1977. Account exec., pub. rels. firm, 1977-79, Mgmt. Recruiters, 1979; owner, operator Holland Exec. Search, Marina Del Rey, Calif., 1979—; pres. Bus. Communications, 1983—; cons. on outplacement to bus.; condr. seminars on exec. search; guest lectr. and instr. on exec. recruiting at community colls. Active Ahead with Horses. Recipient numerous local honors. Mem. Am. Coaster Enthusiasts, LK.A. Can., Mensa, Peruvian Paso Horse Owners N.Am. Office: Holland Exec Search 4748 Admiralty Way Ste 9774 Marina Del Rey CA 90295

HOLLAND, TOM, painter, educator; b. Seattle, Wash., June 15, 1936; m. Judy, 1958; children: Randolph, Brenden, Joel. Student, U. Calif.-Berkeley, 1954-56, Willamette U., Salem, Oreg., 1956-58, U. Calif.-Santa Barbara. Instr. San Francisco Art Inst., 1963-68, 1971-75; asst. prof. UCLA, 1968-70, U California, Berkeley, 1978-79, Cornish Inst., Seattle, Wash., 1978. Exhibited one-man shows Catholic U., Santiago, Chile, 1960, Richmond Art Ctr., Calif., 1962, Laynon Gallery, Palo Alto, Calif., 1963, 64, 65, Hansen Fuller Gallery, 1965, 74, Nicholas Wilder Gallery, L.A., 1965, 67, 69, 76, Ariz. State U., Tempe, 1968, Neuendorf Gallery, Cologne, Germany, 1970, Robert Elkon Gallery, N.Y.C., 1970, 71, Corcoran and Corcoran, Miami, 1972, Multiples, L.A., 1972, Knoedler Contemporary Art, N.Y.C., 1973, 75, Watson de Nagy Gallery, Houston, 1977, Smith Anderson Gallery, Palo Alto, Calif., 1978, Droll Kolbert Gallery, N.Y.C., 1978, San Francisco Art Inst., 1979, Corcoran Gallery, L.A., 1980, 83, 85, 87, 89, Charles Cowles Gallery, N.Y.C., 1981, 83, 84, 85, 88, Fuller Goldeen Gallery, San Francisco, 1982, The Greenberg Gallery, St. Louis, 1983, John Berggruen Gallery, 1984, 86, 88, 89; group shows San Francisco Art Inst., 1963, 67, San Francisco Mus. Modern Art, 1964, 70, La Jolla Mus. Calif., 1965, L.A. County Mus., 1966, Phila. Soc. Arts Invitational, 1968, Corcoran Mus., Washington, 1969, Mus. Modern Art, N.Y.C., 1970, Whitney Mus. Contemporary Art, 1970, 78, Albright-Knox Art Gallery, Buffalo, 1971, Walker Art Ctr., Mpls., 1972, Mus. Modern Art, N.Y.C., 1972, Whitney Mus. Am. Art, N.Y.C., 1973, Corcoran Biennial, Washington, 1975, Richmond Art Ctr., 1976, Nat. Collection Fine Arts, Washington, 1977, Mus. Modern Art, N.Y.C., 1981, Calif. Inst. Tech., Pasadena, 1982; represented permanent collections Oakland Mus. Calif., Stanford U., St. Louis City Mus., Larry Aldrich Mus., Ridgefield, Conn., Mus. Art, San Francisco, Mus. Modern Art, N.Y.C., Chgo. Art. Inst., Walker Art Ctr., Mpls., Guggenheim Mus., N.Y.C., Hirshhorn Mus., Washington, others. Grantee Nat. Endowment for Arts, 1975-76; Fulbright fellow, 1959-60; Guggenheim fellow, 1979. Office: San Francisco Art Inst 800 Chestnut St San Francisco CA 94133-2299 also: 8957 Norma Pl Los Angeles CA 90069

HOLLATZ, SARAH SCHOALES, rancher, business owner; b. N.Y.C., Sept. 1, 1944; d. Dudley Nevison and Virginia Jocelyn (Vanderlip) Schoales; m. David Earl Hollatz, Jan. 27, 1968 (div. June 1985); children: Melissa Virginia, Peter David. BS, U. Wis., 1966; postgrad., U. So. Calif., L.A., 1966. Copywriter Max W. Becker Advt., Long Beach, Calif., 1966-67; advt. dir. officers news USN, Coronado, Calif., 1968-70; with syndicate dept. Morgan Stanley & Co., N.Y.C., 1970-72; lay-out asst. North Castle News, Armonk, N.Y., 1972-75; performer, writer Candy Band, Pound Ridge, N.Y., 1975-82; owner, mgr. Circle Bar Guest Ranch, Utica, Mont., 1983—; bd. dirs. Park Inn, Lewistown, Mont. Artist, composer: Play Me a Song, 1978, Going Home, 1980; composer: (mus. play) Elsie Piddock, 1979, Secret Garden, 1981, Windows, 1989. Soloist Hobson (Mont.) Meth. Ch., 1983—; founder What the Hay, Utica, 1990—. Mem. Mont. Emergency Med. Assn. (bd. dirs. 1990—), Dude Rancher's Assn. (bd. dirs. 1989—). Episcopalian. Home and Office: Circle Bar Guest Ranch Utica MT 59452

HOLLEMAN, ROBERT WOOD, JR., electrical engineer, educator; b. Lakeland, Fla., Apr. 20, 1931; s. Robert Wood Sr. and Anne Carolyn (Jensen) H.; m. Margaret Ann Phillippi, Dec. 20, 1953; children: David Leigh, Linda Lee Demer, Christopher Wood. BSEE in Communications, Auburn (Ala.) U., 1952. Registered elec. engr. Ariz., Fla.; registered quality engr. Calif.; cert. reliability engr. Am. Soc. Quality Control. Engr. Fla. Power Corp., Winter Park, 1955-57, Sperry Rand Corp., 1957-71; engr. Hughes Aircraft Co., Tucson, 1971-89, ret., 1989; profl. engr. A.E.S. Inc., Tucson, 1973—; part-time engr. Multiple Mirror Telescope Obs., Tucson, 1987—; tchr. Pima Community Coll., Tucson, 1975—, U. Ariz. Coll. of Architecture, Tucson, 1977—. Lt. (j.g.) USN, 1948-55. Mem. IEEE (sr., treas. 1982). Episcopalian. Home and Office: 6545 N Camino De Michael Tucson AZ 85718-1941

HOLLENBAUGH, KENNETH M., academic administrator, geology consultant; b. Fostoria, Ohio, Sept. 8, 1934; s. Kenneth and Lavera Ann H.; m. Sue F. George, July 21, 1961; children: Bradley, Gregory, David. BS, Bowling Green State U., 1957; MS, U. Idaho, 1959, PhD, 1968; EM, Harvard U., 1979. Exploration geologist Idaho Bur. of Mines, Moscow, 1958-59; mine engr. Kaiser Cement & Gypsum, Bellingham, Wash., 1960-63; minr mgr. Kaiser Steel Corp., Cushinbury, Calif., 1963-66; rsch. geologist Kaiser Steel Corp., Big Bear, Calif., 1965-66; mineral evaluator Kaiser Steel Corp., Fontana, Calif., 1966-68; rsch. geologist Idaho Bur. Mines, Moscow, 1966-68; prof. Geology Boise State U., 1968—, dean, Grad. Coll., 1975—, assoc. exec. v.p., 1980—. Mem. Boise City Planning & Zoning Com., 1972-76, Boise City Design Review Com., Gov's Task Force Edn., Gov's Task Force on Environment, 1980. Pvt. US Army, 1959-63. Recipient Outstanding Tchr. award Soc. Mining Engrs., 1975, Contbns. to Idaho award Idaho Atty. Gen., 1978. Mem. Am. Inst. Mining Engrs. (chmn.), Am. Assn. for Advancement Sci., Geological Soc. of Am., Idaho Assn. Profl. Geologists (pres., v.p.), Idaho Quartzite Corp. (v.p.), Boise Water Corp.(v.p.), Soc. Mining Engrs., Aurum Corp (v.p.), Rotary Club of Am. Office: Boise State U 1910 University Dr Boise ID 83725-0001

HOLLIDAY, DOC, JR. See EASTMAN, RICHARD DARE

HOLLIGER, FRED LEE, oil company executive; b. Kansas City, Mo., Feb. 4, 1948; s. Ronald and Margorie (Klein) H.; m. Susan Lynn Harris, Oct. 6, 1972; children: Meredith, Allison, Lauren. BS in Petroleum Engring., U. Mo., Rolla, 1970; postgrad., U. Mich., 1978. Petroleum engr. Transok Pipeline Co., Tulsa, 1971; reservoir engr. No. Natural Gas Co., Omaha, 1972-73; project mgr. No. Natural Gas Co., Lyons, Kans., 1974-76; area mgr. No. Natural Gas Co., Great Bend, Kans., 1977-79; gen. mgr. mktg. No. Natural Gas Co., Omaha, 1980-83, v.p. gas supply, 1984-85, v.p. mktg., 1986, pres., COO, 1987-88; exec. v.p., COO Giant Industries, Scottsdale, Ariz., 1989—; dir. Giant Industries. Mem. Nat. Petroleum Refining Assn.

(dir. 1990—), Desert Highlands Golf Club. Office: Giant Industries 23733 N Scottsdale Rd Scottsdale AZ 85255

HOLLINGER, DAVID ALBERT, historian, educator; b. Chgo., Apr. 25, 1941; s. Albert Jr. and Evelyn Dorothy (Steinmeier) H.; m. Joan Heifetz, Sept. 17, 1967; children: Jacob, Julia. BA, U. La Verne, 1963; MA, U. Calif., Berkeley, 1965, PhD, 1970. From asst. to assoc. prof. SUNY, Buffalo, 1969-77; prof. U. Mich., Ann Arbor, 1977-92, U. Calif., Berkeley, 1992—. Author: Morris R. Cohen and the Scientific Ideal, 1975, In the American Province, 1985. Guggenheim Found. fellow, 1983. Mem. Am. Hist. Assn., Am. Studies Assn., Soc. Am. Historians, Orgn. Am. Historians, History Sci. Soc. Office: Dept History U Calif Berkeley CA 94720

HOLLINGSWORTH, JOHN MARK, financial planner; b. Caripe, Venezuela, Jan. 9, 1957; s. Dean Wesley and Jessie (Mitchell) H.; m. Joanna Stocker, Aug. 9, 1980; children: Mindi Jo, Kaci Ann. BBA, Biola U., 1979. CFP. Asst. sales mgr. Wickes Furniture, Anaheim, Calif., 1980-82; account exec. Merrill Lynch, Fullerton, Calif., 1982-84; v.p. investments Prudential Securities, Anaheim, 1984—. Fin. advisor Martin Luther Hosp., Anaheim, 1990—; deacon Calvary Bapt. Ch., Yorba Linda, Calif., 1987—; mem. sch. bd. Calvary Christian Sch., Yorba Linda, 1991—; chmn. Stadium Bus. Forum, Anaheim, 1992. Republican. Home: 4452 Rainbow Ln Yorba Linda CA 92686 Office: Prudential Securities 2390 E Orangewood Ave # 100 Anaheim CA 92806

HOLLINGSWORTH, MARGARET CAMILLE, financial services administrator, consultant; b. Washington, Feb. 20, 1929; d. Harvey Alvin and Margaret Estelle (Head) Jacob; m. Robert Edgar Hollingsworth, July 14, 1960 (div. July 1980); children: William Lee, Robert Edgar Hollingsworth Jr., Barbara Camille, Bradford Damion. AA, Va. Intermont Coll., 1949. Bookkeeper Fred A. Smith Real Estate, Washington, 1949-53; adminstrv. mgr. Airtronic, Inc., Bethesda, Md., 1953-61; pers. adminstr. Sears Roebuck, Washington, 1973-74; adminstrv. mgr., communication mgr. Garvin GuyButler Corp., San Francisco, 1980-88, exec. sec., pers. mgr., 1989—; assoc. Robert Hollingsworth Nuclear Cons., Walnut Creek, Calif., 1975-79. Mem., bd. dirs. Civic Arts, Walnut Creek, 1975. Recipient Spl. Recognition award AEC, 1974. Mem. Commonwealth Club, Beta Sigma Phi (pres. 1954). Democrat. Presbyterian. Home: 1108 Limeridge Dr Concord CA 94518-1923 Office: Garvin GuyButler Corp 456 Montgomery St Ste 1900 San Francisco CA 94104-1252

HOLLINGSWORTH, MEREDITH BEATON, clinical nurse specialist; b. Danvers, Mass., Oct. 5, 1941; d. Allan Cameron and Arlene Margaret (Jerue) Beaton; m. William Paul Hollingsworth, Nov. 19, 1983; stepchild, Brendon R. Diploma, R.I. Hosp. Sch. Nursing, Providence, 1968; BS in Nursing, U. Ariz., 1976; MS in Human Resource Mgmt., Golden Gate U., 1984; enterostomal therapy nursing program, U. Tex., 1988; postgrad., U. N.Mex., 1989—. Cert. enterostomal therapy nurse, health edn. specialist. Commd. ensign USN, 1968, advanced through grades to lt. comdr., 1979; charge nurse USN, USA, PTO, 1968-88; command ostomy nurse, head ostomy clinic Naval Hosp. Portsmouth, Va., 1985-88; pres., chief exec. officer Enterostomal Therapy Nursing Edn. and Tng. Cons. (ETNetc), Rio Rancho, N.Mex., 1989-90; mgr. clin. svcs. we. area Support Systems Internat., Inc., Charleston, S.C., 1990-92; pres., CEO Paumer Assocs. Internat., Inc., Rio Rancho, N.Mex., 1992—; nurse, clin. educator Presbyn. Health Care System, Albuqueque, 1993—. Mem. adminstrv. bd. Baylake United Meth. Ch., Virginia Beach, 1980-83; deacon St. Paul's United Ch., Rio Rancho; active Am. Cancer Soc. Mem. Wound, Ostomy and Continence Nurses Soc. (govt. affairs nat. com., govt. affairs com. Rocky Mountain region, pub. rels. com., pres. Rocky Mountain region), United Ostomy Assn., World Coun. Enterostomal Therapists, N.Mex. Soc. Healthcare Edn. and Tng. of Am. Hosp. Assn., N.Mex. Health Care Assn., Care Star Network. Republican. Office: PO Box 44395 Rio Rancho NM 87174-4395

HOLLINGTON, JAMES EDWARD, lawyer; b. Blakely, Ga., Oct. 4, 1949; s. Edward E. and Ruby Louise (White) H.; m. Deborah Ann Huelsmann, Jan. 14, 1977; 1 child, Ryan Edward. BS in History, Troy (Ala.) State U., 1971; JD, U. Ala., 1974. Bar: N.Mex. 1976, U.S. Dist. Ct. N.Mex. 1981, U.S. Ct. Appeal (10th cir.) 1987, U.S. Supreme Ct. 1989. Adminstr. Calhoun Meml. Hosp., Arlington, Ga., 1975-78; exec. dir. Albany (Ga.) Area Primary Health, 1978-80; pvt. practice Albuquerque, 1980—; mem. State Bd. of Fin., N.Mex., 1991-94, N.Mex. First, 1992; atty. Bernalillo County Bd. Commr., Albuquerque, 1987—. Bd. dirs. New Day, Inc., Albuquerque, 1988—. Mem. ABA, State Bar of N.Mex., Albuquerque Bar Assn. Democrat. Home: 1824 Camino Raso NW Albuquerque NM 87107

HOLLIS, DEAN, food products executive; b. Clearwater, Fla., May 4, 1960; s. Mark C. and Lynn (Darracott) H.; m. Darla Deines, Aug. 1, 1987; children: Darrica Lyn, David William. BS in Psychology, Stetson U., 1982. Supr. Ga. Pacific, Houston, 1982-83; dist. mgr. Ga. Pacific, Atlanta, 1983-85; sales planning mgr. The TreeSweet Cos., Houston, 1985-86; regional mgr. The TreeSweet Cos., Atlanta, 1986-87, Conagra Frozen Foods, Atlanta, 1987-88; salesplanning mgr. Conagra Frozen Foods, St. Louis, 1988-89; dir. sales S.E. Conagra Frozen Foods, Atlanta, 1989-90; dir. sales west Conagra Frozen Foods, Scottsdale, Ariz., 1990-92, v.p. sales west, 1992—. Bd. advisors Stetson U., Deland, Fla., 1988—. Office: Conagra Frozen Foods 1400 E Southern Ave # 250 Tempe AZ 85282

HOLLISON, ROBERT VICTOR, JR., physician, medical executive; b. Honolulu, Nov. 9, 1947; s. Robert Victor and Gladys (Yamanoha) H.; m. Kathleen Mitsu Toyama, Mar. 9, 1968; children: Renee, Keith, Dawn. BA, U. Hawaii, 1969; MD, U. Wash., 1973. Diplomate Am. Bd. Internal Medicine, Am. Bd. Family Practice, Am. Bd. Geriatric Medicine; cert. FAA flight examiner, FAA med. rev. officer for drug screening. Various to chief resident Madigan Army Med. Ctr., Ft. Lewis, Wash., 1975-76; dir. residency tng. Madigan Army Med. Ctr., Ft. Lewis, 1980-82; clin. asst. prof. of family medicine U. Wash. Sch. Medicine, Seattle, 1980-82; chief Hawaii Kai Straub Clinic, Honolulu, 1982-84; pvt. practice Univ. Family Medicine, Honolulu, 1983—; med. dir., cons. Hawaii Job Corps, Honolulu, 1983—; med. dir. Comprehensive Home Svcs. of Hawaii, Honolulu, 1991—; comdr. Tripler USAR Hosp. Augmentation, Honolulu, 1991—; med. dir. The Queen's Health Care Plan, Inc./Island Care, Honolulu, 1991—; asst. prof. U. Hawaii Sch. Medicine, 1982—; med. dir. Island Nursing Home/Oahu Care Facility, Honolulu, 1987—, Occupational Medicine-Kapiolani Med. Ctr. for Women and Children, Honolulu, 1990—. Contbg. author: Family Medicine: Principles and Practices, 1983. Mem. community rels. coun. Hawaii Job Corps, Honolulu, 1985—; mem. Am. Cancer Soc., Honolulu, 1984-86, Hawaii Kai Neighborhood Bd. # 1, Honolulu, 1983-86, chmn. health and safety com., 1983-85. Col. U.S. Army, 1970—. Named to Outstanding Young Men of Am., 1978, 84. Fellow Am. Coll. Physicians, Am. Acad. Family Physicians; mem. Hawaii Acad. Family Physicians (pres. 1992—, pres.-elect 1991-92), Am. Coll. Physician Execs., Hawaii Med. Assn., Res. Officer Assn., Phi Beta Kappa. Office: Univ Family Medicine 1904 University Ave Honolulu HI 96822

HOLLISTER, RIPLEY ROBERT, physician; b. Bryan, Tex., Sept. 10, 1955; s. Robert H. and Dana R. Hollister; m. Norma H. Hollister, Nov. 5, 1977; children: Bethany, Justin, Noelle. BS, U. Calif., Irvine, 1977; MD, U. So. Calif., 1982. Diplomate Am. Bd. Family Practice, Geriatrics. Intern, then resident in family practice Wyo. Med. Ctr., Wyo. Med. Ctr. and U. Wyo., 1982-85; attending physician McNairy County Gen. Hosp., Selmer, Tenn., 1985-90, chief of staff, 1989-90; county med. examiner McNairy County Sheriff Dept., Selmer, 1987-90; pvt. practice Ramer, Tenn., 1985-90, Brush, Colo., 1990—; attending physician East Morgan County Hosp., Brush, 1990-91, Penrose Hosp., St. Francis Hosp., 1992—; family health cons. Ind. Appeal newspaper, Selmer, 1987-90. Elder, ch. pioneer Country Ch. of Foursquare Gospel, Ramer, 1988, Mount Vernon Cumberland Presbyn. Ch., Ramer, 1989-90; active Austin Bluffs Assembly of God Ch., 1992, bd. deacons, 1993; vol. Heritage Dancers White House Ranch, Colorado Springs, Colo., 1992. Mem. Am. Med. Soc., Colo. Med. Soc., Christian Med. Dental Soc. Office: 2141 N Academy Circle # 101 Colorado Springs CO 80909

HOLLOWAY, CINDY, mortgage company executive; b. Queens, N.Y., Aug. 8, 1960; d. Richard Stephen and Beverly Bunny (Harris) Tannenbaum; m. David Milton Holloway (div. Mar. 1986); 1 child, Benjamin Jerome. BA, Calif. State U., Fullerton, 1981. Lic. real estate broker. Waitress Bob's Big Boy, San Bernardino, Calif., 1984-85; receptionist RNG Mortgage Co., San Bernardino, 1985; loan processor Quality Mortgage Co., Colton, Calif., 1985-88, loan officer, 1988-91; loan officer RNG Mortgage, 1991-92; v.p., br. mgr. Mountain West Fin., 1992—. Mem. San Bernardino Bd. Realtors (spl. events com. 1988—, comm. com. 1990—), Nat. Trust for Hist. Preservation, San Bernardino Execs. Assn., Assn. Profl. Mortgage Women (dir. 1989-90, v.p. 1992-93, Affiliate of Yr. 1990). Home: PO Box 3187 Crestline CA 92325-3187

HOLLOWAY, DAVID JAMES, political science educator; b. Dublin, Ireland, Oct. 13, 1943; came to U.S., 1983; s. James Joseph and Gertrude Mary (Kennedy) H.; m. Arlene Jean Smith, June 12, 1976; children: James, Ivor. MA, PhD, Cambridge (Eng.) U., 1964. Asst. lectr. U. Lancaster (Eng.), 1967-69; rsch. assoc. Inst. for Strategic Studies, London, 1969-70; lectr. U. Edinburgh (Scotland), 1970-84, reader, 1984-86; prof. Stanford (Calif.) U., 1986-91, co-dir. Ctr. Internat. Security and Arms Control, 1991—; dir. internat. rels. program Stanford U., 1989—. Author: The Soviet Union and the Arms Race, 1983; co-author: (with S. Drell and P. Farley) The Reagan Strategic Defense Initiative, 1985. Bd. dirs. Ploughshares Found., San Francisco, 1989—. Mem. Am. Polit. Sci. Assn., Am. Assn. for the Advancement of Slavic Studies. Home: 710 Torreya Ct Palo Alto CA 94303-4160 Office: Stanford U Ctr Internat Security Arms Control 320 Galvez St Stanford CA 94305

HOLLOWAY, GEORGE ALLEN, JR., physician, educator; b. N.Y.C., Oct. 14, 1938; s. George Allen and Betsey (Paddock) H.; children: Mara, Brett. B.A. in Chinese Studies, Yale U., 1960; M.D., Harvard U., 1964. Diplomate Am. Bd. Internal Medicine. Fellow in pathology Mass. Gen. Hosp., Boston, 1964-65; intern, then resident I UCLA Med. Ctr., 1965-67; resident II U. Wash. Hosp., Seattle, 1967-68; USPHS fellow in nephrology U. Wash. Hosp., 1968-69; chief dept. medicine U.S. Army Hosp., Camp Zama, Japan, 1969-72; from asst. to assoc. prof. Ctr. Bioengring., U. Wash., Seattle, 1972-88; dir. vascular lab. Maricopa Med. Ctr., 1988—, pres. med. staff, 1990-92, dir. med. rsch. , 1992—; cons. Nuclear Pacific/Med Pacific, Seattle, 1978—; lectr. local and nat. vascular disease and wound healing; adj. prof. of Bioengineering Ariz. State U., 1992—. Contbr. articles to profl. jours., chpts. to books. Developer laser doppler velocimeter, 1976. Med. dir. Pacific West Ski Patrol, Snoqualmie Pass, Wash., 1982-88. Served to maj. U.S. Army, 1969-72. USPHS grantee, 1976; recipient Career Devel. award USPHS, 1980-85. Mem. Am. Assn. Advancement Med. Instrumentation, Biomed. Engring. Soc. (sr.), Am. Soc. Laser Medicine and Surgery, Soc. for Vascular Medicine and Biology, European Microcirculatory Soc., Western Vascular Soc. Home: 3314 E Rock Wren Rd Phoenix AZ 85044-8707 Office: Maricopa Med Center PO Box 5099 Phoenix AZ 85010-5099

HOLLOWAY, ROBERT ANTHONY, financial services executive; b. Oklahoma City, Okla., Aug. 30, 1946; s. Maurice Earl and Gertrude (VanHooser) H. BA in Psychology with honors, Chapman Coll., Orange, Calif., 1979; MA in Clin. Psychology, Chapman Coll., 1981; PhD in Clin. Psychology, Calif. Grad. Inst., L.A., 1982. Cert. sch. tchr. K-12, Calif., Wash., adult edn. tchr. Prodn. contr. Boeing Co., Seattle, 1967-70; pres., chief exec. officer Camelot Communications, Inc., Sacramento, 1986; prin. The Exec. Fin. Group, Sunnyvale, Calif., 1987—; cons. Great Expectations, L.A., 1986-87; presdl. staff duty selection U.S. Army, 1970. Head coach Pop Warner Football, Seattle, 1968-69; active in past various charitable orgns. Capt. U.S. Army, 1964-78. Decorated Purple Heart, Silver Star, Navy Commendation medal, Vietnamese Cross of Gallantry for Valor, others. Office: 872 Spinosa Dr Sunnyvale CA 94087-1865

HOLLOWAY, ROBERT WESTER, radiochemist; b. Morrilton, Ark., Jan. 3, 1945; s. Otho and Bessie Vance (Woolverton) H.; m. Mary Ella Hamel, Dec. 31, 1970; children: David, Jason. BS, Harding Coll., 1967; postgrad., U. Okla., 1968; PhD, U. Ark., 1977. Asst. prof. U. Ark., Pine Bluff, 1976-79; research chemist DuPont Corp., Aiken, S.C., 1979-81; supervisory chemist EPA, Las Vegas, 1981—. Contbr. articles to profl. jours. Served to capt. USAF, 1967-72. Mem. Am. Chem. Soc., Health Physics Soc., Toastmasters, Optimists. Republican. Home: 311 E Desert Rose Dr Henderson NV 89015-8107 Office: EPA PO Box 93478 Las Vegas NV 89193-3478

HOLLOWAY, WILLIAM J., JR., federal judge; b. 1923. A.B., U. Okla., 1947; LL.B., Harvard U., 1950. Ptnr. Holloway & Holloway, Oklahoma City, 1950-51; atty. Dept. Justice, Washington, 1951-52; assoc., ptnr. Crowe and Dunlevy, Oklahoma City, 1952-68; judge U.S. Ct. Appeals (10th cir.), Oklahoma City, 1968—; past chief judge U.S. Ct. Appeals 10th Cir., Oklahoma City. Mem. ABA, Fed. Bar Assn., Okla. Bar Assn., Oklahoma County Bar Assn. Office: US Ct Appeals 10th Circuit PO Box 1767 Oklahoma City OK 73101-1767

HOLLY, JAMES DOUGLAS, brokerage house executive; b. Fresno, Calif., May 29, 1952; s. Marvin R. and Loraine (Reilly) H.; m. Nancy M. Lombardi, Mar. 1, 1975; 1 child, Leanna M. BA, UCLA, 1975. CLU. Underwriter Prudential, Fresno, 1976-79; mgr. sales Northwestern Mut. Life, Fresno, 1980-83; brokerage mgr. Morris Ins. Svcs., Fresno, 1983-85; dist. mgr. Old N.W. Agts., Fresno, 1985—. Mem. Make-A-Wish Found., Rep. Nat. Com., Washington, 1992. Recipient spl. tribute Greater Valley Health Underwriters, 1989, Pioneer award Guard-A-Kid Program, 1992. Mem. Calif. Assn. Health (v.p. 1986), Calif. Assn. Life Underwriters (chmn. 1992-93), Fresno Life Underwriters (nat. committeeman 1991-93, Life Underwriter of Yr. 1992, John Olmstead award 1992), Prodrs. Dairy Bowl (pres. 1990-92), Vol. Bur., Fresno C. of C. (health com. 1992), Ram Huddle Club. Roman Catholic. Office: Old NW Agts 726 W Barstow # 101 Fresno CA 93704

HOLLY, JAN ELISE, mathematician; b. Boulder, Colo., Oct. 22, 1965; d. Richard Lee and Judith Carol (Yeltema) Hutson. BS in Math., U. N.Mex., 1986; MS in Math., U. Ill., 1989, PhD in Math., 1992. Rsch. assoc. Robert S. Dow Neurological Scis. Inst., Portland, Oreg., 1992—. Mem. Am. Math. Soc., Assn. Computing Machinery, Assn. for Symbolic Logic, Math. Assn. Am. Office: RS Doe Neurol Scis Inst 1120 NW 20th Ave Portland OR 97209-1595

HOLMAN, ARTHUR STEARNS, artist; b. Bartlesville, Okla., Oct. 25, 1926; s. Newton Davis and Barbara (Hendry) H. B.F.A., U. N.Mex., 1951; postgrad., Hans Hofmann Sch., 1951, Calif. Sch. Fine Arts, San Francisco, 1953. One-man shows include, Esther Robles Gallery, Los Angeles, 1960, David Cole Gallery, San Francisco, 1962, 80, De Young Mus., San Francisco, 1963, San Francisco Mus., 1963, Gumps Gallery, San Francisco, 1964, 65, 66, 69, 87, Marin Civic Ctr. Gallery, 1970, William Sawyer Gallery, San Francisco, 1971, 73, 74, 76, John Bolles Gallery, Santa Rosa, Calif., 1982, Braunstein, Quay Gallery, San Francisco, 1992; group exhbns. include, San Francisco Mus., 1960, 76, Downey Mus., Los Angeles, 1961, 50 Calif. Artists, Whitney Mus., N.Y.C., Walker Art Ctr., Albright-Knox Gallery, Des Moines Art Ctr., 1962, U.N.C. Annual, 1965, Smithsonian Instn., Washington, 1977, Coll. of Marin, 1983, Hall of Flowers, San Francisco, 1985, 86, 20th Century Landscape Drawings, De Young Mus., San Francisco, 1989, Jan Holloway Gallery, San Francisco, 1989; represented in permanent collections, San Francisco Mus., Oakland Mus., Mills Coll., Stanford U., Eureka Coll., Achenbach Found., San Francisco. Served with USAAF, 1945-46. Address: PO Box 72 Lagunitas CA 94938

HOLMAN, HALSTED REID, medical educator; b. Cleve., Jan. 17, 1925; s. Emile Frederic and Ann Peril (Purdy) H.; m. Barbara Marie Lucas, June 26, 1949 (div. July 9, 1982); children: Michael, Andrea, Alison; m. Diana Barbara Dutton, Aug. 10, 1985; 1 child, Geoffrey. Student, Stanford U., 1942-43, UCLA, 1943-44; MD, Yale U., 1949. Med. resident Montefiore Hosp., N.Y.C., 1952-55; staff physician Rockefeller Inst., N.Y.C., 1955-60; prof. medicine Stanford (Calif.) U., 1960—, chmn. dept. medicine, 1960-71, co-chief div. family and community medicine, 1987—, dir. clin. scholar program, 1969—, dir. Multipurpose Arthritis Ctr., 1977—; pres. Midpeninsula Health Svc., Palo Alto, Calif., 1975-80; mem. adv. bd. Calif Health Facilities Commn., Sacramento, 1978-81, Office Tech. Assessment, U.S. Congress, 1979-81, Inst. Advancement of Health, N.Y.C., 1982—; Guggenhime prof. medicine, 1960—. Author 1 book; contbr. numerous articles to profl. jours. Recipient Bauer Meml. award Arthritis and Rheumatism Found., N.Y., 1964. Master Am. Coll. Rheumatology; fellow ACP; mem. Assn. Am. Physicians, Am. Soc. Clin. Investigation (pres. 1970), Western Assn. Physicians (pres. 1966),. Democrat. Home: 747 Dolores St Stanford CA 94305-8427 Office: Stanford University Stanford Arthritis Ctr 701 Welch Rd Ste 3301 Palo Alto CA 94304-2203

HOLMAN, JOHN FOSTER, investment banker; b. Chgo., Dec. 11, 1946; s. William Judson and Evelyn Mae (Foster) H.; m. Paula Susan Anderson, Aug. 1, 1970 (div. Oct. 1978). BS, Ariz. State U., 1969, MBA, 1971, JD, 1975; Cert. Fin. Planner, Coll. for Fin. Planning, 1991. Bar: Ariz. 1975; cert. fin. planner; registered investment advisor; lic. fed. securities. Congl. legis. intern, 1971; trial atty. Johnson, Tucker, Jessen & Dake, Phoenix, 1975-78, Holman, Meador and Hergott, Phoenix, 1978-80; nat. mktg. dir. Franchise Fin. Corp. Am., Phoenix, 1980-87; mng. dir. Fin. Resource Group, Sausalito, Calif., 1987-89; pres. Holman Internat. Group, Phoenix, 1990—; CEO, Internat. Salvage Corp., 1992—; pres. Fin. Freedom Assocs., Ltd., Phoenix, 1992—; prin. John F. Holman, P.C., 1981—. Founder Am. Wellness Assn., 1989—; mem. camp com. YMCA, Phoenix, 1968—; life mem. Rep. Senatorial Inner Circle, 1984—, Senatorial Commn., 1991; mem. Rep. Presdl. Task Force, 1989—; elder Presbyn. Ch., 1970—; mem. Ariz. Acad. Town Halls, 1969—. Capt. U.S. Army, 1968-76. Recipient Presdl. Order of Merit, 1991. Mem. Fed. Bar Assn., State Bar Ariz., Sales and Mktg. Execs. Phoenix, Ariz. State U. Alumni Assn. (bd. dirs. 1975-81), Internat. Platform Assn., World Record Setting Am. Transcontinental Relay Team, Mt. Kenya Safari Club, Capitol Hill Club, Delta Sigma Pi, Pi Sigma Epsilon. Home and Office: 6530 N 16th St Ste 102 Phoenix AZ 85016-1311

HOLMAN, PAUL DAVID, plastic surgeon; b. Waynesboro, Va., Mar. 13, 1943; s. Wallace D. and Rosalie S. Holman; m. Victoria Lynn Holman, Mar. 1, 1986. B.A., U. Va., 1965; M.D., Jefferson Med. Coll., 1968. Intern, George Washington U. Hosp., 1968-69, resident in gen. surgery, 1969-70, 72-74; resident in plastic surgery Phoenix Plastic Surgery Residency, 1974-76; practice medicine specializing in plastic surgery, Phoenix, 1977—; mem. staff Good Samaritan Hosp., Phoenix, St. Joseph's Hosp., Phoenix, Phoenix Children's Hosp. Served to lt. comdr. USNR, 1970-72. Diplomate Am. Bd. Surgery, Am. Bd. Plastic Surgery. Mem. AMA, ACS, Am. Soc. Plastic and Reconstructive Surgeons, Phi Beta Kappa. Office: 2111 E Highland Ave Ste 105 Phoenix AZ 85016-4732

HOLMBERG, ANGELA BROWN, landscape architect; b. Norman, Okla., Dec. 22, 1956; d. Elbert Edwin and Betty Ruth (De Shazo) Brown; m. William Martin Holmberg, Oct. 8, 1983; 1 child, Daniel Brown. BA in Cartography, East Cen. U., 1979; MS in Landscape Architecture, Okla. State U., 1981. Registered landscape architect, Calif., Okla.; cert. irrigation auditor. Landscape architect Saunders-Thalden Assocs., St. Louis, 1984-86, Austin Tao & Assocs., St. Louis, 1986-87; landscape architect, project mgr. Halsey Design Group, San Diego, 1988-92; pvt. practice Ramona, Calif., 1992—. Mem. Am. Soc. Landscape Architects (sec. St. Louis chpt. 1985).

HOLMER, FREEMAN, retired public administrator; b. St. Paul, Nov. 3, 1917; s. Adolph Frederick and Esther Victoria (Freeman) H.; m. Marcia Kathleen Wright, Jan. 1, 1942; children: William E., Alan F. BA, Concordia Coll., Moorhead, Minn., 1938; MA, U. Oreg., 1946; postgrad., Columbia U., 1946-49. Instr. NYU, N.Y.C., 1946-49; from asst. prof. to assoc. prof. Willamette U., Salem, Oreg., 1949-59; dir. finance and adminstrn. State of Oreg., Salem, 1959-66; dir. environ. protection State of Wis., Madison, 1966-68; assoc. dir. Nat. Govs.' Conf., Washington, 1968-69; vice-chancellor adminstrn. State System of Higher Edn., Eugene, Oreg., 1969-79; govt. affairs coord. Eugene C. of C., 1979-84; city councilor City of Eugene, 1983-90. Editor: Suggested State Legislation, 1969; contbr. articles to profl. jours. Chmn. Western States Water Coun., Salt Lake City, 1965-66; mem. Nat. Coun. on Pub. Works Improvement, Washington, 1985-88, Nat. Coun. on Higher Edn. Systems, Boulder, Colo., 1973-76; pres. Young Republican Fedn. of Oreg., Salem, 1950-51; v.p. Eugene Arts Found., 1992—. Master sgt. U.S. Army, 1942-46. Mem. Town Club of Eugene, Eugene Swim & Tennis Club. Mem. United Ch. of Christ. Home: 996 Lariat Dr Eugene OR 97401-5148

HOLMES, ALBERT WILLIAM, JR., physician; b. Chgo., Feb. 3, 1932; s. Albert William and Eleanor Muir H.; m. Lois Ann Geiger, Sept. 4, 1954; children—Nancy, William, Elizabeth, Robert. Student, U. Chgo., 1947-49; B.A., Knox Coll., 1952; M.D., Western Res. U., 1956. Diplomate Am. Bd. Internal Medicine. Intern Presbyn. Hosp., Chgo., 1956-57; resident Presbyn.-St. Luke's Hosp., Chgo., 1957-59, 61-62; instr. U. Ill., Chgo., 1961-62, asst. prof., 1963-65, assoc. prof., 1966-68, prof. medicine, 1968-70; prof. medicine and microbiology Rush Med. Coll., Chgo., 1971-75; dir. sect. hepatology Rush-Presbyn.-St. Luke's Med. Center, Chgo., 1966-75; asso. chmn. dept. medicine Rush-Presbyn.-St. Luke's Med. Center, 1972-75, acting v.p. research affairs, 1973-74; prof., chmn. dept. internal medicine Tex. Tech U., Lubbock, 1975-83, prof. medicine, 1983-85; prof., chmn. dept. medicine U. Ill., Peoria, 1985-89; prof. medicine U. Calif., San Francisco, 1990—; chief medicine Valley Med. Ctr., 1990—. Contbr. articles in field to profl. jours. Served with U.S. Army, 1959-61. Recipient Alumni Achievement award Knox Coll., 1976; NIH spl. fellow, 1963-66. Fellow A.C.P.; mem. Am. Assn. Study Liver Diseases, Central Soc. Clin. Research, Alpha Omega Alpha. Presbyterian. Home: 1137 W Escalon Ave Fresno CA 93711-2018 Office: Dept of Med Valley Med Ctr Fresno CA 93702

HOLMES, BRUCE SCOTT, computer programmer, environmental cartographer; b. Glendale, Calif., Jan. 3, 1951; s. Kenneth John and Virginia (Waldron) H. AA, L.A. Pierce Coll., Woodland Hills, Calif., 1971; BA, Calif. State U., Northridge, 1974, MA, 1977. Cartographer U.S. Army C.E., Portland, Oreg., 1978-82, park ranger, 1982-83; cons. environ. analyst, Portland and L.A., 1983-86; cons. computer programmer and analyst, L.A., 1986—. Contbr. articles to profl. jours. Mem. S.W. Informix Users Group (exec. com. L.A. 1988—). Home and Office: 8112 Chimineas Ave Reseda CA 91335

HOLMES, DAVID BRUCE, quality control engineer; b. Salt Lake City, Nov. 3, 1952; s. Richard Lehman and Dorothy Hortense (Nusshart) H.; m. Cynthia Jane Brown, May 26, 1973; children: Katherine Lee, Christopher David. Lic., Elkins Inst. Electricity, Mpls., 1972. Cert. sr. reactor operator Nat. Regulatory Commn. Various operator positions Ft. St. Vrain, Pub. Svc. Co. Colo., Denver, 1973-85; quality assurance engr., ops. planner Rancho Seco, SMUD, Sacramento, 85-89; quality assurance engr. comml. nuclear sta. Wash. Pub. Power Supply System, Richland, 1989—. Office: WNP-2 QA MD 956B PO Box 968 Richland WA 99352

HOLMES, DAVID LEE, financial investment advisor; b. Salt Lake City, Oct. 3, 1955; s. Joseph Mark and Mary (Jarvis) H.; m. Deborah Harries, July 9, 1980; children: Kimberly Rachel, David Michael, Daniel Lee, Chelsea Rebecca. BS in Acctg., Brigham Young U., 1980, MBA, 1990. Cert. mgmt. acct. Owner, entrepreneur Innovative Propane Technologies & Land Devel., Provo, Utah, 1980-82; chief acct. MGM Grand Hotel, Reno, 1982-83; v.p. fin. Realty Income Corp., Escondido, Calif., 1983-88; v.p. mktg. Real Property Svcs., Carlsbad, Calif., 1988-89; self-employed Provo, 1989-90; investment advisor Morgan Stanley & Co., L.A., 1990—. Patentee in field. Campaign worker Rep. Party, San Diego, 1988; local com. chmn. Boy Scouts of Am., Ramona, Calif., 1988-89. Mem. Inst. Cert. Mgmt. Accts., Nat. Assn. Accts., Brigham Young U. Mgmt. Soc. Republican. Mormon. Home: 38115 Miramonte Ave Palmdale CA 93551-4444 Office: Morgan Stanley & Co Bldg 2400 1999 Avenue Of The Stars Los Angeles CA 90067-6070

HOLMES, JAMES FREDERICK, electrical engineer, educator; b. Billings, Mont., Sept. 10, 1937; s. James Allen and Minnie L. (Fulford) H.; m. Avon Ferne Opland, June 18, 1959; children: Jeffrey Allen, Randal Frederick, Rustin Freeman. BSEE, U. Wash., 1959, PhD in Elec. Engring., 1968; MSEE, U. Md., 1963. Rsch. engr. Boeing Co., Seattle, 1963-66; predoctoral rsch. assoc. U. Wash., Seattle, 1966-68; asst. prof. Oreg. State U., Corvallis, 1969-74; assoc. prof. Oreg. Grad. Ctr., Beaverton, 1974-75, chmn., prof. dept. applied physics, 1975-88, prof., 1988—. Contbr. articles to profl. jours.; patentee in field. With USN, 1959-63. Fellow Optical Soc. Am.; mem. IEEE, Elks. Republican. Home: 9345 NW Kaiser Rd Portland OR 97231 Office: Oreg Grad Inst Dept Elec Engring & Applied Physics 19600 NW Van Neumann Rd Beaverton OR 97006

HOLMES, PAUL LUTHER, political scientist, educational consultant; b. Rock Island, Ill., Mar. 7, 1919; s. Bernt Gunnar and Amanda Sophia (Swenson) H.; m. Ardis Ann Grunditz, Nov. 1, 1946; children: Mary Ann, David Stephen. B.A., U. Minn., 1940; M.A., Stanford U., 1949, Ed.D., 1968; M.A., George Washington U., 1964. Career officer U.S. Navy, 1941-64, ret. as capt.; adminstr. Laney Coll., Oakland, Calif., 1965-70; dean Contra Costa Coll., San Pablo, Calif., 1970-71; pres. Coll. of Alameda (Calif.), 1971-75, prof. polit. sci., 1975-80; dir. doctoral studies program No. Calif., Nova U., 1975-80; cons. in higher edn., Gig Harbor, Wash., 1981—; regent Calif. Luth. U., 1973-76. Decorated Navy Air, Joint Service medals. Mem. AAUP, Am. Polit. Sci. Assn., Navy League, Stanford Univ. Alumni Assn., Phi Delta Kappa. Lutheran. Club: Rotary (Gig Harbor).

HOLMES, (LLOYD) PAULL, college official; b. Alamosa, Colo., Nov. 14, 1943; s. H.V. and Grace Marie (Tripp) H.; m. Susan R. Ashby, Oct. 9, 1982; children: Jeffery, Michael, Nathaniel, Lucas. BA, Adams State Coll., Alamosa, 1965; MS, U. Utah, 1968. Instr. Adams State Coll., 1967-69; prof. Barton County C.C., Gt. Bend, Kans., 1969-82, asst. dir. computer svcs., 1979-82; dir. computer svcs. San Juan Coll., Farmington, N.Mex., 1982—. Mem. Am. Chem. Soc., N.Mex. Coun. Higher Edn. Computing Svcs. Home: 4116 Windsor Dr Farmington NM 87402 Office: San Juan Coll 4601 College Blvd Farmington NM 87402

HOLMES, RICHARD ALBERT, software engineer; b. Santa Barbara, Calif., May 7, 1958; m. Janet M. Dunbar; children: Brian D., Kevin M. AA in Music summa cum laude, City Coll. San Francisco, 1987; BS in Computer Sci. summa cum laude, Nat. U., 1991. Ind. software cons. San Francisco, 1986-88; software quality assurance contractor Oxford & Assocs., Mountain View, Calif., 1988-89; software engr. Apple Computer, Cupertino, Calif., 1989—. CCSF tchr. & faculty scholar, 1986, 87, Alpha Gamma Sigma scholar, 1987. Mem. IEEE, Assn. for Computing Machinery, Alpha Gamma Sigma (treas. 1986-87). Office: Apple Computer Inc MS 302-4K 20525 Mariani Ave Cupertino CA 95014

HOLMES, RICHARD BROOKS, mathematical physicist; b. Milw., Jan. 7, 1959; s. Emerson Brooks Holmes and Nancy Anne (Schaffter) Winship. BS, Calif. Inst. Tech., 1981; MS, Stanford (Calif.) U., 1983. Sr. systems analyst Comptek Rsch., Vallejo, Calif., 1982-83; staff scientist Western Rsch., Arlington, Va., 1983-85; sr. scientist AVCO Everett (Mass.) Rsch. Lab., 1985-88; prin. rsch. scientist North East Rsch. Assocs., Woburn, Mass., 1988-90; sr. mem. tech. staff Rocketdyne div. Rockwell Internat., Canoga Park, Calif., 1990—; cons. North East Rsch. Assocs., 1990. Contbr. Matched Asymptotic Expansions, 1988; contbr. articles to Phys. Rev. Letters, Phys. Rev., Jour. of the Optical Soc. Am. and IEEE Jour. of Quantum Electronics. Mem. No. Calif. Scholarship Founds., Oakland, 1977; mem. Wilderness Soc., Washington, 1989. Stanford fellow Stanford U., 1982; fellow MIT, 1990; recipient Presdl. Medal of Merit, 1992. Mem. AAAS, Am. Phys. Soc., Optical Soc. Am. Office: Rockwell Internat Rocketdyne Div 6633 Canoga Ave # FA40 Canoga Park CA 91309-2703

HOLMES, ROBERT EUGENE, state legislative consultant, journalist; b. Shelbyville, Ind., June 5, 1928; s. Eugene Lowell and Sarah Lucinda (Hughes) H.; m. Retha Carolyn Richey, June 27, 1955 (div. Sept. 1966); children: Enid Adair Offley, William Houstoun (dec.), Holly Ann Holmes. BA in Polit. Sci., DePauw U., 1950; MA in Journalism, Ind. U., 1953; MA in Communs. and Urban Affairs, Stanford U., 1976. City editor, investigative editor Press-Enterprise, Riverside, Calif., 1957-70; sr. cons. Calif. State Senate Dem. Caucus, Sacramento, 1971-74, dep. dir., 1978-79; press sec. Lt. Gov. of Calif., Sacramento, 1975-77; project dir. Border Area Devel. Study, U.S. Econ. Devel. Adminstrn., Sacramento, 1978; chief cons. Joint Legis. Ethics Com., Calif. Legislature, Sacramento, 1981-82, Joint Com. on Prison Constrn. and Ops., Calif. Legislature, Sacramento, 1983—; rsch. cons. Calif. Rsch. Bur., Calif. State Libr., Sacramento, 1991-92. Author, editor rschr. legis. reports; contbg. editor creative writing quar. Noah's Hotel, Inverness, Calif., 1991-92. Pres., Golden Bear Dem. Club, Sacramento, 1972-74; media dir. Lt. Gov. Campaign, Sacramento and L.A., 1974. Sgt. USMC, 1951-53. Recipient Silver Gavel award ABA, 1969, 1st Place award Calif. Newspaper Pubs. Best Series, 1969, 70, 71, Jack Anderson award Calif. Correctional Peace Officers Assn., 1993; Am. Polit. Sci. Assn. fellow Stanford U., 1970. Mem. ACLU, Calif. Writers Club, Common Cause. Democrat. Home: 416 Florin Rd Sacramento CA 95831 Office: Office Sen Robert Presley State Capitol Sacramento CA 95814

HOLMES, ROBERT WAYNE, service executive, consultant, biological historian; b. Brush, Colo., July 16, 1950; s. George William Jr. and Reba Mary (Sandel) H. BA, Western State Coll., 1972. Exec. Rose Exterminator Co., San Francisco, 1986-92; founder, owner BFE Cons., 1992—. Author: The Killing River. Mem. Smithsonian Instn., Washington, 1986, Sta. KRMA-TV-PBS, Denver, 1987, Ft. Morgan (Colo.) Heritage Found., 1988, Ctr. for Study of Presidency, Wilson Ctr., Nat. Mus. Am. Indian. Mem. AAAS, N.Y. Acad. Scis., Acad. Polit. Sci., Wilson Ctr. Assoc. Ctr. for Study of the Presidency, Am. Mus. Natural History, Denver Mus. Natural History, Nat. Mus. Am. Indian, Nature Conservancy, FPCN, SoAm. Explorers Club.

HOLMES, THOMAS JOSEPH, aerospace engineering consultant; b. Paterson, N.J., Oct. 22, 1953; s. George Murray and Juliette (Schutz) H. BSEE, BS in Aerospace Engring., Pa. State U., 1975; MS in Aerospace and Astron. Engring., Stanford U., 1976; MS in Indsl. Adminstrn., Carnegie-Mellon U., 1989; Hypnotherapist Cert., Palo Alto Sch. Hypnotherapy, 1991. Assoc. engr. Lockheed Missiles & Space Orgn., Sunnyvale, Calif., 1976-78; engr. Jet Propulsion Lab., Pasadena, Calif., 1978-79; sr. engr., project mgr. Systems Control Technology, Palo Alto, Calif., 1979—. Author: Advances in Control and Dynamic Systems, Vol. 23, 1986; contbr. articles to profl. jours. Counselor Parental Stress Hotline, Palo Alto, 1986. Mem. AIAA, IEEE, U.S. Cycling Fedn., Tau Beta Pi. Home: 2253 Harvard St Palo Alto CA 94306-1359 Office: Systems Control Tech 2300 Geng Rd Palo Alto CA 94303-3317

HOLMES, THOMAS LEROY, small business owner; b. Vancouvr, Wash., Apr. 14, 1953; s. Clifford Leroy and Dorothy Ann (Predeek) H.; m. Patricia Lynn Blake, Apr. 12 (div.); 1 child, Blake Leroy. BS in Bus., Oreg. State U., 1975. Outside salesman Empire Pacific Industries, 1975-82; owner, treas. NW Door and Supply, Inc., Tigard, Oreg., 1982—. Office: NW Door and Supply Inc PO Box 68 Tualatin OR 97062

HOLMGREN, RODERICK B., retired journalism educator; b. Chgo., July 26, 1914; s. Warner Elof and Josephine (Peterson) H.; m. Katherine DeWese, June 10, 1938 (dec. Sept. 1988); m. Alma Elizabeth Oberst, Jan. 20, 1990; 1 child, John Edward. BS, Northwestern U., 1937; MA, U. Calif., Berkeley, 1959. Prodr. Univ. Broadcasting Coun., Chgo., 1936-39; news editor Iowa State U., Ames, Iowa, 1939-41, Des Moines Register, Iowa, 1941-42, Chicago Sun, Chgo., 1942-43; regional dir. Office of War Info., Chgo., 1943-45; news editor WCFL, Chgo., 1945-49; editor The Union, Denver, 1950-57; instr. Monterey Peninsula Coll., Monterey, Calif., 1959-79; prof. Grad. Coll. Journalism, Beijing, 1982-84, Beijing Broadcasting Inst., Beijing, 1986; Fulbright lectr. Kabul U., Afghanistan, 1966-67. Editor: The Mass Media Book, 1972; author: The American Character, 1978. Named C.C. Journalism Tchr. of the Yr., L.A., 1972; sr. fellow NEH, 1975-76. Mem. Com. on Environ. Impact Military, Sierra Club Marine Com. (Conservationist of the Yr. Monterey chpt., 1979), Minerals Mgmt. Svc. Home: 3398 Taylor Rd Carmel CA 93923

HOLMLUND, LISA LYNNE, marketing professional; b. Aberdeen, Wash., Oct. 11, 1960; d. Carl Don H. and Sharon Lynne (Markwell) Stein. BA in Communications, Wash. State U., 1983. Intern Jay Rockey Pub. Relations, Seattle, 1982-83; account exec. Arst Pub. Relations, Bellevue, Wash., 1983-86; dir. mktg. com. Princess Cruises & Tours, Seattle, 1986—; cons. Boys and Girls Clubs, King County, Wash., 1984-86; mem. mktg. task force Bellevue C. of C., 1985-86; bd. dirs. Southeast Alaska Tourism Coun. Bd. dirs. Eastside Theater Co., 1985-86. Office: Princess Tours 2815 2d Ave Ste 400 Seattle WA 98121

HOLMQUIST, WALTER RICHARD, research chemist, molecular evolutionist, mathematics educator; b. Kansas City, Mo., Dec. 23, 1934; s. Walter Theodore and Elsie Wilburnia (Seitz) H.; m. Ann Marie Hofer, Sept.8, 1968 (dec. Mar. 1990); children: Laura Marie, Jon Aron. BS, Washington and Lee U., 1957, Calif. Inst. Tech., 1961; PhD in Chemistry, Calif. Inst. Tech., 1966. Lectr. organic chemistry and biochemistry U. Ife, Ibadan, Nigeria, 1966-68; research fellow in biology Harvard U., 1968-70; asst. research chemist Space Scis Lab. U. Calif., Berkeley, 1970-74, assoc. research chemist Space Scis Lab., 1974-80, research chemist, 1980—, math. educator, 1989—; exec. mem. Com. Space Research Interdisciplinary Sci. Commn. on Life Scis. Related to Space, 1982—. Editor: Life Sciences and Space Research, 1976-82; assoc. editor Molecular Phylogenetics and Evolution; mem. editorial bd. Adv. Space Research, Jour. Molecular Evolution, Molecular Biology and Evolution, Molecular Phylogenetics & Evolution, BioSystems. Grantee Nat. Heart and Lung Inst., 1971-73; grantee NSF, 1977-81, 83-87. Mem. Internat. Soc. Molecular Evolution, Am. Assn. Adv. Sci., Am. Chem. Soc., Am. Soc. Biochem. and Molecular Biology, N.Y. Acad. Scis., Calif. Acad. Scis., Am. Inst. Chemists, Internat. Union Pure and Applied Chem., Soc. for Study Evolution, Internat. Soc. Molecular Evolution, Phi Beta Kappa, Sigma Xi. Home and Office: 760 Mesa Way Richmond CA 94805-1743

HOLO, SELMA REUBEN, museum director, educator; b. Chgo., May 21, 1943; d. Samuel and Ghita (Hurwitz) Reuben; m. Sanford Holo, June 14, 1964 (div. 1981); children: Robert, Joshua; m. Fred Croton, June 18, 1989. BA, Northwestern U., 1965; MA, Hunter Coll., 1972; PhD, U. Calif., Santa Barbara, 1980; postgrad., Mus. Mgmt. Inst., 1985. Lectr. Art Ctr. Coll. of Design, Pasadena, Calif., 1973-77; curator of acquisitions Norton Simon Mus., Pasadena, 1977-81; dir. Fisher Gallery and mus. MA art history/mus. studies program U. So. Calif., L.A., 1981—; guest curator, cons. Getty Mus., Malibu, Calif., 1975-76, 81; guest curator Isetan Mus., Tokyo, 1982; cons. Nat. Mus. for Women in Arts, Washington, 1984; reviewer grants Inst. Mus. Svcs., Washington, 1986, 87, Getty Grant Program, 1988-90; panel chmn. Internat. Com. on Exhbn. Exch., Washington, 1984; panelist NEA, Washington, 1985, 91, 92, Idaho Commn. on the Arts; mem. admission panel Mus. Mgmt. Inst., 1990; hon. curator Tokyo Fuji Mus. Author: (catalogues) Goya: Los Disparates, 1976; co-author: La Tauromaquia: Goya, Picasso and the Bullfight, 1986; editor: Keepers of the Flame, The Unofficial Artists of Leningrad, 1990; guest editor New Observations, 1990; contbr. articles to profl. jours. Disting. Scholar fellow La Napoule Art Found., 1988; Kress Found. grantee, N.Y., 1979, Internationes Fed. Republic of Germany grantee, 1985, 92; recipient Fuj Fine Art Award, 1990. Mem. ICOM, Coll. Art Assn. (survey com. mus. studies programs 1986), Am. Assn. Mus., Art Table. Office: U So Calif Fisher Gallery 823 Exposition Blvd Los Angeles CA 90089-0001

HOLST, SANFORD, strategic consulting executive; b. Batavia, N.Y., Nov. 4, 1946; s. William Walker and Catherine (Loggie) H.; children: Suzanne, Kristina. BS in Aero., Astronautics, MIT, 1968; MBA, UCLA, 1970. Engr. advanced design group Lockheed Aircraft Corp., Los Angeles, 1968-71; analyst UCLA, Los Angeles, 1972-73, So. Calif. Assn. Govts., Los Angeles, 1973-78; systems analyst Northwest Industries, Los Angeles, 1978-80; v.p. computer systems dept. Parsons Corp., Pasadena, Calif., 1980-93; pres. The Holst Group, L.A., 1993—. Editor Taurus mag., 1971-72; contbr. articles to various publs. Vice chmn. Beverly Hills (Calif.) Bicentennial Com., 1976. Mem. Phi Kappa Sigma (pres. Alpha Mu chpt. 1967-68). Office: Holst Group 14755 Ventura Blvd Ste 413 Sherman Oaks CA 91403

HOLSTEIN, ROBERT K., finance company executive; b. Seattle, May 18, 1967; s. Robert Holstein and Karen Baker Schoner. AA, North Idaho C.C., 1988; BA in Economics, Chinese, Pacific Lutheran, 1990. With guest svc's Hagadong Hospitality/Coeur D'Alene (Idaho) Resort, 1985-88; gen. mgr. Fujiya Internat. Restaurants, Tacoma, Tokyo, 1988-91; dir. sales, mktg. Premium Computers, Tacoma, 1991—; cons. CIBA, Seattle, 1991—, Tacoma Assn. Realtors, 1990—, New York Life, Tacoma, 1990—; dir. Benner/Holstein, Seattle, 1991—. amb. South Ctr. C.C., 1992, pres. Young Reps., 1985-88. Named Outstanding Spokesman for Freedom Am. Legion, 1983, 84, 85, Outstanding Spokesman for Democracy, Vets. of Foreign Wars, 1984, 85, Champion Phi Rho Pi, 1987. Mem. Tacoma Pierce County C. of C. Office: Premium Computers 3116 Elwood Dr W Tacoma WA 98466

HOLT, EDWARD ALLEN, electric utility official; b. Machias, Maine, Aug. 19, 1946; s. Fred Edward and Helen Louise (Brett) H.; m. Anne Sherwood Willcox, Aug. 2, 1969; children: Sarah Willcox, Meredith Sawin. BA, U. N.H., 1968; M Urban Planning, U. Wash., 1974. Rsch. analyst U. Wash., Seattle, 1974-75; sr. resources planner Math. Scis. N.W., Bellevue, Wash., 1976-78; project mgr. Seattle Energy Office, 1979-81; energy cons. Seattle City Light, 1975-76, project mgr., 1982-83, supr. conservation planning, 1983-85, mgr. planning and program devel., 1985-89, mgr. comml. and indsl. programs, 1989—; mem. sci. and statis. adv. com. N.W. Power Planning Coun., Portland, Oreg., 1981-83; mem. residential and comml. task force Electric Power Rsch. Inst., Palo Alto, Calif., 1990-93; speaker, panelist in field. Contbr. articles to profl. jours. Mem. grievance com. Group Health Coop. Puget Sound, Seattle, 1984—. Staff sgt. USAF, 1968-72. Mellon fellow U. Wash., 1973. Mem. Assn. Demand-Side Mgmt. Profls. Home: 7726 Bagley Ave N Seattle WA 98103 Office: Seattle City Light 1015 3d Ave Seattle WA 98104

HOLT, JAMES FRANKLIN, retired numerical analyst, scientific programmer analyst; b. Alexander, Ark., Aug. 24, 1927; s. Edward Warbritton and Etta Turner (Ludi) H.; m. Gloria Anne Gaishin, May 5, 1963; children: Gregory James, Elizabeth Diana, Debora Anne. BA in Math., UCLA, 1953. With Pacific Mutual Ins. Corp., L.A., 1953-54; assoc. engr. Lockheed Aircraft Corp., Burbank, Calif., 1954-58; mem. tech. staff Space Tech. Labs., El Segundo, Calif., 1958-61, Aerospace Corp., El Segundo, 1961-91. Author: (play) To Play's the Thing, 1963 (French Grand Prix award); internat. expert zeros of arbitrary functions, eigenvalues, non linear boundary value problems, differential algebraic equations, numerical integration methods; papers in field. Mem. Univ. Recreation Assn. UCLA (pres. 1952-53), UCLA Student Exec. Council, Young Reps., L.A., 1960-66. Cpl. USAF, 1945-48. Mem. Aerospace Profl. Staff Assn. (1st v.p. 1985-87). Home: 3534 Mandeville Canyon Rd Los Angeles CA 90049-1022

HOLT, JANET LOUVAU, artist; b. San Diego, Nov. 20, 1929; d. James Steele and Elma Bernice (Vahle) Louvau; m. Jay Earl Jansen, Aug. 18, 1951 (div. 1976); children: Rebecca Jansen Onorato, Jill Jansen Paveza, Juliet Jansen Schlesser; m. Byron Thompson Holt, Apr. 21, 1979. Student, Mills Coll., 1947-49; BA, U. Calif., Berkeley, 1951. Artist Calif., Or, 1954-72; sales agt. Stan Wiley Realtors, Inc., Portland, Oreg., 1972-80, dir., 1980—; designer needlepoint Portland, 1972—; artist Portland, Oreg., 1980—; speaker in field, 1985, 91, 92. Author catalogue; represented in permanent collection Portland Art Mus. and Oreg. Hist. Soc. Docent Portland Art Mus., 1964—, chmn. docent coun., 1990-92, orgn. com., 1992—, bd. dirs. Portland Art Mus., 1993—; pres. Oreg. Found., Inc., Tigard, 1990-92; mem. Nature Conservancy, 1990—. Mem. Colored Pencil Soc. Am. (historian 1990—), Watercolor Soc. Oreg. (historian 1985—), Oreg. Soc. Artists, Arts in Oreg., N.W. Print Coun. (assoc.), Friends of the Print Ctr., Mills Coll. Alumnae.

HOLTEN, VIRGINIA LOIS ZEWE, college president; b. McKeesport, Pa., Mar. 29, 1938; d. Albert J. and Virginia Kathryn (Minnick) Zewe; m. Darold Duane Holten, Dec. 29, 1962; 1 child, Peggy. B.A., Carlow Coll., 1960; M.S., U. N.D., 1962, Ph.D., 1965; diploma U. Glasgow, Scotland, 1975. Researcher Oak Ridge Nat. Lab., 1965-67; assoc. prof. Riverside City Coll., Calif., 1968-78; dean natural sci., 1978-82; v.p. instrn. Victor Valley Coll., Victorville, Calif., 1982-86; supt., pres. Lassen Coll., 1986-90; pres. Solano Coll., 1990—. Contbr. articles to profl. jours. Am. Cancer Soc. postdoctoral fellow, Oak Ridge, 1965-67; named Outstanding Student, Brit. Inst. Mgmt., Glasgow, 1975. Mem. Fairfield C. of C., Vacaville C. of C., Vallejo C. of C., Community Coll. League Calif., Assn. Calif. Community Coll. Adminstrs., Rotary. Home: 1877 Shirley Dr Benicia CA 94510-2670 Office: Solano Community Coll 4000 Suisun Valley Rd Suisun City CA 94585-3197

HOLTH, HENRY ALBERT, arts administrator; b. Camden, N.J., June 6, 1927; s. Adolph Thomas and Hedwig Rosa (Weber) H. BS, Rider Coll., 1951. Gen. mgr. Boston Ballet, 1969-71; mng. dir. Houston Ballet, 1971-76; pres. Dallas Ballet, 1978-83, San Jose (Calif.)/Cleve. Ballets, 1984-86, Ballet of the Ams., El Paso, Tex., 1986—; cons. Soc. for the Performing Arts, Houston, 1977-78, Theater Under the Stars, Houston, 1983, Ballet de las Ams., Juarez, Mex., 1988; panelist Nat. Endowment for the Arts, 1987-88, Tex. Commn. on the Arts, 1988—. Served as pvt. U.S. Army, 1945-47. Home: 120 E Mallard Dr Ste 206 Boise ID 83706-3987 Office: Am Festival Ballet 217 N 10th St Boise ID 83702-5744

HOLTON, WILLIAM CHESTER, engineer, consultant; b. Caldwell, Idaho, May 2, 1939; s. Chester Clayton and Margaret Ann (MacLaren) H.; m. Rhoberta Phaigh Romo, June 1, 1958 (div. Sept. 1976); children: William Lee, Robert Charles, Ronald Clayton. AS, Regents Coll., 1986. lic. FCC. Electronic technician Litton Industries, L.A., 1963-66; applications engr. 3M Co., Camarillo, Calif., 1966-74; program analyst USN, Port Magu, Calif., 1974-75; video supr. U. Calif., Santa Barbara, 1975-77; cons. Great Am. Tech. Services, L.A., 1977—. Creator digitally controlled screenings theater for Steven Spielberg at Universal Studios, first high speed sound-on-film editing suite in People's Republic of China, variable speed projection control system for Eddie Murphy. Mem. Soc. Motion Picture TV Engrs. (voting). Office: Great Am Tech Svcs 4219 W Olive Ave # 109 Burbank CA 91505-4262

HOLTZ, JOSEPH NORMAN, marketing executive; b. Matawan, N.J., Oct. 11, 1930; s. Joseph Antone and Catherine Martina (Crosby) H.; m. Irene Strano, July 15, 1951; children: Joseph Jr., Karl, Gary, Robert, Eric. AA, De Vry Tech. Inst., 1954; student, Monmouth Coll., 1955-56; BBA, Nat. U., 1988, MBA, 1989. Lic. GRI designated real estate agent Nat. Assn. Realtors, MIRM designation Inst. of Residential Mktg. Engr. Bendix Aviation, Red Bank, N.J., 1952-56, Hughes Aircraft Co., L.A., 1956-73; pres. Jo-Rene Assocs., Orange, Calif., 1973-86; asst. v.p. Builders Sales Corp., Santa Ana, Calif., 1986-87; exec. v.p. The Lehnert Group, Irvine, Calif., 1987-88; pres. J.N. Holtz Assocs., Orange, 1988—; v.p., corp. broker Mortgage Outlet Corp., 1992—; corp. broker Shancie Real Estate Corp., 1992—; area dir. Citi-Exec Mgmt. Corp., Costa Mesa, 1993—. Com. mem. United Way, Santa Ana, 1987—. Mem. IEEE, Inst. Residential Mktg., Sales and Mktg. Coun., Phoenix Club, Am. Soc. for Quality Control. Republican. Home: 5045-2 E Almond Ave Orange CA 92669-4207 Office: J N Holtz Assocs PO Box 10014 Santa Ana CA 92711-0014

HOLTZAPFEL, PATRICIA KELLY, health facility executive; b. Madison, Wis., Jan. 29, 1948; d. Raymond Michael and Laura Margaret (Stegner) Kelly; m. Robert Adrian Bunker, Oct. 4, 1975 (div. June 1979); m. Raymond Paul Holtzapfel, Mar. 12, 1983 (div. Feb. 1992). RN, Ariz.; cert. pub. health nurse. Staff nurse Madison Gen. Hosp., 1970-72; bloodmobile staff nurse ARC, Madison, 1972-73; pub. health nurse Dane County Pub. Health Dept., Madison, 1973-75; field health nurse CIGNA Health Plan, Phoenix, 1975-84; dir. nursing Olsten Health Care, Phoenix, 1984-85; mgr. bus. Holtzapfel Phys. Therapy and Pain Control Clinic, Phoenix, 1985-89, bus. cons., 1989-92; supr. CIGNA Healthplan Ariz., Phoenix, 1989-92. Bd. dirs. Deer Valley Vocat. Arts Adv. Coun., Phoenix, 1986-89. Mem. The Exec. Female Assn., Ariz. Networking Council.

HOLTZCLAW, JOYCE MADELYN IRENE, petroleum engineer; b. La Junta, Colo., Aug. 28, 1956; d. Samuel Thomas Baldwin and Dolores (Strickland) Petersen; m. Mark John Holtzclaw, June 2, 1979; 1 stepchild, Bradley Mark. Student, Colo. Sch. Mines, Golden, 1974-75; BS in Mech. Engring., U. Nev., 1987, MBA, 1990. Prodn. technologist Amoco Prodn. Co., Denver, 1976-77; engring. asst. Champlin Petroleum Co., Englewood, Colo., 1977-81; engr. Coseka Resources U.S.A. Ltd., Denver, 1981-84, sr. evaluations engr., 1984-86; corp. planner Sierra Pacific Resources, Reno, Nev., 1989-90; power marketer, contract adminstr. Great Basin Energy Co., sub. Sierra Pacific Resources, Reno, 1990; petroleum engr. Chevron U.S.A. Prodn. Co., Cymric, Calif., 1990—. Coord. mem. Prime-Time Network, U. Nev., 1986-87; mem. Western Indsl. Nev., Reno, 1989-90. Mem. Soc. Mech. Engrs., Soc. Petroleum Engrs. (bd. dirs. 1993), MBA Assn. (pres. 1989-90). Home: 10904 Stony Point Dr Bakersfield CA 93312

HOLUB, ELAINE NATHANSON, public relations executive; b. Tucson, Nov. 4, 1949; d. Robert Morris and Hilda F. (Anser) Nathanson; m. Hugh A. Holub, Oct. 31, 1976; children: Annie, Elizabeth. BA, U. Ariz., 1971. Reporter Ariz. Daily Star, Tucson, 1971-74, 75-76; with pub. rels. Nat. Jewish Hosp., Denver, 1974-75; consumer investigator City of Tucson, 1976-80; pub. rels. coord. So. Ariz. Water Resources Assn., Tucson, 1982-84; sr. v.p. pub. rels. Judith Abrams/Elaine Holub Pub. Rels., Tucson, 1984-91; ptnr. Holub, Peck & Peck Assocs. in Pub. Rels., Inc., Tucson, 1991-93; v.p. Leiss, Holub, Peck & Godwin, Inc., Tucson, 1993—. Pres. bd. dirs. Ednl. Enrichment Found., Tucson, 1989, sec. bd. dirs. 1990. Mem. Pub. Rels. Soc. of Am. (counselors acad., APR accreditation 1987), Rocky Mountain Pub. Rels. Network. Office: Leiss Holub Peck & Godwin Inc 177 N Church Ste 608 Tucson AZ 85701

HOLUB, ROBERT FRANTISEK, nuclear chemist, physicist; b. Prague, Czechoslovakia, Sept. 19, 1937; came to U.S., 1966; s. Stanislav and Marie (Prochazkova) H.; m. Johnna S. Thames, Dec. 27, 1977; children: Robert M., John F., Elisabeth J. BS, Charles U., Prague, 1958, MS, 1960; PhD, McGill U., 1970. Research assoc. Fla. State U., Tallahassee, 1970-73; teaching intern U. Ky., Lexington, 1973-74; rsch. physicist Bur. Mines, U.S. Dept. Interior, Denver, 1974—; cons. Internat. Atomic Energy Agy., Vienna, Austria, 1984-89, key participant radon intercalibration program, 1990—; faculty affiliate Colo. State U., Ft. Collins, 1982—. Patentee continuous working level exposure apparatus. Contbr. articles to sci. jours. NRC Can. scholar, 1967-70. Mem. Am. Phys. Soc., Health Physics Soc., Am. Assn. for Aerosol Rsch.

HOLVE, LESLIE MARTIN, pediatrician; b. Santa Ana, Calif., Sept. 26, 1926; s. Alfred A. and Susanna (Winkler) H.; m. Eleanore L. Holve, Aug. 20, 1950; children: Richard L., Stephen A., Kurt Martin. BS, Occidental Coll., L.A., 1947; MD, U. So. Calif., L.A., 1952. Diplomate Am. Bd. Pediatrics. Intern L.A. County Gen. Hosp., 1951-52, resident, 1952; resident UCLA Med. Ctr., Westwood, Calif., 1954-56; pvt. practice L.A., 1956-78, Santa Monica, Calif., 1978-90; cons., med. dir. St. Johns Hosp., Cleft Palate and Craniofacial Ctr., Santa Monica, Calif., 1964—; med. dir. March of Dimes 99th Birth Defects Ctr., Santa Monica.; assoc. clin. prof. UCLA Med. Ctr., 1960—; chief pediatrics St. John's Hosp., Santa Monica, 1964-70; mem. staff UCLA Med. Ctr., St. John's Hosp., Santa Monica Hosp.; mem. Clin. Faculty Review Com. UCLA, 1991—. Contbr. articles to profl. jours. Mem. Rep. Nat. Conv., Washington, 1977-90. Lt. (j.g.) USN, 1952-54. Named Physician of Yr., St. John's Hosp. and Health Ctr., Santa Monica, 1990. Fellow Am. Acad. Pediatrics; mem. L.A. Pediatric Soc. (pres. 1964-65), Am. Cleft Palate Assn. (pres. 1984-85), AMA, Calif. Med. Assn., L.A. County Med. Assn., Native Sons Golden West, Salerni Collegium, Westwood Rotary. Republican. Office: St Johns Hosp & Health Ctr Cleft Palate Ctr 1328 22d St Santa Monica CA 90404

HOLZER, THOMAS LEQUEAR, geologist; b. Lafayette, Ind., June 26, 1944; s. Oswald Alois and Ruth Alice (Lequear) H.; m. Mary Elizabeth Burbach, June 13, 1968; children: Holly Christine, Elizabeth Alice. BSE, Princeton U., 1965; MS, Stanford U., 1966, PhD, 1970. Asst. prof. geology U. Conn., Storrs, 1970-75; adj. environmentalist Griswold & Fuss, Manchester, Conn., 1973-75; research geol. U.S. Geol. Survey, Menlo Park, Calif., 1975-82, rsch. geologist, 1984-88, 93—; dep. asst. dir. rsch. U.S. Geol. Survey, Reston, Va., 1982-84, chief br. engring. seismology and geology, 1989-93, rsch. geologist, 1993—. Contbr. numerous articles to profl. jours. Coach Am. Youth Soccer Orgn., Palo Alto, Calif., 1979-82. Recipient Superior Svc. award U.S Geol. Survey, 1981, Outstanding Pub. Svc. award U.S. Geol. Survey, 1991. Fellow Geol. Soc. Am. (chmn. engring. geology div. 1988-89); mem. AAAS, Am. Geophys. Union, Assn. Ground Water Scientists and Engrs. Republican. Presbyterian. Home: PO Box 851 Palo Alto CA 94302 Office: US Geol Survey 345 Middlefield Rd Menlo Park CA 94025-3591

HOLZGANG, DAVID ALLAN, systems analyst consultant, writer; b. L.A., Oct. 6, 1941; s. Albert Otto and Marianne Josephine (Kane) H. AB, UCLA, 1964, MBA, 1973. Programmer N.Am. Aviation, Downey, Calif., 1964-66, Planning Rsch. Corp., L.A., 1966-68; project mgr. HW Systems, Inc., L.A., 1968-71; systems analyst Penn Corp. Fin., Santa Monica, Calif., 1973-76; dir. advt. systems Petersen Pub. Co., L.A., 1976-78; from v.p. programming to sr. v.p. ops. Haney Group, Woodland Hills, Calif., 1978-83; mng. gen. ptnr. Cheshire Group, Chatsworth, Calif., 1983-88, San Francisco, 1988-90, Sebastopol, Calif., 1990—; chmn. PostScript stds. com. SPS Assn., Chelmsford, Mass., 1989-90. Author: Display PostScript Programming, 1990,

Programming LaserWriter, 1991, Laser Jet Companion, 2d edit., 1991, Understanding PostScript, 1992; editor PostScript Jour., 1992—; series editor Prima Publs., 1992—. Mem. Apple Developers Assn., Adobe Developers Assn. Office: Cheshire Group 321 S Main St Ste 36 Sebastopol CA 95472

HOM, RICHARD YEE, research engineer; b. Phoenix, July 26, 1950; s. Tommy Look and Betty (Mah) H.; BS in Engring. Sci. and Aero. and Aerospace Tech., Ariz. State U., 1973; m. Kathleen Chien; 1 child, Matthew Thomas Yee. Asst. engr. Sperry Flight System, Phoenix, 1973; sr. engr., composite tool engring. Boeing Comml. Airplane Co., Seattle, 1973-84; specialist engr. 1984-88, sr. specialist engr. rsch. and devel., metall. processing and advanced projects Boeing Aerospace Co., 1984-90, also automation tech.; with customer svcs. and airline support Boeing Comml. Airplane Group, 1990-91; with metallics rsch. and devel. Boeing Def. and Space Group, 1991—. Mem. AIAA, Air Force Assn., Soc. Mfg. Engrs., Aircraft Owners and Pilots Assn. Home: 28704 15th Ave S Federal Way WA 98003-3161 Office: Boeing Def and Space Group M/S 8J-74 PO Box 3999 Seattle WA 98124-2207

HOMAN, RALPH WILLIAM, finance company executive; b. Wilkes-Barre, Pa., June 7, 1951; s. Norman Ryan and Adelaide Bernice (Sandy) H.; m. Donna Marie Webb, Jan. 25, 1975. BS in Acctg., Wheeling Coll., 1977; MBA in Mktg., Nat. U., 1986. Paymaster Dravo Corp., Pitts., 1974-75; tax preparer H&R Block, Wheeling, W.Va., 1977; fin. services exec. NCR Credit Corp., Sacramento, 1977-84; leasing exec. CSB Leasing, Sacramento, 1984-85; pres. Convergent Fin. Svcs., Colorado Springs, Colo., 1985—. Sponsor Harrison High Sch. Key Club; cons. Jr. Achievement, 1990—. Co-winner Name the Plane Contest Pacific Southwest Airlines, 1984. Mem. The 30/40 Something Social Club (founder, pres. Sedonna chpt.), Am. Assn. of Boomers (pres. Pikes Peak chpt. 1992-93), Toastmasters (treas. Oak Creek chpt. 1988-89), Kiwanis (sec. 1988-89, founder, chmn. adult soccer league). Baha'i. Home and Office: Convergent Fin Svcs 5720 Escapardo Way Colorado Springs CO 80917-3340

HOMBURG, JEFFREY ALLAN, geoarchaeologist; b. Oklahoma City, Jan. 30, 1957; s. Leo Paul and Linda Jane (Fisher) St. Onge. BA, U. Okla., 1979; MA, La. State U., 1991. Supr. Archaeol. Rsch. and Mgmt. Ctr., Norman, Okla., 1978-79, Great Plains Mus., Lawton, Okla., 1979-80; crew chief/ project dir. New World Rsch., Inc., Pollock, La., 1980-84; project dir. New World Rsch., Inc., Fort Walton Beach, Fla., 1986-87; rsch. asst. La. State U., Baton Rouge, 1984-86; project dir. Statis. Rsch., Inc., Tucson, 1988—; reviewer Ariz. Archaeol. and Hist. Soc., Tucson, 1990-91. Author: Cultural Resources Survey and Overview for the Rillito River Drainage Area, 1989, Playa Vista Archaeological Project Research Design, 1990, Intermontane Settlement Trends in the Eastern Papagueria, 1993, Archaeological Investigations at the LSU Campus Mounds, 1992, Life in the Ballona: Archaeological Investigations at the Admiralty Site (CA-LAN-47) and the Channel Gateway Site (CA-LAN-1596-H), 1992, Archaeological Investigations at Lee Canyon: Kayenta Farmsteads in the Upper Basin, Coconino County, Arizona, 1992, Late Prehistoric Change in the Ballona Wetland, 1993, Limited Archaeological Testing at the Centinela Site (CA-LAN-60), Los Angeles County, California, 1993, Comments on the Age of the LSU Mounds: A Reply to Jones, 1993. Chmn. tech. standards com. Profl. Disc Golf Assn., Oklahoma City, 1989-93. Sigma Xi rsch. grantee, La. State U., 1986. Mem. Soc. Am. Archaeology, Soc. Archaeol. Sci., Soil Sci. Soc., Soc. Profl. Archaeologists (cert.). Democrat. Lutheran. Home: 5330 E Bellevue St Apt 3 Tucson AZ 85712-4939 Office: Statis Rsch Inc PO Box 31865 Tucson AZ 85751-1865

HOMESTEAD, SUSAN, psychotherapist; b. Bklyn., Sept. 20, 1937; d. Cy Simon and Katherine (Haas) Eichelbaum; m. Robert Bruce Randall, 1956 (div. 1960); 1 child, Bruce David; m. George Gilbert Zanetti, Dec. 13, 1962 (div. 1972); m. Ronald Eric Homestead, Jan. 16, 1973 (div. 1980). BA, U. Miami-Fla., 1960; MSW, Tulane U., 1967. Diplomate Am. Bd. Clin. Social Work; acad. cert. social workers, 1971, LCSW, Va., Calif. Pvt. practice, cons., Richmond, Va., 1971—; psychotherapist, cons. Family and Children's Svcs., Richmond, 1981—, Richmond Pain Clinic, 1983-84; Health Internat. Va., P.C., Lynchburg, 1984-86, Franklin St. Psychotherapy & Edn. Ctr, Santa Clara, Calif., 1988-90; pvt. practice, 1971—; Santa Clara County Children's Svc., 1973-75, 86-88; co-dir. asthma program Va. Lung Assn., Richmond, 1975-79, Loma Prieta Regional Ctr.; chief clin. social worker Med. Coll. Va., Va. Commonwealth U., 1974-79; field supr. 1980 Census, 1981-87. Contbr. articles to profl. jours. Active Peninsula Children's Ctr., Morgan Ctr., Coun. for Community Action Planning, Community Assn. for Retarded, Comprehensive Health Planning Assn. Santa Clara, Mental Health Commn., Children and Adolescent Target Group Calif., Women's Com. Richmond Symphony, Va. Mus. Theatre, mem. fin. com. Robb for Gov.; mem. adv. com. Lung Assn.; mem. steering com. Am. Cancer Soc. Va. div. Epilepsy Found., Am. Heart Assn., Cen. Va. Guild for Infant Survival. Mem. NASW, Va. Soc. Clin. Social Work, Inc. (charter mem., sec. 1975-78), Internat. Soc. Communicative Psychoanalysis & Psychotherapy, Am. Acad. Psychotherapists, Internat. Soc. for the Study of Multiple Personality and Dissociation, Am. Assn. Psychiatric Svcs. for Children.

HOMME, MARC S., lawyer; b. Bismarck, N.D., Oct. 7, 1949; s. Orrin R. and Camille (Wachter) H. BA, U. Colo., 1971; JD, Loyola U., L.A., 1974. Bar: Calif. Pvt. practice Palm Desert, Calif., 1978—; prof. Coll. of the Desert, Palm Desert, Calif., Chapman Coll., Palm Desert. Bd. dirs. Desert Youth Sports. Mem. Calif. Bar Assn., Phi Beta Kappa. Office: 74-361 Hwy 111 #1 Palm Desert CA 92260

HOMMEL, DANIEL JAY, radiation oncologist; b. Denver, June 2, 1955; s. Gunther Heinz and Helen (Wasinger) H.; m. Julie Anne Collier (div. June 1991); children: Stephanie Marie, Brandon Joel. BS in Chemistry magna cum laude, Regis Coll., Denver, 1977; MD, U. Colo., Denver, 1983. Diplomate Am. Bd. Radiology. Intern in internal medicine St. Lukes-Presbyn. Med. Ctr, Denver, 1983-84, resident in radiation oncology, 1984-87; med. dir. dept. radiation oncology Meml. Hosp. Laramie County, Cheyenne, Wyo., 1991—. Contbr. numerous articles to sci. jours. Team physician Colo. High Sch. Football Players, Denver, 1984-87; physician Am. Boxing Fedn.-U.S. AAU, Denver, 1985-87; bd. dirs. Greene County (Ohio) unit Am. Cancer Soc., 1989-81, bd. dirs. Wyo. unit, 1991—, pres. Laramie County unit, 1991—. Maj. M.C., USAF, 1987-91. Regis scholar Regis Coll., 1977. Mem. AMA, Am. Coll. Radiology, Am. Soc. Therapeutic Radiology and Oncology, Am. Soc. Clin. Oncology, N.Am. Hyperthermia Group, Radiation Rsch. Soc., Wyo. Med. Soc. Roman Catholic. Office: Meml Hosp Laramie County Dept Radiation Oncology 300 E 23d St Cheyenne WY 82001-3790

HONAKER, RICHARD HENDERSON, lawyer; b. Laramie, Wyo., Mar. 10, 1951; s. Hayward E. and Faola I. (Henderson) H.; m. Shannon Kathleen Casey, Dec. 24, 1978; children: Heather, Harmony, Dustin. BA cum laude, Harvard U., 1973; JD, U. Wyo., 1976. Bar: Wyo. 1976, U.S. Dist. Ct. Wyo., 1976, U.S. Ct. Appeals (10th cir.) 1977, U.S. Supreme Ct. 1989. Asst. atty. gen. State of Wyo., Cheyenne, 1976-78, state pub. defender, 1979-81; ptnr. Honaker, Hampton & Newman, Rock Springs, Wyo., 1981—. Press sec. to Gov. of Wyo., 1978; mem. Wyo. State Ho. of Reps., Sweetwater County, 1986-93. Mem. Wyo. Bar Assn., Wyo. Trial Lawyers Assn. (v.p. 1985-86, pres. 1986), Assn. Trial Lawyers Am., Am. Bd. Trial Advocates (charter), Christian Legal Soc. Democrat. Office: Honaker Hampton & Newman PO Box 1804 Rock Springs WY 82901

HONBO, CLAYTON K., physician; b. Honolulu, Hawaii, Feb. 9, 1938; s. William S. and Florence O. (Okumoto) H.; m. Lynette K. Honbo, July 11, 1971; children: William, Gregory, Lauren, Daniel. BA, Williams Coll., 1960; MD, Northwestern U., 1964. Diplomate Am. Bd. Ob-Gyn. Intern Cook County Hosp., Chgo., 1964-65, resident, 1966-69; Bd. dirs. Ctl. Pacific Bank. Maj. USAF, 1969-71. Home: 3109 Huelani Pl Honolulu HI 96822 Office: 1380 Lusitana St Ste 1014 Honolulu HI 96813

HONG, NORMAN G. Y., architect; b. Honolulu, May 5, 1947; s. Kwai Ing and Patricia Y.S. (Dye) H.; m. Lorna Sachiko Yano, Aug. 11, 1973; 1 child, Christopher. T.S.C. BArch, U. Hawaii, 1969. Registered architect, Hawaii. Designer, John Tatom Architect, Honolulu, 1969-71; assoc. Group 70 Inc., Honolulu, 1971-77, prin., 1977-80, ptnr., 1980-84, mng. ptnr., 1984-88, pres., chief operating officer, 1989-90, vice chmn., 1990—. Bd. dirs. Manpower Planning Agy. Honolulu, 1972; com. mem. Ann. Gov./Mayor's Prayer, Honolulu, 1984; mem. Mayor's Adv. Com. on Chinatown Gateway, 1987, mem. adv. bd. spl. design dists., 1989—; mem. Epephany Epis. Sch. Bd., 1989-91; mem. Haleiwa Spl. Design Adv. Com., 1986-87, Gov's Congress on Hawaii's Future, 1988; commr. Commn. on Culture and Arts, Honolulu, 1991—. Recipient C.W. Dickey award U. Hawaii, 1967, Cert. Exemplary Performance, Dept. Navy Pacific Divsn., 1984, Chief Engrs. Design Merit award, 1991. Mem. Constrn. Specifications Inst., AIA, Hawaii Soc. AIA (v.p. Hawaii 1987, pres. 1988, sec. Hawaii 1984-86, chmn. long range plan com. 1987, chmn. state conv., 1983), Plaza Club, Honolulu Country Club, Rotary. Mem. Kaimuki Christian Church. Office: Group 70 Inc 924 Bethel St Honolulu HI 96813-4398

HONGO-WHITING, VALERIE ANN, gallery artisan; b. L.A., 1953; m. Ted P. Hucal, 1973 (div. 1976); m. Lawrence R. Whiting, 1985. BS, U. So. Calif., 1974, MPA, 1977; student, Loyola U. Sch. Law, 1982-83. Pers. intern L.A. City Fire Dept., 1971-78; tng. and devel. specialist L.A. Dept. Water and Power, 1978-81; human resources mgr. TRW Def. & Space Systems, Redondo Beach, Calif., 1981-82; bus. mgr. Law Offices of L.R. Whiting, Garden Grove, Calif., 1982-88; owner, designer Gallery Accents, Dana Point, Calif., 1989—. Commd. to design exclusive line of jewelry, 1993. Active Beverly Hills Art League, Laguna Beach Art-A-Fair Coop. With USO, 1967-72. Mem. U. So. Calif. Alumni Assn., Catalina Art Assn. Office: Gallery Accents 32545-B Golden Lantern # 195 Dana Point CA 92629

HONGSERMEIER, MARTIN KARL, software and systems architect, consultant; b. Grand Island, Nebr., Aug. 13, 1953; s. Leo Albert and Ingeborg Albine (Goepfert) H.; m. Dana René Gudde, Oct. 10, 1990. BS in Geophys. Engring., Colo. Sch. Mines, Golden, 1978. Well log computer programmer Birdwell div. Seismograph Svc. Corp., Tulsa, 1979-85; prin. programmer analyst Teledyne Brown Engring., Lawton, Okla., 1985-90; sr. mem. tech. staff Nichols Rsch. Corp., Huntsville, Ala., 1990-91; sr. software engr. Codar Tech., Inc., Longmont, Colo., 1991—; rschr. BitSmith, Lawton, Okla., 1982-92. Bd. dirs. Oak Ridge Property Owners Assn., Kingston, Okla., 1985-86. Mem. IEEE Computer Soc., Assn. for Computing Machinery. Home: PO Box 1461 Longmont CO 80502 Office: Codar Tech Inc 2405 Trade Centre Ave Longmont CO 80503

HONIG, LAWRENCE STERLING, neuroscientist, neurologist; b. Berkeley, Calif., Oct. 26, 1953; s. Arnold and Alice H. AB, Cornell U., 1973; PhD, U. Calif., Berkeley, 1978; MD, U. Miami (Fla.), 1986. Diplomate Am. Bd. Med. Examiners, Am. Bd. Psychiatry and Neurology. Staff scientist MRC Nat. Inst. Med. Rsch., London, 1980; rsch. asst. prof. U. So. Calif., L.A., 1981-83; med. intern Stanford (Calif.) U. Hosp., 1986-87, neurology resident, 1987-90; clin. instr. Stanford U. Med. Sch., 1990-92, clin. asst. prof., 1992—. Author: (with others) Embryonic Mechanisms, 1986, Multiple Sclerosis, 1989; contbr. articles to profl. jours. Anna Fuller Fund fellow Middlesex Hosp. Med. Sch., London, 1978-79, Dana fellow Stanford U., 1990, Walter and Idun Berry fellow, Stanford U., 1991. Fellow Zool. Soc. London; mem. AMA, AAAS, Am. Acad Neurology, Soc. for Neurosci., Sigma Xi. Office: Dept Neurology & Neurol Sci (H3160) Stanford U Med Ctr Stanford CA 94305-5235

HONTON, EDWARD JUDE, technology management executive; b. Terre Haute, Ind., Feb. 9, 1955; s. Edward Franklin and Margaret Angelyn (Dautremont) H. BS in Civil Engring., Ohio State U., 1977, MA in Econs., 1979. Rsch. asst. econs. dept. Ohio State U., Columbus, 1973-79; prin. rsch. scientist Battelle Columbus, 1979-89, mgr. intellectual property, 1989-90; assoc. Resource Dynamics Corp., 1990-93; pres. Foresite, Prineville, Oreg., 1993—. Contbr. articles to profl. publs.; patentee software (Disting. Inventor award 1988, 89). Bd. dirs. Internat. Youth Hostel Fedn., Welwyn Garden City, Eng., 1989—; v.p. Am. Youth Hostels, Inc., Washington, 1982-84, pres. 1984-87, sec. 1987-90, v.p. 1990—; publs. cons. Nat. Park Found., Washington, 1988—; active local community activities, Columbus. Recipient Brown award ASCE, 1977. Home and Office: 246889 Long Hollow Rd Prineville OR 97754

HOOD, JACQUELINE ANN NITZ, management educator; b. Chgo., July 20, 1954; d. John Robert and Marjorie Ann Nitz; m. James Michael Hood, Aug. 19, 1978. BA, No. Ill. U., 1976, MBA, 1981; PhD, U. Colo., 1989. Rsch. asst. No. Ill. U., DeKalb, Ill., 1979-81; acct. exec. AT&T, Chgo., 1981-83; instr. Met. State Coll., Denver, 1985, 86; cons. Browning-Ferris Industries, Denver, 1983; instr. U. Colo., Boulder, 1983-86; asst. prof. Regis U., Denver, 1986-88; cons. S.W. Community Health Svcs., Albuquerque, 1991, Hosp. Home Health Care, Albuquerque, 1992—; asst. prof. U. N.Mex., Albuquerque, 1988—; exec. bd. mem. Women in Mgmt. Div.-Nat. Acad. Mgmt., 1992-95. Contbr. articles to profl. jours. Recipient Rsch. grant Anderson Schs. Mgmt., 1989, 91, 92, Gerald Hart Rsch. fellowship U. Colo., 1987, 88; named Outstanding Young Women of Am., 1987, Outstanding Woman Student, No. Ill. U., 1981. Mem. Acad. Mgmt., Internat. Coun. for Small Bus., U.S. Assn. for Small Bus. and Entrepreneurship. Office: U of New Mexico Anderson Sch of Mgmt Albuquerque NM 87131

HOOD, JOE DON, historian, archaeologist, researcher; b. Bakersfield, Calif., July 12, 1936; s. Joseph D and Eilleen Lenore (Kay) H.; m. Beverly Ann Gould, July 20, 1958; children: Jeffry Robin, Jason Stuart, Jennifer Lyn. BA, Sacramento State Coll., 1958. State park ranger I Calif. State Park System, various parks No. Calif., 1959-66, state park ranger II, 1966-80; state archaeologist Calif. State Park System, Sacramento, 1980-87, state historian II, 1987—. Mem. Internat. Plastic Modelers Soc. Democrat. Home: 106 Fargo Way Folsom CA 95630-2906 Office: Calif State Park System PO Box 942896 Sacramento CA 94296-0001

HOOD, MICHAEL JAMES, theatre educator; b. San Bernardino, Calif., Nov. 29, 1946; s. Howell Badley and Bette B. (Cole) H.; m. Katherine Elizabeth Shryock, Aug. 4, 1968; children: Molly Lorraine, Cole Southford. BA in Theatre, Ariz. State U., 1972; MA in Drama and Communications, U. New Orleans, 1975, MFA in Drama and Communications, 1975. Cert. tchr. Asst. prof. theatre and speech U. Alaska, Anchorage, 1976-80, chair, assoc. prof. theatre and speech, 1980-84, assoc. dean Coll. Art and Scis., 1984-87, chair, prof. theatre and dance, 1987—; pres. N.W. Drama Conf. Inc, Monmouth, Oreg., 1988—; pres. Alaska Theatre of Youth, Anchorage, 1989—. Contbr. articles to profl. jours. With USN, 1964-67. Awards for outstanding direction Am. Coll. Theatre Festival, 1982, 84, 88, 92. Mem. Soc. Am. Fight Dirs., Assn. Theatre in Higher Edn., Assn. for Canadian Studies in U.S. Home: 1942 N Salem Dr Anchorage AK 99508-5181 Office: U Alaska 3211 Providence Dr Anchorage AK 99508-4614

HOOK, RALPH CLIFFORD, JR., business educator; b. Kansas City, Mo., May 2, 1923; s. Ralph Clifford and Ruby (Swanson) H.; m. Joyce Fink, Jan. 20, 1946; children—Ralph Clifford III, John Gregory. BA, U. Mo., 1947, MA, 1948; PhD, U. Tex., 1954. Instr. U. Mo., 1947-48; asst. prof. Tex. A&M U., 1948-51; lectr. U. Tex., 1951-52; co-owner, mgr. Hook Buick Co., also Hook Truck & Tractor Co., Lee's Summit, Mo., 1952-58; assoc. prof. U. Kansas City, 1953-58; dir. Bur. Bus. Research and Services, Ariz. State U., 1958-66, prof. mktg., 1960-68; dean Coll. Bus. Adminstrn., U. Hawaii, 1968-74; prof. mktg. U. Hawaii, 1974—; vis. Disting. prof. N.E. La. U., 1979; dir. Hook Bros. Corp., Hilo Coast Processing Co. Ltd., Pan Pacific Inst. Ocean Scis., Mauna Loa Macadamia Ptnrs., ltd. partnerships; mem. Nat. Def. Exec. Res., Dept. Commerce. Author: (with others) The Management Primer, 1972, Life Sytle Marketing, 1979, Marketing Service, 1983; contbr. (with others) monograph series Western Bus. Roundup; founder, moderator monograph series Western Bus. Roundup radio series, 1958-68. Bd. dirs. Jr. Achievement Hawaii; trustee Tokai U. Honolulu Ctr., 1987—. Served to 1st lt. F.A. AUS, 1943-46; col. Res. Recipient alumni citation of merit U. Mo. Coll. Bus. and Pub. Adminstrn., 1969; Distinguished Service award Nat. Def. Transp. Assn., 1977, God and Service award United Meth. Ch./Boy Scouts Am., 1986; named to Faculty Hall Fame Ariz. State U. Coll. Bus. Assn., 1977, Hawaii Transp. Hall of Fame, 1986. Fellow Internat. Coun. for Small Bus. (pres. 1963); mem. Small Bus. Adminstrn. (chmn. adv. coun. region IX 1982-87), Hawaii World Trade Assn. (pres. 1973-74), Am. Mktg. Assn. (v.p. 1965-67, pres. Central Ariz. chpt. 1960-61, pres. Honolulu chpt. 1991-92), Western Assn. Collegiate Schs. Bus. (pres. 1972-73), Sales and Mktg. Execs. Internat. (life mem.), Acad. Internat. Bus., Nat. Def. Transp. Assn. (Hawaii v.p. 1978-82), Newcomen Soc. N. Am. (Hawaii chmn.), Pi Sigma Epsilon (v.p. for edn. programs 1990—), Mu Kappa Tau (sec.-treas. 1991-94), Beta Gamma Sigma, Omicron Delta Kappa, Beta Theta Pi, Delta Sigma Pi (gold coun.). Methodist. Club: Rotarian. Home: 311 Ohua Ave Apt 1104D Honolulu HI 96815-3636 Office: U Hawaii Coll Bus Adminstrn 2404 Maile Way # 401C Honolulu HI 96822-2282

HOOPER, CATHERINE EVELYN, developmental engineering specialist; b. Bklyn., Nov. 10, 1939; d. Frederick Charles Jr. and Catherine Veronica (Heaney) Podeyn; m. Melvyn Robert Lowney, Nov. 30, 1957 (div. 1970); children: Denise Lowney Andrade, Michele Lowney Budris; m. William White Hooper, Sept. 21, 1974. Student, San Jose (Calif.) City Coll., 1969, De Anza Coll., 1980. Insp. Amelco Semiconductor, Mountain View, Calif., 1966-68; lab. technician Fairchild R & D, Palo Alto, Calif., 1968-73; sr. lab. technician Varian Cen. Rsch., Palo Alto, 1973-84; sr. devel. engr. Hughes Rsch. Labs., Malibu, 1984—. Contbr. articles to profl. jours. Mem. Am. Vacuum Soc., Materials Rsch. Soc., Grad Women in Sci. (L.A. pres. 1990-92), Internat. Soc. Optical Engrs., Sigma Xi (sec. 1987-90). Office: Hughes Rsch Labs 3011 Malibu Canyon Rd Malibu CA 90265-4797

HOOPER, EDWIN BICKFORD, physicist; b. Bremerton, Wash., June 18, 1937; s. E.B. and Elizabeth (Patrick) H.; m. Virginia Hooper, Dec. 28, 1963; children: Edwin, Sarah, William. SB, MIT, 1959, PhD, 1965. Asst. prof. applied sci. Yale U., New Haven, 1966-70; physicist, special asst. sci. and tech. Lawrence Livermore (Calif.) Nat. Lab., 1970—. Contbr. articles to profl. jours. Pres. Danville (Calif.) Assn., 1982-84; pres. Friends Iron Horse Trail, 1984-86; v.p. San Ramon Valley Edn. Found., 1989-90; dir. Leadership, San Ramon Valley, 1990-92. Fellow Am. Phys. Soc. (bd. dirs. div. Plasma Physics 1990-91); mem. AIAA, Am. Assn. for Advancement Sci. Office: Lawrence Livermore Nat Lab 1 637 Livermore CA 94550

HOOPER, HENRY OLCOTT, university dean, physicist; b. Washington, Mar. 9, 1935; s. Olcott Lorin and Eleanor (Drew) H.; m. Donna Faulkingham, June 10, 1956 (div. 1992); children: Deborah, Bruce, Katherine, Michael, Andrew. B.S. in Engring. Physics, U. Maine, 1956; M.S. in Physics, Brown U., 1959, Ph.D., 1961. Asst. prof. Brown U., Providence, 1961-64; asst. prof. physics Wayne State U., Detroit, 1964-66, assoc. prof., 1966-70, prof., 1970-73; prof., chmn. dept. physics U. Maine, Orono, 1973-76, dean Grad. Sch., 1977-80, v.p. acad. affairs, 1979-80; assoc. v.p. acad. affairs, dean Grad. Coll., Grad. Coll. No. Ariz. U., Flagstaff, 1981—, interim v.p. acad. affairs, 1993—; cons. NASA, Huntsville, Ala., 1967-68; mem. rev. panel div. ednl. programs Argonne (Ill.) Nat. Lab., 1982-84; mem. exec. bd. Assoc. Western Univs., 1991—; v.p. Nat. Coun. Univ. Rsch. Adminstrs., 1991-92, pres., 1992-93. Author: College Physical Science, 3d edit., 1974, Physics and the Physical Perspective, 1977, 2d rev. edit., 1980; editor: Conf. Procs. Amorphous Magnetism, 1973. Fellow Am. Phys. Soc.; mem. AAAS, Am. Assn. Physics Tchrs. Home: 1300 University Height Dr S Flagstaff AZ 86001 Office: No Ariz U PO Box 4085 Flagstaff AZ 86011-4085

HOOPER, PAUL F(RANKLIN), American studies educator; b. Walla Walla, Wash., July 31, 1938; s. Dallas Albert and Mary Charlotte (Brewer) H.; m. Gloria Jean Zitterkopf, June 16, 1960; 1 child, Anthony Owen. BA, Ea. Wash. Coll., 1961; MA, U. Hawaii, 1965, PhD, 1972. Rsch. dir. Asia Tng. Ctr. U. Hawaii, Honolulu, 1967-69; dir. minority rsch. office Ho. Reps. Hawaii State Legislature, Honolulu, 1969-72; faculty mem. dept. Am. studies U. Hawaii, Honolulu, 1972—; exec. dir. Internat. Programs U. Hawaii, 1976-77, chmn. dept. Am. studies, 1988—; sr. lectr. Fulbright Program, Beijing, China, 1983-84; exec. asst. to mng. dir. City and County of Honolulu, 1985-86. Author: Elusive Destiny, 1980; editor: Building A Pacific Community, 1982, Remembering the Institute of Pacific Relations, 1993; contbr. articles to profl. jours. NDEA fellow, East-West Ctr. fellow, 1962-66; grantee various founds. and orgns., 1972—. Mem. AAUP, Am. Studies Assn., Fulbright Assn., U.S. Small Bus. Adminstrn. (nat. adv. bd. 1991—). Republican. Office: Dept Am Studies U Hawaii Honolulu HI 96822

HOOPES, SIDNEY LOU, marketing and advertising consultant, environmentalist; b. Monterey, Calif., Oct. 24, 1944; d. Jack Sidney Wayne Combs and Alta Virginia (Lane) Combs-Snow; m. Dan Fredrick Hoopes, Oct. 11, 1969; children: Rachel Virginia, Sarah Elizabeth. BSBA in Mktg., U. Ark., 1964. Market researcher Procter & Gamble, Cin., 1964-65; asst. press sec. U.S. Senator J. W. Fulbright, Washington, 1966-68; adminstr. regional office Tex. Chapparal Basketball Team, Lubbock, 1970-71; office adminstr., sec. Tex. Tech. U., Lubbock, 1971-72; office adminstr. Hoopes Law Office, Idaho Falls, Idaho, 1973-82; cons. mktg. and advt. Idaho Falls, 1983—; field rep. to Richard H. Stallings U.S. Congressman. Environ. educator Sch. Dist. #91, Idaho Falls, 1982-86; treas. Bonneville County Dem. Party, 1975-76, sec., 1988—; chief fund raiser Yellowstone Nat. Park Inst., 1983-84; bd. dirs. Idaho Falls Opera Theatre, 1984—; dist. field. mgr. U.S. Ho. of Reps. in 2d Congl. Dist. of Idaho. Named One of Outstanding Young Women Dems. in Idaho, 1975; proclaimed Sidney Hoopes Appreciation Day, Idaho Falls Opera Theatre, 1989. Mem. Greater Yellowstone Coalition (charter). Episcopalian. Home: 1950 Alan St Idaho Falls ID 83404-5722

HOOPES, SPENCER WENDELL, manufacturing executive; b. Safford, Ariz., Apr. 13, 1947; s. Spencer P. and Mary Anne (Ray) H.; m. Barbara Lynn Colvin, Dec. 14, 1983; 1 child, Lindsay Blair. BA, U. So. Calif., 1969; JD, U. Calif., Davis, 1972. Bar: Calif. 1972, U.S. Dist. Ct. (no. dist.) Calif. 1972, U.S. Ct. Appeals (10th cir.) 1972. Antitrust counsel Safeway Stores, Oakland, Calif., 1972-73; fin. analyst Curtis Fin. Corp., San Francisco, 1973-77; mng. dir. Churchill Internat., San Francisco, 1977-83; chief exec. officer Perstorp Xytec, Inc., Tacoma, 1983—. Patron Mont. Land Reliance, Helena, 1985; active Nature Conservancy, San Francisco, 1983. Capt. USAR, 1972-80. Mem. Calif. Bar Assn., Sierra Club, Young Pres. Orgn. Home: 4 Presidio Ter San Francisco CA 94118-1411 Office: Perstorp Xytec Inc 9350 47th Ave SW Po Box 99057 Tacoma WA 98499

HOOPS, ALAN, health care company executive; b. 1947. Asst. adminstr. Long Beach Mem. Hosp., 1973-77; v.p. Pacificare Health Sys. Inc., Cypress, Calif., 1977-85, sec., from 1982, sr. v.p., 1985-86, COO, exec. v.p., 1986—, CEO, 1993. Office: Pacificare Health Systems Inc 5995 Plaza Dr Cypress CA 90630-5028

HOOPS, WILLIAM JAMES, clergyman; b. Welch, Okla., June 10, 1957; s. Paul Raymond and Berta Lue (Stillwell) H.; m. Susan Denise Towers, May 12, 1983; 1 child, Robert Paul. BA, Okla. Bapt. U., 1983; MDiv, Golden Gate Sem., 1987. Ordained to ministry So. Bapt. Ch., 1987. Ministerial intern 1st Bapt. Ch., Concord, Calif., 1984-87; pastor 1st Bapt. Ch., Marina, Calif., 1987-91; chaplain USAFR, Mather AFB, Calif., 1975—, Fed. Bur. Prisons, Lompoc, Calif., 1991—. Producer TV documentary Insights, 1986-87. Bible tchr. 1st So. Bapt. Ch., Lompoc, 1991—. Capt. USAFR, 1975—. Mem. Calif. So. Bapt. Conv. (revival steering com. 1988-90), Cen. Coast Bapt. Assn. (vice moderator 1987-88, dir. evangelism 1988-91), Pacific Coast Bapt. Assn., Air Force Assn., Res. Officers Assn., Lompoc Fed. Correctional Instn. Employees Club (sec. 1991-92), Cen. Coast Ministerial Alliance (pres. 1988-89).

HOOTNICK, LAURENCE R., electronics company executive; b. 1942; married. With Ford Motor Co., Detroit, 1966-70, RCA Corp., 1970-73; sr. v.p. Intel Corp., San Jose, 1973—; also gen. mgr. Intel Corp. Office: Maxtor Corp 211 River Oaks Pkwy San Jose CA 95134

HOOVER, DONALD BRUNTON, geophysicist, gemologist; b. Cleve., June 17, 1930; s. Paul Leslie and Florence (Brunton) H.; m. Lucille Elizabeth Smith, Jan. 22, 1977. BS, Case Inst. Tech., Cleve., 1952; MSE, U. Mich., 1953; DSc, Colo. Sch. Mines, Golden, 1966. Registered profl. engr., Ohio. Seismic trainee Gulf Rsch. & Devel. Co., Harmarville, Pa., 1953; engr. Gulf Rsch. & Devel. Co., 1956-58; geophysicist U.S. Geol. Survey, Denver, 1960—; advisor geophysics Departmento Nacional de Producao Mineral, Rio de Janeiro, 1969-72; U.S. rep. in geophysics Pan Am. Inst. Geography and History, Mexico City, 1988-90. Author: Topaz; contbr. articles to profl. jours. With U.S. Army, 1954-56. Recipient U.S. Geol. Survey superior performance award, 1990. Fellow Gemmological Assn. Gt. Britain; mem. AAAS, Soc. Exploration Geophysicists (workshop organizer 1989), Assn. Exploration Geochemists, Colo. Soc. for Natural Hazards Rsch. (pres. 1976), Mineral. Soc. Am., Gemmological Assn. (U.K.), Colo. Gemmological Assn. (pres. 1984, 93), Gemmological Inst. Am. Alumni Assn. Office: US Geol Survey MS 964 Box 25046 Denver CO 80225

HOOVER, PEARL ROLLINGS, nurse; b. LeSueur, Minn., Aug. 24, 1924; d. William Earl and Louisa (Schickling) Rollings; m. Roy David Hoover, June 19, 1948 (dec. 1987); children: Helen Louise, William Robert (dec.). Grad. in nursing, U. Minn., 1945, BS in Nursing, 1947; MS in Health Sci., Calif. State U., Northridge, 1972. Dir. affiliate nursing sch. Mooselake (Minn.) State Hosp., 1948-49; nursing instr. Anchor Hosp., County Hosp., St. Paul, 1949-51; student nurse supr. and instr. Brentwood VA Hosp., L.A., 1951-52; sch. nurse L.A. Unified City Schs., 1963-91, part time sch. nurse, 1991—; part time sch. nurse Van Nuys Middle Sch., Calif., 1992—. Camp nurse, United First Meth. Ch. Mem. L.A. Coun. Sch. Nurses, Calif. Sch. Nurses Orgn. Democrat. Methodist. Home: 17851 Lull St Reseda CA 91335-2237

HOOVER, ROBERT CLEARY, bank executive; b. Highland Park, Ill., July 26, 1928; s. Howard Earl and Dorothy (Higgs) H.; m. Beatrice Leona Borroughs, June 21, 1949 (div.); children: Catherine, Robert C. II, Holly; m. Nancy Ellen Pitman, July 25, 1959 (div.); children: John, Elizabeth, Courtney; m. Cecilia Susan Flournoy, July 3, 1981; 1 child, Whitney Suzanne. BA, U. Calif., Berkeley, 1950. Asst. advt. mgr. Hoover Co., North Canton, Ohio, 1951-54; v.p., asst. gen. mgr. Golden State Linen Svc., Oakland, Calif., 1954-61; asst. mgr. Wells Fargo Bank, San Francisco, 1961-66; v.p. Bank Calif. Assn., San Francisco, 1966-84, v.p., spl. asst. to chmn. bd. and chief exec. officer, 1984—. Bd. mem. Providence Hosp., Oakland, 1985-91, Bay Area Tumor Inst., 1975—. Mem. Am. Inst. Banking, Naval War Coll. Found. (life), Navy League United States (life), Naval Order U.S. (life), Bohemian Club, Claremont Country Club, Pacific Union Club. Republican. Episcopalian. Home: 46 Sotelo Ave Piedmont CA 94611-3535

HOOVER, WILLIAM R(AY), computer service company executive; b. Bingham, Utah, Jan. 2, 1930; s. Edwin Daniel and Myrtle Tennessee (McConnell) H.; m. Sara Elaine Anderson, Oct. 4; children—Scott, Robert, Michael, James, Charles. B.S., M.S., U. Utah. Sect. chief Jet Propulsion Lab., Pasadena, Calif., 1954-64; v.p. Computer Scis. Corp., El Segundo, Calif., 1964-69, pres., 1969—, chmn. bd., 1972—, now also chief exec. officer, also bd. dirs. Office: Computer Scis Corp 2100 E Grand Ave El Segundo CA 90245-5098*

HOPE, GERRI DANETTE, telecommunications management executive; b. Sacramento, Feb. 28, 1956; d. Albert Gerald and Beulah Rae (Bane) Hope. AS, Sierra Coll., Calif., 1977; postgrad. Okla. State U., 1977-79. Instructional asst. San Juan Sch. Dist., Carmichael, Calif., 1979-82; telecommunications supr. Delta Dental Svc. of Calif., San Francisco, 1982-85; telecommunications coordinator Farmers Savs. Bank, Davis, Calif., 1985-87; telecommunications officer Sacramento Savs. Bank, 1987—; mem. telecomm. adv. panel Golden Gate U., Sacramento; lectr. in field. Mem. NAFE, Telecommunications Assn. (v.p. membership com. Sacramento Valley chpt.), Am. Philatelic Soc., Sacramento Philatelic Assn., Errors, Freaks and Oddities Club, Philatelic Collectors. Republican. Avocations: writing, computers, philately, animal behavior, participating in Christian ministry. Home: 2229 Woodside Ln # 8 Sacramento CA 95825-7487

HOPFIELD, JOHN JOSEPH, biophysicist, educator; b. Chgo., July 15, 1933; s. John Joseph and Helen (Staff) H.; m. Cornelia Fuller, June 30, 1954; children—Alison (Mrs. Charles C. Lifland), Jessica, Natalie. A.B., Swarthmore Coll., 1954; Ph.D., Cornell U., 1958; DSc (hon.), Swarthmore Coll., 1992. Mem. tech. staff ATT Bell Labs., 1958-60, 73-89; vis. research physicist Ecole Normale Superieure, Paris, France, 1960-61; asst. prof., then asso. prof. physics U. Calif. at Berkeley, 1961-64; prof. physics Princeton U., 1964-80, Eugene Higgins prof. physics, 1978-80; Dickinson prof. chemistry and biology Calif. Inst. Tech., Pasadena, 1980—. Trustee Battelle Meml. Inst., Harvey Mudd Coll., Huntington Med. Rsch. Inst. Guggenheim fellow, 1969, MacArthur Prize fellow, 1983; recipient Golden Plate award Am. Acad. Achievement, 1985, Michelson-Morley prize, 1988, Wright prize, 1989; named Calif. Scientist of Yr., 1991. Fellow Am. Phys. Soc. (Oliver E. Buckley prize 1968, Biol. Physics prize 1985); mem. Nat. Acad. Scis., Am. Acad. Arts and Scis., Am. Philos. Soc., Phi Beta Kappa, Sigma Xi. Home: 931 Canon Dr Pasadena CA 91106-4428 Office: Calif Inst Tech 139-74 Pasadena CA 91125

HOPKINS, ANDREW JAY, geologist; b. Houston, June 25, 1964; s. Roy Thomas and Geraldine L. (Baca) H. BS in Land Use and Geology, Met. State Coll., Denver, 1989. Asst. ranger Boy Scouts Am., Peaceful Valley, Colo., 1983; surveying asst. Rocky Mountain Cons., Denver, 1984; clk., typist Rocky Mountain Mapping Center, USGS, Lakewood, Colo., 1985; clk., typist hazardous waste mgmt. div. EPA, Denver, 1987; phys. sci. technician water resources div. Nat. Water Quality Lab., USGS, Arvada, Colo., 1988-89; engring. technician U.S. Army C.E., Pierre, S.D., 1989; cartographer Def. Mapping Agy., Hydrographic/Topographic Ctr., Louisville, 1989-90; phys. scientist-geologist U.S. Geol. Survey Br. Sedimentary Processes, Lakewood, 1991-92; seasonal maintenance worker Devils Tower Nat. Monument Nat. Pk. Svc., 1993—. Asst. scoutmaster Boy Scouts Am., Lakewood, 1982—. Mem. Colo. Pub. Interest Rsch. Group, Colo. Gem. and Mineral Soc., Colo. Sci. Soc., Sierra Club, Colo. Mountain Club, Jaycees, Toastmasters. Democrat. Presbyterian. Home: 1830 S Valentine St Lakewood CO 80228-3943

HOPKINS, CECILIA ANN, educator; b. Havre, Mont., Feb. 17, 1922; d. Kost L. and Mary (Manaras) Sofos; B.S., Mont. State Coll., 1944; M.A., San Francisco State Coll., 1958, M.A., 1967; postgrad. Stanford U.; Ph.D., Calif. Western U., 1977; m. Henry E. Hopkins, Sept. 7, 1944. Bus. tchr. Havre (Mont.) High Sch., Mateo, Calif., 1942-44; sec. George P. Gorham, Realtor, San Mateo, 1944-45; escrow sec. Fox & Cars 1945-50; escrow officer Calif. Pacific Title Ins. Co., 1950-57; bus. tchr. Westmoor High Sch., Daly City, Calif., 1958-59; bus. tchr. Coll. of San Mateo, 1959-63, chmn. real estate-ins. dept., 1963-76, dir. div. bus., 1976-86, coord. real estate dept., 1986-91; cons. to commr. Calif. Div. Real Estate, 1963-91, mem. periodic rev. exam. com.; chmn. C.C. Adv. Com., 1971-72, mem. com., 1975-91; projector direction Calif. State Chancellor's Career Awareness Consortium, mem. endowment fund adv. com., c.c. real estate edn. com., state c.c. adv. com.; mem. No. Calif. adv. bd. to Glendale Fed. Savs. and Loan Assn.; mem. bd. advisors San Mateo County Bd. Suprs., 1981-82; mem. real estate edn. and rsch. com. to Calif. Commr. Real Estate, 1983-90; mem. edn., membership, and profl. exchange coms. Am. chpt. Internat. Real Estate Fedn., 1985-92. Recipient Citizen of Day award KABL, Outstanding Contbns. award Redwood City-San Carlos-Belmont Bd. Realtors, REEAIS award emeritus, 1993; named Woman of Achievement, San Mateo-Burlingame br. Soroptimist Internat., 1979. Mem. AAUW, Calif. Assn. Real Estate Tchrs. (state pres. 1964-65, life hon. dir. 1962—, outstanding real estate educator of yr. 1978-79), Real Estate Cert. Inst. (Disting. Merit award 1982), Calif. Bus. Edn. Assn. (certificate of commendation 1979), San Francisco State Coll., Guidance and Counseling Alumni, Calif. Real Estate Educators' Assn. (dir. emeritus, hon. dir. 1990), Real Estate Nat. Educators Assn. (award emeritus for outstanding contributions, 1993), Alpha Delta, Pi Lambda Theta, Delta Pi Epsilon (nat. dir. interchpt. rels. 1962-65, nat. historian 1966-67, nat. sec. 1968-69), Alpha Gamma Delta. Co-author: California Real Estate Principles; contbr. articles to profl. jours. Home: 504 Colgate Way San Mateo CA 94402-3206

HOPKINS, EDWINA WEISKITTEL, graphic designer; b. Cin., June 7, 1947; d. Edwin and Moody (Bowling) Campbell; m. Michael J. Weiskittel, May 1966 (dec. May 1970); 1 son, Todd Michael. Student, U. Cin., 1965-66. Asst. to art dir. World Library Publs., Cin., 1965-68; comml. artist Campbell & Assocs. Art Studio, Cin., 1969-73; prodn. mgr. William Wilson Advt. Agy., Palos Verdes, Calif., 1973-74; ptnr. Hopkins & Hopkins Design Studio, Redondo Beach, Calif., 1975-76; owner, graphic designer Winnissa Comml. Art Studio, Rolling Hills, Calif., 1976-81; pres. Winnissa Inc., Redondo Beach, 1981—. U. Cin. hon. scholar, 1965. Mem. NAFE, Nat. Assn. Women Bus. Owners, Redondo Beach C. of C. Home and Office: 718 Avenue D Redondo Beach CA 90277-4924

HOPKINS, HENRY TYLER, art educator, university gallery director; b. Idaho Falls, Idaho, Aug. 14, 1928; s. Talcott Thompson and Zoe (Erbe) H.; children—Victoria Anne, John Thomas, Christopher Tyler. B.A., Sch. of Art Inst., Chgo., 1952, M.A., 1955; postgrad., UCLA, 1957-60; Ph.D. (hon.), Calif. Coll. Arts and Crafts, 1984; chmn. dept. art, UCLA, 1991—. Curator exhbns., publs. Los Angeles County Mus. of Art, 1960-68; dir. Fort Worth Art Mus., 1968-74, San Francisco Mus. of Modern Art, 1974-86; dir., emir. Frederick R. Weisman Collection Art Found., Los Angeles, 1986—; chmn., art dept. Univ. Calif., Los Angeles, 1991—; dir. F.S. Wight Gallery, UCLA, 1991—; lectr. art history, extension U. Calif. at Los Angeles, 1958-68; instr. Tex. Christian U., Fort Worth, 1968-74; dir. U.S. representation Venice (Italy) Bienniel, 1970; dir. art presentation Festival of Two Worlds, Spoleto, Italy, 1970; co-commr. U.S. representation XVI São Paulo (Brazil) Biennale, 1981; cons. Nat. Endowment for Arts, mem. mus. panel, 1979-84, chmn., 1981; cons., mem. mus. panel Nat. Endowment for Humanities, 1976. Contbr. numerous articles to profl. jours., also numerous mus. publs. Served with AUS, 1952-54. Decorated knight Order Leopold II, Belgium); recipient special internat. award, Art L.A., 1992. Mem. Assn. Art Mus. Dirs. (pres. 1985-86), Coll. Art Assn., Am. Assn. Museums, Western Assn. Art Museums (pres. 1977-78). Home: 939 1/2 Hilgard Ave Los Angeles CA 90024-3032 Office: Wight Art gallery UCLA 1100 Dickson Gallery Bldg 405 Hilgard Los Angeles CA 90024

HOPKINS, PAUL NATHAN, physician, researcher; b. Ft. Belvoir, Va., Sept. 13, 1952; s. Robert Clarke and Elizabeth (Ramsey) H.; m. Cynthia Lynn Harvey, July 11, 1986; 1 child, Zachary Harvey. BS, UCLA, 1976, MS in Pub. Health, 1978; MD, U. Utah, 1984. Diplomate Am. Bd. Pub. Health and Preventive Medicine. Resident in internal medicine Mayo Grad. Sch. of Medicine, Rochester, Minn., 1984-85; asst. prof. internal medicine rsch. Sch. of Medicine U. Utah, Salt Lake City, 1986—; adj. asst. prof. dept. food and nutrition U. Utah, 1987—; Lipid faculty Merck, Sharpe Dohme; prin. investigator Drug/Nutrition Studies and Family Studies in Cardiovascular Genetics, Salt Lake City, 1989—. Contbr. articles to profl. jours. Mem. N.Y. Acad. Scis. LDS. Home: 10418 N Hidden Oak Dr Highland UT 84003-9203 Office: Cardiovascular Genetics 410 Chipeta Way Rm 161 Salt Lake City UT 84108-1209

HOPKINS, PHILIP JOSEPH, journalist, editor; b. Orange, Calif., Dec. 10, 1954; s. Philip Joseph and Marie Elizabeth H. BA in Journalism, San Diego State U., 1977. Cert. tissue therapist Center for Decubitis Ulcer Research, 1981. Reporter, La Jolla Light & Journal (Calif.), 1973; editorial cons. San Diego Union, 1974; asst. producer Southwestern Cable TV, San Diego, 1974; corr. Mission Cable TV, San Diego, 1975; photojournalist United Press Internat., San Diego, 1976; editor Rx Home Care mag., L.A., 1981, Hosp. Info. Mgmt. mag., 1981; editor, assoc. pub. Arcade mag., 1982; mng. editor Personal Computer Age, L.A., 1983-84; bur. chief Newsbytes syndicated column, 1985-86; v.p. Humbird Hopkins Inc., L.A., 1978-88; personal fin. writer Hume Pub. Co., 1987-89; writer, editor and researcher Ind. Rsch. and Info. Svc., 1988-90; writer, analyst Geneva Bus. Rsch., 1990; sci. writer, The Cousteau Soc., 1990; pub. cons. U. So. Calif., 1989; sr. info. analyst Kaiser Permanente, 1991—. Recipient 1st and 4th place awards Nikon, Inc., Photo Contest, 1974; 3rd prize Minolta Camera Co. Creative Photography awards, 1975; Best Feature Photo award Sigma Delta Chi Mark of Excellence contest, 1977. Pres. Ind. Writers of So. Calif., 1988. Mem. Computer Press Assn. (life, hon.). Co-author: The Students' Survival Guide, 1977, 78; photographs have appeared in Time and Omni mags., The Mythology of Middle Earth, Parenting Your Aging Parents, Beginners Guide to the SLR, NBC-TV's Saturday Night Live. Office: PO Box 40939 Pasadena CA 91114-7939

HOPKINS, ROBERT ARTHUR, retired industrial engineer; b. Youngstown, Ohio, Dec. 14, 1920; s. Arthur George and Margaret Viola (Brush) H.; m. Mary Madelaine Bailey, Apr. 6, 1946; 1 child, Marlaine Hopkins Kaiser. BBA, Case Western Reserve U., 1949; cert. loss control engr., U. Calif., Berkeley, 1969. Lic. indsl. safety engr. Ins. agt. Nat. Life and Accident Ins. Co., Lorain, Akron, Ohio, 1951-56, San Mateo, Calif., 1951-56; ins. agt., engr. Am. Hardware Mt. Ins. Co., San Jose, Fresno, Calif., 1956-60; loss control engr. Manhattan Guarantee-Continental Ins. Co., Calif., 1967-77. Organizer Operation Alert CD, Lorain, 1951-52; prin. speaker CD, Fresno, 1957; active Pleasant Hill (Calif.) Civic Action Com., 1981-83; civilian coord. Office Emergency Svcs., Pleasant Hill, 1983-85; advisor, coord. airshows and warbird aircraft, 1980—; chmn. bd. Western Aerospace Mus., Oakland, Calif., 1988—; ops. asst. for tower and ops. 50th Anniversary Golden Gate Bridge, San Francisco, 1987; advisor, coord. Travis AFB Air Expo '90, 1990, Naval Air Sta. Alameda (Calif.) 50th Anniversary, 1990; advisor Naval Air Sta. Moffett Field Air Show, 1990, 92; warbird coord. Port of Oakland Airshow, 1987; mem. Smithsonian Mus., Smithsonian Air & Space Mus. With U.S. Army Air Corps, 1942. Recipient Letter of Appreciation Fresno CD, 1957, cert. of appreciation City of Pleasant Hill, 1986. Mem. No. Calif. Safety Engrs. Assn. (v.p., pres., chmn. 1974-77), Confederate Air Force (mem. staff, leader Pacific wing 1980—), Nat. Aero. Assn., Aero. Club No. Calif., Hamilton Field Assn. (dir. ops. Wings of Victory Air Show 1987, coord. 1988, 89—, asst. to pres. 1989—, advisor contr. 1990—), VFW (life, state civil disaster chmn. Area 5 Calif. 1991), Air Force Assn., Kiwanis (chpt. sec.-treas.). Republican. Roman Catholic. Home: 48 Mazie Dr Pleasant Hill CA 94523-3310

HOPKINS, RONALD HERBERT, university official; b. Marshalltown, Iowa, Oct. 16, 1941; s. Richard Herbert and Rosella Eva (Drewelow) H.; m. Mary Judith Cockrill, Sept. 5, 1964; children: Tracy Jo, Kirstin Anne. BS, Iowa State U., 1963; MS, U. Iowa, 1966, PhD, 1967. Rsch. assoc. Stanford (Calif.) U., 1967-68; asst. prof. SUNY, Binghamton, 1968-69; asst. prof., assoc. prof. psychology Wash. State U., Pullman, 1969-74, assoc. prof., prof., chmn. dept. psychology, 1975-86, vice provost, 1986-90, acting provost, 1990-91; grants assoc. NIH, Bethesda, Md., 1974-75, health scientist adminstr., 1975; v.p. for acad. affairs San Diego State U., 1991—; Bd. dirs. Wash. Inst. for Pub. Policy, Olympia, 1986-91, Calif. State U. Inst. for Teaching and Learning, Long Beach, 1992—; presenter in field; prin., co-investigator extramural rsch. grants. Contbr. articles to profl. jours. Chmn. bd. dirs. June Burnett Inst. for Children, San Diego, 1992—. Scholar Iowa State U., 1959-63; fellow NDEA, 1965-67. Mem. Am. Psychol. Soc., Cognitive Sci. Soc., Midwestern Psychol. Assn., Psychonomic Soc., Golden Key (hon.), Sigma Xi. Office: Office Acad Affairs San Diego State U San Diego CA 92182-0713

HOPKINS, STEPHEN DAVIS, retired business executive; b. N.Y.C., Oct. 31, 1907; s. Louis Davis and Margaret Hall (Daly) H.; m. Hildegarde Lupprian, 1942 (dec. 1983). BA, Yale U., 1935. Page N.Y. Stock Exch., 1928; specialist clk. N.Y. Stock Exch., N.Y.C., 1929-31; teller 1st Nat. Bank, Greenwich, Conn., 1935-37; editor Commerce & Fin. mag., 1938-41; chief adminstrv. officer Jensvold Mfg. Co., Olympia, Wash., 1945-46; account exec. Conrad, Bruce & Co., Seattle, 1947-48; investment counsel Pacific Rsch. & Mgmt. Co., Seattle, 1949-63; gen. mgr. plywood coop., Tacoma, 1951-52; writer nat. media on domestic currency consumer point view Deer Lodge, Mont., 1962—; advisor, cons. to U.S. currency mgrs., 1962—; advisor to currency mgrs. Republic of Russia, 1992, 93. Editor: U.S. Coin and Currency Laws from 1775—, Inflation-Watch, 1978-83. Head usher St. George's Episcopal Ch., N.Y.C., 1975-76; mem. western Wash. enrollment and scholarship com. Yale U., 1948-52. 1st lt. C.E., U.S. Army, 1942-45. Mem. Mil. Order World Wars (officer Seattle chpt. 1950). Home and Office: 525 W 3d Ave Anchorage AK 99501

HOPKINS, THOMAS DAVID, educator, consultant; b. El Cerrito, Calif., Jan. 15, 1939; s. Arthur Lorenzo and Ina Grace (Davis) H.; m. E. Jean Morris, Sept. 12, 1960 (div. 1965); children: Cynthia Grace, Susan Jean; m. Rose Annie Smith Connie, Jan. 26, 1967; children: Karen Connie, David Thomas, Kevin John. BA in Edn., Brigham Young U., 1962, MA in Music Theory, 1968; EdD, U. of Pacific, 1977. Instr. clarinet Brigham Young U., Provo, Utah, 1961-62; music tchr., coord. South Sanpete Schs., Ephraim, Utah, 1962-64, North Summit Sch., Coalville, Utah, 1965-67; tchr. music Grantsville (Utah) High Sch., 1964-65; tchr. music Stockton (Calif.) Unified Sch. Dist., 1967-75, tchr. math., algebra, 1976—; tchr. educator Univ. of Pacific, Stockton, 1975-76; ind. cons. in edn., pvt. adminstrn., 1975—. Adult leader backpacking, survival unit Calif. Sierras coun. Boy Scouts Am., 1973-78; tchr., leader backpacking, survival unit Girls' Camp Liahona, Calif. Sierras, 1978-92; asst. dir. Stockton Family History Ctr., 1986—; high councilor, leader LDS Ch., Stockton; music dir. local ch. and musical events, San Joaquin Valley, Calif., 1975-85. With USN, 1957-60. Mem. Calif. Music Educators Assn. (disting. author, lectr. 1978), Phi Delta Kappa (pres., bd. dirs. Univ. of Pacific chpt. 1978-88, area coord. no. Calif. and Nev. chpt. 1990—, curriculum disseminator 1986—). Republican. Home: 125 Erma Ave Stockton CA 95207 Office: Hamilton Middle Sch 2245 E 11th St Stockton CA 95206

HOPKINSON, SHIRLEY LOIS, library science educator; b. Boone, Iowa, Aug 25, 1924; d. Arthur Perry and Zora (Smith) Hopkinson; student Coe Coll., 1942-43; A.B. cum laude (Phi Beta Kappa scholar 1944), U. Colo., 1945; B.L.S., U. Calif., 1949; M.A. (Honnold Honor scholar 1945-46), Claremont Grad. Sch., 1951; Ed.M., U. Okla., 1952, Ed.D., 1957 Tchr. pub. sch. Stigler, Okla., 1946-47, Palo Verde High Sch., Jr. Coll., Blythe, Calif., 1947-48; asst. librarian Modesto (Calif.) Jr. Coll., 1949-51; tchr., librarian Fresno, Calif., 1951-52, La Mesa, Cal., 1953-55; asst. prof. librarianship, instructional materials dir. Chaffey Coll., Ontario, Calif., 1955-59; asst. prof. librarian ship, San Jose (Calif.) State Coll., 1959-64; assoc. prof., 1964-69, prof., 1969—. Dir. NDEA Inst. Sch. Librarians, summer 1966; mem. Santa Clara County Civil Service Bd. Examiners. Mem. ALA, Calif. Library Assn., Audio-Visual Assn. Calif., NEA, AAUP, AAUW (dir. 1957-58), Bus. Profl. Women's Club, Sch. Librarians Assn. Calif. (com. mem., treas. No. sect. 1951-52), San Diego County Sch. Librarians Assn. (sec. 1945-55), Calif. Tchrs. Assn., LVW (bd. dirs. 1950-51, publs. chmn.), Phi Beta Kappa, Alpha Lambda Delta, Alpha Beta Alpha, Kappa Delta Pi, Phi Kappa Phi (disting. acad. achievement award 1981), Delta Kappa Gamma. Author: Descriptive Cataloging of Library Materials; Instructional Materials for Teaching the Use of the Library. Contbr. to profl. publs. Editor: Calif. Sch. Libraries, 1963-64; asst. editor: Sch. Library Assn. of Calif. Bull., 1961-63. Office: 1340 Pomeroy Ave # 408 Santa Clara CA 95051-3658

HOPPENSTEADT, JON KIRK, law librarian; b. Milw., Feb. 24, 1959; s. George Arthur and Sheila Ann (Doyle) H. BA, U. Nev., 1980, '81; MA, Denver U., 1984; JD, U. Minn., 1989. Reference libr. intern Denver U., Englewood (Colo.) Pub. Libr., 1984; indexer, abstractor Info. Access Co., Foster City, Calif., 1984-86; pub. libr. intern Mpls. Pub. Libr., 1987-88; student dir. Legal Assistance to Minn. Prisoners, Mpls., 1988-89; reference libr. Univ. Minn. Law Libr., Mpls., 1987-91; victims' rights advocate unaffiliated, Rohnert Park, Calif., 1992—. Cataloger Westlaw Legal Database Catalog, 1991. Mem. Nat. Orgn. for Victim Assistance, Washington, 1992. Mem. Am. Assn. Law Librs. Democrat. Lutheran. Home and Office: 4889 Fairway Dr Rohnert Park CA 94928-1306

HOPPER, DAVID LEE, neuropsychologist, somnologist; b. Memphis, Aug. 28, 1953; s. Billy Joe and Una Mae (Claussen) H.; m. Clara Santiago, Dec. 28, 1989; children: Michael, Robert, John. BS, La. State U., 1982; MS, Columbia Pacific, 1987, PhD, 1987. Cert. behavioral medicine, somnology, med. psychotherapy, profl. psychotherapy, substance abuse, clin. hypnotherapy, addictions. Dir. Baton Rouge Counseling & Therapy Ctr., 1983-86; pvt. practice Las Vegas, Nev., 1987-89; instr. continuing edn. U. Nev., Las Vegas, 1988—; somnologist Western Region Sleep Disorders Ctr., Las Vegas, 1990-91; med. psychologist-neuropsychologist Univ. Med. Ctr., Las Vegas, 1989-92; advisor rsch. com. Univ. Med. Ctr., Las Vegas, 1990-92; trauma psychologist South Nev. Regional Trauma Ctr., Las Vegas, 1990-92; adj. faculty dept. sci. and health Community Coll. So. Nev.; clin. dir. Behavioral Medicine Cons.; program developer/mental health dir. Vitality Ctr., Elko, Nev.; lectr. in field. Researcher/developer Psychotherapeutic Diagnostic and Treatment Techniques; developer Neurosensory Feedback Coma Stimulation; contbr. articles to profl. publs. Active various civic and community svc. orgns. Fellow Am. Acad. Behavioral Medicine, Am. Acad. Somnology (pres. 1986—), Am. Assn. Profl. Hypnotherapists, Am. Bd. Med. Psychoterapists, Internat. Acad. Behavioral Medicine, Counseling & Psychotherapy; mem. AAAS, APA, Am. Assn. Counseling and Devel., Am. Mental Health Counselors Assn., Am. Acad. Somnology, Am. Pain Soc., Nat. Assn. Alcohol & Drug Abuse Counseling, Assn. Applied Psychophysiology & Biofeedback, N.Y. Acad. Scis. Republican. Roman Catholic. Home: PO Box 29124 Las Vegas NV 89126-3124 Office: Univ Med Ctr 1800 W Charleston Blvd Las Vegas NV 89102-2329

HOPPER, SALLY, state legislator; widowed; children: Nancy, Joan, Caroline, Anne. BA, U. Wyo., 1956. Mem. Colo. Senate, Denver, 1987—; chair Senate Health, Environ., Welfare and Insts. com.; chair Criminal Justice Commn, mem. Judiciary com. Mem. nat. bd. Physically Challenged Access to the Woods; chair bd. Spalding Rehab. Hosp., bd. dirs. Colo. Trail Found. Mem. Kappa Kappa Gamma. Republican. Episcopalian. Home: 21649 Cabrini Blvd Golden CO 80401-9406

HOPPER, WILBERT HILL, oil industry executive; b. Ottawa, Ont., Can., Mar. 14, 1933; s. Wilbert Clayton and Eva (Hill) H.; m. Patricia Marguerite Walker, Aug. 12, 1957; children: Sean Wilbert, Christopher Mark. Student, Scots Coll., Sydney, Australia, Wellington (New Zealand) Coll.; BSc in Geology, Am. U.; MBA, U. Western Ont., London; LLD (hon.), Wilfrid Laurier U. Petroleum geologist Imperial Oil, 1955-57; petroleum economist Foster Assocs., 1959-61; sr. energy economist Nat. Energy Bd., Ottawa, 1961-64; sr. petroleum cons. Arthur D. Little, Inc., Cambridge, Mass., 1964-73; asst. dep. min. energy policy Dept. of Energy, Mines and Resources, Ottawa, 1973-75; pres., chief exec. officer Petro-Can., 1976-79, chmn., ceo, dir., 1979—, also bd. dirs.; chmn., bd. dirs. Westcoast Energy Inc.; vice-chmn., bd. dirs. Panarctic Oils Ltd.; bd. dirs. Can.-China Trade Coun., ICG Propane Inc., Bi-Provincial Upgrader Joint Venture. Mem. bd. govs. Oxford Inst. for Energy Studies, Ottawa; mem. internat. adv. coun. Centre for Global Energy Studies; mem. adv. com. Sch. Bus. Adminstrn., U. Western Ont. Decorated officer Order of Can. Mem. Can. Econ. Assn., Am. Econ. Assn., Can. Soc. Petroleum, Am. Assn. Petroleum Geologists, Can. Inst. for Advanced Rsch., Can. Inst. Mining and Metallurgy, Soc. Petroleum Engrs., Ont. Petroleum Inst. Inc. Office: Petro-Canada, 150-6th Ave SW PO Box 2844, Calgary, AB Canada T2P 3E3

HOPPING, WILLIAM RUSSELL, hospitality industry consultant and appraiser; b. Balt., May 3, 1947; s. Russell Leroy and Janet Louise (Cloud) H. BS in Hotel Adminstrn., Cornell U., 1969; MBA, U. Denver, 1978. Mgr. Sylvania (Ohio) Country Club, 1972-77; sr. cons. Pannell Kerr Forster, Denver, 1978-82; ind. cons. Ginther Wycoff Grp., Denver, 1982-85; pres. W.R. Hopping & Co., Inc., Denver, 1985—. Vol., Big Bros., Inc., Denver, 1990—; chmn. adv. bd. U. Denver Profl. Career Devel. Prog., 1987-88, chmn. task force, Career and Placement Ctr., 1989. 1st lt. U.S. Army, 1970-72. Mem. Appraisal Inst., Internat. Soc. Hospitality Cons. (pres. 1990-91, chmn. 91—), Cornell Soc. Hotelmen (pres. Rocky Mountain chpt. 1984-85). Office: W R Hopping & Co Inc 4170 S Roslyn St Denver CO 80237-2115

HORAN, MARY ANN THERESA, nurse; b. Denver, July 4, 1936; d. John Paul and Lucille (Somma) Perito; m. Stephen F. Horan, Sr., Dec. 28, 1957; children: Seanna, Dana, Michelle, Annette, Stephen Jr., Christine, David. BSN, Loretto Heights Coll., Denver, 1958; postgrad, Pima Community Coll., 1982. RN, Ala. Staff nurse Med. Ctr. Hosp., Huntsville, Ala., 1978-79, Crestwood Hosp., Huntsville, 1980-81, St. Joseph Hosp. Eye Surgery, Tucson, 1981—; v.p. Success Achievement Ctr., Tucson, 1987—; Amway distbr. Horan and Assocs., 1992—. Contbr. articles to nursing jours. Republican. Roman Catholic. Home: 8311 E 3d St Tucson AZ 85710

HORAN, STEPHEN FRANCIS, technical writer, insurance agent; b. Denver, June 15, 1933; s. Daniel Stephen and Rose Bridget (Shanley) H.; m. Mary Ann Theresa Perito, Dec. 28, 1957; children: Seanna, Dana, Michelle, Annette, Stephen Jr., Christine, Dave. Diploma, Interior Command Sch., Gt. Lakes, Mich., 1953, Mech. Design & Draft Sch., Denver, 1956; postgrad., U. Denver, 1957. Sr. tech. writer Missile Systems Corp., Denver, 1961-62; sr. tech. publs. engr. Martin Marietta Co., Denver, 1962-64; chief editorial br. Dugway Proving Ground U.S. Army, Utah, 1964-65, chief svcs. div. Dugway Proving Ground, 1965-68; tech. publs. editorial supr. Deseret Test Ctr. U.S. Army, 1968-73; tech. publs. writer Tropic Test Ctr. U.S. Army, Ft. Clayton, C.Z., Panama, 1973-75; tech. manuals writer Missile Command U.S. Army, Huntsville, Ala., 1978-81; tech. publs. writer, editor Communications Security Log U.S. Army, Ft. Huachuca, Ariz., 1981-92; pres. Success Achievement Ctr., Tucson, 1987—; Amway distributor Horan & Assocs. Amway Distribution, 1992—. Author Tour of Historic Ft. Douglas, 1976. Coach, Dugway Youth Activities, 1968-72, 75-78; pres. Dugway Parish Council, 1975, Dugway Booster Club, 1976. With USN, 1951-54. Mem. Soc. Tech. Writers and Pubs., Author's Resource Ctr., Toastmasters, KC. Roman Catholic. Home and Office: Success Achievement Ctr 8311 E 3d St Tucson AZ 85710

HORN, GILBERT, minister. Exec. dir. Colo. coun. of Chs., Denver. Office: Colo Coun Ch 1370 Pennsyvania Ste 100 Denver CO 80203

HORN, LEWIS MARTIN, computer consultant; b. Bklyn., May 28, 1965; s. Charles and Fay (Zuckerman) H.; m. Jerrel Ruth Bond, July 25, 1992. AA, Broward Community Coll., 1987; BS, Calif. State U., Dominguez Hills, 1993. Cardmember svcs. rep. Am. Express Co., Fort Lauderdale, Fla., 1984-87; sr. cost acct. Am. Comml. Inc., Carson, 1987-92; ind. cons. L.M. Horn & Assocs., Gardena, Calif., 1992—. Author: (computer software) Vic Autodialer, 1984, Comnet BBS, 1985, InterStore, 1992, JV, 1992. Mem. Nat. Assn. Rocketry, Am. Radio Relay League, Sierra Club. Democrat. Home: 24 W 53d St # 4 Long Beach CA 90805 Office: LM Horn Assocs PO Box 3556 Gardena CA 90247

HORN, (JOHN) STEPHEN, congressman, political science educator; b. San Juan Bautista, Calif., May 31, 1931; s. John Stephen and Isabelle (McCaffrey) H.; m. Nini Moore, Sept. 4, 1959; children: Marcia Karen Horn Yavitz, John Stephen. AB with great distinction, Stanford, 1953, postgrad., 1953-54, 55-56, PhD in Polit. Sci, 1958; M in Pub Adminstrn., Harvard, 1955. Congl. fellow, 1958-59; adminstrv. asst. to sec. labor Washington, 1959-60; legislative asst. to U.S. Senator Thomas H. Kuchel, 1960-66; sr. fellow The Brookings Instn., 1966-69; dean grad. studies and research Am. U., 1969-70; pres. Calif. State U., Long Beach, 1970-88, Trustee prof. polit. sci., 1988-93; mem. 103rd Congress from 38th Calif. dist., 1993—; sr. cons., host The Govt. Story on TV, The Election Game (radio series), 1967-69, vice chmn. U.S. Commn. on Civil Rights, 1969-80 (commr. 1980-82); chmn. Urban Studies Fellow Adv. Com., U.S. Dept. HUD, 1969-70; mem. Law Enforcement Ednl. Prog. Adv. Com., U.S. Dept Justice, 1969-70; adv. bd. Nat. Inst. Corrections, 1972-88 (chmn. 1984-87),. Author: The Cabinet and Congress, 1960, Unused Power: The Work of the Senate Committee on Appropriations, 1970, (with Edmund Beard) Congressional Ethics: The View from the House, 1975. Mem. urban studies fellowship adv. bd. Dept. Housing and Urban Devel., 1969-70, chmn., 1969; mem. Pres.-elect Nixon's Task Force on Orgn. Exec. Br., 1968; mem. Kutak Found.; Long Beach area C. of C. (vice chmn. 1984-88), co-founder Western U.S. Com. Arts and Scis. for Eisenhower, 1956; chmn. Am. Assn. State Colls. and Univs., 1985-86; mem. Calif. Ednl. Facilities Authority, 1984-93. USAR, 1954-62. Fellow John F. Kennedy Inst. Politics Harvard U., 1966-67. Fellow Nat. Acad. Pub. Adminstrn.; mem. Stanford Assocs., Stanford Alumni Assn. (pres. 1976-77), Phi Beta Kappa, Pi Sigma Alpha. Republican. Office: 1023 Longworth House Office Bldg Washington DC 20515

HORN, STEVEN WALTER, state agency official; b. Clinton, Iowa, May 14, 1947; s. Walter Edmund and Janice Francis (Soll) H.; m. Karen Sue Blackett, July 15, 1970; children: Tiffany Anne, Melissa Lee, Amanda Sue. BS in Wildlife Biology, Colo. State U., 1969, MS in Zoology, 1974, PhD in Zoology, 1979. Resource conservationist Colo. Soil Conservation Bd., Denver, 1978-83, dir., 1983-87; dep. commr. agr. Colo. Dept. Agr., Denver, 1987-89, exec. dir., 1987—, commr., 1989—. Contbr. articles to profl. publs. Trustee Colo. 4-H Found. With U.S. Army, 1970-72, Vietnam. Recipient numerous grante, awards for conservation and agrl. activities. Mem. AAAS, Animal Behavior Soc., Am. Assn. Manmmalologists, Soc. Vet. Ethology, Assn. Applied Animal Behaviorists, Colo. Farm Bur., Rocky Mountain Farmers Assn., Sigma Xi. Office: Colo Dept Agr 700 Kipling St 4th Fl Lakewood CO 80227

HORNADAY, ALINE GRANDIER, publisher, independent scholar; b. San Diego, Sept. 14, 1923; d. Frank and Lydia Landon (Weir) Grandier; m. Quinn Hornaday, Oct. 9, 1965. BA, Union of Experimenting Colls., San Diego, 1977; PhD, U. Calif., San Diego, 1984. Pub. San Diego Daily Transcript, 1952-72, columnist, 1972-74; dir. San Diego Ind. Scholars, 1985-87; co-pub. Jour. Unconventional History, Cardiff, Calif., 1989—; vis. scholar U. Calif., San Diego, 1984—; speaker at profl. confs. Co-author: The Hornadays, Root and Branch; contbr. articles to profl. jours. Commr. San Diego City Libr. Commn., 1964-70. Mem. San Diego Ind. Scholars, Nat. Coalition Ind. Scholars, Med. Assn. of Pacific, Am. Hist. Assn., Medieval Acad. Am., Nat. Soc. Colonial Dames of Am., Wed. Club (pres. 1964-65). Home and Office: 6435 Avenida Cresta La Jolla CA 92037-6514

HORNBACK, VERNON T., JR., university administrator; b. Bowling Green, Ky., Oct. 3, 1931; s. Vernon Theodore and Elizabeth (Borrone) H.; m. Patricia Barrett, Sept. 1 1962; children: Vernon Theodore III, James Barrett, Robert Borrone. BS, St. Louis U., 1953, MA, 1955, PhD, 1963. Grad. teaching asst. St. Louis U., 1953-55, dir. athletic publicity, 1957-59; instr., asst. prof. So. Ill. U., Edwardsville, 1959-64; asst., assoc. and full prof. dept. English Calif. State U., Sacramento, 1964—; chmn. dept. English Calif. State U., 1969—; cons. writing programs English dept. evaluations, 1980—; cons., reader Ednl. Testing Svc., Emeryville, Calif., 1975—. Contbr. articles to various publs. Chmn. legis. com. Calif. Assn. Tchrs. of English, Sacramento, 1970-76; mem. high sch. equivalency exam evaluation com., Sacramento, 1975; me. readability com. office legis. analyst, Calif. State Legis., 1984—. 1st lt. USAF, 1955-57. Mem. AAUP (pres. chpt. 1963-64), Nat. Coun. Tchrs. English (bd. dirs. 1971-73, 79-81), Calif. Assn. Tchrs. English (bd. dirs. 1971-73, 79-81), Calif. Faculty Assn., English Coun. Calif. State U. (pres. 1971-73, 79-81, exec. com. 1971-77, 79-83), MLA. Democrat. Roman Catholic. Office: Calif State U Sacramento English Dept Sacramento CA 95819

HORNBAKER, LARRY DOUGLAS, academic administrator, fundraiser; b. Hutchinson, Kans., Nov. 3, 1934; s. Cecil Frank and Helen Gertrude (Beard) H.; m. Carolee GrosJean, Mar. 19, 1964; children: Deborah Lee Hornbaker Barnett, Douglas Carroll, David William, Darin Frank. BA, Abilene (Tex.) Christian U., 1965; MBA, Pepperdine U., 1976, EdD, 1986. From asst. campaign mgr. to v.p., gen. mgr. Hallmark Communications, Inc., Abilene, 1963-69; v.p. devel. Pepperdine U., Malibu, Calif, 1969-73, v.p. adminstrn., 1973-74, 75-76, acting v.p. fin., 1974-75, sr. v.p., 1976-89, v.p. corporate rels., 1989-92, exec. vice chancellor, 1992. Bd. dirs. Malibu Township Coun., 1983-84, Malibu Esplanade, 1985—, western div. ARC, L.A., 1991—. Mem. Conejo C. of C. (bd. dirs. 1980-85), Rotary (gov. dist. 5280 1990-91), Regency Club. Republican. Home: 26608 Goldenrod Pl Calabasas CA 91302-2944 Office: Pepperdine U Malibu CA 90263-4898

HORNBEIN, VICTOR, architect; b. Denver, Oct. 26, 1913; s. Samuel and Rose (Frumess) H.; m. Ruth Kriesler, Mar. 20, 1947; children: Victoria Ann, Peter. Student, Atelier Denver, Beaux-Arts Inst. Design, 1930-35. Practice as Victor Hornbein, architect, 1940-60; with firm Victor Hornbein and Edward D. White, Jr., Denver, 1960-76; partner Victor Hornbein and Edward D. White, Jr., 1960-76; prin. Victor Hornbein & Assos., Denver, 1976-80; partner Victor Hornbein & John James, 1980-82; prin. Victor Hornbein, Architect, 1982—; vis. lectr. U. Denver, 1949-52, U. Colo., 1958-59, 68, 75, mem. design rev. bd., 1969-73; design adv. panel region 8 Gen. Services Adminstrn., 1967-70; vol. faculty U. Colo. Sch. Architecture, 1989-90. Major works include: conservatory and edn. bldg. Denver Bot. Gardens, 1966-71, conservatory and edn. bldg. Porter Library, Colo. Women's Coll., Denver, 1962, Bethesda Hosp., Denver, 1970, René Spitz Children's div. Ft. Logan Mental Health Center, Denver, 1965, housing for elderly, 1973, Sanctuary Wellshire Presbyn. Ch., 1980, Orchid and Bromeliad House, Denver Bot. Gardens, 1980, Wellshire Presbyn. Ch., 1985. Pres. Met. Council Community Services, 1957; bd. advisors Wright-Ingraham Inst., 1972—, trustee, 1974—, chmn. bd. trustees, 1975-82. Served with AUS, 1942-45. Decorated Bronze Star. Fellow AIA (pres. Colo. Central chpt. 1971, Silver medal Western Mountain region 1981). Home and Office: Victor Hornbein Architect 266 Jackson St Denver CO 80206-5525

HORNBY-ANDERSON, SARA ANN, metallurgical engineer, marketing professional; b. Plymouth, Devon, Eng., Apr. 17, 1952; came to U.S., 1986; d. Foster John and Joanna May (Duncan) Hornby; m. John Victor Anderson, Sept. 2, 1978 (div. May 1987). BSc in Metallurgy with honors, Sheffield (Eng.) City Poly., 1973, PhD in Indsl. Metallurgy, 1980. Chartered engr. Metallurgist Joseph Lucas Rsch., Solihull, Eng., 1970, William Lee Maleable, Dronfield, Eng., 1972; tech. sales specialist Applied Rsch. Labs, Luton, Beds, Eng., 1973-74; quality assurance metallurgist Firth Brown Tools, Sheffield, 1974-75, rsch. metallurgist high speed steel, 1975; lectr. Sheffield City Poly., 1975-78; grad. metallurgist, strip devel. metallurgist British Steel Corp., Rotherham, Eng., 1978-80; program mgr. Can. Liquid Air, Montreal, 1980-85; group mktg. mgr. Liquid Air Corp., Countryside, Ill., 1986-90; tech. mgr. Liquid Air Corp., Walnut Creek, Calif., 1990—; bd. dirs., chmn. R & D com., mem. publs. com., chmn. promotions and mktg. com. INvestment Casting Inst., Dallas; presenter to confs. in field. Contbr. articles to profl. jours.; patentee in field of metallurgy. Mem. AIME, Inst. Metals (young metallurgists com. 1974-80), Sheffield Metall. Soc. Inst. Metals (sec. 1978-80), Am. Soc. Metals, Am. Foundry Soc., Powder Metals Soc., Am. Iron & Steel Inst. (steering com. 1987—, chmn. topics com. 1988—, sec. 1992, vice chair 1993), Inst. Chartered Engrs. Eng. Mem. Ch. of Eng. Office: Liquid Air Corp 2121 N California Blvd Walnut Creek CA 94596-3572

HORNE, BOYD WILLIAM, academic administrator; b. Ft. Smith, Ark., July 23, 1933; s. Boyd William Horne and Hazel (Speer) Buckner; m. Sara Rosoff, Dec. 19, 1959; children: Philip, Jennifer, Allyson. BA, Fresno State U., 1955; MBA, Claremont Grad. Sch., 1984. Jr. staff analyst Calif. State Dept. Edn., 1960-61, asst. budget analyst, 1961; asst. budget analyst Trustees Calif. State Univs., 1961-63, assoc. budget analyst, 1963-66, sr. budget analyst, 1966-67, supervising budget analyst, 1967-71, asst. chief fiscal svcs., 1971-83, chief fiscal svcs., 1983-86, asst. vice chancellor, 1987-92. Capt. USAF, 1955-58. Mem. Nat. Assn. Coll. and Univ. Bus. Officers (chair large univ. com. 1992). Home: 412 Via El Chico Redondo Beach CA 90277 Office: Trustees Calif State U 400 Golden Shore Long Beach CA 90802

HORNE, FREDERICK HERBERT, academic administrator, chemistry educator; b. Kansas City, Mo., Mar. 11, 1934; s. Corwin Denzel and Ella Mae (Player) H.; m. Clara Ann Johnson, Jan. 31, 1959; children: Frederick John, James Herbert, Nancy Carolyn. AB, Harvard U., 1956; PhD, U. Kans., 1962. NSF postdoctoral fellow Stanford (Calif.) U., 1962-63, instr. chemistry, 1963-64; NSF postdoctoral fellow Mich. State U., East Lansing, 1964-69, assoc. prof., 1969-73, prof., 1973-86, assoc. chmn. dept. chemistry, 1975-82, acctg. mgr. for performing arts, 1980-81, assoc. dean Coll. Natural Sci., 1982-86; prof. Oreg. State U., Corvallis, 1986—, dean Coll. of Sci., 1986—; vis. scientist Lawrence Livermore (Calif.) Lab., 1971, Odense (Denmark) U., 1979; vis. prof. Arya Mehr U., Tehran, Iran, 1975; mem. Nat. Rsch. Coun. Bd. on Sci. and Tech. in Internat. Devel., Washington, 1988—; mem. panel for evaluation of peer rev. process bur. for sci. and tech. AID, 1989; mem. panel on univ. devel. and linkages program Agy. Internat. Devel., 1991—, chair, 1992; mem. panel sci. and tech. coop. in Middle East, NRC, 1991. Contbr. over 40 articles to profl. jours. Bd. dirs. Friends of Chamber Music, Corvallis, 1987—, Oreg. State U.-Corvallis Symphony, 1987-90; mem. exec. adv. bd. Corvallis da Vinci Days, 1988-89, bd. dirs., 1992—. Harvard U. nat. scholar, 1952-55; NSF grad. fellow, 1959-61, Danforth Found. assoc., 1971. Mem. AAAS, Am. Chem. Soc., Materials Rsch. Soc., Am. Indian Sci. and Engring. Soc. (chpt. advisor 1988—, lifetime Sequoyah fellow 1991—), Harvard Club Cen. Mich. (pres. 1981-86), Univ. Club (chmn. pool com. 1973-80), Sigma Xi, Phi Kappa Phi, Phi Lambda Upsilon, Pi Mu Epsilon. Home: 3910 SW Fairhaven Dr Corvallis OR 97333-1432 Office: Oreg State U Coll of Sci Kidder Hall 128 Corvallis OR 97331-4608

HORNER, ALTHEA JANE, psychologist; b. Hartford, Conn., Jan. 13, 1926; d. Louis and Celia (Newmark) Greenwald; children: Martha Horner Hartley, Anne Horner Benck, David, Kenneth. BS in Psychology, U. Chgo., 1952; PhD in Clin. Psychology, U. So. Calif., 1965. Lic. psychologist, N.Y., Calif. Tchr. Pasadena (Calif.) City Coll., 1965-67; from asst. to assoc. prof. Los Angeles Coll. Optometry, 1967-70; supr. Psychology interns Pasadena Child Guidance Clinic, 1969-70; pvt. practice specializing in psychoanalysis and psychoanalytic psychotherapy. N.Y.C., 1970-83; supervising psychologist dept. psychiatry Beth Israel Med. Ctr., N.Y.C., 1972-83, coordinator group therapy tng., 1976-82, clinician in charge Brief Adaptation-Oriented Psychotherapy Research Group, 1982-83; assoc. clin. prof. Mt. Sinai Sch. Medicine, N.Y.C., 1977-91, adj. assoc. prof., 1991—; mem. faculty Nat. Psychol. Assn. for Psychoanalysis, N.Y.C., 1982-83; sr. mem. faculty Wright Inst. Los Angeles Postgrad. Inst., 1983-85; pvt. practice specializing in psychoanalysis and psychoanalytic psychotherapy L.A., 1983—; clin. prof. dept. Psychology UCLA, 1985—. Author: (with others) Treating the Oedipal Patient in Brief Psychotherapy, 1985, Object Relations and the Developing Ego in Therapy, 1979, rev. edit., 1984, Little Big Girl, 1982, Being and Loving, 1978, 3d edit. 1990, Psychology for Living (with G. Forehand), 4th edit., 1977, The Wish for Power and the Fear of Having It, 1989, The Primacy of Structure, 1990, Psychoanalytic Object Relations Therapy, 1991; mem. editorial bd. Jour. of Humanistic Psychology, 1986—, Jour. of the Am. Acad. of Psychoanalysis; contbr. articles to profl. jours. Mem. AAAS, Am. Psychol. Assn., Calif. State Psychol. Assn., Am. Women Sci., Nat. Psychol. Assn. for Psychoanalysis, Am. Acad. Psychoanalysis (sci. assoc.), So. Calif. Psychoanalytic Soc. and Inst. Office: 638 W Duarte Rd Arcadia CA 91007-7605

HORNER, CHARLES ALBERT, air force officer; b. Davenport, Iowa, Oct. 19, 1936; s. Everett Gerald and Mildred Bernice (Baker) H.; m. Mary Jo Gitchell, Dec. 22, 1958; children: Susan Ann, John Patrick, Nancy Jo. BA in Sci., U. Iowa, 1958; MBA, Coll. William and Mary, 1972. Commd 2d lt. USAF, 1958, advanced through grades to gen., 1992; comdr. 405 Tactical Tng. Wing, Luke AFB, Ariz., 1979-80, 474 Tactical Fighter Wing, Nellis AFB, Nev., 1980-81, 833 Air Div., Holloman AFB, N.Mex., 1981-83, USAF Air Def. Weapons Ctr., Tyndall AFB, Fla., 1983-85; dep. chief of staff plans Hdqrs. Tactical Air Command, Langley AFB, Va., 1985-87; comdr. 9th Air Force U.S. Cen. Command, Shaw AFB, S.C., 1987-92; comdr. U.S. Air Force Operation Desert Storm, 1991; comdr. CINCNORAD/USCINCSPACE/AFSPACECOM, Peterson AFB, Colo., 1992—. Home: 216 Otis Cir Colorado Springs CO 80916 Office: Hdqrs NORAD US SPACECOM Ste 116 250 S Peterson Blvd Peterson AFB CO 80914-3010

HORNER, DAVID NORMAN, marketing executive; b. N.Y.C., May 30, 1939; s. Manuel and Gertrude (Bayer) H.; m. Catherine Casson de Valrey, Feb. 18, 1978 (div. 1988); children: John, Julie. BS, U. Fla., 1960; MBA, NYU, 1970. Dir. planning Revlon Inc., N.Y.C., 1967-72; v.p. internat. Helena Rubinstein, N.Y.C., 1973-76, Max Factor, L.A., 1976-78; co-founder, sr. v.p. Giorgio Parfum, L.A., 1979-87; chmn., CEO Horner Enterprises, L.A., 1988—. Lt. U.S. Army, 1960-62. Home: 5313 Ocean Front Walk Marina Del Rey CA 90292-7106 Office: Horner Enterprises 8383 Wilshire Blvd Beverly Hills CA 90211-3403

HORNER, HARRY CHARLES, JR., sales executive, theatrical and film consultant; b. Pitts., Oct. 30, 1937; s. Harry Charles and Sara Marie (Hysong) H.; m. Patricia Ann Hagarty, June 15, 1965 (div. 1981); m. Sharon Kae Wyatt, Dec. 30, 1983; children: Jeffrey Brian, Jennifer Leigh, Mark Gregory. BFA, U. Cin., 1963; postgrad., Xavier U., Cin., 1963-64. Sales mgr. Environ. Care Inc., Calbassas, Calif., 1985—; mgr. Retail Credit Co., Atlanta, 1964-68; ops. mgr. Firestone Tire and Rubber cO., l.a., 1968-80; exec v.p. Romney/Ford Enterprises Inc., Scottsdale, Ariz., 1980-85; pres., chief exec. officer The Cons. Group Cos. Ltd., Palm Desert, Calif., 1984—; pres. E. Valley Theatre Co., Chandler, Ariz., 1984-86. Cons. Ariz. Commn. on Arts, Phoenix, 1983-84. Republican. Mem. LDS Ch. Office: Environ Care Inc 81531 Industrial Pl Indio CA 92201-2098

HORNER, JOHN ROBERT, paleontologist, researcher; b. Shelby, Mont., June 15, 1946; s. John Henry and Miriam Whitted (Stith) H.; m. Virginia Lee Seacotte, Mar. 30, 1972 (div. 1982); 1 child, Jason James; m. Joann Katherine Raffelson, Oct. 3, 1986. DSc (hon.), U. Mont., 1986. Rsch. asst. dept. geology Princeton (N.J.) U., 1975-82; curator paleontology Mus. of the Rockies, Mont. State U., Bozeman, 1982—; adj. asst. prof. dept. geology Mont. State U., 1982—; rsch. scientist Am. Mus. Nat. History, N.Y.C., 1980-82. Co-author: Maia: A Dinosaur Grows up, 1985, Digging Dinosaurs, 1988 (N.Y. Acad. Sci. award 1989), Digging Up Tyrannosaurus Rex, 1993, The Complete T-Rex, 1993; contbr. articles to profl. jours. With USMC, 1966-68; Vietnam. MacArthur fellow, 1986. Home: 9304 Cougar Dr Bozeman MT 59715-9515 Office: Mont State U Mus of the Rockies Bozeman MT 59717

HORNING, ROBERT ALAN, securities broker; b. Bristol, Tenn., Jan. 8, 1954; s. Sanford Lee and Pauline Stern (Marks) H.; m. Phyllis Ann Bockian, Apr. 12, 1981; children: Aaron Marks, Rachel Michelle. BA, U. Tenn., 1976, MA, 1979. Edn. specialist Knoxville (Tenn.) Police Dept., 1979-80; security cons. Sonitrol of Knoxville, 1980-81; sales rep. Guardsmark, Inc., Charleston, W.Va., 1981-84; mgr. in charge Guardsmark, Inc., L.A., 1984-88; v.p. mktg.-western region Fed. Armored Express, L.A., 1988-92; prin. Upton Affiliates, L.A., 1993—. Bd. dirs. B'Nai Tikvah Congregation, L.A., 1989—, v.p. membership, 1991. Mem. Am. Soc. Indsl. Security (chmn. L.A. chpt. 1990), Internat. Platform Assn., Phi Beta Kappa, Omicron Delta Kappa. Democrat. Jewish. Home: 7072 W 85th St Los Angeles CA 90045-2625 Office: Upton Affiliates 7072 W 85th St Los Angeles CA 90045-2625

HOROWITZ, BEN, medical center executive; b. Bklyn., Mar. 19, 1914; s. Saul and Sonia (Meringoff) H.; m. Beverly Lichtman, Feb. 14, 1952; children: Zachary, Jody. BA, Bklyn. Coll., 1940; LLB, St. Lawrence U., 1935; postgrad. New Sch. Social Rsch., 1942. Bar: N.Y. 1941. Dir. N.Y. Fedn. Jewish Philanthropies, 1940-45; assoc., ea. regional dir. City of Hope, 1945-50, nat. exec. sec., 1950-53, exec. dir., 1953-85, gen. v.p., bd. dirs., 1985—, bd. dirs. nat. med. ctr., 1980—; bd. dirs. Beckman Rsch. Inst., 1980—. Mem. Gov.'s Task Force on Flood Relief, 1969-74. Bd. dirs., v.p. Hope for Hearing Found., UCLA, 1972—; bd. dirs. Forte Found., 1987-92, Ch. Temple Housing Corp., 1988—, Leo Baeck Temple, 1964-67, 86-89, Westwood Property Owners Assn., 1991—. Recipient Spirit of Life award, 1970, Gallery of Achievement award, 1974, Profl. of Yr. award So. Calif. chpt. Nat. Soc. Fundraisers, 1977; Ben Horowitz chair in rsch. established at City of Hope, 1981. City street named in his honor, 1986. Jewish. Formulated the role of City of Hope as pilot ctr. in medicine, sci., and humanitarianism, 1959. Home: 221 Conway Ave Los Angeles CA 90024-2601 Office: City of Hope 208 W 8th St Los Angeles CA 90014-3208

HOROWITZ, DANIEL KENT, marketing and advertising executive; b. Columbus, Ohio, Jan. 24, 1962; s. Robert Earl and Suzanne Ruth (Brandwein) H. BS, U. So. Calif., 1984. Asst. L.A. Olympic Orgn. Com., 1984; prodn. coord. Lorimar-Telepictures, L.A., 1985-86; prodn. asst. RKO Pictures, L.A., 1986-87; devel. coord. Think Entertainment, Studio City, Calif., 1987-89; mktg. mgr. Practical Peripherals, Thousand Oaks, Calif., 1989—. Mem. B'nai B'rith Entertainment Unit (founding). Jewish. Office: Practical Peripheals 375 Conejo Ridge Ave Thousand Oaks CA 91361

HOROWITZ, EVAN JOSHUA, SR., aerospace, project and structural engineer, flutter dynamicist, stress analyst; b. Phila., May 3, 1961; s. Seymour Bernard Horowitz. BSME, San Jose State U., 1983; MS in Aerospace Engring., Ga. Inst. Tech., 1984, PhD in Aerospace Engring., 1987. Assoc. engr. Lockheed Aeronautical Systems Co., Burbank, Calif., 1986-90; sr. engr. Beech Aircraft Co., Wichita, Kans., 1990-91; project engr. Sierracin/Sylmar Corp., Sylmar, Calif., 1991-92; sr. structural engr. Elsinore Aerospace Systems, Chatsworth, Calif., 1992—. Republican.

HOROWITZ, MYER, retired university president-education educator; b. Montreal, Que., Can., Dec. 27, 1932; s. Philip and Fanny Cotler H.; m. Barbara Rosen, 1956; children: Carol Anne, Deborah Ellen. BA, Sir George Williams U., 1956; MEd, U. Alta., 1959; EdD, Stanford U., 1965; LLD (hon.), McGill U., 1979, Concordia U., 1982, Athabasca U., 1989, U. B.C., 1990, U. Alta., 1990. Tchr. elem. and high schs., Montreal, Que. area, 1952-60; lectr. in edn. McGill U., 1960-62, asst. prof., 1963-65, assoc. prof., 1965-67, prof., 1967-69, asst. dean, 1965-69; prof., chmn. dept. elem. edn. U. Alta., 1969-72, dean of edn., 1972-75, v.p. (acad.), 1975-79, pres., 1979-89, prof. emeritus, 1990—. Author articles in field. Decorated officer Order of Can. Fellow Can. Coll. Teachers. Jewish. Office: U of Alta, 845B Edn Centre, Edmonton, AB Canada T6G 2G5

HOROWITZ, ZACHARY I., entertainment company executive; b. N.Y.C., Apr. 27, 1953; s. Ben and Beverly (Lichtman) H. BA summa cum laude, Claremont Mens Coll., 1975; JD, Stanford U., 1978. Bar: Calif. 1978. Assoc. Kaplan, Livingston, Goodwin, Berkowitz & Selvin, Beverly Hills, Calif., 1978; sr. atty. CBS Records, Los Angeles, 1978-80, dir. bus. affairs West Coast, 1980-83; v.p. bus. and legal affairs MCA Records, Universal City, Calif., 1983-84, sr. v.p. bus. and legal affairs, 1984-88; sr. v.p. bus. and legal affairs MCA Music Entertainment Group, Universal City, 1988-89, exec. v.p., 1989—; mem. oper. com. Motown Record Co., L.A., 1988-93. Mem. bd. editors Stanford Law Rev., 1977-78. Nat. bd. dirs. City of Hope, 1989—, vice chmn. Music Industry chpt., 1985-86, chmn. maj. gifts com., 1986-90, nat. campaign co-chmn., 1990-91, pres., 1991-92, chmn., 1993—. Mem. Record Industry Assn. Am. (bd. dirs. 1990—). Office: MCA Records Inc 70 Universal City Plz Universal City CA 91608-1002

HORSMA, DAVID AUGUST, material scientist, technical manager; b. Hubbell, Mich., Sept. 3, 1940; s. Hjalmer Richard and Anne Aina (Turi) H.; m. Hazel Geraldine Boomer, Jan. 28, 1966; children: Jennifer, Amy. BS, Mich. Tech. U., 1962; PhD, U. Calif., Davis, 1966; postdoctoral studies, UCLA, 1966-67. Asst. prof. Calif. Poly. U., Pomona, 1967-68; group leader Rohm and Hass Corp., Bristol, Pa., 1968-71; materials engr. Crown Zellerbach Corp., San Leandro, Calif., 1971-72; tech. mgr. Raychem Corp., Menlo Park, Calif., 1972-78; tech. dir. Raychem Corp.-Europe, Brussels, 1978-82, Raychem Corp., Menlo Park, Calif., 1982-89; tech. mgr., scientist advanced packaging systems Raychem Corp., San Jose, Calif., 1989-91, tech. mgr., 1991—. Contbr. articles to profl. jours.; 20 patents in field. Mem. Am. Chem. Soc., Internat. Electronic and Elec. Engring. Soc., Internat. packaging Soc., Soc. for Advanced Materials and Process Engring. Home: 1141 Parkinson Ave Palo Alto CA 94301-3449 Office: Raychem Corp 300 Constitution Dr Menlo Park CA 94025

HORSMAN, JAMES DEVERELL, Canadian provincial government official; b. Camrose, Alta., Can., July 29, 1935; s. George Cornwall and Kathleen (Deverell) H.; m. Elizabeth Marian Whitney, July 4, 1964; children: Catherine Anne, Diana Lynn, Susan Marian. B.Com., LLB, U. B.C. Appointed as Queen's counsel, 1980. Mem. Alta. Legis. Assembly for Medicine Hat, 1975—, minister of advanced edn. and manpower, 1979-82, minister of fed. intergovtl. affairs, 1982-92, atty. gen., 1986-88, dep. govt. house leader, 1982-87, dep. premier, 1989-92, govt. house leader, 1989-92; chmn. Senate Reform Task Force, 1988-90, Constl. Task Force, 1990-91; chmn. Select Spl. Com. on Constl. Reform, 1991-92; mem. Alta. Del. to First Ministers Conf. on Constn., 1981, Can. Del. to GATT, 1986, 88, 90; chmn. Provincial Ministers Responsible for Manpower, 1982; co-chmn. Nat. Conf. State Legislators; hon. dir. State Legis. Leaders Found.; Canadian co-chmn. Mont./Alta. Boundary Adv. Com; co-chmn. Can.-U.S. legis. exchange project Nat. Conf. State Legis. Mem. 1982-91, chmn. bd. govs. Medicine Hat Coll., 1972-74; v.p. Pacific Northwest Econ. Region, 1991—; elder St. John's Ch. Medicine Hat C. of C. (pres. 1971-72). Progressive Conservative. Presbyterian. Clubs: Kinsmen (past pres., past dist. officer), Cypress. Office: Deputy Premier, 319 Legislature Bldg, Edmonton, AB Canada T5K 2B6

HORSTMAN, CAROL BELLHOUSE, lawyer; b. Brantford, Ont., Can., Oct. 14, 1953; came to U.S., 1960, naturalized, 1980; d. Gerald LaVerne and Irma (Vansickle) Bellhouse; m. James K. Horstman, July 2, 1980 (div.); children: Whitney Sarah, Michael Andrew. B.A., Wesleyan U., 1976; J.D., Washington U., St. Louis, 1980. Bar: Ill. 1981, U.S. Dist. Ct. (cen. dist.) Ill. 1981, Colo. 1991. Assoc., Costello, Young & Metnik, Springfield, Ill., 1980-82; sole practice, Springfield, 1982-84, 85—; ptnr. Horstman & Speta, P.C., Springfield, 1984-85. Mem. Ill. Bar Assn., Cen. Ill. Bar Assn., Nat. Assn. Women Bus. Owners, Sangamon County Bar Assn. Office: PO Box A Leadville CO 80461-1017

HORTON, ETHAN SHANE, professional football player; b. Kannapolis, N.C., Dec. 19, 1962. With Kansas City Chiefs, 1985; tight end L.A. Raiders, 1987—. Office: L.A. Raiders 332 Center St El Segundo CA 90245

HORTON, JACK KING, utilities executive; b. Stanton, Nebr., June 27, 1916; s. Virgil L. and Edna L. (King) H.; m. Betty Lou Magee, July 15, 1937; children: Judy, Sally, Harold. A.B., Stanford U., 1936; LL.B., Oakland Coll. Law, 1941. Bar: Calif. 1941. Treasury dept. Shell Oil Co., 1937-42; pvt. law practice San Francisco, 1942-43; atty. Standard Oil Co., 1943-44; sec., legal counsel Coast Counties Gas & Electric Co., 1944-51, pres., 1951-54; v.p. Pacific Gas & Electric Co., San Francisco, 1954-59; pres. So. Calif. Edison Co., 1959-68, chief exec. officer, 1965-80, chmn. bd., 1968-80, chmn. exec. com., 1980-89; former dir. First Interstate Bank of Calif., Pacific Mut. Life Ins., Lockheed Aircraft Corp., First Interstate Bancorp, EEI; former trustee Tax Found. Trustee U. So. Calif., Haynes Found.; pres. bd. Pepperdine U., Exec. Svc. Corp. of So. Calif. Mem. State Bar Calif., Bus. Coun. Clubs: Pacific Union, Bohemian, California, Los Angeles Country,

Cypress Point. Office: So Calif Edison Co 2244 Walnut Grove Ave Rosemead CA 91770-3714

HORTON, LAWRENCE STANLEY, electrical engineer, apartment developer; b. Hanston, Kans., July 25, 1926; s. Gene Leigh and Retta Florence (Abbott) H.; m. Margaret Ann Cowles, Nov. 26, 1946 (dec. 1964); children: Craig, Lawrence Stanley, Steven J.; m. Julia Ann Butler Wirkkula, Aug. 15, 1965; stepchildren: Charles Wirkkula Horton, Jerry Higginbotham Horton. BSEE, Oreg. State U., 1949. Elec. engr. Mountain States Power Co., Calif. Oreg. Power Co., Pacific Power and Light Co., 1948-66; mgr. Ramic Corp., 1966-69; cons. elec. engr. Marquess and Assocs., Medford, Oreg., 1969-85, sec., bd. dirs.; pres., owner Medford Better Housing Assn., 1985—; ptnr. Eastwood Living Group, Jackson St. Properties, T'Morrow Apts., Lake Empire Apts., Johnson Manor, Fountain Pla., Champion Pk.; bd. dirs. Valley of Rogue, developer various apt. complexes, 1969—; bd. dirs. Medford Hist. Commn. Active Medford Planning Commn., Archtl. Review Commn., Housing Authority; bd. govs. State of Oreg. Citizens Utility; pres. United Fund, 1963-64. With USN, 1945-46. Named Rogue Valley Profl. Engr. of Yr., 1969. Mem. IEEE, Nat. Soc. Profl. Engrs., Profl. Engrs. of Oreg., So. Oreg. Rental Owners Assn. (pres.), Rogue Valley Geneol. Soc. (pres.), Medford C. of C. (dir.), Rogue Valley Country Club, Rogue Valley Yacht Club (commodore 1974-55, dir., local fleet capt., champion), Rogue Valley Knife and Fork (pres. elect), San Juan 21 Fleet Assn. (western vice commodore, Top Ten San Juan Sailor West Coast, 1980), Jackson Toastmasters (founder 1957), Univ. Club, Medford Rotary, Kiwanis (life, pres. Crater Golden 1990-91, chmn. Craterlake Ambulance Found.). Republican. Methodist. Grad. instr. Dale Carnegie course, 1955, 56; contbr. elec. articles to profl. assns., 1956-61. Office: Medford Better Housing Assn 1118 Spring St Medford OR 97504-6272

HORTON, MARGUERITE LETITIA, retired human services administrator; b. St. Louis, May 26, 1917; d. Frank Samuel and Violet Marie (Erwin) Allen; m. Ira D. Horton Jr., Apr. 9, 1971. BS, Lincoln U., 1938; MSW, U. Utah, 1966; HHD (hon.), Weber State, 1992. Social caseworker Bur. of Pub. Assistance, L.A., 1949-61; social caseworker Div. of Family Svcs., Ogen, Utah, 1962-64, asst. dir. social svcs., 1966-69, dir. social svcs., 1973-77, ret., 1977; pers. rev. bd. State of Utah, Salt Lake City, 1979-84. Co-writer (play) Black History. Chmn. RSVP, Ogden, 1975-76; chair family svcs. com. Bonneville chpt. ARC, Ogden, 1979-87; mem. sub-com. City Govt. Transition, 1992; mem. LWV, Weber County Orgn. for Elderly, 1985—, Human Rights Coalition, 1990—; exec. com. Women's Hist. Soc., treas. 1984—. Recipient Living Legacy award Nat. Caucus and Ctr. of Black Aged, 1987; named Citizen of Yr., Ogden Bd. Realtors, 1988; inducted into Weber County Registry of Honor, 1992. Mem. AAUW (corr. sec. 1990—), Utah Adv. Coun. on Aging, Weber/Morgan Coun. on Aging (pres. 1988—), Utah Conf. on Human Svcs., Weber County Women's Legis. Coun. (bd. dirs. 1991-93), Ogden Minority Forum (community devel. chair 1989—). Home: 843 Dixie Dr Ogden UT 84405

HORTON, MICHAEL L., mortgage company executive, publishing executive; b. Pasadena, Calif., Oct. 19, 1961; s. Jerry S. and Mary L. Horton. BA in Bus. Econs., Claremont McKenna Coll., 1983. Lic. real estate broker. Gen. mgr. I.W.S., Pasadena, 1976-80; proprietor NBB Svcs. Orgn., Upland, Calif., 1980-85; regional mgr. Sycamore Fin. Group Inc., Rancho Cucamonga, Calif., 1984-87; CEO, pres. Boulder Fin. Corp., Rancho Cucamonga, 1987—, M.C.M. Pub. Corp., Rancho Cucamonga, 1992—. Author: A Real Estate Professional's Guide to Mortgage Finance, 1985; author Mortgage Fin. Newsletter, 1984—; author fin. workshop. Mem. Rep. State Ctrl. Com., Calif., 1980—, Bldg. and Industry Assn., Rancho Cucamonga, 1988—, Res Publica Soc., Claremont, Calif., 1986—; donor mem. L.A. World Affairs Coun., 1988—. Claremont McKenna Coll. scholar, 1981-82; recipient Dons D. Lepper Meml. award Exec. Women Internat., 1981, So. Calif. Edison Bus. Competition award, 1979, 81. Office: Boulder Fin Corp 9121 Haven Ave # 150 Rancho Cucamonga CA 91730

HORTON, SUSANNE PAMELA, nursing administrator; b. St. Johns, Mich., May 29, 1957; d. Victor Lowell and Helanejo (Nielson) Sheline; m. Dallas Hack, Sept. 1976 (div. 1984); children: Dana Sue, Melissa Ann. BSN, Loma Linda U., 1974, MSN, 1976; postgrad., Pepperdine U. RN. Dir. of nurses Corona (Calif.) Community Hosp., 1980-82; relief staff nurse RG Hosp. Knollwood Ctr., Riverside, Calif., 1980-82; pres. Home Outreach Med. Enterprises, Orange, Calif., 1982-87; pvt. duty nurse Integrated Care, Costa Mesa, Calif., 1986-91; supr. August Internat., Orange, 1987-89; dir. White Meml. Med. Ctr., L.A., 1989-90; dir. nurses, mem. utilization rev. Paracelsus Healthcare Corp., Orange, 1990—; guest lectr. Calif. State U., San Bernardino, 1980; cons. Nursing Edn. Am., Covina, Calif., 1981—; instr. U. Phoenix, Fountain Valley, Calif., 1983—; mem. faculty Loma Linda (Calif.) U., 1983—. Contbr. articles to profl. jours. Pianist Costa Mesa Performing Arts Ctr., 1990; mem. Young Reps., Costa Mesa, 1986—. Mem. ANA, Calif. Nurses Assn., Orange County C. of C., Calif. Assn. of Health Svcs. at Home, Am. Cancer Soc., Calif. Soc. for Nursing Svcs. Adminstrn. Office: Orange County Community Hosp 401 S Tustin Ave Orange CA 92666

HORVATH, TERRENCE MICHAEL, manufacturing company executive; b. Marinette, Wis., Jan. 5, 1961; s. Frank Alexander and Marion Lydia (Chervenka) H.; m. Deborah Lynn Otte, Nov. 27, 1987; children: Michael Alexander and Matthew Ryan (twins). BSBA, Ariz. State U., 1983; postgrad., UCLA, 1988. Jr. buyer Caoptol Machine Co., Phoenix, 1981-84; supr. Intel Corp., Albuquerque, 1984-85; buyer Lockheed Calif. Co., Burbank, 1985-86, sr. buyer, 1986-87, subcontract adminstr., 1987-88; sr. subcontract adminstr. McDonnell Douglas Aircraft Co., Long Beach, Calif., 1988-89, McDonnell Douglas Heilcopter Co., Mesa, Ariz., 1989—. Mem. Nat. Assn. Purchasing Mgmt., Purchasing Mgmt. Assn. Ariz. Republican. Roman Catholic. Home: 3006 N Ricardo Mesa AZ 85205-0910 Office: McDonnell Douglas Helicoptr 5000 E Mcdowell Rd Mesa AZ 85205-9707

HORWICH, FRANKLIN M., software company executive; b. Chgo., Sept. 12, 1960; s. Norman and Marcia (Morris) H.; m. Margaret Ann Webb, May 20, 1990. BS, So. Ill. U., 1979; MBA, Wharton U., 1992. Programmer, analyst TenMan Systems, Chgo., 1978-79; dir. data processing Transaction Svcs., Chgo., 1979-83; dir. product devel. Perle Ltd., Chgo., 1983-85; pres. Frank Horwich & Assocs., Chgo., 1985-87; v.p. Secutron Corp., Denver, 1987—; dir. data processing RAF Fin. Corp., Denver, 1988-92. Inventor in field. Vol. Colo. for Clinton, Denver, 1992. Mem. Colorado Mountain Club, Sierra Club. Office: Secutron Corp 3773 Cherry Creek North Dr Denver CO 80209

HORWIN, LEONARD, lawyer; b. Chgo., Jan. 2, 1913; s. Joseph and Jennie (Fuhrmann) H.; m. Ursula Helene Donig, Oct. 15, 1939; children—Noel Samuel, Leonora Marie. LLD cum laude, Yale U., 1936. Bar: Calif. 1936, U.S. Dist. Ct. (cen. dist.) Calif. 1937, U.S. Ct. Appeals (9th cir.) 1939, U.S. Supreme Ct. 1940. Assoc., Lawler, Felix & Hall, 1936-39; ptnr. Hardy & Horwin, Los Angeles, 1939-42; counsel Bd. Econ. Warfare, Washington, 1942-43; mem. program adjustment com. U.S. War Prodn. Bd., 1942-43; attache, legal advisor U.S. Embassy, Madrid, Spain, 1943-47; sole practice, Beverly Hills, Calif., 1948—; dir., lectr. Witkin-Horwin Rev. Course on Calif. Law, 1939-42; judge pro tempore Los Angeles Superior Ct., 1940-42; instr. labor law U. So. Calif., 1939-42. U.S. rep. Allied Control Council for Ger., 1945-47; councilman City of Beverly Hills, 1962-66, mayor, 1964-65; chmn. transp. Los Angeles Goals Council, 1968; bd. dirs. So. Calif. Rapid Transit Dist., 1964-66; chmn. Rent Stabilization Com., Beverly Hills, 1980. Fellow Am. Acad. Matrimonial Lawyers; mem. ABA, State Bar Calif., Order Coif. Clubs: Balboa Bay, Aspen Inst. Author: Insight and Foresight, 1990; contbr. articles to profl. jours. Office: 121 S Beverly Dr Beverly Hills CA 90212-3065

HORWITZ, BARBARA ANN, physiologist, educator, consultant; b. Chgo., Sept. 26, 1940; d. Martin Horwitz and Lillian (Knell) Bloom; m. John M. Horowitz, Aug. 17, 1970. BS, U. Fla., 1961, MS, 1962; PhD, Emory U., 1966. Asst. rsch. physiologist U. Calif., Davis, 1968-72, asst. prof. physiology, 1972-75, assoc. prof., 1975-78, prof., 1978—, chair animal physiology, 1991-93, chair neurobiology, physiology and behavior dept., 1993—; cons. Am. Inst. Behavioral Rsch., Palo Alto, Calif., 1980, Am. Inst. Res., Washington, D.C., 1993—, NSF, Washington, D.C., 1981-84. Contbr. articles to profl. jours. Recipient prize for teaching and scholarly achievement U. Calif., Davis, 1991; USPHS postdoctoral fellow, 1966-68. Fellow AAAS; mem. Am. Physiol. Soc. (edn. & program coms., coun. 1993—), Am. Soc. Zoologists, N.Y. Acad. Scis., N.Am. Assn. for the Study of Obesity (exec. coun. 1988-92), Soc. Exptl. Biol. Medicine (exec. coun. 1990—), Phi Beta Kappa (pres. Davis chpt. 1991-92), Sigma Xi (pres. Davis chpt. 1980-81), Phi Kappa Pi, Phi Sigma (v.p. Davis chpt. 1983—). Office: U Calif Dept Neurobiology Physiology Davis CA 95616

HOSHI, KATSUO KAI, international business executive; b. Satomimura, Kujigun, Ibaraki, Japan, Aug. 28, 1933; s. Takeyasu and Take H.; m. Yukiko Imajima, Mar. 24, 1959; children: Manami Hoshi Hunt, Naomi, Brian D. BA in Fgn. Study, Sophia U., Tokyo, Japan, 1959; MS in Mktg., Calif. State U., 1969. Nat. A/C sales mgr. Olivetti Corp. of Japan, Tokyo, 1961-67; v.p. Kubota Tractor Corp., Compton, Calif., 1969-83, Auburn (Nebr.) Consol. Industries, 1978-83; sr. v.p. Transport Mgmt. System Inc., N.Y.C., 1983-85; exec. v.p. Merzario USA, Inc., N.Y.C., 1985-86; pres. Canon Italia SpA, Verona, Italy, 1986-91, Canon Milano SpA, Milan, Italy, 1988-91, Canon Trading USA, Inc., Irvine, Calif., 1992—; dir. Kubota Tractor Corp., Compton, Calif., 1972-83, Merzario USA, Inc., N.Y.C., 1985-86, Canon Italia SpA, Verona, 1986-91, Canon Trading USA, Inc., Irvine, 1992—. Recipient Nebr. Citizenship award, 1978, Baton Rouge Citizenship award, 1979, scholarship Japan-Am. Soc., 1967. Home: 54 Club Vista San Juan Capistrano CA 92679 Office: Canon Trading USA Inc Irvine CA 92718

HOSIE, STANLEY WILLIAM, foundation executive, writer; b. Lismore, New South Wales, Australia, Apr. 28, 1922; came to U.S., 1945; s. Stanley James and Catherine Clare (Chisholm) H. BA, U. Queensland, Brisbane, Australia, 1945; Lic. in Theology, Cath. U., Washington, 1947, MA, 1948. Dean of studies Marist Coll., Lismore, 1949-57; pres., founder Chanel Coll., Geelong, Victoria, Australia, 1958-62; writer-in-residence Casa Generalitia Societatis Mariae, Rome, 1963-66; exec. dir. The Found. for the Peoples of the South Pacific, Inc., N.Y.C., 1966—; theologian for Conf. of Pacific Cath. Bishops, 2d Vatican Coun., Rome, 1963-65; dir. Am. Coun. for Vol. Internat. Action, N.Y.C., 1976—, treas. 1983-84; dir. Pvt. Agys. Collaborating Together, 1977—; mem. Presdl. Adv. Com. on Vol. Aid, 1988. Author: The Swiss Conspiracy, 1976, The Boomerang Conspiracy, 1978, (biography) Anonymous Apostle, 1966, also numerous screenplays. Recipient Best Article Vatican II award Nat. Cath. Periodicals Assn., 1964. Mem. Writers Guild Am. East, Soc. des Oceanistes, Australian Coll. Edn. Democrat. Roman Catholic. Home: 723 Palisades Beach Rd Santa Monica CA 90402-2621 Office: Counterpart 1634 Eye St Washington DC 20006-9999

HOSIE, WILLIAM CARLTON, food products company executive; b. Stockton, Calif., June 25, 1936; s. Fred A. and Janet (Russell) H.; m. Sherryl Rasmussen, Jan. 12, 1963; children: Shaen Case, Erin Frick. B.S., U. Calif.-Davis, 1960. Field rep. Flotill Inc., Stockton, 1960-61; orchardist Hosie Ranch Inc., Linden, Calif., 1961-83; chmn. bd. dirs. Diamond Walnut Growers Inc., Stockton, 1981—; dir. Sun-Diamond Growers Calif., Pleasanton; advisor U. Calif. Extension-Stockton, 1975—, Calif. Farm Bur., Sacramento, 1976—, Farmer and Mchts. Bank, Linden, 1979; dir. Walnut Mktg. Bd., San Mateo, Calif., 1981—. Pres. Stockton East Water Dist., 1969-79. Served with AUS, 1958-59. Mem. Stockton C. of C. Republican. Club: Rotary Internat. Office: Diamond Walnut Growers Inc 1050 Diamond St Stockton CA 95205

HOSKINS, ALICE ELIZABETH, university official; b. Vernonia, Oreg., Feb. 17, 1934; d. James Arther and Julia Marie (Selig) Davis; m. H.W. Fleskes (div. 1970); m. William Harold Hoskins, Apr. 28, 1973. Student, Pacific U., 1952-53. With Pacific U., Forest Grove, Oreg., 1970-91, dir. alumni rels., 1991—. Office: Office Alumni Rels Pacific U Forest Grove OR 97116

HOSMER, BRADLEY CLARK, air force officer; b. San Antonio, Oct. 8, 1937; s. Clark L. and Elynor H.(Hendrickson); m. Zita Vlavianos, Jan. 4, 1964; children: Basil, Caitlin, Andrew. BS, U.S. Air Force Acad., 1959; MA, Oxford U., 1962; grad., Squadron Officer Sch., 1965, Naval War Coll., 1969, Nat. War Coll., 1975. Commd. 2nd lt. USAF, 1959, advanced through grades to lt. gen., 1986; supt. USAF Acad., North Colorado Springs, Colo., 1991—. Office: HQ USAFA/SUPT 2304 Cadet Dr Ste 342 USAF Academy CO 80840-5001*

HOSSLER, DAVID JOSEPH, lawyer, educator; b. Mesa, Ariz., Oct. 18, 1940; s. Carl Joseph and Elizabeth Ruth (Bills) H.; m. Gretchen Anne, Mar. 2, 1945; 1 child, Devon Annagret. BA, U. Ariz., 1969; JD, 1972. Bar: Ariz. 1972, U.S. dist. ct. Ariz. 1972, U.S. Supreme Ct. 1977. Legal intern to chmn. FCC, summer 1971; law clk. to chief justice Ariz. Supreme Ct., 1972-73; chief dep. county atty. Yuma County (Ariz.), 1973-74; ptnr. Hunt, Stanley and Hossler, Yuma, Ariz., 1974—; instr. in law and banking, law and real estate Ariz. Western Coll.; instr. in bus. law, mktg. Webster U; co-chmn. fee arbitration com. Ariz. State Bar, 1990—. Mem. precinct com., Yuma County Rep. Cen. Com., 1974—, vice chmn., 1982; chmn. region II Acad. Decathalon competition, 1989; bd. dirs. Yuma County Ednl. Found., Yuma County Assn. Behavior Health Svcs., also pres., 1981; coach Yuma High Sch. mock ct. team, 1987—; bd. dirs. Friends of U. Med. Ctr. With USN. Recipient Man and Boy award Boys Clubs Am., 1979, Freedoms Found. award Yuma Chpt., 1988, Demolay Legion of Honor, 1991; named Vol. of Yr., Yuma County, 1981-82. Mem. Assn. Trial Lawyers Am., Am. Judicature Soc., Yuma County Bar Assn. (pres. 1975-76), Navy League, VFW, Am. Legion, U. Ariz. Alumni Assn. (nat. bd. dirs., past pres.), Rotary (pres. Yuma club 1987-88, dist. gov. rep. 1989, dist. gov. 1992-93). Editor-in-chief Ariz. Adv., 1971-72. Episcopalian (vestry 1978-82). Home: 2802 S Fern Dr Yuma AZ 85364-7909 Office: Hunt Stanley & Hossler 330 W 24th St Yuma AZ 85364-6455

HOSTETLER, DAVE, transportation company executive; b. Burlington, Colo., July 24, 1951; s. John Loyd and Elizabeth Louise (Chaffin) H.; m. Lavonne Rae Kranz, Feb. 14, 1978 (div. 1984); children: Scott David, Melissa Ann; m. Betty Jean Mead, Mar. 11, 1989. BA, We. State Coll., Gunnison, Colo., 1973. Pipefitter Ramsey Constrn. and Fabricating, Cheyenne, Wyo., 1978; boilermaker various locations, 1979; owner D & B Svcs., Evanston, Wyo., 1976-84, S & M Transp., Bethune, Colo., 1984—. Office: S & M Transp Box 158 Bethune CO 80805

HOSTETLER, JEFF W., professional football player; b. Johnstown, Pa., Apr. 22, 1961; m. Vicky Nehlen; children: Jason, Tyler, Justin. Attended, Pa. State U.; grad. in fin., W.Va. U. Cert. fin. planner. Player N.Y. Giants, 1984-92; quarterback Superbowl XXV championship team, 1991; with L.A. Raiders, 1993—. Named to Acad. All Am. Season, 1983-84. Address: care LA Raiders 332 Center St El Segundo CA 90245

HOSTETLER, KARL YODER, internist, endocrinologist, educator; b. Goshen, Ind., Nov. 17, 1939; s. Carl Milton and Etta LaVerne (Yoder) H.; m. Margaretha Steur, Dec. 17, 1971; children: Saskia Emma, Kirsten Cornelia, Carl Martijn. BS in Chemistry, DePauw U., 1961; MD, Western Res. U., 1965. Diplomate Am. Bd. Internal Medicine, Am. Bd. Endocrinology and Metabolism. Intern, resident in medicine Univ. Hosp. Cleve., 1965-69; fellow endocrinology Cleve. Clinic Found., 1969-70; postdoctoral fellow, lipid chemistry U. Utrecht, The Netherlands, 1970-73; asst. prof. medicine U. Calif., San Diego, 1973-79, assoc. prof. medicine, 1979-82, prof. medicine, 1982—; founder, sr. v.p. Vical Inc., San Diego, 1987-92. Assoc. editor, Jour. Clin. Investigation, 1992—; contbr. over 100 articles to scholarly and profl. jours. Pres. San Diego County chpt. Am. Diabetes Assn., 1982-83. Recipient fellowship John Simon Guggenheim Found., 1980-81, Japan Soc. for Promotion of Sci., Tokyo, 1986. Mem. Am. Soc. Clin. Investigation, Am. Soc. Biochemistry and Molecular Biology, Western Assn. Physicians, Am. Soc. Microbiology. Office: U Calif San Diego Dept Medicine 0676 La Jolla CA 92093

HOSTETTER, H. CLYDE, writer; b. Mayetta, Kans., July 17, 1925; s. Harvey Edgar and Mae Edna (Charlesworth) H.; m. Carolyne Southerland, July 20, 1952; children: Cynthia, Craig. B of Journalism, U. Mo., 1948. Pub. rels. dir. U.S. Jaycees, Tulsa, 1950-52; assoc. editor Town Jour. Mag., Washington, 1952-55; pub. rels. assoc. Carl Byoir & Assocs., Culver City, Calif., 1955-56; prof. Calif. Poly. State U., San Luis Obispo, Calif., 1956-85; multimedia cons. Govt. of Saudi Arabia, Riyadh, Saudi Arabia, 1976-77, Govt of Indonesia, Medan, Sumatra, Indonesia, 1985-86, Govt. of Afghanistan, Peshawar, Pakistan, 1990; writer Food for Thought, San Luis Obispo, 1985—; pres. Instrnl. Materials Sect. Am. Vocat. Assn., Washington, 1974-75. Author: Star Trek to Hawaii, 1991. Ltjg. USN, 1943-45. Mem. Soc. Profl. Journalists, Am. Assn. Ret. Persons, Kappa Alpha Mu. Home: 48 Los Palos Dr San Luis Obispo CA 93401

HOSTICKA, CARL J., academic administrator, educator, legislator; b. Oak Park, Ill., June 21, 1944; s. Harold E. and Marilyn (Simons) H.; 1 child, Anna Tamura. BA, Brown U., 1965; PhD, MIT, 1976. Assoc. dir. Peace Corps India, 1968-71; prof. U. Oreg., Eugene, 1977—, assoc. v.p., 1989—. State rep. Oreg. Ho. of Reps., Salem, 1983—, majority leader, 1990—. Democrat. Home: PO Box 3236 Eugene OR 97403-0236 Office: U Oreg Dept Public Affairs Eugene OR 97403

HOSTNIK, CHARLES RIVOIRE, lawyer; b. Glen Ridge, N.J., Apr. 8, 1954; s. William John and Susan (Rivoire) H.; m. Gail J. Martinolich, Aug. 23, 1980; children: Katherine M., James M. AB, Dartmouth Coll., 1976; JD, U. Puget Sound, 1979. Bar: Wash. 1980, U.S. Dist. Ct. (we. dist.) Wash. 1980, U.S. Dist. Ct. (ea. dist.) Wash. 1982, U.S. Ct. Appeals (9th cir.) 1983, Hoh Tribal Ct. 1984, Nisqually Tribal Ct. 1984, Puyallup Tribal Ct. 1984, Shoalwater Bay Tribal Ct. 1984, Skokomish Tribal Ct. 1984, and others. Asst. atty. gen. Atty. Gen.'s Office State of Wash., Olympia, 1980-84; assoc. Kane, Vandeberg, Hartinger & Walker, Tacoma, 1984-87, Anderson, Caraher, Brown & Burns, Tacoma, 1988; ptnr. Anderson, Burns & Hostnik, Tacoma, 1988—; trial and appellate judge N.W. Intertribal Ct. System, Edmonds, Wash., 1986—. Author: (chpt.) Washington Practice, 1989. Mem. com. to re-elect justice R. Guy, Olympia and Tacoma, 1990. Mem. N.W. Tribal Ct. Judges Assn. Office: Anderson Burns & Hostnik 4041N Ruston Way Ste 2A Tacoma WA 98402-5392

HOSTROP, RICHARD WINFRED, publishing executive; b. Waterloo, Iowa, Oct. 8, 1925; s. Winfred Ditliv Hostrop and Frances Lucille (Walton) Elkins; m. LeeOna Jean Selland, Dec. 27, 1950; children: Holly Lee, Kristin Ingrid. BA, UCLA, 1950, MA, 1952, PhD, 1966. Tchr. Calif. Pub. Schs., 1948-52; curriculum coord. Green Park Schs., Bakersfield, Calif., 1952-53; prin. Aliso Sch., Carpinteria, Calif., 1953-54; supt. schs. dependent schs. U.S. Dept. Def., Europe, Africa, Asia, 1954-65; registrar Coll. of the Desert, Palm Desert, Calif., 1965-67; pres. Prairie State Coll., Chicago Heights, Ill., 1967-70, ETC Publs., Palm Springs, Calif., 1970—; cons. various acad. orgns. in U.S. and Can. on ednl. mgmt., 1967—. Author: Teaching and the Community College, 1968, Managing Education for Results, 1986; editor: Effective Sch. Administrator, 1991, Outstanding Public and Private Elementary Schools, 1991. Sgt. USAF, 1944-46.

HOTCHKISS, VIVIAN EVELYN, employment agency executive; b. Fulda, Germany, May 5, 1956; came to U.S., 1957; d. Fred Roy and Rosemary (Wehner) Krug. Student, Pierce Coll., 1974-75, Calif. State U., Northridge, 1976, UCLA, 1991-92. Adminstrv. sec. Taurus Fin. Corp., Hollywood, Calif., 1976-79; adminstrv. asst. Peoples Fin. Corp., Encino, Calif., 1979-81, Thor Employment Agy., L.A., 1981-83, Creative Capital Corp., L.A., 1983-85; owner, pres. Bus. Systems Staffing & Assocs., L.A., 1985—; exec. dir. Edn., Counseling & Placement Program, L.A., 1990—. Author: (newsletter) The Leader; contbr. articles to newspaper, 1990. Mem. Execs. Assn. L.A. (membership dir. 1989—, Member of Yr. 1990), Calif. Assn. Pers. Cons., Pers. and Indsl. Rels. Assn. Office: Business Systems Staffing & Assocs Inc 10680 W Pico Blvd Ste 210 Los Angeles CA 90064

HOTCHKISS, WILLIAM ROUSE, hydrologist; b. Schenectady, June 12, 1937; s. Edwin Lyman and Christine Matheson (Rouse) H.; m. Nancy Lee Taplin, June 12, 1965; children: Terry, Seana, Kristi, Alyson, Judi, Heather. Student, Dartmouth Coll., 1955-59; BS in Earth Scis., Mont. State U., 1962, MS in Geology and Math., 1965; PhD in Civil Engring., Colo. State U., 1988. Hydrologist U.S. Geol. Survey, Sacramento, 1965-72; hydrologist U.S. Geol. Survey, Helena, Mont., 1974-78, project leader No. Gt. Plains regional aquifer system assessment, 1978-82; chief Nat. Tng. Ctr. U.S. Geol. Survey, Denver, 1982-88, hydrologist cen. regional staff, 1988—; former instr. geology Calif. State U., Sacramento, Mont. State U.; assoc. prof. civil engring. dept. Colo. State U.; former nat. avalanche advisor Nat. Ski Patrol, Denver, now mem. steering com. Contbr. numerous articles on hydrology and snow avalanches to profl. jours. Recipient citation for svc. and lives saved Nat. Avalanche Found., 1989, Montgomery M. Atwater award, leadership award Lions Club, Helena, 1982, Outstanding Adminstr. award Nat. Ski Patrol, 1982; grantee U.S. Geol. Survey, 1972. Fellow Geol. Soc. Am.; mem. Am. Geophys. Union, Am. Inst. Hydrology (pres. Colo. sect. 1987—), Am. Water Resources Assn. (co-chmn. tech. meeting 1990), Assn. Am. Avalanche Profls., Western Snow Conf., Sigma Xi. Home: 14373 W 3d Ave Golden CO 80401-5212 Office: US Geol Survey WRD MS 406 Box 25046 DFC Lakewood CO 80225-0046

HOTLE, JACKIE LEE, credit union executive; b. Waco, Tex., Aug. 21, 1939; d. Charles Fredrick William and Neva Jean (Jennings) Steffen; m. Tommy Joe Jackson, Nov. 29, 1956 (div. 1970); 1 child, Steven Wade; m. Ronald V. Hotle, Nov. 23, 1974; 1 child, Randel Keith. Student, Durham Bus. Coll., 1958, U. Wis., Madison, 1985. Pres. Waco Telco Fed. Credit Union, 1960-70, Simmons Fed. Credit Union, Dallas, 1970-72, PIA Fed. Credit Union, Dallas, 1972-74, Natrona County Sch. Employee Credit Union, 1981—; v.p., bd. dirs. Wyo. Cen. Fed. Credit Union, Casper, 1986-87; supervisory com. System United Corp. Fed. Credit Union, 1988—; judge Distbv. Edn. Clubs Am., Casper, 1986, 89. Mem. Wyo. Credit Union League, Casper, 1987-93. Mem. Pioneer Chpt. Credit Unions (pres. 1990, 91), Soroptimist Internat. (treas. Cen. Wyo. chpt. 1987-88, pres. 1990, bd. dirs. 1992, treas. children's nutrition svcs. 1991-93). Republican. Episcopalian. Home: 1730 S Spruce St Casper WY 82601-4539 Office: Natrona County Sch Employee Fed Credit Union 1301 S Wisconsin Casper WY 82609-2900

HOTVEDT, KRIS JOANNA, artist; b. Wautoma, Wis., Jan. 29, 1943; d. Arnold Ralph and Joanna Jessie (Walker) Hotvedt; m. Jim Thornton, 1967 (div. 1969). Student, Layton Sch. Art, Milw., 1961-64; BFA, San Francisco Art Inst., 1965; MFA, Instituto Allende San Miguel, Mexico, 1967. Instr. art Pembroke (N.C.) State U., 1967-69; instr. life drawing St. John's Coll., Santa Fe, N.Mex., 1969-79; S.W. rep. Pembroke mag., 1970—. Author: Fry Breads, Feast Days, and Sheeps, 1987, Pueblo & Navajo Indian Life Today, 1993; woodcuts and dwgs. reproduced numerous mags. including Santa Fean and S.W. Art Mag. and Book in Germany; works exhibited at The Gallery on Canyon Road, The Opening Scene, Mesa Fine Arts, Franklin, Mich., Blaire Carnahn Fine Arts, San Antonio, others; author, artist: Coyote Stars the Trees, 1988. Democrat. Home: 2901 Santa Clara SE Albuquerque NM 87106 Office: Vista Grande Design PO Box 15774 Santa Fe NM 87506-5774

HOTZ, HENRY PALMER, physicist; b. Fayetteville, Ark., Oct. 17, 1925; s. Henry Gustav and Stella (Palmer) H.; m. Marie Brase, Aug. 22, 1952; children: Henry Brase, Mary Palmer, Martha Marie. B.S., U. Ark., 1948; Ph.D., Washington U., St. Louis, 1953. Asst. prof. physics Auburn U., Ala., 1953-58, Okla. State U., Stillwater, 1958-64; assoc. prof. Marietta Coll., Ohio, 1964-66; physicist, scientist-in-residence U.S. Naval Radiol. Def. Lab., San Francisco, 1966-67; assoc. prof. U. Mo., Rolla, 1967-71; physicist Qanta Metrix div. Finnigan Corp., Sunnyvale, Calif., 1971-74; sr. scientist Nuclear Equipment Corp., San Carlos, Calif., 1974-79, Envirotech Measurement Systems, Palo Alto, Calif., 1979-82, Dohrmann div. Xertex Corp., Santa Clara, Calif., 1982-86; sr. scientist Rosemount Analytical Div. Dohrmann, 1983-91; cons. Burlingame, Calif., 1991—; cons. USAF, 1958-62; mem. lectr. selection com. for Hartman Hotz Lectrs. in law, liberal arts U. Ark. Served with USNR, 1944-46. Mem. Am. Phys. Soc., Am. Assn. Physics Tchrs., AAAS, Phi Beta Kappa, Sigma Xi, Sigma Pi Sigma, Pi Mu Epsilon, Sigma Nu. Methodist. Lodge: Masons. Home: 290 Stilt Ct Foster City CA 94404-1323 Office: Hotz Assocs 525 Almer Rd Ste 201 Burlingame CA 94010

HOUDASHELT, DERREL WILBUR, environmental safety administrator; b. Fresno, Calif., July 14, 1925; s. Claude Monroe and Goldie Vivien (Brandon) H.; m. Ruth Marion Henning, July 27, 1944; children: Netha L. Thacker, Ellen C. Wyatt, D. Timothy, Heather S., Naomi R. Chronister, Ila Elizabeth (dec.). AA in Physical Sci, San Jose City Coll., 1964. Registered evviron. assessor, Calif.; cert. environ. insp., Calif. Sr. lab technician kaiser Rsch. Lab., San Jose, Calif., 1956-61; jr. engr. Memorex Corp., San Jose, 1961-65; site supr. Lick Obs. U. Calif., San Jose, 1965-66; jr. engr. Standard

Slag Co., Reno, 1966-69; lab. mgr. Titanium West Corp., Reno, 1969-71; gen. mgr. PanCana Industries, Calgary, Alta., Can., 1975-79; project mgr. Dorado Mining Co., Houston, 1980-85; quality control technician Lika Corp., Stockton, Calif., 1986-88; environ. safety officer U. Pacific, Stockton, 1988—; cons. Tuscarora (Nev.) Assocs., 1979, Bell Mining Co., Goldfield, Nev., 1979, Newmont Mining Co., Carlin, Nev., 1980. Author safety manuals. Active Stockton Conservation Com., 1988, Solid Waste Task Force, Stockton, 1989, Community Awareness Emergency Response Com., 1990, Environ. Round Table, Stockton, 1992. With U.S. Army, 1948-49. Recipient Scouter's Key award Boy Scouts Am. Coun., Salinas, Calif., 1957. Mem. Environ. Assessment Assn., Nat. Safety Coun. (campus safety assn.), Calif. EPA, Calif. Campus Environ. Health and Safety Assn., Calif. C. of C. Protestant. Office: U Pacific 3601 Pacific Ave Stockton CA 95211

HOUGH, NANETTE, advertising executive; b. Everett, Wash., Sept. 4, 1933; d. Ray Arthur and Doris Marie (Phillips) Morrison; m. William Doren Jackson, Apr. 17, 1951 (div. 1963); children: William Raymond, Michael Allen, Anne Marie; m. Henry Michael Hough, Aug. 31, 1963; children: Robyn Michelle, Bryan Morrison. Traffic mgr. Sta. KOXR, Oxnard, Calif., 1959-60, Sta. KYA, San Francisco, 1960-63; traffic dept. Sta. KING, Seattle, 1960-63, continuity dir., 1967-69; traffic dept. Sta. KING-TV, Seattle, 1966-67; traffic dept. Sta. KBRC, Mt. Vernon, Wash., 1972-74, sales staff, 1977-82; promotion dir. Skagit Valley Pub. Co., Mt. Vernon, Wash., 1982-89; co-owner The Agy., Mt. Vernon, Wash., 1989—. Mem. Crime Awareness Com., Mt. Vernon, 1979-81, United Way Communicaitons Com., Skagit County, Wash., 1978—, Substance Abuse Coalition, Mt. Vernon, 1983-91. Recipient Citizen of Yr. award Skagit County Assn. Realtors, 1988; Gordon Phillips scholar, 1989. Mem. Internat. Newspaper Mkgt. Assn. (bd. dirs. 1988-89), Northwest Design Assn., Wash. Press Assn. (author newspaper columns), Lincoln Theatre Ctr. Found., Mt. Vernon Women in Bus. (bd. dirs. 1988-90), Skagit Women's Alliance and Network (sec. 1990), Skagit Women in Bus., Mt. Vernon/Burlington/Sedro-Woolley La Conner C. of C., Kiwanis (bd. dirs. Mt. Vernon club 1988-92). Home: 1018 E Fulton St Mount Vernon WA 98273 Office: The Agy 723 S 1st St Ste D Mount Vernon WA 98273-3812

HOUGH, STEVEN HEDGES, lawyer; b. Cleve., May 24, 1938; s. William Rockwell and Virginia Hull (Olds) H.; m. Carolyn Millicent Day, July 29, 1968 (dec. July 1981); children: Glenn, Holly, Heather. BSBA, Chico State Coll., 1961; JD, U. Calif., San Francisco, 1964. Bar: Calif. 1966, U.S. Dist. Ct. (no. dist.) Calif. 1966, U.S. Ct. Appeals (9th cir.) 1966, U.S. Supreme Ct. 1975. Trial atty. L.A. County Pub. Defender, L.A., 1966-76, head dep., 1976—; pres. Criminal Cts. Bar Assn., L.A., 1984; asst. presiding referee state bar ct. State Bar Calif., L.A., San Francisco, 1985-91, chair standing com. on delivery of legal svcs. to criminal defendants, 1978-79; bd. govs. Long Beach (Calif.) Bar Assn., 1990, 91; instr., lectr., panelist trial advocacy clinic, day in ct. program; mtgs. L.A. County Pub. Defenders, marshal program Calif. Youth Authority, Long Beach Police Dept., other orgns. Mem. First Congregational Ch., Santa Ana, Calif., deacon, 1985-87, 91-93; mem. PTA several schs.; referee, coach, bd. dirs. region 5 Am. Youth Soccer Orgn.; referee, coach North Huntington Beach Soccer Club, Coast Soccer League; treas. Orange County Soccer Referees Assn., 1986; sustaining mem. Boy Scouts Am., Girl Scouts U.S.; mem. Westhaven Homeowners Assn., Gifted Children's Assn. Orange County; life mem. So. Calif. Acro Team; fund raising solicitor United Way Crusade, Brotherhood Crusade. Recipient Charitable Giving Hon. award Brotherhood Crusade, 1982. Mem. ABA (criminal law sect.), Criminal Cts. Bar Assn., Calif. Pub. Defenders Assn., Calif. Attys. for Criminal Justice, S.E. Bar Assn., Calif. State Bar Assn., Long Beach Bar Assn. (bd. govs. 1990, 91), South Bar Bar Assn., U.S. Supreme Ct. Bar Assn., Nat. Coll. Criminal Def. Lawyers and Pub. Defenders, Nat. Assn. Criminal Def. Lawyers, Am. Judicature Soc., Am. Contract Bridge League (life master), Mission Viejo Country Club, Hastings Alumni Assn., Univ. Sch. Alumni Assn., Lambda Chi Alph. Republican. Office: LA County Pub Defenders Office 3655 Torrance Blvd Ste 200 Torrance CA 90503-4811

HOUGLUM, PEGGY ANN, physical therpist, athletic trainer; b. Detroit Lakes, Minn., Aug. 19, 1948; d. Edgar Jesness and Margaret Ann (Dugas) H. Student, St. Cloud State U., 1966-68; BS, U. Minn., 1971; MS, Ind. State U., Terre Haute, 1975. Lic. phys. therapist; cert. athletic trainer. Phys. therapist Sister Kenney Rehab. Hosp., Mpls., 1971-73; phys. therapist in pvt. practice Mpls., 1973-74; athletic trainer Ind. State U., 1975-78, Iowa State U., Ames, 1978-81; phys. therapist TRACC, Inc., L.A., 1981, Torrance (Calif.) Meml. Hosp., 1981-87, STAAR Clinic, Fountain Valley, 1987-88, Centinela Med. Ctr., Manhattan Beach, Calif., 1989-92, Gardena (Calif.) Indsl. Medicine, 1992—; instr. Mt. St. Mary's Coll., L.A., 1991—; presenter in field. Clin. editor Jour. Sprot Rehab., 1992—; contbr. articles to profl. jours. Walker, AIDS Project L.A. Walkathon, 1990, 91, 92; vol. Found. for Ednl. Rsch., L.A., 1990. Mem. Am. Phys. Therapy Assn. (sports medicine sect.), Nat. Athletic Trainers Assn. (profl. edn. com. 1987—, curriculum accreditation team officer 1988—, Dist. 8 pub. rels. com.), Calif. Athletic Trainers Assn. Home: 3190 Gardena Gardena CA 90247 Office: Gardena Indsl Medicine 1300 W 155th St # 210 Gardena CA 90247

HOUK, KENDALL NEWCOMB, chemistry educator; b. Nashville, Tenn., Feb. 27, 1943; s. Charles H. and Janet Houk; 1 child, Kendall M.; m. Robin L. Garrell. AB, Harvard U., 1964, MS, 1966, PhD, 1968. Asst. prof. chemistry La. State U., Baton Rouge, 1968-72, assoc. prof., 1972-75, prof., 1975-80; prof. U. Pitts., 1980-86; prof. UCLA, 1986-91, chmn. dept. chemistry and biochemistry, 1991—; dir. chemistry div. nat. Sci. Found., 1988-90. Contbr. numerous articles to profl. jours. Mem. AAAS, Am. Chem. Soc. (James Flack Norris award in physical organic chemistry 1991). Office: UCLA Dept Chemistry and Biochemistry 405 Hilgard Ave Los Angeles CA 90024

HOULDING, VIRGINIA H., physical chemist; b. Berkeley, Calif., June 27, 1953; d. Neal W. and Phyllis V. (Watson) H.; m. John R. Dick III,Nov. 7, 1986; children: Joshua, Justin. BA with honors, U. Calif., Santa Cruz, 1975; PhD, U. So. Calif., 1980. Postdoctoral fellow Calif. Inst. Tech., Pasadena, 1979-81, Swiss Inst. Tech., Lausanne, 1981-83; vis. scientist Solar Energy Rsch. Inst., Golden, Colo., 1983-84; rsch. scientist Allied-Signal, Inc., Morristown, N.J., 1984-89; sr. mem. tech. staff Bandgap Tech. Corp., Broomfield, Colo., 1989-93, quality assurance/quality control mgr., 1993—; pres. Houlding Chem. Cons. Group. Author over 20 tech. papers. Mem. Am. Chem. Soc., Materials Rsch. Soc., Sigma Xi. Office: Bandgap Chem Corp 1861 Lefthand Cir Longmont CO 80501

HOULE, JOSEPH ADRIEN, orthopaedic surgeon; b. Ft. Saskatchewan, Alta., Can., Nov. 3, 1928; came to U.S., 1978; s. Adelard Houle and Bertha (Durocher) Guay; divorced; children: Valerie, Diane, Lorraine, Louis, Doreen, Ludmilla, Virginia; m. Marjorie Elizabeth Tuhy. BSc, cert. in premed., U. Ottawa, 1955; MD, Laval U., 1960, Licentiate Med. Council of Can., 1960. Cert. specialist orthopaedic surgery, Quebec, Can. Intern Hotel Dieu Hosp., Quebec City, Can., 1959-60; resident in gen. surgery St. Vincent de Paul Hosp., Sherbrooke, Que., Can., 1960-61, St. Vincent's Hosp., Bridgeport, Conn., 1961-62; resident in orthopaedic surgery Montreal Children's Hosp., Montreal Gen. Hosp. and Queen Mary's Vet. Hosp., 1962-65; practice medicine specializing in orthopaedic surgery Montreal, Can., 1965-78; chief of orthopaedic surgery Thomas Davis Med. Ctr., Tucson, 1978—. Produced film Mechanical Knee, 1969. Mem. Bd. Med. Examiners of Ariz., 1978. Served to capt. Royal Can. Forces, 1956-67. Mem. AMA, Can. Orthopaedic Assn., Ariz. Orthopaedic Assn., Pima County Med. Soc. Roman Catholic. Home: 3715 N Pantano Rd Tucson AZ 85715-2348 Office: Thomas Davis Med Ctrs 707 N Alvernon Way Tucson AZ 85711-1870

HOULIHAN, PATRICK THOMAS, museum director; b. New Haven, June 22, 1942; s. John T. and Irene (Rourke) H.; m. Betsy Eliason, June 19, 1965; children: Mark T. and Michael D. (twins). BS, Georgetown U., 1964; MA, U. Minn., 1969; PhD, U. Wis., Milw., 1971. Asst. commr. N.Y. State Mus., Albany, 1980-81; dir. Heard Mus., Phoenix, 1972-80, SW Mus., Los Angeles, 1981—. Mem. Am. Assn. Mus. (council mem. 1978-81), Soc. Mus. Anthropology (bd. dirs. 1982—). Office: Millicent Rogers Mus PO Box A Taos NM 87571-0546

HOUPIS, HARRY LOUIS FRANCIS, research physicist; b. Johnson City, N.Y., Jan. 18, 1954; s. Louis Harry and Annamarie Houpis.; m. Carole Lynn Turner, Jan. 28, 1984; children: Demetrius Vesalius, Carissa Selena. BS in Math., MIT, 1976, BS in Physics, 1976; MS in Physics, U. Calif. San Diego, La Jolla, 1978, PhD in Physics, 1981. Asst. rsch. physicist U. Calif. San Diego, La Jolla, 1981-87; vis. rsch. physicist Max Planck Inst. for Aeronomie, Katlenburg-Lindau, Fed. Republic Germany, 1985, Cen. Rsch. Inst. for Physics, Budapest, Hungary, 1986, Supercomputer Computations Rsch. Inst. Fla. State U., Tallahassee, 1986-87; vis. and assoc. rsch. physicist Space Physics Rsch. Lab. U Mich., Ann Arbor, 1987-88; tech. staff Mission Rsch. Corp., Carmel, Calif., 1988-90; dir. we. region Ctr. for Remote Scnsing, Missoula, Mont., 1990—; lectr. in physics Hartnell C.C., Salinas, Calif., 1989-90; proposal referee NASA, NSF, Washington, 1985—; manuscript referee Jour. of Geophys. Rsch. and Icarus, 1981—. Author: The Physics of Comets; contbr. numerous articles to profl. jours. Pub. lectr. San Diego Speakers Bur., 1979-86. Fulbright sr. scholarship Coun. for Internat. Exch. of Scholars, 1985-86; Max Planck Soc. fellowship, Max Planck Inst., 1983, 85. Mem. AIAA, N.Y. Acad. Scis., Am. Geophys. Union, Am. Astron. Soc., Am. Phys. Soc. Home: 3509 Norman Dr Missoula MT 59801 Office: Ctr for Remote Sensing Ste 107 1916 Brooks St Missoula MT 59801 also: Ctr for Remote Sensing Ste 223 5667 Snell Ave San Jose CA 95123

HOUSE, DAVID L., electronics components company executive; b. 1943. With Raytheon, 1965-69, Honeywell, 1969-72, Microdata, 1972-74; v.p., gen. mgr. Intel Corp., 1974—, now sr. v.p. Office: Intel Corp PO Box 58119 Santa Clara CA 95052-8119

HOUSE, ERNEST ROBERT, education educator, educational evaluator; b. Alton, Ill., Aug. 7, 1937; s. Ernest House and Helen Lucille (Schumake) McDaniel) m. Donna Brown, Feb. 1, 1964; children: Kristin, Colby. AB, Washington U., St. Louis, 1959; MS, So. Ill. U., 1964; EdD, U. Ill., 1968. Cert. high sch. tchr., Ill. Tchr. English, Roxana (Ill.) High Sch., 1960-64; cons. Ill. demonstration project for gifted youth U. Ill., Urbana, 1964-65, dir. gifted program evaulation Coop. Ednl. Rsch. Lab., 1967-69, project dir., ednl. specialist, 1969-71, project dir., asst. prof. edn., 1971-75, assoc. prof., 1975-79, prof., 1979-85; vis. prof. U. Colo., Boulder, 1982, prof. edn., 1985—, dir. Lab. for Policy Studies, 1985—; vis. scholar UCLA, 1976, Harvard U., Cambridge, Mass., 1980; mem. lab. rev. panel U.S. Dept. Edn., 1987—. Author: The Politics of Educational Innovation, 1974, (with Steve Lapan) Survival in the Classroom, 1978; Evaluating With Validity, 1980, Jesse Jackson and the Politics of Charisma, 1988, Professional Evaluation: Social Impact and Political Consequences, 1993; mem. editorial bd. Ednl. Evaluation and Policy Analysis, 1971-81, 86—; editor-in-chief New Directions for Program Evaluation, 1982-85; columnist Evaluation Practice, 1984-88. Mem. rsch. staff Senator Adlai Stevenson of Ill., 1970, Ill. lt. gov. Paul Simon, 1972. Recipient Harold D. Lasswell prize Policy Scis. Policy Scis. Jour., 1989, Lazarfield award. Mem. Am. Ednl. Rsch. Assn. (program chmn. 1976, chmn. awards com. 1983), Am. Evaluation Assn., Phi Beta Kappa. Democrat. Office: U Colo Sch Edn CB 249 Boulder CO 80309

HOUSE, GEORGE MICHAEL, museum curator; b. Silver City, N.Mex., Apr. 2, 1955; s. William Winfrey House and Ruth Lestra (Williams) Billings; m. Maria Cedillo Enriquez, Dec. 24, 1983; children: Vanessa Yvette, Joshua Michael, Benjamin Alexander. BA in History and Social Sci., Western N.Mex. U., 1984, MA in History, 1985. With forest svc. USDA, Silver City, N.Mex., 1973, Kingston, N.Mex., 1976; museum curator Space Ctr., Alamogordo, N.Mex., 1985—; cons., instr., rschr., lectr. Space Ctr., Alamogordo, 1985—. Contbr. articles to publs. Sunday sch. tchr. Ch. of Christ, Bayard, N.Mex., 1976-85, Alamogordo, 1985—; juror Otero County Courthouse, Alamogordo, 1990. With USN, 1973-76. Dean Caulkins Meml. scholar Western N.Mex. U., 1983, Bd. of Regents scholar Western N.Mex., 1983. Mem. Pi Gamma Mu (Cert. of Merit 1984). Home: PO Box 382 Alamogordo NM 88311-0382 Office: Space Ctr PO Box 533 Top of NM Hwy 2001 Alamogordo NM 88311-0533

HOUSE, KAREN SUE, nursing consultant; b. San Francisco, July 16, 1958; d. Mathas Dean and Marilyn Frances (Weigand) H. Casa Loma Coll., 1985; AS in Nursing, SUNY at Albany, 1987. Psychiat. charge nurse Woodview Calabasas (Calif.) Hosp., 1985-87, Treatment Ctrs. Am., Van Nuys, Calif., 1987-88; cons., RN Valley Village Devel. Ctr., Reseda, Calif., 1988; plastic surg. nurse George Sanders, M.D., Encino, Calif., 1986—; nurse New Image Found., 1989—, Mid Valley Youth Ctr., 1991—; dir. nursing Encino Surgicenter (Sanders), 1992—; dir. nursing Devel. Tng. Svcs. for Devel. Disabled, 1988—; nurse cons. New Horizons for Developmentally Disabled, 1993. Recipient Simi Valley Free Clinic Scholarship. Home: 26798 Claudette St # 338 Santa Clarita CA 91351-4848 Office: 16633 Ventura Blvd Ste 110 Encino CA 91436-1803

HOUSE, LEO BRANDYBUCK, hydrologist; b. Madison, Wis., May 1, 1954; s. Harold Beauregard and Mary Lee Pflaum (Fix) H.; m. Diane Marie Pett, Dec. 27, 1990. BSCE, U. Wis., 1976, MSCE, 1978. Registered profl. engr., Wis. Hydrologist U.S. Geological Survey, Madison, Wis., 1978—. Mem. ASCE, Am. Water Resources Assn. Office: US Geological Survey PO Box 25046 MS 415 Denver CO 80225

HOUSE, PETER KYLE, geologist; b. Cin., July 1, 1965; s. Robert Eugene and Sue (Stein) H.; m. Carrie Beth Nelson; July 5, 1991. BA, We. Wash. U., 1989, BS magna cum laude, 1989; MS, U. Ariz., 1991. Hydrologist Pima County Flood Control Dist., Tucson, 1989-90; rsch. asst. dept. geosciences U. Ariz., Tucson, 1989—; geologist Ariz. Geol. Survey, Tucson, 1990—. Contbr. articles to profl. jours. Fellowship Dept. Geography, We. Wash. U., 1986. Mem. Geol. Soc. of Am. (student mem.), Am. Geophys. Union (student), Phi Kappa Phi, Sigma xi. Office: U Ariz Dept Geoscis Tucson AZ 85719

HOUSE, R(OLAND) MARK, marketing professional; b. Portland, Oreg., Jan. 3, 1961; s. Robert Louis and Geraldine Elizabeth (Watt) H.; m. Elizabeth Southall Raich, May 2, 1992. BS in Environ. Planning & Mgmt., U. Calif., Davis, 1984; MBA, Golden Gate U., 1988. Sales & mktg. cons. Sir Francis Drake Hotel, San Francisco, 1983-87; assoc. cons. Laventhol & Horwath, San Francisco, 1987-88; pres. 4 House Devel., Inc., Salinas, Calif., 1989—; assoc. cons. Horwath & Horwath Asia Pacific, Hong Kong, 1989; speaker. Bd. dirs. Palma Found., Salinas, 1992—. Mem. Carmel Valley Property Owners Assn., Salinas Valley Builders Exch., Salinas C. of C. Republican. Roman Catholic. Office: 4 House Devel Inc 158 Central Ave Ste # 3 Salinas CA 93901

HOUSER, GERALD BURNETT, university administrator; b. Glendale, Calif., May 15, 1951; s. Willard Alba and Anna Mae (Smidderks) H.; m. Lyndsey Rose Fields, Aug. 30, 1983; children: Graham Fields, Rebecca Rose. BA, Azusa Pacific U., 1973, MA, 1979; postgrad., Fuller Sem., Pasadena, Calif., 1974-76; PhD, U. So. Calif., 1986. Circus clown L.A. Dept. Recreation and Parks, 1969-73; minister of youth Herman Free Meth. Ch., L.A., 1974-77; carpenter L.A., 1976; head resident Azusa (Calif.) Pacific U., 1977-79; area coord. housing U. So. Calif., L.A., 1979-81, asst. dir. career devel. ctr., 1981-87, assoc. dir., 1987-89, dir., 1989—; adj. prof. U. So. Calif., Mount St. Mary's, Azusa Pacific U., L.A., 1979—; individual career counselor, L.A., 1981—; pub. speaker over 100 presentations at confs., cos., orgns., West Coast, L.A., 1979—; cons. Sugar Ray Youth Found., L.A., 1984-85; career cons. over 10 different cos./depts., L.A., 1981—. Contbr. articles to profl. jours. Group leader All Saints Episcopal Ch. Mem. Western Coll. Placement Assn. (workshop chair 1987-89). Democrat. Episcopalian. Office: U So Calif Career Devel Ctr Student Union 111 Los Angeles CA 90089-4897

HOUSTON, C(LARENCE) STUART, radiologist, educator; b. Williston, N.D., Sept. 26, 1927; s. Clarence Joseph and Sigridur (Christianson) H.; m. Mary Isabel Belcher, Aug. 12, 1951; children: Stanley, Margaret, David, Donald. MD, U. Man., Winnipeg, Can., 1951; DLitt, U. Sask., Saskatoon, Can., 1987. Demonstrator in anatomy U. Sask., 1960-61, teaching fellow in radiology, 1963-64, lectr., 1964-65, asst. prof., 1965-67, assoc. prof., 1967-69, prof., 1969—, head dept. med. imaging, 1982-87. Author: To the Arctic by Canoe, 1974, Pioneer of Vision, 1980, Arctic Ordeal, 1984, R.G. Ferguson, Crusader, 1991; editor Jour. Can. Assn. Radiologists, 1976-81. Recipient Roland Michener Conservation award Can. Wildlife Fedn., 1986, Douglas H. Pimlott Conservation award Can. Nature Fedn., 1988, Ralph D. Bird award Man. Naturalists' Soc., 1989, Doris Huestis Speirs award Soc. Can. Ornithologists, 1989, Eugene Eisenmann medal Linnean Soc. N.Y., 1990, Sask. Order of Merit, 1992, Officer of Order of Can., 1993. Mem. Can. Soc. for History of Medicine (pres. 1987-89), Royal Coll. Physicians and Surgeons (mem. coun. 1984-90, chmn. specialty com. 1984-88), Am. Ornithologists' Union (mem. coun. 1978-80, mem. memorials com. 1984—, v.p. 1990-91). Home: 863 University Dr, Saskatoon, SK Canada S7N 0J8 Office: U Hosp, Dept Med Imaging, Saskatoon, SK Canada S7N 0X0

HOUSTON, ELIZABETH REECE MANASCO, educator, consultant; b. Birmingham, Ala., June 19, 1935; d. Reuben Cleveland and Beulah Elizabeth (Reece) Manasco; m. Joseph Brantley Houston; 1 child, Joseph Brantley Houston III. BS, U. Tex., 1956; MEd, Boston Coll., 1969. Cert. elem. tchr., Calif., cert. spl. edn. tchr., Calif., cert. community coll. instr., Calif. Tchr., elem. Ridgefield (Conn.) Schs., 1962-63; staff, spl. edn. Sudbury (Mass.) Schs., 1965-68; staff intern Wayland (Mass.) High Sch., 1972; tchr., home bound Northampton (Mass.) Schs., 1972-73; program dir. Jack Douglas Ctr., San Jose, Calif., 1974-76; tchr. specialist spl. edn., coord. classroom svcs., dir. alternative schs. Santa Clara County Office Edn., San Jose, Calif., 1976—; instr. San Jose State U., 1980-87, U. Calif., Santa Cruz, 1982-85, Santa Clara U., 1991—; cons. Houston Rsch. Assocs., Saratoga, Calif., 1981—; mem. adv. bd. Santa Clara County Justice System. Author: (manual) Behavior Management for School Bus Drivers, 1980, Classroom Management, 1984, Synergistic Learning, 1988, Learning Disabilities in Psychology for Correctional Education, 1992. Recipient President's award Soc. Photo-Optical Instrumentation Engrs., 1979, Classroom Mgmt. Program award Sch. Bds. Assn., 1984, Svc. to Youth award, Juvenile Ct. Sch. Adminstrs. of Calif., 1986, 90, 91, 92; grantee Santa Clara County Office Edn. Tchr. Advisor Program U.S. Sec. Edn., 1983-84. Mem. ASCD, Assn. Calif. Sch. Adminstrs., Coun. Exceptional Children, Juvenile Ct. Sch. Adminstrs. of Calif. (bd. dirs.), Correctional Edn. Assn. Home: 12150 Country Squire Ln Saratoga CA 95070-3444 Office: Santa Clara County Office Edn 100 Skyport Dr San Jose CA 95110-1301

HOUSTON, HARRY ROLLINS, retired obstetrician, gynecologist; b. Bangor, Maine, Mar. 2, 1928; s. Howard Raymond and Ethel Elizabeth (Rollins) H.; m. Bett Grierson, Dec. 17, 1950; children: Susan, James, Barbara. Student, Bates Coll., 1948-51; MD, Tufts U., 1955; postgrad., Hebrew U., Jerusalem, 1993—. Diplomate, Am. Bd. Ob-Gyn. Enlisted USN, 1946, served in PTO, 1946-48, commd. ensign, 1951, advanced through grades to capt., 1970; intern, then resident U.S. Naval Hosp., Chelsea, Mass., 1955-60; chief ob.-gyn. Naval Sta. Hosp., Kodiak, Alaska, 1960-62; chief ob.-gyn. various U.S. Naval Hosps., 1966-76; ret. USN, 1976; pvt. practice Bremerton, Wash., 1976-93; chief ob.-gyn., Harrison Meml. Hosp., Bremerton, 1978-80. Comdr. Peninsula Squadron, CAP, Bremerton, 1966-70. Fellow Am. Coll. Ob.-Gyn.; mem. AMA, Kitsap County Med. Assn., Washington State Med. Assn., Yokosuka (Japan) Lodge, Masons, Naval Coun., Shriners, Scottish Rite. Republican. Presbyterian. Office: Med Office 2625 Wheaton Way Bremerton WA 98310-3318

HOUSTON, JANE HUNT, retired educator; b. Upper Montclair, N.J., Dec. 22, 1919; d. MacLean and Mary Hunt (Young) H. BA, Duke U., 1941; MEd, U. Wyo., 1960. Cert. tchr., Wyo. Field worker Glendale (Calif.) coun. Girl Scouts U.S., 1941-45; exec. dir. Sacramento coun. Girl Scouts U.S., 1945-46, Cheyenne (Wyo.) coun. Girl Scouts U.S., 1946-56; tchr. Laramie County Sch. Dist. #1, Cheyenne, 1956-79; ret., 1979. Co-author: Centennial, Wyoming 1876-1976-the Real Centennial. Bd. dirs. Carbon Power and Light Inc., Saratoga, Wyo., 1983—, Centennial Water and Sewer Dist., 1988—. Mem. LWV, Centennial Valley Hist. Assn. (sec. 1975—), Wyo. State Hist. Soc. (charter), Laramie County Ret. Tchr. (com. chmn. 1980—). Republican. Episcopalian. Office: Centennial Valley Hist Soc PO Box 200 Centennial WY 82055-0201

HOUSTON, JOHN ALBERT, political science educator; b. Spokane, Dec. 24, 1914; s. John Alexander and Ethel (Robinson) H.; m. Marjorie Anne Robinson, Aug. 14, 1939 (dec. Sept. 1968); children—Alexandra Louise (Mrs. Lee Benham), John Alexander II, Ann Celeste; m. Pollyanna Turner, Nov. 1, 1969. A.B. in Econs, Stanford, 1936, M.A. in Internat. Relations, 1947; Ph.D. in polit. sci, U. Mich., 1951. Ins. broker Johnson & Higgins, San Francisco, 1936-37; case aide Calif. Relief Adminstrn., 1938-40; asst., then asso. prof. polit. sci. U. Miss., 1949-54; faculty Knox Coll., Galesburg, Ill., 1954—; prof. polit. sci. Knox Coll., 1957-80, prof. emeritus, 1980—, Philip Sydney Post disting. prof., 1961-80; sec.-treas. Midwest Collegiate Athletic Conf., 1961-67. Author: Latin America in the United Nations, 1956, Book; rev. editor: Midwest Jour. Polit. Sci, 1962-65. Mem. Galesburg Planning Commn., 1956-57. Served to lt. comdr. USNR, 1941-45. Social Sci. Research Council fellow, 1956. Mem. Am. Polit. Sci. Assn., Midwest Conf. Polit. Scientists, Omicron Delta Kappa, Pi Sigma Alpha, Scabbard and Blade, Sigma Alpha Epsilon. Home: 565 Henley Way Ashland OR 97520-3119

HOUSTON, PAUL DAVID, school system administrator; b. Springfield, Ohio, Apr. 10, 1944; s. Paul Doran and Irene Almeda (Sansom) H.; m. Marilyn Kay Bowyer, Aug. 27, 1966 (div. July 1986); children: Lisa Lenore, Suzanne Elizabeth, Caroline Michelle; m. Jovel Kane, June 27, 1988; children: Todd Arnold, Chad Arnold. Tchr., Ohio State U., 1966; MA in Teaching, U. N.C., 1968; Cert. Advanced Study, Harvard U., 1971, EdD, 1973. Tchr. Chapel Hill (N.C.) City Schs., 1968-70; prin. Summit (N.J.) City Schs., 1972-74; asst. supt. Birmingham (Ala.) City Schs., 1974-77; supt. Princeton (N.J.) Regional Schs., 1977-86, Tucson Unified Sch. Dist., 1986-91, Riverside (Calif.) Unified Schs., 1991—; vis. prof. Brigham Young U., Princeton U.; pres. S.W. Regional Labs. Bd., 1989-90. Co-author: Exploding the Myths, 1993; contbr. articles to profl. jours. Pres. N.J. Interscholastic Assn.; bd. dirs. Princeton and Tucson Libr., 1977-87, YMCA, 1977-87. Recipient Richard Green Leadership award, Coun. of Great City Schs., 1991; named Exec. Educator of the Month, Exec. Educator, 1985, 100 Outstanding Exec. Educators in N.Am., 1984, 93. Mem. Am. Assn. Sch. Adminstrs. (Finis E. Engleman scholar 1972), Assn. Calif. Sch. Adminstrn., Rotary (pres. 1983-84), Phi Delta Kappa. Home: 1932 Bronson Way Riverside CA 92506 Office: Riverside Unified Sch Dist 3380 14th St Riverside CA 92501-0400

HOVATTER, KURT EUGENE, counselor; b. Oct. 5, 1954; s. Eugene Hendrik and Loradana Maria (Von Pessler) H. AA in History, Orange Coast Coll., 1974; BA in History, Calif. State U., Long Beach, 1978, BA in Polit. Sci., 1978. Sch. tutor Orange Coast Coll., Costa Mesa, Calif., 1972-74; sch. tutor Newport Mesa Sch. Dist., Costa Mesa, 1973-74, student tchr., 1975-76; food svc. asst. Sears, Costa Mesa, 1976-78; communications technician Continental Telephone Co., Bishop, Calif., 1980-84; youth counselor, social worker Inyo Mono Advocates For Community Action, Bishop, 1984-87; social worker Right Way Homes, Bishop, 1986-88; counselor Warm Beach Conf. Ctr., Stanwood, Wash., 1988—; youth counselor Youth for Christ, Stanwood, 1988—. Performer Camwood Players Community Theatre, Stanwood, 1990—. Republican. Home: 20800 Marine Dr Apt 10 Stanwood WA 98292-7850

HOVE, BRIAN E., bank officer; b. Spokane, Wash., Nov. 15, 1961; s. Henry H. and Virginia M. (Jackson Lisle) H. Mgmt. trainee Nat. Bank of Alaska, Anchorage, 1989-91, loan officer, 1991-92; br. mgr. Nat. Bank of Alaska, Delta Junction, 1992—. Mem. Delta Junction C. of C. (bd. dirs.). Republican. Protestant. Home: PO Box 921 Delta Junction AK 99737 Office: Nat Bank of Alaska PO Box 548 Delta Junction AK 99737

HOVIND, DAVID J., manufacturing company executive; b. 1940. BA, U. Wash., 1964; postgrad., Stanford U., 1984. With PACCAR Inc., Bellevue, Wash., 1964—, sr. v.p., 1986-87, exec. v.p., 1987-93; now pres. PACCAR Inc., 1993—. Office: PACCAR Inc PO Box 1518 777 106th Ave NE Bellevue WA 98004-5001

HOVIS, JAMES BRUNTON, judge; b. Yakima, Wash., Dec. 15, 1922; s. Ford Carpenter and Jean B. (Brunton) H.; m. Lorraine June Focht, June 14, 1947; children: James Brian, Mary Jean, Karen Lorraine, Nancy Elizabeth. BS, U. Wash., 1949, JD, 1950; student, Wash. State Coll., Ctrl. Wash. Coll. Bar: U.S. Dist. Ct. (ea. dist.) Wash. 1952, U.S. Dist. Ct. (we. dist.) Wash. 1971, U.S. Claims Ct. 1968, U.S. Tax Ct. 1977, U.S. Ct. Appeals (9th cir.) 1963, Supreme Ct. Wash. 1950. Assoc. Velikanje & Velikanje, Yakima, Wash., 1950-52; pvt. practice Zillah, Wash., 1950-52; ptnr. Hovis & Kaiser, Yakima, Wash., 1952-54, Brown, Hovis & Cockrill,

Yakima, Wash., 1954-64, Hovis, Cockrill & Roy, Yakima, Wash., 1965-82, Hovis, Cockrill, Weaver & Bjur, Yakima, Wash., 1982-87; U.S. Magistrate judge U.S. Dist. Ct. (ea. dist.), Spokane, Wash., 1987-91, Yakima, Wash., 1991—. Mem. Wash. State Parks & Recreation Commn., 1961-66, chmn., 1962-65, Wash. State Racing Commn., 1983-84; dir. Sundown M Ranch, 1967-87, pres., 1987, Yakima Valley Regional Libr., 1986-87. Office: US Dist Ct 25 S Third St Yakima WA 98901

HOWARD, BRADFORD REUEL, travel company executive; b. Honolulu, Aug. 6, 1957; s. Joseph DeSylva and Marguerite Evangeline (Barker) H.; m. Marcia Andresen, June 23, 1985; 1 child, Evan DeSilva Andresen. BS in Bus., U. Calif., Berkeley, 1979. Owner, operator Howard Janitorial Svcs., Oakland, Calif., 1970-80; prodn. mgr. Oakland Symphony Orch., 1976-80; brand mgr. The Clorox Co., Oakland, 1980-85; gen. mgr., corp. sec. Howard Tours, Inc./Howard Enterprises, Oakland, 1985—; co-owner Howard Mktg. Cons., Oakland, 1985—; cons. Marcus Foster Found., Oakland, 1984-85; pres., gen. mgr. Piedmont (Calif.) Community Theater, 1976-92. Mem. Calif. Alumni Assn. (bd. dirs. 1991—), U. Calif. Bus. Alumni Assn. (v.p. 1986-88, pres. 1988-89, Bay Area chpt. 1983-84), Oakland-Sunrise Rotary (sec. 1985-87, pres. 1987-88), Lake Merrit Breakfast Club. Office: Howard Tours Inc 526 Grand Ave Oakland CA 94610-3515

HOWARD, CHRISTOPHER HOLM, lawyer; b. Cleve., Sept. 28, 1956; s. George Thomas and Karen Miriam (Holm) H.; m. Jaime Vaughn Austen, Dec. 15,1 988; 1 child, Alexandria Vaughn Austen Howard. AB in Polit. Sci., Johns Hopkins U., 1977; JD, Stanford U., 1980. Bar: Wash. 1980, U.S. Dist. Ct. (we. dist.) Wash. 1980, U.S. Ct. Appeals (9th cir.) 1981. Assoc. Reed and McClure, Seattle, 1980-85, dir., 1986-88; shareholder, dir. Weiss Jensen Ellis & Botteri, Seattle and Portland, Oreg., 1988—, dir., 1989—. Bd. dirs. Jack Straw Found., Pub. Radio, Seattle and Everett, Wash. Mem. Wash. State Bar Assn. (interprofl. com. 1990—), Wash. Soc. Hosp. Attys., Wash. Soc. Def. Trial Lawyers, Def. Rsch. Inst. Office: Weiss Jensen Ellis Botteri 3150 1st Interstate Ctr Seattle WA 98104

HOWARD, CHRISTOPHER PHILIP, business consultant; b. N.Y.C., Aug. 6, 1947; s. Murray and Hope (McGurn) H.; m. Danina Mary Hill, June 29, 1987; children: Sean, Stephen, Coby, Katherine, Sara. BA in Econs., Stanford U., 1968; MBA, Santa Clara U., 1970. Cert. mgmt. acct., mgmt. cons. Cons. Ernst & Ernst, CPAs, Phoenix, 1972-74; ops. mgr. Jensen Tools & Alloys Inc., Phoenix, 1974-77; CFO Pioneer Industries, Inc., Phoenix, 1977-80; sr. v.p. Health-Tech Mgmt., Inc., Phoenix, 1980-84; mng. ptnr. Howard and Assocs., Phoenix, 1984-87; consulting mgr. Grant Thornton, CPAs, Reno, 1987-89; mng. ptnr. Howard Consulting Group, Reno, 1989—; faculty mem. U. Nev., Reno, 1991—. 1st lt. USAF, 1970-72. Mem. Inst. Cert. Mgmt. Accts., Inst. Cert. Mgmt. Cons., Stanford Alumni Assn., Sunrise Rotary. Episcopalian. Office: Howard Consulting Group 600 S Arlington Reno NV 89509

HOWARD, GEORGE HARMON, management consultant; b. St. John, Wash., Nov. 14, 1934; s. George Philip and Corrinne Cadwallader (Rippeteau) H.; m. Elizabeth Ann Ogden, Dec. 22, 1956 (dec. July 1991); children: Debra Ann Leming, Keith Philip, Corrie Lou Govostis, Stacia Elizabeth. BA, Wash. State U., 1957; MBA, Harvard U., 1967. Sales rep. Burroughs Corp., Spokane, Wash., 1957; various positions USAF, 1958-77; vice commdr. AF Contract Mgmt. Div., Kirkland AFB, N.Mex., 1978; mgr. corp. devel. Leisure Dynamics, Evergreen, Colo., 1978-80; pres. HBK Assocs., Inc., Evergreen, 1981-87; dir. ops. ILX Lightwave Corp., Bozeman, Mont., 1988-89; sr. cons. Matrix Mgmt. Group, Seattle, 1990—; pres. Howard Farms, Inc., St. John, Wash., 1986—. Co-author: TFX Acquisition, 1966. Instr. Red Rocks Community Coll., Denver, 1986-87; del. Colo. Rep. Conv., Denver, 1984. Recipient Outstanding Sr. award Wash. State U., 1957, Legion of Merit award USAF, 1978, Bronze star USAF, 1968. Mem. Shrine, York Rite Bodies, Masonic Lodge, Order of Eastern Star, Wheatland Grange, Air Force Assn., The Ret. Officers Assn. Republican. Episcopalian. Home: 6358 S 298th Pl Auburn WA 98001-3040 Office: Matrix Mgmt Group 811 1st Ave Seattle WA 98104

HOWARD, JAMES WEBB, investment banker, lawyer, engineer; b. Evansville, Ind., Sept. 17, 1925; s. Joseph R. and Velma (Cobb) H.; m. Phyllis Jean Brandt, Dec. 27, 1948; children: Sheila Rae, Sharon Kae. B.S. in Mech. Engring, Purdue U., 1949; postgrad., Akron (Ohio) Law Sch., 1950-51, Cleve. Marshall Law Sch., 1951-52; M.B.A., Western Res. U., 1962; J.D., Western State Coll. Law, 1976. Registered profl. engr., Ind., Ohio. Jr. project engr. Firestone Tire & Rubber Co., Akron, 1949-50; gen. foreman Cadillac Motor Car div. GM, 1950-53; mgmt. cons. M.K. Sheppard & Co., Cleve., 1953-56; plant mgr. Lewis Welding & Engring. Corp., Ohio, 1956-58; underwriter The Ohio Co., Columbus, 1959; chmn. Growth Capital, Inc., Chgo., 1960—; pvt. practice law San Diego, 1979-85; pres. Meister Brau, Inc., Chgo., 1965-73, The Home Mart, San Diego, 1974-82; mgn. agt., fin. instn. specialist FDIC/RTC, 1985-90; specialist in charge Office of FDIC-DOL, Portland, Oreg., 1986-87. Developer of "Lite" beer. Co-chmn. Chgo. com. Ill. Sesquicentennial Com., 1968. Served with AUS, 1943-46. Decorated Bronze Star, Parachutist badge, Combat Inf. badge. Mem. ASME, Nat. Assn. Small Bus. Investment Cos. (past pres.), State Bar Calif., Grad. Bus. Alumni Assn. Western Res. U. (past gov.), Masons, Tau Kappa Epsilon, Pi Tau Sigma, Beta Gamma Sigma. Methodist.

HOWARD, JANE OSBURN, educator; b. Morris, Ill., Aug. 12, 1926; d. Everett Hooker and Bernice Otilda (Olson) Osburn; B.A., U. Ariz., 1948; M.A., U. N.Mex., 1966, Ph.D., 1969; m. Rollins Stanley Howard, June 5, 1948; children—Ellen Elizabeth, Susan (Mrs. John Karl Nuttall). Instr. U. N.Mex. Sch. Medicine, Albuquerque, 1968-70, mem. staff pediatrics, deaf blind children's program, Albuquerque, 1971-72, asst. dir. N.Mex. programs for deaf blind children, 1972—, instr. psychiatry, instr. pediatrics, coordinator deaf-blind children's program, 1972-76, edn. cons., 1976—, publicity and pub. relations cons., 1983—; Cons. Mountain-Plains Regional Ctr. for Services to Deaf-Blind Children, Denver, 1971-74, Bur. Indian Affairs, 1974. Active Cystic Fibrosis, Mother's March, Heart Fund, Easter Seal-Crippled Children. Recipient fellowships U. N.M., 1965, 66, 66-67, 67-68, U. So. Calif. John Tracy Clinic, 1973. Fellow Royal Soc. Health; mem. Council Exceptional Children, Am. Assn. Mental Deficiency, Nat. Assn. Retarded Children, AAUW, Pi Lambda Theta, Zeta Phi Eta, Alpha Epsilon Rho. Republican. Methodist. Home: 615 Valencia Dr SE Albuquerque NM 87108-3742

HOWARD, JO ANN, business owner; b. L.A., Nov. 22, 1937; d. John George and Lucile Anne (Farish) Heinzman; m. William Harold Howard, Dec. 2, 1958; children: Teri Lynn Wilson, Tracey Ann Currie, Randall William, Richard John. Student, Mt. San Antonio Coll., 1957. Escrow officer, mgr. So. Cities Escrow, Hemet, Calif., 1970-75; escrow officer Hemet Escrow, 1975-76; ptnr. Ramona Escrow, Hemet, 1976-79; pres., supr. Howard Escrow, Hemet, 1979—; pres. Recon Enterprises, Inc., Hemet, 1976—; co-owner J & B Mobile Modular Housing, Hemet, 1986—; pres. Chaparral Accomodators, Inc., Hemet, 1990—. Pres. Sorpotimists Internat., San Jacinto-Hemet Valley, Calif., 1979. Named one of Disting. Pres.'s, Soroptimists, 1978-80; recipient Woman of Distinction award Soroptimist Internat. (San Jacinto-Hemet Valley 1990). Mem. Women's Coun. Bd. Realtors (affiliate, treas.), Hemet-San Jacinto Bd. Realtors (affiliate), San Jacinto C. of C., Hemet C. of C., Calif. Escrow Assn. (pres. Calif. chpt. 1991), Riverside County Escrow Assn. (bd. dirs. 1985—), Escrow Inst. of Calif. (bd. dirs. 1992—). Republican. Presbyterian. Office: Howard Escrow 3292 E Florida Ste D Hemet CA 92544

HOWARD, KAREN LYNN, computer programmer and analyst; b. Goldsboro, N.C., Oct. 17, 1967; d. Charles Ty and Beverly Ann (Schmidt) H. BA with honors in Bus. Adminstrn., U. Puget Sound, 1990. Sales assoc. Best Products, Aurora, Colo., 1983-84; spl. projects asst. to pres. KRM Software Devel. Co., Englewood, Colo., 1984-89; mktg. asst. Riviera Fin. Svcs., Seattle, 1989; adminstrv. coord. Fin. Insights, Tacoma, 1990; devel. excellence ops. trainee Seafirst Nat. Bank, Seattle, 1990, programmer, analyst, 1991, project mgr., 1992—. Agy. coord. Seafirst Adopt-A-Family Program, 1990; dept. coord. Food Lifeline Food Drive, Seattle, 1991; div. coord. Seafirst campaign drive United Way, 1991, 92; v.p., bd. dirs. Pathways for Women, Edmonds, Wash., 1991-92, pres., bd. dirs., 1993—. Recipient Disting. Svc. award Alpha Kappa Psi, 1990; dean's scholar U. Puget Sound, 1990; named Seafirst Outstanding Vol. of Yr., 1992. Mem. Am. Mktg. Assn., Kappa Alpha Theta, Alpha Kappa Psi. Home: 11060 NE 33d Pl Apt E-4 Bellevue WA 98004 Office: Seafirst Nat Bank 800 5th Ave Seattle WA 98104

HOWARD, KATSUYO KUNUGI, counselor, educator, consultant; b. Kushigata, Yamanashi, Japan, Apr. 9, 1945; came to U.S., 1972; m. John P. Howard, Feb. 14, 1976; children: Shinichi, Keiko. BS, Chiba (Japan) U., 1968; MS in Linguistics, Calif. State U., Fresno, 1976, MS in Counseling, 1979. Lic. marriage, family and child counselor, Calif.; cert. tchr., community coll. credential, adult edn., Calif. Instr. Fresno City Coll., 1976-80; advisor Internat. Student Counseling, Calif. State U., Fresno, 1978-80, counselor, 1980-86; coord. SE Asian Student Svcs., Calif. State U., Fresno, 1986—; pvt. practice and cons., Fresno, Calif., 1992—; presenter in field. Author: Passages: An Anthology of the Southeast Asian Refugee Experience, 1990; producer: (video) Pathfinders: Hmong Refugees in Higher Education, 1987. Bd. dirs. The East-/west Ctr. Assn. East-West Community Svcs. Mem. Soc. for Intercultural Edn., Tng. and Rsch., Nat. Assn. for Fgn. Student Affairs, Cen. Valley Asian Pacific Women (bd. dirs.), Japanese Am. Citizen League, Calif. Assn. Marriage and Family Therapists, Cen. Valley Refugee Forum, Am. Assn. for Counseling and Devel., Am. Coll. Pers. Assn., Hmong Am. Women Assn., Asian & Pacific Americans in Higher Edn. Office: Calif State U Fresno Student Union 306 N Jackson Fresno CA 93740-0036

HOWARD, KENNETH JOHN, accounting director; b. San Francisco, Feb. 24, 1946; s. Jerome Francis and Florence Helen (Cleary) H.; m. Sandra Rae Culp, Aug. 21, 1971; children: Jennifer N., Melissa M. BA in Sociology, U. Notre Dame, 1968; MBA in Fin., San Francisco State U., 1972; MPA in Mgmt., Golden Gate U., 1979. CPA, Calif. Auditor U.S. Gen. Acctg. Office, San Francisco, 1972-75, audit mgr., 1976-81; audit mgr. Clorox Co., Oakland, Calif., 1981-82; mgr. gen. acctg. Household Products Div., Clorox Co., Oakland, Calif., 1982-84, mgr. fin. analysis, 1984-85; mgr. cost systems Kingsford Products Div., Clorox Co., Oakland, Calif., 1985; dir. fin. and acctg. Food Svc. Div., Clorox Co., Oakland, Calif., 1986—; instr. in field. Columnist and photographer in field. Bd. dirs. Bay Area coun. Girl Scouts U.S., 1992-94; campaign chair Clorox United Way Campaign, Oakland, 1987-88, com. chair, 1982-86. Recipient numerous awards Internat. Competitions for Underwater Photography, 1976—. Mem. Calif. State Soc. CPAs, Ctrl. Coun. Diving Clubs, Underwater Photographic Soc. Home: 10 Woodside Ct San Anselmo CA 94960 Office: The Clorox Co PO Box 24305 Oakland CA 94623-1305

HOWARD, MARK ALAN, veterinarian; b. Gary, Ind., Mar. 1, 1952; s. John Melville and Isabelle Jean (Foot) H.; m. Kathryn Barbour, May 27, 1977 (div. 1989); children: Christopher Mark, Sara Jean, Kathryn Brit. BS, Colo. State U., 1975, DVM, 1979. Intern Southwest Animal Coll., Lubbock, Tex., 1979-80; staff veterinarian Alameda Vet. Hosp., Lakewood, Colo., 1980-85; hosp. dir. Elmfield Vet. Ctr., Denver, 1986—. Staff Christian Rsch. Assocs., Denver, 1982-85. With USAF, 1970-74. Mem. Am. Vet. Med. Assn., Colo. Vet. Med. Assn., DAVMS. Orthodox Christian. Home: 1212 1/2 S Emerson Denver CO 80212 Office: Elmfield Vet Ctr 2658 W Florida Denver CO 80219

HOWARD, MURRAY, manufacturing, real estate, property management executive, farmer, rancher; b. Los Angeles, July 25, 1914; s. George A. J. and Mabel (Murray) H. B.S., UCLA, 1939. C.P.A., Calif. Mgr. budget control dept. Lockheed Aircraft, 1939-45; pres., chmn. bd. Stanley Foundries, Inc., 1945-59, Howard Machine Products, Inc., 1959—, Murray Howard Realty, Inc., 1959—, Murray Howard Devel., Inc., 1969—, Howard Oceanography, Inc., 1967—, Ranch Sales, Inc., 1968—, Murray Howard Investment Corp., 1961—; owner, gen. mgr. Greenhorn Ranch Co., Greenhorn Creek Guest Ranch, Spring Garden, Calif.; pres., chmn. bd. Murray Howard Cattle Co., Prineville, Oreg.; dir. Airshippers Publ. Corp., LaBrea Realty & Devel. Co., Shur-Lok Corp. Served as mem. Gov. Calif. Minority Com. Mem. Nat. Assn. Cost Accts. (dir., v.p.), NAM (dir.). Office: 1605 W Olympic Blvd Ste 404 Los Angeles CA 90015-3808

HOWARD, ROBERT CAMPBELL, JR., lawyer; b. Bklyn., June 7, 1951; s. Robert Campbell and Helen (Buck) H.; divorced; 1 child, Cordell Campbell; m. Kathy Evenson, May 18, 1991. BA in Polit. Sci., Ariz. State U., 1973, JD, 1976. Bar: Ariz. 1976, U.S. Dist. Ct. Ariz. 1976. Assoc. Combs & Foley, Phoenix, 1976-77, Paul Brodwell, P.C., Phoenix, 1977-78, Law Office Louis Jekel, Scottsdale, Ariz., 1978-80; ptnr. Jekel & Howard, Scottsdale, Ariz., 1980—; judge pro-tempore City of Scottsdale, Ariz., 1983—. Commr. City of Scottsdale Airport, 1985-90, chmn. 1989; bd. dirs. Sereno Soccer League, Phoenix, 1986-89, Phoenix Dist. Tennis Assn., 1989—; mem. Scottsdale Charros, 1986—, pres. 1992-93; bd. dirs. Scottsdale Leadership, 1989—, pres. 1992-93; chmn. Scottsdale Visioning Steering Com., 1990-91. Named Charro of Yr., 1988. Mem. Ariz. Bar Assn., Scottsdale Bar Assn. (pres. 1985). Republican. Presbyterian. Office: Jekel & Howard 7285 E Stetson Dr # E Scottsdale AZ 85251-3423

HOWARD, ROBERT STAPLES, newspaper publisher; b. Wheaton, Minn., Oct. 23, 1924; s. Earl Eaton and Helen Elizabeth (Staples) H.; m. Lillian Irene Crabtree, Sept. 2, 1945; children: Thomas, Andrea, William, David. Student, U. Minn., 1942, 45. Pub. various daily, weekly newspapers, 1946-55; pub. Chester, Pa. Times, 1955-61; Pres. Howard Pubs. (18 daily newspapers), 1961—. With AUS, 1942-43; 2d lt. USAAF, 1944-45. Home: PO Box 1337 Rancho Santa Fe CA 92067-9999 Office: PO Box 570 Oceanside CA 92049-0570

HOWARD, SHERWIN WARD, college president; b. Safford, Ariz., Feb. 19, 1936; s. Fred Pack and Beatrice Sarah (Ward) H.; m. Annette Mina Shoup, June 30, 1961; children: Andrea Lynne, John Stanley, Stephen Ward, David Stowell. BS, Utah State U., 1960, MA, 1963; MFA, Yale U., 1966; PhD, U. Wis., 1980. Asst. to provost, asst. prof. Ohio U., Athens, 1966-69; asst. to pres., assoc. prof. Lawrence U., Appleton, Wis., 1969-80; prof. theatre arts, dean Coll. Arts and Humanities Weber State U., Ogden, Utah, 1980-92; pres. Deep Springs Coll., Dyer, Nev., 1992—. Author: (poems) Sometime Voices, 1988 (Utah Poet of Yr.), also plays and poems. 1st lt. U.S. Army, 1960-62. Mem. Dramatists Guild, Phi Sigma Iota, Pi Lambda Theta. Home and Office: Deep Springs Coll HC 72 Box 45001 Dyer NV 89010-9803

HOWARD, VICTOR, management consultant; b. Montreal, Que., Can., Aug. 12, 1923; s. Thomas and Jean (Malkinson) H.; BA, Sir George Williams U., 1947; BSc, 1948; PhD, Mich. State U., 1954; m. Dorothy Bode, Dec. 25, 1953. Mech. design engr. Canadian Vickers Ltd., Montreal, 1942-46; with Aluminum Co. Can., 1946-48, E.B. Badger Co., Boston, 1948-50; asst. prof. Mich. State U., 1952-56; social scientist Rand Corp., 1956-58; staff exec., personnel dir. System Devel. Corp., Santa Monica, Calif., 1958-66; staff cons. Rohrer, Hibler & Replogle, San Francisco, 1966-69; mng. dir. Rohrer, Hibler & Replogle Internat., London and Brussels, 1969-74, ptnr. 1974, mgr. San Francisco, 1974-88, dir., 1979-88; pres. V. Howard and Assocs., 1988—, The Inst. on Stress and Health in the Work Place, 1988—; vice chair State Bd. Psychology, 1989-93. Fellow Brit. Inst. Dirs.; mem. Am. Psychol. Assn., Western Psychol.Assn., U.S. Power Squadrons (comdr. Sequoia Squadron 1981, dist. comdr. 1987), Calif. State Mil. Res. (col. 1984), Reform Club, Hurlingham (London) Club, Thames Motor Yacht Club (Molesey, Eng.), Order of St. John of Jerusalem (chevalier)Sovereign Mil. Order of the Temple, Masons (33 degree), Shriners, Sigma Xi. Office: 1350 Old Bayshore Hwy Ste 610 Burlingame CA 94010

HOWARD, VOLNEY WARD, JR., wildlife science educator, researcher; b. Catarina, Tex., Apr. 9, 1941; s. Volney Ward and Millicent Beatrice (Zobal) H.; m. Linda Ann Turpen, Aug. 26, 1967; children: Kurtis Sutton, Kimberly Rene. BS, Tex. A & M U., College Station, 1964; MS, N.Mex. State U., 1966; PhD, U. Idaho, 1969. Cert. wildlife biologist. Student trainee Tex. Game, Fish & Oyster Commn., McAllen, summer 1962, Palestine, summer 1963; grad. rsch. asst. dept. animal, range, wildlife sci. N.Mex. State U., Las Cruces, 1964-66; grad. fellow Coll. Forsetry, Wildlife, Range Sci. U. Idaho, Moscow, 1966-69; asst. prof. dept. animal, range, wildlife scis. N.Mex. State U., 1969-73, assoc. prof., 1973-75, assoc. prof. dept. fishsery, wildlife sci., 1975-79, prof., 1979—; cons., Las Cruces, 1974—; sec.-treas. Franklin Arms Co., Las Cruces, 1985-87, pres., 1987—. Contbr. articles and rsch. to profl. publs. Recipient rsch. award Bur. Land Mgmt., U.S. Dept. Interior, Roswell, N.Mex., 1977-81, Outstanding Teaching award Coll. Agr. and Home Econs., Mex. State U., 1991; named Disting. Alumni Coll. Agr. and Home Econs., N.Mex. State U., 1988, Disting. Grad. Tchr., Gamma Sigma Delta, Las Cruces, 1989. Mem. Dona Ana County Associated Sportsmen (bd. dirs. 1982-86), Ducks Unltd. (treas. 1981-85, 10-30 Club award 1981-85), Wildlife Soc. (several local coms.), Soc. Range Mgmt., Nat. Geog. Soc. Democrat. Methodist. Office: NMex State U Dept Fishery & Wildlife Sci PO Box 30003 Las Cruces NM 88003-0003

HOWARD, WALTER EGNER, wildlife biology and ecology educator; b. Woodland, Calif., Apr. 9, 1917; s. Walter Lafayette and May Belle Howard; m. Elizabeth Ann Kendall; children: Thomas Kendall, Kathryn Spencer, John Casey. AB, U. Calif., Berkeley, 1939; MS, U. Mich., 1941, PhD, 1947. Fellow U. Mich., Ann Arbor, 1942, 46-47; from instr. zoology to prof. wildlife biology and vertebrate ecology U. Calif., Davis, 1947-87, prof. emeritus, 1987—; cons. UN, FAO, WHO, internat. assignments. Contbr. numerous articles to profl. jours.; patentee in field. With AUS, 1942-46, PTO. Fulbright scholar, Australia, New Zealand, 1957-58. Fellow AAAS; mem. British Ecol. Soc., Ecol. Soc. Am., Am. Soc. Mammalogists, Wildlife Soc., Western Soc. Naturalists, Soc. Range Mgmt., Sigma Xi, Phi Kappa Phi, Phi Sigma. Lodge: Rotary. Home: 24 College Park Davis CA 95616-3607 Office: U Calif Dept Wildlife Fisheries Biology Davis CA 95616

HOWARD, WILLIAM MATTHEW, business executive, arbitrator, lawyer, author; b. Oak Park, Ill., Dec. 16, 1934; s. William and Martha Geraldine (Herlock) H.; m. Linda Marie Eckelkamp, Dec. 30, 1991; children from previous marriage: Matthew William, Stephanie Sue. BSBA, U. Mo., 1956, JD with honors, 1958; postgrad., U. Nice, France, 1976, U. London, 1977. Bar: Mo. 1958, U.S. Supreme Ct. 1986. Jr. ptnr. Bryan, Cave, McPheeters & McRoberts, St. Louis, 1958-66; asst. to pres. Granite City (Ill.) Steel Co., 1966-69; pres. Thomson Internat. Co., Thibodaux, La., 1969-70; founder, pres., chmn. bd. The Catalyst Group, Phoenix, Ariz., 1970—; adj. faculty U. Mo., Columbia, 1956-58, St. Louis U., 1958-61; chmn. unauthorized practice law com. Mo. Bar, St. Louis, 1964-65; chmn. bd. N.V. Vulcaansoord, Terborg, The Netherlands, 1975-78, E. Chalmers Holdings, Ltd., Glasgow, Scotland, 1977-78; exec. cons. Chem. Bank, Irvine, Calif., 1985-90; vis. lectr. UCLA, 1987; arbitrator Am. Arbitration Assn., N.Y.C., 1987—, N.Y. Stock Exch., 1987—, Nat. Assn. Securities Dealers, Chgo., 1987—, Nat. Futures Assn., Chgo., 1988—, Am. Stock Exch., N.Y.C., 1988—; hearing officer Mo. Dept. Natural Resources, Jefferson City, 1987-89; bd. dirs. Xeric Corp., Denver. Editor newsletter Extras, 1970—; exec. producer: (motion picture) Twice a Woman, 1979; contbr. numerous articles and revs. to various jours. Bd. dirs. U. Mo. Alumni Assn., 1986, Breckenridge (Colo.) Film Festival, 1989, Actors Theatre Phoenix, 1990; mem., pres.' club adv. bd. Phoenix Art Mus., 1990; dir. Scottsdale Cultural Coun., 1991. Mem. Am. Arbitration Assn. (regional adv. com.), Turnaround Mgmt. Assn., Phoenix C. of C., Econ. Club Phoenix, Mensa, Order of Coif. Office: Catalyst Group 2619 Beekman Pl Phoenix AZ 85016-7483

HOWATT, SISTER HELEN CLARE, library director; b. San Francisco, Apr. 5, 1927; d. Edward Bell and Helen Margaret (Kenney) H. BA, Holy Names Coll., 1949; MS in Libr. Sci., U. So. Calif., 1972; cert. advanced studies Our Lady of Lake U., 1966. Joined Order Sisters of the Holy Names, Roman Cath. Ch., 1945. Life teaching credential, life spl. svcs. credential, prin. St. Monica Sch., Santa Monica, Calif., 1957-60, St. Mary Sch., L.A., 1960-63; tchr. jr. high sch. St. Augustine Sch., Oakland, Calif., 1964-69; tchr. jr. high math St. Monica Sch., San Francisco, 1969-71, St. Cecilia Sch., San Francisco, 1971-77; libr. dir. Holy Names Coll., Oakland, Calif., 1977—. Contbr. math. curriculum San Francisco Unified Sch. Dist., Cum Notis Variorum, publ. Music Libr., U. Calif., Berkeley. Contbr. articles to profl. jours. NSF grantee, 1966, NDEA grantee, 1966. Mem. Cath. Libr. Assn. (chmn. No. Calif. elem. schs. 1971-72), Calif. Libr. Assn., ALA, Assn. Coll. and rsch. Librs. Home and Office: Holy Names Coll 3500 Mountain Blvd Oakland CA 94619-1699

HOWD, ROBERT ALLEN, toxicologist; b. McMinnville, Oreg., Nov. 19, 1944; s. Leland Ernest and Dorothy (Capps) H.; m. Sherry Lea Rock, Dec. 23, 1966; 1 child, Jennifer. BA, Linfield Coll., 1966; PhD, U. Wash., 1973. Chemist FDA, Seattle, 1966-68; postdoctoral fellow MIT, Cambridge, 1973-75; biochem. pharmacologist SRI Internat., Menlo Park, Calif., 1975-88; toxicologist, Toxic Substances Control Prog. Calif. Dept. Health Svcs., Sacramento, 1988-91; toxicologist pesticide & environ. toxicology sect. Office of Environ. Health Hazard Assessment, Calif. EPA, Berkeley, 1991—. Contbr. articles to profl. jours.; inventee in field. NIH fellow MIT, 1973-75. Mem. AAAS, Am. Soc. for Pharmacology and Exptl. Therapeutics, Soc. Risk Analysis, Soc. of Toxicology. Office: Calif EPA Office of Environ Health Hazard Assessment 2151 Berkeley Way # 11 Berkeley CA 94704-1011

HOWDEN, FREDERICK MICHAEL, surgeon; b. Seattle, Mar. 30, 1953; s. Frederick James and Patricia Elizabeth (McGoldrick) H.; m. Estelita Aboga Mora, Jan 10, 1985 (div. 1993); 1 child, Maureen Mora. AB, Dartmouth Coll., 1975; MD, Cornell U., 1983. Diplomate Am. Bd. Surgery, Am. Bd. Thoracic Surgery. Surgical intern North Shore U. Hosp., Manhasset, N.Y., 1983-84; surgical resident St. Luke's Roosevelt Hosp. Ctr., N.Y.C., 1984-89; fellow in surgery Med. Coll. Ga., Augusta, 1989-91; staff surgeon Naval Hosp., San Diego, 1991—. Commdr. USNR, 1990—. Assoc. fellow ACS; mem. Soc. Thoracic Surgeons, San Diego County Med. Soc. Republican. Home: 3 Aruba Bend Coronado CA 92118 Office: Naval Hosp San Diego Dept Cardiothoracic Surgery San Diego CA 92134

HOWE, DRAYTON FORD, JR., lawyer; b. Seattle, Nov. 17, 1931; s. Drayton Ford and Virginia (Wester) H.; m. Joyce Arnold, June 21, 1952; 1 son, James Drayton. A.B., U. Calif.-Berkeley, 1953; LL.B., Hastings Coll. Law, 1957. Bar: Calif. 1958, C.P.A. Calif. Atty. IRS, 1958-61; tax dept. supr. Ernst & Ernst, San Francisco, 1962-67; ptnr. Bishop, Barry, Howe, Haney & Ryder, San Francisco, 1968—; lectr. on tax matters U. Calif. extension, 1966-76. Mem. Calif. Bar Assn., San Francisco Bar Assn. (chmn. client relations com. 1977), Calif. Soc. C.P.A.s.

HOWE, JOSEPH WILLIAM, radiologist; b. Galeton, Pa., May 27, 1930; s. Lawrence Evered and Mabel Jane (Howe) H.; m. Mary Dolores Rathfon, May 9, 1953; children: Hollie D. Martin, Daniel W., Steven L., Nancy D. Rawson, Melinda G. Shillig, Jaynan Lotts. Student, Pa. State U., 1949-50, Elizabethtown (Pa.) Coll., 1950; DC, Palmer Coll. Chiropractic, Davenport, Iowa, 1952; cert. in Roentgenology, Nat. Coll. Chiropractic, 1959. Diplomate Am. Chiropractic Bd. Radiology, Nat. Bd. Chiropractic Examiners; lic. chiropractor, Pa., Ohio, Ill., Calif. Pvt. practice New Cumberland, Pa., 1952-54, 56-68; dir. radiology and rsch. Assocs. Diagnostic Ctr., Tallmadge, Ohio, 1968-72; prof., chmn. Roentgenology dept. Nat. Coll. Chiropractic, Lombard, Ill., 1972-76, dir. clin. sci. div., 1976-78; prof., chmn. radiology dept. L.A. Coll. Chiropractic, Whittier, Calif., 1978-87, prof. radiology, dir. radiology residency program, 1987—; pvt. practice Sylmar, Calif., 1978-87, West Las Angeles, 1989—. Contbr. articles to profl. jours. With U.S. Army, 1954-56. Fellow Am. Chiropractic Coll. Radiology; mem. Am. Chiropractic Assn., Coun. Diagostic Imaging, Calif. Chiropractic Assn., Am. Pub. Health Assn. Republican. Mormon. Home and Office: 13403 Lochrin Ln Sylmar CA 91342-1855 also: #202 10474 Santa Monica Blvd Los Angeles CA 90025

HOWE, MARK LEE, archaeologist, researcher; b. Omaha, Nov. 3, 1965; s. Merlin E. and Mary Jo (Peaker) H.; m. Shelley Lynn Wiegert, May 21, 1988. BA, U. Nebr., 1991. Machine operator Metromail Corp., Lincoln, Nebr., 1985-86; dist. mgr. Lincoln Jour.-Star, Lincoln, 1986-88; archeol. aid Midwest Archeol. Ctr., Lincoln, 1988-90; osteologist U. Nebr., Lincoln, 1990; archeol. technician Bur. Land Mgmt., Buffalo, 1991; dist. mgr. Lincoln Jour.-Star, 1990-92, Billings (Mont.) Gazette, 1992; archeol. technician Bur. Land Mgmt., Kremmling, Colo., 1992—; city archeologist, Billings Planning & Preservation Bd., 1992. Mem. Dem. Ctrl. Com., Lincoln, 1991; precinct committeeman, Billings, 1992. Sgt. USMCR, 1984-89. Mem. Nebr. Assn. Profl. Archeologists, Mont. Archeol. Soc., Peabody Mus. Assn., Ft. Phil Kearney/Bozeman Trail Assn. Democrat. Lutheran. Home and Office: PO Box 291 Kremmling CO 80459

HOWE, MARY KRISTIN, counselor; b. Cedar Rapids, Iowa, Mar. 28, 1947; d. Richard Louis and Betty Jane (Davenport) Petersmith; m. Ronald Evans Howe, Aug. 16, 1970; children: Sarah Elizabeth, Rachel Ellen,

Michael Evans. BS, Iowa State U., 1965-69; MEd, U. Manitoba, 1982-84. Lic. marriage and family couselor. Tchr. Filmore Sch., Cedar Rapids, Iowa, 1969-70, Trinity Christian Acad., Dallas, 1970-71; counseling intern U. Winnipeg, Winnipeg, Man., 1984-85, Link Care Ctr., Fresno, Calif., 1985-90, Behavioral Hlth Ctr., Fresno, Calif., 1990—; active support group Evang. Free Ch.; spkr. Hume Lake Christian Camp, Hume, Calif., 1990, Millcreek Response Ctr, Fresno, Calif., 1990—. Mem. Calif. Assn. Marriage Family Therapists. Home: 889 E Portland Fresno CA 93720 Office: Behavioral Health Ctr 4781 E Gettysburg Fresno CA 93720

HOWE, RICHARD CUDDY, state supreme court justice; b. South Cottonwood, Utah, Jan. 20, 1924; s. Edward E. and Mildred (Cuddy) H.; m. Juanita Lyon, Aug. 30, 1949; children: Christine Howe Schultz, Andrea Howe Reynolds, Bryant, Valerie Howe Winegar, Jeffrey, Craig. B.S., U. Utah, 1945, J.D., 1948. Bar: Utah. Law clk. to Justice James H. Wolfe, Utah Supreme Ct., 1949-50; judge city ct. Murray, Utah, 1951; individual practice law Murray, 1952-80; justice Utah Supreme Ct., 1980—. Mem. Utah Ho. of Reps., 1951-58, 69-72, Utah Senate, 1973-78. Named Outstanding Legislator Citizens' Conf. State Legislatures, 1972. Mem. ABA, Utah Bar Assn. Mem. LDS Ch. Office: Utah Supreme Ct 332 State Capitol Salt Lake City UT 84114-1181

HOWE, WARREN BILLINGS, physician; b. Jackson Heights, N.Y., Oct. 25, 1940; s. John Hanna and Francelia (Rose) H.; m. Hedwig Neslanik, Aug. 7, 1971; children: Elizabeth Rose, Sarah Billings. BA, U. Rochester, 1962; MD, Washington U., St. Louis, 1965. Diplomate Am. Bd. Family Practice, Nat. Bd. of Med. Examiners. Intern Phila. Gen. Hosp., 1965-66; resident physician Highland Hosp./U. Rochester, 1969-71; family physician Family Medicine Clinic of Oak Harbor (Wash.), Inc., PS, 1971-92; student health physician, univ. team physician We. Wash. U., Bellingham, 1992—; team physician Oak Harbor High Sch., 1972-92; head tournament physician Wash. State High Sch. Wrestling Championships, Tacoma, 1989—; attending physician Seattle Goodwill Games, 1990; clin. asst. prof. U. Wash. Sch. Medicine, 1975-82. Contbr. articles to profl. jours. and chpts. to books. Bd. dirs. Oak Harbor Sch. Dist. #201, 1975-87; chmn. Oak Harbor Citizen's Com. for Sch. Support, 1988-90. Lt. comdr. USN, 1966-69, Vietnam. Recipient Disting. Svc. award City of Oak Harbor, 1984; Paul Harris fellowship Oak Harbor Rotary Club. Fellow Am. Coll. Sports Medicine (membership chair), Am. Acad. Family Physicians; mem. AMA, Wash. State Med. Assn., Brit. Assn. Sport and Medicine, Am. Med. Soc. for Sports Medicine, Am. Coll. Health Assn. Presbyterian. Home: 4222 Northridge Way Bellingham WA 98226 Office: WWU Student Health Ctr 25 High St Hall Bellingham WA 98225

HOWELL, CHARLES DAVID, mechanical process and piping engineer; b. Camden, N.J., Jan. 16, 1957; s. Donald Francis Sr. and Cora Mae (Stopford) H.; m. Carol Ann DeVaul, Dec. 5, 1987; children: Nancy Marie, David James. AS, Camden County Coll., Blackwood, N.J., 1980; BS magna cum laude, N.J. Inst. Tech., Newark, 1987. Registered profl. engr. Sr. assoc. engr. Stone & Webster Engring., Cherry Hill, N.J., 1980-87; mech. engr. Piping Systems Engring., Inc., Tempe, Ariz., 1987-90, Motorola, Inc., Chandler, Ariz., 1990—. Foster parent East Valley Cath. Social Svcs., Chandler, 1990—; block watch Chandler Police Dept., 1990—; vol. fireman Lindenwold (N.J.) Fire Dept., 1973-80. Named Foster Parent of Yr., KIDS Consortium, Phoenix, 1992. Home: 1611 W Nopal Ct Chandler AZ 85224

HOWELL, JANICE HOPKINS, physician, educator; b. St. John's, Nfld., Can., Nov. 3, 1942; came to U.S., 1989; d. Gerald Thomas and Phyllis Carter (Ross) H.; m. Robert Leo Dey, Dec. 27, 1987; 1 child, Irene. BSc, McGill U., Montreal, Can., 1965; MD, Med. Coll. Pa., Phila., 1977. Instr. anesthesiology Bowman Gray Sch. Medicine, Allied Health, Winston-Salem, N.C., 1969-72, coord. edn., dir. respiratory therapy tng., 1969-72; intern, then resident fellow Montreal (Can.) Children's Hosp., 1977-81; asst. prof. pediatrics McGill U., Montreal, 1982-88; attending physician Montreal Children's Hosp., 1981-88, dir. gen. pediatric clinic, 1985-87, dir. med. ward svcs., 1988-89; assoc. prof. pediatrics Univ. of Colo. Health Scis., Denver, 1989—; assoc. dir. clinic Nat. Jewish Ctr. for Immunology and Respiratory Medicine, Denver, 1989—, med. dir. pediatric psychophysiologic unit, 1989-91, chief pediatric ambulatory svcs., 1989—; cons. Regional Med. Ctr., Chibougamau, Que., Can., 1983-85; course dir., co-dir several continuing med. edn. courses McGill U., 1981-88, coord. pediatric drug therapy, 1990. Mem. editorial rev. bd. Devel. Pharmacology and Therapeutics, 1986—; contbr. articles to profl. jours. Recipient Leadership and Character award Imperial Order Daus. of the Empire, Montreal, 1960; fellow McGill U., 1980-81. Fellow Royal Coll. Physicians and Surgeons Can., Am. Acad. Pediatrics, Fed. Medecins Specialistes Que.; mem. Can. Pediatric Soc., N.Y. Acad. Scis., Am. Coll. Physician Execs., Alpha Omega Alpha. Office: Nat Jewish Ctr Immunology and Respiratory Medicine 1400 Jackson St Denver CO 80206-2761

HOWELL, LLEWELLYN DONALD, management educator, department head; b. Oct. 12, 1940; m. Susana G. Lacayo; 1 child, Joseph L. BS in Sci. Edn. cum laude, SUNY, Brockport, 1963; MA in Govt., Internat. Affairs, Fla. State U., 1967; PhD in Internat. Rels., Syracuse U., 1973. Rsch. and teaching asst. dept. govt. Fla. State U., 1965-66; instr. Peace Corps tng. ctr. U. Hawaii, 1966; instr. polit. sci. Onondaga C.C., Syracuse, 1969; vis. rschr. Inst. S.E. Asian Studies, Singapore, 1970-71; asst. prof. polit. sci. U. Hawaii, Hilo, 1971-74; from asst. prof. to prof. internat. rels. Am. U., Washington, 1974-91, interim chair dept. comparative and regional studies, 1990-91; chair dept. internat. studies Am. Grad. Sch. Internat. Mgmt., Glendale, Ariz., 1991—; lectr. Fgn. Svc. Inst., 1980—; adj. prof. nat. security affairs Naval Postgrad. Sch., Monterey, Calif., 1987; sr. rsch. assoc. Third Point Systems, Monterey, 1984-86; adj. prof. Monterey Inst. Internat. Studies, 1986; dir. Washington Summer Inst. in Quantitative Polit. Rsch., 1981-83; vis. asst. prof. polit. sci. U. Hawaii, Manoa, 1974; prin. investigato NSF, 1991—. Editor Internat. Studies Notes, 1991—; co-editor: International Education: An Agenda for the Future, 1984, Malaysian Foreign Policy, 1990; contbr. articles and revs. to profl. jours. and chpts. to books. Coach boys' baseball and basketball, 1986—. Recipient Fulbright-Hayes award, 1987-88, Summer Rsch. Initiation award NSF, 1974; Shell Internat. Studies fellow, 1970-71. Mem. Internat. Studies Assn., Acad. Internat. Bus., Am. Polit. Sci. Assn., Assn. for Asian Studies, Am. Fgn. Svc. Assn. (assoc.), Malaysia-Am. Soc. (pres. 1981-84, 86-87), Coun. Internat. Bus. Risk Mgmt. Office: Am Grad Sch Internat Mgmt Dept Internat Studies 15249 N 59th Ave Glendale AZ 85306-6011

HOWELL, SCOTT NEWELL, computer company executive, state legislator; b. Provo, Utah, Sept. 28, 1953; s. Varon L. and Kathryn (Tuttle) H.; m. Linda Skanchy, Sept. 8, 1978; children: Bryan, Bradley, Jason, Jeffrey. BA, U. Utah, 1978. With sales IBM Corp., mgr.; mem. Utah State Senate, 1992—; chmn. Nat. Acad. Fin., Salt Lake City, 1991-93. Bd. dirs. UCNCPCA, Salt Lake City, 1992-93, visually handicapped divsn. United Way, Salt Lake City, 1992-93. Democrat. Mormon. Home: 9711 S 3725 E Sandy UT 84092

HOWELL, STEPHEN BARNARD, oncologist, educator; b. Shirley, Mass., Sept. 29, 1944; s. Wallace Egbert and Christine (Gallagher) H.; m. Julianne Howell, 1968; children: Justin, Brett. AB in Biology, U. Chgo., 1966; MD in Immunology, Harvard U., 1970; MD honoris cause, U. Goteborg, Sweden, 1992. Intern Mass. Gen. Hosp., 1970-71, resident, 1971-72; rsch. assoc. lab. cell biology Nat. Cancer Inst., Bethesda, Md., 1972-74; resident U. Calif. Hosps., San Francisco, 1974-75; fellow in oncology Dana Farber Cancer Inst., Boston, 1975-77; asst. prof. medicine U. Calif., San Diego, 1977-80, assoc. prof. medicine, 1981-87, prof. medicine, 1987—; assoc. dir. clinical rsch. U. Calif. Cancer Ctr., San Diego; dir. lab. pharmacology U. Calif., San Diego, 1978—, dir. Clayton Found. Drug Resistance Lab., 1984—; program com. Am. Assn. for Cancer Rsch., 1990; adv. bd. Calif. Collaborative AIDS Treatment Group, 1987-90; chair cancer rsch. coord. com. State of Calif., 1985-89; cons., lectr. Naval Regional Med. Ctr., San Diego, 1984-90; mem. biochem. modulation adv. group div. cancer treatment Nat. Cancer Inst., 1979-88; organizer various confs.; speaker in field. Mem. editorial bd. Jour. Cellular Pharmacology, 1990—, Rgional Cancer Treatment, 1988-90, Cancer Drug Delivery, 1984-88, Cancert Treatment Reports, 1982-84. Fogarty Sr. Internat. fellow, 1984; recipient Milken Family Med. Found. Cancer Rsch. prize, 1989. Mem. Am. Assn. for Cancer Rsch., Am. Soc. for Clin. Oncology, Am. Fedn. for Clin. Rsch., Am. Soc. for Clin. Investigation, Am. Soc. for Clin. Pharmacology and Therapeutics, Phi Beta Kappa, Alpha Omega Alpha. Office: U Calif San Diego Dept Medicine 0812 9500 Gilman Dr La Jolla CA 92093-0001

HOWELL, WILLIAM HAYWOOD, software engineer; b. San Bernardino, Calif., July 19, 1956; s. Fred Stanley and Iris Haywood (Virginia) H.; m. Christine Susan Druga, Dec. 2, 1988 (dec. Dec. 7, 1992). Diploma in elec. tech., DeVry Inst. Tech., 1980. Electronics technician Tektronix, Inc., Wilsonville, Oreg., 1980-82; mfg. engr. Metheus Corp., Hillsboro, Oreg., 1982-83, Support Tech., Inc., Beaverton, Oreg., 1983-85; test engr. Cadre Tech., Inc., Hillsboro, 1985-89; systems engr. Protocol Systems, Inc., Beaverton, 1989—. Mem. Obukan Kendo Club (treas. 1991-92, v.p. 1992-93, pres. 1993—).

HOWES, GLORIA, state legislator. BA, West Tex. U.; MA, U. N.Mex. County mgr. McKinley County, N.Mex., county comr.; mem. N.Mex State Senate from 4th dist. Democrat. Mailing: 509 Lacima Rd Gallup NM 87301-5738 Office: NM State Senate State Capitol Santa Fe NM 85703

HOWITT, DAVID ANDREW, human resources executive; b. N.Y.C., Feb. 11, 1953; s. George and Naomi Doris (Rubenstein) H.; m. Leigh Ann Louise Kulp, Jan. 31, 1976; children: Jennifer Elizabeth, Caitlin Rachel. BS in Bus. and Econs., Lehigh U., 1975. Cert. sr. profl. in human resources. Pers. rep. Mutual Benefit Life Ins. Co., Newark, 1975-80; mgr. human resources C-E Lummus, The Lummus Co., Bloomfield, N.J., 1980-83; dir. human resources Pubrs. Phototype, Inc., Carlstadt, N.J., 1983-85; asst. v.p. human resources Fireman's Fund Ins. Co., Novato, Calif., 1985—. Mem. of corp. United Way of Morris County, Cedar Knolls, N.J., 1986-89. Mem. Soc. for Human Resources Mgmt., No. Calif. Human Resources Coun., Assn. Human Resources Systems Profls. Democrat. Office: Fireman's Fund Ins Co 777 San Marin Dr Novato CA 94998

HOWLAND, JOSEPH EMERY, advertising executive; b. Providence, Apr. 2, 1918; s. Clifford Howard and Margaret Edith (Loughran) H.; m. Virginia Frances Hornby, Aug. 26, 1917 (div. 1969); children: Joy, Hornby; m. Mary Ann Johnson, Nov. 23, 1969. BS, R.I. State U., Kingston, 1940; MS, Mich. State U., 1942; PhD, Cornell U., 1945. Assoc. editor Better Homes & Gardens, Des Moines, 1945-48; asst. pub. House Beautiful, N.Y.C., 1948-56; asst. pres. O.M. Scott & Sons, Marysville, Ohio, 1956-68; prof. horticulture U. Nev., Reno, 1968-73; v.p. mktg. Geo J. Ball, Inc., West Chicago, 1973-78; prof. advt. U. Nev., Reno, 1978-91, prof. emeritus, 1991; prin. Mgmt. Analysis Ctr. Inc., Cambridge Mass., 1968-90; vice chmn. Nev. First Bank System, Reno, 1986-90. Author: Gardens & Outdoor Living, 1957, Horticultural Marketing, 1986; monthly commentator Nursery Mgr., Greenhouse Mgr., SAF Mag., 1969—. Recipient Dupage Horticulture Sch. Spl. award Exec. Com. Bd. Dirs., 1978, Bradford Williams Medal Am. Soc. Landscape Architects, 1983. Fellow Garden Writers Assn. Am.; mem. Reno Advt. Club (Thomas C. Wilson lifetime achievement award, 1989, Men's Garden Club Am. (pres. 1967). Home: 350 W Riverview Cir Reno NV 89509-1125

HOWLAND, PETER MCKINNON, academic administrator; b. Corvallis, Oreg., Apr. 2, 1956; s. James Chase and Ruth Louise (Meisenhelder) H. BA, Linfield Coll., 1978; postgrad., Boise State U., 1981-82; MA in Interdisciplinary Studies, Oreg. State U., 1985. Travel agt. Sather Tours and Travel, Salem, Oreg., 1979-81; office asst. then devel. asst. Linfield Coll., McMinnville, Oreg., 1985-90, devel. asst. for rsch., 1990—. Mem. Pi Sigma Alpha. Republican. Mormon. Office: Linfield Coll Office Devel 900 S Baker St Mcminnville OR 97128

HOWLETT, JOHN DAVID, intergovernmental relations consultant; b. Akron, Colo., July 16, 1952; s. John Butler and Reavis Lavina (Smith) H. BA, U. Nebr., 1975, M in Urban and Regional Planning, 1977. Urban and regional planner Oblinger-McCaleb, Denver, 1979-80; staff project mgr. Greater Denver C. of C., 1980-83; dir. econ. devel. City of Littleton, Colo., 1983-87; dir. civic and econ. devel., interim pres. The Denver Partnership, Denver, 1987-91; mng. assoc. Linton, Mields, Reisler, & Cottone, Ltd., Denver, 1991—; bd. dirs. First Night Colo.; mem. Arapahoe/Douglas Pvt. Industry Coun., Englewood, Colo., 1984-87; mem. steering com. New Bus. and Industry Coun., Denver, 1985-87; mem. exec. com. Met. Denver Network, 1987-91. Mem. profl. adv. coun. Coll. Arch., U. Nebr., Lincoln, 1980—; vice chmn. C-470 Inter-Camber Task Force, Denver, 1984-87; trustee AMC Cancer Rsch. Ctr., Lakewood, Colo., 1985-87; mem. exec. bd. Friends Auraria Libr., Denver, 1989-90; mem. vocat. adv. com. Mental Health Corp., 1990—; bd. dirs. First Night Colo., 1992—. Mem. Am. Planning Assn. (pres. Colo. chpt. 1985-87, Karen Smith Chpt. award 1987), City Club Denver (pres. 1984-85). Democrat. Presbyterian. Home: 3026 W Prentice Ave # L Littleton CO 80123-7722 Office: Linton Mields Reisler & Cotton Ltd 410 17th St Ste 1345 Denver CO 80202-4426

HOWSLEY, RICHARD THORNTON, lawyer, regional government administrator; b. Medford, Oreg., Jan. 31, 1948; s. Calvin Nevil and Arvilla Constance (Romine) H.; m. Susan Erma Johnson, Oct. 23, 1971; children: James Denver, Kelly Ann. BA, Willamette U., 1970; MS, Va. Poly. Inst. and State U., 1974; JD, Lewis and Clark Law Sch., 1984. Bar: Oreg. 1984, Wash. 1985, U.S. Dist. Ct. (we. dist.) Wash., 1985. Tech. editor U.S. Bur. Mines, Arlington, Va., 1971-72; program mgr., sr. planner KRS Assos., Inc., Reston, Va., 1972-74; exec. dir. Rogue Valley Council Govts., Medford, 1974-78; exec. dir. Regional Planning Council of Clark County, Vancouver, Wash., 1978-84; pres. Landerholm, Memovich, Lansverk & Whitesides, Vancouver, 1985-92; pvt. practice, Vancouver, 1992—; vice chmn. Oreg. Council of Govts. Dirs. Assn., 1976-77, chmn., 1977-78; mem. regional adv. com. So. Oreg. State Coll., 1975-78. Mem. Medford-Ashland Air Quality Adv. Com., 1977-78. Carpenter Found. scholar, 1966-70, Leonard B. Mayfield Meml. scholar, 1966-67, Albina Page Found. scholar, 1966-70. Mem. ABA, Oreg. State Bar Assn., Wash. State Bar Assn., Am. Planning Assn., Am. Inst. Cert. Planners, Internat. City Mgmt. Assn. (10-yr. service award), Nat. Assn. Regional Councils (10-yr. service award). Democrat. Methodist. Home: 1616 NW 79th Cir Vancouver WA 98665-6626 Office: Richard T Howsley PS Ste 200 1400 Washington Vancouver WA 98660

HOYE, WALTER BRISCO, retired college administrator; b. Lena, Miss., May 19, 1930; s. William H. and LouBertha (Stewart) H.; m. Vida M. Pickens, Aug. 28, 1954; children—Walter B. II, JoAnn M. B.A., Wayne State U., 1953. Sports/auto editor Detroit Tribune, 1958-65; sports editor Mich. Chronicle, 1965-68; assoc. dir. pub. relations San Diego Chargers Football Co., 1968-76; media liason NFL, 1972-75; community services officer San Diego Coll. Dist., 1976-78; placement officer Ednl. Cultural Complex, San Diego, 1978-80, info. officer, 1980-82, placement officer, adminstrv. asst., 1982-83, placement/program support supr., 1983-91, supr. program support svcs., 1989—; cons. in field. Bd. dirs. San Diego County ARC; active San Diego Conv. and Tourist Bur., Joint Ctr. Polit. Studies, Am. Cancer Soc., San Diego Urban League, Neighborhood Housing Assn., Public Access TV. Named San Diego County Citizen of Month, May, 1979; recipient United Way Award of Merit, 1974. Mem. Internat. Assn. Auditorium Mgrs., Am. Personnel and Guidance Assn., San Diego Career Guidance Assn., Nat. Mgmt. Assn., Assn. Calif. Community Coll. Adminstrs., Calif. Community Coll. Placement Assn., Rocky Mountain Assn. Student Fin. Aid Adminstrs. Home: 6959 Ridge Manor Ave San Diego CA 92120-3146

HOYT, JACK WALLACE, engineering educator; b. Chgo., Oct. 19, 1922; s. Claire A. and Fleta M. (Wheeler) H.; B.S., Ill. Inst. Tech., 1944; M.S., UCLA, 1952, Ph.D., 1962; m. Helen Rita Erickson, Dec. 27, 1945; children: John A., Katheryn M. (Mrs. Richard Everett), Annette M. (Mrs. Walter Butler), Denise M. (Mrs. Paul Kruesi). Research engr. gas turbines Cleve. Lab., NACA, 1944-47; mem. staff Naval Ocean Systems Center, Navy Dept., DOD, San Diego, 1948-79, asso. for sci. fleet engring. dept., 1967-79, now cons.; vis. prof. mech. engring. Rutgers U., New Brunswick, N.J., 1979-81; Benjamin Meaker vis. prof. U. Bristol (Eng.), 1987; prof. mech. engring. San Diego State U., 1981—. Fellow ASME (Freeman scholar 1971); mem. N.Y. Acad. Scis., Soc. Naval Architects and Marine Engrs. Author, patentee in field. Editorial bd. Internat. Shipbldg. Progress, 1965—. Spl. rsch. propulsion and hydrodynamics. Home: 4694 Lisann St San Diego CA 92117-2441

HRDY, SARAH BLAFFER, anthropology educator; b. July 11, 1946; m. Daniel B. Hrdy; 3 children. AB summa cum laude, Radcliffe Coll., 1969; PhD in Anthropology, Harvard U., 1975. Instr. in anthropology U. Mass., Boston, 1973; lectr. in biol. anthropology Harvard U., Cambridge, Mass., 1975-76, postdoctoral fellow in biology, 1977-78; assoc. in biol. anthropology Peabody Mus., Harvard U., 1979; sr. fellow Am. Inst. Indian Studies, New Delhi, India, 1980-81; vis. assoc. prof. Rice U., Houston, 1981-82; prof. in anthropology U. Calif., Davis, 1984—; presenter workshops in field; tchr. hygiene to Spanish-speaking adults El Paraiso, Honduras, 1967; mem. adv. bd. Primates, 1984-90; mem. editorial Cultural Anthropology, 1984—; cons. editor Am. Jour. Primatology, 1980—; assoc. editor Human Evolution, 1985-88, Numan Nature, 1989. Author: The Black-man of Zinacantan: A Central American Legend, 1972, The Langurs of Abu: Female and Male Strategies of Reproduction, 1977, The Woman that Never Evolved, 1981 (Notable Book of Yr., N.Y. Times), Infanticide Comparative and Evolutionary Perspectives, 1984; contbr. articles, revs. to profl. publs.; producer various films in field. Guggenheim fellow, 1987-88; grantee Wenner-Gren Found., 1982, 85, Miller Found., 1971, Smithsonian Instn., 1979, NSF, 1979, U. Calif., 1985, Rockefeller Found., 1985. Mem. NAS, Am. Soc. Naturalists, Am. Soc. Primatologists, Animal Behavior Soc., Am. Anthropol. Soc., Internat. Primatolog. Soc., Calif. Acad. Scis., Am. Acad. Arts and Scis., Phi Beta Kappa. Office: U Calif Dept Anthropology Young Hall Davis CA 95616

HRIBAR, JOHN PETER, SR., engineering administrator, consultant; b. Cleve., Jan. 1, 1936; s. John Frank and Virginia C. (Vito) H.; m. Francine Marie Stepic, Oct. 3, 1964; children: John P. Jr., Wendy M., Tammy J., Tommie J., Francine A. BS in Civil Engring., U. Notre Dame, Ind., 1958. Registered profl. engr., Ohio, Ill., Ind., Wis., Ariz., Calif., Nev. With Howard Needles Tammen & Bergendoff, 1958-92; dep. dir. adminstrv. svcs. Howard Needles Tammen & Bergendoff, Milw., 1977-85; dir. engring. Howard Needles Tammen & Bergendoff, Phoenix, 1990-92; tech. dir., chief civil engr. Frederic R. Harris, Inc., San Pedro, Calif., 1993—. Contbr. articles to profl. jours. Mem. St. Joseph Athletic Assn., Milw., 1981-87, pres. 1986; mem. parish coun. Community of Blessed Sacrament, 1990-93, chmn. 1992-93. Fellow ASCE (chmn. engring. mgmt. div. exec. com. 1987-90, chmn. 1989), Am. Mgmt. Assn., Am. Pub. Works Assn. Roman Catholic. Home: 6002 E Redfield Rd Scottsdale AZ 85254-3102 Office: Frederic R Harris Inc 222 West 6th St San Pedro CA 90731

HRUT, CHRISTOPHER BOLESLAW, sales and marketing executive; b. Szczecin, Poland, Apr. 18, 1958; came to U.S. 1986; s. Zdzislaw and Halina (Maj) H. MSc, Gdansk U., Poland, 1982; Dipl.Eng., Tech. U. Gdansk, 1983; MSc, MIT, 1987; MBA, Harvard U., 1989. Sr. supr. Gdansk Shipyard, 1983-86; exec. asst. Fuji-Xerox, Tokyo, 1988; mng. exec. Network Equip. Technologies, 1989-90; dir. Trimble Navigation & Navigation Techs., Sunnyvale, Calif., 1991—; gen. ptnr. Renaissance Capital, Boston, 1993—; gen. ptnr. European Renaissance Ptnrs.; cons. in field. Contbr. articles to profl. jours. MIT grantee, Harvard Bus. Sch. fellow, Kosciuszko Found. grantee. Mem. Harvard Bus. Sch. Club No. Calif., MIT Club No. Calif., Commonwealth Club of Calif., Harvard U. Club No. Calif., Churchill Club, Kosciuszko Found., Harvard U. Club of Poland (founding chmn. 1991—), Harvard U. Club of Hungary (founding chmn. 1990—), Harvard U. Club of Czechoslovakia (founding chmn. 1990—). Home: 1000 Escalon Ave # E2040 Sunnyvale CA 94086-4125 Office: Navigation Techs 740 E Arques Ave Sunnyvale CA 94086-3833 also: Zaruskiego 26, PL-80-299 Gdansk-Osowa Poland

HSU, CHIEH SU, engineering educator, researcher; b. Soochow, Kiangsu, China, May 27, 1922; came to U.S., 1947.; s. Chung yu and Yong Feng (Wu) H.; m. Helen Yung-Feng Tse, Mar. 28, 1953; children—Raymond Hwa-Chi, Katherine Hwa-Ling. BS, Nat. Inst. Tech., Chungking, China, 1945; MS, Stanford U., 1948, Ph.D., 1950. Project engr. IBM Corp., Poughkeepsie, N.Y., 1951-55; assoc. prof. U. Toledo, 1955-58; assoc. prof. Univ Calif.-Berkeley, 1958-64, prof., 1964—, chmn. div. applied mechanics, 1969-70; mem. sci. adv. bd. Alexander von Humboldt Found. of Fed. Republic Germany, Bonn, 1985—. Author: 98 tech. papers; contbg. author: Thin-Shell Structures, 1974, Advances in Applied Mechanics, vol. 17, 1977; author: Cell-to-Cell Mapping, 1987; tech. editor Jour. Applied Mechanics, N.Y.C., 1976-82; assoc. editor profl. jours. Recipient Alexander von Humboldt award Fed. Republic Germany, 1986; Guggenheim Found. fellow, 1964-65; Miller research prof., U. Calif.-Berkeley, 1973-74. Fellow ASME (Centennial award 1980) Am. Acad. Mechanics; mem. Acoustical Soc. Am., Soc. Indsl. and Applied Math., U. S. Nat. Acad. Engring., Acad. Sinica, Sigma Xi. Office: U Calif Dept Mech Engring Berkeley CA 94720

HSU, SHU-DEAN, hematologist, oncologist; b. Chiba, Japan, Feb. 21, 1943; came to U.S., 1972; s. Tetzu and Takako (Koo) Minoyama; m. San-San Hsu, Mar. 3, 1973; children: Deborah Te-Lan, Peter Jie-Te. MD, Taipei (Taiwan) Med. Coll., 1968. Diplomate Am. Bd. Internal Medicine, Am. Bd. Hematology, Am. Bd. Med. Oncology. Asst. in medicine Mt. Sinai Sch. Medicine, N.Y.C., 1975-77; asst. instr. medicine U. Tex., Galveston, 1977-78; lectr. in medicine Tex. A&M U., Temple, 1978-80; asst. prof. medicine U. Ark., Little Rock, 1980-83; practice medicine specializing in hematology-oncology Visalia (Calif.) Med. Clinic, 1983—; chief hematology and oncology VA Med. Ctr., Temple, Tex., 1978-80. Contbr. articles to profl. jours. Fellow ACP; mem. N.Y. Acad. Scis., Am. Soc. Clin. Oncology, Am. Soc. Hematology, Calif. Med. Assn., Tulare County Med. Soc. Club: Visalia Racquet. Home: 3500 W Hydeway Visalia CA 93291 Office: Visalia Med Clinic PO Box 3347 Olympic Valley CA 96146-3347

HSU, YU-CHIN, computer science educator; b. Taiwan, Republic of China, Apr. 5, 1958; came to U.S., 1991; s. Wan-Sou and Ju-Gee (Lin) H.; m. Chin-Wun Lin, July 19, 1984; children: Joyce, James. BS, Nat. Taiwan U., Taipei, Republic of China, 1981; MS, U. Ill., 1985, PhD, 1987. Assoc. prof. Nat. Tsing Hua U., Hsin Chu, Republic of China, 1987-91, U. Calif., Riverside, 1991—. Author: (with others) High Level Synthesis, 1991; contbr. articles to IEEE Transactions on CAD. Named Outstanding Young Author, IEEE CAS Soc., 1990. Mem. IEEE, Assn. for Computing Machinery. Home: 6160 Port Au Prince Cir Riverside CA 92506 Office: Dept Computer Sci U Calif Riverside Riverside CA 92521

HU, CHI YU, physicist, educator; b. Szchwan, China, Feb. 12, 1933; came to U.S., 1956, naturalized, 1974; s. T.C. and P.S. (Yang) H.; children—Marica, Mark, Albert, Han Chin. B.S., Nat. Taiwan U., 1955; Ph.D., M.I.T., 1962. Research asso. St. John's U., Jamaica, N.Y., 1962-63; asst. prof. physics Calif. State U., Long Beach, 1963-68; asso. prof. Calif. State U., 1968-72, prof., 1972—; NSF vis. prof. UCLA, 1988-90. Contbr. articles to profl. jours. NSF summer fellow, 1965, 76; grantee NSF, 1969-70, 86-88, 88-90, 90—, Calif. State U. Long Beach Found., 1965, 66, 70, 72, Dept. Energy, 1986-88. Mem. Am. Phys. Soc., AAUP, United Profs. Calif. Office: Calif State U Dept Physics Long Beach CA 90840

HU, EDNA GERTRUDE FENSKE, pediatrics nurse; b. Arlington, S.D., June 11, 1922; d. Walter O. and Therese (Kautz) Fenske; m. Patrick P.C. Hu, Nov. 26, 1954; children: Lou Anne Hu Yee, Mark C., Lawrence P. BS in Nursing, U. Colo. Sch. Nursing, 1954. RN, Colo. Staff pediatrics nurse Colo. Gen. Hosp., Denver, 1954-63, night nursing supr., 1963-65; staff nurse alcohol withdrawal unit Denver Gen. Hosp., 1971-73; staff surg. nurse Fitzsimons Army Hosp., Denver, 1973-79; staff nurse VA Hosp., Allens Pk., Mich., 1979-81, Drug and Alcohol Withdrawal and Rehab. Ctr., Ft. Dodge, Iowa, 1981-83; researcher Ft. Collins, Colo., 1988—; researcher effects on memory following long term residence in another culture; instr. English, health care, Asia. Recipient Disting. Alumna award Class of 1954. Mem. ANA, Colo. Nurses Assn., Non-practicing and Part-time Nurses Assn. Home: 2518 Timber Ct Fort Collins CO 80521-3120

HU, JOHN CHIH-AN, chemist, research engineer; b. Nanchang, Hubei, China, July 12, 1922; came to U.S., 1954, naturalized, 1965; s. Chi-Ching and Chao-Xien (Tsen) H.; BS in Chemistry, Nat. Central U., Nanjing, China, 1946; MS in Organic Chemistry, U. So. Calif., 1957, postgrad., 1957-61; PhD (hon.) Marquis Giuseppe Scicluna Internat. Univ. Foundation, 1985; m. Betty Siao-Yung Ho, Oct. 26, 1957; children: Arthur, Benjamin, Carl, David, Eileen, Franklin, George. Dir. rsch. dept. Plant 1, Taiwan Fertilizer Mfg. Co., Chilung, 1947-54; rsch. assoc. chemistry dept. U. So. Calif., L.A., 1957-61; rsch. chemist Chem Seal Corp. Am., Los Angeles, 1961-62; rsch. chemist Products Rsch. & Chem. Corp., Glendale, Calif.,

1962-66; sr. rsch. engr., materials and tech. unit, Boeing Co., Seattle, 1966-71, specialist engr. Quality Assurance Labs., 1971-90, ret., 1990; cons. UN; lectr., China, profl. confs. Fellow Am. Inst. Chemists; mem. Am. Chem. Soc. (chmn. Puget Sound sect. 1988, councilor 1989—), Royal Soc. Chemistry (London), N.Y. Acad. Sci., Phi Lambda Upsilon. Patentee Chromatopyrography; contbg. author: Analytical Approach, 1983, Advances in Chromotography, vol. 23, 1984; contbr. articles on analytical pyrolysis, gas chromatography, mass spectrometry, polymer characterization, chemistry and tech. of sealants and adhesives to profl. publs. in Chinese and English; editor Puget Sound Chemist; referee profl. jours. Analytical Chemistry, Analytica Chimica Acta, Am. Chem. Soc. short courses. Home: 2813 Whitworth Ave S Renton WA 98055-5008

HU, MARY LEE, artist, educator; b. Lakewood, Ohio, Apr. 13, 1943; d. Dana Willis and Virginia Haines (Bennett) Lee; m. Tah-Kai Hu, Sept. 9, 1967 (dec. May 1972). Student, Miami U., Oxford, Ohio, 1961-63; BFA, Cranbrook Acad. Arts, Bloomfield Hills, Mich., 1965; MFA, So. Ill. U., 1967. Instr. So. Ill. U., Carbondale, 1968-69; freelance artist various locations, 1969-75; lectr. U. Wis., Madison, 1976-77; asst. prof. art Mich. State U., East Lansing, 1977-80; assoc. prof. U. Wash., Seattle, 1980-86, prof., 1986—; vis. artist U. Iowa, Iowa City, fall 1975; instr. Kans. State U., Manhattan, summer 1976; dep. v.p. for North Am. World Crafts Coun., N.Y.C., 1982-84. Represented in permanent collections: Columbus (Ohio) Mus. Art, 1975, Am. Craft Mus., N.Y.C., 1985, Renwick Gallery, Washington, 1985, The Art Inst., Chgo., 1989, The Victoria & Albert Mus., London, 1991. Bd. dirs. Wing Luke Asian Mus., Seattle, 1984-88. Fellow Nat. Endowment Arts, 1976, 84, 92. Mem. Am. Crafts Coun. (sec. 1982-83, trustee 1980-84), Soc. N.Am. Goldsmiths (disting., v.p. 1976-77, pres. 1977-80), Artist Blacksmith Assn. N.Am., N.W. Designer Craftsmen, Seattle Metals Guild, N.W. Bead Soc., James Renwick Alliance (hon.). Office: U Wash Sch Art DM-10 Seattle WA 98195

HUACO, GEORGE ARTHUR, sociology educator; b. Oakland, Calif., Dec. 21, 1927; s. Sergio Arturo and Carmen Rosa (Menendez) H.; m. Marcia Brown, 1960 (div. July 1977); m. Letty Whisner, 1978; children: Miriam Komaromy, Valerie D. BA, U. Calif., Berkeley, 1954; MA, UCLA, Berkeley, 1959; PhD, U. Calif., Berkeley, 1963. Asst. prof. Yale U., New Haven, 1963-69; assoc. prof. SUNY, Buffalo, 1969-71; prof. U. N.Mex., Albuquerque, 1971—. Author: The Sociology of Film Art, 1965; contbr. articles to profl. publs. With U.S. Army, 1954-56. Social Sci. Rsch. Coun. N.Y. rsch. fellow, 1967-68; Yale Coun. for Internat. Studies rsch. grantee, 1966. Socialist. Shamanist.

HUACUJA, MANLIO, economist, Mexican specialist, educator; b. Monterrey, Nuevo Leon, Mex., Apr. 24, 1959; came to U.S., 1986; s. Marco-Tulio and Alicia (Gonzalez) H.; m. Cindy Kane, Dec. 7, 1984; 1 child, Kylan. BS, Monterrey Inst. Tech., 1980; MS, Purdue U., 1982. Analyst Vitro Indsl. Group, Monterrey, 1980-81; dept. chief Ministry Planning and Budget, Mexico City, 1983-84; advisor to undersec. Ministry Commerce, Mexico City, 1984-86; mgr. econs. program Pikes Peak Area Coun. Govts., Colorado Springs, Colo., 1987-88; sr. economist Office of Gov., State of Colo., Denver, 1988—; Mexican specialist cons. to various cos., Denver, 1988—; instr. bus. adminstrn. Regis U., Denver, 1989—, U. Denver, 1989—; bus. resource Moran, Stahl & Boyer, Inc., Boulder, Colo., 1990—. Contbr. articles on econ. policy and social issues to profl. jours. Mem. Colo. Adv. Coun. on Mex., 1990—. Mem. Nat. Assn. Bus. Economists, Denver Assn. Bus. Economists. Office: Office of Gov 111 State Capitol Bldg Denver CO 80203

HUANG, CHIEN CHANG, electrical engineer; b. Nanking, Peoples Republic of China, Feb. 16, 1931; came to U.S., 1957; s. Ling-Kuo Huang and Yi-Ching Liu; m. Li-May Tsai, June 2, 1962; children: Frederick G., Lewis G. BSEE, Taiwan Coll. Engring., Tainan, 1954; MSEE, U. Ill., 1959; postgrad., U. Pa., 1960-62. Engr. Burrough Corp., Paoli, Pa., 1960-64; sr. staff engr. Unisys Corp., San Diego, 1974—; sr. engr. Philco Ford Corp., Blue Bell, Pa., 1965-69; staff engr. Fairchild Semiconductor, Mountain View, Calif., 1969-71; sr. staff engr. Am. Micro Systems, Santa Clara, Calif., 1971-74. Contbr. articles to profl. jours. Home: 14481 Maplewood St Poway CA 92064-6446 Office: Unisys Corp 10850 Via Frontera San Diego CA 92127-1788

HUANG, FRANCIS FU-TSE, engineering educator; b. Hong Kong, Aug. 27, 1922; came to U.S., 1945, naturalized, 1960; s. Kwong Set and Chen-Ho (Yee) H.; m. Fung-Yuen Fung, Apr. 10, 1954; children: Raymond, Stanley. BS, San Jose State Coll., 1951; MS, Stanford U., 1952; Profl. M.E., Columbia U., 1964; Cultural Doctorate in Energy Sci. (hon.), World U., Ariz., 1990. Design engr. M.W. Kellogg Co., N.Y.C., 1952-58; faculty San Jose (Calif.) State U., 1958—, assoc. prof. mech. engring., 1962-67, prof., 1967-91, prof. emeritus, 1991, chmn. dept., 1973-81; hon. prof. heat power engring. Taiyuan (People's Republic of China) U. Tech., 1981—. Author: Engineering Thermodynamics—Fundamentals and Applications, 1976, 2d edit., 1988. Capt. Chinese Army, 1943-45. Recipient Disting. Teaching award Calif. State Coll. System, 1968-69; named Outstanding Prof. of Yr., Tau Beta Pi, 1967, 76, Prof. of Yr., Pi Tau Sigma, 1985; NSF faculty fellow, 1962-64. Mem. AAAS, ASME, AIAA, AAUP, Am. Soc. Engring. Edn., N.Y. Acad. Scis., Sigma Xi. Home: 1259 Sierra Mar Dr San Jose CA 95118-1235 Office: San Jose State U Dept Mech Engring San Jose CA 95192

HUANG, H. K., radiological science educator; b. China, Oct. 10, 1939; came to U.S., 1961; BSc, Nat. Taiwan U., Taipei, 1961; MS, Kans. State U., 1963; DSc, George Washington U., 1972; postdoctorate, Georgetown U., 1973. Asst. prof. Georgetown U., Washington, 1975-79, rsch. assoc. prof., 1979-80; assoc. prof. U. Iowa, Iowa City, 1980-82; prof. dept. radiol. scis. UCLA, 1982-92, dir. biomed. physics grad. program, 1984-91, chief div. med. imaging, 1984-91, prof., vice chair dept. radiol. scis., 1991-92; dir. Radiol. Informatics; prof., vice-chmn. dept. radiology, U. Calif., San Francisco. Author: Cross-Sectional Atlas, 1975, Digital Radiology, 1987, Computer in Medical Physics, 1990, Picture Archiving and Communication Systems, 1991. Office: Dept Radiology Univ Calif San Francisco CA 94143-0628

HUANG, JEN-TZAW, pharmaceutical executive; b. Taipei, Taiwan, Oct. 8, 1938; s. C.W. Huang; m. Grace Huang; 1 child, George. BS, Nat. Taiwan U., 1962; MS, U. Houston, 1969; PhD, U. Tex., Houston, 1972. Sr. rsch. scientist Inst. of Neurochemistry, Wards Island, N.Y., 1975-80; assoc. mem. Va. Mason Rsch. Ctr., Seattle, 1980-86; dir. scientific affairs JBC, Inc. Gifu Rsch. Lab., Kaizu, Gufu, Japan, 1986-88; mgr. JBC Inc., USA br., Thousand Oaks, Calif., 1988-91; v.p. FASA Co., Thousand Oaks, 1991—. Contbr. articles to profl. jours. Grantee NIH, 198-, 83. Mem. Regulatory Affairs Profl. Soc., Am. Assn. Lab. Animals Sci. Office: 1378 Oakridge Ct Thousand Oaks CA 91362-1923

HUANG, KUN LIEN, software engineer, scientist; b. Nantou, Taiwan, Jan. 20, 1953; came to U.S., 1984; S. Chai-Chang and Fei-Chei (Chi) H.; m. Sue Hui Lee, Mar. 24, 1981; 1 child, Wayne. BS, Nat. Taipei Inst. Tech., Taiwan, 1973, N.D. State U., 1986; MS, U. Mo., 1988. Mech. engr. Ta Tung Aluminum Co., Taipei, 1975-76; rsch. mgr. Ta Tung Aluminum Co., Tapei, 1976-77, prodn. tech. mgr., 1977-79, quality control mgr., 1979-84; computer programmer U. Mo., Columbia, 1988; systems analyst, programmer NCR Corp., San Diego, 1989-92; database cons. Gamma-Metrics, 1992-93; software engr. Science Applications Internat. Corp., 1993—; cons. Computing Ctr., U. Mo., Columbia, 1987-88. Recipient Nat. scholarship Republic China Jaycees, Taipei, 1972. Mem. AAAS, San Diego Taiwanese Cultural Assn. Republican. Home: 8939 Adobe Bluffs Dr San Diego CA 92129

HUANG, PAN MING, soil science educator; b. Pu-tse, Taiwan, Sept. 2, 1934; arrived in Can., 1965; s. Rong Yi and Koh (Chiu) H.; m. Yun Yin Lin, Dec. 26, 1964; children: Daniel Chian Yuan, Crystal Ling Hui. BSA, Nat. Chung Hsing U., Taichung, Taiwan, 1957; MSc, U. Man., Winnipeg, Can., 1962; PhD, U. Wis., Madison, 1966. Cert. prof. agrologist. Asst. prof. soil sci. U. Sask., Saskatoon, Can., 1965-71, assoc. prof., 1971-78, prof., 1978—; nat. vis. prof., head dept. soil sci. Nat. Chung Hsing U., 1975-76; councilor Clay Minerals Soc., Boulder, Colo., 1985-88. Author: Soil Chemistry, 1991; contbr. over 180 articles to profl. jours. Bd. dirs. Saskatoon Chinese Mandarin Sch., 1977-79, Saskatoon Soc. for Study Chinese Culture, 1983—. 2d lt. Taiwan Mil. Tng. Corps, 1957-59. Grantee The UN Environment Programme, Nat. Scis. and Engring. Rsch. Coun. Can. and numerous other agys., 1965—. Fellow Can. Soc. Soil Sci., Soil Sci. Soc. Am. (rep. clay minerals soc. 1979-83, chmn. dir. 1982-83, bd. dirs. 1983-84, assoc. editor 1987-92, editor spl. publ. 1986, rep. to Inernat. Union Pure and Applied Chemistry 1990—, award com. 1986, Marion L. and Christie M. Jackson Soil Sci. award com. 1990—, fellows com. 1992—), Am. Soc. Agronomy; mem. Internat. Soc. Soil Sci. (chmn. working group 1990—), Am. Chem. Soc., Sigma Xi. Home: 130 Mount Allison Cres, Saskatoon, SK Canada S7H 4A5 Office: U Sask, Dept Soil Sci, Saskatoon, SK Canada S7N 0W0

HUANG, SUNG-CHENG, electrical engineering educator; b. Canton, China, Oct. 26, 1944; came to U.S., 1967; s. Hip-chung Wong and Chung Huang; m. Caroline S. Soong, Sept. 4, 1971; children: Michael, Dennis. BSEE, Nat. Taiwan U., Taipei, 19656; DSc, Wash. U., 1973. Postdoctral rsch. assoc. Biomed. Computer Lab. Wash. U., St. Louis, 1973-74; project engr. Picker Corp., Cleve., 1974-77; asst. prof. Sch. Medicine UCLA, 1977-82, assoc. prof. Sch. Medicine, 1982-86, prof. Sch. Medicine, 1986—; Edward Farber lectr. U. Chgo., 1986. Mem. editorial bd. Jour. Cerebral Blood Flow, 1989-92; dep. chief editor Jour. Cerebral Blood Flow and Metabolism, 1993—; contbr. over 150 articles to scholarly and profl. jours. Recipient George Von Hevesy Prize World Congress of Nuclear Medicine and Biology, 1982; grantee U.S. Dept. Energy, 1977—, NIH, 1977—. Mem. AAAS, IEEE, Soc. Nuclear Medicine, Soc. Cerebral Blood Flow. Office: UCLA Sch Medicine Div Nuclear Medicine and Biophysics 405 Hilgard Ave Los Angeles CA 90024

HUBATA, ROBERT, computer capacity planner; b. Batesville, Ark., Dec. 5, 1942; s. Robert Albert and Emma Jean (Murphy) H.; m. Cecily Myers, Oct. 10, 1962 (div. 1972); 1 child, Rachel Isabelle Ashton-Hubata; m. Corrine Phillips, May 8, 1993. BA in Math., U. Calif., Berkeley, 1967; MS in Statistics, Ariz. State U., Tempe, 1994. Mathematician Chevron Rsch., Richmond, Calif., 1967-69; computer programmer Univ. Computing Co., Chgo., 1969-73; tech. analyst Blue Cross Blue Shield, Chgo., 1973-76; systems programmer Market Rsch. Corp. Am., Chgo., 1976-79; systems analyst Entergy Corp., New Orleans, 1979-90; capacity planner Am. Express, Phoenix, 1990—. Author: Computer Measurement Group Transactions, 1988, SAS Users Group Conference Proceedings, 1990. Mem. Math. Assn. Am., Am. Statis. Assn. Office: Am Express 19640 N 31st Ave Phoenix AZ 85027

HUBBARD, CHARLES RONALD, engineering executive; b. Weaver, Ala., Feb. 4, 1933; s. John Duncan Hubbard and Athy Pauline (Lusk) Thorpe; m. Betty Lou McKleroy, Dec. 29, 1951; 1 son, Charles Ronald Hubbard II. BSEE, U. Ala., 1960. Mktg. mgr. Sperry Corp., Huntsville, Ala., 1969-71, head engring. sect., 1971-74; sr. staff engr. Honeywell Inc., Clearwater, Fla., 1974-76, mgr., 1976-79, chief engr., West Covina, Calif., 1979-83, assoc. dir. engring., 1983-84, assoc. dir. advanced systems, 1984-87, assoc. dir. programs, 1987-88; v.p. govt. systems div. Integrated Inference Machines, Anaheim, Calif., 1988-91; pres. Synergy Computer Systems, Anaheim, 1991—. Served as staff sgt. USAF, 1953-57. Recipient Outstanding Fellow award U. Ala., 1991. Mem. IEEE (sect. chmn. 1972-73). Methodist. Home: 5460 E Willowick Cir Anaheim CA 92807-4642 Office: Synergy Computer Systems 5460 Willowick Cir Anaheim CA 92807

HUBBARD, DONALD, marine artist, writer; b. Bronx, N.Y., Jan. 15, 1926; s. Ernest Fortesque and Lilly Violet (Beck) H.; student Brown U., 1944-45; A.A., George Washington U., 1959, B.A., 1958; student Naval War Coll., 1965-66; m. Darlene Julia Huber, Dec. 13, 1957; children: Leslie Carol, Christopher Eric, Lauren Ivy, Carmeron C. McNall. Commd. ensign U.S. Navy, 1944, advanced through grades to comdr., 1965; served naval aviator, ret., 1967; founder Ocean Ventures Industries, Inc., Coronado, Calif., 1969, operator, 1969-77; marine artist; founder, operator Sea Eagle Pubs., Coronado, 1988; lectr. on marine art; SCUBA instr. Author: Ships-in-Bottles, 2d edition, 1988, A How to Guide to a Venerable Nautical Craft, 1971; Buddleschiffe: Wie Macht Man Sie, 1972; The Complete Book of Inflatable Boats, 1979; Where to Paddle in San Diego County and Nearby Mexico, 1992; editor: The Bottle Shipwright; works featured in Am. Artist of the Bookplate, 1970-90, Cambridge Bookplate Press, 1990; contbr. articles in field to publs. Decorated Air Medal. Mem. Ships-in-Bottles Assn. (pres. N.Am. div. 1982—), Nature Printing Soc., Am. Soc. Bookplate Collectors adn Designers, San Diego Watercolor Soc. (bd. dirs. 1981-82), Marine Hist. Soc., San Diego Maritime Assn. Home and Office: 1022 Park Pl Coronado CA 92118-2822

HUBBARD, GREGORY SCOTT, physicist; b. Lexington, Ky., Dec. 27, 1948; s. Robert Nicholas and Nancy Clay (Brown) H.; B.A., Vanderbilt U., 1970; postgrad. U. Calif., Berkeley, 1975-77; m. Susan Artimissa Ruggeri, Aug. 1, 1982. Lab. engr. physics dept. Vanderbilt U., Nashville, 1970-73; staff scientist Lawrence Berkeley Lab. Dept. Instrument Techniques, Berkeley, Calif., 1974-80; dir. research and devel. Canberra Industries, Inc., Detector Products Div., Novato, Calif., 1980-82; v.p., gen. mgr. Canberra Semicondr., Novato, Calif., 1982-85; cons., owner Hubbard Cons. Services, 1985—; cons. SRI Internat., Menlo Park, Calif., 1979-86, sr. rsch. physicist, 1986-87; div. staff scientist space exploration projects office Ames Rsch. Ctr., NASA, Moffett Field, Calif., 1987-90, chief space instrumentation and studies br. NASA Ames Rsch. Ctr., Moffett Field, 1990-92; deputy chief space projects divsn., NASA Ames Rsch. Ctr., Moffett Field, 1992—; lectr. in field. Recipient Founders Scholarship, Vanderbilt U., 1966. Mem. AIAA, IEEE, Nuclear Sci. Soc., Am. Phys. Soc., Commonwealth Club Calif., Hon. Order Ky. Cols.

HUBBARD, MARK RANDALL, financial executive; b. Monterey, Calif., Sept. 17, 1955; s. William Frederick Jr. and Faye Jo (Browning) H.; m. Francine Elizabeth Vital, Oct. 11, 1980; children: Kevin Michael, Michelle Renee. BSBA, Calif. State U., Northridge, 1980. CPA, Calif. Ptnr. French Hubbard Accountancy Corp., Canoga Park, Calif., 1984-85; CFO Harmony Pictures, Inc., Burbank, Calif., 1985—, Harmony Holdings, Inc., 1991-. Coach local Youth Baseball. Mem. AICPA, Calif. Soc. CPAs, Assn. Ind. Comml. Producers (treas. 1990—) Assn. Ind. Comml. Producers-West (bd. dirs. 1989—, treas. 1989-91), Calif. Advt. Alliance (treas. 1992—), Calif. Film Comsn. (apptd. by Gov. 1993), Mensa, Knollwood Golf Club, River Ridge Golf Club. Republican. Office: Harmony Holdings Inc 2921 W Alameda Ave Burbank CA 91505

HUBBARD, RICHARD WARD, clinical biochemist; b. Battle Creek, Mich., Dec. 24, 1929; s. Ralph Martin and Myrtle (Ward) H.; m. Constance Mae Hubbard, Nov. 18, 1951; children: Robert John, Jeffrey Allen, Karen Ann. BA, Pacific Union Coll., 1951; MS, Purdue U., 1959, PhD, 1961. Analytical chemist Willard Storage Battery Co., East L.A., 1951-53; med. tech. trainee L.A. County Gen. Hosp., 1953-54; instr. biochemistry Dept. Dermatology, U. Mich., Ann Arbor, 1960-63; sr. rsch. chemist Spinco div. Beckman Instruments, Palo Alto, Calif., 1963-67; project leader biochemistry NASA/SRI, Biosatellite Primate Pr., Menlo Park, 1967-70; asst. prof. biochemistry Depts. Pathology and Biochemistry, Loma Linda (Calif.) U., 1970-73, assoc. prof. biochemistry, 1973-89, assoc. rsch. prof. pathology, 1989—; cons., tchr. Beckman Instruments, Palo Alto, 1967-69; cons. biochemistry NASA/Standford Rsch. Inst., Menlo Park, Fla., 1970-72; cons. chromatology Lab. Data Control, Riviera Beach, Calif., 1978-79; scientific advisor Spinco div. Beckman Instruments, Palo Alto, 1986—. Author: Preservation of Biol. Sp., 1972; (with others) Amino Acid Connection, 1988, Monographs on Atherosclerosis, 1990. Mem. Am. Inst. Nutrition, Am. Inst. Clin. Nutrition, Am. Assn. Clin. Chemists (sec. 1980-84), Am. Chem. Soc., Am. Soc. Med. Tech. (chpt. pres. 1983), N.Y. Acad. Sci., Calif. Soc. Med. Tech. (stud bowl dir. 1979-92, Outstanding Mem. 1989), Omicron Sigma, Phi Lambda Upsilon, Sigma Xi. Republican. Seventh-Day Adventist. Home: 1906 Verde Vista Dr Redlands CA 92373

HUBBELL, FLOYD ALLAN, physician, educator; b. Waco, Tex., Nov. 13, 1948; s. F.E. and Margaret (Fraser) H.; m. Nancy Cooper, May 23, 1975; 1 child, Andrew Allan. BA, Baylor U., 1971, MD, 1974; MS in Pub. Health, UCLA, 1983. Diplomate Am. Bd. Internal Medicine. Intern, resident, Long Beach Med. Program U. Calif., Irvine, 1975-78, asst. prof. medicine, 1981-89, assoc. prof. medicine and social ecology, 1989-92; dir. Primary Care Internal Medicine Residency, 1992—. Contbr. articles to profl. jours. Recipient Outstanding Tchr. award U. Calif., Irvine, 1985, 89. Fellow ACP; mem. APHA, Soc. Gen. Internal Medicine, Am. Fedn. for Clin. Rsch. Democrat. Office: U Calif Irvine Med Ctr 101 City Dr Orange CA 92668

HUBBELL, ROBERT NEWELL, psychologist; b. Neenah, Wis., Oct. 23, 1931; s. Ralph Newell and Ruth Elizabeth (Lindsey) H.; m. Joann Marguerite Jansen, Aug. 14, 1954; children: Scott David, Brian Jansen. BS, Northwestern U., 1954; MA, U. Wis., 1961, PhD, 1964. Lic. psychologist, Colo. Dean of men, asst. prof. U. Iowa, 1964-67; Am. Coun. on Edn. intern U. Calif., Santa Barbara, 1967-68; assoc. prof., staff psychologist Colo. State U., Ft. Collins, 1968-72; coord. Community Counseling Ctr., Granby, Colo., 1972-76; coord. mental health svcs. West Cent. Mental Health Ctr., Canon City, Colo., 1976-77; pvt. practice clin. psychology Canon City, 1977—; behavioral sci. intern Nat. Tng. Labs., Bethel, Maine, summer 1968; cons. Pomona Coll., summer 1969, Luth. Ch. Am., 1969-70, Higher Edn. Assocs., 1970-72; adj. prof. Walden U., Naples, Fla., 1971—, Colo. State Penitentiary, 1977-79. Lt. (j.g.) USNR, 1954-57. Contbr. articles to profl. jours. Mem. Biofeedback Soc. Am. (cert.), Am. Soc. Clin. Hypnosis, Nat. Register Health Svcs. Providers in Psychology, Am. Coun. Edn., Colo. Psychol. Assn. Methodist. Home: 2317 Greenway Cir Canon City CO 81212-2036 Office: PO Box 687 Canon City CO 81215-0687

HUBEN, BRIAN DAVID, lawyer; b. Inglewood, Calif., May 14, 1962; s. Michael Gerald and Dorothy (Withers) H.; m. Kathy Henson Johnson, Apr. 6, 1991. BA, Loyola Marymount U., 1984; JD, Loyola Law Sch., 1987. Bar: Calif. 1988, U.S. Dist. Ct. (no., ce., ea. and so. dists.) Calif. 1988, U.S. Ct. Appeals (9th cir.) 1988, D.C. 1989. Assoc. Steinberg, Nutter & Brent, Santa Monica, Calif., 1988-89, Smith & Hilbig, Torrance, Calif., 1989—; del. L.A. County Bar Assn. State Conv., 1990—. Mem. instl. rev. bd. Torrance Meml. Med. Ctr., 1990—. Mem. Calif. Bar Assn., D.C. Bar Assn., L.A. County Bar Assn. Democrat. Roman Catholic. Office: Smith & Hilbig 21515 Hawthorne Blvd Ste 500 Torrance CA 90503-6568

HUBER, COLLEEN ADLENE, artist; b. Concordia, Kans., Mar. 30, 1927; d. Claude Irve and Freda (Trow) Baker; m. Wallace Charles Huber, Oct. 18, 1945 (dec.); children: Wallace Charles II, Shawn Dale, Devron Kelly, Candace Lynette, Melody Ann. Student, UCLA, 1974-78; BA cum laude, Calif. Poly. U., 1983. Co-owner, artist The Rocket (community newspaper), Garden Grove, Calif., 1955-58; quick sketch artist Walt Disney Prodn. Co., Burbank, Calif., 1958-59; v.p., art dir. Gray Pub. Co., Fullerton, Calif., 1968-76; tchr. North Orange County Sch. Dist., La Palma, Calif., 1974-76; art dir. Shoppers Guide, Upland, Calif., 1979-81; pub., owner Community Woman/Huber Ad Agy., Anaheim, Calif., 1976-79; artist Bargain Bulletin Pub., Fallbrook, Calif., 1979-82; graphic artist, designer Van Zyen Pub., Fallbrook, 1982-83; cons. sales East San Diego Mag./Baker Graphics, Rancho San Diego, Calif., 1978-88; owner, artist Coco Bien Objet d'Art, Laguna Beach, Calif., 1986-92; instr. Camp Fire Inc., 1990-92, Coco Bien Objet d'Art, Tenecula, Calif., 1992—; dir. edn. Art Acad., Orange County, 1992—; instr. Lake Elsinore Community Ctr. Author: Gail, 1980 (1st Pl. award 1981, 2d Pl. award 1981); artist: Yearlings (2d Pl. award 1985), Penning (1st Pl. award 1987). Participant Art-A-Fair, Laguna Beach Festival Show. Recipient certs. North Orange County ROP, 1976-77. Fellow Zonta (2d v.p. 1990-91), Laguna Beach C. of C. (docent gallery night 1988); mem. Exec. Women, Calif. Press Women Assn. (chmn. jr. journalism contest Orange County chpt. 1985-86, pres. 1986-87; chair Taste of Valley art show). Republican. Roman Catholic.

HUBER, LINDA RUTH, non-commissioned officer; b. Stafford Springs, Conn., Aug. 3, 1955; d. Joseph Lawrence and Edith Viola (Plante) Young; m. Vernon R. Huber Jr., Dec. 26, 1981; children: James R., Brian D., Chad T., Nicole L., Christopher A. Student, C.C. of Air Force, 1985, Embry-Riddle AU, 1988—. Admission clk. St. Anthony Hosp., St. Petersburg, Fla., 1974-76; customer svc. rep. Zayre Dept. Stores, St. Petersburg, 1976-77; jet engine technician Fighter Interceptor Squadron, Griffiss AFB, N.Y., 1977-79, Logistics Support Squadron, Okinawa, Japan, 1979-81; asst. NCOIC outbound assignments Combat Support Group, McConnell AFB, Kans., 1981-82; jet engine specialist Consolidated Aircraft Maintenance Squadron, Altus AFB, Okla., 1982-84; NCOIC quick engine changes sect. 81 Component Repair Squadron, RAF Bentwaters, UK, 1984-88; NCOIC tech. adminstrn. 355 Component Repair Squadron, Davis-Monthan AFB, Tucson, 1988-92; NCOIC orderly room 355 Ops. Support Squadron, Davis-Monthan AFB, Tucson, 1992—; USAF disaster preparedness support team Combat Support Group, RAF Bentwaters, 1984-88; mem. Desert Shield/Desert Storm support Component Repair Squadron, Davis-Monthan AFB, 1990-91. Coach Pop Warner Mitey Mite Football, Tucson, 1989, Apache Little League Baseball, Tucson, 1988-92; coach (asst.) Pantano Soccer League, Tucson, 1989-92; fundraiser rep. Pop Warner Football, Tucson, 1990-92. Named one of Outstanding Young Men of Am., 1988. Democrat. Lutheran. Office: 355 Ops Support Squadron Davis Monthan AFB Tucson AZ 85707

HUBER, NORMAN FRED, communications executive, educator; b. N.Y.C., Sept. 14, 1935; s. Fred M. Huber and Hetty (Blum) Ryan; m. Marilyn Rose Chicky, June 30, 1962; children: Norman Fred Jr., Cheryle, Karl, Karen, Daniel, Thomas. Student, West Coast U., 1963-64, Orange Coast Coll., 1965-66, UCLA, 1977-78. Mgr. systems engring. IBM Corp., South Bend, Ind., 1955-62; asst. dir. computing Rockwell Internat., Downey, Calif., 1963-69; dir. computing Computer Credit Corp., Los Angeles, 1970-74; v.p. computer services Blue Cross of Calif., Los Angeles, 1974-79; mgr., consultant Coopers & Lybrand, Los Angeles, 1979-80; pres., founder Huber Data Systems Inc., Thousand Oaks, Calif., 1980—; cons., educator Ameritech/Bell Ind., Ill., Mich., Indpls., 1986-92, Bell Atlantic/Southwestern Bell, Silver Spring, Md., Kansas City, Mo., 1986-88, Hughes Aircraft Co., Long Beach, Calif., 1986-93, State of Calif., Sacramento, 1986-91, Communications Engring. Ltd., Hong Kong, 1989-92, Strategic Advancement, Singapore, 1992-93, N.Y. Telephone, White Plains, 1989-92. Author: Data Communications "An Intensive Introduction", 1993, Data Communications "The Business Aspects", 1983, Data Communications "Glossary of Data Communications Terms", 1993, Migration to New Technology, 1992., Advanced Data Communications, 1993; pub. Snoopy Trader, 1986-93. With USN, 1953-55. Mem. IEEE, Data Processing Mgmt. Assn. Republican. Home and Office: 931 Emerson St Thousand Oaks CA 91362-2447

HUBER, NORMAN KING, geologist; b. Duluth, Minn., Jan. 14, 1926; s. Norman and Hedwig Marie (Graessner) H.; m. Martha Ann Barr, June 2, 1951; children: Steven K., Richard N. BS, Franklin and Marshall Coll., 1950; MS, Northwestern U., 1952, PhD, 1956. Registered geologist, Calif. Geologist U.S. Geol. Survey, Menlo Park, Calif., 1954—; authority geology of Sierra Nev. Contbr. articles to profl. jours. With U.S. Army, 1944-46, Europe and Japan. S.F. Emmons fellow Soc. Econ. Geologists, 1953-54. Fellow Geol. Soc. Am. Home: 220 Diablo Ave Mountain View CA 94043-4117 Office: US Geol Survey M/S 975 345 Middlefield Rd Menlo Park CA 94025-3591

HUBER, WAYNE CHARLES, engineering educator; b. Shelby, Mont., Aug. 2, 1941; s. Hubert Henry and Lois Marion (Hendrickson) H.; m. Catherine Ann Forster, June 22, 1968; 1 child, Lydia Ann. BS, Calif. Inst. Tech., Pasadena, 1963; MS, MIT, 1965, PhD, 1968. Registered profl. engr., Fla. Asst. prof. Dept. of Environ. Engring. Scis., U. Fla., Gainesville, 1968-73, assoc. prof., 1973-79, prof., 1979-91; prof., head Dept. of Civil Engring., Oreg. State U., Covallis, 1991—; cons. Nat. Oceanic and Atmospheric Adminstrn., Rockville, Md., 1990-91, Internat. Inst. for Hydraulic and Environ. Engring., Delft, Netherlands, 1988-91, U.S. EPA, Washington, 1978-83. Coauthor: Hydrology and Floodplain Analysis, 1992; contbr. articles to profl. jours. Recipient Lorenz G. Straub award U. Minn., 1969, Outstanding Tech. Achievement award Fla. Engring. Soc., 1985. Mem. ASCE (com. chair 1990-92, Hilgard Hydraulic prize 1973), Internat. Assn. for Hydraulic Rsch., Am. Geophys. Union, Am. Water Resources Assn., Sigma Xi, Tau Beta Pi. Democrat. Home: 1854 NW Jameson Pl Corvallis OR 97330 Office: Oreg State U Dept Civil Engring Corvallis OR 97331-2302

HUBERT, WAYNE PAUL, college dean; b. Bradley, Ill., Sept. 28, 1943; s. Paul Clifford and Dorothy Rita (Dionne) H.; m. Sandra Kay Shaffer, Apr. 30, 1966; children: Lisa Marie Chapman, Jeffrey Wayne, Gregory Scott. BA in English, Loyola U., L.A., 1965; MA in English, Calif. State U., L.A., 1972; PhD in Higher Edn., Claremont (Calif.) Grad. Sch., 1985. English instr. Chaffey High Sch., Ontario, Calif., 1967-71, Montclair (Calif.) High Sch., 1971-76; English instr. Chaffey Coll., Alta Loma, Calif., 1976-92, div.

chair lang. arts, 1988-92, dean arts and humanities, 1992—. Mem. Assn. Calif. Community Coll. Adminstrs. Democrat. Roman Catholic. Home: 12729 Kumquat Ave Chino CA 91710 Office: Chaffey Community Coll 5885 Haven Ave Alta Loma CA 91737

HUCK, LARRY RALPH, manufacturers representative, sales consultant; b. Yakima, Wash., Aug. 10, 1942; s. Frank Joseph and Helen Barbara (Swalley) H.; 1 child, Larry Ralph II. Student Wash. Tech. Inst., 1965-66, Seattle Community Coll., 1966-68, Edmonds Community Coll., 1969-70. Salesman, Kirby Co., Seattle, 1964-68, sales mgr., 1968-69; saleman Sanico Chem. Co., Seattle, 1968-69; salesman Synkoloid Co., Seattle, 1970-71; tech. sales rep. Vis Queen div. Ethyl Corp., Seattle, 1971-75; Western sales mgr. B & K Films, Inc., Belmont, Calif., 1975-77; pres. N.W. Mfrs. Assocs., Inc., Bellevue, Wash., 1977-86; pres. combined sales group, 1984 ; nat. sales mgr. Gazelle, Inc., Tomah, Wis., 1979-81; dir. sales J.M.J. Mktg. E.Z. Frame div., 1984-85; pres. Combined Sales Group, Seattle, 1984; nat. accounts mgr. Upnorth Plastics, St. Paul, 1984-87; pres. Combined Sales Group, Inc., Redmond, Wash., 1987—. V.p. Bellevue Nat. Little League; basketball coord. Cath. Youth Orgn., Sacred Heart Ch.; head baseball coach Pierce Coll., Tacoma. With USMC, 1959-64. Mem. Nat. Coun. Salesmen's Orgns., Mfrs. Agts. Nat. Assn., Am. Hardware Mfrs. Assn., Northwest Mfrs. Assn. (pres.), Hardware Affiliated Reps., Inc., Door and Hardware Inst., Internal Conf. Bldg. Ofcls., Am. Baseball Coaches Assn., Marine Corps Assn., 1st Marine Div. Assn., 3d Marine Div. Assn. (life, v.p.). Roman Catholic. Office: 14925 NE 40th St Redmond WA 98052-5326

HUCK, MATTHEW L., process development engineer; b. Syracuse, N.Y., Apr. 19, 1961; s. Ludwig A. and Margaret (Brooks) H.; m. Wanda Leigh Englert, July 6, 1985 (div. May 1992); 1 child, Brian. BS, Rochester (N.Y.) Inst. Tech., 1983. Photolithographic engr. Am Microsystems Inc, Santa Clara, Calif., 1983-85, sect. mgr., 1985-87; R & D engr. Am Microsystems Inc, Pocatello, Idaho, 1987-90, R & D photolithographic engring. staff, 1990-93; R & D photolithographic engring. sr. staff Am. Microsystems Inc., Pocatello, Idaho, 1993—; sec. Bacus, Inc., San Jose, Calif., 1985-87. Contbr. articles to profl. jours. Mem. Soc. Photo-Optical Instrumentation Engrs. (active BACUS and Microlithography groups). Republican. Home: 2750 Castle Peak Way Pocatello ID 83201 Office: Am Microsystems Inc 2300 Buckskin Rd Pocatello ID 83201

HUCKABEE, PHYLLIS, gas industry professional; b. Andrews, Tex., Aug. 11, 1963; d. Tommie Jack and Sylvia (Wingo) H. BBA in Fin., Tex. Tech U., 1984, MBA, 1986. Clk. loan escrow 1st Fed. Savs. Bank, Lubbock, Tex., 1984; mgmt. trainee El Paso (Tex.) Nat. Gas Co., 1986-87, analyst rate dept., 1987-88, specialist Calif. affairs, 1988-91, rep. Calif. affairs, 1991-92; asst. dir. Cambridge Energy Rsch. Assocs., Oakland, Calif., 1992—. Bd. dirs. El Paso Community Concert Assn., 1988, bd. dirs. Performing Arts Workshop, 1991-92, mem. adv. bd., 1992—; vol. Bus. Vols. for Arts, San Francisco, 1989, East Bay Habitat for Humanity, 1993—; tutor, fundraiser Project Read, San Francisco, 1990. Mem. Internat. Assn. Energy Econs., Women Energy Assocs. (bd. dirs. 1990—), Berkeley Archtl. Heritage Assn. Methodist. Democrat. Home: 1721 McGee Ave Berkeley CA 94703 Office: Cambridge Energy Rsch Assoc 1999 Harrison St Ste 1440 Oakland CA 94612

HUCKEBY, KAREN MARIE, graphic arts executive; b. San Diego, June 4, 1957; d. Floyd Riley and Georgette Laura (Wegimont) H. Student Coll. of Alameda, 1976; student 3-M dealer tng. program, St. Paul, 1975. Staff Huck's Press Service, Inc., Emeryville, Calif., 1968—, v.p., 1975—. Mem. Rep. Nat. Task Force, 1984—; bd. dirs. CitiArts Benefactors, Concord, Calif., 1990—, v.p., treas., 1991—. Recipient service award ARC, 1977. Mem. East Bay Club of Printing House Craftsman (treas. 1977-78), Oakland Mus. Soc., Nat. Trust Historic Preservation, Smithsonian Inst., San Francisco Mus. Soc., Internat. Platform Assn., Am. Film Inst., Commonwealth Club. Home: 1054 Hera Ct Hercules CA 94547-1927 Office: Staff Huck's Press Svc Inc 691 S 31st St Richmond CA 94804-4022

HUDAK, THOMAS MICHAEL, plastic surgeon; b. Akron, Ohio, May 16, 1937; s. Rudolph Michael and Muriel (Creighton) H.; m. Anne Elizabeth Verhey, Aug. 11, 1963 (div.); m. Mary Louise Schmidt, Aug. 16, 1974; children: Michael, Stephen, Allison. BA, U. Mich., 1959, MD, 1963. Intern U. Md., Balt., 1963-64, surg. resident, 1964-68; resident in plastic surgery U. Mich., Ann Arbor, 1968-70; pvt. practice Phoenix, 1970—. Mem. Phoenix Thunderbirds, 1976—, Ariz. Acad., 1991—; pres. The Heart Mus., Phoenix, 1989-91. Recipient Outstanding Paper award Nat. Residents' Conf., Salt Lake City, 1970. Mem. NCCJ (bd. dirs. 1983-88), Am. Soc. Plastic and Reconstructive Surgery, Am. Sc. Aesthetic Plastic Surgery, Reed O. Dingham Soc., Frederick A. Coller Soc., Am. Assn. Hand Surgery., Men's Art Coun., Phoenix Country Club. Republican. Roman Catholic. Office: Plastic Surgery Affiliates 555 W Catalina #319 Phoenix AZ 85013-4416

HUDDLESTON, JACKSON NOYES, JR., business consultant; b. Huntington, W.Va., Jan. 24, 1938; s. Jackson Noyes and Margaret (Bussell) H.; m. Keiko Nakajima, July 12, 1972; children: Shannon Lea Huddleston Lucansky, Sayako. BA, Princeton U., 1960; postgrad., Stanford U., 1960, 63-64, U. Wash., 1960-63. V.p. Chem. Bank, N.Y.C., 1964-79; pres. Chemco Internat. Leasing, N.Y.C., 1978-79; sr. v.p. Am. Express, N.Y.C. and Tokyo, 1979-82; bus. cons., Tokyo and Seattle, 1982—; prof. U. Wash., Seattle, 1983, 89, Hanson prof., 1987-88. Author: Gaijin Kaisha: Running a Foreign Business in Japan, 1990; contbr. articles to profl. jours. Trustee Princeton-in-Asia, Blakemore Found. Scholar Ford Found., 1960, 63-64, NDEA, 1960-63. Mem. Assn. for Asian Socs., Japan-Am. Soc. Seattle, Japan Soc., Am. C. of C. Japan, Internat. House Japan, Fgn. Corrs. Club Japan, Seattle Tennis Club, Central Park Tennis Club. Home: 3536 45th Ave NE Seattle WA 98105-5316 Office: 3536 45th Ave NE Seattle WA 98105-5316

HUDSON, CHRISTOPHER JOHN, publisher; b. Watford, Eng., June 8, 1948; s. Joseph Edward and Gladys Jenny Patricia (Madgwick); m. Lois Jeanne Lyons, June 16, 1979; children: Thomas, Ellen, Ronald, Timothy. BA with honors, Cambridge U., Eng., 1969, MA with honors, 1972. Promotion mgr. Prentice-Hall Internat., Eng., 1969-70; area mgr. Prentice-Hall Internat., Eng., France, 1970-71; mktg. mgr. Prentice-Hall Internat., Englewood Cliffs, N.J., 1971-74, dir. mktg., 1974-76, asst. v.p., 1976; group internat. dir. I.T.T. Pub., N.Y.C., 1976-77; pres. Focal Press, Inc., N.Y.C., 1977-82; v.p., pub. Aperture Found. Inc., N.Y.C., 1983-86; head publs. J. Paul Getty Trust, L.A., 1986—. Author: Guide to International Book Fairs, 1976; pub. Aperture, 1983-86, J. Paul Getty Mus. Jour., 1986—. Mem. adv. coun. Nat. Heritage Village, Kioni, Greece; mem. trade with eastern Europe com. Assn. Am. Pubs., N.Y., 1976-79, internat. fairs com., 1986-88. Mem. Internat. Assn. Mus. Publs. (Frankfurt, Fed. Republic Germany, chmn. 1992-93), U.S. Mus. Publ. Group (chmn. 1989—), Internat. Pubs. Assn., Hellenic Soc. (London), Oxford & Cambridge Club (London), Internat. Assn. Scholarly Pubs. (chmn. internat. contracts com.). Office: J Paul Getty Trust 17985 Pacific Coast Hwy Malibu CA 90265-5799

HUDSON, DONALD J., stock exchange executive; b. Vancouver, B.C., Canada, Sept. 26, 1930. BA in Econs. and Math., U. B.C., 1952; LLD (hon.), Simon Fraser U., 1993. With Shell Oil Co. of Can. Ltd., 1952-53; dir. sales devel. Can. Pacific Airlines, Vancouver, 1953-64; sr. v.p. Pacific div. T. Eaton Co., Ltd., Vancouver, 1964-81; pres. Vancouver Stock Exch., 1982—; bd. dirs. Brit. Pacific Properties Ltd., Norwich Union Life Ins. Soc., Can. Bd., The Can. Journalism Found. Chmn. Internat. Fin. Centre Vancouver, Simon Fraser U. Found. Bd.; mem. Brit. Columbia & Yukon Coun. of the Duke of Edinburgh's Award in Can.; sr. adv. bd. mem. YMCA of Greater Vancouver. Mem. The Niagara Inst. (adv. coun.), Pacific Corridor Enterprise Coun. (bd. dirs.), Vancouver Law Tennis Club, The Vancouver Club. Office: Stock Exch Tower, 609 Granville St, PO Box 10333, Vancouver, BC Canada V7Y 1H1

HUDSON, DONNA LEE, computer science educator; b. Fresno, Calif., July 16, 1946; d. David and Elvera Marie (Hegquist) Harder; m. Samuel Eugene Hudson, Jr., Sept. 9, 1967. BS in Math., Calif. State U., Fresno, 1968, MS in Math., 1972; PhD in Computer Sci., UCLA, 1981. Lectr. Calif. State U., Fresno, 1975-81; asst. prof. U. Calif., Davis, 1981-82, asst. prof. U. Calif., San Francisco, 1982-88, assoc. prof., 1988—, dir. computer ctr. U. Calif., San Francisco, Fresno Med. Edn. Program, 1982—. Contbr. articles to profl. jours. Mem. IEEE, Internat. Soc. Mini and Microcomputers, Am. Math Soc., Assn. for Computing Machinery, N.Am. Fuzzy Info. Processing Soc. (bd. dirs.), Assn. Computing Machinery, Phi Kappa Phi, Beta Gamma Sigma.

HUDSON, EDWARD VOYLE, linen supply company executive; b. Seymour, Mo., Apr. 3, 1915; s. Marion A. and Alma (Von Gonten) H.; student Bellingham (Wash.) Normal Coll., 1933-36, also U. Wash.; m. Margaret Carolyn Greely, Dec. 24, 1939; children—Edward G., Carolyn K. Asst. to mgr. Natural Hard Metal Co., Bellingham, 1935-37; partner Met. Laundry Co., Tacoma, 1938-39; propr., mgr. Peerless Laundry & Linen Supply Co., Tacoma, 1939—; propr. Independent Laundry & Everett Linen Supply Co., 1946-74, 99 Cleaners and Launderers Co., Tacoma, 1957-79; chmn. Tacoma Public Utilities, 1959-60; trustee United Mut. Savs. Bank; bd. dirs. Tacoma Better Bus. Bur., 1977—. Pres., Wash. Conf. on Unemployment Compensation, 1975-76; pres. Tacoma Boys' Club, 1970; v.p. Puget Sound USO, 1972—; elder Emmanuel Presbyn. Ch., 1974—; past campaign mgr., pres. Tacoma-Pierce County United Good Neighbors. Recipient Disting. Citizen's cert. U.S. Air Force Mil. Airlift Com., 1977; U.S. Dept. Def. medal for outstanding public service, 1978. Mem. Tacoma Sales and Mktg. Execs. (pres. 1957-58), Pacific NW Laundry, Dry Cleaning and Linen Supply Assn. (pres. 1959, treas. 1965—), Internat. Fabricare Inst. (dir. dist. 7 treas. 1979, pres. 1982), Am. Security Council Bd., Tacoma C. of C. (pres. 1965), Air Force Assn. (pres. Tacoma chpt. 1976-77, v.p. Wash. state 1983-84, pres. 1985-86), Navy League, Puget Sound Indsl. Devel. Council (chmn. 1967), Tacoma-Ft. Lewis-Olympia Army Assn. (past pres.) Republican. Clubs: Elks (vice chmn. bd. trustees 1984, chmn. 1985-86), Shriners (potentate 1979), Masons, Scottish Rite, Tacoma, Tacoma Country and Golf, Jesters, Rotary (pres. Tacoma chpt. 1967-68), Tacoma Knife and Fork (pres. 1964). Home: 3901 N 37th St Tacoma WA 98407-5636 Office: Peerless Laundry & Linen Supply Co 2902 S 12th St Tacoma WA 98405-2598

HUDSON, JERRY E., university president; b. Chattanooga, Mar. 3, 1938; s. Clarence E. and Laura (Campbell) H.; m. Myra Ann Jared, June 11, 1957; children: Judith, Laura, Janet, Angela. B.A., David Lipscomb Coll., 1959; M.A., Tulane U., 1961, Ph.D., 1965; LL.D. (hon.), Pepperdine U., 1983. Systems engr. IBM, Atlanta, 1961; prof. Coll. Arts and Scis., Pepperdine U., 1962-75; provost, dean Coll. Arts and Scis., Malibu Campus, Pepperdine U., 1971-75; pres. Hamline U., St. Paul, 1975-80, Willamette U., Salem, Oreg., 1980—; dir. Portland Gen. Co., E.I.I.A. Mem. Nat. Assn. Ind. Colls. (bd. dirs.), Phi Alpha Theta. Office: Willamette U Office of Pres 900 State St Salem OR 97301-3922

HUDSON, JOHN IRVIN, retired marine officer; b. Louisville, Oct. 12, 1932; s. Irvin Hudson and Elizabeth (Reid) Hudson Hornbeck; m. Zetta Ann Yates, June 27, 1954; children—Reid Irvin, Lori Ann, John Yates, Clark Ray. B.S. in Bus. Mgmt., Murray State U., 1971. Commd. 2d lt. USMC, 1954, advanced through grades to lt. gen., 1987; comdg. officer Marine Fighter Attack Squadron 115, Vietnam, 1968, Marine Corps Air Sta., Yuma, Ariz., 1977-80; asst. wing comdr. 2d Marine Air Wing, Cherry Point, N.C., 1980-81; comdg. gen. LFTCLANT 4th Marine Amphibious Brigade, Norfolk, Va., 1981-83, 3d Marine Aircraft Wing, El Toro, Calif., 1985-87; dep. chief staff for manpower Hdqrs. USMC, Washington, 1987-89, ret. active duty, 1989; dir. U.S. Marine Corps Edn. Ctr., Quantico, Va., 1983-85. Decorated DFC, DSM, Bronze Star, Air medals, Silver Hawk; flew 308 combat missions in Vietnam in F-4 Phantom. Mem. VFW, Marine Corps Aviation Assn. (life), Marine Corps Assn., Marine Corps Hist. Soc., Order of Daedalians. Home: 12439 E Del Rico Yuma AZ 85365-9446

HUDSON, MICHAEL ELLIOTT, SR., human resource specialist; b. L.A., Jan. 15, 1955; s. Joe Sr. A. and Dorothy (Elliott) H.; m. June Maria Grundy, Dec. 23, 1978; children: Michael Jr., April. BA, Pacific U., 1977; MBA, Loyola Marymount U., 1981. Coord. broadcast ops. St. KLCS-TV, L.A., 1977-88; pers. analyst L.A. Unified Sch. Dist., 1988-89, supr. employment office, 1989-92, personnel analyst, 1992—; with career awareness program Dorsey High Sch., L.A, 1986—; with bus. adv. com. San Pedro (Calif.) Wilmington Skills Ctr., 1989—, Harbor Occupational Ctr., San Pedro, 1989—. Bd. dirs. Consumer Credit Counselors, L.A., 1985-88; mem. Calif. Afro-Am. Mus. Found., L.A., 1988—; mem. Westchester (Calif.) YMCA Men's Club, 1986—. Named Campaign Goal-Buster Weingart Urban Ctr. YMCA, L.A., 1983, 84, 85; recipient Shining Example award ARC, L.A., 1985. Mem. Radio and TV Ednl. Soc. (pres. 1987-88, v.p. 1985-87), Pers. Testing Coun., So. Calif. Pers. Mgmt. Assn., Pers. and Indsl. Rels. Assn. Loyola Marymount U. MBA Alumni Assn., Pacific U. Alumni Assn., Alpha Phi Alpha (career awareness program 1980-83). Home: 5514 Deane Ave Los Angeles CA 90043-2353 Office: L A Unified Sch Dist Employee Rels Office Dept L PO Box 3307 Los Angeles CA 90051

HUDSON, SALLY NEIDLINGER, former legislative aide; b. Boston, Sept. 28, 1929; d. Lloyd Kellock and Marion (Walker) N.; m. John Franklin Hudson, July 31, 1955 (dec. Dec. 1985); children: James, John, William. Student, U. Colo., 1947-51; BS in Pub. Adminstrn., U. San Francisco, 1986; Cert. in Environ. Planning, U. Calif., Davis, 1975. Owner Sporthaus, L.A., 1953-69; ski instr. Squaw Valley (Calif.) Ski Sch., 1969-74; realtor Boice Realty, Truckee, Calif., 1973-80; legis. aide Gov.'s Office of Planning, Sacramento, 1979-81, Calif. State Senate, Sacramento, 1981-85, Calif. State Assembly, Sacramento, 1986-91; dir. Squaw Valley County Water Dist., 1974-80, Tahoe Truckee Sanitation Agy., 1978-80; gov. apptd. to Tahoe Area Land Aquisition Commn., 1982-84. Del. Dem. Cent. Com. Placer County, 1980-84, Nat. Dem. Conv., San Francisco, 1988; mgr. Dukakis for Pres. Campaign Office, Sacramento, 1990. Mem. U.S. Olympic Ski Team, 1952; named Woman of Yr. Far West Ski Assn., 1969; honored mem. U.S. Ski Hall of Fame, 1971. Episcopalian. Home: 2922 Pasatiempo Pl Sacramento CA 95833

HUDSON, STEVEN REX, accountant; b. Portales, N.Mex., Feb. 1, 1956; s. Rex Don and Dolly Pauline (Skinner) H.; m. Tina Marie Campbell, June 25, 1983 (div. July 1990); children: Whitney Beth, Tyler Payne. BBA, Ea. N.Mex. U., 1980. CPA. Bookkeeper McKay & Co., P.C., Clovis, N.Mex., 1977-80, acct., 1980-86, CPA, shareholder, 1986-91; CPA pvt. practice, Portales, N.Mex., 1991—. Dir. Curry County United Way, Clovis, N.Mex., 1985-90; trustee Ea. N.Mex. U., Clovis Campus, 1989, Clovis (N.Mex.) High Plains Hosp., 1990—. Mem. Roosevelt C. of C. (dir. 1992—), AICPA, N.Mex. Soc. CPAs. Republican. Home: 124A Yucca Dr Portales NM 88130 Office: 712 W First Portales NM 88130

HUEBSCHER, FRED, political consultant; b. L.A., Jan. 18, 1960; s. Julian and Eva (Zimbler) H. BA in Polit. Sci., UCLA, 1981. Bus. mgr. L. Zimbler Interiors, L.A., 1981-83; sales rep. Modern Foods, Inc., Vernon, Calif., 1983—; pres. Polit. Scientists, L.A., 1987—. Cons. New Deal Dem. Club, Santa Monica, Calif., 1988—. Mem. ACLU, United Jewish Appeal, Friends of Hollywood Bowl, UCLA Alumni Assn. (life), Sierra Club (life). Home: 1523 N Vista St Los Angeles CA 90046

HUEFNER, SUE HAMILTON PIKE, department secretary; b. Cleve., Mar. 5, 1940; d. Robert Bruce and Helen (Barch) Hamilton; div. 1992; children: Tammerlaine Babette Pike, Terralynn Nanette Pike, Tobias Nathanael Pike, Terry Huefner, Tabithanne Suzette Pike. Student, U. Calif., Irvine, 1986, Fullerton Coll., 1985, 86, 91. Exec. sec. Parker-Hannifin, Cleve., 1958-61; accts. receivable clk. Beckman Instruments, Fullerton, Calif., 1961-62; bus. mgr. A-1 Tub Technician, Brea, Calif., 1990—; dept. sec. Calif. State U., Fullerton, 1978—. Compiler, editor numerous books. Mem. NAFE, Smithsonian Assocs., Human Svcs. Student Assn., Assn. Info. Systems Profls. Internat., Am. Inst. Profl. Bookkeepers, Am. Biog. Rsch. (bd. dirs.). Home: 720 W Whittier Blvd La Habra CA 90631 Office: Calif State Univ 800 N State Coll Fullerton CA 90631

HUESTIS, DOUGLAS WILLIAM, physician, pathologist; b. London, Ontario, Can., Mar. 21, 1925; s. Richard Douglas and Marie Marguerite (Hinde) H.; m. Rosemary Lucille Colford, June 11, 1955; children: Lucy Mary, Marilyn Joan, Andrew Charles, Karen Ann, Peter Douglas. MD, McGill U., Montreal, Que., 1948. Cert. anatomic pathology, clin. pathology. Pathologist, asst. dir. labs. Western Pa. Hosp., Pitts., 1955-60; instr. pathology Univ. Pitts., 1955-60; dir. Chas. Hymen Blood Ctr. Mount Sinai Hosp. Med. Ctr., Chgo., 1960-69; assoc. prof., pathology Chgo. Med. Sch., 1960-66, prof. clin. pathology, 1966-69; prof. pathology, chief transfusion medicine Univ. Ariz., 1969—; med. dir., blood program Southern Ariz. Red Cross, 1970-77; mem. nat. blood. resource program Nat. Heart & Lung Inst., Bethesda, Md., 1970-74; coun. on immunohematology Am. Soc. Clin. Pathologists, Chgo., 1965-70; bd. dirs. Am. Assn. of Blood Banks, Chgo., 1964-70; chmn. med. adv. com. Southern Arizona Red Cross Blood Program, 1987—. Author: Practical Blood Transfusion, 1969, 76, 81, 88; contbr. articles to sci. jours. exch. scientist Soviet-Am. Health Exch. Nat. Insts. of Health, Moscow, 1976; coun. North Am. Internat. Soc. Blood Transfusion, Paris, 1976-82; expert mem. bd. dirs. Vox Sanguinis Found., Basel, Switzerland, 1987—. With Canadian Army, 1944-45. Mem. Am. Assn. Blood Banks (John Elliott award, 1975), Am. Soc. clin. Pathologists, Am. Soc. Apheresis, Internat. Soc. Blood Transfusion (Coun. 1976-82), British Blood Transfusion Soc. Home: 6750 West Camino Del Cerro Tucson AZ 85745

HUETER, JAMES WARREN, painter, sculptor; b. San Francisco, May 15, 1925; m. Alabelle M. Hunter, 1948. BA, Pomona Coll., 1948; MFA, Claremont (Calif.) Grad. Sch., 1951. One-man shows include Pasadena (Calif.) Art Mus., 1955, Heritage Gallery, L.A., 1961, 62, 64, 67, Tobey C. Moss Gallery, L.A., 1984, 86, 88, 91, 93, U. Calif., Davis, 1986, Claremont Grad. Sch., 1989; exhibited in group shows Pasadena Art Mus., 1950-59, L.A. County Mus., 1952, 54-59, 38th Corcoran Biennial, Washington, 1983-84, Albuquerque Mus., 1984, Bklyn. Mus., 1984, San Francisco Mus. Modern Art, 1984. Recipient 1st Prize Purchase award Pasadena Art Mus., 1952, Long Beach (Calif.) State U., 1961, 1st Prize award L.A. County Fair award 1951, L.A. County Mus., 1955, Frye Mus., 1957. Home: 190 E Radcliffe Dr Claremont CA 91711-2832 Office: Tobey C Moss Gallery 7321 Beverly Blvd Los Angeles CA 90036-2503

HUFF, DALE EUGENE, environmental services executive; b. Windsor, Colo., Nov. 1, 1930; s. Floyd Eugene and Katherine Oleva (Parsons) H.; m. Flossie Leone Moses, Nov. 18, 1951; children: Clifford Allen, Herbert Eugene, Dalene Faye, Linda Reneé. BA, Pacific Union Coll., 1963, MA, 1968. Tchr. Pleasant Hill (Calif.) Jr. Acad., 1963-66; prin. Ukiah (Calif.) Jr. Acad., 1966-71; tchr. Paradise (Calif.) Adventist Acad., 1971-80; acct. Loma Linda (Calif.) U., 1980-86, environ. svcs. exec., 1986—. With U.S. Army, 1946-49. Mem. Nat. Exec. Housekeeping Assn. (exec. bd. 1987-90). Republican. Home: 10961 Desert Lawn Dr # 145 Calimesa CA 92320-2242 Office: Loma Linda U Dept Environ Svcs Loma Linda CA 92350

HUFF, DAVID CHARLES, educational administrator; b. El Centro, Calif., Jan. 6, 1950; s. Cecil Clyde and F. Esther (Statler) H.; m. Janis Marie Dickman, Nov. 24, 1973; children: Lisa Marie, Scott Michael, Matthew Charles. AA, Imperial (Calif.) Valley Coll., 1970; BA, Biola Coll., La Mirada, Calif., 1973. Youth pastor 1st Bapt. Ch. Encinitas, Calif., 1973-75; program dir. Camp Bethel, Big Horn Bapt. Youth Found., Dayton, Wyo., 1975-77; prodn. supr. N.W. Wyo. Bd. Coop. Svcs., Thermopolis, 1977-79, supr. maintenance and transp., 1979-92; pastor New Life Chapel of Foursquare Gospel, Thermopolis, 1982-89; pupil transp. specialist Mont. Office Pub. Instrn., Helena, 1992—, pub., founder newsletter The Loading Zone, 1989—; cons. on pupil transp. Wyo. Dept. Edn., Cheyenne, 1987-91; instr. Wyo.-Mont. Safety Coun., Cheyenne, 1991—. Mem. Nat. Assn. State Dirs. Pupil Transp. Svcs. (cons. spl. edn. com. 1991—), Nat. Assn. for Pupil Transp., Mont. Assn. for Pupil Transp., Mont. Operation Lifesaver. Office: Mont Office Pub Instrn State Capitol Helena MT 59620

HUFF, KENNETH O., oilfield executive, geologist; b. Daleville, Ind., Dec. 17, 1926; s. George Byron and Mary Ethel (Smith) H.; m. Donna Mae Zimmerschied, Mar. 25, 1957; children—John, Robert, Donald, Patricia. Student Purdue U., 1944-45, Ball State U., 1947-48; B.S. in Geology, Ind. U., 1956. Well logging engr. Core Labs., Inc., Williston, N.D. and Farmington, N.Mex., 1956-64, lab. mgr., sales engr. Farmington and Casper, Wyo., 1964-67, supr. Rocky Mountain dist., Casper, 1967-69, cons. geologist, 1969-72; pres. cons. geologist Adventures, Inc., Casper, 1972—; mem. dist. export council U.S. Dept Commerce, Wyo., 1977-83. Patentee in field. Served as sgt. U.S. Army, 1944-46, 50-51; Korea. Mem. Soc. Petroleum Engrs., Am. Assn. Petroleum Geologists, Wyo. Geol. Assn. Republican. Club: Petroleum (Casper). Home: 1106 Payne Ave Casper WY 82609-2639 Office: Adventures Inc 535 N Lennox St Casper WY 82601-2144

HUFF, MARILYN L., district judge; b. 1951. BA, Calvin Coll., Grand Rapids, Mich., 1972; JD, U. Mich., 1976. Assoc. Gray, Cary, Ames & Frye, 1976-83, ptnr., 1983-91; judge U.S. Dist. Ct. (so. dist.) Calif., San Diego, 1991—. Contbr. articles to profl. jours. Mem. adv. coun. Calif. LWV, 1987—, Am. Lung Assn.; bd. dirs. San Diego and Imperial Counties, 1989—; mem. LaJolla Presbyn. Ch. Named Legal Profl. of Yr. San Diego City Club and Jr. C. of C., 1990; recipient Superior Ct. Valuable Svc. award, 1982. Mem. ABA, San Diego Bar Found., San Diego Bar Assn. (bd. dirs. 1986-88, v.p. 1988, chmn. profl. edn. com. 1990, Svc. award to legal profession, 1989, Lawyer of Yr. 1990), Calif. State Bar Assn., Calif. Women Lawyers, Am. Bd. Trial Advs., Libel Def. Resource Ctr., Am. Inns of Ct. (master 1987—, exec. com. 1989—), Lawyers' Club San Diego (adv. bd. 1989-90, Belva Lockwood Svc. award 1987), Univ. Club, Aardvarks Lt. Office: US Dist Ct US Courthouse 940 Front St San Diego CA 92189-0010

HUFF, RICKY WAYNE, sales executive; b. Willits, Calif., Sept. 30, 1953; s. Walter Richard and Janine Norma (Iles) H.; m. Donna Elizabeth Todd, Sept. 17, 1977; children: Brianne Ashley, Kendra Danielle. AA, Santa Rosa (Calif.) Jr. Coll., 1973; BA, Chico (Calif.) State U., 1975. Swim instr., lifeguard Chico YMCA, 1973; mall maintenance Chico Plz., 1973-74; warehouseman Stihl. Co., Chico, 1974-75; delivery driver Downey (Calif.) Unified Sch. Dist., 1975-76; regional mgmt. trainee Montgomery Ward, Norwalk, Calif., 1976-78; sr. sales rep. Fisher-Price Toys, East Aurora, N.Y., 1978-86; key account rep. Rubbermaid, Wooster, Ohio, 1986-87; dir. of sales Century Products Co., Macedonia, Ohio, 1987—. Author: (handbook) Contract Services, Retail Service Program, 1986, Independent Sales Force Sales Manual, 1989. Vol. YMCA, Downey, 1977-86, campainer, 1986, wampom bearer YMCA Indian Princesses, Downey, 1992—; bd. dirs. First Presbyn. Ch., Downey, 1987-89. Mem. Western Toy and Hobby Reps Assn., Downey DeMolay (adv. 1976-78), Willits DeMolay (master councilor 1970-71). Republican. Presbyterian. Home: 8120 Pageant St Downey CA 90240 Office: Century Products Co 3166 E Slauson Ave Vernon CA 90058

HUFF, WELCOME REX ANTHONY, chemical researcher; b. Indpls., Mar. 26, 1967; s. Welcome Charles and Judith Kathleen (Payton) H. BS in Chemistry with honors, Ind. U., 1989. Undergrad. researcher G.E. Ewing Group, Ind. U., Bloomington, 1988-89; grad. researcher D.A. Shirley Group, U. Calif., Berkeley, 1989—. Fundraiser Multiple Sclerosis Soc., Monterey, Calif., 1990. H.G. Day Summer Rsch. scholar Ind. U. Chemistry Dept., 1988, H.G. Day Acad. Yr. Rsch. scholar Ind. U. Chemistry Dept., 1988. Mem. AAAS, NRA, Am. Chem. Soc., Am. Phys. Soc., Internat. Platform Assn., Alpha Chi Sigma. Home: 25 Neva Ct Oakland CA 94611 Office: Lawrence Berkeley Lab MS 2-300 1 Cyclotron Rd Berkeley CA 94720

HUFFINGTON, MICHAEL, congressman; b. Dallas, 1947; s. Roy M. Huffington; m. Arianna; 2 children. BS in Engring., Stanford U., BA in Econs.; MBA in Fin., Harvard U. Chmn. Crest Films, Santa Barbara, Calif.; vice chmn. Roy M. Huffington, Inc.; dep. asst. Sec. of Def. for Negotiations Policy, 1986-87; mem. 103rd Congress from 22d Calif. dist., 1993—. Bd. overseers L.A. Music Ctr.; bd. trustees U. Calif. Santa Barbara Found.; bd. dirs. Santa Barbara Zoological Found. Republican. Office: US House of Representatives Washington DC 20515

HUFFMAN, ARLIE CURTIS, JR., geologist; b. Washington, Dec. 26, 1942; s. Arlie Curtis and Margret Hope (Bailie) H.; m. Susan Leslie Keen, June 26, 1965; children: Arlie Curtis III, Melinda Mary. BS, Va. Poly. Inst. and State U., 1965; MS, George Washington U., 1971, PhD, 1974. Geologist US Geol. Survey, Denver, 1974—, sect. leader, 1981, assoc. br. chief, 1981-84, sect. leader, basin coord., 1989—; adj. prof. Colo. State U., Ft. Collins, 1983-85. Contbr. sci. articles to profl. publs. Den Leader Cub Scouts Am., Lakewood, Colo., 1976-77; mem. adminstrv. bd. Applewood Valley United Meth. Ch., Lakewood, 1976-80; v.p. Ops. Applewood Athletic Club, 1992—; treas. Denver Pick and Hammer Inc., 1992—. Capt. USAF, 1965-69. Mem. Am. Assn. of Petroleum Geologists, Soc. Econ. Paleontologists and Mineralogists, Internat. Assn. Sedimentologists, Colo. Sci. Soc., Four Corners Geol. Soc. Methodist. Office: US Geol Survey MS-939 Box 25046 DFC Denver CO 80225

HUFFMAN, EDGAR JOSEPH, oil company executive; b. Hartford City, Ind., Aug. 24, 1939; s. Floyd Edgar and Elizabeth Jean (Rawlings) H.; m. Margaret Mary Brenet, May 3, 1980; children: Donovan L. Walker, Maryanne Ramirez. BBA, Ind. Cen. U., 1961; MA, NYU, 1968. V.p. corp. profitability Valley Nat. Bank, Phoenix, 1978-82, v.p. corp. planning, 1982-85; v.p., chief exec. officer Visa Industries Ariz., Phoenix, 1985—; chmn. bd. dirs. Montessori Day Schs., Inc., Phoenix, 1981; bd. dirs. FCS Labs., Inc., Phoenix, Basic Earth Scis., Calpcco III. Office: Visa Industries Ariz 9215 N 14th St Phoenix AZ 85020-2713

HUFFMAN, LINDA RAE, artist, instructor; b. Pitts., Mar. 5, 1946; d. Raymond Charles and Elizabeth Rose (Kress) Miller; m. James Joseph Short, July 4, 1964 (div. 1978); children:Janine Marie, James Raymond; m. Charles Daryl Huffman, Feb. 14, 1987. Grad. high sch., Chgo. Pvt. oil painting instr. San Diego, 1975-80, Spokane, Wash., 1980-86, Seattle, 1986—. Exhibited in group shows at Simic Galleries, Calif., Queen Elizabeth II Gallery and Mus. Home: 5014 S 3rd Ave Everett WA 98203

HUFFMAN, NONA GAY, financial consultant, retirement planning specialist; b. Albuquerque, June 22, 1942; d. William Abraham and Opal Irene (Leaton) Crisp; m. Donald Clyde Williams, Oct. 20, 1961; children: Debra Gaylene, James Donald. Student pub. schs. Lawndale, Calif. Lic. ins., securities dealer, N.Mex. Sec. City of L.A., 1960, L.A. City Schs. 1960-62, Aerospace Corp., El Segundo, Calif., 1962-64, Albuquerque Pub. Schs., 1972-73, Pub. Service Co. N.Mex., Albuquerque, 1973; rep., fin. planner Waddell & Reed, Inc., Albuquerque, 1979-84; broker Rauscher Pierce Refsnes, Inc., 1984-85; rep., investment and retirement specialist Fin. Network Investment Corp., 1985-89, John Hancock Fin. Svcs., 1989-90; account exec. Eppler, Guerin & Turner, Inc., 1990-91, Fin. Network Investment Corp., Albuquerque, 1991—; instr. on-site corp. training in fin. strategies for retirement, instr. fin. strategies for successful retirement U. N.Mex. Continuing Edn. Mem. Profl. Orgn. Women (co-chmn.), Women in Bus. (Albuquerque chpt.), Internat. Assn. Fin. Planners. Office: Fin Network Investment Corp 8500 Menaul Blvd NE # 195B Albuquerque NM 87112-2298

HUFFNAGLE, NORMAN PARMLEY, physicist; b. Honolulu, Dec. 26, 1941; s. Norman Sylvester and Helen Louise (Parmley) H.; m. Cleda May Walker, June 7, 1980; children: Mitchell Walker, Norman Walker, Donley Walker Jr., Kent Norman, Craig Benjamin, Christian Thomas. BA, Drake U., 1963; MS in Sci. Edn., U. Nebr., 1969. Physicist Mine Def. Lab. USN, Panama City, Fla., 1963-66; mem. tech. staff Hughes Aircraft, Canoga Park, Calif., 1969-72; staff engr. Martin Marietta Corp., Orlando, Calif., 1972-78; mgr. Electro-Optics Systems div. Boeing Mil. Airplane Co., Huntsville, Ala., 1978-83, sr. staff engr. Honeywell Def. Systems div., 1983-85; sect. head Honeywell Precision Weapons div., 1985-87; mgr. advanced concepts Northrop Electro-Mech. Div., Anaheim, Calif., 1987-89; mgr. advanced systems & software requirements Northrop Electronics Systems Div., Hawthorne, Calif., 1989—, mgr. system requirements and modelling, 1990-91, dep. dir. BAT systems engring., 1991-92, mgr. test equipment requirements, 1992—; dir. Village Green Lighting Dist. Contbr. articles to profl. publs. including IEEE Jour., Acoustical Soc. of Am., and USN Auto Testcon; holder 7 patents in sonar, electronics, lasers, fuzing, signal processing, and fiber optics control systems. Mem. Acoustical Soc. Am., Soc. Auto. Test Engring., Martin Marietta Mgmt. Club, Boeing Mil. Airplane Co. Mgmt. Club, Honeywell Mgmt. Club, Sigma Xi. Republican.

HUG, PROCTER RALPH, JR., federal judge; b. Reno, Mar. 11, 1931; s. Procter Ralph and Margaret (Beverly) H.; m. Barbara Van Meter, Apr. 4, 1954; children: Cheryl Ann, Procter James, Elyse Marie. B.S., U. Nev., 1953; LL.B., J.D., Stanford U., 1958. Bar: Nev. 1958. With firm Springer, McKissick & Hug, 1958-63, Woodburn, Wedge, Blakey, Folsom & Hug, Reno, 1963-77; U.S. judge 9th Circuit Ct. Appeals, Reno, 1977—; chmn. 9th Cir. Edn. Com., 1984-89, long range planning com., 1992—; chmn. Nev. State Bar Com. on Jury Inst.; dep. atty. gen., State of Nev.; v.p., dir. Nev. Tel. & Tel. Co., 1958-77. V.p. Young Democrats Nev., 1960-61; chmn. bd. regents U. Nev.; bd. visitors Stanford Law Sch.; mem. Nev. Humanities Commn., 1988—; vol. civilian aid sect. U.S. Army, 1977. Served to lt. USNR, 1953-55. Recipient Outstanding Alumnus award U. Nev., 1967, Disting. Nevadan citation, 1982; named Alumnus of Yr. U. Nev., 1988. Mem. ABA (bd. govs. 1976-78), Am. Judicare Soc. (bd. dirs. 1975-77), Nat. Judicial Coll. (bd. dirs. 1977-78), Nat. Assn. Coll. and Univ. Attys. (past mem. exec. bd.), U. Nev. Alumni Assn. (past pres.), Stanford Law Soc. Nev. (pres.). Office: US Ct Appeals 9th Cir 50 W Liberty St Ste 600 Reno NV 89501-2495

HUGGINS, JOHN JOSEPH, development consultant; b. Incapuquio, Peru, Mar. 15, 1958; came to U.S. 1960; s. William Edward and Jo Ann (Jones) H.; m. Diane L. Skufca, July 3, 1983; children: William James, Robert Parshall. BA, U. Chgo., 1980; M.Pub. Policy, Harvard U., 1985. Chief staff Boston Redevel. Authority, 1985-88; dep. dir. Transit Constrn. Authority, Denver, 1988-89; devel. cons. Denver, 1989-92; dir.mayor's office econ. devel. City of Denver, 1992—. Contbr. articles to profl. jours. Treas. Colo. Dem. Leadership Coun., Denver, 1990. Recipient John F. Kennedy Pub. Svc. award, Boston Redevel. Authority, 1987. Mem. Urban Land Inst. (full). Democrat. Home: 2229 Bellaire St Denver CO 80207-3723

HUGH, GEORGE M., pipeline company executive. COO TransCan. Pipelines Ltd., Calgary, Alta.; bd. dirs. Great Lakes Gas Transmission Co., Detroit, Trans. Que. and Maritimes, Montreal, Foothills Pipeline, Calgary, Alberta Nat. Gas, Calgary. Office: TransCan Pipelines Ltd, PO Box 1000 Sta M, Calgary, AB Canada T2P 4K5 also: 111 -5th Ave SW, Calgary, AB Canada T2P 3Y6

HUGHES, ALLAN BEBOUT, chamber of commerce executive; b. Boston, June 30, 1924; s. Edwin Holt and Gladys B. (Bebout) H.; m. Margery H. Hall, Dec. 27, 1947; children: Katherine, Lee Ann, Melinda, Sally. BA, Depauw U., 1947. Commd. USMCR, 1942, advanced through grades to col., 1970; ret. USMC, 1984; sales rep. ADT Co., Los Angeles, 1954-64; sales mgr. Ernest Paper Co., Los Angeles, 1964-68; mdse. mgr. BM&T Paper Co., Los Angeles, 1968-70; pres. Hughes Paper Co., Anaheim, Calif., 1970-82, Transpark, Inc., Anaheim, 1982-84; exec. dir. C. of C., Anaheim, from 1984. Past pres. Federated C. of C. of Orange County, 1988-91; chmn. bd. Anaheim Meml. Hosp., Calif. Angels Adv. Bd. Home: 18661 Eunice Pl Tustin CA 92680-2441 Office: care Anaheim C of C 100 S Anaheim Blvd Ste 300 Anaheim CA 92805-3899

HUGHES, AUTHOR E., university president, association executive; b. Hoopeston, Ill., Nov. 4, 1929; s. Author Ernest and Nora (Clevel) H.; m. Marjorie Ann Herman, Aug. 21, 1956; children: James Gregory, Timothy Charles, John Andrew, Susan Marie. BS, Ea. Ill. U., 1951; MA, No. Colo. U., 1954; PhD, U. Iowa, 1960; PhD (honorary), Chapman U. High sch. bus. tchr., 1951-54, coll. bus. tchr., 1954-66; dean No. Ariz. U. Coll. Bus., Flagstaff, 1966-69; v.p., provost No. Ariz. U. Coll. Bus., 1969-71; pres. U. San Diego, 1971—; chmn. Nat. Assn. Ind. Colls. and Univs., 1991-92. Co-author: Automated Data Processing, 1969. Bd. dirs. United Way, Am. Cancer Soc., 1985—; mem. Pres.'s Commn. on White House Fellowships. Recipient Regional Brotherhood award NCCJ, Internat. Citizen award World Affairs Coun. San Diego, 1992; named Outstanding Citizen Catholic Community Svcs. Mem. Nat. Assn. Ind. Colls. and Univs. (past chmn.), Assn. Cath. Colls. and Univs. (chair bd. dirs.), Assn. Calif. Ind. Colls. and Univs., San Diego C. of C., Knights of Holy Sepulchre, Beta Gamma Sigma, Delta Pi Epsilon, Delta Sigma Pi. Office: U San Diego Casa de Alcala San Diego CA 92110

HUGHES, BRADLEY RICHARD, marketing executive; b. Detroit, Oct. 8, 1954; s. John Arthur and Nancy Irene (Middleton) H.; m. Linda McCants, Feb. 14, 1977; children: Bradley Richard Jr., Brian Jeffrey. AA, Oakland Coll., 1974; BS in Bus., U. Colo., 1978, BJ, 1979, MBA in Fin. and Mktg., 1981, MS in Telecommunications, 1990. Cert. Office Automation Profl. Buyer Joslins Co., Denver, 1979; mktg. adminstr. Mountain Bell, Denver, 1980-82; ch. cons. AT&T Info. Systems, mktg. exec. AT&T, Denver, 1983-86, acct. exec., 1986-87; mktg. mgr. U.S. West, Denver, 1987—. Bd. dirs. Brandychase Assn.; state del., committeeman Republican Party Colo. Mem. IEEE, Assn. MBA Execs., U.S. Chess Fedn., Internat. Platform Assn., Mensa, Intertel, Assn. Telecommunications Profls., Am. Mgmt. Assn., Am. Mktg. Assn., Info. Industry Assn., Office Automation Soc. Internat., World Future Soc., Triple Nine Soc., Internat. Soc. Philos. Inquiry, Assn. Computing Machinery. Republican. Methodist. Home: 5759 S Jericho Way Aurora CO 80015 Office: US West 1801 California # 1930 Denver CO 80202

HUGHES, C. GETHIN B., bishop. Bishop Diocese of San Diego, 1992—. Office: Diocese of San Diego 2728 6th Ave San Diego CA 92103-6397*

HUGHES, CHARLES WILSON, retired army officer, consultant, purchasing director; b. Greenville, Ky., May 3, 1946; s. Clifton J. and Christine Vive (Critzer) H.; m. Daniele Kay Martin, Oct. 6, 1973; children: Charles William, Jennifer Jill. BS, U. Tenn., Martin, 1967; JD, U. Tenn., Knoxville, 1971. Bar: Tenn. 1971. Commd. 2d lt. U.S. Army, 1971, advanced through grades to maj., 1981; contract officer Rock Island (Ill.) Arsenal, 1971-73; logistics officer Pusan (Republic of Korea) Garrison, 1973-76; chief contracts Def. Contract Office, Woodland Hills, Calif., 1976-80, Def. Contract Adminstrn., El Segundo, Calif., 1986-89; dir. indsl. ops. Würzburg (Fed. Republic Germany) Mil. Command, 1980-83; chief ops., program mgr. Tank Systems, Warren, Mich., 1983-86; logistics officer 63d Army Res. Command, Los Alamitos, Calif., 1989-92; pres. Hughes Assocs., Garden Grove, Calif., 1991—; dir. purchasing Calif. State U., Long Beach, 1992—; cons. DCAS Computer, Garden Grove, 1988-92, USAR, Los Alamitos, 1991-92; special lectr., Calif. State U., 1992—. Editor: Collection of Poems, 1976; also articles. Sr. advisor Jr. Achievement, L.A., 1971-81; scoutmaster troop 147, Boy Scouts Am., 1987-93, dist. commr. Orange County coun., 1988-90. Recipient achievement award Jr. Achievement, Costa Mesa, Calif., 1981; award of merit, Silver Beaver award Boy Scouts Am., 1989, Disting. Scouter award, 1991. Fellow Marne Assn. (recorder 1981-82, Marne Man award 1982); mem. Assn. U.S. Army (sec. 1981-82, svc. award 1982), Ret. Officers Assn., Nat. Contract Mgmt. Assn. (v.p. 1977-78, svc. award 1979), DCAS Computer Users Group (pres. 1986-88, svc. award 1988), Masons, Knights of Malta. Republican. Baptist. Home: 10072 Roselee Dr Garden Grove CA 92640-1826 Office: Calif State U Long Beach Purchasing & Support Svcs 1250 Bellflower Blvd Long Beach CA 90840-0123

HUGHES, DONALD LEWELLYN, insurance broker; b. Cheyenne, Wyo., Apr. 11, 1957; s. Jack D. and Phyllis L. (Rizzuto) H.; m. Glenda Kay Webber, Feb. 14, 1980; children: Nathan John, Bryana Mae. Student, U. Wyo., 1975-76, Brigham Young U., 1976, 79, Laramie County Coll., 1979-80, Am. Coll., Bryn Mawr, Pa., 1988—. Asst. mgr. AT&T, Cheyenne, Wyo., 1979-82; field underwriter N.Y. Life, Cheyenne, 1982-85; employee benefits mgr. Ed Murray & Sons, Inc., Cheyenne, 1985—; seminar instr. Ed Murray & Sons, Cheyenne. Bd. dirs. Meals on Wheels, Cheyenne, 1987-89; mem. Lions. Internat., Cheyenne, 1980-85; elders quorum pres. Ch. of Jesus Christ of Latter-Day Saints, Cheyenne, 1985—, choir dir., 1985—, missionary, Bangkok, Thailand, 1976-78. Full Music scholar U. Wyo., 1975. Mem. Wyo. Life Underwriters (bd. dirs. 1987—, legis. 1987—, lobbyist state legis. 1989). Republican. Office: Ed Murray and Sons PO Box 1388 Cheyenne WY 82003-1388

HUGHES, EDWARD JOHN, religious studies educator; b. N.Y.C., May 15, 1944; s. John Howard and Mary (Chiswell) H.; m. Mary Frances Gozik, Nov. 25, 1972; 1 child, Sean Michael. BA, Manhattan Coll., 1965; MDiv, Pitts. Theol. Sem., 1978; MA in History of Religions, Claremont Grad. Sch., 1981, PhD in History and Philosophy of Religions, 1984. Asst. prof. Muskingum Coll., New Concord, Ohio, 1982-83; instr. Calif. State U., Long Beach, 1984-86, 88-89, asst prof., 1989—; asst. prof. Calif. State U., Chico, 1986-87; asst prof. La Verne (Calif.) U., 1987-88. Author: Wilfred Cantwell Smith: A Theology for the World, 1986; editor: Paths of Faith, 1991. Clara Ibrig Linhardt fellow Claremont Grad. Sch., 1982, Timken-Sturgis fellow, 1980, Thomas Jamison fellow Pitts. Theol. Sem., 1978; named Tchr. of Yr. The Youth Learning Ctr., 1973. Mem. Am. Acad. Religion, Woodrow Wilson Nat. Found. (award 1965), Soc. for Values in Higher Edn. Office: Calif State Univ Dept Religious Studies Long Beach CA 90840

HUGHES, EDWARD JOHN, artist; b. North Vancouver, B.C., Feb. 17, 1913; s. Edward Samuel Daniell and Katherine Mary (McLean) H.; m. Fern Rosabell Irvine Smith, Feb. 10, 1940 (dec. 1974). Grad., Vancouver Sch. Art, 1933. Exhbns. include retrospective, Vancouver Art Gallery, 1967, Surrey Art Gallery, Art Gallery of Greater Victoria, Edmonton Art Gallery, Calgary Glenbow Gallery, 1983-85, Nat. Gallery Can., Beaverbrook Gallery, Fredericton, 1983-85; represented in permanent collections, Nat. Gallery Can., Ottawa, Art Gallery Ont., Toronto, Vancouver Art Gallery, Montreal Mus. Fine Art, Greater Victoria Art Gallery; ofcl. Army war artist, 1942-46. Served with Can. Army, 1939-46. Recipient Can. Council grants, 1958, 63, 67, 70. Mem. Royal Can. Acad. Arts. Presbyterian. Address: 2449 Heather St, Duncan, BC Canada V9L 2Z6

HUGHES, EUGENE MORGAN, university president; b. Scottsbluff, Nebr., Apr. 3, 1934; s. Ruby Melvin and Hazel Marie (Griffith) H.; m. Margaret Ann Romeo; children: Deborah Kaye, Greg Eugene, Lisa Ann, Jeff, Mark, Christi. Diploma, Neb. Western Coll., 1954; BS in Math. magna cum laude, Chadron State Coll., 1956; MS in Math., Kans. State U., 1958; PhD in Math., George Peabody Coll. for Tchrs., Vanderbilt U., 1968. Grad. asst. dept. math. Kans. State U., Manhattan, 1956-57; instr. math. Nebr. State Tchrs. Coll. at Chadron, 1957-58; asst. prof. math., head dept. Chadron State Coll., 1958-66, assoc. prof., 1966-69, prof. math., 1969-70, dir. rsch., 1965-66, asst. to the pres., 1966-68, dean adminstrn., 1968-70; grad. asst. dept. math. George Peabody Coll. for Tchrs., Nashville, 1962-63, 64-65; asst. to undergrad. dean George Peabody Coll. for Tchrs., 1964, asst. to pres., 1964-65; instr. Peabody Demonstration Sch., 1963-64; prof. math. No. Ariz. U., Flagstaff, 1970-93; dean No. Ariz. U. (Coll. Arts and Scis.), 1970-71, provost univ. arts and sci. edn., 1971-72, acad. v.p., 1972-79, pres., 1979-93, pres. emeritus, 1993—; pres. Wichita State U., 1993—; cons. Nebr. Dept. Edn., 1966-70; mem. adv. bd. United Bank Ariz., 1980-82; mem. nat. adv. bd. Ctr. for Study of Sport in Society, 1990; bd. dirs. Ariz. Bank; mem. adv. bd. Bank IV; mem. Christopher Columbus Quincentenary Commn., 1990—. Mem. staff bd. trustees Nebr. State Colls., Lincoln, 1969-70; co-dir. workshop tchr. edn. North Cen. Assn. U. Minn., 1968-70; officer fed. ednl. programs, Nebr., Ariz., 1966—; mem. Ariz. Commn. Postsecondary Edn.; bd. fellows Am. Grad. Sch. Internat. Mgmt., 1980-93; mem. Gov.'s Com. Quality Edn., Chadron Housing Authority, 1968-70, Pres.' Commn. NCAA; pres. bd. dirs. Ariz. State Bd. Edn., 1991, Flagstaff Summer Festival, Ariz. Coun. Humanities and Pub. Policy, Mus. No. Ariz., Grand Canyon coun, Boy Scouts Am.; chair Ariz. Leadership Adv. Coun., 1990-93; mem. Ariz. Town Hall, 1991; commr. Western Interstate Commn. for Higher Edn., 1992-93; mem. Gov.'s Strategic Partnership for Econ. Devel., 1992. Recipient Chief Manuelito award Navajo Tribe, 1976, Disting. Service award Chadron State Coll., 1982, Flagstaff Citizen of Yr., 1988, Disting. Math. Grad. award Kans. State U., 1990; named Hon. Chmn. Black Bd. Dirs., 1989; Ariz. Acad. NSF fellow, 1963, 64. Mem. NEA, Am. Assn. State Colls.and Univs. (past chmn. & mem. com. on grad. studies 1979—, bd. dirs., mem. com. on accreditation, 1980—), Math. Assn. Am. (vis. lectr. secondary schs. Western Nebr. 1962), Ariz. Edn. Assn., North Cen. Assn. Colls. and Secondary Schs. (coord. 1968-72, cons./evaluator 1977—), Nat. Coun. Tchrs. of Math., Flagstaff C. of C., Blue Key, Masons, Elks, Rotary (past pres.), Pi Mu Epsilon, Phi Delta Kappa, Kappa Mu Epsilon, Phi Kappa Phi.

HUGHES, GLENN VERNON, international relations consultant; b. L.A., June 18, 1927; s. Charles LaSalle Hughes and Elsie Agnes (Redman) Hammel; m. Yolanda Corina Morris, Dec. 3, 1960 (div. 1986); children: Glenn III, Sean, Geoffrey, Jennifer. Student, Compton Coll., 1947-48; cert., UCLA, 1970. Profl. designation in pub. rels. Dir. entertainment U.S. Army, Camp Beale, Calif., 1945-47; dir. talent Paramount TV Prodns., L.A., 1949-55; dir. entertainment Hawaiian Village Hotel, Honolulu, 1960-64; coord. spl. events Port of L.A., 1965-70; dir. govt. and community rels. Worldport LA, L.A., 1970-86; pvt. practice internat. rels. cons. L.A., 1986—; cons. Worldport LA, 1986-91, Port of Long Beach, 1992; exec. dir. City of L.A. Sister City Program, 1989—. Author, editor: World In-Sight, 1991; contbr. articles to profl. jours., mags., newspapers. Pres. Seaman's Ctr., L.A., 1975-76; chmn. 32nd Dist. Congl. Youth Award Com., 1985-90, L.A.-Jakarta Sister City, L.A., 1992-93; bd. dirs. Am. Merchant Marine Meml., San Pedro, Calif., 1985. With U.S. Army, 1945-47. Mem. Inst. Noetic Science, Sister Cities Internat., Am. Buddhist Congress, L.A.-Guangzhou China Sister City Assn., Joseph Campbell Libr. Assn., Propeller Club of L.A.-Long Beach (chmn.). Home and Office: 473 Cherry Hills Ln Thousand Oaks CA 91320

HUGHES, JAMES ARTHUR, electrical engineer; b. Wayne, Nebr., Feb. 15, 1939; s. James Wallace and Ruth Genevieve H.; m. Judy Lorraine Gaskins, July 18, 1967; children: Robert Linn, Benjamin Reed, Barnaby James. BSEE, U. Nebr., 1967. Electronic technician, space tech. labs. TRW, Redondo Beach, Calif., 1963-67; mem. tech. staff systems group TRW, 1967-80, sect. mgr. electronics and def. div., 1980-82, systems engr. space and tech. group, 1982--. Designer solid state thermostat, pn generator. Deacon First Bapt. Ch. Lakewood, Long Beach, Calif., 1975-76, 78-80, 87-89; mem. exec. bd. parent-tchr. fellowship, Grace Sch., Rossmoor, Calif., 1981-87. With USN, 1959-63. Mem. AAAS, IEEE, Nat. Soc. Profl. Engrs. Republican. Office: TRW Space and Def One Space Pk S/1869 Redondo Beach CA 90278

HUGHES, JOHN HAROLD, surgeon, educator; b. New Rochelle, N.Y., Feb. 17, 1936; s. Harold Tegai and Ida (Erickson) H.; m. Janet Gail Williams, Mar. 7, 1964; children: Stephen A.T., Megan Elizabeth, John E.Q. BA, Yale U., 1957; MD, Cornell U., 1961. Diplomate Am. Bd. Surgery. Intern in surgery St. Luke's Hosp., N.Y.C., 1961-62, resident in surgery, 1962-66; chief of surgery Ft. Benjamin Harrison, Indpls., 1966-67; surgeon Hardin Meml. Hosp., Kenton, Ohio, 1968-74; asst. prof., dir. clinics Med. Coll. Ohio, Toledo, 1974-77; assoc. prof., dir. emergency svcs. U. Ariz., Tucson, 1977-81; surgeon, prof. surgery Naval Hosp. Long Beach, Calif., 1982-85; surgenprof. surgery Naval Hosp. Oak Knoll, Oakland, Calif., 1990-91; med. dir. Casa Grande (Ariz.) Clinic, 1992-93; pvt. practice Casa Grande, Ariz., 1993—; clin. instr. surgery Columbia U., N.Y.C., 1965-66; clin. lectr. U. Ariz., Tucson, 1981—; clin. prof. surgery U. Health Scis., Bethesda, 1990. Contbr. over 65 articles to profl. jours.; editor emergency medicine jour. Hosp. Medicine, 1979—; editorial reviewer jour. Mil. Medicine, 1987—; book reviewer jour. Profl. Safety, 1981—. Commr. health Hardin County, Ohio, 1969-74; pres. Hardin County Med. Soc., Kenton, Ohio, 1973-74. Capt. USNR, 1982—. Grantee Nat. Cancer Inst., 1976, NIMH, 1979. Fellow ACS; mem. Assn. Mil. Surgeons, Pima County Med. Soc., Tucson Surgical Soc., Sigma Xi. Presbyterian. Home: 7712 E Oakwood Cir Tucson AZ 85715-2338 Office: 210 W Florence Blvd Casa Grande AZ 85222

HUGHES, JUDITH MARKHAM, history educator; b. N.Y.C., Feb. 20, 1941; d. Sanford H. and Sylvia (Kovner) Markham; m. H. Stuart Hughes, Mar. 26, 1964; 1 child, David. BA with high honors, Swarthmore Coll., 1962; MA, Harvard U., 1963, PhD, 1970. Teaching fellow Harvard U., Cambridge, Mass., 1965-66, 67-70, asst. prof. social studies, 1970-75; assoc. prof. history U. Calif., San Diego, 1975-84, prof. history, 1984—. Editorial bd. Diplomatic History, 1976-78, The Psychohistory Review, 1993—; author: To the Maginot Line: The Politics of French Military Preparation in the 1920s, 1971, Emotion and High Politics: Personal Relations at the Summit in Late Nineteenth-Century Britain and Germany, 1983, Reshaping the Psychoanalytic Domain: The Work of Melanie Klein, W.R.D. Fairbairn, and D.W. Winnicott, 1989; contbr. articles, book revs. to scholarly publs. Woodrow Wilson Found. fellow, 1962-63, Nat. Endowment Humanities fellow, 1974. Mem. Am. Hist. Assn., N.Am. Conf. Brit. Studies, Group for Use of Psychology in History, Assn. Internat. Histoire de la Psychanalyse, Western Assn. Women Historians (article prize com. 1985), Phi Beta Kappa. Office: Dept History 0104 9500 Gilman Dr U Calif San Diego La Jolla CA 92093-0104

HUGHES, LINDA J., newspaper publisher; b. Princeton, B.C., Can., Sept. 27, 1950; d. Edward Rees and Madge Preston (Bryan) H.; m. George Fredrick Ward, Dec. 16, 1978; children: Sean Ward, Kate Ward. BA, U. Victoria (B.C.), 1972. With Edmonton Jour., Alta., Can., 1976—, from reporter to asst. mng. editor, 1984-87, editor, 1987-92, pub., 1992—. Southam fellow U. Toronto, Ont., Can., 1977-78. Office: Edmonton Journal, 10006 101st StPO Box 2421, Edmonton, AB Canada T5J 2S6

HUGHES, LOYD RAY, college provost, educator; b. Portales, N. Mex., July 9, 1940; s. Arnel Daniel and Fannie Pearl (Jackson) H.; m. Rita M. Smith, Aug. 20, 1965; children—Shawn, Ladawn, Kevin. Student Eastern N.Mex. U., 1959-61; BS, N.Mex. State U., 1963, MA, 1966; EdD, U. Ill.-Urbana, 1968. Dir. career edn. Yavapai Coll., Prescott, Ariz., 1968-73; dean instrn. Vernon Regional Jr. Coll., Tex., 1973-80; provost Eastern N.Mex. U., Roswell, 1980—. Author: (report) The Area Vocational School, 1966; Ornamental Horticulture, 1968. Contbr. articles to profl. jours. Bd. dirs. Faith Christian Day Sch., Vernon, 1975-77, AWARE-N.Mex., 1984-85; trustee Working Mothers' Day Nursery, 1983-84; campaign vice chair Chaves County United Way, 1990-91; bd. dirs. Counseling Assocs., Roswell, 1989—, Ptnrs.-in-Edn., 1989—. Mem. Tex. Assn. Jr. Coll. Instrs. and Adminstrs., Am. Assn. Higher Edn., Am. Assn. Community and Jr. Colls., N.Mex. Assn. Community and Jr. Colls., Roswell C. of C., Roswell Hispano C. of C., Phi Delta Kappa. Mem. Ch. of Christ. Lodges: Rotary, Elks. Avocations: automotive restoration, handyman.

HUGHES, MARGARET EILEEN, law educator, former dean; b. Saskatoon, Sask., Can., Jan. 22, 1943; d. E. Duncan and Eileen (Shaver) Farmer; m. James Roscoe Hughes, May 21, 1966; children: Shannon Margaret, Krista Lynn. BA, U. Sask., 1965, LLB, 1966; LLM, U. Mich., 1968, MSW, 1968. Asst. prof. law U. Windsor, Ont., Can., 1968-71, assoc. prof. law, 1971-75; exec. interchange Dept. Justice, Ottawa, 1975-77, counsel, 1977-78; prof. law U. Sask., 1978-84; dean law U. Calgary, Alta., Can., 1984-89, prof., 1989—; faculty sr. univ. adminstrs.'s course Centre Higher Edn., R & D, Banff, Can., 1990—; bd. dirs. Indsl. Rels. Rsch. Group, 1990—. Contbr. articles to profl. jours. and chpts. to books. William Cooke fellow U. Mich. Faculty Law, 1966-68. Mem. Law Soc. Alta., Law Soc. Upper Can., Law Soc. Sask., Legal Edn. Soc. Alta. (bd. dirs. 1984-89), Law Soc. Alta. (legal edn. com. 1984-89), Can. Assn. Law Tchrs., Council Can. Law Deans (sec. 1986-87, chmn. 1987-88), Can. Inst. Resources Law (exec. com. 1984-89, bd. dirs. 1984-89), Can. Research Inst. for Law and Family (exec. com. 1986-88, bd. dirs. 1986-89). Office: U Calgary Faculty Law, 2500 University Dr NW, Calgary, AB Canada T2N 1N4

HUGHES, MARY KATHERINE, lawyer; b. Kodiak, Alaska, July 16, 1949; d. John Chamberlain and Marjorie (Anstey) H.; m. Andrew H. Eker, July 7, 1982. BBA cum laude, U. Alaska, 1971; JD, Willamette U., 1974; postgrad. Heriot-Watt U., Edinburgh, Scotland, 1971. Bar: Alaska 1975. Ptnr., Hughes, Thorsness et al, Anchorage, 1974—, mem. mgmt. com., 1991-92; trustee Alaska Bar Found., pres., 1984—; bd. visitors Willamette U., Salem, Oreg., 1980—; bd. dirs. Alaska Repertory Theatre, 1986-88, pres., 1987-88; commr. Alaska Code Revision Commn., 1987—; mem. U. Alaska Found., 1985—, trustee, 1990—; bd. dirs. Anchorage Econ. Devel. Corp., 1989—; mem. adv. bd. Providence Hosp., 1993—. Fellow Am. Bar Found.; mem. Alaska Bar Assn. (bd. govs. 1981-84, pres. 1983-84), Anchorage Assn. Women Lawyers (pres. 1976-77), AAUW, Delta Theta Phi. Republican. Roman Catholic. Club: Soroptimists (v.p. 1986-87, pres. 1986-87). Home: 2240 Kissee Ct Anchorage AK 99517-1003 Office: Hughes Thorsness Gantz Powell & Brundin 509 W 3d Ave Anchorage AK 99501

HUGHES, RICHARD DOUGLAS, military officer; b. Sacramento, Calif., Feb. 26, 1951; s. Douglas Watson and Margaret Jane (Barrett) H.; m. Cynthia Louise Schauer, Jan. 18, 1975; children: Mark Charles, Conrad Scott. BA in Internat. Rels., Calif. State U., Chico, 1976. Commd. 2d lt. USMC, 1976, advanced through grades to maj., 1988. Mem. U.S. Naval Inst., Marine Corps Assn., Marine Corps Res. Officer Assn. Roman Catholic. Office: 1st BPO Co 4th LSB 901 E Mission St San Jose CA 95112-1697

HUGHES, ROBERT LACHLAN, newspaper executive; b. Regina, Saskatchewan, Can., June 1, 1944; s. Robert Wesley and Helen Elizabeth (MacLachlan) H.; m. Barbara Elaine Barootes, June 28, 1980; children: Geoffrey Robert, Ryan Stewart Gordon. Office boy, gen. reporter, police reporter, sports reporter Regina (Sask.) Leader-Post, 1962-69; sports columnist Saskatoon (Sask.) Star-Phoenix, 1969-70, Calgary Albertan, Can., 1970-72; sports editor, columnist Regina Leader-Post, 1972-88, mng. editor, news columnist, 1988—. Recipient Can. 125 medal Govt. of Can., 1992; named to Hall of Fame Can. Football Football Reporters of Can., 1990. Mem. Can. Mng. Editors Assn. (dir. 1989—), Royal United Svcs. Inst.,

Regina Golf Club. Protestant. Office: The Leader-Post, 1964 Park St, Regina, SK Canada S4P 3G4

HUGHES, ROBERT MERRILL, control system engineer; b. Glendale, Calif., Sept. 11, 1936; s. Fred P. and Gertrude G. (Merrill) H.; AA, Pasadena City Coll., 1957; 1 child, Tammie Lynn Cobble. Engr. Aerojet Gen. Corp., Azusa, Calif., 1957-64, 66-74; pres. Automatic Electronics Corp., Sacramento, 1964-66; specialist Perkin Elmer Corp., Pomona, Calif., 1974-75; gen. mgr. Hughes Mining Inc., Covina, Calif., 1975-76; project mgr. L&A Water Treatment, City of Industry, Calif., 1976-79; dir. Hughes Industries Inc., Alta Loma, Calif., 1979—; pres. Hughes Devel. Corp., Carson City, Nev.; chmn. bd. Hughes Mining Inc., Hughes Video Corp. Registered profl. engr., Calif; lic. gen. bld. contractor. Mem. AIME, Nat. Soc. Profl. Engrs., Instrument Soc. Am., Am. Inst. Plant Engrs. Republican. Patentee in field. Home: 10009 Banyan St Alta Loma CA 91737-3603 Office: PO Box 1203 Lahaina HI 96767-1203

HUGHES, ROGER K., dairy and grocery store company executive. Chief exec. officer Hughes Markets, Los Angeles. Office: Hughes Markets 14005 Live Oaks Ave Irwindale CA 91706

HUGHES, STEVEN MICHAEL, occupational safety engineer, supervisor; b. Akron, Ohio, Apr. 27, 1955; s. John Russell and Joanne Carolyn (Lewis) H.; m. Alberta Yvonne Shetron, aug. 25, 1984 (dec. Feb. 1986); m. Jan Murray Beckman, Feb. 25, 1989; children: Stephanie Ray Hughes, Emily Cross-Hughes (stepdaughter). BA in History, U. Akron, 1977; student, U. South Dakota, 1978-81; MA in Bus. Adminstrn., Webster U., 1983; student, U. Calif. Santa Barbara, 1989. Lt., missile maintenance officer USAF, Ellsworth AFB, 1978-81; capt. USAF, McConnell AFB, 1981-86, Vandenburg AFB, 1986-88; safety and training dir. Southwestern Portland Cement, Victorville, Calif., 1989-90; supr. occupational safety Lockheed Advanced Devel. Co., Palmdale, Calif., 1990—; cons. in field. Volunteer Big Bros., Rapid City, S.D., Wichita, Kans., 1978-86; cubmaster Boy Scouts Am., Wichita, 1984-86; First Aid instr. ARC, Palmdale, 1990—. With USAF 1978-88. Recipient Air Force commendation medal USAF, Vandenberg AFB, 1986, 88. Mem. High Desert Safety Assn. (treas. 1990, pres. 1993), Am. Soc. Safety Engrs., Nat. Safety Mgmt. Soc., Air Force Assn., Nat. Mgmt. Assn. Home: 15039 Lofton St Victorville CA 92392

HUGHES, W. JAMES, optometrist; b. Shawnee, Okla., Oct. 15, 1944; s. Willis J. and Elizabeth Alice (Nimohoyah) H. B.A. in Anthropology, U. Okla., 1966, M.A. in Anthropology, 1972; O.D., U. Houston, 1976; M.P.H., U. Tex., 1977. Lic. Optometrist, Okla., Tex., W. Va. Physician's asst., Houston, Dallas, 1969-70; teaching asst. in clin. optics U. Houston, 1973-74, contact lens research asst., 1974; Wesley Jessen Contact Lens Rep., 1974-76; extern eye clinic Tuba City Indian Hosp., 1975; teaching fellow pub. health optometry U. Houston, 1975-76; Indian Health Service optometrist, Eagle Butte, S.D., 1976; optometrist vision care project Crockett Ind. Sch. Dist., 1977; vision care program dir. Bemidji Area Indian Health Service, 1977-78; optometrist Navajo Area Indian Health Service, Chinle Health Ctr., 1978-79; adj. prof. So. Calif. Coll. of Optometry, Los Angeles, U. Houston Coll. of Optometry, 1978—, So. Coll. Optometry, Memphis, 1980—; optometrist Shiprock USPHS Indian Hosp., 1979—, chief vision care program; Navajo area Indian Health Service rep. to optometry career devel. com. USPHS. Served with U.S. Army, 1966-69. Decorated Bronze Star, Purple Heart. Recipient House of Vision award 1974; Community Health Optometry award 1976; Better Vision scholar, 1973-76. Mem. Am. Pub. Health Assn., Am. Optometric Assn., Tex. Optometric Assn. Commd. Officers Soc., Assn. Am. Indian Physicians, Beta Sigma Kappa. Democrat. Roman Catholic. Contbr. articles to profl. jours.

HUGHES, WILLIAM L., hospital administrator; b. Richmond, Ky., July 23, 1952; s. Paul and Joann (Broaddus) H. BS, Ea. Ky. U., 1974, MS, 1976; MPH, Tulane U., 1985, MBA, 1985. Adminstrv. fellow Allegheny Health Svcs., Pitts., 1985; asst. v.p. Bristol Meml. Hosp., Bristol, Tenn., 1985-86; v.p. fin. and chief fin. officer The Hosp. of the Good Samaritan, L.A., 1986-92; v.p. fin., CFO U. Colo. Hosp., Denver, 1992—. Active Big Bros. of L.A., 1989-92; chmn. med. support com. Calif. Spl. Olympics, 1988-90. Capt. U.S. Army, 1976-81. Mem. Am. Hosp. Assn., Healthcare Fin. Mgmt. Assn., Am. Coll. Healthcare Execs. Republican. Episcopalian. Office: Univ Hosp A020 4200 E 9th Ave Denver CO 80262

HUGHS, MARY GERALDINE, accountant, social service specialist; b. Marshalltown, Iowa, Nov. 28, 1929; d. Don Harold, Sr., and Alice Dorothy (Keister) Shaw; A.A., Highline Community Coll., 1970; B.A., U. Wash., 1972; m. Charles G. Hughs, Jan. 31, 1949; children: Mark George, Deborah Kay, Juli Ann, Grant Wesley. Asst. controller Moduline Internat., Inc., Chehalis, Wash., 1972-73; controller Data Recall Corp., El Segundo, Calif., 1973-74; fin. adminstr., acct. Saturn Mfg. Corp., Torrance, Calif., 1974-77; sr. acct., adminstrv. asst. Van Camp Ins., San Pedro, Calif., 1977-78; asst. adminstr. Harbor Regional Ctr., Torrance, Calif., 1979-87; active bookkeeping svc., 1978—; instr. math. and acctg. South Bay Bus. Coll., 1976-77. Sec. Pacific N.W. Mycol. Soc., 1966-67; treas., bd. dirs. Harbor Employees Fed. Credit Union; mem. YMCA Club. Recipient award Am. Mgmt. Assn., 1979. Mem. Beta Alpha. Republican. Methodist. Author: Iowa Auto Dealers Assn. Title System, 1955; Harbor Regional Center Affirmative Action Plan, 1980; Harbor Regional Center - Financial Format, 1978—; Provider Audit System, 1979; Handling Client Funds, 1983. Home and Office: 18405 Haas Ave Torrance CA 90504-5405

HUIGENS, DANIEL DEAN, dentist; b. Osmond, Nebr., May 16, 1953; s. Mickey Helen (White) H.; m. Linda Sue Wilbourn, May 19, 1982 (div. 1991); 1 child, Matthew Blake. BA, U. LaVerne, 1975; BS, U. Okla., 1979, DDS with honors, 1982. EMT Community Ambulance Svc., San Dimas, Calif., 1971-74; emergency room technician San Dimas Community Hosp., San Dimas, Calif., 1974-77; physician assoc. Muskogee Bone and Joint Clinic, 1979-82; dentist Drs. Huigens and Hanawalt, LaVerne, Calif., 1986—; mem. part time staff UCLA Coll. Dentistry. Mem. ADA, Acad. Gen. Dentistry, Calif. Dental Assn., Tri County Dental Soc., Pomona Valley Amatuer Astronomers Assn., LaVerne C. of C., Omicron Kappa Upsilon. Office: Dr Dan Huigens 2450 D St La Verne CA 91750

HULL, CORDELL WILLIAM, business executive; b. Dayton, Ohio, Sept. 12, 1933; s. Murel George and Julia (Barto) H.; m. Susan G. Ruder, May 10, 1958; children: Bradford W., Pamela H., Andrew R. B.E., U. Dayton, 1956; M.S., MIT, 1957; J.D., Harvard U., 1962. Bar: Ohio 1962; Registered profl. engr., Mass. Atty. Taft, Stettinius & Hollister, Cin., 1962-64, C & I Girdler, Cin., 1964-66; gen. counsel, treas., pres. C&I Girdler, Internat., Brussels, 1966-70; v.p. Bechtel Overseas Corp., San Francisco, 1970-73; pres., dir. Am. Express Mcht. Bank, London, 1973-75; v.p., treas. Bechtel Corp. and Bechtel Power, San Francisco, 1975-80; pres. Bechtel Fin. Services, San Francisco, 1975-82; v.p., chief fin. officer Bechtel Group Inc., 1980-85; pres. Bechtel Power Corp., 1987-89; bd. dirs., mem. exec. com. Bechtel Investments Inc., Sequoia Ventures, Inc.; chmn. Bechtel Enterprises; exec. v.p. bd. dirs., mem. exec. com. Bechtel Group, Inc.; mem. svcs. policy adv. com. Office U.S. Trade Rep.; bd. dirs. SRI Internat., trustee. Trustee Dominican Coll., Com. for Econ. Devel.; bd. dirs. Atlantic Coun. U.S., Invest-In-Am.; bd. overseers Exec. Coun. on Fgn. Diplomats. Clubs: Bankers, Knickerbocker, Pacific Union, Links, San Francisco Golf, Menlo Country. Office: Bechtel Group Inc 50 Beale St PO Box 193965 San Francisco CA 94105

HULL, GREGORY STEWART, artist; b. Okmulgee, Okla., Sept. 2, 1950; s. Donald Earl and Betty Mardell (Stewart) H.; m. Graciela Irene Andres, Nov. 9, 1974; children: Elizabeth Maria, Rebekah Ann. BFA, U. Utah, 1973, MFA, 1977. Tchr. continuing edn. Salt Lake City, 1976; teaching asst. U. Utah, 1975-77; represented by Wally Findlay Galleries, Chgo., 1978—. Exhibited in group shows at Salt Lake Art Ctr., 1975 (purchase prize), Davis County Competition, Utah, 1976 (1st prize), Utah Painting and Sculpture, 1976 (best of show), Am. Artists Golden Anniversary Nat. Art Competition, 1987; commd. for numerous portraits. Mem. Plein Air Painters of Am., Met. Opera Guild, U. of Utah Alumni Assn. Home: 2725 Oakmont Dr Flagstaff AZ 86004-7429

HULL, JAN GUNNAR, international consultant; b. St. Malm, Sweden, Apr. 29, 1939; came to U.S., 1986; s. Ture Gunnar and Elly Teresia (Lagerstedt) H.; m. Karin Solveig Anita Karlson, July 12, 1960 (div. 1980); children: Jan Oscar, Sandra Karin Anita; m. Gunnel Viola Catharina Jedberger, Apr. 11, 1981 (dec. Sept. 1992). MBA, Gothenburg (Sweden) Sch., 1963. Devel. engr. Saab/Aircraft, Linköping, Sweden, 1963-65, contracts mgr., 1966-68; fin. mgr. Aerospace div. Saab-Scania, Linköping, Sweden, 1969-71; comml. dir. Europlane Ltd., Weybridge, Eng., 1972-73; mktg. mgr. Datasaab div. Saab-Scania, Linköping, 1974-77; mgr. Fin. Terminal Systems div. Datasaab, Linköping, 1978-81; mgr., pres. Saab-Fairchild, Linköping, 1981-83; v.p. corp. bus. devel. Saab-Scania, Linköping, 1983-86; pres. Hull Venture Contacts, Inc., Cupertino, Calif., 1987—; chmn. Microinvest AB, Linköping, 1989-91, Svenska MicroSystem AB, Linköping, 1989-91, Z Systems, Inc., Cupertino, 1990—. Capt. Swedish AF, 1957-63. Mem. World Forum of Silicon Valley, Swedish-Am. C. of C. (bd. dirs. 1990-92), Kiwanis Club of Palo Alto. Home and Office: 6344 South Haven Oaks Pl Salt Lake City UT 84121

HULL, JEFFERY GORDON, mortgage company executive; b. Fairfax, Va., Dec. 14, 1964; s. Homer E. and Dorothy J. Hull. BS in Mktg., San Diego State, 1987. Account mgr. Beecham Products, Irvine, Calif., 1987-89; v.p. Paramount Mortgage, San Jose, Calif., 1989—. Mem. Calif. Assn. Mortgage Brokers, San Jose Real Estate Bd. Republican. Home: 624 S 14th San Jose CA 95112

HULL, MCALLISTER HOBART, JR., retired university administrator; b. Birmingham, Ala., Sept. 1, 1923; s. McAllister Hobart and Grace (Johnson) H.; m. Mary Muska, Mar. 23, 1946; children: John McAllister, Wendy Ann. B.S. with highest honors, Yale, 1948, Ph.D. in Physics, 1951. From instr. to asso. prof. physics Yale U., 1951-66; prof. physics, chmn. dept. Oreg. State U., 1966-69; prof. physics, chmn. dept State U. N.Y. at Buffalo, 1969-72, dean Grad. Sch., 1972-74, dean. grad. and profl. edn., 1974-77; provost U. N.Mex., 1977-85, counselor to pres., 1985-88, prof. emeritus physics, 1988—; adviser to supt. schs., Hamden, Conn., 1958-65. Author papers, books, chpts. in books, articles in encys. Bd. dirs. Western N.Y. Reactor Facility, 1970-72; trustee N.E. Radio Obs. Corp., 1971-77; pres. Western Regional Sci. Labs., 1977; chmn. tech. adv. com. N.Mex. Energy Research Inst., 1981-83, mem., 1983-88; co-chmn. Nat. Task Force on Ednl. Tech., 1984-86. Served with AUS, 1943-46. Faculty fellow Yale U., 1964-65. Fellow Am. Phys. Soc.; mem. Am. Assn. Physics Tchrs. (chmn. Oreg. sect. 1967-68). Office: U New Mexico Dept Physics and Astronomy Univ Of New Mexico NM 87131

HULL, ROGER KERMIT, military officer; b. Chattanooga, Tenn., Apr. 19, 1946; s. George Fletcher and Dorothy Helen (Suddarth) H.; m. Mary Alison Welter Hull, Dec. 21, 1981; children: Nathan Kyle, Rachel Rebecca. BS in Aviation Mgmt., Auburn U., Ala., 1968; MS in Ops. Rsch., Naval Postgrad. Sch., Monterey, Calif., 1977. Cert. Flight Instructor fixed wing and hot air balloon, airline transport pilot, designated Materiel Profl., USN. Flight student Naval Aviation Sch. Command, Pensacola, Fla., 1968-69; advanced jet flight instructor Naval Aviation Training Command, Kingsville, Tex., 1969-71; combat attack pilot Attack Squadron 146, Lemoore Calif., Vietnam, 1971-74; student Naval Postgrad. Sch., Monterey, Calif., 1974-77; competition parachutist U.S. Parachute Team, Pope Valley, Calif., 1977; dept. head Attack Squadron 56, Yokosuka, Japan, 1977-81; chief operation test dir. Air Test & Eval. Squadron Five, China Lake, Calif., 1981-84; air ops. officer Cruiser Destroyer Group One, San Diego, 1984-87; program mgr. Space & Naval Warfare Systems Command, Washington, 1987-90; commanding officer Naval Weapons Eval. Facility, Albuquerque, N.Mex., 1990-93; small bus. owner "Copy To:", Hanford, Calif., 1975-77; pvt. computer cons., MacPro, Washington, 1987-90; cons. ops. analyst, San Diego, 1984-87. Author: United We Fall, 1977; contbr. articles to profl. jours. Mem. Gov.'s Disting. Pub. Svc. awards Coun., 1991. Capt., USN, 1968—. Recipient World Champion Parachutist, Fed. Aeronautics Internat., Gatton, Autralia, 1977; Indiv. Overall Nat. Champion Parachutist, U.S. Parachute Assn., Talequah, Okla., 1977; Proven Subspecialist Ops. Rsch., USN., 1981; Proven Subspecialist Command & Control, USN, 1988. Mem. U.S. Parachute Assn., Fed. Exec. Bd., Mensa, Military Ops. Rsch. Soc., Armed Forces Communications & Electronics Assn., Omicron Delta Kappa. Office: Vice Commdr Naval Air Warfare Ctr Weapons Divsn Point Mugu Nas CA 93042

HULLAR, THEODORE LEE, university chancellor; b. Mar. 19, 1935; m. Joan J. Miller, Aug. 2, 1958; children: Theodore W., Timothy E. BS with high distinction, U. Minn., 1957, PhD in Biochemistry, 1963. Asst. prof. medicinal chemistry SUNY, Buffalo, 1964-69, assoc. prof., 1969-75, assoc. dean grad. sch., 1969-71; dep. commr. programs and research N.Y. State Dept. Environ. Conservation, 1975-79; assoc. dir. Cornell U. Agrl. Experiment Sta., 1979-81, dir., 1981-84; assoc. dir. research N.Y. State Coll. Agriculture and Life Scis., Cornell U., 1979-81; adj. prof. natural resources Cornell U. Agrl. Experiment Sta., 1979-81; prof. natural resources, dir. research N.Y. State Coll. Agriculture and Life Scis., Cornell U., 1981-84; exec. vice chancellor U. Calif., Riverside, 1984-85, chancellor, prof. biochem., 1985-87; chancellor, prof. environ. toxicology U. Calif., Davis, 1987—; chmn. hazardous waste mgmt. com. So. Calif. Assn. Govs., 1986-87, chmn. air quality task force, 1985-87, mem. regional adv. council, 1985-87; chmn. com. on environment Nat. Assn. State Univs. and Land Grant Colls., 1985—, com. on biotech., 1985—, chmn. program devel. subcom., 1982—, coord. Agr. Rsch. Initiative; chmn. Gov. Deukmejian's Task Force on Toxics, Waste and Tech., 1985-86; chmn. bd. agr. Nat. Rsch. Council; chmn. Calif. Council on Sci. and Tech.; mem. gov. bd. Internat. Irrigation Mgmt. Inst.; lectr. various orgns. Contbr. articles to profl. jours. Commr. Environ. Quality Erie County, N.Y., 1974-75; alternate to Gov. N.Y. on Delaware and Susquehanna River Basin Commns., 1975-79; mem. N.Y. State Agrl. Resources Commn., 1974-75; mem. Arlington Heights Greenbelt Study Com., 1986-87; mem. Monday Morning Group, 1985-87; active various community orgns. NSF postdoctoral fellow SUNY Buffalo, 1963-64. Mem. Am. Chem. Soc., AAAS, Chem. Soc. London, Regional Inst. So. Calif., Greater Riverside C. of C., (bd. dirs. 1985-87), Sigma Xi. Home: 16 College Park Davis CA 95616-3607 Office: U Calif Davis Office of Chancellor Davis CA 95616*

HULLEY, CHARLES BROEKSMIT, investment executive; b. Boston, Dec. 22, 1954; s. John Charles Lincoln Hulley and Laura Fiske (Broeksmit) Thurston; m. Patricia Jean Crooke; Jan 28, 1984; children: Vanessa Claire, Genevieve Ann. BA, U. Calif., Berkeley, 1977; MBA, George Washington U., 1986. Pvt. practice investment advisor London, 1978-83; investment banker Brown Bros. Harriman & co., N.Y., 1986-88; investment exec. Mitsui & Co. (U.S.A.), Inc., San Francisco, 1988—. Active YMCA; com. mem. Asian Art Mus. Mem. Assn. Corp. Growth (bd. dirs. 1992—), Urban Land Inst., Mill Valley Tennis Club, Hurlingham Club, World Trade Club. Episcopalian. Office: 1 California St Ste 3000 San Francisco CA 94111-5467

HULSE, JOHN EDWARD, telephone company executive; b. Hannibal, Mo., June 11, 1933; s. Giles and Edythe (Watt) H.; B.S., U.S.D., 1955; m. Mary Jean Pfeiffer, Aug. 21, 1954; children: Celine, Michelle, Christi, Mary Pat, Michael. Gen. comml. and mktg. mgr. Northwestern Bell Telephone Co., Omaha, 1968-72, dir. mktg. sales project AT&T, N.Y.C., 1972-74, v.p., chief exec. officer, Sioux Falls, S.D., 1974-75, v.p., chief exec. officer, Mpls., 1975-79, sr. v.p., Omaha, 1979-81; exec. v.p., chief fin. officer Pacific Telesis Group (formerly Pacific Tel. & Tel.), San Francisco, 1981-82, vice-chmn. bd., chief fin. officer, 1983—. Trustee San Francisco Ballet Assn.; mem. Merritt/Peralta Found., Fin. Acctg. Found. Mem. Fin. Execs. Inst. (pres. San Francisco chpt. 1986, dir. western area 1987-90), Telephone Pioneers Am. (sr. v.p., pres. elect), San Francisco C. of C. (dir., treas.), World Affairs Council No. Calif, Pvt. Sector Council. Clubs: San Francisco Bankers, Commonwealth, Blackhawk Country. Office: Pacific Telesis Group 130 Kearny St San Francisco CA 94108-4803

HULSE, RALPH ROBERT, management consultant; b. St. Joseph, Mo., Jan. 14, 1935; s. Ralph Raymond and Eva Laduska (Hatfield) H.; m. Gwen Lea Bartosh, May 21, 1956 (div. 1959); m. Jutta-Beaujean, Jan. 14, 1961. AB, Cen. Meth. Coll., 1957; MEd, U. Mo., 1965. Continuing edn. programmer U. Mo., Columbia, 1969-71; dir. edn. tng. North Kansas City (Mo.) Meml. Hosp., 1971-74; mgmt. cons. Lawrence-Leiter, Kansas City, 1974-77; adminstr. U.S. Congress, 6th dist., Mo., 1977-78; bus. cons. Hulse & Assocs., Kansas City, 1978-88; adminstr. Sales Tng. Inst. div. Mile Hi Bus. Coll., Denver, 1988-89; bus. cons., pres. Crystal Devel. Systems, Inc, Denver, 1989—; founder, bd. dirs. Opportunity Industry Inc., St. Joseph, 1965-71; pres. State Adult Edn. Assn., Mo., 1978-79. Contbr. articles to profl. jours. (Nat. Pub. award 1974, 75). Served with U.S. Army, 1959-61. Mem. Colo. Cons. Assn. (founder, pres. 1985-87). Republican. Methodist. Home and Office: 8706 Independence Way Arvada CO 80005-1247

HUMBACH, ROBERT FREDERICK, management consultant; b. Ft. Campbell, Ky., Sept. 1, 1958; s. Robert F. and Joy (Schmidt) H.; m. Michelle Ann Will, Oct. 3, 1987. BS in Bus. Mgmt., Metropolitan State Coll., Denver, 1983. Pres. Ultimate Sports Club, Inc., Denver, 1983-86, Quality Sports Inc., Aurora, Colo., 1986-89; turn-around cons. Johnson West, Denver, 1989; sml. bus. cons. DPC Holdings, Denver, 1989; pres. Dynamics Unltd., Inc., Denver, 1989-91; dist. sales mgr. Stenograph Corp., Mt. Prospect, Ill., 1991—. Tutor, Adult Learning Svc., Denver, 1990. Office: Stenograph Corp 1500 Bishop Ct Mount Prospect IL 60056

HUME, DARRELL J., retail executive; b. 1948. Student, U. Wash. With Nordstrom, Inc., Seattle, 1969—, co-pres., 1991—. Office: Nordstrom Inc 1501 5th Ave Seattle WA 98101*

HUME, KEVIN DEAN, accountant; b. Clinton, Ill., June 10, 1954; s. Harold Dean and Helen (Nichols) H.; m. Kelli Leigh Safarian, June 25, 1988. BA, Eureka Coll., 1976; BS, Ill. State U., 1981; M. in Tax, U. Denver, 1985. CPA, Colo; cert. tax profl. Tax specialist Peat, Marwick, Mitchell, Tulsa, 1981-83; tax mgr. T.A. Myers & Co., Denver, 1983-90; pres. Kevin Hume, CPA, PC, Denver, 1990—; adj. prof. Columbia Coll., Aurora, Colo., 1991-92, Met. State Coll., Denver, 1992; lectr. Nat. Ctr. for Profl. Edn., Zachary, La., 1992; adv. bd. mem. All Care Health Svcs., Inc., Denver, 1992. V.p. membership Camerata (Opera Colo), Denver, 1987-88; tax advisor Saturday Night Live (DCPA), Denver, 1988; mem. Founder's Day Com., U. Denver, 1988. Mem. Inst. Tax Consultants, Nat. Assn. Tax Profls., Internat. Fiscal Assn. Office: 240 Saint Paul # 310 Denver CO 80206

HUMPHERYS, ALFRED GLEN, museum director; b. Montpelier, Idaho, May 7, 1939; s. Alfred and Ivie Mae (Wood) H.; m. Marilyn Stanley, June 6, 1963; children: Alan Glen, Kenneth, Grant Warren. BS in History, Brigham Young U., 1963, MA in History, 1964; PhD in Latin Am. History, U. N.Mex., 1974. Tchr. Glen Hill Sch., Glenwood, Alta., 1964-65; history instr. Ricks Coll., Rexburg, Idaho, 1965-69; ranger historian C&O Canal, Nat. Pk. Svc., Washington, 1966, Custer Battlefield, Nat. Pk. Svc., Crow Agency, Mont., 1967; grad. asst. U. N.Mex., Albuquerque, 1969-73; sgt.-at-arms Utah Senate, Salt Lake City, 1974; curator, dir. Wheeler Historic Farm, Salt Lake City, 1976—; historic cons. Jr. League of Salt Lake City, 1976; exec. dir. Wheeler Farm Friends, Inc., Salt Lake City, 1976—. Author, Contbr. book series: Mountain Men and the Fur Trade, 1968; contbr. articles to profl. jours. Scoutmaster Boy Scouts Am., Midvale, Utah, 1989—. Recipient Wetlands Protection award, EPA, 1989, Outstanding Recreation-Program award, Utah Recreation Assn., 1990. Mem. Utah Conservation Assn. (pres. 1988-89), Utah Mus. Assn. (pres. 1982-83), Assn. of Living History Farms and Agrl. Mus., Internat. Dutch Oven Soc. (bd. dirs. 1987-91). Mem. Ch. of Jesus Christ of Latter Day Saints. Home: 274 E 6790 S Midvale UT 84047-1224 Office: Wheelr Historic Farm 6351 S 9th E Salt Lake City UT 84121-2438

HUMPHREY, JOHN JULIUS, university program director, historian, writer; b. Booneville, Miss., Jan. 22, 1926; s. George Duke and Josephine (Robertson) H.; m. Mary Margaret Ryan, Jan. 19, 1949; children: George Duke II, Laurie Ann. BS, Miss. State U., 1945; BA, U. Wyo., 1946, MA, 1964, postgrad., 1964-68; postgrad., U. Ariz., 1969-71. Pres. J.J. Humphrey Co. Inc., Laramie, Wyo., 1947-68; lectr. History U. Ariz., Tucson, 1969-71, asst. dir. placement, 1969-70, dir. scholarships, awards, 1970-72, dir. office of scholarships and fin. aid, 1972-84, dir. scholarship devel., 1970-91; asst. to pres. western area Cumberland Coll., Williamsburg, Ky., 1991; v.p. bus. affairs Tucson Coll. Arts and Scis., 1992. Sec. Baird Found., Tucson, 1970—, bd. dirs. Bendalin Fund, Phoenix, 1976—, Cacioppo Found., Tucson, 1986—; cons. DeMund Found., St. Louis, 1970—; mem. Pres. Club Ariz. Found., mem. Az Assn. Fin. Aid Officers, 1970-91, pres. 1973-74, pres. Ariz. Coll. & Univ. Found., 1972-73. Recipient Spl. award U. Ariz. Black Student Govt., 1983, Black Alumni, 1990. Mem. Am. Indian Alumni Assn. (Spl. Appreciation for Svc. in Scholarships Native Ams. award 1982). Home: 6901 E Potawatami Dr Tucson AZ 85715-3246

HUMPHREY, KAREN MICHAEL, mayor; b. Cin., Sept. 27, 1945; m. Ken Clarke, Sept. 1973; 4 stepchildren. BA in Humanities magna cum laude, U. So. Calif., 1966. TV news field reporter, anchorperson, producer KFSN-TV, Fresno, Calif., 1970-79; freelance media cons., polit. advisor, 1979-89; mayor City of Fresno, 1989—, mem. planning commn., 1979-81, mem. city coun., 1981-89, mayor, 1989—; mayor Calif. Commn. on Crime Control and Violence Prevention, 1981-83; mem. Fresno-Clovis Met. Solid Waste Commn., chmn., 1981—. Bd. dirs. Fresno Convention and Vis. Bur.; mem. Fresno County Transp. Authority, Fresno County Econ. Devel. Corp., City of Fresno Gen. Employees and Police and Fire Retirement Bds., Fresno-Madera Area Agy. on Aging, Fresno Employment and Tng. Commn., 1981-86. Mem. League Calif. Cities (bd. dirs. 1981-86, 90-91, chair pub. safety com. 1983-86, chair Brown Act com. 1987, mem. task force on revenues and responsibilities 1988-89, pres. S. San Joaquin div. 1986, mem. exec. bd. 1984-87), Nat. League Cities (adv. coun. 1988—, bd. dirs. 1986-88, steering com. human devel. 1984, policy com. on human devel. 1986), Women in Mcpl. Govt. (state coord. 1984-88), Nat. Orgn. to Insure Sound-controlled Environ. (bd. dirs. 1985—), Phi Beta Kappa, Phi Kappa Phi. Office: Office of Mayor City Hall 2600 Fresno St Fresno CA 93721-1824

HUMPHREYS, JOSEPH ROY, consultant; b. San Francisco, Apr. 14, 1938; s. Roy William and Vera Josephine (Lyon) H.; m. Joan Ann Budz, July 17, 1965; children: Josephine, Wendy Lyon, Joseph S. BA, St. Patrick's Coll., Menlo Park, Calif., 1959; MA, U. San Francisco, 1965. Various staff positions Social Security Adminstrn., Balt. and Santa Rosa, Calif., 1965-68; specialist in social legis. Congl. Rsch. Svc., Libr. of Congress, Washington, 1968-73; profl. staff mem. Com. on Fin., U.S. Senate, Washington, 1973-91; ind. cons. San Francisco, 1991—. Mem. Nat. Acad. Social Ins. Democrat. Roman Catholic. Home: 20 Knollview Way San Francisco CA 94131-1216

HUMPHREYS, LYNN MARIE, church official; b. Stillwater, Okla., Feb. 5, 1962; d. Kenneth Lester and Elizabeth Lourie (Hay) H. BA in History and English, Seattle Pacific U., 1984, cert. in profl. teaching, 1984; postgrad., U. Wash., 1987, Ea. Wash. U., 1988. Cert. tchr., Wash. Coord. visitor svcs. Pacific Sci. Ctr., Seattle, 1984-87; computer operator pvt. promotional co. Spokane, Wash., 1987-88; dispatcher Seattle Police Dept., 1989-91; sec., receptionist 1st Presbyn. Ch., 1993—; tchr. social studies Edmonds (Wash.) Sch. Dist., 1985-87. Presbyterian. Home: W 720 Cora Apt 55 Spokane WA 99205

HUMPHRIES, STANLEY, JR., physics educator; b. Paterson, N.J., Feb. 25, 1946; s. Stanley and Katherine (Ehrentraut) H.; children: Colin James, Courtney Elizabeth. BS, MIT, 1968; MS, U. Calif., Berkeley, 1969, PhD, 1971. Postdoctoral researcher Los Alamos (N.Mex.) Nat. Lab., 1971-72; asst. prof. physics Cornell U., Ithaca, N.Y., 1972-77; physicist Sandia Nat. Lab., Albuquerque, 1977-82; prof. nuclear engring. U. N.Mex., Albuquerque, 1982-87, prof., electrical engr., 1987—, dir. Inst. Accelerator Tech.,, 1985-90; pres. Acceleration Assoc., 1989—; cons. Los Alamos Nat. Lab., 1982—, Lawrence Berkeley Nat. Lab., 1987-90, Westinghouse Corp., Pitts., 1984—, Pulsed Scis., Inc., San Leandro, Calif., 1983—, McDonnell-Douglas, St. Louis, 1986—, W.J Schafer Assoc., 1988—. Author: (textbook) Principles of Charged Particle Acceleration, 1986, Charged Particle Beams, 1990; contbr. articles to profl. jours. Grantee U.S. Dept. Energy, 1984-86, Office Naval Research, 1984—, Air Force Office Sci. Research, 1983—, Los Alamos Nat. Lab., 1983—, Sandia Nat. Labs, 1990—. Fellow Am. Phys. Soc., IEEE. Office: U NMex Dept Elec Engring Albuquerque NM 87131

HUMPHRY, DEREK JOHN, association executive, writer; b. Bath, Somerset, Eng., Apr. 29, 1930; came to U.S., 1978; s. Royston Martin and Bettine (Duggan) H.; m. Jean Edna Crane, May 5, 1953 (dec. Mar. 1975); children: Edgar, Clive, Stephen; m. Ann Wickett Kooman, Feb. 16, 1976 (div. 1990); m. Gretchen Crocker, 1991. Student pub. schs. Reporter, Evening News, Manchester, Eng., 1951-55, Daily Mail, London, 1955-63; editor Havering Recorder, Essex, Eng., 1963-67; sr. reporter Sunday Times,

London, 1967-78; spl. writer L.A. Times, 1978-79; founder, exec. dir. Hemlock Soc. N.Am., L.A., 1980-92, pres. 1988-90. Author: Because They're Black, 1971 (M.L. King award 1972), Police Power and Black People, 1972; Jean's Way, 1978, Let Me Die Before I Wake, 1982, The Right to Die, 1986, Final Exit, 1991, Dying With Dignity, 1992, Lawful Exit, 1993. With Brit. Army, 1948-50. Mem. World Fedn. Right-to-Die Socs. (newsletter editor 1979-84, 1992-94, sec.-treas. 1983-84, pres. 1988-90), Ams. Death with Dignity (v.p. 1993). Home: PO Box 10603 Eugene OR 97440-2603

HUNDHAUSEN, ROBERT JOHN, mining engineer; b. Cape Girardeau, Mo., Sept. 28, 1916; s. Herman Henry and Charlotte Virginia (Heekman) H.; married, 1937 (div. 1965); children: Robert J. Jr., Thomas G., William H., Phyllis Hundhausen Taylor; m. Adele Johannah Eck, May 2, 1968. Grad., Colo. Sch. Mines, 1934-38. Mining engr. N.J. Zinc Co., Gilman, Colo., 1938-40; with U.S. Bur. Mines, 1942-55; gen. mgr. Dawn Mining Co., Ford, Wash., 1955-57; prin. Real Estate & Mining, Hayden, Idaho, 1958-81. Contbr. articles to profl. jours.; inventor in field. Mem. AAAS, Am. Inst. Mining Engrs., N.W. Mining Assn., N.Y. Acad. Scis. (life), Colo. Sch. Mines Alumni Assn., Spokane Club, Hayden Lake Country Club, Sigma Xi, Kappa Sigma. Presbyterian. Home: RR 2 Box 164 Hayden ID 83835

HUNING, DEBORAH GRAY, actress, dancer, audiologist; b. Evanston, Ill., Aug. 23, 1950; d. Hans Karl Otto and Angenette Dudley (Willard) H.; divorced; 1 child, Bree Alyeska. BS, No. Ill. U., 1981, MA, 1983. Actress, soloist, dancer, dir. various univ. and community theater depts., Bklyn., Chgo. and Cranbrook, B.C., Can., 1967—; ski instr. Winter Park (Colo.) Recreation Assn., 1975-79; house photographer C Lazy U Ranch, Granby, Colo., 1979; audiologist, ednl. programming cons. East Kootenay Ministry of Health, Cranbrook, 1985-89; ind. video prodn./asst., 1991—; master of ceremonies East Kootenay Talent Showcase, EXPO '86, Vancouver B.C., Can., 1986; creator, workshop leader: A Hearing Impaired Child in the Classroom, 1986. Producer, writer, dir., editor (video) Down With Decibels, 1992; author: Living Well With Hearing Loss: A Guide for the Hearing-Impaired and Their Families, 1992. Sec., treas. Women for Wildlife, Cranbrook, 1985-86; assoc. mem. adv. bd. Grand County Community Coll., Winter Park, Colo., 1975-77; assoc. mem. bd. dirs. Boys and Girls Club of Can., Cranbrook, 1985. Mem. Nat. Assn. Gifted Children, Internat. Marine Animal Trainers Assn.

HUNLEY, W. HELEN, former Canadian provincial government official; b. Acme, Alta., Can., Sept. 6, 1920. Student pub. schs., Rocky Mountain House, Alta.; LL.D., U. Alta., 1985. Telephone operator Carstairs, Acme and Calgary, Alta.; with implement and truck dealership, ins. agy. Rocky Mountain House, 1948-57; owner, mgr. Helen Hunley Agys. Ltd., ins. agy., Rocky Mountain House, 1968-71; town councillor Rocky Mountain House, 1960-66, mayor, 1966-71; mem. Can. Ho. of Commons, 1974-88; elected mem. Legis. Assembly Province of Alta., Edmonton, 1971-79, minister without portfolio, 1971-73, solicitor-gen., 1973-75, minister social services and community Health, 1975-79, lt. gov., 1985-91. Formerly active numerous community affairs and vol. agys., including Can. Red Cross, Can. Boy Scouts, Recreation Bd., Alta. Girls Parliament, Provincial Mental Health Adv. Council; hon. patron numerous assns. Served to lt. Can. Women's Army Corps, 1941-45. Named Knight of Grace of the Most Venerable Order fo the Hosp. of St. John of Jerusalem, Chancellor of the Alta. Order of Excellence, Citizen of Yr. Red Deer C. of C., 1990; Paul Harris fellow Rotary Internat., 1989. Presbyterian. Office: Rocky Mountain House, Edmonton, AB Canada T5K 2B6

HUNNICUTT, RICHARD PEARCE, metallurgical engineer; b. Asheville, N.C., June 15, 1926; s. James Ballard and Ida (Black) H.; B.S. in Metall. Engring., Stanford, 1951, M.S., 1952; m. Susan Haight, Apr. 9, 1954; children—Barbara, Beverly, Geoffrey, Anne. Research metallurgist Gen. Motors Research Labs., 1952-55; sr. metallurgist Aerojet-Gen. Corp., 1955-57; head materials and processes Firestone Engring. Lab., 1957-58; head phys. scis. group Dalmo Victor Co., Monterey, 1958-61, head materials lab., 1961-62; v.p. Anamet Labs., Inc., 1962-82, exec. v.p., 1982—; partner Pyrco Co. Author: Pershing, A History of the American Medium Tank T20 Series, 1971, Sherman, A History of the American Medium Tank, 1978, Patton, A History of the American Main Battle Tank, vol. 1, 1984, Firepower, A History of the American Heavy Tank, 1988, Abrams, A History of the American Main Battle Tank, vol. 2, 1990, Stuart, A History of the American Light Tank, vol. 1, 1992. Served with AUS, 1943-46. Mem. Electrochem. Soc., AIME, Am. Soc. Metals, ASTM, Am. Welding Soc., Am. Soc. Lubrication Engrs. Research on frictional behavior of materials, development of armored fighting vehicles. Home: 2805 Benson Way Belmont CA 94002-2938 Office: 3400 Investment Blvd Hayward CA 94545-3811

HUNNICUTT, ROBERT WILLIAM, engineer; b. Pauls Valley, Okla., Aug. 12, 1954; s. James Warren Hunnicutt. BS, N.Mex. State U., 1980. Sr. assoc. engr. IBM, Tucson, 1980—. Mem. Ariz.-Sonora Desert Mus. Republican. Home: 8383 S Pistol Hill Rd Tucson AZ 85747-9999 Office: IBM Corp Test and Integration Lab 72Y/041-2 Tucson AZ 85744

HUNSAKER, FLOYD B., accountant; b. Collinston, Utah, Sept. 6, 1915; s. Allen G. and Mary Ann (Bowcutt) H.; grad. high sch.; m. Zella D. Hepworth, Mar. 3, 1943; children: Marcia (Mrs. Marvin Bahr), Charlene (Mrs. Abelino Ancira), Sonia (Mrs. Val Fisher), Rhonda (Mrs. Kim Veigel), Tamara (Mrs. Randy Beardall). Lic. ins. salesman, security dealer. Owner, operator dairy farm, Bedford, Wyo., 1946-70; acct., Afton, Wyo., 1959—; owner Credit Bur. Star Valley, Afton, 1967-87; mcpl. judge Town of Afton, 1967-77; local office claimstaker Wyo. Unemployment Compensation Dept., 1975-85. Pres., Holdaway Sch. PTA, 1960; active Boy Scouts Am., 1946-49, 58-67; chmn. Cub Scouts com., 1987—; bd. dirs. Star Valley Sr. Citizens, 1981-83, 84-88; pres. Lower Valley 4-H council, 1961-62, leader, 1959-63; chmn. Star Valley chpt. Am. Revolution Bicentennial Adminstrn., 1975-76, Star Valley chpt. ARC, 1976—; ward pres. Sunday Sch., 1985-87; mem. Wyo. Centennial Com., 1990; subdivider Fertile Acres 1981-88; archtl. designer Star Valley Vets. Meml. Monument, 1990; mem. Lincoln County Selective Ssvc. Bd., 1984—. Pub. Star Valley Bus. Directory, 1990, 91, 92. Recipient 50 Yr. Vol. award ARC, 1992. Served with Devils Brigade, 1941-45; ETO. Mem. Farm Bur. (exec. sec. Lincoln County 1961-66), Internat. Platform Assn., Afton C. of C. (dir. 1973-74), Star Valley C. of C. (dir. 1988—, exec. sec. 1989-90, treas. 1991—), VFW (post svc. officer 1949—, post quartermaster 1959—, dist. comdr. Wyo. 1974-75, 77-78, state dept. jr. vice comdr. 1978-79, sr. vice comdr. 1979-80, state comdr. 1980-81, dist. comdr. 1982-83, 86-88, chmn. state audit com. 1985—), Am. Legion (post svc. officer, adj. treas. 1975—). Mem. Ch. of Jesus Christ of Latter-day Saints. Home: 323 Adams St Afton WY 83110 Office: 498 Washington St Afton WY 83110

HUNSBERGER, CHARLES WESLEY, library director; b. Elkhart, Ind., Sept. 25, 1929; s. Charles August and Emma Edna (Zimmerman) H.; m. Hilda Carol Showalter, July 3, 1949 (div.); children—Jonathan Wesley, Jerald Wayne, Jane Wannette. BA, Bethel Coll., Mishawaka, Ind., 1952; MLS, Ind. U., 1967. Mem. Ft. Wayne (Ind.) Libr. Staff, 1960-62; dir. Columbia (Ind.) City Libr., 1962-64, Monroe County Libr., Bloomington, Ind., 1964-71, Clark County Libr. Dist., Las Vegas, Nev., 1971—; cons. sch., pub. librs., 1968-70; lectr. libr. schs. Ind. U., 1970-71, U. Ariz., 1974, U. Nev., Reno, 1976; mem. Nev. Coun. on Librs., 1973-81, chmn., 1980-81. Mem. Calif. Libr. Assn., ALA, Nev. Libr. Assn. (named Libr. of Yr. 1988), Internat. Assn. of Met. City Librs. (sec./treas., 1992—), Rotary (pres. 1979-80, Las Vegas-Paradise chpt.). Democrat. Home: 1501 Crestview Dr Las Vegas NV 89124 Office: Las Vegas Libr 833 Las Vegas Blvd N Las Vegas NV 89101

HUNSBERGER, ROBERT EARL, mechanical engineer, manufacturing executive; b. San Diego, Nov. 9, 1947; s. Arnold and Edith Mae (Miller) H.; m. Charlotte Louise Herr, Mar. 30, 1968; children: David Arnold, Allen Robert. BS in Mech. Engring., San Diego State Coll., 1969, MBA, 1975. Project engr. Gen. Atomic Co., San Diego, 1970-75; pvt. practice commodity mktg. specialist San Diego, 1975-77; devel. engr. Solar Turbines, Inc., San Diego, 1977-82, project engr., 1982-84, project mgr., 1984-89, mgr. pub. svcs., 1989-92, sourcing mgr., 1992—. Contbr. articles to profl. jours. Leader local Webelos, 1981-82; com. chmn. Boy Scouts Am., Ramona, Calif., 1982-83, cub master, 1983-84, com. mem., 1982—, com. chmn., 1985-86. Recipient Spirit of Courage award San Deigo Inst. Burn Medicine, 1979, Cert. Commendation Calif. Hwy. Patrol, 1979, B.S.A. Dist. Unit award, 1992. Republican. Club: Model A Restorers.

HUNSUCKER, ROBERT DUDLEY, physicist, electrical engineer, educator, researcher; b. Portland, Oreg., Mar. 15, 1930; s. Robert Deets and Johnnie Morris (Kuykendal) H.; m. Judith Mary Cotter, Apr. 28, 1956 (dec. Nov. 1980); children: Edith Louise, Jeanne Marie, Cynthia Lee; m. Phyllis Marie Hoover, July 25, 1981. BS in Physics, Oreg. State U., 1954, MS in Physics, 1958; PhDEE, U. Colo., 1969. Asst. prof. Geophysics Inst. U. Alaska, Fairbanks, 1958-64, assoc. prof. Geophysics Inst., 1971-78, prof. Geophysics Inst., 1978-87; physicist Nat. Bur. Standards, Boulder, Colo., 1964-67; sr. project leader ITS Office of Telecommunications Sci., Boulder, 1967-71; prof. emeritus physics and elec. engring., sr. cons. U. Alaska, Fairbanks, 1988—; radio propagation cons. Author: technical book; assoc. editor URSI Radio Scientist Mag.; contbr. articles to profl. jours. Served to lt. USNR, 1954-57. Fellow AAAS, IEEE (Yr. Alaska sect. 1988, recipient outstanding achievement award IEEE region 6, 1988); mem. Am. Geophys. Union, U.S. Commission Internat. Union of Radio Sci., Sigma Xi, Sigma Pi Sigma, Eta Kappa Nu. Republican. Presbyterian. Lodge: Rotary (bd. dirs. College, Alaska club 1979-81). Office: U Alaska Geophys Inst Fairbanks AK 99775-0800

HUNT, DAVID BRIAN, software test engineer; b. Oak Park, Ill., Jan. 14, 1962; s. Daniel Porter and Norma Rae (Geddes) H.; m. Wendy Dawn Randal, Dec. 22, 1984; children: Hayley Christina, Heather Nicole. BS in Computer Sci., Seattle Pacific U., 1985, MS in Info. System Mgmt., 1990. Computing security adminstr. The Boeing Co., Seattle, 1985-89, project cons., 1989-90; software test engr. Microsoft Corp., Redmond, Wash., 1990—. Presbyterian. Office: Microsoft Corp 10S/1 One Microsoft Way Redmond WA 98052-6399

HUNT, HEBER TRUMAN, academic administrator; b. Salt Lake City, May 30, 1928; s. Jacob Truman and Esther (Canfield) H.; m. GeNeal Richins, Oct. 3, 1955; children: Pamela, Michael, Baylen, Kevin, Ronald, Reneé, Ryan. BS, Brigham Young U., 1954. V.p. Hylon Koburn Chem. Co., Salt Lake City, 1955-57; owner Nat. Supply Co., Salt Lake City, 1957-64; bank examiner State of Utah, Salt Lake City, 1964-66; legis. fiscal analyst State of Utah Legislature, Salt Lake City, 1966-87; v.p. bus. Salt Lake C.C., 1987—. Cpl. U.S. Army, 1952-54. Mem. Rotary. Office: Salt Lake CC 4600 S Redwood Rd Salt Lake City UT 84130

HUNT, ROBERT GORDON, JR., real estate broker; b. Washington, Sept. 20, 1927; s. Robert Gordon and Pauline (Fred) H.; children: Louise Anne, Kenneth Gordon, David Robert. BS, U.S. Naval Acad., 1949; MBA, George Washington U., 1969. Commd. 2d lt. USMC, 1949, advanced through grades to lt. col., 1969; commanding officer H Co., 3d Bn., 3d Marine Regiment, 1954; sr. adv. First Republic of Korean Marine Regiment, 1964; comdg. officer 3d Bn., 27th Marine Regiment, 1968; mgr. Tarzana div. Mut. Devel. Corp., 1971; mgr. Apple Valley div. CRCF United Growth, 1972-76; pres. Bob Hunt Realty, Inc., Apple Valley, Calif., 1976-81; instr. Victor Valley Community Coll., 1980-82. Columnist Hesperia Resorter, 1982-86. Pres. Coalition for Orderly Growth, 1982—. Served with USN, 1945-49. Mem. Nat. Assn. Realtors, Realtors Nat. Mktg. Inst. (cert. comml. investment mem.), Calif. Assn. Realtors (bd. dirs.), Victor Valley Bd. Realtors (treas.), Victorville C. of C., Apple Valley Country Club, Rotary, Optimists (Victor Valley pres. 1975-76). Republican. Episcopalian. Home: 16361 Wintun Rd Apple Valley CA 92307-1548 Office: Bob Hunt Realty 18843 Us Hwy 18 Apple Valley CA 92307-2213

HUNT, ROBERT WILLIAM, theatrical producer, data processing consultant; b. Seattle, June 8, 1947; s. William Roland and Margaret Anderson (Crowe) H.; m. Marcie Loomis, Aug. 24, 1968 (div. Dec. 1975); 1 child, Megan; m. Susan Moyer, June 17, 1989; children: Donovan, Jillian. BA, U. Wash., 1969. CPA, Wash. Data processing cons Arthur Andersen & Co., Seattle, 1968-78; owner, cons. Robert W. Hunt & Assocs., Seattle, 1978—; exec. producer Village Theatre, Issaquah, Wash., 1979—; cons. San Francisco Mus. Modern Art, 1981-90, Mus. of Flight, Seattle, 1983-90, Met. Mus. N.Y.C., 1984-85. Creator arts computer software; producer (mus.) Eleanor, 1987, Heidi, 1989, Charlie and the Chocolate Factory, 1989, Book of James, 1990, Funny Pages, 1991, Jungle Queen Debutante, 1991; creator, writer (pop group music and video) The Shrimps, 1984. Chmn. com. Seattle Arts Commn., 1975-78; treas. Arts Resource Svcs., Seattle, 1976-78; gen. mgr. Musicomedy Northwest, Seattle, 1977-79. Grantee Seattle Arts Commn., 1978-79, Wash. State Arts Commn., 1980—, King County Arts Commn., 1980—, Nat. Endowment for the Arts, 1992—. Mem. Wash. Soc. CPAs., Nat. Alliance of Mus. Theatre Producers (treas., bd. dirs.). Office: Village Theatre 120 Front St N Issaquah WA 98027-3234

HUNT, TIMOTHY ARTHUR, literature professor; b. Calistoga, Calif., Dec. 22, 1949; s. Arthur Lee and Nancy Mae (Rouke) H.; m. Merrill Elizabeth Vargo, Sept. 4, 1971 (div. 1982); m. Susan Diancee Spurlock, Nov. 12, 1982; children: John Howard, Jessica Ann. AB cum laude, Cornell U., 1970, MA, 1974, PhD, 1975. Asst. prof. U. Utah, Eng. Dept., Salt Lake City, 1974-76; lectr. U. Del., Newark, 1976-80; vis. asst. prof. Colby Coll., Eng. Dept., Waterville, Maine, 1980-81; prof. Eng., speech Deep Springs (Calif.) Coll., 1981; dir. communications and humanities Nova U., Nova Coll., 1982-84; instr. U. Wash., Eng. Dept., Seattle, 1984-85; from asst. prof. to assoc. prof. Ind. U.-Purdue U., Fort Wayne, Ind., 1985-87; acad. dean Deep Springs (Calif.) Coll., 1987-90; assoc. prof. Wash. State U., Vancouver, 1990—; coord. humanities Wash. State U., Vancouver, 1990—; curriculum coord. Hon. Program Coun. Ind. U.-Purdue U., Ft. Wayne, 1987, U. Del., 1976-79; dir freshman liberal studies sequence in Am. studies U. Utah, 1974-76. Numerous books, articles, essays, papers, poems, reviews in field. NEH fellow, 1992., grantee, 1986, 87-88,90; grantee Am. Coun. Learned Socs., 1987-88, Ind. U.-Purdue U., 1986, Ind. U. Pres. Coun. Humanities, 1986, U. Utah, 1975; rsch. fellow U. Del., 1977, Cornell U.-Ford Found., 1970-71, 72-74; winner 1st prize Nat. Poetry Competition, Chester H. Jones Found., 1983. Mem. MLA, Am. Lit. Assn., Soc. Textual Scholarship, W. Am. Lit. Assn., Robinson Jeffers Assn. (pres. 1993—). Office: Wash State U 1812 E Mcloughlin Blvd Vancouver WA 98663-3517

HUNT, VIRGINIA, university official; b. Cedar Rapids, Iowa, Dec. 3, 1935; d. Reid Lyttleton and Virginia (Gordon) H. BA in Polit. Sci., U. Iowa, 1957, MPE, 1962; EdD in Adminstrn. and Phys. Edn., U. N.C., 1976. Instr. Oberlin (Ohio) Coll., 1960; tchr. Adm. King High Sch., Lorain (Ohio) City Schs., 1961; from instr. to assoc. prof. Coll. of Wooster, Ohio, 1962-74, dir. women's athletics, 1965-74, acting chmn. dept. phys. edn. and athletics, 1973-74, field hockey coach, 1962-71, volleyball coach, 1967-73; assoc. dir. women's athletics, adj. prof. phys. edn. U. Mich., Ann Arbor, 1976-77; dir. women's athletics Mont. State U., Bozeman, 1977—, adj. prof. phys. edn. and adult and higher edn., 1977—, treas. Univ. Club, mem. faculty coun., 1987—, vice chmn., 1888-89, chmn., 1989-90; dir. various nat., regional, state and conf. championships; mem. long range planning com. Mont. State U., 1991—. Mem. vestry St. James Episcopal Ch., 1979-82, mem. chaplaincy support com., 1980-86, 89—. Mem. Nat. Fedn. Bus. and Profl. Women (pres. Bozeman chpt. 1985-86, editor newsletter 1987-88, dir. Mont./Dist. II chpt. 1986-87, legis. chmn. 1987-88, 88-89, chairperson state nominating com. 1989-90), Am. Coun. on Edn., Nat. Identification Program for Advancement of Women in Higher Edn. (coord. Mont. chpt. 1988—), Nat. Assn. Girls and Women in Sports (chairperson Ohio chpt. 1967-69, sec. affiliated bds. ofcls. 1972-74, chmn. affiliated bds. ofcls, 1975-76, bd. dirs. 1975-76), U.S. Olympic Com. (mem. eligibility com. 1981-84), Assn. for Inter Collegiate Athletics for Women (co-dir. athletics dirs. cong. 1979, dir. athletics dirs. workshop 1979, chmn. ethics and eligibility com. 1980-81, chmn. elect ethics and eligibility com. 1979-80, pres.-elect 1982), Mountain West Athletic Conf. (pres. 1982, 84-85, chmn. compliance com. 1984-85), Big Sky Conf. (chmn. women's com. 1988-89). Democrat. Office: Mont State U 1 Bobcat Circle Bozeman MT 59717-0328

HUNT, WILLIAM E., SR., state supreme court justice; b. 1923. B.A., LL.B., Univ. Mont. Bar: 1955. Justice Mont. Supreme Ct., Helena. Office: Mont Supreme Ct Justice Bldg Helena MT 59620 also: Montana Supreme Ct Helena MT 69620*

HUNTER, DUNCAN LEE, congressman; b. Riverside, Calif., May 31, 1948; m. Lynne Layh, 1973; children: Robert Samuel, Duncan Duane. J.D., Western State U., 1976. Bar: Calif. 1976. Practiced in San Diego; mem. 97th Congress from 42d Dist. Calif., 98th-102nd Congresses from 45th Dist. Calif., 103rd Congress from 52nd Dist. Calif.; mem. Armed Svcs. com., subcom. mil. installations, facilities, rsch., tech., House Rep. rsch. com. Served with U.S. Army, 1969-71, Vietnam. Decorated Air medal, Bronze Star. Mem. Navy League. Republican. Baptist.

HUNTER, FRED, mayor, lawyer; m. Jeanne Hunter; 4 children. Student, Fullerton Community Coll.; JD, Western Sch. Law, 1974. Office Anaheim (Calif.) Police Dept., 1965-75; mem. city coun. City of Anaheim, 1986—, mayor, 1988—. With USN, 1959-62. Office: Office of Mayor 200 S Anaheim Blvd Anaheim CA 92805-3820*

HUNTER, JOHN NATHANIEL, manufacturing executive; b. Elko, Nev., Mar. 11, 1929; s. John N. and Evelyn (Boyer) H.; m. Josephine A. Kegley, June 27, 1959; children: Julene Gordon, Wendi Lane, Elizabeth Kerrigan, John T. Hunter, Mary M. Hunter. BA, Stanford (Calif.) U., 1951. Personnel mgr. Container Corp. of Am., Oakland, Calif., 1953-57, W.P. Fuller Paint Co., San Francisco, 1957-59; pres., chief exec. officer Indsl. Boxboard Corp., Hayward, Calif., 1959—; bd. dirs. 4/1 Enterprises; gen. ptnr. IBC Co., Hayward, 1966—. Pres. Hayward Rotary Club Found., 1991—, West Hayward Owners Assn., 1984—; chmn. Calif. State Affiliates, Hayward, 1987-89; mem. task force Hazardous Waste Minimization, 1993-94, pres. Hayward C. of C. Lt. U.S. Army, 1951-53. Recipient Presdl. award St. Rose Hosp. Found., 1988; Cert. Appreciation Emergency Shelter Inc., 1989, Patron of Youth YMCA, 1987. Mem. Rotary Internat. (bd. dirs., officer, Rotarian of the Year 1991 Hayward chpt.), Tanglewood Racquet Club, Stanford Buck Club, United Employers, Inst. of Packaging Profls., C. of C. (bd. dirs.). Presbyterian. Office: Indsl Boxboard Corp 2249 Davis Ct Hayward CA 94545-1113

HUNTER, M. PENELOPE, university administrator; b. Nashville, Feb. 12, 1954; d. William B. and Margaret A. (Jackson) H.; m. Earl E. Ennor, May 7, 1984. BS, U. Oreg., 1975. Records analyst U. Houston, 1976-77; asst. dir. admissions and placement Coll. of Law Willamette U., Salem, Oreg., 1979-86; gallery organizer Quintana's Gallery, Portland, Oreg., 1986-88; asst. to pres. Haugh, Dean & Powell, Portland, 1988-89; asst. dir. admissions Pacific U., Forest Grove, Oreg., 1989-92, dir. admissions, grad. & profl. programs, 1992—; cons., interviewer Continuing Edn./Optometry, Forest Grove, 1992. Lead paddler Dragon Boat Racing Team, Portland Rose Festival, Internat. Dragon Boat Races, 1991—. Mem. Pacific N.W. Assn. Admissions Counselors. Democrat. Office: Pacific U 2043 College Way Forest Grove OR 97116

HUNTER, MELVIN EUGENE, hospital administrator, writer, researcher; b. Carmel, Calif., Sept. 15, 1946; s. Andrew Jefferson and Hazel (Furrey) H.; Anne Davies, Mar. 22, 1969; children: John Andrew, Bess Anne. BA in History, Calif. Poly Tech. U., 1971; MPA, U. San Francisco, 1975; JD, LaSalle U., L.A., 1989. adj. prof. law LaSalle U., L.A., 1991—. Author: Crested Cactus, 1992; editor Forensic Forum Jour. Forensic Mental Health Assn. Calif.; contbr. articles to profl. jours. Dir. Clin. Safety Project, Atascadero, Calif., 1987—; chair Prison Adv. Bd., San Luis Obispo, Calif.; pres. San Luis Obispo Zool. Soc., 1988; mem. San Luis Obispo Grand Jury, 1989-90. Recipient Safety award Gov. Pete Wilson, 1991, Superior Accomplishment award Calif. Dept. Mental Health, 1992; grantee Calif. Dept. Indsl. Rels., 1992. Mem. Am. Hosp. Assn., Hosp. Risk Mgrs. Home: 4000 Arizona Ave Atascadero CA 93422 Office: Atascadero State Hosp PO Box 7001 Atascadero CA 93423

HUNTER, RICHARD WILLIAM, director of training, researcher; b. Long Beach, Calif., Aug. 26, 1954; s. Lloyd Lawson and Margaret Elizabeth (Upjohn) H. AA, Chemeketa Community Coll., Salem, Oreg., 1972; BS in Sociology, Willamette U., 1976; MSW, Portland (Oreg.) State U., 1978. Researcher Oreg. Gov.'s Commn. on Youth, Salem, 1973-74; counseling coord. Comprehensive Youth Svcs. Ctr., Salem, 1978-79; social worker Salem Pub. Sch. Dist., 1979-81, Oreg. Children's Svcs. Div., Dallas, 1981-85; social worker supr. Oreg. Children's Svcs. Div., Corvallis, 1985-87; dir. tng. rsch. and tng. ctr. on family support and children's mental health Portland State U., 1987—; field instr. Western Oreg. State Coll., Monmouth, 1979-81, Portland State U., 1984-85, instr., 1988—. Author: (monograph) Changing Roles, Changing Relationships: Parent-Professional Collaboration on Behalf of Children with Emotional Disabilities, 1988. Mem. adv. com. Oreg. Justice Juvenile, Salem, 1976-80, Salem Youth Commn., 1972-73; chmn. Oreg. Human Resoures Opportunities Coalition, Salem, 1974-75, Oreg. Alliance Social Svc. Workers, Portland, 1981-83, Coalition in Oreg. for Parent Edn. Bd. Dirs.; mem. adv. bd. Oregon Family Support Network. Mem. NASW, Nat. Fedn. Families for Children's Mental Health, Bertha Capen Reynolds Soc. Democrat. Office: Portland State U Rsch and Tng Ctr 1912 SW 6th Ave Portland OR 97201

HUNTER, ROBERT MADISON, JR., osteopathic physician; b. Fairmont, W.Va., Dec. 29, 1951; s. Robert Madison and Betty Jo (Toothman) H.; m. Carol Lynn Conley, Aug. 4, 1979; children: Robert Madison III, Sean Michael. BS, BA, U. Ariz., 1975; DO, Phila. Coll. Osteo. Medicine, 1983. Intern Tucson Gen. Hosp., 1983-84; physician St. Johns (Ariz.) Health Ctr., 1984-87; physician in pvt. practice Tucson, 1987-88; physician Carondelet Health Svcs., Sierra Vista and Benson, Ariz., 1988-89; med. officer Davis-Monthan AFB, Tucson, 1989—; recreation supr. Ariz. Youth Ctr., Tucson, 1973-74; med. lit. scientist Med. Documentation Svc., Coll. Physicians of Phila., 1977-79; instr. CPR, ARC, Phila., 1981-83; dir. preventive medicine Tucson Gen. Hosp., 1987-88. Asst. editor Jour. of the Coll. of Physicians of Phila., 1978-79. Asst. instr. Rendokan Judo Dojo, Tucson, 1991-92, Black Belt, 1991. USPHS scholar, 1980-83. Mem. Am. Osteo. Assn., NRA, U.S. Judo Fedn., U.S. Judo Assn., Fifth Cavalry Meml. Regiment (quartermaster 1991-92). Office: 355th Med Group Davis-Monthan AFB Tucson AZ 85707

HUNTER, THEODORE PAUL, lawyer, energy consultant; b. St. Clair, Mich., Dec. 14, 1951; s. James Peter and Esther (Breuehner) H.; m. Ramona Holmes, Sept 5, 1977; children: Justin, Brandon. BS with honors, Portland (Oreg.) State U., 1973; JD, U. Wash., 1978. Bar: Wash 1978, U.S. Dist. Ct. (we. dist.) Wash. 1978, U.S. Ct. Appeals (9th cir.) 1979. Ptnr. Lippek, Hunter, Caryl & Raan, Seattle, 1978-83; chief counsel Wash. State Legis. Energy Com., Olympia, 1983-88; dir. Pacific Energy Inst., Seattle, 1988—; legal counsel Western Solar Network, Wash., Oreg., 1980-82; arbitrator King County Superior Cts., Seattle, 1985; prof./instr. Evergreen Coll., Olympia, 1986—. Contbr. articles to profl. jours. Fellow Environ. Law Inst., Washington, 1979. Mem. Washington State Bar Assn. (chair dispute resolution sect.), Environ. Lawyers of Wash., Soc. Profls. in Dispute Resolution, Klapa Sokoli. Democrat. Lutheran. Office: 101 Yesler Way Ste 607 Seattle WA 98104

HUNTER, THOMAS WILLARD, writer; b. Emmett, Idaho, Sept. 22, 1915; s. Stuart M. and Louise (Willard) H.; m. Mary Louise Merrell, Aug. 22, 1945; children: Thomas M., Willard M. BA, Carleton Coll., 1936; postgrad., Harvard Law Sch., 1936-38; MDiv, Andover Newton Theol. Sch., 1973, STM, 1977. Ordained to ministry, United Ch. of Christ, 1973. Staff exec. Oxford Group/Moral Re-Armament, Washington, 1938-56; assoc. gen. sec. Macalester Coll., St. Paul, 1957-59; coord. of devel. Claremont (Calif.) U. Ctr., 1959-66; guest scholar Brookings Instn., Washington, 1966-67; exec. v.p. Ind. Colls. of So. Calif., L.A., 1967-70; pastor Lee (N.H.) Ch. Congl. and Union Congl. Ch. of Madbury (N.H.), 1970-76; asst. to the pres. Sch. of Theology, Claremont, 1976-80; writer, speaker Claremont, 1980—. Author: The Tax Climate for Philanthropy, 1968, The Spirit of Charles Lindbergh, 1993; newspaper columnist, 1983—. Founder 4th of July Citizens Oratory Program, Claremont, 1977—, Ann. Claremont Way of the Cross, Claremont, 1980—, Anual Walk to L.A. from San Gabriel, 1981—; grand marshal Claremont 4th of July Parade, 1987; mem. Claremont United Ch. of Christ, 1961—. Named to Guinness Book of World Records for Longest Oration, 1984, 85. Mem. Univ. Club Claremont, Claremont Rotary. Republican. Home and Office: 525 W 6th St Claremont CA 91711

HUNTER, WALTER RAYMOND, physician; b. Bloomington, Ind., Aug. 2, 1953; s. Richard Raymond and Cecile Ruth (Rogers) H. AB, Ind. U., 1974; MD, Ind. U., Indpls., 1978. Diplomate Am. Bd. Internal Medicine.

Intern internal medicine Youngstown (Ohio) Hosp. Assn., 1978-81, chief resident, 1981-82; internist, chief medicine King Khahid Mil. City Hosp., Saudi Arabia, 1982-83; internist PruCare/Health First Med. Group, Memphis, 1983-85, Lerwick Clinic, St. Louis, 1986, Littleton (Colo.) Clinic, 1987-89; pvt. practice Denver, 1989—; mem. Archdiocesan AIDS Task Force, Denver, 1991—; advisor Archdiocesan Hospice of Peace, Denver, 1992; chmn. ethics com. Mercy Med. Ctr., Denver, 1990—; clin. instr. U. Colo. Sch. Medicine, Denver, 1990—; advisor pastoral care dept. St. Thomas Sem., Denver, 1991—. Columnist The 12 Step Times, 1989—; mem., contbg. editor Partners Mag. Choir mem. St. John's Cathedral Choir, Denver, 1987-92; mem., actor Main St. Players, Littleton, Colo., 1992. Mem. AMA, ACP, Am. Soc. Internal Medicine, Am. Soc. Law, Medicine and Ethics, Nat. Hospice Orgn., Soc. for Health and Human Values, The Hastings Ctr., Kennedy Inst. Ethics. Roman Catholic. Office: Coastal Med Center 9250 A Hwy 17 Bypass Murrells Inlet SC 29576

HUNTING, ANNE RITCHIE, school principal; b. Grants Pass, Oreg., July 1, 1944; d. William Riley Jr. and Allie Brown (Clark) R.; m. Charles James Cooper, Sept. 4, 1968 (div. 1985); children: Holly Anne, Wendy Nicole; William E. Hunting, Dec. 16, 1989. BA in Edn. with honors, Calif. State U., Sacramento, 1981. Cert. elem. tchr., Calif. Prin., dir. El Rancho Schs., Inc., Carmichael, Calif., 1981—; citizen amb. del. People to People Internat., Russia, Lithuania, Hungary, 1993. Mem. Republican Senatorial Inner Circle, Washington, 1992. Mem. Nat. Assn. Edn. for Young Children, Profl. Assn. Childhood Educators, Assn. for Supervision and Curriculum Devel., Sacramento Symphony Assn., AAUW, Crocker Art Museum. Episcopalian.

HUNTINGTON, HILLARD GRISWOLD, economist; b. Boston, Apr. 10, 1944; s. Hillard Bell and Ruth Smedley (Wheeler) H.; m. Honor Mary Griffin, Sept. 30, 1972; children: Honora Redmond, Emma Anne Hillard. BS, Cornell U., 1967; MA, SUNY, Binghamton, 1972, PhD, 1974. Staff economist Fed. Energy Adminstrn., Washington, 1974-77; dir., sr. economist Data Resources, Inc., Washington, 1977-80; exec. dir. Energy Modeling Forum Stanford (Calif.) U., 1980—; vol. U.S. Peace Corps., Pub. Utilities Authority, Monrovia, Liberia, 1967-69; vis. rsch. assoc. Inst. Devel. Studies, U. Nairobi, Kenya, 1972-73; mem. joint U.S.-U.S.S.R. Nat. Acad. Sci. Panel on Energy Conservation, 1986-90; mem. peer rev. panel Nat. Acid Precipitation Assessment Program Task Force, Ctrs. for Excellence Govt. Can.; consultant to Argonne Nat. Lab., Electric Power Rsch. Inst., numerous others. Editor Macroeconomic Impacts of Energy Shocks, 1987, N. Am. Natural Gas Markets: selected tech. studies, 1989. Mem. Internat. Assn. Energy Econs. (v.p. publs. 1990—, program chmn. ann. conf.), Am. Statis. Assn. (com. on energy stats. 1992—), Am. Econ. Assn. Home: 305 Hermosa Way Menlo Park CA 94025-5821 Office: Stanford U 406 Terman Ctr Stanford CA 94305

HUNTLEY, MARK EDWARD, biological oceanographer; b. Seattle, May 7, 1950; s. James Robert Huntley and Patricia Mary (Barricklow) Kissel; m. Patricia Darlene McFarlane, June 21, 1973 (div. 1980); children: Seth, Timothy; m. Kimberly Batcheller Brown, Sept. 19, 1981 (div. 1992); children: Swan Fairchild, Flannery Elizabeth, Zara Edith, Fletcher Wells. BSC with honors, U. Victoria, B.C., Can., 1976; PhD, Dalhousie U., Halifax, N.S., Can., 1980. Postdoctoral fellow Inst. Marine Resources, Scripps Instn. Oceanography, U. Calif. San Diego, La Jolla, Calif., 1980-82, asst. rsch. biologist, 1982-84; adj. lecturer Scripps Instn. Oceanography, U. Calif. San Diego, La Jolla, 1984—; asst. rsch. biologist marine biology rsch. div. Scripps Instn. Oceanography, La Jolla, 1984-87, assoc. rsch. biologist, 1987—; pres. Aquasearch, Inc., San Diego, 1984-88, chief oper. officer, 1988—, also chmn. bd. dirs., 1988—; deputy coord. water rsch. project U. Calif. San Diego, La Jolla, 1988-90; chmn. bd. dirs. Aquasearch, Inc., San Diego, 1984—; chief scientist Rsch. Antarctic Coastal Ecosystem Rates, La Jolla, 1986-87, 89, 91-92; exec. and steering com. mem. Global Ocean Ecosystem Dynamics, Washington, 1989—. Editor: Biological Treatment of Agricultural Wastewater, 1989; inventor Aquasearch Growth Module, 1989. Grantee Nat. Sci. Found. Office Naval Rsch., 1980—. Mem. Am. Soc. Limnology and Oceanography, Oceanography Soc. Office: Scripps Instn Oceanography 0202 La Jolla CA 92093

HUNTLEY, ROBERT JOSEPH, management consultant; b. Rochester, N.Y., May 28, 1924; s. Carroll Thomas and Margaret (Mosier) H.; student U. Redlands, 1943-44; B.S., U. So. Calif., 1947, M.S., 1952, D. Pub. Adminstrn., 1974; m. Patricia Ann Poss, Aug. 25, 1945; children: Timothy Robert, Debra Ann, Jon Joseph. Mem. Budget Bur. City of Los Angeles, 1947-52; asst. adminstrv. officer City of Beverly Hills, Calif., 1952-56; city adminstr. City of Santa Paula, Calif., 1957-58, City of La Habra, Calif., 1959-64; exec. Alpha Beta Acme Markets, La Habra, 1964-67; city adminstr. City of Westminster, Calif., 1967-77; exec. asst. County of Orange (Calif.), 1977-80, chief, labor relations, 1980-82, chief personnel ops., 1982-84; exec. dir. Hughes Enterprises, Laguna Hills, Calif., 1984-85; lectr., U. So. Calif., 1953-58, 70-74, Ventura Coll., 1958; asst. prof. Calif. State U., Fullerton, 1964-65; lectr. Golden West Coll., Orange Coast Coll., Calif. State U. at Davis, prof. Calif. State U. at Long Beach, 1971-79. Mem. pres. Municipal Water Dist. of Orange County, 1989-93, Gov.'s Policy Com. of Local Govt. Reform Task Force, 1973; active United Crusade. Served with USN, 1941-45; PTO. Mem. Am. Acad. Polit. and Social Sci., Am. Soc. Pub. Adminstrn., Western Govtl. Research Assn., Internat. City Mgmt. Assn., League Calif. Cities (exec. com. 1964-72), Blue Key, Pi Sigma Alpha, Phi Kappa Tau. Republican. Roman Catholic. Author: History of Administrative Research, 1952; Public Relations Training, 1954; The American City Manager, 1974. Home: 15172 Vermont St Westminster CA 92683-6136 Office: PO Box 430 Westminster CA 92684-0430

HUNTSBERGER, MICHAEL WILLIAM, radio station manager, consultant; b. Palo Alto, Calif., July 11, 1955; s. Ralph Francis and Margaret Elizabeth (Kroener) H.; m. Karen Elizabeth Berkey, June 18, 1983; 1 child, Eric Thomas. Student, U. Colo., 1973-75; BA, Evergreen State Coll., 1978. Prodn. mgr. Sta. KAOS Evergreen State Coll., Olympia, Wash., 1980, tech. dir., 1980-81, sta. mgr., 1981-82; owner Great Blue Heron Audio Co., Olympia, 1979-84; gen. mgr. Sta. KAOS Olympia Pub. Radio, 1982—; v.p., treas., sec., officer West Coast Pub. Radio, Ashland, Oreg., 1986—; del. Nat. Fedn. Community Broadcasters, Wash., 1983—. Dir. radio theater Alive in Olympia, 1987. De. Thurston County Dem. Conv., Olympia, 1984; mem. Wash. Fair Share, Seattle, 1989, Greenpeace, Washington, 1990. Mem. Nat. Model Railroad Assn. (pacific northwest region), Wash. Pub. Broadcasting Assn. (sec. 1992—). Democrat. Office: KAOS Olympia Pub Radio CAB 301 TESC Olympia WA 98505

HUNTSMAN, EDWARD LOYD, business consultant, marketing executive; b. Farmington, N.Mex., Dec. 19, 1951; s. Arral B and Ann McFarland (Viles) H.; m. Debbie J. Komadina, Aug. 21, 1976; 1 child, Steven Christopher. Student, U. N.Mex., 1973-75; BS in Bus. Adminstrn., Pacific Western U., L.A., 1991, MBA in Mgmt., 1993. Staff instr. U. N.Mex., Gallup, 1976-78; sta. mgr., staff mgr. Frontier Airlines, Denver and Durango, Colo., 1977-85; corp. sales mgr. Tamarron Inn and Country Club, Durango, 1985-86; dir. mktg. Royal West Airlines, Las Vegas, 1986-88; mgr. sales and svc. Am. West Vacations, Tempe, Ariz., 1988-91; bus. and mktg. cons. Total Resource Network, Tempe, 1991—; mktg. cons. Huntsman Graphic Design, Phoenix, 1988—. Photographer: Graphic Art Collateral, 1983. Bd. dirs. McKinley County United Way, Gallup, 1976-78; mem. exec. bd. Boy Scouts Am., Las Vegas, 1986-87; staff instr. Police Athletic League, Albuquerque, 1978-80; mem. Durango Area Mktg. Group, 1985-86; elder Presbyn. Ch. U.S.A., Durango, 1985. Sgt. U.S. Army, 1969-73, Viet Nam and Germany. Decorated Army Commendation medal; recipient Outstanding Leadership award Albuquerque Police Athletic League, 1976, Cert. of Merit for stopping a hijacking attempt Air Transp. Assn. Am./FAA, 1983; col., aide-de-camp to Gov. of N.Mex., 1976. Office: Total Resource Network 2125 E 5th St Ste 103 Tempe AZ 95281

HUPP, HARRY L., federal judge; b. L.A., Apr. 5, 1929; s. Earl L. and Dorothy (Goodspeed) H.; m. Patricia Hupp, Sept. 13, 1953; children: Virginia, Karen, Keith, Brian. AB, Stanford U., 1953, LLB, 1955. Bar: Calif. 1956, U.S. Dist. Ct. (cen. dist.) Calif. 1956, U.S. Supreme Ct. Pvt. practice law Beardsley, Hufstedler and Kemble, L.A., 1955-72; judge Superior Ct. of Los Angeles, 1972-84; appointed fed. dist. judge U.S. Dist. Ct. (cen. dist.) Calif., L.A., 1984—. Served with U.S. Army, 1950-52. Mem. Calif. Bar Assn., Los Angeles County Bar Assn. (Trial Judge of Yr. 1983), Order of Coif, Phi Alpha Delta. Office: US Dist Ct 312 N Spring St Los Angeles CA 90012-4701

HURABIELL, JOHN PHILIP, SR., lawyer, corporate professional; b. San Francisco, June 2, 1947; s. Emile John and Anna Beatrice (Blumenauer) H.; m. Judith Marie Hurabiell, June 7, 1969; children—Marie Louise, Michele, Heather, John Philip Jr. J.D., San Francisco Law Sch., 1976. Bar: Calif. 1977. Sole practice, San Francisco, 1977-86; ptnr. Huppert & Hurabiell, San Francisco, 1985—; pres. San Francisco S.A.F.E., Inc., 1983-88, pres. emeritus 1988—. Treas. Rep. election coms.; 1st v.p. Bling Babies Found., 1989-91; bd. dirs. Calif. State Mining and Mineral Mus., 1990-93. With USN, Vietnam. Decorated Navy Commendation Medal. Mem. ABA, Calif. Bar Assn., San Francisco Bar Assn., Assn. Trial Lawyers Am., Calif. Trial Lawyers Assn., San Francisco Trial Lawyers Assn., Lawyers Club San Francisco, St. Thomas More Soc., St. Francis Hook & Ladder Soc. (trustee). Roman Catholic. Clubs: Press of San Francisco (v.p. 1990-92), Ferrari Club Am., Golden Gate Breakfast Club. Lodge: KC, Alhambra (organizing regional dir. 1983-85). Editor, primary author: C.A.L.U. Business Practices Guidelines, rev. edit., 1980. Avocation: racing vintage automobiles, hunting. Office: Huppert & Hurabiell 1355 Market St Ste 417 San Francisco CA 94103-1317

HURLBERT, ROGER WILLIAM, information service industry executive; b. San Francisco, Feb. 18, 1941; s. William G. and Mary (Greene) H.; m. Karen C. Haslag, Nov. 6, 1982; children: Chula, Monk, Morris. BS in Community Devel., So. Ill. U., 1965. Newspaper editor and reporter various, San Francisco Bay Area, 1958-62; pvt. practice investigation Ill., 1963-65; advisor San Francisco Planning Urban Rsch. Assn., 1969-87; pres. Sage Info. Svcs., San Francisco, 1988—. Compiler Western States Land Data Base, 1972—. Pres. Haight-Ashbury Neighborhood Coun., San Francisco, 1959-61. With U.S. Army, 1966-68, Vietnam. Recipient Cert. of Merit San Francisco Coun. Dist. Merchants Assn., 1972. Mem. Info. Industry Assn., Direct Mktg. Assn., Mail Advt. Svc. Assn. Internat., League of Men Voters (v.p. 1959—). Democrat. Office: Sage Info Svcs 414 Clement St # 5 San Francisco CA 94118-2367

HURLEY, FRANCIS T., archbishop; b. San Francisco, Jan. 12, 1927. Ed., St. Patrick Sem., Menlo Park, Calif., Catholic U. Am. Ordained priest Roman Cath. Ch., 1951; with Nat. Cath. Welfare Conf., Washington, asst. sec., 1958-68; assoc. sec. Nat. Cath. Welfare Conf., now U.S. Cath. Conf., 1968-70; consecrated bishop, 1970; titular bishop Daimlaig and aux. bishop Diocese of Juneau, Alaska, 1970-71; bishop of Juneau, 1971-76, archbishop of Anchorage, 1976—. Office: Archdiocese of Anchorage Chancery Office 225 Cordeva St PO Box 102239 Anchorage AK 99510-0080

HURLEY, JAMES VINCENT, lawyer; b. St. Paul, Jan. 8, 1934; s. William J. and Marian J. (Clark) H.; m. Patricia G. Coleman, June 17, 1967; children: Anne, Mary, Catherine, Susan. BS, Loyola U., Chgo., 1956; M in Bus., U. Wis., 1957, JD, 1961. Bar: Oreg. 1961, U.S. Dist. Ct. Oreg. 1961, U.S. Ct. Appeals (9th cir.) 1967. Assoc. Koerner, Young, et al, Portland, Oreg., 1961-65; ptnr. Holmes, Hurley et al, Bend, Oreg., 1965—. Bd. dirs. Bend-LaPine Sch. Dist. #1, 1973-77, St. Charles Med. Ctr., Bend, 1978-86, bioethics com., 1985—; bd. dirs. St. Charles Med. Ctr. Found., Bend, 1989-90. Mem. ABA, Oreg. State Bar, Cen. Oreg. Bar Assn., Bend C. of C., Phi Delta Phi. Office: Holmes Hurley Bryant et al 40 NW Greenwood Ave Bend OR 97701-2027

HURLEY, MARK JOSEPH, bishop; b. San Francisco, Dec. 13, 1919; s. Mark J. and Josephine (Keohane) H. Student, St. Joseph's Coll., Mountain VIew, Calif., 1939, St. Patrick's Sem., Menlo Park, Calif., 1944; postgrad., U. Calif., Berkeley, 1943-45; PhD, Cath. U. Am., 1947; JCB, Lateran U., Rome, 1963; LLD, U. Portland, 1971. Ordained to priest Roman Cath. Ch., 1944. Asst. supt. schs. Archdiocese, San Francisco, 1944-51; tchr. Serra High Sch., San Mateo, Calif., 1944; prin. Bishop O'Dowd High Sch., Oakland, Calif., 1951-58, Marin Cath. High Sch., Marin County, Calif., 1959-61; supt. schs. Diocese, Stockton, Calif., 1962-65; chancellor, diocesan counsultor Diocese, 1962-65; asst. chancellor Arcdiocese, San Francisco, 1965-67; vicar gen. Arcdiocese, 1967-69; titular bishop Thunusuda; aux. bishop Thunusuda, San Francisco, 1967-69; bishop Santa Rosa, Cal., 1969—; pastor St. Francis Assisi Ch., San Francisco, 1967—; Prof. grad. schs. Loyola U., Balt., 1946, U. San Francisco, 1948, San Francisco Coll. Women, 1949, Dominican Coll., San Rafael, Calif., 1949, Cath. U. Am., 1954; prof. theology Beda Coll. Rome, 1987—, Angelicum U., Rome, 1989—; Del. Conf. Psychiatry and Religion, San Francisco, 1957; mem. bd. Calif. Com. on Study Edn., 1955-60; cons. Congregation for Cath. Edn., 1986—; del.-at-large Cal., White House Conf. on Youth, 1960; Cath. del., observer Nat. Council Chs., Columbus, Ohio, 1964; del. edn. conf. German and Am. educators, Nat. Cath. Edn. Assn., Munich, Germany, 1960; mem. commns. sems., univs. and schs. II Vatican Council, Rome, 1962-65; mem. commn. Christian formation U.S. Cath. Conf. Bishops, 1968; asst. archdiocesan coordinator Campaign on Taxation Schs. Calif., 1958, Rosary Crusade, 1961; adminstr. Cath. Sch. Purchasing Div., 1948-51, St. Eugene's Ch., Santa Rosa, Calif., 1959, St. John's Ch., San Francisco, 1961; mem. U.S. Bishops' Press Panel, Vatican Council, 1964-65, U.S. Bishops' Com. on Laity, 1964, U.S. Bishops' Com. Cath.-Jewish Relationships, 1965—, U.S. Bishops' Com. on Ecumenical and Interreligious Affairs, 1970, Conf. Maj. Superiors of Men, 1970; chmn. citizens Com. for San Francisco State Coll., 1968—; mem. adminstrn. bd. Nat. Council Cath. Bishops, 1970, mem. nominating com., 1971; mem. Internat. Secretariat for Non-Believers, Vatican, 1973; chmn. Secretariat for Human Values, Nat. Conf. Cath. Bishops, Washington, 1975; mem. Secretariat for Non-Believers, Vatican, 1986—; Vatican del. World Intellectual Properties Orgn., Washington, 1990. Syndicated columnist San Francisco Monitor, Sacramento Herald, Oakland Voice, Yakima (Wash.) Our Times, Guam Diocesan Press, 1949-66, TV speaker and panelist, 1956-67; author: Church State Relationships in Education in California, 1948, Commentary on Declaration on Christian Education in Vatican II, 1966, Report on Education in Peru, 1965, The Church and Science, 1982, Blood on the Shamrock, 1989, The Unholy Ghost, 1992. Trustee N.Am. Coll., Rome, 1970, Cath. U. Am., 1978—, Cath. Relief Services, 1979; cons. Congregation for Edn.; mem. Secretariat for Non-Belief, Vatican City; bd. dirs. Overseas Blind Found. Address: 273 Ulloa St San Francisco CA 94127

HURLEY, MARLENE EMOGENE, oil company executive; b. Chamois, Mo., July 23, 1938; d. Eugene Arthur Harrison and Mary Elizabeth (Turner) Meredith; m. Aaron Downs Hurley, Nov. 25, 1956; children: Mitchell Kelly, Aaron Downs Jr. Cert. oil and gas acctg., frontline mgr. Acct. McGrath Constrn. Co., Tulsa, 1964-66, G&T, Inc., G&T Constrn. and Valley Supply Co., Tulsa, 1965-67; acctg. supr. Automation Industries, Inc., Boulder, Colo., 1968-73; office mgr., chief acct. Automotive Svcs., White Rock Investments, JWD Corp., 3 Constrn. Div., Boulder, 1973; freelance acct. various cos., Boulder, 1974-76; treas., contr. Quicksilver, Inc., Colo. X-Ray, Colo. Processor Svc., Broomfield, 1974-79; contr. Hartford House, Ltd., Boulder, 1979-80; adminstrv. asst., mgr. Joint Acct. Payables Freeport McMoran, Inc., McMoran Oil & Gas, Midlands Oil, Lakewood, Colo., 1980-86; chief fin. officer Transp. Engring. Systems, Inc., Broomfield, 1987-88; asst. treas., contr. Altex Industries Inc., Altex Oil, Parrish Oil Tools, Denver, 1989—; cons. Spruce Realty, Boulder, 1974-76, Aaron Associated Affiliates, Lafayette, Colo., 1987-88. Mem. Rebekah lodge (past madam pres. 1966-67). Democrat. Home: RR 7 Box 405 Golden CO 80403-9805 Office: Altex Industries Inc 1430 Larimer St Denver CO 80202-1709

HURRELL, ANN PATRICIA, assistant director, educator; b. York, Eng., Aug. 23, 1942; d. Douglas and Kathleen Robson; m. John Patrick Hurrell, Nov. 23, 1963; children: Helen, Karen, Christopher. Diploma in Math., Aston Tech. Coll., England, 1961; postgrad., UCLA, 1973, AB in Econs., 1977; MBA, Calif. State U., Long Beach, 1987. Cert. early childhood edn. tchr., Calif. Systems analyst Physics and Engring. depts. Oxford (Eng.) U., 1961-66; early childhood tchr. Sheelana Presch., Lomita, Calif., 1970-71; ednl. cons. Sheelana Presch., Palos Verdes, Calif., 1971-78; tchr. St. Peters Sch., San Pedro, Calif., 1978-79, Chadwick Sch., Palos Verdes, 1979-87; asst. dept. adminstr. Kaiser Permanente Med. Group, Harbor City, Calif., 1987-88; dean middle sch. Chadwick Sch., Palos Verdes, 1988-91; asst. dir. Chadwick Mid. Sch., Palos Verdes, 1991—. Contbr. articles to profl. jours. Mem. ASCD, Nat. Mid. Sch. Assn., Assn. Ednl. Therapists. Office: Chadwick Sch 26800 Academy Dr Palos Verdes Peninsula CA 90274-3997

HURST, DEBORAH, pediatric hematologist; b. Washington, May 9, 1946; d. Willard and Frances (Wilson) H.; m. Stephen Mershon Senter, June 14, 1970; children: Carlin, Daniel. BA, Harvard U., 1968; MD, Med. Coll. Pa., 1974. Diplomate Nat. Bd. Med. Examiners, Am. Bd. Pediatrics, Am. Bd. Pediatric Hematology-Oncology. Intern Bellevue Hosp., NYU Hosp., N.Y.C., 1974-75, resident in pediatrics, 1975-76; ambulatory pediatric fellow Bellevue Hosp., N.Y.C., 1976-77; hematology, oncology fellow Bellevue Hosp., Columbia U., N.Y.C., 1977-80; assoc. hematologist Childrens Hosp. Oakland, Calif., 1980-92; asst. clin. prof. U. Calif. San Francisco Med. Ctr., 1992—; assoc. rsch. dir. Miles Biol. Div., Inc., Berkeley, Calif., 1992—; hematology cons. Assn. Asian/Pacific Community Health Orgns., Oakland; dir. Satellite Hematology Clinic/Valley Childrens Hosp., Fresno, Calif., 1984-92; cons. state dept. epidemiology Calif. State Dept. Health, Berkeley, 1992; chelation cons. lead poisoning program Childrens Hosp., Oakland, 1986-92. Contbr. articles to profl. jours. Vol. cons. lead poisoning State Dept. Epidemiology and Toxicology, Berkeley, 1986-92. Fellow Am. Acad. Pediatrics; mem. Am. Soc. Hematology, Hemophilia Rsch. Soc., N.Y. Acad. Sci., Nat. Hemophilia Found., Internat. Soc. Thrombosis and Hemostasis. Office: Miles Biological Div Inc 4th and Parker Sts Berkeley CA 94701

HURT, CHARLIE DEUEL, III, library school director; b. Charlottesville, Va., Sept. 20, 1950; s. Charlie Deuel Jr. and Timie Oletta (Young) H.; m. Susan Edith Scudamore, May 15, 1981. BA, U. Va., 1971; MLS, U. Ky., 1975; PhD, U. Wis., 1981. Engring. librarian U. Va., Charlottesville, 1975-78, automation librarian, 1977-78; asst. prof. McGill U., Montreal, Que., Can., 1981-84, assoc. prof., 1984; assoc. prof. Simmons Coll., Boston, 1984-86; dir., prof. lib. sch. U. Ariz., Tucson, 1986—; prin. Info. Prime, Montreal, 1984—; cons. Scudamore & Assocs. Montreal, 1984-85. Author: Information Sources in Science and Technology, 1988; co-author: Scientific and Technical Literature, 1990; contbr. articles to profl. jours. Hollowell grantee Simmons Coll., 1984. Mem. ALA, IEEE, Am. Math Soc., Assn. Library and Info. Sci. Edn., History Sci. Soc., N.Y. Acad. Sci. Home: 1820 W Wimbledon Way Tucson AZ 85737-9070 Office: U Ariz Sch Libr Sci 1515 E 1st St Tucson AZ 85719

HURTUBISE, MARK, academic administrator; b. Evanston, Ill., Apr. 28, 1948; m. Rowena Yung; children: Monica, Michelle, Justin. BA, St. Joseph's Coll., Ind., 1970; MA, U. Santa Clara, 1979; JD, Lincoln U., 1975; EdD, U. San Francisco, 1988. Assoc. Margolis, Chatzky, Dunnett, Meuhlenbeck, Los Gatos, Calif., 1975-77; dir. legal affairs, acting and asst. dir. div. cont. edn. Coll. of Notre Dame, Belmont, Calif., 1979-87; v.p., dean Sierra Nevada Coll.-Lake Tahoe, Incline Village, Nev., 1987-92, pres., 1993—; devel. officer, in-house legal counsel, cons. Cogswell Poly. Coll., Cupertino, Calif., 1982-87. Author: (with others) Enhancing Departmental Leadership, 1990; contbr. atricles to poetry, law, history and edn. jours. Mem. Incline Village/Crystal Bay Econ. Task Force; vice chmn. San Francisco Archdiocesan Bd. Edn.; founding mem. Nev chpt. UN Assn. U.S.A. Mem. Calif. Acad. Scis., San Francisco Zool. Soc., Soc. for History Edn., Sierra Club, Lake Tahoe Artists Network. Office: Sierra Nevada Coll 800 Coll Dr PO Box 4269 Incline Village NV 89450

HUSBAND, RICK DOUGLAS, air force officer, test pilot; b. Amarillo, Tex., July 12, 1957; s. Douglas Earl and Jane Virginia (Barbagallo) H.; m. Evelyn June Neely, Feb. 27, 1982; 1 child, Laura Marie. BSME cum laude, Tex. Tech U., 1980; MSME with distinction, Calif. State U., Fresno, 1990. Cons. engr. Abrahamson and Assocs., Amarillo, Tex., 1980; commd. 2d lt. USAF, 1980, advanced through grades to maj., 1993; F-4 aircraft comdr. 69 Tactical Fighter Squadron, Moody AFB, Ga., 1982-85; F-4 instr. pilot 35 Tactical Tng. Squadron, George AFB, Calif., 1985-87; exptl. test pilot 6512 Test Squadron, Edwards AFB, Calif., 1988-89, 6515 Test Squadron, Edwards AFB, 1989-92; fixed wing test squadron RAF Boscombe Down, 1992—. Bd. dirs. First United Meth. Ch., Valdosta, Ga., 1984-85, choir mem., 1983-85; choir mem. Ch. of the Valley, Apple Valley, Calif., 1985-87, Antelope Valley Master Chorale, Lancaster, Calif., 1991-92. Mem. Soc. Exptl. Test Pilots, Air Force Assn., Daedalians, Toastmasters, Tau Beta Pi (engring. hon., V.P. 1978-79), Pi Tau Sigma (engring. hon., sec. 1978).

HUSKEY, HARRY DOUGLAS, information and computer science educator; b. Whittier, N.C., Jan. 19, 1916; s. Cornelius and Myrtle (Cunningham) H.; m. Velma Elizabeth Roeth, Jan. 2, 1939; children: Carolyn, Roxanne, Harry Douglas, Linda. BS, U. Idaho, 1937; student, Ohio U., 1937-38; MA, Ohio State U., 1940, PhD, 1943. Temp. prin. sci. officer Nat. Phys. Labs., Eng., 1947; head machine devel. lab. Nat. Bur. Standards, 1948; asst. dir. Inst. Numerical Analysis, 1948-54; asso. dir. computation lab. Wayne U., Detroit, 1952-53; asso. prof. U. Calif., Berkeley, 1954-58, prof., 1958-68, vice chmn. elec. engring., 1965-66; prof. info. and computer sci. U. Calif., Santa Cruz, 1968-85, prof. emeritus, 1985—; dir. Computer Center, 1968-77, chmn. bd. info. sci., 1976-79, 82-83; vis. prof. Indian Inst. Tech., Kanpur; (Indo-Am. program), 1963-64, 71, Delhi U., 1971; cons. computer div. Bendix, 1954-63; vis. prof. M.I.T., 1966; mem. computer sci. panel NSF, Naval Research Adv. Com.; cons. on computers for developing countries UN, 1969-71; chmn. com. to advise Brazil on computer sci. edn. NAS, 1970-72; project coord. UNESCO/Burma contract, 1973-79; mem. adv. com. on use microcomputers in developing countries NRC, 1983-85. Co-editor: Computer Handbook, 1962. Recipient Disting. Alumni award Idaho State U., 1978, Pioneer award Nat. Computer Conf., 1978, IEEE Computer Soc., 1982; U.S. sr.scientist awardee Fulbright-Alexander von Humboldt Found., Mathematisches Institut der Tech. U. Munich, 1974-75, 25th Ann. medal ENIAC; inducted into U. Idaho Alumni Hall of Fame, 1989. Fellow AAAS, IEEE (editorial bd., editor-in-chief computer group 1965-71, Centennial award 1984), Brit. Computer Soc.; mem. Am. Math. Soc., Math. Assn. Am., Assn. Computing Machinery (pres. 1960-62), Am. Fedn. Info. Processing Socs. (governing bd. 1961-63), Sigma Xi. Home: 656 High St Santa Cruz CA 95060-2645 Office: U of Calif Santa Cruz Computer & Info Sci Santa Cruz CA 95064

HUSS, CHARLES MAURICE, municipal building official; b. Chgo., Nov. 11, 1946; s. Charles Maurice and June Pierce (Bailey) H.; m. Winifred Louise Traughber, Dec. 24, 1973; children: Amber Elaine, Ra Ja Lorraine, Micah Alexander, Gabriel Joe, Cameron M., Jordan Charles. AA, Kendall Coll., 1984; student Chukchi Community Coll., 1978-83, Oregon State U., 1985, Western Oreg. State Coll., 1984-89, U. Cin., 1985—, U. Alaska, Western Ill. U., 1987, City U., 1986, Nat. Fire Acad., 1986-88, Ohio U., 1989—. Traffic mgr. The Harwald Co., Evanston, Ill., 1966-67, asst. v.p., 1968-69; traffic mgr. Northwestern U. Press, Evanston, 1969-71; fire chief City of Kotzebue, Alaska, 1971-76, asst. city mgr., 1973-76; dir. maintenance USPHS Hosp., Kotzebue, 1976-79; pres., gen. mgr. Action Builders, Inc., Kotzebue, 1979-82; gen. mgr. Husky Maintenance Svcs., 1982—; chief bldg. insp. City of Kotzebue, 1985—; adj. faculty Nat. Fire Acad., Emmitsburg, Md. Guest essayist Seven Days and Sunday (Kirkpatrick), 1973; contbr. to Alaska Craftsman Home Building Manual. Chmn. Kotzebue Planning Commn., 1978-82, Kotzebue Sch. Bd., 1974-79, 83—; founding vice chmn. Kotzebue chpt. ARC; mem. Alaska Criminal Code Revision Commn., 1976-78; mem. Fire Marshal's Sprinkler Task Force; mem. Alaska Fire Fighter Tng. Commn.; mem. Arctic Fire Mitigation Code Task Force, Statewide Bldg. Code Task Force, Alaska Housing Fin. Corp. Bldg. Inspector Standards Task Force; asst. chief Kotzebue Vol. Fire Dept., 1972-76, 82—; bd. dirs, instr. Alaska Craftsman Home Program 1986—; instr. Kotzebue Regional Fire Tng. Ctr., 1982—. Pullman Found. scholar, 1964-65, Blackburn Coll. scholar, 1964-65, Ill. State scholar, 1964-66. Mem. ASHRAE, Am. Constrn. Inspectors Assn. (registered constrn. inspector, engring. divsn., bldg. divsn.), Alaska Assn. for Computers in Edn., Constrn. Specifications Inst., Internat. Soc. Fire Svc. Instrs., Fire Marshals Assn. N.Am., Bldg. Ofcls. and Code Adminstrs. Internat., Alaska Firefighters Assn., Internat. Assn. Fire and Arson Investigators, Assn. Fire Protection Designers, Western Fire Chiefs Assn., Internat. Conf. Bldg. Ofcls. (cert. bldg. ofcl., fire, plumbing, elec., combination dwelling and mech. insp.), Am. Soc. Safety Engrs., Internat. Assn. Plumbing and Mech. Ofcls., Internat. Assn. Elec. Insps., Internat. Assn. Fire Chiefs, Home Builders Assn. Alaska, Nat. Fire Protection Assn., Soc. Nat. Fire Acad. Instrs., Coalition for Home Fire Safety, Masonry Soc., Kotzebue C. of C. Home and Office: PO Box 277 Kotzebue AK 99752-0277

HUSSEY, DAVID BRADFORD, quality assurance inspector; b. Portsmouth, N.H., June 5, 1960; s. Robert Melvin and Ann Virginia (Brachett) H.; m. Debra Lou Rice, Mar. 3, 1983 (div. May 1987); 1 child, Adrienne Cherie. Mgr. L.P.g. div., H&H Oil Co., Inc. Mgr. H&H Oil Co., Inc.,

Greenland, N.H., 1979-83; quality assurance piping and welding Pullman Power Products, Seabrook, N.H., 1983-85; quality assurance inspector Calvent, San Diego, 1986-87, Remec Microwave Components, San Diego, 1987—. Writer songs Better to Have, 1988, Just a Nobody, 1988, Mother's Birthday Song, 1991, Adrienne's Song, 1992, others. Mem. Union of Concerned Scientists, Cambridge, Mass., 1987—; lectr. to pub. schs. Mem. Planetary Soc. Republican.

HUSTON, HARRIETTE IRENE OTWELL (REE HUSTON), city official; d. Harry C. Otwell and Fannie (Mitchell) Otwell Geffert; m. Dan E. Huston, Jan. 21, 1951; children: Terry Dane, Dale Curtis, Ronald William, Randall Philip. BS, Kans. State Coll., 1951. Cert. life ins. agt., Wash.; cert. wastewater operator in tng., Wash. Tchr. Kans., Ill., 1955-68; assoc. home economist McCall's Patterns Co., N.Y.C., 1959-62; counselor, owner Dunhill of Seattle Personnel, 1968-75; enrollment officer, trainer, adminstrv. sec. Teller Tng. Insts., Seattle, 1975-76; life and health ins. agt. Lincoln Nat. Sales, Seattle, 1976-77; office mgr., adminstrv. sec. ARA Transp. Group, Seattle, 1977-78; asst. to the pres. Pryde Corp., Bellevue, Wash., 1978-80; sr. sec. Municipality of Met. Seattle, 1980-91, project asst., 1992—. Co-author: Homemaking textbook, 1956; contbr. articles to profl. jours.. Sec. exec., mem. gen. bd. Bellevue Christian Ch., Disciples of Christ, 1976-77, 86-87, chmn. flowers com., 1978-83, elder, 1978, deacon, 1987; bd. dirs., sec. Surrey Downs Community Club, Bellevue, 1983-85. Recipient Clothing award check McCall's Patterns Co., N.Y.C., 1962, Certs. of Merit Metro Hdqrs., Seattle, 1981, 82, 83, 86, 89. Club: Bridge (Bellevue). Home: 2424 109th Ave SE Bellevue WA 98004-7332 Office: Municipality of Met Seattle 821 2d Ave Seattle WA 98104

HUSTON, JOHN CHARLES, law educator; b. Chgo., Mar. 21, 1927; s. Albert Allison and Lillian Helen (Sullivan) H.; m. Joan Frances Mooney, Aug. 1, 1954; children: Mark Allison, Philip John, Paul Francis James; m. Inger Margareta Westerman, May 4, 1979. AB, U. Wash., Seattle, 1950; JD, U. Wash., 1952; LLM, NYU, 1955. Bar: Wash. 1952, N.Y. 1964, U.S. Dist. Ct. (we. dist.) Wash. 1953, U.S. Ct. Appeals (9th cir.) 1953, U.S. Tax Ct. 1977. Assoc. Kahin, Carmody & Horswill, Seattle, 1952-53; teaching fellow NYU Law Sch., 1953-54; asst. co-dir. U. Ankara Legal Research Inst., Turkey, 1954-55; asst. prof. NYU, 1953-57; asst. prof. Syracuse U., N.Y., 1957-60, assoc. prof., 1960-65, prof., 1960-67; prof., assoc. dean U. Wash., Seattle, 1967-73, prof. law, 1973—; adj. prof. Asia-Pacific Law Inst., Bond Univ., Australia; of counsel Carney, Badley, Smith & Spellman, Seattle; vis. prof. U. Stockholm, 1986, U. Bergen, 1989, Bond U., Australia, 1991. Author: (with Redden) The Mining Law of Turkey, 1956, The Petroleum Law of Turkey, 1956, (with Mucklestone and Cross) Community Property: General Considerations, 1971, 3d edit., 1984, (with others) Administration of Criminal Justice, 1966, 2d edit., 1969, (with Miyatake & Way) Japanese International Taxation, 1983, supplements, 1993, (with Cross & Shields) Community Property Desk Book, 1989, (with Williams) Handbook on Permanent Establishment, 1993. Served to capt. USAF. Mem. ABA, Wash. State Bar Assn., Seattle-King County Bar Assn., Japanese Am. Soc. Legal Studies, Internat. Fiscal Assn. (past regional v.p.). Office: U Wash Sch Law JB-20 Seattle WA 98105

HUSTON, KENNETH DALE, lawyer; b. Watsonville, Calif., Aug. 2, 1936; s. Charles Edward Huston and Chauncey Elfie (Bivens) Stephen; m. Janet Joyce Markarian, Dec. 31, 1971; children: Jennifer, Brian. Student, U. Okla., 1954-56, U. Utah, 1958-60; BA in Engring. and Math., San Diego State U., 1972; JD, U. San Diego, 1979. Bar: Calif. 1979. Assoc. Higgs, Fletcher & Mack, San Diego, 1980-88; dir. Grace, Neumeyer & Otto, L.A. and San Diego, 1988-89; dir., shareholder Grace, Scocypek, Cosgrove & Schirm, L.A. and San Diego, 1988—; judge pro-tem San Diego Mcpl. Ct. South Bay, Chula Vista, Calif., 1988—. With USN, 1956-78. Mem. Calif. State Bar, San Diego County Bar Assn., San Diego Def. Lawyers. Republican. Office: Grace Scocypek Cosgrove & Schirm 1551 4th Ave Ste 710 San Diego CA 92101

HUSTON-COLLICOTT, TERRI LYNN, artist; b. Laramie, Wyo., Feb. 2, 1959; d. James Robert and Sandra Lynn (Taylor) Wagner; m. Lex Dover Huston, Aug. 21, 1977 (div. Oct. 1984); children: Cortney, Josie, Cameron; m. David Robert Collicott, Mar. 30, 1991. AA, Arapahoe C.C., 1987-89. Graphic artist T. Huston Wearable Art, Jackson, Wyo., 1977—; apt. mgr. Catalina Shores, Las Vegas, Nev., 1989-90, Absolute Rental Properties, Sheridan, Wyo., 1992—; USA/Can. trade show mgr. Huckleberry Mountain Chocolates, 1993—. Executed murals Sweatshop, 1992, DollHouse, 1992, Laundry Ladies, 1992, Santa's Village-North Pole, 1991; artist stationery, Christmas cards Cat Care Soc., 1989. Vol. Colo. Pub. Interest Rsch. Group, Denver, 1990; regional pres. Betterment of Youth, Las Vegas, 1991-92; mem. Nature Conservancy, 1986—, Greenpeace, 1986—, Earth First, Las Vegas, 1991—, Pro-Choice; com. chair Creative Life Ch., 1989-91. Home and Office: 2200 Corner Creek Ln Jackson WY 83001

HUSZTI, JOSEPH BELA, conductor, educator; b. Lorain, Ohio, Sept. 27, 1936; s. Joseph Maynard and Rose (Farkas) H.; m. Melinda Murray, Aug. 15, 1959; 1 child, Heather Christine. MusB, Northwestern U., 1958, MusM, 1959; postgrad., Occidental Coll., UCLA, U. So. Calif., Ohio State U., SUNY, Bingamton; studies with, Todd Duncan, Hellmuth Rilling, Otto Werner Mueller, William Vennard, Howard Swan; student, Baroque Inst., Oberlin Coll., 1992. Prof. Bakersfield (Calif.) Coll., 1959-66, U. Del., Newark, 1966-72, Boston U., 1972-77; prof. music, head voice and choral studies U. Calif., Irvine, 1977—; dir. Young Vocalist Program at Tanglewood, Lenox, Mass., 1973-77; condr., clinician festivals in numerous states and countries, 1965—; participant Bach Festival, U. Oreg., 1979, 82. Condr. (rec.) Boston University at Tanglewood, 1978; dir. (performance video) Madrigal Dinner, 1982 (ACE/Achievement in Cablecasting Excellence award 1982); contbg. author: (book on choral music) In Quest of Answers, 1990; movie credits include To The Limit, 1990; contbr. articles to profl. publs. Condr. first Am. choir to win Ordo I mixed choirs, Llangollen, Wales, 1965; recipient Ecumenical medal Pope Paul VI, 1965, Lauds and Laurels award U. Calif., 1991, Folklore award Béla Bartók Competition, Debrecen, Hungary, 1988, 1st prize Youth Choirs Competition, Llangollen, 1992, World Choral Festival, Seoul, Korea, 1992. Mem. Am. Choral Dirs. Assn. (pres. Del. chpt. 1969-74, pres. Mass. chpt. 1973-75, pres. western divsn. 1979-81). Office: U Calif Sch Fine Arts Music Dept Irvine CA 92717

HUTCHCRAFT, A. STEPHENS, JR., aluminum and chemical company executive; b. Orange, N.J., June 26, 1930; s. A. Stephens and Marguerite (Davis) H.; m. Mary Seaman, May 28, 1955; children: Pamela, Martha, A. Stephens. B.S., Yale U., 1952; postgrad. mgmt. devel., Harvard U., 1964. Registered profl. engr., Calif. Extrusion plant mgr. Kaiser Aluminum & Chem. Corp., Los Angeles, 1964-68; div. mgr. Kaiser Aluminum & Chem. Corp., Oakland, Calif., 1968-70, v.p., mgr. elec. products, 1970-75, v.p. aluminum, reduction and carbon, 1975-80, v.p., gen. mgr. aluminum div., 1980-82, pres., COO, 1982-93, chmn. bd. dirs., CEO, 1993—; dir. Anglesey Aluminum, London, Valco, Ghana. Chmn. western region Nat. Amigos de Ser, Dallas, 1983; bd. dirs. Met. YMCA Alameda County, Calif., Calif. Symphony. Mem. Aluminum Assn. (chmn. 1982—). Republican. Presbyterian. Home: 15 Hillside Dr Danville CA 94526-3714 Office: Kaiser Aluminum & Chem Corp 300 Lakeside Dr Oakland CA 94643-0002

HUTCHERSON, CHRISTOPHER ALFRED, sales executive, sales and recruiting consultant; b. Memphis, June 13, 1950; s. Wayne Alfred Hutcherson and Loretta (Morris) Kindsfather; m. Glenda Ann Champ, May 22, 1971. BS, U. Houston, 1972, M in Adminstrn., 1977, postgrad., 1977-79. Pvt. music instr. Spring Br. and Pasadena Ind. Sch. Dists., Tex., 1968-75; jr. high and high sch. band dir. Deer Park (Tex.) Ind. Schs., 1972-80; recruiter M. David Lowe Personnel, Houston, 1981; sales dir. Instl. Financing Svcs., Benicia, Calif., 1982-85; sales mgr. Instl. Financing Svcs., Benicia, 1985-87; nat. tng. dir. Champion Products and Svcs., San Diego, 1987-88, west coast and midwest sales mgr., 1988-89; pres. Camelot, Inc., Auburn, Calif., 1989-91; pres., chief exec. officer Camelot Telephone Assistance Program, Inc., Folsom, Calif., 1991-92, Nat. Scrip Ctr. Distbrs., Inc., 1992—. Judge Tex. jr. high and high sch. bands, 1974-81; choir dir. St. Hyacinth Ch., Deer Park, 1979-81; vice-chmn. Ch. Coun. St. Hyacinth Ch., 1980. Mem. Kappa Kappa Psi (v.p.). Republican. Roman Catholic. Home: 2491 Frontier Rd Auburn CA 95603-9480

HUTCHESON, JERRY DEE, manufacturing company executive; b. Hammon, Okla., Oct. 31, 1932; s. Radford Andrew and Ethel Mae (Boulware) H.; B.S. in Physics, Eastern N. Mex. U., 1959; postgrad. Temple U., 1961-62, U. N.Mex., 1964-65; m. Lynda Lou Weber, Mar. 6, 1953; children—Gerald Dan, Lisa Marie, Vicki Lynn. Research engr. RCA, 1959-62; sect. head Motorola, 1962-63; research physicist Dikewood Corp., 1963-66; sr. mem. tech. staff Signetics Corp., 1966-69; engring. mgr. Litton Systems, Sunnyvale, Calif., 1969-70; engring. mgr. Fairchild Semiconductor, Mountain View, Calif., 1971; equipment engr., group mgr. Teledyne Semiconductor, Mountain View, 1971-74; dir. engring. DCA Reliability Labs., Sunnyvale, 1974-75; founder, prin. Tech. Ventures, San Jose, Calif., 1975—; chief exec. officer VLSI Research, Inc., 1981—. Democratic precinct committeeman, Albuquerque, 1964-66. Served with USAF, 1951-55. Registered profl. engr., Calif. Mem. Nat. Soc. Profl. Engrs., Profl. Engrs. Pvt. Practice, Calif. Soc. Profl. Engrs., Semiconductor Equipment and Materials Inst., Soc. Photo-Optical Instrumentation Engrs., Am. Soc. Test Engrs., Presbyterian. Club: Masons. Contbr. articles to profl. jours. Home: 5950 Vista Loop San Jose CA 95124-6562 Office: VSLI Rsch 1754 Technology Dr Ste 117 San Jose CA 95110-1308

HUTCHINGS, DALE, county official; b. Bakersfield, Calif., Mar. 23, 1954; s. Cleave and Effie Letha (Wheeler) H.; m. Mary Georgette Coder, Oct. 11, 1975; 1 child, Christina Renee. AA, Bakersfield Jr. Coll., 1982; diploma, Universal Tech. Inst., 1983; BA, Calif. State U., Bakersfield, 1990, MA, 1992. Sales rep. Am. Nat. Ins., Bakersfield, 1976-80; claim adjuster Gen. Adjustment Bureau Bus. Svcs., Ind., Bakersfield, 1985; dist. office adjuster Auto Club of So. Calif., Bakersfield, 1985-87; internrisk mgmt. dept. Am. Soc. Pub. Administrs., Bakersfield, 1990-91; grad. intern County Adminstrv. Office, Bakersfield, 1991—. Vol. fundraiser Kern County Shrine Club, Bakersfield, 1989. Mem. ASPA (bd. dirs. 1991-92, scholar 1990-91), Internat. City Mgrs. Assn., Pub. Risk Mgmt. Assn., Masons (jr. deacon 1989, marshall 1990, 32 degree), Knights Templar Calif. (Sir Knight), Al Malaikah Temple (Noble, fundraiser 1988). Republican. Home: 3014 18th St Bakersfield CA 93301

HUTCHINS, CHARLES LARRY, educational association administrator, consultant; b. Oskaloosa, Iowa, Mar. 12, 1938; s. Charles Eugene and Margaret Emma (Ferguson) H.; m. Carolyn Lyn Moran, Dec. 26, 1962; children: Holly, Julie, Christie. Student, Cornell Coll., Mt. Vernon, Iowa, 1956-58; BA, U. Iowa, 1960, MA, 1961, PhD, 1965. Instr. U. Mo., Columbia, 1961-63; asst. prof. U. Ill., Chgo., 1965-66; exec. dir. Oreg. State System of Higher Edn., Corvallis, Oreg., 1966-68; assoc. dir. Far West Lab., San Francisco, 1968-74; asst. dir. Nat. Inst. Edn., Washington, 1974-78; exec. dir. Mid-Continent Regional Ednl. Lab., Aurora, Colo., 1978-88; cons. and speaker in field. Sr. author: mgmt. tng. system "A"chieving Excellence, 1989; co-author: tng. program Tactics for Thinking, 1987; sr. editor, author: periodical Noteworthy, 1978—. Precinct capt. Arapahoe County Dems., Aurora, 1980-82. Mem. Coun. for Edn., Devel. and Rsch. (chmn. 1988-89), Internat. Soc. Study of Systems, Nat. Rsch. Coun. (com. Fed. role in edn. rsch., 1991-92), Assn. for Supervision and Curriculum Devel., Phi Beta Kappa. Office: Mid-Continent Regional Lab 2550 S Parker Rd Aurora CO 80014-1671

HUTCHINS, EARL LEROY, retired school system administrator; b. Deer Park, Wash., Nov. 26, 1908; s. Harry Merton and May Edith (Burroughs) H.; m. Helen Lucile Weeks, Aug. 27, 1934 (dec. May 1978); children: Linda Mary, Stephen Weeks, Patrick Earl; m. Betty Soule Hazen, June 11, 1979. BA in Edn., Western Wash. U., 1941; MA, Stanford U., 1951. Program dir. State of Wash., Longview, 1957-59; adminstrv. asst. Longview Pub. Schs., 1959-61, asst. supt., 1961-74; retired, 1974. Chmn. publicity com. Longview St. Ctr., 1986-88; pres. Longview Kiwanis Club, 1957. Wash. Edn. Assn. (pres. Skamokawa, Wash. chpt. 1937-38). Home: 575 Peardale Ln # 9 Longview WA 98632-3255

HUTCHINS, JEFFREY CARLTON, protective services official; b. Coronado, Calif., May 28, 1959; s. Carlton Leroy and Lucille (Cash) H.; m. Patricia Lynn Palmer, Feb. 16, 1980; children: Ashleigh Lynne, Emily Erin, Glenell Renee, Kendall Marie. AS in Criminal Justice, Southwestern Calif. Coll., Chula Vista, 1983. Dispatcher City of Coronado Police Dept., 1977-80, police officer, 1980-86, police investigator, 1986-89, police sgt., 1989—; rep. City of San Diego County Disaster Coun., 1986-89; mem. So. Calif. Emergency Svcs. Assn., 1986-89. Cons.: (book) Emergency Planning Guidelines for Local Law Enforcement, 1989. Mem. Calif. Police Officers Assn., Coronado Police Officers Assn. (sec., treas. 1977-80), Fraternal Order of Police, Amateur Radio League, Coronado Kiwanis. Republican. Methodist. Office: Coronado Police Dept 578 Orange Ave Coronado CA 92118-1897

HUTCHINS, JOHN MILTON, lawyer; b. Washington, Dec. 5, 1950; s. Edward John and Majorie Dolores (Wiegert) H.; m. Dale Denise Ockl; 1 child, Adam Edward. BA, U. Colo., 1973, JD, 1976. Bar: Colo. 1976, Tex. 1980, U.S. Ct. Mil. Appeals 1978, U.S. Supreme Ct. 1983. Asst. city atty. City of El Paso, Tex., 1982; asst. Colo. atty. gen. Colo. Office of Atty. Gen., Denver, 1982-84, 1st asst. Colo. atty. gen., 1984-90; asst. U.S. atty. dist. of Colo. U.S. Atty.'s Office, Denver, 1990—. Contbr. articles to profl. publs. Mem. Northglenn (Colo.) City Charter Commn., 1975, Northglenn City Coun., 1976-77; grand juror Adams County, Colo. Grand Jury, Brighton, 1988. Capt. U.S. Army, 1977-81. Mem. Denver Posse of Westerners (sec. 1989-90, v.p. 1992—), State Bar of Tex., Colo. Bar Assn. Republican. Presbyterian. Office: Office of US Atty 1961 Stout St Denver CO 80294

HUTCHINS, SANDRA ELAINE, computer scientist; b. National City, Calif., Jan. 22, 1946; d. Edwin and Elaine (Emerson) H. BA in Applied Physics, U. Calif., San Diego, 1967, PhD in Computer & Info. Scis., 1970. Asst. prof. electronics engr. Purdue U., Lafayette, Ind., 1970-72; sr. staff engr. TRW Def. & Space Systems, Redondo Beach, Calif., 1972-77; mng. engr. rsch. & devel. Linkabit Corp., San Diego, 1977-79; tech. dir. voice processing ITT Def., San Diego, 1979-83, ITT Communication Div., Nutley, N.J., 1979-83; pres. Emerson & Stern Assoc. Inc., San Diego, 1983—; instr. Loyola Marymount U., Westchester, Calif., 1972-80, U. Calif., Davis, 1972-80. Patentee in field, 1971, 83, 87, 88. Grantee NSF, 1971. Mem. IEEE, Assn. Computing Machinery, Eta Kappa Nu, Sigma Xi. Office: 10150 Sorrento Valley Rd San Diego CA 92121-1639

HUTCHINSON, ALLISON MCKENNA, humanities educator; b. Birmingham, Eng., June 5, 1950; came to U.S., 1973; d. Peter and Elizabeth Ellen (Nee) McKenna; m. Thomas Eugene Hutchinson, Aug. 25, 1973; children: Amy-Ellen, Peter, Ian. MA with honors, Glasgow (Scotland) U., 1971; cert. in secondary edn., Notre Dame Coll., Glasgow, 1973; postgrad.Makerer U., Kampala, Uganda, 1972; MEd, U. Oreg., 1974-76. Cert. tchr., Wash., Oreg., Uganda, U.K. Head geography dept. Kamuli Coll., Namasagali, Uganda, 1971-72; social studies tchr. Redmond (Oreg.) High Sch., 1975-76, Barrhead (Scotland) High Sch., 1976-78; instr. Silver Lake Coll., Manitowoc, Wis., 1988—; adult educator Tng. in Positive Parenting Skills, Longview, Wash., 1991—; instr. Lower Columbia Coll., Longview, 1992—; guest lectr. Glasgow U., 1972; cons. Dept. Human Resources, Kelso, Wash., 1991-92; co-chair strategic planning com. Longview Sch. Dist., 1991-92. Founder In Touch with Art Program, Green Bay, Wis., 1986-89, Mornings for Moms, Tacoma, 1981-86; chair activities com. Boy Scouts Am., 1990—; mem. parish coun. St. Rose Cath. Ch., 1989—. Mem. Women in Network (bd. dirs. 1990—), Found. for Global Community, Fellowship of Reconciliation. Office: Lower Columbia Coll Maple St Longview WA 98632

HUTCHINSON, CHARLES SMITH, JR., book publisher; b. Topeka, Oct. 17, 1930; s. Charles S. and Cecil Marguerite (Weidenhamer) H.; m. Elizabeth Dunbar Hall, June 16, 1956; children: Amy Elizabeth, Todd Charles. B.A., Principia Coll., 1952. Editor-in-chief, sec., dir. Burgess Pub. Co., Mpls., 1955-65; editor-in-chief coll. and profl. books Reinhold Book Corp., N.Y.C., 1965-68; editor-in-chief profl. and reference books Van Nostrand Reinhold Co., N.Y.C., 1968-70; pres., chmn. bd. Dowden, Hutchinson and Ross, Inc., Stroudsburg, Pa., 1970-78, v.p., sec., 1978-80; v.p. Hutchinson Ross Pub. Co., 1980-83, Van Nostrand Reinhold Co., N.Y.C., 1984-86; mng. dir. Hutchinson Assocs., Prescott, Ariz., 1987-91; pres. Geosci. Press, Inc., Phoenix, 1989—, Harbinger House, Inc., Tucson, 1992—. Bd. dirs. Hist. Farms Assn., pres., 1985-87. With C.E., U.S. Army, 1952-55. Recipient NuJay award Mpls. Jaycees, 1957. Fellow Geol. Soc. Am.; mem. Rocky Mountain Books Pubs. Assn., Kiwanis (treas. Stroudsburg chpt. 1977-78, v.p. 1978-80, pres. 1980-81, Disting. Pres. award 1981). Home: 5520 N Camino Arenosa Tucson AZ 85718

HUTCHINSON, EDWARD PAUL, air force master sergeant; b. Tucson, May 19, 1961; s. Willard Lafayette and Dorothy Jean (Ellis) H. AAS in Security Adminstrn., Commun. Coll. of the Air Force, Montgomery, Ala., 1989. Cert. peace officer, Ariz.; emergency med. technician. Enlisted U.S. Air Force, 1978, served in U.S., Europe, Asia, Africa, 1978—; Elite Guard flight chief 7001st Spl. Security Squadron, Ramstein Air Base, West Germany, 1983-86; non-commd. officer in charge secure communication 53d Combat Communications Squadron, Robins AFB, Ga., 1987-90; aircraft security flight chief 836th Security Police Squadron, Davis-Monthan AFB, Ariz., 1990-91, non-commd. officer in charge, confinement, 1991; shift comdr. 355th Security Police Squadron, Davis-Monthan AFB, 1991—; res. officer Tucson Police Dept., 1991—; mil. customs insp. U.S. Customs Svc., Nogales, Ariz., 1991—. Troop com. mem. Boy Scouts Am., Robins AFB, 1988-89; vol. emergency med. technician USAF Clinic, Spangdahlem Air Base, West Germany, 1982-83. Decorated Air Force Commendation medal; named to Outstanding Young Men in Am., 1987. Christian. Office: 355th Security Police Sqdn Davis-Monthan AFB Tucson AZ 85707

HUTCHINSON, JOSEPH CANDLER, retired foreign language educator; b. Hazelhurst, Ga., Jan. 10, 1920; s. George Washington and Lillie Arizona (Rowan) H.; m. June Cruce O'Shields, Aug. 12, 1950 (div. 1980); children: Junie O'Shields, Joseph Candler. BA, Emory U., 1940, MA, 1941; PhD, U. N.C., 1950; postgrad. U. Paris, summers 1951, 53. Tchr., Tech. High Sch., Atlanta, 1941-42; instr. French, German, Italian, Emory U., Atlanta, 1946-47; instr. U. N.C., Chapel Hill, 1947-50, asst. prof., 1954, assoc. prof., to 1957; asst. prof. Sweet Briar (Va.) Coll., 1950-51, 53-54; assoc. prof. Tulane U., New Orleans, 1957-59; fgn. lang. specialist U.S. Office Edn., Washington, 1959-64; acad. adv. hdqrs. Def. Lang. Inst., Washington, 1964-74, Monterey, 1974-77, dir. tng. devel. Def. Lang. Inst. Fgn. Lang. Ctr., Monterey, Calif., 1977-82, asst. acad. dean, 1982-85; dean of policy, from 1985-88; vis. prof. U. Va., Charlottesville, 1966, Arlington, 1970, Georgetown U., 1968, Am. U., 1971; cons. Council of Chief State Sch. Officers, 1960, U. Del., 1966, U. Colo., 1968, U. Ill., 1968; U.S. del. Bur. Internat. Lang. Coordination, NATO, 1964-79, 81-82, 86-87. Author: Using the Language Laboratory Effectively: School Executive's Guide, 1964, The Language Laboratory: Equipment and Utilization in Trends in Language Teaching, 1966, others; editor Dialog on Language Instruction, 1986-88; contbr. articles to profl. jours. Served with U.S. Army, 1942-46, 51-53. Decorated Bronze Star. Mem. Am. Council on Edn. (task force on internat. edn. 1973), NEA (sec. dept. fgn. langs. 1961-64), AARP (vote team), Higher Edn. Assn. Monterey Peninsula, Am. Council on Teaching of Fgn. Lang., MLA, Am. Mgmt. Assn., Am. Soc. Tng. and Devel., Nat. Assn. Ret. Fed. Employees (v.p. Monterey chpt. 1990, pres. 1991-92), Monterey Choral Soc., Camerata Singers, Presidio of Monterey Officers and Faculty, Washington Linguistics Club (v.p. 1970-72). Episcopalian.

HUTCHINSON, NANCY ANNE, English language educator; b. Peoria, Ill., May 3, 1947; d. E. John and Alvina K. (Zeeck) Richardson; m. Bennett Buckley Hutchinson, June 27, 1970; 1 child, Amy Ann. BA, Ill. State U., 1969; MA, Abilene Christian U., 1974. Dir. Call For Help, Abilene, Tex., 1975-78, Meth. Svc. Ctr., Abilene, 1978-79; social worker Brentwood Day Care Ctr., Austin, Tex., 1979-80; tchr. of English Cooper High Sch., Abilene, 1980-90; vis. prof. Pepperdine U., Malibu, Calif., 1990—; trainer Big Country Writing Inst., Abilene, 1985—. Del. State Dem. Conv., 1974-80; active Jr. League of Abilene, 1974—. Named to Outstanding Young Women of Am. Mem. AAUW, Nat. Coun. Tchrs. of English, Tex. Coun. Tchrs. of English (v.p. for affiliates), Big Country Tchrs. of English (chmn. nominating com.), NEA, Tex. Edn. Assn. (bldg. rep.), Phi Delta Kappa, Delta Kappa Gamma. Mem. United Methodist Ch. Home: 24303 Baxter Dr Malibu CA 90265-4752 Office: Pepperdine U Dept Communication Malibu CA 90265

HUTCHINSON III, WILLIAM KINSEY, aerospace company executive; b. Carlisle, Pa., Apr. 27, 1953; s. William Kinsey II and Lois Ann (Lackey) H. Student, St. Mary's Internat., Tokyo, 1960-61, Volkshochschule, Karlsruhe, Germany, 1973; BFA, Calif. Inst. of the Arts, Velencia, 1977; MBA, Pepperdine U., 1988. Travel cons. AAA, Washington, 1973-74; park attraction ops. Disneyland, Anaheim, Calif., 1975-78; sales rep. United Airlines, L.A., 1978-84; prin. specialist flight test ops. McDonnell Douglas, Long Beach, Calif., 1984—. Editor: New Students Handbook, 1976, Flight Test Progress Report, 1991—. Mem. Am. Biog. Inst. (bd. of advisors-rsch. 1990—), McDonnell Douglas Mgmt. Club, Am. Film Inst., S.W. Informational Nomad User's Group (v.p. 1992—, editor newsletter 1992—). Democrat. Anglican. Home: 10402 Sande St Cypress CA 90630-4530 Office: McDonnell Douglas 3855 Lakewood Blvd Long Beach CA 90846

HUTCHISON, JOHN NELSON, correspondent; b. Arlington, Iowa, May 1, 1911; s. Orson Ray and Lulu Olive (Webber) H.; m. Sarabel Roberts, Dec. 24, 1937 (dec. June 1990); children: Judith, Susan; m. Vivienne Audrey Barnett, Aug. 15, 1991. BA, U. Ark., 1937. Reporter Cin. Post and Memphis Comml. Appeal, 1937-41, San Francisco News, 1946-48; fgn. svc. officer European Coop. Adminstrn., Paris, 1948-52; dir. Press & Publs., U.S. Info. Agy., Washington, 1952-55; pub. rels. officer United Fund of Bay Area, San Francisco, 1955-59; dir. info. Am. Nat. Red Cross, Washington, 1959-60; fgn. svc. officer U.S. Info. Agy., Washington, London, Manila, Wellington; corr. New Zealand Herald, Christchurch Press, Auckland, Christchurch, 1973—. Co-author: Gods, Men and Wine, 1965, Wines of the World, 1967, The Book of California Wine, 1984; contbg. editor Wines and Vines Mag., 1973—; contbr. more than 1000 articles to newspapers and mags. Lt. col. U.S. Army, 1941-46. Decorated Bronze Star. Mem. Savile Club London. Democrat. Home and Office: 441 Zimpher Dr Sebastopol CA 95472

HUTCHISON, LOYAL DWAYNE, pharmacist; b. Stockton, Calif., Jan. 3, 1933; s. Lester and Muriel (Van Nortwick) H.; m. Jean E. McColl, Jan. 26, 1961; children: Michael, Donald. BS in Pharmacy, U. Pacific, 1966. Pharmacist Fifth St. Pharmacy, Stockton, 1966-76, prin., 1976—; prin. Hutchison Pharmacies Inc., Stockton, 1976—, McKinley Pharmacy, Stockton, 1976—, Lathrop (Calif.) Pharmacy, 1976—. Served with U.S. Army, 1957-59. Fellow Am. Coll. Apothecary; mem. Calif. Pharmacists Assn. (Pac Silver Circle), Am. Pharmacists Assn. Home: PO Box 1737 Stockton CA 95201-1737 Office: Hutchison Pharmacies Inc 1839 S El Dorado St Stockton CA 95206-2099

HUTNER, HERBERT L., financial consultant, lawyer; b. N.Y.C.; s. Nathan M. and Ethel (Helhor) H.; m. Juli Reding, Nov. 28, 1969; children by previous marriage: Jeffrey J., Lynn M. Colwell; 1 stepson, Christopher D. Taylor. B.A., Columbia U., 1928, J.D., 1931. Bar: N.Y. 1932. Ptnr., Osterman & Hutner, mem. N.Y. Stock Exch., N.Y.C., 1945-57; successively pres. N.E. Life Insurance Co., N.Y.C.; chmn. bd. Sleight & Hellmuth Inc., N.Y.C.; chmn. bd. Pressed Metals of Am., Port Huron, Mich.; chmn. bd. Struthers Wells Corp., Warren, Pa., Plateau Mining Co. Inc., Oak Ridge, Tenn.; investor, cons., L.A., 1963—; dir. United Artists Communications, Inc., 1965-87, Todd AO-Glen Glen, 1987—, L.A. Rams, 1972-75, mem. adv. bd., 1991—; chmn. bd. Cellvent, Inc., 1991—. Chmn. pres.'s adv. com. on arts, Kennedy Ctr., 1982-90; founder L.A. Music Ctr.; chmn. profl. sports com. United Way; corporator Eye Rsch. Inst., Boston; mem. internat. adv. com. Up With People. Decorated title DATO, Sultan of Johore, Malaysia, Highest Order of the Crown, 1981. Mem. ASCAP, Deepdale Golf Club (Manhasset, N.Y.). Composer: The Super Bowl Song, Go Rams Go, others.

HUTORON, ADAM NATHAN, accountant; b. Phoenix, Ariz., Mar. 1, 1965; s. Abe and Ruby (Eagle) H. BS, Ariz. State U., 1987. CPA. Staff acct. Peat Marwick Main & Co., Phoenix, 1988-89; sr. assoc. Coopers and Lybrand, Phoenix, 1990—. Mem. AICPA, Ariz. Soc. CPAs, Combined Metro. Phoenix Arts and Scis. Republican. Jewish. Home: 5995 N 78th St Apt 1010 Scottsdale AZ 85250-6122 Office: Coopers and Lybrand 2901 N Central Ave Phoenix AZ 85012-2700

HUTTER, JAMES RISQUE, lawyer; b. Spokane, Wash., Mar. 20, 1924; s. James R. and Esther (Nelson) H.; m. Patricia Ruth Dunlavy, Aug. 12, 1951 (dec.); children: Bruce Dunlavy, Gail Anne, Dean James, Karl Nelson; m. Elizabeth Brown Ruess, Mar. 10, 1990. B.S., UCLA, 1947; J.D., Stanford U., 1950. Bar: Calif. 1951, U.S. Supreme Ct. 1965. Assoc. Gibson, Dunn &

Crutcher, Los Angeles and Beverly Hills, Calif., 1950-58, ptnr., 1959—; dir. Fifield Manors, Los Angeles, 1955—, v.p., 1964-85, pres., 1985—. Bd. dirs., chmn. fin. com. Congl. Found. for Theol. Studies, Nat. Assn. Congl., Christian Chs., 1961-67; mem. San Marino (Calif.) City Planning Commn., 1968-90, chmn., 1976-90. With 104th inf. div. AUS, 1943-46. Decorated Purple Heart. Mem. State Bar Calif. (com. on corps. 1973-76, exec. com. bus. law sect. 1976-78), ABA, Los Angeles County Bar Assn., Beverly Hills Bar Assn. (bd. govs. 1968-70), Am. Judicature Soc., Town Hall, City Club on Bunker Hill, Valley Hunt Club, Phi Delta Phi, Beta Gamma Sigma, Phi Kappa Psi. Home: 1400 Circle Dr San Marino CA 91108-1003 Office: Gibson Dunn & Crutcher 333 S Grand Ave Fl 48 Los Angeles CA 90071-3197

HUTTON, PAUL ANDREW, history educator, writer; b. Frankfurt, Germany, Oct. 23, 1949; naturalized citizen; s. Paul Andrew and Louise Katherine (Johnson) H.; m. Vicki Lynne Bauer, 1972 (div. 1985); 1 child, Laura; m. Lynn Terri Brittner, Dec. 31, 1988; 1 child, Lorena. BA, Ind. U., 1972, MA, 1974, PhD, 1981. Editorial asst. Jour. Am. History, Bloomington, Ind., 1973-77; instr. history Utah State U., Logan, 1977-80, asst. prof., 1980-84; asst. prof. U. N.Mex., Albuquerque, 1984-86, assoc. prof., 1986—. Author: Phil Sheridan and His Army, 1985; editor: Ten Days on the Plains, 1985, Soldiers West, 1987, The Custer Reader, 1992, (series) Eyewitness to the Civil War, 1991—; assoc. editor Western Hist. Quar., 1977-84; editor N.Mex. Hist. Rev., 1985-91. Recipient Evans Biography award Brigham Young U., 1986; Mead disting. rsch. fellow Huntington Libr., 1988. Mem. Orgn. Am. Historians (Ray A. Billington award 1987), Western Hist. Assn. (exec. dir. 1990—), Soc. for Mil. History, Western Writers Am. (Spur award 1986). Home: 29 Encantado Loop Santa Fe NM 87505 Office: U NMex Dept History Albuquerque NM 87131

HWANG, CORDELIA JONG, chemist; b. N.Y.C., July 14, 1942; d. Goddard and Lily (Fung) Jong; m. Warren C. Hwang, Mar. 29, 1969; 1 child, Kevin. Student Alfred U., 1960-62; BA, Barnard Coll., 1964; M.S., SUNY-Stony Brook, 1969. Rsch. asst. Columbia U., N.Y.C., 1964-66; analytical chemist Veritron West Inc., Chatsworth, Calif., 1969-70; asst. lab. dir., chief chemist Pomeroy, Johnston & Bailey Environ. Engrs., Pasadena, Calif., 1970-76; chemist Met. Water Dist. So. Calif., Los Angeles, 1976-79, rsch. chemist 1980-91, sr. chemist 1992—; mem. Joint Task Group on Instrumental Identification of Taste and Odor Compounds, 1983-85, instr. Citrus Coll., 1974-76; chair Joint Task Group on Disinfection by-products: chlorine, 1990. Mem. Am. Chem. Soc., Am. Water Works Assn. (cert. water quality analyst level 3, Calif.-Nev.), Am. Soc. for Mass Spectometry. Office: Met Water Dist So Calif 700 N Moreno Ave La Verne CA 91750-3399

HWANG, KOU MAU, corporate professional; b. Kaoshiung, Taiwan, Sept. 5, 1940; came to U.S., 1966; s. Tien C. and Zui C. (Yu) H.; m. Sue H. Cheng, Sept. 5, 1969; children: Sandy, Carol, Nancy. BS, Kaohsiung Med. Coll., 1964; MS, Ohio State U., 1969, PhD, 1972; postgrad., Yale U., 1974. Teaching asst. Duquesne U., Pitts., 1965-66, Ohio State U., Columbus, Ohio, 1967-71; rsch. fellow Yale Med. Sch., New Haven, 1972-76; asst. prof. M.D. Anderson Hosp./Univ. Tex., Houston, 1976-77, U. So. Calif., L.A., 1977-79; sr. investigator Nat. Cancer Inst., Frederick, Md., 1980-83; sr. scientist Cetus Inc., San Francisco, 1984; sr. dir. Genelabs Inc., Redwood City, Calif., 1985—; vis. prof. Rutger U., Piscataway, N.J., 1985-88; educator Internat. AIDS Confs., U.S., China, 1989; cons., lectr. Kaushiung Med. Coll., Taiwan, 1991-92. Patentee AIDS Therapy, 1989, New Therapy for Herpes Simplex, 1992; inventor in field; contbr. numerous articles to profl. jours. Cultural exch. person Taiwanese Prof. Assn., 1990—. 2nd lt. Taiwanese Army, 1964-65. Rsch. grantee Welch Found., Houston, 1977, Am. Cancer Soc., L.A., 1977-80; sml. bus. grantee U.S. Govt., San Carlo, Calif., 1987-88; recipient Nat. Drug Discovery grants NIAID, Redwood City, 1988-91. Mem. Am. Assn. Cancer Rsch., Am. Chem. Soc., AAAS, Rho Chi. Home: 220 Stanbridge Ct Danville CA 94526 Office: Genelabs Inc 550 Penobscot Dr Redwood City CA 94063

HYBL, WILLIAM JOSEPH, foundation executive; b. Des Moines, July 16, 1942; s. Joseph A. and Geraldine (Evans) H.; m. Kathleen Horrigan, June 6, 1967; children: William J. Jr., Kyle Horrigan; BA, Colo. Coll., 1964; JD, U. Colo., 1967. Bar: Colo. 1967. Asst. dist. atty. 4th Jud. Dist., El Paso and Teller Counties, 1970-72; pres., exec. v.p., dir. Garden City Co., 1973—; dir. Broadmoor Hotel, Inc., 1973—, also vice-chmn., 1987—; chmn., CEO, trustee El Pomar Found, 1973—; pres. U.S. Olympic Com. 1991-92; bd. dirs. Bank One, Colo. Springs, Bank One Colo., Denver, KN Energy Inc., Lakewood, Colo., 1988—; mem. Colo. Ho. Reps., 1972-73; spl. counsel The White House, Washington, 1981. Trustee, vice chmn. Colo. Coll., 1978—; pres., trustee Air Force Acad. Found.; sec., trustee Nat. Jr. Achievement; vice chmn. bd. U.S. Adv. Commn. on Pub. Diplomacy, 1990—; civilian aide to sec. of army, 1986—. Capt. U.S. Army, 1967-69. Republican.

HYBRIDGE, JOHN, career officer; b. Tokyo, Apr. 7, 1948; s. Harley and June (Uchida) H.; m. Helen Manson, Sept. 22, 1972; children: Raquel, Ursela, Pamela. AA, Seattle Community Coll., 1969; BS, Brigham Young U., 1980; MS, Am. Tech. U., Killeen, Tex., 1987. Commd. 2nd lt. U.S. Army, 1977, advanced through grades to maj., 1989; morale support activity officer U.S. Army, Camp Zama, Japan, 1983, postal officer/Honshu, 1983-84; chief, Personnel Mgmt. Br., 2d Armored Div. U.S. Army, Ft. Hood, Tex., 1984-86, chief, Personnel Svcs. Div., 2d Armored Div., 1986, dep. adj. gen. 2d Armored Div., 1986-88, comdr. 502nd Per. Svc. Co. and 2d Armored Div., 1988-89, AG plans officer III Corps, 1989-90; asst. chief of staff, G5 6th Infantry Div. U.S. Army, Ft. Wainwright, Alaska, 1990-92. Vol. Mental Health/Mental Retardation, Temple, Tex., 1986-90, pres. 1989; treas. Am. Tech. U. Counseling Club, Killeen, 1986. Recipient Dick Johnson Scholarship award Am. Tech. U., 1986; decorated Army Commendation Medal with three oak leaf clusters, Army Achievement Medal with oak leaf cluster. Mem. Assn. of the U.S. Army, Tex. Assn. for Counseling and Devel., Mid-Tex. Assn. for Counseling and Devel. Democrat. Home: 23721 100th Ave SE Kent WA 98031-4211 Office: Mervyn's 4126 124th Ave SE Bellevue WA 98006

HYLAND, PENELOPE, writer; b. Columbus, Ohio, Sept. 19, 1953; d. John Roth Hyland and Martha Ann (Burger) Shipman; m. Charles David Moore (div. 1989); children: Jacquetta Nicole, Tara, Chad David, Shaun Dai. BS, U. So. Colo., 1987; MA, Adams State Coll., 1989; D of Clin. Hypnotherapy, Am. Inst. Hypnotherapy, 1990. Cert. hypnotherapist, Edu-Kinesthetics. Neuropsychiat. technician Assocs. for Psychotherapy, Pueblo, Colo., 1987-88; clin. therapist Parkview Anxiety and Depression Unit, Pueblo, Colo., 1990; counselor U. So. Colo., Pueblo, Colo., 1988, acad. advisement coord., 1988-89, psychotherapist, tchr., writer, 1988—; founder, exec. dir. Stop Abusive Family Environments, Pueblo, 1986—. Author: (booklet) A Survival Guide for Battered Women, 1985. Adv. coun. Pueblo County Sheriff Dept., 1992; crisis counselor YWCA Crisis Shelter, Pueblo, 1981-86; leadership com. Bus. Women's Network, Pueblo, 1989-92; campaign advisor Dem. Candidate for Commr., Pueblo, 1990. Named Outstanding Coll. Student, 1989, Outstanding Woman of Yr., U. So. Colo., 1985-86; recipient Honors and Spl. Distinction, U. So. Colo., 1987, Vol. Svc. award YWCA, 1983. Mem. Bus. Women's Network, Psi Chi, Alpha Chi. Office: PO Box 11894 Pueblo CO 81001

HYMAN, KEVIN MICHAEL, communications executive; b. Dallas, Mar. 8, 1950; s. Joseph Raymond and Mary Angela (Dwyer) H.; m. Marjanna Mercer, July 17, 1983; children: Colleen, Chasen, Katelynn. BA in Econs., U. No. Colo., 1972; MA in Econs., U. R.I., 1974. Asst. prof. econs. Nasson Coll., Springvale, Maine, 1974-78; v.p. Boettcher & Co., Colorado Springs, Colo., 1978-85; chief exec. officer, pres. Citizens' Cable, Colorado Springs, Colo., 1985-89; also bd. dirs. Citizens' Cable, Colorado Springs; dir. ops. Cablevision, Colo. Springs, 1989—. Bd. dirs. Better Bus. Bur., Pikes Peak Amateur Hockey Assn., Colorado Springs, coach, 1987-88, rep. 1991—; trustee Bob Johnson Ice Hockey Found.; coord. West El Paso Little League, Colorado Springs, pres. 1993—; dir. Profile Theatre, Portland, Maine, 1974-76. Mem. Colo. C. of C., Colo. Amateur Hockey Assn. Roman Catholic. Club: Plaza (Colorado Springs). Office: Cablevision 213 N Union Blvd Colorado Springs CO 80909-5799

HYNEK, FREDERICK JAMES, architect; b. Minot, N.D., May 24, 1944; s. Frederick Frank and Esther Irene (Hermanson) H.; BArch, N.D. State U., 1967; m. Jane Rebecca Lowitz, June 9, 1966; children: Tyler James, Scott Anthony. Intern archtl. firms in Bismarck, N.D., 1967-72; architect Gerald W. Deines, Architect, Casper and Cody, Wyo., 1972-73; v.p. Gerald Deines and Assos., 1973-77; propr. Fred J. Hynek, AIA/Architect, Cody, 1977-80; pres. Design Group, P.C., Architects/Planners, Cody, 1980-86; pres. CHD Architects, Cody, 1986—; mem. cert. of need rev. bd. State of Wyo., 1984-87, selection com. for archtl. students for Western Interstate Commn. for Higher Edn. Profl. Student Exchange Program, U. Wyo., 1979—; chmn. archtl. adv. commn. City of Cody. Bd. dirs. Cody Stampede, Inc., 1977-82; chmn. Cody Econ. Devel. Council, 1982-84; coach Absaroka Ski Assn., Bill Koch Youth Ski League, 1990—. Served with USAR, 1967-68. Mem. AIA (dir. Wyo. chpt. 1976-83, pres. 1980, 81, sec./treas., 1990-91; conf. chmn. Western Mountain region 1977, mem. awards jury 1981, 92, treas. 1982-86; chmn. design awards jury N.D. 1981, 2 awards for Excellence in Archtl. Design Wyo. chpt.), U.S. Ski Assn., U.S. Ski Coaches Assn., Cody County C. of C. (dir., pres. 1982). Republican. Presbyterian. Clubs: Cody Country Amb. (Amb. of Yr. 1990). Mem. editorial adv. bd. Symposia mag., 1981-82. Home: 708 Southfork Rd Cody WY 82414-8842 Office: 1008 13th St Cody WY 82414

IACANGELO, PETER AUGUST, actor; b. Bklyn., Aug. 13, 1948; s. Peter and Mary Rose (Bordini) I.; m. Melody Rose Marzola, Apr. 5, 1975; children: Peter August III, Perique Ashly, Paxton Aaires. AA in Marine Biology, Suffolk County Community Coll., 1968; BFA, Hofstra U., 1971. Actor South Bronx (N.Y.) Repertory Co., 1971, The Fifteen Cent Token Improvisation, N.Y.C., 1971; actor off-Broadway One Flew Over The Cuckoo's Nest, 1972, Moon Children, 1972-74; actor off-Broadway and N.Y. Shakespeare Festival Comedy of Errors, 1975; actor on-Broadway Three Penny Opera, 1976-77; actor Blood Brothers Warner Bros., N.Y.C. and Hollywood, Calif., 1977; actor Hoodlums Nai Bonet Entertainment, N.Y.C., 1977; ind. actor, 1978—; actor on Broadway Filumena, N.Y.C., 1979-80, Passione, N.Y.C., 1980; tchr. Upward Bound Program, Brunswick, Maine, 1968; owner, tchr., coach Conflict Workshop, N.Y.C., 1971-74; tchr., acting coach Learning Tree U., Northridge, Calif., 1985-86. Contbr. short stories and poems to various mags., 1965—; appeared in numerous prodns. including Tattoo, 1978, Times Square, 1979, Spittoon, 1980-81, Hanky Panky, 1981, Hero at Large, 1979, Archie Bunkers Place, 1981, Hill Street Blues, 1981, St. Elsewhere, 1981, The A Team, 1981, 86, Taxi, 1981, 82, Cagney & Lacey, 1982, Over Here, Mr. President, 1982, The Jeffersons, 1982, 85, Carpool, 1982, Gimmie a Break, 1982, Hardcastle & McCormick, 1983, The Phoenix, Falcon Crest, 1983, Masquerade, 1984, Cheers, 1984, Night Court, 1984, The Fall Guy, 1984, Knots Landing, 1985, Amazing Stories, Who's the Boss, 1985, Our Family Honor, 1985, The Return of Mickey Spillane's Mike Hammer, 1986, The New Mike Hammer, 1986, Easy Street, 1986, The Tortellis, 1986, Santa Barbara, 1986, On The Edge, 1986, 1987, Amen, 1987, Valerie's Family, 1988, Over the Edge, 1988, Nitti, 1988, Killer Instinct, 1989, Gangsters, 1989, Freddy's Nightmares, 1989, Brothers, 1989, Alf, 1989, Mr. Belvedere, 1989, Wolf, 1989, Capital News, 1990, Singer & Sons, 1990, Best Intentions, 1990, Strong Man's Weak Child at L.A.T.C., 1990, (TV shows) They Came From Outer Space, 1991, Babes, 1991, Life Goes On, 1991, Murphy Brown, 1991, Dream On, 1991, Dear John, 1991, Good & Evil, 1991, Walter & Emily, 1991, Quantum Leap, 1992, Down the Shore, 1992, Good Advice, 1992, Love and War, 1993, (feature film) We're Talking Serious Money, 1991, Addams Family II, 1993. Vol. Better Horizons Program, Selden, N.Y., 1967-68, Nat. Fedn. of the Blind, N.Y.C., 1971-73, Spl. Olympics, So. Calif., 1981—; actor benefit performance for N.Y.C. and Mayor John V. Lindsey, 1972; celebrity participant St. Jude's Children's Hosp. Fun Shoot. Recipient certificate Mayor John V. Lindsey, 1972. Mem. AFTRA, NRA, SAG, Actors Equity Assn., Actors Fund Am. (life), West Coast Ind. Chess Masters (pres.), The Universal Coterie of Pipe Smokers, Pipe Collectors Internat. (life). Roman Catholic.

IACHETTI, ROSE MARIA ANNE, educator; b. Watervliet, N.Y., Sept. 22, 1931; d. Augustus and Rose Elizabeth Archer (Orciuolo) Iachetti; BS, Coll. St. Rose, 1961; MEd, U. Ariz., 1969. Joined Sisters of Mercy, Albany, N.Y., 1949-66; tchr. various parochial schs. Albany (N.Y.) Diocese, 1952-66; tchr. Headstart Program, Troy, N.Y., 1966; tchr. fine arts Watervliet Jr. and Sr. High Sch., 1966-67; tchr. W.J. Meyer Sch., Tombstone, Ariz., 1968-71, Colonel Johnston Sch., Ft. Huachuca, Ariz., 1971-78; tchr. Myer Sch., Ft. Huachuca, 1978-89, coord. program for gifted and talented, 1981-85. Ann. chmn. Ariz. Children's Home Assn., Tombstone, 1973-74; trustee Tombstone Sch. Dist. #1, 1972-80; active Dem. Club; mem. Bicentennial Commn. for Ariz., 1972-76, Tombstone Centennial Commn., 1979-80, chmn. Centennial Ball, 1980; pres. Tombstone Community Health Svcs., 1978-80; mem. Tombstone City Coun., 1982-84, Inner Senatorial Cir., 1989-91; governing bd. Southeast Ariz. Area Health Edn. Coun., 1985—; pres. S.E. Health Edn. Coun., 1990-91; patron Our Lady of Santa Rita Abbey, Met. Opera Guild; v.p. Sacred Heart Parish Bd., 1991-92. Mem. Ariz. Edn. Assn. (so. regional dir. 1971-73), Ft. Huachuca Edn. Assn., Tombstone Dist. 1 Edn. Assn. (pres. 1969-71), Ariz. Sch. Bd. Assn., NEA (del. 1971-73), Ariz. Classroom Tchrs. Assn. (del. 1969-71), Internat. Platform Assn., Tombstone Bus. and Profl. Women's Club, Am. Legion Aux., Tombstone Assn. Arts, Inner Senatorial Circle, Pi Lambda Theta, Delta Kappa Gamma, (pres. 1982-84), Phi Delta Kappa (historian 1979-82, 2d v.p. 1982-83). Home: Round Up Trailer Ranch PO Box 725 Tombstone AZ 85638-0725 Office: Myer Sch Fort Huachuca AZ 85613

IAMELE, RICHARD THOMAS, law librarian; b. Newark, Jan. 29, 1942; s. Armando Anthony and Evelyn (Coladonato) I.; m. Marilyn Ann Berutto, Aug. 21, 1965; children: Thomas, Ann Marie. BA, Loyola U., L.A., 1963; MSLS, U. So. Calif., 1967; JD, Southwestern U., L.A., 1976. Bar: Calif. 1977. Cataloger U. So. Calif., L.A., 1967-71; asst. cataloger L.A. County Law Libr., 1971-77, asst. ref. libr., 1977-78, asst. libr., 1978-80, libr. dir., 1980—. Mem. ABA, Am. Assn. Law Librs., Calif. Libr. Assn., So. Calif. Assn. Law Librs., Coun. Calif. County Law Librs. (pres. 1981-82, 88-90). Office: Los Angeles County Law Libr 301 W 1st St Los Angeles CA 90012-3100

IANNETTA, SCOTT KIMON, graphoanalyst; b. Kailua, Hawaii, Oct. 17, 1943; a; children: Lisa, Christina, Leslie, Beau. Cert. graphoanalyst; forensic handwriting examiner. Handwriting expert Honolulu Police Dept., 1983-88; cons. to attys. on jury selection, security profiling, design and coordination of mock trials Kailua, Hawaii, 1988—; instr. U. Hawaii, Manoa, 1983—; researcher Hawwaii State Hosp. Monthly columnist Windward Oahu News, 1986—. Mem. Am. Bd. of Forensic Handwriting Analysts, Internat. Graphoanalysis Soc. (Graphoanalyst of Yr. award 1982, Outstanding Mem. award Hawaii chpt. 1983, President's citation of merit 1984), Am. Handwriting Analysis Found., World Assn. Document Examiners, Nat. Assn. Document Examiners, Am. Soc. for Indsl. Security. Office: Trial Run Ink PO Box 1486 Kailua HI 96734-1486

IANZITI, ADELBERT JOHN, industrial designer; b. Napa, Calif., Oct. 10, 1927; s. John and Mary Lucy (Lecair) I.; student Napa Jr. Coll., 1947, 48-49; m. Doris Moore, Aug. 31, 1952; children: Barbara Ann Ream, Susan Therese Shifflett, Joanne Lynn Lely, Jonathan Peter, Janet Carolyn Kroyer. AA, Fullerton Jr. Coll., 1950; student UCLA, 1950, Santa Monica Community Coll., 1950-51. Design draftsman Basalt Rock Co. Inc. div. Dillingham Heavy Constrn., Napa, 1951-66, chief draftsman plant engring., 1966-68, process designer, 1968-82, pres. employees assn., 1967; now self-employed indsl. design cons. V.p., Justin-Siena Parent-Tchr. Group, 1967. Mem. Aggregates and Concrete Assn. No. Calif. (vice-chmn. environ. subcom. 1976-77), Constrn. Specifications Inst., Native Sons of the Golden West, World Affairs Coun. No. Calif., Internat. Platform Assn., Commonwealth of Calif. Club. Republican. Roman Catholic. Home and Office: 2650 Dorset St Napa CA 94558-6110

IBERALL, ARTHUR SAUL, physicist, publisher; b. N.Y.C., June 12, 1918; s. Benjamin and Anna (Katz) I.; m. Helene Rubenstein, Jan. 28, 1940; children: Eleanora Iberall Robbins, Pamela Iberall Rubin, Althea, Valerie Iberall O'Connor. B.S., CCNY, 1940, postgrad., 1940-41; postgrad., George Washington U., 1942-45; hon. degree, Ohio State U., 1976. Gen. physicist Nat. Bur. Standards, Washington, 1941-53; research dir. ARO Equipment Corp., Cleve., 1953-54; chief physicist Rand Devel. Corp., Cleve., 1954-65; chief scientist, pres. Gen. Tech. Services, Inc., Upper Darby, Pa., 1965-81; editor, pub. CP2: Commentaries-Physical and Philosophical, 1990—; vis. scholar UCLA, 1981-92. Author: Toward a General Science of Viable Systems, 1972, On Pulsatile and Steady Arterial Flow, 1973, Physics of Membrane Transport, 1973, Bridges in Science: From Physics to Social Science, 1974, On Nature, Life, Mind and Society, 1976, What's Wrong with Evolution, 1989, How to Run a Society, 1991; editor: (with J. Reswick) Technical and Biological Problems of Control; A Cybernetic View, 1970, (with A. Guyton) Regulation and Control in Physiological Systems, 1973; assoc. editor: Am. Jour. Physiology, Integrative and Comparative Physiology, 1976-90; contbr. tech. articles to profl. jours. Fellow ASME (chmn. auto. control div. 1973); mem. Am. Phys. Soc., N.Y. Acad. Scis., Biomed. Engring. Soc. (Alza Disting. lectr. 1975), Am. Cybernetic Soc., Microcirculation Soc., Instrument Soc. Am., Biophys. Soc., Sigma Xi. Democrat. Jewish. Club: Cosmos. Home: 5070 Avenida Del Sol Laguna Beach CA 92653-1876

IBSEN, KENNETH HOWARD, biochemistry educator; b. Bklyn., Feb. 4, 1931; s. Niels Christopher and Inga Sophie (Brandt) I.; m. Denise Lee Duke, June 15, 1959 (div. Oct. 1980); children: Kristine Lee, David Allen; m. Dorothy Jeanette Martin, June 30, 1984; 1 child, Kurt Martin. AA, City Coll., Los Angeles, 1951; BS, UCLA, 1955, PhD, 1959. Lab. technician Lieberman Breweries, Vernon, Calif., 1954; research biochemist Vets. Hosp., Sepulveda, Calif., 1959-61; asst. research prof. physiol. chemistry UCLA, 1961-65, from asst. prof. to assoc. prof. biochemistry, 1964-93, asst. dean Coll. Medicine, 1986-93, prof. emeritus, 1993—, dir. acad. affairs, 1993—. Contbr. articles to profl. jours. Mem. AAAS, Am. Chem. Soc., Am. Soc. Biol. Chemists, Sigma Xi. Home: 87 Lakeshore Irvine CA 92714-3324 Office: U Calif Sch Biol Scis Irvine CA 92717

ICE, GEORGE GARY, hydrologist, researcher; b. Stillwater, Okla., Feb. 14, 1950; s. George Emery and Rubye Pearl (Scholl) I.; m. Catherine Ann Roberts, Apr. 16, 1977. BS in Forest Mgmt., U. Calif., Berkeley, 1972, MS in Watershed Mgmt., 1973; PhD in Forest Hydrology, Oreg. State U., 1978. Rsch. hydrologist Nat. Coun. of Paper Industry for Air & Steam Improvement, Corvallis, Oreg., 1977—, mgr. air quality and forest health program western region, 1986—; mem. Tech. Panel on Wetlands, Salem, Oreg., 1989-91, Tech. Specialists Panel on Water Quality, Salem, 1990-91. Zone dir., chmn. Benton Soil and Water Conservation Dist., Corvallis, 1988—. Outstanding Dir. award Soil and Water Conservation Dist., Oreg., 1992; U. Calif. fellow, 1973-74. Mem. Am. Geophys. Union, Am. Water Resource Assn., Soc. Am. Foresters (chmn. Marys Peak chpt. 1993), Nat. Assn. State Foresters (chmn. subcom. on cumulative watershed effects 1990-92), So. Forest Hydrology Group (bd. dirs. at large 1984-86), Watershed Mgmt. Coun. (bd. dirs. at large 1990—). Home: 23834 Mouse Mountain Rd Philomath OR 97370-9703 Office: NCASI 720 SW 4th St Corvallis OR 97333-4426

ICENOGLE, RONALD DEAN, physical chemist, writer; b. Bismarck, N.D., May 5, 1951; s. Grover Donald and Mary Adeline (Parks) I.; m. Maria Cecilia Co, Apr. 26, 1987; 1 child, Paul Steven. BS, Mich. State U., 1974; MS, Cornell U., 1977, PhD, 1981. Rsch. chemist Shell Devel. Co., Houston, 1980-85; writer on philosophy and sci. Spokane, Wash., 1985-87; sr. devel. engr. Teknor Apex Co., Pawtucket, R.I., 1987-89; agt. N.Y. Life Ins. Co., Spokane, Wash., 1991; ind. ins. mktg. agt. Spokane, 1991-92. Co-inventor, 5 U.S. patents low-smoke polypropylene insulation compounds, also fgn. patents granted; contbr. articles to profl. jours. Mem. Am. Chem. Soc., N.Y. Acad. Scis., Internat. Platform Assn., Phi Beta Kappa, Phi Kappa Phi. Republican. Roman Catholic. Home and Office: 2303 W Mission Ave Spokane WA 99201-2926

ICHIKAWA, WAYNE, oral and maxillofacial surgeon; b. Palo Alto, Calif., July 25, 1954; s. Thomas Toshiaki and June Haruko (Jofuku) I.; m. Kathryn Linda Ito, Aug. 22, 1987. AA, Foothill Coll., 1974; BA, U. Calif., Berkeley, 1976; DDS, U. Calif., Los Angeles, 1981; MS, U. Ill., Chgo., 1986. Diplomate Am. Bd. Oral and Maxillofacial Surgery. Practice medicine specializing in oral and maxillofacial surgery San Leandro, Calif., 1985-86, San Jose, Calif., 1986-88, Campbell, Calif., 1988—; intern, then resident in oral and maxillofacial surgery U. Ill. Med. Ctr./VA Hosp., Chgo., 1981-85; adj. asst. prof. dept. oral and maxillofacial surgery U. Pacific, San Francisco, 1987. Contbr. articles to profl. jours. Fellow Am. Assn. Oral and Maxillofacial Surgeons, Am. Coll. Oral and Maxillofacial Surgeons; mem. ADA, Am. Dental Soc. Anesthesiology, Calif. Assn. Oral and Maxillofacial Surgeons, Calif. Dental Assn., No. Calif. Soc. Oral and Maxillofacial Surgeons, Santa Clara County Dental Soc., Western Soc. Oral and Maxillofacial Surgeons. Buddhist. Office: 1580 Winchester Blvd Ste 101 Campbell CA 95008-0519

IDE, TOSHI, computer software company executive; b. Fukuoka, Japan, Jan. 1, 1958; came to U.S., 1987; s. Kazuo and Hisako (Iyadomi) I.; m. Naomi Odashiro, Jan. 12, 1988. Electronics engring., Osaka U., Japan, 1981. Engr. Fostex Corp., Norwalk, Calif., 1982-89; dir rsch. and devel. Dynaware USA, Inc., Foster City, Calif., 1990—. Author: (computer software) Ballade, 1991, F.A.M.E., 1989. Office: Dynaware USA Inc 950 Tower Ln Ste 1150 Foster City CA 94404

IDEMAN, JAMES M., federal judge; b. Rockford, Ill., Apr. 2, 1931; s. Joseph and Natalie Ideman; m. Gertraud Erika Ideman, June 1, 1971. BA, The Citadel, 1953; JD, U. So. Calif., 1963. Bar: Calif. 1964, U.S. Dist. Ct. (cen. dist.) Calif. 1964, U.S. Ct. Mil. Appeals 1967, U.S. Supreme Ct. 1967. Dep. dist. atty. Los Angeles County, 1964-79; judge Los Angeles County Superior Ct., 1979-84; appointed judge U.S. Dist. Ct. (Cen. Dist.) Calif., Los Angeles, 1984—. Served to 1st lt. U.S. Army, 1953-56, col. AUS Ret. Republican. Office: US Dist Ct 312 N Spring St Los Angeles CA 90012-4701

IDLE, DUNNING, V, air force officer; b. Washington, July 29, 1959; s. Dunning IV and Mary Granger (Chapin) I.; m. Lynda Ann Espinoza, Apr. 1, 1989. BS in Astron. Engring., USAF Acad., 1982; MS in Aerospace Engring., U. So. Calif., L.A., 1984; PhD in Aerospace Engring., U. Tex., 1989. Commd. 2d lt. USAF, 1982, advanced through grades to capt., 1989; br. chief USAF Space Div./YOM, El Segundo, Calif., 1982-85, Weapons Lab., Albuquerque, 1989-91, Phillips Lab., Kirtland AFB, N.Mex., 1991—; mission specialist pilot FL500 High Altitude Soaring Project, 1985-88. Co-dir. Tomasita Elem. Sch. Stargazer's Young Astronauts Club, 1991—. Recipient Symons Meml. award Soaring Soc. Am., 1987. Mem. Planetary Soc. Home: 12804 El Vado Ct NE Albuquerque NM 87112 Office: PL/LI0 Kirtland A F B NM 87117

IERARDI, STEPHEN JOHN, physician; b. Honolulu, July 5, 1960; s. Ernest John and Roberta Ann (Hackett) I.; m. Erica Ewing, May 28, 1989; 1 child, Daphne Alexandra. BA in Biology, Williams Coll., 1982; MD, U. Rochester, 1986. Diplomate Am. Bd. Family Physicians. Intern U. Calif. at Irvine Med. Ctr., Orange, 1986-87, resident, 1987-89, chief resident, 1988-89; physician Laguna Hills, Calif., 1989—. Recipient UCI Care awards Univ. Calif. at Irvine Med. Ctr., 1986-89. Fellow Am. Acad. Family Physicians; mem. Assn. Am. Family Physicians (assoc.), Orange County Med. Assn. Home: 115 Cloudcrest Laguna Beach CA 92656-1329 Office: Ste 334 23961 Calle de la Magdalena Laguna Hills CA 92653

IGER, ROBERT A., broadcast executive; b. N.Y.C., 1951; m. Susan Iger; children: Kate, Amanda. Grad. magna cum laude, Ithaca Coll. Studio supr. ABC-TV, 1974-76, dir. programming Wide World of Sports, 1976-85; former v.p. program planning, development ABC Sports, 1985-87, v.p. program planning and acquisition, 1987-88; exec. v.p. ABC TV Network Group, 1988-89, pres., 1993—; pres. ABC Entertainment, 1989-93; exec. v.p. Capital Cities/ABC Inc., N.Y.C., 1993—. Trustee Ithaca Coll. Office: ABC TV Network Group 77 W 66th St New York NY 10023

IGNATOSKI, MICHAEL ALLAN, physical plant director; b. Grand Rapids, Mich., Oct. 17, 1950; s. Herman Valentine and Estelle (Szatan) I.; m. Margaret Anne Watson, Feb. 14, 1975; children: Kelly Marie, Michael Allan II, Penelope Jane, Hilary Anne. BS cum laude, Mich. State U., 1972. Pres. and CEO Quality Asphalt Paving, Inc., Dorr, Mich., 1973-85; maintenance supr. Wayland (Mich.) Union Schs., 1985-89; dir. of bldgs. and grounds Byron Ctr. (Mich.) Pub. Schs., 1989-91; dir. of physical plant Sheridan Coll., Sheridan, Wyo., 1991—; mem. Mich. Sch. Bus. Ofcls., Lansing, 1989-91. Mem. Assn. Physical Plant Adminstrs., Rocky Mountain Physical Pland Adminstrs., Physical Plant Crafts Assn., Wyo.-Mont. Safety Coun. Home: 167 Key Stone Rd Sheridan WY 82801 Office: Sheridan Coll 3059 Coffeen Sheridan WY 82801

IGO, GEORGE JEROME, physics educator; b. Greeley, Colo., Sept. 2, 1925; s. Henry J. and Ida J. (Danielsen) I.; m. Nancy Tebonn, May 12, 1953; children: Saffron, Peter Alexander. AB, Harvard Coll., 1949; MS, U. Calif., Berkeley, 1951, Phd, 1953. Postdoctoral Yale Univ., 1954, Brook Haven Nat. Lab., Upton, N.Y., 1955-57; instr. Stanford Univ., Palo Alto, Calif., 1957-59; guest prof. Univ. Heidelberg, Germany, 1960; staff mem. Lawrence Berkeley (Calif.) Lab., 1961-66, Los Alamos (N.Mex.) Nat. Lab., 1966-68; prof. UCLA, 1969—. With U.S. Army, 1944-46. Recipient Fulbright Travel award, 1960, Saclay, France, 1970, Sr. Scientist award Alexander von Humboldt Found., 1991. Fellow Am. Phys. Soc. Office: UCLA Dept Physics 405 Hilgard Ave Los Angeles CA 90024

IHRIG, EDWIN CHARLES, JR., mathematics educator; b. Washington, June 26, 1947; s. Edwin Charles and Lenore (Kokas) I.; m. Laurie Heather McColgan, July 6, 1974; 1 child, Karen Ann. BS, U. Md., 1969, MA, 1970; PhD, U. Toronto (Can.), 1974. Postdoctoral fellow math. dept. U. New Brunswick, Fredericton, Can., 1974-75; asst. prof. math. dept. Dalhousie U., Halifax, N.S., Can., 1975-76, McMaster U., Hamilton, Ont., Can., 1976-79; assoc. prof. math. dept. Ariz. State U., Tempe, 1979-85, prof. math. dept., 1985—. Contbr. articles to Gen. Relativity, Nuclear Physics, Combinatorics, Differential Geometry, Group Theory. Home: 1032 E Riviera Dr Tempe AZ 85282-5533 Office: Ariz State U Dept Math Tempe AZ 85287

II, JACK MORITO, aerospace engineer; b. Tokyo, Mar. 20, 1926; s. Iwao and Kiku Ii; came to U.S., 1954, naturalized, 1966; BS, Tohoku U., 1949; MS, U. Washington, 1956; M in Aero. Engring., Cornell U., 1959; PhD in Aero. and Astronautics, U. Wash., 1964; PhD in Engring., U. Tokyo, 1979; children: Keiko, Yoshiko, Mutsuya. Reporter, Asahi Newspaper Press, Tokyo, 1951-54; aircraft designer Fuji Heavy Industries Ltd. Co., Tokyo, Japan, 1956-58; mem. staff structures rsch. Boeing Co., Seattle, 1962—. Mem. AIAA, Japan Shumy and Culture Soc. (pres. 1976—), Sigma Xi. Mem. Congregational Ch. Contbr. numerous articles on aerodyns. to profl. jours. Office: The Boeing Co M/S 6M-44 Seattle WA 98124

IKAGAWA, TADAICHI, banking executive; b. Kyoto, Japan, 1939. Grad., Kyoto U., 1961. CEO Sumitomo Bank Calif. Mem. Japanese C. of C. Home: 801 El Camino Del Mar San Francisco CA 94121 Office: Sumitomo Bank of Calif 320 California St San Francisco CA 94104

IKEDA, MOSS MARCUS MASANOBU, educational administrator, lecturer, consultant; b. Los Angeles, Sept. 11, 1931; s. Masao Eugene and Masako (Yamashina) I.; BE, U. Hawaii, 1960, MEd, 1962; postgrad. Stanford U., 1961-62; M in Mil. Art and Sci., U.S. Army Command and Gen. Staff Coll., 1975; grad. U.S. Army War Coll., 1976; EdD, U. Hawaii, 1986; m. Shirley Yaeko Okimoto; children: Cynthia Cecile Ikeda Tamashiro, Mark Eugene, Matthew Albert. Tchr., Farrington High Sch., Honolulu, 1962-64; vice-prin. Kailua Intermediate Sch. 1964-65; adminstrv. intern Central Intermediate Sch., Honolulu, 1965-66; vice-prin. Kaimuki High Sch., Honolulu, 1966-67; prin. Kawananakoa Intermediate Sch., Honolulu, 1967-68, Kailua High Sch., 1969-71, Kalaheo High Sch., Kailua, 1972-77; ednl. specialist Hawaii Dept. Edn., Honolulu, 1977-79; ednl. adminstr. Hawaii Dept. Edn., Honolulu, 1979—; frequent speaker on edn.; lectr. U. Hawaii, 1987—. Bd. dirs. Western Assn. Schs. and Colls. Served with AUS, 1951-57, 68-69, col. U.S. Army ret. Decorated Legion of Merit, Army Commendation medal. Mem. Nat. Assn. Secondary Sch. Prins., Western Assn. Schs. and Colls. (bd. dirs.), Accrediting Commn. for Sch's. (chair), Network for Outcome-Based Schs., Commonwealth Coun. for Ednl. Adminstrn., Assn. U.S. Army, Res. Officers Assn., Go For Broke Assn., Army War Coll. Alumni Assn., Hawaii Govt. Employees Assn., Phi Delta Kappa, Phi Kappa Phi. Home: 47-494 Apoalewa Pl Kaneohe HI 96744 Office: Hawaii Dept Edn 2530 10th Ave Honolulu HI 96816-3097

IKEDA, TSUGUO (IKE IKEDA), social services center administrator, consultant; b. Portland, Oreg., Aug. 15, 1924; s. Tom Minoru and Tomoe Ikeda; m. Sumiko Hara, Sept. 2, 1951; children: Wanda Amy, Helen Mari, Julie Ann, Patricia Kiyo. BA, Lewis & Clark Coll., 1949; MSW, U. Wash., 1951. Social group worker Neighborhood House, Seattle, 1951-53; exec. dir. Atlantic St. Ctr., Seattle, 1953-86; pres. Urban Partnerships, Seattle, 1986-88, Tsuguo "Ike" Ikeda and Assoc., Seattle, 1988—; cons. Seattle, 1988—; cons. Commn. on Religion and Race, Washington, 1973, North Northeast Mental Health Ctr., Portland, 1985; affirmative action cons. Nat. Assn. Social Workers, Washington, 1977; cons./trainer various other orgns. Tsuguo "Ike" Ikeda, Pub. Svc. ann. award established in 1987. Mem. Nat. Task Force to develop standards and goals for juv. delinquency, 1976; mem. Gov.'s Select Panel for social and health svcs., Olympia, Wash., 1977; chmn. Asian Am. Task Force, Community Coll., Seattle dist., 1982, King County Coordinated Health Care Initiative Client Edn., Mktg. Subcom., 1993; div. chmn. social agys. Seattle United Way campaign, 1985; vice-chmn. Wash. State Com. on Vocat. Edn., Olympia, 1985-86, chmn. 1986-87; chmn. regional adv. com. Dept. Social and Health Svcs., 1990-91; mem. Gov. Mike Lawry's Commn. on Ethics Govt., Campaign Practices, 1993—. With Mil. Intelligence Lang. Sch., 1945-46. Recipient cert. appreciation U.S. Dept. Justice, Washington, 1975-76, Am. Dream award Community Coll. Dist., Seattle, 1984, Asian Counseling & Referral Svc., 1991, Wing Luke Mus., 1991-92, Atlantic St. Ctr., 1992, Seattle Chines Post, 1992, Bishop's award, PNW Conf., U. Meth. Ch., Tacoma, Wash., 1984, community service award Seattle Rotary Club, 1985, Oustanding Citizen award Mcpl. League, Seattle and King County, 1986, Outstanding Leadership award Dept. Social and Health Svcs., 1993, community award South Pacific Islander Program Seattle Pub. Schs., 1993, numerous others. Mem. Nat. Assn. Social Workers (chpt. pres., Social Worker of Yr. 1971), Vol. Agy. Exec. Coalition (pres., Outstanding Community Svc. award 1979), Ethnic Minority Mental Health Consortium (chmn., Outstanding Ldr. 1982, David E. "Ned" Skinner Community Svc. award 1990), Minority Exec. Dirs. Coalition (organizer, mem. chmn. 1980-86). Democrat. Methodist.

IKEGAWA, SHIRO, artist; b. Tokyo, July 15, 1933; came to the U.S., 1956; s. Fujinori and Sumie (Mastuki) I.; 1 child, Jima. Student, Tokyo U. Arts; MFA, Otis Art Inst. L.A., 1961. Asst. prof. art Pasadena (Calif.) City Coll., 1961-67, Calif. State U., L.A., 1967-76; prof. art Otis Art Inst., 1979-85; guest prof. Calif. Inst. Arts, 1968-71, Otis Art Inst. L.A., 1967, Calif. State U., San Francisco, 1972, U. Calif., Berkeley, 1973, Vancouver (British Columbia) Sch. Art, 1974, U. Calif., Irvine, 1974-75, Calif. State U., Dominguez Hills, 1985; vis. prof. Claremont (Calif.) Grad. Sch., 1987, U. Calif., Davis, 1989; lectr. in field; juror various art exhibitions. Exhibited works in numerous one-person and group shows including So. Oreg. Coll., Ashland, 1987, Monterey Bay Gallery, Calif., 1987, Soker-Kaseman Gallery, San Francisco, 1985, No. Ariz. U., Flagstaff, 1985, Shinno Gallery, L.A., 1984, Calif. State U., L.A., 1983, Fine Arts Gallery, Laguna Beach, Calif., 1983, L.A. Inst. Contemporary Art, 1980; prin. works represented in pub. and pvt. collections including Pasadena Art Mus., Long Beach Art Mus., Seattle Art Mus., L.A. County Mus., others. Otis Art Inst. grantee, 1960, Calif. State U. L.A. Found. grantee, 1968-72, Ford Found. grantee, 1977, 80; NEA fellow, 1974, 81; recipient numerous awards including Jurors' Award of Merit 2d N.H. Internat. Graphics Annual, 1974, Purchase prize Santa Monica City Coll., 1973, Otis Art Inst., 1969, U. N.D., 1967, Wichita Art Ctr., 1965, Western Mich. U., 1964, Calif. Palace of Legion of Honor, 1964, Seattle Art Mus., 1963, Long Beach Art Mus., 1963, Pasadena Art Mus., 1964, others. Home: 323 E Altadena Dr Altadena CA 91001

ILIFF, WARREN JOLIDON, zoo administrator; b. Madison, Wis., Nov. 5, 1936; s. Warren Jolidon and Wilma Marie (Lowenstein) I.; m. Ghislaine de Brouchoven de Bergeyck, Feb. 13, 1970. A.B., Harvard U., 1958. Helicopter pilot, crop duster Central Am., 1962-66; dir. planning Air Transport Assn., Washington, 1966-67; spl. asst. to dir. Nat. Zoo, Washington, 1967-71; exec. dir. Friends of Nat. Zoo, 1971-73; asst. dir. Nat. Zoo, 1973-75; dir. Washington Park Zoo, Portland, Oreg., 1975-84, Dallas Zoo, 1984-91, Phoenix Zoo, 1991—. Bd. dirs. Wildlife Preservation Trust Internat., 1985—, Jane Goodall Inst., 1985—. Served with USMC, 1958-62. Mem. Am. Assn. Zool. Parks and Aquariums (past pres.), Internat. Union Dirs. Zool. Gardens. Home: 7202 N Red Ledge Dr Paradise Valley AZ 85253 Office: Arizona Zoological Society The Phoenix Zoo PO Box 52191 Phoenix AZ 85072-2191

ILLING, JOSEPH RAYMOND, realtor, food service company owner; b. Chgo., Apr. 4, 1943; m. Barbara Heenan, 1968; children: Joey, Chris, Katie. BA in English, U. Calif., Berkeley, 1970. Founder, prin. Illing Realty, Olympia, Wash., 1979—, Valley Hoe! Bldg. and Grounds Maintenance Svcs., Olympia, 1989—; founder, co-owner Quick's Burgers, Inc., Aberdeen, Wash., 1990—. Author: (poems) The Bedroom of the Sun, 1993; creator, host (cable TV series) The Story of Olympia, 1987-90. Repub. candidate 3rd Congl. Dist., Wash., 1986; founding chmn. Wash. Centennial Organizing Com., 1979-84; founder 1989 Wash. Centennial Com., Olympia, 1979-89, chmn., 1979-82; creator, supr. Day in the Life of Lacey, Wash.; past pres. Lacey's Mus., Arts, and Dance Festival; former commr. Lacey Hist. Commn.; mem. Thurston County Econ. Devel. Coun., St. Michael's Ch.; mem. developers adv. group Gen. Adminstrn., State of Wash.; founder, bd. dirs. To Russia With Love. Mem. Capitol Area Photographic Soc. (founder, past pres.), Olympia Country and Golf Club (memberhsip com. chair, comm. chair, clubhouse renovation com., chmn. bd. dirs.), Wash. Gens., Olympia/Thurston C. of C. (former mem. bus. and econ. devel. com.), Thurston County Bd. Realtors (past chmn. publicity com.). Home: 3002 Country Club Loop NW Olympia WA 98502-3754 Office: Illing Realty 203 4th Ave E Ste 405 Olympia WA 98501-1186

ILSTAD, GEIR ARE, investment banker; b. Norway, Mar. 19, 1955; s. Johan Julius and Rønnaug Synnøve (Kristensen) I.; m. Prudence Burnett Herman, Dec. 1, 1984; children: Bergen Burnett, Alexandra Burnett. Degree in Econs., U. Fribourg, Switzerland, 1980; BS, Menlo Sch. Bus., Atherton, Calif., 1982, MBA, 1982. Prin. Ilstad Group, Menlo Park, 1981; mgr. Bergen Bank A/S, Oslo, 1982-85; prin. TSC Inc., 1984-86, pres. prin. SØR Invest A/S, 1984; project mgr. corp. fin. A.S. Factoring Finans, Oslo, 1985-86; pres., chmn. Prudent Mgmt., Inc., Menlo Park, 1986—. Mem. Nesodden Speed Skating Club, 1969-75, Unge Høyre, Nesodden, Norway, 1971. Served with paratroopers Norwegian Army, 1975-76. Mem. Norwegian Bus. Forum (bd. dirs.), Swedish-Am. C. of C. Home and Office: Prudent Mgmt Inc 12620 Viscaino Ct Los Altos Hills CA 94022

IMAI, KAZUO, electronics company executive; b. Tokyo, Aug. 5, 1946; came to U.S., 1989; s. Kyasaku and Masae (Kudo) I.; m. Hachiko Kamei, June 20, 1971; children: Kyoko, Keisuke. Student, Tech. Sch., Tokyo. Gen. mgr. non-consumer div. Sony UK Ltd., Staines, Eng., 1980-84, bd. dirs., 1984-86; gen. mgr. R & D innovation Sony Corp., Tokyo, 1986-87, gen. mgr. bus. strategy Videocom group, 1987-88; pres. Sony Microsystems, Sony Corp. Am., Palo Alto, Calif., 1989-90; exec. v.p. Sony Trans Com Inc., Irvine, Calif., 1990—. Mem. Inst. Dirs. (London), Mktg. Soc. (London). Office: Sony Trans Com Inc 1833 Alton Ave Irvine CA 92714

IMAMURA, EUGENE HACHIRO, osteopathic physician, surgeon; b. Waipahu, Hawaii. BS, U. Hawaii, 1943; DO, Kansas City Coll. Osteopath, 1953. Intern Waldo Gen. Hosp., Seattle, 1953-54; pvt. practice Seattle, 1955-86, Terrace, 1986—; pres. of staff Waldo Gen. Hosp., Seattle, 1957-58. Life patron Edmonds Art Festival. With U.S. Army, 1944-46. Mem. Am. Osteopathic Assn. (life mem.), UHS Coll. of Osteopathic Med., Wash. Osteopathic Medical Assn., Am. Coll. General Practitioners. Home: 16024 75th Pl W Edmonds WA 98026-4524 Office: 5707 244 St SW Mountlake Terrace WA 98043

IMANA, JORGE GARRON, artist; b. Sucre, Bolivia, Sept. 20, 1930; s. Juan S. and Lola (Garron) I.; grad. Fine Arts Acad., U. San Francisco Xavier, 1950; cert. Nat. Sch. for Tchrs., Bolivia, 1952; came to U.S., 1964, naturalized, 1974; m. Cristina Imana; children—George, Ivan. Prof. art Nat. Sch. Tchrs., Sucre, 1954-56; prof. biology Padilla Coll., Sucre, 1956-60; head dept. art Inst. Normal Simon Bolivar, La Paz, Bolivia, 1961-62; propr., mgr. The Artists Showroom, San Diego, 1973—. Over 86 one-man shows of paintings in U.S., S. Am. and Europe, 1952—, including: Gallery Banet, La Paz, 1965, Artists Showroom, San Diego, 1964, 66, 68, 74, 76, 77, San Diego Art Inst., 1966, 68, 72, 73, Contrast Gallery, Chula Vista, Calif., 1966, Central Public Library, San Diego, 1969, Universidad de Zulia, Maracaibo, Venezuela, 1969, Spanish Village Art Center, San Diego, 1974, 75, 76, La Jolla Art Assn. Gallery, 1969, 72-88, Internat. Gallery, Washington, 1976, Galeria de Arte L'Atelier, La Paz, 1977, Museo Nacional, La Paz, 1987, Casa del Arte, La Jolla, Calif., 1987, Museo Nacional, La Paz, Bolivia, 1988; numerous group shows including: Fine Arts Gallery, San Diego, 1964, Mus. of Modern Art, Paris, 1973, exhibits in galleries of Budapest (Hungary), 1975, Moscow (USSR), 1975, Warsaw (Poland), 1976; represented in permanent collections: Museo Nacional, La Paz, Bolivia, Museo de la Universidad de Potosi, Bolivia, Muse Nacional de Bogota, Colombia, S. Am., Ministerio de Edn., Managua, Nicaragua, Bolivian embassy, Moscow and Washington, also pvt. collections in U.S., Europe and Latin Am.; executed many murals including: Colegio Padilla, Sucre, Bolivia, 1958, Colegio Junin, Sucre, Bolivia, 1959, Sindicato de Construccion Civil, Lima, Peru, 1960. Hon. consul of Bolivia, So. Calif., 1969-73. Served to lt. Bolivian Army, 1953. Recipient Mcpl. award Sucre, Bolivia, 1958. Mem. San Diego Art Inst., San Diego Watercolor Soc., Internat. Fine Arts Guild, La Jolla Art Assn. Home: 3357 Caminito Gandara La Jolla CA 92037-2907

IMIRZIAN, MARLENE SIROUN, architect; b. Detroit, Sept. 24, 1958; d. Kirkor and Hasmig (Berberian) I. BS, U. Mich., 1980; MArch, U. Mich, 1983. With Gunnar Birkerts & Assocs., Architects, Birmingham, Mich., 1978, 1980-81; archtl. designer Smith, Hinchman & Grylls, Inc., Detroit, 1983-84; archtl. designer Smith, Hinchman & Grylls, Inc., Phoenix, 1989-90, design mgr., 1990; archtl. designer William Kessler & Assocs. Inc., Detroit, 1984-89; vis. design critic U. Mich., U. Detroit, 1987, Lawrence Inst. Tech., Southfield, Mich., 1986; thesis com. Ariz. State U. Sch. Architecture, 1990, prof. adv. coun.; speaker Nat. Coun. C.C. Bus. Ofcls. Exhibited in shows at Detroit Artists Market, 1984, Isis Gallery, Mich., 1987, Valley Nat. Bank Ctr., Phoenix, 1991, Scottsdale (Ariz.) Fashion Square, 1991, Valley Bank Ctr., Phoenix, 1992. bd. dirs. Ariz. Women in Architecture. Mem. AIA, City of Phoenix Design Review Standards Com., Friends Belle Isle, Skating Club of Phoenix. Office: Smith Hinchman & Grylls SW 1001 N Central Ave Phoenix AZ 85004-1935

IMMENSCHUH, WILLIAM TABER, aeronautical engineer; b. Monte Vista, Colo., June 12, 1917; s. Aldie Philip and Helen Frances (Taber) I.; m. Julia Watkins, Sept. 23, 1943 (div. 1965); children: Cheryl, William P., Edwin; m. Joan Palmer, Dec. 31, 1969. Tech. Cert., Ryan Sch. Aero. & Engring., San Diego, 1940. Registered profl. engr., Calif. Aero. engr. Ryan Aero. Co., San Diego, 1940-69, Teledyne Ryan Aero. Co., San Diego, 1969-83; ret. Pres. San Diego Aeropace Mus., 1980-92, chmn. bd. dirs., 1992—. Silver Knight, Nat. Mgmt. Assn., San Diego, 1981; recipient Pub. Svc. award, AIAA, 1981, 83, award San Diego Press Club, 1991. Fellow AIAA (assoc. fellow); mem. SAE. Republican. Home: 4621 Euclid Ave San Diego CA 92115-3226 Office: San Diego Aerospace Museum 2001 Pan American Plz San Diego CA 92101-1636

IMMERMAN, WILLIAM JOSEPH, lawyer, motion picture producer; b. N.Y.C., Dec. 29, 1937; s. Nathan and Sadye (Naumoff) I.; children: Scott, Eric, Lara. BS, U. Wis., 1959; JD, Stanford U., 1963. Bar: Calif., 1964. Dep. dist. atty. L.A. County, L.A., 1963-65; v.p. bus. affairs Am. Internat. Pictures, L.A., 1965-72; sr. v.p. 20th Century Fox Film Corp., L.A., 1972-77; producer Warner Bros. Pictures, L.A., 1977-79; pres. Scoric Prodns., Inc., L.A., 1977—, Salem Prodns., Inc., L.A., 1978—, Distbn. Expense Co., L.A., 1986—; of counsel Barash and Hill, L.A., 1983-93; ptnr. Law Offices of Immerman and Kaplan, L.A., 1993—; pres. Immkirk Fin. Corp., 1987—; chmn. Cinema Group, Inc., L.A., 1979-82; vice-chmn. Cannon Pictures, Inc., L.A., 1989-90; cons. to pres. Pathe Comm. Corp., L.A., 1988-89; dir. Heritage Entertainment Corp., L.A., 1987-91. Dir. The Thalians, L.A., 1978—. Capt. USAR, 1959-68. Mem. Assn. Motion Picture and TV Producers (bd. dirs. 1972-77), Ind. Film and Distbr. Assn. (bd. dirs. 1966-70), Acad. Motion Picture Arts and Sci., State Bar Calif, Los Angeles County Bar Assn. Office: Immerman and Kaplan 2029 Century Park E #2050 Los Angeles CA 90067

INABA, LAWRENCE AKIO, educational director; b. Honolulu, May 19, 1932; m. Violet C. Oki, Mar. 19, 1955; 1 child, Lori. BEd, U. Hawaii, 1960, MEd, 1963; PhD, Ohio State U., 1970; EdD, Ashiya U., Japan, 1980. Cert. tchr., Hawaii. Electronics instr. Roosevelt High Sch., Honolulu, 1959-68; rsch., teaching assoc. Ohio State U., Columbus, 1968-70; program specialist vocat. edn. Dept. Edn., Honolulu, 1970-75, adminstr. vocat. edn., 1975-76, ednl. dir., 1976-85; state dir. vocat. edn. U. Hawaii, Honolulu, 1985—; cons. in field. Author: Analysis of Job Tasks, 1973, Effective Use of Advisory Committee, 1975, Content Identification and Vaildation, 1974, Trends and Developments in Vocational Education, 1984. NDEA fellow, 1967. Mem. Hawaii Vocat. Assn., Am. Vocat. Assn., Hawaii Electronics Assn., Am. Tech. Educators Assn., Epsilon Pi Tau (Disting. Svc. award 1988, Laureate citation 1978), Phi Delta Kappa. Home: 3791 Pukalani Pl Honolulu HI 96816-3813 Office: 1117 Kapahulu Ave Honolulu HI 96816

INFANTE, DONALD RICHARD, electronics executive; b. Youngstown, Ohio, May 2, 1937; s. Michael and Fannie Susan (Felice) I.; m. Norma Jean Barchie, May 9, 1959; children: Dean Michael, Renee Louise. BS, Youngstown State U., 1958, D Mil. Sci., 1986; MS in Ops. Rsch., Rensselaer Poly Inst., 1969. Commd. 2d lt. U.S. Army, 1959, advanced through grades to maj. gen., 1986, numerous mgmt. positions, 1959-79; commanding officer 69th Air Def. Brigade U.S. Army, Wurzberg, Fed. Republic Germany, 1979-82; dep., commanding gen. 32nd Army Air Def. Command U.S. Army, Darmstadt, Fed. Republic Germany, 1982-83; project mgr. Patriot Project Office U.S. Army, Redstone Arsenal, Ala., 1983-85, poject mgr. Air Def. Project Office, 1985; commanding gen. U.S. Army, Fort Bliss/El Paso, Tex., 1985-89; retired U.S. Army, 1989; asst. div. mgr. defense electronics systems Hughes Aircraft Co., Fullerton, Calif., 1989-93, div. mgr., 1993—; bd. dirs. U.K. Systems Ltd., London; mem. Hughes Aircraft Air Def. Adv. Coun., Westchester, Calif., 1990—. Contbr. articles to profl. jours. Pres. Kilmer PTA, Vienna, Va., 1970-73, Fairfax County Parents of Spl. Children's Assn., Fairfax, Va., 1972-73; bd. dirs. Armed Svcs. YMCA, Fort Bliss, 1985-89. Decorated Legion of Merit, U.S. Army, 1975, 79, Disting. Svc. medal Pentagon, Washington, 1989; recipient Vol. of Yr. award Nat. Armed Svcs. YMCA, Chgo., 1988, Key to City awards Youngstown City Coun., 1989, El Paso City Coun., 1989. Mem. VFW, Def. Preparedness Assn., Assn. of U.S. Army (Cert. achievement 1989). Republican. Roman Catholic. Home: 7720 E Doheny Ct Anaheim CA 92808-2100 Office: Hughes Aircraft Co PO Box 3310 Bldg 676/D313 Fullerton CA 92634-3310

ING, DENNIS ROY, finance executive; b. Blue Island, Ill., Apr. 20, 1947; s. R.L. and Lois (Wright) I.; m. Phyllis J. Nienhouse, Mar. 11, 1967; 1 child, Laura J. BS in Engring., U. Ill., Chgo., 1972; MBA, De Paul U., 1977. Cons. Chgo. Hosp. Coun., 1972-73; acctg. mgr. Chgo. & North Western Trans. Co., 1973-77; mgmt. cons. Touche Ross & Co., Chgo., 1977-79; from internal auditor mgr. to dir. fin. Amdahl Corp., Sunnyvale, Calif., 1979-86; contr. Amdahl Can. Ltd., Toronto, Ont., 1986-88; v.p. fin. Amdahl Communications, Inc./Amdahl Can. Ltd., Toronto, Ont., 1988—. Chmn. bd. dirs. Christian Challenge Ministries, San Jose, Calif., 1985-90. Sgt. USAF, 1966-70. Mem. Info. Tech. Assn. Can., Fin. Exec. Inst., Can.-U.S. Bus. Assn., Can. Advanced Tech. Assn. (treas. 1992—), Delta Mu Delta. Republican. Home: 5360 Arezzo Dr, San Jose, CA Canada Office: Amdahl Corp Ms 514 1250 E Arques Ave Box 3470 Sunnyvale CA 94088-3010

INGALLS, JEREMY, poet, educator; b. Gloucester, Mass., Apr. 2, 1911; d. Charles A. and May E. (Dodge) Ingalls. AB, Tufts Coll., 1932, AM, 1933; student, U. Chgo., 1938-39; LHD, Rockford Coll., 1960; LittD, Tufts U., 1965. Asst. prof. English lit. Western Coll., Oxford, Ohio, 1941-43; resident poet, asst. prof. English lit. Rockford (Ill.) Coll., 1948-50, successively assoc. prof. English and Asian studies, prof., chmn. div. arts, chmn. English dept., 1950-60; Fulbright prof. Am. lit., Japan, 1957; Rockefeller Found. lectr. Kyoto Am. Studies seminar, 1958. Author: A Book of Legends, 1941, The Metaphysical Sword, 1941, Tahl, 1945, The Galilean Way, 1953, The Woman from the Island, 1958, These Islands Also, 1959, This Stubborn Quantum, 1983, Summer Liturgy, 1985, The Epic Tradition and Related Essays, 1989; translator (from Chinese) A Political History of China, 1840-1928 (Li Chien-Nung), 1956, The Malice of Empire (Yao Hsin-Hung), 1970, (from Japanese) Tenno Yugao (Nakagawa), 1975. Recipient Yale Series of Younger Poets prize, 1941, Shelley Meml. award, 1950, and other awards for poetry; apptd. hon. epic poet laureate United Poets Laureate Internat., 1965; Guggenheim fellow, 1943, Chinese classics rsch. fellow Republic of China, 1945, 46, Am. Acad. Arts and Letters grantee, 1944, Ford Found. fellow Asian studies, 1952, 53. Fellow Internat. Inst. Arts and Letters; mem. MLA (chmn. Oriental-western lit. rels. conf.), Assn. Asian Studies (life), Authors Guild, Poetry Soc. Am., New Eng. Poetry Soc., Dante Soc. Am. (life), Phi Beta Kappa, Chi Omega. Episcopalian. Home: 6269 E Rosewood St Tucson AZ 85711-1638

INGEBRITSEN, STEVEN ERIC, research hydrogeologist; b. San Diego, Apr. 2, 1956; s. Samuel Albert and Ann (Stevens) I.; m. Barbara Sandra Gaal, Oct. 24, 1980; children: Joanna Rose, Ellen Jane. BA, Carleton Coll., 1978; MS, Stanford U., 1983, PhD, 1986. Hydrogeologist U.S. Geol. Survey, Menlo Park, Calif., 1980—; nat. com. Internat. Assn. Volcanology and Chemistry of Earth's Interior, 1991—. Editorial bd. mem. Geothermics, 1991—; author numerous papers in field. Nat. co-chair Stanford-U.S. Geol. Survey Fellowship, 1990—; vol. Sci. Mate Program, 1992—. Mem. Am. Geophysical Union, Geol. Soc. of Am., Geothermal Resources Coun., Sigma Xi. Office: U S Geol Survey 345 Middlefield Rd Menlo Park CA 94025

INGERMAN, MICHAEL LEIGH, business consultant; b. N.Y.C., Nov. 30, 1937; s. Charles Stryker and Ernestine (Leigh) I.; m. Madeleine Edison Sloane; Nov. 24, 1984; children by previous marriage: Shawn Marie, Jenifer Lyn. BS, George Washington U., 1963. Health planner, Marin County, Calif., 1969-70, 70-72; regional cons. Bay Area Comprehensive Health Coun., San Francisco, 1972-73; hosp. cons. Booz, Allen & Hamilton, San Francisco, 1974; health planning coord. Peralta Hosp., Oakland, Calif., 1975-76; pres. Discern, Inc., mgmt. cons., Nicasio, Calif., 1976—; prin. Human Resources Mgmt. Group, San Francisco, 1991—; instr. Golden Gate U., 1981-88. Bd. dirs. Nicasio Land Owners Assn., 1989-91, pres., 1990; coord. Nicasio Disaster Com., 1988-89; nat. bd. dirs. Am. Friends Svc. Com., 1980-81, bd. dirs. John Woolman Sch., 1980-87, 90—, bd. chmn., 1991, Hospice of Marin, 1983-89, pres. bd. dirs., 1988-89; bd. dirs. Vol. Ctr. Marin, 1991—, Friends Assn. Svc. for the Elderly, 1984-89, pres. 1988-89; mem. Marin County Civil Grand Jury, 1977-78, Nicasio Design Rev. Com., 1979-83. Office: Discern Inc Box 786 Nicasio CA 94946

INGERSOLL, ANDREW PERRY, planetary science educator; b. Chgo., Jan. 2, 1940; s. Jeremiah Crary and Minneola (Perry) I.; m. Sarah Morin, Aug. 27, 1961; children: Jeremiah, Ruth Ingersoll Wood, Marion, Minneola, George. BA, Amherst Coll., 1960; PhD, Harvard U., 1965. Rsch. fellow Harvard U., Cambridge, Mass., 1965-66; mem. staff summer study program Woods Hole (Mass.) Oceanographic Inst., 1965, 70-73, 1976, 80, 92; asst. prof. Calif. Inst. Tech., Pasadena, 1966-71, assoc. prof., 1971-76, prof., 1976—; prin. investigator Pioneer Saturn Infrared Radiometer Team, NASA; mem. Voyager Imaging Team, NASA, Cassini Imaging Team; interdisciplinary scientist, Mars Observer Project, Galileo Project, NASA. Bd. trustees Poly. Sch., Pasadena. Fellow AAAS, Am. Geophys. Union; mem. Am. Astron. Soc. (vice chmn. div. planetary sci. 1988-89, chmn. 1989-90). Office: Calif Inst Tech 170-25 Pasadena CA 91125

INGERSOLL, JOHN GREGORY, physicist, energy specialist, educator; b. Athens, Greece, July 25, 1948; came to U.S., 1971; s. Gregory and Catherine (Asteris) I.; m. Sally Lynn Roberts, Apr. 7, 1984. BS, Nat. Tech. U., Athens, 1970; MS, Syracuse U., 1973; PhD, U. Calif., Berkeley, 1978. Instr. physics U. Calif., 1974-75, research asst. Lawrence Berkeley Lab., 1975-77, from asst. research prof. to assoc. research prof. Lawrence Berkeley Lab., 1978-82; sr. staff scientist Hughes Aircraft Co., Los Angeles, 1983—; staff mem., advisor USN Energy Office, Washington, 1988—; cons. Calif. Energy Commn., Sacramento, 1981-82, U.S. Dept. Energy, Washington, 1981-83, Bldg. Industry, N.Y. and Calif., 1982—; prin. investigator Energy Tech. Group UCLA, 1983—; mem. tech. team for devel. of a comml. passenger electric vehicle GM, 1990—. Contvr. over 70 articles on nuclear sci., renewable energy sources, indoor air quality, efficient utilization of energy in bldgs., passive solar systems and solar elec. energy to profl. jours.; contbg. author to 3 books on energy mgmt. in bldgs.; patentee heat pipe devels., nonfreon low power air conditioner for electric vehicles and buses. Mem. Rep. Presdl. Task Force, Calif., 1981-83. Served as lt. USNR, 1982—. Recipient 2d Pl. award Edison Electric Inst., Gen. Motors, and Dept. Energy, 1993; fellow Democritus Nuclear Research Ctr., Athens, 1970, Syracuse U., 1972, Rockefeller Found., 1974. Mem. Gen. Motors team (tasked with development, production, mktg. of passenger electric vehicle). Presbyterian. Home: 21315 Lighthill Dr Topanga CA 90290-9715 Office: Hughes Aircraft Co PO Box 902 El Segundo CA 90245-0902

INGLE, JAMES CHESNEY, JR., geology educator; b. Los Angeles, Nov. 6, 1935; s. James Chesney and Florence Adelaide (Geldart) I.; m. Fredricka Ann Bornholdt, June 14, 1958; 1 child, Douglas James. B.S. in Geology, U. So. Calif., 1959, M.S. in Geology, 1962, Ph.D. in Geology, 1966. Registered geologist, Calif. Research assoc. Univ. So. Calif., 1961-65; vis. scholar Tohoku U., Sendai, Japan, 1966-67; asst., assoc. to full prof. Stanford U., Calif., 1968—; W.M. Keck prof. earth scis. Stanford U., 1984—, chmn. dept. geology, 1982-86; co-chief scientist Leg 31 Deep Sea Drilling Project, 1973, co-chief scientist Leg 128 Ocean Drilling Program, 1989; geologist U.S. Geol. Survey W.A.E, 1978-81. Author: Movement of Beach Sand, 1966; contbr. articles to profl. jours. Recipient W.A. Tarr award Sigma Gamma Epsilon, 1958; named Disting. lectr. Am. Assn. Petroleum Geologists, 1986-87, Joint Oceanographic Institutions, 1991; A.I. Leverson award Am. Assn. Petroleum Geologists, 1988. Fellow Geol. Soc. Am., Calif. Acad. of Scis.; mem. Cushman Found. (bd. dirs. 1984-91), Soc. Profl. Paleontol. and Mineralogists (Pacific sect. 1958—, prs. elect. 1993), Am. Geophys. Union.

INGLE, ROBERT D., newspaper editor; b. Sioux City, Iowa, Apr. 29, 1939; s. Walter J. and Thelma L (McCoy) I.; m. Martha N. Nelson, Sept. 12, 1964 (div. 1984); 1 child, Julia L.; m. Sandra R. Reed, Mar. 2, 1985. B.A. in Journalism and Polit. Sci., U. Iowa, 1962. Various positions Miami Herald, 1962-75, asst. mng. editor, 1975-77, mng. editor, 1977-81; sr. v.p., exec. editor San Jose Mercury News, Calif., 1981—. Pres. Calif. First Amendment Coalition, 1990-92. Mem. AP Mng. Editors Assn., Am. Soc. Newspaper Editors. Office: San Jose Mercury News 750 Ridder Park Dr San Jose CA 95190-0001

INGRAM, CECIL D., accountant, state legislator; b. Blackfoot, Idaho, Dec. 27, 1932; s. Orval Otto and Mary Marjorie (Evans) I.; m. Lois Ann Glenn, Dec. 28, 1952; children: Cynthia, William, Christopher. BBA, U. Oreg., 1962. Contr. transp. & distbn. divsn. Boise (Idaho) Cascade Corp., 1962-91; senator Idaho State Legislature, Boise, 1993—. Capt. U.S. Army, 1953-58, Korea. Mem. Masons. Republican. Baptist. Home: 7025 El Caballo Dr Boise ID 83704

INGRAM, COLIN, writer, editor, book publisher; b. Chgo., July 18, 1936; s. Carl and Florence (Kahn) I.; m. Judy Charleen Bausor, Feb. 21, 1979; children: Rachel Evangeline, Evan Aldwyn. Owner, pub. Monterey Pacific Publs., Marina, Calif., 1981—. Author over 120 books, latest being The Small Business Test, 1991, The Drinking Water Book, 1991; editor over 80 books, latest being Preparing Your Family To Manage Wealth, 1991, From the Hearts of Men, 1992, Voices from the Womb, 1992; contbr. over 200 articles to sci. jours., trade mags., newspapers, and popular publs. Home and Office: PO Box 829 Marina CA 93933

INGRAM, PEGGY JOYCE, educator; b. Wichita Falls, Tex., Feb. 15, 1943; d. Albert Cronjie and Esther (Wiist) Weiss; m. Darwin Keith Ingram, Aug. 19, 1972; 1 child, Lindsey Michelle. Student, Midwestern U., 1961-62; BS, West Tex. State U., 1966; MNS, U. Okla., 1972; postgrad., Ea. N.Mex. U., 1975. Cert. secondary sci. tchr. Tchr. Palo Duro High Sch., Amarillo, Tex., 1966-72, Texico (N.Mex.) High Sch., 1972-73; tchr., chair sci. dept. Clovis High Sch., 1973—; tchr. Ea. N.Mex. U., Clovis, 1981-82; participant NASA Honors Workshop, Jet Propulsion Lab., 1990. Mem. NEA, Clovis Edn. Assn., Nat. Sci. Tchrs. Assn., N.Mex. Acad. of Sci., Delta Kappa Gamma. Democrat. Methodist. Home: 2501 Williams Ave Clovis NM 88101-3330 Office: Clovis High Sch 1900 N Thornton St Clovis NM 88101-4555

INGRAM, ROBERT EDWARD LEE, science educator, assayer; b. Dallas, Oct. 9, 1932; s. Vernon Dewey and Genevieve (Ingram) I.; m. Geryl Lynn Fonnesbeck, July 12, 1956; children: Karene Elise, Alexander Frank, Robert Edward, Christian Vernon, Rosalyn, Harold Lee. Student, Brigham Young U., 1954-55; BA, U. Utah, 1958; MS, Ariz. State U., 1965; postgrad. Oreg. State U., 1970-71. Registered assayer, Ariz. Asst. chemist Marathon Oil Co., Littleton, Colo., 1958-61; grad. asst. Ariz. State U., Tempe, 1961-64; prof. Ariz. Western Coll., Yuma, 1964—; v.p. Ariz. ops. Chemex Labs, Inc., Sparks, Nev., 1991-93; cons. Yuma Proving Grounds, U.S. Army, 1981—, Yuma County Hazardous Materials Disaster Response Team, 1982—; chief chemist Western Am. Mineral and Chem. Cons. Inc., Yuma, 1984—. Author computer program. Scoutmaster, Desert Trails council Boy Scouts Am., 1975-78, commr., 1978—. Served with USN, 1950-54. Recipient Silver Beaver award Boy Scouts Am., 1983. Mem. Astron. Soc. Pacific, Royal Astron. Soc., Geochem. Soc., Am. Inst. Chemists. Democrat. Mem. LDS Church. Office: Ariz Western Coll PO Box 929 Yuma AZ 85366-0929

INGRAM, ROBINA ELAINE, nursing administrator, counselor, clinical nurse; b. San Francisco, Apr. 30, 1956; d. Louis William and Harriet Ann (Austin) I.; m. Gary Hugh McMillan, Aug. 28, 1982 (div. 1993). BSN, U. Calif., San Francisco, 1977; MS in Genetic Counseling, U. Calif., Berkeley, 1985, MPH in Maternal-Child Health, 1986. Clin. nurse ambulatory surgery, intensive care, operating rm. U. Calif. Davis Med. Ctr., Sacramento; orthopedic rsch. nurse Sch. Medicine U. Calif. Davis, Sacramento, relief supr., adminstrv. nurse Cowell Student Health Ctr.; hemophilia region X coord., genetic counselor, clin. nurse Oreg. Hemophilia Ctr., Portland. Contbr. articles to profl. jours. Helen Wallace rsch. grantee, 1985-86. Mem. APHA, AACN (Sacramento chpt. sec. 1979), AAUW (legis. chmn. Davis br., 1985-86, sec. Lake Oswego br. 1987-89, women's issues chmn., books interest group chmn. 1989-91, local arrangements com. assn. conv. 1991), NSCG, Sigma Theta Tau. Home: 440 Boca Ratan Dr Lake Oswego OR 97034-1602

INGRAM, WILLIAM AUSTIN, federal judge; b. Jeffersonville, Ind., July 6, 1924; s. William Austin and Marion (Lane) I.; m. Barbara Brown Lender, Sept. 18, 1947; children: Mary Ingram Mac Calla, Claudia, Betsy Ingram Friebel. Student, Stanford U., 1947; LL.B., U. Louisville, 1950. Assoc., Littler, Coakley, Lauritzen & Ferdon, San Francisco, 1951-55; dep. dist. atty. Santa Clara (Calif.) County, 1955-57; mem. firm Rankin, O'Neal, Luckhardt & Center, San Jose, Calif., 1955-69; judge Mcpl. Ct., Palo Alto-Mountain View, Calif., 1969-71, Calif. Superior Ct., 1971-76; judge U.S. Dist. Ct. (no. dist.) Calif., San Jose, 1976-88, chief judge, 1988-90. Served with USMCR, 1943-46. Fellow Am. Coll. Trial Lawyers. Republican. Episcopalian. Office: US Dist Ct Rm 4050 280 S First St San Jose CA 95113

INGRAO, JEROLD KENNETH, distribution company executive; b. Rochester, N.Y., Aug. 10, 1947; s. Joseph Robert and Mary Rose (Viola) I.; m. Marsha Louise Lalone, Sept. 29, 1973; children: Heather, Travis. BS in Acctg., Calif. State U., 1976. Nat. distbn. mgr. Pioneer Electronics, Long Beach, Calif., 1978-89; v.p. United Whse. and Distbn. Corp., Long Beach, 1989—. Bd. regents LaSalle High Sch., Pasadena, 1991—. Sgt. U.S. Army, 1967-70, Vietnam. Mem. NRA (life), Am. Legion (life), Disabled Am. Vets (comdr.), Ducks Unltd. (sponsor). Republican. Roman Catholic. Office: United Warehouse 2417 E Carson St Long Beach CA 90810

INKELES, ALEX, sociology educator; b. Bklyn., Mar. 4, 1920; s. Meyer and Ray (Gewer) K.; m. Bernadette Mary Kane, Jan. 31, 1942; 1 child, Ann Elizabeth. B.A., Cornell U., 1941, M.A., 1946; postgrad., Washington Sch. Psychiatry, 1943-46; Ph.D., Columbia U., 1949; student, Boston Psychoanalytic Inst., 1957-59; A.M. (hon.), Harvard U., 1957; prof. honoris causa, Faculdade Candido Mendez, Rio de Janerio, 1969. Social sci. research analyst Dept. State and OSS, 1942-46; cons. program evaluation br., internat. broadcasting div. Dept. State, 1949-51; instr. social relations Harvard U., Cambridge, Mass., 1948, lectr., 1948-57, prof. sociology, 1957-71, dir. studies social relations Russian Research Ctr., dir. studies social aspects econ. devel. Ctr. Internat. Affairs, 1963-71, research assoc., 1971—; Margaret Jacks prof. edn., prof. sociology Stanford U., Calif., 1971-78, prof. sociology, 1978-90; sr. fellow Hoover Inst., 1978—; prof. emeritus, 1990—; mem. exec. com. behavioral sci. div. NRC, 1968-75; lectr. Nihon U., Japan, 1985. Author: Public Opinion in Soviet Russia, 1950 (Kappa Tau Alpha award 1950, Grant Squires prize Columbia 1955); (with R. Bauer, C. Kluckhohn) How the Soviet System Works, 1956; (with R. Bauer) The Soviet Citizen, 1959, Soviet Society (edited with H.K. Geiger), 1961; What Is Sociology?, 1964; Readings on Modern Sociology, 1965; Social Change in Soviet Russia, 1968; (with D.H. Smith) Becoming Modern, 1974 (Hadley Cantril award 1974); Exploring Individual Modernity, 1983; contbr. articles to profl. jours.; editor-in-chief: Ann. Rev. Sociology, 1971-79; editorial cons. Internat. Rev. Cross Cultural Studies; editorial bd. Ethos, Jour. Soc. Psychol. Anthropology, 1978; editor Founds. Modern Sociology Series; adv. editor in sociology to Little, Brown & Co. Recipient Cooley Mead award for Disting. Contbn. in Social Psychology, 1982; fellow Ctr. Advanced Study Behavioral Sci., 1955, Founds. Fund Research Psychiatry, 1957-60, Social Scis. Research Council, 1959, Russell Sage Found., 1966, 85, Fulbright Found., 1977, Guggenheim Found., 1978, Bernard van Leer Jerusalem Found., 1979, Rockefeller Found., 1982, Eisenhower Assn., Taiwan, 1984; NAS Disting. Scholar Exchange, China, 1983; grantee Internat. Rsch. and Exchs. Bd., 1989, NSF, 1989. Fellow AAAS (co-chmn. western ctr. 1984-87, chmn. Talcott Parsons award com. 1988—), Am. Philos. Soc., Am. Psychol. Assn.; mem. NIMH Nat. Inst. Aging (monitoring com. health retirement survey 1990—), Nat. Acad. Scis. (corr. human rights com. 1986-88, mem. com. on scholarly communications with People's Republic of China, chmn. panel on social sci. and humanities, NRC panel on issues in democratization 1991—), Am. Sociol. Soc. (council 1961-64, v.p. 1975-76), Eastern Sociol. Soc. (pres. 1961-62), World Assn. Pub. Opinion Research, Am. Assn. Pub. Opinion Research, Inter-Am. Soc. Psychology, Sociol. Research Assn. (exec. com. 1975-79, pres. 1979), Soc. for Study Social Problems. Home: 1001 Hamilton Ave Palo Alto CA 94301-2215 Office: Stanford U Hoover Instn Stanford CA 94305

INKSTER, NORMA, school librarian; b. Springfield, Ill., Jan. 24, 1936; d. Thomas and Rosa (Kornack) Hollinshead; m. Albert Charles Inkster, Sept. 11, 1954. BS in Edn., Ill. State U., 1963; MA in English, U. Ariz., 1970, MLS, 1976. Cert. libr., tchr. Ill. Tchr. 5th grade Crete (Ill.) Elem. Sch., 1957-61; tchr. English Crete-Monee High Sch., 1962-66, Magee Jr. High Sch., Tucson, 1966-82; head libr. Catalina High Sch., Tucson, 1982—. Mem. Ariz. State Libr. Assn. Office: Catalina High Sch 3645 E Pima Tucson AZ 85716

INLOW, RUSH OSBORNE, chemist; b. Seattle, July 10, 1944; s. Edgar Burke and Marigale (Osborne) I.; B.S., U. Wash., 1966; Ph.D., Vanderbilt U., 1975; m. Gloria Elisa Duran, June 7, 1980. Chemist, sect. chief U.S. Dept. Energy, New Brunswick Lab., Argonne, Ill., 1975-78, chief nuclear safeguards br. Albuquerque ops., 1978-82, sr. program engr. Cruise missile systems, 1983-84, program mgr. Navy Strategic Systems, 1984-85, dir. weapon programs div., 1985-88, dir. prodn. ops. div., 1988-90, asst. mgr. safeguards and security, 1990—m apptd. Fed. Sr. Exec. Svc., 1985. Served with USN, 1966-71. Tenn. Eastman fellow, 1974-75. Mem. Am. Chem. Soc., Sigma Xi. Republican. Episcopalian. Contbr. articles to profl. jours. Home: 2024 Monte Largo Dr NE Albuquerque NM 87112-3736

INMAN, CLAUDIA JEAN, real estate executive; b. Portland, Oreg., Oct. 23, 1942; d. Claude John and Dorothy Caroline (Svarvari) Forrette; m. Charles Dibert, June 28, 1970 (div. Dec. 1977); m. Robert Willard Inman, Apr. 12, 1980; 1 child, Brian Dibert. Student, Portland Community Coll., 1970-88, Lewis & Clark Coll., 1979; banking degree, U. Wash., 1983. Proof transit clk. Bank of Calif., Portland, 1960-62, 68-69; proof and transit clk. LaSalle Nat. Bank, Chgo., 1963-65; with computer payroll and ops. Bank of Calif., Portland, 1969, ops. officer, 1974-75, liaison officer, 1975-79, credit officer, 1979-80, corp. loan officer, asst. v.p., 1980-86, asst. v.p. real estate loans, 1986-89, v.p. real estate loans, 1990-93; v.p. comml. loans Bank of Vancouver, Wash., 1993—; bd. dirs. Robert Morris Assocs., Oreg., 1991. Vol. Oreg. Art Mus./Rental Sales Gallery, Portland, 1987—; participant women in the pvt. sector Am. bus./culture class Internat. Devel. Ctr. of Japan, Willamette U., Salem, 1988—. Mem. Oreg. Mortgage Bankers Assn. (com. 1988—), Oreg. Bankers Assn. (com. 1980—), Machinists and Boilermakers FCU (bd. dir. 1983-88), Bank Adminstrn. Inst. (bd. dir. 1984-87), City Club of Portland, Portlandia Club of Portland, Fin. Women Internat. (nat. dir. 1985-86). Democrat. Roman Catholic. Home: 4660 SW Ormandy Way Portland OR 97221-3116 Office: Bank of Vancouver 109 E 13th St Vancouver WA 98666-9988

INOUYE, DANIEL KEN, senator; b. Honolulu, Sept. 7, 1924; s. Hyotaro I. and Kame Imanaga; m. Margaret Shinobu Awamura, June 12, 1949; 1 child, Daniel Ken. A.B., U. Hawaii, 1950; J.D., George Washington U., 1952. Bar: Hawaii 1953. Asst. pub. prosecutor Honolulu, 1953-54, pvt. practice, 1954—; majority leader Territorial Ho. of Reps., 1954-58, Senate, 1958-59; mem. 86th-87th U.S. Congresses from Hawaii, U.S. Senate from Hawaii, 1963—; sec. Senate Dem. Conf., 1978-88; chmn. Dem. Steering Com., Senate Com. on Appropriations; chmn. subcom. def., mem. Commerce Com.; chmn. subcom. on communications Select Com. on Intelligence, 1976-77, ranking mem. subcom. budget authorizations, 1979-84; chmn. Select Com. Indian Affairs; mem. Select Com. on Presdl. Campaign Activities, 1973-74; chmn. Sen. select com. Secret Mil. Assistance to Iran and Nicaraguan Opposition, 1987. Author: Journey to Washington. Active YMCA, Boy Scouts Am. Keynoter; temporary chmn. Dem. Nat. Conv., 1968, rules com. chmn., 1980, co-chmn. conv., 1984. Pvt. to capt. AUS, 1943-47. Decorated D.S.C., Bronze Star, Purple Heart with cluster; named 1 of 10 Outstanding Young Men of Yr. U.S. Jr. C. of C., 1960; recipient Splendid Am. award Thomas A. Dooley Found., 1967 Golden Plate award Am. Acad. Achievement, 1968. Mem. DAV (past comdr. Hawaii), Honolulu C. of C., Am. Legion (Nat. Comdr.'s award 1973). Methodist. Clubs: Lion. (Hawaii), 442d Veterans (Hawaii). Home: 469 Ena Rd Honolulu HI 96815-1749 Office: US Senate 722 Hart Senate Bldg Washington DC 20510-1102*

INSKEEP, ROBERT FORMAN, leadership development consultant; b. Billings, Mont., Dec. 5, 1944; m. Shirleen Jeannette Tripp, Nov. 5, 1966; children: Robert, James, Jaclyn. BBA magna cum laude, Nat. U., 1982, MA in Psychology, 1984. Dir. Leadership Mgmt. Edn. and Tng., San Francisco, 1987-90; pres. Inskeep and Assocs., Sonoma, Calif., 1990—; cons., trainer Office Pers. Mgmt., San Francisco, 1991-93; adj. instr. Am. Mgmt. Assn., 1992-93. Co-author: Leadership Education Awareness Development, 1978, (tng. guide) Performance Evaluation, 1979. Workshop leader Experience Unltd., San Francisco, 1991. With USN, 1967-90. Mem. ASTD, Fleet Res. Assn. Office: Inskeep and Assocs 102 Serres Dr Sonoma CA 95476-3121

INSLEE, JAY R., congressman, lawyer; b. Feb. 9, 1951; s. Frank and Adele Inslee; m. Trudi Anne Inslee; children: Jack, Connor, Joe. BA in Econs., U. Wash., 1973; JD magna cum laude, Willamette U., 1976. Atty. Peters, Fowler & Inslee, Selah, Wash., 1976-92; city prosecutor City of Selah, 1976-82; mem. from 14th dist. Wash. State Ho. of Reps., 1988-92; mem. 100th-103d Congresses from 4th Dist. State of Wash., 1992—. Chair Selah Sch. Bond Com., 1980; bd. dirs. New Valley Osteopathic Hosp., 1978-86. Mem. Wash. State Trial Lawyers Assn. (bd. dirs. 1984-88). Democrat. Office: US Ho of Reps Office of Ho Mems Washington DC 20515

INTRIERE, ANTHONY DONALD, physician; b. Greenwich, Conn., May 9, 1920; s. Rocco and Angelina (Belcastro) I.; m. Carol A. Yarmey, Aug. 1, 1945; children: Sherry Showmaker, Michael, Nancy M., Lisa A. MD, U. Mich., 1944. Intern, New Rochelle (N.Y.) Hosp., 1944-45; pvt. practice, Greenwich, Conn., 1947-53, Olney, Ill., 1956-61, Granite City, Ill., 1961-74, San Diego, 1975—; fellow in internal medicine Cleve. Clinic, 1953-55; fellow in gastroenterology Lahey Clinic, Boston, 1955-56. Capt. M.C., AUS, 1945-47. Fellow Am. Coll. Gastroenterology (assoc.); mem. AMA, ACP (assoc.), Am. Soc. Internal Medicine. Home: 9981 Caminito Chirimolla San Diego CA 92131-2001

INTRILIGATOR, DEVRIE SHAPIRO, physicist; b. N.Y.C.; d. Carl and Lillian Shapiro; m. Michael Intriligator; children: Kenneth, James, William, Robert. BS in Physics, MIT, 1962, MS, 1964; PhD in Planetary and Space Physics, UCLA, 1967. NRC-NASA rsch. assoc. NASA, Ames, Calif., 1967-69; rsch. fellow in physics Calif. Inst. Tech., Pasadena, 1969-72, vis. assoc., 1972-73; asst. prof. U. So. Calif., 1972-80; mem. Space Scis. Ctr., 1978-83; sr. rsch. physicist Carmel Rsch. Ctr., Santa Monica, Calif., 1979—; dir. Space Plasma Lab., 1980—; cons. NASA, NOAA, jet Propulsion Lab; chmn. NAS-NRC com. on solar-terrestrial rsch., 1983-86, exec. com. bd. atmospheric sci. and climate, 1983-86, geophysics rsch. bd., 1983-86, geophysics study com., 1983-86; U.S. nat. rep. Sci. Com. on Solar-Terrestrial Physics, 1979-81; mem. adv. com. NSF Div. Atmospheric Sci. Contbr. articles to profl. jours. Recipient 3 Achievement awards NASA, Calif. Resolution of Commendation, 1982. Mem. NAS-NRC, Am. Phys. Soc., Am. Geophys. Union, Cosmos Club. Home: 140 Foxtail Dr Santa Monica CA 90402-2048 Office: Carmel Rsch Ctr PO Box 1732 Santa Monica CA 90406-1732

INUI, THOMAS SPENCER, physician, educator; b. Balt., July 10, 1943; s. Frank Kazuo and Beulah Mae (Sheetz) I.; m. Nancy Stowe, June 14, 1969; 1 child, Tazo Stowe. BA, Haverford Coll., 1965; MD, Johns Hopkins U., 1969, ScM, 1973. Diplomate Am. Bd. Internal Medicine. Intern Johns Hopkins Hosp., Balt., 1969-70, resident in internal medicine, 1970-73; clin. scholar Johns Hopkins U., Balt., 1971-73, chief resident, instr., 1973-74; chief of medicine USPHS Indian Hosp., Albuquerque, 1974-76; chief gen. medicine, dir. health svc. rsch. Seattle VA Med. Ctr., 1976-86; dir. Robert Wood Johnson clin. scholars program U. Wash., Seattle, 1977-92, prof. dept. medicine and health svcs., 1985-92, head div. gen. internal medicine, 1986-92; prof., chmn. of dept. ambulatory care and prevention Harvard Med. Sch. and Harvard Community Health Plan, Boston, 1992—. Contbr. articles to profl. publs. Surgeon USPHS, 1974-76. Fellow ACP; mem. Soc. Gen. Internal Medicine (pres. 1988-89, mem. coun. 1983-89), APHA (mem. coun. 1988-90), Am. Fedn. Clin. Rsch., Assn. Health Svcs. Rsch., Soc. Tchrs. of Family Medicine, Inst. Medicine, Nat. Acad. Sci., Hastings Ctr. (assoc.), Phi Beta Kappa, Alpha Omega Alpha.

INVERSO, MARLENE JOY, optometrist; b. Los Angeles, May 10, 1942; d. Elmer Encel Wood and Sally Marie (Sample) Hirons; m. John S. Inverso, Dec. 16, 1962; 1 child, Christopher Edward. BA, Calif. State U., Northridge, 1964; MS, SUNY, Potsdam, 1975; OD, Pacific U., 1981. Cert. doctor optometry, Wash., Oreg. English tchr. Chatsworth (Calif.) High Sch., 1964-68, Nelson A. Boylen Second Sch., Toronto, Ont., Can., 1968-70, Gouverneur (N.Y.) Jr.-Sr. High Sch., 1970-74, 76-77; reading resource room tchr. Parishville (N.Y.) Hopkinton Sch., 1974-75; coordinator learning disability clinic SUNY, Potsdam, 1975-77; optometrist and vision therapist Am. Family Vision Clinics, Olympia, Wash., 1982—; mem. adv. com. Sunshine House St. Peter Hosp., Olympia, 1984-86, Pacific U. Coll. Optometry, Forest Grove, Oreg. 1986. Contbr. articles to profl. jours. Mem. Altrusa Svc. Club, Olympia, 1982-86; tchr. Ch. Living Water, Olympia, 1983-88, Olympia-Lacey Ch. of God, 1989—, sec. women's bd., 1990; bd. advisors Crisis Pregnancy Ctr., Olympia, 1987-89; den mother Cub Scouts Am. Pack 202, Lacey, Wash., 1987-88; vol. World Vision Countertop ptnr., 1986—. Fellow Coll. Optometrists in Optometric Devel.; mem. Am. Optometric Assn. (sec. 1983-84), Assn. Children and Adults with Learning Disabilities, Optometric Extension Program, Sigma Xi, Beta Sigma Kappa. Home: 4204 Timberline Dr SE Olympia WA 98503-4443

IPSEN, GRANT RUEL, insurance and investments professional; b. Malad, Idaho, Nov. 6, 1932; s. Nephi Ruel and Ada (Hughes) I.; m. Edna Wayne Hughes, July 27, 1956; children: Edna Gaye, LeAnn, Garin Grant, Shawna Lee, Wayne Ruel. BA, Brigham Young U., 1961. CPA Idaho; CLU, ChFC. Acct. Ernst & Ernst, Boise, Idaho, 1961-64; with sales dept. Mut. of N.Y., Boise, 1964—; mem. Idaho State Senate, 1992—. Active Boy Scouts Am., 1945—; co-convener Boise Religious Freedom com., 1991—. With U.S. Army, 1956-58. Named Agt. of Yr. Boise Assn. Life Underwriters, 1978. Mem. Million Dollar Round Table (life), Brigham Young Univ. Alumni (bd. dirs. 1987-93). Republican. LDS.

IRANI, RAY R., oil and gas and chemical company executive; b. Beirut, Lebanon, Jan. 15, 1935; came to U.S., 1953, naturalized, 1956; s. Rida and Naz I.; children: Glenn R., Lillian M., Martin R. BS in Chemistry, Am. U. Beirut, 1953; PhD in Phys. Chemistry, U. So. Calif., 1957. Rsch. scientist, then sr. rsch. scientist Monsanto Co., 1957-67; assoc. dir. new products, then dir. research Diamond Shamrock Corp., 1967-73; with Olin Corp., 1973-83, pres. chems. group, 1978-80; corp. pres., dir. Olin Corp., Stamford, Conn., 1980-83, COO, 1981-83; chmn. Occidental Petroleum Corp. subs. Occidental Chem. Corp., Dallas, 1983—; CEO Occidental Petroleum Corp., subs. Occidental Chem. Corp., Dallas, 1983-91; chmn. Can. Occidental Petroleum Corp. Ltd., Calgary, 1987—; exec. v.p. Occidental Petroleum Corp., L.A., 1983-84, pres., chief operating officer, 1984-91, chmn., pres., chief exec. officer, 1991—, also bd. dirs.; also chmn. Occidental Chem. Corp., Dallas, Texas; bd. dirs. Am. Petroleum Inst., Oxy Oil & Gas USA Inc., IBP Inc., Island Creek Corp., Occidental Oil & Gas Corp., Occidental Petroleum Investment Corp. Author: Particle Size; also author papers in field; numerous patents in field. Trustee U. So. Calif., Am. U. Beirut, St. John's Hosp. and Health Ctr. Found., Natural History Mus. Los Angeles County; bd. govs. Los Angeles Town Hall, Los Angeles World Affairs Coun. Mem. Nat. Petroleum Coun., Am. Inst. Chemists, Am. Chem. Soc., Sci. Rsch. Soc. Am., Indsl. Rsch. Inst., The Conf. Bd., Calif. Roundtable, Nat. Assn. Mfrs. (bd. dirs.), Am. Petroleum Inst. (bd. dirs.). Office: Occidental Petroleum 10889 Wilshire Blvd Los Angeles CA 90024 also: Can Occidental Petroleum Ltd, 500 635 8th Ave S W, Calgary, AB Canada T2P 3Z1*

IRELAND, ROBERT ABNER, JR, education consultant; b. Winterville, Miss., Nov. 13, 1918; s. Robert A. Sr. and Clara Lee (Johnson) I.; children: Robert A. III (dec.), Daniel G., Merry L., Kathleen, Joseph K., John E., Christopher M. BA, U. Va., 1941; MS, Columbia U., 1947; MA, Pepperdine U., 1974. Cert. counselor, Calif., career counselor. Commd. 2nd lt. U.S. Army, 1941, advanced through grades to lt. col., 1961, ret., 1972, edn. svcs. officer, counselor ednl.-vocat., 1976-80; cons. edn. U.S. Navy, L.A., 1981-93; ind. cons. career devel. L.A., 1988-93. Mem. AACD, APA, Academic and Profl. Soc. in Counseling, Am. Ednl. Rsch. Assn., Nat. Coun. on Measurement in Edn., Nat. Soc. for the Study of Edn., Mil. Testing Assn., Phi Delta Kappa, Chi Sigma Iota, Kappa Delta Pi. Office: Navy Recruiting Dist 5051 Rodeo Rd Los Angeles CA 90016

IRISH, JERRY ARTHUR, academic administrator, religion educator; b. Syracuse, N.Y., Nov. 25, 1936; s. Frank Leonard and Dorothy (Fries) I.; m. Patty Lee Williams; children: Lee Douglas, Jeffrey Scott, Mark Steven. BA in English and Philosophy, Cornell U., 1958; BD, So. Meth. U., 1964; PhD, Yale U., 1967. Instr. religion Stanford (Calif.) U., 1967-68, asst. prof. religious studies, 1968-75; assoc. prof. religion, dept. chmn. Wichita (Kans.) State U., 1975-80; provost, prof. religion Kenyon Coll., Gambier, Ohio, 1980-86; v.p., dean coll., prof. religion Pomona Coll., Claremont, Calif., 1986—; Stauffacher vis. prof. Pomona Coll., 1980. Author: A Boy Thirteen: Reflections on Death, 1975, The Religious Thought of H. Richard Niebuhr, 1983; contbr. articles to jours. and chpts. to books. Served to capt. USMC, 1958-61. Fellow Soc. for Values in Higher Edn.; mem. Am. Acad. Religion(sec. 1975-78). Office: Pomona Coll Office of Dean Summer Hall 201 Claremont CA 91711

IRSFELD, JOHN HENRY, academic administrator, English language educator; b. Bemidji, Minn., Dec. 2, 1937; s. Hubert Louis and Mary Lillian (McKee) I.; m. Margaret Elizabeth Drushel, Aug. 29, 1965 (div. Feb. 1978); 1 child, Hannah Christine; m. Janet Elizabeth Jones, May 5, 1984. BA, U. Tex., 1959, MA, 1966, PhD, 1969. Tchr. Spanish and English Calallen, Tex., 1959-60; teaching asst. U. Texas, Austin, 1960-61, 64-68, teaching assoc., 1968-69; from asst. prof. to assoc. prof. English U. Nev., Las Vegas, 1969-73, prof., 1977—, v.p., dep. to pres., 1990—, dep. to pres., 1987. Author: (novels) Coming Through, 1975, Little Kingdoms, 1976, 89, Rats Alley, 1987. Sgt. inf. U.S. Army, 1961-64. Democrat. Office: U Nev 4505 S Maryland Pky Las Vegas NV 89154-1001

IRVIN, MARK CHRISTOPHER, real estate consultant, broker and developer; b. San Antonio, Oct. 29, 1955; s. Eugene Jr. and Patricia Alice (Blomfield) I.; m. Linda S. Irvin, Nov. 27, 1976; 1 child, Christopher Ross. AS in Bus. and Transp., Eastfield Coll., 1979; BBA, So. Meth. U., 1986. V.p., ptnr. Refrigerated Motor Carriers Assn., Dallas, 1980-87; ptnr. T.S.I., Dallas, 1980-87; owner Irvin Transp. Cons., Dallas, 1980-87; mgr. transp. & tariffs F.F.E. Transport Svcs., Inc., Dallas, 1983-86; ptnr. PICOR Comml. Real Estate Svcs., Tucson, 1987—; mem. designate Cert. Comml. Investment Coun., Chgo., 1986—, Soc. Indsl. & Office Realtors. Mem. external mktg. com. Greater Tucson Econ. Coun., 1992; pres.-elect Boys and Girls Club, Tucson, 1992. Mem. Tucson Brokers Roundtable Assn. (pres. 1987—), Tucson Bd. Realtors (broker), Phi Theta Kappa. Republican. Office: PICOR Comml Real Estate Svc 335 N Wilmot Ste 505 Tucson AZ 85711

IRVINE, JERRY ANDREW (GERALD IRVINE), manufacturing executive, publisher; b. Claremont, Calif., Aug. 10, 1958; s. Robert Gerald and Joan (Granberg) I.; m. Bridget Ann Glidden, Jan. 9, 1988; children: Andrew Steven Irvine, Johnathan Glenn Holguin, Elizabeth Renee Holguin. BS in Econs., Calif. State Polytechnic, 1983. Program advisor Claremont (Calif.) Parks and Recreations, 1973-78; ins. agt. ITT Life, Transamerica Life, L.A., 1978-82; pub. Calif. Rocketry Pub., Claremont, 1979—; pres. U.S. Rockets, Claremont, 1979—; endowment, ins. specialist Irvine Agy., Claremont;

chmn. local and state programs The Public Endowment Strategy, Claremont, 1992—; advisor/sect. leader Polaris Sect. #193 Nat. Assn. Rocketry, Claremont, 1974-84; advisor/program leader Claremont Rocket Soc., 1974—; prefect Lucerne Test Range Prefecture #007 of Tripoli Rocketry Assn., Inc., Claremont, 1985—; spl. effects coord. U.S. Rockets, 1988—. Republican. Lutheran. Office: The Pub Endowment Strategy Box 1240 Claremont CA 91711 also: The Irvine Agy Box 1240 Claremont CA 91711

IRVINE, VERNON BRUCE, accounting educator, administrator; b. Regina, Sask., Can., May 31, 1943; s. Joseph Vern and Anna Francis (Phillip) I.; m. Marilyn Ann Craik, Apr. 29, 1967; children: Lee-Ann, Cameron, Sandra. B. Commerce, U. Sask., 1965; MBA, U. Chgo., 1967; PhD, U. Minn., 1977. Cert. mgmt. acct. Researcher, Sask. Royal Commn. on Taxation, Regina, 1964; lectr. acctg. Coll. Commerce, U. Sask., Saskatoon, 1967-69, asst. prof., 1969-74, assoc. prof., 1974-79, prof., 1979—, head dept. acctg., 1981-84; profl. program lectr. Inst. Chartered Accts., Regina, 1982-84, Soc. Mgmt. Accts., Saskatoon, 1982-84. Co-author: A Practical Approach to the Appraisal of Capital Expenditures, 1981; Intermediate Accounting: Canadian Edition, 1982, 3d edit., 1990; contbr. articles to acctg. jours. Grantee John Wiley & Sons, Ltd., 1981, 85, 87, 88, 92, Soc. Mgmt. Accts. Can., 1979, Pres.'s Fund, U. Sask., 1978, Nelson Can. grantee, 1990. Bd. dirs. Big Sisters of Sask., 1987-90. Fellow Soc. Mgmt. Accts. Can. (bd. dirs. 1979-82, 85-87, 89-92, chmn. Nat. Edn. Svcs. com.); mem. Can. Acad. Acctg. Assn. (sec. 1992—, exec. com., chmn. mem. com. 1989-91), Internat. Acctg. Standards Com. (Can. rep. 1984-87), Internat. Fedn. Accts. Council (tech. advisor 1988-90), Soc. of Mgmt. Accts. of Sask. (pres. 1980-81). Clubs: Sutherland Curling (treas. 1979-83), Saskatoon Golf and Country (bd. dirs. 1988-90). Home: 45 Cantlon Crescent, Saskatoon, SK Canada S7J 2T2 Office: U Sask, Coll Commerce, Saskatoon, SK Canada S7N 0W0

IRWIN, DEBORAH JO, educator, flutist; b. Ellensburg, Wash., Aug. 3, 1952; d. Robert Major and Charlotte Ruth (Klein) Panerio; m. Brent Willard Irwin, June 15, 1974; children: Tony, Nick. BA in Music Edn., Cen. Wash. U., 1974, MA in Music, 1978. Tchr. Federal Way (Wash.) Schs., 1974-75, Auburn (Wash.) Schs., 1975—; prin. flutist Tacoma Concert Band, 1982—, Renton (Wash.) Pks. Band, 1978-82; tchr. The Flute Studio, Federal Way, 1983-84; mem., historian Fireside Concert Series, Auburn, 1983-84. Mem. mus. groups Windsong, Scirrocco. Mem. NEA, Seattle Musicians Union, Seattle Flute Soc. Home: 28012 188th Ave SE Kent WA 98042-5439

IRWIN, JAMES DONHOWE, technical writer; b. Albion, Mich., Mar. 29, 1950; s. Joseph James and Laurentia Mae (Donhowe) I.; m. Mary Jane Boucher, May 21, 1989. BA, U. Mich., 1972, BFA, 1976. Ceramics instr. Interlochen (Mich.) Nat. Music Camp, 1976; profl. artist San Francisco, 1977-83; mgr. software prodn. Software Rsch., Inc., San Francisco, 1984-88; mgr. tech. pubs. Wind River Systems, Inc., Alameda, Calif., 1988—. Office: Wind River Systems Inc 1010 Atlantic Ave Alameda CA 94501

IRWIN, JAMES STUART, family physician; b. Yuma, Ariz., Jan. 14, 1953; s. Ralph T. I.; m. Lorna A. McCauley, May 18, 1974; children: Mavis, Kyle, Ross. BS, U. Ariz., 1974; MD, U. Utah, 1980. Diplomate Am. Bd. of Family Practice. Resident in family practice S.W. Idaho Boise, 1980-83, chief resident, 1983; aux. faculty U. Wash., Seattle, 1989—; chief of staff St. Benedict's Family Med. Ctr., Jerome, Idaho, 1991—; med. cons. Region V Child Devel. Ctr. Twin Falls, Idaho, 1983—. Mem. Internat. Physicians Against Nuclear War, Physicians for Social Responsibility, Audubon Soc., Sierra Club, Alpha Omega Alpha. Home: 76 W 100th N Jerome ID 83338 Office: 112 5th Ave W Jerome ID 83338

IRWIN, R. ROBERT, lawyer; b. Denver, July 27, 1933; s. Royal Robert and Mildred Mary (Wilson) I.; m. Sue Ann Scott, Dec. 16, 1956; children—Lori, Stacy, Kristi, Amy. Student U. Colo., 1951-54, B.S.L., U. Denver, 1955, LL.B., 1957. Bar: Colo. 1957, Wyo. 1967. Asst. atty. gen. State of Colo., 1958-66; asst. div. atty. Mobil Oil Corp., Casper, Wyo. 1966-70; prin. atty. No. Natural Gas Co., Omaha 1970-72; sr. atty. Coastal Oil & Gas Corp., Denver 1972-83, asst. sec. 1972-83; ptnr. Baker & Hostetler, 1983-87; pvt. practice 1987—. Mem. Colo. Bar Assn., Arapahoe County Bar Assn., Rocky Mountain Oil and Gas Assn. Republican. Clubs: Los Verdes Golf, Petroleum, Denver Law (Denver). Office: 9960 E Chenango Ave Englewood CO 80111-3606

ISAAC, ROBERT MICHAEL, mayor, lawyer; b. Colorado Springs, Colo., Jan. 27, 1928; s. Isaac Albert and Sigrid Elvira (Oksa) I.; children from previous marriage: Leslie Ann Isaac Williams, Julia Hermine Isaac Harrington, Melissa Sue Isaac Denton, Tiffany Ann, Chance Robert. Student, U. Colo., 1945-46; BS, U.S. Mil. Acad., 1951; JD, U. So. Calif., 1962. Sales engr. Trane Co., Los Angeles, 1957-62; practice law and dep. city atty. City Colorado Springs, 1962-64; asst. dist. atty. 4th Jud. Dist. Colo., Colorado Springs, 1965-66; judge Colorado Springs Mcpl. Ct., 1966-69; ptnr. Trott, Kunstle, Isaac & Hughes, Colorado Springs, 1969-72, Isaac, Walsh & Johnson, Colorado Springs, 1972-74, Isaac, Johnson & Alpern, 1974-88; councilman City of Colorado Springs, 1975-79, mayor, 1979—; past pres. U.S. Conf. Mayors; mem. adv. bd. Nat. League Cities; mem. adv. commn. Ingergovtl. Rels. Gen. chmn. YWCA/YMCA/USO fund dr., past pres. Pikes Peak Y/USO; past pres. El Paso County Soc. Crippled Children and Adults; past mem. Nat. USO Council; chmn. Pikes Peak Area Council Govts., 1976-78. Served as officer inf. U.S. Army, 1951-57. Mem. Am. Bar Assn., Colo. Bar Assn. Calif. Bar Assn., El Paso County Bar Assn. Episcopalian. Office: Office of the Mayor PO Box 1575 30 S Nevada Ave Ste 401 Colorado Springs CO 80903-1825

ISAACS, JONATHAN WILLIAM, oil company executive; b. Chgo., Apr. 9, 1957; s. Kenneth Sidney and Ruth Elizabeth (Johnson) I.; m. Marcia Eileen Gresback, Jan. 2, 1979 (div. Feb. 1986). BA, Lake Forest Coll., 1980. Prin. Kenisa Oil Co., Northbrook, Ill., 1980—, Kenisa Drilling Co., Denver, 1986—. Mem. NRA, Nat. Skeet Shooting Assn., Ind. Petroleum Assn., Rep. Mens Club, Denver Athletic Club, Exmoor Country Club, Alpha Nu Chi Psi. Republican. Office: Kenisa Drilling Co 410 17th St Denver CO 80202

ISAACSON, ROBERT LOUIS, investment company executive; b. Chgo., Apr. 21, 1944; s. Abe B. and Laverne (Skolka) I. BS, Mich. State U., 1966. Mktg. mgr. Florasynth, Inc., San Francisco, 1966-69; br. mgr. Florasynth, Inc., Lincolnwood and Palo Alto, Calif., 1969-72; br. office mgr. Geldermann, Palo Alto, 1972-76; founder, pres. Commodity Investment Cons., Los Altos, Calif., 1976—, Future Funding Cons., Menlo Park, Calif., 1976—; co-founder, co-chmn. Nat. Assn. Futures Trading Advisors; bd. dirs. Futures Industry Assn. Edn. and Tng., Williams & Clarissa, Inc.; bd. dirs., exec. com., membership com. Nat. Futures Assn.; membership Nat. Futures Assn. Regional Bus. Conduct Com.; v.p. Lind-Waldock Co., Chgo. Contbr. articles to mags and profl. jours. Founder Fun for Lunch Bunch. With U.S. Mil., 1966-72. Recipient Doncheon award Managed Accounts Report, 1984. Mem. San Francisco Futures Soc., Managed Futures Assn. (co-chmn.), Peninsula Commodities Club, Elks, Kiwanis. Home: 380 La Questa Way Woodside CA 94062 Office: Commodity Investment Cons Future Funding Cons 380 La Questa Way Woodside CA 94062

ISABELL, WILLIAM TOMLIN, JR., non-profit development consultant; b. Phoenix, Aug. 5, 1950; s. William Tomlin Isabell and Theresa Marie (Childers) Rote; m. Pamela Diane Morris; 1 child, Paul Taylor. BA, Ariz. State U., 1972. Behavioral health specialist Ariz. State Hosp., Phoenix, 1973-77; dir. spl. projects Conbela Assocs., Seattle, 1978-84; owner Pacific Imaginations Pub., Lahaina, Hawaii, 1985-86; gen. mgr. Rainbow Resources, Everett, Wash., 1987-89; pubs. rep. The Isabell Co., Seattle, 1985—, cons., owner, 1989—. Organizer King County Initiatives for Mental Health Housing, Wash. State, 1991. Recipient Disting. Svc. award Conbela Assocs., Seattle, 1982. Office: The Isabell Co PO Box 17554 Seattle WA 98107

ISBELL, ALAN GREGORY, editor, writer; b. Denver, June 7, 1951; s. Morris Leroy Isbell and Ida Belle (Lanyon) Whittemore; m. Sherry Ann Meiers, July 8, 1972; children: Zane Michael, Evan Kele. AA with honors, Coll. Alameda, 1975; BS, U. Colo., 1978. Reporter Douglas County News Press, Castle Rock, Colo., 1978-80; bur. chief Glenwood Post, Glenwood Springs, Colo., 1980-83; news editor Sun Press, Kaneohe, Hawaii, 1984-86; editor Mauian mag., Lahaina, Hawaii, 1986-87, South Maui Times, Kihei, Hawaii, 1988—; contbg. editor Colorado River Jour., 1981-83; regional correspondent AP, 1981-83; Hawaii correspondent World News, N.Y.C., 1986-88; freelance writer, Maui, 1987-88; Maui news correspondent KGMB-TV, Honolulu, 1987-88, Honolulu Star Bulletin, 1989-90. Recipient award Colo. Press Assn., 1983. Mem. Hawaii Pubs. Assn. (awards 1990, 92, 93), Soc. Profl. Journalists, Maui Assn. Reporters and Editors. Home: 2751 Kauhale St Kihei HI 96753 Office: South Maui Times 1847 Kihei Rd Ste 205 Kihei HI 96753

ISBELL, HAROLD M(AX), writer, investor; b. Maquoketa, Iowa, Sept. 20, 1936; s. H. Max and Marcella E. I.; BA cum laude (scholar), Loras Coll., 1959; MA (fellow), U. Notre Dame, 1962; grad. U. Mich. Grad. Sch. Bank Mgmt., 1982; m. Mary Carolyn Cosgriff, June 15, 1963; children: Walter Harold, Susan Elizabeth, David Harold, Alice Kathleen. Instr., U. Notre Dame, South Bend, Ind., 1963-64; assoc. prof. St. Mary's Coll., 1969-72; asst. prof. San Francisco Coll. for Women, 1964-69; with Continental Bank & Trust Co., Salt Lake City, 1972-83, v.p., 1977-83, comml. credit officer, 1978-83, also dir. Trustee Judge Meml. Cath. High Sch., Salt Lake City, 1977-84; mem. Utah Coun. for Handicapped and Developmentally Disabled Persons, 1980-81; bd. dirs. Ballet West, 1983-90, emeritus, 1990—; founder Cath. Found. Utah, pres. 1984-86, trustee, 1984-89; Mem. MLA, Mediaeval Acad. Am., Am. Assn. for the Advancement of Sci. Democrat. Roman Catholic. Club: Alta. Editor and translator: The Last Poets of Imperial Rome, 1971, Ovid: Heroides, 1990; contbr. to publs. in field of classical Latin lit. and contemporary Am. Lit.

ISBELL, VIRGINIA, state legislator; b. Chinook, Mont., May 8, 1932; d. Domenico Renda and Bessie M. (Newton) Renda; cert. med. sec. No. Mont. Coll., 1953; m. Donald D. Isbell, Oct. 11, 1953; children—David, Daniel, Mahealani, Iwalani, Richard. Tchr., Kona (Hawaii) Schs., 1962-72; mgr. Wilmot Boone, M.D., Allan Hubacker, M.D., Kona Coast Med. Group, Inc., Kailua, Kona, Hawaii, 1972-78; mem. Hawaii Ho. of Reps., 1980—. Bd. dirs. Kona Family YMCA; active ARC. Named Woman of Yr., Mayor's award, 1980. Democrat. Mem. Ch. of Jesus Christ of Latter-day Saints. Club: Soroptimist (past pres.).

ISENBERG, HAROLD, physician; b. Chgo., Oct. 28, 1938; s. Morton Joseph and Helen (Pruzansky) I.; divorced 1982; children: Gerard, Warren. BS in Zoology, U. Ill., 1959; BS in Pharmacy, U. Ill., Chgo., 1963, BS in Dentistry, 1966, DDS, 1966; MD, U. of East, Quezon City, Philippines, 1976. Diplomate Am. Bd. Family Practice. Pharmacist Urban's Pharmacy, and Budlong Drugs, Chgo., 1963-64, Stite's Pharmacy, Macomb, Ill., 1969-72; dentist Barkley Dental Group Ltd., Macomb, 1969-72; intern U. Ill. Coll. Medicine, Peoria, 1977-78, resident in family practice, 1978-80; part-time emergency rm. physician Meth. Med. Ctr., Peoria, Ill., 1977-80; family practice physician Hawthorne Community Med. Group, Torrance, Calif., 1980-91, Cigna Staff Model, Torrance, 1991—; asst. instr. U. Ill., Chgo., 1968-69, Peoria, 1977-80; vol. clin. instr. Harbor UCLA, Torrance, 1983—. Contbg. author: American Academy of Family Practice, 1982; investigator Practical Cardiology jour., 1990. Mem. Simon Wiesenthal Ctr., L.A., 1983—, Music Ctr., L.A., 1986—. Partial Acad. scholar U. of the East, 1973. Fellow Am. Acad. Family Practice; mem. AMA, ADA, Ill. Dental Soc., Prairie Valley Dental Soc., Calif. Med. Soc., Los Angeles County Med. Assn., Rho Chi. Jewish. Office: CIGNA 3333 Skypark Dr Torrance CA 90505-5020

ISENBERG, JAMES ALLEN, mathematics and physics researcher, educator; b. Boston, Mar. 14, 1951; s. Paul Charles and Ruth Selma (Schultz) I.; m. Jillian Bowling, Aug. 26, 1989. AB, Princeton U., 1973; PhD, U. Md., 1979. Postdoctoral fellow U. Waterloo, Ontario, Can., 1979-80, U. Calif., Berkeley, 1980-82; asst. prof. math. U. Oreg., Eugene, 1982-87, assoc. prof. math., 1987-93, prof. math., 1993—; vis. asst. prof. Rice U., Houston, 1983-84, U. Minn., Mpls., 1985; vis. rsch. fellow U. Paris, France, 1986, Ctr. Math. Analysis, Canberra, Australia, 1988, Inst. for Theoretical Physics, U. Calif., Santa Barbara, 1993; vis. prof. U. Calif. San Diego, La Jolla, 1989; conf. organizer Pacific Gravity Meeting, 1985—. Editor: Mathematics in General Relativity, 1988; contbr. articles to profl. jours.; achievements include work on long time behavior of solutions of Einstein's equations, twistor representation of solutions of the Yang Mills equations; use of heat equations to study the relationship between geometry and topology. Prospective student interviewer Princeton U., Eugene, 1974—. Grantee NSF 1983—, Ctr. Nat. Rsch. Sci., Paris, 1986. Mem. Am. Phys. Soc., Am. Math. Soc., Soc. Gen. Relativity & Gravitation. Home: 717 Amelia Ave Brownsville OR 97327 Office: Univ Oregon Dept Math Eugene OR 97405

ISENBERG, PHILLIP L., state legislator; b. Gary, Ind., Feb. 25, 1939; s. Walter M. and Violet R. (Phillips) I.; m. Marilyn Y. Araki, July 13, 1963. B.A., Sacramento Coll., 1961; J.D., U. Calif., Berkeley, 1967. Bar: Calif. 1967. Practice law Sacramento; mem. Sacramento City Council, 1971-75; mayor City of Sacramento, 1975-82;; mem. Calif. Assembly, 1982—. Mem. Calif. Bar Assn. Democrat. Office: State Capitol Rm 6005 Sacramento CA 95814

ISHIMARU, AKIRA, electrical engineering educator; b. Fukuoka, Japan, Mar. 16, 1928; came to U.S., 1952; s. Shigezo and Yumi I.; m. Yuko Kaneda, Nov. 21, 1956; children: John, Jane, James, Joyce. BSEE, U. Tokyo, 1951; PhDEE, U. Wash., 1958. Registered profl. engr., Wash. Engr. Electro-Tech. Lab, Tokyo, 1951-52; tech. staff Bell Telephone Lab, Holmdel, N.J., 1956; asst. prof. U. Wash., Seattle, 1958-61, assoc. prof., 1961-65, prof. elec. engring., 1965—; vis. assoc. prof. U. Calif., Berkeley, 1963-64; cons. Jet Propulsion Lab., Pasadena, Calif., 1964—, The Boeing Co., Seattle, 1984—. Author: Wave Propagation & Scattering in Random Media, 1978, Electromagnetic Wave Propagation, Radiation and Scattering, 1991; editor: Radio Science, 1982; editor-in-chief Waves in Random Media, U.K., 1990. Recipient Faculty Achievement award Burlington Resources, 1990; Boeing Martin professorship, 1993. Fellow IEEE (mem. editorial bd., Region VI Achieveemnt award 1968, Centennial Medal 1984), Optical Soc. Am. (assoc. editor jour. 1983); mem. Internat. Union Radio Sci. (commn. B chmn.). Home: 2913 165th Pl NE Bellevue WA 98008-2137 Office: U Wash Dept Elec Engring FT-10 Seattle WA 98195

ISHLER, MICHAEL WILLIAM, structural engineer; b. Cleve., Dec. 21, 1952; s. William Edward and Elizabeth (Swift) I.; m. Kathleen Ann Abell, Sept. 6, 1975; children: Stephanie Ann, Matthew Scott. BArch, U. Cin., 1977, MS, 1979; SM, MIT, 1981. Sr. engr. Owens Corning Fiberglas, Toledo and Granville, Ohio, 1981-86; assoc. Ove Arup & Ptnrs., London, 1987-88, L.A., 1988-93; consulting structural engr. M.W. Ishler, L.A., 1993—. Inventor double hexagonal mesh air supported fabric roof structure, 1985, parallel compression ring fabric roof structure, 1986. Mem. ASCE (sec.-treas. Toledo chpt. 1983-85, Outstanding Engr. 1985), Structural Engrs. So. Calif., Alpha Rho Chi. Lutheran. Home: 2314 Pearl St Santa Monica CA 90405-2830

ISHMAEL, WILLIAM EARL, land use planner, civil engineer; b. Mt. Sterling, Ky., Mar. 11, 1946; s. Charles William and Alice Clay (Trimble) I. BSCE, Duke U., 1968; MA in Urban Planning, U. Mich., 1975. Registered civil engr., Calif., Ky.; registered planner Am. Inst. Cert. Planners. Petroleum engr. Humble Oil (now Exxon), New Orleans, 1968-69; dep. dir. Richmond Regional Planning Commn., Richmond, Va., 1975-78; sr. planner Nolte and Assocs., Sacramento, 1978—, assoc. of the corp., 1984-90, v.p., mng. prin., Sacramento, 1990—; cons. to City of Lincoln, So. Pacific RR . Mem. City Planning Commn., Sacramento, 1983-89, vice chmn., 1985, chmn. 1986; bd. dirs. Sacramento Heritage, 1983-88, chmn., 1985-86; chmn. Urban Design Task Force for Downtown Sacramento, 1986; active Big Bros., 1978-83. Served to lt. USN, 1969-72. Named Mover and Shaper Heir Apparent, Exec. Pl. Mag., 1986. Mem. Sacramento C. of C. (mem. land use com. 1983—), Am. Planning Assn. (dir. pro tem 1981-83, Disting. Service award 1983), Chi Epsilon. Office: Nolte & Assocs 1750 Creekside Oaks Dr Ste 200 Sacramento CA 95833-3640

ISIDORO, EDITH ANNETTE, horticulturist; b. Albuquerque, Oct. 14, 1957; d. Robert Joseph and Marion Elizabeth (Miller) I. BS in Horticulture, N.Mex. State U., 1981, MS in Horticulture, 1984; postgrad., U. Nev., Reno, 1992—. Range conservationist Soil Conservation Service, Estancia, Grants, N.Mex., 1980-82; lab. aide N.Mex. State U. Dept. Horticulture, Las Cruces, 1982, 83-84; technician N.Mex. State U. Coop. Extension Service, Las Cruces, 1983-84, county agrl. extension agt., 1985; area extension agr. U. Nev., Reno, Fallon, 1985—; hay tester Nev. Agrl. Services, Fallon, 1988-92. Mem. AAUW, Am. Soc. Hort. Sci., Am. Horticulture Soc., Am. Botany Soc., Am. Horticulture Therapy Assn., Alpha Zeta, Pi Alpha Psi. Home: 3900 Sheckler Rd Fallon NV 89406-8202 Office: Churchill County Coop Extension 1450 Mclean Rd Fallon NV 89406-8919

ISLEY, ERNEST D., Canadian provincial official; b. Vermilion, Alta., Can., June 29, 1937; m. Sheila; children—Floyd, Lori, Thea, Tracy. B.Edn. with distinction, U. Alta., 1969. Operator farm, Bonnyville, Alta., Can.; agt. ins. co.; prin. Bonnyville Centralized High Sch., 1971-78, Altario Sch., 1961-71; mem. Alta. Legis. Assembly, 1979—, mem. edn. caucus, agr. caucus coms., select com. of legislature on fisheries, select com. of legislature on surface rights, curriculum policies bd., Port Churchill Devel. Bd.; minister of manpower Province of Alta., Edmonton. Pres., Lakeland Tourist Assn., 1975; chmn. Bonnyville Sr. Citizens Project Com., 1976; dir., v.p. Bonnyville Progressive Conservative Assn., 1974-78; mem. Travel Alta. Zone Assistance Rev. Bd., 1976-78, chmn. bd., 1977-78. Minister Pub. Works, Supply and Services, 1986—. Office: Minister of Agriculture, Legislature Bldg Rm 131, Edmonton, AB Canada T5K 2B6

ISMACH, ARNOLD HARVEY, journalism educator; b. N.Y.C., Dec. 28, 1930; s. Louis and Augusta (Lacher) I.; m. Judy Daniels, June 20, 1959 (div. 1975); children: Richard, Theresa. BA, U. Okla., 1951; MA, UCLA, 1970; PhD, U. Wash., 1975. News editor Union-Bulletin, Walla Walla, Wash., 1954-56; reporter, editor Sun-Telegram, San Bernardino, Calif., 1956-69; prof. journalism U. Minn., Mpls., 1973-85; dean journalism U. Oreg., Eugene, 1985—; cons. Pub. Relations Ctr., Los Angeles, 1970-75; pres. Communications Research Ctr., Mpls., 1973-85. Co-author: (textbooks) New Strategies, 1976, Enduring Issues, 1978, Reporting Processes, 1981. Served to sgt. U.S. Army, 1951-54. Mem. Soc. Profl. Journalists, Assn. for Edn. in Journalism, Am. Assn. Pub. Opinion Rsch., Oreg. Assn. Broadcasters (dir.). Democrat. Home: 5326 Tahsili St Eugene OR 97405-4021 Office: U Oreg Sch Journalism Office of the Dean Eugene OR 97403

ISMAIL, RAGHIB (ROCKET ISMAIL), professional football player; b. Newark, Nov. 18, 1969. Student, U. Notre Dame. With Toronto Argonauts, 1991-93, L.A. Raiders, 1993—. Office: Care L A Raiders 332 Center St El Segundo CA 90249

ISON, LONI SUZANNE, marriage, family and child counselor, educator; b. Pasadena, Calif., Jan. 19, 1954; d. Leonard Henderson and LaVielle (Furlong) LaMont; children: Michael, Nicole. AA, Grossmont Coll., La Mesa, Calif., 1986; BA, Nat. U., 1987, MA, 1990. Psychologist Faith Chapel Family Clinic, La Mesa, 1986-92; pvt. presch. dir. El Cajon, Calif., 1986-92; prof. Christian Heritage Coll., El Cajon, 1992—. Psychologist Royal Family Kids Camp, San Diego, 1990-91; seminar leader La Jolla (Calif.) Presbyn. Ch. Home: 1980 Vista Grande Way El Cajon CA 92019

ISRAEL, JOAN, social worker; b. Bklyn., July 19, 1943; d. Joseph Israel and Irene (Solon) Kansey; m. Ronald Jerome Janesh, June 28, 1980 (div. Feb. 1985); 1 child, Ariel Naomi. BA, Bklyn. Coll., 1965; MSW, U. Mich., 1974. Lic. clin. social worker, Nev. Social worker Alameda County Welfare Dept., Oakland, Calif., 1965-72; group therapist Pacific Ctr. for Human Growth, Berkeley, Calif., 1975-77; individual and group therapist, bd. dir. Bi-Ctr., San Francisco, 1976-78; clin. social worker, supr. Audrey L. Smith Devel. Ctr., San Francisco, 1977-78; psychiat. social worker South Nev. Adult Mental Health Dept., Las Vegas, 1978-84, part-time clin. social worker, 1988—; pvt. practice clin. social worker Las Vegas, 1984—. Contbr. articles to profl. publs. Organizer Drug/Alcohol Abuse Task Force, Las Vegas, 1983-84, Task Force on AIDS, Las Vegas, 1985-86. Mem. NASW (chair nominating com. 1978-80, 82-84, sec. 1984-86, chair com. on inquiry 1988—, legis. chair 1982-84, diplomate clin. social work), Sierra Club. Democrat. Jewish. Office: 3180 W Sahara Ave Ste 25C Las Vegas NV 89102-6005

ISRAEL, PAUL NEAL, computer design engineer; b. Balt., Apr. 22, 1959; s. Sheldon Leonard and Sheila Lee (Goldmacher) I. BS in EECS, U. Calif., Berkeley, 1981. Project mgr. computer sci. dept. U. Calif., Berkeley, 1981-82; design engr. Electronic Signature Lock Corp., Berkeley, 1983; staff engr. Qantel Bus. Systems, Hayward, Calif., 1983-89; sr. hardware design engr. SBE, Inc., Concord, Calif., 1989-90; engring. contractor Renegade Systems, Sunnyvale, Calif., 1990-92; sr. hardware design engr. Unisys Corp., San Jose, Calif., 1992—. Mem. IEEE Computer Soc. (assoc.), Assn. Computing Machinery. Office: Unisys Corp 2700 N 1st St San Jose CA 95134-2028

ISRAEL, RICHARD STANLEY, investment banker; b. Oakland, Calif., Sept. 27, 1931; s. Sybil Noble, July 29, 1962; children: Richard Lee, Lynne, Lawrence. BA, U. Calif., Berkeley, 1953, MA, 1953. Copy editor San Francisco Chronicle, 1953-59; publicist CBS TV Network, L.A., 1959-62; sr. v.p. Rogers & Cowan, Beverly Hills, Calif., 1962-69; v.p. Cantor, Fitzgerald, Beverly Hills, 1969-73; pres. Sponsored Cons. Svcs., L.A., 1973—. Pres. North Beverly Dr. Homeowners Assn., Beverly Hills, 1986-88; v.p. Temple Emanuel, Beverly Hills, 1988-93, L.A. chpt. Juvenile Diabetes Found. Internat, 1987—. With U.S. Army, 1956-58. Recipient Alumni citation U. Calif. Alumni Assn., Berkeley, 1984. Mem. L.A. Venture Assn. (pres. 1987). Democrat. Office: Sponsored Cons Svcs 8929 Wilshire Blvd Ste 214 Beverly Hills CA 90211-1951

ISSARI, MOHAMMAD ALI, film producer, educator, consultant; b. Esfahan, Iran, Oct. 3, 1921; s. Abbas Bek and Qamar (Soltan) I.; m. Joan Gura Aamodt, 1953; children: Scheherezade, Katayoun, Roxana. B.A., U. Tehran, Iran, 1963; M.A., U. So. Calif., 1968; Ph.D., 1979. Films officer Brit. Embassy, Brit. Council Joint Film Div., Tehran, 1944-50; asst. motion picture officer USIS, 1950-65; cons. to various Iranian govt. ministries on film and TV devels., 1950-77; liaison officer Am. and Iranian govt. ofcls., 1950-65; prof. cinema Coll. Communication Arts and Scis. Mich. State U., East Lansing, 1969-81; also dir. instructional film and multimedia prodn. Mich. State U., 1969-78; mass media cons., 1981—; pres. Multimedia Prodn. Svcs., Thousand Oaks, Calif., 1989—; film, public relations adviser to Iranian Oil Operating Cos. in, Iran, 1963-65; spl. cons. on edn. and instructional TV Saudi Arabian Ministry of Info., 1972; tchr. Persian lang. Iran-Am. Soc., Tehran, 1949-59; introduced audio-visual edn. in Iran, 1951; established first film festivals in Iran. Producer, dir. over 1000 ednl., instructional and documentary films, 1956-78; freelance film reporter: Telenews, UPI, Iran, 1959-61; project dir., exec. producer: Ancient Iran Film Series, 1974-78; dir. film prodn. workshops, Cranbrook Inst., Detroit, 1973-74; author: (with Doris A. Paul) A Picture of Persia, 1977, What is Cinema Vérité?, 1979, Cinema in Iran, 1900-1979, 1989; contbr. articles on ednl. communication and audio-visual instruction to periodicals and profl. jours. Founder, exec. sec. Youth Orgn. of Iran, 1951-52; v.p. Rugby Football Fedn., Iran, 1952-53, pres., 1954-55. Recipient Cine Golden Eagle award, 1975, Meritorious Honor award USIA, 1965; decorated Order of Magnum Cap Ord: S.F. Danaie M. Sigillum, King of Denmark, 1960, Order of Cavalieres Italy, 1958, Order of Oranje Nassau Queen Juliana of Holland, 1959, Orders of Kooshesh and Pas HIM Shah of Iran, 1951, 57, Order of Esteghlal King Hussein of Jordan, 1960, Order of Ordinis Sancti Silvestri Papae Pope John 23d, 1959. Mem. Anglo-Iranian Dramatic Soc. (bd. dirs. 1943-50), Mich. Film Assn. (co-founder 1972, bd. dirs. 1972-73), Mid. East Studies Assn., N.Am. Soc. Motion Picture and TV Engrs. (life), Ancient Studies Inst. (co-founder, pres. 1989-93), Bashgahe Esfahan, Inc. (co-founder, pres. 1990-93), Assn. Ednl. Communication and Tech., Delta Kappa Alpha (v.p. 1967). Office: Multimedia Prodn Svcs 982 Golden Crest Ave Newbury Park CA 91320-5814

ISSEL, DANIEL PAUL, professional basketball coach; b. Batavia, IL, Oct. 25, 1948; m. Cheri Issel; children: Sheridan, Scott. Student, U. Ky. Basketball player Ky. Cols., 1970-75, Denver Nuggets, 1975-85; broadcast analyst U. Ky., 1987-88; color analyst, mgr. player edn. and career enhancement programs Denver Nuggets, 1988-92, head coach, 1992—; prin. Courtland Farms Horse Racing. Office: Denver Nuggets 1635 Clay St Denver CO 80204

ISTOCK, STEVEN VERVE, commerical lending officer; b. Detroit, Sept. 12, 1966. BA in Econs. and English, U. Mich., 1989. Credit analyst Security Pacific, L.A., 1989-91, loan officer, 1991-92; comml. loan officer

Bank of Am., L.A., 1992, asst. v.p., 1992—. Mem. L.A. Bank of Am. Speakers Club, People Plus, U. Mich. Alumni Assn., Orchard Lake Country Club. Republican. Presbyterian.

ITALIANO, JULIA ANNE, librarian; b. Redwood City, Calif., Dec. 14, 1958; d. John Duane and Carmen Irene (Chase) Quackenbush; m. Christopher Frank Italiano, Sept. 14, 1985. BA in Geography, San Diego State U., 1981; MLS, U. Hawaii, 1984. Libr. student asst. San Diego U., 1977-81; libr. specialist Stanford (Calif.) U., 1982-83; libr. asst. U. Hawaii, Monoa, 1983-84; libr. Contra Cost County Libr., Pleasant Hill, Calif., 1985—, Dames & Moore, San Francisco, 1988—. Home: 289 Riverwood Cir Martinez CA 94553-4127

ITTNER, PERRY MARTIN, sales and marketing consultant; b. Anaheim, Calif., June 14, 1961; s. Franklin Glenn and Delina (Martin) I.; m. Sylvia Marie Garcia, May 16, 1987; 1 child, Kristina Nicole. Student, Cerritos Coll., 1979-82. Purchasing agt. Shield Healthcare, Inc., Van Nuys, Calif., 1979-85; gen. mgr. Propak div. of Devco Med. Co., Santa Fe Springs, Calif., 1985-86; materials mgr. Reliable Med. Supply, Brea, Calif., 1986-87; dir. sales and mktg. Telesis Rsch. Group, La Crescenta, Calif., 1985-90; mktg. product specialist Interhealth Corp., Whittier, Calif., 1988-89; prin. Psi Healthcare Assocs., Hacienda Heights, Calif., 1990—. Mem. Calif. Assn. of Residential Care Homes, Health Industry Reps. Assn., Noetic Soc., Whittier Optimist Club. Home: 16360 Kennard St Hacienda Heights CA 91745 Office: Psi Healthcare Assocs Ste 193 2110 1/2 Hacienda Blvd Hacienda Heights CA 91745

IULIANO, JAMES P., financial executive; b. Waltham, Mass., Feb. 7, 1959; s. Russell W. and Mary A. (Ridenti) I. BS, Boston Coll., 1981; MBA, Harvard U., 1986. Fin. analyst IBM, Essex Junction, Vt., 1981-86; budget mgr. VLSI Tech., Inc., San Jose, Calif., 1986-87, div. controller, 1987-89, group controller, 1989-90; corp. controller Molecular Devices, Menlo Park, Calif., 1990, chief fin. officer, 1990-92, v.p. ops., chief fin. officer, 1992-93, pres., COO, 1993—. Instr. Jr. Achievement, Milpitas, Calif., 1988-90; tchr. Adult Basic Edn., Burlington, Vt., 1983-84; bd. dirs. Children's Legal Svc., Burlington, Vt., 1983-84; coach Burlington Internat. Games, 1983-85. Mem. Fin. Execs. Inst., Assn. of Biotechnology Fin. Officers, Harvard Community Ptnrs., Harvard Bus. Sch. Alumni Club. Home: 1069 Middlefield Rd Palo Alto CA 94301-3343 Office: Molecular Devices 4700 Bohannon Dr Menlo Park CA 94025-1031

IVANY, J. W. GEORGE, university president; b. Grand Falls, Nfld., Can., May 26, 1938; s. Gordon and Stella (Skinner) I.; m. Marsha Gregory, Mar. 24, 1983; children: Leslie, George, Jessica, Sarah. BS, Meml. U., Nfld., 1960, LLD (hon.), 1991; MA, Columbia U., 1962; PhD, U. Alta., 1965. Asst. prof. U. Alta., 1965-66; assoc. prof. Columbia U., from 1966; dept. head, prof., dean edn. Meml. U., 1974-77; prof., dean edn. Simon Fraser U., 1977-84; acting pres. Sinon Fraser U., 1983; acad. v.p. Simon Fraser U., from 1984; pres. U. Sask., Saskatoon, 1989—. Contbr. articles to profl. jours. Office: U Saskatchewan, Adminstrn Bldg, Saskatoon, SK Canada S7N 0W0

IVES, RICHARD LEE, educator, writer; b. Aberdeeh, S.D., Feb. 8, 1951; s. Lyle Dean and Jean (Pratt) I. BA in English, Ea. Wash. U., 1974; MFA in Creative Writing, U. Mont., 1977. Libr. U. Mont. Libr., Missoula, 1973-83; tchr. writing, lit. Everett (Wash.) C.C., 1983—. Author: Notes from the Water Journals, 1980; editor: From Timberline to Tidepool, 1986, Evidence of Fire, 1989; editor Owl Creek Press, 1979—; translator: Yesterday I Was Leaving, 1987. Grantee NEA, 1985, Artist Trust, 1990, 93.

IVIE, RUSSELL LYN, small business owner; b. Decatur, Ill., Nov. 14, 1953; s. Charles Russell and Edith June (McGuire) I.; m. Vickie Jean Rushing, June 9, 1984; children: Branden Lyn, Adam Christopher. Student, Oreg. Tech. Inst., Klamath Falls, 1971-72; student, sheet metal apprenticeship, Chemeketa CC, 1973-78. Sheet metal journeyman Salem Heating & Sheet Metal, 1975-78; owner, operator Russ Ivie Fireplace Installation, Salem, Oreg., 1974-81; carpet layer Hansen Floor Coverings, Salem, 1981-84; sheet metal journeyman Western States Sheet Metal, Portland, Oreg., 1989; owner, operator Russ Ivie Sheet Metal, Salem, 1989—. Entertainer Block Party-Highland Neighborhood, Salem, 1991-92. Home and Office: Russ Ivie Sheet Metal 4676 Duchess Ct NE Salem OR 97301

IVINS, ORVILLE RUSH, marketing executive; b. Chadron, Nebr., Feb. 10, 1950; s. James Rush and Gloria Ruth (Leetch) I.; m. Kathy Anne Hawkins, Dec. 19, 1969 (div. 1978); 1 child, Cynthia Anne; m. Beverly Kay Weitl, July 18, 1978. BS Bus. Adminstrn., U. N.C., 1974. Store mgr. Am. Stores, La Habra, Calif., 1974-79; merchandising cons. Alta Loma, Calif., 1979-82; sales rep. Lanier Bus. Products, Atlanta, 1982-83; sales mgr. NBI, Inc., Boulder, Colo., 1983-87; sr. account rep. Itek Graphix Inc., Rochester, N.Y., 1987-90; dist. sales mgr. Data Gen., Westboro, Mass., 1990—; mem. Data Gen. Steering Com. (sales tng. 1990-92, new bus. 1991-92), Westboro; guest lectr. Calif. Poly. U., Pomona, 1984-87. Dir. Longmont (Colo.) Jaycees, 1973, treas., 1974, state chmn. Colo. Jaycees, 1975 (exhausted Rooster); apptd. mem. Denver Regional Coun. Govs., 1974. Recipient Nat. project of Yr. for Sr. Citizen Home Energy Renovation project, 1974. Mem. Tri-County Urban and Regional Info. Systems. Republican. Episcopalian. Home: 4095 Fruit St # 627 La Verne CA 91750 Office: Data Gen Corp 1485 Spruce St Ste J Riverside CA 92501

IWAI, THOMAS YOSHIO, JR., aquatic biologist; b. Honolulu, Oct. 23, 1949; s. Thomas Yoshio sr. and Doris Hisae (Yoshida) I.; m. Sharon Nobuko Haruguchi, Aug. 18, 1975; children: Gavin Yoshio, Miki Yoshiko. BA in Zoology, U. Hawaii, 1972, MS in Animal Nutrition, 1975. Rsch. asst. U. Hawaii John A. Burns Sch. Medicine, Physiology Dept., Honolulu, 1972-73; asst. project co-dir., dive coord. U. Hawaii Marine Option Program, Nat. Sci. Found., Honolulu, 1973; U.S. prawn trainee rep., aquaculture prawn farming systems E.W. Ctr. Food Inst., Honolulu, 1973; grad. researcher Office Econ. Opportunity, Am. Taxpayers Marine Aquaculture rsch., Kaneohe, Hawaii, 1973-74; freshwater prawn farm mgr. Ewa Beach Prawn Farm, Ewa, Hawaii, 1974-75; grad. asst. I U. Hawaii, Inst. Marine Biology, Kaneohe, 1974-75; from aquatic biologist II to aquatic biologist IV State of Hawaii Aquatic Resources Div., Anuenue Fisheries Rsch. Ctr., Honolulu, 1976—. Author (with others) Handbook of Mariculture, 1983. Pres. Marine Option Program Alumni Assn., Honolulu, 1990—; v.p. Kaneohe Elem. Sch. PTA, 1990-91, pres. 1991-92. Mem. Internat. Oceanographic Found. Democrat. Home: 44-703 Malulani St Kaneohe HI 96744 Office: Anuenue Fisheries Rsch Ctr Sand Island Area 4 Honolulu HI 96819

IYER, HARIHARAIYER MAHADEVA, geophysicist, researcher; b. Attingal, India, June 21, 1931; came to U.S., 1967, naturalized, 1976; s. Srinivasa Harihara and Parvathy Iyer; m. Krishnaveni, Oct. 20, 1972; children: Swarna Parvathy, Anuradha. B.Sc., Kerala U., Trivandrum, India, 1951, M.Sc., 1953; Ph.D., Imperial Coll., London, 1959. Registered geophysicist, Calif. Scientist, Indian Naval Lab., Cochin, Kerala, India, 1953-56; postdoctoral fellow U. Calif.-San Diego, 1960-61; Gassiot fellow in seismology Brit. Meteorol. Office, Bracknell, Surrey, Eng., 1961-63; sci. officer Bhabha Atomic Research Centre, Bombay, India, 1963-67; geophysicist U.S. Geol. Survey, Menlo Park, Calif., 1967-, asst. br. chief for programs, 1992-; U.S.-India exchange scientist NSF, 1978; cons. UN Devel Program, Pune, India, 1981, Regional Govt. Azores, 1983—; presenter lectures to workshops, symposia, conferences, 1953—; participant adv. panel Sandia Magma Research, 1979, 80; mem. Dept. Energy Induced Seismicity Rev. Panel, 1979; mem. Dept. Energy Consortium on Active and Passive Seismic Methods for Geothermal Exploration, 1977. Author: (with others) Global Geophysics, 1970; editor: (with K. Hirahana) Seismic Tomography: Theory and Practice, 1993. Contbr. papers to sci. jours., books. Fellow Indo Am. Coun. for Internat. Exch. Scholars, Nat. Geophys. Rsch. Inst., India, 1985-86; recipient Krishan Meml. Gold medal Indian Geophys. Union, 1966. Fellow Assn. Exploration Geophysicists; mem. Am. Geophys. Union, Seismol. Soc. Am., Internat. Assn. Seismology and Physics of the Earth's Interior (commn. on microseisms). Democrat. Hindu. Home: 697 Gilbert Ave Menlo Park CA 94025-2731 Office: US Geol Survey MS 977 345 Middlefield Rd Menlo Park CA 94025-3591

IZZO, MARY ALICE, real estate broker; b. Mesa, Ariz., Aug. 5, 1953; d. Edward Lee and Evangeline Lauda (Gorraiz) Meeker; m. Michael David Izzo, Dec. 26, 1971; children: Michael Wade, Clinton Jarred, Antoinette Marie. Student, Pioneer Coll., 1977, Yavapai Coll., 1984. Cert. realtor, Ariz. Real estate sales agt. Babbit Bros., Flagstaff, Ariz., 1970-76; owner Cottonwood (Ariz.) Tees, 1978-84; realtor Weston Realty, Cottonwood, 1985-86, Coldwell Banker Mabery Real Estate, Cottonwood, 1986-89; sales agent, assoc. broker The Glenarm Land Co., Cottonwood, 1989—; office mgr., sec. Izzo & Sons Contracting, 1985-91, Wilhoit Water Co., 1991-93. Auhtor: Current Customer Cook Book, 1984. Bd. dirs. cub scouts Boy Scouts Am., 1984, 87, AYSO Soccer, Verde Valley, Ariz., 1984-87, 92—, also coach tournament traveling team, 1993—; leader youth group, Cottonwood. Mem. Women's Coun. Realtors. Democrat. Roman Catholic. Home: PO Box 2002 Cottonwood AZ 86326-2002 Office: The Glenarm Land Co 408 S Main St Cottonwood AZ 86326-3903

JABARA, MICHAEL DEAN, telecommunications company executive; b. Sioux Falls, S.D., Oct. 26, 1952; s. James M. and Jean Marie (Swiden) J.; m. Gundula Beate Dietz, Aug. 26, 1984; children: James Michael, Jenna Mariel. Student, Mich. Tech. U., 1970-72; BSBA, U. Calif., Berkeley, 1974; MBA, Pepperdine U., 1979. Mgr. Sprint project So. Pacific Communications Corp., 1976-78; network product mgr. ROLM Corp., 1978-81; cons. McGraw Hill Co., Hamburg (Fed. Republic of Germany) and London, 1982-83; founder, chief exec. officer Friend Techs. Inc. (merger VoiceCom Systems, Inc.), San Francisco, 1984-88; pres. VoiceCom Ventures, San Francisco, 1988—; bd. dirs. VoiceCom Systems, Inc. Patentee in field. Mem. Info. Industry Assn. (bd. dirs.), Assn. for Corp. Growth, Pepperdine Bus. Alumni, U. Calif. Berkeley Bus. Alumni, The Classic Cars of the Candy Store (bd. dirs.). Home: 340 St Francis Blvd San Francisco CA 94127-1943 Office: VoiceCom Systems Inc 275 Battery St San Francisco CA 94111

JACKLICH, JOEL, music educator, orchestra conductor; b. Detroit, Mar. 13, 1948; s. Joseph and Valeria (Koss) J.; m. Judy Chandler, July 1, 1976; 1 child, Barbara Diane. BMus cum laude, Western Mich. U., 1970; MFA, U.S. Internat. U., 1980. Cert. C.C. instr., Calif., Ariz., secondary tchr. music K-12, Calif., English tchr., Calif., lang. devel. specialist, Calif. Tchr. music La Mesa (Calif.) Spring Valley Sch. Dist., 1972-73; substitute tchr. San Diego Unified Sch. Dist., 1973-74; prin. staff ballet accompanist sch. performing arts U.S. Internat. U., San Diego, 1973-74; tchr. music, English Cent. Union High Sch., El Centro, Calif., 1974-89; instr. music Imperial (Calif.) Valley Coll., 1975-89, instr. music, head music dept., 1989—; assoc. prof. music Ariz. Western Coll., Yuma, 1985-87; lectr. music Imperial Valley campus San Diego State U., 1988—; adjudicator Music Tchrs. Assn. Calif., 1974—; asst. conductor San Diego Youth Symphony, 1973-77; music dir. Yuma Community Orch., 1985-87, Imperial Valley Chamber Orch. and Chorus, 1974—. Author: A Manual for the Novice Ballet Accompanist, 1980; editor: Composition: A Structural Approach, 1980. Mem. DeAnza Search and Rescue Unit, Imperial, 1988—; project leader guide dogs Imperial County 4-H, 1990—. Named Imperial County Man of Music Imperial Valley Press, 1977; recipient Disting. Svc. award Imperial Valley Coll., 1991. Mem. Music Educators Nat. Conf., Am. Symphony Orch. League, Coll. Music Soc., Conductors Guild (nat. treas. 1975-77), Therapy Dogs Internat. (cert. CGCE Evaluator), Imperial Valley Kennel Club (show chmn. 1984-88, obedience chmn. 1989—), Imperial County Arts Coun., Phi Mu Alpha Sinfonia, Pi Kappa Lambda, Omicron Delta Kappa. Home: 1904 Johnson Ln El Centro CA 92243-9547 Office: Imperial Valley Chamber Orch PO Box 713 El Centro CA 92244-0713

JACKMAN, JAY MYRON, psychiatrist; b. Bklyn., June 4, 1939; s. James Jeremiah and Dora (Emmer) J.; m. Judith Gail Meisels, Nov. 23, 1963 (div. Sept. 1987); children: Tenaya, Rashi, Jason Scott; m. Myra Hoffenberg Strober, Oct. 21, 1990. BA, Columbia U., 1960; MD, Harvard U., 1964. Diplomate Am. Bd. Psychiatry and Neurology; lic. physician, Calif., Hawaii. Rotating intern San Francisco County Gen. Hosp., 1965; psychiat. resident Stanford U., 1969; asst. dir. community psychiatry Mt. Zion Hosp., San Francisco, 1969-70; dir. drug treatment programs Westside Community Mental Health Ctr., San Francisco, 1970-74; pvt. practice San Francisco, 1969-74; dir. Lanakila Clinic Kalihi-Palama Community Mental Health Ctr., Honolulu, 1974-75; pvt. practice Honolulu, 1975-90, Stanford, Calif., 1990—; cons. Salvation Army Addiction Treatment Facility, Honolulu, 1974-81; chmn. Task Force on Drugs, Nat. Coun. Community Mental Health Ctrs., 1971-75; chmn. no. sect. Calif. Assn. Methodone Programs, 1973-74. Contbr. articles on substance abuse to profl. jours. Mem. Mayor's Adv. Com. on Drug Abuse, Honolulu, 1975-77. Mem. Am. Psychiat. Assn. (commn. on drugs 1973-77), Am. Acad. Psychiatry in the Law, Hawaii Psychiat. Assn., No. Calif. Psychiat. Soc., Santa Clara County Bar Assn. (vol., lay mem. fee arbitration com. 1992). Democrat. Jewish.

JACKMAN, MICHELE, management consultant; b. Los Angeles, Aug. 18, 1944; d. Michael and Grace (DeLeo) Pantaleo; m. Jarrell C. Jackman, Sept. 7, 1968; 1 child, Renee Grace. BA in Polit. Sci., U. Calif., Davis, 1966; MSW in Social Policy, Cath. U., 1980; MA in Human Rels. Mgmt., U. Okla., 1980. Social worker Los Angeles County, 1966-70; supr., trainer Santa Barbara (Calif.) County, 1970-74; mgr. Drug/Alcohol program U.S. Army, Western Europe, 1974-78; analyst, cons. Office Dep. Chief of Staff Pers. U.S. Army, Washington, 1978-80; trainer, cons. Profit Systems, Internat., Santa Barbara, 1980—; lectr. organizational psychology U. Calif., Santa Barbara; cons. numerous agys., orgns. Co-author: Choices/Challenges Teacher's Guide, 1985; author: (tape) Humor at the Worplace, 1988, Star Teams, Key Players, 1991; contbr. chpts. to books. Bd. dirs. Women's Community Ctr.; community advisor Jr. League, 1991-93. Recipient Commdr.'s medal for Disting. Civilian Svc. U.S. Army, 1977, Bus. Personality of Yr., 1992 Bus. Digest. Mem. OAS, NAFE, Am. Mgmt. Assn., Nat. Assn. Social Workers (chmn. local chpt.), Am. Soc. Tng. and Devel., UN Instl. Assn., Inst. Noetic Scis., Santa Barbara C. of C. (Bus. award Council of High Edn./Industry 1986), University Club, Native Daus. of Golden West. Office: Profit Systems Internat Tng & Mgmt Systems 5266 Hollister Ave Apt 109 Santa Barbara CA 93111-2066

JACKS, BRIAN PAUL, physician; b. Regina, Can., May 23, 1943; came to U.S., 1968; s. Nathan Benjamin and Ida (Nathanson) J.; m. Carole Marks, June 24, 1968 (div. 1973); m. Brooke Ann Foland, Nov. 14, 1976; 1 child, Erika. Student, Kennedy Collegiate, Windsor, Ont., Can., 1955-61, U. Toronto, Can., 1961-63, 63-67. Psychiat. extern Menninger Inst., Topeka, 1966; intern Vancouver (Can.) Gen. Hosp., B.C., 1967-68; gen. psychiatrist U. So. Calif. Med. Ctr., L.A., 1968-70, child psychiatrist, 1970-72, chief resident in child psychiatry, 1971-72, asst. dir. adolescent psychiatry outpatient svcs., 1972-76, ward chief, 1976-79; examiner Nat. Bd. Psychiatry and Neurology, 1978; pvt. practice Beverly Hills, Calif., 1979—; tchr. in field. Contbr. articles to profl. jours. Bd. dirs. LVN and community workers Advanced Found., L.A. Psychiat. Scvs., Venice, Calif., Kedren Clinic, L.A. City Schs., L.A. Child Guidance Clinic; chmn. Dept. Spl. Edn. U. So. Calif.; probation officer L.A. County Probation Dept.; tchr. Exceptional Found.; student nurse Martin Luther King Hosp.; social worker Dept. Pub. Social Svc. and many others. Fellow Am. Acad. Child Psychiatry; mem. Am. Soc. Adolescent Psychiatry, Am. Psychiat. Assn., So. Calif. Soc. for Adolescent Psychiatry (past pres. 1983-84), So. Calif. Psychiat. Soc., Calif. Soc. Indsl. Medicine, Soc. Calif. Soc. Child Psychiatry (past pres. 1982-83). Office: 435 N Bedford Dr Penthouse Beverly Hills CA 90210

JACKS, RICHARD NELSON, psychologist, educator; b. Lewiston, Idaho, Oct. 31, 1938; s. Wilbur Donwin and Myrtle Elizabeth (Gooch) J.; m. Riett Brown, Mar. 23, 1978; children: Christopher, Eric, Rachel. BA, Ea. Wash. U., 1962, MEd, 1963; PhD, Stanford U., 1972. Mem. faculty, chmn. dept. psychology Olympic Coll., Bremerton, Wash., 1963-69; counselor, mem. faculty Stanford (Calif.) U., 1972-79; dir. counseling, assoc. prof. psychology Whitman Coll., Walla Walla, Wash., 1979—; psychologist Wash. State Penitentary, Walla Walla, 1989—. Contbr. articles to profl. publs. Vice chair Walla Walla County Human Svcs. Adv. Com., 1984-90. Mem. APA, Wash. State Psychol. Assn. Methodist. Home: 516 Catherine Walla Walla WA 99362 Office: Whitman Coll 345 Boyer Walla Walla WA 99362

JACKSON, ALBERT SMITH, electronics engineer; b. Sylvia, Kans., Feb. 2, 1927; s. Oliff Harold and Nellie Blanche (Dewhurst) J.; m. Solace Patricia Smith, June 9, 1951; (div. Aug. 1978); children: Linda Michelle, Jill Sharon, Theresa Louise, Steven Thomas, Craig Michael; m. Elaine Sonia Spontak, Sept. 1, 1978. AA, John Muir Coll., 1948; BSEE, MSEE, Calif. Inst. Tech., 1952; PhDEE, Cornell U., 1956. From instr. to asst. prof. Cornell U., Ithaca, N.Y., 1952-59; dept. mgr. TRW Computers Co., Canoga Park, Calif., 1959-61; pres. Control Tech., Inc., Long Beach, Calif., 1961-65, 71-72; chief scientist Milgo Electronic Corp., Miami, Fla., 1965-71; pres. Opto Logic Corp., Long Beach, 1972-75; engring. mgr. Motorola, Inc., Orange, Calif., 1975—; cons. Naval Research Lab., Washington, 1964-69, Gen. Electric Corp., Ithaca, 1953-59; lectr. UCLA, 1972-77, U. Calif., Irvine, 1965—. Author: Analog Computation, 1960; contbr. articles to profl. jours.; inventor in field. Active Redevel. Agy., Seal Beach, Calif., 1972-74. Served with USN, 1945-46. Named Outstanding Mem. of Extension Faculty, U. Calif.-Irvine, 1985. Mem. IEEE (chmn. profl. group on human factors in engring. 1953-64, regional edn. coordinator 1984-86). Republican. Office: Motorola Inc 101 Pacifica Ste 300 Irvine CA 92718-3330

JACKSON, BETTY EILEEN, music and elementary school educator; b. Denver, Oct. 9, 1925; d. James Bowen and Fannie (Shelton) J. MusB, U. Colo., 1948, MusM, 1949, MusB in Edn., 1963; postgrad. Ind. U., 1952-55, Hochschule für Musik, Munich, 1955-56. Cert. educator Colo., Calif. Tchr., accompanist, tchr. H.L. Davis Vocal Studios, Denver, 1949-52; teaching assoc. U. Colo., Boulder, 1961-63, vis. lectr., summers 1963-69; tchr. Fontana Unified Sch. Dist., Calif., 1963-92, pvt. studio, 1966—; lectr. in music Calif. State U., San Bernardino, 1967-76; performer, accompanist, music dir. numerous musical cos. including performer, music dir. Fontana Mummers, 1980—, Riverside Community Players, Calif., 1984—; performer Rialto Community Theatre, Calif., 1983—; head visual and performing arts com. Cypress Elem. Shc., 1988-92. Performances include numerous operas, musical comedies and oratorios, Cen. City Opera, Denver Grand Opera, Univ. Colo., Ind. Univ. Opera Theater (leading mezzo), 3 tours of Fed. Republic Germany, 1956-58; oratorio soloist in Ind., Ky., Colo., and Calif., West End Opera (lead roles), Riverside Opera (lead roles). Judge, Inland Theatre League, Riverside, 1983-92; mem. San Bernardino Cultural Task Force, 1981-83. Fulbright grantee, Munich, 1955-56; named Outstanding Performer Inland Theatre League, 1982-84; recipient Outstanding Reading Tchr. award, 1990, Tchr. of Yr. nominations, 1990, 91, Honorary Svc. award 1992. Mem. AAUW (bd. dirs., cultural chair 1983-86), NEA, Nat. Assn. Tchrs. Singing (exec. bd. 1985-89), Internat. Reading Assn., Music Educators Nat. Conf., Calif. Tchrs. Assn., Calif. Elem. Educators Assn., Fontana Tchrs. Assn., Music Tchrs. Assn., Arrowhead Reading Coun., San Bernardino Valley Concert Assn. (bd. dirs. 1977-83), Internat. Platform Assn., Nat. Assn. for Preservation and Perpetuation of Storytelling (1990—), Order Eastern Star, Kappa Kappa Iota (v.p. 1982-83), Sigma Alpha Iota (life), Chi Omega. Avocations: community theater and opera, travel, collecting Hummels and plates. Home: PO Box 885 Rialto CA 92377-0885

JACKSON, BEVERLEY JOY JACOBSON, columnist, lecturer; b. L.A., Nov. 20, 1928; d. Phillip and Dorothy Jacobson; student U. So. Calif., UCLA; m. Robert David Jackson (div. Aug. 1964); 1 child, Tracey Dee. Daily columnist Santa Barbara (Calif.) News Press, 1968-92, Santa Barbara Independent, 1992—; nat. lectr. Santa Barbara history, hist. China recreated, also China today; free lance writer, fgn. corr. Bd. dirs. Santa Barbara br. Am. Cancer Soc., 1963—; mem. art mus. coun. L.A. Mus. Art, 1959—, mem. costume coun., 1983—; docent L.A. Mus. Art, 1962-64; mem. exec. bd. Channel City Women's Forum, 1969—; mem. adv. bd. Santa Barbara Mus. Natural History, Coun. of Christmas Cheer, Women's Shelter Bldg., Direct Relief Internat., Nat. Coun. Drug and Alcohol Abuse; mem adv. bd. Hospice of Santa Barbara, 1981—, Stop AIDS Coun., Arthritis Found.; bd. dirs. So. Calif. Com. for Shakespear's Globe Theatre; chmn. Santa Barbara Com. for Visit Queen Elizabeth II, 1982—; founder costume guild Santa Barbara Hist. Soc.; curator Chinese collections Santa Barbara Hist. Mus.; adv. bd. Santa Barbara Choral Soc.; hon. bd. Santa Barbara Salvation Army. Author: Dolls and Doll Houses of Spain, 1970; (with others) I'm Just Wild About Harry, 1979. Home: PO Box 5118 Santa Barbara CA 93150-5118

JACKSON, BO (VINCENT EDWARD JACKSON), professional baseball and football player; b. Bessemer, Ala., Nov. 30, 1962; m. Linda Jackson. Student, Auburn U. Baseball player Kansas City Royals, 1986-91; football player L.A. Raiders, 1987-90; baseball player Chicago White Sox, 1991—. Recipient Heisman Trophy, 1985; mem. NFL Pro Bowl Team, 1990; mem. A.L. All-Star Team, 1989. Office: care Chicago White Sox 333 W 35th St Chicago IL 60616

JACKSON, DAVID ROBERT, executive director; b. Long Beach, Calif., Jan. 15, 1945; s. Harlan Leroy and Helen Louise (Worthen) J.; m. Stacey Ann Bryan, Nov. 13, 1971; children: David, Daniel, Chad, Loren, Darcy. Student, Fullerton Coll., 1963-64, Brigham Young U., 1965-67, Santa Ana Coll., 1977, Orange Coast Coll., 1977, 78. Mgr. trainee Carl Karcher Interprizes, Fullerton, Calif., 1964; asst. mgr. Household Fin. Co., Santa Ana., Calif., 1964-65; pres. Areo Wash Co., Santa Ana., Calif., 1970-79; mgr. Chateau Apres Lodge, Park City, Utah, 1965-69; exec. dir. Fairmont Schs. Inc., Anaheim, Calif., 1979—. Bishop Ch. Jesus Christ Latter Day Saints, Corona, Calif., 1990—; chmn. Orange County 2000, Calif., 1992-93. Mem. Nat. Ind. Private Sch. Assn. (chmn. visitation team, bd. dirs.), Orange County Private Sch. Assn. (pres.), Calif. Assn. Nationally Recognized Schs. Republican. Office: Fairmont Sch 1557 W Mable Anaheim CA 92802

JACKSON, DUANE, agriculturist; b. Frederick, Okla., Feb. 15, 1942; s. Dale L. and E. Lucille J. BS, Okla. State U., 1964; PhD, Tex. A&M U., 1970. Cert. prof. agronomist and soil scientist. Lab. asst. Okla. State U., Stillwater, 1962-64; rsch. and teaching asst., rsch. assoc. Tex. A&M U., College Station, 1966-69; asst. prof. agr. Ohio State U., Columbus, 1970-72; agrl. cons. Ohio Crop Prodn., Columbus, 1972-74; cons. agronomist, entomol. agrl. engr. and soil scientist Field Crop Svc., Sterling, Colo., 1976—; pres. Ind. Agrl. Cons. Colo., 1991. Okla. State U. Sch. Agr. scholar, 1962. Mem. Am. Inst. Biol. Scis., Am. Soc. Agronomy, Gideons, Alpha Zeta. Office: Field Crop Svc PO Box 1055 Sterling CO 80751-1055

JACKSON, DURWARD PRESSLEY, information systems educator; b. Hartsville, S.C., Apr. 12, 1940; s. Erby L. and K. Sue (Duffee) J.; m. Sandra Wright, Sept. 27, 1967 (div. 1976); m. Alice Renfroe, June 8, 1984. BS in Aerospace Engring., U. Ariz., 1964; M of Engring. Adminstrn., U. Utah, 1969; MBA, Golden Gate U., 1978; PhD in Exec. Mgmt., Claremont Grad. Sch., 1983. Mgmt. cons. Touche Ross & Co., Denver, 1969-71; pres., cons. Data Phase, Inc., Park City, Utah, 1971-76; data adminstr. Air Force Flight Test Ctr., Edwards AFB, Calif., 1976-81; prof. Calif. State U., L.A., 1981—, chmn. info. systems dept., 1985-91; cons. Fed. Emergency Mgmt. Agy., Washington, 1982-83, Nat. Fire Info. Coun., Raleigh, N.C., 1983-84. Mem. adv. com. Bus. Forum, 1985—; contbr. articles to profl. jours. Bd. dirs. Antelope Valley-East Kern Water Agy., Quartz Hill, Calif., 1984—. Capt. USAF, 1961-68. Mem. Assn. for Computing Machinery, Data Processing Mgmt. Assn. (bd. dirs. 1988-89). Republican. Office: Calif State Univ LA 5151 State University Dr Los Angeles CA 90032

JACKSON, FRANK THOMAS, engineering manager; b. Union City, N.J., Jan. 16, 1934; s. Frank T. Sr. and Ruth Ann (Broulatour) J.; m. Alice L. Stewart, Aug. 5, 1951; children: Frank T. Jr., John A., Alisa D., Michael P. B in Engring., Long Beach (Calif.) Coll., 1960; JD, Orange Coast Coll., 1987; LLB, Citrus Belt Law Sch., 1985. Engring. mgr. Indsl. Electronic Engring., Van Nuys, Calif., 1966-71; owner, mgr. Lincoln Pub., Anaheim, Calif., 1971-82; sr. design engr. Ford Aerospace, Newport Beach, Calif., 1982-84; engring. mgr. Hartwell Corp., Placenta, Calif., 1984—; cons. Tech Star Co., Anaheim, 1989—, Modern Graphics, Anaheim, 1980—. Author: Military Hardware Handbook, 1974, Engine Specification Manual, 1980, Material & Finishes Handbook, 1980; inventor missile latch; 8 patents in field; contbr. articles to profl. jours. Office: Hartwell Corp 900 S Richfield Rd Placentia CA 92670-6788

JACKSON, HARRY ANDREW, artist; b. Chgo., Apr. 18, 1924; s. Harry and Ellen Grace J.; m. Valentina Moya Lear, Feb. 22, 1974; children: Matthew, Molly, Jesse, Luke, Chloe. LLD (hon.), U. Wyo., 1986. Founder, ptnr. pvt. foundry Camaiore, Italy, 1964—; CEO Harry Jackson Studios (formerly Wyo. Foundry Studios, Inc.), Cody, Wyo., 1965—; founder, ptnr. Jackson-Mariani S.R.L. Fine Art Bronze Foundry, Camaiore, 1985—. Author: Lost Wax Bronze Casting, 1972; one man exhbns. Tibor de Nagy Gallery, N.Y.C., 1952, 53, Martha Jackson Gallery, N.Y.C., 1956, Knoedler Gallery, N.Y.C., 1960, Amon Carter Mus., Fort Worth, 1961, 68, Kennedy

Gallery, N.Y., 1964, 68, 69, Nat. Mus. Am. Art, Smithsonian Instn., Washington, 1964, Whitney Gallery Western Art/Buffalo Bill Hist. Mus., Cody, 1964, 80-81, Mont. Hist. Soc., 1964, Tryon Gallery London, 1969, J. Poole Gallery, London, 1981, S.W. Mus., Los Angeles, 1979, Smith Gallery, 1981, 86, Whitney Gallery, Cody, Wyo., Palm Springs Desert Mus., Camaiore, 1981, Mpls. Inst. Art, 1982, Trailside Gallery, Scottsdale, Ariz., 1983, Met. Mus. Art, N.Y.C. 1987; retrospective exhbn. Palm Springs Desert Mus., 1985, U. Wyo. Art Mus., 1987; represented in permanent collections Am. Mus. of Gt. Britain, U.S. State Dept., Met. Mus. Art, N.Y., Lyndon Baines Johnson Meml. Library, Nat. Cowboy Hall of Fame, Oklahoma City, Wyo. State Mus., Cheyenne, Wyo., Whitney Gallery of Western Art, Buffalo Bill Hist. Ctr., Plains Indian Mus., Cody, Amon Carter Mus., Willaroc Mus., Mont. Hist. Soc., others; commd. works include: mural, Fort Pitts Mus., Pitts., 10-foot Sacagawea polychrome bronze monument, Buffalo Bill Hist. Ctr., Plains Indian Mus., 10-foot Sacagawea polychrome bronze monument, Cen. Wyo. Coll., 1981, The Horseman 21-foot monumental equestrian bronze, Gt. Western Fin. Corp., Beverly Hills, Calif., 1984, 10-foot patinaed Sacagawea Santa Barbara, Calif., 1985, Capezzano-Pianore, Camaiore, 1985; subject of books and catalogues: (by Frank Getlein) Harry Jackson, (by Kennedy Galleries) Monograph Catalogue 1969, (by Pointer & Goddard) Harry Jackson, 1981, (by Wyo. Foundry Studios, Inc.) Harry Jackson, Forty Years of His Work 1941-81, 1981, (by City of Camaiore) Harry Jackson, Thirty Years in Versillia (by Donald Goddard) American Painting, 1990. Served with USMC, 1942-45. Decorated Purple Heart with gold star; recipient 2 Presdl. citations, Gold medal NAD, 1968, Best Cover Art of 1969 award for sculpture of John Wayne, Am. Inst. Graphic Arts, 1969, Presdl. citation R.I. Sch. Design, gov.'s award Gov. of Wyo., 1990; Italian Govt. grantee, Fulbright grantee, 1957; 1 bronze presented as official gifts of state to Queen Elizabeth II by Pres. Gerald Ford, 1976, 2 bronzes presented by Pres. Ronald Reagan, 1982. Fellow Nat. Acad. Western art, Nat. Sculpture Soc., Nat. Acad. Design (academician). Address: PO Box 2836 Cody WY 82414

JACKSON, JAMES OSWALD, health and safety services professional; b. Detroit, Mar. 9, 1940; s. James Elwin and Edna Grace (Tompkins) J.; m. Madelene Keller, June 6, 1968; children: Jeannette M., Rebecca B. BS in Chemistry/Chem. Engring., Detroit Tech. Inst. Technology, 1968; MS in Indsl. Hygiene, Wayne State U., 1970; PhD in Eviron. Health, U. Mich., 1974. Cert. indsl. hygienist. Health sci. technician Gen. Motors Rsch. Labs., Warren, Mich., 1965-68; engr. Mich. Consol. Gas Co., Detroit, 1968-69, Wayne County Health Dept., Detroit, 1969-74; health sci. lab dir. Gulf Oil Corp., Pitts., 1974-76, dir. indsl. hygiene, 1976-79; assoc. prof. U. Ariz., Tucson, 1979-80; indsl. hygiene group leader Los Alamos (N.Mex.) Nat. Lab., 1980-90, HSE dep. div. leader, 1990-92; with health and safety div. Reader Lawrence Livermore (Calif.) Nat. Lab., 1993—; cons. Electric Power Rsch. Inst., Palo Alto, Calif., 1976—, Nat. Inst. Occupational Safety and Health, Cin. and Atlanta, 1973—, various in field, 1968—. Editor and author: Toxicology of Fly Ash, 1990, Biological Effects of Plume Fly Ash, 1991; contbr. articles to profl. jours. Mem. State of N.Mex. Health and Safety Tech. Adv. Com., Santa Fe, 1985-92, Los Alamaos County Emergency Planning Bd., 1987-92; state treas. N.Mex. Citizens for Clear Air and Water, Santa Fe, 1989-92. With U.S. Army, 1963-65, Europe. Recipient Environ. Quality award U.S. EPA, Washington, 1974. Mem. Am. Conf. Gov. Indsl. Hygienists (bd. dirs. 1990-93), Am. Indsl. Hygiene Assn., Ariz. Ctr. for Occupational Safety and Health (bd. dirs. 1980—), Am. Chem. Soc., Am. Acad. Indsl. Hygiene, AAAS; fellow Am. Inst. Chemists. Democrat. Roman Catholic. Home: 866 Waverly Common Livermore CA 94550 Office: Lawrence Livermore Nat Lab PO Box 808 L-384 Livermore CA 94551

JACKSON, JANE W., interior designer; b. Asheville, N.C., Aug. 5, 1944; d. James and Willie Mae (Stoner) Harris; m. Bruce G. Jackson; children: Yvette, Scott. Student, Boston U., 1964; BA, Leslie Coll., 1967; postgrad., Artisan Sch. Interior Design, 1980-82. Tchr. Montessori, Brookline, Mass., 1969-72; interior designer, owner Nettle Creek Shop, Honolulu, 1980-88; owner Wellesley Interiors, Honolulu, 1988—. Active Mayor's Com. for Small Bus., Honolulu, 1984. Mem. Honolulu Club. Democrat. Office: Wellesley Interiors PO Box 1365 Kaneohe HI 96744-1365

JACKSON, JEFFREY CHRYST, lawyer; b. Lynwood, Calif., Mar. 3, 1961; s. Jimmie Lee and Terry Lynn (Chryst) J. BA, Chapman U., 1984; JD, U. San Diego, 1988. Bar: Calif. 1989; U.S. Dist. Ct. (so., cen., ea. dists.) Calif. 1989. Atty. LaPlount and Ricciordulli, San Diego, 1988-91; sr. ptnr. Jackson and Allen, Carlsbad, Calif., 1991—; pres. N.J.H. Enterprises Inc., San Diego, 1991—; chmn. bd. dirs. N.J.H. Enterprises Inc., San Diego, 1991—. Vol. Vols. in Parole, San Diego, 1990—. Mem. Calif. Trial Lawyers Assn., San Diego Trial Lawyers Assn., San Diego County Bar Assn., North County Bar Assn., Bar Assn. No. San Diego County (arbitration). Office: Jackson and Allen 1921 Palomar Oaks Way Ste 205 Carlsbad CA 92008

JACKSON, JEWEL, retired state youth authority executive; b. Shreveport, La., June 3, 1942; d. Willie Burghardt and Bernice Jewel (Mayberry) Norton; children: Steven, June Kelly, Michael, Anthony. With Calif. Youth Authority, 1965—, group supr., San Andreas and Santa Rosa, 1965-67, youth counselor, Ventura, 1967-78, sr. youth counselor, Stockton, 1978-81, parole agt., 1986, treatment team supr., program mgr., Whittier and Ione, 1981-91; retired, 1991; pres. Valley Paralegal Svc., Stockton. Avocations: reading, horseback riding, writing poetry and short stories, stamp collecting. Home: 2416 Hall Ave Stockton CA 95205-7715

JACKSON, JOHN BRINCKERHOFF, writer, educator; b. Dinard, Ile et Vilaine, France, Sept. 25, 1909; s. William Brinckerhoff and Alice (Richardson) J. AB, Harvard Coll., Cambridge, Mass., 1932; DR of Arts, U. N.Mex., Albequerque, 1977. Adjunct prof. U. Calif., Berkeley, Calif., 1961-77; visiting prof. Harvard U. Dept. of Landscape Architecture, 1961-77; lecturer Harvard U. Dept. of Visual and Environmental Studies, 1969; Carl Sauer Memorial Lecturer U. Calif., Berkeley, Calif., 1978; visiting prof. U. Tex., Austin, Tex., 1980; resident Am. Acad. in Rome, 1983; lecturer Cullinen Lectures on Architecture, Rice U., 1986; editor publisher Landscape Mag., Santa Fe, 1951-68. Author: Landscapes, American Space, Necessity for Ruins, Exploring the Venacular Landscape, The Essential Landscape. Maj. Cavalry, 1940-46.

JACKSON, JOSEPH BRIAN, physician, health facility administrator; b. Brunswick, Ga., Dec. 23, 1946; s. J. A. and M. J. (Ross) J.; m. Cathleen Ann Goddard, Feb. 17, 1969 (div. 1982); children: Tracy Rene, Brian Eric. BS in Chemistry, San Diego State U., 1969; MD, Loma Linda U., 1973. Criminalist San Bernardino County (Calif.) Sheriff's Dept., 1969-70; intern, resident Santa Clara Valley Med. Ctr., San Jose, Calif., 1973-74; emergency medicine specialist Sharp Cabrillo Med. Ctr., San Diego, 1975-82, dep. dir. emergency rm., 1980-82; med. dir. East County Community Clinic, El Cajon, Calif., 1982—; pvt. practice Ramona, Calif., 1991-92; chief adult medicine Logan Heights Family Health Ctr., San Diego, Calif., 1992—, pvt. practice, 1991—; investigator CODA trial Phizer Inc., 1991. Mem. Area 5 Emergency Planning Com., San Diego, 1976-78; mem. Robert Wood Johnson Pilot Health Ins. Program, San Diego, 1986-88. Nat. Merit scholar UpJohn Co., 1964. Lutheran. Office: Logan Heights Family Health Ctr 1809 National Ave San Diego CA 92113

JACKSON, KRISTINE CLAIRE, forester, motorcycle rights activist; b. Pontiac, Mich., Sept. 6, 1956; d. John Covert and Dorothy Bonner (Knaggs) J. Student, San Jose State U., 1974-76; BS in Natural Resources Mgmt., Calif. Poly. U., San Luis Obispo, 1980; MS in Forest Econs., U. Idaho, 1984; postgrad., Va. Poly. Inst. and State U., 1989-90. Notary pub., W.Va. Grad. asst. U. Idaho, Moscow, 1981-84; forestry technician Los Padres Nat. Forest, USDA Forest Svc., Santa Barbara, Calif., 1975-76; wilderness ranger Sequoia Nat. Forest USDA Forest Svc., Springville, Calif., 1977-78; forestry technician Clearwater Nat. Forest USDA Forest Svc., Kamiah, Idaho, 1980; rsch. forester Pacific N.W. Rsch. Sta. USDA Forest Svc., Portland, Oreg., 1984-88; rsch. forester Northeastern Forest Expt. Sta. USDA Forest Svc., Princeton, W.Va., 1988-91, mgr. fed. women's program, 1988-91; forester Pacific Southwest region, Calif., 1991—. Contbr. articles to profl. publs. Active in voter registration, 1988—; W.Va. rep. Motorcycle Riders Found., 1990-91; v.p. Am. Bikers Aimed Toward Edn. W.Va., 1990. Recipient cert. of merit USDA Forest Svc., 1986, 90, cert. of appreciation, 1990, 91, 92, Points of Light award, 1991; scholar U. Idaho, 1983, 84. Mem. Soc. Am. Foresters (sec., co-capt. logging team 1978-80, sec. Bay area chpt. 1992), Soc. for Basic Irreproducible Rsch., Am. Brotherhood Aimed Towards Edn. of Calif. (1992—). Home: 236 Arroyo Dr Pacifica CA 94044 Office: USDA Forest Svc 630 Sansome St San Francisco CA 94111

JACKSON, MILES MERRILL, university dean; b. Richmond, Va., Apr. 28, 1929; s. Miles Merrill and Thelma Eugertha (Manning) J.; m. Bernice Olivia Roane, Jan. 7, 1954; children: Miles Merrill III, Marsha, Muriel, Melia. BA in English, Va. Union U., 1955; MS, Drexel U., 1956; postgrad., Ind. U., 1961, 64; PhD, Syracuse U., 1974. Br. libr. Free Libr., 1955-58; acting libr. C.P. Huntington Meml. Libr., Hampton (Va.) U., 1958-59, libr., 1959-63, asst. prof. libr. sci., 1958-62; territorial libr. Am. Samoa, 1962-64; chief libr. Trevor Arnett Libr., Atlanta U., 1964-69; also lectr. Sch. Libr. Sci.; assoc. prof. State U. N.Y., Geneseo, 1969-75; prof. U. Hawaii, 1975—, dean, 1983—, chmn. interdisciplinary program in communication and info. scis., 1985-89; Fulbright lectr. U. Tehran, Iran, 1968, 69; libr. cons., Fiji, Samoa, Papua New Guinea, Micronesia; USIA cons. India, 1983, Pakistan, 1985. Editor: A Bibliography of Materials on Negro History and Culture for Young People, 1968, Comparative and International Librarianship, 1971, International Handbook of Contemporary Developments in Librarianship, 1981, Pacific Island Studies: Review of the Literature, 1986; mem. editorial bd.: Internat. Jour. Info. Mgmt., Internat. Libr. Rev., 1982-87; chmn. bd. Hawaii Lit., Inc., 1985-88; founder, editor: Pacific Info. and Libr. Svcs. Newsletter; contbr. articles to profl. jours.; book reviewer. Bd. dirs. Central YMCA, 1986—, Hawaii Gov.'s Coun. on Literacy, 1986—, Hawaii ACLU, 1990—, office holder in Democratic party of Hawaii, 1992—. With USNR, 1945-48. Recipient Outstanding Alumnus award Va. Union U., 1987; Rsch. grantee Am. Philos. Soc., 1966; Coun. on Libr. Resources fellow, 1970, vis. fellow Republic of China, 1986; Harold Lancour fgn. travel awardee Beta Phi Mu, 1976. Mem. ALA (chmn. Internat. Rels. Roundtable 1988-89), Assn. for Libr. and Info. Sci. Edn. (pres. 1989-90), Coll. Lang. Assn. (hon. mention poetry 1954, 2d prize award short story 1955). Democrat. Office: U Hawaii Sch Library & Info Studies 2550 The Mall Honolulu HI 96822-2274

JACKSON, PETER VORIOUS, III, retired association executive; b. Butte, Mont., May 18, 1927; s. Peter V. and Besse Portia (McLean) J.; m. Johnneta Pierce, Apr. 29, 1949; children: Ward, Michelle (Mrs. Jerry Vanhour), Johnathan. Wheat and cattle rancher, 1949—; mem. Mont. Ho. of Reps., 1971-72; chief Grass Conservation bur. Mont. Dept. Natural Resources, Helena, 1972-74; supr. Conservation Dist. Madison County, Ennis, Mont., from 1957; past exec. dir. Western Environ. Trade Assn., Helena.; exec. v.p. Soc. for Range Mgmt., Denver, 1983-92; ret., 1992; vol. to develop and implement grazing lands conservation initiative Soil Conservation Svc., USDA, 1992—. Author: Montana Rangeland Resources Program, 1970. Mem. Madison County Fair Bd.; pres. Grazing Lands Forum, 1988. Recipient Renner award Soc. Range Mgmt., 1971, Conservation award Mont. Wildlife Fedn., 1966. Mem. Nat. Assn. Conservation Dists. (bd. dirs.), Mont. Assn. Conservation Dists. (exec. v.p. 1974), Soc. for Range Mgmt. (nat. pres., spl. award for outstanding achievement 1992). Lodges: Masons, Elks. Home and Office: PO Box 86 Harrison MT 59735-0086

JACKSON, RICHARD H., geography educator, writer; b. Orem, Utah, Apr. 22, 1941; s. John Henry and Nan Ennice (Ellsworth) J.; m. Mary Wadley, June 3, 1965; children: Joel, John, Mark, Mariah Lynne. BS, Brigham Young U., Provo, Utah, 1965, MS, 1966; PhD, Clark U., Worcester, Mass., 1970. Instr. geography Brigham Young U., 1969-70, asst. prof., 1970-75, assoc. prof., 1975-78, prof., 1979—; cons. Bur. Land Mgmt., Provo, 1976-78. Author: Mormon Role in Settlement of the West, 1978 (award Mormon Hist. Assn. 1979), Land Use in America, 1981, World Regional Geography, 1982, 3d edit., 1990, Cultural Geography, 1990; contbr. numerous articles to profl. jours. Bd. appeals Utah County, 1976-82; councilman City of Orem, 1979-87; bd. dirs. Redd Ctr. for Western History, Brigham Young U., 1978—, Utah Transit Authority, Salt Lake City, 1990—. Recipient Disting. Univ. Svc. award Utah Acad. Scis., Arts and Letters, Salt Lake City, 1985. Mem. Assn. Am. Geographers (Outstanding Tchr. award 1986), Am. Planning Assn., Utah History Assn. (Outstanding Scholarly Article award 1985). Home: 356 S Palisades Dr Orem UT 84058-5740 Office: Brigham Young U 690e SWKT Provo UT 84602

JACKSON, ROBERT D., society executive; b. San Pedro, Calif., Oct. 18, 1943; s. Robert David and Helen Ann (Duval) J.; m. Edith Beth Barschi, Oct. 3, 1982; 1 child, Rachel Elizabeth. BA, U. Calif., Berkeley, 1965; PhD, Harvard U., 1976. V.p. Chem. Banking Corp., N.Y.C., 1976-87; exec. dir. San Francisco Early Music Soc., Berkeley, Calif., 1992—. Treas. Hillside Assn. Berkeley, Calif., 1992. Recipient Grad. Prize fellowship Harvard U., Cambridge, Mass., 1967-75. Home: 1597 Le Roy Ave Berkeley CA 94708

JACKSON, TERRENCE MICHAEL, public defender; b. Omaha, Oct. 15, 1946; s. Robert George and Yvette Suzanne (Meunier) J.; m. Beverly Dianne Baker, Aug. 16, 1985; children: Justine Dianne, Sean Michael. BS in Math., Oreg. State U., 1968; grad., U Oreg., 1969-70; JD, Howard U., 1975. Bar: Nev. 1975, Calif. 1979, U.S. Supreme Ct. 1980. Rsch. asst. U. Nev., Las Vegas, 1969; staff atty. Clark County Legal Svcs., Las Vegas, 1975-76; chief dep. Pub. Defender's Office County of Clark, Las Vegas, 1976—; Bd. dirs. Las Vegas Art mus., 1984, Nev. Attys. for Criminal Justice, 1992-93. Board dirs. Las Vegas Art Mus., 1984; lectr. Nev. State Bar, Las Vegas, 1987, 88; guest lectr. U. Nev., 1991. Fleishman Found. scholar Oreg. State U., 1964-68; NEH grantee, 1980. Democrat. Roman Catholic. Office: Clark County Pub Defender 309 S 3d Las Vegas NV 89155

JACKSON, VIRGINIA ADAMS KNIGHT, lawyer; b. Detroit, Nov. 29, 1951; d. Robert B. and Elizabeth (Klien) Knight; children: Elizabeth, Allison; m. R. Kayle Jackson, Oct. 25, 1986; 1 child, Bridger. JD, Western New Eng. Coll., 1978. Bar: Colo. 1978, Mont. 1978, U.S. Dist. Ct. (Colo.) 1978, U.S. Dist. Ct. (Mont.) 1978. Assoc. Gough, Shanahan, Johnson & Waterman, Helena, Mont., 1978-83; pvt. practice Bozeman, Mont., 1987-92; pub., writer Knight's Headnotes, Helena and Bozeman, 1983—. Bd. mem. Mont. Coun. Internat. Visitors, Bozeman, 1987-89; chairperson Seeley Lake Comunity Coun. Mem. Lions (bd. dirs.). Office: PO Box 918 Seeley Lake MT 59868

JACKSON-SMITH, PRINCESS NADINE, state official, educator, consultant; b. Cordele, Ga., Jan. 25, 1946; d. Robert Ellis and Evelyn Juanita (Horton) Jackson; m. John Austin Rustad, June 15, 1968 (div. 1973); m. Richard Lee Smith, June 25, 1977. BA in English, U. Wash., 1971. Grants coord. community devel. dept. City of Seattle, 1971-72, mgr. capital improvement program, 1972-74; dir. art in pub. places program Arts Commn., Seattle, 1974-76; program coord. Pratt Fine Arts Ctr., City of Seattle, 1976-77; dir. communications Wash. Assn. Community Action Agys., Olympia, 1977-78; pub. info. officer Wash. State Dept. Licensing, Olympia, 1978-86, chief pub. info. officer, 1986-90; dir. pub. affairs Wash. State Ferries, Seattle, 1990—; mem., loaned exec. Wash. State Martin Luther King, Jr. Holiday Commn., Olympia, 1987-89; owner, prin. Communicator Cons., 1988—; adj. faculty South Puget Sound C.C., 1985-90; mem. Jr. League Community Adv. Bd.; mem. the Links, Inc. Speech pub. in Vital Speeches of the Day, 1983. Bd. dirs. United Way, Olympia, 1987-93; bd. dirs., pub. rels. com. chmn. Episcopal Svc. for Youth, Tacoma, 1989-91; mem. King County chpt. ARC, 1991—; pub. rels. chmn. South Sound Options Unltd., Olympia, 1990—. Recipient Outstanding Performance award Seattle Parks Dept., 1977, appreciation award Black Women's Caucus Wash. State, 1979, Leader of 80's award NW Conf. Black Pub. Ofcls., 1979, Profl. Excellence award Wash. Dept. Licensing, 1988, Meritorious Svc. award United Negro Coll. Fund, 1992, Govt. Video Prodn. award Washington Press Assn., 1991. Mem. Wash. Info. Coun. (v.p. 1980-81), Pub. Rels. Soc. Am., Alpha Kappa Alpha. Democrat. Home: 4333 Waldrick Rd SE Olympia WA 98501-9578 Office: Wash State Ferries 801 Alaska Way Seattle WA 98104-1487

JACOB, BETTY MUTHER, international administrator; b. River Forest, Ill., Sept. 5, 1910; d. Albert William and Edith (Ashleman) Muther; m. Philip Ernest Jacob, Dec. 24, 1935 (dec. June 19, 1985); children: Sally, Kirk, Stefan. BA, Wellesley Coll., 1934. Exec. sec. Herbert Hoover's Nat. Student Com. on Food for Small Dem., 1929-41; special asst. dir. gen. UNRRA, 1945-46; special asst. exec. dir. UNICEF, N.Y.C., 1947-54; pres. Cheyney Homesteads, 1955-60; internat. adminstr.&investigator Internat. Studies of Values in Pol., Phila., 1960-70; chancellor Un. of New World, Valais, Switzerland, 1970; res. assoc. & nat. coord. Automation & Indsl. Workers Res. Corp., Honolulu, 1970-80, 1970-80; co-dir., Inst. for Peace Univ. Hawaii, Honolulu, 1986-88; coord. Asia-Pacific Dialogue, Honolulu, 1986-90; internat. adminstr. New Democracy and Local Governance, Honolulu, 1990—. Author: A Peace To End Wars, 1945, This I Believe, 1953, Values & The Active Community, 1971, Automation & Industrial Workers, 1986. Recipient Agnes Baldwin Alexander Humanity Svc. award Nat. Assembly of the Hawaiian Bahais, 1986, Matsunaga Peace Inst. award, 1988, Achievement in Com. Svc. award Hawaii Psychol. Assn., 1992. Mem. Soc. of Friends. Home: 999 Wilder Ave # 1502 Honolulu HI 96822

JACOB, STANLEY WALLACE, surgeon, educator; b. Phila., 1924; s. Abraham and Belle (Shulman) J.; m. Marilyn Peters; 1 son, Stephen; m. Beverly Swarts; children—Jeffrey, Darren, Robert; m. Gail Brandis; 1 dau., Elyse. M.D. cum laude, Ohio State U., 1948. Diplomate: Am. Bd. Surgery. Intern Beth Israel Hosp., Boston, 1948-49; resident surgery Beth Israel Hosp., 1949-52, 54-56; chief resident surg. service Harvard Med. Sch., 1956-57, instr., 1958-59; asso. vis. surgeon Boston City Hosp., 1958-59; Kemper Found. research scholar A.C.S., 1957-60; asst. prof. surgery U. Oreg. Med. Sch., Portland, 1959-66; asso. prof. U. Oreg. Med. Sch., 1966—; Gerlinger prof. surgery Oreg. Health Scis. U., 1981—. Author: Structure and Function in Man, 5th edit, 1982, Laboratory Guide for Structure and Function in Man, 1982, Dimethyl Sulfoxide Basic Concepts, 1971, Biological Actions of DMSO, 1975, Elements of Anatomy and Physiology, 1989; contbr. to: Ency. Brit. Served to capt. M.C. AUS, 1952-54; col. Res. ret. Recipient Gov.'s award Outstanding N.W. Scientist, 1965; 1st pl. German Sci. award, 1965; Markle scholar med. scis., 1960. Mem. Phi Beta Kappa, Sigma Xi, Alpha Omega Alpha. Home: 1055 SW Westwood Ct Portland OR 97201-2708 Office: Oreg Health Scis U Dept Surgery 3181 SW Sam Jackson Park Rd Portland OR 97201

JACOBS, ARTHUR DIETRICH, educator, researcher, health services executive; b. Bklyn., Feb. 4, 1933; s. Lambert Dietrich and Paula Sophia (Knissel) J.; m. Viva Jane Sims, Mar. 24, 1952; children: Archie (dec.), David L., Dwayne C., Dianna K. Hatfield. BBA, Ariz. State U., 1962, MBA, 1966. Enlisted USAF, 1951, commd. 2d lt., 1962, advanced through grades to maj., 1972, ret., 1973; indsl. engr. Motorola, Phoenix, 1973-74; mgmt. cons. state of Ariz., 1974-76; mgmt. cons. Productivity Internat., Tempe, Ariz., 1976-79; faculty assoc. Coll. Bus. Adminstrn., Ariz. State U., Tempe, 1977—; productivity advisor Scottsdale (Ariz.) Meml. Health Services Co., 1979-84; researcher U.S. internment of European-Am. aliens and citizens of European ancestry during World War II. Bd. dirs. United Way of Tempe, 1979-85. Mem. Am. Soc. Quality Control, Ariz. State U. Alumni Assn. (bd. dirs. 1973-79, pres. 1978-79), Inst. Indsl. Engrs. (pres. Central Ariz. chpt. 1984-85), Ops. Research Soc. Am., Sigma Iota Epsilon, Beta Gamma Sigma, Delta Sigma Pi. Club: Optimist (life) (Tempe). Contbr. articles to profl. jours.

JACOBS, BRUCE MARRIN, lawyer; b. Oakland, Calif., July 21, 1926; s. Allen Walter and Celia Teresa (Marrin) J.; m. Jane Gray, June 26, 1954; children: Tracy Ann, Brian G., Nancy C. Fleming. AB, U. Calif., Berkeley, 1947; JD, U. San Francisco, 1953. Bar: Calif. 1953. Assoc. Law Office Robert K. Byers, Gilroy, Calif., 1953-56; ptnr. Byers & Jacobs, Gilroy, 1957-67, Jacobs & Biafore, Gilroy, 1967-74, Jacobs & McDonald, Gilroy, 1974—; dir. Nat. Fiberglass, Gilroy. Bd. pres. Gavilan Community Coll., Gilroy, 1963, trustee, 1963-73; city atty. City of Gilroy, 1966-91. Lt. (j.g.) USN, 1944-49, PTO. Mem. State Bar Calif., Gilroy C. of C. (pres. 1958), Gilroy Rotary (pres. 1957, 59), Gilroy Elks. Republican. Presbyterian. Home: 7820 Santa Theresa Dr Gilroy CA 95020 Office: Jacobs & McDonald PO Box 458 Gilroy CA 95021-0458

JACOBS, DONALD TRENT, health psychologist; b. St. Louis, June 13, 1946; m. Beatrice A. Jacobs, Aug. 17, 1985; 1 child, Jessica. BS, S.W. Mo. U., 1968; MS, Columbia U., 1979, PhD, 1981. Cert. tchr., Calif. Firefighter, EMT Marin County Fire Dept., Mill Valley, Calif., 1975-85; prof. U. Calif., Berkeley, 1985-88; dir. Internat. Soc. for Trauma Patient Comm., Sonoma, Calif., 1991—; advisor Govs. Coun. on Wellness, Calif., 1983-85. Author: Physical Fitness for Firefighters, 1976, Ride and Tie: The Challenge, 1978, Getting Your Executive Fit, 1981, Patient Communication, 1991. Chmn. Am. Heart Assn., Marin, Calif., 1980-81. Lt. USMC, 1969-71. Mem. Calif. Soc. of Clin. Hypnosis (v.p. 1988-89). Home: PO Box 742 Kenwood CA 95452 Office: Hope Counseling Svcs 941 B St Petaluma CA 94950

JACOBS, GEOFFREY LANE, electronics marketing executive; b. Long Beach, N.Y., June 8, 1948; s. Harvey Stanley and Rhoda Lillian (Siegel) J.; m. Susan Lucille Lowden, Jan. 14, 1978; children: Bryan Michael, Spencer Donald. BS in Chem. Engring., U. Rochester, 1970; MS in Chem. Engring., Pa. State U., 1974. Bus. devel. engr. Air Products and Chems., Inc., Allentown, Pa., 1972-77; mktg. mgr. Raychem Corp., Menlo Park, Calif., 1978-80, tech. svcs. mgr., 1980-82, product mgr., 1982-89; mktg. mgr. Micrographic Tech. Corp., Mountain View, Calif., 1990; dir. mktg. Trimble Nav. Ltd., Sunnyvale, Calif., 1991—; mem. Internat. Ozone Inst., 1976-77. Contbr. articles to profl. jours. Mgr., Union City (Calif.) Little League, 1992; mem. Men's Sr. Baseball League, San Jose, Calif., 1988-92. Mem. Chi Phi. Home: 4582 Ojai Loop Union City CA 94587

JACOBS, JOHN HOWARD, association executive; b. Phila., June 7, 1925; s. Howard Elias and Elizabeth Pauline (Dresel) J.; m. Shirley Elizabeth Salini, Apr. 21, 1960. BS in Econs., N.Mex. State U., 1950; LLD (hon.), Golden Gate U., 1985. Adminstrv. officer U.S. Fgn. Service (NATO), London, Paris, 1951-53; gen. mgr. Vis-a-Pack Corp., Beverly, N.J., 1953-58; exec. dir. Red. Agy., City of Stockton, Calif., 1958-66, San Francisco Planning and Urban Research, 1966-81; exec. dir. San Francisco C. of C., 1981-88, pres., 1988-89; chmn. Point Reyes Bird Obs., Pacific Region Nat. Assn. Housing and Redevel. Ofcls., Stockton, 1965-66, mem. nat. bd. govs., San Francisco, 1966-70; bd. dirs. Sta. KQED-TV (Pub.). Trustee emeritus Fine Arts Mus. San Francisco; bd. dirs. SPUR, San Francisco, World Affairs Coun. No. Calif., San Francisco State U. Found.; chmn. pres.'s adv. coun. San Francisco State U.; v.p. San Francisco Devel. Fund. Home: 2823 Octavia St San Francisco CA 94123-4305

JACOBS, KENT FREDERICK, dermatologist; b. El Paso, Tex., Feb. 13, 1938; s. Carl Frederick and Mercedes D. (Johns) J.; m. Sallie Ritter, Apr. 13, 1971. BS, N.Mex. State U., 1960; MD, Northwestern U., 1964; postgrad., U. Colo., 1967-70. Dir. service unit USPHS, Laguna, N.Mex., 1966-67; pvt. practice specializing in dermatology Las Cruces, N.Mex., 1970—; cons. U.S. Army, San Francisco, 1968-70, cons. NIH, Washington, 1983, Holloman AFB, 1972-77; research assoc. VA Hosp., Denver, 1969-70; preceptor U. Tex., Galveston, 1976-77; mem. clin. staff Tex. Tech U., Lubbock, 1977—; asst. clin. prof. U. N.Mex., Albuquerque, 1972—; bd. dirs. First Nat. Bank of Dona Ana County, Las Cruces, N.Mex., 1987—. Novelist; contbr. articles to profl. jours. and popular mags. Trustee Mus. N.Mex. Found., 1987—, mem. bd. regents Mus. N.Mex., 1987—, pres., 1989-91; bd. dirs. Dona Ana Arts Coun., 1992—. Invitational scholar Oreg. Primate Ctr., 1968; Acad. Dermatology Found. fellow, 1969; named Disting. Alumnus N.Mex. State U., 1985. Fellow Am. Acad. Dermatology, Royal Soc. Medicine, Soc. Investigative Dermatology; mem. AMA, Fedn. State Med. Bds. (bd. dirs. 1984-86), N.Mex. Med. Soc., N.Mex. Bd. Med. Examiners (pres. 1983-84), N.Mex. State U. Alumni Assn. (bd. dirs. 1975—), Phi Beta Kappa, Beta Beta Beta. Republican. Presbyterian. Clubs: Mil Gracias (pres. 1972-74), Pres.'s Assocs. Lodge: Rotary. Home: 3610 Southwind Rd Las Cruces NM 88005-5556 Office: # 15-106 2525 S Telshor Blvd Las Cruces NM 88001-9147 also: Mus NM PO Box 2087 Santa Fe NM 87504

JACOBS, PAUL ALAN, lawyer; b. Boston, June 5, 1940; s. Samuel and Sarah (Rodman) J.; m. Carole Ruth Greenstein, Aug. 28, 1962; children: Steven N., Cheryl R., David F., Craig A. BA in Econs. magna cum laude, Tufts U., 1960; JD magna cum laude, U. Denver, 1968. Bar: Colo. 1968, U.S. Dist. Ct. Colo. 1968. Personnel officer First Nat. Bank Denver, 1964-68; assoc. Holme Roberts & Owen, Denver, 1968-73, sr. ptnr., 1973-93; exec. v.p., gen. counsel Colo. Rockies profl. baseball orgn., Denver. Bd. dirs. Anti-Defamation League B'Nai B'rith, Denver, 1987—. Served to 1st lt. USAF, 1960-63. Mem. ABA, Denver Bar Assn., Colo. Bar Assn. Jewish. Home: 4041 S Narcissus Way Denver CO 80237-2025 Office: Colo Rockies Baseball Club 1700 Broadway Denver CO 80290

JACOBS, RALPH, JR., artist; b. El Centro, Calif., May 22, 1940; s. Ralph and Julia Vahe (Kirkorian) J. Paintings appeared in: Prize Winning Art (3 awards), 1964, 65, 66, and New Woman Mag., 1975; one man shows and exhbns. Villa Montalvo, Calif., Stanford Rsch. Inst., Calif., Fresno Art Ctr., Calif., de Young Meml. Mus., Calif., Rosicrucian Mus., Calif., Cunningham Meml. Gallery, Calif., 40th Ann. Nat. Art Exhibit, Utah, Nat. Exhbn. Coun. of Am. Artists Socs., N.Y.C., Am. Artists Profl. League Show, Armenian Allied Arts, Calif., Monterey Peninsula Mus. Art, Calif. Recipient 1st place award Statewide Annual Santa Cruz Art League Gallery, 1963, 64; 2nd place award Soc. Western Artists Ann. M.H. de Young Mus., 1964; A.E. Klumpkey Meml. award, 1965. Address: PO Box 5906 Carmel CA 93921

JACOBS, RALPH RAYMOND, physicist; b. Niagara Falls, N.Y., Dec. 31, 1942; m. Leedia Gordeev, June 5, 1966; children: Aleda Anne, Liana Lizabeth. BS cum laude in Physics, NYU, 1964; MS in Physics, Yale U., 1965, PhM in Physics, 1967, PhD in Physics, 1969. Summer fellow physics dept. NYU, N.Y.C., 1962-63; teaching asst. Yale U., New Haven, 1967-69; mem. tech. staff GTE Labs., Inc., Bayside, N.Y., 1969-72; cons., sr. physicist, project mgr. laser programs U. Calif., Lawrence Livermore Nat. Lab., 1972-80; corp. mgr. for rsch. Spectra-Physics, Inc., San Jose, Mountain View, Calif., 1980-84, engring. mgr. laser products div., 1985-89, dir. corp. tech. devel., 1989-90; dir. new technology initiatives, laser programs U. Calif., Lawrence Livermore Nat. Lab., 1990—; conf. chair Lasers and Electro-Optics Soc. Ann. Meeting, Orlando, Fla., 1989; v.p. for confs. and mem. bd. govs. IEEE/Lasers and Electro-Optics Soc., 1990—. Mem. editorial bd. Laser Focus World, Lasers & Optronics. Recipient GM and NYU Alumni scholarships, Kappa Sigma Frat. Nat. Man of Yr. award, 1963. Fellow IEEE (Lasers and Electro-Optics Soc. v.p. for confs. and bd. govs.), Optical Soc. Am.; mem. Am Phys. Soc., Sigma Pi Sigma (NYU chpt. pres.), Tau Beta Pi (NYU chpt. pres.), Sigma Xi.

JACOBS, RANDALL BRIAN, lawyer; b. N.Y.C., July 8, 1951; s. John and Evelyn (Teper) J.; 1 child, Jillian. BA, Coll. of Idaho, 1972; JD, U. West L.A., 1978. Bar: Calif., D.C., Wis. Lawyer B. Randall Jacobs Law Corp., Santa Monica, Calif., 1978—; real estate broker Morgan Reed & Co., Santa Monica, 1979—; pvt. investigator Randy Brian Assocs., Santa Monica, 1976—. Reserve deputy sheriff, L.A. County Sheriff, L.A., 1979—. Mem. Shom Rim Soc., Nat. Rifle Assn., Masons, Shriners. Office: Law Offices B R Jacobs 2309 Ocean Park Blvd Santa Monica CA 90405-5199

JACOBS, ROBERT COOPER, political scientist, consultant; b. N.Y.C., Jan. 23, 1939; s. Max and Paula (Glotzer) J.; m. Barbara Linda Lax (div.); children: Michael, Deborah; m. Mollie Jenks Edson; children: Elliot, Madeleine, Eleanor. AB, CCNY, 1959; AM, Columbia U., 1961, PhD, 1970. Instr. Colby Coll., Waterville, Maine, 1965-68, asst. prof., 1968-70; from asst. prof. to prof. Cen. Wash. U., Ellensburg, 1970—, dir. law and justice, 1974-88, prof., 1982—; vis. prof. criminal justice Temple U., 1988-89. Contbr. articles to profl. jours. Mem. Kittitas County Juvenile Accountability Bd., Ellensburg, 1975—. N.Y. State Regents scholar, 1955-59; State of N.Y. teaching fellow, 1962-63. Mem. Am. Polit. Sci. Assn., Wash. Assn. Criminal Justice Educators (past pres.), Supreme Ct. Hist. Soc. Democrat. Home: 111 E 10th Ave Ellensburg WA 98926-2909 Office: Cen Wash U Dept of Political Science Ellensburg WA 98926

JACOBS, ROBERT EDWIN, mountaineering guide, adventure travel consultant; b. Salt Lake City, Jan. 8, 1952; s. Winfred Oscar and Katherine Marie (Kaiser) J.; m. Margaret Elaine Keller, m. July 1, 1981 (div. Jan. 1992); 1 child, Ian William. BA in Archeology, English Lit., U. N.Mex., 1974. Horse packer, trail mgr. U.S. Forest Svc., Walla Walla, Wash., 1974-78; owner, operator St. Elias Alpine Guides, McCarthy, Alaska, 1978—; title rschr. Jacobs Land Svcs., Durango, Colo., 1979-81; ski guide, instr. Lone Mountain Ranch, Big Sky, Mont., 1979-81; mem. McGuire Polar Expdn., 1985, Polish-Alaska Mt. Everest Expdn., 1989; cons. Siberia Alaska Trading Co., Anchorage, 1989-92. Author Walk to the Pole jour., 1985 (Press Club award 1986). Supr. Tramway Constrn., McCarthy, 1984. Recipient Nordic Ski Instr. award Profl. Ski Instrs. Assn., 1976. Mem. Am. Mountain Guides Assn. (cert. Alpine guide, sec. 1990—), Am. Alpine Club, Arctic Inst. N.Am., Alaska Wilderness Recreation and Tourism Assn. (past pres. 1986—), Explorers Club. Home: Shushanna Ave McCarthy AK 99588 Office: St Elias Alpine Guides PO Box 111241 Anchorage AK 99511

JACOBS, WILBUR RIPLEY, writer, history educator; b. Chgo.; s. Walter Ripley and Nona Isabel (Deutsch) J.; divorced; children: Elizabeth Shirley Jacobs Hayden, Catherine Elaine,; m. Priscilla Beth Dehmel, Dec. 20, 1982; children: William Ripley, Emily Marilyn. BA with honors, UCLA, MA with honors, PhD; postgrad., Johns Hopkins U. Prof. history U. Calif., Santa Barbara, 1965-88, chmn., dean of students; apt. rsch. scholar Huntington Libr., San Marino, Calif., 1989—; vis. prof. U. Calif., Berkeley, Claremont Grad. Sch., UCLA, Ind. U., U. Mich.; fulbright prof. Australian Nat. U., Canberra.; Am. studies lectr. U. Sidney, Melbourne U., U. Papua New Guinea, U. Queensland; lectr. U. Calif. Alumni Camps; U.S. Dept. State Cultural Exch. Program Yugoslavia, rep. for vis. historians from USSR. Author: Wilderness Politics and Indian Gifts, 1968, (Pacific Coast Am.-Hist. Assn. prize), The Historical World of Frederick Jackson Turner, 1968, Dispossessing the American Indian, 1985, Francis Parkman, The Historian As Hero, 1991; co-author; Turner Bolton and Webb, Three Historians of the Frontier, 1965, Survey of American History, 1949; editor: The Paxton Riots and The Frontier Theory, 1958, Letters of Francis Parkman, 1960 (runner up Pulitzer Prize in history 1961), Indians of the Southern Colonial Frontier, 1969, Benjamin Franklin, Philosopher-Statesman or Materialist, 1972; contbr. numerous articles, essays to profl. jours., newspapers, Encyclopedia Britannica. Mem. exec. bd. dirs. Get Oil Out, Santa Barbara, Throop Unitarian Ch., Pasadena; active Mass. Hist. Soc. Grantee Stanford U., Rockefeller Found., Ford Found., Am. Philos. Soc., Huntington Libr. Mem. Am. Hist. Assn. (Pacific Coast br., pres.), Am. Soc. Ethnohistory (pres.), Am. Soc. Environ. History (pres.), Am. Studies Assn. (pres. So. Calif. br.), Humane Soc. U.S. (nat. bd.), Econ. Roundtable So. Calif., Assocs. Calif. Inst. Tech.

JACOBSEN, GERALD BERNHARDT, biochemist; b. Spokane, Wash., Nov. 25, 1939; s. Hans Bernhardt and Mabel Grace (Swope) J.; m. Sally-Ann Heimbigner, June 7, 1961 (div. 1976); children: Claire Elise, Hans Edward; m. Jean Eva Robinson, Dec. 5, 1976. BA, Whitman Coll., 1961; MS, Purdue U., 1965, PhD, 1970. Postdoctoral fellow Oreg. State U., Corvallis, 1970-73; rsch. chemist Lamb-Weston, Inc., Portland, Oreg., 1973-85, sr. rsch. chemist, 1985—; presenter at profl. confs. Contbr. articles to profl. jours. Grantee NSF, 1960; NIH grad. fellow, 1965; Herman Frasch postdoctoral fellow Oreg. State U., 1970. Mem. AAAS, Am. Oil Chemists Soc., Am. Chemistry Soc., Assn. Ofcl. Analytical Chemists, Sigma Xi. Home: 1204 Knollwood Ct Richland WA 99352-9448 Office: Lamb Weston Tech Ctr 2005 Saint St Richland WA 99352-5306

JACOBSEN, JUDITH EVA, geography educator; b. Miami Beach, Fla., Dec. 27, 1952; d. Lyman William Jacobsen and Carolyn Elise (Comins) Burnham; m. John William Firor, Oct. 15, 1983. BA in Polit. Sci., U. Maine, 1975; JD, Coll. William & Mary, 1978; PhD in Geography, U. Colo., 1989. Bar: Va. 1979. Exec. dir. Carrying Capacity, Inc., Washington, 1981-82; sr. researcher Worldwatch Inst., Washington, 1982-83; asst. prof. U. Wyo., Laramie, 1989-93; cons. Am. Embassy, Lagos, Nigeria, summers 1984-85; adj. prof. U. Denver, 1993—. Author booklets U.S. Carrying Capacity, 1982, Promoting Population Stabilization, 1983, Population Change, Resources and Environment, 1983; contbr. articles to profl. publs., chpts. to books. Trustee Zero Population Growth, Washington, 1984-92, mem. exec. com., 1985-90, pres. bd., 1986-89; v.p. bd., chmn. fundraising Boulder Valley Women's Health Ctr., Boulder, Colo., 1985-87; trustee High County News, 1992—. Mem. Assn. Am. Geographers. Democrat.

JACOBSEN, KIM ANDREW, educational administrator, computer consultant; b. Fresno, Calif., May 17, 1952; s. Elmer Ernest and Violet Marie (Rassmussen) J.; m. Shirley Ann Kuhns, Dec. 18, 1976; children: Timothy Andrew, Kristi Lyn. BA in English, Calif. State U., Fresno, 1975. Cert. tchr. Calif. Payroll clk. Tenneco West, Inc., Del Rey, Calif., 1970-73, office mgr., 1973-76; tchr. Washington Jr. High Sch., Sanger, Calif., 1976-80, tchr. computers, 1980-84; coord. computer edn. Sanger Unified Sch. Dist., 1984—; computer cons., Fresno, 1985—; computer technician, Fresno, 1986—; tchr. computers adult edn. Nat. U., Fresno, 1988; dir. Calif. tech. project Capital Valley Consortium. Editor Instrnl. Svcs., 1986-88. Treas. Little League Baseball, Fresno, 1984—. Calif. Dept. Edn. grantee, 1981, 83. Mem. Computer Using Educator (v.p. 1981-82). Republican. Lutheran. Home: 1757 S Homsy Ave Fresno CA 93727-5976 Office: Sanger Unified Sch Dist 1905 7th St Sanger CA 93657-2897

JACOBSEN, LAREN, programmer/analyst; b. Salt Lake City, June 15, 1937; s. Joseph Smith and Marian (Thomas) J.; B.S., U. Utah, 1963; m. Audrey Bartlett, July 29, 1970 (div.); children—Andrea, Cecily, Julian. Programmer, IBM Corp., 1963-70; systems programmer Xerox Computer Services, 1970-79; sr. systems analyst Quotron Systems, Los Angeles, 1979-86; programmer/analyst Great Western Bank, 1987-92; pres. Prescient Investments Co., 1975-82. Served with USAR, 1961. Mem. Am. Guild Organists (dean San Jose chpt. 1967), Mensa. Home: PO Box 91174 Los Angeles CA 90009-1174

JACOBSEN, MARK LEE, bank officer; b. Twin Falls, Idaho, July 9, 1965; s. Elvernon B. and Kathryn Arlene (Anderson) J. BBA, Idaho State U., 1987. Mgmt. trainee First Security Bank, Boise, Idaho, 1987-88; credit analyst First Security Bank, Boise, 1988-89; credit analyst First Security Bank, Pocatello, Idaho, 1988, comml. loan officer, 1989-90; comml. loan officer First Security Bank, Idaho Falls, Idaho, 1990-91; asst. v.p., asst. mgr. First Security Bank, Burley, Idaho, 1991—; bd. dirs., facilitator, instr. Women's Fin. Info. Programs, Burley, 1991—; instr. Am. Inst. Banking, Burley, 1991—; with Rotary Internat. Group Study Exchange, England, 1992. Capt. Portneuf Valley Paintfest, Pocatello, 1989, 90, Hands Helping Homes, Idaho Falls, 1991; bd. dirs. Mt. Harrison Heritage Found., Burley, 1992, Chief Theatre Found., Pocatello, 1989-91. Mem. Burley Area C. of C., Lions, Alpha Kappa Psi (v.p. 1986-87). Office: First Security Bank PO Box 38 Burley ID 83318

JACOBSEN, REBECCA HANSON, psychologist; b. Dallas, Oreg., Mar. 1, 1949; d. Earl Willard and Virginia (Van Mourik) H.; m. Michael Anthony Jacobsen, Sept. 25, 1970; 1 child, Leif Peter. BA, CCNY, 1972, MS, 1974; MS, U. Ga., 1980, PhD, 1982. Lic. psychologist, Calif. Asst. rsch. scientist N.Y. State Psychiat. Inst., 1974-77; grad. teaching asst. U. Oreg., Eugene, 1978-79; psychology intern. VA Med. Ctr., Durham, N.C., 1980-81; asst. prof. Med. Coll. Ga., Augusta, 1983-86; clin. psychologist VA Med. Ctr., Augusta, 1982-86, V.A. Med. Ctr., Sepulveda, Calif., 1986—; clin. asst. prof. Fuller Theol. Sem., Pasadena, Calif., 1987—, Neuropsychiat. Inst. UCLA, 1991—; postdoctoral fellow tng. program neuropsychology, 1988-90; tng. fellow Ind. Consultation Ctr., Bronx, 1974-77. Contbr. articles to profl. jours. U. Ga. fellow, 1981-82. Mem. Am. Psychol. Assn., Nat. Orgn. VA. Psychologists, Internat. Neuropsychol. Soc., Psychologists in Pub. Svc. Democrat. Avocations: tennis, gourmet food, bird-watching, needlework.

JACOBSEN, RICHARD T., mechanical engineering educator; b. Pocatello, Idaho, Nov. 12, 1941; s. Thorleif and Edith Emily (Gladwin) J.; m. Vicki Belle Hopkins, July 16, 1959 (div. Mar. 1973); children: Pamela Sue, Richard T., Eric Ernest; m. Bonnie Lee Stewart, Oct. 19, 1973; 1 child, Jay Michael; stepchild: Erik David Lustig. BSME, U. Idaho, 1963, MSME, 1965; PhD in Engring. Sci., Wash. State U., 1972. Registered profl. engr., Idaho. Instr. U. Idaho, 1964-66, asst. prof. mech. engring., 1966-72, assoc. prof., 1972-77, prof., 1977—, chmn. dept. mech. engring., 1980-85, assoc. dean engring., 1985-90, assoc. dir. Ctr. for Applied Thermodynamic Studies, 1975-86, dir., 1986—, dean engring., 1990—. Author: International Union of Pure and Applied Chemistry, Nitrogen-International Thermodynamic Tables of the Fluid State-6, 1979; Oxygen-International Thermodynamic Tables of the Fluid State-9, 1987, Ethylene-International Thermodynamic Tables of the Fluid State-10, 1988, ASHRAE Thermodynamic Properties of Refrigerants (2 vols.), 1986; numerous reports on thermodynamic properties of fluids, 1971—; contbr. articles to profl. jours. NSF sci. faculty fellow, 1968-69; NSF rsch. and travel grantee, 1976-83; Nat. Inst. Standards and Tech. grantee, 1974-91, Gas Rsch. Inst. grantee, 1986-91, 1992—, Dept. Energy grantee, 1991—. Fellow ASME (faculty advisor 1972-75, 78-84, chmn. region VIII dept. heads com. 1983-85, honors and awards chmn. 1985-91, K-7 tech. com. thermophys. properties 1985—, chmn. 1986-89, 92—, rsch. tech. com. on water and steam in thermal power systems, 1988—, gen. awards com. 1985-91, chmn. 1988-91, com. on honors 1988—, mem. bd. on profl. practice and ethics, 1991—), N.W. Coll. and Univ. Assn. for Sci. (bd. dirs. 1990—), Idaho Rsch. Found. (bd. dirs. 1991—), Soc. Automotive Engrs. (Ralph R. Teetor Edn. award, Detroit 1968), ASHRAE (co-recipient Best Tech. Paper award 1984), Sigma Xi, Tau Beta Pi, Phi Kappa Phi (Disting. Faculty award 1989). Office: U Idaho Coll Engring Office of Dean Janssen Engring Bldg 125 Moscow ID 83844

JACOBSMEYER, JAY MICHAEL, electrical engineer; b. Okaloosa County, Fla., Mar. 13, 1959; s. John Henry and Patricia Ann (McDonough) J.; m. Joyce Ann Deem, June 20, 1981; children: Abigail Ann, Brian James. BS magna cum laude, Va. Poly. Inst. & State U., 1981; MS, Cornell U., 1987. Registered profl. engr., Colo. Commd. 2nd lt. USAF, 1981-90, advanced through grades to capt., 1985; elec. engr. 3397 Tech. Tng. Squadron, Biloxi, Miss., 1981-82; comm. engr. 1st Combat Comm. Group, Wiesbaden, Germany, 1982-85; communications engr. HQ Air Force Space Command, Colorado Springs, 1987-90; resigned USAF, 1990; staff engr. ENSCO, Inc., Colorado Springs, 1990-91, sr. staff engr., 1991-93; co-founder, chief tech. officer Pericle Comm. Co., 1992—. Patent pending wireless data modem; contbr. articles to profl. publs. Maj. USAFR. Decorated Meritorious Svc. medal, Air Force Commendation medal; named Man of Yr., Va. Poly. Inst. and State U., 1981; rsch. grantee, NSF, USN. Mem. IEEE (sr.), Armed Forces Comm. and Electronics Assn. (v.p. 1989-90), Air Force Assn., Omicron Delta Kappa, Eta Kappa Nu. Home: 2475 Edenderry Dr Colorado Springs CO 80919

JACOBSON, ARTHUR, painter, art educator; b. Chicago, Jan. 10, 1924; s. Harry and Gertrude (Goldenson) J.; m. Ursula Sanbuber Jacobson, July 21, 1955; 1 child, Leah. BS, U. Wis., 1948, MS, 1950. Tchr. Taos (N.Mex.) Valley Art Sch., 1952-53, Philbrook Art Ctr., Tulsa, 1953-54; prof. Ariz. State U., Tempe, Ariz., 1956-86; prof. emeritus Ariz. State U., Tempe, 1986—; guest prof. U. Wis., Madison, 1967-68. One-man shows include Yares Gallery, 1981, Kerr Cultural Ctr., 1989, Ariz. Western Coll., Yuma, 1989, Medford Gallery, Tucson, 1992; represented in permanent collections Phoenix Mus., N.Mex. Mus., Ariz. State U., Hastings Coll., Ariz. Western Coll., Dallas Mus., Pa. Acad. Fine Arts and also pvt. collections. Sgt. U.S. Army, 1943-45. Home: 7209 E Mcdonald Dr Unit 47 Scottsdale AZ 85250-6051

JACOBSON, CRAIG LOWELL, sales and marketing executive; b. Chgo., July 7, 1955; s. Lowell Howard and Eleanor Louise (Waghorne) J.; m. Jane Williams, Apr. 18, 1987. BA in Econs., Vanderbilt U., 1977; MBA, Duke U., 1979. Bus. analyst Am. Hosp. Supply Corp., Evanston, Ill., 1979-84; from sales forecasting mgr. to custom products mgr. Am. Pharm., Glendale, Calif., 1980-84; product dir. Johnson & Johnson, San Diego, 1985-89, internat. sales mgr., 1989—. Inventor MINITWIN orthodontic bracket. Mem. Am. Mgmt. Assn., World Trade Assn. (San Diego chpt.). Home: 403 Gardendale Rd Encinitas CA 92024-1948 Office: "A" Co 11436 Sorrento Valley Rd San Diego CA 92121-1393

JACOBSON, DAWN ADELE, artist, architectural historian; b. Pitts., Jan. 28, 1956; d. Donald Richard and Mary Audrey (McQuaide) Tuttle; m. Stephen Norman, May 14, 1978. BA in History, Calif. State U., Northridge, 1984. Prin. Jacobson Assocs., Vallejo, Calif., 1979—. Democrat. Home: 933 Florida St Vallejo CA 94590

JACOBSON, DONALD THOMAS, management consultant; b. Powers Lake, N.D., June 5, 1932; s. Martin I. and Gladys E. (Thronson) J.; BA, Whitman Coll., 1954; MBA, Stanford U., 1956; m. Andrea Marie Moore, Aug. 14, 1954; 1 child, Kathryn E. Hanson. Sales and mktg. mgmt. Guy F. Atkinson Co., Portland, Oreg., 1959-63; sales control mgr. Boise Cascade Corp., Portland, 1964-66; v.p. and dir. rsch. Lund, McCutcheon, Jacobson, Inc., Portland, 1966-74; pres. Mgmt./Mktg. Assocs., Inc., Portland, 1974—; chmn. Oreg. Bus. Workshops, 1974-76; exec. com., dir. Full-Circle, Inc., 1971-77. Lt. U.S. Army, 1956-59. Decorated commendation ribbon; recipient Oreg. Econ. Devel. award, 1973; Mem. Am. Mktg. Assn. (pres. Oreg. chpt. 1972-73, bd. dirs. 1967-74, 89-93, Oreg. Marketer of Yr. award 1991, chair Internat. Outreach Com., 1992-93), Am. Mgmt. Assn., Inst. Mgmt. Cons. (cert.; founding mem., founder and pres. Pacific N.W. chpt. 1980-81), Mktg. Rsch. Assn., Nat. Assn. Bus. Economists, Portland Metro. C. of C. (bd. dirs. 1987-90, chmn.'s award Outstanding Svc., 1987), Met. Chambers Econ. Devel. Coun. Portland Area (chmn. mktg. task force 1983-85, emerging issues com., 1987-89, labor policy com. 1988-91, chmn. Tri-Met Task Force 1985-88, chmn. transpn. com. 1987-88), The Planning Forum (v.p. Oreg. chpt. 1986-87, bd. dirs., 1986-90), U.S. Dept. Commerce (nat. def. exec. res. 1966—), (chmn. Oreg.-Idaho assn. 1969-70), Oregonians for Cost-Effective Govt. (bd. dirs. 1986-90, bd. advisor 1991-92), Econ. Roundtable (coord. 1982—), Whitman Coll. Alumni Assn. (pres. 1975-77), Stanford U. Bus. Sch. Assn. (founding pres. Portland chpt. 1971-72), Phi Beta Kappa. Republican. Lutheran. Contbr. articles on mgmt. and mktg. to profl. jours. Home: 3635 SW 87th Ave # 18 Portland OR 97225-2838 Office: Mgmt/Mktg Assocs Inc Bank Of Calif Tower Ste 1460 Portland OR 97205

JACOBSON, ERIC SCOTT, lawyer; b. Santa Monica, Calif., Aug. 20, 1952; s. Jerome P. and Hortense A. Jacobson; m. Lucia M. Tobin, May 5, 1978; children: McKim R., Gabriella L. BA, Antioch Coll., 1974; JD, U. So. Calif., L.A., 1977. Bar: Calif. 1977. Assoc. Edwin M. Rosenberg, P.C., L.A., 1977-80; pvt. practice L.A., 1980—; dir. West Coast studies Right On Rsch., San Francisco, 1974-84. Commr. Roller Games Internat., L.A., 1981-88. Clore Warne Intern fellow Constitutional Rights Found., L.A., 1975. Office: 3580 Wilshire Blvd # 2030 Los Angeles CA 90010-2529

JACOBSON, FRANK JOEL, cultural organization adminisrator; b. Phila., Sept. 14, 1948; s. Leonard and June Anette (Groff) J.; m. Stephanie Lou Savage, July 5, 1970; children: Aaron Jeffery, Adam Michael, Ashley Celeste. BA, U. Wis., 1970; MFA, Boston U., 1973. Mng. dir. Mont. Repertory Theater, Missoula, Mo., 1973-75; asst. prof. drama U. Mont., Missoula, 1973-75; program dir. Western States Arts Found., Denver, 1975-77, dir. programs, 1977-78, gen. mgr. budget/planning, 1978-79; exec. dir. Arvada (Colo.) Ctr. for the Arts & Humanities, 1979-85; dir. theatres and arenas City & County of Denver, 1985-87; pres., CEO Scottsdale (Ariz.) Cultural Coun., 1987—; bd. dirs. Met. Denver Arts Alliance, pres., 1979-85, Rocky Mountain Arts Consortium, pres., 1979-80. Contbr. articles to profl. jours. Mem. panel theater program NEA, Washington, 1990-92; bd. dirs. Scottsdale Focus, 1988-92, Arizonans for Cultural Devel., 1992—. Named one of Outstanding Men in Am., Jaycees, 1980. Mem. Am. Theatre Assn. (bd. dirs. 1976-78), Mont. State Theatre Assn. (bd. dirs., pres. 1974-75), Rocky Mountain Theatre Assn. (bd. dirs., pres. 1976-78), Assn. for Performing Arts Presenters (bd. dirs. 1984-87). Office: Scottsdale Cultural Coun 7383 E Scottsdale Mall Scottsdale AZ 85251-4414

JACOBSON, JON STANLEY, history educator; b. Oxnard, Calif., Feb. 12, 1938; s. Stanley Joel and Niona Elizabeth (Lindquist) J.; m. Patricia A. O'Brien, Aug. 26, 1989; children: Kirsten, Margreta. BA, U. Calif., Berkeley, 1959, MA, 1960, PhD, 1965. Asst. prof. history U. Calif., Irvine, 1965-72, assoc. prof., 1972—. Author: Locarno Diplomacy, 1972; contbr. articles to profl. jours. Recipient George Louis Beer prize Am. Hist. Assn., 1972. Office: U Calif Dept History Irvine CA 92717

JACOBSON, JUDITH HELEN, state senator; b. South Bend, Ind., Feb. 26, 1939; d. Robert Marcene and Leah (Alexander) Haxton; m. John Raymond Jacobson, 1963; children—JoDee, Eric, Wendy. Student U. Wis.-Milw. and Madison, 1957-60. Mem. Mont. Senate, 1980—. Mem. Nat. Conf. State Legislators (human resources com. 1981—, del. Mont. Med. Aux. (legis. chmn. 1981—). Democrat. Lutheran. Office: Mt State Senate State Capitol Helena MT 59620

JACOBSON, RAYMOND EARL, electronics company executive; b. St. Paul, May 25, 1922; s. Albert H. and Gertrude W. (Anderson) J.; BE with high honors, Yale U., 1944; MBA with distinction, Harvard U., 1948; B.A. (Rhodes scholar), Oxford U., 1950, M.A., 1954; m. Margaret Maxine Meadows, Dec. 22, 1959 (dec. 1987); children: Michael David, Karl Raymond, Christopher Eric. Asst. to gen. mgr. PRD Electronics, Inc., Bklyn., 1951-55; sales mgr. Curtiss-Wright Electronics Div., Carlstadt, N.J., 1955-57; dir. mktg. TRW Computers Co., Los Angeles, 1957-60; v.p. ops. Electro-Sci. Investors, Dallas, 1960-63; pres. Whitehall Electronics, Inc., Dallas, 1961-63, dir., 1961-63; chmn. bd. Gen. Electronic Control, Inc., Mpls., 1961-63, Staco, Inc., Dayton, Ohio, 1961-63; pres. Maxson Electronics Corp., Gt. River, N.Y., 1963-64, Jacobson Assocs., San Jose, Calif., 1964-67; co-founder, pres., chmn., chief exec. officer Anderson Jacobson, Inc., San Jose, 1967-88; chmn. Anderson Jacobson, SA, Paris, 1974-88; mng. dir. Anderson Jacobson, Ltd., London, 1975-85; chmn. Anderson Jacobson Can., Ltd./Ltée, Toronto, 1975-85, Anderson Jacobson, GmbH, Cologne, 1978-83, CXR Corp., San Jose, 1988—; bd. dirs. Tamar Electronics, Inc., L.A., Rawco Instruments, Inc., Dallas, 1960-63; lectr. engring., UCLA, 1958-60; mem. underwriting Lloyd's London, 1975—. Committeeman, Eagle Scout Boy Scouts Am. Lt. (j.g.) USNR, 1943-46. Mem. Am. Assn. Rhodes Scholars, Harvard Bus. Sch. Assn., Sigma Xi, Tau Beta Pi. Republican. Lutheran. Clubs: Yale, Courtside Tennis, Seascape Swim and Racquet. Home: 1247 Montcourse Ln San Jose CA 95131-2420 Office: CXR Corp 521 Charcot Ave San Jose CA 95131-1118

JACOBSON, STEVE EVAN, production company executive; b. St. Louis, May 8, 1955; s. Leonard and June Annette (Groff) J.; m. Jane Elizabeth Heal, Sept. 5, 1980. BA, U. So. Calif., L.A., 1977. Prodn. asst. on-air promotion ABC, L.A., 1978; writer Walt Disney Prodns., Burbank, Calif., 1978-79; freelance producer on-air promotion NBC, Burbank, 1979-81, writer, producer on-air promotion, 1981-83, mgr. on-air promotion, 1983-88; v.p. on-air promotion CBS, L.A., 1988-93; pres. Pittard-Sullivan-Fitzgerald, Inc. and Nu Pictures, Inc., 1993—. Co-producer (film) Junior High School, 1978 (over 40 internat. awards 1978-79). Recipient Bronze award Broadcast Designers Assn., 1988, 90, 93, Finalist award Internat. Film & TV Festival, N.Y., 1988. Mem. Broadcast Promotion & Mktg. Execs., U. So. Calif.-Cinema/TV Alumni Assn. Office: Pittard Sullivan Fitzgerald 6430 Sunset Blvd Ste 200 Hollywood CA 90028

JACOBSON, THOMAS ERNEST, physician; b. Berlin, Germany, Aug. 8, 1931; came to U.S., 1940; s. Max and Alice (Lowner) J.; children by previous marriage: Gail Ellen, Lauren Kay, Randall Allen. AB, U. Mich., 1952; MD, Howard U., 1956. Diplomate Am. Bd. Internal Medicine, Sub-bd. Cardiol. Intern Meadow Brook Hosp., L.I., 1956-57; resident State U. Iowa Hosps., Iowa City, 1959-60, Met. Hosp., N.Y.C., 1960-61; fellow in cardiology Mt. Sinai Hosp., N.Y.C., 1961-62; practice internal medicine Encino, Calif., 1962-67; practice medicine specializing in cardiology Tarzana, Calif., 1967—; mem. attending staff Cedars of Lebanon Hosp., L.A.; dir. coronary unit West Park Hosp., Canoga Park, 1969—; co-dir. coronary care unit West Hills Hosp., Canoga Park, 1970; clin. instr. medicine U. Calif., L.A., 1966—. Capt. USAF, 1957-59. Grantee Regional Med. Program, 1968-70; recipient Heart Recognition award L.A. Heart Assn., 1969. Fellow ACP, N.Am. Soc. for Pacing and Electrophysiology, Am. Coll. Chest Physicians, Am. Coll. Cardiology; mem. AMA, L.A. County Med. Assn. (sec.-treas. San Fernando Valley br. 1977), Mt. Sinai Alumni, Phi Delta Epsilon. Office: 5th Fl 7230 Medical Center Dr West Hills CA 91307

JACOBSON-BARNES, DARRYL LYNN, insurance agency executive; b. Phila., Apr. 4, 1957; d. Stanley Irwin and Marcia Grace (Krokow) Jacobson; m. Robert Alan Barnes, Oct. 12, 1985. BS in Biology, U. Ariz., 1977; postgrad., Am. Coll., Bryn Mawr, Pa., 1984-86. CLU. Multi-line sales rep. Met. Life Ins. Co., Tucson, Scottsdale, Ariz., 1978-83; field trainer Bankers Life Nebr., Scottsdale, 1983; field supt. agys. Sentry Ins., Scottsdale, 1983-85; group rep. Crown Life Ins. Co., Phoenix, 1986-87; owner, mgr. Darryl Jacobson-Barnes & Assoc., Mesa, Tempe, Ariz., 1985—, All-Star Ins. Agy., Tempe, 1990—; ptnr. HSG Co. subs. Harris Scholnik, Phoenix, 1988-90; pub. speaker, 1987—; testified on health care related bills and reform to U.S. Congress and State Legislature, 1988—. Vol. healthcare cons. Congressman Kyl's Reelection Com., Phoenix, 1992; chmn. March of Dimes Teamwalk, 1983; founder Women's Tips Group, Scottsdale, 1983; participant Sen. DeConcini's Vision 2000 Group, 1992. Recipient cert. of appreciation Scottsdale C. of C. Mem. Nat. Assn. Health Underwriters (lobbyist 1981—, legis. chmn. 1985—, founder health care coalition 1990—, participant Capital Conf. 1991—), Nat. Assn. Life Underwriters (various bd. offices Scottsdale 1981-85), Leading Prodrs. Round Table. Republican. Jewish. Office: All-Star Ins Agy 2426 E Wesleyan Dr Tempe AZ 85282

JACOBY, ERIKA, social worker; b. Miskolc, Hungary, May 1, 1928; came to U.S. 1949; d. Jeno and Malvina (Salamonovits) Engel; m. Emil Jacoby, Sept. 24, 1950; children: Jonathan D., Benjamin M., Michael D. BA, Calif. State U., Northridge, 1971; MSW, U. So. Calif., L.A., 1975. Tchr. Adat Ari El Religious Sch., North Hollywood, Calif., 1961-73; tchr./counselor Camp Ramah, Ojai, Calif., summers 1961-72; clin. social worker Family Svc. of L.A., Van Nuys, 1975-80; psychiatric social worker Kaiser Psychiatry, Van Nuys, 1980—; clin. social worker in pvt. practice North Hollywood, Calif., 1975—; lectr. in field; conductor workshops in field. Contbr. articles to profl. jours. Mem. Nat. Assn. Social Workers, Common Cause, Hadassah, Amnesty Internat., Adat Ari El. Democrat. Jewish. Office: Kaiser Permanente 13746 Victory Blvd Van Nuys CA 91401-2391

JACOBY, JOHN FREEDLEY, business owner; b. Phila., Mar. 26, 1945; s. James Dillon and Mary Louise (Javoronok) J.; m. Kwai-Chu Leung, Nov. 9, 1969. AA, Napa Valley Coll., 1992; student, U. Calif. Berkeley, 1992. Merchant seaman Sun Oil Co., Marcus Hook, Pa., 1963; agent Gen. Steamship Corp., San Francisco, 1967-81; CEO Borgen Shipping Co., San Francisco, 1981; v.p. Winfield Fin. Corp., Moraga, Calif., 1982-83; loans officer Union Corp., San Francisco, 1983-88; prin., operator Jacoby & Assocs., Vallejo, Calif., 1988—.

JACOBY, PETER FREDRICKSON, music educator; b. Laramie, Wyo., July 27, 1947; s. Glenn J. and Dorothy (Fredrickson) J.; m. Margaret E. Judd, Mar. 5, 1973 (div. 1983). BA in Music magna cum laude, U. Wyo., 1969; Diploma, U. Vienna Acad. Music, Austria, 1975. Opera coach Zurich Opera House, Switzerland, 1975-76; gen. ptnr. E.L. Price Assoc., San Francisco and Chgo., 1976-78; exec. dir. The Prelude Co., San Francisco, 1978-80; pres., chief exec. officer Bighorn Energy Co., Ft. Collins, Colo., 1980—; exec. v.p. Newcomb Securities Co., N.Y.C., 1981-84; sr. mgr. E.L. Price Bank, Galveston, Tex., 1983-87, also bd. dirs.; pres., chief exec. officer Code A Check, Inc., Cheyenne, Wyo., 1988-89; prof. Sch. Music U. Houston, 1989—. Bd. dirs. Van Ness Arts Ctr., San Francisco, 1978-79, Ft. Collins Art Inc., 1981-82. Sgt. U.S. Army, 1969-71. Republican. Episcopalian. Home: 3912 Roseneath Dr Houston TX 77021-1544 Office: U Houston Sch Music Houston TX 77204-4893

JACOBY, SANFORD MARK, management educator, historian; b. N.Y.C., May 13, 1953; s. Arthur and Doris (Alexander) J.; m. Susan Bartholomew, Sept. 9, 1984; children: Alexander, Margaret. AB magna cum laude, U. Pa., 1973; PhD in Econs., U. Calif., Berkeley, 1981. Asst. prof. UCLA Grad. Sch. Mgmt. and History Dept., 1980-85, assoc. prof., 1985-90, prof., 1990—; rsch. assoc. UCLA Inst. Indsl. Rels., 1980-90, assoc. dir., 1990—; vis. scholar Cornell U., Ithaca, N.Y., 1989-90. Author: Employing Bureaucracy, 1985 (Terry prize 1986); editor: Masters to Managers, 1991, National Labor, Global Capital; mem. editorial bd. Calif. Mgmt. Rev., 1983—, Indsl. Rels. Jour., 1985—, Labor History, 1991—; contbr. articles to profl. jours.; coauthor numerous books. Rsch. fellow NEH, 1989; recipient Nevins prize Econ. History Assn., 1982, Yardley prize U. Pa., 1974. Mem. Am. Soc. Assn., Indsl. Rels. Rsch. Assn. (chair nominating com. 1987), Am. Econ. Assn., Orgn. Am. Historians, Soc. for the Advancement of Socioecons. Office: UCLA Grad Sch Mgmt 405 Hilgard Ave Los Angeles CA 90024-1481

JACQUEZ, JOSEPHINE, educator; b. Las Vegas, N.Mex., May 2, 1930; d. Conrad and Juanita (Sandoval) Aragon; m. Sebastian Jacquez, Aug. 18, 1970; 1 child, Yvette Marie. BA, Immaculate Heart Coll., L.A., 1966; postgrad., U. Fullerton, Pepperdine U. 2nd grade tchr. Canal Zone, Panama, 1966-70; 5th grade tchr. L.A. Pub. Schs., 1970-75; reading resource tchr. Lynwood, Calif., 1975-81, bilingual resource tchr., 1981-87, 1st grade tchr., 1987-88; adult edn. tchr. Montebello, Calif., 1988-90, 1st grade tchr., 1990—; religious educator De Paul Sem., 1990. Sch. rep. Washington Sch. Tchrs. Union, Lynwood, 1976; rep. Montebello Tchrs. Union, 1990-92; vol. ARC. Recipient PTA Svc. award, Montebello, 1989, Red Cross award Whittier divsn. ARC, 1989. Mem. Delta Kappa Gamma (pres. 1984, corr. sec., Gold pin 1988). Democrat. Roman Catholic. Home: 7302 Pellet St Downey CA 90241 Office: Bandini Elem Sch 2318 Couts Ave Commerce CA 90040

JAEGER, JEFF TODD, professional football player; b. Tacoma, Wash., Nov. 26, 1964. With Cleve. Browns, 1987; kicker L.A. Raiders, 1989—. Office: L.A. Raiders 332 Center St El Segundo CA 90245

JAEGER, SHARON ANN, educator, poet, publisher; b. Douglas, Ariz., Jan. 15, 1945; d. Paul and Catherine (Simon) Jaeger. BA summa cum laude, U. Dayton, 1966; MA in English, Boston Coll., 1971; DA in English, SUNY-Albany, 1982; MA in Comparative Lit. and Lit. Theory, U. Pa., 1990, Co-instr. creative writing, instr. writing ctr. Rensselaer Polytech. Inst., Troy, N.Y., 1978-79; tutor writing workshop SUNY, Albany, 1979-80; co-editor Sachem Press, Old Chatham, N.Y., 1980—; editor Intertext, Anchorage, 1982—; Fulbright lectr. U. Nova de Lisboa and U. de Aveiro, Portugal, 1983-84; poetry reader throughout country, 1979—; coord. Jawbone Reading Series, Albany, 1981-82; co-instr. writers' workshop, Appalachian Writers Assn., Johnson City, Tenn., July 1983; freelance editor Phila. Mus. Art, 1987; vis. asst. prof. Haverford Coll., 1987-88; vis. lectr. U. Pa., 1988, 90—; reporter Valdez Vanguard, 1989; editor The Cordova Times, 1990. Author: (poetry) Filaments of Affinity, 1989, The Chain of Dead Desire, 1990; co-translator Rainer Maria Rilke, Duino Elegies, 1991; contbr. poetry to anthologies and periodicals, article and book reviews to profl. jours. Vol. DeWitt Nursing Home, N.Y.C., 1973-75. Recipient 1st place award Ezra Pound Competition for Literary Translation, 1988, 90, 91, 93, 1st place award McKinney Literary Competition, 1979, Best of Issue award Western Poetry Quar., 1978, first place William Carlos Williams award, 1992, Alpha Sigma Tau Honor Key award U. Dayton, Ohio, 1966, Profl. Journalist award Alaska Press Club, 1990, 3 Profl. Journalist awards Sigma Delta Chi, 1989; Austrian Govt. scholar U. Salzburg, summer 1966; research fellow U. Pa., Phila., 1982-83; Presdl. fellow SUNY, 1979-82. Mem. Comparative Lit. Assn. of Students (pres. U. Pa. 1982-83), Poetry Soc. Am., Acad. Am. Poets, Am. Comparative Lit. Assn., Modern Lang. Assn., Rhetoric Soc. Am., Northeast Modern Lang. Assn., Associated Writing Programs, Fulbright Alumni Assn.

JAFFER, ADRIAN MICHAEL, physician; b. Cape Town, S. Africa, Aug. 24, 1943; came to U.S., 1969; s. George Daniel Jaffer and Theresa (Kourie) Binsted; children: Brendan, Terence. MBchB, U. Cape Town Med. Sch., 1966. Diplomate Am. Coll. Physicians. Intern Loyola Univ. Hosp., Maywood, Ill., 1969-70; resident Northwestern U., Chgo., 1970-72; fellow Harvard U., Boston, 1972-73, Scapps Clinic & Rsch., LaJolla, Calif., 1973-75, Northwestern U., Chgo., 1975-76; pvt. practice LaJolla, 1976—; assoc. clin. prof. U. Calif. San Diego, LaJolla, 1976—. Contbr. articles to profl. jours. Mem. AMA, Am. Coll. Rheumotology, Am. Acad. Allergy. Office: 9850 Genesee Ave # 860 La Jolla CA 92037-1214

JAGER, FRED GERRIT, corporate finance executive; b. Chgo., Sept. 30, 1938; s. Fred M. and Barbara Agnus (Jaeger) J.; m. Judith Ann Tucker, Aug. 20, 1960 (div. Oct. 1981); children: David Scott, Mary Elizabeth, Patrick Tucker; m. Marcia Jane Wise, June 8, 1985. Student, Iowa State U., 1956-58, Naperville Coll., 1958; BA, U. Iowa, 1960. With fin. sales Pritchard & Co., Denver, 1960-62; intelligence officer USN, Morocco, England, U.S., 1962-69; exec. v.p., chief operating officer Career Acad., Inc., Milw., 1969-72; pres. Jager & Co., Inc., Denver, 1972-86, Geneva Bus. Svcs., Irvine, Calif., 1986—; speaker numerous groups, 1969—; dir. 4 pub., 13 pvt. corps. Contbr. over 400 articles to profl. jours. Founder, pres. Colo. Crime Commn., Denver, 1978; pres. Colo. Assn. Children with Learning Disabilities, Denver, 1978-79; trustee Nat. Asthma Ctr., Denver, 1977, Denver Zoo, 1976-86, Colo. Spl. Olympics, Denver, 1980-86. Mem. Internat. Assn. Corp. Growth (v.p. 1989-91), Internat. Forum for Corp. Dirs. (chmn. 1992-93). Home: 407 Emerald Bay Laguna Beach CA 92651-1214 Office: Geneva Bus Svcs Inc 5 Park Plaza Irvine CA 92714

JAGER, MERLE LEROY, aerospace engineer; b. Eugene, Oreg., Sept. 22, 1942; s. Earl Christian and Alma Marie (Jensen) J.; m. Shannon Kay Jacobsen, Mar. 18, 1967; children: Holly, Peter, Melanie, Marissa,. BS in Mech. Engring., Oreg. State U., 1965; MS in Aeronautical Engring., U. So. Calif., 1967. Aerodynamicist Lockheed-Calif. Co., Burbank, 1965-68; rsch. engr. The Boeing Co., Seattle, 1968-70; aerodynamics engr. Gates Learjet Corp., Torrance, Calif., 1970; project engr. Irvin Industries, Inc., Gardena, Calif., 1971-73; aerodynamics mgr. Northrop Corp., Hawthorne, Calif., 1973-91; mgr. flight mechanics Northrop Corp., Pico Rivera, Calif., 1991—. Patentee in field. Treas. Goldenwest Assn., Westminster, Calif., 1976-78; tribal chief YMCA Indian Princess Program, Huntingdon Beach, Calif., 1986-87; bishopric counselor Mormon Ch., Westminster, 1986—. Mem. AIAA, Tau Beta Pi, Pi Tau Sigma, Sigma Tau. Republican. Home: 15282 Notre Dame St Westminster CA 92683-6117 Office: Northrop Corp Aircraft Div Advanced Tech./Design Ctr 8900 E Washington Blvd Pico Rivera CA 90660

JAGER, TAMMY S., lawyer; b. Fontana, Calif., Nov. 4, 1963; d. Jacob Herbert and Norma Lee (Willis) J. BA in Psychology, Calif. State U., 1986; JD, U. La Verne, 1989. Bar: Calif. 1989. Sec. Reardon, McCallum & Co., Upland, Calif., 1979-84; counselor Ontario (Calif.) Community Hosp., 1985-86; interviewer Office Pub. Defender San Bernardino County, Calif., 1985-86; assoc. Covington and Crowe, Ontario, 1989—. Mem. Calif. Young Lawyers Assn., Calif. Trial Lawyers Assn., San Bernardino County Bar Assn., Western San Bernardino County Bar Assn., U. La. Verne Coll. of Law Alumni Assn. (bd. dirs.), Delta Theta Phi (dist. chancellor). Office: Covington & Crowe 1131 W 6th St Ste 300 Ontario CA 91762-1118

JAIN, CHANDRA PRABHA, chemist; b. Kanpur, India, Mar. 11, 1948; came to U.S., 1968; d. Tilak P. and Akshama R. (Jain) Oswal; m. Staish K. Jain, Sept. 30, 1968; children: Ravi, Kiran. BSc, Christ Church Coll., Kanpur, 1966; MSc, M.E. Coll., Gwalior, India, 1968; MA, Calif. State U., Fullerton, 1976. Assoc. chemist Beckman Inst. Inc., Fullerton, 1977-79, chemist, 1979-81; sr. chemist Beckman Inst. Inc., Brea, Calif., 1981-86, staff scientist, 1986-88, project scientist, 1988-91, sr. project scientist, 1991-92, dept. mgr., 1992—. Patentee in field. Judge high sch. sci. fair, Orange County, 1990—. Mem. Am. Assn. Clin. Chemistry, Am. Chem. Soc. Office: Beckman Instrument Inc 200 S Kraemer Blvd Brea CA 92621-6209

JAIN, MUKESH K., publisher; b. Ambala, Haryana, India, Aug. 3, 1948; came to U.S., 1970; s. Digamber K. and Padma R. Jain; m. Namita Jain, Dec. 9, 1979; children: Monika, Ambika. BS, Roorkee U., India, 1970; MBA, Okla. State U., 1973. Mgr. fin. Litton Industries, Sunnyvale, Calif., 1973-88; pub. Asian Humanities Press, Fremont, Calif., 1989—. Mem. Assn. for Asian Studies, Am. Booksellers Assn., Internat. Assn. Ind. Pubs. Office: Asian Humanities Press PO Box 3523 Fremont CA 94539

JAKOBSEN, JAKOB KNUDSEN, mechanical engineer; b. Bording Sogn, Denmark, Aug. 7, 1912; came to U.S., 1952, naturalized, 1958; s. Laust Peder and Inger Marie (Kristensen) J.; m. Eva Koch, Nov. 19, 1941 (dec. 1983); children—Marianne Gyrithe (Mrs. Earl C. Green), Peter Laust (dec. 1969), Claus Michael, Suzanne Elizabeth (Mrs. Paul B. Marsh), Niels-Olaf Sejten, Lars Jakob. M.S. in Mech. Engring, Royal Tech. U. Denmark, 1941. Registered profl. engr., Mich., Calif. Asst. to prof. machine design Royal Tech. U., Denmark, 1941; mech. engr. turbines Brown Boveri et Cie, Switzerland, 1941-43; project engr. co-generation steam power sta. Pub. Power Utilities of Copenhagen, Denmark, 1943-45; mech. engr., asst. to chief engr. turbo-supercharge two-stroke marine Diesel engines Burmeister & Wain, Copenhagen, 1945-52; gas turbine engr. Clark Bros. div. Dresser Industries, Olean, N.Y., 1952-55; staff engr. automotive research Chrysler Corp., Detroit, 1955-60; sr. tech. specialist for R&D of liquid rocket engines for space program Rocketdyne div. Rockwell Internat., Canoga Park, Calif., 1960-77; cons. to industry on rocket engines, aircraft aux. power units, co-generation power plants, aircraft environ. control systems, 1977—. Author: NASA monograph Rocket Engine Turbopump Inducers, 1971; Contbr. articles profl. jours. Mem. AIAA, NSPE, ASTM (com. for erosion by cavitation and impingement 1964—), ASME (recipient Melville Gold medal 1964), Soc. Automotive Engrs., Danish Inst. Civil Engrs. Republican. Lutheran. Home: 10531 Etiwanda Ave Northridge CA 91326-3113

JALAJAS, EMIL WALTER PETER, geochemist; b. Orange, N.J., Mar. 28, 1960; s. Arvo Andres and Nancy Jane (Keene) J.; m. Robin Lyn Blackmore, July 9, 1988; 1 child, Erik Robert. AB in Geochemistry, Occidental Coll., L.A., 1981; MS in Geol. Scis., U. So. Calif., 1986. Registered geologist, Calif.; registered environ. assessor, Calif. Assoc. Ecology & Environment, Inc., L.A., 1986-87; sr. scientist Geraghty & Miller, Inc., West Covina, Calif., 1987—; engr. in tng. Calif., 1991. Contbr. articles to profl. jours. Recipient Richter fellowship Occidental Coll., 1980, Achievement Rewards for Coll. Scientists, 1979-80. Mem. Assn. Ground-Water Scientists and Engrs., Am. Chem. Soc. (founding author Environ. Cons. Corner, So. Calif. sect.), Groundwater Resources Assn. Calif. (founding officer So. Calif. br., v.p.).

JALLINS, RICHARD DAVID, lawyer; b. L.A., Mar. 21, 1957; s. Walter Joshua and Elaine Beatrice (Youngerman) J.; m. Katherine Sue Pfeiffer, June 12, 1982; children: Stephen David, Rachel Marie. BA, U. Calif., Santa Barbara, 1978; JD, Calif. Western Sch. Law, 1981. Bar: Calif. 1988, U.S. Dist. Ct. (so. dist.) Calif. 1988. Panel atty. Bd. Prison Terms, Sacramento, 1989—, Appellate Defenders, Inc., San Diego, 1989-91, Calif. Dept. Corrections, Parole Hearings Divsn., Sacramento, 1992—. Mem. ABA, Calif. Prisoners Rights Union, San Diego County Bar Assn., Phi Alpha Delta. Home: 11857 Via Hacienda El Cajon CA 92019-4096

JAMAR, PETER NORTON, urban planner; b. Duluth, Minn., Jan. 4, 1957; s. Norton and Joan Helen (Hanson) J. BA, Gustavus Adolphus Coll., 1979; postgrad., U. Colo., 1979-81. Town planner Town of Vail, Colo., 1980-83; dir. planning Berridge Assocs., Inc., San Francisco, 1983-87; pres. Peter Jamar Assocs., Inc., Vail, 1987—; cons. in field. Mem. Urban Land Inst., Am. Planning Assn., Am. Inst. Cert. Planners (cert.), Coldstream Assn. (bd. dirs. 1987-90), Cascade Club. Office: Peter Jamar Assocs Inc 108 S Frontage Rd W Vail CO 81657

JAMES, ARLO DEE, state legislator, retired mining maintenance executive; b. Murray, Utah, Sept. 16, 1931; s. Leonard Wilson and Ida Lucille (Dalton) J.; m. Helen Nancy Beutsis, May 13, 1952; children: Sandy, George, Mary, David. Grad. high sch., Sandy, Utah, 1950; cert. master supervisor, U. Utah, cert. middle mgmt.; cert. diesel engr. (hon.), I.T.S., Kearns, Utah, 1978; D of Engine (hon.), Perfect Circle Corp., 1979. Heavy eqipment operator Kennecott Copper Corp., Bingham Canyon, Utah, 1951-76, sr. shop foreman, 1976-78, asst. shop gen. foreman, 1978-80, shop gen. foreman, 1980-81, field repair gen. foreman, 1981-84; mem. Utah Ho. Reps., Salt Lake City, 1977-93. Chmn. Kearns (Utah) Community Coun., 1977-92; voter dist. chair Kearns Dist. 3150, 1956-93; legis. dist. chair Kearns Dist. 48, 1980-93. With USAF, 1951-52. Named Mr. Kearns, Kearns County Ofcls., 1982, 84, Legislator of Yr. State of Utah, 1986; recipient Golden Rule award J.C. Penney Corp., 1984. Mem. Am. Legion. Democrat. Mormon.

JAMES, DAVID LEE, lawyer, international advisor, educator; b. Chgo., Aug. 23, 1933; s. Roy L. and Ethel (Wells) J.; m. Sheila Feagley, May 26, 1962; children: Pamela, James, Winifred, Paul, Brian, Adam. A.B., Harvard U., 1955; J.D., U. Chgo., 1960; grad. exec. program, Stanford U., 1979. Bar: N.Y. 1961, N.J. 1967, Hawaii 1976, Ill. 1987. With various law firms N.Y.C., 1960-67; counsel and asst. gen. counsel, asst. sec. Texasgulf Inc., 1967-75; gen. counsel, sec. Dillingham Corp., Honolulu, 1975-77, v.p., gen. counsel, sec., 1977-84; v.p. legal affairs, sec. Dillingham Corp., San Francisco, 1984-85; asst. gen. counsel, asst. sec. Crown Zellerbach Corp., San Francisco, 1985-86; sr. ptnr., sr. corp. atty. Arnstein & Lehr, Chgo., 1987-90; chmn. bus. programs East-West Ctr., Honolulu, 1990-92; chief party and sr. law devel. advisor U.S. Agy. Internat. Devel. and Govt. of Indonesia, Jakarta, Indonesia, 1992-93; pres. Bus. Strategies Internat., Cambridge, Mass., 1993—; hon. consul of Malaysia, Hawaii, 1977-84; adv. bd. Internat. and Comparative Law Ctr., Southwestern Legal Found., Dallas, 1976-91; adv. com. Law of Sea Inst., Honolulu, 1977-84. Author Doing Business in Asia, 1993; contbr. various articles on bus. and legal subjects. Bd. dirs. Chgo. Chamber Orch., 1988-90, pres. 1989-90, Jr. Achievement Hawaii, 1976-84, Hawaii Opera Theatre, 1981-84, Friends of East-West Ctr., 1982-84; mem. Morristown (N.J.) Bd. Edn., 1967-68. Served to lt. (j.g.) USNR, 1955-57. Clubs: Pacific, Outrigger Canoe (Honolulu), World Trade (San Francisco).

JAMES, DON, university athletic coach; m. Carol Hoobler; children: Jeff, Jill, Jeni. M.Ed., U. Kans., 1957. Grad. asst. U. Kans., 1956-57; tchr., coach Southwest Miami (Fla.) High Sch., 1957-59; asst. coach Fla. State U., 1959-66, U. Mich., 1966-68, U. Colo., 1968-70; head football coach Kent State U., 1971-74; head football coach U. Wash. Huskies, 1974—, head coach Divsn. 1A football champions (tied with U. Miami), 1991; coach North-South Shrine Game, Miami, 1973, Ohio Shrine Game, 1973, 74, Am. Bowl, 1976, East-West Shrine Game, San Francisco, 1979, Japan Bowl, 1979. Served with Transp. Corps U.S. Army, 1954-56. Named Coach of Yr. Mid Am. Conf., 1972, Ohio Coach of Yr. Coll. Football Coaches Assn., 1972, Coach of Week UPI, 1977, Nat. Coach of Yr. Am. Football Coaches Assn., 1978, Nat. Coach of Yr. Athlon Publs., 1981, Pre-Season Coach of Yr. Playboy Mag., 1982; U. Wash. Rose Bowl Champions, 1978, 82, Sun Bowl Champions, 1979, Pac-10 Champions, 1980, 81, Aloha Bowl Champions, 1982, Orange Bowl Champions, 1985, Freedom Bowl Champions, 1985. Mem. Omega Delta Kappa. Lodge: Rotary. Office: U Wash Athletic Dept Graves Bldg Seattle WA 98195

JAMES, EARL DENNIS, geologist, consultant; b. Glendale, Calif., Oct. 16, 1952; s. Gardner Francis and Patricia Eva (Schlegel) J.; m. Elizabeth Ann McDonald, Apr. 27, 1991. BS in Geology, Calif. State U., Hayward, 1977, MS Geology, 1982. Geologist Chevron U.S.A., San Francisco, 1977-87, Kennedy/Jenks/Chilton, San Francisco, 1987-89; prin. geologist Erler & Kalinowski, Inc., San Mateo, Calif., 1989—. Mem. Am. Assn. Petroleum Geologists (speaker L.A. 1986), Geothermal Resources Coun. (sec. 1986-87), Nat. Water Well Assn., World Affairs Coun., Commonwealth Club San Francisco. Home: 1516 Shrader St San Francisco CA 94117

JAMES, GEORGE BARKER, II, apparel industry executive; b. Haverhill, Mass., May 25, 1937; s. Paul Withington and Ruth (Burns) J.; m. Beverly A. Burch, Sept. 22, 1962; children: Alexander, Christopher, Geoffrey, Matthew. AB, Harvard U., 1959; MBA, Stanford U., 1962. Fiscal dir. E.G. & G. Inc., Bedford, Mass., 1963-67; fin. exec. Am. Brands Inc., N.Y.C., 1967-69; v.p. Pepsico, Inc., N.Y.C., 1969-72; sr. v.p., chief fin. officer Arcata Corp., Menlo Park, Calif., 1972-82; exec. v.p. Crown Zellerbach Corp., San Francisco, 1982-85; sr. v.p., chief fin. officer Levi Strauss & Co., San Francisco, 1985—; bd. dirs. Pacific States Industries, Inc., Basic Vegetable Products, Inc., Canned Foods Inc., Fibreboard Corp. Author: Industrial Development in the Ohio Valley, 1962. Mem. Andover (Mass.) Town Com., 1965-67; mem. Select Congl. Com. on World Hunger; mem. adv. coun. Calif. State Employees Pension Fund.; chmn. bd. dirs. Towle Trust Fund; trustee Nat. Corp. Fund for the Dance, Cate Sch., Levi Strauss Found., Stern Grove Festival Assn.; mem. San Francisco Com. on Fgn. Rels.; trustee Zellerbach Family Fund, San Francisco Ballet Assn.; bd. dirs. Stanford U. Hosp., World Affairs Coun.; mem. San Francisco Film Commn. Served with AUS, 1960-61. Clubs: Pacific Union, Family (San Francisco); Menlo Circus (Atherton, Calif.); Harvard (Boston and N.Y.C.); Harvard (San Francisco) (bd. dirs.); N.Y. Athletic Club. Home: 207 Walnut St San Francisco CA 94118-2012 Office: Levi Strauss & Co Levi's Pla 1155 Battery St San Francisco CA 94111-1230

JAMES, HERB MARK (JAY JAMES), foundation and insurance executive, free trade consultant; b. Trail, B.C., Can., Jan. 30, 1936; s. George William and Violet Ethyl (Corbin) J. Student, bus. adminstrn. Simon Fraser U., 1965-69; m. Patricia Helen Boyd, Nov. 1, 1958; 1 child, Brad Mark. Founder, Internat. Sound Found., Ottawa, Can., 1967—, Blaine, Wash., 1975—; cons. Fed. Bus. Dev. Bank; mem. bus. adv. bd. U.S. Senate, 1981—; mem. Can. Internat. Devel. Agy.; founder Better Hearing Better Life projects, Fiji, Kenya, Cayman Islands, Nepal, Costa Rica, Pakistan, Guatemala, Mex. Musician B. Pops Orch. Govt. of Can. grantee, 1973-83. Founder Can.-Mex. Free Trade Adjustment Group. Mem. Christian Bus. Men's Assn., Blaine C. of C., Masons, Shriners, Demolay. Office: PO Box 1587 Blaine WA 98230-1587

JAMES, MARION RAY, magazine publisher and editor; b. Bellmont, Ill., Dec. 6, 1940; s. Francis Miller and Lorraine A. (Wylie) J.; m. Janet Sue Tennis, June 16, 1960; children: Jeffrey Glenn, David Ray, Daniel Scott, Cheryl Lynne. BS, Oakland City Coll., Ind., 1964; MS, St. Francis Coll., Fort Wayne, Ind., 1978. Sports and city editor Daily Clarion, Princeton, Ind., 1963-65; English tchr. Jac-Cen-Del High Sch., Osgood, Ind., 1965-66; indsl. editor Whirlpool Corp., Evansville and LaPorte, Ind., 1966-68, Magnavox Govt. and Indsl. Electronics Co., Fort Wayne, 1968-79; editor, pub. Bowhunter mag., Fort Wayne, Ind., 1971-88, Kalispell, Mont., 1989—; instr. Ind.-Purdue U., Ft. Wayne, 1980-88. Author: Bowhunting for Whitetail and Mule Deer, 1975, Successful Bowhunting, 1985, My Place, 1991; editor: Pope and Young Book World Records, 1975, 2nd edit., 1993, Bowhunting Adventures, 1977. Recipient Best Editorial award United Community Svc. Publs., 1970-72; named Alumnus of Yr., Oakland City Coll., 1982, to Hall of Fame, Mt. Carmel High Sch., Ill., 1983. Mem. Outdoor Writers Assn. Am., Fort Wayne Assn. Bus. Editors (Fort Wayne Bus. Editor of Yr. 1969, pres. 1975-76), Toastmasters (Able Toastmaster award), Alpha Phi Gamma, Alpha Psi Omega, Mu Tau Kappa. Home: 600 Bayou Rd Kalispell MT 59901-6526

JAMES, PAUL GORDON, biochemist; b. Roxboro, N.C., June 25, 1958; s. Charlie Gordon and Marion (Dixon) J. BS, U. Fla., 1981; PhD, Ga. State U., 1988. Rsch. technologist ARC, Atlanta, 1983-86; rsch. technician III Ga. State U., Atlanta, 1986-89; scientist Glycomed, Inc., Alameda, Calif., 1989—. Contbr. articles to profl. jours.; co-patentee in blotting fluorescent materials. Named Young Lion of God Designee, Fellowship of Christian Athletes, 1977. Mem. AAAS, Am. Soc. Microbiology, Am. Chem. Soc., N.Y. Acad. Scis. Methodist. Office: Glycomed Inc 860 Atlantic Ave Alameda CA 94501

JAMES, ROBERT PAUL, physics educator; b. Westfield, Vt., Jan. 21, 1927; s. Walter A. and Pauline P. James; m. Helen M. Foster, May 25, 1987; 1 child, Rebecca P. BS in Edn., Ga. So. Coll., 1953; MS in Physics, UCLA, 1961. Insp. Retail Credit Co., Macon, Ga., 1952-53; high sch. tchr. Avondale High Sch., Avondale Estates, Ga., 1953-57; physic instr. L.A. City Coll., 1957-63; prof. physics Grossmont Coll., El Cajon, Calif., 1963—. Author physics lab. manual, 1978. With Merchant Marine, 1944-48. Mem. Sierra Club (outings leader 1970—). Home: 3818 Riviera Dr San Diego CA 92109 Office: Grossmont Coll 8800 Grossmont Coll Dr El Cajon CA 92020

JAMES, WAYNE EDWARD, electrical engineer; b. Racine, Wis., Apr. 2, 1950; s. Ronald Dean James and Arlene Joyce (Mickelsen) Dawson; m. Bertie Darlene Tague, July 18, 1972; children: Terry Scott, Kevin Arthur. BS in Electronic Engring. Tech., U. So. Colo., 1976. Electronic technician Lawrence Livermore (Calif.) Nat. Lab., 1976-80; electronic technician Inmos Corp., Colorado Springs, Colo., 1980-86, assoc. CAD engr., 1986-87; CAD engr. United Techs. Microelectronics Ctr., Colorado Springs, 1988—. Sec.-treas. Stratmoor Hills Vol. Fire Dept., Colorado Springs, 1983, 84, lt., 1985, capt., 1986. Served with USN, 1968-72. Named Fireman of Yr., Stratmoor Hills Vol. Fire Dept., 1983. Lutheran. Office: United Techs Microelectronics Ctr 1575 Garden Of The Gods Rd Colorado Springs CO 80907-3415

JAMES, WILLIAM LANGFORD, aerospace engineer; b. Southampton, Va., Jan. 13, 1939; s. Leroy and Worthie (Murphy) J.; m. Elaine Cecilia Reed; children: William Jr., Terri Lynne. Student, Va. State Coll., 1956, Hampton Inst., 1958; BS, Calif. State U., Los Angeles, 1962, MS, 1964; postgrad., U. Nev., Reno, 1984; spl. engring. studies, UCLA, 1970-82. Rsch. engr. non-metallic materials lab. N.Am. Aviation, L.A., 1960-67; rsch. analyst tech. staff The Aerospace Corp., El Segundo, 1967-75, materials engr., 1975-85; project engr. program mgmt. office The Aerospace Corp., El Segundo, Calif., 1985—. Contbr. numerous articles and reports to profl. publs.; patentee in field. Recipient numerous awards for USAF space contributions. Mem. AAAS, Soc. Advancement Material and Process Engring. (vice-chmn. 1987-89). Home: PO Box 19735 Los Angeles CA 90019-0735 Office: Aerospace Corp M5 712 M5 712 Los Angeles CA 90009

JAMIN, MATTHEW DANIEL, lawyer, magistrate; b. New Brunswick, N.J., Nov. 29, 1947; s. Matthew Bernard and Frances Marie (Newburg) J.; m. Christine Frances Bjorkman, June 28, 1969; children: Rebecca, Erica. BA, Colgate U., 1969; JD, Harvard U., 1974. Bar: Alaska 1974, U.S. Dist. Ct. Alaska 1974, U.S. Ct. Appeals (9th cir.) 1980. Staff atty. Alaska Legal Svcs., Anchorage, 1974-75; supervising atty. Alaska Legal Svcs., Kodiak, Alaska, 1975-81; contract atty. Pub. Defender's Office State of Alaska, Kodiak, 1976-82; prin. Matthew D. Jamin, Atty., Kodiak, 1982; ptnr. Jamin & Bolger, Kodiak, 1982-85, Jamin, Ebell, Bolger & Gentry,

Kodiak, 1985—; part-time U.S. magistrate U.S. Cts., Kodiak, 1984—. Part-time instr. U. Alaska Kodiak Coll., 1975—; pres. Threshhold Svcs., Inc., Kodiak, 1985-92. Mem. Alaska Bar Assn. (Professionalism award 1988), Kodiak Bar Assn. Office: US Dist Ct 323 Carolyn St Kodiak AK 99615-7394

JAMISON, JOHN, mortgage banker, author; b. Asheville, N.C., Sept. 19, 1938; s. John R. and Alice (Wild) J.; m. Laura Rayburn, Nov. 26, 1983. BA, Vanderbilt U., 1960; ThM, So. Seminary, Louisville, 1965. Chaplain U. Md., College Park, 1965-69; gen. mgr. Flintridge Corp., Phoenix, 1969-71; asst. v.p. Kissell Co., Phoenix, 1971-77; v.p. United Mortgage Co., Denver, 1977-78, Rainier Mortgage Co., Seattle, 1978-82; pres. Comml. Mortgage of Santa Barbara, Calif., 1983-87; v.p. City Commerce Bank, Santa Barbara, 1987-91; pres. Loan Svc. Assocs., San Francisco, 1991—. Contbr. articles to various profl. jours. Pres. Washington Coalition for Affordable Housing, Seattle, 1980-81; bd. dirs. Tri-County Red Cross, Santa Barbara, 1990-91. Capt. USAR, 1960-68. Mem. Coun. for Innovative Housing Solutions (pres. 1991—), Flat Earth Soc. (sec. 1987-91), Phi Beta Kappa.

JAMISON, JOHN LOCKWOOD, management consultant; b. St. Louis, July 9, 1966; s. Rex Lindsay and Dorothy Tufts (Lockwood) J. BA, Swarthmore Coll., 1989. Software developer Lockheed Missiles & Space Co., Palo Alto, Calif., 1983-88; system and network mgr. Swarthmore (Pa.) Coll., 1988-89; mgmt. cons. Andersen Cons., San Francisco, 1989—.

JANECKY, DAVID RICHARD, geochemist; b. Meeker, Colo., Apr. 24, 1953; s. Richard Myron and Lois Margaret (McKenzie) J.; m. Louise Adele Anderson, Dec. 20, 1986; children: Gregg David, Grant Frederick. Student, U. Bergen, Norway, 1973-74; AB, U. Calif., 1975; postgrad., U. Calif., Santa Barbara, 1975-76, Stanford U., 1977-78; PhD, U. Minn., 1982. Teaching asst. U. Calif., Santa Barbara, 1975-76; rsch. asst. Stanford U., 1976-78; rsch. asst. U. Minn., Mpls., 1978-82, rsch. assoc., 1982-84; staff mem. Los Alamos (N.Mex.) Nat. Lab., 1985—. Contbr. articles to profl. jours. Post-doctoral rsch. fellow Los Alamos Nat. Lab., 1984-85; grantee NSF, 1978-84, U.S. Dept. Energy/Office Basic Energy Scis., 1985—, Inst. Geophysics and Planetary Physics, 1986-92, U.S. Dept. Energy/Office Tech. Devel., 1992—. Fellow Soc. Econ. Geology; mem. Am. Geophys. Union, Geochem. Soc., Internat. Assn. Geochemistry and Cosmochemistry, Norway Geol. Soc., Oceanography Soc. Democrat. Methodist. Office: Los Alamos Nat Lab Isotope and Environ Geochemistry Group INC-9 MS J514 Los Alamos NM 87545

JANES, ROBERT ROY, museum director, archaeologist,; b. Rochester, Minn., Apr. 23, 1948; m. Priscilla Bickel; children: Erica Helen, Peter Bickel. Student, Lawrence U., 1966-68, BA in Anthropology cum laude, 1970; student, U. of the Ams., Mexico City, 1968, U. Calif., Berkeley, 1968-69; PhD in Archaeology, U. Calgary, Alta., Can., 1976. Postdoctoral fellow Arctic Inst. N.Am., U. Calgary, 1981-82; adj. prof. archaeology U. Calgary, 1990—; founding dir. Prince of Wales No. Heritage Centre, Yellowknife, N.W.T., 1976-86, project dir. Dealy Island Archaeol. and Conservation Project, 1977-82; founding exec. dir. Sci. Inst. of N.W.T.; sci. advisor Govt. of N.W.T., Yellowknife, 1986-89; dir., chief exec. officer Glenbow Mus., Calgary, 1989—; adj. prof. anthropology U. Calgary, 1990—. Author manuscripts, monographs, book chpts.; contbr. articles to profl. jours. mem. First Nations/CMA Task Force on Mus. and First Peoples, 1989-92. Recipient Nat. Pks. Centennial award Environment Can., 1985, Can. Studies Writing award Assn. Can. Studies, 1989, Disting. Alumni award Alumni Assn. of U. Calgary, 1989, L.R. Briggs Disting. Achievement award Lawrence U., 1991; Can. Coun. doctoral fellow, 1973-76; rsch. grantee Govt. of Can., 1974, Social Scis. and Humanities Rsch. Coun. Can., 1988-89. Fellow Arctic Inst. N.Am. (bd. dirs. 1983-90, vice chmn. bd. 1985-89, hon. rsch. assoc. 1983-84, chmn. priorities and planning com. 1983-84, mem. exec. com. 1984-86, adv. editor Arctic jour. 1987—), Am. Anthrop. Assn. (fgn. fellow); mem. Soc. for Am. Archaeology, Can. Archaeol. Assn. (v.p. 1980-82, pres. 1984-86, co-chmn. fed. heritage policy com. 1986-88), Current Anthropology (assoc.), Can. Mus. Assn. (hon. life mem., cert. accreditation 1982, Outstanding Achievement award in Mus. Mgmt. 1992), Am. Assn. Mus., Alta. Mus. Assn. (moderator seminars 1990, Merit award 1992), Internat. Coun. Mus., Can. Art Mus. Dirs. Orgn. (mem.-at-large bd. dirs.), Mus. West (bd. dirs.), U. Calgary's Pres.'s Circle, Ranchmen's Club, Calgary Philharmonic Soc., Sigma Xi. Home: Box 32 Site 32, RR 12, Calgary, AB Canada T3E 6W3 Office: Glenbow Mus-AB Inst, 130 9 Ave SE, Calgary, AB Canada T2G 0P3

JANIGIAN, BRUCE JASPER, lawyer, educator; b. San Francisco, Oct. 21, 1950; s. Michael D. Janigian and Stella (Minasian) Amerian; m. Susan Elizabeth Frye, Oct. 4, 1986; children: Alan Michael, Alison Elizabeth. AB, U. Calif., Berkeley, 1972; JD, U. Calif., San Francisco, 1975; LLM, George Washington U., 1982. Bar: Calif. 1975, U.S. Supreme Ct. 1979, D.C. 1981. Dir. Hastings Rsch. Svcs., Inc., San Francisco, 1973-75; judge adv. in Spain, 1976-78; atty. advisor AID U.S. State Dept., Washington, 1979-84; dep. dir., gen. counsel Calif. Employment Devel. Dept., Sacramento, 1984-89; Fulbright scholar, vis. prof. law U. Salzburg, Austria, 1989-90; chmn. Calif. Agrl. Labor Rels. Bd., 1990—; prof. law McGeorge Sch. Law, U. Pacific, Sacramento, 1986—, Inst. on Internat. Legal Studies, Salzburg, Austria, summer 1987, London Inst. on Comml. Law, summers 1989, 92, 93; vis. scholar Hoover Inst. War, Revolution and Peace, Stanford U., 1991-92. Editor: Financing International Trade and Development, 1986, 87, 89, International Business Transactions, 1989, 92, International Trade Law, 1993. Coordinating fund raiser March of Dimes, Sacramento, 1987. Capt. USNR, 1975-79, mem. Res. Fulbright scholar, 1989-90; decorated Meritorious Achievement medal. Mem. Calif. Bar Assn., D.C. Bar Assn., Sacramento Bar Assn. (exec. com. taxation sect. 1988-89), Sacramento Met. C. of C. (award for program contbns. and community enrichment 1989), Nat. Rep. Lawyers Assn., Naval Res. Officers Assn., Marine Meml. Assn., Fulbright Assoc. (life), Knights of Vartan, Phi Beta Kappa. Home: 1631 12th Ave Sacramento CA 95818 Office: Agrl Labor Rels Bd 915 Capitol Mall Sacramento CA 95814-4810

JANIS, BRIAN CHARLES, freelance photographer; b. San Diego, Mar. 5, 1959; s. Henry Charles and Arlene Elizabeth (Carroll) J.; m. Susana Georgina Meza, Apr. 15, 1990. BA in Econ., Rutgers Coll., 1981. Nat. cert. photofinishing engr. Pres. Phototechnick, Easton, Pa., 1981-83; dir. photo ops. Greyhound Expo Svcs., Las Vegas, Nevada, 1983-85; ptnr. Media Group, Las Vegas, Nevada, 1985-87; pres. Brian Janis/Phototechnik, Las Vegas, Nevada, 1987—; assoc. editor On Dirt Motorsports, Calabasis, Calif., 1985—; staff photographer Globe Photos, Inc., N.Y.C., Hollywood, Calif., 1987—, Las Vegas Bus. Press, 1989—; contbg. photographer NV Motion Picture Div., Las Vegas, 1988—. Photog. coverage of various entertainment figures for the pub. industry including Bill Cosby, Sam Kinison, Johnny Mathis, Siegfried & Roy among others; contbr. articles to profl. jours. Active pub. information com. Opportunity Village (good samaritan award), Las Vegas, 1985—. Mem. Am. Soc. Mag. Photographers, Profl. Photographers Am., Pub. Rels. Soc. Am., Las Vegas Advt. Fedn., Advt. Photographers of Am. Office: Brian Janis/Phototechnik 3180 E Desert Inn Rd Ste 212 Las Vegas NV 89121-3857

JANKE, DAVID CURTIS, computer company executive; b. Ogden, Utah, Aug. 25, 1949; s. John Erwin and Vera (Stoker) J.; m. Michelle Morrison, Aug. 10, 1974; children: Clark, Richard, Spencer, Cameron. BSEE, Stanford U., Palo Alto, Calif., 1971; MBA, Brigham Young U., 1975. Project engr. Kaiser Aluminum and Chem. Corp., Ravenswood, W.Va., 1975-77; engring. econ. Kaiser Aluminum and Chem. Corp., Oakland, Calif., 1977-79; project mgr. Kaiser Aluminum and Chem. Corp., Tacoma, 1979-81, mgr. engring. and maintenance, 1981-83; mgr. engring. and maintenance Kaiser Aluminum and Chem. Corp., Spokane, Wash., 1983-85; project mgr. Eaton-Kenway, Salt Lake City, 1985-88; program mgr. Evans and Sutherland Computer Corp., Salt Lake City, 1988-89, dir. internat. bus., 1989—. Scoutmaster, com. chmn. Boy Scouts Am., Sandy, Utah, 1975-91. Mem. IEEE, Phi Beta Kappa, Tau Beta Pi, Eta Kappa Nu. Republican. Mem. LDS Ch. Office: Evans and Sutherland Corp 600 Komas Dr Salt Lake City UT 84158

JANKE, NORMAN CHARLES, engineering geologist; b. Milw., Sept. 5, 1923; s. Charles Augustus and Normana (Westness) J.; 1 child, Garth. MS, U. Chgo., 1952; PhD, UCLA, 1963. Registered geologist, engring. geologist, Calif. Instr. Fresno (Calif.) State Coll., 1955, Sacramento State Coll., 1956-83; cons., 1952—; trustee Moss Landing (Calif.) Marine Lab., 1967-71. Contbr. articles to profl. jours. Maj. Calif. State Mil. Res., 1980-87. Mem. ASTM, Assn. Engring. Geologists, N.Y. Acad. Scis., Soc. Explosives Engrs., Soc. Mining Engrs., Soc. Am. Mil. Engrs., Sigma Xi. Home and Office: 2670 Fair Oaks Blvd Sacramento CA 95864-4933

JANKURA, DONALD EUGENE, hotel executive, educator; b. Bridgeport, Conn., Dec. 20, 1929; s. Stephen and Susan (Dirga) J.; m. Elizabeth Deborah Joynt, June 20, 1952; children: Donald Eugene Jr., Stephen J., Daria E., Diane E., Lynn M. BA in Hotel Adminstrn., Mich. State U., 1951. Asst. sales mgr. Pick Fort Shelby Hotel, Detroit, 1951-53; steward Dearborn Inn and Colonial Homes, Dearborn, Mich., 1953-54, sales mgr., 1954-60, resident mgr., 1960-62; gen. mgr. Stouffer's Northland Inn, Southfield, Mich., 1962-64; staff adviser Stouffer Motor Inns, Cleve., 1964-66, v.p., 1966-68; v.p. Assoc. Inns & Restaurants Co. Am., Denver, 1968-76, exec. v.p., 1976-81, sr. v.p., 1981-91; pres. Waverly Hospitality Assocs., Parker, Colo., 1991—; dir. Sch. Hotel and Restaurant Mgmt. U. Denver, 1988-91; disting. spl. lectr. hospitality U. New Haven, Conn.; pres. Am. Hotel Assn. Directory Corp., 1986; guest lectr. Mich. State U., 1964, Fla. Internat. U., 1968, Cornell U., 1983, Denver U., 1986-87; mem. industry adv. bd. U. Denver, Mich. State U.; bd. dirs. Vend Right Service Co., Kansas City, Kans., Beverage Retailers Ins. Co., Washington; mem. adv. bd. Acad. Travel and Tourism-Nat. Acad. Found., Denver, 1991—. Named to Hall of Fame Colo. Hotel and Lodging Assn., 1992; named Alumnus of Yr. Mich. State U. Hotel Sch., 1986. Mem. Am. Hotel and Motel Assn. (dir. 1978-80, vice chmn. industry adv. council 1980-81, sec.-treas. 1985, v.p. 1986, pres. 1987—) Colo./Wyo. Hotel and Motel Assn. (dir., bd. dirs. 1984—, Disting. Svc. award 1983), Coalition Lic. of Beverage Retailers Assn. (bd. dirs. 1987—), Hotel Sales Mgmt. Assn. (bd. dirs. 1984—), Council Hotel, Restaurant and Instnl. Educators, Internat. Platform Assn., Internat. Soc. Hospitality Cons., Pinery Country Club, Pres.'s Club, Masons, Phi Kappa Tau. Episcopalian. Home and Office: 7445 E Windlawn Way Parker CO 80134-5941

JANOUSEK, ARNOLD LEE, computer information services administrator; b. Kanona, Kans., Jan. 9, 1930; s. Fred and Edyithe Louise (Rohr) J.; m. Eleanor Ruth Deeter, Dec. 29, 1957 (div. 1991); children: Guy M., Cecile N. Janousek Befort, Jenifer L. BS, Ft. Hays Kans. State U., 1952, MS, 1956. Instr. computer sci. U. Kans., Lawrence, 1957-63; project systems analyst Trans World Airlines, Kansas City, Mo., 1963-84; instr., computer info. svcs. dir. Haskell Indian Jr. Coll., Lawrence, 1984-92; computer specialist Billings (Mont.) Bur. Indian Affairs-Info. Mgmt. Ctr., 1992—. Sgt. U.S. Army, 1952-54. Mem. Masons (32 degree, past master lodge 9). Mormon. Office: Bur Indian Affairs IMC 316 N 26 Billings MT 59101

JANSEN, GUSTAV RICHARD, academic administrator, educator; b. N.Y.C., May 19, 1930; s. Gustav Enoch and Ruth Miriam (Olson) J.; m. Coerene Miller, July 5, 1953; children: Norman, Barbara, Kathryn, Ellen. Student, Wagner Coll.; BA, Cornell U., 1950, PhD, 1958. Assoc. chemist Am. Cyanamid, Stamford, Conn., 1953-54; rsch. biochemist E.I. DuPont De Nemours, Wilmington, Del., 1958-62; rsch. fellow Merck Inst., Rahway, N.J., 1962-69; prof., dept. head Colo. State U., Ft. Collins, 1969-90, prof. emeritus, 1990—; mem. human nutrition bd. Sch. Counselors, USDA, Washington, 1986-91. 2d lt. USAF, 1950-53. Fellow Inst. Food Techologists (exec. com. 1989-91); mem. AAAS, NAS (com. mil. nutrition rsch.), Am. Inst. Nutrition, Am. Soc. for Biochemistry and Molecular Biology, Nat. Assn. Scholars. Republican. Methodist. Home: 1804 Seminole Dr Fort Collins CO 80525-1536 Office: Colo State U Dept Food Sci and Human Nutrition Fort Collins CO 80523

JANTZEN, JENS CARSTEN, mathematician, educator; b. Stoertewerker-Koog, Schleswig-Holstein, Fed. Republic of Germany, Oct. 18, 1948; came to U.S., 1988; s. Ewald and Annelene (Steensen) J. PhD, U. Bonn, Fed. Republic of Germany, 1973. Asst. prof. U. Bonn, 1973-78, assoc. prof., 1978-85; prof. U. Hamburg, Fed. Republic of Germany, 1985-88; prof. math. U. Oreg., Eugene, 1988—. Author: Moduln mit einem hoechsten Gewicht, 1979, Einhuellende Algebren Halbeinfacher Lie-Algebren, 1983, Representations of Algebraic Groups, 1987. Mem. Am. Mat. Soc., German Math. Soc. Home: 124 High St Eugene OR 97401-2306 Office: U Oreg Dept of Math Eugene OR 97403-1222

JANTZEN, J(OHN) MARC, educator; b. Hillsboro, Kans., July 30, 1908; s. John D. and Louise (Janzen) J.; m. Ruth Patton, June 9, 1935; children: John Marc, Myron Patton, Karen Louise. A.B., Bethel Coll., Newton, Kans., 1934; A.M., U. Kans., 1937, Ph.D., 1940. Elementary sch. tchr. Marion County, Kans., 1927-30, Hillsboro, Kan., 1930-31; high sch. tchr., 1934-36; instr. sch. edn. U. Kans., 1936-40; asst. prof. Sch. Edn., U. of Pacific, Stockton, Calif., 1940-42; assoc. prof. Sch. Edn., U. of Pacific, 1942-44, prof., 1944-78, prof. emeritus, 1978—, also dean sch. edn., 1944-74, emeritus, 1974—, dir. summer sessions, 1940-72; condr. overseas seminars; past chmn. commn. equal opportunities in edn. Calif. Dept. Edn., 1959-69; mem., chmn. Commn. Tchr. Edn. Calif. Tchrs. Assn., 1956-62; mem. Nat. Coun. for Accreditation Tchr. Edn., 1969-72. Bd. dirs. Ednl. Travel Inst., 1965-89. Recipient Hon. Service award Calif. Congress of Parents and Tchrs., 1982; Paul Harris fellow Rotary Found., 1980; named Outstanding Rotarian of the Yr. North Stockton, Calif. Rotary Club, 1989-90. Mem. NEA, Am. Edn. Rsch. Assn., Calif. Edn. Rsch. Assn. (past pres. 1954-55), Calif. Coun. for Edn. Tchrs., Calif. Assn. of Colls. for Tchr. Edn. (sec., treas. 1975-85), Phi Delta Kappa. Methodist. Lodge: Rotary. Home: 117 W Euclid Ave Stockton CA 95204-3122

JAQUITH, GEORGE OAKES, ophthalmologist; b. Caldwell, Idaho, July 29, 1916; s. Gail Belmont and Myrtle (Burch) J.; BA, Coll. Idaho, 1938; MB, Northwestern U., 1942, MD, 1943; m. Pearl Elizabeth Taylor, Nov. 30, 1939; children: Patricia Ann Jaquith Mueller, George, Michele Eugenie Jaquith Smith. Intern, Wesley Meml. Hosp., Chgo., 1942-43; resident ophthalmology U.S. Naval Hosp., San Diego, 1946-48; pvt. practice medicine, specializing in ophthalmology, Brawley, Calif., 1948—; pres. Pioneers Meml. Hosp. staff, Brawley, 1953; dir., exec. com. Calif. Med. Eye Council, 1960—; v.p. Calif. Med. Eye Found., 1976—. Sponsor Anza council Boy Scouts Am., 1966—. Gold card holder Rep. Assocs., Imperial County, Calif., 1967-68. Served with USMC, USN, 1943-47; PTO. Mem. Imperial County Med. Soc. (pres. 1961), Calif. Med. Assn. (del. 1961—), Nat., So. Calif. (dir. 1966—, chmn. med. adv. com. 1968-69) Soc. Prevention Blindness, Calif. Assn. Ophthalmology (treas. 1976—), San Diego, Los Angeles Ophthal. Socs., Los Angeles Research Study Club, Nathan Smith Davis Soc., Coll. Idaho Assocs., Am. Legion, VFW, Res. Officers Assn., Basenji Assn., Nat. Geneal. Soc., Cuyamaca Club (San Diego), Elks, Phi Beta Pi, Lambda Chi Alpha. Presbyterian (elder). Office: PO Box 511 665 S Western Brawley CA 92227-0511

JARAMILLO, MARI-LUCI, educational services corporation executive; b. Las Vegas, N.Mex., June 19, 1928. B.A., N.Mex. Highland U., 1955, M.A., 1959; Ph.D., U. N.Mex., 1970. Lang. arts cons. Las Vegas Sch. System, 1965-69; asst. dir. instructional services Minority Group Ctr., 1969-72; assoc. prof., chmn. dept. elem. edn. U. N.Mex., 1972-75, coordinator Title VII tchr. tng., 1975-76, assoc. prof. edn., 1976-77, prof., 1977, spl. asst. to pres., 1981-82, assoc. dean Coll. Edn., 1982-85, v.p. for student affairs, 1985-87; asst. v.p., dir. Ednl. Testing Service, Emeryville, Calif., 1987-93; ambassador to Honduras, Tegucigalpa, 1977-80; dep. asst. sec. for inter-Am. affairs Dept. State, Washington, 1980-81. Contbr. articles to jours., chpts. to books. Trustee Tomas Rivera Ctr. Mem. Nat. Assn. Bilingual Edn., Latin Am. Assn., Am. Assn. Colls. for Tchr. Edn., Nat. Council La Raza.

JARCHO, LEONARD W., retired neurology educator; b. N.Y.C., Aug. 12, 1916; s. Julius and Susana (Wallenstein) J.; m. Ann Elizabeth Adams, Apr. 11, 1956; children: John Adams, Daniel Gordon, William Stephen. AB, Harvard U., 1936; MA, Columbia U., 1937, MD, 1941. Intern in medicine Beth Israel Hosp., Boston, 1942; asst. resident medicine Mt. Sinai Hosp., N.Y.C., 1946-47; fellow in medicine Johns Hopkins Sch. Medicine, Balt., 1946, 47-52; instr. medicine Johns Hopkins Sch. Medicine, 1952; clin. clk. neurology Nat. Hosp. Queen Sq., London, 1958; fellow in neuropathology Mass. Gen. Hosp., Boston, 1959; from asst. prof. to prof. neurology U. Utah, Salt Lake City, 1959-81, prof. emeritus, 1981—. With U.S. Army, 1943-46.

JARDINE, LESLIE JAMES, nuclear engineering executive; b. Valparaiso, Ind., Mar. 18, 1945; s. James Ray Jardine and Dorthy Pearl (Wunder) Cota; m. Kathleen M. Miller, Mar. 30, 1962; 1 child, Renee Ann. BS in Chemistry, Ind. State U., 1967; MS in Nuclear Engring., U. Calif., 1969, PhD in Nuclear Engring., 1971. Rsch. asst., rsch. engr. Lawrence Berkeley (Calif.) Lab., 1969-74; nuclear engring. group leader Argonne (Ill.) Nat. Lab., 1975-82; project engr., project mgr. Bechtel Nat., Inc., San Francisco, 1982-89; project mgr. Lawrence Livermore (Calif.) Nat. Lab., 1989—; mem. rev. com. materials scis. div. Argone Nat. Lab., 1988—. Author: Tables of Isotopes, 1988. Patrol dir. Nat. Ski Patrol, Downers Grove, Ill., 1981-82. Mem. Am. Nuclear Soc. (Edward Teller award 1971), Nat. Ski Patrol, Masons. Office: Lawrence Livermore Nat Lab PO Box 808 Livermore CA 94551-0808

JARMAN, DONALD RAY, public relations professional; b. Benton Harbor, Mich., May 6, 1928; s. Ray Charles and Grace Marie (Timanus) J.; m. Bo Dee Foster, July 7, 1950 (div. 1985); children: Mark, Katharine Law, Luanne Miller; m. Sharon Lee Becker, Feb. 16, 1991. BA, Chapman U., 1950; MDiv, Lexington Theol. Sem., 1953; D in Ministry, Sch. of Theology, 1970. Cert. Fund. Raising Exec., Nat. Soc. Fund. Raising Execs. Pastor Sharpsberg (Ky.) Christian, 1950-53, First Christian Ch., Santa Maria, Calif., 1953-58, St. Claire St. Ch. of Christ, Kirkcaldy, Scotland, 1958-61, So. Bay Christian, Redondo Beach, Calif., 1961-71; dir. human value in health care Eskaton, Charmichael, Calif., 1971-73; exec. dir. Northwestern NBA Svc., Portland, Oreg., 1973-85; dir. pub. relations and mktg. Retirement Housing Found., Long Beach, Calif., 1985-89; dir. community relations S.W. Diversified, Signal Hill, Calif., 1989—; pres. So. Calif. Mins., 1967; chmn. Pacific S.W. Region Christian Ch., 1968; mem. gen. bd. Disciples of Christ, 1969-70; exec. dir. Signal Hill Econ. Devel. Bd., 1992. Editor: Reachout, 1973-84, Hill Street News; editor-in-chief: December Rose, 1985-89; columnist NW Senior News, 1980-84. Pres. Signal Hill C. of C., 1992-93 (named Most Valuable Mem. 1991); treas. Hist. Soc., Signal Hill, 1990-92. Recipient Master Make-up Technician award Portland Opera, 1983, Outstanding Older American award City of Signal Hill, Calif., 1993. Mem. Rotary (pres. Progress, Oreg. 1983-84, pres. Signal Hill, 1993—), Masons, Chapman Univ. Alumni Assn. (pres.-elect 1993—). Democrat. Office: SW Diversified 2501 Cherry #160 Signal Hill CA 90806

JARMON, LAWRENCE, developmental communications educator; b. L.A., Nov. 7, 1946; s. Robert and Movella (Young) J. BA, Calif. State U., 1969, MA in Adminstrn. Health and Safety, 1988; MS, U. Wash., 1972; EdD in Edn. Adminstrn., Wash. State U., 1975. Athletic dir., instr. dept. phys. edn. L.A. SW Coll., 1975-85, agy. dir. summer programfor disadvantaged youth, 1975-91, asst. dean instruction, 1976, project adminstr. NCAA, 1977-79; instr. health edn. Golden West Coll., Huntington Beach, Calif., 1978; instr. dept. English Calif. State U., L.A., 1986; instr. dept. edn. Nat. U., L.A., 1986-88; prof. developmental comm. L.A. SW Coll., 1988—. Author numerous booklets, manuscripts and manuals on sports programs and edn. qualifications and policies. Active Black Edn. Com., L.A. Unified Sch. Dist., Involvement for Young Achievers, L.A., L.A. Police Dept. Football Centurions, Paradise Ch. Found., L.A., Pop Warner Little Scholars, Phila., Employee Assistance Program Liaison Officer, L.A.,. Mem. Am. Alliance Health, Phys. Edn. and Recreation, Am. Alliance Health Edn., Am. Assn. Sch. Adminstrs., Calif. State Alumni Assn., U. Wash. Alumni Assn., Wash. State Alumni Assn., Calif. Assn. Health, Phys. Edn. and Recreation, Calif. State Athletic Dirs. Assn., L.A. Jr. C. of C., Kappa Alpha Psi, Nat. Interscholastic Athletic Adminstrs. Assn., Phi Delta Kappa. Office: LA SW Coll 1600 South Imperial Hwy Los Angeles CA 90047

JAROS, DEAN, university official; b. Racine, Wis., Aug. 23, 1938; s. Joseph and Emma (Kotas) J. B.A., Lawrence Coll., Appleton, Wis., 1960; M.A., Vanderbilt U., 1962, Ph.D., 1966. Asst. prof. polit. sci. Wayne State U., Detroit, 1963-66; from asst. prof. to prof. polit. sci. U. Ky., 1966-78, assoc. dean Grad. Sch., 1978-80; dean Grad. Sch. No. Ill. U., DeKalb, 1980-84; dean Grad. Sch. Colo. State U., Ft. Collins, 1984-91, assoc. provost, 1991—. Author: Socialization to Politics, 1973, Political Behavior: Choices and Perspectives, 1974, Heroes Without Legacy, 1993, also articles.; Mem. editorial bds. profl. jours. Mem. Exptl. Aircraft Assn. Office: Colo State U Grad Sch Fort Collins CO 80523

JAROSLOVSKY, ALAN, judge; b. Des Moines, Iowa, May 11, 1948; s. Louis and Ruth (Grossmark) J. BA, UCLA, 1970; JD, Golden Gate U., 1977. Bar: Calif. 1977. Pvt. practice Santa Rose, Calif., 1978-87, U.S. Bankruptcy judge, 1987—. Author: Practical Bankruptcy Procedure, 1993. Dir. Calif. Rural Legal Assistance, 1981. Lt. USN, 1970-73, Vietnam. Mem. Sonoma County Bar Assn. (pres. 1987). Democrat. Jewish. Office: US Bankruptcy Ct 99 South E St Santa Rosa CA 95404

JARRELL, WESLEY MICHAEL, soil and ecosystem science educator, researcher, consultant; b. Forest Grove, Oreg., May 23, 1948; s. Burl Omer and Edith LaVerne (Sahnow) J.; m. Linda Ann Illig, June 24, 1972; children: Benjamin George, Emily Theresa. BA, Stanford U., 1970; MS, Oreg. State U., 1974, PhD, 1976. Grad. rsch. asst. Oreg. State U., 1971-76; asst. prof. soil sci. U. Calif., Riverside, 1976-83, assoc. prof., 1983-88; dir. Dry Lands Res. Inst., 1985-88; assoc. prof. Oreg. Grad. Inst., Portland, 1988-91, prof., 1991—; dept. head, internat. cons. agr., 1992—. Mem. AAAS, Soil Sci. Soc. Am., Am. Soc. Agronomy. Democrat. Lutheran. Contbr. articles to profl. jours. Home: 1920 NW 110th Ct Portland OR 97229-4852 Office: Oreg Grad Inst Environ Sci Engring 20000 NW Walker Dr Portland OR 97222

JARRETT, RONALD DOUGLAS, nurse, legal assistant; b. Oceanside, Calif., Oct. 31, 1952; s. William Douglas and Francia Elizabeth (Ladd) J.; m. Lois Ellen Shurmaster, Dec. 23, 1984; 1 child, Emily Rose. ASN, Cabrillo Coll., 1981; student, SUNY, Albany, 1984-88; JD, Lincoln Law Sch. Sacramento, 1993. RN, Calif. Hosp. corpsman USN, 1970-74; psychiat. technician County Mental Health Dept., Santa Cruz, Calif., 1974-81; staff nurse ICU/CCU Watsonville (Calif.) Community Hosp., 1981-84; RN, ICU, CCU Dominican Santa Cruz Hosp., Santa Cruz, Calif., 1983-85; staff nurse ICU U. Calif.-Davis Med. Ctr., Sacramento, 1986-87; staff nurse ICU/emergency room Calif. Healthcare Cons., Sacramento, 1987-90; nurse ICU, critical care unit, emergency room Yolo Gen. Hosp., Woodland, Calif., 1990-91; with Nursing Svcs. Internat., 1991-92; law clk. Klauschie & Shannon, 1992—; affiliate faculty Am. Heart Assn., Salinas, Calif., 1979-84; assoc. faculty Cabrillo Coll. nursing dept., Aptos, Calif., 1983-85; med. record rev. Cigna. Served to HM3 USN, 1970-73. Fellow Ancient Mystical Order Rosae Crucis; mem. Sacramento PC Users Group. Republican. Home: 9400 Marcola Ct Sacramento CA 95826-5221 Office: 2720 Gateway Oaks Dr Ste 310 Sacramento CA 95833

JARVIS, BARBARA ANN, transportation executive; b. San Francisco, May 5, 1946; d. Steve and Irma Vivian (Ford) Jarvis; m. Andre Pardow Mitchell (div. Jan. 1973); children: Kristin Dion, Damien Pardow Mitchell; m. Michal Kamionko, Nov. 15, 1987. Student, Skyline City Coll., 1975. Entertainment booking agt. Joe Tex, singer, San Francisco, 1979-82; entertainment booking agt., pres., owner MJM Prodns., San Francisco, Sacramento, 1982-84; dir. transp. Kaiser Permanente Med. Ctr., San Francisco, 1982—. Bd. dirs. HIV Continuum, San Francisco, 1989; transp. dir. San Francisco Kaiser Neighborhood & Health Plan Mem. Free Svc., 1984-89. Recipient State of Calif. Gov.'s award for best transp. program in Calif., 1990. Mem. Nat. Assn. Health Svcs. Execx., Joint Institutional Transp. Brokers' Assn. (pres.), Institutional Mcpl. Parking Assn. (speaker, Award Transp. Excellence IMPC Conv. 1989), Rides for Bay Area Commuters (advisor to new TSM mgrs. 1984—, bd. dirs. Trip Reduction Ordinance for City of San Francisco, Achievement Award in Transp. 1989, Best Transp. Program of 1989-90 Yr. award 1990), San Francisco Tennis Club. Democrat. Roman Catholic. Office: Kaiser Permanente Med Ctr 2425 Geary Blvd San Francisco CA 94115-3395

JARVIS, CHRISTOPHER JOHN, newspaper reporter; b. Seattle, Sept. 3, 1957; s. Richard B. and Elizabeth (de Grace) J. BA, Western Wash. U., 1980. Reporter Sta. KBFW, Bellingham, Wash., 1976-79, Juneau (Alaska) Empire, 1982-84, Anchorage Times, 1984-85; news dir. Sta. KJNO, Juneau, 1981-82; reporter Jour. Am., Bellevue, Wash., 1987—. Mem. subcom. Bellevue Mcpl. Emergency Plan, 1992. Recipient Best Series award Alaska Press Club, 1984, 1st place for reporting award King County Fire Dist. 36, 1991, others. Mem. Soc. Profl. Journalists (various awards), Pacific N.W.

Newspaper Guild (unit chmn. 1988-90). Democrat. Roman Catholic. Home: 4724 7th Ave NE Seattle WA 98105 Office: Jour Am 1705 132d Ave NE Bellevue WA 98005

JARVIS, DONALD BERTRAM, judge; b. Newark, Dec. 14, 1928; s. Benjamin and Esther (Golden) J.; BA, Rutgers U., 1949; JD, Stanford U., 1952; m. Rosalind C. Chodorcove, June 13, 1954; children: Nancie, Brian, Joanne. Bar: Calif. 1953. Law clk. Justice John W. Shenk, Calif. Supreme Ct., 1953-54; assoc. Erskine, Erskine & Tulley, 1955; assoc. Aaron N. Cohen, 1955-56; law clk. Dist. Ct. Appeal, 1956; assoc. Carl Hoppe, 1956-57; adminstrv. law judge Calif. Pub. Utilities Commn., San Francisco, 1957-91, U.S. Dept. of Labor, 1992—. mem. exec. com. Nat. Conf. Adminstrv. Law Judges, 1986-88, sec. 1988-89, vice-chair, 1990-91, chair-elect, 1991-92, chair 1992-93; pres. Calif. Adminstrv. Law Judges Coun., 1978-84; mem. faculty Nat. Jud. Coll., U. Nev., 1977, 78, 80. Chmn. pack Boy Scouts Am., 1967-69, chmn. troop, 1972; class chmn. Stanford Law Sch. Fund, 1959, mem. nat. com., 1963-65; dir. Forest Hill Assn., 1970-71. Served to col. USAF Res., 1949-79. Decorated Legion of Merit. Mem. Am. Bar Assn., State Bar Calif., Bar Assn. San Francisco, Calif. Conf. Pub. Utility Counsel (pres. 1980-81), Nat. Panel Arbitrators, Am. Arbitration Assn., Air Force Assn., Res. Officers Assn., De Young Museum Soc. and Patrons Art and Music, San Francisco Gem and Mineral Soc., Stanford Alumni Assn., Rutgers Alumni Assn., Phi Beta Kappa (pres. No. Calif. 1973-74), Tau Kappa Alpha, Phi Alpha Theta, Phi Alpha Delta. Home: 530 Dewey Blvd San Francisco CA 94116-1427 Office: 211 Main St San Francisco CA 94105

JAUREGUI, RON JOSEPH, lawyer, consultant; b. Whittier, Calif., Mar. 19, 1963; s. Fred Jr. and Paula (Massei) J. BA, Claremont McKenna Coll., 1985; JD, UCLA, 1990. Bar: Calif. 1991. V.p. legal affairs and trade devel. Calif. World Trade Ctrs., Inc., Long Beach, 1992—. Participant Leadership Inst., Hispanic Devel. Coun., United Way program, Irvine, Calif., 1991; participant leadership devel. program Mexican-Am. Legal Def. and Edn. Fund, Santa Ana, Calif., 1992. Riordan fellow UCLA Anderson Grad. Sch. Mgmt., 1992. Mem. N.Am. Free Trade Agreement, Calif. Hispanic C. of C. (vol. 1992), Hispanic C. of C. (co-founder internat. affairs com. 1991—). Democrat. Roman Catholic. Home: 1845 Calle Belleza Rowland Heights CA 91748 Office: Calif World Trade Ctrs Inc One World Trade Ctr Ste 807 Long Beach CA 90831

JAY, CHRISTOPHER EDWARD, stockbroker; b. Walla Walla, Wash., May 2, 1949; s. Orville Elmo and Juanita Hope (Beckius) J.; m. Mardra Marguerite Jones, July 25, 1981; children: Pohaku Kepano, Hope Lauren, Christopher James. BS, Lewis and Clark Coll., 1972; MA, U. Nev., 1975. V.p. Merrill Lynch & Co., Anchorage, 1975—, now 1st v.p. Dist. chair Rep. Cen. Com., Anchorage, 1980-81; bd. trustees Lewis and Clark Coll., Portland, Oreg., 1988—; bd. dirs. Anchorage Mus. History and Art, 1988-90, KSKA Pub. Radio, Anchorage, 1991—. Mem. Rotary (pres. Anchorage chpt. 1989-90, Paul Harris fellow 1989). Presbyterian. Home: 11060 Hideaway Lake Dr Anchorage AK 99516 Office: Merrill Lynch & Co 3601 C St 14th Fl Anchorage AK 99503

JAY, DAVID JAKUBOWICZ, management consultant; b. Danzig, Poland, Dec. 7, 1925; s. Mendel and Gladys Gitta (Zalc) Jakubowicz; came to U.S., 1938, naturalized, 1944; BS, Wayne State U., 1948; MS, U. Mich., 1949, postgrad., 1956-57; postgrad. U. Cin., 1951-53, MIT, 1957; m. Shirley Anne Shapiro, Sept. 7, 1947; children: Melvin Maurice, Evelyn Deborah. Supr. man-made diamonds GE Corp., Detroit, 1951-56; instr. U. Detroit, 1948-51; asst. to v.p. engring. Ford Motor Co., Dearborn, Mich., 1956-63; project mgr. Apollo environ. control radiators N.Am. Rockwell, Downey, Calif., 1963-68; staff to v.p. corporate planning Aerospace Corp., El Segundo, Calif., 1968-70; founder, pres. PBM Systems Inc., 1970-83; pres. Cal-Best Hydrofarms Coop., Los Alamitos, 1972-77; cons. in field, 1983—. Pres., Community Design Corp., Los Alamitos, 1971-75; life master Am. Contract Bridge League. Served with USNR, 1944-46. Registered profl. engr., Calif., Mich., Ohio. Fellow Inst. Advancement Engring.; mem. Art Stamp and Stencil Dealers Assn. (pres. 1993—), Inst. Mgmt. Sci. (chmn. 1961-62), Western Greenhouse Vegetable Growers Assn. (sec.-treas. 1972-75), Tau Beta Pi. Jewish. Patentee in air supported ground vehicle, others. Home: 13441 Roane Santa Ana CA 92705-2271

JAYME, WILLIAM NORTH, writer; b. Pitts., Nov. 15, 1925; s. Walter A. and Catherine (Ryley) J.; student Princeton, 1943-44, 47-49. With Young & Rubicam Advt., Inc., 1949, Charles W. Gamble & Assos., 1949-50; asst. circulation promotion mgr. Fortune mag., 1950-51, Life mag., 1951-53, copy dir., sales and advt. promotion CBS Radio Network, N.Y.C., 1953-55; sr. copywriter McCann-Erickson, Inc., 1955-58; established own advt. creative service, 1958-71; pres. Jayme, Ratalahti, Inc., 1971—; lectr. direct mktg. Stanford U., Radcliffe Coll., worldwide mktg. confs. Producer U.S. Army radio program Music Motorized, 1945-46; editor, producer Time, Inc. TV programs Background for Judgment, 1951, Citizen's View of '52; script editor CBS Radio-UPA motion picture Tune in Tomorrow, 1954; creator promotions that launched Smithsonian, New York, Bon Appetit, Food & Wine, California, American Health, Air & Space, other nat. mags.; author script adaptations for Studio One and other TV programs, articles and stories in periodicals. Served as sgt., 2d Armored Div., AUS, 1944-46. Democrat. Episcopalian. Club: Century Assn.,(N.Y.C.). Author: (with Roderick Cook) Know Your Toes and Other Things to Know, 1963; (with Helen McCully, Jacques Pepin) The Other Half of the Egg, 1967; (opera libretto, with Douglas Moore) Carry Nation. Address: 1033 Bart Rd Sonoma CA 95476

JAYMES, DOROTHY L., health science administrator; b. New Orleans, Mar. 10, 1934; d. Hampton Moten and Beulah Mae (Houston) Moten Jones; m. Herbert Harrison, div.; children: Brenda Joyce, Beulah Mae, Mary Patricia, Breeman Joseph; m. Charles Royal, June 1968 (dec.). Student, Patten Bible Coll., 1979-81; BS, U. San Francisco, 1983; postgrad., City Coll. San Francisco, 1985-86. Owner, operator kindergarten New Orleans, 1960-62; asst. mgr. Houston For Music Sch. and Wholesale Retail Store, New Orleans, 1960-65; teller Bank Am., San Francisco, 1966-67; inventory clk. Tenneco Chems., Inc., San Francisco, 1967-70; coding clk. Assigned Risk Auto Ins., San Francisco, 1970-72; specialist health and homemaking Dept. Social Svcs., San Francisco, 1975-77; para profl. Woodrow Wilson High Sch., San Francisco, 1975; sec., book-keeper A&B Floor Coverings Co., San Francisco, 1975-77; dept. head Mcpl. Lost & Found Dept., San Francisco, 1977-78; spl. currier Dept. Social Svcs., San Francisco, 1978-79; mng. supr. San Francisco Mcpl. Elderly & Handicapped Programs, 1979-90; asst. to mgr. San Francisco Dept. City Planning, 1990-91, phys. plant mgr. and safety officer, 1992—; owner, operator Retail Furniture and Appliance store, New Orleans, 1992; apptd. rep. Am. Disabled Com., 1991—. Voters registrator Local 400, AFL/CIO, San Francsico, 1977—, shop steward Local 400 & 790, 1977-83, trustee, exec. bd. Local 790, 1983—; mem. Nat. Dem. Fund Raiser, Washington, 1980—, Regional Transit Authority Tech. Adv. Com., 1980-91, Joint Labor Mgmt. Team, 1989-91, Organizing Com. for the Pvt. Sector, 1991; del. San Francisco Labor Counsel, 1982—, San Francisco Organizing Project, 1983-88; negotiator City of San Francisco, 1980-91. Recipient Spl. Recognition for Civil and Pub. Servant and Ednl. Achievement award U. San Francisco, 1983, Religious and Civic Leadership award 3d Bapt. Ch., 1986, Leadership Achievement plaque Local 790 SEIU AFL/CIO, 1990; grantee Regional Transit Authority; San Francisco Mcpl. Ry. Presisio Div. lounge and lunchroom named in her honor, 1990; grantee BEOG, 1981-83, St. Ignatius, 1986-90. Mem. Ams. For Change (charter, presdl. task force), Order Eastern Star (past Worthy Matron, past Grand Dep., Silver Star 1960), Pleasure Treasure Club (pres. 1983), Sew and Save Club (sec. 1961-65), Silver's Social Lodge, Golden Gate Nat. Park Assn., Commonwealth Club, Zeta Phi Beta. Baptist. Home: 1665 Golden Gate Ave Apt 12 San Francisco CA 94115-4546 Office: Dept City Planning 450 Mcallister St San Francisco CA 94102-4516

JAYNE, CHARLOTTE, foundation executive; b. South Bend, Ind., Aug. 3, 1939; d. John K. and Lida G. (Jayne) Crippen; m. Raymond Dewitt Drake II, Sept. 23, 1959 (div. 1968); children: Jayne Rae Wyrick, Raymond Dewitt Drake III. AB, Monmouth (Ill.) Coll., 1958. Part-owner, v.p. Carlten Assocs., Newport Beach, Calif., 1980—; exec. dir., founder Parkinson's Ednl. Program, Newport Beach, 1982—; part-owner Wise Port, Newport Beach, 1986—; part-owner, v.p. Garland Drake Internat., Newport Beach, 1988—. Author: The Fourth Dimension, 1991; editor: (newsletter) PEP Exchange, 1981—. Mem. Nat. Orgn. Rare Disorders (bd. dirs.), Nat. Coalition for Rsch. in Neurol. and Communicative Disorders, Nat. Assn. Cosmetology Schs., Beauty and Barber Supply Inst. 555 Club, C. of C. Home: 1800 Park Newport 202 Newport Beach CA 92660 Office: Parkinsons Ednl Program 3900 Birch St Ste 105 Newport Beach CA 92660

JAYNES, PHIL, safety consultant; b. Chgo., May 10, 1923; s. Philip Somers and Katherine (Barrett) J.; m. Amy Walter, Dec. 11, 1949; children: Edie O'Laughlin, Phyllis Lappin, Wendy Neves, Lisa Johnson. BA, U. Chgo., 1948; MA, Loyola U., Chgo., 1963. Cert. safety profl., citizen ambassador. Sr. safety engr. Inland Steel Co., East Chicago, Ind., 1949-85; safety dir. No. Am. Refractories Co., Gary, Ind., 1987; pres., safety cons. Phil Jaynes & Assocs., Highland, Ind.-Sacramento, 1972—; mem. U.S. Safety and Health Mission to Peoples' Republic of China, 1983, to Czechoslovakia, Hungary, and Poland, 1992; safety cons. Internat. Exec. Svc. Corps, Peoples Republic of China, 1985-86, Brazil, 1988. Producer, author: (safety movie) Saved By the Belt, 1984. Chmn. Little Calumet River Commn. State of Ind., 1973-75; pres. Unitarian Universalist Community Ch., Sacramento, 1990-92; dir. Natomis Community Coun., Sacramento, 1989. 1st lt. USAAF, 1942-46. Mem. ASTM (sec. F-23 1982-85), Am. Soc. Safety Engrs. (legis. coord. Sacramento chpt. 1991, dir. 1991), Am. Indsl. Hygiene Assn., Nat. Safety Coun., System Safety Soc., Sacramento Area Coun. for Safety and Health. Republican. Office: Phil Jaynes & Assocs 7414 Sun Point Ln Sacramento CA 95828-6219

JAYNES, STEVEN MARK, project accountant; b. Oceanside, Calif., June 18, 1958; s. Gordon Kelsey and Charlotte Jane (Kardell) J.; m. Cathy Jo Heying, Dec. 14, 1990; children: Kerry Sweeney, Mary Sweeney. Student, U. Alaska, 1976-80; B., Pacific U., 1980; postgrad., U. Alaska, 1983-87, Seattle U., 1988-89, City U., 1993—. Environ. reclaimer NANA Devel. Corp., Anchorage, 1977; mgmt. trainee McDonald's Corp., Anchorage, 1975-77; staff mgmt. Up With People, Tucson, 1980-82; accounting security ARCO Alaska, Inc. (AGA), Anchorage, 1982-84; acct./counsel adminstrv. asst. Frontier Cos. of Alaska, Anchorage, 1984-87; project acct. Fletcher Indsl. Inc., Seattle, 1987—. Editor: Pacific University Directory, 1979. Bd. dirs. exec. com. Pacific U., Forest Grove, Oreg., 1979. Recipient Honor award Americas Names & Faces, 1980. Office: Fletcher Indsl Inc 425 Pontius Ave N Seattle WA 98109-5423

JEANLOZ, RAYMOND, geophysicist; b. Winchester, Mass., Aug. 18, 1952. BA, Amherst Coll, 1975; PhD in Geology and Geophysics, Calif. Inst. Tech., 1979. Asst. prof. Harvard U., 1979-81; from asst. prof. to assoc. prof. U. Calif., Berkeley, 1982-85, prof., 1985—. Recipient Mineral Soc. Am. award, 1988; MacArthur grantee, 1988. Fellow AAAS, Am. Geophysics Union (J.B. Macelwane award 1984); mem. Am. Acad. Arts and Scis. Office: U Calif Dept Geology Berkeley CA 94720-4767

JEDENOFF, GEORGE ALEXANDER, steel consultant; b. Petrosovodsk, Russia, July 5, 1917; came to U.S., 1923, naturalized, 1928; s. Alexander N. and Barbara Vacilivna (Sepiagina) J.; m. Barbara Jane Cull, Feb. 27, 1943; children: Nicholas, Nina. A.B. in Mech. Engring. magna cum laude, Stanford, 1940, M.B.A., 1942. With U.S. Steel Corp., 1942-74; indsl. engr. U.S. Steel Corp. (Columbia-Geneva Steel div.), Pittsburg, Calif., 1942-43; gen. foreman U.S. Steel Corp. (Columbia-Geneva Steel div.), 1946-52, asst. supt. sheet finishing, 1952-53, cold reduction, 1953-54, supt. cold reduction, 1954, asst. gen. supt., 1955-58, gen. supt., 1959; gen. supt. U.S. Steel Corp. (Geneva Works), Utah, 1960-67, Gary, Ind., 1967-69; gen. mgr. heavy products U.S. Steel Corp., Pitts., 1969-70; v.p. (Western Steel ops.), 1970-73; pres., dir. USS Engrs. & Cons., Inc. (subsidiary), Pitts., 1974; pres., chief operating officer, dir. Kaiser Steel Corp., Oakland, Calif., 1974-77; dir. Kaiser Internat. Shipping Corp., Kaiser Resources Ltd. (Can.), Hamersley Holdings (Melbourne), Australia, Kaiser Industries, 1974-77; now cons. steel industry and gen. mgmt. Active Boy Scouts Am., 1960—; pres. Utah Valley United Fund, 1966, N.W. Ind., 1968; co-chmn. Urban Coalition, Gary, 1968; mem. health and med. com. Am. Bur. Med. Aid to China, 1974; Bd. dirs. Mercy Hosp., Gary, 1967-69; mem. adv. council Brigham Young U., 1965-73; bd. dirs. Keep Am. Beautiful; chmn. East Bay major gifts com. Stanford U., 1978.; bd. govs. Stanford Assocs., 1984-86. Served to lt. USNR, 1943-46. Recipient Jesse Knight Indsl. Citizenship award Brigham Young U., 1966; Disting. Service award Stanford Bus. Sch. Alumni Assn., 1978; named Man of Year Utah Harvard Club, 1967. Mem. Iron and Steel Soc. of AIME, Am. Iron and Steel Inst., Assn. Iron and Steel Engrs. (pres. 1977), Western Pa. Safety Coun. (exec. com. 1970-74), Engrs. Soc. Western Pa., Bituminous Coal Operators Assn. (dir. 1974-77), Am. Assn. Engring. Socs. (commn. internat. relations), Oakland C. of C. (dir. 1976-79), Ind. C. of C. (dir. 1967-69), Stanford U. Bus. Sch. Alumni Assn. (nat. pres. 1956-57), Phi Beta Kappa, Tau Beta Pi. Clubs: Alta (Salt Lake City); Claremont (Oakland); Pacific-Union (San Francisco).

JEFFE, DOUGLAS IVAN, public affairs executive; b. L.A., Jan. 17, 1943; s. Harry and Mary (Cornblith) J.; m. Sherry Bebitch, Sept. 15, 1968. BA, UCLA, 1965. Dir. pub. affairs Calif. Dem. Party, L.A., 1963-66; founding ptnr. Pacific Mgmt. Assocs., L.A., 1967-68; sr. cons. Calif. State Assy., Sacramento, 1968-74; exec. v.p. Braun Ketchum, L.A., 1974—. Contbr. articles to profl. jours. Vice chair L.A. Taxpayers Assn.; Pres. L.A. Theatre Wks.; del. Dem. Nat. Conv., Miami, Fla., 1972. Office: Braun Ketchum 11755 Wilshire Blvd Los Angeles CA 90025

JEFFERIES, JOHN TREVOR, astronomer, astrophysicist, observatory administrator; b. Kellerberrin, Australia, Apr. 2, 1925; came to U.S., 1956, naturalized, 1967; s. John and Vera (Healy) J.; m. Charmian Candy, Sept. 10, 1949; children: Stephen R., Helen C., Trevor R. MA, Cambridge (Eng.) U., 1949; DSc, U. Western Australia, Nedlands, 1962. Sr. research staff High Altitude Obs., Boulder, Colo., 1957-59, Sacramento Peak Obs., Sunspot, N.Mex., 1957-59; prof. adjoint U. Colo., Boulder, 1961-64; prof. physics and astronomy U. Hawaii, Honolulu, 1964-83, dir., Inst. Astronomy, 1967-83; dir. Nat. Optical Astronomy Obs., Tucson, 1983-87; astronomer Nat. Optical Astronomy Obs., 1987-92; cons. Nat. Bur. Standards, Boulder, 1960-62; disting. vis. scientist Jet Propulsion Lab., 1991—. Author: (monograph) Spectral Line Formation, 1968; contbr. articles to profl. jours. Guggenheim fellow, 1970-71. Mem. Internat. Astron. Union, Am. Astron. Soc. Home: 1652 E Camino Cielo Tucson AZ 85718-1105 Office: Nat Optical Astronomy Obs PO Box 26732 Tucson AZ 85726-6732

JEFFERS, L(ESLIE) JOY, educational administrator; b. Union City, Ind., June 18, 1961; d. Emory Defoe and Linda Mae (Hoover) Jeffers; m. David William Haggard, July 23, 1988; children: Ian David Jeffers-Haggard, Ava Joy Jeffers-Haggard. A in Mgmt. Scis., Purdue U., 1989. Camp counselor YMCA, Ft. Wayne, Ind., 1979-80, gymnastics instr., 1980-82; bartender, waitress Azteca Restaurant, Ft. Wayne, 1982-84; customer svc. rep. Aetna Ins. Co., Ft. Wayne, 1984-87; dir. fin. aid Denver Inst. Tech., 1987—. Mem. Colo. Pvt. Schs. Assn., Rocky Mountain Assn. Student Fin. Aid Adminstrs., Colo. Assn. Fin. Aid Adminstrs., Nat. Assn. Fin. Aid Adminstrs. Democrat. Office: Denver Inst Tech 7350 N Broadway Denver CO 80221

JEFFERSON, GALEN, apparel executive; b. 1950. Student, Boston U., U. Wash. With Nordstrom Inc., 1974—; co-pres. Nordstrom Inc., Seattle, 1991—. Office: Nordstrom Inc 1501 5th Ave Seattle WA 98101*

JEFFERSON, JOHN DANIEL, political activist; b. Oakland, Calif., May 14, 1948; m. Eloise Glenn; children: Angela, Justin. AA in Social Scis. cum laude, Laney Jr. Coll., Oakland, Calif., 1974; BA in Polit. Sci. and History cum laude, San Francisco State U., 1976, MA in Polit. Sci., 1980. Congl. intern Oakland, Calif., 1977-78; urban intern U.S. Dept. H.U.D., 1980-81; multifamily housing rep. U.S. HUD, 1980-81, various positions, 1982-87, resigned, 1987; precinct committeman, dep. registrar Ariz. State Rep. Party, 1987; pres., owner Global Enterprises, Phoenix, 1985-91; Rep. activist, dir. S.W. region Vet. Coalition Bush-Quale '92 Campaign, 1991-92; Rep. polit. activist, 1992—. Elected vice chmn. Ariz. Black Rep. Coun., 1987; vol. Bush for Pres. campaign, 1987-88; mem. Nat. Urban Issues Task Force, 1988; del. Ariz. GOP Conv., 1988, Nat. GOP Conv., 1988; state chmn. Black Arizonians for Bush-Quayle, 1988; chmn. Ariz. Black Rep. Coun., 1988-90; mem. exec. com. Ariz. State GOP, 1988-90; co-chmn. State GOP Outreach Com., 1989-90; polit. appointee, spl. asst. Small Bus. Adminstrn., 1991-92, liaison to Schedule C Assn., 1991-92. With U.S. Mil., 1970-72. Mem. Phi Alpha Theta, Phi Sigma Alpha.

JEFFERSON, MYRA LAVERNE TULL, sales executive; b. Chester, Pa.; d. Clarence Ernest and Mary Marie (Gaines) Tull; m. Bernard Carr Jefferson III, Mar. 11, 1983. BS in Computer Sci., Roosevelt U., 1987; postgrad., Chaminade U., 1986-87. Computer programmer Integrated Computer Techs., Phila., 1979-83; cons. Honolulu, 1983-88; data base mgr. E.S.R.D. Network Coordinating Council, Honolulu, 1984-88; comptr. Static Control Products, Phoenix, 1989-93; pres. Lion-S Sales and Svcs., 1991—; cons. NCC #1 Med. Rev. Bd., Honolulu, 1985, Thrifty Constrn. Co., Honolulu, 1986-87, Computer Support, 1985. Apptd. by mayor City Mesa Human Svcs. Adv. Bd.; apptd. by gov. Econ. Security Adv. Bd.; treas. bd. Mesa Community Action Network; bd. dirs. WOW Project; alumnae Mesa Leadership Tng. Program, Valley Leadership Program, black bd. dirs. project. Recipient award for Outstanding Contributions to Data Processing, 1987, Profl. and Scholastic Achievement award, 1986, award for Outstanding Achievement in Data Processing Profession, 1986. Mem. AAUW, Math. Assn. Am., Am. Math. Soc., Women in Computing, Am. Assn. Ind. Investors. Office: PO Box 3149 Tempe AZ 85280-3149

JEFFERY, JAMES NELS, protective services official; b. Torrance, Calif., May 16, 1944; s. Daryl Fredrick and Mildred Evelyn (Sogard) J. AA, Long Beach City Coll., 1964; student, Calif. State U., Long Beach, 1964-65, Calif. State U., Sacramento, 1979-80. Capt., firefighter L.A. Fire Dept., 1965-87; dir. Long Beach (Calif.) Search & Rescue Unit, 1968—; asst. chief fire div. Calif. Office Emergency Svcs., Riverside, 1987—; rep. Firescope Communications, Riverside, 1979—. Co-author emergency plans. Chmn. svc. com. Boy Scouts Am., Long Beach, 1979-81, tng. com., 1982—; bd. dirs. Long Beach Community Episepsy Clinic, 1971-72. Recipient Disting. Svc. award Long Beach Jaycees, 1977, Community Svc. award Long Beach Fire Dept., 1978, Silver Beaver award Boy Scouts Am., 1983, Commendation Mayor City of L.A., 1985. Mem. Calif. State Firemen's Assn., Calif. Fire Chiefs Assn., Nat. Coord. Coun. on Emergency Mgmt., Nat. Eagle Scout Assn., So. Calif. Assn. Foresters and Fire Wardens, Lions, Elks. Republican. Lutheran. Home: 3916 Cerritos Ave Long Beach CA 90807-3608 Office: Office Emergency Fire Svcs PO Box 92257 Long Beach CA 90809-2257

JEFFERY, JOHN EDWARD, retired research chemist; b. Winnipeg, Man., Can., June 21, 1915; came to U.S., 1920; s. Isaac and Marguerite Elizabeth (Giles) J.; m. Ruth Norine Settergren, Jan. 2, 1942; children: Lynn, Robert, Jill, Sherry. BS in Chemistry, U. Wash., 1938, MS, 1941. Rsch. chemist Atlas Powder Co., Tamaqua, Pa., 1941-45; rsch. chemist, analytical group leadder ITT Rayonier Inc., Shelton, Wash., 1945-78; ret., 1978. Contbr. articles to profl. jours.; patentee delay electric blasting. Pres. Shelton Sch. Bd., 1952, Shelton Hosp., 1956. Mem. Am. Chem. Soc., Kiwanis, Moose, Elks. Episcopalian. Home: SE 323 Stotsbery Rd Shelton WA 98584

JEFFREDO, JOHN VICTOR, aerospace engineer, manufacturing company executive, inventor; b. Los Angeles, Nov. 5, 1927; s. John Edward and Pauline Matilda (Whitten) J.; m. Elma Jean Nesmith, (div. 1958); children: Joyce Jean Jeffredo Ryder, Michael John; m. Doris Louise Hinz, (div. 1980); children: John Victor, Louise Victoria Jeffredo-Warden; m. Gerda Adelheid Pillich, 1980. Grad. in Aeronautical Engring. Cal-Aero Tech. Inst., 1948; AA in Machine Design, Pasadena City Coll., 1951; grad. in Electronics The Ordnance Sch. U.S. Army, 1951; AA in Am. Indian Studies, Palomar Coll., 1978; postgrad. U. So. Calif., 1955-58; MBA, La Jolla U., 1980, PhD in Human Rels., 1984. Design engr. Douglas Aircraft Co., Long Beach and Santa Monica, Calif., 1955-58; devel. engr. Honeywell Ordnance Corp., Duarte, Calif., 1958-62; cons. Honeywell devel. labs., Seattle, 1962-65; supr. mech. engr. dept. aerospace div. Control Data Corp., Pasadena, Calif., 1965-68; project engr. Cubic Corp., San Diego, 1968-70; supr. mech. engring. dept. Babcock Electronics Co., Costa Mesa, Calif., 1970-72; owner, operator Jeffredo Gunsight Co., Fallbrook, Calif., 1971-81; chief engr. Western Designs, Inc., Fallbrook, 1972-81, exec. dir., 1981-88, chief exec. officer, 1988—; owner, operator Western Designs, Fallbrook, 1981-87, Western Design Concepts, Inc., 1987—; exec. dir. JXJ, Inc., San Marcos, Calif., 1981-88, chief exec. officer, 1988—; mgr. Jeffredo Gunsight div., 1981-89, owner, 1989—, chief engr. JXJ, Inc., 1987-92, owner, 1989-92 (merger JXJ, Inc. and Western Design Concepts, Fallbrook, Calif.); owner, mgr. Energy Assocs., San Diego, 1982-86; pres. Jeffredo Internat., 1984-88; founder, chief exec. officer John-Victor Internat., San Marcos, Calif., Frankfurt, Fed. Republica Germany, 1988—; engring. cons. Action Instruments Co., Inc., Gen. Dynamics, Alcyon Corp., Systems Exploration, Inc. (all San Diego), Hughes Aircraft Co., El Segundo, Allied-Bendix, San Marcos; bd. dirs. Indian World Corp., JXJ., Inc., John-Victor Internat. Author: Wildcatting; contbr. articles to trade jours. and mags.; guest editorial writer Town Hall, San Diego Union; patentee agrl. frost control, vehicle off-road drive system, recoil absorbing system for firearms, telescope sight mounting system for firearms, breech mech. sporting firearm, elec. switch activating system, 33 others. Mem. San Diego County Border Task Force on Undocumented Aliens, 1979-80, 81-82; chmn. Native Californian Coalition, 1982—; bd. dirs. Nat. Geog. Soc., 1968. With U.S. Army, 1951-53. Recipient Superior Svc. Commendation award U.S. Naval Ordnance Test Sta., Pasadena, 1959. Mem. AIAA (sr. mem.), IEEE, Am. Soc. for Metals, Soc. Automotive Engrs., Nat. Rifle Assn. (life), San Diego Zool. Soc., Sierra Club (life), The Wilderness Soc. Avocations: sculpture, chess, music, conservation, travel. Home: 1629 Via Monserate Fallbrook CA 92028-9305 Office: PO Box 669 San Marcos CA 92079-0669

JEFFREY, JOHN ORVAL, lawyer; b. Portsmouth, Va., Aug. 6, 1963; s. Orval L. and Mary L. (Coakley) J. BA, U. Dayton (Ohio), 1985; diploma internat. legal studies, U. San Diego, Paris, 1987; JD, Southwestern U., L.A., 1988. Bar: Calif. 1988, U.S. Dist. Ct. (cen. dist.) Calif. 1988. Assoc. Shield & Smith, L.A., 1989-90, Hewitt, Kaldor & Prout, L.A., 1990—. Campaign worker John Glenn Campaign for Pres., N.H., 1984; vol. Amnesty Internat. Mem. ABA (tort and ins. sect. internat. law sect., litigation sect., entertainment/sports law sect.), Assn. So. Calif. Def. Coun., Internat. Bar Assn., L.A. County Bar Assn. (evaluation profl. standards com., legis. activity), Phi Alpha Delta, Alpha Nu Omega. Democrat. Office: Hewitt Kaldor and Prout 4605 Lankershim Blvd Ste 540 North Hollywood CA 91602

JEFFREY, RENWICK BYRON, small business owner; b. Cedar Rapids, Iowa, Aug. 17, 1935; s. Carl Everett and Ruth Viola (Thompkins) J.; m. Nancy Adele, Feb. 15, 1986; children by previous marriage: Allyson Cecile, Valorie Ann, Ryan Barrett. AA in Social Sci., Am. River Coll., Sacramento, 1962; BA in Sociology, Calif. State U., Sacramento, 1965. Sales rep. Burroughs Wellcome Co., Chico, Calif., 1965-71, spl. rep. trainer, 1969-72; spl. rep. hosps. Burroughs Wellcome Co., San Francisco, 1971-77, Fresno, Calif., 1977-87; pres. Fur-Pets-Only, Visalia, Calif., 1987—. Author: Role of Antihistamines in Therapy of Allergies and Colds, 1978. Pub. rels. dir. Butte County Pharmacy Assn., Chico, 1968-70; v.p. Homeowners Assn., Redwood Shores, Calif., 1973; pres. Belmont (Calif.) Little League, 1972. Mem. Western World Pet Supply Assn., Rotary Internat. Republican. Episcopalian. Home: 3507 W Howard Visalia CA 93277 Office: Fur Pets Only 650 S Bridge St Visalia CA 93277

JEFFREY, RONALD JAMES, youth director, educator; b. Cheyenne, Wyo., Mar. 11, 1949; s. John Thomas and Lillian Leola (Carter) J.; m. Marilyn Mansell, Dec. 10, 1977; children: Keeya, Kaylee. BS, Chardon St. Coll., 1972; MS, U. No. Colo., 1976. Dir. Office of Youth Alterntives, Cheyenne, 1971—; cons. various human svc. groups, Cheyenne, 1972—, Title IV Sch. Adminstrn. State of Colo., 1973-74; instr. Laramie County Community Coll., Cheyenne, 1973-85, U. Wyo., Laramie, 1977-90; bd. dir. Rocky Mountain Fed. Bank, Cheyenne; guest speaker various group, 1980—. Author: A Guide for the Family Therapist, 1984; co-author: The Family: A Living Kaleidoscope, 1981; editor (manual) "We Care" Volunteer Training, 1981. Mem. Wyo. Youth Initiative, Cheyenne, Wyo. African/Am. Hist. Com., Cheyenne, Adult Learning Ctr. Adv. Bd.; bd. dir. United Way, Cheyenne, 1987—. Recipient George Washington Honor medal Feedom Found., 1977, Jefferson award Jefferson Com., 1980. Mem. Wyo. Assn. of Marriage and Family (past pres. 1987-89), Phi Delta Kapp. Democrat. Methodist. Office: Office Youth Alternatives 1328 Talbot Ct Cheyenne WY 82001-2648

JEFFRIES, RUSSELL MORDEN, communications company official; b. Carmel, Calif., July 15, 1935; s. Herman M. and Louise (Morden) J.; m. Barbara Jean Borcovich, Nov. 24, 1962; 1 child, Lynne Louise. AA, Hartnell Coll., 1971. Sr. communications technician AT&T, Salinas, Calif., 1955-91; mayor City of Salinas, 1987-91. Pres. El Gabilan Sch. PTA,

Salinas, 1971-74, Salinas Valley Council PTA, 1975-76; mem. Salinas City Sch. Bd., 1975-81; mem. Salinas City Council, 1981-87; bd. dirs. Community Hosp. Salinas Found., 1987--, Salinas-Kushikino Sister City, 1987--, pres. 1992-93, John Steinbeck Ctr. Found., 1987--, Food Bank for Monterey County, 1992—; hon. bd. dirs. Monterey Film Festival, 1987, Calif. Rodeo Assn., 1987; mem. ctrl. bd. Calif. Regional Water Quality, 1992—. Recipient hon. service award PTA, Salinas, 1976; cert. of appreciation Calif. Dept. Edn., 1980, Salinas City Sch. Dist., 1981, Calif. Sch. Bds. Assn., 1981, Steinbeck Kiwanis, Salinas, 1987; named hon. mem. Filipino community Salinas Valley, 1988. Mem. Salinas C. of C., Native Sons Golden West, K.C., Rotary, Moose. Republican. Roman Catholic. Home: 204 E Curtis St Salinas CA 93906-2804

JELEN, JAROSLAW ANDRZEJ, mathematician, researcher; b. Nowy Targ, Cracow, Poland, Sept. 14, 1943; came to Can., 1984; s. Henryk and Maria (Cieslewicz) J.; m. Alicja Barbara Solecka, Feb. 13, 1971; 1 child, Marek. MS in Math., U. Wroclaw, Poland, 1969; PhD, Acad. Mining and Metallurgy, Cracow, Poland, 1978. Programmer, computer factory, Wroclaw, 1969-71; research scientist Petroleum Inst., Cracow, 1971-78; asst. prof. U. Cracow, 1979-84; research scientist Nova Husky Research Co. Ltd., Calgary, Alta., Can., 1985. Contbr. articles to profl. jours. Co-inventor in area of oil and gas exploitation. Mem. Am. Math. Soc. Roman Catholic. Avocations: downhill skiing, swimming, hiking. Home: 35 Sanderling Hill NW, Calgary, AB Canada T3K 3B6

JELLICO, JOHN ANTHONY, artist; b. Koehler, N.Mex., June 26, 1914; s. Michael and Matilda (Saban) J.; children: Janice, Carol, Kenneth. Diploma, Art Inst. Pitts., 1937; cert., Phoenix Art Inst., 1939. Illustration dept. head Art Inst. of Pitts., 1946-50, asst. dir., 1950-56; dir. Colo. Inst. of Art, Denver, 1956-62, pres., 1962-75; co-owner art gallery, Santa Fe, N.Mex. Contbg. editor Am. Artist, N.Y.C., 1969-81; assoc. editor Southwestern Art, Austin, 1974-77; author: How to Draw Horses, 1946, 5 text books; executed murals St. Patrick's Ch., Raton, N.Mex., 1937, 3d Air Force Chapels, 1942-46. Staff sgt. USAF, 1942-46. Scholarship Art Inst. of Pitts., 1935; invited to hang four paintings at White House, 1975-77. Home: 291 W Belleview Ave Englewood CO 80110-6633 Office: Jellico Studio Western Art Englewood CO 80110

JELLICO, NANCY ROSE, painter, sculptor; b. LaGrange, Ga., Sept. 22, 1939; d. James Davis and Mary Myrtle (Capley) Norris; m. John Anthony Jellico, Dec. 22, 1960 (div. 1981); children: Janice Lee, Carol Anne, Kenneth Alan; m. Glenn Howard Hildebrandt, May 2, 1987 (div. 1992). Diploma, Colo. Inst. Art, 1960. registrar Colo. Inst. Art., Denver, 1961-64, instr., 1964-65. Group exhibits include Steamboat Springs, Colo., 1990, 91, Denver, 1990, Great Falls, Mont., 1990, Tucson Mus. Art, 1991, 92, 93, Murisaki Gallery, Tokyo, 1992, numerous others; commd. works include The Upjohn Co., Kalamazoo, 1983-90, St. Thomas Theol. Sem., Denver, 1985, 88, 90, Pro Rodeo Hall Fame & Mus. Am. Cowboy, Colorado Springs, 1983; illustrator featured articles numerous publs. including Art of the West mag., 1990, Equine Images mag., 1989, Cowboy Internat. mag., 1987, Southwest Art mag., 1986. Mem. Pastel Soc. Am. (assoc.), Nat. Soc. Painters in Casein and Acrylic (assoc.), Pastel Soc. S.W., Knickerbocker Artists (assoc.). Office: Jellico Art Studio 1449 W Littleton Blvd # 204 Littleton CO 80120-2127

JELLINEK, ROGER, editor; b. Mexico City, Jan. 16, 1938; came to U.S., 1961; s. Frank Louis Mark and Marguerite Lilla Donne (Lewis) J.; m. Margherita DiCenzo, Dec. 22, 1963 (div. 1985); children: Andrew Mark, Claire; m. Eden-Lee Murray, 1985; 1 child, Everett Peter Murray. Student, Bryanston Sch., Dorset, Eng., 1951-56; MA, Cambridge U., Eng., 1961. Assoc. editor Random House, 1963-64; editor Walker & Co., 1964-65; editor N.Y. Times Book Rev., 1966-70, dep. editor, 1970-73; editor in chief Times Books, Quadrangle/N.Y. Times Book Co., 1974-78, sr. editor, 1978-81, editor Lamont newsletter and yearbook, 1981-91; pres. Clairemark, Ltd., Palisades, N.Y., 1981—. Editor Atlantic Realm Project. With Royal Marines, 1956-57; 2d lt. Brit. Intelligence Corps., 1957-58. Mellon fellow Yale, 1961-63. Home and Office: 45-112 Seabury Pl Kaneohe HI 96744

JENCKES, THOMAS ALLEN, utility environmental program administrator; b. Providence, Aug. 9, 1939; s. Thomas Allen and Marjorie Jane (Blanchard) J.; children: Katharine, Stuart. BS in Physics with honors, U. R.I., 1969; MS in Environ. Health, Temple U., 1970, PhD, 1975; MA in Mgmt., JFK U./NTL Inst., 1991. Radiation safety and environ. engr. Met. Edison Co., Reading, Pa., 1973-78; radiation protection advisor Pacific Gas & Electric Co., San Francisco, 1978-80, supervising nuclear plant ops. engr., 1980-81; supervising engr. R&D dept. Pacific Gas & Electric Co., San Ramon, Calif., 1981-82, project mgr. Carrisa Plains 30 Mwe Solar Thermal Power Plant, 1982-84, supervising engr. tech. info. svcs., 1984-92, mgr. EPRI Tech. Transfer, 1992, environ. program mgr. R&D dept., 1992—. Chmn. dept. engring. rsch. United Way Campaign, 1986; prs. Mt. Diablo Unified Sch. Dist. Edn. Fund, 1984-85; vol. United Way Campaign, 1991. With USN, 1960-67. USPHS fellow, Phila., 1979-82. Mem. Electric Power Rsch. Inst. (tech. info. coord. com. 1983—), Edison Electric Inst. (health physics com. 1974-79), Sigma Pi Sigma, Phi Kappa Phi. Office: Pacific Gas & Electric Co 3400 Crow Canyon Rd San Ramon CA 94583

JENES, THEODORE GEORGE, JR., retired military officer; b. Portland, Oreg., Feb. 21, 1930; s. Theodore George and Mabel Marie (Moon) J.; m. Beverly Lorraine Knutson, Jan. 29, 1953; children—Ted, Mark. BS, U. Ga., 1956; MS, Auburn U., 1969; grad., Army Command and Gen. Staff Coll., Armed Forces Staff Coll., Air War Coll.; LLD (hon.), U. Akron, 1986. Enlisted U.S. Army, 1951, commd. 2d lt., 1953, advanced through grades to lt. gen., 1984, various assignments, 1953-75; comdr. 3d Brigade, 2d Inf. Div., Republic of Korea, 1975-76, 172d Inf. Brigade, Ft. Richardson, Alaska, 1978-81, 4th Inf. Div., Ft. Carson, Colo., 1982-84; comdg. gen. 3d U.S. Army, Ft. McPherson, Ga., 1984-87; commander U.S. Army Forces Ctrl. Command, Ft. McPherson, Ga., 1984-87; dep. comdg. gen. hdqrs. U.S. Army Forces Command, Ft. McPherson, Ga., 1984-87, ret., 1987; cons. Burdeshaw and Assocs., 1987-88; gen. mgr. Seattle Tennis Club, 1988—. Decorated D.S.M., Legion of Merit, Bronze Star, Meritorious Service medal, Air medal, Army Commendation medal, Vietnamese Cross of Gallantry with Silver Star. Mem. Assn. of U.S. Army, Rotary. United Methodist. Home: 809 169th Pl SW Lynnwood WA 98037-3307

JENKINS, BETTY JEAN, human services administrator; b. Fargo, N.D., Mar. 5, 1940; d. Emil and Esther M. (Flamer) Sunderland; m. Leslie Thomas Jenkins, July 2, 1966 (div. 1986); children: Kaaren E., Ralph T. Jenkins. BS in Sociology, U. Hawaii, Hilo, 1989; MPH, U. Hawaii, 1990. Intern healthy aging project Hawaii State Dept. of Health, Honolulu, 1990; policy analyst Hawaii Med. Svc. Assocs., Honolulu, 1991-92; long term care channeling specialist, case mgr. State of Hawaii Dept. Human Svcs., Honolulu, 1992—. Contbr. chpt. in book. Mem. Hawaii Assn. Case Mgrs. (bd. dirs.), Soc. Pub. Health Educators, Phi Kappa Phi. Baptist. Home: 1726 A Elua St Honolulu HI 96819 Office: Hawaii Dept Human Svcs 810 N Vineyard Blvd Honolulu HI 96817

JENKINS, BRUCE STERLING, federal judge; b. Salt Lake City, Utah, May 27, 1927; s. Joseph and Bessie Pearl (Iverson) J.; m. Margaret Watkins, Sept. 19, 1952; children—Judith Margaret, David Bruce, Michael Glen, Carol Alice. B.A. with high honors, U. Utah, 1949, LL.B., 1952, J.D., 1952. Bar: Utah 1952, U.S. Dist. Ct. 1952, U.S. Supreme Ct. 1962, U.S. Circuit Ct. Appeals 1962. Pvt. practice law Salt Lake City, 1952-59; assoc. firm George McMillan, 1959-65; asst. atty. gen. State of Utah, 1952; dep. county atty. Salt Lake County, 1954-58; bankruptcy judge U.S. Dist. Ct., Dist. of Utah, 1965-78; judge U.S. Dist. Ct. of Utah, 1978—, chief judge, 1984—. Research, publs. in field; contbr. essays to Law jours.; bd. editors: Utah Law Rev, 1951-52. Mem. Utah Senate, 1959-65, minority leader, 1963, pres. senate, 1965, vice chmn. commn. on orgn. exec. br. of Utah Govt., 1965-66; mem. adv. com. Utah Tech. Coll., 1967-72; mem. instl. council Utah State U., 1976. Served with USN, 1945-46. Mem. Utah State Bar Assn., Salt Lake County Bar Assn., Am. Bar Assn., Fed. Bar Assn., Order of Coif, Phi Beta Kappa, Phi Kappa Phi, Phi Eta Sigma, Phi Sigma Alpha, Tau Kappa Alpha. Democrat. Mormon. Office: US Dist Ct 251 US Courthouse 324 S State St Ste 105 Salt Lake City UT 84111-2321

JENKINS, CAREN, legislative research analyst; b. Phila., Aug. 14, 1958; d. Arthur B. and Eileen C. (Rosenthal) J. BS, Pa. State U., 1980; MA, Golden Gate U., 1983. With pub. rels. dept. Fed. Emergency Mgmt. Agy., Ft. Indiantown Gap, Pa., 1980; coord. History, Arts and Sci. Commn., Daly City, Calif., 1981-84; exec. dir. Brewery Arts Ctr., Carson City, Nev., 1984-89; sr. rsch. analyst Legis. Counsel Bur., Carson City, 1989—; cons. North San Mateo County Ctr. for Arts, Daly City, Calif., 1983-84; prin. staff legis. com. on health care, assembly natural resources Nev. Ho. of Reps., Carson City, 1991-93; mem. prin. staff transp. com. Nev. Senate, 1991-93. Contbr. articles on pub. policy issues to profl. publs. Bd. dirs. Pub. Access TV, Carson City, 1985-89, Carson City Mainstreet, 1987-91, Very Spl. Arts Nev., Reno, 1988-90. Mem. Carson City C. of C. (bd. dirs. 1984-89), Pa. State U. Alumni Assn. Jewish. Home: 194 Galena Way Carson City NV 89706-1902

JENKINS, EVERETT WILBUR, JR., lawyer; b. Oklahoma City, Nov. 28, 1953; s. Everett Wilbur and Lillie Belle (Ingram) J.; m. Monica Lynn Endsley, June 3, 1978; children: Ryan, Camille, Jennifer, Cristina. BA, Amherst Coll., 1975; JD, U. Calif., Berkeley, 1978. Bar: Calif. 1979. Dep. county counsel Contra Costa County, Martinez, Calif., 1980-81; dep. city atty. City of Richmond, Calif., 1981-84; asst. city atty. City of Richmond, 1984—; bd. atty. West County Agy., Richmond, 1981-90; authority atty. Solid Waste Mgmt. Authority West Contra Costa, Richmond, 1985-87, 88-91; legal rep. tech. adv. com. Contra Costa County Solid Waste Commn., Martinez, Calif., 1986-87; pub. mem., 1987-88. Rep. Contra Costa County Hazardous Materials Commn., Martinez, 1987-88; bd. dirs. West Contra Costa YMCA, Richmond, 1987—, chair program com., 1991-92. vice chair bd. dirs., 1992—, chair community gifts campaign, 1992— (named Rita Davis Vol. of the Yr., 1993). Mem. State Bar Calif. (exec. bd. pub. law sect. exec. com. 1987-91, editor Pub. Law News 1988-91, liaison to bd. govs. 1991-92), Charles Houston Bar Assn. Democrat. Office: City Atty's Office 2600 Barrett Ave # 330 Richmond CA 94804-1661

JENKINS, JAMES STANLEY, architect; b. Rockford, Ill., Aug. 8, 1935; s. Amey W. and Patricia Dawn (Snively) J.; m. Patricia Eleanor Erickson, Oct. 6, 1956; children: Lynn Christine, Laura Catherine, Lisa Caroline. Cert. in bldg. consgrn., Chog. Tech. Coll., 1962; cert. in landscape design, Nat. Landscape Inst., 1967; cert. in architecture, Ctr. Degree Studies, Scranton, Pa., 1989. Registered architect, Ill., Wash., Calif., Oreg., Idaho. Constrn. adminstr. Bradley & Bradley, Inc., Rockford, 1965-70; project mgr. Harry Weese, Ltd., Chgo., 1970-76, Project Control, Inc., Chgo., 1976-78; pres. Mohawk Design, Inc., Wheaton, Ill., 1978-82; sr. project dir. John Graham Co., Seattle, 1982-86; project mgr. Unico Properties, Inc., Seattle, 1986-89; devel. coord. The Hearthstone, Seattle, 1989-91; owner rep. pvt. residence constrn. Medina, Wash., 1991—. Cpl. USMC, 1956-59. Mem. AIA, Nat. Coun. Archtl. Registration Bds., Bldg. Owners and Mgrs. Inst. (real property adminstr.). Republican. Lutheran. Home: 5605 101st St SW Mukilteo WA 98275

JENKINS, JANET E., state legislator, lawyer; b. Omaha, Jan. 22, 1941; d. Albert Eldon and Callie Elizabeth (Cowan) Clark; children: Jay Allen, John Richard, Janell Elizabeth, Lucille Jenkins. BS, So. Oreg. State Coll., 1962; JD magna cum laude, Gonzaga U., 1982. Bar: Idaho; cert. libr. Sch. libr. Corbett (Oreg.) Sch. Dist., 1972-76; tchr. Gresham (Oreg.) Sch. Dist., 1975-77, Wood River Jr. High Sch., Hailen, Idaho, 1978; law clerk U.S. Dist. Ct. (ea. dist.) Wash., Spokanne, 1982-83; atty. Hannon, Jenkins & Assocs., Coeur d'Alene, Idaho, 1983-88, Jenkins & Leggett, Coeur d'Alene, 1989-92; mem. Idaho Ho. Reps., 1990—; pvt. practice atty. Coeur d'Alene, 1993—. Mem. AAUW, NOW, Idaho State Bar. Democrat. Methodist. Home: 1627 Boyd Coeur D Alene ID 83814

JENKINS, JEFFREY M., educator; b. L.A., Mar. 13, 1963; s. Harley L. and Judy A. (Pasos) J. BA, Loyola Marymount U., L.A., 1985. Cert. tchr., Calif. Tchr. Daniel Murphy High Sch., L.A., 1990—, dir. campus ministry, 1991—. Roman Catholic.

JENKINS, MARGARET AIKENS, educational administrator; b. Lexington, Miss., May 14, 1925; d. Joel Bryant and Marie C. (Threadgill) Melton; m. Daniel Armstrong, May 21, 1944 (div. 1950); children: Marie Cynthia, Marsha Rochelle; m. Gabe Aikens, June 29, 1954 (div. 1962); m. Herbert Jenkins, May 21, 1966. Student, Chgo. Conservatory of Music, 1959, Moody Bible Inst., Chgo., 1959, Calif. State U.-Northridge, 1984; HHD (hon.), Payne Acad., 1984, Pentecostal Bible Coll., 1988, So. Calif. Sch. Ministry, 1990, Liberty U., 1990—. Clk., U.S. Signal Corps, Chgo., 1944, Cuneo Press, Chgo., 1948-52, Ford Aircraft, Chgo., 1952-58, Corps of Engrs., Chgo., 1958-64; progress control clk. Def. Contract Adminstrn. Service Region, Los Angeles, 1966-73; founder, adminstr. Celeste Scott Christian Sch., Inglewood, Calif., 1976—; founder, pres. Mary Celeste Scott Meml. Found., Inc., Inglewood, 1973—; pub., writer, founder Magoll Records, Chgo., 1958-64, M&M Aikens Music, 1957—; mem. Inglewood Coalition Against Drugs, 1987—; radio broadcast Look and Live Sta. KTYM, Inglewood, Calif., 1986—; Mayor of Inglewood Ann. Prayer Breakfast Com., 1988. Recipient Cert. Appreciation, Mayor of Inglewood, 1984, Mayor of Los Angeles, 1980, State Senator, 1975, State Rep., 1976, Congressional Cert. of Appreciation, 1993; named Woman of Yr., Los Angeles Sentinel, 1982, Inglewood C. of C., 1982, Presdl. Commemorative Honor Roll, 1991, Outstanding Christian Woman of Faith World Won for Christ Ministries, Englewood, Calif., 1993. Mem. Broadcast Music Inc., Am. Fedn. TV and Radio Artists, Nat. Assn. Pentecostal Women and Men Inc. Avocations: religion, writing and recording music, education. Home: 11602 Cimarron Ave Hawthorne CA 90250-1916 Office: Celeste Scott Christian Sch 930 S Osage Ave Inglewood CA 90301-4188

JENKINS, ROBERT LEE, management consultant; b. Portland, Oreg., June 21, 1932; s. Joseph A. and Elfreda (Carlsen) J.; m. Carolyn E. Osborne, July 8, 1955; children: Craig H., Brian G. AB, Harvard U., 1954. Cons. Office of Graham Parker, N.Y.C. and Rome, 1957-63; gen. mgr., dir. devel. H.J. Heniz Co., Pitts. and Brussels, 1963-73; gen. mgr. Macke Co., Washington, 1973-75; dir. devel. Continental Grain Co., San Francisco, 1976-80; gen. ptnr. Mgmt. Resource Ptnrs., San Francisco, 1981—; bd. dirs. Supreme Casting Ltd., L.A., Bayline Mgmt., Inc., Redwood Shores, Calif. Capt. USMC, 1954-57. Mem. Assn. Corp. Growth Dirs., Internat. Exec. Svc. Corps, USMC Command and Staff Coll. Home: 36 Irving Ave Atherton CA 94027 Office: Mgmt Resource Ptnrs Ste 100 3 Lagoon Dr Redwood Shores CA 94065

JENKINS, RONALD PATRICK, air force officer; b. Edwards AFB, Calif., Jan. 11, 1960; s. Ronald Emmet and Myrtis Barbara (McLain) J.; m. Brenda-Lyn Anne Oliver, Oct. 27, 1984; children: Ronald Joseph, Megan Marie, Kristin Michelle, Christopher Patrick, Caitlin Anne. BBA, The Citadel, 1982; MBA, Webster U., 1987; student, USAF Squadron Officer Sch., 1987. Commd. comdr. USAF, 1983, advanced through grades to capt., 1986; dep. missile combat crew comdr. USAF, McConnell AFB, Kans., 1983, standardization evaluation dep. crew comdr., 1983-85; missile combat crew comdr. USAF, Little Rock, Ark., 1986, instr. missile combat crew comdr., 1987; flight comdr. missile combat crew comdr. USAF, Malstrom AFB, Mont., 1987-88, evaluator missile combat crew comdr, 1988-89, emergency war order instr., 1989-90; satellite planning/analysis officer USAF, Falcon AFB, Colo., 1990-91, undergrad. space trainee, 1991-92, satellit ops. flight comdr., 1992-93, chief opers. tng., 1993, exec. officer 50th space wing, 1993—; chief pubs. br., Malmstrom AFB, 1988-89; computer facility mgr., Malmstrom AFB, 1989-90. Big brother Big Bros. and Big Sisters, Wichita, Kans., 1984-85. Decorated Airman's Medal for Heroism. Mem. Air Force Assn.

JENKINS, ROYAL GREGORY, manufacturing executive; b. Springville, Utah, Dec. 11, 1936; s. Chester W. and Sarah E. (Finch) J.; m. Donna Jeanne Jones, Aug. 3, 1957; children: Brad, Kent. BS in Engring., San Jose State U., 1959; MBA, U. Santa Clara, 1968. With Lockheed Corp., Sunnyvale, Calif., 1959-64; contr. ICORE Industries, Sunnyvale, 1964-68; div. v.p. fin. Dart Industries, Los Angeles, 1968-74; dir. planning, div. v.p. Avery Label Group, Avery Internat., Los Angeles, 1974-81, group v.p. Materials Group, Painesville, Ohio, 1981-87, sr. v.p. tech. and planning, Pasadena, Calif., 1987-88, sr. v.p. fin., 1988—; CFO, Avery Dennison Corp. Republican. Avocation: golf. Office: Avery Dennison 150 N Orange Grove Pasadena CA 91103

JENKINS, SAMUEL LEROY, insurance executive; b. Walsenburg, Colo., May 5, 1928; s. William H. and Mary (Irons) J.; m. Ferol M. Deaderick, Dec. 29, 1960; children: Mary Marguerite, Thelma Kathleen, John James. BS in Edn. with honors, U. Idaho, 1952. Regional supr. Pacific Mutual Life Ins. Co., Phoenix, 1958-60; pres. Phillip S Hack & Co., Phoenix, 1960-69; sr. v.p., regional mgr. Martin E. Segal Co., Denver, 1969—. Vice chmn. Denver Coun. of Govts., 1975-77; city councilman Greenwood Village Colo., 1972-77, mayor, 1977-81; vice chmn. Denver Regional Coun. of Govs., 1975-77. Capt. USMC, 1952-55. Named Citizen of Yr. Bd. of Realtors, 1979. Mem. Valley Country Club, Sertoma Club, 1st Marine Div. Assn., others. Democrat. Methodist. Home: 4951 S Clinton St Englewood CO 80111 Office: The Segal Co 6300 S Syracuse Way Englewood CO 80111

JENKINS, SPEIGHT, opera company executive, writer; b. Dallas, Jan. 31, 1937; s. Speight and Sara (Baird) J.; m. Linda Ann Sands, Sept. 6, 1966; children: Linda Leonie, Speight. B.A., U. Tex.-Austin, 1957; LL.B., Columbia U., 1961; DMus (hon.), U. Puget Sound, 1992; HHD, Seattle U., 1992. News and reports editor Opera News, N.Y.C., 1967-73; music critic N.Y. Post, N.Y.C., 1973-81; TV host Live from the Met, Met. Opera, N.Y.C., 1981-83; gen. dir. Seattle Opera, 1983—; classical music editor Record World, N.Y.C., 1973-81; contbg. editor Ovation Mag., N.Y.C., 1980—, Opera Quar., Los Angeles, 1982—. Served to capt. U.S. Army, 1961-66. Recipient Emmy award for Met. Opera telecast La Boheme TV Acad. Arts and Scis., 1982. Mem. Phi Beta Kappa Assocs. Presbyterian. Home: 903 Harvard Ave E Seattle WA 98102-4561 Office: Seattle Opera Assn PO Box 9248 Seattle WA 98109-0248

JENKINS, WILLIAM WALTER, psychologist, consultant; b. Phila., Sept. 10, 1943; s. William and Emily Elizabeth (Bachman) J.; m. Doreen Gayle Meyers, may 30, 1976; children: Eran Scott, Joshua Ian, Tracey Lynn. BS, Temple U., 1968; MEd, Pa. State U., 1974, PhD, 1982. Lic. psychologist, Ariz. Commd. 1st lt. USAF, 1970; advance through grades to lt. col. USNG, 1993; program coord. psychology dept. Phila. State Hosp., 1975-78; psychologist base svc. unity MH/MR, Bellefonte, Pa., 1978-82; program dir. Stress Control Svcs., Inc., Middletown, Pa., 1982-84; sr. staff psychologist Deveraux Ctr., Scottsdale, Ariz., 1985-87; clin. dir. Alamo Juvenile Instn., Phoenix, 1987-88; program dir. children's treatment unit Ariz. State Hosp., Phoenix, 1988-91; pvt. practice cons. psychology Scottsdale, Ariz., 1985—; cons. psychologist Community Care Network, Scottsdale, 1990-92; Prehab of Mesa (Ariz.), 1990—, Maricopa Clin. Mgmt., 1992-93; cons. Sta. WITF-PBS, Harrisburg, Pa., coord. community responses TV series on grief and loss Begin with Goodbye, 1982; cons. Continuing Porfl. Edn. Devel. Project, University Park, Pa., GE, Phila, Ariz. Dept. Corrections, Phoenix, Charter counseling Ctr., Phoenix; lectr. personality devel. and disorders in children Psychiat. Technician Tng. Program, 1988-91. Contbr. articles to profl. jours. Facilitator support group for parents of young head injured children St. Joseph's Hosp., 1986-87. Diplomate Am. Bd. Vocat. Experts; mem. APA, N.G. Assn., Pa. State U. Alumni Assn., Phi Kappa Phi. Jewish. Home: 15233 N 62 Pl Scottsdale PA 85254

JENNERICH, EDWARD JOHN, college administrator; b. Bklyn., Oct. 22, 1945; s. William James and Anna Johanna (Whicker) J.; m. Elaine Zaremba, May 27, 1972; children—Ethan Edward, Emily Elaine. B.A., Trenton State Coll., 1967; M.S.L.S., Drexel U., 1970; Ph.D., U. Pitts., 1974. Cert. tchr., learning resources specialist. Tchr. U.S. history Rahway High Sch., N.J., 1967-70; librarian Westinghouse High Sch., Pitts. Pub. Sch., 1970-74; adminstrv. intern U. Pitts, 1973; chmn. dept. library sci. Baylor U., Waco, Tex., 1974-83; dean Sch. Library Sci. So. Conn. State U., New Haven, 1983-84; v.p. acad. affairs Va. Intermont Coll., Bristol, 1984-87; grad. dean Seattle U., 1987-89; assoc. provost for acad. adminstrn., dean Grad. Sch., 1989—. Co-author: University Administration in Great Britain, 1983, The Reference Interview as a Creative Art, 1987; contbr. articles to profl. jours. Bd. dirs. Waco Girls Club, Tex., 1977-83. Recipient Eileen Tosney Adminstrv. Excellence award Am. Assn. Univ. Adminstrs., 1985. Mem. Am. Assn. Univ. Adminstrs. (bd. dirs. 1980-82, 83-86, 89—, exec. com. 1982-87, chmn. overseas liaison com. 1982-87), Assn. for Coll. and Rsch. Librs. (exec. bd. dirs. 1984-88), ALA (office for libr. personnel resources 1980-82), Fulbright Adminstrv. Exch. (rev. panel 1983-86), Phi Delta Kappa. Republican. Episcopalian. Home: 6935 NE 164th St Bothell WA 98011-4282 Office: Seattle U Office of Assoc Provost Seattle WA 98122

JENNETT, SHIRLEY SHIMMICK, hospice executive, nurse; b. Jennings, Kans., May 1, 1937; d. William and Mabel C. (Mowry) Shimmick; m. Nelson K. Jennett, Aug. 20, 1960 (div. 1972); children: Jon W., Cheryl L.; m. Albert J. Kukral, Apr. 16, 1977 (div. 1990). Diploma, Rsch. Hosp. Sch. Nursing, Kansas City, Mo., 1958. RN, Mo., Colo., Tex., Ill. Staff nurse, head nurse Rsch. Hosp., 1958-60; head nurse Penrose Hosp., Colorado Springs, Colo., 1960-62, Hotel Dieu Hosp., El Paso, Tex., 1962-63; staff nurse Oak Park (Ill.) Hosp., 1963-64, NcNeal Hosp., Berwyn, Ill., 1964-65, St. Anthony Hosp., Denver, 1968-69; staff nurse, head nurse, nurse recruiter Luth. Hosp., Wheat Ridge, Colo., 1969-79; owner, mgr. Med. Placement Svcs., Lakewood, Colo., 1980-84; vol., primary care nurse, admissions coord., team mgr. Hospice of Metro Denver, 1984-88, dir. patient and family svcs., 1988, exec. dir., 1988—; mem. adv. com. Linkages Assn. for Older Adults, Denver, 1989-90. Community liaison person U. Phoenix, 1988-90. Mem. Nat. Hospice Orgn. (bd. dirs. 1992—), Colo. Hospice Orgn. (bd. dirs., pres. 1991-93), NAFE. Republican. Mem. Ch. of Religious Sci. Office: Hospice of Metro Denver 3955 E Exposition Ave Ste 500 Denver CO 80209-5033

JENNI, DONALD ALISON, zoology educator; b. Pueblo, Colo., June 20, 1932; s. George Luis and Genevieve Agnes (Cox) J.; m. Mary Anne Hovland, Aug. 16, 1956; children—Robert Walter, William George, Karen Elizabeth, Thomas Iver; m. Catherine Brinckerhoff Cory, Jan. 3, 1986. B.S., Oreg. State U., 1953; M.S., Utah State U., 1955; Ph.D., U. Fla., 1961. Asst. prof. zoology U. Fla., 1961-62; asst. prof. Eastern Ill. U., 1962-64; vis. scientist U. Leiden, Netherlands, 1964-66; assoc. prof. U. Mont., 1966-71, prof., 1971—, chmn. dept. zoology, 1972-75, 85-88, dean biol. scis., 1988-91; vis. prof. Cornell U., 1975, U. Wash., 1979. Served with USAF, 1955-57. NIH fellow, 1964-66; NSF research grantee, 1970, 73, 74, 85; NATO and NRC travel grantee, 1970-72; Boone and Crockett Club research grantee, 1981-83; Camp Fire Research Fund grantee, 1983-87; NSF Young Scholars grantee, 1991, 92; NSF Travel grantee, 1985, 92. Mem. Am. Ornithologists Union, Animal Behavior Soc., Ecol. Soc. Am., Assn. Tropical Biology, Wilson Ornithol. Soc., Cooper Ornithol. Soc. Office: U Mont Div Biol Scis Missoula MT 59812

JENNINGS, CHARLES WAYNE, art educator, artist; b. Battlecreek, Mich., Feb. 20, 1944; s. Verl Wayne and Helen Louise (Davis) J.; children: Christine Lynn, Andrew Aaron. BA in Art, Wheaton Coll., 1966; MA in Art, No. Ill. U., 1968, MFA, 1968. Profl. freelance artist San Luis, Calif., 1968—; prof. art Cal Poly State U., San Luis, 1968—, chmn. dept. art and design, 1986—; graphic designer CW Jennings Design, San Luis, 1980-90. Work in permanent collection Nat. Air and Space Mus. Smithsonian Inst. Home: 210 Squire Canyon Rd San Luis Obispo CA 93401 Office: Calif Poly State U Dept Art & Design San Luis Obispo CA 93407

JENNINGS, EMMIT M., surgeon; b. Tucumcari, N.Mex., Oct. 12, 1922; s. Felix Carlow and Rose (Wich) J.; m. Laura-Jean Cameron. Sept. 23, 1950; children: Katherine, John, Patrick, Teresa, Margaret, Colleen, Maureen. BS, Notre Dame, 1945; MD Sch. of Medicine, St. Louis U., 1946. Diplomate Am. Bd. Surgery, Am. Coll. Surgeons. Physician family practice, Tucumcari, 1950-51; chief of surgery U.S. Army, Ft. Huachuea, 1951-53; fellowship thoracic surgery, L.A., 1953-54; pvt. practice Gen. Surgery, Roswell, N. Mex., 1954-93; pres. N. Mex. Med. Soc., 1967-68, N. Mex. Physicians Liability Co., Albuquerque, 1986-93; del. from N. Mex. AMA, 1968-76. Mem. City Coun. of Roswell, 1960-64; commr. Chaveg County 1989-92; senator State of N. Mex., Santa Fe, 1993—. Capt. U.S. Army, 1943-46, 1951-53. Recipient A.H. Robbins award for Community Svc., 1980; named Man of the Yr. Jaycees, Roswell, 1957. Mem. Am. Legion, Knights of Columbus, Elks. Republican. Roman Catholic. Home: 1901 W 4th St Roswell NM 88201 Office: 212 W 1st St Roswell NM 88201

JENNINGS, JAY BRADFORD, security company executive; b. Phoenix, Apr. 6, 1957; s. John Edward and Joan (Jackson) J.; m. Kay Frances Parcks, Nov. 20, 1982. BS in Gen. Bus., U. Ariz., 1979. Sec.-treas. Assoc. Security Co., Phoenix, 1979; dir. security Safeguard Security, Phoenix, 1982-84, v.p.,

1987—; pres. East Valley Security Alliance, Phoenix, 1985-87; bd. dirs. Nurses PRN Corp. Pres. 10/30 Internat., Phoenix, 1987, Ariz. Family Bus. Alliance, Phoenix, 1989; bd. dirs. Children in Need Found., Phoenix, 1988-89; vol. Fiesta Bowl, 1989—, Am. Cancer Soc., 1989—, Boys and Girls Club Met. Phoenix, 1992—. Recipient Zajac Outstanding Achievement award 20/30 Internat., 1988, Ben Rosner Excellence award 20/30 Internat., 1987, Outstanding Contbn. award Children's Crisis Nursery, 1987, Barry Goldwater Man of Yr. award 20/30 Internat., 1989. Mem. Nat. Fire Protection Assn., Security Alliance (bd. dirs. 1986-87, pub. relations award 1987), Ariz. Burglar and Fire Alarm Assn., Am. Soc. Indsl. Security, Nat. Burglar and Fire Alarm Assn., Sigma Alpha Epsilon (sec. 1976-77). Republican. Lutheran. Office: Safeguard Security Svcs 4801 E Indian School Rd Phoenix AZ 85018-5498

JENNINGS, JUDITH MADRONE, city official; b. Teaneck, N.J., May 21, 1949; d. Frank Gouverneur and Ethel Kathleen (Richards) J. BA, CUNY, N.Y.C., 1971. Cert. elec. inspector. Electrician Internat. Brotherhood of Elec. Workers, Oakland, Calif., 1978-86; elec. inspector City of Oakland, Calif., 1986—. Mem. Internat. Assn. Elec. Inspectors (cert.), Internat. Brotherhood of Elec. Workers. Office: City of Oakland 1330 Broadway Oakland CA 94612

JENNINGS, LEE NEWLIN, musician, choral music conductor; b. Salt Lake City, Jan. 6, 1932; s. Ralph St. Clair Jennings and Lauda (Newlin) Jennings Cone; m. Gladys Norine Phelps, Aug. 20, 1953; children: Patricia Joan Jennings Siltala, Bruce Ira, Sharon Elizabeth Jennings Bowler, Kent Stanley, NancyLee Jennings Van Zwol. AB, Westminster Coll., 1953; teaching cert., U. Utah, 1959; MusM, U. Idaho, 1969; postgrad., U. Wash., 1970-75. Cert. tchr., Idaho, Wash. Choral music tchr. Ind. Sch. Dist. Boise, 1962-68; choir dir. Southminster Presbyn. Ch., Boise, 1962-64; dir. of music 1st Presbyn. Ch., Boise, 1964-68; choral music tchr. Seattle pub. schs., 1968-75; minister of music John Knox Ch., Seattle, 1968-76; tchr. music Evergreen Sch. Dist., Vancouver, Wash., 1976-88, tchr. history, 1988—; dir. of music Columbia Presbyn. Ch., Vancouver, 1976—; bd. dirs. Music Week Inc., Boise, 1966-68, Vancouver Symphony Orch., 1988-91; placement dir. Puget Sound Choral Conductors Guild, Seattle, 1973-76; adjudicator, clinician Pacific Basin Choral Festival, Honolulu, 1990; invited performer Expo 86, Vancouver, B.C., Can., 1986, Expo 88, Brisbane, Australia, 1988, Pacific Rim Choral Festival, Sydney, Australia, 1994. Host tchr. Jr. Achievement, Portland, Oreg., 1988—. With U.S. Army, 1955-57. Mem. Presbyn. Assn. Musicians, Am. Choral Dirs. Assn. Office: Columbia Presbyn Ch 805 Columbia Ridge Dr Vancouver WA 98664

JENNINGS, MARCELLA GRADY, rancher, investor; b. Springfield, Ill., Mar. 4, 1920; d. William Francis and Magdalene Mary (Spies) Grady; student pub. schs.; m. Leo J. Jennings, Dec. 16, 1950 (dec.). Pub. relations Econolite Corp., Los Angeles, 1958-61; v.p., asst. mgr. LJ Quarter Circle Ranch, Inc., Polson, Mont., 1961-73, pres., gen. mgr., owner, 1973—; dir. Giselle's Travel Inc., Sacramento; fin. advisor to Allentown, Inc., Charlo, Mont.; sales cons. to Amie's Jumpin' Jacks and Jills, Garland, Tex. investor. Mem. Internat. Charolais Assn., Los Angeles County Apt. Assn. Republican. Roman Catholic. Home and Office: 509 Mt Holyoke Ave Pacific Palisades CA 90272-4328

JENNINGS, PAUL CHRISTIAN, engineering educator; b. Brigham City, Utah, May 21, 1936; s. Robert Webb and Elva S. (Simonsen) J.; m. Millicent Marie Bachman, Aug. 28, 1981; m. Barbara Elaine Morgan, Sept. 3, 1960 (div. 1981); children: Kathryn Diane, Margaret Ann. BSCE, Colo. State U., 1958; MSCE, Calif. Inst. Tech., 1960, PhD, 1963. Prof. civil engring., applied mechanics Calif. Tech. Inst., Pasadena, 1966—, chmn. div. engring, applied sci., 1985-89, v.p., provost, 1989—; mem. faculty bd. Calif. Tech. Inst., 1974-76, steering com., 1974-76, chmn. nominating com., 1975, grad. studies com., 1978-80; cons. in field. Author: (with others) Earthquake Design Criteria. Contbr. numerous articles to profl. jours. Served to 1st lt. USAF, 1965-66. Recipient Walter Huber award ASCE, 1973, Newmark medal, 1992, Achievement in Acadamia award Coll. Engring., Colo. State U., 1992; Erskine fellow U. Canterbury, New Zealand. Fellow AAAS, New Zealand Soc. Earthquake Engring.; mem. ASCE, Seismol. Soc. Am. (pres. 1980), Earthquake Engring. Research Inst. (pres. 1981-83). Club: Athenaeum (Pasadena). Home: 516 S Catalina Ave Pasadena CA 91106-3307 Office: Calif Inst Tech Mail Code 206-31 Pasadena CA 91125

JENNINGS, TIMOTHY ZEPH, rancher, state senator; b. Roswell, N.Mex., Sept. 4, 1950; s. James Traynor and Frances Mitchell (Schultz) J. Student N.Mex. State U., 1968-69; B.S. in Bus. Adminstrn., Creighton U., 1972. With Bill Deane Goodyear, San Jose, Calif., 1973; operator Penasco River Ranch, Roswell, 1973—; v.p. First Roswell Co.; mem. N.Mex. Senate, 1978—, mem. conservation com., edn. com. Mem. Chaves County Bd. Commrs., 1974-78; mem. N.Mex. Standards and Goals Com. for Juvenile Justice, 1974-76. Democrat. Roman Catholic. Lodge: Elks. Home: PO Box 1797 Roswell NM 88202-1797

JENNISON, BRIAN L., environmental specialist; b. Chelsea, Mass., June 13, 1950; s. Lewis L. and Myra S. (Piper) J. BA, U. N.H., 1972; PhD, U. Calif., Berkeley, 1977; cert. hazardous materials mgr., U. Calif., Davis, 1986. Teaching, rsch. asst. U. Calif., Berkeley, 1972-77; staff rsch. assoc. Dept. of Molecular Biology, Berkeley, 1978-80; instr. dept. biology Calif. State U., Hayward, 1977; sr. biologist San Francisco Bay Marine Rsch. Ctr., Emeryville, Calif., 1980-81; inspector I Bay Area Air Quality Mgmt.Dist., San Francisco, 1981-83, inspector II, 1983-88; enforcement program specialist Bay Area Air Quality Mgmt. Dist., San Francisco, 1988-92; dir. air quality mgmt. div. Washoe County Dist. Health Dept., Reno, Nev., 1992—; cons. U.S. Army Corps of Engrs., L.A., 1980, San Francisco, 1981; instr. U. Calif., Berkeley extension, 1990—, Assoc. Bay Area Govs., 1990—. Contbr. articles to profl. jours. Sustaining mem. Rep. Nat. Com., Washington. Postdoctoral fellow, Harbor Br. Found., 1977-78. Mem. Air and Wast Mgmt. Assn., Navy League of U.S. (life), U.S. Naval Inst. (assoc.), Am. Assn. Advance Sci., Phi Beta Kappa. Republican. Office: Washoe County Dist Health Dept PO Box 11130 Reno NV 89520

JENSEN, ARTHUR ROBERT, psychology educator; b. San Diego, Aug. 24, 1923; s. Arthur Alfred and Linda (Schachtmayer) J.; m. Barbara Jane DeLarme, May 6, 1960; 1 child, Roberta Ann. B.A., U. Calif., Berkeley, 1945; Ph.D., Columbia U., 1956. Asst. med. psychology U. Md., 1955-56; research fellowInst. Psychiatry U. London, 1956-58; prof. ednl. psychology U. Calif., Berkeley, 1958—. Author: Genetics and Education, 1972, Educability and Group Differences, 1973, Educational Differences, 1973, Bias in Mental Testing, 1979, Straight Talk about Mental Tests, 1981; Contbr. to profl. jours., books. Guggenheim fellow, 1964-65, fellow Ctr. Advanced Study Behavioral Scis., 1966-67. Fellow AAAS, Am. Psychol. Assn., Eugenics Soc.; mem. Psychonomic Soc., Am. Soc. Human Genetics, Soc. for Social Biology, Behavior Genetics Assn., Psychometric Soc., Sigma Xi. Office: U Calif Sch Edn Berkeley CA 94720

JENSEN, CARL MARTIN, communications educator; b. Bklyn., July 25, 1929; s. Martin Gert and Anna (Haakenson) J.; m. Donna Jackson, 1950 (div.); m. Patricia Marell Annan, Nov. 27, 1954 (div.); m. Sandra J. Scott, June 21, 1977; children: Carl Martin Sherman, Lisa Annan, Pia Christina, John Christian. BA in Sociology, U. Calif., Santa Barbara, 1971; MA in Sociology, U. Calif., 1972, PhD in Sociology, 1977. Writer, editor Arcata (Calif.) Union, 1947-51; reporter Miami (Fla.) Daily News, 1954-55; owner, pub. North Dade Times, North Miami Beach, Fla., 1955-56; copy editor Wall St. Jour., San Francisco, 1956; v.p., account supr. Batten, Barton, Durstine, Osborn, San Francisco, L.A., 1956-70; prof. Sonoma State U., Rohnert Park, Calif., 1973—; mktg. cons. 1971-73, 84—; founder, bd. dirs. Project Censored, Rohnert Park, Lincoln Steffens Journalism Awards, Santa Rosa, Junk News Awards; speaker in field; guest radio, TV news and talk shows. Author: Censored! The News That Didn't Make The News -- And Why, 1993; Contbr. articles to mags. and newspapers. Bd. dirs. Malibu Canyon Property Owners Assn., 1967-68; pres. Malibu Dem. Club, 1962. 1st lt. USAF, 1951-54. Recipient Copy awards Advt. Assn. of West L.A., 1964-65, Rsch. Commendation award Assn. for Edn. in Journalism and Mass Communications, 1988, Giraffe award Giraffe Project, 1988, Unimpeachable Source award Media Alliance, 1989, Univ. Prof. of Jour. award Calif. Newspaper Pub's. Assn., 1992, Hugh Hefner First Amendment award Playboy Found., 1992. Mem. Media Alliance (Meritorious Achievement), Investigate Reporters and Editors, Soc. Profl. Journalists (Freedom of Info. award 1990), Sonoma County Press Club, Fairness and Accuracy in Reporting. Democrat. Lutheran. Office: Sonoma State U Rohnert Park CA 94928

JENSEN, CHARLES HOWARD, JR., environmental geologist; b. Denver, May 7, 1967; s. Charles Howard Sr. and Christine Estelle (Petri) J. BS, Tex. Christian U., 1989. Geologist Groundwater Tech., Inc., Englewood, Colo., 1989—. Recipient Youth on the Move award KCNC-TV, 1985, Outstanding Student Leadership award Tex. Christian U., 1989. Mem. Eagle Mountain Lake Beach Club (co-founder). Roman Catholic.

JENSEN, CHRISTOPHER LARS, U.S. air force officer; b. Red Deer, Alta., Can., Mar. 29, 1961; came to U.S., 1967, naturalized citizen, 1976.; s. Gordon Lars and Sophie Lillian (Tcacik) J.; m. Cheryl Ann Valgren, Aug. 14, 1982; children: Kayla Marie, Kyle Christopher. AS in Electronics Tech., Community Coll. of Air Force, 1987; BS, NYU, 1989. With USAF, 1979—, commd. 2d lt., 1989; defensive fire control technician 5th BMW USAF, Minot AFB, N.D., 1979-82, defensive fire supr. 5th BMW, 1982-86, quality assurance evaluator 5th BMW, 1986-88; wing avionics instr. B-52H 3450th TTG USAF, Lowry AFB, Colo., 1988-89; dep. missile combat crew comdr. 321SMS/DO USAF, F.E. Warren AFB, Wyo., 1990-91, with OSCAR flight DMCCC 321SMS/DO, 1990-91; crewmem. quarter 90th Missle Wing USAF, F.E. Warren AFB, 1992, crewmem. quarter 20th AF, 1992; fireout investigator 5 BMW, Minot AFB, 1986-88; competitor Olympic Arena, Strategic Air Command Missle Combat Competition 25th Anniversary, 1992. Pres. Minot AFB Overachievers Club, 1982-88; treas. NCOA, Minot AFB, 1986-88; com. mem. Minot Festival of the Parks, 1985-88. Mem. F.E. Warren AFB Officers Club (named one of Outstanding Young Men Am. 1987, 88, 89, 90). Office: USAF 321 SMS/D0 F E Warren AFB WY 82005

JENSEN, D. LOWELL, federal judge, lawyer, government official; b. Brigham, Utah, June 3, 1928; s. Wendell and Elnora (Hatch) J.; m. Barbara Cowin, Apr. 20, 1951; children: Peter, Marcia, Thomas. A.B. in Econs, U. Calif.-Berkeley, 1949, LL.B., 1952. Bar: Calif. 1952. Dep. dist. atty. Alameda County, 1955-66, asst. dist. atty., 1966-69, dist. atty., 1969-81; asst. atty. gen. criminal div. Dept. Justice, Washington, 1981-83, assoc. atty. gen., 1983-85, dep. atty. gen., 1985-86; judge U.S. Dist. Ct. (no. dist.) Calif., San Francisco, 1986—; mem. Calif. Council on Criminal Justice, 1974-81; past pres. Calif. Dist. Atty.'s Assn. Served with U.S. Army, 1952-54. Fellow Am. Coll. Trial Lawyers; mem. Nat. Dist. Atty.'s Assn. (victim/witness commn. 1974-81), Boalt Hall Alumni Assn. (past pres.). Office: US Dist Ct 450 Golden Gate Ave PO Box 36060 San Francisco CA 94102

JENSEN, DALLIN W., lawyer; b. Afton, Wyo., June 2, 1932; s. Louis J. and Nellie B. Jensen; m. Barbara J. Bassett, Mar. 22, 1958; children—Brad L., Julie N. B.S., Brigham Young U., 1954; J.D., U. Utah, 1960. Bar: Utah 1960, U.S. Dist. Ct. Utah 1962, U.S. Ct. Appeals (10th cir.) 1974, U.S. Ct. Appeals D.C. 1980, U.S. Supreme Ct. 1971. Asst. atty. gen. Utah Atty. Gen., Salt Lake City, 1960-83, solicitor gen., 1983-88; shareholder Parsons, Behle & Latimer, Salt Lake City, 1988—; alt. commr. Upper Colo. River Commn., 1983—; mem. Colo. River Basin Salinity Adv. Council, 1975—; spl. legal cons. Nat. Water Commn., Washington, 1971-73; mem. energy law center adv. council U. Utah Coll. Law, 1976—. Edit. bd. Rocky Mountain Mineral Law Found., 1983-85. Author: (with Wells A. Hutchins) The Utah Law of Water Rights, 1965. Contbr. articles on water law and water resource mgmt. to profl. jours. Served with U.S. Army, 1955-57. Mem. Ch. Jesus Christ Latter-day Saints. Home: 3565 S 2175 E Salt Lake City UT 84109-2902 Office: 201 S Main St Ste 1800 PO Box 11898 Salt Lake City UT 84147-0898

JENSEN, EDMUND PAUL, bank holding company executive; b. Oakland, Calif., Apr. 13, 1937; s. Edmund and Olive E. (Kessell) J.; m. Marilyn Norris, Nov. 14, 1959; children: Juliana L., Annika M. BA, U. Wash., 1959; postgrad., U. Santa Clara, Stanford U., 1981. Lic. real estate broker, Oreg., Calif. Mgr. fin. plan and evaluation Technicolor, Inc., Los Angeles, 1967-69; group v.p. Nat. Industries & Subs, Louisville, 1969-72; v.p. fin. Wedgewood Homes, Portland, 1972-74; various mgmt. positions U.S. Bancorp, Portland, 1974-83; pres., COO U.S. Bancorp, Inc., Portland, 1983-93; vice chmn., COO U.S. Bancorp, Inc., Portland, 1993—; bd. dirs. U.S. Nat. Bank of Oreg., U.S. Bank Washington. Chmn. United Way, 1986, N.W. Bus. Coalition, 1987; bd. dirs. Saturday Acad., Portland, 1984—, Visa U.S.A., Visa Internat., Marylhurst Coll., Oreg. Bus. Coun., Oreg. Downtown Devel. Assn., Oreg. Ind. Coll. Found., 1983—, treas., 1986—, chmn., 1988—; bd. dirs. Portland Art Mus., 1983—, vice chmn., 1989—. Mem. Portland C. of C. (bd. dirs. 1981—, chmn. 1987), Assn. Res. City Bankers, Assn. for Portland Progress (pres. 1988), Waverly Country Club, Multnomah Athletic Club, Arlington Club. Office: US Bancorp PO Box 8837 Portland OR 97208-8837

JENSEN, GARY JON, computer consultant; b. N.Y.C., Apr. 20, 1949; s. Grover Cullen and Ingrid (Didrickson) J. BS in Chemistry summa cum laude, Wagner Coll., N.Y.C., 1971; postgrad., Columbia U., 1971-72; MS in Nuclear Engring., Westinghouse Nuclear Engring., Idaho Falls, 1981. Rsch. tech. NYU Med. Ctr., 1972-73; asst. scientist Technicon Instruments Corp., Tarrytown, N.Y., 1973-78, scientist, 1978-80; sr. scientist Westinghouse Electric Corp., Idaho Falls, Idaho, 1980-91; gen. mgr. Techstar Tech. Skills Tng. & Rsch., Pocatello, Idaho, 1991—; cons. in field, Idaho Falls, 1988—. Editor: Building With Words, 1989, Leading By Example, 1989, Building the Management Team, 1990, Department of Energy Facility Surveillance, 1990, Conduct of Operations: A Philosophic Approach, 1991. Home: 3099 Sunnybrook Ln Idaho Falls ID 83404-7480

JENSEN, GERALD RANDOLPH, graphics designer; b. Kalispell, Mont., Aug. 12, 1924; s. Hans Clemen and Mabel (Everson) J.; m. Helen Jeanne Levine, Dec. 11, 1943; 1 child, Marjorie Jeanne. MA, Union U., 1976, PhD, 1978; LittD, Internat. Acad. World Frat. of Scholars, London. Regional and nat. dir. Youth & Christian Edn. Internat., Four Square Los Angeles, 1946-54; dir. San Francisco Youth for Christ, San Francisco, 1955-60; v.p. Sacred Records, Whittier, Calif., 1960-63; dir. pub. Full Gospel Bus. Men's Fellowship, Los Angeles, 1962-69; pres. Triangle Prodns., Burbank, Calif., 1970-79, Claiborne-Jensen Advt., Arcadia, Calif., 1980-82, Jerry Jensen & Assoc., Santa Fe Springs, Calif., 1982-85; editor Full Gospel Bus. Men's Fellowship, Costa Mesa, Calif., 1985—; bd. dirs. High Adventure Ministries, Van Nuys, Calif., 1970-89, Found. for Airborne Relief, Long Beach, Calif., 1986-89, Ambassadors of Aid, Vancouver, British Columbia, 1978-89, Friends in the West, Seattle, 1969-89, Internat. Bible Inst., Santa Fe Springs, Calif., 1982-92. Bd. regens Golden State U., Los Angeles, 1979-89; advt. & pub. relations Orange County Jesus Rally, Anaheim, Calif., 1980-81. Recipient Award of Merit Golden State U., 1986. Mem. Evang. Press Assn., Am. Mgmt. Assn. Republican. Home: 5772 Garden Grove Blvd Trlr 482 Westminster CA 92683-1859 Office: 3150 Bear St Costa Mesa CA 92626-2926

JENSEN, HELEN, musical artists management company executive; b. Seattle, June 30, 1919; d. Frank and Sophia (Kantosky) Leponis; student pub. schs., Seattle; m. Ernest Jensen, Dec. 2, 1939; children: Ernest, Ronald Lee. Co-chmn., Seattle Community Concert Assn., 1957-62; sec. family concerts Seattle Symphony Orch., 1959-61; hostess radio program Timely Topics, 1959-60; gen. mgr. Western Opera Co., Seattle, 1962-64, pres. 1963-64; v.p., dir., mgr. pub. rels. Seattle Opera Assn., 1964-83, preview artists coord., 1981-84; bus. mgr. Portland (Oreg.) Opera Co., 1968, cons., 1967-69; owner, mgr. Helen Jensen Artists Mgmt., Seattle, 1970-92. First v.p. Music and Art Found., 1981-84, pres. 1984-85. Recipient Cert., Women in Bus in the Field of Art, 1973, award Seattle Opera Assn., 1974, Outstanding Svc. award Music and Art Found., 1984, Women of Achievement award Women in Communications, 1992. Mem. Am. Guild Mus. Artists, Music and Art Found. (life), Seattle Opera Guild (life, bd. dirs. 1988-92, pres., award of distinction 1983, parliamentarian 1987-89), Ballard Symphony League (sec.), Portland Opera Assn., Portland Opera Guild, Seattle Civic Opera Assn. (pres. 1981—), 200 Plus One, Aria Preview, Lyric Preview Group (chmn. 1988-92), Past Pres. Assembly (pres. 1977-79, parliamentarian 1987-89), Pres.'s Forum (1st v.p. 1990-91, program vice chmn. 1987-88, pres. 1991-92), North Shore Performing Arts Assn. (pres. 1981), Women of Achievement (past pres's. assembly, chmn.), Pres.'s Forum (pres. 1991-92), Woman's Century Club (chmn. art, drama, music dept. 1992-93), Helen Jensen Hiking Club. Home: 19029 56th Ln NE Seattle WA 98155-3156 Office: 716 Joseph Vance Bldg Seattle WA 98101

JENSEN, JAKKI RENEE, retail company executive; b. Eugene, Oreg., Mar. 1, 1959; d. Philip William Jensen and Mary Katherine (Sommers) Henderson; m. Johnny Claiborne Hawthorne, May 7, 1983. Student, Oreg. State U., 1977-78; student (hon.), Portland State U., 1978-81. With Nordstrom Inc., Beaverton, Oreg., 1981—; mgr. cosmetics Nordstrom Inc., Beaverton, 1984; mgr. cosmetics Nordstrom Inc., Walnut Creek, Calif., 1984-86, buyer cosmetics, 1986-88; buyer cosmetics Nordstrom Inc., San Francisco, 1988-93; area mdse. mgr. Nordstrom Own Product, San Francisco, 1993—. Affiliate, vol. San Francisco Soc. for Prevention of Cruelty to Animals, 1990—. Republican. Home: 118 Costanza Dr Martinez CA 94553 Office: 865 Market St San Francisco CA 94103-1901

JENSEN, JAMES LESLIE, chemistry educator, dean; b. Tulare, Calif., Oct. 17, 1939; s. Lester Eugene and Mabel Irene (Brown) J.; m. Nancy Ruth Peterson, Aug. 13, 1960; children: Randall Mark, Linda Suzanne. BA in Chemistry, Westmont Coll., 1961; MA in Chemistry, U. Calif., Santa Barbara, 1963; PhD in Organic Chemistry, U. Wash., 1967. Instr. chemistry Westmont Coll., Santa Barbara, Calif., 1962-64, U. Wash., Seattle, 1968; from asst. prof. to prof. Calif. State U., Long Beach, 1968—, assoc. dean Sch. Natural Scis., 1983-93, dean Coll. Nat. Scis. and Math., 1993—; vis. scientist Brandeis U.-W.P. Jencks Lab., Waltham, Mass., 1974-75; vis. prof. U. Calif. Irvine, 1981-82; chmn. various univs. and schs. dept. coms.; lectr. over 40 univs. and profl. confs., U.S., U.K., France, Italy, Sweden. Reviewer NSF, Jour. Am. Chem. Soc., Jour. Organic Chemistry; contbr. 25 articles to profl. jours. Weyerhauser fellow, U. Wash., 1966-67; scholar Westmont Coll., 1957-58, 60-61; recipient Merit award Long Beach Heart Assn., 1970, Disting. Service award Am. Heart Assn., 1971; grantee: NSF, NIH. Mem. AAAS, Am. Sci. Affiliation, Internat. Union of Pure and Applied Chemistry, Am. Chem. Soc. (organic div.), Royal Soc. Chemistry (organic chemistry div., fast reactions groups), Nat. Assn. for Sci., Tech., Soc., Sigma Xi, Phi Beta Kappa, Phi Lambda Upsilon. Republican. Office: Calif State U Dept Chemistry Long Beach CA 90840

JENSEN, JAN CAIN, school system administrator; b. San Antonio, Nov. 5, 1943; d. Paul Smith and Silva Jeanetta (Snyder) Blair; m. Stephen Scott Cain, Dec. 24, 1965 (div. Apr. 1971); m. G. Eric Jensen, Mar. 17, 1984. BA, U. Colo., 1965; MA, U. Denver, 1968, cert. advanced studies, 1972, postgrad., 1992—. Cert. elem. tchr., libr., secondary prin., supt., Colo. Circulation asst. Littleton (Colo.) Pub. Libr., 1961-65; sales, modeling May D&F Dept. Store, Denver, 1963-65; from tchr. to libr. media specialist Jefferson County Schs., Golden, Colo., 1965-79; libr. media specialist Jefferson County Schs., Golden, 1981-91; bus. ptnr. Consortium Communications, Denver, 1979-81; asst. prin. Evergreen (Colo.) High Sch., 1991—; cons. Littleton Pub. Schs., U. No. Colo., Boulder Valley Schs., Aurora Pub. Schs., St. Brain Schs., 1989-91; grad. teaching asst. U. Denver, 1988-89; dir. ASAP Telefacsimile Network, Arvada, Colo., 1988-91; media cons., Montevideo, Uruguay, 1972. Author: Colorado Libraries, 1990. Tech. chair Colo. Ednl. Media Assn., Denver, 1989-91; pres. MeadowCreek Homeowners Assn., Lakewood, Colo., 1979-81; adv. com. Gov's. Telecom. Task Force, Colo., 1990-91; sponsor student rep. The Pres. White House Conf., 1991. Recipient Excellence in Online Edn. award DIALOG Info. Svc., Washington, 1990, Model Sch. Program award Colo. Alliance Rsch. Libr., Colo., 1991; named to Arvada Sr. High Sch. Staff Hall of Fame, 1990-91, Sch. Libr. Media Specialist of Yr. 3M Co. and Assoc., 1990-91. Mem. ASCD, Am. Assn. Sch. Libr. (Model Sch. Libr. award 1991), Am. Libr. Assn., Colo. Edn. Media Assn. (bd. dirs. 1971-75, 88—, State Model Sch. Libr. award 1990), Colo. Assn. Sch. Exec., Phi Delta Kappa. Presbyterian. Home: 23916 W Currant Dr Golden CO 80401 Office: Evergreeen High School 5301 S Olive Rd Evergreen CO 80439

JENSEN, JORGENE MARIE, import company executive; b. Parkers Prairie, Minn., May 8, 1943; d. Bill Clement and Viola Marie (Buse) Danelke; m. Dan D. Jensen, Nov. 14, 1982; children: Bill Allen, Susanne Allen. B, U. Minn., 1966, MBA, 1978. Instr. various community colls. Mpls., 1970-77; owner Color Consultation, Mpls., 1972-79, Fashion Consultation, Mpls., 1972-77; CEO, owner Kimono Kountry, La Jolla, Calif., 1972-77, Design Room La Jolla, 1980—, Hat Designs by Jorgene, La Jolla, 1983—, Jorgene Internat., La Jolla, 1985—; lectr., cons. Mesa Coll., San Diego; cons. City Colls., Sna Diego, TV Sta. 8, TV Sta. 39; adv. bd. San Diego C.C. Dist. Fashion, social editor La Jolla Mag., 1985-87. Originator, organizer, sponsor La Jolla Easter Hat Parade, 1985-92; bd. dirs. San Diego Symphony, 1985-92, La Jolla Opera Guild, 1985-92, San Diego Opera Assn., 1985-92. Mem. Internat. Fashion Group San Diego, Charter 100, Club Altura. Office: Jorgene Internat 2509 Caminito Muirfield La Jolla CA 92037

JENSEN, JUDY DIANNE, psychotherapist; b. Portland, Oreg., Apr. 8, 1948; d. Clarence Melvin and Charlene Augusta (Young) J.; m. Frank George Cooper, Sept 4, 1983; stepchildren: Pamela Cooper, Brian Cooper. BA in Sociology and Anthropology with honors, Oberlin Coll., 1970; MSW, U. Pitts., 1972; postgrad., U. Wis., 1977. Lic. clin. social worker, marriage and family therapist, Oreg. Social worker Day Hosp. Western Psychiat. Inst. and Clinic, Pitts., 1972-73, South Hills Child Guidance Ctr., Pitts., 1973-74; mem. drug treatment program Umatilla County Mental Health Clinic, Pendleton, Oreg., 1975-77; social worker Children's Services Div. State of Oreg., Pendleton, 1978-80, therapist intensive family services project, 1980—, dir. intensive family services project, 1986—; pvt. practice Pendleton, 1980—. NIMH grantee, 1970-72; NDEA fellow 1977; Gen. Motors scholar Oberlin Coll., 1966-70. Mem. Am. Assn. Marriage and Family Therapists (clin.), Nat. Assn. Social Workers. Home: 325 NW Bailey Ave Pendleton OR 97801-1604 Office: PO Box 752 Pendleton OR 97801-0752

JENSEN, LAWRENCE ROBERT, lawyer; b. Oakland, Calif., Apr. 7, 1959; s. Robert Johan and Dolores Fawn (Freeland) J.; m. Susan Kim McShane, Aug. 23, 1983 (div. 1986); m. Terry Ann Hutson, July 29, 1989 (div. 1993). BA in Psychology with honors, U. Calif., Santa Cruz, 1984; JD cum laude, Santa Clara U., 1987. Bar: Calif. 1987, U.S. Dist. Ct. (no. dist.) Calif. 1987, U.S. Ct. Appeals (9th cir.) 1991. Assoc. Howell & Hallgrimson, San Jose, 1987-89, Law Offices of Joseph DiCiuccio, San Jose, 1989-90, Hallgrimson, McNichols, McCann & Inderbitzen, San Jose, 1990-92, Liccardo, Rossi, Sturges & McNeil, San Jose, 1992—. Bd. dirs. ACLU, No. Calif. Affiliate, 1987-89, 92—, Santa Clara Valley chpt., 1986-89, 92—, San Jose Northside Neighborhood Assn., 1992—. Recipient Cert. of Recognition State Bar Bd. Govs., 1989. Mem. Santa Clara County Bar Assn., Calif. Trial Lawyers Assn., Santa Clara County Trial Lawyers Assn. Office: 1960 The Alameda Ste 200 San Jose CA 95126

JENSEN, NELS NORDY, JR., college official; b. Oak Park, Ill., Oct. 30, 1942; s. Nels N. and Josephine (Smith) J.; m. Alice P. Haeker, June 25, 1966; children: Eric, Gregory, Brent, Kurt. BA, Ariz. State U., 1964. Dir. sports info. N.Mex. State U., Las Cruces, 1964-65, San Jose (Calif.) State U., 1965-68, Ariz. State U., Tempe, 1968-71; editor NCAA News, NCAA, Kansas City, Mo., 1971-72; dir. conf. rels. Western Athletic Conf., Littleton, Colo., 1972-85; dir. pub. rels. Colo. Sch. Mines, Golden, 1985—. Pres. Golden-Applewood Midget Football Assn., 1975-76; mem. citizen's budget adv. com. Jefferson County R-1 Sch. Dist., 1979; co-chmn. Golden High Sch. Parents Assn., 1986-87. Recipient Presdl. citation Nat. Invitational Tourney, 1985. Mem. Pub. Rels. Soc. Am., Golden C. of C. (bd. dirs. 1988-89, cert. of recognition 1989), Coll. Sports Info. Dirs. Am. (pres. 1984-85), Denver C. of C. (metro sports com. 1986-91), Rotary (bd. dirs., head youth and group exchs. Golden), Foothills Art Ctr. (v.p., bd. dirs., edn. com., 1990—), Pi Sigma Alpha. Presbyterian. Office: Colo Sch Mines 1500 Illinois St Golden CO 80401-1887

JENSEN, TOMMY GERT, oceanographer; b. Copenhagen, Denmark, Mar. 4, 1954; came to U.S., 1985; s. Knud Erik and Paula Bertha (Rasmussen) J.; m. Louise Marie Mattacchione, Oct. 18, 1989; 1 child, Gianna Majbritt Mattacchione. BS, U. Aarhus, Denmark, 1978; Cand. Sci. in Phys. Oceanography, U. Copenhagen, 1981, Lic. Sci. in Phys. Oceanography, 1986; PhD in Geophys. Fluid Dynamics, Fla. State U., 1989. Asst. Greenland Geol. Inst., Copenhagen, 1978; rsch. asst. Nordic Coun. for Phys. Oceanography, various, Scandinavia, 1979-83; rsch. fellow U. Copenhagen, 1983-85, lectr., 1985; rsch. asst. Fla. State U., Tallahassee, 1985-89; rsch. assoc. Colo. State U., Fort Collins, 1989—; reviewer NSF, Washington, 1991—, Gulf of Maine Regional Marine Rsch. Program, 1993—, Jour. Geophys.

Rsch., 1987—, Jour. Oceanography, 1991—, Jour. Phys. Oceanography, 1992—; internat. lectr. U. Sao Paulo, Brazil, 1990; mem. users exec. com. Supercomputer Computations Rsch. Inst., Fla. State U., 1987-89; mem. sci. team Computer Hardware Advance Math. and Model Physics, U.S. Dept. Energy, 1992—. Contbg. author: Modelling Marine Systems II, 1989 (Sigma Xi award 1989); contbr. articles to profl. jours;. Recipient fellowships Nordic Coun. for Phys. Oceanography, 1980, U. Copenhagen, 1983, NATO Sci. Fellowship prog., 1984, NATO Advanced Study Inst., 1985, Super Computer Rsch. Inst., Fla. State U., 1987. Mem. Am. Geophys. Union, The Oceanography Soc., Phi Kappa Phi, Chi Epsilon Pi. Home: 1319 Clementine Ct Fort Collins CO 80526 Office: Dept Atmospheric Science Colo State Univ Fort Collins CO 80523

JENSEN, WALLACE M., bank officer, consultant; b. Salt Lake City, Sept. 24, 1947; s. W. Merrill and Lois (Forslund) J.; m. Pamely Gay Ahlquist, May 6, 1972; children: W. Merlin, Mollie, Miles, Mathew, Madison. BS in Fin., U. Utah, 1971. Asst. v.p. Comml. Security Bank, Salt Lake City, 1972-82; exec. v.p. Bajan Svcs., Inc., Salt Lake City, 1982-88; sr. lending officer USAA Fin. Svcs. Assn., Salt Lake City, 1988-92, USAA Credit Card Bank, Salt Lake City, 1989-92; v.p., chief lending officer Everest Nat. Fin., Salt Lake City, 1992—; pres. Homeshare Gen. Owners Assn., Park City, Utah, 1984-88; owner Jensen & Assocs., Salt Lake City, 1984—. Bd. dirs., treas. S.L. Neighborhood Housing Svcs., Inc., Salt Lake City, 1990—. Mem. Utah Assn. Fin. Svcs. (chmn. com.), New Zealand Mission Soc., Sugar House C. of C. (chmn. bd.), Rotary. Republican. Mem. LDS Ch. Office: Everest Nat Fin 2180 S 1300 Bast Ste 260 Salt Lake City UT 84106

JENSEN, WILLARD SCOTT, warehouse executive; b. Logan, Utah, Dec. 9, 1941; s. W. Gail and Clarice Julia (Gessel) J.; m. Marilyn Waters, June 23, 1974; children: Corby Scott, Eric. Grad., high sch., 1960. V.p. Backus Inc., Ogden, Utah, 1965-77, Video Dynamics Inc., Ogden, 1977-80; pres. Data Decisions Corp., Ogden, 1977-82; gen. mgr. CSA Transport, Salt Lake City, 1982-85; co-owner, gen. mgr. Wholesale Transfer & Warehouse, Salt Lake City, 1985—; cons. Home Furnishing Dealers and Mfrs. Mem. Furniture Shippers Assn., Furniture Club. Office: Wholesale Transfer & Warehouse Inc 2700 S 600 W Salt Lake City UT 84115

JENSON, CHARLES DAVID, computer scientist; b. Ft. Riley, Kans., Nov. 19, 1952; s. Charles D. and Geniel (Wood) J.; m. Judy Thurston, Apr. 17, 1976; children: Teri, Jacque, Zakary Daniel, Mikel David, Kayle Torsten. BS in Computer Sci., Brigham Young U., 1978. Programmer Digital Micro Systems, Orem, Utah, 1977, Brigham Young U., Provo, Utah, 1977-78; programmer analyst Tex. Instruments, Inc., Austin, 1978-79; assoc. systems programmer Sperry Univac, Salt Lake City, 1979-81; sr. devel. engr. Novell, Inc., Orem, 1981-83; sr. project engr. Technadyne Engrng. Cons., Inc., Albuquerque, 1983-91; systems programmer EG&G/EM, Albuquerque, 1993—; cons., Technadyne/Sandia Labs., Albuquerque, 1983—. Author computer software for pharmacy prescription control, Korean lang. terminal, others. Scoutmaster, Albuquerque area Boy Scouts Am., 1987. Mem. N.Mex. Rail Runners (pres. 1992—). Republican. Home: 6700 Beck NE Albuquerque NM 87109 Office: EG&G/EM Kirtland Ops PO Box 4339 Sta A Albuquerque NM 87196-9999

JENSTAD, NELS LINDEN, songwriter, musician; b. Mpls., Mar. 15, 1956; s. Donald Linden and Elizabeth Marie (Holmes) J. Student, Contra Costa Coll., 1976-79, Saddleback Coll., 1980-82, 85. Prodn. mgr. Contra Costa Symphony Assn., Inc., Orinda, Calif., 1976-79; songwriter, performer Nels Jenstad Music Prodns., throughout Calif., 1975—; pub. D-Force Press, San Juan Capistrano, Calif., 1989—; owner, mgr. N. Jenstad Music Pub., San Juan Capistrano, 1990—; composer, arranger, performer, mem. exptl. chorus div. Contra Costa County, 1978. Composer, performer: Stroxe, 1978, 80, Blue Trees, 1981-85; composer, art dir. LP album Synthesis Limited, 1986, cassette albums; composer, performer Sincere Fibers, 1983-86, World Processor, CHAO-5, 1988-89, Man Against Nature, 1990—, Crayon Revolution, 1992—, Swing House, 1992—. Composer-in-residence, Musical Arts Contra Costa County, 1978. Mem. ASCAP, Internat. Platform Assn. Lutheran. Office: Nels Jenstad Music 31921 Camino Capistrano San Juan Capistrano CA 92675-3210

JENTSCH, WILLIAM AUGUST, JR., petroleum engineer; b. Wichita Falls, Tex., Jan. 24, 1958; s. William August Sr. and Patricia Ann (McDonald) J. BSME, Tex. A&M U., 1981; postgrad., UCLA, 1992—. Registered profl. engr., Tex. Prodn. engr. Sun Exploration & Prodn. Co., Midland, Tex., 1981-87; project coord. Sun Exploration & Prodn. Co., Dallas, 1987-88; dist. mech. and ops. engr. Oryx Energy Co., Valencia, Calif., 1988-91; sr. facilities and prodn. engr. Arco Oil and Gas, Bakersfield, Calif., 1991—. Vol. Republican Party, Midland, 1981-87, Gov. Clements Re-election Campaign, Midland, 1982; cons. Jr. Achievement, Richardson, Tex., 1987-88; com. mem. Boy Scouts Am., Dist. Com., Midland, Buffalo Trails, 1987, 88. Recipient Eagle Scout award, Boy Scouts Am., Wichita Falls, 1974. Mem. ASME, NSPE, Soc. Petroleum Engrs. (Computer Applications jour. rev. chmn. 1992—), Midland A&M Club (v.p. activities 1985-87), Am. Petroleum Inst. (bd. dirs. San Joaquin Valley chpt. 1992-93), Midland Jaycees, Midland C. of C. (com. mem. 1986-87), Young Execs. Am. (bd. dirs. 1990, 91). Republican. Roman Catholic.

JEPPSON, ROBERT BAIRD, JR., management consultant; b. Rexburg, Idaho, Apr. 23, 1920; s. Robert Baird and Elsie (Smith) J.; B.S., U. Calif., 1942; grad. Advanced Mgmt. Program, Harvard U., 1963; m. Edith Abigail French, Jan. 9, 1947; children: Jane Elizabeth, James Robert, Virginia K. Commd. ensign U.S. Navy, 1942, advanced through grades to capt., 1962; ret., 1969; bus. mgr. Reno Radiol. Assocs., 1969-78; broker Alpine Realty Assos., 1971—; mgmt. cons., 1978—; gen. mgr., partner BHLS Investments. Republican. Mormon. Home: 2675 Everett Dr Reno NV 89503-3912 Office: PO Box 7011 Reno NV 89510

JEPSEN, CARL HENRY, dentist, behavioral scientist, lecturer; b. Tacoma, Wash., Aug. 27, 1940; s. Martin Hansen and Rilda (Bigalow) J.; m. Judi Marlene Shoe, June 21, 1965 (div. 1980); children: Christopher Paul Jepsen, Mark Andrew Jepsen. DDS, U. Wash., Seattle, 1965; PhD in Human Behavior, U.S. Internat. U., San Diego, 1983. Preventive dentistry officer USN Naval Air Station, San Diego, 1965-67; pvt. practice Coronado, Calif., 1967-85, San Diego, 1982—; pres., founder Inst. Behavioral Rsch. in Health Care, San Diego, 1984—; dir. Dental Fears Treatment Program Scripps Ctr. for Dental Care, Lajolla, Calif., 1991—; editorial bd. Jour. Dental Practice Adminstrn., 1989-91, Motivational Dentistry, 1989-90, Jour. Mich. Dental Assn., 1991—, Jour. Calif. Dental Assn., 1993; lectr. various Univ., Dental meetings, 1967—. Author: Precision Communication, 1990, Neutralize Dental Fear, 1990; contbr. author: Dentistry; contbr. articles to profl. jours. Pres. Big Brothers of San Diego County, 1973, Balboa Tennis Club, 1984-85. Recipient Headliner award, San Diego Press Club, 1974, Hon. Dept. Sheriff of San Diego County, 1974—. Mem. Am. Dental Assn., Am. Acad. Gen. Dentistry, Am. Acad. Dental Practice Adminstrn., Assn. for Humanistic Psychology, Acad. Guided Imagery. Republican. Home: 4632 Van Dyke Ave San Diego CA 92116-4842 Office: Carl H Jepsen DDS PhD 1916 3d Ave San Diego CA 92101

JERISON, HARRY JACOB, psychology educator; b. Bialystok, Poland, Oct. 13, 1925; came to U.S., 1929; m. Irene Landkof, Dec. 17, 1950. BS in Biol. Scis., U. Chgo., 1947, PhD in Psychology-Biol. Scis., 1954. Lectr. in psychology U. Ind., South Bend, 1951-52; rsch. psychologist Aero Medi. Lab., Dayton, Ohio, 1949-57; from assoc. prof. to prof., dir. behavior rsch. lab. Depts. Psychology and Biology Antioch Coll., Yellow Springs, Ohio, 1957-69; prof. biobehavioral scis. and psychology UCLA, 1969-92, prof. emeritus, 1993—; vis. scientist Applied Psychology Unit Med. Rsch. Coun., Cambridge, Eng., 1978-79; acad. visitor Dept. Zoology Oxford U., 1986; vis. prof. Istituto de Antropologia Universita di Firenza, Italy, 1986-87, Dept. Psychology U. Hawaii, 1987, Max-Planck-Inst. f. Biologische Kybernetik, Tubingen, Fed. Republic of Germany, 1989, Dept. Psychology Univ. Coll., London, 1993—; dir. Evolutionary Biology Intelligence NATO ASI, 1986-87; James Arthur lectr. Am. Mus. Natural History, N.Y.C., 1989. Fellow Ctr. Advanced Study Behavioral Scis., Stanford, Calif., 1967-68; scholar in residence Rockefeller Found. Study and Conf. Ctr., Bellagio, Italy, 1983. Home: 503 W Rustic Rd Santa Monica CA 90402-1115 Office: UCLA Psychiat Dept Los Angeles CA 90024

JERMINI, ELLEN, academic administrator; b. Krefeld, Germany, Aug. 25, 1939; came to U.S., 1986.; d. Maximilian and Mathilde (Wachtberger) Wilms; m. Helios Jermini, 1961 (div. June 1989); children: Mariella Arnoldi, Diego Jermini. PhB, U. Healing, 1984, M in Healing Sci., 1985, PhD, 1986; PhB, U. Philosophy, 1992. Sec. Germany, Switzerland, 1962; pub. translator, 1984—; seminar organizer Europe, 1983—; dir. U. Philosophy/European Found., 1986—; pres. U. Healing, Campo, Calif., 1986—, U. Philosophy, Campo, 1986—; abbot Absolute Monastery, Campo, 1986—. Editor: (newsletter Italian) The Absolute, (newsletter German) The Absolute; author: Practitioner's Manual. Speaker various univs. and orgns. in Calif. and N.Y., 1989-92, St. Petersburg, Moscow, 1991, various seminars and workshops. Home and Office: Univ of Healing 1101 Far Valley Rd Campo CA 91906

JERNIGAN, JAMES LEROY, optical engineer; b. San Antonio, Nov. 8, 1936; s. James Sinkler and Beatrice M. (Trafton) J.; m. Carol Ann Roe, June 6, 1961; children: Deborah S., James D., Stephen S., Daniel K., Matthew J., Ruth H., Naomi E. BS in Physics, Brigham Young U., 1965. Physicist Naval Weapons Ctr., China Lake, Calif., 1965-79; optical physicist White Sands (N.Mex.) Missile Range, 1979-82; optical engr., researcher Phys. Sci. Lab. N.Mex. State U., Las Cruces, N.Mex., 1982-89; sr. staff engr. TRW, Las Cruces, 1989; sr. optical engr. IIT Rsch. Inst., Las Cruces, 1989-92; v.p., chief scientist JTI Systems, Inc., Albuquerque, 1992—. Contbr. articles to profl. jours.; patentee in field. Pres. Inyokern (Calif.) C. of C., 1975. Mem. Optical Soc. Am. Office: JTI Systems Inc. 1009 Bradbury Dr SE Albuquerque NM 87106-4302

JERRYTONE, SAMUEL JOSEPH, beauty school executive, educator; b. Pittston, Pa., Mar. 21, 1947; s. Sebastian and Susan Teresa (Chiampi) J.; m. Barbara Ann Musto, Feb. 1, 1969; children: Sandra, Cheryl, Samuel, Sebastian. Assoc. in Bus., Scranton (Pa.) Lackawanna Jr. Coll., 1966. Mgr. House of Jerrytone Beauty Salon, West Pittston, Pa., 1967-68; regional sales dir. United Republic Life Ins., Harrisburg, Pa., 1970-76; night instr. Wilkes-Barre (Pa.) Vo-Tech High Sch., 1976-78; spl. sales agt. Franklin Life Ins. Co., Wilkes-Barre, 1978-80; instr. Jerrytone Beauty Sch., Pittston, Pa., 1968-69, supr., 1969—; prof. sch. evaluator Nat. Accrediting Com. Arts and Scis., Washington, 1984—; mem. adv. craft com. Wiles-Barre Vo-Tech High Sch., 1988—. Mem. com. Rep. Presdl. Task Force, Washington, 1984. Mem. Pa. Hairdressers Assn., Nat. Accrediting Com. Cosmetology, Am. Coun. Cosmetology Educators, Masons (3d degree award 1983, 32d degree award Lodge Coun. chpt. consistory 1984), Shriners (Irem temple). Roman Catholic. Office: Jerrytone Beauty Sch 2101 S Decatur Blvd Ste 20 Las Vegas NV 89102-8506

JERSEY, BRAD DOUGLAS, airline executive; b. New Brighton, Pa., May 12, 1960; s. Willard Darryl and Ruth Alyce (Pugh) J. BA in Psychology Econs., Washington and Jefferson U., 1982. Acct. exec. Keebler Co., Pitts., 1982-84; acct. exec. Airborne Express, Pitts., 1984-85, sr. acct. exec., 1985-86, dist. mgr., 1986-88; mgr. nat. accts. Am. Airlines, Dallas, 1988-89; regional mgr. Am. Airlines, Chgo., 1989-90; div. mgr. Am. Airlines, L.A., 1990-91, regional dir. So. Calif., 1991—. Bd. dirs. Orange County Sports Assn. Mem. British Am. C. of C., Orange County C. of C., Orange County Sports Coun., Elks. Republican. Office: Am Airlines 770 City Dr Orange CA 92668

JERVIS, JANE LISE, academic administrator, historian; b. Newark, N.J., June 14, 1938; d. Ernest Robert and Helen Jenny (Roland) J.; m. Kenneth Albert Pruett, June 20, 1959 (div. 1974); children: Holly Jane Pruett, Cynthia Lorraine Pruett; m. Norman Joseph Chonacky, Dec. 26, 1981; children: Philip Joseph Chonacky, Joseph Norman Chonacky. AB, Radcliffe Coll., 1959; MA, Yale U., 1974, MPhil, 1975, PhD in History of Sci., 1978. Tech. writer Raytheon Co., Wayland, Mass., 1959-62, Texaco Experiment, Inc., Richmond, Va., 1962; freelance sci. editor and writer, 1962-72; edn. advisor, adminstr. U. Md. Program/USAF, France, 1964-65; lectr. in history Rensselaer Poly. Inst., 1977-78; dean Davenport Coll., lectr. in history of sci., Yale Coll. Seminar program Yale U., 1978-82; dean students., assoc. prof. history Hamilton Coll., 1982-87; dean coll., lectr. in history Bowdoin Coll., 1988-92, acting pres., 1990; pres. Evergreen State Coll., Olympia, Wash., 1992—; outside examiner coll. of sci. in society Wesleyan U., 1980, 81; cons. Portland Sch. Art., 1992. Author: Cometary Theory in 15th Century Europe; contbr. articles to profl. jours.; book reviewer; presenter in field. Trustee Maine Hist Assn., 1991-92; chair Maine selection com. Rhodes Scholarship Trust, 1990-92, chair Northwest selection com., 1992—. Office: Evergreen State Coll Office of President Olympia WA 98505

JESENA, ALFONSO T., JR., environmental engineer; b. Iloilo City, The Philippines, Feb. 11, 1946; came to U.S., 1972; s. Alfonso C. and Ramona T. Jesena; m. Mae S. Jesena, Sept. 9, 1973; children: Anita Louise, Christine. BSCE, Western Inst. Tech., Iloilo City, 1966; BS in San. Engring., Nat. U., Manila, 1971, postgrad., 1972; MPH, U. Okla., 1976. Registered profl. engr., Okla. Civil engr. Western Stell Inc./Certeza Surveying Co., Manila, 1965-72; san. engr. U.S. Army, San Francisco, 1976-78; environ. planner USN Facilities Engrng. Command, San Bruno, Calif., 1978-80, gen. engr., 1980-90, environ. engr., constrn. mgr., 1990—. Capt. USAF, 1972-76. Mem. Soc. Am. Mil. Engrs., Am. Water Works Assn., Okla. Water Pollution Control Assn. Roman Catholic. Home: 98 Wakefield Ave Daly City CA 94015-4448 Office: USN Facilities Engring Command Code 1824 AJ PO Box 727 San Bruno CA 94066-0720

JESKE, KEITH WILLIAM, real estate and mortgage executive; b. Milw., June 16, 1950; s. Gilbert F. and Betty A. (Langdon) J.; children: KC William, Camie Sloan; m. Christy Sue Bynum, Feb. 12, 1993. AA, San Bernardino Valley Coll., 1971; BA, Point Loma, San Diego, 1973; JD, UCLA, 1976. CEO Keith Jeske Realty, Las Vegas, Nev., 1976—, Levin Mortgage, Las Vegas, 1991—; cons. Consumer Credit Counselors, L.A., 1974-78, Planning Commn., Culver City, Calif., 1975-77. Author: Goal Mind, 1988; contbr. articles to profl. jours. Mediator Community Mediation of San Diego, 1990; educator, arbitrator Alternative Dispute Resolutions, Las Vegas, 1992. Named Sales Person of Yr., Beverly Hills, 1973, Mgr. of Yr., Bd. of Realtors, L.A., 1979. Mem. Nat. Assn. Realtors, Calif. Assn. Realtors, L.A. Bd. Realtors, Culver City Bd. Realtors, Las Vegas Bd. Realtors, Mortgage Brokers Assn. Home: 994 Bel Air Cir Las Vegas NV 89109

JESSING, THEODORE CHARLES, business owner, consultant; b. Klamath Falls, Oreg., Oct. 18, 1949; s. Louis Christopher and Patricia Gene (McEnery) J.; m. Constance Cadrecha Jessing (Div); 1 child: Mathau Jacob Allen Jessing; m. Judy Fay Miller; children: Louis, Lambert, Theodore "Tyrone", Alina. AS, Chemeketa Community Coll., Salem, Oreg., 1988. Salesperson Camera and Computer Emporium, Portland, Oreg., 1978-80, Byte N.W. Inc., Beaverton, Oreg., 1980-82; owner S.O.L.V.E., LaFayette, Oreg., 1983—. Office: SOLVE 788 Adams Lafayette OR 97127

JESSUP, W. EDGAR, JR., lawyer; b. L.A., Sept. 9, 1922; s. Walter E. and Marian (Moses) J.; m. Audrey B. Vail; children: Bryn W., Holden D. ScB in Engring. magna cum laude, Brown U., 1943; JD, U. So. Calif., L.A., 1949. Bar: Calif. 1950, U.S. Dist. Ct. (cen. dist.) Calif. 1950, U.S. Claims Ct. 1976, U.S. Tax Ct., 1952. Founding ptnr. Ervin, Cohen & Jessup, Beverly Hills, Calif., 1953—; lectr. Sch. Engring. U. So. Calif., 1950-58, Sch. Law, 1965-76; bd. dirs. Logicon, Inc., L.A., Magnetika, Inc., L.A. Author: Law & Specifications for Engineers & Scientists, 1963; contbr. articles to profl. jours. Bd. dirs. Assn. Alumni Brown U., Providence, 1985-89; chmn. bd. dirs. Westside Family YMCA, West Los Angeles, Calif., 1988-93; bd. dirs. Brentwood (Calif.) Westwood Symphony, 1953—; bd. mgrs. L.A. Metro YMCA, 1988-93. Lt. USNR, 1943-46, ETO, PTO. Mem. ABA, State Bar Calif., L.A. Bar Assn., Beverly Hills Bar Assn., Brown U. Club So. Calif. (pres. 1984-91), Calif. Yacht Club (former flag officer), Order of Coif, Tau Beta Pi, Phi Kappa Phi, Phi Alpha Delta. Office: Ervin Cohen & Jessup 9401 Wilshire Blvd Beverly Hills CA 90212-2928

JESSUP, WARREN T., lawyer; b. Eureka, Calif., Aug. 1, 1916; s. Thurman W. and Amelia (Johnson) J.; m. Evelyn Via, Sept. 13, 1941; children: Thurman W., Paul H., Stephen T., Marilyn R. Jessup Huffman. B.S., U. So. Calif., 1937; J.D., George Washington U., 1942. Bar: D.C. 1941, Calif. 1947, U.S. Dist. Ct. (cen., so., no. dists.) Calif. 1947, U.S. Ct. Appeals (Fed. cir.) 1947, U.S. Supreme Ct. 1947. Engr. Gen. Electric Co., 1937-38, patent dept., 1938-42; mem. patent div. USN, 1944-46; patent counsel 11th Naval Dist., 1946-50; mem. Huebner, Beehler, Worrel & Herzig, 1950-56; ptnr. Herzig & Jessup, 1957-59; individual practice law, 1959-68; mem. firm Jessup & Beecher, Sherman Oaks, also, L.A., 1968-85, Jessup Beecher & Slehofer, Westlake Village, Calif., 1985—; instr. patent law, grad. div. Law Sch. U. So. Calif.; instr. bus. law U. Calif. at L.A. Author: Patent Guide for Navy Inventors, 1950; Contbr. to: Ency. of Patent Practice and Invention Mgmt. Chmn. citizens adv. com. Point Mugu State Park, 1973; mem. Ventura County Mental Health Adv. Bd., 1977-82, chmn., 1979. Served from ensign to lt. comdr. USN, 1942-46; comdr. Res. Mem. Patent Law Assn. Los Angeles (pres. 1974-75), NSPE, Am. Intellectual Property Law Assn., Conejo Valley Bar Assn. (pres. 1987), Conejo Valley Hist. Soc. (bd. dirs. 1971-83), Order of Coif, Tau Beta Pi, Eta Kappa Nu, Phi Kappa Phi, Phi Delta Phi. Baptist. Office: Jessup Beecher & Slehofer 875 Westlake Blvd Ste 205 Thousand Oaks CA 91361

JESTE, DILIP VISHWANATH, psychiatrist, researcher; b. Pimpalagaon, India, Dec. 23, 1944; came to U.S., 1974; naturalized Feb., 1980; m. Sonali D. Jeste, Dec. 5, 1971; children: Shafali, Neelum. B in Medicine & Surgery, U. Poona, India, 1966; D. Psychiat. Medicine, Coll. Physicians and Surgeons, 1970; MD, U. Bombay, 1970. Cer. Am. Bd. Psychiatry and Neurology, 1979; lic. physician, D.C., Md., Calif. Hon. asst. prof. KEM Hosp., G.S. Med. Coll., Bombay, 1971-74; staff psychiatrist St. Elizabeth's Hosp., Washington, 1977-82, chief movement disorder unit, 1982-86; clin. assoc. prof. psychiatry Walter Reed Med. Ctr., Bethesda, Md., 1981-84; assoc. clin. prof. psychiatry and neurology George Washington U., Washington, 1984-86; prof. psychiatry and neuroscis. U. Calif., San Diego, 1986—; chief psychiatry svc. San Diego VA Med. Ctr., San Diego, 1989-92; dir. geriatric psychiatry clin rsch ctr. U. Calif. and VA Med. Ctr., San Diego, 1992—; vis. scientist dept. neuropathology Armed Forces Inst. of Pathology, Washington, 1984-86; co-dir. Med. Students' Psychiatry Clerkship Program, 1987-91; ad-hoc mem. Vets. Adminstrn. Neurobiology Grant Rev. Bd., 1984—; participant numerous meeting and confs.; lectr. in field. Co-author: Understanding and Treating Tardive Dyskinesia, 1982; editor: Neuropsychiatric Movement Disorders, 1984, Neurpsychiatric Dementias, 1986, Psychosis and Depression in the Elderly, 1988; contbr. articles to numerous profl. jours, reviewer numerous profl. jours. Mem. Acad. Geriatric Resource Com., U. Calif., 1986-87, mem. com. on joint doctoral program in clin. psychology, 1986-87, mgmt. com. faculty compensation fund com., 1988-89, chmn. Psychiat. Undergrad. Edn. Com., 1987. Recipient Merit award NIMH, 1988; recipient numerous grants in field. Fellow Indian Psychiatric Soc. (recipient Sandoz award 1973), Am. Psychiatric Assn. (co-chmn. Tardive Dyskinesia task force 1984-92), Am. Coll. Neuropsychopharm. (co-chmn. fin. com. 1988-89); mem. Soc. for Neurosci., Internat. Brain Rsch. Orgn., Soc. Biolog. Psychiatry (A.E. Bennett Neuropsychiatric Rsch. award 1981), Am. Acad. Neurology, Am. Geriatrics Soc., Calif. Psychiatric Soc., Am. Assn. Geriatric Psychiatry, West Coast Coll. Biolog. Psychiatry, San Diego Soc. Psychiatric Physicians, Assn. Scientists of Indian Origin in Am. (pres. neurosci. chpt. 1988—, named Outstanding Neuroscientist 1988). Office: Vets Affairs Med Ctr 3350 La Jolla Village Dr V116A San Diego CA 92161

JEWETT, LUCILLE MCINTYRE (MRS. GEORGE FREDERICK JEWETT, JR.), civic worker; b. St. Louis, Jan. 1, 1929; d. Charles Edwin and Elizabeth (Newbery) McIntyre; student U. Puget Sound, 1950; m. George Frederick Jewett, Jr., July 11, 1953; children: Mary Elizabeth Coombs, George Frederick III. Mem. Jr. League, Tacoma; mem. World Svc. Coun., YWCA, Achievement Rewards for Coll. Scientists; trustee San Francisco Ballet Assn.; mem. nat. coun. Sch. Am. Ballet, N.Y.C., 1986—; collectors com. Nat. Gallery Art, Washington; trustee U. Puget Sound, Tacoma; mem. Henry Luce Fdn., Asian Scholars Selection Com. Mem. Order St. John of Jerusalem, Francisca Club, Pi Beta Phi. Presbyterian. Home: 2990 Broadway St San Francisco CA 94115-1062

JEX, MICHAEL WILLIAM, hospital executive; b. Blackfoot, Idaho, Aug. 23, 1957; s. William M. and Anna R. (Cook) J.; m. Kathryn Rees, Dec. 31, 1985. AA, Ricks Coll., Rexburg, Idaho, 1980; student, Brigham Young U., 1982. Cert. patient accounts mgr. Patient accounts mgr. American Fork (Utah) Hosp., 1986-89, Utah Valley Regional Med. Ctr., Provo, 1989; dir. patient account svcs. So. Region, Intermountain Helath Care, Inc., Salt Lake City, 1989—. Mem. Am. Guild Patient Account Mgmt. (bd. dirs. 1990-91, treas. Mountain West chpt. 1992—), Utah Hosp. Assn. (Utah state uniform billing com. 1989—, Utah state bus. office com. 1991—). Office: Utah Valley Region Med Ctr Patient Accounts 1034 North 500 West Provo UT 84604

JIALANELLA, JOHN JAMES, financial planner; b. Massillon, Ohio, Nov. 29, 1941; s. Samuel J. and Margaret D. (Fryer) J.; divorced; children: Robert, Crystal, Thomas. Student, Kent State U., 1960-62. CFP. Store mgr. Kroger Co., Canton, Ohio, 1962-74; dist. mgr. IDS Fin. Svcs., Canton, 1974-84, Dana Point, Calif., 1984-88; br. mgr. LPL Fin. Svcs., Dana Point, 1988—. Cpl. USMC, 1960-64. Mem. Internat. Assn. Fin. Planners, Dana Point Boating Singles (pres. 1988-92). Home and Office: 34091-B Calle La Primavera Dana Point CA 92620

JIMÉNEZ, FRANCISCO, academic administrator; b. San Pedro Tlaquepaque, Mexico, June 29, 1943; came to U.S., 1947; s. Francisco and Maria (Hernandez) Gonzalez J.; m. Laura Catherine Facchini, Aug. 17, 1968; children: Francisco Andres, Miguel Antonio, Tomas Roberto. BA, Santa Clara (Calif.) U., 1966; MA, Columbia U., 1969, PhD, 1973; postgrad., Harvard U., 1989. Preceptor Columbia U., N.Y.C., 1969-70, assoc. of Spanish, 1971-72, asst. prof., 1972-73; asst. prof. Santa Clara U., 1973-77, assoc. prof., 1977-81; prof. San Filippo Univ., 1981—; instr. ctr. for continuing edn. Santa Clara U., Mexico City, 1975-77; assoc. v.p. for acad. affairs Santa Clara U., 1990—; vis. prof. U. Mexico, 1987; mem. Accrediting Commn. for Sr. Colls. and Univs., 1989—; bd. dirs. Western Assn. of Schs. and Colls. Accrediting Commn. Author: Los episodios nacionales, 1974, Viva la lengua, 1975, 87, Mosaico de la Vida, 1981, several short stories which have been reprinted in numerous anthologies of Am. Lit.; editor: The Identification and Analysis of Chicano Literature, 1979, The Bilingual Review, 1973—, Poverty and Social Justice, 1987, (with others) Hispanics in the United States: An Anthology of Creative Literature, 1980, 82; contbr. numerous articles to profl. jours. Chmn. Calif. Commn. on Tchr. Credentialing, 1976-86; vice chair Calif. Coun. for Humanities, 1987—; bd. dirs. Far West Lab. Ednl. R&D, 1988—, elected chair, 1991—; bd. dirs. Western Assn. Schs. and Colls. Accrediting Commn., 1992—; mem. accrediting commn. Sr. Colls. and Univs., 1989—. Woodrow Wilson fellow, 1966. Mem. Am. Assn. for Higher Edn., MLA, Nat. Chicano Coun. Higher Edn., Assn. Calif. Tchrs. Fgn. Langs., Pacific Coast Coun. Latin Am. Studies, Am. Assn. Tchrs. Spanish and Portuguese, Nat. Assn. Chicano Studies, Western Assn. Schs. and Colls. (bd. dirs. 1992—). Democrat. Roman Catholic. Home: 624 Enos Ct Santa Clara CA 95051-6207 Office: Santa Clara U Office Acad Affairs Santa Clara CA 95053

JIMMINK, GLENDA LEE, elementary school educator; b. Lamar, Colo., Feb. 13, 1935; d. Harold Dale and Ruth Grace (Ellenberger) Fasnacht; m. Gary Jimmink, Oct. 24, 1964 (div. 1984); 1 child, Erik Gerard. BA, U. LaVerne, Calif., 1955. Tchr. elem. grades Pomona (Calif.) Unified Sch. Dist., 1955-61, Palo Alto (Calif.) Unified Sch. Dist., 1961-65, San Rafael (Calif.) Sch. Dist., 1966—; curriculum coun. San Rafael Sch. Dist., 1983-89, mentor tchr., 1989-90, mem. social studies steering com., 1990—, advisor Black Student Union; charter mem. Marin County Curriculum Connection, 1991—. Artist, pub. (calendar) Dry Creek Valley, 1987; author: World Geography Resource Handbook for Tchrs., 1990, others. Mem. Marin Arts Coun., San Rafael, 1988—, Big Bros.-Big Siters, San Rafael, 1986-93, PTA, San Rafael, 1988—, Earthwatch, 1990—. Mem. NEA, Calif. Tchrs. Assn., San Rafael Tchrs. Assn., Nat. Wildlife Soc., Sierra Club. Office: Davidson Mid Sch 225 Woodland Ave San Rafael CA 94901-5098

JIRIKOWSKI, GUSTAV FRIEDRICH, neuroscientist; b. Vienna, Austria, July 14, 1954; came to U.S., 1984; s. Harald and Eva (Lewinsky) J.; m. Gerhild Polak, June 7, 1980; children: Gunther, Martin, Ursula. PhD, U. Salzburg, Austria, 1981. Rsch. asst. dept. zoology U. Salzburg, 1976-78; rsch. assoc. dept. anatomy U. Ulm, Germany, 1978-84, assoc. prof. dept. anatomy and cell biology, 1986-89; asst. prof. dept. anatomy U. N.C., Chapel Hill, 1984-86; rsch. scientist dept. neuropharmacology Scripps Rsch. Inst., La Jolla, Calif., 1989—; sci. dir. Cyto GmbH, Giessen, Germany,

1987—; docent U. Ulm, 1988; dir. R & D Cytech Internat., Sarasota, Fla., 1991—; with Max Planck Inst. Psychiatry, Munich, 1993-94. Author, editor: Role of Oxytocin in Sexual Behavior, 1992; inventor immunoassay system. Minna Jamnes Heineman Found. fellow, 1984, Fogarty fellow NIH, 1985; recipient Heisenberg Found. award, 1989. Mem. Internat. Brain Rsch. Orgn., Internat. Assn. Histochemists, Soc. for Neurosci.

JOANOU, PHILLIP, advertising executive; b. Phoenix, June 5, 1933; s. Paul and Alice (Lukken) J.; m. Michelle Mason, Aug. 18, 1956; children: Janet, Phillip, Jennifer, Kathleen. B.S., U. Ariz., 1956. Exec. v.p. Galaxy Inc., Los Angeles, 1958-60; sr. account exec. Erwin Wasey Co., 1960-64; account supr. Dancer, Fitzgerald, Sample Co., Los Angeles, 1964-67; v.p. Grey Co., Los Angeles, 1966-68, Doyle, Dane & Bernbach Inc., Los Angeles, 1968-71; exec. v.p., dir. Nov. Group, N.Y.C. and Washington, 1971-72; pres., dir. Dailey & Assocs., L.A., 1973-83, chmn., chief exec. officer, 1984—; instr. mktg. U. So. Calif., 1975-76, dir. inst. advt. studies, 1976-77. Mem. Washington Com. to Re-elect Pres. Nixon, 1971-72; advisor Pres. Ford Election Com., 1976, Pres. Reagan Campaign, 1980; bd. dirs. Crippled Children's Soc., Crippled Children's Hosp., L.A, 1980—; founder, dir. Partnership For A Drug Free Am.; pres. La Canada Ednl. Found. trustee Art Ctr Coll. Served to capt. USAR, 1957-58. Recipient Pvt. Sector Initiative award Pres. Reagan, 1987; named Advt. Leader of the West, Am. Advt. Fedn., 1992. Mem. Western States Advt. Assn. (dir. 1975—, pres. 1980-81, Advt. Man of Yr. 1983), Am. Assn. Advt. Agencies (gov. 1980-81, bd. dirs. 1981-83), Mktg. Execs. Club, Los Angeles Advt. Club (dir., Merit of Achievement award 1988), World Affairs Council. Republican. Episcopalian. Club: California. Office: Dailey & Assocs 3055 Wilshire Blvd Los Angeles CA 90010-1108

JOAQUIM, RICHARD RALPH, hotel executive; b. Cambridge, Mass., July 28, 1936; s. Manuel and Mary (Marrano) J.; m. Nancy Phyllis Reis, Oct. 22, 1960; 1 child, Vanessa Reis. BFA, Boston U., 1955, MusB, 1959. Social dir., coord. summer resort, Wolfeboro, N.H., 1957-59; concert soloist N.H. Symphony Orch., Vt. Choral Soc., Choral Arts Soc., Schenectady Chamber Orch., 1957-60; coord. performance functions, mgr. theatre Boston U., 1959-60, asst. program dir., 1963-64, dir. univ. programs, 1964-70; gen. mgr. Harrison House of Glen Cove; dir. Conf. Svc. Corp., Glen Cove, N.Y., 1970-74, sr. v.p., dir. design and devel.; v.p. Arltec, also mng. dir. Sheraton Internat. Conf. Ctr., 1975-76; v.p., mng. dir. Scottsdale (Ariz.) Conf. Ctr. and Resort Hotel, 1976—; pres. Internat. Conf. Resorts, Inc., 1977, chmn. bd., 1977—; pres. Western Conf. Resorts; concert solist U.S. Army Field Band, Washington, 1960-62. Creative arts cons., editorial cons., concert mgr. Commr. recreation Watertown, Mass., 1967—; mem. Spl. Study Com. Watertown, 1967—, Glen Cove Mayor's Urban Renewal Com., Nat. Com. for Performing Arts Ctr. at Boston U., Jacob K. Javits Fellows Program Fellowship Bd. Bd. dirs. Nat. Entertainment Conf.; trustee Boston U., 1983—, Hotel and Food Adminstrn. Program Adv. Bd., Boston U., 1986—, Ariz. Opera Co. With AUS, 1960-62. Recipient Disting. Alumni award Boston U., 1991. Mem. Assn. Coll. and Univ. Concert Mgrs., Am. Symphonic League, Am. Fedn. Film Socs., Assn. Am. Artists, Am. Pers. and Guidance Assn., La Chaine des Rotisseurs, Knights of the Vine, Order of St. John, Nat. Alumni Council Boston U. Clubs: The Lotos (N.Y.). Office: Scottsdale Conf Ctr & Resort Hotel 7700 E Mccormick Pky Scottsdale AZ 85258-3431

JOBELMANN, HERMAN FREDERICK, musician, music union administrator; b. Portland, Oreg., May 20, 1913; s. Fred William Jobelmann and Matilda Miriam (Singer) Chapman; m. India Mabel Keplinger, Apr. 20, 1984. Grad., Lincoln High Sch., Portland, 1934. Pit musician various theatres, Portland, 1933-38; prin. bass Portland, Oreg. Symphony, 1934-83, Metro. Opera Nat., N.Y.C., 1965-67; libr., bass Sarah Caldwell's Boston Opera, 1968-70; prin. bass Roger Wagner Chorale, 1970-71, Clebanoff Strings, 1972; double bass Hollywood (Calif.) Studios, 1971-73; pres. local 99 Am. Fedn. Musicians, Portland, 1986—; adj. prof. Lewis and Clark Coll., Portland, Marylhurst Coll., Portland, Reed Coll., Portland. Mem. Portland Oreg. Visitor's Assn., Portland C. of C. Mem. Masons, Shriners. Democrat. Presbyterian. Home: 11955 SW Morning Hill Dr Tigard OR 97223 Office: Am Fedn Musicians 325 NE 20th Ave Portland OR 97232

JOBES, PATRICK CLARK, sociology educator; b. L.A., Dec. 31, 1941; s. Ralph Clark Jobes and Dorothy Marie (Johnston) Richards; m. Sarah Owens, June 22, 1965 (div. June 1988); children: Genevieve, Peter. BA, U. Colo., MA; PhD, U. Wash., 1970. Asst. prof. U. Colo., Boulder, 1969-72; asst. prof. Mont. State U., Bozeman, 1972-75, assoc. prof., 1976-82, prof., 1983—; cons. Dept. Energy, USDA, Washington, 1979-81, Mountain West Resources, Billings, Mont., 1981-83, Nat. Park Svc., Denver, 1989-92; com. chair Rural Migration, USDA, Washington, 1986, 92. Contbr. book chpts. and articles to profl. jours. Chair Dist. 47 Sch. Bd., Gallating County, 1976-83, Environ. Info. Ctr., Bozeman, 1984-86. Fellowship NIMH, 1968-69; grantee NSF, 1971-72, USDA, 1972—. Mem. Am. Sociol. Assn. (com. on environ. sociology 1972-75), Rural Sociol. Soc. (treas., chair elections com. 1987—), Pacific Sociol. Assn. (com. acad. freedom, 1983-85). Democrat. Roman Catholic. Office: Dept Sociology Mont State U Bozeman MT 59717

JOBS, STEVEN PAUL, computer corporation executive; b. 1955; adopted s. Paul J. and Clara J. (Jobs); m. Laurene Powell, Mar. 18, 1991. Student, Reed Coll. With Hewlett-Packard, Palo Alto, Calif.; designer video games Atari Inc., 1974; co-founder Apple Computer Inc., Cupertino, Calif., chmn. bd., 1975-85, former dir.; pres. NeXT, Inc., Redwood City, Calif., 1985—. Co-designer: (with Stephan Wozniak) Apple I Computer, 1976. Office: NeXT Inc 900 Chesapeake Dr Redwood City CA 94063

JOCHUM, LESTER H., dentist; b. Chgo., Nov. 19, 1929; s. J. Harry and Hilma O. (Swanson) J.; m. Anne Elizabeth Cannon, Sept. 20, 1952 (div. Apr. 1983); 1 child, David S. Student U. Wyo., 1947-48; BS in Bus. Adminstrn. with honors, Oreg. State U., 1952; pre-dental student Portland State Coll., 1959-60; B.S. with honors in Sci., U. Oreg., 1963, D.M.D., 1964. Staff acct. Pacific Telephone and Telegraph Co., San Francisco, 1952-59; gen. practice dentistry, San Jose, Calif., 1965-83; dental cons. Delta Dental Plan of Calif., Sacramento, 1983—; ptnr. Trinity Imports. Contbr. articles Calif. Wine Press; also others. Asst. chief Santa Clara Reserve Police Dept., Calif., 1976-83. Active No. Calif. diocese Episc. Ch. Served with U.S. Army, 1952-54. Mem. Sacramento Dist. Dental Soc., Calif. Dental Assn., ADA, Phi Kappa Phi, Psi Omega, Alpha Phi Omega, Lambda Chi Alpha (ritual chmn. 1951, soc. chmn. 1952). Republican. Office: Delta Dental Plan of Calif 7667 Flosom Blvd. Sacramento CA 95826

JOCKERS, MATTHEW LEE, English language educator; b. Bronxville, N.Y., Nov. 28, 1966; s. Robert Lee and Gail Anne (Perrault) J. BA, Mont. State U., 1989; MA, U. No. Colo., 1993; postgrad., So. Ill. Univ., 1993—. Guide Soda Fork Outfitters, Jackson Hole, Wyo., 1985-88, Mountain Sky Guest Ranch, Livingston, Mont., 1991; tutor Greeley, Colo., 1991-93; English tchr. U. of No. Colo., Greeley, 1990—. Author: Mercenaries Guide to English Composition, 1991, James Joyce's Ulysses Explicator, 1992; asst. editor Colo. North Rev., 1992. Grad. fellowship U. No. Colo., 1991, 92; Mae Cross scholar, 1992. Mem. English Grad. Student Orgn. (pres. 1991-92), Sigma Tau Delta. Republican. Home: Rt 85 Box 4322 Livingston MT 59047

JOFFE, BENJAMIN, mechanical engineer; b. Riga, Latvia, Feb. 23, 1931; came to U.S., 1980, naturalized, 1985; s. Alexander and Mery (Levenson) J.; m. Frida Erenshteyn, Aug. 6, 1960; children: Alexander, Helena. ASME, Mech. Tech. Sch., Krasnoyarsk, USSR, 1951; BSME, Polytechnic Inst. Moscow, 1959; MSME, Polytechnic Inst. Riga, 1961; PhD, Acad. Scis., Riga, 1969. Design engr. Electromachine Mfg. Corp., Riga, 1955-59, head engring. dept., 1959-62; sr. design engr. Acad. Scis., Riga, 1962-67; sr. scientist Inst. Physics, Riga, 1967-78; chief design engr. Main Design Bur., Riga, 1978-80; sr. design engr. Elec-Trol, Inc., Saugus, Calif., 1980-81; sr. design engr. VSI Aerospace div. Fairchild, Chatsworth, Calif., 1981-85; mech. engring. mgr. Am. Semiconductor Equipment Tech., Woodland Hills, Calif., 1985-90; mem. tech. staff Jet Propulsion Lab. Calif. Inst. Tech., Pasadena, 1991—. Author: Mechanization and Automatization of Punching Presses at the Plants of the Latvian SSR, 1963, Mechanization and Automatization of Processes of Plastic Parts Production at the Plants of the Latvian SSR, 1964, Mechanization and Automatization of Control and Measuring Operations, 1966, and 5 sci. engring. books; contbr. numerous articles to profl. jours. Recipient Honored Inventor award Latvian Republic, Riga, 1967, 1st prize Latvian Acad. Scis., 1972, Latvian State award in engring. scis., 1974. Mem. ASME (dir. exec. bd.). Republican. Home: 22314 James Alan Cir Chatsworth CA 91311-2054 Office: Calif Inst Tech Jet Propulsion Lab 4800 Oak Grove Dr Pasadena CA 91109-8099

JOHANNSEN, DAVID CHARLES, physicist, aerospace engineer; b. Pasadena, Calif., Oct. 3, 1957; s. Charles Edward and Mary Jane (Boies) J. BS with honor, Calif. Inst. Tech., 1979; MS, U. Calif., Riverside, 1981, PhD, 1983. Mem. tech. staff Hughes Aircraft Co., El Segundo, Calif., 1982-83; rsch. physicist Allied Corp., Westlake Village, Calif., 1983-84; engring. specialist Northop Electronics Div., Hawthorne, Calif., 1984-87; project engr. Aerospace Corp., El Segundo, 1987—; vis. asst. prof. Loyola Marymount U., L.A., 1982. Author: (with others) Tunable Solid State Lasers, 1985. Mem. L.A. Conservancy, Pasadena Hist. Soc., Pasadena Heritage. Mem. Optical Soc. Am. Republican.

JOHANOS, DONALD, orchestra conductor; b. Cedar Rapids, Iowa, Feb. 10, 1928; s. Gregory Hedges and Doris (Nelson) J.; m. Thelma Trimble, Aug. 27, 1950; children—Jennifer Claire, Thea Christine, Gregory Bruce (dec.), Andrew Mark, Eve Marie; m. Corinne Rutledge, Sept. 28, 1985. Mus.B., Eastman Sch. Music, 1950, Mus.M., 1952; D.F.A. (hon.), Coe Coll., 1962. Tchr. Pa. State U., 1953-55, So. Meth. U., 1958-62, Hockaday Sch., 1962-65. Mus. dir., Altoona (Pa.) Symphony, 1953-56, Johnstown (Pa.) Symphony, 1955-56, asso. condr., Dallas Symphony Orch., 1957-61, resident condr., 1961-62, mus. dir., 1962-70, assoc. condr., Pitts. Symphony, 1970-79, mus. dir., Honolulu Symphony Orch., 1979—, artistic dir., Hawaii Opera Theater, 1979-83, guest condr., Phila. Orch., Amsterdam Concertgebouw Orch., Pitts. Symphony, Rochester Philharm., New Orleans Philharm., Denver Symphony, Vancouver Symphony, Chgo. Symphony, San Francisco Symphony, Netherlands Radio Philharm., Swiss Radio Orch., Mpls. Symphony, Paris Opera, Boston Symphony, San Antonio Symphony, Orchestre Nat. de Lyon, others; recordings for Marco Polo, Naxos, Turnabout, Candide, others. Advanced study grantee Am. Symphony Orch. League and Rockefeller Found., 1955-58. Mem. Am. Fedn. Musicians Internat. Congress of Strings (dir.). Office: Honolulu Symphony Orch 1441 Kapiolani Blvd Ste 1515 Honolulu HI 96814-4495

JOHANSEN, MARJORIE HARKINS, librarian; b. Salem, Oreg., Sept. 9, 1938; d. Lewis Charles Harkins and Marjorie (Fossum) Boring; 1 child, Christopher. BA, Oreg. State U., 1960; MLS, San Jose State U., 1981. Reference libr. Burlingame (Calif.) Pub. Libr., 1982-86, San Francisco (Calif.) State U., 1987-90; bus. reference libr. San Mateo (Calif.) Pub. Libr., 1990—. Mem. ALA, Calif. Libr. Assn. Democrat. Episcopalian. Office: San Mateo Pub Libr 55 W 3d Ave San Mateo CA 94402

JOHANSEN, NILS IVAR, geotechnical engineer, educator, consultant; b. Oslo, Dec. 25, 1941; came to U.S., 1964; s. Ivar Helge and Elisabeth Jenny (Axelsen) J.; m. Ann Loretta Matthew, Aug. 5, 1967; 1 child, Elizabeth Ann. B.S.C.E., Purdue U., 1966, M.S.C.E., 1967, Ph.D., 1971. Registered profl. engr., Alaska, Ind. Hwy. engr. I, Ind. State Hwy. Commn., Lafayette, 1967-71; asst. prof., dept. head mineral engring. U. Alaska, Fairbanks, 1971-76, assoc. prof. geol. engring., 1976—; project engr. Shannon & Wilson, Inc., Fairbanks, 1982-83; program evaluator geol. engring. Accredidation Bd. for Engring. and Tech., N.Y.C., 1982—; acad. skills coord. U. So. Ind., 1989; head Dept. of Min. Expl. and Mining Tech., 1990—; dir. Office of Faculty Devel., 1992—. Contbr. articles to profl. jours. Mem. exec. bd. Boy Scouts Am., 1979—. Served with Norwegian Army, 1960-62. Fellow ASCE; mem. AIME (vice chmn. Alaska 1976-77), Nat. Assn. of Devel. Edn., Norwegian Soc. Chartered Engrs., Assn. U.S. Army, U.S. Field Arty. Assn., Ind. Acad. Sci. (chmn. engring. sect. 1991, 92, 93), Sigma Xi, Tau Beta Pi, Chi Epsilon, Sigma Gamma Epsilon. Home: PO Box 82018 Fairbanks AK 99708-2018 Office: Geol Engring Dept U Alaska Fairbanks AK 99775

JOHANSON, DONALD CARL, physical anthropologist; b. Chicago, Ill., June 28, 1943; s. Carl Torsten and Sally Eugenia (Johnson) J. ; m. Lenora Carey, 1988. BA, U. Ill., 1966; MA, U. Chgo., 1970, PhD, 1974; DSc (hon.), John Carroll U., 1979; D.Sc. (hon.), Coll. of Wooster, 1985. Mem. dept. phys. anthropology Cleve. Mus. Natural History, 1972-81, curator, 1974-81; pres. Inst. Human Origins, Berkeley, Calif., 1981—; prof. anthropology Stanford U., 1983-89; adj. prof. Case Western Res. U., 1978-81, Kent State U., 1978-81. Co-author: (with M.A. Edey) Lucy: The Beginnings of Humankind, 1981 (Am. Book award 1982), Blueprints: Solving the Mystery of Evolution, 1989 (with James Shreeve) Lucy's Child: Discovering a Human Ancestor, 1989, (with Kevin O'Farrell) Journey from the Dawn: Life with the World's First Family, 1981, Lucy in Disguise, 1982; host PBS Nature series; prodr.: (films) The First Family, 1990; contbr. numerous articles to profl. jours. Recipient Jared Potter Kirtland award for outstanding sci. achievement Cleve. Mus. Natural History, 1979, Profl. Achievement award, U. Chgo., 1980, Gold Mercury Internat. ad personem award Ethiopia, 1982, Humanist Laureate award Acad. of Humanism, 1983, Disting. Svc. award Am. Humanist Assn., 1983, San Francisco Exploratorium award, 1986, Internat. Premio Fregene award, 1987; grantee Wenner-Gren Found., NSF, Nat. Geog. Soc., L.S.B. Leakey Found., Cleve. Found., George Gund Found., Roush Found. Fellow AAAS, Calif. Acad. Scis., Rochester (N.Y.) Mus., Royal Geog. Soc.; mem. Am. Assn. Phys. Anthropologists, Internat. Assn. Dental Research, Internat. Assn. Human Biologists, Am. Assn. Africanist Archaeologists, Soc. Vertebrate Paleontology, Soc. Study of Human Biology, Societe de l'Anthropologie de Paris, Centro Studi Ricerche Ligabue (Venice), Founders' Coun., Chgo. Field Mus. Natural History (hon.), Assn. Internationale pour l'etude de Paleontologie Humaine, Mus. Nat. d'Histoire Naturelle de Paris (corr.), Explorers Club (hon. dir.), Nat. Ctr. Sci. Edn. (supporting scientist). Office: Inst Human Origins 2453 Ridge Rd Berkeley CA 94709

JOHANSON, JERRY RAY, company executive; b. Murray, Utah, Aug. 29, 1937; s. Albert F. and Elizabeth (Cox) J.; m. Harlean Marie Shepherd, July 12, 1957; children: Kerry, Bryan, Michael, Cynthia, Elizabeth. PhD, U. Utah, 1962. Registered profl. engr., Calif., Mass. Sr. technologist U.S. Steel Applied Rsch. Lab., Monroeville, Pa., 1962-66; pres. Jenike & Johanson, Inc., North Billerica, Mass., 1966-85, JR Johanson, Inc., San Luis Obispo, Calif., 1985—. Patentee in field. Mem. ASME (exec. com. 1972-73, Henry Hess award 1966), Am. Soc. Chem. Engrs., Inst. Briquetting and Agglomeration (Neal Rice award 1989). Mormon. Office: JR Johansen Inc 712 Fiero Ln # 37 San Luis Obispo CA 93401-7944

JOHANSON, WILLIAM RICHARD, physics educator; b. Oakland, Calif., Aug. 8, 1948; s. Raymond Richard and B. Louise J. BS in Physics, U. Hawaii, 1972; MS in Physics, U. Calif., Riverside, 1974, PhD in Physics, 1978. Postdoctorate Argonne (Ill.) Nat. Lab., 1978-81, Los Alamos (N. Mex.) Nat. Lab., 1982-83; asst. prof. Pomona Coll., Claremont, Calif., 1983-89; assoc. prof. Santa Clara (Calif.) Univ., 1989—, dept. chair, 1990—. Contbr. articles to numerous scholarly jours. With USAF, 1967-71. Mem. Am. Assn. of Physics Tchrs., Am. Physical Soc., Coun. on Undergraduate Rsch., Sigma Xi. Office: Santa Clara Univ Dept of Physics Santa Clara CA 95053

JOHNS, LINDA ANN, artist; b. Elmira, N.Y., Jan. 5, 1961; d. Wilbur Wilcox and Margaret Louise (Stull) J.; m. Harold Frank Friebe, Mar. 9, 1991. BFA, Ringling Sch. Art, Sarasota, Fla., 1986. Illustrator Pan Am World Svcs., Poulsbo, Wash., 1982-83; graphic artist The Weekly, Seattle, 1984-87; graphic artist, mgr. Key Strokes, Bellevue, Wash., 1987-89; dir. prodns. Communique, Kirkland, Wash., 1989-91. Exhibited in group shows Edmonds (Wash.) Art Festival, 1986—, Longacres Equine Art Show, Renton, Wash., 1986—, Mercer Island (Wash.) Art Festival, 1989—. Methodist. Home and Studio: 14211 SE 37th St Bellevue WA 98006

JOHNS, ROY (BUD JOHNS), publisher, author; b. Detroit, July 9, 1929; s. Roy and Isabel Johns; m. Judith Spector Clancy, 1971 (dec. 1990); m. Frances Moreland, 1992. BA in English and Econs., Albion (Mich.) Coll., 1951. Various editorial positions Mich. and Calif. daily newspapers, 1942-60; bur. chief Fairchild Pubs., 1960-69; dir. corp. communications Levi Strauss & Co., 1969-81, corp. v.p., 1979-81; pres. Synergistic Press, Inc., San Francisco, 1968—; bd. dirs. Apple-Wood Books, Bedford, Mass., Documentary Rsch., Inc., Buffalo; founder, ptnr. Apple Tree Press, Flint, Mich., 1954-55; cons. on communications, publishing and related areas. Author: The Ombibulous Mr. Mencken, 1968, Bastard in the Ragged Suit, 1977; co-editor and author introduction: What is This Madness?, 1985; scriptwriter, exec. producer: What is This Madness?, 1976; exec. producer: The Best You Can Be, 1979 (CINE Golden Eagle award 1980); editor: Old Dogs Remembered, 1993; free-lance writer numerous mag. articles. Dir. Greenbelt Alliance, San Francisco, 1982—, pres. 1990—;mem. Nat. Coun. of Mus. of Am. Indian, N.Y.C., 1980-90; dir. The San Francisco Contemporary Music Players, 1981—, others in past. Home and Office: 3965 Sacramento St San Francisco CA 94118-1627

JOHNSON, ALAN BOND, federal judge; b. 1939. BA, Vanderbilt U., 1961; JD, U. Wyo., 1964. Pvt. practice law Cheyenne, Wyo., 1968-71; assoc. Hanes, Carmichael, Johnson, Gage & Speight P.C., Cheyenne, 1971-74; judge Wyo. Dist. Ct., 1974-85; judge U.S. Dist. Ct. Wyo., 1986—, part-time fed. magistrate, 1971-74; substitute judge Mcpl. Ct., Cheyenne, 1973-74. Served to capt. USAF, 1964-67, to col. Wyo. Air N.G., 1973-90. Mem. ABA, Wyo. State Bar, Laramie County Bar Assn. (sec.-treas. 1968-70), Wyo. Jud. Conf. (sec. 1977-78, chmn. 1979), Wyo. Jud. Council. Office: O'Mahmey Fed Bldg Rm 210 2120 Capitol Ave Ste 2242 Cheyenne WY 82003 also: PO Box 888 Cheyenne WY 82003

JOHNSON, ALICE ELAINE, retired academic administrator; b. Janesville, Wis., Oct. 9, 1929; d. Floyd C. and Alma M. (Walthers) Chester; m. Richard C. Johnson, Sept. 25, 1948 (div. 1974); children: Randall S., Nile C., Linnea E. BA, U. Colo., 1968. Pres., administrator Pikes Peak Inst. Med. Tech., Colorado Springs, Colo., 1968-88; mem. adv. com. to Colo. Commn. on Higher Edn., 1979-80, State Adv. Council on Pvt. Occupational Schs., Denver, 1978-86; mem. tech. adv. com. State Health Occupations, 1986-88; bd. dirs. All Souls Unitarian Ch., Colorado Springs, 1990—, mem. celebration team, 1990-91, pres. bd. trustees, 1991—. Mem. Colo. Pvt. Sch. Assn. (pres. 1981-82, bd. dirs. 1976-88, Outstanding Mem. 1978, 80), Phi Beta Kappa. Democrat. Unitarian.

JOHNSON, ANTHONY RICHARDO, military officer; b. Mexia, Tex.; s. Willie Larcie and Betty Jean (Cotton) J.; m. Terryе Lynne Dickerson. BS in History, USAF Acad., 1976; MBA, Columbia Pacific U., 1985; MAS in Aeronautical Sci., Embry-Riddle Aeronautical U., 1989. Commd. 2d lt. USAF, 1976, advanced through grades to lt. col., 1980; wing combat crew instr. USAF, Minot AFB, N.D., 1980-81; airborne missile ops. commdr. USAF, Ellsworth AFB, S.D., 1981-83, Airborne Launch Control System upgrade instr., 1983-84, chief Airborne Launch Control System standardization/evaluation, 1984-86, system safety program mgr., 1986-87, chief small ICBM flight test integration br., 1988-90, chief small ICBM system test div., 1990-91, dir. small ICBM system test integration, 1991-92; dir. systems, concepts and plans USAF, Norton AFB, Calif., 1992-93, dep. program mgr. rapid execution and combat targeting, 1993—. Recipient CAP award, Rapid City, S.D., 1982. Mem. Assn. Grads. Indsl. Coll. of Armed Forces, Tuskegee Airmen Internat. Home: 2778 Irvington Ave San Bernardino CA 92407-2141 Office: USAF BMO/MME-1 Norton AFB CA 92409-6468

JOHNSON, ARTHUR WILLIAM, JR., planetarium executive; b. Steubenville, Ohio, Jan. 8, 1949; s. Arthur William and Carol (Gilcrest) J.; B.Mus., U. So. Calif., 1973. Lectr., Griffith Obs. and Planetarium, 1969-73; planetarium writer, lectr. Mt. San Antonio Coll. Planetarium, Walnut, Calif., 1970-73; dir. Fleischmann Planetarium, U. Nev., Reno, 1973—. Organist, choirmaster Trinity Episcopal Ch., Reno, 1980—; bd. dirs. Reno Chamber Orch. Assn., 1981-87 , 1st v.p., 1984-85. Nev. Humanities Com., Inc. grantee, 1979-83. Mem. Am. Guild Organists (dean No. Nev. chpt. 1984-85), Internat. Planetarium Soc., Cinema 360, Inc. (treas. 1985-90, pres. 1990—), Pacific Planetarium Assn. (pres. 1980), Planetarium Assn. Can., Rocky Mountain Planetarium Assn., Lions (pres. Reno Host Club 1991-92), Reno Advt. Club (dir. Sheep Dip Show 1988, 90, 92), Sigma Xi (pres. U. Nev. chpt. 1989-91). Republican. Episcopalian. Writer, producer films: (with Donald G. Potter) Beautiful Nevada, 1978, Riches: The Story of Nevada Mining, 1984. Office: Fleischmann Plantarium University of Nevada 1650 N Virginia St Reno NV 89557

JOHNSON, BEVERLY ANN, camera operator; b. Annapolis, Md., Apr. 22, 1947; m. Michael Hoover. Mem. search and rescue fire crew Yosemite/Nat. Park Svc., 1971-76; ski instr. Yosemite Park and Curry Co., Yosemite, 1970-75; stuntman Universal/Columbia Pictures, others, 1971-77; camera operator ABC, CBS, NBC and others. audio technician (film) Endless Summer II; filmed overland expeditions to North and South Pole. Office: EDI Box 130 Kelly WY 83011

JOHNSON, BRUCE PAUL, electrical engineer, educator; b. Lewiston, Maine, Aug. 8, 1938; s. Albert Samuel and Francis Katherine (Powers) J.; m. Marcia Ann Duarte, Feb. 3, 1961; children: Michael, Robyn, Samuel, Rebecca. BS in Physics, Bates Coll., 1960; MS in Physics, U. N.H., 1962; PhD in Physics, U. Mo., 1967. Instr. physics Hobart/William Smith Coll., Geneva, N.Y., 1962-64; advanced scientist Gen. Elec. Med. Systems, Milw., 1967-70; group leader Solid State Lamp Project Gen. Elec., Cleve., 1970-74; from assoc. prof. to prof. elec. engring. and computer sci. U. Nev., Reno, 1974—, chmn. dept., 1978-83, 91—; cons. Solid State Farms, Reno, 1986-88, Xebec Corp., Reno, 1984-86, Caddo Enterprises, 1987-91, Hytek Microsystems, 1991—; mem. U.S. Metric Bd., Washington, 1978-82. Contbr. over 50 articles to sci. and engring. jours. Fellow NSF, 1961, NSF, NASA, Los Alamos Research Lab., Air Force Office Sci. Research, Cal-Trans, Strategic Highway Rsch. Program and pvt. industry. Mem. IEEE (pres. no. Nev. sect. 1985-86, Region 6 student activities coord. 1990—), Am. Soc. Engring. Edn., Internat. Soc. Mini and MicroComputers, Masons, Sig.na Xi (pres. Nev. chpt. 1984-85), Eta Kappa Nu (bd. dirs. 1990-92, v.p. 1993—). Republican. Home: 3190 W 7th St Reno NV 89503-3103

JOHNSON, BYRON JERALD, state supreme court judge; b. Boise, Idaho, Aug. 2, 1937; s. Arlie Johnson and V. Bronell (Dunten) J.; children: Matthew, Ethan, Elaine, Laura; m. Paticia G. Young, 1984. AB, Harvard U., 1959, LLB, 1962. Bar: Idaho, 1962. Justice Idaho Supreme Ct., Boise, 1988—. Pres. Boise Art Assn., 1967-69; del. Dem. Nat. Conv., 1968; mem. Dem. Nat. Com., Dem. Nat. Charter Commn., 1974; bd. dirs. ARC, Boise, Phila., Salvation Army; campaign chmn. Boise United Fund. Mem. Nat. Assn. Estate Planning Couns. (bd. dirs., pres. 1971-72). Office: US Supreme Ct Idaho 451 W State St Boise ID 83720-0001

JOHNSON, CAGE SAUL, hematologist, educator; b. New Orleans, Mar. 31, 1941; s. Cage Spooner and Esther Georgianna (Saul) J.; m. Shirley Lee O'Neal, Feb. 22, 1968; children: Stephanie, Michelle. Student, Creighton U., 1958-61, MD, 1965. Intern U. Cin., 1965-66, resident, 1966-67; resident U. So. Calif., 1969-71; instr. U. So. Calif., L.A., 1971-74, asst. prof., 1974-80, assoc. prof., 1980-88, prof., 1988—; chmn. adv. com. Calif. Dept. Health Svcs., Sacramento, 1977—; dir. Hemoglobinopathy Lab., L.A., 1976—; bd. dirs. Sicke Cell Self-Help Assn., L.A., 1982-86. Contbr. numerous articles to profl. jours. Dir. Sickle Cell Disease Rsch. Found., L.A., 1986—; active Nat. Med. Fellowships, Inc., Chgo., 1979—; chmn. rev. com. NIH, Washington, 1986—. Major U.S. Army, 1967-69, Viet Nam. Fellow N.Y. Acad. Scis., Am. Coll. Angiology; mem. Am. Soc. Hematology, Am. Fedn. Clin. Rsch., Western Soc. Clin. Investigation, Internat. Soc. Biorheology, E.E. Just Soc. (sec.-treas. 1985—). Office: U So Calif 2025 Zonal Ave Los Angeles CA 90033-4526

JOHNSON, CAROLYN ELIZABETH, librarian; b. Oakland, Calif., May 29, 1921; d. Ferdinand Orin and Clara Wells (Humphrey) Hassler; m. Benjamin Alfred Johnson, Feb. 12, 1943; children: Robin Rebecca, Anne Elizabeth, Delia Mary. BA, U. Calif.-Berkeley, 1946; cert. librarian Calif. State U., Fullerton, 1960; M.L.S., Immaculate Heart Coll., 1968. Asst. children's libr. Fullerton Pub. Libr., Calif., 1951-59, coord. children's svcs., 1959-81, city librarian, 1981-90; ret., 1990; apptd. curator Mary Campbell collection hist. children's lit. Fullerton Pub. Libr., 1990; instr. Rio Hondo City Coll., Whittier, Calif., part time 1970-72, Calif. State U.-Fullerton, 1972-77; ; vice chmn. 3d Pacific Rim Conf. Council, 1983-86; mem. Korczak award com. U.S. Bd. Books for Young People, 1988. Author: The Art of Walter Crane, 1988. Mem. Library Tech. Tng. Adv. Com., Fullerton Coll., 1970; founding bd. dirs. Youth Sci. Ctr., Fullerton, 1958; chmn. adv. bd. YMCA Child Devel. Ctr., 1992—. Named Profl. Woman of Yr., N. Orange County YWCA, 1986, Woman of Yr. Fullerton C. of C., 1990. Mem. ALA, Calif. Library Assn. (chmn. children's service div.), Orange County Library

Assn. (v.p.), So. Calif. Coun. on Lit. for Children and Young People (pres. 1979-81, Dorothy C. McKenzie award 1987), PTA (life), AAUW, LWV, Phi Beta Kappa, Theta Sigma Phi. Methodist. Home: 644 Princeton Cir E Fullerton CA 92631-2728

JOHNSON, CHARLES FOREMAN, architect, architectural photographer, planning, architecture and systems engineering consultant; b. Plainfield, N.J., May 28, 1929; s. Charles E. and E. Lucile (Casner) J.; student Union Jr. Coll., 1947-48; B.Arch., U. So. Calif., 1958; postgrad. UCLA, 1959-60; m. Beverly Jean Hinnendale, Feb. 19, 1961 (div. 1970); children: Kevin, David. Draftsman, Wigton-Abbott, P.C., Plainfield, 1945-52; architect, cons., graphic, interior and engring. systems designer, 1953—; designer, draftsman with H.W. Underhill, Architect, Los Angeles, 1953-55; teaching asst. U. So. Calif., Los Angeles, 1954-55; designer with Carrington H. Lewis, Architect, Palos Verdes, Calif., 1955-56; grad. architect Ramo-Wooldridge Corp., Los Angeles, 1956-58; tech. dir. Atlas weapon system Space Tech. Labs., L.A., 1958-60; advanced planner and systems engr. Minuteman Weapon System, TRW, Los Angeles, 1960-64, div. staff ops. dir., 1964-68; cons. N.Mex. Regional Med. Program and N.Mex. State Dept. Hosps., 1968-70; prin. Charles F. Johnson, architect, Los Angeles, 1953-68, Sante Fe, N.Mex., 1968-88, Carefree, Ariz., 1988—; free lance archtl. photographer, Sante Fe, 1971—; tchr. archtl. apprentice program, 1974—; program writer, workshop leader, keynote speaker Mich. Archtl. Design Competition, 1993. Major archtl. works include: residential bldgs. in Calif., 1955-66; Bashein Bldg. at Los Lunas (N.Mex.) Hosp. and Tng. Sch., 1969, various residential bldgs., Santa Fe, 1973—, Kurtz Home, Dillon, Colo., 1981, Whispering Boulders Home, Carefree, 1981, Hedrick House, Santa Fe, 1983, Kole House, Green Valley, Ariz., 1984, Casa Largo, Santa Fe (used for film The Man Who Fell to Earth), 1974, Rubel House, Santa Fe, 1986, Smith House, Carefree, Ariz., 1987, Klopfer House, Sante Fe, 1988, Janssen House, Carefree, 1988, Art Start Gallery, 1988, Dr. Okun's House, 1990, Luterback home, Carefree, 1993. Pres., Santa Fe Coalition for the Arts, 1977; set designer Santa Fe Fiesta Melodrama, 1969, 71, 74, 77, 78, 81; designed Jay Miller & Friends Fiesta float 1970-88 (winner of 20 awards); presenter design workshop, keynote address, agrl. design competition, Mich., 1993. Mem. Desert Mountain Gulf Club, Delta Sigma Phi. Contbr. articles on facility planning and mgmt. to profl. publs.; contbr. archtl. photographs to mags. in U.S., Eng., France, Japan and Italy, contbr. articles on facility mgmt., planning info. systems, etc. to profl. jours. Internat. Recognized for work in organic architecture and siting buildings to fit the land; named among top 100 Architects, Archtl. Digest, 1991. Avocations: music, photography, collecting architecture books, Frank Lloyd Wright works. Home: PO Box 6070 1598 Quartz Valley Dr Carefree AZ 85377

JOHNSON, CHARLES WAYNE, mining engineer, mining executive; b. Vinita, Okla., Feb. 7, 1921; s. Charles Monroe and Willie Mae (Hudson) J.; m. Cleo Faye Wittee, 1940 (div. 1952); m. Genevieve Hobbs, 1960 (dec. Sept. 1985); m. Susan Gates Johnson, Apr. 19, 1986 (div. 1992); 1 child, Karen Candace Limon. BE, Kensington U., 1974, ME, 1975, PhDE, 1976. Owner El Monte (Calif.) Mfg. Co., 1946-49; co-owner Anjo Pest Control, Pasadena, Calif., 1946-56, Hoover-Johnson Cons. Co., Denver, 1956-59; pres. Vanguard Chem. Co., Denver, 1957-61, Mineral Products Co., Boise, Idaho, 1957-61; owner Crown Hill Meml. Park, Dallas, 1959-61, Johnson Engring., 1961—; pres. Crown Minerals, Victorville, Calif., 1985-92; owner J&D Mining Co., Victorville, 1977—. Contbr. articles to profl. pubs.; patentee in field. Active Rep. VIP Club. Served with USN, 1941-45. Recipient Outstanding Achievement award East Pasadena Bus. Assn., 1948. Mem. Ch. Ancient Christianity. Office: Johnson Engring PO Box 1423 Thermal CA 92274

JOHNSON, CHARLES WILLIAM, state supreme court justice; married. BA in Econs., U. Wash., 1973; JD, U. Puget Sound, 1976. Pvt. practice law Pierce County, Wash., 1977-90; judge Supreme Ct. of Wash., Olympia, 1991—; pub. defender for indigent criminal defendants; prosecutor, defender in superior ct. hearings; pro tem judge in Pierce County. Mem. Wash. State Bar Assn., Tacoma-Pierce County Bar Assn. Office: Supreme Ct Wash PO Box 40929 Olympia WA 98504-0929*

JOHNSON, CHRISTOPHER RAY, medicine, computer science, mathematics, and bioengineering educator; b. Kansas City, Kans., Jan. 17, 1960; s. Raymond Lee Johnson and Sherlie (Steffans) Baker; m. Katharine A. Coles, Nov. 25, 1989. BS, Wright State U., 1982; MS, U. Utah, 1984, PhD, 1990. Asst. prof. physics Westminster Coll., Salt Lake City, 1985-89; asst. prof. computer sci. U. Utah, Salt Lake City, 1992—; adj. asst. prof. math. U. Utah, Salt Lake City, 1990—, adj. asst. prof. bioengring., 1991—. Recipient various grants and fellowships. Mem. Am. Phys. Soc., N.Y. Acad. Sci., Engrs. in Medicine and Biology. Office: Dept Computer Sci 3190 MEB U Utah Salt Lake City UT 84112

JOHNSON, DALE GEDGE, pediatric surgeon; b. Salt Lake City, Sept. 27, 1930; s. Morris C. and Leah (Gedge) J.; m. Beverly Clark, Dec. 22, 1952; children: Pam, Paul, Charlotte, Peter. BS, U. Utah, 1953, MD, 1956. Diplomate Am. Bd. Surgery; cert. spl. competence pediatric surgery. Tech. asst. dept. anatomy Harvard U. Sch. of Medicine, Boston, 1957-58; investigator in exptl. surgery Walter Reed Army Inst., Washington, 1961-63; assoc. in rsch. surgery U. Pa., Phila., 1963-64, asst. prof. pediatric surgery, 1966-71; assoc. prof. surgery U. Utah Coll. of Medicine, Salt Lake City, 1971-76, assoc. prof. pediatrics, 1971-77, prof. surgery, 1976—, prof. pediatrics, 1977—; surgeon-in-chief Primary Children's Med. Ctr., Salt Lake City, 1971—; vis. prof. Project Hop Med. Relief Project, Krakow, Poland, 1980, 81, 83, 88, 89; editorial cons. Pediatric Surgery Internat., 1986—. Contbr. numerous articles to profl. jours. and 24 chpts. to med. textbooks; assoc. editor: Jour. of Pediatric Surgery, 1976-79, Clin. Pediatrics, 1980-84, Pediatric Surgery Internat., 1986—. Mem. Mormon Tabernacle Choir, Salt Lake City, 1971-80; bd. dirs. Salt Lake Repertory Orch., Salt Lake City, 1976-77, Am. Cancer Soc., 1972-78. Capt. U.S. Army Med. Corps, 1961-63. Named Outstanding Alumnus, Children's Hosp. of Phila., 1990; recipient Polish Order of Merit Silver medal, 1991, Sword of Hope award Am. Cancer Soc., 1991. Fellow Am. Coll. Surgeons; surg. fellow Am. Acad. Pediatrics, Am. Surg. Assn., Soc. Univ. Surgeons, AMA, Brit. Assn. Pediatric Surgeons; mem. Pacific Assn. Pediatric Surgeons (pres. 1990-91), Am. Pediatric Surg. Assn. (sec. 1973-76, pres. 1985-86). LDS. Office: 100 N Medical Dr Ste 2600 Salt Lake City UT 84113-1100

JOHNSON, DANIEL ARTHUR, health care executive; b. Wadena, Minn., Sept. 11, 1953; s. William Arthur and Lois Eileen (Vikan) Johnson; m. Margaret Claudia Brophy; Aug. 24, 1984; children: Augene Vikan, Augusta Martine. BA, St. Olaf Coll., 1976; AS in Nursing, Met. C.C., Mpls., 1979; MBA, U. Alaska, 1993. RN Minn., Alaska. Nurse Alaska Area Native Health Svc., Anchorage and Barrow, Alaska, 1980-81; community health aide coord., inst. Tannan Chiefs Conf., Tok, Alaska, 1982-84; emergency med. svcs. dir. Fairbanks (Alaska) North Star Borough, 1984-86; community health aide, program adminstr. Yukon Koskokwin Health Corp., Bethel, Alaska, emergency med. svcs. dir., advance life support instr., 1988; ctr. coord. U. Alaska Fairbanks Rural Alaska Health Edn. Ctr., 1989-90; dir. Rural Alaska Health Professions Found., Fairbanks, 1990—; mem. U. Wash. Rural Health Rsch. Ctr. Adv. Bd., Seattle, 1990—, U. Alaska Fairbanks Instl., Rev. Bd., 1990—, Alaska Interagy. Primary Care Com., Juneau, 1992; chmn. 1992 Alaska Rural Health Conf., Anchorage. Author: Alaska Health Career Guide, 1989. Pres. Interior Region Emergency Med. Svcs. Coun., Inc., Fairbanks, 1992—; bd. dirs. So. Region Emergency Med. Svcs. Coun., Inc., Anchorage, 1987-88, Interior Ambulance Rescue, Inc., Fairbanks, 1992—. Mem. Alaska Emergency Med. Svcs. Assn. (v. chmn. 1986-87), Nat. Assn. of Area Health Edn. Ctr. Dirs. (exec. com. bd. dirs.). Office: Rural Alaska Health Professions Found UAF 113 Red Bldg Fairbanks AK 99775

JOHNSON, DANIEL FREDRICK, minister of music; b. Jamestown, N.Y., June 13, 1953; s. Theodore Elliot and Helen Elizabeth (Burgh) J. Student, North Park Sem., Chgo., 1977, Hartt Sch. Music, Hartford, Conn., 1977-78; BA, North Park Coll., Chgo., 1980; postgrad., Fuller Theol. Sem., Menlo Park, Calif., 1989. Commd. and lic. min. Evang. Covenant Ch., 1991. Steward The Masters Sch., Simsbury, Conn., 1978-79; min. music Hilmar (Calif.) Covenant Ch., 1980—; mem. faculty Pacific Sch. Religion, Berkeley, Calif., summers 1986-89, 92-93; singer Covenant Ministers Nat. Chorus, 1991—; performer, dir. Vineyard Pastoral Music Ministry, San Leandro, Calif., 1986-90; coord. Centennial Performing Arts Camp, Chgo., Mpls., 1984-85; music and Bible dir. Camp Squanto, West Swanzey, N.H., 1974-79; instr. aerobics, Hilmar, 1984—. Contbr. articles to demoninational publs. Emotional support vol. Stanislaus Community AIDS Project, Modesto, Calif., 1987-90; urgent action vol. Amnesty Internat., Nederland, Colo., 1987—; sect. leader Hilmar Community Band, 1991—. Mem. Evang. Covenant Ch. Ministerium, Sacred Dance Guild (v.p. 1986-90, coord. chpt. newsletter 1986-88), Choral Condrs. Guild, Christians in Arts Networking. Home: 20336 Topaz Circle Hilmar CA 95324 Office: Hilmar Covenant Ch 8515 Lander Ave Hilmar CA 95324

JOHNSON, DANIEL LEE, SR., state agency administrator; b. Yuba City, Calif., July 6, 1936; s. John Clem J. and Verginia Nellie (Hammons) Clark; children: Daniel Lee Jr., Michael Kevin, Theodore Allen. Student, Yuba Coll., 1955, U. Calif., Davis, 1974. Drafting aide Div. Hwys., State of Calif., Marysville, 1956-57, drafting aide II, 1957-59, delineator, 1959-73; graphic artist Caltrans, Marysville, 1973-84, sr. delineator, 1984-91, asst. adminstr., 1991—; freelance artist, 1955-92; chmn. bd. dirs. Caltrans Disabled Adv. Com., 1985-86, dist. chmn., 1981-88, mem. adv. bd., 1988—. With U.S. Navy, 1951-61. Named Citizen of Yr. Citizens Right to Keep and Bear Arms, 1989, 90, 91, 92; recipient Sustained Superior Accomplishment award Caltrans Disabled Adv. Com., 1990, Theo Wormland Kunstpreis, 1993. Mem. NRA (charter founder second amendment task force 1993), Citizens Rights to Keep and Bear Arms, Moose (gov. 1982-83, editor Moose Call Bull. 1971—, state publicity chmn. 1990-91, Moose of Yr. 1990, 1st place award Calif.-Nev. assn. 1990-93, Internat. award of Excellence 1990-93, Community Svc. award 1990, Internat. Shining Star recipient 1993). Republican. Methodist. Office: Calif Dept Transp 703 B St Marysville CA 95901-5566

JOHNSON, DANIELLE VERSTAEN, translator; b. Waregem, Belgium, July 1, 1950; came to U.S., 1986; d. Henri Marcel Verstaen; m. Jon Kellerman Johnson, July 27, 1987; 1 child, Marieke. LLD, U. Ghent, Belgium, 1974. Atty. Wakken, Belgium, 1974-84; atty., advisor Nato-Shape Support Group, Belgium, 1985-86; CEO Coforex, Wakken, Belgium, 1984—; translator, CEO E.F.F. Svcs., Lakewood, Colo., 1987—; exec. trainer Moran, Stahl & Boyer, Boulder, Colo., 1987—. Mem. Am. Translators Assn. Home and Office: EFF Svcs 651 Cody St Lakewood CO 80215

JOHNSON, DAVID SELLIE, civil engineer; b. Mpls., Apr. 10, 1935; s. Milton Edward and Helen M. (Sellie) J. BS, Mont. Coll. Mineral Sci. Tech., 1958. Registered profl. engr., Mont. Trainee Mont. Dept. Hwys., Helena, 1958-59, designer, 1959-66, asst. preconstrn. engr., 1966-68, regional engr., 1968-72, engring. specialities supr., 1972-89, preconstrn. chief, 1989—, forensic engr., 1965—, traffic accident reconstructionist, 1978—. Contbr. articles on hwy. safety to profl. jours. Adv. bd. mem. Helena Vocat.-Tech. Edn., 1972-73. Fellow Inst. Transp. Engrs.; mem. Nat. Acad. Forensic Engrs. (diplomate), Mont. Soc. Profl. Engrs., NSPE, Transp. Rsch. Bd., Wash. Assn. Tech. Accident Investigators, Corvette Club. Mem. Algeria Shrine Temple. Club: Treasure State (Helena) (pres. 1972-78). Lodges: Elks, Shriners. Home: 1921-6 Ave Helena MT 59601 Office: Mont Dept Transp 1921-6 Ave Helena MT 59601

JOHNSON, DELMAS WAYNE, engineer; b. Montpelier, Idaho, June 10, 1965; s. Wayne D. and Julia Annis (Kearl) J.; m. Julianne Newman, Feb. 8, 1991. BS, Brigham Young U., 1990, postgrad., 1993—. Design engr. Allied Signal-Aftermarket, Clearfield, Utah, 1991-92, Beehive Machinery, Sandy, Utah, 1992—. Mem. Coll. Reps., Brigham Young U., 1988-90. Republican. Mem. LDS Ch. Home: 1600 E 3970 S # 3 Salt Lake City UT 84124

JOHNSON, DENNIS NEAL, manufacturing company executive, consultant; b. Portland, Oreg., July 31, 1942; s. Emil John and Evelyn (Rund) J.; m. Antoinette Heraut, Aug. 15, 1981; children: Tracey, Christopher, Shelley, Stacey. BS, City U., Seattle, 1982, MBA, 1993. Sales rep. Sears, Roebuck & Co., Moses Lake, Wash., 1963-66; sales mgr. Sears, Roebuck & Co., Seattle, 1966-71, dist. mgr., 1971-85; owner, pres. Deanto Inc., Seattle, 1985-89; chief operating officer, gen. mgr. Ramco Constrn. Tools, Inc., Kent, Wash., 1989—. Mem. Mensa, Am. Soc. Materials, Constrn. Industry Mfr. Assn., World Trade Club (bd. dirs. Seattle club). Office: Ramco Construction Tools 21213 76th Ave S Kent WA 98032

JOHNSON, DONALD WALLACE, III, business educator; b. Fort Lauderdale, Fla., July 7, 1959; s. Elliot Max and Irean (Dorithy) J.; children: Dempsey Donald, Donald Wallace IV. BA, Fla. State U., 1976, PhD, 1987; MSW, U. Hawaii, 1984; hotel and motel mgmt. cert., Linsey Hopkins, Miami, Fla., 1974. Intern, investigator State Atty. Office 5th Dist., Daytona Beach, Fla., 1983-87; chief exec. officer Heartline Found., Sparks, Nev., 1987—; dean of studies Sch. Bus., Sparks, 1987—. With U.S. Army, 1976-82. Republican. Roman Catholic. Home and Office: 1395 S Wells Ave Reno NV 89502

JOHNSON, DORIS ANN, educational administrator; b. Marinette, Wis., Dec. 4, 1950; d. Jerome Louis and Jean Fern (Henry) La Plant; m. Daniel Lee Leonard, June 10, 1972 (div. June 1987); children: Jeremiah Daniel, Erica Leigh, Wesley Cyril; m. Paul Robert Johnson, Oct. 21, 1989; stepchildren: Kindra Michelle, Tanya Marie. Student, U. Wis., Oshkosh, 1969-70; BA in Edn., U. Wis., Eau Claire, 1973; MS in Edn., U. Wis., Whitewater, 1975; postgrad., Oreg. State U., 1988—. Reading specialist Brookfield (Wis.) Cen. High Sch., 1975-79; lead instr. N.E. Wis. Tech. Coll., Marinette, 1979-87; dir. adult basic edn. Umpqua C.C., Roseburg, Oreg., 1987—; founding bd. dirs. Project Literacy, Umpqua Region, Roseburg, 1989—; mem. adv. bd. Umpqua Community Action Network, Roseburg, 1987—; mem. State Dirs. of Adult Edn., Oreg., 1987—, vice chair, 1992-93, chair, 1993—; mem. Adminstrn. Assn., Roseburg, 1989—. Co-author literacy module Communication Skills, 1988; author ednl. curriculum. Bd. dirs. St. Joseph Maternity Home, Roseburg, 1987-90, founding mem.; mem. Literacy Theater, Roseburg, 1988—; mem. Project Leadership, Roseburg, 1988-89. state legalization assistance grantee Fed. Govt., 1988—, homeless literacy grantee Fed. Govt., 1990-91, family literacy grantee Fed. Govt., 1991—, intergenerational literacy grantee State of Oreg., 1991, literacy expansion grantee Fed. Govt., 1992-93, literacy outreach grantee Fed. Govt., 1992-93, staff devel. spl. projects grantee Fed. Govt., 1992-93. Fellow Nat. Inst. Leadership Devel., Am. Assn. Adult and Continuing Edn., Oreg. Assn. Disables Students, Oreg. Developmental Edn. Studies, Oreg. Assn. for Children with Learning Disabilities, Tchrs. of English to Speakers of Other Langs., Western Coll. Reading and Learning Assn., Am. Assn. Women in Coll. and Jr. Coll. Republican. Lutheran. Home: 761 Garden Grove Roseburg OR 97470 Office: Umpqua CC PO Box 967 Roseburg OR 97470

JOHNSON, DOUGLAS WALTER, artist; b. Portland, Oreg., July 8, 1946; s. Herbert Walter Johnson and Barbara Elizabeth (Speer) Hall. Student, San Jose (Calif.) State Coll. Artist Jamison Gallery, Santa Fe, 1971-77, Horwich Gallery, Santa Fe, 1977-86, Gerald Peters Corp., Santa Fe, 1986—. Executed mural El Dorado Hotel, 1986; exhibited in numerous group shows.

JOHNSON, E. ERIC, insurance executive; b. Chgo., Feb. 7, 1927; s. Edwin Eric and Xenia Alice (Waisanen) J.; m. Elizabeth Dewar Brass, Sept. 3, 1949; children: Christal L. Johnson Neal, Craig R. BA, Stanford U., 1948. Dir. group annuities Equitable Life Assurance Soc., San Francisco, 1950-54; div. mgr. Equitable Life Assurance Soc., L.A., 1955-59; v.p. Johnson & Higgins of Calif., L.A., 1960-67, dir., 1968-87, chmn., 1986-87; chmn. TBG Fin., L.A., 1988—; bd. dirs. Showscan Corp., Law Environ. Group, 1989-93; exec. v.p. Johnson & Higgins, N.Y.C., 1984-87. Bd. dirs. Sta. KCET, pub. TV, L.A., 1977—, chmn., 1992—; vice chmn. adv. bd. UCLA Med. Ctr., 1983—; bd. dirs. Johnson Comprehensive Cancer Ctr., UCLA, 1985—, Stanford U. Grad. Sch. Bus., 1986-91; trustee Nuclear Decommissioning Trust, Rosemead, Calif., 1986. Mem. Calif. Club., L.A. Country Club, Vintage Club, Riviera Tennis Club, Links Club N.Y.C., Beach Club, So. Calif. Tennis Assn. (exec. com.). Office: TBG Fin 2029 Century Park E Los Angeles CA 90067-2901

JOHNSON, EARVIN (MAGIC JOHNSON), television sports announcer; b. Lansing, Mich., Aug. 14, 1959; s. Earvin and Christine Johnson; m. Cookie Kelly; 1 son, Earvin. Student, Mich. State U., 1976-79. Basketball player L.A. Lakers, 1979-91; sportscaster NBC-TV, 1993—; gold medalist, U.S. Olympic Basketball Team, 1992. Author: (autobiography) Magic, 1983; (autobiography, with Roy S. Johnson) Magic's Touch, 1989; What You Can Do to Avoid AIDS, 1992; My Life, 1992. Mem. NCAA Championship Team, 1979, Nat. Basketball Assn. All-Star Team, 1980, 82-92, Nat. Basketball Assn. Championship Team, 1980, 82, 85, 87, 88; named Most Valuable Player, Nat. Basketball Assn. Playoffs, 1980, 82, 87, Nat. Basketball Assn., 1987, 89, 90, All-Star Game, 1990, 92, Player of the Year, Sporting News, 1987; recipient Schick Pivotal Player award, 1984; holder NBA rec. most career assists. Office: Box 32 Inglewood CA 90312-0032

JOHNSON, EDWARD LEE, urologist; b. Lindsborg, Kans., Nov. 26, 1931; s. C.D. Leonard and Adeline E. (Spongberg) J.; m. Alice L. Vornoff, May 25, 1958; children: Bruce, Tamara, Allison, Lance. BA, Bethany Coll., Lindsborg, 1953; MD, U. Kans., 1957. Med. dir. Kansas City (Mo.) Gen. Hosp., 1963; chief urology Children's Mercy Hosp., Kansas City, 1963; pvt. practice Albuquerque, 1964—; clin. instr. surgery U. N.Mex., Albuquerque, 1964—. Editor Clin. Urol. Forum; contbr. articles to profl. jours. Named Outstanding Alumnus, Bethany coll., Lindsborg, 1974. Mem. Am. Assn. Clin. Urologists (pres. 1990-91), Internat. Soc. Advanced Humanistic Studies (pres. 1988), Am. Coll. Gynecology (past pres. N.Mex. chpt. 1988), N.Mex. Med. Soc. (past pres. 1986-87), Albuquerque-Bernalillo County Med. Soc. (pres. 1980), Elks, Rotary. Republican. Lutheran. Office: 7000 Cutler Ave NE Ste 24E Albuquerque NM 87110-4405

JOHNSON, ELIZABETH HILL, foundation administrator; b. Ft. Wayne, Ind., Aug. 21, 1913; d. Harry W. and Lydia (Buechner) Hill; m. Samuel Spencer Johnson, Oct. 7, 1944 (dec. 1984); children: Elizabeth Katharine, Patricia Caroline. BS summa cum laude, Miami U., Oxford, Ohio, 1935; MA in English Lit., Wellesley Coll., 1937; postgrad., U. Chgo., 1936. Cert. tchr., Ohio. Pres., co-founder S.S. Johnson Found., Calif. Corp., San Francisco, 1947—. Mem. Oreg. State Bd. Higher Edn., Eugene, 1962-75, Oreg. State Edn. Coord. Com., Salem, 1975-82, Assn. Governing Bds., Washington, 1970-80, chairperson, 1975-76; mem. Oreg. State Tchr. Standards and Practices Commn., Salem, 1982-89; bd. dirs. Lewis and Clark Coll., Portland, Oreg., 1985—, Pacific U., Forest Grove, Oreg., 1982—, Sunriver Prep. Sch., 1983-92, Oreg. Hist. Soc., Portland, 1985—, Cen. Oreg. Dist. Hosp., Redmond, 1982—, Oreg. High Desert Mus., 1984—, Bend, Oreg. Health Decisions, 1986-92. Lt. USNR, 1943-46. Named Honoree March of Dimes White Rose Luncheon, 1984; recipient Aubrey Watzek award Lewis and Clark Coll., 1984, Cen. Oreg. 1st Citizen award, Abrams award Emanuel Hosp., 1982, Pres. award Marylhurst Coll., 1991, Thomas Jefferson award Oregon Historical Soc., 1993. Mem. Am. Assn. Higher Edn., Am. Assn. Jr. Colls., ASCD, Soroptimists (hon.), Francisca Club, Town Club, Univ. Club, Waverley Club, Beta Sigma Phi, Phi Beta Kappa, Phi Delta Kappa, Delta Gamma. Republican. Lutheran. Home: 415 SW Canyon Dr Redmond OR 97756-2028 Office: S S Johnson Found 441 SW Canyon Dr Redmond OR 97756-2028

JOHNSON, ERIC ELLIOTT, electrical and computer engineer, educator, consultant; b. Iowa City; s. Malcolm Kaye and Patty McKinley (Hake) J.; m. Donna Lynn Summers. BS in Physics, BSEE, Washington U., St. Louis, 1979, MScEE, 1980; PhD, N.Mex. State U., 1987. Sr. engr. Lockheed, Johnson Space Ctr., Las Cruces, N.Mex., 1984-86; instr. dept. elec. and computer engring. N.Mex. State U., Las Cruces, 1986-87, asst. prof., 1987-92, assoc. prof., 1992—; cons. Planning Rsch. Crop., Sierra Vista, Ariz., 1984-90, Sci. Applications Internat. Corp., 1991—; CEO Johnson Rsch., Las Cruces, 1990—; summer fellow IBM, Austin, Tex., 1990; founder Parallel Architecture Rsch. Lab., N.Mex. State U. Inventor in field; contbr. articles and reports to profl. jours. Faculty adviser to student orgn., leader academic stress workshops. Capt. U.S. Army, 1980-84. Rsch. grantee Army Rsch. Office, AT&T Found., others. Mem. IEEE, IEEE Computer Soc., Assn. Computing Machinery (Computer Architecture and Computer Performance Measurement Spl. Interest Groups), Phi Kappa Phi, Tau Beta Pi, Eta Kappa Nu, Sigma Xi. Office: NMex State U Dept 3-0 Thomas Brown 106 Las Cruces NM 88003

JOHNSON, F. BRENT, microbiologist, educator; b. Monroe, Utah, Mar. 31, 1942; s. Horace Jay and Ida (Christiansen) J.; m. Paula Dawn Forbush, June 18, 1965; children: Brian, Matthew, Christopher, Wesley, Stephanie. Student, Coll. So. Utah, 1960-61; BS, Brigham Young U., 1966, MS, 1967, PhD, 1970. NIH predoctoral fellow Brigham Young U., Provo, Utah, 1966-70, asst. prof. microbiology, 1972-75, assoc. prof., 1975-80, prof., 1980—; postdoctoral fellow NIH, Bethesda, Md., 1970-72; lab. dir. Richards Lab., Inc., Pleasant Grove, Utah, 1986—; lab. dir. MicroVir Labs., Inc., Orem, Utah, 1989—, also pres., chmn. bd.; pres., chmn. bd. Johnson Biorsch. & Devel. Corp., Orem. Contbr. articles to profl. jours. USAF fellow, 1977, rsch. grantee, 1978-82, NIH, 1973-76. Mem. Am. Soc. for Microbiology, AAAS, Sigma Xi, Phi Kappa Phi. LDS Ch. Office: Brigham Young U 887 WIDB Provo UT 84602

JOHNSON, FERD, cartoonist retired, color artist; b. Spring Creek, Pa., Dec. 18, 1905; s. John F. and Bessie A. Johnson; m. Doris Lee White, Feb. 24, 1930; 1 child, Thomas (dec.). Student, Chgo. Acad. Fine Arts, 1923. Color artist, Chgo. Tribune, 1923, asst. to, Frank Willard (Moon Mullins), 1923-58; sports illustrator: Westbrook Pegler, 1925-30; cartoonist: Texas Slim; syndicated, Tribune Media Svcs. 1925-27, 40-58, Moon Mullins, 1958-91; oil paintings represented in various So. Calif. galleries. Mem. Nat. Cartoonist Soc., Comics Coun.

JOHNSON, GAREY ANTONY, manufacturers representative; b. Benton Harbor, Mich., Sept. 14, 1947; s. Wilce Meeks and Magnolia Morris. BSEE, Mich. Tech., 1972; M of Internat. Mgmt., AGSIM, 1978; MS in Systems Mgmt., U. So. Calif., 1983, D of Pub. Adminstrn., 1992. Mktg. mgr. Spelly Corp., Deer Valley, Ariz., 1978-79; internat. mktg. mgr. Signetics Corp., Sunnyvale, Calif., 1979-81; sr. field sales engr. PMI Corp., Santa Clara, Calif., 1981-85; strategic accounts mgr. Weitek Corp., Sunnyvale, 1985-91; dir. The Johnson Group, 1991—; cons. domestic policy; pub. speaker in field. Contbr. articles to Thunderbird Internat., Microelectrical Fabrication, Arms Sales to Saudi Arabia. Mem. Big Bros.; com. mem. World Affairs Coun., San Francisco; motivational speaker to high schs. Capt. USAF, 1972-77. Recipient City Commn. citation Benton Harbor City Coun., 1974. Fellow IVS Armed Forces and Soc.; mem. Am. Soc. for Pub. Adminstrn. Home and Office: 1146 Chantal Way Redwood City CA 94061

JOHNSON, GARY KENT, management education company executive; b. Provo, Utah, Apr. 16, 1936; s. Clyde LeRoy and Ruth Laie (Taylor) J.; m. Mary Joyce Crowther, Aug. 26, 1955; children—Mary Ann Johnson Harvey, Gary Kent, Brent James, Jeremy Clyde. Student Brigham Young U., 1954-55, U. Utah, 1955-58, 60-61, U. Calif.-Berkeley, 1962. Sales rep. Roche Labs., Salt Lake City, 1958-61, sales trainer, Denver, 1962, sales trainer, Oakland, Calif., 1962, div. mgr., Seattle, 1962-69; sec.-treas. Western Mgmt. Inst., Seattle, 1969-71; pres. WMI Corp., Bellevue, Wash., 1971—, Provisor Corp., 1983-86; speaker, cons. various nat. orgns. Bd. dirs. Big Bros.; del. King County Republican Com. Served with U.S. N.G., 1953-61. Walgreen scholar, 1955-58; Bristol scholar, 1958. Mem. Am. Soc. Tng. and Devel., Internat. Platform Assn., Phi Sigma Epsilon. Mormon. Club: Bellevue Athletic. Author: Select the Best, 1976; Antitrust Untangled, 1977; The Utilities Management Series, 1979; Performance Appraisal, A Program for Improving Productivity, 1981, QSE Quality Service Everytime, 1990. Office: WMI Corp 1309 114th Ave SE Ste 212 Bellevue WA 98004-6903

JOHNSON, GINA CURRY, pharmacist; b. Vallejo, Calif., May 2, 1960; d. Fred Eugene and Arline Mae (Grenier) C.; m. Darrell Wayne Johnson, Oct. 5, 1985. PharmD, U. Pacific, Stockton, Calif., 1983. Cert. nutrition support pharmacist. Profl. rep. Merck, Sharp & Dohme, Sacramento, 1983-85; pharmacist Rogue Valley Physicians Svc., Medford, Oreg., 1985-87, Rogue Valley Med. Ctr., Medford, 1987-88; clin. pharmacist U. Hosp., Denver, 1988-92; adj. asst. prof. Pharmacy U. Colo., Denver, 1990-92; clin. pharmacist Calif. Infusion Svc., Sausalito, 1992—. Author (book chpt.) Nutrition Support Compendia, 1992. Mem. Am. Soc. Hosp. Pharmacists (Colo. chpt. com. chair 1990-91), Am. Soc. for Parenteral and Enteral Nutrition (Colo. chpt. sec. 1989-91, bd. dirs. 1991—).

JOHNSON, GWENAVERE ANELISA, artist; b. Newark, S.D., Oct. 16, 1909; d. Arthur E. and Susie Ellen (King) Nelson; m. John Wendell Johnson, Dec. 17, 1937; 1 child, John Forrest. Student, Mpls. Sch. Art, 1930; BA, U. Minn., 1937; MA, San Jose State U., 1957. Cert. gen. elem., secondary, art tchr., Calif. Art tchr., supr. Austin (Minn.) Schs., 1937-38; art tchr. Hillbrook Sch., Los Gatos, Calif., 1947-52; art tchr., supr. Santa Clara (Calif.) Pub. Schs., 1952-55; art tchr., dept. chmn. San Jose (Calif.) Unified Schs., 1955-75; owner Tree Tops studio, San Jose, 1975— Juried shows: Los Gatos Art Assn., 1976-79, 85-88, Artist of Yr., 1988 (1st and 2d awards), 83, 84 (Best of Show awards), Treeside gallery, 1991, Los Gatos, 1980, 81 (1st awards); Livermore Art Assn., 1977 (2d award), Los Gatos Art Mus., 1981 (1st award), 82 (2d award), 91 (best of show award), Rosicrucean Mus., 1983, Centre d'Art Contemporian, Paris, 1983; creator Overfelt portrait Alexian Bros. Hosp., San Jose, Calif., 1977; exhibited in group shows Triton Art Mus., 1983-93, ann. Garden Art Show, 1981-92. Recipient Golden Centaur award Acad. Italia, 1982, Golden Album of prize winning Artists, 1984, Golden Flame award Academia Italia, 1986, others. Mem. San Jose Art League, Los Gatos Art Assn. (Artist of Yr. 1988, 2d, 3d awards), Santa Clara Art Assn. (Artist of Yr. 1983, 3 First awards 1989, 2d award in spl. merit achiever's exhbn. 1992, 3 First awards in merit achiever's exhbn. 1993), Soc. Western Artists, Nat. League Am. Penwomen (corr. sec., Merit Achiever award). Home and Office: 2054 Booksin Ave San Jose CA 95125-4909

JOHNSON, HEIDI SMITH, English language educator; b. Mpls., June 1, 1946; d. Russell Ward and Eva Ninette (Holmquist) Smith; m. Alan C. Sweeney, Dec. 21, 1968 (div. 1977); m. Robert Allen Johnson, July 17, 1981. BA, U. Calif., Riverside, 1969; MA, No. Ariz. U., 1992. Park ranger U.S. Nat. Parks Svc., Pinnacles Nat. Monument, 1972-73; aide Petrified Forest Mus. Assn., Ariz., 1973-75; dispatcher police dept. U. Ariz., Tucson, 1975-76; communications operator II dept. ops. City of Tucson, 1976-78; dispatcher Tucson Police Dept., 1978-82, communications supr., 1982-85, communications coord., 1985; substitute tchr. Bisbee (Ariz.) Pub. Schs., 1985-91; instr. English Cochise Community Coll., Douglas, Ariz., 1990-92; tchr. English/creative writing Bisbee High Sch., 1992—; GED tchr. Cochise County Jail, 1988-89. Assoc. editor Ariz. Fossil Record. Trustee Bisbee Coun. on Arts and Humanities, 1986-88; pres. Cooper Queen Libr. Bd., Bisbee, 1988-91; book sales chmn. Shattuck Libr., Bisbee Mining Mus., 1987-92. Mem. Mid-Am. Paleontol. Soc., N.Mex. Geol. Soc., Ariz. Geol. Soc., Paleontol. Soc. So. Ariz., So. Calif. Palentol. Soc. Roman Catholic. Home: PO Box 1221 Bisbee AZ 85603-2221

JOHNSON, HERMAN LEONALL, research nutritionist; b. Whitehall, Wis., Apr. 1, 1935; s. Frederick E. And Jeanette (Severson) J.; m. Barbara Dale Matthews, July 3, 1960 (dec. May 1971); m. Barbara Ann Badger, Apr. 3, 1976. BA in Chemistry, North Cen. Coll., Naperville, Ill., 1959; MS in Biochemistry & Nutrition, Va. Poly. Inst. and State U., 1961, PhD in Biochemistry and Nutrition, 1963. Rsch. biochemist S.R. Noble Found., Ardmore, Okla., 1963-65; nutrition chemist U.S. Army Med. Rsch., Denver, 1965-74; nutrition physiologist Letterman Army Rsch., Presidio San Francisco, 1974-80, Western Human Nutrition Rsch. Ctr. USDA, Presidio San Francisco, 1980—. Contbr. numerous articles to profl. jours. Trustee 1st Meth. Ch., Rohnert Park, Calif., 1985—. Served with Med. Service Corps, U.S. Army, 1954-56. Named one of Outstanding Young Men of Am., 1975; NIH traineeship Va. Poly. Inst. and State U., Blacksburg, 1961-63. Mem. AAAS, Am. Inst. Nutrition, Am. Soc. Clin. Nutritionists, Am. Coll. Nutritionists, Am. Coll. Sports Medicine, Sebastopol Spinners, Sigma Xi, Phi Lambda, Phi Sigma. Republican. Home: 256 Alden Ave Rohnert Park CA 94928-3704 Office: USDA Western Human Nutrition Rsch Ctr PO Box 29997 San Francisco CA 94129-0997

JOHNSON, J. MICHAEL, SR., gemologist; b. Salt Lake City, Mar. 31, 1935; s. J. Irwin and Anne (Freeman) J.; m. Mary Louise Stanley, May 26, 1956 (div. June 1974); children: J. Michael Jr., Christopher W., Stanley E., Nicholas A.; m. Rita Anastasia Francis, Jan. 8, 1988. BS, Purdue U., 1956; AA in Real Estate, Saddleback Coll., Mission Viejo, Calif., 1976; diploma gemology, Gemological Inst. Am., Santa Monica, Calif., 1991. Grad. gemologist; lic. real estate broker, Calif.; sr. mem. designate Nat. Assn. Jewelry Appraisers. Engr. specialist N.Am. Aviation (Apollo), Downey, Calif., 1963-69; sr. engr. specialist Philco-Ford Aeronutronic, Newport Beach, Calif., 1969-71; chief engr. J.M. Johnson Assocs., San Clemente, Calif., 1971-74; real estate broker Laguna Beach (Calif.) Bd. Realtors, 1974-84; co-author, instr. Real Estate Exch. Counselors Course, Newport Beach, 1977-78; instr. real estate Saddleback C.C., Mission Viejo, 1975-78; pres. Conejo Maico Enterprises, Newport Beach, 1982-88; founder, owner Imperial Gems S.W. Gemological Lab., Huntington Beach, Calif., 1988—; pres., founder South Coast Exchangors, San Clemente, Calif., 1976-78, Saddleback Problem Solvers, Mission Viejo, 1977-80, Nat. Coun. Exchangors, L.A., 1977-78; tchr. classes and seminars relating to consumer understanding of jewelry and gemology, 1989-90. Contbr. articles on gem and jewelry appraisal to profl. jours. Founder, comdr. Flotilla 29 USCG Aux., Dana Point, Calif., 1974-78; mem. USCG Aux., 1968-88. Capt. U.S. Army, 1953-63, Korea. Mem. Am. Legion, Nat. Assn. Jewelry Appraisers, Gemological Inst. Am. Alumni, Purdue Alumni. Republican. Office: Imperial Gemological SW Geol Lab PO Box 6903 Huntington Beach CA 92615

JOHNSON, JACK STODDARD, physician, surgeon; b. Tremonton, Utah, Nov. 28, 1932; s. Heber Guy and Emorett (Stoddard) J.; m. Mary Carol Hoppins, May 28, 1962; children: Gregory T, Julie Ellen, Hyte, John, Marc, Suzanne, Paul. Student, LDS Sem., Garland, Utah, 1951; U S Army Nutrition Food Sch., Ft. Lewis, Washington, 1954, LDS Inst. Religion, Salt Lake City, 1956; student, U. Utah; MD, George Washington U., 1960. Diplomate Am. Bd. Family Practice, Nat. Bd. Med. Examiners. Intern LDS Hosp., Salt Lake City, 1960-61, resident, 1961-62; pvt. practice Tremonton, Utah, 1963—; researcher Johnson Med. Rsch. Ctr., Tremonton; clin. instr. U. Utah Med. Sch., Salt Lake City, 1965-80, asst. prof. dept. community and family medicine, bd. dirs., mem. adv. bd., 1980—; med. dir. Box Elder County Nursing Home, Tremonton, 1978—. Contbr. articles to profl. jours. Bd. dirs. Box Elder Sch. Dist. Found., Emergency Med. Svcs. Dist. 1, Utah, 1975-87, Box Elder chpt. ARC, 1963-79, Utah Arthritis Found., Utah Mental Health Clinic; chmn. Bear River Ednl. Endowment Assn., 1980-88, 90-91. Mem. AMA (del. Utah hosp. sect.), Am. Soc. Internal Medicine, Am. Soc. Abdominal Surgeons, Am. Acad. Family Physicians, Utah Med. Assn., Utah Acad. Family Physicians (pres. 1975-76), Utah Heart Assn., Intermountain Geoege Washington U. Alumni Assn. (pres. 1967-72), Bear River C. of C. Republican. Mem. LDS Ch. Office: 13 N 2D E Tremonton UT 84337

JOHNSON, JAMES BASS, work process improvement consultant, trainer; b. L.A., Nov. 12, 1949; s. Herbert Elroy Jr. and Cornelia (Wales) J.; m. Anne Johnson, July 28, 1990; children: Jason F., Dorothy W. BS in Math., Harvey Mudd Coll., 1971. Sci. programmer Logicon, Inc., San Pedro, Calif., 1972; systems rep. Burroughs Corp., San Francisco, 1973-75; data processing mgr. Victoria Sta. Inc., San Francisco, 1976-78; MIS dir. Tannery West Corp., San Francisco, 1978-80; systems cons. Bank of Am., San Francisco, 1980-82; dist. support mgr. Wang Labs., San Francisco, 1982-85, sales rep., 1985-88; prin. Work Design Assocs., Berkeley, Calif., 1988—. Author: How to Improve Work Processes, 1993. Unitarian. Office: Work Design Assocs 2552 LeConte Ave # 1W Berkeley CA 94709

JOHNSON, JAMES DANIEL, theoretical physicist; b. Toledo, Mar. 21, 1944; s. James Elmer and Gwendolin (Dale) J.; m. Suzanne Darling, June 11, 1966; 1 child, Ian Christopher. B.S., Case Inst. Tech., 1966; M.A., SUNY-Stony Brook, 1968, Ph.D., 1972. Research assoc. Rockefeller U., N.Y.C., 1972-74; research assoc. Los Alamos Nat. Lab., Los Alamos, N.Mex., 1974-76, staff mem., 1976-89, acting head Sesame Library, 1982-85, project mgr. carbon project, 1984-89, dep. group leader, 1989—; head Sesame Libr., 1989—. Contbr. articles to profl. jours. Adult advisor Gt. S.W. Area council Boy Scouts Am., 1980-83; adult advisor sr. high youth group United Ch. of Los Alamos, 1982-85; active Los Alamos Light Opera Orgn., Los Alamos Little Theater; mem. U.S. Del. to Nuclear Testing Talks, 1988-89. Recipient Disting. Performance award Los Alamos Nat. Lab, 1988; NSF fellow 1966-71; Air Force grantee, 1980-82. Mem. Am. Phys. Soc., AAAS. Democrat. Club: Los Alamos Ski. Home: 321 Manhattan Loop Los Alamos NM 87544-2918 Office: Los Alamos Nat Lab T-1 MS B221 Los Alamos NM 87545

JOHNSON, JAMES DAVID, concert pianist, educator; b. Greenville, S.C., Aug. 7, 1948; s. Theron David and Lucile (Pearson) J.; m. Karen Elizabeth Jacobson, Feb. 1, 1975. MusB, U. Ariz., 1970, MusM, 1972, D of Mus. Arts, 1976; MusM, Westminster Choir Coll., 1986. Concert pianist, organist Pianists Found. Am., Boston Pops Orch., Royal Philharm., Nat. Symphony Orch., Leningrad Philharmonic, Victoria Symphony, others, 1961—; organist, choirmaster St. Paul's Episcopal Ch., Tucson, 1968-74, First United Meth. Ch., Fairbanks, Alaska, 1974-89; prof. music U. Alaska, Fairbanks, 1974-91, chair music dept., 1991. Recordings include Moszkowski Etudes, 1973, Works of Chaminade Dohnanyi, 1977, Mendelssohn Concerti, 1978, Beethoven First Concerto, 1980, Beethoven, Reinecke, Ireland Trios with Alaska Chamber Ensemble, 1988, Kabalevsky Third Concerto, Muczynski Concerto, Muczynski Suite, 1990, Beethoven Third Concerto, 1993. Recipient Record of Month award Mus. Heritage Soc., 1979, 80; finalist mus. amb. program USIA, 1983. Mem. Music Tchrs. Nat. Assn., Phi Kappa Phi, Pi Kappa Lambda. Episcopalian. Office: U Alaska-Fairbanks Dept Music Fairbanks AK 99775

JOHNSON, JAMES GIBSON, JR., community recycling specialist; b. Flagstaff, Ariz., Feb. 26, 1938; s. James Gibson and Inga Anette J.; m. Faye Bodian, Aug. 23, 1973; children: Jill Johnson, Ginger Johnson, Jonathan Johnson. BA, U. Colo., 1960. Editor, pub. Town and Country Rev., Boulder, Colo., 1963-78; owner James G. Johnson and Assocs., Boulder, Colo., 1978-87; exec. dir. Eco Cycle Recycling, Boulder, Colo., 1987-89; community recycling specialist Office of Energy Conservation, State of Colo., Denver, 1989—. Mem. Open Space Bd. Trustees, Boulder, 1980-85, chmn., 1984-85; mem. Boulder County Pks. and Open Space Bd., 1985—, chmn., 1987-89. Democrat. Home: 630 Northstar Ct Boulder CO 80304-1021 Office: Colo Office of Energy Conservation 1675 Broadway Ste 1300 Denver CO 80202

JOHNSON, JAMES LAWRENCE, clinical psychologist, writer; b. Devils Lake, N.D., Sept. 17, 1953; s. Lawrence Tillman and Irene (Fah) J.; m. Paula Lou Sechler, Aug. 28, 1981; children: Daniel, Michael, Alisha. BA, U. N.D., 1975; MA, Azusa Pacific U., 1980; PhD, U.S. Internat. U., San Diego, 1990. Lic. marriage, family, child counselor and psychologist. Writer, editor Campus Crusade for Christ, San Bernardino, Calif., 1975-77; marriage, family, child counselor Foothill Community Mental Health Ctr., Glendora, Calif., 1978-81; social worker Le Roy Boys Home, LaVerne, Calif., 1981-83; counselor Creative Counseling Ctr., Pomona and Claremont, Calif., 1983—, Covina (Calif.) Psycholog. Group, 1981—; freelance writer, 1977-78, 90—; counselor trainer Stephen Ministries, Covina, 1985-86. Contbr. numerous articles to profl. and popular jours. Editor, advisor 1st Bapt. Ch., Covina, 1988, cabinet leader singles ministries, 1980-82. Mem. APA (clin.), Calif. Assn. Marriage and Family Therapists (clin.), Christian Writers' Fellowship, Psi Chi. Office: Creative Counseling Ctr 250 W 1st St Ste 214 Claremont CA 91711-4743

JOHNSON, JAMES RALPH, artist, writer; b. Fort Payne, Ala., May 20, 1922; s. James Andrew and Vera Sue (Small) J.; m. Betty Ann Johnson, Dec. 24, 1942 (div. Oct. 1961); children—JoAnn Johnson Harrell, Glen, David; m. Burdetta Fay Beebe, Oct. 11, 1961. B.S. in Econs., Howard Coll., Birmingham, Ala., 1943. Instr. art workshop, Santa Fe and Albuquerque, 1972—. Author: Animals and Their Food, 1972; Zoos of Today, 1971; Photography for Young People, 1971; Southern Swamps of America, 1970; Everglades Adventure, 1970; Animal Paradise, 1969; Moses' Band of Chimpanzees, 1969; Ringtail, 1968; Blackie-The Gorilla, 1968; Pepper, 1967; Advanced Camping Techniques, 1967; The Wolf Cub, 1966; Anyone Can Backpack in Comfort, 1965; Anyone Can Camp in Comfort, 1964; Camels West, 1964; Utah Lion, 1962; Anyone Can Live Off the Land, 1961; Best Photos of the Civil War, 1962; Wild Venture, 1961; Horsemen Blue & Gray, 1960; Big Cypress Buck, 1957; The Last Passenger, 1956; Lost on Hawk Mountain, 1954; Mountain Bobcat, 1953; (with B. F. Beebe) American Bears, 1965; American Wild Horses, 1964. Contbr. articles to profl. jours. Served to maj. USMC, 1942-64. Recipient Jr. Book award cert. Boys Clubs Am., 1965. Mem. Am. Indian and Cowboy Artists, Nat. Western Artists Assn., Artists Equity, Outdoor Writers Am., Western Writers Am., Western Writers Assn., Santa Fe Artists Soc. Home: PO Box 5295 Santa Fe NM 87502-5295

JOHNSON, JAMES WILLIAM, III, journalism educator; b. Flushing, N.Y., Feb. 6, 1938; s. James William Jr. and Edith C. (Horne) J.; m. Marilyn Dale Moyer, May 26, 1967; 1 child, Thayer Jay. BA, U. Ariz., 1961. Editor, reporter Oakland (Calif.) Tribune, 1961-79; assoc. prof. U. Ariz., Tucson, 1979—; cons. Contra Costa Times, Walnut Creek, Calif., 1989. Contbr. numerous articles to mags. Recipient Nat. Teaching award Poynter Inst. for Media Studies, 1983, Ariz. Journalism Tchr. of Yr. Ariz. Newspapers Assn., 1983. Mem. Soc. Profl. Journalists (pres. Southern Ariz. chpt. 1989, nat. health and welfare com.), Contra Costa Press Club (pres. 1968), Sigma Chi. Republican. Methodist. Home: 4177 N Via Villas Tucson AZ 85719 Office: U Ariz Dept Journalism Franklin Bldg Rm 101M Tucson AZ 85721

JOHNSON, JENNIFER J., public relations executive, editor; b. Ames, Iowa, Aug. 2, 1962; d. Ernest Walter and Cynthia Ann (Nold) J.; m. R. Scott Carter, Oct. 16, 1987. BA, Brigham Young U. Staff editor Wicat Systems, Provo, Utah, 1984-86; campus writer Newsweek Mag., Provo, Utah, 1985-86; exec. dir. Lan Times Mag. Novell, Inc., Provo, Utah, 1986-88; account exec. Dahlin, Smith & White, Salt Lake City, 1988-90; pub. rels. dir. Penna, Powers, Cutting & Haynes, Salt Lake City, 1990-91; dir. industry rels. Dahlin, Smith & White, Salt Lake City, 1991—. Contbr. articles to profl. jours. Recipient Distinction, Merit and Excellence awards, Soc. Tech. Communications, 1987, Golden Spike awards, 1989, 90. Mem. Pub. Rels. Soc. Am. (v.p., pres. Intermountain chpt., newsletter editor 1988-89), Soc. Tech. Communication, Internat. Assn. Bus. Communicators (Regional Silver award, 1989). Democrat. Home: 722 E 800 S Salt Lake City UT 84102-3518 Office: Dahlin Smith White 5 Triad Ctr Ste 375 Salt Lake City UT 84180-1103

JOHNSON, JEROME LINNÉ, cardiologist; b. Rockford, Ill., June 19, 1929; s. Thomas Arthur and Myrtle Elizabeth (Swanson) J.; m. Molly Ann Rideout, June 27, 1953; children: Susan Johnson Nowels, William Rideout. BA, U. Chgo., 1951; BS, Northwestern U., 1952, MD, 1955. Diplomate Nat. Bd. Med. Examiners. Intern U. Chgo. Clinics, 1955-56; resident Northwestern U., Chgo., 1958-61; chief resident Chgo. Wesley Meml. Hosp., 1960-61; mem., v.p. Hauch Med. Clinic, Pomona, Calif., 1961-88; pvt. practice cardiology and internal medicine Pomona, 1988—; clin. assoc. prof. medicine, U. So. Calif., L.A., 1961—; mem. staff Pomona Valley Hosp. Med. Ctr., chmn. coronary care com. 1967-77; mem. staff L.A. County Hosp. Citizen ambassador, People to People; mem. Town Hall of Calif., L.A. World Affairs Coun. Lt. USNR, 1956-58. Fellow Am. Coll. Cardiology, Am. Geriatrics Soc., Royal Soc. Health; mem. Galileo Soc., Am. Heart Assn. (bd. dirs. L.A. County div. 1967-84, San Gabriel div. 1963-89), Am. Soc. Internal Medicine, Inland Soc. Internal Medicine, Pomona Host Lions. Home: 648 Delaware Dr Claremont CA 91711-3457

JOHNSON, JOAN, state senator; b. Denver, Oct. 4, 1943. BA, U. Colo., 1965. Mem. state senate dist. 24; pub. rels. cons., writer Creative Assocs. Unltd., Englewood, Colo.; Mem. Colo. Adv. Com. on Intergovtl. Rels., Gov.'s AIDS Coun., Gov.'s Task Force on Food Safety, Colo. Hazard Mitigation Coun. Mem. Nat. Fedn. Press Women (Nat. Comm. award), Colo. Press Women (State Comm. award), Westminster Newcomers Club, Colo. Press Assn. (assoc.), Colo. Broadcasters (assoc.); bd. trustees Adams County Libr. Roman Catholic. Democrat. Address: 7951 York St Apt 1 Denver CO 80229

JOHNSON, JOHN DAVID, pediatrician; b. Palo Alto, Calif., Sept. 14, 1938; s. Willis Hugh and Elizabeth Ann (Schma) J.; m. Margaret Jane Grider, June 19, 1960; children: William Todd, Timothy Hugh, Kelly Lynn. AB, Wabash Coll., 1960; MD, Stanford U., 1965. Diplomate Am. Bd. Pediatrics, Am. Bd. Neonatal and Perinatal Medicine. Intern in pediatrics Johns Hopkins Hosp., 1965-66, resident in pediatrics, 1966-67; resident in pediatrics Stanford U. Hosp., 1969-70; asst. prof. pediatrics Stanford (Calif.) U. Sch. Medicine, 1970-77, assoc. prof., 1977-79; assoc. prof. pediatrics and ob-gyn U. N.Mex. Sch. Medicine, Albuquerque, 1979-83, prof. pediatrics and ob-gyn, 1983—, chmn. pediatrics, 1986-93; chief staff U. N.Mex. Med. Ctr., Albuquerque, 1989-91. Contbr. articles to profl. jours. Lt. col. UPHS, 1967-69. Rsch. grant NIH, 1983-90. Mem. Soc. for Pediatric Rsch. (pres. 1984, sec. treas. 1977-82), Am. Pediatric Soc., Am. Acad. Pediatrics, Western Soc. Pediatric Rsch. (pres. 1987), Perinatal Rsch. Soc. (pres. 1989-90), N.Mex. Pediatrics Soc. (exec. com. 1989-91), N.Mex. Med. Soc. Office: U NMex Sch Medicine Ambulatory Care Ctr Albuquerque NM 87131

JOHNSON, JOHN EDLIN, JR., neuroscientist; b. Ft. Worth, Aug. 21, 1945; s. John E. and Mary (Thompson) J.; m. Susan Edwards, June 15, 1968; 1 child, Cynthia Brooke. BS in Psychology, Zoology, U. Wash., 1968; MS in Psychology, Tulane U., 1970, PhD in Neurosci., 1973. Fellow NASA, Mt. View, Calif., 1973-76; staff fellow NIH, Balt., 1976-80; asst. prof. neurology Johns Hopkins Med. Sch., Balt., 1979-89; vis. scholar U. Calif., Berkeley, 1990-91; pres. Sci. Design & Info., Redwood City, Calif., 1991—; editor-in-chief Microscopy Rsch. and Technique, 1983—, SYNAPSE, 1987—. Editor 6 textbooks on microscopy and pathology. 1st lt. USAF, 1973-80. Home: 165 Cervantes Rd Redwood City CA 94062 Office: Sci Design & Info PO Box 5247 Redwood City CA 94063

JOHNSON, JOHN PHILIP, geneticist, researcher; b. Wabash, Ind., June 6, 1949; s. Melvin Leroy and Cleo Pauline (Aldrich) J.; m. Sheryl Kay Kennedy, June 3, 1978; children: Craig Eric, Lindsay Sara. BS, U. Mich., 1971, MD, 1975. Diplomate Am. Bd. Pediatrics, Am. Bd. Med. Genetics. Intern, 2d-yr. resident Children's Hosp. Los Angeles, 1975-77; 3d yr. resident in pediatrics U. Utah, Salt Lake City, 1977-78, fellow in genetics, 1980-82, asst. prof. pediatrics, 1982-85; pediatrician Family Health Program, Salt Lake City, 1978-80; assoc. dir. med. genetics, attending/active staff physician Children's Hosp. Oakland, Calif., 1985-92; dir. med. genetics, attending/active staff physician Children's Hosp., Oakland, 1992—; clinic physician Utah State Tng. Sch., American Fork, 1982-85; attending and staff physician Primary Children's Med. Ctr., Salt Lake City, 1978-80. Contbr. articles to med. jours. Recipient William J. Branstrom award U. Mich., 1967. Fellow Am. Acad. Pediatrics; mem. Am. Soc. Human Genetics, Soc. for Pediatric Rsch., Alpha Omega Alpha. Home: 1638 Harlan Dr Danville CA 94526-5310 Office: Children's Hosp 747 52nd St Oakland CA 94609

JOHNSON, JOHN RECTER, medical foundation administrator; b. Greeley, Colo., Oct. 20, 1923; s. Recter William and Elsie Martha (Bales) J.; m. Phyllis Jean Hackman, Sept. 2, 1944; children: Steven, Kristina. AB, Stanford U., 1947. Asst. dir. Coro Found., San Francisco, 1947-52; asst. city mgr. City of Menlo Park (Calif.), 1952-58, city mgr., 1958-64; exec. adminstr. Palo Alto (Calif.) Med. Clinic/Found., 1964-87; v.p. adminstrn. Palo Alto Med. Found., 1987-91; ret., 1991; cons. Med. Group Mgmt. Assn., Denver, 1975—. Trustee Palo Alto Med. Found., 1987—, Channing House, Palo Alto, 1965—; pres. Stanford (Calif.) U. Alumni Assn., 1974, Foothills Tennis/Swim Club, Palo Alto, 1960, Palo Alto Club, 1975. Coro Found. scholar, 1947. Mem. Med. Group Mgmt. Assn. (pres. 1988-89). Democrat. Home: 985 San Mateo Dr Menlo Park CA 94025-5639

JOHNSON, JOHNNY BURL, business owner, architect; b. Bryan, Tex., Mar. 2, 1944; s. L. W. and Lois (Moon) J.; m. Stephanie L. Bates, Dec. 26, 1964; 1 child, Jennifer Lea-Bates. BArch, Tex. A&M U., 1969. Designer William E. Nash, Architect, Bryan, 1967-69; architect, planner R. Keith Hook & Assocs., Inc., Colorado Springs, Colo., 1969-80; co-owner Becker & Johnson, Inc., Colorado Springs, 1980-86, owner, 1986—; mem. com. Colorado Springs Park Bd.; mem. sch. and park fee adv. bd. City of Colorado Springs, 1978-84. Mem. Fine Arts Ctr., Colorado Springs, Pikes Peak Hist. Commn., Colorado Springs. Mem. AIA (pres. So. Colo. chpt. 1978-79), Colo. Soc. Architects (sec. 1979-80), Homebuilders Assn., Urban Land Inst., Urban Transp. Inst., Colorado Springs C. of C., Sertoma (pres. Cheyenne Mountain chpt. 1990—). Republican. Home: 4600 J C Nichols Pky # 512 Kansas City MO 64112-1607 Office: Becker & Johnson Inc 955 S Union Blvd Colorado Springs CO 80910-3574

JOHNSON, KEITH RONALD, obstetrician-gynecologist; b. Chgo., Mar. 19, 1929; s. Clarence Albert and Alma Alice (Semrad) J.; m. Esther Louise Rieve, June 26, 1954; children: Robert, Jeffrey, Cynthia. BS, U. Ill., 1950; MD, U. Ill., Chgo., 1954. Diplomate Am. Bd. Obstetrics and Gynecology. Intern L.A. City Hosp., 1954-55; resident in ob/gyn San Diego County Gen. Hosp./Mercy Hosp., 1957-60; pvt. practice specializing in ob/gyn. La Mesa, Calif., 1960—. Lt. USNR, 1955-57. Fellow Am. Coll. Obstetricians and Gynecologists, Internat. Coll. Surgeons; mem. Calif. Med. Assn., San Diego Med. Assn., Am. Assn. Gynecol. Laparoscopists, Rotary. Republican. Office: 8881 Fletcher Pky Ste 285 La Mesa CA 91942-3136

JOHNSON, KEVIN, systems director; b. Jersey City, Apr. 2, 1964; s. Harold James and Doris Elizabeth (Conley) J. BS, St. Peter's Coll., Jersey City, 1986; doctoral student, Calif. Sch. Profl. Psychology, 1987-88, U. Lisbon (Portugal), 1988; cert., Inst. Rational-Emotive Therapy, N.Y.C., 1986. Dir. svcs. Nat. Found. Dentistry for the Handicapped, Jersey City, 1986-87; systems adminstr. Boalt Hall Sch. of Law, U. Calif., Berkeley, 1988-92; dir. computer and information systems Sch. of Pub. Health U. Calif., Berkeley, 1992—; cons. Lex-Tech. Inc., Berkeley, 1988-89, LAW Svcs., Oakland, Calif., 1989, Stratford Assocs., Berkeley, 1989—. Editor articles in profl. jours. Prodn. staff Citiarts/Theatre Concord (Calif.), 1989; Am. sign lang. instr. Concord Leisure Svcs., 1988-89; asst. dir. Calif. Shakespeare Festival, Orinda, 1991. Scholar, St. Peter's Coll., 1982, Inst. for the Advancement Human Behavior, 1988; fellow U. Lisbon, 1988. Mem. Am. Psychol. Assn., Calif. State Psychol. Assn.

JOHNSON, LARRY DEAN, chemist, administrator; b. Denver, Sept. 11, 1953; s. Elwood V. and Maxine R. (Provenzano) J.; m. Donna M. Walsh, Apr. 8, 1978; children: Nicholas, Megan. BS in Chemistry, Colo. State U., 1975; MBA, Ariz. State U., 1990. Chemist Atomic Energy Commn., Idaho Falls, Idaho, 1975-77; analytical chemist Dept. Energy, Argonne, Ill., 1977-78, Dept. Treasury, Chgo., 1978-79; chemist Magma Copper Co., San Manuel, Ariz., 1979-80; sr. analytical chemist Rockwell Internat., Golden, Colo., 1980-82; nuclear chemist Ariz. Pub. Svc., Phoenix, 1982-84, nuclear safety engr., 1984-90, chemistry mgr., 1990—; mem. EPRI secondary water chemistry com., Palo Alto, Calif., 1992—. Office: Ariz Pub Svc PO Box 52034 Sta 7295 Phoenix AZ 85072-2034

JOHNSON, LAWRENCE M., banker; b. 1940. Student, U. Hawaii. With Bank of Hawaii, Honolulu, 1963—, exec. v.p., 1980-84, vice chmn., 1984-89, pres., 1989—; pres. Bancorp Hawaii, Inc. Office: Bancorp Hawaii Inc PO Box 2900 Honolulu HI 96813 also: 130 Merchant St Honolulu HI 96813*

JOHNSON, LAYMON, JR., utility marketing analyst; b. Jackson, Miss., Sept. 1, 1948; s. Laymon and Bertha (Yarbrough) J.; m. Charlene J. Johnson, Nov. 13, 1982. B in Tech., U. Dayton, 1970; MS in Systems Mgmt., U. So. Calif., 1978. Mem. tech. staff Rockwell Internat., Canoga Park, Calif., 1975-77; sr. dynamics engr. Gen. Dynamics, Pomona, Calif., 1978-83; fin. systems specialist Northrop Corp., Pico Rivera, Calif., 1983-90; utility mktg. analyst dept. water and power City of L.A., 1991—. Lt. comdr. USNR, 1970-92. Mem. Naval Res. Assn., Assn. Mil. Surgeons U.S., Los Angeles County Mus. Art, Music Ctr. L.A., Smithsonian Assocs., Nat. Hist. Soc., ISSM Triumvirate, Tau Alpha Pi. Democrat. Roman Catholic.

JOHNSON, LEE CARROLL, electronics company executive; b. Monroe, Ind., Sept. 29, 1933; s. Thetus Jesse and Vida Louise (Ward) J.; m. Donna Lee Heald, Nov. 25, 1951; children: Marga Lynn Johnson Cullumber, Shelon Lee. BEE, Purdue U., 1953; LLB, LaSalle U., Chgo., 1966. V.p., dir. bus. devel. ITT Aerospace, Ft. Wayne, Ind., 1952-74; v.p., gen. mgr. govt. electronics group Motorola Corp., Scottsdale, Ariz., 1974-88; cons. Motorola Tng. and Edn. Ctr., Schaumburg, Ill. Patentee in field. Mem. fin. com. Devereux Found., Scottsdale, 1981-88. Mem. IEEE, Air Force Assn., Navy League, Assn. of U.S. Army, NRA (life), Aircraft Owners and Pilots Assn., Assn. Old Crows. Republican. Methodist. Home and Office: 9090 N 86th Pl Scottsdale AZ 85258-1934

JOHNSON, LEIGH THORNTON, administrative assistant to Congressman; b. Oakland, Calif., Feb. 23, 1943; s. Corwin Southwick and Lena (Thornton) J. BS, South Oreg. State Coll., 1966. Owner Leigh's Sports and Hardware, Ashland, Oreg., 1968-72; state rep. Oreg. Legis., Salem, 1971-74; owner Pony Express Food and Brew, Ashland, 1975-83; adminstv. asst. Congressman Bob Smith, Medford, Oreg., 1982—, Washington, 1982—; mem. Oreg. State Marine Bd., Salem, 1980-83. With USNG, 1968-72. Recipient Outstanding Young Man of Yr. Ashland C. of C., 1971. Mem.

Rotary Internat. Republican. Office: Congressman Bob Smith 259 E Barnett Ste E Medford OR 97501

JOHNSON, LEONIDAS ALEXANDER, optometrist; b. Chgo., Jan. 16, 1959; s. Leon and Dolores J.; m. Crystal Dwaun Ellington, June 23, 1990. BA in Biology, Ill. Wesleyan U., 1981; BS in Visual Sci., So. Calif. Coll. of Optometry, Fullerton, 1983, OD, 1985; student, Grace Theol. Sem., Long Beach, Calif., 1986-89, Biola U., La Mirada, Calif., 1991—. Registered Optometrist. Optometrist Larry Gotlieb, O.D., Redondo Beach, Calif., 1985-86, James Moses, O.D., Inglewood, Calif., 1986-87, Eyecare U.S.A., Montclair, Calif., 1987-89, Pearle Visioncare, Brea, Calif., 1989—; quality assurance com. mem. Eyecare U.S.A., 1988-89. Contbr. article to profl. jour. Deacon Friendship Bapt. Ch., Yorba Linda, Calif. Mem. Am. Optometric Assn., Calif. Optometric Assn., Nat. Optometric Assn., Ill. Wesleyan Minority Alumni Network (mentor). Home: PO Box 9746 Brea CA 92622-9746 Office: Pearle Visioncare 2027 Brea Mall # 1046 Brea CA 92621-5730

JOHNSON, LINDA SUE, state legislator, hospital administrator; b. Ft. Worth, Dec. 4, 1950; d. William Jr. and Helen Adelene (Loya) McCormick; m. Jerry Eugene Johnson, May 24, 1974 (div. 1984); children: Jeremy Scott, Nicholas Adam, Jennifer Leigh. BA in Biology, U. Tex., 1972; ADN, Shoreline C.C., Seattle, 1986; M in Healthcare Adminstrn., U. Wash., 1988. RN. Physician's asst. CHildren's Med. Ctr., Austin, Tex., 1973; collections corr. Sears Roebuck & Co., Seattle, 1973-77; nurse Northwest Hosp., Seattle, 1985-88; intern Univ. Hosp., Seattle, 1987-88; clin. mgr. ops. Evergreen Urgent Care Ctr., Woodinville, Wash., 1988-90; dir. med. staff Evergreen Hosp. Med. Ctr., Kirkland, Wash., 1990—; mem. Wash. Ho. Reps., Olympia, 1993—. Trustee, pres. Trustees Assn. Tech. and Community Colls., Olympia, 1990-92; trustee Shoreline C.C., 1987-92; active PTA. Mem. Am. Coll. Healthcare Execs., Wash. Stata Nurses Assn. (legis. com. 1991-93), Citizen Steering Com. Democrat. Office: Wash State Legislature JWB 304 Olympia WA 98504

JOHNSON, LINN VALEN, pilot; b. Joliet, Ill., Aug. 5, 1942; s. Norman Boyd and Laurell Eugenia (Nelson) J.; m. Diane Jane Purcell, May 14, 1966 (div. Nov. 1975); children: Jeffrey Valen, Douglas David. BA, U. Puget Sound, 1966; exch. student, Kita-Kyushu U., Japan, 1964. Cert. FAA comml. pilot., flight engr. Airplane cleaner United Airlines, Seattle, 1960-61; kitchen helper United Airlines, 1962; cargo agt. Pan Am. Airways, Seattle, 1963, 65; pilot Western Airlines, L.A., 1972-87, Delta Air Lines, Atlanta, 1987—; com. rels. chmn. Air Line Pilots Assn., Seattle, 1974-79, aeromed. chmn., 1986-89; pilot rep. Western Al Health Svc., L.A., 1985-87; Western regional chmn. Delta Pilots Asst. Com., Salt Lake City, 1987-88. Editor: The Bird Word Quarterly News, 1986-91. Founder Tomlinson Meml. Scholar, 1988—; pres. PTA, Puyallup, Wash., 1978, 79 (Golden Acorn award 1979); chmn. Pierce County Airport Dist. Prop, Puyallup, 1980; mem. Election Campaign for Gov., Tacoma, 1978. Capt. USAF, 1966-72. Scholar Women's Soc. of C.S., Des Moines, 1961.

JOHNSON, LLOYD WARREN, artist, real estate investor; b. N.Y.C., June 5, 1941; Carl Gustave and Edna Lillian (Klein) J. BS, N.Y. Inst. Tech., 1964. Paintings in many group exhibitions including Pietrantonio Gallery, Interchurch Ctr., Union Carbide Gallery, Artists Equity Gallery, Brooklyn Union Gas Co. Gallery, also colls., librs. and regional mus. Treas. Anna Meltzer Art Soc., N.Y.C., 1970-74, pres. 1974-75. Mem. Artists Equity of N.Y.

JOHNSON, LOIS EILEEN, artist; b. Shafter, Calif., July 20, 1942; d. Pete S. and Martha (Sawatski) Unruh; m. William Howard Johnson, Aug. 13, 1960 (div. 1987); 1 child, Cindy Eileen. Student, Fresno City Coll., 1959-60, North Tex. State U., 1962-63, No. Ariz. U., 1970-75, Scottsdale Artists' Sch., 1984-87. art cons. grades 7 and 8 Auberry (Calif.) Elem. Sch., 1987-92, pvt. portrait com., 1979-82. Exhibited in group shows at Husberg Fine Art and El Prado Galleries, Sedona, Ariz., 1970-79, O'Brien's Art Emporium, Scottsdale, 1982-93, Georgetown U. Art Gallery, Washington, 1992, SUNY Butler Gallery, 1992, Port History Mus., Phila., 1992, Ellis Island, N.Y., 1992, JFK Mus. and Libr., Boston, 1992, Nat. Hist. Mus., L.A., 1993, Transamerica Twr., San Francisco, 1993, Cambria (Calif.) Coast Gallery, 1990-93, others; represented in permanent collections Valley Nat. Bank, U.S. Dept. Justice, Wickenburg Art Mus., others. Host Internat. Coll. Students, Dallas, Tex. and Flagstaff, Ariz., 1962-78; co-founder Campus Ambs., Flagstaff, 1965-78; fundraiser in community, 1966—. Recipient scholarship Nat. Portrait Seminar, Washington, 1983, 1st Pl. Best and Brightest Competition, Scottsdale (Ariz.) Art Sch., 1986, 2d Pl. Immigration and Naturalization Svc. Internat. Competition, U.S. Dept. Justice, Washington, 1992. Home: 33535 S J & E Rd Auberry CA 93602

JOHNSON, LOIS JEAN, music educator; b. Los Angeles, Jan. 13, 1950; d. Kenneth Franklin and Iona Jean (Miller) J. BA, Brigham Young U., 1971, MusM, 1975; postgrad., Ind. U. Grad. teaching asst. Brigham Young U., Provo, Utah, 1972-75, instr. voice, 1975—; instr. music study Vienna, Austria, 1978; chief registrar vital stas. City-County Health Dept., Provo, 1979-85; mus. dir. Utah Valley Choral Soc., Provo, 1980—, trustee, 1983—; mus. dir. Promised Valley Playhouse, Salt Lake City, 1984; dir. choral activities, chair Fine Arts Dept. American Fork (Utah) High Sch., 1985—, chmn. fine arts dept., 1986—; recitalist, soloist Mormon Tabernacle Choir, Salt Lake City, 1972-91. Mem. NEA, Am. Choral Dirs. Assn. (pres. Utah chpt. 1991-93), Nat. Assn. Tchrs. Singing (v.p. local chpt. 1983-84), Utah Edn. Assn., Music Educator Nat. Conf., Utah Music Educators Assn. Republican. Mormon. Home: 835 N 750 W Provo UT 84604-3213 Office: Am Fork High Sch 510 N 600 E American Fork UT 84003-1999

JOHNSON, LOREN RAY, real estate investor; b. Seattle, Aug. 11, 1951; s. Gerald Richard Johnson and Vena (Welch) Danek; m. Celia Marie Merritt, Dec. 29, 1975; children: Cameron, Charisse, Chana. Ed., Shoreline C.C., Olympic C.C., Nat. Assn. Realtors; grad., Realtors Inst. Br. mgr., v.p. Century 21 Larkin Realty Inc., Bremerton, Wash., 1976-80; pres. Century 21 Cameron Real Estate, Inc., Port Orchard, Wash., 1980—; pres. Olympic Property Mgmt., 1993—; sec.-treas. Sta. 1400-AM, Kitz Radio, Silverdale, Wash., 1991—. Dir. communications Am. Cancer Soc., Bremerton, 1992. Bahai. Office: Century 21 Cameron R E Inc 4108 Bethel Rd SE Port Orchard WA 98366

JOHNSON, MAGIC See JOHNSON, EARVIN

JOHNSON, MARC, corporate executive; b. Xenia, Ohio, Dec. 12, 1943; s. Carl Andrew and Gertrude Virginia (Moon) J. Student, Miami U., Oxford, Ohio, 1960, Cornell U., 1961-63. Gen. mgr. Johnson Enterprises, Dayton, Ohio, 1963-64; regional sales mgr. Hartcrest Co., Columbus, Ohio, 1964-68; nat. project engr. Guerdon Corp., Louisville, 1969; nat. sales mgr. Alpine div. Skyline Corp., 1969-70; plant mgr., voting mem. exec. com. Automated Structures Corp., Charlottesville, Va., 1970-71; pvt. practice cons. with Native Am. tribes, 1971-83; exec. v.p. Associated Contractors, Hawaii, 1981-83; founder, chmn., CEO The Store, Present Industries Inc., Laramie, 1983—. Author (column) Housing in Hawaii, Hawaii Tribune-Herald, 1982-83. Com. chmn. Pres'. Coun. on Housing, Washington, 1970-71. Ellsworth M. Statler scholar Cornell U., N.Y., 1961-63. Office: 7075 Salt Creek Route 4 Casper WY 82601

JOHNSON, MARIAN ILENE, university educator; b. Hawarden, Iowa, Oct. 3, 1929; d. Henry Richard and Wilhelmina Anna (Schmidt) Stoltenberg; m. Paul Irving Jones, June 14, 1958 (dec. Feb. 1985); m. William Andrew Johnson, Oct. 3, 1991. BA, U. La Verne, 1959; MA, Claremont Grad. Sch., 1962; PhD, Ariz. State U., 1971. Cert. tchr., Iowa, Calif. Elem. tchr. Cherokee (Iowa) Sch. Dist., 1949-52, Sioux City (Iowa) Sch. Dist., 1952-56, Ontario (Calif.) Pub. Schs., 1956-61, Reed Union Sch. Dist., Belvedere-Tiburon, Calif., 1962-65, Columbia (Calif.) Union Sch. Dist., 1965-68; prof. edn. Calif. State U., Chico, 1972-91. Contbr. articles to profl. jours. Mem. Internat. Reading Assn., Phi Delta Kappa, Delta Kappa Gamma. Home: 26437 S Lakewood Dr Sun Lakes AZ 85248-7246

JOHNSON, MARTIN CHESTER, controller; b. Mpls., Feb. 5, 1954; s. Chester Otto and Marian Ruth (Swanson) J.; m. Gail Anne Simi, June 4, 1988; 1 child, Amelia Christine. BA in Geology, Augustana Coll., 1976; MS, U. Iowa, 1978; MBA, Northwestern U., 1985. Geologist Lindgren Exploration Co., Wayzata, Minn., 1978-79, Milchem, Inc., Houston, 1979-82; mgr. adminstrn. Geonomics, Inc., Campbell, Calif., 1986-88; controller On-Site Techs., Inc., Campbell, 1988-90; controller, chief fin. officer Balzer/Shopes Inc., Brisbane, Calif., 1990-92; controller Sunpower Corp., Sunnyvale, Calif., 1992—. Mem. Inst. Mgmt. Accts., Geol. Soc. Am., Soc. Econ. Geologists. Democrat. Lutheran. Home: 1845 S Bascom Ave # 14B Campbell CA 95008

JOHNSON, MELINDA See CUMMINGS, SPANGLER

JOHNSON, MILTON H., dentist; b. Great Falls, Mont., Feb. 25, 1923; s. Arthur and Irene (Nara) J.; m. Joann R. Carlson, Apr. 28, 1946; children: Karen, Nancy., Bruce, Linda. DMD, U. Oreg., 1946. Pvt. practice dentist Portland, Oreg., 1946-51, Vancouver, Wash., 1953-92; asst. prof. dentistry U. Oreg., Portland, 1946-80; faculty U. Wash. Dental, Seattle, 1978-80. Elder Presbyn. Ch., Vancouver, Wash. Capt. USAF, 1951-53. Fellow Am. Acad. Gen. Dentistry, Internat. Coll. Dentists; mem. Am. Dental Assn., Wash. STate Dental Assn. (treas. 1975), Wash. Acad. Gen. Dentistry (pres. 1978). Republican.

JOHNSON, MIRIAM MASSEY, sociology educator; b. Atlanta, Jan. 12, 1928; d. Herbert Neal and Leola (Paullin) Massey; m. Guy Benton Johnson Jr., July 21, 1951; children: Frank Shannon, Rebekah Paullin. PhD, Harvard U., 1955. Instr. U. Oreg., Eugene, 1959-63, 73-75, asst. prof., 1975-80, assoc. prof., 1980-88, prof., 1988—, retired emeritus, 1993; acting dir. Ctr. for Study of Women in Soc., U. Oreg., 1986-88, 91. Author: (with Jean Stockard) Sex Roles: Sex Inequality and Sex Role Development, 1980, Gender and Society, 1991; author: Strong Mothers Weak Wives, 1988. Rockefeller Found. grantee, 1988-89. Office: U Oreg Dept Sociology Eugene OR 97403

JOHNSON, NOEL LARS, biomedical engineer; b. Palo Alto, Calif., Nov. 11, 1957; s. LeRoy Franklin and Margaret Louise (Lindsley) J.; m. Elise Lynnette Moore, May 17, 1986; children: Margaret Elizabeth, Kent Daniel. BSEE, U. Calif., Berkeley, 1979; ME, U. Va., 1982, PhD, 1990. Mgr. automated infusion systems R&D hosp. products div. Abbott Labs., Mountain View, Calif., 1986—. Contbr. articles to profl. jours. Fellowship NIH 1980-85; rsch. grantee Abbott Labs. 1989. Mem. IEEE, Biomed. Engring. Soc., Am. Soc. Anesthesiologists, Sigma Xi, Delta Chi (founder, 1st pres. chpt. U. Calif. at Berkeley). Home: 6649 Canterbury Ct San Jose CA 95129-3871 Office: Abbott Labs Hosp Products Divsn 1212 Terra Bella Ave Mountain View CA 94043-1899

JOHNSON, PATRICIA GAYLE, corporate communication executive, writer; b. Conway, Ark., Oct. 23, 1947; d. Rudolph and Frances Modene (Hayes) J. Student U. Calif., Irvine, 1965-68. Advance rep. Disney on Parade, Los Angeles, 1971-75; mktg. dir., dir. field ops. Am. Freedom Train, 1975-77; publ. rels. mgr. Six Flags, Inc., Los Angeles, 1977-81; mgr. corp. communications Playboy Enterprises, Inc., Los Angeles, 1981-82; external rels. mgr. Kal Kan Foods, Inc., Los Angeles, 1982-86; v.p. Daniel J. Edelman, Inc., 1986-88; sr. v.p. Amies Advt. and Pub. Rels., Irvine, 1988-89; dir. pub. rels. World Vision, Monrovia, Calif., 1989-92; v.p. The Bohle Co., L.A., 1992—; lectr. U. So. Calif., UCLA, Calif. State U., Northridge, Calif. State U., Dominguez Hills. Mem. Pub. Rels. Soc. Am. (past officer), Pub. Affairs Council, Delta Soc. (advisor). Mem. Foursquare Gospel Ch. Collaborator TV scripts; contbr. articles to various consumer and profl. mags. Office: World Vision 919 W Huntington Dr Monrovia CA 91016-3111

JOHNSON, PAUL E., mayor; m. Christa Johnson; 2 children. Student, U. Phoenix. Rep. Dist. 3 City of Phoenix, 1986—; mayor City of Phoenix, 1990—. Address: Office of the Mayor 251 W Washington St Phoenix AZ 85003

JOHNSON, PAUL RONALD, economist; b. Sydney, Australia, Apr. 6, 1955; came to U.S., 1989; s. Ronald Thomas and Joan Therese (Reilley) J.; m. Lydia Wai-Chong Leong, July 4, 1987. BA, Macquarie U., 1978; MA, U. Rochester, 1983, PhD, 1985. Rsch. officer Res. Bank, Australia, 1978; lectr. York U., Toronto, Can., 1983-85; fin. officer Australian Treasury, Canberra, 1986-89; lectr. Nanyang Technol. U., Singapore, 1987-88; asst. prof. U. Alaska, Anchorage, 1989—. Contbr. articles to profl. jours. Mem. Am. Econ. Assn., Asian Studies Assn., Acad. Internat. Bus., Atlantic Econ. Assn. Baptist. Office: U Alaska Ctr Internat Bus 3211 Providence Dr Anchorage AK 99508

JOHNSON, PHYLLIS JEAN, tour company owner, tour guide; b. Denver, Aug. 28, 1937; d. Paul Houtchens and Helen Mason Gilman (Dow) Parker; m. Lavern O. Johnson, June 21, 1959 (div. 1973); children: Beverly Ann, Brian Paul, Christina Lynn, David Keith. MusB, U. Denver, 1959; cert., Internat. Guide Acad., 1989. Music tchr., performer Denver, 1954—; sec., office mgr. Johns Manville Corp., Williams Fin. Co., Denver, 1973-85; hostess, driver, guide Historic Denver, Inc., 1984-91; driver, guide Rocky Mountain Park Tours, Estes Park, Colo., 1985-90; step-on guide, tour escort various cos., Denver, 1984—; tchr. Colo. history Internat. Guide Acad., Denver, 1990; owner, driver, guide Colo. Bug Tours, Denver, 1991—. Concert artist Mu Phi Epsilon ann. concert, 1990; host, coord., tchr. youth flute camp, 1989; vol. Alry Flute Choir, Denver, 1992. Mem. Profl. Guide Assn. Am. (conv. booth coord. 1991), Denver Musicians Assn.

JOHNSON, QULAN ADRIAN, software engineer; b. Great Falls, Mont., Sept. 17, 1942; s. Raymond Eugene and Bertha Marie (Nagengast) J.; m. Helen Louise Pocha, July 24, 1965; children—Brenda Marie, Douglas Paul, Scot Paul, Mathew James. B.A. in Psychology, Coll. Gt. Falls, 1964. Lead operator 1st Computer Corp., Helena, Mont., 1966-67; v.p., sec.-treas. Computer Corp. of Mt., Great Falls, 1967-76, dir., 1971-76; sr. systems analyst Mont. Dept. Revenue, Helena, 1976-78; software engr. Mont. Systems Devel. Co., Helena, 1978-80; programmer/analyst III info. systems div. Mont. Dept. Adminstrn., Helena, 1980-82; systems analyst centralized services Dept. Social and Rehab. Services State of Mont., 1982-87, systems and programming mgr. info systems, Blue Cross and Blue Shield of Montana, Helena, 1987—. Mem. Assn. for Systems Mgmt., Mont. Data Processing Assn., Data Processing Mgmt. Assn., Mensa. Club: K.C. (rec. sec. 1975-76). Home: 2231 8th Ave Helena MT 59601-4841 Office: Blue Cross & Blue Shield Info Systems 404 Fuller Ave Helena MT 59601-5006

JOHNSON, RANDALL DAVID (RANDY JOHNSON), professional baseball player; b. Walnut Creek, Calif., Sept. 10, 1963. Student, U. So. Calif. With Montreal (Can.) Expos, 1988-89; pitcher Seattle (Wash.) Mariners, 1989—. Named to All-Stars, 1990, 93. Office: Seattle Mariners PO Box 4100 411 1st Ave South Seattle WA 98104

JOHNSON, RAYMOND A., apparel executive; b. 1942. Grad., Western Wash. U. With Nordstrom Inc., 1969—; co-pres. Nordstrom Inc., Seattle, 1991—. Office: Nordstrom Inc 1501 5th Ave Seattle WA 98101*

JOHNSON, RAYMOND W. (PADRE JOHNSON), artist, minister; b. Mpls., June 27, 1934; s. Raymond Wendell and Lorena Sylvia (Harbrecht) J.; divorced; children: Raymond, Richard. BA, Gustavus Adolphus Coll., 1956; MDiv., Luth. Sch. Theology, 1960; postgrad., U. Minn., 1971-72; D in Ministry, United Theol. Sem., 1978. Ordained to ministry Luth. Ch., 1960. Med. technician Pub. Hosp., Moline, Ill., 1956-58; campus pastor Middlebury (Vt.), Dartmouth (N.H.) Colls., 1960-66; chaplain USN, Charleston, S.C., 1966; chaplain, field med. officer Navy Spl. Forces, USN, Vietnam, 1967-68; chaplain Blue Angels flight squadron Navy Spl. Forces, USN, Pensacola, Fla., 1968-69; dir. devel. gov.'s crime commn. State of Minn., St. Paul, 1969-72; community devel. specialist Nat. Tech. Services Found., Mpls., 1972-74; resident minister Jonathan Ecumenical Community Ch., Mpls., 1974-79. Author: Postmark Mekong Delta, 1968, Journeys with the Global Family, 1992, Portrait-Faces of the Gobal Human Family; exhibits include UN, N.Y., Premier Exhbn., Portrait of the Human Family; contbr. articles to profl. jours. Sponsor Nat. Coun. of Chs. Served lt. USN, 1966-69, Vietnam; comdr. USNR, 1979—. Decorated Legion of Merit, Silver Star with oak leaf cluster, Cross of Gallantry, Purple Heart with oak leaf cluster. Recipinet Gold medal Internat. Art Honor Soc., 1984; named one of 10 Outstanding Young Men of Am. U.S. Jaycees. Avocation: sports, mountain climbing. Home and Office: PO Box 146 Cody WY 82414-0146

JOHNSON, RICHARD KARL, hospitality company executive; b. Gaylord, Minn., May 27, 1947; s. Karl S. and Mildred (Tollefson) J.; m. Eva Margaret Wick, Oct. 12, 1973; children: Michelle, Richard, Ryan. BA, Gustavus Adolphus U., St. Peter, Minn., 1969. Gen. mgr. Green Giant Restaurants, Inc., Mpls., 1969-71, Mpls. Elks Club, Mpls., 1971-73; dir. concept devel. Internat. Multifoods, Mpls., 1972-75; v.p. concept devel. A&WFood Svcs. Can., North Vancouver, B.C., 1975-81; dir. food and beverages Ramada, Reno, 1981-82; pres., owner R.K. Johnson & Assoc., Reno, 1981—; owner D.J. Mgmt., 1990—; asst. gen. mgr. Gold Dust West Casino, Reno, 1983-85; gen. mgr. P&M Corp., Reno, 1985-86; v.p. ops. C.P.S.W. Inc., Reno and Tempe, Ariz., 1986-87, Lincoln Fairview, Reno, 1987-89; v.p. corp. affairs Myers Realty, 1991—. Mem. Aircraft Owners and Pilots Assn., Nat. Restaurant Assn., Nev. Realtor, Elks Club. Lutheran. Home: 825 Meadow Springs Dr Reno NV 89509-5913 Office: RK Johnson & Assoc 825 Meadow Springs Dr Reno NV 89509-5913

JOHNSON, ROB CARL, insurance agent; b. Sedro-Woolley, Wash., Feb. 15, 1952; s. Hubert Carl and Genevieve Louise (Walker) J.; m. Ruth A.C. Correa, Oct. 19, 1980; children: Genevieve, Lars. BA, U. Wash., 1974; postgrad., Western Wash. U., 1977. CLU; ChFC. Ins. agt. Equitable Life, Mount Vernon, Wash., 1977-83, Whitfield's, Marysville, Wash., 1983—; agts. forum del. Equitable Life, Seattle, 1985-90. Del. Wash. Ho. of Reps. (40th dist. fin. insts. com.); vol. Peace Corps, Truk Island, 1975; bd. dirs. Skagit County Housing Authority, Mount Vernon, 1989—. Mem. Nat. Assn. of Life Underwriters, Nat. Assn. of Health Underwriters. Democrat. Lutheran. Office: Whitfield's PO Box 128 Marysville WA 98270

JOHNSON, ROBERT ALAN, chemical engineer; b. Salt Lake City, Apr. 4, 1923; s. J. Herman and Hazel Florence (Woodruff) J.; m. Helen Patricia Colberg, July 23, 1948; children: Brian W., Cynthia A. Johnson Smalley, David S. BSChemE, U. Nebr., 1947. Registered profl. engr., Calif. Employee Standard Oil Co., Whiting, Ind., 1947-50, Casper, Wyo., 1950-57; project chem. engr. Standard Oil Co., Whiting, Ind., 1957-61; prin. process engr. CF Braun & Co., Alhambra, Calif., 1961-88; chief process engr. RM Parsons Co., Pasadena, Calif., 1988—. Deacon, ruling elder La Canada Presbyn. Ch., 1975. Mem. Am. Inst. Chem. Engrs., Am. Chem. Soc., Casper Engrs. Club (founder 1954, pres. 1957), Sigma Xi, Sigma Phi Epsilon, Pi Mu Epsilon. Home: 2026 Tondolea Ln La Canada Flintridge CA 91011-1552

JOHNSON, ROBERT BRITTEN, geology educator; b. Cortland, N.Y., Sept. 24, 1924; s. William and Christine (Hofer) J.; m. Garnet Marion Brown, Aug. 30, 1947; children: Robert Britten, Richard Karl, Elizabeth Anne. Student, Wheaton (Ill.) Coll., 1942-43, 46-47; AB summa cum laude, Syracuse U., 1949, MS, 1950; PhD, U. Ill., 1954. Asst. geologist Ill. Geol. Survey, 1951-54; asst. prof. geology Syracuse U., 1954-55; sr. geologist and geophysicist C.A. Bays & Assn., Urbana, Ill., 1955-56; from asst. prof. to prof. engring. geology Purdue U., 1956-66, head, engring. geology dept., 1964-66; prof. geology DePauw U., 1966-67, head, dept. geology, 1966-67; prof. geology Colo. State U., 1967-88, acting chmn. dept. geology, 1968, chmn. dept., 1969-73, prof. in charge geology programs, dept. earth resources, 1973-77, acting head dept. earth resources, 1979-81, prof. emeritus, 1988—; geologist U.S. Geol. Survey, 1976-88; cons. in field, 1957—; instr. Elderhostel programs, 1991—. Active local Boy Scouts Am., 4-H Club, Sci. Fair, dist. schs. Served with USAAF, 1943-46. Fellow Geol. Soc. Am. (E.B. Burwell Jr. Meml. award 1989); mem. Assn. Engring. Geologists (Claire P. Holdredge Outstanding Publ. award 1990), Internat. Assn. Engring. Geology, Phi Beta Kappa. Republican. Home: 2309 Moffett Dr Fort Collins CO 80526-2122

JOHNSON, ROBERT HERSEL, journalist; b. Colorado City, Tex., May 28, 1923; s. Robert Hersel and Leah (Sikes) J.; m. Luise Putcamp, Jr., Feb. 24, 1945; children: Robert Hersel, III, Luise Robin, Jan Leah, Stephanie Neale, Jennifer Anne. B.S. in Journalism, So. Methodist U., 1947. Reporter Phoenix Gazette, 1940-42; asst. sports editor Ariz. Republic, Phoenix, 1942-43; newscast writer Sta. KOY, Phoenix, 1943; reporter Dallas Times-Herald, 1946; with AP, 1946—, Utah-Idaho bur. chief, 1954-59, Ind. bur. chief, 1959-62, Tex. bur. chief, 1962-69, gen. sports editor, 1969-73, mng. editor, 1973-77, asst. gen. mgr., spl. asst. to pres., 1977-84, N.Mex. bureau chief, 1984-88; prof. journalism N.Mex. State U., Las Cruces, 1988, U. N.Mex., Albuquerque, 1989; exec. dir. N.Mex. Found. for Open Govt., Albuquerque, 1989—; Mem. Newspaper Readership Council, 1977-82. Served to capt. USMCR, 1943-46, 51-52. Home: PO Box 877 Placitas NM 87043-0877

JOHNSON, ROBERT LESLIE, management consultant, educator, engineer; b. Attleboro, Mass., Feb. 20, 1923; s. John Edward and Ada Emily (Chadwick) J.; m. Floriene Smalley, Mar. 8, 1946; 1 child, Debra Denise. BS, Ind. U., 1956; MBA, Ohio State U., 1959; cert. in econs., U. Calif., Berkeley, 1962; postgrad., Santa Clara (Calif.) U., 1978. Cert. econs. and bus. tchr., Calif.; registered profl. engr., Calif. Systems analyst Western Electric, Indpls., 1955-56, N.Am. Aviation, Columbus, Ohio, 1956-57; fin. exec. State of Ohio, Columbus, 1957-59; sr. systems analyst Lockheed Missiles & Space Co., Sunnyvale, Calif., 1959-62; head project mgmt. United Tech. Corp., Sunnyvale, 1962-65; sr. staff dep. dir. SRI Internat., Menlo Park, Calif., 1965-71; dir. policy mgmt. City of San Jose, Calif., 1971-79; exec. cons., chair faculty strategic mgmt. U. Phoenix, San Jose, 1980—; pvt. practice cons. engr., Sunnyvale, 1959—; mem. adj. faculty mgmt. and econs. Pepperdine U., San Jose, 1980-83; asst. prof. pub. adminstrn. Calif. State U. System, 1978-84. Contbr. numerous articles to profl. jours. Math. lab aide Ardenwood Sch., Fremont, Calif.; mem. Rep. Presdl. Task Force; pres., bd. dirs. ASPA, San Jose, 1972-79. Master sgt. USAF, capt. USAFR, ret. USAF scholar Ind. U., 1954-56. 4em. NRA, Fed. Emergency Mgmt. Agy. Execs. (exec. reservist), Ret. Officers Assn. (life), Res. Officers Assn. (life), Air Force Assn., San Jose Ret. Employees Assn., Calif. Rifle and Pistol Assn, Marines Meml. Club, San Jose Mgmt. Assn. Home: 836 Shetland Pl Sunnyvale CA 94087-4841

JOHNSON, ROBERT WAYNE, government official; b. Lovelock, Nev., Mar. 6, 1951; s. Dorsey Edward and Geneva Mae (Shearer) J.; m. Mary Lucy Serrano, May 19, 1974; children: Gabriel, Carolynn. BS, U. Nev., 1973, MS, 1977. Rsch. asst. U. Nev., Reno, 1974-75; agrl. economist U.S. Bur. Reclamation, Sacramento, 1975-79; economist U.S. Bur. Reclamation, Boulder City, Nev., 1979-81, chief econ. resources bd., 1981-87; chief contracts and repayment U.S. Bur. Reclamation, Washington, 1987-88; regional supr. water, land and power U.S. Bur. Reclamation, Boulder City, 1988-91, asst. regional dir., 1991—; instr. Golden Gate U., Las Vegas, Nev., 1981-87; speaker, panel am. Am. Soc. Pub. Adminstrs., Las Vegas, 1991; speaker Ariz. Agribus. Coun., Phoenix, 1991; participant Western States Water Coun. Workshops, Park City, Utah, 1992. Contbg. author: Water Marketing, 1989; also articles. Recipient performance awards U.S. Bur. Reclamation, 1977, 78, 81, 84-86, 88, 90, Professorial Lectr. award Golden Gate U., San Francisco, 1987; fellow U. Nev., 1974-75; profl. water exch. fellow U.S. Bur. Reclamation, Canberra, Australia, 1992. Memm. Colorado River Water Users Assn., Assn. Calif. Water Agys., Nev. Water Resources Assn. (speaker 1989—). Home: 2001 Grafton Ave Henderson NV 89014 Office: US Bur Reclamation PO Box 427 Boulder City NV 89005

JOHNSON, RODNEY DALE, law enforcement officer, photographer; b. Montebello, Calif., May 14, 1944; s. Albert Gottfreid and Maxine Elliot (Rogers) J.; m. Karen Rae Van Antwerp, May 18, 1968; 1 child, Tiffany Nicole. AA, Ela Community Coll., 1973; postgrad. Law Enforcement Spl., FBI, Acad., 1976; BA, U. of La Verne, 1978. Cert. tchr. police sci., Calif. Dep., Los Angeles County Sheriff, 1969-75, dep. IV, 1976-78, sgt., 1978—; fire arms inst., Hacienda Heights, Calif., 1975—; photographer Weddings and Portraits, 1983—; photography instr., Hacienda Heights, 1983—; pres. Wheelhouse Enterprises, Inc., Whittier, 1971-86; instr. State Sheriff's Civil Procedural Sch. Los Medanos Coll., Concord, Calif., 1985-88. Creator and actor, Cap'n Andy, 1973-80; song writer for Cap'n Andy theme, 1972. Sgt. USMC, 1965-69, Vietnam, master gunnery sgt. Res., 1969—; intelligence chief, Persian Gulf. Recipient Service award Trinity Broadcasting Network, 1979. Mem. Profl. Peace Officers Assn., Sheriff's Relief Assn., Assoc. Photographers Internat. Republican. Mem. Assembly of God. Club: Faithbuilders (pres. 1981-87), (Pomona).

JOHNSON, ROGER W., computer manufacturing company executive; b. 1935. BA, Clarkson Coll. of Tech., 1956; MBA, U. Mass., 1963. With GE Co., 1956-69; with The Singer Co., 1969-74, v.p. ops. bus. machines div.;

with Memorex Corp.; with System Devel. Corp., 1978-81, pres. products group; pres. office systems group Burroughs Corp., 1981-82; pres., chief oper. officer Western Digital Corp., 1982-83, also chief exec. officer, 1983—, also chmn. bd., 1984—, now chmn. bd., pres., chief exec. officer. Office: Western Digital Corp PO box 19665 Irvine CA 92714*

JOHNSON, RONALD DOUGLAS, business executive; b. Klamath Falls, Oreg., Sept. 16, 1949; s. Clifford Douglas and Anna Elizabeth (Fine) J.; m. Wendi Susan Brown, Aug. 20, 1972; children: Bryan Douglas, Timothy Christopher, Michael Casey. BA in Polit. Sci., Wash. State U., 1975, MA in Pub. Adminstrn., 1976, MA in Agrl. Econs., 1981. Rsch. asst. Wash. Water Rsch. Ctr., Pullman, 1974-75; mgmt. trainee Potlatch Corp., 1971-74; intern Gov. Daniel J. Evans, Olympia, Wash., 1975; rsch. asst. Wash. State U., Pullman, 1976-79; asst. mgr. Reardan Grain Gowers Assn., Wash., 1980-82; gen. mgr. Bean Growers Warehouse Assn., Twin Falls, Idaho, 1982-84; dry bean group mgr. Rogers NK Seed Co., Boise, Idaho, 1984—; bd. dirs. Consolidated Agrl. Inc., Twin Falls, 1986—. With U.S. Army, 1968-70, Viet Nam. Commn. Econ. Assistance grantee Oreg. State U., 1978, Washington Water Rsch. grantee, Wash. State U., 1976. Home: 10464 Shadybrook Dr Boise ID 83704-3944 Office: Rogers Bros Seed Co 1755 Westgate Dr Boise ID 83704-7174

JOHNSON, RONALD GLENN, arts administrator; b. L.A., Dec. 3, 1949; s. Edward Andrew and Elizabeth Jane (Freeman) J.; m. Jane E. Walker, Aug. 16, 1969; children: Andrew Edward, Robin Winfield. MusB, W.Va. U., 1975, MusM, 1977. Freelance musician L.A., 1977-85; edn. coord. San Diego Symphony Orch., 1985-86, artistic adminstr., 1986-87, mgr., 1987-89; ops. mgr. Mainly Mozart Festival, San Diego, 1989-90; exec. dir. Eugene (Oreg.) Symphony Orch., 1990—. Sgt. U.S. Army, 1970-73. Mem. Am. Symphony Orch. League, Northwest Assn. Symphony Orchs. (pres.). Office: Eugene Symphony Orch 45 W Broadway Ste 201 Eugene OR 97401-3002

JOHNSON, RONALD WEBSTER, university administrator, financial aid director; b. Bklyn., Jan. 6, 1948; s. Charles and Lorna Mae (Williams) J.; m. Barbara Ann Thibodeaux, July 8, 1988; children from previous marriage: Matthew Webster, Nicholas Michael; 1 stepchild, Eric Von Lewis. Student, Santa Barbara Community Coll., 1967-69; BSBA, San Jose State U., 1971; postgrad., Golden Gate U., 1971-72. Dir. fin. aid Golden Gate U., San Francisco, 1971-74; asst. dir. of counseling U. Calif., Davis, 1974-81, acting dir. of fin. aid, 1980-81, dir. of fin. aid, 1981—; fin. aid cons. Dept. of Health, Edn. and Welfare, Region IX, Famous Beauty Coll., Hayward, Calif., 1973-75. Race promotor, organizer First July 4th Davis Criterium Bike Race, 1976-78; past pres., race dir. Peugeot Davis Bike Club, 1978; fund raiser Am. Heart Assn., Am. Cancer Soc., Assn. Univ. Women, 1977-86; past pres., mem. Blacks for Effective Community Action, 1983-86, chair scholarship com., 1990; coach Am. Youth Soccer Orgn., 1981-87; chair Yolo County Bd. Suprs. Maternal Child and Adolescent Health Com., 1984—; mem. Coll. Entrance Exam. Bd., Coll. Scholarship Svc. Assembly, Creative Edn. Found. Mgmt. fellow Student Affairs/Bus. and Fin. U. Calif., Davis, 1979. Mem. Nat. Assn. Student Fin. Aid Adminstrs. (fed. aid program com. 1984-86, instr. student fin. aid tng. program 1977-78, instr. basic edn. opportunity grant tng. program 1977-78), Western Assn. of Student Fin. Aid Adminstrs. (summer inst. coord. 1984-87, western regional assbembly fin. aid com. 1984-87, speaker Mont./Idaho state assn. ann. conf. 1985, ann. conf. com. 1983-84, tng. com. chairperson 1984-86, v.p. 1984-85, coll. bd. conf. panel participant 1983-88, lead instr. summer inst. 1983, regional rev. panelist for the office of edn. 1973-74, Recognition award 1987), Calif. Assn. Student Fin. Aid Adminstrs. (v.p. 1987, fed. issues com. chair 1987, U. Calif. segmental rep. 1984, ann. conf. panelist 1984-88, conf. program com. 1989, Segmental Leadership award 1984, 91), Nat. Notary Assn., Am. Soc. Tng. and Devel., Calif. Coll. Pers. Assn., Nat. Assn. Colls. and Univ. Bus. Officers. Democrat. Methodist. Office: U Calif Fin Aid Office 125 North Hall Davis CA 95616

JOHNSON, STEWART WILLARD, civil engineer; b. Mitchell, S.D., Aug. 17, 1933; s. James Elmer Johnson and Grace Mahala (Erwin) Johnson Parsons; m. Mary Anis Giddings, June 24, 1956; children: Janelle Chiemi, Gregory Stewart, Eric Willard. BSCE, S.D. State U., 1956; BA in Bus. Adminstrn. and Polit. Sci., U. Md., 1960; MSCE, PhD, U. Ill., 1964. Registered profl. engr., Ohio. Commd. 2d lt. USAF, 1956, advanced through grades to lt. col.; prof. mechs. and civil engring. Air Force Inst. Tech. USAF, Dayton, Ohio, 1964-75; dir. civil engring. USAF, Seoul, Republic of Korea, 1976-77; chief civil engring. research div. USAF, Kirtland AFB, N.Mex., 1977-80; ret. USAF, 1980; prin. engr. BDM Corp., Albuquerque, 1980—; cons. in space sci., lunar basing NASA, U. N.Mex., N.Mex. State U., Los Alamos Nat. Labs., 1986—; adj. prof. civil engring. U. N.Mex., 1987—; prin. investigator devel. concepts for lunar astron. obs. U. N.Mex., N.Mex. State U., NASA, 1987—; tech. chmn. Space '88 and Space '90 Internat. Confs.; gen. chair Space '94 Internat. Conf., Albuquerque; vis. lectr. Internat. Space U., Japan, 1992; invited lectr., vis. lectr. in field. Editor Engineering, Construction, and Operations in Space, I and II; contbr. articles to profl. jours. Pres. ch. council Ch. of Good Shepherd United Ch. Christ, Albuquerque, 1983-85, chair bd. deacons, 1991-93; trustee Lunar Geotech. Inst., 1990—; mem. adv. bd. Lab. for Extraterrestrial Structures Rsch. Rutgers U., 1990—. Fellow Nat. Acad. Scis. NRC, 1970-71. Mem. AIAA (Engr. of Yr. region IV 1990), AAAS, ASCE (chmn. exec. com. aerospace div. 1979, tech. activities com. 1984, chmn. com. space engring. and constrn. 1987—, mem. nat. space policy com. 1988—, chmn. 1990—, Outstanding News Corr. award 1981, Aerospace Scis. and Tech. Applications award 1985, 90, Edmund Friedman Profl. Recognition award 1989), Am. Geophys. Union, Sigma Xi, Pi Sigma Alpha. Republican. Mem. United Ch. of Christ. Office: BDM Internat Inc 1801 Randolph Rd SE Albuquerque NM 87106-4295

JOHNSON, SUZANNE, public relations specialist; b. N.Y.C., May 30, 1952; d. John Henry and Matilda Elvira (Rodriguez) O'Neil; m. Allan Frederic Johnston, May 14, 1988; children: David, Jeffrey. Student, St. Louis U., Madrid, 1972-73; BA, Stephens Coll., 1974; MA, Ohio State U., 1979; postgrad., Columbia Basin Coll., 1993—. Stringer United Press Internat., Madrid, 1972-73; congl. aide Detroit, 1974-76; various broadcast positions Columbus, Ohio, 1977-82; news dir. Sta. WSNY, Columbus, 1982-84; faculty lectr. Sch. Journalism Ohio State U., Columbus, 1984; dir. corp. community affairs Battelle Meml. Inst., Columbus, 1984-87; exec. asst. to pres. Whitman Coll., Walla Walla, Wash., 1987-90; exec. dir. Tri-Cities Regional Consortium for Ednl. Progress, Kennewick, Wash., 1992—; sr. dir. communications Kaiser Engrs., Richland, Wash., 1992-93; specialist pub. rels. Los Alamos (N.Mex.) Nat. Lab., 1993—. Author: Teen Pregnancy Manual, 1991. Bd. dirs. Econ. Devel. Adv. Bd., Richland, 1990-93, Columbia Basin Coll. Found., Pasco, Wash., 1992-93. Mem. Soc. Profl. Journalists (bd. dirs.). Episcopalian.

JOHNSON, SYLVIA SUE, university administrator, educator; b. Abiline, Tex., Aug. 10, 1940; d. SE Boyd and Margaret MacGilliuray (Withington) Smith; m. William Ruel Johnson; children: Margaret Ruth, Laura Jane, Catherine Withington, Mac Gilliuray. BA, U. Calif., Riverside, 1962; postgrad., U. Hawaii, 1963. Elem. edn. credential, 1962. Mem. bd. regents U. Calif.; mem. steering com. Citizens University Com., chmn. 1978-79; bd. dirs., charter mem. U. Calif.-Riverside Found., chmn. nominating com., 1983—; charter mem. Affiliates of U. Calif.-Riverside, Friends of UCR Bot. Gardens; pres., bd. dirs. Friends of the Mission Inn, 1969-72, 73-76, Mission Inn Found., 1977—, Calif. Bapt. Coll. Citizens Com., 1980—; v.p. Riverside Community Hosp. Aux., Riversity Community Hosp. Founders Club; bd. dirs. Riverside Community Hosp., 1980—, Riverside Jr. league, 1976-77, Nat. Charity League, 1984-85, Riverside Art Alliance, 1968-69; mem. Riverside Com. to Rev. Sign Ordinance Moratorium, Com. to Rev. Mgmt. Structure of Mission Inn, Salvation Army Alternatives for Transient Housing, Riverside Art Ctr. Capitol Campaign Com.; co-chmn. Riverside Com. for Sign Control; mem. chancellors blue ribbon com., devel. com. Calif. Mus. Photography. Mem. U. Calif.-Riverside Alumni Assn. (bd. dirs. 1966-68, v.p. 1968-70).

JOHNSON, THEODORE, physician; b. Ames, Iowa, Apr. 30, 1925; s. Birger Lars and Elizabeth (Schulze) J.; m. Hope Polishuk, Aug. 1951; children: Theodore E., Jeffrey L., Christian E. BS, Mont. State U., 1948; MD, Temple U., 1953. Intern Thomas D. Dee Hosp., Ogden, Utah, 1954; physician Weber County, Ogden, Utah, 1954-59; pvt. practice Ogden, 1955-59; asst. editor JAMA AMA, Chgo., 1959-60; pvt. practice Glenview, Ill., 1964-77; asst. dir. AMA Commn. Cost of Med. Care, Chgo., 1960-63; med. dir. Raleigh Hills Hosp., Spokane, Wash., 1977-84; pvt. practice Spokane, 1977-84; clin. dir. LOU Wash. State Hosp., Medical Lake, 1986-88, clin. dir. ITA, 1990—; clin. instr. Abraham Sch. Medicine, Chgo., 1975-77; asst. physician Alcohol Treatment Ctr., Luth. Gen. Hosp., Park Ridge, Ill., 1967-77, chmn. dept. family practice, 1969; chmn. med. staff Wash. State Hosp., Medical Lake, 1987-89. Pub. health officer Glenview, Ill., 1964-67. Lt. USN, 1943-46, USNR, 1946-66. Mem. AMA, Wash. Med. Assn., Spokane Med. Soc. (pres. 1985), Am. Assn. Marriage and Family Therapists, Am. Soc. Addiction Medicine. Office: Wash State Hosp PO Box A Medical Lake WA 99022-0045

JOHNSON, THOMAS WEBBER, JR., lawyer; b. Indpls., Oct. 18, 1941; s. Thomas W. and Mary Lucinda (Webber) J.; m. Sandra Kay McMahon, Aug. 15, 1964 (div. 1986); m. Deborah Joan Collins, May 17, 1987 (div. 1990); m. Barbara Joyce Walter, Mar. 13, 1992. BS in Edn., Ind. U., 1963, JD summa cum laude, 1969. Bar: Ind. 1969, Calif. 1970. Law clk. Ind. Supreme Ct., Indpls., 1968-69; assoc. Irell & Manella law firm, L.A., 1969-76, ptnr., 1976-84; ptnr. Irell & Manella law firm, Newport Beach, Calif., 1984—; chmn. Com. on Group Ins. Programs for State Bar of Calif., San Francisco, 1978-79; lectr. for Practicing Law Inst., Calif. Continuing Edn. of the Bar, Calif. Judges Assn., seminars on ins. and bus. litigation. Editor-in-chief: Ind. Law Review, 1968-69; contbr. articles to profl. jours. With USNR, 1959-65. Named Outstanding Grad. Province XII, Phi Delta Phi legal fraternity, 1969. Mem. ABA (lectr.), Calif. Bar Assn., Fed. Bar Assn., Orange County Bar Assn., Newport Beach Country Club, Balboa Bay Club (Newport Beach); Masons. Republican. Mem. Christian Ch. Office: Irell & Manella 840 Newport Center Dr Ste 500 Newport Beach CA 92660-6324

JOHNSON, TORRENCE VAINO, astronomer; b. Rockville Centre, N.Y., Dec. 1, 1944; s. Vaino Oliver and Priscilla Welch (Sneed) J.; m. Mary Eleanor Zachman, Mar. 31, 1967; children: Aaron Torrence, Eleanor Nancy. B.S. with honors, Washington U., St. Louis, 1966; Ph.D., Calif. Inst. Tech., 1970. Research assoc. Planetary Astronomy Lab., MIT, 1969-71; resident research assoc. NRC, Jet Propulsion Lab., Pasadena, 1971-73, sr. scientist, mem. tech. staff, 1973-74; group supr. Optical Astronomy Group, 1974-85, project scientist Project Galileo, 1977—, research scientist, 1980-81, sr. research scientist, 1981—; vis. assoc. prof. Calif. Inst. Tech., 1981-83; cons. Jet Propulsion Lab., Pasadena, 1971. NASA trainee Calif. Inst. Tech., 1966-69, Exceptional Svc. medal NASA, 1991; recipient Exceptional Achievement medal NASA, 1980, 81. Fellow Explorers Club, Am. Geophys. Union (pres. planetology sect. 1990-92); mem. AAAS, Am. Astron. Soc. (sec.-treas. div. planetary sci. 1977-80), Internat. Astron. Union, Planetary Soc. (founding mem.), Sigma Xi. Office: 183-501 Jet Propulsion Lab 4800 Oak Grove Dr Pasadena CA 91109-8099

JOHNSON, VERNER CARL, geology educator; b. Chgo., Sept. 14, 1943; s. Rudolph V. and Mabel R. (Reinhardt) J. BA, So. Ill. U., 1967, MS, 1970; PhD, U. Tenn., 1975. Geologist Tenn. Valley Authority, Knoxville, 1971; lectr. Calif. State U., Northridge, 1972-74; project geophysicist Gulf Rsch. and Devel., Houston, 1974-76; staff geoscientist Bendix Field Engring., Grand Junction, Colo., 1977-83; asst. prof. Mesa State Coll., Grand Junction, 1984-88, assoc. prof., 1988—; cons. Walter Fees and Assocs., Grand Junction, 1983. Contbr. articles to profl. jours. Pres. Handicapped Student Scholarship Assn., Grand Junction, 1984—. Mem. Am. Assn. Petroleum Geologists, Geol. Soc. Am., Am. Geophys. Union, Nat. Ground Water Assn., Soc. Exploration Geophysicists, Computer Oriented Geol. Soc., Grand Junction Geol. Soc., Sigma Gamma Epsilon (faculty chpt. adv.). Office: Mesa State Coll Dept Geology Grand Junction CO 81502

JOHNSON, WALTER CURTIS, JR., biophysics educator; b. Princeton, N.J., Feb. 11, 1939; s. Walter Curtis and Caroline (Shirk) J.; m. Susan Margaret Scheller, Aug. 27, 1960; children: Walter C. III, Heather L. BA in Chemistry, Yale U., 1961; PhD in Phys. Chemistry, U. Wash., 1966; postgrad., U. Calif., Berkeley, 1966-68. Grad. rsch. asst. dept. chemistry U. Wash., Seattle, 1961-66; NSF postdoctoral fellow U. Calif., Berkeley, 1966-68; asst. prof. dept. biochemistry and biophysics Oreg. State U., Corvallis, 1968-72, assoc. prof., 1972-78, prof., 1978—; panelist NIH Spl. Panel for Equipment, Washington, 1979, 83, NSF Biol. Instrumentation, Washington, 1980-83; adv. bd. Biopolymers, 1987—; mem. NIH BBCA Study Sect., Washington, 1988-92. Contbr. articles to profl. jours., publs. Recipient grad. fellowship NSF, Seattle, 1963-65, postdoctoral fellowship Berkeley, 1966-68, Rsch. Career Devel. award PHS, Corvallis, 1970-74. Home: 1265 NW Heather Dr Corvallis OR 97330-3010 Office: Dept Biochem/Biophys Oregon State U 2011 Ag-Life Sci Corvallis OR 97331

JOHNSON, WALTER EARL, geophysicist; b. Denver, Dec. 16, 1942; s. Earl S. and Helen F. (Llewellyn) J.; Geophys. Engr., Colo. Sch. Mines, 1966; m. Ramey Kandice Kayes, Aug. 6, 1967; children—Gretchen, Roger, Aniela. Geophysicist, Pan. Am. Petroleum Corp., 1966-73; seismic processing supr. Amoco Prodn. Co., Denver, 1973-74, marine tech. supr., 1974-76, div. processing cons., 1976-79, geophys. supr. No. Thrust Belt, 1979-80; chief geophysicist Husky Oil Co., 1981-82, exploration mgr. Rocky Mountain and Gulf Coast div., 1982-84; geophys. mgr. ANR Prodn. Co., 1985—; pres. Sch. Lateral Ditch Co.; cons. engr. Bd. dirs. Rocky Mountain Residence, nursing home. Registered profl. engr., cert. geologist, Colo. Mem. Denver Geophys. Soc., Soc. Exploration Geophysicists. Republican. Baptist. Office: 600 17th St Ste 800 Denver CO 80202-5401

JOHNSON, WARREN LYLE, educator; b. Mpls., Oct. 14, 1939; s. Paul A. and Irene (Lazorik) Wilson; m. Lana-Jean Cole, June 24, 1967; 1 child, Kenneth Lee. BS, Ea. N.Mex., 1962; MA, Boston U., 1984; postgrad., Air War Coll., 1976; diploma, Def. Systems Coll., 1989; student, Royal Mil. Coll., Swindon, Eng., 1989. Polit. intern State of N.Mex., Santa Fe, 1962-63; commd. 2d lt. USAF, 1964, advanced through grades to major, 1976, ret., 1984; educator State of N.H., Concord, 1984-85; analyst U.S. Govt., Boston, 1985-86, U.S. Govt., U.S. Embassy, Bonn, Germany, 1986-88; reQ officer U.S. Govt., USAF Hqrs. Europe, 1988-90; educator Albuquerque Pub. Sch., 1991—; lead negotiator U.S. Govt., Germany, 1986-90, with spl. projects, Washington, 1990. Editor concept paper. V.p. Shenandoah Neighborhood Assn., Albuquerque, 1991—; mem. Mayors Adv. Bd. ram, Albuquerque, 1991-92. Decorated Cross of Gallantry, Bronze Star, Meritorious Svc; NAS grantee, 1993-94. Mem. Am. Polit. Sci. Soc., Ret. Officers Assn., Vietnam Vets. Am. (state rep. 1986—, state edn. chmn.), DAV, Masons (32d degree). Democrat. Lutheran.

JOHNSON, WAYNE EATON, writer, editor; b. Phoenix, May 9, 1930; s. Roscoe and Marion (Eaton) J.; children: Katherine, Jeffrey. BA, U. Colo., 1952; postgrad., Duke U., 1952-53; postgrad. (KLM polit. reporting fellow 1957), U. Vienna, Austria, 1955-56; MA, UCLA, 1957. Reporter Internat. News Service, Des Moines, 1958, Wheat Ridge (Colo.) Advocate, 1957, Pueblo (Colo.) Chieftain, 1959; reporter Denver Post, 1960, editorial writer, music critic, 1961-65; arts and entertainment editor Seattle Times, 1965-92, drama critic, 1980-92; instr. journalism Colo. Woman's Coll., 1962. Author: Show: A Concert Program for Actor and Orchestra, 1971, America! A Concert of American Images, Words and Music, 1973, From Where the Sun Now Stands: The Indian Experience, 1973; editor, co-publisher: Secrets of Warmth, 1992, Footprints on the Mountains, 1993. Served with CIC AUS, 1953-55, Korea. Home: 11303 Durland Pl NE Seattle WA 98125-5926

JOHNSON, WAYNE HAROLD, librarian, county official; b. El Paso, Tex., May 2, 1942; s. Earl Harold and Cathryn Louise (Greeno) J.; m. Patricia Ann Froedge, June 15, 1973; children: Meredith Jessica (dec.), Alexandra Noëlle Victoria. BS, Utah State U., 1968; MPA, U. Colo., 1970; MLS, U. Okla., 1972. Circulation libr. Utah State U., Logan, 1968, adminstrv. asst. libr., 1969; with rsch. dept. Okla. Mgmt. and Engring. Cons., Norman, 1972; chief adminstrv. svcs. Wyo. State Libr., Cheyenne, 1973-76, chief bus. officer libr. archives and hist. dept., 1976-78, state libr., 1978-89; county grants mgr. Laramie County, Wyo., 1989—. Trustee Bibliog. Ctr. for Rsch., Denver, pres., 1983, 84; mem. Cheyenne dist. Longs Park coun. Boy Scouts Am., 1982-86; active Cheyenne Frontier Days, 1975—; mem. admissions and allocation com. United Way, 1991—; mem. Ho. of Reps., Wyo. Legislature, 1993—. Served with USCG, 1960-64. Mem. Aircraft Owners and Pilots Assn., Cheyenne C. of C. (chmn. transp. com. 1982, 83). Republican. Presbyterian. Club: No. Colo. Yacht. Lodges: Masons, Kiwanis (bd. dirs. 1986, 87). Office: 2101 Oneil Ave Cheyenne WY 82001-3550

JOHNSON, WILLIAM HARRY, international management consultant; b. Ridley Park, Pa., Oct. 1, 1941; s. Harry Brown and Lydia Florence (Round) J.; m. Anna Marie Castellanos, Oct. 19, 1984. BS, Drexel U., Phila., 1963; MBA, Drexel U., 1967. Mgmt. exec. DuPont Co., Wilmington, Del., 1963-69; bus. analysis mgr. Imperial Chem. Ind., Wilmington, 1970-76; mgr. analysis and acquisitions Fluor Daniel Corp., Irvine, Calif., 1976-78; fin. analysis mgr. Alexander Proudfoot, Chgo., 1978-79; exec. v.p., chief fin. officer Sego Internat., Niagara Falls, Ont., Can., 1980-82; exec. v.p., gen. mgr. Sci. Mgmt. Corp., Basking Ridge, N.J., 1982-87; exec. mgr. McDonnell Douglas Corp., Long Beach, Calif., 1987—; bd. dirs. Clariton Recycling Assn., Inc., Clariton, Pa., Madden Assocs., Buffalo Grove, Ill., KABB Inc., El Segundo, Calif., Sego Internat., Penn Bus. Resources, Santa Ana, Calif. Contbr. articles to profl. jours.; author: Explosives Distributors, 1967. Mem. Rep. Nat. Com., Washington, El Segundo Residents Assn. Recipient Presdl. Achievement award, Rep. Nat. Com., 1988, Outstanding Achievement award, Sego Internat., 1981. Mem. Inst. Indsl. Engrs., Am. Mgmt. Assn., Nat. Productivity Assn. of Can. (dir. 1980-85), Nat. Assn. Accts., Nat. Petroleum Refinery Assn., Am. Mktg. Assn., Internat. Productivity Orgn., Drexel U. Alumni Assn. (bd. dirs.), Highlander Clan, Lions (Kowloon, Hong Kong). Republican. Presbyterian. Home: 807 Hillcrest St El Segundo CA 90245-2025 Office: McDonnell Douglas 3855 N Lakewood Blvd Long Beach CA 90846-0001

JOHNSON, WILLIAM HUGH, JR., hospital administrator; b. N.Y.C., Oct. 29, 1935; s. William H. and Florence P. (Seinsoth) J.; m. Gloria C. Stube., Jan. 23, 1960; children: Karen A., William H. III. B.A., Hofstra U., 1957; M.Ed., U. Hawaii, 1969. Commd. 2d lt. U.S. Army, 1957, advanced through grades to lt. col., 1972, health adminstr., world wide, 1957-77, health adminstr., world wide, ret., 1977; chief exec. officer U. N. Mex. Hosp., Albuquerque, 1977—; asst. prof. U.S. Mil. Acad., West Point, N.Y., 1962-65; mem. clin. faculty U. Minn., Mpls., 1980-83; preceptor Ariz. State U., Tempe, 1982-83; pres. Albuquerque Area Hosp. Council, 1980; bd. dirs. Bank Am. of N.Mex. Vice pres. Vis Nurse Service, Albuquerque, 1979; mem. exec. bd., Albuquerque Com. on Devel.; pres. Magnifico Arts Fiesta; bd. dirs. Good Will N.Mex. Decorated Army Commendation Medal with 2 oak leaf clusters, Order of Merit (Rep. of Vietnam), Legion of Merit. Mem. Am. Hosp. Assn. (governing bd. met. hosp. sect. 1982-86, chmn. com. AIDS, mem. regional policy bd. 1982-86, 88—), Am. Coll. Hosp. Adminstrs., Coun. Tchg. Hosps. (bd. dirs.), N.Mex. Hosp. Assn. (bd. dirs. 1983, chmn.), Nat. Assn. Pub. Hosps., Greater Albuquerque C. of C. (bd. dirs., econ. planning coun.), N.Mex. Assn. Commerce and Industry (treas.), Albuquerque Conv. and Visitors Bur. (bd. dirs.). Roman Catholic. Home: 7920 Sartan Way NE Albuquerque NM 87109-3128 Office: U NMex Hosp Office of Chief Exec Officer 2211 Lomas Blvd NE Albuquerque NM 87106-2745

JOHNSON, WILLIAM LEWIS, materials science educator; b. Bowling Green, Ohio, July 26, 1948; s. Melvin Carl and Martha Maxine (Roller) J.; m. Rachel Marie Newman, Jan. 21, 1984. B.A., Hamilton Coll., 1970; Ph.D., Calif. Inst. Tech., 1974. Staff IBM Watson Research Ctr., Yorktown Heights, N.Y., 1975-77; asst. prof. materials sci. Calif. Inst. Tech., Pasadena, 1977-80, assoc. prof., 1980-84, prof., 1984—; R.F. Mettler Prof. materials sci., 1989— ; cons. Lawrence Livermore Lab., 1979—, Dresser Industries, Irvine, Calif., 1978—, Gen. Motors Research, Warren, Mich., 1983—, Hughes Research Ctr., Malibu, Calif., 1981—. Co-author: Glassy Metals I, 1981; Properties of Amorphous Metals, 1983; Physical Metallurgy, 1983, ASM Metals Handbook-Metallic Glasses, 1990. U.S. Steel fellow, 1971; Alexander von Humboldt fellow, 1988; recipient Southworth Physics prize Hamilton Coll., 1970. Mem. Metals Soc. of AIME, Am. Phys. Soc., AAAS, Materials Rsch. Soc., Phi Beta Kappa, Sigma Xi. Lutheran. Home: 3546 Mountain View Ave Pasadena CA 91107-4616 Office: Calif Inst of Tech Div Engring & Applied Scis Mail Code 138 78 Pasadena CA 91125

JOHNSON, WILLIAM POTTER, newspaper publisher; b. Peoria, Ill., May 4, 1935; s. William Zweigle and Helen Marr (Potter) J.; m. Pauline Ruth Rowe, May 18, 1968; children: Darragh Elizabeth, William Potter. AB, U. Mich., 1957. Gen. mgr. Bureau County Rep., Inc., Princeton, Ill., 1961-72; pres. Johnson Newspapers, Inc., Sebastopol, Calif., 1972-75, Evergreen, Colo., 1974-86, Canyon Commons Investment, Evergreen, 1974—; pres., chmn. bd. dirs. Johnson Media, Inc., Winter Park, Colo., 1987—. Author: How the Michigan Betas Built a $1,000,000 Chapter House in the '80s. Alt. del. Rep. Nat. Conv., 1968. Lt. USNR, 1958-61. Mem. Colo. Press Assn., Nat. Newspaper Assn., Suburban Newspapers Am., Oro Valley Country Club, El Conquistador Country Club, Beta Theta Pi. Roman Catholic. Home: 445 W Rapa Pl Tucson AZ 85737-9601 Office: PO Box 409 Winter Park CO 80482-0409

JOHNSTON, CAMERON I., accountant; b. Seattle, Aug. 8, 1955; s. George Donald and Kathryn L. (Flynn) J. BS in Acctg., Ctrl. Wash. U., 1987, BS in Bus. Adminstrn., 1991. CPA. Acct. Aurora Antique Pavilion, Edmonds, Wash., 1989-93; software installation specialist Convergent Dealership Systems, Hunt Valley, Md., 1988-89; ptnr. Mad Hatter Antiques, Kent, Wash., 1992—; sec., treas. Panorealm, Inc., Woodinville, Wash., 1992—. Mem. Wash. Soc. of CPAs, Ctrl. Wash. U. Alumni Assn. Home: 3607 Wetmore Everett WA 98201 Office: Aurora Antique Pavilion Ste 201 24111 Hwy 99 Edmonds WA 98026

JOHNSTON, CAROL STRICKLAND, nutrition educator, dietitian; b. Evanston, Ill., Apr. 19, 1957; d. Griffin Junior and Genelle (Alexander) Strickland; m. Dale Edward Johnston, Oct. 18, 1980 (div. 1984); m. Raymond A. Nippress, June 2, 1988; children: Jesse James, Jacob Russell. BS, U. Mich., 1979; MA, U. Tex., 1983, PhD, 1986. Registered dietitian. Statis. clk. Tex. Dept. Health, Austin, 1979-80; instr. Austin Community Coll., 1983-86; assoc. prof. nutrition Ariz. State U., Tempe, 1986—; speaker Ariz. State U. Speakers Bur., 1986—. Contbr. articles to profl. jours. Fellow Am. Coll. Nutrition; mem. Am. Inst. Nutrition. Democrat. Methodist. Office: Ariz State U Dept Family Resources Tempe AZ 85287

JOHNSTON, CHARLES LELAND, III, investment advisor, vintner, winery owner; b. L.A., Oct. 10, 1946; s. Charles Leland and Evelyn (Apel) J.; m. Judith Sumner Pratt, June 20, 1969 (div. Dec. 20, 1972); 1 child, Sarah Mare; m. Lisa Cumilla Peacock, June 12, 1982; 1 child, Tanya Simone. AA, N. Mex. Mil. Inst., 1966; BA, U. Ariz., 1969; B in Internat. Mgmt., Am. Grad. Sch. of Internat. Bus. Mgmt., 1970; student, U. Mo., U. Calif., Riverside, UCLA. Export mgr. Sunkist Growers Inc., Ontario, Calif., 1970-80; v.p. mktg. and sales Continental Flavors, Brea, Calif., 1980-82; v.p. investments Dean Witter Reynolds, Inc., Napa, Calif., 1982—; co-owner Good N Airy Angel, Calistoga, Calif., 1987—; owner Helena View Johnston Winery, Calistoga, Calif., 1992—; cons. Internat. Beverage Industry, Napa, 1982-90. Mem. Am. Enology Assn., Calif. Cert. Organic Farmers Assn., Calif. Farm Bur., Napa Valley Mus. Assn., Napa Landmarks Assn., St. Helena Wine Libr. Assn., Calistoga C. of C., Napa Valley Grape Growers Assn., Napa Valley Opera House (past pres., bd. dirs.) 1988—, Com. on Foreign Rels. (San Francisco chpt.). Republican. Methodist. Home: PO Box 658 Napa CA 94559 Office: Dean Witter Reynolds 1004 Seminary St PO Box 3440 Napa CA 94558

JOHNSTON, CRAIG ALAN, pharmacologist, educator; b. Butte, Mont., May 25, 1955; s. Clayton Alan and Elisabeth Jean (Nutting) J.; m. Sharon Rae Estabrook, Aug. 7, 1976; children: Hope Alicia, Christopher Alan. BS in Chemistry, MIT, 1977; PhD in Phrmacology/Toxicology, Mich. State U., 1982, PhD in Neuroscis., 1982. Staff fellow Lab. Reproductive and Developmental Toxicology Reproductive Neuroendocrinology Sect., NIEHS, Research Triangle Park, N.C., 1983-85; sr. staff fellow Reproductive Neuroendocrinology Sect. Lab. Molecular and Integrative Neurosci., NIEHS, 1985-87; asst. prof. Wash. State U., Pullman, 1987-90; asst. prof. pharmacology Sch. Pharmacy & Allied Health Scis. U. Mont., Missoula, 1990—; lectr. in field; regional ednl. counselor for admissions for MIT; mem. biotech. roundtable Missoula Econ. Devel. Corp.; legal cons., testimony expert Tech. Advisors Svc. for Attys. High sch. Sunday sch. tchr., head ushering com., mem. nurture com., elder First Presbyn. Ch. of Missoula. Recipient numerous awards and scholarships; grantee NIMH. Mem. AAAS, Am. Assn. Colls. Pharmacy, Am. Diabetes Assn., Brit. Brain Rsch. Assn. (hon.), European Brain and Behavior Soc. (hon.), Internat. Soc. Neuroendocrinology, Internat. Brain Rsch. Orgn., N.Y. Acad. Sci., Soc. Neurosci., Endocrine Soc., World Fedn. Neuroscientists, Soc. for Exptl. Biology and Medicine, Mont. Acad. Sci. (sect. v.p.), Sigma Xi (v.p.), Kappa Psi (grand coun. dep., chmn. nat. scholarship com.), Rho Chi. Republican. Presbyterian. Home: 1721 Humble Rd Missoula MT 59801-5089 Office: Sch Pharmacy Allied Health Scis U Mont Missoula MT 59812-1075

JOHNSTON, DICK, Canadian provincial government minister. Mem. Province of Alta. Legislative Assembly from Lethbridge-East; formerly minister of advanced edn., now provincial treas. Office: Provincial Treas, 224 Legislature Bldg, Edmonton, AB Canada T5K 2B6

JOHNSTON, GWINAVERE ADAMS, public relations consultant; b. Casper, Wyo., Jan. 6, 1943; d. Donald Milton Adams and Gwinavere Marie (Newell) Quillen; m. H.R. Johnston, Sept. 26, 1963 (div. 1973); children: Gwinavere G., Gabrielle Suzanne; m. Donald Charles Cannalte, Apr. 4, 1981. BS in Journalism, U. Wyo., 1966; postgrad., Denver U., 1968-69. Editor, reporter Laramie (Wyo.) Daily Boomerang, 1965-66; account exec. William Kostka Assocs., Denver, 1966-71, v.p., 1969-71; exec. v.p. Slottow, McKinlay & Johnston, Denver, 1971-74; pres. The Johnston Group, Denver, 1974-92; chair, CEO The Johnston-Wells Group, Denver, 1992—; adj. faculty U. Colo. Sch. Journalism, 1988-90. Bd. dirs. Leadership Denver Assn., 1975-77, 83-86, Mile High United Way, 1989—, Colo. Jud. Inst., 1991—. Mem. Pub. Rels. Soc. Am. (pres. Colo. chpt. 1978-79, bd. dirs. 1975-80, 83-86, nat. exec. com. Counselor's Acad. 1988-93, profl. award, Disting. Svc. award 1992), Colo. Women's Forum, Rocky Mountain Pub. Rels. Group (founder), Denver Athletic Club, Denver Press Club. Republican. Home: 717 Monaco Pky Denver CO 80220-6040 Office: The Johnston-Wells Group 1512 Larimer St Ste 720 Denver CO 80202-1622

JOHNSTON, LOGAN TRUAX, III, lawyer; b. New Haven, Dec. 9, 1947; s. Logan Truax Jr. and Elizabeth (Josey) J.; m. Paula Ann Parker, Aug. 26, 1972; children: Charlotte Hathaway, Logan Truax IV, Owen Conrad. BA, Yale U., 1969; JD, Harvard U., 1973. Bar: Ill. 1973, Ariz. 1984, U.S. Ct. Appeals (2d cir.) 1982, U.S. Ct. Appeals (7th cir.) 1973, U.S. Ct. Appeals (9th cir.) 1986, U.S. Ct. Appeals (fed. cir.) 1990, U.S. Supreme Ct. 1991. Assoc. Winston & Strawn, Chgo., 1973-79, ptnr., 1979-83; ptnr. Winston & Strawn, Phoenix, 1983-89; mng. ptnr. Johnston Maynard Grant & Parker, Phoenix, 1989—; spl. asst. state's atty. Du Page County, Ill., Wheaton, 1976-77; cons. Community Legal Svcs., Phoenix, 1984—. Served with U.S. Army N.G., 1970-76. Mem. ABA, Maricopa County Bar Found., Maricopa County Bar Assn., Ariz. Bar Found., Ariz. State Bar Assn., Plaza Club. Presbyterian. Office: Johnston Maynard Grant & Parker 3200 N Central Ave Phoenix AZ 85012-2417

JOHNSTON, MARJORIE DIANE, computer programming executive, analyst; b. Fullerton, Calif., Sept. 19, 1943; d. Earl Lawrence Whipple and Ruth Juanita (Long) Purcell; children: Stephen, Deborah. Grad computer programming LaSalle U., Chgo., 1973. Computer programmer Los Alamos (N.Mex.) Nat. Lab., 1972-81, sr. analyst, programmer, cons., 1989—; contract programmer Computer Assistance, Inc., Tulsa, 1981-82; profl. svcs. analyst Control Data Corp., Denver, 1982-84, Los Alamos, 1984-89. Mem. Rebekah, Order Eastern Star (past matron). Home: 950 Santa Clara Pl Los Alamos NM 87544-3209

JOHNSTON, PATRICIA KATHLEEN, college dean; b. Seattle, May 21, 1936; d. Robert Leonard and Dorothy Evelyn (Crow) Pearson; m. Edward Paul Johnston, Sept. 3, 1955; children: Linda Suzanne Johnston Murosako, Martin Edward. BA, Walla Walla Coll., 1958; MPH, Loma Linda U., 1978; MS, U. Wash., 1979; DrPH, UCLA, 1987. Registered dietitian. Instr. Loma Linda (Calif.) U., 1979-81, asst. prof., 1981-88, assoc. prof., 1988—, dir. DrPH program, 1987-90, chmn. nutrition dept., 1990—, assoc. dean Sch. Pub. Health, 1990—; chmn. program 2d Internat. Congress on Vegetarian Nutrition, Washington, 1992, editor proc.; speaker in field. Contbr. articles to profl. jours.; editor jour. Vibrant Life, 1988—. Recipient Danforth Found. award Auburn Acad., 1953, Honored Student award L.A. Nutrition Coun., 1985, G. Emmerson award UCLA, 1985. Mem. APHA, Am. Dietetic Assn., Am. Soc. Bone and Mineral Rsch., Calif. Nutrition Coun., Soc. Nutrition Edn., Assn. Grad. Faculties in Pub. Health Nutrition, Omicron Nu, Delta Omega (nat. merit award 1981). Seventh Day Adventist. Office: Loma Linda U Sch Pub Health Loma Linda CA 92350

JOHNSTON, ROBERT KENT, provost, seminary dean, educator; b. Pasadena, Calif., June 9, 1945; s. Roy Gunnar and Naomi Mae (Harmon) J.; m. Catherine M. Barsotti; children: Elizabeth Amy, Margaret Nell. A.B., Stanford U., 1967; B.D., Fuller Theol. Sem., Pasadena, 1970; postgrad., North Pk. Theol. Sem., Chgo., 1970-71; Ph.D., Duke U., 1974. Ordained to ministry Evang. Covenant Ch., 1975. Youth pastor Pasadena, 1967-69; asst. min. Edgebrook Covenant Ch., Chgo., 1970-71; asst. prof. Western Ky. U., Bowling Green, 1974-78, assoc. prof., 1978-82; dean, assoc. prof. theology North Pk. Theol. Sem., Chgo., 1982-85, dean, prof. theology, 1985-93; provost North Pk. Coll. and Theol. Sem., Chgo., 1988-93; provost, prof. theology and culture Fuller Theol. Sem., Pasadena, Calif., 1993—; vis. prof. New Coll., Berkeley, Calif., 1980-81; mem. bd. of the ministry, pastoral rels. commn., exec. com. of ministerium Evang. Covenant Ch., 1982-93. Author: Evangelicals at an Impasse, 1979, Psalms for God's People, 1980, The Christian at Play, 1983; editor: The Use of the Bible in Theology: Evangelical Options, 1985; co-editor: The Variety of American Evangelicalism, 1991, Studies in Old Testament Theology, 1992, Servant Leadership, Vols. 1-2, 1993. Mem. North Suburban Spl. Edn. Dist. Governing Bd., 1987-89; mem. sch. bd. Dist. 39, Wilmette, Ill., 1987-91; bd. dirs. Centro de Estudios Teologicos del Pacto Evangelico, L.A., 1988-93. James B. Duke fellow Duke U., 1971-74. Mem. Am. Acad. Religion (co-chair evang. theology group 1986-90), Am. Theol. Soc. (east coast and midwest sects.), Assn. Theol. Schs. in U.S. and Can. (commn. on accrediting 1988-93), Bonhoeffer Soc., Phi Beta Kappa. Democrat. Office: Fuller Theol Sem 135 N Oakland Ave Pasadena CA 91182

JOHNSTON, ROGER GLENN, chemist, biotechnology and laser scientist; b. Lincoln, Nebr., Feb. 15, 1954; s. Glenn Hanford and Janet Frances (Hutchinson) J. BA, Carleton Coll., 1977; MS, PhD, U. Colo., 1983. Postdoctoral fellow life scis. div. Los Alamos (N.Mex.) Nat. Lab., 1984-85, staff mem., 1985-90, staff mem. chem. and laser sci. div., 1990—; pvt. biotechnology cons., 1990—. Patentee in field; contbr. articles to profl. jours. Recipient R & D 100 award for laser interferometry, 1992, Best of What's New award for Biotech., Popular Sci., 1992, Excellence in Enterprise award for tech. transfer, 1992. Mem. Am. Phys. Soc. (life), U.S. Biometrics Consortium. Home: 2462 36th St Los Alamos NM 87544-1547 Office: Los Alamos Nat Lab CLS-2 MS J565 Los Alamos NM 87545

JOHNSTON, ROSS W., engineering executive; b. Phila., Pa., May 7, 1947; s. Ross Dudley and Virginia Mary (Lucas) J.; m. Barbara E. Greso, Aug. 15, 1970; 1 child, Jay R. BS in Mech. Engring., U. Pitts., 1969. Sr. engr. Univac, Blue Bell, Pa., 1970-74; mgr. continuation engring. Control Data, Valley Forge, Pa., 1974-76, product devel. mgr., 1976-83; unit mgr. RCA, Camden, N.J., 1983-86; dir. advanced devel. Seagate Tech., Scotts Valley, Calif., 1986-88; v.p. engring., founder R-Byte Inc., San Jose, Calif., 1988-92; v.p. engring. Advanced Computer Link Inc., San Jose, Calif., 1992—; mem. Am. Nat. Standards Com. X3B5. Patentee in field. Republican. Lutheran. Home: 1770 Jarvis Rd Santa Cruz CA 95065-9704 Office: ACL Inc R-Byte Inc 2674 N First St San Jose CA 95134

JOHNSTON, VIRGINIA EVELYN, editor; b. Spokane, Wash., Apr. 26, 1933; d. Edwin and Emma Lucile (Munroe) Rowe; student Portland Community Coll., 1964, Portland State U., 1966, 78-79; m. Alan Paul Beckley, Dec. 26, 1974; children—Chris, Denise, Rex. Proofreader, The Oregonian, Portland, 1960-62, teletypesetter operator, 1962-66, operator Photon 200, 1966-68, copy editor, asst. women's editor, 1968-80; spl. sects. editor (UPDATE), 1981-83, 88—; editor FOODday, 1982—; pres. Matrix Assos., Inc., Portland, 1975—, chmn. bd., 1979—; cons. Dem. Party Oreg., 1969, Portland Sch. Dist. No. 1, 1978. Mem. Eating and Drinking Soc. Oreg. (past pres.), We. Culinary Inst. (mem. adv. bd.), Portland Culinary Alliance (mem. adv. bd.), Internat. Food Media Conf. (mem. adv. bd.). Democrat. Editor Principles of Computer Systems for Newspaper Mgmt., 1975-76. Home: 4140 NE 137th Ave Portland OR 97230-2624 Office: 1320 SW Broadway Portland OR 97201

JOHNSTON, WALT, artist; b. Washington, Mar. 4, 1932; s. Laurence P. and Ruth Susanna (Streightiff) J.; m. Betty Reynolds (div. 1967); children: Susan, Alison; m. Susan Marean Springer, Aug. 7, 1971; 1 child, Nancy Marean. Student, Art Inst. Chgo., U. Chgo.; studied art with Eliot O'Hara. Artist in tempera and watercolor; exhbns. include Carnegie Inst., Pitts., 1948, Butler Inst., Youngstown, Ohio, 1967, N.Mex. State Fair Profl. Fine Art Exhibit, 1968, 76, 88, Nat. Acad. Design, N.Y.C., 1970, 71, Soc. Graphic Artists-Kennedy Galleries, N.Y.C., 1972, Audubon Artists N.Y., 1984, Knickerbocker Artists N.Y., 1984, Boston Printmakers, 1984, The Classic Invitational, Albuquerque, 1989. Address: 9404 Dona Marguerita Albuquerque NM 87111

JOHNSTON, WALTER WESLEY, computer information disciplines analyst; b. Chgo., May 20, 1946; s. Walter George and Elsie Marie (Subert) J. BS in Maths., No. Ill. U., 1967; postgrad., U. Ill., 1967-68; MA in Maths., Sangamon State U., 1974, MA in History, 1981. With State of Ill., 1969-85, mgr. data procesing for health services Dept. Pub. Health, 1977-84, mgr. Info. Ctr., 1984-85; data base analyst Chevron, Inc., San Ramon, Calif., 1985-93, info. disciplines analyst, 1993—; geneal. researcher, lectr., 1975-85. Contbr. articles to profl. jours.; editor and pub. Butson Family Newsletter, 1979-87. Mem. Ill. Hist. Soc. (life), Ill. Geneal. Soc. (life, long-range planning com. 1980-84, chmn. honors and awards com. 1983-84, chmn. computer com. 1983-84), Chgo. Hist. Soc. (life), Chgo. Geneal. Soc. (life), Sangamon County Geneal. Soc. (life, 2d v.p. 1976, trustee 1978-80), Ont. Hist. Soc. (life), Ont. Geneal. Soc. (life), Am. Assn. Artificial Intelligence, Sangamon County Hist. Soc. (life), Brown County (Minn.) Hist. Soc. (life), Royal Inst. Cornwall (life), Devon and Cornwall Record Soc., Internat. Neural Network Soc., Inst. Noetic Scis.

JOHNSTON, CLINT, electric power industry executive. Pres. Bechtel Nat. Inc., San Francisco. Office: Bechtel Nat Inc 50 Beale St Box 3965 San Francisco CA 94119

JOHNSTONE, KENNETH ERNEST, electronics and business consultant; b. L.A., Sept. 13, 1929; s. John Ernest and Lorena Hayes (Patterson) J.; m. Edna Mae Iverson, Aug. 20, 1950; children: Bruce, Kent, Anita, Christian, Daniel, Carol, Karen. BSEE, U. Wash., 1966. Registered profl. engr., Wash. Electronics technician The Boeing Co., Seattle, 1955-66, engr., 1966-75; engring. mgr. Boeing Aerosystems Internat., Seattle, 1975-85; ptnr. North Creek Engring., Lynnwood, Wash., 1985-87; pres. SensorLink Corp., Lynnwood, 1987-90; electronics and bus. cons. Bellingham, Wash., 1991—; internat. lectr. in field. Mem. IEEE (sr.), Tau Beta Pi. Home and Office: 3765 E Smith Rd Bellingham WA 98226-9504

JOHNSTONE, SALLY MAC, educational association administrator, psychology educator; b. Macon, Ga., Dec. 8, 1949; d. Ralph E. and Maxine A. J.; m. Stephen R. Tilson, 1977; 1 child, Emma. BS, Va. Poly. Inst., 1974, MS, 1976; PhD, U. N.C., 1982. Lectr. European div. U. Md., Heidelberg, Fed. Republic of Germany, 1982-84; instr. psychology U. Md., College Park, 1984-89, asst. dean, 1984-86, dir. Ctr. for Instructional Telecom., 1986-89; dir. Western Coop. for Ednl. Telecom., Boulder, Colo., 1989—; cons. Grand Valley State U., Grand Rapids, Mich., 1989, Can. Distance Learning Devel. Centre, Edmonton, Alta., Can., 1989, Program for Educating Nurses via Satellite Links, Charleston, W.Va., 1986-89, Fairleigh Dickinson U., Teaneck, N.J., 1990, Northwest Legis. Leadership Forum, Seattle, 1990, Pacific Northwest Econ. Region, Whistler, B.C., 1991, Calif. State U. System, 1993; invited panelist U.S. Dept. Edn., Washington, 1990—, Aspen Inst., Washington, 1990, Pacific Northwest Econ. Region, 1991-92; presenter Pacific Rim Pub. U. Pres. Conf. Asia Found., Bangkok, Thailand, 1990, workshops Pacific Telecom Coun., Honolulu, 1991, Nat. U. Continuing Edn. Assn., Miami, Fla.; keynote speaker Mountain States Community Coll. Assn., Farmington, N.Mex., 1991; speaker EDUCOM, San Diego, 1991, edn. commn. States' Legislator's Workshop, Cin., 1992, State Higher Edn. Exec. Officer's Meeting, Jackson, Wyo., 1992, Calif. State U. Project DELTA Workshop, Sacramento, 1993, higher edn. conf. NEA, New Orleans, 1993, meeting Nat. Assn. State Univs. & Land Grant Colls. Distance Edn. & Telecomm. Working Group; witness U.S. Senate Subcom. Edn., Humanities and Arts, Washington, 1991; leader faculty devel. workshop Athabasca U., Alta., Can., 1992; study advisor Corp. Pub. Broadcasting, 1993. Mem. Ednl. Access Com., Prince George's County, Md., 1986-89; sci. fair judge U. Hills. Elem. Sch., Md., 1986-89. Annenberg/CPB Project grantee, 1988, 91-93, U.S. Dept. Edn. grantee, 1991; recipient Disting. Rsch. award Nat. U. Continuing Edn. Assn., 1989. Mem. Am. Psychology Assn., Internat. Teleconferencing Assn.

JOHNSTONE, WILLIAM MERVYN, small business owner, writer; b. Orilla, Ont., Can., Nov. 1, 1946; m. Susan Margaret Chestnut; children: Melanie Beth, Mervyn Scott. Student, U. Waterloo, Ont., Can., 1970-72. Tchr., coord. demonstrations IBM Can. Ltd., Toronto, Ont., Can., 1967-70; computer programmer Dominion Life Assurance, Waterloo, 1973-75; freelance novelist Ibiza, Spain, 1975-77; communications mgr. Comshare Ltd., Toronto, 1978-81; owner, gen. mgr. Spark Communications Ltd., Victoria, B.C., Can., 1982—; founding ptnr. Beacon Hill Comm. Group, Inc., 1991—. Contbr. articles to nat. mags.; editor newsletters and manuals. Mem. Periodical Writers Assn. Can. (regional bd. dirs. B.C. chpt. 1986-87), Amnesty Internat. (C.Am. network coord. Victoria chpt. 1984—).

JOINER, DENNIS ASHLEY, personnel management consultant; b. Reno, Mar. 20, 1953; s. Virgil Lafayette and Rebecca Elizabeth (Moon) J.; m. Sharon Corinne Dunn, Jan. 26, 1980; 1 child, Kimberly Ann. BA in Psychology, Calif. State U., Sacramento, 1975, MS in Counseling, 1978. Pers. analyst Calif. State Pers. Bd., Sacramento, 1977-80; cons., owner Dennis A. Joiner & Assocs., Fair Oaks, Calif., 1980—. Contbr. numerous articles to profl. jours. Mem. Internat. Pers. Mgmt. Assn. Assessment Coun. (dir. 1987-92, pres. 1990-91),Pers. Testing Coun. No. Calif. (bd. dirs. 1988, 89, pres. 1987). Home and Office: Dennis A Joiner & Assocs 4975 Daru Way Fair Oaks CA 95628

JOKLIK, GÜNTHER FRANZ, mining company executive; b. Vienna, Austria, May 30, 1928; came to U.S., 1953; s. Karl Friedrich and Helene (Giessl) J.; m. Pamela Mary Fenton, Dec. 22, 1962; children: Carl Duncan, Katherine Pamela, Paul Richard. B.Sc. with 1st class honors, U. Sydney, Australia, 1949; 1989-93; Ph.D., U. Sydney, Australia, 1953. Exploration geologist Kennecott Corp., N.Y.C., 1954-62, v.p., 1974-79; pres. Kennecott Corp., Salt Lake City, 1980-89, pres., chief exec. officer, 1989—; exploration mgr. Australia div. AMAX, Inc., Greenwich, Conn., 1963-71, v.p., 1972-73; sr. v.p. metals and mining Standard Oil Co. (parent), Cleve., 1982-89; dir. First Security Corp., Salt Lake City; mem. Nat. Strategic Materials Adv. Com., 1984-89. Contbr. articles to profl. jours. Fulbright scholar Columbia U., 1953-54. Mem. AIME, Internat. Copper Assn. (bd. dirs. 1982—), Copper Devel. Assn. (chmn. 1985-87), Nat. Acad. Engring., Australasian Inst. Mining and Metallurgy, Am. Mining Congress (bd. dirs. 1985—). Clubs: Alta (Salt Lake City); Tokeneke (Darien, Conn.). Office: Eagle Gate Twr Ste 700 60 East South Temple Salt Lake City UT 84111

JOLLEY, DONAL CLARK, artist; b. Zion Nat. Pk., UT, Oct. 20, 1933; s. Donal Jones and Nora (Crawford) J.; m. Doris Kay Dean, May 31, 1960 (div. 1969); m. Virginia E. Harrison, Nov. 14, 1970; children: Karen E., Donal Dean, Keith P. BS, Brigham Young U., Provo, UT, 1959. Illustrator Space Tech. Lab., Redondo Beach, Calif., 1960-61; illus. The Aerospace Corp., El Segundo, Calif., 1961-71; pvt. practice Rimforest, Calif., 1971—; tchr. San Bernardino Valley Coll., 1972-76. Prin. works Canyonland Memories, 1980, Jolley, 1989. Decorated Army Commendation Medal, U.S. Army, 1957; recipient Nat. Watercolor Soc. members cash award, Palm Springs, Calif., 1980, gold medal WC AICA, 1990, bronze medal, 1992. Mem. Watercolor West, Nat. Watercolor Soc. (1st v.p.), Am. Indian and Cowboy Artists. Home: 26375 Apache Trl Rimforest CA 92378-9999 Office: Studio/Gallery 26375 Apache Trl Rimforest CA 92378-9999

JOLLY, MICHAEL JOHN, college administrator; b. Oct. 24, 1960; s. John T. and Lois E. (Sumpter) J. BS, Adams State Coll., 1984, MA, 1985. Dir. housing Adams State Coll., Alamosa, Colo.; student counselor, lab. instr. Adams State Coll. Mem. Am. Coll. Pers. Assn., Colo. Assn. Counseling Devel., Am. Mental Health Counseling Assn., Colo. Coll. Student Devel. Assn., Phi Delta Kappa. Office: Adams State Coll Office of Housing # 1 Petteys Hall Alamosa CO 81102

JONAS, JOAN, artist; b. N.Y., 1936. B.A. in Art History, Mt. Holyoke Coll., 1958; postgrad. Sch. of Mus. Fine Arts, 1958-61; M.F.A., Columbia U., 1965. Outdoor exhbns. include: Jones Beach Piece, Jones Beach State Park, Nassau County, N.Y., 1970, Delay, Delay, Tiber River, Rome, 1972; exhbns. include: Oad Lau, St. Peter's Ch., N.Y., 1968, Organic Honey's Vertical Roll, Leo Castelli Gallery, N.Y., 1973, Sonnabend Gallery, N.Y., 1979, Univ. Art Mus., U. Calif.-Berkeley, 1980, Anthology Film Archives, N.Y., 1982; filmography include: Wind, 1968; Paul Revere, 1971; Veil, 1971; Songdelay, 1973; selected videography incudes: Left Side Right Side, 1972; Barking, 1973; Glass Puzzle, 1974; Good Night Good Morning, 1976; I Want to Live in the Country (and Other Romances), 1977-78. Home: 112 Mercer St New York NY 10012

JONCKOWSKI, LYNN (JONNIE), bull rider; b. Fargo, N.D., July 22, 1954. Appeared on David Letterman's Late Night; featured on CBS TV's Street Stories, 48 Hours, Hard Copy, George Michael's Sports Machine, Jane Pauley, Linda Ellerbe, Charlie Rose, Bob Eubanks. Vol. spokesperson Mont. Mental Health Assn. and Light Hearth Group Home; supporter, spokesperson Zoo Mont.; motivational speaker for youth and high sch. groups. Qualified pentathlon U.S. Olympic Trials, 1976; named Woman of the '80s, CNN; inductee Nat. Cowgirl Hall of Fame and Western Heritage Ctr., 1991. Mem. Profl. Womens Rodeo Assn. (World Bull Riding Champion 1986, 88). Home: PO Box 20797 Billings MT 59104

JONES, ARTHUR FRANCIS, surgeon; b. Utica, N.Y., May 13, 1946; s. Arthur Hywel and Ellen Joanna (Burke) J.; m. Patricia Ann Barton, Aug. 24, 1968 (div. Apr. 1981); children: David A., Eric W.; m. Wanda Lea Stewart, June 4, 1983; 1 child, Christopher. AB, Hamilton Coll., 1967; MD cum laude, Yale U., 1971. Diplomate Am. Bd. Surgery. Intern U. Colo., Denver, 1971-72, resident in surgery, 1972-73, 75-79; ptnr., surgeon Foothills Surg. Assocs., Wheat Ridge, Colo., 1979—; chmn. dept. surgery Luth. Med. Ctr., Wheat Ridge, 1989-90. Maj. U.S. Army, 1973-75. Fellow ACS (pres. Colo. chpt. 1991); mem. Denver Acad. Surgery, Southwestern Surg. Soc., Alpha Omega Alpha. Unitarian. Office: Foothills Surg Assocs 8550 W 38th Ste 308 Wheat Ridge CO 80033

JONES, BOB GORDON, bishop; b. Paragould, Ark., Aug. 22, 1932; s. F.H. and Helen Truman (Ellis) J.; m. Judith Munroe, Feb. 22, 1963; children: Robert Gordon, Timothy Andrew. B.B.A., U. Miss., 1956; M.Div., Episcopal Sem. S.W., 1959, D.D. hon., 1978. Asst. to dean Trinity Cathedral, Little Rock, 1959-62; vicar St. George-in-Arctic, Kotzebue, Alaska, 1962-67; rector St. Christopher's Ch., Anchorage, 1967-77; bishop Episcopal Diocese Wyo., Laramie, 1977—; chmn. bd. Cathedral Home Children, Laramie, 1977—; mem. exec. com. Provence N.W., Helena, Mont., 1980-83, Coalition 14, Phoenix, 1982-84. Pres. Arctic Circle C. of C., Kotzebue, 1966; mem. exec. com. Alaska C. of C., Juneau, 1967; chmn. allocations com. United Way, Anchorage, 1973-75; pres. United Way Anchorage, 1975-76. Served with USN, 1950-55, Korea. Republican. Lodges: Lions; Elks. Home: 104 W 4th St Box 1007 Laramie WY 82070-5005 Office: Episcopal Diocese of Wyo 104 S 4th St Box 1007 Laramie WY 82070*

JONES, CHARLES IRVING, bishop; b. El Paso, Tex., Sept. 13, 1943; s. Charles I. Jr. and Helen A. (Heyward) J.; m. Ashby MacArthur, June 18, 1966; children: Charles I. IV, Courtney M., Frederic M., Keith A. BS, The Citadel, 1965; MBA, U. N.C., 1966; MDiv, U. of the South, 1977, DD, 1989. CPA. Pub. acctg. D.E. Gatewood and Co., Winston-Salem, N.C., 1966-72; dir. devel. Chatham (Va.) Hall, 1972-74; instr. acctg. U. of the South, Sewanee, Tenn., 1974-77; coll. chaplain Western Ky. U., Bowling Green, 1977-81; vicar Trinity Episcopal Ch., Russelville, Ky., 1977-85; archdeacon Diocese of Ky., Louisville, 1981-86; bishop Episcopal Diocese of Mont., Helena, 1986—; bd. dirs. New Directions Ministries, Inc., N.Y.C.; mem. standing com. Joint Commn. on Chs. in Small Communities, 1988-91, Program, Budget and Fin., 1991—; v.p. province VI Episcopal Ch., 1991—, mem. Presiding Bishop's Coun. Advice, 1991—. Author: Mission Strategy in the 21st Century, 1989, Total Ministry: A Practical Approach, 1993; bd. editors Grass Roots, Luling, Tex., 1985-90; contbr. articles to profl. jours. Founder Concerned Citizens for Children, Russelville, 1981; bd. dirs. St. Peter's Hosp., Helena, 1986—. With USMCR, 1961-65. Mem. Aircraft Owners and Pilots Assn. Office: Diocese Mont 515 N Park Ave Helena MT 59601-2798

JONES, CHARLES J., consultant; b. Marshfield, Oreg., Jan. 29, 1940; s. Charles J. Cotter and Lois C. (Smith) Meltebeke; m. Sharon S. Madsen, Mar. 29, 1969; children: Mary E., Judith A., Kari C., April M., Autumn C. AS in Fire Sci. Tech., Portland Community Coll., 1974; BS in Fire Adminstrn., Eastern Oreg. State Coll., 1983; diploma, Nat. Fire Acad., 1983, 85; MPA, Lewis and Clark Coll., 1989. Cert. class VI fire officer, Oreg., hazardous materials instr., fire instr. I; lic. real estate agt., Oreg. From firefighter to capt. Washington County Fire Dist., Aloha, Oreg., 1964-74, battalion chief, 1974-81, dir. comms., dir. research and devel., 1981-85, dir. strategic planning, 1986-88; cons. Tualatin Valley Fire & Rescue, Aloha, 1989-90; pres., CEO Jones Internat. Ltd.; basic and advanced 1st aid instr. ARC, 1965-80; cons. Washington County Consol. Communications Agy., 1983-86, chmn. 9-1-1 mgmt. bd., 1982-83; mem. adv. bd. Washington County Emergency Med. Svcs., 1981-83; owner/instr. internat. vocat. inst. and family tree learning ctrs. Jones Internat., Ltd., 1990—. Editor local newsletter Internat. Assn. Firefighters, 1970; contbr. articles on fire dept. mgmt. to jours. Active Community Planning Orgn., Washington County, 1979-90, chmn. 1988-89. With USAF, 1957-59. Mem. Oreg. Fire Chiefs Assn. (chmn. seminar com. 1982-83, 89, co-chmn. 1981, 84, 86, 87, 88). Republican. Mem. Infinity Universal Ch. Office: Jones Internat Ltd PO Box 1508 Beaverton OR 97075-1508

JONES, CHRISTOPHER VYN, management sciences educator, consultant; b. Wilbraham, Mass., Nov. 25, 1958; s. Robert Warren and Ann Dorothy (Marx) J. BS, Cornell U., 1980, M of Engring., 1981, MS, 1983, PhD, 1985. Asst. prof. Wharton Sch. U. of Pa., Phila., 1985-90; assoc. prof. Simon Fraser U., Burnaby, B.C., Can., 1990—; cons. Chesapeake Decision Scis., New Providence, N.J., 1983—. Author: (chpt.) Handbook of Operations Research, 1992; assoc. editor Ops. Rsch. Soc. Am. Jour. on Computing, 1992—; contbr. articles to profl. jours. Recipient grant NSF, 1990, grant Natural Sci. and Engring. Rsch. Coun. Can., 1991. Mem. Ops. Rsch. Soc. of Am., Inst. Mgmt. Sci., Assn. for Computing Machinery. Democrat. Office: Simon Fraser Univ, Burnaby, BC Canada

JONES, CLEON BOYD, research engineer; b. Norwalk, Calif., Nov. 9, 1961; s. Cleon Earl and Marjorie Helen (McDade) J. BS in Math., Biola U., 1983. Rsch. libr. Christian Rsch. Inst., San Juan Capistrano, Calif., 1981-84; flight control engr. Leading Systems, Inc., Irvine, Calif., 1984-90; rsch. engr. Dynamic Rsch., Inc., Torrance, Calif., 1990—. Mem. AIAA. Republican. Home: 12464 Fallcreek Ln Cerritos CA 90701

JONES, D. MICHAEL, banker; b. Tacoma, June 25, 1942; s. Delbert Edward and Marilyn Maurine (Myers) J.; m. Linda R. Lavigne, June 7, 1964; 1 child, Karee Michele. BA in Econs., Wash. State U., 1964. CPA, Wash. Acct. Deloitte Haskins & Sells, Seattle, 1964-68, princ., 1968-72; treas. Old Nat. Bancorp., Spokane, Wash., 1973-76, exec. v.p., 1976-81, pres., 1982-87; pres. Moore Fin. Group Inc. (now West One Bancorp), Boise, ID, 1987—; bd. dirs. Columbia Paint Co., Spokane. Bd. dirs. Spokane City Libraries, 1974-78, Leadership Spokane, 1982-84; sec. treas., bd. dirs. Spokane Unltd., 1980-86. Recipient Outstanding Alumnus award, Wash. State U., 1986. Mem. Am. Inst. CPA's, Wash. Soc. CPA's, Spokane C. of C. (sec. treas. 1985-86). Episcopalian. Clubs: Spokane (pres. 1984-85); Hayden Lake (Idaho) Country (pres. 1982-83). Office: West One Bancorp PO Box 8247 Boise ID 83733-0001*

JONES, DANIEL LEE, software development company executive; b. Sterling, Colo., Feb. 17, 1954; s. Gerald Dean and Joyce Elaine (Pyle) J.; m. Laurie Elaine Ganong, Sept. 6, 1975; 1 child, Jonathon Alexander. AB cum laude, Dartmouth Coll., 1976; MA in Physics, U. Calif., Davis, 1977, PhD in Physicis, 1979. Assoc. in physics U. Calif., Davis, 1976-79; physicist Argonne (Ill.) Nat. Lab., 1979-82; mem. tech. staff TRW, Inc., Redondo Beach, Calif., 1982-84; chief scientist, co-founder Affine Scis. Corp., Newport Beach, Calif., 1984-85; chief scientist Peripheral Systems, Inc., Van Nuys, Calif., 1985-89, Jones & Jones, Sterling, Colo., 1989—; v.p., co-founder Jones

Techs. Inc., Sterling, 1991—, also bd. dirs.; sec. Jones Techs. Inc., Sterling, 1991—; cons. Davis Polk & Wardwell, N.Y.C., 1987-91. Author (newspaper column) Your Computer, 1991—; contbr. articles to profl. jours. Dist. accountability com. RE-1 Valley Schs., Sterling, 1991—, dist. tech. com., 1991—. Recipient Rufus Choate scholar Dartmouth Coll., 1972, Outstanding Contbrn. Inst. of Internal Auditors, 1987-88; tech. transfer grantee TRW, Inc., 1982. Mem. IEEE, IEEE Computer Soc., Assn. for Computing Machinery, Soc. for Indsl. and Applied Math., Uni-Forum. Republican. Methodist. Home: 510 Glenora St Sterling CO 80751 Office: Jones Techs Inc 301 Poplar St Ste 6 West Sterling CO 80751

JONES, DARYL EMRYS, university administrator, English educator; b. Washington, July 26, 1946; s. William Emrys and Willa Jean (Hibbard) J.; m. Martha Ann Bilton, June 11, 1979. BA, Mich. State U., 1968, MA, 1970, PhD, 1974. Prof. English Tex. Tech U., Lubbock, 1973-86, chmn. English dept., 1982-86; prof. English, dean Coll. Arts and Scis. Boise (Idaho) State U., 1986-91, interim exec. v.p., 1991—. Author: The Dime Novel Western, 1978, Someone Going Home Late, 1990; author numerous poems and book revs. NDEA fellow, 1969-71, Creative Writing fellow NEA, 1985. Mem. Tex. Assn. Creative Writing Tchrs. (pres. 1984-86), Tex. Joint Coun. Tchrs. of English (pres. South Plains area coun. 1983-84), Tex. Inst. Letters (Natalie Ornish Poetry award 1990), Coun. Colls. Arts and Scis., Internat. Coun. Fine Arts Deans, Idaho Humanities Coun., Phi Beta Kappa, Phi Kappa Phi. Home: 1375 E Monterey Dr Boise ID 83706-5078 Office: Boise State U Exec VP 1910 University Dr 1910 University Dr Boise ID 83725

JONES, DAVID JOHN, aerospace executive; b. Pueblo, Colo., Jan. 21, 1934; s. David John and Clare Elizabeth (Bronish) J.; m. Margaret Alice Hoagland; children—David Robert, Pamela Ruth. A. Engring., Pueblo Jr. Coll., 1954; B.S. in Aero. Engring., U. Colo., 1956; Exec. Program, Stanford U., 1977. Engr., Ryan Aero., 1956-59; program mgr. Convair div. Gen. Dynamics Corp., 1959-71, program mgr. space, 1971-75, dir. conventional applications of Tomahawk Cruise Missile, 1975-79, dir. advanced space systems, 1979-80; dir. space techs. System Devel. Corp., Santa Monica, Calif., 1980-82, dep. gen. mgr. Space and Control Systems div., 1987, v.p., gen. mgr. Command and Control div., Camarillo, Calif., 1987-89; v.p. Def. Electronics, Paramax System Corp., Great Neck, N.Y., 1989—; mem. planning com. on space NASA, 1975-76. Cons. Jr. Achievement Project Bus., 1980—; mem. San Diego council Boy Scouts Am., 1967-70, San Diego Multiple Sclerosis Com., 1973; bd. dirs. Moorpark Coll., 1988—. Assoc. fellow AIAA (dir., Nat. Service award San Diego chpt. 1977, 80); mem. Aerospace Industries Assn., Nat. Mgmt. Assn., Assn. U.S. Army, Am. Def. Preparedness Assn., Assn. Unmanned Vehicle Systems, Porsche Club Am., Unisys Mgmt. Assn. Contbr. articles to profl. jours.

JONES, DEAN CLARENCE, social services executive, educator; b. Denver, Apr. 22, 1932; s. Henry Isaac and Jessie May (Houchens) J.; m. Stella Belle Bean, Feb. 2, 1951; children: Steven, Kathy. BA, Warner Pacific U., 1954, Seattle Pacific U., 1961; MA, U. Wash., 14967, PhD, 1971. Pastor Ch. of God, Baker, Rainier, Oreg., 1954-58; caseworker State of Wash., Seattle, 1962-65; asst. prof. Seattle Pacific U., Seattle, 1968-70, U. Utah, Salt Lake City, 1970-71, Ind. U.-Purdue U., Indpls., 1971-77; asst. to dept. chair Bowman Gray Sch. of Medicine, Winston-Salem, N.C., 1977-79; asst. prof. U. Wash., Seattle, 1979-82; dir. Operation Nightwatch, Denver, St. Louis, 1982-86, Tacoma, 1986—. Contbr. articles to profl. jours. Bd. dirs. Comprehensive Mental Health, Tacoma. Mem. Pierce County Alliance (adv. bd. mem.), Kiwanis (bd. dirs.), Ministerial Alliance Groups. Office: Operation Nightwatch PO Box 1181 Tacoma WA 98401-1181

JONES, DENNIS PIERCE, educational research center executive; b. Hastings, Nebr., Mar. 20, 1940; s. Pierce Carter and Ellen Geraldine (Corner) J.; m. M. Elizabeth Doherty, Aug. 17, 1963; children: Douglas Lee, Daniel Wayne. BS in Mgmt. Engring., Rensselaer Poly. Inst., 1961, MS in Mgmt. Engring., 1964. Asst. to bus. mgr. Rensselaer Poly. Inst., Troy, N.Y., 1963-68, asst. dir. planning, 1968-69; staff analyst Nat. Ctr. for Higher Edn. Mgmt. Systems, Boulder, Colo., 1969-75, assoc. dir., 1975-83, v.p. planning and evaluation, 1983-85, pres., 1985—; mem. adv. panel on univ. sci. stats. NSF, Washington, 1977—; mem. spl. study panel on ednl. indicators U.S. Dept. Edn., Washington, 1989-91. Author: (monographs) Data and Information for Executive Decisions in Higher Education, 1982, Higher Education Budgeting at the State Level, 1984; contbr. numerous articles to profl. jours. Chmn. accountability and accreditation com. St. Vrain Valley Schs., Longmont, Colo., 1979-86; mem. Colo. Task Force on Excellent Schs., Denver, 1989-91. Mem. Assn. for Instnl. Rsch., Assn. for Study Higher Edn., Am. Assn. Higher Edn. Office: Nat Ctr Higher Edn Mgmt Sys PO Drawer P Boulder CO 80301-9752

JONES, DONALD FORSYTH, food equipment company executive; b. Chgo., Mar. 28, 1942; s. H. Carter and Dorothy S. (Simons) J.; m. Jeri Lynn Riha, July 3, 1965; children: Marcus, David. BS in Indsl. Engring., Calif. State Poly. U., 1965. Test engr. Boeing Co., Seattle, 1965-70; plant mgr. Western Kraft Corp., Portland, Oreg., 1970-78; gen. mgr. Spear & Jackson, Ltd., Eugene, Oreg., 1978-80; pres. J.V. Northwest, Inc., Portland, 1980—. Contbr. articles to mags. Republican. Mem. Christian Ch. (Disciples of Christ). Home: 17405 Wren Ct Lake Oswego OR 97034-6670 Office: JV Northwest Inc 28120 SW Boberg Rd Wilsonville OR 97070-9205

JONES, DONALD L., lawyer; b. Ft. Worth, Tex.. BA in History, U. Tex., 1965; JD, U. N.Mex., 1969. Bar: N.Mex. 1969. Pvt. practice Albuquerque, 1969—; lawyer Rodey, Dickason, Sloan, Akin and Robb, P.A., Albuquerque, 1991-92. Legal intern City of Albuquerque, 1967, N.Mex. Jaycees, 1970-71, bd. dirs. 1971-72; mem. N.Mex. chpt. Nat. Assn. Indsl. and Office Pks., 1986-91, sec., dir. 1987; pres. Albuquerque Youth Symphony Parents Assn., 1987-88; chmn. Charter Rev. Task Force City Albuquerque, 1988-89; mem. The League Women Voters of Albuquerque/Bernalillo County, 1991-92. Mem. ABA (real property probat and trust sect.), State Bar Assn. N.Mex., Albuquerque C. of C. (bd. dirs. 1984-85, 90-92, chmn. local gov. affairs com. 1984, v.p. govtl. affairs divsn. 1985, vice chmn. westside divsn. 1990—, vice chmn. govt. divsn. 1991-92, co-chmn. equal access to justice campaign, 1992). Address: 1012 Lomas Blvd NW Albuquerque NM 87102

JONES, DONALD RAY, entrepreneur; b. Phoenix, July 19, 1947; m. Rose Fryer, Nov. 15, 1969; children: Duryea, Tramar. Student, Phoenix Coll., 1972-74. Sales rep. Consumer Product Co., 1973-81; dir. mktg. maj. auto dealer, 1983-84; founder, pres. DRJ & Assocs., Inc., Phoenix, 1984—. Mem. adv. bd. Sta. KPNX Broadcasting, South Mountain Community Coll., Foster Care Rev. Bd., edn. bd. Antioch Missionary Bapt. Ch. With U.S. Army, 1967-69, Vietnam. Office: DRJ & Assocs PO Box 2314 Phoenix AZ 85002-2314

JONES, DONNA MARILYN, real estate broker, legislator; b. Brush, Colo., Jan. 14, 1939; d. Virgil Dale and Margaret Elizabeth (McDaniel) Wolfe; m. Donald Eugene Jones, June 9, 1956; children: Dawn Richter, Lisa Shira, Stuart. Student, Treasure Valley Community Coll., 1981-82; grad., Realtors Inst. Cert. residential specialist. Co-owner Parts, Inc., Payette, Idaho, 1967-79; dept. mgr., buyer Lloyd's Dept. Store, Payette, Idaho, 1979-80; sales assoc. Idaho-Oreg. Realty, Payette, Idaho, 1981-82; mem. dist. 13 Idaho Ho. of Reps., Boise, 1987-90, mem. dist. 10, 1990—; assoc. broker Classic Properties Inc., Payette, 1983-91; owner, broker ERA Preferred Properties Inc., 1991—. Co-chmn. Apple Blossom Parade, 1982; mem. Payette Civic League, 1968-84, pres. 1972; mem. Payette County Planning and Zoning Commn., 1985-88, vice-chmn. 1987; field coordinator Idaho Rep. Party Second Congl. Dist., 1986; mem. Payette County Rep. Cen. Com. 1978—; precinct II com. person, 1978-79, state committeewoman, 1980-84, chmn. 1984-87; outstanding county chmn. region III Idaho Rep. Party Regional Hall of Fame, 1985-86; mem. Payette County Rep. Women's Fedn., 1988—, bd. dirs., 1990—; mem. Idaho Hispanic Commn., 1989—, Idaho State Permanent Bldg. Adv. Coun., 1990—; mem Idaho Hispanic Commn., 1989—; apptd. Idaho State Permanent Bldg. Fund Adv. Coun.; committeperson Payette County Cen.; bd. dir. Payette County Rep. Women's Fedn., 1988—; chmn. Ways and Means Idaho House of Reps., 1993—; Idaho chmn. Am. Legis. Exchange Coun., 1991—. Recipient White Rose award Idaho March of Dimes, 1988; named Payette/Washington County Realtor of Yr., 1987. Mem. Idaho Assn. Realtors (legis. com. 1984-87, chmn. 1986, realtors active in politics com. 1982—, polit. action com. 1986, polit. affairs com. 1986-88, chmn. 1987, bd. dirs. 1984-88), Payette/Washington County Bd. Realtors (v.p. 1981, state dir. 1984-88, bd. dirs 1983-88, sec. 1983), Bus. and Profl. Women (Woman of Progress award 1988, 90, treas. 1988), Payette C. of C., Fruitland C. of C., Wiesr C. of C.. Republican. Home: 1911 1st Ave S Payette ID 83661-3003 Office: ERA Preferred Properties 1610 6th Ave S Payette ID 83661-3348

JONES, DOROTHY JOANNE, social services professional; b. L.A.; d. Joseph Anthony and Florence (Chaffin) Ghiotto; divorced; children: Teri McKane, Carole Thompson, Christopher Jones. BA, La Verne U., 1980; MS, Calif. State U., Fullerton, 1983. Lic. marriage, family/child counselor. Dep. sheriff L.A. County Sheriff Office, 1972-76; dir. A.I.C., L.A., 1976-80; mgr. McDonnell Douglas, Long Beach, Calif., 1980-93; pvt. practice Los Alamitos, Calif., 1985—. Author: When to Say No, 1983. Mem. Ctr. for Performing Arts, L.A., 1976—, Transpacific Mgmt., Long Beach, 1982—. Recipient Spl. Svc. award Assn. Labor and Mgmt., Orange County, Calif., 1983. Mem. Employee Assistance Profls. Assn. (pres. 1980-82), Alcoholism Info. Ctr. (v.p. 1980-91), Counseling Assocs. (v.p. 1976-83), Calif. Assn. Marriage and Family Therapists. Democrat. Episcopalian. Office: Ste 201 10741 Los Alamitos Los Alamitos CA 90720

JONES, DOUGLAS CLYDE, author; b. Winslow, Ark., Dec. 6, 1924; s. Marvin Clyde and Bethel Mae (Stockburger) J.; m. Mary Arnold, Jan. 1, 1949; children: Mary Glenn, Martha Claire, Kathryn Greer, Douglas Eben. B.A. in Journalism, U. Ark., 1949; M.S. in Mass Communications, U. Wis., Madison, 1962. Commd. U.S. Army, 1949, advanced through grades to lt. col., 1968; service in W. Ger. and Korea; chief armed forces news br. Dept. Def., 1966-68, ret., 1968; prof. U. Wis. Sch. Journalism, Madison, 1968-74. Painter of plains Indians, 1974-75; novelist, 1976—; author: Treaty of Medicine Lodge, 1966, Court Martial of G.A. Custer, 1976 (Spur award Western Writers Am. 1976), Arrest Sitting Bull, 1977, Creek Called Wounded Knee, 1978, Winding Stair, 1979, Elkhorn Tavern, 1980 (Friends of Am. Writers award 1980), Weedy Rough, 1981, The Barefoot Brigade, 1982, Season of Yellow Leaf, 1983, Gone the Dreams and Dancing, 1984 (Spur award Western Writers Am. 1985), Roman, 1986 (Spur award 1986); (short stories) Hickory Cured, 1987, Remember Santiago, 1988, Come Winter, 1989, The Search for Temperance Moon, 1991, This Savage Race, 1993. Served with U.S. Army, 1943-45, World War II, PTO. Decorated Commendation medal (3) Legion of Merit. Recipient Chancellor's award U. Wis., 1987, Owen Wister award for body of work Western Writers Am., 1993. Home: 1424 Harold St Fayetteville AR 72703

JONES, EBON RICHARD, retail executive; b. Oak Park, Ill., Aug. 23, 1944; s. Ebon Clark and Marilyn B. (Dow) J.; m. Sally Samuelson, Jan. 27, 1968; children: Stephanie Blythe, Heather Denise. B.A., Priceton U., 1966; M.B.A., Stanford U., 1968. Adminstrv. asst. Nat. Air Pollution Control Adminstrn., Washington, 1968-70; cons. McKinsey & Co., San Francisco and Paris, 1970-83; exec. v.p. Safeway Stores Inc., Oakland, Calif., 1983-86, group v.p., 1986-88, exec. v.p., 1988—. Bd. dirs. San Francisco Zool. Soc., 1979—, chmn. bd., 1979-85, pres., 1985-90; trustee Crystal Springs Uplands Sch., 1986—; mem. bd. govs. Uniform Code Coun., 1984—. Lt. USPHS, 1968-70. Mem. Phi Beta Kappa. Home: 58 Chester Way San Mateo CA 94402-1043 Office: Safeway Stores Inc 201 4th St Oakland CA 94660-0001

JONES, EDWARD LOUIS, historian, educator; b. Georgetown, Tex., Jan. 15, 1922; s. Henry Horace and Elizabeth (Steen) J.; m. Dorothy M. Showers, Mar. 1, 1952 (div. Sept. 1963); children: Cynthia, Frances, Edward Lawrence; Lynne Ann McGreevy, Oct. 7, 1963; children Christopher Louis, Teresa Lynne. BA in Philosophy, U. Wash., 1952, BA in Far East, 1952, BA in Speech, 1955, postgrad., 1952-54; JD, Gonzaga U., 1967. Social worker Los Angeles Pub. Assistance, 1956-57; producer, dir. Little Theatre, Hollywood, Calif. and Seattle, 1956-60; research analyst, cons. to Office of Atty. Gen., Olympia and Seattle, Wash., 1963-66; coordinator of counseling SOIC, Seattle, 1966-68; lectr., advisor, asst. to dean U. Wash., Seattle, 1968—; instr. Gonzaga U., Spokane, Wash., 1961-62, Seattle Community Coll., 1967-68; dir. drama workshop, Driftwood Players, Edmonds, Wash., 1975-76. Author: The Black Diaspora: Colonization of Colored People, 1988, Tutankhamon: Son of the Sun, King of Upper and Lower Egypt, 1978, Black Orators' Workbook, 1982, Black Zeus, 1972, Profiles in African Heritage, 1972, From Rulers of the World to Slavery, 1990, President Zachary Taylor and Senator Hamlin: Union or Death, 1991, Why Colored Americans Need an Abraham Lincoln in 1992, 1992; editor pub. NACADA Jour. Nat. Acad. Advising Assn., 1981—, Afro-World Briefs newsletter, 1985—. V.p. Wash. Com. on Consumer Interests, Seattle, 1966-68. Served to 2d lt. Fr. Army, 1940-45. Recipient Outstanding Teaching award U. Wash., 1986, Tyee Inst. Yr. U. Wash., 1987, appreciation award Office Minority Affairs, 1987, acad. excellence award Nat. Soc. Black Engrs., 1987, Appreciation award Fla. chpt. Nat. Bar Assn., 1990; Frederick Douglass scholar Nat. Coun. Black Studies, 1985, 86. Mem. Nat. Assn. Student Personnel Adminstrs., Smithsonian Inst. (assoc.), Am. Acad. Polit. and Social Sci., Nat. Acad. Advising Assn. (bd. dirs. 1979-82, Cert. of Appreciation 1982, editor Jour. 1981—, award for Excellence 1985), Western Polit. Sci. Assn. Democrat. Baptist. Office: U Wash Seattle WA 98195

JONES, ELIZABETH ANNE, skin care company executive, herbalist; b. Port Chester, N.Y., May 7, 1941; d. Harold Dean and Virginia (Hale) Cater; m. Peter Rood, June 15, 1963 (div. Mar. 1970); m. Lawrence E. Jones, Sept. 7, 1986. BS, Skidmore Coll., 1963; secondary teaching credential, U. Calif., Berkeley, 1970; elem. teaching credential, Sonoma State U., 1975. Cert. profl. herbalist Calif. Sch. Herbal Studies; cert. profl. aromatherapist Pacific Inst. Aromatherapy. Head tchr. children's workshop Primary Sch., Petaluma, Calif., 1973-76; tchr. English and art Ana High Sch., Sebastopol, Calif., 1977-79; dir. Shining Earth Pottery Studio, Petaluma, 1976-80; tchr. Cheney Valley Elem. Sch., Petaluma, 1979-81; pres. Body Love Natural Cosmetics Inc., Petaluma, Santa Cruz, Calif., 1981—; tchr. aromatherapy Dominican Hosp., Capitola, Calif., 1992, Santa Cruz Parks and Recreation Dept., 1992. Contbr. articles to various publs.; inventor amazing grains, aroma oil, herbal facial steams, also others. Caregiver Hospice, Petaluma, 1984-84, Hosp., Santa Rosa, Calif., 1984-86; visitor to elderly I-You Venture, Santa Cruz, 1992—. Recipient award Coun. on Econ. Priorities, 1991, Nat. Anti-Vivisection Soc., 1992. Mem. Am. Aromatherapy Assn., Am. Herbalist Guild, Women's Network (v.p. 1991-92), Sierra Club. Home: 925 King St Santa Cruz CA 95060 Office: Body Love Natural Cosmetics 303 Potrero St Sts 4 and 19 Santa Cruz CA 95060

JONES, GALEN RAY, physician assistant; b. Salt Lake City, Feb. 1, 1948; s. Leonard Ray and Veda (Whitehead) J.; m. Patricia Ann Poulson, Jan. 21, 1972; children: Brian, Marci, Natalie. Grad., Med. Field Svc. Sch. Ft. Sam Houston, San Antonio, 1971; BS, U. Utah, 1982. Missionary Ch. of Jesus Christ of Latter Day Saints, Alta., Sask., Can., 1967-69; asst. mgr. Cowan's Frostop Hamburger Stand, Salt Lake City, 1969-70; with Safeway Stores, Inc., Salt Lake City, 1970; o.r. tech. Latter Day Saint Hosp., Salt Lake City, 1973-75; physician asst. Lovell Clinic Inc., Lovell, Wyo., 1975-77, Family Health Care, Inc., Tooele, Utah, 1977-86, West Dermatology and Surgery Med. Grp., Redlands, Calif., 1986—; maturation lectr. Tooele Sch. Dist., 1978-86; course dir., instr. EMT, North Big Horn County Search and Rescue, 1976; instr. EMT, Grantsville Ambulance Inc., 1979-85; lectr. on skin care and changes to sr. citizen groups, hosp. auxs., health fairs, 1986—; high sch. sophomore sem. tchr. religion, 1991-93. Chmn. County Health Teen Pregnancy Prevention Project, Tooele, 1980-81; adv. bd. State Dept. Health-Rural Health Network, Salt Lake City, 1985-86; health lectr. County Health & Edn. Dept. Progs., Tooele, 1977-86; mormon bishop/pastor Lakeview Ward, Latter Day Saints Ch., Tooele, 1982-86; mem. Utah Acad. Physician Assts. (pres. 1980-81, editor newsletter 1979-80). With U.S. Army, 1971-73. U. Utah grantee, 1966, 67, 69. Fellow Am. Acad. Physician Assts., Calif. Acad. Physicians Assts.; mem. Moreno Valley C. of C. Republican. Mem. Ch. of Jesus Christ of Latter Day Saints Ch. Home: 101 Channing St Redlands CA 92373-4862

JONES, GERALD JOSEPH, former broadcasting executive; b. Saginaw, Mich., May 22, 1920; s. LaVern Pierce and Yvonne Maria (Berthaud) J.; student Los Angeles Jr. Coll., 1939; m. Madelyn Fio Rito, Nov. 15, 1970; children by previous marriage—Jennifer Jones Batteau, Steven G. Account exec. Murray Dymock, 1946, West-Holliday, 1947-50, The Katz Agy., Inc., 1950-60, v.p., 1967-78, West Coast mgr., 1977-78, v.p. sta. and industry relations, 1978-80. Served to flight lt. RCAF, 1941-45. Decorated D.F.C.; col. Staff of Gov. John McKeithen, La., 1971. Mem. Pacific Pioneer Broadcasters, So Calif. Advt. Golfers Assn. Republican. Clubs: Bel Air, Woburn Golf and Country (Milton Keynes, Eng.), Milline (sec. 1963-66); Thunderbird Country Club. Home: 40995 Thunderbird Rd Rancho Mirage CA 92270

JONES, GERRE LYLE, marketing and public relations consultant; b. Kansas City, Mo., June 22, 1926; s. Eugene Riley and Carolyn (Newell) J.; m. Charlotte Mae Reinhold, Oct. 30, 1948; children: Beverly Anne Jones Putnam, Wendy S. Jones Stout. BJ, U. Mo., 1948, postgrad., 1953-54. Exec. sec. Effingham (Ill.) C. of C., 1948-50; field rep. Nat. Found. Infantile Paralysis, N.Y.C., 1950-57; dir. pub. relations Inst. Logopedics, Wichita, Kans., 1957-58; owner Gerre Jones & Assocs., Pub. Relations, Kansas City, Mo., 1958-63; info. officer Radio Free Europe Fund, Munich, Federal Republic of Germany, 1963-65, spl. asst. to dir. pub. relations, 1965-66; exec. asst. pub. affairs Edward Durell Stone, 1967-68; dir. mktg. and communications Vincent C. Kling & Ptnrs., Phila., 1969-71; mktg. cons. Ellerbe Architects, Washington, 1972; v.p. Gaio Assocs., Ltd., Washington, 1972-73, exec. v.p., 1973-76; exec. v.p. Bldg. Industry Devel. Services, Washington, 1973-76; pres. Gerre Jones Assocs. Inc., Albuquerque, 1976-89, ret., 1989; sr. v.p. Barlow Assocs., Inc., Washington, 1977-78; lectr. numerous colls. and univs. Author: How to Market Professional Design Services, 1973, 2d edit., 1983, How to Prepare Professional Design Brochures, 1976, (with Stuart H. Rose) How to Find and Win New Business, 1976, Public Relations for the Design Professional, 1980; contbr. articles to profl. jours. Served with USAAF, 1944-45, maj. USAF (ret.). Mem. Internat. Radio and TV Soc., Nat. Assn. Sci. Writers, AIA (hon.), Sigma Delta Chi, Alpha Delta Sigma, Phi Delta Phi. Republican. Clubs: Kansas City Press; Overseas Press; Deadline (N.Y.C.). Lodge: Masons.

JONES, HAROLD ROGER, real estate company executive; b. Oakland, Calif., Oct. 15, 1947; ss. Charles Roger and Sachie (Yamauchi) J.; m. Lana Mei Yong, Aug. 18, 1968; children: Adam, Kehaulani, Aaron, Noelani. BBA, U. Hawaii, 1970; MA, Internat. Sch. Theology, Honolulu, 1988. Cert. real estate broker, Hawaii, Internat. Properties Specialist. Campus dir. Campus Crusade for Christ, Mesa, Ariz., 1970-73; area dir. Campus Crusade for Christ, Honolulu, 1973-76; Here's Life dir. Campus Crusade for Christ, Beirut and, Cyprus, 1977-80; realtor assoc. Locations Inc., Honolulu, 1981-83; tng. dir. Luke & Luke Realty, Inc., Honolulu, 1983-85, v.p., 1985-87; pres. ERA Jones Realty, Honolulu, 1987-92, Coldwell Banker McCormack, Honolulu, 1992—; cons. SE Asian Settlement Com., Honolulu, 1982—. Mem., minority floor leader, whip Hawaii Ho. of Reps., 1982-88; Hawaii nat. committeeman Rep. Nat. Com., 1988-92; trustee Internat. Coll., Honolulu, 1984-89. With USN, 1965-67. Named Legislator of Yr., Am. Legis. Coun., 1986. Mem. Nat. Assn. Realtors, Hawaii Assn. Realtors, Maui Bd. Realtors, Honolulu Bd. Realtors (strategic planning com. 1989—), Inernat. Real Estate Fedn., FIABCI (bd. dirs. Hawaii chpt.). Office: 841 Bishop St Ste 2300 Honolulu HI 96813

JONES, HENRIK, cable television executive; b. Mpls., Oct. 19, 1960; s. Waring and Yoyo (Tesdorpf) J. BA, Brown U., 1983; MBA, Harvard U., 1991. Trainee JP Morgan & Co., N.Y.C., 1984, asst. treas., 1985, asst. v.p., 1986-89, v.p., 1989; analyst Fidelity Investments, Boston, 1990; ptnr. InterMedia Ptnrs., San Francisco, 1991—. Treas. Creative Arts Workshops for Homeless Children, N.Y.C., 1986-89. Mme. The Players Club. Home and Office: InterMedia Ptnrs 235 Montgomery St San Francisco CA 94104

JONES, J. GILBERT, research consultant; b. San Francisco, June 1, 1922; s. Enoch Roscoe L. Sr. and Remedios (Ponce de Leon) J.; student U.S. Mcht. Marine Acad., 1942-44, San Francisco City Coll., 1942-44, 46-47; AB, U. Calif., Berkeley, 1949, MA, 1952. Lic. pvt. investigator. Ins. insp. Ins. Cos. Insp. Bur., San Francisco, 1959-62; pub. rels. cons., San Francisco, 1962-67; ins. insp. Am. Svc. Bur., San Francisco, 1967-72; propr., mgr. Dawn Universal Internat. San Francisco, 1972—, Dawn Universal Security Svc., San Francisco, 1983—. Mem. Calif. Rep. Assembly, 1978—; sponsor Nat. Rep. Congl. Com. Mem. SAR, Sons. Spanish-Am. War Vets. Soc., World Affairs Coun. N. Calif., U. Calif. Alumni Assn. Office: PO Box 424057 San Francisco CA 94102

JONES, JACK BRISTOL, education educator; b. Las Cruces, N.Mex., Apr. 16, 1931; s. John Keith and Elsie Dean (Bristol) J.; m. Joy Elaine Moffett, Dec. 18, 1954; children: Sherri E. Callinan, Candi Marie, Craig Britol. BA, U. Calif., Santa Barbara, 1957, MA, 1965; EdD, U. Ariz., Tucson, 1970; PhD, Calif. Western U., 1979. Cert. elem. and secondary tchr., adminstr., reading specialist. Sgt. Santa Barbara Police Dept., 1955-61; elem. tchr. Goleta (Calif.) Sch. Dist., 1962-66; grad. asst. U. Ariz., Tucson, 1966-68; instr. Ventura (Calif.) Community Coll., 1968-69; prof. education Calif. Poly. State U., San Luis Obispo, 1969—. Author: Tips for Tutors, 1980; editor Calif. Reader, 1975-80. Vice-comdr. San Luis Obispo County Sheriff's Aero Squadron, 1977-80; comdr. San Luis Obispo County Sheriff's Res., 1980-85. lst lt. U.S. Army, 1950-53, col. Res., 1964-87. Decorated Legion of Merit. Mem. Internat. Reading Assn., Calif. Prof. Reading (pres. 1975-76), Calif. Reading Assn. (pres. 1981-82, Margaret Lynch Svc. award 1984), Orgn. Tchr. Educators in Reading (pres. 1987-88), Res. Officers Assn., San Luis Obispo Hist. Arms Soc. (founder, prs. 1983-86), Rotary, Elks, Phi Delta Kappa. Republican. Episcopalian. Office: Calif Poly State U San Luis Obispo CA 93407

JONES, JAMES HAROLD, pharmaceutical company executive; b. Harrison, Ark., Aug. 26, 1930; s. Charlie and Pearl M. (Wood) J.; m. Peggy Lou Bort, Apr. 2, 1960; children: James Bort, Cliff Ownbey, Lee Christopher, Kenneth Carson. BBA, U. Ark., 1953; cert. banking, So. Meth. U., 1960; advanced mgmt. degree, Harvard U., 1966. From asst. cashier to v.p. Republic Nat. Bank Dallas, 1954-63, sr. v.p., 1963-67, exec. v.p., 1967-69; chmn., pres., chief exec. officer First Commerce Corp., New Orleans, 1969-75; dep. chmn., pres., chief exec. officer Bancal Tri-State Corp., San Francisco, 1975; chmn., pres. First Resources Corp., San Mateo, Calif., 1975—; chmn., chief executive officer Jameson Pharm. Corp., Burlingame, Calif., 1983—; Bd. dirs. Wal-Mart Stores, Inc. Trustee Pub. Affairs Research Council La., Inc., 1972-75, chmn. Greater New Orleans devel. com., 1972-75; dir. United Way Greater New Orleans, 1973-75, chmn. various fund drives 1972-74; dir. Greater New Orleans Area C. of C., 1970-74, mem. many coms., 1970-75; dir. Greater New Orleans Tourist and Conv. Commn., 1970-75; mem. adv. bd. La. Found. for Pvt. Colls., 1972-75; devel. council U. Ark., Fayetteville, 1973—; v.p. New Orleans Area Council Boy Scouts Am., 1972-75; active Nat. Council Boy Scouts Am., 1974; nat. bd. Childrens' Charities Am., 1974-75; bd. dirs. New Orleans Philharmonic, 1971-75; hon. bd. mem. Big Bros. Am.; active Hillsborough (Calif.) Sch. Found., 1982-84; dir. bd. deacons, chmn. fin. com. First Baptist Ch. of Burlingame. Recipient Hornblower award New Orleans Pub. Rels. Soc. Am., 1974, Svc. award Nat. Cystic Fibrosis Rsch. Found., Svc. award New Orleans C. of C., 1972, Carnation award for Otstanding Svc. Vol. and Info. Agy. Mem. Commonwealth Club of Calif., Newcomen Soc., Ark. U. Alumni Assn. (life, bd. dirs. 1963-66), Phi Lamda Chi. Home: 862 Chiltern Rd Burlingame CA 94010-7028 Office: Jameson Pharm Corp 855 Mahler Rd Burlingame CA 94010-1603

JONES, JAN LAVERTY, mayor; m. Ted Jones. Grad. Stanford Univ. Mayor, City of Las Vegas. Office: Office of Mayor City Hall 10th Fl 400 Stewart Ave Las Vegas NV 89101-2942*

JONES, JANET BENSON (J.B.), clinical social worker, consultant. BA in Counseling and Communicative Arts, U. Redlands, 1973; Emergency Med. Technician, Barstow Jr. Coll., 1975; MSW, U. Denver, 1981. Lic. clin. social worker. Dir., designer CARE-line phone hotline Barstow (Calif.) Mental Health Ctr., 1973-74; social svc. worker San Bernardino (Calif.) Dept. Social Svcs., 1974-77; house parent Group Homes of Greater Waterbury, Conn., 1978-79; case worker Big Sisters of Colo., Denver, 1979-80; social worker Office of Refugee Resettlement Region VIII U.S. HHS, Denver, 1980-81; interviewer CREDCO of Colo., Denver, 1982-84; EPA site supr Community Corp., Adams County and Denver, 1984-86; social work cons. Curtis Park Community Ctr., Denver, 1986-87; sch. social worker Adams County Sch. Dist. 50, Westminster, Colo., 1986-87, Jefferson County Pub. Schs., Arvada and Lakewood, Colo., 1987-88; social worker Spring Wind Group Home, Denver, 1988-89; sch. social worker Denver Pub. Schs., 1989—. Mem. NASW (bd. dirs.). Office: Denver Pub Schs 900 Grant St Denver CO 80203-2996

JONES, JANETTE LEE, artist; b. Vallejo, Calif., Nov. 11, 1953; d. Robert Elwood and Margaret (Barber) Matney; m. Ronnie Dean Jones, May 17, 1975; children: Kelly Rebecca, Emily Nicole. AA, Solano C.C., 1973; student, Stanislaus State Coll., 1973-74. Gallery dir. Vacaville (Calif.) Art League, 1989—. One-woman show Village Gallery, Fair Oaks, Calif., 1992; exhibited in group shows including Yolo State Fair, Woodland, Calif., 1992. Organizer, active Yolo Hospice Art Auction Benefit, Woodland, 1990-92, 93, Yolo Friends of Art Scholarship, 1992; active, donator Children's Network Solano County, Vacaville, 1989—; active Yolo Cancer Soc. Auction, 1989-92. Mem. Watercolor Artists of Sacramento Horizons (Honorable Mention Open show 1991), Vacaville Art League (bd. dirs. 1991). Democrat. Home and Studio: 112 Almond Dr Winters CA 95694

JONES, JERVE MALDWYN, construction company executive; b. Los Angeles, Sept. 21, 1918; s. Oliver Cromwell and Zola (Hill) J.; m. Alice Castle Holcomb, Apr. 12, 1942; children—Jay Gregory, Janey Lee Matt, Joel Kevin. B.S. in Civil Engring., U. So. Calif., 1939. Registered profl. engr., Calif. Stress analyst Northrop Aircraft, L.A., 1940-43; ptnr. Jones Bros. Constrn. Co., Beverly Hills, Calif., 1946-56; pres., chief exec. officer Peck/Jones Constrn. Corp. (formerly Jones Bros. Constrn. Co.), Beverly Hills, Calif., 1956—; cons. Jerve M. Jones Assocs., Beverly Hills, 1970—; chmn. Jones Constrn. Mgmt., Beverly Hills, 1983—. Bd. dirs. Huntington Library, San Marino, Calif., 1984—, Pepperdine U., Malibu, Calif., Boy Scouts Am., L.A., Santa Monica Hosp. Found., YMCA Met. L.A.; chmn. L.A. Music Ctr., United Fund Campaign; life mem. Town Hall Calif., L.A., adv. bd. UCLA Med. Ctr.; mem. State Calif. Strong Motion Instrumentation Program, Dept. Mines and Geology. With USNR, 1943-46, PTO. Recipient Civil Engring. Alumnus of Yr. award U. So. Calif., 1985, Bronze Hat award United Contractors Assn., 1985, Disting. Scout award, 1989. Mem. Constrn. Mgmt. Assn. Am. (nat. pres. 1984, Founders award 1985), Archtl. Guild, Archimedes Circle, Constrn. Industry Commn. (chmn. 1980-84), Assoc. Gen. Contractors Am., Los Angeles Area C. of C. (dir.). Republican. Episcopalian. Clubs: Los Angeles Country, California. Lodge: Rotary (dir. 1962-68). Office: Peck/Jones Constrn Corp 10866 Wilshire Blvd Fl 7 Los Angeles CA 90024-4300

JONES, JOANNA PATRICIA, educator, child development consultant; b. Chgo., Dec. 23, 1935; d. John Edward Payne and O'Deal Pauline (Dammann) Fear; m. Leon Koenen (div.); 1 child, Diana Suzanne; m. Paul Jones, Nov. 19, 1972; children: Glenn, Randy, Bonnie, Paula. BA, Colgate U., 1958; BS, Pacific Oaks Coll., 1959, MA, 1971; MA, Claremont Grad. Sch., 1969, PhD, 1981. Mem. staff, tchr. Pacific Oaks Coll., Pasadena, Calif., 1959-71; dir. edn. Orange County Head Start, Orange, Santa Ana, Calif., 1965-71; instr. Mt. Sac Coll., Walnut, Calif., 1966-70, 89—; prof. Chaffey Coll., Rancho Cucamonga, Calif., 1971—; mem. edn. staff Claremont (Calif.) Grad. Sch., 1972-74; trainer child devel. assoc. Los Angeles County Head Start, 1980-85; instr. Fontera (Calif.) Woman's Prison, 1985-88; cons. Far West Lab. for Edn. Rsch., San Francisco, 1965-71. Contbr. articles to profl. jours.; presenter in field, Taiwan, Japan, Australia. Co-founder Prevention of Child Abuse, Pomona, Calif., 1983; chair Cultural Arts Com., Pomona, 1988—. Mem. Assn. for Childhood Edn. Internat., Nat. Assn. Edn. Young Children, Internat. Play Assn., UCLA Alumni Assn., Pi Lambda Theta. Home: 1295 Loma Vista Pomona CA 91768 Office: Chaffey Coll Child Devel Dept 5885 N Haven Rancho Cucamonga CA 91701

JONES, JOEL MACKEY, educational administrator; b. Millersburg, Ohio, Aug. 11, 1937; s. Theodore R. and Edna Mae (Mackey) Jones; children: Carolyn Mae, Jocelyn Corinne. BA, Yale U., 1960; MA, Miami U., Oxford, Ohio, 1962; PhD, U. N.Mex., 1966. Dir. Am. studies U. Md., Balt., 1966-69; chmn. Am. studies U. N.Mex., Albuquerque, 1969-73, asst. v.p. acad. affairs, 1973-77, dean faculties, assoc. provost, prof. Am. studies, 1977-85, v.p. adminstrn., 1985-88; pres. Ft. Lewis Coll., Durango, Colo., 1988—. Contbr. numerous essays, articles and chpts. to books. Founder Rio Grande Nature Preserve Soc., Albuquerque, 1974—; bd. dirs., mem. exec. com., United Way, Albuquerque, 1980-83; nat. bd. cons. NEH, 1978—; bd. dirs. Mercy Hosp., 1990—, 1st Nat. Bank; mem. ACE Commn. on Leadership. Farwell scholar Yale U., New Haven, 1960; Sr. fellow NEH, 1972, Adminstrv. fellow Am. Coun. Edn., Washington, 1972-73. Mem. Am. Studies Assn., Am. Assn. Higher Edn. Home: 35 Lewis Mountain Ln Durango CO 81301 Office: Ft Lewis Coll Office of Pres Durango CO 81301-3999

JONES, JOHN FINBAR, dean, social work educator; b. Dublin, Ireland, Mar. 29, 1929; s. John Patrick and Kathleen Mary (O'Brien) J.; m. Lois Key McCleskey, Aug. 3, 1974; children: Sean Christopher, Kristin Victoria. BA, U. Coll. Dublin, 1953; MSW, U. Mich., 1966; MPA, PHD, U. Minn., 1968. Lectr. U. Hong Kong, 1968-70; assoc. prof. social work U. Wis., Milw., 1970-71; founding dean, prof. Sch. Social Devel. U. Minn., Duluth, 1971-76; prof., dir. univ. studies in social work Chinese U. of Hong Kong, 1976-87; dean, prof. Grad. Sch. Social Work U. Denver, 1987—; mem. Adv. Commn. on Social Work, Hong Kong, 1977-87. Author: Education in Depth, 1979, (with others) Citizens in Service, 1976; editor: Social Development, 1981, The Common Welfare, 1981. Fellow United Coll., Chinese U., Hong Kong, 1976-87; trustee Chinese U. Coun., Hong Kong, 1980-83. Mem. NASW (pres. Mpls. chpt. 1972-75), Internat. Coun. Social Welfare (exec. mem. Vienna, Austria 1982-86), Am. Assn. for Protecting Children (chair Denver 1987—), Am. Humane Assn. (bd. dirs. Denver 1987—). Roman Catholic. Home: 7759 S Ivy Way Englewood CO 80112-2457 Office: U Denver Grad Sch Social Work Spruce Hall S Denver CO 80208

JONES, JOHN WESLEY, entrepreneur; b. Wenatchee, Wash., Nov. 15, 1942; s. Richard F. and Hazel F. (Hendrix) J.; m. Melissa L. Meyer, June 22, 1968 (div. 1982); children: John E., Jennifer L.; m. Deborah G. Matthews, Apr. 24, 1993. BA in Bus./Econs., Western Wash. U., Bellingham, 1966. Trainee Jones Bldg., Seattle, 1967-69; mgr. Jones Bldg., 1969-78; owner/mgr. N.W. Inboards, Bellevue, Wash., 1974-78, Jones Bldg., Seattle, 1978-86; pvt. investor Bellevue, 1987—; trustee BOMA Health & Welfare Trust, 1982-86, chmn. 1986; mem. Seattle Fire Code Adv. Bd., 1979-86. With USMCR, 1966-72. Mem. Seattle Bldg. Owners and Mgrs. Assn. (trustee 1979-86), Bldg. Owners & Mgrs. Internat., N.W. Marine Trade Assn., Am. Assn. Individual Investors, Seattle Yacht Club. Republican. Home: 61 Skagit Key Bellevue WA 98006-1021 Office: 12819 SE 38th St # 288 Bellevue WA 98006-1395

JONES, JOHNNIE A., III, lawyer, legal educator; b. Roswell, N.Mex., Mar. 25, 1953; s. Johnnie Jr. and Inez (Palmer-Espy) J.; divorced; children: Jacqueline Inez, Marquis Aaron. BA, U. N.Mex., 1975, MA with hons., 1979; JD, Antioch U., 1985; postgrad., Georgetown U. Bar: N.Mex. 1986, U.S. Dist. Ct. N.Mex. 1986, U.S. Ct. Appeals (10th cir.) 1986, D.C. 1987, U.S. Supreme Ct. 1989. Jud. intern to presiding justice Superior Ct., Washington, 1985; law clk. to presiding justice Dist. Ct., Albuquerque, 1986; asst. dist. atty. Bernalillo County, Albuquerque, 1986—; legal instr. Albuquerque Tech. Inst. Community Coll., 1979—. Recipient Civic award Sec. of N.Mex., 1987, Kiwanis Club, 1987. Mem. ABA, Nat. Bar Assn., Albuquerque Bar Assn., Assn. Trial Lawyers Am., Am. Judicature Soc., N.Mex. Black Lawyers Assn., Moot Ct., U.S. Jaycees, Pi Alpha Alpha, Phi Delta Phi. Home: 7301 Churchill Rd SW Albuquerque NM 87121-2260 Office: Dist Atty's Office 111 Union Square St SE Albuquerque NM 87102-3432

JONES, KENNETH MERLE, rehabilitation services professional; b. Glenns Ferry, Idaho, May 9, 1937; s. Frank Cassius and C. Virginia (Parker) J.; m. N. Jeannette Sutton, Sept. 30, 1962. BS in Edn., U. Idaho, 1969, MEd, 1975; cert., U. San Francisco, 1972. Lic. profl. counselor, Idaho. Vocat. trainer Idaho State Sch. and Hosp., Nampa, Idaho, 1969-72; exec. dir. Vocat. Devel. ctr., Boise, Idaho, 1972-73; facility supr. Idaho Vocat. Rehab., Boise, 1973-76, chief field svcs., 1976-86, chief mgmt. svc., 1986—; cons. Com. on Acreditation Rehab. Facilities, Tucson, 1972-74; bd. dirs. Devel. Disabilities Coun., Boise, 1976-80; apptd. by gov. state dir. Internat. Yr. of Disabled, Boise, 1980. Pres. Mayors Com. on Employment of Persons with Disabilities, Boise, 1989-90; Boise liaison Nat. Orgn. Disability, 1989-93. With U.S. Army, 1959-62. Mem. Nat. Rehab. Assn (pres. local chpt. 1983, 89, pres. pacific region 1990-92), NRA Adminstrn. Assn. (Profl. of Yr. 1989). Home: 4400 Goldenrod Ave Meridian ID 83642-5604 Office: Idaho Div Vocat Rehab Ste 150 LBJ 650 W State Boise ID 83720-3650

JONES, KENTON RUSH, civil engineer; b. Davenport, Iowa, Aug. 24, 1967; s. Brian Marshall Jones and Judith Alleen (Grier) Munson. BS, San Diego State U., 1990, postgrad., 1992—. Cert. engr.-in-tng. Project engr. Chilcote, Inc., San Diego, 1990; civil engr. Rick Engring., Inc., San Diego, 1990-91; assoc. civil engr. County of San Diego, 1991—. Mem. Chi Epsilon (life, chpt. pres. 1990). Republican. Methodist.

JONES, LAURIE GANONG, audit consultant; b. Owatonna, Minn., Feb. 22, 1954; d. Harvey Mathias and Elaine Ione (Mauren) Ganong; m. Daniel Lee Jones, Sept. 6, 1975; 1 child, Jonathon Alexander. AB in Econs., U. Calif., Davis, 1979; MBA, Pepperdine U., Malibu, Calif., 1987. Cert. internal auditor, cert. info. systems auditor. EDP auditor Nat. Blvd. Bank, Chgo., 1980-82; sr. EDP auditor Carnation Co., L.A., 1982-85, Wickes Cos., Santa Monica, Calif., 1985-87; sr. audit mgr. Watt Industries, Santa Monica, 1987-89; dir. audit svcs. Canaudit, Inc., Simi Valley, Calif., 1988-93; prin. Jones & Jones, Sterling, Colo., 1989—; pres. Jones Techs, Inc., Sterling, Colo., 1991-92; dir. support svcs. Sykes Enterprises, Charlotte, N.C., 1992—; guest lectr. Calif. Poly. Inst., Pomona, 1985-87, Calif. State U., Long Beach and Domingez Hills, Calif., 1985-87; ocnf. speaker Inst. Internal Auditors, Orlando, Fla., L.A., 1988—. Author: (monograph) Internal Audit Involvement in the Joint Venture Process, 1990, The Successfull In Charge Auditor, 1990, Introduction to Internal Auditing, 1990, 11A Cash Operations Practice Set, 1991, 11A Risk Assessment Tool Kit, 1990. Disaster preparedness coord. Watt Industries, Santa Monica, 1988-89. Named Bus. Person of the Year Logan County C. of C., 1992. Mem. EDP Auditors Assn. (3d pl. rsch. award 1988), Inst. Internal Auditors (bd. govs. L.A. 1987-89, bd. govs. Denver 1990, internat. bd. regents 1988-91, outstanding rsch. paper 1988, outstanding mem. 1988). Republican. Methodist. Sterling Country Club. Office: Sykes Enterprises Inc 301 Poplar Sterling CO 80751

JONES, LILLIE AGNES, retired educator; b. Leroy, Iowa, Nov. 25, 1910; d. Orace Wesley and Lorena Floy (Buffum) Davis; m. John Hammond Jones, May 27, 1938; children: John Harry, Mary Agnes Jones Edwards. BA, Colo. State Coll. Edn., 1937. Cert. elem. tchr., Colo. Elem. tchr. Weld County Sch. Dist. 81, Kersey, Colo., 1930-34, Weld County Sch. Dist. 121, Erie, Colo., 1934-38, Longmont (Colo.) Pub. Schs., 1955-59, Adams County Sch. Dist. 12, Thornton, Colo., 1959-67, Littleton (Colo.) Pub. Schs., 1967-69; Farmington (N.Mex.) Pub. Schs., 1969-76, ret., 1976; cataloger Longmont Pub. Libr., 1953-55. Kersey High Sch. scholar, 1928. Mem. AAUW (life, past treas. Longmont), Nat. Ret. Tchrs. Assn., N.Mex. Ret. Tchrs. Assn. (life), Pub. Employees Retirement Assn., Colo. Ret. Sch. Employees Assn., Alpha Delta Kappa (rec. sec. Farmington 1975-76, sec. Sun City, Ariz. 1980, historian 1982). Democrat. Home: Sun Grove Resort Village 10134 W Mohawk Ln # 1017 Peoria AZ 85382-2205

JONES, MARGUERITE ROSE (MARGIE JONES), social welfare coordinator; b. Seattle, Feb. 25, 1938; d. Steven M. and Marguerite Alvina (Krueger) Martini; m. LeRoy A. Jones, Feb. 6, 1960; children: Karen Marie, Steven LeRoy, Christopher Micheal, Barbara Susan. BA in Speech Communications, Wash. State U., 1960; postgrad., Cen. Wash. U., 1976-81. Cert. tchr., Wash. Tchr. Wenatchee (Wash.) Dist. Schs., 1960-62; lab. instr. Wenatchee Valley Coll., 1964-65; substitute tchr. Wenatchee Sch. Dist., 1971-77; instr., tech. aide Wenatchee Valley Coll., 1977-82; coord. Allied Arts of North Cen. Wash., Wenatchee, 1984-86; exec. dir. YWCA of Wenatchee Valley, 1986-89; coord. Big Bros./Big Sisters program Children's Home Soc. of Wash., 1989—; workshop instr. Wenatchee Valley Coll.; cons. in field. Mem. adv. bd. Heritage Coll. North Cen. Campus, 1983-84; bd. dirs. Wenatchee Valley Coll. Found., 1983-89. Mem. AAUW (state program v.p. 1989-91, state membership v.p. 1982-84, nat. governance task force 1989-91, grantee 1991), Bus. & Profl. Womens Club, Kiwanis. Roman Catholic. Home: 711 Gellatly Ave Wenatchee WA 98801-3103

JONES, MARK ALAN, broadcast technician; b. San Francisco, 1957; m. Stephanie Phillips, 1983. BA in Communication Studies, Calif. State U., 1979. Chief operator Sta. KXPR, Sacramento, 1979-80, with ops./prodn.dept., 1980-93. Recipient pub. radio program award for Excellence, Corp. Pub. Broadcasting, 1981. Office: Stas KXPR/KXJZ Inc #B 3416 American River Dr Sacramento CA 95864

JONES, MARK LOGAN, educational association executive, educator; b. Provo, Utah, Dec. 16, 1950; s. Edward Evans and Doris (Logan) J. BS, Ea. Mont. Coll., 1975; postgrad. in labor relati, Cornell U.; postgrad., SUNY, Buffalo. Narcotics detective Yellowstone County Sheriff's Dept., Billings, Mont., 1972-74; math tchr. Billings (Mont.) Pub. Schs., 1975-87; rep. Nat. Edn. Assn. of N.Y., Buffalo, Jamestown, 1987-91, Nat. Edn. Assn. Alaska, Anchorage, 1991—. Photographs featured in 1991 N.Y. Art Rev. and Am. Artist. Committeeman Yellowstone Dem. Party, Billings, 1984-87; exec. com. Dem. Cen. Com., Billings, 1985-87; bd. dirs. Billings Community Ctr., 1975-87; concert chmn. Billings Community Concert Assn., 1980-87; bd. dirs. Chautauqua County Arts Coun. With U.S. Army, 1970-72. Recipient Distinguished Svc. award, Billins Edn. Assn., 1985, Mont. Edn. Assn., 1987. Mem. Billings Edn. Assn. (bd. dirs. 1980-82, negotiator 1981-87, pres. 1982-87), Mont. Edn. Assn. (bd. dirs. 1982-87), Ea. Mont. Coll. Tchr. Edn. Project, Accreditation Reviewer Team Mont. Office Pub. Edn., Big Sky Orchard, Masonic, Scottish Rite. Home: PO Box 102904 Anchorage AK 99510-2904 Office: Nat Edn Assn Alaska 1411 W 33d Ave Anchorage AK 99503

JONES, MICHAEL OWEN, folklore educator; b. Wichita, Kans., Oct. 11, 1942; s. Woodrow Owen and Anne Elizabeth (Blackford) J.; m. Jane Dicker, Aug. 1, 1964; 1 child, David Owen. BA in History, Art and Internat. Rels., U. Kans., 1964; MA in Folklore, Ind. U., 1966, PhD in Folklore and Am. Studies, 1970. Prof. history and folklore U. Calif., L.A., 1968—, dir. folkore and mythology ctr., 1984-91. Author: Exploring Folk Art, 1987, Craftsman of the Cumberlands, 1988, (with others) People Studying People, 1980; co-editor: Foodways and Eating Habits, 1981, Inside Organizations, 1988; editor: Putting Folklore to Use, 1993. Mem. Calif. Coun. for the Humanities, San Francisco and L.A., 1988-92. Fellow Am. Folklore Soc., Soc. for Applied Anthropology, Finnish Acad. Sci. and Letters; mem. Am. Culture Assn. (governing bd. 1985-86), So. Calif. Culinary Guild, Orgn. Devel. Network, Acad. Mgmt., Calif. Folklore Soc. (pres. 1981-83), Am. Folklore Soc. Office: U Calif Folklore Mythology Ctr 1037 GSM 405 Hilgard Ave Los Angeles CA 90024-1301

JONES, NANCY C., construction executive; b. Cody, Wyo., Mar. 16, 1942; d. John Carl and Catherine (Schaff) Buckingham; m. William D. Norman, Feb. 5, 1965 (div. 1972); 1 child, Kelly Blue; m. Raymond M. Jones, May 31, 1974; children: Dan, Stephen, Renee, Kelly, Susie. Student, Colo. State U., 1963-65. Owner J.B. Blue Restaurant, Gillette, Wyo., 1968-74; pres. WoodBuck, Inc., Sheridan, Wyo., 1973—; bd. dirs. Shayne and Shortco, Inc., Belen, N.Mex., 1983—. Republican. Roman Catholic. Home: 361 S 26th Ave Brighton CO 80601 Office: Shayne & Shortco Inc PO Box 6399 Sheridan WY 82801-1799

JONES, NANCY LYNNE, computer services executive; b. Larned, Kans., Nov. 27, 1938; d. Jack Edward Doerr and Grace May (Linder) Turner; m. Alva Ray Jones Jr., Dec. 28, 1957; children: Jeffrey Ray, Michael Alan (dec.), Elizabeth Kay, Douglas Edward. BA in Music, San Jose State U., 1975. Tchr., pianist Nancy L. Jones Piano Studio, Eugene, Oreg., 1954—; owner Bits & Bytes Computer Svcs., Eugene, 1987—; pianist, teacher Music Acad. of the West, 1955-56. Composer: 20th Century piano compositions, 1990, Perfect Peace (mixed chorus), 1974; author: (book, tape) Mental Illness Heal Yourself, 1993. Mem. Music Tchrs. Nat. Assn. (nat. cert. 1991), Am. Bus. Women's Assn.

JONES, PALMER THOMASON, editor; b. Memphis, Tenn., May 1, 1959; d. John Joseph and Sally (Palmer) T.; m. John Harrison, Apr. 27, 1985. BA in English, Grinnell Coll., 1981. Rsch. assoc. Miss. River Mus., Memphis, 1981-82; asst. registrar Memphis Brooks Mus. Art, 1982-84; mng. editor Orange Coast Mag., Costa Mesa, Calif., 1985-89, editor, 1989-92; pvt. practice book editing Newport Beach, Calif., 1991-92. Tutor Laubach Libr., Costa Mesa, Calif. 1991-92. Mem. Orange County Press Club (Best Feature Story hon. mention, 1990).

JONES, PETER C., computer scientist; b. Boston, Apr. 19, 1960; s. Paul E. and Janet F. (Wright) J. BA, Harvard Coll., 1978. Sr. software engr. Digital Equipment Corp., Maynard, Mass., 1978-80; cons. Arthur D. Little, Inc., Cambridge, Mass., 1980-84; pres. Amplex Systems, Honolulu, 1984—; chief info. officer Divsn. Community Hosps., State of Hawaii, 1991—; cons. oil ministry, Saudi Arabia, 1981-84, New Zealand Telecom, 1987, USDA, Washington, 1986-89. Author: (with Paul E. Jones) Data Theory, 1991. Office: 1270 Queen Emma St Ste 1200 Honolulu HI 96813-9999

JONES, PHILLIP LAWRENCE, physicist; b. Schenectady, N.Y., Mar. 12, 1962; s. Lawrence Sutton J. and Joan Leila (Heimlich) Semle; m. Joy Ellen Traver, Aug. 3, 1985; 1 child, Laura Elizabeth. BS cum laude, SUNY, Albany, 1985, MS, 1987, PhD, 1990. Rsch. assoc. Inst. for Study of Defects in Solids, Albany, 1985-88; rsch. intern IBM T.J. Watson Rsch. Lab., Yorktown Heights, N.Y., 1988-90; process engr. III Lam Rsch. Corp., Fremont, Calif., 1991—. Contbr. articles to profl. jours. Vol. N.Y. Pub. Interest Rsch. Group, Albany, 1982-84, ACLU, Albany, 1990-92, Sierra Club, 1991—. Fellow Inst. for Study of Defects in Solids, 1987. Mem. Am. Phys. Soc., Soc. of Physics Students (pres. Albany chpt. 1985), Sigma Pi Sigma, Sigma Xi (assoc.). Office: Lam Rsch Corp 4650 Cushing Pkwy M/S A551 Fremont CA 94538

JONES, RANDALL LEE, German language educator; b. Cedar City, Utah, Feb. 21, 1939; s. Wayne K. and Aleda (Christiansen) J.; m. Janet Loraine Taylor, May 24, 1962; children: Kendall, Jeffrey, Michael, Loraine, Scott. BA, Brigham Young U., 1963, MA, 1964; MA, Princeton U., 1966, PhD, 1970. Asst. prof. Cornell U., Ithaca, N.Y., 1968-72, 74-78; assoc. prof. Brigham Young U., Provo, 1978-82, prof., 1982—, dean Coll. of Humanities, 1981—. Editor: (concordance) Standard Edition of Freud, 1980, Goethe's Faust-Part I, 1990, (electronic book) Electronic Library: Goethe, 1991. Recipient Barker lectureship Brigham Young U., Provo, 1987, David Kennedy fellowship, Brigham Young U., Provo, 1989-91. Mem. Am. Assn. Tchrs. German, Assn. for Computers and the Humanities (exec. sec. 1988—), Modern Lang. Assn. (com. chair 1986-90). Democrat. LDS Ch. Office: College of Humanities 2054 JKHB Provo UT 84602

JONES, RICHARD ARGUSTIA, computer science educator, writer; b. Portsmouth, Va., Mar. 26, 1945; s. Gus and Bertie (Sills) J.; m. Carol Marie Stahmer, May 17, 1972; children: Graham, Shauna, Lindsey. BA in Math., Minot (N.D.) State Coll., 1970; MS in Teaching, Drake U., 1972; M Spl. Studies, U. Denver, 1987; M Telecom., 1992. Systems engr. IBM, Kansas City, Mo., 1973-75; tchr. Loretto Acad., Kansas City, 1976-77; graphic artist Portfolio Graphic Arts, Washington, 1977-78; instr. Westmar Coll., Le Mars, Iowa, 1980-83; tchr. math. Kent Denver Sch., Englewood, Colo., 1986-90; instr. computer sci. Teikyo Loretto Heights U., Denver, 1990—. Contbr. poetry and short story to various publs. Sgt. USAF, 1965-69. Recipient medal Freedoms Found., 1968; scholar United Negro Coll. Fund, 1962. Mem. Planetary Soc. Democrat.

JONES, RICHARD HUTTON, history educator; b. Rye, Colo., Aug. 11, 1914; s. John Wiley and Jessie (Hutton) J.; m. Alyce Decker, Aug. 15, 1935; 1 child, Robert Charles. BA, U. No. Colo., 1934, MA, 1937; PhD, Stanford U., 1947; LLD, Reed Coll., 1982. High sch. tchr. Ft. Lupton, Colo., 1934-38; instr. Stanford U., 1940-41; mem. faculty Reed Coll., Portland, Oreg., 1941-86; Richard F. Scholz prof. history Reed Coll., 1962-83; dir. Nat. Endowment Humanities Inst., 1978; profector Oreg. Shakespearean Festival, 1964; chmn. com. European history Coll. Entrance Exam. Bd., 1961-69, mem. com. exams., 1965-68; spl. cons. Ednl. Assocs., Inc., 1968-70; vis. scholar Wolfson Coll., Cambridge, Eng., 1983; curator Pub. Papers of Mark O. Hatfield, 1985—; faculty summer inst. in Hellenic studies Anatolia Coll., Greece, 1986-90; introductory speaker for drama Tygres Heart Shakespeare Co., 1992. Author: The Royal Policy of Richard II, 1966; editor: Areopagitica Press, 1986-91; contbg. editor: medieval sect. London Times Atlas of World History, 1978. Pub. mem. Oreg. Legis. Interim Com. Lbor, 1958-60; mem. Oreg. Commn. Constl. Revision, 1961, 62; exec. sec. Citizens Com. Constl. Revision, 1963-65; Oreg. chmn. Rep. Com. Arts and Scis., 1965-66; chmn. Oreg. Reps. for McCarthy; mem. Oreg. Gov.'s Com. on Humanities, 1965-66; mem. adv. coun. Oreg. Commn. for Humanities, 1973-82; mem. State Panel of Fact Finders, 1976—; mem. citizen amb. dels. to USSR, Sweden, France and Eng., 1988, 90, to three Baltic Republics, 1993. Social Sci. Rsch. Coun. faculty fellow, 1951-53, Ford Found. fellow, 1953-54, sr. fellow law and behavioral sci. U. Chgo. Sch. Law, 1956-57. Mem. Am. Arbitration Assn. (panel on arbitrators). Home: 3908 SE Reedway St Portland OR 97202-7530

JONES, RICHARD LAWRENCE, former college dean, legislative staff member; b. Hartford, Wis., May 29, 1933; s. Lawrence Evan and Ruth Margaret (Wolkow) J.; m. Valeria Elizabeth Morgan, June 18, 1955; children: Richard Kelly, Robert Evan. AA, UCLA, 1953, AB, 1955, MA, 1959, EdD, 1972. Cert. tchr., Calif. Assoc. dir. bands U. Calif., L.A., 1957-59; dir. bands Newport Harbor High Sch., Newport Beach, Calif., 1959-60; prof. Long Beach (Calif.) City Coll., Calif., 1960-66, spl. assignment, 1966-68, dean, 1968-92, dean external rels., 1985-92; dist. dir. for Congressman Stephen Horn, U.S. House of Reps.; guest speaker and conf., workshop, seminar panelist, 1958—; adminstr. cable TV game show series Long Beach City Coll., 1988-91; dir. Western States Marching Band Workshops, 1958-67. Composer, arranger, performer for a various musical groups. Bd. dirs. Am. Cancer Soc.; den father, committeeman Boy Scouts of Am., Eagle Scout; bd. dirs. Cambodian Assn. of Am., Goodwill Industries of So. L.A. County, United Way Harbor/S.E. Region, Long Beach Pub. Corp. for the Arts, Global Edn. Program in So. Calif., Nat. Coun. for Community Svcs., Long Beach Regional Arts Coun., Long Beach Symphony Assn., Nat. Conf. Christians & Jews; bd. dirs., pres. Family Svc. of Long Beach; area chair Keep Good Schs. Coms.; bd. dirs. Long Beach Centennial Celebration, mem. edn. com., pub. rels. com.; mem. Long Beach Regional Adult and Vocat. Edn. Adv. Com., Long Beach Regional Adult and Vocat. Edn. Coun., Calif. Community Colls. Chancellors Task Force on Contract Edn.; trustee St. Mary Med. Ctr. Music scholar UCLA, 1951-55, USN scholar, 1951-55; recipient Pres. award Family Svc. Long Beach, 1993. Mem. NEA, Internat. Bus. Assn., Calif. Community Coll. Community Svcs. Assn. (regional rep., legis. com.), Calif. Community Coll. Continuing Edn. Assn. (past pres.), Assn. Calif. Community Coll. Adminstrs. (legis. com.), Calif. Jr. Coll. Music Educators Assn. (past pres.); Calif. Tchrs. Assn., Coll. Band Dirs. Nat. Assn. (chair jr. coll. div.), Community Coll. Pub. Rels. Orgn., So. Calif. Jr. Coll. Music Educators (past pres.), Long Beach City Coll. Adminstrs. Assn. (past pres.), Long Beach Coll. Alumni Assn., Long Beach City Coll. Faculty/Staff Assn., Long Beach City Coll. Faculty Coun. (com. chair), Long Beach City Coll. Helm Assn., Long Beach Sch. Adminstrs., Suprs. and Cons. Assn. , Tchrs. Assn. of Long Beach, UCLA Doctoral Alumni Assn., Long Beach Area C. of C. (bd. dirs., bus. and arts com., bus. devel. focus group, chmn. edn. and job devel. com., govt. rels. com., long range planning implementation task force, long range strategic planning task force, mktg. coun., new resident guide task force, pub. rels. com.), Lakewood C. of C., Signal Hill C. of C., Kiwanis Internat., Phi Delta Kappa. Republican. Office: Congressman Stephen Horn 4010 Watson Plz Dr Ste 160 Lakewood CA 90712

JONES, RICHARD THEODORE, biochemistry educator; b. Portland, Oreg., Nov. 9, 1929; s. Lester Tallman and Olene (Johnson) J.; m. Marilyn Virginia Beam, June 20, 1953; children: Gary Richard, Alan Donald, Neil William. Student, Calif. Inst. Tech., 1948-51, Ph.D., 1961; B.S., U. Oreg., 1953, M.S., M.D., 1956. Student asst. dept. physiology U. Oreg. Med. Sch., Portland, 1953-56; asst. prof. med. sch. U. Oreg., 1961-64, assoc. prof. exptl. medicine and biochemistry, 1964-67, prof., 1967—, chmn. dept. biochemistry and molecular biology, 1967-93; acting pres. U. Oreg. Health Scis. Center, 1977-78; intern Hosp. U. Pa., 1956-57; research asst. dept. chemistry Calif. Inst. Tech., 1959-60; Mem. biochemistry tng. com. Nat. Inst. Gen. Med. Scis., NIH, 1968-73, med. sci. tng. com., 1971-74; comprehensive sickle cell centers ad hoc rev. com. Nat. Heart, Lung and Blood Inst., 1974-77; biochemistry test com. Nat. Bd. Med. Examiners, 1968-74, FLEX com. Nat. Bd. Med. Examiners, 1982—. Contbr. articles to profl. jours. Mem. Am. Soc. Biochem. and Molecular Biology, AAAS, Sigma Xi, Alpha Omega Alpha, Tau Beta Pi. Home: 2634 SW Fairmount Blvd Portland OR 97201-1433 Office: 3181 SW Sam Jackson Park Rd Portland OR 97201-3098

JONES, ROBERT ALONZO, economist; b. Evanston, Ill., Mar. 15, 1937; s. Robert Vernon and Elsie Pierce (Brown) J.; m. Ina Turner Jones; children: Lindsay Rae, Robert Pierce, Gregory Alan, William Kenneth. AB, Middlebury Coll., 1959; MBA, Northwestern U., 1961, LLD (hon.) Middlebury

(Vt.) Coll., 1992. Economist Hahn, Wise & Assoc., San Carlos, Calif., 1966-69; sr. rsch. officer Bank of Am., San Francisco, 1969-74; v.p., dir. fin. forecasting Chase Econometrics, San Francisco, 1974-76; chmn. bd. Money Market Svcs., Inc., Belmont, Calif., 1974-86; chmn. bd. MMS Internat., Redwood City, Calif., 1986-89, chmn. emeritus, 1989—; chmn. bd. dirs. Market News Svc., N.Y.C.; chmn. bd. trustees Geonomics Inst., Middlebury, 1986—; chmn. bd. Jones Internat., 1989—; bd. dirs. Market News Svc., Inc., N.Y.C., chmn. bd., 1993—; chmn. bd. Market Broadcasting Corp., Incline Village, N.Y.; dean coun. Harvard U. Div. Sch., Cambridge, Mass., 1991—; instr. money and banking, Am. Inst. Banking, San Francisco, 1971, 72. Councilman, City of Belmont (Calif.), 1970-77, mayor, 1971, 72, 75, 76; dir. San Mateo County Transit Dist., 1975-77; chmn. San Mateo County Coun. of Mayors, 1975-76; trustee Incline Village Gen. Improvement Dist., 1984-85. Author: U.S. Financial System and the Federal Reserve, 1974, Power of Coinage, 1987. 1st lt. USAR, 1961-68. Named Hon. Life Mem. Calif. PTA, ordo honorum Kappa Delta Rho Nat. Fraternity; recipient Ernst & Young Entrepreneur of the Yr. award, 1986. Mem. Nat. Assn. Bus. Economists, San Francisco Bond Club. Republican. Methodist.

JONES, ROBERT CLIVE, judge; b. Las Vegas, Nev., July 21, 1947; s. Robert E. and Meryl (Dunn) J.; m. Anita Michele Bunker, Mar. 26, 1970; children: JaNae, Justin, Melissa, Kimberly. BS with honors, Brigham Young U., 1971; JD with honors, UCLA, 1975. Bar: Nev. 1976, U.S. Dist. Ct. Nev. 1976, U.S. Tax Ct. 1979; CPA, Nev. Acct. Laventhol & Horwath, Las Vegas, 1971-72, Touche Ross, Los Angeles, 1974-75, Haskins & Sells, Las Vegas, 1976; assoc. Albright & McGimsey, Las Vegas, 1976; ptnr. Jones & Holt, Las Vegas, 1977-83; chief judge U.S. Bankruptcy Ct., Dist. of Nev., Las Vegas, 1983—. Mem. Order of Coif. Office: US Dist Ct 300 Las Vegas Blvd S Las Vegas NV 89101-5812

JONES, ROBERT EDWARD, federal judge; b. Portland, Oreg., July 5, 1927; s. Howard C. and Leita (Hendricks) J.; m. Pearl F. Jensen, May 29, 1948; children—Jeffrey Scott, Julie Lynn. B.A., U. Hawaii, 1949; J.D., Lewis and Clark Coll., 1953; LL.D. (hon.), City U., Seattle, 1984. Bar: Oreg. 1953. Trial atty. Portland, Oreg., 1953-63; judge Oreg. Circuit Ct., Portland, 1963-83; justice Oreg. Supreme Ct., Salem, 1983-90; judge U.S. Dist. Ct. Oreg., Portland, 1990—; mem. faculty Nat. Jud. Coll., Am. Acad. Jud. Edn.; pres. Oreg. Circuit Judges Assn., 1967—, Oreg. Trial Lawyers Assn., 1959; former mem. Oreg. Evidence Revision Commn., Oreg. Ho. of Reps.; former chair Oreg. Commn. Prison Terms and Parole Standards; adj. prof. Northwestern Sch. Law, Lewis and Clark Coll. 1963—, Willamette Law Sch., 1988—. Bd. overseers Lewis and Clark Coll. Served to capt. JAGC, USNR. Recipient merit award Multnomah Bar Assn., 1979; Citizen award NCCJ, Legal Citizen of the Yr. award Law Related Edn. Project, 1988; Service to Mankind award Sertoma Club Oreg.; James Madison award Sigma Delta Chi; named Disting. Grad., Northwestern Sch. Law. Mem. State Bar Oreg. (former chmn. continuing legal edn. com.). Office: US Dist Ct House 620 SW Main St Portland OR 97205-3023

JONES, ROBERT EUGENE, systems engineering executive; b. St. Paul, Dec. 16, 1923; s. Keith Andrew and Gertrude Mabel (Colwell) J.; m. Barbara Mason, June 6, 1944 (div. 1963); children: Douglas; m. Joy Hewins, Dec. 28, 1964; children: Keith, Christopher, David. BA, U. N.C., 1948; MA, U. Colo., Boulder, 1962, PhD, 1966. Asst. dir. US Bi-Nat. Ctr., San Jose, Costa Rica, 1948-50; prodn. control mgr. Brown Brockmeyer Electric Mfg., Dayton, Ohio, 1950-51; systems analyst Wright Patterson AFB, Dayton, 1951-52; chief mgmt. engring. br. Air Def. Command, Colorado Springs, Colo., 1952-60; dir. systems evaluation N. Am. Aerospace Def. and Space Command, Colorado Springs, 1960-84; asst. to v.p. Teledyne Brown Engring., Colorado Springs, 1984-86; project mgr., Rockwell Internat., 1986—; lectr. U. Colo., Colorado Springs, 1966-72. Contbr. in field. Chmn. dist. com. Pikes Peak coun.l Boy Scouts Am., Colorado Springs, 1960-74; bd. dirs. Broadmoor Ski Racing Acad., Colorado Springs, 1981-84; 19th Mtn. divsn. Italian campaign. With U.S. Army, 1943-46. Recipient Meritorious Civilian Svc. award Sec. of the Air Force, 1973, Exceptional Civilian Svc. award, Sec. of Air Force, 1983. Mem. N.Y. Acad. Sci., Ops. Rsch. Soc. Am., Am. Econ. Assn., AAAS. Episcopalian. Office: Rockwell Internat 1250 Academy Park Loop Colorado Springs CO 80910-3708

JONES, ROBERT RICHARD, insurance and financial consultant, educator; b. Canton, Ohio; s. Robert Hall Jones and Clara Maybelle Channell; children: Melinda, Christopher. BA, UCLA, 1951; postgrad., Asia Inst., 1952; MA, NYU, 1962; postgrad., U. Pa., 1974; CLU, Am. Coll., 1978; D of Bus. Adminstrn., Golden Gate U., 1991. Spl. events officer, news corr. U.S. Dept. State, 1948-51; news corr. U.N. Internat. Info. Adminstrn./Voice of Am., N.Y.C., 1948-53; various to nat. sales dir. N.Y. Life Ins. Co., N.Y.C., 1953-66; various to pres., CEO Fla. Growth Fund, Jacksonville, 1966-69; asst. v.p., dir. of manpower devel. Aetna Variable Annuity Life, Washington and Hartford, Conn., 1969-72; nat. dir. of specialized mktg. ITT Hartford, 1972-78; owner, prin. Robert R. Jones & Assocs., Burlingame, Calif., 1978—; prof. Coll. of Notre Dame MBA Grad. Program, Belmont, Calif., 1987—; sr. ins. cons. SRI, Internat., Fin. Industries Ctr., Internat. Mgmt. and Econs. Group, Menlo Park, Calif., 1982-83, per diem cons. 1983—. Contbr. articles to profl. jours. Commr. City of Burlingame (Calif.), 1991—. With USN, 1943-51, numerous theaters. Named NBC Radio scholar UCLA, 1949-50, J.N. Flint scholar, 1950, others; recipient Disting. Svc. and Leadership awards Internat. Assn. for Fin. Planning, San Francisco, 1984-85. Mem. Nat. Assn. Securities Dealers (registered prin.), Nat. Assn. Life Underwriters (bd. dirs.), Am. Soc. Life Underwriters (bd. dirs., ethics chmn.). Office: Robert R Jones & Assocs PO Box 489 Burlingame CA 94010

JONES, ROBERT THOMAS, aerospace scientist; b. Macon, Mo., May 28, 1910; s. Edward Seward and Harriet Ellen (Johnson) J.; m. Megan Lillian More, Nov. 23, 1964; children: Edward, Patricia, Harriet, David, Gregory, John. Student, U. Mo., 1928; Sc.D. (hon.), U. Colo., 1971. Aero. research scientist NACA, Langley Field, Va., 1934-46; research scientist Ames Research Center NACA-NASA, Moffet Field, Calif., 1946-62; sr. staff scientist Ames Research Center, NASA, 1970-81, research assoc., 1981—; scientist Avco-Everett Research Lab., Everett, Mass., 1962-70; cons. prof. Stanford U., 1981. Author: (with Doris Cohen) High Speed Wing Theory, 1960, Collected Works of Robert T. Jones, 1976, Wing Theory, 1987; contbr. (with Doris Cohen) articles to profl. jours. Recipient Reed award Inst. Aero. Scis., 1946; Inventions and Contbns. award NASA, 1975; Prandtl Ring award Deutsche Gesellschaft für Luft and Raumfahrt, 1978; Pres.'s medal for disting. fed. service, 1980; Langley medal Smithsonian Instn., 1981; Excalibur award U.S. Congress, 1981. Fellow AIAA (hon.); mem. NAS (award in aero. engring. 1989), NAE, Am. Acad. Arts and Scis. Home: 25005 La Loma Dr Los Altos CA 94022-4507

JONES, ROGER CLYDE, electrical engineer, educator; b. Lake Andes, S.D., Aug. 17, 1919; s. Robert Clyde and Martha (Albertson) J.; m. Katherine M. Tucker, June 7, 1952; children: Linda Lee, Vonnie Lynette. B.S., U. Nebr., 1949; M.S., U. Md., 1953; Ph.D. U. Md., 1963. With U.S. Naval Research Lab., Washington, 1949-57; staff sr. engr. to chief engr. Melpar, Inc., Falls Church, Va., 1957-58; cons. project engr. Melpar, Inc., 1958-59, sect. head physics, 1959-64, chief scientist for physics, 1964; prof. dept. elec. engring. U. Ariz., Tucson, 1964-89; dir. quantum electronics lab. U. Ariz., 1968-88, adj. prof. radiology, 1978-86, adj. prof. radiation-oncology, 1986-88, prof. of radiation-oncology, 1988-89, prof. emeritus, 1989—; tech. dir. H.S.C. and A., El Paso, 1989—; guest prof. in exptl. oncology Inst. Cancer Research, Aarhus, Denmark, 1982-83. Patentee in field. Served with AUS, 1942-45. Mem. Am. Phys. Soc., Optical Soc. Am., Bioelectromagnetics Soc., IEEE, AAAS, NSPE, Am. Congress on Surveying and Mapping, Eta Kappa Nu, Pi Mu Epsilon, N.Mex. Acad. Sci. Home: 5809 E 3d St Tucson AZ 85711 Office: U Ariz Dept Elec and Computer Engring Tucson AZ 85721

JONES, ROGER WAYNE, electronics executive; b. Riverside, Calif., Nov. 21, 1939; s. Virgil Elsworth and Beulah (Mills) J.; m. Sherill Lee Bottjer, Dec. 28, 1975; children: Jerrod Wayne, Jordan Anthony. BS in Engring., San Diego State U., 1962. Br. sales mgr. Bourns, Inc., Riverside, 1962-68; sales and mktg. mgr. Spectrol Electronics, Industry, Calif., 1968-77, v.p. mktg., 1979-81; mng. dir. Spectrol Reliance, Ltd., Swindon, England, 1977-79; sr. v.p. S.W. group Kierulff Electronics Corp., L.A., 1981-83; v.p. sales and mktg. worldwide electronic techs. div. Beckman Instruments, Fullerton, Calif., 1983-86; pres., ptnr. Jones & McGeoy Sales, Inc., Newport Beach, Calif., 1986—. Author: The History of Villa Rockledge, A National Treasure in Laguna Beach, 1991. Republican. Home: 4 Royal St George Newport Beach CA 92660 Office: 5100 Campus Dr Newport Beach CA 92660

JONES, RONALD H., computer information systems executive; b. San Diego, Feb. 11, 1938; s. Henry G. and Geneva H. (Hodges) J.; m. Carol Sue Carmichael, Dec. 9, 1967. BS, San Diego State Coll., 1959, MS, 1961. Project mgr. UNIVAC, San Diego, 1961-67, Computer Scis. Corp., San Diego, 1967-75; v.p. Interactive, Inc., San Diego, 1975-92; owner Consulting Co., San Diego, 1992—; ind. cons., programmer various mfg. & distbg. cos., San Diego, 1992—. Contbr. articles to profl. jours. Advisor San Diego State Univ.; Rep. nat. committeeman, 1979—. Mem. Am. Prodn. & Inventory Control Soc., Assn. Computing Machinery, Calpirg & Ucan. Presbyterian. Home and Office: 2484 Pine St San Diego CA 92103-1042 Office: Johnstone Supply 4320 Pacific Hwy San Diego CA 92110

JONES, RONALD VANCE, broadcast executive; b. Livingston, Mont., Apr. 20, 1940; s. Glenn Llewellyn and Heretha (Emmett) J.; m. Angelina Lee Vicedomini, May 19, 1974. Student in journalism, U. Mont., 1960-61; diploma in radio/TV, N.W. Schs., 1963. Announcer KPRK Radio, Livingston, Mont., 1956-64, KCHY Radio, Cheyenne, Wyo., 1964; announcer, sales rep. KXXL Radio, Bozeman, Mont., 1964-70, ops. and sales mgr., 1967-68; sales rep. KOOK Radio, Billings, Mont., 1970-71; gen. mgr. KXLF Radio, Butte, Mont., 1971-74, KBOM Radio, Bismarck, N.D., 1974; sales mgr. KYYA Radio, Billings, 1975-87, gen. mgr., 1987—. Mem. mktg. com. Big Sky Internat. Air Show, Billings, 1988-90; bd. dirs. Consumer Credit Counseling Svc., Billings; bd. dirs. Park County Jaycees, Livingston, 1960-64. Sgt. USNG, 1957-63. Mem. Billings Radio Broadcasters Assn., Billings C. of C. (mem. com.), Billings Ad Club (v.p., bd. dirs. 1978-86). Republican. Office: KYYA Radio 1645 Central Ave Billings MT 59102-5197 Home: PO Box 355 Laurel MT 59044-0355

JONES, RUSSELL DEAN, real estate developer; b. L.A., Aug. 17, 1933; s. Fred S. and Rose Marie (Mauler) J.; m. Hae Young Lee; children: Kellianne P. Jones Wilder, Katelyn M. BBA, Loyola U., L.A., 1954; JD, Loyola U., 1957. Bar: Calif.; lic. real estate broker, Calif. Asst. city adminstr. City of Culver City, Calif., 1958-60; sr. asst. city mgr. City of Santa Monica, Calif., 1960-64; city adminstr. City of Placentia, Calif., 1964-67; asst. dir. Calif. Dept. Housing & Community Devel., Sacramento, 1967-68; v.p. Boise Cascade Bldg. Co., L.A., 1968-72; pres. Russell D. Jones Group, L.A., 1972-81; v.p. hotel devel. Marriott Corp., L.A., 1981-90; pres. Russell D. Jones & Assocs., Rancho Palos Verdes, Calif., 1991—; lectr. in field. Mem. Gov.'s Adv. Com. on Factory Built Housing, Sacramento, 1969-72; mem. subdivision adv. com. Dept. Real Estate, Sacramento, 1968-71. Named Alumnus of the Yr., Alpha Delta Gamma, 1964. Mem. State Bar of Calif., Western Govtl. Rsch. Assn., Loyola Marymount U. Alumni Assn. (bd. dirs. 1981-84), Bldg. Industry Assn. Calif. (v.p. 1971-72), Alpha Delta Gamma (nat. pres. 1956-57). Republican. Roman Catholic. Home and Office: 4129 Admirable Dr Palos Verdes Peninsula CA 90274-6031

JONES, SAMUEL VADAKEDATH, ministries executive; b. Kumbanad, Kerala, India, Feb. 9, 1933; came to U.S., 1959; s. Varughis Vadakedath and Mariamma (Cherian) Samuel; m. Annette Louise McCullough, Aug. 14, 1965; children: Elizabeth, Mark. BA, Agra U., Gorakhpur, India, 1956; MDiv, Asbury Theol. Sem., 1960; MSW, Scarritt Coll., 1963; ThD, Kingsway Sem., 1987. Ordained to ministry Nepal Border Bible Fellowship, 1958. Field rep. St. Thomas Ch. of Kerala, Tibet, 1957-58; profl. svc. staff Billy Graham Assn., Mpls., 1959-87, activities, internat. crusade assoc., 1965-69, film distbn., 1969-71; exec. dir. Hong Kong office Billy Graham Assn., 1972-81; internat. conf. dir., Amsterdam Horizon Internat. Ministries, San Diego, 1987-91; frequent speaker on missions and cross-cultural issues; cons. Billy Graham Assn., 1992—. Contbr. articles to mags. Pres. Internat. Student Fellowship, Mpls., 1969; bd. dirs. for several civic orgns. Mem. Kiwanis (charter mem., Outstanding Svc. award Hong Kong club 1979, life mem., treas., pres. Hong Kong club 1978-79). Democrat. Home: 4353 Arden View Ct Arden Hills MN 55112

JONES, SANDRA LOU, college program director; b. Golden, Colo., July 13, 1944; d. John R. and Evelyn M. (Anderson) Hampton; m. Jerry Schloffman, June 29, 1963 (div. 1980); children: Jerry Jon, Heather Nicole; m. Stuart A. Jones, May 15, 1982. Student, Colo. State U., 1962-63. Sec. Adams State Coll., Alamosa, Colo., 1963-65; adminstrv. sec. Met. State Coll., Denver, 1965-75, adminstrv. officer, 1975-80, asst. dir. Contract Personnel, 1980-82, dir. Contract Personnel, 1982-87, dir. Personnel, Payroll, 1987—. Bd. dirs. Cardinals Aurora (Colo.) Youth League, 1978-84, Hinkley High Athletic Boosters, Aurora, 1985-90; adminstrv. bd. Burns Meml. United Meth. Ch., Aurora, 1984—. Mem. Colo. Higher Edn. Pers. Assn. (pres.-elect), Coll. and Univ. Pers. Assn. Methodist. Home: 684 Dearborn St Aurora CO 80011-6917

JONES, SCOTT AUSTIN, software developer, microcomputer consultant; b. Phoenix, Aug. 22, 1962; s. Travis Hayhurst and Mary Louise (Coy) J. BA, U. Ariz., Tucson, 1988. Sr. programmer analyst Alpha Therapeutic Corp., L.A., 1988-90; owner Austin Software Design, L.A., Grand Junction, 1989—; cons., Austin Software Design, L.A., Grand Junction; software reviewer, Assn. of Shareware Profls. Author: Recursive Realm, 1989, 90, 91. Mem. Assn. of Shareware Profls. Office: Austin Software Design PO Box 30133 Grand Junction CO 81503-3200

JONES, SHARON ELAINE, lawyer; b. Chgo., Aug. 3, 1955; d. Raymond L. and Lillian (Taylor) J. BA, Harvard U., 1977, JD, 1982. Bar: Ill. 1982, U.S. Dist. Ct. (no. dist.) Ill. 1982, Calif. 1990, U.S. Dist. Ct. (cen. dist.) Calif. 1990, U.S. Ct. Appeals (7th cir. and 9th cir.) 1985, 1990. Assoc. Lord, Bissell & Brook, Chgo., 1982-85; asst. U.S. atty. no. dist. Ill. U.S. Atty.'s Office, Chgo., 1985-89; of counsel Orrick, Herrington & Sutcliffe, L.A., 1989—. Office: Orrick Herrington & Sutcliffe 777 S Figueroa St Ste 3200 Los Angeles CA 90017-2513

JONES, THOMAS ROBERT, social worker; b. Escanaba, Mich., Jan. 3, 1950; s. Gene Milton and Alica Una (Mattson) J.; m. Joy Sedlock. BA, U. Laverne, 1977; MSW, U. Hawaii, 1979. Social work assoc. Continuing Care Svcs., Camarillo, Calif., 1973-78; psychiat. social worker Camarillo State Hosp., 1980-84; psychotherapist Terkensha Child Treatment Ctr., Sacramento, Calif., 1984-86; psychiat. social worker Napa (Calif.) State Hosp., 1986-87, Vets. Home Calif., Yountville, 1987—. Mem. Nat. Assn. Social Workers, Soc. Clin. Social Work, Am. Orthopsychiat. Assn., Acad. Cert. Social Workers, Assn. for Advancement Behavior Therapy. Home: PO Box 1095 Yountville CA 94599-1095 Office: Vets Home of Calif Yountville CA 94599

JONES, THORNTON KEITH, research chemist; b. Brawley, Calif., Dec. 17, 1923; s. Alfred George and Madge Jones; m. Evalee Vestal, July 4, 1965; children: Brian Keith, Donna Eileen. BS, U. Calif., Berkeley, 1949, postgrad., 1951-52. Research chemist Griffin Chem. Co., Richmond, Calif., 1949-55; western product devel. and improvement mgr. Nopco Chem. Co., Richmond, Calif., 1955; research chemist Chevron Research Co., Richmond, 1956-65, research chemist in spl. products research and devel., 1965-1982; product quality mgr. Chevron USA, Inc., San Francisco, 1982-87, ret. Patentee in field. Vol. fireman and officer, Terra Linda, Calif., 1957-64; mem. adv. com. Terra Linda Dixie Elem. Sch. Dist., 1960-64. Served with Signal Corps, U.S. Army, 1943-46. Mem. Am. Chem. Soc., Forest Products Research Soc., Am. Wood Preservers Assn., Alpha Chi Sigma. Republican. Presbyterian.

JONES, VERNON QUENTIN, surveyor; b. Sioux City, Iowa, May 6, 1930; s. Vernon Boyd and Winnifred Rhoda (Bremmer) J.; student UCLA, 1948-50; m. Rebeca Buckovecz, Oct. 1981; children: Steven Vernon, Gregory Richard, Stanley Alan, Lynn Sue. Draftsman III Pasadena (Calif.) city engr., 1950-53; sr. civil engring. asst. L.A. County engr., L.A., 1953-55; v.p. Treadwell Engring. Corp., Arcadia, Calif., 1955-61, pres., 1961-64; pres. Hillcrest Engring. Corp., Arcadia, 1961-64; dep. county surveyor, Ventura, Calif., 1964-78; propr. Vernon Jones Land Surveyor, Riviera, Ariz., 1978—; city engr. Needles (Calif.), 1980-87; instr. Mohave Community Coll., 1987—. Chmn. graphic tech. com. Ventura Unified Sch. Dist., 1972-78, mem. career adv. com., 1972-74; mem. engring. adv. com. Pierce Coll., 1973; pres. Mgmt. Employees of Ventura County, 1974. V.p. Young Reps. of Ventura County, 1965. Pres., Marina Pacifica Homeowners Assn., 1973. Mem. League Calif. Surveying Orgns. (pres. 1975), Am. Congress on Surveying and Mapping (chmn. So. Calif. sect. 1976), Am. Soc. Photogrammetry, Am. Pub. Works Assn., County Engr. Assn. Calif. Home: 913E San Juan Ct Riviera AZ 86442-5618

JONES, WANDA CAROL, nurse; b. Riverside, Calif., Jan. 2, 1956; d. Wallace Campbell and Erma Frances (Elliott) Wendelstadt; m. Rodney Jay Shelton, Feb. 16, 1980 (dec.); 1 child from previous marriage, Wendy Mae Cox; m. Jimmy L. Jones, July 30, 1992. Cert. in voc. nursing, United Health Careers, 1982; AS, San Bernardino Valley Coll., 1987. RN, Calif. Tchr. piano Fontana, Calif., 1969-75; underwriter Prudential Ins. Co., San Bernardino, Calif., 1977; newspaper editor Allied Constrn. Ind., San Bernardino, 1979-82; nursing asst. San Bernardino County Med. Ctr., 1982-83; voc. nurse Remedy Health Svcs., San Bernadino, 1983; voc. nurse Kaiser Permanente, Fontana, 1983-87, RN, 1987—. Mem. choir Calvary Bapt. Ch. Mem. NAFE, United Nurses Assn. Calif., Grange Club, Order of Rainbow for Girls, Alpha Gamma Sigma.

JONES, WENDELL OREN, information technology executive; b. Alpena, Ark., Apr. 13, 1941; s. Stephen Decatur and Millie (Hopper) J.; m. Grace Bougere, June 23, 1963; children: Daniel, Brian, Kimberly. BS, U. Ark., 1962; MBA, U. Ga., 1970, PhD, 1978. Post-doctoral fellow Cornell U., Ithaca, N.Y., 1980-81; assoc. prof. U.S. Mil. Acad., West Point, N.Y., 1981-85; gen. mgr. Info. Systems Devel. Ctr., Ft. Lee, Va., 1986-88; dir. corp. info. systems McDonnell Douglas Corp., St. Louis, 1988-89; gen. mgr. McDonnell Douglas Info. Svcs. Co., Long Beach, Calif., 1989—. Col. U.S. Army, 1962-78. Home: 16236 Santa Barbara Ln Huntington Beach CA 92649-2177 Office: McDonnell Douglas 3300 E Spring St Long Beach CA 90806-2428

JONES, WILLIAM CHARLES, library-media specialist; b. Princeton, N.J., Feb. 28, 1937; s. George Edward and Margaret Louise (Fetzing) J.; m. Elizabeth Ann Brooks, Oct. 10, 1971; 1 child, Courtney Elizabeth. BA, U. Denver, 1959, MA, 1966; Ednl. Specialist, U. Colo., 1970. Tchr. Mapleton Pub. Schs., Adams County, Colo., 1960-69, libr., 1969-85, library-media coord., 1985—; editor Colo. Bibliography project Grubstake, Colo. Ednl. Media Assn., Denver, 1975-77; Colo. editor young adult lit. project ALA, Chgo., 1978. Co-author: Denver: A Pictorial History, 1973, Photo by McClure, 1983, Buckwalter: Pioneer Photojournalist, 1989, William Henry Jackson's Colorado, 1992; contbr. articles to profl. jours. Trustee Colo. R.R. Mus., Golden, 1968—; mem. Colo. Hist. Soc., Denver, 1960—, Colo. Corral of Westerners, Denver, 1987—, Historic Denver, 1970—. Mem. NEA, Nat. Rwy. Hist. Soc. (regional v.p. 1968-84), Colo. Ednl. Media Assn. Methodist. Home: 7 Blue Sage Littleton CO 80127-5797 Office: Mapleton Pub Schs 591 E 80th Ave Denver CO 80229-5899

JONES, WILLIAM EDWARD, air force officer; b. Memphis, Apr. 18, 1942; s. Raymond Frederick and Marjorie (Hutchinson) J.; m. Terry Bevis, July 17, 1965; 1 child, Gary. BS in Bus. Adminstrn. and Mgmt., U. Tenn., 1964; grad., Air Command and Staff Coll., Maxwell AFB, 1976, Indsl. Coll. Armed Forces, Maxwell AFB, 1977; grad. with distinction, Air War Coll., Maxwell AFB, 1983; grad. Sr. Official in Nat. Security, Harvard U., 1989. Commd. 2d lt. USAF, advanced through grades to maj. gen., 1992; various operational ground and staff positions, HQ, maj. commands and unit level operation USAF, various U.S. and overseas, 1965-83; dir. command automation 17th AF USAF, Sembach Air Base, Fed. Republic Germany, 1983-84; comdr. 600th tactical control group USAF, Hessich-Oldendorf, Fed. Republic Germany, 1984-85; dir. programs HQ USAFE USAF, Ramstein Air Base, Fed. Republic Germany, 1985-86; vice comdr. 487th Tactical Missile Wing USAF, Camiso Air Base, Italy, 1986-87; comdr. 501st Tactical Missile Wing USAF, RAF Greenham Common, Eng., 1987-88; dir. forces HQ USAF Pentagon USAF, Washington, 1988-90; dep. chief staff for plans Hdqs. Air Force Space Command, Colorado Springs, Colo., 1990-92, dep. chief staff for ops., 1992-93; dir. forces Hdqs. USAF, Washington, 1993—. Decorated Legion of Merit with device, Def. Meritorious Svc. medal, Meritorious Svc. medal with 4 devices. Mem. Air Force Assn. Home: 481 Selfridge Cir Colorado Springs CO 80916-5170 Office: USAF DCS/Plans Hdqs AFSPACEOM Peterson AFB CO 80916

JONES, WILLIAM HAWOOD, electrical engineer; b. Cooper, Tex., Jan. 20, 1927; s. Paul Adair and Demily (Delores) J.; m. Margaret Nadean Pittman, Oct. 20, 1947; children: Bonnie Jean, Margaret Angela. BSEE, Okla. U., 1951; MSEE, Syracuse U., 1962. Registered profl. engr., N.Y., Okla. Engr. GE, Syracuse, N.Y., 1952-65, Honeywell/Control Data, Oklahoma City, 1965-79; engr., mgr. Magnex Corp. subs. Exxon, San Jose, Calif., 1979-82; engr. Atasi Corp., San Jose, 1982-86; engr., mgr. Konica Tech. Inc., Sunnyvale, Calif., 1986—. Inventor, patentee in field. Mem. IEEE, Etta Kappa Nu. Office: Jones Consulting 6525 NW 115th St Oklahoma City OK 73162-2932

JONES-DAVIS, GEORGIA, newspaper book review editor; b. L.A., Apr. 29, 1951; d. Raymond and Frances Esther (Weinberg) Jones; m. Howard Louis Davis, May 3, 1987; 1 child, Emily Hannah. BA, UCLA, 1974, postgrad., 1974-75. Editorial asst. L.A. Herald Examiner, 1978-80; feature writer, book reviewer Herald Examiner, 1979-84; feature writer, book reviewer, freelance worker L.A.; asst. book editor L.A. Herald Examiner, 1980-83, feature desk copy editor, 1983-84; asst. book rev. editor L.A. Times, 1984—, book reviewer, 1984—. Active animal welfare, Delta Res., L.A., 1980—; mem. NOW. Mem. Nat. Book Critic Cir., PEN. Democrat. Office: LA Times Book Rev Times Mirror Sq Los Angeles CA 90053

JONES-SCHENK, JANEA, nursing administrator; b. Hugoton, Kans., Aug. 14, 1952; d. Orville Bruce and Patricia Earline (Green) Jones; m. Paul Schenk, Aug. 7, 1977; children: Hillary Jane, Morgan Andrew. AA, Mesa Coll., Grand Junction, Colo., 1972; student, U. Colo., 1973-74; BSN magna cum laude, Westminster Coll., Salt Lake City, 1977; postgrad., U. Utah, 1987; M in Nursing Adminstrn., U. Phoenix, 1992. Staff nurse orthopedics St. Marks Hosp., Salt Lake City, 1977-78; staff nurse emergency rm. St. Marks Hosp., 1978-80, nursing supr., 1980-81, head nurse, 1981-83; asst. dir. nursing HCA St. Marks Hosp., Salt Lake City, 1983-89; pres. JJS Assocs., Park City, Utah, 1990—; guest lectr. U. Utah Coll. Nursing, 1988-90. Mem. bd. dirs. HCA St. Marks Women's Ctr., Salt Lake City, 1989; co-chmn. Parks and Recreation Adv. Bd., Park City, 1990. Mem. ANA, NOW, Am. Orgn. Nurse Execs., Utah Nurses Assn., Utah Nurses Found. (bd. dirs. 1992), Utah Tennis Assn., Alpha Chi, Sigma Theta Tau. Democrat. Office: JJS Assocs 1500 Lucky John Dr Park City UT 84060-6910

JONGEWARD, GEORGE RONALD, systems analyst; b. Yakima, Wash., Aug. 9, 1934; s. George Ira and Dorothy Marie (Cronk) J.; m. Janet Jeanne Williams, July 15, 1955; children: Mary Jeanne, Dona Lee, Karen Anne. BA, Whitworth Coll., 1957; postgrad., Utah State U., 1961. Sr. systems analyst Computer Scis. Corp., Honolulu, 1969-71; cons. in field Honolulu, 1972-76; prin. The Hobby Co., Honolulu, 1977-81; sr. systems analyst Computer Systems Internat., Honolulu, 1981—; instr. EDP Hawaii Pacific Coll., Honolulu, 1982—. Mem. car show com. Easter Seal Soc., Honolulu, 1977-82; active Variety Club, Honolulu, 1978-81. Mem. Mensa (local pres. 1967-69). Republican. Presbyterian. Club: Triple-9. Home: 400 Hobron Ln Apt 2611 Honolulu HI 96815-1206 Office: Computer Systems Internat 841 Bishop St Ste 501 Honolulu HI 96813-3991

JONKER, PETER EMILE, gas company executive; b. The Hague, The Netherlands, Sept. 15, 1948; came to U.S., 1966, naturalized, 1985; s. Jacob and Jurrina (Wories) J.; m. Janet Lynn Gotfredson, Sept. 6, 1974; children: Jeffrey, Annelies. BSChemE cum laude, U. So. Calif., 1971, MSChemE, 1972; JD with honors, Western State U., Fullerton, Calif., 1979. Bar: Calif. 1979. Research engr. Union Oil Co., Los Angeles, 1972-75; regulations coordinator Union Oil Co., L.A., 1975-79, atty., 1979; mgr. govtl. and pub. affairs Western Liquefied Nat. Gas, L.A., 1979-81; mgr. environ. permitting Tosco Corp., L.A., 1981-83; mgr. regional pub. affairs So. Calif. Gas. Co., L.A., 1983-85, mgr. rate design, demand forecast and analysis, 1986-88, mgr. fed. energy affairs, 1988-90, mgr. support svcs., 1990-92; mgr. policy and planning So. Calif. Gas Co., L.A., 1992—; mem. So. Coast Air Quality Mgmt. Dist. Adv. Council, Los Angeles, 1983-85. Editor Western State Law Rev., 1976-79; contbr. articles to profl. jours. Trustee, deacon San Marino

(Calif.) Presbyn. Community Ch., 1980—; councilman U. So. Calif. Engring. Student Council, Los Angeles, 1971-72, dir. Engring. Alumni Assn., 1971-72; fgn. del. White House Conf., Washington, 1971. Mem. Am. Gas Assn., Air & Waste Mgmt. Assn. (v.p. West coast chpt. 1984, 85), Fed. Energy Bar Assn., Pacific Coast Gas Assn., Tau Beta Pi (pres., v.p. Calif. Delta chpt. 1970-71). Republican. Home: 2450 Melville Dr San Marino CA 91108-2616 Office: So Calif Gas Co 555 W 5th St Los Angeles CA 90013-1010

JONSSON, RICHARD EUGENE, bilingual educator; b. Cleveland Heights, Ohio, Feb. 10, 1935; s. John Eric Walter and Anna Patricia (McGrath) Johnson; m. Betty Lasap Calado, Aug. 14, 1984; 1 child, Brenda Anne. BA in Social Studies, U. Americas, Puebla, Mex., 1960; postgrad., U. Stockholm, 1961-62; MA in English Lit., Northeastern U., 1973. Asst. field dir. Nat. ARC, 1963-66; libr. asst. art, music and recreation dept. San Diego Pub. Libr., 1974-76; classical music announcer Sta. WDCS-FM, Portland, Maine, 1979-80; bilingual tutor Anchorage Sch. Dist., 1980—. Author poetry, other publs. With USAF, 1954-58. Roman Catholic. Home: 223 Fawn Ct Anchorage AK 99515-3471 Office: Anchorage Sch Dist 4600 Debarr Rd Anchorage AK 99508-3195

JOOST-GAUGIER, CHRISTIANE LOUISE, art history educator; b. St. Maxime, France; d. Louis Clair and Agnes (Larsen) G.; children: Leonarda, Nathalie. BA with honors, Radcliffe Coll., 1955; MA, Harvard U., 1959, PhD, 1973. Asst. prof. Mich. State U., East Lansing, 1960-61, Tufts U., Medford, Mass., 1968-73; assoc. prof., dept. chmn. N.Mex. State U., Las Cruces, 1975-81, prof., dept. chmn., 1980-85; prof., dept. chmn. U. N.Mex., Albuquerque, 1985-87, prof., 1987—. Author: Selected Drawings of Jacopo Bellini, 1980; contbr. articles to profl. jours. Vassie James Hill fellowship AAUW; grantee Am. Philos. Soc., Am. Coun. of Learned Socs., Delmas, Fulbright; Fulbright fellow U. Munich, 1958-60. Mem. Renaissance Soc. Am. (coun. mem. 1980-84), Coll. Art Assn. Am. (bd. dirs. 1980-86), Soc. Archtl. Historians, Am. Assn. for Italian Studies, Nat. Coun. Arts Adminstrs. (bd. dirs. 1979-85), Sixteenth Century Soc., Internat. Soc. for the Classical Tradition. Office: U NMex Dept Art and Art History Albuquerque NM 87131

JOPLIN, ALBERT FREDERICK, transportation executive; b. Victoria, B.C., Can., Feb 22, 1919; s. Albert Edward and Emily Eliza (Norford) J.; m. Margaret Brigid McMorragh-Kavanaugh, May 26, 1947 (dec.); 1 child, Mary Lynn Barbara; m. Dorothy Anne Cook, July 29, 1977. BASc in Civil Engring., U. B.C., 1948. With Can. Pacific Ltd., 1947-87, spl. engr., Calgary, 1962-65, devel. engr., Vancouver, 1965-66, mgr. spl. projects, 1966-68, system mgr. planning and devel., Montreal, Que., 1968-69, dir. devel. planning, 1969-71, v.p. mktg. and sales CP Rail, 1971-74, v.p. operation and maintenance, 1974-76; gen. mgr. Marathon Realty, 1965-66; pres., chief exec. officer Canadian Pacific (Bermuda) Ltd., 1976-84; Shaw Industries, Ltd., Toronto, Ont., Straits Oil and Gas Ltd., pres. Straits Oil and Gas U.S.A. Ltd., Sydney; chmn., bd. dirs. Leaders Equity Corp., Vancouver, Advanced Smelters Tech. Inc.; pres., chief exec. officer Cen. Ocean Industries Ltd. Commr., gen. dir. Can. Pacific Pavilion Expo '86, 1984-87; assoc. mem. Boy Scouts Can. Served with RCAF, 1941-45. Mem. Assn. Profl. Engrs. B.C. (life), Engring. Inst. Can. (life), Can. Soc. Civil Engrs. (life), Internat. Soc. for Planning and Strategic Mgmt., Can. Maritime Law Assn., Vancouver Maritime Arbitrators Assn., Inst. Corp. Dirs. Can., Air Force Officers Assn., Indian Ocean Flying Boat Assn., Terminal City Club (Vancouver), Jericho Officers' Mess Club (Vancouver), Royal Montreal Golf Club, Traffic Club, Mount Stephen Club (Montreal), Canadian Railway Club, Western Canada Railway Club, Mid-Ocean Club, Bermuda Maritime Museum (life), Vancouver Maritime Mus., Nat. Trust (Bermuda), Rotary (Vancouver, B.C., Paul Harris fellow), Order of St. John, Beta Theta Pi. Home: 4317 Staulo, Vancouver, BC Canada V6N 3S1 Office: PO Box 43, 200 Granville St, Vancouver, BC Canada V6C 2R3

JORDAHL, GEIR ARILD, photographer, educator; b. Kristiansund, Norway, Jan. 27, 1957; came to U.S., 1961; s. Sigurd and Solveig Ingvarda (Pedersen) J.; m. Kathleen Patricia O'Grady, Sept. 24, 1983. BA, Calif. State U., Hayward, 1979; MFA, Ohio U., 1983. Life C.C. teaching credential, Calif. Teaching assoc. Ohio U., Athens, 1980-82; instr. photography Chabot Coll., Hayward, Calif., 1983—; owner, mgr. Geir & Kate Jordahl, Photography, Hayward, 1983—; ind. curator, Hayward, 1984—; coord. PhotoCen. Photography Programs, Hayward, 1983—; artist-in-residence Yosemite (Calif.) Nat. Park, 1993; mem. curatorial com. Hayward Forum for Arts/Sun Gallery, 1992. Exhibited in numerous shows including Kans. City (Mo.) Art Inst., 1987, Ohio State Art Gallery, Newark, 1987, Mus. Art U. Oreg., Eugene, 1988, Mus. for Photography, Braunschweig, Germany, 1988, Ansel Adams Gallery, Yosemite, 1989, Mus. Modern Art, Tampere, Finland, 1989, Trenton (N.J.) Mus. Art, 1991, Ansel Adams Ctr. for Photography, San Francisco, 1990, Photo Forum Gallery, Pitts., 1992; contbr. to profl. publs.; photographer various catalogues. Precinct capt. Hayward Dem. Com., 1992. Recipient purchase award Hayward Area Forum Arts, 1986, Ohio State U., 1987, Yosemite Nat. Park and Curry Co., 1992, award of excellence Calif. State Fair, 1987, 89, One of Top 100 New Photographers award Maine Photog. Workshops and Kodak Corp., 1987, Innovative New Program award Calif. Parks and Recreation Soc., 1990; scholar Calif. State U., 1975, Ohio U., 1981, Oslo Internat. Summer Sch., 1982, exch. scholar U. Trondheim, Norway, 1983, Peder P. Johnsen scholar Sons of Norway, 1983. Mem. Soc. Photog. Edn., Internat. Assn. Panoramic Photographers, Friends of Photography, San Francisco Camerawork. Home and Studio: PO Box 3998 144 Medford Ave Hayward CA 94540

JORDAN, DANNY JOSEPH, accountant; b. Detroit, Jan. 15, 1948; s. Homer Augustine and Gertrude Jean (Nuttle) J.; m. Rita Rosina Slagel, Dec. 28, 1973. BS in Acctg., Sacramento State U., 1971; MBA in Fin., U. Calif., Berkeley, 1977. CPA, Calif. Sr. auditor Arthur Andersen & Co., San Francisco, 1971-74; asst. controller Cen. Banking System, Oakland, Calif., 1974-75; acctg. mgr., controller Pacific Union Assurance Co., San Francisco, 1975-77; asst v.p. fin., controller West Coast Life Ins. Co., San Francisco, 1977-78; controller, chief fin. officer L.K. Lloyd & Assocs., San Francisco, 1978-80; supr., mgr., ptnr. Greene, Nakahara & Arnold, Oakland, 1980-85; ptnr. Jordan & Decker, Mill Valley, Calif., 1985—; bd. dirs. Cost, Inc. Oakland, Calif., Calif. No. Fin. consumer Svcs, Oakland, Ham Enterprises, Richmond, M.K. Blake Estate Co., Berkeley, Calif.; mem. adminstv. com. Calif. Soc. CPAS Group Ins. Trust, Redwood City, 1980—, chmn., 1990-92. Mem. Calif. Soc. CPAs, AICPA, Calif. Soc. CPAs, Nat. Assn. Accts. (v.p. 1987). Republican. Home: 94 Nelson Ave Mill Valley CA 94941-2122 Office: Jordan & Decker PO Box 1755 Mill Valley CA 94942-1755

JORDAN, ELLEN RAUSEN, law educator, consultant; b. Denver, Feb. 6, 1943; d. Joseph and Sarah (Ratner) Rausen; m. Carl Parsons Jordan, Aug. 20, 1967; children: Daniel Victor, Timothy Julian. BA, Cornell U., 1964; JD, Columbia U., 1972. Bar: Md. 1972. Analyst Nat. Security Agy., Ft. Meade, Md., 1964-66; programmer Bankers Trust Co., N.Y.C., 1966-69; sole practice, Cumberland, Md., 1972-75; asst. prof. law U. Ga., Athens, 1976-79, assoc. prof., 1980-85, prof., 1985-91, assoc. dean Sch. of Law, 1983-86; dean Sch. of Law, U. Calif., Davis, 1991-92; prof. of law, 1992—; vis. asst. prof. U. Va., Charlottesville, 1979-80; cons. U.S. Dept. Justice, Washington, 1980-81, Adminstrv. Conf. of U.S., Washington, 1982-83; acting assoc. v.p. academic affairs, U. Ga., 1986-88. Contbr. articles to profl. jours. Legal History fellow U. Wis., 1983. Mem. ABA, Assn. Am. Law Schs (exec. com. 1986-89), Phi Beta Kappa. Home: 2 Sequoia Pl Woodland CA 95695 Office: UC Davis School of Law King Hall Davis CA 95616

JORDAN, FRANK GEORGE, computer consultant; b. Mitchell, Ind., Nov. 23, 1931; s. Frank George and Millison (Lagle) J.; m. Carolyn Hazel Carey, June 21, 1952; children: Christopher David, Catherine Diane, Michael Steven. BA in Math., Occidental Coll., 1953. Cert. data processor. Computer programmer Douglas Aircraft Corp., Santa Monica, Calif., 1953-63; systems engr. IBM Corp., L.A., 1963-88; pres. VM/FJ Cons., L.A., 1989—. Reader Recording for the Blind, Hollywood, Calif., 1989—. Mem. Assn. for Computing Machinery, Ind. Computer Cons. Assn. (bd. dirs. 1992).

JORDAN, FRANK M., mayor; b. San Francisco, CA; three sons: Jim, 24, Frank J. Jordan, 22, and Thomas, 16. Former chief of police, San Francisco, 1986-1990; mayor City of San Francisco, 1992—. Office: Office of Mayor 200 City Hall 400 Van Ness Ave San Francisco CA 94102*

JORDAN, JACK TERRELL, systems, telecommunications analyst; b. Corpus Christi, Tex.; s. James M. and Ann Jordan; m. Susan K. Soy, July 2, 1988. BS in TV prodn., U. Tex., 1979; MBA, UCLA, 1981. Broadcast engr. Sta. WNET-TV, N.Y.C., 1975, Sta. ABC-TV, N.Y.C., 1976, Sta. KLRN-TV, Austin, Tex., 1977-79; systems analyst Western prodn. div. Exxon Co. USA, Thousand Oaks, Calif., 1982-86; systems analyst Am. Honda, Torrance, Calif., 1986—. Office: 1910 Holly Hill Dr Austin TX 78746

JORDAN, JAMES DOUGLAS, JR., chemical dependency consultant; b. Bklyn., Oct. 1, 1965; s. James Douglas Sr. and Vergia (Kemp) J. BS, Coll. of Notre Dame, Belmont, Calif., 1987, MA in Psychology, 1993. Leadership devel. specialist Regional Leadership, Menlo Park, Calif., 1986-88; counselor Community Living Ctrs., Redwood City, Calif., 1987-89, client program coord., 1989-90; juvenile group supr. San Mateo Probation Dept., Belmont, Calif., 1988-93; supervising case mgr. Community Living Ctrs., Redwood City, 1990-92; exec. cons. Chem. Dependency Cons. and Mktg. Group, San Jose, Calif., 1992—. Author papers. Rschr. Congl. Election Com., Sunnyvale, Calif., 1988-91; dir. pub. rels. Omega Youth Club, East Palo Alto, Calif., 1991—. Mem. Coll. of Notre Dame Alumni Assn. (bd. dirs. 1988-91), Delta Epsilon Sigma, Kappa Gamma Pi. Office: Chem Dependency Consulting and Mktg Group 5339 Prospect Rd # 409 San Jose CA 95129

JORDAN, JEFFREY GUY, foodservice marketing executive; b. Oshkosh, Wis., May 21, 1950; s. Berwin Russell and Delores Suzanne (Tomlitz) J. BS, U. Wis., Oshkosh, 1973; postgrad., UCLA, 1978. Analyst corp. planning and rsch. May Co. Dept. Store, L.A., 1973-77; dir. mktg. svcs. DJMC Advt., L.A., 1977-80; dir. mktg. Wienerschnitzel, Internat., Newport Beach, Calif., 1980-84, York Steakhouse Restaurants (Gen. Mills), Columbus, Ohio, 1984-85, Paragon Restaurant Group, San Diego, 1985-87; v.p. mktg. Paragon Steakhouse Restaurants, Inc., San Diego, 1987—; cons., presenter U.S. Internat. U., San Diego, 1989. Mem. Conv. and Visitors Bur., San Diego; vol. Boys' Club of Am., Oshkosh, 1973-74; fundraising coord. Am. Cancer Soc., L.A., 1976. Mem. Am. Mktg. Assn., Multi Unit Foodservice Operators Assn., San Diego Advt. Assn. (creative exec. 1986-88), San Diego C. of C. Republican. Lutheran. Office: 6620 Convoy Ct San Diego CA 92111-1009

JORDAN, LAWRENCE WILLIAM, engineering educator; b. Lakewood, Ohio, Mar. 8, 1931; s. Lawrence William and Virginia Lee (Little) J.; m. Donna Faye Craig, June 15, 1957; children: Craig Robert, Juli Claire, Lori Elaine. BChemE, Ohio State U., 1956, MSc, 1957, PhD, 1959; JD, UCLA, 1971. Bar: Calif. 1972, U.S. Ct. Appeals (9th cir.) 1973, U.S. Supreme Ct. 1981; registered profl. engr., Ohio, Calif., Oreg. Research engr. Calif. Research, La Habra, 1959-67; research chemist Aerojet-Gen., Downey, Calif., 1967-68; assoc. Bullivant, Wright et al, Portland, Oreg., 1971-74, Norman Stoll, Portland, 1974-77; city atty. Lake Oswego, Oreg., 1977-79; asst. adminstr. Oreg. Dept. Commerce, Salem, 1979-81; pres. SITEC, Salem, 1981-89; prof. of engring., dept. chair Coll. of Marin, Kentfield, Calif., 1989—. Author: Azeotropy: The Binary Systems, 1961, Continuing Legal Education Family Law, 1973 (award 1974). Mem. Orange (Calif.) City Council, 1964-72; mem. Salem Planning Commn. 1984-86. Fellow Proctor & Gamble Co., 1957, Dow Chem. Corp., 1958, Ford Found., 1970; Wilson scholar UCLA, 1968. Mem. State Bar Calif., Salem C. of C. (greeter, com. chmn. 1984-85), Tau Beta Pi, Pi Mu Epsilon, Sigma Xi, Phi Lambda Upsilon. Home: PO Box 42 Kentfield CA 94914-0042 Office: Coll of Marin 835 College Ave Kentfield CA 94904

JORDAN, LOIS HEYWOOD, real estate developer; b. Salem, Oreg., Apr. 22, 1913; d. Frank Hall and Winnifred E.(Heywood) Reeves; m. Edmund A. Jordan, Nov. 19, 1936 (dec. Dec. 1982); children: Jolie Mae, E. Andrew Jr., Jennifer Loie. Student, Oreg. State U., 1931-33, N.W. Sch. of Art, Portland, Oreg. Dress designer Portland, 1933-36, real estate developer, 1955—; pres. Jordan Developers, Portland, 1987—. Pres. Alameda Sch. PTA, Portland, 1960; v.p. Ainsworth Sch. PTA, Portland, 1964; pres. Alameda Garden Club, Portland, 1956, Women's Convalescent Home, Portland, 1957; v.p. sec. SW Hills Residential League, Portland, 1968; v.p. Friends Marquam Ravine, Portland, 1976; bd. dirs. Friendly House, Portland, 1986. Mem. Multnomah Athletic Club, Pi Beta Phi (mgr. Oreg. State chpt. 1932-33). Republican. Prebyterian. Office: Jordan Developers 1650 NW 113th Ave Portland OR 97229-5006

JORDAN, RAYMOND ALAN, forensic engineer, consultant; b. Haldimand County, Ont., Can., Dec. 18, 1942. B Engring. Sci., U. Western Ont., 1966; MS, Tex. A&M U., 1974. Registered profl. engr., Ariz., Ont.; cert. safety profl. Commd. 2d lt. Can. Armed Forces, 1966, advanced through grades to maj., served as aerospace engr., 1966-83, ret., 1983; co-founder, v.p. Microstar Software Ltd., Nepean, Ont., 1983-85; engring. cons. Arndt and Assocs., Tempe, Ariz., 1985-87; pres. Jordan Cons. Svcs., Phoenix, 1987—; prin. Jordan Fine Arts, Phoenix, 1987—; chief exec. officer The Jordan Group, Phoenix, 1991—; aerospace engring. adv. bd. Can. Armed Forces, 1975-77; cons. Ambon Internat., Phoenix, 1991—. Contbr. articles to profl. publs. Mayor Community Coun., Medley, Alta., Can., 1977; mem. minister's adv. com. on further edn., Province of Alta., 1978. Recipient Can. Merit award Govt. of Can., 1978, Cert. of Merit, Aerospace Engring. Test Establishment, Cold Lake, Alta., 1978. Mem. Am. Soc. Safety Engrs., Nat. Forensics Ctr., Internat. Soc. Air Safety Investigators, Alpha Pi Mu. Office: The Jordan Group 9402 S 43d Pl Phoenix AZ 85044

JORDAN, RAYMOND BRUCE, health services consultant; b. Holland, Mich., Mar. 10, 1912; s. Albert Raymond and Aimee (Best) J.; m. Dorothy Caig, June 6, 1942. B.A., Sacramento State Coll., 1952; M.B.A., Stanford U., 1959. Pub. acct., Calif. Acct., auditor State Bd. Equalization, Calif. Dept. Employment, 1947-48, mgmt. analyst, 1948-52, chief analyst, 1952-59; chief mgmt. analyst Hdqrs. Office, Calif. Dept. Mental Hygiene, 1959-63; bus. adminstr. Atascadero State Hosp., 1963-68, Patton State Hosp., San Bernardino, Calif., 1968-70; mgmt. cons. hosps., Victoria, B.C., Can., 1970-72; instr. Sacramento City Coll., 1951-62; cons. Govt. Iran, faculty, U. Tehran, 1956; instr. U. Calif.-Davis, 1963, Cuesta Coll., San Luis Obispo, 1967-68, Monterey Peninsula Coll., 1974-76; adj. prof. Golden Gate U., Monterey and San Francisco Campus, 1974-84; chmn. grievance rev. bd. Monterey Peninsula Unified Sch. Dist., 1976. Pres., Monterey County Ombudsman Program, 1976-79; founder, adv. bd. mem. Monterey County Sr. Hearing Ctr., 1977-78; treas. Experience, Inc., 1973-78; bd. dirs. Monterey County Sr. Aide Program, 1976-78; mem. adv. bd. Alliance on Aging, 1976-78; founder, pres. Concerned Sr. Citizens, Monterey Peninsula Club, 1974-77; mem. adv. group Monterey Sr. Day Care Ctr., 1977-78. Recipient Bronze Achievement award Mental Hosp. Service, 1963. Served with U.S. Army, 1943-46. Club: Toastmasters. Author: Management Analysis in Health Services, 1982; Supervision—Effective Management, 1982; contbr. articles to profl. jours. Home: 33 Linda Ave Apt 1908 Oakland CA 94611-4818

JORDAN, ROBERT LEON, lawyer, educator; b. Reading, Pa., Feb. 27, 1928; s. Anthony and Carmela (Votto) J.; m. Evelyn Allen Willard, Feb. 15, 1958; children—John Willard, David Anthony. BA, Pa. State U., 1948; LLB, Harvard U., 1951. Bar: N.Y. 1952. Assoc. White & Case, N.Y.C., 1953-59; prof. law UCLA, 1959-70, 75-91, prof. law emeritus, 1991—, assoc. dean Sch. Law, 1968-69; vis. prof. law Cornell U., Ithaca, N.Y., 1962-63; coreporter Uniform Consumer Credit Code, 1964-70, Uniform Comml. Code Articles 3, 4, 4A, 1985-90; Fulbright lectr. U. Pisa, Italy, 1967-68. Coauthor: (with W.D. Warren) Commercial Law, 1983, 3d edit., 1992, Bankruptcy, 1985, 3d edit., 1993. Lt. USAF, 1951-53. Office: UCLA Sch Law 405 Hilgard Ave Los Angeles CA 90024-1476

JORDAN, SHARON LEE, librarian, educator; b. Long Beach, Calif., Jan. 19, 1946; d. Harold Wilson and Nina Pearl (Campbell) Chapman; m. Frank Cody Jordan, Jan. 1, 1984. BA, Calif. State U., Chico, 1968, MA, 1975; MLS, San Jose State U., 1980. Life K-14 teaching credentials, Calif. Tchr. Coacti-Anderson (Calif.) Union High Sch., 1969-79; data processor, sr. computer programmer Lockheed Missiles & Space Co., Sunnyvale, Calif., 1980-83; dist. libr. Highland Sch. Dist., Cowiche, Wash., 1983-88; libr., tchr. Port Townsend (Wash.) Sch. Dist., 1988—. Mem. NEA, Wash. Edn. Assn. (former v.p., sec., treas., grievance chmn., assembly rep., head negotiator Cowiche), Wash. Libr. Media Assn. (conf. presenter), Escapees (winter grievance chmn.), Ladies Aux. VFW, Order Ea. Star, Phi Kappa Phi, Phi Delta Kappa. Republican. Home: PO Box 429 Chimacum WA 98325 Office: Port Townsend High Sch 1500 Van Ness Port Townsend WA 98368

JORDAN, WILLIAM SPENCER, administrator, economic counselor; b. Mpls., Oct. 6, 1939; m. Rosalie A. Jordan, May 26, 1984; children: Scott, Dan, Emlyn, Lauri. Student, Albuquerque Police Acad., 1963-64, U. N.Mex., 1974-77, Liberty U., Lynchburg, Va., 1989-91. Police officer Albuquerque Police Dept., 1963-68; owner, operator Albuquerque Motor Escort and Security, Inc., 1968-75; svc. technician Wa-co Heating and Air Cooling, Inc., Albuquerque, 1975-77; maintenance supr. Richardson Ford, Albuquerque, 1977-84, Jordan Maintenance and Consultation, Albuquerque, 1984-90; adminstrv. dir., econ. counselor Jordan Consortium, Albuquerque, 1991—; vol. Creative Alternatives for Spl. Adults. With USN, 1957-60. Home and Office: 3554 Dakota NE Albuquerque NM 87110-2118

JORDANIA, VAKHTANG, conductor, educator; b. Tbilisi, Georgia, USSR, Dec. 9, 1942; came to U.S., 1983; s. Givi and Varvara J.; children: Georgi, Nina, Maria, Dimitri. Student, Tbilisi Conservatory, 1966, Leningrad (USSR) Conservatory, 1969; MusD, Moscow Conservatory, 1971, People's Artist, 1983. Asst. condr. Leningrad Philharm., 1970-71, assoc. condr., 1971-73; condr., artistic dir. Leningrad Radio Orch., 1973-74; prof. music Saratov (USSR) Conservatory, 1974-76; condr., music dir. Saratov Philharm., 1974-76; condr., artistic dir. Kharkov (USSR) Philharm., 1976-83; guest condr. Shaw Concerts, Inc., N.Y., 1983-85; condr., artistic dir. Chattanooga Symphony and Opera Assn., 1985-91; condr., music dir. Spokane Symphony, 1991—; prin. guest condr. K.B.S. Philharm., Seoul, Republic of Korea, 1990—; music dir. St. Petersburg Royal Festival Orch., Kharkov Philharm., Kharkov Opera. Condr. (record) Elmar Olivera-Tchaikovsky competition, 1978, Michaela Martin-Tchaikovsky competition, 1978; (album) Shostakovich Symphonies 6 and 9, USSR State Symphony Orch., Leningrad Chamber orch., 1972; (movie) Dersu Ursula, 1980; other recordings. Recipient 1st place USSR Nat. Audition for Internat. Competition, 1971, Herbert Von Karajan prize, 1971. Office: Spokane Symphony W 621 Mallon Ste 203 Spokane WA 99201

JORGENSEN, DONALD ALLAN, health facility administrator, immunologist; b. Omaha, Feb. 6, 1952; s. Allan Herbert and Virginia (Vance) J.; m. Mary Patricia Simpson, Sept. 5, 1975; children: Jason Allan, Katherine Marie, Jacob John. BS in Biology, George Mason U., 1974. From lab. technician to v.p. Kent Labs., Redmond, Wash., 1974—. Contbr. articles to profl. jours. Office: Kent Labs 23404 NE 8th St Redmond WA 98053-7227

JORGENSEN, ERIK HOLGER, lawyer; b. Copenhagen, July 18, 1916; s. Holger and Karla (Andersen) J.; children: Jette Friis, Lone Olesen, John, Jean Ann. JD, San Francisco Law Sch., 1960. Bar: Calif. 1961. Pvt. practice law, 1961-70; ptnr. Hersh, Hadfield, Jorgensen & Fried, San Francisco, 1970-76, Hadfield & Jorgensen, San Francisco, 1976-88 . Pres. Aldersly, Danish Retirement Home, San Rafael, Calif., 1974-77, Rebild Park Soc. Bay Area chpt., 1974-77. Fellow Scandinavian Am. Found. (hon.); mem. ABA, Assn. Trial Lawyers Am., San Francisco Lawyers Club, Bar Assn. of San Francisco, Calif. Assn. Realtors (hon. life bd. dirs.). Author: Master Forms Guide for Successful Real Estate Agreements, Successful Real Estate Sales Agreements, 1989; contbr. articles on law and real estate law to profl. jours. Office: 350 California St San Francisco CA 94104-1402

JORGENSEN, GORDON DAVID, engineering company executive; b. Chgo., Apr. 29, 1921; s. Jacob and Marie (Jensen) J.; BS in Elec. Engring., U. Wash., 1948, postgrad. in bus. and mgmt., 1956-59; m. Nadina Anita Peters, Dec. 17, 1948 (div. Aug. 1971); children: Karen Ann, David William, Susan Marie; m. Barbara Noel, Feb. 10, 1972 (div. July 1976); m. Ruth Barnes Chalmers, June 15, 1990. With R.W. Beck & Assos., Cons. Engrs., Phoenix, 1948—, ptnr., 1954-86; pres. Beck Internat., Phoenix, 1971—. Served to lt. (j.g.) U.S. Maritime Service, 1942-45. Recipient Outstanding Service award Phoenix Tennis Assn., 1967; Commendation, Govt. Honduras, 1970. Registered profl. engr., Alaska, Ariz., Calif., Colo., Nev., N.Mex., N.D., Utah, Wash., Wyo. Mem. IEEE (chmn. Wash.-Alaska sect. 1959-60), Nat. Soc. Profl. Engrs., Am. Soc. Appraisers (sr. mem.), Ariz. Cons. Engrs. Assn., Ariz. Soc. Profl. Engrs., Internat. Assn. Assessing Officers, Southwestern Tennis Assn. (past pres.), U.S. Tennis Assn. (pres. 1987-88, chmn. U.S. Open com.); chmn. U.S. Davis Cup com.; chmn. Internat. Tennis Fed., Davis Cup com. Presbyterian (elder). Project mgr. for mgmt., operation studies and reorgn. study Honduras power system, 1969-70. Home: 74-574 Palo Verde Indian Wells CA 92210 Office: RW Beck & Assocs 3003 N Central Ave Phoenix AZ 85012-2902

JORGENSEN, JOYCE ORABELLE, artist, writer; b. Newell, Iowa, Feb. 26, 1928; d. James G. and Elsie C. (Haahr) Andersen; m. John G. Jorgensen, Apr. 27, 1949 (dec. Dec. 1958); children: Richard Kirsten John (dec.); m. L.A. Johnson, Jan. 1, 1965 (div. Jan. 1968); 1 child, Brian. Pvt. art study, Arthur Schweider, 1945-46. Co-pub. and editor Orleans (Nebr.) Chronicle, 1949-53, Ouray County Herald, 1954-56; operator Little Studio & Gallery, Ouray, Colo., 1954-56; pvt. sec., office mgr. Atty. Gen., Juneau, Alaska, 1957-58; freelance artist, instr., operator Jorgensen Studio and Gallery J, Ouray, 1959-68; editor Ouray County Plaindealer, 1967-70, pub., editor, 1970-90; established, pub., editor The Ridgway (Colo.) Sun, 1980-90. sec. Ouray City Planning and Zoning Commn., 1969-70; chmn. Ouray Bd. of Zoning Appeals, 1971-75; bd. dirs., creator Ouray County Arts Coun. and Artists Alpine Holiday, 1961-62; originator, dir. Small Sch's. Art Program, 1963-64; originator, mem. com. to Restore Ouray City Hall Facade, 1974-78, 1987-88; Colo. Press Assoc. State Chmn. to Nat. Newspaper Assoc., 1978-79. Recipient Gov's award in Arts and Humanities, 1974, Outstanding Communicator award Denver Press Club for Bill Daniels Comm. Ctr., B.P.O.E. (Elks) Disting. Citizenship award, 1986; named Ouray County Woman of the Yr., 1974, Outstanding Communicator Sigma Delta Chi (Colo. chpt.), Soc. Prof. Journalists, 1974. Home and Office: 540 8th Ave Ouray CO 81427

JORGENSEN, JUDITH ANN, psychiatrist; b. Parris Island, S.C.; d. George Emil and Margaret Georgia Jorgensen; B.A., Stanford U., 1963; M.D., U. Calif., 1968; m. Ronald Francis Crown, July 11, 1970. Intern, Meml. Hosp., Long Beach, 1969-70; resident County Mental Health Services, San Diego, 1970-73; staff psychiatrist Children and Adolescent Services, San Diego, 1973-78; practice medicine specializing in psychiatry, La Jolla, Calif., 1973—; staff psychiatrist County Mental Health Services of San Diego, 1973-78, San Diego State U. Health Services, 1985-87; psychiat. cons. San Diego City Coll., 1973-78, 85-86; asst. prof. dept. psychiatry U. Calif., 1978—, assoc. prof. dept. psychiatry, 1991—; chmn. med. quality rev. com. Dist. XIV, State of Calif., 1982-83. Mem. Am. Psychiat. Assn., San Diego Soc. Psychiat. Physicians (chmn. membership com. 1976-78, v.p. 1978-80, fed. legis. rep. 1985-87, fellowship com. 1989), Am. Soc. Adolescent Psychiatry, San Diego Soc. Adolescent Psychiatry (pres. 1981-82), Calif. Med. Assn. (alternate del.), Soc. Sci. Study of Sex, San Diego Soc. Sex Therapy and Edn. (cert. sex therapist), San Diego County Med. Soc. (credentials com. 1982-84). Club: Rowing. Office: 470 Nautilus St Ste 211 La Jolla CA 92037-5970

JORGENSEN, LOU ANN BIRKBECK, social worker; b. Park City, Utah, May 14, 1931; d. Robert John and Lillian Pearl (Langford) Birkbeck; student Westminster Coll., 1949-51; B.S., U. Utah, 1953, M.S.W., 1972, D.S.W., 1979; grad. Harvard Inst. Ednl. Mgmt., 1983; m. Howard Arnold Jorgensen, June 9, 1954; children: Gregory Arnold, Blake John, Paul Clayton. Social work adminstr. nursing home demonstration project, dept. family and community medicine U. Utah Med. Ctr., Salt Lake City, 1972-74; mental health ednl. specialist Grad. Sch. Social Work, U. Utah, 1974-77, 77-80, asst. prof., 1974-80, assoc. prof., 1980-89, dir. doctoral program, 1984-89, assoc. dean, 1986—; regional mental health cons. Bd. dirs. Info. and Referral Ctr., 1975-82, United Way of Utah, 1976-82, Pioneer Trail Parks, 1977-83, Rowland Hall-St. Marks Sch., 1980-86; Salt Lake County housing commr., 1980-86, Utah State Health Facilities Bd., 1991—; pres. Human Svcs. Conf. for Utah, 1979-80; bd. dirs. Alzheimer Assn., Utah chpt., 1990—, Salt Lake County Coalition Bus. and Human Svcs., 1990—, Town Club 1990-93, Valley Mental Health. Mem. Coun. on Social Work Edn., Commn. Women in High Edn., Nat. Assn. Social Workers (pres. Utah chpt. 1978-79), Adminstrs. of Public Agys. Assn., Human Svcs. Assn. Utah, Jr. League of Salt Lake City, Phi Kappa Phi. Republican. Episcopalian. Clubs: Town, Eastern Star. Author: Explorations in Living, 1978, Social Work in Business and Industry, 1979; Handbook of the Social Services, 1981; contbr. articles to profl. jours. Home: 1458 Kristianna Cir Salt Lake City UT 84103 Office: U Utah Grad Sch Social Work Salt Lake City UT 84112

JORGENSEN, MARK CHRISTOPHER, state park naturalist; b. San Diego, Aug. 24, 1951; s. Francis Peter and Emily Josephine (Parrott) J.; m. Bonnie Louise Bird, Aug. 2, 1975 (div. 1982); 1 child, Kristofer Bird; m. Kelley Lynn Blackledge, Jan. 30, 1988; children: Jack Ryan, Carly Elizabeth. AA, Grossmont Jr. Coll., El Cajon, Calif., 1971; BS in Environ. Resources, Sacramento State U., 1973. Seasonal/Bighorn researcher Anza-Borrego Desert State Park, Borrego Springs, Calif., 1972-75; state pk. ranger San Diego Coast Dist., Carlsbad, Calif., 1975-76, Channel Coast Dist., Ventura, Calif., 1976-78, Ocotillo Wells State Vehicle Recreation Area, Borrego Springs, 1978-80; naturalist Anza-Borrego Desert State Pk., 1980—; cons. Riyahd Devel. Authority, Saudi Arabia, 1984-85; advisor Bighorn Inst., Palm Desert, Calif., 1983—; contractor Forest Svc., USDA, Bishop, Calif., 1974-75. Co-author: Anza-Borrego Desert, 1982; editor guidebooks: Weekender's Guide, 1986, Anza-Borrego Region, 1988; editor color book: Forgotten Artist, 1989 (Benjamin Franklin Gold award 1989). Bd. dirs., sec. Borrego Springs Children's Ctr., 1988—; tech. staff Desert Bighorn Coun., Inc., Riverside, Calif., 1983—. Mem. Anza-Borrego Desert Natural History Assn. (bd. advisor 1980—), Desert Protective Coun. Democrat. Office: Anza-Borrego Desert Pk PO Box 299 Borrego Springs CA 92004-0299

JORGENSEN, PAUL ALFRED, English language educator emeritus; b. Lansing, Mich., Feb. 17, 1916; s. Karl and Rose Josephine (Simmons) J.; m. Virginia Frances Elfrink, Jan. 3, 1942; children: Mary Catherine, Elizabeth Ross Jorgensen Howard. A.B., Santa Barbara State Coll., 1938; M.A., U. Calif. at Berkeley, 1940, Ph.D., 1945. Instr. English Bakersfield (Calif.) Jr. Coll., 1945-46, U. Calif., Berkeley, summer 1946, U. Calif., Davis, 1946-47; mem. faculty UCLA, 1947—, prof. English, 1960-81, prof. emeritus, 1981—; vis. prof. U. Wash., summer 1966; mem. editorial com. U. Calif. Press, 1957-60; mem. Humanities Inst. U. Calif., 1967-69; mem. acad. adv. council Shakespeare Globe Ctr. N.Am. Author: Shakespeare's Military World, 1956, (with Frederick B. Shroyer) A College Treasury, rev. edit, 1967, (with Shroyer) The Informal Essay, 1961, Redeeming Shakespeare's Words, 1962; editor: The Comedy of Errors, 1964, Othello: An Outline- Guide to the Play, 1964, (with Shroyer) The Art of Prose, 1965, Lear's Self-Discovery, 1967, Our Naked Frailties: Sensational Art and Meaning in Macbeth, 1971, William Shakespeare: The Tragedies, 1985; mem. bd. editors Film Quar, 1958-65, Huntington Library Quar, 1965-83, Coll. English, 1966-70; mem. adv. com. Publs. of MLA of Am, 1978-82. Guggenheim fellow, 1956-57; Regents' Faculty fellow in humanities, 1973-74. Mem. Modern Lang. Assn., Shakespeare Assn. Am. (bibliographer 1954-59), Renaissance Soc. Am., Philol. Assn., Pacific Coast (exec. com. 1962-63), Internat. Shakespeare Assn. Episcopalian. Home: 234 Tavistock Ave Los Angeles CA 90049-3229

JORGENSEN, TILTON DENNIS, healthcare executive; b. Turlock, Calif., Apr. 8, 1945; s. Tilton Roy and Dona Marie (Harmon) J.; m. Carol Ann Lipsky, 1970 (div. 1972); m. Katharine Susan Strong, Apr. 30, 1983. BBA, Gonzaga U., 1967. Mktg. rep. IBM, L.A., 1968-69; v.p., gen. mgr. Newhall (Calif.) Ambulance, Inc., 1970-77; instr. in emergency med. tech. Coll. of the Canyons, Valencia, Calif., 1972-77; v.p., gen. mgr. Profl. Ambulance Svc., Glendale, Calif., 1974-77; dir. emergency med. svcs. Nat. Med. Enterprises, Inc., L.A., 1977-78, v.p. equipment ops., 1979-82; v.p. emergency med. svcs. Nat. Med. Enterprises, Inc., New Orleans, 1982-84; v.p. internat. div. Nat. Med. Enterprises, Inc., Santa Monica, Calif., 1984-86; v.p. adminstrn. Nat. Med. Enterprises Hosp. Group, Santa Monica, 1986-92; sr. v.p. support svcs. NME Ops. Nat. Med. Enterprises, Inc., 1992—. Office: Nat Med Enterprises Inc 2700 Colorado Ave Santa Monica CA 90404-3570

JOSEPH, EZEKIEL (ED JOSEPH), manufacturing company executive; b. Rangoon, Burma, June 24, 1938; s. Joe E. Joseph and Rachel Levi; m. Sheila G. Rabinovitch, Feb. 17, 1963; children: Renah, Heather, Jerald. Mktg. mgr. Gen. Electric Corp., Waynesboro, Va., 1968-75; dir. Actron div. McDonnell Douglas Corp., Monrovia, Calif., 1975-78; pres. Joseph Machinery Inc., Huntington Beach, Calif., 1978-84, Xtalite Display Systems Inc.), Huntington Beach, 1985-88, Secure Optical Systems Inc., Anaheim, Calif., 1992—; pres. Retract-a-Roof Inc., Huntington Beach. Pres. Temple Beth David, Huntington Beach, 1990—. Mem. Austin Healey Assoc. Democrat. Home: 16242 Typhoon Ln Huntington Beach CA 92649-2542 Office: Secure Optical Systems Inc Unit D 1571 S Sunkist Anaheim CA 92806

JOSEPH, GEORGE MANLEY, retired judge; b. Caldwell, Idaho, Aug. 31, 1930; s. Ben Manley and Mabel Gertrude (Newburn) J.; m. Elizabeth Lyle Starr, dec. 21, 1954; children: Sarah Katherine, Amy Elizabeth, Abigail Serena, Benjamin Manley, Jonathan Lyle. BA, Reed Coll., 1951; JD, U. Chgo., 1955; LLM, NYU, 1959. Law clk. Oreg. Supreme Ct., Salem, Oreg., 1955-56; law prof. Ohio No. U., Dickinson Sch. Law, U. Ark., 1956-63; dep. dist. atty. Multnomah County, Portland, Oreg., 1963-66; pvt. practice Portland, 1966-74; county counsel Multnomah County, Portland, 1975-77; judge Oreg. Ct. of Appeals, Salem, 1977-80; chief judge Ct. of Appeals Oreg., Salem, 1981-92. Alumni trustee Reed Coll., Portland, 1972-75, trustee, 1975-80; chmn. City-Coun ty Charter Commn., Portland, 1971-74; bd. vis. Willamette U. Sch. Law, Salem, 1980-92; vis. com. mem. Oriental Inst. U. Chgo., 1986—. Mem. Oreg. State Bar Assn., ABA, Multnomah Bar Assn., Council of Chief Judges (exec. com. vice-chmn. 1983-84, chmn. 1984-85). Home: 7110 SE 29th Ave Portland OR 97202-8730

JOSEPH, GREGORY NELSON, television columnist; b. Kansas City, Mo., Aug. 25, 1946; s. Theodore Leopold and Marcella Kathryn (Nelson) J.; m. Mary Martha Stahler, July 21, 1973; children: John, Jacqueline, Caroline. AA, Met. C.C., Kansas City, 1967; BA with honors, U. Mo., Kansas City, 1969. Intern, cub reporter Kansas City Star-Times, 1965-67; feature writer, asst. city editor The Pasadena (Calif.) Union, 1971-73; investigative reporter The Pasadena Star-News, 1973-75; bus. writer The Riverside (Calif.) Press Enterprise, 1975-76; reporter, consumer writer, feature writer, TV critic The San Diego Tribune, 1976-90; TV columnist The Ariz. Republic, Phoenix, 1990—. Recipient various writing awards Copley Newspapers, Pasadena and San Diego, 1971-73, 83, Pub. Awareness award San Diego Psychiat. Physicians. Mem. SAG, NATAS (bd. govs. 1990-92), TV Critics Assn., Phi Kappa Phi. Roman Catholic. Home: 4864 W Alice Ave Glendale CA 85302 Office: The Ariz Republic 120 W Van Buren St Phoenix AZ 85004

JOSEPHSON, DAVID LANE, engineer, industrialist; b. New Haven, June 17, 1956; s. Stanley Davis and Carolyn Virginia (Buck) J. Student, U. Calif., Berkeley, 1975-79. Chief engr. KALX Radio, U. Calif., Berkeley, 1975-79; systems engr. High Life Helicopters, Puyallup, Wash., 1979-81; mgr. systems group EG&G Geometrics, Inc., Sunnyvale, Calif., 1981-85; dir. China ops. EG&G Inc., Beijing, China, 1985-87; chief internat. liaison EG&G Inc., Wellesley, Mass., 1987-88; mgr. mil. geophysics EG&G Geometrics, Inc., Sunnyvale, 1988-91; dir. Josephson Engring., San Jose, Calif., 1984—; tech., export advisor Inst. for Def. Analyses, Alexandria, Va., 1987—, U.S. Dept. Commerce. Contbr. articles to profl. jours. Mem. steering com. San Francisco Bay Area emergency airlift vols., 1992—. Mem. Audio Engring. Soc. (dir. San Francisco sect. 1988—). Democrat. Office: Josephson Engring 2660 John Montgomery Dr # 25 San Jose CA 95148-1009

JOSEPHSON, DIANA HAYWARD, aerospace executive; b. London, Oct. 17, 1936; came to U.S., 1959; d. Robert Hayward and Barbara (Clark) Bailey. BA with honors, Oxford U., Eng., 1958, MA, 1962; M in Comparative Law, George Washington U., 1962. Bar: Eng. and Wales 1959, D.C. 1963. Assoc. Covington & Burling, Washington, 1959-68; asst. dir. Office of the Mayor, Washington, 1968-74; exec. dir. Nat. Capital Area ACLU, Washington, 1975-78; dep. asst. adminstr. policy and planning, satellites NOAA, U.S. Dept. Commerce, Washington, 1978-82; pres. Am. Sci. and Tech. Corp., Bethesda, Md., 1982-83, Space Am., Bethesda, 1983-85; v.p. mktg. Arianespace, Inc., Washington, 1985-87; v.p. Martin Marietta Comml. Titan Inc., Washington, 1987-89; dir. bus. devel. Martin Marietta Advanced Launch Systems, Denver, 1989-90, Martin Marietta Civil Space and Communications Co., Denver, 1990-93; dep. under sec. for oceans and atmosphere Nat. Ocean and Atmospheric Adminstrn., U.S. Dept. Commerce, Washington, 1993—; mem. Space Applications Bd., Nat. Rsch. Coun., 1988-89, comml. space transp. adv. commn., U.S. Dept. Transp., Washington, 1984-85. Mem. D.C. Law Revision Commn., Washington, 1975-78, D.C. Internat. Women's Yr. State Coordinating Com., 1977. Recipient Gold medal for Disting. Svc., U.S. Dept. Commerce, 1981. Mem. Am. Astronautical Soc. (bd. dirs. 1985-88), Nat. Space Club (bd. govs.), Women in Aerospace, Washington Space Bus. Roundtable (adv. bd. 1985-87), Am. Inst. Aeronautics and Astronautics. Office: Nat Oceanic & Atmospheric Adminstrn US Dept Commerce Washington DC 20235

JOSEPHSON, HAROLD ALLAN, real estate developer; b. Montreal, Que., Can., July 21, 1944; s. Joseph and Edith (Marco) J.; m. Sheila Gloria Laing, July 4, 1966 (div. July 1976); children: Daniel, Robert.; MBA with distinction, Harvard U., 1971. V.p. Marcil Mortgage Corp., Montreal, 1976-78; prin. Josephson Properties, Montreal, 1978-83, Los Angeles, 1983—. Mem. Urban Land Inst., Nat. Assn. Indsl. and Office Parks, Internat. Council Shopping Ctrs. Jewish. Club: Beverly Hills Country (Los Angeles), Regency (Los Angeles). Office: 2029 Century Park E # 1200 Los Angeles CA 90067-2957

JOSEPHSON, LINDA SUSAN, company executive; b. Cleve., Sept. 25, 1950; d. Robert Heidler Josephson and Ruth Lerner Shiffman Gardocki; m. Norm Lowell Buske, Aug. 25, 1980; 1 child, Orion Josephson Buske. AB, Barnard Coll., 1972; MS, Portland State U., 1976. Programmer Pacific Engring., Portland, 1977-78; dir. Search/Tides Found., Davenport, Wash., 1991—; cons., rschr. Search Tech. Svcs., Davenport, Wash., 1979—. Choreographer modern dance: Photo Electric Effect, 1987, Labor and Materials, 1988, Unlikeness, 1989, Three Poems, 1991. Dir. Namasté Modern Dance Theatre, Spokane, 1988—. Office: Search Tech Svcs HCR Box 17 Davenport WA 99122

JOSHI, SATISH DEVDAS, organic chemist; b. Bombay, Maharashtr, India, Sept. 29, 1950; came to U.S., 1982; s. Devdas Ganesh and Premlata (Prabhu) J.; m. Shima Janakimohan Bhadra, May 2, 1974; children: Shruti, Shilpa. BS, Bombay U., 1970, MS, 1972; PhD in Chemistry, Bombay U., Bombay, 1977. Rsch. fellow State U. Gent, Belgium, 1979-81, Louvain Med. Sch., Brussels, Belgium, 1981-82; rsch. assoc. Mt. Sinai Sch. Medicine, N.Y.C., 1982-85; group leader Bachem, Inc., Torrance, Calif., 1985-87; dir. Bachem Biosci. Inc., Phila., 1987-89; pres., chief exec. officer Star Biochems., Torrance, 1989-91; dir. peptide tech. Mallinchrodt Inc., St. Louis, 1991—. Mem. AAAS, ACS, Am. Peptide Soc., Torrance C. of C. Home: 1928 Via Estudillo Palos Verdes Estates CA 90274 Office: Star Biochemicals 20916 Higgins Ct Torrance CA 90501-1722

JOSHUA, AARON, investment company executive; b. Los Angeles, Aug. 26, 1957; s. Elmo and Pineniece Penny (Starks) J.; m. Valeri Janien. BBA, Whittier Coll., 1978, MBA, 1980. Life ins. Agt. ITT Ins. Corp., Marina del Ray, Calif., 1980—; gen. ptnr. fin. planning and asset. mgmt. Internat. Mgmt. Assocs., Beverly Hills, Calif., 1980—; gen. ptnr. Hollywood Knights, Ltd., 1990—; SEC investment adviser. Mem. Am. Mgmt. Assn., Hollywood C. of C., Beverly Hills C. of C. (edn. com.), Inglewood C. of C., Internat. Assn. Fin. Planning, Inglewood Rotary, Internat. Assn. Fin. Planning. Republican. Baptist. Office: 1635 Cahuenga Blvd Ste 600 Los Angeles CA 90028

JOVENE, NICHOLAS ANGELO, JR., construction company official; b. Bklyn., Jan. 19, 1938; s. Nicholas Angelo and Nancy Theresa (Aiello) J.; m. Delores Zimmermann, June 18, 1960; children: Deborah R. Jovene Ritter, Margaret L. Jovene Norris, Christine D., Nicholas Angelo III. BS, L.I. U., 1961. Field engr. Turner Constrn. Co., N.Y.C., 1960-63; field engr. J.R. Stevenson Corp., N.Y.C., 1963-68, v.p., 1968-78; pres. Romney Corp., Denver, 1982-86; project mgr. Hensel Phelps Constrn. Co., Greeley, Colo., 1978-82, 86—. Mem. City and County of Denver Bd. Appeals, 1991-93; mem. rev. com. City and County of Denver Bldg. Dept., 1992. With USAR, 1957-64. Recipeint hon. citation Gov. of Colo., 1991. Mem. Assoc. Gen. Contractors (apprenticeship com. Denver 1992), Am. Arbitration Assn. (arbitrator). Roman Catholic. Home: 1512 Larimer St Apt 10 Denver CO 80202 Office: Hensel Phelps Constrn Co PO Box 0 420 6th Ave Greeley CO 80632-0710

JOVICK, ROBERT L., lawyer; b. Butte, Mont., Oct. 2, 1950; m. Stacy Towle, June 23, 1976; children: Janelle, Torey, Jay. BS in Indsl. Engring., Mont. State U., 1972; JD, U. Mont., 1975. Bar: Mont. 1975, U.S. Dist. Ct. Mont. 1975. Pvt. practice Livingston, Mont., 1975—; city atty. City of Livingston, 1975—. Sec. Livingston Community Trust, 1987—. Mem. Livingston Golf Club (pres. 1990). Methodist. Office: PO 1245 227 S 2d St Livingston MT 59047

JOY, BRENT MICHAEL, sales executive; b. Minneola, Kans., Mar. 17, 1963; s. George Wayne and Rosalie (Barrett) J.; m. Megen Elizabeth Gaddy, Aug. 17, 1985; children: Brandon, Amanda, Casey. Student, Colo. State U., 1981-82, U. Colo., 1984. Sales mgr. Associated Bus. Products, Denver, 1984-86; stock broker Dean Witter Reynolds, Denver, 1986-89; ctrl. sales mgr. Lewan & Assocs., Colorado Springs, Colo., 1989—. instr. Winter Park Handicaped Ski Program, Winter Park, Colo., 1987-90. Mem. Woodmoor Country Club, President's Club (cabinet mem.). Republican. Office: Lewan & Assocs. 1830 Palmer Park Blvd Colorado Springs CO 80909

JOY, CARLA MARIE, educator; b. Denver, Sept. 5, 1945; d. Carl P. and Theresa M. (Lotito) J. AB cum laude, Loretto Heights Coll., 1967; MA, U. Denver, 1969, postgrad., 1984—. Instr. history Community Coll. Denver; prof. history Red Rocks Community Coll., Lakewood, Colo., 1970—; cons. for innovative ednl. programs; reviewer fed. grants, 1983-89; mem. adv. panel Colo. Endowment for Humanities, 1985-89. Contbr. articles to profl. publs. Instr. vocat. edn. Mile High United Way, Jefferson County, 1975; participant Jefferson County Sch. System R-1 Dist., 1983-88; active Red Rocks Community Coll. Speakers Bur., 1972-89, strategic planning com., 1992—; chair history discipline The Colo. Core Transfer Consortium Project, 1986—. Cert. in vocat. edn. Colo. State Bd. Community Colls. and Occupational Edn., 1975; mem. evaluation team for Colo. Awards, edn. and civic achievement for Widefield Sch. Dist. #3, 1989; mem. Red Rocks Community Coll.-Jefferson County Sch. System R-1 Articulation Team, 1990—. Ford Found. fellow, 1969; recipient cert. of appreciation Kiwanis Club, 1981, Cert. of Appreciation Telecommunication Coop. for Colo's. Community Colls., 1990-92; Master Tchr. award U. Tex. at Austin, 1982. Mem. Am. Hist. Assn., Nat. Council for Social Studies, Nat. Geog. Soc., Inst. Early Am. History and Culture, Nat. Edn. Assn., Colo. Edn. Assn., Colo. Council for Social Studies, The Smithsonian Assocs., Denver Art Mus., Denver Mus. of Nat. Hist., Community Coll. Humanities Assn., Orgn. Am. Historians, The Colo. Hist. Soc., Colo. Endowment for the Humanities, Phi Alpha Theta. Home: 1849 S Lee St Apt D Lakewood CO 80232-6252 Office: Red Rocks Community Coll 13300 W 6th Ave Golden CO 80401-5398

JOY, TIMOTHY JOHN, English language instructor; b. Portland, Oreg., Dec. 27, 1956; s. Harry Bernard and Bernice Madeline (Lienert) J.; m. Kimberly Ann Hills, June 28, 1980; children: Megan Nicole, Ryan Benjamin, Caitlin Elizabeth, Emma Elyse. BS, Portland State, 1983. Shipping, receiving mgr. Acad. Book Ctr., Portland, Oreg., 1977-79; bus. devel. mgr. Kidney Assn. of Oreg., Lake Oswego, 1979-80; asst. textbook mgr. Portland State Bookstore, 1980-83; instr. English La Salle High Sch., Milwaukie, Oreg., 1983—; copy editor KidsCare, Clackamas, Oreg., 1988-89. Contbr. essays and stories to lit. mags. Chmn. Kidney Assn. Oreg. Fundraising, Milwaukie, 1978, 79, 83. Mem. Nat. Coun. Tchrs. English. Democrat. Roman Catholic. Home: 9306 SE Windsor Dr Milwaukie OR 97222-4287 Office: La Salle High Sch 11999 SE Fuller Rd Portland OR 97222-1291

JOYCE, CRAIG DOUGLAS, lawyer; b. Phila., Mar. 28, 1951; s. Louis C. and Rachel (Zimmerman) J.; m. Holly A. Schwenker, Dec. 18, 1977; children: Heather, Tyler, Colin, Madeleine. AB, Rutgers Coll., 1973; MLS, Rutgers U., 1975; JD, U. Denver, 1980. Bar: Colo. 1980. Assoc. DeMuth, Kemp & Backus, Denver, 1980-82, Roath & Brega, Denver, 1982-84; ptnr. Walters & Theis, Denver, 1984-93, Walters & Joyce, Denver, 1993—; adj. prof. law U. Denver, 1990—; faculty mem. Nat. Inst. for Trial Advocacy Western Regional Program, 1992—. Mem. ABA, Colo. Bar Assn., Denver Bar Assn., Colo. Trial Lawyers Assn. Home: 4041 Montview Blvd Denver CO 80207 Office: Walters & Joyce 2015 York St Denver CO 80205

JOYCE, ROBIN HANK, advertising executive; b. Las Vegas, Jan. 16, 1960; s. James Austin and Nedra (Norton) J.; m. Patricia Kay Wilson, Sept. 5, 1982; children: Jillian Allene, Miles Austin. Student, U. Nev., 1983. Asst. sports info. dir. U. Nev., Reno, 1982-84; account exec. Joyce Advt., Reno, 1983-86; pub. rels. dir. Joyce Advt., Las Vegas, 1986-90, v.p., 1990—; chmn. Century Campaign Communications Com. U. Nev., 1991—. Rep. World Vision Community Outreach Program, Las Vegas, 1988—; mem. MADD Red Ribbon Campaign Com., Las Vegas, 1989—; bd. dirs. Big Bros./Big Sisters of Las Vegas, 1988-90; founders bd. Boys and Girls Club Las Vegas, 1990—; mem. So. Nev. adv. bd. U. Nev. Century Campaign; bd. dirs. Crisis Pregnancy Ctr. Las Vegas, 1992—; mem. adv. bd. D.A.R.E. of So. Nev. Mem. Pub. Rels. Soc. Am. (v.p. fin., pub. rels.). Republican. Office: Joyce Advt 602 S 10th St Las Vegas NV 89101-7001

JOYCE, STEPHEN MICHAEL, lawyer; b. Los Angeles, Mar. 19, 1945; s. John Rowland and Elizabeth Rose (Rahe) J.; m. Bernadette Anne Novey, Aug. 18, 1973; children: Natalie Elizabeth, Vanessa Anne. BS, Calif. State U., Los Angeles, 1970; JD, U. San Fernando, 1976. Bar: Calif. 1976, U.S. Dist. Ct. (cen. dist.) Calif. 1977, U.S. Ct. Claims 1981. Sole practice Beverly Hills, Calif., 1976-81; pvt. practice Beverly Hills, 1982-84; ptnr. Gold & Joyce, Beverly Hills, 1984-88; personal atty. to Stevie Wonder and various other celebrities, 1977—. Contbr. articles to profl. jours. Served to pvt. USAR, 1963-69. Mem. ABA, Calif. Bar Assn., Los Angeles County Bar Assn., Beverly Hills Bar Assn., Los Angeles Trial Lawyers Assn. Democrat. Roman Catholic. Club: Calabasas (Calif.) Athletic. Home: 4724 Barcelona Ct Calabasas CA 91302-1403 Office: 16530 Ventura Blvd Ste 600 Encino CA 91436-2006

JOYNER, DARLA JEAN, trade association executive; b. Sioux Falls, S.D., Dec. 4, 1947; d. John Jay and Darlene Dorothy (Loe) Anderberg; m. John A. Joyner, Dec. 7, 1968; children: Jay Arthur, Amy Renee, Evan James. AA, Arapahoe Community Coll., 1974; postgrad., Met. State Coll., Denver, 1974-78; cert., Inst. Organizational Mgmt., Boulder, Colo., 1986. Layout artist JC Penney, Denver, 1973-74; gen. mgr. Bozeman (Mont.) Area C. of C., 1978-83, exec. v.p., chief exec. officer, 1983—; state adv. coun. Mont. Small Bus. Administrn.; S.W. Mont. adv. bd. Horizon Airlines. Editor Ignacio Chieftain mag., 1971-72, Beverage Analyst Mag., 1972-73. Trustee Belgrade (Mont.) City-County Planning Bd., 1986-90, Belgrade Sch. Dist., 1990—; bd. dirs. Big Bros. and Sisters, Bozeman; bd. dirs., steering com. Mike Mansfield Found. Sgt. USMC, 1966-69. Mem. Am. C. of C. Execs (del. 1989-90), Mountain States Assn. C. of C. (pres. bd. dirs. 1990-91), Mont. Assn. Chamber Execs. (pres. 1987-88), Bus. Profl. Women (v.p. Bozeman chpt. 1982-83, Outstanding Young Woman award 1983, Woman of Achievement award 1985), Gallatin Performing Art Ctr. (sec., bd. dirs. 1989—), Mont. SBA (adv. coun. 1992—), Mont. State Rural Devel. Coun. (exec. com.), Mus. Rockies, Rotary.

JUAREZ, MARETTA LIYA CALIMPONG, social worker; b. Gilroy, Calif., Feb. 14, 1958; d. Sulpicio Magsalay and Pelagia Lagotom (Viacrusis) Calimpong; m. Henry Juarez, Mar. 24, 1984. BA, U. Calif., Berkeley, 1979; MSW, San Jose State U., 1983. Lic. clin. social worker. Mgr. Pacific Bell, San Jose, Calif., 1983-84; revenue officer IRS, Salinas, Calif., 1984-85; social worker Santa Cruz (Calif.) County, 1985, Santa Clara County, San Jose, 1985—. Recipient award Am. Legion, 1972. Mem. Nat. Assn. Social Workers, Nat. Council on Alcoholism. Democrat. Roman Catholic.

JUBA, GEORGE E., judge; b. Washougal, Wash., Jan. 11, 1928; s. Dmitrov and Kathrine (Cymbyluk) J.; m. Sue Marie Mellor, Sept. 5, 1952 (dec. 1982); children: Karen Sue Hansen, David George; m. Terrie Jo Blinn, June 6, 1987. BA, Willamette U., 1952, JD, 1956. Bar: Oreg. 1956, U.S. Dist. Ct. Oreg. 1956, U.S. Ct. Appeals (9th cir.) 1957. Assoc. Miller, Nash, et al., Portland, Oreg., 1956-57; asst. U.S. atty. Dept. Justice, Portland, 1957-59; spl. agt. FBI, Denver and New Orleans, 1959-62; chief dep. Office of Dist. Atty., Portland, 1962-65; dist. judge Dist. Ct., Portland, 1965-70; clerk ct. U.S. Dist. Ct. Oreg., Portland, 1970-71, magistrate judge, 1971—. With USN, 1946-48, China. Mem. Oreg. Bar Assn., Multnomah County Bar Assn., Multnomah Athletic Club. Republican. Protestant. Office: U S Dist. Ct 512 US Courthouse 620 S W Main St Portland OR 97205

JUBERG, RICHARD KENT, mathematician, educator; b. Cooperstown, N.D., May 14, 1929; s. Palmer and Hattie Noreen (Nelson) J.; m. Janet Elisabeth Witchell, Mar. 17, 1956 (div.); children: Alison K., Kevin A., Hilary N., Ian C.T.; m. Sandra Jean Vakerics, July 8, 1989. BS, U. Minn., 1952, PhD, 1958. Asst. prof. U. Minn., Mpls., 1958-65; sci. faculty fellow Univerista di Pisa, Italy, 1965-66; assoc. prof. U. Calif., Irvine, 1966-72, U. Sussex, Eng., 1972-73; prof. U. Calif., Irvine, 1974-91, prof. emeritus, 1991—; vis. prof. U. Goteborg, Sweden, 1981; mem. Courant Inst. Math. Scis., NYU, 1957-58. Contbr. articles to profl. jours. With USN, 1946-48, Guam. NSF Faculty fellow, Univ. Pisa, Italy, 1965-66. Mem. Am. Math. Soc., Tau Beta Pi. Democrat. Office: U Calif Math Dept Irvine CA 92717

JUDD, DAVID LOCKHART, physicist, educator; b. Chehalis, Wash., Jan. 8, 1923; married, 1945; 2 children. AB, Whitman Coll., 1943; DSc (hon.), Whitman Coll, 1973; MS, Calif. Inst. Tech., 1947, PhD in Physics, 1950. Staff mem. physics divsn. Los Alamos Sci. Lab., 1945-46; staff mem. theoretical physics Nuclear Energy Divsn. Rand Corp., 1949-51, group leader theoretical physics, 1951-66, from dept. head to head physics divsn., 1963-70, assoc. dir., 1967-70; sr. rsch. physicist Lawrence Berkeley Lab, 1970—, lectr., 1953-62; sr. lectr. dept. physics U. Calif., Berkeley, 1962—; cons. Northrop Aircraft Co., 1947-49, Radiation Lab., U. Calif., 1950-51, Rand Corp., 1951-55, W.M. Brobeck & Assocs., 1960; mem. adv. com. Electronuclear and Physics divsn., Oak Ridge Nat. Lab., 1963-65. Contbr. articles on theoretical and mathematical physics, accelerator theory, ion optics, plasma and particle physics, nonlinear mechanics, to profl. jours. Fellow Am. Phys. Soc.; mem. Sigma Xi. Office: Dept Physics U Calif 366 Le Conte Hall Berkeley CA 94720

JUDD, LEONARD R., copper mining industry executive; b. 1939. BSME, U. Ariz., 1962, MBA, 1968. With Phelps Dodge Corp., Phoenix, 1961—, gen. supt., asst. mgr., 1977-80, corp. v.p., 1980-82, v.p., mgr. western ops., 1982-83, sr. v.p., 1983-87, exec. v.p., 1987-89, pres., COO, 1989-91, also bd. dirs. Office: Phelps Dodge Corp 6218 N 47th St Paradise Valley AZ 85253

JUDD, O'DEAN P., physicist; b. Austin, Minn., May 26, 1937. MS in Physics, UCLA, 1961, PhD in Physics, 1968. Staff physicist and project dir. Hughes Rsch. Lab., Malibu, Calif., 1959-67; postdoctoral fellow UCLA Dept. Physics, 1968-69; researcher Hughes Rsch. Lab., Malibu, Calif., 1969-72; researcher, group leader Los Alamos Nat. Lab., 1972-82, chief scientist for def. rsch. and applications, 1981-87; chief scientist Strategic Def. Initiative Orgn., Washington, 1987-90; energy and environ. chief scientist, lab. fellow Los Alamos (N.Mex.) Nat. Lab., 1990—; mem. numerous govt. coms. related to def. and nat. security policy; advisory com. to SDIO; adj. prof. of physics U. N.Mex., Albuquerque. Patentee in sci. and tech.; contbr. numerous articles to sci. and def.-related jours. Fellow IEEE; mem. AAAS, Am. Phys. Soc. Office: Los Alamos Nat Lab MS A107 Los Alamos NM 87544-2648

JUDD, RICHARD D(ONALD), lawyer; b. Sapulpa, Okla., July 1, 1940; s. Donald H. and Mabel M. (Green) J.; m. Jamy Crawford, June 13, 1962 (div. Mar. 1976); m. Janis Ball Newens, May 29, 1976. AB, Williams Coll., 1962; LLB, U. Colo., 1965. Bar: Colo. 1965, U.S. Dist. Ct. Colo. 1965, U.S. Ct. Appeals (10th cir.) 1965. Assoc. Dawson, Nagel, Sherman & Howard, Denver, 1965-66, Inman, Flynn & Coffee, Denver, 1966-69; ptnr. Reno & Judd, Denver, 1970-74; pvt. practice Denver, 1975-80; ptnr. Baker & Hostetler, Denver, 1980-89, Rossi & Judd, A Profl. Corp., Denver, 1989—. Mem. ABA, Colo. Bar Assn., Denver Bar Assn., Denver Law Club. Clubs: University (Denver); Boulder (Colo.) Country. Office: Rossi & Judd A Profl Corp 4250 Republic Pla 370 17th St Denver CO 80202-5656

JUDD, ROBERT HARRIS, writer; b. Cleve., June 16, 1939; s. Clarence Howard and Cora Elisabeth (Harris) J.; married, Sept. 23, 1982 (div. May 1992). BA with honors, Williams Coll., 1961. Copywriter J. Walter Thompson, N.Y.C., 1961-65; creative dir. J. Walter Thompson, London, 1965-70; creative dir. J. Walter Thompson, N.Y.C., 1970-78, v.p., creative dir., 1982; v.p., creative dir. J. Walter Thompson, London, 1983-88; creative dir. Kenyon & Ekhart, N.Y.C., 1982. Co-author: (with Debora Phillips) How to Fall Out of Love, 1978, Sexual Confidence, 1980; author: Formula One, 1989, Indy, 1990, Monza, 1991, Phoenix, 1992, Silverstone, 1993, Burn, 1993. Mem. Am. Racing Press Assn., Mystery Writers Am., Author's Guild, Hampstead Cricket Club, Soc. of Authors (recipient of Miller award for Excellence in Journalism, 1992).

JUDD, THOMAS ELI, electrical engineer; b. Salt Lake City, Apr. 12, 1927; s. Henry Eli Judd and Jennie Meibos; m. Mary Lu Edman, June 21, 1948; children: Shauna, Kirk E., Blake E., Lisa. BSEE, U. Utah, 1950. Registered profl. engr., Utah. Mech. engr. Utah Power & Light Co., Salt Lake City, 1950-55; chief engr. Electronic Motor Car Corp., Salt Lake City, 1955-56, Equi-Tech Corp., Salt Lake City, 1978-79; hydraulic devel. engr. Galigher Co., Salt Lake City, 1956-58; pres. Toran Corp., Salt Lake City, 1958-71, T M Industries, Salt Lake City, 1971-78; chief exec. officer, mgr. Ramos Corp., Salt Lake City, 1979—; project cons. Eimco Corp., Salt Lake City, 1966; design cons. to tech. cos. Patentee in field in U.S. and fgn. countries; contbr. editor U.S. Rail News, 1982—. Cons. Nat. Fedn. Ind. Bus., 1983—. With USNR, 1945-46, PTO. Mem. Tau Beta Pi. Republican. Mormon. Home: 129 W Harris Ave Salt Lake City UT 84115 Office: Ramos Corp 125 Harris Ave Salt Lake City UT 84115-5204

JUDGE, BRIAN ROBERT, environmental specialist; b. Fontana, Calif., Oct. 26, 1959; s. Crawford McCoulough and Joan Marie (Pilgrim) J.; m. Cheryl Anne Kruschke, June 18, 1983; children: Jenna Louise, Kaitlyn Marie. BS in Geology, U. Calif., Santa Barbara, 1989. Geologist Summit Engring., Reno, Nev., 1989-91; environ. specialist Tahoe Regional Planning Agy., Zephyr Cove, Nev., 1991—. Democrat. Home: PO Box 10888 Zephyr Cove NV 89448 Office: Tahoe Regional Planning Agy PO Box 1038 Zephyr Cove NV 89448

JUDGE, GEORGE GARRETT, economics educator; b. Carlisle, Ky., May 2, 1925; s. William Everett and Etna (Perkins) J.; m. Sue Dunkle, Mar. 17, 1950; children: Lisa C., Laura S.; m. Margaret C. Copeland, Oct. 8, 1976. BS, U. Ky., 1948; MS, Iowa State U., 1949, PhD, 1952; Asst. prof. U. Conn., Storrs, 1951-55; prof. U. Okla., Stillwater, 1955-58; vis. prof. Yale U., New Haven, 1958-59; prof. econs. U. Ill., Urbana, 1959-86; prof. U. Calif., Berkeley, 1986—; vis. disting. prof. U. Ga., 1977-79; cons. Internat. Wool Secretariat, London, 1976-77. Author: Learning and Practicing Econometrics, 1992, Improved Methods of Inference, 1986, Introduction to the Theory and Practice of Econometrics, 1982, 88, Theory and Practice of Econometrics, 1980, 85, Pre-Test and Stein Rule Estimators, 1978, Allocation Over Space and Time, 1975, Spatial Equilibrium, 1972; Markov Processes, 1970. Served with USAAF, 1943-45; PTO. Fellow Social Sci. Research Council, 1958-59, NSF, 1965-66; NSF grantee, 1976-77. Fellow Econometric Soc.; mem. Am. Statis. Assn., Am. Econ. Assn. Club: Dial. Avocations: golf, sailing. Office: U Calif 207 Giannini Berkeley CA 94720

JUDKOFF, RONALD DENNIS, architectural engineer, scientist, researcher; b. N.Y.C., May 8, 1947; s. Irving and Eleanor (Abramson) J.; m. Carolyn Stoloff, June 29, 1980; 1 child, Jennifer E.O. Student, La Sorbonne, 1967-68; BA, Tufts U., 1969; MArch, Columbia U., 1977. Constrn. supr. Peace Corps, Senegal and Upper Volta, 1971-73; resident mgr. div. constrn. N.Y.C. Dept. Engring., 1975; constrn. mgr. Steele Point Devel. Corp., Tortola, British Virgin Islands, 1976; teaching asst. in heating, ventilating and air conditioning Columbia U. Grad. Sch. Architecture and Planning, N.Y.C., 1976-77; staff engr. Brookhaven Nat. Lab., Upton, N.Y., 1977-78; sr. archtl. engr. Nat. Renewable Energy Lab., Golden, Colo., 1978—; energy cons. for AID, Tunisia, 1982, Sheladia Inc., Bamako, Mali, 1983, Rsch. Triangle Inst., Marrakech, Morocco, 1984-86, Bldg. Rsch. Establishment, London, 1987; mem. experts group Internat. Energy Agy., Paris, 1985—. Mem. tech. editorial bd. Home Energy mag., 1990; contbr. numerous articles to profl. jours. Sr. patroller Nat. Ski Patrol, Denver, 1984—; safety chmn. Colo. Whitewater Assn., Denver, 1986-90; mem. Colo. Tech. Adv. Bd. on Weatherization, Denver, 1988—; mem. Colo. Gov.'s Com. on Home Energy Rating Systems, Denver, 1988—. Devel. grantee Am. Embassy, Dakar, Senegal, 1972; scholar Columbia U. Grad. Sch. Architecture and Planning, 1974-77; fellow Columbia U. Grad. Sch. Internat. Affairs, 1975-76. Mem. Union of Concerned Scientists, ASHRAE (com. chmn. 1988—), Internat. Solar Energy Soc., Sierra Club, Colo. Mountain Club. Office: Nat Renewable Energy Lab 1617 Cole Blvd Golden CO 80401

JUDSON, CHERYL JEAN, college administrator, management consultant; b. Mpls., Mar. 6, 1947; d. Peter Joseph and Eileen Clair (Smith) Lynch; divorced. BA, U. Minn., Duluth, 1969; MA, Mich. State U., 1972; PhD, Oreg. State U., 1981. Dir. admissions St. Martins Acad., Rapid City, S.D., 1972-75; vets. coord. Oreg. Inst. Tech., Klamath Falls, 1975-77; asst. dir. fin. aid Oreg. State U., Corvallis, 1978-84; dir. fin. aid Met. State Coll. of Denver, 1984-92, asst. v.p. fin. aid, 1993—; mem. nat. adv. bd. Am. Coll. Testing, Iowa City, Iowa, 1987-89, mem. regional adv. bd., 1984-87. Author monograph. Title IX coord. LWV, Klamath Falls, Oreg., 1975. Named to Outstanding Young Women of Am., 1982. Mem. Nat. Assn. Fin. Aid Adminstrs. (editorial bd. 1981-88, assoc. editor 1988-89), Colo. Assn. Fin. Aid Adminstrs., Rocky Mt. Assn. Student Affairs Adminstrs., Rocky Mountain Dressage Soc. (treas. 1990-92), N.Am. Trail Ride Conf. Home: 10955 Gray Cir Westminster CO 80030 Office: Met State Coll Denver PO Box 173362 Campus Box 2 Denver CO 80217-3362

JUDSON, KATHRYN DANIELS, writer, photographer; b. Portland, Oreg., Sept. 21, 1956; d. Dorin Slater and Kathryn Rose (Meyer) Daniels; m. David L. Judson, June 7, 1989. BA, Coll. of Idaho, 1978. Cast mem. Up With People, US & Can. Tour, 1979-80; reporter, assoc. editor Argus Observer, Ontario, Oreg., 1981-85; columnist Argus Observer, Ontario, 1985, columnist, reporter, 1988-91; free lance writer, 1981—; state ambassador Oregon Pavilion Expo '86, Vancouver, B.C., 1986; editor In Ontario Schs., 1992—; speaker, schools clubs in Oregon, Idaho, S. Dakota, 1981—. Mem. Malheur County Family Protection Coun., 1980s; officer Sister City Youth Club, Ontario, Oreg., 1980s; bd. dirs. Buckle Buddies traffic safety program, 1980s. Named Outstanding Chemistry Student, Am. Chem. Soc., Ontario, 1973, Hon. Chpt. Farmer, Future Farmers Am., Ontario, 1983; grantee NSF, 1973, Oreg. Coun. for Humanities, 1991-92. Office: PO Box 878 Ontario OR 97914

JUDSON, ROBERT EDWARD, marketing professional, advertising consultant; b. New Haven, Sept. 3, 1946; s. Ralph W. and Gladus E. (Stackpole) J.; m. Monica Elena Vocos, Jan. 13, 1989; children from previous marriage: Kimberly, Beth, Chamer. BS in Psychology, U. Tex., Arlington, 1972; MS in Ops. Rsch., U. Mich., 1975, MA in Psychology, 1977. Program evaluator City of Dallas, 1975-77; account exec. S.W. Rsch., Dallas, 1977-78; v.p. GMA Rsch., Portland, Oreg., 1978-81; v.p., account exec. Burke Mktg. Rsch., Santa Monica, Calif., 1981-86, v.p., mgr. Communicus div., 1986-91; owner Communicus Cons., 1991. Contbr. articles to profl. jours. NIMH fellow, 1973-76. Mem. Am. Mktg. Assn. (bd. dirs. So. Calif. chpt. 1983-86), Inst. Mgmt. Sci., Advt. Rsch. Found., Sierra Club. Home: 48 Ozone Ave # C Venice CA 90291-2410 Office: Communicus 501 Santa Monica Blvd Ste 405 Santa Monica CA 90401-2415

JUENGER, FRIEDRICH KLAUS, lawyer, educator; b. Frankfurt am Main, Germany, Feb. 18, 1930; came to U.S., 1955, naturalized, 1961; s. Wilhelm and Margarete J.; m. Baerbel Thierfelder, Sept. 15, 1967; children: J. Thomas, John F. Referendarexamen (Studienstiftung des deutschen Volkes scholar), J.W. Goethe-Universität, 1955; MCL, U. Mich., 1957; JD (Harlan-Fiske-Stone scholar), Columbia U., 1960. Bar: N.Y. 1962, Mich. 1970, U.S. Supreme Ct. 1970. Assoc. Cahill, Gordon & Reindel, N.Y.C., 1960-61, Baker & McKenzie, N.Y.C., Chgo., Madrid, 1961-66; assoc. prof. law Wayne State U., Detroit, 1966-68; prof. Wayne State U., 1968-75; vis. prof. Albert-Ludwigs U., Freiburg, Ger., 1972-73, 74, U. Calif., Davis, 1975-93; Edward L. Barrett prof., 1993—; vis. prof. Max-Planck Inst. für ausländisches und internationales Privatrecht, Hamburg, Fed. Republic of Germany, 1981-82, U. Jean Moulin, Lyon, France, 1984; lectr. Hague Acad. Internat. Law, 1983, Uruguayan Fgn. Rels. Inst., 1987; Eason-Weimann vis. prof. comparative law Tulane U., 1989; vis. prof. J.W. Goethe Universitat, Frankfurt am Main, Germany, 1992; sec. State Adv. Commn. Pvt. Internat. Law. Author: (with L. Schmidt) German Stock Corporation Act, 1967, Zum Wandel des Internationalen Privatrechts, 1974, Choice of Law and Multistate Justice, 1993; editor: Columbia Law Rev., 1959-60; bd. editors Am. Jour. Comparative Law, 1977—; contbr. articles on the conflict of laws, fgn. and comparative law to legal jours. Recipient Faculty Rsch. award Wayne State U., 1971, Disting. Teaching award U. Calif., Davis, 1985, Gen. Reporter on Judgments Recognition 12th Internat. Congress of Comparative Law, Australia, 1986, Fulbright lecturing award, 1987; Fulbright scholar, 1953-55; Rsch. grantee Volkswagen Found., 1972-73, Humboldt Found. Rsch. grantee Albert-Ludwigs-U. Freiburg, Fed. Republic Germany, 1990; Fulbright sr. rsch. fellow, 1981-82. Mem. ABA, Assn. of Bar of City of N.Y., Am. Fgn. Law Assn., Am. Law Inst., Am. Soc. Internat. Law, Am. Soc. Comparative Law (pres.), Assn. Can. Law Tchrs., Gesellschaft für Rechtsvergleichung, Internat. Acad. Comparative Law (assoc. mem.), Internat. Law Assn. (com. on internat. litigation), Soc. Pub. Tchrs. of Law, Academia Mexicana de Derecho Internacional Privado y Comparado (hon.). Office: U Calif King Hall Davis CA 95616

JUKKOLA, GEORGE DUANE, obstetrician-gynecologist; b. Aliquippa, Pa., Feb. 28, 1945; s. Waino Helmer and Bedlia (Pyle) J.; m. Gretchen Louise Strom, Feb. 14, 1970 (div. 1984): children: David, Jeffrey; m. Wendee Leigh Bookhart, Apr. 23, 1988 (div. 1993). BA in Psychology, U. Calif., Berkeley, 1970; MD, U. Pitts., 1975. Diplomate Am. Bd. Ob-Gyn. Caseworker Pa. Dept. Welfare, Rochester, 1971; resident in ob.-gyn. Akron (Ohio) Med. Ctr., 1975-78; pvt. practice Riverside, Calif., 1978—; co-founder, Family Birthing Ctr. Riverside, 1981-87; mng. ptnr. Parkview Profl. Ctr., Riverside, 1984—; chief dept. ob.-gyn. Parkview Community Hosp., Riverside, 1986-91, vice-chief of staff, 1992-93; chmn. ob-gyn. dept. Moreno Valley Med. Ctr., 1991—, dir. perinatal svcs., 1992—; guest lectr. Riverside Community Coll., 1984, 85. With USAF, 1965-69. Decorated Air medal with 4 oak leaf clusters. Fellow Am. Coll. Ob.-Gyn.; mem. AMA, Calif. Med. Assn. (mem. survey team), Riverside County Med. Assn., Am. Assn. Individual Investors, Victoria Club Riverside, Inland Physicians Med. Group (v.p. 1987-88), Mensa. Republican. Unitarian-Universalist. Home: 10252 Victoria Ave Riverside CA 92503-6100 Office: 3900 Sherman St Ste F Riverside CA 92503-4062

JULIEN, ROBERT MICHAEL, anesthesiologist, author; b. Port Townsend, Wash., Mar. 24, 1942; s. Frank Felton and Mary Grace (Powers) J.; m. Judith Dianne DeChenne, Feb. 14, 1963; children: Robert Michael, Scott M. BS in Pharmacy, U. Wash., 1965, MS in Pharmacology, 1968, PhD, 1970; MD, U. Calif.-Irvine, 1977. Diplomate Am. Bd. Anesthesiology. Intern, Good Samaritan Hosp., Portland, Oreg., 1977-78; resident Oreg. Health Scis. U., 1978-80; asst. prof. pharmacology U. Calif.-Irvine, 1970-74, asst. clin. prof., 1974-77; assoc. prof. anesthesiology and pharmacology U. Oreg., Portland, 1980-83; staff anesthesiologist St. Vincent Hosp., Portland, 1983—; cons., lectr. DuPont Labs., Wilmington, Del., 1981—. Author: Primer of Drug Action, 1975, 6th edit., 1991, Understanding Anesthesiology, 1984., Drugs and the Body, 1987. Recipient Service award Am. Epilepsy Soc., 1975. Mem. Am. Soc. Anesthesiologists, Am. Assn. Pharmacology and Exptl. Therapeutics, Soc. Neurosci., Oreg. Med. Assn., Western Pharmacology Soc. Roman Catholic. Club: Oswego Lake (Lake Oswego, Oreg.). Home: 1212 SW Hessler Dr Portland OR 97201-2807 Office: St Vincent Hosp Dept Anesthesia 9205 SW Barnes Rd Portland OR 97225-6622

JUMAO-AS, ALEX BARONDA, engineer; b. Surigao City, The Philippines, June 12, 1961; came to U.S., 1982; s. Gaudencio Tamosa and Adelaida (Baronda) J.; m. Remedios Panoncillo, Jan. 28, 1981; children: Real James, Rylan Justin. BS in Indsl. Engring. with high honors, U. San Jose Recoletos, Cebu City, Philippines, 1982; grad. mech. and elec. tech. with high honors, U. Alaska, 1988, AAS in Archtl. and Engring. with honors, 1989. Drafter Dept. Interior Bur. Land Mgmt., Anchorage, 1983-84, Raj Bhargava Assocs., Anchorage, 1984; asst. engr., drafter Unicom, Inc., Anchorage, 1984-93; civil engr. Raytheon Svc. Co., Anchorage, 1993—; adj. instr. U. Alaska, 1989-91; v.p. Unicom, Inc. Anchorage Employee Svc. Assn., 1985-86. Mem. Metro Cebu Jaycees, Am. Inst. Design and Drafting, Pundok Bisaya (Cebuano Filipino Assn. Alaska) (v.p.). Roman Catholic. Home: 8412 Barnett Dr Anchorage AK 99518-2900 Office: Raytheon Svc Co 550 W 7th Ave Anchorage AK 99501

JUMONVILLE, FELIX JOSEPH, JR., physical education educator, realtor; b. Crowley, La., Nov. 20, 1920; s. Felix Joseph and Mabel (Rogers) J.; m. Mary Louise Hoke, Jan. 11, 1952; children: Carol, Susan. BS, La. State U., 1942; MS, U. So. Calif., 1948, EdD, 1952. Assoc. prof. phys. edn. Los Angeles State Coll., 1948-60; prof. phys. edn. Calif. State U., Northridge, 1960-87, emeritus prof. phys. edn., 1987—; owner Felix Jumonville Realty, Northridge, 1974-82, Big Valley Realty, Inc., 1982-83, Century 21 Lamb Realtors, 1983-86, Cardinal Realtors, 1986-87; varsity track and cross-country head coach L.A. State Coll., 1952-60, Calif. State U., Northridge, 1960-71. Served with USCGR, 1942-46. Mem. Assn. Calif. State Univ. Profs., AAHPER, Pi Tau Pi, Phi Epsilon Kappa. Home: 2001 E Camino Parocela Apt 98N Palm Springs CA 92264-8283

JUNAK, STEVEN ALAN, botanist; b. Chgo., Apr. 25, 1949; s. Walter J. and Josephine H. Junak. BA in Environ. Biology, U. Calif., Santa Barbara, 1972, MA in Botany, 1987. Instr. botany continuing edn. div. Santa Barbara Community Coll., 1975-81, 84-85; herbarium botanist Santa Barbara Botanic Garden, 1976-87, herbarium curator, 1987—. Contbr. articles to profl. jours. Mem. adv. coun. Santa Cruz Island Found., 1991-93. Nature Conservancy grantee, 1988. Fellow Linnean Soc. London; mem. Am. Soc. Plant Taxonomists, Calif. Botanical Soc. (2d v.p. 1992-93), So. Calif. Botanists, Torrey Botanical Club. Democrat. Roman Catholic. Office: Santa Barbara Botanic Garden 1212 Mission Canyon Rd Santa Barbara CA 93105-2126

JUNDIS, ORVY LAGASCA, writer, consultant; b. Bato, Leyte, Philippines, Sept. 30, 1943; s. Andrew Acenas and Aurora Fernandini (Lagasca) J.; m. Edna Claire Salaver, Mar. 15, 1971 (div. June 1983); children: Elrik Mikhael, Maya Rebecca, Franz Gilchrist; m. Editha Erlina Diez, Feb., 9, 1993. AA in Liberal Arts, cert. social work, City Coll. San Francisco, 1983; BA in Humanities, New Coll. Calif., San Francisco, 1984. Free-lance writer San Francisco, 1968—; writer, editorial cartoonist Mabuhay Republic Newspaper, San Francisco, 1970-88; art advisor Top Illustrators and Cartoonists, various locations, 1971—; pres. Internat. Guild Fine Art Painters, various locations, 1971—; fgn. corr. Philippine Press, Manila, 1971—; contbg. editor Chelsea House Pub., N.Y.C., 1976; sr. writer Witty World Internat. Mag., North Wales, Pa., 1987—; cons. Philippine Kommix Industry, Philippines, 1971—, Marvel Comics, N.Y.C., 1973-79, Japanese Comic Book Industry, Tokyo, 1973—; bd. dirs. Philippine Am. Hist. Archives, San Francisco; lectr. San Francisco (Calif.) State U., 1992, San Francisco (Calif.) Art Inst., 1991, 92. Author, editor: Liwanag, 1975, World Encyclopedia of Comics, 1976; contbr., editorial bd.: Without Names, 1985; contbr. to profl. jours. Coord. Philippine Am. Community Endeavor, 1968—; co-founder Sch. Ethnic Studies, San Francisco (Calif.) State Coll., 1968; educator Chinese Cultural Ctr., San Francisco, 1984; advisor for anti-drugs comic book Pilipino Early Intervention Project, San Francisco, 1987; designer AIDS edn. poster Westbay Pilipino Multi Svc. Ctr., San Francisco, 1989. Cpl. USAR, 1965-71. Recipient Commendation Philippine Consulate, San Francisco, 1970, Oakland (Calif.) Mus., 1982, Mayor of San Francisco, 1990, cert. recognition Acad. Am. Poets, City Coll. San Francisco, 1984. Mem. Kearny St. Workshop, Poetry for the People, Liwanag Artists, Kommix Barkada, Bay Area Pilipino Am. Writers (editorial bd.), Manilatown Oral Historians (advisor). Democrat. Office: Philippine Am Hist Archives PO Box 12174 San Francisco CA 94112

JUNE, JEFFREY ALLEN, fishery consultant, marine biologist; b. Burbank, Calif., July 30, 1950; s. Coleman Ashely and Jessie Dee (Lamme) J.; m. Amandalei Bennett, June 12, 1991. AA in Chemistry, Los Angeles Valley Jr. Coll., Van Nuys, Calif., 1968; BA in Zoology, BS in Fisheries, Humboldt State U., Arcata, Calif., 1973; MS in Fisheries, U. Wash., 1981. Vol. Peace Corps, Lima, Peru, Palay, Micronesia, 1974-78; stream ecologist Weyerhaeuser Co., Seattle, 1978-79; chief scientist Nat. Marine Fisheries Svc., Seattle, 1979-85; ptnr., owner Natural Resources Cons., Inc., Seattle, 1985—; v.p. Pacific Observers, Inc., Seattle, 1989—; pres., CEO, Eco-Sound Products, Inc., Seattle, 1990—. Vice pres. Adopt A Beach, Inc., Seattle, 1990-92, pres., 1992—. Fellow Am. Inst. Fishery Rsch. Biologists. Home: 2133 NW 98th St Seattle WA 98117 Office: Natural Resources Cons Inc 4055 21st Ave W Seattle WA 98199

JUNE, ROY ETHIEL, lawyer; b. Forsyth, Mont., Aug. 12, 1922; s. Charles E. and Elizabeth F. (Newnes) J.; m. Laura Brautigam, June 20, 1949; children—Patricia June, Richard Tyler. B.A., U. Mont., 1948, B.A. in Law, 1951, LL.B., 1952. Bar: Mont. 1952, Calif. 1961. Sole practice, Billings, Mont., 1952-57, Sanders and June, 1953-57; real estate developer, Orange County, Calif., 1957-61; ptnr. Dugan, Tobias, Tornay & June, Costa Mesa, Calif., 1961-62; city prosecutor, Costa Mesa, 1962-63, asst. city atty., 1963-67, city atty., 1967-78; sole practice, Costa Mesa, 1962—. Atty. Costa Mesa Hist. Soc., Costa Mesa Playhouse Patron's Assn., Red Barons Orange County, Costa Mesa Meml. Hosp. Aux., Harbor Key, Child Guidance Ctr. Orange County, Fairview State Hosp. Therapeutic Pool Vols., Inc.; active Eagle Scout evaluation team, Harbor Area Boy Scouts Am., YMCA; atty. United Fund/Community Chest Costa Mesa and Newport Beach; bd. dirs. Boys' Club Harbor Area, bd. dirs. Mardan Ctr. Ednl. Therapy, United Cerebral Palsy Found. Orange County. Served with USAF, World War II. Decorated Air medal with oak leaf cluster, D.F.C. Mem. Mont. Bar Assn., Calif. Bar Assn., Orange County Bar Assn., Harbor Bar Assn., Costa Mesa C. of C. (bd. dirs.). Clubs: Masons, Scottish Rite, Shriners, Santa Ana Country, Amigos Viejos, Los Fiestadores. Office: 2960 D Harbor Blvd PO Box 3050 Costa Mesa CA 92626-3929

JUNG, DONALD T., pharmacokineticist; b. L.A., Apr. 10, 1953; s. Benson and Betty T.Y. (Dear) J.; m. Young Mi Lee, Mar. 31. 1984; children: Stacy T., Brian P. BS in Biochemistry, U. Calif., Davis, 1974; MS in Pharm. Chemistry, U. Calif., San Francisco, 1978; PhD Pharm. Sci., U. Ariz., 1980. Teaching asst. Sch. Pharmacy U. Calif., San Francisco, 1975-77; rsch. and teaching asst. Coll. Pharmacy U. Ariz., Tucson, 1979-80; asst. prof. Coll. Pharmacy U. Ill., Chgo., 1981-87, coord. Clin. Pharmacokinetics Lab. Coll. Pharmacy, 1987, adj. prof. pharmacodynamics Coll. Pharmacy, 1987—; vis. prof. BioFarmasi, Fakultas Farmasi U. Gadjah Mada, Yogyakarta, Indonesia, 1985; sr. staff researcher Syntex Rsch., Palo Alto, Calif., 1987—; cons. Hoechst-Roussel Pharms. Inc., Somerville, N.J., 1980, FDA, 1986-87. Contbr. articles to profl. jours. Calif. Heart Assn. fellow, 1974, U. Calif. San Francisco Regent's fellow, 1974-75; U. Ariz. Grad. Academic scholar, 1979-80. Mem. Am. Pharm. Assn., Am. Assn. Pharm. Scientists, Acad. Pharm. Scis., Phi Kappa Phi, Rho Chi.

JUNG, EUGENE, tax manager; b. San Francisco, Apr. 9, 1957; s. Horatio CM. and Jane J. (Tong) J.; m. Erin Lorraine Dunn, Aug. 24, 1991. BA in Architecture, U. Calif. Berkeley, 1978; MBA in Taxation, Golden Gate U., 1990. Sr. tax acct. Arthur Young & Co., San Francisco, 1981-83, Pacific Bell, San Francisco, 1983-85; corp. tax mgr. Western Temp. Svcs., Inc., Walnut Creek, Calif., 1986—. Mem. Tax Execs. Inst. (mem. fed. tax com.). Office: Western Temp Svcs Inc 298 N Wiget Ln Walnut Creek CA 94598-9280

JUNG, HENRY HUNG, mechanical engineer; b. Hong Kong, Aug. 3, 1957; s. Cheuk-Sun and Siu-Kuen (Ma) J.; m. Mi-Ying Miranda, Mar. 28, 1986. BS MechE, Ariz. State U., 1980; MS MechE, U. Ill., 1983. Engr. Lockheed Aircraft, Burbank, Calif., 1981-82; researcher U. Ill., Champaign-Urbana, 1982-83; engr. Pratt & Whitney Aircraft, West Palm Beach, Fla., 1983-84; sr. scientist Lockheed Missiles & Space Co., Palo Alto, Calif., 1984—. Mem. ASME, AIAA, N.Y. Acad. Scis., Sigma Xi, Tau Beta Pi, Pi Tau Sigma. Home: 21486 Holly Oak Dr Cupertino CA 95014-4928

JUNG, TIMOTHY TAE KUN, otolaryngologist; b. Seoul, Korea, Dec. 1, 1943; came to U.S., 1969; s. Yoon Yong and Helen Chung-Hyuk (Im) J.; m. Lucy Moon Young, Sept. 10, 1972; children: David, Michael, Karen. BS, Seoul Nat. U., 1966, Loma Linda U., 1971; MD, Loma Linda U., 1974; PhD, U. Minn., 1980. Diplomate, Am. Bd. Otolaryngology. Med. intern Loma Linda (Calif.) U. Med. Ctr., 1974-75; fellow in surgery U. Minn. Med. Sch., Mpls., 1975-76; fellow in otolaryngology U. Minn. Med. Sch., 1976-80, asst. prof. otolaryngology, 1980-84, clin. asst. prof., dir. prostaglandin lab., 1984-85; assoc. prof., dir. otolaryngology rsch. Loma Linda U., 1985-90, prof., dir. otolaryngology rsch., 1990-92, clin. prof., assoc. dir. otolaryngology rsch., 1992—; mem. deafness and communications disroders rev. com. Nat. Inst. Deafness and Communications, NIH, 1989-92. Contbr. numerous chpts. to med. books, over 100 articles and abstracts to med. jours. Sgt. Korean army, 1966-69. Recipient Edmund Price Fowler award. Fellow ACS, Triological Soc., Am. Acad. Otoalryngology (honor award 1990); mem. AMA, Am. Otol. Soc., Am. Neurotol. Soc., Soc. Univ. Otolaryngologists, Assn. Rsch. in Otolaryngology, Centurions, Collegium Otorhinolaryngogium Amicetiae Sacrum, Alpha Omega Alpha. Seventh-day Adventist. Home: 11790 Pecan Way Loma Linda CA 92354-3452 Office: 3975 Jackson St Ste 202 Riverside CA 92503

JUNGBLUTH, CONNIE CARLSON, real estate entrepreneur; b. Cheyenne, Wyo., June 20, 1955; d. Charles Marion and Janice Yvonne (Keldsen) Carlson; m. Kirk E. Jungbluth, Feb. 5, 1977; children: Tyler, Ryan. BS, Colo. State U., 1976. CPA, Colo. Sr. acct. Rhode Scripter & Assoc., Boulder, Colo., 1977-81; mng. acct. Arthur Young, Denver, 1981-85; asst. v.p. Dain Bosworth, Denver, 1985-87; v.p. George K. Baum & Co., Denver, 1987-91; with KC Ventures, Napa, Calif., 1991-93; pvt. real estate interests Napa, 1992—. Active Denver Estate Planning Coun., 1981-85; organizer Little People Am., Rocky Mountain Med. Clinic and Symposium, Denver, 1986; adv. bd. Children's Home Health, Denver, 1986-89; fin. adv. bd. Gail Shoettler for State Treas., Denver, 1986; campaign chmn. Kathi Williams for Colo. State Legislature, 1986; mem. Sch. Dist. 12 Colo. Edn. Found. Bd., 1991, Napa Sch. Dist. Elem. Site Com., 1992—. Named one of 50 to watch, Denver mag., 1988. Mem. AICPA, Colo. Soc. CPAs (strategic planning com. 1987-89, instr. bank 1983, trustee 1984-87, pres. bd. trustees 1986-87, bd. dirs. 1987-89, chmn. career edn. com. 1982-83, Pub. Svc. award 1985-87), Colo. Mcpl. Bond Dealers, Metro North C. of C. (bd. dirs. 1987-90), Am. Hort. Soc., Denver City Club (bd. dirs. 1987-88), Pi Beta Phi.

JUNGBLUTH, KIRK E., real estate appraiser; b. Lima, Ohio, Apr. 5, 1949; s. Harold A. and Marjorie J. (Brown) J.; m. Connie Carlson, Feb. 5, 1977; children: Tyler, Ryan. Student, Mesa Coll., Grand Junction, Colo., 1967-69, Regis Coll., Denver. Lic. real estate appraiser, Calif. Loan officer, real estate appraiser Home Fed. Savs. & Loan, Ft. Collins, Colo., 1973-76; real estate appraiser Jungbluth & Assocs., Ft. Collins, 1976-83; pres., bd. dirs. Security Diamond Corp., Denver, 1982-90; nat. sales dir. InfoAm. Computers, Denver, 1982-90; chmn. bd. dirs., chief exec. officer U.S. Capital Lending Corp., Denver, 1987-90, Capital Real Estate & Devel. Corp., Denver, 1988-90; ct.-appointed receiver Dist. Ct. State of Colo., 1990; real estate appraiser World Savs. & Loan Assn., Walnut Creek, Calif., 1992—. Sec.-treas. St. Peters Luth. Ch., Ft. Collins, Colo., 1980-81, pres., 1982-84. Sgt. USMC, 1969-71. Republican.

JUNGKIND, WALTER, design educator, consultant; b. Zurich, Switzerland, Mar. 9, 1923; came to Can., 1968; s. Oskar and Frieda (Leuthold) J.; m. Jenny Voskamp, 1953; children—Christine, Stefan, Brigit. Nat diploma, Kunstgewerbeschule, Zurich, 1943; nat diploma, Regent Street Poly tech., London, 1953. Freelance designer London, 1955-68; lectr. London Coll. Printing and Graphic Arts, 1960-65, sr. lectr., 1965-68; assoc. prof. dept. art and design U. Alta., Edmonton, Can., 1968-72, prof., 1972-90, prof. emeritus, 1990—; Design cons. pub. works Province of Alta., 1972-75; chmn. Canadian Adv. Com. Standards Council Can., 1978—. Initiator and curator internat. exhbn. Graphic Design for Pub. Service, 1972, Language Made Visible, 1973. Recipient Design Can. award Nat. Design Council Can., 1979, 1984; Chmns. award Nat. Design Council Can., 1982. Fellow Soc. Indsl. Artists and Designers Gt. Britain, Soc. Graphic Designers Can. (pres. 1978-82); mem. Internat Council Design Assns. (pres. 1974-76, Design for Edn. award 1972, Nat. Design Coun. awards 1982-85). Home: 6304-109th Ave, Edmonton, AB Canada T6A 1S2

JUNGREN, JON ERIK, civil engineer; b. Malmo, Sweden, Oct. 19, 1927; came to U.S., 1966; s. Axel Bernhard and Lilly Ottonie (Eliasson) Ljungren; m. Elaine Berry, May 13, 1977. BS, Chalmers Inst. Technology, Gothenburg, Sweden, 1951; MS, Chalmers Inst. Technology, 1952; BA, Royal Inst. Technology, Stockholm, Sweden, 1954; PhD, Columbia Pacific U., 1985. Registered civil engr., Calif., Ariz. Br. mgr. Jacobsen & Widmark, Lund, Sweden, 1954-59; pres., owner Civilingnjoren SVR Jan Ljunggren AB, Lund, 1959-66; supervising engr. Bechtel Corp., San Francisco, 1966-74; engring. mgr. Morrison Knudsen, Holland, U.S.A., 1974-83; chmn. Jungren & Duran, Inc., Santa Ana Heights, Calif., 1983—; cons. engr. Assn. of Calif.

Legis. Com., 1987-90. Contbr. articles to profl. jours. Recipient Archtl. award, 1959, 66. Mem. ASCE, Am. Cons. Engrs. Coun., Cons. Engrs. Assn. Calif., Am. Concrete Inst., Internat. Conf. Bldg. Ofcls., Masons, Mensa. Democrat. Home: 2420 Miseno Way Costa Mesa CA 92627 Office: Jungren & Duran Inc 20341 Irvine Ave Ste 5 Santa Ana Heights CA 92707-5628

JUNK, VIRGINIA WICKSTROM, family and consumer studies educator; b. Cin., Dec. 14, 1945; d. Raymond John Wickstrom and Clara Anna (Walter) Woodcock; m. William Stanley Junk, Sept. 11, 1965; children: Clifford Raymond, Laura Ann. BS in Home Econs., U. Idaho, 1967, MS in Home Econs., 1983, PhD in Edn., 1986. Cert. home economist. Home econs. tchr. Genesee (Idaho) Sch. Dist., 1967-68; salesperson Oak Ridge Realty, San Jose, Calif., 1976-80; buyer Stretch and Sew Fabrics, Eugene, Oreg., 1972-73; substitute tchr. Berryessa Sch. Dist., San Jose, 1975-80; rsch. scientist Stanford U., Palo Alto, Calif., 1989-90; asst. prof. U. Idaho, Moscow, 1986-91, assoc. prof., 1992—; chair USDA HATCH Project, U. Idaho Experiment Sta., Moscow, 1991-92. Contbr. articles to profl. publs.; reviewer peer jours.; editor (proceedings) Am. Assn. of Housing Educators, 1991. Idaho chair Teenage Pregnancy Task Force, Boise, 1987-88; Idaho rep. Teenage Pregnancy Western Region Com., Seattle, 1987-89; mem. Gov.'s Subcom. on Teenage Pregnancy, Boise, 1988-89; advisor Phi Upsilon Omicron, Moscow, 1986-92. Mary Hall Nicholls scholar U. Idaho Home Econs. Dept., 1982-83. Mem. Soc. Consumer Affairs Profl., Am. Soc. on Aging, Am. Home Econ. Assn., A. Coun. on Consumer Interests (reviewer 1993-94), Am. Assn. Housing Edn. (proceedings editor 1991), Phi Upsilon Omicron, Phi Delta Kappa, Gamma Sigma Delta. Republican. Episcopalian. Office: U Idaho Sch Family & Consumer Scis Moscow ID 83843

JURECKI, CASIMER JOHN JOSEPH, financial analyst; b. Cleve., Apr. 5, 1952; s. Casimer Joseph and Helen Ann (Hertvik) J.; m. Marcella Loubet, July 16, 1988. BA, Cleve. State U., 1976; MBA, Calif. State U., L.A., 1984. Accounts analyst Am. Greetings Corp., Cleve., 1977-79; regional credit mgr. Carnation Co., L.A., 1979-84, fin. analyst, 1984-86; sr. fin. analyst Carnation Co., Glendale, Calif., 1986-91; mgr. fin. planning and analysis Abex Aerospace, Oxnard, Calif., 1991-92; bus. cons. Hiram Walker Internat. Liqueurs, L.A., 1992—. Mem. So. Calif. Food Mfrs. Credit Assn. (v.p. 1978-79), Santa Anita Catholic Singles (pres.'s award 1987), U.S. Assn. Evening Students (Roy J. Barry award 1981), Assn. MBA Execs., Choice L.A. Retreat Program. Republican. Roman Catholic. Home: 15737 Covello St Van Nuys CA 91406-3120 Office: Hiram Walker Internat Liqueurs 10 Universal City Plz Universal City CA 91608

JUREWICZ, BENJAMIN RAYMOND, engineering executive; b. Wilkes-Barre, Pa., June 10, 1942; s. Benjamin Jacob and Sophie Ann (Blocki) Urevitch; m. Mary Dolan Jurewicz, Nov. 29, 1969; children: Justin, Matthew, Elizabeth. AB in Math., Kings Coll., Wilkes-Barre, 1965; BS in Aero. Engring., Pa. State U., 1965; MS in Aero. and Astro. Engring., MIT, 1966; MBA, U. Conn., 1972; EAA in Aero. and Astro. Engring., MIT, 1967; postgrad., U. Va., 1988. Program mgr. devel. engring. United Aircraft Corp., East Hartford, Conn., 1967-76; chief product planning Hamilton Standard, Windsor Locks, Conn., 1977, mgr. inventory system requirements, 1978, chief advanced systems, 1979-85; v.p. engring. Sperry, Charlottesville, Va., 1985-87, v.p. mktg., 1988; dir. systems divsn. Thiokol Corp., Ogden, Utah, 1989—; cons. Ctr. for Innovative Tech., Va., 1988-89. Contbr. articles on lasers to profl. jours.; patent applications. Town commr. City of South Windsor, Conn., 1972-82; elected mem. Town Dem. Party, South Windsor, 1982-89. Evan Pugh scholar Pa. State U., 1965; NASA fellow MIT, 1965-67. Fellow AIAA (assoc., chmn. Utah chpt. 1991-92, chmn. Conn. chpt. 1984-85, mem. tech. coms. 1986—); mem. Assn. Unmanned Vehicles, NSIA (mem. submarine, ship system and fire control tech. com. 1986-88), Submarine League, USN League (v.p. Conn. 1983-85), Tau Beta Pi, Phi Mu Epsilon, Sigma Gamma Tau, Phi Kappa Phi, Beta Gamma Sigma. Office: Thiokol Corp Brigham City UT

JURGENS, LEONARD JOHN, range conservationist; b. Pickrell, Nebr., May 2, 1933; s. Wilke J. and Freda C. (Wolken); married; children: Glenn S., Mark A., Yvonne L. BS in Agronomy, U. Nebr., 1959. Range conservationist USDA Soil Conservation Svc., Burwell, Nebr., 1959-64, Franklin, Nebr., 1964-66; area range conservationist USDA Soil Conservation Svc., Emporia, Kans., 1966-81; state range conservationist USDA Soil Conservation Svc., Bismarck, N.D., 1981-85, Lakewood, Colo., 1985—; adj. prof. U. Emporia, 1970-81. With U.S. Army, 1953-55. Mem. Soc. Range Mgmt., SRM (pres. 1976 K-O sect., Colo. sect.). Home: 9518 Dudley Dr Broomfield CO 80021-4357 Office: USDA Soil Conservation Svcs 655 Parfet St Rm 200ec Westminster CO 80215-5517

JUSINSKI, LEONARD EDWARD, physicist, consultant; b. Oakland, Calif., Aug. 12, 1955; s. Leonard George and Kathleen Teresa (Vincent) J.; m. Mary Jane Blair, June 19, 1977; children: Jennifer, Kristin, Blair, Michelle. BS, U. San Francisco, 1977. Engr. Varian Assocs., Palo Alto, Calif., 1982; physicist SRI Internat., Menlo Park, Calif., 1983—; founder Soft Bus. Systems, Fremont, Calif., 1992—. Contbr. 60 articles to profl. jours. Capt. USAF, 1977-81. Home: 3432 Little Ct Fremont CA 94538-2914 Office: SRI Internat Molecular Physics Lab 333 Ravenswood Ave Menlo Park CA 94025-3493

JUSTIN, JOSEPH EUGENE, retired military officer, business consulting executive; b. Orange, N.J., June 3, 1945; s. James Fredrick and Elizabeth (McCartney) J.; children: James Kenneth, Joseph Patrick. BS, USAF Acad., 1969; MS, Ohio State U., 1973; MA, U. So. Calif., 1980; MBA, UCLA, 1989. Commd. 2d lt. USAF, 1969, advanced through grades to maj., 1980; lead project engr. USAF Avionics Lab. USAF, Wright-Patterson AFB, Ohio, 1970-74; exchange officer USAF Systems Commd. USAF, F.E. Warren AFB, Cheyenne, Wyo., 1974; mgr. guidance improvement program USAF Ballistic Missiles Office, Norton AFB, Calif., 1975-77, chief flight test integration div., 1985-89; pres. JE Justin & Assocs., bus. cons., 1989—; asst. prof. astronautics USAF Acad., Colorado Springs, Colo., 1977-81; research fellow USAF Hdqrs.-Rand Corp., Santa Monica, Calif., 1981-82; dir. space system studies Hdqrs. USAF, Washington, 1982-85. Mem. AIAA (sr.), Air Force Assn. (life), Air Force War Coll. Assn. (life), USAF Acad. Assn. Grads. (life), Ohio State U. Alumni Assn. (life), USAF Rsch., Acad. of Country Music, Assocs. Assn., Naval Inst. Home: PO Box 2256 2768 Snowflower Dr Running Springs CA 92382

JUVET, RICHARD SPALDING, JR., chemistry educator; b. Los Angeles, Aug. 8, 1930; s. Richard Spalding and Marion Elizabeth (Dalton) J.; m. Martha Joy Myers, Jan. 29, 1955 (div. Nov. 1978); children: Victoria, David, Stephen, Richard P.; m. Evelyn Raeburn Elthon, July 1, 1984. B.S., UCLA, 1952, Ph.D., 1955. Research chemist Dupont, 1955; instr. U. Ill., 1955-57, asst. prof., 1957-61, assoc. prof., 1961-70; prof. analytical chemistry Ariz. State U., Tempe, 1970—; vis. prof. UCLA, 1960, U. Cambridge, Eng., 1964-65, Nat. Taiwan U., 1968, Ecole Polytechnique, France, 1976-77, U. Vienna, Austria, 1989-90; mem. air pollution chemistry and physics adv. com. EPA, HEW, 1969-72; mem. adv. panel on advanced chem. alarm tech., devel. and engring. directorate Def. Systems div. Edgewood Arsenal, 1975; adv. panel on postdoctoral associateships NAS/NRC, 1991—. Author: Gas-Liquid Chromatography, Theory and Practice, 1962; Editorial advisor to: Jour. Chromatographic Sci., 1969-85, Jour. Gas Chromatography, 1963-68, Analytica Chimica Acta, 1972-74, Analytical Chemistry, 1974-77, biennial reviewer in, 1962-76. NSF sr. postdoctoral fellow, 1964-65; recipient Sci. Exchange Agreement award Czechoslovakia, Hungary, Romania and Yugoslavia, 1977. Fellow Am. Inst. Chemists; mem. AAAS, Am. Chem. Soc. (nat. chmn. div. analytical chemistry 1972-73, nat. sec.-treas. div. analytical chemistry 1969-71, div. com. on chem. edn., subcom. on grad. edn., 1988—, councilor 1978-89, coun. com. analytical reagents 1985—, chmn. U. Ill. sect. 1968-69, sec. 1962-63, co-author Reagent Chemicals 7th edit., 1986, 8th edit., 1993, directorate div. officers' caucus 1987-90), Internat. Platform Assn., Internat. Union of Pure and Applied Chemistry, Am. Radio Relay League, Sigma Xi, Phi Lambda Upsilon, Alpha Chi Sigma (profl. rep.-at-large 1989—, chmn. expansion com. 1990-92). Presbyn. (deacon 1960—, ruling elder 1972—, commr. Grand Canyon Presbytery 1974-76). Home: 4821 E Calle Tuberia Phoenix AZ 85018-2932 Office: Ariz State U Dept Chemistry Tempe AZ 85287-1604

KACHOUEI, MAHMOUD H., mechanical and nuclear engineer; b. Isfahan, Iran; came to U.S., 1974; s. Abbas Ali; m. Parvin M. Mohammad Sadeghi, 1984. BS in Physics, U. Isfahan, 1971; BS in Nuclear Engring., U. Okla., 1977; MS in Mech. Engring., Calif. State U., Los Angeles, 1980; cert. control systems, UCLA, 1981, cert. advanced microprocessor, 1983. Registered profl. engr., Calif., Md., Va., Wash., Oreg., Tenn., Pa., Ariz., N.Mex. Sr. mech. engr. Wed Enterprises, Glendale, Calif., 1979-83; sr. mech. engr. Holmes & Narver Inc., Orange, Calif., 1984; sr. control systems engr., mech. engr. Bechtel Power Co., Norwalk, Calif., 1984—. Recipient 2 medallions for disting. engring. on Epcot Ctr. and Disneyland project, Tokyo, 1982, 83, Wed Enterprises. Mem. NSPE. Address: PO Box 3171 Glendale CA 91221-0171

KACMARCIK-BAKER, MARY ELIZABETH, university official; b. Lowell, Mass., Sept. 30, 1960; d. William Francis and Frances Catherine (Niedziela) Kacmarcik; m. Robert Thomas Baker, Mar. 16, 1991. BA, U. Mass., 1982; MA, Bowling Green State U , 1985; postgrad., Pepperdine U., 1991—. Leadership cons. Alpha Chi Omega, Indpls., 1982-83; dir. student orgns. West Chester (Pa.) U., 1985-86; asst. dean for student activities Iowa State U., Ames, 1986-88; dir. orientation Calif. State U., L.A., 1988-91, exec. dir. Alumni Assn., 1991—. Mem. alumni coun. Calif. State U. Recipient Disting. Advisor award Iowa State U., 1987, Norman K. Russell award Nat. Orientation Dirs. Assn., 1991, Colleague's award Pepperdine U., 1991, 92. Mem. Coun. for Advancement and Support Edn., Alpha Chi Omega (U. So. Calif. chpt. adv.). Mem. Co. Office: Calif State U Alumni Office 5154 State University Dr Los Angeles CA 90032

KACZYNSKI, WILLIAM F., investment executive; b. Evergreen Park, Ill., Dec. 25, 1959; s. William F. Sr. and Virginia Mae (Frenette) K. BS in Accountancy, U. Ill., 1983; M of Mgmt., Northwestern U., Evanston, Ill., 1992. CPA, Ill. Staff acct. Price Waterhouse & Co., Chgo., 1983-84; field analyst Fidelcor Bus. Credit Corp., Chgo., 1984-85; account exec. Fidelcor Bus. Credit Corp., L.A., 1985-86; sr. client fin. analyst Heller Fin., Inc., L.A., 1986-87, mgr. client exams, 1987-88, asst. v.p., underwriter, 1988; asst. v.p., underwriter Heller Fin., Inc., Chgo., 1989, v.p., sr. underwriter, 1989-90, v.p. portfolio mgmt., 1990-91; v.p. Heller Equity Capital Corp., 1991-92; sr. v.p. Heller Fin., L.A., 1992—. Mem. AICPA. Republican. Roman Catholic. Home: 25225 W Carson Way Stevenson Ranch CA 91381 Office: Heller Fin Inc 505 N Brand Blvd Glendale CA 91203

KADEG, ROGER DAN, environmental chemist, engineer; b. Seattle, Apr. 23, 1951; s. John Alfred and Delores Betty (Bell) K. BS in Physics cum laude, Seattle Pacific U., 1973; MS in Chemistry, U. Wash., 1975, MSE in Environ. Engring., 1979. Quality assurance/quality control chemist Union Carbide-Linde div., Seattle, 1975-77; EPA rsch. assoc. U. Wash., Seattle, 1977-79; asst. engr. to prin. engr. Environ. div. Ebasco Svcs., Inc., Bellevue, Wash., 1980—; contbr. to U.S. EPA Sediment Quality Criteria Tech. Com. Prin. author handbook: Sediment Toxicity Handbook, Environmental Toxicity Handbook - EPA; contbr. articles to profl. jours. Exec. coun. So. Seattle Fellowship of Singles, 1986-90; trustee Highline Bapt. Ch., 1980-85, edn. bd., 1985-91. Recipient Pub. Svc. Group Achievement award, NASA, 1989. Mem. Soc. of Environ. Toxicology and Chemistry, Assn. N.W. Environ. Profls., Photographic Soc. Am., Three Tree Community Ch. Republican. Baptist. Home: 15248 29th Ave S Seattle WA 98188 Office: Ebasco Environ 10900 NE 8th St Bellevue WA 98004

KADNER, CARL GEORGE, biology educator emeritus; b. Oakland, Calif., May 23, 1911; s. Adolph L. and Otilia (Pecht) K.; m. Mary Elizabeth Moran, June 24, 1939; children: Robert, Grace Wickersham, Carl L. BS, U. San Francisco, 1933; MS, U. Calif., Berkeley, 1936, PhD, 1941. Prof. biology Loyola Marymount U., Los Angeles, 1936-78, prof. emeritus, 1978—; trustee Loyola U., Los Angeles, 1970-73. Served to maj. U.S. Army, 1943-46. Mem. Entomol. Soc. Am. (emeritus), Sigma Xi, Alpha Sigma Nu. Republican. Roman Catholic. Home: 8100 Loyola Blvd Los Angeles CA 90045-2639

KAGEL, JOHN, lawyer; b. Berkeley, Calif., Jan. 19, 1940; s. Sam and Sophie Rae (Hornstein) Kagel; m. Mary Pat Radocy, Feb. 15, 1987; children: Susan, Andrew, Megan, Molly, Patrick. AB, U. Calif., Berkeley, 1961, LLB, 1964. Bar: Calif. 1965, U.S. Ct. Appeals 1965, U.S. Ct. Claims 1967, U.S. Dist. Ct. (no. dist.) 1968, U.S. Supreme Ct. 1968. Sports reporter San Francisco Examiner, 1959-64; ptnr. Kagel and Kagel, San Francisco, 1968—; arbitrator, mediator, U.S. and Can. Contbr. articles to profl. publs. Bd. dirs. Juvenile Diabetes Found. Internat., Greater Bay Area Chpt. Capt. JAGC, U.S. Army, 1965-67. Recipient Sally Siegel Friend of Edn. award Palo Alto Tchrs./Sch. Bd., 1985, Willoughby Abner award Soc. Profls. in Dispute Resolution, 1988. Mem. ABA, Am. Arbitration Assn. (achievement award 1989), Nat. Acad. Arbitrators, Calif. State Bar Assn., San Francisco Bay Club (racquetball award 1991). Office: Kagel & Kagel 544 Market St Ste 401 San Francisco CA 94104-5423

KAGEMOTO, HARO (HARO), filmmaker; b. Tokyo, Jan. 9, 1952; came to U.S. 1956.; s. Herbert Yoshito and Nobuye Shirley (Furukawa) K.; m. Patricia Mae Jow, Sept. 21, 1991. Cert., Sch. Modern Photography, N.J., 1972; BFA, U. Hawaii, 1977; MFA, SUNY-New Paltz, 1979. Instr. Communications Village, Kingston, N.Y., 1977-79; vis. artist U. Calif. Ext., Berkeley, 1980-82; vis. lectr. San Francisco State U., 1982-83; asst. dir. Wonderland Prodns., San Francisco, 1983-88; dir. Wonderland Prodns., Oakland, Calif., 1989—. Dir. video documentary: Visitations, 1989, Ancient Meso-America, 1990; editor video shor: Hendrix Experience, 1988; author poetry collection: Orion's Winter, 1975. Mem. Am. Film Inst. Home: 2806 Truman Ave Oakland CA 94605-4847

KAGEYAMA, DAVID KENJI, graphic and industrial designer; b. Seattle, June 2, 1948; s. Noboru and Natsuko (Tanaka) K.; m. Norma Jean Dill, July 25, 1981; 1 child, Joshua Kenichi. AAS, Seattle Cen. Community Coll., 1976; student, U. Wash., 1966-68. Artist Charles Okada, Artist, Seattle, 1976; owner David Kageyama Designer, Seattle, 1976—; instr., cons. U.S. Nat. Park Svc. Region X, Seattle, 1987—; instr. U. Wash. Expetl. Coll., Seattle, 1980-82. Bd. dirs. Seattle Cherry Blossom and Japanese Cultural Festival, 1981—, chmn., 1988, 89, 91, 92, treas., 1993; mem. fin. com. Asian Counseling and Referral Svc., Seattle, 1989—, chmn. ann. Community Recognition Dinner, 1991; chmn. City of Seattle Dept. Neighborhoods, Citywide Review Team, 1992, 93. Recipient Behind the Scenes award King County Domestic Violence Coalition, Seattle, 1983, Founders award NW Women's Law Ctr., Seattle, 1987, Svc. award Consulate Gen. of Japan, Seattle, 1989, Cert. of Appreciation, Seattle Cherry Blossom and Japanese Cultural Festival, 1982, James K. Fukuda Meml. award Am. Cultural Exchange, 1992. Mem. Am. Mensa Ltd. (bd. dirs. 1987-89, membership officer 1987-89, nat. membership enhancement officer 1989-91), Mensa of Western Wash. (pres. 1983-87, Cert. of Appreciation 1982). Office: PO Box 9767 Seattle WA 98109-0767

KAGIWADA, REYNOLD SHIGERU, advanced technology manager; b. L.A., July 8, 1938; s. Harry Yoshifusa and Helen Kinue (Imura) K.; m. Harriet Hatsune Natsuyama, Aug. 19, 1961; children: Julia, Conan. BS in Physics, UCLA, 1960, MS in Physics, 1962, PhD in Physics, 1966. Asst. prof. in residence physics UCLA, 1966-69; asst. prof. physics U. So. Calif., 1969-72; mem. tech. staff TRW, Redondo Beach, Calif., 1972-75, scientist, sect. head, 1975-77, sr. scientist, dept. mgr., 1977-83, lab. mgr., 1984-87, project mgr., 1987-88, MIMIC chief scientist, 1988-89, asst. program mgr., 1989-90; advanced technology mgr. TRW, Redondo Beach, 1990—. Presented papers at numerous profl. meetings, co-author over 44 articles to profl. jours.; patentee for eight solid state devices. Recipient Gold Medal award TRW, 1985, Ramo Tech. award, 1985, Transfer award. Fellow IEEE (v.p. IEEE MTT-S Adminstrn. Com. 1991, pres. 1992); mem. Assn. Old Crows, Sigma Pi Sigma, Sigma Xi. Home: 3117 Malcolm Ave Los Angeles CA 90034-3406 Office: TRW-ESG Bldg MS Rm 1470 One Space Park Bldg Redondo Beach CA 90034

KAHAN, SHELDON JEREMIAH, musician, singer; b. Honolulu, Mar. 5, 1948; s. Aaron Kahan and Marianne (Royjiczek) Sann. Student, Tel Aviv U., 1967-69, Merritt Coll., 1972-74. Guitarist The Grim Reapers, Miami Beach, Fla., 1965-66; bassist The Electric Stage, Jerusalem, 1969-71; music dir., musician Fanfare, L.A., 1974-75, Jean Paul Vignon & 1st Love, L.A., 1975-76; musician Jenny Jones & Co., L.A., 1976; musician, vocalist Fantasy, L.A., 1977-79; leader, musician, vocalist Fortune, L.A., 1980-83; bassist Johnny Tillotson Show, Nev., 1983; ptnr., musician, vocalist Heartlight, L.A., 1983-84; leader, musician, vocalist The Boogie Bros., L.A., 1984—; arranger, conductor L.A. Rock Chorus, 1988; musician, vocalist Jeremiah Kahan, L.A., 1988; bass player LIX, L.A., 1990—; solo act Sheldon Kahan, L.A., 1990—; spokesman Moore Oldsmobile & Cadillac, Valencia, Calif., 1987. Compiled musical work copyrighted in Libr. of Congress: "Sheldon Jeremiah Kahan The Early Years-Vol.I"; producer/disc jockey Kaleidoscope Radio Mag., Am. Radio Network; one-man show El Capitan, Irvine, Calif., 1990, Sagebrush Cantina, Calabassas, Calif., 1990, Don Jose, Artesia, Calif., Pineapple Hill, Tustin, Calif, 1991, The Fling, Tustin, 1992, Beverly Garland, N. Hollywood, Calif., Brian Patch, Garden Grove, Calif., Sugar Suite, Granada Hills, Calif, 1993; albums include "Out of the Shadows", 1992, "City Lights", 1993. Mem. AFTRA, Am. Fedn. Musicians. Democrat. Jewish. Home: 391512 Fredonia Dr Los Angeles CA 90068-1213

KAHAN, WILLIAM M., mathematics educator, consultant; b. Toronto, Ont., Can., June 5, 1933; s. Myer and Gertrude (Rosenthal) K.; m. Sheila K. Strauss, Sept. 5, 1954; children: Ari J., Simon H. BA in Math., U. Toronto, 1954, MA in Math., 1956, PhD in Math., 1958; DEng (hon.), Chalmers Tech. U., Sweden, 1993. Lectr. U. Toronto, Can., 1954-58, from asst. prof. to prof., 1960-68; postdoctoral rsch. student math. lab. Cambridge (Eng.) U., 1958-60; vis. prof. Stanford (Calif.) U., 1966; cons. IBM, N.Y.C. and Austin, Tex., 1967—, calculator div. Hewlett-Packard, Cupertino, Calif. and Corvallis, Oreg., 1974-80, Intel, Santa Clara, Calif., 1977—; cons. Co-inventor Intel 8087, 1980; contbr. articles to profl. jours. Am. Math. Soc., Assn. Computing Machinery (1st G. E. Forsythe Meml. award 1972, A. M. Turing prize 1990), Soc. for Indsl. and Applied Math., IEEE Computer Soc. (affiliate mem., mem. tech. standards com. 1985, 88). Jewish. Office: U Calif Dept Elec Engring & Computer Sci Berkeley CA 94720

KAHLER, JAMES FREDERICK, health care executive; b. Detroit, Mar. 13, 1943; s. Curtis Ibsen and Lottie (Black) K.; m. Patricia Irene Gilmore, Aug. 24, 1963 (div. Feb. 1974); 1 child, Kimberly Rene. BA, No. Mich. U., 1965; cert. phys. therapy, Mayo Clinic, 1968; MBA, Chaminade U., 1989. Dir. phys. therapy Marquette (Mich.) Gen. Hosp., 1968-76; phys. therapist, cons. Hilo (Hawaii) Hosp., 1976-78; v.p. patient care svcs. Rehab. Hosp. of the Pacific, Honolulu, 1978-90; v.p. outpatient svcs. Home Health Svcs. Hale Makua, Kahului, Hawaii; pres. Hawaii Assn. For Home Care; bd. dirs. Kuakini-At Home Adv. Bd., Honolulu; adv. bd. Kapiolani C.C., Honolulu, 1987—; adv. bd. dirs. Hawaii Assisted Tech. Svc. Bd. dirs. Medicredit Fed. Credit Union, Honolulu, 1989, MADD, Honolulu, 1989, Am. Arthritis Found., Honolulu, 1986; treas. Diocese of No. Mich., Marquette, 1976. Mem. Am. Mgmt. Assn., Am. Phys. Therapy Assn. (pres. No. Mich. chpt. 1969-75, Hawaii chpt.), Assn. for Advancement of Tech., Am. Coll. Health Care Execs., Nat. Assn. for Home Care. Episcopalian. Office: Hale Makua Home Health 140 Hoohana St # 212 Kahului HI 96732-2099

KAHN, ALICE JOYCE, columnist; b. Chgo., Dec. 22, 1943; d. Herman and Idell (Avonovitch) Nelson; m. Edward Paul Kahn, Aug. 14, 1966; children: Emma Ruby, Hannah Rose. BA in English Lit., Columbia U., 1965; BS in Nursing, Calif. State U., Hayward, 1973; nurse practitioner degree, U. Calif., San Francisco, 1976. Cert. secondary tchr., Calif.; RN; cert. family planning nurse practitioner; cert. adult health nurse practitioner. Tchr. English San Lorenzo (Calif.) Unified Schs., 1966-69; RN Alameda County Health Dept., Oakland, Calif., 1973-74; nurse practitioner Krause, Watanabe & Silverstein, Berkeley, Calif., 1975-86; columnist East Bay Express newspaper, Oakland, 1984-86, San Francisco Chronicle, 1986—; syndicated columnist L.A. Times Syndicate, 1988—. Author: Multiple Sarcasm, 1985, My Life As a Gal, 1987, Luncheon At the Cafe Ridiculous, 1990; contbr. articles to Vogue, Elle, Savvy, Playboy, Calif., L.A. Times Mag., 1986—. Mem. med. bd. Berkeley Free Clinic, 1969-72; chief medic Berkeley Womens Health Collective, 1981-74; food server McGee Ave. Bapt. Ch., Berkeley, 1989. Recipient Meritorious Achievement award for free-lance writing Media Alliance, San Francisco, 1985, Cert. of Excellence for features Greater L.A. Press Club, 1987. Mem. Newspaper Guild. Office: San Francisco Chronicle 901 Mission St San Francisco CA 94103-2988

KAHN, EARL LESTER, market research executive; b. Kansas City, Mo., May 30, 1919; s. Samuel and Sarah (Kaufman) K. BA, Harvard U., 1940; MA, U. Chgo., 1947. Pres. Social Research, Inc., Chgo., 1946-74; chmn. bd. KPR Assocs., Inc., Scottsdale, Ariz., 1974-88. Contbr. articles to profl. jour. Served to capt. USAF, 1942-46. Mem. Am. Mktg. Assn, Am. Sociol. Assn. Home: 5608 N Scottsdale Rd Paradise Valley AZ 85253-5912

KAHN, HOWARD ALAN, foundation administrator; b. Culver City, Calif., July 24, 1956; s. Eugene and Mary (Axler) K.; m. Elizabeth Robbins Burges, Sept. 24, 1983. BA, U. Calif., Berkeley, 1979; MA, U. Minn., 1981. Dir. govt. svcs. Jurgovan and Blair, Inc., Santa Rosa, Calif., 1982-84; prin. Howard Kahn Assocs., Inc., 1984-91; CEO Health Plan San Mateo, Calif., 1986-91; pres. Calif. Wellness Found., Woodland Hills, 1991—; acting chmn. Found. Consortium Sch.-Linked Svcs., Sacramento, 1992; founding mem. Philanthropy Task Force Rebuild L.A., 1992; mem. U. Calif. Berkely 50th anniversary hon. com., 1992. Bd. dirs. Friends Outside Nat. Orgn., 1990—. Humphrey Inst. fellow U. Minn., 1991; recipient Commendation award Bd. Suprs. San Mateo County, 1991. Mem. Group Health Assn. Am. (com. mem.), Am. Pub. Health Assn., S. Calif. Assn. for Philanthropy, N. Calif. Grantmakers.

KAHN, IRWIN WILLIAM, industrial engineer; b. N.Y.C., Feb. 3, 1923; s. Milton and Clara (Clark) K.; B.S., U. Calif.-Berkeley, 1949; student Cath. U., 1943-44; m. Mildred Cross, May 14, 1946 (dec. May 1966); children: Steven Edward, Michael William, Evelyn Ruth, Joanne Susan; m. 2d, Marajayne Smith, Oct. 9, 1979. Chief indsl. engr. Malsbary Mfg. Co., Oakland, Calif., 1953-57, Yale & Towne Mfg. Co., San Leandro, Calif., 1957-60; sr. indsl. engr. Eitel McCulloch, San Carlos, Calif., 1961-62, Lockheed, Sunnyvale, Calif., 1962-69; v.p. Performance Investors, Inc., Palo Alto, 1969-74; with Kaiser-Permanente Services, Oakland, 1974-76; nat. mgr. material handling Cutter Labs., Berkeley, Calif., 1976-83; sr. mgmt. engr. Children's Hosp. Med. Ctr., Oakland, 1983; sr. indsl. engr. Naval Air Rework Facility, Alameda, Calif., 1983-85, Naval Supply Ctr., Oakland, 1985-88; vis. lectr. U. Calif., Berkeley, 1986; tchr. indsl. engring. Laney Coll., Oakland, 1967—, Chabot Coll., Hayward, Calif.; pres. East Bay Table Pad Co., 1990. Chmn. Alameda County Library Adv. Commn., 1965—. Served with AUS, 1943-46. Registered profl. engr., Calif. Mem. Am. Inst. Indsl. Engrs. (chpt. pres. 1963-64, chmn. conf. 1967 nat. publ. dir. aerospace div. 1968-69), Calif. Soc. Profl. Engrs. (pres. chpt.). Club: Toastmasters (dist. gov. 1960-61).

KAHN, JOEL SHELDON, physician; b. Washington, Sept. 27, 1956; s. Werner David and Gladys (Homer) K.; m. Ann Reimers, Feb. 6, 1982; 1 child, Ashley Elizabeth. BS, George Washington U., 1977; MD, U. Md., 1981. Diplomate Am. Bd. Emergency Medicine. Surg. resident physician Cedars-Sinai Med. Ctr., L.A., 1981-83; pvt. practice, emergency physician Calif., 1983—. Editor (newspaper) The Aesculapian, 1979-81. Chmn. Second Undergrad. Conf. on Bioethics, Washington, 1977. Mem. Am. Coll. Emergency Physicians, Phi Beta Kappa, Alpha Chi Sigma. Democrat. Jewish. Home: 4 Delamesa West Irvine CA 92720

KAHN, KENNETH ALLEN, health care quality consultant; b. Albuquerque, Nov. 10, 1926; s. Albert and Marcella (Ehrlich) K.; m. Diana Sonya Zimmerman, Aug. 16, 1958; children: Beverly, Michael. BA, Johns Hopkins U., 1949; MD, U. Colo., 1953; fellowship internal medicine, U. Minn., 1954-57; fellowship in cardiology, Stanford U., 1957-59. Diplomate Am. Bd. Internal Medicine. Pvt. practice Associated Internists, Boulder, Colo., 1959-80; assoc. med. dir. Colo. Found. Med. Care, Denver, 1974-92; pres. Kahn-sults, Ltd., Boulder, 1992—; bd. dirs. Cob Personalize Edn. Physicians, 1986-92, Total Long Term Care, Denver; pres. Colo. Found. Med. Care, Denver, 1973-74. Panelist Health Care Financing Adminstrn., Case Mix, Reimb. and Quality Project. With USNR, 1944-46. Fellow ACP (Colo. chpt. Laureate award 1990); mem. Colo. Med. Soc. (pres. 1973-74, Disting. Svc. award 1974), Alpha Omega Alpha. Home and Office: Kahn-sults Ltd 760 Flagstaff Rd Boulder CO 80302

KAHN, LINDA MCCLURE, maritime industry executive; b. Jacksonville, Fla.; d. George Calvin and Myrtice Louise (Boggs) McClure; m. Paul Markham Kahn, May 20, 1968. B.S. with high honors, U. Fla.; M.S., U. Mich., 1964. Actuarial trainee N.Y. Life Ins. Co., N.Y.C., 1964-66, actuarial asst., 1966-69, asst. actuary, 1969-71; v.p., actuary US Life Ins., Pasadena, Calif., 1972-74; mgr. Coopers & Lybrand, Los Angeles, 1974-76, sr. cons., San Francisco, 1976-82; dir. program mgmt. Pacific Maritime Assn., San Francisco, 1982—. Bd. dirs. Pacific Heights Residents Assn., sec.-treas., 1981; trustee ILWU-PMA Welfare Plan, SIU-PD-PMA Pension and Supplemental Benefits Plans, 1982-90, Seafarers Med. Ctr., 1982-90, others. Fellow Soc. Actuaries (chmn. com. on minority recruiting 1988-91, chmn. actuary of furture sect.), Conf. Actuaries in Pub. Practice; mem. Internat. Actuarial Assn., Internat. Assn. Cons. Actuaries, Actuarial Studies Non-Life Ins., Am. Acad. Actuaries, Western Pension Conf. (newsletter editor 1983-85, sec. 1985-88, treas. 1989-90), Actuarial Club Pacific States, San Francisco Actuarial Club (pres. 1981), Met. Club, Commonwealth Club, Soroptimists Club (v.p. 1973-74). Home: 2430 Pacific Ave San Francisco CA 94115-1238 Office: Pacific Maritime Assn 550 California St San Francisco CA 94104-1060

KAHN, MARIO SANTAMARIA, international marketing executive; b. Manila, Jan. 16, 1956; came to U.S., 1980; s. Rene L. and Dolores (Santamaria) K.; m. Maria Victoria Legaspi, Dec. 28, 1987; 1 child, Marc Daniel. AB in Mktg. & Comm., De La Salle U., Manila, 1977; MA in Comm. Mgmt. cum laude, U. So. Calif., 1982; postgrad., Stanford U., 1989. Assoc. prof. De La Salle U., Manila, 1978-80; account mgr. McCann-Erickson, Manila, 1977-80; teaching asst. U. So. Calif., L.A., 1980-82; new store planning mgr. Dayton-Hudson Corp., Mpls., 1982-85; regional mktg. mgr. Europe/Middle East/Australasia Sunkist Soft Drinks Internat. Sunkist Growers, Inc., Ontario, Calif., 1986—; advt. cons. J. Romero & Assocs., Manila, 1992—. Mem. Am. Mktg. Assn., Am. Mgmt. Assn., Stanford Alumni Assn., Annenberg Alumni Assn., De La Salle Alumni Assn. Office: Sunkist Growers Inc 720 E Sunkist St Ontario CA 91761

KAHN, MICHAEL ALEXANDER, lawyer; b. Buffalo, Feb. 4, 1949; s. Otto Albert and Eleanor Ruth (Pick) K.; m. Nancy A. Oliveria, Aug. 28, 1971; children: Matthew Jason, Lauren Elizabeth. BA, UCLA, 1970; MA in Polit. Sci. and JD, Stanford (Calif.) U., 1973. Bar: Calif. Supreme Ct. 1973, U.S. Ct. Appeals (9th cir.) 1973, U.S. Dist. Ct. (no. dist.) Calif. 1973, U.S. Dist. Ct. (ea. dist.) Calif. 1979, U.S. Dist. Ct. (so. dist.) Calif. 1980, U.S. Dist. Ct. (cen. dist.) Calif. 1983, U.S. Supreme Ct. 1982. Law clk. to Hon. Ben C. Duniway U.S. Ct. Appeals (9th cir.), San Francisco, 1973-74; assoc. Steinhart, et al, San Francisco, 1974-79; sr. ptnr. Folger & Levin, San Francisco, 1979—; mme. No. Dist. Calif. Task Force for Dispute Resolution, San Francisco, 1982—; mem. bd. visitors Stanford U. Law Sch., 1990—; mem. adv. group Civil Justice Reform Act 1990; mem. adv. coun. Ctr. for Study of Presidency, 1991—. Panelist Ctr. for the Study of the Presidency on Eisenhower and Civil Rights, Austin, Tex., 1990—; bd. dirs. Legal Aid Soc. San Francisco, 1991—; arbitrator San Francisco Superior Ct., 1981—; mem. Calif. Senate Commn. on Property Tax Equity and Revenue, 1990—; mem. Calif. State Ins. Commr. Task Force on Environ. Liability Inst., 1993—; chmn. unfair practices com. Calif. Ins. Commr. Task, 1991—. Irving Hellman Jr. scholar Stanford U. Mem. ABA, Am. Law Inst., Am. Assn. Ltd. Ptnrs. (bd. dirs.), World Affairs Coun., Commonwealth Club, Supreme Ct. Hist. Soc. Home: 3933 Clay St San Francisco CA 94118-1623 Office: Folger & Levin 275 Battery St San Francisco CA 94111-3305

KAHN, MIRIAM, anthropology educator; b. N.Y.C., Mar. 30, 1948; d. Ludwig Werner and Tatyana (Uffner) K.; m. Richard Lee Taylor, Oct. 26, 1985; 1 child, Rachel Kahn Taylor. BA, U. Wis., 1970; MA, Bryn Mawr (Pa.) Coll., 1974, PhD, 1980. Asst. to Margaret Mead Am. Mus. of Natural History, N.Y.C., 1970-71; exhibit researcher and designer Field Mus. of Natural History, Chgo., 1973; asst. prof. Vanderbilt U., Nashville, 1980-81, The New Sch. of Music, Phila., 1985-86; asst. prof., curator Asian and Pacific ethnology Burke Mus. U. Wash., Seattle, 1986—, assoc. prof., 1991—; cons. Seattle Art Mus., 1988—. Author: Always Hungry, Never Greedy, 1986; co-editor: Continuity and Change in Pacific Foodways, 1988; contbr. articles to profl. jours. Inst. for Intercultural Studies grantee, 1970, 76, Field Mus. of Natural History grantee, 1973, Nat. Mus. of Can. grantee, 1974, Bryn Mawr Coll. grantee, 1974, Werner-Gren Found. for Anthropol. Rsch., 1976, 79, NIMH grantee, 1976, Am. Friends Svc. Com. grantee, 1979, NSF grantee, 1981, 88, Wash. Commn. for the Humanities grantee, 1986, U. Wash. grantee, 1989. Home: 2806 NW 60th St Seattle WA 98107-2508 Office: U Wash Dept of Anthropology Seattle WA 98195

KAHN, PAUL MARKHAM, actuary; b. San Francisco, May 8, 1935; s. Sigmund Max and Alexandrina K. (Strauch) K.; m. Linda P. McClure, May 20, 1968. BS, Stanford U., 1956; MA, U. Mich., 1957, PhD, 1961. Asst. actuary Equitable Life Assurance Soc., N.Y.C., 1961-71; v.p., life actuary Beneficial Standard Life, Los Angeles, 1971-75; v.p., actuary Am. Express Life Ins. Co., San Rafael, Calif., 1975-77, P.M. Kahn & Assocs., 1977—; prof. actuarial math. San Fransisco State U. Editor Dictionary of Actuarial and Life Ins. Terms, 1972, 2d edit., 1983, Credibility: Theory and Practice, 1975, Computational Probability, 1980. Fellow Soc. Actuaries (Triennial prize 1961-64), Can. Inst. Actuaries, Conf. of Cons. Actuaries; mem. Am. Acad. Actuaries, Internat. Actuarial Assn., Inst. Actuaries (Eng.), Spanish Actuarial Inst., Swiss Actuarial Assn., German Actuarial Assn., Italian Actuarial Inst., Am. Antiquarian Soc. Clubs: Grolier (N.Y.C.) Zamorano (Los Angeles), Roxburghe, Concordia-Argonaut, Comml. (San Francisco); Pacific, Waikiki Yacht (Honolulu). Address: 2430 Pacific Ave San Francisco CA 94115

KAHN, ROBERT IRVING, management consultant; b. Oakland, Calif., May 17, 1918; s. Irving Herman and Francesca (Lowenthal) K.; m. Patricia E. Glenn, Feb. 14, 1946; children: Christopher, Roberta Anne. BA cum laude, Stanford U., 1938; MBA, Harvard U., 1940; LLD (hon.), Franklin Pierce Coll., 1977. Exec. researcher R.H. Macy's, Inc., N.Y.C., 1940-41; controller Smith's, Oakland, 1946-51; v.p., treas. Sherwood Swan & Co., Oakland, 1952-56; prin. Robert Kahn & Assocs. (mgmt. cons.), Lafayette, Calif., 1956—; pres. Kahn & Harris Inc. (investment bankers), San Francisco, 1974-90; v.p. Hambrecht & Quist (investment bankers), San Francisco, 1977-80; cons. to comdg. gen. U.S. Army and Air Force Exch. Svc., 1987—; bd. dirs. Components Corp. Am.; bd. dirs., v.p. Lipps Inc., Marc Paul Inc., Piedmont Grocery Co. Pub. newsletter Retailing Today, 1965—; author: weekly newspaper column Pro and Kahn, 1963-77, 86-89; mem. editorial bd. Jour. of Retailing; editor ethics dept. Jour. Mgmt. Consulting. Mem. Nat. Eagle Scout Assn., Boy Scouts Am., past dir. Oakland Coun.; past bd. dirs. Oakland Area ARC; past bd. dirs., officer San Francisco Bay Girl Scout Coun., Fannie Wall Day Home and Nursery; bd. dirs., officer, mem. exec. com. Unitd Way Bay Area, 1946-81, chmn. allocations, membership, fin., by-laws, and personnel coms.; trustee Kahn Found.; past sec. League to Save Lake Tahoe; founder Lafayette Forward, 1970, sec., 1976—; mem. adv. com. Retail Mgmt. Inst. Santa Clara U., 1983—. With USAAF, 1941-46; with USAF, 1951-52; lt. col. Res. ret. Recipient Mortimer Fleishhacker award as outstanding vol. United Way Bay Area, 1980, Best Article award Jour. Mgmt. Cons., 1985; founding mem. Baker Scholar Harvard Bus. Sch., 1939. Mem. Assn. Mgmt. Cons. (pres. 1977), Inst. Mgmt. Cons. (a founder), Nat. Retail Fedn. (assoc. cons. mem.), Mensa, Phi Beta Kappa. Home: 3684 Happy Valley Rd Lafayette CA 94549-3040 Office: PO Box 249 Lafayette CA 94549

KAHN, SHERWIN ALLEN, chiropractic physician; b. Muskogee, Okla., Oct. 21, 1953; s. Ezie and Florence (Hoffman) K. BA in Psychology, UCLA, 1976; D of Chiropractic, Logan Coll., 1989. Diplomate Nat. Bd. Chiropractic Examiners. Program mgr. UCLA-ACTION Program, L.A., 1972-74; rsch. assoc. UCLA, 1975-77; owner The Candy Kettle, Maui, Hawaii, 1977-79; sales mgr. Charles Bohannon Realty, Maui, Hawaii, 1977-79; prodn. mgr. Media Home Entertainment, Beverly Hills, Calif., 1979-81, Modern Videofilm, Hollywood, Calif., 1981-83; owner Hollywood Candy Studio, L.A., 1983-85; owner, clinic dir. ChiroPractice, Santa Rosa, Calif., 1990—. Dir. Visions in Youth, Santa Rosa, 1992. Mem. Santa Rosa C. of C., Active 20/30 Club, Psi Chi Honor Soc. Office: ChiroPractice 825 Sonoma Ave Santa Rosa CA 95405

KAIL, JOSEPH GERARD, computer sales executive, marketing executive; b. Cin., Dec. 23, 1946; s. Henry Thomas and Cosma (Contadino) K.; m. Patricia Lynne Riedel, June 28, 1969; children: Robert, Daniel, Joseph. BS, Xavier U., Cin., 1969, MEd, 1973. Tchr., athletic coach Alter High Sch., Kettering, Ohio, 1969-77; sales rep. Philips Bus. Systems, Inc., Cin., 1977-78, Hewlett-Packard Co., Dayton, 1978-81; dist. sales mgr. Hewlett-Packard Co., Pitts., 1981-83; sales mgr. Rocky Mountain area Hewlett-Packard Co., Denver, 1983-87, western regional sales mgr. bus. computer systems, 1988-91, western regional mktg. mgr. computer systems, 1991-92, am. mktg. mgr. computer systems organization, 1992—. Com. mem. troop 986, Boy Scouts Am., Denver, 1984-88, Highlands Ranch High Sch. Boosters, Denver, 1988. Republican. Roman Catholic. Office: Hewlett-Packard Co 24 Inverness Dr E Englewood CO 80112-5624

KAISCH, KENNETH BURTON, psychologist, priest; b. Detroit, Aug. 29, 1948; s. Kenneth R. Kaisch and Marjorie F. (Howe) Bourke; m. Suzanne Carol LePrevost, Aug. 31, 1969; 1 child, Samuel. BA, San Francisco State U., 1972; MDiv, Ch. Divinity Sch. Pacific, 1976; MS, Utah State U., 1983, PhD in Clin. Psychology, 1986. Ordained deacon Episcopal Ch., 1976, priest, 1977; lic. clin. psychologist, Calif. Intern local parish, 1973-76; ordinand tng. program Ch. of the Good Shepherd, Ogden, Utah, 1976-77; pastor St. Francis' Episc. Ch., Moab, Utah, 1977-80, St. John's Episc. Ch., Logan, Utah, 1980-84; psychol. asst. Peter Ebersole, Ph.D., Fullerton, Calif., 1984-86; intern in clin. psychology Patton State Hosp., Calif., 1985-86; psychol. asst. Ronald Wong Jue, Ph.D., Fullerton and Newport Beach, Calif., 1986-88; pvt. practice clin. psychologist Calif., 1988—; clin. dir. Anxiety Clinic; exec. dir. Contemplative Congress, Fullerton, Calif., 1988-91; founder, pres. OneHeart, Contemplative Visions, Fullerton, 1990—; supply priest Episc. Diocese of L.A.; invited lectr. Acad. Sch. Profl. Psychology, Moscow, 1992, 93. Co-author: Fundamentals of Psychotherapy, 1984; contbr. numerous articles to profl. jours. Mem. St. Andrew's Episc. Ch., Fullerton. Mem. APA, Calif. Psychol. Assn., Assn. of Transpersonal Psychology, Anxiety Disorders Assn. Am., Nat. Register of Health Svc. Providers in Psychology, Phi Kappa Phi, Rotary (bd. dirs., past officer). Episcopalian. Office: 2555 E Chapman Ave Ste 617 Fullerton CA 92631-3622

KAISER, ERNEST PHILIP, management consultant; b. Oak Park, Ill., Nov. 22, 1935; s. John and Anne Margaret (Kreuser) K.; children: Anne Margaret, Philip August. Student, U. Alaska, 1965, postgrad., 1968. Asst. engr. U. Alaska, Fairbanks, 1967-70; mng. dir. Coral Constrn. Co. Ltd., Suva, Fiji, 1970-73; chief engr. Ramada Chori, Tokyo, 1974-75; dir. devel. Ramada Europe, Brussels, 1975-76; prin. Ernest Kaiser and Assocs., Fairbanks and Phoenix, Ariz., 1976-79; project mgr. Kitchell CEM, Phoenix, 1980-82; gen. mgr. W.F. Conelly Constrn. Co., Phoenix, 1983-85; ptnr. Capital Improvement Assocs, Inc., Phoenix, 1986—; panelist Am. Arbitration Assn., Phoenix, 1986—. Contbr. articles to profl. jours. With USAF 1952-56. Recipient Cert. of Appreciation award Pacific Area Travel Assn., 1983, Honor award Am. Inst. Architects, 1991. Mem. Aircraft Owners and Pilots Assn., Am. Mensa, U. Alaska Alumni Assn., Phoenix Zoo. Home: 2138 E Myrtle Ave Phoenix AZ 85020

KAISER, JOHN RAYMOND, wheat farmer; b. Denver, Feb. 5, 1955; s. Bernard Thomas and Rita Margaret (Pretz) K.; m. Debora Louise Zima, Mar. 24, 1984; 1 child, Paul Anthony. AS, Laramie County Community Coll., 1977; BS, U. Wyo., 1979. Wheat farmer Kaiser Farms, Cheyenne, Wyo., 1979—; participant Am. Cyanamid/Nat. Assn. Wheatgrowers Ambassador Program, 1992. Wyo. Leadership Edn. and Devel. fellow, 1988-90; named Monsanto Young Farmer Nat. Assn. Wheat Growers, New Orleans, 1988. Mem. Nat. Young Farmers Edtl. Assn. (bd. dirs., lesser developed country spokesperson 1992—), Wyo. Wheat Growers Assn. (bd. dirs. 1991—, registered lobbyist 1991), Wyo. Agrl. Leadership Coun., Wyo. Young Farmers Ednl. Assn. (pres. 1992-93), Laramie County Young Farmers (pres. 1988-92). Republican. Roman Catholic. Home and Office: 1860 Milton Dr Cheyenne WY 82001-1645

KAISER, JONI ANN, social services executive; b. Reno, Nev., July 12, 1955; d. John Joseph and Phyllis Ann (Baker) K.; m. Thomas John Lake, Aug. 28, 1982; children: Greg, Sally, Karen. BA in Social Work, Antioch Coll., 1977; M Nonprofit Adminstrn., U. San Francisco, 1988. Lic. social worker, Nev. Program assoc. Am. Friends Svc. Com., Reno, 1976-77; co-founder, exec. dir. Com. to Aid Abused Women, Sparks, Nev., 1977—; bd. dirs., past pres. Truckee Meadows Human Svcs. Assn., Reno, 1982—; bd. dirs., past pres., treas. Nev. Network Against Domestic Violence, Reno, 1980-91; past pres., bd. dirs. No. Nev. Task Force on Child Abuse and Neglect, Reno, 1981-85. mem. Anne Martin Women's Polit. Caucus, Reno, 1982-91; councilwoman City of Sparks, 1989; mem. Western Indsl. Nev., Reno, 1989—; trustee Washoe County Libr. Bd., Reno, 1992—. Recipient Woman Helping Women award Soroptimists of Truckee Meadows, 1982, So. Reno Soroptimists Club, 1990; recipient Woman of Yr. award Reno Bus. and Profl. Women, 1983; named to Hall of Fame Nev. Women's Fund, 1987. Mem. Nat. Soc. Fund Raising Execs. (charter, chair Philanthropy Day com. 1992). Democrat. Office: Com to Aid Abused Women 101 15th St Sparks NV 89431

KAKFWI, STEVE, Canadian government official. Mem. Legis Assembly, 1987-91; Min. Justice, Personnel, Intergovernmental and Aboriginal Affairs; former pres. Dene Nation. Office: Minister of Justice, PO Box 1320, Yellowknife, NT Canada X1A 2L9

KAKITA, LEONORE SETSUKO, dermatologist; b. Oakland, Calif., Aug. 27, 1940; d. Hajime and Grace Chiyo (Takata) Uyeyama; m. Edward Y. Kakita, Aug. 17, 1968; children: Neil, Grant, Garrett. BS, U. Calif., Berkeley, 1963; MD, U. Calif., L.A., 1967. Diplomate Am. Bd. Dermatology; Am. Bd. Medical Examiner. Intern Children's Hosp. of L.A., 1967-68; resident dermatology U. Calif., L.A., 1968-71; pvt. practice Descanso Dermatology Med. Group, La Canada, Calif., 1971-82; pvt. practice La Canada, 1982-86, Glendale, Calif., 1986—; clin. instr. divsn. dermatology Sch. Medicine, UCLA, 1971-76, asst. clin. prof., 1976—; tech. cons. RBRUS dermatology Phase I, II, III, Sch. Pub. Health, Harvard U., 1989—, Dermatology Svcs., Inc. Mem. editorial advisory bd. Derm Coding Advisory, 1993. Bd. dirs. Japanese Am. Nat. Mus., L.A., 1991—. Mem. AMA (Physician's Recognition award 1971—), Am. Acad. Dermatology (com. on dir. access 1985, adv. coun. 1985-91, com. on health care delivery systems 1986-89, adv. coun. on Am. Acad. Dermatology electons 1988-89, adv. coun. exec. bd. Dist. VIII 1986-87, adv. coun. vice chmn. 1988-91, coun. on communications coun. 1987-91, AMA/CPT panel derm-specific vignette validator panel 1992, relative value study com. 1992—, RUC com. and RVS update com. 1992—, ad hoc com. on dermatologic cost effectiveness 1993, chmn. com. on gov. and private reimbursement, 1993), Am. Soc. Dermatol. Surgery, Calif. Congress Dermatol. Soc. (v.p. 1983-84, pres. 1984-86, dermatol. rep. Calif. medicare carrier adv. com.), Calif. Med. Assn. (specialty socs. com. 1983—, sci. adv. panel on dermatology 1983—, alt. del. for specialty soc. del. for dermatology 1988-89, 90-92, reference com. J, med. staff affairs 1990-92, ad hoc com. on policy rev. 1991-92, Physician's Recognition award 1971—), Internat. Soc. Dermatol. Soc., L.A. County Med. Assn. (strategic planning com. 1987-91, com. on plan oversight 1990-91, bd. dirs. LACMA Ins. Svcs., Inc. 1990—, LAMAC task force on non-geographic dists., 1992-93, com. assn. elections, 1986-91), L.A. Met. Dermoatol. Soc., Pacific Dermatol. Assn. (membership com. 1984-86, chmn. membership com. 1987, program chmn. 1994), Women's Dermatol. Soc., Japanese Am. Med. Assn. Home: 5700 Catherwood Dr La Canada CA 91011 Office: Ste 402 1818 Verdugo Blvd Glendale CA 91208

KALB, BENJAMIN STUART, television producer, director; b. Los Angeles, Mar. 17, 1948; s. Marcus and Charlotte K. BS in Journalism, U. Oreg., 1969. Sportswriter, Honolulu Advertiser, 1971-76; traveled with tennis profl. Ilie Nastase; contbr. articles N.Y. Times, Sport Mag. and Tennis U.S.A., 1976; editor Racquetball Illustrated, 1978-82; segment producer PM Mag. and Hollywood Close-Up, 1983-86; exec. producer Ben Kalb Prodns., 1986—; instr. sports in soc. U. Hawaii, 1974-75. Producer (video) The Natural Way to Meet the Right Person, 1987; producer, dir. (video) Casting Call: Director's Choice, 1987, The Natural Way to Meet The Right Person (Best Home Videos of Yr. L.A. Times), (TV pilot and home video) Bizarro, 1988, (infomercial) How To Start Your Own Million Dollar Business, 1990; segment dir. (home video) Movie Magic, 1990, (TV show) Totally Hidden Video; writer-segment dir. (home video) Making of The American Dream Calendar Girl, 1991; producer, host (cable TV show) Delicious Sports, 1987-88; segment dir. Totally Hidden Video (Fox TV Network), 1991-92. Served with Hawaii Army N.G., 1970-75. Named Outstanding Male Grad. in Journalism, U. Oreg., 1969. Mem. Sigma Delta Chi (chpt. pres. 1968). Democrat. Jewish. Contbr. articles to mags. and newspapers. Home: 1429 S Bundy Dr # 4 Los Angeles CA 90025-2108 Office: Ben Kalb Prodns 1341 Ocean Ave Ste 160 Santa Monica CA 90401-1066

KALENSCHER, ALAN JAY, surgeon; b. Bklyn., July 9, 1926; s. Abraham and Julia (Horwitz) K.; BS, Union Coll., Schenectady, 1945; MD, N.Y. U., 1949; m. Hannah Blaufox, June 18, 1949; children: Judith Lynne, Mark Robert. Intern Morrisania City Hosp., N.Y.C., 1949-50; surg. resident Maimonides Med. Ctr., Bklyn., 1950-51, 54; asst., then chief resident Bronx Mcpl. Hosp. Ctr., 1954-56; mem. faculty surgery dept. Albert Einstein Coll. Medicine, 1956-59; practice medicine specializing in surgery, Sacramento, 1959-84; chief med. cons. Disability Evaluation Div. Calif. State Dept. Soc. Svcs., 1984—; attending surgeon Sacramento Med. Ctr.; commr. Bd. Med. Quality Assurance Calif.; clin. faculty dept. surgery U. Calif. Coll. Medicine, Davis, 1970-75 . Served with USNR, 1943-45, 51-53; ETO, Korea. Recipient citation N.Y.C. Cancer Com., 1959. Diplomate Am. Bd. Surgery, Nat. Bd. Med. Examiners (examiner 1957-59). Fellow Am. Soc. Contemporary Medicine and Surgery; mem. AAAS, Calif. Med. Assn., Sacramento County Med. Soc., Am. Diabetes Assn., Am. Mensa Ltd.

KALIHER, MICHAEL DENNIS, historian; b. Santa Monica, Calif., Nov. 7, 1947; s. Eugene Charles and Phyllis Joan (McCrary) K. BA, U. Ariz., 1990. Pres. Klamath County (Oreg.) Hist. Soc., 1985; founder Native Am. History Week, Klamath County Mus., 1985-86. Contbr. articles to various hist. jours. Mem. Thoreau Soc., Pi Lambda Theta, Phi Alpha Theta. Roman Catholic. Home: 1218 Essex Ln Newport Beach CA 92660-5616

KALIS, BARBARA HARRIET, interior designer; b. N.Y.C., Oct. 28, 1943; d. Harry Charles and Vera Grace (Allen) Schefer; m. Bruno Kalis, June 27, 1964. BA in Lit. and Edn., SUNY at New Paltz, 1965; AA in Interior Design, Bellevue Community Coll., 1980. Tchr. Mt. Prospect (Ill.) Sch. Dist., 1965-67, Des Plaines (Ill.) Sch. Dist., 1967-71; adminstrv. asst. Ford Motor Co., Cologne, Germany, 1972-74; tchr. Genovevastr. Gymnasium, Cologne, Germany, 1974-77; interior design Barbara Kalis Interior Designer, Bellevue, Wash., 1980—. Designer of Street of Dreams Home, 1992 (Best of Show award 1992). Pres., sec. Bellevue Civitan, 1989—; pres. programs for social concerns Meth. Ch., Bellevue, 1978—. Mem. N.W. Soc. Interior Designers (chair exec. bd. 1986-90, pres. 1987-90), U.S. Power Squadron (membership com. 1992—), Porsche Club of Am. (sec. 1988), Leads (asst. dir. 1992—). Office: 12244 SE 25th St Bellevue WA 98005

KALKBRENNER, EDWARD JOSEPH, JR., pilot, aviation consultant; b. Belleville, Ill., Dec. 8, 1942; s. Edward Joseph Sr. and Bessie Marie (Johnston) K.; m. Mary Susan Kenny, Aug. 21, 1965 (div. Sept. 1981); children: Melissa Jane, Cynthia Marie Buschmann; m. Karen Kathleen Moore, June 12, 1982; stepchildren: Dawn Marie Hilterbrand, Tiffany Anne Boehm. BSEE, St. Louis U., 1964, MBA, 1982. Elec. engr. IBM, Owego, N.Y., 1969-70; mktg. rep. IBM, St. Louis, 1970-73; systems mgr. Chemtech Industries, Inc., St. Louis, 1973-75, Rueckert Meat Co., St. Louis, 1975-76; chief pilot Southwestern Bell Telephone Co., St. Louis, 1976-84; corp. pilot U.S. West, Inc., Englewood, Colo., 1984—; v.p. Kalkbrenner & Assocs., Inc., Aurora, Colo., 1985—, Mgmt. Synergy, Inc., Denver, 1986—; v.p. Customers First, Inc. Active in ch. and fundraising orgns. Capt. USAF, 1964-69, Vietnam. Roman Catholic. Home: 15941 Sampson Rd Littleton CO 80127

KALLAY, MICHAEL FRANK, II, medical devices company official; b. Painesville, Ohio, Aug. 24, 1944; s. Michael Frank and Marie Francis (Sage) K.; BBA, Ohio U., 1967; m. Irma Yolanda Corona, Aug. 30, 1975; 1 son, William Albert. Salesman, Howmedica, Inc., Rutherford, N.J., 1972-75, Biochem. Procedures/Metpath, North Hollywood, Calif., 1975-76; surg. specialist USCI div. C. R. Bard, Inc., Billerica, Mass., 1976-78; western and central regional mgr. ARCO Med. Products Co., Phila., 1978-80; Midwest regional mgr. Intermedics, Inc., Freeport, Tex., 1980-82; Western U.S. mgr. Renal Systems, Inc., Mpls., 1982—; pres. Kall-Med, Inc., Anaheim Hills, Calif., 1982—. Mem. Am. Mgmt. Assn., Phi Kappa Sigma. Home and Office: PO Box 17248 7539 E Bridgewood Dr Anaheim CA 92817-7248

KALLENBERG, JOHN KENNETH, librarian; b. Anderson, Ind., June 10, 1942; s. Herbert A. and Helen S. K.; m. Ruth Barrett, Aug. 19, 1965; children: Jennifer Anne, Gregory John. A.B., Ind. U., 1964, M.L.S., 1969. With Fresno County Library, Fresno, Calif., 1965-70, dir., 1976—; librarian Fig Garden Pub. Library br., 1968-70; asst. dir. Santa Barbara (Calif.) Pub. Library, 1970-76; mem. Calif. Libr. Svcs. bd., 1990—, v.p. 1992—; Beth Ann Harnish lectr. com., 1988-91, chmn., 1989-90. Mem. Calif. Library Assn. (councilor 1976-77, v.p., pres. 1987), Calif. County Librs. Assn. (pres. 1977), Calif. Libr. Authority for Systems and Svcs. (chmn. authority adv. coun. 1978-80), Kiwanis (pres. Fresno 1981-82, lt. gov. div. 5, 1991-92). Presbyterian. Office: Fresno County Free Libr 2420 Mariposa St Fresno CA 93721-2285

KALLMAN, ROBERT FRIEND, research radiation biologist, educator; b. N.Y.C., May 21, 1922; s. Morris and Eva (Cohn) K.; m. Frances Lou Green, June 4, 1948 (dec. Mar. 1966); children: Timothy R., Robin L.; m. Ingrid Moelhede Christensen, Apr. 19, 1969; 1 child, Lars. AB, Hofstra Coll., 1943; MS, NYU, 1949, PhD, 1952. Instr. in biology Bklyn. Coll., 1947-48; teaching fellow NYU, 1948-50; asst. rsch. physiologist U. Calif., San Francisco, 1952-56; rsch. assoc. Stanford (Calif.) U. Sch. Medicine, 1956-59, asst. prof., 1959-64, assoc. prof., 1964-72, prof., 1972-92, prof. emeritus, 1992—; cons. dept. radiation oncology editoral bds. Proc. Soc. Exptl. Biology and Med., 1987-90, Cancer Rsch., 1988-91, Internat. Jour. Radiation Oncology, 1980—. Contbr. articles to profl. jours. With U.S. Army, 1943-45. Recipient USPHS Rsch. Ctr. Devel. award NIH, 1962-72; numerous grants. Fellow N.Y. Acad. Scis.; mem. Am. Assn. for Cancer Rsch., Radiation Rsch. Soc. (pres. 1976-77), Cell Kinetics Soc. (councillor 1989-92), Soc. Analytical cytology, Soc. Exptl. Biology and Medicine, Am. Soc. for Therapeutic Radiology and Oncology. Democrat. Jewish. Home: 735 San Rafael Pl Stanford CA 94305 Office: Stanford U Sch Medicine Dept Radiation Oncology Boswell Bldg AO-38 Stanford CA 94305-5105

KALM, WILLIAM DEAN, information system executive; b. Mason City, Iowa, Aug. 28, 1951; s. Walter Leslie and Ruth Louise (Beier)K.; m. Linda Marlene Murphy, Dec. 12, 1987; 1 child, Andrew William. BS, Iowa State U., 1973, MS, 1977. Ptnr. Andersen Cons., Phoenix, 1977—. Mem. Ctr. Against Sexual Assault (bd. treas. 1986-88), Phoenix, Earlview Homeowners Assn. (bd. chmn. 1981-87), Phoenix. Recipient Appreciation Plaque Soc. for Info. Mgmt., Phoenix, 1988, Appreciation cert. Ctr. Against Sexual Assault, Phoenix, 1988. Mem. Soc. for Info. Mgmt. (chmn. 1985-90), No. Ariz. U.-CIS adv. coun. (chmn. 1988-90), Healthcare Fin. Mgrs. Assn.(com. 1982-86), Renaissance Club, Ariz. Club. Home: 11410 N 44th St Phoenix AZ 85028-2239

KALOOGIAN, HOWARD JAMES, lawyer; b. Detroit, Dec. 30, 1959; s. Harry and Sarah (Ayanian) K. BA in Polit. Sci. and Bus., Mich. State U., 1981; JD, Pepperdine U., 1984. Bar: Calif. 1985, U.S. Tax Ct. 1985, U.S. Dist. Ct. Mich., U.S. Dist. Ct. Calif., Mich. 1987; lic. ins. agt., securities broker. Probate atty. May & May, Southfield, Mich., 1984-85; estate planner, atty. Terry Knight & Assoc., Troy, Mich., 1985-87, Robert Armstrong & Assoc., San Diego, 1987-88; atty. self-employed Carlsbad, Calif., 1988—; radio talk show host KCEO, Carlsbad, 1988-91; adj. prof. law Western State U., San Diego, 1992—; cons. Cranbrook Estates, Carlsbad, 1989—. Contbr. articles to profl. jours. Co-chair Mich. Reagan-Bush Campaign; del. Rep. Conv., 1980; chair 74th Congl. Caucus, Rep., Carlsbad, 1991; county chair Bill Allen for U.S. Senate, San Diego, 1992, Lead or Leave, San Diego, 1992; deacon, bd. trustees, fin. chair Palomar Hgts. Ch., San Marcos, Calif., 1992. Recipient City wide Appreciation Cert., City of Oceanside, 1991, Vol. Appreciation Cert., Am. Lung Assn. of San Diego County, 1990, Vol. Appreciation Cert., Sr. Citizen Legal Clinic, 1989, Appreciation Cert., San Diego Haven, 1990. Mem. Western Ctr. for Law and Religious Freedom, Federalist Soc. for Law and Pub. Policy, San Diego County Bar Assn. (exec. com. chair 1990), Delta Theta Phi Legal Frat. Republican. Assembly of God. Office: Law Office Howard Kaloogian 701 Palomar Airport Rd #160 Carlsbad CA 92009

KALTENBACH, CARL COLIN, agriculturist, educator; b. Buffalo, N.Y., Mar. 22, 1939; s. Carl H. and Mary Colleen (McKeag) K.; m. Ruth Helene

Johnson, Aug. 22, 1964; children: James Earl, John Edward. BS, U. Wyo., 1961; MS, U. Nebr., 1963; PhD, U. Ill., 1967. Prof. animal sci. U. Wyo., Laramie, 1969-89, head dept. animal sci., 1978-80, assoc. dir. coll. agr., 1980-84, assoc. dean and dir., 1984-89; vice dean coll. agriculture, dir. agrl. experiment sta. U. Ariz., Tucson, 1989—; chmn. Exptl. Sta. Com. on Orgn. and Policy, 1986-87. Contbr. more than 200 articles to profl. jours. Recipient Young Scientist award West Sect. Am. Soc. Animal Sci., 1976, Faculty award merit Gamma Sigma Delta, 1980; named Outstanding Alumnus U. Wyo. Coll. Agriculture, 1991. Mem. AAAS, Soc. Study Reproduction (treas. 1980-83), Am. Soc. Animal Sci., Soc. for Study of Fertility. Office: U Arizona 314 Forbes Bldg Tucson AZ 85721

KALUSTIAN, LISA ANN, communications executive; b. L.A., Oct. 30, 1963; d. Martin and Alice Arpy (Hovanesian) K. MPA, U. So. Calif., 1993, postgrad., 1992—. Referral specialist Calif. Self-Help Ctr., L.A., 1984-86; assoc. The Wessell Co., Burbank, Calif., 1987-90; mgr. industry practice comm. Heidrick & Struggles, L.A., 1991—. Pres. Friends of Coro, L.A., 1990-91. Fellow Coro So. Calif., 1986-87. Mem. Women in Pub. Affairs, Town Hall Calif., L.A. Jr. C. of C., Coro Nat. Alumni Assn. (chmn. membership affiliations 1990-92), Phi Beta Kappa. Office: Heidrick & Struggles 300 S Grand Ave Ste 2400 Los Angeles CA 90071

KALVINSKAS, JOHN JOSEPH, chemical engineer; b. Phil., Jan. 14, 1927; s. Anthony and Anna (Slezute) K.; m. Louanne Marie Adams, Sept. 3, 1955; 1 son, Adrian John. B.S. in Chem. Engring., MIT, 1951, M.S., 1952; Ph.D. in Chem. Engring., Calif. Inst. Tech., 1959. Chem. engr. DuPont, Gibbstown, N.J., 1952-55, 59-60; with Rockwell Internat., El Segundo, Calif., 1960-70; pres. Resource Dynamics Corp., Los Angeles, 1970-74; corp. research dir. Monogram Industries, Inc., Los Angeles, 1972; project mgr. Holmes & Narver, Inc., Anaheim, Calif., 1974; project mgr. Jet Propulsion Lab., Calif. Inst. Tech., Pasadena, 1974—; cons. to industry. Patentee in field (8). Co-author: Nuclear Rocket Propulsion, 1962. Contbr. articles to profl. jours. Mem. Town Hall Calif., 1967—. Served with USN, 1944-46; Guam. Recipient cert. of recognition NASA, 1976-84; Stauffer Found. teaching fellow, 1957-58. Mem. Am. Chem. Soc. (sec. 1966, 67, trustee, 1968-71), Am. Inst. Chem. Engrs., N.Y. Acad. Scis., Sigma Xi, Kappa Kappa Sigma. Republican. Roman Catholic. Club: MIT of So. Calif. (Los Angeles). Home: 316 Pasadena Ave Apt 3 South Pasadena CA 91030-2939 Office: Jet Propulsion Lab 4800 Oak Grove Dr Pasadena CA 91109-8099

KAMEMOTO, GARETT HIROSHI, reporter; b. Honolulu, Oct. 30, 1966; s. Fred I. and Alice T. (Asayama) K. BA, U. Hawaii, 1989. Reporter Sta. KHVH, Honolulu, 1989-92; Sta. KGMB-TV, Honolulu, 1992—. Home: 3664 Waaloa Way Honolulu HI 96822 Office: KGMB-TV 1534 Kapiolani Blvd Honolulu HI 96814

KAMEN, MARTIN DAVID, physical biochemist; b. Toronto, Aug. 27, 1913. BS with honors, U. Chgo., 1933, PhD, 1936, ScD (hon.), 1969; PhD (hon.), U. Paris, 1969; ScD (hon.), Washington U., St. Louis, 1977, U. Ill., Chgo., 1978, U. Freiburg, Germany, 1979, Weizmann Inst., Rehovot, Israel, 1987, Brandeis U., 1988. Fellow nuclear chemistry Radiation Lab. U. Calif., 1937-39, research assoc., 1939-41; marine test engr. Kaiser Cargo., Calif., 1944-45; assoc. prof. biochemistry Wash. U., 1945-46; assoc. prof. chemistry and chemist Mallinckrodt Inst., 1945-57; prof. biochemistry Brandeis U., 1957-61; prof. chemistry U. Calif., San Diego, 1961-74, chmn. dept., 1971-73, prof. biol. scis., 1974-78, prof. emeritus biol. scis., 1978—; prof. emeritus biol. scis. U. So. Calif., Los Angeles, 1978—. NSF sr. fellow, 1956, Guggenheim fellow, 1956, 72; recipient C.F. Kettering Award Am. Soc. Plant Physiologists, 1969. Fellow Am. Inst. Chemists, Am. Philos. Soc.; mem. Nat. Acad. Sci., Am. Chem. Soc. (award 1963), Am. Soc. Biol. Chemists (Merck award 1982), Am. Acad. Arts and Sci. (John Scott award Phila. 1989, Einstein award).

KAMERMAN, KENNETH M., business and management consultant; b. N.Y.C., June 21, 1931; m. Merilee J. Dannemann, Apr. 28, 1991. BS in Textile Engring., U. Lowell, 1953; MBA, U. N.Mex., 1970. Mgr. customer rels. Lytle Corp., Albuquerque, 1956-61; bus. mgr. Teaching Machines Inc., Albuquerque, 1961-65; adminstrv. mgr. Westinghouse Learning Corp., Albuquerque, 1965-71; mgr. pers. and adminstrv. svcs. Bellamah Corp., Albuquerque, 1972-78; v.p. Honor Corp., Albuquerque, 1979-81; firm adminstr. Rogoff, Diamond & Walker, Albuquerque, 1981-82; v.p. Battery Power Specialists, Albuquerque, 1982-87; assoc. broker Lee A. Welsh Real Estate Inc., Albuquerque, 1987-91; bd. dirs. Design Products Inc., Learning Mgmt. Corp. Vice chmn. Rep. Cen. Com., Bernalillo County, N.Mex., 1978-81, mem. 1976—; state senator, 1986-93; chmn. Police Adv. Bd., Albuquerque, 1978-80; sec. bd. trustees Bernalillo County Mental Health/Mental Retardation Ctr., 1981-86, v.p. 1984, pres. 1985; treas. N.Mex. Rep. Legis. Campaign Com., 1987-90. USN, 1953-56. Home: 3125 Tennessee St NE Albuquerque NM 87110-2432 Office: PO Box 21787 Albuquerque NM 87154-1787

KAMILLI, ROBERT JOSEPH, geologist; b. Phila., June 14, 1947; s. Joseph George and Marie Emma (Clauss) K.; m. Diana Ferguson Chapman, June 28, 1969; children: Ann Chapman, Robert Chapman. BA summa cum laude, Rutgers U., 1969; AM, Harvard U., 1971, PhD, 1976. Geologist Climax Molybdenum Co., Empire, Colo., 1976-79, asst. resident geologist, 1979-80; project geologist Climax Molybdenum Co., Golden, Colo., 1980-83; geologist U.S. Geol. Survey, Saudi Arabian Mission, Jeddah, 1983-87, mission chief geologist, 1987-89; rsch. geologist U.S. Geol. Survey, Tucson, Ariz., 1989—; adj. prof. U. Colo., Boulder, 1981-83. Mem. editorial bd. Econ. Geology; contbr. articles to profl. jours. Henry Rutgers scholar Rutgers U., 1968-69. Fellow Geol. Soc. Am., Soc. Econ. Geologists; mem. Sigma Xi, Phi Beta Kappa. Home: 5050 N Siesta Dr Tucson AZ 85715-9652 Office: US Geol Survey Tucson Field Office U Ariz Gould-Simpson Bldg #77 Tucson AZ 85721

KAMINE, BERNARD SAMUEL, lawyer; b. Oklahoma City, Dec. 5, 1943; s. Martin and Mildred Esther Kamine; m. Marcia Phyllis Haber, Sept. 9, 1982; children: Jorge Hershel, Benjamin Haber, Tovy Haber. BA, U. Denver, 1965; JD, Harvard U., 1968. Bar: Calif. 1969, Colo. 1969, U.S. Supreme Ct. 1973. Dep. atty. gen. Calif. Dept. Justice, L.A., 1969-72; asst. atty. gen. Colo. Dept. Law, Denver, 1972-74; ptnr. Kamine, Steiner & Ungerer (and predecessor firms), L.A., Calif., 1976—; instr. Glendale (Calif.) U. Coll. Law, 1971-72; judge pro tem Mcpl. Ct., 1974—, Superior Ct., 1989—; arbitrator Contract Arbitration Com. Calif. Pub. Works, 1990—; mem. adv. com. legal forms Calif. Jud. Coun., 1978-82; lectr. Calif. Continuing Edn. of the Bar Programs, 1979-85. Contbr. chpts. to legal texts, articles to profl. jours. Mem. L.A. County Dem. Cen. Com., 1982-85; mem. Pacific S.W. Regional Bd. Anti-Defamation League, 1982—, exec. com., 1988—, treas., 1990-92, sec. 1992—. Lt. col. USAR, 1969—. Mem. ABA, Calif. State Bar Assn. (chair conf. dels. calendar coordinating com. 1991-92), L.A. County Bar Assn. (chair Superior Cts. com. 1977-79, chair constrn. law subsect. of real property sect. 1981-83), Engring. Contractors' Assn. (bd. dirs. 1985—, rep. Am. Pub. Works Assn.-Associated Gen. Contractors Joint Coop. Com. that pubs. Standard Specifications for Pub. Works Constrn. 1984—, affiliate chair 1992—), Bd. Registered Constrn. Insps., Am. Arbitration Assn. (arbitrator 1976—, mem. regional constrn. industry arbitration adv. com. 1987—), Res. Officers Assn. (pres. chpt. 1977-78), Omicron Delta Kappa. Office: 350 S Figueroa St Ste 250 Los Angeles CA 90071-1286

KAMINS, PHILIP E., diversified manufacturing company executive; b. 1936. Salesman H. Muehlstein, 1957-62; founder Kamco Plastics Inc., Sun Valley, Calif., 1965-71; pres., CEO PMC Inc., Sun Valley, Calif., also bd. dirs. Office: PMC Inc 12243 Branford St Sun Valley CA 91352-1097

KAMINSKI, BRUCE DAVID, lawyer; b. Santa Monica, Calif., Sept. 20, 1958; s. Henry Joseph Kaminski and Sandra Lorraine (Newton) Gleeson; m. Katherine K. Andritsakis, Jan. 4, 1992. BA, Stanford U., 1980; JD, Santa Clara U., 1983. Bar: Calif. 1983. Assoc. Weintraub, Genshlea, Hardy, Erich & Brown, Sacramento, 1983-86; Assoc. Rader, Rader, Goulart & Gray, Sacramento, 1987-90, ptnr., 1991—. Vol. atty. Voluntary Legal Svcs. Program, Sacramento, 1987—. Mem. Calif. Bar Assn., Sacramento Bar Assn., Sacramento Barristers Club, Stanford Alumni Club Sacramento (bd. dirs. 1985-92, pres. 1988-89), Tenn. Squires. Republican. Roman Catholic. Home: 2508 Rio Bravo Cir Sacramento CA 95826 Office: Rader Rader Goulart & Gray 2617 K St Ste 200 Sacramento CA 95816

KAMM, HERBERT, journalist; b. Long Branch, N.J., Apr. 1, 1917; s. Louis and Rose (Cohen) K.; m. Phyllis I. Silberblatt, Dec. 6, 1936; children: Laurence R., Lewis R., Robert H. Reporter, sports editor Asbury Park (N.J.) Press, 1935-42; with AP, 1942-43; with N.Y. World-Telegram and Sun, 1943-66, successively rewrite man, picture editor, asst. city editor, feature editor, mag. editor, 1943-63, asst. mng. editor, 1963, mng. editor, 1963-66; exec. editor N.Y. World Jour. Tribune, 1966-67; editorial cons. Scripps-Howard Newspapers, 1967-69; assoc. editor Cleve. Press, 1969-80, editor, 1980-82, editor emeritus, 1982; edit. dir. Sta. WJW-TV, Cleve., 1982-85; instr. journalism Case Western Res. U., 1972-75, Calif. Poly., San Luis Obispo, 1991—. Radio and TV news commentator and panelist, 1950-85, TV talk show host, 1974-85; contbr. articles mags., syndicates. Bd. overseers Case Western Res. U., 1974-78. Herb Kamm scholarship in journalism established Kent State U., 1983; inducted Cleve. Journalism Hall of Fame, 1986. Mem. AFTRA, Soc. Profl. Journalists (pres. Calif. Missions chpt. 1986-87). Clubs: City of Cleve. (pres. 1982), Silurians. Home: 147 River View Dr Avila Beach CA 93424-2307

KAMMAN, ALAN BERTRAM, communications consulting company executive; b. Phila., Jan. 25, 1931; s. Daniel Lawrence and Sara Belle K.; m. Madeleine Marguerite Pin, Feb. 15, 1960; children: Alan Daniel, Neil Charles. BCE, Swarthmore Coll., 1952. With Bell Tel. Co. Pa., Phila., 1952-69; with Arthur D. Little, Inc., Cambridge, Mass., 1969-85, v.p. telecommunications scis., 1977-81, v.p. corp. staff, 1981-85; pres. Telematix Intern. Ltd., Boston, 1985-87, Gand A Unltd., 1985-88; nat. dir. telecommunications markets KPMG Peat Marwick, Lexington, Mass., 1987-91; mng. dir. Global Consulting Group, St. Helena, Calif., 1991—; chmn. adv. bd. grad. program telecommunications U. San Francisco, Intelevent, Europe, Telecom 75, Telecom 79, Telecom 83, Telecom 91, Telecommunications Mag.; world rep. KPMG Peat Marwick to Internat. Telecommunications Union, UN. Contbr. articles to jours. in field. Bd. dirs. U.S. Coun. World Communications Yr. Fellow Royal Geog. Soc. (London), Appalachian Club (v.p. ops., bd. dirs.), World Link. Office: 3594 Siverado Trail Saint Helena CA 94574

KAMP, RONALD CARL, lawyer; b. Peoria, Oct. 18, 1934; s. Carl Edward and Margaret Bernadine (LeSeure) K.; m. Roberta Hulda Hensley, Mar. 9, 1963; children: David Edward, Douglas Kyle, Diane Carrie. BSME, U. Ill., 1956, MS, 1959; JD, George Washington U., 1963; MBA, U. Chgo., 1969; AAS in ELT, Oakton Comm. Coll., 1985. Bar: Ill. 1963, Va. 1963. Engr. trainee Hiram Walker & Sons, Inc., Peoria, Ill., 1956-58; patent examiner U.S. Patent Office, Washington, 1959-61; patent agt. Office Naval Rsch., Washington, 1961-63; patent atty. Internat. Harvester Co., Chgo., 1963-64, sr. patent atty., 1965-81; asst. patent counsel LeTourneau-Westinghouse, Peoria, 1964-65; group patent counsel FMC Corp., Chgo., 1981-88; mgr. West Coast patent dept. FMC Corp., Santa Clara, Calif., 1988—; bd. dirs. Corey Steel, Cicero, Ill. Patentee in field. Chmn. Wilmette (Ill.) Vol. Blood Program, 1976-81. Mem. ABA, ASME, Soc. Automotive Engrs., Am. Intellectual Property Law Assn., Va. Bar Assn., Ill. Bar Assn., Patent Law Assn. Chgo., Peninsula Intellectual Property Law Assn., San Francisco Intellectual Property Law Assn. Republican. Home: 116 Clover Way Los Gatos CA 95032-5621

KAN, KENNY WAI, actuary; b. Kuala Lumpur, Malaysia, May 19, 1966; came to U.S., 1985; s. Tong Fong and Sau Kee (Yap) K.; m. Henrietta Lu, 1992. BBA, U. Tex., 1987, assoc., 1988; internat. West Coast coord., Buck Cons., San Francisco, 1990—. CPA, Md. Analyst Buck Cons., Dallas, 1988-89; sr. analyst, assoc. Towers Perrin, San Francisco, 1989-92; mng. ptnr. 80 Percenters, San Francisco, 1990—; internat. coord. West Coast Buck Cons., San Francisco, 1992—; adminstrv. v.p. Bus. Roundtable, 1990-91; founder Silver Tongues, 1990—; speaker in field various confs. and seminars. Contbr. articles to profl. jours.; speaker numerous orgns., profl. groups. Mem. AICPA, Soc. Actuaries (assoc.), Asian Bus. League, World Affairs Coun., Schwabmasters (founder, mentor 1990—), Toastmasters (area bd. govs. dist. 4, Phoenix award 1990, Get into Action award 1990, Disting. Toastmaster award 1991).

KANDELL, MARSHALL JAY, public relations counselor; b. Bklyn., Dec. 5, 1937; s. Harry and Mollie Rebecca (Remstein) K.; m. Judith Ann Zeve, May 28, 1961; children: Paul Bryon, Robin Pilar. AA in Journalism, Los Angeles City Coll., 1958; student Calif. State U., Los Angeles, 1963-65. Cert. tchr. community colls., Calif. Pub. rels. staff City of Hope (Calif.) Nat. Med. Ctr., 1966-68; v.p. Roger Beck Pub. Rels., Sherman Oaks, Calif., 1968-71; account supr. Laurence Laurie & Assoc., L.A., 1971-72; community rels. dir. St. Mary Med. Ctr., Long Beach, Calif., 1972-75; dir. pub. rels. Cedars-Sinai Med. Ctr., L.A., 1975; founder Marshall Jay Kandell Pub. Rels., Huntington Beach, Calif., 1976-91; pub. rels. dir. Housing Authority City of L.A., 1991—; vis. faculty mem. Calif. State U., Long Beach; mem. founding faculty Coastline Community Coll. Pres. Encino Jaycees, 1970-71; pres. Community Vol. Office, Long Beach, 1975-76; bd. dirs. Long Beach chpt. ARC, 1974-75, Civic Ctr. Barrio Housing Corp., Santa Ana, Calif., 1985-93; mem. Citizen's Adv. Commn. 1984 Olympic Games, adv. panel Jewish Family Svc. of Orange County, Calif.; v.p. Irvine Jewish Community, 1973; founding mem., v.p. Congregation B'nai Tzedek, Fountain Valley, Calif., 1976. Served in USAF, 1958-63. Recipient Disting. Service award Encino Jaycees, 1972; MacEachern award Acad. Hosp. Pub. Relations, 1973-74; Best written story award Press Club Greater Los Angeles, 1965. Mem. Pub. Relations Soc. Am. Democrat. Jewish. Home: 18882 Deodar St Fountain Valley CA 92708-7223

KANDLER, JOSEPH RUDOLPH, financial executive; b. Vienna, Austria, Dec. 13, 1921; came to Can., 1952; s. Franz and Maria Franziska (Stanzel) K.; m. Lubomyra-Melitta Melnechuk, June 15, 1963. D.Rerum Commercialium, Sch. Econs., Vienna, 1949; Chartered Acct., Inst. Chartered Accts. Alta., 1965. Sales exec. Philips, Vienna, 1951; acct. Brown & Root, Ltd. Edmonton, Alta., Can., 1952-54, 56, chief acct., 1957-64; v.p. fin. Healy Ford Ctr. and Assoc. Cos., Edmonton, 1964-89; pres. Sentha Investments, Ltd., Edmonton, 1978—. Bd. dirs. Edmonton Symphony, 1969-72, Alta. Cultural Heritage Council, 1973-81, Edmonton Opera, 1982-84, Tri-Bach Festival, 1982-84; founder Johann Strauss Found., Alta., bd. dirs. 1975-84, pres. 1975-78, founder, pres. B.C. chpt., 1985—; bd. govs. U. Alta., 1982-86, mem. senate, 1973-79, 82-86; mem. adv. com. on cultural and convention ctr. City of Edmonton, 1974-78, vice-chmn., 1976-78. Recipient Achievement award for svc. to community Govt. Alta., 1975, Johann Strauss medal in gold Vienna Tourist Bd., 1989, Knight's Cross of Honor 1st Class Republic of Austria, 1990, Golden Emblem of Honor City of Vienna, 1991. Mem. Inst. Chartered Accts. Alta., Mensa. Address: Sentha Investments Ltd, 392 Lang Rd C-10 RR 4, Ganges, BC Canada V0S 1E0

KANDLER, PAUL ALFRED, ophthalmologist; b. N.Y.C., Nov. 30, 1939; s. Paul and Edith (Reichhard) K.; m. Mary Kathryn Gibbons, May 7, 1966; 1 child, Kirsten. BA, Johns Hopkins U., 1961; MD, U. Md., 1965. Commd. ens. USN, 1964, advanced through grades to comdr., 1974; intern U.S. Naval Hosp., Great Lakes, Ill., 1965-66; med. officer USS Delta AR-9, Alameda, Calif., 1966-68, USN Dispensary, Treasure Island, Calif., 1968-69; resident in ophthalmology U.S. Naval Hosp., Oakland, Calif., 1969-72; chief of ophthalmology U.S. Naval Hosp., Great Lakes, 1972-74; asst. prof. surgery Chgo. Med. Sch., 1973-74; ret. USN, 1974; pvt. practice ophthalmology Monterey, Calif., 1975—. Fellow Am. Acad. Ophthalmology; mem. Calif. Med. Assn., Monterey Peninula Country Club, Beach and Tennis Club Pebble Beach. Home: 3580 Edgefield Pl Carmel CA 93923 Office: 1011 Cass St Monterey CA 93940

KANE, BARTHOLOMEW ALOYSIUS, state librarian; b. Pitts., Nov. 2, 1945; s. Bartholomew A. and Ruth M. (Loerlein) K.; divorced; 1 child, Leah. BA in Journalism, Pa. State U., 1967; MLS, U. Pitts., 1971; cert., Modern Archives Inst., 1987. Cert. Preservation Inst. Nat. Archives, 1990. Dir. Bradford Meml. Library, El Dorado, Kans., 1972-74; researcher Hawaii Dept. Planning and Econ. Devel., Honolulu, 1974-75, state librarian, 1982—; librarian Hawaii State Library System, Lanai City, 1975-79, Honolulu, 1979-82; adj. faculty mem. U. Hawaii, Manoa, 1986, 88, 92. Mem. Gov.'s Coun. on Literacy, 1985—. Hazel McCoy fellow Friends of Library of Hawaii, 1971. Mem. ALA, Hawaii Libr. Assn. Democrat. Home: 44-130 Puuohalai Pl Kaneohe HI 96744 Office: Hawaii State Pub Libr System 465 S King St B-1 Honolulu HI 96813

KANE, CAROLINE MARIE, biochemistry educator; b. Warren, Ohio, June 9, 1949; d. John Baxter and Phyllis Jean (Mattson) Kane; m. Michael J. Chamberlin, Jan. 31, 1981. BS, Ohio U., 1970; MS, N.C. State U., 1972; PhD, U. Calif., Berkeley, 1979. Postdoctoral reschr. NIEHS Core Grant, U. Calif., Berkeley, 1979; NIH postdoctoral fellow Div. Genetics, Fred Hutchinson Cancer Rsch. Ctr., Seattle, 1980-81; postdoctoral fellow U. Calif., Berkeley, 1981-83, asst. rsch. biochemist, 1983-89, adj. asst. prof. biochemistry, 1989—; co-organizer Keystone Symposium on Transcript Elongation and Termination, 1991; co-dir. Howard Hughes Med. Inst. Award for Undergrad. Biol. Sci. Edn. Initiative, Berkeley, 1992—. Contbr. articles to profl. jours. NSF grantee, 1992—. Mem. Am. Soc. for Cell Biology, Am. Soc. for Microbiology, Am. Soc. for Biochemistry and Molecular Biology, Sigma Xi, Phi Beta Kappa, Phi Kappa Phi. Office: Univ of Calif Dept Molecular and Cell Biology 401 Barker Hall Berkeley CA 94720

KANE, JAMES PATRICK, utility company manager; b. Rahway, N.J., Nov. 16, 1946; s. John Francis and Marcella Ann (Moore) K.; m. Su Ann Roberts, June 1, 1968; children: Jennifer Jill, Christopher Matthew. BA in Edn., Ariz. State U., 1969, postgrad. sch. mgmt., 1986—. Groundman Ariz. Pub. Service, Phoenix, 1970-72, assoc. engr., 1972-75; supt. Vanguard Concrete, Edmonton, Alta., Can., 1975-77; mktg. rep. Ariz. Pub. Service, Flagstaff, 1977-80; mktg. supr. Ariz. Pub. Service, Phoenix, 1981-82; dist. mgr. Ariz. Pub. Service, Yuma, 1982-84; gen. mgr. S.W. Gas Corp., Phoenix, 1984-93, v.p., 1993—; expert witness Ariz. Corp. Commn., Phoenix, 1985, 87. Bd. dirs. Phoenix Urban League, 1987—, Ariz. State U. West, Phoenix, 1987—; grad. Valley Leadership Orgn., Phoenix, 1986—. Served with U.S. Army, 1968-70. Named Football All-American, UPI, Tempe, 1968. Mem. Am. Gas Assn., Pacific Gas Assn. Republican. Club: Ariz. State U. Lettermans. Home: 5104 N 32d St # 226 Phoenix AZ 85018 Office: SW Gas Corp PO Box 26500 Tucson AZ 85726-6500

KANE, JOHN LAWRENCE, JR., federal judge; b. Tucumcari, N.Mex., Feb. 14, 1937; s. John Lawrence and Dorothy Helen (Bottler) K.; children: Molly Francis, Meghan, Sally, John Pattison. B.A., U. Colo., 1958; J.D., U. Denver, 1961. Bar: Colo. 1961. Dep. dist. atty. Adams County, Colo., 1961-62; assoc. firm Gaunt, Byrne & Dirrim, 1961-63; ptnr. firm Andrews and Kane, Denver, 1964; pub. defender Adams County, 1965-67; dep. dir. eastern region of India Peace Corps, 1967-69; with firm Holme Roberts & Owen, 1970-77, ptnr., 1972-77; judge U.S. Dist. Ct. Colo., Denver, 1978-88, U.S. sr. dist. judge, 1988—; adj. prof. law U. Denver; vis. lectr. Trinity Coll., Dublin, Ireland, winter 1989. Contbr. articles to profl. jours. Recipient St. Thomas More award Cath. Lawyers Guild, 1983, Info. Agy. Outstanding Svc. award, 1985, Outstanding Alumnus award U. Denver, 1987, Lifetime Jud. Achievement award Nat. Assn. Criminal Def. Lawyers, 1987, Civil Rights award B'nai B'rith, 1988, . Fellow Internat. Acad. Trial Lawyers, Am. Bd. Trial Advs. (hon.). Roman Catholic. Office: US Dist Ct C-550 US Courthouse 1929 Stout St Denver CO 80294-2900

KANE, KAREN MARIE, public affairs consultant; b. Colorado Springs, Colo., Mar. 7, 1947; d. Bernard Francis and Adeline Marie (Logan) K. Student, Mills Coll., Oakland, Calif., 1965-66; BA, U. Wash., 1970, MA, 1973, PhC, 1977, postgrad. Pub. affairs cons., housing subcom. Seattle Ret. Tchrs. Assn., 1981-84; pub. affairs cons. 1st U.S. Women's Olympic Marathon Trials, 1982-83, Seattle, 1985—. Contbr. articles to newsletters and mags. Vol. city coun. campaigns, Seattle; bd. mem. Showboat Theatre Found., 1984—; preservation chmn. LWV, Seattle, 1989—, Allied Arts of Seattle, 1987; sec. bd. trustees, mem. exec. com., mem. Mayor's Landmark Theatre Adv. Group, 1991—; mayoral appointee as commr. on Pike Pl. Market Hist. Commn., Seattle, 1992—. Recipient Award of Honor, Wash. Trust for Hist. Preservation, 1990, Recognition award Found. for Hist. Preservation and Adaptive Reuse, Seattle, 1991; Am. Found. grantee, 1989, 91. Mem. Am. Assn. Univ. Women, Mills Coll. Alumnae Assn., U. Wash. Alumni Assn., Nat. Trust for Hist. Preservation, Hist. Hawai'i Found., Found. for San Francisco's Archtl. Heritage, Internat. Platform Assn. Office: Allied Arts of Seattle 105 S Main St Seattle WA 98104-2515

KANE, KATHERINE D., historical society official; b. Peoria, Ill., May 15, 1950; d. John L. and Virginia Hays (Harris) Deffenbaugh; m. Frank Kane, Aug. 28, 1971. BA, U. Denver, 1972; MA, U. Colo., 1985. Coord. spl. projects Denver Art Mus., 1978-82; dir. pub. svcs. Colo. Hist. Soc., Denver, 1982-91, dir. collections svcs., 1991—; mem. faculty Mus. Archives Inst., Sturbridge, Mass., 1987—; curator various exhibits, 1986—. Editor: Colorado Museum Directory, 1984; contbr. numerous articles to profl. publs. NEH grantee, 1986, 88, 92. Mem. Am. Assn. Mus., Am. Assn. State and Local History (regional awards chmn. 1988-92), Colo.-Wyo. Assn. Mus. (chmn. 1990-92, program chmn. 1993), Soc. Colo. Archivists (program chmn., mem. coun. 1987-89). Mem. Am. Assn. Museums, Am. Assn. State and Local History (regional award chmn. 1988-92), Colo.-Wyo. Assn. Museums (chmn. 1990-92), Soc. Colo. Archivists (program chmn., mem. coun. 1987—). Office: Colo Hist Soc 1300 Broadway Denver CO 80203-2104

KANE, THOMAS REIF, engineering educator; b. Vienna, Austria, Mar. 23, 1924; came to U.S., 1938, naturalized, 1943; Ernest Kanitz and Gertrude (Reif) K.; m. Ann Elizabeth Andrews, June 4, 1951; children: Linda Ann, Jeffrey Thomas. BS, Columbia U., 1950, MS, 1952, PhD, 1953; D Tech. Scis. (hon.), Tech. U. Vienna, Austria, 1990. Asst. prof., assoc. prof. U. Pa., Phila., 1953-61; prof. Sch. Engring. Stanford U., Calif., 1961—; cons. NASA, Harley-Davidson Motor Co., AMF, Lockheed Missiles and Space Co., Vertol Aircraft Corp., Martin Marietta Co., Kellet Aircraft Co. Author: (vol. 1) Analytical Elements of Mechanics, 1959, (vol. 2), 1961, Dynamics, 1972, Spacecraft Dynamics, 1983; Dynamics: Theory and Applications, 1985; contbr. over 150 articles to profl. jours. Served with U.S. Army, 1943-45, PTO. Recipient Alexander von Humboldt prize, 1988. Fellow ASME, Am. Astronautical Soc. (Dirk Brouwer award 1983); mem. Sigma Xi, Tau Beta Pi. Office: Stanford U Dept Mech Engring Durand Blg 265 Stanford CA 94305

KANEGIS, ARTHUR L.D., film producer, screenwriter; b. Washington, Nov. 4, 1947; s. Leon and Lillian (Hayman) K.; m. M. Susan Grabill, Sept. 2, 1967; children: Robin Aura, Bethany Star Bellon; m. Molly Post. BA, Earlham Coll., Richmond, Ind., 1969. Audio-visual documentary producer, writer Am. Friends Svc. Com., Phila., 1969-77; media dir. Ctr. for Def. Info., Washington, 1977-85; pres. Future Wave Inc., Santa Fe, 1985—; producer 2020 Prodns., Inc., Santa Fe, 1987—; audio-visual producer, speechwriter McGovern for Pres., Washington, 1972; juror Cine Film Festivals, 1984-88. Produced several documentaries including The Automated Airwar, 1970, Sharing Global Resources, The Post War War, War Without Winners II, 1982, The Weapons Bazaar, 1985; feature films OOOPS!, 1991, Astrocops, 1993; author: The Bully Proof Shield, 1991; contbr. articles to profl. jours. Recipient 1st place blue ribbon Am. Film Festival, 1980. Mem. Ind. Feature Film Producers, World Federalist Assn., World Future Soc. Quaker. Office: 2020 Prodns Inc 105 Camino Teresa Santa Fe NM 87501-4703

KANEHANN, JOSEPH ANTHONY, development and marketing professional, investor; b. Allentown, Pa., Mar. 19, 1929; s. William Nicholas and Mary Catherine (McDermott) K.; m. Margaret Ann Somers, Jan. 25, 1958; children: Mary Beth, J. Patrick, David Casey. BS in Chemistry, Lehigh U., 1950, MS in Chemistry, 1951; MBA, NYU, 1955. Chemist Mobil Oil Co., Bklyn., 1951-56; ptnr., dir. W.E. Hill & Co., N.Y.C., 1958-68; v.p. I.C.I. Am., Stamford, Conn., 1968-71, Allied Chem., Morristown, N.J., 1971-73; corp. exec. staff assoc. Gen. Electric, Fairfield, Conn., 1973-82; v.p. Hydril Co., L.A., 1982-86; v.p., s.v.p. Everest & Jennings, L.A., 1986-91; v.p. DA Internat., L.A., 1991—; dir. GCI Corp., San Francisco, Calif., 1989-90, E & J Asia, Tokyo, 1987-91, E & J Avenues, L.A., 1988-91, chair TK World Trading, N.Y.C., 1981-83. Capt. USAF, 1956-58. Mem. Am. Chem. Soc., Assn. of Corp. Growth. Republican. Roman Catholic. Home: 27940 Winding Way Malibu CA 90265 Office: DA Internat LTD 72 Mamaroneck Ave White Plains NY 10601

KANEHIRO, KENNETH KENJI, insurance educator, risk analyst, consultant; b. Honolulu, May 10, 1934; s. Charles Yutaka and Betty Misako (Hoshino) K.; m. Eiko Asari, June 23, 1962; 1 child, Everett Peter. B in Counseling Psychology, U. Hawaii, 1956, grad. cert. in Counseling Psychology, 1957; grad. cert. in Counseling Psychology, The Am. Inst., 1971. Chartered property and casualty underwriter. Claims adjustor Cooke Trust Co., Honolulu, 1959-62, underwriter, 1962-66; account supr. Alexander & Baldwin, Honolulu, 1966-68; spl. risk exec. Hawaiian Ins. & Guaranty, Honolulu, 1968-71; br. mgr. Hawaiian Ins. & Guaranty, Hilo, Hawaii, 1971-72, Marsh & McLennan, Inc., Hilo, 1972-78; sr. mktg. rep. Occidental Underwriters, Honolulu, 1978-87; pvt. practice Honolulu, 1987—; coord. Ins. Sch. of Pacific, Honolulu, 1978—; lectr. ins. Hawaii Dist. Cts., 1986—; mem. arbitration panel Hawaii Family Ct.; cons. Dai Tokyo Royal State Ins. Co., 1992—. Bd. dirs. The Children's House, Pearl City, Hawaii, 1987—; ins. cons. Arcadia Retirement Residence, Honolulu, 1987—; risk mgr. Aloha coun. Boy Scouts Am., Honolulu, 1980—, adult leader, Hilo and Honolulu, 1956—; bd. govs. U. Hawaii Founders Alumni Assn., Honolulu, 1991; edn. chmn. Gen. Ins. Assn. Hawaii, Hilo, 1971-77. With U.S. Army, 1957-59. Mem. Soc. Chartered Property and Casualty Underwriters (pres. 1986-87, CPD award 1988, 92), Soc. Ins. Trainers and Educators (Outstanding Vol. award 1990). Home: 1128 Ala Napunani St Apt 705 Honolulu HI 96818-1606

KANENAKA, REBECCA YAE, microbiologist; b. Wailuku, Hawaii, Jan. 9, 1958; d. Masakazu Robert and Takako (Oka) Fujimoto; m. Brian Ken Kanenaka, Nov. 10, 1989; 1 child, Kent Masakazu. Student, U. Hawaii, Manoa, 1976-77; BS, Colo. State U., 1980. Lab. asst. Colo. State U., Ft. Collins, 1979-80; microbiologist Foster Farms, Livingston, Calif., 1980-81; microbiologist Hawaii Dept. Health, Lihue, 1981-86, Honolulu, 1986—. Mem. AWWA, Am. Soc. Microbiology (Hawaii chpt.), Nat. Registry of Microbiologists, Hawaii Pub. Health Assn. Clubs: Brown Bag (Lihue) (pres. 1985-86); Golden Ripples (4-H leader). Home: 1520 Liholiho St Apt 502 Honolulu HI 96822 Office: Hawaii Dept Health Lab 1250 Punchbowl St Honolulu HI 96813-2428

KANESTA, NELLIE ROSE, chemical dependency counselor; b. Zuni, N.Mex., Aug. 8, 1939; d. Paxton E. and Bessie (Thompson) Boone; m. Patrick Tsethlikia, Apr. 10, 1959 (div. Mar. 1973); children: Nina, Frederick William, Pamela, Judson, Marie Christine, Paxton, Clifford. Student, U. N.Mex., Gallup, 1973-80, 86-87, U. Minn., Duluth, 1987-88. Alcoholism counselor Zuni (N.Mex.) Indian Hosp., 1985-86; counselor Friendship Svcs., Inc., Gallup, N.Mex., 1986-87; trainer Hazelden Found., Center City, Minn., 1987-88; intense residential guidance counselor Ramah (N.Mex.) Navajo Dormitory, 1988-89; Title V counselor, dir. Pine Hills (N.Mex.) Schs., 1989-91, phys. ednl. aide, 1992-93, group home life skills counselor, 1993—; counselor Zuni PHS Indian Hosp., 1985, Regional Conf. on Children of Alcoholics, Albuquerque, 1985; insvc. tng. confs. Western N.Mex. U., 1986, Native Am. Cultural Issues in Substance Abuse, Coll. of Santa Fe, 1986, Chem. Dependency and Intervention, The N.Mex. Alcoholism and Drug Abuse Counselors, 1986, In-Svc. Tng. on Battered Families and Its Relation to Alcohol/Drug Abuse, 1987, N.Mex. Alcoholism and Drug Abuse Counselors Assn., 1986-88, Hazelden Chem. Dependency Counselor Tng. Program, 1988. Home: PO Box 206 Pinehill NM 87357-0206 Office: Ramah Navajo Sch Bd Inc PO Drawer H Pine Hill NM 87357

KANG, CHANG-YUIL, immunologist; b. Pusan, Korea, Nov. 28, 1954; came to U.S., 1982; s. Hee-Kyong and Yang-Hee (Oh) K.; m. Young-Youn Lee, Jan. 17, 1984; children: Stephen, Catherine. BS, Seoul (Korea) Nat. U., 1977, MS, 1981; PhD, SUNY, Buffalo, 1987. Diplomate pharmacist, Dept. Health and Human Svc., Korea. Dept. asst. Seoul Nat. U., 1981-82; rsch. affiliate Roswell Park Cancer Inst., Buffalo, 1983-86, postdoctoral rsch. fellow, 1986-87; scientist I IDEC Pharm. Corp., La Jolla, Calif., 1987-89, scientist II, 1989-92, scientist III, 1992—. Inventor AIDS vaccine, 1991; contbr. articles to profl. jours. With Korean Marine Corps, 1977-79. NIH grantee, 1990-91, 91-92, 92-94. Mem. Am. Assn. Immunologists. Home: 1736 Buttercup Rd Encinitas CA 92024 Office: IDEC Pharm Corp # 160 11099 N Torrey Pines Rd La Jolla CA 92037

KANIA, ALAN JAMES, administration consultant, journalist; b. Lawrence, Mass., Nov. 30, 1949; s. Frank J. and Genievieve (Martin) K. Student, Boston U., 1967-69; BS, Emerson Coll., Boston, 1971; MPA, U. Colo., Denver, 1985. Exec. dir. Ctr. For Wild Horse and Burro Rsch, Inc., 1970-86; cons. various orgns., 1983-86; mktg. and found. cons. St. Anthony Hosp. Systems, 1981-87; contract health care cons. Boulder (Colo.) County Health Dept., 1986-87; asst. dir. mktg. Bethesda Psychealth System, 1987-88, mktg. cons., 1988-89; adminstrn. cons. various orgns., 1989—; sr. editor The Daily Jour., 1990; master plan adminstr. U.S. Forest Svc., Colo. Trail Found., 1990-92; exec. editor Health Care Strategic Mgmt., 1992—; condr. seminars, confs. Am. Hosp. Assn., 1985, 88, Grantsmanship Ctr. Workshop, 1984, 85. Author: John Otto of Colorado National Monument, 1984, Bench and the Bar, 1991; editor Trail and Timberline mag., 1984; exec. editor Health Care Strategic Mgmt. Bd. dirs. Parker Fire Dist., 1987—, Colo. Trail Found., 1987-90, Parker Fire Protection Dist., bd. dirs. pension fund; mem. coun. cir. Internat. Soc. for Protection of Mustangs and Burros, treas.; mem. program com. Acad. for Health Care Mktg.; chmn. strategic planning St. Anthony Found., 1986-87; spl. advisor Western Colo. Hist. Mus. and Inst., 1986; pub. rels. cons. Cath. Svc. Assn., 1986; mem. winterization com. Community Action Program, 1986; dir. Grand Junction Day Care Task Force, 1986. Recipient Journalism awards for Excellence and Best in Show Soc. for Tech. Communications, 1983, Gold Leaf awards Colo. Hosp. Assn., Best External Publication award, 1982, 83, Best AV presentation award, 1982, 83, Best TV Commercial award, 1983, News awards Colo. Media, Agencies, Clients, 1985, 88, 1st prize Colo. Soc. for Profl. Journalists, 1988, 89. Mem. Boulder County Horsemen's Assn. (publicity chmn.), Internat. Assn. Bus. Communicators, Profl. Photographers Am., Brit. Kinematography, Sound and TV Soc., Colo. Horseman's Coun., Carriage Assn. Am., Denver Press Club, Colo. Mountain Club, Appalachian Mountain Club, Colo. Driving Soc., Metro State Coll. Soc. Profl. Journalists, Sigma Delta Chi. Home: 5931 N Thunderhill Rd Parker CO 80134-5836

KANIECKI, MICHAEL JOSEPH, bishop; b. Detroit, Apr. 13, 1935; s. Stanley Joseph and Julia Marie (Konjora) K. BA, Gonzaga U., 1958, MA in Philosophy, 1960; MA in Theology, St. Mary's, Halifax, Can., 1966. Ordained priest, 1965; consecrated bishop, 1984. Missionary Alaska, 1960-83; coadjutor bishop Diocese of Fairbanks, Alaska, 1984-85, bishop, 1985—. Address: 1316 Peger Rd Fairbanks AK 99709*

KANN, MARK ELIOT, political science educator; b. Chgo., Feb. 24, 1947; m. Kathy Ellen Michael, Feb. 13, 1969; 1 child, Simon Michael. BA in Polit. Sci., U. Wis., Madison, 1968; MA in Polit. Sci., U. Wis., 1972, PhD in Polit. Sci., 1975. Tchr. Chgo. Pub. Schs., 1968-71; prof. U. So. Calif., L.A., 1975—, dir. Ctr. for Excellence in Teaching, 1990-93, assoc. dean Grad. Studies, 1990-93, Salvatori prof. Am. Studies, 1993—. Author: On the Man Question: Gender and Civic Virtue in America, 1991, Middle Class Radicalism in Santa Monica, 1986, The American Left: Failures and Fortunes, 1982; editor: The Future of American Democracy, 1983, Humanities in Society, 1981-84; co-editor: The Problem of Authority in America, 1981; contbr. articles to profl. jours. Recipient Nat. Endowment for Humanities, 1989, William Andrews Clark Meml. Libr., postdoctoral fellowship, 1988. Office: U So Calif University Park Los Angeles CA 90089-0044

KANTER, JAY IRA, film company executive; b. Dec. 12, 1926. Began career with MCA, Inc.; then pres. First Artists Prodn. Co., Ltd.; v.p. prodn. 20th Century-Fox, 1975-76, sr. v.p. worldwide prodns., 1976-79; v.p. The Ladd Co., 1979-84; pres. worldwide prodns. motion picture div. MGM-United Artists Entertainment Co., 1984-85; pres. worldwide prodns. United Artists Corp., 1985; pres. Worldwide Prodn. MGM Pictures, Inc., Culver City, Calif., 1986-89; chmn. prodn. Pathé Entertainment Co., Beverly Hills, Calif., 1989—; COO, chmn. prodn. MGM Comm., 1991—. Office: MGM Comm Inc 2500 Broadway St Santa Monica CA 90404-3061

KANTER, MICHAEL HOWARD, pathologist; b. Chgo., Mar. 21, 1956; s. Morton Lee and Audrey Lee (Wilsey) K.; m. Sandra May Spitzer, May 15, 1983; children: Melanie, Robert. BS in Cybernetics, UCLA, 1976; MD, U. Calif., San Francisco, 1980. Diplomate Am. Bd. Anatomic and Clin. Pathology and Transfusion Medicine. Resident in pathology Harbor-UCLA Med. Ctr., Torrance, 1980-83, chief resident in pathology, 1983-84; pathologist, dir. blood bank So. Calif. Kaiser Permanente Med. Group, L.A., 1984—. Contbr. sci. articles to profl. pubs. Grantee Kaiser Permanente Rsch. Program, 1988. Mem. Coll. Am. Pathologists, N.Y. Acad. Scis., L.A. Soc. Pathologists, Am. Assn. Blood Banks (inspector 1984-90), Nat. Blood Found. (grant review com.). Office: Kaiser Permanente Med Group 6041 Cadillac Ave Los Angeles CA 90034-1700

KANTOR, BRUCE HOWARD, insurance broker; b. Bklyn., Mar. 11, 1944; s. Milton S. and Sophia (Panitz) K.; m. Sherrie Rubinson, Aug. 22, 1965; children: Analisa, Jamie. BA in English, U. Colo., Denver, 1964. CLU; registered health underwriter. Mgr. MR R Shop, Denver, 1965-70; owner, mgr. Bruce H. Kantor, CLU Ins. Broker, Denver, 1970—. Contbr. articles to profl. publs. Trustee C.C. Aurora (Colo.) Found., 1990—. Fellow Life Underwriter Tng. Coun.; mem. Nat. Assn. Life Underwriters (nat. trustee 1986-87, vice chmn. Legislature Coun.), Assn. Health Ins. Agts., Colo. Assn. Life Underwriters (pres. 1985), Colo. Assn. Health Undderwriters (pres. 1993-94), Soc. CLU's (bd. dirs. Rocky Mountain chpt. 1991-94), Am. Philatelic Soc., Rotary (pres. Aurora 1991, Paul Harris fellow 1992). Republican. Jewish. Home: 2191 S Dallas St Denver CO 80231 Office: 1745 Stout St Ste 200 Denver CO 80202

KANTOR, IGO, film and television producer; b. Vienna, Austria, Aug. 18, 1930; came to U.S., 1947; s. Samuel and Miriam (Sommerfreund) K.; m. Enid Lois Dershewitz, June 24, 1962; children: Loren, Mark, Lisa. AA, UCLA, 1950, BS, 1952, MS in Polit. Sci., 1954. Fgn. corr. Portuguese Mag. Flama, L.A., 1949-57; music supr., editor Screen Gems, Columbia, L.A., 1954-63; post-prodn. supr. various ind. cos. L.A., 1963-64; music supr.-editor Universal-MCA, L.A., 1964-66; pres., film editor Synchrofilm, Inc., L.A., 1966-74; pres., producer Duque Films, Inc., L.A., 1971-78; ind. producer Jerry Lewis Films, Film Ventures, L.A., 1979-84; pres., producer Laurelwood Prodns. Inc., L.A., 1984-87, Major Arts Corp., L.A., 1987—; pres. Jubilee Holding Co., L.A., 1988—. Producer Legends of the West with Jack Palance (TV spl. series), 1992, United We Stand, 1988, Act of Piracy, 1987, The Golden Eagle Awards, 1986, It's A Wondeful World, 1986, The Grand Tour, 1985, Shaker Run, 1984, From Hawaii with Love, 1983, Night Shadows, 1983, Kill and Kill Again, 1981, Hardly Working, 1980, Good Luck, Miss Wyckoff, 1979, many others. Named Emmy nominee, 1967, 68, 69, 70. Mem. Acad. Motion Picture Arts & Scis. (exec. sound bd. 1969-71), Dirs. Guild Am. (assoc. dir.). Democrat. Jewish. Home: 11501 Duque Dr Studio City CA 91604-4279 Office: Major Arts Corp 9100 Wilshire Blvd Beverly Hills CA 90212-3403

KANTZ, PAUL THOMAS, biology educator; b. Jacksonville, Tex., Jan. 21, 1941; s. Paul Thomas K. and Katherine Virginia (Smith) Conner; m. Nancy J. Raley; children: Thomas Sinclair, Katherine Ellen, Karen Elizabeth. BA, U. Tex., 1963, MA, 1965, PhD, 1967. Asst. prof. Sacramento State Coll., 1967-71, assoc. prof., 1971-78; prof. Calif. State U., Sacramento, 1978—, chmn. dept. biol. scis., 1988-90; mem. steering com. inst. for teaching and learning Calif. State U., 1989-90; bd. dirs. Moss Landing (Calif.) Marine Labs., 1975-86. Co-author: Morphological and Taxonomic Investigations of Nostoc and Anabaena, 1969; editor: Subject Matter Assessment for Life Sciences, 1990. Mem. N.Y. Acad. Scis., Am. Inst. Biol. Scis., AAAS, Am. Botan. Soc., Am. Phycological Soc., British Phycological Soc., Sigma Xi. Home: 525 42d St Sacramento CA 95819 Office: Calif State U Dept BioSci 6000 J St Sacramento CA 95819-2605

KAO, CHENG CHI, electronics executive; b. Taipei, Taiwan, Republic of China, Aug. 3, 1941; s. Chin Wu and Su Chin (Wu) K.; m. Susan Lin, July 4, 1970; children: Antonia Hueilan, Albert Chengwei, Helen Siaolan. BS, Taiwan U., 1963; AM, Harvard U., 1965, PhD, 1969. Research fellow Harvard U., Cambridge, Mass., 1969-70; scientist Xerox Corp., Webster, N.Y., 1970-75; mgr. Internat. Materials Research, Inc., Santa Clara, Calif., 1976-78; exec. v.p. President Enterprises Corp., Tainan, Taiwan, 1979-85; pres. Kolyn Enterprises Corp., Los Altos, Calif., 1979—. Contbr. articles to profl. jours. Bd. dirs. Taipei Am. Sch., 1980-82. Mem. IEEE, Chinese Inst. Elec. Engring. (bd. dirs. 1982-85), Sigma Xi. Club: Am. in China (Taipei), Palo Alto Hills Golf and Country. Office: Kolyn Enterprises Corp 4962 El Camino Real Ste 119 Los Altos CA 94022-1410

KAO, PHILIP MIN-SHIEN, operations research specialist; b. L.A., Dec. 16, 1963; s. Donald and Jennie (Chen) Kao; m. Lori Suzanne Wilson, June 25, 1989. BA, U. Calif., San Diego, 1985. Student engr. Hughes Aircraft Co., Fullerton, Calif., 1983-85; rsch. asst. Hybritech Inc., San Diego, 1986; rsch. assoc. Salk Inst. Biotech. Ind. Assocs., La Jolla, Calif., 1986-90; analytical chemist Alliance Pharm. Corp., San Diego, 1990-91; network adminstr. Ligand Pharms., Inc., San Diego, 1991—. Contbr. articles to profl. jours. Mem. Am. Chem. Soc., AAAS, Assn. Am. Clin. Chemistry. Office: Ligand Pharms Inc 9393 Towne Centre Dr Ste 100 San Diego CA 92121-3016

KAPLAN, CRAIG ANDREW, cognitive scientist, writer; b. Berkeley, Calif., Oct. 22, 1963; s. Melvin Jordan and Margaret Anne (Bohannon) K. Diploma, Philips Exeter Acad., 1981; BA, U. Calif., Santa Cruz, 1985; MS, Carnegie Mellon U., 1987, PhD, 1989. Scientist Santa Teresa Labs. IBM, San Jose, Calif., 1989-90, tech. asst. to exec. Santa Teresa Labs., 1990-91, scientist, author, 1991—; lectr. U. Calif., Santa Cruz, 1991. Contbr. articles to profl. jours.; patentee in field. Mem. Assn. for Computing Machinery, Sigma Xi (assoc.). Home: 120 20th Ave B Santa Cruz CA 95062 Office: IBM Santa Teresa Labs 555 Bailey Ave San Jose CA 95161

KAPLAN, DONALD ROBERT, biologist, educator; b. Chgo., Jan. 17, 1938; married; 2 children. B.A., Northwestern U., 1960; Ph.D. in Botany, U. Calif., Berkeley, 1965. Asst. prof. biol. scis. U. Calif., Irvine, 1965-68; from asst. to assoc. prof. botany U. Calif., Berkeley, 1968-77, prof. botany, 1977—. NSF fellow, Royal Bot. Garden, 1965. Fellow Linnean Soc. London; mem. AAAS, Bot. Soc. Am. (Merit award 1984), Internat. Soc. Plant Morphology, Am. Soc. Cell Biology. Office: U Calif Dept Botany III Genetics & Plant Biology Berkeley CA 94720

KAPLAN, DONALD SHELDON, real estate developer and rehabilitator, property management company executive; b. L.A., Aug. 1, 1938; s. Adolph Iven and Ruth Janet (Rose) K.; m. Marsha Lynn Le Van, June 12, 1960 (div. July 1980); children: Lisa Ann, Drew Jason; m. Joanne Natalie Cossu, Apr. 19, 1981; children: Alyson Ilene, Tara Ruth. Student, L.A. City Coll., 1957-58, Pacific State U., 1959-60. Pres. DSK Devel. Co., Inc., 1964--, Assured Maintenance Corp., Inc., 1974--, DSK Mgmt. Co., Inc., 1983--, New Renaissance Investmens, Inc., 1986--, Kaplan Enterprises, Inc., L.A., 1986--. Home: 5699 Kanan Rd Apt 234 Agoura Hills CA 91301-3328 Office: Kaplan Enterprises Inc 5699 Kanan Rd Agoura Hills CA 91301-3328

KAPLAN, GARY, executive recruiter; b. Phila., Aug. 14, 1939; s. Morris and Minnie (Leve) K.; m. Linda Ann Wilson, May 30, 1968; children: Michael Warren, Marc Jonathan, Jeffrey Russell. BA in Polit. Sci., Pa. State U., 1961. Tchr. biology N.E. High Sch., Phila., 1962-63; coll. employment rep. Bell Telephone Labs., Murray Hill, N.J., 1966-67; supr. recruitment and placement Unisys, Blue Bell, Pa., 1967-69; pres. Electronic Systems Personnel, Phila., 1969-70; staff selection rep. Booz, Allen & Hamilton, N.Y.C., 1970-72; mgr. exec. recruitment M&T Chems., Rahway, N.J., 1972-74; dir. exec. recruitment IU Internat. Mgmt. Corp., Phila., 1974-78; v.p. personnel Crocker Bank, Los Angeles, 1978-79; mng. v.p. ptnr. western region Korn-Ferry Internat., Los Angeles, 1979-85; pres. Gary Kaplan & Assocs., Pasadena, Calif., 1985—. Mgmt. columnist, Radio and Records newspaper, 1984-85. Chmn. bd. dirs. Vis. Nurse Assn., L.A., 1985-87; bd. dirs. The Wellness Community-Nat. Capt. Adj. Gen. Corps., U.S. Army, 1963-66. Mem. Calif. Exec. Recruiters Assn. (bd. dirs.), Am. Compensation Assn. Home: 1735 Fairmount Ave La Canada Flintridge CA 91011-1632 Office: Gary Kaplan & Assocs 201 S Lake Ave Pasadena CA 91101-3004

KAPLAN, GEORGE WILLARD, urologist; b. Brownsville, Tex., Aug. 24, 1935; s. Hyman J. and Lillian (Bennett) K.; m. Susan Gail Solof, Dec. 17, 1961; children: Paula, Elizabeth, Julie, Alan. BA, U. Tex., 1955; MD, Northwestern U., 1959, MS, 1966. Diplomate Am. Bd. Urology. Intern Charity Hosp. of La. at New Orleans, 1959-60; resident Northwestern U., 1963-68; instr. Med. Sch. Northwestern U., Chgo., 1968-69; clin. prof., chief pediatric urology Sch. Medicine U. Calif., San Diego, 1970—; trustee Children's Hosp. and Health Ctr., San Diego, 1978-90, Am. Bd. Urology, Bingham Farms, Mich., 1991—; del. Am. Bd. Med. Specialties, Evanston, Ill., 1992—. Author: Gentiourinary Problems in Pediatrics; asst. editor Jour. Urology, Balt., 1982-89; assoc. editor Child Nephrology and Urology, Milan, Italy, 1988—; contbr. articles to profl. publs. Pres. med. staff Children's Hosp., San Diego, 1980-82. Lt. USN, 1960-63. Recipient Joseph Capps prize Inst. of Medicine, 1967. Fellow ACS (pres. San Diego chpt. 1980-82), Am. Acad. Pediatrics (chmn. sect. on urology 1986); mem. AMA, Soc. for Pediatric Urology (pres. 1993), Am. Urol. Assn., Soc. Internat. Urologie, Soc. Univ. Urologists. Republican. Jewish. Office: 7930 Frost St Ste 407 San Diego CA 92123

KAPLAN, HELEN, social worker; b. Miami, Fla., Aug. 4, 1948; d. Paul and Lilyan (Field) Sobel; m. Peter L. Kaplan, Nov. 25, 1970; children: Ben, Joshua. BA in Social Work, Colo. State U., 1988; MSW, Denver U., 1989. Bereavement counselor Larimer County Hospice, Ft. Collins, Colo., 1979-1981; clinical internship Catholic Community Svc., Greeley, Colo., 1986-87; internship McKee Med. Ctr., Loveland, Colo., 1988; clinical internship Weld Mental Health, Greeley, 1989; social worker, counselor Poudre RI Sch. Dist., Ft. Collins, 1990—; allocations panel vol. United Way, Ft. Collins, 1981-84; crisis intervention vol. Crisis & Info. Ctr., 1982-84. Mem. Internat. Reading Assn., Nat. Assn. Social Workers, Phi Kappa Phi, Alpha Lambda Delta, Phi Eta Sigma, Golden Key Nat. Hon. Soc.

KAPLAN, HENRY GEORGE, oncologist, educator; b. Staten Island, N.Y., Feb. 3, 1947; s. Alfred H. and Dorothy (Avins) K.; m. Susan V. Dorfman, June 29, 1969; 1 child, Elizabeth. AB in Chemistry, U. Rochester, 1968, MD, 1972. Intern U. Wash., Seattle, 1972-73, resident, 1973-74; chief resident medicine U. Wash., Seattle, Md., 1976-77; asst. prof. medicine U. Wash., Seattle, 1979-81, clin. asst. prof., 1981-88, clin. assoc. prof., 1988—; clin. assoc. oncology Nat. Cancer Inst., Bethesda, Md., 1974-76; asst. prof. Med. Sch. Brown U., Providence, 1979-80; chief oncology Swedish Hosp. Med. Ctr., Seattle, 1986—. Surgeon USPHS, 1974-76. Mem. ACP, Am. Fedn. Clin. Rsch., Am. Assn. Cancer Rsch., Am. Soc. Clin. Oncology, Alpha Omega Alpha. Office: Swedish Hosp Tumor Inst 1221 Madison St Seattle WA 98104

KAPLAN, IRVING EUGENE, human ecologist, psychologist; b. Phila., May 1, 1926; s. Abraham and Bertha (Posner) K.; m. Harriet Bromberg, Sept. 29, 1951; children: Addie Eve, Meryl Denise. BS, L.I. U., 1950; MA, New Sch. Social Rsch., 1953; PhD, U.S. Internat. U., 1971. Lic. psychologist, Calif. Depth interviewer Dr. Ernest Dichter, N.Y.C., 1950-52; employment interviewer N.Y. State Employment Svc., N.Y.C., 1952-56; rsch., program dir. U.S. Naval Personnel Rsch. Activity, San Diego, 1957-66; cons. psychologist San Diego, 1957—, human ecologist, designer, 1962—; cons., writer Ctr. for Study Dem. Instns., Santa Barbara, Calif., 1964-78, UN Law of Sea, N.Y.C. and Jamaica, N.Y., 1970—, Found. Reshaping the Internat. Order, Rotterdam, The Netherlands, 1980-82, UN Comm. Peaceful Uses of Outer Space, N.Y.C. and Vienna, Austria, 1982, Sri Lanka Inst. Advanced Study, 1982; designer in field; rsch. in climatic change. Contbr. articles to profl. jours. Served with USN, 1944-46. Mem. AAAS, Am. Geophys. Union, Am. Psychol. Assn. Home and Office: 3121 Beech St San Diego CA 92102-1535

KAPLAN, JULIUS DAVID, art educator; b. Nashville, Tenn., July 22, 1941; s. Abraham Morris and Ada Sarah (Berlin) K.; m. Robin Lillian Reiser, Mar. 1, 1970. BA, Wesleyan U., 1963; MA, Columbia U., 1965, PhD, 1972. Asst. prof. Colby Coll., Waterville, Maine, 1966, UCLA, 1969-77; assoc. to full prof. Calif. State U., San Bernardino, 1977—, chair art dept., 1979-84, assoc. dean grad. program, 1986-89; dean. grad. studies and rsch. Calif. State U., 1989-91, dean grad. studies, rsch. & faculty devel., 1991—; grad. fellowship adv. com. Calif. Student Aid, Sacramento, 1988-91, visual arts panel Dorland Mountain Colony, Temecula, Calif., 1988—; mem. Arlt com. Coun. Grad. Schs., 1991—. Author: Gustave Moreau, 1982, (with others) The Dictionary of Art, 1990. Recipient Excellence in Teaching award C. of C., 1987; grantee Nat. Endowment for the Arts, 1981-88. Mem. Coll. Art Assn., Art Historians of So. Calif., Calif. Faculty Assn., L.A. County Mus. Art, L.A. Music Ctr. Opera Guild, Phi Kappa Phi. Democrat. Jewish. Office: Calif State U 550 University Pky San Bernardino CA 92407

KAPLAN, MARJORIE ANN PASHKOW, school district administrator; b. Bronx, N.Y., Apr. 10, 1940; d. William B. and Laura (Libov) Pashkow; m. Marvin R. Kaplan, Aug. 12, 1982 (dec. 1980); children: Eliot, Mara; m. Timothy Sweeney, 1985 (div. 1986). BA, Smith Coll., 1962; MA, Ariz. State U., 1974, PhD, 1979. Presch. dir., tchr. Temple Beth Israel, Phoenix, 1967-72; tchr. Washington Sch. Dist., Phoenix, 1972-74, coord., 1974-75, prin., 1975-81; asst. supt. Paradise Valley Unified Sch. Dist., Phoenix, 1981-83, supt., 1984-92; supt. Shawnee Mission Unified Sch. Dist., Overland Park, Kans., 1992—. Named Supt. of Yr., Ariz. Sch. Bd. Assn., 1987-88; named to Top 100 Educators, Exec. Educator mag., 1986. Mem. Am. Assn. Sch. Adminstrs. (Ariz. Supt. of Yr. 1992). Office: Shawnee Mission Unified Sch Dist 512 7235 Antioch Shawnee Mission KS 66214

KAPLAN, MARTIN NATHAN, electrical and electronic engineer; b. Beloit, Wis., Nov. 14, 1916; s. Abraham Louis and Eva (Schomer) K.; m. Florence Helen Grumet (div. 1956); 1 child, Kathy Sue; m. Sylvia Greif, Dec. 7, 1963. BSEE, U. Wis., 1942. Sr. electronics engr. Convair, San Diego, 1951-56; rsch. engr. AMF/Sunstrand, Pacoima, Calif., 1956-59; sr. rsch. engr. Ryan Electronics, San Diego, 1959-63; sr. design engr. N.Am. Aviation, Downey, Calif., 1963-66; rsch. specialist Lockheed, Burbank, Calif., 1966-70; mem. tech. staff Aerospace Corp., El Segundo, Calif., 1980-82; rsch. scientist Motorotor, North Hollywood, Calif., 1983—. Lt. (j.g.) USNR, 1943-46. Mem. IEEE (life), Am. Phys. Soc. (life). Home and Office: Motorotor 11610 Cantlay St North Hollywood CA 91605-3940

KAPLAN, MIKE, film producer, independent film and video distributor; b. Providence, Mar. 16, 1943; s. Julius and Ida (Rabinovitz) K. BA, U. R.I., 1964. Assoc. editor Ind. Film Jour., N.Y.C., 1964-65; publicist MGM, N.Y.C., 1965-68, publicity coord., 1968, nat. publicity dir., 1968-71; v.p.Polaris Prodn. Stanley Kubrick, London, 1971-73; internat mkgt. exec. Warner Bros., L.A., London, 1973-74; pres. Circle Assocs. Ltd., U.S., London, 1973—, Lion's Gate Distbn., 1975-80; mktg. v.p. Lion's Gate Films (Robert Altman), 1975-80; producer, pres. Circle Assoc. Ltd., L.A., 1978—; v.p. mktg. Northstar Internat., Hal Ashby, L.A., 1981-83; pres. mktg. Alive Films, L.A., 1985-87. Producer: (film) The Whales of August, 1987; (video) Oak Grove Sch., 1988; assoc. prodr.: (film) Short Cuts, 1992; co-prodr., co-dir. (documentary) Luck, Trust and Ketchup: Robert Altman in Carver Country, 1993; actor: Buffalo Bill and The Indians, Welcome To L.A., Choose Me, The Player. Recipient Best Film award Nat. Media Awards, Retirement Rsch. Found., 1987, Key Art award Hollywood Reporter, 1976, 87. Mem. Acad. Motion Picture Arts and Scis., Screen Actors Guild, Publicists Guild. Office: Circle Assocs PO Box 5730 Santa Monica CA 90409-5730

KAPLAN, MILTON EMANUEL, retired accountant, tax consultant; b. N.Y.C., Oct. 5, 1914; s. Meyer and Ida (Weinstein) K.; m. Lillian Nathanson Kaplan, Aug. 31, 1937 (dec. Sept. 1990). BBA, CCNY, 1937. CPA, N.Y. Acct. Schnur, Jaffe & Co., N.Y.C., 1937-38, City of N.Y., 1938-41; pvt. practice N.Y.C., 1953-60; internal revenue agt. U.S. Dept. Treasury, N.Y.C., 1941-53, 60-63; internat. examiner U.S. Dept. Treasury, Washington, 1963-71; strike force rep. U.S. Dept. Justice and U.S. Dept. Treasury, Washington and N.Y.C., 1971-74; large case examiner U.S. Dept. Treasury, Mineola, N.Y., 1974-77, ret., 1977. Treas. Israel Ctr., Flushing, N.Y., 1950-74, Congregation Sholom, Seal Beach, Calif., 1977—, Golden Rain Found., Seal Beach, 1987—; mem. appeals bd. City of Seal Beach, 1980—; pres. Mut. 7 Bd., Seal Beach, 1983-87; fin. cons. Leisure World Emergency Meals, 1982—. Recipient Outstanding Svc. award U.S. Dept. Justice Organized Crime and Racketeering Sect., 1974, Albert Gallatin award U.S. Sec. Treasury, 1977, Merit award U. Judaism, 1993. Mem. B'nai Brith (pres. 1982-84, Akiba award 1988), KP (life).

KAPLAN, OZER BENJAMIN, environmental health specialist, consultant; b. Santiago, Chile, Jan. 3, 1940; naturalized U.S. citizen, 1969; s. David and Raquel (Klorman) K.; m. Adele M. Brandt, Jan. 12, 1974. Student, U. Chile, 1958-59; BS, Calif. Polytech. U., 1964; MS, U. Calif., Davis, 1966, PhD, 1969; MPH, UCLA, 1973. Teaching and rsch. asst. U. Calif., Davis, 1968-69; assoc. prof. soil sci. N.C. A & T State U., Greensboro, 1969-70; assoc. prof. biology Morris Coll., Sumter, S.C., 1970-71; ind. cost/benefit cons. L.A., 1971-72; mem. environ. health task force Inland Counties Health Systems Agy., San Bernardino, Calif., 1974-76; environ. health planning coord. San Bernardino County, Calif., 1974-80; ind. cons. environ. health San Bernardino, 1987—. Author: Septic Systems Handbook, 1986, 2d edit. 1990. V.p. Citizens Against Pass Area Prisons, Riverside County, Calif., 1982-86, Pass Citizens for Sound Planning, Riverside County, 1986-91. Mem. Fedn.

Am. Scientists, Am. Soc. Agronomy, Soil Sci. Soc. Am., Calif. Environ. Health Assn. (chmn. land use com., chmn. environ. health sect., Cert. of Appreciation 1976, 77), Nat. Environ. Health Assn., Common Cause, Pub. Citizens, Sigma Xi, Phi Kappa Phi. Home and Office: PO Box 522 Calimesa CA 92320-0522

KAPLAN, RICHARD EMANUEL, academic administrator; b. Phila., July 4, 1938; s. Albert and Eleanor K.; m. Mimi Joy Greenfield, Aug. 14, 1960; children: Hilary Jane ; David Michael. BS, MS, MIT, 1961, ScD, 1964. Asst. prof. U. So. Calif., L.A., 1964-68, assoc. prof., 1968-74, prof., 1974-82, dir. engring. computer lab, 1982-84, dept. chmn., 1983-87, assoc. dean, 1984-87, v. provost, 1987—. Home: 2165 Fern Dell Pl Los Angeles CA 90068 Office: Univ So Calif Adminstrn Bldg 300 Los Angeles CA 90089-4019

KAPLAN, ROBERT B., linguistics educator, consultant, researcher; b. N.Y.C., Sept. 20, 1929; s. Emanuel B. and Natalie K.; m. Audrey A. Lien, Apr. 21, 1951; children—Robin Ann Kaplan Gibson, Lisa Kaplan Morris, Robert Allen. Student, Champlain Coll., 1947-48, Syracuse U., 1948-49; B.A., Willamette U., 1952; M.A., U. So. Calif., 1957, Ph.D., 1962. Teaching asst. U. So. Calif., Los Angeles, 1955-57, instr. coordinator, asst. prof. English communication program for fgn. students, 1965-72, assoc. prof., dir. English communication program for fgn. students, 1972-76, assoc. dean continuing edn., 1973-76, prof. applied linguistics, 1976—, dir. Am. Lang. Inst., 1986-91; instr. U. Oreg., 1957-60; cons. field service program Nat. Assn. Fgn. Student Affairs, 1964-84; pres.-elect faculty senate U. So. Calif., 1988-89, pres., 1989-90; adv. bd. internat. comparability study of standardized lang. exams. U. Cambridge Local Exams. Syndicate. Author: Reading and Rhetoric: A Reader, 1963; (with V. Tufte, P. Cook and J. Aurbach) Transformational Grammar: A Guide for Teachers, 1968; (with R.D. Schoesler) Learning English Through Typewriting, 1969; The Anatomy of Rhetoric: Prolegomena to a Functional Theory of Rhetoric, 1971; On the Scope of Applied Linguistics, 1980; The Language Needs of Migrant Workers, 1980; (with P. Shaw) Exploring Academic English, 1984; (with U. Connor) Writing Across Languages: Analysis of L2 Text, 1987; (with W. Grabe) Introduction To Applied Linguistics, 1991; editorial bd. Standpoints, Jour. Asian Pacific Communication, Internat. Educator, BBC English Dictionary, Second Lang. Instruction/Acquisition Abstracts, Jour. of Second Lang. Writing; contbr. articles to profl. jours., U.S. Australia, Brazil, Can., Chile, Germany, Holland, Japan, Mexico, N.Z., Philippines and Singapore; mem. editorial bd. Oxford Internat. Encyclopedia Linguistics; editor in chief Ann. Rev. Applied Linguistics, 1980-91; contbr. notes, revs. to profl. jours. U.S. and abroad. Bd. dirs. Internat. Bilingual Sch. L.A., 1986-91, Internat. Edn. Research Found., 1986—. Served with inf. U.S. Army, Korea. Fulbright sr. scholar, Australia, 1978, Hong Kong, 1986, New Zealand, 1992. Mem. Am. Anthrop. Assn., AAAS, Am. Assn. Applied Linguistics (v.p., pres. 1992-94) AAUP, Assn. Internationale de Linguistique Applique, Assn. Internationale Pour La Researche et La Diffusion Des Methodes Audio-Visuelles et Structuro-Globales, Assn. Tchrs. English as Second Lang. (chmn. 1968-69), Calif. Assn. Tchrs. English to Speakers Other Langs. (pres. 1970-71), Can. Council Tchrs. English, Nat. Assn. Fgn. Student Affairs (nat. pres. 1983-84), Linguistics Soc. Am., Tchrs. English to Speakers of Other Langs. (1st v.p., pres. 1989-91). Office: U So Calif Dept Linguistics Los Angeles CA 90089-1693

KAPLAN, ROBERT MARSHALL, investment company executive; b. Montreal, Que., Can., Nov. 11, 1936; came to U.S., 1959; s. Albert Oscar and Alice Lillian (Westbury) K.; m. Candace Kay Holt, June 12, 1981; children: Matthew Dana, Meredith Leigh. MBA, Harvard U., 1961; PhD, Mich. State U., 1967. Prof. U. No. Iowa, Cedar Falls, 1971-76, U. Vermont, Burlington, 1976-80; 2nd v.p. Shearson Lehman Hutton, Phoenix, 1981-86; sr. v.p. Drexel Burnham Lambert, Phoenix, 1986-89, Bateman Eichler Hill Richards, Phoenix, 1989—. Author: (books) Marketing Concept in Action, 1964, Salesmanship, 1968; contbr. articles to profl. jours. Bd. dirs. Sun Angel Found., Phoenix, men's league Scottsdale Ctr. for the Arts. Mem. Harvard Bus. Sch. Alumni (pres., bd. dir.). Home: 5546 E Sanna St Paradise Vly AZ 85253-1621 Office: Paine Webber Inc 10220 W Bell Rd Sun City AZ 85351-1177

KAPLAN, RUTH ELIZABETH, private investigating company executive; b. Galveston, Tex., June 1, 1930; d. John Lewis and Katie Irene (Ellis) Swann; m. Alan Millard Kaplan, May 2, 1955; children: Gina Marlene Kaplan, Nicol Charmaine Kaplan Stevenson. MMus, St. Louis Inst. Music, 1949; student, Am. U., Germany, 1957-58, U. Nev., Las Vegas, 1983. Lic. pvt. investigator, Nev. Vocalist numerous TV and radio stas., Harlingen, Weslaco, Tex., 1945-56; vocalist, instrumentalist Kay's Serenaders, Harlingen, 1949-56; talk show host Woman's World Armed Forces TV, Spangdahlem, Germany, 1957-73; asst. fashion coord. Broadway S.W., Las Vegas, 1975-77; co-owner, dep. dir. Atty.'s Investigative Cons., Las Vegas, 1978—; freelance model Joske's, San Antonio, 1951; freelance vocalist and model, Sacramento, 1956; piano and voice tchr., vocalist, model in Germany, Eng., U.S., 1957-73; guest star performer Horace Heidt, Tex., 1947. Named 1st pl. female vocalist for Tex., Ted Mack Amateur Hour, 1946. Mem. Fin. Investigators Network Internat., Pi Mu (nat. coun. 1946-49). Home: 580 N Hollywood Blvd Las Vegas NV 89110 Office: Attys' Investigative Cons PO Box 43029-4500 Las Vegas NV 89116

KAPLAN, SAMUEL, pediatric cardiologist; b. Johannesburg, South Africa, Mar. 28, 1922; came to U.S., 1950, naturalized, 1958; s. Aron Leib and Tema K.; m. Molly Eileen McKenzie, Oct. 17, 1952. MB, BcH., U. Witwatersrand, Johannesburg, 1944, MD, 1949. Diplomate: Am. Bd. Pediatrics. Intern Johannesburg, 1945; registrar in medicine, 1946; lectr. physiology and medicine U. Witwatersrand, 1946-49; registrar in medicine U. London, 1949-50; fellow in cardiology, research assoc. U. Cin., 1950-54, asst. prof. pediatrics, 1954-61, assoc. prof. pediatrics, 1961-66, prof. pediatrics, 1967-87, asst. prof. medicine, 1954-67, assoc. prof. medicine, 1967-82, prof. medicine, 1982-87; prof. pediatrics UCLA, 1987—; cons. NIH; hon. prof. U. Santa Tomas, Manila. Mem. editorial bd. Circulation, 1974-80, Am. Jour. Cardiology, 1976-81, Am. Heart Jour, 1981—, Jour. Electrocardiology, 1977—, Clin. Cardiology, 1979—, Jour. Am. Coll. Cardiology, 1983-87, Progress Pediat. Cardiology, 1990—. Cecil John Adams fellow, 1949-50; grantee Heart, Lung and Blood Inst. of NIH, 1960—. Mem. Am. Pediatric Soc., Am. Soc. Pediatric Research, Am. Heart Assn. (med. adv. bd. sect. circulation), Am. Fedn. Clin. Research, Am. Coll. Cardiology, Internat. Cardiovascular Soc., Am. Acad. Pediatrics, Am. Assn. Artificial Internal Organs, Midwest Soc. Pediatric Research (past pres.), Sigma Xi, Alpha Omega Alpha; hon. mem. Peruvian Soc. Cardiology, Peruvian Soc. Angiology, Chilean Soc. Cardiology, Burma Med. Assn. Office: UCLA Sch Medicine Dept Pediatric Cardiology Los Angeles CA 90024

KAPLOWITZ, KAREN (JILL), lawyer; b. New Haven, Nov. 27, 1946; d. Charles Cohen and Estelle (Gerber) K.; m. Alan George Cohen, Aug. 17, 1980; children: Benjamin, Elizabeth. BA cum laude, Barnard Coll., 1968; JD, U. Chgo., 1971. BarL Calif. 1971, U.S. Dist. Ct. (cen. dist.) Calif. 1971. Assoc. O'Melveny & Myers, L.A., 1971-74; ptnr. Bardeen, Bersch & Kaplowitz, L.A., 1974-80, Alschuler, Grossman & Pines, L.A., 1980—. Contbr. articles to profl. jours. Mem. vis. com. U. Chgo. Law Sch., 1990-93. Mem. Assn. Bus. Trial Lawyers (bd. govs.), Calif. Women Lawyers (Fay Stender award 1982), Women Lawyers Assn. L.A. Home: 216 Marguerita Ave Santa Monica CA 90402-1622 Office: Alschuler Grossman & Pines 1880 Century Park E Fl 12 Los Angeles CA 90067-1600

KAPLOWITZ, RICHARD ALLEN, academic dean; b. Bklyn., Dec. 12, 1940; s. Joseph and Sonya (Taub) K.; m. Lisette Feldstein, Dec. 22, 1964 (div. Oct. 1990); children: David, Robert. BA, Bklyn. Coll., 1961; MA, Columbia U., 1962; EdD, Harvard U., 1970. Tchr. various schs. N.Y., France, 1962-67; founding dir. Weekend Coll., C.W. Post U., Greenvale, N.Y., 1970-72; dean continuing edn. Merrimack Coll., North Andover, Mass., 1974-80; dir. human resource devel. Raytheon Co., Andover, Mass., 1980-82; pres. Teem Inc., Andover, 1982-90; dean New England Inst., Boston, 1985-87, chair grad. div. Notre Dame Coll., Manchester, N.H., 1988-90; v.p. enrollment mgmt. Pacific Grad. Sch. Psychology, Palo Alto, Calif., 1990—. Author: Selecting Academic Administrators, 1973, Selecting College and University Personnel: The Quest and the Questions, 1988; contbr. articles to profl. jours. Pres. Greater Lawrence Mental Health and Retardation Bd., 1977-79; overseer Lawrence Gen. Hosp., 1980-90. Mem. Assn. Continuing Higher Edn. (bd. dirs. 1979-82). Jewish. Avocation: flying. Home: 181 El Carmelo Palo Alto CA 94306 Office: Pacific Grad Sch of Psychology 935 E Meadow Mountain View CA 94303

KAPP, ELEANOR JEANNE, impressionistic artist, writer, researcher; b. Hagerstown, Md., Oct. 16, 1933; d. James Norman and Nellie Belle (Welty) Weagley; m. Alan Howard Kapp, Sept. 25, 1972. Cert., L.A. Interior Design, 1969; student, U. Utah, 1976-82. Artist Farmers Ins. Group, L.A., 1960-63; interior designer W&J Sloane, Beverly Hills, Calif., 1965-70; ski resort exec. Snowpine Lodge, Alta, Utah, 1970-84; dir. mktg. and pub. rels. Alta Resort Assn., 1979-84; free-lance photographer Alta, 1979—; bus. owner Creative Art Enterprises, Sandy, Utah, 1984-85; artist-resident Blackhawk Graphic Gallery, Danville, Calif., 1991—; owner Art of Jeanne Kapp, Lafayette, Calif., 1985—. Author, pub.: The American Connection, 1985, 91; author, prodr. (documentary) A Look at China Today, 1981; photographer: Best of the West, 1983. Promotion liaison Alta Town Coun., 1980-84; floral decorator Coun. State Govts., Snowbird, Utah, 1976; photographer Utah Dems., Salt Lake City, 1981; exhibit curator Salt Lake County Libr. System, 1982, founder Alta Br. Libr., 1982; fundraiser Friends of Libr., Alta, 1982; mem. Alta Town-Libr. Adv. Bd., 1983. Recipient Cert. of Appreciation, Salt Lake County Libr. System, 1981, Cert. of Recognition, Gov. Cal Rampton, Salt Lake City, 1972-74, Calendar Cover award Utah Travel Coun., 1981, Internat. Invitational Art Exhibit, Centre Internat. D'Art Conempor., Paris, 1983. Mem. Diablo Art Assn. (pub. rels. chmn. 1987, Hon. Mention award 1989), Concord Art Assn. (1st place award 1991), Alamo and Danville Artist's Soc. (cir. leader 1990—, Hon. Mention award 1991), Las Junas Artist Assn. (juror's asst. 1992, 2d Place award 1992). Home: 411 Donegal Way Lafayette CA 94549

KAPPEN, CLAUDIA THERESE, molecular biologist; b. Remscheid, Germany, Apr. 5, 1958; came to U.S., 1988; d. Hermann-Josef and Ursula Elisabeth (Müller) K.; m. Thomas Risse-Kappen, Aug. 8, 1980. MSc, U. Cologne (Germany), 1983, PhD, 1987. Postdoctoral fellow dept. biology Yale U., New Haven, 1988-90, postdoctoral assoc. dept. biology, 1990-92; asst. prof., assoc cons dept. biochemistry/molecular biology Mayo Clinic, Scottsdale, Ariz., 1992—; spokesperson for profl. women in sci. and tech. Profl. Women in Sci. and Tech., Germany, 1981-88; invited speaker on topics of sci. and tech. multiple orgns. and instns., 1984-88. Mem. subcom. on women in sci. German Fedn. Univ. Women, Germany, 1984-88. Postdoctoral fellow German Rsch. Soc., 1988-90. Mem. AAAS, Soc. for Devel. Biology, Neurosci. Soc. Roman Catholic. Home: Dr # 338 10080 E MountainView Lake Scottsdale AZ 85258 Office: Mayo Clinic/Rsch 13400 E Shea Blvd Scottsdale AZ 85259

KARABATSOS, ELIZABETH ANN, aerospace industry executive; b. Geneva, Nebr., Oct. 25, 1932; d. Karl Christian and Margaret Maurine (Emrich) Brinkman; m. Kimon Tom Karabatsos, Apr. 21, 1957 (div. Feb. 1981); children: Tom Kimon, Maurine Elizabeth, Karl Kimon. BS, U. Nebr., 1954; postgrad., Ariz. State U., 1980; Cert. contemporary exec. devel., George Washington U., 1985. Instr. bus. Fairbury (Nebr.) High Sch., 1954-55; staff asst. U.S. Congress, Washington, 1955-60; with Karabatsos & Co. Pub. Relations, Washington, 1960-73; conf. asst. to asst. adminstr. and dep. adminstr. Gen. Services Adminstrn., Washington, 1973-76; dir. corr. Office Pres.-Elect, Washington, 1980; assoc. dir. adminstrv. services Pres. Personnel-White House, Washington, 1981; dept. asst.to Sec. and Dep. Sec. Def., Washington, 1981-86, asst. to, 1987-89; dir. govt. and civic affairs McDonnell Douglas Helicopter Co., Mesa, Ariz., 1989-90, gen. mgr. gen. svcs., 1990-92, co. ombudsman, community rels. exec., 1992—; bd. dirs. S.W. Inst. Dispute Resolution. Mem. Nat. Mus. Women in Art, Washington; bd. dirs. East Valley Partnership, U.S. C. of C. Com. on Labor & Tng.; mem. Gov.'s Sci. and Tech. Com., Mem. Ariz. Com. Employer Support for the Guard and Res., 1991; active Gov. Com. for Ariz. Clean and Beautiful, World Affairs Coun. of Ariz., Valley Contbrs. Assn. Mem. AAUW, Women in Def. (nat. & Ariz. chpts.), Mesa C. of C. (bd. dirs.), Order Eastern Star, Pi Omega Pi, Pi Beta Phi. Episcopalian. Home: 7818 E Montebello Ave Scottsdale AZ 85250-6173

KARAHALIOS, SUE M. COMPTON, secondary education educator; b. Newport, R.I., May 8, 1949; d. Raymond F. and Elsie R. (Hall) Compton; divorced; children: Herb, Nicole, Korren, Corey. BS, U. New Orleans, 1970; MEd, Western Wash. U., 1979; postgrad., U. Wash. Cert. tchr., Wash. Instr. Skagit Valley Coll., Oak Harbor, Wash., 1971—; tchr. Oak Harbor Sch. Dist., 1971—; mem. Wash. State Ho. Reps., 1993—. Contbr. articles to profl. jours. Named Tch. of the Yr., Oak Harbor, 1979; recipient gifted grant 1988. Mem. NEA, Wash. Edn. Assn. (pres.), Oak Harbor Edn. Assn., Phi Delta Kappa, Delta Kappa Gamma.

KARAKEY, SHERRY JOANNE, financial and real estate investment company executive, interior designer; b. Wendall, Idaho, Apr. 16, 1942; d. John Donald and Vera Ella (Frost) Kingery; children: Artist Roxanne, Buddy (George II), Kami JoAnne, Launi JoElla. Student, Ariz. State U., 1960. Corp. sec., treas. Karbel Metals Co., Phoenix, 1963-67; sec. to pub. Scottsdale (Ariz.) Daily Progress, 1969-72; with D-Velco Mfg. of Ariz., Phoenix, 1959-62, dir., exec. v.p., sec., treas., 1972-87; mng. ptnr. Karitage, Ltd., Scottsdale, 1987—.

KARALASH, BEVERLY KAY, sales executive; b. South Bend, Ind., Nov. 15, 1958; d. Joseph Louis and Betty Lou (Walkowski) Elias; m. Daniel Michael Karalash, Dec. 12, 1981; 1 child, Morgan Danielle. BS, Mich. State U., 1981; postgrad., Cen. Mich. U., 1986-87. Med. technologist Lee Meml. Hosp., Dowagiac, Mich., 1981; sales rep. Consolidated Biomed. Lab., Sacramento, 1982-83, Roche Biomed. Labs., Mich., 1983-87; sr. sales specialist Roche Biomed. Labs., Sacramento, 1988, assoc. dist. sales mgr., 1989, dist. sales mgr., 1990; dist. sales mgr. MetWest Clin. Labs., Sacramento, 1991—. Mem. Officer's Wive's Club, U.S., 1982-91. Named one of Outstanding Young Women of Am., 1987. Roman Catholic. Home: 14 Sedley Ct Sacramento CA 95823

KARASA, NORMAN LUKAS, home builder, geologist; b. Balt., June 10, 1951; s. Norman and Ona K.; m. Lois J. Hansen, Jan. 4, 1974; children: Andrew, Jane. AB in Geology, Rutgers U., 1973; MS in Geophysics, U. Wyo., 1976; MBA in Fin., U. Colo., Colorado Springs, 1990. Systems mgr. Brit. Petroleum, N.Y.C., 1973-74; seismic processing leader Phillips Petroleum, Bartlesville, Okla., 1976-79; geophysicist Phillips Petroleum, Houston, 1979-80; internat. spl. project geophysicist Marathon Oil, Findlay, Ohio, 1980-82; internat. exploration geophysicist Marathon Oil, Houston, 1982-85, internat. reservoir geologist/geophysicist, 1985-86; home builder, designer, owner Monument (Colo.) Homes, 1986—, developer, 1992—; lic. stock broker, ins. advisor Prin. Group, Colo., 1987—. Active Boy Scouts Am., Colo., 1987—. Mem. Home Builder Assocs. Presbyterian. Office: Monument Homes PO Box 1423 Monument CO 80132

KARATZ, BRUCE E., business executive; b. Chgo., Oct. 10, 1945; s. Robert Harry and Naomi Rae (Goldstein) K.; m. Janet Louise Dreisen, July 28, 1968; children: Elizabeth, Matthew, Theodore. BA, Boston U., 1967; JD, U. So. Calif., 1970. Bar: Calif. 1971. Assoc. Keatinge & Sterling, Los Angeles, 1970-72; assoc. corp. counsel Kaufman and Broad, Inc., Los Angeles, 1972-73; dir. forward planning Kaufman and Broad, Inc., Irvine, Calif., 1973-74; pres. Kaufman and Broad Provence, Aix-en-Provence, France, 1974-76, Kaufman and Broad France, Paris, 1976-80, Kaufman and Broad Devel. Group, Los Angeles, 1980-86; pres., chief exec. officer Kaufman and Broad Home Corp., Los Angeles, 1986—, also bd. dirs.; bd. dirs. MacFrugal's Bargains, Close-Outs, Inc., Honeywell Corp. Mem. bd. govs. Cedars Sinai Med. Ctr., L.A., 1983—; founder Mus. Contemporary Art, L.A., 1981; trustee Pitzer Coll., Claremont, Calif., 1983—; bd. dirs. Coro Found., 1981; trustee, pres. Wilshire Blvd. Temple. Mem. Young Pres.' Orgn. Democrat. Office: Kaufman & Broad Home Corp 10877 Wilshire Blvd Los Angeles CA 90024-4341*

KARL, GEORGE, professional basketball coach; b. Penn Hills, Pa., May 12, 1951; m. Cathy Karl; children—Kelci Ryanne, Coby Joseph. Grad., U. N.C., 1973. Guard San Antonio Spurs, NBA, 1973-78, asst. coach, head scout, 1978-80; coach Mont. Golden Nuggets, Continental Basketball Assn., 1980-83; dir. player acquisition Cleve. Cavaliers, 1983-84, coach, 1984-86; head coach Golden State Warriors, Oakland, Calif., from 1986, Albany (N.Y.) Patrons, 1988-89, 90-91, Real Madrid, Spain, 1991-92, Seattle Supersonics, 1992—. Named Coach of Yr., Continental Basketball Assn., 1981, 83. Mem. Continental Basketball Assn. Office: care Seattle Supersonics 190 Queen Anne Ave N Seattle WA 98109-4926

KARLEN, PETER HURD, lawyer, writer; b. N.Y.C., Feb. 22, 1949; s. S. H. and Jean Karlen; m. Lynette Ann Thwaites, Dec. 22, 1978. BA in History, U. Calif., Berkeley, 1971; JD, U. Calif., Hastings, 1974; MS in Law and Soc., U. Denver, 1976. Bar: Calif. 1974, U.S. Dist. Ct. (so. dist.) Calif. 1976, U.S. Dist. Ct. (no. dist.) Calif. 1983, Hawaii 1989, U.S. Supreme Ct. 1990, Colo. 1991. Assoc. Sankary & Sankary, San Diego, 1976; teaching fellow Coll. of Law U. Denver, 1974-75; lectr. Sch. of Law U. Warwick, United Kingdon, 1976-78; pvt. practice La Jolla, Calif., 1979-86; prin. Peter H. Karlen, P.C., La Jolla, 1986—; adj. prof. U. San Diego Sch. of Law, 1979-84; mem. adj. faculty Western State U. Coll. of Law, San Diego, 1976, 79-80, 88, 92—. Contbg. editor Artweek, 1979—, Art Calendar, 1989—, Art Cellar Exch. mag., 1989—; mem. editorial bd. Copyright World, 1988—; contbr. numerous articles to profl. jours. Mem. ABA, Am. Soc. for Aesthetics, San Diego County Bar Assn., Brit. Soc. Aesthetics. Office: 1205 Prospect St Ste 400 La Jolla CA 92037-3682

KARLESKINT, BARRY MICHAEL, retail store executive, landscape contractor; b. Santa Maria, Calif., May 25, 1941; s. John Peter and Mary Alward (Fitzgerald) K.; student Calif. State Poly. U., 1959-62; m. Brenda Signorelli, July 20, 1963; children: Kenneth Brian, Robert Jasen, Ann Marie. Foreman, Landscape Dept., Karleskint's Florist & Nursery, San Luis Obispo, 1962-67; v.p. Landscape Dept., Karleskint-Crum, Inc., San Luis Obispo, Calif., 1969-91, v.p., retail gen. mgr., 1975, pres., 1980-85, gen. mgr. 1985-91; pres., dir. Canyon Leasing Co., 1984—; pres. KC Stores Inc., San Luis Obispo, 1985—, also bd. dirs.; instr. San Luis Coastal Sch. Dist. Adult Sch., 1977-78; gen. ptnr. Suburban Assocs.; cons. in field. Mem. organizing com. Obispo Beautiful Assn., 1970; mem. San Luis Obispo City Joint Use Adv. Com., 1985-89; pres. Mission-Nativity Parents Assn., 1974-76, mem. sch. bd., 1974-76; pres. Nativity of Our Lady Cath. Ch. Council, 1977; mem. San Luis Obispo City Parks and Recreation Commn., 1981-89; com. chmn. 1987-89; mem. San Luis Obispo City Tree Com., 1981-84; mem. San Luis City Planning Commn., 1989— (com. chmn. 1992—). Served with U.S. Army, 1962, USAR, 1962-66, USNG, 1966-68. Cert. nurseryman, Calif. Mem. Calif. Assn. Nurserymen (chpt. dir. 1978-80), Calif. Landscape Contractor's Assn. (chpt. dir. 1964-66), alif. State Sheriff's Assn., Controller's Roundtable San Luis Obispo, Roman Catholic. Clubs: San Luis Obispo Swim (pres. 1977-78); KC, Old Mission Sch. Booster (sec. 1961-63), Rotary (pres.-elect 1992-93). Home: 623 Jeffrey Dr San Luis Obispo CA 93405-1021 Office: 1422 Monterey St San Luis Obispo CA 93401-2996

KARLIN, SAMUEL, mathematics educator, researcher; b. Yonova, Poland, June 8, 1924; s. Morris K.; m. Elsie (div.); children—Kenneth, Manuel, Anna. B.S. in Math., Ill. Inst. Tech., 1944; Ph.D. in Math., Princeton U., 1947; D.Sc. (hon.), Technion-Israel Inst. Tech., Haifa, 1985. Instr. math. Calif. Inst. Tech., Pasadena, 1948-49; asst. prof. Calif. Inst. Tech., 1949-52, assoc. prof., 1952-55, prof., 1955-56; vis. asst. prof. Princeton U., N.J., 1950-51; prof. Stanford U., Calif., 1956—; Andrew D. White prof.-at-large Cornell U., 1975-81; Wilks lectr. Princeton U.., 1977; pres. Inst. Math. Stats., 1978-79; Commonwealth lectr. U. Mass., 1980; 1st Mahalanobis meml. lectr. Indian Statis. Inst., 1983, prin. invited speaker XII Internat. Biometics Meeting, Japan; prin. lectr. Que. Math. Soc., 1984; adv. dean math. dept. Weizmann Inst. Sci., Israel, 1970-77; Britton lectr. McMaster U., Hamilton, Ont., Can., 1990. Author: Mathematical Methods and Theory in Games, Programming, Economics, Vol. I: Matrix Games, Programming and Mathematical Economics, 1959, Mathematical Methods and Theory in Games, Programming, Economics, Vol. II: The Theory of Infinite Games, 1959, A First Course in Stochastic Processes, 1966, Total Positivity Vol. I, 1968; (with K. Arrow and H. Scarf) Studies in the Mathematical Theory of Inventory and Production, 1958; (with W.J. Sudden) Tchebycheff Systems: With Applications in Analysis and Statistics, 1966; (with H. Taylor) A First Course in Stochastic Processes, 2d edit., 1975, A Second Course in Stochastic Processes, 1980, An Introduction to Stochastic Modeling, 1984; (with C.A. Micchelli, A. Pinkus, I.I. Schoenberg) Studies in Spline Functions and Approximation Theory, 1976; editor: (with E. Nevo) Population Genetics and Ecology, 1976; (with T. Amemiya and L.A. Goodman) Studies in Econometric, Time Series, and Multivariate Statistics, 1983; (with K. Arrow and P. Suppes) Contributions to Mathematical Methods in the Social Sciences, 1960; (with K. Arrow and H. Scarf) Studies in Applied Probability and Management Sciences, 1962; (with S. Lessard) Theoretical Studies on Sex Ratio Evolution, 1986; editor: (with E. Nevo) Evolutionary Processes and Theory, 1986; sr. editor Theoretical Population Biology, Jour. D'Analyse; assoc. editor Jour. Math. Analysis, Lecture Notes in Biomath., Jour. Applied Probability, Jour. Multivariate Analysis, Jour. Approximation Theory, SIAM Jour. Math. Analysis, Jour. Linear Algebra, Computers and Math. with Applications, Ency. of Math. and Its Applications, Advanced in Applied Math.; contbr. articles to profl. jours. Recipient Lester R. Ford award Am. Math. Monthly, 1973, Robert Grimmett Chair Math., Stanford U., 1978, The John Von Neumann Theory prize, 1987, U.S. Nat. Medal Sci., 1989; Proctor fellow, 1945, Bateman Research fellow, 1947-48; fellow Guggenheim Found., 1959-60, NSF, 1960-61; Wald lectr., 1957. Fellow AAAS, Internat. Statis. Inst., Inst. Math. Stats.; mem. NAS (award in applied math. 1973), Am. Math. Soc., Am. Acad. Arts and Scis., Am. Soc. Human Genetics, Genetic Soc. Am., Am. Naturalist Soc., Human Genome Orgn., London Math. Soc. (elected hon. 1991). Office: Stanford U Bldg 380 Stanford CA 94305

KARLOVICH, ROBERT JOSEPH, engineering executive; b. Carlisle, Pa., Oct. 8, 1964; s. Edward James and Barbara Jane (Schlemmer) K. BSME, Pa. State U., 1988. Co-op engr. GM Design Staff, GM Tech. Ctr., Warren, Mich., 1985-87; product engr. AMP Inc., Harrisburg, Pa., 1988-89, devel. engr., 1989-91; design engr. Foxconn Internat. Inc., Sunnyvale, Calif., 1991-92, strategic account mgr., 1992—; summer engr. AMP Inc., Harrisburg, 1987; guest lectr. San Jose (Calif.) State U., 1992. Inventor, patentee in field. Chmn. Industry/ASME Adv. Coun., Santa Clara Valley, Calif., 1992—; publicity chmn. Bay Area Tech. Conf., Belmont, Calif., 1992, Micro Electromechanical Systems Tech. Conf., Berkely, 1993. Mem. ASME (Santa Clara Valley sect., mentor 1992, industry rels. chair 1992—, exec. com. Susquehanna Valley sect. 1991, vice chmn. Task Force 2001 1992—), Internat. Inst. Connector and Interconnection Tech., Pa. State U. Alumni Assn., Silcon Valley Club (bd. dirs. 1992—). Office: Foxconn Internat Inc 930 W Maude Ave Sunnyvale CA 94086

KARLTON, LAWRENCE K., federal judge; b. Bklyn., May 28, 1935; s. Aaron Katz and Sylvia (Meltzer) K.; m. Mychelle Stiebel, Sept. 7, 1958. Student, Washington Sq. Coll.; LL.B., Columbia U., 1958. Bar: Fla. 1958, Calif. 1962. Acting legal officer Sacramento Army Depot, Dept. Army, Sacramento, 1959-60; civilian legal officer Sacramento Army Depot, Dept. Army, 1960-62; individual practice law Sacramento, 1962-64; mem. firm Abbott, Karlton & White, 1964, Karlton & Blease, until 1971, Karlton, Blease & Vanderlaan, 1971-76; judge Calif. Superior Ct. for Sacramento County, 1976-79, U.S. Dist. Ct. (ea. dist.) Calif., Sacramento, 1979—; formerly chief judge U.S. Dist. Ct., Sacramento. Co-chmn. Central Calif. council B'nai B'rith Anit-Defamation League Commn., 1964-65; treas. Sacramento Jewish Community Relations Council, chmn., 1967-68. Mem. Am. Bar Assn., Sacramento County Bar Assn. Club: B'nai B'rith (past pres.). Office: US Dist Ct 2012 US Courthouse 650 Capitol Mall Sacramento CA 95814-4708*

KARNIK, AVINASH RAMKRISHNA, electronics engineer; b. Bombay, May 31, 1940; came to U.S., 1964; s. Ramkrishna W. and Ashalata R. K.; m. Aruna A. Wadhavkar, Jan. 12, 1969; children: Jwala, Prachi. BE, U. Bombay, 1961; M Tech., Indian Inst. Tech., Bombay, 1963; PhD, U. Rochester, 1969. Rsch. scientist Xerox Corp., Webster, N.Y., 1969-71, devel. engr., 1972-74, mgr. systems, 1976-81; mgr. process rsch. Rank Xerox, Eng., 1974-76; project mgr. Electrosystems div. Aerojet, Azusa, Calif., 1981-82, mgr. electronics, 1982-84, chief engr. for design, 1984-86, chief engr. for systems, 1986-91; instrument mgr. jet propulsion lab, 1991. Contbr. articles to profl. jours.; inventor blade for metering liquid devel. Founder Rochester chpt. Assn. Indians in Am., 1976; mem. conv. exec. com. Brihan Maharashtra Mandal, L.A., 1991. Mem. Sigma Xi. Office: Jet Propulsion Lab 4800 Oak Grove Dr Pasadena CA 91109-8099

KARP, AARON S., artist; b. Altoona, Pa., Dec. 7, 1947; s. Max and Betty Rae (Helf) K. BA, SUNY, Buffalo, 1969; MFA, Ind. U., 1973. Dir. gallery East Carolina U., Greenville, N.C., 1977-79; asst. prof. art U. N.Mex., Albuquerque, 1979-84; artist-in-residence Roswell (N.Mex.) Mus. and Art Ctr., 1981. One-man shows, 1984, SUNY, Albany, 1990, Barclay Simpson Gallery, Lafayette, Calif., 1990, Janus Gallery, Santa Fe, 1990, Katharine Rich Perlow Gallery, N.Y.C., 1991, Rosischon Gallery, Denver, 1991, Helander Gallery, Palm Beach, Fla., 1992, Amarillo Art Ctr., Tex., 1992, Barclay Simpson, 1992, Janus, Sante Fe, 1992; exhibited in group shows, 1979—, including Guggenheim Mus., N.Y.C., 1982, Mus. Fine Art, Santa Fe, 1987, Eve Mannes Gallery, Atlanta, 1990; represented in permanent collections U. N.Mex. Art Mus., Gray Mus., East Carolina U., Ackland Art Ctr., U. N.C., Mus. Fine Arts, Sante Fe, Albuquerque Mus., various corps., also numerous others. Recipient Exxon Corp. purchase award Guggenheimm Mus., 1983; grantee U. N.Mex., 1979, 80, 82, 84. Home and Studio: 7811 Guadalupe Trail NW Albuquerque NM 87107

KARP, RICHARD ALAN, computer scientist; b. Chgo., May 1, 1944; s. Mark Lawrence and Mildred Marcia (Citron) K.; m. Nancy Kay Hood, Sept. 6, 1974; children: John Lee, Michael David. BS, Calif. Inst. of Tech., 1964; MS, U. Wis., 1966; PhD, Stanford U., Palo Alto, Calif., 1980. V.p. software, founder Sequoia Systems Inc., Marlborough, Mass., 1980-82; v.p. software Tri-Data Corp., Mountain View, Calif., 1982-85; pres. ISON Technologies Corp., Mountain View, 1985—; cons. Control Data Corp., Durango Systems, Palo Alto, 1978-80, Data Delecta, various Swedish mcpl. and govt. orgns., Stockholm, 1984-85; mem., rep. U.S. and Internat. Stds. Orgns., 1970-74. Author: Proving Operating Systems Correct, 1982; inventor concurrent system design. Vol. Peace Corps, Baguio City, Manila Philippines, 1966-69; v.p. So. Calif. Peace Corps. Svc. Coun., L.A., 1970-73. Recipient Disting. Svc. So. Calif. Peace Corps. Svc. Coun., 1973. Mem. Assn. for Computing Machinery, Math. Assn. of Am. Office: ISON Technologies Corp 1940 Colony St Mountain View CA 94043

KARPAN, KATHLEEN MARIE, state official, lawyer, journalist; b. Rock Springs, Wyo., Sept. 1, 1942; d. Thomas Michael and Pauline Ann (Taucher) K. B.S. in Journalism, U. Wyo., 1964, M.A. in Am. Studies, 1975; J.D., U. Oreg., 1978. Bar: D.C. 1979, Wyo. 1983, U.S. Dist. Ct. Wyo., U.S. Ct. Appeals (D.C. and 10th cirs.). Asst. news editor Cody Enterprise, Wyo., 1964; press asst. to U.S. Congressman Teno Roncalio U.S. Ho. of Reps., Washington, 1965-67, 71-72, adminstrv. asst., 1973-74; asst. news editor Wyo. Eagle, Cheyenne, 1967; free-lance writer, 1968; teaching asst. dept. history U. Wyo., 1969-70; desk editor Canberra Times, Australia, 1970; dep. dir. Office Congl. Relations, Econ. Devel. Adminstrn. U.S. Dept. Commerce, Washington, 1979-80, atty. advisor Office of Chief Counsel, Econ. Devel. Adminstrn., 1980-81; campaign mgr. Rodger McDaniel for U.S. Senator, Wyo., 1981-82; asst. atty. gen. State of Wyo., Cheyenne, 1983-84, dir. Dept. Health and Social Services, 1984-86, sec. of state, 1987—. Del. Dem. Nat. Conv., San Francisco, 1984, Atlanta, 1988, N.Y.C., 1992; mem. bd. govs. Nat. Dem. Leadership Coun., drafting com. Dem. Nat. Platform, Santa Fe, 1992. W.R. Coe fellow, 1969. Mem. Wyo. Bar Assn., Bus. and Profl. Women, Rotary, Zonta. Roman Catholic. Home: 410 W 2d Ave Cheyenne WY 82001 Office: Wyo Sec of State State Capitol Cheyenne WY 82002

KARPELES, DAVID, museum director; b. Santa Barbara, Calif., Jan. 26, 1936; s. Leon and Betty (Friedman) K.; m. Marsha Mirsky, June 29, 1958; children: Mark, Leslie, Cheryl, Jason. BS, U. Minn., 1956, postgrad., 1956-59; MA, San Diego State U., 1962; postgrad., U. Calif., Santa Barbara, 1965-69. Dir., founder Karpeles Manuscript Libr. Mus., Montecito, Calif., 1983—, Santa Barbara, Calif., 1988—, N.Y.C., 1990—, Tacoma, Wash., 1991—, Jacksonville, Fla., 1992—. Creator program to provide ownershp of homes to low-income families. Recipient Affordable Housing Competition award Gov. Edmund G. Brown Jr., State of Calif., Dept. Housing and Community Devel., 1981. Jewish. Home: 465 Hot Springs Rd Santa Barbara CA 93108

KARPENKO, VICTOR NICHOLAS, mechanical engineer; b. Harbin, China, Jan. 23, 1922; s. Nicholas Stephan and Sophia Andrea (Kootas) K.; came to U.S., 1941, naturalized, 1943; student San Francisco State Coll., 1941-42, Oreg. State Coll., 1943; B.S. in Mech. Engring., U. Calif., Berkeley, 1948; m. Lydia Kamotsky, June 23, 1950; children—Victor, Mark, Alexandra. Staff engr. Atomic Products Equipment div. Gen. Electric Co., San Jose, Calif., 1956-57; project engr. nuclear explosives engring. Lawrence Livermore (Calif.) Lab., 1957-65, sect. leader nuclear explosives engring., 1965-66, div. leader Nuclear Test Engring. div., 1966-76, project mgr. Mirror Fusion Test Facility, 1976-85; div. head Magnet System Superconducting Super Collider, Univ. Research Assn., Berkeley, Calif., 1986-87, cons., 1987—; ptnr. devel. cryogenic equipment PHPK Tech. Inc., Columbus, Ohio, 1992—; mem. fusion reactor safety com. Dept. Energy; mem. Containment Evaluation Panel, ERDA. Dist. chmn. U. Calif. Alumni Scholarship Program, 1976-80; com. mem. U. Calif. Alumni Scholarship Program, 1972-76; pres. San Ramon AAU Swim Club, 1964. Served with AUS, 1943-46. Registered profl. mech. and nuclear engr., Calif. Mem. Am. Nuclear Soc., Calif. Alumni Assn. Republican. Greek Orthodox. Home: 613 Bradford Pl Danville CA 94526-2357

KARPILOW, CRAIG, physician; b. San Francisco, Oct. 23, 1947; s. David and Babette (David) K.; BSc, U. Alta. (Can.), 1967; MA, U. So. Calif., 1970; M.D., Dalhousie U., 1974. Diplomate Canadian Coll. of Family Practice. Intern, Dalhousie U., Halifax, N.S., Can., 1974-75; resident in family practice medicine Meml. U. Nfld., St. John's, 1975-77; practice medicine specializing in family medicine and occupational medicine, 1978-81; practice occupational medicine, Snohomish, Wash., 1981-83; med. health officer Storey County, Nev., 1978-80; med. dir. Med. Ctr., Dayton, 1978-81; pres. Internat. Profl. Assocs. Ltd., 1978—; med. dir./clin. N.W. Occupational Health Ctrs., Seattle, 1983-84; ptnr. physician, co-dir. CHEC Med. Ctr., Seattle, 1984-85; head dept. occupational and diagnostic medicine St. Cabrini Hosp., Seattle, 1984-86; med. dir. N.W. Indsl. Svcs., 1985-86, Queen Anne Med. Ctr., Seattle, 1985—, Travel Med. and Immunization Clinic of Seattle, 1986—; ptnr. Clin. Assocs., 1990—. Diplomate Am. Bd. Family Practice; licenciate Med. Coll. Can. Fellow Am. Acad. Family Practice, Am. Coll. Occupational & Environmental Medicine, Royal Soc. Tropical Medicine, Am. Coll. Occupational Medicine (recorder Ho. of Dels./bd. dirs. 1990-91); mem. AMA, Am. Soc. Tropical Medicine and Hygiene, Wash. State Med. Assn. King County Med. Soc., Wash. Acad. Family Physicians (rsch. collaborative, dir. Com. on Rsch.), Am. Coll. Occupational and Environ. Medicine (chmn. internat. occupational medicine sect.), N.W. Occupational Med. Assn. (bd. dirs. 1985-92, pres. 1990-91), Can. Soc. for Internat. Health, Can. Pub. Health Assn., Am. Com. Clin., Tropical and Travel Medicine, Can. Soc. of Northwest, Marimed Found. Pacific N.W. (adv. bd.), Seattle Swiss Soc., Finnish Soc., Corinthian Yacht Club, Nature Conservancy, Rotary (bd. dirs., chmn. internat. rels. com., chmn. Hepatis Project), U. So. Calif. Alumni assn., Kappa Sigma. Office: 509 Olive Way Ste 803 Seattle WA 98101-1769

KARPMAN, ROBERT RONALD, orthopedic surgeon; b. Phila., Nov. 18, 1952; s. Sol H. and Tillie C. (Ginsburg) K.; m. Laurel Ann Brody, May 29, 1977; children: Hannah Elizabeth, Jodi Gayle. BA magna cum laude, LaSalle Coll., Phila., 1973; MD, U. Pa., Phila., 1977; MBA, U. Phoenix, 1992. Diplomate Am. Bd. Orthopedic Surgeons. Intern U. Ariz. Health Scis. Ctr., Tucson, 1977-78, resident in orthopedic surgery, 1978-81; gen. surgery intern U. Ariz., Tucson, 1977-78; pvt. practice Phoenix, 1981-86; resident in orthopedic surgery U. Ariz., Tucson, 1978-81; dir. acad. affairs Maricopa Med. Ctr., Phoenix, 1992—; adj. prof. dept. biomed. engring. Ariz. State U., Phoenix, 1991—; clin. assoc. prof. surgery Coll. Medicine U. Ariz., Tucson, 1989—. Editor: Musculoskeletal Disorders in Aging, 1989; contbr. 25 articles to profl. jours., 1981. Fellow ACS, Am. Acad. Orthopedic Surgeons; mem. Am. Orthopedic Foot and Ankle Soc., Gerontol. Soc. Am., Ariz. Geriatrics Soc. (pres. 1990-91). Jewish. Office: Maricopa Med Ctr 2601 E Roosevelt Box 5099 Phoenix AZ 85010

KARR, CHERYL LOFGREEN, film producer, consultant; b. Norco, Calif., Oct. 6, 1954; d. Ted Lee and Charlotte Dorae (Mackinga) Lofgreen; m. Paul Michael James Karr, Apr. 21, 1977. AA, Brigham Young U., 1975, BA, 1978, MA, 1983. Instr. radio and TV prodn. Brigham Young U., Provo, Utah, 1976-77; writer, dir. Paul S. Karr Prodns., Phoenix, 1978-80; mng. editor Weeknight TV News Mag., Provo, 1981-82; gen. mgr. CCN Cable Network, Provo, 1982-83; news reporter The Daily Herald, Provo, 1984; v.p. prodn. Alpine Film and Video Exchange, Inc., Orem, Utah, 1984-86; producer, dir. Sta. KBYU-TV, Provo, 1984—; instr. English, Utah Valley Community Coll., Orem, 1986—; pres. SEEN-BY-SCENE PRODNS., Orem, 1987—; cons. Film Video Services, Phoenix, 1985-87, Producers Consortium, Orem, 1986—, Skaggs Retail Inst., Provo, 1987—; producer, dir. hdqrs. USMC, Washington, Count Me In, Spl. Svcs. Media Campaign, 1989; producer, dir., writer State of Utah, Earthquake Awareness Media Campaign, 1989; assoc. producer feature film Rockwell, 1990. Writer (documentary) Escape from Ground Zero, 1983; producer, writer (documentary) Tonga: A King and Its People, 1987; writer Yue-Sai Kan, Inc. CCTV, 1986—; writer, dir. (documentary) Islands of Love: People of Faith, 1992. Recipient Prodn. Excellence award Phototec, 1978, Nat. TV award Women in Communications, 1983, Golden Microphone award Brigham Young U., 1984, Cine Golden Eagle, 1993, Gold Camera award, 1993, Angel award, 1993, Emmy award, 1993. Mem. Am. Film Inst. Republican. Mormon. Home: 1045 N 300 E Orem UT 84057-3324 Office: Seen-By-Scene Prodns 1363 W 1600 N Orem UT 84057-2431

KARRAKER, NANEEN, criminologist, consultant; b. N.Y.C., July 6, 1949; d. Charles William and Celine Baekeland (Roll) K.; m. Richard Henry Schooler, Aug. 29, 1980; children: Benjamin, Nicholas. BA, U. Calif., Berkeley, 1971; MA, Calif. State U., San Francisco, 1978. Project dir. Am. Friends Svc. Com., San Francisco, 1972-74; dir., coord. West office Unitarian Universalist Svc. Committee, San Francisco, 1975-85; asst. dir. West office Nat. Ctr. on Institutions and Alternatives, San Francisco, 1985-91; asst. dir. Ctr. on Juvenile and Criminal Justice, San Francisco, 1991-92; dir. Criminal Justice Consortium, Oakland, Calif., 1992—; bd. dirs. Legal Svcs. for Prisoners with Children, San Francisco, 1990—; criminal justice com. Am. Friends Svc. Com., 1975-92; mem. Mayor's Com. on Jail Overcrowding, San Francisco, 1980-84. Author: Alternatives to Incarceration, 1980. Cons., vol. Supr. Nancy Walker, San Francisco, 1987-91. Office: Criminal Justice Consortium 1212 Broadway # 830 Oakland CA 94612

KARRAS, DONALD GEORGE, tax administrator; b. Sioux City, Iowa, Dec. 23, 1953; s. George D. and Mary T. (Kyriakos) K.; m. Donna Lynn Ciripompa, Mar. 6, 1982; children: Dane Anthony, Dillon James. BA, Augustana Coll., 1977; MBA, U. S.D., 1980, JD, 1981. CPA, S.D. Bar: S.D. 1981. Instr. U. S.D. Sch. Bus., Vermillion, 1980-81; tax sr. acct. Deloitte Haskins & Sells, Denver, 1981-84; tax mgr. The Anschutz Corp., Denver, 1984-87; dir. taxes Kennecott Corp., Salt Lake City, 1988-92; v.p. Taxes Newmont Mining Corp., Denver, 1992—. Mem. Colo. Pub. Expenditure Coun. Mem. ABA, S.D. Bar Assn., Am. Hellenic Ednl. Progressive Assn., Tax Execs. Inst., Inc., Am. Mining Congress (tax com.), Rocky Mountain Mineral Law Found., Colo. Mining Assn., Internat. Fiscal Assn. Republican. Greek Orthodox. Home: 632 13th Ave Salt Lake City UT 84103 Office: Newmont Mining Corp One Norwest Ctr 1700 Lincoln St Denver CO 80203

KARRAS, NOLAN ELDON, investment advisor; b. Ogden, Utah, Dec. 30, 1944; s. Orien John and Afton Elaine (Green) K.; m. Lynda Frances Purrington, Nov. 22, 1967; children: Brett N., Jodie Lynn, Darrin O. BS, Weber State U., 1970; MBA, U. Utah, 1977; HHD (hon.), Coll. of E. Utah, 1990. CPA, Colo., Utah; registered investment adv., Utah. Acct. Arthur Andersen & Co., Denver, 1970-72, Peat, Marwick & Mitchell, Salt Lake City, 1972-75, Schmitt, Griffiths & Smith, Ogden, 1975-79; fin. v.p. Jack B. Parson Cos., Ogden, 1979-93; registered rep. Investment Mgmt. & Rsch., Roy, Utah, 1985—; pres. Superior Air Handling Corp., Cldarfield, Utah, 1990-91; bd. dirs. Pacificorp, Utah Power & Light. Mem. Utah Ho. of Reps., Salt Lake City, 1981-90, majority leader, 1987-88, speaker, 1989-90; trustee Salt Lake City Olympic Bid Com., 1989-90. With USAR, 1963-69. Recipient Outstanding Legislator award AFL-CIO, 1986, Disting. Alumnus award Weber State U., 1990, Outstanding Alumnus award Beta Alpha Psi, 1988-89. Mem. AICPA (Pub. Svc. award 1987), Utah Assn. CPAs (Disting. Svc. award 1987), Ogden/Weber C. of C. (bd. dirs. 1989-93). Republican. Mormon. Home: 2195 W 4250 S Roy UT 84067-2023 Office: 4695 S 1900 W # 3 Roy UT 84067

KARROS, ERIC PETER, professional baseball player; b. Hackensack, N.J., Nov. 4, 1967. Student, UCLA. 1st baseman L.A. Dodgers, 1992—. Named Nat. League Rookie of the Year, 1992. Office: Dodger Stadium 1000 Elysian Park Ave Los Angeles CA 90012

KASAMA, HIDETO PETER, accountant, real estate consultant; b. Tokyo, Nov. 21, 1946; came to U.S., 1969; s. Toshiyoshi and Hamako (Yoshioka) K.; m. Evelyn Patricia Cruz (div. Apr. 1990); children: Jennifer, Nicole, Leona; m. Heidi W. Snare, June 29, 1991. BABA, Seattle U., 1971, MBA, 1973. CPA. Mgmt. trainee Security Pacific Bank, Seattle, 1972-74; audit supr. Ernst & Young, Seattle, 1974-79; pres. KASPAC Corp., Seattle, 1979-89; mng. ptnr. Kasama & Co., Seattle, 1980—. Contbr. articles to newspapers. Mem. AICPA, Wash. Soc. CPA's, Columbia Tower Club (founder). Home: 725 9th Ave S Edmonds WA 98020-3311 Office: Kasama & Co 3147 Fairview Ave E Ste 110 Seattle WA 98102

KASARI, LEONARD SAMUEL, quality control professional, concrete consultant; b. Los Angeles, Sept. 22, 1924; s. Kustaa Adolph and Impi (Sikio) K.; m. Elizabeth P. Keplinger, Aug. 25, 1956; children: Lorraine Carol, Lance Eric. Student, Compton Coll., 1942-43, UCLA, 1964-70. Registered profl. engr., Calif. Gen. construction Los Angeles, 1946-61; supr. inspection service Osborne Labs., Los Angeles, 1961-64; mgr. customer service Lightweight Processing, Los Angeles, 1965-77; dir. tech. service Crestlite Aggregates, San Clemente, Calif., 1977-78; quality control mgr. Standard Concrete, Santa Ana, Calif., 1978-92. Camp dir. Torrance YMCA, High Sierras, Calif., 1969-80, mem. bd. mgrs., 1970—. Served with USN, 1943-46. Recipient Sam Hobbs Svc. award ACI-So. Calif., 1992; named Hon. Life Mem. Calif. PTA, 1983. Mem. Am. Concrete Inst., So. Calif. Structural Engrs. Assn. Democrat. Lutheran. Office: 2450 W 233rd St Torrance CA 90501-5730

KASIK, DAVID JOSEPH, computer scientist; b. Council Bluffs, Iowa, May 21, 1949; s. John Joseph and Elisabeth Bonifacia (Ehrenfeld) K.; m. Peggy Lynn Burwell, June 17, 1972; children: Jennifer, Rebecca. BA, Johns Hopkins U., 1970; MS, U. Colo., 1972. Computer graphics researcher Battelle-Columbus, Ohio, 1972-77; user interface researcher Boeing Computer Svcs., Seattle, 1977-84, devel. tools mgr., 1984-89; tools and system architect Electronic Data Systems, Seattle, 1988-91; sr. prin. scientist Boeing Comml. Airplanes, Seattle, 1991—; instr. user interface Spl. Interest Group in Computer Graphics, SIGCHI, AUSGRAPH, 1982-87. Editor workshop procs. Computer Graphics Future, 1974; contbr. articles to profl. jours. Mem. Citizen's Adv. Com. on Edn., Renton, Wash., 1985-86; mem. food drive com. St. Joseph's Ch., Issaquah, Wash., 1988—. Mem. Assn. Computing Machinery, Spl. Interest Group in Computer Graphics (exhibits chair 1980, exhibits liaison 1981-92, spl. recognition award 1992), Good Earth Handball (capt. 1984—). Roman Catholic. Home: 3903 219th Ave SE Issaquah WA 98027

KASKEL, NEAL T., financial services executive; b. Buffalo, Oct. 6, 1943; s. David and Bertha (Perlmuter) K.; m. Geraldine Slutsky, Apr. 3, 1966; children: Amy Melissa, Robert Jason. BS, DePaul U., 1966; MBA, Northwestern U., 1972. Market rsch. analyst D'Arcy Advt., Chgo., 1965-67; rsch. supr. Foote, Cone & Belding, Chgo., 1967-72; market rsch. mgr. Armour-Dial, Phoenix, 1972-74, Hunt-Wesson Foods, Fullerton, Calif., 1974-79; dir. mktg. svcs. FHP, Fountain Valley, Calif., 1979-81; mktg. mgr. TCM div. Smith Internat., Tustin, Calif., 1981-83; v.p. Geneva Cos., Irvine, Calif., 1983—; adj. prof. Calif. State U., Fullerton, 1975—, U. LaVerne, Fountain Valley, 1990—, U. Phoenix, Fountain Valley, 1990—. Bd. mem. Jewish Family Svc., Orange County, Calif., 1980-84; exec. bd. mem. Jewish Fedn., Orange County, 1984—; pres. Congregation B'Nai Tzedek, Fountain Valley, 1984-87; trustee Sch. Assets Mgmt. Inc., Fountain Valley, 1989-91. Lt. USNR, 1968-74. Mem. Am. Mktg. Assn. Home: 18880 Mt Morgan Cir Fountain Valley CA 92708-6517 Office: Geneva Cos 5 Park Plz Irvine CA 92714-5995

KASMER, JOSEPH, writer; b. East Stroudsburg, Pa., Jan. 5, 1951; s. Joseph and Agnes (Oliver) Kascmer. BSC in Physics, Pa. State U., 1972. Staff writer Picker Corp., Cleve., 1972-74; exhibit editor Calif. Acad. Scis., San Francisco, 1975-76; script developer Deterline Prodns., Palo Alto, Calif., 1977-78; staff writer Sybex Books, Berkeley, Calif., 1982-83; mng. editor Hands On Jour., Cambridge, Mass., 1986-87; instr. Peralta Coll., Oakland, Calif., 1989-91, UCLA, 1993—, San Diego State U., 1993—; cons. and lectr. in field; seminar leader Media Alliance Pub. Ctr., San Francisco, 1988-89. Author: Easy Guide Series, 1983, Using Pagemaker, 1988, Teach Yourself QuarkXPress, 1992, The Windows Desktop Sourcebook, 1993. Home and Office: Studio K PO Box 3562 San Diego CA 92163

KASPER, CHRISTINE ELEANA, nursing educator; b. Chgo., Mar. 16, 1953; d. John Michael and Olga (Kozor) K.; m. Ramiro G. Iturralde, June 25, 1978; 1 child, Alexandra Vitoria Iturralde. BSN, U. Evansville (Ind.), 1975; MSN, Rush U., Chgo., 1976; PhD, U. Mich., 1982. RN, Ill., Mich., Wis., Calif. Tchr./practitioner Rush Presbyn.-St. Luke's Hosp., Chgo., 1976-77; predoctoral fellow U. Mich., Ann Arbor, 1978-82; teaching asst. U. Mich., 1978-81; postdoctoral fellow Rush Med. Coll., Chgo., 1982-84; asst. prof. nursing U. Wis., Madison, 1984-88, UCLA, 1988—. Contbr. articles to profl. jours. Grantee NASA, NIH; recipient Rackman Dissertation/Thesis award, 1980, Nat. Rsch. Svc. award DHHS, 1978-81. Mem. Am. Coll. Sports Medicine, Am. Nurses Assn., Biophys. Soc., Midwest Nurses Rsch. Soc., N.Y. Acad. Sci., Am. Soc. Gravitational and Space Biology, Sigma Theta Tau. Russian Orthodox. Office: UCLA Sch Nursing 10833 Le Conte Ave Los Angeles CA 90024-6918

KASSAN, STUART S., rheumatologist; b. White Plains, N.Y., Nov. 19, 1946; s. Robert Jacob and Rosalind (Suchin) K.; m. Gail Karesh, Apr. 4, 1971; children: Michael Andrew, Merrill Alissa. BA, Case Western Res., 1968; MD, George Washington U., 1972. Diplomate Am. Bd. Internal Medicine, Am. Bd. Rheumatology, Am. Bd. Geriatrics. Intern and resident Grady Meml. Hosp., Altanta, 1972-74; clin. fellow NIH, Bethesda, Md., 1974-76; fellow Hosp. for Spl. Surgery, Cornell Med. Ctr., N.Y.C., 1976-78; head rheumatology clinic VA Med. Ctr., Denver, 1978-80; asst. clin. prof. medicine U. Colo. Health Scis. Ctr., Denver, 1978-84, assoc. clin. prof. medicine, 1984—; med. dir. rehab unit. Luth. Med. Ctr., Wheatridge, Colo., 1983-87; med. dir. rehab. unit St. Anthony Hosp., Denver, 1987—; cons. Annals Internal Medicine, Phila., 1986—; vis. alumni scholar George Washington U. Sch. Medicine, 1986; nat. med. adv. bd. Sjögren's Found., Port Washington, N.Y., 1987—. Co-editor: Sjögren's Syndrome, 1987; contbr. over 25 articles to profl. jours. Bd. dirs. Rocky Mountain chpt. Arthritis Found., Denver, 1978-90 (Polachek fellow, 1976-77). With USPHS, 1974-76. Fellow Am. Coll. Physicians, Am. Coll. Rheumatology (network physician 1989—); mem. Harvey Soc. Jewish. Office: Colo Arthritis Assoc 4200 W Conejos Pl Ste 314 Denver CO 80204-1311

KASSER, IVAN MICHAEL, entrepreneur; b. Budapest, Hungary, Dec. 9, 1940; came to U.S., 1956; s. Alexander and Elizabeth (Aranyi) K.; m. Lynn von Kersting, Feb. 2, 1974 (div. Sept. 1979); m. Beth Louise Chadwick, Aug. 4, 1985; children: Violet, Michael. BS, MIT, 1960, MS, 1961; D of Engring., U. Grenoble, France, 1964; MBA, Harvard U., 1968. Registered profl. engr., N.J. Fin. analyst W.R. Grace & Co., N.Y.C., 1968-71; pres. Technopulp, Inc., Montclair, N.J., 1971-81; chmn. Booher Lumber Co., Syracuse, N.Y., 1972-81; pres. Holualoa Mgmt. Corp., Kailua-Kona, Hawaii, 1985—; chmn. salary commn., 1989-92; vice chmn. A.L.L., Inc.; edn. counselor MIT. Mem. Am. Hungarian Assn. (bd. dirs.), Kona Family YMCA (bd. dirs. 1988-91), Aloha Performing Arts Ctr. (bd. dirs., fin. com. chmn. 1990-91), Kasser Art Found. (bd. dirs.). Home and Office: Holualoa Ariz Inc 75 5706 Hanama Pl Ste 205 Kailua Kona HI 96740

KASSICIEH, SULEIMAN KHALIL, management educator; b. Jerusalem, May 6, 1952; came to U.S., 1971; s. Khalil Suleiman and Raoufeh (Nasri) K.; m. Heyam Baddour, May 28, 1983; children: Charles, Christina. BS, U. N.Mex., 1973, MBA, 1975; PhD, U. Iowa, 1978. Prof. Ill. State U., Normal, 1979-81, U. N.Mex., Albuquerque, 1981—; disting. found. prof. Anderson Sch. Mgmt., 1990—; cons. Sandia Nat. Lab., 1992—. Contbr. 100 articles to profl. jours. Republican. Greek Orthodox. Office: U NMex Anderson Sch Mgmt Albuquerque NM 87131

KASSIS, NOURA I., nursing educator; b. Aleppo, Syria, Sept. 7, 1943; parents: Iskendar and Maggy (Marangozian) K. BSN, Am. U. Beirut, 1965; MSN, UCLA, 1967; EdD, Nova U., 1983. Instr. Mt. San Antonio Coll., Walnut, Calif. Mem. ANA, Calif. Nurses, Nat. League Nursing, CTA. Home: 826 W Pepperdine Ln Claremont CA 91711-2502

KASSNER, MICHAEL ERNEST, materials science educator, researcher; b. Osaka, Japan, Nov. 22, 1950; (parents Am. citizens); s. Ernest and Clara (Christa) K.; m. Marcia J. Wright, Aug. 19, 1972 (div. Dec. 1976). BS, Northwestern U., 1972; MS, Stanford U., 1979, PhD, 1981. Metallurgist Lawrence Livermore (Calif.) Nat. Lab., 1981-90, head phys. metallurgy and joining sect., 1988-90; lectr. San Francisco State U., 1983; prof. Naval Postgrad. Sch., Monterey, Calif., 1984-86; assoc. prof. Oreg. State U., Corvallis, 1990—; temproary assignment as project mgr. Office Basic Energy Scis., U.S. Dept. Energy, 1991—; vis. scientist dept. material sci. Stanford U., 1981-83, dept. physics U. Groningen, The Netherlands, 1985-87; vis. scholar Dept. Materials, Sci. and Engring. Stanford U. Author over 100 sci. articles; editor various sci. jours. Served to lt. USN, 1972-76. Fulbright scholar, The Netherlands, 1983-84. Mem. ASME, Am. Soc. Metals, The Metall. Soc., Materials Research Soc., Sigma Xi. Roman Catholic. Home: PO Box 269 Otter Rock OR 97369-0269

KASZNIAK, ALFRED WAYNE, neuropsychologist; b. Chgo., June 2, 1949; s. Alfred H. and Ann Virginia (Simonsen) K.; B.S. with honors, U. Ill., 1970, M.A., 1973, Ph.D., 1976; m. Mary Ellen Beaurain, Aug. 26, 1973; children—Jesse, Elizabeth. Instr. dept. psychology Rush Med. Coll., Chgo., 1974-76, asst. prof. dept. psychology, 1976-79; from asst. prof. to assoc. prof. dept. psychiatry U. Ariz. Coll. Medicine, Tucson, 1979-82, assoc. prof. dept. psychology and psychiatry, 1982-87; prof. depts. psychology, neurology and psychiatry, 1987—; chmn. U. Ariz. Commn. on Gerontology, 1990-93, acting head U. Ariz. dept. psychology, 1992-93 ; dir. U. Ariz. Coordinated Clin. Neuropsychology Program; staff psychologist Presbyn.-St. Luke's Hosp., Chgo., 1976-79, Univ. Hosp., Tucson, 1979—; mem. human devel. and aging study sect. div. research grants NIH, 1981-86. Trustee So. Ariz. chpt. Nat. Multiple Sclerosis Soc., 1980-82; mem. med. and sci. adv. bd. Nat. Alzheimer's Disease and Related Disorders Assn., 1981-84; mem. VA Geriatrics and Gerontology Adv. Com., 1986-89, Ariz. Gov.'s Adv. Com. on Alzheimer's Disease, 1988-92; mem. med. adv. bd. Fan Kane Fund for Brain-Injured Children, Tucson, 1980-92. Grantee Nat. Inst. Aging, 1978-83, 89—, NIMH, 1984—, Robert Wood Johnson Found., 1986-89. Fellow Am. Psychol. Assn. (Disting. Contbr. award div. 20 1978); mem. AAAS, Internat. Neuropsychol. Soc., Soc. for Neurosci., Gerontol. Soc. (rsch. fellow 1980). Author 2 books; editorial cons. Jour. Gerontology, 1979-92; mem. editorial bd. Psychology and Aging, 1984-87; The Clin. Neuropsychologist, 1986—, Jour. Clin. and Exp. Neuropsychol., 1987-90, Jour Gerontology, 1988-92, Neuropsychology, 1992-93; contbr. articles to profl. jours. Home: 2327 E Hawthorne St Tucson AZ 85719-4944 Office: U Ariz Dept Psychology Tucson AZ 85721

KATCHUR, MARLENE MARTHA, nursing administrator; b. Belleville, Ill., Dec. 20, 1946; d. Elmer E. and Hilda B. (Gutherz) Wilde; m. Raymond J. Katchur, Feb. 22, 1969; 1 child, Nickolas Phillip. BSN, So. Ill. U., 1968; MS in Health Care Adminstrn., Calif. State U., L.A., 1982. RN; cert. critical care nurse. Staff nurse, head nurse, nursing supr. U. So. Calif Med. Ctr. LA County, 1968-81, assoc. dir. nursing, internal medicine nursing, 1981-83, mem. staff internal medicine nursing, info. systems dept., 1983-89, patient-centered info. systems cons., 1989-90, nursing info. systems cons. for pediatrics, psychiatry and ICU, 1990-92, psychiat. nursing svcs. human resources and info. systems, 1992—. Mem. Sheriff's Relief Assn. Mem. AACCN, NAFE, AAUW, Nat. Critical Care Inst. Edn., Am. Heart Assn., So. Ill. U. Alumni Assn. (life), Health Svcs. Mgmt. Forum, Orgn. Nurse Execs. Calif. (membership com.), Am. Soc. Profl. and Exec. Women, Soc. Clin. Data Mgmt. Systems (bd. dirs. 1990-91), Soc. Med. Computer Observers (charter), Am. Legion Aux., Nat. Hist. Soc., Job's Daus. (past honor queen). Office: U So Calif Med Ctr LA County 1200 N State St Los Angeles CA 90033-4525

KATHER, GERHARD, air force base administrator; b. Allenstein, Germany, Jan. 30, 1939; came to U.S., 1952, naturalized, 1959; s. Ernst and Maria (Kempa) K.; m. Carol Anne Knutsen, Aug. 18, 1962; children: Scott

T., Cynthia M., Tracey S., Chris A.; m. Mary Elsie Frank, Oct. 25, 1980. BA in Govt., U. Ariz., 1964; MPA, U. So. Calif., 1971; cert. in personnel adminstrn., U. N.Mex., 1987. Tchr. social studies, Covina, Calif., 1965-67; tng. officer Civil Personnel, Ft. MacArthur, Calif., 1967-70; chief employee tng. and devel. Corps Engrs., L.A., 1970-72; chief employee tng. and devel. Frankfurt Area Army Personnel Office, 1972-73; chief employee rels. and tng. brs. Corps Engrs., L.A., 1973-74; chief employee devel. and tng. Kirtland AFB, N.Mex., 1974-87; labor relations officer, Kirtland AFB and detachments in 13 U.S. cities, 1987-90; ret., 1990; project coord., adv. Protection and Advocacy System, 1991—. Mem. adv. com. Albuquerque Tech.-Vocat. Inst., 1982-92, U. N.Mex. Valencia Campus, 1985-92; mem. Coalition for Disability Rights, 1988—; chmn. Comprehensive Accessibility Network, 1990—; adv. coun. N.Mex. Disability Prevention, 1992—. Served with USAF, 1958-64. Named Prominent Tng. and Devel. Profl., H. Whitney McMillan Co., 1984; Outstanding Handicapped Fed. Employee of Yr., all fed. agys., 1984; recipient Govt. Employees Ins. Co. GEICO Pub. Svc. award for work in phys. rehab., 1988. Mem. Am. Soc. Tng. and Devel. (treas. chpt. 1984-85), Paralyzed Vets. Am. (bd. dirs. 1986-87, pres. local chpt. 1986-87, 1990-92), Toastmasters Internat. (chpt. treas., v.p., pres. 1967-70), Vietnam Vets. of Am., Phi Delta Kappa. Democrat. Roman Catholic. Office: 1720 Louisiana Blvd NE Ste 204 Albuquerque NM 87110-7070

KATHKA, DAVID ARLIN, state parks and cultural resources administrator, state archivist; b. Columbus, Nebr.; s. Arlin Arthur and Edith Ferne (Wilcox) K.; m. Anne Condon Butler, Aug. 15, 1965. BA, Wayne (Nebr.) State Coll., 1964, MA, 1966; PhD in History, U. Mo., 1976. Tchr. Ravenna (Nebr.) Pub. Schs., 1964-65; instr. Midwestern Coll., Denison, Iowa, 1966-68; prof. history Western Wyo. Coll., Rock Springs, 1972-87, dean acad. affairs, 1980-84, interim pres., 1984-85, v.p. acad. affairs, 1985-87; dir. State Parks and Cultural Resources Div., State of Wyo., Cheyenne, 1987—; adj. prof. U. Wyo., Laramie, 1976—; vis. instr. U. Mo., St. Louis, 1971-72; cons. various Wyo. govt. agys.; mem. gov.'s Blue ribbon Task Force on Cultural Resources, Wyo. Trails adv. com. Author hist. papers; contbr. hist. articles to mags. Mem. Wyo. Centennial Commn., 1986-87, Rock Springs Library Bd., 1984-87, Gov.'s Com. on Hist. Preservation, 1982; v.p. Rocky Mountain Region Kidney Found., Denver, 1976-77. Recipient Wyo. Humanities award for exemplary svc., 1990. Mem. Orgn. Am. Historians, Am. Assn. State and Local History (Commendation 1982), Wyo. State Hist. Soc. (pres. 1984-85, Wyo. Humanities award 1990). Democrat. Office: State of Wyo Divsn Parks & Cultural Resources 2301 Central Ave Cheyenne WY 82002-0001

KATHOL, ANTHONY LOUIS, financial executive; b. San Diego, June 12, 1964; s. Cletus Louis and Regina Antoinette (Ellrott) K.; m. Kathleen Marie Moore, Jan. 23, 1988; children: Nicole Kathleen, Natalie Antoinette. BS, U. So. Calif., 1986; MBA, U. San Diego, 1988. Fin. aid analyst U. San Diego, 1986-87; bookkeeper Golden Lion Tavern, San Diego, 1987-88; fin. and budget coord. Santa Fe Pacific Realty Corp. (name now Catellus Devel. Corp.), Brea, Calif., 1988-91; mgr. fin. analysisSW U.S. Catellus Devel. Corp., Anaheim, Calif., 1992—. Calif. Bldg. Industry Assn. fellow, 1986, U. San Diego fellow, 1987. Mem. U. San Diego Grad. Bus. Students Assn., K.C. (fin. sec. 1990-91), Tau Kappa Epsilon. Republican. Roman Catholic. Home: 3805 Maxon Ln Chino CA 91710-2073 Office: Catellus Devel Corp 1065 N Pacificenter Dr # 200 Anaheim CA 92806

KATIMS, MILTON, symphony conductor and violist, consultant; b. N.Y.C., June 24, 1909; s. Harry and Caroline (Spiegel) K.; m. Virginia Peterson, Nov. 7, 1940; children: Peter Michael, Pamela Artura Katims Steele. BA, Columbia U., 1930; hon. doctorate in Music, Whitworth Coll., 1967, Seattle U., 1974, Cornish Coll. Arts, Seattle, 1975. Asst. condr., solo violist Sta. WOR, N.Y.C., 1935-43; 1st violist NBC Symphony, N.Y.C., 1943-47; 1st violist, condr. NBC, N.Y.C., 1947-54; condr., music dir. Seattle Symphony, 1954-76; artistic dir. U. Houston Sch. Music, 1976-84; guest condr., performer on 5 continents, 1952—. Contbr. editions and transcriptions to Internat. Music; recorded chamber music for RCA, Columbia, Vox, Mercury, Pantheon. Mem. music adv. panel U.S. Dept. State and USIA, Washington, 1962-67. Recipient Medal of Excellence Columbia U., 1954, Alice M. Ditson award, 1963; Man of Yr. award City of Seattle, 1966. Mem. Am. String Assn. (hon., Disting. Svc. award 1988, Seattle Ctr. honor 1992). Home: Fairway Estates 8001 Sand Point Way NE Seattle WA 98115

KATO, EILEEN A., lawyer; b. Ogden, Utah, Sept. 5, 1950; d. Akio George and Sadie (Aoki) K. BS, San Jose State U., 1976, MBA, 1977; JD, U. Santa Clara, 1980. Bar: Calif. 1981, Pa. 1981, U.S. Dist. Ct. (no. dist.) Calif. 1981, U.S. Tax Ct. 1981, U.S. Ct. Appeals (9th cir.) 1982, Wash. 1983, U.S. Dist. Ct. (we. dist.) Wash. 1983, U.S. Dist. Ct. (ea. dist.) Wash. 1989. Assoc. Office of Chief Counsel, IRS, San Francisco, 1980-83; sr. trial atty. Office of Chief Counsel, IRS, Seattle, 1983-89; assoc. Miller, Nash, Wiener, Hager & Carlsen, Seattle, 1989-92, Hiscock & Barclay, Seattle, 1992—; spl. asst. to U.S. Atyy, 1984-89; cons. Nise Prodns., Inc., 1988—, On-Air Entertianment, 1988—; judge pro tempore King County Superior Ct., 1993—, Seattle Dist. Ct., Seattle Mcpl. Ct., 1992—, magistrate pro tempore, 1992—; judge pro tempore King County Superior Ct., 1993—. Arbitrator Better Bus. Bur., 1984—; active Japanese Am. Citizens League, 1993—; mem. N.W. Minority Job Fair Com., workshop co-chair; bd. dirs. Empty Space Theatre, 1992—, Northwest Asian Am. Theatre, 1993—, New Beginnings Shelter for Battered Women and Children, 1993—, N.W. Asian Am. Theatre; bd. trustees ednl. opportunity program U. Wash., 1993—. Mem. ABA (bus., taxation and sports and entertainment sect.), Seattle King County Bar Assn. (creditor-debtor, corp. and bus. sect., assn. legal clinic 1993—, chair ethnic diversity in legal profession com. 1993—), Asian Bar Assn. Wash. (instr. community law program 1990—, jud. rating com. 1992—, exec. bd.), Wash. Women Lawyers (CLE/program com. 1993—), Nat. Asian Pacific Am. Bar Assn. (bd. govs.), Womens Bus. Exchange, Wash. State Trial Lawyers Assn. (northwest minority law student job fair com. 1990—, women in the law com. 1993—, women and Wash. State Trial Lawyers Assn. com.), Greater Seattle Bus. Assn. Office: Hiscock & Barclay Ste 3900 AT&T Gateway Tower 700 5th Ave Seattle WA 98104-5390

KATSH, SEYMOUR, pharmacology educator; b. Bklyn., Jan. 13, 1918; s. Julius and Sara (Levine) K.; m. Grace Finkelstein, Apr. 17, 1946; children: Sara, Judith, Naomi. BA, NYU, 1944, MS, 1948, PhD, 1950. Fellow NYU, Brookhaven, Calif. Tech., Carnegie, 1945-58; from asst. prof. to prof. pharmacology dept. U. Colo., Denver, 1958-83, acting dept. chmn., 1964-67, assoc. dean grad. and rsch. affairs, 1969-83, prof. emeritus, assoc. dean emeritus, 1983—; program dir. NSF, Washington, 1967-68; cons. Ford Found., N.Y.C., 1963-64, Govt. India, New Delhi, 1963-64, NIH, Bethesda, Md., 1965-74, Agy. for Internat. Devel., Washington, 1972-74;. Contbr. articles to profl. jours. Office: U Colo Pharmacology Dept Box B 216 4200 E 9th Ave Denver CO 80262

KATZ, ALAN STEWART, service executive, lawyer; b. Niagara Falls, N.Y., Jan. 27, 1953; s. Samuel Eaton and Ethyl (Nimelman) k.; m. Jerry Margaret Simmons, Nov. 26, 1988. BA, UCLA, 1975; JD, U. Calif., Davis, 1979; M in Urban Studies, Occidental Coll., 1982. Bar: Calif. 1979, U.S. Ct. Appeals (D.C. dist.) 1979. Atty. U.S. Securities & Exchange Commn., Washington, 1979-81; dep. dir. Bradley for Gov., L.A., 1982; v.p. Multiple Svcs., Inc., Ins. Mktg., L.A., 1983-87, '89-90; chief of staff Office of Lt. Gov., L.A., Sacramento, 1987-89; prin. Centerstone Ins. & Fin. Svcs. (formerly West Coast Multiple Svcs.), Woodland Hills, Calif., 1990—. Author: (booklet) Consumer Edn. Handbook: Understanding Health Ins.; contbr. articles to profl. pubs. V.p. Westside Fair Housing Coun., L.A., 1983-87; pres. Am. Jewish Congress, Pacific S.W. Region, L.A., 1984-86; mem. Santa Monica (Calif.) City Coun., 1985-88, Calif. Econ. Devel. Commn., 1989—. Mem. Nat. Assn. Health Underwriters (registered health underwriter, chair legis. coun. 1993—), L.A. Assn. Health Underwriters (Paladin award 1992), Calif. Assn. Health Underwriters (v.p. 1989-91, pres. 1992—, Pres. award 1990, 92). Democrat. Jewish. Office: Centerstone Ins and Fin Svcs 20750 Ventura Blvd Ste 350 Woodland Hills CA 91364

KATZ, ELIAS, psychologist, consultant; b. N.Y.C., Sept. 22, 1912; s. Samuel and Fannie (Huss) K.; m. Florence Ludins, Dec. 7, 1937; 1 child, Jonathan. BA, CCNY, 1932, MSEd, 1933; PhD, Tchrs. Coll. Columbia, N.Y.C., 1942; diploma, Ctr. Tng. Community Psychiatry, Berkeley, Calif., 1972. Lic. psychologist, marriage and family counselor. Tchr. N.Y. City Schs., N.Y.C., 1934-42; clin. psychologist VA, N.Y.C., 1946-49, U. Calif. Med. Ctr., San Francisco, 1953-71; asst. dir. Ctr. Tng. in Community Psychiatry, Berkeley, Calif., 1968-76; co-founder, co-dir. Creative Growth, Oakland, Calif., 1974-82; co-founder, co-dir. Nat. Inst. Art and Disabilities, Richmond, Calif., 1984-90, exec. dir., 1990-92, pres., 1992—; pvt. practice clin. psychology Calif., 1949—. Author: Children's Preferences for Art, Retarded Adult in Community, 1968; co-author: Freedom to Create, 1987, Art and Disabilities, 1990, The Creative Spirit, 1990. Co-founder, pres. Enabled Artists United, Richmond, 1989. 2d lt. U.S. Army, 1943-46. Recipient Spl. Recognition award Calif. Psychol Assn., 1987, Calif. State Coun. Devel. Disabilities, 1991; NEA grantee, 1990; named Outstanding Vol. J.C. Penney, 1992. Fellow APA, Am. Assn. Mental Retardation; mem. Nat. Register Health Profls., Alameda County Phychol. Assn., Coun. Exceptional Children. Home: 2839 Ashby Ave Berkeley CA 94705 Office: Nat Inst Art & Disabilities 551-23 RD St Richmond CA 94705

KATZ, JERRY PAUL, corporate executive; b. L.A., Jan. 24, 1944; s. Samuel and Dorothy Rose (Solovay) K.; m. Judy Simmering, Sept. 10, 1985 (div. 1988); m. Julie Stacey, Aug. 26, 1990. AA, East L.A. Coll., 1964; BS, BA, Calif. State U., 1970. Registered sanitarian, Calif. Sanitarian L.A. County Health Dept., L.A., 1971-73; dir. Compton (Calif.) Model Cities Vector Control, 1973-74; health officer Lynwood (Calif.) City, 1974-76; pres., chief exec. officer Associated Industries, L.A., 1976—; cons., bd. dirs. All Am. Fire Protection, L.A., 1987—. Founding mem. Moore St. Homeowners Assn., Monterey Park, Calif., 1989—; mem. Nature Conservancy, World Wildlife Fund. Recipient World Record (2) hang gliding Nat. Assn. Aeronautics, 1977; named for Distance-Altitude Gain, Guinness Book of World Records, London, 1977. Mem. Nat. Glass Assn., Surfrider Found., U.S. Hangliding Assn., Sea Shepard Soc. Office: Associated Industries 5140 Via Corona St Los Angeles CA 90022-2007

KATZ, JOHN W., lawyer, state official; b. Balt., June 3, 1943; s. Leonard Wallach and Jean W. (Kane) K.; m. Joan Katz, June 11, 1969 (div. 1982); 1 child, Kimberly Erin. BA, Johns Hopkins U., 1965; JD, U. Calif., Berkeley, 1969. Bar: Alaska, Pa., U.S. Dist. Ct. D.C. 1971, U.S. Ct. Appeals (D.C. cir.), U.S. Tax Ct., U.S. Ct. Claims, U.S. Ct. Mil. Justice, U.S. Supreme Ct. Legis. and adminstrv. asst. to Congressman Howard W. Pollock of Alaska, Washington, 1969-70; legis. asst. to U.S. Senator Ted Stevens of Alaska, Washington, 1971; assoc. McGrath and Flint, Anchorage, 1972; gen. counsel Joint Fed. State Land Use Planning Commn. for Alaska, Anchorage, 1972-79; spl. counsel to Gov. Jay S. Hammond of Alaska, Anchorage and Washington, 1979-81; commr. Alaska Dept. Natural Resources, Juneau, 1981-83; dir. state fed. relations and spl. counsel to Gov. Bill Sheffield of Alaska, Washington and Juneau, 1983-86; dir. state-fed. relations, spl. counsel to Gov. Steve Cowper of Alaska, Washington, 1986-90, Gov. Walter J. Hickel of Alaska, Washington, 1990—; mem. Alaska Power Survey Exec. Adv. Com. of FPC, Anchorage, 1972-74; mem. spl. com. hard rock minerals Govs. Council of Sci. and Tech., Anchorage, 1979-80; guest lectr. on natural resources U. Alaska, U. Denver. Contbr. articles to profl. jours.; columnist Anchorage Times. Acad. supr. Alaska Externship Program, U. Denver Coll. Law, 1976-79; mem. Reagan-Bush transition team for U.S. Dept. Justice, 1980. Recipient Superior Sustained Performance award Joint Fed. State Land Use Planning Commn. for Alaska, 1978. Republican. Office: State of Alaska Office of Gov 444 N Capitol St NW # 336 Washington DC 20001-1512

KATZ, PERRY MARC, motion picture company executive; b. N.Y.C., Aug. 31, 1951; s. Arthur E. and Shirley (Cohen) K. BA in Psychology with honors, CUNY, 1974; MBA, NYU, 1976. Project mgr. Eric Marder and Assocs., N.Y.C., 1975-78; sr. rsch. exec. Grey Advt., N.Y.C., 1978-80; dir. rsch. Columbia Pictures Industries, L.A., 1980-82; pres. Creative Mktg. Assocs., L.A., 1982-83; v.p. rsch. Metro-Goldwyn-Mayer/United Artists, L.A., 1983-87; sr. v.p. mktg. MCA/Universal Pictures, L.A., 1987—. Mem. Acad. Motion Picture Arts and Scis., Motion Picture Assn. Am. (rsch. com.), Am. Film Inst. (3d decade coun. adv. bd.), So. Calif. Rsch. Soc., Film Info. Coun., Motion Picture Pioneers, Inc. Office: MCA/Universal Pictures 100 Universal City Plz Universal City CA 91608-1002

KATZ, VERA, mayor, former college administrator, state legislator; b. Dusseldorf, Germany, Aug. 3, 1933; came to U.S., 1940; d. Lazar Pistrak and Raissa Goodman; m. Mel Katz (div. 1985); 1 child, Jesse. BA, Bklyn. Coll., 1955, postgrad., 1955-57. Market research analyst TIMEX, B.T. Babbitt, N.Y.C., 1957-62; mem. Oreg. Ho. of Reps., Salem; former dir. devel. Portland Community Coll., from 1982; mayor City of Portland, Oreg., 1993—; mem. Gov.'s Council on Alcohol and Drug Abuse Programs, Oreg. Legis., Salem, 1985—; mem. adv. com. Gov.'s Council on Health, Fitness and Sports, Oreg. Legis., 1985—; mem. Gov.'s Commn. on Sch. Funding Reform; mem. Carnegie task Force on Teaching as Profession, Washington, 1985-87; vice-chair assembly Nat. Conf. State Legis., Denver, 1986—. Recipient Abigail Scott Duniway award Women in Communications, Inc., Portland, 1985, Jeanette Rankin First Woman award Oreg. Women's Polit. Caucus, Portland, 1985, Leadership award The Neighborhood newspaper Portland, 1985, Woman of Achievement award Commn. for Women, 1985, Outstanding Legis. Advocacy award Oreg. Primary Care Assn., 1985, Service to Portland Pub. Sch. Children award Portland Pub. Schs., 1985. Fellow Am. Leadership Forum (founder Oreg. chpt.); mem. Dem. Legis. Leaders Assn., Nat. Bd. for Profl. Teaching Standards. Democrat. Jewish. Office: Office of the Mayor 1220 S.W. Fifth Ave. Portland OR 97204

KATZBECK, KAREN LYNN, accounting executive; b. Chgo., Aug. 11, 1951; d. Frank A. and Lorraine S. (Williams) K.; m. Carl A. Petersen, June 17, 1972 (div. June 1975); m. Jack L. Shishido, Dec. 10, 1982 (div. Oct. 1991). BS, U. Ill.-Chgo., 1976. CPA. Mem. tax staff Price Waterhouse, Chgo., 1977-78, tax sr./mgr., Tokyo, 1978-82, tax mgr., L.A., 1982-83, sr. mgr., 1984-85; mgr. internat. tax Walt Disney Prodns., Burbank, Calif., 1985-88; chief fin. officer Santiago Air Conditioning, 1988-89; v.p. fin., adminstrn. Houlihan, Lokey, Howard & Zukin, Inc., L.A., 1989-93; exec. dir. Cox, Castle and Nicholson, L.A., 1993—. Active Asia Pacific Coun. Am. Chambers, Tokyo, 1979-82. Recipient Pres.'s Leadership award Am. C. of C. in Japan, 1980. Mem. AICPA, Calif. CPA Soc., Am. Soc. Women CPAs, Japan-Am. Soc., Century City C. of C. Office: Cox Castle & Nicholson 2049 Century Park E 28th Fl Los Angeles CA 90067

KATZENSTEIN, DAVID ALLENBERG, internal medicine educator, virologist; b. Hartford, Conn., Jan. 3, 1952; s. Henry Sour and Constance (Allenberg) K.; m. Sharon Suzette Mayes, Dec. 25, 1983; 1 child, Melissa Sanders-Self. BA, U. Calif.-San Diego, La Jolla, 1973, MD, 1977. Diplomate Am. Bd. Internal Medicine, Am. Bd. Infectious Disease. Intern U. N.Mex., Albuquerque, 1977-78; resident in internal medicine U. Calif.-San Diego, 1978-80; fellow in infectious disease U. Calif.-Davis, Martinez, 1981-83; asst. prof. U. Minn., Mpls., 1984-86; lectr. U. Zimbabwe, Harare, 1986-87; rsch. fellow Ctr. for Biologics Evaluation and Rsch., FDA, Bethesda, Md., 1987-89; physician specialist Stanford (Calif.) U. Med. Ctr., 1989-91, asst. prof. medicine, 1991—, assoc. med. dir. Ctr. for AIDS Rsch., 1989—. Contbr. articles to med. jours. Mem. Infectious Disease Soc. Am., Internat. AIDS Soc., Am. Soc. for Microbiology. Office: Stanford U Med Ctr S-156 Div Infectious Disease Stanford CA 94305

KATZER, ELAINE, artist, sculptor; b. L.A., Feb. 17, 1933; d. Erwin and Eloise (Bouchey) K.; children: Robin Corona, Jenny Wren Armstrong, Eric Amrstrong. Diploma, Chouinard Art. Inst., 1955; M in Art, Calif. State U., Long Beach, 1969. Prof., Art Dept. Foothill Coll., Los Altos Hills, Calif., 1971-74; illustrator, L.A. Zoo City of L.A., Dept. of Recreation and Parks, L.A., 1978-80; illustrator, Cabrillo Marine Mus. City of L.A., Dept. of Recreation and Parks, San Pedro, Calif., 1981-83; illustrator, sculptor, Griffith Park Rangers City of L.A., Dept. of Recreation and Parks, L.A., 1983-85; freelance artist sculptor, illustrator, painter, 1985—. Executed murals Chula Vista Libr., 1977, Bellflower Libr., Calif., 1974, Melbourne Zoo, Victoria, Australia, 1980, Brown Pelican Diving, Cabrillo, 1982, Glendale Fed. Bank, San Diego, 1983, Encino, Calif., 1985, Manhattan Village Mall, Calif., Griffith Park Ranger Station, L.A., 1985; work represented in permanent collections at Sunbird Gallery, Los Altos Hills, Joan Crawley Galleries Scottsdale, Ariz., Santa Fe, Three Horse Gallery, Franklin, Tex. Recipient Design Woman of the Year award L.A. County Fine Art Mus., 1981, Artist In Residence award Arts Victoria, 1978, Transindental Meditation award Art & Peace, 1982. Home: 894 Summerland San Pedro CA 90731

KATZUNG, BERTRAM GEORGE, pharmacologist; b. Mineola, N.Y., June 11, 1932; m. Alice V. Camp; children: Katharine Blanche, Brian Lee. BA, Syracuse U., 1953; MD, SUNY, Syracuse, 1957; PhD, U. Calif., San Francisco, 1962. Prof. U. Calif., San Francisco, 1958—, v. chmn. Dept. Pharmacology, 1983—. Author: Drug Therapy, 1991, Basic and Clinical Pharmacology, 1992, Pharmacology, Examination and Board Review, 1993; contbr. articles to profl. jours. Markle scholar. Mem. AAAS, AAUP, Am. Soc. Pharmacology and Experimental Therapeutics, Biophysical Soc., Fed. Am. Scientists, Internat. Soc. Heart Rsch., Soc. Gen. Physiologists, Western Pharmacology Soc., Phi Beta Kappa, Alpha Omega Alpha, Golden Gate Computer Soc. Office: UCSF Dept Pharmacology PO Box 0450 San Francisco CA 94143-0450

KAUFFMAN, ERLE GALEN, geologist, paleontologist; b. Washington, Feb. 9, 1933; s. Erle Benton and Paula Virginia (Graff) K.; m. Claudia C. Johnson, Sept. 1989; children from previous marriage: Donald Erle, Robin Lyn, Erica Jean. BS, U. Mich., 1955, MS, 1956, PhD, 1961; MSc (hon.), Oxford (Eng.) U., 1970; DHC, U. Göttingen, Germany, 1987. Teaching fellow, instr. U. Mich., Ann Arbor, 1956-60; from asst. to full curator dept. paleobiology Nat. Mus. Natural History Smithsonian Instn., Washington, 1960-80; prof. geology U. Colo., Boulder, 1980—, chmn. dept. geol. scis., 1980-84, interim dir. Energy, Minerals Applied Rsch. Ctr., 1989-91; adj. prof. geology George Washington U., Washington, 1962-80; cons. geologist, Boulder, 1980—. Author, editor: Cretaceous Facies, Faunas and Paleoenvironments Across the Cretaceous Western Interior Basin, 1977; contbg. editor: Concepts and Methods of Biostratigraphy, 1977, Fine-grained Deposits and Biofacies of The Cretaceous Western Interior Seaway, 1985, High Resolution Event Stratigraphy, 1988, Paleontology and Evolution: Extinction Events, 1988, Extinction Events in Earth History, 1990, Evolution of the Western Interior Basin, 1993; also jour. articles. Recipient U.S. Govt. Spl. Svc. award, 1969, NSF Best Tchr. award U. Colo., 1985 R.C. Moore medal Soc. Sedimentary Geology, 1991; named Disting. Lectr. Am. Geol. Inst., 1963-64, Am. Assn. Petroleum Geologists, 1984, 85, 91, 92; Fulbright fellow, Australia, 1986. Fellow Geol. Soc. Am., AAAS; mem. Paleontol. Soc. (councilor under 40, pres. elect 1981, pres. 1982, past pres. 1983, chmn. 5 coms.); mem. NRC (rep.), Palaeontol. Assn., Internat. Paleontol. Assn. (v.p. 1982-88), Paleontol. Research Instn., Am. Assn. Petroleum Geol., Soc. Sedimentary Geology (com. mem., Spl. Svc. award 1985, Best Paper award 1985), Rocky Mountain Assn. Geologists (project chief) (Scientist of Yr. 1977), Paleontol. Soc. Wash. (pres., sec., treas.), Geol. Soc. Wash. (councilor), Md. Acad. Scis. (hon. Paleontology sect.), Sigma Xi, Phi Kappa Phi, Sigma Gamma Epsilon. Democrat. Home: Flagstaff Star Rte 3555 Bison Dr Boulder CO 80302 Office: U Colo Dept Geol Scis Campus Box 250 Boulder CO 80309

KAUFFMAN, JEFFREY LAYNE, SR., minister; b. Plymouth, Ind., Sept. 3, 1961; s. Ronald Lynn and Sara Lea (Blackford) K.; m. Barbara Carol Hendricks, June 30, 1984; children: Jeffrey Layne Jr., Elyse Joy, David Raymond, Jonathon Ronald. Diploma, Moody Bible Inst., 1980, Word of Life Bible Inst., 1983. Ordained to ministry Bapt. Ch. Student staff evangelist Open Air Campagners, N.Y.C., 1980-83, Chgo., 1980-83; dir. student outreach Moody Bible Inst., Chgo., 1981-83; youth pastor Tippecanoe (Ind.) Community Ch., 1984-85; asst. pastor El Dorado Bapt. Ch., Phoenix, 1985-86; sr. pastor El Dorado Bapt. Ch., 1986-88, Cactus Bapt. Ch., Phoenix, 1988—; mem. Southwest Conservation Bapt. New Ch. Com., Phoenix, 1988—; mem.-at-large Conservative Bapt. Pastor's fellow, Phoenix, 1990; mem. Conservative Bapt. Ordination Com., Phoenix, 1991—. Coach Paradise Valley Parks Recreation, Northeast Phoenix, 1990-91. Mem. Nat. Assn. Evangelicals, Greater Phoenix Assn. Evangelicals. Republican. Home: 3932 E Captain Dreyfus Ave Phoenix AZ 85032-6641 Office: Cactus Bapt Ch 13244 N 21st Pl Phoenix AZ 85022-5111

KAUFFMAN, WILLIAM RAY, lawyer; b. Chambersburg, Pa., Nov. 11, 1947; s. Harold William and Margaret Lenna (McCann) K.; children: Michael Harold, Scott William. BA, Gettsburg (Pa.) Coll., 1969; JD, U. Pitts., 1972. Bar: Pa. 1972, Kans. 1977, U.S. Dist. Ct. Kans. 1977, U.S. Supreme Ct. 1980, Alaska 1986. Dir. employee rels. Shippensburg (Pa.) State Coll., 1972-74; asst. atty. gen., regional legal counsel Pa. State Colls. and Univ. System, Millerville, 1974-76; gen. counsel Kans. Bd. of Regents, Topeka, 1976-86; gen. counsel U. Alaska, Fairbanks, 1986-88, v.p., gen. counsel, 1988—; mem. adj. faculty U. Alaska Fairbanks, 1990—. Incorporator, bd. dirs. Pioneer Village, Inc., Topeka, 1979-84; bd. dirs. Presbyn. Hospitality House, Fairbanks, 1988-92, State of Alaska Phys. Therapy and Occupational Therapy Bd., Juneau, Alaska, 1989-92. Mem. Alaska Bar Assn., Nat. Assn. Coll. and Univ. Attys. (bd. dirs. 1989-92), Am. Corp. Coun. Assn., Nat. Pub. Employer Labor Rels. Assn. Office: U Alaska 910 Yukon Dr Ste 203 Butrovich Bldg Fairbanks AK 99775

KAUFMAN, ALBERT I., lawyer; b. N.Y.C., Oct. 2, 1936; s. Israel and Pauline (Pardes) K.; m. Ruth Feldman, Jan. 25, 1959; 1 son, Michael Paul. A.A., L.A. City Coll., 1957; B.A., U. San Fernando Valley, 1964, J.D., 1966. Bar: Calif. 1967, U.S. Ct. Appeals (9th cir.) 1968, U.S. Supreme Ct. 1971, U.S. Dist. Ct. (cen. dist.) Calif. 1967, U.S. Tax Ct. 1971, U.S. Ct. Internat. Trade 1981. Sole practice, Encino, Calif., 1967—; judge pro tem L.A. Mcpl. Ct., 1980—, L.A. Superior Ct., 1991—; family law mediator L.A. Superior Ct., 1980—. Mem. Pacific S.W. regional bd. Anti-Defamation league of B'nai B'rith, 1970-91. Served with USAF, 1959-65, to col. CAP, 1956—. Recipient Disting. Svc. award B'nai B'rith, 1969; Exceptional Service award CAP, 1977. Mem. ABA, L.A. County Bar Assn., San Fernando Valley Bar Assn., Calif. Trial Lawyers Assn., L.A. Trial Lawyers Assn. Republican. Clubs: Toastmasters, Westerners 1117 (pres. 1969), B'nai B'rith (pres. 1971-72). Office: 17609 Ventura Blvd Suite 201 Encino CA 91316

KAUFMAN, HERBERT MARK, educator; b. Bronx, N.Y., Nov. 1, 1946; s. Henry and Betty (Fried) K.; m. Helen Laurie Fox, July 23, 1967; 1 child, Jonathan Hart. BA, SUNY, Binghamton, 1967; PhD, Pa. State U., 1972. Economist Fed. Nat. Mortgage Assn., Washington, 1972-73; asst. prof. Ariz. State U., Tempe, 1973-76; econs. prof. Ariz. State U., 1980-88; fin. prof. Ariz. State U., Tempe, 1988—, chair dept. fin., 1991—; exec. dir. Ctr. for Fin. System, chmn. dept. fin. Ariz. State U., 1988—; cons. World Bank, Washington, 1985-86, Gen. Acctg. Office, Washington, 1985, Congl. Budget Office, Washington, 1980. Author: Financial Markets, Financial Institutions and Money, 1983, (with others) The Political Economy of Policy Making, 1979, Money and Banking, 1991; contbr. articles to profl. jours. Mem. Am. Econ. Assn., Am. Fin. Assn., Nat. Assn. of Bus. Economists. Home: 1847 E Calle De Caballos Tempe AZ 85284-2505 Office: Ariz State U Dept Fin Tempe AZ 85287

KAUFMAN, IRVING, engineer, educator; b. Geinsheim, Germany, Jan. 11, 1925; came to U.S., 1938, naturalized, 1945; s. Albert and Hedwig Kaufmann; m. Ruby Lee Dordek, Sept. 10, 1950; children—Eve Deborah, Sharon Anne, Julie Ellen. B.E., Vanderbilt U., 1945; M.S., U. Ill., 1949, Ph.D., 1957. Engr. RCA Victor, Indpls., Ind. and Camden, N.J., 1945-48; instr., research assoc. U. Ill., Urbana, 1949-56; sr. mem. tech. staff Ramo-Wooldridge & Space Tech. Labs., Calif., 1957-64; prof. engring. Ariz. State U., 1965—; founder, dir. Solid State Research Lab., 1968-78; collaborator Los Alamos Nat. Lab., 1989, 91; vis. scientist Consiglio Nazionale delle Ricerche, Italy, 1973-74; vis. prof. U. Auckland, N.Z., 1974; liaison scientist U.S. Office Naval Rsch., London, 1978-80; lectr. and cons. elec. engring. Contbr. articles to profl. jours. Recipient Disting. Research award Ariz. State U. Grad. Coll., 1986-87; Sr. Fulbright research fellow Italy, 1964-65, 73-74, Am. Soc. for Engring. Edn./Naval Rsch. Lab. fellow, 1988. Fellow IEEE; mem. Am. Phys. Soc., Electromagnetics Acad., Gold Key (hon.), Sigma Xi, Tau Beta Pi, Eta Kappa Nu, Pi Mu Epsilon. Jewish. Office: Ariz State U Dept Elec and Computer Engring Tempe AZ 85287-5706

KAUFMAN, JONATHAN ALLAN, public relations executive; b. N.Y.C., May 31, 1943; s. Stephen Allan and Jean (Friedman) K.; m. Jill J. Horowitz, July 17, 1982. BA, Carleton Coll., 1966; MA, Syracuse U., 1967. Vol. VISTA, N.Y.C., 1967-69; rsch. dir. Nat. Welfare Rights Orgn., Washington, 1969-71; polit. campaign mgr. various, San Francisco, 1971-77; exec. dir. Calif. Tax Reform Assn., San Francisco, 1972-77; asst. mgr. Household Fin. Corp., San Francisco, 1977-79; account exec. Solem & Assocs., San Francisco, 1979-84, v.p., 1984-86, exec. v.p., 1986—. Contbr. articles to profl. jours. Pres. Ann Martin Children's Ctr., Oakland, Calif.; mem. bd. Jewish Bulletin of No. Calif., San Francisco; bd. dirs. Am. Israel Pub. Affairs

Com. of No. Calif., San Francisco. Andrew W. Mellon Fellow, Syracuse U., 1966, Max Bondy Citizenship award Windsor Mt. Sch., Lenox, Mass., 1962. Mem. Am. Assn. Polit. Cons. Jewish. Home: 107 Alvarado Rd Berkeley CA 94705-1510 Office: Solem & Assocs 545 Mission St Fl 5 San Francisco CA 94105-2931

KAUFMAN, JULIAN MORTIMER, broadcasting company executive, consultant; b. Detroit, Apr. 3, 1918; s. Anton and Fannie (Newman) K.; m. Katherine LaVerne Likins, May 6, 1942; children: Nikki, Keith Anthony. Grad. high sch., Newark. Pub. Elizabeth (N.J.) Sunday Sun, Inc., 1937-39; account exec. Tolle Advt. Agy., San Diego, 1947-49; pub. Tucson Shopper, 1948-50; account exec. ABC, San Francisco, 1949-50; mgr. Sta. KPHO-TV, Phoenix, 1950-52; gen. mgr., v.p. Bay City TV Corp., San Diego, 1952-85; v.p. Jai Alai Films, Inc., San Diego, 1961—; TV cons. Julian Kaufman, Inc., San Diego, 1985—; dir. Spanish Internat. Broadcasting, Inc., L.A. Contbr. articles to profl. jours.; producer (TV show) Pick a Winner. Mem. Gov.'s adv. bd., Mental Health Assn., 1958—; bd. dirs. Francis Parker Sch., San Diego Better Bus. Bur., 1979-84, San Diego Conv. and Visitors Bur., World Affairs Coun., Pala Indian Mission. Served with USAAF, 1942-46. Recipient Peabody award, 1975, Emmy award, 1980. Mem. San Diego C. of C., Advt. and Sales Club, Sigma Delta Chi. Republican. Clubs: San Diego Press, University (San Diego). Home: 3125 Montesano Rd Escondido CA 92029-7302 Office: 8253 Ronson Rd San Diego CA 92111-2004

KAUFMAN, MARCUS MAURICE, retired judge, lawyer; b. Norfolk, Va., June 19, 1929; s. Samuel Kaufman and Mary (Vitsky) Rushall; m. Eileen Fern Wilkin, Sept. 3, 1950; children: Sharon Kaufman Granowitz, Joel Alan (dec.), Ellen Kaufman Wolf. BA, UCLA, 1951; JD, U. So. Calif., 1956. Bar: Calif. 1956, U.S. Supreme Ct. 1991, U.S. Ct. Appeals (9th cir.) 1991. Rsch. atty. Calif. Supreme Ct., 1956-57; law instr. U. So. Calif. Law Sch., 1957-58; ptnr. Kaufman and Wagner, San Bernardino, Calif., 1958-70; assoc. justice Calif. Ct. Appeal, San Bernardino, 1970-87, Calif. Supreme Ct., San Francisco, 1987-90; of counsel Buchalter, Nemer, Fields and Younger, Newport Beach, CA, 1990—; mem. faculty Calif. Jud. Edn. and Rsch. Found., 1974-87; law lectr. Rutter Group and local bar assns., 1983—; pres., bd. dirs. Legal Aid Soc., San Bernardino, 1961-63; mem. State Bar disciplinary com., San Bernardino, 1962-64, chmn., 1964-66; bd. dirs. Criminal Justice Legal Found., 1991—; mem. Am. Jur. Editorial Adv. Bd., 1991—. Co-author: California Practice Guide: Bad Faith, 1986; editor in chief U. S.C. Law Sch. Law Rev., 1955-56; author numerous legal opinions for cts. publs., 1970-90. Mem. and chmn. San Bernardino County Air Pollution Control Hearing Bd., 1967-70; chmn. troup com. Boy Scouts Am., San Bernardino, 1968. 1st lt. U.S. Army, 1951-53, Korea. Mem. ABA, Calif. State Bar Assn., San Bernardino County Bar Assn. (sec. 1963-64), L.A. County Bar Assn., Orange County Bar Assn., Orange County Legion Lex Inn of Ct., Calif. Judges Assn., Legion Lex U. So. Calif. Law Ctr. (life), Order of Coif, Hadassah (Arrowhead chpt. San Bernardino, assoc.), Jewish War Vets., B'nai Brith, Phi Beta Kappa. Republican. Jewish. Office: Buchalter Nemer Fields & Younger 660 Newport Center Dr Newport Beach CA 92660-6401

KAUFMAN, ROBERT JAMES, sales executive, promotions consultant, restaurantmanager; b. San Jose, Calif., May 4, 1966; s. S. Fred and Madeline (Soares) K. BA in Advt., San Jose State U., 1989. Asst. v.p. Engelter, Cross and Tapson Promotions and Mktg., San Jose, Calif., 1989-91; v.p. Rose Promotions, Los Gatos, Calif., 1991; mgr. Steamers Restaurant, Los Gatos, Calif., 1983—; sales exec., mktg. dir. Cable Connection, Los Gatos, Calif., 1991—; cons. Rose Promotions, Los Gatos, 1991—, Engelter Enterprises, San Jose, 1991—. Coach Pop Warner Football, Los Gatos, 1989, 90. Mem. Sigma Alpha Epsilon (Man of Yr. 1989). Democrat. Jewish. Office: Cable Connection 102 Cooper Ct Los Gatos CA 95030

KAUFMAN, S. HARVARD, psychiatrist; b. Milw., Dec. 16, 1913; s. Nathan and Helen (Greenberg) K.; m. Leone Van Gelda, Apr. 28, 1934 (dec. June 10, 1985); children: Elizabeth Sarah, Mark; m. Leona M. Dairymple, Nov. 29, 1986. BS, U. Wis., 1934, MD, 1936. Diplomate Am. Bd. Neurology and Psychiatry. Intern Milw. County Hosp., 1936-37; resident Milw. Sanitarium, Wauwatosa, Wis., 1937-38, Worcester (Mass.) State Hosp., 1938-41; fellow forensic U. Pa., Phila., 1941-43; dir. Western State Psychiat. Inst., Pitts., 1943-45; juvenile psychiatrist Allegheny Juvenile Ct., Pitts., 1944-45; instr. U. Pitts., 1944-45; dir. Seattle Clinic, 1945-49; dir., asst. prof. child psychiatry, clin. prof. U. Wash., 1949-55, 60—; psychiat. cons. Shoreline Sch. dist., Seattle, 1958-71, Children's Indsl. Home, Tacoma, Wash., 1992—; examining psychiatrist, Seattle VA Hosp. Co-author: K-F-D, 1970, 72; contbr. numerous articles to profl. jours. Mem. Seattle Ctrl. Sch. Coun., 1965-68. Fellow Am. Psychiat. Assn., Am. Acad. Child and Adolescent Psychiatry. Democrat. Jewish. Office: 710 10th Ave E Seattle WA 99102-4506

KAUFMAN, SHELLEY S., psychologist; b. Syracuse, N.Y., July 16, 1953; d. Elliott Alexander and Arlene Phyllis (Wolfe) K.; m. Timothy James Burke, Nov. 27, 1977; children: Marin, David. BA, Ariz. State U., 1975, MA, 1977, M Counseling, 1978, PhD, 1984. Lic. psychologist, Ariz. Tchr. Alief Ind. Sch. Dist., Houston, 1975-76; elem. sch. counselor Chandler (Ariz.) Unified Sch. Dist., 1978-80, 85-86; child therapist Jane Wayland Ctr., Phoenix, 1986-87, psychologist, 1987-88; psychologist Inst. Neurodevelopmental Tng., Phoenix, 1988; outpatient clin. dir. Wayland Family Ctrs., Phoenix, 1988-90; dir. clin. svcs. Jewish Family and Children's Svc., Phoenix, 1990-91; pvt. practice Phoenix, 1991—; cons. NOVA, Phoenix, 1989-90, Terros, Phoenix, 1989-90; faculty assoc. Ariz. State U., Tempe, 1987-89; assoc. med. staff St. Luke Hosp., Phoenix, 1989—, Charter Hosp. East Valley, Chandler, Ariz., 1989—. Grad. Students Assn. rsch. grantee, 1983. Mem. Am. Psychol. Assn., N.Y. Acad. Scis., Phi Delta Kappa. Democrat. Jewish. Home: 1966 E Kentucky Ln Tempe AZ 85284-1731 Office: 512 E Van Buren St Bldg 5 Phoenix AZ 85004-2234

KAUFMANN, THOMAS DAVID, economist, educator; b. Rye, N.Y., July 23, 1922; s. Fritz and Irma (Heiden) K.; B.A., Oberlin Coll., 1943; M.P.A., Harvard U., 1947, M.A., 1947, Ph.D., 1949; m. Maureen Liebl, June 4, 1983; children—Peter F., David T. Economist, U.S. del. NATO and OEEC, Paris, 1949-56; dir. new bus. Amax, Inc., N.Y.C., 1956-67; v.p. Alumax, Inc., Greenwich, Conn., 1967-69; dir. bus. planning Hunter-Douglas, London, 1969-75; trader Asoma, N.Y.C., 1975-77; cons. Daniel K. Ludwig, N.Y.C., 1977-82; prof. mineral econs. Colo. Sch. Mines, Golden, 1982-92. Contbr. articles to profl. jours. Served with U.S. Army, 1943-46. Mem. Am. Econ. Assn., Mineral Econs. & Mgmt. Soc., Am. Arbitration Assn., Phi Beta Kappa. Jewish. Home: 1966 Mt Zion Dr Golden CO 80401-1736 Office: Colo Sch Mines Golden CO 80401

KAUKONEN, JORMA L., foundation administrator, retired foreign service officer; b. Ironwood, Mich., Oct. 24, 1910; s. Jacob L. and Ida (Palmquist) K.; m. Beatrice Levine, Dec. 26, 1936; children: Jorma Ludwig, Benson Lee. AB, UCLA, 1933; postgrad., George Washington U., 1935-36, Am. U., 1937-39, U. Mich., 1945. Health edn. specialist USPHS, 1938-40; info. specialist Social Security Bd., 1940-42; sr. adminstrv. officer War Manpower Commn., 1943-44; labor advisor U.S. Mil. Govt., Seoul, Korea, 1946-49; chief Asian sect. Bur. Labor Stats. U.S. Dept. Labor, 1949-52, Asian specialist, 1952-54, Far East specialist Office Internat. Labor Affairs, 1956-57; Pakistan rep. to Asia Found., 1955-56; labor attaché Am. Embassy, Manila, Philippines, 1957-60, 1st sec., labor attache, 1960-62; labor attaché, 1st sec., polit. officer U.S. Embassy, Stockholm, 1967-70; labor attaché, 1st sec., econ. officer U.S. Embassy, Ottawa, Ont., Can., 1967-70; ret., 1970. Pres. Palo Alto-Stanford (Calif.) chpt. Finlandia Found., 1974-84, nat. trustee, 1984—, also past sec., past pres.; bd. dirs. Finnish Am. Home Assn., Sonoma, Calif.; active various community orgns., Mill Valley, Calif. Served to lt. (j.g.) USNR, 1944-46. Mem. Finnish Brotherhood Lodge of Berkeley, Belvedere Tennis Club (past. pres.). Home: 30 Underhill Rd Mill Valley CA 94941

KAUNE, JAMES EDWARD, ship repair company executive, former naval officer; b. Santa Fe, N.Mex., Mar. 4, 1927; s. Henry Eugene and Lucile (Carter) K.; B.S., U.S. Naval Acad., 1950; Naval Engr. degree Mass. Inst. Tech., 1955; B.S. in Metallurgy, Carnegie-Mellon U., 1960; m. Pauline Stamatos, June 24, 1956; children—Bradford Scott, Audrey Lynn, Jason Douglas. Commd. ensign U.S. Navy, 1950, advanced through grades to capt., 1970; asst. gunnery officer U.S.S. Floyd B. Parks, 1950-52; project officer U.S.S. Gyatt, Boston Naval Shipyard, 1955-57; main propulsion officer U.S.S. Tarawa, 1957-58; asst. planning officer Her Majesty's Canadian Dockyard, Halifax, N.S., Can., 1960-62; repair officer U.S.S. Cadmus, 1962-64; fleet maintenance officer Naval Boiler and Turbine Lab., 1964-68; various shipyard assignments, 1968-70, material staff officer U.S. Naval Air Forces Atlantic Fleet, 1971-74; production officer Phila. Naval Shipyard, 1974-79; comdr. Long Beach Naval Shipyard, Calif.; exec. v.p. Am. Metal Bearing Co., Garden Grove, Calif., from 1979; gen. mgr. San Francisco div. Topp Shipyards, Alameda, Calif., v.p. engring. Point Richmond Shipyard (Calif.); v.p. engring., mktg. Service Engring. Corp, San Francisco. Mem. Am. Soc. Naval Engrs., Am. Soc. Quality Control, Soc. Naval Architects and Marine Engrs., U.S. Naval Inst., Am. Soc. Metals. Episcopalian. Club: Masons. Contbr. articles to profl. jours. Home: 403 Camino Sobrante Orinda CA 94563-1844 Office: Svc Engring Corp Pier 50 San Francisco CA 94107

KAUPINS, GUNDARS EGONS, education educator; b. Mpls., Dec. 29, 1956; s. Alfreds and Skaidrite (Akots) K. BA, Wartburg Coll., 1979; MBA, U. No. Iowa, 1981; PhD, U. Iowa, 1986. Grad. asst. U. No. Iowa, Cedar Falls, 1979-81; employee rels. asst. Norand Corp., Cedar Rapids, 1983; grad. asst. Univ. Iowa, Iowa City, 1981-86; assoc. prof. Boise (Idaho) State U., 1986—; cons. in field. Contbr. articles to profl. jours. Recipient rsch. grants Boise State U., 1987-89, Ponder scholarship U. Iowa, 1983-85; named Adv. of the Yr., Boise State U., 1989. Mem. Soc. for Human Resource Mgmt. (sec., v.p. 1982-83), ASTD (sec. 1989), Assn. of Mgmt., Acad. of Mgmt., Am. Psychol. Assn. Home: 1829 W Boise Ave Apt F Boise ID 83706-3403 Office: Boise State U Dept Mgmt Boise ID 83725

KAUR, SWARAJ, research biochemist; b. Lucknow, India, Jan. 30, 1955; came to U.S., 1984; d. Kartar Singh and Joginder Kaur. MusB, Bhatkande Music U., Lucknow, India, 1971; MusM, Bhatkande Sangeet MahaVidyalaya, Lucknow, India, 1974; MS in Biochemistry, Lucknow U., 1975, PhD, 1981; MBA, Nat. U., San Diego, 1989. Jr. rsch. fellow Coun. Sci. and Indsl. Rsch., Lucknow, 1976-78, sr. rsch. fellow, 1978-80; sr. rsch. fellow Indian Coun. Med. Rsch., Lucknow, 1980-81, rsch. assoc., 1982-84; postdoctoral rsch. toxicologist U. Calif., Riverside, 1984-86; sr. project scientist Alpha Therapeutic Corp., L.A., 1986-88, prin. scientist, 1988-91, sr. prin. scientist, 1992-93, assoc. dir., 1993—; presenter at symposia and sci. confs., 1979—. Contbr. articles to profl. jours. Mem. Sigma Xi. Sikh. Home: 10395 Vernon Ave Montclair CA 91763-4508 Office: Alpha Therapeutic Corp 5555 Valley Blvd Los Angeles CA 90032

KAUTZ, JUDITH ANN, administrator; b. Muscatine, Iowa, Sept. 22, 1943; d. Richard Carl and Mary Elda (Stein) K; children: Jess Calvin, William Noa. BS, U. Ariz., 1967; MPH, U. Tex., 1973, PhD, 1977; MBA, U. Hawaii, 1986. Computer programmer M.D. Anderson Hosp., Houston, 1968-69; systems analyst Med. Computer Systems, Houston, 1969-71, Baylor Coll. Medicine, Houston, 1971-73; stat. cons. U. Tes., Houston, 1973-76; asst. prof. Northwestern U., Chgo., 1976-78; asst. prof. Baylor Coll. Medicine, 1978-83, asst. to v.p., 1982-83; biostat. Kuakini Hosp., Honolulu, 1983-85; mgmt. cons. U. Rsch. Corp., Bethesda, Md., 1987-89; assoc. dean U. Hawaii Coll. Bus. Adminstrn., Honolulu, 1989—; bd. dirs. Hawaii Soc. Corp. Planners, Honolulu; regional adv. bd. Biometric Soc., Washington, 1979-81; vice chair info. tech. adv. com. U. Hawaii, 1990—; adv. com. Tech. Transfer and Faculty Entrepreneurship, 1992—. Contbr. articles to profl. jours.; contbr. editor: Current Index Stats., 1976-83. Active Nature Conservancy, 1983—; pres. parent/faculty assn. Assets Sch., Honolulu, 1991—; mediator Neighborhood Justice Ctr., Honolulu, 1991—. Mem. Am. Stat. Assn., Pacific Club, Assn. Mgmt. Sci., Women Acad. Adminstrn., PEO, Kappa Kappa Gamma, Beta Gamma Sigma. Home: 1005 Kailua Rd Apt D Kailua HI 96734-4365 Office: U Hawaii Coll Bus Adminstrn 2404 Maile Way Honolulu HI 96822-2282

KAUZLARICH, SUSAN MARY, educator, researcher; b. Worchester, Mass., Sept. 24, 1958; d. James Joseph and Sally Ann (Smith) K.; m. Peter Klavins, May 7, 1988. BS, Coll. William & Mary, 1980; PhD, Mich. State U., 1985. Postdoctoral researcher Ames Lab., Iowa State U., 1985-87; asst. prof. solid state chem. U. Calif., Davis, 1987-92, assoc. prof., 1992—. Com. mem. Minority Undergrad. Rsch. Apprenticeships in Letters and Sci. Mem. AAAS, Am. Chem. Soc., Materials Rsch. Soc., Sigma Xi, Iota Sigma Pi. Office: Univ Calif Dept Chemistry Davis CA 95616

KAWACHIKA, JAMES AKIO, lawyer; b. Honolulu, Dec. 5, 1947; s. Shinichi and Tsuyoko (Murashige) K.; m. Karen Keiko Takahashi, Sept. 1, 1973; 1 child, Robyn Mari. BA, U. Hawaii, Honolulu, 1969; JD, U. Calif., Berkeley, 1973. Bar: Hawaii 1973, U.S. Dist. Ct. Hawaii 1973, U.S. Ct. Appeals (9th cir.) 1974, U.S. Supreme Ct. 1992. Dep. atty. gen. Office of Atty. Gen. State of Hawaii, Honolulu, 1973-74; assoc. Padgett, Greeley & Marumoto, Honolulu, 1974-75, Law Office of Frank D. Padgett, Honolulu, 1975-77, Kobayashi, Watanabe, Sugita & Kawashima, Honolulu, 1977-82; ptnr. Carlsmith, Wichman, Case, Mukai & Ichiki, Honolulu, 1982-86, Bays, Deaver, Hiatt, Kawachika & Lezak, Honolulu, 1986—; mem. Hawaii Bd. of Bar Examiners, Honolulu; arbitrator Cir. Ct. Arbitration Program State of Hawaii, Honolulu, 1986—. Mem. Disciplinary Bd. Hawaii Supreme Ct., 1991—; mem. U.S. Dist. Ct. Adv. Com. on the Civil Justice Reform Act of 1990, 1991—. Mem. ABA, Hawaii Bar Assn. (bd. dirs. Honolulu chpt. 1975-76, young lawyers sect. 1983-84, 92-93, treas. 1987-88), 9th Crct. Jud. Conf. (lawyer rep., Honolulu chpt. 1988-90), Assn. Trial Lawyers Am. Office: Bays Deaver Hiatt Kawachika & Lezak Alii Pl 16th Fl 1099 Alakea St Honolulu HI 96813

KAWAHARA, RONALD AKIRA, accountant, real estate executive; b. Wailuku, Hawaii, Nov. 27, 1943; s. Archer A. and Bessie K. (Saito) K.; divorced; 1 child, Robert S. BBA, U. Hawaii, 1968. CPA; cert. property mgr. Auditor Haskins & Sells, CPAs, Kahului, Hawaii, 1968-70; pres. Ronald A. Kawahara & Co. CPAs Inc., Lahaina, Hawaii, 1970—, Destination Maui, Inc., Lahaina, 1974—. Pres. Maui United Way, 1982, West Maui Taxpayers Assn., 1990-92. With U.S. Army, 1965-67. Mem. AICPA, Inst. Real Estate Mgmt., Maui Bd. Realtors, Maui County Bd. Taxation Rev. (chmn.), Rotary (sec.), Toastmasters (pres. Lahaina club 1991), La Chaine de Rotisseurs. Home: 1619 Lokia St Lahaina HI 96761

KAWANO, RANDALL TOSHIO, banker; b. Honolulu, Sept. 27, 1959; s. Toshio and Tokiye (Kato) K.; m. Suzanne C. Harada, Feb. 15, 1986; 1 child, Jordan T. BBA in Acctg. with distinction, U. Hawaii, 1982; grad. honors, Sch. for Bank Adminstrn., 1989. CPA, Hawaii; cert. mgmt. acct. Auditor Ernst and Whinney, Honolulu, 1983-84; acctg. officer First Hawaiian Creditcorp., Honolulu, 1984-86; asst. v.p. and asst. contr. City Bank, Honolulu, 1986-89, v.p., asst. contr., 1989-92, sr. v.p., contr., 1992—. Contbr. articles to profl. jours. Mem. AICPA, Hawaii Soc. CPAs, Inst. Mgmt. Accts. (dir. student rels. Hawaii chpt. 1990-91, v.p. profl. edn.), Nat. Assn. Bank Cost and Mgmt. Accts., Bank Adminstrn. Inst. (Hawaii chpt. v.p. edn.), Fin. Execs. Inst. Office: City Bank 201 Merchant St Honolulu HI 96813-2992

KAY, ALAN COOKE, chief judge; s. Harold Thomas and Ann (Cooke) K. BA, Princeton U., 1957; LLB, U. Calif., Berkeley, 1960. Assoc. Case, Kay & Lynch, Honolulu, 1960-64, ptnr., 1965-86; judge U.S. Dist. Ct. Hawaii, Honolulu, 1987—. Mem. steering com. Fuller Theol. Sem. Hawaii, 1985-86; pres., trustee Hawaii Mission Children's Soc., Honolulu, 1980-86; bd. dirs. Good News Mission, 1980-86, Econ. Devel. Corp. Honolulu, 1985-86, Legal Aid Soc., Honolulu, 1968-71. Mem. ABA, Hawaii Bar Assn. (exec. com. 1972-73, bd. dirs. real estate sect. 1983-86), 9th Cir. Dist. Ct. Judges Assn., Am. Inns of Ct. (counselor Aloha Inn 1987—). Republican. Office: US Dist Ct PO Box 50128 Honolulu HI 96850-0001*

KAY, FENTON RAY, habitat biologist; b. Pacolma, Calif., Oct. 10, 1942; s. Lyle E. Kay and Donna F. (Estill) Allan; m. Carol Ann Rolph, June 13, 1971 (div. Jan. 1985); children: Aelene B., Jennifer M.; m. Peggy Foley, Sept. 2, 1990; 1 stepchild, Mark Williams. BS in Biology, U. Nev., 1967, MS in Zoology, 1969; PhD in Biology, N.Mex. State U., 1974, postgrad., 1982-83. Mem. faculty Calif. State U., Los Angeles, 1976-78; sr. ecologist H.D.R. Scis. Div., Santa Barbara, Calif., 1978-79; sr. subject matter specialist OAO Kentron Internat., White Sands Missile Range, N.Mex., 1979-82; ops. mgr. OAO Corp., White Sands Missile Range, N.Mex., 1982-83; treas. CEI Corp., Las Cruces, N.Mex., 1979-82; habitat staff biologist Nev. Dept. Wildlife, Reno, 1984-90; prin. ecologist Kayrat Svcs., 1990-92; supr. natural resources databases Ariz. Game and Fish Dept., 1992-93; sr. environ. scientist Proteus Corp., Albuquerque, 1993—; mem. faculty Truckee Meadows Community Coll., Reno, 1984-89, W. Nev. Community Coll., 1988, U. Nev., Reno, 1988; cons. Nev. State Mus., Carson City, 1983-84; vis. scientist Tall Timbers Rsch. Sta., Tallahassee, 1977. Author: (computer program) Butler-Adventure, 1983, Keno-Game, 1984; contbr. articles to profl. jours. Active Citizen's Adv. Com. on Endangered Species, Las Vegas, 1968. Postdoctoral trainee NIH, 1974-76; named Outstanding Centennial Alumnus N.M. State U., 1988. Mem. Am. Soc. Mammalogists, Ecol. Soc. Am., Herpetologists' League, So. Nev. Herpetol. Soc. (founder 1967), Soc. Conservation Biology, Desert Tortoise Coun., Sigma Xi (grantee 1973). Democrat. Office: Proteus Corp 10010 Indian School Rd NE Albuquerque NM 87112

KAY, HERMA HILL, law educator; b. Orangeburg, S.C., Aug. 18, 1934; d. Charles Esdorn and Herma Lee (Crawford) Hill. BA, So. Meth. U., 1956; JD, U. Chgo., 1959. Bar: Calif. 1960. Law clk. to Justice Roger Traynor, Calif. Supreme Ct., 1959-60; asst. prof. law U. Calif., Berkeley, 1960-62; assoc. prof. U. Calif., 1962, prof., 1963, dir. family law project, 1964-67, Jennings prof., 1987—, dean, 1992—; co-reporter uniform marriage and div. act Nat. Conf. Commrs. on Uniform State Laws, 1968-70; vis. prof. U. Manchester, Eng., 1972, Harvard U., 1976; mem. Gov.'s Commn. on Family, 1966. Author: Text Cases and Materials on Sex-based Discrimination, 3d edit., 1988, Supplement, 1992; (with R. Cramton, D. Currie and L. Kramer) Conflict of Laws: Cases, Comments, Questions, 5th edit., 1993; contbr. articles to profl. jours. Trustee Russell Sage Found., N.Y., 1972-87, chmn. bd., 1980-84; trustee , bd. dirs. Equal Rights Advs. Calif., 1976—, chmn., 1976-83; pres. bd. dirs. Rosenberg Found., Calif., 1987-88, bd. dirs. 1978—. Recipient Rsch. award Am. Bar Found., 1990, award ABA Commn. Women in Profession, 1992; fellow Center Advanced Study in Behavioral Scis., Palo Alto, Calif., 1963-64. Mem. Calif. Bar Assn., Bar U.S. Supreme Ct., Calif. Women Lawyers (bd. govs. 1975-77), Am. Law Inst. (mem. coun. 1985-), Assn. Am. Law Schs. (exec. com. 1986-87, pres.-elect 1988, pres. 1989, past pres. 1990), Am. Acad. Arts and Scis., Order of Coif (nat. pres. 1983-85). Democrat. Office: U Calif Law Sch Boalt Hall Berkeley CA 94720

KAYE, IVAN NATHANIEL, writer; b. L.A., Aug. 24, 1932; s. Harry and Babette Dorothy (Richman) K. BA in History, U. Mich., 1954; MS in Journalism, Columbia U., 1958; postgrad., U. Calif., Berkeley, 1960, Harvard U., 1964-65. Reporter/writer UPI, Madison, Wis., 1958-60; Washington corres. Madison Capital Times, 1962-64; writer Newsweek Mag., N.Y.C., 1970-72; sci. writer People Mag., N.Y.C., 1974-82. Author: Good Clean Violence, A History of College Football 1973; articles pub. in Sports Illustrated, Harvard Mag., N.Y. Times, Michigan Alumnus, many others. With U.S. Army, 1954-56. Congl. fellow Am. Polit. Sci. Assn., 1960-61. Address: 950 6th St Boulder CO 80302

KAYE, JHANI, radio station manager, director; b. Maywood, Calif., June 18, 1949; s. Jimmie Eccak and Betty Jo (Holland) Kazaroff. BA, UCLA, 1971. Lic. 1st class radio. Music dir. Sta. KFXM, San Bernardino, Calif., 1969-73; announcer Stas. KUTE-FM/KKDJ-FM, L.A., 1972-74; asst. program dir. Sta. KROQ, L.A., 1973-74, Sta. WCFL, Chgo., 1980-82, Sta. KFI, L.A., 1982; program dir. Sta. KINT-FM, El Paso, Tex., 1975-80; sta. mgr., program dir. Sta. KOST-FM, L.A., 1982—. Appeared in TV series Falcon Crest, 1985; dir. TV commls., 1986—; voice-over motion picture The Couch Trip, 1987. Named Radio Program Dir. of Yr., Gavin Report, 1987, 90, Billboard Mag., 1990, Radio Sta. of Yr., Nat. Assn. Broadcasters, 1990, 91. Office: Sta KOST(FM) 610 S Ardmore Ave Los Angeles CA 90005

KAYFETZ, VICTOR JOEL, journalist, editor, translator; b. N.Y.C., July 20, 1945; s. Daniel Osler and Selma Harriet (Walowitz) K.; B.A., Columbia U., 1966; postgrad. U. Stockholm (Sweden), 1966-67; M.A. in History, U. Calif.-Berkeley, 1969. Teaching asst. in Swedish, U. Calif., Berkeley, 1969-70; tchr., adminstr. Swedish adult edn. programs, 1970-75; corr. Reuters, Stockholm, 1975-78; sub-editor Reuters World Ser., London, 1978; corr. London Fin. Times, Stockholm, 1979-80; free lance translator Swedish, Danish, Norwegian, 1967—; free lance journalist, editor Swedish and Am. mags., Stockholm, 1979-80, San Francisco, 1980—. Henry Evans traveling fellow, 1966-67; Nat. Def. Fgn. Lang. fellow, 1967-69; Thord Gray fellow Am.-Scandinavian Found., 1970. Mem. Swedish Am. C. of C., Swedish Bus. and Soc. Research Inst., Soc. Advancement Scandinavian Study, Am. Scandinavian Found., World Affairs Council No. Calif., Sierra Club, Phi Beta Kappa. Author: Sweden in Brief, 1974, 80; Invest in Sweden, 1984, Skanska, the First Century, 1987; editor, translator numerous books, ann. reports, mags. for Swedish govt. agys. interest orgns., univs., insl. corps., banks. Office: Scan Edit 870 Market St Ste 1284 San Francisco CA 94102-2907

KAYLAN, HOWARD LAWRENCE, musical entertainer, composer; b. N.Y.C., June 22, 1947; s. Sidney and Sally Joyce (Berlin) K.; m. Mary Melita Pepper, June 10, 1967 (div. Sept. 1971); 1 child, Emily Anne; m. Susan Karen Olsen, Apr. 18, 1982; 1 child, Alexandra Leigh. Grad. high sch., Los Angeles. Lead singer rock group The Turtles, Los Angeles, 1965-70, Mothers of Invention, Los Angeles, 1970-72, Flo and Eddie, 1972—; radio, TV, recording entertainer various broadcast organizations, Los Angeles, 1972—; screenwriter Larry Gelbart, Carl Gotleib prodns., Los Angeles, 1979-85; producer children's records Kidstuff Records, Hollywood, Fla., 1980—; singer, producer rock band Flo and Eddie, Los Angeles, 1976—; singer, producer The Turtles (reunion of original band), Los Angeles, 1980—; actor, TV and film Screen Actors Guild, Los Angeles, 1983—; background vocalist various albums for Bruce Springsteen, John Lennon, numerous other performers; syndicated talk show host Unistar Radio Network, 1989—; radio personality Sta. WXRK-FM, N.Y.C., 1990-91, KLOU, St. Louis, 1993. Contbr. articles to Creem Magazine, Los Angeles Free Press, Rockit Magazine, Phonograph Record; screenwriter motion picture Death Masque, 1985; actor motion picture Get Crazy, 1985; performed at the White House, 1970. Recipient 8 Gold and Platinum LP album awards while lead singer, 1965—, Fine Arts award, Bank of Am., L.A., 1965, Spl. Billboard Mag. award, 1992; recorded numerous top ten hit songs during sixties with Turtles. Mem. AFTRA, Screen Actors Guild, Am. Fedn. Musicians, AGVA. Democrat.

KAYSER, DAVID WILLIAM, archaeologist; b. Chgo., June 22, 1939; s. Clio George Kayser and Mary E. (Granda Merva; m. Linda Monzingo, 1973 (div. 1974); m. Mary Jo Woodfin-Lass, 1979 (div. 1982); life ptnr. Sylvia Hawley; 1 child, Benjamin H. Student, Ariz. State U., 1962-68, U. Nev., 1991, 92. Chief excavation crew Tumacacon Nat. Monument, Nat. Park Svc., 1965; archaeologist ruins stblzn. unit Nat. Park Svc., Chaco Canyon, N.Mex., 1966; survey archaeologist Ariz. State Mus., U. Ariz., Tucson, 1967, asst. ethnographer, 1969; archaeologist, curator II Lab. Anthropology Mus. N.Mex., Santa Fe, 1969-78; asst. state monument dir. monuments div. Mus. N.Mex., 1973; archaeologist, soil technician U.S. Soil Conservation Svc., Reserve, N.Mex., 1980; archaeologist, dir. Taos (N.Mex.) Archaeol. Rsch. Assocs., 1981-82; curator El Rincon Trading Post and Mus., Taos, 1982-85; archaeologist Bur. Land Mgmt., U.S. Dept. Interior, Socorro, Carlsbad, Farmington, N.Mex., 1985-91, Bakersfield, Calif., 1991—; founder Archaeol. Svcs., Santa Fe, 1973-75; co-founder Taos Archaeol. Rsch. Assocs., 1981-82. Author: (monograph) The Mesa Top Mogollon: Excavations, 1974, Archaeological Survey of West Central New Mexico, 1989; co-editor: Archeology of the Gallisteo Basin, New Mexico, 1976; author more than 100 articles on archaeology, ethnogeology, cultural history, and history of greater southwestern U.S. Comdr. Royal Rangers, Christian Family Ch., Taos, 1985-86. With USMC, 1958-62. Recipient spl. achievement award Bur. Land Mgmt., 1986, 91; J.R. Reynolds scholar Ariz. State U., 1966. Mem. Am. Assn. Conservation Archaeologists, Soc. for Calif. Archaeology. Home: PO Box 80564 Bakersfield CA 93380 Office: US Dept Interior Bur Land Mgmt 4301 Rosedale Hwy Bakersfield CA 93380

KAYTON, MYRON, engineering company executive; b. N.Y.C., Apr. 26, 1934; s. Albert Louis and Rae (Danoff) K.; m. Paula Erde, Sept. 5, 1954; children: Elizabeth Kayton Kerns, Susan Kayton Barclay. BS, The Cooper Union, 1955; MS, Harvard U., 1956; PhD, MIT, 1960. Registered engr., Calif. Sect. head Litton Industries, Woodland Hills, Calif., 1960-65; dep. mgr. NASA, Houston, 1965-69; mem. sr. staff TRW, Inc., Redondo Beach, Calif., 1969-81; pres. Kayton Engring. Co., Inc., Santa Monica, Calif., 1981—; chmn. bd. dirs. WINCON Conf., L.A., 1985-92; founding dir. Caltech-MIT Enterprise Forum, Pasadena, Calif., 1984—; tchr. tech. courses UCLA Extension, 1969-88. Author: Avionic Navigation Systems, 1966,

Navigation: Land, Sea, Air and Space, 1990; contbr. numerous articles on engrng., econs. and other profl. subjects. Founding dir. UCLA Friends of Humanities, 1971-75; West coast chmn. Cooper Union Fund Campaign, 1989—. Fellow NSF, Washington, 1956-57, 58-60; recipient Gano Dunn medal The Cooper Union, N.Y.C., 1975. Fellow IEEE (pres. aerospace 1993—, exec. v.p. aerospace 1991-92, v.p. tech. ops., 1988-90, nat. bd. govs. 1983—, vice chmn. L.A. coun. 1983-84, M.B. Carlton award 1988, disting. lectr.); mem. ASME, Harvard Grad. Soc. (coun. mem. chmn. nominating com. 1988-91), Inst. Navigation, Soc. Automotive Engr., Harvard Club So. Calif. (pres. 1979-80), MIT Club (L.A.). Office: Kayton Engring Co PO Box 802 Santa Monica CA 90406-0802

KAZAN, BENJAMIN, research engineer; b. N.Y.C., May 8, 1917; s. Abraham Eli and Esther (Bookbinder) K.; m. Gerda B. Mosse, Nov. 4, 1988; 1 child from previous marriage, David Louis. BS in Physics, Calif. Inst. Tech., 1938; MA in Physics, Columbia U., 1940; PhD in Physics, Tech. U. Munich, 1961. Radio engr. Dept. Def., Ft. Monmouth, N.J., 1940-50; rsch. engr. RCA Labs., Princeton, N.J., 1950-58; head solid state display group Hughes Rsch. Lab., Malibu, Calif., 1958-61; head imaging sect. Electro-Optical Systems, Pasadena, Calif., 1961-68; head exploratory display group T.J. Watson Rsch. Ctr., Yorktown Heights, N.Y., 1968-74; prin. scientist Xerox Rsch. Ctr., Palo Alto, Calif., 1974-85; cons. display and imaging tech., 1985—; cons. Advisory Group Electron Devices, Dept. Def., 1973-82; adj. prof. U. R.I., Kingston, 1970-74. Author: (with others) Storage Tubes, 1952; Electronic Image Storage, 1968. Editor: Advances in Image Pickup and Display series, 1972-84; assoc. editor Advances in Electronics and Electron Physics series, 1984—; contbr. articles to profl. jours.; patentee in field. Recipient Silver medal Am. Roentgen Ray Soc., 1957. Fellow IEEE (assoc. editor Jour. Electron Devices 1979-83), Soc. Info. Display (editor jour. 1974-78); mem. Am. Phys. Soc., Sigma Xi, Tau Beta Pi. Home: 557 Tyndall St Los Altos CA 94022-3920 Office: Xerox Rsch Ctr 3333 Coyote Hill Rd Palo Alto CA 94304-1314

KAZLAUSKAS, EDWARD JOHN, educator; b. Cleve., Jan. 4, 1942; s. Frank and Anna (Gregitis) K. AB, John Carroll U., 1963; MLS, U. Ill., 1964; PhD, U. So. Calif., 1975. Asst. U. Ill. Libr., Urbana, 1963-64; libr. Fla. Atlantic U., Boca Raton, 1964-66; systems analyst Calif. State U., Northridge, 1966-70; prof. U. So. Calif., L.A., 1970—; cons. Paramount Pictures, L.A., 1988-91, La Canada (Calif.) Sch. Dist., 1990-91, TRW, Inc., L.A., 1985-91, UN, Cairo, 1983, UN (ACCIS), 1992. Author: Administrative Uses of Computers, 1991, Information Management Software, 1989, Managing Information Systems, 1986. Mem. Am. Soc. for Info. Sci. (dir. 1987-89), Spl. Libr. Assn., Assn. Sch. Bus. Ofcls., Internat. Coun. Computers in Edn. Roman Catholic. Office: U So Calif WPH 1004d Los Angeles CA 90089-0031

KAZLE, ELYNMARIE, producer; b. St. Paul, June 22, 1958; d. Victor Anton and Marylu (Gardner) K. BFA, U. Minn., Duluth, 1982; MFA, Ohio U., 1984. Prodn. mgr. Great Lakes Shakespeare, Cleve., 1983; prodn. stage mgr. San Diego (Calif.) Opera, 1984, PCPA Theaterfest, Santa Maria, Calif., 1986-87; stage mgr. Bklyn. Acad. Music, 1987; assoc. producer Am. Theater Actors, N.Y.C., 1988—; prodn. stage mgr. Time Flies When You're Alive, West Hollywood, Calif., 1988—; asst. advt. display Wall St. Jour., L.A., 1988-89; West Coast adminstr. Soc. Stage Dirs. and Choreographers, 1991-93. Editor, pub. (newsletter) The Ohio Network, 1984-90; prodr. Santa Monica Playhouse, 1989—. Trustee Theatre/L.A., 1992—. Mem. Stage Mgrs. Assn., Stage Mgrs. Assn. L.A., U.S. Inst. for Theatre Tech. (bd. dirs. 1990—), Actors Equity Assn., Phi Kappa Phi, Delta Chi Omega (past pres. 1978). Office: Santa Monica Playhouse 1211 4th St Santa Monica CA 90401-1326

KEABLES, MICHAEL JOHN, geography educator; b. Denver, May 19, 1955; s. John Mayoll and Barbara Jean (Boettcher) K.; m. Dawn Alexandria Errickson, July 15, 1978; children: Paul Michael, Kevin Andrew. BA, U. Colo., 1978; MS, U. Wis., 1982, PhD, 1986. Lectr. dept. geography U. Wis., Madison, 1983-85, U. Md., Catonsville, 1985-86; asst. prof. dept. geography U. Denver, Colo., 1986-92; assoc. prof. dept. geography U. Denver, 1992—; prin. investigator rsch. grant U.S. Geol. Survey, 1990. Contbr. articles to profl. jours. Panelist State Auditors Office-Air Pollution Programs, Denver, 1991; mem. Coop. Decision Making-Denver (Colo.) Pub. Schs., 1992. Mem. Assn. Am. Geographers, Am. Meteorol. Soc., Am. Geophysical Union, Nat. Geographic Soc., Nat. Coun. for Geographic Edn. (Teaching Achievement award 1990), Sigma Xi. Democrat. Episcopalian. Office: Univ Denver Dept Geography 2130 S Race St Denver CO 80208

KEALIINOHOMOKU, JOANN WHEELER, anthropologist, dance ethnologist, educator; b. Kansas City, Mo., May 20, 1930; d. George V. and Leona Lavena (Moore) Wheeler; 1 child, Halla K. BSS, Northwestern U., 1955; MA, 1965; PhD, Ind. U., 1976. Mem. faculty No. Ariz. U., Flagstaff, 1970-72, 75-87 , assoc. prof. anthropology, 1980-87 ; sr. research assoc. Ctr. for Colo. Plateau Studies No. Ariz. U., 1987—, ind. scholar, 1987—; mem. faculty World Campus Afloat, fall 1972, 73, Semester-at-Sea, 1989; resident scholar Sch. Am. Research, Santa Fe, 1974-75; vis. faculty U. Hawaii, Hilo, spring 1973, summer 1973, 74, U. Hawaii-Manoa, fall 1981, spring, 1991, NYU, summer 1980, 84, U. N.C., Greensborough, summer 1990, Tex. Woman's U., summer 1992. Bd. dirs. Native Americans for Community Action, Flagstaff Indian Center, 1977-82, sec., 1980-82. Grantee, Am. Philos. Soc., 1966, 69-70, Wenner Gren Found., Ariz. Humanities Coun., 1991; Weatherhead fellow Sch. Am. Research, 1974-75; research fellow East-West Center, 1981; NEH grantee, 1986. Fellow Current Anthropology; mem. Soc. Ethnomusicology (councilor; co founder Southwestern chpt.), Dance Research Center (charter), Congress on Research in Dance (bd. dirs. 1974-79), Cross-Cultural Dance Resources (co-founder 1981). Contbr. articles to profl. jours. Home and Office: 518 S Agassiz St Flagstaff AZ 86001-5711

KEAN, MICHAEL HENRY, publishing company executive; b. Phila., Feb. 7, 1945; s. Milton Charles and Dorothy (Dash) K.; m. Constance Gordon, Sept. 15, 1968; children: Megan C., Adam C. BA, Pa. State U., 1966; MA, Ohio State U., 1968, PhD, 1972. Rsch. asst. evaluation ctr. Ohio State U., Columbus, 1967-68, rsch. asst. dept. edn. devel., 1968-70; asst. to supt. Sch. Dist. Phila., 1970-73, exec. dir. office rsch. evaluation and testing, 1973-81; dir. midwest region Ednl. Testing Svc., Evanston, Ill., 1981-83; publ. CTB/ McGraw-Hill, Monterey, Calif., 1983-88; v.p. mktg. CTB Macmillan/ McGraw-Hill, Monterey, 1988-90, v.p. pub. and govt. affairs, 1990—; chmn. Large City Rsch. Dirs., 1978-79; vis. scholar ctr. for study of evaluation UCLA, 1977. Author: Sherlock Holmes: Vintage and Spirited, 1993; co-author: Debates on Evaluation, 1990; editor: Three Porges Parodies and a Pastiche, 1989; editor-in-chief: (journal) New Dimensions for Testing and Measurement, 1981-84. Bd. dirs. Boys & Girls Club. Monterey Peninsula, Seaside, Calif., 1984—, Sabin-McEwen Inst., Carmel, Calif., 1984-85, Pa. State Coll. Edn. Alumni Soc., University Park, Pa., 1975-81; steering com. community leadership program U. Pa., Phila., 1972-81. Mem. Am. Edn. Rsch. Assn. (v.p. 1979-81, Div. H. Svc. award 1989), Assn. Am. Publ. (chmn. test com. 1985—), Baker St. Irregulars, Diogenes Club, Phi Delta Kappa (rsch. adv. com. 1982—). Office: CTB Macmillan/McGraw-Hill 20 Ryan Ranch Rd. Monterey CA 93940-5703

KEARNEY, JOSEPH LAURENCE, athletic conference administrator; b. Pitts., Apr. 28, 1927; s. Joseph L. and Iva M. (Nikirk) K.; m. Dorothea Hurst, May 13, 1950; children: Jan Marie, Kevin Robert, Erin Lynn, Shawn Alane, Robin James. B.A., Seattle Pacific U., 1952, LL.D., 1979; M.A., San Jose State U., 1964; Ed.D., U. Wash., 1970. Tchr., coach Paradise (Calif.) High Sch., 1952-53; asst. basketball coach U. Wash., 1953-54; coach, tchr. Sunnyside (Wash.) High Sch., 1954-57; prin. high sch., coach Onalaska (Wash.) High Sch., 1957-61; prin. Tumwater (Wash.) High Sch., 1961-63; asst. dir. Wash. High Sch. Activities Assn., 1963-64; athletic dir., assoc. dir. U. Wash., 1964-76; athletic dir. intercollegiate athletics Mich. State U., East Lansing, 1976-80, Ariz. State U., Tempe, 1980; commr. Western Athletic Conf., Denver, 1980—. Pres. Community Devel. Assn., 1957-61; bd. dirs. U.S. Olympic Com., 1985—, mem. games preparation com., 1985—. Recipient Disting. Service award Mich. Assn. Professions, 1979. Mem. Nat. Football Found. (ct. of honors com.), Nat. Collegiate Athletic Assn., Nat. Assn. Collegiate Dirs. Athletics (Corbett award 1991), Collegiate Commrs. Assn. (pres.). Home: 7361 S Monroe Ct Littleton CO 80122-2220 Office: Western Athletic Conf 14 W Dry Creek Cir Littleton CO 80120-4478

KEARNS, HOMER H., school system administrator. AA in Spanish, West Hills Coll., Coalinga, Calif., 1962; BA in Spanish and Life Sci., Calif. State U., Fresno, 1964, MA in Adminstrn., 1970; PhD in Adminstrn. Higher Edn. and Sociology, Mich. State U., 1971. Tchr., head tchr., prin. Clovis (Calif.) Unified Sch. Dist, 1964-70; asst. prof. edn. dept. cirriculum and instrn. coll. edn., assoc. dir. Northwest Community Edn. Devel. ctr. U. Oreg., Eugene, 1971-72; supt. schs. Sisters (Oreg.) Sch. Dist., 1972-75, Redmond (Oreg.) Sch. Dist., 1975-81; county supt. schs. Deschutes County Edn. Svc. Dist., Bend, Oreg., 1978-81; assoc., dep. supt. Salem-Keizer Pub. Schs., Salem, Oreg., 1981-86, supt. schs., 1986—; mem. exec. com. Coalition for Equitable Sch. Funding, 1988-91; bd. dirs. Marion & Polk Schs. Credit Union, Salem Econ. Devel. Corp., Northwest Regional Ednl. Lab., chair bd. equity com. Bd. dirs. Salem Family YMCA; past bd. dirs. Oreg. Congl. Awards Coun., Cascade Child Treatment Ctr.; bd. dirs. Salem Sch. Found.; active Oreg. 2000 Com., United Way, County Planning Commn., Econ. Devel. Strategic Planning Group; mem. panel Gannet Found. Named Supt. of Yr., Oreg. Counseling Assn., 1988. Mem. Am. Assn. Sch. Adminstrs. (chair suburban supts. adv. com. 1990, exec. com. 1992—), Oreg. Assn. Sch. Execs. (bd. dirs., pres. 1990, chair sch. funding coalition 1992, Supt. of Yr. award with AASA 1990), Rotary Internat., Willamette U. Cardinal Roundtable, City Club. Office: Salem/Keizer SD 24J PO Box 12024 Salem OR 97309*

KEARSE, DAVID GRIER, stage and screen writer; b. Annapolis, Md., June 24, 1937; s. Francis Grier and Esther Carlisle (McCusker) K. BA, U. Miami, 1959; postgrad., Columbia U., 1959-60, NYU, 1988-89. Reporter, editor Capital Gazette Press, Annapolis, 1961-67; critic, copy editor The Balt. Sun, 1967-78; creative dept. Young and Rubicam Advtg., N.Y.C., 1978-83; with pub. rels. dept. Stephen W. Brener Assoc., N.Y.C., 1985-89; ind. screenwriter Hollywood, Calif., 1989—. Author: (musical) Miranda, 1991; author, dir. (play) Once Bitten, 1978; author: (screenplay) Alfredo's Sunset, 1991; dir.: The Winter's Tale, 1978, Playformers, 1989. Co-founder Annapolis Fine Arts Festival, 1963; AIDS vol. Roosevelt Hosp., N.Y.C., 1988-89; mem. Spiritual Adv. Com. AIDS Project L.A.; assoc. Episcopal Order Holy Cross. Mem. The Dramatists Guild, Writers Guild Am. (assoc.). Republican.

KEARY, GERALDINE (GERI), artist; b. Salt Lake City, Feb. 22, 1935; d. Morgan James and Edith Mary (King) Magness; m. Robert Patrick Keary, Apr. 22, 1954; children: Judy Lynn, Kenneth Patrick, Michele. Student, Diablo Valley Coll., 1974, 75, 76,, Diablo Valley Coll., 77, 78, 79, 83. Exhibited in group shows, Pleasanton Mus., Martinez City Hall, Bankers Gallery, San Francisco (award); represented in permanent collections in the U.S and Europe. Bd. dirs. Martinez (Calif.) Arts Assn., 1970-73, Pleasant Hill (Calif.) Civic Arts, 1987-91. Named Yachtsman of Yr., Martinez (Calif.) Yacht Club, 1983, Best of Class, Alameda County Fair, Plesanton, Calif., 1990-91, Best of Show, Contra Costa County Fair, Antioch, 1992; recipient Purchase award Triton Mus., Santa Clara, Calif., 1992, Merit award Calif. State Fair, Sacramento, 1992. Mem. Soc. Western Artists (v.p. 1991, pres. 1992), Nat. League Am. Pen Women, Artists Adv. Bd. State Fair. Church of Jesus Christ of Latter Day Saints. Home: 3870 Canyon Way Martinez CA 94553

KEASLEY, DAWN DELAYNE, military officer; b. Homestead AFB, Fla., Jan. 14, 1967; d. Joe Benjamin and Vera (Davis) K. BS, USAF Acad., 1989; MS, Lesley Coll., 1993. Commd. 2d lt. USAF, 1989, advanced through grades to capt., 1993; convoy comdr. 88th Missile Security Squadron USAF, Cheyenne, Wyo., 1991—, OIC of camper support 88th Missile Security Squadron, 1991-92, squadron sec. com. 88th Missile Security Squadron, 1992; group OPSEC/COMSEC, energy conservation 90th Security Police Group, Cheyenne, 1991—. Vocalist Adult Gospel Choir, Vogelweh, Fed. Republic Germany, 1980-85, Expressions of Christ Gospel Choir, Vogelweh, 1983-85. Mem. Air Force Assn., Laramie County Peace Officer Assn. Office: USAF 88th Missile Security Squad 88 MLSS/CC F E Warren AFB WY 82005

KEATING, JOY MARIE, hospital administrator; b. Seattle, Oct. 4, 1944; d. Albert Franklin Amundsen and Wilma Ruth (Radley) Haughn; m. Richard William Nyholm, Apr. 23, 1963 (div. July 1975); children: John Derek, Troy David, Allison Joy; m. Douglas Arthur Keating, May 8, 1976. ADN, U. Alaska, 1976; BS in Pub. Adminstrn., Kennedy-Western U., 1986, MS in Pub. Adminstrn., 1988. RN Cen. Peninsula Hosp. Soldotna/Luth. Hosp. and Homes Soc., Alaska, 1976-77; nurse counselor and bush nurse Kenai Peninsula Borough Sch. Dist., Soldotna, 1979-83; home health nurse, nurse supr. dept. corrections State of Alaska, Kenai, 1983-87; hosp. adminstr. Valdez Community Hosp. Valdez (Alaska) Community Hosp/Luth. Health Systems Mgmt. Co., 1987-90; v.p. programs Correctional Med. Ctrs. Am., Portland, Oreg., 1990-91; dir. health svcs. Marian Retirement Ctr., Sublimity, Oreg., 1990—; mem. exec. bd. Marian Retirement Ctr., 1990—; cons., speaker in field. Author sch. health curriculum and correctional healthcare programs; contbr. articles to profl. jours. Pres. bd. dirs. Emergency Assistance of Valdez, Alaska, 1987-89; mem. Care Providers, Valdez, 1987-89. Mem. Health Assn. Alaska (bd. dirs. 1987-89, mem. legis. affairs com. 1987-89), Am. Hosp. Assn., Am. Correctional Health Assn., Oreg. Long Term Care Nurses Assn. (dir. 1991-92, chmn. pub. rels. com. 1992, pres. 1992-93), Rotary (sec. 1988-89). Home: 2198 Joplin St S Salem OR 97302-2260 Office: Marian Retirement Ctr 390 SE Church St Sublimity OR 97385-9714

KEATING, LARRY GRANT, electrical engineer, educator; b. Omaha, Jan. 15, 1944; s. Grant Morris and Dorothy Ann (Kauffold) K.; m. Barbara Jean Merley, Dec. 21, 1968. LLB, Blackstone Sch. Law, 1968; BS, U. Nebr., 1969; BS summa cum laude, Met. State Coll., 1971; MS, U. Colo., Denver, 1978. Chief engr. broadcast electronics 3 radio stas., 1965-69; coord. engrng. reliability Cobe Labs., Lakewood, Colo., 1972-74; quality engr. Statitrol Corp., Lakewood, Colo., 1974-76; instr. electrical engring. U. Colo., Denver, 1976-78; from asst. prof. to prof. Met. State Coll., Denver, 1978—, chmn. dept., 1984—; cons. Transplan Assocs., Boulder, Colo., 1983-84. 1st lt. U.S. Army, 1962-70. Recipient Outstanding Faculty award U. Colo., Denver, 1980, Outstanding Alumnus award Met. State Coll., 1985. Mem. IEEE (sr.), Instrument Soc. Am. (sr.), Robotics Internat. (sr.), Am. Soc. Engring. Edn., Nat. Assn. Radio and Telecommunications Engrs. (cert. engr.), Order of the Engr., Eta Kappa Nu, Tau Alpha Pi, Chi Epsilon. Home: 6455 E Bates Ave # 4108 Denver CO 80222-7135 Office: Met State Coll PO Box 173362 Campus Box 29 Denver CO 80217-3362

KEATING, THOMAS FRANCIS, state senator; b. Langdon, N.D., Nov. 26, 1928; s. Thomas Delbert and Olive Mary (Bear) K.; student Eastern Mont. Coll., 1951; B.A. in Bus. Adminstrn., U. Portland, 1953; m. Anna Louise Walsh, Aug. 22, 1953; children—Thomas J., Patrick, Michael, Kathryn, Terence. Landman, Mobil Oil Corp., Billings, Mont., 1954-61, Oklahoma City, 1961-66, Burlington No. R.R., Billings, 1966-67; Mont., landman, Billings, 1967-81; mem. Mont. Senate, 1981—. Served with USAF, 1946-49. Mem. Mont. Assn. Petroleum Landmen (pres. 1969), Am. Assn. Petroleum Landmen (dir. 1971-73), Ind. Petroleum Assn., Billings C. of C. Republican. Roman Catholic. Home: PO Box 20522 Billings MT 59104-0522

KEATS, DONALD HOWARD, composer, educator; b. N.Y.C., May 27, 1929; s. Bernard and Lillian K.; m. Eleanor Steinholz, Dec. 13, 1953; children: Jeremy, Jennifer, Jeffrey, Jocelyn. Mus.B., Yale U., 1949; M.A., Columbia U., 1951; Ph.D., U. Minn., 1962; student, Staatliche Hochschule fur Musik, Hamburg, Germany, 1954-56. Teaching fellow Yale U. Sch. Music, New Haven, Conn., 1949-50; instr. music theory U.S. Naval Sch. Music, Washington, 1953-54; post music dir. Ft. Dix, N.J., 1956-57; faculty Antioch Coll., Yellow Springs, Ohio, 1957-76; prof. Antioch Coll., 1967-76, chmn. music dept., 1967-71; vis. prof. music U. Wash. Sch. Music, 1969-70, Lamont Sch. Music, U. Denver, 1975-76; composer-in-residence Colo. Music Festival, 1980, Arcosanti, 1986; vis. composer Aspen Music Festival, 1987; prof. music, composer-in-residence Lamont Sch. Music, U. Denver, 1975—, Phipps Prof. in the humanities, 1982-85. Pianist concerts of own music, London, 1973, Tel Aviv, 1973, Jerusalem, 1973, N.Y.C., 1975, Denver, 1984, 91; Composer: Divertimento For Winds and Strings, 1949, The Naming of Cats, 1951, The Hollow Men, 1951, String Quartet 1, 1952, Concert Piece for Orchestra, 1952, Variations for Piano, 1955, First Symphony, 1957, Piano Sonata, 1960, An Elegiac Symphony, 1962, Anyone Lived in a Pretty How Town, 1965; ballet New Work, 1966; Polarities for Violin and Piano, 1968-70, String Quartet 2, 1965, A Love Triptych, 1970, Dialogue for Piano and Winds, 1973, Diptych for Cello and Piano, 1975, Upon the Intimation of Love's Mortality, 1975, Branchings for Orch, 1976, Epithalamium for Violin, Cello and Piano, 1977, Four Puerto Rican Love Songs: Tierras del Alma for soprano, flute and guitar, 1978, Musica Instrumentalis I for chamber group, 1980, Concerto for Piano and Orch., 1990, Revisitations for Violin, 'Cello and Piano, 1992. Served with U.S. Army, 1952-54. Recipient ASCAP awards, 1964—; awards from Ford, Danforth and Lilly founds., Nat. Endowment for Arts; winner Rockefeller Found. Symphonic Competitions, 1965, 66; Guggenheim fellow Europe, 1964-65, 72-73; Nat. Endowment for Arts grantee, fellow, 1975; Fulbright Scholar, 1954-56. Mem. ASCAP, Coll. Music Soc., Am. Music Center, Phi Beta Kappa. Home: 9261 E Berry Ave Englewood CO 80111-3507 Office: U Denver Lamont Sch Music Denver CO 80208

KEAY, LOU CARTER, public relations executive, writer; b. Oceanside, Calif., Mar. 28, 1927; d. Frank Leslie and Ota Belle (McCain) C.; m. David Warren Keay, June 11, 1948 (dec.); children: David Leslie, Monica Lou Keay Andrews. Student, Tex. Woman's U., Denton, 1944-46, Emerson Coll., Boston, 1947-48; cert. pub. rels. mgmt., Tex. U., Austin, 1958; student, UCLA, 1979, 80, 81. TV writer WBAP-TV, Ft. Worth, 1950-56; TV continuity dir. KDUB-TV, Lubbock, Tex., 1959-62; pub. rels. dir. United Fund, Lubbock, 1962-64, The Mus. Tex. Tech. U., 1964-71; owner Apropos Pub. Rels., Lubbock and L.A., 1964—; ptnr. Triad Publs., Media Tours, Investment Mgmt. Assocs.; nat. chmn. Calif. Writers' Roundtable Contests, L.A., 1984—; bd. dirs. Judy Lopez Found., L.A., 1985—, pres., 1992—; columnist. Author: Beggars Would Ride, 1953; editor: American Museums Association Proceedings, 1970; contbr. to Erotic Interludes, 1987. Founder Greater Ft. Worth Community Theatre (name now Scott Theatre), 1951. Recipient Berke Found. poetry award, N.Mex., 1970, 71, world poetry awards, Calif., 1971, 72, 73. Mem. Women's Nat. Book Assn. (bd. dirs. L.A. chpt., past nat. sec. 1988-90), Calif. Writers Club (bd. dirs. L.A. chpt. 1989), Book Publicists So. Calif., Intertel, Mensa Internat., Nat. Writers Club. Republican. Episcopalian. Home: 11684 Ventura Blvd Ste 807 Studio City CA 91604-2652 Office: Sony Pictures Entertainment 3400 W Riverside Dr Ste 5034 Burbank CA 91505-4627

KEDING, ANN MAXWELL, freelance copywriter; b. Ft. Benning, Ga., Aug. 31, 1944; d. Porter Bill and Clyrene (Stull) Maxwell; children from previous marriage: Robert, Jeff. BA in Psychology, Calif. State U., Fullerton, 1973, MA in Psychology, 1975; postgrad., U. So. Calif., 1980-83. Instr. psychology Calif. State U., Fullerton, 1974-76, Golden West Coll., Huntington Beach, Calif., 1976-78; mktg. sch. project dir. Foote, Cone & Belding, L.A., 1978-80; copywriter Yuguchi & Krogstad, L.A., 1980-82, Hamilton Advt., L.A., 1982-84, Grey Advt., L.A., 1984-85; freelance copywriter L.A., Eugene, Calif. and Oreg., 1985—; tenured instr. U. Oreg., Eugene, 1992—. Co-author: How to Produce Creative Advertising, 1991; writer TV commls., advt. campaigns, brochures. Mem. adv. coun. L.A. Commn. on Assaults Against Women, 1985—. Recipient Pub. Citation Govt. Calif., 1985, Humanitarian award L.A. Commn. Assaults Against Women, 1986; Gannett fellow, 1987, 88, Jonathan Marshall award for teaching innovations, Sch. Journalism, 1992. Mem. Am. Acad. Advt., Calif. State U. Fullerton Alumni Assn., Phi Kappa Phi (bd. dirs. 1974-75). Office: U Oreg Sch Journalism Eugene OR 97403

KEEFFE, EMMET BRITTON, medicine educator; b. San Francisco, Apr. 12, 1942; s. Emmet Britton and Corinne M. (Walsh) K.; m. Melenie M. Laskey, June 18, 1966; children: Emmet III, Brian, Meghan. BS, U. San Francisco, 1964, secondary teaching credential, 1965; MD, Creighton U., 1969. Intern straight medicine Oreg. Health Sci. U., Portland, 1969-70, resident, 1970-73, fellow gastroenterology, 1973-74; asst. prof. medicine Oreg. Health Sci. U., 1979-83; assoc. prof. medicine Oreg. Health Sci. U., Portland, 1983-89, prof. med., 1989-92; fellow gastroenterology U. Calif., San Francisco, 1977-79, clin. prof. medicine, 1992—; chief divsn. gastroenterology, hepatology Calif. Pacific Med. Ctr., San Francisco, 1992—, med. dir. liver transplant program, 1992—. Author: Flexible Sigmoidoscopy, 1985; contbr. 80 book chpts.and articles to profl. jours. lt. comdr. USN, 1974-77. Fellow ACP, Am. Coll. Gastroenterology; mem. AAAS, AMA, Am. Liver Found. (bd. dirs., 1991—), Am. Gastroenterologic Assn., Am. Assn. Study Liver Diseases, Am. Soc. Gastrointestinal Endoscopy (sec. 1991—), Am. Soc. Transplant Physicians, Am. Fedn. Clin. Research, North Pacific Soc. of Internal Medicine, Internat. Liver Transplantation Soc., Pacific Interurban Clin. Club, Western Gut Club (pres. 1991). Home: 22 Weatherly Dr Mill Valley CA 94941 Office: Calif Pacific Med Ctr 2340 Clay Ste 423 San Francisco CA 94115

KEELER, DAVID LEE, computer systems firm owner; s. Russell Julius and Dorothy Marie (Ewbank) K. Field svc. Cutler-Hammer (Eaton Corp.), Milw., 1978-80; field supt. Cutler-Hammer (Eaton Corp.) at China Steel Corp., Kaoshiung, Taiwan, 1980; field svc. engr. Square D Co., Palatine, Ill., 1980-85; field svc. sales Siemens Energy and Automation, Inc., Atlanta, 1985-88; ptnr., mktg. mgr. Vision 21 Systems, Fountain Valley, Calif., 1988-92, Orange, Calif., 1992—. Bd. dirs. Eastmont Villas Community Assn., Anaheim, Calif., 1988-90, 92—, So. Calif. Chinese Alliance, L.A., 1989; mem. Orange County and Calif. State Dem. Cen. Com., 1991-92, 93-95. With USN, 1970-73. Mem. Assn. for Computing Machinery (voting), Nat. Computer Graphics Assn. (voting), Nat. Rifle Assn.

KEELER, ORVILLE ALAN, engineer; b. Great Bend, Kans., June 3, 1938; s. Orville A. and Neva Gladys (Wilson) K.; m. Mary Martha Kongs, Aug. 22, 1970; children: Mark Alan, Timothy Andrew. BS in Milling Tech., Kans. State U., 1961. Mgmt. trainee Internat. Milling Co., Mpls., 1961-63; underwriter N.Y. Life Ins. Co., Kansas City, Mo., 1963-64; claims adjuster St. Paul Fire & Marine Ins. Co., Colorado Springs, Colo., 1964-66, Royal Globe Ins. Co., Denver, 1965-66; devel. engr. Gates Rubber Co., Denver, 1966—. Chmn. Castlewood Fire Protection Dist., Englewood, Colo., 1983—; chmn. 39th Legis. Dist., Arapahoe County, Colo., 1986-92. Mem. Elks, Sigma Phi Epsilon (alumni bd. dirs. 1991—). Republican. Presbyterian. Home: 6090 E Fair Ave Englewood CO 80111-4250 Office: Gates Rubber Co 1001 S Broadway Denver CO 80217-5887

KEENA, BETTY KAREN, accountant; b. Wichita, Kans., Apr. 22, 1942; d. Raymond Thomas and Evelyn Ann (Koehler) Fairbanks; 1 child, Michael Alan. Grad., Met. State Coll., 1971; MPA, U. Colo., 1979. CPA, Colo. Statis. clk. Met. State Coll., Denver, 1968-70, asst. to dean, 1970-71, asst. to v.p., 1971-73, dir. instnl. rsch., 1973-77, assoc. v.p., 1977-80; acct. Rosemary Weiss & Co., Denver, 1981, Combellick O'Connor & Reynolds, Englewood, Colo., 1982-85; owner Stricklin Loomis & Keena, Denver, 1985-87, B.K. Keena, CPA, Denver, 1987—. Contbr. articles to newpapers and mags. Councilman City of Englewood, 1979-82; mem. Citizen Fact Finding Com., Littleton, Colo., Econ. Devel. Task Force, Englewood. Mem. South Met. Denver C. of C. (bd. dirs. 1986-91, vice chmn. communication 1987-88, chmn. bd. dirs. 1989-90). Office: Ste 770 3333 S Bannock Englewood CO 80110

KEENAN, EDWARD JOSEPH, management consultant; b. N.Y.C., Oct. 3, 1932; s. Edward Joseph and Leona (Tansey) K.; married; 2 children. BA, U. Minn., 1967; MA in Edn., Chapman Coll., 1977; MBA, Pepperdine U., 1984; PhD in Bus. Adminstrn., Kensington U., 1989. Served with U.S. Air Force, 1951-71; ptnr. Edman-Keenan & Assocs., San Bernardino, Calif., 1971-73; adminstr. for pvt. law firms, Los Angeles and Beverly Hills, Calif., 1973-78; cons. to law firms, small bus., and hosps., 1978—; instr. law office mgmt. U. So. Calif., U. West Los Angeles, Calif. State U., Long Beach; cons. in field. Mem. Am. Inst. Indsl. Engrs., Assn. Legal Adminstrs. (charter; pres. Beverly Hills chpt. 1977-78), Cons. Roundtable So. Calif. (chair prof. devel. com.), Hosp. Mgmt. Systems Soc. Republican. Lodges: Elks, Moose, K.C.

KEENAN, ROBERT, architect; b. Rochester, N.Y., Jan. 8, 1950; s. John Lawrence and Frances (Hartigan) K.; m. Marianne Julia Janko, Sept. 9, 1989; 1 child, Robert John. BA, Fordham U., 1971; MArch, Harvard U., 1976. Registered architect, Mass., Calif.; cert. nat. coun. archtl. registration bds. Architect Archtl. Resources Cambridge Inc., Cambridge, Mass., 1977-79, Hoskins, Scott, Taylor & Ptnrs., Boston, 1979-81; architect Harry Weese & Assocs., Chgo., 1981-89, v.p., 1983-89; chief architect Metro Rail Transit Cons., 1986-89; architect, urbam designer Bechtel Corp., San Francisco, 1989—; chief architect Bay Area Transit Cons., 1989-91; chief architect for expansion/renovation Athens Metro System, 1991—; speaker, session chmn. Internat. Conf. on Tall Bldgs, Singapore, 1984. Prin. works include Regis

Coll. Athletic Facility, Weston, Mass., Singapore Mass Rapid Transit System, So. Calif. Metro Rail Project, L.A., Bay Area Rapid Transit System, San Francisco, Athens Metro Project, Athens, Greece. Mem. AIA. Republican. Roman Catholic. Office: Bechtel Corp/Job # 21710 PO Box 193965 50 Beale St San Francisco CA 94119-3965

KEENE, CLIFFORD HENRY, medical administrator; b. Buffalo, Jan. 28, 1910; s. George Samuel and Henrietta Hedwig (Yeager) K.; m. Mildred Jean Kramer, Mar. 3, 1934; children: Patricia Ann (Mrs. William S. Kneedler), Martha Jane (Mrs. William R. Sproule), Diane Eve (Mrs. Gordon D. Simonds). AB, U. Mich., 1931, MD, 1934, MS in Surgery, 1938; DSc, Hahnemann Med. Coll., 1973; LLD, Golden Gate U., 1974. Diplomate Am. Bd. Surgery, Am. Bd. Preventive Medicine (occupational medicine). Resident surgeon, instr. surgery U. Mich., 1934-39; cons. surgery of cancer Mich. Med. Soc. and Mich. Dept. Health, 1939-40; pvt. practice surgery Wyandotte, Mich., 1940-41; med. dir. Kaiser-Frazer Corp., 1946-53; instr. surgery U. Mich., 1946-54; med. adminstrv. positions with Kaiser Industries and Kaiser Found., 1954-75, v.p., 1960-75; v.p., gen. mgr. Kaiser Found. Hosps. and Kaiser Found. Health Plan, 1960-67; med. dir. Kaiser Found. Sch. Nursing, 1954-67; dir. Kaiser Found. Research Inst., 1958-75; pres. Kaiser Found. Hosps. Health Plan, Sch. Nursing, 1968-75, dir., 1960-80; chmn. editorial bd. Kaiser Found. Med. Bull., 1954-65; lectr. med. econs. U. Calif.-Berkeley, 1956-75; mem. vis. com. Med. Sch., Stanford U., 1966-72, Harvard U., 1967-71, 79-85, U. Mich., 1973-78; Mem. Presdl. Panel Fgn. Med. Grads. (Nat. Manpower Commn.), 1966-69. Contbr. papers to profl. lit. Bd. visitors Harvard Bus. Adv. Council, 1972, Charles R. Drew Post-grad. Med. Sch., 1972-79; trustee Amman Civil Hosp., Jordan, 1973, Community Hosp. of Monterey Peninsula, 1983-92. Lt. col. M.C. AUS, 1942-46. Recipient Disting. Service award Group Health Assn. Am., 1974; Disting. Alumnus award U. Mich. Med. Center, 1976; Disting. Alumnus Service award U. Mich., 1985. Fellow ACS; mem. Am. Assn. Indsl. Physicians and Surgeons, Nat. Acad. Scis., Inst. Medicine, Calif. Acad. Medicine, Frederick A. Coller Surg. Soc., Calif., Am. med. assns., Alpha Omega Alpha (editorial bd., contbr. to Pharos mag. 1977—). Home: 3978 Ronda Rd PO Box 961 Pebble Beach CA 93953

KEENE, MICHAEL ANDREW, molecular biologist; b. Abington, Pa., Aug. 23, 1956; s. Robert Clinton and Flora Martha (Etherington) K.; m. Mary Jane Pennington, Apr. 27, 1985. BA in Biochemistry, Princeton U., 1977; MBA, U. Iowa, 1992; PhD in Biochemistry and Molecular Biology, Harvard U., 1983. Postdoctoral fellow Fred Hutchinson Cancer Research Ctr., Seattle, 1983-86; research assoc. Howard Hughes Med. Research Unit, U. Utah, Salt Lake City, 1986-88; group leader, diagnostic research Integrated DNA Techs., Inc., Iowa City, 1988-90; asst. rsch. scientist U. Iowa Coll. Medicine, 1990-92; v.p. corp. devel. Intech One-Eighty Corp., North Logan, Utah, 1993—. Contbr. numerous articles to profl. sci. jours. Recipient Nat. Research Service award Nat. Inst. Health, 1983-86. Mem. AAAS, Am. Soc. Cell Biology (legis. alert com. 1985-92), Genetics Soc. Am., Photog. Soc. Am. (bd. dirs. 1985-86), Seattle Photog. Soc. (bd. dirs., competition chmn. 1985-86), Photog. Soc. Am. (bd. dirs. 1988-89), Salt Lake Photochrome Club (bd. dirs., competition chmn. 1987-88), Am. Philatelic Soc., Sigma Xi. Home: 2121 E Lonsdale Salt Lake City UT 84121-4952 Office: Ste 108 1780 N Research Park Way North Logan UT 84321

KEENE BLAKELY, NANCY ALICE, employment compensation specialist; b. San Francisco, Jan. 7, 1958; d. Eugene Harold and Alice Louise (Games) Keene; m. Dennis Edward Schroader, Oct. 22, 1977 (div. Oct. 4, 1982); chldren: Dennis Edward Jr., Diana Suzanne; m. Marc Edwin Blakely, Jan. 25, 1992. AA, Pierce Coll., 1992. Exec. sec. Prudential Ins. Co., Tacoma, 1975-81; comml. lines asst. Hutchinson & Teel Ins., Tacoma, 1985-86; surplus lines asst. Sedgwick-James, Tacoma, 1986-87; mktg. supr. Grange Ins. Assn., Seattle, 1987-92, employment compensation specialist, 1992—; bd. dirs. Adminstrv. Mgmt. Soc., Seattle, 1991-92. Letter-of-the-month writer Planned Parenthood, Pierce, Colo., 1990-92. Recipient People Accepting the Challenge of Excellence award, 1991, Trustee scholarship U. Puget Sound, 1976. Mem. Nat. Assn. Ins. Women (cert. profl. ins. woman). Office: Grange Ins Assn 200 Cedar St Seattle WA 98121

KEENE-BURGESS, RUTH FRANCES, army official; b. South Bend, Ind., Oct. 7, 1948; d. Seymour and Sally (Morris) K.; m. Leslie U. Burgess, Jr., Oct. 1, 1983; children: Michael Leslie, David William, Elizabeth Sue, Rachael Lee. BS, Ariz. State U., 1970; MS, Fairleigh Dickinson U., 1978; grad., U.S. Army Command and Gen. Staff Coll., 1986. Inventory mgmt. specialist U.S. Army Electronics Command, Phila., 1970-74, U.S. Army Communications-Electronics Material Readiness Command, Fort Monmouth, N.J., 1974-79; chief inventory mgmt. div. Crane (Ind.) Army Ammunition Activity, 1979-80; supply systems analyst Hdqrs. 60th Ordnance Group, Zweibruecken, Fed. Republic Germany, 1980-83; chief inventory mgmt. div. Crane (Ind.) Army Ammunition Activity, 1983-85, chief control div., 1985; inventory mgmt. specialist 200th Theater Army Material Mgmt. Ctr., Zweibruecken, 1985-88; analyst supply systems U.S. Armament, Munitions and Chem. Command, Rock Island, Ill., 1988-89; specialist logistics mgt. U.S. Army Info. Systems Command, Ft. Huachuca, Ariz., 1989—. Mem. Federally Employed Women (chpt. pres. 1979-80), NAFE, Soc. Logistics Engrs., Assn. Computing Machinery, Am. Soc. Public Adminstrn., Soc. Profl. and Exec. Women, Assn. Info. Systems Profls., AAAS, NOW. Democrat.

KEENER, JOHN WESLEY, management consultant; b. Macedonia, Iowa, Apr. 10, 1927; s. Elza Lee and Florence Evelyn (Rhoades) K.; m. Loucille Clementine Wiedower, Nov. 19, 1949; children: Tonya Florence, Jonellyn Christine. BSEE, La. Tech., 1945; postgrad., St. Mary's Coll., 1945, Air War Coll., 1971. Owner 4K Motors, Medford, Oreg., 1948-51; purchasing agt. White City Lumber, Medford, 1951-52; asst. mgr. Woodbury & Co., Medford, 1952-57, Am. Steel & Supply, Medford, 1957-68; gen. mgr. Am. Steel & Supply, Medford and Redding, Calif., 1968-73, Medford, 1973-85; owner Rogue Pacific, Medford, 1985-91; mgmt. cons. Medford, 1991—; pres., bd. dirs. Jackson C.C. Found., Medford; cons. Oreg. div. Aeronautics, Salem, Oreg. Mem. Medford Planning Commn., 1972-75; chmn. Jackson County Econ. Devel., Medford, 1991; mem. County Airport Adv. Com., Medford, 1983—; chief instr. Oreg. Air Search and Rescue. With USN, 1944-46, Col. USAF-CAP, 1972—. Recipient Commendation for Community Svc. Gov. Oreg., 1992, Community Leader Spirit award Broadcasters, 1987. Mem. Loyal Order of Moose, Oreg. Wing Civil Air Patrol (comdr. 1981-82), Pacific Regional Civil Air Patrol (commendation 1981, nat. life saving awards (2)), Jackson County Airport Com. (past chmn., mem.), Rogue Valley Country Club. Republican. Methodist. Office: PO Box 22 Medford OR 97501

KEEP, JUDITH N., federal judge; b. 1944. B.A., Scripps Coll., 1966; J.D., U. San Diego, 1970. With Defenders Inc., 1971-73; pvt. practice law, 1973-76; asst. U.S. atty. Calif., 1976; judge Mcpl. Ct., San Diego, 1976-80, U.S. Dist. Ct. (so. dist.) Calif., San Diego, 1980—. Office: US Dist Ct 940 Front St San Diego CA 92189-0010

KEESE, JOHN STANLEY, airline pilot, consultant; b. Lovington, N.Mex., Apr. 20, 1952; s. James Richard and Jean Mavis (Moore) K.; m. Kristine Kay Kolb, Jan. 22, 1972; children: Sarah Jean, Rachel Leigh, Elizabeth Ann, Martha Katherine, Hannah Marie. BSChemE, San Jose (Calif.) State U., 1975; postgrad., Calif. State U., Fresno, 1981-83, Air Command & Staff Coll., 1983, Calif. State Poly. Inst., Pomona, 1984. Commd. 2d lt. USAF, 1976, advanced through grades to maj., 1987, 1st lt., student pilot 71st Student Squadron & 355th TAC Ftr, 1976-77; capt., A-7D aircraft comdr. USAF-23d Tact. Fighter Wing, England AFB, La., 1978-80; capt., F-4G pilot, flight lead USAF-37th Tact. Fighter Wing, George AFB, Calif., 1981-83; maj., flight comdr., F-117A & A-7D pilot USAF-4450th Tact. Group, Nellis AFB and Tonopah Test Range, Nev., 1984-89, 1989; semi-conductor process engr. AMI, Inc. (now Gould Semiconductor), Santa Clara, Calif., 1976-77; co-pilot DC 9 Am. Airlines, Inc., L.A., 1989-90, co-pilot Boeing 737, 1990-91, co-pilot DC-10, 1991—; cons. McClendon Assocs., Bedford, Tex., 1989-91. Elder chmn. Victor Valley Bible Ch., Victorville, Calif., 1982-84; worship dir. Las Vegas (Nev.) Bible Ch., 1984-88. Home: 4610 Stanton Way Bakersfield CA 93309

KEHLER, DOROTHEA FAITH, educator; b. N.Y.C., Apr. 21, 1936; d. Nathan and Minnie (Coopersmith) Gutwill; (widowed 1981); children: Paul Dolid, Eve Boyd, Jessica, Ted. BA, CCNY, 1956; MA, Ohio U., 1967, PhD, 1969. Instr. MacMurray Coll., Ill., 1964-65; instr. Ohio U., Athens, 1965-66, teaching fellow, 1966-68; lectr. San Diego State U., 1969-70, asst. prof., 1970-85, assoc. prof., 1985-88, prof., 1988—. Author: Problems in Literary Research, 1975, 2d edit., 1981, 3d edit., 1987; editor: In Another Country: Feminist Perspectives on Renaissance Drama, 1991. Nat. Endowment for the Humanities fellow Harvard U., 1983; Folger Libr. Inst. grantee, 1988; San Diego State U. scholar, 1990—. Mem. ACLU, MLA, NOW, Internat. Shakespeare Assn., Rocky Mountain Modern Lang. Assn., Southeastern Renaissance Conf., Renaissance Conf. So. Calif., Philol. Assn. of Pacific Coast, Shakespeare Assn. Am., Amnesty Internat. Democrat. Office: San Diego State U English Dept San Diego CA 92182-0295

KEHLMANN, ROBERT, artist, critic; b. Bklyn., Mar. 9, 1942. BA, Antioch Coll., 1963; MA, U. Calif., Berkeley, 1966. One-man shows include: Richmond Art Ctr., Calif., 1976, William Sawyer Gallery, San Francisco, 1978, 82, 86, Galerie M, Kassel, Fed. Republic Germany, 1985, Anne O'Brien Gallery, Washington, 1988, 90 Dorothy Weiss Gallery, San Francisco, 1993; group shows include: Am. Craft Mus., N.Y.C., 1978, 86, Corning (N.Y.) Mus. Glass, 1979, Tucson Mus. of Art, 1983, Kulturhuset, Stockholm, Sweden, 1985; represented in permanent collections at Corning Mus. Glass, Leigh Yawkey Woodson Art Mus., Hessisches Landes Mus., W.Ger., Bank of Am. World Hdqrs., San Francisco, Toledo Mus. Art, Hokkaido Mus. Modern Art, Sapporo, Japan, Huntington Mus. of Art, W.Va., Am. Craft Mus., N.Y.C., Musée des Arts Décoratifs, Lausanne, Switzerland; instr. glass design Calif. Coll. Arts and Crafts, Oakland, 1978-80, 91, Pilchuck Glass Ctr., Stanwood, Wash., 1978-80. Author: Twentieth Century Stained Glass: A New Definition, 1992; contbg. editor: New Glass Work mag.; editor: Glass Art Soc. Jour.,1981-84. Nat. Endowment Arts grantee, 1977-78. Mem. Glass Art Soc. (bd. dirs. 1980-84, 89-92). Office: Dorothy Weiss Gallery 256 Sutter St San Francisco CA 94108

KEHOE, VINCENT JEFFRÉ-ROUX, photographer, author, cosmetic company executive; b. Bklyn., N.Y., Sept. 12, 1921; s. John James and Bertha Florence (Roux) K.; m. Gena Irene Marino, Nov. 2, 1966. Student, MIT, 1940-41, Lowell Technol. Inst., 1941-42, Boston U., 1942; BFA in Motion Picture and TV Prodn., Columbia U., 1957. Dir. make-up dept. CBS-TV, N.Y.C., 1948-49, NBC Hallmark Hall of Fame series, 1951-53; make-up artist in charge of make-up for numerous film, TV and stage prodns., 1942—; dir. make-up Turner Hall Corp., 1959-61, Internat. Beauty Show, 1962-66; pres., dir. research Research Council of Make-up Artists, Inc., 1963—; chief press officer at Spanish Pavilion, N.Y. World's Fair, 1965; free-lance photographer, 1956—. Contbr. photographs to numerous mags. including Time, Life, Sports Illustrated, Argosy, Popular Photography; author: The Technique of Film and Television Make-up for Color, 1970, The Make-up Artist in the Beauty Salon, 1969, We Were There: April 19, 1775, 1974, A Military Guide, 1974, 2d rev. edit., 1993, The Technique of the Professional Makeup Artist, 1985, Special Make-up Effects, 1991; author-photographer bullfighting books: Aficionado! (N.Y. Art Dirs. Club award 1960), Wine, Women and Toros (N.Y. Art Dirs. award 1962); producer: (documentary color film) Matador de Toros, 1959. Served with inf. U.S. Army, World War II, ETO. Decorated Purple Heart, Bronze Star, CIB; recipient Torch award Council of 13 Original States, 1979. Fellow Co. Mil. Historians; mem. Soc. for Preservation of Colonial Culture (curator, life), Tenth Foot Royal Lincolnshire Regimental Assn. (life; Hon. Col. 1968), Soc. Motion Picture and TV Engrs. (life), Acad. TV Arts and Scis., Soc. for Army Hist. Research (Eng.) (life), Brit. Officers Club New England (life), 10th Mountain Div. Assn., 70th Inf. Div. (life), DAV (life), Nat. Rifle Assn. (life). Home and Office: PO Box 850 Somis CA 93066-0850

KEIM, MICHAEL RAY, dentist; b. Sabetha, Kans., June 8, 1951; s. Milton Leroy and Dorothy Juanita (Stover) K.; m. Christine Anne Lorenzen, Nov. 20, 1971; children: Michael Scott, Dawn Marie, Erik Alan. Student, U. Utah, 1969-72; DDS, Creighton U., 1976. Pvt. practice Casper, Wyo., 1976—. Mem. organizing bd. dirs. Ctrl. Wyo. Soccer Assn., 1976-77; mem. Casper Mountain Ski Patrol, Nat. Ski Patrol System, 1980—, avalanche ski mountaineering advisor No. Div. Region III, 1992—; bd. dirs., dep. commr. for fast pitch Wyo. Amateur Softball Assn., 1980-84; bd. dirs. Ctrl. Wyo. Softball Assn., 1980-84. Recipient Purple Merit Star for Saving a Life, 1992. Mem. ADA, Fedn. Dentaire Internat., Pierre Fauchard Acad., Wyo. Acad. Gen. Dentistry (sec.-treas. 1980-82, pres. 1982-87), Wyo. Dental Assn. (bd. dirs. 1992—, chmn. conv. 1993), Wyo. Dental Polit. Action Com. (sec.-treas. 1985—), Cen. Wyo. Dental Assn. (sec.-treas. 1981-82, pres. 1982-83), Wyo. Dental Hist. Assn. (bd. dirs. 1989—), Kiwanis (v.p. Casper Club 1988-89, bd. dirs. 1986—, pres.-elect 1989-90, pres. 1990-91, internat. del. 1989-91), Creighton Club (pres. 1982-84). Methodist. Home: 58 Jonquil St Casper WY 82604-3863 Office: 1749 S Boxelder St Casper WY 82604-3538

KEIM, ROBERT THOMAS, educator, consultant; b. St. Marys, Pa., Jan. 12, 1949; s. Robert Charles and Ida Florence (Radin) K.; m. Judy Conti, Sept. 12, 1970; children: Amanda Marie, Valerie Rita. BS in Math. and Computer Sci., U. Pitts., 1970, MBA, 1971, PhD in Mgmt. Info. Systems, 1976. Asst. prof. Fla. State U., Tallahassee, 1974-79; rsch. assoc. Ariz. State U., Tempe, 1979-82; asst. prof. info. systems Ariz. State U., 1979-84, assoc. prof. info. systems, 1984—, dir. Decision Systems Rsch. Ctr., 1988-92; dir. Divsn. Info. Mgmt. and Systems Tech. (InMaST), 1992—. Author: Business Computers, 1985; contbr. articles to acad. and profl. jours. Mem. Assn. Systems Mgmt. (internat. dir. 1986-89, Achievement award 1985, Disting. Svc. award 1986), Inst. Mgmt. Sci., Decision Scis. Inst., Mng. Apple Computers in Info. Systems (MacIS). Democrat. Roman Catholic. Home: 1039 W Natal Ave Mesa AZ 85210-7653 Office: Decision Systems Rsch Ctr Ariz State U Tempe AZ 85287-4206

KEIM, TERRY, writer; b. West Point, N.Y., Feb. 22, 1958; d. Robert Raymond and Nell (Caver) K.; m. Robert Wayne Renchler, Oct. 7, 1989. BA in Studio Fine Arts, U. N.Mex., 1982. Pub. affairs specialist Bur. Land. Mgmt., Roswell, N.Mex., 1987-89; freelance writer Hines, Oreg., 1989—; reporter, photographer Burns (Oreg.) Times-Herald, 1990—. Publicist Harney Hosp. Found., Burns, 1990—. Mem. Nat. Fedn. Press Women, Oreg. Press Women. Home and office: PO Box 305 Hines OR 97738

KEIPER, MARILYN MORRISON, educator; b. South Gate, Calif., June 12, 1930; d. David Cline and Matilda Ruth (Pearce) M.; m. Edward E. Keiper, June 18, 1962; children: Becky S. Swickard, Edward M. BA, Calif. State U., L.A., 1954; postgrad., UCLA, 1968. Elem. tchr. Rosemead (Calif.) Sch. Dist., 1954—. 2d reader 1st Ch. Christ Scientist, Arcadia, Calif., 1991—; mem., cons. Janson Adv. Group, Rosemead, 1985—; bd. dirs. Janson PTA, Rosemead, 1985—. Fellow Rosemead Tchrs. Assn., Delta Kappa Gamma.

KEIR, GERALD JANES, newspaper editor; b. Ludlow, Mass., Aug. 22, 1943; s. Alexander J. and Evelyn M. (Buckley) K.; m. Karen Mary Devine, July 22, 1972; children: Matthew J., Katherine B., Megan E. BA, Mich. State U., 1964, MA, 1966. Reporter Honolulu Advertiser, 1968-74, city editor, 1974-86, mng. editor, 1986-89, editor, 1989—. Co-author text: Advanced Reporting: Beyond News Events, 1985. Bd. dirs. Aloha United Way. Recipient Nat. Reporting award Am. Polit. Sci. Assn., 1971, Benjamin Fine Nat. award Am. Assn. Secondary Sch. Prins., 1981; John Ben Snow fellow, 1983, NEH fellow, 1973. Mem. Am. Soc. Newspaper Editors, Assoc. Press Mng. Editors, Am. Assn. Pub. Opinion Rsch. Soc. Profl. Journalists, Asian-Am. Journalists Assn., Social Sci. Assn., Pacific Club. Office: Honolulu Advertiser PO Box 3110 605 Kapiolani Blvd Honolulu HI 96802

KEISLING, PHILLIP A., state official; b. Portland, Oreg., June 23, 1955; s. Les and Ione Keisling; m. Pam Wiley, Sept. 4, 1988. BA, Yale U., 1977. Speech writer Gov. Tom McCall, Salem, Oreg., 1978; reporter Willamette Week, Portland, 1978-81; editor Washington Monthly mag., 1982-84; sr. legis asst. Oreg. Speakers of the Ho., Salem, 1985-88; state rep. State of Oreg., Salem, 1989-91, sec. of state, 1991—; mem. State Land Bd., Salem, 1991—, Hanford Waste Bd., Portland, 1991—. Chair Brooklyn Neighborhood Assn., Portland, 1986-88; del. local dist. Dem. Precinct Com., Portland, 1989-91. Office: Office Sec of State State Capitol Rm 136 Salem OR 97310*

KEISTER, JEAN CLARE, lawyer; b. Warren, Ohio, Aug. 28, 1931; d. John R. Keister and Anna Helen Brennan. JD, Southwesten, 1966. Bar: Calif. 1967, U.S. Supreme Ct. 1972, U.S. Dist. Ct. (so. dist.) Calif. 1988. Legal writer Gilbert Law Summaries, L.A., 1967; isntr. Glendale (Calif.) Coll. Law, 1968; pvt. practice Glendale, 1967—. Mem. Themis Soc., 1989-93. Recipient Golden Poet award World of Poetry. Mem. Burbank Bar Assn. (sec. 1993), Burbank C. of C. Office: 224 E Olive Ave Ste 219 Burbank CA 91502-1234

KEITH, BRUCE EDGAR, political analyst, genealogist; b. Curtis, Nebr., Feb. 17, 1918; s. Edgar L. and Corinne E. (Marsteller) K.; m. Evelyn E. Johnston, Oct. 29, 1944; children: Mona Louise, Kent Marsteller, Melanie Ann. AB with high distinction, Nebr. Wesleyan U., 1940, MA, Stanford U., 1952; grad. Command and Staff, Marine Corps Schs., 1958, Sr. Resident Sch., Naval War Coll., 1962; PhD, U. Calif.-Berkeley, 1982. Commd. 2d lt. U.S. Marine Corps, 1942, advanced through grades to col., 1962, ret., 1971, comdg. officer 3d Bn., 11th Marines, 1958-59, ops. officer, Pres. Dwight D. Eisenhower visit to Okinawa, 1960, G-3 ops. officer Fleet Marine Force, Pacific, Cuban Missile Crisis, 1962, mem. U.S. del. SEATO, Planning Conf., Bangkok, Thailand, 1964, G-3, Fleet Marine Force, Pacific, 1964-65, head Strategic Planning Study Dept., Naval War Coll., 1966-68, genealogist, 1967—, exec. officer Hdqrs. Marine Corps programs, Washington, 1968-71; election analyst Inst. Govtl. Studies, U. Calif.-Berkeley, 1974-86, polit. analyst, 1986—; teaching asst. U. Calif.-Berkeley, 1973-74. Bd. dirs., Bay Area Funeral Soc., 1980-83, v.p., 1981-83. Decorated Bronze Star, Navy Commendation medal, Presdl. Unit citation with 3 bronze stars. Recipient Phi Kappa Phi Silver medal Nebr. Wesleyan U., 1940, Alumni award, 1964. Mem. Am. Polit. Sci. Assn., Acad. Polit. Sci., Am. Acad. Polit. and Social Sci., Marine Corps Assn., Ret. Officers Assn. Phi Kappa Phi, Pi Gamma Mu. Republican. Unitarian. Clubs: Commonwealth of Calif. (San Francisco), Marines' Meml. (San Francisco). Lodge: Masons. Contbg. author: The Descendants of Daniel and Elizabeth (Disbrow) Keith, 1979-81; History of Curtis, Nebraska-The First Hundred Years, 1984; author: A Comparison of the House Armed Services Coms. in the 91st and 94th Congresses: How They Differed and Why, 1982; The Johnstons of Morning Sun, 1979; The Marstellers of Arrellton, 1978; The Morris Family of Brookville, 1977; Japan-the Key to America's Future in the Far East, 1962; A United States General Staff: A Must or a Monster?, 1950; co-author: California Votes, 1960-72, 1974; The Myth of the Independent Voter, 1992; Further Evidence on the Partisan Affinities of Independent " Leaners," 1983. Address: PO Box 156 El Cerrito CA 94530-0156

KEITH, DONALD MALCOLM, physician; b. Cordova, Alaska, May 18, 1932; s. Russell Monroe and Alverra Corinne (Anderson) K.; m. Betty Mae Riggers, Aug. 14, 1955; children: Heather Adair Moe, Allison Marie Ramsey. BS, Pacific Luth. Coll., 1954; MD, U. Wash., 1958. Diplomate Am. Bd. Family Practice. Family physician Ballenger Rd. Med. Ctr., Seattle, 1960-64; pvt. practice Seattle, 1965-86, 89—; family physician Highland Clinic, Seattle, 1986-89; pvt. practive Seattle, 1990—; clin. assoc. U. Wash. Sch. Medicine, Seattle, 1969-72, clin. instr., 1973-74, clin. asst. prof., 1975-87, clin. assoc. prof., 1987—; bd. dirs. Am. Bd. Family Practice, Wash. Physicians Health Program. Recipient Mead Johnson Grad. Tng. award Am. Acad. Gen. Practice, 1959, Disting. Alumnus award Pacific Luth. U., 1983, U. Wash. Sch. Medicine, 1986. Fellow Am. Acad. Family Physicians (bd. dirs. 1987-90); mem. AMA, Wash. Acad. Family Physicians (pres. 1974-75, Family Physician of Yr. 1980), King County Acad. Family Physicians (pres. 1969-70, Clin. Tchr. award 1986), Wash. State Med. Assn. (pres. 1982-83), King County Med. Soc. (pres. 1976). Republican. Lutheran. Office: 17191 Bothell Way NE Seattle WA 98155

KEITH, KENT MARSTELLER, academic administrator, corporate executive, government official, lawyer; b. N.Y.C., May 22, 1948; s. Bruce Edgar and Evelyn E. (Johnston) K.; m. Elizabeth Misao Carlson, Aug. 22, 1976. BA in Govt., Harvard U., 1970; BA in Politics and Philosophy, Oxford U., Eng., 1972, MA, 1977; JD, U. Hawaii, 1977. Bar: Hawaii 1977, D.C. 1979. Assoc. Cades, Schutte, Fleming & Wright, Honolulu, 1977-79; coord. Hawaii Dept. Planning and Econ. Devel., Honolulu, 1979-81, dep. dir., 1981-83, dir., 1983-86; energy resources coord. State of Hawaii, Honolulu, 1983-86, chmn. State Policy Coun., 1983-86; chmn. Aloha Tower Devel. Corp., 1983-86; project mgr. Mililani Tech. Park Castle and Cooke Properties Inc., 1986-88, v.p. pub. rels. and bus. devel., 1988-89, pres. Chaminade U. Honolulu, 1989—; bd. dirs. Grove Farm Co., Inc., 1990-93. Author: Jobs for Hawaii's People: Fundamental Issues in Economic Development, 1985, Hawaii: Looking Back from the Year 2050, 1987, For the Love of Students, 1992; contbr. articles on ocean law to law jours. Pres. Manoa Valley Ch., Honolulu, 1976-78; mem. platform com., Hawaii Dem. Conv., 1982, 84, 86; trustee Hawaii Loa Coll., 1986-89, vice chmn. 1987-89; mem. Diocesan Bd. Edn., 1990-93, chmn. 1990-93; bd. dirs. St. Louis Sch., 1990—, Hanahauoli Sch., 1990—; chmn. Manoa Neighborhood Bd., 1989-91. Rhodes scholar, 1970; named one of 10 Outstanding Young Men of Am., U.S. Jaycees, 1984. Mem. Am. Assn. Rhodes Scholars, Internat. House of Japan, Nature Conservancy, Pla. Club, Pacific Club, Harvard Club of Hawaii (Honolulu, bd. dirs. 1974-78, sec. 1974-76), Rotary (Honolulu). Home: 2626 Hillside Ave Honolulu HI 96822 Office: Chaminade U Honolulu 3140 Waialae Ave Honolulu HI 96816-1578

KEITH, NORMAN THOMAS, aerospace company administrator; b. Antioch, Calif., Jan. 12, 1936; s. Dean Theodore and Edna Margaret (Doty) K.; m. Marla Mildred Osten, Sept. 9, 1962. B of Tech., Tex. State Tech. Inst. Cert. profl. mgr. Field service engr. Gen. Dynamics Corp., San Diego, 1955-66, supr. Data Ctr., 1966-76, chief data systems, 1976-81, chief property adminstrn., 1981-83, motivational mgr., 1983-86, sr. program adminstr., 1986-90, mgr. total quality mgmt.Convair divsn., 1990—. Contbr. articles to profl. jours. Mem. mil. adv. bd. congressman Ron Packard, 1983-86; sgt. Res. Dep. Sheriff's Office, San Diego County; bd. dirs. San Dieguito Boys/Girls Clubs, Encinitas, 1966-69; loaned exec. United Way, San Diego, 1980-81. Mem. Nat. Mgmt. Assn. (bd. dirs., pres.), Nat. U. Alumni Assn. (life), Woodbury Coll. Alumni Assn., San Diego State U. Alumni Assn., Hon. Dep. Sheriff's Assn. (bd. dirs.). Republican. Lutheran. Lodges: Lions (sec. 1962-63), Elks. Home: 620 Cole Ranch Rd Encinitas CA 92024-9726 Office: Gen Dynamics Convair Div 5001 Kearny Villa Rd San Diego CA 92123-1499

KEITH, PAULINE MARY, artist, illustrator, writer; b. Fairfield, Nebr., July 21, 1924; d. Siebelt Ralph and Pauline Alethia (Garrison) Goldenstein; m. Everett B. Keith, Feb. 14, 1957; 1 child, Nathan Ralph. Student, George Fox Coll., 1947-48, Oreg. State U., 1955. Illustrator Merlin Press, San Jose, Calif., 1980-81; artist, illustrator, watercolorist Corvallis, Oreg., 1980—. Author 5 chapbooks, 1980-85; editor: Four Generations of Verse, 1979; contbr. poems to anthologies and mags.; one-woman shows include Roger's Meml. Libr., Forest Grove, Oreg., 1959, Corvallis Art Ctr., 1960, Human Resources Bldg., Corvallis, 1959-61; juried community shows include Hewlett-Packard Co., 1984-85, Corvallis Art Ctr., 1992, Chintimini Sr. Ctr. 1992. Co-elder First Christian Ch. (Disciples of Christ), Corvallis, 1988-89, co-deacon 1980-83, elder, 1991-93; sec. Hostess Club of Chintimini Sr. Ctr., Corvallis, 1987, pres. 1988-89. Recipient Watercolor 1st price Benton County Fair, 1982, 83, 88, 89, 91, 2d prize, 1987, 91, 3d prize, 1984, 90, 92. Mem. Oreg. Assn. Christian Writers, Internat. Assn. Women Mins., Linn-Benton Diabetes Assn., Am. Legion Aux. (elected poet post II Corvallis chpt. 1989-90,elected sec. 1991-92, chaplain 1992-93). Republican. Office: PO Box 825 Corvallis OR 97339-0825

KEITH, ROBERT ALLEN, psychology educator; b. Brea, Calif., Mar. 16, 1924; s. Albert Henry Keith and Delphene Ruth (Morgan) Parker;m. Nanette Hardesty, Sept. 1, 1949; children: Leslie Susan Keith Berclaz, Claudia Lynn Keith Lorenzana. BA, U. Calif., L.A., 1948, MA, 1951, PhD, 1953. Lic. psychologist, Calif.; diplomate in clin. psychology. Clin. psychology intern L.A. Psychiat. Svcs., 1950-53; dir. counseling svcs. Claremont (Calif.) Coll., 1953-59; from asst. to assoc. prof. psychology Claremont Grad. Sch., 1953-89; dir. rsch. div. Casa Colina Hosp., Pomona, Calif., 1968—. Contbr. articles related to med. rehab. to profl. jours. Lt. USNR, 1943-46, PTO. Harvard U. fellow, 1960-61; Rehab. Psychol. fellow, 1984, World Rehab. Fund of London fellow, 1987. Fellow Am. Psych. Assn., Am. Assn. U. Profs., Am. Congress Rehab. Medicine, Assn. for Health Svcs. Rsch., Am. Pub. Health Assn.

KEITHCART, KERRY EDWARD, air force officer; b. Bethesda, Md., July 6, 1954; s. Raymond Edward and Colleen (Moore) K. BS, USAF Acad.,

1976; MA in Guidance and Counseling, Rider Coll., 1983; MA in Marriage-Family-Child Counseling, Chapman Coll., 1989; postgrad., Calif. Grad. Sch., 1988—. Commd. 2d lt. USAF, 1976, advanced through grades to maj., 1992; instr., pilot USAF, Mather AFB, Calif., 1983-86; glider pilot USAF Acad. USAF, Colorado Springs, Colo., 1986-89; pilot 312th Airlift Squadron USAF, Travis AFB, Calif., 1990—; guest instr. marriage and family counseling USAF Acad.; adj. counselor McGuire AFB Social Actions. ARC vol. in sensitivity tng. for Spl. Olympics. Decorated Air Medal. Mem. ACA, Am. Orthopsychiat. Assn., Am. Assn. Marriage and Family Therapy, Assn. Grads. USAF Acad., Soaring Soc. Am., U.S. Tennis Assn.

KELEN, JOYCE ARLENE, social worker; b. N.Y.C., Dec. 5, 1949; d. Samuel and Rebecca (Rochman) Green; m. Leslie George Kelen, Jan. 31, 1971; children: David, Jonathan. BA, Lehman Coll., 1970; MSW, Univ. Utah, 1974, DSW, 1980. Recreation dir. N.Y.C. Housing Authority, Bronx, 1970-72; cottage supr. Kennedy Home, Bronx, 1974; sch. social worker Davis County Sch. Dist., Farmington, Utah, 1976-86; clin. asst. prof. U. Utah., Salt Lake City, 1976—; sch. social worker Salt Lake City Sch. Dist., 1986—; cons. in field, Salt Lake City, 1981—. Editor: To Whom Are We Beautiful As We Go?, 1979; contbr. articles to profl. jours. Utah Coll. of Nursing grantee, 1985. Mem. Nat. Assn. Social Workers (chairperson Gerontology Council, 1983-84, Utah Sch. Social Worker of Yr., 1977), NEA, Utah Edn. Assn., Davis Edn. Assn. Democrat. Jewish. Home: 128 M St Salt Lake City UT 84103-3854 Office: Franklin Elem Sch 1100 W 400 S Salt Lake City UT 84104-2334

KELEN, JULIA LAURA, radio station executive; b. N.Y.C., May 25, 1950; d. Emery Imre and Betty (Stones) Kelen; m. Craig Partridge, Oct. 16, 1977; children: Jesse, Clea. BA, U. Wash., 1973. Pres. Growing Family, Inc., Seattle, 1974-75; typographer Health Printers, Seattle, 1975-76; owner Julia Kelen Graphics, Seattle, 1976-82; announcer KEZX-AM Radio, Seattle, 1987-88; tng. and ops. mgr. KAOS-FM Radio, Olympia, Wash., 1988—. Editor tng. manual: Radio for Everyone, 1992. Mem. pub. rels. com. Olympia Waldorf Sch., 1988-89. Office: KAOS-FM Radio Evergreen State Coll CAB 301 Olympia WA 98505

KELL, ERNEST EUGENE, JR., mayor, contractor; b. N.D., July 5, 1928; s. Ernest Eugene and Katherine (Moynier) K.; m. Jacqueline Kell; children: Julie, Brian. Owner, operator Western Detailing Service, Inc., Anaheim, Calif., 1955-71; gen. contractor Long Beach, Calif., 1971—; councilman 5th dist. City Long Beach, Calif., 1975—, mayor, 1984—. Commr. Los Angeles County Transp. Commn., 1982-84; trustee Mosquito Abatement Dist., Los Angeles County, 1977—; chmn. Californians for Consumers No-Fault. Mem. Calif. Steel Detailers Assn. (pres.). League of Calif. Cities. Democrat. Lodge: Lions. Home: 3471 Marna Ave Long Beach CA 90808-3126 Office: City of Long Beach Office of Mayor 333 W Ocean Blvd Long Beach CA 90802-4664*

KELLAM, NORMA DAWN, medical/surgical nurse; b. Benton Harbor, Mich., June 13, 1938; d. Edgar Arnold and Bernice (Cronk) K. AA, San Bernardino Valley Coll., 1958; student, Calif. State Coll., Long Beach, 1961-1964, 1965, 1966, 1967; BS, San Diego State Coll., 1961; MS, Calif. State U., Fresno, 1972. Nursing instr. Porterville (Calif.) State Hosp., 1968-69; staff nurse Northside Psychiat. Hosp., Fresno, 1969-72; nursing instr. Pasadena (Calif.) City Coll., 1972-73; night shift lead Fairview Devel. Ctr., Costa Mesa, Calif., 1973—. Contbr. articles to newspapers. Recipient Cert. of Appreciation for vol. work Interstitial Cystitis Assn. Mem. Calif. Nurses Assn., Phi Kappa Phi.

KELLEHER, MATTHEW DENNIS, mechanical engineering educator; b. N.Y.C., Feb. 1, 1939; s. James Finbar and Mary Florence (Fitzgerald) K.; m. Jean Esther Jolliffe, May 31, 1969; children: Genevieve Jean, Veronica Jane. BS in Engring. Sci., U. Notre Dame, 1961, MSME, 1963, PhD, 1966. Registered profl. engr., Calif. Asst. prof. U. Notre Dame, Ind., 1965-66; Ford Found. fellow Dartmouth Coll., Hanover, N.H., 1966-67; assoc. scientist Avco Everett Research Lab., summer 1967; asst. prof. Naval Postgrad. Sch., Monterey, Calif., 1967-72, assoc. prof., 1972-82, prof. mech. engring., 1982—; cons. Lawrence Livermore (Calif.) Nat. Lab., 1985—; chmn. Mech. Engring. Dept., 1992—; Apple Computer Co., Cupertino, Calif.; sr. acad. visitor Dept. Engring. Sci. Oxford (Eng.) U., 1988-89. Contbr. articles to profl. jours. Chmn. Lower Carmel Valley adv. com. to Monterey County Planning Commn., 1981—. NSF grantee, 1973; Office Naval Research grantee, 1981—. Fellow ASME; mem. Sigma Xi. Roman Catholic. Home: 25000 Outlook Dr Carmel CA 93923-8939 Office: Naval Postgrad Sch Mech Engring Dept Monterey CA 93943

KELLEHER, RICHARD CORNELIUS, marketing and communications executive; b. Buffalo, Nov. 21, 1949; s. Cornelius and Lucile Norma (White) K.; m. Sherri Fae Anderson, Mar. 17, 1981 (div. 1991); children: Erin Marie, Shawn Michael. BA, U. New Mex., 1975; MBA, U. Phoenix, 1984. Reporter, photographer Daily Lobo, Albuquerque, 1973-75; mgn. editor News Bulletin, Belen, New Mex., 1975-77; various corp. mktg. titles AT&T Mountain Bell, Denver, 1978-84; exec. editor Dairy Mag., Denver, 1984-86; communications dir. Am. Heart Assn., Phoenix, 1987-90; cons. Kelleher Communications & Mktg., Phoenix, 1990—; spl. writer Denver Post, 1977-82, Denver Corr. Billboard Mag., 1977-82. Mem. Gov.'s Roundtable on Employee Productivity, Gov. of Ariz., 1990-91; vol. communications Am. Cancer Soc., 1990-92. Recipient Harvey Communications Study award, 1986. Mem. Pub. Rels. Soc. Am., Toastmasters. Home: 12331 N 19th St Apt 233 Phoenix AZ 85022

KELLEHER, ROBERT JOSEPH, federal judge; b. N.Y.C., Mar. 5, 1913; s. Frank and Mary (Donovan) K.; m. Gracyn W. Wheeler, Aug. 14, 1940; children: R. Jeffrey, Karen Kathleen. A.B., Williams Coll., 1935; LL.B., Harvard U., 1938. Bar: N.Y. 1939, Calif. 1942, U.S. Supreme Ct 1954. Atty. War Dept., 1941-42; Asst. U.S. atty. So. Dist. Calif., 1948-50; pvt. practice Beverly Hills, 1951-71; U.S. dist. judge, 1971—. Mem. So. Calif. Com. Olympic Games, 1964; capt. U.S. Davis Cup Team, 1962-63; treas. Youth Tennis Found. So. Calif., 1961-64. Served to lt. USNR, 1942-45. Mem. So. Calif. Tennis Assn. (v.p. 1958-64, pres. 1983-85), U.S. Lawn Tennis Assn. (pres. 1967-68), Internat. Lawn Tennis USA, Internat. Lawn Tennis of Great Britain, Internat. Lawn Tennis of france, Internat. Lawn Tennis of Can., Internat. Lawn Tennis of Mex., Internat. Lawn Tennis of Australia, Internat. Lawn Tennis of India, Internat. Lawn Tennis of Israel, All Eng. Lawn Tennis and Croquet (Wimbledon), Harvard Club (N.Y. and So. Calif.), Williams Club (N.Y.), L.A. Country Club, Delta Kappa Epsilon. Home: 15 St Malo Bch Oceanside CA 92054-5854 Office: US Dist Ct 255 East Temple Ste 830 Los Angeles CA 90012-4701

KELLEHER, RONALD RAY, sales executive; b. Spokane, Wash., Sept. 27, 1951; s. Raymond Charles and Ruby Ruth (Sauer) K.; m. Barbara Earline Stennett, Mar. 30, 1980; children: Justin, Rebekah. BS in Mktg., Wash. State U., 1973. Sales rep. coffee Procter & Gamble, L.A., 1973-74; dist. field rep. coffee Procter & Gamble, Portland, Oreg., 1975; unit mgr. coffee Proctor & Gamble, Sacramento, 1976-79; assoc. dist. mgr. food svc. Procter & Gamble, Portland, 1980-83; unit mgr. beverage Procter & Gamble, L.A., 1984-87; unit mgr. Crush Proctor & Gamble, L.A., 1987-89, gen. unit mgr. food, 1989-90, unit sales mgr. food/beverage, 1990—; dir. Guidelines Internat., Laguna Hills, Calif.; pres. Master's Mgmt. Devel., Mission Viejo, Calif., 1990—; exec. dir. Marketplace Forum, Mission Viejo, Calif., 1992—. Pub., author: (newsletter) Wheat and Chaff, 1991, Marketplace Forum, 1992; (book) Life-Time Management, 1992. Republican. Office: Masters Mgmt Devel PO Box 2804 Mission Viejo CA 92690

KELLER, ARTHUR MICHAEL, computer science researcher; b. N.Y.C., Jan. 14, 1957; s. David and Luba K. BS summa cum laude, Bklyn. Coll., 1977; MS, Stanford U., 1979, PhD, 1985. Instr. computer sci. Stanford (Calif.) U., 1979-81, rsch. asst., 1977-85, acting asst. chmn. dept. computer sci., 1982, rsch. assoc., 1985, 89-91, vis. asst. prof., 1987-89, rsch. scientist, 1991-92, sr. rsch. scientist, 1992—; sr. rsch. scientist Advanced Decision Systems, Mountain View, Calif., 1989-92; chief tech. advisor Persistence Software, San Mateo, Calif., 1992—; systems analyst Bklyn. Coll. Computer Ctr., 1974-77; summer rsch. asst. IBM, Thomas J. Watson Rsch. Ctr., Yorktown Heights, N.Y., 1980; acad. assoc. San Jose Rsch. Lab., 1981; asst. prof. U. Tex., Austin, 1985-88, adjunct asst. prof., 1988-89; mem. program com. Internat. Conf. on Data Engring., L.A., 1986, 87, 89, Internat. Conf. on Very Large Data Bases, Amsterdam, The Netherlands, 1989. Author: A First Course in Computer Programming Using Pascal, 1982. Mem. IEEE (vice chmn. com. database engring. Computer Soc. 1986-87), Assn. Computing Machinery, TeX Users Group (fin. com. 1983-85, internat. coord. 1985-87), Chai Soc. (communications officer 1987-89, v.p. publicity 1989-90). Home: 3881 Corina Way Palo Alto CA 94303-4507 Office: Stanford U Dept Computer Sci Stanford CA 94305-2140

KELLER, GEORGE MATTHEW, retired oil company executive; b. Kansas City, Mo., Dec. 3, 1923; s. George Matthew and Edna Louise (Mathews) K.; m. Adelaide McCague, Dec. 27, 1946; children: William G., Robert A., Barry R. BS in Chem. Engring., MIT, 1948. Engr. Standard Oil Calif. (now Chevron Corp.), San Francisco, 1948-63, fgn. ops. staff, 1963-67, asst. v.p., asst. to pres., 1967-69, v.p., 1969-74, dir., 1970-88, vice-chmn., 1974-81, chmn., chief exec. officer, 1981-88; bd. dirs. 1st Interstate Bancorp., 1st Interstate Bank Calif., Boeing Co., McKesson Corp., SRI Internat., Met. Life Ins. Co., Chronicle Pub. Co. Trustee Notre Dame Coll., Belmont, Calif., MIT, Cambridge, Mass. Served to 1st lt. USAAF, 1943-46. Mem. Bus. Coun. Office: Chevron Corp 555 Market St San Francisco CA 94105-2801

KELLER, J(AMES) WESLEY, credit union executive; b. Jonesboro, Ark., Jan. 6, 1958; s. Norman Grady and Norma Lee (Ridgeway) Patrick; m. Patricia Marie Delavan, July 7, 1979. Student, U. Miss., 1976-78; BS in Bus. and Mgmt., Redlands U., 1991. Sr. collector Rodkwell Fed. Credit Union, Downey, Calif., 1978-79; acct. Lucky Fed. Credit Union, Buena Park, Calif., 1979-84; pres., chief exec. officer Long Beach (Calif.) State Employees Credit Union, 1984—. Mem. Credit Union Exec. Soc., Calif. Credit Union League (bd. govs. Long Beach chpt., treas. 1985-86), So. Calif. Credit Union Mgr.s Assn., U. Redlands Whitehead Leadership Soc., Nat. Assn. State Charted Credit Unions (bd. dirs.), Kiwanis. Republican. Baptist. Home: 872 E Bernard Dr Fullerton CA 92635-1933 Office: Long Beach State Employees Credit Union 3840 N Long Beach Blvd Long Beach CA 90807-3391

KELLER, KENT EUGENE, advertising and public relations executive; b. Oil City, Pa., Oct. 5, 1941; s. George W. and Lois (Wallace) K.; divorced; children: Eric Trent, Todd Jason. BA, Kent State U., 1963; cert., Chrysler Inst., Detroit, 1968, UCLA, 1973. Editor Oil City (Pa.) Derrick, 1959-60; various mgmt. positions Chrysler Corp., Twinsburg, Ohio, 1960-64, prodn. cont. mgr., 1964-67; group mgr. Chrysler Corp. AMG, Detroit, 1967-69; dir. advt. and pub. rels. Zero Corp., Burbank, Calif., 1969-75; exec. v.p. Basso & Assocs. Inc., Newport Beach, Calif., 1975-80; pres. Jason Trent & Co., Inc., Fountain Valley, Calif., 1980—; pub. rels. counsel Electronic Convs. Inc., L.A., 1980-85; bd. dirs. Neurosci. Tech. Inc., Tarzana, Calif.; cons. Global Engring., Irvine, Calif., 1989—; co-founder Strategic Concepts, Fountain Valley, Calif., 1990. Editor (industry report) TOLD Report, 1985—, (mag.) Zero Dimensions, 1969-75. Mem. Town Hall of Calif., L.A., 1980—. Mem. Bus. & Profl. Advt. Assn., Pub. Rels. Soc. Am., Back Bay Club. Republican. Presbyterian. Home: 18072 Darmel Pl Santa Ana CA 92705-1916

KELLER, MICHAEL CROSLEY, correctional facilities official; b. Salem, Oreg., Aug. 3, 1949; s. John L. and E. Ruth (Simmons) K.; m. Renée L. Romanko, June 30, 1975 (dec.Apr. 1984); m. Edie Ann Cannon, Mar. 25, 1989; children: Aaron Crosley, Alexis Catherine. BS, Western Oreg. State Coll., 1978; postgrad., Somona State U., 1978-84. Substitute tchr. Apache County Schs., Ganado, Ariz., 1972; correctional officer San Quentin (Calif.) State Prison, 1978-80, correctional sgt., 1980-82, correctional counselor, 1982-84, employee rels. officer, 1984-85; watch comdr., lt. Correctional Tng. Facility, Soledad, Calif., 1988-93; capt. North Kern State Prison, Delano, Calif., 1993—; asst. negotiator Dept. of Pers. Adminstrn., Sacramento, 1985. With U.S. Army, 1973-76, Korea. Republican. Office: North Kern State Prison PO Box 567 Delano CA 93216-0567

KELLER, ROBERT LEE, kennel executive, video producer; b. Detroit, Aug. 21, 1945; s. Herbert Olen Keller and Dorothy Lee (Richardson) Smith; m. Edith Ann Head, Oct. 12, 1963; children: Juliette Ann Keller McNew, Victoria Marie. Student, Mt. San Antonio Coll., Walnut, Calif., 1963-65. Materials analyst Gen. Dynamics/Pomona, Calif., 1963-68, systems analyst, 1968-73; mgr. data processing Packers Cold Storage, Fullerton, Calif., 1973-76; owner, mgr. Starline Kennels, Stanton, Calif., 1974—; exec. dir. Kit Collectors Internat., Stanton, 1980—; exec. producer Starline Prodns., Stanton, 1988—; cons. Revell/Monogram, Morton Grove, Ill., 1983—; producer Kit Collectors Expn., Buena Park, Calif., 1975—; video editor Western Photographer, San Diego, 1989—; pub. jour. Vintage Plastic, 1980-87. Author: Kit Collectors Pricing Guide, 1980, 2d edit., 1981; producer, dir. TV series The Model Club, 1989, Young Talent Showcase '90; contbr. articles to profl. publs. Mem. Orange County (Calif.) Animal Control Adv. Com., 1974-76. Mem. Nat. Fedn. Local Cable Programmers, Internat. Plastic Modelers Soc. (hon.), Orange County Kennel Owners (sec. 1987—), Miniature Schnauzer Club So. Calif. (hon., pres. 1971-72). Republican. Office: Kit Collectors Internat PO Box 38 Stanton CA 90680-0038

KELLER, ROBERT LEE, economic developer, planner; b. Durham, N.C., 1946; s. Robert s. and Maren (L.) K. BA in Math., Econs., U. Calif., Berkeley, 1968; MA in Econs., U. Mich., 1970. Planner, trainer Fed. Office of Econ. Opportunity, Seattle, 1970-73; grant writer, cons. Am. Indian Programs, Seattle, 1973-77; mgmt. cons., trainer AK Fedn. of Natives, Seattle, 1978-81; contracts adminstr. Fairbanks (Alaska) Native Assn., 1982-84; non-profit orgns. mgmt. cons. Redmond, Wash., 1984-85; econ. devel. dir. Fairbanks Native Assn., 1985-91; cons. in mgmt. and devel. Alaska Native Villages, Fairbanks, 1992—; leadership inst. C. of C., Fairbanks, 1988-89. Patentee in field. Evang. chmn. Fairbanks Luth. Ch., 1990. Class Champion Model Ships award State Fair, Fairbanks, 1988. Home: Box 75161 Fairbanks AK 99707

KELLER, ROBERT SCOTT, writer; b. Portland, Oreg., June 5, 1945; s. Stuart Robert and Royce Myrtle (Latham) K.; m. Tana Nancy Thiele, Dec. 15, 1986; 1 child, Aaron Charles. BA in Molecular Biology, Harvard U., 1967. Tchr. Peace Corps, Monrovia, Liberia, 1967-69, Washington Pub. Sch., 1970-71; musician various orgns., Washington, 1971-80, Eugene, Oreg., 1971-80; tchr. Willamette Sci. & Tech. Ctr., Eugene, 1981-82; editor Home Computer Mag., Eugene, 1983-86, Programmer's Jour., Eugene, 1986-87, Microsoft Press, Redmond, Wash., 1989-90, Borland Internat., Scotts Valley, Calif., 1989-90; pres. Spirit Software, Eugene, 1988—; sr. writer Microsoft, Redmond, 1990—. Contbr. articles profl. jours.; author software. NSF grantee, 1966. Home: 7816 NE 12th St Bellevue WA 98004-3116 Office: Microsoft 1 Microsoft Way Redmond WA 98052-6393

KELLER, SUSAN AGNES, insurance officer; b. Moline, Ill., July 12, 1952; d. Kenneth Francis and Ethel Louise (Odendahl) Hulsbrink; m. Kevin Eugene Keller, June 20, 1981; 1 child, Dawn Marie. Grad. in Pub. Relations, Patricia Stevens Career Coll., 1971; grad. in Gen. Ins., Ins. Inst. Am., 1986. CPCU; lic. ins. and real estate agt.; notary public. Comml. lines rater Bitiminous Casualty Corp., Rock Island, Ill., 1973-78; with Roadway Express, Inc., Rock Island, 1978-81; front line supr. Yellow Freight System, Inc., Denver, 1982-83; supr. plumbing and sheet metal prodn. Bell Plumbing and Heating, Denver, 1983-84; v.p. underwriting farm/ranch dept. Golden Eagle Ins. Co., San Diego, 1985—; cons. real estate foreclosure County Records Svc., San Diego, 1986-89; tchr. Ins. Inst. of Am., 1991. Vol. DAV, San Diego, 1985—; tchr. IEA and CPCU courses. Mem. Soc. Chartered Property and Casualty Underwriters (bd. dirs.), Profl. Women in Ins., NAFE. Roman Catholic. Home: 449 Jamul Ct Chula Vista CA 91911-2504 Office: Golden Eagle Ins Co 7175 Navajo Rd San Diego CA 92119-1642

KELLER, WILLIAM D., federal judge; b. 1934. BS, U. Calif., Berkeley, 1956; LLB, UCLA, 1960. Asst. U.S. atty. U.S. Dist. Ct. (so. dist.) Calif., 1961-64; assoc. Dryden, Harrington, Horgan & Swartz, Calif., 1964-72; U.S. atty. U.S. Dist. Ct. (cen. dist.) Calif., Los Angeles, 1972-77, judge, 1984—; ptnr. Rosenfeld, Meyer & Susman, Calif., 1977-78; pvt. practice law Calif., 1978-81; ptnr. Hahn & Cazier, Calif., 1981-84. Office: US Dist Ct 312 N Spring St Los Angeles CA 90012-4701

KELLERAN, REBECCA JOHNSTON, remodeling company executive; b. Atlanta, Apr. 30, 1943; d. John Roland and Maxine (Maynard) Johnston; m. Bruce Russell Kelleran, June 28, 1963; children: Jeffrey R., Amy E. Student, U. Wash., 1961-62, Wash. State U., 1962-63. Prin. Showplace Kitchens & Baths, Redmond, Wash., 1983—. Con., case aide vols. King County Juvenile Ct., Seattle, 1966. Mem. N.W. Chpt. Nat. Kitchen and Bath Assn. (v.p. 1989-90, pres. 1990-91, long range planning chairperson 1991-92, Dealer mem. of yr. 1990, seminar speaker 1990).

KELLERMAN, FAYE MARDER, novelist, dentist; b. St. Louis, July 31, 1952; d. Oscar and Anne (Steinberg) Marder; m. Jonathan Seth Kellerman, July 23, 1972; children: Jesse Oren, Rachel Diana, Ilana Judith. AB in Math, UCLA, 1974, DDS, 1978. Author: The Ritual Bath, 1986 (Macavity award best 1st novel 1986), Sacred and Profane, 1987, The Quality of Mercy, 1989, Milk and Honey, 1990, Day of Atonement, 1991, False Prophet, 1992; contbr. short stories to Sisters in Crime vols. 1 & 3, Ellery Queen Mag., A Woman's Eye, Women of Mystery, the year's 2d finest crime: mystery stories. UCLA rsch. fellow, 1978. Mem. Mystery Writers of Am., Womens' Israeli Polit. Action Com., Sisters in Crime. Jewish.

KELLEY, BRUCE DUTTON, pharmacist; b. Hartford, Conn., Jan. 4, 1957; s. Roger Weston and Elizabeth Morrill (Atwood) K.: m. DawnReneé Cinocco, Jan. 19, 1990. Student, U. Hartford, 1975-77; BS in Pharmacy, U. Colo., 1985, postgrad. in Russian, 1985—. RPh, Colo. Various part time jobs while attending school, 1975-85; pharmacist King Soopers, Inc., Boulder, Colo., 1990—; asst. tour leader in Russia U. Tex., El Paso, 1991; Russia asst. guide, U. Ariz., Tucson, 1992 (summer). Vol. Warderburg Student Health Ctr., U. Colo., Boulder, 1981-83, Am. Diabetes Assn. Mem. NRA, Am. Fedn. Police, Am. Pharm. Assn., Elks Club, Nat. Eagle Scout Assn. Republican. Home: 6152 Willow Ln Boulder CO 80301 Office: King Soopers Inc 6550 Lookout Rd Boulder CO 80301

KELLEY, GEORGE GREGORY, business educator, management consultant; b. Renton, Wash., Dec. 28, 1956; s. George Gregory Kelley and Treva Elizabeth (Grim) Gomez; m. Nancy Arlene Wahl, June 17, 1986; children: Erin Elizabeth Alice, Nancy Ann Kelley Hendrickson. BA in History and Govt., Seattle U., 1988; MS and MBA in Mgmt., Mktg., and Info. Systems, Marylhurst Coll., 1990; MA in History and Govt., U. Portland, 1992. Legal asst. King County Prosecuting Atty., Seattle, 1978-81; asst. br. mgr. ITT Fin. Svcs., Seattle, 1983-84, Fin. One, Seattle, 1984-85; corp. credit mgr. Landa, Inc., Portland, Oreg., 1986-88; mgmt. cons. N.W. Small Bus. Inst., Portland, 1988—; prof. bus. and mgmt. Marylhurst (Oreg.) Coll., 1990—; exec. v.p., chief operating officer Tel-Mar Corp., Kirkland, Wash., 1991. Editor: (newsletter) Marylhurst Network, 1990. Mem. Marylhurst Coll. Mgmt. Assn. (pres., faculty advisor 1992), Am. Mgmt. Assn. Democrat. Mem. LDS Ch. Home: 14639 SE Main Portland OR 97233 Office: Marylhurst Coll Marylhurst OR 97036

KELLEY, JACQUELYN LARSON, gerontologist; b. Palo Alto, Calif., Oct. 28, 1945; d. John Monroe and Glendora Drusilla (Sampson) Larson; m. Stephen Earl Kelley, Dec. 24, 1963 (div. 1993); children: Kristina Leona Jane, Stephenie Victoria. AA, Coll. San Mateo, 1974; BS summa cum laude, Coll. Notre Dame, Belmont, Calif., 1980; postgrad., San Francisco State U., 1980-82, Coll. Notre Dame, 1992—. ESL aide Cabrillo Unified Sch. Dist., Half Moon Bay, Calif., 1975-76; community services specialist Ret. Sr. Vol. Program, Menlo Park, Calif., 1980-82, dir., 1982-83; dir. vol. services Vis. Nurse Assn. San Francisco, 1983-85; gerontology specialist San Jose (Calif.) Office on Aging, 1986-90, gerontology supr., 1990-92; analyst San Jose Dept. Human Resources, Retirement Benefits, 1992—; lectr. San Jose State U., 1991-93. Founder Ocean Shore Resident's Assn., Half Moon Bay, 1976; founder Friends of RSVP Inc., Redwood City, Calif., 1983. Mem. Internat. Soc. for Retirement Planning (chpt. pres., bd. dirs. 1985—, v.p. 1991—), Nat. Coun. Aging, Am. Soc. on Aging (com. chmn. 1984-87, chmn. retirement program planning com. 1988-90, chair recration and leisure planning com. 1990—), Assn. Profl. Vol. Mgrs. (founder, chmn. 1984-87, trainer), Nat. Recreation and Park Assn. (aging task force 1990—, founding pres. aging and leisure sect. 1991—), Calif. Park and Recreation Soc. (bd. dirs., founder, pres. aging sect. 1988—), Alpha Gamma Sigma, Delta Epsilon Sigma, Kappa Gamma Pi. Democrat. Lutheran. Home: 2221 Lake Rd # 3 Belmont CA 94002

KELLEY, JAMES LEE, hospitality marketing executive; b. Mt. Pleasant, Mich., Apr. 21, 1947; s. Homer and Jean Genevieve (Brady) K. Student, Northwood Inst., 1965-66, Ferris State Coll., 1966-68; cert., Delta Coll., 1973. Mgr. Red Roof Inns, Columbus, 1975-76; sales mgr. Hospitality Inns, Ohio and Ga., 1976-78; regional sales dir. Hospitality Inns, Cleve., 1978-79; no. div. sales dir. Harley Hotels, Cleve., 1979-80; sales mgr. N.Y. Statler Hotel, N.Y.C., 1980-81; dir. sales Americana Hotels, Inns & Resorts, Chgo., Orlando, Fla., and N.J., 1981-84; dir. mktg. Claremont Resort, Spa and Tennis Club, Oakland, Calif., 1984-91; corp. dir. mktg. Harsch Investments, Portland, Oreg., 1988-91; pres., CEO Kelley Mktg., San Francisco, 1992—. Bd. dirs. Bread and Roses, Mill Valley, Calif., 1991—. Fellow Hotel Sales Mgmt. Assn. (Bronze Adrian Bell 1990, Gold Adrian Bell 1990); mem. Sales and Mktg. Exec. San Francisco. Democrat. Office: Kelley Mktg #402 500 Beale St San Francisco CA 94105-2030

KELLEY, JAMES TERRY, quality assurance/regulatory affairs specialist; b. Oklahoma City, June 27, 1953; s. James Lloyd and Dorthea Lee (Moore) K.; m. Catherine Ann Barney, Sept. 14, 1985; children: Joshua Isaiah, Jared Eto. Grad. high sch., Oklahoma City, 1971. Mgr. Bixlers Drive-In, Oklahoma City, 1968-71; quality control engr. Honeywell Informational Systems, Oklahoma City, 1971-75; quality control supr. CCC divsn. Bendix, San Diego, 1979-80; survey mgr. Interocean Systems, Inc., San Diego, 1980-81; regulatory affairs/quality assurance mgr. CooperVision, Inc., San Diego, 1981-85; v.p. quality assurance/regulatory affairs Technivision, Inc., San Diego, 1985-88; quality assurance engr. Camino Labs., Inc., San Diego, 1988-89; regulatory affairs/quality assurance supr. Signet Armorlite, Inc., San Marcos, Calif., 1989—. Inventor, patentee cooling jacket design; co-inventor, co-patentee optical system design auto perimeters. With USN, 1975-79. Home: 13516 Silver Lake Dr Poway CA 92064 Office: Signet Armorlite Inc 1001 Armorlite Dr San Marcos CA 92069

KELLEY, KEVIN PATRICK, security, safety, risk management administrator; b. Indpls., Apr. 21, 1954; s. Everett Lee and Emily Louise (Bottoms) K.; m. Kathie Jo Fluegeman, Oct. 13, 1984. BS, Calif. State U., Long Beach, 1984; cert. mgmt. supervision, UCLA, 1984. Mgmt. asst. FBI, Los Angeles, 1973-79; security/safety supr. U. Calif., 1979-82; security/safety adminstr. Micom Systems, Inc., Chatsworth, Calif., 1982-83; loss prevention, safety auditor Joseph Magnin, Inc., San Francisco, 1983-84; loss prevention, safety adminstr. Wherehouse Entertainment, Inc., Gardena, Calif., 1984-86; risk control cons. Indsl. Indemnity Co., Los Angeles, 1986-87, Kemper Group, City of Industry, Calif., 1987-90; account mgr. loss control engring. Tokio Marine Mgmt. Inc., Pasadena, Calif., 1990—; commr. pub. safety City of Norwalk, Calif., 1984-86. Mem. security com. Los Angeles Olympic Organizing Com., 1984. Mem. Am. Soc. Indsl. Security (cert., Peter Updike Meml. scholar 1985), Am. Soc. Safety Engrs., Chief Spl. Agts. Assn., Risk Ins. Mgmt. Soc., Nat. Safety Mgmt. Soc. (sec. 1985-86), Am. Heart Assn. (governing bd. chmn. 1986-88), Ins. Inst. Am. (cert.). Republican. Roman Catholic. Lodges: Rotary, Kiwanis.

KELLEY, LISA STONE, public guardian, conservator; b. Sacramento, Calif., Mar. 10, 1947; d. John William and Coral Frances (Roberts) Stone; m. Charles B. Kelley, Oct. 7, 1967 (div. Feb. 1987); children: Brian Christopher, Darren Matthew. Student, Sacramento City Coll., 1965-67, AA in Social Sci., 1978; BA in Social Work with honors, Calif. State U., Sacramento, 1982, MSW with honors, 1985. Lic. clin. social worker, Calif. Pharmacy clerk S. Sacramento Pharmacy, 1966-68; temp. med. asst. Sacramento, 1978-80; adv., counselor El Dorado Women's Info. Ctr., Placerville, Calif., 1982; dep. patients rights adv. Sacramento County Office Patients Rights, 1983-84; sch. social worker Elk Grove (Calif.) Unified Sch. Dist., 1984-85; mental health counselor Sacramento Mental Health Ctr., 1986; dep. pub. guardian/conservator Sacramento County, 1986—. Mem. NASW, Sacramento County Employees Orgn., Am. Orthopsychiat. Assn., Menninger Found., Calif. State U. Alumni Assn., Phi Kappa Phi. Democrat. Office: Sacramento County Pub Guardian/Conservator 4875 Broadway Ste I Sacramento CA 95820-1500

KELLEY, MARK ALAN, trust company executive; b. St. Louis, Sept. 7, 1951; s. James A. and Kathleen M. (Goetz) K.; m. Joan B. Baldzikowski,

Aug. 6, 1984. BA, U. Denver, 1973, M in Taxation, 1977. CPA, Colo.; Cert. Fin. Planner. Ins. auditor State Compensation Ins. Fund, Denver, 1973-76, Pueblo, Colo., 1976-79; pvt. practice Boulder, Colo., 1979-91; v.p. First Trust Corp., Denver, 1981—. Treas. Big Sisters of Colo., Denver, 1990-93. Mem. AICPA, Internat. Assn. Fin. Planning, Colo. Soc. CPAs. Republican. Buddhist. Office: First Trust Corp 717 17th St Ste 2300 Denver CO 80202-3323

KELLEY, RICHARD ROY, hotel executive; b. Honolulu, Dec. 28, 1933; s. Roy Cecil and Estelle Louise (Foote) K.; m. Jane Zieber, June 21, 1955 (dec. 1978); children: Elizabeth, Kathryn, Charles, Linda J., Mary Colleen; m. Linda Van Gilder, June 23, 1979; children: Christopher Van Gilder, Anne Marie. BA, Stanford U., 1955; MD, Harvard U., 1960. Pathologist Queen's Med. Ctr., Honolulu, 1962-70, Kapiolani Maternity Hosp., Honolulu, 1961-70; asst. prof. pathology John A. Burns Med. Sch., U. Hawaii, Honolulu, 1968-70; chmn., CEO Outrigger Hotels Hawaii, Honolulu, 1970—; bd. dirs. First Hawaiian Bank, Outrigger Internat. Travel, Inc. Bd. dirs. Straub Med. Rsch. and Edn. Found., Assets Sch., Hawaii Conv. Park Coun.; trustee, past chmn. Punahou Sch.; bd. govs. Ctr. for Internat. Comml. Dispute Resolution; adv. bd. Travel Industry Mgmt. Sch., U. Hawaii, Am. Hotel and Motel Assn. Ednl. Inst.; chmn. bd. councilors Hawaii Pacific div. Am. Cancer Soc.; chair commn. on performance standards. Named Marketer of Yr., Am. Mktg. Assn., 1985, Communicator of Yr., Internat. Bus. Communicators, 1987; named to Hawaii Bus. Hall of Fame, 1993. Mem. Am. Hotel and Motel Assn., Hawaii Bus. Roundtable (bd. dirs.), Hawaii Visitors Bur. (bd. dirs., chmn. 1991-92), Waikiki Oahu Visitors Assn., Waikiki Improvement Assn., Chief Execs. Orgn., Japan Assn. Travel Agts., Japan Hawaii Econ. Coun., Pacific Asia Travel Assn., World Pres.'s Orgn., Pacific Peace Found., Waialae Country Club, World Travel and Tourism Coun., Oahu Country Club. Office: Outrigger Hotels Hawaii 2375 Kuhio Ave Honolulu HI 96815-2939

KELLEY, ROBERT FRANKLIN, systems analyst, consultant; b. Chgo., July 2, 1961; s. Jerry Dean and Jean (Laine) K. BA in Philosophy, Western Md. Coll., 1985; MBA in MIS, Ind. U., 1989. Human resource specialist Marriott Corp., Gaithersburg, Md., 1985-86; mgr. in tng. Courtyard by Marriott, Fairfax, Va., 1986-87; software applications specialist Hewlett-Packard, Palo Alto, Calif., 1989—. counselor Camp Allen for the Physically Handicapped, Manchester, N.H., 1977; track coach for disadvantaged youth Rockville (Md.) Recreation, 1980. Home: 408 Grant Ave Apt 309 Palo Alto CA 94306 Office: Hewlett-Packard 3000 Hanover St # 20bj Palo Alto CA 94304-1112

KELLEY, ROBERT OTIS, medical science educator; b. Santa Monica, Calif., Apr. 30, 1944; s. David Otis and Onetia May (Nettles) K.; married; children: Jennifer Leigh, Karin Michelle. BS, Abilene Christian U., 1965; MA, U. Calif., Berkeley, 1966, PhD, 1969. Asst. prof. U. N.Mex. Sch. of Medicine, Albuquerque, 1969-74, assoc. prof., 1974-79, prof., 1979—, chmn. dept. anatomy, 1981—; vis. scientist Okazaki (Japan) Nat. Labs., 1984-85, speaker U. N.Mex. Speakers Bur., 1969—; mem. study sect. NIH, Bethesda, Md., 1982-86; anatomy com. Nat. Bd. Med. Examiners, Phila., 1992—. Author: Basic Histology, 1989; editor Cell and Tissue Rsch., 1970—, Anat. Record, 1970—; contbr. articles to profl. jours. Patroller Nat. Ski Patrol, 1970—. Recipient Rsch. Career Devel. award NIH, 1972-77, Kaiser award U. Calif., Irvine, 1976; Internat. Exch. Scholar NSF; NIH grantee, 1970—;. Mem. Biophys. Soc., Am. Soc. Cell Biology, Soc. for Devel. Biology, Electron Microscopy Soc. Am. (bd. dirs. 1987—), Am. Assn. Anatomists (mem. exec. com. 1988—). Democrat. Protestant. Office: U NMex Sch Medicine Dept Anatomy Albuquerque NM 87131

KELLEY, ROBERT PAUL, JR., management consultation executive; b. Mansfield, Ohio, Mar. 27, 1942; s. Robert Paul and Rachel Marie Kelley; BBA, Notre Dame U., 1964; MBA, Harvard U., 1969; m. Mimi Grant, June 15, 1975; children: Robert, Laura, Elizabeth. Mktg. cons., supr. Laventhol & Horwath, L.A., 1972-73; dir. mktg., entertainment and mdsg. Knott's Berry Farm, Buena Park, Calif., 1974-76; sr. v.p. mktg. Am. Warranty Corp., L.A., 1978-80; co-founder Gen. Group of Cos., 1981; chief exec. officer Strategy Network Corp.; dir. Orange County sect. So. Calif. Tech. Exec.'s Network, 1984-85, pres., chief exec. officer, 1985—; co-founder, chief exec. officer ABL Health Care Execs. Network, 1989; chmn. bd. Micro Frame Techs., Inc. Author: The Board of Directors and its Role in Growing Companies, 1984. Served with USNR, 1964-67. Home: 6004 E West View Dr Orange CA 92669-4314 Office: 17772 17th St Ste 200 Tustin CA 92680

KELLEY, TERRY WAYNE, mechanical engineer; b. Eugene, Oreg., May 30, 1952; s. Edgar Harold and Esther Gwendolyn (Hansen) K.; m. Norma Kay Eberli, June 8, 1974; children: Stephanie Lynn, Sarah Elizabeth. BS in Mech. Engring., Oreg. State U., 1974, MS in Mech. Engring., 1975. Registered profl. engr., Calif. Engr. geothermal div. Unocal, Santa Rosa, Calif., 1975-78, prodn. engr., 1980-83, mech. engring. supr., 1983-93, advising prodn. engr., 1993—; project engr. Philippine Geothermal Inc., Manila, 1978-80; problem writer Nat. Coun. of Examiners for Engring. and Surveying Profl. Engrs. licensing exam., 1983-92. Mem. Geothermal Resource Coun., ASME, Pi Tau Sigma, Tau Beta Pi, Phi Kappa Phi. Democrat. Lutheran. Office: Unocal Geothermal 3576 Unocal Pl Santa Rosa CA 95403-1774

KELLNER, JAMIE, broadcasting executive. With CBS, 1969; former v.p. first-run programming, devel., sales Viacom Enterprises; pres. Orion Entertainment Group, 1979-86; pres., CEO Fox Broadcasting Co., L.A., 1986-93. Office: Fox Inc PO Box 900 10201 W Pico Blvd Beverly Hills CA 90213-0900

KELLNER, RICHARD GEORGE, mathematician, computer scientist; b. Cleve., July 10, 1943; s. George Ernest and Wanda Julia (Lapinski) K.; BS, Case Inst. Tech., 1965; MS, Stanford U., 1968, PhD, 1969; m. Charlene Ann Zajc, June 26, 1965; children: Michael Richard, David George. Staff mem. Los Alamos (N.M.) Scientific Lab., 1969-79, Los Alamos Nat. Lab., 1983-88; co-owner, dir. software devel. KMP Computer Systems, Inc., Los Alamos, 1979-84; mgr. spl. projects KMP Computer Systems div. 1st Data Resources Inc., Los Alamos, 1984-87; with microcomputer div., 1988; owner CompuSpeed, 1986—; co-owner Computer-Aided Communications, 1982-84; v.p. Applied Computing Systems Inc., 1988—; cons., 1979—. Recipient Commendation award for outstanding support of operation Desert Storm. Mem. IEEE, Assn. Computing Machinery, Math. Assn. Am., Soc. Indsl. and Applied Math., Am. Math. Soc. Home: 4496 Ridgeway Dr Los Alamos NM 87544-1960 Office: Applied Computing Systems Inc 120 Longview Dr Los Alamos NM 87544-3093

KELLOGG, BRENT NELSON, dentist; b. Seattle, Nov. 25, 1951; s. Richard Webster and Lois (Nelson) K.; m. Kathleen Julie Johanson, Mar. 23, 1974 (div. June 1986); m. Denise Marie Shostad, Dec. 6, 1986; children: Leigh Marie, Richard Lee. BA in Zoology, U. Wash., 1974, DDS, 1978. Pvt. practice Everett, Wash., 1978—; instr. part-time U. Wash. Dental Sch., Seattle, 1979-80. Mem. ADA, Wash. State Dental Assn., Snohonish County Dental Assn., Acad. Gen. Dentistry, U.S. Naval Inst., Mill Creek Country Club, Omicron Kappa Upsilon. Republican. Home: 1300 141st St SE Bothell WA 98012-1362 Office: 1809 100th Pl SE Everett WA 98208-3829

KELLOGG, FREDERICK, historian; b. Boston, Dec. 9, 1929; s. Frederick Floyd and Stella Harriet (Plummer) K.; m. Patricia Kay Hanbery, Aug. 21, 1954 (dec. 1975); 1 child, Kristine Marie Calvert. AB, Stanford U., 1952; MA, U. So. Calif., 1958; PhD, Ind. U., 1969. Instr., Boise State U., 1962-64, asst. prof., 1964-65; vis. asst. prof. U. Idaho, 1965; asso. prof. Boise State U., 1966-67; instr. history U. Ariz., 1967-68, asst. prof., 1968-71, asso. prof., 1971—. Founder, chmn. Idaho Hist. Conf., 1964. U.S.-Romania Cultural Exchange Research scholar, 1960-61; Sr. Fulbright-Hays Research scholar, Romania, 1969-70. Recipient Am. Council Learned Socs. Research grant, 1970-71; Internat. Research and Exchanges Bd. Sr. Research grant, 1973-74. Mem. Am. Hist. Assn., Am. Assn. Advancement Slavic Studies, Am. Assn. Southeast European Studies. Author: A History of Romanian Historical Writing, 1990; mng. editor Southeastern Europe, 1974—; contbr. articles to academic publs. Office: U Ariz Dept History Tucson AZ 85721

KELLOGG, GREGG BARNUM, computer scientist; b. Newport Beach, Calif., Feb. 27, 1957; s. Gladstone Berkshire and Laura Elizabeth (Barnum) K.; m. Anh Ngoc Pham, July 27, 1991; 1 child, Andy. BS in Math., Humboldt State U., 1979; MS in Computer Sci., UCLA, 1981. Engr., mgr. Hewlett Packard Co., Cupertino, Calif., 1981-87; engr. Next Computer, Inc., Redwood City, Calif., 1987-91; engr., mgr. EO Inc., Mountain View, Calif., 1991—. Mem. IEEE. Office: EO Inc 800 A E Middlefield Rd Mountain View CA 94043

KELLSHAW, TERENCE, bishop; b. Manchester, Eng., Oct. 4, 1936; m. Hazel Frederica Johnson, Nov. 3, 1963; 4 children. Student in theology, London Univ., attended Oakhill Theol. Coll.; D. Ministry, Pitts. Theol. Coll., 1985. Ordained deacon, The Ch. of Eng., 1967, priest, 1968. Med. technologist; sr. med. technologist Makerere Univ., Uganda; asst., Christ Ch., Clifton, Bristol, 1967-71, St. John's, Woking, Surrey, 1971-73, rector, inner-city parish group, from 1973; prof. pastoral theology Trinity Episc. Sch. for Ministry, Ambridge, Pa., from 1980; interim pastor Ch. of the Ascension, Pitts., 1984-85; bishop Diocese of the Rio Grande Episcopal Ch., Albuquerque, 1989—. Office: Rio Grande Episc Diocese 4304 Carlisle Blvd NE Albuquerque NM 87107-4811

KELLY, BRIAN FRANCIS, engineer, consultant; b. Glasgow, Scotland, Mar. 21, 1952; came to U.S., 1975; s. James Henry and Mary (McGoldrick)K.; m. Margaret Marina Hirsch, Sept. 15, 1991. BS in Elec. and Electronic Engring., Heriot-Watt U., Edinburgh, Scotland, 1975. Chief engr. Village Recorder, L.A., 1977-80; engr. Rupert Neve Inc., L.A., 1980-82; audio engr. Sprocket Systems/Lucasfilm Ltd., San Rafael, Calif., 1982-85, asst. chief engr., 1985-89; project mgr. LucasArts, Nicasio, Calif., 1989-92; pres. BKMS, El Cerrito, Calif., 1992—; lectr. in field; judge sci. fair Marin County Edn. Dept., Marin County, Calif. 1988-91. Mem. IEEE, Audio Engring. Soc., Soc. Motion Pictures and T.V. Engrs. Office: BKMS PO Box 1063 El Cerrito CA 94530

KELLY, BRIAN MATTHEW, industrial hygienist; b. Ogdensburg, N.Y., June 16, 1956; s. Lauris F. and Catherine M. (McEvoy) K. BA, SUNY, Oswego, 1978; BS, Clarkson U., 1981; MS in Indsl. Safety, Cen. Mo. State U., 1990. Cert. indsl. hygienist Am. Bd. Indsl. Hygiene; cert. accident investigator U.S. Dept. Energy, NASA and Nuclear Regulatory Commn. Maintenance engr. Kelly Sales Corp., Madrid, N.Y., 1978-80, carpenter, 1981-82; hygienist indsl. hygiene and toxicology ES&H assessment dept. 7001 Sandia Nat. Labs., Albuquerque, 1983—; mem. tech. adv. bd. Albuquerque (N.Mex.) Tech. Vocat. Inst., 1989—. Mem. Air Pollution and Hazardous Waste Mgmt. Assn., Am. Chem. Soc. (div. chem. health and safety), Am. Inst. Chemists, Am. Indsl. Hygienists Assn., N.Y. Acad. Scis., Am. Soc. Safety Engrs., Am. Welding Soc., Am. Acad. Indsl. Hygiene, Nat. Fire Protection Assn., Gamma Sigma Epsilon, Phi Kappa Phi. Republican. Roman Catholic. Home: 1455 Beall St Bosque Farms NM 87068-9536 Office: Sandia Nat Labs ES&H Assessment Dept 7001 PO Box 5800 Albuquerque NM 87185-5800

KELLY, CAROLYN SUE, newspaper executive; b. Pasco, Wash., Oct. 25, 1952; d. Jerald Davin and Margaret Helen (Nibler) K. BBA, Gonzaga U., 1974; MBA, Seattle U., 1985. CPA, Wash. Acct. Brajcich & Loeffler, Spokane, Wash., 1972-74; auditor Peat, Marwick, Mitchell & Co., Seattle, 1974-77; fin. analyst Seattle Times, 1977-81, asst. circulation mgr., 1981-83, spl. project advt. mgr., 1983-86, dir. mktg. and new bus., 1986-89, v.p., chief fin. officer, 1989—. Bd. dirs. Econ. Devel. Coun., Seattle, 1992, Campfire, Artists Unltd. Mem. Fin. Execs. Office: Seattle Times PO Box 70 Seattle WA 98111

KELLY, CHARLES EUGENE, II, gastroenterologist, researcher; b. Salina, Kans., Sept. 4, 1958; s. Charles Eugene and Byrdie Inez (Sowell) K. BA in Chemistry, U. Kans., 1980, MD, 1984; postgrad in internal medicine, U. Mich., 1984-87. Gastroenterology fellow Stanford U. Med. Ctr., 1987—. Recipient Nat. Rsch. Sci. award NIH, 1990. Mem. Am. Coll. Physicians (assoc.), Am. Gastroenterology Assn. (assoc.). Baptist. Office: Stanford U Med Ctr Gastroenterology Office 300 Pasteur Dr S-069 Stanford CA 94305

KELLY, DAVID RICHARD, accountant; b. Oakland, Calif., June 9, 1940; s. David Philip and Annetta Marie K.; m. Margo Ann Lourdeaux, May 9, 1964; children: Brian D., Timothy A. BS in Econs., Bus. Adminstrn., St. Mary's Coll., Moraga, Calif., 1962; MBA, U. Calif., Berkeley, 1971. CPA, Calif. Staff acct. Price Waterhouse, San Francisco, 1962-65, Victor Equipment Co., San Francisco, 1965-66; staff acct., mgr. taxes Hood & Strong, San Francisco, 1966-69; pvt. practice acctg. Walnut Creek, Calif., 1970-74; officer Kelly Tama Shiffman, Inc., CPA's, Walnut Creek, 1974—. Chmn. planned giving com. Children's Hosp. Med. Ctr. Found., Oakland, 1981-82, 87-93, trustee, 1988—; bd. dirs. (hon.) Contra Costa County Dist. Council Soc. St. Vincent de Paul; alumni ex-officio mem. Bd. Regents, bd. trustees St. Mary's Coll., 1979-80; treas. St. Mary's East Bay Scholarship Fund, Inc., 1982—, Family Aid to Cath. Edn., Roman Cath. Diocese, Oakland, Calif., 1990—; mem. budget and fin. coms. Mt. Diablo Family YMCA, 1982-84, bishop's com. for charity Roman Catholic Diocese Oakland, Calif., 1988-90; past treas. Easter Seal Soc. Contra Costa County; past bd. dirs. Diablo Valley Estate Planning Council; mem. bd. regents St. Mary's Coll. High Sch., Berkeley, Calif., 1988—; dir. Contra Costa Coun., 1990—. Mem. Am. Inst. CPA's, Calif. Soc. CPA's (statewide dir. 1977-80, pres. East Bay chpt. 1978-79, task force for community service, 1982, task force CPA requirements 1985), St. Mary's Coll. Nat. Alumni Assn. (bd. dirs. 1972—, pres. 1979-80). Democrat. Roman Catholic. Office: Kelly Tama Shiffman Inc 2121 N California Blvd Ste 900 Walnut Creek CA 94596-7306

KELLY, DENNIS RAY, sales executive; b. Olympia, Wash., Aug. 20, 1948; s. William E. and Irene (Lewis) K.; m. Pamela Jo Kresevich, Mar. 16, 1974. BA, Cen. Wash. U., 1972; postgrad., U. Wash., 1977-78. Sales rep. Bumble Bee Sea Foods, Seattle, 1972-74; retail sales mgr. Pacific Pearl Sea Foods, Seattle, 1974-76; regional sales mgr. Castle & Cooke Foods, Seattle, Phila., and N.Y.C., 1976-80; v.p. sales mktg. Frances Andrew Ltd., Seattle, 1980-82; regional sales mgr. Tenneco West, Seattle, 1982-85; sales and mktg. mgr. for western U.S. David Oppenheimer, Seattle, 1985—. Alumni advisor Cen. Wash. U., Ellensburg, 1979-87, alumni bd. dirs., 1986—, fund drive chmn., 1988, mem. sch. community group bd.; mem. Statue of Liberty Ellis Island Found.; chmn. ann. fund drive Cen. Wash. U., bd. dirs., 1992. Mem. New Zealand-Am. Soc., Mfrs. Reps. Club Wash. (bd. dirs.). Republican. Home: 2821 2d Ave Ste 1204 Seattle WA 98121

KELLY, DONALD IGNATIUS, management consultant; b. Bklyn.; s. Henry and Mary (Sullivan) K.; children: Kurt, Kimberly. AB, The Citadel, 1951-55; law student, U. West L.A. Sch. Law, 1981-82. Owner Kelly Indsl. Supply Co., N.Y.C.; dist. mgr. Firestone Tire and Rubber Corp., Akron, Ohio; v.p. Uniroyal, N.Y.C., Mark C. Bloome, L.A., Dunlop Tire & Rubber Corp., London, Eng.; pres. Sebring Tire & Rubber Corp., Akron, PacMetro NT&T Div., L.A., 1980—; cons. D.K. Internat., L.A., 1981—, Take One Prodns., L.A., N.Y.C., 1981—, PacMet. Entertainment, L.A., N.Y.C., 1981—, various other companies, 1981—; franchise mgr. Digitcom AT&T. Author: (novel and movie) War Games, (TV presentations) Star Search, Starcare, Battle of the Video Games, others, 1980-85. 1st lt. USAF. Roman Catholic. Home: 6565 Sunset Blvd Apt 318 Hollywood CA 90028 Office: PacMetro NT&T Div 12923 Venice Blvd Culver City CA 90006

KELLY, FLORENCE ANN, writer, poet; b. Columbia, S.C., May 24, 1948; d. George Lafayette Austin and Minna Florence (Bolding) K. BA with honors, Columbia U., 1970; postgrad., U. Houston, 1982. Sec. Mass. Mut. Life Ins., 1983-84, Statesman Nat. Life Ins., Houston, 1985, O'Keefe Real Estate, Surprise, Ariz., 1987; adminstrv. asst. Periodontics Ltd., Phoenix, 1987-90; with Executemps, Phoenix, 1991—; with PAMS Temp. Agy., 1993—. Author poetry. Organizer New Alliance Party/Dem. Party high conservative br., N.Y.C. Houston and Phoenix, 1980-90. Recipient Am. Legion award for Citizenship, 1966, William W. Fairlough award Pelham Manor Club, N.Y., 1966, others.

KELLY, FRANK KING, foundation administrator; b. Kansas City, Mo., June 12, 1914; s. Francis Michael and Martha Oneita (King) K.; m. Barbara Allen Mandigo, Dec. 5, 1941; children: Terence F., Stephen D. AB, U. Mo., Kansas City, 1937; LHD, U. Santa Barbara, 1993. Reporter, editor The Kansas City Star, 1937-41; editor, feature writer AP, N.Y.C., 1941-46; info. specialist Nat. Housing Agy., N.Y.C., 1946-47; speech writer Pres. Harry S. Truman, Washington, 1948; asst. dir. research div. Dem. Nat. Com., Washington, 1948; prof. Boston U., 1948; asst. to U.S. senate majority leader, dir. Senate Majority Policy Com., Washington, 1949-52; U.S. dir. Internat. Press Inst., N.Y.C., 1952-53; v.p. Fund for Republic and Ctr. for Study Dem. Instns., Santa Barbara, Calif., 1956-75; sr. v.p. Nuclear Age Peace Found., Santa Barbara, 1982—; advisor Acad. World Studies, San Francisco; cons. Santa Barbara Community Coll.; hon. chmn. Univ. Religious Ctr., U. Calif., Santa Barbara; participant White House Conf. Internat. Cooperation, Washington, 1965; speaker Conf. on Human Responsibilities for Peace, UN U. for Peace, Costa Rica, 1989, Summit Meeting Humanity, 1993. Author: An Edge of Light, 1949, Reporters Around the World, 1957, Your Freedoms: The Bill of Rights, 1964, The Martyred Presidents, 1967, Your Laws, 1970, The Fight for the White House, 1961, Court of Reason, 1981, The 100% Challenge: The United States Academy of Peace, 1983, Searching for a President in a Nuclear Age, 1988, Star Ship Invincible, 1979, Waging Peace in a Nuclear Age, 1988, Waging Peace II: Vision and Hope for the 21st Century, 1992; contbr. articles to Fantasy Commentator. Dir. Harriman for Pres. Com., Washington, 1952, Work Tng. Program, Santa Barbara, 1964—, UN Assn., Santa Barbara, 1980—, Calif. Council, UN U., 1987—; speech writer for Pres. Truman's 1948 Presdl. Campaign; bd. dirs. Nat. Peace Acad. Campaign., 1978-84; past pres. Cath. Social Services, Santa Barbara; founder Nat. Coun. of Citizens, 1991. Served with U.S. Army, 1943-45. Nieman fellow Harvard U., 1942-43. Democrat. Roman Catholic. Clubs: Harvard, Channel City (Santa Barbara). Home: 34 E Padre St Santa Barbara CA 93105-3530 Office: Nuclear Age Peace Found 1187 Coast Village Rd Ste 123 Santa Barbara CA 93108-2737

KELLY, GABRIELLE MARY, film production executive; b. Galway, Ireland, Apr. 16, 1953; d. Gabriel Francis and Nora (Geraghty) K.; m. Allan Avrum Goldstein, May 30, 1986; children: Fiona Ann, Eamon Saul. BA in Am. Lit. with honors, U. Sussex, Brighton, Eng., 1976. Rsch. asst. BBC London/WGBH Boston, 1973-75; copy editor N.Y. Rev. of Books, N.Y.C., 1975-78; head devel. Lumet-Allen Co., N.Y.C., 1978-83; prodr. Paramount & Columbia Pictures, N.Y.C. & L.A., 1983-85; prodr., writer CBS Films, N.Y.C., 1985-86; v.p. prodn. Bud Yorkin Prodns., 1988-89; v.p. creative affairs Robert Evans Co., Paramount Pictures, L.A., 1990—. Democrat. Roman Catholic. Home: 2509 Greenvalley Rd Los Angeles CA 90046

KELLY, JAMES P., computer company executive; b. Jersey City, N.J., Feb. 27, 1942; s. James Patrick and Rosetta Cecilia (Nestor) K.; m. Sharon Martin, Jan. 30, 1965 (div. Nov. 1979); children: James, Thomas, Colleen, Shannon. BS in Math., St. Peter's Coll., 1964; MBA in Fin., Rutgers U., 1968. Programmer Prudential Ins. Co., Newark, 1966-68; sr. sales rep. computer systems div. RCA, Newark, 1968-71, Sperry Univac, N.Y., N.J., 1971-73; sales mgr. Sperry Corp., N.Y., N.J., 1973-77; br. mgr. Sperry Corp., Montclair, N.J., 1977-79; regional dir. Martin Marietta Corp., N.Y.C., 1979-82; nat. sales dir. Martin Marietta Corp., Bethesda, Md., 1982-85, Unisys Corp., Phila., 1985-88; v.p. mktg. & sales Unisys Corp., Santa Ana, Calif., 1988-92; pres. On Line Computer Systems, Newport Beach, Calif., 1992—. Lt. U.S. Army, 1964-66. Home: 24341 Santa Clara Ave # 3 Dana Point CA 92629-3049 Office: On Line Computer Systems 610 Newport Ctr Dr Newport Beach CA 92660

KELLY, JEROME BERNARD, insurance company executive; b. Kankakee, Ill., Oct. 4, 1954; s. Joseph B. and Mary J. (Demerly) K.; m. Barbara Fawcett, June 21, 1986; children: Anna, Sarah. BA, Regis Coll., 1980; MBA, U. Phoenix, 1989. V.p. Shearson Hayden Stone, Denver, 1977-83, E.F. Hutton, Denver, 1983-85; portfolio mgr. 17th St. Fin. Mgmt., Denver, 1985-87; stockbroker Dain Bosworth, Denver, 1987-88; owner J.B. Kelly Ins. Agy., Denver, 1988—. Bd. dirs. United Cerebral Palsy Assn. Denver, 1987-90. Mem. Colo. Bus. Sch. Club (pres. 1988-89), Trout Unltd., Nat. Assn. of Securties Dealers (bd. arbitration 1987—), Am. Arbitration Assn. (panel arbitrators 1990—). Office: JB Kelly Ins Agy 1863 S Pearl St Denver CO 80210

KELLY, LEONTINE T. C., clergywoman; b. Washington; d. David D. and Ila M. Turpeau; m. Gloster Current (div.); children: Angella, Gloster Jr., John David; m. James David Kelly (dec.); 1 child, Pamela (adopted). Student W.Va. State Coll.; grad. Va. Union U., 1960; MDiv, Union Theol. Sem., Richmond, Va., 1976. Formerly sch. tchr.; former pastor Galilee United Meth. Ch., Edwardsville, Va.; later mem. staff Va. Conf. Council on Ministries; pastor Asbury United Meth. Ch., Richmond, 1976-83; mem. nat. staff United Meth. Ch., Nashville, 1983-84; bishop Calif.-Nev. Conf., San Francisco, 1984-88. Adj. prof. Pacific Sch. Religion, Berkeley, Calif., 1992—. Office: 316 N El Camino Real Apt 112 San Mateo CA 94401-2529

KELLY, NANCY KAREN, civic worker; b. Salt Lake City, Dec. 29, 1935; d. Martin Julius and Nancy Blanche (Wyant) Sather; m. James Patrick Kelly, June 29, 1967 (div. 1988); children: Kathryn Kling, Mark Kling, Lisa Bergland, James Kelly. BA, Augustana Coll., 1960; MS, U. S.D., 1964; MA, U. Nebr., 1973. Tchr. English Sioux Falls (S.D.) Sch. Dist., 1960-67; tchr., head dept. English Houston Sch. Dist., 1967-69; supr. early intervention program Suffolk County (N.Y.) Assn. Retarded Citizens, 1973-75; instr. Allegheny C.C., Pitts., 1977-78; legal advocate Hunnicutt Law Firm, Tustin, Calif., 1981-82; bd. dirs. Three Rivers Youth and Foster Grandparents Orgn., Pitts., 1979-84; mem. Pa. Gov.'s Com. on Mental Health and Mental Retardation, 1980-84; county and state chmn. Pa. Assn. Retarded Citizens, 1979-84; chair. Adv. Com. on Spl. Edn., Tustin, 1988—. Contbr. articles to profl. publs. Chair project rev. Health Systems Agy., Pitts., 1977-84; mem. Area Bd. Devel. Disabilities, Tustin, 1991—; chair voter registration 69th Assembly Dist., Tustin, 1990—. Mem. LWV. Home: 17381 Norwood Park Pl Tustin CA 92680

KELLY, PAUL HAMILTON, life insurance company official; b. Sugar City, Idaho, Sept. 9, 1937; s. Howard G. and Irene (Hamilton) K.; m. Deanne Packer, Dec. 20, 1961; children: Joan, David, Kathryn, Ruth, Joseph, Anne. Student, Ricks Coll., Rexburg, Idaho, 1955-57; BS, Brigham Young U., 1962. CLU. Commd. 2d lt. USAF, 1963, advanced through grades to capt., 1967; assigned to Italy, The Philippines, Calif., S.D., 1963-74; resigned, 1974; life underwriter Mut. N.Y., Idaho Falls, Idaho, 1978—. Mem. exec. bd. Grand Teton coun. Boy Scouts Am., 1984—. Mem. Soc. CLU's and Chartered Fin. Cons. (exec. bd. Idaho Falls 1990—), North Ea. Idaho Assn. Life Underwriters (pres. 1985-86), Ricks Coll. Alumni Assn. (pres. 1984-89). Republican. Mem. LDS Ch. Office: Mut NY 1920 E 17th St Ste 110 Idaho Falls ID 83404-8036

KELLY, PAUL JOSEPH, JR., lawyer; b. Freeport, N.Y., Dec. 6, 1940; s. Paul J. and Jacqueline M. (Nolan) K.; BBA, U. Notre Dame, 1963; JD, Fordham U., 1967; m. Ruth Ellen Dowling, June 27, 1964; children—Johanna, Paul Edwin, Thomas Martin, Christopher Mark, Heather Marie. Bar: N.Mex. 1967. Law clk. Cravath, Swaine & Moore, N.Y.C., 1964-67; assoc. firm Hinkle, Cox, Eaton, Coffied & Hensley, Roswell, 1967-71, ptnr., 1971-92; judge U.S. Ct. Appeals (10th cir.), Santa Fe, 1992—; mem. N.Mex. Bd. Bar Examiners, 1982-85; mem. N.Mex. Ho. of Reps., 1976-81, chmn. consumer and public affairs com., mem. judiciary com. Mem. N.Mex. Pub. Defender Bd.; bd. of vis.itors, Fordham U. Sch. of Law, 1992—; pres. Roswell Drug Abuse Com., 1970-71; mem. Appellate Judges Nominating Commn., 1989-92. Pres. Chaves County Young Reps., 1971-72; vice chmn. N.Mex. Young Reps., 1969-71, treas., 1968-69. Bd. dirs. Zia council Girl Scouts Am., Roswell Girls Club, Chaves County Mental Health Assn., 1974-77; bd. dirs. Santa Fe Orch., 1992—, Roswell Symphony Orch. Soc., 1969-82, treas., 1970-73, pres., 1973-75; mem. Eastern N.Mex. State Fair Bd., 1978-83. Mem. ABA, Fed. Bar Assn., State Bar N.Mex. (v.p. young lawyers sect. 1969, co-chmn. ins. sub-com. 1972-73, mem. continuing legal edn. com. 1970-73). Roman Catholic (pres. parish council 1971-76). K.C. Office: US Court Appeals 10th Circuit Montoya Bldg S Federal Plz PO Box 10113 Santa Fe NM 87504-6113

KELLY, TIM DONAHUE, state senator; b. Sacramento, Aug. 15, 1944. Former legis. aide to Calif. and Nev. Legislatures; mortgage banker; mem. Alaska Ho. of Reps., 1976-78, Alaska Senate, 1978—, senate pres., 1989-90. With USMC, Alaska Air NG. Office: State Capitol Juneau AK 99801-1182

KELLY, WILLIAM BRET, insurance executive; b. Rocky Ford, Colo., Sept. 28, 1922; s. William Andrew and Florence Gail (Yant) K.; m. Patricia Ruth Ducy, Mar. 25, 1944; children: Eric Damian, Kathryn Gail Kelly Schweitzer. BA cum laude, U. Colo., 1947. CPCU. With Steel City Agys., Inc., and predecessor, Pueblo, Colo., 1946—, pres., 1961-76, chmn. bd., 1977—; dir. United Bank Pueblo, 1963—, chmn. bd., 1983-88; mem. Pub. Expenditure Coun., 1984—; v.p. Colo. Ins. Edn. Found., 1981, pres., 1982. Mem. Pueblo Area Coun. Govts., 1971-73, Colo. Forum 1985—, trustee Pueblo Bd. Water Works, 1966-80, pres., 1970-71; pres. Pueblo Single Fund Plan, 1960-61, Pueblo Heart Coun., 1962, Family Svc. Soc. Pueblo, 1963; mem. 10th Jud. Dist. Nominating Com., 1967-71; trustee U. So. Colo. Found., 1967—, v.p., 1991, 92; trustee Jackson Found., 1972—, Farley Found., 1979—, Roselawn Cemetery Assn., 1982—, Kelly-Ducy Found., 1983—; sch. bus. adv. coun. mem. U. So. Colo., 1989—; hon. parade marshall Colo. State Fair, 1991. With inf. AUS, 1943-45. Decorated Silver Star, Bronze Star with oak leaf cluster, Purple Heart with oak leaf cluster; recipient Disting. Svc. award U. Colo., 1992; honored for community svc. Parkview Episcopal Med. Ctr., 1992. Mem. Soc. CPCU's, Pueblo C. of C. (past pres.), Pueblo Kiwanis (past pres.), Pueblo Country Club (treas. 1964-66), So. Colo. Press Club (Outstanding Community Svc. award 1991), Phi Beta Kappa. Democrat. Home: 264 S Sifford Ct Pueblo West CO 81007-2843 Office: 1414 W 4th St Pueblo CO 81004-1270

KELLY, WILLIAM STATES, data network engineer; b. Frederick, Md., Oct. 15, 1956; s. William Tolson III and Jane Randall (States) K. BS, Union Coll., Schenectady, 1978; MS, U. Ariz., 1983. City planner Bur. Planning, Schenectady, 1978-79; grad. teaching asst. systems engring. dept. U. Ariz., Tucson, 1981-83; systems engr. Gen. Dynamics, San Diego, 1983-85; staff engr. Martin Marietta, Littleton, Colo., 1985-88; data network engr. Covia/United Airlines, Englewood, Colo., 1988—; mem. user adv. coun. Quintessential Solutions, Inc., San Diego, 1991—; mem. user group AT&T-Accunet, Bridgewater, N.J., 1991; presenter C.A.C.I. Simulation Conf., 1988. Contbr. articles to profl. publs. Mem. Orchard Creek Park Assn., Greenwood Village, Colo., 1990—. Home: 5875 S Long Ln Greenwood Village CO 80121 Office: Covia/United Airlines 5350 S Valentia Way Englewood CO 80111

KELMAN, BRUCE JERRY, toxicologist, consultant; b. Chgo., July 1, 1947; s. LeRoy Rayfield and Louise (Rosen) K.; m. Jacqueline Anne Clark, Feb. 5, 1972; children: Aaron Wayne, Diantha Renee, Coreyanne Louise. BS, U. Ill., 1969, MS, 1971, PhD, 1975. Diplomate Am. Bd. Toxicology. Postdoctoral rsch. assoc. U. Tenn., Oak Ridge, 1974-76, asst. prof., leader prenatal toxicology group, 1976-79; mgr. devel. toxicology sect. Battelle NW, Richland, Wash., 1980-84, assoc. mgr. biology and chemistry dept., 1984-85, mgr., 1985-89, mgr. new products devel. Life Scis. Ctr., 1989-90; mgr. Internat. Toxicology Office, Battelle Meml. Inst., Richland, 1986-89; mng. scientist, mgr. toxicology dept. Failure Analysis Assocs., Inc., Menlo Park, Calif., 1990—; mem. Nation Rsch. Coun. com. on possible effects of electromagnetic fields on biologic systems, 1993-94; adj. prof. N.Mex. State U., Las Cruces, 1983—. Co-editor: Interactions of Biological Systems with Static and ELF Electric and Magnetic Fields, 1987; mem. editorial bd. Trophoblast Rsch., 1983—, Biological Effects of Heavy Metals, 1990. Mem. adv. coun. Seattle Fire Dept., 1988-90; mem. Wash. Gov.'s Biotech. Targeted Sector Adv. Com., 1989-90. Fellow Am. Acad. Vet. and Comparative Toxicology; mem. Soc. Toxicology (founding pres. molecular biology splty. sect. 1988-89, pres. metals splty. sect. 1985-86, cert. of recognition 1989), Am. Soc. for Exptl. Pharmacology and Therapeutics, Soc. for Exptl. Biology and Medicine (award of merit 1980), Teratology Soc., Wash. State Biotech. Assn. (bd. dirs. 1989-90). Office: Failure Analysis Assocs Inc 149 Commonwealth Dr PO Box 3015 Menlo Park CA 94025

KELSEY, EDITH JEANINE, psychotherapist, consultant; b. Freeport, Ill., Oct. 15, 1937; d. John Melvin and Florence Lucille (Ewald) Anderson; m. Craig Ken Kelsey, Dec. 12, 1960; children: Steven Craig, Kevin John. Student, Pasadena Coll., 1955-58; BA in Psychology, Calif. State U., San Jose, 1980; MA in Counseling Psychology, Santa Clara U., 1984. Lic. marriage, family and child counselor. Counselor, cons. Omega Assocs. Santa Clara (Calif.) U., 1981-85, dir. research, 1982-84; intern in counseling Sr. Residential Services, San Jose, 1983-84; psychotherapist Process Therapy Inst., Los Gatos, Calif., 1983-86, Sexual Abuse Treatment Ctr., San Jose, 1984-87; cons. in field, Santa Clara Valley, 1982—; trainer, cons. Omega Assoc., 1987-88; teaching asst. Santa Clara U., 1987-88; pvt. practice psychotherapy, cons., tng., 1987—. Contbr. articles to profl. jours. Vol. Parental Stress Hotline, Palo Alto, Calif., 1980-85. Mem. Am. Assn. Marriage and Family Therapists, Calif. Assn. Marriage and Family Therapists (clin.). Democrat. Presbyterian. Home: 431 Casita Ct Los Altos CA 94022 Office: 153 Forest Ave Palo Alto CA 94301-1615

KELTNER, JOHN WILLIAM, mediation, arbitration consultant; b. Literberry, Ill., June 20, 1918; s. Claude Eugene and Geno Blanche (Lewis) K.; m. Alberta Isabelle Cochran, Jan. 1, 1941 (div. 1972); children: Mary Jean, Lewis Dean; m. Maria Leigh Steinhauer, June 3, 1979. B.Ed., Ill. State U., 1940; MA, Northwestern U., 1943, PhD, 1947. Cert. secondary tchr., Ill. Various acad. teaching positions, 1940-46; asst. prof. speech Iowa State Tchrs. Coll. (now No. Iowa U.), 1946-46; assoc. prof. speech U. Okla., 1949-54; head dept. speech Kans. State U., 1954-58; commr. Fed. Mediation and Conciliation Svc., 1958-63, tng. officer, 1960-63, ad hoc mediator, 1963-71; dept. head speech comm. Oreg. State U., 1963-71, prof. speech communication, 1963-86; founder, dir. Self Awareness and Interpersonal Communication Workshops, 1972-92; prin. Consulting Assocs., Corvallis, Oreg., 1964—; mediator in family and divorce disputes, 1975—; prof. emeritus speech communication Oreg. State U., 1987—; arbitrator, mediator in lab.-mgmt. rels. et al., 1963—; pres. SAIC, Inc., 1985-90; bd. dirs. Linn-Bentcam County Ct. mandated mediation com., 1991—. Author: Group Discussion Processes, 1957, Interpersonal Speech Communication, 1970, Elements of Interpersonal Communication, 1973, Instructor's Manual, Interpersonal Speech Communication, 1970, Instructor's Manual, Elements of Interpersonal Communication, 1973, Mediation: Toward A Civilized System of Dispute Resolution, 1987, The Management of Struggle: Elements of Dispute Resolution through Negotiation, Mediation, and Arbitration, 1993, others; editor: Reading and Resource Book on Self Awareness and Interpersonal Communication, 1981, 82, 83, 84, others; TV prodr. Mem. Neighborhood Dispute Resolution, Corvallis, 1992—. Mem. Soc. Profls. in Dispute Resolution (Svc. award 1981), Am. Arbitration Assn., Speech Communication Assn., Western Speech Communication Assn. (pres. 1971-73, honorary award 1988). Home: 2770 SW De Armond Corvallis OR 97333 Office: Consulting Assocs Box 892 Corvallis OR 97339

KELTNER, LEILA HOCKING, health facility administrator, physician; b. Eugene, Oreg., Apr. 12, 1954; children: Reed, Tiel, Mera, Case. BS, MS, Oreg. State U., 1978; ND, Case Western Res., 1982, PhD, 1985, MD, 1986. Intern Emanuel Hosp., Portland, 1987; dir. Benton County Community Child Care, 1974-76; instr. Oreg. State U., Corvallis, 1977-79; dir. Ronald Mcdonald House, Cleve., 1982-83; cons. EPISTAT, Portland, Oreg., 1984—; resident in internal medicine Emanuel Hosp., Portland, 1987-88, staff physician Child Abuse and Response Evaluation Svcs. program, 1988—; med. dir. Outside-In Health Clinic, Portland, 1988—, Multnomah County Health Dept., Portland, 1988—. Active Govs. Commn. on Maternal Drug Abuse, Portland, 1989—. Nat. Libr. Medicine fellow. Mem. AMA, Sigma Theta Tau, Phi Beta Kappa. Home: 5225 SE Morrison Portland OR 97215-1845 Office: EPISTAT PO Box 18225 Portland OR 97218

KELTON, ARTHUR MARVIN, JR., real estate developer; b. Bennington, Vt., Sept. 12, 1939; s. Arthur Marvin and Lorraine (Millington) K.; m. Elaine White, Nov. 1, 1986; 1 child, Ashley. BA, Dartmouth Coll., 1961. Ptnr. Kelton and Assocs., Vail, Colo., 1966-77; pres. Kelton, Garton and Assocs. Inc., Vail, 1977-84, Kelton, Garton, Kendall, Vail, 1984—. Head agt. Dartmouth Alumni Fund, Hanover, N.H., 1985-90, class pres., 1990—; pres. Vail Valley Med. Ctr. Found., 1991—. Republican. Congregationalist. Home: 1034 Homestake Cir Vail CO 81657-5111 Office: Kelton Garton Kendall 288 Bridge St Vail CO 81657-4523

KEMP, DAVID WESTLEY, communications executive, police officer; b. San Diego, Dec. 10, 1958; s. George Washington and Marjorie Jean (Erickson) K. BBA, San Diego State U., 1981; AA in Criminal Justice, Rancho Santiago Coll., 1982. Owner Countryside Landscaping, Santa Ana, Calif., 1976-78; dep. sheriff Orange County, Santa Ana, 1977—; technician Motorola MSS, Westminster, Calif., 1979-81, Santa Ana, 1981-82; pres. internat. radiotelephone AT&T, Santa Ana, 1981-85; pres. Internat. Satellite, Santa Ana, 1982—; mgr. Western Mobile Telephone, Anaheim, Calif., 1987-88; supr., tech. svc. Global Telecommunications, PAC-TEL Cellular, Anaheim, 1988-91; cable TV cons. Internat. Satellite, 1982—; CEO Corp. Investigations, Eugene, Oreg., 1992—. Patentee multi plexor systems for satellite and cable TV. Mem. Nat. Assn. Bus. Radio Users, Orange County Dep. Sheriff's Assn. (mem. adv. com., youth com. 1989—). Republican. Office: Global Telecommunications 1990 S Anaheim Blvd Anaheim CA 92805-6600

KEMP, EDDY NELSON, investment advisory firm executive; b. Pike County, Ohio, June 29, 1938; s. Edward Clifton and Eulah Jessie (Martin) K.; m. Therese Helene Cisowski, June 25, 1960; children: Gregory, Christine, Brian. BA, Ball State U., 1965. CPA, registered investment advisor, Hawaii. Mgr. tax dept. Peat, Marwick, Mitchell & Co., Honolulu, 1965-74; dir. fin. and adminstrn. Estate of James Campbell, Honolulu, 1974-82; pres., part owner R.K. Marine, Inc., Honolulu, 1982-84; pres., owner E.N. Kemp & Assocs., Inc., Kaneohe, Hawaii, 1982—; cons. Bowen & Hunsaker, CPAs, Honolulu, 1992—, Tax Strategies, Honolulu, 1984-92; dir. Tropical Clothing Co., Honolulu, 1988—. Envisioned, researched, co-designed and supervised constrn. of world's largest passenger catamaran. Mem. Kahaluu (Hawaii) Neighborhood Bd., 1988; pres. 15th House Dist., Rep. Party of Hawaii, Honolulu, 1990, chmn. 8th Senatorial Dist., 1992, 23rd Senatorial Dist., 1993; dir. Alger Found., Honolulu, 1986-90. With USAF, 1956-61. Mem. AICPAs, Fin. Execs. Inst. (treas., sec., 2d v.p., 1st v.p., pres., dir. 1981-88), Hawaii Soc. CPAs (various coms. 1969-93), Investment Soc. Hawaii. Home and Office: E N Kemp & Assocs Inc 47-449 Ahuimanu Pl Kaneohe HI 96744

KEMP, JEANNE FRANCES, office manager; b. L.A., Dec. 8, 1942; d. Damian Thomas and Helen Catherine (Bohin) Hanifee; m. Don H. Kemp, Dec. 16, 1966 (div. 1972). AB, San Francisco State U., 1965. Food svc. technician United Air Lines, San Francisco, 1961-65; clk. N.Y. Life Ins., San Francisco, 1965-66; inventory clk. Ingersoll-Rand, San Francisco, 1966; advt./order clk. Patrick's Stationers, San Francisco, 1966-67; sec. Dartmouth Travel, Hanover, N.H., 1967-68, Olsten Temp. Svcs., N.Y.C., 1968-70; office mgr. Brown U. Devel., N.Y.C., 1970-73; asst. dir. Cen. Opera Svc., N.Y.C., 1974-85; office mgr., sec. Payne, Thompson, Walker & Taaffe, San Francisco, 1986—. Editor: Career Guide...Singers, 1985, Operas...for Children, 1985; asst. editor COS Bull., 1976-85; editorial asst.: Who's Who in Opera, 1975. Democrat. Roman Catholic. Office: Payne Thompson Walker & Taaffe 235 Montgomery St Ste 760 San Francisco CA 94104-2910

KEMP, PATRICK SAMUEL, retired accountant, educator; b. Galveston, Tex., Aug. 2, 1932; s. Samuel Herbert and Florence (Moor) K.; m. Carol Margaret Boren, Aug. 22, 1959; children: Robert Wade, Cathleen Anne. BA, Rice U., 1953; MPA, U. Tex., 1956; PhD, U. Ill., 1959. Staff acct. Arthur Young & Co., Houston, 1954-55; instr. U. Ill., Urbana, 1956-59; asst. prof. acctg. Emory U., 1959-61, assoc. prof., 1961-62; assoc. prof. U. Richmond, 1962-65, prof., 1965-68; prof. Va. Poly. Inst. and State U., 1968-74, Oreg. State U., 1974-90. Author: Accounting For The Manager, 1970, (with Mary Ellen Phillips) Advanced Accounting, 1989. Mem. AICPA, Inst. Mgmt., Oreg. Soc. CPAs, (instr. continuing profl. edn. program), Alpha Kappa Psi, Beta Alpha Psi, Beta Gamma Sigma.

KEMP, PAUL JAMES, chemist; b. Inglewood, Calif., June 26, 1942; s. Elkan Vern and Nettie Emerine (Sisam) K.; m. Hsu-nii Hsieh, Mar. 15, 1990; children: James Joseph, Eran Sulfon, SeanPaul James, Hong-ru Hsieh. BSc, Iowa State U., 1965; MS, Oreg. State U., 1969. Water system operator Deep Springs Coll., Via Dyer, Nev., 1960-63; analytical chemist Dept. Geology, Iowa State U., Ames, 1963-65; chief chemist, dir. Psychon Labs., Corvallis, 1965-69; chief exec. officer, gen. mgr. Outrite Plastics, Boise, Idaho, 1969-75; chief chemist Lens Inc., Honolulu, 1975-77; dist. mgr. Olin Water Svcs., San Francisco, 1977-81; reg. mgr. Midland Rsch. Labs., Inc., Haleiwa, Hawaii, 1981-89; indsl. applications chemist Brewer Environ. Ind., Inc., Honolulu, 1989—; tech. advisor Lens Inc., 1977—, Sunset Terrace Homeowners Assn., Haleiwa, 1977—; sysop Sunset Beach Water Log, CBBS, Haleiwa, 1983—. Contbr. articles to profl. jours. Mem. Am. Chem. Soc., Am. Waterworks Assn., Water Environment Fedn., Hawaiian Sugar Technologists. Republican. Presbyterian. Office: Brewer Environ Ind 311 Pacific St Honolulu HI 96817-5038

KEMPE, DOUGLAS WALTON, minister; b. Idaho Falls, Idaho, Feb. 12, 1955; s. Eugene Roger and Lois Juanita (Petersen) K.; m. Deirdre Meehan, Aug. 5, 1980; children: Maria Colleen, Gavin Meehan, Declan Walton. BA in Psychology cum laude, Calif. Luth. U., 1977, secondary teaching credential, 1978; MDiv, Pacific Luth. Theol. Sem., 1984. Ordained minister Evang. Luth. Ch. in Am., 1984. Athletic trainer Calif. Luth. U., Thousand Oaks, 1974-78; tchr. Payette (Idaho) Pub. Schs., 1978-79, Ontario (Oreg.) Pub. Schs., 1979; lead pastor Bethlehem Luth Ch., Billings, Mont., 1984-92; on call chaplain St. Vincent's Hosp., Billings, 1990-92; lead pastor Redeemer Lutheran Ch., Boise, Idaho, 19926; corp. rep. St. John's Luth. Home, Billings, 1984-92; edn. ministries team Pacific N.W. Synod Lutheran Ch. Am., Seattle, 1985-88; chair Growth in Mission Mont. Synod, Evang. Lutheran Ch. Am., Great Falls, Mont., 1986-89, chair companion synod, 1990-92, worship coord. Boise River Fest., 1993, coord. Boise Assn. Chs. Boise State U. Career Fair, 1993. Designer: (stained glass window) Word of God, 1988. Host, fundraiser Children's Commn. Ten. of No. Ireland, 1985—; swim instr. YMCA, Billings, 1988-92; chair tchr. appreciation Washington Sch. PTA, Billings, 1989-91; key communicator Billings (Mont.) Pub. Schs., 1991-92. Named Outstanding Young Man of Am., 1985.

KEMPF, MARTINE, voice control device manufacturing company executive; b. Strasbourg, France, Dec. 9, 1958; came to U.S., 1985; d. Jean-Pierre and Brigitte Marguerite (Klockenbring) K. Student in Astronomy, Friedrich Wilhelm U., Bonn, Fed. Republic of Germany, 1981-83. Owner, mgr. Kempf, Sunnyvale, Calif., 1985—. Inventor Comeldir Multiplex Handicapped Driving Systems (Goldenes Lenkrad Axel Springer Verlag 1981), Katalavox speech recognition control system (Oscar, World Almanac Inventions 1984, Prix Grand Siecle, Comite Couronne Francaise 1985). Recipient Medal for Service to Humanity Spinal Cord Soc., 1986; street named in honor in Dossenheim-Kochersberg, Alsace, France, 1987; named Citizen of Honor City of Dossenheim-Kochersberg, 1985, Outstanding Businessperson of Yr. City of Sunnyvale, 1990. Office: 1080 E Duane Ave Ste E Sunnyvale CA 94086-2628

KEMPSON, DAVID JOHN, environmental engineer, industrial hygienist; b. Elizabeth, N.J., Jan. 19, 1963; s. David Michael and Rita (Riker) K. BSME, Lehigh U., 1985. Engr. aid landfill site Wehran Engring., Edison, N.J., 1985; air compliance engr. Ariz. Dept. Environ. Quality, Phoenix, 1990—. 1st lt. USAF, 1986-90. Mem. Am. Conf. Govtl. Indsl. Hygienists, Assn. Med. Surgeons U.S. Republican. Roman Catholic. Home: 2437 W Kilarea Mesa AZ 85202 Office: Ariz Dept Environ Quality OAQ 2005 N Central Ave Phoenix AZ 84004

KEMPTHORNE, DIRK ARTHUR, U.S. senator; b. San Diego, Oct. 29, 1951; s. James Henry and Maxine Jesse (Gustason) K.; m. Patricia Jean Merrill, Sept. 18, 1977; children: Heather Patricia, Jeffrey Dirk. BS in Polit. Sci., U. Idaho, 1975. Exec. asst. to dir. Idaho Dept. Lands, Boise, 1975-78; exec. v.p. Idaho Home Builders Assn., Boise, 1978-81; campaign mgr. Batt for Gov., Boise, 1981-82; lic. securities rep. Swanson Investments, Boise, 1983; Idaho pub. affairs mgr. FMC Corp., Boise, 1983-86; mayor Boise, 1986-93; U. S. Senator from Idaho, 1993—; 1st v.p. Assn. of Idaho Cities, 1990-93; chmn. U.S. Conf. of Mayors Standing Com. on Energy and Environment, 1991-93, mem. adv. bd., 1991-93; sec. Nat. Conf. of Rep. Mayors and Mcpl. Elected Officials, 1991-93. Pres. Assn. Students U. Idaho, Moscow, 1975; chmn. bd. dirs. Wesleyan Presch., Boise, 1982-85; mem. magistrate commn. 4th Jud. Dist., Boise, 1986-93; mem. task force Nat. League of Cities Election, 1988; bd. dirs. Parents and Youth Against Drug Abuse, 1987—. Recipient Idaho Citizen of Yr. award The Idaho Statesman, 1988. Republican. Methodist. Office: U S Senate Office of Senate Members Washington DC 20510

KENAGY, JOHN WARNER, surgeon; b. Lincoln, Nebr., May 28, 1945; s. Wyman Black and Sylvia (Adams) K.; m. Barbara Penterman, Feb. 1968 (div. 1975); 1 child, Jennifer; m. Jonell Day, Apr. 21, 1978; children: Susanne, Emma, John Wyman. BS, U. Nebr., 1967, MD, U. Nebr., Omaha, 1971. Diplomate Am. Bd. Surgery; splty. cert. in gen. vascular surgery. Intern, Hosps. of U. Wash., Seattle, 1971-72, resident in surgery, 1971-76; surgeon Longview Surgical Group, Longview, Wash., 1976—; clin. instr. surgery U. Wash., Seattle, 1979-82, clin. asst. prof. surgery, 1982-89, clin. assoc. prof., 1989—; dir. peripheral vascular svcs. St. Johns Hosp., Longview, 1979-88, chmn. credentials com., 1989-90; dir. trauma svcs. St. Johns Med. Ctr., 1990-92. Editor current concepts in vascular diagnosis St. Johns Vascular Lab., Longview, 1979-88; contbr. articles to profl. jours. Chmn. bd. dirs. Cowlitz Med. Service, Longview, 1985-86. Regents scholar U. Nebr., Lincoln, 1963-67. Fellow ACS, Henry Harkins Surg. Soc. (trustee 1983-84), Seattle Surg. Soc.; mem. Internat. Cardiovascular Soc., Pacific N.W. Vascular Soc. (pres.-elect 1986-87, pres. 1987-88, chmn. com. on standards 1989-91), North Pacific Surg. Soc., Med. Group Mgmt. Assn., Am. Coll. Physician Execs., Alpha Omega Alpha, Theta Nu, Phi Gamma Delta. Republican. Office: Longview Gen & Thoracic Surgery 900 Fir St Ste 1J Longview WA 98632-2544

KENDALL, JOHN MICHAEL, army officer; b. Ft. Benning, Ga., Apr. 15, 1949; s. Maurice Wesley and Aura Charlene (Gross) K.; m. Lori Renee Huebschman, Mar. 9, 1974; children: Kristi, John, Katie. BS, U.S. Mil. Acad., 1971; MA, Duke U., 1979, PhD, 1982. Commd. 2d lt. U.S. Army, 1971, advanced through grades to lt. col., 1989; asst. prof. history U.S. Mil. Acad. U.S. Army, West Point, N.Y., 1979-82; dep. comdr. UN Command Security Force U.S. Army, Panmunjom, Korea, 1985-86; dep. chief of staff, then bn. comdr. U.S. Army, Ft. Lewis, Wash., 1988-90; exec. officer to comdr. Army forces ctrl. command U.S. Army, Riyadh, Saudi Arabia, 1990-91; chief ops. I Corps U.S. Army, Ft. Lewis, 1991-92; comdr. detachment 3 joint task force-full accounting MIA/POW resolution U.S. Army, Vientiane, Laos, 1993—. Author: Inflexible Response, 1982; editor: Speeches of General Thurman, 1986, Motorized Experience, 1989. Active Tacoma area Boy Scouts Am., 1988—; trustee Beckonridge Community Assn., University Place, Wash., 1992. Decorated Legion of Merit, Bronze Star medal. Mem. Mil. History Soc., Meriweather Soc. Am., Seattle-Tacoma Geneal. Soc. Home: 9007 Ridgeview Cir W Tacoma WA 98466 Office: US Army Hdqrs I Corps Fort Lewis WA 98433

KENDALL, JOHN WALKER, JR., medical educator, researcher, university dean; b. Bellingham, Wash., Mar. 19, 1929; s. John Walker and Mathilda (Hansen) K.; m. Elizabeth Helen Meece, Mar. 19, 1954; children—John, Katherine, Victoria. B.A., Yale Coll., 1952; M.D., U. Wash., 1956. Intern and resident in internal medicine Vanderbilt U. Hosp., Nashville, 1956-59; fellow in endocrinology Vanderbilt U. Hosp., 1959-60, U. Oreg. Med. Sch., Portland, 1960-62; asst. prof. medicine Oreg. Health Scis. U., Portland, 1962-66, assoc. prof. medicine, 1966-71, prof. medicine, 1971—, head div. metabolism, 1971-80; dean Sch. Medicine, Oreg. Health Scis. U., Portland, 1983-92, dean emeritus, 1992—; assoc. chief staff-research VA Med. Ctr., Portland, Oreg., 1971-83, dep. chief of staff, 1993—; cons. Med. Research Found. Oreg., Portland, 1975-83; sec., bd. dirs. Oreg. Found. Med. Excellence, Portland, 1984-89, pres., 1989-91. Served to lt. comdr. M.C., USN, 1962-64. Mem. AMA (mem. governing coun. med. sch. sect. 1989—, chair 1991-92, alt. del. 1992-93, AMA rep. Coun. Grad. Med. Edn. 1993—), Assn. Am. Physicians, Am. Soc. Clin. Investigation, Am. Fedn. Clin. Research, Western Soc. Clin. Research (councillor 1972-75), Endocrine Soc., Multnomah County Med. Soc. (treas. 1989, pres.-elect 1990 , pres. 1991), Med. Rsch. Found. (Mentor award 1992). Presbyterian. Lodge: Rotary. Home: 3131 SW Evergreen Ln Portland OR 97201-1816 Office: Oreg Health Scis U Sch Medicine 3181 SW Sam Jackson Park Rd Portland OR 97201-3011

KENDIG, JOAN JOHNSTON, neurobiology educator; b. Derby, Conn., May 1, 1939; d. Frank and Agnes (Kerr) Johnston; children: Scott Johnston Kendig, Leslie Anne Kendig. BA, Smith Coll., 1960; PhD, Stanford U., 1966. Rsch. assoc. Stanford U. Med. Sch., 1968-71, asst. prof. biology in anesthesia, 1971-76, assoc. prof., 1976-86, prof., 1986--; mem. physiology study sect. NIH, 1981-85. NIH neurosci. grantee, 1973—; Javits neurosci. investigator, 1988—. Mem. Soc. for Neurosci., Biophys. Soc., Am. Soc. Pharmacology and Therapeutics, Assn. U. Anesthesiologists. Office: Stanford U Med Sch Dept Anesthesia Stanford CA 94305

KENDLER, HOWARD H(ARVARD), psychologist, educator; b. N.Y.C., June 9, 1919; s. Harry H. and Sylvia (Rosenberg) K.; m. Tracy Seedman, Sept. 20, 1941; children—Joel Harlan, Kenneth Seedman. A.B., Bklyn. Coll., 1940; M.A., U. Iowa, 1941, Ph.D., 1943. Instr. U. Iowa, 1943; research psychologist OSRD, 1944; asst. prof. U. Colo., 1946-48; assoc. prof. NYU, 1948-51, prof., 1951-63; chmn. dept. Univ. Coll., 1951-61; prof. U. Calif., Santa Barbara, 1963-89, prof. emeritus, 1989—, chmn. dept. psychology, 1965-66; project dir. Office Naval Research, 1950-68, USAAF, 1951-53; mem. adv. panel psychobiology NSF, 1960-62; tng. com. Nat. Inst. Child Health and Human Devel., 1963-66; cons. Dept. Def., Smithsonian Instn., 1959-60, Human Resources Research Office, George Washington U., 1960; vis. prof. U. Calif., Berkeley, 1960-61, Hebrew U. Jerusalem, 1974-75, Tel Aviv U., 1990; chief clin. psychologist Walter Reed Gen. Hosp., 1945-46. Author: Basic Psychology, 1963, 2d edit., 1968, 3d edit., 1974, Basic Psychology: Brief Version, 1977, Psychology: A Science in Conflict, 1981, Historical Foundations of Modern Psychology, 1987; co-author: Basic Psychology: Brief Edition, 1970; co-editor: Essays in Neobehaviorism: A Memorial Volume to Kenneth W. Spence; assoc. editor: Jour. Exptl. Psychology, 1963-65; contbr. to profl. jours., books. Served as 1st lt. AUS. Fellow Center for Advanced Studies in Behavioral Scis., Stanford, Calif., 1969-70; NSF grantee, 1954-76. Mem. Am. psychol. assn. (pres. div. exptl. psychology 1964-65, pres. div. gen. psychology 1967-68), Western psychol. assn. (pres. 1970-71), Soc. Exptl. Psychologists (exec. com. 1971-73), Psychonomic Soc. (governing bd. 1963-69, chmn. 1968-69), Sigma Xi. Home and Office: 4596 Camino Molinero Santa Barbara CA 93110

KENDRICK, WILLIAM MARVIN, school system administrator; m. Carol Kendrick; children: Julie, Jeffrey, Jay. BA, Western Wash. U., 1953; MA, UCLA, 1960; postgrad., San Diego State Coll., 1965, Northwestern U., 1968. Dir. Supplementary Edn. Ctr. Dept. Edn., San Diego County, Calif., 1962-67; dir. curriculum and instrnl. svcs. Evanston (Ill.) Sch. Dist. # 65, 1967-69; v.p. Croft Ednl. Svcs., 1969-72; supt. Salem (Oreg.)-Keizer Pub. Schs., 1972-86, Seattle Pub. Schs., 1986—; vis. lectr. edn. Western Wash. U., Bellingham, Wash., 1963; lectr. in edn. San Diego State Coll., 1966. Bd. dirs. United Way of King County; mem. corp. bd. YMCA Greater Seattle. Recipient Disting. Educator award Western Washington U., Disting. Alumnus award Western Washington U., Nat. Sch. Supt. award Nat. Community Edn. Assn., Outstanding Leadership in Edn. of Lang. Minority Students award Western Oreg. State Coll. Inst. on Lang. and Culture. Office: Seattle Pub Schs 815 4th Ave N Seattle WA 98109-3902

KENISON, LYNN T., chemist; b. Provo, Utah, Feb. 20, 1943; s. John Silves and Grace (Thacker) K.; m. Daralyn Wold, June 10, 1969; children: Marlene, Mark, Evan, Guy, Amy, Suzanne. BS in Chemistry, Brigham Young U., 1968, MS in Chemistry, 1971. Tchr. Weber County Sch. Dist., Ogden, Utah, 1968-69; bench chemist (drugs) Salt Lake City/County Health Dept., 1971-74; chemist U.S. Dept. Labor, OSHA Salt Lake Tech. Ctr., 1974—, bench chemist, 1974-77, supr., br. chief, 1977-84, sr. chemist, 1984—; tech. writer OSHA. Editor: Review Methods and Analytical Papers Before Publication, 1984—; tech. writer. Councilman West Bountiful City, Utah, 1980-83, 85-89; scouting coord. Boy Scouts Am., cub master local pack; full-time missionary LDS Ch., Ark., Mo., Ill., 1962-64. Mem. Am. Indsl. Hygiene Assn., Fed. Exec. Assn. (Disting. Svc. award, Jr. Award for Outstanding Fed. and Community Svc.), Toastmasters Internat. (treas. Salt Lake City chpt. 1987-88). Home: 1745 N 600 W West Bountiful UT 84087-1150 Office: US Dept of Labor OSHA Salt Lake Tech Ctr 1781 S 300 W Salt Lake City UT 84165-0200

KENNARD, JOYCE, state judge. Former judge L.A. Mcpl. Ct., Superior Ct., Ct. Appeal, Calif.; assoc. justice Calif. Supreme Ct., San Francisco, 1989—. Office: Calif Supreme Ct South Tower 303 2nd St San Francisco CA 94107*

KENNEDY, CHARLENE FARRINGTON, head reference librarian; b. Cin., Sept. 17, 1947; d. Charles Winifred and Margaret Irene (Hurd) Farrington; m. Timothy Louis Kennedy, May 12, 1977 (div. 1981). BS in Sociology, U. Wis., 1969, MLS, 1971. Libr. intern Milw. Cen. Libr., 1969-71; reference libr. Atkinson Br. Libr., Milw., 1972-73; reference libr. sci. and bus. dept. Milw. Cen. Libr., 1973-78; reference libr., coord. on-line svcs. City of Carlsbad, Calif., 1978-85, head spl. reference svcs., 1985—. Contbr. articles to profl. jours. Mem. Soroptomist Internat., Carlsbad, 1987. Mem. Calif. Libr. Assn., San Diego On-Line Users Group, North San Diego County Genealogical Soc., Bus. and Profl. Women (pres. Carlsbad chpt. 1983). Office: Carlsbad City Libr 1250 Carlsbad Village Dr Carlsbad CA 92008-1991

KENNEDY, DAN F., telecommunications company executive; b. Columbia Falls, Mont., Aug. 19, 1957; s. R. Glenn and Betty (Terry) K.; m. Janet C. Welsh, May 1, 1987; children: David, Rachel. BA in Bus. Adminstrn. and Acctg., U. Mont., 1979. CPA, Alaska. Audit mgr. Ernst & Young, Anchorage, 1979-85; v.p. fin. Matanuska Telephone Assn., Palmer, Alaska, 1986—. Pres., Big Bros./Big Sisters of Anchorage, 1982-84; bd. dirs. Big Bros./Big Sisters of Am., Phila., 1985-86; campaign chmn. United Way of Mat-Su Borough, Palmer, 1989. Named Big Brother of Yr., 1984. Mem. AICPA, Alaska Soc. CPAs, Wasilla Rotary Club (sec. 1987-89, pres. 1992, Rotarian of Yr. 1987, 90). Republican. Roman Catholic. Home: PO Box 510 Palmer AK 99645 Office: Matanuska Telephone 1740 S Church 1740 S Chugach Palmer AK 99645

KENNEDY, DEBRA JOYCE, marketing professional; b. Covina, Calif., July 9, 1955; d. John Nathan and Drea Hannah (Lancaster) Ward; m. John William Kennedy, Sept. 3, 1977 (div.); children: Drea, Noelle. BS in Communications, Calif. State Poly. U., 1977. Pub. rels. coord. Whittier (Calif.) Hosp., 1978-79, pub. relations mgr., 1980; pub. rels. dir. San Clemente (Calif.) Hosp., 1979-80; dir. pub. rels. Garfield Med. Ctr., Monterey Park, Calif., 1980-82; dir. mktg. and community rels. Charter Oak Hosp., Covina, 1983-85; mktg. dir. CPC Horizon Hosp., Pomona, 1985-89; dir. mktg. Sierra Royale Hosp., Azusa, 1989-90; mktg. rep. PacifiCare, Cypress, 1990-92; regional medicare supr. Health Net, Woodland Hills, Calif., 1992—. Mem. Am. Soc. Hosp. Pub. Rels., Healthcare Mktg. Assn., Healthcare Pub. Rels. and Mktg. Assn., Covina and Covina West C. of C., West Covina Jaycees. Republican. Methodist. Club: Soroptimists. Contbr. articles to profl. jours.

KENNEDY, DONALD, environmental studies educator; b. N.Y.C., Aug. 18, 1931; s. William Dorsey and Barbara (Bean) K.; children: Laura Page, Julia Hale; m. Robin Beth Wiseman, Nov. 27, 1987; stepchildren: Cameron Rachel, Jamie Christopher. AB, Harvard U., 1952, AM, 1954, PhD, 1956; DSc (hon.), Columbia U., Williams Coll., U. Mich., U. Ariz., U. Rochester, Reed Coll. Mem. faculty Stanford (Calif.) U., 1956-60, 1960-77, prof. biol. scis., 1965-77, chmn. dept., 1965-72, sr. cons. sci. and tech. policy Exec. Office of Pres., 1976, commr., 1977-79; provost Stanford U., 1979-80; pres. Stanford (Calif.) U., 1980-92; pres.-emeritus, Bing prof. environ. studies Stanford U., 1992—; bd. overseers Harvard U., 1970-76; bd. dirs. Health Effects Inst., Clean Sites Inc., Calif. Nature Conservancy, Nat. Commn. on Pub. Svc., Carnegie Commn. on Sci., Tech. and Govt. Mem. editorial bd. Jour. Comparative Physiology, 1965-76, Jour. Neurophysiology, 1969-75, Science, 1973-77; contbr. articles to profl. jours. Fellow AAAS, Am. Acad. Arts and Scis.; mem. NAS, Am. Philos. Soc. Office: Stanford U Inst for Internat Studies Encina Hall 201 Stanford CA 94305

KENNEDY, HAROLD LAVERNE, heavy duty wheel and brake parts distribution company executive; b. Casper, Wyo., Oct. 12, 1962; s. Keith Edgar and Barbara Ann (Tromble) K. Grad. high sch., Casper, Wyo. Mechanic Van's Body and Repair, Casper, 1979; attendant-mgr. V-1 Oil Co., Casper, 1979-81; mechanic Melrose Trucking, Casper, 1981; parts counter S.W. Kenworth Inc., Casper, 1981-82; shipping/receiving Elder Quinn & McGill Inc., Casper, 1982-90; pres. KKT Inc DBA Timpte Quinn & McGill Inc., Casper, 1990—. EMT Evansville Vol. Fire Dept., Casper, 1982-85; supt. Faith Assembly of God, Casper, 1991—. Mem. Breakfast Optimist Club, Wyo. Trucking Assn., Fellowship of Christian Athletes. Republican. Office: Timpte Quinn & McGill Wyo 664 Circle Dr Casper WY 82601-1611

KENNEDY, JAMES WILLIAM, JR. (SARGE KENNEDY), special education administrator, consultant; b. Santa Rosa, Calif., Oct. 6, 1940; s. James William and Kay Jean (Eaton) k.; m. Lorene Adele Dunaway, May 12, 1962 (dec. Sept. 1971); children: Sean, Erin, Mark; m. Carolyn Judith Nighsonger, Mar. 1972 (div. Dec. 1979); m. Patricia Carter Critchlow, Nov. 5, 1988; 1 child, Joy. BA, San Francisco State U., 1964, MA, 1970. Tchr., prin., coord. spl. edn., dir. spl. edn. local plan area Napa County (Calif.) Schs., 1968-83; spl. edn. compliance cons. overseas dependent schs. Mediterranean region Dept. Def., 1983-84; dir. special programs and svcs. Tehama County Dept. Edn., Red Bluff, Calif., 1985—. Editor Calif. Fed. Coun. Exceptional Children Jour. 1971-77, 81-83. Mem. Wilson Riles Spl. Edn. Task Force, Calif., 1981-82, Spl. Edn. Fiscal Task Force, Calif., 1987-89. Mem. Coun. for Exceptional Children (sgt. at arms 1980—), Calif. Fedn. Coun. for Exceptional Children (treas. 1990—), Profl. Football Researcher's Assn., San Francisco State Alumni Assn., Phi Delta Kappa. Democrat. Office: Tehama County Dept Edn PO Box 689 Red Bluff CA 96080-0689

KENNEDY, JOHN EDWARD, art dealer, appraiser, curator; b. Glens Falls, N.Y., Apr. 21, 1930; s. John Edward and Veronica Irene (Young) K.; m. Katherine Joan Donovan, July 14, 1956 (div. June 1973); children: Amy Joan Rosato, Gavin John; m. Ann Swift Kimball, Apr. 2, 1975. AB with hons., Boston Coll., 1951; JD, Harvard U., 1956; grad., U.S. Army Command and Gen. Staff Coll., 1964. Bar: Mass. 1956. Asst. counsel New England Mut. Life Ins., Boston, 1956-64; counsel Pa. Life Ins. Co., Beverly Hills, Calif., 1964-68; investment banker Smith Barney and Co., L.A. and N.Y.C., 1968-70; real estate developer Calif. and Hawaii, 1970-80; v.p. Galerie De Tours, Carmel, Calif., 1980-88; curator Gallery Americana, Carmel, 1988-92; patron Monterey Peninsula Mus. of Art., 1988—, Carmel Art Assn., 1985—. Trustee Harrison Meml. Library, Carmel, 1986-88; commr. Planning commn., Carmel, 1988—, chmn., 1992—. With U.S. Army, 1952-53, Korea, Lt. Col., U.S. Army Res., 1969. Decorated Bronze Star for Valor, Purple Heart with cluster; recipient Disting. Mil. Svc. medal Republic of Korea, 1953. Mem. Am. Soc. of Appraisers (cert.), New England Appraisers Assn. (cert.), Am. Planning Assn., Marines Meml. Club. Republican. Episcopalian. Home: PO Box 1844 Carmel CA 93921 Office: New Masters Gallery Dolores & 7th Carmel CA 93921

KENNEDY, JOHN HARVEY, chemistry educator; b. Oak Park, Ill., Apr. 24, 1933; s. John Harvey and Margaret Helen (Drenthe) K.; m. Joan Corinne Hipsky, June 9, 1956 (div. Mar. 1969); children: Bruce Laurence, Bryan Donald, Brent Peter, Jill Amy.; m. Victoria Jane Matthew, July 2, 1970; 1 child, Karen Anne. BS, UCLA, 1954; AM, Harvard U., 1956, PhD, 1957. Sr. research chemist E.I. du Pont de Nemours, Wilmington, Del., 1957-61; asst. prof. chemistry U. Calif., Santa Barbara, 1961-63, 67-69, assoc. prof., 1969-76, prof., 1976—, chmn. dept., 1982-85; assoc. prof. Boston Coll., Chestnut Hill, 1963-64; head inorganic chemistry Gen. Motors, Santa Barbara, 1964-67; cons. Eveready Battery Co., Cleve., 1983—; vis. prof. U. N.C., Chapel Hill, 1980-81, Japan Soc. Promotion of Sci., Nagoya, 1984-85, Leningrad State U., 1989, China Academy of Scis., 1990. Author: Analytical Chemistry, Principles, 1990, Analytical Chemistry, Practice, 1990; contbr. articles to profl. jours.; patentee in field. Mus. dir. Christ the King Episcopal Ch., Santa Barbara, 1982—. Mem. Am. Chem. Soc., Electrochem. Soc. Democrat. Home: 5357 Agana Dr Santa Barbara CA 93111-1601 Office: U Calif Dept Chemistry Santa Barbara CA 93106

KENNEDY, JON, health services executive; b. Oakland, Calif., Jan. 20, 1950; s. Van Dusen and Beth (Cunningham) K.; m. Alexandra Banks, June 19, 1971; 1 child, Taylor. BA in Psychology, U. Calif., Santa Cruz, 1971; MA in Counseling Psychology, U. Santa Clara, 1975. Lic. marriage and family counselor. Counselor Do It Now Found., Santa Cruz, Calif., 1972, Santa Cruz (Calif.) Community Counseling Ctr., Inc., 1973-76; pvt. practice counseling Santa Cruz, 1976-81; asst. dir. Lawrence & Assocs., Santa Clara, Calif., 1982; dir. Human Affairs Internat., San Jose, Calif., 1982-89; pres. Human Affairs Internat. of Calif., Campbell, Calif., 1989—; Bd. mem. HAI of Calif., Campbell, 1989—, Santa Cruz Community Counseling Ctr., Inc., 1973-75. Office: Human Affairs Internat CA 2105 S Bascom Ave Ste 295 Campbell CA 95008-3277

KENNEDY, L. THOMAS, restaurateur and developer; b. Metropolis, Ill., Oct. 5, 1934; s. Nellis Lowell and Dora Esther (Womack) K.; m. Binni Jo Lewis, June 10, 1955; children: Lori Ann, Scott Thomas. Owner Kennedy's Kwik Inn, Colorado Springs, Colo., 1956—, A&W Drive-In, Security, Colo., 1959-77; developer Security (Colo.) Shoppette, 1983-84, Ivywild Plaza, Colorado Springs, 1986—. Treas. Ch. Christ, Security, 1965-77; cons. Widefield High Sch. Adv. Council, Security, 1974-76. Mem. Colo. A&W Operators Assn. (bd. dirs., v.p. 1970-75, pres. 1974-75), Security Businessmen's Assn. (pres. 1969-70). Republican. Clubs: Broadmoor Figure Skating (bd. dirs. 1968-72); Adaman (Colorado Springs) (named Mem. of Year 1979). Home: 2607 Leo Dr Colorado Springs CO 80906-1012 Office: Kwik Inn 385 Main St Colorado Springs CO 80911-1798

KENNEDY, ORIN, film company executive; b. N.Y.C., May 24, 1939; s. Solomon Fuchs and Gertrude Krex. BFA, N.Y. Sch. Interior Design, 1963. Prodn. assoc. Fries Entertainment, Los Angeles, 1976-84; exec. location mgr. Metro-Goldwyn-Mayer subs. United Artists Entertainment, Culver City, Calif., 1984-85; exec. location mgr. The Twilight Zone TV series CBS Entertainment, Los Angeles, 1985-86; exec. location mgr. LA Law TV series 20th Century Fox Film Corp., Los Angeles, 1986—, exec. location mgr. Picket Fences TV series, 1991—.

KENNEDY, PETER SMITHSON, personnel consultant; b. Bluffton, Ohio, Dec. 16, 1934; s. Harold James and Ruby Marie (Amstutz) K.; m. Barbara Ann Lindholm, Mar. 15, 1958 (div. 1972); children: Cheryl Lynn, David Michael, Jeanie Marie. BS, Bluffton (Ohio) Coll., 1956. Supr. Avco Fin., 1956-69; owner Kennedy-Blackman, San Diego, 1970-76; dir., pres. Bus. & Mgmt. Profiles, Inc., San Diego, 1977—; dir. Allen-West Pubs., San Diego, San Diego Employers Assn.; cons. Nat. Assn. Mail Advt., San Diego, 1985—. Author: The B&MP Approach to Successful Hiring, 1986. Pres. The Exec. Assn. of San Diego, 1984-85. Mem. Am. Personnel and Guidance Assn. Republican. Methodist. Office: Bus & Mgmt Profiles 8322 Clairemont Mesa Blvd # 202 San Diego CA 92111

KENNEDY, RAYMOND MCCORMICK, JR., interior designer; b. Glendale, Calif., Sept. 19, 1930; s. Raymond McCormick and June (Sparks) K.; adopted son Myrtle Abrahamson Kennedy. BA in Architecture, U. Calif.-Berkeley, 1956. Draftsman, Bechtel Corp., San Francisco, 1956-58; draftsman/designer Maher & Martens, Architects, San Francisco, 1956; free lance designer, San Francisco, 1966-67; designer Bernard J. Block, Architect, San Francisco, 1967-69; v.p. Rodgers Assocs., San Francisco, 1969-77; pres. RMK Design, Inc., San Francisco, 1977-83; pres. Kennedy-Bowen Assocs., Inc., San Francisco, 1983—; mem. faculty Acad. of Art Coll., San Francisco, 1982-86, mem. adv. coun., 1991—. Bd. dirs. San Francisco Easter Seals Soc., 1974-79; bd. dirs., pres. Design Found., Inc., 1986-87. Served with U.S. Army, 1952-54. Fellow Am. Soc. Interior Designers (dir., v.p. No. Calif. chpt. 1983, sec. bd. 1984, pres. 1987-88, nat. bd. dirs. 1989—, nat. v.p. 1990, nat. pres. 1991-92); mem. Golden Gate U. Assn., Am. Inst. Architects (affiliate), Internat. Furnishings and Design Assn., Nat. Trust for Hist. Preservation, Assocs. for San Francisco's Archtl. Heritage, Commonwealth Club, Press Club (San Francisco). Office: Kennedy-Bowen Assocs Inc 930 Lombard St San Francisco CA 94133-2218

KENNEDY, RICHARD JEROME, writer; b. Jefferson City, Mo., Dec. 23, 1932; s. Donald and Mary Louise (O'Keefe) K.; m. Lillian Elsie Nance, Aug. 3, 1960; children: Joseph Troy, Matthew Cook. BS, Portland State U., 1958. Author: (novel) Amy's Eye, 1985 (Internat. Rattenfanger Lit. prize, Fed. Republic Germany 1988), also 18 children's books including Richard Kennedy: Collected Stories, 1988 and 3 musicals. With USAF, 1951-54. Home and Office: 415 W Olive St Newport OR 97365-3716

KENNEDY, RICHARD TERRANCE, computer systems analyst; b. Seattle, Dec. 6, 1953; s. Francis Joseph and Giulia Mary (Reano) K.; m. Heidi E. Morgan, Aug. 1, 1992; children: Jamie Michael Morgan, Jesse Lloyd Bjelland, Kendle Llee Bjelland. BA in Geography and BS in Maths., U. Wash., 1976; MS in Geodetic Sci., Ohio State U., 1978. Cartographer CIA, Washington, 1974-75; teaching asst. Ohio State U., Columbus, 1976-77; computer systems analyst The Boeing Co., Seattle, 1978—; Editor: One Hundred Years of the Waterland Community: A History of Des Moines, Washington, 1989. Council mem. City of Des Moines, 1986—; mayor pro tem, 1988-89, mayor 1992—; chair Zenith Community Mcpl. Corp., Des Moines, 1982-86; bd. dirs. Assn. Wash. Cities, Olympia, 1990-91, Airport Communities Coalition, Normandy Park, 1993—. U.S. Army ROTC scholar, 1972-76. Mem. Magic Lantern Soc. of U.S. and Can., Hist. Soc. of Fed. Way, Greater Des Moines Hist. Soc. (life, bd. dirs. 1990—), Nat. Geographic Soc. (life), Des Moines Waterland Commodores, Theta Delta Chi (rec. sec. 1973-74), Phi Beta Kappa. Presbyterian. Home: 1017 S 251st St Des Moines WA 98198-8548 Office: City of Des Moines 21630 11th Ave S Des Moines WA 98198-6398

KENNEDY, SANDRA DENISE, state representative; b. Oklahoma City, Dec. 25, 1957; d. Leland and Doll B. (Alford) K.; 1 child, Mahogany Renee Cherry. Student, Phoenix Coll., 1975-76, So. Mountain Community Coll. and Ariz. State U., 1976-86. Acct. Kennedy and Assocs., Phoenix, 1983—; state rep. Ariz. Ho. of Reps., Phoenix, 1986—; del. Fgn. Relations Conf. Am. Council Young Polit. Leaders, Washington, 1987, alternate del. Commn. Internat. Trade State Fed. Assembly, Washington, 1987. Bd. dirs. Ariz. Cactus Pine Girl Scouts, Phoenix, 1987—. Mem. Nat. Conf. State Legislators, Nat. Black Caucus Stte Legislators, Order Women Legislators, Nat. Assn. Exec. Women Inc. Baptist. Home: 2333 E Wier Ave Phoenix AZ 85040-2657 Office: Arizona State Senate 2317 E Weir Ave Phoenix AZ 85040

KENNEDY, SHEILA GRACE, medical social worker; b. San Jose, Calif., May 17, 1949; d. Irwin Thomas and Martha Ruth (Markey) O'Connell; m. Timothy Anthony Kennedy, Apr. 4, 1975; children: Maureen, Timmy, Patrick. BA in Social Work, Coll. Notre Dame, 1971; MA in Counseling Psychology, U. Santa Clara, 1977. Elem. sch. tchr. St. Louise de Marillac Sch., Covina, Calif., 1971-72; dir. social svcs. and hospice Sequoia Hosp., Redwood City, Calif., 1972-89; hospice dir. Kaiser Med. Ctr., Redwood City, Calif., 1990—. Mem. adv. bd. peer counseling for srs. San Carlos (Calif.) Sr. Ctr., 1986-88; bd. dirs. San Mateo (Calif.) County com. on child abuse, 1981-83, Parish bd. edn., Nativity Ch., 1984—, pres. 1988; v.p. bd. dirs. Am. Cancer Soc., San Mateo County, Burlingame, Calif., 1983-85, pres. bd. dirs., 1985-87. Named Woman of Yr. Notre Dame High Sch., San Jose, 1989. Mem. Nat. Assn. Social Workers, Am. Hosp. Assn., Hosp. Social Work Dirs. Democrat. Roman Catholic. Home: 67 Lorelei Ln Menlo Park CA 94025-1715 Office: Kaiser Med Ctr 1150 Veterans Blvd Redwood City CA 94063-2087

KENNEDY, THOMAS CRAWFORD, history educator; b. Glace Bay, Can., Aug. 12, 1932; came to U.S., 1932; s. Malcolm MacDonald and Annie Jean (Harris) K.; m. Barbara Anne Kennedy, Aug. 25, 1956 (div. 1974); children: Douglas, Elizabeth, David; m. Melody Ann Washburn, May 29, 1976 (div. 1980); 1 stepchild, Ivan; m. Judy Marie Caturia, June 8, 1985; stepchildren: Jamie, Jesse. BA in History, Antioch Coll., Yellow Springs, Ohio, 1958; MA in History, Stanford (Calif.) U., 1959, PhD in History, 1961. Instr. in history Stanford U., 1961-62; prof. of history U. Wyo., Laramie, 1962—. Author: Charles A. Beard and American For Policy, 1975; contbr. chpts. to books and articles to profl. jours. Sgt. U.S. Army, 1952-54. Fellowship Woodrow Wilson Found., 1958-60, Fulbright-Hays, 1965, Hamline U., 1981, West Point Mil. History Workshop, 1982. Mem. Orgn. of Am. Historians, Soc. for Historians of Am. Fgn. Rels. (membership com. 1980—). Democrat. Episcopalian. Office: U Wyo Dept History Laramie WY 82071

KENNEDY, V. WAYNE, academic administrator; b. Balt., Apr. 2, 1938; s. Michael V. and Henrietta (Kostkowski) K.; m. Flora Louise Seegmuller, Sept. 25, 1959; children: Michael, Kelly. BS, U. Md., 1961. Faculty rsch. asst. U. Md., College Park, 1961-65, asst. comptroller, 1965-69; asst. dean U. Md. Sch. of Medicine, Balt., 1969-73; assoc. dean, assoc. vice chancellor Sch. Medicine U. Calif. San Diego, La Jolla, 1973-81, dir. planning and budget, 1981-82, vice chancellor resource mgmt. and planning, 1982-85, vice chancellor, adminstr., 1985-93; sr. v.p. bus. and fin. Office of the Pres. Office of the Pres., U. Calif. San Diego, La Jolla, 1993—. Mem. Assn. Am. Med. Colls. (chmn. group on bus. affairs, Washington, 1976-77), Coun. on Govt. Rels. (bd. dirs. 1979-86, 91—, chmn. bd. mgmt. 1983-85). Office: Univ California San Diego 109 University Center La Jolla CA 92093-0057

KENNEDY, WILLIAM THOMAS, airline personnel administrator; b. Yokahama, Japan, Oct. 19, 1952; s. William James and Marie Angela (Lombardi) K.; m. Elaine Bryant, May 24, 1975; children: Travis W., Nicole E. BA, U. S.C., 1974; MEd, Colo. State U., 1978. Grad. sch. asst. Colo. State U., Ft. Collins, 1976-78; coord. student group activities Miami U., Oxford, Ohio, 1978-80; cons. Auraria Higher Edn. Ctr., Denver, 1980-81; flight attendant Frontier Airlines, Denver, 1981-83, supr. inflight svcs., 1983-84; supr. inflight svcs. United Airlines, Denver, 1984-87, staff rep. flight officer employment, 1987-91, sr. staff rep. flight ops. pers., 1991—. With USN, 1974-76. Roman Catholic. Office: United Airlines Flight Ctr Denver CO 80207

KENNEDY-MINOTT, RODNEY, international relations educator, former ambassador; b. Portland, Oreg.; s. Joseph Albert and Gainor (Baird) Minott; children: Katharine Pardow, Rodney Glisan, Polly Berry. AB, Stanford U., 1953, MA, 1956, PhD, 1960. Instr. history Stanford U., 1960-61, asst. prof., asst. dir. history of western civilization program, 1961-62, asst. dir. summer session, 1962-63, dir. summer session, 1963-65; assoc. prof. Portland State U., 1965-66; assoc. prof., assoc. dean instrn. Calif. State U., Hayward, 1966-67, prof., 1967-77, head div. humanities, 1967-69; ambassador to Sweden and chmn. Swedish Fulbright Com., 1977-80; adj. prof. Monterey Inst. Internat. Studies, Calif., 1981; exec. v.p. Direction Internat., Washington, 1982-83; sr. research fellow Hoover Instn., 1981-82, 85—; chmn. Alpha Internat., Washington, 1983-85; congl. staff mem., 1965-66; sr. fellow Ctr. Internat. Rels., UCLA, 1986—; prof. nat. security affairs tng. U.S. Naval Postgrad. Sch., Monterey, Calif., 1990—. Author: Peerless Patriots: The Organized Veterans and the Spirit of Americanism, 1962, The Fortress That Never Was: The Myth of Hitler's Bavarian Stronghold, 1964, The Sinking of the Lollipop: Shirley Temple v. Pete McCloskey, 1968, Regional Force Application: The Maritime Strategy and Its Affect on Nordic Stability, 1988, Tension in the North: Sweden and Nordic Security, 1989, Lonely Path to Follow: Non-aligned Sweden, United States/NATO, and the U.S.S.R., 1990. Mem. adv. bd. Ctr. for the Pacific Rim U. San Francisco, 1988—. Served with U.S. Army, USAR, 1946-52. Mem. Am. Hist. Assn., Orgn. Am. Historians, World Affairs Council No. Calif., Internat. Studies Assn., Am. Fgn. Service Assn. (assoc.), Internat. Inst. for Strategic Studies, Swedish-Am. C. of C. Clubs: Marines Meml. Assn. (San Francisco). Office: Dept Nat Security Affairs US Naval Postgrad Sch Monterey CA 93943

KENNEL, CHARLES FREDERICK, physicist, educator; b. Cambridge, Mass., Aug. 20, 1939; s. Archie Clarence and Elizabeth Ann (Fitzpatrick) K.; m. Ellen Lehman; children: Matthew Bochner, Sarah Alexandra. A.B. (Nat. scholar 1955-59), Harvard U., 1959; Ph.D. in Astrophys. Scis. (W.C. Peyton Advanced fellow 1962-63), Princeton U., 1964. Prin. research scientist Avco-Everett Research Lab., Mass., 1960-61, 64-67; vis. scientist Internat. Center Theoretical Physics, Trieste, Italy, 1965; mem. faculty U. Calif., Los Angeles, 1967—; prof. physics U. Calif., 1971—, chmn. dept., 1983-86; mem. Inst. Geophysics and Planetary Physics, 1972—, acting assoc. dir. inst., 1976-77; mem. space sci. bd. NRC, 1977-80, chmn. com. space physics, 1977-80; Fairchild prof. Calif. Inst. Tech., 1987; mem. space and earth scis. adv. com. NASA, 1986-89; mem. NRC Bd. Physics and Astronomy, 1987—, chmn., 1992—; chmn. plasma sci. NRC, mem. DOE fusion policy adv. com., 1990; Fulbright lectr. Brazil; visitor U.S.-USSR Acads. Exch., 1988-90; disting. vis. prof. U. Alaska, 1988-89, 90—; advisor U.S. Arctic Commn., 1993—; cons. in field. Co-author: Matter in Motion, The Spirit and Evolution of Physics, 1977; co-editor: Solar System Plasma Physics, 1978. Bd. dirs. Los Angeles Jr. Ballet Co., 1977-83, pres., 1979-80; bd. dirs. Inst. for Theoretical Physics, Santa Barbara, Calif., 1986-90. NSF postdoctoral fellow, 1965-66, Sloan fellow, 1968-70, Fulbright scholar, 1985, Guggenheim fellow, 1987. Fellow Am. Geophys. Union, Am. Phys. Soc. (pres. div. plasma physics 1989), AAAS; m. NAS, Am. Astron. Soc., Internat. Union Radio Sci., Internat. Acad. Astronautics. Office: U Calif Dept Physics Los Angeles CA 90024

KENNER, LAUREL, aerospace writer; b. Santa Monica, Calif., May 18, 1954; d. John Drewson and Mildred May (Bame) Kenner. BA, UCLA, 1977. Govt. reporter Newhall Signal, Valencia, Calif., 1983-86; news reporter AP, L.A., 1986; reporter Daily Breeze, Torrance, Calif., 1987-88; aerospace writer Copley L.A. Newspapers, T rance, 1989—. Recipient Verbatim award AP News Execs. Coun., 1989, 1st and 3rd Place Copley Ring of Truth awards, 1993. Mem. Aviation and Space Writers Assn. (regional awards 1990). Office: Copley LA Newspapers 5215 Torrance Blvd Torrance CA 90503-4009

KENNERKNECHT, RICHARD EUGENE, sales executive; b. Glendale, Calif., Apr. 29, 1961; s. Richard and Sharon Mavis (Zane) K. Profl. sporting clays shooter, exhbn. shooter; pres. FDC, Inc., Lost Hills, Calif., 1989-91. Mem. U.S. Sporting Assn.(mem. team USA 1988, 89, all- Am. team 1988, 89, 90), U.S. Sporting Clays Assn. (mem. rules and ethics com., capt. team Perazzi), Verdugo Hills Ducks Unltd. (founding mem.), Nat. Sporting Clays Assn. (mem. nat. adv. coun., 1991-92), Olin Winchester (adv. coun., 1991—), Shooting Sports of the Calif. Waterfowl Assn. (dir.), Western Outdoor News (outdoor columnist). Republican. Episcoplian. Home: 1940 Rustic Dr Casper WY 82609 Office: Def Tech Corp Am PO Box 240 2136 Oil Dr Casper WY 82602

KENNETT, WILLIAM ERIC, geologist; b. San Francisco, May 30, 1914; s. John Dennis and Gerda (Johanson) K.; m. Frances Louise Archer, May 31, 1942; children: Karen Kennett Sanders, Kathryn Kennett Torrington. AA in Sci., Modesto Jr. Coll., 1935; BA in Geology, U. Calif., Berkeley, 1938. Registered geologist, Calif.; registered petroleum engr., Calif. Geologist U.S. Geol. Survey, Medford, Oreg., 1938; from geologist to geol. supr. The Superior Oil Co., Calif., 1939-56; geol. mgr. Calif. Phillips Petroleum, L.A., Santa Barbara, Calif., 1956-70; chief exploration geologist USA Phillips Petroleum, Bartlesville, Okla., 1970-72; chief geologist Phillips Petroleum Far East, Singapore, 1972-76; v.p. Phillips Petroleum New Zealand, Wellington, 1976-79; v.p. ops. Ogle Resources, Santa Barbara, 1980-88; cons. water resources pvt. practice, Santa Barbara, 1988—. Mem. Santa Barbara Com. on Foreign Rels., 1981—, Downtown Parking Com., City of Santa Barbara, 1989—, Allied Neighborhood Assn., Santa Barbara, 1991—; pres. Braemar Ranch Homeowners' Assn., Santa Barbara, 1989—. Mem. U. Calif. Alumni Club (v.p. Santa Barbara), 1992—. Republican. Methodist. Home and Office: PO Box 3682 Santa Barbara CA 93130-3682

KENNEY, JOHN WILLIAM, III, chemistry educator; b. Long Beach, Calif., Aug. 15, 1950; s. John William Jr. and Janice (Kendrick) K.; m. M. Inga Samuelsen, Sept. 11, 1982; children: Clarissa Eileen, Charlotte Elizabeth. BS in Chemistry, U. Nev., 1972; PhD in Chemistry, U. Utah, 1979. Postdoctoral assoc. in chem. physics Wash. State U., Pullman, 1979-81; assoc. prof. chemistry Eastern N.Mex. U., Portales, 1982—. Contbr. articles to profl. jours. Troop leader Sangre de Cristo council Girl Scouts U.S., 1985—, mem. cadette/sr. planning bd. advisers, 1988—; adviser Ea. N.Mex. U. chpt. Alpha Lambda Delta, 1988—. Recipient Teola Artman award Sangre de Cristo coun. Girl Scouts U.S., 1988, Outstanding Vol. award, 1988, Girl Scout Honor Pin, 1990, Favorite Faculty award Ea. N.Mex. U. Alpha Lambda Delta, 1988; named one of Outstanding Young Men of Am., 1982-84; grantee Universal Energy Systems/USAF Office of Sci. Rsch., 1987-88, 1991-93. Mem. AAAS, Am. Vacuum Soc. (rsch. awards 1986-91), Am. Chem. Soc. (co-chmn. South Plains sect. 1989, rsch. award 1986), Phi Kappa Phi (sec. Ea. N.Mex. U. chpt. 1988-90, pres. Ea. N.Mex. U. chpt. 1990-92). Democrat. Lutheran. Home: 1112 Leo Dr Portales NM 88130-6120

KENNEY, MARIANNE, educator; b. Idaho Falls, Idaho, Jan. 11, 1933; d. Karl and Rose Katherine (Keller) Wolff; m. Bruce Warren Kenney, June 23, 1956; children: Karl Herbert, Peter James, Mary-Rose, Joseph Paul. BS in Elem. Edn., U. Idaho, 1955; MEd in Counseling/Guidance, U. Nev. at Las Vegas, 1971. Cert. elem. edn. tchr., counseling, edn. adminstrn. Elem. tchr. Elk River (Idaho) Sch. Dist., 1953-54; elem. tchr. Clark County Sch. Dist., Las Vegas, 1955-60, English tchr. jr. high, 1968-72, core tchr., 1972-75, Title I reading tchr., 1975-77, sch. counselor, 1977-79, dean of students, 1979-85, chpt. 1 reading tchr., 1985—. Author: Clark County School District Language Arts Guide, 1977, Clark County School District Elementary

Counselors' Guide, 1979. Mem. Las Vegas Child Welfare Bd., 1977-85, chmn., 1980. Fulbright fellow, India, 1976; Edn. scholar U. Idaho, Moscow, 1954; recipient Ivy Leaf award Alpha Phi, 1954. Mem. Alpha Delta Kappa Internat. (exec. bd. 1985-87, southwest regional grand v.p. 1987-89, southwest regional scholar Mexico 1990), Phi Delta Kappa.

KENNEY, WILLIAM FITZGERALD, lawyer; b. San Francisco, Nov. 4, 1935; s. Lionel Fitzgerald and Ethel Constance (Brennan) K.; m. Susan Elizabeth Langfitt, May 5, 1962; children: Anne, Carol, James. BA, U. Calif.-Berkeley, 1957, JD, 1960. Bar: Calif. 1961. Assoc. Miller, Osborne Miller & Bartlett, San Mateo, Calif., 1962-64; ptnr. Tormey, Kenney & Cotchett, San Mateo, 1965-67; pres. William F. Kenney, Inc., San Mateo, 1968—; gen. ptnr. All Am. Self Storage, 1985—, Second St. Self Storage, 1990—. Trustee San Mateo City Sch. Dist., 1971-79, pres., 1972-74; pres. March of Dimes, 1972-73; bd. dirs. Boys Club of San Mateo, 1972-90, Samaritan House, 1989—, Lesley Found., 1992—. With U.S. Army, 1960-62. Mem. State Bar of Calif. (taxation com. 1973-76), San Mateo County Bar Assn. (bd. dir. 1973-75), Calif. Assn. Realtors (legal affairs com. 1978—), San Mateo C. of C. (bd. dirs. 1987-93), Self Storage Assn. (we. region, pres. 1989-90, nat. bd. dirs. 1990—). Republican. Roman Catholic. Club: Rotary (pres. 1978-79). Lodge: Elks (exalted ruler 1974-75). Home: 221 Clark Dr San Mateo CA 94402-1004 Office: William F Kenney Inc 120 N El Camino Real San Mateo CA 94401-2705

KENNY, ALAN DENNIS, sales account manager, computer educator; b. Quebec City, Quebec, Can., Nov. 12, 1963; s. Thomas Geer and Charlene Mae (Hecker) K. Student, U.S. Naval Acad., 1982, U. Minn., 1983-89. Engring. technician Honeywell, Inc., Hopkins, Minn., 1984-89; sales acct. mgr. Gen Rad, Inc., Chgo., 1989-90, Milpitas, Calif., 1990—. Contbr. articles to profl. jours. With USN, 1982. Recipient Spl. Achievement award Honeywell, Inc., 1985, 87, 88, Creative Sci. award 3M, Inc., 1981, Honeywell Math and Sci. Excellence scholarship, 1982. Mem. Ins. Environ. Scis. Office: Gen Rad Inc 510 Cottonwood Dr Milpitas CA 95035

KENNY, MICHAEL H., bishop; b. Hollywood, Calif., June 26, 1937. Ed., St. Joseph Coll., Mountain View, Calif., St. Patrick's Sem., Menlo Park, Calif., Cath. U. Am. Ordained priest Roman Cath. Ch., 1963; ordained bishop of Juneau, Alaska, 1979—. Office: Diocese of Juneau 419 6th St#200 Juneau AK 99801-1072 Home: 2960 Howell Ave Juneau AK 99801*

KENOFF, JAY STEWART, lawyer; b. L.A., Apr. 29, 1946; s. Charles Kapp and Martha (Minchenberg) K.; m. Pamela Fran Benyas, Sept. 1, 1979 (div. Dec. 1981); m. Luz Elena Chavira, June 9, 1991. AB, UCLA, 1967; MS, U. So. Calif., L.A., 1972; JD, Harvard U., 1970. Bar: Washington 1970, Calif. 1971, U.S. Ct. Appeals (9th cir.) 1974, U.S. Dist. Ct. (so., cen. dists. Calif.) 1974, U.S. Ct. Mil. Appeals 1974. Assoc. Wyman, Bautzer, Rothman & Kuchel, Beverly Hills, Calif., 1974-76, Epport & Delevie, Beverly Hills, 1977-78; ptnr. Bushkin, Gaims, Gaines & Jonas, L.A., 1978-86; prof. Sch. of Law Northrup U., Inglewood, Calif., 1981-85; ptnr. Kenoff & Machtinger, L.A., 1986—; judge pro tem L.A. Mcpl. Ct., 1985—; arbitrator, mediator Ctr. for Comml. Mediation, L.A., 1986—; mediator L.A. Superior Ct., 1987—, mem. settlement panel, 1987—. Author: Entertainment Industry Contracts, 1986; contbg. editor Entertainment Law & Finance. Commdr. USN Navy Judge Adv. Corps, USNR, 1968-91. Mem. Beverly Hills Bar Assn., Harvard-Radcliffe Club. Democrat. Jewish. Office: Kenoff & Machtinger Bldg 1250 1999 Avenue Of The Stars Los Angeles CA 90067-6037

KENT, CHRISTOPHER ANDREW, history educator; b. Winnipeg, Man., Can., Oct. 28, 1940; s. Cecil Charles and Elizabeth McTaggart (Frame) K.; m. Mary Carolyn Marino, Oct. 26, 1977; 1 child, Andrew Michael. BA, U. Toronto (Ont., Can.), 1963, MA, 1964; DPhil, U. Sussex, Brighton, Eng., 1969. Asst. prof. Prince of Wales Coll., Charlottetown, P.E.I., Can., 1968-69, U. P.E.I., Charlottetown, 1969-70; asst. prof. U. Sask., Saskatoon, Can., 1970-73, assoc. prof., 1973-78, prof., 1978—, dept. head, 1987-90. Author: Brains and Numbers, 1976; editor Can. Jour. History, 1977-83; mem. editorial bd. Canadian Jour. History, Victorian Studies, Victorian Rev., Victorian Periodicals Rev. Mem. Victorian Studies Assn. (pres. 1986-88), Rsch. Soc. for Victorial Periodicals (bd. dirs. 1977—), Jane Austen Soc. N.Am. Office: U Sask, Dept History, Saskatoon, SK Canada S7N 0W0

KENT, DARREL ARTHUR, systems engineer; b. Colby, Kans., June 14, 1954; s. Norman Kent and LaVaughn (Hudson) Durkin; m. Diana Lynn Goodholm, Feb. 3, 1954; children: Nicole Christine, Jonathan Arthur, Jessica Suzanne. Student, Regis Coll., Denver, 1980-82, Community Coll., Westminster, Colo., 1982-84. Computer operator Mountain Bell Telephone Co., Denver, 1972-76, computer specialist, 1976-79, asst. mgr., 1979-82; systems programmer Mountain Bell/U.S. West, Denver, 1982-86; systems engr. Nat. Advanced Systems, Englewood, Colo., 1986-89; sr. systems engr. Hitachi Data Systems, Englewood, 1989—, dist. systems specialist, 1992—, cons. capacity planning, 1992—. Coach Little League Baseball Assn., Thornton, Colo., 1990-91; cubmaster Boys Scouts Am., Cub Scout Pack 564, Thornton, 1990—. Mem. Rocky Mountain Computer Measurement Group (founding dir. 1988-91), Computer Measurement Group (nat. adv. bd. 1990-91, author 1989). Mem. Christian Reformed Ch. Home: 5214 E 114th Pl Thornton CO 80233 Office: Hitachi Data Systems 5251 DTC Pkwy Ste 990 Englewood CO 80111-2738

KENT, JAMES GUY, health care executive, kinesiologist; b. Jacksonville, N.C., Nov. 8, 1952; s. David Wolfe and Lucille (Epstein) K.; m. Rochelle Sue Halfon, June 16, 1979; children: Ashley, Jason, Bryan. BA, Calif. State U., Northridge, 1974; MS, UCLA, 1979; PhD, Pacific Western U., L.A., 1982. Dir. Wilshire Phys. Therapy, L.A., 1977-80; pres., founder Integrated Rehab. Corp. and predecessor cos., Marina Del Rey, Calif., 1980-92; clin. assoc. prof. Calif. Coll. Podiatric Medicine, L.A., 1984-85, clin. instr., 1983-84; co-founder Phys. Therapy Program Coll. Osteo. Medicine Pacific, Pomona, Calif., 1992. Editorial bd. Sports Medicine Digest, 1981-86. Sponsor Student Internships, UCLA, 1979-84; bd. dirs. Switzer Ctr. for Children, Torrance, Calif., 1988-91. Mem. Am. Coll. Sports Medicine, Am. Acad. Forensic Scis., Nat. Assn. Rehab. Facilities, Am. Congress Rehab. Medicine, Internat. Soc. Biomechanics, N.Am. Soc. Pediatric Exercise Medicine. Office: 924 Westwood Blvd Ste 800 Los Angeles CA 90024-2929

KENT, SUZIE BERRYHILL, health physicist; b. Jeffersonville, Ind., Sept. 2, 1946; d. Leon John and Jane Elizabeth (Mitchell) Berryhill; m. Robert Taylor Kent, Jan. 5, 1968; children: Mitchell Gregory Kent, ELizabeth Bedingfield Kent. BA, U. Tex., 1968; MS in Health Professions, S.W. Tex. State U., 1990. Environ. chemist Tex. Dept. Health, Austin, 1969-80, health physicist, 1980-90; reactor health physicist U. Calif., Irvine, 1990-91; pub. health physicist Orange County Health Care Agy., Santa Ana, Calif., 1991—; com. mem., task force Conf. Radiation Control Program Dirs., Frankfort, Ky., 1982—. Capt. Austin Aqua Festival, Austin, Tex., 1980-85; sec. Balcones Hills Women's Club, Austin, 1986; lectr., religion tchr. St. John Neumann Parish, Irvine, Calif., 1990—. Fellow Tex. Pub. Health Assn., Austin, Tex. Mem. Health Physics Soc. (chmn.-elect edn. commn. So. Calif. chpt.), Bioelectromagnetics Soc., Tex. Pub. Health Assn. Roman Catholic. Office: Orange County Health Care Agy Environmental Health 2009 E Edinger Santa Ana CA 92705

KENT, THEODORE CHARLES, psychologist; m. Shirley, June 7, 1948; children: Donald, Susan, Steven. BA, Yale U., 1935, MA, Columbia U., 1940, MA, Mills Coll., 1953, PhD, U. So. Calif., 1951; Dr. Rerum Naturalium, Johannes Gutenberg U., Mainz, Germany, 1960. Diplomate in clin. psychology. Clin. psychologist, behavioral scientist USAF, 1951-65, chief psychologist, Europe, 1956-60; head dept. behavioral sci. U. So. Colo., Pueblo, 1965-78, emeritus, 1978—; staff psychologist Yuma Behavioral Health, Ariz., 1978-82, chief profl. svcs., 1982-83; dir. psychol. svcs. Rio Colo. Health Systems, Yuma, 1983-85; clin psychologist, dir. mental health Ft. Yuma (Calif.) Indian Health Svc., USPHS, 1985-88; exec. dir. Human Sci. Ctr., San Diego, 1982—. Columnist Yuma Daily Sun, 1982-86. Author (tests) symbol arrangementtest, 1952, internat. culture free non-verbal intelligence, 1957, self-other location chart, 1970, test of suffering, 1982; (books) Skills in Living Together, 1983, Conflict Resolution, 1986, A Psychologist Answers Your Questions, 1987, Behind The Therapsist's Notes, 1993; plays and video Three Warriors Against Substance Abuse. Named Outstanding prof. U. So. Colo., 1977. Fellow Am. Psychol. Assn. (disting. visitor undergrad. edn. program); mem. AAAS, Deutsche Gesellschaft fur Antropologie, Internat. Assn. Study of Symbols (founder, 1st pres. 1957-61), Japanese Soc. Study KTSA (hon. pres.), Home and Office: PO Box 270169 San Diego CA 92198-2169

KENWORTH, KURT HAROLD, manufacturing executive; b. Chgo., Mar. 12, 1931; s. Walter M. and Clare D. (Boehm) K.; m. Suzanne Davids, Oct. 17, 1963 (div. 1973); m. Marcia L. Tillotson, Apr. 13, 1973; children: Kelly, Todd, Caryl, Kathryn, Jennifer, Julie. AA, Pasadena City Coll., 1953; BS, UCLA, 1955; MBA, Harvard U., 1958. Product mgr. Ducommun Corp., L.A., 1958-63; mgr. nat. sales Bobrick Corp., North Hollywood, Calif., 1963-71; sr. v.p. Mobex Corp., Fullerton, Calif., 1971-76; pres. Alaco Ladder Co., Chino, Calif., 1976—; com. mem. Ansi Ladder Standards, N.Y.C., 1984; mem. Nat. Fire Protection Standards Coms., Quincy, Mass., 1989-92. Contbr. articles to profl. jours. Mem. Chino Valley C. of C. (bd. dirs. 1990). Office: Alaco Ladder Co 5167 G St Chino CA 91710

KENY, SHARAD VASANT, mathematics educator and researcher; b. Panaji, Goa, India, Jan. 21, 1946; d. Vishnu Roulu and Mandabai Vishnu Rao; m. Vasant Yeshwant Keny, May 26, 1969; children: Hemant, Shilpa, Ameet, Shveta. BS, Bombay U., 1966, MS, 1968; MA, UCLA, 1973; PhD, 1976. Instr. Dhempe Coll., Bombay, 1968-69, UCLA, Los Angeles, 1976-77; asst. prof. Calif. State U., Long Beach, Calif., 1977-86; adj. prof. Calif. State U., Fullerton, 1980-81, Golden West Coll., Huntington Beach, Calif., 1981-83, Orange Coast Community Coll., Costa Mesa, Calif., 1983-85; asst. prof. Whittier (Calif.) Coll., 1986-88, assoc. prof., 1988—; adj. prof. Cypress (Calif.) Coll., 1990-91; curriculum cons. La Serna High Sch., Whittier, Calif., 1989-90. Contbr. articles to profl. jours. Mem. Brahan Maharashtra Mandal, 1990, Maharashtra Mandal, 1974-90. Mem. Math. Assn. of Am., Am. Math. Soc., Indian Math. Soc., Maharashrian Assn. of L.A., Shantivan L.A. Home: 7901 Lemonwood Cir Buena Park CA 90623-1834 Office: Whittier Coll 13406 Philadelphia St Whittier CA 90601-4413

KENYON, DAVID V., federal judge; b. 1930; m. Mary Cramer; children: George Cramer, John Clark. B.A., U. Calif.-Berkeley, 1952; J.D., U. So. Calif., 1957. Law clk. presiding justice U.S. Dist. Ct. (cen. dist.) Calif., 1957-58; house counsel Metro-Goldwyn-Mayer, 1959-60, Nat. Theatres and TV Inc., 1960-61; pvt. practice law, 1961-71; judge Mcpl. Ct. L.A., 1971-72, L.A. Superior Ct., 1972-80, U.S. Dist. Ct. (cen. dist.) Calif., L.A., 1980—. Office: US Dist Ct 312 N Spring St Los Angeles CA 90012-4701

KENYON, KENNETH JAMES, research librarian; b. Phila., Oct. 30, 1930; s. H. Edison and Astrid (Sorensen) K.; m. Mary Ann Strong, Mar. 28, 1959; children—Kenneth, Jr., Norman. A.A., Los Angeles City Coll., 1961; student Santa Ana Coll., 1963, UCLA, 1964. Record librarian ABC, Hollywood, Calif., 1953-55; with camera dept. Walt Disney Prodns., 1955-56; research librarian 20th Century Fox Film Corp., Beverly Hills, Calif., 1957-70, head research dept., 1970-92; archivist Ronald Reagon Presdl. Libr., 1992—. Mem. Rep. Nat. Com. Served with USMC, 1948-52. Mem. Spl. Libraries Assn., Acad. Motion Picture Arts and Scis., TV Acad. Arts and Scis., Am. Film Inst., Am. Legion, UCLA Alumni Assn., USMC Combat Corrs. Assn. Lodges: Masons, VASA. Office: 20th Century Fox Rsch Libr PO Box 900 Beverly Hills CA 90213-0900

KEOGH, HEIDI HELEN DAKE, publishing executive; b. Saratoga, N.Y., July 12, 1950; d. Charles Starks and Phyllis Sylvia (Edmunds) Dake; m. Randall Frank Keogh, Nov. 3, 1973; children: Tyler Cameron, Kelly Dake. Student, U. Colo., 1972. Reception, promotions Sta. KLAK, KJAE, Lakewood, Colo., 1972-73; account exec. Mixed Media Advt. Agy., Denver, 1973-75; writer, mktg. Jr. League Cookbook Devel., Denver, 1986-88; chmn., coordinator Colorado Cache & Creme de Colorado Cookbooks, 1988-90; speakers bur. Mile High Transplant Bank, Denver, 1983-84, Writer's Inst., U. Denver, 1988; bd. dirs. Stewart's Ice Cream Co., Inc., Jr. League, Denver. Contbr. 6 articles to profl. jours. Fiscal officer, bd. dirs. Mile High Transplant Bank; blockworker Littleton (Colo.) Rep. Com., 1980-84, Heart Fund and Am. Cancer Soc., Littleton, 1978—; fundraising vol. Littleton Pub. Schs., 1980—; vol. Hearts for Life, 1991—, Oneday, 1992, Denver Ballet Guild, 1992—. Mem. Jr. League Denver (pub. rels. bd., v.p. ways and means 1989-90, planning coun./ad hoc 1990-92), Community Emergency Fund (chair 1991-92), Jon D. Williams Cotillion at Columbine (chmn. 1991—), Columbine Country Club, Gamma Alpha Chi, Pi Beta Phi Alumnae Club (pres. Denver chpt. 1984-85, 93-94). Episcopalian. Home: 63 Fairway Ln Littleton CO 80123-6648

KEOGH, RICHARD JOHN, management analyst; b. Woonsocket, R.I., Sept. 23, 1932; s. Michael Joseph and Dora Marie (Rumgay) K. BBA, U. Mass., 1958; MA, Pepperdine U., 1974. Lic. explosive disposal technician, Mass.; expert witness explosives, Hawaii. Commd. 2d lt. U.S. Army, 1958, advanced through grades to maj., 1967; stationed at Korea, S.C., Ala., 1958-73; ret. USAR, 1979; disposal specialist USN, Lualualei, Hawaii, 1973-76; mgmt. analyst Marine Corps Air Sta., Kaneohe Bay, Hawaii, 1976—. Contbr. articles to profl. jours. Pres. Assn. of Owners Palms Condominium, Honolulu, 1978-80. With USAR, 1973-79. Decorated 3 Bronze Stars, 2 Purple Hearts, 2 Air medals, Cross of Gallantry; recipient Founders award, Order of the Arrow Boy Scouts Am., 1989, FBI Cert. of Appreciation, 1991. Mem. Internat. Assn. Bomb Technicians and Investigators (life), Disabled Am. Vets. (life), Nat. Auto Pistol Collectors Assn., Ohio Gun Collectors Assn., Bay Colony Weapons Collectors, Gun Owners Action League. Home: 431 Nahua St Apt 203 Honolulu HI 96815-2915 Office: Marine Corps Air Sta Compt Dept Kailua HI 96863

KEPNER, RITA MARIE, sculptor, writer, editor, educator, public affairs officer, marketing and communications professional; b. Binghamton, N.Y., Nov. 15, 1944; d. Peter Walter and Helena Theresa (Piotrowski) Kramnicz; m. John C. Matthiesen; 1 child, Stewart. Student, Elmira Coll., 1962-63; BA, SUNY, 1966; postgrad., Okla. U., 1988, Seattle Pacific U., 1991, Western Wash. U., 1991, 92, diplome of merit (hon.), Acad. Bedriacense, Calvatore, Italy, 1984. Instr. exptl. coll. U. Wash., 1972-74; instr. sculpture internship program Evergreen Coll., Olympia, Wash., 1974-78; informal visual arts amb. between U.S. and Poland, 1976-81; pres. fed. women's program coun. Seattle dist., 1985-86; fed. women's program mgr., Schweinfurt, Fed. Republic Germany, 1986-87, Wiesbaden, Fed. Republic Germany, 1988; artist-in-residence City of Seattle, 1975, 77-78; del. Internat. Sculptors Conf., Toronto, Ont., Can., 1978; writer, editor, pub. affairs specialist Seattle dist. U.S. Army C.E.; pub. affairs officer Wiesbaden Milcom Hdqrs., 1987-88, editor, Schweinfurt, 1986-87; instr. writing & editing for mgrs. Dept. of Navy, Bremerton, Wash., 1991—; apptd. disaster assistance employee region 10, Fed. Emergency Mgmt. Agy. One-woman shows include Willoughby Wallace Meml. Gallery, Branford, Conn., 1967, Penryn Gallery, Seattle, 1970, 73, 76, Haines Gallery, Seattle, 1975, Zoliborz Gallery, Warsaw, Poland, 1981, Yorkshire 510, Norman, Okla., 1988; group shows include SUNY, Binghamton, 1966, Manawata Art Gallery, Palmerston North, N.Z., 1976, Modern Art Mus., Seattle, 1976, Portland (Oreg.) Art Mus., 1976, Hajnowka (Poland) Gallery, 1977, Die Roemer Gallery, Wiesbaden, Fed. Republic Germany, 1988, Blue Heron Gallery, Port Hadlock, Wash., 1991-92, Quimper Arts, Port Townsend, Wash., 1993; major works include Peace Pipe, Zalaegerszeg, Hungary, Human Forms in Balance, City of Seattle, 1975, Unity, City of Znin, Poland, 1976, Rough to Smooth, Seattle Pub. Libr., 1978; contbr. articles to N.W. Arts, Seattle Post-Intelligencer, Leonardo mag., Polska Panorama, Poland mag. Founder Bainbridge Island Arts Coun., 1984; VISTA vol., 1982-84; bd. dirs. Aradia Med. Clinic, Seattle, 1972-74; founder Chimacum (Wash.) Sch. Dist. Learning Boosters, 1989; loaned exec. to govt. campaigns United Way, 1989; trainer for campaign coords. and key workers, 1989; 1st aid trainer Medic I, Seattle, 1989-91; elected chair Marrowstone Island Groundwater Com.; mem. adv. com. Seawater Intrusion Team Dept. of Ecology, Wash. State. Recipient merit award for superior journalistic achievement U.S. Army CE, 1984, 85, 2d place news category competition award, 1985, 86; suggestion award Dept. Army, 1984, ofcl. commendation Dept. of Army, 1985, 86, 87, 90, Dept. of Navy, Puget Sound Naval Shipyard, 1990, 91, Specialist Achievement award, 1991; cert. achievement Washington Assn. Educators of the Talented and Gifted, 1990; Kosciuszko Found. grantee, 1975, 76, 79, 81. Mem. Internat. Artists Cooperation (Edewecht, Fed. Republic Germany), N.W. Multihull Assn. (commodore 1974), Marrostone Island Community Assn. (pres. 1993). Holder USCG capt. lic. for passenger carrying aux. sailing vessels up to 50 tons, 1980—. Home: 6681 Flagler Rd Nordland WA 98358-9629

KERASOTE, THEODORE JOHN, environmental writer, natural history photographer; b. N.Y.C., Mar. 17, 1950; s. George and Elpis (Cladis) K. BA in English Lit., Colgate U., 1972; MA in English Lit., U. Colo., 1983. Freelance writer and photographer, 1968—; editor environ. affairs Sports Afield, N.Y.C., 1979—; staff writer Outside mag., 1983-86. Author: Navigations, 1988, Bloodties, 1993; contbr. numerous photographs and articles to popular and profl. publs. Mem. Outdoor Writers Assn. Am., Soc. Environ. Journalists, Nikon Profl. Svcs., Am. Alpine Club. Office: Box 100 Kelly WY 83011

KERCHNER, CHARLES TAYLOR, educator; b. Chgo., Feb. 18, 1940; s. Charles W. and Dorothy (Taylor) K.; m. Leanne Bauman, Sept. 5, 1962; children: Paige, Charles Arthur. BS, U. Ill., 1962, MBA, 1964; PhD, Northwestern U., 1976. Reporter, news editor, asst. to gen. mgr. St. Petersburg Times, Fla., 1964-71; assoc. dir. Ill. Bd. Higher Edn., Chgo., 1971-73; dir. fed. projects City Colls. of Chgo., 1973; grad. fellow, project dir., asst. prof. Northwestern U., Evanston, Ill., 1974-76; asst. prof. to prof. edn. and dir. The Claremont Grad. Sch. Ednl. Leadership Program, 1976—. Co-author: The Changing Idea of a Teachers Union, 1988; editor/contbr.: The Politics of Choice and Excellence, 1989, A Union of Professionals, 1993; contbr. articles to profl. jours. Nat. Inst. Edn. grantee, Stuart Found. grantee, Carnegie Corp. N.Y. grantee, others. Mem. Am. Ednl. Rsch. Assn., Indsl. Rels. Rsch. Assn., Politics of Edn. Assn. (bull. editor 1985-87). Democrat. Presbyterian. Office: The Claremont Grad Sch 150 E 10th St Claremont CA 91711-6160

KERFOOT, BRANCH PRICE, electronics scientist; b. N.Y.C., May 9, 1925; s. Branch Price and Henrietta (Bartlett) K.; m. Carol Saindon, Feb. 13, 1965; 1 child, B. Price III. BE, Yale U., 1945; MSE, U. Mich., 1947, PhD, 1955; JD, Western State U., 1987. Registered profl. engr., Calif. Engr. RCA Missile and Radar Div., Moorestown, N.J., 1949-57; tchr. Pasadena (Calif.) City Coll., 1958; prin. engr. Ford Aeronautronic Div., Newport Beach, Calif., 1958-68; prin. scientist McDonnell Douglas Electronics, Huntington Beach, Calif., 1968-90; ret., 1990; founder Natural Resource Geophysics, Inc., Newport Beach; bd. dirs. Inventors Forum, Irvine, Calif., 1989—. Patentee fluid-flow drag reducer; author: Kerfoot & Related Families' Ancestors, 1992; contbr. tech. articles to profl. publs. Adviser Jr. Achievement; trustee Newport Harbor Art Mus., 1973-76; active Soc. of Cin., 1950—; active Baronial Order of the Magna Charta, 1992—. Lt. comdr. USNR, 1943-46, PTO. Mem. IEEE (life sr.), USNR Assn. (life), Order Founders and Patriots Am., Electric Automobile Assn., Balboa Bay Club, Classic Car Club Am., Rolls Royce Owners Club, Sigma Xi, Kappa Sigma. Republican. Home: 1420 Antigua Way Newport Beach CA 92660-4914

KERMAN, BARRY MARTIN, ophthalmologist, educator; b. Chgo., Mar. 31, 1945; s. Harvey Nathan and Evelyn (Bialis) K.; B.S., U. Ill., 1967, M.D. with high honors, 1970. Diplomate Am. Bd. Ophthalmology; m. Pamela Renee Berliant, Aug. 18, 1968 (div. 1989); children: Gregory Jason, Jeremy Adam. Intern in medicine Harbor Gen. Hosp., Torrance, Calif., 1970-71; resident in ophthalmology Wadsworth VA Hosp., L.A., 1971-74; fellow in diseases of the retina, vitreous and choroid Jules Stein Eye Inst. UCLA, 1974-75; fellow in ophthalmic ultrasonography Edward S. Harkness Eye Inst., Columbia U., N.Y.C. and U. Iowa Hosps., Iowa City, 1975; asst. prof. ophthalmology UCLA, 1976-78, Harbor Gen. Hosp., 1976-78; asst. clin. prof. ophthalmology UCLA, 1978-83, assoc. clin. prof., 1983—, dir. ophthalmic ultrasonography lab., 1976—; cons. ophthalmologist, L.A., 1976—; mem. exec. bd. Am. Registry Diagnostic Med. Sonographers, 1981-87. With USAFR, 1971-77. Fellow Am. Acad. Ophthalmology; mem. Calif. Med. Assn., L.A. County Med. Assn., L.A. Soc. Ophthalmology, Am. Inst. Ultrasound in Medicine, Am. Soc. Ophthalmic Ultrasound, Am. Assn. Ophthalmic Standardized Echography, Societas Internat. Pro Diagnostica Ultrasonica in Opthalmic. Contbr. articles to profl. jours. Office: 2080 Century Park E Ste 800 Los Angeles CA 90067

KERMAN, THEA, lawyer; b. N.Y.C., Nov. 21, 1949; d. Samuel and Faye (Rogoff) K. BS, Cornell U., 1971; JD, NYU, 1974. Bar: N.Y. 1975, U.S. Dist. Ct. (so. and ea. dist.) N.Y. 1975, U.S. Ct. Appeals (2d cir.) 1975, Calif. 1976. Assoc. Linden & Deutsch, N.Y.C., 1974-77, Poletti, Freidin, Prashker, Feldman & Gartner, N.Y.C., 1978; counsel Marvel Comics Group, N.Y.C., 1979-81; assoc. Frankfurt, Garbus, Klein & Selz, N.Y.C., 1982-85, Marshall, Morris, Wattenberg & Platt, N.Y.C., 1985-88; asst. gen. counsel Tri-Star Pictures, Inc., Burbank, Calif., 1988-90; sole practitioner L.A., 1991—. Mem. ABA, Assn. of the Bar of the City of N.Y. Democrat. Jewish. Home: 720 Huntley Dr West Hollywood CA 90069-5038 Office: 720 Huntley Dr Ste 213 Los Angeles CA 90069

KERN, DONALD MICHAEL, internist; b. Belleville, Ill., Nov. 21, 1951; s. Donald Milton Kern and Dolores Olivia (Rust) Cohoon. BS in Biology, Tulane U., 1973; MD magna cum laude, U. Brussels, 1983. ECFMG cert.; lic. Calif. Intern in surgery Berkshire Med. Ctr., Pittsfield, Mass., 1983-84; intern in psychiatry Tufts New England Med. Ctr., Boston, 1984-85; resident in internal medicine Kaiser Found. Hosp., San Francisco, 1985-87; with assoc. staff internal medicine Kaiser Permanente Med. Group, Inc., San Francisco, 1987-89; assoc. investigator AIDS Clin. Trial Unit Kaiser Permanente Med. Ctr., Stanford U., Nat. Inst. Allergy & Infectious Disease, San Francisco, 1988-90; mem. staff internal medicine Kaiser Permanente Med. Group, South San Francisco, 1989—. Mem. Am. Coll. Physicians. Democrat. Roman Catholic. Office: Kaiser Permanente Med Group Inc 1200 El Camino Real South San Francisco CA 94080-3299

KERN, PAUL ALFRED, advertising company executive, research consultant, realtor; b. Hackensack, N.J., Mar. 17, 1958; s. Paul Julian and Edith Helen (Colten) K. BS in Commerce, U. Va., 1980; MBA, U. So. Calif., 1983. Sales rep. Procter & Gamble, Cin., 1980-81; rsch. svcs. mgr. Opinion Rsch., Long Beach, Calif., 1984; consumer planning supr. Dentsu, Young & Rubicam, L.A., 1984-85; rsch. exec. DJMC Advt., Inc., L.A., 1986; realtor assoc. Tarbell Realtors, Santa Ana, Calif., 1988-89; corp. pres. Jennskore, Inc., Torrance, Calif., 1989—, also bd. dirs.; bd. dirs. Applicon, Inc., Hillsdale, N.J., Kernakopia, Hillsdale; cons. Venture Six Enterprises, Encino, Calif., 1985—, DFS/Dorland, Torrance, 1986, IMI Machinery Inc., Charleston, S.C., 1987—. Coach, supr. Little League Football, Alexandria, Va., 1981; active Surf and Sun Softball League (1987 champions). Recipient Most Calls Per Day award Procter and Gamble, 1980. Mem. Profl. Research Assn., Am. Mktg. Assn., Am. Film Inst., Internat. Platform Assn., U.S. Tennis Assn. (Michelob Light 4.5 Team Championship 1982), U. Va. Alumni Assn, Nat. Assn. Realtors, Calif. Assn. of Realtors, S. Bay Rd. of Realtors (Torrance-Lomita), Carson Bd. of Realtors. Club: Alta Vista Racquet. Home: 516 S Irena Ave Redondo Beach CA 90277-3820 Office: 34-455 Suncrest Dr Cathedral City CA 92234

KERN, ROBERT WILLIAM, education educator; b. St. Louis, Aug. 8, 1934; s. Russell and Mary (Wilson) K.; m. Susan Brake, Mar. 10, 1989; children from previous marriage: Jonathan, Joshua. BA, Antioch Coll., 1957; MA, U. Chgo., 1961, PhD, 1966. Lectr. Ind. U., Gary, 1962, U. Calif., Riverside, 1965-66; prof. U. Mass., Amherst, 1966-68, U. N.Mex., Albuquerque, 1968—; prof. Guadalajara U., Mex., 1971, U. Amsterdam, The Netherlands, 1972, Nat. U. Spain, Madrid, 1976. Author: Liberals, Reformers and Caciques in Restoration Spain, 1973, Red Years/Black Years, 1978; editor: Labor in New Mexico, 1983, Historical Dictionary of Modern Spain, 1988 (Choice award 1990); co-editor: European Women on the Left, 1982. Mem. AAUP (pres. 1990), Am. Hist. Assn., Soc. Spain and Portugal Hist. Studies. Home: 6404 Katson NE Albuquerque NM 87109 Office: U NM Mesa Vista Hall Albuquerque NM 87131

KERN, THOMAS RAYMOND, wholesale distribution executive; b. Albany, Oreg., Aug. 6, 1958; s. Thomas Eugene and Delores Jane (Shortridge) K.; m. Sonya Leigh Mitchell, Sept. 15, 1989. Student, Oreg. State U., 1976-77. Exec. recruiter DHRG, Inc., Dallas, 1978-80, dir. info. systems, 1980-82; sales mgr. Magnetic Supply, Houston, 1982-84; mgr. bus. devel. Plateau Elec. Constructors, Salt Lake City, 1984-86; pres., chmn. PacServe, Inc., Portland, Oreg., 1987—; chmn. Northrup Properties Corp., 1987—. Mem. Perry Ctr. for Children, Portland, 1990. Mem. Nat. Assn. Credit Mgrs., Nat. Fedn. Ind. Businessmen. Republican. Methodist.

KERN, WILLIAM HENRY, pathologist; b. Nuernberg, Germany, Dec. 25, 1927; came to U.S., 1952; s. Wilhelm and Julie (Maedl) K.; m. Lynn Williams, Aug. 14, 1966; children: Julie Lynn, Lisa Catherine. MD, U. Munich, Germany, 1952. Lic. Phys./Surgeon, Calif. Pres. L.A. Soc. Pathologists, 1968; dir. dept. Pathology Hosp. Good Samaritan, L.A., 1966-91; clin. prof. Pathology U. Southern Calif., L.A., 1970—; chmn. medical staff Hosp. Good Samaritan, L.A., 1972-74, 87-89; pres. Am. Soc. Cytology, 1980-81, L.A. Acad. Medicine, L.A., 1980-81; trustee Hosp. Good Samaritan, 1972-89; bd. dirs./vice chmn. Am. Red Cross L.A. Chpt., 1983-86. Contbr. over 100 articles in profl. jours. Capt. U.S. Army, 1956-58. Recipient Papanicolaou award, 1987; grants for cancer rsch. 1963-70. Mem. Saddle & Sirloin Club (pres. 1970), Jonathan Club, Rancheros Visitadores. Home: 2321 Chislehurst Dr Los Angeles CA 90027-1046

KERNKAMP, PETER HAROLD, private investigator, planning consultant; b. Worthington, Minn., Aug. 2, 1953; s. James H. and Alfreda R. (Koba) K.; m. Melinda Jane Sheehan, Apr. 9, 1992. BS, Mankato State U., 1978. Grantsman intern City of Lakeville, Minn., 1978; town planner Town of Silt, Colo., 1979; planner City of Gillette, Wyo., 1980-85, City of Colorado Springs, Wyo., 1985-92; pvt. investigator Manitou Springs, Colo., 1992—; planning cons. in pvt. practice Manitou Springs, 1992—. Precinct chmn. Dem. Farmer Labor Party, St. Paul, 1976. Mem. Am. Planning Assn., Colorado Springs C. of C. (Bus. Climate Improvement award 1991). Democrat. Unitarian. Office: 331-C El Paso Blvd Manitou Springs CO 80829

KERNODLE, UNA MAE, educator; b. Jackson, Tenn., Mar. 4, 1947; d. James G. and Mary E. (McLemore) Sikes. B.S. in Home Econs., U. Tenn., 1969; M.Edn., U. Alaska, 1974. Tchr., head dept. vocat. edn. and electives Chugiak High Sch., Anchorage; edn. cons. State of Alaska, Anchorage Talent Bank; presenter Gov.'s Conf. on Child Abuse, Alaska Vocat. Edn. Assn. Conf., Alaska Home Econs. Inst., 1989; state officer Alaska Home Econs. Recipient Gruening award, 1989. Mem. Am. Home Econs. Assn., Anchorage Assn. Edn. Young Children, NEA, Am. Vocat. Assn. Democrat. Baptist. Office: Chugiak High Sch PO Box 770218 Eagle River AK 99577-0218

KERNS, GERALD ARTHUR, securities firm executive; b. Plano, Ill., Dec. 2, 1929; s. Levi John and Mae Louise (Antoine) K.; m. Aloysia Ann Ryan, Sept. 26, 1959; children: Tracy Kerns Smith, Carolyn Kerns Ranieri, Connor, Chandler. BA in Econs., U. Notre Dame, 1951. V.p. Tamak Inc., Portland, Oreg., 1959-82, Equitable Savs., Portland, Oreg., 1974-82, Far West Fed. Bank, Portland, Oreg., 1982-85, IRA Inst., Portland, Oreg., 1985; pres. Mktg. One Securities, Inc., Portland, Oreg., 1985—; dir. The IRA Inst., Portland, 1984-86. Lt. (j.g.) USCG, 1951-53. Mem. Investment Co. Inst. (mem. joint com.), Sierra Club. Office: Mktg One Securities Inc 851 SW 6th Ave Portland OR 97204

KERNS, PEGGY SHOUP, state representative; b. Columbus, Ohio, Mar. 17, 1941; d. Ronald Traxler and Marie (Strausbaugh) Shoup; m. Pat L.J. Kerns, Nov. 9, 1963; children: Jerry, Deborah. BA, Duquesne U., 1963. Editor co. newspaper Samsonite Corp., Denver, 1978-83; mgr. customer svc. dept. Mt. Med. Equipment, Littleton, Colo., 1983-88; state rep. State of Colo., 1989—; mem. bd. trustees Humana Hosp., Aurora, Colo., 1984—. Mem. coun. City of Aurora, 1983-89, mayor pro tem., asst. minority leader, 1993—. Named Bus. and Profl. Women's Woman of Yr., 1991, Legislator of Yr., 1989. Mem. AAUW, LWV, Aurora C. of C. (Woman of Yr. 1989), BPW. Democrat. Roman Catholic. Home: 1124 S Oakland St Aurora CO 80012-4260 Office: State Ho Reps State Capitol Denver CO 80201

KERNS, ROBERT MICHAEL, oil company executive; b. Newark, Ohio, Sept. 21, 1955; s. Robert Myron and Claudia Eula (Holman) K.; m. Glenna Diane Lucas, July 4, 1984 (div. 1988). BS in Math./Physics, Ill. Inst. Tech., Chgo., 1977; PhD in Math., U. Chgo., 1981. Instr. U. So. Calif., L.A., 1981-82; staff Congressman Robert K. Dornan, Washington, 1982; sr. assoc. Richter & Combs Investment Bankers, Encino, Calif., 1983-86; stockbroker Dean Witter Reynolds, Inc., L.A., 1986-87; br. mgr. Titan Capital Corp., Tustin, Calif., 1987-88; CFO Whitworth Energy Resources, Ltd., Woodland Hills, Calif., 1988—. Contbr. articles to profl. jours. So. Calif. chmn. Pat Buchanan for Pres., Glendale, Calif., 1992; campaign staff Robert K. Dornan for U.S. Senator, L.A., 1982; chpt. pres. Calif. Rep. Assy., 1984-85; chpt. pres. Calif. Young Reps., 1987-88. Fellow Nat. Hon. Physics Soc., Nat. Hon. Chem. Soc.; mem. E Clampus Vitas, Pi Kappa Phi. Home: 606 Knob Hill Ave Redondo Beach CA 90277 Office: Whitworth Energy Resources 20335 Ventura Blvd #235 Woodland Hills CA 91364

KERR, GIB, financial planner; b. Ottawa, Ont., Can., Apr. 21, 1927; came to U.S., 1966; s. Francis and Gladys (Larmondra) K.; m. Shirley Cochrane, June 15, 1952 (div. Apr. 1971); children: Judith Ann, Brian Jeffrey, Barry Philip, Sandra Gail, Randolph James (dec.). Grad. high sch., Ottawa. CLU; CFP; ChFC. Lab asst. E.B. Eddy Pulp and Paper Co., Hull, Quebec, Can., 1946-47; spl. svcs. mgr. Bell Telephone Co. of Can., Ottawa, 1947-57; owner, operator Spotlight Studios, Ottawa, 1957-58; corp. pres., career mgr. G.K.E. Inc., Ottawa, L.A., 1957-70; entertainer L.A., 1970-77, fin. planner, 1977—; personal mgr. for Rich Little, 1958-69. Author: Budget for the Lazy Person, 1988, (tng. manuel) Who's The Boss, 1989, Talk, 1986. Bd. dirs. Beverlywood Mental Health Ctr., L.A., 1989-91. Mem. Inst. Cert. Fin. Planners (v.p. L.A. soc. 1991—), West Los Angeles Le Tip (pres. 1988-90). Home and Office: 5625 Cambridge Way Apt 102 Culver City CA 90230-6766

KERR, GREGORY ALAN, sales executive, financial systems consultant; b. Denver, Oct. 24, 1950; s. Victor William and Lois Fern (Bell) K.; m. Abrilita Jaime Averell, Oct. 22, 1972 (div. Nov. 1982); m. Maureen Ann Worman, Apr. 20, 1985; 1 child, Christopher Allen Minard. AA, Glendale (Calif.) C.C., 1983; BS, Ariz. State U., 1988. Avionics technician Lockheed Internat., Bandar Abass, Iran, 1976-77; avionics instr. Lockheed-Calif. Co., Burbank, 1977-78; sr. programmer Data Systems Support, Woodland Hills, Calif., 1978-80; computer systems analyst TRW Datacom Internat., L.A., 1980-81; fin. systems analyst Valley Nat. Bank, Phoenix, 1981-84; project mgr., corp. officer First Interstate Bank, Phoenix, 1984-87; mgr., bus. cons., sales supporter Digital Equipment Corp., Tempe, Ariz., 1987—; mem. exec. com. MoneyNET Nat. Users Group, Chgo., 1986-87; conf. coord. MoneyNET Users Group, Scottsdale, Ariz., 1987; mem. bd. officers Phoenix chpt. DECUS User Soc., 1992—. Vol. Ariz. Spl. Olympics, Tempe, 1983—; Webelos leader, asst. cubmaster, mem. pack com. Cub Scouts Am., Phoenix, 1989—; mem. troop com. Grand Canyon coun. Boy Scouts Am., 1992—. Mem. Internat. Platform Assn., Nat. Pks. and Conservation Assn., DevilWest-Ariz. State U. Alumni Assn. (bd. dirs.), Beta Gamma Sigma, Sigma Iota Epsilon. Republican. Roman Catholic. Office: Digital Equipment Corp 1901 W 14th St Tempe AZ 85281-6983

KERR, JAMES W., pipe line company executive; b. Hamilton, Ont., Can., Mar. 11, 1914; s. George Robert and Helen Robertson (Bews) K.; m. Ruth Eleanor Marrs, Oct. 5, 1940; children: David, Barbara. B.Sc., U. Toronto. Various positions with Canadian Westinghouse Co., 1937-58, v.p., gen. mgr. apparatus products group, 1956-58; pres., chief exec. officer TransCan. PipeLines, Toronto, 1958-61; chmn. bd., pres. TransCan. PipeLines, 1961-68, chmn., chief exec. officer, 1968-79, cons. and dir., 1979-84, cons., 1984—; bd. dirs. Internat. Minerals and Chem. Corp. (Can.) Ltd.; dir. emeritus Can. Imperial Bank Commerce, Gt. Lakes Gas Transmission Co.; hon. pres. Internat. Gas Union. Hon. gov. Queen Elizabeth Hosp., Toronto; past chmn. Salvation Army Territorial Adv. Bd. Exec. Served as squadron leader RCAF, 1942-45. Mem. Bd. Trade Met. Toronto (past pres.), Am. Gas Assn., Can. Gas Assn. (past pres.), Engring. Inst. Can., Assn. Profl. Engrs. Province Ont., Can. Acad. Engring. Clubs: York, Toronto, Hamilton, Rosedale Golf.

KERR, JAMES WILFRID, artist; b. N.Y.C., Aug. 7, 1897; s. James Fairbairn and Leah M. (Galer) K.; grad. Poppenhusen Inst., 1914, N.Y. Sch. Fine and Applied Arts, 1923; m. Rose R. Netzorg, June 24, 1922; children: Andra Gail (dec.), Paul F. (adopted). Dir., Art Summer Sch., Detroit, 1923-24; artist, lectr., art adminstr., 1923—; painter in oils, tchr.; one-man and group shows include: Galeria Del Sol, Allied Artists Am., NAD, Am. Vets. Soc., N.J. Painters and Sculptors Soc., Carnegie Inst. Pitts., 1949 (by invitation), Conn. Acad. Fine Arts, Davenport (Iowa) Mus., Houston Mus., Irvington (N.J.) Mus., Norfolk Mus. Arts and Scis., Dialists Exhibit, N.J. Artists, Newark Mus., Ridgewood, N.J., Salmagundi Club, N.Y.C., Delgado Mus., New Orleans, Art U.S.A., Madison Sq. Garden, N.Y.C., 1958, Richmond Mus., Artists Equity Assn. show Botts Meml. Hall, Albuquerque, 48th-50th Fiesta shows at Mus. Fine Arts, Santa Fe, Springville, Utah, 1962-63, 1st Air Force Acad. Exhbn., 1962-63, Juried Arts Nat. Exhbn., Tyler, Tex., 1963, Western Mich. U., Kalamazoo, 1983; represented in permanent collections: Mus. City N.Y., Joslyn Art Mus., Omaha, Newark Mus., Mus. Albuquerque, Fla. So. Coll., Lakeland, N.Mex. State Fair, Fergusson Library, Albuquerque, Waldwick (N.J.) Elem. Sch., Western Mich. U. Trustee, Mus. Albuquerque. Recipient awards, prizes N.J. State Exhibit, Montclair, 1943 (hon. award); NAD, 1945 (1st Altman prize); Plainfield (N.J.) Art Assn. (hon. award), 1946; prize Oil, Morristown (N.J.) Art Assn.; Irvington Art and Mus. Assn., 1st prize in Oil, 1948, 49; Ridgewood (N.J.) Art Assn., 1st prize Oil, 1948; Art Council N.J., 2d Oil prize, 1948; Am. Vets. Soc. Artists purchase award, 1951; Ridgewood (N.J.) Art Assn. (hon. award), 1952; citation Fla. So. Coll., Lakeland, 1952; 1st prize 50th Fiesta Show, Mus. N.Mex., 1963; purchase prize N.Mex. State Fair, 1963, grand award, 1964; silver medal Am. Vets. Soc. Artists, 1963; prizes Ouray County Ann. Exhbn., 1964, State Fair, 1966; The Rose M. Kerr and James W. Kerr Found. named in his honor at Western Mich. U. Served with USN, World War I. Mem. Allied Artists Am. (treas. 1952, mem. jury awards oil painting 1958, dir. 1955, chmn. membership com. 1955), Internat. Assn. Plastic Arts (Joint com. for Am. participation), Assn. Artists N.J. (dir.), Artists Equity Assn. (chmn. nat. mus. com., co-chmn. nat. artists-museums com. 1958, nat. treas. 1959), Dialists (N.J.), Grand Central Galleries (artist-mem.), Irvington (N.J.) Art and Mus. Assn. (artist mem.), N.J. Soc. Painters and Sculptors, New Mexican Art League (dir. 1966), Ridgewood Art Center (past pres.), Salmagundi Club (artist mem.), Art Assn. New Orleans, Artists Equity Assn. (nat. treas. 1952-55), Am. Vets. Soc. Artists (pres. 1958-60), Albuquerque Mus. Assn. (pres. 1967-68, dir.), Smithsonian Instn. Archives Am. Art, Pres.'s Club Western Mich. U. Co-artist, author: Historic Design for Modern Use; also articles on art for School Arts mag. and Everyday Art mag. Lectr. women's clubs, high schs., colls., univs., art clubs and assns. on painting, graphic arts, modern movements in arts, and psychology related to art, radio and TV. Address: 7017 Bellrose Ave NE Albuquerque NM 87110

KERR, JIMMIE BARRY, small business owner, mayor; b. Tucson, Apr. 20, 1934. BS, Ariz. State U., 1958. Mayor City of Casa Grande, Ariz., 1967-75, 85—; owner Kerr Enterprises, Casa Grande, 1959—; elected to Casa Grande City Coun. for a four-yrs. term; mem. Pinal County Bd. Suprs., 1977-85. Past bd. dirs., mem. Ariz. State U.; mem. Casa Grande Hist. Soc., Casa Grande Friends of the Arts, Gov.'s Regional Jetport Commn. Named an Outstanding Young Man of Casa Grande Jaycees, 1969, 70, Outstanding Young Man of Ariz. 1970. Mem. Nat. League Cities Energy Environment (natural resources policy com., bd. dirs. Pinal County govtl. alliance), Cen. Ariz. Assn. of Govts. (founding), Ariz. Acad. (past bd. dirs.), Casa Grande Humane Soc., Casa Grande C. of C. (bd. dirs. 1985—), Ariz. Inst. Study Am. Wars, USAF Vets., League of Ariz. Cities and Towns (exec. com.), Am. Legion, Elks. Office: PO Box 883 Casa Grande AZ 85222

KERR, KLEON HARDING, former state senator, educator; b. Plain City, Utah, Apr. 26, 1911; s. William A. and Rosemond (Harding) K.; m. Katherine Abbott, Mar. 15, 1941; children: Kathleen, William A., Rebecca Rae. AS, Weber Coll., 1936; BA, George Washington U., 1939; MS, Utah State U., Logan, 1946. Tchr., Bear River High Sch., Tremonton, Utah, 1940-56, prin. jr. high sch., 1956-60, prin. Bear River High Sch., 1960-71; city justice Tremonton, 1941-46; sec. to Senator Arthur V. Watkins, 1947. Mayor, Tremonton City, 1948-53; mem. Utah Local Govt. Survey Commn., 1954-55; mem. Utah Ho. of Reps., 1953-56; mem. Utah State Senate, 1957-64, chmn. appropriation com., 1959—, majority leader, 1963; mem. Utah Legis. Council. Author: (poetry) Open My Eyes, 1983, We Remember, 1983, Trouble in the Amen Corner, 1985, Past Imperfect, 1988, A Helping Hand, 1990, Sound of Silence, 1991, Power Behind the Throne, 1992, Unreachable Goal?, 1993; (history) Those Who Served Box Elder County, 1984, Those Who Served Tremonton City, 1985, Diamond in the Rough, 1987, Facts of Life, 1987, Gettin' and Givin', 1989. Dist. dir. vocat. edn. Box Elder Sch. Dist. Recipient Alpha Delta Kappa award for outstanding contbn. to edn., 1982, award for outstanding contbrs. to edn. and govt. Theta Chpt. Alpha Beta Kappa, 1982, Excellence Achieved in Promotion of Tourism award, Allied Category award Utah Travel Counc., 1988, Merit award, 1993, Andy Rytting Community Svc. award, 1991; named Tourism Ambassador of Month, 1986. Mem. NEA, Utah, Box Elder edn. assns., Nat., Utah secondary schs. prins. assns., Bear River Valley. C. of C. (sec., mgr. 1955-58), Lions, Kiwanis, Phi Delta Kappa. Mem. Ch. of Jesus Christ of Latter-day Saints. Home: PO Box 246 Tremonton UT 84337-0246

KERRICK, DAVID ELLSWORTH, lawyer; b. Caldwell, Idaho, Jan. 15, 1951; s. Charles Ellsworth and Patria (Olesen) K.; m. Juneal Casper, May 24, 1980; children: Peter Ellsworth, Beth Anne, George Ellis, Katherine Leigh. Student, Coll. of Idaho, 1969-71; BA, U. Wash., 1972; JD, U. Idaho, 1980. Bar: Idaho 1980, U.S. Dist. Ct. Idaho 1980, U.S. Ct. Appeals (9th cir.) 1981. Senator State of Idaho, 1990—, majority caucus chmn., 1992—. Mem. ABA, Assn. Trial Lawyers Am., Idaho Bar Assn. (3d dist. pres. 1985-86), Idaho Trial Lawyers Assn., Canyon County Lawyers Assn. (pres. 1985). Republican. Presbyterian. Lodge: Elks. Office: PO Box 44 Caldwell ID 83606

KERSCH, JENNIFER LYNN, budget analyst; b. Fullerton, Calif., June 28, 1968; d. Vincent Carl and Marie Violet (Granato) Thoemmes; m. Timothy Steven Kersch, May 23, 1992. BA in Econs., U. Calif., Irvine, 1990. Fin. systems advisor Thoemmes Cabinet Makers, LaHabra, Calif., 1986-90; fin. assoc. Northrop Corp., Hawthorne, Calif., 1990-91; budget analyst Northrop Corp., Pico Rivera, Calif., 1991—. Tutor Huntington Beach (Calif.) Tutor Ctr., 1992. Republican. Roman Catholic. Home: 119 7th St # 9 Seal Beach CA 90740 Office: Northrop Corp 8900 E Washington Blvd Pico Rivera CA 90660

KERSCHNER, LEE R(ONALD), educational administrator; b. May 31, 1931; m. Helga Koller, June 22, 1958; children: David, Gabriel, Riza. B.A. in Polit. Sci. (Univ. fellow), Rutgers U., 1953; M.A. in Internat. Relations (Univ. fellow), Johns Hopkins U., 1958; Ph.D. in Polit. Sci. (Univ. fellow), Georgetown U., 1964. From instr. to prof. polit. sci. Calif. State U., Fullerton, 1961-69, prof., 1988—; state univ. dean Calif. State Univs. and Colls. Hdqrs., Long Beach, 1969-71, asst. exec. vice chancellor, 1971-76, vice chancellor for adminstrv. affairs, 1976-77, vice chancellor acad. affairs, 1987-92; exec. dir. Colo. Commn. on Higher Edn., Denver, 1977-83, Nat. Assn. Trade and Tech. Schs., 1983-85, Calif. Commn. on Master Plan for Higher Edn., 1985-87; interim pres. Calif. State U., Stanislaus, 1992—; cons. in field. Mem. exec. com. Am. Jewish Com., Denver, 1978-83; internat. bd. dirs. Amigos de las Americas, 1982-88 (chmn. 1985-87). Served with USAF, 1954-58; col. Res., ret. Home: PO Box 748 Weimar CA 95736-0748 Office: Calif State U Stanislaus 801 W Monte Vista Ave Turlock CA 95380

KERSEY, TERRY L(EE), astronautical engineer; b. San Francisco, June 9, 1947; s. Ida Helen (Schmeichel) K. Houseman, orderly Mills Meml. Hosp., San Mateo, Calif., 1965-68; security guard Lawrence Security, San Francisco, 1973-74; electronic engr. and technician engring. research and devel. dept. McCulloch Corp., Los Angeles, 1977; warehouseman C.C.H. Computax Co., Redondo Beach, Calif., 1977-78; with material ops. and planning customer support dept. Allied-Signal Aerospace Co., Torrance, Calif., 1978-91; security guard Guardsmark Inc., L.A., 1993; electronic technician J. W. Griffin, Venice, Calif., 1993—. Participant 9th Space Simulation conf., Los Angeles, 1977, 31st Internat. Astronautical Fedn. Congress., Tokyo, 1980, Unispace 1982 for the U.N., Vienna. Served to sgt. USAF, 1968-72, Vietnam. Decorated Vietnam Service medal with 2 bronze stars, Republic of Vietnam Campaign medal, Air Force commendation medal for Vietnam campaign Service. Mem. AAAS, AIAA (mem. space systems tech. com. 1981—, mem. aerodynamics com. 1980—, Wright Flyer Project Aerodynamics com. 1980—, pub. policy com. 1989—), Nat. Space Inst., Am. Astronautical Soc., The Planetary Soc., Internat. L5 Soc., Ind. Space Rsch. Group, IEEE Computer Soc., Space Studies Inst. (sr. assoc.). Zen Buddhist.

KERSTEN, TIMOTHY WAYNE, economics educator, consultant; b. Algona, Iowa, Nov. 18, 1944; s. Harold Arthur and Marcella (Heger) K.; m. Carol Ann Oliver, Dec. 22, 1967; one child, Jeffrey Alexander. BA, Calif. State U., Sacramento, 1967; MA, U. Oreg., 1971, PhD, 1973. Asst. prof. econs. Calif. Poly. State U., San Luis Obispo, 1971-75, assoc. prof., 1976-80, prof., 1981—, chmn. senate, 1980-82; mem. state-wide acad. senate Calif. State U., 1983—, chmn. faculty affairs com., 1984-86, mem. govtl. affairs com., 1986-89, chmn., 1990-91, vice chmn., 1992—, mem. exec. com., 1991-92. Author: Instructors Guide to Accompany Contemporary Economics, 1975. Mem. citizens adv. com. San Luis Obispo City Council, 1976-77. Fellow U.S. Govt., 1969-71. Mem. Am. Econ. Assn., Omicron Delta Epsilon, Phi Mu Alpha Sinfonia. Office: Calif Poly State U Dept Econs San Luis Obispo CA 93407

KERSTIENS, FRANCIS LYLE, electrical engineer; b. Colorado Springs, Colo., Dec. 7, 1950; s. Francis Louis and Marjorie Ann (Heye) K.; m. Debora Marie Oehlkers, Apr. 27, 1972 (div. May, 1990); children: Erica Lee, Eron Lyle. BSEE, U. New Mex., 1986. Reactor operator U.S. Navy USS James Monroe, 1971-78; accelerator operator Los Alamos (New Mex.) Nat. Lab., 1978-79, quality assurance specialist, 1979-86, instrumentation engr., 1986—. With USN, 1971-78.

KERTZ, MARSHA HELENE, accountant, educator; b. Palo Alto, Calif., May 29, 1946; d. Joe and Ruth (Lazear) K. BSBA in Acctg., San Jose State U., 1976, MBA, 1977. CPA, Calif., cert. tax profl. Staff acct. Steven Kroff & Co., CPA's, Palo Alto, 1968-71, 73-74; contr. Rand Teleprocessing Corp., San Francisco, 1972; auditor, sr. acct. Ben F. Priest Accountancy Corp., Mountain View, Calif., 1974-83; tchr. San Jose Unified Regional Occupation Program, San Jose, 1977; pvt. practice accounting San Jose, 1977—; lectr. San Jose State U., 1977—. Mem. AICPA, Nat. Soc. of Tax Profls., Am. Inst. Tax Studies, Am. Acctg. Assn., Calif. Soc. CPAs, Beta Alpha Psi, Beta Gamma Sigma. Democrat. Jewish. Home: 4544 Strawberry Park Dr San Jose CA 95129 Office: San Jose State U Acctg & Fin Dept San Jose CA 95192

KERVER, THOMAS JOSEPH, editor, consultant; b. Cleve., Nov. 9, 1934; s. William F. and Hope M. (Roberts) K.; m. Elizabeth G. Galloway, Apr. 12, 1969 (div. Apr. 1990); children: Kenneth, Stephen, Suzanne, Sarah. BA, Xavier U., 1956; M of Mil. Arts and Scis., U.S. Army Gen. Staff Coll., 1968; MA in Polit. Sci., U. Wis., 1972, MA in Journalism, 1972. Commd. 2d lt. U.S. Army, 1956, advanced through grades to lt. col., 1976; pres. Kerver People, Ft. Collins, Colo., 1976-80; dir. communications, publicity Colo. Bankers Assn., Denver, 1980-82; sr. editor Cardiff Pub. Co., Englewood, Colo., 1982-90; bus. editor Cablevision Mag., Denver, 1990—; prof. journalism Colo. State U., Ft. Collins, 1978-80; vice chmn. Larimer County Budget Adv. Com., Ft. Collins, 1978-79; chmn. Larimer Conty Pvt. Industry Coun., Ft. Collins, 1979-80. Contbr. articles to profl. jours. Organizer Larimer County Dem. Party, Ft. Collins, 1976-80; cons. Nat. Urban Indian Coun., Denver, 1980-81; organizer, affiliate Clinton for Pres. Campaign, Denver, 1992. Decorated Bronze Star (4), Legion of Merit (2); recipient Presdl. Citation award Pres. Jimmy Carter, 1980, Cert. of Distinction award Nat. Alliance Bus., 1980. Mem. Cable/Satellite Broadcasters Assn. Asia (chartered), Soc. Satellite Profls. Roman Catholic. Home: 7652 E Nassau Ave Denver CO 80237 Office: Capital Cities/ABC Inc Cable Pub Group 600 S Cherry # 400 Denver CO 80222

KERWIN, KENNETH HILLS, II, technology and management consultant, electronics systems and electro-optics specialist; b. San Francisco, Apr. 11, 1939; s. Kenneth H. and Helen E. (Schraubstädter) K.; m. Norma Larsen, Nov. 3, 1974. B in Physics, Pomona Coll., 1961; postgrad., Stanford U., 1968-70. Process engr. Data Disc, Inc., Palo Alto, Calif., 1964-67; rsch. engr. Stanford Rsch. Inst., Menlo Park, Calif., 1967-75; dir. Electronics Facility U. Calif., Santa Cruz, 1975-78, lectr. in physics, 1976-78; mgr. of engring. Balzers Corp., Hudson, N.H., 1978-81; v.p. tech. Ferrofluidics Corp., Nashua, N.H., 1981-86; engring. mgr. Thermal Tech., Inc., 1987-89; proprietor Kerwin & Assocs., Forestville, Calif., 1961—; co-founder Data Disc, Inc., 1959-60, 64-67; founding dir. Diskos Electronics Corp., Mountain View, Calif., 1968-72, Quantum Electro-Optical Devel. Corp., San Jose, Calif., 1989-91, Modular Process Tech. Corp., Santa Clara, Calif., 1991-92. Inventor TV instant replay, thin-film memory discs, fully-automated growth of semiconductor crystals, (with others) instruments for vision rsch./med. practice. 1st lt. S.C., U.S. Army 1961-64. Republican. Christian. Office: PO Box 1309 Forestville CA 95436-1309

KESEY, KEN, writer; b. La Hunta, Colo., Sept. 17, 1935; s. Fred and Geneva (Smith) K.; m. Norma Faye Haxby, May 20, 1956; children: Shannon, Zane, Jed (dec. 1984) Sunshine. B.S., U. Oreg., 1957; postgrad., Stanford U., 1958-60. Pres. Intrepid Trips, Inc., 1964; editor, pub. mag. Spit in the Ocean, 1974—. Author: One Flew Over the Cuckoo's Nest, 1962, Sometimes a Great Notion, 1964, Garage Sale, 1973, Demon Box, 1986; co-author Caverns, 1990, Little Tricker the Squirrel Meets Big Double The Bear, 1990, The Further Inquirey, 1990, The Sea Lion, 1991, Salior Song, 1992. Address: 85829 Ridgeway Rd Pleasant Hill OR 97455

KESKA, JERRY KAZIMIERZ, mechanical engineering educator; b. Wilkowisko, Poland, Feb. 14, 1945; came to U.S., 1984, naturalized, 1990; s. Jan and Stefania (Kawecka) K.; m. Jadwiga T. Sadowy, Sept. 11, 1966; children: Agnieszka, Marek. BSME, MS, State U. Krakow (Poland), 1970, PhD, 1974. Rsch. and teaching asst. State U. Krakow, 1965-70, lectr., 1970-74, asst. prof. Coll. Engring., 1974-75, assoc. prof. Lab. Multiphase Flow and Instrumentation, 1975-81; staff sr. scientist dept. mech. engring. State U. Karlsruhe (Germany), 1981-84; sr. project engr. rsch. dept. Copeland Corp., Sidney, Ohio, 1984-87; sr. systems engr. rsch. div. Technicon Instruments Corp., Tarrytown, N.Y., 1987-88; assoc. prof. mech. engring. dept. U. Nebr., Lincoln, 1988-92; sr. rsch. engr. Pacific N.W. Labs., Battelle, Richland, Wash., 1992—; vis. prof. dept. mech. engring. State U. Karlsruhe, 1975-76, Franzius Inst., State U. Hannover (Germany), 1980-81; lab. head Lab. Multiphase Flow and Instrumentation, Krakow, 1975-81; prin. investigator U. Nebr., Lincoln, 1988-92; chmn. internat. symposium Slurry Transport, Krakow, 1979. Author: (with others) Slurry Pipelines, 1976, Creation of Underground Cavern, 1978, Engineering Handbook, Sect. 8, Vol. 2, 1980; contbr. monographs and articles to profl. jours.; patentee in field. Deutsches Akademische Austauschdienst fellow, Bad Goesberg, Germany, 1975, Mina-James-Heinemann fellow, Hannover, Germany, 1980; recipient Gold medal Internat. Invention Exhbn., Brno, Czechoslovakia, 1980, Summer Faculty rsch. award Argonne Nat. Lab., 1990. Mem. ASME, Am. Soc. Engring. Edn., Am. Inst. Chem. Engrs., Am. Soc. Civil Engrs. Home: PO Box 573 Richland WA 99352 also: 2348 Hood Ave # 3 Richland WA 99352 Office: Battelle PNL Battelle Blvd Richland WA 99352

KESSEL, BRINA, educator, ornithologist; b. Ithaca, N.Y., Nov. 20, 1925; d. Marcel and Quinta (Cattell) K.; m. Raymond B. Roof, June 19, 1957 (dec. 1968). B.S. (Albert R. Brand Bird Song Found. scholar), Cornell U., 1947, Ph.D., 1951; M.S. (Wis. Alumni Research Found. fellow), U. Wis.-Madison, 1949. Student asst. Patuxent Research Refuge, 1946; student teaching asst. Cornell U., 1945-47, grad. asst., 1947-48, 49-51; instr. biol. sci. U. Alaska, summer 1951, asst. prof. biol. sci., 1951-54, assoc. prof. zoology, 1954-59, prof. zoology, 1959—, head dept. biol. scis., 1957-66; dean U. Alaska (Coll. Biol. Scis. and Renewable Resources), 1961-72, curator terrestrial vertebrate mus. collections, 1972-90, curator ornithology collection, 1990—, adminstrv. asso. for acad. programs, grad. and undergrad., dir. acad. advising, office of chancellor, 1973-80; project dir. U. Alaska ecol. investigation for AEC Project Chariot, 1959-63; ornithol. investigations NW Alaska pipeline, 1976-81, Susitna Hydroelectric Project, 1980-83. Author book, monographs; contbr. articles to profl. jours. Fellow AAAS, Am. Ornithologists' Union (v.p. 1977, pres.-elect 1990-92, pres. 1992—), Arctic Inst. N.Am.; mem. Wilson, Cooper ornith. socs., Soc. for Northwestern Vertebrate Biology, Pacific Seabird Group, Assn. Field Ornithologists, Sigma Xi (pres. U. Alaska 1957), Phi Kappa Phi, Sigma Delta Epsilon. Home: PO Box 80211 Fairbanks AK 99708-0211 Office: Am Ornithologists Union US Nat Museum of Nat History Washington DC 20560

KESSEL, HARLAN ROBERT, publisher, investor; b. St. Paul, Minn., Feb. 15, 1928; s. Robert Lyle and Lily Marie (Anderson) K.; m. Esther Ann Partanen, Feb. 6, 1950; children: Joanna Libby Curtis, Lori Alene Torrano. BA, U. Calif., Berkeley, 1954. Owner H.R. Kessel Painting Co., San Francisco, 1949-58; mgr. libr. div. G.P. Putnam's Sons, N.Y.C., 1958-61; mktg. dir. Collier Macmillan Co., N.Y.C., 1961-63, U. Calif. Press, Berkeley, 1963-85; dir. East Bay Regional Park Dist., Oakland, Calif., 1975-92; v.p.

Western Heritage of Calif., Berkeley, 1981—. President MGO Dem. Club, Oakland, 1972-74. With USN, 1946-48. pres. Alameda County Historical Soc., 1993—. Mem. Calif. Native Plant Soc. (v.p. Berkeley chpt. 1980-87), Citizens for Urban Wilderness Areas (bd. dirs. 1984—), Lake Merritt Breakfast Club (editor Oakland chpt. 1990—), Book Club of Calif. (editor-in-chief San Francisco chpt. 1990—).

KESSELHAUT, ARTHUR MELVYN, financial consultant; b. Newark, May 18, 1935; s. Harry and Rela (Wolk) K.; m. Nancy Slater, June 17, 1956; children—Stuart Lee, Amy Beth. B.S. in Bus. Adminstrn, Syracuse (N.Y.) U., 1958; postgrad., NYU. With Coopers & Lybrand, N.Y.C., 1958-64; treas., chief fin. officer and sr. v.p. Anchor Group, Elizabeth, N.J., 1964-79; treas., sr. v.p. also Anchor Capital Fund, Anchor Daily Income Fund, Inc., Anchor Growth Fund, Inc., Anchor Income Fund, Inc., Anchor Spectrum Fund, Inc., Fundamental Investors, Inc., Westminster Fund, Washington Nat. Fund, Inc., Anchor Pension Mgmt. Co.; sr. v.p. corp. devel. USLIFE Corp., N.Y.C., 1979-82, exec. v.p.; chief operating officer, 1982-86; pres., chief exec. officer, dir. USLIFE Equity Sales Corp, 1985-86; exec. v.p. Pacific Mut. Life Ins. Co., Newport Beach, Calif., 1986-92; chmn., CEO, bd. dirs. Pacific Equities Network, Calif.; bd. dirs. Mut. Svc. Corp., United Planners Group, So. Calif. Entrepreneurship Acad. Commr., Dana Point, Calif. With U.S. Army. Home: 34300 Lantern Bay Dr Villa 69 Dana Point CA 92629

KESSLER, A. D., business, financial, investment and real estate advisor, consultant, educator, lecturer, author, broadcaster, producer; b. N.Y.C., May 1, 1923; s. Morris William and Belle Miriam (Pastor) K.; m. Ruth Schwartz, Nov. 20, 1944 (div. 1974); children: Brian Lloyd, Judd Stuart, Earl Vaughn; m. Jaclyn Jeanne Sprague. Student U. Newark, 1940-41, Rutgers U., 1941-42, 46, Albright Coll., 1942, Newark Coll. Engring., 1946; MBA, Kensington U., 1976, PhD in Mgmt. and Behavioral Psychology, 1977. Sr. cert. rev. appraiser; cert. bus. counselor; cert. exchangor; registered mortgage underwriter; registered investment advisor. Pvt. practice real estate, ins. and bus. brokerage, N.J., Pa., Fla., N.Y., Nev., Calif., Hong Kong, 1946—; pres. Armor Corp. , 1947-68; pres. Folding Carton Corp., Am., N.Y.C., 1958-68; exec. v.p. Henry Schindall Assocs., N.Y.C., 1966-67; tax rep. Calif. State Bd. Equalization, 1968-69; aviation cons. transp. div. Calif., Dept. Aeros., also pub. info. officer; 1969-71; FAA Gen. Aviation Safety Counselor; broker, mgr. La Costa (Calif.) Sales Corp., 1971-75; chmn. bd. Profl. Ednl. Found., 1975—, Timeshare Resorts Internat., 1975—, Interex, Leucadia, Calif., 1975-82, The Kessler Orgn., Rancho Santa Fe, Calif., 1975—, The Kessler Fin. Group, Fin. Ind. Inst., 1977—; pres. Ednl. Video Inst., 1978—, Fin. Planning Inst., 1975—, Rancho Santa Fe Real Estate & Land, Inc., 1975—; treas., exec. bd. dirs. Nat. Challenge Com. on Disability, 1983—; dir. Practice Mgmt. Cons. Abacus Data Systems, 1984—; broker mgr. Rancho Sante Fe Acreage & Homes, Inc., 1987-89; mktg. dir. Commercial Real Estate Services, Rancho Santa Fe, 1987—; cons. broker Glenct. Properties Ptnrs., 1989-90; dir. U.S. Advisors, 1989—; pub., editor in chief Creative Real Estate Mag., 1975—; pub. Creative Real Estate Mag. of Australia and New Zealand; founder, editor Moderator of Tape of the Month Club; founder, producer, chmn. Internat. Real Estate Expo; chmn. bd. The Brain Trust, Rancho Santa Fe, Calif., 1977—; fin. lectr. for Internat. Cruise Ships, Cunard Line, Norwegian Am. Cruises, P&O, Princess, others; lectr. life enrichment and stress mgmt. Internat. Cruise Ships; Calif. adj. faculty, prof. fin. Clayton U., St. Louis; developer, operator Barnegat Baywood Seaplane Base, Barnegat Bay, N.J.; owner, operator Skyline Airport, Hunterdon County, N.J. Scoutmaster Orange Mountain coun. Boy Scouts Am., 1955-62; harbor master N.J. Marine Patrol, 1958-67; dep. sheriff, Essex County, N.J., 1951-65; mem. pres.' adv. bd. Seton Hall U., 1961-64; chmn. Stop Smoking, 1990, Quick Study, 1990; feature broadcaster/producer Kalaidascope Radio Mag., Am. Radio Network, 1990—. Served with USAF, 1942-45. Decorated D.F.C., Air medal, Purple Heart; named to French Legion of Honor, Order of Lafayette; named a flying col, a.d.c., Gov. of Ga., 1957. Mem. Am. Soc. Editors and Pubs., Author's Guild, Internat. Platform Assn., Nat. Speakers Assn., Nat. Press Photographers Assn., Guild Assn. Airport Execs., Aviation and Space Writers Assn., Nat. Assn. of Real Estate Editors, Internat. Exchangors Assn. (founder), Air Force Assn. (dep. comdr. N.J. chpt. 1955-57). Clubs: Nat. Press, Overseas Press, La Costa Country, Cuyamaca, Rancho Santa Fe Country, Passport. Lodges: Masons, Shriners. Author: A Fortune At Your Feet, 1981, How You Can Get Rich, Stay Rich and Enjoy Being Rich, 1981, Financial Independence, 1987, The Profit, 1987; author, instr. Your Key to Success seminar, 1988; editor: The Real Estate News Observer, 1975—; fin. editor API, 1978—; fin. columnist Money Matters, 1986—; syndicated columnist, radio and tv host of "Money Making Ideas," 1977—; songwriter: Only You, 1939, If I'm Not Home For Christmas, 1940, Franny, 1940, Flajaloppa, 1940, They've Nothing More Dear Only They've Got It Here, 1941, The Summer of Life, 1956; producer (movies) The Flight of the Cobra, Rena, We Have Your Daughters, Music Row; speaker for radio and TV as The Real Estate Answerman, 1975—;show) Ask Mr. Money. Inventor swivel seat, siptop, inflatumbrella. Home: Box 1144 Rancho Santa Fe CA 92067-1144

KESSLER, LAUREN JEANNE, educator, writer; b. N.Y.C., Apr. 4, 1950; d. Sidney and Margarita (Falk) K.; m. Thomas Arthur Hager, July 7, 1984; children: Jackson, Zane. BJ, Northwestern U., 1971; MS, U. Oreg., 1975; Phd, U. Wash., Seattle, 1980. Govt. reporter Burlingame (Calif.) Villager, 1972-73; asst. prof. Linfield Coll., McMinnville, Oreg., 1975-79; freelance mag. writer, 1978—; asst. prof. Sch. of Journalism U. Oreg., Eugene, 1980-84, assoc. prof. Sch. of Journalism, 1984-91, prof. Sch. of Journalism, 1991—. Author: The Dissident Press, 1984, When Worlds Collide, 1984, 88, 92, Mastering the Message, 1989, Aging Well, 1990, After All These Yrs., 1990, The Search, 1991, Stubborn Twig, 1993; contbr. articles to profl. jours. Mem. Journalism History (editorial bd.), Oreg. Hist. Soc. (adv. bd.), Media History Inst. (founder). Office: U Oreg Sch of Journalism Eugene OR 97405

KESSLER, LYNN ELIZABETH, state legislator; b. Seattle, Feb. 26, 1941; d. John Mathew and Kathryn (Berry) Eisen; m. Keith L. Kessler, Dec. 24, 1980; children: William John Moore, Christopher Scott Moore, Bradley Jerome Moore, Jamie. Attended, Seattle U., 1958-59. Mem. Wash. Ho. of Reps., 1993—, mem. higher edn., energy and utilities, fin. instns. and ins. coms. Exec. dir. United Way Grays Harbor, 1984-92; mem. adv. coun. Head Start, 1986-89, Cervical Cancer Awareness Task Force, 1990-91, vocat. adv. coun. Hoquiam High Sch., 1991—, strategic planning com. Grays Harbor Community Hosp., 1991-92, Grays Harbor Food Bank Com., 1991-92, Grays Harbor Dem. Ctrl. Com.; vice-chair Grays Harbor County Shorelines Mgmt. Bd., 1988-90; chair Disability Awareness Com., 1988-90, Youth 2000 Com., 1990-91; pres. Teenage Pregnancy, Parenting and Prevention Adv. Coun., 1989-91; v.p. Grays Harbor Econ. Devel. Coun., 1990-92; trustee Grays Harbor Coll., 1991—, Aberdeen YMCA, 1991—. Mem. Aberdeen Rotary (pres. 1993—). Home: 62 Kessler Lane Hoquiam WA 98550 Office: Wash State Legislature John L O'Brien Bldg Rm 439 Olympia WA 98504

KESSLER, MELODY SHERYL, infosystems professional; b. Flushing, N.Y., Aug. 17, 1968; d. Melvin Lewis and Susan Penny (Linke) K. BSBA, U. Ariz., 1990. Infosystems engring. analyst Motorola, Inc., Tempe, Ariz., 1990—. Mem. Tempe Sister City Orgn., 1985—, chair Oktoberfest Parade (opening ceremonies, 1992; alumni advisor Sigma Delta Tau, 1992—. Mem. Am. Prodn. and Inventory Control Soc. Home: 631 E Manhatton Dr Tempe AZ 85282

KESSLER, PETER BERNARD, computer scientist, researcher; b. N.Y.C., Apr. 5, 1952; s. Richard Howard and Marian Judith (Singer) K.; m. Monica Elaine McHenney, Dec. 27, 1984; children: Jacob Mitchell, Samuel Morris, Ryan Michael. BS, Yale Coll., 1973; MS, U. Calif., Berkeley, 1980, PhD, 1984. Mem. rsch. staff Xerox Palo Alto (Calif.) Rsch. Ctr., 1985-90; staff engr. Sun Microsystems Labs., Inc., Mountain View, Calif., 1990—. Reviewer various confs. and jours.; contbr. articles to profl. jours. Judge paper airplanes Palo Alto Jr. Mus., 1990-92. Mem. Assn. for Computing Machinery, Computer Profls. for Social Responsibility. Office: Sun Microsystems Labs Inc 2550 Garcia Ave MTV 29-112 Mountain View CA 94043-1100

KESSLER, ROBERT ALLEN, data processing executive; b. N.Y.C., Feb. 2, 1940; s. Henry and Caroline Catherine (Axinger) K.; m. Marie Therese Anton, Mar. 17, 1967; children: Susanne, Mark. BA in Math., CUNY, 1961; postgrad., UCLA, 1963-64. EDP analyst Boeing Aircraft, Seattle, 1961-62; computer specialist System Devel. Corp., Santa Monica, Calif., 1962-66; mem. tech. staff Computer Scis. Corp., El Segundo, Calif., 1966-67, sr. mem. tech. staff, 1971-72, computer scientist, 1974-81; systems mgr. Xerox Data Systems, L.A., 1967-71; prin. scientist Digital Resources, Algiers, Algeria, 1972-74; sr. systems cons. Atlantic Richfield, L.A., 1981—. Mem. Big. Bros. L.A., 1962-66; precinct cpat. Goldwater for Pres., Santa Monica, 1964; mem. L.A. Conservacy, 1987. Mem. Assn. Computing Machinery. Home: 6138 W 75th Pl Los Angeles CA 90045-1634 Office: ARCO 515 S Flower St Los Angeles CA 90071-2200

KESSLER, WALTER ARNOLD, food products executive; b. San Jose, Calif., Aug. 24, 1953; s. W. Arnold and Elizabeth (Waspi) K. AA, San Joaquin Delta Coll., 1973; BS, Fresno State Coll., 1973. Ptnr. Bay Meadow Farms, Galt, Calif., 1986—; bd. dirs., pres., 1980-81. Bd. dirs., pres. Barnyard Olympics, Galt, 1980—, Galt Community Coun., 1984—, chmn. 1985-86. Recipient Am. Farmer award Future Farmers Am., 1973, YOung Guernsey Breeder award Am. Guernsey Assn., 1989; named Outstanding Guernsey Young Breeder Calif., 1984. Mem. Am. Guerney Assn. (bd. dirs.-at-large 1985), Calif. Guernsey Cattle Club (bd. dirs. 1983—, pres. 1981—), Western Guenrsey Sires (pres. 1988—, rep.), Western United Dairymen, Calif. Tax Reduction Movement, Calif. Assn. Family Farmers.

KESTEN, PHILIP REED, physicist; b. N.Y.C., June 24, 1956; s. Seymour Ronald and Rose Edith (Posner) K.; m. Kathleen O'Shea, June 22, 1986; 1 child, Samuel O'Shea. BS in Physics, MIT, 1978; MS in Physics, U. Mich., 1980, PhD in Physics, 1985. Postdoctoral fellow Brandeis U., Waltham, Mass., 1985-88, lectr. physics, 1989-90; asst. prof. physics Santa Clara (Calif.) U., 1990—; cons. Pyramid Tech. Cons., Inc., Waltham, 1985-86. Contbr. articles to profl. jours. Mem. Am. Phys. Soc., Nat. Coun. on Undergrad. Rsch., Sigma Xi, Sigma Pi Sigma. Office: Santa Clara U Physics Dept Santa Clara CA 95053

KESTER, DALE EMMERT, pomologist, educator; b. Audubon, Iowa, July 28, 1922; s. Raymond and Fannie (Ditzenberger) K.; m. Daphne Dougherty; children: William Raymond, Nancy Inman. BS in Horticulture, Iowa State Coll., 1947; MS in Horticulture, U. Calif., Davis, 1949, PhD in Plant Physiology, 1951. Rsch. asst. dept pomology U. Calif., Davis, 1947-51, lectr., jr. pomologist, 1951-53, asst. prof., asst. pomologist, 1953-60, assoc. prof., assoc. pomologist, 1960-69, prof., pomologist, 1969-91, prof. emeritus, 1991—; vis. scholar dept. genetics U. Wis., Madison, 1962-63, Volcanic Rsch. Inst., Bet Dagan, Israel, 1975. Author: (with H. Hartmann) Plant Propagation: Principles and Practices, 1959, 5th revised edit., 1990; contbr. numerous articles to profl. and popular publs. 1st lt. USAF, 1943-45, ETO. Fellow Am. Soc. Hort. Sci. (Stark award 1980); mem. Internat. Plant Propagators Soc. (sec. 1961), Phytopath. Soc., Alpha Zeta, Gamma Sigma Delta, Phi Beta Kappa, Pi Alpha Xi. Republican. Presbyn. Home: 750 Anderson Rd Davis CA 95616-3511 Office: U Calif Dept Pomology Davis CA 95616

KESTER, JAMES RAYMOND, sales executive; b. Garden City, Kans., Apr. 21, 1941; s. Luther Raymond and Ruth (Dunn) K. m. Barbara Maglaras, May 12, 1979; children: Janice, Marcia. AA, Kemper Mil. Sch., 1961; BS, Ft. Hays U., 1964, MS, 1967. Tchr. Hugoton (Kans.) Grade Sch., 1964-66; sales/nat. acct. Cities Service Oil, Tulsa, 1967-69, planning analyst, 1971-72; mfr. rep. Stryker Corp., Kalamazoo, 1972-74; midwest region mgr. McGhan Medical-3M, Santa Barbara, Calif., 1974-79; nat. ophthalmology and otology specialist & trainer MgGhan Med.-3M, Santa Barbara, Calif., 1978-79; mfr. rep Med. Optics Cntr., Irvine, Calif., 1979-81; Midwest region mgr. Am./Allergan Med. Optics, Irvine, 1981-86; dir internat. bus. devel. Allergan Med. Optics, Irvine, 1986-88, dir. sales ops. and worldwide tng., 1988-91, dir. of sales, 1991-92, worldwide key acct. mgr., 1993—; cons. Itanen and Assocs., Irvine, 1986-88; speaker 23 internat. surg. seminars in Africa, Europe and Asia, 1986—. Mem. activity com. South Fla. coun. Boy Scouts Am., 1969, scoutmaster Hugoton, 1964-66; mem. Rep. Senatorial Inner Circle. Named Grad. Asst. Ft. Hays St. U. 1966-67. Mem. Jaycees, Internat. Platform Assn. Office: Allergan Med Optics 9701 Jeronimo Rd Irvine CA 92718-2076

KETCHAM, HENRY KING, cartoonist; b. Seattle, Mar. 14, 1920; s. Weaver Vinson and Virginia Emma (King) K.; m. Alice Louise Mahar, June 13, 1942 (dec.); 1 son, Dennis L.; m. Jo Anne Stevens, July 1, 1959 (div.); m. Rolande Praeprost, June 9, 1970; children: Dania King, Scott Henry. Student, U. Wash., 1938. Represented by Internat. Mgmt. Group Inc., Cleve. Animator, Walter Lantz Prodns., Universal Studios, Hollywood, Calif., 1938-39, Walt Disney Prodns., 1939-41, free lance cartoonist, 1946-51; creator: Dennis the Menace, 1950 (distributed by N.Am. Syndicate); also creator Half Hitch, 1971-75. Donor Hank Ketcham Collection, Boston U. Libraries. Author: Dennis the Menace cartoon book collections, 1954—, I Wanna Go Home, 1965, Well, God, I Goofed Again, 1975, Someone's in the Kitchen with Dennis, 1978 (autobiography) The Merchant of Dennis, 1990, (anthology) His First 40 Years, 1991; illustrator Dennis the Menace, Prayers and Graces, 1993; author 1/2 hour animation spl. for TV: Mayday for Mother; designer: Dennis The Menace Playground, Monterey, Calif. Trustee Community Hosp. of Monterey Peninsula. Served as chief photographer specialist USNR, 1941-45; creative work Navy War Bond, Tng. Film Program 1942-45. Recipient Billy de Beck Award for outstanding cartoonist of yr., 1952, Silver T-Sq. award Nat. Cartoonist Soc., 1978; nominated Outstanding Comic Book Humor Cartoonist Yr., 1974. Mem. Nat. Cartoonists Soc., Phi Delta Theta. Clubs: Golf Club de Geneva; Old Baldy (Saratoga, Wyo.); Cypress Point Golf (Pebble Beach); Royal and Ancient Golf (St. Andrews, Scotland); Old Capital (bd. govs.) (Monterey, Calif.). Address: 512 Pierce St Monterey CA 93940

KETCHERSID, WAYNE LESTER, JR., medical technologist; b. Seattle, Oct. 16, 1946; s. Wayne Lester and Hazel May (Greene) K.; m. Wilette LaVerne Mautz, Oct. 6, 1972; 1 son, William Les. BS in Biology, Pacific Luth. U., 1976, BS in Med. Tech., 1978; MS in Adminstrn., Cen. Mich. U., 1990. Cert. med. technologist; cert. clin. lab. dir. Nat. Cert. Agy. for Med. Lab. Pers. Staff technologist Tacoma Gen. Hosp., 1978-79, chemistry supr., 1979-81, head chemistry, 1981-83; head chemistry Multicare Med. Ctr., 1984-86, mgr., 1986—. Mem. Nat. Rep. Com.; bd. trustees Polit. Action Com., 1991—. Served with U.S. Army, 1966-68. William E. Slaughter Found. scholar, 1975-76. Mem. Am. Assn. Clin. Chemistry, Am. Hosp. Assn., Am. Soc. Med. Tech. (cert., chmn. region IX adminstrn. 1984—, nat. del. 1984—, vice chmn. govt. affairs com. 1991-92, chmn. 1992—, nominee Mem. of Yr. 1992), Wash. State Soc. Med. Tech. (chmn. biochemistry sect. 1983-86, dist. pres. 1986—, cert. merit 1983, 84, 86, 88, pres. 1988-89, 89-90, mem. of the yr., 1990, chmn. govt. affairs com. 1991-92, chmn. 1992—), Am. Coll. Health Care Execs., Am. Soc. Clin. Pathologists (med. technologist), N.W. Med. lab. Symposium (chmn. 1986-88, 90, 92). Lutheran. Contbr. articles to profl. jours. Office: Multicare Med Ctr 315 S K St Tacoma WA 98405-4234

KETCHUM, MILO SMITH, civil engineer; b. Denver, Mar. 8, 1910; s. Milo Smith and Esther (Beatty) K.; m. Gretchen Allenbach, Feb. 28, 1944 (dec. Dec. 21, 1990); children: David Milo, Marcia Anne, Matthew Phillip. B.S., U. Ill., 1931, M.S., 1932; D.Sc. (hon.), U. Colo., 1976. Asst. prof. Case Sch. Applied Sci., Cleve., 1937-44; engr. F.G. Browne, Marion, Ohio, 1944-45; owner, operator Milo S. Ketchum, Cons. Engrs., Denver, 1945-52; partner, prin. Ketchum, Konkel, Barrett, Nickel & Austin, Cons. Engrs. and predecessor firm, Denver, 1952—; prof. civil engring. U. Conn., Storrs, 1967-78; emeritus U. Conn., 1978—; mem. Progressive Architecture Design Awards Jury, 1958, Am. Inst. Steel Constrn. Design Awards Jury, 1975, James F. Lincoln Arc Welding Found. Design Awards Jury, 1977; Stanton Walker lectr. U. Md., 1966. Author: Handbook of Standard Structural Details for Buildings, 1956; editor-in-chief Structural Engineering Practice, 1981-84; contbr. engring. articles to tech. mags. and jours. Recipient Disting. Alumnus award U. Ill., 1979. Mem. Am. Concrete Inst. (hon., bd. dirs., Turner medal 1966), ASCE (hon., pres. Colo. sect.), Am. Cons. Engrs. Coun., Nat. Acad. Engring., Am. Engring. Edn., Internat. Assn. Shell and Space Structures, Structural Engrs. Assn. Colo. (pres.), Cons. Engrs. Coun. Colo. (pres.), Sigma Xi, Tau Beta Pi, Chi Epsilon, Phi Kappa Phi, Alpha Delta Phi.

KETCHUM, ROBERT GEORGE, college administrator; b. Spokane, Wash., Feb. 21, 1951; s. Robert Harris and Mary Catherine (Bach) K.; m. Heather Dawn Matheson, Feb. 17, 1985; 1 child, Tiernan Robert. BA, Ea. Wash. U., 1973, MEd, 1976; PhD in Edn., Wash. State U., 1985; postgrad., Maharishi European Rsch. U., 1976-77. Indsl. arts tchr. Sandy (Oreg.) Elem. Schs., 1973-75; instr. indsl. tech. dept. Ea. Wash. U., Cheney, 1977-78; dir. Spokane office Am. Fedn. for Sci. of Creative Intelligence, 1978-80; instr. tech. tng. program Maharishi Internat. U., Fairfield, Iowa, 1980-81, dir. tech. tng. program, 1981-82, dir. tech. tng. programs, asst. prof. tech. tng., 1985-90; dir. workforce tng. and community edn. North Idaho Coll., Coeur d'Alene, 1990—. Mem. ASCD, ASTD, Am. Vocat. Assn., Epsilon Pi Tau, Phi Delta Kappa. Home: 1376 Circle Dr Hayden ID 83835-9503 Office: North Idaho Coll 1000 W Garden Ave Coeur D Alene ID 83814-2161

KETTEMBOROUGH, CLIFFORD RUSSELL, computer scientist, consultant; b. Pitesti, Arges, Romania, June 8, 1953; came to U.S., 1983; s. Petre and Constanta (Dascalu) I. MS in Math., U. Bucharest, Romania, 1976; MS in Computer Sci., West Coast U., L.A., 1985; MS in Mgmt. Info. System, West Coast U., Los Angeles, 1986; PhD in Computer and Info. Sci., Pacific Western U., 1988; MBA, U. LaVerne, 1992. Lic. mathematician. Mathematician, programmer Nat. Dept. Chemistry, Bucharest, 1976-80; sr. programmer, analyst Nat. Dept. Metallurgy, Bucharest, 1980-82; sr. software engr. Xerox Corp., El Segundo, Calif., 1983-88; computer and info. scientist Jet Propulsion Lab. NASA, Pasadena, Calif., 1988-89; sr. engr. Rockwell Internat., Canoga Park, Calif., 1989-91, cons., 1991-93; mgr. micro devel. Transam. Corpp., L.A., 1993—. Contbr. articles to profl. jours. Sec. Romanian Nat. Body Bldg. Com., Bucharest, 1980-82; pres., chmn. Bucharest Mcpl. Body Bldg. Com., 1978-82. Served to lt. Romanian Army, 1978. Mem. IEEE, No. Assn. Am., Assn. Computing Machinery. Republican. Home: 6004 N Walnut Grove Ave San Gabriel CA 91775-2530

KETTER, DAVID E., lawyer; b. Ft. Benning, Ga., Jan. 1, 1945; s. Victor Eugene and Ruth Maxine (Ratekin) K. BA, Augustana Coll., Rock Island, Ill., 1967; MA, U. Ill., 1968; JD, Georgetown U., 1975. Bar: Iowa 1975, Ill. 1975, U.S. Dist. Ct. (so. dist.) Ill. 1975, U.S. Ct. Appeals (7th cir.) 1975, Wash. 1977, U.S. Dist. Ct. (we. dist.) Wash. 1978, U.S. Tax Ct. 1978, U.S. Ct. Appeals (9th cir.) 1978. Assoc. Klockau, McCarthy, Lousberg, Ellison & Rinden, Rock Island, 1975-77, Law Offices of W.V. Clodfelter, Seattle, 1977-78; pvt. practice Seattle, 1979-83; ptnr. Simburg, Ketter, Sheppard & Purdy, Seattle, 1984—; pres. Harper Farms, Inc., Seattle, 1979—. Trustee Fulghum Found., Seattle, 1990—; trustee New City Theatre, Seattle, 1978-93; pres. Sidney Fund, Seattle, 1979—. Mem. ABA, Ill. Bar Assn., Wash. Bar Assn., Seattle/King County Bar Assn., Omicron Delta Kappa. Office: Simburg Ketter Sheppard & Purdy 999 3rd Ave Ste 2525 Seattle WA 98104-4089

KETTERING, JAMES DAVID, microbiologist; b. Pekin, Ill., Mar. 27, 1942; s. Floyd Ransum and Elizabeth (McLyea) K.; m. Betty Jane Stevens, June 9, 1963; children: Brian Dean, Pamela Sue, David Eric. BA, Andrews U., 1964; MS, Loma Linda U., 1968, PhD, 1974. Microbiologist Indsl. Bio-Test Corp., Northbrook, Ill., 1964-66; instr. Loma Linda (Calif.) U., 1968-74, asst. prof., 1974-80, assoc. prof., 1980-89, prof. microbiolgy, 1989—; postdoctoral fellow Calif. Dept. Health, Berkeley, 1975-77; cons. Loma Linda U. Med. Ctr., 1984—. Author textbooks; contbr. articles to med. jours. Mem. Am. Soc. Microbiology, Am. Soc. Virology, Infectious Diseases Soc., Am. Assn. Dental Schs., Am. Assn. Dental Rsch., Sigma Xi, Omicron Kappa Epsilon. Republican. Seventh-day Adventist. Home: 11980 Canary Ct Grand Terrace CA 92324-5317 Office: Loma Linda Univ Dept Microbiology Loma Linda CA 92350

KETTERMAN, GREG SCOTT, mechanical engineer, consultant; b. Plentywood, Mont., Mar. 6, 1959; s. Leo Duane and Twila Noreen (Johnsboen) K. BSME, Calif. Poly. U., 1983. Evaluation engr. Honeywell, Gardena, Calif., 1983-84; design engr. TRW, Redondo Beach, Calif., 1984-87; engring. cons. Long Beach, Calif., 1987—; design engr. Stars and Stripes Design Team, San Diego, 1988. Patentee in field. Home and Office: 3215 Hackett Ave Long Beach CA 90808

KEYES, SAUNDRA ELISE, newspaper editor; b. Salt Lake City, June 28, 1945; d. Vernon Harrison and Mildred (Wilkins) K.; m. William J. Ivey, June 13, 1969 (div. 1976). BA, U. Utah, 1966; MA, Ind. U., 1969, PhD, 1976. Tchr. Salt Lake City Pub. Schs., 1966-67; asst. prof. Fisk U., Nashville, 1971-76; reporter, city editor The Tennessean, Nashville, 1976-83; staff writer The Courier-Jour., Louisville, 1983-84; dep. mng. editor Orlando (Fla.) Sentinel, 1985-88; mng. editor Phila. Daily News, 1988-90; exec. editor, sr. v.p. Press-Telegram, Long Beach, Calif., 1991-93; mng. editor The Miami Herald, 1993—. Ford Found. fellow, 1978. Mem. Am. Soc. Newspaper Editors.

KEYS, DONALD FRASER, educational organization administrator; b. L.A., June 9, 1924; s. Gilbert Schurman and Margaret (Snell) K.; m. Betty Jane Pedersen, Aug. 29, 1950 (div. 1966); children: Fraser Thuesen, Christopher Webster. Student, Pasadena Jr. Coll., 1939-42, U. So. Calif., 1950. Engr., announcer Sta. KWSD, Mt. Shasta, Calif., 1948-53; communiations technician U.S. Forest Svc., Santa Barbara, Calif., 1953-55; field rep. Calif. United World Federalists, L.A., 1955-56; UN observer Lucis Trust, N.Y.C., 1957; exec. dir. Nat. Com. For a Sane Nuclear Policy, N.Y.C., 1958-67, Internat. League for Human Rights, N.Y.C., 1968-69; UN rep. World Assn. World Federalists, N.Y.C., 1969-82; pres., exec. dir., founder Planetary Citizens, N.Y.C., 1974-84, Mt. Shasta, 1984—; cons., writer UN Delegations, 1969-86; bd. dirs. Alcyone Light Ctr., Hilt, Calif., 1986-90, The Baconian Found., Ashland, Oreg., 1987-90, Josephine Taylor Found., Mt. Shasta, 1990-91. Author: (books) Earth at Omega: The Passage to Planetization, 1982; co-editor Disarmament: The Human Factor, 1981. Sgt. USAF, 1943-45. Office: Planetary Citizens PO Box 1045 Mount Shasta CA 96067

KEYSER, RICHARD LEE, hospital executive; b. Gary, Ind., Nov. 4, 1941; s. Edward Arnold and Mildred Lee (Hernly) K.; m. Joan Carolyn Whitson, Apr. 2, 1967; children: Brian Lester, Lauren Elizabeth. B in Acctg., U. Ill, 1963, M in Acctg., 1964. Mgr. Arthur Andersen & Co., San Francisco, 1965-71; health svcs. coord. Sisters of Mercy, Burlingame, Calif., 1971-76; v.p. ops. Health Care Devel., Newport Beach, Calif., 1976-77; sr. v.p. Amherst Assocs., Walnut Creek, Calif., 1977-83; pres. Mercy Hosp. and Med. Ctr., San Diego, 1983—; bd. dirs. Community Care Network, San Diego, 1984-88. Mem. budget panel United Bay Area Crusade, San Francisco, 1972-73. Mem. Am. Coll. Hosp. Adminstrs., Am. Hosp. Assn., Calif. Hosp. Assn., Calif. Assn. Hosps. and Health Systems (bd. dirs. 1987-89), Calif. Assn. Cath. Hosps. (bd. dirs. 1984—), Hosp. Coun. San Diego/Imperial Counties (trustee 1985-89), Rotary. Republican. Presbyterian. Office: Mercy Hosp & Med Ctr 4077 5th Ave San Diego CA 92103-2180

KEYSTON, STEPHANI ANN, small business owner; b. Baytown, Tex., Aug. 6, 1955; d. Herbert Howard and Janice Faye (Stowe) Cruickshank; m. George Keyston III, Oct. 8, 1983; children: Jeremy George, Kristopher Samuel. AA with honors, Merced Coll., Merced, Calif., 1975; BA in Journalism with distinction, San Jose State U., 1976. Reporter, Fresno (Calif.) Bee, 1974-75; reporter, photographer Merced (Calif.) Sun-Star, 1974-77; pub. info. officer Fresno City Coll. (Calif.), 1977-80; dir. communications Aerojet Tactical Systems Co., Sacramento, 1980-83; co-owner, v.p. Keyco Landscape Contractor Inc., Auburn, Calif., 1984—. Co.-coordinator Aerojet United Way Campaign, 1981; Aerojet Tactical Systems Co. coordinator West Coast Nat. Derby Rallies, 1981-83. Mem. Internat. Assn. Bus. Communicators (dir. Sacramento chpt. 1983), Citrus Heights C. of C. (v.p. 1983). Republican. Home: 13399 Lakeview Pl Auburn CA 95602 Office: Keyco Landscape Contractor Inc 6216 Main Ave Ste B-2 Orangevale CA 95662

KHACHATOURIANS, GEORGE GHARADAGHI, microbiology educator; b. Nov. 21, 1940; s. Sumbat and Mariam (Ghazarian) K.; m. Lorraine M. McGrath, Oct. 14, 1974; 1 child, Ariane K. BA, Calif. State U., San Francisco, 1966, MA, 1969; PhD, U. B.C., Vancouver, 1971. Postdoctoral fellow Biol. Div. Oak Ridge (Tenn.) Nat. Lab., 1971-73; rsch. assoc. U. Mass. Med. Sch., Worcester, 1973-74; asst. prof. microbiology dept. U. Saskatchewan, Sask., Can., 1974-77, assoc. prof., 1977-80, prof., 1980-81, prof. applied microbiology and food sci., 1981—; resident prof. U. B.C., Vancouver, 1992; mem. Gov. of Can. Fed. Task Force on Biotech., Ottawa, Ont., Can., 1980-81, Operating Grants Panel, Can. Agr., 1981-84, Biomed. Grants Panel, Sask. Health Rsch., 1988—; bd. dirs. PhilomBios Inc.; pres. Khachatourians Enterprises Inc.; founding dir. BioInsecticide Rsch. Labs., U. Sask, 1982—; vis. prof. U. B.C., Vancouver, 1992. Contbg. author ency. chpts.; co-editor: (book series) Food Biotechnology-Microorganisms, 1993.

Recipient grants Nat. Sci. Engring. Coun., Ottawa, Can., 1974—, Sask. Agr. Rsch. Found., 1981-85, Nat. Rsch. Coun., 1977-88, Agrl. Devel. Found., Regina, Sask., 1985—. Mem. Am. Soc. Microbiology, Can. Soc. Microbiology, Soc. Indsl. Microbiol., Am. Entomol. Soc. Home: 1125 13th St East, Saskatoon, SK Canada S7H 0C1 Office: Applied Microb & Food Sci, U Saskatchewan, Saskatoon, SK Canada S7N 0W0

KHAJAWALL, ALI MOHAMAD, psychiatrist; b. Srinagar, Kashmir, Mar. 28, 1944; s. Gulam Rasool and Sitara (Begum) K.; m. Farida Rajab, Apr. 24, 1979; 1 child, Farhad Ali. FAC, S.P. Coll., Srinagar, 1961; MBBS, Srinagar Med. Coll., 1966. Intern Cook County Hosp., Chgo., 1973-74; resident Mo. Inst. Psychiatry, 1974-78; asst. prof. U. So. Calif., L.A., 1983-84, U. Calif., Irvine, 1984-86; cons. Med. Bd. Calif., Sacramento, 1986-87; cons. surveyor HCFA, Washington, 1987-91; cons. psychiatrist forensic outpatient L.A. County, 1991; cons. reviewer CMRI, San Francisco, 1992; sr. psychiatrist MSH, Norwalk, Calif., 1978—. Mem. Heritage Found., Washington, 1989; spokesman Kashmiri Am. Coun., Washington, 1990; 1st sec. Kashmir Am. Mission; del. Rep. Presdl. Campaign, Washington, 1992. Lt. col. MC, USAR, 1982—. Recipient Congl. award of merit U.S. Rep. Chmn., Washington, 1984—. Mem. AMA, AMSUS, USAA, IMA. Home: 1538 S Sunbluff Dr Diamond Bar CA 91765 Office: Met State Hosp 11400 Norwalk Blvd Norwalk CA 90650

KHALSA, SAT TARA SINGH, information entrepreneur, corporate executive; b. Polson, Mont., Mar. 5, 1953; s. Norman F. and Mary Elsie (Wood) Hefty; m. Sat Tara Kaur, Jan. 5, 1975; children: Shabad Ratan Kaur Khalsa, Sat Santokh Singh Khalsa. BA, U. Chgo., 1975, MA, 1978. Rsch. asst. U. Chgo. (Ill.) Dept. Psychiatry, 1975-78; rsch. assoc. Nat. Coop. Study of Sickle Cell Disease, Chgo., 1979-81; programmer Image Producers, Northbrook, Ill., 1981-82; founder, chief exec. officer Kriya Systems Inc., Chgo., 1982-85; founder, ptnr. Infotel Ptnrs., Chgo., Aspen, 1985-87; pvt. practice personal computer industry cons. Chgo., 1987-88; founder, chief exec. officer Room Svc. Cinema, Hamilton, Mont., 1990—; chmn., CEO InfoNow Corp.; commencement convocation speaker U. Chgo., 1975. Ring leader (computer software) Typing Tutor, 1982, 1985. Dir. Sikh Dharma of Ill., Chgo., 1980—, 3HO Found. of Ill., Chgo., 1980—. Recipient scholarship U. Chgo., 1971-74, fellowship Am. Cancer Soc., 1970, champion first pl. award Ill. Div. Amateur Fencers League of Am., 1972. Mem. Assn. Computing Machinery, IEEE, Social Venture Network, Khalsa Coun. of Sikh Dharma, Reality Club. Sikh. Home: 3897 Promontory Ct Boulder CO 80304

KHALSA, SHAKTI PARWHA KAUR, not for profit foundation executive; b. Mpls., June 19, 1929; d. Jacob Garon and Fay Weinberg. Student, UCLA, 1947-48. Exec. sec., dir. 3HO Found., L.A., 1969—; exec. fin. sec. Sikh Dharma, L.A., 1971—; tchr. yoga, 1969—. Editor: Golden Temple Conscious Cookbook; sr. editor mag. Beads of Truth, 1971—; founder, editor newspaper, Still Keeping Up, 1980—. Minister Sikh Dharma religion, 1975—. Office: 3 HO Foundation PO Box 351149 Los Angeles CA 90035-9549

KHAN, AHMED MOHIUDDIN, financial/insurance executive; b. Hyderabad, Andhra Pradesh, India, Nov. 14, 1955; s. Mohammad Mominuddin and Mehar-Unnisa Begum Hyderabad; m. Marjorie L. Klein-Khan, Mar. 31, 1983; 1 child, Yosuf F. MBA, U. Palm Beach, 1975; doctoral studies, Calif. Coast U. Inventory auditor RGIS, Inc., Chgo., 1975-78; staff acct. Somerset, Inc., Chgo., 1979-84; fin. cons. Provident Mutual Fin. Svc., Inc., Phoenix, 1985-91; regional mgr. fin. svcs. US Life/Old Line Life Ins. Co. of Am., Phoenix, 1992—; pres. Khan and Assocs., Fin./Ins. Svcs., Phoenix, 1993—. Named to Execs. Hall of Fame, 1991. Mem. India Assn., U.S.A., Assn. MBA Execs., Nat. Assn. Life Underwriters, Ariz. Assn. Life Underwriters, Millon Dollar Round Table. Democrat. Islam. Home and Office: 4643 E Grandview Rd Phoenix AZ 85032

KHAN, SARBULAND BILL, inventor, entrepreneur, consultant; b. Zanzibar, E. Africa, Apr. 11, 1951; came to U.S., 1984; s. Gulkhan Yusufzai and Sarfiraz (Abdulhakim) Awan; m. Stella Conner, May 12, 1979 (div. Nov. 1989); 1 child, Zenobia. Cert. telecommunications, Garrettsgreen Tech. Coll., Birmingham, Eng., 1969; cert. advanced level physics, Handsworth Tech. Coll., Birmingham, 1973. Telecommunications technician G.P.O. (name now Brit. Telecom), W. Midlands, Eng., 1968-71; sr. instr., co-owner Aston Martial Arts Centre, Birmingham, 1972-75; exec. dir. Dianetics & Scientology Centre, Birmingham, 1976-82, Am. Sun Solar, Inc., Redondo Beach, Calif., 1984-86; Hubbard adminstrv. tech. instr., supr. Singer Consultants, Beverly Hills, Calif., 1985-86; bus. cons., supr. W.I.S.E. Corp., L.A., 1986-88; pvt. practice rsch., discovery and mktg. L.A., 1987—. Author: How to Invent and Get Rich; patentee disposable diaper, biodegradable plastic, soft drink, tools and accesssories. Dancer Ballroom and Latin Am. Gold Medalist, 1970-71. Mem. Internat. Platform Assn., Planetary Soc., Children Internat., Millionaires Club of Hollywood (founder, chmn.). Home and Office: 1539 N Alexandria Ave Apt 310 Los Angeles CA 90027-5242

KHANNA, HARI NARAYAN, mechanical engineer, industrial engineer; b. Mathura, U.P., India, Aug. 8, 1944; came to U.S., 1968; s. Jagat Narain and Tara Devi (Tandon) K.; m. Manju Lata Kapur, June 9, 1971. BSc in Mech. Engring., Agra (India) U., 1966; M Engring., Roorkee (India) U., 1968. Registered mech. and indsl. engr., Ariz.; cert. mfg. mgmt. engr., energy mgr. Indsl. engr. Marpak Inc., Skokie, Ill., 1969, Allison Steel, Phoenix, 1970-71, Garland Steel, Phoenix, 1971-74, Cudahy Foods, Phoenix, 1974; rsch. analyst Ariz. Dept. Transp., Phoenix, 1974-76, state planner, 1976-79, sr. state planner, 1979-91, transp. engr., 1991—; cons. St. Lukes Hosp., Phoenix, 1969-70, John C. Lincoln Hosp., Phoenix, 1970, Revelon Inc., Phoenix, 1971-72; part time faculty Maricopa Community Coll. Math Learning Ctr., 1993—, South Scottsdale Kumon Learning Ctr., 1993—. Editor Valley Leader newsletter, 1984, 93—; mem. editorial bd. Energy Engr. Jour., 1981-86. Co-founder, pres. Ariz. chpt. Assn. Energy Engrs., Phoenix, 1980, 82-83; co-founder, pres. Tempe Leadership, 1984, 87-88, bd. mem., 1985-91; bd. mem. Valley Leadership, Inc., Phoenix, 1984-90, 92—, Golden Gate Community Ctr. United Way, Phoenix, 1985-90; mem. vol. Valley Big Bros., Phoenix, 1983-84; mem. mgmt. assistance program United Way, 1988-90, coord. com. Valley of the Sun United Way, 1985-87. Recipient Outstanding Svc. award Toastmaster Club, Dist. 3, Ariz., 1978-79, Disting. Svc. award Ariz. chpt. Assn. Energy Engrs., Phoenix, Ariz., 1988. Mem. Am. Arbitration Assn. (arbitration panel), Inst. Indsl. Engrs., Inst. Transp. Engrs., Valley Leadership Alumni Assn. (bd. dirs. 1991-92). Home: 4714 S Kenneth Pl Tempe AZ 85282-7126 Office: Ariz Dept Transp 206 S 17th Ave Phoenix AZ 85007-3213

KHOSLA, VED MITTER, oral and maxillofacial surgeon, educator; b. Nairobi, Kenya, Jan. 13, 1926; s. Jagdish Rai and Tara V. K.; m. Santosh Ved Chabra, Oct. 11, 1952; children: Ashok M., Siddarth M. Student, U. Cambridge, 1945; L.D.S., Edinburgh Dental Hosp. and Sch., 1950, Coll. Dental Surgeons, Sask., Can., 1962. Prof. oral surgery, dir. postdoctoral studies in oral surgery Sch. Dentistry U. Calif., San Francisco, 1968—; chief oral surgery San Francisco Gen. Hosp.; lectr. oral surgery U. of Pacific, VA Hosp.; vis. cons. Fresno County Hosp. Dental Clinic.; Mem. planning com., exec. med. com. San Francisco Gen. Hosp. Contbr. articles to profl. jours. Examiner in photography and gardening Boy Scouts Am., 1971-73, Guatemala Clinic, 1972. Granted personal coat of arms by H.M. Queen Elizabeth II, 1959. Fellow Royal Coll. Surgeons (Edinburgh), Internat. Assn. Oral Surgeons, Internat. Coll. Applied Nutrition, Internat. Coll. Dentists, Royal Soc. Health, AAAS, Am. Coll. Dentists; mem. Brit. Assn. Oral Surgeons, Am. Soc. Oral Surgeons, Am. Dental Soc. Anesthesiology, Am. Acad. Dental Radiology, Omicron Kappa Upsilon. Club: Masons. Home: 1525 Lakeview Dr Burlingame CA 94010-7330 Office: U Calif Sch Dentistry Oral Surgery Div 3D Parnassus Ave San Francisco CA 94117-4342

KIANG, ASSUMPTA (AMY KIANG), brokerage house executive; b. Bejing, Aug. 15, 1939; came to U.S., 1962; d. Pei-yu and Yu-Jean (Liu) Chao; m. Wan-lin Kiang, Aug. 14, 1965; 1 child, Eliot Y. BA, Nat. Taiwan U., 1960; MS, Marywood Coll., Scranton, Pa., 1964; MBA, Calif. State U., Long Beach, 1977. Data programmer IBM World Trade, N.Y.C., 1963; libr. East Cleve. Pub. Libr., 1964-68; lectr. Nat. Taiwan U., Taipei, 1971-73; with reference dept. U.S. Info. Svc., Taipei, 1971-74; v.p. Merrill Lynch, Santa Ana, Calif., 1977—. Founder Pan Pacific Performing Arts Inc., Orange County, Calif., 1987; treas. women league Calif. State. U., Long Beach, 1980-82. Mem. Chineses Bus. Assn. Soc. Calif. (chmn. 1987—, v.p. 1986-87), U.C.I. Chancellor's Club, Old Ranch Country Club. Democrat. Roman Catholic. Office: Merrill Lynch 2670 N Main St Santa Ana CA 92701-1224

KIBBLE, EDWARD BRUCE, insurance-investment advisory company executive; b. Seattle, May 11, 1940; s. Francis Bruce and Doris Kibble; m. Carol Kibble, July 8, 1961; 3 children. BA, U. Wash., 1972. CLU. Agt. Equitable of Iowa, Seattle, 1962-72; co-founder, co-chmn. Kibble & Prentice, Inc., Seattle, 1972—; bd. dirs. Kibble & Prentice/KPI-Western Ins., Seattle, Drug Emporium, Bellevue, Wash. Contbr. articles to profl. jours. Bd. dirs. Jr. Achievement Greater Puget Sound, Seattle Pacific Found. Mem. Assn. for Advanced Life Underwriting (bd. dirs.), Nat. Assn. Life Underwriters (Seattle Life Underwriter of Yr. award), Million Dollar Round Table, Estate Planning Coun. Seattle (exec. com.), Wash. Athletic Club, Columbia Tower Club, Rainier Club, Seattle Yacht Club, Rotary (bd. dirs. Seattle). Republican. Office: 600 Stewart St Ste 1000 Seattle WA 98101-1265

KICE, JOHN LORD, chemistry educator; b. Colorado Springs, Colo., Feb. 18, 1930; s. William Branson and Ruth Creevey (Lord) K.; m. Mary Ellen Bass, June 16, 1953; children: Virginia, Joanne. AB, Harvard U., 1950, PhD, 1954. Sr. chemist Rohm & Haas Co., Phila., 1953-56; asst. prof., then assoc. prof. chemistry U. S.C., Columbia, 1956-60; from assoc. prof. to prof. chemistry Oreg. State U., Corvallis, 1960-70; chmn. dept. chemistry U. Vt., Burlington, 1970-75; chmn. dept. chemistry Tex. Tech U., Lubbock, 1975-82, assoc. v.p. for rsch., 1982-85; chair dept. chemistry U. Denver, 1985-88, dean natural scis., math. and engring., 1988—. Co-author textbook: Modern Principles of Organic Chemistry, 1966, 2d edit., 1974, also papers in field. Fellow Alfred P. Sloan Found., 1957-61, spl. fellow NIH, 1968-69. Fellow Japan Soc. for Promotion of Sci.; mem. Am. Chem. Soc. (chmn. Colo. sect. 1990), Coun. for Chem. Rsch. (governing bd. 1991—). Office: U Denver Faculty Natural Scis Denver CO 80208

KICKBUSH, BILL E., theatrical lighting designer; b. Pasadena, Calif., Oct. 1, 1950; s. Anselm Harold Charles and Virginia Rose (Holdhusen) K.; m. Deborah Joyce Hadley, July 15, 1972 (div. 1979); children: Brandon Wesley, Brian Anthony. BA, San Diego State U., 1973; postgrad., Concordia Theol. Sem., 1974-76. Dancer, instr. San Diego Ballet, 1967-71, Ballet Usiu, San Diego, 1971-74; co. mgr. Springfield (Ill.) Ballet, 1976-81; freelance lighting designer various locations, 1981—; prodn. stage mgr., lighting designer State of Ala. Ballet, Birmingham, 1982-84, Ballet Miss., Jackson, 1984-89; lighting designer Nev. Dance Theatre, Las Vegas, 1989—; bd. dirs. Modern Dance Collective, Jackson, 1988-89. Lutheran. Home: 7957 Lions Rock Way # 202 Las Vegas NV 89128-3832 Office: Nev Dance Theatre 4505 S Maryland Pky Las Vegas NV 89154-0002

KIDD, ALVIN CURTIS, utilities services representative; b. L.A., Oct. 22, 1958; s. Robert Lager (dec.) and Fannie Bruce (Brown) Taite; m. Vanessa Gale Pittman, Dec. 30, 1983 (div. Oct. 1989); children: Deronn Curtis, Karmen Marie. BA in Social Welfare, San Diego State U., 1980; BS in Bus. Mgmt., SUNY, Albany, 1992; MA in Counselor Edn., San Diego State U., 1993. Human svcs. tech. Peachtree/Parkwood Hosp., Atlanta, 1981-83; telemarketing sales rep. MCI Telecommunications Corp., Atlanta, 1982-84; recruitment coord. ARC, Atlanta, 1983-84; meter svcs. rep. San Diego (Calif.) Gas and Electric Co., 1985—; mem. contbn. club San Diego Gas and Electric Co., 1985—, speaker's corp., 1990—, ambassador, 1990—. Bd. dirs. Campfire Coun. San Diego, Jackie Robinson YMCA, Urban League of San Diego, 1993; vol. Sickle Cell Found., San Diego, 1989—, United Negro Coll. Fund Scholarship Telethon, San Diego, 1990—, Lincoln Prep Sch. Mentor Program, San Diego, 1991—; mem. Bonita (Calif.) Ch. of Religious Sci., 1989—. With USNR, 1985—. Recipient letter of appreciation Nat. Naval Officer's Assn., San Diego, 1989; decorated Naval Achievement medal 1990, Meritorious Svc. medal 1993; named Outstanding Young Men of Am., 1989. Mem. Nat. Assn. Black Psychologist (San Diego chpt.), Nat. Naval Officer's Assn. (San Diego chpt.) 1989—. Home: PO Box 16202 San Diego CA 92116 Office: San Diego Gas & Electric Co PO Box 1831 San Diego CA 92112

KIDD, BETTY JEAN, human resources professional; b. Dayton, Ohio, Aug. 27, 1938; d. Gustin McKinley and Bernice (Payley) Riber; m. Donald Hallahan, June 4, 1960 (div. 1975); 1 child, Heather Hallahan Trzeciak; m. William Norman Kidd, Jan. 10, 1980. Exec. sec. Top Value Enterprises, Dayton, Ohio, 1956-75, adminstrv. asst., 1975-77; office mgr. T.V. Travel. Inc., Dayton, Ohio, 1977-81, accounts receivable/credit mgr., 1981-86; sec. to pres. Transco Products Inc., Camarillo, Calif., 1986-90, pers. mgr., 1990—; human resource mgr. Datron/Transco Inc., Simi Valley, Calif. Office: Datron/Transco Inc 200 2 Los Angeles Ave Simi Valley CA 93065

KIDD, LYNDEN LOUISE, medical facility executive; b. Casper, Wyo., May 7, 1959; d. David Thomas and Sally Louise (Noble) K. AA, Stephens Coll., 1979; BA in Polit. Sci., Comm., U. Wyo., 1981, JD, 1986. Adminstrv. dir. Wyo. Med. Ctr., Casper, 1986-92, v.p. med. affairs, 1992—. Mem. Wyo. Heritage Soc., 1987-89, Gov. Coun. Sports, Fitness, Wyo., 1991—; chair, mem. Leadership Casper, 1989-91; bd. dirs., campaign chair United Way, Casper, 1989—; bd. dirs. Casper Classic, Inc., 1989-92. Mem. Am. Coll. Med. Staff Affairs, Nat. Health Lawyers Assn., Wyo. Hosp. Assn., C. of C. (bd. dirs. 1991—), Phi Alpha Delta. Home: 3850 E 14th Unit F Casper WY 82609 Office: Wyo Med Ctr 1233 E 2d Casper WY 82601

KIDD, MELVIN DON, banker; b. Crowell, Tex., Oct. 10, 1937; s. Ewing Wilson and Joan (Solomon) K.; m. Sarrah Dee Whitley, Feb. 1, 1957; children: Vickye L. Kidd Faulk, Joan Renai, Sarah Dion. Student, Angelo State Coll., San Angelo, Tex., 1961-63, SW Grad. Sch. Banking, Dallas, 1972. Br. mgr. Pioneer Fin. Co., San Angelo, 1957-60, Southwestern Investment Co., Amarillo, Tex., 1960-67; v.p. Bank Commerce, Abilene, Tex., 1967-70, Coronado State Bank, El Paso, Tex., 1970-72; pres., chief exec. officer Western Commerce Bank, Carlsbad, N.Mex., 1973—, chmn. bd. dirs.; chmn. bd. dirs.; sr. chmn. bd. Western Bank Las Cruces, N.Mex.; vice chmn., chief exec. officer Western Bank Alamogordo, N.Mex.; pres. Western Bancshares Alamogordo, Inc., Western Commerce Bancshares Carlsbad (N.Mex.) Inc., Western Bancshares Clovis (N.Mex.), Inc., Western Bancshares Las Cruces, Inc.; bd. dirs. Western Bank Clovis; past chmn. Albuquerque dist. adv. coun. SBA. Past pres. Eddy County Sheriff's Posse, Eddy County United Way; past chmn. President's Assn N.Mex. State U., Carlsbad, past pres. bd. regents; mem. N.Mex. State U. Found.; bd. dirs. Carlsbad Dept. Devel., Western States Sch. Banking; chmn. bd. trustees N.Mex. Sch. Banking. With USMCR. Mem. N.Mex. Bankers Assn. (past pres.), Carlsbad C. of C. (past pres.). Republican. Methodist. Home: PO Box 1358 Carlsbad NM 88221-1358 Office: Western Commerce Bank 127 S Canyon St Carlsbad NM 88220-5732

KIDD, MICHAEL DENNIS, contracting company executive; b. Silvercreek, N.Y., July 31, 1951; s. John Patrick and Dee Claudia (Canli) K.; m. Janet Marlene Line, Sept. 1, 1974; children: Eric, Russell. BS in Sociology, Calif. Poly. U., Pomona, 1973. Owner, mgr. Southland Developer Svc., Covina, Calif., 1973-76; supr. Metalclad Insulation Corp., St. Joseph, Ariz., 1976-78; estimator Metalclad Insulation Corp., Fresno, Calif., 1978-85; v.p. Insulation Contracting and Supply Corp., Fresno, 1985—, also bd. dirs.; pres. Profl. Asbestos Removal Corp., Fresno, 1986—, also bd. dirs. Mem. ASHRAE, Nat. Asbestos Coun., Nat. Insulation and Abatement Contractors Assn. (asbestos abatement com. 1987—), Western Insulation Contractors Assn. (asbestos dir. 1990-91). Office: Profl Asbestos Removal Corp 2706 S Railroad Ave Fresno CA 93725

KIDD, REUBEN PROCTOR, management engineer; b. Bedford, Va., Feb. 18, 1913; s. Oscar Kibbler and Estelle (Johnson) K.; B.S., Va. Poly. Inst., 1936; m. Margaret Jerome, June 23, 1952. Pres., Frito Corp. of Roanoke (Va.), 1947-49; indsl. engr. USAF, Sacramento, 1956-73; chmn. bd. USDR, Inc., Sacramento, 1961-69, MEN Internat., Inc., Mpls., 1977—; owner The Kidd Cos., operator Precision Tune-Up, Sacramento, 1974—. Served to capt. U.S. Army, 1942-46, to maj., 1949-51. Decorated Silver Star; registered profl. engr., Calif. Republican. Presbyterian. Home: 5809 Northgrove Way Citrus Heights CA 95610-6522 Office: Precision Tune-Up 6241 Spruce Ave Sacramento CA 95841-2052

KIDDE, ANDREW JUDSON, sales executive, consultant; b. N.Y.C., Nov. 6, 1948; s. Fred Judson and Ellice (Welch) K.; m. Monica Bertell (div. 1981); m. Linda Jean Olsen, Feb. 24, 1983; children: Judson F., Briana P. BA in History, Polic. Sci., Hawthorne Coll., 1971; AA in Hotel Adminstrn., LaSalle U., 1993. Banquet mgr. Sheraton Hotel, Manchester, N.H., 1967-71; asst. dir. sales Hilton Hotel Corp., N.Y.C., 1971-75; regional dir. sales Ramada Inns, Detroit, 1975-77; regional sales mgr. Westin Hotels, Inc., Detroit, 1977-79; pres. Kidde & Assocs., San Diego, 1979-82; nat. sales mgr. Las Vegas (Nev.) Hilton, 1982-85; dir. sales, mktg. Madison Hotels, Washington, 1986-89; sr. nat. sales mgr. Walt Disney Resorts, Anaheim, Calif., 1989—. Recipient Nat. Hotel Sales award Guinness Book, 1985. Mem. Greater Washington D.C. Soc. of Assn. Execs. (assoc.), Am. Soc. Assn. Execs. (assoc.), Profl. Conv. Mgmt. Assn. (assoc.). Republican. Home: 1395 Corte Almeria Oceanside CA 92057

KIDDE, JOHN EDGAR, food company executive; b. Kansas City, Mo., May 4, 1946; s. Gustave E. and Mary Sloan (Orear) K.; m. Donna C. Peterson, Aug. 4, 1973; children: Kari Lauren, Laurie Catherine, Kellie Ann. BA, Stanford U., 1968; MBA, Northwestern U., 1971. Corp. banking officer First Interstate Bank, L.A., 1971-73; v.p. ops. Colony Foods, Inc., Newport Beach, Calif., 1973-78; pres. Western Host Food Svcs., Inc., Newport Beach, 1978-81, Giuliano's Delicatessen & Bakery,Inc., Carson, Calif., 1981-90; pres., chief exec. officer Sona & Hollen Foods, Inc., Los Alamitos, Calif., 1990—, bd. dirs. Mem. adv. bd. Restaurant Institutions mag., 1975-78. Bd. trustees Harbor Day Sch., 1990—; mem. alumni admissions com. Phillips Acad., 1981—. 1st lt. U.S. Army, 1969-70. Mem. Stanford Club Orange County, Stanford Buck Club. Republican. Episcopalian. Home: 3907 Inlet Isle Dr Corona Del Mar CA 92625-1605 Office: Sona & Hollen Foods Inc 3712 Cerritos Ave Los Alamitos CA 90720-2487

KIDDOO, ROBERT JAMES, engineering service company executive; b. Kansas City, Mo., July 8, 1936; s. Robert Leroy and Margaret Ella (Wolford) K.; m. Patricia Anne Wakefield, Apr. 17, 1957; children: Robert Michael, Stacey Margaret Kiddoo-Lee. BSBA, UCLA, 1960; MSBA, Calif. State U., Northridge, 1969; MBA, U. So. Calif., 1972, D of Bus. Adminstrn., 1978. Cert. mgmt. acct. Asst. v.p., nat. div. loan officer Crocker-Citizen's Nat. Bank, L.A., 1958-69; v.p., chief fin. officer, dir. corp. sec. Kirk-Mayer, Inc., L.A., 1969-87; prof. acctg. and MIS Calif. State U., Northridge, 1970—; region adminstr. mgr. CDI Corp.-West, Chatsworth, Calif., 1990; exec. v.p. Kirk-Mayer, Inc., L.A., 1990—. With U.S. Army, 1955-56. Mem. Mensa, Ltd., Beta Gamma Sigma, Beta Alpha Psi.

KIDNEY, GARY WAYNE, college administrator; b. Mt. Ayr, Iowa, Aug. 16, 1953; s. George Ford and Edith Lorene (Hoyt) K.; m. Debra Ann Lauer, Dec. 22, 1979; children: Brandon Alexander, Joshua David. BS in Polit. Sci., Ariz. State U., 1975, BA in Edn., 1976, MA in Edn., 1977. Tchr. Mesa (Ariz.) Pub. Schs., 1976-82; customer svc. rep. Radio Shack/Tandy Corp., Phoenix, 1982-83; ednl. computer specialist Maricopa Community Coll., Phoenix, 1983-85; dir. acad. computing Santa Monica (Calif.) Coll., 1985-92, U. Houston, Clear Lake, Tex., 1991—. Author: Just Enough Basic, 1985. Deacon Van Nuys (Calif.) Ch. of Christ, 1990—. Mem. Calif. Dirs. Acad. Computing (v.p. 1990-91, pres. 1992—). Democrat. Office: Santa Monica Coll 1900 Pico Blvd Santa Monica CA 90405-1628

KIEDA, DAVID BASIL, physics educator; b. Johnson City, N.Y., Mar. 22, 1960; s. Walter Basil and Theresa (Muzek) K.; m. Lisa Dale Goldstein, Aug. 15, 1988. BS in Physics, Mass. Inst. of Tech., 1982; PhD in Physics, U. Pa., 1989. Rsch. asst. U. Pa., Phila., 1983-88; rsch. assoc. Dept. Physics U. Utah, Salt Lake City, 1988-90, asst. prof. Physics, 1990—; cons. Salt Lake Knee & Sports Medicine, Salt Lake City, 1990—; pres. Wildcat Cons. Contbr. articles to profl. jours. NCAA Div III Champion Hammer Thrower, 1982, New Eng. Div. III Champion, 1980-82. Mem. AAAS, Am. Physical Soc. (travel grant 1987), Sigma Xi. Office: U Utah Dept Physics 201 JFB Salt Lake City UT 84112

KIEFER, JOHN ROBERT, environmental engineer, consultant; b. Cleve., Aug. 17, 1951; s. John Michael and Mary Louise (Billings) K.; m. Kathleen Balmes, Aug. 29, 1987; 1 child, Caitlin Joyce. BS, Cornell U., 1973; MS, Stanford U., 1975. Registered profl. engr., Calif. Environ. engr. URS Rsch. Co., San Mateo, Calif., 1973-78; staff engr. Woodward-Clyde Cons., San Francisco, 1978-80; sr. engr. Utah Internat. Inc., San Francisco, 1980-86, mgr. environ. svcs., 1986; cons. engr. Greenbrae, Calif., 1986—; assoc. Forensic Mgmt., San Mateo, 1990—. Contbr. articles to profl. jours. Vol. instr. YMCA, San Francisco, 1980-87. Mem. ASCE, Nat. Groundwater Assn. Home: 290 N Almenar Dr Greenbrae CA 94904

KIEFER, ROBERT JOHN, mechanical engineer; b. Cleve., Dec. 7, 1936; s. Paul Everette and Beulah Elizabeth (Moore) K.; m. Barbara Gayle Niemiec, June 14, 1958 (div. Aug. 1981); children: Kelly Jane, Paul Joseph; m. Aura Ann Knosby, Sept. 4, 1983 (div. Dec. 1989); children: Kimberly Fenske, Kerri Fenske. BSME, MSME, Ohio State U., 1959. Registered profl. engr., mechanical, nuclear, Ohio, Calif. Project officer Air Force Weapons Lab, Albuquerque, N.Mex., 1959-62; mgr., fuel applications engring. Gen. Atomic Co., San Diego, Calif., 1962-76; mgr. tech. tng. Scientific Atlanta, San Diego, 1976-93; staff cons. Air Force Space Div., L.A., 1976-87. Contbr. articles to profl. jours. Lt. col. USAFR, 1959-87. Mem. Soc. Am. Mil. Engrs. (gold medal, 1959), Sigma Xi, Pi Tau Sigma, Tau Beta Pi, Am. Soc. Mechanical Engrs., Inst. Environ. Scis., NSPE. Republican. Baptist. Home: 10215 Saunders Dr San Diego CA 92131-1313

KIEFFER, SUSAN WERNER, geology educator; b. Warren, Pa., Nov. 17, 1942. BS in Physics and Math., Allegheny Coll., 1964; MS in Geol. Scis., Calif. Inst. Tech., 1967, PhD in Planetary Scis., 1971; DSc (hon.), Allegheny Coll., 1987. Postdoctoral research geochemist UCLA, 1971-73, asst. prof. geology, 1973-79; geologist U.S. Geol. Survey, Flagstaff, Ariz., 1979-90; prof. geology Ariz. State U., Tempe, 1988—, Regents prof., 1991-93; prof., head dept. geol. sci. U. B.C., Vancouver, Can., 1993—. Co-editor: (with A. Navrotsky) Microscopic to Macroscopic: Atomic Environments to Mineral Thermodynamics, 1985. Alfred P. Sloan Found. fellow, 1977-79; W.H. Mendenhall lectr., U.S. Geol. Survey, 1980; recipient Disting. Alumnus award Calif. Inst. Tech., 1982, Meritorious Svc. award Dept. Interior, 1986, Spendiarov award Soviet Acad. of Scis., 1990. Fellow Am. Geophys. Union, Am. Acad. Arts and Scis., Mineral. Soc. Am. (award 1980), Geol. Soc. Am. (Day medal 1992), Meteoritical Soc.; mem. NAS. Office: U BC, Dept Geol Sci, 6339 Storres Rd, Vancouver, BC Canada V6T 1Z4

KIEHN, MOGENS HANS, aviation engineer, consultant; b. Copenhagen, July 30, 1918; came to U.S., 1957; s. Hans-Christian and Lydia-Thea (Theillx Burban de Parmer) K.; m. Ase Rasmusen, Apr. 28, 1942; children: Marianne, Hans, Lars. BSME, U. Tech. Engring., Copenhagen, 1941; MS, Copenhagen U., 1942; degree in Army Intelligence, Def. Indsl. Security Inst., 1972. Registered profl. engr., Ariz. Pres. Hamo Engring., Copenhagen, 1939-49, Evanston, Ill., 1958-78; engr. Sundstrand, Rockford, Ill., 1957-58; pres. Kiehn Internat. Engring., Phoenix, 1980—; chmn., pres. ETO Internat. Engring., Phoenix, 1980—; tech. engring. cons. Scandinavian Airlines, Sundstrand Engring., McDonnell Douglas, Ford, GM, Chrysler, Honeywell, Motorola, Gen. Electric, Hughes Aircraft; chmn. bd. Internat. Tech. Engring. Recipient 32 patents including rehab. hosp. lighting for highmast, drafting machine, tooling machinery, parts for aircraft, garbage and pollution machine, optical coupler, also others. With Finnish Army, 1939, Danish Underground, 1940-45, Morocco French Fgn. Legion, 1948-53, Vietnam. Mem. AIII, NSPE, Soc. Illuminating Engrs., Nat. Geog. Soc., Am. Fedn. Police, East Africa Wildlife Soc., Internat. Intelligence and Organized Crime Orgn., Adventures Club Denmarkk, Honors Club Internat. Office: Internat Tech Engring PO Box 1561 Scottsdale AZ 85252

KIEHNE, ANNA MARIE, financial systems analyst; b. Preston, Minn., Dec. 15, 1947; d. Alvin H. and Anna Mae (Goldsmith) K.; m. Lyman Loveland, June 15, 1991. BBA, Winona (Minn.) State U., 1969; M in Internat. Bus., West Coast U., 1992. Adminstrv. acct. ECA/Intercomp, Denver, 1981-82; staff acct. Plaza Mortgage, L.A., 1982-83; systems analyst Home Savs. of Am., L.A., 1983-87; assoc. systems analyst Cray Rsch., Inc., Mpls., 1988-89; v.p. Bowest Corp., La Jolla, Calif., 1989-90; cons., 1990—. Mem. Sister City Internat. Commn., Richfield, Minn., 1989. Mem. Nat. Assn. Accts., Am. Mgmt. Assn. Democrat. Lutheran. Home: 1148 Grape St San Marcos CA 92069-3178

KIELAROWSKI, HENRY EDWARD, marketing executive; b. Pitts., Dec. 29, 1946; s. Henry Andrew Kielarowski and Evelyn Marie Kline Boileau; m. Lynda Blair Powell, Aug. 1971 (div. 1976); children: Amorette, Blair. BA, Duquesne U., Pitts., 1969; MA, Duquesne U., 1974, PhD, 1974. Pres. Communicators, Inc., Pitts., 1974-76; mktg. specialist McGraw-Hill, Inc., N.Y.C., 1976-81; mktg. dir. Fidelity S.A., Allison Park, Pa., 1981-86; exec. v.p. ARC Systems, Inc., Pitts., 1986-88; v.p. product devel. First Deposit Corp., San Francisco, 1988—. Author: Microcomputer Consulting in the CPA Environment, 1987; contbr. articles to profl. jours. Mem. Am. Mktg. Assn. (mktg. excellence award 1988), Direct Mktg. Assn. Democrat. Home: 107 Lyon St San Francisco CA 94117-2112

KIELHORN, RICHARD WERNER, chemist; b. Berlin, Germany, June 17, 1931; s. Richard H. and Auguste (Lammek) K.; m. Anneliese Heinrich, Aug. 9, 1952; children: Anita, Margit. BS, Chem. Tech. Sch., Berlin, 1953. Lab. tech. Zoellner Werke, Berlin, 1950-57, Montrose Chem. Corp., Henderson, Nev., 1957-78; chief chemist Stauffer Chem. Corp., Henderson, 1978-88, Pioneer Chlor Alkali Co., Henderson, 1988-92; tax cons. H&R Block, Las Vegas, Nev., 1972—, instr, 1978—. Mem. ASTM, Am. Chem. Soc., Am. Soc. Quality Control, Am. Water Works Assn., Nat. Soc. Tax Profls. Home: 1047 Westminster Ave Las Vegas NV 89119-1825 Office: Exec Tax Svc 3170 W Sahara Ave Las Vegas NV 89102

KIELSMEIER, CATHERINE JANE, school system administrator; b. San Jose, Calif; d. Frank Delos and Catherine Doris (Sellar) MacGowan; M.S., U. So. Calif., 1964, Ph.D., 1971; m. Milton Kielsmeier; children—Catherine Louise, Barry Delos. Tchr. pub. schs. Maricopa, Calif.; sch. psychologist Campbell (Calif.) Union Sch Dist., 1961-66; asst. prof. edn. and psychology Western Oreg. State Coll., Monmouth, 1966-67, 70; asst. research prof. Oreg. System Higher Edn., Monmouth, 1967-70; dir. spl. services Pub. Schs., Santa Rosa, Calif., 1972-91; cons., 1991—. Mem. Sonoma County Council Community Services, 1976-91, bd. dirs. 1976-82, Sonoma County Orgn. for Retarded/Becoming Independent, 1978-91, bd. dirs. 1978-82. Mem. Council for Exceptional Children, Laubach Literacy Internat., Commonwealth of Calif. Office: 7495 Poplar Dr Forestville CA 95436-9672

KIEMELE, LAURIE ANN, educator; b. Reedsburg, Wis.; d. LeRoy and Joanne Gay (Heckman) K. BA in Edn., Pacific Luth. U., 1986. Cert. tchr., Wash. Tchr. Sumner (Wash.) Sch. Dist., 1988-89; tchr. intermediate sch. Univ. Pl. Sch. Dist., Tacoma, Wash., 1989—; coach Narrows View Drill Team, Tacoma, 1991-92. Supt. Sunday sch. Olympic View Bapt. Ch., Tacoma, 1991-92. Republican. Office: Narrows View Intermediate Sch 7813 44th St W Tacoma WA 98466

KIENHOLZ, LYN SHEARER, arts projects coordinator; b. Chgo.; d. Mitchell W. and Lucille M. (Hock) Shearer; student Sullins Coll., Md. Coll. Women. Assoc. producer Kurt Simon Prodns., Beverly Hills, Calif., 1963-65; owner, mgr. Vuokko Boutique, Beverly Hills, 1969-75; bd. dirs. L.A. Inst. Contemporary Art, 1976-79, Fellows of Contemporary Art, 1977-79, Internat. Network for Arts, 1979-89, L.A. Contemporary Exhbns., 1980-82; exec. sec., bd. dirs. Beaubourg Found. (now George Pompidou Art and Culture Found.), 1977-81; visual arts adv. Performing Arts Coun., L.A. Music Ctr., 1980-89; bd. govs. Calif. Inst. Tech. Baxter Art Gallery, 1980-85; adv. bd. dirs. Fine Arts Communications, pub. Images & Issues mag., 1981-85; founder, chmn. bd. Calif./Internat. Arts Found., 1981—; bd. dirs., western chmn. ArtTable 1983-89; bd. dirs. Galef Inst., 1992—; exec. bd. Sovereign Fund, 1981-93; exec. bd. dirs. Scandinavia Today, 1982-83, Art L.A., 1987, 88, 89; mem. adv. bd. Otis/Parsons Sch. Design, 1983-85, U. So. Calif. dept. fine arts, 1983-85; bd. dirs. UK/LA Festival of Britain, 1986-88, 92—; hon. bd. dirs. L'Ensemble des Deux Mondes, Paris, 1986-91; mem. Comité Internat. pour les Museés d'Art Moderne, 1985—, bd. dirs., 1991—; Bd. dirs. Arts, Inc., 1987-89. Co-host radio program ARTS/L.A., 1987-91; contbg. editor Calif. mag., 1984-89. Address: 2737 Outpost Dr Los Angeles CA 90068

KIER, RAYMOND EDWARD, motel and restaurant owner; b. Denver, Jan. 21, 1942; s. Edward L. Kier and Georgine E. (Traber) Bond. BA, Oberlin Coll., 1963; MBA, NYU, 1965; profl. acctg. program, Northwestern U., Chgo., 1970. CPA, Calif., Ariz., Utah. Vol. Peace Corps, Santiago, Chile, 1966-68; acct. Arthur Young & Co., San Francisco, 1969-73; contr. Kaiser Aetna, Oakland, Calif., 1973-76; gen. mgr. Tomahawk Trucking, Vernal, Utah, 1976-81; account exec. Waddell & Reed, Kansas City, Mo., 1981-84; exec. v.p. Vernal Area C. of C., 1984-92, sec. Found., 1990-92, bd. dirs., 1982-84; owner Sage Motel and Restaurant, Vernal. Sec.-treas. Dinosaur Roundup Rodeo Assn., Vernal, 1985-92; mem. Unitah County Econ. Devel. Bd., Vernal, 1986-89. Fellow NYU Grad. Sch. Bus., 1964-65; recipient Outstanding Pub. Svc. award Vernal Area, 1992. Mem. Rotary (pres. Vernal 1978-79), Dinaland Country Club (sec. 1984-86). Home: 393 S 400 W Vernal UT 84078-3011 Office: Sage Motel and Restaurant 54 W Main Vernal UT 84078

KIERSCH, GEORGE ALFRED, geological consultant, emeritus educator; b. Lodi, Calif., Apr. 15, 1918; s. Adolph Theodore and Viola Elizabeth (Bahmeier) K.; m. Jane J. Keith, Nov. 29, 1942; children—Dana Elizabeth Kiersch Haycock, Mary Annan, George Keith, Nancy McCandless Kiersch Bohnett. Student, Modesto Jr. Coll., 1936-37; B.S. in Geol. Engring., Colo. Sch. Mines, 1942; Ph.D. in Geology, U. Ariz., 1947. Geologist 79 Mining Co., Ariz., 1946-47; geologist underground explosion tests and Folsom Dam-Reservoir Project U.S. C.E., Calif., 1948-50; supervising geologist Internat. Boundary and Water Commn., U.S.-Mex., 1950-51; asst. prof. geology, asst. prof., dir. mineral survey U. Ariz., Tucson, 1951-55, dir. Mineral Resources Survey Navajo-Hopi Indian Reservation, 1952-55; exploration mgr. resources survey So. Pacific Co., San Francisco, 1955-60; assoc. prof. geol. sci. Cornell U., Ithaca, N.Y., 1960-63, prof., 1963-78, prof. emeritus, 1978—, chmn. dept. geol. scis., 1965-71; geol. cons., Ithaca, 1960-78, Tucson, 1978—; chmn. coordinating com. on environment and natural hazards, Internat. Lithosphere Program, 1986-1991. Author: Engineering Geology, 1955, Mineral Resources of Navajo-Hopi Indian Reservations, 3 vols., 1955, Geothermal Steam-A World Wide Assessment, 1964; author: (with others) Advanced Dam Engineering, 1988; editor/author: Heritage of Engineering Geology--First Hundred Years 1888-1988 (vol. of Geol. Soc. Am.), 1991; editor: Case Histories in Engineering Geology, 4 vols., 1963-69; mem. editorial bd. Engring. Geology/Amsterdam. Mem. adv. council to bd. trustees Colo. Sch. Mines, 1962-71; mem. nine coms. NAE/NAS, 1966-88; reporter coordinating com. 1 CC1 Nat. Hazards U.S. GeoDynamics Com., 1985-90. Capt. C.E., U.S. Army, 1942-45. Recipient award for best articles Indsl. Mktg. Mag., 1964; NSF sr. postdoctoral fellow Tech. U. Vienna, 1963-64. Fellow ASCE, Geol. Soc. Am. (chmn. div. engring. geology 1960-61, mem. U.S. nat. com. on rock mechanics 1980-86, Disting. Practice award 1986, Burwell award 1992); mem. Soc. Econ. Geologists, U.S. Com. on Large Dams, Internat. Soc. Rock Mechanics, Internat. Assn. Engring. Geologists (U.S. com. 1980-86, chmn. com. 1983-87, v.p. N.Am. 1986-90), Assn. Engring. Geologists (1st recipient Claire P. Holdredge award 1965, hon. mem. 1985). Republican. Episcopalian. Clubs: Cornell (N.Y.C.); Statler, Tower (Ithaca); Mining of Southwest (Tucson). Home and Office: 4750 N Camino Luz Tucson AZ 85718-5819

KIERSTINE, JULIE ANNETTE, opera singer; b. San Francisco, Apr. 13, 1960; d. Larry Wesley and Wilmette Anne (Rachac) K. BA in Music, U. Calif. San Diego, La Jolla, 1984; M. Music in Vocal Performance, New Eng. Conservatory of Music, 1986. Mem. Phyllis Curtin seminar Tanglewood Music Festival, Lenox, Mass., 1984; Am. Lyric Theatre artist Lake George Opera Festival, Glens Falls, N.Y., 1987, 88; guest artist Grand Teton Music Festival, Jackson Hole, Wyo., 1991; artist-in-residence Opera San José (Calif.), 1992-93; guest artist Colo. Symphony, Denver, 1992, Cleve. Chamber Symphony, 1993. Vol. Dem. Nat. Com., San Mateo, Calif. Named nat. finalist Met. Opera Auditions, N.Y.C., 1989, study grantee Met. Opera, 1989, 91, 92. Office: Thea Dispeker Artists Rep 59 E 54th St New York NY 10022

KIEST, ALAN SCOTT, social services administrator; b. Portland, Oreg., May 14, 1949; s. Roger M. and Ellen K.; 1 child, Jennifer S. BA in Polit. Sci., U. Puget Sound, Tacoma, 1970; MPA, U. Wash., 1979. Welfare eligibility examiner Wash. Dept. Social and Health Services, Seattle, 1970-72, caseworker, 1972-76, service delivery coordinator, 1976-82; community svcs. office adminstr. Wash. Dept. Social and Health Svcs., Seattle, 1982—; planning commr. City of Lake Forest Park, 1989, mem. city coun., 1990, chair city fin. com., 1992; mem. King County Managed Health Care Oversight Com., 1993—. Mem. Suburban Cities Assn. (mem. transp. planning subcom. 1990—). Home: 18810 26th Ave NE Seattle WA 98155-4146 Office: Wash Dept Social and Health Svcs 11536 Lake City Way NE Seattle WA 98125-5395

KIESWETTER, JAMES KAY, history educator; b. Dodge City, Kans., Mar. 8, 1942; s. Orville James and Ruth Margaret (Bredahl) K. BM, U. Colo., 1963, MA, 1965, PhD, 1968. Asst. prof. history Eastern Wash. U., Cheney, 1968-71, assoc. prof., 1971-76, prof., 1976—. Author: Metternich's Intervention Policy, 1970, Political Career of Etienne-Denis Pasquier, 1977; contbr. articles to profl. publs. Bd. dirs. Spokane Humane Soc., 1986—, Spokane Rose Soc., 1983-86. Recipient Faculty Achievement award Burlington No. Found., 1986. Mem. Am. Hist. Assn., Soc. French Hist. Studies, Western Soc. French History. Office: Eastern Wash U Dept History MS #27 Cheney WA 99004

KIKUCHI, RYOICHI, physics educator; b. Osaka, Japan, Dec. 25, 1919; came to U.S., 1950; m. Toshiko Sono; children: John M., Ann K. Snyder. BS, Tokyo U., 1942, PhD, 1951. Research assoc. MIT, Cambridge, 1951-53; asst. prof. U. Chgo., 1953-55; research physicist Armour Research Found., Chgo., 1955-56; assoc. prof. Wayne State U., Detroit, 1956-58; sr. scientist Hughes Research Labs., Malibu, Calif., 1958-85; research prof. U. Wash., Seattle, 1985-89; adj. prof. UCLA, 1975-86, 89—; vis. prof. Purdue U., West Lafayette, Ind., 1977-93, Tohoku U., Sendai, Japan, 1982, Technische Hugeschool, Delft, The Netherlands, 1980, 81. Contbr. articles to profl. jours. Recipient A. Von Humboldt Sr. U.S. Scientist award, Bonn, Fed. Republic of Germany, 1985. Mem. Am. Phys. Soc. Office: UCLA Dept Materials Sci & Engring 5732 Boelter Hall Los Angeles CA 90024

KILBURN, KAYE HATCH, medical educator; b. Logan, Utah, Sept. 20, 1931; d. H. Parley and Winona (Hatch) K.; m. Gerrie Griffin, June 7, 1954; children: Ann Louise, Scott Kaye, Jean Marie. BS, U. Utah, 1951, MD, 1954. Diplomate Am. Bd. Internal Medicine, Am. Bd. Preventive Medicine. Asst. prof. Med. Sch. Washington U., St. Louis, 1960-62; assoc. prof., chief of medicine Durham (N.C.) VA Hosp., 1962-69; prof., dir. environ. medicine Duke Med. Ctr., Durham, 1969-73; prof. U. Mo., Columbia, 1973-77; prof. Mt. Sinai Sch. of Medicine CUNY, 1977-80; Ralph Edgington prof. U. So. Calif. Sch. Medicine, L.A., 1980—; v.p. Neurotest Inc., 1988—; pres. Workers Disease Detection Svcs. Inc. Editor-in-chief Archives of Environ. Health, 1986—; editor Jour. Physicology, 1970—, Environ. Rsch., 1975—, Am. Jour. Indsl. Medicine, 1980—; contbr. over 180 articles to profl. jours. Capt. M.C., U.S. Army, 1958-60. Home: 3250 Mesaloa Ln Pasadena CA 91107-1129 Office: U So Calif Sch Medicine 2025 Zonal Ave Los Angeles CA 90033-4526

KILCREASE, DAVID PARKER, physicist, computer analyst; b. Jacksonville, Fla., Aug. 7, 1952; s. Cecil Calvert and Mary Lou (Brown) K.; m. Patricia Ann Flaherty, June 15, 1980. BS in Chemistry, U. Fla., 1978, PhD in Physics, 1991. Chemist Inst. for Food and Agrl. Sci., Gainesville, Fla., 1976-82; computer analyst, project mgr. Stenis Space Ctr.-Naval Oceanographic Office, Miss., 1991-92; rschr. Los Alamos (N.Mex.) Nat. Lab., 1992—. Contbr. articles to profl. jours. Fellow British Interplanetary Soc.; mem. Am. Phys. Soc. Office: Los Alamos Nat Lab B212 Los Alamos NM 87545

KILE, RAYMOND LAWRENCE, aerospace project manager, consultant; b. Tucson, Oct. 3, 1946; s. Roddy Lloyd and Polly Ann (Vardalakes) K.; m. Sharon Kate Durham, June 5, 1969; 1 child, Kasey Sheridan. BSEE, U.S. Air Force Acad., 1969; MSEE, U. Mo., 1972. Commd. 2d lt. USAF, 1969, advanced through grades to capt., 1986, engr., 1969-78; software developer Westinghouse Hanford, Richland, Wash., 1978-79; communications mgr. Wash. Pub. Power Supply System, Richland, 1980-82; dir. projects Contel Info. Systems, Denver, 1982-86; cost estimation tech. mgr. Hughes Aircraft Co., Aurora, Colo., 1986—; software cons. USAFR Contract Mgmt. Div., 1978-90, USAF/SC, 1991—, pvt. practice, 1988—; guest lectr. USAF Software Devel. Courses, 1987—, Chapman Coll., Colo. Springs, Colo., 1988; FAA flight instr.; owner RKK Engring. and Svc., 1992—; guest lectr. U. Colo., 1992—. Author: (software) REVIC (cost estimating program), 1986, 87, 88, 89, 90, 91. Lt. col. USAFR, 1981—. Mem. Res. Officers Assn. (life), Assn. Grads. USAF Acad., Air Force Assn., Airplane Owners and Pilots Assn., NRA (life). Republican. Home: 1539 E Nichols Cir Littleton CO 80122-2940 Office: Hughes Aircraft Co 16800 E Centretech Pky Aurora CO 80011-9046

KILEY, ALLAN JAMES, dentist; b. Portland, Oreg., Sept. 23, 1946; s. Allan Jack and Mary Alice (Kastel) K.; m. Diane Louise Henry, Aug. 16, 1969; children: AnnMarie, Kathleen Theresa. Student, U. San Francisco, 1964-67; DMD, U. Oreg. Dental Sch., 1971. Dentist, capt. U.S. Army, Aberdeen Proving Ground, Md., 1971-73; owner, dentist Jim Kiley, DMD, PC, Hillsboro, Oreg., 1973—. Mem., officer Active 20-30 Club, Hillsboro, 1973-88; mem., pres. Washington County Dental Aid for Children, Washington County, Oreg., 1974-82, 84-91. Named Dentist of Yr., Washington County Dental Aid for Children, 1989. Mem. Am. Dental Assn., Acad. Gen. Dentistry. Roman Catholic. Office: Jim Kiley DMD PC 730-C SE Oak St Hillsboro OR 97123

KILEY, ROBERT RALPH, political consultant; b. Honolulu, Apr. 21, 1948; s. Kenneth John and Dorothy Irene (Ambrozich) K.; m. Debra Nelson, 1975 (div. 1984); 1 child, Kristin Leigh; m. Barbara Lynn Weber, Mar. 16, 1985; 1 child, Tiryn Marie. AA, Fullerton Coll., 1971; BA, U. So. Calif., 1975. Specifications coord. Hughes Aircraft, Fullerton, Calif., 1967-70; adminstrv. aide Hon. Robert H. Finch for Senate, Fullerton, 1975-76; field supr. Rep. Nat. Com., Washington, 1976; exec. dir. Rep. Party Orange County, Orange, Calif., 1976-80; pres., cons. Robert Kiley & Assocs., Yorba Linda, Calif., 1980—; lead advanceman Pres. and Mrs. Ronald Reagan, Washington, 1984-88; v.p. Am. Campaign Schs., Yorba Linda, 1989—. Bd. dirs. Bd. Psychology, Sacramento, 1984—; chmn. legis. com., Sacramento, 1986—. Named one of Outstanding Young Men Am., 1977; recipient Cert. Appreciation Anaheim Lions Club, 1987, Calif.-Nev. Lions Internat., 1988. Mem. U. So. Calif. Alumni Assn. (life). Office: 5028 Vista Montana Yorba Linda CA 92686-4508

KILEY, THOMAS, rehabilitation counselor; b. Mpls., Aug. 18, 1937; s. Gerald Sidney and Veronica (Kennedy) K.; m. Jane Virginia Butler, Aug. 25, 1989; children: Martin, Truman, Tami, Brian. BA in English, UCLA, 1959; MS in Rehab. Counseling, San Francisco State U., 1989. Cert. rehab counselor, nat. and Hawaii. Former rsch. profl., businessman various S.E. Asian and Hawaiian cos.; sr. social worker Episcopal Sanctuary, San Francisco, 1986-88; dir. social svcs. Hamilton Family Ctr., San Francisco, 1988-89; rehab. specialist Intracorp, Honolulu, 1989-91; pres., prin. rehab. counselor Heritage Counselling Svc., Honolulu, 1991—. Mem. ACA, Nat. Assn. Rehab. Profls. in Pvt. Sector, Am. Rehab. Counselors Assn. (profl.), Nat. Rehab. Assn., Rehab. Assn. Hawaii, Phi Delta Kappa. Office: Heritage Counselling Svcs PO Box 3098 Mililani HI 96789-0098

KILGORE, JOE EVERETT, JR., army officer; b. Chattanooga, Dec. 11, 1954; s. Joe Everett and Jewell Yvonne (Nunley) K.; m. Mary Nijhuis, Aug. 21, 1982. BA in Biology, U. Tenn., Chattanooga, 1976; MS in Systems Mgmt., U. So. Calif., 1980; MA in Internat. Rels., Salve Regina Coll., Newport, R.I., 1990; MS in Nat. Security, U.S. Naval War Coll., Newport, 1990. Cert. diving officer and civilian diving instr. Commd. 2d lt. U.S. Army, 1976, advanced through grades to lt. col., 1987; platoon leader 101st Airborne Div., Ft. Campbell, Ky., 1976-79; detachment comdr. 1st bn. 7th Spl. Forces Group, Ft. Bragg, N.C., 1980-83, co. comdr. hdqs., 1983-84; plans and ops. officer U.S. Army Western Command, Ft. Shafter, Hawaii, 1985-89; comdr. A Co., 2d bn. 1st Spl. Forces Group, Ft. Lewis, Wash., 1990-91, exec. officer 2d bn., 1991—; exec. officer 1st Spl. Forces Group, 1992; inspector gen. USSOCOM, 1993; dir. tng. Down Under Divers, Waipahe, Hawaii, 1985-89; instr. scuba diving Aquidneck Island Divers, Salve Regina Coll., 1989-90. Contbr. articles to mil. publs. Advisor Explorer Post 5101, Boy Scouts Am., Chattanooga, 1972-76; dir. Explorer Olympics, U. Tenn., 1975; instr. oxygen first aid Divers Alert Network, Chapel Hill, N.C., 1991; speaker jr. ROTC program, Oahu, Hawaii, 1985-89. Mem. Nat. Assn. Underwater Instrs. (life, instr.), Spl. Forces Assn. (life, membership com. 1991-92), Assn. U.S. Army, Res. Officers Assn., Am. Legon, N.Am. Fishing Club (life charter), BNat. Rifle Assn. (life), Beta Beta Beta. Methodist. Home: 930 Symphony Isles Blvd Apollo Beach FL 33572 Office: USSOCOM ATTN SOIG Mac Dill AFB FL 33601

KILKENNY, JOHN F., federal judge, lawyer; b. Heppner, Oreg., Oct. 26, 1901; s. John Sheridan and Rose Ann (Curran) K.; m. Virginia Brannock, Oct. 14, 1931; children: John Michael, Karen Margaret. LLB, U. Notre Dame, 1925; LLD (hon.), U. Portland, Oreg., 1976. Bar: Oreg. 1926, U.S. Dist. Ct. Oreg. 1927, U.S. Ct. Appeals (9th cir.), 1933, U.S. Supreme Ct. 1954. Assoc. Raley, Kilkenny & Raley and predecessor firm Raley, Raley & Steiwer, Pendleton, Oreg., 1926-31, ptnr., 1931-52; ptnr. Kilkenny, Fabre & Kottkamp, Pendleton, 1952-59; judge U.S. Dist. Ct. Oreg., Portland, 1959-69, U.S. Ct. Appeals (9th cir.), Portland, 1969—; pres., dir. Happy Canyon Co., Pendleton, 1939-40; mem. Oreg. Bd. Bar Examiners, 1951-52. Author: Shamrocks and Shepherds: The Irish of Morrow County, 1969. V.p. Irish-Am. Hist. Soc., 1942-57; charter mem. Oreg. Hist. Soc., 1975—; trustee U. Portland, Oreg. State Libr., Umatilla County Libr. Recipient Outstanding Citizen award U. Portland, 1967, Disting. Citizen award, 1972, Cert. of Commendation Am. Assn. State and Local History, 1973, Heritage award Oreg. Hist. Soc., 1975, Medal of honor DAR, 1976, Disting. Alumnus award U. Notre Dame and Notre Dame Law Sch., 1985; named hon. lifetime dir. Hist. Soc. U.S. Dist. Ct. Oreg., 1983; John F. Kilkenny U.S. P.O. and Courthouse, Pendleton renamed in his honor, 1984. Fellow Am. Coll. Trial LAwyers, Am. Bar Found.; mem. ABA, Am. Jusicature Soc., Oreg. State Bar Assn. (pres. 1943-44, Award of Merit 1981), Notre Dame Law Assn. (bd. dirs. 1952-72), University Club, Knights of Malta, Elks (life). Republican. Roman Catholic. Home: 821 SW Davenport St Portland OR 97201-2219 Office: US Ct Appeals 212 Pioneer Courthouse 555 SW Yamhill St Portland OR 97204-1336

KILKENNY, TIMOTHY RHODES, nutritionist; b. Walnut Creek, Calif., Aug. 3, 1957; s. Paul Edward and Eunice Anne (Crapuchettes) K. AA, Diablo Valley Coll., 1978; BS, Donsbach U., 1981. Various positions Pleasant Hill, 1974-76; bulk food dept. mgr. The Grist Mill, Pleasant Hill, 1976-77; various positions Calif., 1977-82; bulk food dept. mgr. Harvest House, Inc., Concord, Calif., 1982-87; asst. produce dept. mgr. Good Nature Grocery, Walnut Creek, Calif., 1987-91; mem., participant Organic Retail Assn., San Francisco, 1988-91; retail seminar organizer Calif. Cert. Organic Farmers, Santa Cruz, Calif., 1991, mktg. com. mem., 1988-91; produce dept. mgr. Elmwood Natural Foods, Berkeley, Calif., 1991; produce dept. tem mem. Whole Foods Market, Berkeley, Calif., 1992—. Patentee in field; author Haiku poetry books. Mem., participant Green Party of Contra Costa County, Lafayette, Calif., 1991-92; supporting mem. Mount Diablo Peace Ctr., Walnut Creek, 1984-92. Roman Catholic. Home: 817 Slater Ave Pleasant Hill CA 94523

KILLIAN, ALLAN JOSEPH, electrical engineer consultant; b. Pasadena, Calif., Aug. 2, 1946; s. Joseph Oschenschlager and Jeanellen (O'Connor) K.; m. Jahanna DeLano Edgell, 1968 (div. 1980); children: Kendra, Katreena; m. Diana E. Schmidt, 1987; children: Jennifer, Jessica. BS in Physics, Harvey Mudd Coll., 1968; PhD, MS in Elec. Engring., U. Nev., 1968-73. Founder, tech. advisor IMSAI Mfg. Corp., San Leandro, Calif., 1974-79; founder, v.p. engring, v.p. mfg. MicroPro Internat. Corp., San Rafael, Calif., 1979-87; cons. engr. Fit-heuristix, Nicasio, Calif., 1987-90; founder, pres. Killian Assocs., Nicasio, Calif., 1990—; tech. advisor Fut-heuristix, Nicasio, Calif., 1987-92. Co-inventor: Multi-processor, 1977; designer IMSAI-8080 microcomputer, 1976. Mem. Profl. and tech. Cons. Assn., Spare Internat. Home and Office: 45 Via Del Sol Nicasio CA 94946-9707

KILLIAN, GEORGE ERNEST, association executive; b. Valley Stream, N.Y., Apr. 6, 1924; s. George and Reina (Moeller) K.; m. Janice E. Bachert, May 26, 1951 (dec.); children: Susan E., Sandra J.; m. Marilyn R. Killian, Sept. 1, 1984. BS in Edn., Ohio No. U., 1949; EdM, U. Buffalo, 1954; PhD in Phys. Scis., Ohio Northern U., 1989. Tchr.-coach Wharton (Ohio) High Sch., 1949-51; insp. USN, Buffalo, 1951-54; dir. athletics Erie County (N.Y.) Tech. Inst., Buffalo, 1954-69; asst. prof. health, phys. edn., recreation Erie County (N.Y.) Tech. Inst., 1954-60, asso. prof., 1960-62, prof., 1962-69; exec. dir. Nat. Jr. Coll. Athletic Assn., Colorado Springs, Colo., 1969—. Editor: Juco Rev., 1960—. Served with AUS, 1943-45. Recipient Bd. Trustees award Hudson Valley C. of C., 1969, Erie County Tech. Inst., 1969, Service award Ohio No. U. Alumni, 1972, Service award Lysle Rishel Post, Am. Legion, 1982; named to Ohio No. U. Hall of Fame, 1979. Mem. U.S. Olympic Com. (dir.), Am. Legion, Internat. Basketball Fedn. (pres. 1990—), Phi Delta Kappa, Delta Sigma Phi. Clubs: Masons, Rotary. Home: 325 Rangely Dr Colorado Springs CO 80921-2655 Office: Nat Jr Coll Athletic Assn PO Box 7305 Colorado Springs CO 80933

KILLIAN, RICHARD M., library director; b. Buffalo, Jan. 13, 1942; m. Nancy Killian; children from previous marriage: Tessa, Lee Ann. BA, SUNY, Buffalo, 1964; MA, Western Mich. U., 1965; grad. advanced mgmt. library adminstrn., Miami U., Oxford, Ohio, 1981; grad. library adminstrn. devel. program, U. Md., 1985. Various positions Buffalo and Erie County Pub. Libraries, 1963-74, asst. dep. dir., personnel officer, 1979-80; dir. Town of Tonawanda (N.Y.) Pub. Library, 1974-78; asst. city librarian, dir. pub. svcs. Denver Pub. Library, 1978-79; exec. dir. Nioga Library System, Buffalo, 1980-87; library dir. Sacramento (Calif.) Pub. Library, 1987—. Mem. ALA, Calif. Library Assn., Rotary. Home: 3501 H St Sacramento CA 95816-4506 Office: Sacramento Pub Libr 828 I St Sacramento CA 95814-2589*

KILLINGER, KERRY KENT, bank executive; b. Des Moines, June 6, 1949; m. Debbie Rousch. BBA, U. Iowa, 1970, MBA, 1971. Exec. v.p. Murphey Favre, Inc., Spokane, 1976-82; exec. v.p. Wash. Mutual Savs. Bank, Seattle, 1982-88, pres., 1988—, chief exec. officer, 1990—, chmn., 1990—. Bd. dirs. Seattle Repertory Theatre, 1990—, Washington Roundtable, 1990—, Downtown Seattle Assn., 1991—, Leadership Tomorrow, 1991—, Wash. Savs. League, 1992—, Savs. and Community Bankers Am.; mem. Thrift Instn. Adv. Coun. to Fed. Res. Bd., 1993—; co-chmn. AIDS Walk-a-thon, Seattle, 1990. Mem. Soc. Fin. Analysts, Life Mgmt. Inst., Seattle C. of C. (bd. dirs. 1991), Rotary. Office: Wash Mut Savs Bank Ste 1500 1201 3d Ave Seattle WA 98101-3015

KILLINGSWORTH, COLLEEN, public relations practitioner; b. Reno, Feb. 14, 1964; d. Ben Wade and Delores Ann (Clark) K. BA in Journalism, U. Nev., 1987. Communications dir. Sierra Nev. Girl Scout Coun., Reno, 1987-88; lead rep. St. Mary's Regional Med. Ctr., Reno, 1988—; pub. info. chmn. Am. Cancer Soc., Reno, 1989-91; south pacific dist. dir. Pub. Rels. Student Soc., Am., Reno, 1987-88. Recipient Gold Spirit award Excellence Communications Cath. Health Assn. U.A., 1991, award Merit Silver State IABC, 1991, Hon. mention, 1991. Mem. Am. Mktg. Assn. (v.p. communications 1991-92), Am. Hosp. Assn., Pub. Rels. Soc. Am. (accredited, pres. elect 1992, pres. 1993), Phi Beta Phi. Republican. Methodist. Office: St Mary's Regional Med Ctr 235 W 6th St Reno NV 89520

KILLINGSWORTH, KATHLEEN NOLA, artist, real estate agent; b. Eglin AFB, Fla., Sept. 5, 1952; d. Marlin Donald Evans and Winnifred Irene (Pelton) Yow; m. Thomas Marion, Dec. 31, 1973 (div. Feb. 1976). Grad. high sch., Myrtle Point, Oreg. Food svc. Internat. Trade Club, Mobile, Ala., 1970-73; food and beverage Gussies Restaurant and Night Club, Coos Bay, Oreg., 1973-77, Libr. Buttery and Pub, Las Vegas, Nev., 1977-79; beverage dir. Laughlin's (Nev.) Riverside Resort, 1979-80; food and beverage Hyatt Regency Maui, Lahaina, Hawaii, 1980-92; realtor assoc. Wailea (Hawaii) Properties, 1990; sole propr. K N Killingsworth Enterprises, Lahaina, 1990—; assoc. Kona Coast Resort II, 1992—; vol. Lahaina Arts Soc., 1992—; mem. Hui No'eau Visual Arts Ctr., Makawao, Maui, Hawaii, 1992—. Artist numerous watercolors; photographer nature greeting cards. Vol. The Word For Today, Lahaina, 1983-87, Kumalani Chapel, Kapalua, Hawaii, 1983-87, Maui Special Olympics, 1993—; founding mem. & vol. Maui Community Arts & Cultural Ctr.; supporter Teen Challenge, Lahaina, 1987—. Mem. Lahina Arts Soc., 1992—. Republican. Office: K N Killingsworth Enterprises PO Box 5369 Lahaina HI 96761

KILLUS, JAMES PETER, JR., atmospheric scientist, consultant, writer; b. Nashville, June 1, 1950; s. James Peter Sr. and Lanis Sue (Embry) K. BS in Engring., Rensselner Poly. Inst., 1972, M of Engring., 1974. Teaching asst.

Rensselaer Poly. Inst., Troy, N.Y., 1971-74; instr. Jr. Coll. of Albany, N.Y., 1973-74; staff scientist to sr. scientist Systems Applications, San Rafeal, Calif., 1975-85; cons. Berkeley, Calif., 1985—; cons. EPA, 1989—. Author: (novel) Book of Shadows, 1983, Sunsmoke, 1985. Mem. IEEE, AAAS, Am. Chem. Soc., Sci. Fiction Writers of Am. Home: 433 Michigan Ave Berkeley CA 94707-1713

KILMER, MAURICE DOUGLAS, marketing executive; b. Flint, Mich., Sept. 14, 1928; s. John Jennings and Eleanor Minnie (Gerholz) K.; m. Vera May Passino, Mar. 30, 1950; children: Brad Douglas, Mark David, Brian John, David Scott, Karen Sue. B of Indsl. Engring., Gen. Motors Inst., 1951; MBA, U. Minn., 1969. Quality svcs. mgr. ordnance div. Honeywell, Hopkins, Minn., 1964-69; product assurance dir. peripheral ops. Honeywell, San Diego, 1969-71; pres. Convenience Systems, Inc., San Diego, 1972-75; salesman real estate Forest E. Olson Coldwell Banker, La Mesa, Calif., 1976-77; resident mgr. Forest E. Olson Coldwell Banker, Huntington Beach, Calif., 1977-78; mgmt. cons. Century 21 of the Pacific, Santa Ana, Calif., 1978-83; dir. broker svcs. Century 21 of the Pacific, Anaheim, Calif., 1983-85; exec. dir. Century 21 of S.W., Phoenix, 1985-86; sales assoc. Century 21 Rattan Realtors, San Diego, 1986-82; diamond dir. Life Trends Internat., San Diego, 1992—. With U.S. Army, 1951-52. Mem. Am. Soc. for Quality Control, San Diego Bd. Realtors. Republican. Home: 668 Corte Raquel San Marcos CA 92069-7320 Office: Life Trends Internat 668 Corte Raquel San Marcos CA 92069-7320

KILMER, NEAL HAROLD, physical scientist; b. Orange, Tex., Apr. 24, 1943; s. Harold Norval and Luella Alice (Sharp) K. BS in Chemistry and Math., Northwestern Okla. State U., 1964; MS in Chemistry, Okla. State U., 1971; PhD in Chemistry, Mich. State U., 1979. Rsch. assoc. N.Mex. Petroleum Recovery Rsch. Ctr. N.Mex. Inst. Mining & Tech., Socorro, 1979-81, rsch. chemist, 1981-85, lectr. I geol. engring., 1984, asst. prof. mining engring., 1985-86; phys. scientist Phys. Sci. Lab. N.Mex. State U., Las Cruces, 1986—. Contbr. articles to profl. jours. Mem. Am. Chem. Soc., Am. Inst. Physics, Soc. Photo-Optical Instrumentation Engrs., Optical Soc. Am., Sigma Xi, Pi Mu Epsilon, Phi Lambda Upsilon. Presbyterian. Home: 2200 Corley Dr Apt 14G Las Cruces NM 88001 Office: Phys Sci Lab PO Box 30002 Las Cruces NM 88003-0002

KILMER, PATRICIA MARIE, principal; b. Pasco, Wash., Nov. 7, 1959; d. L.A. and Margaret L. (O'Brien) Merk; m. Dan Kilmer, Mar. 26, 1983; 1 child, Kellan. Student, Spolane (Wash.) Community Coll, 1980; BA in Edn., Western Wash. U., 1982; MA in Edn., Seattle Pacific U., 1990. Cert. prin. Tchr. Arlington (Wash.) Sch. Dist., 1982-90; prin. Ocean Shores (Wash.) Elem., 1990—, Ocean City Elem. Sch., 1992—; dir. chpt. 1 and 2 Learning Assistance program and Highly Capable program North Beach Sch. Dist.; supt. selection com. mem. Banquet decorations/decorations Food Bank Vols., Arlington, 1989; chmn. Frontier Days Fun Run, Arlington, 1988; vol. Beach Clean Up Crew, Ocean Shores, 1990; co-creator, mem. St. Jerome's Folk Choir. Named one of Outstanding Young Women in Am., 1989. Mem. ASCD, Wash. Assn. Sch. Adminstrs., N.W. Women Ednl. Adminstrn., Ptnrs. in Edn. (founder), PTA (nomination com. 1989-90, chairperson 1990), Gray-Pac's Prin.'s Assn. (pres.), Kiwanis (v.p., key advisor 1990—, chairperson scholarship com. , pub. newsletter, v.p.), Delta Kappa Gamma (fund raising chairperson 1989). Home: Po Box 1605 Ocean Shores WA 98569-1605 Office: Ocean Shores Elem 300 Mt Olympus Ave SE Ocean Shores WA 98569-9746

KIM, EDWARD KUI NAM, JR., insurance company executive; b. Honolulu, Oct. 24, 1952; s. Edward K.N. Kim and Marisa Poliandri; m. Elisabeth Anne Watson, July 12, 1961; children: Brandon Edward, Sienna Elise. Student, U. Hawaii, 1970-72. Agt. Crown Life Ins. Co., Honolulu, 1970-74; mktg. agt. Lincoln Nat. Life Ins. Co., Honolulu, 1974-76; v.p. Pacific Guardian Life Ins. Co., Honolulu, 1981-83; pres. Hawaii Pacific Ins. Corp., Honolulu, 1976—. Appeared as actor and model in over 50 commls. and TV. Mem. Million Dollar Round Table (life), Nat. Assn. Life Underwriters. Home: 1311 Kaeleku St Honolulu HI 96825 Office: Hawaii Pacific Ins Corp 1600 Kapiolani Blvd Ste 624 Honolulu HI 96814

KIM, EDWARD WILLIAM, ophthalmic surgeon; b. Seoul, Korea, Nov. 25, 1949; came to U.S., 1957; s. Shoon Kul and Pok Chu (Kim) K.; m. Carole Sachi Takemoto, July 24, 1976; children: Brian, Ashley. BA, Occidental Coll., Los Angeles, 1971; postgrad. Calif. Inst. Tech., 1971; MD, U. Calif.-San Francisco, 1975; MPH, U. Calif.-Berkley, 1975. Diplomate Nat. Bd. Med. Examiners, Am. Bd. Ophthalmology. Intern, San Francisco Gen. Hosp., 1975-76; resident in ophthalmology Harvard U.-Mass. Eye and Ear Infirmary, Boston, 1977-79; clin. fellow in ophthalmology Harvard U., 1977-79; clin. fellow in retina Harvard, 1980; practice medicine in ophthalmic surgery, South Laguna and San Clemente, Calif., 1980—; vol. ophthalmologist Eye Care Inc., Ecole St. Vincent's, Haiti, 1980, Liga, Mex., 1989; chief staff, South Coast Med. Ctr., 1988-89; asst. clin. prof. dept. ophthalmology, U. Calif., Irvine. Founding mem. Orange County Ctr. for Performing Arts, Calif., 1982, dir. at large, 1991; pres. Laguna Beach Summer Music Festival, Calif., 1984. Reinhart scholar U. Calif.-San Francisco, 1972-73; R. Taussig scholar, 1974-75. Fellow ACS, Am. Acad. Ophthalmology, Royal Soc. Medicine, Internat. Coll. Surgeons; mem. Calif. Med. Assn., Keratorefractive Soc., Orange County Med. Assn., Mensa, Expts. in Art and Tech. Office: Harvard Eye Assocs 665 Camino De Los Mares Ste 102 San Clemente CA 92672-2845

KIM, IRVING ILWOONG, hospital business executive; b. Seoul, Republic of Korea, Sept. 25, 1940; came to U.S., 1970; s. Man Yee and Soon Yee (Yoo) K.; m. Sonja Lee, Sept. 14, 1969; children: Daniel, Michael. B.Th., Korean Union Coll., Seoul, 1967; BS, Korea U., Seoul, 1964; postgrad. in bus., Wayne State U., 1976. Asst. controller Highland Park (Mich.) Gen. Hosp., 1970-73; dir. finance Mt. Carmel Mercy Hosp., Detroit, 1974-81; controller Nat. Med. Enterprises Hosps., L.A., 1981-88; dir. patient fin. svcs. McKenzie-Willamette Hosp., Springfield, Oreg., 1989—. Pres. Korean Assn. of Greater Detroit, 1977-78, chmn. bd. dirs., 1979-80. Named for Outstanding Achievement, Korean Nat. Cultural Ministry, Seoul, 1979. Mem. Healthcare Fin. Mgmt. Assn. (advanced). Seventh-Day Adventist. Home: 37004 Conley Rd Springfield OR 97478 Office: McKenzie Willamette Hosp 1460 G St Springfield OR 97477-4197

KIM, JAMES HYUNG JIN, investment banker. BA, Ea. Wash. U., 1967; postgrad., Am. Inst. of Banking, 1970-73. V.p., mgr. Rainier Bank, Seattle, 1968-88, Security Pacific Asian Bank, L.A., 1988-90; pres. Premier Capital Internat. Inc., Seattle, 1991; dir. Princeton Pacific Group; mem. adv. bd. Whitworth Inst. for Internat. Mgmt. Cert. Internat. Exec. for Export Mgmt. Am. Soc. of Internat. Execs., 1967. Mem. Am. Fin. Assn., Bankers Club (pres. 1971-72), Korean Am. Assn. (pres. 1978-79), Wash. Athletic Club. Office: Premier Capital Internat 550 Kirkland Way # 405A Kirkland WA 98033

KIM, JAY, congressman; b. Korea, 1939; m. June, 1961; children: Richard, Kathy, Eugene. BS, U. So. Calif., MCE; MPA, Calif. State U. Mem. City Coun. city of Diamond Bar, Calif., 1990, mayor, 1991; mem. 103rd Congress from 41st dist. Calif., 1993—; pres., founder Jaykim Engrs. Inc. Recipient Outstanding Achievement in Bus. and Community Devel. award, Engr. of Yr. award, Caballero de Distinction award, Engr. Bus. of the Yr. award, others. Republican. Methodist. Office: US House of Representatives Office of House Members Washington DC 20515

KIM, JOUNG-IM, communication educator, consultant; b. Taejon, Choognam, Republic of Korea, May 8, 1947; came to U.S., 1975; d. Yong-Kap Kim and Im-Soon Nam; m. James Andrew Palmore, Jr., Jan. 21, 1989. BA in Libr. Sci., Yonsei U., Seoul, Korea, 1970, postgrad., 1974-75; postgrad., U. Hawaii at Manoa, 1975, MA in Sociology, 1978; PhD in Comm., Stanford U., 1986. Rschr. Korean Inst. Family Planning, Seoul, 1974-75; spl. resource person UN/East-West Ctr., Honolulu, 1976; rsch. asst. East-West Ctr., Honolulu, 1977-78; rsch., teaching asst. Stanford (Calif.) U., 1979-83, instr., 1984; asst. prof. U. Hawaii at Manoa, Honolulu, 1984—, also mem. faculty Ctr. Korean Studies; cons. UN Econ. and Social Commn. for Asia and Pacific, Bangkok, 1979, 84-86, 89, 90-92; cons. UN Devel. Program, Devel. Tng. Comm. Planning, Bangkok, 1984, UN Population Funds, N.Y.C., 1991, 92. Contbr. articles to profl. jours., monographs, and chpts. to books. Grantee East-West Ctr., 1972, 75-78; Population Libr. fellow U. N.C., 1973; Stanford U. fellow, 1978-79, 83, 84. Mem. Internat. Comm. Assn., Internat. Network for Social Newtwork Analysis. Office: U Hawaii at Manoa 2560 Campus Rd # 336 Honolulu HI 96822

KIM, MATTHEW HIDONG, physicist, researcher; b. Seoul, Korea, Sept. 21, 1958; came to U.S., 1962; s. Shoon Kyung and Jeung Hi (Hahn) K. BS in Engring. Physics, Cornell U., 1980; MS in Physics, U. Ill., 1981, PhD in Physics, 1988. Rsch. scientist Bandgap Tech. Corp., Broomfield, Colo., 1989—. Referee Jour. Applied Physics, 1991—, Applied Physics Letters, 1991—; contbr. over 20 articles to profl. jours. Mem. Am. Phys. Soc., N.Y. Acad. Scis., Tau Beta Pi. Office: Bandgap Tech Corp 325 Interlocken Pkwy Broomfield CO 80021

KIM, PAUL MYUNGCHYUN, law enforcement officer, educator; b. Seoul, Korea, July 23, 1951; came to U.S., 1967; s. John Young and Soo Bok Kim; m. Sue Edwards, May 5, 1972 (div. Nov. 1980); m. Jane Kang, June 20, 1985; children: Michael, Jennifer, Adam, Amanda. BS cum laude, Pepperdine U., 1975, MPA, 1978; cert., FBI Nat. Acad. Cert. police mgr.; cert. ct. and adminstrv. hearing interpreter, Calif.; cert. community coll. tchr. Patrolman LaHabra (Calif.) Police Dept., 1975-77; police officer L.A. Police Dept., 1977-81, detective, 1981-85, sgt., 1985-89, lt., 1989—; bd. dirs. Korean Christian Broadcasting, L.A. Bd. govs. Calif. Community Colls., Sacramento. Capt. USMC, 1972-75. Recipient Presdl. citation Pres. of Korea, 1983; named Policeman of Yr., Mayor of L.A., 1991. Mem. Rotary (charter sec.). Republican. Roman Catholic. Home: 12227 Leayn Ct North Hollywood CA 91605 Office: LA Police 150 N Los Angeles St Los Angeles CA 90012

KIM, STEPHEN TAE, stockbroker; b. Seoul, Republic of Korea, Jan. 15, 1965; came to U.S., 1977; s. Jae B. and Veronica (Kang) K. BA in Econs., U. Calif., Irvine, 1988. Export market/sales Tubesales, L.A., 1989-91; fin. cons. Merrill Lynch, Santa Ana, Calif., 1991—; guest speaker Korean-Am. Small Bus. Assn., L.A., 1992; corp. guest speaker U. So. Calif. Asian Am. Bus. Assn., L.A., 1992. Mem. Korean Am. Young Profl. Assn., U. Calif. Irvine Korean Am. Student Alumni Assn. Republican. Office: Merrill Lynch 2670 N Main St Santa Ana CA 92701

KIM, SUNG JIN, entrepreneur, consultant; b. Seoul, Korea; came to U.S., 1977; s. Sam Soowoo and Barbara Kim. BS, U. of Pacific, 1990. Auditor Coopers & Lybrand, Sacramento, 1990-91; asst. contr. Schutter & Glickton Attys., Honolulu, 1991; office mgr. Yempuku & Goo, AAL, ALC, Honolulu, 1991—; owner Tutors Unlimited, Honolulu, 1990—; ptnr., owner Kim & Lum Acctg. Svcs., Honolulu, 1992—. Office: Yempuku & Goo Ste 930 841 Bishop St Honolulu HI 96813

KIM, YONGMIN, electrical engineering educator; b. Cheju, Korea, May 19, 1953, came to U.S., 1976; s. Ki-Whan and Yang-Whi (Kim) K.; m. Eunai Yoo, May 21, 1976; children: Janice, Christine, Daniel. BEE, Seoul Nat. U., Republic of Korea, 1975; MEE, U. Wis., Madison, 1979, PhD, 1982. Asst. prof. U. Wash., Seattle, 1982-86, assoc. prof., 1986-90, prof., 1990—; cons. MITRE Corp., McLean, Va., 1990, Lotte-Canon, Seoul, 1991, Seattle Silicon, Bellevue, Wash., 1990—, U.S. Army, 1989—, Neopath, Inc., Bellevue, Wash., 1989-90, Trinius Ptnrs., Seattle, 1989-91, Samsung Advanced Inst. Tech., Suwon, Republic of Korea, 1989-92, Daewoo Telecom Co., Seoul, 1989-91, Aptec Systems, Portland, Oreg., 1992—, Optimedx, Seattle, 1992—; bd. dirs. Image Computing Systems Lab., 1984—, Ctr. for Imaging Systems Optimization, 1991. Contbr. numerous articles to profl. jours., chpts. in books; editor Proceedings of the Annual International Conference of the IEEE EMBS, vol. 11, 1989, Proceedings of the SPIE Medical Imaging Conferences, vol. 1232, 1990, vol. 1444, 1991, vol. 1653, 1992, vol. 1897, 1993. Mem. various nat. coms.; chmn. numerous confs. Recipient Career Devel. award Physio Control Corp., 1982; grantee NIH, 1984—, NSF, 1984—, U.S. Army, 1986—, USN, 1986—; Whitaker Found. biomed. engring. grantee, 1986. Mem. IEEE (sr., Early Career Achievement award 1988, Disting. Speaker 1991), Assn. Computing Machinery, Soc Photo-Optical Instrumentation Engrs., Tau Beta Pi, Eta Kappa Nu. Presbyterian. Subspecialties: computer engring., high-performance image computing workstations, image processing, computer graphics, medical imaging, and multimedia workstations. Home: 4431 NE 189th Pl Seattle WA 98155

KIMBALL, CURTIS ROLLIN, investment advisor, appraiser; b. Grand Rapids, Mich., Dec. 21, 1950; s. Rollin Hibbard and Jane Ann (Walterman) K.; m. Marilyn M. Quaderer; 1 child, Neil Curtis. B.A., Duke U., 1972; M.B.A., Emory U., 1984. Comml. lending and trust portfolio mgr. Wachovia Bank and Trust Co., N.A., Winston-Salem, N.C., 1972-81; v.p., trust mgr. bus. owner services group Citizens and So. Nat. Bank, Atlanta, 1981-88, prin. Willamette Mgmt. Assocs., Inc., Portland, Oreg., 1988—. Mem. activities council, Portland Art Mus. Fellow Inst. Chartered Fin. Analysts; sr. mem. Am. Soc. Appraisers (pres. Atlanta chpt. 1985-86); mem. Nat. Assn. Bus. Econs. (pres. Portland chpt. 1992-93). Republican. Episcopalian. Avocations: running; fencing; tennis. Office: Willamette Mgmt Assocs Inc 111 SW 5th Ave Ste 2150 Portland OR 97204

KIMBALL, DONALD W., electric utility corporate executive; b. Deadwood, S.D., Apr. 17, 1947; s. Garrett J. and Marietta (Alexander) K.; m. A. Sue Eide, Sept. 19, 1964; children: Lisa Gray, Tammi Bymers. BSEE, Colo. State U., 1974. Lineman Butte Electric Corp., Newell, S.D., 1965-68; journeyman lineman Pourdre Valley Rural Electric, Ft. Collins, Colo., 1968-69; engr. Pourdre Valley Rural Electric, F. Collins, Colo., 1969-74; systems engr. Grand Valley Rural Power, Grand Juction, Colo., 1974-76, Heartland Consumers Power Dist., Madison, S.D., 1976-77; spl. projects enrg. East River Electric Power Corp., Madison, S.D., 1977; mgr. Clay Union Electric, Vermillion, S.D., 1978-88, Union County Electric Corp., Elk Point, S.D., 1984-88; exec. v.p., gen. mgr. Ariz. Electric Power Corp., Benson, Ariz., 1988—; bd. dirs., officer Heartland Consumers Power, Madison, S.C., 1979-88; cons. City of Elk Point, S.D., 1984-88; bd. dirs. Ariz. Power Polling Assn., Phoenix, Grand Canyon State Electric Coop. Assn., Inc.; pres. Western Power Producers, 1991. Democrat. Lutheran. Home: 6828 E Calle Luciente Tucson AZ 85715-3208 Office: Ariz Electric Power Corp PO Box 670 Benson AZ 85602-0670

KIMBALL, K. RANDALL, broadcasting executive; b. Salt Lake City, June 3, 1951; s. Ralph Taylor and Marie (Seegmiller) K.; m. Rebecca Joye Cummings, Nov. 17, 1973; children: Jenifer, Nicklaus, Stefanie. BS in Acctg., U. Utah, 1975. Staff acct. Bonneville Internat. Corp., Salt Lake City, 1975-78; bus. mgr. B.I.C. KAAM-KAFM-Radio, Dallas, 1978-80, KCPX Inc. AM/FM Radio, Salt Lake City, 1980-84; controller Thomas, Phillips, Clawson Advt., Salt Lake City, 1984-85; bus. mgr. United TV Inc.-KTVX, Salt Lake City, 1985—. Contbr. articles to profl. jours. Mem. Broadcast Cable Fin. Mgmt. Assn. Mem. LDS. Home: 1361 Ridgemark Dr Sandy UT 84092 Office: United TV Inc KTVX 1760 Fremont Dr Salt Lake City UT 84104

KIMBALL, RICHARD NEPHI, engineering educator; b. Salt Lake City, July 19, 1936; s. Stanley Wallace Pratt and Agnes Josephine (Berg) Kimball; m. Nancy Joan Bryan, June 29, 1961; children: Jana, Rolaine, LaDawn, LaNeta, Shari, Bryan. BS, Utah State U., 1963, MS, 1965; Engr. in Civil Engring. degree, Stanford U., 1972. Registered profl. engr., Utah, land surveyor. Rsch. asst. Agrl. Rsch. Svc., Logan, Utah, 1960-61; lectr. Utah State U., Logan, 1964-65; asst. prof. So Utah State Coll. (name now So. Utah U.), Cedar City, 1965-74, prof. dept. engring., 1985—; owner R.N. Kimball Assocs., Cedar City, 1973—; pres. Color County chpt. Utah Coun. Land Surveyors. County chmn. Reagan for Pres. Campaign, Iron County, Utah, 1980. With U.S. Army, 1961-62. NSF sci. faculty fellow, 1969-71, Ideal Cement Co. fellow, 1963-64. Mem. ASCE, Sons of Utah Pioneers (pres. 1988). Republican. Mem. Ch. of Latter-day Saints. Home: 425 S 300 W Cedar City UT 84720-3233 Office: So Utah U Engring Dept Cedar City UT 84720

KIMBELL, MARION JOEL, retired engineer; b. McDonough, Ga., Sept. 7, 1923; s. Charles Marvin and Mary (McMillian) K.; BS in Civil Engring., U. Houston, 1949, MChem Engring., 1953; m. Judy Weidner, Dec. 18, 1946; children: Nancy, Susan, Candice. Civil engr. U.S. Dept. Interior, Lemmon, S.D., 1954; chief piping engr. M.W. Kellog Co., Paducah, Ky., 1955; nuclear engr. Westinghouse Atomic Power Div., Pitts., 1956-59; control systems prin. engr. Kaiser Engrs., Oakland, Calif., 1959-80; control systems supervising engr. Bechtel Inc., San Francisco, 1980-86; ret., 1986; control systems tchr. Laney Coll. cons. engr. NASA, Gen. Atomic Co.; advisory bd. Chabot Collage on radiation tech. Served as sgt. U.S. Army, 1943-46. Registered profl. nuclear engr., Calif.; control systems engr., Calif. Mem. Instrument Soc. of Am. (sr. mem. exec. com.). Clubs: Moose. Contbr. articles to profl. jours. Home: 22324 Ralston Ct Hayward CA 94541-3336

KIMBERLEY, A. G., JR., management executive; b. Portland, Oreg., Oct. 29, 1939; s. A. Gurney and Meta (Horgan) K.; m. M. Susan Solie, Sept. 15, 1949 (div.); children: John Langton, Thea Ness; m. Roxanne Johannesen, Mar. 26, 1952. BS, Lewis & Clark Coll., 1959-62; postgrad., U. Oreg., 1963. Mgr. meat and dairy div. Hudson House Co., Portland, 1963-64; pres. Wall-Western Inc., Portland, 1964-92, Kimberley Indsl., Portland, 1982-92; owner Kimberley Boxwood Farm, Wilsonville, Oreg., 1987—, A. G. Kimberley & Co., 1992—. Republican. Episcopalian. Home: 16720 SW Wilsonville Rd Wilsonville OR 97070-9511

KIMBLE, MARK STEPHEN, editor; b. Mpls., Feb. 1, 1952; s. William Earle and Jean Margaret (Cayia) K.; m. Jane Ellen Deerr, May 18, 1974 (div. 1981); m. Jennifer Lynn Boice, May 21, 1989. BA in Journalism, U. Ariz., 1974. Reporter AP, Miami, Fla., 1974; reporter Tucson Citizen, 1974-81, asst. city editor, 1981-84, city editor, 1984-91, asst. mng. editor, 1991—. Vol. Pima County Victim Witness, Tucson, 1990—. Mem. Investigative Reporters and Editors, Soc. Profl. Journalists (v.p. So. Ariz. chpt. 1989—). Office: Tucson Citizen PO Box 26767 Tucson AZ 85726-6767

KIMBRELL, GRADY NED, author, educator; b. Tallant, Okla., Apr. 6, 1933; s. Virgil Leroy Kimbrell and La Veria Dee Underwood; m. Marilyn Louise King, May 30, 1953 (div.); m. Mary Ellen Cunningham, Apr. 11, 1973; children: Mark Leroy, Lisa Christine, Joni Lynne. BA, Southwestern Coll., Winfield, Kans., 1956; MA, Colo. State Coll., 1958. Cert. tchr. (life), Calif., Colo.; cert. adminstr., Calif. Bus. tchr. Peabody (Kans.) High Sch., 1956-58; bus. tchr. Santa Barbara (Calif.) High Sch., 1958-65, coordinator work edn., 1965-75, dir. research and evaluation, 1975-88; cons., textbook researcher and author. Author: Introduction of Business and Office Careers, 1974, The World of Work Career Interest Survey, 1986; co-author: Succeeding in the World of Work, 1970, 5th rev. edit., 1992, Entering the World of Work, 1974, 3rd rev. edit., 1988, The Savvy Consumer, 1984, Marketing Essentials, 1991, Office Skills for the 1990's, 1992, Advancing in the World of Work, 1992, Exploring Business and Computer Careers, 1992. Served as cpl. U.S. Army, 1953-55. Mem. NEA, Calif. Assn. Work Experience Educators (life, v.p. 1968-70), Nat. Work Experience Edn. Assn., Calif. Tchrs. Assn., Coop. Work Experience Assn. Republican.

KIMME, ERNEST GODFREY, communications engineer; b. Long Beach, Calif., June 7, 1929; s. Ernest Godfrey and Lura Elizabeth (Dake) K.; BA cum laude, Pomona Coll., 1952; MA, U. Minn., 1954, PhD, 1955; m. Margaret Jeanne Bolen, Dec. 10, 1978; children by previous marriage: Ernest G., Elizabeth E., Karl Frederick. Mem. grad. faculty Oreg. State U., Corvallis, 1955-57; mem. tech. staff Bell Telephone Labs., Murray Hill, N.J., 1957-65, supr. mobile radio rsch. lab., 1962-65; head applied sci. dept. Collins Radio Co., Newport Beach, Calif., 1965-72; rsch. engr. Northrop Electronics, Hawthorne, Calif., 1972-74; sr. staff engr. Interstate Electronics Corp., Anaheim, Calif., 1974-79; dir. advanced systems, dir. advanced comm. systems, tech. dir. spl. comm. programs Gould Navcomm Systems, El Monte, Calif., 1979-82; pres. Cobit, Inc, 1982-84; tech. staff Gen. Rsch. Corp., Santa Barbara, 1984-87; v.p. engring. Starfind, Inc., Laguna Niguel, Calif., 1987-88; dir. engring. R&D Unit Instruments, Orange, Calif., 1988-89; staff scientist Brunswick Def. Systems, Costa Mesa, Calif., 1989-90; v.p. engring. Redband Techs., Inc., 1990—; prin. assoc. Ameta Cons. Technologists; v.p. A.S. Johnston Drilling Corp., Woodland Hills, Calif.; adj. prof. U. Redlands, Golden Gate Univ., 1989—; mem. adj. faculty math. U. Redlands, 1990—. Mem. AAAS, IEEE, Soc. Indsl. and Applied Math., Aircraft Owners and Pilots Assn., Phi Beta Kappa, Sigma Xi. Contbr. articles to profl. jours. Home: 301 N Starfire St Anaheim CA 92807-2928

KIMMEL, ROBERT O., marketing executive; b. Bklyn., Aug. 31, 1928; s. Philip Murray and Katherine (Mittleman) K.; BEE cum laude, Bklyn. Poly Inst., 1951; children by previous marriage: Kenneth, Jeanne; m. Barbara Gajdik, Oct. 12, 1969; children: Katherine Nicole, Todd Philip. Field eng. Gen. Electric Co., 1951-53; sales engr. Raytheon Co., Los Angeles, 1953-60; regional mktg. mgr. Hughes Aircraft Co., Torrance, Calif., 1960-69; v.p. ABC Electronic Sales, Inc., Williston Park, N.Y., 1969-84; pres. R. O. Kimmel Assocs., Inc.; dir. Acro-Com, KW Internat. Co. Mem. IEEE, Tau Beta Pi, Eta Kappa Nu.

KIMMEY, MICHAEL BRYANT, gastroenterology educator; b. Grand Junction, Colo., Aug. 15, 1953; s. Bernard Augustus and Marilyn (Withrow) K.; m. Cynthia Grant Campbell, Feb. 14, 1984; children: Philip, Peter. AB magna cum laude, Washington U., St. Louis, 1975, MD, 1979. Intern, resident U. Wash., Seattle, 1979-82, acting instr. medicine, 1982-86, acting asst. prof. medicine, 1986-87, asst. prof. medicine, 1987—, assoc. prof. medicine, 1992—, dir. therapeutic endoscopy, 1987—, dir. gastrointestinal endoscopy, 1992—. Recipient Acad. Achievement award Mo. State Med. Assn., 1978, George F. Gill prize for rsch. in pediatrics Washington U., St. Louis, 1979. Fellow Am. Coll. Gastroenterology; mem. ACP, Am. Gastroenterological Assn., Am. Soc. for Gastrointestinal Endoscopy, Pacific N.W. Gastroenterology Soc., King County Med. Soc., Phi Beta Kappa. Home: 4007 45th Ave NE Seattle WA 98105-5452 Office: U Washington 1959 NE Pacific St RG 24 Seattle WA 98195-0001

KIMPTON, DAVID RAYMOND, natural resource consultant, writer; b. Twin Falls, Idaho, Feb. 19, 1942; s. Lloyd and Retura (Robins) K.; m. Joanna Peak, June 2, 1984; foster children: Donnie, Derrick, Dustin. BS in Forestry, U. Idaho, 1964. Forester U.S. Forest Svc., Panguitch, Utah, 1966-68; with dept. interdisciplinary natural resources U.S. Forest Svc., Ely, Nev., 1968-71; with dept. interdisciplinary natural resources U.S. Forest Svc., Stanley, Idaho, 1971-72, dist. forest ranger, 1972-78; dist. forest ranger U.S. Forest Svc., Mountain City, Nev., 1978-84; natural resource cons. Idaho, 1984-92; range conservationist U.S. Forest Svc., Stanley, Idaho, 1992—; incident comdr. U.S. Forest Svc., Western States, 1978-86; botanist pvt. and govtl., Idaho, Nev., 1985-92; naturalist schs., pvt., govt., Idaho, Nev., 1988-92; bd. dirs. Salmon River Emergency Med. Clinic, Stanley, Idaho, 1984-86, v.p., 1987-92; bd. dirs. v.p. Idaho Mountain Health Clinics, Boise, 1985-92. Author Mining Law jour., 1990; author Life Saving Rescue mag., 1989. Pres. Meth. Youth Found., Twin Falls, 1960; treas., v.p. Chrisman Bd. Dirs., Moscow, Idaho, 1960-63; bd. dirs. Vol. Fire Dept., Ely, 1968-71, Salmon River Emergency Med. Clinic, Stanley, 1973-77, v.p., 1978; bd. dirs. Sawtooth Valley Meditation Chapel, 1974-76, Stanley Community Bldg., 1977-78; mem. Sawtooth Valley Assn., Stanley, 1971-72, Vol. Fire Dept., Stanley, 1975-78, Mountain Search and Rescue, Stanley, 1972-78; com. mem. Coalition of Taxpayers, Stanley, 1990—. With U.S. Army, 1965-66, Vietnam. Recipient Presdl. Unit Citation award Pres. Johnson, 1965; named Outstanding Young Man Am., Bd. Nat. Advs., 1971, Outstanding Mem., White Pine Jaycees, 1969. Mem. Idaho Wildlife, Sawtooth Wildlife Coun. Mem. Christian Ch. Home and Office: PO Box 32 Stanley ID 83278

KIMSEY, RUSTIN RAY, bishop. s. Lauren Chamness K.; m. Gretchen Beck Rinehart, 1961; 2 children. BS U. Oreg., 1957, BD Episcopal Theol. Sem., 1960. Ordained priest, Episcopal Ch., 1960; vicar, St. John Ch., Hermiston, 1960-61; priest in charge, St. Paul NYSSA, 1961; vicar, St. Albany, 1961-67; rector, St. Stephen, Baker, 1967-71, St. Paul, the Dalles, 1971-80; consecrated bishop of Eastern Oreg., 1980; bishop, Episcopal Diocese Eastern Oreg., The Dalles, 1980—. Office: Episcopal Diocese Ea Oreg PO Box 620 The Dalles OR 97058-0620*

KINASHI, DOREEN ANN, systems analyst, writer, editor; b. Plainfield, N.J., Jan. 2, 1957; d. Chester Paul and Helen Carol (Barsh) Cichurski; m. Yasuhiro Kinashi, Apr. 25, 1987; 1 child, Jason Philip. BSW, U. Evansville, Ind., 1979. Applications engr., support rep. NBI Inc. Govt. Systems, Washington, 1983-85; def. systems analyst Ultrasystems Inc., Irvine, Calif., 1985—; course instr. Def. Intelligence Agy., Washington, 1983-85. Author: Trends in Computer Ergonomic, 1984, Military Software Applications, 1987. Intelligence officer USAFR, Fayetteville, N.C., 1979-83, San Bernardino, Calif., 1985-87; jr. v.p. Res. Officers Assn., Arlington, Va., 1984; pres. Air Force Jr. Officers Com., Fayetteville, N.C., 1979-80. Capt. USAF, 1979-83.

Mem. Nat. Historic Preservation Soc., AAUW. Home: 10426 Mount Sunapee Rd Vienna VA 22182-1523

KINCHELOE, LAWRENCE RAY, state official; b. Twin Falls, Idaho, Jan. 1, 1941; s. Kenneth Kincheloe and Wilma Gladys (Barnett) Routt; m. Sharon Kathleen Moseley, July 14, 1964; children—Gerry, Corey, Michelle, Lawrence, Jeffrey. BA, Mont. State U., 1963; MA, Pacific Luth. U., 1978. Assoc. supt. Dept. Corrections, Wash. State Penitentiary, Walla Walla, 1978-82, warden, 1982-89; dir. Div. of Prisons, Olympia, Wash., 1989-91; supt. Spring Creek Correctional Ctr., Seward, Ak, 1992—. Served to maj. U.S. Army, 1963-78. Decorated Silver Star, Bronze Star with oak leaf cluster, Legion of Merit, Air medal with oak leaf cluster, Army Commendation medal (2); Vietnamese Cross of Gallantry (3). Mem. Am. Corrections Assn., N.Am. Assn. Wardens, West Cen. Wardens and Supts. Assn. Home: PO Box 2109 Seward AK 99664 Office: Alaska Dept Corrections PO Box 2109 Seward AK 99664

KIND, KENNETH WAYNE, lawyer, real estate broker; b. Missoula, Mont., Apr. 1, 1948; s. Joseph Bruce and Elinor Joy (Smith) K.; m. Diane Lucille Jozaitis, Aug. 28, 1971; children: Kirstin Amber, Kenneth Warner. BA, Calif. State U.-Northridge, 1973; JD, Calif. Western U., 1976. Bar: Calif. 1976, U.S. Dist. Ct. (ea., so., no. dists.) Calif., 1976, U.S. Cir. Ct. Appeals (9th cir.); lic. NASCAR driver, 1987. Mem. celebrity security staff Brownstone Am., Beverly Hills, Calif., 1970-76; tchr. Army and Navy Acad., Carlsbad, Calif., 1975-76; real estate broker, Bakersfield, Calif., 1978—; sole practice, Bakersfield, 1976—; lectr. mechanic's lien laws, Calif., 1983—. Staff writer Calif. Western Law Jour., 1975. Sgt. U.S. Army, 1967-70. Mem. ABA, VFW, Nat. Order Barristers. Libertarian. Office: 5225 Business Center Dr Ste 370 Bakersfield CA 93309-1625

KINDEL, JOSEPH MARTIN, physicist, consultant; b. Barberton, Ohio, Mar. 10, 1943; s. Joseph Elias Kindel and Violette Isabelle (Voris) Alexander; m. Mary Elizabeth Mackovic Ramsey, Nov. 18, 1961 (div. Mar. 1981); children: Kenneth Brian, Robert Michael; m. Carolyn Macdonald, Mar. 7, 1982; children: Christopher Macdonald, David Macdonald. BS, U. Akron, 1965; MS, UCLA, 1966, PhD, 1970. Rsch. assoc. Princeton (N.J.) U., 1970-71; staff mem., dep. group leader Los Alamos (N.M.) Nat. Lab., 1971-78, assoc. group leader, 1979-86, coord. new initiatives, 1989—; group project leader TRW, Redondo Beach, Calif., 1978-79; div. mgr. Mission Rsch. Corp., Los Alamos, 1986-89; indsl. partnership coord. Nuclear Weapons Tech. Directorate Los Alamos Nat. Lab., 1992—; chmn. new initiatives working group Los Alamos Nat. Lab., 1991—; mem. microstructure scis. tech. adv. bd. Semicondr. Rsch. Corp., 1991—, Transp. Rsch. Bd.; co-organizer internat. confs.; invited speaker numerous confs. Referee numerous jours. including Phys. Rev. Letters; contbr. articles to profl. jours. Grantee Centre Europeen De Atomique Et Moleculaire, Paris, 1989, 91. Fellow Am. Phys. Soc. (past com. mem., fellowship com.); mem. AAAS. Home: 107 Sierra Vista Dr Los Alamos NM 87544-3426 Office: Nuclear Weapons Tech MS A105 Los Alamos NM 87545

KINDRICK, ROBERT LEROY, academic administrator, educator; b. Kansas City, Mo., Aug. 17, 1942; s. Robert William and Waneta LeVeta (Lobdell) K.; B.A., Park Coll., 1964; M.A., U. Mo., Kansas City, 1967; Ph.D., U. Tex., 1971; m. Carolyn Jean Reed, Aug. 20, 1965. Instr., Central Mo. State U., Warrensburg, 1967-69, asst. prof., 1969-73, assoc. prof., 1973-78, prof. English, 1978-80, head dept. English, 1975-80; dean Coll. Arts and Scis., also prof. English, Western Ill. U., Macomb, 1980-84; v.p. acad. affairs, prof. English, Emporia State U., Kans., 1984-87; provost, v.p. academic affairs, prof. English, Eastern Ill. U., Charleston, 1987-91; provost, v.p. acad. affairs and prof. English U. Mont., 1991—. Chmn. bd. dirs. Mo. Com. for Humanities, 1979-80, Ill. Humanities Coun., 1991. Pres. Park Coll. Young Dems., 1963; v.p. Mo. Young Dems., Jefferson City, 1964; campus coordinator United Way, Macomb, Ill., 1983; mem. study com. Emporia Arts Council, 1985-86. U. Tex. fellow, 1965-66; Am. Council Learned Socs. travel grantee, 1975; Nat. Endowment for Humanities summer fellow, 1977; Mediaeval Acad. Am. grantee, 1976; Mo. Com. Humanities grantee, 1975-84; Assn. Scottish Lit. Studies grantee, 1979. Mem. Mo. Assn. Depts. English (pres. 1978-80), Mo. Philological Assn. (founding pres. 1975-77), Medieval Assn. Midwest (councillor 1977—, ex officio bd. 1980—, v.p. 1987-88, exec. sec. 1988—), Ill. Medieval Assn. (founding exec. sec. 1983-93), Mid-Am. Medieval Assn., Rocky Mountain MLA, Assn. Scottish Lt. Studies, Early English Text Soc., Société Rencesvals, Medieval Acad. N.Am. (exec. sec. com. on ctrs. and regional assns.), Internat. Arthurian Soc., Sigma Tau Delta, Phi Kappa Phi. Club: Rotary (editor Warrensburg club). Author: Robert Henryson, 1980; A New Classical Rhetoric, 1980, Henryson and the Medieval Arts of Rhetoric, 1993; editor: Teaching the Middle Ages, 1981—; editor Studies in Medieval and Renaissance Teaching, 1975-80; contbr. articles to profl. jours. Home: PO Box 9398 Missoula MT 59807 Office: U Mont Main Hall Missoula MT 59812

KING, ALEXANDER LOUIS, pediatrician; b. Trenton, N.J., June 9, 1914; s. Edgar Emmanuel and Mildred Gertrude (Alexander) Klinkowstein; m. Carol Jean Leona Siegert, Jan. 23, 1958; 1 child, Susan Alexis. BA, Johns Hopkins U., 1933, MD, 1937. Diplomate Am. Bd. Pediatrics. Asst. prof. pediatrics Med. Sch. Wayne U., Detroit, 1946-47; dir. pediatrics Kaiser Found. Hosp., Oakland, Calif., 1950-65; sr. cons. pediatrics Kaiser Hosps., Oakland and Walnut Creek, Calif., 1965-79; blood bank physician Alameda-Contra Costa Med. Assn. Blood Bank, Oakland, 1980—. Capt. USMC, 1942-46. Fellow Am. Acad. Pediatrics; mem. Calif. Med. Assn., No. Calif. Am. Acad. Pediatrics. Home: 33 La Cresta Rd Orinda CA 94563 Office: Alameda Contra Costa Med Assn Blood Bank 6230 Claremont Ave Oakland CA 94563

KING, BRUCE, governor; b. Stanley, N.Mex., Apr. 6, 1924; s. William and Molly (Schooler) K.; m. Alice Marie Martin, June 1, 1947; children: Bill, Gary. Student, U. N.Mex., 1943-44. Rancher, farmer Stanley; mem. Santa Fe County Commn., 1955-58, chmn., 1957-58; mem. N.Mex. Ho. of Reps., 1959-68, speaker, 1963-68; pres. N.Mex. Constl. Conv., 1969; gov. State of N.Mex., 1971-75, 79-83, 91—; co-owner King's Butane Co., Stanley. Mem. Gov.'s Task Force on Edn., 1968; mem. v.p. N.Mex. Soil and Water Conservation Commn.; mem. steering com. Edn. Commn. States, 1971—; chmn. Four Corners Regional Commn., 1972, Nat. Oil and Gas Compact Commn., 1973; vice chmn. Western Gov.'s Conf., 1973, chmn., 1974; mem. nat. adv. com. Dem. Party; chmn. N.Mex. Dems., 1966; bd. dirs. Edgewood Soil Conversation Commn. With F.A., AUS, 1944-46, PTO. Office: Office of the Gov State Capital Bldg 4th Fl Santa Fe NM 87503

KING, CALVIN, entrepreneur, consultant; b. Shreveport, La., Apr. 2, 1951; s. Samuel Leroy and Evelyn Cynthia (Jones) K. AA Arts and Humanities, Laney Coll., 1981, AA Social Sci., 1983, AA Language Arts, 1985, AA Theater Arts, 1989. Assoc. The Heritage Group, Walnut Creek, Calif., 1974—; pres., CEO Magnetic Phi Radio and TV Announcing Inc., Oakland, Calif., 1988—; supervisor Loomis Armored Inc, Oakland, Calif., 1991—; musician, poet free-lance, Oakland, 1970—; model, actor, Laney Coll., Yosson Enterprises, Oakland, San Francisco, 1981—; actor, dir. The Mahdi Theater, Oakland, 1989—; rschr., dir., Expressions for Art and Humanities, Oakland, 1989—. Author (book of poetry) Africa Sweet Africa Me Africa Me, 1991, (short story) Three Coins for the Fisherman, 1990. Minister Imam Nation of Islam, San Francisco, 1975—; minister in training The Allen Temple Baptist Ch., 1981— (diploma); fruit of Islam, Nation of Islam mosque 26 (uniform); asst. coach Peralta Coll. dist., Oakland, 1986-87; active spl. svcs. Rainbow Coalition State of Calif., 1984; del. Students for Mr. Jesse Jackson campaign, State of Calif., 1989. Pvt. U.S. Army, 1975-76. Mem. Pre-Paid Legal Svcs. (assoc., license), The Fed Bear Sports Club (diploma), Nirvana Found. for Psychic Rsch. (life), Am. Legion (life), Phi Beta Lambda, Epsilon Alpha Phi (past pres., past v.p. state chpt.). Republican. Islam. Home and Office: 706 34th St Ste 3 Oakland CA 94609

KING, CHARLOTTE ELAINE, program analyst; b. Baker, Oreg., Apr. 10, 1945; d. Melvin Howard and Rella Maxine (Gwilliam) Wright; m. Craig Seldon King, April 14, 1965; children: Andrea Karen, Diana Susan. Clerical positions various firms, Idaho, Va., Conn., 1964-71; nursing sec. VA, San Diego, 1974-77; sec. USN, Agana, Guam, 1972-73; procurement clk. USN, Bremerton, Wash., 1977-80; procurement clk. USN, San Diego, 1980, support svcs. supr., 1980-83, div. dir., 1983-87, program analyst, 1987—. Recipient Model Agy. cup USN, San Diego, 1986. Republican. Office: USN Pub Works Ctr Code 192 PO Box 113 San Diego CA 92140-0113

KING, DANIEL RICHARD, airspace manager, mayor; b. Tularosa, N.Mex., Feb. 16, 1940; s. Dan. W. and Ruthena C. (Champion) K.; m. Patricia A. Lambert, Aug. 29, 1964; children: Dan P., Scott J. BSBA, N.Mex. State U., 1963. V.p. Security Bank and Trust, Alamogordo, N.Mex., 1971-73, First State Bank, Cuba, N.Mex., 1973-74; owner, mgr. The Metalworks, Alamogordo, 1974-78; asst. chief pilot Air N.Mex., Santa Fe, 1979-80; pilot Black Hills Aviation, Alamogordo, 1978-81; dir. of ops., chief pilot Airways of N.Mex., Alamogordo, 1981-83; pilot Alamogordo, 1983-84; airspace mgr. 49 Tactical Fighter Wing, Holloman AFB, N.Mex., 1984-89; chief airspace mgmt. 833 Air Div., Holloman AFB, 1989—. City commr. City of Alamogordo, 1989—, mayor, 1990—. With USAF, 1963-69. Decorated D.F.C. Mem. Air Force Assn. Home: 1217 New York Ave Alamogordo NM 88310-6728 Office: 49 OSS/OSTA Holloman Air Force Base NM 88330

KING, DAVID, data processing executive; b. Eastleigh, Hampshire, Eng., Dec. 3, 1940; came to U.S., 1970; s. Shirley Walter and Flora Ellen (Worboys) K.; children: Sean David (dec.), Melanie Rachel. Cert. electronic engring., Medway Coll., Rochester, Eng., 1964; grad., Harrow Tech. Coll., Middx, Eng., 1967; postgrad., Open Univ., Milton Keynes, U.K., 1975—. Electronic engr. Elliott Automation, London and Rochester, Kent, Eng., 1960-64; cons. Howard Engrs., London, 1964-68; project mgr. IBM U.K. Ltd., Stirling Forest, N.Y., and Havant, U.K., 1968-75; pres. InFotech, Pasadena, Calif., 1975-79; v.p data processing Security Pacific Nat., Glendale, Calif., 1979-84; v.p. computer systems Citicorp, Santa Monica, Calif., 1984-86, N.Y.C., 1986-91; v.p. systems, programming Sunamerica Inc., L.A., 1991—; instr. computer programs UCLA, 1980-84; guest lectr. Pepperdine U., 1993—; mem. exec com. UCLA Info. Systems Assocs., chmn. elect, 1994. Author: Current Practices in Software Development, 1984, Creating Effective Software, 1988, Project Management Made Simple, 1992; contbr. articles to profl. jour. Mem. IEEE, British Inst. Radio and Electronic Engrs., Soc. Info. Mgmt., Assn. Computing Machinery. Office: Sunamerica Inc 11601 Wilshire Blvd Los Angeles CA 90025

KING, DAVID BURNETT, history educator; b. Phila., Jan. 31, 1930; s. Karl Burnett and Edith (Loveless) K.; m. Mary Brownson, Mar., 1952 (div. 1962); children: Laura, Bonnie, Thomas; m. Paula Richter, Mar., 1963 (div. 1967); 1 child, Stephen; m. Juanita Parot, Sept. 3, 1974; 1 child, Hannah. BA, Hamilton Coll., 1951; MA, Rutgers U., 1955; postgrad., U. Heidelberg, 1957-58; PhD, Cornell U., 1962. Vis. instr. Culver (Ind.) Mil. Acad., 1964-65; from instr. to asst. prof. history Oreg. State U., Corvallis, 1962-64, from assoc. to prof. history, 1965—; head honors program Oreg. State U., 1967-68. Author: The Crisis of Our Time: Reflections on the Course of Western Civilization, 1988. 1st lt. U.S. Army, 1951-54. Schurman fellow Heidelberg U., 1957-58, Andrew White fellow Cornell U., 1958-59; Fulbright grantee Bonn, 1981. Mem. German Studies Assn., AAUP (v.p. Corvallis chpt. 1966-67). Home: 7950 NW Oxbow Dr Corvallis OR 97330-2830 Office: Oreg State U History Dept Corvallis OR 97331

KING, DAVID W., state treasurer; b. Albuquerque, June 28, 1946; m. Martha Lynn King; children: Shannon, David II, Kevin Sam. BS, N.Mex. State U., 1969, MS in Agrl. Dcons., 1970; computer short course, Rochester, N.Y., 1074. Ptnr. King Bros. and Sons Ranch, Stanley, N.Mex., 1964—, Pine Canyon Ranches, Inc. and King Land and Cattle Co., Stanley, 1969—; dir. state planning office State of Mex., Santa Fe, 1971-74; state dir. farmers home adminstrn. USDA, Albuquerque, 1977-78; gov.'s cabinet sec. Dept. Fin. and Adminstrn., chmn. state investment coun. State of Mex., 1979-80, gov.'s cabinet sec. Gen. Svcs. Dept., 1983-85; dept. state treas. Office State Treas., 1986-90; state treas. State of N.Mex., Stanley, 1991—; exec. sec., gov.'s liaison Gov.'s N.Mex. Border Commission., 1071-75, 79-80. Mem. goodwill ambs. N.Mex. Amigos, 1973-86, Community Coun. of Albuquerque, 1974-79, N.Mex. Rural Devel. Coun., 1980-85; mem. resource conservation and devel. dist. exec. com. HUB, 1974-75; commn. mem. Internat. Space Hall of Fame., Alamogordo, N.Mex., 1975-81; supr. legal polit. subdiv. Edgewood Soil and Water Conservation Dist., 1976—; chmn. State Resource Conservation and Devel. Coun., 1971-77, N.Mex. Mortgage Fin. Authority, 1991—, Ednl. Assistance Found. Bd., 1991—; pres. N.Mex. Assn. Conservation Dists., 1977-79, nat. bd. dirs., 1980-81, N.Mex. State U. Bd. Regents, 1982-89; coord. 1st internat. border govs. conf. Mex. and U.S. El Paso, Tex. and Juarez Mex., 1980; mem., officer exec. bd. State Bapt. Ch., 1972-75; Sun. sch. dir. Calvary Bapt. Ch., 1983-85, Rodeo Road Bapt., 1985-88; elected to So. Bapt. conv. Nat. Christian Life Commn., Nashville, 1976-84; vice chmn. Border Devel. Authority, 1991—. Recipient State Minority and Human Devel. award N.Mex. State Conf. NAACP, 1972, Nat. Disting. Svc. award Nat. Assn. Conservation Dists., 1980-81, Supreme Ct. Excellence award State of Mex., 1985; named an Outstanding State Employee Soil Conservation Soc. Am., 1975. Mem. N.Mex. Technet (founding mem.), Rotary (past moriarty pres.), Omicron Delta Epsilon. Home: PO Box 85 Stanley NM 87056-0085 Office: N Mex State Treas PO Box 608 Santa Fe NM 87504-0608*

KING, FRANK, investment company executive; b. Redcliff, Alta., Can.; married; 4 children. BSChemE, U. Alta., 1958; LLD (hon.), U. Calgary, 1988. Chem. engr. various cos., 1958-72; pres. Met. Investment Corp., 1972—; pres., CEO Turbo Refining and Mktg. Co. Ltd., The Inmark Group, Avanti Petroleums Ltd.; also bd. dirs. other cos., Can. Chmn., chief exec. officer XV Olympic Winter Games Organizing Com.; active many community/sports programs. Decorated Officer Order of Can., Olympic Order in gold; recipient Air Can. Amateur Sports award, Premier's Award of Excellence, 1981, Champion d'Afrique Gold medal. Mem. Assn. Profl. Engrs., Geologists and Geophysicists of Alta., World Pres. Orgn., Calgary Booster Club (hon., life), Men's Can. Club (hon., life), Can. 125 Corp. (co-pres.), Lions (hon., life). Office: 837-2 Ave SW, Calgary, AB Canada T2P 0E6

KING, FRANK WILLIAM, writer; b. Port Huron, Mich., Oct. 1, 1922; s. William Ernest and Catherine Theresa (Smith) K.; student U. Utah, 1963-65, Santa Monica City Coll., 1941, 48-49; BA, Marylhurst Coll., 1979; MA, U. Portland, 1982; m. Carma Morrison Sellers, Sept. 16, 1961; children: Rosanne, Jeanine Nell, Melanie, Lisa June; one stepson, Michael Sellers. Air traffic contr. FAA, Salt Lake City, Albuquerque and Boise, Idaho; 1949-65, info. officer Western Region, L.A., 1965-68; pub. affairs officer L.A. Dist. C.E., U.S. Army, 1968-69, Walla Walla (Wash.), 1969-77, N. Pacific div., Portland, Oreg., 1977-79; dir. pub. rels. U. Portland, 1979-80; adj. asst. prof. communications U. Portland, 1982-83; instr. Portland Community Coll., 1980-87; freelance writer, 1980—. Exec. asst. L.A. Fed. Exec. Bd., 1965-67; chmn. Walla Walla County Alcoholism Adminstrv. Bd., 1974-75; vice-chmn. Walla Walla County Human Services Adminstrv. Bd., 1976-78, chmn., 1977-78. Served with USMCR, 1942-45. Decorated Air medal; William Randolph Hearst scholar, 1965. Mem. Soc. Profl. Journalists, Pub. Relations Soc. Am. (accredited), Kappa Tau Alpha. Democrat. Roman Catholic. Home and Office: 310 N Fawn Dr Otis OR 97368-9323

KING, FREDERIC, health services management executive, educator; b. N.Y.C., N.Y., May 9, 1937; s. Benjamin and Jeanne (Fritz) K.; m. Linda Ann Udell, Mar. 17, 1976; children by previous marriage—Coby Allen, Allison Beth, Lisa Robyn, Daniel Seth. B.B.A. cum laude, Bernard M. Baruch Sch. Bus. and Public Adminstrn., CUNY, 1958. Dir. adminstrn. Albert Einstein Coll. Medicine, Bronx, N.Y., 1970-72; assoc. v.p. health affairs Tulane Med. Ctr., New Orleans, 1972-77; dir. fin. Mt. Sinai Med. Ctr., N.Y.C., 1977-78; v.p. fin. Cedars-Sinai Med. Ctr., Los Angeles, 1978-82; pres. Vascular Diagnostic Services, Inc., Woodland Hills, Calif., 1982-84; exec. dir. South Bay Ind. Physicians Med. Group Inc., Torrance, Calif., 1984—; assoc. adj. prof. Tulane U. Sch. Pub. Health; asst. prof. Mt. Sinai Med. Ctr.; instr. Pierce Coll., Los Angeles; Bd. dirs pres./chmn. Ohr Eliyahu Acad.; dir. Pacific Jewish Ctr. Served with U.S. Army, 1959-62. Mem. Am. Pub. Health Assn., Healthcare Forum, Am. Hosp. Assn., Pres.'s Assn., Calif. Assn. Hosps. and Health Systems. Republican. Jewish. Home: 1116 Rose Ave Venice CA 90291-2835

KING, GUNDAR JULIAN, university dean; b. Riga, Latvia, Apr. 19, 1926; came to U.S., 1950, naturalized, 1954; s. Attis K. and Austra (Dale) Kenins: m. Valda K. Andersons, Sept. 18, 1954; children: John T., Marita A. Student, J.W. Goethe U., Frankfurt, Germany, 1946-48; BBA, U. Oreg., 1956; MBA, Stanford U., 1958, PhD, 1964; DSc (hon.), Riga Tech. U., 1991; D Habil. Oecon., Latvian Sci. Coun., 1992. Asst. field supr. Internat. Refugee Orgn., Frankfurt, 1948-50; br. office mfr. Williams Form Engring. Corp., Portland, Oreg., 1952-54; project mgr. Market Rsch. Assocs., Palo Alto, Calif., 1958-60; asst. prof., assoc. prof. Pacific Luth. U., 1960-66, prof., 1966—, dean Sch. Bus. Adminstrn., 1970-90; vis. prof. mgmt. U.S. Naval Postgrad. Sch., 1971-72, San Francisco State U., 1980, 87-88; internat econ. mem. Latvian Acad. Scis., 1990—; regent Estonian Bus. Sch., 1991—. Author: Economic Policies in Occupied Latvia, 1965; contbr. articles to profl. publs. Mem. Gov.'s Com. on Reorgn. Wash. State Govt., 1965-88; mem. study group on pricing U.S. Commn. Govt. Procurement, 1971-72; pres. N.W. Univs. Bus. Adminstrn. Conf., 1965-66; mem. bd. regents Estonian Bus. Sch., Tallinn, 1991—. With AUS, 1950-52. Fulbright-Hayes scholar, Thailand, 1988. Mem. AAUP (past chpt. pres.), Am. Mktg. Assn. (past chpt. pres.), Assn. Advancement Baltic Studies (pres. 1970), Western Assn. Collegiate Schs. Bus. (pres. 1971), Latvian Acad. Scis., Alpha Kappa Psi, Beta Gamma Sigma. Home: PO Box 44401 Tacoma WA 98444-0401 Office: Pacific Luth U Tacoma WA 98447

KING, HELEN EILEEN, service executive; b. Sunnyslope, Alberta, Can., June 3, 1920; d. Elvin Cyril and Pearl Marion (Archibald) White; m. Charles Lester King, Dec. 20, 1949; children: Gail, Carol, Laura. BEd, U. Alberta, 1947; postgrad., Pasadena Coll., 1948, U. Colo., 1979. Cert. elem. and secondary tchr., Can. Tchr. various sch. dists., Alberta, Can., 1941-45, C.N. Coll., Red Deer, Alberta, 1947-48; English tchr. Centro Boliviano Am., La Paz, Bolivia, 1954; forest fire lookout U.S. Forest Svc., Coeur d'Alene, Idaho, 1950, Grand Canyon, Ariz., 1974; mgr. Campus Natural Food Shoppe, Boulder, Colo., 1981-82; pres. Bus. and Postal Svcs., Boulder, 1982—; pres. Neola, Inc., Boulder, 1992—; mem. Alberta Tchrs. Assn., Edmonton, 1941-48. Vol. coord. Boulder County Safe house, Boulder, 1979; bd. dirs. Images in Motion differently abled Dance Group, Boulder, 1985—. Named Eco Hero, Boulder Daily CAmera, 1990, Colo. Recycler of Yr., Recycle Now, Denver, 1990. Mem. Nat. Fedn. Ind. Bus., Associated Mail Receiving Agy., Hill Merchants Assn., Nat. Health Fedn. Office: Bus and Postal Svcs 1085 14th St Boulder CO 80302

KING, INDLE GIFFORD, industrial designer, educator; b. Seattle, Oct. 23, 1934; s. Indle Frank and Phyllis (Kenney) K.; m. Rosalie Rosso, Sept. 10, 1960; children: Indle Gifford Jr., Paige Phyllis. BA, U. Wash., 1960, MA, 1968. Indsl. designer Hewlett-Packard, Palo Alto, Calif., 1961-63; mgr. indsl. design Sanborn Co., Boston, 1963-65; mgr. corp. design John Fluke Electronics Mfg. Co., Everett, Wash., 1965—; prof. indsl. design Western Wash. U., Bellingham, 1985—; cons. in field. Contbr. articles to profl. jours.; designer patents in field. Coach Mercer Island (Wash.) Boys' Soccer Assn., 1972-77; pres. Mercer Island PTA, 1973; advisor Jr. Achievement, Seattle, 1975-78. Mem. Idsl. Design Soc. Am. (Alcoa award 1965, v.p. Seattle chpt. 1986-88), Mercer Island Country Club. Office: John Fluke Co 6920 Seaway Blvd Everett WA 98203-5800

KING, IVAN ROBERT, astronomy educator; b. Far Rockaway, N.Y., June 25, 1927; s. Myram and Anne (Franzblau) K.; m. Alice Greene, Nov. 21, 1952 (div. 1982); children: David, Lucy, Adam, Jane. AB, Hamilton Coll., 1946; AM, Harvard U., 1947, PhD, 1952. Instr. astronomy Harvard U., 1951-52; mathematician Perkin-Elmer Corp., Norwalk, Conn., 1951-52; methods analyst U.S. Dept. Def., Washington, 1954-56; with U. Ill., 1956-64; assoc. prof. astronomy U. Calif., Berkeley, 1964-66, prof., 1966—, chmn. astronomy dept., 1967-70; mem. faint object camera team Hubble Space Telescope. Contbr. numerous articles to sci. jours. Served with USNR, 1952-54. Mem. AAAS (chmn. astronomy sect. 1974), NAS, Am. Acad. Arts & Scis., Am. Astron. Soc. (councillor 1963-66, chmn. div. dynamical astronomy 1972-73, pres. 1978-80), Internat. Astron. Union. Office: Univ of Calif Dept of Astronomy Berkeley CA 94720

KING, JANE CUDLIP COBLENTZ, volunteer educator; b. Iron Mountain, Mich., May 4, 1922; d. William Stacey and Mary Elva (Martin) Cudlip; m. George Samuel Coblentz, June 8, 1942 (dec. June 1989); children: Bruce Harper, Keith George, Nancy Allison Coblentz Patch; m. James E. King, August 23, 1991. BA, Mills Coll., 1942. Mem. Sch. Resource and Career Guidance Vols., Inc., Atherton, Calif., 1965-69, pres., chief exec. officer, 1969—. Proofreader, contbr. Mills Coll. Quarterly mag. Life gov. Royal Children's Hosp., Melbourne, Australia, 1963—; v.p. United Menlo Park (Calif.) Homeowner's Assn.; nat. pres. Mills Coll. Alumnae Assn., 1969-73, bd. trustees 1975-83. Named Vol. of Yr., Sequoia Union High Sch. Dist., 1988, Golden Acorn award for outstanding svc. Menlo Park C. of C., 1991. Mem. AAUW, Atherlons, Palo Alto (Calif.) Area Mills Coll. Club (pres. 1986), Phi Beta Kappa. Republican. Episcopalian. Home: 1109 Valparaiso Ave Menlo Park CA 94025-4412

KING, JANE LOUISE, artist; b. South Bend, Ind., Aug. 9, 1951; d. Bill and Anne Luciel (Hopkins) Berta; m. Gerald William King Jr., July 7, 1983; children: Kelly Anne, Dinah Jolene. Student, Ind. U., South Bend, 1969-70, Ind. U., 1970-71; BFA, Ohio State U., 1973. Ind. artist Colo., 1974—; instr. Sangre de Cristo Art Ctr., Pueblo, Colo., 1982, Art Studio, Longmont, Colo., 1989. Exhibited oil and pastel paintings in numerous exhibitions including 5th Ann. Internat. Exhibit Kans. Pastel Soc., 10th Ann. Pastel Soc. Am., N.Y., Colo. State Fair, Poudre Valley Art League; prin. works represented in numerous pvt. collections. Leader 4-H Club, Longmont, 1986—; sec. Longmont Artists Guild Gallery, 1988-89, bd. dirs., 1989; supt. 1st Bapt. Ch., Longmont, 1990-91. Mem. Colo. Artists Assn., Longmont Artists Guild (Grumbacher award 1992), Longmont Arts Coun., Knickerbocker Artists N.Y., Audubon Artists N.Y. Republican. Home: 1508 Kempton Ct Longmont CO 80501

KING, JANET CARLSON, nutrition educator, researcher; b. Red Oak, Iowa, Oct. 3, 1941; d. Paul Emil and Norma Carolina (Anderson) Carlson; m. Charles Talmadge King, Dec. 25, 1967; children: Matthew, Samuel. BS, Iowa State U., 1963; PhD, U. Calif., Berkeley, 1972. Dietitian Fitzsimmons Gen. Hosp., Denver, 1964-67; NIH postdoctoral fellow dept. nutrition sci. U. Calif., Berkeley, 1972-73, asst. prof. nutrition dept. nutrition sci., 1973-78, assoc. prof. nutrition dept. nutrition sci., 1978-83, prof. nutrition dept. nutrition sci., 1983—, chair dept. nutrition sci., 1988—; Frances E. Fischer Meml. nutrition lectr. Am. Dietetic Assn. Found., 1985, Lotte Arnrich Nutrition lectr. Iowa State U., 1985; Massee lectr. N.D., 1991. Contbr. articles to Jour. Am. Diet. Assn., Am. Jour. Clin. Nutrition, Jour. Nutrition, Nutrition Rsch., Obstetrics and Gynecology, Brit. Jour. Obstetrics and Gynaecology. Recipient Lederle Labs. award in human nutrition Am. Inst. Nutrition, 1989. Mem. Am. Dietetic Assn., Calif. Dietetic Assn., Am. Inst. Nutrition, AAAS, Sigma Xi. Office: U Calif Dept Nutritional Sci 119 Morgan Hall Berkeley CA 94720

KING, JONATHAN DAVID, microcomputer administrator; b. Wabash, Ind., Nov. 10, 1958; s. David Solomon King and Marilyn (Fenstermaker) Garrison. BA, U. N.Mex., 1981. Tech. programmer Honeywell DASD, Albuquerque, 1986-89; project coord. Reference Software Internat., Albuquerque, 1989-92; microcomputer adminstr. Arthur Andersen & Co., Albuquerque, 1992—. Home: 408 Maple SE #27 Albuquerque NM 87106

KING, LIONEL DETLEV PERCIVAL, retired nuclear physicist; b. Williamstown, Mass., Dec. 29, 1906; s. James Percival and Edith Marianne (Seyerlen) K.; m. Edith Marie Bork, Dec. 25, 1925 (dec. 1969); children: Nicholas S. P., Lidian King Watson; m. Jacqueline Cyzmoure, Jan. 1, 1970 (dec. 1973); m. Edna Johnson, Apr. 22, 1974 (dec. 1977); m. Elizabeth Dyar Russell, Apr. 30, 1978. BSME, U. Rochester, 1930; PhD in Physics, U. Wis., 1937. Asst. in physics U. Rochester, N.Y., 1930-31, MIT, Cambridge, 1931-33, U. Wis., Madison, 1935-37; instr. physics Purdue U., Lafayette, Ind., 1937-42; fellow U.S. Corps of Engrs., 1942-43; group leader Los Alamos (N.Mex.) Sci. Lab., 1943-57, asst. div. leader, 1958-59, chmn. rover flight safety, 1960-69, rsch. advisor, 1969-73, retired, 1973; lectr. Atoms for Peace Conf., Geneva, 1955, U.S. tech. dir., 1958; advisor U.S. del. to UN, 1958; cons. Los Alamos Sci. Lab., 1973-78. Active Oppenheimer Meml. Com., 1969— (chmn. 1974-76); chmn., treas. and sec. El Cajon Grande Tesuque Ditch Assn., 1975-79, mayordomo, 1979—. Fellow AAAS, Am. Nuclear Soc. (chmn. prog. com. 1954-57, honors and awards com. 1954-57, bd. dirs. 1954-59), Am. Phys. Soc., Sigma Xi. Home: RR 4 Box 16B Santa Fe NM 87501-9804

KING, MACLELLAN EDGAR, JR., telephone company executive; b. N.Y.C., Aug. 14, 1937; s. MacLellan Edgar and Betty Jane (Hellebush) K.; m. Elizabeth Hellyer, Sept. 17, 1960; children: Elizabeth, Blair, Stephanie. BS, U.S. Naval Acad., 1959; MBA, U. Chgo., 1972. Various mgmt. positions AT&T, 1964-83; v.p. Pacific Telephone & Telegraph, San Francisco, 1983-84, Pacific Bell, San Ramon, Calif., 1984-91, Pacific Telesis, San Francisco, 1991-93; pres., CEO Nev. Bell, Reno, 1993—. Pres. Leffingwell Forest Preserve Assn., Old Mission, Mich., 1980-82; mem. adv. bd. Bay Area Engrs., San Francisco, 1981—; bd. dirs. Stanford Mid Peninsula Urban Coll., Palo Alto, Calif., 1983-85; chair bd. trustees Athenian Sch., Danville, Calif., 1988—. Lt. USN, 1959-64. Republican. Office: Nevada Bell E Plumb Ln Reno NV 89502

KING, MARCIA, management consultant; b. Lewiston, Maine, Aug. 4, 1940; d. Daniel Alden and Clarice Evelyn (Curtis) Barrell; m. Howard P. Lowell, Feb. 15, 1969 (div. 1980); m. Richard G. King Jr., Aug., 1980. BS, U. Maine, 1965; MSLS, Simmons Coll., 1967. Reference, field advisory and bookmobile libr. Maine State Libr., Augusta, 1965-69; dir. Lithgow Pub. Libr., Augusta, 1969-72; exec. sec. Maine Libr. Adv. Com., Maine State Libr., 1972-73; dir. Wayland (Mass.) Free Pub. Libr., 1973-76; state libr. State of Oreg., Salem, 1976-82; dir. Tucson Pub. Libr., 1982-91; mgmt. cons. King Assocs., Tucson, 1991—. Past chmn. bd. dirs. Tucson United Way; chmn. adv. bd. com. Sta. KUAT (PBS-TV and Radio); mem. adv. bd. Resources for Women, Inc., Salvation Army. Mem. ALA, Pub. Library Assn., Ariz. State Library Assn., AAUW, Assn. Specialized and Coop. Library Agys. Unitarian. Office: King Assocs 7130 N Camino Caballos Tucson AZ 85743

KING, NICOLETTE JANE, ophthalmic lens company executive; b. Woking, Surrey, Eng., Oct. 10, 1962; came to U.S., 1986; d. Raymond Cecil and Kathleen (Watson) K.; m. Richard Henry Stanton, Sept. 18, 1987; 1 child, Caitlin King. BA/MA, St. Hilda's Coll., Oxford U., Eng., 1984; MBA, Stanford U., 1988. Assoc. cons. Bain and Co., London and Paris, 1984-86; cons. Bain and Co., San Francisco, 1988-89; mgr. strategic planning Pilkington Visioncare, Menlo Park, Calif., 1989-91; dir. laminate program Sola Optical, subs. Pilkington Visioncare, Petaluma, Calif., 1991—. Home: 37 Magnolia Ave San Anselmo CA 94960 Office: Sola Optical USA 1500 Cader Ln Petaluma CA 94953

KING, OSCAR LLOYD, astrodynamicist; b. Galveston, Tex., July 5, 1922; s. Oscar Lloyd and Lillie Dale (Johnson) K.; m. Ruth Norma, Feb. 1958. BA in Physics, Dartmouth Coll., 1948; postgrad., UCLA, 1950-66; MS in Engring., Cath. U. of Am., 1976. With USN, 1940-46; physicist GS-7 USN, China Lake, Calif., 1948-50; assoc. engr. North Am. Aviation, Downey, Calif., 1954-55, 61-66; rsch. analyst Douglas Aircraft, Santa Monica, Calif., 1956-59; sr. engr. McDonnell Douglas, St. Louis, 1966-68; satellite engr. Telesat-Canada, Ottawa, 1970-71; tech. staff Computer Sci. Corp., Silver Spring, Md., 1973-75; rsch. specialist Boeing, Kent, Wash., 1978-80, Wichita, Kans., 1983-88; staff engr. Martin Marietta, Denver, 1981-82; astrodynamicist Par Govt. Systems, Colorado Springs, 1989-90; cons. astrodynamics Correa Enterprises, Albuquerque, N.Mex., 1992—; pres. Wichita Astron., 1987; instr. Ferguson-Florisant Sch., St. Louis, 1967. Creator: Interplanetary Rendezvous Trajectory Software, 1992; author: Charts on Interrelationships of Math to Human Endeavor and Space Exploration Disciplines, 1991, 92. Tchr. Calif. Mus. of Sci. and Industry, L.A., 1965; mathematician Denver Pub. Librs., 1991. Mem. AIAA. Democrat. Home: 4264 S Nucla Way Aurora CO 80013-2927

KING, RAY JOHN, electrical engineer; b. Montrose, Colo., Jan. 1, 1933; s. John Frank and Grace (Rankin) K.; m. Diane M. Henney, June 20, 1964; children: Karl V., Kristin J. BS in Electronic Engring., Ind. Inst. Tech., 1956, BS in Elec. Engring., 1957; MS, U. Colo., 1960, PhD, 1965. Instr. Ind. Inst. Tech., 1956-58, asst. prof., 1960-62, acting chmn. dept. electronics, 1960-62; research asso. U. Colo., 1962-65; research assoc. U. Ill., 1965; assoc. prof. elec. engring. U. Wis., Madison, 1965-69; prof. U. Wis., 1969-82, assoc. dept. chmn. for research and grad. affairs, 1977-79; staff rsch. engr. Lawrence Livermore Nat. Lab. (Calif.), 1982-90, sr. scientist high power microwaves program, 1989-90; co-founder KDC Tech. Corp., 1983, v.p., 1990—, cons.; vis. Erskine fellow U. Canterbury, N.Z., 1977; guest prof., Fulbright scholar Tech. U. Denmark, 1973-74. Author: Microwave Homodyne Systems, 1978; contbr. articles to profl. jours.; patentee in field. NSF Faculty fellow, 1962-65. Fellow IEEE; mem. IEEE Soc. on Antennas and Propagation (adminstrv. com. 1989-91, chmn. wave propagation stds. com. 1986-89, gen. chmn. symposium 1989), IEEE Soc. Microwave Theory and Techniques, IEEE Soc. Instrumentation and Measurements, Forest Products Rsch. Soc., Soc. for Advancement Materials and Processing, Electromagnetics Acad., Internat. Sci. Radio Union (commns. A, B, F), Sigma Xi, Iota Tau Kappa, Sigma Phi Delta. Home: 2595 Raven Rd Pleasanton CA 94566-4605 Office: KDC Tech Corp 2011 Research Dr Livermore CA 94550-3803

KING, ROBERT LUCIEN, lawyer; b. Petaluma, Calif., Aug. 9, 1936; s. John Joseph and Ramona Margaret (Thorson) K.; m. Suzanne Nanette Parre, May 18, 1956 (div. 1973); children: Renee Michelle, Candyce Lynn, Danielle Louise, Benjamin Robert; m. Linda Diane Carey, Mar. 15, 1974 (div. 1981); 1 child, Debra; m. J'an See, Oct. 27, 1984 (div. 1989); 1 child, Jonathan F.; m. Marilyn Collins, June 15, 1991. AB in Philosophy, Stanford U., 1958, JD, 1960. Bar: Calif., N.Y. 1961. Asst. U.S. atty. U.S. Atty's. Office (so. dist.), N.Y.C., 1964-67; assoc. Debevoise & Plimpton, N.Y.C., 1960-64, 67-70, ptnr., 1970-89; mng. ptnr. Debevoise & Plimpton, L.A., 1989—; lectr. Practicing Law Inst., N.Y.C., ABA, Asia/Pacific Ctr. for Resolution of Internat. Bus. Disputes; bd. dirs. L.A. Ctr. Internat. Comml. Arbitration. Fellow Am. Coll. Trial Lawyers; mem. ABA, Assn. Bar City N.Y., Calif. Bar Assn., L.A. County Bar Assn., Assn. Bus. Trial Lawyers. Democrat. Home: 10000 Tikita Pl Toluca Lake CA 91602-2920 Office: Debevoise & Plimpton Ste 3700 601 S Figueroa St Los Angeles CA 90017

KING, SAMUEL PAILTHORPE, judge; b. Hankow, China, Apr. 13, 1916; s. Samuel W. and Pauline (Evans) K.; m. Anne Van Patten Grilk, July 8, 1944; children—Samuel Pailthorpe, Louise Van Patten, Charlotte Lelepoki. B.S., Yale, 1937, LL.B., 1940. Bar: D.C., Hawaii bars 1940. Practiced law Honolulu, 1941-42, 46-61, 70-72, Washington, 1942; atty. King & McGregor, 1947-53, King & Myhre, 1957-61; judge 1st Circuit Ct. Hawaii, 1961-70, Family Ct., 1966-70; judge U.S. Dist. Ct. for Hawaii, 1972—, chief judge, 1974-84; Faculty Nat. Coll. State Judiciary, 1968-73, Nat. Inst. Trial Advocacy, 1976, U. Hawaii Law Sch., 1980-84. Co-translator, co-editor: (O. Korschelt) The Theory and Practice of Go, 1965. Served with USNR, 1941-46; capt. Res. ret. Fellow Am. Bar Found.; mem. ABA, Hawaii Bar Assn. (pres. 1953), Order of Coif. Republican (chmn. Hawaii central com. 1953-55, nat. com. 1971-72). Episcopalian. Home: 1717 Mott Smith Dr Honolulu HI 96822-2873 Office: US Dist Ct PO Box 50128 Honolulu HI 96850-0001

KING, SAMUEL PAILTHORPE, JR., lawyer; b. Honolulu, June 16, 1947; s. Samuel Pailthorpe Sr. and Anne Van Patten (Grilk) K.; m. Adrienne Caryl Sepaniak, Oct. 19, 1974; children: Christopher E.S., Samuel Wilder II. BS in Econs., Yale U., 1969; JD, U. Colo., 1973. Bar: Hawaii 1974, U.S. Ct. Appeals (9th cir.) 1974, U.S. Supreme Ct., 1978. Ptnr. King & King, Honolulu; arbitrator Court program and AAA, Honolulu, 1985—. vice chancellor Episc. Diocese Honolulu, 1989-93. Mem. Hawaii Assn. Criminal Def. Lawyers (pres. 1988, sec. 1989—). Republican. Home: 1163 Kaäeleku St Honolulu HI 96825 Office: 735 Bishop St # 308 Honolulu HI 96813

KING, W. DAVID, professional hockey coach; b. North Battleford, Sask., Can., Dec. 22, 1947. Head coach Team Can. Internat. League, 1984-92; head coach Calgary (Can.) Flames, 1992—. Office: Calgary Flames, PO Box 1540 Sta M, Calgary, AB Canada T2P 3B9

KINGMAN, DONG, artist, educator; b. Oakland, Calif., Apr. 1, 1911; s. Dong Chuan-Fee and Lew Shee K.; m. Wong Shee, Sept. 1929 (dec. June 1954); children—Eddie, Dong Kingman Jr.; m. Helena Kuo, Sept. 1956. Student, Lingnan, Hong Kong, 1924-26; LHD (hon.), Acad. Art Coll., San Franciso, 1987. Tchr. art San Diego Art Gallery, 1941-43; tchr. Famous Artists Schs., Westport, Conn., Columbia U., Hunter Coll.; Lectr. tour around world sponsored by internat. cultural exchange program Dept. State, 1954. Represented in permanent collections, Whitney Mus. Am. Art, Am. Acad. Arts and Letters, Bklyn. Mus., Toledo Mus. Art, Joslyn Art Mus., Omaha, Mus. Fine Arts, Boston, Met. Mus. Art, Mus. Modern Art, N.Y.C., U. Nebr., Wadsworth Atheneum, Bloomington (Ill.) Art Assn., San Francisco Mus., Mills Coll., De Young Mus., Albert Bender Collection, Eleanor Roosevelt Collection, Chgo. Art Inst., N.Y. State Tchrs. Coll., Springfield (Ill.) Art Assn., Cranbrook Acad. Art, Butler Art Inst., Ft. Wayne Mus., Addison Gallery, U.S. Dept. State, many others; executed murals, Bank of Calif., San Francisco, N.Y. Hilton Hotel, R.H. Macy & Co., Franklin Sq., N.Y., Boca Raton Hotel, Fla., Hyatt Regency Hotel, Hong Kong, Ambassador Hotel, Kowloon, Hong Kong, Lincoln Savs. Bank, N.Y.C.; illustrator: The Bamboo Gate (Vanya Oakes), 1946, China's Story (Enid LaMonte Meadowcroft), 1946, Nightingale (Andersen), 1948, Johnny Hong in Chinatown (Clyde Robert Bulla), 1952, Caen's and Kingman's San Francisco (Herb Caen), 1964, City on the Golden Hill (Herb Caen), 1967; author: (with Helena Kuo Kingman) Dong Kingman's Watercolors, 1980, Paint the Yellow Tiger, 1991; Painted: (with Helena Kuo Kingman) title paintings for 55 Days at Peking, movie title paints for Flower Drum Song, 1964, movie poster Universal Studio Tour. Served in U.S. Army. Recipient award Chgo. Internat. Watercolor Exhbn., 1944, Gold medal of honor Audubon Artists Exhbn. 1946, award, 1956; Joseph Pennel Meml. medal Phila. Watercolor Club, 1950, award, 1968; Watercolor prize Pa. Acad., 1953, Am. Watercolor Soc. award, 1956, 60, 62-65, 67, 72, High Wings Medal award, 1973, V.K. McCracken Young award, 1976, Ford-Times award, 1978, Barse Miller Meml. award, 1979, Dolphin Medal award, 1987; 150th Anniversary Gold Medal award Nat. Acad. Design, 1975, Walter Bigg Meml. award, 1977; Key to City of Omaha, 1980, Key to City of Cin., 1980; San Diego Watercolor Soc. prize, 1984, 1st prize for Ch. No. 1, San Francisco Art Assn., 1936; named Hon. Admiral of Navy, Omaha, 1979, Hon. Citizen of Louisville, 1980, Hon. Capt. of Belle of Louisville, 1980, Man of Yr. Chinatown Planning Coun., N.Y.C., 1981, Man of Yr. Oakland (Calif.) Chinese Community Coun., 1985, Man of Yr. Rotary Club 1991, Man of Yr. Chinese Affirmative Action, San Francisco, 1991, Guest of Honor for Opening Internat. Book Fair, Hong Kong, 1991, judge Miss Universe and Miss U.S.A., 1963-85; Guggenheim fellow, 1942-43. Home: 21 W 58th St New York NY 10019-1604 Office: care Stary Sheet Gallery 14988 Sand Canyon Ave Irvine CA 92718-9999

KINGMAN, ELIZABETH YELM, anthropologist; b. Lafayette, Ind., Oct. 15, 1911; d. Charles Walter and Mary Irene (Weakley) Yelm; m. Eugene Kingman, June 10, 1939; children—Mixie Kingman Eddy, Elizabeth Anne Kingman. BA U. Denver, 1933, MA, 1935. Asst. in anthropology U. Denver, 1932-34; mus. asst. Ranger Naturalist Force, Mesa Verde Nat. Park, Colo., 1934-38; asst. to husband in curatorial work, Indian art exhibits Philbrook Art Ctr., Tulsa, 1939-42, Joslyn Art Mus., Omaha, 1947-69; tutor humanities dept. U. Omaha, 1947-50; chmn. bd. govs. Pi Beta Phi Settlement Sch., Gatlinburg, Tenn., 1969-72; asst. to husband in exhibit design mus. of Tex. Tech. U., 1970-75, bibliographer Internat. Ctr. Arid and Semi-Arid Land Studies, 1974-75; librarian Sch. Am. Research, Santa Fe, 1978-86; research assoc., 1986—; v.p. Santa Fe Corral of the Westerners, 1985-86. Mem. Archeol. Inst. Am. (v.p. Santa Fe chpt. 1981-83), LWV, Santa Fe Hist. Soc. (sec. 1981-83). Presbyterian. Home: 604 Sunset St Santa Fe NM 87501-1118 Office: Sch Am Rsch 660 Garcia St Santa Fe NM 87501

KINGORE, EDITH LOUISE, retired geriatrics and rehabilitation nurse; b. Parsons, Kans., Nov. 18, 1922; d. George Richard and Josephine (Martin) K. Diploma, Mo. Meth. Hosp., St. Joseph, 1955. RN. Staff nurse El Cerrito Hosp., Long Beach, Calif., 1966-69; nurse Alamitos-Belmont Convalescent Hosp., Long Beach, 1973-75; staff nurse Freeman Hosp., Joplin, Mo., 1975-76, Oak Hill Osteo. Hosp., Joplin, 1976-77; surg. care and rehab. nurse St. Francis Med. Ctr., Cape Guiardo, Mo., 1977-78; psychiat. nurse Western Mo. Mental Health Ctr., Kansas City, Mo., 1978; pvt. duty nurse, 1978-83. Historian South Coast Ecumenical Coun., 1992-93. Mem. Woman's Music Club of Long Beach. Home: 3333 Pacific Pl Apt 418 Long Beach CA 90806-1261

KINGRY, BARBARA ANNE, technical center administrator; b. Hazleton, Pa., Feb. 7, 1939; d. Marvin Frederick and Ruth Anna (Wheeler) Siebel; m. Wayne H. Kingry, Jr., June 27, 1975 (dec. Dec. 1989); children: Sean M., James Goldey. BA, Trenton State Coll., 1957; MEd, Lesley Coll., Cambridge, Mass., 1986. Registered respiratory therapist. Dept. dir. North Platte (Nebr.) Community Hosp., 1974-75; newborn coord. Children's Hosp., Denver, 1975-79; edn. coord. Rose Med. Ctr., Denver, 1979-81; program dir. respiratory tech. program Pickens Tech., Aurora, Colo., 1981-86; mktg. rep. Foster Med. Corp., Denver, 1986-87; staff therapist Porter Meml. Hosp., Denver, 1987-88; dir., br. mgr. Pediatric Svcs. Am., Denver, 1988-90; dir. clin. edn. T.H. Pickens Tech. Ctr., Aurora, Colo., 1991, div. coord. health occupations, 1991—; site evaluator Joint Rev. Com. for Respiratory Therapy Edn., Euless, Tex. Met. coun. mem. Am. Lung Assn., 1987-91. Mem. Am. Assn. Respiratory Care (program com. 1992), Colo. Soc. Respiratory Care (dir. at large 1983-86, 90-92, sec. 1980-81, program com. 1982-92), Colo. Assn. Respiratory Educators (chair 1991—). Methodist. Home: 11478 S Marlborough St Parker CO 80134 Office: T H Pickens Tech Ctr 500 Buckley Rd Aurora CO 80011

KINGSBURY, CAROLYN ANN, software systems engineer; b. Newark, Ohio, Aug. 4, 1938; d. Cecil C. Layman and Orpha Edith (Hisey) Layman Dick; m. L.C. James Kingsbury, Apr. 25, 1959; children: Donald Lynn, Kenneth James. BS in Math., BS in Info. and Computer Scis., U. Calif., Irvine, 1979; postgrad. West Coast U., 1982-84. Systems engr., analyst Rockwell Internat., Downey, Calif., 1979-84, system and software engr. Northrop Corp., Pico Rivera, Calif., 1984-89; systems engr. Hughes Aircraft Co., Long Beach, Calif., 1989-90, Fullerton, Calif., 1990-91. Pres. PTA, Manhattan Beach, Calif., 1971-73; Cub Scout den mother Boy Scouts Am., Manhattan Beach, 1972-73. Recipient Service award Calif. Congress Parents and Tchrs., 1973, Leadership Achievement award YWCA, Los Angeles, 1980, 84, NASA Achievement awards, 1983. Mem. NAFE, AAUW, Nat. Mgmt. Assn., Newtowners Club (pres. 1962). Republican. Home: 11392 Stonecress Ave Fountain Valley CA 92708-2450

KINGSBURY, WILLIAM CHARLES, JR., political consultant; b. San Jose, Calif., Apr. 15, 1936; s. William C. and Ruth (Garnsey) K.; m. Jerilee Douglas, June 19, 1965 (div. 1967); m. Susan White, Oct. 2, 1971; 1 child, Michael Charles. BA, Upper Iowa U., 1979; MA, Auburn U., 1980; student, Calif. So. Law Sch., 1992—. Comd. 2d lt. USAF, 1961, advanced through grades to col., 1979; commdr. 351st Strategic Missile Wing, Whiteman AFB, Mo., 1982-83; chief of staff Under Sec. of Def., Washington, 1983-86; ret. USAF, 1986; strategy cons. Bob Ryan for Congress, Las Vegas, Nev., 1986; campaign mgr. Hamby for Congress, Concord, N.C., 1986; nat. campaign staff Laxalt for Pres., Washington, 1987-88; cons. Marshall Coleman for Gov., McLean, Va., 1989; polit. cons. Kingsbury & Assoc., Redlands, Calif., 1990—. Cons. Nev. Rep. Com., Las Vegas, 1987—, Clark County Rep. Com., Las Vegas, 1987—. Decorated Def. Superior Svc. medal, Legion of Merit, Meritorious Svc. medal. Mem. Air Force Assn., Order of Daedalians, Ret. Officers Assn., Am. Legion. Republican. Episcopalian. Home: 117 E Cypress Ave Redlands CA 92373 Office: Kingsbury & Assocs 117 E Cypress Ave Redlands CA 92373

KINGSLEY, GEORGE MILLIS, JR., insurance company executive; b. Cleve., Nov. 13, 1931; s. George Millis Sr. and Dorothy Mae (Loomis) K.; m. Virginia Stevenson, June 11, 1955; children: Karen Dorothy, George Millis III, David Maitland. AB, Dartmouth Coll., 1954; MBA, Harvard U., 1958. CLU. Agt. Northwestern Mutual, Cleve., 1958-62; supr. Mass. Mutual, Cleve., 1962-65, The New Eng., Cleve., 1965-68; v.p. The New Eng., Boston, 1968-72; gen. agt. The New Eng., Buffalo, 1972-82; regional v.p. The New Eng., Irvine, Calif., 1982-86; gen. agt. The New Eng., San Diego, 1986-90; cons. GMK & Assocs., San Diego, 1990—; instr. Am. Coll., Buffalo, 1980-82, Northeastern U., Boston, 1970. Speaker convs.; contbr. articles to profl. jours. Pres. Dartmouth Alumni Club, Cleve., 1960. 1st lt. U.S. Army, 1954-56. Mem. Cleve. Life Underwriters (pres. 1971-72), Buffalo Life Underwriters (pres. 1979-80), Western N.Y. Gen. Agt. Assn. (pres. 1975), New Eng. Gen. Agts. Assn. (pres.-elect 1982), Park Country Club (pres. 1978-79). Episcopalian. Home: 12389 Avenida Consentido San Diego CA 92128

KINGSTON, GEORGE, professional hockey team coach. Formerly sports dir. Norwegian Ice Hockey Fedn.; coach, nat. hockey team, Norway; head coach San Jose Sharks, San Jose, Calif., 1991—. Office: care San Jose Sharks 10 Almaden Blvd Ste 600 San Jose CA 95113-2226

KINKADE, KATE, publishing executive, magazine editor, insurance executive; b. N.Y.C., Jan. 22, 1951; d. Joel M. and Peeta S. (Sherman) Sandleman; m. Patrick Ramsey, June 27, 1981; children: Jamaa Ramsey, Kikanza Ramsey. BS in Speech, Emerson Coll., Boston, 1972; postgrad., Am. Coll., Bryn Mawr, Pa. CLU. Mgr. sales Equitable Life Ins., L.A., 1973-76; agy. v.p. Lincoln Nat. Life Ins. Co., Encino, Calif., 1976-80; chief exec. officer TIME Fin. Svcs., Reseda, Calif., 1980—; editor-in-chief Calif. Broker, Burbank, Calif., 1981—; exec. v.p. Life Underwriters Assn., Encino, 1978-81. Contbr. articles to profl. jours. Treas., trustee Labor Community Strategy Ctr., Van Nuys, Calif.. Recipient Asst. Prodn. awards Equitable Life, 1973, 77, Lincoln Nat. Life, 1978, 80, Pacific Mut. Life, 1983. Mem. Assn. CLU's. Democrat. Office: TIME Fin 18107 Sherman Way Ste 205 Reseda CA 91335-4572

KINLEN, JAMES GILBERT, publishing executive; b. Breckenridge, Pa., Aug. 25, 1933; s. George Sylvanius Kinlen and Bernice Carson; m. Rozonna Kinlen, Mar. 28, 1959; children: Christopher James, Leslie Loree. Student, Wayne State U. Mgr. State Securities, Dallas, 1956-66, Gen. Tire Co., Denver, Albuquerque, 1966-71; owner, pres. FLYING Review Publs., Albuquerque, 1972—; pres. Aviation Factors, Albuquerque, 1976—. Mem. Albuquerque C. of C., 1985-90. Staff sgt. U.S. Army, 1952-55, Korea. Recipient Cert. of Merit, Nat. Aeronautic Assn., 1990, Journalism award Ziff Daivs Pub., 1976; named Man of Yr., Mo. Pilots Assn., 1985. Mem. U.S. Pilots Assn. (bd. dirs., Mem. of Yr. 1986), N.Mex. Pilots Assn. (bd. dirs.), Irish Am. Soc., Air Force Assn., Aircraft Owners and Pilots Assn., VFW, Am. Legion. Republican. Methodist. Home: 4801 Charlotte Ct NE Albuquerque NM 87109 Office: FLYING Review PO Box 9191 Albuquerque Airport Albuquerque NM 87119

KINNEE, SANDY, artist; b. Port Huron, Mich., Mar. 30, 1947; s. Floyd Amos Jr. and Annabel Victoria (O'Hare) K.; m. Gale Barbara Murray, Jan. 22, 1977; 1 child, Lauren Murray Kinnee. BFA, U. Mich., 1969; MFA, Wayne State U., 1976. instr. Colo. Coll., 1986, 79, 92-93, U. Colo., Colo. Springs, 1978-80, Colo. Springs Fine Arts Ctr., 1977-78. Prin. works represented in numerous one-man shows including Zurich, Switzerland, 1992, 1/1 Gallery, Denver, 1992, Peter M. David Gallery, Mpls., 1990, Marcus/Gordon, Pitts., 1987, Mather Gallery Case Western Res. U., Cleve., 1982, Creighton U., Omaha, 1981; prin. works reperesented in numerous pub. and pvt. collections including Met. Mus. Art, N.Y.C., State Office Bldg., Columbus, Ohio, Allen Art Mus., Oberlin, Ohio, Evergreen State Coll., Olympia, Wash., N.Mex. Mus., Santa Fe, Portland (Oreg.) Art Mus., Madison (Wis.) Art Ctr. Founder, dir. Early Bird Field Hockey, Colo. Springs, 1987—. Pollack-Krasner Found. grantee, 1987; Printmakers fellow Western States Art Found., 1979. Mem. U.S. Field Hockey Assn. Home: 1202 N Institute St Colorado Springs CO 80903-2625

KINNEY, GREGG ALAN, management consultant, financial consultant; b. Denver, July 7, 1948; s. John Charles and Mildred Fay (Brandt) K.; m. Julie Jean Reed, Mar. 15, 1948; children: Karen Jean, Steven Reed. BS in Bus. and Indsl. Adminstrn., U. Kans., 1970; grad., Colo. Graduate Sch. of Banking, 1982. Lic. real estate broker, Colo. Asst. cashier Affiliated First Colo. Bank & Trust, Denver, 1973-76; cashier Affiliated First Nat. Bank in Loveland, Loveland, Colo., 1977-79; sr. v.p. Omnibank Aurora, Aurora, Colo., 1979-83; dir., pres., CEO Omnibank Arapahoe, N.A., Englewood, Colo., 1983-84; dir. Bergen Pk. Nat. Bank, Evergreen, Colo., 1985-90, Douglas County Nat. Bank, Parker, Colo., 1985-90; owner Advanced Fin. Mgmt., Evergreen, 1985—. With USAR, 1970-76. Office: Advanced Fin Mgnt 31202 Island Dr Evergreen CO 80439-8900

KINNEY, JAY MACNEAL, editor, author, illustrator; b. Cleve., July 18, 1950; s. Del Jay and Analee (Lathrop) K.; m. Dixie Leone Tracy, July 8, 1978. Student, Baldwin Wallace Coll., Berea, Ohio, 1968-69, Pratt Inst., Bklyn., 1969-72. Prodn. asst. Whole Earth, Sausalito, Calif., 1980-83; editor Coevolution Quar., Sausalito, Calif., 1983-85; editor-in-chief Gnosis Mag., San Francisco, 1985—; pres. The Lumen Found., San Francisco, 1984—. Contbg. editor Whole Earth Rev., 1985—; editor/author comic art pubs.; contbr. articles to profl. jours.; freelance illustrator. Office: Gnosis Mag PO Box 14217 San Francisco CA 94114

KINNEY, LISA FRANCES, state senator; b. Laramie, Wyo., Mar. 13, 1951; d. Irvin Wayne and Phyllis (Poe) K.; m. Rodney Philip Lang, Feb. 5, 1971; children: Cambria Helen, Shelby Robert, Eli Wayne. BA, U. Wyo., 1973, JD, 1986; MLS, U. Oreg., 1975. Reference libr. U. Wyo. Sci. Libr., Laramie, 1975-76; outreach dir. Albany County Libr., Laramie, 1975-76, dir., 1977-83; mem. Wyo. State Senate, Laramie, 1984—, minority leader, 1992—, with documentation office Am. Heritage Ctr. U. Wyo., 1991—. Author: (with Rodney Lang) Civil Rights of the Developmentally Disabled, 1986; (with Rodney Lang and Phyllis Kinney) Manual For Families with Emotionally Disturbed and Mentally Ill Relatives, 1988, rev. 1991; Lobby For Your Library; Know What Works, 1992; contbr. articles to profl. jours; editor, compiler pub. relations directory for ALA, 1982. Bd. dirs. Big Bros./Big Sisters, Laramie, 1980-83. Recipient Beginning Young Profl. award Mt. Plains Libr. Assn., 1980; named Outstanding Wyo. Libr. Wyo. Libr. Assn., 1977, Outstanding Young Woman State of Wyo., 1980. Mem. ABA, Nat. Confs. of State Legislatures (various coms. 1985-90), Laramie C. of C., Snowy Range Internat. Folk Dance Club (pres. 1980-87), Zonta (v.p. 1989-91). Democrat. Avocations: photography, dance, reading, traveling, languages. Home and Office: 2358 Jefferson St Laramie WY 82070

KINNEY, RALEIGH EARL, artist; b. Brainerd, Minn., Mar. 11, 1938; s. Earl Martin and Nancy Ann (Wolleat) K.; m. Darlene Joyce Fox, Sept. 12, 1964; children: Rodney Eric, Aaron Weston. BS, St. Cloud (Minn.) State U., 1965, MA, 1968. Cert. tchr. Art tchr. St. Cloud Jr. High Sch., 1965-70; art tchr., dept. chmn. St. Cloud Sr. High Sch., 1970-80; ind. instr. watercolor workshop, 1980—. Contbr. artist North Light Pub., 1993. Served with USN, 1957-61. Named Artist of Yr. Phoenix C. of C., 1987. Mem. Ariz. Watercolor Soc. (signature), Midwest Watercolor Soc. (v.p. 1976-77, signature). Republican. Home: 1947 E Manhatton Dr Tempe AZ 85282-5815

KINNIE, ROBERT H., retail company executive. Chmn., pres., chief exec. officer Can. Safeway, Ltd., Winnipeg, Man. Office: Can Safeway Ltd, 150 6th Ave SW, Calgary, AB Canada T2P 2S6 also: Mac Donalds Consol Ltd, 840 Cambie St, Vancouver, BC Canada V6B 4S8 also: Safeway Stores Inc 201 4th St Oakland CA 94660

KINNISON, HARRY AUSTIN, transportation engineer; b. Springfield, Ohio, Oct. 2, 1935; s. Errett Lowell and Audrey Muriel (Smith) K. BSEE, U. Wyo., 1964; M. in Transp. Engring., Seattle U., 1983; PhD in Civil Engring., U. Tenn., 1987. Enlisted USAF, 1958, commd. 2d lt., 1964, advanced through grades to capt., 1968, released from active duty, 1968; electronics engr. 1839th Electronics Installation Group, Keesler AFB, Biloxi, Miss., 1972-77; staff engr. Casper (Wyo.) Air Facilities Sector FAA, 1977; test engr. Boeing Aerospace Co., Seattle, 1977-81; grad. rsch. engr. U. Tenn. Transp. Ctr., Knoxville, 1983-87; avionics engr. Boeing Comml. Airplane Co., Seattle, 1981-83, 87-89, maintenance programs engr. customer svcs. div., 1989—. Mem. Inst. Transp. Engrs. (assoc.), Transp. Rsch. Bd. (assoc.), Inst. Elec. and Electronics Engrs. Republican. Mem. Christian Ch. Home: 11630 SE 219th Pl Kent WA 98031 Office: Boeing Comml Airplane Group PO Box 3707 M/S 2J52 Seattle WA 98124

KINNISON, ROBERT WHEELOCK, accountant; b. Des Moines, Sept. 17, 1914; s. Virgil R. and Sopha J. (Jackson) K.; m. Randi Hjelle, Oct. 28, 1971; children—Paul F., Hazel Jo Huff. B.S. in Acctg., U. Wyo., 1940. C.P.A., Wyo., Colo. Ptnr. 24 hour auto service, Laramie, Wyo., 1945-59; pvt. practice acctg., Laramie, Wyo., 1963-71, Las Vegas, Nev., 1972-74, Westminster, Colo., 1974-76, Ft. Collins, Colo., 1976—. Served with U.S. Army, 1941-45; PTO. Mem. Wyo. Soc. C.P.A.s, Am. Legion (past comdr.), Laramie Soc. C.P.A.s (pres. 1966), VFW. Clubs: Laramie Optimist (pres. 1950), Sertoma. Home: PO Box 168 Fort Collins CO 80522-0168 Office: 2050 Airway Ave Fort Collins CO 80524

KINSELL, JEFFREY CLIFT, investment banker; b. Santa Barbara, Calif., Sept. 13, 1951; s. Clift Seybert and Shirlee Grace (Burwash) K.; m. Sondra A. Kinsell, May 21, 1987; children: Amy Elizabeth, Pamela Suzanne. BS in Biology, Tulane U., 1973; MBA in Fin., Acctg., UCLA, 1976. Assoc. mcpl.

sales and trading First Boston Corp., N.Y.C., 1976-78; v.p. First Boston Corp., San Francisco, 1978-88; v.p., western regional mgr. Paine Webber Capital Markets, Inc., San Francisco, 1988—. Mem. San Francisco Mcpl. Bond Club, Beta Beta Beta, Sigma Alpha Epsilon. Republican. Episcopalian. Home: 93 La Espiral Rd Orinda CA 94563-1852 Office: Paine Webber Inc 100 California St Ste 1245 San Francisco CA 94111-4517

KINSELLA, WILLIAM PATRICK, author, educator; b. Edmonton, Alta., Can., May 25, 1935; s. John Matthew and Olive Mary (Elliot) K.; m. Mildred Irene Clay, Sept. 10, 1965 (div. 1978); children: Shannon, Lyndsey, Erin; m. Ann Ilene Knight, Dec. 30, 1978. BA, U. Victoria, B.C., Can., 1974; MFA, U. Iowa, 1978; DLitt, Laurentian U., Sudbury, Ont., Can., 1990, U. Victoria, 1991. Prof. U. Calgary, Alta., Can., 1978-83; freelance author White Rock, B.C., Can., 1983—. Author: Dance Me Outside, 1977, Scars, 1978, Shoeless Joe Jackson Comes to Iowa, 1980, Born Indian, 1981, Shoeless Joe, 1982, Mocassin Telegraph, 1983, The Thrill of Grass, 1984, The Alligator Report, 1985, The Iowa Baseball Confederacy, 1986, The Fencepost Chronicles, 1986, Five Stories, 1987, Red Wolf, Red Wolf, 1987, The Further Adventures of Slugger McBatt, 1988, The Miss Hobbema Pageant, 1989, Two Spirits Soar: The Art of Allen Sapp, 1990, Box Socials, 1991; co-author: (poetry with Ann Knight) The Rainbow Warehouse, 1989, The Dixon Cornbelt League, 1993. Houghton Mifflin Lit. fellow, 1982; recipient Fiction award Can. Authors Assn., 1982, Vancouver Writing award, 1987, Stephen Leacock medal, 1987; named Author of Yr., Can. Libr. Assn., 1987. Mem. Enoch Emery Soc., Am. Amateur Press Assn.

KINSEY, BARBARA CUTSHALL, counselor, consultant; b. Abington, Pa., Sept. 24, 1947; d. Frankland Lester and Margaret R. (Zartman) Cutshall; m. William Gayne Kinsey, Oct. 7, 1972; children: Valerie Lauren, Michael Charles. BA, U.S. Internat. U., 1969; MA, U. San Francisco, 1985. Lic. marriage, family and child counselor, Calif. Therapist Adult & Child Guidance, San Jose, Calif., 1984-91; pvt. practice San Jose, 1989—, marriage, family and child counselor, 1989-; pvt. practice cons., San Jose and Milpitas, Calif., 1991—; practicum supr. Santa Clara U., 1991—. Mem. Calif. Assn. Marriage, Family and Child Therapists Bd. (supr. Youth and Family Assistance, Redwood City, Calif.). Office: 888 Saratoga Ave Ste 23 San Jose CA 95129-2639 also: 830 Hillview Ct Ste 260 Milpitas CA 95035

KINSLER, BRUCE WHITNEY, air traffic controller, consultant, air traffic control engineer, air defense engineer; b. Ukiah, Calif., Jan. 11, 1947; s. John Arthur and Mary Helen (Hudson) K.; m. Mickey Kinsler, Apr. 1, 1969 (div. Nov. 1976); 1 child, Arthur Todd; m. Segundina L. Pangilinan, May 27, 1978; 1 stepchild, Stephanie Camalig. AA, El Camino Coll., 1979; BA, Calif. State U., Long Beach, 1984. Air traffic controller FAA, various locations, 1971-81; cen. sta. mgr. Times Mirror Security Communications, Irvine, Calif., 1982-84; supr. office services Law Offices Paul, Hastings, Janofsky & Walker, L.A., 1984-85; air traffic control tng. Hughes Aircraft Co., Fullerton, Calif., 1985-88, sr. project. engr. (C3I), 1990—; engr., scientist space sta. div. McDonnell Douglas, Huntington Beach, Calif., 1989-90; mem. citizens adv. com. Calif. Dept. Transp., Sacramento, 1982—. Author air traffic control tng. manuals. Res. dep. sheriff Orange County. With USNR, 1986—. Mem. Nat. Air Traffic Com. (nat. com.), Air Traffic Control Assn., Human Factors Soc. (pres. elect ORange county chpt.). Democrat. Home: 283 Longbranch Circle Brea CA 92621-3437

KINSMAN, ROBERT PRESTON, biomedical plastics engineer; b. Cambridge, Mass., July 25, 1949; s. Fred Nelson and Myra Roxanne (Preston) K. BS in Plastics Engring., U. Lowell, 1971; MBA, Pepperdine U., 1982. Cert. biomed. engr., Calif.; lic. real estate sales person, Calif. Product devel. engr., plastics divsn. Gen. Tire Corp., Lawrence, Mass., 1976-77; mfg. engr. Am. Edwards Labs. divsn. Am. Hosp. Supply Corp., Irvine, Calif., 1978-80, sr. engr., 1981-82; mfg. engring. mgr. Edwards Labs., Inc. subs. Am. Hosp. Supply Corp., Añasco, P.R., 1983; project mgr. Baxter Edwards Critical Care divsn. Baxter Healthcare Corp., Irvine, 1984-87, engring. and prodn. mgr., 1987—; mem. mgmt. adv. panel Modern Plastics mag., N.Y.C., 1979-80. Instr. first aid ARC, N.D., Mass., Calif., 1971—; vol. worker VA, Bedford, Mass., 1967-71; pres., bd. dirs. Lakes Homeowners Assn., Irvine, 1985-91; bd. dirs., newsletter editor Paradise Park Owners Assn., Las Vegas, Nev., 1988—; bd. dirs. Orange County, Calif. chpt. Am. Heart Assn., 1991—, v.p. bd. dirs., 1993—, mem. steering com. Heart and Sole Classic fundraiser, 1988—, subcom. chmn., 1989, event chmn., 1991-92, mem. devel. com. Calif. affiliate. Capt. USAF, 1971-75. Recipient Cert. of Appreciation, VA, 1971, Am. Heart Assn., 1991, 92, 93. Mem. Soc. Plastics Engrs. (sr., Mem. of Month So. Calif. sect. 1989), Am. Mgmt. Assn., Arnold Air Soc. (comptr. 1969, pledge tng. officer 1970), Plastics Acad., Demolay, Profl. Ski Instrs. Am., Mensa, Am. Legion, Elks, Phi Gamma Psi. Office: Baxter Edwards Critical-Care 17221 Red Hill Ave Irvine CA 92714-5686

KIPP, JUNE CAROL, health science laboratory administrator; b. Johnstown, Penn., Apr. 11, 1932; d. John Claude and Margaretta Olive (Firth) Saylor; m. David Franklin Kipp Sr., Aug. 18, 1951; children: Peggy Carol, David Franklin Jr., Matthew. AA, Lamar (Colo.) Coll., 1974; postgrad., U. Colo., Denver, 1978. Rsch. tech. Eli Lilly Co., Indpls., 1950-51; blood bank tech. Charleroi-Monessen Hosp., Penn., 1957-60; chief tech. Windber Hosp, Penn., 1960-70; technologist Nuclear Test Site, Mercury, Nev., 1970-71; blood bank tech ARC, Johnstown, Penn., 1971-72; chief tech. S.E. Colo. Hosp., Springfield, 1972-76; lab. supr. Smith Kline Clin. Labs., Denver, 1976-81, Indian Pub. Health Svc., Chinle, Ariz., 1982—. Mem. Am. Med. Tech. Assn., Colo. Med. Tech. Assn. (sec. 1977-81), Ariz. Med. Tech. Assn. Republican. Mem. Ch. of the Brethren. Office: Indian Pub Health Svc PO Drawer PH Chinle AZ 86503

KIPPING, VERNON LOUIS, film consultant, marine scientist; b. Cape Girardeau, Mo., Oct. 19, 1921; s. Theodore Frederick and Augusta (Meyer) K.; m. Anna Ruth Uelsmann, Mar. 26, 1944; children: Theodore Paul, John Louis, Douglas Kim. Student, S.E. Mo. State U., 1940-41; AA, Multnomah Coll., 1948; JD, U. San Francisco, 1951. Fingerprint examiner FBI, Washington, 1941-43; with radio communications FBI, Portland, Oreg., 1943-44; spl. employee FBI, Portland, 1946-48; spl. employee San Francisco, 1948-71, 72-76, Chgo., 1971-72; freelance film cons. San Francisco, 1976—; testified as expert witness Patricia Hearst trial. Owner 19 U.S. and internat. patents motion picture tech., marine sci.; invented means to convert still photos of Patricia Hearst's bank robbery into motion picture and produced said films which were admitted as evidence in Hearst trial. Member San Francisco Neighborhood Libr. Coun., 1989-91; mem. adv. coun. TV Sch. Napa Valley Coll., 1990—. Sgt. USAAF, 1944-46, PTO. Recipient Spl. prize San Francisco Film Festival, 1967. Mem. AAAS, Soc. Motion Picture and TV Engrs. (program chmn. 1977-79, mgr. 1979-81, membership chmn. 1981-85, spl. events chmn. 1985-88, sec., treas. 1988-90, chmn. 1990-92, past chmn. 1992—, edn. com. 1990—, past audio-visual conf. chmn., Citation for Outstanding Svc. 1986), Silicon Valley Engring. Coun. Republican. Club: No. Calif. Imperial Owners (San Francisco) (v.p. 1979-83, pres. 1983-87). Home and Office: 540 Melrose Ave San Francisco CA 94127-2220

KIPPUR, MERRIE MARGOLIN, lawyer; b. Denver, July 24, 1962; d. Morton Leonard and Bonnie (Seldin) Margolin; m. Bruce R. Kippur, Sept. 7, 1986. BA, Colo. Coll., 1983; JD, U. Colo., 1986. Bar: Colo. 1986, U.S. Dist. Ct. Colo. 1986, U.S. Ct. Appeals (10th cir.) 1987. Assoc. Sterling & Miller, Denver, 1985-88, McKenna & Cuneo, Denver, 1989—; lectr. trial practice, chapter 9 bankruptcy, RESPA. Author: Student Improvement in the 1980's, 1984, (with others) Ethical Considerations in Bankruptcy, 1985, Partnership Bankruptcy, 1986, Colorado Methods of Practise, 1988. Contract Liaison Jr. League Denver, 1992-94. Mem. ABA, Colo. Bar Assn., Colo. Women's Bar Assn., Colo. Trial Lawyers Assn., Denver Bar Assn., Am. Judicature Soc., Am. Bankruptcy Inst., Gamma Phi Beta, Phi Delta Phi, Pi Gamma Mu. Democrat. Office: McKenna & Cuneo 303 E 17th Ave #600 Denver CO 90203

KIRBENS, SAMUEL MORRIS, judge; b. Lincoln, Nebr., Dec. 15, 1918; s. Michael and Rose (Greenspan) Kirshenbaum; m. Betty Fine, Feb. 1, 1948 (div. 1974); children: Drew J., Andrea Gail Kirbens Greenberg; m. Gloria Elaine Burns, Jan. 17, 1979. Ba, U. Nebr., 1940, JD, 1942. Atty. Columbia Pictures Corp., Hollywood, Calif., 1946-52; pvt. practice Denver, 1952-65; judge Denver County Ct., 1965-85; pvt. practice Laguna Hills, Calif., 1987-93; judge pro tem Orange County Superior Ct., Santa Ana, Calif., 1987-90, arbitrator-mediator, 1987-90; instr. Dale Carnegie Courses, Denver, 1952-74; v.p. Laguna Canyon Conservancy Environ. Group, 1990-93. Editor Nebr. U. Law Rev., 1941-42. Chmn. Denver Mayor's Townhall meetings, 1963-65; chmn. U. Calif. Irvine and Leisure World Lecture Series, Laguna Hills, 1989-93. Sgt. USAF, 1942-45, ETO. Recipient Ross Essay award ABA, 1968. Mem. Nebr. Bar Assn., Calif. State Bar, Colo. State Bar., Orange County Bar Assn. Home: 3486-1C Bahia Blanca W Laguna Hills CA 92653

KIRCH, PATRICK VINTON, anthropology educator; b. Honolulu, July 7, 1950; s. Harold William and Barbara Ver (MacGarvin) K.; m. Debra Connelly, Mar. 3, 1979 (div. 1990). BA, U. Pa., 1971; MPhil, Yale U., 1974, PhD, 1975. Assoc. anthropologist Bishop Mus., Honolulu, 1975-76, anthropologist, 1976-82, head archaeology div., 1982-84, asst. chmn. anthropology, 1983-84; dir., assoc. prof. Burke Mus. U. Wash., Seattle, 1984-87, prof., 1987-89; prof. U. Calif., Berkeley, 1989—; curator Hearst Mus. Anthropology, 1989—; adj. faculty U. Hawaii, Honolulu, 1979-84; mem. lasting legacy com. Wash. State Centennial Commn., 1986-88; pres. Soc. Hawaiian Archaeology, 1980-81. Author: The Anthropology of History in the Kingdom of Hawaii, 1992, Feathered Gods and Fishhooks, 1985, Evolution of the Polynesian Chiefdoms, 1984; editor: Island Societies, 1986; contbr. articles to profl. publs. Grantee NSF, 1974, 76, 77, 82, 87, 88, 89, NEA, 1985, NEH, 1988, Hawaii Com. for Humanities, 1981; Rsch. grantee Nat. Geographic Soc., 1986, 89. Fellow NAS, Am. Acad. Arts and Scis., Am. Anthrop. Assn.; mem. Assn. Field Archaeology, Polynesian Soc., Seattle C. of C., Sigma Xi. Democrat. Office: U Calif Dept Anthropology Berkeley CA 94720

KIRCHER, MARVIN LARRY, public affairs executive; b. Chgo., July 10, 1950; s. Daniel D. and Gloria (Bresloff) K.; m. Margaret M. DiFrank, Oct. 7, 1978; 1 child, Adam. BA in Media Communications, Gov.'s State U., Park Forrest, Ill., 1985. Aide Thornton Twp., South Holland, Ill., 1977-85; v.p. Whiteco Metrocom, Tucson, 1985—. Treas. Am. Cancer Soc. of Ariz., 1988-90; pres. Tucson Bus. Com. For Arts, 1988-90; mem. adv. bd. Kuat Pub. Broadcasting, Tucson, 1988-90; apptd. by Gov. Ariz. Commn. on the Arts, 1989. Mem. Pub. Rels. Soc. Am. (bd. dirs. 1988-90), Ariz. Outdoor Advt. Assn. (pres. 1990—), Ariz. Hwy. Users Fedn. (bd. dirs. 1989—), Tucson C. of C. Office: Whiteco Metrocom PO Box 7395 Tucson AZ 85725-7395

KIRCHKNOPF, ERIN MASSIE, accountant, controller; b. Quantico, Va., Sept. 12, 1963; d. Thornton and Patricia Adele (Padgett) Boyd; m. Timothy Wayne Massie, Nov. 6, 1982 (div.); children: Laila Jasmyn, Alexander Jordan; m. Tristan Andreas Kirchknopf, Dec. 28, 1991. AS in Bus., Coll. of Alameda, Calif., 1989; student, Tidewater Community Coll., Virginia Beach, Va., 1984, Am. Inst. Banking, Washington, 1981-83, San Francisco State U., 1990—. Asst. bookkeeper C.D.P.C. Constrn. Co., Washington, 1978-81; asst. head teller Nat. Savs. & Trust Bank, Washington, 1981-83; controller Va. Beach Air Conditioning Corp., Virginia Beach, 1983-86, Terra Nova Industries, Walnut Creek, Calif., 1986-89; acct. Lawrie Devel. Corp., Danville, Calif., 1989-90; owner, acct. Erin Boyd Massie Co., San Francisco, 1989-90; controller Plath & Co. Inc., San Francisco, 1990—; notary pub., Va., Calif. Bd. dirs. Community Media Svcs., Inc., Washington, 1981-85; founding mem. Dunwood Civic Assn., Virginia Beach, 1985; mem. NOW. Mem. Nat. Notary Assn., Women Constrn. Owners & Execs., Am. Soc. Notaries, Inst. Mgmt. Accts., Phi Beta Lambda. Office: Plath & Co Inc 1458 Howard St San Francisco CA 94103

KIRCHNER, ERNST KARL, company executive; b. San Francisco, June 18, 1937; s. Karl Ewald and Theresa (Muller) K.; m. Ursula Martha Karmann, Sept. 3, 1960; children: Mark Ernst, Christl Elaine, Steven Thomas. BSEE, Stanford U., 1959, MSEE, 1960, PhD in EE, 1963. Tech. staff Teledyne MEC, Palo Alto, Calif., 1965-72; project engr. Teledyne MEC, Palo Alto, 1972-79, staff engr., 1979-81, mgr., 1981-82, ops. mgr., 1982-83, sr. mgr., 1983-84; mgr. engring. Teledyne Microwave, Mountain View, Calif., 1984-87; dir. engring. Teledyne Microwave, Mountain View, 1987-88, v.p. bus. devel., 1988—; v.p. delay device product line Teledyne Microwave, 1990—; tchr. U. Ariz., Tucson, 1963-65. Contbr. articles to profl. jours.; patentee in field. Com. mem. Town of Atherton, Calif., 1986-87; deacon, elder Menlo Park Presbyn. Ch.; bd. mem., vice chmn. Christian Found. for Mindanao; bd, dirs. Hope Unltd. Internat. Lt. U.S. Army, 1963-65. Recipient Army commendation medal and citation, U.S. Army, 1965. Mem. IEEE, Am. Phys. Soc., Am. Mktg. Assn., Assn. of Old Crows, Kappa Kappa Psi, Tau Beta Pi, Sigma Xi. Republican. Home: 41 Ashfield Rd Menlo Park CA 94027-3805 Office: Teledyne Microwave 1290 Terra Bella Ave Mountain View CA 94043-1885

KIRK, BRADLEY REED, lawyer; b. Flint, Mich., June 2, 1964; s. Jerry Reed and Luci (Shabaz) K. BA in Math., Westmont Coll., 1986; postgrad., Fuller Sem., 1987-88; JD magna cum laude, Pepperdine U., 1992. Bar: Calif. 1992. Presch. tchr. for handicapped L.A. Unified Sch. Dist., 1988-89; extern for Judge Pamela Ann Rymer U.S. Ct. Appeals, 9th cir., 1991; assoc. Morrison & Foerster, Irvine, Calif., 1992—. Assoc. editor Pepperdine Law Rev., 1991-92. Vol. Union Rescue Mission, L.A., 1988-92. Odell McConnell scholar, 1991-92, Presdl. Leadership scholar, 1983-86, Dean's Scholarship, 1989-92. Home: 2018 Westwind Santa Ana CA 92704 Office: Morrison & Foerster 19900 MacArthur Blvd Irvine CA 92715

KIRK, CARMEN ZETLER, data processing executive; b. Altoona, Pa., May 22, 1941; d. Paul Alan and Mary Evelyn (Pearce) Zetler. BA, Pa. State U., 1959-63; MBA, St. Mary's Coll. Calif., 1977. Cert. in data processing. Pub. sch. tchr. State Ga., 1965-66; systems analyst U.S. Govt. Dept. Army, Oakland, Calif., 1967-70; programmer analyst Contra Costa County, Martinez, Calif., 1970-76; applications mgr. Stanford (Calif.) U., 1976-79; pres. Zetler Assocs., Inc., Palo Alto, Calif., 1979—; cons. State Calif., Sacramento, 1985-88. Author: (tech. manuals) Comparex, 1982-83. Office: Zetler Assocs Inc PO Box 50395 Palo Alto CA 94303-0395

KIRK, CASSIUS LAMB, JR., lawyer, investor; b. Bozeman, Mont., June 8, 1929; s. Cassius Lamb and Gertrude Violet (McCarthy) K.; A.B., Stanford U., 1951; J.D., U. Calif., Berkeley, 1954. Bar: Calif. 1955. Assoc. firm Cooley, Godward, Castro, Huddleson & Tatum, San Francisco, 1956-60; staff counsel for bus. affairs Stanford U., 1960-78; chief bus. officer, staff counsel Menlo Sch. and Coll., Atherton, Calif., 1978-81; chmn. Eberli-Kirk Properties, Inc., Just Closets, Menlo Park, 1981—; mem. faculty Coll. Bus. Adminstrn. U. Calif., Santa Barbara, 1967-73; mem. adv. bd. Allied Arts Guild, Menlo Park. With U.S. Army, 1954-56. Mem. Calif. Bar Assn., Stanford Assocs., Order of Coif, Phi Alpha Delta. Republican. Club: Stanford Faculty. Home: 1330 University Dr Apt 52 Menlo Park CA 94025-4241 Office: 3551 Haven Ave Unit N Menlo Park CA 94025-1009

KIRK, HENRY PORT, administrator; b. Clearfield, Pa., Dec. 20, 1935; s. Henry P. and Ann (H.) K.; m. Mattie F., Feb. 11, 1956; children: Timothy, Mary Ann, Rebecca. BA, Geneva Coll., 1958; MA, U. Denver, 1963; EdD, U. Southern Calif., 1973. Counselor, ednl. Columbia Coll., Columbia, Mo., 1963-65; dean Huron (S.D.) Coll., 1965-66; assoc. dean Calif. State U., L.A., 1966-70; dean El Camino Coll., Torrance, Calif., 1970-81; v.p. Pasadena (Calif.) City Coll., 1981-86; pres. Centralia (Wash.) Coll., 1986—. Contbr. articles to profl. jours. Mem. hist. commn., City Chehalis, 1990, pres. econ. devel. coun., 1992; campaign chmn., United Way, Centralia, 1989-90. Recipient PTK Bennett Disting. Pres. award, 1990; Exemplary Contbn. to Resource Devel. award NCRD, 1993. Mem. Wash. Assn. Community Colls., Torrance Rotary Club (pres. 1987-88), Centralia Rotary Club (pres. 1990-91), Phi Theta Kappa, Phi Delta Kappa. Presbyterian. Office: Centralia Coll 600 W Locust St Centralia WA 98531-4099

KIRK, JAMES ALBERT, religious studies educator; b. L'Anse, Mich., Jan. 20, 1929; s. Orman Albert and Gladys E. (Tremaine) K.; m. Lois Eileen Grubaugh, Aug. 19, 1956; children: Robert A., Aletha K., Ann L. BA, Hillsdale Coll., 1951; ThM, Iliff Sch. of Theology, 1954, ThD, 1959. Ordained to ministry Congregational Ch., 1954. Minister 1st Congregational Ch., Arriba, Colo., 1951-59; instr. U. Denver, 1959-60, asst. prof., 1960-68, assoc. prof., 1968-77, prof., 1977-93; dir. PhD's Iliff/Denver U., 1982-85; retired, 1993; vis. faculty U. Pitts., 1989. Author, compiler: Stories of the Hindus, 1972; co-author: Religion and the Human Image, 1977. Rsch. fellow U. Madras (India), 1967-68, Doshisha U., Kyoto, Japan, 1968. Mem. Am. Acad. Religion (pres. Rocky Mountain Region 1969-70), Assn. for Asian Studies, Internat. Assn. Buddhist Studies, The Asia Soc., Highlands Inst. Am. Religious Thought. Mem. United Ch. of Christ. Home: 1919 E Cornell Ave Denver CO 80210-6306

KIRK, JAMES WILLIAM, communications company administrator; b. Rochester, Pa., Dec. 7, 1930; s. John Alfred and Genevieve Thelma (Umstead) K.; m. E. Leonora Krings, Sept. 16, 1956; children: Susan, James. BS in Indsl. Mgmt., U. Md., 1957; JD, U. Md., Balt., 1962. Engr. AT&T, Balt., 1957-68, mgr. prodn. control, 1968-85; mgr. AT&T, Phoenix, 1985-92. Mem. Bd. Edn., Harford County, Md., 1979-84, pres., 1984; mem. Housing Commn., Harford County, 1977-79, pres., 1979. 2d lt. U.S. Army, 1951-55, Korea.

KIRK, JANET BROWN, artist, educator, art gallery owner; b. Cisco, Tex., Oct. 3, 1929; d. Olen Benjamin Brown and Evelyn (White) Pitman; m. Glenn L. Kirk, Aug. 5, 1949; children: David Patrick, Dennis Paul, Steven Lloyd, Lisa Evelyn Nave. Student, U. Colo., 1973, 74, 76, Metro State Coll., 1978, 80, Rocky Mountain Sch. Art., 1982. instr. art classes and workshops, Wyo., Colo., 1982—; gallery affiliations Cornerstone Gallery, Longmont, 1970-92, Wild Basin Gallery, Allenspark, Colo., 1988-91, Eastin Gallery, Allenspark, 1992—, Profl. Galleries, St. Cloud, Minn., 1989—, J. Michaels Gallery, Edina, Minn., 1989—, San Juan Art Ctr., Ridgeway, Colo., 1992, Gwendolyn's Art Gallery Ltd., Lake City, Colo., 1993—. Exhibited in one person shows Niwot (Colo.) Art Gallery, 1982, Santa Fe Gallery, Odessa, Tex., 1984, Cornerstone Gallery, Longmont, Colo., 1988; exhibited in group shows The COORS Show, Golden, Colo., 1988, Colo. Artists ABS Shows, Loveland, 1988, 89, Denver, 1991, Colo. Watercolor Soc. Show, Botanical Gardens, Denver, 1992, Colo. Artists Guild State Hist. Mus. Show, Denver, 1992, New England Art Inst. State of the Arts 1993, Boston, 1993; represented in permanent collections Citi-Corp., USA, Energy Div., Denver, John Cox Drilling Co., Midland, others. Bd. mem. Longmont (Colo.) Coun. for the Arts, 1990-91; speaker and demonstrator in field. Recipient Purchase award Glenwood Springs (Colo.) Art Show, 1992. Mem. Am. Watercolor Soc. (assoc.), Nat. Watercolor Soc. (assoc.), Southwest Watercolor Soc. (assoc.), Colo. Watercolor Soc., Western Colo. Watercolor Soc., Colo. Art Guild, Coun. on Arts and Humanities (bd. mem. 1990-92), Colo. Artists Assn. (regional rep. 1982-86, exec. bd. mem. 1986—, Juror's Choice award State Conv. 1991, Spl. Merit award State Conv. 1992). Home: 719 W Third Ave Longmont CO 80501

KIRK, REA HELENE (REA HELENE GLAZER), school administrator, educator; b. N.Y.C., Nov. 17, 1944; d. Benjamin and Lillian (Kellis) Glazer; 3 stepdaughters. B.A., UCLA, 1966; M.A., Eastern Mont. Coll., 1981; postgrad. U. So. Calif. Life cert. spl. edn. tchr., Calif., Mont. Spl. edn. tchr., Los Angeles, 1966-73; clin. sec. speech and lang. clinic, Missoula, Mont., 1973-75; spl. edn. tchr., Missoula and Gt. Falls, Mont., 1975-82; br. mgr. YWCA of L.A., Beverly Hills, Calif., 1989-91; sch. adminstrn. Adv. Schs., 1991; dir. Woman's Resource Ctr., Gt. Falls, Mont., 1981-82; dir. Battered Woman's Shelter, Rock Springs, Wyo., 1982-84; dir. Battered Victims Program Sweetwater County, Wyo., 1984-88, Battered Woman's Program, San Gabriel Valley, Calif., 1988; mem. Wyo. Commn. on Aging, Rock Springs; mem. Community Action Bd. City of L.A.; edn. coord. Adv. Schs. of Calif., 1991—. Pres., bd. dirs. battered woman's shelter, Gt. Falls, Woman's Resource Ctr., Gt. Falls; founder, advisor Rape Action Line, Gt. Falls; founder Jewish religious svcs., Missoula; 4-H leader; hostess Friendship Force; Friendship Force ambassador, Wyo., Fed. Republic Germany, Italy; mem. YWCA Mont. and Wyo. Recipient Gladys Byron scholar U. So. Calif., 1992, honors Missoula 4-H; recognized as significant Wyo. woman as social justice reformer and peace activist Sweetwater County, Wyo.; nominated Wyo. Woman of the Yr., 1981, 82. Mem. Council for Exceptional Children (v.p. Gt. Falls 1981-82), Assn. for Children with Learning Disabilities (Named Oustanding Mem. 1982), Phi Delta Kappa, Delta Kappa Gamma, Psi Chi. Democrat. Jewish.

KIRK, SAMUEL ALEXANDER, psychologist, educator; b. Rugby, N.D., Sept. 1, 1904; s. Richard B. and Nellie (Boussard) K.; m. Winifred Eloise Day, June 25, 1933; children: Jerome Richard, Nancy Lorraine. Ph.B., U. Chgo., 1929, M.S., 1931; Ph.D., U. Mich., 1935; L.H.D., Lesley Coll., 1969; D.L., U. Ill., 1983. Research psychologist Wayne Country Tng. Sch., Northville, Mich., 1931-34, mental hygienist, 1934-35; dir. div. edn. for exceptional children State Tchrs. Coll., Milw., 1935-42, 46; chmn. grad. sch. vis. lectr. U. Mich, 1942; prof. edn. and psychology U. Ill., 1947-68, prof. emeritus, 1968—; dir. Inst. Research Exceptional Children, 1952-68; prof. spl. edn. U. Ariz., Tucson, 1968-86. Author: (with Hegge and W.D. Kirk) Remedial Reading Drills, 1936, Teaching Reading to Slow-Learning Children, 1940, (with Johnson) Educating the Retarded Child, 1951, (with Karnes and Kirk) You and Your Retarded Child, 1955, Early Education of the Mentally Retarded, 1958, Educating Exceptional Children, 1962, 2d edit, 1972, (with Gallagher) Educating Exceptional Children, 1979, 83, 86, 89, (with Gallagher and Anastasiow) Educating Exceptional Children, 1993, (with Wiener) Behavioral Research on Exceptional Children, 1964, (with J.J. McCarthy and Kirk) The Illinois Test of Psycholinguistic Abilities, rev. edit., 1968, (with Kirk) Psycholinguistic Learning Disabilities, 1971, (with Lord) Exceptional Children: Resources and Perspectives, 1974, (with J.M. McCarthy) Learning Disabilities, 1975, (with Kleibahn and Lerner) Teaching Reading to Slow and Disabled Readers, 1978, (with Chalfant) Academic and Developmental Learning Disabilities, 1984, (with Kirk and Minskoff) Phonic Remedial Reading Lessons, 1985, The Foundations of Special Education: Selected Papers and Speeches of Samuel A. Kirk, 1993; contbr. articles to profl. pubs. Served as maj. AUS, 1942-46. Recipient 1st internat. award for profl. service in mental retardation Joseph P. Kennedy Jr. Found., 1962, J.E. Wallace Wallin ann. award Council for Exceptional Children, 1966, recognition award for early childhood edn., 1981, ann. award Assn. Children with Learning Disabilities, 1966, ann. award Caritas Soc., 1966, Internat. Milestone award Internat. Fedn. Learning Disabilities, 1975, Disting. Service award Am. Assn. Speech and Hearing, 1976, Disting. Citizen award U. Ariz. Alumni Assn., 1977, award for outstanding leadership Ill. Council Exceptional Children, 1980, recognition award Pa. Assn. Children with Learning Disabilities, 1980, Ariz. Div. Devel. Disability, 1980, Helen T. Devereaux Meml. award, 1981. Fellow Am. Psychol. Assn. (Edgar Bell award 1980); Am. Assn. for Mental Deficiency (award 1969); mem. Internat. Council Exceptional Children (pres. 1941-43), Nat. Soc. Study Edn. (chmn. 1950 yearbook com), Brit. Assn. Spl. Edn. (hon. v.p. 1962), Sigma Xi. Home: 7500 N Calle Sin Envidia Tucson AZ 85718-7300

KIRKENDALL, JEFFREY LAWRENCE, real estate executive; b. Lynwood, Calif., Feb. 20, 1954; s. Richard S. and Marilyn E. K. BS in Bus. Adminstrn. Mktg., San Diego State U., 1976. Broker assoc. Grubb & Ellis Comml. Brokerage, San Diego, 1976-80; v.p., regional mgr. Meyer Investment Properties, Denver, 1980-85; pres. Moore Comml. Co. & Moore Asset Mgmt. Inc., Denver, 1987-90; real estate exec. D.C. Burns Realty & Trust Co., Denver, 1990—. Bd. dirs. Aspen Child Devel. Ctrs., Englewood, Colo., Human Svcs., Inc., Denver; mem. exec. com. Denver Bd. Realtors Comml. Div. Mem. FIABCI U.S.A., World Trade Ctr. Office: DC Burns Realty & Trust Co 1625 Broadway Denver CO 80202-4731

KIRKER, JACK M., telecommunications company executive; m. Joanne Kirker; 3 children. Degree in bus. adminstrn.; grad. advanced mgmt. program, Harvar Bus. Sch. Formerly gen. mgr. GE Transp. Systems Bus. Div., Transp. Equipment Products Div.; pres. GTE Automatic Electric Inc., Northlake, Ill., from 1981, AG Communications Systems Corp. (formerly GTE Communication Systems Corp.), Phoenix, 1984—. Office: AG Communications Systems 2500 W Utopia Rd Phoenix AZ 85027-4199

KIRKING, CLAYTON CARROLL, information specialist, librarian; b. Coeur d'Alena, Idaho, July 29, 1949; s. Hilbert Clifton and Mary Evelyn (Taber) K. BFA, Pacific Luth. U., 1971; MLS, U. Wash., 1974. Libr. fine arts dept. Tacoma Pub. Libr., 1975-79, head fine arts div., 1979-81; dir. librs., info. specialist Phoenix Art Mus., 1981—, assoc. curator Latin Am. art, 1992—. Co-editor: Grant Development for Large and Small Libraries, 1990. Mem. ALA, Spl. Librs. Assn., Art. Librs. Soc. of N.Am., Friends of Mex. Art, Ariz. Mus. of Mex. Art, Art Libr. Soc. of N.Am. (pres. Ariz. chpt. 1983-84). Home: 2303 E Mitchell Dr Phoenix AZ 85016-6615 Office: Phoenix Art Mus 1625 N Central Ave Phoenix AZ 85004-1685

KIRKLAND, JAMES IAN, paleontologist, educator, geologist; b. Weymouth, Mass., Aug. 24, 1954; s. Robert and Mary Ellen (Provan) K.; m.

Susan Marie Copley, May 21, 1988; 1 child, Kelsey Lynn. BS, N.Mex. Tech., 1977; MS, No. Ariz. U., 1983; PhD, U. Colo., 1990. Teaching asst. No. Ariz. U., Flagstaff, 1977-79; rsch. asst. Mus. of No. Ariz., Flagstaff, 1979-81; teaching asst. U. Colo., Boulder, 1981-84, rsch. asst., 1985-87; instr. U. Nebr., Lincoln, 1987-89; paleontologist Dinamation Internat.Soc., Fruita, Colo., 1990—; rsch. assoc. Mus. of Western Colo., Grand Junction, 1989—, Mus. of No. Ariz., Flagstaff, 1990—. Contbr. articles to profl. jours. NSF grantee, 1990. Mem. Soc. of Vertebrate Paleontology, Paleontol. Soc., Paleontol. Assn. Office: Dinamation Internat Soc 145 N Mesa PO Box # 307 Fruita CO 81521

KIRKLAND, JOHN CLARENCE, lawyer; b. Omaha, Nebr., Dec. 28, 1963; s. John and Marilou (Witt) K. AB, Columbia U., 1986; JD, UCLA, 1990. Bar: Calif. 1990. Assoc. Cadwalader, Wickersham & Taft, L.A., 1990—. Editor: UCLA Journal of Environmental Law and Policy, 1990. Mem. ABA, Assn. Trial Lawyers Am., L.A. County Bar Assn., L.A. Trial Lawyers Assn. Home: 16178 W Sunset Blvd Pacific Palisades CA 90272-3436 Office: Cadwalader Wickersham & Taft 660 S Figueroa St Los Angeles CA 90017-5700

KIRKORIAN, DONALD GEORGE, college official, management consultant; b. San Mateo, Calif., Nov. 30, 1938; s. George and Alice (Sergius) K. BA, San Jose State U., 1961, MA, 1966, postgrad., 1968; postgrad., Stanford U., 1961, U. So. Calif., 1966; PhD, Northwestern U., 1972. Producer Sta. KNTV, San Jose, Calif., 1961; tchr. L.A. City Schs., 1963; instrnl. TV coord. Fremont Union High Sch. Dist., Sunnyvale, Calif., 1963-73; assoc. dean instrn. learning resources Solano Community Coll., Suisun City, Calif., 1973-85, dean instrnl. services, 1985-89; dean learning resources and staff devel., 1989—; owner, pres. Kirkorian and Assocs., Suisun City; field cons. Nat. Assn. Edn. Broadcasters, 1966-68; extension faculty San Jose State U., 1968-69, U. Calif. Santa Cruz, 1970-73, U. Calif. Davis, 1973-76; chmn. Bay Area TV Consortium, 1976-77, 86-87; mem. adv. panel Speech Communication Assn./Am. Theater Assn. tchr. preparation in speech, communication, theater and media, N.Y.C., 1973-77. Author: Staffing Information Handbook, 1990, NAtional Learning Resources Directory, 1991, 93; editor: Media Memo, 1973-80, Intercom: The Newsletter for Calif. Community Coll. Librs., 1974-75, Update, 1980-90, Exploring the Benicia State Recreation Area, 1977, California History Resource Materials, 1977, Time Management, 1980; contbr. articles to profl. jours. Chmn. Solano County Media Adv. Com., 1974-76; bd. dirs. Napa-Solano United Way, 1980-82; mem. adv. bd. Calif. Youth Authority, 1986-93. Mem. Nat. Assn. Ednl. Broadcasters, Assn. for Edn. Communications and Tech., Broadcast Edn. Assn., Calif. Assn. Ednl. Media and Tech. (treas.), Western Ednl. Soc. for Telecommunications (bd. dirs. 1973-75, pres. 1976-77, State Chancellor's com. on Telecommunications 1982-86), Learning Resources Assn. Calif. Community Colls. (exec. dir. 1976—, sec.-treas.), Assn. Calif. Community Coll. Adminstrs. (bd. dirs. 1985-91), Phi Delta Kappa. Home: 1655 Rockville Rd Suisun City CA 94585-1373 Office: Solano Community Coll 4000 Suisun Valley Rd Suisun City CA 94585-3197

KIRKPATRICK, RICHARD ALAN, internist; b. Rochester, Minn., Jan. 17, 1947; s. Neal R. and Ethel C. (Hull) K.; m. Susan Baxter; children: James N., Ronald S., David B., Mary J., Scott B. BA in Chemistry with honors, U. Wash., 1968, BS in Psychology, 1968, MD, 1972. Diplomate Am. Bd. Internal Medicine. Intern, resident in internal medicine Mayo Grad. Sch., Rochester, 1972-76, spl. resident in biomed. communications, 1974-75; pvt. practice specializing in internal medicine Longview, Wash., 1976—; sr. ptnr. Internal Medicine Clinic of Longview; mem. clin. faculty U. Wash.; dir. cardiac rehab. program St. John's Hosp. . Editor: Drug Therapy Abstracts, Wash. Internists; mem. editorial adv. bd. Your Patient and Cancer, Primary Care and Cancer; weekly med. TV talk show host, 1978—; contbr. articles to med. jours. Mem. City Coun., Longview; mem. S.W. Wash. Symphony; bd. dirs. S.W. Wash. Youth Symphony; pres., bd. dirs. Sta. KLTV. Fellow ACP; mem. Wash. State Soc. Internal Medicine (trustee, past pres.), Am. Geriatrics Soc., Am. Soc. Echocardiography, Am. Soc. Internal Medicine, Wash. Med. Assn. (coun. med. svc.), Am. Cancer Soc. (local bd. dirs.), Am. Soc. Clin. Oncology, AMA, Am. Med. Writers Assn. Office: PO Box 578 748 14th Ave Longview WA 98632

KIRKPATRICK, SUSAN ELIZABETH D., political scientist; b. Niagara Falls, N.Y., Oct. 6, 1950; d. George Leo Jr. and Bette (Wadsworth) Dischinger; m. Allan Thomson Kirkpatrick, July 1, 1972; children: Anne Thomson, Robert Wadsworth. BA, U. Mich., 1971; MEd, Harvard U., 1975; ABD, Colo. State U., 1990. Social studies tchr. Walsingham Acad., Williamsburg, Va., 1972-74; adminstr. Wentworth Inst. Tech., Boston, 1977-80; polit. scientist Colo. State U., Fort Collins, 1987-91; asst. prof. polit. sci. U. No. Colo., Greeley, 1992—. City coun. mem. City of Fort Collins, 1986-93, mayor, 1990-93; exec. bd. Colo. Mcpl. League, 1990-93. Mem. Jr. League Fort Collins (newsletter editor 1984), Am. Polit. Sci. Assn., Women in Mcpl. Govt. (sec. 1989), Fort Collins C. of C. (chmn. advocacy com. 1989). Home: 2312 Tanglewood Dr Fort Collins CO 80525

KIRKS, JAMES HARVEY, JR., librarian and administrator; b. L.A., Sept. 16, 1937; s. James Harvey Sr. and Grace Edna (Whitney) K.; m. Barbara Aileen Barry, June 1962 (div. July 1982); children: Cara Lynn, Laura Lee. AA, Compton Coll., 1957, UCLA, 1958; BA, UCLA, 1959; MS in LS, U. So. Calif., 1962. Head of reference, circulation and audiovisual City of Inglewood (Calif.) Pub. Libr., 1962, head of extension svcs., 1964-66; dir. pub. svcs. Arcadia (Calif.) Pub. Libr., 1966-70; city librarian Port Angeles (Wash.) Pub. Libr., 1970-73; dir. North Olympic Libr. System, Port Angeles, 1973-75; coord. North State Coop. Libr. System, Willows, Calif., 1975—. Contbr. articles to profl. jours. Pres. United Way, Clallum County, Wash., 1973; Port Angeles Symphony Orch., 1975, Faith Luth. Ch., Chico, Calif., 1981-82. With Signal Corps, U.S. Army, 1962-64, France. Mem. ALA (various coms.), Calif. Libr. Assn. (various coms.), Congress of Calif. Pub. Libr. System (pres. 1980s), Aid Assn. for Luths. (pres. br. 1990—), Rotary Internat. (bd. dirs. 1974). Home: 11 Hemming Ln Chico CA 95926 Office: North State Coop Lib System 259 N Villa Ave Willows CA 95988-2607

KIRMACI, ISMAIL, electrical engineer; b. Ankara, Turkey, Mar. 9, 1953; came to U.S., 1974; s. Orhan and Melahat (Tamturk) K.; m. Stephanie Ruth Evans, Apr. 21, 1984; children: Kent Orhan, Elyse Ayshe. BSEE, Robert Coll., Istanbul, Turkey, 1974; MSEE, U. Fla., 1978. Equipment engr. Dunlop Tire Factory, Birmingham, Eng., 1972; test engr. Sait Electronics, Brussels, 1973; staff elec. engr. Vector, an Aydin Corp., Newtown, Pa., 1974-75; sr. elec. engr. S.T.I Inc., Ft. Walton Beach, Fla., 1978-80; engring. mgr. Amedyne, Inc., Irvine, Calif., 1980-84; sr. scientist Pacific Semicondr. Equipment, Anaheim, Calif., 1984-88; cons. Pacific Semicondr. Equipmment, Anaheim, Calif., 1988—; prin. engr. Orthodyne Electronics, Costa Mesa, Calif., 1988—; cons. Ikegami Tsushinki Co., Ltd., Mito, Japan, 1980-83, Asymtek, Vista, Calif., 1984, Benchmark Techs., N.H., 1983-84. Contbr. articles to profl. jours. Home: 8292 Indianapolis Ave Huntington Beach CA 92646 Office: Orthodyne Electronics 2300 Main St Sect B Irvine CA 92714-6223

KIRSCH, ALAN, optometrist; b. Bklyn., May 3, 1953; s. Daniel and Marilyn (Horowitz) K.; m. Sindy Sue Lieberman, Nov. 29, 1980; children: Joshua Reuben, Rachel Alana. BA, SUNY, Plattsburgh, 1975; D in Optometry, Ill. Coll. Optometry, 1979. Assoc. optometrist in pvt. office, Glendale Heights, Ill., 1979-82; optometrist Eyecare, U.S.A., Sacramento, 1982-87, in pvt. office, Sacramento, 1987-89; owner Eyelusions Optometric Ctr., Sacramento, Calif., 1989—. Bd. dirs. Congregation B'Nai Israel, Sacramento, 1992. Mem. Calif. Optometric Assn., Calif. Optometric Assn. Office: Eyelusions/Optometric Ctr 7465 Rush River Dr # 410 Sacramento CA 95851

KIRSCHNER, MELVIN HENRY, physician; b. N.Y.C., Aug. 13, 1926; s. Philip S. and Belle (Lobel) K.; m. Geraldine Lee Williams, Dec. 30, 1961; children: Darin Markley, Corey Alan, Todd Andrew. BA, UCLA, 1948, BS, 1949; MPH, U. Calif., Berkeley, 1955; MD, U. So. Calif., 1960. Sanitarian Tulare (Calif.) County Health Dept., 1949-51, Oakland (Calif.) City Helath Dept., 1951-52, 55; cons. pub. health sanitarian Calif. State Health Dept., Berkeley, 1952-54; sanitary engr. Calif. State Health Dept., 1956-59; intern L.A. County Hosp., 1960-61; pvt. family practice Van Nuys, Calif., 1961—; chmn. Unihealth Bioethics Inst.; med. dir. San Fernando Valley Home Health Agy., Encino, Calif., 1968-71, Sheraton Convalescent Hosp., Sepulveda, Calif., 1968—, Beverly Manor Convalescent Hosp., Panorama City, Calif., 1967-92; dir. biomed. ethics Valley Hosp. Med. Ctr., Van Nuys, 1986—, Panorama Hosp. Med. Ctr., 1982-91; chmn. family practice com. Valley Presbyn. Hosp., 1992. With USN, 1944-46. Mem. Am. Acad. Family Physicians (diplomate), AMA, Am. Pub. Health Assn., Nat. Coun. Against Health Fraud, Calif. Med. Assn., Calif. Acad. Family Practice, L.A. Co-med. Assn. (chmn. biomed. ethics com.). Office: 14411 Gilmore St Van Nuys CA 91401-1430

KIRSCHNER, RICHARD MICHAEL, naturopathic physician, speaker, author; b. Cin., Sept. 27, 1949; s. Alan George and Lois (Dickey) K.; 1 child, Aden Netanya; m. Lindea Bowe. BS in Human Biology, Kans. Newman Coll., 1979; D in Naturopathic Medicine, Nat. Coll. Naturopathic Medicine, 1981. Vice pres. D. Kirschner & Son, Inc., Newport, Ky., 1974-77; co-owner, mgr. Sunshine Ranch Arabian Horses, Melbourne, Ky., 1975-77; pvt. practice Portland, Oreg., 1981-83, Ashland, Oreg., 1983—; seminar leader, trainer Inst. for Meta-Linguistics, Portland, 1981-84; cons. Nat. Elec. Contractors Assn., So. Oreg., 1985-86, United Telephone N.W., 1986; speaker Ford Motor Co., Blue Cross-Blue Shield, Balfour Corp., NEA, AT&T, Triad Systems, Supercuts, 1986-89, Hewlett-Packard, Pepsi Co., George Bush Co., 1990-91, Goodwill Industries Am., Motorola, 1992; speaker, trainer R & R Prodns., Ashland, 1984—, Careertrack Seminars, Boulder, Colo., 1986—. Co-author audio tape seminar How To Deal with Difficult People, 1987, video tape seminar, 1988; author (audio tape seminar) How To Find and Keep a Mate, 1988, (videotape seminar) How to Find a Mate, 1990, (videotape seminar) How To Deal with Difficult People, 1992. Spokesman Rogue Valley PBS, 1986, 87. Mem. Am. Assn. Naturopathic Physicians (bd. dirs., chmn. pub. affairs), Wilderness Soc., Nat. Speakers Assn., Internat. Platform Assn. Republican. Office: R&R Prodns PO Box 896 Ashland OR 97520-0030

KIRSHBAUM, HOWARD M., state judge; b. Oberlin, Ohio, Sept. 19, 1938; s. Joseph and Gertrude (Morris) K.; m. Priscilla Joy Parmakian, Aug. 15, 1964; children—Audra Lee, Andrew William. B.A., Yale U., 1960; A.B., Cambridge U., 1962, M.A., 1966; LL.B., Harvard U., 1965. Ptnr. Zarlengo and Kirshbaum, Denver, 1969-75; judge Denver Dist. Ct., Denver, 1975-80, Colo. Ct. Appeals, Denver, 1980-83; justice Colo. Supreme Ct., Denver, 1983—; adj. prof. law U. Denver, 1972—; dir. Am. Law Inst. Phila., Am. Judicature Soc., Chgo., 1983-85, Colo. Jud. Inst. Denver, 1979-89; pres. Colo. Legal Care Soc., Denver, 1974-75. Bd. dirs. Young Artists Orch., Denver, 1976-85; pres. Community Arts Symphony, Englewood, Colo., 1972-74; dir. Denver Opportunity, Inc., Denver, 1972-74; vice-chmn. Denver Council on Arts and Humanities, 1969. Mem. ABA, Denver Bar Assn. (trustee 1981-83), Colo. Bar Assn., Am. Judicature Soc. Office: Supreme Ct Colo 2 E 14th Ave Denver CO 80203-2116

KIRSHBAUM, JACK D., pathologist; b. Chgo., Dec. 31, 1902; s. David and Regina (Uno) K.; m. Florence R. Kirshbaum, Dec. 27, 1931; children: Gerald, Robert, Richard. MD, U. Ill., 1929, MS, 1934. Inter Cook County Hosp., Chgo., 1929-30, intern in pathology, 1932-41; instr. medicine U. Ill., 1932-34; prof. pathology, head dept. Chog. Med. Sch., 1946-47; sr. pathologist Nagasaki, Japan, 1968-70, Atomic Bomb Casualty Commn.; asst. prof. pathology Loma Linda, 1949-59; sr. pathologist Hadassah Hosp., Israel, 1978-79; mem. staff Emeritus Desert Hosp. Comdr. Jewish War Vets., Calif., 1947-48. Col. U.S. Army, 1942-47. Fellow ACP, Coll. Am. Pathologists; mem. U.S. Acad. Pathology, Can. Acad. Pathology, L.A. County Med. Assn., L.A. Pathology Soc., Calif. Pathology Soc., Am. Bd. Pathologists, Colo. Assn. Sch. Execs., Soc. Clin. Pathologists, Israel Red Cross Magen David (life), Hadassah (life fellow, assoc.), B'Nai Brith, Sigma Xi. Home: 229 Toro Cir Palm Springs CA 92264-9317

KIRSLIS, PETER ANDRE CHRISTOPHER, computer science research and development specialist; b. Cambridge, Mass., Feb. 9, 1954. BA in Applied Math. cum laude, Harvard U., 1975; MS in Computer Sci., U. Ill., 1977, PhD in Computer Sci., 1986. Mem. tech. staff AT&T Bell Labs., Murray Hill, N.J., 1978-81, Denver, 1986—; rsch. analyst U. Ill., Urbana, 1981-86; tech. staff mem. Digital Tech., Inc., Champaign, 1982, Interactive Systems Corp., Estes Park, Colo., 1983. Co-author (chpt. in book) A Distributed Unix System, 1987; contbr. articles to profl. jours. Mem. IEEE Computer Soc., Assn. Computing Machinery, Rocky Mountain Harvard U. Alumni Assn. (chmn. scholarship 1987-89). Office: AT&T Bell Labs 11900 N Pecos St Denver CO 80234

KIRTS, WAYNE CHARLES, interior designer; b. Terre Haute, Ind., Aug. 9, 1934; s. Harold Murray and Juanita June (DuChane) K.; m. Melinda Suzanne Peacock, Jan. 18, 1959 (div. 1963); children: Daren Arthur Laurence. Student, Ind. State U., 1952-54; student, U. Cin., 1954-55; BA, UCLA, 1957. Interior designer Adele Faulkner, FASID, Inc., L.A., 1957-67; interior designer Arthur Elrod, AID, Inc., Palm Springs, Calif., 1957-67, Virginia Douglas, AID, Inc., Bel Air, Calif., 1967-81, Kirts Assocs., Beverly Hills, Calif., 1967-81; owner, interior designer Kirts Assocs., Scottsdale, Ariz., 1981-86, San Diego, 1986—; owner DuChane Antiques, La Mesa, Calif.; instr. interior design UCLA, 1973-81, Mesa Community Coll., San Diego, 1987—, Univ. Calif., San Diego, Scottsdale (Ariz.) Community Coll., 1983-86. Author interior design program U. Calif.-San Diego; contbr. articles to profl. jours. Mem. Am. Soc. Interior Designers (chpt. v.p. 1969-71, 1st v.p. 1987-88, pres. 1989-91).

KISCHER, CLAYTON WARD, embryologist, educator; b. Des Moines, Mar. 2, 1930; s. Frank August and Bessie Erma (Sawtell) K.; m.Linda Sese Espejo, Nov. 7. 1964; children: Eric Armine, Frank Henry. BS in Edn., U. Omaha, 1953; MS, Iowa State U., 1960, PhD, 1962. Asst. prof. biology Ill. State U., 1962-63; rsch. assoc. Argonne (Ill.) Nat. Lab., 1963; asst. prof. zoology Iowa State U., 1963-64; NIH postdoctoral fellow in biochemistry M.D. Anderson Hosp, Houston, 1964-66; chief sect. electron microscopy S.W. Found. Rsch. and Edn., San Antonio, 1966-67; assoc. prof. anatomy U. Tex. Med. Br., Galveston, 1967-77; assoc. prof. anatomy U. Ariz. Coll. Medicine, Tucson, 1977-92, prof. emeritus, 1993—; cons., dir. Scanning electron microscopy lab. Shrine Burns Inst., Galveston, 1969-73. Contbr. articles to profl. jours. Cubmaster pack 107 Island Dist., Galveston, 1974-76; bd. dirs. YMCA. With USN, 1947-49. NIH Rsch. grantee, 1968-89; Morrison Trust grantee, 1975-76. Mem. SAR, AAAS, Galveston Rsch. Soc. (pres. 1971-72), Am. Soc. Cell Biology, Electron Microscopy Soc. Am., Soc. Developmental Biology, Am. Assn. Anatomists, Tex. Soc. Electron Microscopy (hon.) (editor newsletter 1969-73, pres. 1975-76), Ariz. Soc. Electron Microscopy (pres. 1980-81), Gamma Pi Sigma. Home: 6249 N Camino Miraval Tucson AZ 85718-3024 Office: U Ariz Coll Medicine Dept Anatomy Tucson AZ 85724

KISER, NAGIKO SATO, librarian; b. Taipei, Republic of China, Aug. 7, 1923; came to U.S., 1950; d. Takeichi and Kinue (Sōma) Sato; m. Virgil Kiser, Dec. 4, 1979 (dec. Mar. 1981). Secondary teaching credential, Tsuda Coll., Tokyo, 1945; BA in Journalism, Trinity U., 1953; BFA, Ohio State U., 1956, MA in Art History, 1959; MLS, cert. in library media, SUNY, Albany, 1974. Cert. community coll. librarian, Calif., cert. jr. coll. tchr., Calif., cert. secondary edn. tchr., Calif., cert. tchr. library media specialist and art, N.Y. Pub. rels. reporter The Mainichi Newspapers, Osaka, Japan, 1945-50; contract interpreter U.S. Dept. State, Washington, 1956-58, 66-67; resource specialist Richmond (Calif.) Unified Sch. Dist., 1968-69; editing supr. CTB/McGraw-Hill, Monterey, Calif., 1969-71; multi-media specialist Monterey Peninsula Unified Sch. Dist., 1975-77; librarian Nishimachi Internat. Sch., Tokyo, 1979-80, Sacramento City Unified Sch. Dist., 1977-79, 81-85; sr. librarian Camarillo (Calif.) State Hosp. and Devel. Ctr., 1985—. Editor: Short Form Test of Academic Aptitude, 1970, Prescriptive Mathematics Inventory, 1970, Tests of Basic Experience, 1970. Mem. Calif. State Supt.'s Regional Coun. on Asian Pacific Affairs, Sacramento, 1984-91. Library Media Specialist Tng. Program scholar U.S. Office Edn., 1974. Fellow Internat. Biog. Assn. (life), mem. ALA, Calif. Libr. Assn., Med. Libr. Assn., Asunaro Shogai Kyoiku Kondankai (Lifetime Edn. Promoting Assn., Japan), The Mus. Soc., Internat. House of Japan, Matsuyama Sacramento Sister City Corp., Japanese Am. Citizens League, UN Assn. U.S., Ikenobo Ikebana Soc. Am., L.A. Hototogisu Haiku Assn., Ventura County Archeol. Soc. Mem. Christian Science Ch. Office: Camarillo State Hosp & Devel Ctr Profl Libr PO Box 6022 Camarillo CA 93011-6022

KISER, ROBERTA KATHERINE, chiropractic assistant, education educator; b. Alton, Ill., Aug. 13, 1938; d. Stephen Robert and Virginia Elizabeth (Lasher) Golden; m. James Robert Crisman, sept. 6, 1958 (div. May 1971); 1 child, Robert Glenn; m. James Earl Kiser, Dec. 19, 1971; 1 child, James Jacob. BEd, So. Ill. U., 1960. Cert. tchr., Ill., Calif. Librarian Oaklawn (Ill.) Elem. Sch., 1960-62, Alsip (Ill.) Elem. Sch., 1966-69; tchr. Desert Sands Unified Sch. Dist., Indio, Calif., 1969-79; prin. Mothercare Infant Sch., Rancho Mirage, Calif., 1980-89; substitute tchr. Greater Coachella Valley Sch., Calif., 1989-91; med. acct. Desert Health Care, Bermuda Dunes, Calif., 1990-92; mentor tchr., computing, typing skils Wilde Woode Children's Ctr., Palm Springs, Calif., 1990-92; chiropractic asst. Rapp Chiropractic Health Ctr, Palm Desert, Calif., 1992—. V.p. Palm Desert (Calif.) Community Ch. Montessori Sch. Bd., 1982-85. Republican. Presbyterian. Home: 39-575 Keenan Dr Rancho Mirage CA 92270 Office: Rapp Chiropractic Health Ctr 44-855 San Pablo Ave Palm Desert CA 92260

KISH, MARIE DE ALCUAZ, art expert; b. San Mateo, Calif., Dec. 8, 1955; d. Luis G. and Jeanne (Francisco) de Alcuaz; m. John Theodore Kish, Jan. 29, 1989; 1 child, Robert Mencken. BA, U. Calif., Davis, 1978; AM, U. So. Calif., 1981. Curator of art Fisher Gallery, U. So. Calif., L.A., 1980-85; art curator L.A. Mcpl. Art Gallery, 1985-90; freelance art expert Saratoga, Calif., 1990—; guest curator Taipei (Taiwan) Fine Arts Mus., 1987. Author: Ceci n'est pas le Surrealism, 1984, Contemporary Southern California Art, 1987. Chair Affirmative Action Com., L.A., 1985-87. Mem. Am. Assn. Mus., Calif. Arts Assn. Home and Office: L A Mcpl Art Gallery 20800 4th St Apt 2 Saratoga CA 95070-5802

KISHI, GLEN YO, physician; b. Walnut Creek, Calif., Aug. 6, 1958; s. Tadashi and Yoshiko (Nakamura) K.; m. Margaret Marie Charlebois, Feb. 18, 1989; 1 child, Patrick Gregory. BS in Chem. Engring., U. Calif., Davis, 1981; MD, U. Calif., Irvine, 1985. Diplomate Am. Bd. Ob/Gyn. Intern, then resident in ob.-gyn. Phoenix Integrated Residency in Ob.-Gyn., 1985-89; attending staff Maricopa Med. Ctr., Phoenix, 1989—. Mem. AMA, Phi Kappa Phi, Tau Beta Pi, Pi Mu Epsilon. Republican. Office: Maricopa Med Ctr Dept Ob-Gyn 2601 E Roosevelt St Phoenix AZ 85008-4973

KISHIMOTO, YORIKO, business consultant; b. Shizuoka, Japan, Sept. 8, 1955; m. Leland D. Collins; 2 children. BA, Wesleyan U., 1977; MBA, Stanford U., 1981. Bus. fellow Nomura Rsch. Inst., Kamakura, Japan, 1979-81; prin. Japan Pacific Assocs., Palo Alto, Calif., 1982—; speaker numerous internat confs. Pacific Rim. Pub. Biotech. in Japan News Svc., 1982-92; co-author: The Third Century, 1988; editor, co-pub. Biotech. in Japan Yearbook, 1990. Mem. Alliance Forum (co-founder), Coalition for The Presidio Pacific Ctr. Office: Japan Pacific Assocs Ste 2 467 Hamilton Ave Palo Alto CA 94301

KISNER, NED BERNARD, paint manufacturing company executive; b. Santa Ana, Calif., Oct. 18, 1938; s. Virgil O. and Lois A. (Wisehart) K.; m. Diane C. Hock, June 11, 1960; children: Bradley S., Janet L. Andersen, Ken D., Mardy K. BSME, Oreg. State U., 1960; MBA, Calif. State U., Fullerton, 1964. Plant supt. Dow Chem., Pittsburg, Calif., 1964-67; plant mgr. The Flecto Co., Oakland, Calif., 1967-73; gen. mgr. Midland div. Dexter Corp., Hayward, Calif., 1973-81; pres. Triangle Coatings, San Leandro, Calif., 1981—. Patentee mercury cell lead-in device. Founder Program Advocating Responsible Legislation for the Environment, chmn., 1989-91. Capt. USMC, 1960-63. Mem. San Leandro Mfrs. Assn. (bd. dirs. 1986—, pres. 1992—), Golden Gate Paint and Coatings Assn. (bd. dirs. 1976—, pres. 1991-92), Nat. Paint and Coatings Assn. Republican. Office: Triangle Coatings 1930 Fairway Dr San Leandro CA 94577

KISSLINGER, CARL, geophysicist, educator; b. St. Louis, Aug. 30, 1926; s. Fred and Emma (Tobias) K.; m. Millicent Ann Thorson, Mar. 27, 1948; children: Susan, Karen, Ellen, Pamela, Jerome. B.S., St. Louis U., 1947, M.S., 1949, Ph.D., 1952. Faculty St. Louis U., 1949-72, prof. geophysics, geophys. engring., 1961-72, chmn. dept. earth and atmostpheric scis., 1963-72, prof. geophysics, 1972—; dir. Coop. Inst. Research in Environ. Scis., U. Colo., Boulder, 1972-79; UNESCO expert in seismology, chief tech. adviser Internat. Inst. Seismology and Earthquake Engring., Tokyo, 1966-67; chmn. com. seismology NRC-Nat. Acad. Scis., 1970-72; mem. U.S. Geodynamics Com., 1975-78; U.S. nat. corr. Internat. Assn. Seismology and Physics of Earth's Interior, 1970-72; mem. Internat. Union Geodesy and Geophysics, bur., 1975-83, v.p., 1983-91; mem. Gov.'s Sci. Adv. Council, State of Colo., 1973-77, com. on scholarly communication with People's Republic of China, Nat. Acad. Scis., 1977-81, NRC/Nat. Acad. Scis. adv. com. to U.S. Geol. Survey, 1983-88; governing bd. Am. Inst. Physics, 1989—. Recipient Alumni Merit award St. Louis U., 1976, Alexander von Humboldt Found. Sr. U.S. Scientist award, 1979, U.S. Geol. Survey's John Wesley Powell award, 1992, Disting. Svc. award U. Colo., 1993, Commemorative medal USSR Acad. Scis., 1985. Fellow Am. Geophys. Union (bd. dirs. sect. seismology 1970-72, fgn. sec. 1974-84), Geol. Soc. Am., Assn. Exploration Geophysics (India), AAAS; mem. Soc. Exploration Geophysicists, Seismol. Soc. Am. (dir. 1968-74, pres. 1972-73), Austrian Acad. Sci. (corr.), Phi Beta Kappa, Sigma Xi. Club: Cosmos. Home: 4165 Caddo Pky Boulder CO 80303-3602

KISTNER, DAVID HAROLD, biology educator; b. Cin., July 30, 1931; s. Harold Adolf and Hilda (Gick) K.; m. Alzada A. Carlisle, Aug. 8, 1957; children—Alzada H., Kymry Marie Carlisle. A.B., U. Chgo., 1952, B.S., 1956, Ph.D., 1957. Instr. U. Rochester, 1957-59; instr., asst. prof. biology Calif. State U., Chico, 1959-64, assoc. prof., 1964-67, prof., 1967-92, prof. emeritus, 1992—, sr. rschr. univ. found.; rsch. assoc. Calif. State U. Found., Chico, 1992—, Field Mus. Natural History, 1967—, Atlantica Ecol. Rsch. Sta., Salisbury, Zimbabwe, 1970—; CEO Kistner family Trust, 1982—; dir. Shinner Inst. Study Interrelated Insects, 1968-75. Author: (with others) Social Insects, Vols. 1-3; editor Sociobiology, 1975-82; contbr. articles to profl. jours. Patron Am. Mus. Natural History; life mem. Republican Nat. Com., 1980—. Recipient Outstanding Prof. award Calif. State Univs. and Colls., L.A., 1976; John Simon Guggenheim Meml. Found. fellow, 1965-66; grantee NSF, 1960—, Am. Philos. Soc., 1972, Nat. Geog. Soc., 1988. Fellow Explorers Club, Calif. Acad. Scis.; mem. AAUP, AAAS, Entomol. Soc. Am., Pacific Coast Entomol. Soc., Kans. Entomol. Soc., Am. Soc. Naturalists, Am. Soc. Zoologists, Soc. Study of Systematic Zoology, Internat. Soc. Study of Social Insects, Mus. Nat. Hist. (life), Chico State Coll. Assocs. (charter). Home: 3 Canterbury Cir Chico CA 95926-2411

KITA, GEORGE ISAO, lawyer; b. Orange County, Calif., July 22, 1964; m. Isabel Barrales, Dec. 29, 1990. Student, Pierce Coll., 1982-85; BA, Calif. State U., L.A., 1988; JD, U. Calif., San Francisco, 1991. Bar: Calif., 1991. Sports stringer L.A. Daily News, Van Nuys, Calif., 1982-84; law clk. Calif. Atty. Gen.'s Office, San Francisco, 1989-90 summers; judicial extern, clk. to presiding justice Calif. State Ct. of Appeals, San Francisco, 1990; assoc. Medearis & Grimm, Lawyers, L.A., 1992—. Vol. Jr. Traffic Police, Honolulu, 1976, Mayor's Beautification Program, Honolulu, 1976, March of Dimes Walk-a-thon, Honolulu, 1979; block capt. Neighborhood Watch, 1985-88; project chmn. Operation Identification, 1986-87; founder, chief coord. No Drugs in City Terr., 1986-87; chmn. E. L.A. We Turn in Pushers, 1987-88, San Francisco, 1988-91, nat. v.p., bd. dirs., 1991—; vol. San Francisco Marathon, 1990, San Francisco Aids Walk-a-Thon, 1990, Art Torres for L.A. County Supr., 1990; street law tchr. Horace Mann Middle Sch., 1991; chmn., chief coord., host Upland BBQ fundraiser Sen. David Roberti, pres. pro tem re-election campaign, 1992. Recipient Criminal Justice Leadership award Calif. Contract Cities Assn., 1987, cert. appreciation Calif. State Ct. of Appeals, 1990; named to Outstanding Young Men of Am., 1989. Mem. Japanese Am. Bar Assn. (jud. selection com., Asian concerns com.), Los Angeles County Bar Assn., San Bernardino County Bar Assn., Greater Bay Area (Scholarship award 1989), Asian Pacific Bar So. Calif., Japanese Am. Bar So. Calif. Democrat. Office: Meadaris & Grimm Lawyers 1331 Sunset Blvd Los Angeles CA 90026

KITADA, SHINICHI, biochemist; b. Osaka, Japan, Dec. 9, 1948; came to U.S., 1975; s. Koichi and Asako Kitada. MD, Kyoto U., 1973; MS in Biol. Chemistry, UCLA, 1973, PhD, 1979. Intern Kyoto U. Hosp., Japan, 1973-74; resident physician Chest Disease Research Inst., 1974-75; rsch. scholar lab. nuclear medicine and radiation biology UCLA, 1979-87, rsch. scholar Jules Stein Eye Inst., 1988-91; rsch. biochemist La Jolla (Calif.) Cancer Rsch. Found., 1992—. Author papers in field. Japan Soc. Promotion Sci. fellow

1975-76. Mem. Am. Oil Chemists Soc., N.Y. Acad. Scis., Sigma Xi. Home: 920 Kline St Apt 301 La Jolla CA 92037 Office: La Jolla Cancer Rsch Found 10901 N Torrey Pines Rd La Jolla CA 92037

KITCHEN, JOHN MARTIN, historian, educator; b. Nottingham, Eng., Dec. 21, 1936; s. John Sutherland and Margaret Helen (Pearson) K. B.A. with honors, U. London, 1963, Ph.D., 1966. Mem. Cambridge Group Population Studies, Eng., 1965-66; mem. faculty Simon Fraser U., Burnaby, B.C., Can., 1966—. Author: The German Officer Corps 1890-1914, 1968, A Military History of Germany, 1975, Fascism, 1976, The Silent Dictatorship, 1976, The Political Economy of Germany 1815-1914, 1979, The Coming of Austrian Fascism, 1980, Germany in the Age of Total War, 1981, British Policy Towards the Soviet Union During the Second World War, 1986, The Origins of the Cold War in Comparative Perspective, 1988, Europe Between the Wars, 1988, A World in Flames, 1990. Fellow Inter-Univ. Seminar on Armed Forces and Soc. Fellow Royal Hist. Soc., Royal Soc. Can. Office: Simon Fraser U, Dept History, Burnaby, BC Canada V5A 1S6

KITCHEN, MARK SCOTT, college administrator, dean of college; b. Cheyenne, Wyo., Aug. 20, 1953; s. Otis Mead and Doris Charlene (Scott) K.; m. Sandra Gail Siel, June 23, 1984; children: Katherine Anne, Scott Edward. BA, U. Wyo., 1975. News editor Lovell (Wyo.) Chronicle, 1975-77; dir. pub. info. N.W. Community Coll., Powell, Wyo., 1977-80, asst. to pres. for coll. rels., 1980-85, asst. to pres. info., alumni and devel., 1985-90; dean of coll. rels. and devel. N.W. Coll., Powell, Wyo., 1990—, interim pres., summer 1991. Editor Northwest Alumni News, 1980—. Pres. Powell Valley C. of C., 1984; chmn. N.W. Civic Orch. and Chorus Bd. Dirs., Powell, 1986; mem. Park County (Wyo.) Arts Coun., 1987-88; v.p. Friends of Sta. KEMC Bd. Dirs., Billings, Mont., 1990. Recipient Pacemaker award Wyo. Press Assn., 1990, 1st prize Paragon award in newsletter category Nat. Coun. Community Rels., 1987. Mem. Coun. for Advancement and Support of Edn. (adv. contest judge 1985, Award of Merit newsletter 1986), Nat. Coun. Mktg. and Pub. Rels. (dist. IV exec. coun. 1989-92). Home: 275 Stockade Ct Powell WY 82435-2202 Office: NW Coll 231 W 6th St Powell WY 82435-1898

KITTLE, PAUL EDWIN, pediatric dentist; b. Meriden, Conn., Mar. 6, 1948; s. Paul Edwin and Mary Lee (Conway) K.; m. Linda Susan Holthaus, Mar. 2, 1973; children: Christopher Paul, Zachary Joseph. BA in Biology, U. Conn., 1970; DDS, Creighton U., 1975; Cert. in Pedodontics, U. Texas, 1981. Diplomate Am. Bd. Pediatric Dentistry. Commd. capt. U.S. Army, Ft. Riley, Kans., 1975; advanced through grades to col. U.S. Army, 1992; intern U.S. Army, Ft. Riley, Kans., 1976; gen. dental officer U.S. Army, Butzbach, Fed. Republic Germany, 1976-79; pediatric dental resident U.S. Army, San Antonio, 1979-81; chief pediatric dentist U.S. Army, Baumholder, Fed. Republic Germany, 1981-85, Ft. Leavenworth, 1985-89; asst. dir. pediatric dental residency program U.S. Army, Ft. Lewis, Wash., 1989-91, dir. pediatric dental residency program, 1991-93. Republican. Unitarian. Office: US Army Dentac Fort Lewis WA 98431

KITTO, FRANKLIN CURTIS, computer systems specialist; b. Salt Lake City, Nov. 18, 1954; s. Curtis Eugene and Margaret (Ipson) K.; m. Collette Madsen, Sept. 16, 1982; children: Melissa Erin, Heather Elise, Stephen Curtis. BA, Brigham Young U., 1978, MA, 1980. Tv sta. operator Sta. KBYU-TV, Provo, Utah, 1973-78; grad. teaching asst. Brigham Young Univ., 1978-80; cable TV system operator Instructional Media U. Utah, Salt Lake City, 1980-82, data processing mgr., 1982-83, media supr., 1983-85, bus. mgr., 1985-87; dir. computer systems tng. MegaWest Systems, Inc., Salt Lake City, 1987-90, dir. new product devel., 1990-91, mgr. tng. and installation, 1991-93, mgr. rsch. and devel., 1993—; tng. and installation mgr. Total Solutions, Am. Fork, Utah, 1993—. Recipient Kiwanis Freedom Leadership award, Salt Lake City, 1970, Golden Microphone award Brigham Young U., 1978. Mem. Assn. Ednl. Communications and Tech., Utah Pick Users Group (sec. 1983-87, pres. 1987-89, treas. 1989-90), Am. Soc. Tng. and Devel., Assn. for Computer Tng. and Support, Phi Eta Sigma, Kappa Tau Alpha. Mormon. Home: 10931 S Avila Dr Sandy UT 84094-5965 Office: Total Solutions 117 S 700 E American Fork UT 84003

KITTREDGE, WILLIAM ALFRED, humanities educator; b. Portland, Oreg., Aug. 14, 1932; s. Franklin Oscar and Josephine (Miessner) K.; m. Janet O'Connor, Dec. 8, 1952 (div. 1968); children: Karen, Bradley. BS, Oreg. State U., 1953; MFA in Creative Writing, U. Iowa, 1969. Rancher Warner Valley Livestock, Adel, Oreg., 1957-67; prof. U. Mont., Missoula, 1969—. Author: We Are Not In This Together, 1984, Owning It All, 1987, Hole in the Sky, 1992. With USAF, 1954-57. Recipient award for lit. Gov. of Mont., 1987; named Humanist of Yr. State of Mont., 1988. Home: 143 S 5th E Missoula MT 59801 Office: U Mont Missoula MT 59801

KIUCHI, TAKASHI TACHI, electronics company executive; b. Hamburg, Fed. Republic Germany, June 1, 1935; came to U.S., 1969-76, 88—; s. Nobutane and Tayo (Shidachi) K.; m. Kyoko Tsutsumi, Mar. 8, 1965; children: Shintaro, Reijiro, Eriko, Junzaburo. BA, Keio U, Tokyo, 1958; MA, U. B.C., Vancouver, Can., 1960; program for sr. execs., MIT, 1980. Exec. v.p. Mitsubishi Electric Am., L.A., 1974-76; pres., chmn. Mitsubishi Electric Am., Cypress, Calif., 1988—; gen. mgr. Mitsubishi Electric Corp., Tokyo, 1981-87. Co-author: Management Challenge, 1985. Home: 17 Hilltop Cir Palos Verdes Peninsula CA 90274 Office: Mitsubishi Electric Am 5665 Plaza Dr Cypress CA 90630-0007

KIVELSON, MARGARET GALLAND, physicist; b. N.Y.C., Oct. 21, 1928; d. Walter Isaac and Madeleine (Wiener) Galland; m. Daniel Kivelson, Aug. 15, 1949; children: Steven Allan, Valerie Ann. AB, Radcliffe Coll., 1950, AM, 1951, PhD, 1957. Cons. Rand Corp., Santa Monica, Calif., 1956-69; asst. to geophysicist UCLA, 1967-83, prof., 1983—, also chmn. dept. earth and space scis., 1984-87; prin. investigator of magnetometer, Galileo Mission, Jet Propulsion Lab., Pasadena, Calif., 1977—; overseer Harvard Coll., 1977-83; mem. adv. coun. NASA, 1987—; chair atmospheric adv. com. NSF, 1986-89, Com. Solar and Space Physics, 1977-86, com. planetary exploration, 1986-87, com. solar terrestial phys., 1989-92. Editor: The Solar System: Observations and Interpretations, 1986; contbr. articles to profl. jours. Named Woman of Yr., L.A. Mus. Sci. and Industry, 1979, Woman of Sci., UCLA, 1984; recipient Grad. Soc. medal Radcliffe Coll., 1983, 350th Anniversary Alumni medal Harvard U. Fellow AAAS, Am. Geophysics Union; mem. Am. Phys. Soc., Am. Astron. Soc. Office: UCLA Dept Earth & Space Scis 6843 Slichter Los Angeles CA 90024-1567

KIVER, EUGENE PAUL, geology educator; b. Cleve., Feb. 26, 1937; s. Eugene F. and Olga (Kutchinsky) K.; m. Barbara E. Wrenn, Mar. 28, 1964; children: Mark, Rebecca, Phillip. BA, Case Western Res. U., 1964; PhD, U. Wyo., 1968. Prof. geology Eastern Wash. U., Cheney, 1968—; geologist Dept. Resources, State of Wash., 1976-79, U.S. Bur. Reclamation, Grand Coulee, Wash., 1983-86. Author: Geologic Story of National Parks and Monuments, 1985. Mem. Geol. Soc. Am., Sigma Xi (sec. Eastern Wash. U.-Spokane chpt. 1975—). Home: 22202 S Frog Hollow Ln Cheney WA 99004-9796 Office: Eastern Wash U Cheney WA 99004

KIZZIAR, JANET WRIGHT, psychologist, author, lecturer; b. Independence, Kans.; d. John L. and Thelma (Rooks) Wright; m. Mark Kizziar. BA, U. Tulsa, 1961, MA, 1964, EdD, 1969. Sch. psychologist Tulsa Pub. Schs.; pvt. practice psychology Tulsa, 1969-78, Bartlesville, Okla., 1978-88. Co-host: Psychologists' Corner program, Sta. KOTV, Tulsa.; author: (with Judy W. Hagedorn) Gemini: The Psychology and Phenomena of Twins, 1975, Search for Acceptance: The Adolescent and Self Esteem, 1979. Sponsor Youth Crisis Intervention Telephone Center, 1972-74; Bd. dirs. March of Dimes, Child Protection Team, Women and Children in Crisis, United Fund, YMCA Fund, Mental Health of Washington County., Alternative High Sch. Named Disting. Alumni U. Tulsa, Outstanding Young Woman of Okla. Mem. APA, NOW, Internat. Twins Assn. (pres. 1976-77). Home: 9427 N 87th Way Scottsdale AZ 85258-1913 Office: PO Box 5227 Scottsdale AZ 85261-5227

KLAAR, RICHARD, aerospace engineer; b. Novi Vrbas, Vodjvodina, Yugoslavia, Oct. 6, 1941; s. Richard and Katharina (Greiling) K.; m. Kay Murray, Apr. 26, 1964; children: Richard Raymond, Raymond Richard. Diploma, Metals Engring. Inst., 1986. Welding technician Seatrain Shipbldg., N.Y.C., 1973-75; foreman welding Nat. Steel & Shipbldg. Co., San Diego, 1975-76, gen. foreman welding, 1976-77, welding engr., 1977-82, welding engr. sr., 1982-87; mfg. tech. engr. Gen. Dynamics space systems div., San Diego, 1987-88, mfg. engring. specialist, 1988—. Mem. welding adv. bd. San Diego Community Coll., 1980-89. Mem. Am. Soc. Nondestructive Testing, Am. Soc. Metals, Nat. Mgmt. Assn., Am. Welding Soc., Soc. Mfg. Engrs. Republican. Home: 19476 Corey Rd Loranger LA 70446

KLAHR, GARY PETER, lawyer; b. N.Y.C., July 9, 1942; s. Fred and Frieda (Garson) K. Student Ariz. State U., 1958-61; LL.B. with high honors, U. Ariz., 1964. Bar: Ariz. 1967, U.S. Dist. Ct. Ariz. 1967. Assoc., Brazlin & Greene, Phoenix, 1967-68; sr. ptnr. Gary Peter Klahr, P.C., Phoenix, 1968—. Mem. Phoenix City Council, 1974-76; mem. CODAMA, bd. dirs., 1975-89, pres. 1980-81; mem. City Lic. Appeals Bd., 1987—, vice-chmn, 1988-92, chmn., 1993—; bd. dirs. 7th Step Found., 1978-84, pres. 1980-82; bd. dirs. Tumbleweed Runaway Center, 1972-76; chmn. Citizens Criminal Justice Comn., 1977-78; co-chmn. delinquency subcom. Phoenix Forward Task Force; vol. Juvenile Ct. referee, 1969; vol. adult probation officer; vol. counselor for Dept. Corrections youth programs, Phoenix; ex-officio mem., spl. cons. Phoenix Youth Commn.; mem. citizen adv. council Phoenix Union High Sch. Dist., 1985-90, elected governing bd., 1991—, v.p., 1992—; review bd. Phoenix Police Dept., 1985—; bd. dirs. Metro Youth Ctr., 1986-87; bd. dirs. Svc./Employment/Redevel. (SER) Jobs for Progress, Phoenix, 1985-90, pres., 1986-87; v.p. local chpt. City of Hope, 1985-86; Justice of the Peace Pro Tem Maricopa County Cts., 1985-89; juvenile hearing officer Maricopa County Juvenile Ct., 1985-89; v.p., co-founder Community Leadership for Youth Devel. (CLYDE); co-chmn. Phoenix Union High Sch. Citizens Adv. Com., 1970-72; del. Phoenix Together Town Hall on Youth Crime, 1982. Named 1 of 3 Outstanding Young Men Phoenix Jr. C. of C., 1969; Disting. Citizen award Ariz. chapt. ACLU, 1976. Mem. ABA, ACLU (v.p. cen. chpt. Ariz. 1990—), Ariz. State Bar (past sec., bd. dirs. young lawyers sect., co-chmn. unauthorized practice com. 1988-89, mem. other coms.), Maricopa County Bar Assn. (past sec. and bd. dirs. young lawyers sect.), Am. Judicature Soc., Jewish Children's and Family Service, Common Cause, NAACP, Ariz. Consumers Council, Phoenix Jaycees, Order of Coif, Phi Alpha Delta. Democrat. Jewish. Contbr. numerous articles to profl. jours.; asst. editor Ariz. Law Rev. 1963-64. Office: 917 W Mcdowell Rd Phoenix AZ 85007-1729

KLAKEG, CLAYTON HAROLD, cardiologist; b. Big Woods, Minn., Mar. 31, 1920; s. Knute O. and Agnes (Folvik) K.; student Concordia Coll., Moorhead, Minn., 1938-40; BS, N.D. State U., 1942; BS in Medicine, N.D. U., 1943; M.D., Temple U., 1945; MS in Medicine and Physiology, U. Minn.-Mayo Found., 1954; children: Julie Ann, Robert Clayton, Richard Scott. Intern, Med. Ctr., Jersey City, 1945-46; mem. staff VA Hosp., Fargo, N.D., 1948-51; fellow in medicine and cardiology Mayo Found., Rochester, Minn., 1951-55; internist, cardiologist Sansum Med. Clinic Inc., Santa Barbara, Calif., 1955—; mem. staff Cottage Hosp., St. Francis Hosp. Bd. dirs. Sansum Med. Rsch. Found., pres., 1990. Served to capt. M.C., USAF, 1946-48. Diplomate Am. Bd. Internal Medicine. Fellow ACP, Am. Coll. Cardiology, Am. Coll. Chest Physicians, Am. Heart Assn. (mem. council on clin. cardiology); mem. Calif. Heart Assn. (pres. 1971-72, Meritorious Service award 1968, Disting. Service award 1972, Disting. Achievement award 1975), Santa Barbara County Heart Assn. (pres. 1959-60, Disting. Service award 1958, Disting. Achievement award 1971), Calif. Med. Assn., Los Angeles Acad. Medicine, Santa Barbara County Med. Assn., Mayo Clinic Alumni Assn., Santa Barbara Soc. Internal Medicine (pres. 1963), Sigma Xi, Phi Beta Pi. Republican. Lutheran. Club: Channel City. Contbr. articles to profl. jours. Home: 5956 Trudi Dr Santa Barbara CA 93117-2175 Office: Sansum Med Clinic Inc PO Box 1239 Santa Barbara CA 93102-1239

KLAMMER, JOSEPH FRANCIS, management consultant; b. Omaha, Mar. 25, 1925; s. Aloys Arcadius and Sophie (Nadolny) K.; BS, Creighton U., 1948; MBA, Stanford, 1950; cert. in polit. econs. Grad. Inst. Internat. Studies, U. Geneva, 1951. cert. mgmt. cons. Adminstrv. analyst Chevron Corp., San Francisco, 1952-53; staff asst. Enron Corp., Omaha, 1953-57; mgmt. cons., bd. dirs. Cresap, McCormick and Paget, Inc., San Francisco, 1957-75, v.p., mgr. San Francisco region, 1968-75; mgmt. cons., prin. J.F. Klammer Assocs., San Francisco, 1975—. Past mem. bd. dirs. Conard House. Apptd. and attended U.S. Mil. Acad., West Point, N.Y.; served to 1st lt. USAAF, 1943-46; lt. col. USAF (ret.). Rotary Found. fellow, 1950-51. Republican. Roman Catholic. Clubs: Univ., Omaha, Alpha Sigma Nu. Home: 1998 Broadway St San Francisco CA 94109 Office: 1 Market Plz San Francisco CA 94105-1019

KLARITCH, THOMAS MICHAEL, SR., financial executive; b. Jamaica, N.Y., Oct. 30, 1957; s. Richard Joseph and Delores Gladys (Albano) K.; m. Darlene Helen Korb, Feb. 12, 1983; children: Erica Ann, Thomas Michael Jr., Nicholas James, Adam Joseph. Student, N.Y. Inst. Tech., Old Westbury, N.Y., 1978; BS, SUNY, 1980. CPA, Pa. Dept. mgr. Korvettes, Inc., Huntington Station, N.Y., 1974-78; high shortage analyst Gimbel Bros., N.Y., 1981-82; internal auditor Allied Stores Corp., N.Y., 1982-83; mgr. pvt. practice Winthrop U. Hosp., Mineola, N.Y., 1983-86; O/P contr. Fair Oaks Hosp., Summit, N.J., 1986-88; asst. contr. HCA LAS Encinas Hosp., Pasadena, Calif., 1988-89; chief fin. officer, contr. HCA Montevista Hosp., Las Vegas, Nev., 1989—; acting adminstr. HCA Montevista Hosp., Las Vegas, Nev., 1990-91; mem. budget com. Hosp. Corp. Am., Nashville, 1991; dir. compliance Behavioral Healthcare Corp., 1993—. Treas. Woodland Ridge Community Assn., Henderson, Nev., 1989-90, v.p. 1992—. Fellow Healthcare Fin. Mgmt. Assn.; mem. Pa. Inst. CPA, Healthcare Fin. Mgmt. Assn., Healthcare Fin. Mgmt. Assn. (Nev. chpt. pres. elect 1993—). Republican. Roman Catholic. Office: HCA Montevista Hosp 5900 W Rochelle Ave Las Vegas NV 89103-3327

KLASSEN, ALVIN HENRY, mathematics educator; b. San Bernardino, Calif., July 18, 1949; s. Herman Arthur and Elsie Frieda (Lille) K. BA, Calif. State U., 1971; MA, San Diego State U., 1990. Auditor May Co., Riverside, Calif., 1973-75; comdr. USNR, 1984—; comdg. officer USNR CA unit, Santa Ana, Calif., 1990—; math. instr. San Diego State U., 1989—; tennis ofcl. U.S. Tennis Assn., White Plains, N.Y., 1985—, Internat. Tennis Fedn., 1991—; physics instr., dept. chmn. NROTC Prep. Sch., USN, summers 1988—. Judge, math. div. Greater San Diego Sci. and Engring. Fair, 1988—. Lt. USN, 1975-84. Decorated D.S.M., Navy Achievement medal. Mem. Naval Res. Assn. (Diamond in the Rough award 1990, v.p. 1990—, Jr. Officer of Yr. 1989), Am. Math. Soc., Math. Assn. Am., San Diego County Tennis Umpires Assn., U.S. Tennis Assn., Internat. Tennis Fedn. (ofcl. 1991—). Lutheran. Home: 13119 Bonita Vista St # 232 Poway CA 92064-5721 Office: San Diego State U 5300 Campanile Dr San Diego CA 92115-1338

KLATT, GORDON ROY, surgeon; b. St. Paul, Dec. 1, 1942; s. Roy Paul and Elizabeth (Gartner) K.; children: Lisa Mary, Julie Ann, David Christopher. BS in Biolog, Coll. of St. Thomas, St. Paul, 1964; MD, U. Minn., 1968. Diplomate Am. Bd. of Surgery, Am. Bd. Colon and Rectal Surgery. Commd. 2d lt. U.S. Army, 1966, advanced through grades to lt. col., 1976, off active duty, 1977; intern Fitzsimons Army Med. Ctr., Denver, 1968-69; resident in gen. surgery Madigan Army Med. Ctr., Tacoma, 1969-73; gen. surgeon Madigan Army Med. Ctr./U.S. Army, Okinawa, Japan, 1973-76; fellow colorectal surgery U. Minn., Mpls., 1977-78; pvt. practice Tacoma, 1978—; commdr. 6250th U.S. Army Hosp., 1985-87, 50th Gen. Hosp., 1987-90; chmn. Coalition for a Tobacco-Free Pierce County, Tacoma, 1988-91; co-chmn. tobacco addiction coordinating coun. State of Wash., Olympia, 1988-91; med. dir. Multicare Health Systems Cancer Program, 1991—. Bd. dirs. Tacoma Philharmonic, 1979-81, . Am. Cancer Soc., Pierce County unit, Tacoma, 1978—; chmn. tobacco free Wash. com., Seattle, 1986-90. Col. USAR. Mem. Fellow ACS, Am. Soc. Colon and Rectal Surgeons; mem. AMA, Wash. State Med. Assn., Pierce County Med.Soc. (pres. 1990), N. Pacific Surg. Assn., Pan Pacific Surg. Assn., Kiwanis. Home: 1120 Cliff Ave #404 Tacoma WA 98402-9999 Office: Mt Rainier Surg Assocs 902 S L St Ste 202 Tacoma WA 98405-4040

KLATT, JOHN PAUL, engineering consultant; b. Bloomington, Ill., Mar. 5, 1958; s. Richard Paul and Mary Therese (Stahl) K.; m. Maureen Denise Janeczek, Sept. 19, 1987. BS in Engring., U. Ill., 1980, MS in Engring., 1986. Devel. engr. Ferro Corp., Crooksville, Ohio, 1981-84; sr. rsch. engr. Lockheed Missile and Space, Sunnyvale, Calif., 1987-91; cons. engr. Ceramic Answers Cons., San Jose, Calif., 1991—. Author: Applied Ceramics, 1992; contbr. articles to profl. jours. Mem. Am. Ceramic Soc., Soc. for the Advancement of Material and Process Engring. Office: Ceramic Answers Cons 3391 Valley Forge Way San Jose CA 95117

KLAUSNER, JACK DANIEL, lawyer; b. N.Y.C., July 31, 1945; s. Burt and Marjory (Brown) K.; m. Dale Arlene Kreis, July 1, 1968; children: Andrew Russell, Mark Raymond. BS in Bus., Miami U., Oxford, Ohio, 1967; JD, U. Fla., 1969. Bar: N.Y. 1971, Ariz. 1975, U.S. Dist. Ct. Ariz. 1975, U.S. Ct. Appeals (9th cir.) 1975, U.S. Supreme Ct. 1975. Assoc. counsel John P. McGuire & Co., Inc., N.Y.C., 1970-71; assoc. atty. Hahn & Hessen, N.Y.C., 1971-72; gen. counsel Equilease Corp., N.Y.C., 1972-74; assoc. Burch & Cracchiolo, Phoenix, 1974-78; ptnr. Burch & Cracchiolo, 1978—; judge pro tem Maricopa County Superior Ct., 1990—, Ariz. Ct. Appeals, 1992—. Bd. dirs. Santos Soccer Club, Phoenix, 1989-90; bd. dirs., pres. south Bank Soccer Club, Tempe, 1987-88. Home: 8373 S Forest Ave Tempe AZ 85284-2375 Office: Burch & Cracchiolo 702 E Osborn Rd Phoenix AZ 85014-5241

KLAWE, MARIA MARGARET, administrator; b. Toronto, Ontario, Can., July 5, 1951; d. Janusz Josef and Kathleen Wreath (McCaughan) K.; m. Nicholas John Pippenger, May 12, 1980; children: Janek, Sasha. BS, U. Alberta, Edmonton, Can., 1973; PhD, U. Alberta, 1977. Asst. prof. Oakland U., Dept. Math. Sci., Rochester, Mich., 1977-78, U. Toronto, Dept. Computer Sci., Can., 1979-80; rsch. staff mem. IBM Rsch., San Jose, Calif., 1980-89; mgr., discrete math. IBM Rsch., 1984-85, mgr., dept. math., related computer sci., 1985-87; prof., dept. head dept. computer sci. U. B.C., Vancouver, 1988—; mem. Premier's Adv. Coun. on Sci. and Tech., 1992—, Provincial Adv. Com. on Edn. Tech., 1993—; dir. Computing Rsch. Assn., Washington, 1990—, vice-chair, 1993—; mem. adv. bd. univ. rels. IBM Toronto Lab., 1989—, sci. adv. bd., Dimacs NSF Sci. Tech. Ctr., New Brunswick, N.J., 1989—. Editor: (jours.) Combinatorica, 1985—, Siam Jour. on Computing, 1986-93, Siam Jour. on Discrete Math., 1987-93; contbr. articles to profl. jours. Dir. Sci. World, Vancouver, 1990—; vol. Scientists in Schs., B.C., 1989—; mem. Prov. Adv. Coun. Edn. Tech., 1993—. Nat. Rsch. Coun. Can. fellow, 1973-77; INCO scholar, 1968-71. Mem. Am. Math. Soc., Math. Assn. Am., Can. Math. Soc. (bd. dirs.), Can. Heads Computer Sci. (pres. 1990-91), ACM, Assn. Women Math. (exec. com.), Soc. Ind. Applied Math. (coun. mem.). Office: U BC, Dept Computer Sci, Vancouver, BC Canada V6T 1Z2

KLEBANOFF, SEYMOUR JOSEPH, medical educator; b. Toronto, Ont., Can., Feb. 3, 1927; s. Eli Samuel and Ann Klebanoff; m. Evelyn Norma Silver, June 3, 1951; children: Carolyn, Mark. MD, U. Toronto, 1951; PhD in Biochemistry, U. London, 1954. Intern Toronto Gen. Hosp., 1951-52; postdoctoral fellow Dept. Path. Chemistry, U. Toronto, 1954-57, Rockefeller U., N.Y.C., 1957-62; assoc. prof. medicine U. Washington, Seattle, 1962-68, prof., 1968—; mem. adv. coun. Nat. Inst. Allergy and Infectious Diseases, NIH, 1987-90. Author: The Neutrophil, 1978; also 197 jour. articles. Recipient Merit award NIH, 1988, Mayo Soley award Western Soc. for Clin. Investigation, 1991. Fellow AAAS; mem. NAS, Am. Soc. Clin. Investigation, Am. Soc. Biol. Chemists, Assn. Am. Physicians, Infectious Diseases Soc. Am., Endocrine Soc., Reticuloendothelial Soc. (Marie T. Bonazinga rsch. award 1985), Inst. Medicine. Home: 509 Mcgilvra Blvd E Seattle WA 98112-5047 Office: Univ Wash Dept Medicine SJ-10 Div of Allergy & Infectious Dis Seattle WA 98195

KLEE, VICTOR LA RUE, mathematician, educator; b. San Francisco, Sept. 18, 1925; s. Victor La Rue and Mildred (Muller) K.; m. Elizabeth Bliss; children—Wendy Pamela, Barbara Christine, Susan Lisette, Heidi Elizabeth; m. Joann Polack, Mar. 17, 1985. B.A., Pomona Coll., 1945, D.Sc. (hon.), 1965; Ph.D., U. Va., 1949; Dr. honoris causa, U. Liège, Belgium, 1984. Asst. prof. U. Va., 1949-53; NRC fellow Inst. for Advanced Study, 1951-52; asst. prof. U. Wash., Seattle, 1953-54, asso. prof., 1954-57, prof. math., 1957—, adj. prof. computer sci., 1974—, prof. applied math., 1976-84; vis. asso. prof. UCLA, 1955-56; vis. prof. U. Colo., 1971, U. Victoria, 1975, U. Western Australia, 1979; cons. IBM Watson Research Center, 1972; cons. to industry; mem. Math. Scis. Research Inst., 1985-86; sr. fellow Inst. for Math. and its Applications, 1987. Contbr. articles to profl. jours. Recipient Research prize U. Va., 1952, Vollum award for disting. accomplishment in sci. and tech. Reed Coll., 1982, David Prescott Burrows Outstanding Disting. Achievment award Pomona Coll., 1988, Max Planck rsch. prize, 1992; NSF sr. postdoctoral fellow; Sloan Found. fellow U. Copenhagen, 1958-60; fellow Center Advanced Study in Behavioral Scis., 1975-76; Guggenheim fellow, Humboldt award U. Erlangen-Nürnberg, 1980-81, Fulbright award U. Trier, 1992; sr. fellow Inst. Mathematics and Its Applications, 1987. Fellow AAAS (chmn. sect. A 1975); mem. Am. Math. Soc. (asso. sec. 1955-58, mem. exec. com. 1969-70), Math. Assn. Am. (pres. 1971-73, L.R. Ford award 1972, Disting. Service award 1977, C. B. Allendoerfer award 1980), Soc. Indsl. and Applied Math. (mem. council 1966-68), Assn. Computing Machinery, Ops. Rsch. Soc. Am., Math. Programming Soc., Internat. Linear Algebra Soc., Phi Beta Kappa, Sigma Xi (nat. lectr. 1969). Home: 13706 39th Ave NE Seattle WA 98125-3810 Office: U Wash Dept Mathematics GN 50 Seattle WA 98195

KLEESE, WILLIAM CARL, genealogy research consultant; b. Williamsport, Pa., Jan. 20, 1940; s. Donald Raymond and Helen Alice (Mulberger) K.; m. Vivian Ann Yeager, June 12, 1958; children: Scott, Jolene, Mark, Troy, Brett, Kecia, Lance. BS in Wildlife Biology, U. Ariz., 1975, MS in Animal Physiology, 1979, PhD in Animal Physiology, 1981. Sales rep. Terminix Co., Tucson, 1971-72; pest control operator, 1973-75; fire fighter Douglas Ranger Dist. Coronado Nat. Forest U.S. Forest Svc., 1975, biol. technician Santa Catalina ranger dist., 1975-76; lab. technician dept. animal scis. U. Ariz., 1977-78, rsch. technician dept. pharmacology and toxicology, 1978, rsch. asst. dept. biochemistry, 1979-81, rsch. specialist muscle biology group, 1981—; genealogy rsch. cons. Tucson, 1988—. Author: Introduction to Genealogy, 1988, Introduction to Genealogical Research, 1989, The Genealogical Research, Neophyte to Graduate, 1992, Genealogical Research in the British Isles, 1991; contbr. numerous articles to profl. jours. Chaplain Ariz. State Prisons, Tucson, 1988—. Mem. Ariz. Genealogy Adv. Bd. (com. chmn. 1990-92), Herpetologists League, Lycoming County Geneal. Soc., Nat. Geneal. Soc., Nat. Wildlife Fedn., Pa. Geneal. Soc., Soc. for the Study of Amphibians and Reptiles, Soc. of Vertebrate Paleontology, Ariz. State Geneal. Soc. (pres. 1990-93). Republican. Mormon. Home: 6521 E Fayette St Tucson AZ 85730-2220 Office: 6061 E Broadway Blvd Ste 128 Tucson AZ 85711-4020

KLEHS, HENRY JOHN WILHELM, civil engineer; b. Dornbusch bez Stade, Germany, Dec. 7, 1910; s. Frederick and Anna (Mahler) K.; B.S., U. Calif., 1935; m. Clodell Peters, July 17, 1948; came to U.S., 1920, naturalized through father, 1922. Engr. So. Pacific Transp. Co., 1936-75, supr. hazardous materials control, until 1975; ret., 1975. Mem. Calif. Fire Chiefs Assn., Internat. Assn. Fire Chiefs, Steuben Soc. Am., Am. Ry. Engring Assn., ASCE. Home: 604 Glenwood Isle Alameda CA 94501-5605

KLEIBER, DOUGLAS HAROLD, information systems consultant; b. Portland, Oreg., July 28, 1955; s. Harold Adolf an Adeline Margaret (Berg) K.; m. Sue Louise Coleman, Aug. 28, 1982; children: Daniel Douglas, Joseph Richard, Maria Louise. AA, N. Seattle Community Coll., 1984; BA in Bus. summa cum laude, Seattle U., 1987. Free lance musician Gresham, Oreg., 1974-80; acct. Skipper's Inc., Seattle, 1981, computer programmer, 1982-85, data processing mgr., 1986-88; free lance info. systems cons. Seattle, 1992-92; prin. Deterministics, 1992—. Republican. Lutheran. Home: 21137 SE 28th Pl Issaquah WA 98027-7416

KLEIMAN, HARLAN PHILIP, film company executive; b. N.Y.C., Nov. 9, 1940; s. Ira Arthur Kleiman and Dorothy Rosen; m. Sondra Lee (divorced); m. Sandy Charles, May 12, 1985. BA, Hunter Coll., 1962; MS in Indsl. adminstrn., Yale U., 1964. Founder, exec. dir. Long Wharf Theater, New Haven, Conn., 1964-68; producer Off Broadway, N.Y.C., 1968-72; v.p. Video Corp. Am., N.Y.C., 1972-74, HBO, N.Y.C., 1974-76; sr. v.p. cable div. Warner Communications, N.Y.C., 1976-79; pres. Harlan Kleiman Co., L.A., 1979-87; chmn. bd. dirs. Filmstar Inc., L.A., 1987-92; pres. Strategic Fin. Group, Encino, 1991—. Recipient ACE award Best Dramatic TV Spl., Nat. Cable TV Assn., 1984. Mem. Hollywood Radio & TV Soc., Am. Film

Mktg. Assn. Home: 15700 Dickens St Encino CA 91436-3123 Office: Strategic Fin Group 15840 Ventura Blvd Ste 419 Encino CA 91436

KLEIN, ARNOLD WILLIAM, dermatologist; b. Mt. Clemens, Mich., Feb. 27, 1945; m. Malvina Kraemer. BA, U. Pa., 1967, MD, 1971. Intern Cedars-Sinai Med. Ctr., Los Angeles, 1971-72; resident in dermatology Hosp. U. Pa., Phila., 1972-73, U. Calif., Los Angeles, 1973-75; pvt. practice dermatology Berverly Hills, Calif., 1975—; assoc. clin. prof. dermatology/medicine U. Calif. Ctr. for Health Scis; mem. med. staff Cedars-Sinai Med. Ctr.; asst. clin. prof. dermatology Stanford U., 1982-89; asst. clin. prof. to assoc. clin. prof. dermatology/medicine, UCLA; Calif. state commr., 1983-89; med. adv. bd. Skin Cancer Found., Lupus Found. Am., Collagen Corp.; presenter seminars in field. Reviewer Jour. Dermatologic Surgery and Oncology, Jour. Sexually Transmitted Diseases, Jour. Am. Acad. Dermatology; mem. editorial bd. Men's Fitness mag., Shape mag., Jour. Dermatologic Surgery and Oncology; contbr. numerous articles to med. jours. Mem. AMA, Calif. Med. Assn., Am. Soc. Dermatologic Surgery, Internat. Soc. Dermatologic Surgery, Calif. Soc. Specialty Plastic Surgery, Am. Assn. Cosmetic Surgeons, Assn. Sci. Advosors, Los Angeles Med. Assn., Am. Coll. Chemosurgery, Met. Dermatology Soc., Am. Acad. Dermatology, Dermatology Found., Scleroderma Found., Internat. Psoriasis Found., Lupus Found., Am. Venereal Disease Assn., Soc. Cosmetic Chemists, AFTRA, Los Angeles Mus. Contemporary Art (founder), Dance Gallery Los Angeles (founder), Am. Found. AIDS Research (founder, dir.), Friars Club, Phi Beta Kappa, Sigma Tau Sigma, Delphos. Office: 435 N Roxbury Dr Ste 204 Beverly Hills CA 90210-5087

KLEIN, DAVID, foreign service officer; b. N.Y.C., Sept. 2, 1919; s. Sam and Fannie H. (Falk) K.; m. Anne L. Cochran, Mar. 14, 1953; children: Peter S., Steven C., John W., Barbara J., Richard L., Suzanne G. BA, Bklyn. Coll., 1939; MBA, Harvard U., 1948; MA, Columbia U., 1952; postgrad., U. Md., 1964-66; grad., Nat. War Coll., 1966. Fgn. service officer, 1947-75; vice consul Lourenco Marques, 1947-49; 3d sec., econ. officer Rangoon, Burma, 1949-51; Russian lang. and area studies Dept. State, 1951-52; 2d sec., consular/econ. officer Moscow, 1952-54; Regensburg-Soviet studies, 1954-55; polit./econ. officer Berlin, 1955-57; 1st sec., polit. officer Bonn, Germany, 1957-60; Soviet desk Dept. State, 1960-62; sr. mem. for European affairs Nat. Security Council, 1962-65; counselor econ. affairs Moscow, 1966-67; counselor polit. affairs, 1967-68; polit. adviser Berlin, 1968-71, U.S. minister to, 1971-74; asst. dir. ACDA, Washington, 1974-75; exec. dir. Am. Council on Germany, 1975-88, dir., 1975-88; exec. dir. John J. McCloy Fund, 1975-88; pres. German-Am. Partnership Program, 1976-85; spl. asst. for fgn. affairs for pres. Fairleigh Dickinson U., N.J., 1986-90; advisor on internat. programs U. Tulsa, 1990-93; instr. govt. and politics U. Md., 1969-71; vis. prof. U. San Diego, 1989—, U. Calif., San Diego, 1990—; chmn. bd. Zeiss Avionics, Calif.; cons. in field. Author: The Basmachi, a Study in Soviet Nationalities, 1952, Berlin: From Symbol of Confrontation to Keystone of Security, 1989. Bd. dirs. Deutsches Haus, NYU, 1977-90; vice chmn. bd. trustees Mercer County Community Coll., West Windsor, N.J., 1978-84; mem. adv. bd. Byrnes Internat. Ctr. U. S.C., 1987-91; mem. bd. visitors internat. program U. Calif., San Diego. Served to col. AUS, 1941-46. Decorated Legion of Merit; recipient Superior Svc. award U.S. Dept. State, 1964; twice Baker Scholar Harvard U.; twice Disting. Order of the Cross (Fed. Republic of Germany), Disting. Svc. award City of West Berlin. Mem. Am. Fgn. Service Assn., Council on Fgn. Rels., Harvard Bus. Club (v.p. Washington chpt. 1965-66), Century Assn., Univ. Club (N.Y.C.). Unitarian. Office: 6535 Caminito Kittansett La Jolla CA 92037-5813

KLEIN, EDITH MILLER, lawyer, former state senator; b. Wallace, ID, Aug. 4, 1915; d. Fred L.B. and Edith (Gallup) M.; m. Sandor S. (deceased 1970). BS in Bus., U. ID, 1935; teaching fellowship, Wash. State U., 1936; JD, George Wash. U., 1946, LLM, 1954. Bar: D.C. 1946, Idaho 1947, N.Y. 1955, U.S. Supreme Ct. 1954. Pers. spec. Labor and War Depts., Wash., 1942-46; practice law Boise, ID, 1947—; judge Mcpl. Ct., Boise, 1947-49; mem. Idaho Ho. Reps., 1948-50, 64-68, Idaho Senate, 1968-82; atty. FCC Wash., 1953-54; FHA N.Y.C., 1955-56. Trustee Boise State U. Found. Inc., 1973—; regent Pioneer chpt. DAR, 1991-93; pres. Boise Music Week, 1991-93. Named Woman of Yr. Boise Altrusa Club, 1966, Boise C. of C., 1970, Disting. Citizen, Idaho Statesman 1970, Woman of Progress, Idaho Bus. Prof. Women, 1978; recipient Women Helping Women award Soroptomist Club, 1980, Stein Meml. award Y.M.C.A., 1983, Silver and Gold award for Outstanding Svc., U. Idaho, 1985, March of Dimes award to Honor Outstanding Women, 1987, Cert. of Appreciation by Boise Br., AAUW, 1990, Morrison Ctr. Hall of Fame award, 1990. Mem. Bd. Harry W. Morison Found. Inc., 1978—, Bd. Community Health Sci. Assn., Inc., 1982—, St. Alphonsus Regional Med. Ctr. Found. Bd., 1982—, ID Law Enforcement Planning Comm., 1972-82, ID Gov.'s Comm. on Status of Women, 1965-79, 1982-92 (chmn. 1964-72), ID Endowment Investment Bd., 1979-82, Nat. Adv. Comm. on Regional Med. Programs, 1974-76, ID Gov.'s Coun. on Comprehensive Health Planning 1969-76. Republican. Congregationalist. Home: 1588 Lenz Lane PO Box 475 Boise ID 83701 Office: 1400 West One Plaza PO Box 2527 Boise ID 83701

KLEIN, (MARY) ELEANOR, retired clinical social worker; b. Luzon, Philippines, Dec. 13, 1919; came to U.S., 1921; (parents Am. citizens); d. Roy Edgar and Edith Lillian Hay; m. Edward George Klein, June 24, 1955. BA, Pacific Union Coll., 1946; MSW, U. So. Calif., 1953. Lic. clin. social worker. Social worker White Meml. Hosp., Los Angeles, 1948-56; clin. social worker UCLA Hosp. Clinics, 1956-65, supr. social worker, 1965-67, assoc. dir., 1967-73, dir., 1973-82. Bd. dirs., treas. Los Amigos de la Humanidad, U. So. Calif. Sch. Social Work; hon. life mem. bd. dirs. Calif. div. Am. Cancer Soc., mem. vol. bd. Calif. div., 1964—, del. nat. dir., 1980-84, chmn. residential crusade for Orange County (Calif.) unit, 1985-86; bd. dirs. Vol. Ctr. Orange County West, 1988—, sec., 1991—. Recipient Disting. Alumni award Los Amigos de la Humanidad, 1984, Outstanding Performance award UCLA Hosp., 1968, various service awards Am. Cancer Soc., 1972-88. Fellow Soc. Clin. Social Work; mem. Nat. Assn. Social Workers (charter), Am. Hosp. Assn., Soc. Hosp. Social Work Dirs. (nat. pres. 1981, bd. dirs. 1978-82, life mem. local chpt.), Am. Pub. Health Assn. Democrat. Adventist. Home: 1661 Texas Cir Costa Mesa CA 92626-2238

KLEIN, HERBERT GEORGE, newspaper editor; b. Los Angeles, Apr. 1, 1918; s. George and Amy (Cordes) K.; m. Marjorie G. Galbraith, Nov. 1, 1941; children—Joanne L. (Mrs. Robert Mayne), Patricia A. (Mrs. John Root). AB, U. So. Calif., 1940; Hon. Doctorate, U. San Diego, 1989. Reporter Alhambra (Calif.) Post-Advocate, 1940-42, news editor, 1946-50; spl. corr. Copley Newspapers, 1946-50, Washington corr., 1950; with San Diego Union, 1950-68, editorial writer, 1950-52, editorial page editor, 1952-56, assoc. editor, 1956-57, exec. editor, 1957-58, editor, 1959-68; mgr. communications Nixon for Pres. Campaign, 1968-69; dir. communications Exec. Br., U.S. Govt., 1969-73; v.p. corp. relations Metromedia, Inc., 1973-77; media cons., 1977-80; editor-in-chief, v.p. Copley Newspapers, Inc., San Diego, 1980—; publicity dir. Eisenhower-Nixon campaign in Calif., 1952; asst. press sec. Vice Pres. Nixon Campaign, 1956; press sec. Nixon campaign, 1958; spl. asst., press sec. to Nixon, 1959-61; press sec. Nixon Gov. Campaign, 1962; dir. communications Nixon presdl. campaign, 1968; mem. Advt. Council, N.Y. Author: Making It Perfectly Clear, 1980. Trustee U. So. Calif.; chmn. Holiday Bowl; bd. dirs. Clair Burgener Found., Greater San Diego Sports Assn.; mem. exec. com. San Diego unit Am. Cancer Soc., Super Bowl XXII, Olympic Tng. Site com.; bd. dirs. San Diego Econ. Devel. Com. Served with USNR, 1942-46; comdr. Res. Recipient Fourth Estate award U. So. Calif., 1947, Alumnus of Yr. award U. So. Calif., 1971, Gen. Alumni Merit award, 1977, Spl. Service to Journalism award, 1969; Headliner of Yr. award Greater Los Angeles Press Club, 1971, San Diego State Univ.'s First Fourth Estate Award, 1986. Mem. Am. Soc. Newspaper Editors (past dir.), Calif. Press Assn., Pub. Relations seminar, Gen. Alumni U. So. Calif. (past pres.), Alhambra Jr. C. of C. (past pres.), Greater San Diego C. of C. (exec. com.), Sigma Delta Chi (nat. com. chmn., gen. activities chmn. nat. conv. 1958), Delta Chi. Presbyn. Clubs: Commonwealth, Bohemian, Fairbanks Country. Lodges: Kiwanis, Rotary (hon.). Home: 5110 Saddlery Sq PO Box 8935 Rancho Santa Fe CA 92067 Office: Copley Press Inc 350 Camino De La Reina San Diego CA 92108-3003

KLEIN, JAMES MIKEL, music educator; b. Greenville, S.C., Aug. 27, 1953; s. Rubin Harry Klein and Billie (Mikel) Newton. BM, U. Tex., 1975, MM, 1977; MusD, U. Cincinnati, 1981. Prin. trombone player Austin (Tex.) Symphony Orch., 1973-77; conducting asst. U. Tex., Austin, 1975-77, U. Cin., 1977-78; dir. instrumental music Valparaiso (Ind.) U., 1978-84; prof. music Calif. State U. Stanislaus, Turlock, 1984—; mem. faculty Nat. Luth. Music Camp, Lincoln, Nebr., 1985-86; guest conductor, clinician, adjudicator various states, internationally, 1978—; trombone player Modesto (Calif.) Symphony Orch., 1984—; conductor Stanislaus Youth Symphony, Modesto, 1985; music dir. Modesto Symphony Youth Orch., 1986—; site adminstr. Nat. Honors Orch., Anaheim, Calif., 1986, Indpls., 1988; faculty, coord. instrumental music Calif. State Summer Sch. of Arts, 1987-88. Pres. Turlock Arts Fund for Youth, 1986-88; mem. internat. Friendship Com., subcom., City of Modesto, 1990-92; vol. Big Bros. Am. Recipient Meritorious Prof. award Calif. State U., Stanislaus, 1988, Outstanding Young Man Am. award, 1990. Mem. Music Educators Nat Assn., NAt. Sch. Orch. Assn., Am. Fedn. Musicians (local 1), Condrs. Guild, Am. Symphony Orch. League, Calif. Orch. Dir.'s Assn. (pres.-elect 1988-90, pres. 1990-92). Home: 840 Georgetown Ave Turlock CA 95380-0804 Office: Calif State U Dept Music 801 W Monte Vista Ave Turlock CA 95380-0299

KLEIN, LEANDER FRANCIS, accountant, real estate broker; b. Hague, N.D., Sept. 1, 1932; s. Roy C. and Kathryn (Buechler) K.; m. Alice Louella Badgett, Sept. 18, 1954; children: Cindy Sipes, Byron, Neva. BA in Bus. Adminstrn., Wash. State Coll., 1956. Lic. tax acct., real estate broker. Unit mgr. Mannings Inc., Seattle and Portland, Oreg., 1956-63; asst. mgr. Holland House, Portland, 1963-64; dist. mgr. Fred Meyer Inc., Portland and Seattle, 1964-69; ind. tax acct., real estate broker Portland and Florence, Oreg., 1969—. Co-author: (instrn. manual) On to Success in Real Estate, 1970. Pres. St. Mary's Parish Coun., Florence, 1989—, Florence Area Ambs., 1991—; treas. Florence Stop Crime, 1986—. Mem. Oreg. Soc. Tax Cons., Rotary (treas. 1978—, Paul Harris fellow 1991). Republican. Roman Catholic. Home and Office: 06064 Santa Rd Florence OR 97439

KLEIN, PHILIP ALEXANDRE, editor, publisher; b. Washington, June 6, 1966; s. Fred Robert and Solange Yvonne (Gouyer) K. BA in Lit. magna cum laude, U. Colo., 1988; MA in Lit., U. Wash., 1991. Rsch. asst. Smithsonian Instn./Air and Space, Washington, 1978-79; diplomatic liaison Pub. Comms. Inc., Washington, 1982-83; editorial staff Walkabout, U. Colo., Boulder, 1985; fundraiser Pacific Sci. Ctr., Seattle, 1989; rsch. interviewer Seattle Social Devel. Project, 1989-91, ABT/Summer Tng. and Edn. Program, Seattle, 1989, U. Wash. Sch. Social Work, Seattle, 1990-91; founder Sound Opportunities-Guide to Employment, Seattle, 1989—; editor, dir., pub. Sound Opportunities/Non-profit Community Network, Seattle, 1989—. Author: Seattle City Steamscapes, 1990, Nonprofit Resource Directory for Washington State, 1992-93. V.p. The Benefit Gang-Vol. Network, Seattle, 1991—; founder Harmonious Assn. Radical Philanthropists, Seattle, 1992—. Mem. Wash. Commn. for Humanities. Democrat. Office: Sound Opportunities 2708 Elliott Ave Seattle WA 98121

KLEIN, RALPH, provincial legislator, former city mayor; b. Calgary, Alta., Can.; ; m. 2nd, Colleen, 1972; 5 children. Dir. pub. rels. Alta. div. Red Cross; dir. pub. rels. Calgary United Way Fund, 1966-69; with CFCN, 1969-80; newsreader radio div., later television reporter, 1969-80; mayor City of Calgary, 1980-89; legislator Calgary-Elbow constituency Alta. Legislature, Edmonton, 1989—; minister of environment Alta. Legislature, 1989—. Office: Office of the Premier, 307 Legislature Bldg, Edmonton, AB Canada T5K 2B6

KLEIN, RAYMOND MAURICE, lawyer; b. Phila., Jan. 31, 1938; s. Maurice J. and Fay (Clearfield) K.; m. Roberta Steinberg, Apr. 8, 1984; children: Seth Grossman, Micah Grossman. AB, Williams Coll., 1959; JD, Harvard U., 1962. Bar: Pa. 1962, Calif. 1968, U.S. Supreme Ct. 1966. Lawyer Fed. Home Loan Bank Bd., Washington, 1963-67; ptnr. Hahn Cazier, L.A., 1967-78; lawyer Klein Law Corp., L.A., 1978-89, 93—; of counsel Davis Wright Tremaine, L.A., 1989-93; lectr. C. of C., Calif., 1988—, Young Pres.' Orgn., Ohio, 1990, Law Sch. for Entrepreneurs, L.A., 1990—. Author: Putting a Lid on Legal Fees: How to Deal Effectively with Lawyers, 1987. Mem. ABA, Calif. State Bar Assn., L.A. Bar Assn. Home: 908 Kenfield Ave Los Angeles CA 90049-1405 Office: Davis Wright Tremaine 1000 Wilshire Blvd Los Angeles CA 90017-2457

KLEIN, RICHARD LEWIS, urologist; b. Cleve., June 15, 1945; s. Harold and Jean K.; m. Gail Klein, June 13, 1971; children: Rebecca, Joshua. BA, Washington U., St. Louis, 1967; MD, St. Louis U., 1971. Diplomate Am. Bd. Urology. Intern in surgery Mt. Zion Hosp., San Francisco, 1971-72; resident in surgery Mt. Zion Hosp., 1972-73; resident in urology Meml. Hosp., Danville, Va., 1973-76; urologist in pvt. practice San Francisco, 1976-88; urologist Friendly Hills Med. Group, La Habra, Calif., 1989—; chief of urology Friendly Hills Med. Group, 1989—, Davies Med. Ctr., San Francisco, 1986-89; clin. instr. urology U. Calif., San Francisco, 1986-89. Fellow ACS, Internat. Coll. Surgeons; mem. Am. Urologic Assn. Office: Friendly Hills Med Group 951 S Beach Blvd La Habra CA 90631-6418

KLEIN, ROBERT GORDON, state judge; b. Honolulu, Nov. 11, 1947; s. Gordon Ernest Klein and Clara (Cutter) Elliot; m. Aleta Elizabeth Webb., July 27, 1986; children: Kurt William, Eric Robert. BA, Stanford U., 1969; JD, U. Oreg., 1972. Dep. atty. gen. State of Hawaii, 1973, with state campaign spening commn., 1974, with state dept regulatory agys., 1975-78; judge State Dist. Ct. Hawaii, 1978-84; judge cir. ct. State of Hawaii, 1984-92, supreme ct. justice, 1992—. Office: Supreme Ct PO Box 2560 Honolulu HI 96813

KLEIN, SNIRA L(UBOVSKY), Hebrew language and literature educator; came to U.S., 1959, naturalized, 1974; d. Avraham and Devora (Unger) Lubovsky; m. Earl H. Klein, Dec. 25, 1975. Tchr. cert., Tchrs. Seminar, Netanya, Israel, 1956; B. Rel. Edn., U. Judaism, 1961, M in Hebrew Lit., 1963; BA, Calif. State U., Northridge, 1966; MA, UCLA, 1971, PhD, 1983. Teaching asst. UCLA, 1969-71, vis. lectr., 1985-91; instr., continuing edn. U. Judaism, Los Angeles, 1971-76; instr. U. Judaism, L.A., 1975-84, adj. asst. prof., 1984—. Mem. Assn. for Jewish Studies, Nat. Assn. of Profs. of Hebrew, World Union of Jewish Studies. Jewish. Office: U Judaism 15600 Mulholland Dr Los Angeles CA 90077-1599

KLEINBERG, KENNETH ALLAN, entertainment lawyer; b. Ohio, May 2, 1942; s. Arthur and Irene (Silberman) K.; m. Helen Adams, Aug. 9, 1964; children: Lewis, Jody, Elliott. BA with honors, UCLA, 1964, JD, 1967. Bar: D.C. 1968, Calif. 1968. Assoc., ptnr., mng. ptnr., head motion picture/TV dept. Mitchell, Silberberg & Knupp, Los Angeles, 1969-85; exec. v.p., bd. dirs. United Artists Corp., Los Angeles, 1985-86; pres., chief officer Weintraub Entertainment Group, Inc., Los Angeles, 1986-90; co-instr. Am. Film Inst., Los Angeles, 1984-85. Co-chmn. Am. Cinematheque, Los Angeles, 1985-87. Mem. Beverly Hills Bar Assn., L.A. County Bar Assn., L.A. Copyright Soc., Acad. Motion Pictures Arts and Scis. Office: 1880 Century Park E Ste 1150 Los Angeles CA 90067

KLEINFELD, ANDREW JAY, federal judge; b. 1945. BA magna cum laude, Wesleyan U., 1966; JD cum laude, Harvard U., 1969. Law clk. Alaska Supreme Ct., 1969-71; U.S. magistrate U.S. Dist. Ct. Alaska, Fairbanks, 1971-74; pvt. practice law Fairbanks, 1971-86; judge U.S. Dist. Ct. Alaska, Anchorage, 1986-91, U.S. Ct. Appeals (9th cir.), San Francisco, 1991—. Contbr. articles to profl. jours. Mem. Alaska Bar Assn. (pres. 1982-83, bd. govs., 1981-84), Tanana Valley Bar Assn. (pres. 1974-75). Republican. Office: US Ct Appeals 9th Cir Courthouse Square 250 Cushman St Ste 3-A Fairbanks AK 99701

KLEINROCK, LEONARD, computer scientist; b. N.Y.C., June 13, 1934; s. Bernard and Anne (Schoenfeld) K.; m. Stella Schuler, Dec. 1, 1967; children—Nancy S., Martin C. BEE, CCNY, 1957; M.S., MIT, 1959, Ph.D., 1963. Asst. elec. engr. Photobell Co. Inc., 1951-57; research engr. Lincoln Labs., M.I.T., 1957-63; mem. faculty UCLA, 1963—, prof. computer sci., 1970—, chair dept. computer sci., 1991—; pres., co-founder Linkabit Corp., 1968-69; chief exec. officer Tech. Transfer Inst., 1976—; cons. in field, prin. investigator govt. contracts. Author: Queueing Systems, Vol. I, 1975, Vol. II, 1976, Communication Nets: Stochastic Message Flow and Delay, 1964, Solutions Manual for Queueing Systems, Vol. I, 1982, Vol. II, 1986; also articles. Recipient Paper award ICC, 1978, Leonard G. Abraham paper award Communications Soc., 1975, Outstanding Faculty Mem. award UCLA Engring. Grad. Students Assn., 1966, Townsend Harris medal CCNY, 1982, L.M. Ericsson Prize Sweden, 1982, 12th Marconi award, 1986; Guggenheim fellow, 1971-72. Fellow IEEE (Disting. lectr. 1973, 76); mem. NAE, Ops. Research Soc. Am. (Lanchester prize 1976), Assn. Computing Machinery (SIG com. award 1990), Internat. Fedn. Info. Processes Systems, Amateur Athletic Union. Jewish. Home: 318 N Rockingham Ave Los Angeles CA 90049-2636 Office: UCLA Dept Computer Sci 405 Hilgard Ave 3732 Boelter Hall Los Angeles CA 90024-1596

KLEINSMITH, BRUCE JOHN See NUTZLE, FUTZIE

KLEINSMITH, GENE, artist; b. Madison, Wis., Feb. 22, 1942; BA, Augustana Coll., Sioux Falls, S.D., 1963; MA, U. No. Ariz., Flagstaff, 1969; children: Jon Darin, Paul, Christin. Tchr. art high schs. in S.D., Colo., Minn. and Calif., 1963-71; mem. faculty San Bernardino Valley Coll., eves. 1967-71; instr. Victor Valley Coll., Victorville, Calif., 1971—, chmn. art dept., also coord. artist-in-residence programs; lectr., condr. workshops in field; keynote presenter, 1987, Nat. Council on Edn. Ceramic Arts, Boston, 1984; presenter Nat. Council on Edn. for Art, Atlanta, 1983. One-man shows include U. Minn., Mankato, 1967, U. Calif., Riverside, 1969, U. S.D., 1976, No. Ariz. U., 1980, Olive Tree Gallery, Ft. Collins, Colo., 1966, Yavapai Coll., Prescott, Ariz., 1976, Apple Valley, Calif., 1977, Hi-Desert Symphony, Victor Valley, 1979, The Gallery in Flagstaff, Ariz., 1986; group and invitational exhbns. include Gallery II, Charlottesville, Va., 1983, Gallery II, St. George, Utah, 1984, Nat. Council on Edn. for Art, Atlanta, 1983, Faculty exhbns. Victor Valley, 1990; represented in permanent collections Mpls. Art Inst., Valparaiso (Ind.) U., Gustavus Adolphus Coll., St. Peter, Minn., No. Ariz. U., Ariz. Western Coll., Yuma, U. S.D., U. Minn., Mankato, Miami-Dade Community Coll., Gallery II, West Charlottesville, Va., Gallery II West, Beverly Hills, Calif., Rodell Gallery, Los Angeles, Pompidou Ctr., Paris, Topkapi Palace, Istanbul, Turkey; one man show Art of the Olympiad at Marcia Rodell Gallery, Los Angeles, 1984; also pvt. collections; feature artist La Ceramique Moderne, Paris, 1985; presenter workshops; internat. lectr. Faculty fellow Victor Valley Coll., 1973; keynote speaker Internat. Identitic Ceramique, Auxerre, France, 1985. Mem. Nat. Council Art Adminstrs., Nat. Council Edn. for the Arts (mem. exhbns.), Am. Crafts Council, Calif. Art Italy, Paris, Inst. Art History (lectr. 1987), Athens, Greece. Art Mus., Phi Delta Kappa, Kappa Delta Pi. Author: Earth, Fire, Air and Water, 1974, Clay's The Way, 3d edit., 1988; writer Ceramics monthly mag.; contbg. writer TV series Search, Humanities Through The Arts; internat. presenter in field; contbr. articles to profl. jours. Office: PO Box 9400 Victorville CA 92392

KLEMIC, GEORGE GERARD, federal agency official, educator; b. Tamaqua, Pa., Oct. 8, 1949; s. George and Sophie P. (Kornak) K.; m. Virginia Albarracin, Jan. 2, 1971; children: George Gerard, Robert, Michael. BA in German, La Salle U., Phila., 1971; MS in Adminstrn., Cen. Mich. U., 1989; postgrad., Nova U., 1990. Revenue officer IRS, Phila., 1972-78; chief tech. and office compliance br. IRS, Parkersburg, W.Va., 1979-82; group mgr. IRS, San Mateo, Calif., 1982-83; chief field br. IRS, San Francisco, 1983-85; chief spl. procedures br. IRS, San Jose, Calif., 1985-87; supervisory program analyst IRS, Washington, 1988-90, exec. asst. to the asst. regional commr., 1990—. Mem. Acad. Mgmt. Roman Catholic. Office: IRS 1650 Mission St San Francisco CA 94103-2490

KLEMM, LEROY HENRY, chemistry educator; b. Maple Park, Ill., July 31, 1919; s. Henry Joseph and Anna R. K.; m. Christine Jones, Dec. 27, 1945; children: Richard A., Rebecca J., Ann C. BS in Chemistry, U. Ill., 1941; MS in Chemistry, U. Mich., 1943, PhD, 1945. Teaching fellow U. Mich., Ann Arbor, 1941-44; rsch. chemist Pan Am. Refining Corp., Texas City, Tex., 1944-45; rsch. assoc. Ohio State U., Columbus, 1945-46; instr. Harvard U., Cambridge, Mass., 1946-47; instr., asst. prof. Ind. U., Bloomington, 1947-52; asst., assoc. prof. Chemistry U. Oreg., Eugene, 1952-63, prof. of Chemistry, 1963—; vis. prof. U. Cin., 1965-66; vis. prof. and sr. assoc. Australian Govt., 1979-80, 86. Mem. editorial adv. bd. Jour. Heterocyclic Chemistry, 1971—. Author: 162 publs. dealing with organic chemistry rsch., 1941—. Vol. USCG, 1944-45. Recipient Guggenheim Rsch. fellow, London and Zurich, 1958-59; NATO and Fulbright rsch. grantee, Denmark and Holland, 1972-73. Fellow AAAS; mem. Chem. Soc. (counsellor 1982-88), Oreg. Acad. of Sci. (various offices 1952—). Democrat. Presbyterian. Office: U Oreg Dept Chemistry Eugene OR 97403

KLEPINGER, BRIAN WILEY, foundation administrator; b. Omaha, Dec. 20, 1937; s. Forest Harold and Gwenevere Iris (Wiley) K.; m. Judith R. Hassig, Aug. 26, 1961 (div. 1975); children: Eric, Lisa; m. Katherine A. Cattanach, Nov. 24, 1979 (div. 1990). BA, Cornell Coll., Mt. Vernon, Iowa, 1960; MA, U. Chgo., 1962; PhD, U. Minn., 1980. Dir. Coun. Social Planning, Fremont, Calif., 1964-66; exec. dir. Poudre-Thompson Community Action Program, Ft. Collins, Colo., 1966-67; prof. U. Denver, 1967-86; vis. prof. U. Bristol (Eng.), 1980-81; v.p. program Colo. Trust, Denver, 1986-90; exec. officer Denver Zool. Found., 1990—; bd. dirs. Legal Ctr., Denver. Author: The Leadership Behavior of Executives of Social Service Organizations, 1980; contbr. articles to profl. jours. Bd. dirs. Denver Zool. Found., 1987-90, Metro Denver Gives, 1988-90; mem. com. Mile High United Way, Denver, 1987-89. Commd. officer USPHS, 1962-64. Woods Found. fellow, 1961-62. Fellow Am. Assn. Zool. Pks. Aquariums; mem. Colo. Assn. Founds. (exec. 1989-90). Office: Denver Zoo City Park Denver CO 80205

KLEPINGER, JOHN WILLIAM, trailer manufacturing company executive; b. Lafayette, Ind., Feb. 7, 1945; s. John Franklin and R. Wanda (North) K.; m. Mary Patricia Duffy, May 1, 1976; 1 child, Nicholas Patrick. BS, Ball State U., 1967, MA, 1968. Sales engr. CTS Corp., Elkhart, Ind., 1969-70; exec. v.p. Woodlawn Products Corp., Elkhart, 1970-78; v.p. Period Ind., Henderson, Ky., 1976-78, Sotebeer Constrn. Co., Inc., Elkhart, 1978-81; gen. mgr. Wells Industries Inc., Ogden, Utah, 1981—; regional dir. Zion's First Nat. Bank, Ogden, 1986—. Bd. dirs. St. Benedict's Hosp., Ogden, 1986—, chmn. 1987—. Named Ogden Bus. Man of Yr., Weber County Sch. Dist., 1984. Mem. Weber County Prodn. Mgrs. Assn. (pres. 1984-85, 92-93), Weber County Indsl. Devel. Corp. (bd. dirs. 1984—), Weber/Morgan Pvt. Industry Coun., Nat. Assn. Pvt. Industry Couns. (pres., bd. dirs. 1986—), Nat. Job Tng. Partnership Inc. (bd. dirs. 1986-89), Nat. Alliance Bus. (bd. dirs. 1987-90), Ogden Area C. of C. (bd. dirs., treas. 1986—), Utah Job Tng. Coord. Coun., Exch. Club (bd. dirs. Ogden chpt. 1984-86). Roman Catholic. Home: 5181 Aztec Dr Ogden UT 84403-4606 Office: Wells Industries Inc PO Box 1619 Ogden UT 84402-1619

KLEPPER, HARRY GEORGE, minister, educator; b. York, Pa., Jan. 29, 1907; s. George F. and Amanda Jane (Kunkel) K.; m. Elsie Madeline Delaney, May 28, 1929; children: Harry Lee, Josephine Jane, Charles A., Peter I., Julian C. Student mech. engring., Pa. State U., 1939-40; BA, Southwestern Bible Sch., 1948. Crew mgr. Shredded Wheat, Phila., 1926-28; salesman Gen. Foods, Phila., 1928-42, Balt. Life Ins., 1942-45; minister Shamrock Assembly of God Ch., Beaumont, Tex., 1945-52; sales mgr. Combined Ins. Co. Am., Chgo., 1952-59; dir., owner Hogar de Ninos Desamparados, Urubamba, Peru, 1959-84; instr. Bible Sch. Southwestern U., Waxahachie, Tex., 1945-49. Co-editor with Elsie D. Klepper: Step by Step, 1965, Our Little Indians, 1966. Exec. dir. United Srs., Denver, 1987—. With U.S. Army, 1925-26. Mem. Srs. Inc. Republican. Seventh Day Adventist. Home and Office: PO Box 4265 601 W 11th Ave Apt 513 Denver CO 80204

KLEPPER, JOHN CHRISTIAN, oil spill response company executive; b. N.Y.C., Jan. 23, 1945. BS in Meteorology and Oceanography, SUNY, N.Y.C., 1968; cert. in advanced environ. engring., Johns Hopkins U., 1972; MBA, Monmouth (N.J.) Coll., 1985. Masters lic. USCG. Ops. mgr. SERVS Alyeska Pipeline Svc. Co., Valdez, Alaska, 1991—; commr. Bd. Pilots for Bays San Francisco, San Pablo, Suisun, 1986-90, pres., 1989; mem. Alaska Bd. Marine Pilots, 1992—. Office: SERVS Alaska Pipeline Svc PO Box 109 Valdez AK 99686

KLEPPINGER, MOSELLE LEE, public relations professional; b. Worland, Wyo., Mar. 2, 1956; d. Kenneth Myron and Moselle Loretta (Shelton) K.; m. Tim Lee Romanek, May 28, 1983 (div. 1987). BS, U. Wyo., 1978, MA, 1980, postgrad., 1980—. Pub. rels. officer Natrona County Sch. Dist., Casper, Wyo., 1976; corr., intern Casper Star-Tribune, 1976-78; corr., intern KTWO-TV, Casper, 1978-79, reporter, 1979-87; asst. dir. pub. rels. Casper Coll., 1987—; bd. dirs. Conv. and Visitors Bur., Casper C. of C., mem. mktg.

com., 1992—. Participant Leadership Casper, 1990-91, co-chair, 1991-92; bd. dirs. Cultural Affairs Com. Chamber, Casper, 1988—, Troopers Drum and Bugle Corps, Casper, 1989—, Big Bros.-Big Sisters, Casper, 1991—; mem. Stage III Community Theatre, Casper, 1980—, bd. dirs., 1980-87, pres., 1984-87. Recipient Hist. award Wyo. State Hist. Soc., 1987. Mem. Casper Area Mktg. Profls., Soroptimist Internat. (exec. bd. cen. Wyo. chpt. 1990—). Methodist. Home: 933 S Center St Casper WY 82601 Office: Casper Coll 125 College Dr Casper WY 82601

KLEWENO, GILBERT H., lawyer; b. Endicott, Wash., Mar. 21, 1933; s. Melvin Lawrence and Anna (Lust) K.; m. Virginia Symms, Dec. 28, 1958; children: Stanley, Douglas, Phillip. BA, U. Wash., 1955; LLR, U. Idaho, 1959. Bar: Wash. 1960. Assoc. Read & Church, Vancouver, Wash., 1960-68, Boettcher & LaLonde, Vancouver, Wash., 1968—; part-time U.S. Magistrate Judge, 1979. Chmn. Bd. Adjustors, Vancouver, Civil Svc. Commn., Vancouver. Mem. Wash. State Bar Assn., Elks, Gyro Club. Office: Boettcher LaLonde Kleweno 610 Esther St Vancouver WA 98666

KLIEBACK, HY, financial planner; b. Hartford, Conn., Oct. 29, 1931; s. Jacob and Sophie (Zeleznick) K.; m. Lois Bernadine Krauss, Mar. 5, 1950; children: Randi Joy Klieback Ward, Dale Ellen Klieback Strong. Student, UCLA. CFP. Sales mgr. Martin Karn and Assocs.; mgr. nat. sales Davenport Dillard, Roslyn, Md., 1969-70; exec. v.p. Am. Fiduciary Corp., Boston, 1970-83; pres., CEO Comtemporary Fin. Advisors, Phoenix, 1983-91; sr. acct. exec. The Acacia Group, Phoenix, 1991—; weekly guest talk shows Stas. KFYI, KTAR, TALK-NET. Mem. LUTC, Scottsdale Country Club. Jewish. Home: 7007 Via de Manana Scottsdale AZ 85258-3904 Office: The Acacia Group 3500 E Camelback Rd Phoenix AZ 85018

KLIEN, WOLFGANG JOSEF, architect; b. Hollabrunn, Austria, Sept. 29, 1942; s. Josef and Maria (Kainz) K.; Dipl. Ing., Vienna Tech. U., 1967; m. Charlotte Olga Kutscherer, Aug. 14, 1968; children: Christina Olga, Angelika Maria. Designer, E. Donau, Architect, Vienna, 1968; with C. Nitschke & Assos., Architects, Columbus, Ohio, 1968-71; project architect GSAS Architects, Phoenix, 1971-75, 77-78; prodn. architect Harry Glueck, Vienna, 1976-77; v.p. architecture Am. Indian Engring. Inc., Phoenix, 1978-81; pres. S.W. Estate Group, Inc., real estate devel., San Diego, 1980-82; pres., tech. dir., branch mgr. Ariz. br. office SEG-S.W. Estate Group, Inc., Phoenix, 1982-86; prin. Klien & Assoc., Architecture, Planning, Devel. Cons., Phoenix, 1986—, Atlantic-Pacific Trading Corp., Internat. Trade, Phoenix, 1986-88; pres., gen. mgr. Polybau, Inc., Hayward, Calif., 1988-90; pres. Libra Cons., INc., Phoenix, 1989—; ptnr. Heart Devel. Co., LLC, dBa Heart Homes, 1993—. Recipient Great Silver Medal of Merit, Republic of Austria, 1993. Mem. AIA, Austro-Am. Council West, Austrian Soc. Ariz. (founder 1985, v.p. 1985-86, pres. 1987—). Roman Catholic. Home: 214 E Griswold Rd Phoenix AZ 85020-3623 Office: 4501 N 22d St Phoenix AZ 85016

KLIMA, ROGER R., physiatrist; b. Prague, Czechoslovakia; came to U.S., 1982; s. Josef and Radka Klima. BA, Zatlanka Coll., Prague, 1971; MD, Charles U., Prague, 1978. Diplomate Am. Bd. Phys. Medicine and Rehab. Resident in surgery Charles U., 1978-79, resident in orthopedic surgery, 1979-81; fellow, clin. clk. Beverly Hills Med. Ctr. and Cedars-Sinai Med. Ctr., L.A., 1984-86; resident in surgery U. Medicine and Dentistry-N.J. Med. Sch., Newark, 1986-87; resident in phys. medicine and rehab. U. Medicine and Dentistry-N.J. Med. Sch./Kessler Inst., Newark and West Orange, 1987-90; mem. phys. medicine and rehab. faculty Stanford U. and Affiliated Hosps., Stanford, Calif., 1990—; dir. phys. medicine and rehab. outpatient svcs. Palo Alto VA Med. Ctr., 1992—; clin. instr. in phys. medicine and rehab. U. Medicine and Dentistry-N.J.Med. Sch., 1989-90, Stanford U. Sch. Medicine, 1990—. Contbr. articles to profl. jours. Mem. Am. Acad. Phys. Medicine and Rehab. (liaison resident physician coun. 1989-90), Assn. Acad. Physiatrists, N.J. Soc. Phys. Medicine and Rehab., N.J. Assn. Electromyography. Office: Stanford U Med Ctr Divsn Phys Medicine and Rehab Rm NC 104 Stanford CA 94305

KLIMKO, RONALD JAMES, music educator; b. Lena, Wis., Dec. 13, 1936; s. Robert Lewis and Evelyn Mary (Rosera) K.; m. Kathleen Screnson, Oct. 15, 1963 (div. July 1983); children: Karl Nicholas, Christopher Anthony, Julie Marie, Benjamin Andrew; m. Kathryn Paxton George, July 27, 1985; children: Kimberly George, Elizabeth Francene George. B in Mus. Edn., Milton Coll., 1959; postgrad., George Washington U., 1961; MusM, U. Wis., 1963, PhD, 1968. Asst. prof. music Moorhead (Minn.) State Coll., 1966-67, Ind. State U., Terre Haute, 1967-68; prof. music U. Idaho, Moscow, 1968—; vis. prof. Ind. U., Bloomington, 1980, Colo. U., Boulder, 1990-91; bassonist Madison (Wis.), 1961-66, Spokane (Wash.) Symphony, 1968-90. Author: Bassoon Performance Practices in U.S. and Canada, 1974, (with Marc Apfelstadt) Bassoon Performance and Teaching Mateirals, Methods, and Techniques, 1993. Mem. Am. Fedn. Musicians, Internat. Double Reed Soc. (Bassoon editor 1981—). Democrat. Home: 1020 W Cayuse Dr Moscow ID 83843-2461 Office: U Idaho Lionel Hampton Sch Music Moscow ID 83843

KLIMOSKI, DAVID BRUCE, chemical engineer; b. Denver, June 20, 1946; s. Stephen and Helen (Schon) K.; m. Marilyn Simpson, Aug. 29, 1970; children: Lorraine, Bryce. BS in Chem. Engring., U. Colo., 1968; postgrad., U. Calif., Berkeley, 1970-72. Registered profl. engr., Calif.; cert. pers. cons.; cert. employment specialist. Design engr. Chevron USA, San Francisco, 1968-73; project engr. Procon div. U.O.P., Walnut Creek, Calif., 1973-77; project mgr. Enserv Corp., Concord, Calif., 1978-79; owner Profl. Design Svcs., Concord, Calif., 1979—; v.p. F. Lehman Assocs., Inc., Concord, Calif., 1985—; owner Continental Tng. Ctr., Concord, Calif., 1984—; dir. Chief Equip. Corp., Denver, 1968—. Mem. Am. Inst. Chem. Engrs., Am. Instrument Soc., Calif. Assn. for Pers. Cons. (v.p. 1990-92, treas., dir. 1985-89), Calif. Inst. for Educating Pers. Cons. (trustee 1988-90), Calif. Assn. Rehab. Profls. Office: Continental Tng Ctr 1333 Willow Pass Rd #203 Concord CA 94520

KLIMOW, SERGEI NICHOLAS, corporate executive; b. Johnson City, N.Y., Dec. 2, 1939; s. Nicholas Ivan and Elizabeth (Molnar) K.; m. Mary Ruth Thier, Sept. 11, 1965; children: Nicole Elizabeth, Katherine Danielle. BA, Colgate U., 1961; LLB, Syracuse U., 1964, JD, 1968. Cert. N.Y. State Dept. Audit and Control Fin. Sch.; cert. mortgage banker. Assoc. Twining & Fischer, Binghamton, N.Y., 1964-67; atty. Broome County, Binghamton, 1968-70; pres. First Svc. Corp., Phoenix, 1970-75; assoc. Shimmel, Hill, Bishop & Gruender, Phoenix, 1975-78; pres. Sergei N. Klimow P.C., Phoenix, 1978-92; CEO WFI, Inc., Tempe, Ariz., 1991—; cons., dir. Shibaura Internat., Inc., Osaka, Japan and Phoenix; bd. dirs. Interco, Ltd., Tempe; lectr. in field. Contbr. articles to profl. jours. Com. chmn. Glendale Union High Sch. Dist. Bond Elections, Phoenix, 1986; past v.p. Phoenix Credit Bur.; past chmn. City of Phoenix Employee Rels. Bd.; mem. City of Phoenix North Mountain Village Planning Commn., 1985-88. Recipient Maroon citation Colgate U., Hamilton, N.Y., 1991; named Boss of Yr. Maricopa County Legal Secs. Assn., Phoenix, 1987, Friend of Sunnyslope High Sch., Phoenix, 1986. Mem. ABA (internat. law sect.), Internat. Bar Assn., State Bar of Ariz. (corp., real estate, internat. sects.), N.Y. State Bar (exec. com. 1967-70), Maricopa County Bar, Phoenix C. of C. (Phoenicians com. 1980-90), Colgate Univ. Alumni Club (past pres.), Desert Highlands Golf Club (Scottsdale, Ariz.), Desert Forest Golf Club (Carefree, Ariz.). Republican. Byzantine Catholic. Home: # 401 10040 E Happy Valley Rd Scottsdale AZ 85255 Office: WFI Inc 1705 W 4th St Tempe AZ 85281

KLINE, FRED WALTER, communications company executive; b. Oakland, Calif., May 17, 1918; s. Walter E. and Jean M. Kline; m. Verna Marie Taylor, Dec. 27, 1952; children—Kathleen, Nora, Fred Walter. B.A. in Calif. History, U. Calif.-Berkeley, 1940. With Walter E. Kline & Assocs. and successor Fred Kline Agy., Inc., from 1937; chmn. bd., pres. Kline Communications Corp., Los Angeles, 1956—; pres. Capitol News Service. Commr. Los Angeles County Fire Services Commn., Calif. Motion Picture Devel. Council; cons., advisor Calif. Film Commn.; former fed. civil def. liaison; developer state-wide paramedic rescue program; Calif. chmn. Office of Asst. Sec. Def.; mem. Calif. Com. for Employer Support of Guard and Res.; mem. Los Angeles Film Com. Served with USAAF, World War II; brig. gen. Calif. Mil. Dept. Recipient Inter-Racial award City of Los Angeles, 1963, named Man of Yr., 1964. Mem. Acad. Motion Picture Arts and Scis., Radio and TV News Assn. So. Calif., Pub. Relations Soc. Am., Calif. Newspaper Pubs. Assn., Cath. Press Council (founding mem.), Pacific Pioneer Broadcasters, Footprinters Internat., Am. Mil. Govt. Assn. (past pres.), Navy League, Calif. State Police Officers Assn., Internat. Assn. Profl. Firefighters (hon. life), Peace Officers Assn. Los Angeles County (life), Internat. Assn. Chiefs of Police, Internat. Assn. Fire Chiefs, Calif. Fire Chiefs Assn., Fire Marshals Assn. N.Am., Nat. Fire Protection Assn., Nat. Fin. Writers Assn., Hollywood C. of C., Nat. Fire Sci. Acad., Calif. State Mil. Forces, Calif. Pubs. Assn., So. Calif. Cable Club. Sigma Delta Chi. Clubs: Greater Los Angeles Press, Media (Los Angeles), Sacramento Press. Columnist Calif. newspapers. Office: 1180 Weber Way Sacramento CA 95822

KLINE, PAMELA IRIS, consulting company executive; b. Pitts., Aug. 23, 1958; d. Robert Edward and Rae R. Kline. Cert., U. Paris, Sorbonne, 1979; AB magna cum laude, Harvard U., 1980, MBA, 1984. Asst. staff mgr. Bell of Pa., Phila., 1980-82; product mgr. Visa Internat., San Francisco, 1983; v.p. Prognostics, Palo Alto, Calif., 1984-91; dir. Diefenbach/Elkins, San Francisco, 1991-92; prin. Regis McKenna, Inc., 1992—. Vol. San Jose Civic Lights, 1987; dir. Harvard/Radcliffe Fundraising, Boston, 1980—; chmn. Harvard/Radcliffe Schs. com., San Mateo County, 1985—. Mem. Young Profl. Woman Assn., Radcliffe Club (dir. 1987—), Harvard Club. Republican. Home: 570 Beale St Apt 416 San Francisco CA 94105-2025 Office: Regis McKenna Inc 1755 Embarcadaro Rd Palo Alto CA 94303

KLINE, RICHARD STEPHEN, public relations executive; b. Brookline, Mass., June 20, 1948; s. Paul and Helen (Chartoff) K.; m. Carroll Potter, (dec. Apr. 1984); m. Sharon Tate, June 16, 1985; stepchildren: Allison, Kevin. BA, U. Mass., Amherst, 1970. Reporter, photographer Worcester (Mass.) Telegram & Gazette, 1970-71; account exec. Wenger-Michael Advt., L.A., 1971; pub. rels. dir. Oakland (Calif.) Symphony Orch., 1972; asst. v.p., dir. promotions Gt. Western Savs. and Loan, Beverly Hills, Calif., 1972-75; v.p., dir. mktg. Union Fed. Savs. and Loan, L.A., 1975-78; chmn. bd. dirs. Berkhemer & Kline, L.A., 1978-88, Berkhemer Kline Golin/Harris, L.A., 1988-93; chief oper. officer Golin/Harris Comm., L.A., 1992—; former instr. Am. Savs. and Loan Inst.; bd. dirs. Golin/Harris Communications; exec. com. Santa Barbara Old Spanish Days Fiesta Rodeo, 1992. Past pres., mem. exec. com. Big Bros. L.A.; bd. dirs. Am. Cancer Soc., L.A., Solvang (Calif.) TheatreFest; mem. Town Hall Forum, L.A.; commr. Parks and Recreation, City of Oakland, 1973-74; bd. dirs. United Way, 1988—, TheaterFest, 1990—; bd. dirs. Golin/Harris Communications, 1990—. Recipient Pres.'s Club award Big Bros. Greater L.A., 1987, 88, Best in West Pub. Svc. award Am. Advt. Fedn., San Francisco, 1975. Mem. Nat. Investor Rels. Inst., Pub. Rels. Soc. Am. (Disting. Community Svc. award 1987), Internat. Assn. Bus. Communicators, Motor Press Guild, Newcomen Soc., Nat. Cattlemen's Assn., Calif. Cattlemen's Assn., Am. Quarter Horse Assn., We. Horse Show Exhibitors Assn., Publicity Club L.A., Jonathan Club (pub. rels. com.). Office: Berkhemer Kline Golin/Harris One Bunker Hill 601 W 5th St 4th Fl Los Angeles CA 90071

KLINE, ROBERT MARK, protective services official; b. Troy, N.Y., Mar. 31, 1955; s. Ronald Harry and Elaine Violet (Mansfield) K.; m. Linda Loraine Page, Aug. 21, 1977; children: Tamara Loraine, Holly Marie. AS in Criminal Justice, Grossmont Coll., 1975. Police officer Coronado (Calif.) Police Dept., 1987—. Office: Coronado Police Dept 578 Orange Ave Coronado CA 92118-1897

KLINEDINST, JOHN DAVID, lawyer; b. Washington, Jan. 20, 1950; s. David Moulson and Mary Stewart (Coxe) K.; m. Cynthia Lynn DuBain, Aug. 15, 1981. BA in History, Washington and Lee U., 1971, JD, 1978; MBA in Fin. and Investments, George Washington U., 1975. Bar: Calif. 1979, U.S. Dist. Ct. (so. dist.) Calif. 1979, U.S. Ct. Appeals (9th cir.) 1987. With comml. lending dept. 1st Nat. Bank Md., Montgomery County, 1971-74; assoc. Ludecke, McGrath & Denton, San Diego, 1979-80; ptnr. Whitney & Klinedinst, San Diego, 1980-81, Klinedinst & Meiser, San Diego, 1981-86, Klinedinst, Fliehman, Mckillop and Jones, San Diego, 1986—; also bd. dirs. Klinedinst, Fliehman & McKillop, San Diego. Mem. Law Coun., Washington and Lee U., 1993—. Recipient Disting. Alumnus award Washington and Lee U., 1993. Mem. ABA, Calif. Bar Assn., San Diego Bar Assn., San Diego Def. Lawyers, Washington and Lee U. Alumni Assn. (bd. dirs. 1986—, pres. 1989-90), Washington and Lee U. Club (pres. San Diego chpt. 1980-87), Washington and Lee U. Law Campaign (vice chmn. 1991—), Washington and Lee Law Coun., ARC of San Diego/Imperial (bd. dirs. 1991—), LaJolla Beach and Tennis Club, Phi Kappa Psi. Republican. Episcopalian. Home: 6226 Via Dos Valles Rancho Santa Fe CA 92067-9999 Office: Klinedinst Fliehman McKillop & Jones 501 W Broadway Ste 600 San Diego CA 92101-3544

KLINESTIVER, JOHN GARTH, human resources executive; b. Lawrence, Kans., Apr. 1, 1952; s. John Paul and Marian Virginia (Bates) K.; m. Beverly Elaine Glass, Apr. 16, 1988; children: Julia Harm, Laura Glass. BA in Psychology and Sociology, Calif. State U., Chico, 1976; MS in Indsl./Orgnl. Psychology, Calif. State U., San Francisco, 1978. Compensation analyst CBS, Emeryville, Calif., 1978-79; sr. benefits analyst Stanford (Calif.) U., 1979-83; mgr. compensation and benefits Fujitsu Am., San Jose, Calif., 1983-86, dir. compensation and benefits, 1986-89, v.p. human resources, 1989—. Mem. Japan Am. Human Resources Assn. (chmn. 1990—).

KLINGE, CARL GEORGE, plastics engineer, consultant; b. Dubuque, Iowa, May 2, 1952; s. George Karl and Gertrude Rose K.; married. BS in Engring. Ops., Iowa State U., 1974. From engring. trainee to night plant engr. Armour Food Corp. (Greyhound Corp.), Phoenix, 1974-79; plant engr. N.W. Packing Co., Vancouver, Wash., 1979; pres. EDT Corp., Vancouver, 1979—. Mem. Soc. Plastic Engrs., Plane Bearing Standards Assn. Office: EDT Corp 1006J NE 146th St Vancouver WA 98685-1401

KLINGENSMITH, ARTHUR PAUL, relocation and redevelopment consultant; b. L.A., May 23, 1949; s. Paul Arthur and Hermine Elinore K.; m. Donna J. Bellucci, Apr. 26, 1976 (div. Jan. 1981). AA in Social Sci., Indian Valley Jr. Coll., 1976; BA in Indsl. Psychology, San Francisco State U., 1979; MA in Indsl. Psychology, Columbia Pacific U., 1980. Enlisted USAF, Biloxi, Miss.; advanced through grades to staff sgt. USAF; instr. radio ops. USAF, Biloxi, 1968-72; air traffic control operator USAF, Hamilton AFB Novato, Calif., 1972-74; resigned USAF, 1974; elec. technician Calif. Dept. Transp., Oakland, 1975-78; right of way agt. Calif. Dept. Transp., San Francisco, 1978-85; sr. right of way agt. Calif. Dept. Transp., Sacramento, 1985-87, computer researcher, 1985-87; v.p., cons. Associated Right of Way Svcs., Inc., 1989-92; pvt. practice relocation and redevel. cons., 1987—. Mem. Internat. Right of Way Assn. (instr. 1982—), Am. Arbitration Assn., Marin County Bd. Realtors, Assn. Humanistic Psychology, Nat. Assn. Housing and Redevel. Ofcls., Inst. Noetic Scis., Am. Planning Assn. Republican. Office: Arthur P Klingensmith & Assocs PO Box 574 Sausalito CA 94966

KLINGER, ANN, county official; b. Sayre, Okla., Mar. 11, 1933; d. George Thomas Broddrick and Vivan (Reyburn) Hagan; m. Daniel Klinger; children: Daniel Wayne, Anne Eileen. AA, Merced Coll. Mem. Merced County Bd. Suprs., 1976, re-elected, 1980-84, 88, supr., chmn., 1978, 81, 87, 92; chmn. Merced Community Med. Ctr., 1979, 82, 87, Merced County Assn. Govts. and Solid Waste Adv. Bd., 1980, 87-88, Castle Joint Powers Authority, 1991-92; speaker in field. Mem. Commn. on Govt. Reform Task Force on Welfare, 1978; chmn. panel on Future Configuraton of Publicly Funded Health Svcs., 1978-79; dir. spl. adv. com. State Dept. Health Svcs., 1978-79; mem. capital financing adv. com. Dept. Health Svcs. State of Calif. Health and Welfare, 1981; mem. pilot project adv. com. State Dept. of Health Svcs., 1978-79; mem. U.S. Treasury Adv. Group on Fed.-State-Local Fiscal Rels., 1984-85; chmn. governing bd. No. San Joaquin Valley Systems Agy., 1984-86; mem., bd. dirs. Nat. Assn. Regional Couns., 1990-91; bd. dirs. NACo, 1980—, chair health Policy project Brandeis U. and Kellogg Found., 1990-91, chair refugee subcom., 1991-92; mem. Rsch. and Tech. Focus Gruop, 1991-92; presdl. appointee Adv. Commn. on Intergovernmental Rels., 1991-92; mem. nat. adv. bd. on immigrant policy project Nat. Conf. of State Legislatures, 1992; mem. sr. adv. group on Fed.-State-Local Cooperation in Water Governanace ACIR, 1991-92, mem. medicaid subcom.; mem., bd. dirs. Calif. Coun. on Partnerships, 1990-92; mem. Govt. Tech. Conf. Adv. Bd., 1991-92; mem. NAACP, Castle Air Mus. Found. Recipient CAP World Woman award Calif.-Nev. Community Acton Assn., 1979, Leadership/Vol. of Yr. award Health Systems Agy., 1982-83, Civic Participation award Dist. Bus. ans Profl. Women, 1984, Pub. Svc. award Merced Pomona Grange # 23, 1986, Disting. Svc. award Nat. Tng. and Employment Profls., 1990, Jefferson-Jackson award Merced County Dem. Cen. Com., 1991, Medallion NAACP, 1991; named Outstanding Woman Merced County, 1981, Gift Honoree Edn. Found. Program AAUW, 1985. Mem. LWV, SPCA, County Suprs. Assn. Calif. (bd. dirs. 1991-92), Calif. Hosp. Assn. (trustee 1984-87), Air Force Assn., Am. Legion Aux., Black-Am. Polit. Action Calif., Merced C. of C. (Athena award, 1986, Spl. Recognition award 1992), County Hispanic C. of C. (Spl. Recognition award 1992), Merced County C. of C. (Amb. of Goodwill 1992), Calif. Elected Women's Assn. Edn. and Rsch., Calif. Firfighters Hist. Soc., Calif. Women Agr., Farm Bur., Hist. Soc., Merced Bus. and Profl. Women (Women of Achievement 1978), Old Timers Assn., Merced County Geneal. Soc., Merced Trade Club (ann. sponsor), Merced Women's Club (hon. life 1991), Soroptimist (Women of Achievement 1982). Democrat. Home: 1680 Bette St Merced CA 95340 Office: Merced County Bd Suprs 2222 M St Merced CA 95340

KLINGER, HARRY ERNEST, pastor, writer; b. Edmonton, Alta., Can., May 6, 1956; s. Ernest and Linda (Merz) K.; m. Doris Lindner; children: Andrea, Melanie, Thomas, Annette. BA, U. Alta., 1977, MBA, 1983. Cert. gen. acct. Client svcs. officer Royal Trust Corp., Edmonton, 1978-80; analyst Internat. Pipe Line Co., Edmonton, 1982-88, supr. bus. systems, 1988-91; pastor Ch. of God, Barrhead, Alta., 1991—. Author: Found in Christ, 1986, One Day in the Life of Christ, 1987. Home and Office: 5227-47th St, Barrhead, AB Canada T7N 1H3

KLINK, PAUL L., computer company executive; b. Auburn, N.Y., July 28, 1965; s. Charles Lawrence and Regina Joyce (Maniscalco) K. Student, SUNY, Cayuga, 1979-84. Pres., chief exec. officer Info. Tech., Honolulu, 1979—; v.p. Direct Mktg. Mgrs. divsn. Milizi Valenti Gabriel DDB Needham, Honolulu; 2d. v.p. external AD/steeringcom. Japanese C.of C., 1992-93. Contbr. and edited articles for profl. jours. Co-chmn. Aloha United Way, Honolulu, 1989—; active computer affairs Friends of Rep. Paul O'Shiro, Ewa Beach, Hawaii, 1988—, Friends of Gov. John Waihee, Honolulu, 1988—, Friends of Mayor Frank Fasi, Honolulu, 1988—; bd. dirs. Postal Customers Com., 1992-93. Mem. Info. Industry Assn. (dir. membership 1989—), Direct Mktg. and Advt. Assn. Hawaii (bd. dirs.), Database Mgmt. Assn. Hawaii (direct mktg. com.), Puualoa Rifle and Pistol Club, Mensa, Honolulu Club, La Marianas Sailing Club. Office: Info Tech USA Inc 330 Saratoga Rd # 88817 Honolulu HI 96815-9998

KLINNER, ALVIN RICHARD, financial executive; b. Glen Ullin, N.D., Jan. 28, 1930; s. Herman Joseph and Elizabeth Magdelan (Hoerner) K.; m. Chestine Wanda Smith, Dec. 31, 1956 (div. May 1976); children: Devnee, Bobbi, Steven; m. Patricia Ann Krueger, July 22, 1978 (div. Feb. 1989). AAS, Yakima Valley Jr. Coll., 1955; BBA, U. Wash., 1957, MBA, 1971. Cert. systems profl. Inst. Cert. Computer Profls. Mgr. gen. and cost acctg. Gen. Electric Co., Richland, Wash., 1957-64; mgr. adminstrn. Battelle-N.W., Richland, 1965-81; mgr. fin. info. programs Wash. Pub. Power Supply System, Richland, 1981—. Treas. Gesa Fed. Credit Union, Richland, 1968-74, pres., 1975; bd. dirs. Carondelet Psychiat. Care Ctr. (formerly Mid Columbia Mental Health and Psychiat. Hosp.), Richland, 1985-93, chmn. bd., 1990-93; bd. dirs. Our Lady of Lourdes Health Ctr., 1993—. With U.S. Army, 1950-53, Korea. Mem. Assn. Systems Mgmt. (div. dir. 1983-85, div. 20 chmn. 1984-85, Columbia chpt. pres. 1985-86, internat. dir. 1991—). Office: WPPSS MD 120 PO Box 968 Richland WA 99352-0968

KLIPPERT, RICHARD HOBDELL, JR., engineering executive; b. Oakland, Calif., Jan. 25, 1940; s. Richard Hobdell and Carol Ione (Knight) K.; m. Penelope Ann Barker, Sept. 5, 1979; children—David, Deborah, Candice, Kristina. BS in Bus., Oreg. State U., 1962; postgrad. in polit. sci. U. Calif.-Berkeley, 1968-69, in polit. sci. and mgmt. George Washington U., 1972-73; grad. Naval War Coll., 1973. Commd. ensign USN, 1962, advanced through grades to comdr., 1971, ret., 1982, expert: Antisubmarine Warfare; mem. Combat Search and Rescue, Southeast Asia, 1964-67; exec. officer H.S. Squadron, 1974; mem. Flag Staff, 1974-79; chief engr. Light Airborne Multipurpose System MK-III, Washington, 1979-82; sr. engr., mgr. IBM, Boulder, Colo., 1982-83, engring. mgr., 1983-84, mgr. HH-60 systems engring., 1984-85, mgr. V-22 engring., 1985-88, program mgr. Document Mgmt. Systems Integration, 1988—, Pub. Solutions, 1989—, program mgr. USDA SCOAP/ASCS Programs, 1992; loaned exec. Boulder County United Way. Author: The Moon Book, 1971. Contbr. papers to tech. lit. Decorated Silver Star, Navy Commendation; recipient Outstanding Achievement and Golden Circle awards IBM, 1986. Mem. Soc. Naval Engrs., Assn. Image and Info. Mgmt., Soc. Automotive Engrs., Naval Inst., Sigma Chi. Republican. Avocations: golf, tennis, photography, bridge. Home: PO Box 615 Niwot CO 80544-0615 Office: IBM Diagonal Hwy Boulder CO 80301-1492

KLIVINGTON, KENNETH ALBERT, research administrator; b. Cleve., Sept. 23, 1940; s. Albert Cecil and Evelyn Louise (Groom) K.; m. Karen Jensen, Jan. 4, 1968 (div. Sept. 25, 1976); 1 child, Jason; m. Marie Rose Lopez, Nov. 17, 1976. SB, MIT, 1962; MS, Columbia U., 1964; PhD, Yale U., 1967. Asst. rsch. neuroscientist U. Calif., San Diego, 1967-68; dir. R & D Fisher/Jackson Assocs., N.Y.C., 1968-69; vis. rsch. scientist U. Calif., San Diego, 1973; sr. staff officer Nat. Acad. Scis., Washington, 1975-76; program officer & adminstr. Alfred P. Sloan Found., N.Y.C., 1969-81; v.p. R & D, dir. rsch. Electro-Biology, Inc., Fairfield, N.J., 1981-84; asst. to pres. Salk Inst., San Diego, 1984-93; v.p. sci. Fetzer Inst., Kalamazoo, Mich., 1993—; cons. in field; fellow, chmn. rsch. adv. com. Fetzer Inst., Kalamazoo, 1990-93. Author: Science of Mind, 1989, The Brain, Cognition and Education, 1986; contbr. articles to profl. jours. Mem. Soc. for Neurosci., Cognitive Sci. Soc., Bioelectromagnetic Soc., Internat. Brain Rsch. Orgn. Office: The Salk Inst 10010 N Torrey Pines Rd La Jolla CA 92037-1099

KLOBE, TOM, art gallery director; b. Mpls., Nov. 26, 1940; s. Charles S. and Lorna (Effertz) K.; m. Delmarie Pauline Motta, June 21, 1975. BFA, U. Hawaii, 1964, MFA, 1968; postgrad., UCLA, 1972-73. Vol. peace corps Alang, Iran, 1964-66; tchr. Calif. State U., Fullerton, 1969-72, Santa Ana (Calif.) Coll., 1972-77, Orange Coast Coll., Costa Mesa, Calif., 1974-77, Golden West Coll., Huntington Beach, Calif., 1976-77; art gallery dir. U. Hawaii, Honolulu, 1977—; acting dir. Downey (Calif.) Mus. Art, 1976; cons. Judiciary Mus., Honolulu, 1982—, Visual and Performing Arts Ctr., Maui, Hawaii, 1984—; exhibit designer Inst. for Astronomy, Honolulu, 1983-86; juror Print Casebooks. Recipient Best in Exhbn. Design award Print Casebooks, 1984, 86, 88, Vol. Svc. award City of Downey, 1977; Exhbn. grantee NEA, 1979—, State Found. Culture and the Arts, 1977—. Mem. Hawaii Mus. Assn., Nat. Assn. Mus. Exhbn. Roman Catholic. Office: U Hawaii Art Gallery 2535 The Mall Honolulu HI 96822-2233

KLOBUCHER, JOHN MARCELLUS, judge; b. Spokane, Wash., July 12, 1932; m. Virginia Rose Nilles; children—Marcella Marie, John Marcellus II, Christopher. Student Wash. State U., 1952; student Gonzaga U., 1954-57, J.D., 1960. Bar: Wash. 1960, U.S. Dist. Ct. (ea. dist.) Wash. 1961, U.S. Ct. Appeals (9th cir.) 1972. Law clk. to judge U.S. Dist. Ct. (ea. dist.) Wash., 1960-61; dep. pros. atty. criminal div. Spokane County Pros. Atty.'s Office, 1961-63; ptnr. Ennis & Klobucher, Spokane, 1963-78, Murphy, Bantz, Jansen, Klobucher, Clemons & Bury, Spokane, 1981; U.S. bankruptcy judge Eastern Dist. Wash., Spokane, 1981—. Served with U.S. Army, 1953-54. Mem. Wash. State Bar Assn., Spokane County Bar Assn. (pres. 1981), Inland Empire Fly Fishing (pres. 1977). Home: E 11320 17th Spokane WA 99206 Office: US Bankruptcy Ct PO Box 2164 Spokane WA 99210-2164

KLOHA, LARRY CARL, architect; b. Mesa, Ariz., Jan. 15, 1953; s. Carl Henry and Dortha Aramenta (Pritchard) K.; m. Mary Margaret Sumner, Nov. 14, 1987; 1 child, Michael Sumner. BArch, Ariz. State U., 1978. Lic. architect, Calif. Project architect Ware & Malcomb Architects, Irvine, Calif., 1978-84; sr. assoc. Ware & Malcomb Architects, San Diego, 1984-91; prin. architect Larry Kloha Architects, San Diego, 1991—; Mem. Bldg. Industry Assn., San Diego, 1985-90. Cited for Best Indsl. Project, City of Chula Vista, Calif., 1991. Democrat. Home and Office: 9281 Adolphia St San Diego CA 92129

KLOHS, MURLE WILLIAM, consulting chemist; b. Aberdeen, S.D., Dec. 24, 1920; s. William Henry and Lowell (Lewis) K.; m. Dolores Catherine Borm, June 16, 1946; children: Wendy C., Linda L. Student Westmar Coll., 1938-40; BSc, U. Notre Dame, 1947. Jr. chemist Harrower Lab., Glendale,

Calif., 1947, Rexall Drug Co., L.A., 1947-49; sr. chemist Riker Labs., Inc., L.A., 1949-57, dir. medicinal chemistry, Northridge, Calif., 1957-69, mgr. chem. rsch. dept., 1969-72, mgr. pharm. devel. dept., 1972-73, mgr. tech. liaison and comml. devel., 1973-82; cons. chemist, 1982—. Contbr. articles to profl. jours. Served to lt. USNR, 1943-46. Riker fellow Harvard U., 1950. Mem. Am. Chem. Soc., Am. Pharm. Assn., Adventures Club (L.A.). Home and Office: 19831 Echo Blue Dr Lake Wildwood Penn Valley CA 95946

KLONER, ROBERT A., cardiologist, researcher, educator; b. Buffalo, Oct. 8, 1949; s. Philip and Shirley (Miller) K.; m. Judith A. Kloner, July 24, 1977; children: Alissa, Susan. BS, Northwestern U., 1971, PhD, 1974, MD, 1975. Med. house officer Peter Bent Brigham Hosp., Boston, 1975-76, from asst. resident to sr. resident, 1976-78, rsch. clin. fellow in cardiology, 1979; clin. fellow in medicine Harvard Med. Sch., Boston, 1975-78, rsch. fellow in medicine, 1978-79, asst. prof. medicine, 1979-84, assoc. prof. medicine, 1984; prof. medicine Wayne State U., Detroit, 1985-88, U. So. Calif., L.A., 1988—; dir. rsch. Heart Inst. Hosp. of Good Samaritan, L.A., 1988—. Editor: The Guide to Cardiology, 1984, 90; editorial bd. maj. cardiology jours. including Circulation, Circulation Rsch., Jour. Am. Coll. Cardiology, Am. Jour. Cardiology, Am. Heart Jour.; co-editor Stunned Mycardium, 1993; contbr. numerous articles to profl. jours. Recipient Sheard-Sanford award ASCP, 1976, Merck award for Outstanding Achievement in Study of Medicine, 1975. Fellow Am. Coll. Cardiology; mem. Am. Heart Assn. (established investigator award 1981-86), N.Y. Acad. Scis., Am. Fedn. Clin. Rsch., Am. Soc. Clin. Investigators, Alpha Omega Alpha. Office: Hosp Good Samaritan Heart Inst 616 Witmer St Los Angeles CA 90017-2395

KLOPP, KENNETH HAP, business consultant; b. Spokane, Feb. 7, 1942; s. Kenneth H. and Dolores A. (Rowland) K.; m. Margot Ann Latimer, June 18, 1964; children: Kelly, Matt. AB, Stanford U., 1964, MBA, 1966. V.p. adminstrn. White Pine Sash, Spokane, 1963-66; pres., chief exec. officer North Face, Berkeley, Calif., 1967-88; pres. HK Cons., Berkeley, 1988—; CEO Mountain Travel, 1993—; bd. dirs. Helly-Hansen, Seattle, North Face, Nara Sports Gmbh, Munich; lectr. Bus. Sch. Stanford U., 1976—, U. Calif., 1983—, Carnegie Hall, 1988. Author: The Adventure of Leadership, 1992; contbr. column to profl. publs., 1989—. Bd. dirs. Mex. Arts Mus., San Francisco, 1980-85, Builders-A Non Profit Berkeley Indsl. Devel. Orgn., 1982-86; bd. advisors Mont. State U., Missoula, 1990—. Mem. Internat. Explorers Soc. (bd. dirs., Explorer award 1982). Democrat. Office: HK Cons 1815 4th St Ste F Berkeley CA 94710-1910

KLOSS, GENE (ALICE GENEVA GLASIER), artist; b. Oakland, Calif., July 27, 1903; d. Herbert P. and Carrie (Hefty) Glasier; m. Phillips Kloss, May 19, 1925. A.B., U. Calif., 1924; student, Calif. Sch. Fine Arts, 1924-25. Illustrator: The Great Kiva (Phillips Kloss), 1980; One-man shows Sandzen Meml. Gallery, Lindsborg, Kans., Albany Inst. History and Art, 1953, Tulsa, Scottsdale, Ariz., Albuquerque, 1956, Findlay Galleries, Chgo., 1957, Mus. N.Mex., 1960, W. Tex. Mus., 1964, Mus. Arts and Scis., Grand Junction, Colo., 1967, Mus. Okla., 1970, Brandywine Galleries, Albuquerque, 1971, Bishop's Gallery, 1972, Gallery A, Taos, N.Mex., 1973, Wichita (Kans.) Art Assn., 1974, Pratt Graphic Center, N.Y.C., 1976—, Muckenthaler Cultural Center, Los Angeles, 1980, Mus. of Tex. Tech U., 1984, Corcoran Gallery, Washington, 1989; exhibited in Three Centuries Art U.S., Paris, 1938; exhibited 3-man show, Pratt Graphic Center, N.Y., 1975; represented in collections, Library Congress, Carnegie Inst., Smithsonian Instn., N.Y. Pub. Library, Met. Mus., Pa. Acad. Fine Arts, Chgo. Art Inst., Corcoran Gallery, Washington, San Francisco Mus., Honolulu Acad. Fine Arts, Dallas Mus., Mus. N.Mex., Tulsa U., Kans. State Coll., Pa. U. John Taylor Arms Meml., Met. Mus., Peabody Mus., Mus. Tokyo, Auchenback Found. for Graphic Arts, San Francisco, Nat. Gallery, U. N.Mex. Mus., Copley Library, La Jolla, Calif., others; executed 1953 membership prints for, Albany Print Club and for Soc. Am. Graphic Artists, gift plate for, Print Makers of Calif., 1956; exhibited with, Audubon Soc., 1955; etcher, painter in oil, watercolor. Recipient Eyre Gold medal Pa. Acad. Fine Arts, 1936; asso. mem. award Calif. Soc. Etchers, 1934; honorarium Cal. Soc. Etchers, 1940, 41, 44; 3d award oils Oakland Art Gallery Ann., 1939; Purchase prize Chgo. Soc. Etchers, 1940; best black and white Tucson Fine Arts Assn., 1941; 1st prize Print Club, Phila., 1944; Purchase prize Library Congress, 1946; 1st prize prints N.Mex. State Fair, 1946; Ann. Exhibit Meriden, Conn., 1947; Open award Calif. Soc. Etchers, 1949-51; Henry B. Shope prize Soc. Am. Etchers, 1951; hon. mention, 1953; 1st prize prints Arts and Crafts Assn., Meriden, Conn., 1951; 1st prize Chgo. Soc. Etchers, 1952; Phila. Sketch Club prize, 1957; Fowler purchase prize Albany Print Club, 1959; purchase prize, 1961; Annoymous prize NAD, 1961. N.A. Mem. NAD, Soc. Am. Graphic Artists, Print Club of Albany, Phila. Water Color Club, MBLS (adv.).

KLOTT, DAVID LEE, lawyer; b. Vicksburg, Miss., Dec. 10, 1941; s. Isadore and Dorothy (Lipson) K.; m. Maren J. Randrup, May 25, 1975. BBA summa cum laude, Northwestern U., 1963; JD cum laude, Harvard U., 1966. Bar: Calif. 1966, U.S. Ct. Claims. 1968, U.S. Supreme Ct. 1971, U.S. Tax Ct. 1973, U.S. Ct. Appeals (Fed. cir.) 1982. Ptnr. Pillsbury, Madison & Sutro, San Francisco, 1966—; mem. tax adv. group to sub-chpt. C J and K, Am. Law Inst.; tchr. Calif. Continuing Edn. of Bar, Practising Law Inst., Hastings Law Sch., San Francisco; bd. dirs. Marin Wine and Food Soc. Commentator Calif. Nonprofit Corp. Law; bd. dirs. Joan Shorenstein Barone Found. for Harvard; counsel Drum Found.; bd. dirs. Marin Wine and Food Soc. Mem. ABA (tax exempt financing com.), Calif. State Bar Assn. (tax sect.), San Francisco Bar Assn., Am.-Korean Taekwondo Friendship Assn. (1st dan-black belt), Harvard Club, Northwestern Club, Olympic Club, City Club of San Francisco (founding mem.), Bay Club (charter mem.), Harbor Point Racquet and Beach Club, Internat. Wine and Food Soc., Beta Gamma Sigma, Beta Alpha Psi (pres. local chpt.). Office: Pillsbury Madison & Sutro 235 Montgomery St Ste 1616 San Francisco CA 94104

KLOWDEN, MARC JEFFERY, entomology educator; b. Chgo., June 6, 1948; s. Sam and Ruth (Ziskind) K.; m. Anne Janet Weitzman, Aug. 30, 1970; children: Daniel, Amanda. BS, U. Ill., Chgo., 1970, MS, 1973, PhD, 1976. Asst. entomologist U. Ga., Athens, 1976-81; asst. prof. U. Idaho, Moscow, 1981-83, assoc. prof., 1983-88, prof., 1988—. Contbr. articles to profl. jours. Mem. AAAS, Entomolog. Soc. Am., Soc. Vector Ecology, Am. Soc. Zoologists, Am. Mosquito Control Assn., Sigma Xi. Office: U Idaho Div Entomology Moscow ID 83843

KLUCK, CLARENCE JOSEPH, physician; b. Stevens Point, Wis., June 20, 1929; s. Joseph Bernard and Mildred Lorraine (Helminiak) K.; divorced; children: Paul Bernard, Annette Louise Kluck Winiston, David John, Maureen Ellen. BS in Med. Sci., U. Wis., 1951, MD, 1954. Resident San Joaquin Hosp., French Camp, Calif., 1955-56; asst. instr. medicine Ohio State U., Columbus, 1958-60; physician, chief of medicine Redford Med. Ctr., Detroit, 1960-69; practice medicine specializing in internal medicine Denver, 1969-83; med. dir. Atlantic Richfield Co., Denver, 1983-85; corp. med. dir. Cyprus Minerals Co., Englewood, Colo., 1985-92; pres. Kluck Med. Assocs., Englewood, 1992—; bd. dirs. Climbo Catering, Detroit, 1967-69, Met. Labs., Denver, 1970-81, Provest, Inc., Denver, 1985—; pres., CEO, chmn. bd. Corpcare, Inc., Englewood, 1992; CEO, pres. Corpcare Med. Assocs., P.C., 1992. Contbr. articles to profl. jours. Served to capt. U.S. Army, 1956-58. Recipient Century Club award Boy Scouts Am., 1972. Fellow Am. Occupational Med. Assn., Am. Coll. Occupational and Environ. Medicine, Am. Coll. Occupational Medicine; mem. Am. Acad. Occupational Medicine, Rocky Mountain Acad. Occupational Medicine (bd. dirs. 1985-88), Arapahoe County Med. Soc., Denver Med. Soc. (bd. dirs. 1973-74, council mem. 1981-87), Colo. Med. Soc. (del. 1973-74, 81-87), Am. Mining Congress Health Commn., Am. Soc. Internal Medicine, Colo. Soc. Internal Medicine. Roman Catholic. Clubs: Flatirons (Boulder, Colo.); Metropolitan. Home: 1900 E Girard Pl Englewood CO 80110-3151 Office: 6750 Stapleton Dr S Denver CO 80216

KLUDT, GAYLE CATHERINE, middle school educator; b. San Francisco, Aug. 12, 1948; d. Henry Adolf and Jean Veronica (Arjo) Schuback; m. Kenneth Arthur Kludt, July 19, 1969. BA in Sociology, San Jose State U., 1970, teaching credential, 1971, MA in Edn., 1981. Tchr. San Jose (Calif.) Unified Sch. Dist., 1972—. Rep. San Jose Tchrs. Assn., 1973-91; liaison Castillero Home & Sch. Club, San Jose, 1984-92; liaison Los Alamitos PTA, hon. life mem., San Jose, 1974-82. Mem. San Jose Mus. of Art, San Jose Symphony Assn., San Jose Hist. Mus., San Jose State U. Alumni Assn. (pres. 1991-93, v.p. 1989-91, rep. coun. 1988-92. Democrat. Office: Castillero Middle Sch 6385 Leyland Park Dr San Jose CA 95120

KLUG, JOHN JOSEPH, secondary education educator, director of dramatics; b. Denver, Apr. 27, 1948; s. John Joseph Sr. and Dorthea Virginia (Feely) Carlyle. BA in English, U. N.C., 1974; MA in Theatre, U. Colo., 1984. Tchr. Carmody Jr. High Sch., Lakewood, Colo., 1976-78; tchr. Golden (Colo.) High Sch., 1978—, dir. of dramatics, 1978—; producer, dir. Children's Theatre Tours, 1978—; theatrical cons., 1983—; improvisational workshop leader, 1983—. Playwright, editor: Children's Theatre scripts, 1982—. Home: 4565 King St Denver CO 80211-1357 Office: Golden High Sch 701 24th St Golden CO 80401-2398

KLUGHERZ, MARY BERNADETTE, marketing consultant, educator; b. Palo Alto, Calif., Nov. 21, 1955; d. Charles Robert and Elizabeth Francis (Finnochio) K.; m. Thomas Michael Jahnke, June 25, 1988; 1 child, Mark Ryan. AA in Liberal Arts, De Anza Coll., 1975; BS in Recreation and Leisure Studies, San Jose State U., 1977. Program dir. Recreation Svcs. Agy., Europe, Stuttgart, Fed. Republic Germany, 1978-79; dir. mktg. and sales Alaska Travel Adventures, Juneau, 1979-84; dir. mktg. Alaska State Div. Tourism, Juneau, 1984-88; sr. mktg. cons. McDowell Group, Ketchikan, Alaska, 1988—; adj. faculty mem. U. Alaska, S.E., Ketchikan, 1988—; bd. dirs. S.E. Alaska Tourism Coun., Juneau, 1983-84; dir. VIP program U. Alaska, Ketchikan, 1988—. Coord. TV commls. for Alaska for Nat. Campaign, 1985 (Best of 50 States award); coord., co-author mktg. plan for Alaska, 1986 (Best of 50 States award 1986). Bd. dirs., past pres. Juneau Jazz & Classics, 1986, 87, 88; bd. dirs. Jr. Achievement, Ketchikan, 1992—. Recipient Outstanding Svc. to Alaska Visitor Industry award Alaska Visitors Assn., 1988. Mem. LWV, Rotary. Office: McDowell Group Box 3379 Ketchikan AK 99901

KLUSENDORF, ROY EARL, marketing executive; b. Royal Oak, Mich., Feb. 28, 1939; s. Earl Edward Augustus and Lydia (Stolzenfeld) K.; m. Linda Jo Brooks, June 9, 1978; children: Terri, Tami, Tim, Glenn, Kevin, Tom, Eric, Sabrina. BS in Engring. Physics, Mich. Technol. U., 1961; MBA in Quantitative Mgmt., U. Houston, Clear Lake, Tex., 1978. Sr. mgr. Apollo Program GE, Houston, 1965-78; bus. devel. mgr. Aerospace and Defense, various locations, Tex., 1978-88; dir. bus. devel. Astro Aerospace Corp., Carpinteria, Calif., 1989—; chmn. Rsch. and Devel. Com. Astro Aerospace, Carpinteria, Calif. Contbr. to Advanced Devel. Mgr. and Leader, Flight hardware Systems for Space Programs, NASA and DOD Missions Skylab Checkout Mgr. Recipient Apollo Skylab Appreciation Cert., Nat. Aeronautics and Space Agy. (NASA), Houston, Johnson Space Ctr. Mem. AIAA, Am. Astronautical Soc., Armed Force Communications Electronics Assn., U.S. Space Found. Episcopalian. Home: 2012 Dwight Ave Camarillo CA 93010-3855 Office: Astro Aerospace 6384 Via Real Carpinteria CA 93013-2920

KLUSMIRE, JON DALTON, editor, writer; b. Aspen, Colo., June 4, 1956; s. Newton Eldo and Jeanette (Munroe) K.; m. Leslie Anne Halterman, Dec. 27, 1986; children: Devin Wilkinson, Ansel, Mariah. BA, Western State Coll., 1980. Mem. advt. staff Central Phoenix Sun, 1980-81; reporter, bur. mgr. The Weekly Newspaper, Glenwood Springs, Colo., 1982-83, editor, 1983-86; media dir., staff writer/editor Rocky Mountain Inst., Snowmass, Colo., 1986-89; editor Trilogy Mag., Glenwood Springs, Colo., 1989—; We. Colo. corr. Colo. Bus. mag., Lakewood, 1993—; columnist Aspen (Colo.) Times, 1993—. Author: Colorado, A Compass American Guidebook, 1991; co-author: The Sacred Circle: A Healing Way for the Sickness of Alcoholism, 1992, Resource Efficient Housing Guide, 1987; editor: Financing Economic Renewal, 1988, Business Opportunities Casebook, 1988; contbr. articles and poetry to various publs. Bd. dirs. Sta. KDNK Pub. Radio, Carbondale, Colo., 1987-88, Garfield County United Way, 1989-91. Recipient 1st pl. Best News Story Colo. Press Assn., 1982, 3rd pl. Best Coverage of Energy Nat. Newspaper Assn., 1986. Home: 1101 8th St Glenwood Springs CO 81601-3531 Office: Trilogy PO Box 2253 Glenwood Springs CO 81602-2253

KLYCINSKI, FREDERICK ALLEN See ALLEN, RICK

KMET, JOSEPH PAUL, military officer, pharmacist; b. Chgo., Jan. 11, 1942; s. John Norman Kmet and Elizabeth Charlotte (Posh) Miller; m. Rebecca Eugenia Patterson, Mar. 29, 1969. BS in Pharmacy, U. Ariz., 1971; MS in Nuclear Pharmacy, U. So. Calif., 1973; MS in Computer Sci., Corpus Christi U., 1984. Lic. pharmacists. Enlisted USN, 1959, advanced through grades to lt. comdr., 1971-93; intern pharmacist Coronado Drug, Inc., Tucson, Ariz., 1967-71; pharmacist Defender Drug, Tucson, 1971-72; resident in nuclear pharmacy William Beaumont Hosp., Royal Oak, Mich., 1973; pharmacist Vet.'s Administrn. Hosp. Ctr., West Los Angeles, CAlif., 1973-75; nuclear pharmacist dept. radiology, pharmacy Naval Regional Med. Ctr., San Diego, 1975-82; asst. chief pharmacy svc. Naval Regional Med. Ctr., Corpus Christi, Tex., 1982-85; head mgmt. info. dept. Naval Med. Command, Norfolk, Va., 1985-89; pharmacist Naval Hosp., Portsmouth, Va., 1989-90; chief pharmacy svc. Naval Hosp., Lemoore, Calif., 1990-93, ret., 1993. Judge Greater San Diego Sci. and Engring. Fair, 1980-82. Mem. Aircraft Owners and Pilots Assn., NRA (life), Am. Soc. Hosp. Pharmacists, Soc. Nuclear Medicine. Republican. Episcopalian.

KMET, REBECCA EUGENIA PATTERSON, pharmacist; b. Ellisville, Miss., June 17, 1948; d. Eugene Roberts and Ruth Winn (Pettis) Patterson; m. Joseph Paul Kmet, Mar. 29, 1969. BS in Pharmacy, U. Ariz., 1971; MBA, Nat. U., 1981. Pharmacist Santa Monica (Calif.) Bldg. Profl. Pharmacy, 1972-73, Vets. Hosp., West Los Angeles, Calif., 1973-74, Kaiser Med. Ctr., San Diego, Calif., 1979-82, Farmersville Drug Store, Farmersville, Calif., 1991—. Community svc. vol. Lt. USN, 1975-78. Recipient Presdl. Achievement award Rep. Party Nat. Congl. com. Mem. Navy League, Naval Hist. Found., Marine Corps Hist. Found., Rho Chi, Kappa Epsilon, NSDAR. Republican. Episcopalian. Home: 985 Murphy Dr Lemoore CA 93245-2181

KNACK, MARTHA CAROL, anthropology educator; b. Orange, N.J., Jan. 27, 1948; d. Howard Lauren and Dorothy (Place) K. AB cum laude, U. Mich., 1969, AM, 1970, PhD, 1975. Asst. prof. U. Tex., Odessa, 1975-77; asst. prof. U. Nev., Las Vegas, 1977-81, assoc. prof., 1981-87, chairperson dept. anthropology, 1982-86, prof., 1987—; cons. Pyramid Lake Tribe, Nixon, Nev., 1983—. Author: Life is with People: Household Organization of the Contemporary Southern Paiute Indians, 1980; As Long the River Shall Run: An Ethnohistory of the Pyramid Lake Reservation, 1984; contbr. article to profl jours. Office: U Nev Dept Anthropology Ethnic Studies 4505 Maryland Pkwy Las Vegas NV 89154

KNAPP, CLEON TALBOYS, business executive; b. Los Angeles, Apr. 28, 1937; s. Cleon T. and Sally (Brasfield) K.; m. Elizabeth Ann Wood, Mar. 17, 1979; children: Jeffrey James, Brian Patrick, Aaron Bradley, Laura Ann. Student, UCLA, 1955-58. With John C. Brasfield Pub. Corp. (purchased co. in 1965, changed name to Knapp Comm Corp. 1977, sold to Condé Nast Publs. in 1993); pres. Talwood Corp., Knapp Found., L.A.; chmn. Knapp Press; bd. dirs., bd. trustees Otis-Parsons Art Ctr., The Music Ctr. L.A., Mus. Contemporary Art, L.A. County Mus. Art, Art Ctr. Coll. Design; bd. visitors John E. Anderson Grad. Sch. of Mgmt., UCLA. Chmn. bd. dirs. Damon Runyon-Walter Winchell Cancer Rsch. Fund. Mem. Bel Air Country Club, Wilshire Country Club, Regency Club, Country Club of the Rockies. Office: Talwood Corp 10100 Santa Monica Blvd Ste 2000 Los Angeles CA 90067

KNAPP, EBER GUY, accountant; b. Seattle, Sept. 18, 1916; s. Eber G. and Ernestine C. (Venter) K.; student Wilson's Bus. Coll., 1938-39, U. So. Calif., 1946-47; m. M. Lorraine Knapp, July 2, 1947; children—Candyce Lorraine, Ardyce Christine, Carol Lynn. Accredited in acctg. Owner, Knapp's Tax & Bus. Service, Westminster, Calif., 1959—; overall coordinator Orange County (Calif.) Am. Assn. Ret. Persons Tax-Aide Program, 1979-88. Mem. Vice chmn. Mobile Home Commn., Westminster, Calif. Served with U.S. Army, 1941-45. Mem. Am. Legion, Calif. Assn. Ind. Accts. (charter), Nat. Assn. Pub. Accts., VFW. Republican. Mem. Christian Ch. Author: Groom's Survival Handbook, or How to Teach Your Bride to Cook, 1982. Home: 7152 Santee Ave PO Box 1 Westminster CA 92684

KNAPP, GAYLE, molecular biologist, educator; b. Norwich, N.Y., July 31, 1949; d. Carlton Morgan and Annette Rose (Giza) Knapp. AB in Chemistry, Barnard Coll., 1971; PhD in Biochemistry, U. Ill., 1977. Postdoctoral fellow U. Calif., San Diego, 1977-81; asst. prof. microbiology, U. Ala. at Birmingham, 1981-88, assoc. scientist Comprehensive Cancer Ctr., U. Ala., Birmingham, 1983-88; asst. prof. biochemistry Utah State U., Logan, 1988-93; sr. scientist Nat. Ctr. Design of Molecular Function, Utah State U., Logan, 1993—. Mem. AAAS, Nat. Ctr. Design of Molecular Function, Am. Chem. Soc., Am. Soc. Microbiologists, N.Y. Acad. Sci., Sigma Xi. Office: Utah State Univ Nat Ctr for Design Molecular Function Logan UT 84322

KNAPP, KENNETH J., public relations company executive, writer; b. Monroe, Mich., July 15, 1946; s. Kenneth J. Knapp and Donna J. (Richards) Roka; m. Diane Knapp (div. 1967); 1 child, Kenneth J. III; m. Roberta J. Knapp; children: K. Jeffery, Rachel Lynn. AS, Genesee C.C., Flint, Mich., 1970; BS in Natural Sci., Mich. State U., 1973. Owner, mgr. Knapp Comm., Jackson, Sheridan, Wyo., 1977—; pres. Rising Trout Pub. Co. Inc., Jackson, 1978-83, Ptarmigan Inc., Sheridan, 1988—; co-owner Knapp Fly Fishing Expdns., Jackson, 1978-83; writer, wildlife cons. CBS News, N.Y.C., 1982-83; writer, photographer U.S. Forest Svc., Sheridan, 1988-89. Author: Wyoming Fishing Guide, 1978, (booklet) Wildlife of the Bighorns, 1989. Scouting coord. Boy Scouts Am., Sheridan, 1986—, adult advisor Order of Arrow, 1988—; pres. Wyo. Western Film Festival, Sheridan, 1989-90. With USMC, 1963-65. Mem. Outdoor Writers Assn. Am. (bd. dirs. 1982-85, color scenic photographer 1st place ann. award 1983, citation 1985), Bighorn Audubon Soc. (v.p. 1990—), Nat. Eagle Scouts Assn., Brotherhood Order of Arrow (chpt. advisor), KC (4th degree), Phi Kappa. Republican. Roman Catholic. Home and Office: PO Box 725 Sheridan WY 82801

KNAPP, ROBERT STANLEY, English language educator; b. Alamosa, Colo., Mar. 29, 1940; s. Stanley Osgood and Pearl (Betts) K.; m. Christine Knodt, June 17, 1965. BA, U. Colo., 1962; MA, U. Denver, 1963; PhD, Cornell U., 1968. Instr. Princeton U., 1966-68, asst. prof., 1968-74; asst. prof. English Reed Coll., Portland, 1974-77; assoc. prof. English Reed Coll., 1977-83, prof. English, 1983—. Author: Shakespeare - the Theater and the Book, 1989; contbr. articles to profl. jours. NEH fellow, 1979-80. Mem. MLA, Shakespeare Assn. Am. Home: 3735 SE Woodstock Blvd Portland OR 97202-7537 Office: Reed Coll 3203 SE Woodstock Blvd Portland OR 97202-8199

KNAPP, THOMAS EDWIN, sculptor, painter; b. Gillette, Wyo., Sept. 28, 1925; s. Chester M. and Georgia Mabel (Blankenship) K.; m. Dorothy Wellborn; children: Gordon, Kathy, Dan, Kent, Keith. Student, Santa Rosa Jr. Coll., 1952-53; A.A., Calif. Coll. Arts and Crafts, 1953-54; student, Art Ctr. Sch., Los Angeles, 1954-55. Animation artist Walt Disney Studios, Burbank, Calif., 1954-56, Portrait & Hobby Camera Shops, WyoFoto Studies, Cody, Wyo., 1956-64; owner Rocky Mountain Land Devel. Corp., Cody, Wyo., 1965-66; comml. artist Mountain States Telephone Co., Albuquerque, 1966-69; lectr. at art seminars. Exhibited one-man shows, Cody County Art League, 1968, Jamison Gallery, Santa Fe, 1969, Mesilla Gallery, 1971, Inn of Mountain Gods, Mescalero Apache Reservation, N.Mex., Mountain Oyster Club, Tucson, Dos Pajaros Gallery, El Paso, (with Dorothy Wellborn) joint shows, Rosquist Gallery, Tucson, (with Michael Coleman), Zantman Gallery, Palm Desert Calif.; one and two person shows nationally with Dorothy Bell Knapp through 1988; group shows, Saddleback Inn, Santa Ana, Calif., Zantman Gallery, Carmel, Calif., Borglum Meml. Sculpture Exhbn. Nat. Cowboy Hall of Fame, Oklahoma City, 1975-76, Maxwell Gallery, San Francisco, 1975; represented permanent collections, Whitney Gallery Western Art, Cody, Senator Quinn Meml. Auditorium, Spencer, Mass., Heritage Mus., Anchorage, Indpls. Mus. Art, Mescalero Tribe, N.Mex.; works include Dance of the Mountain Spirits (Blue Ribbon award 1976), Laguna Eagle dancer (spl. award 1974, Blue Ribbon Los Angeles Indian Art Show, 1975-76), Santa Clara Buffalo dancer (Spl. award San Antonio Indian Nat. show 1974, Spl. award Los Angeles Indian show 1976), Mandan chieftan (Spl. award San Diego Indian show 1974, Spl. award Los Angeles Indian show 1976); commd. to sculpt bronze statue of Tex. ranger Capt. Bill McMurrey, now in Tex. Ranger Mus., San Antonio, bronze Giant Galapagos Tortoise in collection of Gladys Porter Zoo, Brownsville, Tex., El Paso Mus. of Art, Mus. of Native Am. Cultures, Spokane, Wash., Cherokee Nat. Hist. Mus., Talequah, Okla., Diamond M. Found. Mus., Snyder, Tex., Buffalo Bill Hist. Ctr., Cody, Wyoming; lifesize Tex. Ranger (horseback) in bronze installed El Paso Mus. Art, 1989; commissioned giant Galapagos Tortoise in bronze for installation Sculpture Pk., Loveland, Colo., 1990, 13-foot bronze endangered salt water crocodile for Gladys Porter Zoo, Brownsville, Tex., 1990, heroic size bronze commd. for Rose Bowl, Tournament of Roses, 1992, heroic size Cahuilla Indian woman The Reed Gatherer, Waring Plaza, Palm Desert, Calif. Active Boy Scouts Am., 1947-68, World Wildlife Fund. Served with USN, World War II, Korea. Decorated Air medal; recipient Order Arrow award Boy Scout Am., 1968. Mem. N.Mex. Amigos, Mensa, New York Zool. Soc. Home and Office: Drawer 510 Ruidoso Downs NM 88346

KNATZ, GERALDINE, environmental scientist, city official, educator; b. Paterson, N.J., Oct. 18, 1951; d. Charles Henry and Agnes Veronica (MacCormack) K.; m. John Charles Mulvey, Aug. 8, 1987. BA in Zoology, Rutgers U., Newark, 1973; MS in Environ. Engring., U. So. Calif., 1977; PhD in Biol. Scis., U. Sso. Calif., 1979. Marine biology Tetra-Tech, Pasadena, Calif., 1976-77; environ. scientist Port of Long Beach, Calif., 1977-81, mgr. environ. planning, 1981-88, dir. planning, 1988—; instr. environ. engring. U. So. Calif., L.A., 1981—, mem. sea grant adv. com., 1986—; adj. prof. pub. adminstrn. Calif. State U., Long Beach, 1985—; profl. assoc. East-West Ctr., Honolulu, Beijing, 1984-86; mem. study com. on landslide access to ports NRC-Transp. Rsch. Bd., 1991-92. Author: Illustrated Key to the Planktonic Copepoda of San Pedro Bay, 1980; also numerous articles. Bd. dirs. Harbor Area YwCA, San Pedro, Calif., 1985-91, pres. bd., 1991. Recipient Young Careerist award Bus. and Profl. Women Calif., 1980, resolutions for community achievements Calif. Senate and City of L.A., 1984. Mem. Am. Assn. Port Authorities (sec. harbors, navigation and environ. com. 1991—), Assn. Environ. Profls. (Calif. bd. dirs. 1985-87), Women's Transp. Seminar, Phi Beta Kappa. Roman Catholic. Office: Port of Long Beach 925 Harbor Plz Long Beach CA 90802

KNEBEL, FLETCHER, writer; b. Dayton, Ohio, Oct. 1, 1911; s. A.G. and Mary (Lewis) K.; m. Constance Wood, 1985; child by previous marriage—Jack G. A.B., Miami U., Oxford, Ohio, 1934. With Coatesville (Pa.) Record, 1934, Chattanooga News, 1934-35, Toledo News Bee, 1936; with Cleve. Plain Dealer, 1936-50; Washington corr., 1937-50; corr. Washington bur. Cowles Publs., 1950-64; syndicated columnist Potomac Fever, 1951-64. Author: Night of Camp David, 1965, The Zinzin Road, 1966, Vanished, 1968, Trespass, 1969, Dark Horse, 1972, The Bottom Line, 1974, Dave Sulkin Cares!, 1978, Crossing in Berlin, 1981, Poker Game, 1983, Sabotage, 1986; co-author: No High Ground, 1960, Seven Days in May, 1962, Convention, 1964, Before You Sue, 1987. Served as lt. USNR, 1942-45. Mem. Phi Beta Kappa, Sigma Chi. Club: Gridiron. Address: 1070 Oilipuu Pl Honolulu HI 96825

KNEBEL, JACK GILLEN, lawyer; b. Washington, Jan. 28, 1939; s. Fletcher and Amalia Eleanor (Rauppius) K.; m. Linda Karin Ropertz, Feb. 22, 1963; children: Hollis Anne (dec.), Lauren Beth. BA, Yale Coll., 1960; LLB, Harvard U., 1966. Bar: Calif. 1966, U.S. Dist. Ct. (no. dist.) Calif. 1966, U.S. Ct. Appeals (9th cir.) 1966. Assoc. McCutchen, Doyle, Brown & Enersen, San Francisco, 1966-74, ptnr., 1974—; bd. dirs. San Francisco Lawyers Com. for Urban Affairs, 1980-81, mem. exec. com., 1991—; mem. adv. coun. Hastings Coll. Trial Advocacy, San Francisco, 1981-91, chair, 1990-91. Bd. dirs., pres. Orinda (Calif.) Assn., 1972-74, Sea Ranch (Calif.) Assn., 1978-79; co-chmn. Citizens to Preserve Orinda, 1983-85. Lt. (j.g.) USN, 1960-66. Fellow Am. Coll. Trial Lawyers; mem. ABA, Maritime Law Assn. of U.S. Democrat. Mem. United Ch. of Christ. Home: 5 Tarabrook Dr Orinda CA 94563-3120 Office: McCutchen Doyle Brown & Enersen Three Embarcadero Ctr San Francisco CA 94111

KNECHT, BEN HARROLD, surgeon; b. Rapid City, S.D., May 3, 1938; s. Ben and Ona K.; m. Jane Bowles, Aug. 27, 1961; children: John, Janelle. BA, U. S.D., 1960; MD, U. Iowa, 1964. Diplomate Am. Bd. Surgery. Intern Los Angeles County Gen. Hosp., 1964-65; resident in surgery U. Iowa Sch. Medicine, Iowa City, 1968-72; surgeon Wenatchee (Wash.) Valley Clinic, 1972—; dir. emergency room Cen. Wash. Hosp., Wenatchee, 1972-79, chief surgery, 1983-86; chmn. claims rev. panel Wash. State Med. Assn., Seattle, 1979—, profl. liability com. risk mgmt., 1985-90; clin. assoc. prof. surgery U. Wash.; mem. adv. risk mgmt. com. Wash. State Physicians Ins. Subscribers, 1990—, regional adv. com. Nat. Libr. Medicine, 1991—. Fundraiser Cen. Wash. Hosp. Found., 1987; del. Gov.'s Conf. on Librs., 1991. Lt. comdr. USN, 1965-68, Vietnam. Mem. AMA (alt. del. 1985-87, del. 1988—, surg. caucus exec. com. 1991—), ACS (bd. dirs. Wash. chpt. 1981-84), North Pacific Surg. Assn., Wash. State Med. Assn. (trustee 1980—), Chelan-Douglas County Med. Soc., Rotary (chmn. youth com. 1976-78). Office: Wenatchee Valley Clinic 820 N Chelan Ave Wenatchee WA 98801-6601

KNECHT, RAYMOND LAWRENCE, sugar company executive; b. Phila., Apr. 19, 1948; s. Raymond L. and Mary Emma (Goldsmith) K.; m. Eileen Elizabeth Conn, Oct. 10, 1970; children: Katherine, John. BS, Tulane U., 1970. Chemist, ops. mgr. Colonial Sugars Co., Gramercy, La., 1971-74, 77-81; quality assurance mgr. North Am. Sugars, Mobile, Ala., 1974-77; ops. mgr. Nat. Sugar Refining Co., Phila., 1981; sr. process engr. Amstar, Chalmette, La., 1981-83; process mgr. Amstar, N.Y.C., 1983-85; sr. v.p. ops. C & H Sugar Co., Crockett, Calif., 1985—; referee U.S. Nat. Com. on Sugar Analysis, New Orelans, 1976-81. Author: (with others) Sugar: Users Guide to Sucrose, 1990; contbr. articles to profl. jours. Pres. Vallejo (Calif.) C. of C., 1988; trustee Sutter Solano Med. Ctr., Vallejo, 1990—; dir. Silverado Coun., Boy Scouts of Am., Vallejo, 1987. Home: 615 La Cadena St Vallejo CA 94590-3451 Office: C & H Sugar Co 830 Loring Ave Crockett CA 94525-1171

KNEEBONE, ALICE JEANNETTE, child care coordinator; b. Boulder, Colo., July 28, 1956; d. John William and Miriam Alice (Alcorn) K. AS in Med. Assistance, Parks Coll., 1981. Proof operator, asst. supr. Nat. State Bank, Boulder, 1975-80; child care coord. Mothers of Presch. Children, Boulder, 1982—, Moments with Mothers, Boulder, 1992—; child care coord. Doorways Internat., Inc., Boulder, 1982—, bd. dirs. officer; sec., shipping and receiving mgr. Video Accessory Corp., Boulder, 1984-91; office mgr. Arapahoe Chiropractic Clinic, Boulder, Colo., 1991-92; Home Day Care, 1992—. Author ednl. materials for working mothers; dancer, co-leader Polynesian Dance Troop, 1974—, Hawaiian-Tahitian Dance Troop, 1989—. Tchr. Sunday sch. 1st Presbyn. Ch., Boulder, 1980—; med. asst. blood bank Health Fair, Boulder, 1983; election judge Boulder County Clk. and Recorder Office, 1992—; vol. asst. Home Health Care, 1992—; vol. preparation com. Vacation Bible Sch. Mem. Nat. Assn. Med. Assts., Boulder Assn. Med. Assts., 1st Priority Christian Singles, 20/30 Something Christian Singles Social Club, 20/30 Something Christian Singles (Bible Study), Neighborhood Eco-Cycle Block (asst. to coord.), Ivy Rebekah Lodge (jr. past noble grand of ivy 1993, elevator fund raising 1991—, rep. to dist. 8 odd fellows orgn., chmn. hosp./shut-in visitation, program com. 1991-92, bereavement com. 1992-93), Odd Fellows (UN pilgrimage for youth fund raising 1992—, elevator fund raising 1991—, delgate to internat. order, 1993—). Republican. Office: Internat 1st Presbyn Ch Boulder Moments with Mothers/Doorways 1820 15th St Boulder CO 80302-5494 also: Calvary Bible Evang Free Ch Mothers of Presch Children 3245 Kalmia Ave Boulder CO 80304 also: Arapahoe Chiropractic Clinic 2500 Broadway Boulder CO 80304

KNEECE, DANIEL RUFUS, III, cinematographer; b. Columbia, S.C., Sept. 13, 1956; s. James Frank and Emaleen (Corley) K. Cert. in Cinema, U. So. Calif., 1976; AA, U. S.C., Allendale, 1976; B in Media Arts, U. S.C., 1978, M in Media Arts, 1980. Cameraman Sta. WIS-TV, Columbia, 1979-80; cinematographer Daniroo Ltd., Hollywood, Calif., 1980-88; freelance cinematographer L.A., 1988—; cons. Hollywood South Studio Complex, Columbia, 1979-84; advisor Trident Tech. Coll., Charleston, S.C., 1986-88; steadicam instr. Cinema Products, L.A., 1988—. Camera operator (steadicam) for motion pictures including Blue Velvet, 1985 (Oscar nomination 1986), Raw Deal, 1986, Weeds, 1987, Staying Together, 1987, Child's Play II, 1989, Solar Crisis, 1989, Wild At Heart, 1989 (winner Palme d'Or Cannes 1990), Cold Dog Soup, 1989, Peter Gunn, 1989, Days of Thunder, 1990, Distant Shores, 1990, Mr. Destiny, 1990, Dying Young, 1991, Double Impact, 1991, Nightmare 6-Freddy's Dead, 1991, Night on Earth, 1991, Neil Simon's Broadway Bound, 1991, People Under the Stairs, 1991, Samantha, 1991, The Vagrant, 1991, Richochet, 1991, Imax, (TV show) Twin Peaks, 1990, Twin Peaks movie, 1991, Star Trek VI, 1991, The Public Eye, 1991, Passed Away, 1991, also camera operator and asst. on numerous commls.; animator (films) El Gato, 1979, Cera, 1980. Recipient Regional Student Oscar nomination Acad. Motion Picture Arts and Scis., 1980; Disting. Alumnus honoree U. S.C., 1991. Mem. Soc. Motion Picture and TV Engrs., Soc. Oper. Cameramen, Steadicam Operators Assn., Internat. Photographers Guild, Audio Engring. Soc., S.C. Motion Picture and TV Assn. Office: 7095 Hollywood Blvd Ste 460 Los Angeles CA 90028-6035

KNIERIM, KIM PHILLIP, lawyer; b. Tacoma, Nov. 18, 1945; s. Oscar Fitzpatrick and Dorothy Margaret (King) K.; m. Pamela Gail Waller. B.S. in Sociology, U. Wash., Seattle, 1968; J.D., Columbia U., 1974. Dir. human resources planning N.Y. Telephone Co., 1969-71; atty. Pillsbury, Madison & Sutro, San Francisco, 1974-76, Fulop, Polston, Burns & McKittrick, Beverly Hills, Calif., 1976-81, Gordon, Weinberg & Zipser, Los Angeles, 1982-84, Wood, Lucksinger & Epstein, Los Angeles, 1984-85; pvt. practice L.A., Pasadena, 1985-88; of counsel Arthur K. Snyder Law Corp., L.A., 1988—; judge pro tem Beverly Hills Mcpl. Ct., 1979-87, Los Angeles Mcpl. Ct., 1985—; guest lectr. Pepperdine U. Law Sch., Los Angeles, 1981; mem. Los Angeles City Atty.'s Regulatory Reform Task Force, 1982-86; mem. U.S. Army War Coll. Nat. Security Seminar, 1984. Legal editor: Century 21 Brokers Guide to Working With Developers, 1988-91. Chmn. pub. affairs Planned Parenthood N.Y.C., 1971-74; gen. counsel Los Angeles Ballet, 1979-80; chmn. bd. Bethune Ballet, 1981-82, pres., 1982-83, bd. dirs., 1983—. Served with RNSC, 1957-63; with USNR, 1969. Decorated Nat. Def. Service medal; Order Hosp. St. John Jerusalem (Anglican); Harlan Fiske Stone scholar, 1971-72, James Kent scholar 1972-74; teaching fellow Columbia U., 1973-74. Mem. ABA (vice chmn. young lawyers div. com. jud. tenure, selection and performance 1980-81), Calif. State Bar (del. 1980-87), L.A. County Bar Assn. (arbitrator 1979-88), Beverly Hills Bar Assn. (chmn. environ. law com. 1979-82, vice chmn. resolutions com. 1983-86), Pasadena Bar Assn., Beverly Hills Barristers (gov. 1979-81), U.S. Combined Tng. Assn., Calif. Dressage Soc. (demonstration rider 1989—), U.S. Dressage Fedn. (qualified rider 1989), West Hills Hunt Club (riding chmn. 1987-89, pres. 1989-90, dir. 1990-91), Brit. United Svcs. Club, Paddock Riding Club, Univ. Club Pasadena, and others. Home: 279 Camino Del Sol South Pasadena CA 91030-3560 Office: Wells Fargo Ctr 355 S Grand Ave Bldg 3788 Los Angeles CA 90071-1597

KNIERIM, ROBERT VALENTINE, electrical engineer, consultant; b. Oakland, Calif., Sept. 27, 1916; s. Otto Valentine and Edith May (Bell) K.; m. Esther Perry Bateman, July 10, 1954; children: Kathleen Dianne, David Lyell, Daniel Goddard. BS, U. Calif., Berkeley, 1941; postgrad., U. Pitts., 1942, U. Colo., 1944-45, Raytheon Field Engring Sch, 1945. Registered profl. elec. engr., Calif. Student engr. Westinghouse Corp., East Pittsburgh, Pa., 1942; marine elec. engr. U.S. Maritime Commn., Oakland, 1943-44; elec. engr. U.S. Bur. Reclamation, Denver, 1944-45, Sacramento, 1945-48; field engr. Raytheon Corp., Waltham, Mass., 1945; electronics engr. Sacramento Signal Depot, 1948-49; assoc. elec. engr. Calif. Office Architecture and Constrn., 1949-57, sr. elec. engr., 1957-76; cons. engring., 1976. Mem. Century Club of Golden Empire Council Boy Scouts Am., 1969—, instnl. rep., 1948-54, dist. chmn. camping and activities com., 1951-54. Mem. Sacramento Engrs. Club (charter), IEEE (sr., life), Nat. Rifle Assn. (life), Sierra Club (life, chpt. treas. 1962-65), Nat. Assn. Corrosion Engrs. (life), Calif. Alumni Assn. (life), Eta Kappa Nu, Alpha Phi Omega (life). Republican. Congregationalist. Lodge: Masons. Home and Office: Cons Elec Engring 10325 SW Ashton Circle Wilsonville OR 97070-9532

KNIGHT, CONSTANCE BRACKEN, writer; b. Detroit, Oct. 30, 1937; d. Thomas Francis and Margaret (Kearney) Bracken; m. James Edwards Knight, June 14, 1958 (div. Feb. 1968); children: Constance Lynne Knight Campbell, James Seaton, Keith Bracken. Student, Barry Coll., 1955-56; AA, Marymount Coll., 1957; postgrad., Fla. State U., 1958-60. Columnist, feature writer Miami Herald, Ft. Lauderdale, Fla., 1954-55, 79-80; pub. rels. dir. Lauderdale Beach Hotel, 1965-67; columnist, feature writer Ft. Lauderdale News/Sun-Sentinel, 1980-81; owner Connie Knight and Assoc. Pub. Rels., Ft. Lauderdale, 1981-85; editor, pub. Vail (Colo.) Mag., 1986-89, contbg. freelance writer, 1989—; editorial cons. Vail Valley Mag., 1993—; instr. Colo. Mountain Coll., Vail, 1979; copywriter Colo. Ski Heritage Mus., Vail, 1986—. Mem. Planning and Environ. Commn., Vail, 1990-92. Mem. Soc. Profl. Journalists, N.Am. Ski Journalists (treas. 1990-93). Office: 385 Gore Creek Dr Ste 201 Vail CO 81657

KNIGHT, DENNIS FRED, lecturer, teacher; b. Wiley, Tex., Feb. 23, 1926; s. Dennis and Ethel Knight; m. Hazel Irene Thomas, May 10, 1953 (dec. Oct. 1964); children: Tim T., Dennis H., Debra Ann. BA in Bus., New Mex. Highlands U., 1953; BS in Logistics, Weber State U., 1975. Doodlebugger Tex. Oil Co., Menard, Tex., 1943-44; carpenter pvt. practice Seminole, Tex., 1946-50; foreman Mobil Oil Corp., Seminole, 1953-62; co-owner Hi Country Sporting Goods Store, Las Vegas, New Mex., 1962-65; doodlebugger Amerada Petroleum Corp., Seminole, 1965-66; logistician, inventory control USAF, Hill AFB, Utah, 1966-91. Campaign aide Gaines County Dems., Seminole, 1948-55; worker Utah Reps., Weber County, Utah, 1986-92; vol. Utah Sr. Citizen Legislature, Salt Lake City, 1988-92. With USNR, 1944-46, PTO. Mem. Toastmasters Internat. (area gov. 1990-91, div. coord. 1991-92), MENSA (proctor). Home: 3800 S 1900th W Apt 107 Roy UT 84067-3141

KNIGHT, GORDON RAYMOND, electronics executive; b. Oakland, Calif., Oct. 6, 1940; s. Bert Norman and Ruth Edna (Sommers) K.; m. Nancy Elisabeth Hennings, June 10, 1962 (div. Dec. 1980); m. Doris Yuan-Ping Ma, Dec. 19, 1981; children: Gregory, Marshall, Michael. SB, MIT, 1962; MS, Stanford U., 1964, PhD, 1967. Engr. Lockheed Missiles and Space Co., Sunnyvale, Calif., 1962-63; sr. engr. Sylvania Electronic Def. Labs., Mountain View, Calif., 1963-69, Ampex Corp., Redwood City, Calif., 1969-70; mgr. Rsch. Ctr. Xerox, Palo Alto, Calif., 1970-80; founder, dir. engring. Optimen Corp., Sunnyvale, 1980-86; co-founder, v.p. engring. Maxoptix/Maxtor Corp., San Jose, Calif., 1986—. Republican. Office: Maxoptix Corp 2520 Junction Ave San Jose CA 95134

KNIGHT, JAMES RODNEY, JR., financial consultant; b. Salt Lake City, July 16, 1949; s. James Rodney Sr. and Arlene (Karren) K.; m. Monica Lee Nance, Aug. 15, 1974; children: Lindsey, Jamie, Nicole, Michael. BS in Fin., U. Utah, 1972. CFP. Real estate salesman Sweetwater Park, Salt Lake City, 1972-75; real estate broker J.R. Knight & Assoc., Reno, Nev., 1975-80; fin. cons. Am. Planning Group, Reno, Nev., 1980-82, Clark Fin. Corp., Salt Lake City, 1982-86; pres., fin. cons. Physician Fin. Svcs., Salt Lake City, 1986—. Varsity scout coach Boy Scouts Am., Centerville, Utah, 1987-90. Mem. Internat. Assn. for Fin. Planning (bd. dirs. 1986—, pres. 1990-91, chmn. 1991-92), Centerville/Farmington Rotary. Republican. Mem. LDS Ch. Office: Physician Fin Svcs 2040 E 4800 S Salt Lake City UT 84117

KNIGHT, JEFFREY RICHARD, systems requirements analyst; b. Salt Lake City, Apr. 22, 1962; s. Richard M. and Donna H. (Hallman) K. BBA, Calif. State Poly. Inst. U., 1984, MBA, 1986. With Unisys, Camarillo, Calif., 1985—; pres. Co. Activities Coordinating Com., Camarillo, 1991-93. Chmn. Calif. State Poly. Inst. U. Rose Float Com., 1984-85. Mem. Co. Mgmt. Assn., Thailand Darts Assn., Rose Float Alumni Assn. (treas. 1985-86, bd. dirs. 1987-88, pres. 1991-93), Southern Calif. Darts Assn. Republican. Home: 1340 E Hillcrest Dr Apt 4 Thousand Oaks CA 91362-2559 Office: Unisys 5151 Camino Ruiz Camarillo CA 93012-8625

KNIGHT, PHILIP H(AMPSON), shoe manufacturing company executive; b. Portland, Oreg., Feb. 24, 1938; s. William W. and Lota (Hatfield) K.; m. Penelope Parks, Sept. 13, 1968; children: Matthew, Travis. B.B.A., U. Oreg.; M.B.A., Stanford U. C.P.A., Oreg. Chmn., chief exec. officer, past pres. Nike, Inc., Beaverton, Oreg., 1967—. Bd. dirs. U.S.-Asian Bus. Coun., Washington, 1st lt. AUS, 1959-60. Named Oreg. Businessman of Yr., 1982, One of 1988's Best Mgrs., Bus. Week Magazine. Mem. AICPA. Republican. Episcopalian. Office: Nike Inc 1 Bowerman Dr Beaverton OR 97005*

KNIGHT, THOMAS J., JR., computer consultant; b. San Antonio, Oct. 21, 1955; s. Thomas Jefferson and Martha Lena (Craig) K.; m. Lois Ann Simmons, July 13, 1985; 1 child, Thomas Jefferson III. BS, Baylor U., 1978; M. Pub. Adminstrn., Golden Gate U., 1988. Commd. 2d lt. USAF, 1978, advanced thru grades to capt., 1988; chief of adminstrn. USAF 780th Radar Squadron, Fortuna AFB, N.D., 1978-79; squadron sect. comdr. USAF 325th Component Repair Squadron, Tyndall AFB, Fla., 1979-82; protocol officer USAF HQ Tactical Air Command, Langley AFB, Va., 1982-85; exec. officer USAF 487th Tactical Missile Wing, Comiso AS, Italy, 1985-86, USAF 57th Fighter Weapons Wing, Nellis AFB, Nev., 1986-90; resigned USAF, 1990; cons. Waco, Tex., 1990; software support mgr. Entré Computer Ctr., Waco, 1990—. Local commr. Panama City (Fla.) Boy Scouts Am., 1979-80. Mem. Air Force Assn. Presbyterian.

KNIGHT, THOMAS JOSEPH, history educator; b. Denton, Tex., Aug. 5, 1937; s. Thomas Daniel Knight and Laura Jo (Savage) Knight Myrick; m. Barbara Lorraine Jones, Dec. 29, 1955; children: Russell Alan, Karen Jeanne. BA, North Tex. State U., Denton, 1959; postgrad., U. Minn., 1959-61; PhD, U. Tex., 1967. Instr. history U. Nebr., Lincoln, 1964-65; asst. prof. humanities Mich. State U., East Lansing, 1966-68; asst. prof., then assoc. prof. Pa. State U., Harrisburg, 1968-76; assoc. dean, prof. social scis. Pa. State U., University Park, 1976-82; dean, prof. history U. W.Va., Morgantown, 1982-86, Colo. State U., Ft. Collins, 1986—; cons. Orgn. Econ. Coop. and Devel., Paris, 1982. Author: Latin America Comes of Age, 1979, Technology's Future, 1982. Trustee Univ. Press Colo., Niwot, 1989—. Mem. World History Assn., Nat. Assn. Sci., Tech. and Society, Am. Acad. Polit. and Social Sci., Phi Alpha Theta. Democrat. Unitarian. Home: 2006 Brookwood Dr Fort Collins CO 80525-1212 Office: Colo State U Dept History Fort Collins CO 80523

KNIGHT, VICK, JR. (RALPH KNIGHT), fundraising counselor, educator, dean; b. Lakewood, Ohio, Apr. 6, 1928; s. Vick Ralph and Janice (Higgins) K. BS, U. So. Calif., 1952; MA, L.S. State Coll., 1956; postgrad. Whittier Coll., 1959-61, Long Beach State Coll., 1960-61, Calif. State Coll.-Fullerton, 1961-64, Claremont U., 1963-65; EdD, Calif. Coast U., 1991; m. Beverly Joyce McKeighan, Apr. 14, 1949 (div. 1973); children: Stephen Foster, Mary Ann; m. Carolyn Schlee, June 6, 1981. Producer-dir. Here Comes Tom Harmon radio series ABC, Hollywood, Calif., 1947-50; tchr., vice-prin. Ranchito Sch. Dist., Pico Rivera, Calif., 1952-59; prin. Kraemer Intermediate Sch., Placentia, Calif., 1959-64; dir. instructional svcs. Placentia Unified Sch. Dist., 1964-65, asst. supt., 1965-71; program dir. World Vista Travel Svcs., 1970-72; bd. dir. grad. extension La Verne Coll., 1971-73; v.p. Nat. Gen. West Investments, 1971-74; bd. dir. community rels. and devel. Childrens Hosp. of Orange County (Calif.), 1974-84; sr. dir. curriculum and edn. svcs. Elsinore Union High Sch. Dist., Lake Elsinore, Calif., 1985-88; exec. dir. Elsinore Valley Community Devel. Corp., 1989-92; dean Sch. Edn. Newport U., Newport Beach, Calif., 1992—; pres. Aristan Assocs.; bd. dir. Key Records, Hollywood. Dist. chmn. Valencia council Boy Scouts Am.; chmn. Cancer Soc. Ptnrs. of Ams., also chmn. Sister City Com.; chmn. of Community Chest Drives; chmn. adv. com. Esperenza Hosp.; mem. Educare; hon. life mem. Calif. PTA. Bd. dirs. U. Calif.-Irvine Friends of Library, pres., 1975-77; bd. trustees Lake Elsinore Unified Sch. Dist., 1991, pres. 1993; bd. dirs. Muckenthaler Cultural Groups Found.; chmn. bd. William Claude Fields Found. Club With USN, 1946-48. Recipient Disting. Citizen award Whittier Coll., 1960; Educator of Yr. award Orange County Press Club, 1971, Author and Book award U. Calif., 1973, Children's Lit. award Calif. State U.-Fullerton, 1979, Bronze Pelican award Boy Scouts Am. Mem. Nat. Sch. Pub. Rels. Assn. (regional v.p.), U.S. Jr. C. of C. (bd. dir., Young Man of Calif. 1959), Calif. Jr. C. of C. (state v.p.), Pico Rivera Jr. C. of C. (pres.), Audubon Soc., Western Soc. Naturalists, Calif. Tchrs. Assn., NEA, Internat. Platform Assn., ASCAP, Soc. Children's Book Writers, Authors Guild, Authors League Am., Anti-Slubberdegullion Soc., Bank Dicks, Assn. Hosp. Devel., Art Experience, Good Bears of World, Los Compadres con Libros, Blue Key, Skull and Dagger, Les Amis du Vin, Phi Sigma Kappa, Alpha Delta Sigma, E Clampus Vitus, Theta Nu Epsilon, Kiwanian (pres.), Mason, Canyon Lake Home Owners Club (pres. 1989—), West Atwood Yacht (commodore) Club. Writer weekly Nature Notebook newspaper columns, 1957—, wine columnist Riverside Press-Enterprise, 1991—; fine arts editor Placentia Courier; editor curriculum guides: New Math., Lang. Arts, Social Scis., Pub. Rels., Biol. Sci. Substitute Tchrs; author: (ecology textbooks) It's Our World; It's Our Future; It's Our Choice, Snakes of Hawaii, Earle the Squirrel, Night the Crayons Talked; My Word!; Send for Haym Salomon!. Joby and the Wishing Well; Twilight of the Animal Kingdom; A Tale of Twos, Who's Zoo, A Navel Salute, Friend or Enema?, John Sevier: Citizen Soldier, also math. instrn. units; contbr. articles to various jours. Home: 22597 Canyon Lake Dr S Sun City CA 92587-7573

KNIGHT, WILLIAM J. (PETE KNIGHT), state legislator, retired military officer; b. Noblesville, Ind., Nov. 18, 1929; s. William T. and Mary Emma (Illyes) K.; m. Helena A Stone, June 7, 1958; children: William Pete, David, Stephen; m. Gail A. Johnson, Sept. 3, 1983. BS, Air Force Inst. Tech., 1958; student, Indsl. Coll. Armed Forces, 1973-74. Commd. 2d lt. USAF, 1953, advanced through grades to col., 1971; fighter pilot Kinross AFB, Mich., 1953-56; exptl. test pilot Edwards AFB, Calif., 1958-69; exptl. test pilot, Viet Nam, 1969-70; dir. test and deployment F-15 program, 1976; dir. Flight Attack System Program Office, 1977-79; vice comdr. Air Force Flight Test Ctr. Edwards AFB, 1979-82; ret. USAF, 1982; mayor City of Palmdale, Calif., 1988-92; elected rep. Calif. State Assembly, 1992—; v.p. Eidetics Internat., Torrance, Calif., 1988-92. Decorated D.F.C. with 2 oak leaf clusters, Legion of Merit with 2 oak leaf clusters, Air medal with 11 oak leaf clusters, Astronauts Wings; recipient Octave Chanute award, 1968, Harmony trophy, 1968, citation of honor Air Force Assn., 1969; winner Allison Jet Trophy Race, 1954;p named to Nat. Aviation Hall of Fame, 1988, Lancaster Aerospace Walk of Honor, 1990. Fellow AIAA (assoc.), Soc. Exptl. Test Pilots (past pres.); mem. Air Force Assn., Internat. Order of Characters, Aerospace Primus Club, Daedalians, Elks. Holder world's speed record for winged aircraft, 4520 m.p.h., 1967. Home: 220 Eagle Ln Palmdale CA 93551-3613 Office: Calif State Assemby Sacramento CA 94249-0001

KNIGHTEN, ROBERT LEE, software engineer, mathematician; b. Coos Bay, Oreg., May 7, 1940; s. Darrel Clayborn and Emily Ella (Williams) K.; m. Carol Susan Marians, June 1, 1963; children: Rachel Sylvia, Daniel Joseph. BS, MIT, 1966, PhD, 1962. Instr. U. Chgo., 1966-68; prof. U. Ill., Chgo., 1968-71, U. P.R., Rio Piedras, 1971-83; software engr. Sof Tech, Waltham, Mass., 1983-86, Prime Computer, Framingham, Mass., 1986-88, Encore Computer, Marlboro, Mass., 1988-91, Intel Supercomputer, Beaverton, Oreg., 1991—; chmn. POSIX P1003.14 IEEE, 1989—. Mem. IEEE Computer Soc., Am. Math Assn., Math Assn. of Am., Assn. for Computer Mach., Soc. for Indusl. Applied Math. Home: 12905 SW Butner Rd Beaverton OR 97005 Office: Intel Supercomputer 15201 NW Greenbrier Pky Beaverton OR 97006

KNIGHTON, ROBERT SYRON, neurosurgeon, educator; b. Vallejo, Calif., Aug. 17, 1914; s. David William and Mae Virginia (Clauson) K.; m. Cora Louise Taylor, Sept. 9, 1939; children—Robert W., George L., James E., Joan L., Thomas D. B.S., Pacific Union Coll., 1939; M.D., Loma Linda U., 1942. Diplomate Am. Bd. Neurol. Surgery. Intern Los Angeles County Hosp., 1942-43; resident in neurosurgery White Meml. Hosp., Los Angeles, 1943-44, 46-47; NRC fellow Montreal Neurol. Inst., Que., Can., 1947-48; chief div. neurosurgery Henry Ford Hosp., Detroit, 1952-71, chmn. dept. neurology and neurosurgery, 1971-79, emeritus chmn. dept. neurology and neurosurgery, cons., 1979—; prof. neurosurgery, chmn. div. neurosurgery Loma Linda U., Calif., 1981—; chief neurosurgeon Jerry L. Pettis VA Hosp., Loma Linda, Calif., 1982—; clin. prof. surgery U. Mich., Ann Arbor, 1971-79. Editor: Reticular Formations of Brain, 1957, Pain, 1966; contbr. papers to profl. publs. Served to capt. U.S. Army, 1944-46; ETO. Fellow ACS; mem. Soc. Neurol. Surgeons, Am. Assn. Neurol. Surgeons, Am. Acad. Neurol. Surgeons (v.p. 1977), Neurosurg. Soc. Am. (pres. 1975), Calif. Med. Assn., San Bernardino County Med. Soc. Home: 9388 Avenida San Timoteo Beaumont CA 92223-4314 Office: Loma Linda U Div Neurol Surgery 11234 Anderson St Loma Linda CA 92354-2870

KNIGHTON, WALTER BERKETT, IV, chemist, educator; b. West Chester, Pa., Dec. 24, 1955; s. Walter Berkett III and Charlotte (Darlington) K.; m. MaryAnne Coppersmith, Aug. 26, 1978; children: Kelsey, Cale, Wade. BS in Chemistry, Mont. State U., 1978, MS in Phys. Chemistry, 1980, PhD in Analytical Chemistry, 1984. Asst. prof. Franklin and Marshall Coll., Lancaster, Pa., 1984-87; adj. asst. prof. Mont. State U., Bozeman, 1984, 87, rsch. assoc., 1988-92, rsch. assoc. prof., 1993—. Contbr. articles to profl. jours. Grantee Gen. Telephone and Electric, 1984, EG&G Idaho Inc., 1992; A. Paul Thompson scholar, 1977-78, B.L. Johnson Meml. scholar, 1976. Mem. Am. Chem. Soc., Am. Soc. Mass Spectrometry, Sigma Xi. Office: Mont State U Dept Chemistry Bozeman MT 59717

KNITTLE, WILLIAM JOSEPH, JR., media executive, psychologist, religious leader; b. Santa Monica, Calif., June 11, 1945; s. William Joseph Knittle and Lahlee (Duggins) Morrell; m. Linda Catherine Black, Apr. 19, 1969 (div. Aug. 1977); 1 child, Kristen Elizabeth; m. Alexis Carrell Upton, Sept. 30, 1977; 1 child, Jonathan Kynan. BA in English, Loyola U., Los Angeles, 1966, MA in Communication Arts, 1970, MA in Counseling Psychology, 1973; PhD in Communication Theory and Social Psychology, Lawrence U., Santa Barbara, Calif., 1976; D of Dharma in Asian Religion and Philosophy, U. Oriental Studies, 1980; MBA, U. La Verne, 1983. Ordained Sramanera, Buddhist monk, 1976, ordained Bikkhu, 1977. Assoc. editor Black Belt mag., 1960-65; asst. news dir. Sta. KHJ-TV, Los Angeles, 1966-67; news editor Sta. KFWB Radio, Los Angeles, 1967-69; dir. news and pub. info. Loyola Marymount U., Los Angeles, 1969-75; gen. mgr. Media Five, Los Angeles, 1976-79, v.p., 1981-83; assoc. dir. div. of continuing edn. U. La Verne, Calif., 1979-81; pres. Western News Assocs., Los Angeles, 1983—; asst. to dean UCLA Sch. Medicine, 1985-86; advt./mktg. dir. summer sessions UCLA, 1986—; founder Realization Therapy, 1977. Author: Survival Strategies for the Classroom Teacher, 1982; columnist various newspapers, mags., 1970—; Hollywood corr. Columbia mag., 1974-87; contbr. articles to profl. jours. Asst. abbot Internat. Buddhist Med. Ctr., L.A., 1976-81; bd. mem. Dharma Vijaya Buddhist Vihara, L.A., 1985—; mem. So. Calif. Buddhist Sangha Coun., L.A. Buddhist Union. Recipient Martial Arts Pioneer award Am. Tae Kwon Do-Kung Fu Assn., 1976, Nat. Headliners award Wash. Press Club, 1968, Internat. Journalism award Sigma Delta Chi, 1968. Mem. AAAS, Assn. for Transpersonal Psychology, Inst. for Holistic Edn., Soc. Interdisciplinary Study of Mind, Internat. Brotherhood of Magicians, Internat. Imagery Assn., Am. Soc. Tng. and Devel., Nat. Book Critics Circle, Investigative Reporters and Editors, Am. Fedn. Police (chaplain 1985—), Nat. Police Acad. Home and Office: Western News Assocs PO Box 24130 Los Angeles CA 90024-0130

KNIZE, RANDALL JAMES, physics educator; b. Tacoma, Feb. 4, 1953; s. Howard James and Nathalie (Gage) K. BA, MS, U. Chgo., 1975; MA, Harvard U., 1976, PhD, 1981. Staff physicist Princeton (N.J.) U., 1980-88; asst. prof. physics U. So. Calif., L.A., 1988—. Patentee hydrogen in metals; contbr. papers to sci. jours. NSF fellow, 1975-79. Mem. Am. Phys. Soc. Office: U So Calif Dept Physics MC 0484 Los Angeles CA 90089

KNOEPFLER, PETER TAMAS, psychiatrist, organizational consultant; b. Vienna, Austria, Mar. 14, 1929; came to U.S., 1947, naturalized, 1962; s. Joseph and Claire (Farkas) K.; m. Gayle Kurth, July 3, 1960; children: David, Daniel, Paul. B.S., Calif. Inst. Tech., 1950; M.A., Columbia U., 1951; M.D., Cornell U., 1955. Diplomate Am. Bd. Psychiatry and Neurology. Intern Meth. Hosp. of Bklyn., 1955-56; resident Albert Einstein Coll. Medicine, N.Y.C., 1956-57, 59-61; practice medicine specializing in psychiatry Bellevue, Wash., 1970—; assoc. med. dir. U. Utah Student Health Service, Salt Lake City, 1962-69; staff psychiatrist Menninger Found., Topeka, 1969-70; mem. faculty Menninger Sch. Psychiatry, 1969-70; med. dir. Eastside Community Health Center, Bellevue, 1970-73; mem. staff Fairfax Hosp., Kirkland, Wash., Overlake Hosp., Bellevue, Snoqualmie Valley Hosp.; clin. assoc. prof. psychiatry and behavioral scis. U. Wash., Seattle, 1970-79; clin. prof. psychiatry U. Wash., 1979—; adj. faculty Union Grad. Sch., Yellow Springs, Ohio, 1974—, Antioch West, 1979—; lectr., cons. in field; instr. Am. Group Psychotherapy Ann. Inst., 1976-79; cons. AEC, 1966-68, Planned Parenthood of Bellevue, 1971—, Youth Eastside Services, Bellevue, 1970—, Rosehill Inst., Toronto, Ont., Can., 1973—, Peace Corps, 1964-66, Little Sch. Bellevue, 1972-74, Juvenile Ct. Kings County, Wash., 1972—, Skid Road Community Council, Seattle, 1973-76, Rice Inst., 1975—; mem. exec. med. com. Planned Parenthood Seattle, King County, 1974—. Editorial bd.: Adolescent Psychiatry, 1974—, Jour. Sex Edn. and

Therapy. Mem. adv. bd. Solo Ctr., Seattle, 1974-77; mem. Radio Emergency Associated Citizens Team, 1977-79; bd. dirs. Eliot Inst., Friends of King County Library; bd. dirs. Unitarian Universalist Assn., vice chmn., 1975-77; bd. dirs. Seabeck Christian Conf. Group. Served to capt. M.C. USAF, 1957-59. Recipient Vol. of Yr. award Planned Parenthood of King County, 1980; named Physician of Yr., 1974, Citizen of Day. Fellow Am. Psychiat. Assn. (life), Am. Soc. Adolescent Psychiatry (life, exec. com. 1973-75); mem. Soc. Sci. Study Sex (pres. western region 1989), Am. Assn. Sex Educators, Counsellors and Therapists (dir. 1979-84, treas. N.W. region 1976-79), Am. Soc. Clin. Hypnotists, Internat. Soc. Adolescent Psychiatry (sci. adv. com.), Am. Group Psychotherapy Assn. (dir. 1979-81), N.W. Group Psychotherapy Assn. (pres. 1978-81), N.W. Soc. Adolescent Psychiatry (pres. 1973-75), Internat. Assn. Yoga Therapists. Office: 1621 114th Ave SE Ste 221 Bellevue WA 98004-6979

KNOLLER, GUY DAVID, lawyer; b. N.Y.C., July 23, 1946; s. Charles and Odette Knoller; children—Jennifer Judy, Geoffrey David. B.A. cum laude, Bloomfield (N.J.) Coll., 1968; J.D. cum laude, Ariz. State U., 1971. Bar: Ariz. 1971, U.S. dist. ct. Ariz. 1971, U.S. Sup. Ct. 1976. Trial atty. atty. gen.'s honor program Dept. Justice, 1971-72; atty., adv., NLRB, 1972-73, field atty. region 28, Phoenix, 1972-74; assoc. Powers, Ehrenreich, Boutell & Kurn, Phoenix, 1974-79; ptnr. Froimson & Knoller, Phoenix, 1979-81; sole practice, Phoenix, 1981-84; ptnr. Fannin, Terry & Hay, P.A., 1984-85; sole practice, Phoenix, 1985—; of counsel Burns & Burns. Mem. bd. visitors Ariz. State U. Coll. Law, 1975-76; pres. Ariz. Theatre Guild, 1990, 91. Fellow Ariz. Bar Found.; mem. ABA, State Bar Ariz. (chmn. labor relations sect. 1977-78), Ariz. State U. Coll. Law Alumni Assn. (pres. 1977). Office: 3550 N Central Ave Ste 1401 Phoenix AZ 85012

KNOOP, VERN THOMAS, civil engineer, consultant; b. Paola, Kans., Nov. 19, 1932; s. Vernon Thomas and Nancy Alice (Christian) K. Student, Kans. U., 1953-54; BSCE, Kans. State U., 1959. Registered profl. engr., Calif. Surveyor James L. Bell, Surveyors and Engrs., Overland Park, Kans., 1954; engr. asst. to county engr. Miami County Hwy. Dept., Paola, 1955; engr. State of Calif. Dept. Water Resources, L.A., 1959-85, sr. engr., 1986-88; chief, water supply evaluations sect. State of Calif. Dept. Water Resources, L.A., Glendale, 1989—; hydrology tchr. State of Calif. Dept. Water Resources, L.A., 1984; mem. Interagency Drought Task Force, Sacramento, 1988-91. Mem. Jefferson Ednl. Found., Washington, 1988-91, Heritage Found., Washington, 1988-91, Nat. Rep. Senatorial Com., Washington, 1990-91, Rep. Presdl. Task Force, Washington, 1990-91. With U.S. Army, 1956-57. Decorated Good Conduct medal U.S. Army, Germany, 1957. Mem. ASCE (dir. L.A. sect. hydraulics/water resources mgmt. tech. group 1985-86, chmn. 1984-85), Profl. Engrs. in Calif. Govt. (dist. suprs. rep. 1986—), Singles Internat. Baptist. Home: 116 N Berendo St Los Angeles CA 90004-4785 Office: State of Calif Dept Water Resources 770 Fairmont Ave Glendale CA 91203-1035

KNOPF, KENT RONALD, health facility administrator; b. Bellflower, Calif., Apr. 8, 1963; s. Keith Ronald and Florice Fern (Moffett) K. ASN, N.Y. State Regents, Albany, 1991; BS in Biology, Calif. State U., Long Beach, 1988, BA in Comm., 1988. RN. Adminstr. Bellwood Gen. Hosp., Bellflower, 1986-88; dir. cardiac svcs. Los Cerritos Med. Group, Cerritos, Calif., 1988-90; pres. Profl. Healthcare Assocs., Corona, Calif., 1990—. Mem. ANA, Am. Heart Assn. (instr. 1990-92), Calif. Nurses Assn., Pacific Harbor Assocs. (capt. 1990—). Office: Profl Healthcare Assocs 2621 Green River Rd Ste 105-150 Corona CA 91720

KNOTT, WILEY EUGENE, electronic engineer; b. Muncie, Ind., Mar. 18, 1938; s. Joseph Wiley and Mildred Viola (Haxton) K.; 1 child, Brian Evan. BSEE, Tri-State U., 1963; postgrad. Union Coll., 1970-73, Ga. Coll., 1987. Assoc. aircraft engr. Lockheed-Ga. Co., Marietta, 1963-65; tech. publs. engr. GE, Pittsfield Mass., 1965-77, sr. publs. engr., 1977-79, group leader, 1967-79; specialist engr. Boeing Mil. Airplane Co., Wichita, Kans., 1979-81, sr. specialist engr., 1981-84, 89-90, logistics mgr., 1984-85, customer support mgr., 1985-89; base mgr. Castle AFB, 1990-91; facilities plant ops. and maintenance engr. Everett (Wash.) div. Boeing Comml. Airplane Group, 1991-92, lead engr. 1992—; part-time bus. cons., 1972—. Active Jr. Achievement, 1978-79, Am. Security Council, 1975-90, Nat. Rep. Senatorial Com., 1979-86 , Nat. Rep. Congl. Com., 1979-87, Rep. Nat. Com., 1979-87 , Rep. Presdl. Task Force, 1981-86, Joint Presdl./Congl. Steering Com., 1982-86, Rep. Polit. Action Com., 1979-86, Mus. of Aviation, 1987—; state advisor U.S. Congl. Adv. Bd., 1981-86; adviser Jr. Achievement, 1978-79. With AUS, 1956-59. Mem. Am. Def. Preparedness Assn. (life), Am. Mgmt. Assn., Soc. Logistics Engrs., U.S. Golf Assn. (assoc.), Fraternal Order Police (assoc.), Am. Fedn. Police (assoc.), Am. Assn. Retired Persons, Air Force Assn. (life), Assn. Old Crows, Boeing Mgmt. Club, Nat. Audubon Soc. Methodist.

KNOTT, WILLIAM ALAN, library director, library management and building consultant; b. Muscatine, Iowa, Oct. 4, 1942; s. Edward Marlan and Dorothy Mae (Holzhauer) K.; m. Mary Farrell, Aug. 23, 1969; children: Andrew Jerome, Sarah Louise. BA in English, U. Iowa, 1967, MA in L.S., 1968. Asst. dir. Ottumwa (Iowa) Pub. Libr., 1968-69; libr. cons. Iowa State Libr., Des Moines, 1968-69; dir. Hutchinson (Kans.) Pub. Libr. and S. Cen. Kans. Libr. System, Hutchinson, 1969-71; dir. Jefferson County Pub. Libr., Lakewood, Colo., 1971—. Served with U.S. Army, 1965-67. Mem. ALA, Colo. Libr. Assn. Author: Books by Mail: A Guide, 1973; co-author: A Phased Approach to Library Automation, 1969; editor: Conservation Catalog, 1982. Office: Jefferson County Pub Libr 10200 W 20th Ave Lakewood CO 80215-1402

KNOWLES, JAMES KENYON, applied mechanics educator; b. Cleve., Apr. 14, 1931; s. Newton Talbot and Allyan (Gray) K.; m. Jacqueline De Bolt, Nov. 26, 1952; children: John Kenyon, Jeffrey Gray, James Talbot. SB in Math., MIT, 1952, PhD, 1957; DSc (hon.), Nat. U. Ireland, 1985. Instr. math. MIT, Cambridge, 1957-58; asst. prof. applied mechanics Calif. Inst. Tech., Pasadena, 1958-61, assoc. prof., 1961-65, prof. applied mechanics, 1965—, William R. Kenan, Jr. prof., 1991—; cons. in field. Contbr. articles to profl. jours. Recipient Eringen medal Soc. Engring. Sci., 1991. Fellow ASME, Am. Acad. Mechanics. Home: 522 Michillinda Way Sierra Madre CA 91024-1066 Office: Calif Inst Tech Div Engring and Applied Sci 104-44-1201 E California Blvd Pasadena CA 91125-0001

KNOWLES, RALPH LEWIS, architectural engineer, educator; b. Cleve., Dec. 9, 1928; s. Tom and Florence Kathleen (Ritchie) K.; m. Mary Elizabeth Rogers, Apr. 2, 1955; children: Elizabeth Leigh, John Lewis, Lauren Anne. B in Architecture, N.C. State U., 1954; M of Architecture, MIT, 1959. Registered architect. Asst. prof. of Architecture Auburn (Ala.) U., 1959-63, U. So. Calif., L.A., 1963; assoc. prof. of Architecture U. So. Calif., 1964-68, prof. of Architecture, 1968—; cons. to pvt. archtl. and planning firms, 1959—; solar policy and design cons., 1968—; lectr. Circa 50 and 100 lecture series, 1981-90. Author: (books) Sun, Wind, Water, 1967, Form and Stability, 1968, Energy and Form: An Ecological Framework for Settlement, 1969, Sun, 1976, Energia E Forma, 1981, Sun Rhythm Form, 1981; co-author (with Richard Berry) Solar Envelope Concepts: Moderate Density Building Applications, 1979; contbr. numerous articles to profl. jours. With USN, 1946-48. Recipient Grand Nat. award 4th Ann. Ruberoid Competition, 1962, award for Teaching Excellence, U. So. Calif., 1970, AIA Medal for Rsch., 1974, Design Arts Grants Recognition, Nat. Endowment for the Arts, 1980; grantee Fulbright Teaching fellowship, Slovak Tech. U., Bratislava, 1993, Container Corp. Am., 1961-62, L.A. Dept. Water & Power, 1968, Albert C. Martin and Assocs., L.A., 1979, Solar EnergyRsch. Inst., 1979-81. Office: U So Calif Sch Architecture Los Angeles CA 90089-0291

KNOWLES, RANDALL GENE, financial planner; b. Great Falls, Mont., Nov. 15, 1951; s. Vernon James and Joyce Ann (Zbinden) K.; m. Sheryl Jean Sanders, Jan. 2, 1971; children: Karen Angela Knowles-Hermann, Jennifer Kim. BS in Econs., Mont. State U., 1974. Registered fin. planner. Banker First Bank & First Inter-State, Great Falls, Mont., 1976-81; ins. agt. Lincoln. Nat. Life, Ft. Wayne, Ind., 1981—; assoc., invesmtent advisor Profl. Fin. Planning, Ft. Wayne, Ind., 1990—; pres. Mont. Fringe Benefits, 1989—; mem. Life Underwriters Tng. Coun., Washington, 1988—. Contbr. articles to profl. jours. Donor ARC, Great Falls, 1992. Mem. Nat. Life Underwriters Assn., Internat. Assn. Registered Fin. Planners, S.C.O.R.E., Nat. Rifle Assn. (estate planner 1989—), Toastmasters (pres. 1986, lt. gov. 1987, Toastmaster of Yr. 1987), Kiwanis (pres. 1985), Masons, Shriners, Scottish Rite. Home and Office: 3017 9th Ave S Great Falls MT 59405-3421

KNOWLES, RICHARD THOMAS, state legislator, retired army officer; b. Chgo., Dec. 20, 1916; s. John T. and Signe (Almcrantz) K.; m. Elizabeth Wood Chaney, 1974; children: Diane T. Knowles Buchwald, Katherine T. Knowles Buck, Rebecca T. Ebershoff, Richard J., Stanley W. Crosby III, Steven Chaney. Student, U. Ill., 1939-42; student Command and Gen. Staff Coll, Armed Forces Staff Coll., 1956, U.S. Army War Coll., 1959. Commd. 2d lt. U.S. Army, 1942, advanced through grades to lt. gen., 1970; exec., bn. comdr. 96th F.S. Bn., Far East Command, 1950-51; student, then instr. Command and Gen. Staff Coll., Ft. Leavenworth, Kan., 1951-55; chief budget and plans br. Office Dep. Chief of Staff, Personnel, U.S. Army, Washington, 1956-58; chief Establishments Bur., Hdqrs. U.S. Army Element, SHAPE, 1959-60, mil. asst. Office Chief of Staff, 1960-62; comdg. officer 3d U.S. Army Missile Command, Ft. Bragg, N.C., 1962-63; div. arty. comdr., asst. div. comdr. 11th Air Assault Div., Ft. Benning, Ga., 1963-65; asst. div. comdr. 1st Cav. Div., (airmobile), Ft. Benning, Vietnam, 1965-66; chief of staff II Field Force, Vietnam, 1966; comdg. gen. 196th Light Inf. Brigade, Vietnam, 1966-67, Task Force Oregon, Vietnam, 1967; asst. dep. chief of staff for mil. operations U.S. Army, Washington, 1967-70; asst. to chmn. Joint Chiefs of Staff, Washington, 1970-72; comdg. gen. I Corps Group, Korea, 1972-73; dep. comdr. 8th Army, Korea, 1973-74; ret., 1974; mgr. support services Northrop, Saudi Arabia, 1976-79; owner, operator The General's Store, 1980—; mem. N.Mex. Ho. of Reps. Mem. commn. Conguistador council Boy Scouts Am. Decorated D.S.M. with 3 oak leaf clusters, Silver Star, Legion of Merit with two bronze oak leaf clusters, D.F.C. with bronze oak leaf cluster, Bronze Star with V device and oak leaf cluster, Air medal with 25 oak leaf clusters, Purple Heart, Vietnam Nat. Order 5th Class, Vietnam Gallantry Cross with 2 bronze palms, Vietnam Armed Forces Honor medal 1st Class, Order of Nat. Security Merit Guk-Seon medal Republic of Korea). Mem. Roswell C. of C. (pres.' club). Club: Rotary. Home: PO Box 285 Roswell NM 88202-0285

KNOX, CHUCK (CHARLES ROBERT KNOX), professional football coach; b. Sewickley, Pa., Apr. 27, 1932; s. Charles McMeehan and Helen (Keith) K.; m. Shirley Ann Rhine, Aug. 2, 1952; children: Christeen, Kathy, Colleen, Chuck. BA, Juniata Coll., 1954; postgrad., Pa. State U., 1955. Asst. football coach Wake Forest Coll., 1959-60, U. Ky., 1961-62, N.Y. Jets, 1963-66, Detroit Lions, 1967-72; head football coach Los Angeles Rams, 1973-78; head football coach, v.p. football ops. Buffalo Bills, 1978-82; head football coach Seattle Seahawks, 1983-91, Los Angeles Rams, 1992—. Named NFL Coach of Yr., Sporting News, 1973, 80, NFL Coach of Yr., Seattle Gold Helmet Com., 1983, 84. Lutheran. Club: Big Canyon Country. Office: care L A Rams 2327 W Lincoln Ave Anaheim CA 92801*

KNOX, RICHARD MARSHALL, software author, manufacturing executive; b. San Francisco, Apr. 15, 1933; s. George Livingston and Faith (Van Horn) K.; m. Frances Driscoll (div. 1980); children: Katherine, Robert, Russell, Barbara; m. Valentine Venyaminovna Zubareva, Nov. 10, 1981; children: George Livingston Knox, Valentina Zena Knox. BSME, Stanford U., 1955, MSME, 1959. Registered profl. engr., Calif. Project engr. Marquardt, Van Nuys, Calif., 1959-69; pres. Knox Data Inc., Valencia, Calif., 1969—, Knox Graphic Scis., Valencia, 1991—. Patentee in field. Capt. USAF, 1956-59. Office: Knox Graphic Scis 28170 Crocker #204 Valencia CA 91355

KNOX, SUSAN HIRSCH, occupational therapist; b. New London, Conn., Nov. 2, 1940; d. Fredrick Geake and Elizabeth Mellick (Smyth) Hirsch; m. Robert Leslie Knox, Jan. 3, 1965. BFA, U. N.Mex., 1962; MA, U. So. Calif., 1968, postgrad., 1989—. Registered occupational therapist. Vol. Peace Corps, Peru, 1963-65; occupational therapist Children's Hosp. L.A., 1967-73, dir. occupational therapy, 1973-82; sr. occupational therapist Glendale (Calif.) Adventist Med. Ctr., 1982—; clinic coord. Hyland Clinic, Van Nuys, Calif., 1982—; pvt. practice L.A., 1982—; mem. program com. Blind Children's Ctr., L.A., 1991—; profl. adv. bd. No. L.A. Regional Ctr., L.A., 1985-88; clin. faculty U. So. Calif., L.A., 1967—. Recipient traineeship Vocat. Rehab. Adminstrn., 1968, Dept. Edn., 1989-90, Health and Human Svcs., 1990-91. Fellow Am. Occupational Therapy Assn. (rep. 1976-80, 85-89, recorder 1983-85, Svc. award 1991, exec. bd. dirs. 1983-85); mem. Autism Soc., Occupational Therapy Assn. Calif. (sec. 1982-85, exec. bd. dirs. 1976-90, 82-90, Practice award 1988, Excellence award 1991), Sensory Integration Internat. (bd. dirs. 1982-86), Calif. Found. for Occupational Therapy (treas. 1984—). Home and Office: 3458 La Sombra Dr Hollywood CA 90068

KNUDESON, JASON, clergyman; b. Portland, Oreg., July 27, 1963; s. Dale and Shirley (Noseda) K.; m. Daryl Carnegie, Nov. 25, 1990; children: Sean, Casey. AA, Portland C.C., 1983; BS, Warner Pacific Coll., Portland, 1987; MDiv, North Park Theol. Sem., Chgo., 1991. Lic. min. Evang. Covenant Ch.; ordained minister, 1993. Intern pastor West Hills Covenant Ch., Portland, 1988-90; sr. pastor Sunset Covenant Ch., Portland, 1991—; active West Portland Pastors Prayer Meetings, 1989—; prayer chmn. Kroeze Bros. Crusade, Hillsboro, Oreg., spring 1992. Mem. Alpha Chi. Office: Sunset Covenant Ch 18555 NW Rock Creek Blvd Portland OR 97229

KNUDSON, MELVIN ROBERT, management consultant, business executive; b. Libby, Mont., Oct. 27, 1917; s. John and Serina (Bakken) K.; B.S. in Wood Chemistry, Oreg. State U., 1942; m. Melba Irene Joice, Mar. 5, 1946; children—Mark Bradley, Kevin Marie, Kari Lynne. Mgr. quality control J. Neils Lumber Co., Libby, Mont., 1946-55; mgr. research and devel. St. Regis Paper Co., Libby, 1955-65, div. dir. tech. devel., Tacoma, Wash., 1965-69, div. dir. short and long-range planning, 1969-70; exec. v.p. Property Holding and Devel. Co., Tacoma, 1970-75; exec. v.p. and gen. mgr. U.S. Computers, Inc., Tacoma, 1975-79; corp. mgmt., orgn., univ. governance and adminstrn. cons., 1979—; owner Knudson Travel, Tacoma, 1981—; pres., incorporator, Larex Internat. Corp.; adv. bd. Coll. Engring., Wash. State U., 1967—, chmn., 1971-73. Trustee 1st Luth. Ch., Libby, 1948-56, chmn., 1954-56; trustee Sch. Dist. #4, Libby, 1964-65; trustee Christ Luth. Ch., Tacoma, 1966-71, com. chmn.; trustee Greater Lakes Mental Health Clinic, 1969-73, com. chmn., 1970-73; bd. regents Pacific Luth. U., Tacoma, 1969—, chmn., 1976-81; mem. Steilacoom Improvement Com., 1971-73; chmn. Pacific Luth. U. Pres. Search Com., 1974-75; dir. Wauna Dance Club, 1976-79; dir. Pacific Luth. Univ. "Q" Club, 1976-86; bd. dirs. Tenzler Library, Tacoma, 1980-83, Crime Stoppers, 1981-84, Operation Night Watch, 1989. Served to lt. col. F.A., Paratroops, U.S. Army, 1941-46. Recipient Disting. Service award Pacific Luth. U., 1986. Mem. Wash. Realtors Assn., Wash. Securities Sales, Am. Governing Bds., Center for Study of Democratic Institutions. Republican. Clubs: Tacoma Country and Golf, Normana Male Chorus (Norwegian Singers Assn. Am.). Patentee high-temperature wood-drying process, patentee Ultrarefined Arabinogalactan product; developer domestic natural gum. Home: 6928 100th St SW Tacoma WA 98499-1819 Office: 1103 A St Ste 200 Tacoma WA 98438-1301

KNUDSON, THOMAS JEFFERY, journalist; b. Manning, Iowa, July 6, 1953; s. Melvin Jake and Coreen Rose (Nickum) K. B.A. in Journalism, Iowa State U., 1980. Reporter/intern Wall Street Jour., Chgo., summer 1979; staff writer Des Moines Register, 1980—. Author: (series) A Harvest of Harm: The Farm Health Crisis, 1984 (Pulitzer prize 1985); (series) Majesty and Tragedy; The Sierra in Peril, 1991 (Pulitzer Prize 1992). Recipient James W. Schwartz award Iowa State U., 1985, Nat. Press Club Robert Kozik award, 1992. Office: Sacramento Bee PO Box 15779 21st and Q Sts Sacramento CA 95852

KNUPP, LARRY SHELDON, judge; b. Whittier, Calif., Apr. 7, 1940; s. Wilber Sheldon and Mary Elmyra (Montgomery) K.; m. Jacque Lu Aldridge, Aug. 11, 1963; children: David, Linda. BA, Pomona Coll., 1961; JD, U. Calif., Berkeley, 1964. Bar: Calif. 1965. Ptnr. Knupp Knupp & Smith, Whittier, 1965-75; commr. Whittier Mcpl. Ct., Whittier, 1975-88, judge, 1989—. Mem. Sertoma Club (treas. 1988—). Republican. Home: Whittier Mcpl Ct 7339 Painter Ave Whittier CA 90601

KNUPP, PATRICK MICHAEL, applied mathematician consultant; b. Lebanon, Oreg., May 28, 1953; s. William Walter and Gisela Maria (Arendt) K.; m. Jennifer Sue Johns, July 13, 1985; 1 child, Kevin Johns Knupp. BS in Physics, Mont. State U., 1975; MA in Math., Wash. State U., 1978; PhD in Math., U. N.Mex., 1989. Systems analyst Physics Internat. Co., San Leandro, Calif., 1979-83, Kaman Scis. Corp., Albuquerque, 1983-88; cons. Ecodynamics Rsch. Assocs., Albuquerque, 1988—. Co-author: (with S. Steinberg) Fundamentals of Grid Generation; contbr. articles to profl. jours. Mem. Soc. for Indsl. and Applied Math., Sigma Xi. Office: Ecodynamics Rsch Assocs PO Box 9229 Albuquerque NM 87119

KNUSSMANN, WILLARD THEODORE, mechanical engineer; b. St. Louis, Aug. 3, 1942; s. Willard Ralph and Dorothy Lorretta (Mattes) K.; div.; children: Amy, Kristen, Jill. BSME, U. Mo., Rolla, 1965; MS in Engring. Mgmt., U. Mo., 1972; MBA, So. Ill. U., 1977; doctoral studies, St. Louis U., 1980-81. Registered profl. engr., Mo., Fla. Constrn. engr. Monsanto Co., St. Louis, 1969-71; mech. design engr. Monsanto Co., St. Peters, Mo., 1969; mgr. of engring. Monsanto Co., River, Conn., 1971; resident constrn. engr. Anheuser Busch Cos., St. Louis, 1971-79, sr. resident constrn. engr., 1979-83, engring. constrn. mgr., 1983—; instr. East Idaho Tech. Coll., 1990-91; cons. in field. Lt. (j.g.) USN, 1965-69, Vietnam. Mem. ASME. Lutheran.

KNUTESON, HAROLD DOUGLAS, electronic design and fabrication company executive; b. Spanish Fork, Utah, June 19, 1953; s. Harold and Donna Faye (Gardner) K.; m. Debra Ann Reed, 1972 (div. 1978); 1 child, Joey; m. Eileen Farley, Nov. 23, 1979; children: Cory, Kiel, Kira, Kayla, Kelsey. AS, Utah Tech. Coll., 1978. Electronics designer Tex. Instruments, Ridgecrest, Calif., 1978-81; mgr. Rocky Mountain Engring., Salt Lake City, 1981; sr. designer Computer Video Systems, Inc., Salt Lake City, 1981-82; sr. designer, computer cons. Eaton Corp., Salt Lake City, 1980-86; pres., chief exec. officer Artwerk Specialties, Salt Lake City, 1981—; exec. v.p. Cimsoft, Salt Lake City, 1984-86; regional mgr. Chinook Tech., Salt Lake City, 1987-89; pres., chief exec. officer The Diversified Group of Cos., Inc., Salt Lake City, 1990—; cons. Ashworth Acctg., Salt Lake City, 1987—, Mountain Tech., West Valley, Utah, 1987—. Author: I Have Two Hearts, 1987; inventor IC Spacesaver, 1984, Surface Mount Electronic Library, 1985. Recipient Disting. Leadership award Am. Biog. Inst., 1990. Mem. Blue Chips, Salt Lake Practical Shooters. Republican. Mormon. Home: 13201 S 3300 W Riverton UT 84065-6346 Office: Artwerk Specialties PO Box 897 Riverton UT 84065-0897

KNUTH, ELDON LUVERNE, engineering educator; b. Luana, Iowa, May 10, 1925; s. Alvin W. and Amanda M. (Becker) K.; m. Marie O. Parrat, Sept. 10, 1954 (div. 1973); children: Stephen B., Dale L., Margot O., Lynette M.; m. Margaret I. Nicholson, Dec. 30, 1973. B.S., Purdue U., 1949, M.S., 1950; Ph.D. (Guggenheim fellow), Calif. Inst. Tech., 1953. Aerothermodynamics group leader Aerophysics Devel. Corp., 1953-56; asso. research engr. dept. engring. UCLA, 1956-59, asso. prof. engring., 1960-65, prof. engring. and applied sci., 1965-91, prof. emeritus, 1991—, head chem., nuclear thermal div. dept. engring., 1963-65, chmn. energy kinetics dept., 1969-75, head molecular-beam lab., 1961-88; Gen. chmn. Heat Transfer and Fluid Mechanics Inst., 1959; vis. scientist, von Humboldt fellow Max-Planck Inst. für Strömungsforschung, Göttingen, Fed. Republic Germany, 1975-76. Author: Introduction to Statistical Thermodynamics, 1966; also numerous articles. Served with AUS, 1943-45. Mem. AIAA, Am. Soc. Engring. Edn., Am. Inst. Chem. Engrs., Combustion Inst., Soc. Engring. Sci., AAAS, Am. Phys. Soc., Am. Vacuum Soc., Sigma Xi, Tau Beta Pi, Gamma Alpha Rho, Pi Tau Sigma, Sigma Delta Chi, Pi Kappa Phi. Club: Gimlet (Lafayette, Ind.). Home: 18085 Boris Dr Encino CA 91316-4350

KNUTSON, ELLIOT KNUT, savings and loan association executive; b. Norma, N.D., May 25, 1924; s. Engvald and Cora (Knudson) K.; m. Patricia Loma Eaton, Aug. 19, 1944; children: Patrick, Dale, Dana. Grad., Mohall (N.D.) High Sch., 1942. Asst. v.p. Seattle First Nat. Bank, 1946-62; chmn., chief exec. officer Wash. Fed. Savs. & Loan, Seattle, 1962—. With USMC, 1943-46. Office: Wash Fed Savs & Loan Assn 425 Pike St Seattle WA 98101-2334

KNUTSON, JACK ROSS, electrical engineer; b. Kentfield, Calif., Dec. 9, 1955. BSEE, San Francisco State U., 1983; MSEE, San Jose State U., 1992. Registered profl. engr. Marine engr. Nat. Maritime, San Francisco, 1973-84; design engr. Tex. Instruments, Inc., Dallas, 1984-89; sr. application engr. ULSI Tech., Inc., San Jose, 1989-90; sr. design engr. Adaptec, Inc., Milpitas, Calif., 1990-92; cons. Resource Engring., Fremont, Calif., 1992—. Inventor hardware cursor control, 1989. Active East Bay Activity Ctr., Fremont, 1992. Mem. IEEE.

KNYCHA, JOSEF, journalist; b. Summerside, P.E.I., Can., Apr. 19, 1953; s. Michael Stanley and Marjorie Mary (Gallant) K. Student pub. schs., Auburn, N.S., Can. Reporter Halifax Herald Ltd., N.S., 1971-81; editor The Mirror, Cameron Publs., Kentville, N.S., 1981-82, editor The Register, 1982-84; bus./markets/automotive editor Star-Phoenix, Saskatoon, Sask., Can., 1984-89, asst. news editor, 1990—; editor Cross Country Publs., Brandon Man., 1989-90. Southam fellow U. Toronto. Mem. Automobile Journalists Assn. Can. (bd. dirs.), N.Y. Times Spl. Features Coun. Home: 705 Eastlake Ave, Saskatoon, SK Canada S7N 1A2 Office: The Star-Phoenix, 204 5th Ave N, Saskatoon, SK Canada S7K 2P1

KO, SEUNG KYUN, educator, consultant; b. Seoul, Korea, July 13, 1936; came to U.S., 1957; s. Byong Ryon and Hung Sun (Song) K.; m. Sook Jin Bae, Aug. 29, 1972; children: Young Min, Young Eun. BA, Coll. of Wooster, Ohio, 1962; MA, U. Pa., 1963, PhD, 1969. Instr. Lake Superior State Coll., Sault Ste Marie, Mich., 1967-68; asst. prof. Maryville (Tenn.) Coll., 1968-69; rsch. commr. Ministry of Fgn. Affairs, Seoul, 1972; lectr. Seoul Nat. U., 1972; assoc. prof. Hawaii Loa Coll., Kaneohe, 1972-78, prof., 1978—. Contbr. articles to profl. jours. Pres. Korean Sr. Citizens Coll., Honolulu, 1985. Mem. United Korean Soc. Hawaii (v.p., pres. Honolulu chpt. 1984). Home: 45-209 A Lilipuna Rd Kaneohe HI 96744 Office: Hawaii Pacific U Hawaii Loa Campus 45-045 Kam Hwy Kaneohe HI 96744

KOBIN, WILLIAM H., television station executive; b. Indpls., Feb. 26, 1929; s. Henry V. and Florence (Solomon) K.; m. Anne Hendrickson, Oct. 22, 1957; children—Christopher, Melissa, Matthew, Jennifer. B.A., U. Calif.-Berkeley, 1950; postgrad. NYU. Assoc. producer Dumont News, 1953-56; producer CBS News, 1956-61; ABC News, 1961-63; v.p. programming NET, 1963-72; v.p. Future Works div. CTW, 1972-77; pres., gen. mgr. Twin Cities Pub. TV, St. Paul, 1977-83; pres., chief exec. officer Community TV of So. Calif., 1983—. Bd. dirs. Minn. Dance Theatre, Spring Hill Conf. Ctr. Served with AUS, 1951-53. Recipient 2 Emmy nominations. Mem. Internat. Broadcast Inst., Central Ednl. Network (exec. com.). Home: 2632 Westridge Rd Los Angeles CA 90049-1234 Office: Sta KCET 4401 W Sunset Blvd Los Angeles CA 90027-6090

KOBLIN, DONALD DARYL, anesthesiologist, researcher; b. Chgo., Sept. 1, 1949; s. Alvin and Vera Koblin. BS, UCLA, 1971; PhD, U. Calif., Santa Cruz, 1975; MD, U. Miami, Fla., 1983. Diplomate Am. Bd. of Anesthesiology. Fellow Caltech, Pasadena, Calif., 1975-76; chemist U. Calif., San Francisco, 1976-81; resident in anesthesia Pa. State U., Hershey, 1983-86; assoc. prof. U. Calif., San Francisco, 1986—. Contbr. numerous articles to profl. jours. Mem. Am. Soc. Anesthesiologist, Internat. Anesthesia Rsch. Soc. Office: VA Hosp Dept Anesthesia 4150 Clement St San Francisco CA 94121-1598

KOBLIN, RONALD LEE, business management and development consultant; b. Santa Monica, Calif., Nov., 1946; s. Bernard Lewes and Sadie Irene K.; student U. Oreg., 1965, U. Ariz., 1967; B.A., Calif. State U., Northridge, 1969, postgrad., 1970-71; postgrad. U. So. Calif., 1971. With field advt. Procter & Gamble, 1969; urban planner cities of Compton and Simi Valley, Calif., 1970-72; dir. planning and constrn. Nat. Med. Enterprises, Beverly Hills, Calif., 1972-74; dir. planning and devel. Am. Nat. Group, Beverly Hills, 1974-75, v.p./cons. planning and devel.; founder, pres., vice chmn. bd. dirs. Art Showcases, Inc., Glendale, Calif., 1976-82; founder, owner Firstworld Travel of Century City, Inc., 1982—; cons. in bus. devel., mgmt. and sales; founder, pres. The Lewes Group, Inc. (formerly Concept Implementation Co.), 1982—, founder, pres. Softouch InfoCenters, Inc., 1990; hon. instr. Calif. State Poly. U., 1990. Office: PO Box 115 La Canada Flintridge CA 91012-0115

KOBZA, DENNIS JEROME, architect; b. Ullysses, Nebr., Sept. 30, 1933; s. Jerry Frank and Agnes Elizabeth (Lavicky) K.; B.S., Healds Archtl. Engring., 1959; m. Doris Mae Riemann, Dec. 26, 1953; children—Dennis Jerome, Diana Jill, David John. Draftsman, designer B.L. Schroder, Palo Alto, Calif., 1959-60; sr. draftsman, designer Ned Abrams, Architect, Sunnyvale, Calif., 1960-61, Kenneth Elvin, Architect, Los Altos, Calif., 1961-62; partner B.L. Schroder, Architect, Palo Alto, 1962-66; pvt. practice architecture, Mountain View, Calif., 1966—. Served with USAF, 1952-56. Recipient Solar PAL award, Palo Alto, 1983, Mountain View Mayoral award, 1979. Mem. C. of C. (dir. 1977-79, Archtl. Excellence award Hayward chpt. 1985, Outstanding Indsl. Devel. award Sacramento chpt., 1980) , AIA (chpt. dir. 1973), Constrn. Specifications Inst. (dir. 1967-68), Am. Inst. Plant Engrs., Nat. Fedn. Ind. Bus. Orgn. Club: Rotary (dir. 1978-79, pres. 1986-87). Home: 3840 May Ct Palo Alto CA 94303-4545 Office: 2083 Old Middlefield Way Mountain View CA 94043

KOCAOGLU, DUNDAR F., engineering manager, industrial engineer, civil engineer, educator; b. Turkey, June 1, 1939; came to U.S., 1960; s. Irfan and Meliha (Uzay) K.; m. Alev Baysak, Oct. 17, 1968; 1 child, Timur. BSCE, Robert Coll., Istanbul, Turkey, 1960; MSCE, Lehigh U., 1962; MS in Indsl. Engring., U. Pitts., 1972, PhD in Ops. Rsch., 1976. Registered profl. engr., Pa., Oreg. Design engr. Modjeski & Masters, Harrisburg, Pa., 1962-64; ptnr. TEKSER Engring. Co., Istanbul, 1966-69; project engr. United Engrs., Phila., 1964-71; rsch. asst. U. Pitts., 1972-74, vis. asst. prof., 1974-76, assoc. prof. indsl. engring., dir. engring. mgmt., 1976-87; prof., dir. engring. mgmt. program, Portland State U., 1987—; pres. TMA-Tech. Mgmt. Assocs., Portland, Oreg., 1973—, pres. Portland Internat. Conf. Mgmt. Engring. and Tech., 1990—. Author: Engineering Management, 1981; editor: Management of R&D and Engineering, 1992; co-editor: Technology Management—The New International Language, 1991; series editor Wiley Series in Engring. and Tech. Mgmt.; contbr. articles on tech. mgmt. to profl. jours. Lt. C.E., Turkish Army, 1966-68. Fellow IEEE (Centennial medal 1984, editor-in-chief trans. on engring. mgmt. 1986—); mem. Inst. Mgmt. Scis. (chmn. Coll. Engring. Mgmt. 1979-81), Am. Soc. Engring. Edn. (chmn. engring. mgmt. div. 1982-83), IEEE Engring. Mgmt. Soc. (fellow, publs. dir. 1982-85), ASCE (mem. engring. mgmt. adminstrv. com. 1988—), Muhendis, Ilim Adamlari ve Mimarlar Dernegi Soc. Turkish Engrs. and Scientists (hon.), Am. Soc. Engring. Mgmt. (dir. 1981-86), Omega Rho (pres. 1984-86).

KOCEN, LORRAINE AYRAL, accountant; b. Levittown, N.Y., July 20, 1956; d. Edward Joseph and Joan Dorothy (Destefanis) Ayral; m. Ross Kocen, Oct. 4, 1981; 1 child, Daniel. BS, Hofstra U., 1978; MBA, U. Minn., 1985. Engr. Sperry Systems Mgmt., Great Neck, N.Y., 1978-81; fin. analyst ITT Consumer Fin. Corp., Mpls., 1981-84; cost acct. Mercy Med. Ctr., Mpls., 1984-85, contr., 1985-86; bus. segments acct. GTE, Thousand Oaks, Calif., 1986-88, Cerritos project acct., 1988-90, Cerritos project adminstr., 1990-92, fin. adminstr., 1992—. Asst. editor newsletter Healthcare Fin. Mgmt. Assn., Mpls., 1985-86. Mem. archtl. com. Foxmoor Hills Homeowners Assn., Westlake, Calif., 1989. Office: GTE 1 GTE Pl Thousand Oaks CA 91362

KOCH, CHARLES STEPHEN, hospital executive, economist; b. Freemont, Ohio, Nov. 18, 1948; s. Norbert Urbin and Rita Ann (Rimelspach) K.; m. Marlene Marie Dollbaum, Aug. 2, 1991; 1 child from previous marriage, Colleen Moneghn. BBA, U. Toledo, 1971; MA in Health Care Adminstrn., George Washington U., 1974. Asst. dir. Donald N. Sharp Meml. Hosp., San Diego, 1974-77, asst. dir., chief fin. officer, 1977-81, sr. v.p., adminstr., 1986—, also bd. dirs.; assoc. adminstr. Sutter Meml. Hosp., Sacramento, 1981-86. Co-author: Physician Involvement in Product Line Marketing, 1987; also articles. Bd. dirs. San Diego Blood Bank, 1988-92, chmn. planning com., 1990-92; bd. dirs. Calif. Hosp. and Health Systems, 1992; chair Hosp. Coun. San Diego and Imperial Counties, 1992. Mem. San Diego Taxpayers Assn. (bd. dirs. 1992). Home: 12903 Via Grimaldi Del Mar CA 92014 Office: Sharp Meml Hosp 7901 Frost St San Diego CA 92123

KOCH, DORIE JO, special education educator; b. Bloomington, Minn., Sept. 5, 1959; d. Hartley Ralph Koch and Josephine J. (Johnson) Quale. Student, Golden West Coll., 1980-81. Cable analyst Trionics Inc., Los Alamitos, Calif., 1981-82; instrnl. asst. Orange County Dept. Spl. Edn., Costa Mesa, Calif., 1986—. Author: (poetry) Half Moon: Harvest for the Fools, 1982; lyrics writer, 1978-92. Mem. Profl. Assault Response Team. Recipient Gold medallion, cert. NASA Saturn Project, Calif., 1982. Mem. Audubon Soc. Home: 10362 Lassen St Los Alamitos CA 90720

KOCH, GERALD DOUGLAS, social services administrator; b. Detroit, June 17, 1943; s. Albert Edward and Marjory M. (Mirovsky) K.; m. April Lee Wittrock, Aug. 14, 1965 (div. Jan. 1981); children: Bethany Lynne, Nathan Douglas; m. Janice Eva Faulk, Oct. 2, 1981; stepchildren: Ted Wilson, James Miller, DeAnna Miller Smith. BA, Asbury Coll., Wilmore, Ky., 1965; MSW, Ind. U., 1970. Cert. social worker. Social worker I Ky. State Hosp., Danville, 1965-67; casework supr. The Salvation Army, Indpls., 1967-68, 70-72; settlement dir. The Salvation Army, Chgo., 1973-78; dir. social svcs. The Salvation Army, Kansas City, Mo., 1978-80, Denver, 1980—; field instr. social work edn. U. Wyo, 1984, 85, U. Colo., Denver, 1987-89, U. No. Colo., 1988; tchr. tng. sessions for human svcs. cert., 1985, 89. Bd. dirs. Denver Santa Claus Shop, 1980—, Denver Emergency Housing Coalition, 1980—, LOVE Inc Met. Denver, 1987-89, Met. Denver Emergency Food and Shelter Bd., 1989—; mem. housing task force Denver Dept. Social Svcs., 1989—. Recipient Albert Schweitzer award Emergency Assistance Coalition, Kansas City, 1980, citation Dept. Health and Hosps., Denver, 1984. Mem. Nat. Orgn. Social Workers, Rocky Mountain Brassworks (horn player), 50 for Housing, Piton Found., Colo. Coalition for Homeless. Republican. Home: 4749 S Sherman St Englewood CO 80110-6834 Office: The Salvation Army 2136 Champa St Denver CO 80205-2530

KOCH, NEAL DAVID, journalist; b. Paterson, N.J., July 13, 1954; s. Abraham Victor and Wally V. (Dannenberg) K.; m. Sally Klein, Nov. 8, 1992. BA, Haverford (Pa.) Coll., 1976; JD, Case Western Res. U., 1979; MSc, Columbia U., 1982. Assoc. editor Wall St. Letter, N.Y.C., 1982-83; staff writer L.A. Herald Examiner, 1983-87; sr. editor Channels mag., L.A., 1987-90; freelance journalist N.Y. Times, L.A. Times, Columbia Journalism Rev., L.A., 1991—; freelance journalist Bus. Week, 1982; judge New Orleans Press Club ann. awards, L.A., 1986, Kern County (Calif.) Press Club ann. awards, 1987. Recipient Best Bus. Story of Yr. award Valley Press Club, L.A., 1985, Greater L.A. Press Club, 1986, Laurel Columbia Journalism Rev., 1986. Mem. PEN.

KOCH, NORMAN EDWARD, education educator; b. Portland, Oreg., June 17, 1934; s. Peter and Anna M. (Harding) K.; m. Jane Ann Rapp, Mar. 18, 1958 (div. Aug. 1980); m. Modeen Snedaker, Apr. 27, 1985; children: Johanna M. Koch Dillard, Gretchen L. BA, Cen. Wash. U., 1956, MS, 1958; EdD, U. Oreg., 1966. Cert. sch. adminstr., Wash. Tchr. Wash. State pub. schs., 1955-60; sch. adminstrs. Kennewick (Wash.) pub. schs., 1960-64; asst. prof. Wash. State U., Pullman, 1966-68; prof. and chmn. elem. edn. dept. Western Oreg. State Coll., Monmouth, 1968—; cons. Oreg. Literacy Coalition, Salem, 1988—. Author: Small Schools and The Realities, 1968, Better Than Basals, 1989. Recipient Teaching Rsch. Div. award Oreg. State System of Higher Edn. Mem. Internat. Reading Assn. (state chmn. 1971-76, mem. tchr. edn. com. 1975-80), Oreg. Reading Assn. (chmn. rsch. com. 1980-85), Oreg. Mid. Level Assn. (bd. dirs.), Masons, Shriners, Phi Gamma Delta. Home: 989 Nandina Ct NE Salem OR 97303-3407 Office: Western Oreg State Coll Monmouth OR 97361

KODIS, MARY CAROLINE, marketing consultant; b. Chgo., Dec. 17, 1927; d. Anthony John and Callis Ferebee (Old) K.; student San Diego State Coll., 1945-47, Latin Am. Inst., 1948. Controller, div. adminstrv. mgr. Fed. Mart Stores, 1957-65; controller, adminstrv. mgr. Gulf Mart Stores, 1965-67; budget dir., adminstrv. mgr. Diana Stores, 1967-68; founder, treas., controller Handy Dan Stores, 1968-72; founder, v.p., treas. Handy City Stores, 1972-76; sr. v.p., treas. Handy City div. W.R. Grace & Co., Atlanta, 1976-79; founder, pres. Hal's Hardware and Lumber Stores, 1982-84; retail and restaurant cons., 1979—. Treas., bd. dirs. YWCA Watsonville,1981-84, 85-87; mem. Santa Cruz County Grand Jury, 1984-85. Recipient 1st Tribute to Women in Internat. Industry, 1978; named Woman of the Yr., 1986. Mem. Ducks Unltd. (treas. Watsonville chpt. 1981-89). Republican. Home and Office: 302 Wheelock Rd Watsonville CA 95076-9714

KOEHLER, AGNES THERESA, real estate sales executive, business executive; b. Hixton, Wis., June 8, 1921; d. August Carl and Hildegard (Capaul) K.; m. Bernard Van Eperen, Oct. 4, 1941 (div. 1978); children: David, Shari, Gary. Student, Tchrs. Coll., Oshkosh, Wis., 1940. Lic. real estate broker and sales, assessor. Real estate agt. Moder Realty, Appleton, Wis., 1965-66, Schwartzbauer Realty, Appleton, 1967-68, Kennedy Realty, Appleton, 1969-71; v.p., co-owner Van Eperen Painting, Inc., Appleton, 1960-77; assessor Town of Menasha, Wis., 1975-76; real estate broker Farrow Realty, Carlsbad, Calif., 1979; pres. Aux. Wis. Painting & Decorating Contractor, Appleton, 1966. Artist various oils. Co-founder Fox Cities NOW, Appleton, 1973; mem. Menasha Planning Commn., 1975. Mem. LWV, Am. Assn. Retired Persons, United We Stand Am., San Diego Now, North Coast Dem. Club, San Diego Welcome Wagon, San Diego Floral Assn.. Home: 2147 Bulrush Ln Cardiff By The Sea CA 92007-1407

KOEHLER, GUSTAV ADOLPHUS, state official; b. Culver City, Calif., Oct. 26, 1944; m. Cheryl Haden, Apr. 22, 1980 (div.); children: Lydia, Maxwell. AA, Mesa Jr. Coll., San Diego, 1963; BA, Calif. State U., San Diego, 1965; MA, Calif. State U., San Jose, 1968; PhD, U. Calif., Davis, 1974. Prin. cons. Calif. Rsch. Assocs., 1978-79; consumer rsch. specialist Calif. Dept. Consumer Affairs, Sacramento, 1979-84; govt. rsch. specialist Calif. Emergency Med. Svcs. Authority, Sacramento, 1984-93; policy analyst Calif. Rsch. Bur., Sacramento, 1993—; adj. prof. pub. adminstrn. U. So. Calif., Sacramento, 1978-79, Golden Gate U., Sacramento, 1987-89; pres. Policy Resources Inst., Sacramento; reviewer Ctrs. for Disease Control, Sacramento. Contbr. articles to profl. jours.; 7 one-man art shows Sacramento galleries, 1980—. Co-chmn., assoc. pub. comm. officer Emergency Med. Comm. Com., 1992. Mem. AAAS, Am. Polit. Sci. Assn., Am. Soc. for Pub. Adminstrn., Assn. for Politics and Life Scis. Tibetan Buddhist.

KOELMEL, LORNA LEE, data processing executive; b. Denver, May 15, 1936; d. George Bannister and Gladys Lee (Henshall) Steuart; m. Herbert Howard Nelson, Sept. 9, 1956 (div. Mar. 1967); children: Karen Dianne, Phillip Dean, Lois Lynn; m. Robert Darrel Koelmel, May 12, 1981; stepchildren: Kim, Cheryl, Dawn, Debbie. BA in English, U. Colo., 1967. Cert. secondary English tchr. Substitute English tchr. Jefferson County Schs., Lakewood, Colo., 1967-68; sec. specialist IBM Corp., Denver, 1968-75, pers. administr., 1975-82, asst. ctr. coord., 1982-85, office systems specialist, 1985-87, backup computer operator, 1987—; computer instr. Barnes Bus. Coll., Denver, 1987-92; owner, mgr. Lorna's Precision Word Processing and Desktop Pub., Denver, 1987-89; computer cons. Denver, 1990—. Editor newsletter Colo. NCHA, 1992—. Organist Christian Sci. Soc., Buena Vista, Colo., 1963-66, chmn. bd. dirs.,Thornton, Colo., 1979-80. Mem. NAFE, Nat. Secs. Assn. (retirement ctr. chair 1977-78, newsletter chair 1979-80, v.p. 1980-81), U. Colo. Alumni Assn., Alpha Chi Omega (publicity com. 1986-88). Republican. Club: Nat. Writers. Lodge: Job's Daus. (recorder 1953-54).

KOELSCH, M. OLIVER, federal judge; b. Boise, Idaho, Mar. 5, 1912; m. Virginia Lee Daley, Oct. 30, 1937; children: children: Katherine (Mrs. John Kriken), John, Jane (Mrs. Dennis P. Houghton). BA, U. Wash., 1932, LLB, 1935. Assoc. Davidson & Davidson, Boise, 1936-39, Oleary & Koelsch, Boise, 1939-50; judge U.S. Ct. Appeals, San Francisco, 3d jud. dist., State of Idaho, 1951-59; sr. judge 9th cir. U.S. Ct. Appeals, Seattle, 1959—; asst. prosecutor Ada County, Idaho, 1939-45. Mem. Am. Judicature Soc. Office: US Ct Appeals 816 US Courthouse 1010 5th Ave Seattle WA 98104-1130

KOEPP, JANE ELIZABETH, tax accountant, auditor; b. Milw., June 24, 1947; d. Dwight William and Elizabeth L. (Birkenheier) Van Dale; m. Richard Raymond Koepp, May 31, 1969; children: Richard W., Kristin E., Jeffrey S. BS, Carroll Coll., 1969. Tax preparer Rosenberg Acctg., Mich., 1985-87; tax preparer All State H & R Block, Madison Heights, Mich., 1986-87, Doylestown, Pa., 1988-89; tax acct., mgr. tax office Ron Williams Acctg., Doylestown, 1989-92; enrolled agt., audit rep. Warrington, Pa., 1990-92; tax acct., auditor, enrolled agt. Income Tax Ctr. (divsn. Bus. Adv. & Tax. Svc. Inc.), Colorado Springs, Colo., 1993—. Mem. Nat. Soc. Tax Preparers, Accreditation Coun. for Accountancy and Taxation (accredited tax advisor 1991—). Home: 680 Carlson Dr Colorado Springs CO 80919

KOEPPEL, GARY MERLE, writer, publisher, art gallery owner; b. Albany, Oreg., Jan 20, 1938; s. Carl Melvin and Barbara Emma (Adams) K.; m. Emma Katerina Koeppel, May 20, 1984. BA, Portland State U., 1961; MFA, State U. Iowa, 1963. Writing instr. State U. Iowa, Iowa City, 1963-64; guest prof. English, U. P.R. San Juan, 1964-65; assoc. prof. creative writing Portland (Oreg.) State U., 1965-68; owner, operator Coast Gallery, Big Sur, 1971—, Pebble Beach, Calif., 1986—, Maui, Hawaii, 1985—, Hana, Hawaii, 1991—, Lahaina, Hawaii, 1992; owner Coast Pub. Co., Coast Seri Graphics, 1991—; editor, pub. Big Sur Gazette, 1978-81; producer, sponsor Maui Marine Art Expo., Calif. Marine Art Expo., Paris Marine Art Expo., Hawaiian Cultural Arts Expo., 1993. Author: Sculptured Sandcast Candles, 1974. Founder Big Sur Vol. Fire Brigade, 1975; chmn. coordinating com. Big Sur Area Planning, 1972-75; chmn. Big Sur Citizens Adv. Com., 1975-78. Mem. Internat. Soc. Appraisers, New England Appraisal Soc., Big Sur C. of C. (pres. 1974-75, 82-84), Big Sur Grange, Audubon Soc., Cousteau Soc., Phi Gamma Delta, Alpha Delta Sigma. Address: Coast Gallery PO Box 223519 Carmel CA 93922

KOERBER, JOHN ROBERT, computer programmer; b. L.A., Aug. 17, 1955; s. Thomas Joseph and Betty (Turner) Koerber; m. Kimberly Sue Rider, Mar. 15, 1986. BS, Yale U., 1977. Computer technician Tech Mart, Tarzana, Calif., 1977-79; programmer, ptnr. J&J Computer Svc., Northridge, Calif., 1979-80; sr. programmer Mitec Computer Bus. Systems, Chartsworth, Calif., 1980-87; sr. software engr. Dracon div. Harris Corp., Camarillo, Calif., 1987-88; programmer, cons. Sailing Computer Systems, Chatsworth, 1988—. Mem. IEEE (affiliate, Commns. Soc.), Assn. for Computing Machinery. Democrat. Home: 10444 Canoga Ave #34 Chatsworth CA 91311 Office: Sailing Computer Systems 10258 Glade Ave Chatsworth CA 91311

KOERNER, JANE GOETZE, editor, writer; b. Kansas City, Mo., Nov. 18, 1950; d. Robert Gaver and Mary (Parnell) Goetze; m. William C. Koerner, July 12, 1976 (div. 1990). BA in History, Colo. Coll., 1972. Freelance writer, 1978—; editor Springs Mag., Colorado Springs, Colo., 1982-86; cons. Hewlett Packard, Colorado Springs, 1987; publs. editor Colo. Coll., Colorado Springs, 1987—. Contbr. numerous articles to mags. Election judge County of El Paso, Manitou Springs, Colo., 1980—; precinct capt. Dem. Party, Manitou Springs, 1984-88. Mem. Colo. Mountain Club (conservation chmn. 1992-95, vice chmn. 1983-85, program chmn. 1983-86), Sierra Club. Office: Colo Coll 14 E Cache La Poudre St Colorado Springs CO 80903-3243

KOESTEL, MARK ALFRED, economic, environmental geologist; b. Cleve., Jan. 1, 1951; s. Alfred and Lucille (Kemeny) K.; m. Deborah Leigh Caswell, Sept. 5, 1988. BS, U. Ariz., 1978. Registered profl. geologist Wyo., Alaska, Ind.; registered environ. assessor, Calif. Sr. geologist Union Oil Co. of Calif., Tucson and Denver, 1978-86; mgr. geology Harmsworth Assocs., Laguna Hills, Calif., 1986-88; sr. project mgr. Applied GeoSystems, Irvine, Calif., 1988-90; geologic, environ. cons. Laguna Hills, Calif., 1990—. Contbr. articles to profl. jours. N.Mex. state rep. Minerals Exploration Coalition, Tucson and Denver, 1982. Sci. Found. scholarship No. Ariz. U., 1969, Acad. Achievement scholarship, 1970, Disting. Scholastic Achievement scholarship, 1971. Mem. Am. Inst. of Profl. Geologists (cert.), Soc. of Mining Engrs., Aircraft Owners and Pilots Assn., Geol. Soc. of Am., Nat. Geographic Soc. Home: 22891 Caminito Azul Laguna Hills CA 92653

KOESTER, BERTHOLD KARL, lawyer, retired honorary consul Federal Republic of Germany; b. Aachen, Germany, June 30, 1931; s. Wilhelm P. and Margarethe A. (Witteler) K.; m. Hildegard Maria Buettner, June 30, 1961; children: Georg W., Wolfgang J., Reinhard B. JD, U. Muenster, Fed. Republic Germany, 1957. Cert. Real Estate Broker, Ariz. Asst. prof. civil and internat. law U. Muenster, 1957-60; atty. Cts. of Duesseldorf, Fed. Republic Germany, 1960-82; v.p. Bank J. H. Vogeler & Co., Duesseldorf, 1960-64; pres. Bremer Tank-u., Kuehlschiffahrtsges.m.b.H., 1964-72; atty., trustee internat. corps., Duesseldorf and Phoenix, 1973-82, Phoenix, 1983—; of counsel Tancer Law Offices, Phoenix, 1978-86; prof. internat. bus. law Am. Grad. Sch. Internat. Mgmt., Glendale, Ariz., 1978-81; with Applewhite, Laflin & Lewis, Real Estate Investments, Phoenix, 1981-86, ptnr., 1982-86, Beucler Real Estate Investments, 1986-88, Scottsdale, Ariz.; chief exec. officer, chmn. bd. German Consultants in Real Estate Investments, Phoenix, 1989—; hon. consul Fed. Republic of Germany for Ariz., 1982-92; chmn., chief exec. officer Arimpex Hi-Tec, Inc., Phoenix, 1981—; bd. dirs. Ariz. Ptnrship for Air Transp., 1988-92; chmn. Finvest Corp., Phoenix, 1990—. Contbr. articles to profl. jours. Pres. Parents Assn. Humboldt Gymnasium, Duesseldorf, 1971-78; active German Red Cross, from 1977. Mem. Duesseldorf Chamber of Lawyers, Bochum (Fed. Republic Germany) Assn. Tax Lawyers, Bonn German-Saudi Arabian Assn. (pres. 1976-79), Bonn German-Korean Assn., Assn. for German-Korean Econ. Devel. (pres. 1974-78), Ariz. Consular Corps (sec., treas. 1988-89), German-Am. C. of C., Phoenix Met. C. of C., Rotary (Scottsdale, Ariz.). Home: 6201 E Cactus Rd Scottsdale AZ 85254-4409

KOESTER, RUDOLF, educator; b. Mar. 16, 1936; s. Eric A. and Irmgard (Petzel) K.; m. Elizabeth Margriet Dane, Jan. 12, 1973. BA, UCLA, 1958, MA, 1959; PhD, Harvard U., 1964. Asst. prof. UCLA, 1964-69; assoc. prof. U. Nev., Las Vegas, 1969-76, prof., 1976—. Author: Hermann Hesse, 1975, Joseph Roth, 1982, Hermann Broch, 1987; contbr. articles to profl. jours. Baldwin Prize fellow in Germanics, Harvard U., 1959-60. Mem. Phi Beta Kappa. Home: 2349 Palora Ave Las Vegas NV 89109-1819

KOETHKE, CHARLES RICHARD, advertising specialist, consultant; b. Lewiston, Idaho, Feb. 13, 1945; s. George Richard and Bonna Jean (Lister) K.; m. Diana Kaye White, Mar. 8, 1966 (div. Apr. 1978); children: Timothy Richard, Richard Darin, Karie Jean, Michele Pamela; m. Sara Ann Savisky, Sept. 27, 1980. Grad. high sch., Ravenswood, W.Va. and Lewiston, Idaho. With Nu-Lawn Chem. Co., Redwood City, Calif., 1964, Potlatch Corp., Lewiston, 1964-67, Pacific Gamble Robinson, Lewiston, 1967-68; restaurant mgr. W. T. Grant & Co., Santa Rosa, Calif., 1968-70; owner Koethke's Grocery & Fountain, Lewiston, 1970-71; retail advt. sales dept. Lewiston Morning Tribune, Lewiston, 1971-72; classified advt. mgr. Lewiston Morning Tribune, 1972-77; classified advt. mgr., asst. computer technician The Daily News, Longview, Wash., 1978—. Bd. dirs. Daily News Fed. Credit Union, Longview, 1983—, McClelland Arts Ctr., Longview, 1984—. Mem. Pacific N.W. Assn. Newspaper Classified Advt. Mgrs. (bd. dirs. 1980-82, 89—, v.p. 1983-84, 92-93, 93—, pres. 1984-85), Newspaper Pubs. Assn. (Wash., Oreg., Idaho, Mont., classified cons. 1987-90). Democrat. Home: 705 S 6th Ave Kelso WA 98626-2532 Office: The Daily News 770 11th Ave Longview WA 98632-2412

KOETSCH, PHILIP WAYNE, electronics executive; b. Vanceburg, Ky., Nov. 25, 1935; s. Clarence Robert and Ethel Louise (Phillips) K.; m. Joyce Moore, May 30, 1957; children: Karen, Tanya, Sharon, Christopher. BSEE, U. S C., 1959, MSEE, 1960. Engr. Westinghouse Corp., Pitts., 1960-63; sr. engr. Lockheed Aircraft Corp., Marietta, Ga., 1963-66; cons. Rockford, Ill., 1966-70; design supr. Honeywell, San Diego, 1970-71; test systems mgr. NCR, San Diego, 1971-76; chief engr. ACDC Electronics, Oceanside, Calif., 1976-80; v.p. engring. Powertec Inc., Chatsworth, Calif., 1980—. Contbr. tech. papers to profl. publs.; patentee in field. Mem. IEEE, Am. Elec. Assn., Tau Beta Pi, Sigma Pi Sigma, Pi Mu Epsilon, Omicron Delta Kappa. Office: 1355 Dell Ave Campbell CA 95008

KOETSER, DAVID, export company executive; b. Amsterdam, The Netherlands, July 22, 1906; came to U.S., 1939; s. Joseph and Mathilda Pauline (Hollander) K. Grad., Lyceum, Amsterdam, 1926. Owner Music Pub. Co., Amsterdam, 1935-39; exec. sec. The Netherlands C. of C., 1947-56; owner D.K. Co., Inc., San Francisco, 1957-84. Contbr. articles to profl. jours. Moderator U.S. Small Bus. Adminstrn., Score workshops, San Francisco, 1987—. Staff sgt. CIC, 1942-45, ETO. Mem. Holland Am. Soc. (treas. 1950—), World Trade Club (entertainment com. 1960—), Internat. Exporters Assn. (pres. 1965, recipient Pres. E award). Home and Office: 100 Thorndale Dr Apt 341 San Rafael CA 94903-4574

KOFSKY, FRANK JOSEPH, history educator, author; b. L.A., Nov. 18, 1935; s. Philip and Charlotte (Carash) K.; m. Bonnie Helen Davis. BS in Physics, Calif. Inst. Tech., 1957; postgrad., U. Calif., Berkeley, 1961; MA in History, Calif. State U., L.A., 1965; Phd in History, U. Pitts., 1973. Instr. in history Calif. Inst. of the Arts, L.A., 1964-65; instr. Calif. State U., L.A., 1964-65, 68-69, U. Pitts., 1965-66, Carnegie-Mellon Inst., Pitts., 1966-67; asst. prof. Immaculate Heart Coll., L.A., 1968-69; prof. Calif. State U., Sacramento, 1969—. Author: Black Nationalism..., 1970, Lenny Bruce..., 1975, Harry S. Truman and War Scare of 1948..., 1993, The Macintosh; columnist Sacramento Bee, 1969-81, others. Speaker Physicians for Social Responsibility Napa, Calif., 1986, Sacramento, Calif., 1991, Beyond War, Napa, 1987, SANE, Contra Costa County, Calif., 1988, Beyond War, Petalumna, Calif., 1987, Talking About Vietnam, Calif. Coun. for the Humanities, 1990, Rethinking the Cold War, Madison, Wis., 1991, SANE-Freeze, Sacramento, Calif., 1992, Sacramento Renaissance, 1993. Harry S. Truman Libr. Inst. sr. scholar, 1990-91; Calif. State U. grantee, 1985-86, 1990-92; Am. Coun. Learned Soc. Rsch. fellow, 1991. Mem. Am. Hist. Assn., Orgn. Am. Historians. Office: Calif State U Dept History 6000 J St Sacramento CA 95819-2605

KOGA, ROKUTARO, astrophysicist; b. Nagoya, Japan, Aug. 18, 1942; came to U.S., 1961, naturalized, 1966; s. Toyoki and Emiko (Shinra) K.; m. Cordula Rosow, May 5, 1981; children: Evan A., Nicole A. B.A., U. Calif.-Berkeley, 1966; Ph.D., U. Calif.-Riverside, 1974. Research fellow U. Calif.-Riverside, 1974-75; research physicist Case Western Res U., Cleve., 1975-79, asst. prof., 1979-81; physicist Aerospace Corp., Los Angeles, 1981—. Mem. Am. Phys. Soc., Am. Geophys. Union, IEEE, N.Y. Acad. Scis., Sigma Xi. Contbr. articles to profl. confs.; research on gamma-ray astronomy, solar neutron observation, space scis., charged particles in space and the effect of cosmic rays on microcircuits in space. Home: 7325 Ogelsby Ave Los Angeles CA 90045-1356 Office: Aerospace Corp Space Scis Labs Los Angeles CA 90009

KOGER, RONNY STEWART, career non-commissioned officer; b. Coco Solo, Panama Canal Zone, Mar. 23, 1953; s. Stewart Gamble and Hildegard Elizabeth (Jager) K.; m. Janet Lee Lloyd, Aug. 1972 (div. July 1983); 1 child, Brian Daniel; m. Sheri Jerome, Aug. 29, 1992. Cert. master-fire direction personnel. Enlisted U.S. Army, 1972, advanced through ranks to sgt., 1982; battery chief computer Lone Star Battery 1st Bn. 18th F.A., Ft. Sill, Okla., 1972-74; fire direction computer Alpha Battery 3rd Bn. 37th F.A., Herzo Base, Germany, 1974-76; bn chief fire direction computer 1st Bn. 14th F.A., Ft. Hood, Tex., 1976-79; bn. chief, fire direction computer 1st Bn. 14th F.A., Garlstedt, Germany, 1979-82; instr. gunnery dept. U.S. Army F.A. Sch., Ft. Sill, 1982-83, sr. instr., 1983-84; sr. enlisted adv. Readiness Group of San Francisco, 1984-88; bn. chief fire direction computer 7th Bn. 8th F.A., Schofield Banks, Hawaii, 1988-92; retire, 1992. Recipient Meritorious Svc. medal, Army Commendation medal, Army Acheivement medal, Good Conduct medal, Nat. Defense Svc. medal, Non-commisioned Officer Edn. ribbon, Army Svc. ribbon, Overseas Svc. ribbon. Mem. U.S. Army Field Artillery Assn. (St. Babaras medal 1984). Republican. Roman Catholic. Home: 2400 Natoma Station Dr Folsom CA 95630

KOH, EUSEBIO LEGARDA, mathematics educator; b. Manila, Oct. 4, 1931; s. Enrique Legarda and Felisa Un (Makabuhay) K.; m. Donelita Mesina Viardo, Feb. 21, 1958; children—Eudonette, Elizabeth, Ethel, Denise. B.S. in Mech. Engring. cum laude, U. Philippines, Quezon City, 1954; M.S. in Mech. Engring., Purdue U., 1956; M.S., Birmingham, 1961; Ph.D., SUNY-Stony Brook, 1967. Research engr. Internat. Harvester Co., Chgo., 1956-57; asst. prof. mech. engring. U. Philippines, 1959-64, head dept., 1963-64; assoc. prof. math. U. Regina, Sask., Can., 1970-75, prof., 1975—, head dept. math., 1977-79; guest prof. math. Techn. Hochschule, Darmstadt, Fed. Republic Germany, 1975-76; prof. math. U. Petroleum/ Minerals, Dhahran, Saudi Arabia, 1979-81. Contbr. research papers to profl. jours. Pres., Philippine Assn. Sask., 1971, bd. dirs., 1984; editor Philippine Newsletter, 1985. Colombo Plan scholar Brit. Council, 1960; Travel fellow Nat. Research Council, Fed. Republic Germany, 1975; research grantee Nat. Sci. and Engring. Research Council, 1971—; named Outstanding Prof., U. Philippines Student Union, 1962, Outstanding Filipino-Can. in Edn., The Pinoy Digest, 1990. Mem. Soc. Indsl. and Applied Math., Am. Math. Soc., Math. Assn. Am., Can. Applied Math. Soc., Philippine Am. Acad. Sci. and

Engring. (founding). Avocations: chess, bridge, tennis, golf. Office: U of Regina, Dept of Math and Stats, Regina, SK Canada S4S 0A2

KOHAN, DENNIS LYNN, protective services official, consultant; b. Kankakee, Ill., Nov. 22, 1945; s. Leon Stanley and Nellie (Foster) K.; m. Julianne Johnson, Feb. 14, 1976 (dec. Sept. 1985); children: Toni, Bart, Elyse; m. Betsy Burns, Mar. 8, 1986; 1 child, David. BA, Ill. Wesleyan U., 1967; MPA, Gov.'s State U., 1975; postgrad., John. Marshall Law Sch., 1971-74. Police officer Kankakee County, 1967-75; loan counselor, security officer Kankakee Fed. Savs. & Loan, Kankakee, 1975-76; mgr. Bank Western, Denver, 1976-85; mgr. real estate lending dept. Cen. Savs., San Diego, 1985-87; maj. loan work-out officer Imperial Savs., San Diego, 1987-88; cons. Equity Assurance Holding Corp., Newport Beach, Calif., 1987-88; compliance officer Am. Real Estate Group and New West Fed. Savs. and Loan, Irvine, Calif., 1988-90; co-founder Consortium-Real Estate Asset Cons., Costa Mesa, Calif., 1990-91; investigator, criminal coord. U.S. Govt., Newport Beach, Calif., 1991—; instr. U. No. Colo. Coll. Bus., Greeley, 1981-85; chmn. bd. North Colo. Med. Ctr., Greeley, 1983-85; pres. bd. Normedco, Greeley, 1984-85. Vol. cons., chmn. ARC, Colo., 1979-85; campaign mgr. Donley Senatorial campaign, Colo., 1982, Kinkade City Coun. campaign, Colo., 1983; chmn. Weld County Housing Authority, 1981. Staff sgt. U.S. Army, 1969-71, Vietnam. Mem. Nat. Assn. Realtors, Shriners, Kiwanis. Office: Costa Mesa CA 92323

KOHL, JOHN PRESTON, management educator; b. Allentown, Pa., Dec. 26, 1942; s. Claude Evan and Edna Lenoir (Woodland) K.; m. Nancy Ann Christensen, Mar. 11, 1967; children—John P. Jr., Mark C. B.A., Moravian Coll., 1964; M.Div., Yale U., 1967; M.S. in Mgmt., Am. Tech. U., 1974, M.S. in Counseling, 1976; Ph.D. in Bus. Adminstrn., Pa. State U., 1982. Ordained to ministry United Ch. of Christ, 1967. Minister, Christ Congl. Ch., New Smyrna Beach, Fla., 1968-71, First Congl. Ch., Hutchinson, Minn., 1971-73; instr. Pa. State U., University Park, 1978-82; asst. prof. mgmt. U. Tex., El Paso, 1982-85; assoc. prof. mgmt. San Jose State U., Calif., 1985-87; prof. mgmt., chmn. dept. mgmt. U. Nev., Las Vegas, 1988—; cons. in field. Co-author: (text) Personnel Management, 1986. Served to capt. U.S. Army, 1973-78; to lt. col. USAR, 1978—. Decorated Nat. Def. Service medal, Meritorious Service medal, Army Commendation medal. Mem. Acad. Mgmt. Contbr. articles to profl. publs. Home: 7545 Tara Ave Las Vegas NV 89117-2922 Office: U Nev Las Vegas Coll Bus Econs Las Vegas NV 89154

KOHLENBERGER, JIM, political advisor; b. Fullerton, Calif., Feb. 14, 1962; s. David and Charm (Cavaghan) K.; m. Cynthia Elizabeth Pierce, Oct. 7, 1990; 1 child, Christopher. BS in Physics, U. Calif., Irvine, 1985. Community programs coord. U.S. Sen. Alan Cranston, Washington, 1987-90, legis. asst., 1985-91; So. Calif. field dir. U.S. Sen. Alan Cranston, L.A., 1991—; bd. dirs. Dem. Nat. Talent Pool, Washington; west coast dir. Capitol Govt. Tng. and Dispatch Program, Washington, 1988. Founder Smithsonian Institution Young Benefactors, Washington, 1990; pres. D.C. Hugh O'Brian Youth Leadership Conf., Washington, 1987-88. Recipient Lauds and Laurels for Univ. Svc. award U. Calif., 1985; named one of Outstanding Young Men of Am., 1985, 86. Mem. Washington D.C. Jr. C. of C. (bd. dirs. 1988-89), U. Calif. Irvine Alumni Assn. (founder, pres. Washington chpt. 1986-89), U. Calif. Washington D.C. Area Alumni Assn. (chmn. 1987-90). Home: 3805 Forest Ave Yorba Linda CA 92686

KOHLER, DOLORES MARIE, gallery owner; b. Rochester, N.Y., June 26, 1928; d. Thomas Beranda and Kathryn (Held) White; m. Reuel S. Kohler, June 27, 1946; children: Richard, Kathryn Kohler Farnsworth, Linda Kohler Barnes, Pamela Kohler Conners. BMus, U. Utah, 1976. Lic. real estate broker, lic. cert. gen. real estate appraiser. Broker Kohler Investment Realty, Bountiful, Utah, 1962—; registered rep. Frank D. Richards, Salt Lake City, 1986—; appraiser FHA/HUD, 1962—; owner Marble House Gallery, Salt Lake City, 1987—; owner Sandcastle Theaters, Bountiful, 1976—. Composer songs, 1973—. Music chmn. N. Canyon Stake LDS Ch., Bountiful, 1989-93; sec. North Canyon 3d Ward Sunday Sch., 1993—. Mem. Salt Lake Bd. Realtors, Salt Lake Art Dealers Assn. (v.p. 1988-90, pres. 1990-91), Nat. Assn. Real Estate Appraisers, Inst. Real Estate Mgmt. (pres. 1984), Mu Phi Epsilon. Home: 2891 S 650 E Bountiful UT 84010-4455 Office: Marble House Gallery 44 Exchange Pl Salt Lake City UT 84111-2713

KOHLER, ERIC DAVE, history educator; b. Cin., Oct. 24, 1943; s. Walter Joseph and Irmgard (Marx) K.; m. Kathryn D. K. Kohler, June 22, 1968. AB, Brown U., 1965; MA, Stanford U., 1967, PhD, 1971. Vis. asst. prof. history Calif. State U., Humboldt, 1970-71; asst. prof. U. Wyo., Laramie, 1971-78, assoc. prof., 1978—, acting head history dept., 1989-90. Chair Ivinson Hosp. La Grande Fleur Charity Ball, 1993. Recipient Deutcher Akademischer Austauchdienst award, 1968, U. Wyo. Faculty Devel. award, 1972. Mem. Am. Cath. Hist. Assn., Am. Hist. Assn., Am. Assn. for History of Medicine, German Studies Assn. (program dir. 1989). Club: Laramie Country. Office: U Wyo Dept History PO Box 3198 Laramie WY 82071-3198

KOHLER, JOHN MICHAEL, accountant; b. Richland, Wash., May 18, 1949; s. John Paul and Catherine P. (Larrabee) K.; m. Robin P. Hultner, Apr. 3, 1948; children: Amy P., J. Jesse, Adam S., Tiffany E. BBA, Gonzago U., 1971. CPA, Wash., Idaho. Systems analyst Gonzag U., Spokane, 1969-72; trust tax officer Old Nat. Bank, Spokane, 1972-74; acct. LaMaster & Daniels, Spokane, 1974-76; pvt. practice Spokane, 1976—; tchr. City U., Spokane, 1980-85. Pres. Soccer Referres Assn.; coach, dir. Spokane Youth Sport Assn. Mem. AICPA, Wash. Soc. CPAs, Inst. of Mgmt. Accts., Data Processing Mgmt. Assn. (pres., sec. treas. Inland Empire chpt.). Office: W 222 Mission Ste 230 Spokane WA 99201

KOHLER, PETER OGDEN, physician, educator, university president; b. Bklyn., July 18, 1938; s. Dayton McCue and Jean Stewart (Ogden) K.; m. Judy Lynn Baker, Dec. 26, 1959; children: Brooke Culp, Stephen Edwin, Todd Randolph, Adam Stewart. BA, U. Va., 1959; MD, Duke U., 1963. Diplomate Am. Bd. Internal Medicine and Endocrinology. Intern Duke U. Hosp., Durham, N.C., 1963-64, fellow, 1964-65; clin. assoc. Nat Cancer Inst., Nat Inst. Child Health and Human Devel., NIH, Bethesda, Md., 1965-67, sr. investigator, 1968-73, head endocrinology service, 1972-73; resident in medicine Georgetown U. Hosp., Washington, 1969-70; prof. medicine and cell biology Baylor Coll. Medicine, Houston, 1973-77; chief endocrinology div. and med. service, prof., chmn. dept. medicine U. Ark., 1977-86, interim dean, 1985-86; chmn. Hosp. Med. Bd., 1980-82, chmn. council dept. chmn., 1979-80; prof., dean Sch. Medicine, U. Tex., San Antonio, 1986-88; pres. Oreg. Health Scis. U., Portland, 1988—; cons. endocrinology merit rev. bd. VA, 1985-86; mem. endocrinology study sect. NIH, 1981-85, chmn., 1984-85; mem. bd. sci. counselors NICHD, 1987-92, chair, 1990-92; chair task force on health care delivery Assn. of Acad. Health Ctrs., 1991-92; bd. dirs. Std. Ins. Co., Health Bridge N.W., HealthChoice; mem. adv. bd. Loaves and Fishes, 1989; mem. gov.'s adv. com. Commn. on Tech. Edn., 1989—, Oreg. Health Coun., 1992. Editor: (with G.T. Ross) Diagnosis and Treatment of Pituitary Tumors, 1973, Clinical Endocrinology, 1986; assoc. editor: Internal Medicine, 1983, 87, 90; contbr. articles to profl. jours. With USPHS, 1965-68. NIH grantee, 1973—; Howard Hughes Med. Investigator, 1976-77; recipient NIH Quality awards, 1969, 71, Disting. Alumnus award Duke Med. Sch., 1992. Fellow ACP; mem. Am. Soc. Clin. Investigation, Am. Fedn. Clin. Research (mem. nat. council 1977-78, pres. so. sect. 1976), So. Soc. Clin. Investigation (council 1979-82, pres. 1983, Founder's Medal 1987), AMA (William Beaumont award 1988), Am. Bd. Internal Medicine (endocrinology subspecialty bd. 1983-91, chair 1987-91, mem. bd. govs. ABIM 1987—), Am. Soc. Cell Biology, Assn. Am. Physician, Am. Diabetes Assn., Endocrine Soc. (coun. 1990—), Oreg. Health Coun., Raven Soc., Sigma Xi, Alpha Omega Alpha, Phi Beta Kappa, Omicron Delta Kappa, Phi Eta Sigma. Methodist. Office: Oreg Health Scis U Office of Pres 3181 SW Sam Jackson Park Rd Portland OR 97201-3098

KOHLER, WILLIAM CHARLES, life insurance agency executive, business consultant; b. Buffalo, Nov. 4, 1929; s. William David and Elizabeth (Barnes) K.; m. Mary Lou Sublett, Feb. 7, 1970; 1 child, Elizabeth Marie. BA, U. Buffalo, 1956; postgrad., Santa Ana Coll., 1964-65, Saddleback Coll., 1966-68. Enlisted USMC, 1948, advanced through grades to capt., 1967, assignment in Korea, 1951, assignments in Japan, 1950, 60, 63, assignments in the Philippines, 1962, assignments in Vietnam, ret., 1973; advt. sales rep. Golden West Pub. Co., Mission Viejo, Calif., 1973-74; agt. Penn. Mut. Life Ins. Co., Irvine, Calif., 1974-80, Mut. Trust Life Ins. Co., Tustin, Calif., 1980-83; ind. life ins. agt. Tustin, 1983; supr. agy. Transam. Life Cos., El Toro, Calif., 1983—; v.p., treas. Pro Futures Inc. Bd. dirs. Saddleback Valley YMCA, 1971-73; mem., pres. Saddleback Valley Unified Sch. Dist. Bd. Edn., Mission Viejo, 1975-81; pres., trustee Coastline Regional Occupational Program, Costa Mesa, Calif., 1976-82. Recipient Merit award Orange County Sch. Bd. Assn., 1980; named Man of Yr. Saddleback Valley YMCA Men's Club. Mem. M.C. League Assn., Ret. Officers Assn., Exch. Club (charter, pres. Saddleback Valley 1972-73, area gov. Calif. 1973-75, dist. bd. dirs. 1975-80, chmn. membership expansion 1974-75, 80-81, pres. Calif.-Nev. dist. 1981-82, Pub. Rels. award 1971-73, 79, nat. bd. dirs. 1983-85, regional nat. v.p. 1985-87, pres., bd. dirs. Child Abuse Prevention Ctrs. 1983—, Golden award San Bernardino, Calif. 1986), Saddleback Valley Hi-12 Club, Masons. Republican. Home: 25212 Pike Rd Laguna Beach CA 92653-5142

KOHN, ALAN J., zoology educator; b. New Haven, Conn., July 15, 1931; s. Curtis and Harriet M. (Jacobs) K.; m. Marian S. Adachi, Aug. 29, 1959; children: Lizabeth, Nancy, Diane, Stephen. AB in Biology, Princeton U., 1953; PhD in Zoology, Yale U., 1957. Asst. prof. zoology Fla. State U., Tallahassee, 1958-61; asst. prof. zoology U. Wash., Seattle, 1961-63, assoc. prof. zoology, 1963-67, prof., 1976—; Bd. dirs. Coun. Internat. Exchange Scholars, Wash., 1986-90. Author: A Chronological Taxonomy of Conus, 1758-1840, 1992; author: (with others) The Natural History of Enewetak Atoll, 1987; mem. editorial bd. Am. Zoologist, 1973-77, Am. Naturalist, 1976-78, Malacologia, 1974—, Jour. Exptl. Marine Biology and Ecology, 1981-84, Coral Reefs, 1981-87, Am. Malacological Bull., 1983—; contbr. articles to profl. jours. Sr. Post-Doctoral fellow Smithsonian Inst., Wash., 1990, John Simon Guggenheim fellow, 1974-75, Nat. Rsch. Coun. fellow, 1967; numerous rsch. grants Nat. Sci. Found., 1960—. Mem. Internat. Soc. Reef Studies, Am. Assn. Advancement Sci., Am. Soc. Zoologists (treas. 1971-74), Am. Soc. Limnology & Oceanography, Am. Soc. Naturalists, Ecol. Soc. Am., Am. Malacological Union (pres. 1982-83), Soc. Systematic Zoology, Linnean Soc. London, Marine Biol. Assn. India, British Ecol. Soc., Marine Biol. Assn. U.K., Malacological Soc. London, Malacological Soc. Japan, Australian Coral Reef Soc., Pacific Sci. Assn., Hawaiian Acad. Scis., Sigma Xi (pres. U. Wash. chpt. 1971-72). Home: 18300 Ridgefield Rd NW Seattle WA 98177-3224 Office: Dept Zoology U Wash Seattle WA 98195

KOHN, GERHARD, psychologist, educator; b. Neisse, Germany, Nov. 18, 1921; s. Erich and Marie (Prager) K.; m. Irene M. Billinger, Feb. 9, 1947; children—Mary, Eric. B.S., Northwestern U., 1948, M.A., 1949, Ph.D., 1952; postgrad. U. So. Calif., 1960. Instr., Northwestern U., 1947-49; instr., counselor, dir. pub. relations Kendall Coll., Evanston, Ill., 1947-51; psychologist, counselor Jewish Vocat. Services, Los Angeles, 1951-53, Long Beach Unified Sch. Dist., Calif., 1953-61; instr. Long Beach City Coll., 1955-61; asst. prof. psychology Long Beach State U., 1955-56; counselor, instr. Santa Ana Coll., Calif., 1961-65; prof. Calif. State U., Fullerton, 1971-72; lectr. Orange Coast Coll., 1972-75; asst. clin. prof. psychiatry U. Calif.-Irvine; dir. Reading Devel. Ctr., Long Beach, 1958-88, Gerhard Kohn Sch. Ednl. Therapy, 1967-85; exec. dir. Young Horizons; pvt. practice psychology, 1958—; fir juvenile diversion program Long Beach Area, 1982—; cons. HEW, Bur. Hearing and Appeals, Social Security Adminstrn., Long Beach/Orange County B'nai B'rith Career and Counseling Svcs. (cons. to Long Beach Coun.), Long Beach Coun. of Parent Coop. Nursery Sch., Orange County Headstart, Orange County Coop. Pre-Schs. With AUS, 1942-47. Mem. NEA, Am. Pers. and Guidance Assn., Nat. Vocat. Guidance Assn., Am. Psychol. Assn., Calif. Psychol. Assn. (dir. 1976-79, 91—, sec. 1980-81), Orange County Psychol. Assn. (dir., pres. 1974), Long Beach Psychol. Assn. (pres. 1985, 86, sec. 1989, treas. 1991, chmn. govtl. affairs com.), L.A. County Psychol. Assn. (treas., sec.), Calif. Assn. Sch. Psychologists, Elks, Phi Delta Kappa, Psi Chi. Office: 117 E 8th St Long Beach CA 90813

KOHN, JEROME MILTON, life insurance agent; b. Far Rockaway, N.Y., Nov. 8, 1915; s. Jerome and Frieda (Quittner) K.; m. Betty Sanders, Mar. 16, 1941; children: Leslie Clemens, Sandra Kohn, Jay Kohn. BS, U. Va., 1936; JD, U. Mont., 1938. Chartered life underwriter. Pvt. practice in law Billings, Mont., 1938-42; ptnr. Wholesale Distbn. Firm, Billings, 1944-55; agt. and gen. agt. Am. Nat. Ins. Co., Billings, 1955—; exec. sec. LUPAC-Mont., Billings, 1982—. Lt. USNR, 1942-45. Mem. Optimist Internat., Elks. Democrat. Jewish. Home: 2707-13th St West #1 Billings MT 59102 Office: PO Box 1923 Billings MT 59103

KOHN, MICHAEL BUNDY, art gallery director, owner; b. L.A., Sept. 20, 1958; s. Robert Melvin and Joyce Elizabeth (Spivack) K. BFA, UCLA, 1980; MA, NYU, 1984. Curatorial intern Guggenheim Mus., N.Y.C., 1983; U.S. editor Flash Art Mag., N.Y.C., 1983-85; owner, operator Michael Kohn Gallery, Santa Monica, Calif., 1985—; teaching asst. NYU, 1983; instr. Art Ctr. Coll. Design, Pasadena, Calif., 1986. Contbr. articles to mags. Mem. Santa Monica Art Dealers Assn. Democrat. Jewish. Office: Michael Kohn Gallery 920 Colorado Ave Santa Monica CA 90401-2717

KOHN, MISCH HARRIS, artist, retired art educator; b. Kokomo, Ind., Mar. 26, 1916; s. Jacob and Anna (Kaplan) K.; m. Lore Lisa Traugott, May 19, 1945; children: Jessica, Tamara. BFA, John Herron Art Inst., Indpls., 1939; DFA (hon.), Ind. U., 1991. Assoc. prof. art Ill. Inst. Tech., Chgo., 1953-65, prof., 1965-72; prof. Calif. State U., Hayward, 1972-86, prof. emeritus, 1986—; head dept. visual design Inst. Design, Chgo., 1951; instr. U. Wis., summer 1957; mem. artists adv. com. John Simon Guggenheim Meml. Found., 1962-74; instr. exptl. printmaking U. Chgo., 1969; mem. Pennell Fund com. Libr. Congress, 1972. One-man shows, 1942—, including Art Inst. Chgo., 1951, 61, 70, Los Angeles County Mus. Art, 1957, Cin. Art Mus., 1961, John Herren Mus., 1961, Bklyn. Mus., 1981, numerous colls. and univs.; retrospective exhbn. Mary Porter Sesnon Art Gallery, U. Calif., Santa Cruz, 1985, KALA Inst. Gallery, Berkeley, Calif., 1988; represented in permanent collections Mus. Modern Art, Bklyn. Mus., Met. Mus. Art, Nat. Gallery, Libr. Congress, Smithsonian Instn., Art Inst. Chgo., Bibliotheque Nat., many others. Recipient Alice McFadden Eyre gold medal Pa. Acad.d, Pennell medal, 1952; Burr Meml. gold medal Phila. Free Libr., 1960, prize Bklyn. Mus. Nat. Print Exhibit, 1968; fellow Ford Found., 1959, grantee 1960; Gubbenheim fellow, 1952, 55, Tamarind fellow, 1960; grantee Nat. Endowment for Arts, 1980. Fellow Acad. Fine Arts of Design (hon., Florence, Italy); mem. NAD, Am. Graphic Arts Soc., Print Coun. Am., Phila Print Club (Internat. Graphic Arts Soc. prize 1969). Home: 1860 Grove Way Castro Valley CA 94546

KOHN, ROBERT SAMUEL, JR., real estate investment consultant; b. Denver, Jan. 7, 1949; s. Robert Samuel and Miriam Lackner (Neusteter) K.; m. Eleanor B. Kohn; children: Joseph Robert, Randall Stanton, Andrea Rene. BS, U. Ariz., 1971. Asst. buyer Robinson's Dept. Store, L.A., 1971; agt. Neusteter Realty Co., Denver, 1972-73, exec. v.p., 1973-76; pres. Project Devel. Svcs., Denver, 1976-78, pres., CEO, 1978-83; pres. Kohn and Assocs., Inc., 1979-83; pres. The Burke Co., Inc., Irvine, Calif., 1983-84, ptnr., 1984-91; sr. mktg. assoc. Sliff Thorn & Co., Phoenix, 1992—, Iliff, Thorn & Co., Phoenix, 1992—; owner RSKJ, Inc. Mem. Bldg. Owners and Mgrs. Assn. (pres. 1977-78, dir. 1972-78, dir. S.W. Conf. Bd. 1977-78), Denver Art Mus., Denver U. Libr. Assn., Central City Opera House Assn., Inst. Real Estate Mgmt., Newport Beach Tennis Club. Republican. Jewish. Home: 3140 E Vermont Ave Phoenix AZ 85016

KOHN, ROGER ALAN, surgeon; b. Chgo., May 1, 1946; s. Arthur Jerome and Sylvia Lee (Karlen) K.; m. Barbara Helene, Mar. 30, 1974; children: Bradley, Allison. BA, U. Ill., 1967; MD, Northwestern U., 1971. Diplomate Am. Bd. Opthalmology. Internship UCLA, 1971-72; residency Northwestern U., Chgo., 1972-75; fellowship U. Ala., Birmingham, 1975, Harvard Med. Sch., Boston, 1975-76; chmn. dept. ophthalmology Kern Med. Ctr., Bakersfield, Calif., 1978-87; asst. prof. UCLA Med. Sch., 1978-82, assoc. prof., 1982-86, prof., 1986—. Author: Textbook of Ophthalmic Plastic and Reconstructive Surgery, 1988; contbr. numerous articles to profl. jours.; author chpts. in 13 additional textbooks; patentee in field. Bd. dirs. Santa Barbara (Calif.) Symphony, 1990—. Capt. USAR, 1971-77. Named applied to med. syndrome Kohn-Romano Syndrome. Mem. Am. Soc. Ophthalmic Plastic and Reconstuctive Surgery (cert.), Pacific Coast Ophthal. Soc. (bd. dirs. 1986—, 1st v.p. 1990). Jewish. Office: 525 E Micheltorena Ste 201 Santa Barbara CA 93103

KOHNE, RAYMOND ERNEST, physician, educator; b. Orangeville, Ontario, Canada, Oct. 7, 1962; came to the U.S., 1981; s. Ernest Herman and Milda Lena (Thonigs) K.; m. Cathy Lynette Proctor, Aug. 11, 1985. BS, Andrews U., 1985, MS, 1988; MD, Loma Linda U., 1992. Researcher Andrews U., Berrien Springs, Mich., 1985-88, flight instr., 1985-90; resident Loma Linda (Calif.) Med. Ctr., 1992-93; intern in radiology Loma Linda U. Med. Ctr., 1993—; instr. anatomy Loma Linda U. Med. Ctr., 1992—. Contbr. articles to profl. jours. Mem. Radiologic Soc. North Am., AMA, San Bernadino Med. Assn., Housestaff Assn., Sigma Xi, Alpha Omega Alpha. Office: Loma Linda Med Ctr 11234 Andersant St Loma Linda CA 92324

KOHNE, RICHARD EDWARD, retired consulting engineering and construction company executive; b. Tientsin, China, May 16, 1924; s. Ernest E. and Elizabeth I. (Antonenko) K.; m. Gabrielle H. Vernaudon; children—Robert, Phillip, Daniel, Paul, Renee. B.S., U. Calif., Berkeley, 1948. Structural engr. hydro projects Pacific Gas & Electric Co., San Francisco, 1948-55; with Morrison-Knudsen Engrs., Inc., San Francisco, 1955—, regional mgr. for Latin Am., then v.p., 1965-71, exec. v.p. world-wide ops. in engrng. and project mgmt., 1971-79, pres., chmn., chief exec. officer, 1979-88; chmn., chief exec. officer Morrison-Knudsen Internat. Co., Inc., San Francisco, 1988-90, chmn. emeritus, 1990—. Decorated Chevalier Nat. Order of Leopold (Zaire). Mem. ASCE, U.S. Com. Large Dams, Cons. Engrs. Assn. Calif., World Trade Club (San Francisco). Democrat. Roman Catholic. Home and Office: 1827 Doris Dr Menlo Park CA 94025-6101

KOHO, CLARENCE HERBERT, agriculture laboratory executive, biologist, researcher; b. Pocatello, Idaho, May 17, 1931; s. Harold Baker and Margaretta (Howard) K.; m. Anne Marie Smith, March 24, 1956 (div. May 8, 1988); children: Kim, Brian, Kyle. AA, Coll. of San Mateo, 1964; BS, Fla. Inst. Tech., 1972; PhD (hon.), Polymer Studies Inst., Calif. State Univ., Fresno, 1986. With U.S. Army, 1949-56; coatings cons. Rocketdyne, Santa Sussanna, Calif., 1956-64; environ. control cons. W.R. Grace, St. Louis, 1964-72; owner C.H. Koho Labs, Las Vegas, Nev., 1972—. Mem. Elks. Republican. Presbyterian. Home: 4754 E Flamingo Rd Las Vegas NV 89121

KOIZUMI, CARL JAN, nuclear geophysicist; b. Reno, Jan. 7, 1943; s. Shoichi and Ann (Oshima) K.; m. Jean Anna Edman, June 3, 1968; 1 child, Emi Marie. BS, U. Nev., 1965, MS, 1973, PhD, 1977; MS, Ariz. State U., 1967. Rsch. geophysicist Bendix Field Engring., Grand Junction, Colo., 1977-81; rsch. physicist Gearhart Industries, Austin, Tex., 1982-86; staff scientist Rockwell Hanford, Richland, Wash., 1986-87; prin. scientist Westinghouse Hanford Co., Richland, Wash., 1987-93, RUST-Geotech, Grand Junction, Colo., 1993—; mem. task group Am. Soc. for Testing and Materials, Phila., 1979-86; mem. com. Am. Petroleum Inst., Houston, 1982-92; pub. reports U.S. Dept. Energy; presnter articles for symposium proceedings, papers at profl. soc. meetings. Contbr. articles to profl. jours. Mem. Am. Physical Soc. (life), Soc. Profl. Well Log Analysts, Minerals and Geotech. Logging Soc., Nature Conservancy, Sigma Xi, Sigma Pi Sigma, Pi Mu Epsilon. Republican. Home: 3954 N Seville Circle Grand Junction CO 81506 Office: RUST Geotech PO Box 1400 Grand Junction CO 81502

KOKALJ, JAMES EDWARD, aerospace administrator; b. Chgo., Oct. 29, 1933; s. John and Antoinette (Zabukovec) K. AA in Engring., El Camino Coll., Torrance, Calif., 1953. Dynomometer lab. technician U.S. Electric Motors, L.A., 1953-54; devel. lab. technician AiResearch divsn. Garrett, L.A., 1956-59; tech. rep. McCulloch, L.A., 1959-65; dist. mgr. Yamaha Internat., Montebello, Calif., 1965-67; salesman Vasek Polak BMW, Manhattan Beach, Calif., 1967-68; sr. svc. rep. Stratos-We. div. Fairchild, Manhattan Beach, 1968-70; asst. regional mgr. we. states J.B.E. Olson div. Grumman, L.A., 1970-71; gen. mgr. Internat. Kart Fedn., Glendora, Calif., 1971-73; logistics support data specialist Northrop Aircraft, Hawthorne, Calif., 1974—. Author: Technical Inspection Handbook, 1972; contbr. articles to profl. jours. With USN, 1954-56. Mem. U.S. Naval Inst., Internat. Naval Rsch. Orgn. Republican. Roman Catholic. Home: 805 Bayview Dr Hermosa Beach CA 90254-4147 Office: Northrop Aircraft Div 1 Northrop Ave Hawthorne CA 90250

KOLAKOWSKI, MARILYN, computer graphics specialist; b. Alliance, Ohio, Sept. 18, 1953; d. Eugene Dominic and Mary Stephanie (Galanzosky) K. Student, No. Mich. U., Marquette, 1971-73, El Centro Coll., Dallas, 1980-81, City Coll., San Francisco, 1989-90. Graphics specialist Bevilacqua-Knight Inc., Oakland, Calif., 1985-88; cons. Levi Strauss & Co., San Francisco, 1988—. Home: 138 Monte Cresta Ave Oakland CA 94611

KOLANOSKI, THOMAS EDWIN, financial company executive; b. San Francisco, Mar. 1, 1937; s. Theodore Thaddeus and Mary J. (Luczynski) K.; m. Sheila O'Brien, Dec. 26, 1960; children: Kenneth John, Thomas Patrick, Michael Sean. BS, U. San Francisco, 1959, MA, 1965. Cert. fin. planner. Educator, counselor, administr. San Francisco Unified Sch. Dist., 1960-79; adminstr. Huntington Beach (Calif.) Union, 1969-79; v.p. fin. svcs. Waddell & Reed, Inc., Ariz., Nev., Utah, So. Calif., 1969—. Fellow NDEA, 1965. Mem. Nat. Assn. Secondary Sch. Prins., Internat. Assn. of Fin. Planners, Nat. Assn. Securities Dealers. Republican. Roman Catholic. Home: 1783 Panay Cir Costa Mesa CA 92626-2348 also: 10218 N Central Phoenix AZ 85021

KOLB, KEN LLOYD, writer; b. Portland, Oreg., July 14, 1926; s. Frederick Von and Ella May (Bay) K.; m. Emma LaVada Sanford, June 7, 1952; children: Kevin, Lauren, Kimrie. BA in English with honors, U. Calif., Berkeley, 1950; MA with honors, San Francisco State U., 1953. Cert. jr. coll. English tchr. Freelance fiction writer various nat. mags., N.Y.C., 1951-56; freelance screenwriter various film and TV studios, Los Angeles, 1956-81; freelance novelist Chilton, Random House, Playboy Press, N.Y.C., 1967—; instr. creative writing Feather River Coll., Quincy Calif., 1969; minister Universal Life Ch. Author: (teleplay) She Walks in Beauty, 1956 (Writers Guild award 1956), (feature films) Seventh Voyage of Sinbad, 1957, Snow Job, 1972, (novels) Getting Straight, 1967 (made into feature film), The Couch Trip, 1970 (made into feature film), Night Crossing, 1974; contbr. fiction and humor to nat. mags. and anthologies. Foreman Plumas County Grand Jury, Quincy, 1970; chmn. Region C Criminal Justice Planning commn., Oroville, Calif., 1975-77; film commr. Plumas County, 1986-87. Served with USNR, 1944-46. Establishment Ken Kolb Collection (Boston U. Library 1969). Mem. Writers Guild Am. West, Authors Guild, Mensa, Phi Beta Kappa, Theta Chi. Democrat. Club: Plumas Ski (pres. 1977-78). Home and Office: PO Box 30022 Cromberg CA 96103

KOLBE, JAMES THOMAS, congressman; b. Evanston, Ill., June 28, 1942; s. Walter William and Helen (Reed) K.; m. Sarah Marjorie Dinham, Apr. 16, 1977. BA in Polit. Sci., Northwestern U., 1965; MBA in Econs., Stanford U., 1967. Asst. to coordinating architect Ill. Bldg. Authority, Chgo., 1970-72; spl. asst. to Gov. Richard Ogilvie Chgo., 1972-73; v.p. Wood Canyon Corp., Tucson, 1973-80; mem. Ariz. Senate, 1977-83, majority whip, 1979-81; cons. Tucson, 1983-85; mem. 99th-103rd Congresses from 4th dist. Ariz., 1985—; mem. appropriations com., 1987—, mem. budget com. Trustee Embry-Riddle Aero. U., Daytona Beach, Fla.; bd. dirs. Community Food Bank, Tucson; Republican precinct committeeman, Tucson, 1974—. Served as lt. USNR, 1977-79, Vietnam. Mem. Am. Legion, VFW. Republican. Methodist. Office: Office of House Members 405 Cannon House Office Bldg Washington DC 20515-0305*

KOLBE, JOHN WILLIAM, newspaper columnist; b. Evanston, Ill., Sept. 21, 1940; s. Walter William and Helen (Reed) K.; m. Mary Bauman, Feb. 24, 1993; stepchildren: Erin Simmons, James Simmons; children by previous marriage: Karen, David. BS in Journalism, Northwestern U., Evanston, Ill., 1961; MA in Polit. Sci., U. Notre Dame, 1962. Feature writer, polit. reporter Rockford (Ill.) Register-Republic, 1964-68; press aide Ogilvie for Gov. campaign, Chgo., 1968; asst. press sec. Office Gov., Springfield, Ill., 1969-73; polit. reporter, columnist Phoenix Gazette, 1973—. Elder Valley Presbyn. Ch., Scottsdale, Ariz., 1978-81; mem. adv. com. Morrison Inst., Ariz. State U., Tempe, 1982—. Lt. (j.g.) USNR, 1962-64. Recipient Best Column of Yr. award Ariz. Press Club, 1976, 80, 84. Office: Phoenix Newspapers 120 E Van Buren St Phoenix AZ 85004

KOLDE, BERT, professional sports team executive. Vice chmn. Portland Trail Blazers. Office: Portland Trail Blazers Port of Portland Bldg 700 NE Multnomah St Ste 600 Portland OR 97232

KOLDOVSKY, OTAKAR, pediatrics and physiology educator; b. Olomouc, Czechoslovakia, Mar. 31, 1930; came to U.S., 1968; s. Kvetoslav and Marie (Loukotska) K.; m. Eva Libicka, May 6, 1971. MD, Charles U., Prague, Czechoslovakia, 1955; PhD, Inst. Physiology, Prague, Czechoslovakia, 1962. Rsch. assoc. dept. Pediatrics Stanford (Calif.) U., 1965; vis. scientist dept. Clin. Biochemistry Lund (Sweden) U., 1967-68; from asst. prof. to prof. Pediatrics Rsch. U. Pa., Phila., 1969-79; prof. Pediatrics and Physiology U. Ariz., Tucson, 1980—. Author (books) Utiliz of Nutrients During Postnatal Development, 1967, Functional Development of the Gastrointestinal Tract in Mammals, 1968, Development of the Small Intestinal Function in Mammals and Man, 1969. Recipient Nutrition award Am. Acad. of Pediatrics, 1986, Harry Schwachman award, 1991. Office: U Ariz 1501 N Campbell Ave Tucson AZ 85724-0001

KOLFF, WILLEM JOHAN, surgeon, educator; b. Leiden, Holland, Feb. 14, 1911; came to U.S., 1950, naturalized, 1956; s. Jacob and Adriana (de Jonge) K.; m. Janke C. Huidekoper, Sept 4, 1937; children: Jacob, Adriana P., Albert C., Cornelis A., Gualtherus C.M. Student, U. Leiden Med. Sch., 1930-38; M.D. summa cum laude, U. Groningen, 1946; M.D. (hon.), U. Turin, Italy, 1969, Rostock (Germany) U., 1975, U. Bologna, Italy, 1983; D.Sc. (hon.), Allegheny Coll., Meadville, Pa., 1960, Tulane U., 1975, CUNY, 1982, Temple U., 1983, U. Utah, 1983; D. of Tech. Scis. (hon.), Tech. U. Twente, Enscheded, the Netherlands, 1986; D.Sc. (hon.), U. Athens, 1988. Internist, head med. dept. Mcpl. Hosp., Kampen, Holland; dir. div. artificial organs Cleve. Clinic Found., 1950-67; privaat docent, dept. medicine U. Leiden, 1950-67; prof. surgery U. Utah Coll. Medicine, Salt Lake City, 1967—, Disting. prof. medicine and surgery, 1979—; prof. internal medicine U. Utah Coll. Medicine, 1981—, dir. Inst. for Biomed. Engring., dir. div. artificial organs, 1967-86. Decorated commandeur Orde Van Oranje Netherlands, 1970; Orden de Mayo al Merito en el Grado de Gran Official Argentina, 1974; recipient Landsteiner medal for establishment blood banks during war in Holland Netherlands Red Cross, 1942, 1st Edwin Cohn-De Laval award World Apheresis Assn., 1990, Federa prize Fedn. Scientific Med. Assn., 1990; Cameron prize U. Edinburgh (Scotland), 1964; 5,000 award Gairdner Found., 1966; Valentine award N.Y. Acad. Medicine, 1969; 1st Gold medal Netherlands Surg. Soc., 1970; Leo Harvey prize Technion, Israel, 1972; Sr. U.S. Scientist award Alexander Von Humboldt Found., 1978; Austrian Gewerbeverein's Wilhelm-Exner award, 1980; John Scott medal City of Phila., 1984; named to Nat. Inventors Hall of Fame, 1985; recipient Japan prize Japan Found. Sci. and Tech., 1986, Research prize Netherlands Royal Inst. Engrs., 1986; recipient 1st Jean Hamburger award Internat. Soc. Nephrology, 1987; named to On the Shoulders of Giants Hall of Fame, Cleve., 1989. Mem. AMA (Sci. Achievement award 1982), AAUP, Am. Physiol. Soc., Soc. Exptl. Biology and Medicine, AAAS, Nat. Acad. Engring. (City of Medicine award 1989), N.Y. Acad. Scis., Am. Soc. Artificial Internal Organs, Nat. Kidney Found., European Dialysis and Transplant Assn., ACP, Austrian Soc. Nephrology (hon.), Academia Nacional de Medicine (Colombia) (hon.), NAE. Lodge: Rotary. Office: U Utah Med Ctr College Engring & Medicine 2460 A MEB Salt Lake City UT 84112

KOLIN, ALEXANDER, retired biophysics researcher; b. Odessa, Ukraine, USSR, Mar. 12, 1910; came to U.S., 1934; s. Rudolph and Luba (Gershberg) K.; m. Renée Bourcier, 1951. Student, Inst. Tech. and U. Berlin, Berlin, 1929-33; PhD in Physics, German U. Prague, Czechoslovakia, 1934. Rsch. fellow in biophysics Michael Reese Hosp., Chgo., 1935-37; physicist to hosp. Mt. Sinai Hosp., N.Y.C., 1938-41; rsch. fellow NYU Med. Sch., N.Y.C., 1941-42, asst. prof. physics, 1945; instr. CCNY, 1941-44; instr. Columbia U., N.Y.C., 1944-45, rsch. assoc., 1941-46; assoc. prof. U. Chgo., 1947-56; prof. UCLA, 1956-77, prof. emeritus, 1977—. Author: Physics, Its Laws, Ideas, Methods, 1951; inventor electromagnetic flow meter, method of analysis isoelectric focusing, also others; discoverer electromagnetophoresis phenomenon. Recipient John Scott medal City of Phila., 1965, Albert F. Sperry medal Instrument Soc. Am., 1967, Alexander von Humboldt award Fed. Republic Germany, 1977; rsch. grantee Office Naval Rsch., NIH, also others, 1954—. Mem. AAAS, Am. Phys. Soc., Am. Physiol. Soc., Biophys. Soc., Electrophoresis Soc. (hon. life, Founders' award 1980), Sigma Xi (pres. UCLA chpt. 1966-67). Office: UCLA School of Med 100 Stein Pla Los Angeles CA 90024

KOLKEY, DANIEL MILES, lawyer; b. Chgo., Apr. 21, 1952; s. Eugene Louis and Gilda Penelope (Cowan) K.; m. Donna Lynn Christie, May 15, 1982; children: Eugene, William, Christopher, Jonathan. BA, Stanford U., 1974; JD, Harvard U., 1977. Bar: Calif. 1977, U.S. Dist. Ct. (cen. dist.) Calif. 1979, U.S. Dist. Ct. (no. dist.) Calif. 1980, U.S. Dist. Ct. (ea. dist.) Calif. 1978, U.S. Ct. Appeals (9th cir.) 1979, U.S. Supreme Ct., 1983. Law clk. U.S. Dist. Ct. judge, N.Y.C., 1977-78; assoc. Gibson Dunn & Crutcher, L.A., 1978-84, ptnr., 1985—; arbitrator bi-nat. panel for U.S.-Can. Free Trade Agreement, 1990—; commr. Calif. Law Revision Commn., 1992—. Contbr. articles to profl. publs. Co-chmn. internat. rels. sect. Town Hall of Calif., L.A., 1981-90; chmn. internat. trade legis. subcom., internat. commerce steering com. L.A. Area C. of C., 1983-91 (mem. law & justice com., 1993—); mem. adv. coun. and exec. com. Asia Pacific Ctr. for Resolution of Internat. Bus. Disputes, 1991—; bd. dirs., L.A. Ctr. for Internat. Comml. Arbitration, 1986—, treas., 1986-88, v.p. 1988-90, pres., 1990—; assoc. mem. cen. com. Calif. Rep. Party, 1983—, dep. gen. coun. credentials com., Republican Nat. Convention, 1992, alt. Calif. Delegation, 1992; mem. L.A. Com. on Fgn. Rels., 1983—; mem. L.A. World Affairs Council; gen. counsel Citizens Rsch. Found., 1990—. Mem. ABA, Internat. Bar Assn., L.A. County Bar Assn. (exec. com. internat. law sect. 1987—, vice chmn. 1989-91, chmn. 1991-92), Am. Arbitration Assn. (panel of arbitrators 1993—, arbitrator large complex case dispute resolution program), Chartered Inst. Arbitrators, London (assoc.), Friends of Wilton Park So. Calif. (chmn. exec. com.). Jewish. Office: Gibson Dunn & Crutcher 333 S Grand Ave Los Angeles CA 90071-1504

KOLLER, DUNCAN G., military officer; b. Felixstowe, Suffolk, Eng., Dec. 20, 1946; came to U.S., 1956; s. Carl Anthony and Grace Florence (Bunkell) K.; m. Cheryl Victoria Baccash, June 14, 1969; children: David Andrew, Elisha Anne. BS, Oreg. State U., 1969; MA in Edn., Chapman Coll., 1978; EdD, U. So. Calif., 1992. Commd. 2d lt. USAF, 1969, advanced through grades to col., 1991; squadron exec. officer 315th Security Police Squadron, Phan Rang, Vietnam, 1971-72; squadron comdr. Keesler Tech. Tng. Ctr., Biloxi, Miss., 1978-82; staff officer Hdqr. UN Command, Seoul, Korea, 1982-84; course dir. Armed Forces Staff Coll., Norfolk, Va., 1984-87; dep. base comdr. 8th Tactical Fighter Wing, Kunsan AB, Korea, 1987-88; joint sec. Hdqr. U.S. Pacific Command, Honolulu, 1989-92; prof. aerospace sci. Oreg. State U., Corvallis, 1992—. Pres. Radford High Sch. PTO, Honolulu, 1991-92. Decorated Bronze star. Mem. Phi Delta Kappa, Rotary. Episcopalian. Office: DET 685 AFROTC Oreg State U Corvallis OR 97331

KOLODNY, STEPHEN ARTHUR, lawyer; b. Monticello, N.Y., June 25, 1940; s. H. Lewis and Ida K.; children: Jeffery, Lee. BA in Bus. Adminstrn., Boston U., 1963, LLB, 1965. Bar: Calif. 1966, U.S. Dist. Ct. (cen. dist.) Calif. 1966. Sole practice L.A., 1966—; lectr. on family law subjects. Author: Tort Remedies for Child Stealing; contbg. author symposium book; contbr. articles to profl. jours. Mem. ABA (family law sect., author ABA Advocate), Internat. Acad. Matrimonial Lawyers (bd. mgrs.), Am. Acad. Matrimonial Lawyers (pres., v.p. membership), Calif. State Bar Assn. (cert. family law specialist, lectr. State Bar panel, CEB programs, mem. family law sect.), Los Angeles County Bar Assn. (lectr., mem. & past chmn. family law sect.), Beverly Hills Bar Assn. (lectr., mem. family law sect.), Am. Acad. Matrimonial Lawyers.

KOLPAS, SIDNEY J., mathematician, educator; b. Chgo., Oct. 19, 1947; s. Irving and Molly Lou (Lubin) K.; m. Laurie Ann Puhn, June 27, 1971; children: Allison, Jamie. BA magna cum laude, Calif. State U., Northridge, 1969, MS, 1971; EdD, U. So. Calif., L.A., 1979. Tchr. Luther Burbank (Calif.) Jr. High Sch., 1971-79; tchr., author Tandy Corp., L.A., 1979-85; tchr. John Burroughs High Sch., Burbank, 1979-90; adj. instr. Coll. of the Canyons, Valencia, Calif., 1985-90; ind. cons. L.A., 1979—; instr. Glendale (Calif.) Coll., 1990—; statis. cons. U. So. Calif., L.A.; math. and computer sci. mentor Burbank Unified Sch. Dist., 1985-89; tchr. math. Korean Coll. Prep. Sch., 1989; instr. Moorpark (Calif.) Coll., 1990; tchr. computer programming L.A. Valley Jr. Coll., 1976-77. Author: Topics in Mathematics, 1971, A Theory of Motivation in Mathematics, 1972, Model 3 TRSDOS and Disk Basic, 1979, Computer Applications in Patient Care, 1986, Quest for James Coffin, 1990, The Pythagorean Theorem: 8 Classic Proofs, 1991; contbr. articles to profl. jours. Recipient Teaching award McLuhen Found., L.A., 1984, Honors Teaching award NASA/Nat. Coun. Tchrs. Math., 1987, teaching commendation L.A. County, 1992, Disting. Prof. award Glendale Coll. chpt. Alpha Gamma Sigma, 1993; named Outstanding Tchr., Kiwanis, 1985, Woodrow Wilson Master Tchr., Woodrow Wilson Nat. Fellowship Found., Princeton, 1988, Ministerial and Burbank Tchr. of Yr., 1992. Mem. Nat. Coun. Tchrs. Math., Calif. Math. Coun. (com. chmn. 1985—), Foothill Math. Coun. (pres. 1989-90, 92-93), L.A. County Math. Tchrs. Assn. (bd. dirs. 1985-87), Phi Delta Kappa, Phi Eta Sigma, Alpha Mu Gamma. Democrat. Jewish. Office: Glendale Coll 1500 N Verdugo Glendale CA 91208-5378

KOLSRUD, HENRY GERALD, dentist; b. Minnewaukan, N.D., Aug. 12, 1923; s. Henry G. and Anna Naomi (Moen) K.; m. Loretta Dorothy Cooper, Sept. 3, 1945; children—Gerald Roger, Charles Cooper. Student Concordia Coll., 1941-44; DDS, U. Minn., 1947. Gen. practice dentistry, Spokane, Wash., 1953—. Bd. dirs. Spokane County Rep. Com., United Crusade, Spokane. Capt. USAF, 1950-52. Mem. ADA, Wash. State Dental Assn., Spokane Dist. Dental Soc. Lutheran. Clubs: Spokane Country, Spokane, Empire. Lodges: Masons, Shriners. Home: 2107 W Waikiki Rd Spokane WA 99218-2780 Office: 3718 N Monroe St Spokane WA 99205-2895

KOLSTAD, ROBERT BRUCE, computer scientist; b. Montevideo, Minn., Aug. 21, 1953; s. Clayton Robert and Joanne Marie (Peterson) K. B in Applied Sci., So. Meth. U., 1974; MSEE, U. Notre Dame, 1976; PhD, U. Ill., 1982. Sr. engr., mgr. Convex Computer Corp., Dallas, 1982-88; sr. software engr. Prisma, Inc., Colorado Springs, 1988-89, v.p. software, 1989; sr. staff engr. Sun Micro Systems, Colorado Springs, 1989-91; program mgr. Berkeley Software Design, Inc., Colorado Springs, 1991—; sec., bd. officer USENIX, Berkeley, 1986-92. Patentee in field. Recipient Orange County Community Svc. award, 1989, UNIX Personality of the Yr. award, 1988; named to Guiness Book of World Records. Home and Office: 7759 Delmonico Dr Colorado Springs CO 80919

KOLTAI, STEPHEN MIKLOS, mechanical engineer, consultant, economist; b. Ujpest, Hungary, Nov. 5, 1922; came to U.S., 1963; s. Maximilian and Elisabeth (Rado) K.; m. Franciska Gabor, Sept. 14, 1948; children: Eva, Susy. MS in Mech. Engring., U. Budapest, Hungary, 1948, MS in Econs., MS, BA, 1955. Engr. Hungarian Govt., 1943-49; cons. engr. and diplomatic service various European countries, 1950-62; cons. engr. Pan Bus. Cons. Corp., Switzerland and U.S., 1963-77, Palm Springs, Calif., 1977—. Patentee in field. Charter mem. Rep. Presdl. task force, Washington, 1984—.

KOLTHOFF, CAROL COTTONE, artist, educator; b. San Pedro, Calif., May 24, 1954; d. Leo Peter and Elsie (Donatoni) Cottone; m. David Lee Kolthoff. Student, Marymount Coll., 1972-73; BFA, Calif. State U., Long Beach, 1977, MFA, 1980; postgrad., Loyola Marymount U., 1977-80. Art instr. L.A. County Mus. Art, 1980; art instr., lectr. Calif. State U., Long Beach, 1981-83; art instr. L.A. City Coll., 1982-83; assoc. prof. Orange Coast Coll., Costa Mesa, Calif., 1983-84; art instr. Monterey (Calif.) Peninsula Coll., 1987-89, San Diego Mus. Art, 1990, Southwestern Coll., Chula Vista, Calif., 1991—. Cover artist Bird World mag., 1992; poster artist San Diego Zoo, 1992. Docent edn. dept. Monterey Bay Aquarium, 1988-89. Mem. Artists' Equity, San Diego Watercolor Soc., Western Fedn. Watercolor Socs.

KOMATSU, S. RICHARD, architect; b. San Francisco, May 5, 1916; s. Denzo and Tome (Fujimoto) K.; m. Chisato Frances Kuwata, Aug. 6, 1943; children: Richard Shigeto, Kathryn Kay. BArch, U. Calif., Berkeley, 1938; cert. in interior design, San Francisco Archtl. Club, 1939; cert. in machine design, Lawrence Inst. Tech., Detroit, 1944. Registered architect, Calif.; cert. architect Nat. Coun. Archtl. Registration Bds. Landscape planner Golden Gate Internat. Expn., San Francisco, 1938-39; designer/architect Charles F. Strothoff, Architect, San Francisco, 1939-42, 46-52; asst. project engr. Fed. Pub. Housing Authority, Detroit, 1944; designer Harley, Ellington & Day, Architects, Detroit, 1944; assoc./architect Donald L. Hardison & Assocs., Richmond, Calif., 1952-57; sec./prin. Hardison and Komatsu Assocs., San Francisco, 1957-79; pres./prin. Hardison Komatsu Ivelich & Tucker, San Francisco, 1979-88, cons., 1988—; pvt. practice cons. S. Richard Komatsu, Architect, El Cerrito, Calif., 1988—; invited speaker nat. conv. Nat. Assn. Home Builders, Chgo., 1966, confs. ASCE, San Francisco, 1972, Calif. and Nev. Water Pollution Control Assn., South Lake Tahoe, Calif., 1972; vis. archtl. adviser Cogswell Coll., San Francisco, 1981-82. Prin. works include 47 water treatment plants and related facilities, East Bay Mcpl. Utility Dist., 1964-84 (Gov.'s award 1974), main office complex, Turlock (Calif.) Irrigation Dist., 1988, 24 water treatment plants and related facilities, Contra Costa Water Dist., Concord, Calif., 1967-88 (Concord award 1972), pre-design of 6 water reclamation plants, 3 pumping plants, 1 dechlorination facility for Clean Water Program Greater San Diego, 1990-92; design advisor adminstrn., ops., and lab. bldg., wastwater treatment plant City of Santa Rosa, Calif., adminstrn. bldg. Dublin San Ramon (Calif.) Svcs. Dist., plant ops. ctr. Delta Diablo Sanitation Dist., Calif., 1991-92; contbr. articles to jours. in field. Bd. dirs. Richmond (Calif.) Art Ctr., 1956-60; mem. Planning Commn., City of El Cerrito, 1962-75, chmn. 1966-67, Design Rev. Bd., El Cerrito, 1969-78, chmn. 1973-77, Japanese Am. Citizens League, Contra Costa chpt., 1950—, pres., 1957, bd. dirs., 1956-60 (Silver Pin Achievement award 1966). With U.S. Army, 1944-46. Recipient Cons. Engrs. award Fairfield-Suisun Wastewater Mgmt. Facilities, 1978, AIA award Student Ctr. Complex U. Calif., 1978, Gold Nugget award Southeast Water Pollution Control Plant, 1984. Fellow (emeritus) AIA (East Bay chpt., bd. dirs. 1968-69, chmn. numerous coms.); mem. Am. Water Works Assn. (invited speaker various confs.). Republican. Presbyterian. Address: 1323 Devonshire Dr El Cerrito CA 94530

KOMDAT, JOHN RAYMOND, data processing consultant; b. Brownsville, Tex., Apr. 29, 1943; s. John William and Sara Grace (Williams) K.; m. Linda Jean Garrette, Aug. 26, 1965 (div.); m. Barbara Milroy O'Cain, Sept. 27, 1986; children: Philip August, John William. Student U. Tex., 1961-65. Sr. systems analyst Mass. Blue Cross, Boston, 1970-74; pvt. practice data processing cons., San Francisco, 1974-80, Denver, 1981—; prin. systems analyst mgmt. info. svcs. div. Dept. of Revenue, State of Colo., 1986-89; prin. systems analyst Info. Mgmt. Commn. Staff Dept. Adminstrn. State Colo., 1989—; mem. Mus. Modern Art, CODASYL End User Facilities Com., 1974-76, allocation com. Mile High United Way. Served with U.S. Army, 1966-70. Mem. IEEE, AAAS, Assn. Computing Machinery, Denver Downtown Dem. Forum (mem. exec. com.), Denver Art Mus., Friend of Pub. Radio, Friend of Denver Pub. Libr., Colo. State Mgrs. Assn, Nature Conservancy. Democrat. Office: PO Box 9757 Denver CO 80209

KOMENICH, KIM, photographer; b. Laramie, Wyo., Oct. 15, 1956; s. Milo and Juanita Mary (Beggs) K. BA in Journalism, San Jose State U., 1979. Reporter/photographer Manteca (Calif.) Bulletin, 1976-77; staff photographer Contra Costa Times, Walnut Creek, Calif., 1979-82, San Francisco Examiner, 1982—; lectr. San Francisco Acad. Art. John S. Knight fellow Stanford U., 1993—; recipient 1st Pl. award UPI, 1982, 85, Nat. Headliner award, 1983, 88, 87 1st Pl. award World Press Photo Awards, 1983, 1st Pl. award AP, 1985, 87, Pulitzer prize, 1987, others. Mem. Nat. Press Photographers Assn. (2d Pl. award 1982), San Francisco Bay Area Press Photographers Assn. (Photographer of Yr. award 1982, 84), Sigma Delta Chi (Disting. Service award 1986). Office: San Francisco Examiner 110 5th St San Francisco CA 94103-2972

KOMISAR, JEROME BERTRAM, university administrator; b. Bklyn., Jan. 31, 1937; s. Harry and Fanny (Neumann) K.; m. Natalie Rosenberg, Sept. 8, 1957; children: Harriet, Wade, Frances, Aurenna. BS, NYU, 1957; MA, Columbia U., 1959, PhD, 1968. Asst. prof. econs. Hamilton Coll., Clinton, N.Y., 1961-66; asst. prof., then assoc. prof. mgmt. SUNY, Binghamton, 1966-74, asst. to pres., 1971-74; vice chancellor faculty and staff rels. SUNY System, 1974-81, provost, 1982-85, pres. Rsch. Found., 1982-90, exec. vice chancellor, 1985-90, acting chancellor, 1987-88; acting pres. SUNY, New Paltz, 1979-80; pres. U. Alaska System, Fairbanks, 1990—; Alaska commr. We. Interstate Commn. for Higher Edn., 1990—; chmn. Alaska Aerospace Devel. Corp., 1991—. Author: Work Scheduling in the Wholesale Trades in Manhattan's Central Business District, 1962, Social Legislation and Labor Force Behavior, 1968; co-author: (with John S. Gambs) Economics and Man, 1964. Bd. dirs. Sta. WAMC-FM, Albany, 1982-90; chair bd. overseers Rockefeller Inst., 1987-88. Office: U Alaska System 202 Butrovich Bldg 910 Yukon Dr Fairbanks AK 99775

KOMPALA, DHINAKAR SATHYANATHAN, chemical engineering educator, biochemical engineering researcher; b. Madras, India, Nov. 20, 1958; came to U.S., 1979; s. Sathyanathan and Sulochana Kompala; m. Sushila Viswamurthy Rudramuniappa, Nov. 18, 1983; children: Tejaswi Dina, Chytanya Robby. BTech., Indian Inst. Tech., Madras, 1979; MS, Purdue U., 1982, PhD, 1984. Asst. prof. chem. engring. U. Colo., Boulder, 1985-91, assoc. prof., 1991—; vis. assoc. chem. enging. Calif. Inst. Tech., 1991-92. Editor Cell Separation Sci. and Tech., 1991; contbr. articles to profl. jours. Recipient NSF Presdl. Young Investigators award, 1988-93; NSF Biotech. Rsch. grantee, 1986-89, 89-92, Dept. Commerce Rsch. grantee, 1988, The Whitaker Found. grantee, 1990-93. Mem. Am. Inst. Chem. Engrs., Am. Chem. Soc. (program chair biochem. tech. divsn. 1993). Office: U Colo PO Box 424 Boulder CO 80309-0424

KONDAPAVULUR, VENKATESWARA RAO TIRUMALA, research engineer; b. Vijayawada, India, Aug. 7, 1962; came to U.S., 1984; s. Chalamayya and Sarojini (Inampudi) K.; m. Nagamani Narra, July 3, 1988. BTech., Indian Inst. Tech., Madras, 1984; MS, Purdue U., 1985; PhD, U. Calif., Berkeley, 1988. Grad. asst. Purdue U., West Lafayette, Ind., 1984-85; grad. student rsch. asst. Lawrence Berkeley Lab., 1986-88, postdoctoral fellow, 1988-89; asst. rsch. engr. U. Calif., Berkeley, 1989—. Contbr. articles to profl. publs. IBM fellow, 1987. Mem. Am. Soc. Metals Internat., Minerals, Metals and Materials Soc. (assoc.), Am. Soc. Testing Materials, Materials Rsch. Soc., Alpha Sigma Mu, Phi Kappa Phi. Home: 3400 Richmond Pky Apt 1918 San Pablo CA 94806-5224 Office: Lawrence Berkeley Lab MS 62-203 1 Cyclotron Rd Berkeley CA 94720

KONDRASUK, JACK N. (JOHN KONDRASUK), educator; b. Eau Claire, Wis., Jan. 23, 1942; s. Frank Mathew and Ruthann (Norton) K. Student, Coll. St. Thomas, 1960-61; BS, U. Wis., Eau Claire, 1964; MA, U. Minn., 1966, PhD, 1972. Pers. adminstr. Honeywell, Inc., Mpls., 1967-68; instr. U. Minn., Mpls., 1969; mgmt. edn. specialist Control Data Corp., Mpls., 1969-71; mgmt. cons. J.N. Kondrasuk Co., Mpls., 1971-73; psychologist Persona Corp., Portland, Oreg., 1973; cons. Rohrer, Hibler & Repogle, Inc. (now called RHR Internat.), Portland, Oreg., 1973-74; asst. to pres. U. Portland, 1980-81, asst./assoc. prof., 1975—; vis. prof. Novgorod (Russia) Poly. Inst., 1993. Contbr. articles to profl. jours. Mem. adv. group City of Portland, 1978, State of Oreg., Salem, 1987-88; mem. Clackamas County Econ. Devel. Commn., 1992—. Mem. Am. Soc. Tng. & Devel. (pres. 1987, nat. coms. 1987—, regional conf. chair 1984-86), Soc. Human Resource Mgmt. (sr. profl. in human resources, tng. com. 1988—), N.W. Human Resource Mgmt. Assn. (chair 1979), Acad. Mgmt. (div. newsletter editor 1982), Soc. Indsl. Orgnl. Psychology, Am. Psychol. Soc. Office: U Portland Sch Bus 5000 N Willamette Blvd Portland OR 97203-5750

KONG, LAURA S. L., seismologist; b. Honolulu, July 23, 1961; d. Albert T.S. and Cordelia (Seu) K.; m. Kevin T.M. Johnson, Mar. 3, 1990. ScB, Brown U., 1983; PhD, MIT/Woods Hole Oceanog. Inst., 1990. Grad. rschr. Woods Hole (Mass.) Oceanog. Instn., 1984-90; postdoctoral fellow U. Tokyo, 1990-91; geophysicist Pacific Tsunami Warning Ctr., Ewa Beach, Hawaii, 1991-93; seismologist U.S. Geol. Survey Hawaiian Volcano Obs., 1993—; mem. grad. faculty dept. geology & geophysics U. Hawaii. Contbr. articles to profl. jours.; speaker in field. Mem. equal employment opportunity adv. bd. Nat. Weather Svc. Pacific Region, Honolulu, 1992-93, Asian-Am./Pacific Islander spl. emphasis program mgr., 1992-93. Rsch. fellow Japan Govt.-Japan Soc. for Promotion of Sci., 1990; recipient Young Investigator grant Japan Soc. for Promotion of Sci., 1990. Mem. Am. Geophys. Union, Seismol. Soc. Am., Hawaii Ctr. for Volcanology, Sigma Xi. Office: US Geol Survey Hawaiian Volcano Obs PO Box 51 Hawaii National Park HI 96718

KONIECZNY, JAMES MICHAEL, podiatrist, surgeon; b. Phila., June 14, 1960; s. Henry James and Mary Bernadette (Maguire) K. BS in Biology, Marine Sci., E. Stroudsburg State U. of Pa., 1982; DPM, Calif. Coll. Podiatric Medicine, 1989. Bd. eligible Am. Bd. Podiatric Surgery. Marine biologist and species collector Ichthyological Assocs., Del., 1982; marine biologist Dynamic Marine Assocs., Marathon, Fla., 1982-85; resident in podiatric surgery Calif. Coll. Podiatric Medicine/Kaiser Vallejo, San Francisco, 1989-91; staff podiatrist USPHS/Indian Health Svc., Phoenix, 1991-93, Kaiser Sunnyside Med. Ctr., Clackamas, Oreg., 1993—. Co-prodr. slide series on geriatric foot care. Trustees scholar Calif. Coll. Podiatric Medicine, 1989. Mem. Am. Podiatric Med. Assn., Am. Coll. Foot Surgeons, Commd. Officers Assn., Am. Diabetes Assn., Assn. Mil. Surgeons of the U.S., Sigma Pi, Pi Delta. Office: Kaiser Sunnyside Med Ctr 10180 SE Sunnyside Rd Clackamas OR 97015

KONKEL, R(ICHARD) STEVEN, environmental and social science consultant; b. Denver, June 27, 1950; s. E. Vernon and Rojean (Templeman) K.; m. Jane Frances Ohlert, July 14, 1984; children: Kaitlin Brooke and Britt Edward (twins). BS in Archtl. Engring., U. Colo., 1972; M in City Planning, Harvard U., 1975; PhD in Urban and Environ. Planning, MIT, 1991. Economist, planner Edward C. Jordan Co., Portland, Maine, 1975-77; cost-benefit analyst Oak Ridge (Tenn.) Nat. Lab., 1977-79; prin. economist Konkel Environ. Cons., San Francisco, 1980-82; policy analyst State of Alaska Office of Gov. and Dept. Commerce and Econ. Devel., Juneau, 1982-84; pres. Konkel & Co., Cambridge, Mass., 1984-91; sr. rsch. sci. energy environ. policy and dispute resolution Battelle Pacific Northwest Lab., 1992—; Coord. MIT faculty seminar on risk mgmt., 1988-89. Author: Environmental Impact Assessment Rev., 1987; co-editor: MIT Faculty Seminar on Risk Management, 1989. Co-chair Juneau Energy Adv. Com., 1984. Research grantee Nat. Inst. Dispute Resolution, Washington, 1986-87. Mem. Am. Inst. Cert. Planners (charter), Am. Planning Assn., Am. Econ. Assn., Internat. Assn. Energy Econs., Assn. Environ. and Resource Economists. Home: 8508 W Entiat Pl Kennewick WA 99336 Office: Battelle Pacific Northwest Lab Energy and Eviron Scis Bldgs PO Box 999 Richland WA 99352

KONKOL, PETER ADAM, engineer; b. Yonkers, N.Y., May 25, 1933; divorced; children: Deborah, Joliene. B of Engring., N.Y. Maritime Coll., 1955. Cert. mech. engr. Ariz., Ky., N.Y. Engr. trainee GE, 1955-56, mfg. engr., 1958-70; mfg. engr. Honeywell Computer, Phoenix, 1970-81, mgr. mfg. engring., 1981-84; pres. Enginnered Adaptation Inc., Phoenix, 1984-89; mfg. engr. Honeywell Air Transport, Phoenix, 1989-92; pres. Engineered Adaptation Inc., 1992—. With U.S. Army, 1956-58. Mem. Am. Soc. Mech. Engr., (assoc.), Ariz. Printed Circuits Assn. (sec./treas. 1986—), Soc. Mfg. Engrs. Office: Engineered Adaptation Inc PO Box 82580 Phoenix AZ 85071

KONNICK, RONALD JOHN, data processing executive, consultant; b. East Chicago, Ind., May 18, 1943; s. Michael and Sophie (Kostrubala) K.; m. Marie Anne Kwiecien, Dec. 9, 1972; children: Eric, Bryan. BSEE, Carnegie-Mellon U., 1966; MS in Indsl. Engring., Wayne State U., 1972; MBA, Calif. Poly. State U., 1974. Indsl. engr. Carrier Corp., LaPuente, Calif., 1973-76; sr. indsl. engr. Harris Corp., Quincy, Ill., 1976-78; dir. mgmt. info. service IML Freight, Salt Lake City, 1978-84; site mgr. data ctr. Sun Carriers, Salt Lake City, 1985-88; v.p. info. systems Savage Industries, Salt Lake City, 1988—; instr. data processing U. Phoenix, Salt Lake City, 1984—. Chmn. 4th of July com. City of Sandy, Utah, 1980-81. Mem. Data Processing Mgmt. Assn. (bd. dirs. 1984-92), Inst. Cert. Computer Profls. (cert., award for excellence 1979). Roman Catholic. Home: 1943 Sunridge Cir Sandy UT 84093-7049 Office: Savage Industries 275 W 2755 S 5250 S 300 W Salt Lake City UT 84107

KONNYU, ERNEST LESLIE, former congressman; b. Tamasi, Hungary, May 17, 1937; came to U.S., 1949; s. Leslie and Elizabeth Konnyu; m. Lillian Muenks, Nov. 25, 1959; children: Carol, Renata, Lisa, Victoria. Student, U. Md., 1960-62; BS in Acctg., Ohio State U., 1965. Mem. Calif. Assembly, Sacramento, 1980-86, 100th Congress from 12th Calif. dist., 1985-86; owner Premier Printing, San Jose, Calif., 1990—; chmn. Assembly

Rep. Policy Com. of State Assembly, Sacramento, 1985-86; vice chmn. Assembly Human Services, Sacramento, 1980-86; vice chmn. Policy Research Com., Sacramento, 1985-86. Mem. Rep. State Cen. Com., Calif., 1977-88, Rep. Cen. Com., Santa Clara County, Calif., 1980-86; mem. adv. bd. El Camino Hosp., Mountain View, Calif., 1987. Served to maj. USAF, 1959-69. Recipient Nat. Def. Medal, 1968, Disting. Service award U.S. Jaycees, 1969, Nat. Security award Am. Security Council Found., 1987; named lifetime senator U.S. Jaycees, 1977. Republican. Roman Catholic.

KONOWALOW, DANIEL DIMITRI, research scientist; b. Cleve., Apr. 28, 1929; s. Dimitry and Mary (Ehnatt) K.; m. Marcy Ellen Rosenkrantz, July 24, 1978. BSc, Ohio State U., 1953; PhD, U. Wis., 1961. Chemist E.I. du Pont de Nemours, Wilmington, Del., 1960-62; asst. dir. Theoretical Chem. Inst. U. Wis., Madison, 1962-65; asst. prof. SUNY, Binghamton, 1965-70, assoc. prof., 1970-80, prof., 1980-89; sr. scientist U. Dayton (Ohio) Rsch. Inst., 1987—; with Air Force Phillips Lab., Edwards AFB. Contbr. articles on molecular structure and spectra to profl. jours. Dem. committeeman Broome County, Binghamton, N.Y., 1968-74. 1st Lt. U.S. Army, 1953-55. Mem. AAAS, Am. Physics Soc., Am. Chem. Soc. (chmn. Mojave Desert sect. 1992, councilor Binghamton sect. 1980-87, sec. 1975-78), Scabbard and Blade, Sigma Xi, Phi Eta Sigma, Phi Lambda Upsilon. Home: 5020 W Ave K-8 Lancaster CA 93536 Office: AF Phillips Lab OLAC PL/RKFE 9 Antares Rd Edwards CA 93524

KONTIS, KRIS JOHN, molecular biologist, neurobiologist; b. North Hollywood, Calif., June 7, 1954; s. Charles N. and Frieda Evangeline (Ermedes) K.; m. Linda Joyce Iseley, Aug. 24, 1985; children: Michael, Troy, Angela, Philip, Katrin. BA, Calif. State U., Northridge, 1981; PhD, U. Calif., Irvine, 1989. Tutor, lab. asst. Glendale (Calif.) Community Coll., 1978-79; microbiologist Applied Biol. Scis. Lab., Glendale, 1978-81, 81-82; grad. teaching asst. U. Calif., Irvine, 1982-87, postdoctoral fellow, 1989—; cons. CBC Labs., Buena Park, Calif., 1986—. Nat. Multiple Sclerosis Soc. fellow, 1989—. Mem. AAAS, Am. Soc. for Microbiology, Sigma Xi, Soc. Neurobiology. Republican. Office: U Calif Dept Microbiology Molecular Genetics Irvine CA 92717

KONTNY, VINCENT, engineering and construction company executive; b. Chappell, Nebr., July 19, 1937; s. Edward James and Ruth Regina (Schumann) K.; m. Joan Dashwood FitzGibbon, Feb. 20, 1970; children: Natascha Marie, Michael Christian, Amber Brooke. BSCE, U. Colo., 1958, DSc honoris causa, 1991. Operator heavy equipment, grade foreman Peter Kiewit Son's Co., Denver, 1958-59; project mgr. Utah Constrn. and Mining Co., Western Australia, 1965-69, Fluor Australia, Queensland, Australia, 1969-72; sr. project mgr. Fluor Utah, San Mateo, Calif., 1972-73; sr. v.p. Holmes & Narver, Inc., Orange, Calif., 1973-79; mng. dir. Fluor Australia, Melbourne, 1979-82; group v.p. Fluor Engrs., Inc., Irvine, Calif., 1982-85, pres., chief exec. officer, 1985-87; group pres. Fluor Daniel, Irvine, Calif., 1987-88, pres., 1988—; pres. Fluor Corp., Irvine, 1990—. Contbr. articles to profl. jours. Mem. engrng. devel. coun., U. Colo.; mem. engring. adv. coun., Stanford U. Lt. USN, 1959-65. Mem. Am. Assn. Cost Engrs., Australian Assn. Engrs., Am. Petroleum Inst. Republican. Roman Catholic. Club: Cet. (Costa Mesa, Calif.). Office: Fluor Corp. 3333 Michelson Dr Irvine CA 92730

KONWIN, THOR WARNER, financial executive; b. Berwyn, Ill., Aug. 17, 1943; s. Frank and Alice S. (Johnson) K.; m. Carol A. Svitak, Aug. 2, 1967 (div. Feb. 1990); 1 child, Christopher Vernon; m. Virginia Colburn, May 21, 1993. AA, Morton Jr. Coll., 1966; BS, No. Ill. U., 1967; MS, Roosevelt U., 1971. Acct. Beckerman & Terrill, CPA's, Chgo., 1967-68; cost acct. Sunbeam Corp., Chgo., 1968-72; controller Gen. Molded Products, Inc., Chgo., 1972-75, Sunbeam Appliance Co., Chgo., 1975-81; chief fin. officer Bear Med. System, Inc., Riverside, Calif., 1981-84, Bird Products Corp., Palm Springs, Calif., 1984—; gen. ptnr., 1985—; pres. B&B Ventures Ltd., Riverside, 1987—; chief exec. officer Med One Fin. Group, Salt Lake City; pres. Tags Antiques, Inc., Palm Springs; bd. dris. Bird Med. Techs., Inc., Palm Springs, Bird Products Corp., Palm Springs, Bird Internat., Inc., Riverside, B&B Ventures, Inc., Riverside, Equilink, Inc. Riverside, Stackhouse, Inc., Riverside, Med One Fin. Group, Salt Lake City; CEO Equitable Inc., Palm Springs, Calif., 1990—; adv. coun. U. Calif. Grad. Bus. Sch., Riverside, 1988—. Served with U.S. Army, 1969-71. Home: 45500 Verde Santa Palm Desert CA 92260 Office: Bird Products Corp 3101 E Alejo Rd Palm Springs CA 92262-6267

KOOB, ROBERT DUANE, chemistry educator, educational administrator; b. Graetinger, Iowa, Oct. 14, 1941; s. Emil John and Rose Mary (Slinger) K.; m. E. Yvonne Ervin, June 9, 1960; children—Monique, Gregory, Michael, Angela, Julie, Eric, David. B.A. in Edn., U. No. Iowa, 1962; Ph.D. in Chemistry, U. Kans., 1967. From asst. prof. to prof. chemistry N.D. State U., Fargo, 1967-90, chmn. dept. chemistry, 1974-78, 79-81, dir. Water Inst., 1975-85, dean Coll. Sci. and Math., 1981-84, v.p., 1985-90, interim pres., 1987-88; v.p. for acad. affairs, sr. v.p. Calif. Poly. State U., San Luis Obispo, 1990—; cons. TransAlta, Edmonton, Alta., Can., Alta. Research Council, Mitre Corp., Washington; bd. dirs. State Bank Fargo, Fargo Cass County Econ. Devel. Corp. Contbr. articles to profl. jours. Vice pres. Crookston Diocesan Sch. Bd., Minn., 1982; pres. elem. sch. bd. St. Joseph's Ch., Moorhead, Minn., 1982, parish council, 1983; pres. bd. Shanley High Sch., Fargo, 1985. Grantee in field. Roman Catholic. Office: Calif Poly State U San Luis Obispo CA 93407

KOOKER, DAVID MERRILL, information systems specialist; b. Lafayette, Ind., Dec. 15, 1964; s. Douglas Edward Kooker and Ellyn (Smolik) Riddle. AA in Bus., Copiah-Lincoln Jr. Coll., Wesson, Miss., 1989; BS in Bus., Belhaven Coll., Jackson, Miss., 1990. Computer technician Sci. Applications, Tucson, Ariz., 1987-90; dir. data processing Estes Homebldg., Tucson, 1990—. With U.S. Army, 1983-87. Mem. Tucson Bowl Friday Night League, Phi Theta Kappa. Republican. Home: PO Box 16031 Tucson AZ 85732 Office: Estes Homebldg 5780 N Swan Rd Tucson AZ 85718

KOOMEY, JONATHAN GARO, energy and environmental analyst; b. N.Y.C., Feb. 15, 1962; s. Richard Alan Koomey and Cynthia Carol Chaffee. AB in History of Sci., Harvard U., 1984; MS in Energy and Resources, U. Calif., Berkeley, 1986, PhD in Energy and Resources, 1990. Rschr. Lawrence Berkeley Lab., 1984-90, postdoctoral rsch. fellow, 1990-91, staff scientist, 1991—. Co-author: Energy Policy in the Greenhouse, 1989; also articles. Office: Lawrence Berkeley Lab Bldg 90-4000 1 Cyclotron Rd Berkeley CA 94720

KOON, RAY HAROLD, management and security consultant; b. Little Mountain, S.C., Nov. 19, 1934; s. Harold Clay and Jessie Rae (Epting) K.; m. Bertha Mae Gardner, Aug. 19, 1958; children: Shari Madilyn Koon Goode, Schyler Michele, Kamela Suzanne. BSBA, Old Dominion U., 1957; postgrad., Columbia (S.C.) Coll., 1957-58. Lic. pvt. pilot. Office services supr. FBI, Norfolk, Va., 1953-61, Las Vegas, 1961-62; agt. State Gaming Control Bd., Carson City, Nev., 1962-64, coord., 1967-80, chief of investigations, 1980-83; prodn. control mgr. Colite Industries, Inc., West Columbia, S.C., 1964-67; pres., bd. dirs. Global Advisors, Ltd., Carson City, 1983; dir. gaming surveillance Hilton Hotels Corp., Beverly Hills, Calif., 1983-86; pres., bd. dirs. JRJ Enterprises, Las Vegas, 1986-88; pres. Assoc. Cons. Enterprises, Las Vegas, 1983—; pres. Assoc. Gaming Cons., Las Vegas, 1983—, chief exec. officer, 1990—; bd. dirs. Sta. KNIS-FM Radio, Carson City, 1968-84, also sec., Casino Mgmt. Internat., Carson City, 1993—. Editor, pub. Ray Koon's Gaming Gram, 1986—; columnist Casino Gaming Internat., 1990-92. Chief vols. Warren Engine Co. 1, Carson City Fire Dept., 1962-83; mem. Carson City Sheriff's Aero Squadron, 1983—, past comdr.; mem. exec. bd. Nev. Bapt. Conv. With U.S. Army, 1957-59. Mem. Nev. Arbitration Assn. (bd. dirs. 1986-90), Las Vegas C. of C. (mem. commerce crime prevention and legis. action coms. 1989-90), Zelzah Shrine Aviation Club (past comdr.), Toastmasters, Masons. Republican. Office: Assoc Cons Enterprises 3271 S Highland Dr Ste 705A Las Vegas NV 89109-1051

KOON, ROBIN CHARLES, retail pharmacy executive; b. Pasadena, Calif., Apr. 22, 1953; s. Charles John and Helene (Wickham) K.; m. Laura Lynn Robertson, Aug. 27, 1983; children: Casey Charles, Perry William. BSM, Pepperdine U., 1993. Lic. pharmacy technician. Store mgr. Imperial Drugs, L.A., 1977-81; mem. store mgmt. Thrifty Drugs, L.A., 1987-88; pharmacy technician Horton & Converse Pharmacies, Newport Beach, Calif., 1981-87, mgr. chain ops., 1988—. Unit commr. Boy Scouts Am., Hollywood, Calif., 1984—. Mem. Calif. Pharmacy Assn., Orgn. Pharmacy Technicians, Optimists (v.p. Hollywood club 1986—). Home: 2730 N Kenneth Rd Burbank CA 91504 Office: Horton Converse Pharmacies 1617 Westcliff Newport Beach CA 92660

KOONCE, JOHN PETER, investment company executive; b. Coronado, Calif., Jan. 8, 1932; s. Allen Clark and Elizabeth (Webb) K.; B.S., U.S. Naval Acad., 1954; postgrad. U. So. Calif., 1957, U. Alaska, 1961, U. Ill., 1968-69; M.S. in Ops. Research, Fla. Inst. Tech., 1970; postgrad. Claremont Grad. Sch., 1970; m. Marilyn Rose Campbell, Sept. 21, 1952; children—Stephen Allen, William Clark, Peter Marshall. Indsl. engr. Aluminum Co. Am. Lafayette, Ind., 1954-56; electronic research engr. Autonetics Div. N.Am. Aviation, Downey, Calif., 1956-57; systems field engr. Remington Rand Univac, Fayetteville, N.C., 1957-59; project engr. RCA Service Co., Cheyenne, Wyo., 1959-60, project supr., Clear, Alaska, 1960-62, project supr., Yorkshire, Eng., 1962-64, re-entry signature analyst, Patrick AFB, Fla., 1964-66; mem. tech. staff TRW Systems Group, Washington, 1966-68; mgr. ops research systems analysis Magnavox Co., Urbana, Ill., 1968-69; tech. advisor, EDP, to USAF, Aerojet Electro Systems Co., Azusa, Calif., Woomera, Australia, 1969-72; investment exec. Shearson Hammill, Los Angeles, 1972-74; investment exec. Reynolds Securities, Los Angeles, 1974-75; v.p. investments Shearson Hayden Stone, Glendale, Calif., 1975-77; v.p. accounts Paine, Webber, Jackson & Curtis Inc., Los Angeles, 1977-82; pres. Argo Fin. Corp., Santa Monica, Calif., 1982-83, Fin. Packaging Corp., Flintridge, Calif., 1983—; fin. lectr. cruise ship Island Princess; tchr. investments Citrus Coll., Azusa, Calif., Claremont (Calif.) Evening Sch. Vice pres. Claremont Republican Club, 1973, pres., 1974. Chmn., Verdugo Hosp. Assos., 1979. Recipient Merit certificate RCA, 1966. Mem. Nat. Assn. Security Dealers, Internat. Assn. Fin. Planners, Navy League U.S., Naval Acad. Alumni Assn. Clubs: Masons (past master 1987, pres. dist. officers assn.), 32d Degree, Kiwanis, Marbella Golf & Country. Host, commentator, Sta. KWHY-TV, Los Angeles, (weekly) West of Wall Street, 1986-87; contbr. articles to bus. jours. Home: 5228 Escalante Dr La Canada Flintridge CA 91011-1326 Office: 15233 Ventura Blvd # 404 Sherman Oaks CA 91403-2201

KOONTZ, ALFRED JOSEPH, JR., financial and operating management executive; b. Balt., Mar. 6, 1942; s. Alfred J. and Mary Agnes (Valis) K.; m. Kay Francis Frank, Aug. 4, 1962; children—Debbie Kay, Denise Marie, Stacey Lynn, Alfred Joseph, III. B.S. in Bus. Adminstrn, Pa. State U., 1964. C.P.A., Md. Mgr. Price Waterhouse & Co., Balt., 1964-73; sr. mgr. Price Waterhouse & Co., N.Y.C., 1973-74, Morristown, N.J., 1974-75; v.p. fin Piper Aircraft Corp., Lock Haven, Pa., 1975-80; sr. v.p. fin. Piper Aircraft Corp., 1980-85, sr. v.p. fin., treas., 1985-86; exec. v.p., chief operating officer Piper Aircraft Corp., Vero Beach, Fla., 1987-88; pres., dir. Piper Acceptance Corp., Lakeland, Fla., 1985-88; sr. v.p. fin. and adminstrn., treas., bd. dirs. Todd Shipyards Corp., Seattle, 1988-91; exec. v.p., CFO Pay'N Pak Stores Inc., Bellevue, Wash., 1992—. Mem. AICPA, Md. Assn. CPAs, Inst. Mgmt. Accts. Home: 14565 SE 56th St Bellevue WA 98006-4389 Office: Pay 'n Pak Stores Inc Ste 900 10900 NE 8th St Ste 900 Bellevue WA 98004

KOONTZ, MARGARET ANN, research biologist, educator; b. Wooster, Ohio, Sept. 26, 1947; d. Philip Grant and Florence Rebekah (Eyre) Koontz; m. Loren J. Siebert, Sept. 10, 1988. BA, Coll. of Wooster, 1969; MS, U. Wash., 1974, PhD, 1977, postgrad., 1993—. Teaching asst. zoology dept. U. Wash., Seattle, 1970-76, rsch. asst. zoology dept., 1976-77, acting asst. prof. zoology dept., 1978; postdoctoral fellow Max Planck Inst. for Behavioral Physiology, Seewiesen, Fed. Republic of Germany, 1978-80; sr. fellow ophthalmology dept. U. Wash. Sch. Medicine, Seattle, 1981-89, rsch. assoc., 1989-91, rsch. asst. prof., 1991-93. Contbr. articles to profl. jours. NIH grantee U. Wash., 1989-93. Mem. Soc. for Neurosci., Assn for Rsch. in Vision and Ophthalmology. Office: U Wash Dept Ophthalmology RJ-10 Seattle WA 98195

KOOVSHINOFF, DIMITRI, musician, educator, artist; b. San Francisco, Mar. 10, 1930; s. Dimitri and Margaret (Znamensky) K.; m. Irene Xenia Ivanoff, Apr. 1, 1956; 1 child, Nicholas. BS, Juilliard Sch., 1952, MS, 1953; diploma, Staatliche Hochschule Musik, Freiburg, Germany, 1953-54. Cert. music tchr., Calif. Concert pianist U.S. Dept. State, Germany, 1953-54; tchr. Wilson Sch. Music, Yakima, Wash., 1954-56; educator San Ramon Valley Unified Sch. Dist., Danville, Calif., 1957—; mem. textbook selection com. Contra Costa County Edn. Office, Pleasant Hill, Calif., 1965. Artist various works (recipient 17 awards 1982-92). Named Tchr. of Yr., Contra Costa County, 1985-86; Juilliard scholar, 1948-52; Fulbright grantee, 1953. Mem. Bodega Bay Art Alliance, Alamo Danville Art Assn., Danville Tchrs. Orgn. (pres. 1958-59), Redwood Palette Club (exhibit chmn. 1991-92). Home: 294 Via Cima Ct Danville CA 94526 Office: Charlotte Wood Sch 600 El Capitan Dr Danville CA 94526

KOP, TIM M., psychologist; b. Aug. 3, 1946; s. Michael and Antoinette Wanda (Stahurski) K.; m. Yoshino Fujita, Aug. 9, 1975; children: Maile K., Geoffrey M. BA in Psychology, U. Hawaii, 1972; MA in Edn., Mich. State U., 1976; MS in Psychology, Columbia Pacific U., 1989, PhD in Psychology, 1991. Air traffic controller FAA, Honolulu, 1968-74; with U.S. Dept. Def., 1974—; pres. PAOA, Inc., Honolulu, 1986—; cons. Tripler Army Med. Ctr., Honolulu, 1990-92, State of Hawaii, 1992—. Author: Neural Programming, 1991, Normal Language Learning, 1989, Normal Language Learning and Aphasia, 1988; editor: North Korean Military Forces, 1979; author manuscript: Counterinsurgency along the Thai-Malaysian Border, 1982. Vice pres. Waiau Gardens Community Assn., Pearl City, Hawaii, 1986-88. Capt. U.S. Army, 1965-68, 78. Recipient Sec. of the Navy Award for group achievement U.S. Sec. of Navy, 1982. Fellow Am. Orthopsychiat. Assn.; mem. APA, Am. Psychological Soc., Am. Assn. Artificial Intelligence, U. Hawaii Alumni Assn. (life), Assn. of Mil. Surgeons of U.S. (life). Democrat. Office: Century Ctr Ste 3-520 1750 Kalakaua Ave Honolulu HI 96826-3766

KOPEČEK, JINDŘICH, biomedical scientist, biomaterials and pharmaceutics educator; b. Strakonice, Bohemia, Czechoslovakia, Jan. 27, 1940; came to U.S., 1986; s. Jan and Herta Zita (Krombholz) K.; m. Marie Porcari, Aug. 11, 1962 (Div. 1984); 1 child, Jana; m. Pavla Hrušková, Apr. 27, 1985. MS in Polymer Chemistry, Inst. Chem. Tech., Prague, Czechoslovakia, 1961; PhD in Polymer Chemistry, Inst. Macromolecular Chemistry, Prague, 1965; DSc in Chemistry, Czechoslovak Acad. Scis., Prague, 1990. Rsch. sci. officer Inst. Macromolecular Chemistry, Prague, 1965-67, 68-72, head lab. of med. polymers, 1972-80; postdoctoral fellow NRC, Ottawa, Can., 1967-68; head lab. of biodegradable polymers Inst. Macromolecular Chemistry Czechoslovak Acad. of Scis., Prague, 1980-88; co-dir. Ctr. Controlled Chem. Delivery U. Utah, Salt Lake City, 1986—, prof. bioengring. and pharmaceutics, 1989—; vis. prof. Université Paris-Nord, Paris-Viletaneuse, 1983, U. Utah, 1986-88; adj. prof. material sci. U. Utah, 1987—; invited lectr. internat. meetings, univs. Editorial bd. mem. 11 sci. jours., U.S., U.K., The Netherlands, Poland, 1973—; contbr. over 200 articles to sci. publs. Recipient best sci. papers award Praesidiums of the Czechoslovak and USSR Acads. of Sci., 1977, awards Chem. Sec. of Czechoslovak Acad. Scis., 1972, 75, 77, 78, 85; rsch. grantee NIH, U. Utah, industry, 1986—, Czechoslovak Acad. of Sci., 1970-88. Mem. AAAS, Am. Chem. Soc., Am. Assn. Pharm. Scis., Am. Assn. Cancer Rsch., Biomaterials Soc., Soc. for Molecular Recognition, Controlled Release Soc. (bd. govs. 1988-91, v.p. 1993—). Office: U Utah Dept Bioengring 2480 MEB Salt Lake City UT 84112

KOPEL, ROBERT FRANK, anesthesiologist; b. Detroit, Mar. 2, 1954; s. Howard Frank and Sylvia Sara (Grushko) K.; m. Ann Elizabeth Snyder, May 4, 1986; children: Eric Frank, Laura Ellen. BA, UCLA, 1978; MD, U. Autonoma De Guadalajara, Mex., 1982. Paramedic UCLA Emergency Medicine Ctr., 1974-78; rotating resident Prince George's Hosp. Ctr., Cheverly, Md., 1982-83, internal medicine resident, 1983-86, sexual assault physician, 1984-86, emergency rm. physician, chief med. resident, 1985-86, critical care physician, 1986; critical care medicine fellow U. Va. Sch. Medicine, Charlottesville, Va., 1986-88; critical care physician Greater S.E. Community Hosp., Washington, 1987-88; anesthesiology resident UCLA Hosp. and Clinics, 1988-91; staff anesthesiologist Hoag Meml. Hosp. Presbyn., Newport Beach, Calif., 1991—; asst. clin. prof. anesthesiology UCLA Hosp. and Clinics, 1991—; pres. Prince George's Hosp. Housestaff Assn., 1984-85. Contbr. articles to profl. jours. BCLS instr. Am. Heart Assn., L.A., 1977—, ACLS instr., 1986—. Mem. ACP, Am. Coll. Chest Physicians, Am. Soc. Anesthesiologists, Calif. Soc. Anesthesiologists, Soc. Critical Care Medicine, Phi Delta Epsilon, Zeta Beta Tau (trustee 1977—, v.p. 1975-76). Democrat. Jewish. Home: 2732 Hilltop Dr Newport Beach CA 92660 Office: Hoag Meml Hosp Presbyn Dept Anesthesiology 301 Newport Blvd Newport Beach CA 92663

KOPER, ALEX, dentist, educator; b. St. Louis, Nov. 15, 1917; s. Abram and Miriam Koper; m. Corrine Meta Nagin, Aug. 29, 1948; children: Alex II, Lisa R., Claudia J. BS, U. So. Calif., L.A., 1942, DDS, 1942. Diplomate Am. Bd. Prosthodontics. Pvt. practice prosthodontics, 1946—; prof. dentistry U. So. Calif., L.A., 1966—; cons. USAF, 1981-85; lectr. in field. Contbr. articles to profl. jours. Capt. USAF, 1942-46. Fellow Am. Coll. Prosthodontics (past pres.), Am. Coll. Dentists, Acad. Prosthodontics, Internat. Coll. Dentists, Am. Acad. Crown & Bridge Prosthetics; mem. Pacific Coast Prosthodontists (past pres.), Fedn. Prosthodontic Orgns. (past pres.). Home: 520 N Bristol Ave Los Angeles CA 90049-2610 Office: 11645 Wilshire Blvd Ste 1158 Los Angeles CA 90025-1786

KOPETSKI, MIKE, congressman; b. Oreg., Oct. 27, 1949; 1 child, Matthew. BA, Am. U.; JD, Lewis & Clark Coll. Congl. aide Senate Watergate Com., Washington, 1973-74; del. Dem. Nat. Conv., 1976; adminstr. coms. Oreg. State Legis., 1977-79, 81, state rep., 1985-89; cons. labor, mgmt. and edn.; community organizer Oreg. Law Related Edn. Project, 1986; v.p. Currier-McCormick Communications, 1989-90; mem. 102nd-103rd Congresses from 5th Oreg. dist., Washington, D.C., 1991—, Ways and Means Com., Washington, D.C.; pres. House of Reps. 1st term Dem. class, 1992; v.p. Ho. Reps. 1st term Dem. Class, 1991. Office: US Ho of Reps 218 Cannon Office Bldg Washington DC 20515 also: The Equitable Ctr Bldg 530 Center St NE Ste 340 Salem OR 97301 also: 615 High St Oregon City OR 97045

KOPF, JOHN OSCAR, scientist; b. Kings County, N.Y., Feb. 21, 1938; s. Oscar Emil and Elizabeth Kopf; m. Margaret E. Rutherford, Sept. 9, 1961; children: Elizabeth, Eric. BA, U. Conn., 1960, MA, 1962; PhD, Mich. State U., 1968. Engr. Lawrence Berkley Labs., Berkley, Calif., 1968-73; scientist Tymnet, Cupertino, Calif., 1973-75, sr. scientist, 1975-80; sr. staff scientist Tymnet (Tymshare), San Jose, Calif., 1980-84, Tymnet (McDonald Douglas), San Jose, 1984-88, BT N.Am., San Jose, 1988—. Office: BT NAm 2560 North 1st St San Jose CA 95161-9019

KOPICKI, BENJAMIN F., columnist; b. Huntingdon, Pa., Apr. 14, 1960; s. Derald Kopicki and Gladys Mae (Hoffman) Matter; life ptnr. Michael Thomas Wilson. BA in English magna cum laude, U. Mich., 1982; MA in Journalism, Columbia U., 1984; postgrad., U. Ariz., 1990—. Writer Village Voice, N.Y.C., 1984-86; freelance writer L.A., 1986-90; columnist The Jazz Report, Scottsdale, Ariz., 1990—; lectr. UCLA, 1988-90; guest columnist N.Y. Times, L.A. Times, Rolling Stone. Author: How They Got the Blues: Jazz Greats of the 20th Century, 1988, Am I Blue?: A Novice's Guide to Jazz, 1990. Big brother Big Bros. L.A., 1988-90; sec. Ariz. for Clinton Campaign Team, 1992; vol. Scottsdale After Sch. Ctr., 1992—. Mem. Jazz Journalists Assn. Am. Office: Werik Plz 13610 N Scottsdale Rd Ste 10 Scottsdale AZ 85254-4063

KOPLIN, DONALD LEROY, health products executive, consumer advocate; b. Greenleaf, Kans., Dec. 31, 1932; s. Henry G. Koplin and Edith Mary Stevens; m. Patricia Joynes, June 2, 1962 (div. Aug. 1974); children: Marie Claire, Marie Joelle (adopted). Student, U. San Diego, 1956-59, 67-68. Electronics test insp. Gen. Dynamics, San Diego, 1956-59; cryptographer Dept. of State, Washington, 1959-67; communications program officer Dept. of State, France, Angola, Madagascar, Qatar, India, Oman, Benin and the Bahamas, 1977-86; tech. writer Ryan Aero. Corp., San Diego, 1967-68; comml. dir., tech. advisor, pub. rels. officer Societe AGM, San Francisco, Athens, Greece, Antananarivo and Morondava, Dem. Republic of Madagascar, 1968-72; founder, dir. Soc. Bells, Cyclone & Akai, Antananarivo, 1972-74; founder, ptnr., assoc. editor Angola Report, Luanda, 1974-75; polit. reporter Angola Report, Reuters, AP, UPI Corr., BBC, Luanda; supr. Tex. Instruments, Lubbock, 1976-77; exec. Dial A Contact Lens, Inc., La Jolla, Calif., 1986-90, Assn. for Retarded Citizens, San Diego, 1991-92, Club Med, Copper Mountain, Colo., 1992—. Active San Diego Zool. Soc. With USN, 1951-55, Korea and Japan. Mem. Internat. Platform Assn., Am. Fgn. Svc. Assn.civ. Republican. Roman Catholic. Home: 436 Rosemont St La Jolla CA 92037-6058

KOPP, DAVID EUGENE, manufacturing company executive; b. St. Louis, Apr. 21, 1951; s. Doyle Eugene and Irene Audrey (Gloyeske) K. BA in English, U. South Fla., 1975. Supr. Titleist Golf Co., Escondido, Calif., 1979-80; supr. Imed Corp., San Diego, 1980-82, process engr., 1982-83, sr. process engr., 1983-85; area mgr. Husky Injection Molding Systems Inc., Newport Beach, Calif., 1985-91; dir. sales Tech C.B.I. Inc., Scottsdale, Ariz., 1991—. Mem. Soc. Plastic Engrs. (affiliate, bd. dirs., student liaison person Canoga Park, 1985-87). Republican. Roman Catholic. Home: 9980 N 106th St Scottsdale AZ 85258 Office: TECH CBI Inc 7975 N Hayden Rd Ste D-100 Scottsdale AZ 85258

KOPP, HARRIET GREEN, communication specialist; b. N.Y.C., June 18, 1917; m. George A. Kopp, 1948 (dec. 1968); m. Kurt Friedrich, 1972. MA, Bklyn. Coll., 1939; diploma in edn. of deaf, Columbia U., 1939, PhD, 1962. Scientist Bell Telephone Labs., 1943-46; mem. faculty Eastern Mich. U., 1946-48; adj. prof. Wayne State U., Detroit, 1948-70; dir. communication clinics Rehab. Inst. Met. Detroit, 1955-59; dir. programs deaf and aphasic Detroit Bd. Edn., 1959-70; prof., chmn. communication disorders San Diego State U., 1970-80; acting dean Coll. Human Svcs., 1980-83; prof. emerita San Diego State U., 1983—; mem. Nat. Adv. Com. on Deaf, 1965-72, chmn., 1970-72; mem. Nat. Adv. Com. on Handicapped, 1972-73; adv., rev. panels Bur. Educationally Handicapped, HEW, 1963-83. Author: (with R. Potter, G.A. Kopp) Visible Speech, 1948, 68, Some Applications of Phonetic Principles, 1948, 65, 62, 68, 70, 78, 85, 86; editor: Curriculum, Cognition and Content, 1968, 75, Reading: Cognitive Input and Output, 49th Claremont Reading Conf. Yearbook, 1982, Bilingual Problems of the Hispanic Deaf, 1984. Chair quality of life bd. City of San Diego, 1978-92. Recipient Outstanding Faculty award San Diego State U., 1983. Mem. Am. Speech and Hearing Assn. (fellow 1962), AAAS, A.G. Bell Assn. (dir. 1964-68, chmn. editorial bd. 1966-75), Conf. Execs. Schs. for Deaf, Council Exceptional Children, Calif. Speech and Hearing Assn., Phi Kappa Phi. Address: 6711 Golfcrest Dr San Diego CA 92119

KOPP, QUENTIN L., lawyer, state legislator; b. Syracuse, N.Y.; m. Mara Sikaters; children: Shepard, Bradley, Jennifer. Student, Dartmouth Coll.; JD, Harvard U. Sr. ptnr. Kopp & DiFranco; mem. Calif. State Senate, 1986—, mem. various coms.; commentator Sta. KTVU-TV. Bd. suprs. rep. San Francisco Bay Conservation and Devel. Commn., 1972-78, Met. Transp. Commn., 1976-86, chmn., 1983-85, Bay Area Air Quality Mgmt. Dist., 1978-84; pres. San Francisco Bd. Suprs., 1976-78, 1982; founding mem. San Francisco/San Mateo Joint County Task Force, 1982-86; originator, chmn. Bay Area Super Bowl Task Force; ex officio mem. Calif. Transp. Commn.; bd. dirs. Bay Area Rapid Transit Dist., 1973-74, Golden Gate Bridge, Hwy. and Transp. Dist., 1977-86, v.p., 1984-86, peninsula divsn. League Calif. Cities, 1977-79, pres., 1976-77. Lt. USAF, 1952-54. Mem. Calif. Jr. Bar Assn. (past pres.), San Francisco Jr. Bar Assn. (past pres.), Lawyer's Club, Olympic Club, St. Francis Yacht Club, Marines Meml. Club (hon. life). Office: Office of State Senate 363 El Camino Real #205 South San Francisco CA 94080

KOPPEL, THOMAS PAUL, freelance writer; b. N.Y.C., Sept. 13, 1943; s. Edwin and Margaret (Gillan) K.; m. Christel Renate Schwarz, Dec. 28, 1965 (div. 1970); m. Anna Mary Palovcik, July 18, 1992. BA in Econs., U. Pa., 1966; PhD in Polit. Sci., U. Wis., 1972. Asst. prof. polit. sci. Western Ill. U., Macomb, 1971-72, SUNY, Stony Brook, 1972-73; writer, analyst Deadline Data on World Affairs, Bridgeport, Conn., 1973-81; freelance mag. writer Ganges, B.C., Can., 1982—; guest reporter Rabochaya Gazeta, Kiev, USSR, 1989-90. Contbr. articles to profl. jours., popular mags., newspapers. Mem. Periodical Writer's Assn. Can. Home: Box 944, Ganges, BC Canada V0S 1E0

KOPPES, STEVEN NELSON, public information officer, science writer; b. Manhattan, Kans., Aug. 28, 1957; s. Ralph James and Mary Louise (Nelson) K.; m. Susan Camille Keaton, May 18, 1984. BS in Anthropology cum laude, Kans. State U., 1978; MS in Journalism, Kans. U., 1982. Rsch. asst. dept. anthropology Kans. State U., Manhattan, 1979; reporter The Morning Sun, Pittsburg, Kans., 1981-83; co-mgr. Doc's B.R. Others Restaurant, Tempe, Ariz., 1983-85; info. specialist Ariz. State U. New Bur., Tempe, 1985-87, asst. dir., 1987—. Contbr. to Ariz. State U. Rsch. Mag., 1984—; contbr. articles to various publs. Bd. dirs. Children's Mus. of Metro Phoenix, 1988. Recipient award of excellence Internat. Assn. Bus. Communicators, 1991, award of merit, 1989-91. Mem. Nat. Assn. Sci. Writers, Ariz. Archaeol. Soc. (bd. dirs. Phoenix chpt. 1987-88). Office: New Bur Ariz State U Tempe AZ 85287-1803

KORAN, DENNIS HOWARD, publisher; b. L.A., May 21, 1947; s. Aaron Baer and Shirley Mildred (Kassan) K.; m. Roslynn Ruth Cohen, Apr. 6, 1979; 1 child, Michael; stepchildren: Jeff, Beth, Judy. Student, U. Leeds, Eng., 1966-67, UCLA, 1979-80; BA, U. Calif., Berkeley, 1980; postgrad., Loyola U., L.A., 1982-84, 86-89. Co-founder, co-editor Cloud Marauder Press, Berkeley, 1969-72, Panjandrum/Aris Books, San Francisco, 1973-81; founder, editor Panjandrum Books, San Francisco, 1971—, Panjandrum Press, Inc., San Francisco, 1971—; co-dir. poetry reading series Panjandrum Books, 1972-76. Author: (book of poetry) Vacancies, 1975, After All, 1993; editor Panjandrum Poetry Jour., 1971—; co-editor Cloud Marauder, 1969-72; author poetry pub. various jours. Liaison between U.S. Govt. and Saminole Indians VISTA, Sasakwa, Okla., 1969-70. Nat. Endowment for Arts Lit. Pub. grantee, 1974, 76, 79, 81, 82, 84, Coord. Coun. for Lit. Mags., 1971-80. Mem.Lovers of the Stinking Rose, Poets and Writers. Office: Panjandrum Books 5428 Hermitage Ave North Hollywood CA 91607

KORB, LAWRENCE JOHN, metallurgist; b. Warren, Pa., Apr. 28, 1930; s. Stanley Curtis and Dagna (Pedersen) K.; B.Chem.Engring., Rensselaer Poly. Inst., Troy, N.Y., 1952; m. Janet Davis, Mar. 30, 1957; children: James, William, Jeanine. Sales engr. Alcoa, Buffalo, 1955-59; metall. engr. N. Am. Rockwell Co., Downey, Calif., 1959-62; engring. supr. metallurgy Apollo program Rockwell Internat. Co., Downey, 1962-66, engring. supr. advanced materials, 1966-72, engring. supr. metals and ceramics space shuttle program, 1972-88; cons., 1988—; mem. tech. adv. com. metallurgy Cerritos Coll., 1969-74. Served with USNR, 1952-55. Registered profl. engr., Calif. Fellow Am. Soc. Metals (chmn. aerospace activity com. 1971-76, judge materials application competition 1969, handbook com. 1978-83, chmn. handbook com. 1983, chmn. publs. coun. 1984). Republican. Author articles, chpts. in books. Home: 251 S Violet Ln Orange CA 92669-3740

KORB, ROBERT WILLIAM, materials and processes engineer; b. Warren, Pa., Mar. 12, 1929; s. Dallas Weigand and Evelyn Eleanor (Peterson) K.; m. Diane Marie Goldsberry, Oct. 14, 1964 (div. 1972); 1 child, Karen; m. Setsu Campbell, Aug. 9, 1980; children: Theresa Campbell, Mark Campbell, Laura Campbell. BS in Chemistry, U. Nev., 1951. Chemist Rezolin, Inc., Santa Monica, Calif., 1956-57; mem. tech. staff Hughes Aircraft Co., Culver City, Calif., 1957-64; mem. tech. staff Hughes Aircraft Co., Fullerton, Calif., 1971-74, group head materials engring., 1974-79, sect. head materials and processes engring., 1979—; mem. tech. staff TRW Systems, Redondo Beach, Calif., 1964-71. Contbr. articles to profl. jours.; patentee flexible cable process. 1st lt. USAF, 1951-56. Mem. Inst. for Interconnecting and Packaging Electronic Circuits (co. rep.), Soc. for Advancement Materials and Process Engring. Republican. Home: 12 Palmatum Irvine CA 92720 Office: Hughes Aircraft Co Bldg 607/B214 1901 W Malvern Ave Fullerton CA 92634

KORDUCKI, BARBARA JOAN, former orchestra executive, educator, real estate agent, development consultant; b. Milw., May 2, 1956; d. Edward and Rita Korducki. BA in Mass Communication, U. Wis., Milw., 1980; MPA, Seattle U., 1986. News reporter, pub. affairs producer Sta. WUWM, Milw., 1979-81; cons. Adams & Assocs., Seattle, 1981-82; pub. rels. and projects coord. Nat. Multiple Sclerosis Soc., Seattle, 1982-85; pub. rels. and mktg. specialist Planned Parenthood of Seattle-King County, Seattle, 1985-87; mng. dir. N.W. Chamber Orch., Seattle, 1987-90; devel. cons., real estate agt. Seattle, 1990—; pres., founder Puget Sound Multi-Family Partnerships, Inc., Seattle, 1993—; adj. lectr. journalism Seattle U., 1989-90; mem. mktg. task force Bus. Vols. for Arts, 1989-90, 92—. Exec. producer (ednl. mus.) Henry's Tune, 1990-91. Pub. rels. cons. Seattle Urban League/King County Coalition on Teen Pregnancy, 1985-87; bd. dirs. Wash. Literacy, 1982-85; spl. events com. Nat. Multiple Sclerosis Soc., Seattle, 1987-88; panelist Puget Power Blue Ribbon Commn., 1986-87; project advisor Leadership Tomorrow, Seattle, 1986; fundraiser Black and Latino Adolescent Alcohol and Drug Endeaver, 1990-92; pres. Charlestown Park Homeowner's Assn., 1990—; mem. Alki Beach Community Coun., 1992—; fundraiser Mike Lowry Dem. for Gov., 1992-93. Mem. N.W. Devel. Officers Assn., Pub. Rels. Soc. Am. (cert., chmn. Wash. awards 1987-90, co-chmn. Totem awards 1984-86), Seattle Women's Sailing Assn., King County Assn. Realtors (polit. adv. com.), Seattle Sailing Club (bd. dirs. 1986-87), King County Assn. Realtors. Democrat. Office: Re/Max Northwest 300 NE 97th Seattle WA 98165

KORF, RICHARD EARL, computer science educator; b. Geneva, Dec. 7, 1956; s. Earl Watkin and Suzanne Michelle (Nacouz) K. BS in Elec. Engring. and Computer Sci., MIT, 1977; MS in Computer Sci., Carnegie-Mellon U., Pitts., 1980; PhD in Computer Sci., Carnegie-Mellon U., 1983. Asst. prof. Columbia U., N.Y.C., 1983-85; asst. prof. UCLA, L.A., 1985-88, assoc. prof., 1988—. Author: Learning to Solve Problems by Searching for Macro-Operators, 1985; contbr. articles to profl. jours. NSF rsch. grantee, 1984—; recipient Devel. award IBM Corp., 1985; named Presdl. Young Investigator NSF, 1986. Mem. Am. Assn. Artificial Intelligence. Democrat. Presbyterian. Home: 10470 Colina Way Los Angeles CA 90077-2040 Office: UCLA Dept Computer Sci Los Angeles CA 90024

KORINS, LEOPOLD, stock exchange executive. Pres. Pacific Stock Exch., San Francisco, now chmn., chief exec. officer. Office: Pacific Stock Exch 301 Pine St San Francisco CA 94104-7065

KORMONDY, EDWARD JOHN, university official, biology educator; b. Beacon, N.Y., June 10, 1926; s. Anthony and Frances (Glover) K.; m. Peggy Virginia Hedrick, June 5, 1950 (div. 1989); children: Lynn Ellen, Eric Paul, Mark Hedrick. BA in Biology summa cum laude, Tusculum Coll., 1950; MS in Zoology, U. Mich., 1951, PhD in Zoology, 1955. Teaching fellow U. Mich., 1952-55; instr. zoology, curator insects Mus. Zoology, 1955-57; asst. prof. Oberlin (Ohio) Coll., 1957-63, assoc. prof., 1963-67, prof., 1967-69, acting assoc. dean, 1966-67; dir. Commn. Undergrad. Edn. in Biol. Scis., Washington, 1968-72; dir. Office Biol. Edn., Am. Inst. Biol. Scis., Washington, 1968-71; mem. faculty Evergreen State Coll., Olympia, Wash., 1971-79, interim acting dean, 1972-73, v.p., provost, 1973-78; sr. profl. assoc., directorate sci. edn. NSF, 1979; provost, prof. biology U. So. Maine, Portland, 1979-82; v.p. acad. affairs, prof. biology Calif. State U., Los Angeles, 1982-86; sr. v.p., chancellor, prof. biology U. Hawaii, Hilo/West Oahu, 1986-93. Author: Concepts of Ecology, 1969, 76, 83, General Biology: The Integrity and Natural History of Organisms, 1977, Handbook of Contemporary World Developments in Ecology, 1981; high school textbook Biology, 1984, 88; International Handbook of Pollution Control, 1989; contbr. articles to profl. jours. Served with USN, 1944-46. U. Ga. postdoctoral fellow radiation ecology, 1963-64; vis. research fellow Center for Bioethics, Georgetown U., 1978-79; research grantee Nat. Acad. Scis., Am. Philos. Soc., NSF, Sigma Xi. Fellow AAAS; mem. Ecol. Soc. Am. (sec. 1976-78), Nat. Assn. Biology Tchrs. (pres. 1981), Nat. Sci. Tchrs. Assn., So. Calif. Acad. Scis. (bd. dirs. 1985-86), Sigma Xi.

KORN, DAVID, educator, pathologist; b. Providence, Mar. 5, 1933; s. Solomon and Claire (Liebman) K.; m. Phoebe Richter, June 9, 1955; children: Michael Philip, Stephen James, Daniel Clair. B.A., Harvard U., 1954, M.D., 1959. Intern Mass. Gen. Hosp., Boston, 1959-60; resident Mass. Gen. Hosp., 1960-61; research asso. NIH, 1961-63; mem. staff Lab. Biochem. Pharmacology; also asst. pathologist NIH, 1963-68; prof., chmn. dept. pathology Sch. Medicine, Stanford, 1968-84; physician-in-chief pathology Stanford Hosp., 1968-84, dean Sch. Medicine, 1984-85, v.p., dean, 1986—; cons. pathology Palo Alto VA Hosp., 1968-84; dean Stanford Sch. Med.; sr. surgeon USPHS, 1961-66; mem. cell biology study sect. NIH, 1973-77, chmn., 1976-77; mem. bd. sci. counselors, div. cancer biology and diagnosis Nat. Cancer Inst., 1977-82, chmn., 1980-82; chmn. Nat. Cancer Adv. Bd., 1984-91. Mem. editorial bd. Human Pthology, 1969-74; assoc. editor, 1974-88; mem. editorial bd. Jour. Biol. Chemistry, 1973-79. Recipient Young Scientist award Md. Acad. Sci., 1967. Mem. Am. Soc. Biol. Chemists, Am. Assn. Pathologists, Am. Soc. Cell Biology, Am. Soc. Microbiology, Fedn. Am. Soc. Exptl. Biology (bd. dirs., mem. exec. com.), Inst. of Medicine. Home: 905 Estudillo Rd Palo Alto CA 94305-1055 Office: Stanford U Sch Medicine Office of Dean 300 Pasteur Dr Stanford CA 94305-1901

KORN, GRANINO ARTHUR, engineer; b. Berlin, Germany, May 7, 1922; came to U.S., 1939; s. Arthur and Elizabeth Korn; m. Theresa M. McLaughlin, Sept. 3, 1948; children: Anne Marie, John McLaughlin. BA, Brown U., 1942, PhD, 1948; MA, Columbia U., 1943. Project engr. Sperry Gyroscope Co., Garden City, N.Y., 1946-48; head analysis group Curtiss-Wright Corp., Columbus, Ohio, 1948-49; staff engr. Lockheed Aircraft Co., Burbank, Calif., 1949-53; pvt. practice L.A., 1953-57; prof. elec. engring. U. Ariz., Tucson, 1957-83; prin. G.A. and T.M. Korn Indsl. Cons., Tucson, 1983—. Author numerous engring. texts and handbooks, 1952—; editor: Digital Computer User's Handbook, 1962; editorial bd.: Simulation, 1958—, Mathematics and Computers in Simulation, 1962-84. With USN, 1944-46. Recipient Sr. Scientific award Simulation Councils, 1958, Alexander von Humboldt Found. Prize, 1976. Fellow IEEE; mem. Soc. for Computer Simulation (life, tech. excellence award 1988), Internat. Assn. for Mathematics and Computers in Simulations, Sigma Xi. Office: GA and TM Korn Indsl Cons 6801 E Opatas St Tucson AZ 85715-3339

KORN, JERRY ARLEN, importer; b. San Pedro, Calif.; s. Irving and Kay (Kolchin) K.; divorced; children: Brian, Leslie. BS in Real Estate, San Diego State U., 1976. Owner 3 gift shops, 1969-85; pvt. practice real estate broker Escondido, Calif., 1976—; importer Royal Meerschaum Pipe Co., San Marcos, Calif., 1989—. Reserver sheriff, San Diego, 1980. With U.S. Army, 1967-69, Vietnam. Decorated Silver Star, Purple Heart. Home: PO Box 4051 Carlsbad CA 92018 Office: Royal Meerschaum Pipe Co PO Box 9 San Marcos CA 92079

KORN, WALTER, writer; b. Prague, Czechoslovakia, May 22, 1908; came to U.S., 1950, naturalized, 1956; s. Bernard and Clara (Deutsch) K.; m. Herta Klemperer, Dec. 24, 1933. Dr.Comm., Charles U., Prague, 1938; postgrad. London Sch. Econs., 1949-50; cert. systems and procedures Wayne State U., 1957; cert. polit. sci. New Sch., N.Y.C., 1972-73. Dir. mktg. Kosmos Works, Prague, 1934-39; contract mgr. Cantie Switches, Chester, Eng., 1941-44; dir. UNRRA, U.S. Zone Occupation, Germany, 1945-47; country dir. Orgn. for Rehab. and Tng., Geneva, 1948-49; contract mgr. Royal Metal Mfg. Co., N.Y.C., 1951-55; bus. mgr. J. Community Ctr., Detroit, 1956-59; dir. adminstrn. Am. Joint Distbn. Com., Tel Aviv, 1960-64; exec. asst. Self Help/United Help, N.Y.C., 1965-69; housing mgmt. cons. Exec. Dept. Div. Housing and Community Renewal, State N.Y., N.Y.C., 1970-76; lectr. housing for aged and housing fin., 1958-74; lectr. Brit. Allied Council, Liverpool, Eng., 1942-44. Nat. field rep. United Jewish Appeal, 1968—; mem. Vols. for Internat. Tech. Assistance, 1968-71. Served to capt. Czechoslovakian Army, 1938. Mem. Acad. Polit. Sci., Acad. Polit and Social Sci., Am. Judicature Soc., Amnesty Internat., World Affairs Coun. Clubs: Princeton of N.Y.; Commonwealth of Calif.; Press (San Francisco); Masons. Author: On Hobbies, 1936; Earn as You Learn, 1948; The Brilliant Touch, 1950; Modern Chess Openings, 13th edit., 1990; America's Chess Heritage, 1978, American Chess Art, 1975; Moderne Schach Eroeffnungen I and II, 1968, 75, 91; contbr. essay on chess to Ency. Brit., 1974. Home: 816 N Delaware St Apt 207 San Mateo CA 94401-1543

KORNBERG, ARTHUR, biochemist; b. N.Y.C., N.Y., Mar. 3, 1918; s. Joseph and Lena (Katz) K.; m. Sylvy R. Levy, Nov. 21, 1943 (dec. 1986); children: Roger, Thomas Bill, Kenneth Andrew; m. Charlene Walsh Levering, 1988. BS, CCNY, 1937, LLD (hon.), 1960; MD, U. Rochester, 1941, DSc (hon.), 1962; DSc (hon.), U. Pa., U. Notre Dame, 1965, Washington U., 1968, Princeton U., 1970, Colby Coll., 1970; LHD (hon.), Yeshiva U., 1963; MD honoris causa, U. Barcelona, Spain, 1970. Intern in medicine Strong Meml. Hosp., Rochester, N.Y., 1941-42; commd. officer USPHS, 1942, advanced through grades to med. dir., 1951; mem. staff NIH, Bethesda, Md., 1942-52, nutrition sect., div. physiology, 1942-45; chief sect. enzymes and metabolism Nat. Inst. Arthritis and Metabolic Diseases, 1947-52; guest research worker depts. chemistry and pharmacology coll. medicine NYU, 1946; dept. biol. chemistry med. sch. Washington U., 1947; dept. plant biochemistry U. Calif., 1951; prof., head dept. microbiology, med. sch. Washington U., St. Louis, 1953-59; prof. biochemistry Stanford U. Sch. Medicine, 1959—, chmn. dept., 1959-69; Mem. sci. adv. bd. Mass. Gen. Hosp., 1964-67; bd. govs. Weizmann Inst., Israel. Author: For the Love of Enzymes, 1989; contbr. sci. articles to profl. jours. Served lt. (j.g.), med. officer USCGR, 1942. Recipient Paul-Lewis award in enzyme chemistry, 1951; co-recipient of Nobel prize in medicine, 1959; recipient Max Berg award prolonging human life, 1968, Sci. Achievement award AMA, 1968, Lucy Wortham James award James Ewing Soc., 1968, Borden award Am. Assn. Med. Colls., 1968, Nat. medal of sci., 1979. Mem. Am. Soc. Biol. Chemists (pres. 1965), Am. Chem. Soc., Harvey Soc., Am. Acad. Arts and Scis., Royal Soc., Nat. Acad. Scis. (mem. council 1963-66), Am. Philos. Soc., Phi Beta Kappa, Sigma Xi, Alpha Omega Alpha. Office: Stanford U Med Ctr Dept Biochemistry Stanford CA 94305-5425*

KORNELL, JIM, artificial intelligence researcher; b. Burbank, Calif., July 25, 1951; s. Hal Kornell and Mary (Serruys) Kornell Alfonte; m. Jane Hankey, Apt. 1972 (div. 1976); m. Ellen Kindl, Dec. 10, 1979; children: Nate, Max, Sam, Amy, Will. BS in Computer Sci., U. Calif., Santa Barbara, 1978. Software engr. Raytheon Electronic systems, Goleta, Calif., 1978-81; project engr. Delco Electronics, Goleta, Calif., 1981-83; dir. machine intelligence lab. Gen. Rsch. Corp., Santa Barbara, Calif., 1983-92; prin. Syukhtun Rsch., Santa Barbara, Calif., 1992—. Author: Knowledge Acquisition Guidebook, 1992; (with others) Knowledge Acquisition for Knowledge Based Systems, 1989; editor Santa Barbara Athletic Assn., 1988-91; author systems Eucalyptus, 1990, Katalyst, 1992. Convener Open Alternative Sch., Santa Barbara, 1983, 85, 89; v.p., bd. dirs. Forest Project, Santa Barbara, 1990—. Mem. Am. Assn. Aritifical Intelligence, Cognitive Sci. Soc. Office: Syukhtun Rsch 2740 Williams Way Santa Barbara CA 93105

KORNEY, ELLEN LEMER, interior designer; b. N.Y.C., Dec. 27, 1943; d. Gerald J. and Gladys (Rosenberg) Halbreich; m. Albert Lemer, Apr. 16, 1969 (div. Jan. 1982); 1 child, Alison Hope; m. Michael Stanley Korney, Dec. 25, 1988. BA, Hofstra U., 1965; cert., N.Y. Sch. Interior Design, 1970-71. Asst. Virginia F. Frankel Interiors, N.Y.C., 1971; pres. Ellen Terry Lemer Ltd., N.Y.C., 1971-89; owner Ellen Lemer Korney Assocs., L.A., 1989—; instr. UCLA Extension, 1989, Parsons Sch. of Design, N.Y.C., 1987; guest lectr. Marymount Manhattan, N.Y.C., 1986. Contbr. articles to: Showcase of Interior Design, 1992, Very Small Spaces, 1988; contbr. articles to profl. jours. Mem. Allied Bd. of Trade, Met. Mus., L.A. County Mus. Art, Armand Hammer Mus., Am. Soc. Interior Designers (profl. mem., bd. dirs. L.A. 1990—, N.Y.C. 1986-89, 1st place award design competition residential L.A., 1991, Presdl. Citation 1991). Republican. Office: Ellen Lemer Korney Assocs 10170 Culver Blvd Culver City CA 90232

KORNFELD, PETER, internist; b. Vienna, Austria, Mar. 16, 1925; came to U.S., 1939; s. Otto and Rosa (Weitzmann) K. BA summa cum laude, U. Buffalo, 1948; MD, Columbia U., 1952. Diplomate Am. Bd. Internal Medicine. Intern Mt. Sinai Hosp., N.Y.C., 1952-53; asst. resident, then chief resident in internal medicine Mt. Sinai Hosp., 1955-56; postdoctoral fellow cardiovascular physiology, physician Nat. Heart Inst. at Columbia U./Presbyn. Hosp., N.Y.C., 1953-54; pvt. practice, N.Y., N.J., 1956-88; clin. prof. medicine Stanford U. Sch. Medicine, Univ. Hosp., 1991—; cons. physician N.Y. State Bur. Disability Determination, 1960-87, Hackensack (N.J.) Hosp. Med. Ctr., 1988-91; dir. Myasthenia Gravis Clinic, Englewood (N.J.) Hosp., 1965-91; mem. nat. med. adv. bd. Myasthenia Gravis Found., 1970-91; attending physician Englewood Hosp., Mt. Sinai Hosp.; clin. prof. Mt. Sinai Sch. Medicine, CUNY, 1968-92. Contbr. numerous articles to med. jours. Grantee, NIH, 1966-70, Hoffman-LaRoche, Inc., 1966-73, Muscular Dystrophy Assn., 1978-81, 81-82, Rosenstiel Found., 1979-82; recipient Globus award, Mt. Sinai Jour. Medicine, 1976-77. Fellow ACP, Am. Coll. Cardiology (assoc.), N.Y. Acad. Sci., N.Y. Acad. Medicine; mem. AMA, Am. Fedn. Exptl. Biology, Am. Fedn. Clin. Rsch., Harvey Soc., Am. Diabetes Assn, Am. Heart Assn., Phi Beta Kappa, Alpha Omega Alpha, Sigma Xi.

KORODY, ANTHONY VINCENT, corporate event producer, photographer; b. L.A., Mar. 4, 1951; s. Paul Alexander and Erica K.; m. Jaimie C. Korody, Mar. 13, 1982; 2 children. Student, U. So. Calif., 1970-72. Freelance photographer Black Star, Life, Newsweek, 1970; picture editor Daily Trojan, 1971; founder, chief exec. officer Fourth Estate Press, 1971—; photographer, co-founder SYGMA Agence de Press, Paris, 1973—; freelance photographer People, Time, Fortune, Newsweek, 1978-88; co-founder, v.p., dir. Image Stream, Inc., Los Angeles, 1978-86; contbg. photographer People Weekly Mag., 1979-87; lectr. Art Center; producer events for Apple Computer, Michelin, Toro, Taco Bell, Computerland, numerous others. Represented in permanent collections Time-Life Bldg., N.Y.C., Ronald Reagan Libr., Sylmar, Calif., ACT Hdqrs.; exhibited in group show 100 Time Magazine Covers, Cochran Gallery, Washington. Named Inc. 500 chief exec. officer, 1983, 84, 85. Mem. Nat. Press Photographers Assn., Sigma Delta Chi. Republican. Roman Catholic. Office: Fourth Estate Press PO Box 24B63 Los Angeles CA 90024

KOROPP, PHYLLIS KLEHM, photographer; b. Shanghai, China, Dec. 21, 1921; came to U.S., 1941; d. Henry Ferdinand and Kathleen Baker (Atkins) Merrill; m. Karl Klehm, June 20, 1954 (dec. Dec. 1960); children: Keith, Brook; m. Robert G. Koropp, Nov. 25, 1978. BA, Principia Coll., 1950; AM, Washington U., St. Louis, 1972. Sec. Harvard U., 1942, Helio Aircraft Co., Canton, Mass., 1950-52; asst. registrar Principia Coll., Elsah, Ill., 1961-63, registrar, 1963-70, asst. prof. art history, 1967-78; photographer Robert Koropp Photography, Denver, 1978—; bd. dirs., sec. Gilpin County Arts Assn., Central City, Colo.; mem. Colo. Photographic Arts Ctr. Ch. coms. Sixth Ch. of Christ Scientist, Denver, 1992, 2d reader, 1988-90; juror Denver Peoples Fair, 1986. Home and Office: 24326 Winder Pl Golden CO 80403

KOSECOFF, JACQUELINE BARBARA, health services researcher; b. Los Angeles, June 15, 1949; d. Herman Plaut and Betty (Bass) Hamburger; m. Robert Henry Brook, Jan. 17, 1982; children: Rachel Brook, Davida Brook. BA, UCLA, 1970; MS, Brown U., 1971; PhD, UCLA, 1973. Prof. medicine and pub. health UCLA, 1976—; pres. Value Health Scis., Santa Monica, Calif., 1988—; v.p. Value Health, Inc., Avon, Conn. Author: An Evaluation Primer, 1978, How to Evaluate Education Programs, 1980, Evaluation Basics, 1982, How to Conduct Surveys, 1985; contbr. numerous articles to profl. publs. Regents scholar UCLA, 1967-71; NSF fellow, 1971-72. Mem. Am. Pub. Health Assn., Assn. for Health Services Research. Democrat. Jewish. Home: 1278 N Norman Pl Los Angeles CA 90049-1541

KOSHALEK, RICHARD, museum director, consultant; b. Wausau, Wis., Sept. 20, 1941; s. H. Martin and Ethel A. (Hochtritt) K.; m. Elizabeth J. Briar, July 1, 1967; 1 child, Anne Elizabeth. Student, U. Wis., 1960-61, MA, 1965-67; BA, U. Minn., 1965. Curator Walker Art Ctr., Mpls., 1967-72; asst. dir. NEA, Washington, 1972-74; dir. Ft. Worth Art Mus., 1974-76, Hudson River Mus., Westchester, N.Y., 1976-80, Mus. Contemporary Art, L.A., 1980—; mem. Pres'. Coun. on Arts Yale U., New Haven, Conn., 1989—; mem. internat. bd. Biennale di Venezia, Italy, 1992—; mem. internat. adv. bd. Wexner Ctr. Ohio State U., Columbus, 1990—; cons. in field. Co-curator (exhibitions and books) Panza Collection, 1986, Ad Reinhardt, 1991, Arata Isozaki, 1991, Louis I. Kahn, 1992, Robert Irwin, 1993. Mem. Chase Manhattan Bank Art Com., N.Y.C., 1986; chmn. architect selection Walt Disney Concert Hall, L.A., 1988—; mem. Yale U. Pres.' Coun. com., Art Gallery and Brit. Art Ctr., New Haven, Conn., 1989; adv. Neighborhood Revitalization bd. for Pres. Clinton, Little Rock, Ark., 1993; mem. adv. bd. Am. Ctr. in Paris, 1993—, Internat. Moscow Biennale, 1993—. Fellow NEA, Washington, 1972, Durfee Found., L.A., 1992. Mem. Am. Inst. Graphic Arts (bd. dirs. 1992—), Am. Assn. Mus. Dirs., City Club L.A. (bd. dirs.). Office: Mus Contemporary Art 250 S Grand Ave Los Angeles CA 90012

KOSHLAND, DANIEL EDWARD, JR., biochemist, educator; b. N.Y.C., Mar. 30, 1920; s. Daniel Edward and Eleanor (Haas) K.; m. Marian Elliott, May 25, 1945; children: Ellen, Phyllis, James, Gail, Douglas. BS, U. Calif., Berkeley, 1941; PhD, U. Chgo., 1949; PhD (hon.), Weizmann Inst. Sci., 1984; ScD (hon.), Carnegie Mellon U., 1985; LLD (hon.), Simon Fraser U., 1986; LHD (hon.), Mt. Sinai U.; LLD (hon.), U. Chgo., 1992. Chemist Shell Chem. Co., Martinez, 1941-42; research asso. Manhattan Dist. U. Chgo., 1942-44; group leader Oak Ridge Nat. Labs., 1944-46; postdoctoral fellow Harvard, 1949-51; staff Brookhaven Nat. Lab., Upton, N.Y., 1951-65; affiliate Rockefeller Inst., N.Y.C., 1958-65; prof. biochemistry U. Calif., Berkeley, 1965—, chmn. dept., 1973-78; fellow All Souls, Oxford U., 1972; Phi Beta Kappa lectr., 1976; John Edsall lectr. Harvard U., 1980; William H. Stein lectr. Rockefeller U., 1985; Robert Woodward vis. prof. Harvard U., 1986. Author: Bacterial Chemotaxis as A Model Behavioral System, 1980; mem. editorial bd. jours. Accounts Chem. Rsch., Jour. Biol. Chemistry, Jour. Biology, Biochemistry; editor jour. Procs. NAS, 1980-85; editor Sci. mag., 1985—. Recipient T. Duckett Jones award Helen Hay Whitney Found., 1977, Nat. Medal of Sci., 1990, Merck award Am. Soc. Biochemistry and Molecular Biology, 1991; Guggenheim fellow, 1972. Mem. NAS, Am. Chem. Soc. (Edgar Fahs Smith award 1979, Pauling award 1979, Rosentiel award 1984, Waterford prize 1984), Am. Philos. Soc., Am. Soc. Biol. Chemists (pres.), Am. Acad. Arts and Scis. (coun.), Acad. Forum (chmn.), Japanese Biochem. Soc. (hon.), Royal Swedish Acad. Scis. (hon.), Alpha Omega Alpha. Home: 3991 Happy Valley Rd Lafayette CA 94549-2423 Office: U Calif Dept Molecular Cell & Molecular Biology Berkeley CA 94720-0001

KOSHLAND, MARIAN ELLIOTT, immunologist, educator; b. New Haven, Oct. 25, 1921; d. Waller Watkins and Margaret Ann (Smith) Elliott; m. Daniel Edward Koshland, Jr., May 25, 1945; children—Ellen R., Phyllis A., James M., Gail F., Douglas E. B.A., Vassar Coll., 1942, M.S., 1943; Ph.D., U. Chgo., 1949. Research asst. Manhattan Dist. Atomic Bomb Project, 1945-46; fellow dept. bacteriology Harvard Med. Sch., 1949-51; asso. bacteriologist biology dept. Brookhaven Nat. Lab., 1952-62, bacteriologist, 1963-65; assoc. research immunologist virus lab. U. Calif., Berkeley, 1965-69, lectr. dept. molecular biology, 1966-70, prof. dept. microbiology and immunology, 1970-89, chmn. dept., 1982-89, prof. dept. molecular and cell biology, 1989—; mem. Nat. Sci. Bd., 1976-82; mem. adv. com. to dir. NIH, 1972-75; mem. coun. Nat. Inst. Allergy and Infectious Diseases NIH, 1991—. Contbr. articles to profl. jours. Mem. NAS, Nat. Acad. Arts and Scis., Am. Acad. Microbiology, Am. Assn. Immunologists (pres. 1982-1983), Am. Soc. Biol. Chemists. Home: 3991 Happy Valley Rd Lafayette CA 94549 Office: U Calif Dept Molecular/Cell Biology 439 LSA Berkeley CA 94720

KOSINSKI, RICHARD JOHN, advertising executive; b. Glen Ridge, N.J., Apr. 6, 1965; s. Robert Edward and Madelaine (Kaufmann) K. BA, U. Ariz. Sales rep. Procter & Gamble Co., San Ramon, Calif., 1987-89, Wall St. Jour., San Francisco, 1989—. Tutor Project READ, San Francisco, 1991. Mem. San Francisco Advt. Club (v.p. 1993-94), U. Ariz. Alumni Assn. (dir. recruiting 1990-92), Dolphin Club, Toastmasters (exec. v.p. 1988). Republican. Presbyterian.

KOSKI, JOHN ARTHUR, minister, private school administrator, exercise physiologist; b. Ann Arbor, Mich., Mar. 30, 1950; s. William Arthur and Lucille Marie (Yungen) K.; m. Jenny Craney, June 16, 1984 (div. Apr. 1993); children: Isaac Simeon, Timothy John. AA, Christ for the Nations Inst., Dallas, 1984; BS, Oreg. State U., 1972; MS, U. Mich., 1974; postgrad., La. State U., 1986-88. Ordained to ministry Assembly of God Ch., 1987. Grad. asst. U. Mich., Ann Arbor, 1972-74; phys. dir. Bay City (Mich.) YMCA, 1974-75; health fitness dir. Metro YMCA, Singapore, 1975-77; bicycling evangelist traveled through 36 countries, 1977-81; prof. Jimmy Swaggart Bible Coll., Baton Rouge, 1984-88; min. Assembly of God, Harlem, Mont., 1988-93; assoc. pastor Abundant Life Christian Ch., Pueblo, Colo., 1993—; adminstr. Abundant Life Christian Sch., Pueblo, 1993—; Pres. Harlem Ministerial Assn., 1991-92, sec. Assembly of God sect., 1991-92. Mem. Am. Coll. Sports Medicine. Republican. Home: 1625 Bonforte Blvd 8B Pueblo CO 81001-1667 Office: Abundant Life Ministries PO Box 11010 1001 Constitution Ave Pueblo CO 81001-1010

KOSLOW, IRA LAWRENCE, personal manager musicians, executive producer videos; b. N.Y.C., Jan. 10, 1945; s. Irving and Clare Rita (Bernstein) K.; children: Jessica Koslow, Tim Rogers. BS, CUNY, 1965; MA, UCLA, 1966, C-Phil, 1969. Asst. prof. Calif. State Coll., Long Beach, 1969-73; v.p. Peter Asher Mgmt., L.A., 1975—. Assoc. producer cable spl. James Taylor In Concert, 1979, Linda Ronstadt Mad Love, 1980; exec. producer cable spl. Linda Ronstadt's What's New, 1985, Carole King's Going Home, 1989. Office: Peter Asher Mgmt 644 N Doheny Dr West Hollywood CA 90069-5596

KOSS, MARY LYNDON PEASE, psychology educator; b. Louisville, Sept. 1, 1948; d. Richard Charles and Carol (Bade) Pease; m. Paul G. Koss, Aug. 3, 1968; children: John Bade, Paul Shanor. AB, U. Mich., 1970; PhD, U. Minn., 1972. Lic. psychologist, Ariz. Asst. prof. psychology St. Olaf Coll., Northfield, Minn., 1973-76; prof. psychology Kent (Ohio) State U., 1976-88; prof. dept. family and community medicine U. Ariz. Coll. Medicine, Tucson, 1988—. Grantee NIMH, 1978—, Nat. Inst. Justice, 1985—. Mem. Am. Psychol. Assn. Democrat. Unitarian.

KOSSE, KRISZTINA MARIA, museum curator, archaeologist; b. Budapest, Hungary, Dec. 8, 1943; d. Elemer S. and Aranka (Gallai) Krudy; m. Alan D. Kosse, Nov. 25, 1971; 1 child, Jennifer. Student, U. Budapest, 1963-64; MA with honors, U. Edinburgh, Scotland, 1969; PhD, U. London, 1977. Intern Brit. Mus., Eng., 1968; program planner Iowa Dept. of Transp., 1977-80; curator of collections Maxwell Mus. of Anthropology U. N.Mex., Albuquerque, 1980—. Author: Settlement Ecology of Körös and Linear Pottery Cultures in Hungary, 1979. Abercrombie grantee U. Edinburgh, 1968. Mem. Soc. Am. Archaeology, N.Mex. Assn. of Mus. (treas. 1991-93). Office: U NMex Maxwell Mus of Anthropology Albuquerque NM 87131

KOST, GERALD JOSEPH, cardiovascular scientist; b. Sacramento, July 12, 1945; s. Edward William and Ora Imogene K.; m. Angela Louise Baldo, Sept. 9, 1972; children: Christopher Murray, Laurie Elizabeth. BS in Engring., Stanford U., 1967, MS in Engring., 1968; PhD in Bioengring., U. Calif., San Diego, 1977; MD, U. Calif., San Francisco, 1978. Diplomate Nat. Bd. Med. Examiners, Am. Bd. Pathology. Resident dept. medicine UCLA, 1978-79, resident dept. neurology, 1979-80; resident dept. lab. medicine U. Wash., Seattle, 1980-81, chief resident dept. lab. medicine, 1981-82, cardiopulmonary-bioengring. and clin. chemistry researcher, 1982-83; asst. prof. pathology U. Calif., Davis, 1983-87, assoc. prof., dir. clin. chemistry, faculty biomed. engring., 1987-93, prof., 1993—; vis. prof. and Lilly scholar, 1990; numerous sci. cons., nat. and internat. speaker, invited lectr. Contbr. numerous articles to profl. and sci. jour.; various video and audio prodns. Recipient over 40 awards, honors and research grants including Bank Am. Fine Arts award 1963, Millberry Art award, 1970, Nat. Research Service award Nat. Heart, Lung and Blood Inst., 1972-77, Young Investigator award Acad. Clin. Lab. Physicians and Scientists, 1982, 83, Nuclear Magnetic Resonance award U. Calif., Davis, 1984-88; S.A. Pepper Collegiate scholar, 1963; Fellow Stanford U., 1967-68, Internat. scholar MOP, Venezuela, 1967, NIH, 1970, Highest Honor Calif. Scholarship Fedn.; grantee Am. Heart Assn./U. Calif., Davis, others. Mem. Am. Assn. Clin. Chemistry, Acad. Clin. Lab. Physicians and Scientists, Am. Heart Assn., Biomed. Engring. Soc., Am. Soc. Testing Materials (hon.), Soc. Magnetic Resonance in Medicine, Internat. Trumpet Guild, Sigma Xi, Phi Kappa Phi.

KOSTER, JAMES EDWARD, nuclear physicist; b. Lancaster, Pa., July 24, 1963; s. Charles James and Nancy Virginia (Sheppard) K.; m. Holly Ann Shamberger, July 17, 1982; 1 child, Brandon James. BS summa cum laude, Tex. Christian U., 1985; PhD, N.C. State U., 1990. Postdoctoral fellow Duke U., Durham, N.C., 1990-91, Los Alamos (N.Mex.) Nat. Lab., 1991—; sci. demonstrator local schs. and clubs, N.C., N.Mex., 1990—. Asst. Tiger Scouts, Los Alamos, 1991-92; coach YMCA, 1992, Los Alamos Youth Soccer League, 1992. Mem. Soc. of Physics Students (pres. 1984-85), Am. Phys. Soc., Sigma Pi Sigma, Sigma xi.. Democrat. Office: Los Alamos Nat Lab MS H803 Los Alamos NM 87545

KOSTNER, JACLYN PATTI, educator, writer, speaker, consultant; b. Akron, Ohio, Mar. 27, 1945; d. Pete and Carolyn (Naglic) Patti; 1 child, James Andrew. BA, U. Akron, 1967; MEd., Colo. State U., 1983; PhD in Speech Communication, Univ. Denver, 1990. Tchr. bus. N.E. High Sch., Pasadena, Md., 1967, Athens-Draughon Bus. Coll., Athens, Ga., 1967, McAuley High Sch., Cin., 1971-72; tchr. bus., coord. Scarlet Oaks Joint Vocat. Sch., Cin., 1972-73; instr. bus. Barnes Bus. Coll., Denver, 1974-76; pres., owner Finishing Touches, Englewood, Colo., 1976-78; bus. and med. office cons., 1976-78; tchr. bus. Smoky Hill High Sch., Aurora, Colo., 1976-89; pres., chief exec. officer Multi-Site Team Effectiveness, 1989—; lectr. profl. groups. Mem. Med. Office Asst.'s Adv. Bd., Community Coll. Denver, 1976; pres. bus. adv. com. Cherry Creek Schs., 1983-84; mem. Superintendent's Com. in Excellence, 1983-84; mem. Subcom. to Study the Content of the Curricular Program, 1983-84; mem. Secondary Computer Edn. Coun., 1983-84; co-chmn. Smoky Hill Computer Edn. Com., 1983-84; mem. com. to Plan Needs/Design of District's Fourth High Sch., 1983-84; chmn. Life Skills/Concepts task force, mem. staff devel. com., mem. composer Curriculum com., 1988-89; vol. chairperson Gary Morris Celebrity Golf Classic, 1990; sec. adv. bd. Arapahoe Community Coll., 1990. Mem. NEA, Nat. Bus. Edn. Assn., Mountain Plains Bus. Edn. Assn., Colo. Vocat. Assn., Colo. Educators For and About Bus., Nat. Speaker's Assn., Colo. Speaker's Assn., Cherry Creek Tchrs. Assn., Am. Vocat. Assn., South Metro Denver C. of C., Greater Denver C. of C. (coun.), Chief Exec. Officer Exchange, Internat. Telecommunication Assn., U.S. Figure Skating Assn., Delta Pi Epsilon, Phi Delta Kappa. Club: Denver Figure Skating. Author: Broncos: From Striped Socks to Super Bowl and Beyond, 1980, Houghton-Mifflin Typewriting-Keyboard Mastery and Applications, 1st and 2d yr. texts, 1984, Houghton Mifflin Keyboarding, 1987, Houghton-Mifflin Info. Processing, 1st and 2d yr. texts, 1989, TNT-Teams and Technology Dissertation, 1990; contbr. articles in field; presenter rsch. studies to profl. assns. Office: 8378 E Jamison Cir S Englewood CO 80112-2756

KOSTOULAS, IOANNIS GEORGIOU, physicist; b. Petra, Pierias, Greece, Sept. 12, 1936; came to U.S., 1965, naturalized, 1984; s. Georgios Ioannou and Panagiota (Zarogiannis) K.; m. Katina Sioras Kay, June 23, 1979; 1 child, Alexandra. Diploma in Physics U. Thessoloniki, Greece, 1963; MA, U. Rochester, 1969, PhD, 1972; MS, U. Ala., 1977, Instr. U. Thessaloniki, 1963-65; teaching asst. U. Ala., 1966-67, U. Rochester, 1967-68; guest jr. research assoc. Brookhaven Nat. Lab., Upton, N.Y., 1968-72; research physicist, lectr. UCLA, U. Calif.-San Diego, 1972-76; sr. research assoc. Mich. State U., East Lansing, 1976-78, Fermi Nat. Accelerator Lab., Betavia, Ill., 1976-78; research staff mem. MIT, Cambridge, 1978-80; sr. system engr., physicist Hughes Aircraft Co., El Segundo, Calif., 1980-86; sr. physicist electro-optics and space sensors Rockwell Internat. Corp., Downey, Calif., 1986—. Contbr. articles to profl. jours. Served with Greek Army, 1961-63. Research grantee U. Rochester, 1968-72. Mem. Am. Phys. Soc., Los Alamos Sci. Lab. Exptl. Users Group, Fermi Nat. Accelerator Lab. Users Group, High Energy Discussion Group of Brookhaven Nat. Lab., Pan Macedonian Assn., Save Cyprus Council Los Angeles, Sigma Pi Sigma. Club: Hellenic U. Lodge: Ahepa. Home: 2404 Marshallfield Ln # B Redondo Beach CA 90278-4406 Office: Rockwell Internat Co MC EA28 Space System Div 12214 Lakewood Blvd Downey CA 90242-2693

KOSTRIKIN, MARYBETH ELAINE, excavating company executive; b. Clarkston, Wash., Nov. 22, 1954; d. William Bruce and Rachel Ann (Osborn) Hodgson; m. David Kostrikin, Jan. 6, 1983; children: Troy James Pierson, Rachel Anne. Student, U. Idaho, 1972-75, Clackamas C.C., Oregon City, Oreg., 1976, 77. Meter reader, energy specialist Canby (Oreg.) Utility Bd., 1978-84; sec. Kostco Landscape Mgmt., Canby, 1983-91; v.p. KLM Excavating, Inc., Canby, 1991—. Mem. Nat. Fedn. Ind. Bus. Republican. Baptist.

KOTLER, PAMELA LEE, health analyst; b. Phila., Jan. 2, 1946; d. Harry Winfield and Mary Ellen (Warren) Taylor; m. Barry Lee Kotler, Mar. 19, 1967; children: Joshua, Jenny. BA, Juniata Coll., Huntingdon, Pa., 1967; MA, San Francisco State U., 1978; PhD, UCLA, 1986. Rsch. asst. Calif. Dept. Health Svcs., Human Population Lab., Berkeley, Calif., 1982-86; rsch. assoc. U. Calif., Berkeley, 1986-89; sr. med. econ. analyst Kaiser Found. Health Plan, Oakland, Calif., 1989—. Author: Having It All: Multiple Roles and Mortality, 1989; contbr. articles to profl. jours., chpts. to books. Counselor Suicide Prevention, Berkeley, 1980-85, bd. dirs., 1983-85. Mem. AAAS, Am. Pub. Health Assn., N.Y. Acad. Sci. Office: Kaiser Found Health Plan 1950 Franklin St Oakland CA 94612-5103

KOTLER, RICHARD LEE, lawyer; b. L.A., Apr. 13, 1952; s. Allen S. Kotler and Marcella (Fromberg) Swarttz; m. Cindy Jasik, Dec. 9, 1990; 1 child, Kelsey Elizabeth. BA, Sonoma State Coll., 1976; JD, Southwestern U., 1979. Bar: Calif. 1980, U.S. Dist. Ct. (cen. dist.) Cal. 1980. Sole practice Newhall, Calif., 1980-83, 88—; sr. ptnr. Kotler & Hann, Newhall, 1983-88; pvt. practice Law Offices of Richard L. Kotler, Newhall, 1984-86; judge pro temp Municipal Ct., 1981-84, Superior Ct., 1985—. Chmn. Santa Clarita Valley Battered Women's Assn., Newhall, 1983-87; bd. dirs. Santa Clarita Valley Hotline, Newhall, 1981-83. Recipient Commendation award Los Angeles County, 1983. Mem. Santa Clara Valley Bar Assn. (v.p. 1985—), Los Angeles Astronomy Soc., Newhall Astronomy Club. Lodge: Kiwanis (interclub chmn. S.C.V. club). Office: 23942 Lyons Ave Ste 202 Santa Clarita CA 91321-2444

KOTO, PAUL, multicultural educator; b. Denver, Aug. 3, 1948. BA in Philosophy, U. Colo., 1971. Mgr. ops. Disney Prodns., Denver, 1971-74; with computer ops. dept. US WEST, Denver, 1974-79, computer programmer, 1979-85, fin. comptroller, 1985-89, systems analyst, 1989—, pluralism facilitator, 1989—. Mem. Am. Soc. Quality Control, Am. Legion. Home: PO Box 2662 Denver CO 80202 Office: US WEST 5325 Zuni St Denver CO 80221

KOTTENSTETTE, CHRISTOPHER JOSEPH, paramedic, administrator; b. Salt Lake City, July 24, 1962; s. Thomas Francis and Bettye Jean (Johns) K.; m. Cathi Lynn Jacobs, June 6, 1987; children: Matthew Thomas, Anne-Marie Lynn. Cert. EMT-P, Neonatal Resusitation, BLS instr., ACLS instr., Pre-Hosp. Trauma Life Support instr., Pediatric Advanced Life Support instr., supr. Supr., salesperson Dairy Queen, Ft. Collins, Colo., 1978-86; paramedic supr. Reed Ambulance, Inc., Denver, 1981-86, Poudre Valley Hosp., Ft. Collins, 1986—; owner Emergency Med. Cons., Ft. Collins, 1987—; flight paramedic No. Colo. Med. Ctr., Greeley, Colo., 1990—; featured in TV series Rescue 911, 1991. Mem. EMT Assn. Colo. Home and Office: Emergency Med Cons 2925 Worthington Ave Fort Collins CO 80526-2657

KOTTKE, FREDERICK EDWARD, economics educator; b. Menominee, Mich., Sept. 6, 1926; s. Edward Frederick and M. Marie (Braun) K.; BS, Pepperdine U., 1950; postgrad, U. Wis., 1950-52; MA, U. So. Calif., 1957, PhD, 1960; m. Lillian Dorathy Larson, Aug. 27, 1950; children: Karin Lee, Kurt Edward. Lectr., Pepperdine U., 1952-53; asst. prof. U. So. Calif., 1956-63; assoc. prof. econs., chmn. dept., speaker of gen. faculty Stanislaus State Coll., Calif. State U., Turlock, Calif., 1963-68, prof., also chmn. div. arts and scis., 1968—, prof. emeritus econs., 1992—; pres. KK Economic Consultants, Inc.; independent tax adviser, managerial adviser, 1960—; speaker in field. Chmn., Stanislaus County United Crusade, 1964-65; pres., Stanislaus State Coll. Found., 1972; trustee Emanuel Med. Ctr., 1974—; v.p. Good Shepherd Lutheran Ch., 1985-89. Served with USNR. 1943-46. Recipient Pologrammatic award Pepperdine Coll., 1952, Outstanding Prof. award Calif. State U., Stanislaus, 1987-88. Haynes Found. Postgrad. Research award U. So. Calif., 1959. Mem. Am., Western econ. assns., Nat. Tax Assn. (com. for fed. taxation 1989-90), Am. Finance Assn., C. of C., Omicron Delta Epsilon. Lodge: Kiwanis. Author: An Economic Analysis of Toll-Highway Finance, 1956, An Economic Analysis of Financing an Interstate Highway System, 1959; contbr. to econ. newsletter. Home: 1890 N Denair Ave Turlock CA 95380-1816 Office: Calif State U Stanislaus 801 W Monte Vista Ave Turlock CA 95380-0299

KOTTLOWSKI, FRANK EDWARD, geologist; b. Indpls., Apr. 11, 1921; s. Frank Charles and Adella (Markworth) K.; m. Florence Jean Chriscoe, Sept. 15, 1945; children: Karen, Janet, Diane. Student, Butler U., 1939-42; A.B., Ind. U., 1947, M.A., 1949, Ph.D., 1951. Party chief Ind. Geology Survey, Bloomington, summers 1948-50; fellow Ind. U., 1947-51, instr. geology, 1950; adj. prof. N.Mex. Inst. Mining and Tech., Socorro, 1970—; econ. geologist N.Mex. Bur. Mines and Mineral Resources, 1951-66, asst. dir., 1966-68, 70-74, acting dir., 1968-70, dir., 1974-91, state geologist, 1989-91, emeritust dir., state geologist, 1991—; geologic cons. Sandia Corp., 1966-72. Contbr. articles on mineral resources, stratigraphy and areal geology to tech. jours. Mem. Planning Commn. Socorro, 1960-68, 71-78, chmn., 86-90; mem. N.Mex. Energy Resources Bd.; chmn. N.Mex. Coal Surface Mining Commn.; sec. Socorro County Democratic Party, 1964-68. Served to 1st lt. USAAF, 1942-45. Decorated D.F.C.; decorated Air medal; recipient Richard Owen Disting. Alumni award in Govt. and Industry U. Ind., 1987. Fellow AAAS, Geol. Soc. Am. (councilor 1979-82, exec. com. 1981-82); mem. AIME, Am. Assn. Petroleum Geologists (hon. mem., dist. rep. 1965-68, Disting. Svc. award, editor 1971-75, pres. energy minerals divsn. 1987-88), Assn. Am. State Geologists (pres. 1985-86), Soc. Econ. Geologists, Am. Inst. Profl. Geologists (Pub. Svc. award 1986), Am. Commn. Stratigraphic Nomenclature (past sec., chmn.), Cosmos Club, Sigma Xi. Home: 703 Sunset St Socorro NM 87801-4657 Office: NMex Bur Mines NMex Tech Campus Sta Socorro NM 87801

KOUSSER, J(OSEPH) MORGAN, history educator; b. Lewisburg, Tenn., Oct. 7, 1943; s. Joseph Maximillian and Alice Holt (Morgan) K.; m. Sally Ann Ward, June 1, 1968; children: Rachel Meredith, Thaddeus Benjamin. AB, Princeton U., 1965; M.Phil., Yale U., 1968, PhD, 1971; MA, Oxford U., Eng., 1984. Instr. Calif. Inst. Tech., Padadena, 1969-71, asst. prof., 1971-75, assoc. prof., 1975-79, prof., 1979—; vis. prof. U. Mich., Ann Arbor, 1980, Harvard U., Cambridge, Mass., 1981-82, Oxford U., 1984-85; expert witness Minority Voting Rights Cases; researcher. Author: Shaping of Southern Politics, 1974; editor: Region, Race and Reconstruction, 1982. Guggenheim Found. fellow, 1984-85, Woodrow Wilson Ctr. fellow, 1984-85; grantee NEH, 1974, 82. Mem. Orgn. Am. Historians, Am. Hist. Assn., Social Scis. History Assn., So. Hist. Assn. Democrat. Office: Calif Inst of Tech 228-77 Caltech Pasadena CA 91125

KOUYMJIAN, DICKRAN, art historian, Orientalist, educator; b. Tulcea, Romania, June 6, 1934; came to U.S. (parents Am. citizens), 1939; s. Toros S. and Zabelle I. (Calusdian) K.; m. Angèle Kapoïan, Sept. 16, 1967. BS in European Cultural History, U. Wis., 1957; MA in Arab Studies, Am. U., Beirut, 1961; PhD in Near East Lang. and Culture, Columbia U., 1969. Instr. English Columbia U., N.Y.C., 1961-64; dir. Am. Authors, Inc., N.Y.C., 1965-67; asst. prof. and asst. dir. Ctr. for Arabic Studies Am. U., Cairo, 1967-71; assoc. prof. history Am. U. Beirut, 1971-75; prof. art history Am. U., Paris, 1976-77; prof. history and art, dir. Armenian Studies program Calif. State U., Fresno, 1977—; dir. Sarkis and Meline Kalfayan Ctr. for Armenian Studies, Calif. State U., Fresno, 1990—; Fulbright disting. lectr., prof. Armenian and Am. Lit., Yerevan (Armenia, USSR), 1987; cons. archaeology UNESCO, Paris, 1976; prof., chairholder Armenian Sect., Inst. Nat. des Langs. et Civilisations Orientales, U. Paris, 1988-91; 1st incumbent Haig & Isabel Berberian endowed chair Armenian Studies Calif. State U., Fresno, 1989—. Author: Index of Armenian Art, part I, 1977, part II, 1979, The Armenian History of Ghazar P'arpetzi, 1986, Arts of Armenia, 1992; co-author: (with A. Kapoïan) The Splendor of Egypt, 1975; author and editor: William Saroyan: An Armenian Trilogy, 1986, William Saroyan: Warsaw Visitor and Tales of the Vienna Streets, 1990; editor: (books) Near Eastern Numismatics, Iconography, Epigraphy and History, 1974, Essays in Armenian Numismatics in Honor of C. Sibilian, 1981, Armenian Studies: In Memoriam Haïg Berbérian, 1986; editorial bd. Armenian Rev., 1974—, Ararat Lit. mag., 1975—, Revue des Etudes Arméniennes, 1978—, NAASR Jour. Armenian Studies; contbr. articles to profl. jours. Served with U.S. Army, 1957. Recipient Outstanding Prof. award Am. U., Cairo, 1968-69, 69-70, Outstanding Prof. of Yr. faculty award Calif. State U., 1985-86, Hagop Kevorkian Disting. Lectureship in Near Eastern Art and Civilization, NYU, 1979; Fulbright fellow, USSR, 1986-87; grantee NEH, Paris, 1980-81. Mem. Am. Oriental Soc., Am. Numismatic Soc., Mid. East Studies Assn. (charter), Coll. Arts Assn., Soc. Armenian Studies (charter, pres. 1985-86), Société Asiatique, Medieval Acad., Assn. Internat. des Etudes Arméniennes, others. Home: 30 rue Chevert, 75007 Paris France Office: Calif State U Armenian Studies Program Fresno CA 93740-0004

KOUYOUMJIAN, AIDA MARDIROS, English as a second language educator, translator, writer; b. Felloujah, Iraq, Dec. 14, 1928; came to U.S., 1952; d. Mardiros Hagop and Mannig (Dobajian) K.; m. William Cedric Shanafelt, Apr. 27, 1956 (div. 1970); children: Armen Bruce Shanafelt, Aram Brian Shanafelt, Roger Haig Shanafelt. BA in Edn., U. Wash., 1956, Tchr. Cert., 1968; MA in Edn., Seattle Pacific U., 1985. Cert. tchr., Wash. Tchr. Mercer Island (Wash.) Sch. Dist., 1969-75; coord. ESL program Issaquah (Wash.) Sch. Dist., 1978—; translator Social and Health Svcs., Kent and Bellevue, Wash., 1989—, Turner Broadcasting System for Larry King during Goodwill Games, 1990; adj. faculty Seattle Pacific U., 1990—. Author: Between Two Rivers, 1978 (Pacific N.W. Writers Conf. Non-Fiction award 1978); contbr. articles to profl. jours. chmn. Armenian Women's Orgn., Seattle, 1968-70; pres. Armenian Cultural Assn., Seattle, 1987-89; precinct com. woman Republican Party, Mercer Island, 1990—; v.p. Eastside Rep. Club, Wash. Fulbright scholar U. Wash. Seattle, 1952-56, NSF fellow, 1974-75; recipient Edn. Accomplishments/Civic Contbns. award U.S. Dept. Edn., Region X, 1989. Mem. Wash. Assn. ESL Speakers, Wash. Assn. Bilingual Edn., Kiwanis. Armenian Orthodox and Covenant. Office: Issaquah Sch Dist 565 NW Holly Issaquah WA 98027

KOUZI, SAMIR, medicinal chemist; b. Beirut, Lebanon, May 1, 1961; s. Abdelhafiz Jamil and Mahassen Amin (Anouti) K.; m. Christina Lim, Aug. 2, 1989. BSc in Pharmacy, King Saud U., Saudi Arabia, 1984; PhD, U. Miss., 1991. Rsch. asst. U. Miss., University, 1985-87, 89-90, teaching asst., 1988, 91; rsch. assoc. U. Wash., Seattle, 1992—. Contbr. articles to profl. jours. Rho Chi grad. scholar, 1989. Mem. Am. Chem. Soc. (treas. 1988), Am. Pharm. Assn., N.Y. Acad. Scis., Sigma Xi, Rho Chi. Office: Univ of Wash Medicinal Chemistry BG-20 Seattle WA 98195

KOVACH, RONALD, sporting goods chain executive, outdoor educator; b. N.Y.C., Dec. 22, 1946; s. Edward Joseph and Louise Christine (Ragno) K.; m. Linda Cathrine Clark, May 5, 1969; children: Meredith Alexa, Matthew Alexander. BA with honors, U. Calif., Riverside, 1968, MA, 1970; postgrad., UCLA, 1970-74. Asst. v.p. Big 5 Sporting Goods, El Segundo, Calif., 1972—; dir., founder Eagle Claw Saltwater Fishing Schs., Huntington Beach, Calif., 1989—; ind. cons. to sporting goods industry Huntington Beach, 1992—; bd. dirs. Penn Fishing U.; lectr., condr. seminars, Huntington Beach, 1985—; freelance photojournalist, Huntington Beach, 1985—. Author: Bass Fishing in California: Secrets of the Western Pros, 1985, Trout Fishing in California: Secrets of the Top Western Anglers, 1987, Saltwater Fishing in California: Secrets of the Pacific Experts, 1989; contbr. numerous articles to various publs. Organizer Proposition 132, Calif. anti-gill net initiative, 1990. Calif. State scholar U. Calif., 1970; rsch. NIMH fellow UCLA, 1972. Mem. Nat. Resource Def. Coun., Cousteau Soc., Greenpeace, Calif. Trout, Bass Anglers Sportsman Soc., Outdoor Writers Am. Assn., Outdoor Writers Calif. Home and Office: 17911 Portside Cir Huntington Beach CA 92649

KOVACHY, EDWARD MIKLOS, JR., psychiatrist; b. Cleve., Dec. 3, 1946; s. Edward Miklos and Evelyn Amelia (Palenscar) K.; m. Susan Eileen Light, June 21, 1981; children: Timothy Light, Benjamin Light. BA, Harvard U., 1968, JD, 1972, MBA, 1972; MD, Case Western Reserve U., 1977. Diplomate Nat. Bd. Med. Examiners. Resident in psychiatry Stanford U. Med. Ctr., Stanford, Calif., 1977-81; psychiatrist pvt. practice, Menlo Park, Calif., 1981—; mediator, mgmt. cons. Columnist The Peninsula Times Tribune, 1983-85. Bd. trustees Mid Peninsula High Sch., Palo Alto, Calif., 1990—. Mem. Am. Psychiat. Assn., Physicians for Social Responsibility, Assn. Family and Conciliation Cts., No. Calif. Psychiat. Soc., San Francisco Acad. Hypnosis. Presbyterian. Office: Edward M. Kovachy, Jr 1187 Univ Dr Menlo Park CA 94025

KOVASH, JON ROBERT, public radio news director, journalist; b. Dickinson, N.D., May 28, 1949; s. L. Jerry and Agnes (Ficek) K.; m. Nancy Ellen Kurtz, Oct. 16, 1975; 1 child, Josephine. Student, Casper (Wyo.) Coll., 1968-69, Community Coll., Denver, 1969-70, Metro State Coll., Denver, 1970-72. Editor student publ. The Paper/Metro State Coll., Denver, 1970-72, Aspen (Colo.) Today, 1973-74, Aspen (Colo.) Daily News, 1982-83; news dir. KOTO Pub. Radio, Telluride, Colo., 1987—; freelance journalist. Mem. Western Colo. Congress, Montrose, Colo. Mem. Colo. Pub. Radio (chair com. on news networking 1990—), High Plains News Svc. (adv. com. 1992—). Home: 113 S Townsend Telluride CO 81435 Office: KOTO-FM Telluride CO 81435

KOVEL, LEE RALPH, advertising agency executive, screenwriter; b. Cleve., June 27, 1951; s. Ralph Mallory and Terry Ellen (Horvitz) K. BBA, U. Denver, 1973. Copywriter Marsteller, Inc., N.Y.C., 1973-75, McCann-Erickson, N.Y.C., 1976-78; v.p., assoc. creative dir. Young and Rubicam, N.Y.C., 1978-84; sr. v.p., group creative dir. J. Walter Thompson Adv., N.Y.C., 1984-89; ptnr., exec. creative dir. Lord, Dentsu & Ptnrs., L.A., 1989—. Screenwriter episodes for TV series Equalizer including Marathon Detente, 1988, Thank Your Unlucky Stars, 1988. Recipient Bronze award Cannes Film Festival, 1983, Clio award, 1986, Effie award Am. Mktg. Assn., 1988. Mem. Writers Guild Am. Jewish. Home: 2335 Eastern Canal Venice CA 90291 Office: Lord Dentsu & Ptnrs 4751 Wilshire Blvd Los Angeles CA 90010-3827

KOVTYNOVICH, DAN, civil engineer; b. Eugene, Oreg., May 17, 1952; s. John and Elva Lano (Robie) K. BCE, Oreg. State U., 1975, BBA, 1976. Registered profl. engr., Calif., Oreg. V.p. Kovtynovich, Inc., Contractors and Engrs., Eugene, 1976-80, pres., chief exec. officer, 1980—. Fellow ASCE; mem. Am. Arbitration Assn. (arbitrator 1979—), N.W. China Coun., Navy League of U.S., Eugene Asian Coun. Republican. Office: Kovtynovich Inc 1595 Skyline Park Loop Eugene OR 97405-4466

KOWALCZEWSKI, DOREEN MARY THURLOW, communications company executive; b. London, May 5, 1926; came to U.S., 1957, naturalized, 1974; d. George Henry and Jessie Alice (Gray) Thurlow; BA, Clarke Coll., 1947; postgrad. Wayne State U., 1959-62, Roosevelt U., 1968; m. Witold Dionizy Kowalczewski, July 26, 1946; children: Christina Julianna, Janet Alice, Stephen Robin. Agy. supr. MONY, N.Y.C., 1963-67; office mgr. J.B. Carroll Co., Chgo., 1967-68; mng. editor Sawyer Coll. Bus., Evanston, Ill., 1968-71; mgr. policyholder svc. CNA, Chgo., 1971-73; EDP coord. Canteen Corp., Chgo., 1973-75; mgr. documentation and standards LRSP, Chgo., 1975-77; data network mgr. Computerized Agy. Mgmt. Info. Svcs., Chgo., 1977-86; founder, chmn. Tekman Assocs., 1982—; chpt. sec. Soc. Tech. Communications, 1988-90. Bd. dirs. Wash. E. chpt. LWV, 1993—. Pres., Univ. Park Assn., 1980-84. Mem. Bus. Profl. Women, Women's Bus. Exch., Assn. Profl. Writing Cons., Soc. Tech. Communications, Mensa. Bd. dirs. Lake View Estates, 1993—.

KOWALSKI, KAZIMIERZ, computer science educator, researcher; b. Turek, Poland, Nov. 7, 1946; came to U.S., 1986; s. Waclaw and Helena (Wisniewska) K.; m. Eugenia Zajaczkowska, Aug. 5, 1972. MSc, Wroclaw (Poland) U. Tech., 1970, PhD, 1974. Asst. prof. Wroclaw U. Tech., 1970-76, assoc. prof., 1976-86; assoc. prof. Pan Am. U., Edinburg, Tex., 1987-88; prof. computer sci. Calif. State U.-Dominguez Hills, Carson, 1988—; lectr. U. Basrah, Iraq, 1981-85; cons. XXCal, Inc., L.A., 1987-91; conf. presenter in field. Co-author: Principles of Computer Science, 1975, Organization and Programming of Computers, 1976; also articles. Recipient Bronze Merit Cross, Govt. of Poland, 1980. Mem. IEEE Computer Soc., The N.Y. Acad. Scis., Assn. for Computing Machinery, Am. Assn. for Artificial Intelligence, Sigma Xi. Home: 5042 Raton Cir Long Beach CA 90807-1140 Office: Calif State U 1000 Victoria Carson CA 90747

KOWALSKI, KENNETH R., Canadian government official; b. Bonnyville, Alta., Can., Sept. 27, 1945; m. Jeannine Kowalski; children: Lori Anne, Michael Paul. BA in History, U. Alta., 1966, MA in East Asian History, 1970. Tchr. social studies Lorne Jenken High Sch., Alta., 1969-74; dir. decentralization program Alta. Transp., 1977-79; exec. asst. to dep. premier Minister of Agr., Alta., 1975-77; chmn. regional transp. services, 1977-79, MLA Barrhead, 1979-86; MLA, chmn. Legis.'s Heritage Savs. Trust Fund Select com. Minister Environment, Alta. Pub. Safety Services, 1982-86; minister of Environment Minister Alta. Pub. Safety Services, 1986-88; minister of Career Devel. and Employment Alta. Pub. Safety Svcs., 1988-89, minister Responsible for Lotteries, 1988-89, Minister of Pub. Works, Supply and Svcs., 1989—; Minister Responsible for Lotteries, Major Exhibitions/ Fairs Wild Rose Found., 1988-89, minister of Pub. Affairs Bur., Pub. Safety

Svcs., 1989-92; min. of Gaming and Racing Commns. Alta. Pub. Safety Svcs., 1991-92; dep. premier, govt. house leader, min. pub. works, supply and svcs., responsible for lotteries and gaming, Pub. Affairs Bur. ACCESS Corp., 1992—; standing policy com. of cabinet: priorities, fin. and coordination, social planning. Home: Box 1600, Barrhead, AB Canada T0G 0E0 Office: Rm 408 Legislature Bldg, Edmonton, AB Canada T5K 2B6

KOZINSKI, ALEX, federal appeals court judge; b. Bucharest, Romania, July 23, 1950; came to U.S., 1962; s. Moses and Sabine (Zapler) K.; m. Marcy J. Tiffany, July 9, 1977; children: Yale Tiffany, Wyatt Tiffany, Clayton Tiffany. AB in Econs. cum laude, UCLA, 1972, JD, 1975. Bar: Calif. 1975, U.S. Ct. Appeals (9th cir.) 1978, U.S. Ct. Customs and Patent Appeals 1978, U.S. Customs Ct. 1978, D.C. 1978, U.S. Dist. Ct. (cen. dist.) Calif. 1979, U.S. Supreme Ct. 1979, U.S. Ct. Appeals (D.C. cir.) 1980, U.S. Dist. Ct. D.C. 1980, U.S. Ct. Appeals (2d and 4th cirs.) 1980. Law clk. to Hon. Anthony M. Kennedy U.S. Ct. Appeals (9th cir.), 1975-76; law clk. to Chief Justice Warren E. Burger U.S. Supreme Ct., 1976-77; assoc. Forry Golbert Singer & Gelles, Los Angeles, 1977-79, Covington & Burling, Washington, 1979-81; dep. legal counsel Office of Pres.-elect Reagan, Washington, 1980-81; asst. counsel Office of Counsel to Pres., White House, Washington, 1981; spl. counsel Merit Systems Protection Bd., Washington, 1981-82; chief judge U.S. Claims Ct., Washington, 1982-85; judge U.S. Ct. Appeals (9th cir.), 1985—; lectr. law U. So. Calif., 1992. Contbr. articles to legal jours.; mng. editor: UCLA Law Rev., 1974-75, assoc. editor, 1973-74. Mem. ABA, Fed. Bar Assn., Bar Assn. D.C., D.C. Bar, State Bar Calif., Nat. Lawyers Club, Order of Coif. Club: Nat. Lawyers (Washington). Office: US Ct Appeals 125 S Grand Ave Ste 200 Pasadena CA 91105-1652

KOZLOV, ALEXANDER IGOR, mechanical engineer; b. Redwood City, Calif., Jan. 4, 1956; s. Igor Alexander and Anna S. (Boormistroff) K.; m. Roseanna K. Marchetti, Aug. 4, 1985; children: Raissa A., Milena A. AS in Mech. Engring., Can. Coll., 1976; BSME, Calif. Polytechnic Inst., 1979. Registered profl. engr., Calif. Project mgr. Critchfield Mech. Inc., Menlo Park, Calif., 1984—; mng. engr. Critchfield Mech. Inc., San Diego, 1990—; pres. Kozlov Engring. Co., San Diego, 1992—; staff engr. U.S. Army, U.S., 1982-84. Maj. U.S. Army Corp. Engrs., 1979-84. Decorated commendation medal with second oak leaf cluster. Mem. ASHRAE, Soc. Mil. Engrs., Alpha Sigma (pres. 1978-79). Office: Critchfield Mech Inc 750 B St Ste 2880 San Diego CA 92101

KOZOLCHYK, BORIS, law educator, consultant; b. Havana, Cuba, Dec. 6, 1934; came to U.S., 1956; s. Abram and Chana (Brewda) D.; m. Elaine Billie Herman, Mar. 5, 1967; children: Abbie Simcha, Raphael Adam, Shaun Marcie. DCL, U. Havana, 1956; Diplome, Faculte Internat. de Droit, Luxembourg, 1958; LLB, U. Miami, 1959; LLM, U. Mich., 1960, SJD, 1966. Teaching asst. Sch. of Law U. Miami, Fla., 1957-59; asst. prof. law Sch. of Law So. Meth. U., Dallas, 1960-64; resident cons. The Rand Corp., Santa Monica, Calif., 1964-67; dir. Law Reform Project USAID, San Jose, Costa Rica, 1967-69; prof. law Coll. of Law U. Ariz., 1969—; teaching asst. Faculte Internat. de Droit Campare, 1958; vis. prof. law Nat. U. of Mex., 1961; vis. exch. prof. law Nat. U. of Chile, Santiago, 1962; guest lectr. Latin Am. Law seminar Stanford (Calif.) U., 1964; guest lectr. extension grad. seminar on Latin Am. law UCLA, 1965; Bailey vis. prof., Tucker lectr. La. State U., 1979; vis. prof. U. Aix en Provence, France, 1985; cons. on legal system U.S. Agy. Internat. Devel., 1974-77; legal cons. Overseas Pvt. Investment Corp., 1974—; cons. uniformity of comml. laws Orgn. of Am. States and U.S. State Dept., 1974-77; expert witness on banking and comml. law and custom issues; advisor Libr. Congress Law div.; Joseph Bernfeld Meml. lectr. L.A. Bankruptcy Forum, 1989. Author of books; bd. mem. Am. Jour. of Comparative Law; mem. editorial bd. Internat. Banking Law Jour.; founder, faculty advisor Ariz. Jour. of Internat. and Comparative Law, 1982-86; contbr. articles to profl. jours. and publs. Selected Nat. U. Mex. rep. First Mexican Congress Comml. Law, 1974; pres. Ariz. Friends of Music, 1975-76; mem. Tucson com. on fgn. rels.; hon. chmn. community rels. com. JFSA; mem. adv. com. Ariz.-Mex. Commn. Govs.; legal advisor Ariz.-Mex. Banking Com.; del. U.S. Coun. on Internat. Banking to ICC; adv. mem. U.S. del. to UNCITRAL Internat. Contract Law, 1989; pres., bd. dirs. Nat. Law Ctr. for InterAm. Free Trade, 1992—. NSF rsch. grantee, 1973-75; recipient Extraordinary Teaching and Rsch. Merit award Coll. Law, U. Costa Rica, 1969, Community Svc. award Tucson Jewish Community Coun., 1979, Commendation award U.S. Dept. Justice, 1979, Disting. Svc. award Law Coll. Alumni Assn., 1990; named to Hall of Fame of Profs. of Comml. Law, Nat. U., Mex., 1987. Mem. ABA (task force for the revision of UCC article 5), State of Ariz. Bar, Inter-ABA (co-chmn. comml. law and procedure sec. 1973-78, Best Book award 1973), Am. Soc. of Internat. Law, Internat. Acad. Comml. and Comsumer Law (pres. 1988-90), Am. Acad. Fgn. Law (founding), Am. Law Inst. (consultative com. to UCC articles 3, 4, 4a and 5), Nat. Mexican Notarial Bar Assn. (hon. life 1982), Internat. Acad. Comml. and Consumer Law (elected pres. 1988), Sonora Bar Assn. (1st Disting. Svc. award 1989). Home: 7401 N Skyline Dr Tucson AZ 85718-1166 Office: U Ariz Coll of Law Tucson AZ 85721

KRAFT, C. WILLIAM, III, lawyer; b. Upper Darby, Pa., Apr. 10, 1943; s. C. William Jr. and Frances (Mc Devitt) K.; m. Christa Schuster, May 28, 1966; children: William H., Laurie R. BA, U. Pa., 1965; JD, Villanova U., 1968. Bar: Pa. 1968, U.S. Ct. Appeals (3d cir.) 1969, Colo. 1982, U.S. Ct. Appeals (10th cir.) 1983, U.S. Supreme Ct. 1985. Law clk. to presiding justice U.S. Ct. Appeals (3d cir.), Phila., 1968-69; assoc. Beasley, Hewson, Casey, Kraft & Colleran, Phila., 1969-76; ptnr. Kraft & Beebe, Media, Pa., 1976-80; assoc. gen. counsel ConRail, Phila., 1980-82; gen. counsel Burlington No. R.R., Denver, 1982-86; ptnr. Kraft & Johnson, Denver, 1987-91, Kraft, Johnson & Belt, Denver, 1991-93, Kraft & Belt, Denver, 1992—. Bd. of editors Villanova Law Rev., 1967-68. Supr. Edgmont Twp., Pa., 1977-82. Mem. Colo. Bar Assn., Nat. Assn. R.R. Trial Counsel, Def. Research Inst. Republican. Presbyterian. Club: Hiwan Golf. Home: 13305 S Resort Dr Conifer CO 80433-5201 Office: # 1140 1900 Grant Bldg Denver CO 80203

KRAFT, GEORGE HOWARD, physician, educator; b. Columbus, Ohio, Sept. 27, 1936; s. Glen Homer and Helen Winner (Howard) K.; m. Mary Louise Wells, Oct. 2, 1965; children: Jonathan Ashbrook, Susannah Mary. AB, Harvard U., 1958; MD, Ohio State U., 1963, MS, 1967. Cert. Am. Bd. Phys. Medicine and Rehab., Am. Bd. Electrodiagnostic Medicine (bd. dirs. 1993—). Intern U. Calif. Hosp., San Francisco, 1963-64, resident, 1964-65; resident Ohio State U., Columbus, 1965-67; assoc. U. Pa. Med. Sch., Phila., 1968-69; asst. prof. U. Wash., Seattle, 1969-72, assoc. prof., 1972-76, prof., 1976—, chief of staff Med. Ctr., 1993—; dir. electrodiagnostic medicine U. Wash. Hosp., 1987—, dir. Multiple Sclerosis Clin. Ctr., 1982—, co-dir. Muscular Dystrophy Clinic, 1974—; assoc. dir. rehab. medicine Overlake Hosp., Bellevue, Wash., 1989—; bd. dirs. Am. Bd. Electrodiagnostic Medicine, 1993—. Cons. editor Phys. Med. and Rehab. Clinics, 1990—, EEG and Clin. Neurophysiology, 1992—; assoc. editor Jour. Neurologic Rehab., 1988—; mem. editorial bd. Am. Jour. Phys. Medicine and Rehab., 1987—; contbr. articles to profl. jours. Mem. adv. com. World Rehab. Fund, N.Y.C., 1988—; mem. adv. com. on patient mgmt. tech. Nat. Multiple Sclerosis Soc., N.Y.C., 1990—, chmn., 1993—, med. adv. bd., exec. com. med. adv. bd., 1991—, mem. clinic com., 1993—; bd. sponsors Wash. Physicians for Social Responsibility, Seattle, 1986—. Lt. comdr. USN, 1967-69. Rsch. grantee Rehab. Svcs. Adminstrn., 1978-81, HEW, 1976-79, Nat. Inst. Handicapped Rsch., 1984-88, Nat. Multiple Sclerosis Soc., 1990-92. Fellow Am. Acad. Phys. Medicine and Rehab. (pres. 1984-85, Zeiter award 1991); mem. Am. Assn. Electrodiagnostic Medicine (cert., pres. 1982-83), Assn. Acad. Physiatrists (pres. 1980-81), Am. Acad. Clin. Neurophysiology (treas. 1989-93, pres.-elect 1993—), Am. Congress Rehab. Medicine, Am. Acad. Neurology, Internat. Rehab. Medicine Assn. Episcopalian. Office: U Wash Dept Rehab 1959 NE Pacific St Seattle WA 98195-0001

KRAFT, RICHARD JOE, sales executive; b. Toppenish, Wash., Apr. 20, 1944; s. Joseph Nian and Rose Goldie (Merrick) K.; m. Karolyn Idell Keyes, Oct. 9, 1963 (div. 1982); children: Craig J., Jeffrey Eugene; m. Margaret Celeste Porter, Apr. 9, 1983. Student, Yakima Valley Coll., 1962-63; student, U. Wash., 1964-70. Project engr. Gray & Osborne Consulting Engrs., Seattle, 1965-76; project engr., constrn. cons. Pool Engring., Ketchikan, Alaska, 1976-81; project mgr. Cape Fox Corp., Ketchikan, 1982; project engr. Buno Constrn., Woodinville, Wash., 1983, Straiger Engring. Svcs., Ketchikan, Sitka, Alaska, 1984; owner Kraft Constrn. Svcs., Kirkland, Wash., 1984-85; dir. mcpl. projects ESM, Inc., Renton, Wash., 1985-86; estimator Active Constrn., Inc., Gig Harbor, Wash., 1987; sr. sales engr. Advanced Drainage Systems, Inc., Woodinville, 1987-93; project mgr. TY-Matt, Inc., Ketchikan, 1993—; storm sewer/sanitary specification subcom. Am. Pub. Works Assn., Wash. state chpt., 1985—. Pres. Snohomish (Wash.) Camp, Gideons Internat., 1990—; pres. exec. com. Maltby (Wash.) Congl. Ch. Mem. Utility Contractors Assn. Wash. (bd. dirs. 1990-92). Mem. Christian Ch. Home: PO Box 6384 Ketchikan AK 99901 Office: TY-Matt Inc PO Box 9470 Ketchikan AK 99901

KRAFT, ROBERT PAUL, astronomer, educator; b. Seattle, June 16, 1927; s. Victor Paul and Viola Eunice (Ellis) K.; m. Rosalie Ann Reichmuth, Aug. 28, 1949; children—Kenneth, Kevin. B.S., U. Wash., 1947, M.S., 1949; Ph.D., U. Calif.-Berkeley, 1955. Postdoctoral fellow Mt. Wilson Obs., Carnegie Inst., Pasadena, Calif., 1955-56; asst. prof. astronomy Ind. U., Bloomington, 1956-58, Yerkes Obs., U. Chgo., Williams Bay, Wis., 1958-59; staff Hale Obs., Pasadena, 1960-67; prof., astronomer Lick Obs., U. Calif., Santa Cruz, 1967-92; astronomer, prof. emeritus, 1992—; acting dir. Lick Obs., 1968-70, 71-73, dir., 1981-91; dir. U. Calif. Observatories, 1988-91; chmn. Fachbeirat, Max-Planck-Inst., Munich, Fed. Republic Germany, 1978-88; bd. dirs. Cara corp. (Keck Obs.), Pasadena, 1985-91; bd. dirs. AURA. Contbr. articles to profl. jours. Jila vis. fellow U. Colo., Nat. Bur. Standards, Boulder, 1970; Fairchild scholar Calif. Inst. Tech., Pasadena, 1980, Tinsley prof. U. Tex., 1991-92. Mem. Nat. Acad. Scis., Am. Acad. Arts and Scis., Am. Astron. Soc. (pres. 1974-76, Warner prize 1962), Internat. Astron. Union (v.p. 1982-88, pres.-elect 1994-97, pres. 1997-2000), Astron. Soc. Pacific (bd. dirs. 1981-87). Democrat. Unitarian. Office: U Calif Lick Observatory Santa Cruz CA 95064

KRAFT, SCOTT COREY, correspondent; b. Kansas City, Mo., Mar. 31, 1955; s. Marvin Emanuel and Patricia (Kirk) K.; m. Elizabeth Brown, May 1, 1982; children: Kate, Kevin. BS, Kans. State U., 1977. Staff writer Associated Press, Jefferson City, Mo., 1976-77, Kansas City, 1977-79; corr. Associated Press, Wichita, Kans., 1979-80; nat. writer Associated Press, N.Y.C., 1980-84; nat. corr. L.A. Times, Chgo., 1984-86; bur. chief L.A. Times, Nairobi, Kenya, 1986-88, Johannesburg, South Africa, 1988—. Recipient Disting. Reporting in a Specialized Field award Soc. of the Silurians, 1982, Peter Lisagor award Headline Club Chgo., 1985, Feature Writing finalist Pulitzer Prize Bd., 1985, Sigma Delta Chi award, 1993. Office: LA Times, PO Box 5660, Johannesburg 2000, South Africa

KRAFT, TANYA ALINE, elementary school educator; b. Abilene, Tex., May 16, 1957; d. Jerrold Keith and Janice Elaine (Wood) Johnson; m. Richard Lee Kraft, July 14, 1984; children: Richard Devin, Kelsey Brynn. Student, Baylor U., 1975-77; BE, N.Mex. State U., 1979; postgrad., Va. Commonwealth U., 1983, Ea. N.Mex. U. Cert. elem. tchr. Elem. tchr. Roswell (N.Mex.) Ind. Schs., 1979-89; workshop dir. Roswell Ind. Schs.; guest speaker, Roswell Civic Clubs. Author: A Day On the Plantation, 1983 (a social studies unit). Tchr., choir mem. First Bapt. Ch., Roswell; mem. Community Bible Study, Roswell. Mem. Alpha Delta Kappa (pres. 1990-92), Pi Beta Phi (pres. 1984-87), Xi Kappa Beta Sigma Phi (corr. sec. 1990). Republican. Home: 205 Tierra Berrenda Dr Roswell NM 88201-7869

KRAFT, WILLIAM ARMSTRONG, retired priest; b. Rochester, N.Y., Apr. 13, 1926; s. William Andrew and Elizabeth Ruth (Armstrong) K. BA, St. Bernard Coll., 1947; ThM, Immaculate Heart Theol. Coll., 1951; D of Ministry, Claremont Sch. of Theology, 1981. Ordained priest Roman Cath. Ch., 1951. Dir. and founder of Newman Apostolate Diocese of San Diego, Calif., 1951-63; dir. of pub. rels. Diocese of San Diego, 1956-63, dir. of cemeteries, 1964-70, exec. dir. of devel., 1979-91; founding pastor St. Therese of Child Jesus Parish, San Diego, 1956-70, Good Shepherd Parish, San Diego, 1970-77; pastor St. Charles Borromeo Parish, San Diego, 1977-79; bd. dirs. Cath. Charities, San Diego; bd. of consultors Diocese of San Diego, 1985-91, mem. Presbyteral Coun., 1985-91, mem. bldg. commn., 1977-91. Bd. dirs. Am. Nat. Red Cross, San Diego, 1956-63, Legal Aid Soc., San Diego, 1956-65, Travelers' Aid Soc., San Diego, 1956-65; mem. Presdl. Task Force, Washington, 1984—. Named Prelate of Honor to Pope, Pope John Paul II, Vatican City, 1985, Knight Comdr. of Equestrian, Pope John Paul II, Vatican City, 1984, Order of Holy Sepulchre, Knights of Columbus 4th degree. Mem. Benevolent and Protective Order of Elks, Univ. Club Atop Symphony Towers, Nat. Cath. Conf. for Total Stewardship (bd. dirs.), Nat. Cath. Devel. Conf., Nat. Soc. Fund Raising Execs. (cert.). Republican. Home: 6910 Cibola Rd San Diego CA 92120-1709

KRAG, OLGA, interior designer; b. St. Louis, Nov. 27, 1937; d. Jovica Todor and Milka (Slijepcevic) Golubovic. AA, U. Mo., 1958; cert. interior design UCLA, 1979. Interior designer William L. Pereira Assocs., L.A., 1977-80; assoc. Reel/Grobman Assocs., L.A., 1980-81; project mgr. Kaneko/Laff Assocs., L.A., 1982; project mgr. Stuart Laff Assocs., L.A., 1983-85; restaurateur The Edge, St. Louis, 1983-84; pvt. practice comml. interior design, L.A., 1981—, pres., R.I., 1989—. Mem. invitation and ticket com. Calif. Chamber Symphony Soc., 1980-81; vol. Westside Rep. Coun., Proposition 1, 1971; asst. inaugural presentation Mus. of Childhood, L.A., 1985. Recipient Carole Eichen design award U. Calif., 1979. Mem. Am. Soc. Interior Designers, Inst. Bus. Designers, Phi Chi Theta, Beta Sigma Phi. Republican. Serbian Orthodox. Home and Office: 700 Levering Ave Apt 10 Los Angeles CA 90024-2797

KRAHMER, DONALD L., JR., financial services company executive; b. Hillsboro, Oreg., Nov. 11, 1957; s. Donald L. and Joan Elizabeth (Karns) K.; m. Suzanne M. Blanchard, Aug. 16, 1986; children: Hillary, Zachary. BS, Willamette U., 1981, MM, 1987, JD, 1987. Bar: Oreg. 1988. Fin. analyst U.S. Bancorp, Portland, 1977-87; intern U.S. Senator Mark Hatfield, 1978; legis. aide State Sen. Jeannette Hamby, Hillsboro, Oreg., 1981-83, State Rep. Delna Jones, Beaverton, Oreg., 1983; bus. analyst Pacificorp, Portland, 1987; mgr. mergers/acquisitions Pacificorp Fin. Svcs., Portland, 1988-89; dir. Pacificorp Fin. Svcs., 1990; CEO, pres. Atkinson Group, Portland, 1991—; atty. Black Helterline, Portland, 1991—; bd. dirs., sec. Marathon Fin. Assocs., Portland, 1989; bd. dirs. Self-Enhancement, Inc., Willamette Forum; adv. bd., editor Oreg. Enterprise Forum, 1991—. Treas. Com. to Re-Elect Jeannette Hamby, 1986; bd. dirs. Am. Diabetes Assn., Portland, 1990—; chmn. Atkinson Grad. Sch. Devel. Com., Salem, 1989-92; founder Conf. of Entrepreneurship, Salem, 1984, chmn. breakfast forum, 1993. Recipient Pub.'s award Oreg. Bus. Mag., 1987, Founders award Willamette U., 1987, award Scripps Found., 1980, others. Mem. ABA, Oreg. Bar Assn., Multnomah County Bar Assn., Washington County Bar Assn., Portland Soc. Fin. Analysts, Japan-Am. Soc. Oreg., Assn. Investment Mgmt. and Rsch. (exec. com. fin. insts. sect.), City Club. Republican. Lutheran. Home: 16230 SW Copper Creek Dr Portland OR 97224-6500 Office: Black Helterline 1200 Bank of Calif Tower 707 SW Washington Portland OR 97205

KRAL, IVAN, composer, songwriter; b. Prague, Bohemia, Czech Republic, May 12; came to U.S., 1966; s. Karel and Otylie (Hajtmarova) K.; m. Lynette Avonne Bean, Jan. 1, 1987. BA in Liberal Arts, SUNY, Geneseo, 1970. Owner Crepes de Marle, Seattle. Musician with Patti Smith Group, Iggy Pop, John Waite, John Cale, Joy Rider, Eastern Bloc, Ratlin' Sabres, Sky Cries Mary, Native; songwriter Dancing Barefoot, Every Step of the Way, She's the One, Bang Bang, among others; co-scored film Diner; producer, dir. film Black Generation; scored music for play Full Pocket; producer of N.Y. bands The Band of Outsiders, The Vipers, and Joy Rider. Home: 1522 Post Alley # 314 Seattle WA 98101

KRAMARSIC, ROMAN JOSEPH, engineering consultant; b. Mokronog, Slovenia, Feb. 15, 1926; came to U.S., 1957; s. Roman and Josipina (Bucar) K; m. Joanna B. Ruffo, Oct. 29, 1964; children: Joannine M., Roman III. Student, U. Bologna, Italy, 1947-48; BS, U. Toronto, Can., 1954, MS, 1956; PhD, U. So. Calif., 1973. Registered profl. engr., Ont., Can. Rsch. engr. Chrysler Rsch., Detroit, 1957-58; chief design engr. Annin Corp., Montebello, Calif., 1959-60; mgr. Plasmadyne Corp., Santa Ana, Calif., 1960-62; sr. rsch. engr. NESCO, Pasadena, Calif., 1962-64; asst. prof. U. So. Calif., L.A., 1971-77; mgr. engring. div. MERDI, Butte, Mont., 1977-78; sr. rsch. engr. RDA, Albuquerque, 1978-85; sr. staff mem. BDM, Albuquerque, 1985-90; owner Dr. R.J. Kramarsic's Engring. Svcs., Albuquerque, 1985—; cons. various tech. cos., So. Calif., 1964—; mem. various govt. coms. evaluating high power lasers. Author tech. presentations; contbr. articles to profl. jours. Violinist Albuquerque Civic Light Opera, 1980-85. Mem. ASME (sr.), AIAA (sr.), ASM Internat., Nat. Ski Patrol (aux. leader 1990—). Roman Catholic. Office: Kramarsic's Engring Svcs PO Box 2265 Albuquerque NM 87103-2265

KRAMER, ALEXANDER GOTTLIEB, financial director; b. DesPlaines, Ill., Sept. 21, 1964; s. Gottlieb G. and Norma L. Kramer. BA in Econ. Devel. and Internat. Rels., Lake Forest Coll., 1987; M in Internat. Fin., Am. Grad. Sch. Internat. Mgmt., Glendale, Ariz., 1990. Asst. to dir. parliamentary affairs Spanish Parliament, Madrid, 1985-87; intern to chief polit. consular U.S. Dept. State, Rabat, Morocco, 1987-88; project mgr. H. Shapiro & Assocs., Inc., Chgo., 1988-90; dir. fin. and logistics Pacific Inter-Trade Corp., Westlake Village, Calif., 1990—; prof. internat. fin. West coast U., L.A., 1991—; lectr. Pepperdine U., Malibu, Calif., 1992; corp. advisor World Trade Ctr., Ventura Calif.; mem. Calif. USSR Trade Assn. Mem. Peruvian Arts Soc., Phi Sigma Iota. Home: 7266 Franklin Ave 306 Los Angeles CA 90046 Office: Export SBOC Sr Counsel Internat 110 E 9th St # 669A Los Angeles CA 90079

KRAMER, BARRY ALAN, psychiatrist; b. Phila., Sept. 9, 1948; s. Morris and Harriet (Greenberg) K.; m. Paulie Hoffman, June 9, 1974; children—Daniel Mark, Steven Philip. B.A. in Chemistry, NYU, 1970; M.D., Hahnemann Med. Coll., 1974. Resident in psychiatry Montefiore Hosp. and Med. Ctr., Bronx, N.Y., 1974-77; practice medicine specializing in psychiatry, N.Y.C., 1977-82; staff psychiatrist L.I. Jewish-Hillside Med. Ctr., Glen Oaks, N.Y., 1977-82; asst. prof. SUNY, Stony Brook, 1978-82; practice medicine specializing in psychiatry, L.A., 1982—; asst. prof. psychiatry U. So. Calif., 1982-89, assoc. prof. clin. psychiatry, 1989—; ward chief Los Angeles County/U. So. Calif. Med. Ctr., 1982—; mem. med. staff USC U. Hosp., Cedars Sinai Hosp.; cons. Little Neck Nursing Home (N.Y.), 1979-82, L.I. Nursing Home, 1980-82; dir. ECT U. So. Calif. Sch. Medicine, 1990. Reviewer: Am. Jour. Psychiatry, Hospital and Community Psychiatry; mem. editorial bd. Convulsive Therapy; contbr. articles to profl. jours., papers to sci. meetings. NIMH grantee, 1979-80; fellow UCLA/U. So. Calif. Long-Term Gerontology Ctr., 1985-86. Mem. AMA, Am. Psychiat. Assn., AAAS, Internat. Soc. Chronobiology, Assn. Convulsive Therapy (editorial bd.), Soc. Biol. Psychiatry, Calif. Med. Assn., Los Angeles Med. Assn., Am. Assn. Geriatric Psychiatry, West Coast Coll. Biol. Psychiatry, Gerontol. Soc. Am., So. Calif. Psychiat. Soc. (chair ETC com.). Jewish. Office: Los Angeles County-U So Calif Med Ctr 1934 Hospital Pl Los Angeles CA 90033-1071 also: PO Box 5792 Beverly Hills CA 90209

KRAMER, DONOVAN MERSHON, SR., newspaper publisher; b. Galesburg, Ill., Oct. 24, 1925; s. Verle V. and Sybil (Mershon) K.; m. Ruth A. Heins, Apr. 3, 1949; children: Donovan M. Jr., Diana Sue, Kara J. Kramer Bugbee, Eric H. BS in Journalism, Pub. Mgmt., U. Ill., 1948. Editor, publisher, ptnr. Fairbury (Ill.) Blade, 1946-63, Forrest (Ill.) News, 1953-63; ptnr. Gibson City (Ill.) Courier, 1952-63; pres., publisher, editor Casa Grande (Ariz.) Valley Newspapers, Inc., 1963—; mng. ptnr. White Mt. Pub. Co., Shou Low, Ariz., 1978—. Written and edited numerous articles and newspaper stories including many award-winners such as Sweepstakes award in Ill. and Ariz. Mem., chmn. Econ. Planning and Devel. Bd. State of Ariz., Phoenix, 1976-81; pres. Indsl. Devel. Authority of Casa Grande, 1977—; founding pres. Greater Casa Grande Econ. Devel. Found., bd. dirs., 1982-83, 91; gov. apptd. bd. mem. Ariz. Dept. Transp., 1992—. Sgt. U.S. Army Air Corps, 1943-46, PTO. Recipient Econ. Devel. plaque City of Casa Grande, 1982. Mem. Ariz. Newspapers Assn. (pres. 1980, Master Editor-Pub. 1977), Community Newspapers of Ariz. (pres. 1970-71), Inland Newspapers Assn., Am. Newspapers Assn., Cen. Ariz. Project Assn., Nat. Newspapers Assn., Greater Casa Grande C. of C. (pres. 1981-82, Hall of Fame 1991), Soc. Profl. Journalists. Republican. Lutheran. Home: 1125 E Cottonwood Ln Casa Grande AZ 85222 Office: Casa Grande Valley Newspapers Inc 200 W 2nd St Casa Grande AZ 85222

KRAMER, GORDON, mechanical engineer; b. Bklyn., Aug. 1937; s. Joseph and Etta (Grossberg) K.; m. Ruth Ellen Harter, Mar. 5, 1967 (div. June 1986); children: Samuel Maurice, Leah Marie; m. Eve Burstein, Dec. 17, 1988. BS Cooper Union, 1959; MS, Calif. Inst. Tech., 1960. With Hughes Aircraft Co., Malibu, Calif., 1959-63; sr. scientist Avco Corp., Norman, Okla., 1963-64; asst. div. head Batelle Meml. Inst., Columbus, Ohio, 1964-67; sr. scientist Aerojet Electrosystems, Azusa, Calif., 1967-75; chief engr. Beckman Instrument Co., Fullerton, Calif., 1975-82; prin. scientist McDonnell Douglas Microelectronics Co., 1982-83, Kramer and Assocs., 1983-85; program mgr. Hughes Aircraft Co., 1985—; cons. Korea Inst. Tech. NSF fellow, 1959-60. Mem. IEEE. Democrat. Jewish. Home: 153 Lakeshore Dr Rancho Mirage CA 92270 Office: 2000 E El Segundo Blvd El Segundo CA 90245-4599

KRAMER, GORDON EDWARD, manufacturing executive; b. San Mateo, Calif., June 22, 1946; s. Roy Charles and Bernice Jeanne (Rones) K.; BS in Aero. Engring., San Jose State Coll., 1970; m. Christina Hodges, Feb. 14, 1970; children: Roy Charles, Charlena. Purchasing agent Am. Racing Equipment, Brisbane, Calif., 1970-71, asst. to v.p. mktg., 1971-72; founder, pres. Safety Direct Inc., hearing protection equipment, Sparks, Nev., 1972—; dir. Hodges Transp., Condor Inc.; mem. adv. bd. to pres. Truckee Meadows Community Coll., 1991—. Named Nev. Small Businessperson of Yr., Nev. Small Bus. Adminstrn., 1987, Bus. Person of Yr. Sparks Community C. of C., 1987. Mem. Am. Soc. Safety Engrs., Safety Equipment Distributors Assn., Indsl. Safety Equipment Assn., Nat. Assn. Sporting Goods Wholesalers, Nat. Sporting Goods Assn., Nev. State Amature Trapshooting Assn. (dir. 1978-79), Pacific Internat. Trapshooting Assn. (Nev. pres. 1979-80, 80-81), Advanced Soccer Club (pres.1985-86). Republican. Methodist. Rotary Club (pres. Spark Club 1988-89). Office: Safety Direct Inc 56 Coney Island Dr Sparks NV 89431-6316

KRAMER, HUGH E., marketing educator; b. Apr. 17, 1929; m. Edith W. Held, Aug. 4, 1966; children: Vera, Edith Evelyne. Diplom, Goethe U., Germany, 1952; dr. rer. pol., Franzens U., Graz, Austria, 1960. Prin. Kramer Advertising Agy., Frankfurt, 1955-62; advt. cons. L.A., 1962-64; instr. U.S. Def. Lang. Inst., Monterey, Calif., 1964; sr. economist Copley PRESS AND Copley Internat. Corp., LaJolla, Calif., 1965-66; assoc. prof. internat. bus. The Am. U., Washington, 1967-69; vis. assoc. prof. U. Hawaii, Honolulu, 1969—, from vis. assoc. prof. to prof., dept. chmn., 1969—; vis. prof. Boston U., U. N.S.W., Sydney, Australia, Monterey Inst. Internat. Stdies, Japan Am. Inst. Mgmt. Sci., Honolulu; mgmt. cons. Schleicher Electronics, Berlin. Contbr. to numerous books and academic jours.; patentee electronic invention in advertising, 1960. U. N.S.W. fellow, Lima Grad. Sch. Mgmt. fellow, NYU fellow. Mem. Am. Mktg. Assn. (founding pres. Honolulu chpt. 1970-71), Acad. Mgmt., Acad. Internat. Bus., Rotary, Elks. Office: U Hawaii Coll Bus Administn 2404 Maile Way Honolulu HI 96822-2282

KRAMER, JAMES JOSEPH, artist, painter; b. Columbus, OH, Oct. 24, 1927; s. James Joseph and Louise Julia (Eireman) K.; m. Barbara Peters, Apr. 11, 1959; children: Susan Kramer Erickson, Joan Kramer Busick. Student, OH State U., 1950, Cleve. Sch. of Art, Cleve., 1949. Archtl. Lic. Exhibited w/ Ohio Watercolor Soc., Columbus, OH, 1948-50; pvt. archtl. practice Columbus, OH, 1950-57; architect Hertzka and Knowles, Arch., San Francisco, CA, 1957-59; assoc. Burde, Shaw and Assoc., Arch., Carmel, CA, 1959-70; retired from arch. Carmel, CA, 1970-76; artist, painter Santa Fe, N.Mex., 1976—; instr. Valdes Art Workshop, Santa Fe, N.Mex., 1985—, Scottsdale Artists Sch., Scottsdale Ariz., 1986-88, Ghost Ranch Workshop, Abiquiu, N.Mex., 1980, Mont. Art Edn., Assn., Great Falls, Mont., 1974. Recipient Silver Medal, Nat. Acad. of West Art, Okla. City, 1989, Frederic Remington award for artistic merit, 1991, Calif. Art Club, L.A., 1974, Gold Medal, 1973, Best of Show, Mother Lode Art Assn., Sonora, Calif., 1971. Mem. Nat. Acad. of Western Art, Santa Fe Watercolor Soc. (founding mem. 1989).

KRAMER, JOANN MARY, insurance agency executive; b. Bristol, Pa., Jan. 18, 1956; d. Vincent Louis and Alberta (Hoynoski) gardener; m. Robert E. Kramer, June 16, 1973; children: Jody, Vincent. BS, Mission Viejo (Calif.) C.C., 1978. Mgr. Bob's Custom Cycle Works, Morrisville, Pa., 1973-75; office mgr. Futuristic Custom Paint Studios, Orange, Calif., 1975-78; sales rep. Tandy Corp., Cherry Hill, N.J., 1983-84; appraiser Kramer Real Estate Appraisers, Fountain Hills, Ariz., 1985-86; sales, mgmt. Kramer & Kramer

Agy., Mesa, Fountain Hills, and Scottsdale, Ariz., 1986—, pres., 1987—; sales rep. Western Fidelity, Scottsdale, 1986-87; sales, mgmt. Am. Svc. Life, Mesa, Ariz., 1987-91, United Benefit Life, Fountain Hills, 1991—; pres. Lifestyle Consumer Benefits, Fountain Hills, 1990—, Health Ins. Rating program, Phoenix, Ariz., 1991. Democrat. Roman Catholic. Home: 15414 E Thistle Dr Fountain Hills AZ 85268

KRAMER, LAWRENCE STEPHEN, journalist; b. Hackensack, N.J., Apr. 24, 1950; s. Abraham and Ann Eve (Glasser) K.; m. Myla F. Lerner, Sept. 3, 1978; children: Matthew Lerner, Erika. B.S. in Journalism, Syracuse U., 1972; M.B.A., Harvard U., 1974. Reporter San Francisco Examiner, 1974-77; reporter Washington Post, 1977-80; exec. editor Trenton Times, N.J., 1980-82; asst. to exec. editor Washington Post, 1982, asst. mng. editor, 1982-86; exec. editor San Francisco Examiner, 1986-91. Recipient W.R. Hearst Found. award 1971-72. Mem. Soc. Profl. Journalists. Home: 8 Auburn Ct Belvedere Tiburon CA 94920-1349

KRAMER, LORNE C., protective services official. BA in Pub. Mgmt., U. Redlands, 1977; MPA with honors, U. So. Calif., 1979; Advanced Exec. Cert., Calif. Law Enforcement Coll., 1987; grad., Nat. Exec. Inst., 1993. Comdr. L.A. Police Dept., 1963-91; chief police Colorado Springs (Colo.) Police Dept., 1991—; Cons., instr. drugs and gangs Nat. Inst. Justice, office juvenile justice U.S. Dept. Justice. Active Colo. State DARE Adv. Bd.; bd. dirs. Ctr. Prevention Domestic Violence, Pikes Peak Mental Health. Mem. Colo. Assn. Chiefs Police (bd. dirs., major cities rep.), Internat. Assn. Chiefs Police (juvenile justice com.), Police Exec. Rsch. Forum. Office: Police Dept 224 E Kiowa St Colorado Springs CO 80903*

KRAMER, MICHAEL JEFFREY, physicist, inventor; b. Bronx, N.Y., Feb. 20, 1952; s. Nathan Raymond and Victoria (Perl) K.; m. Nina Postolovskaya, Apr. 11, 1992. BS in Chem. Physics, Mich. State U., 1975; MS in Physics, San Francisco U., 1985. Instr. physics San Francisco State U., 1977-79; chief instrumentation technologist San Francisco State U. Sch. of Sci., 1983-85; sr. scientist Lockheed-Palo Alto (Calif.) Rsch. Labs., 1986—. Vol. crisis counselor The Open Door, East Lansing, Mich., 1972-75, Suicide Prevention Crisis Ctr., San Mateo, Calif., 1988-89, Suicide and Crisis Svc., San Jose, 1989-90; artist, organizer Classical Recitals for Srs., San Francisco Bay Area, 1989—. Mem. Optical So. No. Calif. Home: 5280 Amelia Dr San Jose CA 95118 Office: Lockheed Palo Alto Rsch Lab 3251 Hanover St Palo Alto CA 94304

KRANTZ, WILLIAM BERNARD, chemical engineering educator; b. Freeport, Ill., Jan. 27, 1939; s. Peter Thomas and Caroline (Dorer) K.; m. June Clair Gaspar, Sept. 7, 1968; 1 child, Brigette. BA, St. Joseph Coll., Rensselaer, Ind., 1961; BS, U. Ill., 1962; PhD, U. Calif., Berkeley, 1968. Registered profl. engr., Colo. Fulbright lectr. chem. engring. Istanbul (Turkey) Tech. U., 1974-75; NSF-NATO sr. fellow U. Essex, Colchester, Eng., summer 1975; Fulbright rsch. fellow Aachen (Fed. Republic of Germany) Tech. U., 1981-82; Keating-Crawford prof. Notre Dame U., South Bend, Ind., fall 1985; Fulbright Rsch. fellow and Guggenheim fellow U. Oxford, Eng., 1988-89; asst. prof. U. Colo., Boulder, 1968-73, assoc. prof., 1974-79, prof., 1980—, pres.'s teaching scholar, 1990—; co-dir. NSF Industry/U. Coop. Rsch. Ctr. Separations Using Thin Films, 1990—; program dir. NSF, Washington, 1977-78; cons./advisor various orgns. including U.S. Coun. for Internat. Exch. of Scholars, Dow Chem. Co., Midland, Mich., 1969-71, U.S. Dept. Energy, Laramie, Wyo., 1979-81, U.S. Nat. Bur. Standards, Boulder, 1979-80, Martin Marietta Corp., Denver, 1982, Bend (Oreg.) Rsch. Inc., 1990—. Contbr. numerous articles to profl. publs. Recipient Innovation in Coal Conversion award Pitts. Internat. Coal Conf., 1987, Spl. Achievement award, Outstanding Performance award NSF, Cert. of Appreciation U.S. Dept. Energy; Pres. teaching scholar U. Colo., 1990—. Fellow AAAS (pres. southwestern and Rocky Mountain div. 1993—); mem. Am. Inst. Chem. Engrs. (chmn. tech. program com.), Am. Soc. Engring. Edn. (George Westinghouse award 1980), Am. Chem. Soc., Fulbright-Hays Alumni Assn., Union Concerned Scientists, Sigma Xi (nat. rsch. lectr. 1984-87), Alpha Chi Sigma. Roman Catholic. Home: 35412 Boulder Canyon Dr Boulder CO 80302-9658 Office: Univ Colo Dept Chem Engring Campus Box 424 Boulder CO 80309-0424

KRANWINKLE, CONRAD DOUGLAS, lawyer; b. Elgin, Ill., Oct. 27, 1940; s. Conrad David and Helen Elvira (Walgren) K.; m. Susan Hall Warren, Aug. 24, 1962; children: Mark Conrad, Jane Shafer. BA, Northwestern U., 1962; JD, U. Mich., 1965. Bar: Calif. 1966, U.S. Dist. Ct. (cen. dist.) Calif. 1966, U.S. Ct. Appeals (9th cir.) 1966. Law clk. to chief justice U.S. Supreme Ct., Washington, 1966-67; ptnr. Munger, Tolles & Olson, L.A., 1967-88, O'Melveny & Myers, L.A., 1989—; vis. prof. law U. Mich., winter 1993; bd. dirs. Fremont Gen. Corp., L.A., 1973—; dir. Calif. C. of C., 1990—. Pres. Poly. Sch. Bd. Trustees, Pasadena, Calif., 1986-88; mgr. Republican Gubernatorial Campaign, Calif., 1973-74; chmn. U.S. Senate Campaign, Calif., 1978. Mem. Am. Law Inst., Calif. C. of C. (bd. dirs. 1990—), Calif. Club, Valley Hunt Club, Lake Arrowhead Country Club. Office: O'Melveny & Myers 400 S Hope St Los Angeles CA 90071-2801

KRASILOVSKY, ALEXIS RAFAEL, director, producer; b. Juneau, Alaska, July 5, 1950; d. M. William and Phyllis Krasilovsky. Student, U. Florence, 1968-69; BA cum laude, Yale U., 1971; postgrad., NYU, 1975; MFA, Calif. Inst. of the Arts, 1984. Chairperson Internat. Women's Film Festival, AFI, Washington, 1975; bus. adminstr. The Holographic Film Co., N.Y.C., 1979-80; producer, dir. Rafael Film, L.A., 1982—; asst. prof. Calif. State U., Northridge, Calif., 1987-91, assoc. prof., 1991—; dir. The Street Gallery, L.A., 1987. Co-editor (news mag.) Behind the Lens, 1986; author: Some Women Writers Kill Themselves, 1983, Some Men, 1985, Abuse of Privacy, 1990; filmmaker: Exile, Beale Street, What Memphis Needs. Recipient Streisand Ctr. award, 1983; NEA grantee, 1977-78, Creative Artists Pub. Svc. Program grantee, 1973-74; Walter Lantz Prodns. scholar, 1983-84; Brody Arts Fund Media fellow, 1988, Western Regional Media Arts fellow, 1991. Mem. NOW, PEN, Assn. of Ind. Video and Filmmakers (founder), Women in Film, Behind the Lens: An Assn. Profl. Camera Women. Office: Calif State U Radio TV Film Dept 18111 Nordhoff St Northridge CA 91330-0001

KRASNER, OSCAR JAY, business educator; b. St. Louis, Dec. 3, 1922; s. Benjamin and Rose (Persov) K.; BS in Pub. Adminstrn., Washington U., St. Louis, 1943; MA in Mgmt. with honors, U. Chgo., 1950; MS in Quantitative Bus. Analysis, U. So. Calif., 1965, DBA in Mgmt., 1969; m. Bonnie Kidder, June 4, 1944; children: Bruce Howard, Glenn Evan, Scott Allan, Steve Leland, Michael Shawn, Bettina Jeanine. Mem. staff Exec. Office of Sec., U.S. Dept. Navy, 1944-56; supervising cons. Bus. Research Corp., Chgo., 1956-57; mem. staff flight propulsion div. Gen. Electric Co., Cin., 1957-61, mgr. VTOL project planning, 1959-61; exec. adviser long range planning space div. N.Am. Rockwell Corp., Downey, Calif., 1962-64, dir. tech. resources analysis exec. offices, 1964-70; pres. Solid State Tech. Corp. Calif., 1968-71; prof. mgmt. Pepperdine U., Los Angeles, 1970-92; pres. Rensark Assocs., 1976-92; dir. Quadrant Tech. Corp. Active community orgns.; mem. nat. adv. bd. Nat. Congress Inventor Orgns., 1983-84; bd. dirs. Long Beach (Calif.) JCC, 1969-70; People-to-People Del. to Peoples' Republic China, 1987, Russia, 1991; mem. adv. bd. Cen.for New Venture Alliance, Calif. State U., Hayward; founder Rsch. Inst. Spl Entrepreneurs. Served with Anti-Aircraft, AUS, 1942-44. Recipient Edwin M. Appel prize Price-Babson Inst. for Entrepreunrial Studies, 1990. Mem. Am. Acad. Mgmt., MBA Internat. (chmn. 1976-77), AIAA, AAAS, World Future Soc., Beta Gamma Sigma. Home and Office: 7656 N Sonoma Way Tucson AZ 85743

KRAUS, JEFFREY MILES, risk control specialist; b. L.A., Feb. 3, 1953; s. Samuel and Naomi (Cholden) K.; m. Joyce Gonzales, Aug. 18, 1984. BS, Calif. State U., Northridge, 1975. Tech. rep. Fireman's Fund Ins. Co., L.A., 1976-79; sr. loss prevention specialist Great Am. Ins. Co., Woodland Hills, Calif., 1979; sir. safety svcs. Bayly, Martin & Fay Ins. Brokers, L.A., 1979-86; account exec. Osterloh & Durham Ins. Brokers, Van Nuys, Calif., 1986-87; sr. loss control specialist Reliance Ins. Co., Redding, Calif., 1987-89; unit mgr. Crawford & Co. Risk Control Svcs., Lafayette, Calif., 1989—; chief fin. officer Four Seasons Pacifica, San Clemente, Calif., 1984—. Mem. Am. Soc. Safety Profls. (cert.), Nat. Fire Protection Assn., Calif. Environ. Health Assn. (cert. specialist). Office: Crawford & Co Risk Control 3687 Mt Diablo Blvd Ste 200 Lafayette CA 94549-3748

KRAUS, JOHN WALTER, former aerospace engineering company executive; b. N.Y.C., Feb. 5, 1918; s. Walter Max Kraus and Marian Florance (Nathan) Sandor; m. Janice Edna Utter, June 21, 1947 (dec. Feb. 1981); children: Melinda Jean Kraus Peters, Kim Kohl Kraus; m. Jean Curtis, Aug. 27, 1983. BS, MIT, 1941; MBA, U. So. Calif., 1972. Registered indsl. engr., Ohio, Calif. From indsl. engr. to indsl. engring. mgr. TRW, Inc., Cleve., 1941-61; spl. asst. Atomics Internat., Chatsworth, Calif., 1961-65; br. chief McDonnell Douglas Astronautics Co., Huntington Beach, Calif., 1966-74; sr. mgr. McDonnell Douglas Space Systems Co., Huntington Beach, Calif., 1983-93; pres. Kraus and DuVall, Inc., Santa Ana, Calif., 1975-83; retired, 1993; cons. Tech. Assocs. So. Calif., Santa Ana, 1974-75. Author: (handbook) Handbook of Reliability Engineering and Management, 1988. Mem. Am. Soc. Quality Control (sr.), Am. Def. Preparedness Assn. (life, chmn. tech. div. 1954-57), Nat. Soc. Profl. Engrs. (life). Republican. Home: 2001 Commodore Rd Newport Beach CA 92660-4307

KRAUS, PANSY DAEGLING, gemology consultant, editor, writer; b. Santa Paula, Calif., Sept. 21, 1916; d. Arthur David and Elsie (Pardee) Daegling; m. Charles Frederick Kraus, Mar. 1, 1941 (div. Nov. 1961). AA, San Bernardino Valley Jr. Coll., 1938; student Longmeyer's Bus. Coll., 1940; grad. gemologist diploma Gemological Assn. Gt. Britain, 1960, Gemological Inst. Am., 1966. Clk. Convair, San Diego, 1943-48; clk. San Diego County Schs. Publs., 1948-57; mgr. Rogers and Boblet Art-Craft, San Diego, 1958-64; part-time editorial asst. Lapidary Jour., San Diego, 1963-64, assoc. editor, 1964-69, editor, 1970—, sr. editor, 1984-85; pvt. practice cons., San Diego, 1985—; lectr. gems, gemology local gem, mineral groups; gem & mineral club bull. editor groups. Mem. San Diego Mineral & Gem Soc., Gemol. Soc. San Diego, Gemol. Assn. Great Britain, Mineral. Soc. Am., Epsilon Sigma Alpha. Author: Introduction to Lapidary, 1987; editor, layout dir.: Gem. Cutting Shop Helps, 1964, The Fundamentals of Gemstone Carving, 1967, Appalachian Mineral and Gem Trails, 1968, Practical Gem Knowledge for the Amateur, 1969, Southwest Mineral and Gem Trails, 1972, Introduction to Lapidary, 1987; revision editor Gemcraft (Quick and Leiper), 1977; contbr. articles to Lapidary jour., Keystone Mktg. catalog. Home and Office: PO Box 600908 San Diego CA 92160-0908

KRAUSE, KURTH WERNER, aerospace executive; b. Milw., July 21, 1940; s. Eugene Ralph and Dorothy Mildred (Raffel) K.; m. Susan Ruth Firle, June 15, 1963; children: Scott Alan, Sheryl Lynn Krause Gildea. BS in Math. and Physics, U. Wis., 1962; postgrad., MIT, 1966-67; cert. sr. mgmt. program, UCLA, 1985; cert., Stanford Exec. Inst., 1986. Project engr. AC Spark Plug div. GM, Milw., 1963-65; staff engr. MIT Instrumentation Lab., Cambridge, Mass., 1965-67; mem. tech. staff TRW, Houston, 1967-68, sect. head, 1969-73, dept. head, 1974-75; project mgr. TRW, Redondo Beach, Calif., 1975-79; asst. v.p. Ultrasystems, Inc., Irvine, Calif., 1979-83; dir. aerospace systems Intermetrics, Inc., Huntington Beach, Calif., 1983-84, gen. mgr. aerospace systems group, 1984—; mem. strategic adv. bd. So. Calif. Tech. Execs. Network, Tustin, Calif., 1986—; mem. Air Force Assn./USAF Space and Missile Ctr. Exec. Forum, El Segundo, Calif., 1989—. Contbr. articles to profl. jours. Hon. bd. dirs. Discovery Mus. of Orange County, Santa Ana, Calif., 1990—. Recipient Apollo Achievement award NASA, Washington, 1969, cert. of commendation MIT, Cambridge, 1969, Skylab award NASA Manned Flight Awareness, Johnson Space Ctr., 1974, Apollo/Soyuz Test Project NASA Flight Crew, Johnson Space Ctr., 1975. Mem. AIAA, Am. Electronics Assn., So. Calif. Tech. Execs. Network, USAF Space and Missile Systems Ctr. Exec. Forum, Mesa Verde Country Club (CFO 1980-81), Alpha Delta Phi (pres. Wis. chpt. 1961-62). Republican. Office: Intermetrics Inc 5312 Bolsa Ave Huntington Beach CA 92649

KRAUSE, L. WILLIAM, manufacturing company executive; b. Phila., May 20, 1942; s. Lester William and Helen Louise (Plantulli) K.; m. L. Gay Allebaugh, Aug. 5, 1967. BS, The Citadel, 1963. Gen. mgr. Gen. System div. Hewlett/Packard, 1967-81; chief exec. officer, chmn. bd. 3Com Corp., Santa Clara, Calif., 1981—. Mem. Am. Electronics Assn. (chmn., mem. exec. com.). Office: 3Com Corp 5400 Bayfront Plz Santa Clara CA 95051-0823

KRAUSE, THOMAS EVANS, record promotion consultant; b. Mpls., Dec. 17, 1951; s. Donald Bernhard and Betty Ann (Nokleby) K.; m. Barbara Ann Kaufman, Aug. 17, 1974 (div. Apr. 1978); m. Nicole Michelle Purkerson, Aug. 13, 1988; 1 child, Andrew Todd Evans. Student, Augsburg Coll., 1969-73; BA, Hastings Coll., 1975. Lic. 3d class with broadcast endorsement FCC. Air personality Sta. KHAS Radio, Hastings, Nebr., 1974-75; air personality, news dir. Sta. KWSL Radio, Sioux City, Iowa, 1975-76; asst. program dir. Sta. KISD Radio, Sioux Falls, S.D., 1976-78; music dir. Sta. KVOX Radio, Fargo, N.D., 1978; program dir. Sta. KPRQ Radio, Salt Lake City, 1978-79; air personality Sta. KIOA Radio, Des Moines, 1980; program dir., ops. mgr. Sta. KKSS Radio, Sioux Falls, 1981-83; program dir. Stas. KIYS/KBBK Radio, Boise, Idaho, 1983-87; program dir., ops. mgr. Sta. WSRZ AM/FM Radio, Sarasota, Fla., 1988-90; owner, cons. Tom Evans Mktg., Seattle, 1990—; editor Northwest Log, Seattle, 1991—; co-founder Sta. KCMR Radio, Augsburg Coll., Mpls., 1973; TV show coord./host Z-106 Hottraxx, Sarasota, 1988-90; regional talent scout Platinum Mgmt., L.A., 1990—; air personality/guest disc jockey various radio stas., Pacific NW, 1990—; host Am. Music Report, Sta. KIX-106 Radio, Canberra, Australia, 1992—. Contbr. articles to various trade publs., mags. Steering com. mem. Hitmakers Conf., Seattle, 1992; bd. judges Loyola U. Marconi Awards, Chgo., 1992; mem., advisor Wash. Music Industry Coalition, Seattle, 1992; bd. dirs. Habitat for Humanity, Snohomish County, Wash., 1992, Martin Luther King Day Celebration, Sarasota County, Fla., 1989-90; dist. coord. Carter for Pres., Nebr. 1st Dist., 1975-76; hon. chairperson March of Dimes WalkAm., Sioux Falls, 1977; media vol., MC or spokesperson M.S. Soc., MDA, Am. Diabetes Assn., Human Soc., others. Mem. Free Methodist Ch. Office: Tom Evans Mktg 16426 65th Ave W Lynnwood WA 98037

KRAUSER, JARY J., small business owner, president; b. Portland, Oreg., June 4, 1962; s. Gary Lee Krauser and Donna Joanne (Lowery) Stroup. BS, Oregon State U., 1985; postgrad. in Internat. Studies, Shur Da U., Taipei, Taiwan, 1985. Researcher Land Conservation and Devel., Salem, Oreg., 1982-83; capt. fishing vessel Alaska Fisheries, Prince William Sound, Alaska, 1983-85; gen. mgr. Rockland Industries, Salem, 1985-87; founder, pres. Ischo Enterprises, Seattle, 1987-88; gen. mgr. Puentes Bros., Seattle, 1988—; owner, pres. Symbiotic Enterprises, Seattle, 1989—; cons. Zero Gravity Inc., Salem, 1987—, Jenco Enterprises, Seattle, 1991—. Vol. Goodwill Games, Seattle, 1990. Recipient scholarship Oregon State U., 1980-85, High Sch. State Track 3000 meter champion, Oreg., 1980; named Nat. All-Am. Track team, The Athletic Congress, 1980-81. Mem. World Trade Club, Wash. Athletic Club, Oregon State Flying Club. Office: Puentes Bros 309 Cloverdale Rd Ste 224 Seattle WA 98108

KRAUSS, MICHAEL EDWARD, linguist; b. Cleve., Aug. 15, 1934; s. Lester William and Ethel (Sklarsky) K.; m. Jane Lowell, Feb. 16, 1962; children: Marcus Feder, Stephen Feder, Ethan, Alexandra, Isaac. Bacc. Phil. Islandicae, U. Iceland; BA, U. Chgo., 1953, Western Res. U., 1954; MA, Columbia U., 1955; Cert. d'études supérieures, U. Paris, 1956; PhD, Harvard U., 1959. Postdoctoral fellow U. Iceland, Reykjavik, 1958-60; rsch. fellow Dublin Inst. Advanced Studies, Ireland, 1956-57; vis. prof. MIT, Cambridge, 1969-70; prof. linguistics Alaska Native Lang. Ctr., U. Alaska, Fairbanks, 1960—, dir., 1972—, head Alaska native lang. program, 1972—; panel mem. linguistics NSF. Author: Eyak Dictionary, 1970, Eyak Texts, 1970, Alaska Native Languages: Past, Present and Future, 1980; editor: In Honor of Eyak: The Art of Anna Nelson Harry, 1982, Yupik Eskimo Prosodic Systems, 1985; mem. editorial bd.: Internat. Jour. Am. Linguistics, Arctic Anthropology; edited dictionaries and books in Alaska Eskimo and Indian langs. Halldor Kiljan Lexness fellow Scandinavian-Am. Found., Iceland, 1958-60, Fulbright fellow Leningrad, USSR, 1990; Fulbright study grantee Iceland, 1958-60; grantee NSF, 1961—, NEH, 1967; named Humanities Forum, 1981; recipient Athabaskan and Eyak rsch. award NSF, 1961—. Mem. Linguistics Soc. Am. (chair com. endangered langs. and preservation 1991—), Am. Anthropol. Assn., Soc. Study Indigenous Langs. of the Ams. (pres. 1991). Jewish. Office: U Alaska Alaska Native Lang Ctr Fairbanks AK 99775-0120

KRAVITZ, ELLEN KING, musicologist, educator; b. Fords, N.J., May 25, 1929; d. Walter J. and Frances M. (Prybylowski) Kokowicz; m. Hilard L. Kravitz, Jan. 9, 1972; 1 child, Julie Frances; stepchildren: Kent, Kerry, Jay. BA, Georgian Ct. Coll., 1964; MM, U. So. Calif., 1966, PhD, 1970. Tchr. 7th and 8th grade music Mt. St. Mary Acad., North Plainfield, N.J., 1949-50; cloistered nun Carmelite Monastery, Lafayette, La., 1950-61; instr. Loyola U., L.A., 1967; asst. prof. music Calif. State U., L.A., 1967-71, assoc. prof., 1971-74, prof., 1974—; founder Friends of Music at Calif. State U., L.A., 1976. Author: Finding Your Way Through Music in World Culture, 1993; editorial bd. Jour. Arnold Schoenberg Inst., Los Angeles; jour. editor Vol. I, No. 3, 1977, Vol. II, No. 3, 1978; author: (with others) Catalog of Schoenberg's Paintings, Drawings and Sketches. Mem. Schoenberg Centennial Com., 1974, guest lectr., 1969—. Recipient award for masters thesis U. So. Calif., 1966. Mem. Am. Musicol. Soc., L.A. County Mus. Art, L.A. Music Ctr., Mu Phi Epsilon, Phi Kappa Lambda. Home: PO Box 5360 Beverly Hills CA 90209

KRAVITZ, HILARD L(EONARD), physician; b. Dayton, Ohio, June 26, 1917; s. Philip and Elizabeth (Charek) K.; divorced; children: Kent C., Kerry, Jay; m. Ellen King, Jan. 9, 1972; 1 child, Julie Frances. BA, U. Cin., 1939, MD, 1943. Lic. physician, Calif., Ohio. Resident in internal medicine Miami Valley Hosp., VA Hosp., Dayton, 1946-49; practice medicine specializing in internal medicine Dayton, 1950-54, Beverly Hills and Los Angeles, Calif., 1955—; practice medicine specializing in internal medicine and cardiology Los Angeles, 1955—; attending physician Cedars-Sinai Med. Ctr., 1955—; cons., med. dir. Adolph's Ltd., Los Angeles, 1955-74; mem. exec. com. Reiss-Davis Clinic, Los Angeles, 1966-70; chmn. pharmacy and therapeutic com. Cent City Hosp., Los Angeles, 1974-79; mem. pain commn. service Dept. Health and Human Services, Washington, 1985-86. Patentee sugar substitute, 1959, mineral-based salt, 1978. V.p. Friends of Music Calif. State U., Los Angeles, 1979-81. Served to capt. U.S. Army, 1944-46, ETO. Decorated Bronze Star with oak leaf cluster; Fourragere (France). Mem. AMA, Calif. Med. Assn., Los Angeles County Med. Assn., Am. Soc. Internal Medicine, Calif. Soc. Internal Medicine (del. 1974). Jewish. Office: 436 N Bedford Dr #211 Beverly Hills CA 90210

KRAVJANSKY, MIKULAS, artist; b. Rudnany, Czechoslovakia, May 3, 1928; came to U.S., 1978; s. Imrich and Anna (Kubicekova) K.; m. Ruzena Horvath, Jan. 4, 1958; 1 child, Vladimir. BA P.S.V., Acad. Muzas Arts, Czechoslovakia, 1957. Scenographer State Theatre of J.Z., Czechoslovakia, 1957-62, Nat. Theatre Czechoslovakia, Bratislava, 1958-68; head of art and design Czechoslovakian Tel., Bratislava, 1962-68; asst. master Humber Coll., Toronto, Ont., Can., 1969-75; creator, dir. Black Box Theatre Can., Toronto, 1969-78; pres. Kravjansky Arts Inc., Pampano Beach, Fla., 1978-88, Napa, Calif., 1988—; asst. prof. Acad. of Muzas Art, Bratislava, 1962-68. Bd. dirs. Assn. Slovak Artists, Bratislava, 1965-68. Recipient Golden medal Bienale of Art, Sao Paulo, 1958. Mem. Kiwanis Internat. (bd. dirs. 1989-90). Home: 23 S Newport Dr Napa CA 94559

KRAW, GEORGE MARTIN, lawyer, essayist; b. Oakland, Calif., June 17, 1949; s. George and Pauline Dorothy (Herceg) K.; m. Sarah Lee Kenyon, Sept. 3, 1983. A degree, U. Calif.-Santa Cruz, 1971; student, Lenin Inst., Moscow, 1971; MA, U. Calif.-Berkeley, 1974, JD, 1976. Bar: Calif. 1976, U.S. Dist. Ct. (no. dist.) Calif. 1976, U.S. Supreme Ct. 1980, D.C., 1992. Pvt. practice, 1976—; ptnr. Kraw & Kraw, San Jose, 1988—; co-chair individual rights & constl. law com. Santa Clara County Bar Assn., 1992—. Mem. ABA, Am. Soc. Law, Medicine and Ethics, Nat. Assn. Health Lawyers, Inter-Am. Bar Assn., Union Internationale des Avocats. Office: Kraw & Kraw 333 W San Carlos St Ste 1050 San Jose CA 95110-2711

KREBS, EDWIN GERHARD, biochemistry educator; b. Lansing, Iowa, June 6, 1918; s. William Carl and Louise Helena (Stegeman) K.; m. Virginia Frech, Mar. 10, 1945; children: Sally, Robert, Martha. AB in Chemistry, U. Ill., 1940; MD, Wash. U., St. Louis, 1943; DSc, U. Geneva, 1979. Intern, asst. resident Barnes Hosp., St. Louis, 1944-45; rsch. fellow biol. chemistry Wash. U., St. Louis, 1946-48; asst. prof. biochemistry U. Wash., Seattle, 1948-52, assoc. prof. biochemistry, 1952-57, prof. biochemistry, 1957-66, prof. biochemistry, dean for planning Sch. Medicine, 1966-68; prof., chmn. dept. biol. chemistry, Sch. Medicine U. Calif., Davis, 1968-76; prof., chmn. dept. pharmacology U. Wash., Seattle, 1977-83; investigator, sr. investigator Howard Hughes Med. Inst., Seattle, 1983-90, sr. investigator emeritus, 1991—; prof. biochemistry and pharmacology U. Wash., Seattle, 1984—; mem. Phys. Chemistry Study Sect. NIH, 1963-68, Biochemistry Test Com. Nat. Bd. Med. Examiners, 1968-71, rsch. com. Am. Heart Assn., 1970-74, bd. sci. counselors Nat. Inst. Arthritis, Metabolism and Digestive Diseases, NIH, 1979-84, Internat. Bd. Rev., Alberta Heritage Found. for Med. Rsch., 1986, External Adv. Com. Weis Ctr. for Rsch., 1987-91. Mem. editorial bd. Jour. Biol. Chemistry, 1965-70; mem. editorial adv. bd. Biochemistry, 1971-76; mem. editorial and adv. bd. Molecular Pharmacology, 1972-77; assoc. editor Jour. Biol. Chemistry, 1971—; mem. internat. adv. bd. Advances in Cyclic Nucleotide Rsch., 1972—; editorial advisor Molecular and Cellular Biochemistry, 1987—. Recipient Nobel Prize in Medicine or Physiology, 1992, Disting. lectureship award Internat. Soc. Endocrinology, 1972, Gairdner Found. award, Toronto, Ont., Can., 1978, J.J. Berzelius lectureship, Karolinska Institutet, 1982, George W. Thorn award for sci. excellence, 1983, Sir Frederick Hopkins Meml. lectureship, London, 1984, Rsch. Achievement award Am. Heart Assn., Anaheim, Calif., 1987, 3M Life Scis. award FASEB, New Orleans, 1989, Albert Lasker Basic Med. Rsch. award, 1989, CIBA-GEIGY-Drew award Drew U., 1991, Steven C. Beering award, Ind. U., 1991, Welch award in chemistry, 1991, Welch Found., Louisa Gross Horwitz award Columbia U., 1989; John Simon Guggenheim fellow, 1959, 66. Mem. NAS, Am. Soc. Biol. Chemists (pres. 1986, ednl. affairs com. 1965-68, councillor 1975-78), Am. Acad. Arts and Scis., Am. Soc. Pharmacology and Exptl. Therapeutics. Office: U Wash Dept Pharmacology Howard Hughes Med Inst SL-15 Seattle WA 98195

KREBS, ERNST THEODOR, JR., biochemist; b. Carson City, Nev., May 17, 1912; s. Ernst Theodor and Ida Mae (Greene) K. Student, Hahnemann Med. Coll., 1938-41; AB, U. Ill., 1942; postgrad. U. Calif. Med. Sch., 1943-45; DSc, Am. Christian Coll., 1973. Pres. John Beard Meml. Found., San Francisco, 1961—. Author: The Unitarian or Trophoblastic Thesis of Cancer, 1951, The Unitarian or Trophoblastic Fact of Cancer, 1992. Mem. Sigma Xi. Republican. Lutheran. Home: 1348 S Van Ness Ave San Francisco CA 94110 Office: John Beard Meml Found PO Box 685 San Francisco CA 94101

KREBS, ROGER DONAVON, architect; b. Waverly, Iowa, Nov. 22, 1949; s. Martin Andrew and Ruby Lylas (Homan) K.; m. Deborah Lynn Homerstad; children: Gretchen Marie, Emma Louise, Amanda Lylas. BA, Rice U., 1973, BArch, 1974. Registered architect, Wyo. Archtl. designer John F. Houchins, Houston, 1974-77; archtl. designer Gorder South Group, Casper, Wyo., 1977-78, project architect, 1978-83; architect VA Med. Ctr., Salt Lake City, 1984-85, supervisory architect, 1985—. Prin. works include Wyo. Womens Ctr., Casper Events Ctr.

KREBS, STEPHEN JEFFREY, agriculture educator; b. Belvedere, Ill., July 29, 1950; s. Leo Gerard and Jean Catherine (Fiedler) K.; m. Julie Anderson, May 6, 1989. BS in Plant Sci., U. Calif., Davis, 1976, MS in Horticulture, 1977, PhD in Agrl. Ecology, 1993—. Viticulturist San Pasqual Vineyards, Escondido, Calif., 1977-79, Mayacamas Vineyards, Napa, Calif., 1980-83; researcher Mitchell-Beazley Pubs., London, 1984-85; viticulturist Matanzas Creek Winery, Santa Rosa, Calif., 1985; program coord. viticulture and winery tech. Napa Valley Coll., Napa, Calif., 1986—; advisor La Comunidad Drop-out Prevention Program, Migrant Edn., Healdsberg (Calif.) High Sch., 1986—. Researcher: Vines, Grapes and Wines, 1984-85. Big Bro., Big Bros./Big Sisters, Napa, 1983. Recipient Scholarships, U. Calif.-Davis Dept. Viticulture and Enology, 1989-90, Wine Spectator, N.Y.C., 1990-91. Mem. Am. Soc. Enology and Viticulture (Myron Nightengale Scholarship 1990-91), Farm Bur., Vineyard Tech. Group, Napa Valley Grape Growers. Office: Viticulture and Winery Tech Napa Valley Coll Napa CA 94558

KREGER, MELVIN JOSEPH, tax lawyer; b. Buffalo, Feb. 21, 1937; s. Philip and Bernice (Gerstman) K.; m. Patricia Anderson, July 1, 1955 (div. 1963), children: Beth Barbour, Arlene Roux; m. Renate Hochleitner, Aug. 15, 1975. JD, Mid-valley Coll. Law, 1978; LLM in Taxation, U. San Diego, 1988. Bar: Calif. 1978, U.S. Dist. Ct. (cen. dist.) Calif. 1979, U.S. Tax Ct. 1979; cert. specialist in probate law, trust law and estate planning law, Calif., cert. specialist in taxation law, Calif. Life underwriter Met. Life Ins. Co., Buffalo, 1958-63; bus. mgr. M. Kreger Bus. Mgmt., Sherman Oaks, Calif., 1963-78, enrolled agt., 1971-78; sole practice North Hollywood, Calif.,

1978—. Mem. Nat. Assn. Enrolled Agts., Calif. Soc. Enrolled Agts., State Bar of Calif., L.A. Bar Assn., San Fernando Valley Bar Assn. (probate sect.). Jewish. Office: 11424 Burbank Blvd North Hollywood CA 91601-2397

KREIDLER, MIKE, congressman, optometrist; b. nr. Tacoma, Wash., Sept. 28, 1943; m. Lela Kreidler; children: Kelli, Lora, Michael. BS, Pacific U., Oregon, 1967, MD in Optometry, 1969; MPH, UCLA, 1972. Dr. of Optometry Group Health Coop. of Puget Sound, Olympia, Wash., 1972—; mem. 87th-95th Congresses from 22d Wash. dist., 1977-84; U.S. senator from Wash. 95th-103rd Congresses from 22d dist. Wash., 1985-93; mem. 103rd Congress from 9th Wash. dist., Washington, D.C., 1993—; dir. 1st Community Bank of Wash., Lacey; mem. Gov's. Health Care Cost Control & Access Commn.; mem. energy and commerce com., vets. affairs com. Mem. Sch. Bd. North Thurston County, 1973-77. Lt. col. USAR, Persian Gulf. Mem. Lacey Rotary, Harmony Masonic Lodge, Thurston County Shrine, Olympia Rain Runners. Democrat. Office: US Ho of Reps 1535 Longworth HOB Washington DC 20515

KREIDLER, TERRY JAMES, geologist; b. Detroit, Apr. 15, 1948; s. James Frederick and Florence Emily (Matthes) K.; m. Suzanne Marie Rectenwald, June 20, 1970 (div. 1973); life ptnr. Darlene Beth Schriner. BS in Geology, Bowling Green State U., 1970; postgrad., No. Ariz. U., 1970-73. Geologist Fugro Inc. (named changed to Ertec), Long Beach, Calif., 1973-75, AGIP Mining Co., Denver, 1975-78, U.S. Bur. Mines, Denver, 1978—. Author reports in field; co-author Geol. Survey bulls.; editor U.S. Bur. Mines, 1981—. Mem. Ariz. Geol. Soc., Assn. Earth Sci. Editors. Home: 1027 Indian Peaks Rd Golden CO 80403-9417 Office: US Bur Mines Denver Fed Ctr PO Box 25086 Denver CO 80225

KREIL, CURTIS LEE, research chemist; b. Milw., Aug. 22, 1955; s. Hugo Harvey and Sofia (Patelski) K. AA, U. Wis. Ctr., West Bend, 1975; BS in Chemistry, U. Wis., Madison, 1977; PhD in Chemistry, U. Calif., Los Angeles, 1983. Tech. prodn. asst. DIMAT Inc., Cedarburg, Wis., 1973-75; rsch. asst. U. Wis., Madison, 1975-77; rsch. fellow Columbia U., N.Y.C., 1976; rsch. asst. U. Calif., L.A., 1977-82; sr. rsch. chemist 3M, St. Paul, 1983-86; quality assurance supr. 3M, Camarillo, Calif., 1986-90, tech. mgr., 1990—; chmn. photochemistry chpt. 3M Tech. Forum, St. Paul, 1984-85; chmn. 3M Tech. Forum, Camarillo, 1989-90. Contbr. articles to profl. jours.; inventor electron beam adhesion-promoting treatment of polyester film base for silicone release liners, electron beam adhesion promoting treatment of polyester film base. 1st lt. CAP. Recipient Merck Index award Merck & Co., 1977; grad. fellow NSF, 1977-80. Mem. Am. Chem. Soc., Aircraft Owners and Pilots Assn., Exptl. Aircraft Assn. (v.p. 1991), 3M Aviation Club (pres. 1985-86), Phi Beta Kappa. Office: 3M 350 Lewis Rd Camarillo CA 93012-8485

KREIMAN, ROBERT THEODORE, manufacturing company executive; b. Kenosha, Wis., Sept. 16, 1924; s. Theodore Frederick and May Ellen (Engelhardt) K.; m. Shirley Elizabeth Gregor, Dec. 18, 1953; children: Jody Elizabeth, Jacqueline May. Student, Stanford U., 1943-44; BBA, U. Wis., 1949; Exec. MBA, UCLA, 1969. Mgr. AV sales Bell & Howell Co., Chgo., 1949-58; v.p. AV systems Argus Cameras, Ann Arbor, Mich., 1959-62; v.p. Technicolor Inc., Hollywood, Calif., 1962-70, Suburban Gas, Pomona, Calif., 1970-72; pres., CEO Deluxe Gen., Hollywood, Calif., 1972-80, Pace Internat. Corp., Culver City, Calif., 1968—. Capt. U.S. Army, 1943-46, ETO. Office: Pace Internat Corp 3727 S Robertson Culver City CA 90232

KREITLER, RICHARD ROGERS, company executive; b. Summit, N.J., Nov. 15, 1942; s. Carl John and Juliette (Rogers) K.; m. Donna Chapman, June 24, 1966 (div. Aug. 1984); m. Joy Stringfellow, Oct. 22, 1987; children: Kent, Kim, Ryan McIntire. BA, Washington and Lee U., 1965; MA, George Washington U., 1966. Tchr. Pembroke Country Day Sch., Kansas City, Mo., 1966-67; salesman B. C. Christopher & Co., Kansas City, 1967-70; v.p. Faulkner, Dawking & Sullivan, N.Y.C., 1970-72, Donaldson, Lufkin Jenrett, N.Y.C., 1972-75; sr. v.p. White Weld, N.Y.C., 1975-76; v.p. Goldman Sachs, N.Y.C., 1976-80; gen. ptnr. Dakota Ptnrs., Ketchum, Idaho, 1980—; Faulkner, Dawkins & Sullivan. Trustee Sun Valley (Idaho) Sky Edn. Found., 1984-87, Ketchum Sun Valley Community Sch., 1986-89. Mem. Sun Valley Golf Club. Republican. Episcopalian. Avocations: golf, tennis, skiing, bicycling. Home: 449 Wood River Dr Ketchum ID 83340 Office: Dakota Ptnrs 620 Sun Rd Ketchum ID 83340

KREITZBERG, FRED CHARLES, construction management company executive; b. Paterson, N.J., June 1, 1934; s. William and Ella (Bohen) K.; m. Barbara Braun, June 9, 1957; children: Kim, Caroline, Allison, Bruce, Catherine. BSCE, Norwich U., 1957. Registered profl. engr., Ala., Alaska, Ariz., Ark., Calif., Colo., Conn., Del., D.C., Fla., Ga., Idaho, Ill., Ind., Kans., Ky., Md., Mass., Minn., Miss., Mo., Nebr., Nev., N.C., N.H., N.J., N.Mex., N.Y., Ohio, Okla., Oreg., Pa., S.D., Tenn., Va., Vt., Wash., W.Va., Wis., Wyo. Asst. supt. Turner Constrn. Co., N.Y.C., 1957; project mgr. Project Mercury RCA, N.J., 1958-63; schedule cost mgr. Catalytic Constrn. Co., Pa., 1963-65, 65—; cons. Meridien Engring., 1965-68; prin. MDC Systems Corp., 1968-72; owner, pres., chief exec. officer, bd. dirs. O'Brien-Kreitzberg and Assocs. Inc., San Francisco, 1972—; lectr. Stanford (Calif.) U., U. Calif., Berkeley. Author: Crit. Path Method Scheduling for Contractor's Mgmt. Handbook, 1971; tech. editor Constrn. Inspection Handbook, 1972; contbr. articles to profl. jours. bd. dirs. Partridge Soc.; trustee Norwich U. 2d lt. C.E., U.S. Army, 1957-58. Recipient Disting. Alumnus award Norwich U., 1987; named Boss of Yr., Nat. Assn. Women in Constrn., 1987; named in his honor Kreitzberg Amphitheatre, 1987, Kreitzberg Libr. at Norwich U., 1992; Bay Area Discovery Mus.-Birthday rm. and snack bar named in honor of Kreitzberg family, 1989. Fellow ASCE (Constrn. Mgr. of Yr. 1982), Internat. Leaders in Achievement; mem. Am. Arbitration Assn., Constrn. Mgmt. Assn. Am. (founding, bd. dirs.), Soc. Am. Value Engrs., Community Field Assn., Ross Hist. Soc., N.J. Soc. Civil Engrs., N.J. Soc. Profl. Planners, Project Mgmt. Inst., Constrn. Industry Pres. Forum, Tamalpa Runners Club, Palm Springs (Calif.) Tennis Club, Marin Tennis Club. Home: 19 Spring Rd Box 1200 Ross CA 94957 Office: O'Brien-Kreitzberg & Assocs Inc 188 The Embarcadero San Francisco CA 94105-1231

KREITZER, DAVID MARTIN, artist; b. Ord, Nebr., Oct. 23, 1942; s. David and Norma (Buls) K.; m. Ana Bueno, Apr. 1, 1972 (div. 1978); 1 child, Anatol Christian; m. Jacalyn Bower, Nov. 26, 1987; 1 child, Fredricka Jacalyn. BS, Concordia Coll., Seward, Nebr., 1965; MA, San Jose State U., 1967. Exhibited in group and one-man shows including Maxwell Gallery, San Francisco, 1968-72, Akrum Gallery, L.A., 1970-89, Adele M. Gallery, Dallas, 1972-90, Summa Gallery, N.Y.C., 1988-90, Stary-Sheets Gallery, L.A., 1992. Bd. dirs. Music and Arts for Youth, San Luis Obispo, Calif., 1983-85. Recipient Ciba-Geigy award 1971, Gold medal San Francisco Art Dirs. Club, 1970. Mem. Christian Ch. Home: 1442 12th St Los Osos CA 93402-1711

KREJCI, ROBERT HENRY, aerospace engineer; b. Shenandoah, Iowa, Nov. 15, 1943; s. Henry and Marie Josephine (Kubicek) K.; m. Carolyn R. Meyer, Aug. 21, 1967; children—Christopher S., Ryan D. B.S. with honors in Aerospace Engring., Iowa State U., Ames, 1967, M.Aerospace Engring., 1971. Commd. 2d lt. U.S. Air Force, 1968, advanced through grades to capt., 1978; lt. col. Res.; served with systems command Space Launch Vehicles Systems Program Office, Advanced ICBM program officer; research assoc. U.S. Dept. Energy Lawrence Livermore lab.; dept. mgr. advanced tech. programs Strategic div. Thiokol Corp., 1978-84, mgr. space programs, 1984-85, mgr. Navy strategic programs, 1986—. Decorated A.F. commendation medal, Nat. Def. Service medal. Mem. AIAA. Home: 885 N 300 E Brigham City UT 84302-1310 Office: Thiokol Corp PO Box 689 Brigham City UT 84302-0689

KRELL, GEORGE FREDERICK, university administrator; b. Liberal, Kans., Sept. 17, 1938; s. George Berthold and Margaret Janette (Long) K.; m. Carolyn Dale Pfaff, Dec. 26, 1963 (div. Dec. 1976); children: George Christopher, Michael Andrew, Ellen Ann; m. Kathleen Jean Hinman, May 13, 1977. BS in Civil Engring., U. Wyo., 1964, MS in Indsl. Edn., 1979, EdD in Edn. Adminstrn., 1986. Design engr. City of L.A., 1964-65; dist. engr. Shell Oil Co., L.A., 1965-70; owner, mgr. Coast to Coast Hardware, Rock Springs, Wyo., 1970-77; mgr. facilities engring. U. Wyo., Laramie, 1979-85, assoc. dir. phys. plant, 1985-88, dir. phys. plant, 1988—; roofing cons. City of Cheyenne (Wyo.), 1984, City of Laramie, 1983. Mem. Selective Svc. Bd., Rock Springs, Wyo., 1975; bd. dirs. UniWyo Fed. Credit Union, Laramie, 1985; mem. City Planning Commn., Laramie, 1989—. Mem. Rocky Mountain Phys. Plant Adminstrs. (v.p. 1990, pres. 1991), Assn. Phys. Plant Adminstrs. Univs. and Colls. (bd. dirs. 1992—), Phi Delta Kappa, Kappa Delta Phi. Republican. Methodist. Home: 2013 Thornburgh Dr Laramie WY 82070 Office: U Wyo Phys Plant PO Box 3227 Laramie WY 82071-3227

KREMPEL, RALF HUGO BERNHARD, artist, art gallery owner; b. Groitzsch, Saxony, Germany, June 5, 1935; came to U.S., 1964; s. Curt Bernhard and Liesbeth Anna Margarete (Franz) K.; m. Barbara von Eberhardt, Dec. 21, 1967 (div. 1985); 1 child, Karma. Student, Wood and Steel Constrn. Coll., Leipzig, German Democratic Republic, 1955. Steel constructor worldwide, 1955-73; co-owner San Francisco Pvt. Mint, 1973-81; prin. artist San Francisco Painter Magnate, 1982—; dir. Stadtgalerie Wiprechtsburg Groitzsch, Germany, 1991—. Exhbns. Centre Internat. d'Art Contemporain, 1985, Art Contemporain Cabinet des Dessins, 1986, Galerie Salammbo-Atlante, 1987— and others; inventor, designer Visual Communication System. Home: 2400 Pacific Ave San Francisco CA 94115-1275 Office: San Francisco Painter Magnate Rincon Ctr San Francisco CA 94119-3368 also: Brühl 2, 04539 Groitzsch Germany

KREMPEL, ROGER ERNEST, consultant; b. Waukesha, Wis., Oct. 8, 1926; s. Henry and Clara K.; m. Shirley Ann Gray, June 16, 1948; children—John, Sara, Peter. Student Ripon Coll., 1944, Stanford U., 1945; BCE, U. Wis.-Madison, 1950. Registered profl. engr., Wis., Colo.; registered land surveyor, Wis. Asst. city engr., Manitowoc, Wis., 1950-51; city engr. dir. pub. works, Janesville, Wis., 1951-75; dir. water utilities, pub. works Ft. Collins, Colo., 1975-84, dir. natural resources, streets and stormwater utilities, Ft. Collins, 1984-88; pub. works mgmt. cons., 1988-93; lectr. various univ., coll., nat. confs. and seminars. Contbr. articles to profl. pubs. Served with U.S. Army, 1944-46. Recipient numerous tech. and profl. awards, Distin. Svc. citation U. Wis. Coll. Engring., 1989. Fellow ASCE (life); mem. Am. Pub. Works Assn. (life mem., past pres. Colo. and Wis. chpts., mem. rsch. found.), Pub. Works Hist. Soc. (v.p.), Nat. Soc. Profl. Engrs., Wis. Soc. Profl. Engrs. (past pres.), Am. Acad. Environ. Engrs. (diplomate), Colo. Engrs. Coun. (pres. 1990-91), Am. Soc. Civil Engrs. (mgmt. award 1990)

KREPS, DAVID MARC, economist, educator; b. N.Y.C., Oct. 18, 1950; s. Saul Ian and Sarah (Kaskin) Kreps; m. Anat Ruth Admati, Jan. 4, 1984; 1 child, Tamar. AB, Dartmouth Coll., 1972; MA, PhD, Stanford U., 1975. Asst. prof. Stanford U., 1975-78, assoc. prof., 1978-80, prof., 1980-84, Holden prof., 1984—; rsch. officer U. Cambridge, Eng., 1978-79, fellow commoner Churchill Coll., Cambridge, 1978-79; vis. prof. Yale U., New Haven, 1982, Harvard U., Cambridge, Mass., 1983, U. Paris, 1985; vis. prof. U. Tel Aviv, 1989-90, sr. prof. by spl. apppintment, 1991—. Author: Notes on the Theory of Choice, 1988, A Course in Microeconomic Theory, 1990, Game Theory and Economic Modelling, 1990; co-editor Econometrica, 1984-88. Alfred P. Sloan Found. fellow, 1983, John S. Guggenheim fellow, 1988. Fellow Econometric Soc. (coun. 1987—); mem. Am. Econ. Assn. (J.B. Clark medal 1989), Am. Acad. Arts and Scis. Office: Stanford U Grad Sch of Bus Stanford CA 94305

KRESA, KENT, aerospace executive; b. N.Y.C., Mar. 24, 1938; s. Helmy and Marjorie (Boutelle) K.; m. Joyce Anne McBride, Nov. 4, 1961; 1 child, Kiren. B.S.A.A., MIT, 1959, M.S.A.A., 1961, E.A.A., 1966. Sr. scientist research and advanced devel. div. AVCO, Wilmington, Mass., 1959-61; staff mem. MIT Lincoln Lab., Lexington, Mass., 1961-68; dep. dir. strategic tech. office Def. Advanced Research Projects Agy., Washington, 1968-73; dir. tactical tech. office Def. Advanced Research Project Agy., Washington, 1973-75; v.p., mgr. Research & Tech. Ctr. Northrop Corp., Hawthorne, Calif., 1975-76; v.p., gen. mgr. Ventura div. Northrop Corp., Newbury Park, Calif., 1976-82; group v.p. Aircraft Group Northrop Corp., L.A., 1982-86, sr. v.p. tech. devel. and planning, 1986-87, pres., chief operating officer, 1987-90, pres., chief exec. officer, 1990—; bd. dirs. John Tracy Clinic.; mem. Chief of Naval Ops. exec. panel Washington, Def. Sci. Bd., Washington, DNA New Alternatives Working Group, L.A., Dept. Aeronautics and Astronautics Corp. Vis. Com. MIT. Recipient Henry Webb Salsbury award MIT, 1959, Arthur D. Flemming award, 1975; Sec. of Def. Meritorious Civilian Service medal, 1975, USN Meritorious Pub. Service citation, 1975, Exceptional Civilian Service award USAF, 1987. Fellow AIAA; mem. Naval Aviation Mus. Found., Navy League U.S., Soc. Flight Test Engrs., Assn. of U.S. Army, Nat. Space Club, Am. Def. Preparedness Assn. Club: Mountaingate Country. Office: Northrop Corp 1840 Century Park E Los Angeles CA 90067-2101*

KRETZINGER, RIK J., chemical company executive; b. Johnson AFB, Japan, June 8, 1953; came to U.S., 1955; s. Ronald J. and Martha (Havens) K.; m. Denise Lacanette, Aug. 19, 1978; children: Joel Ryan, Katie Lynn. BS, Calif. Poly. U., 1976. Sales rep. Moyer Chemicals, Fresno, Calif., 1976-78; tech. sales rep. Union Carbide Corp., N.Y.C., 1978-83; regional sales mgr. ADM-Citric Group, Pleasanton, Calif., 1983—. Republican. Presbyterian. Home: 4109 Holland Dr Pleasanton CA 94588-4419

KREVANS, JULIUS RICHARD, university administrator, physician; b. N.Y.C., May 1, 1924; s. Sol and Anita (Makovetsky) K.; m. Patricia N. Abrams, May 28, 1950; children: Nita, Julius R., Rachel, Sarah, Nora Kate. B.S. Arts and Scis, N.Y. U., 1943, M.D., 1946. Diplomate: Am. Bd. Internal Med. Intern, then resident Johns Hopkins Med. Sch. Hosp., mem. faculty, until 1970, dean acad. affairs, 1969-70; physician in chief Balt. City Hosp., 1963-69; prof. medicine U. Calif., San Francisco, 1970—, dean Sch. Medicine, 1971-82, chancellor. Contbr. articles on hematology, internal med. profl. jours. Served with M.C. AUS, 1948-50. Mem. A.C.P., Assn. Am. Physicians. Office: U Calif Office of Chancellor 3D Parnassus Ave San Francisco CA 94143-0001*

KRICK, IRVING PARKHURST, meteorologist; b. San Francisco, Dec. 20, 1906; s. H. I. and Mabel (Royal) K.; m. Jane Clark, May 23, 1930; 1 dau., Marllynn; m. Marie Spiro, Nov. 18, 1946; 1 son, Irving Parkhurst II. B.A., U. Calif., 1928; M.S., Cal. Inst. Tech., 1933, Ph.D., 1934. Asst. mgr. radio sta. KTAB, 1928-29; meteorologist, 1930—; became mem. staff Calif. Inst. Tech., 1933, asst. prof. meteorology, 1935-38, assoc. prof., prof. and head dept., 1938-48; organizer, pres. Am. Inst. Aerological Rsch. and Water Resources Devel. Corp., 1950; pres. Irving P. Krick Assocs., Inc., Irving P. Krick, Inc., Tex., Irving P. Krick Assocs. Can. Ltd.; now, chmn. emeritus, sr. cons. strategic Weather Svc. Krick Ctr. Weather R & D, Palm Springs, Calif.; established meteorology dept. Am. Air Lines, Inc., 1935, established Internat. Meteorol. Cons. Svcs., 1946, mng. dir.; cons. in field, 1935-36; mem. sci. adv. group Von Kármán Army Air Force, 1945-46. Pianist in concert and radio work, 1929-30; Co-author: Sun, Sea and Sky, 1954; Writer numerous articles on weather analysis, weather modification and forecasting and its application to agrl. and bus. industries. Served as lt. Coast Arty. Corps U.S. Army, 1928-36; commd. ensign USNR, 1938; maj., then lt. col. USAAF, 1943; Weather Directorate, Weather Central Div. unit comdr. of Long Range Forecast Unit A 1942-43; dep. dir. weather sect. U.S. Strategic Air Forces Europe, 1944; chief weather information sect. SHAEF 1945. Decorated Legion of Merit, Bronze Star with Oak leaf cluster U.S.; Croix de Guerre France; recipient Distinguished Service award Jr. C. of C.; chosen one of 10 outstanding men under age 35 by U.S. Jr. C. of C. Fellow AIAA (assoc.), Royal Soc. Arts; mem. AAAS, Royal Meteorol. Soc., Am. Meteorol. Soc., Am. Geophys. Union, Sigma Xi. Republican. Home: Apt 13 1200 S Orange Grove Blvd Pasadena CA 91105-3353 Office: Krick Ctr Weather R & D 610 S Belardo Rd Palm Springs CA 92264

KRIEGER, DAVID MALCOLM, peace foundation executive, lawyer; b. L.A., Mar. 27, 1942; s. Herbert D. and Sybil Krieger; m. Carolee Kehaulani Gamble, Aug. 14, 1967; children: Jeffrey, Jonathon, Mara. BA, Occidental Coll., 1963; MA, U. Hawaii, 1967, PhD, 1968; JD cum laude, valedictorian, Santa Barbara Coll. Law, 1987. Bar: Calif., 1987. Asst. prof. polit. sci. U. Hawaii, Honolulu, 1969-70; asst. prof. internat. rels. San Francisco State U., 1970-72; researcher Ctr. for Study of Dem. Instns., Santa Barbara, 1972-74; project coord. Found. Reshaping the Internat. Order, Rotterdam, The Netherlands, 1980-81; pres. Nuclear Age Peace Found., Santa Barbara, 1982—. Editor: The Tides of Change, 1974, Disarmament and Development, 1980, Waging Peace II, Ideas for Action, 1988, Vision and Hope for the 21st Century, 1992; author: Countdown for Survival, 1981, Disarmament and Development: The Challenge of the Control and Management of Dual-Purpose Technologies, 1981, The Oceans: A Common Heritage, 1975, Preventing Accidental Nuclear War, 1984, A Magna Carta for the Nuclear Age, 1992; contbr. articles to profl. publs. 2d lt. U.S. Army, 1968-69. Office: Nuclear Age Peace Found Ste 123 1187 Coast Village Rd Santa Barbara CA 93108

KRIEGER, MICHAEL RAYMOND, computer manufacturing executive, writer; b. Bklyn., Feb. 4, 1954; s. Joseph Ezra and Sally (Gelberg) K.; m. Barbara Gale Rothman, Sept. 27, 1981; children: Rachael, Zachary. Student, Polytech. Inst. N.Y., 1970-72, New Sch. Social Rsch., N.Y.C., 1972-73, Actor's Studio, N.Y.C., 1974-75. Programmer, analyst Inflight Motion Pictures, Queens, N.Y., 1975-77; pres., CEO Solution Bus. Systems, Port Washington, N.Y., 1978-84; v.p. devel. Techland Systems, N.Y.C., 1984-86; dir. advanced systems AST Computer, Irvine, Calif., 1986-93; dir. Ziff-Davis Mag. Network, Foster City, Calif., 1993—; mem. mktg. com. Common-Users Group, Chgo., 1977-93; founding mem. Extended Industry Standard Architecture Consortium Bd., Houston, 1988-93. Author: Smartsizing, 1993; editorial advisor System 3X World, 1989. Recipient Product of Yr. award Lan Mag., 1993. Democrat. Office: Ziff Davis Pub Co 950 Tower Ln Foster City CA 94404

KRIEGER, MURRAY, English educator, author; b. Newark, Nov. 27, 1923; s. Isidore and Jennie (Glinn) K.; m. Joan Alice Stone, June 15, 1947; children: Catherine Leona, Eliot Franklin. Student, Rutgers U., 1940-42; M.A., U. Chgo., 1948; Ph.D. (Univ. fellow), Ohio State U., 1952. Instr. English Kenyon Coll., 1948-49, Ohio State U., 1951-52; asst. prof., then asso. prof. U. Minn., 1952-58; prof. English U. Ill., 1958-63; M.F. Carpenter prof. lit. criticism U. Iowa, 1963-66; prof. English, dir. program in criticism U. Calif. at Irvine, 1966-85; prof. English UCLA, 1973-82; univ. prof. U. Calif., 1974—, co-dir. Sch. Criticism and Theory, 1975-77, dir., 1977-81, hon. sr. fellow, 1981—; assoc. mem. Ctr. Advanced Study, U. Ill., 1961-62; dir. U. Calif. Humanities Rsch. Inst., 1987-89. Author: The New Apologists for Poetry, 1956, The Tragic Vision, 1960, A Window to Criticism: Shakespeare's Sonnets and Modern Poetics, 1964, The Play and Place of Criticism, 1967, The Classic Vision, 1971, Theory of Criticism: A Tradition and Its System, 1976, Poetic Presence and Illusion, 1979, Arts on the Level, 1981, Words About Words About Words: Theory, Criticism and the Literary Text, 1988, A Reopening of Closure: Organicism Against Itself, 1989, Ekphrasis: The Illusion of the Natural Sign, 1992, The Ideological Imperative: Repression and Resistance in Recent American Theory, 1993; editor: (with Eliseo Vivas) The Problems of Aesthetics, 1953, Northrop Frye in Modern Criticism, 1966, (with L.S. Dembo) Directions for Criticism: Structuralism and its Alternatives, 1977, The Aims of Representation: Subject/Text/History, 1987. Served with AUS, 1942-46. Recipient rsch. prize Humboldt Found., Fed. Republic Germany, 1986-87, medal U. Calif. at Irvine, 1991; Guggenheim fellow, 1956-57, 61-62; Am. Council Learned Socs. postdoctoral fellow, 1966-67; grantee NEH, 1971-72; Rockefeller Found. humanities fellow, 1978; resident scholar Rockefeller Study Ctr., Bellagio, 1990. Fellow Am. Acad. Arts and Scis. (council and exec. com. 1987-88); mem. MLA, Internat. Assn. Univ. Profs. English, Acad. Lit. Studies. Home: 407 Pinecrest Dr Laguna Beach CA 92651-1471 Office: U Calif Dept English & Comparative Lit Irvine CA 92717

KRIEGER, TILLIE, librarian, consultant; b. Detroit; d. Louis and Ethel (Plotkin) K.; m. Berthold Stein (div. 1956); 1 child, Joshua Marc. BA in History, UCLA, 1962; MLS in Libr., U. So. Calif., 1964; PhD, U. Ill., 1981. Law libr. U. Calif., Davis, 1966-67; acquisitions libr. Ariz. State U., Tempe, 1967-69; asst. dir. Nat. Serials Pilot Project, Washington, 1969-70; libr. Libr. of Congress, Washington, 1970-73; dir. law classification project U. Ill., Champaign, 1976-79; dir. libr. Ctr. for Study Youth Devel., Boys Town, Nebr., 1979-80; prof. La. State U., Baton Rouge, 1981-87; mgr. periodicals Coll. S.I., N.Y., 1987-90; legis. cons. State of La., Baton Rouge, 1985. Compiler: Subject Headings for the Literature of Law, 4th edit., 1990. Mem. ALA (various coms.), Spl. Librs. Assn. (chair info. tech. group 1989, co-chair planning com. ann. meeting 1989), Oreg. Libr. Assn. Democrat. Jewish. Home: 2591 Polk St Eugene OR 97405-1838

KRIEGER, WILLIAM CARL, English language educator; b. Seattle, Mar. 21, 1946; s. Robert Irving Krieger and Mary (McKibben) Durfee; m. Patricia Kathleen Callow, Aug. 20, 1966; children: Richard William, Robert Irving III, Kathleen Elizabeth. BA in English, Pacific Luth. U., 1968, MA in Humanities, 1973; PhD in Am. Studies, Wash. State U., 1986. Instr. Pierce Coll., Tacoma, 1969—, chmn. English dept., 1973-79, 81-84, chmn. humanities div., 1979-81, prof. English, 1969—; adj. prof. hist. and English Cen. Wash. State U., 1980; vis. prof. hist. and English So. Ill. U., Carbondale, 1981-84, Pacific Luth. U., Tacoma, 1981-84; head coach Gig Harbor High Sch. Wrestling, 1990—; bd. dirs. Thoreau Cabin Project, Tacoma, 1979—; project dir. Campus Wash. Centennial Project, Tacoma, 1984-89; spl. cons. Clover Park Sch. Dist., Tacoma, 1985; lang. arts cons. Inst. for Citizen Edn. in Law, U. Puget Sound Law Sch., 1990. Apptd. Wash. St. Centennial Commn., Constitutions Com, Pierce County Centennial Com. Recipient Disting. Achievement award Wash. State Centennial Commn., 1989, Outstanding Achievement award Pierce County Centennial Commn., 1989, Centennial Alumni recognition Pacific Luth. U., 1990; named Outstanding Tchr. Nat. Inst. Staff and Orgnl. Devel., 1992. Mem. Thoreau Soc. (life), Community Coll. Humanities Assn. (standing com. 1982-83), Am. Studies Assn., Wash. Community Coll. Humanities Assn. (bd. dirs. 1982-84, grantee, 1984), Western Wash. Ofcls. Assn. Home: 4415 68th Street Ct NW Gig Harbor WA 98335-8312 Office: Pierce Coll 9401 Farwest Dr SW Tacoma WA 98498-1999

KRIENKE, CAROL BELLE MANIKOWSKE (MRS. OLIVER KENNETH KRIENKE), realtor, appraiser; b. Oakland, Calif., June 19, 1917; d. George and Ethel (Purdon) Manikowske; student U. Mo., 1937; BS, U. Minn., 1940; postgrad. UCLA, 1949; m. Oliver Kenneth Krienke, June 4, 1941 (dec. Dec. 1988); children: Diane (Mrs. Robert Denny), Judith (Mrs. Kenneth A. Giss), Debra Louise (Mrs. Ed Paul Davalos). Demonstrator, Gen. Foods Corp., Mpls., 1940; youth leadership State of Minn. Congl. Conf., U. Minn., Mpls. 1940-41; war prodn. worker Airesearch Mfg. Co., Los Angeles, 1944; tchr. L.A. City Schs., 1945-49; realtor DBA Ethel Purdon, Manhattan Beach, Calif., 1949; buyer Purdon Furniture & Appliances, Manhattan Beach, 1950-58; realtor O.K. Krienke Realty, Manhattan Beach, 1958—. Manhattan Beach bd. rep. Community Chest for Girl Scouts U.S., 1957; bd. dirs. South Bay council Girl Scouts U.S.A., 1957-62, mem. Manhattan Beach Coordinating Coun., 1956-68, South Coast Botanic Garden Found., 1989—, Long Beach Area Childrens Home Soc. (v.p., 1967-68, pres. 1979; charter mem. Beach Pixies, 1957—, pres. 1967; chmn. United Way, 1967); sponsor Beach Cities Symphony, 1953—, Little League Umpires, 1981-91. Mem. DAR (life, citizenship chmn. 1972-73, v.p. 1979, 83—), Calif. Retired Tchrs. Assn. (life), Colonial Dames XVII Century (charter mem. Jared Eliot chpt. 1977, v.p., pres. 1979-81, 83-84), Friends of Library, Torrance Lomita Bd. of Realtors, South Bay Bd. Realtors, Nat. Soc. New England Women (life, Calif. Poppy Colony), Internat. Platform Assn., Soc. Descs. of Founders of Hartford (life), Friends of Banning Mus., Hist. Soc. of Centinela Valley, Manhattan Beach Hist. Soc., Manhattan Beach C. of C. (Rose and Scroll award 1985), U. Minn. Alumni (life). Republican. Mem. Community Ch. (pres. Women's Fellowship 1970-71). Home: 924 Highview Ave Manhattan Beach CA 90266-5813 Office: OK Krienke Realty 1716 Manhattan Beach Blvd Manhattan Beach CA 90266-6220

KRIKOS, GEORGE ALEXANDER, pathologist, educator; b. Old Phaleron, Greece, Sept. 17, 1922; came to U.S., 1946; s. Alexios and Helen (Spyropoulou) K.; m. Aspasia Manoni, June 22, 1949; children: Helen, Alexandra, Alexios. D.D.S., U. Pa., 1949; Ph.D., U. Rochester, 1959; Ph.D. hon. doctorate, U. Athens, Greece, 1981. Asst. prof. pathology U. Pa. Sch. Dentistry, 1958-61, assoc. prof., 1961-67, prof., 1967-68, chmn. dept., 1964-68; assoc. prof. oral pathology U. Pa. Grad. Sch., 1962-68, prof. oral pathology, 1968; prof. pathobiology Sch. Dentistry, U. Colo., Denver, 1968-75, chmn. dept. pathobiology, 1968-73, prof. oral biology, 1975-86, clin. prof. oral biology, 1986-91, prof. oral biology emeritus, 1991—; asst. dean basic sci. affairs Sch. Dentistry, U. Colo., 1973-75, asso. dean oral biology affairs, 1975-76; vis. prof. Sch. Dentistry, U. Athens, 1980-81; mem. dental study sect. NIH, 1966-70; mem. cancer com. Colo.-Wyo. Regional Med. Program, 1970-72; cons. oral pathology Denver VA Hosp., 1970-72. Served with AUS, 1949-54. Mem. Am. Soc. Investigative Pathology, Internat. Assn.

Dental Rsch., Sigma Xi. Home: 350 Ivy St Denver CO 80220-5855 Office: U Colo Sch Dentistry 4200 E 9th Ave Denver CO 80262-0001

KRILL, PAUL JOSEPH, editor; b. Englewood, N.J., Dec. 4, 1960; s. Edward Paul and Rita (McGrath) K. AA, County Coll. Morris, Randolph, N.J., 1981; BA, William Paterson Coll., 1984. Staff writer Star-Gazette, Hackettstown, N.J., 1984-86, N.J. Herald, Newton, 1986-88, Lion Tech. Cons., Lafayette, N.J., 1988-89; sr. editor Open Systems Today, San Jose, Calif., 1989—. Exec. bd. Morris County Cath. Singles, Denville, N.J., 1989. Mem. N.J. Press Assn. Republican.

KRIMM, DAVID ROBERT, investment company executive; b. Ann Arbor, Mich., Oct. 12, 1953; s. Samuel and Marilyn (Neveloff) K. AB, Brown U., 1975; M. in Pub. and Pvt. Mgmt., Yale U., 1981. Assoc. investment brokering Donaldson, Lufkin & Jenrette, N.Y.C., 1981-83; sr. assoc. The Mac Group, San Francisco, 1983-87; v.p., mgr. corp. svcs. Charles Schwab & Co., San Francisco, 1987-92; dir. retirement plan mktg. G.T. Global Fin. Svcs., San Francisco, 1992—. Home: 100 Parker Ave San Francisco CA 94118-2664

KRIPPNER, STANLEY CURTIS, psychologist; b. Edgerton, Wis., Oct. 4, 1932; s. Carroll Porter and Ruth Genevieve (Volenberg) K.; m. Lelie Anne Harris, June 25, 1966; stepchildren: Caron, Robert. BS, U. Wis., 1954; MA, Northwestern U., 1957, PhD, 1961; PhD (hon.), U. Humanistic Studies, San Diego, 1982. Speech therapist Warren Pub. Schs. (Ill.), 1954-55, Richmond Pub. Schs. (Va.), 1955-56; dir. Child Study Ctr. Kent State U. (Ohio), 1961-64; dir. dream lab. Maimonides Med. Ctr., Bklyn., 1964-73; prof. of psychology Saybrook Inst., San Francisco, 1973—; disting. prof. psychology Calif. Inst. Integral Studies, San Francisco, 1991—; vis. prof. U. P.R., 1972, Sonoma State U., 1972-73, Univ. Life Scis., Bogotá, Colombia, 1974, Inst. for Psychodrama and Humanistic Psychology, Caracas, Venezuela, 1975, West Ga. Coll., 1976, John F. Kennedy U., 1980-82; lectr. Acad. Pedagogical Scis., Moscow, 1971, Acad. Scis., Beijing, China, 1981. Author: (with Montague Ullman) Dream Telepathy, 1973, rev. edit., 1989, Song of the Siren: A Parapsychological Odyssey, 1975; (with Alberto Villoldo) The Realms of Healing, 1976, rev. edit., 1987, Human Possibilities, 1980, (with Alberto Villoldo) Healing States, 1987; (with Jerry Solfvin) La Science et les Pouvoirs Psychiques de l'Homme, 1986, (with Joseph Dillard) Dreamworking, 1988, (with David Feinstein) Personal Mythology, 1988, (with Patrick Welch) Spiritual Dimensions of Healing, 1992, (with Dennis Thong and Bruce Carpenter) A Psychiatrist in Paradise, 1993; editor: Advances in Parapsychological Research, Vol. 1, 1977, Vol. 2, 1978, Vol. 3, 1982, Vol. 4, 1984, Vol. 5, 1987, Vol. 6, 1990, Psychoenergetic Systems, 1979; co-editor: Galaxies of Life, 1973, The Kirlian Aura, 1974, The Energies of Consciousness, 1975, Future Science, 1977, Dreamtime and Dreamwork, 1990; mem. editorial bd. Gifted Child Quar., Internat. Jour. Paraphysics, Jour. Humanistic Psychology, Jour. Transpersonal Psychology, Revision Jour., Jour. Theoretical Parapsychology, Jour. Indian Psychology, Psi Research, Metanoia, Dream Network Bulletin, Humanistic Psychologist, Internat. Jour. Psychosomatics, Jour. Creative Children and Adults, InterAm. U. Press; contbr. 500 articles to profl. jours. Mem. adv. bd., bd. dirs. A.R.E. Clinic, Acad. Religion and Psychical Rsch., Survival Rsch. Found., Aesculapian Inst. for Healing Arts, Hartley Film Found., Inst. for Multilevel Learning, Internat. Horizon Ednl. Audio Recordings, Forest Inst. Profl. Psychology, Humanistic Psychology Ctr. N.Y. Recipient Svc. to Youth award YMCA, 1959; recipient citation of merit Nat. Assn. Gifted Children, 1972, citation of merit Nat. Assn. Creative Children and Adults, 1975, cert of recognition Office of Gifted and Talented, U.S. Office Edn., 1976, Volker Medal South Africa Soc. Psychical Rsch., 1980. Fellow Am. Soc. Clin. Hypnosis, Am. Psychol. Assn., Am. Psychol. Soc., Soc. Sci. Study Sex; mem. AAAS, Am. Soc. Psychical Rsch., N.Y. Soc. Clin. Psychologists (assoc.), Am. Acad. Social and Polit. Sci., Am. Ednl. Rsch. Assn., Am. Assn. of Counseling and Devel., Internat. Council Psychologists, Assn. for Study of Dreams, Soc. for the Anthropology Consciousness, Internat. Kirlian Rsch. Assn., Com. for Study Anomalistic Rsch., Inter-Am. Psychol. Assn., Assn. Humanistic Psychology (pres. 1974-75), Assn. Transpersonal Psychology, Internat. Psychomatics Inst., Internat. Soc. Hypnosis, Internat. Soc. for Study Multiple Personality and Dissociative States, Nat. Assn. for Gifted Children, Sleep Rsch. Soc., Soc. Sci. Exploration, Biofeedback Soc. Am., Coun. Exceptional Children, Soc. Accelerative Learning and Teaching, Soc. Gen. Systems Rsch., Swedish Soc. Clin. and Exptl. Hypnosis, Western Psychol. Assn., World Coun. for Gifted and Talented Children, Internat. Soc. Gen. Semantics, Menninger Found., Nat. Soc. Study of Edn., Parapsychol. Assn. (pres. 1983), Soc. Clin. and Exptl. Hypnosis, Soc. for Sci. Study of Religion, World Future Soc. Home: 79 Woodland Rd Fairfax CA 94930-2153 Office: Saybrook Inst 1550 Sutter St San Francisco CA 94109-5307

KRISE, THOMAS WARREN, military officer; b. Fort Sam Houston, Tex., Oct. 27, 1961; s. Edward Fisher and Elizabeth Ann (Bradt) K.; m. Patricia Lynn Love, Sept. 5, 1987. BS, USAF Acad., 1983; MSA, Cen. Mich. U., 1986; MA, U. Minn., 1989. Commd. 2d lt. USAF, 1983, advanced through grades to capt.; dep. missile comdr. 742d Strategic Missile Squadron, Minot AFB, N.D., 1983-85, missile crew comdr., 1985-86, ICBM flight comdr., 1986-87; instr. of English USAF Acad., Colorado Springs, 1989-91, asst. prof. English, 1991—. Editorial reviewer How to Run a USAF Squadron, 1991, Chernobyl & Nuclear Deterrence, 1991; asst. editor War, Literature and the Arts, 1991—; contbr. articles to profl. jours. Adult literacy tutor Coalition for Adult Literacy, Colorado Springs, 1989-91, literacy tutor trainer, 1990—, Adult Literacy Network, Colorado Springs, 1991—. Recipient Pres.' Student Leadership award U. Minn., 1989; Summer Inst. grant Nat. Endowment for the Humanities, Johns Hopkins U., 1990, Seiler Rsch. grant F.J. Seiler Rsch. Lab., A.F. Systems Command, 1991. Mem. SAR (Pikes Peak chpt. pres. 1991-92), Toastmasters Internat. (U. Minn. chpt. pres. 1988-89), Colorado Springs Adult Literacy Network (pres. 1991—), Assn. of Grads. USAF Acad. (bd. dirs. 1991—), Phi Kappa Phi. Episcopalian. Home: Quarters 4411-F U S A F Academy CO 80840 Office: Dept English USAF Acad Ste 6D35 2354 Fairchild Dr USAF Acad CO 80840

KROGH, PETER SUNDEHL, III, family physician; b. Chgo., Jan. 29, 1953; s. Peter Sundehl Krogh Jr. and Audrey Rose (Kalal) Morgan; m. Cynthia Marie Umano, Mar. 4, 1978. BS, USAF Acad., 1975; MD, Rush Med. Coll., 1979. Diplomate Am. Acad. Family Practice. Commd. 2nd lt. USAF, 1975, advanced through grades to lt. col., 1991; family physician resident David Grant USAF Med. Ctr., Travis AFB, Calif., 1979-82, family physician, 1986—; family physician Scott USAF Med. Ctr., Scott AFB, Ill., 1982-84, Iraklion USAF Hosp., Iraklion AB, Crete, 1984-86. Mem. Uniformed Svcs. Acad. Family Physicians, Am. Acad. Family Physicians, Soc. Tchrs. Family Medicine. Republican. Mem. Evangelical Free Ch. Office: USAF David Grant Med Ctr/SGHF Travis AFB CA 94535

KROHN, JERRY FRANK, automotive executive; b. Milw., Dec. 13, 1938; s. Gerhardt Herman and Elizabeth S. (Ziech) K.; m. Judith Ann Fischer, Aug. 29, 1959; children: Mark, Paul, Allison, April, Jerry Jr. Student, U. Wis., 1960, Stout State U., 1965. Head of dept. auto aircraft Boys' Tech. High Sch., Milw., 1963-67; sr. staff instr. Caterpillar Inc., Peoria, Ill., 1967-70; engine dir. mgr. Caterpillar Inc., Bristol, Conn., 1970-73; sr. staff engr. Caterpillar Inc., Geneva, Switzerland, 1974-81; fuels and lube engr. Caterpillar Inc., Peoria, Ill., 1981; Indonesia rep. Caterpillar Inc., Singapore, 1981-85; dist. mgr. Caterpillar Inc., Taipai, Taiwan, 1985-87; engine div. mgr. Caterpillar Inc., Seattle, 1987-91, Pacific Machinery, Guam, 1991—. Contbr. articles to profl. publs. Bd. edn. Luth. Ch., Maltby, Wash., 1987-91; scout master Boy Scouts Am., Geneva, 1976-81; bd. vice chmn. Christian Salvation Svc., Taipei, 1986—. Republican. Home and Office: 196 E Harmon Ind Pk Rd Harmon GU 96911

KROHN, KENNETH ALBERT, radiology educator; b. Stevens Point, Wis., June 19, 1945; s. Albert William and Erma Belle (Cornwell) K.; m. Marijane Alberta Wideman, July 14, 1968; 1 child, Galen. BA in Chemistry, Andrews U., 1966; PhD in Chemistry, U. Calif., 1971. Acting assoc. prof. U. Wash., Seattle, 1981-84, assoc. prof. radiology, 1984-86, prof. radiology and radiation oncology, 1986—, adj. prof. chemistry, 1986—; guest scientist Donner Lab. Lawrence Berkeley (Calif.) Lab., 1980-81; radiochemist, VA Med. Ctr., Seattle, 1982—. Contbr. numerous articles to profl. jours.; patentee in field. NDEA fellow. Fellow AAAS; mem. Am. Chem. Soc., Radiation Rsch. Soc., Soc. Nuclear Medicine, Acad. Coun., Sigma Xi. Home: 11322 23d Ave NE Seattle WA 98125 Office: Imaging Rsch Lab RC-05 U Washington Seattle WA 98195

KROKENBERGER, LINDA ROSE, chemist, environmental analyst; b. Ridley Park, Pa., July 17, 1954; d. Roy Frank and Rose Marie (Kraffert) K. BS in Chemistry, Syracuse U., 1976. Radiopharm. chemist Upstate Med. Ctr., SUNY, Syracuse, 1976-78; chemist, asst. mgr. lab. IT Corp., Cerritos, Calif., 1978-86; mgr. data control Enseco-Cal Lab., West Sacramento, Calif., 1987; asst. mgr. lab. Sci. Applications Internat. Corp., San Diego, 1987-89; ind. cons. in environ. analytical chemistry and compliance Poway, Calif., 1989—. Recipient Citizenship award DAR, 1972. Republican. Methodist. Home and Office: 12974 Cree Dr Poway CA 92064-3830

KROLL, ROBERT ALAN, veterinarian, researcher; b. L.A., Oct. 12, 1960; s. Benjamin and Shirley Marcel (Sherman) K. BS cum laude, Calif. State Poly. U., 1983; DVM with honors, U. Minn., St. Paul, 1988; postgrad., U. Mo., 1989-92, Oreg. Health Scis. U., 1992—. Intern in small animal surgery and medicine Kans. State U., Manhattan, 1988-89; resident in comparative neurology U. Mo., Columbia, 1989-92; postdoctoral rsch. fellow neuro-oncology Oreg. Health Scis. U., Portland, 1992—; cons. neurology Portland, 1992—. Contbg. author: Current Veterinary Therapy XI, 1992, Consultations in Feline Internal Medicine, vol. 2, 1993; mem. editorial bd. monthly newsletter Vector: Companion Animal Medicine News, 1990-92; contbr. articles to profl. jours. Mem. AVMA, Am. Animal Hosp. Assn., Internat. Brain Rsch. Orgn., Vet. Cancer Soc., Soc. for Neurosci., Phi Zeta, Gamma Sigma Delta. Office: Oreg Health Scis U Dept Neurology L603 3181 SW Sam Jackson Park Rd Portland OR 97201-3098

KRONENBERG, JACALYN, oncological and pediatrics nurse; b. N.Y.C., July 21, 1949; d. Martin Jerome and Joyce (Weinberg) Jacobs; m. Robert Kronenberg, Jan. 23, 1971 (div.); 1 child, Joshua Louis. BA, William Paterson Coll. of N.J., 1971; ADN, Phoenix Coll., 1977. RN, Calif.; cert. IV nurse, chemo, ACLS. Asst. charge nurse Phoenix Gen. Hosp.; nurse Ariz. State Crippled Children's Hosp., Tempe; maternal, child nurse Desert Samaritan Hosp., Mesa, Ariz.; nurse mgr. PPS Inc., Phoenix, Med-Pro 2000, Phoenix; clin. nurse II Phoenix Children's Hosp.; nurse mgr. adolescent unit Shriners Hosp., L.A. Nursing Lab. Tech. scholar, 1976. Mem. Oncology Nursing Soc., Phoenix Oncology Nurses Soc., Pediatric Oncology Nurse Soc., ANA, Calif. Nurses Assn., Nursing Diagnosis Assn. of North Am., IV Nursing Soc. Office: 3160 Geneva St Los Angeles CA 90020-1199

KRONENBERG, JOHN ROBERT, magistrate; b. Spokane, Wash., Mar. 15, 1923; s. George C. and Agnes Isabel (Monaghan) K.; m. Marilyn Elizabeth Miller, Feb. 24, 1962; children—John, Karl, Kathryn. LL.B., Loyola U., Los Angeles, 1958. Bar: Calif. 1959, U.S. Dist. Ct. (cen. dist.) Calif. 1959. Dep. pub. defender Los Angeles County (Calif.) Pub. defender, 1959-73; magistrate U.S. Dist. Ct. (cen. dist.) Calif., 1973—. Served with U.S. Army, 1943-45. Roman Catholic. Office: US Courthouse 312 N Spring St Los Angeles CA 90012-4701

KRONK, BERNARD J., marketing executive; b. Amsterdam, N.Y., June 14, 1933; m. Donna Campbell Dybas, Sept. 6, 1958; children: David, Kathleen. BA in Mktg., Syracuse U., 1960; BS in Wood Product Engring., N.Y. State Coll. Forestry, 1960. Sales rep. Midstate Wholesale Corp., Binghamton, N.Y., 1962-66; sales mgr. Midstate Wholesale Corp., Syracuse, N.Y., 1966-70; mgr. eastern region Triangle Pacific Corp., Dallas, 1970-72, mgr. western region, 1972-74; pres., owner Mktg. Enterprises West, Inc., Thousand Oaks, Calif., 1974—. Served with U.S. Army, 1953-55. Mem. Calif. Bass Fedn. (pres. 1987-89). Office: Mktg Enterprises West Inc 954 Calle Angosta Thousand Oaks CA 91360-2210

KROPLA, STEVEN MARK, human resources executive; b. Decatur, Ill., Oct. 17, 1955; s. Charles Joseph and Dolores Elaine (Wikowsky) K.; m. Diane Elizabeth McCowan, Sept. 24, 1983. Student, Ea. Ill. U., 1975-76; BS in Journalism, So. Ill. U., 1979; MS, Chapman U., 1991. Cert. sr. profl. in human resources. News intern Herald & Rev., Decatur, Ill., 1973-75; reporter Daily Times/Courier, Charleston, Ill., 1975-76, Daily Egyptian, Carbondale, Ill., 1977-78; curriculum design specialist, pers. tng. and devel. Brown & Root Inc., Houston, 1979, curriculum design supr., pers. tng. and devel., 1979-80, documentation specialist, computer svcs., 1980-81; program devel. specialist, orgn. devel. and tng. Pool Well Servicing Co., Houston, 1982-83, project mgr., orgn. devel. and tng., 1983-86; human resources mgr. Pool Arctic Alaska, Anchorage, 1986—; tng. cons., Houston, 1981-82; computer cons., Anchorage, 1989—. Author: Even You can Juggle!, 1980; contbr. articles to profl. publs. Account exec. United Way of Anchorage, 1989-91; del. U.S.-USSR Trade Mission, Alaska State C. of C., Magadan, Khabarovsk, Irkutsk, USSR, 1990. Scholarship Scripps-Howard Found., So. Ill. U., 1978. Mem. Petroleum Club of Anchorage, Internat. Assn. of Drilling Contractors (chmn. Alaska chpt. safety com. 1990-92) Soc. for Human Resources Mgmt., Anchorage Soc. for Tng. and Devel., Am. Soc. Safety Engrs. Home: 2300 Ariel Circle Anchorage AK 99515 Office: Pool Arctic Alaska 5801 Silverado Way Anchorage AK 99518

KROPOTOFF, GEORGE ALEX, civil engineer; b. Sofia, Bulgaria, Dec. 6, 1921; s. Alex S. and Anna A. (Kurat) K.; came to Brazil, 1948, to U.S., 1952, naturalized, 1958; BSCE, Inst. Tech., Sofia, 1941; postgrad. in computer sci. U. Calif., 1968; Registered profl. engr., Calif.; m. Helen P., July 23, 1972. With Standard Eletrica S.A., Rio de Janeiro, 1948-52, Pacific Car & Foundry Co., Seattle, 1952-64, T.G. Atkinson Assocs., Structural Engrs., San Diego, 1960-62, Tucker, Sadler & Bennett A-E, San Diego, 1964-74, Gen. Dynamics-Astronautics, San Diego, 1967-68, Engring. Sci., Inc., Arcadia, Calif., 1975-76, Incomtel, Rio de Janeiro, Brazil, 1976, Bennett Engrs., structural cons., San Diego, 1976-82; project structural engr. Hope Cons. Group, San Diego and Saudi Arabia, 1982-84; cons. structural engr. Pioneered engring. computer software. With U.S. Army, 1941-45. Fellow ASCE; mem. Structural Engrs. Assn. San Diego (assoc.), Soc. Am. Mil. Engrs., Soc. Profl. Engrs. Brazil. Republican. Russian Orthodox. Home: 9285 Edgewood Dr La Mesa CA 91941-5612

KROTKI, KAROL JOZEF, sociology educator, demographer; b. Cieszyn, Poland, May 15, 1922; emigrated to Can., 1964; s. Karol Stanislaw and Anna Elzbieta (Skrzywanek) K.; m. Joanna Patkowski, July 12, 1947; children—Karol Peter, Jan Jozef, Filip Karol. B.A. (hons.), Cambridge (Eng.) U., 1948, M.A., 1952; M.A., Princeton U., 1959, Ph.D., 1960. Civil ser. Eng., 1948-49; dep. dir. stats. Sudan, 1949-58; vis. fellow Princeton U., 1958-60; research adviser Pakistan Inst. Devel. Econs., 1960-64; asst. dir. census research Dominion Bur. Stats., Can., 1964-68; prof. sociology U. Alta., 1968-83, univ. prof., 1983-91, univ. prof. emeritus, 1991—; vis. prof. U. Calif., Berkeley, 1967, U. N.C., 1970-73, U. Mich., 1975; coord. program socio-econ. rsch. Province Alta., 1969-71; dir. Can. Futures Rsch. Inst., Edmonton, 1970—; cons. in field. Author 11 books and monographs; contbr. numerous articles to profl. jours. Served with Polish, French and Brit. Armed Forces, 1939-46. Recipient Achievement award Province of Alta., 1970, Commemorative medal for 125th Anniversary of Can., 1992; grantee in field. Fellow Am. Statis. Assn., Royal Soc. Can. (v.p. 1986-88), Acad. Humanities and Social Scis. (v.p. 1984-86, pres. 1986-88); mem. Fedn. Can. Demographers (v.p. 1977-82, pres. 1982-84), Can. Population Soc., Association des Demographes du Quebec, Soc. Edmonton Demographers (founder, pres. 1990—), Cen. and E. European Studies Soc. (pres. 1986-88), Population Assn. Am., Internat. Union Sci. Study Population, Internat. Statis. Inst., Royal Statis. Soc. Roman Catholic. Home: 10137 Clifton Pl, Edmonton, AB Canada T5N 3H9 Office: U Alta, Dept Sociology, Edmonton, AB Canada T6G 2H4

KROUT, BOYD MERRILL, psychiatrist; b. Oakland, Calif., Jan. 31, 1931; s. Boyd Merrill and Phoebe Lenore (Colby) K.; m. Helena Luise Keel, Aug. 25, 1965. AB, Stanford U., 1951, MD, 1955. Diplomate Am. Bd. Psychiatry and Neurology. Intern San Francisco Hosp., 1954-55; resident Boston U. Hosps., 1958-60, Boston Va Hosp., 1960-61; asst. to clin. prof. UCLA Sch. Medicine, 1961—; chief physician Harbor/UCLA Med. Ctr., Torrance, 1961—. Capt. USAF, 1955-58. Fellow Am. Psychiat. Assn., So. Calif. Psychiat. Soc. (councillor 1988-91), Am. Psychiat. Soc.; mem. L.A. County Med. Soc. Republican. Office: Harbor/UCLA Med Ctr 1000 Carson St Torrance CA 90509

KRUCKY, ANTON CHALMERS, information systems company executive; b. Tokyo, Oct. 30, 1952; s. Anton and Evelyn (Chalmers) K.; m. Dana Anderson; May 12, 1984. BA in Criminology, U. Md., 1974. Systems engr. IBM Corp., San Francisco, 1977-78, mktg. rep., 1978-82; mktg. mgr. IBM Corp., Seattle, 1982-85; exec. asst. IBM Corp., White Plains, N.Y., 1985-86; br. mgr. IBM Corp., Honolulu, 1986-90, gen. mgr., 1990—; adv. bd. mem. Hawaii Pacific U., Honolulu, 1987—; exec. bd. mem. Hawaii Computer Job Tng. Ctr., Honolulu, 1986—; commr. Commn. on Judicial Discipline, 1991. Bd. dirs., exec. bd. mem. Aloha United Way, Honolulu, 1986—; mem. exec. advisory bd. Hawaii Spl. Olympics, Honolulu, 1986—; bd. regents Chaminade Univ., 1992—. Mem. Honolulu C. of C. (exec. adv. bd.), Oahu Country Club, Rotary. Office: IBM 1240 Ala Moana Blvd Honolulu HI 96814-4220

KRUEGER, J. FRANN, editor; b. Wayne, N.H., June 1, 1947; d. Francis M. and Geneva P. (Robinson) Sullivan; m. T.A. Lopez, Sept. 1, 1969 (div. 1980); children: Amy, Karen, Andrew. BSN, U. Nebr., 1968. Med. group mem. Med. Clinic, Pomona, Calif., 1976-82, H. Rahman, M.D., Pomona, Calif., 1982-85; editor Walnut, Calif., 1985—; bus. cons. in med./legal field.

KRUEGER, KURT EDWARD, environmental management company official; b. Santa Monica, Calif., June 24, 1952; s. Richard L. and Peggy J. (Cisler) K.; m. Maureen S. Catland, Aug. 4, 1973; children: Corey Edward, Brendan Kurt, Alyssa Marie. BA in Biology, Calif. State U., Northridge, 1978; MS in Environ. and Occupational Health & Safety, Calif. State U., 1980; MBA, Pepperdine U., 1988. Registered environ. health specialist. Regional health and safety coord. Internat. Tech. Corp., Wilmington, Calif., 1979-82, mgr. emergency response program, 1982-85, ops. mgr., 1985-88, gen. mgr., 1988-89; dir. health and safety Internat. Tech. Corp., Torrance, Calif., 1989—. Mem. Am. Indsl. Hygiene Assn. (cert.), Masons. Office: Internat Tech Corp 23456 Hawthorne Blvd Ste 220 Torrance CA 90505-4738

KRUEGER, LARRY EUGENE, import/export company executive, lawyer; b. Pasco, Wash., Apr. 22, 1944; s. Albert H. and Mabel K. (Mosgaard) K.; m. Barbara Kay Strunk, Apr. 9, 1966; children: Kelli Kay, Eric Alan. AA cum laude, Columbia Basin Coll., 1965; BA in Edn. magna cum laude, Gonzaga U., 1966, JD, 1971; MS in Counseling, Whitworth Coll., 1984. Bar: Wash. 1972, U.S. Dist. Ct. (ea. dist.) Wash. 1973. Pvt. practice, Deer Park, Wash., 1973-76, Spokane, Wash., 1978—; rep. west coast CMA, Inc., Honolulu; CEO, sr. ptnr. N.W. Investment, Trade and Liquidation Groups; v.p., CEO Sta. KRUE-TV Internat. Inc., Salem, Oreg., The Country Connection. Legal dir. County Homes Kiwanis Club, Spokane; leader 5th dist. Rep. Cen. Com., Spokane, 1973-76; bd. dirs. Family Counseling Svc., Spokane, 1976, Antonian Sch. Spl. Children, Spokane, 1978—; mem. Council of Twelve Chs., 1987—. Capt. U.S. Army, 1963-73. Pasco Kiwanis scholar, 1965, Gonzaga U. Law Sch. scholar, 1966-67; named to Outstanding Young Men of Am. U.S. Jaycees, 1979. Mem. Wash. State Bar Assn., Wash. State Trial Lawyers Assn., ABA, Am. Trial Lawyers Assn., Spokane County Bar Assn., Phi Theta Kappa, Phi Alpha Delta, Kappa Delta Pi, Eagles. Home: N 7006 Colton F 101 Spokane WA 99208 Office: PO Box 18589 Spokane WA 99208-0589

KRUGER, CHARLES HERMAN, JR., mechanical engineer; b. Oklahoma City, Oct. 4, 1934; s. Charles H. and Flora K.; m. Nora Nininger, Sept. 10, 1977; children—Sarah, Charles III, Elizabeth, Ellen. S.B., M.I.T., 1956, Ph.D., 1960; D.I.C., Imperial Coll., London, 1957. Asst. prof. MIT, Cambridge, 1960; research scientist Lockheed Research Labs., 1960-62; prof. mech. engring. Stanford (Calif.) U., 1962—, chmn. dept. mech. engring., 1982-88, sr. assoc. dean engring., 1988-93, vice provost, dean rsch. and grad. policy, 1993—; vis. prof. Harvard U., 1968-69, Princeton U., 1979-80; mem. Environ. Studies Bd. NAS, 1981-83; mem. hearing bd. Bay Area Air Quality Mgmt. Dist., 1969-83. Co-author: Physical Gas Dynamics, 1965, Partially Ionized Gases, 1973, On the Prevention of Significant Deteriorization of Air Quality, 1981; asso. editor: AIAA Jour, 1968-71; contbr. numerous articles to profl. jours. NSF sr. postdoctoral fellow, 1968-69. Mem. AIAA (medal, award 1979), Combustion Inst., ASME, Am. Phys. Soc., Materials Res. Soc. Office: Stanford U Bldg 10 Stanford CA 94305-2061

KRUGER, PAUL, nuclear civil engineering educator; b. Jersey City, June 7, 1925; s. Louis and Sarah (Jacobs) K.; m. Claudia Mathis, May 19, 1972; children: Sharon, Kenneth, Louis. BS, MIT, 1950; PhD, U. Chgo., 1954. Registered profl. engr., Pa. Rsch. physicist GM, Detroit, 1954-55; mgr. dept. chemistry Nuclear Sci. and Engring. Corp., Pitts., 1955-60; v.p. Hazleton Nuclear Sci. Corp., Palo Alto, Calif., 1960-62; prof. civil engring. Stanford (Calif.) U., 1962-87, prof. emeritus, 1987—; cons. Elec. Power Rsch. Inst., Palo Alto, 1975—, Los Alamos (N.Mex.) Nat. Lab., 1985—. Author: Principles of Activation Analysis, 1973, Geothermal Energy, 1972. 1st lt. USAF, 1943-46, PTO. Recipient achievement cert. U.S. Energy R & D Adminstrn., 1975. Fellow Am. Nuclear Soc.; mem. ASCE (divsn. chmn. 1978-79). Home: 819 Allardice Way Stanford CA 94305-1050 Office: Stanford U Civil Engring Dept Stanford CA 94305

KRUGER, PAUL ROBERT, insurance broker; b. Ft. Dodge, Iowa, Nov. 16, 1957; s. Robert Wayne and Corinne Maxine (Wierson) K.; m. Lisa Diane Rousselle, June 9, 1990; 1 child, Whitney Katherine. BSBA in Fin. and Mktg., Iowa State U., 1980. Claims rep. IMT Ins. Co., Des Moines, 1981-82; sales mgr. JCPenney Fin. Svcs., Plano, Tex., 1982-89, GranTree Furniture Rental, Aurora, Colo., 1989-90; sales rep. Sentry Ins., Denver, 1990—; with Preferred Risk Ins., Englewood, Colo., 1991—; ins. broker The Urman Co., Englewood, 1992—. Mem. Life Underwriting Tng. Coun., Boulder C. of C., Apt. Assn. Met. Denver (social com. 1989-90, amb. club 1989-90, trade show com. 1989-90), Boulder Jaycees (bd. dirs. 1983-84), Phi Kappa Tau (song leader 1979-80, pledge trainer 1977-78, asst. treas. 1978-79). Republican. Mem. Ch. of Nazarene. Home: 3350 Kassler Pl Westminster CO 80030-2747

KRUGMAN, STANLEY LEE, international management consultant; b. N.Y.C., Mar. 2, 1925; s. Harry and Leah (Greenberg) K.; m. Helen Schorr, June 14, 1947; children: Vicky Lee, Thomas Paul; m. Carolyn Schambra, Sept. 17, 1966; children: David Andrew, Wendy Carol; m. Gail Jennings, Mar. 17, 1974. B Chem. Engring., Rensselaer Poly. Inst., 1947; postgrad., Poly. Inst. Bklyn., 1947-51, Columbia U. Process devel. engr. Merck & Co., Rahway, N.J., 1947-51; sr. process and project engr. C.F. Braun & Co., Alhambra, Calif., 1951-55; with Jacobs Engring. Co., Pasadena, Calif., 1955-76; from chief engr. to v.p. engring. and constrn. to v.p. gen. mgr. to exec. v.p. to pres., also dir.; exec. v.p., dir. Jacobs Engring. Group Inc., Pasadena, Calif., 1974-82; pres., dir. Jacobs Constructors of P.R., San Juan, 1970-82; pres. Jacobs Internat. Inc., 1971-82, Jacobs Internat. Ltd., Inc., Dublin, Ireland, 1974-82; dep. chmn. Jacobs LTA Engring., Ltd., Johannesburg, South Africa, 1981-82; pres. Krugman Assocs., Inc., 1982—; internat. mgmt. cons.; dir. Mediscan Tech., Inc. Served to lt. (j.g.) USNR, 1944-46, PTO. Mem. Am. Inst. Chem. Engrs., Am. Chem. Soc., Ireland-U.S. Council of Industry. Presbyterian. Home and Office: 24452 Portola Rd Carmel CA 93923-9327

KRULAK, VICTOR HAROLD, newspaper executive; b. Denver, Jan. 7, 1913; s. Morris and Besse M. (Ball) K.; m. Amy Chandler, June 1, 1936; children—Victor Harold, William Morris, Charles Chandler. B.S., U.S. Naval Acad., 1934; LL.D., U. San Diego. Commd. 2d lt. USMC, 1934; advanced through grades to lt. gen.; service in China, at sea, with USMC (Fleet Marine Forces), 1935-39; staff officer, also bn. and regimental comdr., World War II; chief staff (1st Marine Div. Korea); formerly comdg. gen. (Marine Corps Recruit Depot), San Diego; formerly spl asst. to dir., joint staff counterinsurgency and spl. activities (Office Joint Chiefs Staff); comdg. gen. Fleet Marine Force Pacific, 1964-68; ret., 1968; v.p. Copley Newspaper Corp., 1968-79; pres. Words Ltd. Corp., San Diego. Decorated D.S.M., Navy Cross, Legion of Merit with 3 oak leaf clusters, Bronze Star, Air medal, Purple Heart (2) U.S.; Cross of Gallantry; Medal of Merit Vietnam; Distinguished Service medal (Korea), Order of Cloud and Banner, Republic of China. Mem. U.S. Naval Inst., U.S. Marine Corps Assn., Am. Soc. Newspaper Editors, InterAm. Press Assn., U.S. Strategic Inst. (vice chmn.). Home: 3665 Carleton St San Diego CA 92106-2163 Office: Words Ltd 3045 Rosecrans St San Diego CA 92110-4827

KRUMM, JOHN MCGILL, bishop; b. South Bend, Ind., Mar. 15, 1913; s. William F. and Harriett Vincent (McGill) K. A.A., Pasadena Jr. Coll.,

1933; A.B., U. Calif., 1935; B.D., Va. Theol. Sem., 1938, D.D. (hon.), 1974; Ph.D., Yale U., 1948; S.T.D. (hon.), Kenyon Coll., Gambier, Ohio, 1962; D.D. (hon.), Berkeley Div. Sch., Gen. Theol. Sem., 1975; L.H.D. (hon.), Hebrew Union Coll., Cin. Ordained to ministry Episcopal Ch., 1938; vicar Episc. chs., Compton, Lynwood and Hawthorne, Calif., 1938-41; asst. rector St. Paul's Ch., New Haven, 1941-43; rector Ch. of St. Matthew, San Mateo, Calif., 1943-48; dean St. Paul's Cathedral, Los Angeles, 1948-52; chaplain Columbia U., 1952-65; rector Ch. of Ascension, N.Y.C., 1965-71; bishop of So. Ohio, Episc. Ch., 1971-80; suffragan bishop in Europe Paris, 1980-83; assisting bishop Los Angeles, 1983—, St. Paul's Ch., Tustin, Calif., 1983—; vis. lectr. N.T., Berkeley Div. Sch., New Haven, 1942-53; vis. lectr. ch. history Va. Theol. Sem., Alexandria, 1942; instr. Prospect Hill Sch., New Haven, 1942-43; instr. religion U. So. Calif., 1950-52; chmn. clergy div. Univ. Religious Conf., L.A.; pres. San Mateo-Burlingame (Calif.) Coun. Chs., 1947-48, Ch. Fedn. L.A., 1951-52; chmn. nat. coun. Panel of Ams., 1952-61; interim pastor St. James' Ch., N.Y.C., 1990-91; interim bishop in Europe, Paris, 1992; interim rector Trinity Ch., Boston, 1992-93. Author: (with J.A. Pike) Roadblocks to Faith, 1953, Modern Heresies, 1961, The Art of Being a Sinner, 1967, Why Choose the Episcopal Church, 1974, (with others) Denver Crossroads, 1979, Letters from Lambeth, 1988, Flowing Like A River, 1989, The Offensive Cross, 1992. Trustee Mt. Holyoke Coll., 1962-72, Bexley Hall of Colgate-Rochester, Kenyon Coll., Children's Hosp., Cin., 1971-80; chmn. Canterbury Irvine Found., U. Calif., Irvine, 1984-92. Democrat. Clubs: Century Assn. (N.Y.C.); University (Cin.). Office: St Paul's Ch 1221 Wass St Tustin CA 92680-2897

KRUPINSKI, ELIZABETH ANNE, psychologist, educator; b. Rome, N.Y., Dec. 4, 1960; d. Joseph Alexander and Carole Anne (Pietrucha) K. BA, Cornell U., 1984; MA, Montclair State Coll., 1987; PhD, Temple U., 1992. Rsch. specialist U. Pa., Phila., 1987-92; instr. Temple U., Phila., 1988-92; asst. rsch. prof. U. Ariz., Tucson, 1992—; cons. U. Iowa, Iowa City, 1992—, UCLA, 1992—, Lawrence Livermore Labs., Calif., 1992—. Contbr. articles to profl. jours. Mem. Am. Psychol. Soc., Applied Vision Assn. Democrat. Roman Catholic. Home: 9225 E Tanque Verde Rd 1103 Tucson AZ 85749 Office: U Ariz Health Scis Ctr Dept Radiology Tucson AZ 85724

KRUPP, EDWIN CHARLES, astronomer; b. Chgo., Nov. 18, 1944; s. Edwin Frederick and Florence Ann (Olander) K.; m. Robin Suzanne Rector, Dec. 31, 1968; 1 son, Ethan Hembree. B.A., Pomona Coll., 1966; M.A., UCLA, 1968, Ph.D. (NDEA fellow, 1970-71), 1972. Astronomer Griffith Obs., Los Angeles Dept. Recreation and Parks, 1972—, dir., 1976—; mem. faculty El Camino Coll., U. So. Calif., extension divs. U. Calif.; cons. in ednl. TV Community Colls. Consortium; host teleseries Project: Universe. Author: Echoes of the Ancient Skies, 1983, The Comet and You, 1986 (Best Sci. Writing award Am. Inst. Physics 1986), The Big Dipper and You, 1989, Beyond the Blue Horizon, 1991, The Moon and You, 1993; editor, co-author: In Search of Ancient Astronomies, 1978 (Am. Inst. Physics-U.S. Steel Found. award for Best Sci. Writing 1978), Archaeoastronomy and the Roots of Science; editor-in-chief Griffith Obs., 1984—. Mem. Am. Astron. Soc. (past chmn. hist. astronomy div.), Astron. Soc. Pacific (past dir., recipient Klumpke-Roberts outstanding contbns. to the public understanding and appreciation of astronomy award 1989), Internat. Astron. Union, Explorers Club, Sigma Xi. Office: Griffith Observatory 2800 E Observatory Rd Los Angeles CA 90027-1299

KRUSE, F. MICHAEL, territory judge. Now chief justice High Ct. Am. Samoa, Pago Pago. Office: High Ct Am Samoa Pago Pago AS 96799

KRYNICKI, BETH ANN, stage manager; b. Seattle, Oct. 4, 1969; d. Paul Francis and Jean (Seinsheimer) K. BA, U. Mich., 1991. Prodn. intern Intiman Theatre, Seattle, 1988; stage mgr. U. Mich., Ann Arbor, 1988-91; asst. stage mgr. Spoleto Festival USA, Charleston, S.C., 1989, 91, 93, supertitle supr., 1992; asst. stage mgr. Seattle Opera, 1991-92, prodn. supr. edn. program, 1992; stage mgr. Chautauqua (N.Y.) Opera, 1992-93; asst. stage mgr. Va. Opera, 1992-93; lighting and set designer Basement Arts, Ann Arbor, 1990, 91; designer database formatting Seattle Opera Running Sheets, 1991-92. Vol. Seattle Opera, 1983-90; refugee tutor svc. credit program Lakeside Sch., Seattle, 1985. Mem. Golden Key. Home: 11215 NE 58th Pl Kirkland WA 98033

KUAN, PUI, nuclear engineering; b. Szechuan, People's Republic of China, Nov. 4, 1945; came to U.S., 1966; s. Chao-Hsiang and Ya-Chih (Wei) K.; m. Habibah Hassan, Apr. 17, 1986. BS in Astronomy, Calif. Inst. Tech., 1970; MA in Astronomy, U. Calif., Berkeley, 1972, PhD in Astronomy, 1973; MBA, Columbia U., 1991. Postdoctoral fellow Kitt Peak Nat. Obs., Tucson, 1974-76; scientist Energy Inc., Idaho Falls, Idaho, 1977-80; sr. engrng. specialist Idaho Nat. Engrng. Lab., Idaho Falls, 1980—. Mem. Am. Nuclear Soc., Am. Astron. Soc. Home: 1699 Laguna Dr Idaho Falls ID 83404-7416 Office: Idaho Nat Engrng Lab PO Box 1625 Idaho Falls ID 83415-3890

KUANG, YANG, mathematics educator; b. Gaoan, Jiangxi, People's Republic of China, Sept. 2, 1965; came to U.S., 1988; s. Shu Gao Kuang and Juan Aoyang; m. Al Jun Zhang, Nov. 17, 1988. BS, U. Sci. and Tech. of China, Hefei, Anhui, 1984; MS, U. Oxford, Eng., 1985; PhD, U. Alta., Edmonton, Can., 1988. ORS rsch. fellow U. Oxford, Eng., 1984-85; Killam fellow U. Alta., Edmonton, Can., 1985-88; asst. prof. Ariz. State U., Tempe, 1988-92, assoc. prof., 1992—. Author: Delay Differential Equations with Applications in Population Dynamics, 1992. Mem. affirmative action com. grad. and undergrad. coms. dept. math. Ariz. State U., Tempe, 1988-91. Recipient NSF travel award, 1990-93, NSF rsch. grant, 1991—. Mem. Soc. Indsl. and Applied Math. (symposium organizer 1990-91), Am. Math. Soc. Home: 1405 E El Parque Dr Tempe AZ 85282-2651 Office: Ariz State U Dept Math Tempe AZ 85287

KUBA, GALEN MASASHI, civil engineer; b. Hilo, Hawaii, Dec. 30, 1951; s. Riichi and Ellen Eiko (Nakao) K.; m. Carole Chieko Uemura, Nov. 26, 1977; children: Chelsi Lyn, Kevin Riichi. BSCE, U. Hawaii, 1973. Registered profl. engr., Hawaii. Civil engr. Inaba Engrng., Hilo, 1973-74; civil engr. County of Hawaii Dept. Pub. Works, Hilo, 1974-85, solid waste divsn. chief, 1985-93, acting engrng. divsn. chief, 1993—. Mem. Govtl. Refuse, Collecting and Disposal Assn., Hawaii Soc. Profl. Engrs. (bd. dirs. 1990-93), Lehua Jaycees (pres. 1983), U. Hawaii Alumni Assn. Office: County of Hawaii Dept Pub Works 25 Aupuni St Hilo HI 96720

KUBE, DANIEL CORNELIUS, airspace operations manager; b. Grangeville, Idaho, Apr. 7, 1934; s. Harry Ernest and Violet May (Dahl) K.; m. Sonja Estlund, May 29, 1955; children: Danna, Stephanie, Todd. Student, Wash. State U., 1952-57, U. No. Colo., 1972-76. Navigation specialist FAA, Drummond, Mont., 1961-62; radar specialist FAA, Grand Junction, Colo., 1962-71; automation specialist FAA, Longmont, Colo., 1971-83, asst. mgr. tng., 1983-85, telecomm. mgr., 1985-90, nat. airspace ops. mgr., 1990—; project mgr. FAA, Boston and Nashua, N.H., 1988-89; field support engr. FAA, Pomona, N.J., 1984. Officer Jaycees, Grand Junction, 1965-69, Am. Luth. Ch., Colo., 1977-81. Office: FAA 2211 17th Ave Longmont CO 80501

KUBIDA, WILLIAM JOSEPH, patent lawyer; b. Newark, Apr. 3, 1949; s. William and Catherine (Gilchrist) K.; m. Mary Jane Hamilton, Feb. 4, 1984; children: Sara Gilchrist, Kathleen Hamilton. B.S.E.E., U.S. Air Force Acad., 1971; JD, Wake Forest U., 1979. Bar: N.C. 1979, U.S. Patent Office 1979, Ind. 1980, U.S. Dist. Ct. (no. dist.) Ind. 1980, U.S. Dist. Ct. (so. dist.) Ind. 1980, U.S. Ct. Appeals (7th cir.) 1981, U.S. Dist. Ct. (Ariz.) 1982, U.S. Ct. Appeals (9th cirs. and fed.) 1982, Ariz. 1982, Colo. 1990, U.S. Dist. Ct. Co., 1990, U.S. Ct. Appeals (10th cir.) 1990. Patent and trademark lawyer Lundy and Assocs., Ft. Wayne, Ind., 1979-81; patent atty. Motorola, Inc., Phoenix, 1981-85; Intellectual Property Counsel Nippon Motorola, Ltd., Tokyo, 1985-87; ptnr. Lisa & Kubida, P.C., Phoenix, 1987-89; engring. law counsel Digital Equipment Corp., Colorado Springs, Colo., 1989-92; of counsel Holland & Hart, Denver and Colorado Springs, 1992—. 1st lt. USAF, 1971-76. Mem. Am. Intellectual Property Law Assn. (computer software sect.), Am. C. of C. (patents, trademarks and lic. sect., Japan), Licensing Exec. Soc. (Pacific Rim subcom.), Country Club Colo., Mensa, Phi Delta Phi. Republican. Presbyterian. Home: 4165 Regency Dr Colorado Springs CO 80906-4368

KUBIN, PATRICK LUDWIG, lawyer; b. Portland, Oreg., Oct. 16, 1959; s. Carl James and Lois Patricia (Graf) K.; m. Jill Marie Johanson, Oct. 10, 1987. BA, U. Portland, 1982; JD, Willamette U., 1986. Pvt. practice Milton-Freewater, Oreg., 1986-88; assoc. Walstead, Mertsching, Husemoen, Donaldson & Barlow, Longview, Wash., 1988—. Editor Willamette U. Law Sch. newspaper The Lawyer, 1984-85. Bd. dirs. Toutle River Boys Ranch, Silver Lake, Wash., 1991—. Mem. Rotary. Home: 2151 Maple St Longview WA 98632 Office: Walstead Mertsching et al 1000 12th Ave # 2 Longview WA 98632

KUBO, EDWARD HACHIRO, JR., lawyer; b. Honolulu, July 9, 1953; s. Edward H. and Rose M. (Coltes) K.; children: Diana K., Dawn M., Edward H. III. BA in Polit. Sci., U. Hawaii, 1976; JD, U. San Diego, 1979. Bar: Hawaii 1979. Dep. pros. atty. Honolulu City Prosecutor's Office, 1980-83, 85-90; assoc. Carlsmith & Dwyer, Honolulu, 1983-85; asst. U.S. atty. U.S. Atty.'s Office, Honolulu, 1990—; instr. Honolulu Police Dept. Acad., Waipahu, Hawaii, 1986-89. Mem. Hawaii Bar Assn., Order of Barristers. Home: 92-922 Welo St Apt 63 Ewa Beach HI 96707

KUBO, JACQUELINE LEA HANAKO, elementary education educator; b. Hilo, Hawaii, Aug. 31, 1966; d. Kiyoshi and Barbara Ann (Varize) K. BA in Speech/Comm., U. Hawaii, 1989, MEd, 1992—. Cert. in elem. edn., Hawaii. Elem. educator Mt. View (Hawaii) Elem. Sch., 1990, Pahoa (Hawaii) High and Elem. Sch., 1990-92, Waiakea Intermediate Sch., Hilo, Hawaii, 1992—; instr. after sch. instrnl. program Waiakea Intermediate Sch., Hilo, 1992—. V.p. precinct, Hilo, 1992; youth leader Dem. party, Hilo, 1992; U.S. rep. Festival Dela Cancion Infantil Iberio Americana, Madrid, 1978. Named Miss Hawaii Teenworld, 1981, Miss Master Dancer, Judi's Polynesian Studio, 1983. Mem. NEA, Hawaii State Tchr. Assn. Democrat. Roman Catholic.

KUBOTA, MITSURU, chemistry educator; b. Eleele, Hawaii, Sept. 25, 1932; s. Giichi and Kiyono (Naskashima) K.; m. Jane Kinue Taketa, June 30, 1956; children: Lynne K., Keith N. BA, U. Hawaii, 1954; MS, U. Ill., 1957, PhD, 1960. Prof. chemistry Harvey Mudd Coll., Claremont, Calif., 1959—; vis. prof. U. Venice, Italy, 1988, Cambridge (Eng.) U., 1989. 1st lt. U.S. Army, 1954-56. Faculty fellow NSF, 1966, career devel. award, 1981; Fulbright advanced rsch. fellow, Sussex, Eng., 1973, Spl. fellow NIH, 1974. Fellow Royal Soc. Chemistry, AAAS; mem. Am. Chem. Soc. (Rsch. award 1992), Sigma Xi. Office: Harvey Mudd Coll 301 East 12th St Claremont CA 91711

KUCHARSKI, DANIEL THOMAS, marketing professional; b. Pitts., Oct. 11, 1952; s. Walter Stanley and Marie Victoria (Gutowski) K.; m. Christina Sue Nagala, Aug. 12, 1978; 1 child, Matthew James. BA in Polit. Sci., Gannon U., 1974; MPA, W.Va. U., 1975. Town mgr. Town of Duncan, Ariz., 1977-78; regional planner Health Systems Agy. Southeast Ariz., Tucson, 1978-79; bus. mgr. Cochise Behavioral Health Svcs., Sierra Vista, Ariz., 1979-80; dir. Cochise County Assn. for Handicapped, Bisbee, Ariz., 1980-81; mktg. rep. Ariz. Lottery, Tucson, 1981—. Mem. Sabar Shrine Mounted Patrol (capt.).

KUCHEMAN, CLARK ARTHUR, religion educator; b. Akron, Ohio, Feb. 7, 1931; s. Merlin Carlyle and Lucile (Clark) K.; m. Melody Elaine Frazer, Nov. 15, 1986. BA, U. Akron, 1952; BD, Meadville Theol. Sch., 1955; MA in Econs., U. Chgo., 1959, PhD, 1965. Instr., then asst. prof. U. Chgo., 1961-67; prof. Claremont (Calif.) McKenna Coll., 1967—, Claremont Grad. Sch., 1967—. Co-author: Belief and Ethics, 1978, Creative Interchange, 1982, Economic Life, 1988; contbg. editor: The Life of Choice, 1978; contbr. articles to profl. jours. 1st lt. USAF, 1955-57. Mem. Am. Acad. Religion, Soc. Christian Ethics, Hegel Soc. Am., N.Am. Soc. for Social Philosophy. Democrat. Mem. United Ch. of Christ. Home: 10160 60th St Riverside CA 92509-4745 Office: Claremont McKenna Coll Dept Philosophy and Religion Pitzer Hall Claremont CA 91711

KUCHLER, SANDRA ROSE, dean; b. Madison, Wis., Oct. 30, 1948; d. William R. and Rose Suzanne (Stumpf) Gersbach; 1 child, Nicholas R. Naidl. AB, San Diego State U., 1979, MS in Counseling, 1981; ABD, Claremont Grad. Sch., 1990. Asst. dean San Diego State U., San Marcos, Calif., 1981-91; dir. devel. svcs. Calif. State U., San Marcos, 1991-92, assoc. dean students, 1993—. Mem. steering com. Women's Opportunity Week, San Diego, 1982-88; bd. dirs. Girl's Club of Vista, Calif., 1982-88, 1st v.p., 1986-88. Nat. Acad. Advising Assn. grantee, 1989. Mem. Women's Coun. of State, Nat. Assn. Women in Edn., Nat. Acad. Advising Assn., Nat. Assn. Student Personnel Adminstrs. Office: Calif State U San Marcos CA 92096-0001

KUCZUN, ANN-MARIE, fine artist, illustrator; b. Springfield, Mass., Sept. 25, 1935; d. Theodore B. and Mary Louise (Rzeszutek) Yamer; m. Sam Kuczun, June 21, 1959; children: Theodore S., Kyle S. BS, Bay Path Coll., Longmeadow, Mass., 1954; postgrad., U. Colo., 1980-82. Editor trade mag. John H. Breck, Inc., Springfield, Mass., 1954-56; copywriter, actor in commls. Sta. WWLP TV, Springfield, 1956-58; advt. asst. Gibney and Barrecca, Inc., Springfield, 1958-59; painter Mpls., 1963-66; illustrator U. Colo., Boulder, 1982—; mgr. Pearl Gray, Denver, 1984-85; painter, printmaker Boulder, 1966—. Mag. editor Buxton, Inc., West Springfield, 1958; painter illustrations in the Art of Collage, 1978, cover illustrations Instream Flow Protection in the West, 1989, Down the Colorado, 1989, Searching Out the Headwaters, 1993. Bd. dirs. Boulder Ctr. Visual Arts, 1973-75; mem. Boulder C. of C. Cultural Affairs Coun., 1978. Honored by Art-in-Embassies Program with painting on loan to U.S. Amb. residence in Nicosia, Cyprus, 1991-93. Orthodox Catholic. Home and Office: 930 Miami Way Boulder CO 80303-6405

KUDLA, JAMES MATTHEW, U.S. naval officer; b. Passaic, N.J., Aug. 2, 1950; s. Matthew and Sophie (Sobczyk) K.; m. Loretta Marie Gilbert, Apr. 7, 1979; children: Matthew, Rachel. BA, Rutgers U., 1972; MA, Am. U., 1988. Commd. ensign USN, 1972, advanced through grades to comdr., 1990; shipboard duty USS Leahy, USS Tarawa, 1974-79; pub. affairs officer Navy Info. Office, N.Y.C., 1979-82, Office of Info. Navy Dept., Washington, 1984-85; spokesman Comdr. Task Force Sixty, Naples, Italy, 1982-84; pub. affairs officer Dep. Chief Naval Oper. Submarines, Washington, 1985-87; spokesman-Pacific Rim issues Dept. Def., Washington, 1988-89; exec. asst. to asst. sec. def. pub. affairs The Pentagon, Washington, 1989-91; dep. spokesman U.S. Pacific Fleet, Honolulu, 1991—. Mem. Soc. Profl. Journalists, Nat. Eagle Scout Assn. Home: 1A Kamakani Pl Honolulu HI 96818 Office: Cmdr in Chief US Pacific Fleet Box 0130 Honolulu HI 96870

KUDO, EMIKO IWASHITA, former state official; b. Kona, Hawaii, June 5, 1923; s. Tetsuzo and Kuma (Koga) Iwashita; BS, U. Hawaii, 1944; MS in Vocational Edn., Pa. State U., 1950; postgrad. U. Hawaii, U. Ore., others; m. Thomas Mitsugi Kudo, Aug. 21, 1951; children: Guy J.T., Scott K., Candace F. Tchr. jr. and sr. high sch., Hawaii, 1945-51; instr. home econs. edn. U. Hawaii Tchrs. Coll., Honolulu, 1948-51, Pa. State U., State College, 1949-50; with Hawaii Dept. Edn., Honolulu, 1951-82, supr. sch. lunch svc., 1951-64, home econ. edn., 1951-64, dir. home econ. edn., 1964-68, adminstr. vocat.-tech. edn., 1968-76, asst. supt. instructional svcs., 1976-78, dep. supt. State Dept. Edn., 1978-82; cons. Am. Samoa vocat. edn. state plan devel., 1970-71, vocat. edn. U. Hawaii, 1986, internat. secondary program devel. Ashiya Ednl. System, Japan, 1986-91; state coord. industry-labor-edn., 1972-76; mem. nat. task force edn. and tng. for minority bus. enterprise, 1972-73; steering com. Career Info. Ctr. Project, 1973-78; co-dir. Hawaii Career Devel. Continuum project, 1971-74; mem. Nat Accreditation and Instl. Eligibility Adv. Council, 1974-77, cons., 1977-78; mem. panel Internat. Conf. Vocat. Guidance, 1978, 80, 82, 86, 88; state commr. edn. commn. of the states, 1982-90; mem. Hawaii edn. coun., 1982-90; dir. Dept. Parks and Recreation, City and County of Honolulu, 1982-84. Exec. bd. Aloha council Boy Scouts Am., 1978-88. Japan Found. Cultural grantee, 1977; Pa. State U. Alumni fellow, 1982; bd. trustees St. Louis High Sch., 1988—; mem. Gov.'s Commn. on Sesquicentennial Observance of Pub. Edn. In Hawaii, 1990-91; mem. commn. state rental housing trust fund 1992-93. Mem. Pa. State U. Disting. Alumni, Western Assn. Schs. and Colls. (accreditation team mem. Ch. Coll. of Hawaii 1972-73), Am. Vocat. Assn., Hawaii Practical Arts and Vocat. Assn., NEA, Hawaii Edn. Assn. (trustee 1992—), Hawaii State Ednl. Officers Assn., Am., Hawaii home econ. assn., Nat., Hawaii assns. for supervision and curriculum devel., Am. Tech. Edn. Assn., Hawaii Recreation and Park Assn., Omicron Nu, Pi Lambda Theta, Phi Delta Kappa, Delta Kappa Gamma. Author handbooks and pamphlets in field. Home and Office: 217 Nenue St Honolulu HI 96821-1811

KUDO, FRANKLIN TY, automotive retailing executive; b. Honolulu, Oct. 3, 1950; s. Charles Toshio and Fujie (Hayakawa) K.; m. Lei Yukie, Aug. 24, 1978 (div. Aug. 1984; 1 child, Lindsey A. BS in Acctg., U. Colo., 1972; MBA, U. Wash., 1974; cert. in systems analysis, Roosevelt U. Cert. advanced real estate agt. Sr. acct. KPMG, Peat, Marwick CPAs, Honolulu, 1974-78; sr. v.p., contr. Aloha Motors, Inc., Honolulu, 1978-83; pres. Virtual Mgmt. Svcs. Inc., Honolulu, 1983; v.p., gen. mgr. Mazda Hawaii Inc., Honolulu, 1983-87; pres., chief oper. officer Tony Mgmt. Group, Honolulu, 1987—; bd. dirs. Tony Honda Pearlridge, Honolulu, Pacific Oldsmobile GMCVW Inc., Pacific Nissan, Inc., Los Gatos (Calif.) Honda, Huntington Beach (Calif.) Acura, Pacific Mazda Subaru, Inc. Treas., bd. dirs. Hawaii Svcs. on Deafness, 1986-91; v.p., bd. dirs. Hawaii Children's Mus., 1989—; bd. dirs. Kuakini Med. Hosp., Better Bus. Bureau, 1992—, Manoa Valley Theatre, 1991—. Mem. AICPAs, Hawaii Soc. CPAs, Hawaii Auto Dealers Assn.(v.p., bd. dirs. 1992—), Hawaii Exec. Coun., Pacific Club, Young Pres.'s Orgn. Democrat. Home: 98-1910 N Kaahumanu St Pearl City HI 96782 Office: 719 Kamehamelia Hwy 3d Fl Pearl City HI 96782

KUEBLER, RICHARD ARTHUR, theatre educator, consultant; b. Lincoln, Nebr., July 31, 1947; s. Richard Arthur Sr. and Phyllis Darlene (Belka) K. BA, Wayne (Nebr.) State Coll., 1970; MFA, U. Nebr., 1980, postgrad., 1980-81. Dir., actor Nettlecreek Players, Inc., Hagerstown, Ind., summers 1975-76; dir. of theatre Kearney (Nebr.) Pub. Schs., 1971-78; dir., actor Kearney Pks. & Recreation, summers 1973-77; workshop and tour dir. U. Nebr., Lincoln, 1978-80, teaching asst., 1979-80; scenic supr. Doane Coll., Crete, Nebr., 1980-81; dir. theatre Northeastern Jr. Coll., Sterling, Colo., 1981—; state festival chmn., adjudicator Colo. Community Theatre Coalition, Sterling, 1989-90; regional adjudicator Am. Coll. Theatre Festival; state theatre chmn. Colo. Community Coll./Occupational Edn. System, Denver, 1988-89; drama chmn. Sterling Arts Coun., 1990—; mem. theatre grant rev. panel Colo. Coun. on the Arts and Humanities, 1990—, community theatre liaison to the organizational assistance program; U.S. rep. The Enniskillen (No. Ireland) Internat. Community Theatre Festival, 1990, The Dundalk (Republic Ireland) Internat. Amateur Theatre Festival, 1990; mem. community theatre liaison Alliance for Colo. Acts; mem. coll./univ. adv. panel to the Denver Ctr. Theatre Comp.; guest dir. U. Wyo., summer 1993. Dir. (play) Luann Hampton Laverty Oberlander, 1980 (Best Dir.), Vanities, 1989 (Best Dir. 1989), The Shadow Box, 1990 (Best Dir.). Pres. Prairie Players, Sterling, 1986-90; bd. dirs. Colo. Community Theatre Coalition, 1989-90, state ajudicator; bd. dirs. Sterling Arts Coun., 1988—; sponsor Northeastern Jr. Coll. Players, 1981-90. Formfit-Rogers scholar, 1965, Knights of Ak-Sar-Ben scholar, 1974, Alliance of Colo. Theatre award, 1992; named Bd. Mem. of Yr. Colo. Community Theatre Coalition, 1990, Highe Edn. Theatre Edn. of Yr. Mem. Am. Assn. Community Theatre (rep. region VII 1989-90). Home: 116 S 3D Ave # 7 Sterling CO 80751 Office: Northeastern Jr Coll ES French Hall Sterling CO 80751

KUEHN, GLENN DEAN, biochemistry educator, researcher; b. Terry, Mont., Apr. 13, 1942; s. Gust and Freida Georgia (Scheid) K.; m. Donna Faye Reuther, June 12, 1965; children: Tara Lynn. BA in Math. and Chemistry, Concordia Coll., 1964; PhD in Biochemistry, Wash. State U., 1968. Postdoctoral fellow NIH UCLA, 1968-70; asst. prof. biochemistry N.Mex. State U., Las Cruces, 1970-75, assoc. prof. biochemistry, 1975-80, MBRS program dir., 1976—, prof. chemistry, 1980—, staff mem. Plant Genetic Engrng. Lab., 1983—. Contbr. articles to profl. jours. Grantee NIH, 1970—, NSF, 1973-80, Am. Cancer Soc., 1970-76, 81-83, USDA, 1986—, U.S. Geol. Survey, 1987—; Roche Research Found. fellow, 1978. Mem. AAAS, NIH (mem. Study sect. 1988-92), Am. Soc. Biochemists and Molecular Biologists, Am. Chem. Soc., Sigma Xi, Alpha Xi Sigma. Lutheran. Home: 2032 Crescent Dr Las Cruces NM 88005-3321 Office: NMex State U Grad Program Molecular Biology Dept 3C PO Box 30001 Las Cruces NM 88003-8001

KUEHN, KLAUS KARL ALBERT, ophthalmologist; b. Breslau, Germany, Apr. 1, 1938; came to U.S., 1956, naturalized, 1971; s. Max and Anneliese (Hecht) K.; m. Eileen L. Nordgaard, June 22, 1961 (div. 1972); children—Stephan Eric, Kristina Annette; m. Lynda O. Hubbs, Oct. 2, 1974. Student, St. Olaf Coll., 1956-57; B.A., B.S., U. Minn., 1961; M.D., 1963. Diplomate Am. Bd. Ophthalmology. Resident in ophthalmology UCLA Affiliated Hosps., 1968-71; practice medicine specializing in ophthalmology, San Bernardino, Calif., 1971—; chief ophthalmology dept. San Bernardino County Med. Ctr., 1979-80; assoc. clin. prof. ophthalmology Jules Stein Eye Inst. and UCLA Med. Ctr., 1978-81. Served to capt. U.S. Army, 1963-64. Fellow Am. Acad. Ophthalmology; mem. AMA, Calif. Med. Assn., Calif. Assn. Ophthalmology (bd. dirs.). Office: 902 E Highland Ave San Bernardino CA 92404

KUEHNERT, ROBERT GERHARDT, retired psychiatrist; b. Crystal Lake, Ill., Dec. 6, 1916; s. Frederich Gerhardt and Clara (Erbe) K.; m. Nannette June Hodges Liefer; m. Dorothy Ruth Coyne, Aug. 11, 1965; children: Michael Lawrence Ford, John Webber Ford, William Joseph Ford, David Kevin Kuehnert, Marshall Andrew Kuehnert, Deborah Ruth Ford, Matthew Robert Kuehnert. BS, U. Ill., 1942, MD, 1942. Cert. Am. Bd. Psychiatry and Neurology, 1950. Psychiatrist State of Calif., L.A. and Vacaville, 1951-81. Comdr. USN, 1942-47, with USNR, 1947-76. Life fellow Am. Psychiat. Soc.

KUESTER, KRISTEN, rolfer, educator; b. Dearborn, Mich., Nov. 12, 1953; d. Kenneth James and Dorothy Louise (Graether) K.; m. Gene Youngblood. BFA, Mich. State U., 1975; MFA, Sch. of the Art Inst., Chgo., 1980; student, Rolf Inst., Boulder, Colo., 1987. Cert. rolfer. Arts educator various colls. and univs., Chgo., 1975-80, U. Mass., Amherst, 1981-82, Southwestern Coll., Santa Fe, 1990-91; movement re-educator Scherer's Acad., Santa Fe, 1989—; rolfer, movement re-educator in pvt. practice Santa Fe, 1987—; founder N.Mex. Women Movement Re-Educators, Santa Fe, 1990—. Sculptor.

KUH, ERNEST SHIU-JEN, electrical engineering educator; b. Peking, China, Oct. 2, 1928; came to U.S., 1948, naturalized, 1960; s. Zone Shung and Tsia (Chu) K.; m. Bettine Chow, Aug. 4, 1957; children: Anthony, Theodore. BS, U. Mich., 1949; MS, MIT, 1950; PhD, Stanford U., 1952. Mem. tech. staff Bell Tel. Labs., Murray Hill, N.J., 1952-56; assoc. prof. elec. engrng. U. Calif., Berkeley, 1956-62, prof., 1962—, Miller rsch. prof., 1965-66, William S. Floyd Jr. prof. engrng., 1990-92, William S. Floyd Jr. prof. engrng. emeritus, 1993—, chmn. dept. elec. engrng. and computer sci., 1968-72, dean Coll. Engrng., 1973-80; cons. IBM Research Lab., San Jose, Calif., 1957-62, NSF, 1975-84; mem. panel Nat. Bur. Standards, 1975-80; vis. com. Gen. Motors Inst., 1975-79, dept. elec. engrng. and computer sci. MIT, 1986-91; mem. adv. council elec. engrng. dept. Princeton (N.J.) U., 1986—; mem. bd. councilors sch. engrng. U. So. Calif., 1986-91; mem. sci. adv. bd. Mills Coll., 1976-80. Co-author: Principles of Circuit Synthesis, 1959, Basic Circuit Theory, 1967, Theory of Linear Active Network, 1967; Linear and Nonlinear Circuits, 1987. Recipient Alexander von Humboldt award, 1980, Lamme medal Am. Soc. Endrng. Edn., 1981, U. Mich. Disting. Alumnus award, 1970, Berkeley citation, 1993; Brit. Soc. Engring. and Rsch. fellow, 1982. Fellow IEEE (Edn. medal 1981, Centenial medal 1984, Circuits and Systems Soc. award. 1988), AAAS; mem. Nat. Acad. Engrng., Academia Sinica, Sigma Xi, Phi Kappa Phi. Office: U Calif Elec Engrng and Computer Sci Depts Berkeley CA 94720

KUHL, FREDERICK WILLIAM, English and journalism educator; b. Camrose, Alta., Can., Mar. 8, 1923; parents Am. citizens; s. Edward and Frances Leopoltine (Roth) K.; m. Beverly Jean Allen, May 5, 1950; children: Katherine A-F., William E., Suzanne J. BS, U. Oreg., 1947, MS, 1961; EdD, Nova U., 1981. Cert. jr. coll. tchr., community coll. supr.; cert. naval intelligence profl. Asst. dir. pub. info. Aluminum Co. Am., Vancouver, Wash., 1947-51; dir. pub. info. Housing Authority-Urban Redevel., Portland, Oreg., 1951-52; reporter, columnist, city editor Enterprise-Courier, Oregon City, Oreg., 1952-56; corr. The Portland Oregonian, Oregon City, 1953-56, 60-61; tchr. English and journalism Clackamas High Sch., Milwaukie, Oreg., 1957-59; pub. info. dir. English and journalism Willamette U., Salem, Oreg., 1960-61; tchr. English and journalism David Douglas High Sch., Portland,

1961-65; dir. pub. info., prof. English and journalism American River Coll., Sacramento, 1965—; editorial cons. Goodyear Pub. Co., L.A., 1975-76, Wadsworth Pub. Co., Belmont, Calif., 1976-77, Peek Pub. Co., Palo Alto, Calif., 1989-91; staff instr. Unit Pub. Affairs Sch., Calif. N.G., Sacramento, 1982-90. Contbr. chpts. to books. Chair bd. edn. Faith Luth. Ch. and Sch., Fair Oaks, Calif., 1972-74, 89-91; mem. adv. com. Martin Manor, Sacramento, 1985—; editorial advisor Calif. N.G. mag. Grizzly, 1982—. Lt. (j.g.) U.S. Navy, 1943-46, PTO, lt. comdr. USNR ret. Recipient Commendation medal, medal of Merit, Mil. Dept., State of Calif., 1992, Pres.'s award Vancouver Jaycees, 1950; named Man of Yr., Optimist Internat., 1955. Mem. Assn. for Edn. in Journalism and Mass Communication, Soc. Profl. Journalists, C.C. Journalism Assn., Naval Intelligence Profls., Naval Res. Assn. (life), The Res. Officers Assn. (life), Kappa Tau Alpha. Democrat. Lutheran. Home: 6701 Rappahannock Way Carmichael CA 95608 Office: Am River Coll 4700 College Oak Dr Sacramento CA 95841

KUHL, RONALD WEBSTER, marketing executive; b. Chgo., Dec. 12, 1938; s. Robert Emerson and Kathleen (Webster) K.; m. Mary Walls, Sept. 28, 1968; children: David Douglas, Kevin Lathrop. BS in Econs., U. Pa., 1960; MBA, Harvard U., 1964. Account exec. Young & Rubicam Advt., N.Y.C., 1964-71; v.p. mgmt. supr. Young & Rubicam Advt., San Francisco, 1988-90; mgr. promotion and design The First Ch. of Christ Scientist, Boston, 1971-75; account exec. BBDO Advt., San Francisco, 1975-77; acct. supr. Ketchum Communications, San Francisco, 1977-80; dir. mktg. ComputerLand Corp., Hayward, Calif., 1985-88; v.p. mktg. communications Ventura Software Inc., San Diego, 1990-92; v.p. mktg. Castelle, Santa Clara, Calif., 1992—. 1st lt. U.S. Army, 1960-62. Office: Castelle 3255-3 Scott Blvd Santa Clara CA 95054

KUHL, WAYNE ELLIOTT, physician; b. Des Moines, Mar. 8, 1947; s. Leonard Peter and Florence Agnes Kuhl; m. Judith A. Kuhl, Aug. 3, 1968; children; Jason, Aaron, Brian. BS, Loras Coll., 1969; MD, U. Iowa, 1972. Staff emergency physician St. Joseph Hosp. & Med. Ctr., Phoenix, 1972-73; fellow in internal medicine Mayo Clinic, Rochester, Minn., 1974-77; physician in internal medicine Phoenix Med. Assocs., Ltd., 1977—; pres. Mamakai Med. Asscs., Phoenix, 1989; team physician Phoenix Cardinal NFL Football Team, 1990—. Fellow ACP; mem. AMA, Am. Soc. Internal Medicine, Nat. Football League Physicians Soc., Paradise Valley C. of C. (bd. dirs. 1989—), Thunderbirds (bd. dirs. Phoenix chpt. 1982—). Fellow ACP; mem. AMA, Sm. Soc. Internal Medicine, Nat. Football League Physicians Soc., Paradise Valley C. of C. (bd. dirs. 1989—), Thunderbirds (bd. dirs. Phoenix chpt. 1982—). Republican. Roman Catholic. Office: Physicians Med Assocs Ltd 3600 N 3d Ave Phoenix AZ 85013 Home: 3501 E Rose Ln Paradise Vly AZ 85253-3735

KUHLMAN, WALTER EGEL, artist, educator; b. St. Paul, Nov. 16, 1918; s. Peter and Marie (Jensen) K.; m. Nora McCants; 1 son, Christopher; m. Tulip Chestman, April 9, 1979. Student, St. Paul Sch. Art, 1936-40; BS, U. Minn., 1941; postgrad., Tulane U., Academié de la Grand Chaumierè, Paris, Calif. Sch. Fine Arts. mem. faculty Calif. Sch. Fine Arts, Stanford (Calif.) U. Ariz., St. Paul Sch. Art, U. Mich., Ann Arbor, Santa Clara (Calif.) U., Sonoma State U., Rohnert Park, Calif., 1969-88. One-man shows include Calif. Palace of Legion of Honor, 1956, 64, Walker Art Ctr., Stanford U., 20-yr. Retrospective De Saisset Mus., 1969, The New Arts Gallery, Houston, Santa Barbara (Calif.) Mus. Art, La Jolla (Calif.) Mus. Contemporary Art, Jonson Gallery, Charles Campbell Gallery, San Francisco, 1981, 83, 85; 40-yr. Retrospective Univ. Gallery, Sonoma State U., 1988, The Carlson Gallery, 1989; group shows include Smithsonian Inst., Washington, San Francisco Mus. Modern Art, anns. 1948-56, Calif. Palace of Legion of Honor, Realities Novelles, Petit Palais, Paris, 1950, Sao Paulo (Brazil) Bienniale, N.Y. World's Fair, Bolles Gallery, Charles Campbell Gallery, Mus. Modern Art, Rio de Janeiro, Oakland Mus., 1973, U. Calif., Davis, Calif. Palace of Legion of Honor, Roswell Mus., N.Mex., Santa Fe Mus. Fine Arts, Bolles Gallery, San Franciso; represented in permanent collections N.Y. Met. Mus. Art, Phillips Meml. Gallery, Washington, Nat. Mus. Am. Art, Washington, San Francisco Mus. Modern Art, Oakland Mus., Rice U., Santa Fe Fine Arts, Mus. Modern Art, Sao Paulo, Roswell Mus., Johnson Gallery, Albuquerque, Minn. Mus. Art., Art Inst. Calif., Mus. Modern Art, Rio de Janeiro, Brit. Mus., London Permanent Coll. of Laguna (Calif.) Mus. Art. Recipient Maestro award Calif. Arts Coun., Outstanding Calif. Working Artist and Tchr. award; fellow Tiffany Found., Graham Found., Cummington Found. Studio: Industrial Center Bldg 480 Gates Rd Sausalito CA 94965

KUHN, CHARLES CLAYTON, human resources executive, technical management specialist; b. Pitts., Apr. 30, 1942; s. Howard Clayton and Lois (Fleming) K.; m. Andrea Thomas, June 15, 1963; children: Charles C. Jr., Elizabeth M.C. Kuhn Martinez. BS in Physics, Coll. Advance Sci., 1963. Engr. Sprague Elec. R&D, Concord, N.H., 1963-66, RCA Hybrid R&D, Indpls., 1966-69; product engr. Tex. Instruments, Dallas, 1969-70; mfg. mgr. TRW, Lawndale, Calif., 1971-81; dir. adminstrn. Elmo Semiconductor Corp., Burbank, Calif., 1981-89; pres. Microsemi Assembly and Test, Inc., Riverside, Calif., 1989—. Pres. Early Childhood Edn., Redondo Beach, Calif., 1973-74; cubmaster Boy Scouts of Am., Redondo Beach, 1972-75. Office: ATK Inc 6240 Sandoval Ave Riverside CA 92509

KUHN, CRAIG CAMERON, state official; b. Portland, Oreg., Apr. 2, 1962; s. John Marvin and Floris Adene (Watkins) Brown. BS, U. Oreg., 1984; MS, Portland State U., 1992. Mail clk., sec. Oreg. Dept. Commerce, Salem, 1985-86; copy writer Lee Graphics Design, Salem, 1986-87; com. asst. Oreg. Legislature, Senate, Labor, Salem, 1987; safety and wellness coord. Oreg. Dept. Ins. and Fin., Salem, 1987-90, staff devel. mgr., 1990-91, safety and health mgr., 1992—; econs. cons., safety cons. Oreg. Dept. Ins. and Fin., Salem, 1988—, tng. cons., 1991-92; intercultural facilitator Portland State U., 1991. Asst. dir. Salem Senate-Aires, 1984—, chief choreographer, 1987—; author newsletter About Baritones, 1988; author: (fiction) Aftermath, 1986. Active theater restorations Save the Elsimore and Grand Theater, Salem, 1991, 92. Mem. ASTD, Salem Senate-Aires (program v.p. 1988-89, asst. music v.p. 1990), Courthouse Athletic Club, Delta Tau Delta (social chmn. 1983-92). Mem. The Way. Home: 4911 Elkhorn Ct SE Salem OR 97301 Office: Oreg Dept Ins and Fin 100 L & I Bldg Salem OR 97310

KUHN, DONALD MARSHALL, marketing professional; b. Miami, Fla., Nov. 2, 1922; s. Paul Carlton Kuhn and Helen (Merrick) Bond; m. Jane Emma Williams, Dec. 24, 1948 (dec. 1988); children: Marshall Merrick, Richard Williams, Diane Joan, Paul Willard; m. Kay Bardsley, Feb. 25, 1990. BA in Journalism and Drama, U. Miami, 1949. Cert. fundraising executive. Advt. copywriter Sears Roebuck and Co., Chgo., 1949-50; dir. pub. relations Tb Inst. Chgo. and Cook County, 1950-54; dir. fundraising Dade County Tb Assn., Miami, 1955-59, Minn. Tb and Health Assn., St. Paul, 1959-60, Mich. Lung Assn., Lansing, 1960-68, Am. Lung Assn., N.Y.C., 1968-78; nat. founder, dir. regional fin. program Rep. Nat. Com., Washington, 1978-79; exec. v.p., dir. fundraising div. Walter Karl, Inc., Armonk, N.Y., 1979-90, cons., 1990-93; cons. May Devel. Svcs., Greenwich, Conn., 1993—; mem. direct mktg. task force Am. Red Cross, Washington, 1983-84; mem. direct mail task force Am. Heart Assn., Dallas, 1982. Editor: Non-profit Council Info. Exchange, 1987-90; contbr. articles to Fundraising Mgmt. Mag. Bd. dirs. Isadora Duncan Internat. Inst., N.Y.C., 1987—. Mem. Nat. Soc. Fundraising Execs. (bd. dirs. 1978-80), Direct Mktg. Assn. (mem. operating com., non-profit coun. 1987-90, recipient non-profit coun. fundraising achievement award 1991). Republican. Congregational. Home and Office: 6305 S Geneva Cir Englewood CO 80111-5437

KUHN, FRANK STUART, real estate executive; b. Dubuque, Iowa, July 31, 1928; s. Carl Henry and Winifred Grace (Krapfel) K.; m. Leone S. Holmes (div. 1976); m. Janet Clark (div. 1991); children: Jeffrey S., Lisa A., Kristina A., Katherine H., Stephen M. BA, Yale U., 1950; MBA, Stanford U., 1952. Cert. counselor of real estate. Analyst Matson Nav. Co., San Francisco, 1955-60; broker, salesman Harrigan-Weidenmuller Co., San Francisco, 1960-64; gen. mgr. Fritz Properties, San Francisco, 1964-69; regional mgr. Dillingham Devel. Co., San Francisco, 1969-70; v.p. BankAm. Realty Svcs., Inc., San Francisco, 1970-73, Urban Investment & Devel. Co., San Francisco, 1973-75; prin. FSK Realty Svcs., Inc., San Francisco, 1975—; pres. NBS Realty Advisors, Inc., San Francisco, 1987—. Participant in various civic activities. Capt. USN, 1952-55, USNR ret. Mem. Am. Soc. Real Estate Counselors, Pacific-Union Club, San Francisco Golf Club, Ross Valley Tennis Club. Republican. Home: 1215 Greenwich St 4-B San Francisco CA 94109

KUHN, MARY CROUGHAN, educator; b. Rinard, Ill., Nov. 1, 1914; d. Ulysses Samuel and Susan Winnifred Croughan; m. Wolfgang E. Kuhn, Aug. 22, 1938; children: Suanna Breed, Elizbeth Bacchetti, Virginia Day. BA, U. Colo., 1958; Cert. d'etudes francaise, U. Tours, France, 1964; MA, Stanford U., 1968. Elem. tchr. cert. lifetime. Reading specialist. Tchr. supr. Kindergarten Co-op, Urbana, Ill., 1945-55; tchr. Kindergarten Co-op., Boulder, Colo., 1955-57, Cupertino (Calif.) Sch. Dist., 1959-82; bd. dirs. Co-op Kindergarten, Urbana, Ill., 1949-55, Boulder, Colo., 1955-57; mem. Children's Theatre Group, Urbana, 1950-55; master tchr., supr. student tchrs. Cupertino, Calif., 1971-81. Author: Second Harvest, 1987. Girl scout leader, Urbana, Ill., 1949-55, Boulder, Colo., 1958. Named Tchr. of Year PTA and Calif. Tchrs. Assn., Cupertino, 1964. Mem. AAUW (bd. dirs. 1968-90), LWV, Writer's Club (Los Altos, Calif.), Stanford Faculty Women's Club. Home: 612 Alvarado Row Stanford CA 94305-8506

KUHNS, CRAIG SHAFFER, business educator; b. Spokane, Wash., Apr. 14, 1928; s. Theodore Lewis and Audrey Grace (Shaffer) K. BS, U. Calif., Berkeley, 1950, BA, 1954, MBA, 1955. Analyst Standard Oil Co. of Calif., San Francisco, 1955-57; bus. educator U. Calif./San Jose State U., 1958-63, City Coll. of San Francisco, 1963—; exec. mng. dir. Blumentec Corp., USA, San Francisco, 1989—; adj. faculty U. San Francisco, 1977-90; bd. dirs. Blumentec Corp. USA. 1st lt. U.S. Army, 1951-52, col. Mil. Intelligence USAR, 1953-80, col. AUS, ret. Mem. Calif. Alumni Assn., U.S. Army War Coll. Alumni Assn., Res. Officers Assn., Japan Soc. Republican. Home: 8 Locksley Ave # 8A San Francisco CA 94122-3850 Office: City Coll of San Francisco 50 Phelan Ave San Francisco CA 94112

KUHNS, DAVID GEORGE, writer, producer, editor, consultant; b. Milw., Oct. 22, 1956; s. Gene Lee and Marilyn Esther (Carlson) Hamblin K.; m. Ilene Fluckiger, Sept. 29, 1981; children: Kristian, Camilla, Sarah, Seth. BA in English with honors, Brigham Young Univ., 1980; degree in German, Goethe Inst., Munich, 1981. Area bureau chief Fond du Lac (Wis.) Reporter, 1981-84; editor Crittenden Newsletters, Novato, Calif., 1984-85; sen. editor Hall Fin. Group, Dallas, 1985-86; v.p. comms. The Myers Group, Dallas, 1986-87; sen. v.p. The Recorp Cos., Phoenix, 1987-88; sen. conf. producer Northwest Ctr. for Profl. Edn./ Inst. Internat. Rsch., 1988-90; writer, conference producer, real estate, health care & fin. cons. pvt. practice, Kirkland, Wash., 1990—. bishopric coun., elder's quorum pres., Ch. of Jesus Christ of Latter Day Saints, 1992—, missionary, 1976-78; coach Kirkland Nat. Little League, 1992—, Lake Wash. Youth Soccer Assn., 1990—. Mem. FIFA/ U.S. Soccer Assn. (referee 1990—). Office: 13815 123d Ave NE Kirkland WA 98034

KUHRAU, EDWARD W., lawyer; b. Caney, Kans., Apr. 19, 1935; s. Edward E. and Dolores (Hardman) K.; m. Janiece Christal, Dec. 8, 1959; children: Quentin, Clayton; m. Eileen Engeness, Oct. 30, 1983; 1 child, Edward. BA, U. Tex., 1960; JD, U. So. Calif., 1965. Bar: Calif. 1966, Wash. 1968, Alaska 1977, U.S. Dist. Ct. (so. dist.) Calif. 1966, U.S. Dist. Ct. (we. dist.) Wash., U.S. Dist. Ct. Alaska 1968, U.S. Ct. Appeals (9th cir.) 1966. Assoc. Adams, Duque & Hazeltine, Los Angeles, 1965-66, Louis Lee Abbot, Los Angeles, 1966-67, Perkins, Coie, Stone, Olsen & Williams, Seattle, 1968-72; ptnr. Perkins, Coie, Stone, Olsen & Williams, Seattle, 1973—, ptnr. in charge Anchorage office, 1977-78, partner in charge and chmn. real estate dept., Seattle, 1971-90. Editor-in-chief Wash. Real Property Deskbook, 1979, 81, 86; contbr. articles to profl. jours. Mem. Seattle Sch. Bd. Adv. Com., 1970-71. Served with USAF, 1955-58. Mem. ABA, Wash. Bar Assn. (chmn. real property, probate and trust sect.), Alaska Bar Assn., State Bar Calif., Seattle-King County Bar Assn., Am. Coll. Real Estate Lawyers, Pacific Real Estate Inst. (pres., founding trustee 1989—), Internat. Council Shopping Centers, Order of Coif. Clubs: Wash. Athletic, Seattle Yacht. Office: Perkins Coie 1201 3d Ave 40th Fl Seattle WA 98101

KUJAWA, WALTER ANDREW, II, architect; b. St. Paul, Mar. 11, 1955; s. Walter Andrew and Geraldine Vera (Baloga) K. BSAD, MIT, 1977. Registered architect, Nebr. Staff Leo A. Daly, Planning, Architecture, Engring., Omaha, 1978-83, assoc., asst. team mgr., 1983-86; assoc., project mgr. Leo A. Daly/Alfred A. Yee, Honolulu, 1986-90, sr. architect, 1987-90; mgr. planning and design Lanai Co./Castle & Cooke Properties, Inc., Honolulu, 1990—; grad. asst. Dale Carnegie Seminars, Omaha, 1985-86. Mem. Alpha Tau Omega (Beta Gamma chpt., v.p. 1975). Democrat. Roman Catholic. Home: 46-359 Haiku Rd # B-6 Kaneohe HI 96744 Office: Castle & Cooke Properties Inc 650 Iwilei Rd Honolulu HI 96817

KUKKONEN, CARL ALLAN, microelectronics and computer research director; b. Duluth, Minn., Jan. 25, 1945; s. Carl Allan and Shirley Minette (Miller) K.; m. Noreen Dorothy Cullen, June 22, 1968; children: Carl, Daniel. AA, Foothill Coll., 1966; BS in Physics, U. Calif., Davis, 1968; MS in Physics, Cornell U., 1970, PhD in Physics, 1975. Rsch. assoc. Purdue U., West Lafayette, Ind., 1975-77; sr. rsch. scientist Ford Motor Co., Dearborn, Mich., 1977-80, prin. rsch. engr., 1980-84; mgr. supercomputing project, dir. ctr. space microelectronics tech. Jet Propulsion Lab. Calif. Inst. Tech., Pasadena, Calif., 1984—; pres. Ultrabyte, Inc., La Canada, Calif., 1984-89. Contbr. articles to profl. jours. Mem. Am. Phys. Soc., Nat. Assn. of Watch and Clock Collectors. Office: Jet Propulsion Lab 4800 Oak Grove Dr Pasadena CA 91109-8099

KUKLIN, JEFFREY PETER, lawyer, talent agency executive; b. N.Y.C., Dec. 13, 1935; s. Norman Bennett and Deane (Cable) K.; m. Jensina Olson, Nov. 18, 1960; 1 son, Andrew Bennett; m. 2d, Ronia Levene, June 22, 1969; children—Adam Blake, Jensena Lynne, Jeremy Brett. A.B., Columbia U., 1957, J.D., 1960. Bar: N.Y. 1962, U.S. Supreme Ct. 1965, Calif. 1973. Atty., TV sales adminstrn. NBC-TV, N.Y.C., 1966-67; asst. to dir. bus. affairs CBS News, N.Y.C., 1967-69; atty., assoc. dir. contracts ABC-TV, N.Y.C. and Los Angeles, 1969-73; v.p. bus. affairs and law Tomorrow Entertainment, Inc., Los Angeles, 1973-75; v.p. legal and bus. affairs Billy Jack Enterprises, Inc., Los Angeles, 1975-76; atty., bus. affairs exec. William Morris Agy., Inc., Beverly Hills, Calif., 1976-79, head TV bus. affairs, 1979-81, v.p., head TV bus. affairs, 1981—. Mem. ABA, Acad. TV Arts and Scis., Los Angeles Copyright Soc. Office: 151 S El Camino Dr Beverly Hills CA 90212-2775

KULAKOWSKI, LOIS LINDER, environmental educator; b. Hartley, Iowa, Mar. 4, 1939; d. Arthur Joseph and Ina Pauline (Boles) Linder; m. John Edward Kulakowski, Sept. 21, 1963; children: Susan Lin, Lora Ann. BS, U. Colo., 1961. Tchr. Lincoln Unified Sch. Dist., Stockton, Calif., 1961-62, Arapahoe Sch. Dist. # 6, Littleton, Colo., 1963-68; environ. cons. Tucson, 1983—; asst. dir. So. Ariz. Water Resources Assoc., Tucson, 1992-93; environ. researcher S.W. Environ. Svc., Tucson, 1983-88; edn. cons. So. Ariz. Water Resources Assn., Tucson, 1984-92; edn./tech. liaison Spare the Air campaign, Tucson, 1989-90. author games: Conserve, 1980, Water Trivia, 1988. Vice chmn. EPAC/Pima Assn. Govts., Tucson, 1987—; environ. specialist LWV, Tucson, 1983-91; adv. coun. Commn. on Ariz. Environ., Phoenix, 1987—; mem. Met. Energy Commn., Tucson, 1989-91, Environ. Edn. Com., Ariz. Dept. Edn., 1991-92. Mem. Nature Conservancy, Wilderness Soc., Natural Resources Def. Coun., LWV, Negative Population Growth, Natural Parks and Conservation Assn.

KULHAVY, RAYMOND WILLIAM, psychology educator; b. San Diego, Dec. 20, 1940; s. Lumir Oldrich and Virginia Dawn (Walker) K.; m. Linda Claire Caterino, July 17, 1977; children: Nicole Dawn Marie, Kathryn Elisabeth Dawn. AB, Calif. State U., San Diego, 1967, MA, 1968; PhD, U. Ill., 1971. Lic. psychologist, Ariz. Rsch. scientist USN, San Diego, 1975; with Ariz. State U., Tempe, 1971-72, prof. psychology, 1979-88, regents prof., 1989—; vis. scholar U. Newcastle, N.S.W., Australia, 1986-87; sr. Fulbright fellow U. Rome, 1986. Editor: Contemporary Edn. Psychology Jour., 1989; contbr. numerous articles to profl. jours. Recipient Palmer O. Johnson award AERA, 1974. Fellow Am. Psychol. Soc., Nat. Consortium for Instruction and Cognition; mem. Psychonomic Soc., AAAS. Office: Ariz State U Psychology in Edn Dept Tempe AZ 85287-0611

KULKOSKY, PAUL JOSEPH, psychology educator; b. Newark, N.J., Mar. 3, 1949; s. Peter Francis and Rose Mary (Leonetti) K.; m. Tanya Marie Weightman, Sept. 16, 1978. BA, Columbia U., N.Y.C., 1971, MA, 1972; PhC, U. Wash., 1974, PhD, 1975. Research assoc. Cornell U., White Plains, N.Y., 1980-81, instr. psychiatry, 1981-82; asst. prof. psychology U. So. Colo., Pueblo, 1982-86, assoc. prof., 1986-89, chmn. dept. psychology, 1988-91, prof., 1989—; bd. advisors Pueblo Zool. Soc., 1984-85, 1988-91, bd. dirs., 1985-88; editorial cons. to pubs. Ad hoc reviewer NIMH, 1989, 91, Nat. Ins. House N.Z., 1991, New Zealand Lottery Health Rsch. Com., 1992; contbr. chpts. to books, articles to profl. jours.; referee psychol. jours. Liaison Rocky Mountain region Coun. Undergrad. Psychology Programs, 1990-91. Named Hon. Affiliate Prof. Am. U., Washington, 1977-80; research grantee NIH, 1984—; staff fellow Nat. Inst. Alcohol Abuse and Alcoholism, 1976-80. Mem. AAAS (vice chair psychol. scis. sect. Southwestern and Rocky Mountain div. 1990-91, chmn. 1991-92, exec. com., Colo. rep. 1991—), Am. Psychol. Soc., Consortium of Aquariums, Univs. and Zoos, N.Y. Acad. Scis., Internat. Brain Rsch. Orgn., Soc. Neurosci., Internat. Soc. Biomed. Rsch. on Alcoholism (charter), Psychonomic Soc., Soc. Study Ingestive Behavior (charter), U. So. Colo. Club, Sigma Xi (treas. 1986—, Outstanding Faculty Rsch. award 1985-91), Colo.-Wyo. Acad. Sci., others. Home: 417 Tyler St Pueblo CO 81004-1405 Office: U So Colo 2200 Bonforte Blvd Pueblo CO 81001-4901

KULL, WILLIAM FRANKLIN, civil engineer, land surveyor; b. Houston, Nov. 21, 1956; s. William Fredrick and Rita Francis (Natiello) K. BS in Civil Engring., U. Santa Clara, 1979. Registered civil engr., land surveyor, Calif. Jr. engr. Nowack & Assocs., San Jose, Calif., 1978-82; sr. engr. Sandis & Assocs., Mountain View, Calif., 1982-87; prin. engr. Civil Cons. Group, Cupertino, Calif., 1987-88; founder, prin. Giuliani & Kull Inc., Cupertino, 1988—. Mem. ASCE. (assoc. 1978—). Republican. Episcopalian. Home: 8406 Oak Crest Ct Oakdale CA 95361 Office: Giuliani & Kull Inc 20431 Stevens Creek Blvd Cupertino CA 95014-2254

KULONGOSKI, THEODORE R., state attorney general, lawyer; b. St. Francois County, Mo., Nov. 5, 1940; married; 3 children. Grad., U. Mo., law degree, 1970. Ptnr. Kulongoski, Durham, Drummonds, and Colombo, Portland, Oreg., 1974-87; dir., Oreg. ins. commr., Oreg. corp. commr., dir. Oreg. fin. institutions, dir. Oreg. workers' compensation program Oreg. Dept. Ins. and Fin., 1987-91; exec. dir. Met. Family Svcs., 1991-93; atty. gen. Oreg., 1993—; gen. counsel Oreg. AFL-CIO; mem. Oreg. legis., 1975-83; chair Ho., Senate labor coms., senate banking and ins. com., mem. Ho. and Senate jud. coms., environ. and energy coms., agriculture and forestry coms. Dem. Party nominee Gov. Oreg., 1982. With USMC. Office: 100 Justice Bldg Salem OR 97310

KULURIS, BRADLEY EUGENE, food service professional; b. Orange, Calif., June 17, 1957; s. Bill and Joan (Moberg) K.; m. Patricia Dee, Apr. 1, 1978; children: Courtney, Nicole, Dustin, Taryn, Stephen. Student, U. Calif., Irvine, 1975-78, Calif. State U., Bakersfield, 1979-80, Bakersfield (Calif.) C.C., 1980. Gen. mgr. McDonalds, L.A., 1973-81, Chuck E. Cheese, Costa Mesa, Calif., 1981-83; v.p. ops. Ben Copy, Long Beach, Calif., 1983-85, Pro AM/CBA Devel., Santa Ana, Calif., 1985-87, El Pollo Loco, Lakewood, Calif., 1987-89; market mgr. Taco Bell Corp., Phoenix, 1989—. Recipient Eagle Scout, Boy Scouts Am., Orange County, 1970; named Employer of Yr., Kern County, 1980. Mem. Am. Mgmt. Assn., Nat. Restaurant Assn., Ariz. Restaurant Assn. Republican. Roman Catholic. Office: Taco Bell Corp 17901 Von Karman Irvine CA 92714

KUMAGAI, LYNN YASUKO, software design engineer; b. L.A., Oct. 14, 1964; d. Fred A. and Sachiko (Imamura) K. BS in Computer Sci. and Math. magna cum laude, Calif. State U., Fullerton, 1985, MS, 1988; postgrad., UCLA, 1991—. Software engr. Software Engring. divsn. Hughes Aircraft Co., Fullerton, Calif., 1984-90; software design engr. Command and Control Systems div. Hughes Aircraft Co., Fullerton, 1990—. Fellowship Hughes Aircraft Co., 1986-88, 91—. Mem. IEEE, Assn. of Computing Machinery, Internat. Neural Network Soc., Calif. Scholarship Fedn., Calif. State U. Fullerton Alumni Assn., Phi Kappa Phi. Office: Hughes Aircraft Co 618/Q315 1901 W Malvern Ave Fullerton CA 92634

KUMAR, ANIL, nuclear engineer; b. Agra, India, Aug. 3, 1952; came to U.S., 1988; s. Vedprakash and Satyawati (Sudhir) Parashar; m. Geeta Sharma, Nov. 29, 1979; 1 child, Amitabh. MSc in Physics, Agra U., 1973; PhD in Nuclear Engring., U. Bombay, India, 1981. Sci. officer Bhabha Atomic Rsch. Ctr., Bombay, 1974-81; sr. researcher Ecole Poly. Fed. Lausanne, Switzerland, 1982-88; devel. engr. UCLA, 1988-90, sr. devel. engr., 1990—. Contbr. articles to Jour. Fusion Energy, Nuclear Sci. and Engring., Fusion Tech., Fusion Engring. and Design, Atom Kern Energie, proc. internat. confs. and symposia. Mem. Am. Nuclear Soc., Am. Phys. Soc., Soc. Indsl. and Applied Math. Office: UCLA 43-133 Eng IV 405 Hilgard Ave Los Angeles CA 90024

KUMAR, RAJENDRA, electrical engineering educator; b. Amroha, India, Aug. 22, 1948; came to U.S., 1980; s. Satya Pal Agarwal and Kailash Vati Agarwal; m. Pushpa Agarwal, Feb. 16, 1971; children: Anshu, Shipra. BS in Math. and Sci., Meerut Coll., 1964; BEE, Indian Inst. Tech., Kanpur, 1969, MEE, 1977; PhD in Electrical Engring., U. New Castle, NSW, Australia, 1981. Mem. tech. staff Electronis and Radar Devel., Bangalore, India, 1969-72; rsch. engr. Indian Inst. Tech., Kanpur, 1972-77; asst. prof. Calif. State U., Fullerton, 1981-83, Brown U., Providence, 1980-81; prof. Calif. State U., Long Beach, 1983—; cons. Jet Propulsion Lab., Pasadena, Calif., 1984-91. Contbr. numerous articles to profl. jours.; patentee; efficient detection and signal parameter estimation with applications to high dynamic GPS receivers; multistage estimation of received carrier signal parameters under very high dynamic conditions of the receiver; fast frequency acquisition via adaptive least squares algorithms. Recipient Best Paper award Internat. Telemetering Conf., Las Vegas, 1986, 10 New Technology awards NASA, Washington, 1987-91. Mem. IEEE (sr.), NEA, AAUP, Calif. Faculty Assn., Auto Club So. Calif. (Cerritos), Sigma Xi, Eta Kappa Nu, Tau Beta Pi (eminent mem.). Home: 13910 Rose St Cerritos CA 90701-5044 Office: Calif State U 1250 N Bellflower Blvd Long Beach CA 90840-0001

KUMLER, ROSE MARIE, career counselor, educator; b. Detroit, Dec. 22, 1935; d. Charles and Aida (Oliveri) Fiorini; m. Frank Wozniak, May 17, 1958 (div. 1975); children: Corrine, Paul. BBA, Western Internat. U., 1982; MA, U. Phoenix, 1985. Lic. career counselor, Ariz. Sales rep. Vestal Labs., Phoenix, 1978-79; personnel cons. Ford Personnel Cons. Inc., Phoenix, 1979-81; owner, career counselor Specialized Employment Evaluation Devel., Phoenix, 1980—; dist. supr. Grand Canyon Color Lab., Phoenix, 1981-83; acad. dean Lamson Colls., Glendale, Ariz., 1983-86, instr. Phoenix Coll., Ottawa U., Phoenix, 1986—; speaker in field, 1987—. Chair subcom. of task force Ariz. Gov.'s Offices Women's Svcs.; active Ariz. Affirmative Action Assn., 1990—. Mem. Fellow Impact (mem. strategic planning com. 1988, edn. com. 1988), The Network, Ariz. Career Devel. Assn., Am. Bus. Women's Assn. (sec. 1975), Soroptimist (judge 1988). Roman Catholic. Home and Office: 13630 N 34th Pl Phoenix AZ 85032-6108

KUMMER, GLENN F., mobile home company executive; b. Park City, Utah, 1933. B.S., U. Utah, 1961. Sr. acct. Ernst & Ernst, 1961-65; trainee Fleetwood Enterprises Inc., Riverside, Calif., 1965-67, purchasing mgr., 1967-68, plant mgr., 1968-70, gen. mgr. recreational vehicle div., 1970-71, asst. v.p. ops. to v.p. ops., 1971-72, sr. v.p. ops., 1972-77, exec. v.p. ops., 1977-82, pres., 1982—, dir. Office: Fleetwood Enterprises Inc 3125 Myers St PO Box 7638 Riverside CA 92513*

KUMP, MICHAEL ROY, engineering executive; b. San Angelo, Tex., Feb. 7, 1953; s. Jessie LeRoy and Maurine Mae (Speer) K. BSEE, Rice U., 1975; MSEE, Stanford U., 1977, PhD, 1988. Device test engr. Am. MicroSystems, Inc., Santa Clara, Calif., 1977-79; process simulation mgr. Tech. Modeling Assocs., Palo Alto, Calif., 1980-88, v.p. engring., 1988—, bd. dirs., bd. sec. Baptist.

KUMPE, DAVID ALLEN, radiologist; b. Covington, Ky., Nov. 30, 1941; s. Carl William and Ruth Rose (Lang) K.; m. Rosemarie Wipfelder, May 9, 1971; children: Carl Christian, David Christoph. AB in Chemistry and Zoology, Oberlin Coll., 1963; MD, Harvard U., 1967. Diplomate Am. Bd. Radiology. Intern Columbia Presbyn. Med. Ctr., N.Y.C., 1967-68; resident Mass. Gen. Hosp., Boston, 1968-71; asst. prof. U. Md. Hosp., Balt., 1973-74, assoc. prof. radiology, 1976-77; fellow in neuroradiology and angiography

Rontgendiagnostiches Zentralinstitut Kantonsspital, Zurich, Switzerland, 1975-76; cons. in radiology Fitzsimons Army Med. Ctr., Denver, 1978—; dir. interventional radiology U. Colo. Health Sci. Ctr., Denver, 1979—, prof. radiology and surgery, 1988—; mem. evaluation com. sci. exhibits on cardiovascular radiology RSNA, 1988-92, chmn. program subcom., 1993—; lectr. in field. Co-editor jours.: Vascular Surgery, 1984, 89, 93, Vascular Diseases: Surgical and Interventional Therapy, 1992; appeared on various TV programs, Denver. Lt. comdr. USPHS, 1971-73. Recipient 1st place award Rocky Mountain Radiol. Soc., 1988; prin. investigator Upjohn Co., 1986-88, Abbott Labs., 1987-88. Fellow Soc. Cardiovascular and Interventional Radiology; sr. mem. Am. Soc. Neuroradiology; mem. Radiol. Soc. N.Am., Am. Coll. Radiology, Western Angiographic Soc., Colo. Radiol. Soc. (sec. 1986-87), N.Y. Acad. Scis. Lutheran. Office: U Colo Health Scis Ctr Dept Radiology A030 4200 E 9th Ave Denver CO 80262

KUNG, LILA MARIE, product development and marketing consultant; b. Highland Park, Mich., Dec. 17, 1954; d. Mieczyslaw and Lidia (Bednarska) Kobylak; divorced; children: Yung-Shin, Yung-Ting. SB in Math., MIT, 1975; postgrad., U. Calif., Berkeley, 1977-78. Engr. Lockheed Co., Sunnyvale, Calif., 1981-83; high tech. product devel. and mktg. cons., Santa Clara, Calif., 1983—. Author: U.S. Markets for Process Control Instrumentation, 1991, World Markets for Analytical Instrumentation in Process Control, 1991, World Process Flow Control Markets, 1992, World Transducer/Sensor Technology Assessment, 1992, World Proximity and Displacement Sensor Markets, 1992. Bd. dirs. Sunnyvale Christian Women's Club, Westwood Open Classroom, Santa Clara. Mem. Math. Assn. Am. (lectr. 1983—), MIT Alumni Assn., MIT Club No. Calif. Home and Office: 2321 Glendenning Ave Santa Clara CA 95050

KUNG, PANG-JEN, materials scientist, electrical engineer; b. I-Lan, Taiwan, May 13, 1959; s. Ching-Yu and A-Se (Yu) K.; m. Tzyy-Yun Tzeng, May 18, 1986. MS in Chem. Engring., Nat. Tsing Hua U., 1983; MS in Elec. Engring., Auburn U., 1988; ME in Metall. Engring., Carnegie Mellon U., 1991, PhD in Materials Sci, 1993. Jr. engr. Tatung Co., Taipei, Taiwan, 1979-80; teaching asst. Nat. Tsing Hua U., Hsin-Chu, Taiwan, 1981-82, rsch. asst., 1982-83; assoc. scientist Indsl. Tech. Res. Inst., Hsin-Chu, 1985-86; teaching and rsch. asst. Auburn (Ala.) U., 1986-89; rsch. asst. Carnegie Mellon U., Pitts., 1989-91; staff rsch. asst. Los Alamos (N.Mex.) Nat. Lab., 1991-92, postdoctoral rsch. fellow, 1993—; chmn. acad. affairs Tatung Inst. Tech., Taipei, 1979-80; tech. info. editor Indsl. Tech. Rsch. Inst., Hsin-Chu, 1985-86; translator tech. articles Super Tech. Books Co., Taipei, 1986. Author, editor: Unit Operation in Chemical Engineering, 1986; contbr. articles to Jour. Applied Physics, Applied Physics Letter, Physical Review B, Jour. Materials Rsch., Jour. Vacuum Sci. & Tech. 2d lt. Chinese Air Force, 1983-85. Recipient Editor's Choice award Nat. Poetry Assn., 1989, 90; Am.-Chinese Engr. scholar Am.-Chinese Assn. Engrs., 1980; Liang Ji-Duan fellow Carnegie Mellon U., 1991. Mem. AAAS, IEEE, SPIE, ASM, Materials Rsch. Soc., Am. Vacuum Soc., Am. Ceramic Soc., Soc. for Applied Spectroscopy,. Internat. Soc. for Hybrid Microelectronics, N.Y. Acad. Scis. Home: 3974B Alabama Ave Los Alamos NM 87544-1639 Office: Los Alamos Nat Lab PO Box 1663 Los Alamos NM 87545-0001

KUNKEE, RALPH EDWARD, viticulture and enology educator; b. San Fernando, Calif., July 30, 1927; s. Azor Frederick and Edith Electa (Engle) K. AB, U. Calif., Berkeley, 1950, PhD, 1955. Research biochemist E.I. Du Pont De Nemours, Wilmington, Del., 1955-60; prof. enology U. Calif., Davis, 1963-92, prof. emeritus, 1992; cons. UNFAO, Bangalore, India, 1986. Co-author: Technology of Winemaking, 1971. Fulbright fellow, Mainz, Fed. Republic Germany, 1970-71, France fellow, Montpellier, France, 1977-78. Mem. Am. Chem. Soc., Am. Soc. Microbiology, Am. Soc. Enology and Viticulture (sec./treas. 1983-85). Home: 820 Radcliffe Dr Davis CA 95616-0941 Office: U Calif Dept Viticulture and Enology Davis CA 95616

KUNKEL, RICHARD LESTER, public radio executive; b. Syracuse, N.Y., Nov. 12, 1944; s. Lester DeLong Kunkel and Margaret Fanny Ralph; m. Mary Joan Goldsworthy, Aug. 10, 1968; children: Richard J., Charles J., Joseph B. BS, Syracuse U., 1967, MS, 1969. Lic. real estate broker, N.C. Program dir. Sta. WNBI, Northland Broadcasting, Park Falls, Wis., 1969-72; instr., prodn. dir. Sta. WMKY, Morehead (Ky.) State U., 1972-77; radio mgr. Maine Pub. Broadcasting Network, Orono, 1977-78; instr., sta. mgr. Sta. KNTU, U. North Tex., Denton, 1978-84; v.p., dean Southeastern Ctr. for Arts, Atlanta, 1985-88; gen. mgr. Sta. KPBX-FM, Spokane, Wash., 1988—; cons., 1978—. With Army N.g., 1968-74. Recipient Addy award 1975. Home: 18212 N Atlantic Rd Colbert WA 99005 Office: Sta KPBX-Spokane Pub Radio 2319 N Monroe St Spokane WA 99205

KUNKEL, SCOTT WILLIAM, strategic management, entrepreneurship educator; b. St. Louis, May 26, 1945; s. Robert Scott and Mary (Muldowney) K.; m. Charlotte Elizabeth Bruce, May 21, 1966; children: Mary Charlotte, Deborah Ann. BBA in Accountancy, Memphis State U., 1974, MS in Finance, 1979; PhD in Bus. Adminstrn., U. Ga., 1991. Asst. v.p., controller First Fed. Savs. & Loan, Memphis, 1976-79; v.p. Maury County Fed. Savs. & Loan, Columbia, Tenn., 1979-81, Great Southern Fed. Savs. & Loan, Gainesville, Ga., 1981-82; assoc. prof. Brenau Coll., Gainesville, 1982-88; asst. prof. U. Nev., Reno, 1988-92, U. San Diego, 1992—. Mem. U.S. Assn. Small Bus. and Entrepreneurship, The Inst. Mgmt. Sci., Acad. Mgmt., Western Acad. Mgmt. Republican. Roman Catholic. Office: U San Diego Sch Bus San Diego CA 92110-2492

KUNST, JENNIFER LYNNE, psychological assistant; b. Cranford, N.J., Dec. 28, 1966; d. J. Bernhard and Linda (Wittich) K. BA in Psychology and Music, Wheaton Coll., 1988; MDiv, Fuller Theol. Sem., 1993. Registered psychol. asst., Calif. Dir. music 1st United Meth. Ch., Temple City, Calif., 1988-90; clin. trainee Sycamores, Altadena, Calif., 1989-90, Rodiger Ctr., Pasadena, Calif., 1990-91; residence dir. Southwestern Acad., San Marino, Calif., 1988—; staff intern Pasadena Presbyn. Ch., 1990—; psychiat. assoc. Kaiser Permanente, L.A., 1991—; guest lectr. Huntington Meml. Hosp., Pasadena, 1990-92; student rep. Fuller Sem., Pasadena, 1988—. Contbr. articles to profl. publs. Mem. APA, Religious Assn., Christian Assn. for Psychol. Studies, Soc. Personality Assessment, Psi Chi. Home: 104 D N Atlantic Blvd Alhambra CA 91801 Office: Fuller Grad Sch Psychology Box 1207 Pasadena CA 91132

KUNZ, PHILLIP RAY, sociologist, educator; b. Bern, Idaho, July 19, 1936; s. Parley P. and Hilda Irene (Stoor) K.; m. Joyce Sheffield, Mar. 18, 1960; children: Jay, Jenifer, Jody, Johnathan, Jana. B.S., Brigham Young U., 1961, M.S. cum laude, 1962; Ph.D. (fellow), U. Mich., 1967. Instr. Eastern Mich. U., Ypsilanti, 1964, U. Mich., Ann Arbor, 1965-67; asst. prof. sociology U. Wyo., Laramie, 1967-68; prof. sociology Brigham Young U., Provo, Utah, 1968—; acting dept. chmn. Brigham Young U., 1973; dir. Inst. Geneal. Studies, 1972-74; cons. various ednl. and research instns., 1968—; missionary Ch. Jesus Christ LDS, Ga. and S.C., 1956-58, mem. high coun., 1969-70, bishop; mission pres. La. Baton Rouge Mission, 1990-93. Author 6 books; contbr. articles on social orgn., family relations and deviant behavior to profl. jours.; contbr. book revs. to profl. jours. Housing commr. City of Provo, 1984—. Served with AUS, 1954-56. Recipient Karl G. Maeser research award, 1977. Mem. Am. Sociol. Assn., Rocky Mountain Social Sci. Assn., Am. Council Family Relations, Rural Sociol. Soc., Am. Soc. Criminology, Soc. Sci. Study of Religion, Religious Research Assn., Sigma Xi, Phi Kappa Phi, Alpha Kappa Delta. Democrat. Home: 3040 Navajo Ln Provo UT 84604-4820 Office: Brigham Young Univ Dept Sociology Provo UT 84602

KUO, PING-CHIA, historian, educator; b. Yangshe, Kiangsu, China, Nov. 27, 1908; s. Chu-sen and Hsiao-kuan (Hsu) K.; m. Anita H. Bradley, Aug. 8, 1946. A.M., Harvard U., 1930, Ph.D., 1933. Prof. modern history and Far Eastern internat. relations Nat. Wuhan U., Wuchang, China, 1933-38; editor China Forum, Hankow and Chungking, 1938-40; counsellor Nat. Mil. Council, Chungking, China, 1940-46, Ministry Fgn. Affairs, 1943-46; participated in Cairo Conf. as spl. polit. asst. to Generalissimo Chiang Kai-shek, 1943; during war yrs. in Chungking, also served Chinese Govt. concurrently in following capacities: mem. fgn. affairs com. Nat. Supreme Def. Council, 1939-46; chief, editorial and pubs. dept. Ministry Information, 1940-42, mem. central planning bd., 1941-45; tech. expert to Chinese delegation San Francisco Conf., 1945; chief trusteeship sect. secretariat UN, London; (exec. com. prep. commn. and gen. assembly), 1945-46; top-ranking dir. Dept. Security Council Affairs, UN, 1946-48; vis. prof. Chinese history San Francisco State Coll., summers 1954, 58; assoc. prof. history So. Ill. U., 1959-63, prof. history, 1963-72, chmn. dept. history, 1967-71, prof. emeritus, 1972—; sr. fellow Nat. Endowment for Humanities, 1973-74; Pres. Midwest Conf. Asian Studies, 1964. Author: A Critical Study of the First Anglo-Chinese War, with Documents, 1935, Modern Far Eastern Diplomatic History (in Chinese), 1937, China: New Age and New Outlook, 1960, China, in the Modern World Series, 1970; Contbr. to Am. hist. pubs. and various mags. in China and Ency. Brit. Decorated Kwang Hua medal A-1 grade Nat. Mil. Council, Chungking, 1941; Auspicious Star medal Nat. Govt., Chungking, 1944; Victory medal, 1945. Mem. Am. Hist. Assn., Assn. Asian Studies. Club: Commonwealth (San Francisco). Home: 8661 Don Carol Dr El Cerrito CA 94530-2752

KUPCHAK, KENNETH ROY, lawyer; b. Forrest Hills, Pa., May 15, 1942; s. Frank V. and Anne B. (Ruzanic) K.; m. Patricia K. Geer, Jan. 27, 1967; children: Lincoln K., Robinson K. AB, Cornell U., 1964; BS, Pa. State U., 1965; JD in Internat. Affairs, Cornell U., 1971. Bar: Hawaii 1971, U.S. Dist. Ct. Hawaii 1971, U.S. Supreme Ct. 1988. Meteorology staff U. Hawaii, Honolulu, 1968; ptnr. Damon Key Bocken Leong & Kupchak, Honolulu, 1971—, also bd. dirs.; chief minority counsel 8th legis. Hawaii Ho. of Reps., Honolulu, 1974-75; legis. coord. Hawaii State Assn. Counties, Honolulu, 1988; bd. dirs. Dinwiddie Constrn. Co., San Francisco, Wright Schuchart, Inc., Seattle, Fletcher Constrn. Co. U.S.A., Ltd., Del. Co-author: Fifty State Construction Lien and Bond Laws, 1992; contbr. articles to profl. jours. Chair agenda com. C.Z.M. Statewide Adv. Com., Hawaii, 1980-92; pres., bd. dirs. Health and Community Svc. Coun. Hawaii, Honolulu, 1982-88; trustee Moanalua Gardens Found., 1985-88, Operation Raleigh (N.C.) U.S.A., 1986-90; bd. dirs., chair program com. Hawaii Nature Ctr., 1989—; chair Hawaii State Commn. on Korean and Vietnam War Meml., 1992—. Capt. USAF, 1964-68, Vietnam. Mem. ABA, Hawaii Bar Assn., Internat. Bar Assn., USAF Assn., Cornell Law Alumni Assn. (exec. com. 1990—), Oahu Country Club, Volcano Golf and Country Club. Office: 1600 Pauahi Tower 1001 Bishop St Honolulu HI 96813-3429

KUPFER, JOHN CARLTON, physicist, engineer; b. L.A., Feb. 12, 1955; s. Donald Harry and Romaine Faye (Littlefield) K.; m. Joan Marie Todd, Apr. 11, 1987. BA in Physics cum laude, Rice U., 1977; MS in Physics, U. Ariz., 1981, PhD in Physics, 1985. Mem. tech. staff Rockwell Internat., Anaheim, Calif., 1985—. Mem. Am. Phys. Soc., Materials Rsch. Soc., Sigma Pi Sigma.

KUPPERSTEIN, EDWARD RAYMOND, broadcast executive; b. Boston, Dec. 27, 1933; s. Barney and Lottie (Bohrer) K. BA, Harvard U., 1955; MusM, New Eng. Conservatory, 1957. Dir. pub. relations, dir. spl. student dept., dir. of placement New Eng. Conservatory, Boston, 1959-65; asst. mgr. Detroit Symphony Orch., 1966-67; gen. mgr. Greater Miami (Fla.) Philharm., 1967-69, Tucson Symphony Orch., 1972-75; exec. producer Tucson Ballet, 1975; promotion cons. Ariz. Opera Co., Tucson, 1976-81; radio music dir. KUAT Comm. Group, Tucson, 1976-83, radio program dir., 1983-90, radio sta. mgr., 1990—; ind. pub. relations and promotion cons., Miami, 1969-72; promotion and prodn. cons., Tucson, 1975—. Commentator, reviewer, reporter, interviewer (radio, TV, print media) Nat. Pub. Radio, Voice of Am., BBC, other nationally distributed services. Ford Found. fellow, 1965-66. Mem. Pi Kappa Lambda. Home: SUPO 20714 Tucson AZ 85720 Office: U Ariz KUAT Comm Group Tucson AZ 85721

KURAISHI, AKARI LUKE, real estate company executive; b. Nagano, Japan, July 29, 1959; came to U.S. 1984; s. Atsushi and Kuniko (Tomita) K.; m. Hiromi Lydia Hatae, Oct. 10, 1987; children: Katrina Ayumi, Kristin Kasumi. BA, Nat. Def. Acad., Yokosuka, Japan, 1982; MBA, U. Dallas, 1986. Registered Internat. Mem. of Internat. Real Estate Inst. Mgr. Gateway Travel & Tours, Dallas, 1985-87; with portfolio investments dept. Mitsui Real Estate Sales USA Co., Ltd., L.A., 1987-90; mgr., 1990-91; asst. v.p. Mitsui Real Estate Sales USA Co., Ltd., L.A., 1991-93, v.p., 1993—; v.p. Santa Ana (Calif.) Corp., 1992—, Santa Ana Mgmt. Corp., 1992—; sec. MI Ptnrs. Co., Ltd., L.A., 1993—; sec. MI Ptnrs. (L.A.) Co., Ltd., 1993—. Mem. NRA, Orange County Japanese Am. Assn. Home: 2348 E Trenton Ave Orange CA 92667-4454 Office: Mitsui Real Estate Sales USA Co Ltd 601 S Figueroa St # 4600 Los Angeles CA 90017-5751

KURASHIGE, BRETT MITSUAKI, management consultant, military officer; b. Honolulu, Nov. 3, 1959; s. Irwin Mitsugi and Joan (Yabusaki) K.; m. Melvina Fushikoshi, July 1, 1989. BA cum laude, Tufts U., 1981; B in Gen. Sci., Roosevelt U., 1988; MS in Info. Systems, Hawaii Pacific U., 1993; MBA, U. Hawaii, 1993. Programmer Bancard Assn. of Hawaii, Honolulu, 1987-88; data processing mgr. Plumbing Spltys. and Supplies, Inc., Honolulu, 1988-90; sr. network engr. Martin Marietta Corp., Camp Smith, Hawaii, 1990-92; sr. mgmt. cons. Deloitte and Touche, Honolulu, 1992—; cons. Plumbing Spltys. and Supplies, Inc., Honolulu, 1990-91. Intern Office of Senator Daniel K. Inouye U.S. Senate, Washington, 1978. Lt. comdr. USNR, 1983—. Mem. Armed Forces Comm. and Electronics Assn., Naval Res. Assn., Hawaii Soc. Corp. Planners, Hawaii Novell Users Group, Data Processing Mgmt. Assn. (program chmn.), Hawaii Tufts Alumni Admissions (program chmn.), Omicron Delta Epsilon. Democrat. Home: 55 S KuKui St # D-1514 Honolulu HI 96813 Office: Deloitte & Touche 1132 Bishop St Ste 1200 Honolulu HI 96813

KUREY, KRISTINE MARIE, small business owner; b. Appleton, Wis., Mar. 7, 1954; d. Donald Joseph and Marilyn Annette (Sigl) K.; m. James Howard Reed, July 11, 1987. BJ, U. Wis., 1976. Editor, writer, photographer New Glarus (Wis.) Post, 1976-78; account exec. James Neal Harvey Advt., N.Y.C., 1978-81; news writer Sta. KYXI, Portland, Oreg., 1981-82; nat. sales mgr. Sta. KTBY-TV, Anchorage, 1982-84; owner Kurey Co., Seattle, 1984—. Mem. Wash./Oreg. Splty. Advt. Assn. (founder, pres. 1988-90). Republican. Roman Catholic. Office: Kurey Co 1700 Westlake Ave N #308 Seattle WA 98109

KURIAN, GEORGE, engineering executive; b. Vellore, India, Nov. 29, 1966; came to U.S., 1986; s. P. Chacko and Molly Rebecca (Mathew) K. BSEE, Princeton (N.J.) U., 1990. Applications engr. Oracle Corp., Redwood Shores, Calif., 1990-91, sr. applications engr., 1991-92, project mgr., 1992—. Vol. Project Literacy, Redwood City, Palo Alto, 1991; founding mem. Oracle Vols., Redwood Shores, 1991—; mem. World Affairs Coun., No. Calif., 1991—, Alliance Francaise, Palo Alto, 1991—. Rsch. grant Phillips Corp., 1989-90; scholarships Princeton U., 1986-90. Mem. MIT-Stanford Venture Lab. for Young Entrepreneurs, Phi Beta Kappa, Sigma Xi, Tau Beta Pi. Methodist. Office: Oracle Corp Box 659304 500 Oracle Pkwy Redwood Shores CA 94065

KURKI, ALLAN W., school system administrator; b. Tampere, Finland, May 18, 1938; m. Suzanne 1965. BS in Aeronautics, St. Louis U., 1960; MBA with honors, U. Pitts., 1962, MS, 1966; EdD, U. Kans., 1975; MLA, Baker U., Kansas City, 1984. Aeronautical engr. Transp. Material Command, St. Louis, 1960-61; teaching fellow U. Pitts., 1962-64; chmn., Dept. of Bus. Mgmt. Point Park Coll., Pitts., 1966-68; sen. mgmt. economist Midwest Rsch. Inst., Kansas City, Mo., 1968-71; faculty, Bus. Mgmt. Johnson County C.C., Overland Park, Kans., 1971-77; cluster dean Oakton C.C., Morton Grove, Ill., 1977-79; v.p., Acad. Affairs Johnson County C.C., 1979-86; superintendent, pres. Antelope Valley C.C., Lancaster, Calif., 1986—. Task Force mem. Johnson County Cultural/Civic Ctr., 1979-86; bd. of deacons Village Presbyn. Ch., 1979-86; citizen's adv. bd. Lancater Community Hosp., 1986—; elder Lancaster Presbyn. Ch., 1986—. Mem. Am Cancer Soc. (bd. dirs., unit pres. 1989-91), United Way (Antelope Valley Region bd. dirs, chair 1991-92), Lancaster C. of C. (bd. dirs., prison com., personnel com., edn. com., v.p. 1990-91, pres. elect 1991-92), Palmdale Regional Airport Commn. (bd. dirs.), Antelope Valley Cultural Found. (bd. dirs.), Domestic Violence Coun. (bd. dirs., pres. 1989-92), Lancaster West Rotary (bd. dirs., club pres. 1990-91, Paul Harris fellow, 1990, Rotary Dist. 5260 sec. 1991-92), Eyeopener Toastmasters Club 1675 (CTM designation, club pres. 1991). Home: 43548 37th St W Lancaster CA 93536 Office: Antelope Valley Coll Office of President 3041 W Ave K Lancaster CA 93536-5426

KURLAND, MICHAEL JOSEPH, writer, editor; b. N.Y.C., Mar. 1, 1938; s. Jack and Stephanie (Yacht) K.; m. Diana Jacquelyn Pearson, Nov. 28, 1988. Student, Hiram Coll., 1955-56, U. Md., Baumholder, Germany, 1961-62, Columbia U., 1962-64. Writer, novelist Crawdaddy Mag., 1963—; mng. editor Crawdaddy Mag., N.Y.C., 1972-74; dir. Squirrel Hill Theater, Berkeley, Calif., 1976-78; pres., editor PennyFarthing Press, Berkeley, 1978-82; editor Angevin Press, L.A., 1990—; with Sharon Jarvis Literary Agts., Pa.; cons. editor Doubleday, 1978; columnist Berkeley Barb., 1968. Author: Ten Little Wizards, The Star Griffin, A Plague of Spies, 1969 (MWA Edgar scroll), The Infernal Device, 1979 (MWA Edgar scroll), The Last President, 1980, A Study in Sorcery, 1989, Button Bright, 1990, Spy Masters' Handbook, 1990, A Gallery of Rogues, 1993, many others. Mem. Authors Guild, Mystery Writers of Am.

KURNICK, ALLEN ABRAHAM, retired biochemist, nutritionist; b. Kaunas, Lithuania, Mar. 15, 1921; came to U.S., 1938; s. Harry and Rose (Narver) K.; m. Nita Binder, Sept. 6, 1942 (dec. May 1979); children: Eileen R. Kurnick Laudau, Marc B.; m. Younghi Kim, Apr. 15, 1983; 1 child, Kimberley Kim Joseph. BS, Calif. State U., 1953; MS, Tex. A & M U., 1955, PhD, 1957. Asst. prof. dept. poultry sci. U. Ariz., Tucson, 1957-59, prof., head poultry sci. dept., 1959-62, mem. grad. faculty, 1959-62; mgr. tech. svcs. chem. div. Hoffmann-LaRoche, Pasadena, Calif., 1962-66; mgr. tech. svcs. chem. div. Hoffmann-LaRoche, Nutley, N.J., 1966-80, gen. mgr., v.p. chem. div., 1980-81, v.p., dir. rsch. nutrition and vitamin divsn., 1981-86; ret., 1986. Contbr. numerous articles to profl. publs. Bd. dirs. Animal Health Inst., Washington, 1977-80, Internat. Poultry Sci. Assn., 1976-8; mem. nutrition coun. Am. Feed Mfrs., 1976. Cpl. USAF, 1943-46. NIH fellow, 1955-57. Fellow AAAS; mem. Am. Chem. Soc., Am. Inst. Nutrition. Home: 2431 Unicornio St Rancho La Costa CA 92009

KURNICK, JOHN EDMUND, hematologist, educator; b. N.Y.C., Feb. 9, 1942; s. Nathaniel B. and Dorothy (Manheimer) K.; m. Luann Fogliani, July 9, 1969; children: David, Katherine. BA, Harvard U., 1962; MD, U. Chgo., 1966. Diplomate Am. Bd. Internal Medicine, Am. Bd. Oncology, Am. Bd. Hematology. Intern U. Wash., Seattle, 1966-67; resident Stanford U., Palo Alto, Calif., 1967-68; asst. prof. medicine U. Colo. Med. Ctr., Denver, 1973-78; chief hematology VA Hosp., Denver, 1973-78; pvt. pracice Downey, Calif., 1979—; assoc. clin. prof. medicine U. Calif., Irvine, 1979—; lectr., expert witness in field. Contbr. articles to med. jours. Maj. Med. Corps., USAR, 1970-73. Fellow U. Colo., 1968-70. Fellow ACP; mem. Am. Soc. Hematology, Am. Soc. Clin. Oncology, Western Soc. Clin. Rsch., Internat. Soc. Hematology, Am. Fedn. Clin. Rsch., Am. Assn. Cancer Edn. Democrat. Office: 11411 Brookshire Ave Downey CA 90241

KURODA, YUTAKA, management consultant; b. Kobe, Hyogo, Japan, Dec. 16, 1950. BS, Waseda U., Tokyo, 1973; MS, Stanford U., 1982. Adv. systems engr. IBM Japan, Tokyo, 1973-85; product mgr. IBM Asia Pacific Group Hdqrs., Tokyo, 1985-88; sr. cons. SRI Internat., Menlo Park, Calif., 1988 --. Home: 4769 Williams Rd San Jose CA 95129-3232 Office: SRI Internat 333 Ravenswood Ave Menlo Park CA 94025-3493

KURRI, JARI, professional hockey player; b. Helsinki, Finland, May 18, 1960; m. Tina Kurri; children: Joonas, Ville. Hockey player Jokerit, Finland, 1977-80, Edmonton Oilers, Alta., Can., 1980-90; with Milan Devils, Italian Hockey League, from 1990, L.A. Kings, Inglewood, Calif., 1991—; mem. NHL All-Star team, 1982-88. Recipient Lady Byng Meml. Trophy, 1985. Office: care LA Kings Gt Western Forum PO Box 17013 Inglewood CA 90308-7013

KURSEWICZ, LEE Z., marketing consultant; b. Chgo., Oct. 26, 1916; s. Antoni and Henryka (Sulkowska) K.; ed. Chgo. and Bata ind. schs.; m. Ruth Elizabeth Venzke, Jan. 31, 1940; 1 son, Dennis. With Bata Shoe Co., Inc., 1936-78, plant mgr., Salem, Ind., 1963-65, v.p., mng. dir., Batawa, Ont., Can., 1965-71; v.p., dir. Bata Industries, Batawa, 1965-71, plant mgr., Salem, 1971-76; pres. Bata Shoe Co., Inc., Belcamp, Md., 1976-77, sr. v.p., dir., 1977-79; gen. mgr. Harford Insulated Panel Systems div. Hazleton Industries, 1981-82. City mgr. City of Batawa, 1965-71; vice chmn. Trenton (Ont.) Meml. Hosp., 1970-71; pres. Priestford Hills Community Assn., 1979-80; chmn. adv. bd. Phoenix Festival Theatre, Hartford County Community Coll., 81; vice chmn. Harford County chpt. ARC, 1980-81, chmn., 1982-83; chmn. Harford County Econ. Devel. Adv. Bd., 1983-85; mem. Susquehanna Region Pvt. Industry Council, 1983-85. Mem. Am. Mgmt. Assn. Clubs: Rotary, Bush River Yacht (commodore 1956), Bush River Power Squadron (comdr. 1957), Western Hills Country of Salem (pres. 1975), Trenton Country (pres. 1968-69), Md. Country. Home and Office: 29707A Niguel Rd Laguna Beach CA 92677-2050

KURTZ, BRUCE, historian, curator; b. Bozeman, Mont., May 18, 1943; s. James Lewis and Mary Hester (Decker) K. BFA, San Francisco Art Inst., 1964; MA, U. Iowa, 1966, MFA, 1967. Curator 20th Century art Phoenix Art Mus., 1985—; instr. art history So. Ill. U., Carbondale, 1967-69; assoc. prof. art history Hartwick Coll., Oneonta, N.Y., 1969-85. Author: Paikvision, Artforum, 1982, Visual Imagination: An Introduction to Art, 1987, Contemporary Art: 1965-90, 1991; contb. The Writings of Robert Smithson, 1979; contbr. articles to profl. jours.; exhbns. organized: Altered Egos: Samaras, Sherman, Wegman, 1986, Keith Haring, Andy Wahol, and Walt Disney, 1991. Recipient Art Ctitic's Fel grant, Nat. Endowment Arts, 1975, 76. Mem. Nat. Arts Club, Assn. Int. Critiques Art. Office: Phoenix Art Museum 1625 N Central Ave Phoenix AZ 85004-1685

KURTZ, F. ANTHONY, savings and loan association executive; b. Chgo., 1941. Grad., Calif. State U., Northridge, 1963. CFO, sr. v.p. HF Ahmanson/Home Savings Am., L.A., 1968-91; pres., COO Downey Savings and Loan Assn., Newport Beach, Calif., 1991—; bd. dirs. Am. Ind. Reinsurance Co., Nat. Am. Ins. Co., N.Y., Stuyesant Life Ins. Co. Mem. AICPA. Office: Downey Savings & Loan Assn 3501 Jamboree Rd Newport Beach CA 92658*

KURTZ, JOHN CALDWELL, computer software company executive; b. Madison, Wis., Jan. 24, 1941; s. Chester Mott and Esther (Caldwell) K.; m. Meeley Turner, Dec. 22, 1963 (dec. July 1971); 1 child, John T.; m. Roxanne Van Horne, Sept. 16, 1971; children: Michael W., Rebecca L., Jennifer A. Cert. in data processing, U. N.Mex., 1966. Programmer Calif. Blue Shield, San Francisco, 1967-68; dept. head El Paso C.C., Colorado Springs, Colo., 1969-70; programming supr. Nat. Fedn. Ind. Bus., San Mateo, Calif., 1971-80; sr. support analyst Wang Labs., Denver, 1981; v.p. GPB Cons., T, 1982-83; owner, pres. The Software Connection, Denver, Incline Village, Nev., 1984—. Author computer system Kwic-File. Home: PO Box 5209 Incline Village NV 89450 Office: The Software Connection PO Box 5696 Incline Village NV 89450

KURTZIG, SANDRA L., software company executive; b. Chgo., Oct. 21, 1946; d. Barney and Marian (Boruck) Brody; children: Andrew Paul, Kenneth Alan; B.S. in Math., UCLA, 1967; M.S.in aeronaut. engring., Stanford U., 1968. Math analyst TRW Systems, 1967-68; mktg. rep., Gen. Electric Co., 1969-72; chmn. bd., chief exec. officer, pres. ASK Computer Systems, Mountain View, Calif., 1972-85, chmn. bd., 1986-89, chmn., pres., chief exec. officer, 1989-92; chmn., founder The ASK Group, Inc., 1993—; pres. ASK Computer Systems. Cited one of 50 most influential bus. people in Am., Bus. Week, 1985. Office: The ASK Group Inc 2440 W El Camino Real Mountain View CA 94040-1400

KURTZMAN, RALPH HAROLD, biochemist, researcher; b. Mpls., Feb. 21, 1933; s. Ralph Harold, Sr. and Susie Marie (Elwell) K.; m. Nancy Virginia Leussler, Aug. 27, 1955; children: Steven Paul, Sue. BS, U. Minn., 1955; MS, U. Wis., 1958, PhD, 1959. Asst. prof. U. R.I., Kingston, 1959-62, U. Minn., Morris, 1962-65; biochemist U.S. Dept. Agriculture, Albany, Calif., 1965—; instr. U. Calif., Berkeley, 1981-82; cons. Bliss Valley Farms, Twin Falls, Idaho, 1983-84. Inventor: mushroom substrate (compost) preperation, 1982, decaffeination of beverages, 1973; contbr. articles to profl. jours. Chmn. Berkeley YMCA Camp Program Com., 1971-72; official Amateur Athletic Union (swimming), San Francisco, 1973-80; treas. Calif. Native Plant Soc., 1970. Mem. Am. Mushroom Inst., Mushroom Growers of Great Britain, Mycological Soc. Am., Sigma Xi. Home: 445 Vassar Ave Berkeley CA 94708 Office: US Dept Agriculture Western Regional Rsch Ctr 800 Buchanan St Albany CA 94708

KURUTZ, KATHERN DARRAH, museum educator; b. L.A., Mar. 5, 1953; married Oct. 4, 1980. BA in Psychology, U. San Francisco, 1974; MS in Indsl.-Organizational Psychology, San Francisco State U., 1981. Presch. tchr. Jewish Community Ctr., San Francisco, 1974; dir. Arlene Lind Gallery, San Francisco, 1974-80; curator of edn. Crocker Art Mus., Sacramento, 1980—; advisor Calif. State Dept. Edn., Sacramento, 1984—, Calif. Arts Coun., Sacramento, 1983—, Sacramento Regional Getty Inst. for Educators on the Visual Arts, Sacramento, 1987—. Author: Sacramento's Pioneer Patrons of Art, 1985, rev. 1990; reviewer Calif. History jour., 1985, 87. Docent Calif. Hist. Soc., San Francisco, 1978-80. Kellogg Found. Smithsonian fellow, Portland, 1984, Field Mus. fellow, Chgo., 1984. Mem. Am. Assn. Mus. (speaker & panelist ann. confs. 1983—), Cultural Connections (program chair 1987-89), Sacramento Book Collectors Club (v.p. 1992, pres. 1993). Office: Crocker Art Mus 216 O St Sacramento CA 95814-5399

KUSHLA, JOHN DENNIS, forester, researcher; b. Norristown, Pa., Feb. 3, 1955; s. Walter and Helen K.; m. Michele Ankenmann, Apr. 1, 1989; 1 child, Melanya Eve. BS in Forest Sci. with honors, Pa. State U., 1977; MS in Forest Sci., minor in Soil Sci., U. Fla., 1979. Grad. rsch. asst. U. Fla., Gainesville, 1977-79; supr. soil and water Union Camp Corp., Savannah, Ga., 1980-90; grad. rsch. asst. Oreg. State U., Corvallis, 1990—, mgr. environ. remote sensing applications lab., 1992—; pvt. practice soil cons., Savannah, 1987-90. Contbr. articles Soil Sci. Soc. Am. Jour. Mem. Am. Soc. Agronomy, Am. Soc. Photogrammetry and Remote Sensing, Soc. Am. Foresters, Soil Sci. Soc. Am., Phi Kappa Phi, Xi Sigma Pi, Gamma Sigma Delta, Alpha Zeta. Office: Oreg State U Peavy Hall A 108 Corvallis OR 97331

KUSKO, BRUCE HARRIS, research physicist, lecturer; b. N.Y.C., Mar. 25, 1953; s. George and Helen (Barrow) K; m. Gabriella Nina Battaglia, Nov. 8, 1987; 1 child, Jonathan Feodor. BS in Physics, CCNY, 1975; MA in Physics, U. Calif., Davis, 1978, PhD in Physics, 1983. Sr. guest physicist Laboratoire de Recherche des Musees de France, Paris, 1988-90; rsch. physicist Crocker Nuclear Lab. U. Calif., Davis, 1978-88, dir. Crocker Hist. and Archeol. Project Crocker Nuclear Lab., 1990—. Author: (with others) Proton Milliprobe Analysis of the Hand-Penned Annotations in Bach's Calov Bible, 1985; contbr. articles to profl. jours. Fulbright rsch. scholar, Paris, 1988-89, NATO sr. guest scientist, 1989-90; recipient high level scientific fellowship French Ministry Fgn. Affairs, 1989-90. Mem. Am. Phys. Soc., N.Y. Acad. Scis., Soc. Archeol. Scis., Sigma Xi (life). Office: U Calif Crocker Nuclear Lab Crocker Hist & Archeol Project Davis CA 95616-8569

KUSMIAK, EUGENE, computer software developer; b. N.Y.C., Apr. 7, 1959; s. Eugene and Iona (Ziegler) K. BA in Sociology, Harvard Coll., 1982. Computer programmer Shawmut Mills, Stoughton, Mass., 1979-80; cons. Bank St. Coll., N.Y.C., 1981-85, Intentional Edns., Watertown, Mass., 1982-83, Broderbund Software, San Rafael, Calif., 1984, Quantum Corp., Milpitas, Calif., 1985-88, Lerner Rsch., Mountain View, Calif., 1987-91, Gregory Assocs., San Jose, Calif., 1991—, Smart TV, Palo Alto, Calif., 1991—. Programmer: (word processor) Bank Street Writer, 1982, (computer games) Macintosh Chuck Yeager AFT, 1988, IBM PC Chuck Yeager AFT II, 1989, Sega Genesis F-22 Interceptor, 1991. Mem. Triple Nine Soc. Home: 64-B Mountain View Ave Mill Valley CA 94941

KUSTER, ROBERT KENNETH, scientist; b. Los Angeles, July 11, 1932; s. Arthur Rollo Kuster and Ermine Rosebud (Prittchett) Woodward. AS, Gavilan Coll., 1974, AA in Humanities, 1981; student, San Jose State U., 1955, 1974-76, UCLA, 1977. Installer Western Electric Co., Inc., Corpus Christi, Tex., 1951-52, 1955, San Jose, Calif., 1957-58, 1960-83; ptnr., scientist, cons. WE-Woodward's Enterprises, Morgan Hill, Calif., 1975—; technician AT&T Tech., Inc., San Jose, 1983-85; scientist pvt. practice, Gilroy, 1978—. Served to sgt. U.S. Army Corps Engrs., 1952-54. Mem. AAAS, Astron. Soc. Pacific, Calif. Acad. Scis., N.Y. Acad. Scis., Am. Legion, VFW. Baptist. Lodge: Elks. Home: 420 W 9th St PO Box 1113 Gilroy CA 95021 Office: Woodward's Enterprises 179 Bender Cir Morgan Hill CA 95037-3533

KUSWA, GLENN WESLEY, physicist, technical advisor; b. Milw., Dec. 11, 1940; s. Webster S. and Elvira (Lipman) K.; m. Patricia Sue Bedwell, June 4, 1966; children: Kevin, Erika. B.S., U. Wis.-Madison, 1962, Ph.D., 1970. Staff mem. Sandia Nat. Labs., Albuquerque, 1970-74; program mgr. Atomic Energy Commn., Washington, 1975-76; dept. mgr. particle beam fusion research Sandia Nat. Labs., 1976-82, mgr. future planning group, 1984-06, mgr. tech. transfer and mgmt. dept., 1986—; tech. adviser Dept. Energy, Washington, 1982-84; bd. pres. New Mexico Bus. Innovation Ctr., 1989-92; mem. bd. New Mexico Mus. Natural History Found., 1989—; sec. energy adv. bd. Dept. of Energy, 1992—. Contbr. articles to profl. jours. Bd. dirs. Planned Parenthood Assn., Albuquerque, 1982, Chamber Orch., Albuquerque, 1982. Recipient Spl. Service award Energy Research and Devel. Adminstrn., 1976. Mem. Am. Phys. Soc., IEEE (officer plasma scis. div. 1980-82), Sigma Xi. Democrat. Unitarian. Home: 1115 San Rafael NE Albuquerque NM 87122 Office: Sandia Nat Labs Kirtland AFB Albuquerque NM 87185

KUTER, KAY E., writer, actor; b. L.A., Apr. 25, 1925; s. Leo E. and Evelyn Bell (Edler) K. BFA, Carnegie Inst. Tech., 1949. Actor L.A., 1944—. Author: Carmen Incarnate, 1946, One Man's Treasure, 1992; editor: The Jester, 1956-60, The Jester 50th Anniversary, 1976. Bd. dirs. Family Svc. of L.A., 1950-70. Mem. SAG (bd. dirs. 1970-73, AEA, AFTRA, Book Publicists of So. Calif., Nat. Soc. Hist. Preservation, Smithsonian, Carnegie Mellon U. Westcoast Drama Alumni Clan (founding mem.), Pacific Pioneer Broadcasters, Carnegie Mellon U. Alumni Assn. (regional v.p. 1976-79, Svc. award 1979), Masquers Club (bd. dirs. 1953-75, rec. sec. 1956-70, corr. sec. 1957-69, v.p. 1971-75). Democrat. Home: 6207 Satsuma Ave North Hollywood CA 91606

KUTTNER, STEPHAN GEORGE, legal history educator; b. Bonn, Germany, Mar. 24, 1909; s. George and Gertrude Hedwig (Schocken) K.; m. Eva Susanne Illch, Aug. 22, 1933; children: Ludwig, Andrew, Susanne, Angela, Barbara, Thomas, Michael, Francis, Philip; came to U.S., 1940, naturalized, 1945. Diploma in Law, U. Frankfurt, Germany, 1928; J.U.D., U. Berlin, 1930; S.J.D. (hon.), U. Bologna, Italy, 1952; J.C.D. (hon.), U. Louvain, Belgium, 1955; LL.D., Holy Cross Coll., 1956, Loyola Coll., Balt., 1960, LaSalle Coll., Phila., 1962; Hon. Dr., U. Paris, 1959, U. Genoa, 1966, U. Milan, 1967, U. Salamanca, 1968, U. Strasbourg, 1970, U. Montpellier, 1972; L.H.D., Cath. U. Am., 1972, U. Madrid, 1978; LL.D., U. Cambridge, Eng., 1978, Lateran U. Rome, 1989; S.T.D. (hon.), Wurzburg, 1982. Asst. Sch. Law, U. Berlin, 1929-32; research assoc. Vatican Library, 1934-40, hon. assoc., 1955—; assoc. prof. Pontifical Inst. Law, Rome, 1937-40; vis. prof. history of canon law Cath. U. Am., Washington, 1940-42, prof., 1942-64; Riggs prof. Roman Cath. studies Yale U., 1964-70, prof. law, 1970-77, prof. law emeritus, 1977—; dir. Robbins Collection U. Calif.-Berkeley, 1970-89 ; pres. Inst. Rsch. and Study in Medieval Canon Law, 1955-91, chmn., bd. dirs., 1991—; Walker Ames prof. history U. Wash., 1949; assoc. mem. All Souls Coll., Oxford Hilary and Trinity, 1951; chmn. Internat. Congress Medieval Canon Law, Bologna, 1952, Louvain, 1958, Boston, 1963, Strasburg, 1968, Toronto, 1972, Salamanca, 1976, Berkeley, 1980, Cambridge, Eng., 1984; hon. cons. Roman and canon law Library Congress, 1943-70; mem. Pontifical Commn. for the Revision of the Code of Canon Law, 1967-83, Pontifical Commn. Hist. Scis., 1965-90. Author: Repertorium der Kanonistik, 1937; The History of Doctrines and Ideas of Canon Law in the Middle Ages, 1980, rev. 1992; Medieval Councils, Decretals, and Collections of Cannon Law, 1980, rev. 1992; Gratian and the Schools of Law, 1983, Studies in the History of Medieval Canon Law, 1991. Co-founder, editor Traditio, 1943-71; editor Seminar, 1953-56, Monumenta Juris Canonici, 1965—, Bull. Medieval Canon Law, 1971—; mem. editorial bd. various Am. and fgn. learned jours. Author monographs, pamphlets, booklets in English and other langs. Guggenheim fellow, 1956, 67; recipient prize for disting. achievement in humanities Am. Council Learned Socs., 1959. Fellow Medieval Acad. Am. (pres. 1974), Am. Acad. Arts and Scis., Am. Philos. Soc.; corr. fellow Acad. Gottingen, Acad. Sci. Bologna, Brit. Acad., Bavarian Acad. Munich, Acad. Lincei Rome, Acad. Lisbon, Royal Hist. Soc., Order Pour le Merite for Arts and Scis., Institut de France; mem. Cath. Hist. Assn. (pres. 1958), Soc. d'Histoire de Droit de Paris, Canon Law Soc. (v.p. 1963), Associazione Internationale di Diritto Canonico (v.p. 1973), Am. Cath. Commn. on Cultural Affairs (chmn. 1963), Phi Beta Kappa. Office: U Calif Law Sch 393 Boalt Hall Berkeley CA 94720

KUTVIRT, DUDA CHYTILOVA (RUZENA), scientific translator; b. Pilsen, Czechoslovakia, Sept. 17, 1919; came to U.S., 1949; d. Frantisek and Ruzena (Vitousek) Chytil; m. Otakar Kutvirt, July 10, 1942 (dec.); children: Thomas (dec.), Daniel. BA, Smith Coll., 1940; MA, Mills Coll., 1942. Rsch. asst. U. Rochester Med. Sch., 1942-44; scientific translator Eastman Kodak Rsch. Labs., Rochester, 1944-45, 61-78. Voter registrar LWV, Albuquerque, 1980—, Rochester, 1955-70; vol. U. N.Mex. Hosp. Svc. League, Albuquerque, 1979—. Home: 5 Pool NW Albuquerque NM 87120

KUTYNA, DONALD JOSEPH, air force officer; b. Chgo., Dec. 6, 1933; s. Frank A. and Isabel E. (Kmiec) K.; m. Lucille Mae Moellering, June 6, 1957; children: Dale J., Douglas J. Student, U. Iowa, 1951-53; BS, U.S. Mil. Acad., 1957; MA in Aero./Astronautics, MIT, 1965. Commd. 2d lt. USAF, 1957, advanced through grades to gen., 1990; pilot trainee Vance AFB, Enid, Okla., 1958; comdr. B-47 crew March AFB, Riverside, Calif., 1958; test pilot Edwards AFB, Calif., 1965-69; pilot 44th Tactical Fighter Squadron, Royal Takhli AFB, Thailand, 1969-70; planner R&D Pentagon, Washington, 1971-72; exec. officer Undersec. of Air Force, Washington, 1973-76; dep. program mgr. Air Force Electronics Systems Div., Bedford, Mass., 1976-82; mgr. Dept. Def. Space Shuttle Program, L.A., 1982-84; dir. space systems Pentagon, Washington, 1984-86; vice comdr. Space Div., L.A., 1986-87; comdr. USAF Space Command, Peterson AFB, Colo., 1987-90; comdr.-in-chief N.Am. Aerospace Def. Command, U.S. Space Command, Peterson AFB, 1990-92. Recipient Space award Nat. Geog. Soc., 1987, James V. Hartinger award Nat. Security Indsl. Assn., 1990. Mem. Air Force Assn. (Schriever award 1991).

KUURE, BOJAN MARLENA, operating room nurse; b. Jakobstad, Finland, Nov. 14, 1942; d. Anders Arne and Aina Viktoria (Back) Sundqvist; m. Arvo Antero Kuure, Nov. 3, 1965; 1 child, Saara Bojan. Diploma, Helsingfors Svenska Sjukvardsinstitut, Helsinki, Finland, 1964; specialty nursing in anesthesia and surgery, Helsingfors Svenska Sjukvards, Helsinki, Finland, 1967-68; Aprubatur in Edn., U. Helsinki, 1972. Staff nurse U. Finland Hosp., 1964-68, specialty nurse, 1968-70; tchr. dir. Nursing Inst., Helsinki, 1970-72; oper. rm. nurse Island Hosp., Anacortes, Wash., 1972-83, surg. dir., 1983. Vol. Interplast, Inc., Healing the Children. Mem. Am. Assn. Oper. Rm. Nurses, Oper. Rm. Mgrs. Wash., Wash. State Coun. Peri-op Nursing, Wash. Orgn. Nurse Execs. Home: 1201 5th St Anacortes WA 98221

KUWABARA, DENNIS MATSUICHI, optometrist; b. Honolulu, July 20, 1945; s. Robert Tokuichi and Toshiko (Nakashima) K.; m. Judith Naomi Tokumaru, June 28, 1970; children: Jennifer Tomiko, Susan Kazuko. BS, So. Calif. Coll. Optometry, 1968, OD cum laude, 1970. Pvt. practice optometry Waipahu, Honolulu, Hawaii, 1972—; pres. 1st Study Club for Optometrists, Honolulu, 1982-83; chmn. Bd. Examiners in Optometry, Honolulu, 1982-90; state dir. Optometric Extension Found., Honolulu, 1980-88. Served to lt. Med. Service Corps, USN, 1970-72. Named Outstanding Young Person of Hawaii, Hawaii State Jaycees, 1979. Fellow Am. Acad. Optometry; mem. Hawaii Optometric Assn. (pres. 1979-80, Man of Yr. award 1976, Optometrist of Yr. 1983), Am. Optometric Assn., Armed Forces Optometric Soc. Home: 94-447 Holaniku St Mililani Town HI 96789 Office: 94-748 Hikimoe St Waipahu HI 96797 also: 1441 Kapiolani Blvd Ste 710 Honolulu HI 96814

KUWAYAMA, GEORGE, curator; b. N.Y.C., Feb. 25, 1925; s. Senzo and Fumiko Kuwayama; m. Lillian Yetsuko Yamashita, Dec. 5, 1961; children: Holly, Mark, Jeremy. B.A., Williams Coll., 1948; postgrad., NYU, 1948-54; M.A., U. Mich., 1956. Curator Oriental art L.A. County Mus. Art, L.A., 1959-70, sr. curator Far Ea. art, 1970—; lectr. U. So. Calif., UCLA; organizer spl. exhbns. Author: Far Eastern Lacquer, 1980, Shippo: The Art of Enameling in Japan, 1980; author, editor: Japanese Ink Painting, 1983, The Quest for Eternity, 1987, Ancient Mortuary Traditions of China, 1991, New Perspective on the Art of Ceramics in China, 1992; author, co-editor: Imperial Taste, 1989. Served with parachute inf. U.S. Army, 1944-46. Charles Freer scholar U. Mich., 1955-56; Inter-Univ. fellow Ford Found., 1957-58; rsch. travel grantee Nat. Endowment for Arts, 1974, 88. Mem. Assn. for Asian Studies, Am. Oriental Soc. (Louise Hackney fellow 1956), Coll. Art Assn., Japan Soc., Internat. House Japan, China Colloquium, Far Ea. Art Coun. Democrat. Methodist. Home: 1417 Comstock Ave Los Angeles CA 90024-5316 Office: LA County Mus Art 5905 Wilshire Blvd Los Angeles CA 90036-4523

KUYPER, PETER WALK, motion picture company executive; b. L.A., Apr. 4, 1942; s. A.B. and Mina (Walk) K.; m. Christine Anne Thomas, Feb. 27, 1966; children: Jonathan, Peter Jr., T. Christopher, Katherine. BA, Pomona Coll., 1964; MBA, U. Chgo., 1966. Master's lic. U.S. Coast Guard. V.p. Paramount TV, L.A., 1968-72, Paramount Pictures Corp., N.Y., 1972-78; pres. Newport (R.I.) Comm., 1978-80; v.p. MGM Film Co., N.Y.C., 1980-82; pres. MGM/United Artists Home Entertainment, N.Y.C., 1982-87; chmn. Motion Picture Licensing Corp., L.A., 1987—. Mem. Royal Prince Alfred Yacht Club, Calif. Yacht Club, N.Y. Athletic Club. Office: Motion Picture Licensing Corp 13315 Washington Blvd Los Angeles CA 90066

KUZELL, WILLIAM CHARLES, physician, instrument company executive; b. Great Falls, Mont., Dec. 13, 1914; s. Charles R. and Theresa (O'Leary) K.; m. Françoise Lavelaine de Maubeuge, Oct. 15, 1945; children: Anne Frances Kuzell Hackstock, Elizabeth Jacqueline, Charles Maubeuge. Exchange student, Lingnan U., Canton, China, 1934-35, U. de Grenoble, summer 1935; BA, Stanford U., 1936, MD, 1941. Diplomate: Am. Bd. Internal Medicine. Research assoc. therapeutics Stanford U., 1948-56, physician in charge arthritis clinic, 1956-59, clin. prof. medicine emeritus, 1986—; chief div. rheumatology Presbyn. Med. Center, San Francisco, 1959-85; dir. emeritus Kuzell Inst. for Arthritis and Infectious Disease Research, Calif. Pacific Med. Ctr., San Francisco, 1985—; chmn. bd., chief exec. officer Oxford Labs., Inc., Foster City, to 1974; guest lectr. Japan Rheumatism Assn., 1964. Editor: Stanford Med. Bull, 1950-53. Pres., No. Calif. chpt. Arthritis Found., 1971-72, chmn. bd., 1972-80. Served to capt. M.C. AUS, 1942-46. Named Man of Yr. in Medicine Shoong Found. Hall of Fame, 1980; recipient Disting. Service award Arthritis Found., 1981. Fellow ACP, Am. Coll. Rheumatology; mem. AMA, Japan Rheumatism Assn. (hon.), Sigma Xi, Sigma Nu, Nu Sigma Nu. Clubs: Olympic, Presidio Golf. Home: 25 W Clay St San Francisco CA 94121-1230 Office: 450 Sutter St Rm 1035 San Francisco CA 94108-3912

KUZMA, GEORGE MARTIN, bishop; b. Windber, Pa., July 24, 1925; s. Ambrose and Anne (Marton) K. Student, Benedictine Coll., Lisle, Ill.; BA, Duquesne U., postgrad.; postgrad., U. Mich.; grad., SS Cyril and Methodius Byzantine Cath. Sem. Ordained priest Byzantine Cath. Ch., 1955. Asst. pastor SS Peter and Paul Ch., Braddock, Pa., 1955-57; pastor Holy Ghost Ch., Charleroi, Pa., 1957-65, St. Michael Ch., Flint, Mich., 1965-70, St. Eugene Ch., Bedford, Ohio, 1970-72, Annunciation Ch., Anaheim, Calif., 1970-86; rev. monsignor Byzantine Cath. Ch., 1984, titular bishop, 1986, consecrated bishop, 1987; aux. bishop Byzantine Cath. Diocese of Passaic, N.J., 1987-90; bishop Van Nuys, Calif., 1991—; judge matrimonial tribunal, mem. religious edn. commn., mem. commn. orthodox rels. Diocese of Pitts., 1955-69; judge matrimonial tribunal, vicar for religious Diocese of Parma, 1969-82; treas., bd. dirs., chmn. liturgical commn., mem. clergy & seminarian rev. bd., liaison to ea. Cath. dirs. religious edn., bd. dirs. diocesan credit union, chmn. diocesan heritage bd., chmn. diocesan ecumenical commn. Diocese of Van Nuys, 1982-86; vicar gen. Diocese of Passaic; episcopal vicar for Ea. Pa.; chmn. Diocesan Retirement Plan Bd.; pres. Father Walter Cizsek Prayer League; chaplain Byzantine Carmelite Monastery, Sugarloaf, Pa. Assoc. editor Byzantine Cath. World; editor The Apostle. With USN, 1943-46, PTO. Office: Pastoral Ctr 18024 Parthenia St Northridge CA 91325-3150*

KVENVOLDEN, KEITH ARTHUR, geochemist; b. Cheyenne, Wyo., July 16, 1930; s. Owen Arthur and Agnes B. Kvenvolden; m. Mary Ann Lawrence, Nov. 7, 1959; children: Joan Agnes, Jon William. Geophys. Engr., Colo. Sch. Mines, 1952; MS, Stanford U., 1958, PhD, 1961. Registered geologist, Calif. Jr. geologist Socony Mobil Oil Co., Caracas, Venezuela, 1952-54; sr. rsch. technologist Mobil Oil Corp., Dallas, 1961-65; rsch. sci. Ames Rsch. Ctr. NASA, Mountain View, Calif., 1965-75, br. chief Ames Rsch. Ctr., 1971-75, div. chief Ames Rsch. Ctr., 1974-75; geologist U.S. Geol. Survey, Menlo Park, Calif., 1975-92, sr. scientist, 1992—; cons. prof. geology Stanford (Calif.) U., 1967—; adj. prof. geology Calif. State U., Hayward, 1978-88; courtesy prof. oceanography Oreg. State U., Corvalis, 1988—. Editor: Geochemistry and the Origin of Life, 1974, Geochemistry of Organic Molecules, 1980; contbr. articles to profl. jours. With U.S. Army, 1952-54. Gilbert fellow U.S. Geol. Survey, 1989; recipient Meritorious Svc. award U.S. Dept. of Interior. Fellow AAAS, Geol. Soc. Am., Explorers Club, Am. Geophys. Union; mem. Internat. Assn. Geochemistry and Cosmochemistry, Am. Assn. Petroleum Geologists, Geochemical Soc. (chmn. Organic Geochemical div., Best Paper award 1971). Office: US Geol Survey M/S 999 345 Middlefield Rd Menlo Park CA 94025-3591

KVERNDAL, ROALD, maritime ministry consultant; b. Bromley, Kent, Eng., July 8, 1921; came to U.S. 1961; s. Olaf Gunvald and Valgjerd (Wroldsen) K.; m. Ruth Louise Ursin, June 27, 1953; children: Olaf, Evelyn, Jeanette, Marianne. Inter-BA, U. London, 1939; Marine Law Deg., Dept. Commerce Oslo, 1942; ThM, Ind. Theol. Sem., Oslo, 1953; ThD, Oslo U., 1984. Consular sec. Govt. Norway, Rouen, France, 1948-49; seafarers' chaplain Norwegian Seamen's Mission, 1954-69; theol. researcher Norwegian Rsch. Coun., Oslo, 1969-72; pastor Am. Luth. Ch., various locations U.S.A., 1972-83; exec. sec. Internat. Coun. Seamen's Agencies, Bellevue, Wash., 1979-91; maritime cons. Luth. World Fedn., Luth. Coun. in USA and Evang. Luth. Ch. in Am., 1984—. Author: Sjömannsetikk (Maritime Ethics), 1971, Seamen's Missions: Their Origin & Early Growth, 1986; editor Watermarks, 1979-91; contbr. articles to profl. jours. Lt. Norwegian Free Forces, 1943-45. Mem. Am. Soc. Missiology, Internat. Assn. for Mission Studies, Internat. Assn. for Study of Maritime Mission (internat. pres. 1990—), Soc. for Nautical Rsch., Luth. Assn. Maritime Ministry (hon. sec.). Lutheran. Office: Lutheran Maritime Ministry 2513 162d Ave NE Bellevue WA 98008

KWAN, EDDY, research mechanician, consultant; b. Hong Kong, Apr. 30, 1959; came to U.S., 1967; s. Kim Lun and Sue (Wong) K.; m. Mary Yuen, May 20, 1990. BA in Maths., U. Calif., Berkeley, 1983. Design engr. Petrogen Inc., Richmond, Calif., 1978-81; sr. lab. mechanician U. Calif., Berkeley, 1983—; design cons. Bio-Rad, Cambridge, Mass., 1990—. Inventor underwater steel cutting system with gasoline and oxygen. Mem. U. Calif. Alumni Assn. Baptist. Office: U Calif 54 Mulford Hall Berkeley CA 94720

KWOK, SUN, astronomer; b. Hong Kong, Sept. 15, 1949; arrived in Canada, 1967.; s. Chuen-Poon and Pui-Ling (Chan) K.; m. Shiu-Tseng Emily Yu, June 16, 1973; children: Roberta Wing-Yue, Kelly Wing-Hang. BSc, McMaster U., Hamilton, Ont., Can., 1970; MSc, U. Minn., Mpls., 1972, PhD, 1974. Postdoctoral fellow U. British Columbia, Vancouver, Can., 1974-76; asst. prof. U. Minn., Duluth, 1976-77; rsch. assoc. Centre for Rsch. in Exptl. Space Sci., Toronto, Ont., Can., 1977-78, Herzberg Inst. of Astrophysics, Ottawa, Ont., Can., 1978-83; asst. prof. U. Calgary, Calgary, Alta., Can., 1983-85, assoc. prof., 1985-88, prof., 1988--; vis. fellow Joint Inst. Lab. Astrophysics, Boulder, Colo., 1989-90; project specialist Internat. Adv. Panel, World Bank, 1984; mem. grant selection com. Natural Sci. and Engring. Rsch. Coun., Ottawa, Can., 1985-88; mem. Nat. Facilities Bd. Nat. Rsch. Coun., Ottawa, Can., 1986-89. Editor (books) Late Stages of Stellar Evolution, 1987, Astronomical Infrared Spectroscopy, 1993, Future Observational Directions, 1993; contbr. over 130 articles to scholarly and profl. jours. Natural Sci. and Engring. Rsch. Coun. grantee, 1984--, NASA grantee, 1990; Nat. Inst. for Standards and Tech. vis. fellowship, 1989-90. Mem. Internat. Astron. Union, Can. Astron. Soc., Am. Astron. Soc. Home: 139 Edgeland Rd NW, Calgary, AB Canada T3A 2Y3 Office: Univ of Calgary, Dept of Physics & Astronomy, Calgary, AB Canada T2N 1N4

KWONG, JAMES KIN-PING, geological engineer; b. Kowloon, Hong Kong, Sept. 12, 1954; came to U.S., 1985; s. Joseph and Mary (Sung) K.; m. Annie May-Ching Loh, June 7, 1980; 1 child, John Richard. BSc with honors, U. London, Eng., 1977; MSc, U. Leeds, Eng., 1978, PhD, 1985. Registered profl. civil engr., Hawaii; chartered engr., Eng. Engring. geologist Maunsell Cons., Hong Kong, 1978-80, Palmer & Turner Geotechnics, Hong Kong, 1980-82; cons., rsch. assoc. U. Guelph, Ont., Can., 1982-85; project mgr. Geolabs Hawaii, Honolulu, 1985-87, Dames & Moore, Honolulu, 1987-91; v.p. Pacific Geotech. Engrs., Inc., Honolulu, 1991—; guest lectr. dept. civil engring. U. Hawaii, Honolulu, 1990—. Contbr. articles to profl. jours. Recipient J.F. Kirkaldy's prize U. London, 1977. Mem. ASCE (exec. bd., pres.-elect Hawaii sect. 1989—), NSPE, Cons. Engrs. Coun. Hawaii (bd. dirs.), Can. Geotech. Soc., Instn. Mining and Metallurgy. Office: Pacific Geotech Engrs Inc # 101 1030 Kohou St Honolulu HI 96817-4434

KYL, JON, congressman; b. Oakland, Nebr., Apr. 25, 1942; s. John and Arlene (Griffith) K.; m. Caryll Louise Collins, June 5, 1964; children: Kristine Kyl Gavin, John Jeffry. BA, U. Ariz., 1964, LLB, 1966. Atty. Jennings, Strouss & Salmon, Phoenix, 1966-86; mem. 100th-103rd Congresses from 4th Ariz. dist., 1987—. Past chmn. Phoenix C. of C.; founding dir. Crime Victim Found., Phoenix Econ. Growth Corp.; past bd. dirs. Ariz. Acad.; past chmn. Young Rep., 1969-70; gen. counsel Ariz. Rep. Party. Mem. Ariz. State Bar Assn. Office: 2440 Rayburn Bldg Washington DC 20515

KYLE, BEVERLY ANN, property/procurement clerk; b. Denver, May 10, 1950; d. Thomas Eugene and Ruth Elaine (Harrington) Hamilton; m. James Robert Kyle, Oct. 22, 1972 (div. June 1976). AA, Ea. N.Mex. U., 1985; BA, Metro State Coll. Denver, 1992. Property/procurement clk. U.S. Postal Svc., Denver, 1981—; bd. mem. affirmative action/women's program com. U.S. Postal Svc., Denver, 1990—. With USAF, 1977-79. Mem. Soc. Human Resource Mgrs. (chpt. v.p. 1990-91). Home: 3450 E 128th Pl Thornton CO 80234

KYLE, JEANNE ELLEN, administrative assistant; b. Toledo, Ohio, Jan. 19, 1954; d. Paul Mac and Wiletta Ruth (Stowers) Spresser; m. Arthur Daniel Bronkhurst, Aug. 30, 1974 (div. 1982); children: Tim, Sarah; m. Kevin Patrick Kyle, Sept. 17, 1983; 1 child, Amorette. Student, Devry Inst. of Tech., Phoenix, 1987-90, Calif. State U., Long Beach, 1991-92. Adminstrv. supr. Compex, Culver City, Calif., 1978-80, 82-87; desktop pub. staff Grubb & Ellis Co., Phoenix, 1987-91; adminstrv. asst. The Carson Cos., Rancho Dominguez, Calif., 1991—; staff desk top pub. Matlow Kennedy Corp., Long Beach, 1991; Macintosh insvc. trainer Grubb & Ellis Co., various cos. 1990—. Ptnr. of conscience L.A. chpt. Amnesty Internat., 1991—. Democrat. Home: 19838 Grace Haven Way Yorba Linda CA 92686 Office: The Carson Cos 18710 Wilmington Ave #200 Rancho Dominguez CA 90220

KYLE, ROBERT TOURVILLE, utility company executive retired; b. Deadwood, S.D., Jan. 15, 1910; s. Robert Doughty and Mellanie Irene (Detourville) K.; m. Colette Bertha Hart, May 29, 1937; 1 child, Robert Hart. BE, John Hopkins U., 1931; MBA, Northeastern U., Boston, 1965. Registered profl. engr., Calif., N.H., N.J. Rsch. engr. Am. Gas Assn., Cleve., 1931-35; gas engr. Iroquois Gas Corp., Buffalo, 1935-47; br. mgr. Gen. Controls Co., Cleve., 1947-48; v.p. The Gas Machinery Co., Cleve., 1948-59; sr. cons. Commonwealth Svcs., N.Y.C., 1959-61; v.p. Orange & Rockland Utilities, Boston, 1961-72, Bay State Gas Co., Boston, 1961-74; pres. Kyle Assocs., Inc., San Diego, 1974-86. Inventor 8 patents in field. Pres. R.B. Community Coun., San Diego, 1982-83. Mem. Am. Gas Assn., Continuing Edn. Ctr. (v.p. 1977—), Rotary Club. Home: 18024 Sencillo Dr San Diego CA 92128-1323

KYTE, LYDIANE, botanist; b. L.A., Jan. 6, 1919; d. Aurele and Helen Scott (Douglas) Vermeulen; m. Robert McClung Kyte, June 2, 1939; children: Katherine Liu, Bobbin Cave, William Robert Kyte. BS, U. Wash., 1964. Supt. Weyerhaeuser Co., Rochester, Wash., 1972-77; lab mgr. Briggs Nursery, Olympia, Wash., 1977-80; owner Cedar Valley Nursery, Centralia, Wash., 1980—; cons. Internat. Exec. Service Corps, Brazil, 1987, Egypt, 1990. Author: Plants From Test Tubes: An Introduction to Micropropagation, 1983, 2d rev. edit., 1988. Mem. Internat. Plant Propagators' Soc., Tissue Culture Assn., Internat. Assn. Plant Tissue Culture, Am. Assn. for Hort. Sci., Am. Assn. Univ. Women. Home and Office: Cedar Valley Nursery 3833 Mcelfresh Rd SW Centralia WA 98531-9510

LAALY, HESHMAT OLLAH, research chemist, roofing consultant, author; b. Kermanshah, Iran, June 23, 1927; came to Germany, 1951, Can., 1967, U.S., 1984; s. Jacob and Saltanat (Afshani) L.; m. Parvaneh Modarai, Oct. 7, 1963; (div. 1971); children: Ramesh, Edmond S.; m. Parivash M. Farahmand, Feb. 7, 1982. BS in Chemistry, U. Stuttgart, Germany, 1955; MS in Chemistry, U. Stuttgart, Republic of Germany, 1958, PhD in Chemistry, 1962. Chief chemist Kress Sohne, Krefeld, Germany, 1963-67; analytical chemist Gulf Oil Research Ctr., Montreal, Que., Can., 1967-70; material scientist Bell-Northern Research, Ottawa, Ont., Can., 1970-71; research officer NRC of Can., Ottawa, 1972-84; pres. Roofing Materials Sci. and Tech., L.A., 1984—; Patentee in field. Author: The Science & Technology of Traditional and Modern Roofing Systems, 1992(World Lifetime Achievement award ABI, 1992); patentee bi-functional photovoltaic single ply roofing membrane. Mem. AAAS (Can. chpt.), ASTM, Inst. Roofing and Waterproofing Cons., Single-Ply Roofing Inst., Assn. Profl. Engrs. Ontario, Am. Chem. Soc., Internat. Union of Testing and Rsch. Labs. for Material and Structures (tech. com. 75), Constrn. Specifications Inst., Nat. Roofing Contractors Assn., UN Indsl. Devels. Orgn., Internat. Conf. Bldg. Ofcls., Roofing Cons. Inst., Can. Standard Assn., Can. Gen. Standards Bd. Office: Roofing Materials Sci & Tech 9037 Monte Mar Dr Los Angeles CA 90035-4235

LABA, MARVIN, management consultant; b. Newark, Mar. 17, 1928; s. Joseph Abraham and Jean Cecil (Saunders) L.; m. Sandra Seltzer, Apr. 16, 1961 (div. May 1974); children: Stuart Michael, Jonathan Todd; m. Elizabeth Luger, June 11, 1974 (div. 1979). BBA, Ind. U., 1951. Buyer Bamberger's (Macy's N.J.), Newark, 1951-67; v.p., mdse. adminstr. Macy's N.Y., 1967-73; v.p., gen. mdse. mgr. Howland/Steinback, White Plains, N.Y., 1973-75, Pomeroy's, Levittown, Pa., 1975-76; v.p., gen. mdse. mgr., sr. v.p., exec. v.p. May Co. Calif., North Hollywood, 1976-79; pres., chief exec. officer G. Fox & Co. (div. of the May dept. stores), Hartford, Conn., 1979-82; pres. Richard Theobald & Asocs., L.A., 1983; pres., chief exec. officer Marvin Laba & Assocs., L.A., 1983—. With U.S. Army, 1946-48. Office: Marvin Laba & Assoc 6255 W Sunset Blvd Ste 617 Los Angeles CA 90028-7466

LABADIE, GEORGE SHERMAN, retired art director; b. Dewey, Okla., Jan. 31, 1916; s. John and Minnie (Lunney) L.; m. Jeanne Elizabeth Woodson, June 24, 1939; children: John Woodson, Lynn Joyce Labadie Todd. Student, Sacramento Jr. Coll., 1934-37, Chouinard Art Inst., 1937-39, Art Ctr. Sch., 1938-39, UCLA, 1948. Art dir. Bishop-Conklin Co., L.A., 1940-42, 45-47, Mayers Co., L.A., 1947-49, Russel Harte & Assocs., L.A., 1949-52; sr. art dir. Erwin Wasey, Inc., L.A., 1952-58; exec. art dir. Donahue & Coe, Inc., L.A., 1958-62; advt. mgr. Equity Funding Corp. Am., Beverly Hills, Calif., 1964-65; pres., owner George S. Labadie Agy., Beverly Hills, 1966-72; exec. art dir. Mulle Breen & Rossi, Inc., Beverly Hills, 1972-90; retired, 1981; instr. Calif. Art Inst., Calabasas, 1987—; producer videos Art Video Prodns., Canoga Park, Calif., 1989-90; instr. workshops in field. Contbr. paintings to profl. mags. Recipient awards San Diego Watercolor Soc., 1982, Old Forge Arts Guild, 1982, 84, 86, Houston Watercolor Soc., 1987, 90, Allied Artists Am., 1987, La. Watercolor Soc., 1989. Mem. Allied Artists Am. (award 1987), Am. Watercolor Soc., Nat. Watercolor Soc. (bd. dirs., treas. 1987-88), Midwest Watercolor Soc. (award 1986, 88, 90), Watercolor West (award 1986, 88), West Coast Watercolor Soc. Republican. Home: 22940 Calabash St Woodland Hills CA 91364-2714

LABBE, ARMAND JOSEPH, museum curator, anthropologist; b. Lawrence, Mass., June 13, 1944; s. Armand Henri and Gertrude Marie (Martineau) L.; m. Denise Marie Scott, Jan. 17, 1969 (div. 1972). BA in Anthropology, Univ. Mass., 1969; MA in Anthropology, Calif. State U., 1986; lifetime instr. credential in anthropology, State Calif. Curator collections Bowers Mus., Santa Ana, Calif., 1978-79, curator anthropology, 1979-86, chief curator, 1986-91, dir. rsch. and collections, 1991—; tchr. Santa Ana Coll., 1981-86, Calif. State U., Fullerton, 1982, 83, 88, U. Calif., Irvine, 1983, 87, 91, 93; trustee Balboa Arts Conservation Ctr., San Diego, 1989—, Ams. Found., Greenfield, Mass., 1985—, Quintcentenary Festival Discovery, Orange County, Calif., 1990-91; mem. adv. bd. Élan Internat., Newport Beach, Calif., 1992—; inaugural guest lectr. Friends of Ethnic Art, San Francisco, 1988. Author: Man and Cosmos, 1982, Ban Chiang, 1985, Colombia Before Columbus, 1986 (1st prize 1987), Leigh Wiener: Portraits, 1987, Colombia Antes de Colón, 1988 (honored at Gold Mus. Bogotá, Colombia, 1988), Images of Power: Master Works of the Bowers Museum of Cultural Art, 1992; co-author Tribute to The Gods: Treasures of the Museo del Oro, Bogotá, 1992. Cons. Orange County Coun. on History and Art, Santa Ana, 1981-85; mem. Task Force on County Cultural Resources, Orange County, 1979; cons., interviewer TV prodn. The Human Journey, Fullerton, 1986-89. With USAF, 1963-67. Recipient cert. of Recognition Orange County Bd. Suprs., 1982, award for outstanding scholarship Colombian Community, 1987; honored for authorship Friends of Libr., 1987, 88. Fellow Am. Anthrop. Assn.; mem. AAAS, Am. Assn. Mus., N.Y. Acad. Scis., S.W. Anthrop. Assn. Office: Bowers Mus 2002 N Main St Santa Ana CA 92706-2731

LABOWITZ, AARON PAUL, information systems executive; b. Panorama City, Calif., July 8, 1968; s. David Alan Labowitz and Michelle (Aaron) Merritt. BA in Econs., U. Calif., Santa Cruz, 1990; postgrad., U. So. Calif., 1993—. Graphics specialist The Santa Cruz (Calif.) Operation, 1990-91, program coord., 1991-92, mktg. analyst, 1992-93, info. systems mgr., 1993—. Active Big Bros./Big Sisters, 1991-93. Home: 14429 1/2 Benefit St Sherman Oaks CA 91423 Office: The Santa Cruz Operation 4000 Encinal St Santa Cruz CA 95061

LACEY, RONALD EDWARD, minority outreach advisor; b. Chgo., Apr. 6, 1958; s. Marion and Grace (Taylor) L.; m. Rochelle Rhone, Oct. 6, 1979 (div. Sept. 1983); children: Isaiah, Rhonda, Seriáh. Student, Yuba C.C., Marysville, Calif., 1985-87; BA, Chico State U., 1990. Outreach advisor Butte C.C., Oroville, Calif., 1991—; instr. Butte C.C., Oroville, 1991—. Activist Pan African Union, Chico, Calif., 1989; actor Martin Luther King Prodn. Co., Chico, 1989; big brother C.A.V.E., Chico, 1988; baseball mgr. Chico Little League, 1989—. With USN, 1976-80. Minority Equity fellow Chico State U., 1990, Lt. Rawlins award Chico State U., 1990.

LACHANCE, MURDOCK HENRY, materials consultant; b. Detroit, Dec. 12, 1920; s. Henry Andrew and Alpha Evangeline (Carlson) LaC.; 1 child, Julie Kay. BS, Mich. Tech. U., 1942, MS, 1947. Flight instr. Purdue Aero. Corp., West Lafayette, Ind., 1942-44; commd. ensign USN, 1944; prin. physical metalurgist Battelle Meml. Inst., Columbus, Ohio, 1947-57; rsch. metallurgist Whirlpool Rsch. Lab., St. Joseph, Mich., 1957-62; sr. scientist Xerox Electro-Optical Systems, Pasadena, Calif., 1962-83; freelance cons. in materials and failure analysis Pasadena, 1983—. Author and patentee in field. Mem. Sigma Xi (Calif. Inst. Tech. chpt.). Home: 260 S Chester Ave Pasadena CA 91106-3109

LACHMAN, ALAN B., dermatologist, surgeon; b. New Haven, Nov. 26, 1935; s. Sander E. and Goldye (Cummins) L.; m. Margaret Frances Lachman, Nov. 16, 1963; children: Tim, Lisa, Patrick, Elizabeth. BS, Haverford Coll., 1957; MD, U. Md., Balt., 1962. Diplomate Nat. Bd. Med. Examiners, Am. Bd. Dermatology. Internship in internal medicine U. Md. Hosp., Baltimore, Oreg., 1962-63; resident in internal medicine VA Hosp., Portland, 1965-66; residency in dermatology U. Oreg. Health Scis. Ctr., Portland, 1966-69; pres. Cedar Hills Dermatology Clinic, P.C., Portland, Oreg., 1969-; clin. prof. dermatology Oreg. Health Scis. U., Portland, 1970—; sr. cons. dermatology U.S. Vets. Hosp. & Clinics, Portland, 1980—. Contbr. articles to profl. jours. Sr. asst. surgeon USPHS, 1963-65. Fellow Am. Acad. Dermatology; mem. AMA, Oreg. Dermatology Soc., Pacific Dermatology Assn., Pacific N.W. Dermatology Soc., Oreg. Med. Assn., Washington County Med. Soc., Alpha Omega Alpha. Home: 2630 NW 144th Ave Beaverton OR 97006-5470 Office: Cedar Hills Dermatology 1585 SW Marlow Ave # 212 Portland OR 97225-5198

LACHMAN, BRANTON GEORGE, lawyer, science educator, pharmacist; b. Altadena, Calif., Nov. 7, 1952; s. Richard George and Blanche Marie (Bayless) L.; m. Sally Reid Johnson, Jan. 10, 1981; children: Hannah, Rose. BA, Calif. State U., Fullerton, 1975; PharmD in Pharmacy, U. So. Calif., L.A., 1979; JD (valedictorian), Western State U., 1992. Bar: Calif. 1992, U.S. Dist. Ct. (ctrl. dist.) Calif., 1992, U.S. Ct. Appeals (9th cir.) 1993; lic. pharmacist, Calif. Pvt. practice Riverside, Calif., 1979-81; hosp. pharmacist Western Med. Ctr., Santa Ana, Calif., 1981-83; clin. asst. prof. U. So. Calif., 1981-92; tchr. music Yucaipa (Calif.) High Sch., 1983-84; v.p. Pontil, Inc., Corona, Calif., 1984-89; clin. pharmacist PHI Health Care Mgmt. Inc., Laguna Hills, Calif., 1989-90; sci. educator Corona-Norco Unified Sch. Dist., 1990-92; assoc. Brunick, Alvarez & Battersby, San Bernardino, Calif., 1993—; adj. prof. Law Western State U., 1993—; reviewer Accreditation Evaluation Svc., Sacramento, 1985-90; guest cons. USPHS/NIH, Washington, 1989; cons. Women's Lifecare Program, Corona, 1990-92. Author: Community Pharmacy Practice Clerkship, 1983; columnist, 1979-90, Comment Home Education and Fundamental Rights: Can Johnny's Parents Teach Johnny?; contbr. articles to profl. jours.; editor-in-chief Western State U. Law Rev., 1991. Founding mem. Corona Peace Watch, 1987; judge sci. fair Corona-Norco Unified Sch. Dist., 1986, 89; treas. Hedrick for Sch. Bd., Corona, 1988, 92; pres. Corona Fine Arts Com., 1985. Mem. Am. Pharm. Assn. (officer 1987-89), Calif. State Bar Assn., Calif. Pharmacist Assn. (officer 1979-90), Riverside County Bar Assn., Peter M. Elliot Inn of Ct. Republican. Office: Brunick Alvarez & Battersby 1839 Commercenter West San Bernardino CA 92412

LACK, LARRY HENRY, small business owner; b. Richland, Wash., Aug. 27, 1952; s. Eugene Herman and Myrtle (Wellman) L.; m. Patricia Ann Henry, Aug. 19, 1978; children: Vicki Marie, Rachel Ann. Enlisted USAF, 1970, disabled vet., 1978; aircraft mechanic Ill., S.C., Okla. AFBs., 1970-78; inventor, prin. Lack Industries, Inc., Shreveport, La., 1979-85, Phoenix, 1985—; CEO Stellar Internat., Phoenix, 1991-92; cons. U.S. Air Force, Altus AFB, 1978-80, Cates & Phillips Patent Attys., Phoenix, 1985—; pres. La. Innovators Tech., Shreveport, 1981-82; lectr. Glendale Community Coll. 1987-88; guest lectr. Ariz. State U., 1989-90; authored legislation to regulate invention promotion cos. in Ariz., 1989. Patentee in field. Republican. Home: 223 Hardscrabble Rd Pine AZ 85544 Office: 3135 S 48th St Ste 3 Tempe AZ 85282-3160

LACKEY, ROBERT THOMAS, ecologist, educator; b. Kamloops, B.C., Can., May 18, 1944; s. Thomas A. and June M. (Cox) L.; m. Lana J. Apparius, June 24, 1967; children: Christopher, Karen. B.S. in Fisheries, Humboldt State U., 1967; M.S. in Zoology, U. Maine, 1968; Ph.D. in Fisheries and Wildlife, Colo. State U., 1971. Cert. fisheries scientist. Assoc. prof. Va. Poly. Inst. and State U., Blacksburg, Va., 1971-79; prof. Oreg. State U., Corvallis, 1982—; leader US FWS Nat. Water Resources Analysis Group, Kearneysville, W.Va., 1979-81; air pollution effects br. U.S. EPA, Corvallis, 1981-84, assoc. br. chief 1984-87, chief terrestrial br., 1987-89, dep. lab. dir. environ. rsch. lab., 1989—; assoc. dir. Ctr. for Analysis Environ. Change, 1991-. Contbr. articles to tech. jours. Fellow Am. Inst. Fishery Rsch. Biologists, mem. Ecol. Soc. Am., Am. Fisheries Soc. (cert. fisheries scientist, assoc. editor 1978-80). Office: US EPA 200 SW 35th St Corvallis OR 97333-4901

LACOMBE, RITA JEANNE, bank consultant; b. Panama City, Fla., Sept. 28, 1947; d. Robert Rosairio and Virginia May (Mauldin) L. AA, Los Angeles Pierce Coll., 1967; BSBA, Calif. State U., Northridge, 1969; postgrad., Stanford U., 1986. Br. mgr. Security Pacific Nat. Bank, San Fernando Valley, Calif., 1970-78; bankcard compliance officer, asst. v.p. Security Pacific Nat. Bank, Woodland Hills, Calif., 1978-82; sect. mgr., v.p. Security Pacific Nat. Bank, Los Angeles, 1982-87; sr. sales rep. corp. microcomputer sales ComputerLand, L.A., 1987-88; corp. sales rep. microcomputer sales ComputerLand, Northridge and Laguna Hills, Calif., 1988-89; sr. mgmt. cons. fin. industries group Deloitte & Touche, CPA, L.A., 1989—. Membership chair Sierra Club, Los Angeles, 1982. Mem. Nat. Assn. Female Execs. Democrat. Roman Catholic.

LA CROIX, SUMNER JONATHAN, economics educator; b. Hartford, Conn., Dec. 28, 1954; s. Harold Francis and Miriam Alma (McDermott) La C. BA, U. Va., 1976; MA, U. Wash., 1979, PhD, 1981. Asst. prof. dept. economics U. Hawaii, Honolulu, 1981-86, assoc. prof., 1986-90, prof., 1990—; vis. lectr. U. Canterbury, Chirstchurch, New Zealand, 1984, Australian Grad. Sch. of Mgmt., Sydney, Australia, 1987; vis. prof., Fudan U., Shanghai, China, 1990. Contbr. articles to profl. jours. Treas. Life Found., Honolulu, 1984-86; chmn. Hawaii Names Project, Honolulu, 1988-90. Recipient Puhlick Vol. award Life Found., Honolulu, 1991. Mem. Am. Econ. Assn., Western Econ. Assn., Econ. History Assn., Cliometric Soc. Democrat. Office: U Hawaii Dept Econs Honolulu HI 96822

LACY, LEE MARVA LOU, educator; b. Longview, Tex., Dec. 28, 1942; d. Louis and Grace Tecumseh (Davis) Armstrong; BS in Math., Prairie View (Tex.) A&M U., 1965; MA in Secondary Math. Edn. (grantee Roosevelt Sch. Dist. 1977-78), Ariz. State U., 1978; m. Troy Lee Lacy, June 20, 1965; children: Corwyn Enrico, Aimee Siubhan, Gardenia Catriona. Tchr. math. schs. in Tex., Nebr., Md. and Ariz., 1965-68, 69-77; sr. gen. edn. instr., counselor Washington Jobs Corps, 1968; tchr. math., spl. tchr. for gifted C.O. Greenfield Jr. High Sch., Phoenix, 1978-82; math and gifted resource tchr. T.B. Barr Sch., Phoenix, 1982-85; instr. math. South Mountain C.C. at Ariz. State U., Tempe, 1985-87, Glendale C.C. MCCCD, 1987—; faculty assoc. Prairie View A&M U., 1981-83; vis. math. tchr. South Mountain C.C., Phoenix, 1982-85; workshop leader, cons. in field. Vol., Arthritis Found., Leukemia Soc.; v.p., trustee sanctuary choir First Instl. Bapt. Ch., Phoenix. Mem. Nat. Council Tchrs. Math., NEA, Assn. Supervision and Curriculum Devel., Ariz. Edn. Assn., Ariz. Assn. Tchrs. Math., Roosevelt Classroom Tchrs. Assn., Ariz. State U. Alumni Assn., Am. Math. Assn. 2-Yr. Colls., Math. Assn. Am., Maricopa County NAACP, Delta Sigma Theta Alumnae. Baptist. Home: 9404 S Kenneth Pl Tempe AZ 85284-4104 Office: Glendale CC Faculty Office Bldg 04-120 Glendale AZ 85302

LADD, ALAN WALBRIDGE, JR., motion picture company executive; b. L.A., Oct. 22, 1937; s. Alan Walbridge and Marjorie Jane (Harrold) L.; m. Patricia Ann Beazley, Aug. 30, 1959 (div. 1983); children: Kelliann, Tracy Elizabeth, Amanda Sue; m. Cindra Kay, July 13, 1985. Motion picture agt. Creative Mgmt., L.A., 1963-69; v.p. prodn. 20th Century-Fox Film Corp., L.A., 1973-74; sr. v.p. 20th Century-Fox Film Corp. (Worldwide Prodns. div.), Beverly Hills, Calif., 1974-76; pres. 20th Century-Fox Pictures, 1976-79, Ladd Co., Burbank, Calif., 1979-83; pres., chief oper. officer MGM/UA Entertainment Co., 1983-86; chief exec. officer MGM/UA Entertainment Co, from 1986, also chmn. bd. dirs.; chmn., chief exec. officer Metro-Goldwyn-Mayer Pictures, Inc., Culver City, Calif., until 1988; pres., chmn. Pathe Entertainment, L.A., 1989-90; co-chmn. MGM-Pathe, L.A., 1990-93, MGM, L.A., 1990-93; chmn., CEO MGM-Pathe Communications, L.A., 1991—. Producer: (films) Walking Stick, 1969, A Severed Head, 1969, TamLin, 1970, Villian Zee and Co, 1971, Fear is the Key, 1973; exec. producer: (films) Nightcomers, 1971, Vice Versa, 1988. Served with USAF, 1961-63. Office: MGM 2500 Broadway St Santa Monica CA 90404

LADEHOFF, ROBERT LOUIS, bishop; b. Feb. 19, 1932; m. Jean Arthur Burcham; 1 child, Robert Louis Jr. Grad., Duke U., 1954, Gen. Theol. Sem., 1957, Va. Theol. Sem., 1980. Ordained deacon, priest The Episcopal Ch., 1957;. Priest in charge N.C. parishes, 1957-60; rector St. Christopher's Ch., Charlotte, N.C., 1960-74, St. John's Ch., Fayetteville, 1974-85; bishop, co-adjutor of Oreg., 1985, bishop, 1986—. Office: Diocese of Oreg PO Box 467 Lake Oswego OR 97034-0467*

LADOUCEUR, PATRICIA ALLAIRE, family services program administrator; b. L.A., June 15, 1955; d. Leo Frederick and Marjorie Ruth (Rabey) L. BA in Communications, U. Calif. San Diego, La Jolla, 1978; MA in Sociology, U. Oreg., 1981; MA in Clin. Psychology, John F. Kennedy U., 1985; PhD in Sociology, U. Oreg., 1984. Lic. marriage, family and child therapist, Calif. Teaching asst. U. Oreg., Eugene, 1982-83; rsch. cons. Nat. Coun. Crime and Delinquency, Inc., San Francisco, 1983-84, project mgr., 1984-87; staff therapist Psychotherapy Inst., Berkeley, Calif., 1986-89; pvt. practice psychotherapy Berkeley, 1987—; program coord. Youth and Family Svcs. Solano County, Inc., Vallejo, Calif., 1987-89, program dir., 1989—; mem. Children's Network adv. com. to County Bd. Suprs., Solano County, 1990. Contbr. articles on troubled youth to profl. jours. Nat. Inst. Justice fellow, 1983-84; Alcohol Rsch. Group fellow, Berkeley, 1983-84. Mem. Calif. Assn. Marriage and Family Therapists. Office: 2424 Dwight Way Ste 6 Berkeley CA 94704-2365

LAFON, RICHARD HARLAND, health care management consultant; b. Ronceverte, W.Va., June 4, 1948; s. Richard Harland and Faye Elouise (Armstrong) LaF.; children: J'nette Chere, Sarah Beth. BA in Polit. Sci., Calif. State U., L.A., 1974. Diplomate Am. Bd. Vocat. Experts; cert. rehab. counselor, cert. ins. rehab. specialist, nat. bd. cert. counselor; expert vocat. witness. Asst. regional mgr. Internat. Rehab. Assocs., Arcadia, Calif., 1974-76; pres. Comprehensive Rehab. Svcs., Arcadia, 1976-81, Comprehensive Rehab. Svcs. of Fla., Roanoke, Va., 1981-82; prin. LaFon Mgmt. & Cons., Lake Arrowhead, Calif., 1982—; exec. dir. Nat. Assn. of Rehab. Profls. in Pvt. Sector, Lake Arrowhead, 1984-90; vocat. expert, health care mgmt. cons. Lake Arrowhead, 1990—; presenter tng. on advt. and mktg. in rehab., other health care svcs. With U.S. Army, 1966-69. Decorated Combat Infantryman's Badge, Purple Heart, Bronze Star with V. Mem. DAV (life), Nat. Rehab. Counselors Assn., Nat. Rehab. Assn., Am. Counseling Assn., U.S. C. of C., Lake Arrowhead C. of C. Office: PO Box 1767 26139 Hwy 189 Lake Arrowhead CA 92352-1767

LA FORCE, JAMES CLAYBURN, JR., economist, educator; b. San Diego, Dec. 28, 1928; s. James Clayburn and Beatrice Maureen (Boyd) La F.; m. Barbara Lea Latham, Sept. 23, 1952; children: Jessica, Allison, Joseph. B.A., San Diego State Coll., 1951; M.A., UCLA, 1958, Ph.D., 1962. Asst. prof. econs. UCLA, 1962-66, assoc. prof., 1967-70, prof., 1971-93, prof. emeritus, 1993—, chmn. dept. econs., 1969-78, dean Anderson Sch. Mgmt., 1978-93; acting dean Hong Kong U. Sci. & Tech., 1991—; bd. dirs. Rockwell Internat., Eli Lilly & Co., Jacobs Engring. Group Inc., Shearson V.I.P. Separate Account, The Blackrock Funds, Imperial Credit Industries, Inc., Payden & Rygel Investment Trust, Providence Investment Coun. Mut. Funds; chmn. adv. com. Calif Workmen's Compensation, 1974-75. Author: The Development of the Spanish Textile Industry 1750-1800, 1965, (with Warren C. Scoville) The Economic Development of Western Europe, vols. 1-5, 1969-70. Bd. dirs. Nat. Bur. Econ. Rsch., 1975-88, Found. Francisco Marroquin, Mgmt. Edn. Assocs., The G. and R. Loeb Found., The Lynde and Harry Bradley Found.; trustee Inst. Contemporary Studies, 1974—, Pacific Legal Found., 1981-86; trustee Found. for Rsch. in Econs. and Edn., 1970—, chmn., 1977—; bd. overseers Hoover Inst. on War, Revolution and Peace, 1979-85, 86-93; mem. nat. coun. on humanities NEH, 1981-88; chmn. President's Task Force on Food Assistance, 1983-84. Social Sci. Research Council research tng. fellow, 1958-60; Fulbright sr. research grantee, 1965-66; Am. Philos. Soc. grantee, 1965-66. Mem. Econ. History Assn., Mont Pelerin Soc., Phi Beta Kappa. Office: UCLA Anderson Grad Sch Mgmt 405 Hilgard Ave Los Angeles CA 90024-1301

LAFRANCE, LEO JAMES, mechanical engineering educator, consultant; b. Muskegon, Mich., Dec. 22, 1942; s. Raymond Roland and Margaret Cleo (Schultz) LaF.; divorced; children: Evan James, Janine Marie, Clare Pauline. AS in Pre-Engring., Muskegon C.C., 1963; BSME, Mich. State U., 1965, MSME, 1967; PhD in Mech. Engring., Purdue U., 1974. Profl. engr., N.Mex. Product engr. Corning Glass Works, Albion, Mich., 1967-71; prin. engr. Borg-Warner, York, Pa., 1974-76; asst. prof. mech. engring. N.Mex. State U., Las Cruces, 1976-80, assoc. prof., 1980—, assoc. dept. head, 1988-92. Contbr. articles to profl. jours. Mem. ASME (profl. devel. chmn. Region XII 1990-92, chmn. Rio Grande sect. 1991-92), NSPE, Soc. Mfg. Engrs., Am. Soc. for Engring. Edn. Home: 2292 LaPaloma Dr Las Cruces NM 88011-5079 Office: NMex State U Mech Engring Dept Box 3001/Dept 3450 Las Cruces NM 88003-0001

LAGASSE, BRUCE KENNETH, structural engineer; b. Bklyn., Feb. 1, 1940; s. Joseph F. Lagasse and Dora S. Gould. BSME, U. Calif., Berkeley, 1964. Structures engr. Rockwell Internat., Canoga Park, Calif., 1964-69; mem. tech. staff Hughes Aircraft Co., Los Angeles, 1969-70; scientist/engr. Hughes Aircraft Co., El Segundo, Calif., 1972—; sr. engr. Litton Ship Systems, Los Angeles, 1971-72; lectr. Hughes Aircraft Co., El Segundo, 1980—; cons. in field, Van Nuys, Calif., 1979—. Libertarian state chmn., Los Angeles, 1977-79, nat. committeeman, Washington, 1979-81. Mem. ASME. Home: 7247-C Balboa Blvd Van Nuys CA 91406

LAGER, DOUGLAS ROY, property tax consultant; b. Eau Claire, Wis., Dec. 10, 1947; m. Barbara Joyce Johnston, Oct. 6, 1985; 1 child, Jeffrey D. BSBA in Acctg., Rockhurst Coll., Kansas City, Mo., 1971. Cert. gen. appraiser, Colo. Head dept. personal property Jackson County Assessor, Kansas City, Mo., 1971-74; property assessment specialist Wis. Dept. Revenue, Madison, 1974-80; property tax cons. Property Tax Svc., Mpls., 1980-84, Denver, 1984-87; property tax cons. Avtax, Inc., Denver, 1987—. Home: 9 White Alder Littleton CO 80127 Office: Avtax Inc 5690 DTC Blvd Ste 290 Englewood CO 80111

LAGERLOF, RONALD STEPHEN, sound recording engineer; b. Long Beach, Calif., Mar. 24, 1956; s. Paul Richard and Harriett Jane Lagerlof; m. Janice Martin, June 7, 1989; 1 child, Jackson Martin. Chief rec. engr. Wishbone Rec., Muscle Shoals, Ala., 1978-79; tech. engr. TM Communications, Dallas, 1980-81; gen. mgr. Studio Svcs., Inc., Dallas, 1984-85; head tech. engr. Dallas Sound Lab., 1985-87; studio mgr. Motown/Hitsville Studios, West Hollywood, Calif., 1987-89; dir. tech. ops. Soundworks West, West Hollywood, 1989-90; ops. mgr. Skywalker Sound divsn. Lucasfilm, Marin County, Calif., 1990-92; owner Visioneering Design Co., Woodland Hills, Calif., 1992—; cons. digital audio-for-video installations Pacific Ocen Post and Record Plant studios. Engr. LP rec. Family Tradition, 1979 (gold record 1980); re-rec. engr. (TV spl.) Motown Merry Christmas, 1987 (Emmy nomination 1988); songwriter copyrighted and pub. works. Mem. Audio Engring. Soc., Soc. Motion Picture and TV Engrs.

LAGORIO, IRENE ROSE, artist, writer; b. Oakland, Calif., May 2, 1921; d. Marcello Natalino and Argentina Maria (Sarmoria) L. BA, U. Calif., Berkeley, 1942, MA, 1943; postgrad., Columbia U., 1945, 46. Art instr. Napa (Calif.) Jr. High, Jr. Coll., 1943-45; supervising tchr. Oakland (Calif.) Pub. Schs., 1945-50; guest lectr. Holy Names Coll., Oakland, 1971, U. Calif. Extension, Berkeley, 1972-73; ednl. curator Calif. Palace of Legion of Honor, San Francisco, 1950, dir. AFGA, 1950-56; pres. Carmel (Calif.) Art Assn., 1972; art critic, writer, illustrator The Herald Newspaper, Monterey, Calif., 1974-89; freelance artist, writer Carmel, 1989—. Artist (mosaic murals) Moon Vista, 1968, Galaxy, 1962, (serigraph) Vainglory, 1955, (mixed media) Articles of Constraint, 1953; one-woman shows include Galleria Pro-Padova, Padua, Italy, 1967, P.G. Mus. of Natural History, Pacific Grove, Calif., 1970, U. Teknik, Trabazon, Turkey, 1967; author: Art History's Innovators, 1992; contbr. poems Ventana Mag.; author: (poetry) Oakland A's in Verse, 1990. Grantee Chapelbrook Found., 1968; recipient Best of Show award Monterey Mus. of Art, 1971. Mem. Earthquake Engring. Rsch. Inst., Ars Associated Found. (v.p.), Am.-Italian Hist. Assn., Phi Beta Kappa. Home: PO Box 153 Carmel CA 93921-0153 Office: 1st and Mission Sts Carmel CA 93921

LAGREEN, ALAN LENNART, public relations executive, radio personality; b. Burbank, Calif., May 20, 1951; s. Lennart Franklin and Mary (Cassara) LaG.; m. Wendy Diane Gilmaker, June 28, 1975; 1 child, Cara Diane. BA, U. So. Calif., L.A., 1972. Pub. rels. asst. Dames & Moore, L.A., 1972-75; asst. pub. Orange County Illustrated, Newport Beach, Calif., 1975; asst. exec. dir. Toastmasters Internat., Santa Ana, Calif., 1975-86; meetings and conv. mgr. Fluor Corp., Irvine, Calif., 1986-87; v.p. mktg. CCRA, Inc., Santa Ana, 1987—; morning radio personality Sta. KSBR-FM Jazz Radio, Mission Viejo, Calif. Home: 120 W 20th St Santa Ana CA 92706-2722

LAI, HIM MARK, writer; b. San Francisco, Nov. 1, 1925; s. Mark Bing and Hing Mui (Dong) L.; m. Laura Jung, June 12, 1953. AA, San Francisco Jr. Coll., 1945; BS in Engring., U. Calif., Berkeley, 1947. Mech. engr. Utilities Engring. Bur., San Francisco, 1948-51, Bechtel Corp., San Francisco, 1953-84; lectr. Chinese Am. history San Francisco State U., 1969, 72-75, U. Calif., Berkeley, 1978-79, 84; researcher, writer on Chinese Am. history San Francisco, 1967—; dir. Chinese of America 1785-1980 Exhbn. Chinese Culture Found. San Francisco, 1979-80, adv. bd. Chinese Am. Women's Project, 1981-83, coord. Chinese Am. search for roots program, 1991—; cons. proposed El Pueblo de L.A. State Hist. Park Chinese Am. Mus., 1987, 89, Asian Am. Studies Program Chinese Materials Rsch. Collection, U. Calif., Berkeley, 1986-88; adj. prof. Asian Am. studies dept. San Francisco State U., 1990—; coord. Chinese Community Hour, Cantonese radio program, 1971-84. Co-author: Chinese of America, 1785-1980: Exhibition Catalog, 1980, Island:Poetry and History of Chinese Immigrants on Angel Island, 1910-1940, 1980; author: A History Reclaimed: An Annotated Bibliography and Guide of Chinese Language Materials on the Chinese of America, 1986,

From Overseas Chinese to Chinese American: History of Development of Chinese American Society During the Twentieth Century, 1992; co-editor: Collected Works of Gilbert Woo, 1991; mem. editorial bd. Amerasia Journal, 1979—, Chinese America: History and Perspective, 1986—; contbr. articles to profl. jours. Mem. Chinese Hist. Soc. Am. (bd. dirs. 1972-81, 84, 85-91, 93), Chinese Culture Found. San Francisco (bd. dirs. 1975-85, 87—, bd. chairperson 1983, 84, 85, 89). Home: 357 Union St San Francisco CA 94133

LAI, NGAI CHIN, physiologist; b. Singapore, Sept. 14, 1956; came to U.S. 1979; s. Shee Ngee and Shook Chin (Kiew) L.; m. Maria Kathy Zuazua, Oct. 21, 1982. BA, Our Lady of the Lake U., San Antonio, 1982; MS, Scripps Instn. Oceanography, San Diego, 1987; PhD, Scripps Inst. Oceanography, San Diego, 1989. Enumerator Ministry of Nat. Devel., Singapore, 1973; armored engr. Ministry of Def., Singapore, 1976-78; teaching asst. Our Lady of the Lake U., San Antonio, 1980-82; lab. asst. S.W. Found. Biol. Ctr., San Antonio, 1982; rsch. asst. Scripps Instn. of Oceanography, San Diego, 1984-89, postgrad. rschr., 1989; resident rsch. assoc. NRC, Washington, 1990; rsch. physiologist VA Med. Ctr., San Diego, 1991—; cons. NOAA, 1987; lectr. U. San Diego, 1989-92; rsch. fellow Scripps Instn. of Oceanography, 1991—; ind. investigator S.W. Fisheries Sci. Ctr., San Diego, 1990-92; mentor Scripps Undergrad. Rsch. Fellowship Program, 1990. Contbr. articles to profl. jours.; referee Can. Jour. Zoology, 1991, Environ. Biology of Fishes, 1992. Sigma Xi judge San Diego County High Sch. Sci. Fair, 1991. Presdl. scholar Our Lady of the Lake U., 1980-82. Mem. Am. Chem. Soc., Am. Soc. Zoologists, Sigma Zeta, Alpha Chi, Sigma Xi. Home: 10545 Ponder Way San Diego CA 92126 Office: VA Med Ctr 3350 LaJolla Village San Diego CA 92161

LAI, WAIHANG, educator; b. Hong Kong, Jan. 7, 1939; s. Sing and Yu-ching L.; came to U.S., 1964; BA, Chinese U. Hong Kong, 1964; MA, Claremont Grad. Sch., 1967; m. Celia Cheung, Aug. 13, 1966. Asst. prof. art Maunaolu Coll., Maui, Hawaii, 1968-70; assoc. prof. art Kauai (Hawaii) Community Coll., 1970—. Vis. prof. art Ariz. State U., Tempe, summer 1967. Recipient NISOD Excellence award U. Tex., 1993. Mem. Am., Kauai (pres. 1974—) watercolor socs., Phila. Watercolor Club, Hawaii Computer Art Soc., Kauai Oriental Art Soc. (pres. 1981—). Author: The Chinese Landscape Paintings of Waihang Lai, 1966, The Watercolors of Waihang Lai, 1967; illustrator: The Tao of Practice Success, 1991, Advertisements for Acupuncturists, 1992. Home: PO Box 363 Lihue HI 96766-0363 Office: Kauai Community Coll Lihue HI 96766

LAIDIG, ELDON LINDLEY, financial planner; b. Oberlin, Kans., Jan. 20, 1932; s. Ira Lawless and Minnie Lorene (Williams) L.; m. Mary Jane Urban, Feb. 13, 1953 (dec. June 1981); 1 child, Larry Wayne; m. Lois Audrey Davey Cameron, Feb. 11, 1983. BS, Ft. Hay Kans. State U., 1954; MS, U. Tex., 1960, PhD, 1967. CFP. Jr. high prin. Jefferson County Pub. Schs., Arvada, Colo., 1963-88; pvt. practice fin. planner Personal Benefit Svcs., Arvada, 1988—. Author: The Influence of Situational Factors on Administrative Behavior, 1967, An Organizational Manual, 1979; editor various local and state newsletters. Bd. dirs. Highlander's Inc., Denver, 1978-83, Arvada Coun. for the Arts and Humanities, 1982, chmn., 1988-93; pres. Jefferson County Sch. Adminstrs., Lakewood, Colo., 1971-72; elder Arvada Presbyn., 1964—; v.p. Arvada Sister Cities Internat., 1992—. Named as Comdg. Officer of Outstanding Coast Guard Unit, 2nd Coast Guard Dist., 1968; recipient Disting. Svc. citation U.S. Dept. of Def., 1974, Unit citation Def. Civil Preparedness Agy., 1974, Don Kemp award for outstanding fundraising Arvada Ctr. for the Arts & Humanities, 1983. Mem. Arvada Hist. Soc. (v.p.. 1983-85), Res. Officers Assn. (pres. Denver chpt. 1974, pres. Dept. of Colo. 1978, nat. councilman 1979), Arvada Sentinel and N.W. Metro C. of C. (Arvada Man of Yr. 1990), Rotary (bd. dirs. Arvada chpt. 1989-90). Home: 7038 Ammons St Arvada CO 80004-1849 Office: Personal Benefit Svcs 5400 Ward Rd Arvada CO 80002-1819

LAIDLAW, DAVID HALES, computer graphics researcher, consultant; b. Binghamton, N.Y., Mar. 24, 1961; s. Charles Dean and Patricia Huntley (Hales) L.; m. Barbara Jane Meier, Sep. 16, 1989. ScB summa cum laude, Brown U., 1983, ScM, 1985; MS, Calif. Inst. Tech., 1992. Rsch. asst. Brown U., Providence, R.I., 1983-85; computer graphics software engr. Stellar Computer, Inc., Newton, Mass., 1986-88, visualization software engr., 1988-89; rsch. asst. Calif. Inst. Tech., Pasadena, 1989-91; cons. Advanced Visual Systems, Inc., Waltham, Mass., 1991—; computer graphics cons. Stardent Computer, Inc., Sunnyvale, Santa Barbara, Calif., Concord, Mass., 1989—. Co-creator (film) Topology and Mechanics: Linear Oscillators and the Hypersphere, 1983, Topology and Mechanics: Flows on the Torus, 1983, The Hypersphere: Foliations and Projections, 1985; covers and illustrations for many books and mags., 1983-90; contbr. articles to profl. jours., 1986-90. Fellow Calif. Inst. Tech., 1989. Mem. IEEE, Assn. Computing Machinery, Special Interest Group for Graphics, Sigma Xi. Democrat. Home: 1146 Heather Sq Pasadena CA 91104-3708 Office: Calif Inst of Tech 350-74 Pasadena CA 91125

LAIDLAW, DOUGLAS MCNEILL, JR., printing industry executive; b. L.A., Nov. 16, 1954; s. Douglas McNeill and Jean Metcalf (Monroe) L.; m. Kathleen Mary Laudenback, Sept. 20, 1986; 1 child, Douglas McNeill III. BSBA, U. So. Calif., L.A., 1978. Prodn. mgr. MacDermott & Chant, Welshpool, Wales, 1977; field rep. Southland Corp., L.A., 1978-80; pres. Creative Web Systems, Rancho Dominguez, Calif., 1980-91, Laidlaw & Assocs., Redondo Beach, Calif., 1991—. Mem. Printing Industries Assn., Nat. Assn. Printers and Lithographers (bd. dirs. 1989—, Soderstrom Soc.), Graphic Arts Tech. Found., Printing Industries Assn. So. Calif. (bd. dirs., exec. vice chmn. 1986—), Printing Industries of Calif. (bd. dirs. 1988—), Graphic Arts Literacy Alliance (bd. dirs. 1988—). Republican. Office: Laidlaw & Assocs Ste 1 230 S Guadalupe Ave Redondo Beach CA 90277

LAIDLAW, HARRY HYDE, JR., entomology educator; b. Houston, Apr. 12, 1907; s. Harry Hyde and Elizabeth Louisa (Quinn) L.; BS, La. State U., 1933, MS, 1934; PhD (Univ. fellow, Genetics fellow, Wis. Dormitory fellow, Wis. Alumni Rsch. Found. fellow), U. Wis., 1939; m. Ruth Grant Collins, Oct. 26, 1946; 1 child, Barbara Scott Laidlaw Murphy. Teaching asst. La. State U., 1933-34, rsch. asst., 1934-35; prof. biol. sci. Oakland City (Ind.) Coll., 1939-41; state apiarist Ala. Dept. Agr. and Industries, Montgomery, 1941-42; entomologist First Army, N.Y.C., 1946-47; asst. prof. entomology, asst. apiculturist U. Calif.-Davis, 1947-53, assoc. prof. entomology, assoc. apiculturist, 1953-59, prof. entomology, apiculturist, 1959-74, asso. dean Coll. Agr., 1960-64, chair agr. faculty, staff, 1965-66, prof. entomology emeritus, apiculturist emeritus, 1974—; coord. U. Calif.-Egypt Agrl. Devel. Program, AID, 1979-83. Rockefeller Found. grantee, Brazil, 1954-55, Sudan, 1967; honored guest Tamagawa U., Tokyo, 1980. Trustee, Yolo County (Calif.) Med. Soc. Scholarship Com., 1965-83. Served to capt. AUS, 1942-46. Recipient Cert. of Merit Am. Bee Jour., 1957, Spl. Merit award U. Calif.-Davis, 1959, Merit award Calif. Central Valley Bee Club, 1974, Merit award Western Apicultural Soc., 1980, Gold Merit award Internat. Fedn. Beekeepers' Assns., 1986; recipient Disting. Svc. award Ariz. Beekeepers Assn., 1988. Cert. of Appreciation Calif. State Beekeepers' Assn., 1987, award Alan Clemson Meml. Found., 1989: NIH grantee, 1963-66; NSF grantee, 1966-74. Fellow AAAS, Entomol. Soc. Am. (C.W. Woodworth award Pacific br. 1981, honoree spl. symposium 1990); mem. Am. Inst. Biol. Scis., Am. Soc. Naturalists, Am. Soc. Zoologists, Internat. Bee Rsch. Assn., Nat. Assn. Uniformed Svcs., Ret. Officers Assn. (2d v.p. Sacramento chpt. 1984-86), Scabbard and Blade, Sigma Xi (treas. Davis chpt. 1959-60, v.p. chpt. 1966-67), Alpha Gamma Rho (pres. La. chpt. 1933-34, counsellor Western Province 1960-66). Democrat. Presbyterian. Author books, the most recent being: Instrumental Insemination of Honey Bee Queens, 1977; Contemporary Queen Rearing, 1979; author slide set: Instrumental Insemination of Queen Honey Bees, 1976. Achievements include determination of cause of failure of attempts to artificially inseminate queen honey bees; invention of instruments and procedures to consistently accomplish same; elucidation of genetic relationships of individuals of polyandrous honey bee colonies; design of genetic procedures for behavioral study and breeding of honey bees for general and specific uses. Home: 761 Sycamore Ln Davis CA 95616-3432 Office: U Calif Dept Entomology Davis CA 95616

LAIRD, ANDREW KENNETH, radio broadcast engineer; b. Stockton, Calif., May 28, 1943; s. Andy George and Helene (Nielsen) L.; m. Diane Louise Bradley, Nov. 7, 1981; 1 stepchild, Jason McCoy. BS in Physics, Coll. of Principia, 1965; postgrad., U. Denver, 1965-66. Staff engr. Sta. KWGN-TV, Denver, 1966-67; chief engr. Sta. KLAK-AM-FM, Denver, 1967-72, Sta. KDAY, L.A., 1972-88; v.p. engring./radio group Heritage Media Corp., Bellevue, Wash., 1988—; cons. Laird Audio/Studio Design, L.A., 1976-88. Columnist Radio & Record Mag., 1974-76; contbr. articles to profl. jours. Staff sgt. Colo. Air N.G., 1966-72. Mem. Soc. Broadcast Engrs., Profl. Broadcast Engrs. (cert.). Office: Heritage Media Corp 15375 SE 30th Pl # 300 Bellevue WA 98007

LAIRD, FRANK N., political science educator; b. Ashtabula, Ohio, Dec. 12, 1952; s. Frank Earl and Mary Yolanda (Fiori) L.; m. Pamela Walker, June 17, 1989. BA, Middlebury Coll., 1975; postgrad., Edinburgh (Scotland) U., 1975-76; PhD, MIT, 1985. Postdoctoral rsch. fellow Harvard U., Cambridge, Mass., 1985-87; asst. prof. U. Denver, 1987—; cons. Sigma Xi, New Haven, Conn., 1985. Contbr. articles to profl. jours. Mem. Am. Polit. Sci. Assn., AAAS, Soc. for Risk Analysis, Assn. for Pub. Policy Analysis and Mgmt., Soc. for Social Studies of Sci. Office: U Denver Grad Sch Internat Studies Denver CO 80208

LAIRD, JERE DON, news reporter; b. Topeka, Aug. 8, 1933; s. Gerald Howard and Vivian Gertrude (Webb) L.; m. Alexandra Berezowsky, Aug. 4, 1957; children: Lee, Jennifer, Christopher. BA in Journalism, U. Nev., 1960. Disc jockey Sta. KHBC Radio, Hilo, Hawaii, 1949-50; announcer, chief engr. Sta. KOLO Radio, Reno, Nev., 1951-58; program dir. Sta. KOLO-TV, Reno, 1958-60; news reporter Sta. KCRA Radio and TV, Sacramento, Calif., 1960-61, Sta. KRLA Radio, L.A., 1962-63; news reporter, editor Sta. KNXT-TV, L.A., 1964-68; news reporter, fin. editor Sta. KNX-CBS Radio, L.A., 1968—; fin. reporter Sta. KCBS-TV, L.A., 1990—; lectr. U. So. Calif., L.A., 1984-85; instr. Calif. State U., Northridge, 1978-79. Cpl. U.S. Army, 1953-55. Recipient Emmy award, L.A., 1964, Peabody award, U. Ga., 1984, Best Bus. News award, L.A. Press Club, 1983, 84, 86, 87, 88, 89, Martin K. Gainsburgh award, Fiscal Policy Coun., Fla., 1978. Mem. Radio TV News Assn. (bd. dirs. 1966-68, Golden Mike award 1984), Sigma Delta Chi. Office: Sta KNX-CBS 6121 W Sunset Blvd Los Angeles CA 90028-6455

LAIRD, MARY See WOOD, LARRY

LAIRD, PAMELA SUE, marketing consultant; b. Conneaut, Ohio, Aug. 6, 1955; d. Howard Duane and Joan Elaine (Walrath) L.; m. Paul Lyman Bixby, June 14, 1979 (div. June 1983); m. Mark Peter Jacobsen, May 30, 1987. BSJ, Northwestern U., 1978, M in Mgmt., 1979. Asst. brand mgr. Procter & Gamble, Cin., 1979-81; brand mgr. Clorox Co., Oakland, Calif., 1981-84; mgr. new bus. DHL Worldwide Express, Redwood City, Calif., 1984-86; pres., owner PSL Mktg. Resources, San Francisco, 1986—. Bd. dirs. Leadership San Francisco Coun., 1989—, v.p., 1991, pres. 1992, Jr. League San Francisco, Advs. for Women, San Francisco. Recipient Bus. Achievement award San Francisco C. of C., 1991. Mem. San Francisco C. of C. (bd. dirs. 1992). Office: 10 Lombard St # 400 San Francisco CA 94111-1109

LAIRD, RODNEY ALAN, manufacturing engineer; b. St. Louis, June 21, 1961; s. John Major Jr. and Carol Yvonne (Christy) L.; m. Sarah Elizabeth Hickey, Feb. 17, 1990; 1 child, Peter Robert Alan. BA in Physics, Grinnell Coll., 1983; BSME, Washington U., St. Louis, 1985; MS in Mfg. Systems Engring., Stanford U., 1991. Process devel. engr. Hewlett Packard, Palo Alto, Calif., 1985-91; sr. mfg. engr. Acuson, Mountain View, Calif., 1991—. Vol. tutor Menlo-Atherton High Sch., Menlo Park, Calif., 1992. Mem. Surface Mount Tech. Assn. Office: Acuson 1220 Charleston Rd Mountain View CA 94039

LAITIN, HOWARD, aerospace executive, educator; b. Bklyn., Nov. 18, 1931; s. Jerome S. and Shirley (Fitzig) L.; m. Elizabeth Watson, Sep. 3, 1961; children: Kenneth, Steven, Linda. BA, Bklyn. Coll., 1952; MA, Harvard U., 1953, PhD, 1956. Registered profl. engr., Calif. Med. economist Hosp. Coun. Greater N.Y., N.Y.C., 1954-56; rsch. dir. Michael Saphier & Assoc., N.Y.C., 1956; project dir. Army Med. Svc., Washington (D.C.), San Antonio, 1957-59; sr. economist Rand Corp., Santa Monica, Calif., 1959-62; clin. assoc. prof. UCLA, 1959-76; mgr. Hughes Aircraft Co., Culver City, CAlif., 1962-82; adj. prof. U. So. Calif., Los Angeles, 1966-89; chief scientist Hughes Aircraft Co., El Segundo, Calif., 1982—; advisor/cons. various govtl's offices, Rand Corp., Hudson Inst., S.W. Found. among others. Author/Co-author in field. Chmn. exec. bd. Gov.'s Task Force on Solid Waste Mgmt., Sacramento, 1969-70, Solid Waste Mgmt. & Resource Recovery Adv. Coun., State of Calif., 1970-73; active Calif. State Assembly's Sci. Tech. Adv. Coun., Sacramento, 1970-72, Exec. Coun. Solid Waste Mgmt. Com., County of Los Angeles, 1972-92. Lt. col. U.S. Army, 1956—, Rsch. Devel. Adv. Coun. Nat. Air Pollution Adminstrn., Washington (D.C.). Recipient Honorary Svc. award Calif. Congress of Parents and Tchrs.; L.A. County Bd. Suprs., Calif. State Assembly, Torrance City Coun. commendations; N.Y. State, Charles Hayden, Thayer scholar. Mem. Phi Beta Kappa, Alpha Kappa Delta. Office: Hughes Aircraft Co PO Box 902 El Segundo CA 90245-0902

LAITONE, EDMUND VICTOR, mechanical engineer; b. San Francisco, Sept. 6, 1915; s. Victor S. L.; m. Dorothy Bishop, Sept. 1, 1951; children: Victoria, Jonathan A. BSME, U. Calif., Berkeley, 1938; PhD in Applied Mechanics, Stanford U., 1960. Aero. engr. Nat. Adv. Com. for Aeros., Langley Field, Va., 1938-45; sect. head, flight engr. Cornell Aero. Lab., Buffalo, 1945-47; prof. U. Calif., Berkeley, 1947—; cons. aero. engr. Hughes Aircraft & Douglas Aircraft, 1948-78; U.S. acad. rep. to flight mechanics AGARD/NATO, 1984-88; chmn. engring. dept. U. Calif. Extension, Berkeley, 1979—. Author: Surface Waves, 1960; author, editor: Integrated Design of Advanced Fighter Aircraft, 1987; contbr. articles to Jour. Aero. Scis., Aircraft and Math. Jour. Named Miller Rsch. prof., 1960, U.S. Exch. prof., Moscow, 1964; vis. fellow Balliol Coll., 1968; vis. prof. Northwestern Poly. Inst., Xian, China, 1980. Fellow AIAA (San Francisco region chmn. 1960-61, assoc. fellow 1964-88); mem. Am. Math Soc., Am. Soc. for Engring. Edn. Home: 6915 Wilson Way El Cerrito CA 94530-1853 Office: U of Calif Dept Mech Engring Berkeley CA 94720

LAIWALA, SADRUDIN, software engineer; b. Surat, Gujarat, India, Apr. 26, 1955; came to U.S., 1981; s. Nooruddin and Zarintaj Laiwala; m. Norjehan Jivani; July 19, 1981; children: Sarah, Nadeem. BE in Civil Engring., Regional Coll. Engring. & Tech., Surat, 1978; BS in Computer Sci., San Francisco State U., 1985. System engr. Electronics Data Systems, Rancho Cordova, Plano, Calif., Tex., 1985-87; software engr. Everex Systems Inc., Fremont, Calif., 1987-89, Cornerstone Tech. Inc., San Jose, Calif., 1989-91; sr. software engr. Sigma Designs Inc., Fremont, 1991, Orchid Tech., Fremont, 1991—; owner, dir. Roshan Diamonds, Freemont, 1991—. Muslim. Home: 5316 Shamrock Common Fremont CA 94555 Office: Orchid Tech 45365 Northport Loop W Fremont CA 94538

LAKE, DAVID S., publisher, lawyer; b. Youngstown, Ohio, July 17, 1938; s. Frank and Charlotte (Stahl) L.; m. Sandra J. Levin, Dec. 18, 1960 (div. Aug. 14, 1987); children: Joshua Seth, Jonathan Daniel. B.A. in Math, Youngstown State U., 1960; J.D. cum laude, Cleve. State U., 1965. Bar: Ohio 1965, D.C. 1970, U.S. Supreme Ct. 1969. Gen. counsel World Pub. Co., Cleve., 1965-68; dir. devel. Cath. U. Am., Washington, 1968-69; v.p., gen. counsel Microform Pub. Corp., Washington, 1969-70; dir. spl. projects Library Resources, Inc., Chgo., 1970-72; gen. mgr., partner Nat. Textbook Co., Skokie, Ill., 1972-76; pres. David S. Lake Pubs., Belmont, Calif., 1976-89, pres, owner, 1984-89; owner Lake Pub. Co., Belmont, 1989—. Contbr. to: Cleve. Marshall Law Rev, 1964. Served with USMC, 1960-62. Jewish. Office: Lake Pub Co 500 Harbor Blvd Belmont CA 94002-4021

LAKE, F(INLEY) EDWARD, diversified company financial executive; b. Newark, June 24, 1934; s. Finley S. and Dorothy (Davis) L.; m. Carol June Freeberg, Sept. 20, 1958; children: David Alan, Jeffrey Dean. BA, Mich. State U., 1956; MBA, U. Chgo., 1970. CPA, Mich. Fin. asst. The Dial Corp. (formerly Greyhound Corp.), Chgo., 1963-66, asst. treas., 1966-68; treas. The Dial Corp., Phoenix, 1968-75, v.p., treas., 1975-87, v.p. fin., 1987—; pres. Nat. Assn. Corp. Treas., 1986-87. Bd. dirs. Am. Heart Assn., 1989—. Office: The Dial Corp Dial Tower Phoenix AZ 85077

LAKE, KEVIN BRUCE, medical association administrator; b. Seattle, Jan. 25, 1937; s. Winston Richard and Vera Emma (Davis) L.; B.S., Portland State U., 1960; M.D., U. Oreg., 1964; m. Suzanne Roto, Oct. 25, 1986; children from previous marriage: Laura, Kendrick, Wesley. Intern, Marion County Gen. Hosp. and Ind. Med. Center, Indpls., 1964-65; resident U. Oreg. Hosps. and Clinics, 1968-70; fellow in infectious and pulmonary diseases, 1970-71; fellow in pulmonary diseases U. So. Calif., 1971-72, instr. medicine, 1972-75, asst. clin. prof., 1975-79, assoc. clin. prof., 1979-84, clin. prof., 1986—; dir. med. edn. and research La Vina Hosp., 1972-75; dir. respiratory therapy Methodist Hosp., Arcadia, Calif., 1975—; mem. staff Los Angeles County/U. So. Calif. Med. Center, Santa Teresita Hosp., Duarte, Calif., Huntington Meml. Hosp., Pasadena, Calif.; attending physician, mem. med. adv. bd. Foothill Free Clinic, Pasadena. Mem. exec. com. Profl. Staff Assn. U. So. Calif. Sch. Medicine; 2d v.p. bd. mgmt. Palm St. br. YMCA, Pasadena, 1974, 1st v.p., 1975, chmn., 1976-78, met. bd. dirs., 1976-84; bd. dirs. Mendenhall Ministries, La Vie Holistic Ministries, Hospice of Pasadena, Hastings Found. co-pres. PTA, Allendale Grade Sch., Pasadena, 1975-76; deacon Pasadena Covenant Ch., 1976-79. Served to lt. U.S. Navy, 1965-68. NIH grantee, 1971-72. Fellow A.C.P., Am. Coll. Chest Physicians; mem. Am. Thoracic Soc., Calif. Thoracic Soc., Oreg. Thoracic Soc., Trudeau Soc., Am. Soc. Microbiology, N.Y. Acad. Scis., Calif. Med. Assn., Los Angeles County Med. Assn. Democrat. Contbr. articles to profl. jours. Home: 875 S Madison Ave Pasadena CA 91106-4404 Office: 50 Alesandro Pl Ste 330 Pasadena CA 91105-3179

LAKE, RANDALL, artist; b. Longbeach, Calif., Aug. 2, 1947. Student, Acad. Julian, Paris, 1968, Atelier 17 W. Stanley Hayter, Paris, 1972-73, Ecole Nat Sup. des Beaux Arts, Paris, 1972; BA cum laude, U. Colo., 1968; MFA, U. Utah, 1977. Dean Guthrie Inst. Fine Arts, 1973-80; assoc. art instr. U. Utah, Salt Lake City, 1978. One-man show John Pence Gallery, San Francisco, 1984-88, 90; exhibited in group shows at Arlington Gallery, Santa Barbara, Calif., 1989, James/Schubert Gallery, Houston, Eccles Community Art Ctr., Ogden, Utah, 1987, Cliff Lodge, Snowbird, Utah, 1986, Utah Arts Coun. Chase Home, Salt Lake City, 1986, 28th Ann. Catalina (Calif.) Festival of Art Invitational, 1986, John Pence Gallery, San Franisco, 1985, Utah Arts Coun., Salt Lake City, 1985, Nora Eccles Harrison Mus. Art, Logan, Utah, Mus. of Fine Art, Salt Lake City, 1984, Salon de Mai Mus. Modern Art, Paris, 1972, Salon D'Automne, Grand Palais, Paris, 1970; portrait of Gov. Nellie T. Ross in Wyo. State Capitol, 1981, portrait of Mayor Ted Wilson, Salt Lake City, 1986; pvt. collections; permanent collections including Springville (Utah) Mus., Am. Libr. of Paris. Recipient purchase award Mus. Fine Arts, Salt Lake City, 1984; John and Anna Lee Stacey scholar, N.Mex., 1978; grantee Karolyi Found., Vence, France, 1973; studio grantee Cité Internat. des Arts, Paris, 1970-71. Mem. Assn. Anciens Cité Internat. Arts. Home: 158 E 200 S Salt Lake City UT 84111-1520

LAKE, STANLEY JAMES, security consulting company executive, motel chain executive, locksmith; b. Oklahoma City, June 3, 1926; s. Clyde Edward Lake and Helene Frances (Herndon) Hunnicut; m. Lila Marguarite Mosley, Mar 29, 1947 (div. Aug. 1952); children: Katherine, Marilyn, Stanley James II; m. Norma Jean Phelps, Jan. 21, 1960. Student, Mont. State U., 1946-48. Owner, mgr. Lake Oil Co., Glendive, Mont., 1949-53, Lake Mining Co., Salt Lake City, 1954-57, Lake Realty Co., Denver, 1958-63, Stanlake Corp., Denver, 1964—, Stanlake Luxury Budget Motels, Denver, 1979—, Lake's Security and Lock Svc., Englewood, Colo., 1979—; co-owner, instr. Colo. Karate Assn., Denver, 1965-73. Originator modular budget motel concept, 1963. Chmn. bd. for karate Rocky Mountain region AAU, 1972-73. With USAAC, 1945-46. Recipient Presdl. award for teaching karate to disadvantaged and civic orgns., 1972, numerous others. Mem. Assn. Locksmiths Am. (cert. master locksmith), Rocky Mountain Locksmiths Assn., Japan Karate Assn. Rocky Mountain Area (chmn. bd. 1970-73), Masons, Shriners. Republican. Methodist. Home: 6026 S Elizabeth Way Littleton CO 80121-2816 Office: Lake's Security & Lock Svc 6200 S Syracuse Way Ste 125 Englewood CO 80111-4738

LAKOFF, EVELYN, music association executive; b. Bklyn., Apr. 8, 1932; d. Boris and Ray (Feldman) Schleifer; m. Sanford Allan Lakoff, June 4, 1961. BA, Queens Coll., 1953; MA in Music Edn., Columbia U., 1955; MA in Musicology, Harvard U., 1963. Pres. San Diego (Calif.) Early Music Soc.; music tchr. N.Y.C. 1955-60, Northport, N.Y., 1965-67. Office: San Diego Early Music Soc 3510 Dove Ct San Diego CA 92103-3904

LAKSHMINARAYANAN, VASUDEVAN, physiological optics scientist; b. Madras, India, Apr. 21, 1957; came to U.S., 1978; s. Ramabhadra and Jayalakshmi Vasudevan; m. Lorraine L. Janeczko, June 10, 1990. BSc, U. Madras, 1976, MSc, 1978; PhD, U. Calif., Berkeley, 1985. Postgrad. researcher U. Calif., Berkeley, 1985-86, asst. rsch. scientist, 1986-91; prin. clin. rsch. assoc. Allergan Therapeutics, Irvine, Calif., 1991-93; adj. assoc. prof. cognitive sci. U. Calif., Irvine, 1993—. Contbr. articles and abstracts to profl. jours. and chpts. to books. Fellow Am. Acad. Optometry; mem. Assn. Rsch. in Vision and Ophthalmology, Optical Soc. Am., SPIE, Sigma Xi.

LALA, TAPAN KANTI, computer and communications engineering manager, consultant, researcher. BEE, Jadaupur U., Calcutta, India, 1972; MSEE, Queen's U., Kingston, Ont., Can., 1977; postgrad., U. Toledo, 1977-79. Instr., teaching asst. U. Toledo, 1975-79, Queen's U., 1975-79; design engr. AVCO Corp., Everett, Mass., 1979-81; mem. tech. staff Mitre Corp., Bedford, Mass., 1981, AT&T Bell Labs., Holmdel, N.J., 1981-84; prin. engr. Motorola, Cupertino, Calif., 1984-85; sr. engr. Fujitsu Am., San Jose, Calif., 1985-86; mgr., group leader Granger Assoc., San Jose, 1986; mgr. NEC Am., San Jose, 1986—; pres. Lala-D-Net, San Jose, 1990—. Merit-Cum-Means scholar Govt. India, Jadaupur U., 1967-72, grad. fellow, 1974-75. Mem. IEEE, IEEE Computer Soc., IEEE Communication Soc. (assoc. editor), IEEE Engring. Mgmt. Soc. (program com. Silicon Valley chpt.), SPIE, Internat. Soc. Optical Engring. Home: 15771 Simoni Dr San Jose CA 95127-2751 Office: NEC Am 110 Rio Robles San Jose CA 95134-1899

LALONDE, ROBERT FREDERICK, state senator; b. Bay City, Mich., Dec. 1, 1922; s. Joseph and Mildred Amanda (Brimmer) LaL.; m. Betty Ellen Schwartz, Aug. 2, 1941; 1 child, Rose Marie Tibbits. BGE in Bus., U. Omaha, 1965. Airport mgr. Jackson Hole Airport, Jackson, Wyo., 1972-80; county commr. Teton County, Jackson, 1982-86, rental property owner, 1970-88; Wyo. state senator Jackson, 1989—. Author: The Dangerous Trilogy, 1973. Chmn. Teton County Rep. Com., Jackson, 1975-77; del. Rep. Nat. Conv., Detroit, 1980; mem. Electoral Coll., Cheyenne, Wyo., 1980; sec. Wyo. Rep. party, 1980-82; chmn. Teton County Plnaning Commn., Jackson, 1973-78. Col. USAF, 1943-70. Mem. Am. Legion (comdr. 1989—), Wyo. Airport Operators Assn. (founder, pres. 1973-75, disting. svc. award 1979), Jackson Hole C. of C. (pres. 1977-79, citizen of yr. 1975, disting. svc. award 1980), Rotary (pres. 1976-77). Christian Scientist. Home: PO Box 1707 Jackson WY 83001

LA LUMIA, FRANK MUNZUETO, artist; b. Chgo., Aug. 9, 1948; s. Frank Sr. and Pearle (Grater) LaL.; m. Sally Jorgenson, Jan. 19, 1981 (div. Sept. 1986). BS, Bradley U., 1970. pvt. tchr. workshops, nationwide. Mem. Nat. Watercolor Soc. Home: PO Box 3237 Santa Fe NM 87501-0237

LAM, LUI (LEI LIN), physicist; b. Lianxian, China, Nov. 17, 1944; came to U.S., 1966; s. Lap-Chung and Lai-Jane (Wong) L.; m. Heung-Mee Lee, July 1, 1972; 1 child, Charlene. B.S., U. Hong Kong, 1965; M.S., U. of B.C., 1968; M.A., Columbia U., 1969, Ph.D., 1973. Research assoc. City Coll. CUNY, 1972-75; research scientist U. Instelling Antwerpen, Belgium, 1975-76, U. Saarlandes, Saarbrucken, Fed. Republic Germany, 1976-77; assoc. research prof. Inst. Physics, Academia Sinica, Beijing, China, 1978-83, adj. prof., 1984—; prof. City Coll. and Queensborough Community Coll. CUNY, 1984-87, San Jose U., 1987—; founder, co-editor Springer Series on Partially Ordered Systems, 1987—, Woodward Conf. Series, 1988—; elected mem. planning and steering com. Internat. Liquid Crystal Conf., 1984-90. Co-editor: Wave Phenomena, 1989, Nonlinear Structures in Physical Systems, 1990, Solitons in Liquid Crystals, 1992, Modeling Complex Phenomena, 1992, Liquid Crystalline and Mesomorphic Polymers, 1993; assoc. editor Jour. Molecular Crystal and Liquid Crystals, 1981—; editorial mem. Liquid Crystals, 1986-90. Li Po Kwai scholar U. Hong Kong, 1963-65; Eugene Higgin fellow Columbia U., 1966-67, Nordita fellow, 1976. Mem. Am. Phys. Soc., Internat. Liquid Crystal Soc. (founder, bd. dir., chmn. conf. com. 1990—). Office: San Jose State U Dept Physics San Jose CA 95192-0106

LAMAR, DONOVAN EUGENE, educator; b. Detroit, Feb. 9, 1956; s. Charles Jr. and Delgreta (Dobbs) LaM.; divorced; 1 stepchild, Kathryn LyNae Cameron. A Gen. Studies, Glendale Coll., 1983; BA, Ottawa U., 1988, MA, 1992; postgrad., No. Ariz. U., 1992—. Cert. tchr., C.C. tchr., Ariz. Asst. mgr. ITT Grinell Corp., Phoenix, 1978-80; student advisor, program advisor, evening adminstr. Gateway C.C., Phoenix, 1981—; program advisor, specialties coord., dir. peer assistance South Mountain C.C., Phoenix, 1981—; substitute tchr. Issac Jr. High Sch. Dist., Phoenix, 1988-89; cons. mgr. human resources D.E.L. Cons., Phoenix, 1986—. Mem. Valley Citizens League, Phoenix, 1989; adv. mem. New Turf Gang Prevention Program, Phoenix, 1991; bd. dirs. Jr. Achievement Cen. Ariz., 1992, mem. curriculum com., Phoenix, 1991—; bd. dirs. Black Bd. Dirs., Phoenix, 1991—. With USNG, 1981-87. Recipient Innovator of Yr. award League of Innovations in C.C., 1991-92. Mem. Nat. Coun. on Black Am. Affairs. Office: South Mountain C.C. 7050 S 24th St Phoenix AZ 85040

LAMB, BERTON LEE, II, policy analyst, researcher; b. Torrance, Calif., July 4, 1945; s. Berton Lee and Phyllis Jean (Schultz) L.; m. Susan Elizabeth Snow, June 22, 1968; 1 child, Kara Lee. BA, Calif. Luth. U., 1967; MA in Internat. Polits., San Francisco State U., 1970; PhD in Polit. Sci., Wash. State U., 1976. Instr. polit. sci. George Fox Coll., Newberg, Oreg., 1969-72; rsch. asst. Water Rsch. Ctr. Wash. State U., Pullman, 1974-75; asst. prof. polit. sci. Ea. Ky. U., Richmond, 1975-76; water res. policy specialist U.S. Fish and Wildlife Svc., Ft. Collins, Colo., 1976-79, policy analyst Nat. Ecology Rsch. Ctr., 1979-86, leader water resources analysis sect., Nat. Ecology Rsch. Ctr., 1986-90; project leader Nat. Ecology Rsch. Ctr., Ft. Collins, Colo., 1990—. Editor: Water Quality Administration, 1980; co-editor: Water Resources Administration. Symposium in Public Administration Review, 1976; bd. editors P.A. Times, 1988-91; author chpts. in Instream Flow Protection in the West, 2d edit., 1993 and Inland Fisheries Management, 1993; contbr. articles to Water Resources Bull., Water Resources Rsch., Jour. Water Resources Planning and Mgmt., Social Sci. Micro-Computer Rev., The Environ. Profl., Boston Coll. Environ. Affairs law Rev. and others. Pres. Trinity Luth. Ch. Coun., Ft. Collins, 1981-82. Future faculty fellow Am. Luth. Ch., 1973; faculty devel. grantee George Fox Coll., 1972; scholar, diplomat Internat. Studies Assn.-Dept. of State, 1973; rsch. fellow Nat. Resources Law Ctr., Sch. of Law, U. Colo., 1990. Mem. Am. Soc. Pub. Adminstrs. Western Social Sci. Assn. (exec. coun. 1989—). Lutheran. Office: US Fish and Wildlife Svc Nat Ecology Rsch Ctr 4512 Mcmurray Ave Fort Collins CO 80525-3400

LAMB, DARLIS CAROL, sculptor; b. Wausa, Nebr.; d. Lindor Soren and June Berniece (Skalberg) Nelson; m. James Robert Lamb; children: Sherry Lamb Sobh, Michael, Mitchell. BA in Fine Arts, Columbia Pacific U., San Rafael, Calif., 1988; MA in Fine Arts, Columbia Pacific U., 1989. Exhibited in group shows at Nat. Arts Club, N.Y.C., 1983, 85, 89, 90, 91, 92 (Catherine Lorillard Wolfe award sculpture 1983), N.Am. Sculpture Exhibit, Foothills Art Ctr., Golden, Colo., 1983, 84, 86, 87, 90, 91, Pub. Svc. Colo. award 1990), Nat. Acad. Design, 1986, Nat. Sculpture Soc., 1985, 91 (C. Percival Dietsch Sculpture Prize 1991), Loveland Mus. and Gallery, 1990, 91, Allied Artists of Am., 1992, others; represented in permanent collections: Nebr. Hist. Soc., Am. Lung Assn. of Colo., Benson Park Sculpture Garden, Loveland, others. Mem. Am. Artists Profl. League, Catherine Lorillard Wolfe Art Club, N.Am. Sculpture Soc. Office: PO Box 9043 Englewood CO 80111

LAMB, MILDRED SHIMONISHI, retired administrative secretary; b. Vacaville, Calif., May 12, 1913; d. Yojiro and Noriye (Takei) Kubota; m. Toshio Shimonishi, June 19, 1938 (dec. Apr. 1963); children: Don, Joyce Takanashi, Sam, Naomi, Terashima, Cheri Mitsuno; m. William L. Lamb, Jan. 29, 1974 (dec. Aug. 1977). AA, Long Beach (Calif.) Jr. Coll., 1935. Sec. to security officer U.S. Naval Air Stat., Japan, 1955-57; sec. to provost marshal U.S. Marine Corp Facility, Japan, 1957-58; stenographer-receptionist Calif. State Disability Ins., Long Beach, 1958-76; retired, 1976. Author: And Then a Rainbow, 1990. Mem. Woman's Club Bellflower (fin. sec. and treas. 1983-92, Woman of Yr. award 1989-90), Gen. Fedn. Women's Club. Republican. Presbyterian. Home: 10548 Semora St Bellflower CA 90706-7142

LAMB, WILLIS EUGENE, JR., physicist, educator; b. Los Angeles, Calif., July 12, 1913; s. Willis Eugene and Marie Helen (Metcalf) L.; m. Ursula Schaefer, June 5, 1939. BS, U. Calif., 1934, PhD, 1938; DSc (hon.), U. Pa., 1953, Gustavus Adolphus Coll., 1975, Columbia U., 1990; MA (hon.), Oxford (Eng.) U., 1956, Yale, 1961; LHD (hon.), Yeshiva U., 1965. Mem. faculty Columbia U., 1938-52, prof. physics, 1948-52; prof. physics Stanford U., 1951-56; Wykeham prof. physics and fellow New Coll., Oxford U., 1956-62; Henry Ford 2d prof. physics Yale U., 1962-72, J. Willard Gibbs prof. physics, 1972-74; prof. physics and optical scis. U. Ariz., Tucson, 1974—, Regents prof., 1990—; Morris Loeb lectr. Harvard U., 1953-54; Gordon Shrum lectr. Simon Fraser U., 1972; cons. Philips Labs., Bell Telephone Labs., Perkin-Elmer, NASA; vis. com. Brookhaven Nat. Lab. Recipient (with Dr. P. Kusch) Nobel prize in physics, 1955, Rumford premium Am. Acad. Arts and Scis., 1953; Rsch. Corp. award, 1954, Yeshiva award, 1962; Guggenheim fellow, 1960-61, Sr. Alexander von Humboldt fellow, 1992-93. Fellow Am. Phys. Soc., N.Y. Acad. Scis.; hon. fellow Inst. Physics and Phys. Soc. (Guthrie lectr. 1958), Royal Soc. Edinburgh (fgn. mem.); mem. Nat. Acad. Scis., Phi Beta Kappa, Sigma Xi. Office: U Ariz Optical Scis Ctr Tucson AZ 85721

LAMB-BRASSINGTON, KATHRYN EVELYN, writer, genealogist; b. Yakima, Wash., Apr. 3, 1935; d. Victor Earl and Anna (Kauzlarich) Lamb; m. Donald Morley Brassington, Dec. 27, 1956 (div. 1968); children: Andrew Stuart, Perry Sanford, Van Victor, Keith Bennett. Student, Wash. State U., 1954-55, U. Wash., 1955-56. Author: A Leg of Lamb, 1985; assoc. editor quar. newsletter Lamb's Pastures. Mem. DAR, Towne Family Assn., Colonial Dames 17th Century, Nat. Soc. Women Descendants of Ancient and Honorable Artillery Co. Republican. Presbyterian. Home: 4509 Somerset Pl SE Bellevue WA 98006-3020

LAMBERT, JOHN PAUL, production supervisor; b. Boston, July 30, 1964; s. Paul Eugene and Pauline Ann (Beaulieu) L. BSME, U. Mass., 1986; MBA, Loyola-Marymount U., L.A., 1993. Prodn. supr. Gillette Co., Santa Monica, Calif., 1990—. 1st lt. U.S. Army, 1986-90, Fed. Republic Germany. Mem. Beta Gamma Sigma.

LAMBERT, L. GARY, French educator; b. Ogden, Utah, Nov. 9, 1937; s. Leo Alexander and Melba Dorothy (Jensen) L; m. Margaret Ann Corcoran, June 14, 1961; children—Eric, Gretchen, Brig, Inger, Kira, Jacob, Mari. B.A., U. Calif.-Berkeley, 1963; M.A., U. Calif.-Santa Barbara, 1965; Ph.D., Rice U., 1969. Summer teaching staff Rice U., Houston, 1967, 68; faculty mem. Alliance Francaise, Houston, 1966; asst. prof. Brigham Young U., Provo, 1969-74, assoc. prof., 1974—, dept. chmn., 1983-89. Gov.'s appointee Utah Humanities Coun. 1989—; active Fulbright Screening Com., 1992—. Mem. Inst. Internat. Edn., Rocky Mountain MLA, Assn. Study 18th Century Studies, Jean-Jacques Rousseau Soc., Pi Delta Phi (nat. bd. dirs. 1992), French Honor Soc. Mormon. Office: Brigham Young U French and Italian Dept 4012 JKHB Provo UT 84602

LAMBERT, MARTHA LOWERY, state legislator; b. Douglasville, Ga., Mar. 27, 1937; d. Edmond Davis and Mary (Daniel) Lowery; m. Paul Dean Lambert, June 13, 1959; children: Melanie Lynn, Kurt Phillip, Brett Cameron, Matthew Dean. Mem. N.Mex. Ho. of Reps., Santa Fe, 1981—; part-owner Premier Foods Inc., Albuquerque, 1989—. Pres. Albuquerque Dist. Dental Aux., 1971, Albuquerque Fed. Rep. Women, 1975; alt. del. Nat. Rep. Conv., Kansas City, Mo, 1976, Houston, 1992. Home: 616 Running Water Cir SE Albuquerque NM 87123-4162 Office: Premier Foods Inc 3900 2nd St NW Albuquerque NM 87107-2242

LAMBERT, RICHARD WILLIAM, mathematics educator; b. Gettysburg, Pa., May 1, 1928; s. Allen Clay and Orpha Rose (Hoppert) L.; m. Phyllis Jean Bain, Sept. 2, 1949 (div. May 1982); children: James Harold, Dean Richard; m. Kathleen Ann Waring, Aug. 30, 1982; stepchildren: Gregory Scott Gibbs, LeAnn Marie Gibbs. BS, Oreg. State U., 1952; MA in Teaching Math., Reed Coll., 1962. Instr. Siuslaw High Sch., Florence, Oreg., 1954-55, David Douglas High Sch., Portland, Oreg., 1955-67; instr. Mt. Hood Community Coll., Gresham, Oreg., 1967-87, ret., 1987. NSF grantee, 1959, 60, 62. Mem. Nat. Coun. Tchrs. of Maths., Am. Math. Assn., Am. Math. Assn. of Two Yr. Colls., Oreg. Coun. Tchrs. of Maths. Democrat. Methodist. Home: 11621 SE Lexington St Portland OR 97266-5933

LAMBERT, STEVEN JUDSON, geochemist, researcher; b. Riverside, Calif., Nov. 6, 1948; s. Squire Valentine and Ruth Mildred (McQueen) L. BA with honors, U. Calif., Riverside, 1970; MS, Calif. Inst. Tech., 1971, PhD, 1976. Cert. profl. geol. scientist. Chemist Naval Weapons Ctr., Corona, Calif., summer 1968; exploration geologist Standard Oil Co. of Calif., Bakersfield, summer 1970; rsch. fellow Calif. Inst. Tech., Pasadena, 1975-76; geologist, geochemist Sandia Nat. Labs., Albuquerque, 1976—. Contbr. articles to profl. jours. Vol. youth leader Boy Scouts Am., Riverside and Albuquerque, 1967-89; vol. docent Rio Grande Zool. Park, Albuquerque, 1986—. Fellow NSF, 1971-73, 75, 75-76; grantee Dept. Energy, 1991—. Mem. Am. Geophys. Union, Am. Inst. Profl. Geologists, Geochem. Soc., Geol. Soc. Am., Phi Beta Kappa, Sigma Xi. Office: Sandia Nat Labs Geochem Dept 6118 Box 5800 Albuquerque NM 87185

LAMBIE, MARGARET MCCLEMENTS, physicist; b. Ayr, Scotland; came to U.S., 1965; d. John Morgan and Jane McKinley (Braney) McClements; m. Andrew Don Lambie, Sept. 8, 1955 (div. June 1973); children: Jane Anne, Robert Alexander, John McClements, Andrew Warren; m. Charles William Hennel, Aug. 1, 1992. BSc with honours, U. Glasgow, Scotland, 1953; diploma, Imperial Coll., London, 1964; PhD, U. London, 1965. Asst. prof. natural philosophy U. Glasgow, 1953-55; rsch. fellow physics dept. Imperial Coll., 1955-58; prof. applied math. U. Malaya, Kuala Lumpur, Malaysia, 1963-64; propr. Margaret Lambie & Assocs., Portland, Oreg., 1965-74; energy devel. specialist U.S. Dept. Energy, Washington, 1978-80; physicist for power system modelling Bonneville Power Adminstrn., Portland, 1971-73, computer analyst, 1973-78, hydroelectric specialist, 1980-86, cogeneration specialist, 1986—; chmn. hydroelectric com. PNUCC, 1980-83; mem. adv. com. Oreg. PUC, 1988-89; lead on BPA Generation Strategy, 1993. Contbr. articles on resource assessment, devel., financing, and regulatory issues to profl. jours. Mem. Oreg. Gov.'s Coun. on Nursing, 1968-69; session clk. 1st Presbyn. Ch., Portland, 1989. Recipient performance award Bonneville Power Adminstrn., 1988, 89, 90. Mem. Assn. Energy Engrs., Women's Advt. Club (v.p. Portland 1985), Multnomah Athletic Club. Office: Bonneville Power Adminstrn 905 NE 11th St PO Box 3621 RMGB Portland OR 97208

LAMEIRO, GERARD FRANCIS, research institute director; b. Paterson, N.J., Oct. 3, 1949; s. Frank Raymond and Beatrice Cecilia (Donley) L.; BS, Colo. State U., 1971, MS, 1973, PhD, 1977. Sr. scientist Solar Energy Rsch. Inst., Golden, Colo., 1977-78; asst. prof. mgmt. sci. and info. systems Colo. State U., Fort Collins, 1978-83, mem. editorial bd. energy engring., 1978-82, editorial bd. energy econs. policy and mgmt., 1981-82, lectr. dept. computer sci., 1983, lectr. dept. mgmt., 1983; pres. Successful Automated Office Systems, Inc., Fort Collins, 1982-84; product mgr. Hewlett Packard, 1984-88; computer networking cons., 1988-89, Ft. Collins.; mem. editorial bd. The HP Chronicle, 1986-88, columnist, 1988, mgmt. strategist, 1988-91; dir. Lameiro Rsch. Inst., 1991—. Mem. editorial bd. Hp Chronicle, 1986-88, Energy Engring., Policy and Mgmt., 1981-82, Energy Engring., 1978-82. Mem. P-resdl. Electoral Coll., 1980. Recipient nat. Disting. Svc. award Assn. Energy Engrs., 1981, Honors Prof. award Colo. State U., 1982; Colo. Energy Rsch. Inst. fellow 1976; NSF fellow 1977. Mem. Assn. for Computing Machinery, Assn. Energy Engrs. (pres. 1980, Nat. Distinguish Service award 1981, internat. bd. dirs. 1980-81), Am. Mgmt. Assn., Am. Soc. for Tng. and Devel., Am. Mktg. Assn. (exec.), Am. Soc. For Quality Control, IEEE Computer Soc., Inst. Indsl. Engrs., U.S. C. of C., Crystal Cathedral Golden Eagles Club, The Heritage Found., Sigma Xi, Phi Kappa Phi, Beta Gamma Sigma, Kappa Mu Epsilon. Roman Catholic. Contbr. articles in mgmt. and tech. areas to profl. jours. Home: PO Box 9580 Fort Collins CO 80525-0500 Office: 3313 Downing Ct Fort Collins CO 80526-2315

LAMEIRO, PAUL AMBROSE, manufacturing executive; b. Bay Shore, N.Y., July 31, 1957; s. Frank R. and Beatrice C. Lameiro. BS in Physics, Colo. State U., 1982. Engr. Hewlett Packard, Loveland, Colo., 1977-91; pres. Wavefront Acoustics, Aurora, Colo., 1983—. Mem. Audio Engring. Soc. Office: Wavefront Acoustics 18012 E Loyola Pl Aurora CO 80013

LAMELL, PHILIP ALAN, banker; b. Chgo., Feb. 5, 1946; s. Harvey and Marie (Beegun) LaM.; m. Jill Harriett Lanoff, Aug., 1970 (div. 1984); children—Jodi, Jason; m. Sandra Lee, May 20, 1984; 1 child, Jeremy. B.S., U. Ill.-Chgo., 1968. Trust officer First Chicago Bank, 1969-76, First Nat. Bank Barrington (Ill.), 1976-79; portfolio mktg. mgr. Valley Nat. Bank, Phoenix, 1979-83, v.p., mgr. investor and shareholder relations, 1983-87, v.p. spl. project trust, planning and mktg., 1987-88; v.p., sr. portfolio mgr. Valley Capital Mgmt., 1988—. Mem. planning commn. Village of Arlington Heights, Ill., 1975-79; bd. mgmt. YMCA, Scottsdale, Ariz., 1980—; bd. dirs. The Found. for the Conservation of Ariz.'s Wildlife, 1990. Mem. Phoenix Soc. Fin. Analysts, Nat. Investor Relation Inst. (treas. Ariz. 1984, pres. 1986), Bank Investor Relations Inst. Office: PO Box 71 (Valley Nat) 241 N Central Phoenix AZ 85001

LAMKA, NANCY CAROLYN, educator; b. Portland, Oreg., July 21, 1944; d. Theodore William and Delma Irene (Sullivan) Schaer; m. Charles Dewane Lamka, Jan. 2, 1966; children: Peter Elisha, Joshua David. BS, U. Puget Sound, 1966. Cert. tchr., Oreg., Wash. Primary tchr. Portland Pub. Schs., 1966-70; tchr. Montessori Schs., Beaverton, Oreg., 1978; tutor, primary tchr. Evergreen Jr. High, Hillsboro, 1987; lang. specialist Indian Ft. St. James, Can., 1983-86; phys. edn. tchr. K-3 Hope Christian Sch., Aloha, Oreg., 1988, 1st grade tchr., 1989-92; tchr. Little Light, Ghana, 1992—, Austria, Hungary, Romania, 1992—; speaker in field, U.S., Europe, Africa, 1985-86, 92; guest speaker Abide in the Vine Sta. KPDQ Radio, 1986. Author: (children's music book) Steps to Joy, 1988; performer representing Nat. Songwriters Conv., 1979; recorded 3 easy listening albums, 2 children's albums; author children's sci. books, 1993; composer of ballet to tour schs. and chs., 1994; contbr. articles to profl. jours. V.p. Little Light Ministries Unltd., 1977-86; worker campaigns for Sen. Chuck Hanlon; helper Keep Our Earth Clean, 1966-67, 91-92. Mem. Am. Christian Schs. Inc. (fellow tchr. 1991-92). Full Gospel Fundamentalist. Home: 17795 NW Emmaus Ln Portland OR 97231

LAMMERS, ANN CONRAD, counselor, writer; b. Bryn Mawr, Pa., June 23, 1945; d. Howard Melvin Jr. Lammers and Louise Carey (Martien) Kelsey; m. Antone Gerhardt Singsen III, June 12, 1965 (div. Apr. 1977); children: Ann Hope Singsen, Molly McKee Singsen. Student, Brown U., 1963-65; BA, Barnard Coll., 1967; MDiv, Gen. Theol. Sem., N.Y.C., 1982; PhD, Yale U., 1987. German tchr. Valhalla (N.Y.) High Sch., 1967-69; textbook editor Harcourt Brace Jovanovich Inc., N.Y.C., 1974-79; counselor Episcopal Social Svc., Inc., Bridgeport, Conn., 1983-86; asst. prof. theology and ethics Church Divinity Sch. of the Pacific, Berkeley, Calif., 1986-90; MS in Counseling Calif. State U., Hayward, 1992; teaching fellow Yale Divinity Sch., New Haven, 1983-86; vis. asst. prof. Christian ethics Santa Clara Univ. (Calif.), 1990-91; marriage, family and child counselor intern in pvt. practice, 1992—. Editor: (textbook series) Unsere Freunde, Die Welt der Jugend, 1979, (essays) Civitas, 1986; translator: Rabbit Island, 1978. Grad. fellow Episcopal Ch. Found., N.Y.C., 1983, 84, 85, Yale U., 1982-86. Mem. Phi Beta Kappa. Democrat. Episcopalian. Home: 720 Evelyn Ave Albany CA 94706-1707

LAMMERS, JOHN CHARLES, public health educator; b. St. Charles, Mo., June 21, 1944; s. John Vallee and Elnor Viola (Ritter) L.; m. Jan Page Marshal, Jan. 14, 1972 (div. Nov. 1975); 1 child, Emily Louise; m. Barbara Jan Wilson, Aug. 10, 1991. BA in Psychology, Calif. State U.-Humboldt, Arcata, 1976; MA in Sociology, U. Calif., Davis, 1979, PhD in Sociology, 1983. Fellow Stanford (Calif.) U., 1983-85; asst. prof. U. Louisville, 1985-88; asst. prof. U. Calif., Berkeley, 1988-89, L.A., 1989—; health economist VA we. region, San Francisco, 1989—; asst. prof. exec. health adminstrn. program U. Colo., Denver, 1989—; mem. faculty Pub. Health Leadership Inst.; cons. Unihealth Am., L.A., 1990—. Contbr. articles to profl. jours. Bd. mem. Metro United Way, Louisville, 1985-88. Regents fellow U. Calif., 1982-84. Mem. Am. Sociol. Assn., Assn. Vol. Action Scholars, Am. Soc. Socio-Econs. Democrat. Home: 711 W Ortega # 10 Santa Barbara CA 93101 Office: UCLA Sch Pub Health Los Angeles CA 90024-1772

LAMONICA, JOHN, food executive; b. Bklyn., Apr. 26, 1954; s. Lou and Alda (Merola) L.; m. Nancy Lamonica. BS in Acctg., Bklyn. Coll., 1977. With N.S.L. Enterprises, 1982—; with Aniellos Pizza, 1979—, Lamonicas N.Y. Pizza, 1980—; restaurant cons. Developer of new pizzas in field. Republican. Mem. Beverly Hills Gun Club, Shelby Am. Club. Office: 1066 Gayley Los Angeles CA 90024

LAMONT, DUANE RICHARD, software design engineer; b. Renton, Wash., Nov. 26, 1965; s. Duane Vernon and Evelyn May (Page) LaM.; m. Cheryl Ann Madison, Mar. 2, 1992. BS in Computer Sci., U. Wash., 1987. Video game programmer Spectral Assocs., Tacoma, Wash., 1982-83; graphics programmer Innovis Interactive Techs., Federal Way, Wash., 1988-89; database specialist Planning Rsch. Corp., Aiea, Hawaii, 1989-90; comm. engr. Amdahl Corp., Sunnyvale, Calif., 1990-91; software design engr. Intelect, Inc., Mililani, Hawaii, 1992—; owner Dot C Software, Kailua, Hawaii, 1992—. Designer (video game) Lancer, 1983. Recipient Tech. Benefitting Mankind award ComputerWorld/Smithsonian, Washington, 1989. Mem. Assn. Computing Machinery, Spl. Interest Group for Graphics, Digital Equipment Corp. Users' Soc. Democrat. Home: 148 Kuukama St Kailua HI 96734 Office: Intelect Inc 200 Kahelu Ave Mililani HI 96789

LA MONT, TAWANA FAYE, video director; b. Ft. Worth, May 12, 1948; d. Jerry James and Roberta Ann (Wilkinson) La M. AA, Antelope Coll., Lancaster, Calif., 1979; BA in Anthropology, UCLA, 1982. Forest technician region #9, trail constrn. supr. U.S. Forest Svc., Pear Blossom, Calif., 1974-79; trail constrn. supr., maintenance asst. Calif. State Parks, 1979-81; cable TV installer Sammons Comm., San Fernando, Calif., 1982-84, camera operator, 1984-87; video studio and ENG remotes dir., mgr., program mgr. channels 6 and 21 Sammons Comm., Glendale, Calif., 1987—; video dir. LBW & Assocs. Internat., Ltd., 1988—; mem. ednl. access channel satellite program evaluation com., Glendale and Burbank, 1990—; mem. Foothill Community TV Network, Glendale and Burbank, 1987—. Prodr., dir. (homeless video) Bittersweet Streets, 1988; cameraperson Rockin in A Hard Place, 1988—; dir., editor over 1000 videos. Active Glendale Hist. Soc., 1992—; bd. dirs. Am. Heart Assn., 1992—, ARC, 1993—. Recipient Award of Appreciation Bur. of Census, 1990, LBW & Assocs. Internat., 1988, Award of Outstanding Pub. Svc. U.S. Social Security Dept. Health Human Svc., 1989, award of appreciation USMC, 1991. Mem. Am. Women in Radio and TV, Wildlife Waystation, Alpha Gamma. Democrat. Home: PO Box 142 Lake Hughes CA 93532-0142

LAMOREAUX, JOYCE, educational institute executive; b. Dec. 26, 1938. Officer SW Steel Rolling Mills & Affiliates, L.A., 1963-72; founder Chela Ctr., Pompano, Fla., 1972-75; exec. v.p. Word Masters, Inc., Seattle, 1975-85; pres. OMNIESS, Inc., 1986-92, OMNI Learning Inst., 1975—; cons. in field; lectr. in field. Author: Philosophy of Holism, The Power of Intuition, Multidimensional Health Care, 1990; co-author: Intuitive Management Workbook; contbr. articles to profl. jours.; holder patent pending in vibrational medicine process. Office: OMNI Learning Inst PO Box 553 Port Townsend WA 98368

LAMORENA, ALBERTO C., III, judge; b. Agana, Guam, Nov. 29, 1949; s. Alberto Tominez and Fe Garta (Cristobal) L. Student, St. Louis U., 1967-69; degree in polit. sci., U. Ill., 1971; postgrad. in acctg., U. Tex., 1974; JD, Drake U., 1977. Assoc. Kearney Lee Hammer P.C., Agana, 1977-80; pvt. practice Agana, 1980-85; ptnr. Lamorena and Ingles P.C., Agana, 1985-88; presiding judge Superior Ct. of Guam, Agana, 1988—; mem. Guam Legislature, Agana, 1979-88, chmn. ways and means com., vice chmn. crimimal justice com., 1979-83, minority leader, 1987-88; advisor Filipino Community of Guam, 1979-88, Ilocano Community of Guam, 1979-88; chmn. Guam Legal Svcs., 1983-85, bd trustees; assoc. prof. U. Guam, 1986-89; chmn. Judicial Coun. Guam, nat. judicial leader, Guam bd. examiners, public defender; pres., founder, Pacific Judicial Coun., 1991—; chmn. criminal justice automation commn., 1991—; judicial rep. Commn. on Self Determination. Chmn. bd. trustees Guam Legal Svcs., 1983-85. Mem. ABA (judicial adminstrn. divsn.), Am. Judges Assn., Conf. Chief Justices, Guam Bar Assn., Fed. Bar Assn., Am. Judicature Soc., Pacific Jud. Coun. (founder, pres.), South Pacific Judicial Conf. Pacific Inst. Judicial Adminstrn., Supreme Ct. Rules Commn. (Guam),. Office: Judicial Ctr 120 W O'Brien Dr Agana GU 96910

LAMOURE, MARTIN SCOTT, chemist; b. Honolulu, Aug. 21, 1954; s. John Edward and Harriet Adel (McBain) LaM.; m. Tina Leilani Fields, Sept. 11, 1982; children: Tyler (dec. Apr. 1989), Matthew. BS in Med. Tech., Calif. State U., Dominguez Hills, 1979. Cert. med. technologist; cert. clin. lab. technologist, Calif. Med. technologist blood bank dept. Meml. Hosp. Med. Ctr. of Long Beach, 1979-80; med. technologist toxicology dept. Swedish Med. Ctr., Seattle, 1980-81; med. technologist Palmdale (Calif.) Hosp. Med. Ctr., 1981-90, chemistry supr., 1990—; quality control cons. Sierra Med. Group, Lancaster, 1984. Mem. Nat. Rep. Senatorial Com., Washington, 1992. Mem. NRA, Aircraft Owners and Pilots Assn. Republican. Office: Palmdale Hosp Med Ctr 1212 E Ave S Palmdale CA 93550

LAMOUREUX, CHARLES HARRINGTON, botanist, arboretum administrator; b. West Greenwich, R.I., Sept. 14, 1933; s. Emile and Cora May (Harrington) L.; m. Florence May Kettelle, Aug. 28, 1954; children: Mark Harrington, Anne Maile. BS in Botany, U. R.I., 1953; MS in Botany, U. Hawaii, 1955; PhD in Botany, U. Calif., Davis, 1961. From asst. to assoc. prof. botany U. Hawaii, Honolulu, 1959-71, prof., 1971—, chair dept. botany, 1962-65, 76-78, acting assoc. dean curriculum coll. arts and scis., 1976-77, 83, project coord. instrnl. assistance unit, 1977-79, assoc. dean acad. affairs coll. arts and scis., 1985-91, dir. Lyon arboretum, 1992—; rsch. assoc. botany Bernice P. Bishop Mus., Honolulu, 1963—; vis. asst. prof. botany U. B.C., Can., summer 1963; vis. colleague dept. botany Canterbury U., Christchurch, New Zealand, 1965-66; mem. sci. adv. com. Pacific Tropical Bot. Garden (name changed to Nat. Tropical Bot. Garden), 1967—, The Nature Conservancy Hawaii, 1980—; dir. summer inst. sci. amd math. tchrs. U.S. children Far East NSF, Chofu, Japan, 1968-71, reviewer, mem. various rev. panels; faculty mem. ctr. Pacific islands studies U. Hawaii, 1971—; guest scientist Nat. Biol. Inst. Indonesia, Bogor, 1972-73, 79-80; mem. adv. com. plants and animals quarantine br. Hawaii State Dept. Agr., 1973-79, 89—; mem. tech. com. endangered Hawaiian plants Hawaii State Divsn. Forestry and Wildlife, 1976—; study lectr./leader Smithsonian Assocs. Study Tours S.E. Asia, 1985, 86, 88, 89, 90, 91, 92, Melanesia, 1987; report reviewer U.S. Congl. Office Tech. Assessment; rschr. in field; bot. and ecol. cons. to various businesses and agys. including State Hawaii Dept. Bus. and Econ. Devel., UNESCO, UN Devel. Programme. Author: Trailside Plants of Hawaii's National Parks, 1976, (U.S. Nat. Pk. Svc. Dir.'s award, Nat. Pks. Coop. Assn. Award of Excellence 1977-78), rev. edit., 1982; bd. editors Pacific Sci., 1965—, editor-in-chief, 1985-86; mem. editorial com. Allertonia, 1977-90; manuscript reviewer for various jours. and presses; contbr. articles to profl. jours. Active Hawaii Audubon Soc., 1959—, past pres., 1st v.p., Hawaiian Bot. Gardens Found., 1959-67, trustee, 1st v.p.; life mem. Conservation Coun. Hawaii, 1959—, state bd. dirs., mem. com. flora conservation, Hawaiian Bot. Soc., 1959—, trustee endowment fund, past pres., v.p., sec., treas., newsletter editor; mem. adv. com. Hawai'i Earth Day, 1990; bd. dirs. Friends Foster Garden, 1992—. Mem. Bot. Soc. Am., Am. Assn. Bot. Gardens and Arboreta, Hawaiian Acad. Sci. (councillor 1991—), Pacific Sci. Assn. (life, standing com. botany 1971—), Internat. Assn. Plant Taxonomists, Internat. Assn. Wood Anatomists. Home: 3426 Oahu Ave Honolulu HI 96822 Office: Harold L Lyon Arboretum 3860 Manoa Rd Honolulu HI 96822

LAMOUREUX, KIMBERLY ANN, insurance company official; b. St. Louis, Nov. 7, 1963; d. John Alexander and Marilyn Kay (Oney) Lamoureux. AS in Law Enforcement, Mo. So. State Coll., 1986, BS in Criminal Justice, 1986. Trainee Travelers Ins. Co., St. Louis, 1987-88, claims rep., 1987, property specialist, 1987-90, liability supr., 1990—. Mem. Mo. So. State Coll. Alumni Assn. Home: 6422 E Otero Pl Englewood CO 80112 Office: Travelers Ins Co PO Box 17360 Denver CO 80217

LAMPL, ANNIE WAGNER, psychotherapist; b. Vienna, Austria, Oct. 27, 1917; came to U.S., 1939; d. Carl and Martha (Frankel) Wagner; m. Josef Lampl, Jan. 26, 1939; children: John W., Lanny J. MS in Psychology, Goddard U., 1968. Lic. marriage, family, child counselor, Calif. Counselor Epihap Industry, L.A., 1963-68; sr. counselor Braille Inst., L.A., 1969—;

counselor Handicapped of the Valley, L.A., 1971—, So. Calif. Counseling Ctr., L.A., 1971—. Recipient Penney Vol. award, 1990, Vol. award State of Calif., 1991. Mem. Analytical Psychology Club, Jung Inst. Home: 1785 Bel Air Rd Los Angeles CA 90077

LAMPSON, FRANCIS KEITH, metallurgical engineer; b. Mpls., Aug. 7, 1924; s. Albert Dean and May (Miner) L.; m. Margaret Elaine Snyder, Sept. 30, 1945; children: Michael, Jan Colleen, Andrea, Kevin. BS in Metall. Engring., U. Ill., 1949. Jr. mgr. N.E.P.A., Fairchild Engring. & Airplane Corp., Oak Ridge, Tenn., 1949-51; exptl. metallurgist Allison div. GMC, Indpls., 1951-54; metallurgist, group leader Marquardt Co., Van Nuys, Calif., 1954-57; tech. rep. Pacific Coast Allegheny Ludlum Steel Corp., L.A., 1957-65; dir. materials engring. Marquardt Co., Van Nuys, Calif., 1965-91; pres. F.K. Lampson Assocs., Northridge, Calif., 1975—. Recipient Disting. Merit award, U. Ill., 1983, Engr. '80 Merit award, San Fernando Valley Engring. Coun., 1980. Fellow ASM (trustee 1978-81), Masons, Shriner. Republican. Baptist. Home: 10000 Aldea Ave Northridge CA 91325-1661

LANCASTER, NICHOLAS, educator, researcher; b. Hemel Hempstead, Eng., Dec. 12, 1948; s. Roger Dudley and Pamela Rosemary (Grindley) L.; m. Judith Mary Botting, May 6, 1972. BA with honors, Cambridge U., 1971, MA, 1975, PhD, 1977. Lectr. U. Malawi, Zomba, Malawi, 1973-78; asst. lectr. U. Witwatersrand, Johannesburg, South Africa, 1978-79; rsch. officer Desert Ecol. Rsch. Unit, Gobages, Namibia, 1980-82; lectr., sr. rsch. officer U. Cape Town, South Africa, 1983-85; faculty rsch. assoc. Ariz. State U., Tempe, 1986-88, vis. asst. prof., 1989-90; assoc. rsch. prof. Desert Rsch. Inst., Reno, 1991—; Author: Late Quaternary Paleoenvironments of Southern African, 1988, The Namib Sand Sea, 1989; mem. editorial bd. Geomorphogy, 1991—. Named Outstanding faculty U. Nev., 1992; grantee NSF, 1989-91, 92—, Nat. Geog. Soc., 1990—. Fellow Royal Geog. Soc., Geol. Soc. of Am.; mem. Assn. Am. Geographers, Internat. Assn. Sedimentologists, Am. Quaternary Assn., Sigma Xi. Office: Desert Rsch Inst 7010 Dandini Blvd Reno NV 89512

LANCE, PEGGY ANN, real estate company executive; b. Cin., Feb. 10, 1936; d. Clay H. and Laura (Ross) Byers; m. William J. Lance, June 11, 1955 (div. June 1962); children: Michael, Gregory. BA in Physics cum laude, Calif. State U., Dominguez Hills, 1980, BA in Philosophy summa cum laude, 1980. Lic. real estate broker, real estate appraiser, Calif., cert. general, Calif. V.p., CEO TLI Techs., Anaheim, Calif., 1987-90; pres., CEO Isar, Inc., L.A., 1978-93; pres. Calif. Real Estate Svcs., L.A., 1991—. Housing dir. Family Assistance Program, L.A., 1991—. Office: PO Box 46 Los Angeles CA 90078

LAND, DAVID BENJAMIN, obstetrician and gynecologist; b. Reading, Pa., May 18, 1950; s. Edward Herbert and Marjorie (Kline) L. BS in Chemistry, U. Miami, Fla., 1972; BS in Pharmacy summa cum laude, U. Tex., 1977; DO cum laude, Tex. Coll. Osteopathic Med., Ft. Worth, 1985. Registered pharmacist, Tex. Indsl. auctioneer David Weis Co., L.A., 1972-74; pharmacist Revco Drug/K-Mart, Ft. Worth, Tex., 1977-81; intern West Allegheny Hosp., Oakdale, Pa.; resident Mich. Health Ctr., Detroit, 1986-90; v.p., dir. residency clinic Physician's Svc. Corp., Detroit, 1991—; staff gynecologist Northeastern Regional Hosp., Las Vegas, N.Mex., 1992—. Recipient Merck Sharpe & Dohme Excellence in Rsch. award, 1990. Mem. Am. Osteo. Assn., Tex. Coll. Osteo. Medicine Alumni Assn., N.Mex. Osteo. Med. Assn., Am. Coll. Osteo. Obstetricians and Gynecologists, Am. Soc. Colposcopic Pathologists, Rho Chi. Democrat. Jewish. Home: 752 Diane Ave Las Vegas NM 87701 Office: Rio Vista OB Gyn P.A. 105 Mills Dr #100 Las Vegas NM 87701

LAND, KENNETH DEAN, test and balance agency executive, energy and environmental consultant; b. Central City, Nebr., Oct. 5, 1931; s. Adrew Kenneth Land and Marie Eveline (Weaver) Gehrke; m. Christa Cawthern. AAME, El Camino Coll., 1957; student, Long Beach City Coll., 1958, Calif. State Coll., Long Beach, 1959. Gen. mgr. Air Heat Engrs., Inc., Santa Fe Springs, Calif., 1956-61; sales and estimating engr. Thermodyne Corp., Los Alamitos, Calif., 1962-64; pres., founder Air Check Co., Inc., Santa Ana, Calif., 1964-69; chief engring. technician Nat. Air Balance Co., Los Angeles, 1969-73; gen. mgr. B&M Air Balance Co., South El Monte, Calif., 1973-78; chief exec. officer, founder Land Air Balance Tech. (LABTECH), Las Vegas, Nev., 1978—; bd. dirs. Energy Resources and Mgmt., Inc., 1980—, San-I-Pac, Internat., Inc., 1980—, Energy Equities Group, Inc., 1990—,; founder, pres. Utility Connection, 1990—. Active Las Vegas Founders Club-Las Vegas Invitational PGA Tournament, 1983—, player, 1992; trustee Assoc. Air Balance Coun.-Sheet Metal Workers Internat. Apprenticeship Tng. Fund; mem. Citizens Against Govt. Waste, 1990—, YNOT Night for YMCA, 1987—; mem., co-founder The Golf Com., operators golf tournaments for Am. Cancer Soc., 1990, 91, Nev. Child Seekers, 1992-93, Am. Diabetes Assn., 1992. With USN, 1951-54. Mem. ASHRAE (pres. so. Nev. chpt. 1983-84, editor chpt. bull. 1979-89, Citizen of Yr. 1989), CSI (co-founder Las Vegas chpt., pres. 1989-90, editor, founder chpt. bull. 1987-90, S.W. regional mem. chmn. 1990-91), Assn. Energy Engrs., Am. Soc. Profl. Cons., Associated Air Balance Coun. (cert. test and balance engr. 1966—, pres. 1988-89, bd. dirs. 1982-90, mem. numerous coms.), Sheet Metal Workers Internat. Tng. Fund, Internat. Conf. Bldg. Officials, Internat. Assn. Plumbing and Mech. Officials, Nat. Fedn. Ind. Businessmen, Rotary (So. El Monte Club 1977-78, bull. editor, Las Vegas S.W. Club 1978—, bd. dirs. 1983-85, 88-90, photographer 1987-90, chmn. internat. svc., 4 Paul Harris fellowships), Citizens for Pvt. Enterprise, Nev. Taxpayers Assn., UNLV Golf Found., UNLV Presdl. Assocs. Group, Nev. Devel. Assn., Nev. Nuclear Waste Study Com. adv. coun., Sheet Metal and Air Conditioning Contractors Assn. (nat. and so. Nev. chpt. bd. dirs.), Associated Gen. Contractors (nat. and Las Vegas chpt.), Nat. Energy Mgmt. Inst. (cert., co-chmn. Nev. adv. coun., instr. Energy Mgmt. Tng. 1991), Nev. Energy Resources Assn., Las Vegas C. of C., Nat. Inst. Bldg. Scis., Nev. Assn. Ind. Businessman, Nat. Fire Protection Assn., Am. Soc. Hosp. Engrs., Las Vegas Country Club. Office: Land Air Balance Tech Inc PO Box 26389 Las Vegas NV 89126-0389

LANDAR, HERBERT JAY, linguistics educator, author; b. N.Y.C., Dec. 7, 1927; s. Leo and Mildred (Mann) L.; m. Muriel Anne Epstein; children: Clifford, Nancy, Stephen. BA, Queens Coll., 1949; MA, Yale U., 1955, PhD, 1960. Instr. Reed Coll., Portland, Oreg., 1957-59; prof. linguistics Calif. State U., L.A., 1960—; vis. prof. Ind. U., Bloomington, 1976-77, Université Blaise Pascal, Clermont-Ferrand, France, 1987-88. Author: Language and Culture, 1966, (in Japanese) Kotoba-To Bunka, 1977; contbr. numerous articles to profl. jours. Cpl. U.S. Army, 1950-52. Guggenheim Found. fellow, 1967-68; Fulbright Commn. grantee, 1987-88. Home: 220 San Anselmo Ave San Francisco CA 94127-2030 Office: Calif State U 5151 State University Dr # 637A Los Angeles CA 90032-4221

LANDAU, CHARLES ROBERT, software architect; b. Des Moines, May 22, 1950; s. William Acton and Delisca (Danforth) L. BSEE, MIT, 1972, MSEE, 1972. Rsch. engr. Lawrence Livermore (Calif.) Lab., 1972-76; computer scientist Tymshare, Inc., Cupertino, Calif., 1976-85; scientist Key Logic, Santa Clara, Calif., 1985-91; sr. software engr. Integrated Systems, Inc., Santa Clara, 1991; v.p. MACS Lab., Inc., Santa Clara, 1990—; cons. in field; software designer Tandem Computers, Inc., Cupertino, 1992—. Contbr. articles to profl. jours. Mem. Assn. Computing Machinery. Home: 2454 Brannan Pl Santa Clara CA 95050 Office: Tandem Computers Inc Loc 3-22 19333 Vallco Pkwy Cupertino CA 95014

LANDAU, HENRY GROH, geoenvironmental consulting engineer; b. N.Y.C., Mar. 1, 1943; s. Henry G. and Ann Marie (Skvarich) L.; m. Joyce Kathryn Van de Merlen, July 27, 1965; children: Greg, Amy, Michael. BS in Civil Engring., CCNY, 1965; MS in Geotech. Engring., Purdue U., 1966, PhD in Engring., 1973. Profl. engr., Wash., N.Y., Alaska. Civil engr. Geotechnica, Sao Paulo, Brazil, 1966-67; officer U.S. Army C.E., South Vietnam, 1967-70; sr. engr. Dames & Moore, Seattle, 1973-82; sr. prin. Landau Assocs., Inc., Edmonds, Wash., 1982—; vis. prof. Fed. U., Paraiba, Brazil, 1978-79; mem. Gov.'s Sci. Adv. Bd., Olympia, Wash., 1987-90, chmn., 1990—. Contbr. articles to profl. jours. Tutor math. & sci. Edmonds Sch. Dist.; scout leader Boy Scouts Am., Edmonds, 1986-90. 1st lt. U.S. Army, 1967-70, Vietnam. Mem. ASCE, Soc. Am. Mil. Engrs., Assn. Groundwater Scientists & Engrs. Office: Landau Assocs Inc 23107 100th Ave W Edmonds WA 98020

LANDER, JAMES FRENCH, government scientific administrator, geophysicist, researcher; b. Bristol, Va., Aug. 24, 1931; s. Richard Foster and Gertrude Elanore (Conklin) L.; m. Corinne Johnson Earle, June 18, 1960; children—Jamie Lander Powell, James F., Jr., Vivian Gail. B.A., Pa. State U., 1958; M.S., Am. U., 1962, M.A., 1972. Geophysicist, U.S. Coast and Geodetic Survey, Washington, 1958-72; chief seismol. investigations br. Nat. Earthquake Info. Ctr., Washington and Boulder, Colo., 1965-72; dir. World Data Ctr.-A For Solid Earth Geophysics, Boulder, 1973-83; dep. dir. Nat. Geophys. Data Ctr. NOAA, Boulder, 1972-87; rsch. assoc. in tsunamis U. Colo., 1988—. Author: United States Tsunamis 1690-1988; (with Alexander and Downing) Inventory of Natural Hazards Data Resources in the Federal Government, 1979. Editor: U.S. Earthquakes, 1961, 62. Mem. U.S. Japan Wind and Seismic Effect Panel, 1982—. Served with U.S. Army, 1951-54. Fellow Dept. Commerce Sci., 1970-71. Mem. Pan Am. Union Inst. for Geography and History (U.S. rep.), Internat. Union Geol. and Geophysics (mem. com. on data, tsunami commn., 1991—), Seismol. Soc. Am., Am. Geophys. Union, Sigma XI. Office: U Colo Campus Box 449 University Of Colorado CO 80309

LANDERS, BILLY N., JR., medical/surgical nurse, administrator; b. Wewoka, Okla., Sept. 3, 1949; s. Billy N. Sr. and A. Marie (Pointer) L. AAS, N.Mex. Jr. Coll., Hobbs, 1972. Nat. cert. orthopedic physician asst. Staff nurse in emergency room, critical care med.-surg. unit Lea Gen. Hosp. System, Hobbs; supr. orthopedic assts. Norte Vista Med. Ctr., Ltd., Hobbs; clin. asst., surg. asst. Midland (Tex.) Orthopedic Clinic, Inc.; mgr. orthotics div., purchasing agt., clin. surg. asst. Bone and Joint Ctr. Southeastern N.Mex. Ltd., Hobbs. Asst. scoutmaster Boy Scouts Am., Hobbs, also chmn. com. High Adventure Explorer Post, adv. OA Lodge, 1990—, mem. med. staff 17th World Scout Jamboree, Republic of Korea, 1991. Mem. ANA, Nat. League Nursing, Am. Nurses Found., Am. Soc. Orthopedic Physician Assts., Nat. Assn. Orthopedic Nurses (charter mem., nat. budget and fin. com.), Nat. Nurses Assn., N.Mex. Nurses Assn., Wilderness Edn. Assn., N.Mex. Jr. Coll. Alumni Assn. (bd. dirs. 1990—). Home: PO Box 2514 Hobbs NM 88241-2514

LANDERS, VERNETTE TROSPER, educator, author; b. Lawton, Okla., May 3, 1912; d. Fred Gilbert and LaVerne Hamilton (Stevens) Trosper; m. Paul Albert Lum, Aug. 29, 1952 (dec. May 1955); 1 child, William Tappan; m. 2d, Newlin Landers, May 2, 1959 (dec. Apr. 1990); children: Lawrence, Marlin. AB with honors, UCLA, 1933, MA, 1935, EdD, 1953; Cultural doctorate (hon.) Lit. World U., Tucson, 1985. Tchr. secondary schs., Montebello, Calif., 1935-45, 48-50, 51-59; prof. Long Beach City Coll., 1946-47; asst. prof. Los Angeles State Coll., 1950; dean girls Twenty Nine Palms (Calif.) High Sch., 1960-65; dist. counselor Morongo (Calif.) Unified Sch. Dist., 1965-72, coordinator adult edn., 1965-67, guidance project dir., 1967; clk.-in-charge Landers (Calif.) Post Office, 1962-82; ret., 1982. V.p., sec. Landers Assn., 1965—; sec. Landers Vol. Fire Dept., 1972—; life mem. Hi-Desert Playhouse Guild, Hi-Desert Meml. Hosp. Guild; bd. friends Copper Mountain Coll., 1990-91; bd. dirs., sec. Desert Emergency Radio Service; mem. Rep. Senatorial Inner Circle, 1990-92, Regent Nat. Fedn. Rep. Women, 1990-92, Nat. Rep. Congl. Com., 1990-91, Presdl. Task Force, 1990-92; lifetime mem. Girl Scouts U.S., 1991. Recipient internat. diploma of honor for community service, 1973; Creativity award Internat. Personnel Research Assn., 1972, award Goat Mt. Grange No. 818, 1987; cert. of merit for disting. svc. to edn., 1973; Order of Rose, 1978, Order of Pearl, 1989, Alpha Xi Delta; poet laureate Center of Internat. Studies and Exchanges, 1981; diploma of merit in letters U. Arts, Parma, Italy, 1982; Golden Yr. Bruin UCLA, 1983; World Culture prize Nat. Ctr. for Studies and Research, Italian Acad., 1984; Golden Palm Diploma of Honor in poetry Leonardo Da Vinci Acad., 1984; Diploma of Merit and titular mem. internat. com. Internat. Ctr. Studies and Exchanges, Rome, 1984; Recognition award San Gorgonio council Girl Scouts U.S., 1984—; Cert. of appreciation Morongo Unified Sch. Dist., 1984, 89; plaque for contribution to postal service and community U.S. Postal Service, 1984; Biographee of Yr. award for outstanding achievement in the field of edn. and service to community Hist. Preservations of Am.; named Princess of Poetry of Internat. Ctr. Cultural Studies and Exchange, Italy, 1985; community dinner held in her honor for achievement and service to Community, 1984; Star of Contemporary Poetry Masters of Contemporary Poetry, Internat. Ctr. Cultural Studies and Exchanges, Italy, 1984; named to honor list of leaders of contemporary art and lit. and apptd. titular mem. of Internat. High Com. for World Culture & Arts Leonardo Da Vinci Acad., 1987; named to honor list Foremost Women 20th Century for Outstanding Contbn. to Rsch., IBC, 1987; ABI medal of honor 1987, Golden Acad. award, Presdl. Order of Merit Pres. George Bush-Exec. Coun. of Nat. Rep. Senatorial Com., Congl. cert. of Appreciation U.S. Ho. of Reps.; other awards and certs. Life fellow Internat. Acad. Poets, World Lit. Acad.; mem. Am. Personnel and Guidance Assn., Internat. Platform Assn., Nat. Ret. Tchrs. Assn., Calif. and Nat. Assn. for Counseling and Devel., Am. Assn. for Counseling and Devel. (25 yr. membership pin 1991), Am. Biog. Research Assn. (life dep. gov.), Internat. Biog. Ctr. Eng. (dep. dir. gen. of the Ams. 1987), Nat. Assn. Women Deans and Adminstrs., Montebello Bus. and Profl. Women's Club (pres.), Nat. League Am. Pen Women (sec. 1985-86), Leonardo Da Vinci Acad. Internat. Winged Glory diploma of honor in letters 1982), Landers Area C. of C. (sec. 1985-86, Presdl. award for outstanding service), Desert Nature Mus., Phi Beta Kappa, Pi Lambda Theta (mortar bd., prytakean UCLA, UCLA Golden Yr. Bruin 1983), Sigma Delta Pi, Pi Delta Phi. Clubs: Whittier Toastmistress (Calif.) (pres. 1957); Homestead Valley Women's (Landers). Lodge: Soroptimists (sec. 29 Palms chpt. 1962, life mem., Soroptimist of Yr. local chpt. 19, Woman of Distinction local chpt. 1987-88). Author: Impy, 1974, Talkie, 1975, Impy's Children, 1975; NineteO Four, 1976, Little Brown Bat, 1976; Slo-Go, 1977; Owls Who and Who Who, 1978; Sandy, The Coydog, 1979; The Kit Fox and the Walking Stick, 1980; contbr. articles to profl. jours., poems to anthologies. Guest of honor ground breaking ceremony Landers Elem. Sch., 1989, dedication ceremony, 1991. Home: 632 N Landers Ln PO Box 3839 Landers CA 92285

LANDERSMAN, STUART DAVID, naval tactical consultant; b. Bklyn., May 26, 1930; s. Joseph David and Thelma (Domes) L.; m. Martha Britt Morehead, Sept. 2, 1955; children: David Wesley, Mark Stuart. BA, Dakota Wesleyan U., Mitchell, S.D., 1953; MS, George Washington U., 1967. Commd. ens. USN, 1953, advanced through grades to capt., 1974, retired, 1982; engr. Applied Physics Lab., Johns Hopkins U., Laurel, Md., 1982—; convoy commodore USN, Royal Navy, Can. Armed Forces, 1984-92. Author books on shiphandling, naval tactics, principles of naval warfare; contbr. articles to mags. Decorated Bronze Star, (3) Legion of Merit. Home: 13220 Cooperage Ct Poway CA 92064-1213 Office: JHU/APL Rep COMNAVSURFPAC NAB Coronado San Diego CA 92155-5035

LANDING, BENJAMIN HARRISON, pathologist, educator; b. Buffalo, Sept. 11, 1920; s. Benjamin Harrison Sr. and Margaret Catherine (Crohen) L.; m. Dorothy Jean Hallas; children: Benjamin H., Susan L. Phillips, William M., David A. AB, Harvard U., 1942, MD, 1945. Diplomate Am. Bd. Pathology (anatomic pathology and pediatric pathology). Intern pathology Children's Hosp., Boston, 1945-46, asst. resident, then resident pathology, 1948-49; resident pathology Boston Lying-in Hosp., 1949, Free Hosp. for Women, Brookline, Mass., 1949; pathologist Children's Med. Ctr., Boston, 1950-53, Cin., 1953-61; pathologist-in-chief Children's Hosp., L.A., 1961-88, rsch. pathologist, 1988—; emeritus prof. pathology and pediatrics Sch. Medicine U. So. Calif., 1991—; asst. pathologist Harvard U. Med. Sch., Boston, 1950-53; from asst. to assoc. prof. U. Cin. Coll. of Medicine, 1953-61; prof. pathology and pediatrics U. So. Calif. Sch. of Medicine, L.A., 1961-91. Author: Butterfly Color/Behavior Patterns, 1984; author chpts. in books; contbr. articles to profl. jours. Chmn. Pacific S.W. Dist. Unitarian-Universalist Assn., 1968-70; pres. Burbank (Calif.) Unitarian Fellowship, 1964-66. Capt. USMC, 1946-48. Mem. Soc. for Pediatric Pathology (pres. 1973-74), Internat. Pediatric Pathology Soc. (pres. 1980). Democrat. Unitarian-Universalist. Home: 4513 Deanwood Dr Woodland Hills CA 91364-5622 Office: Childrens Hosp LA Box 103 4650 W Sunset Blvd Los Angeles CA 90027-6016

LANDIS, ELLEN JAMIE, art curator; b. Chgo., May 6, 1941; d. Alvin and Sadie (Reingold) L.; m. Frederick Cohn, Nov. 4, 1984; 1 child, David. BA, U. Calif., Berkeley, 1962; student, U. Vienna (Austria, 1960-61; MA, NYU, 1965. Asst. curator exhbns. and publs. L.A. County Mus. of Art, L.A., 1967-68; curator B.G. Cantor Collection & Art Found., Beverly Hills, Calif., 1968-70; curatorial cons. Robert Gore Rifkind Art Collection, Beverly Hills, 1970; curator painting and sculpture Balt. Mus. of Art, 1970-71; curator Robert Gore Rifkind Art Collection, Beverly Hills, 1974-75; instr. art history and appreciation Yuba Coll., Marysville, Calif., 1976-77; curator art Albuquerque Mus., 1977—. Author: (exhbn. catalogs) Here & Now, 1981, West/Southwest, 1982; editor: (exhbn. catalogs) Hiroshige, 1983, Printers' Impressions, 1990; adv. bd. Artspace Mag., 1978—. Juror Art in Pub. Places, Albuquerque, 1981, One Percent for Art, Albuquerque, 1978, N.Mex. Women in the Arts, Albuquerque, 1979, Suntran, Albuquerque, 1980; bd. trustees Comprehensive Art Pubs., Ohio, 1980—; bd. dirs. Performing Arts Collective, Albuquerque, 1979-81. Recipient Chris award Film Coun. Greater Columbus (Ohio), 1969. Mem. Am. Assn. Museums, N.Mex. Assn. Museums, ICOM, Coll. Art Assn., Sculpture. Home: 7112 Osuna Rd NE Albuquerque NM 87109-2945 Office: Albuquerque Museum 2000 Mountain Rd NW Albuquerque NM 87104-1459

LANDIS, FRED SIMON, film producer; b. Temuco, Chile, Dec. 9, 1943; came to U.S., 1957; s. Albert E. and Gertrude Jaqueline (Steudler) L.; m. Caroline Ann Brawner, May 1, 1983 (div. 1986). BS, U. Ill., 1968, MA, 1971, PhD, 1975. Media cons. Exec. Office of Mayor, Washington, 1977-79, PNP Party, Kingston, Jamaica, 1980, Rep. of Grenada, St. George's, 1983; cons., video producer Sistema Sandinista de Radio y TV, Managua, Nicaragua, 1980-81; prof. of media Chapman Coll., L.A., 1980-82, Calif. State U., L.A., 1981-82, San Francisco State U., 1984-85; film producer Instituto Cubano de Radio & TV, Havana, 1982-84; owner, dir. Brazil Video, San Diego, 1986—; dir. Indochina Resource Ctr., Washington, 1976-77; cons. U.S. Sen. Select Com. on Intelligence, Washington, 1975-76; tchr. of media and politics U. Ill., Urbana, 1971-75; dir. Ctr. for Chilean Documentation, Urbana, 1973-75; polit. commentator, talk show host KPFA, San Francisco, 1984-85, KPFK, L.A., 1982, U. Pasadena TV, 1987. Author: Psychological Warfare and Media Ops, 1976; co-author: (book and play) Death in Washington, 1980, (book) Global Kommunikationsstukturen, 1980, War in the South Atlantic, 1982. William A. Dougherty fellow U. Ill., 1974; Fund for Investigative Journalism grantee, 1976. Mem. AAUP, Am. Polit. Sci. Assn., Am. Soc. Cybernetics, Latin Am. Studies Assn., Am. Film Inst., U. Ill. Alumni Assn., Flemengo Country Club Rio de Janeiro, Phi Kappa Phi. Mem. Socialist Party of Chile. Lutheran.

LANDIS, RICHARD GORDON, retired food company executive; b. Davenport, Okla., Apr. 5, 1920; s. John William and Venna Marie (Perrin) L.; m. Beth L. Throne, Nov. 6, 1943; children: Gary Perrin, Dennis Michael, Kay Ellen. BA, U. LaVerne, 1942; postgrad., Claremont U., 1947; LLD (hon.), U. LaVerne, 1981. Mgmt. Delmonte Corp, San Francisco, 1942-83, pres., 1971-77, pres. & chief exec. officer, 1977-78, chmn. & chief exec. officer, 1978-81; pres. Pacific div. R.J. Reynolds, Inc., San Francisco, 1981-83; chancellor U. LaVerne, Calif.; bd. dirs. Oregon Steel, Portland, Stanford Rsch. Internat., Menlo Park, Calif. Mem. Commn. of Calif., 1984—; chmn. Pacific Basin Econ. Coun., 1975-83; officer Boy Scouts Am., 1946—, Invest in Am.; Lt. USAF, 1942-46. Mem. Pacific Union Club, Bohemian Club, St. Francis Yacht Club, Claremont C. of C., Peachtree C. of C. Republican. Office: 120 Montgomery St Ste 1880 San Francisco CA 94104-4303

LANDOVSKY, JOHN, artistic director; b. Riger, Latvia, Jan. 2, 1935; came to U.S., 1950; s. Jains and Olga (Kalnins) L. Dancer Weirttenberg Stadiis Opera House, Stuttgart, Fed. Republic Germany, 1965, Internat. Ballet Co., Chgo., 1960-70, Lyric Opera of Chgo., 1960-70; asst. prof. U. Ill., Urbana, 1976-80; director Duluth (Minn.) Ballet Co., 1980-82, Ballet Hawaii, Honolulu, 1982, Hawaii State Ballet, Honolulu, 1982—. Office: Hawaii State Ballet 1418 Kapiolani Blvd Honolulu HI 96814-3603

LANDRE, DEBRA ANN, mathematics educator; b. Quantico, Va., Sept. 15, 1955; d. Thomas F. and Joy L. (Carstens) L. BA in French and Math., Bradley U., 1976, MS in Edn., 1977; MS in Math., Ill. State U., 1979. Math. instr. Bradley U., Peoria, Ill., 1977-79, Ill. Valley Community Coll., Peru, 1980, Ill. Wesleyan U., Bloomington, 1981; computer sci. instr. Lincoln Coll., Bloomington, 1981-85; math. instr. Ill. State U., Normal, 1979-85; pres. Quality Input Inc., Normal, 1983-85; dir. acad. computing San Joaquin Delta Coll., Stockton, Calif., 1985-88; math. instr. San Joaquin Delta Coll., Stockton, 1988—. Author: Explorations in Elementary Algebra, 1992, Explorations in Intermediate Algebra, 1992, Explorations in College Algebra, 1992, Explorations in Statistics and Probability, 1992; co-author: Mathematics: Theory into Practice, 1980, Microprocessor-Based Operations: Systems Software, 1985, Microprocessor-Based Operations, 1985, Data Acquisition, 1985, Explorations in Elem. Algebra, 1992, Explorations in Intermediate Algebra, 1992, Explorations in Coll. Algebra, 1992, Explorations in Statistics and Probability 1992.; contbr. articles to profl. jours. Mem. Calif. Assn. Dirs. Acad. Computing (pres. 1988-90), Calif. Ednl. Computer Consortium (bd. dirs. 1987-90, editor 1988-90), No. Calif. Community Coll. Comptuer Consortium (sec./editor 1986-91), Calif. Math. Coun. (editor exec. bd. 1990—, pres. elect 1991—), Phi Delta Kappa. Office: San Joaquin Delta Coll 5151 Pacific Ave Stockton CA 95207-6370

LANDRETH, LIBBIE, park ranger; b. Wichita, Kans., June 23, 1952; d. Jack Evans and Betty Lee (Stephens) L. BA in Human Devel./Psychology, U. Kans., 1975; MS in Park Adminstrn., U. Wyo., 1979. Cert. in human devel., pyschology, park adminstrn. (outdoor recreation). Rsch. asst. Ctr. for Applied Behavior Analysis, Lawrence, Kans., 1975; recreation supr. Lawrence Parks and Recreation Dept., 1976; teaching asst. Dept. Recreation and Park Adminstrn., Laramie, Wyo., 1977; park ranger Nat. Park Svc., Shenandoah Nat. Park, Luray, Va., 1976-79, Nat. Park Svc., Grant-Kohrs Ranch Nat. Hist. Site, Deer Lodge, Mont., 1979-81; supervisory park ranger interpretation Nat. Park Svc., Great Sand Dunes Nat. Monument, Mosca, Colo., 1981—; Southwest Park and Monuments Assn. coord. Great Sand Dunes, Mosca, 1986—. Author: Exploring the Dunes, 1988, (booklet) Wild Basin Self-Discovery Guide, 1977; editor: Montville Trail Guide, 1987, (newspaper) Sand Dunes Breezes, 1989—. Vol. coord. Great Sand Dunes, Mosca, 1983—; vol. Nat. Park Svc. Rocky Mountain Nat. Park, Estes Park, Colo., 1977-78. Mem. Kans. Trail Coun., Shenandoah Natural History Assn., P.E.O., Friends of the Dunes. Presbyterian. Office: Nat Park Svc Great Sand Dunes 11999 Hwy 150 Mosca CO 81146

LANDRUM, LARRY JAMES, computer engineer; b. Santa Rita, N.Mex., May 29, 1943; s. Floyd Joseph and Jewel Helen (Andreska) L.; m. Ann Marie Hartman, Aug. 25, 1963 (div.); children: Larry James, David Wayne, Andrei Mikhail, Donal Wymore; m. 2d, Mary Kathleen Turner, July 27, 1980. Student N.Mex. Inst. Mining and Tech., 1961-62, N. Mex. State U., 1963-65; AA in Data Processing, Eastern Ariz. Coll., 1971; BA in Computer Sci., U. Tex., 1978. Tech. svc. rep. Nat. Cash Register, 1966-73; with ASC super-computer project Tex. Instruments, Austin, 1973-80, computer technician, 1973-75, tech. instr., 1975-76, product engr., 1976-78, operating system programmer, 1978-80; computer engr. Ariz. Pub. Svc., Phoenix, 1980-84, sr. computer engr., 1984-87, lead computer engr., 1987-88, sr. computer engr., 1988-90, sr. control systems engr., 1990—; pres., chmn. bd. dirs. Glendale Community Housing Devel. Orgn., 1993—; instr. computer fundamentals Eastern Ariz. Coll., 1972-73, Rio Salado C.C., Phoenix, 1985-86; mem. bd. trustees Epworth United Meth. Ch., 1987-89, chmn. 1988; mem. community devel. adv. com. City of Glendale (Ariz.), 1988-90, chmn., 1991-92; local arrangements chmn. Conf. on Software Maintenance, 1988. Mem. IEEE Computer Soc., Assn. Computing Machinery, Mensa, Phi Kappa Phi. Methodist. Home: 6025 W Medlock Dr Glendale AZ 85301-7321 Office: Ariz Nuclear Power Project PO Box 52034 Phoenix AZ 85072-2034

LANDSBOROUGH, RON JAMES, health care executive; b. Jerome, Idaho, Oct. 9, 1955; s. James Ron and Lola Cora (Kinsey) L. BS in Engring., Ariz. State U., 1981, M in Health Service Adminstrn., 1985. Registered profl. engr., Calif. Indsl. mfg. engr. Gen. Instrument Corp., Chandler, Ariz., 1981; systems engr. Samaritan health Service, Phoenix, 1982-85; healthcare systems cons. Shared Med. Systems, Phoenix, 1985-90; healthcare industry specialist Gateway Data Scis., Tempe, Ariz., 1990-91; sr. sales rep. IBAX Healthcare Systems, Orange, Calif., 1991—; cons. Ariz. Dept. Transp., Phoenix, 1980; bd. dirs. Tee-Vision Inc., Phoenix; owner, pres. Wholesale Travel, Tour and Cruise, Scottsdale, Ariz. Author: Proceedings of the Summer Regional Conference of the Hospital Management Systems Society of the American Hospital Association, 1984, Hospital and Health Services Administration, 1985. Mem. Am. Coll. Healthcare Execs., Healthcare Fin. Mgmt. Assn., Health Adminstrs. Forum, Active 20/30 Internat., Soc. for

Arts Phoenix, Toastmasters. Republican. Methodist. Home and Office: 1623 E Broadmor Dr Tempe AZ 85282

LANDSBURG, STEVEN ELLIOT, economics and mathematics educator; b. Phila., Feb. 24, 1954; s. Norman and Vivian Leatrice (Klein) L.; m. Lauren Jan Feinstone, Aug. 14, 1983; 1 child, Cayley Elizabeth. MA, U. Rochester, 1974; PhD, U. Chgo., 1979. Asst. prof. U. Iowa, Iowa City, 1981-85; vis. asst. prof. U. Rochester (N.Y.), 1986-88; assoc. prof. Colo. State U., Ft. Collins, 1989—; vis. asst. prof. Cornell, Ithaca, N.Y., 1983, U. Rochester, 1983-84, vis. assoc. prof. 1991—; rsch. assoc. Inst. for Def. Analysis, Princeton, N.J., 1987, Queens U., Kingston, Ont., Can., 1986; visitor Inst. for Advanced Study, Princeton, 1982, 83, 88; mem. Rochester Ctr. for Econ. Rsch., Rochester, 1987—. Author: Price Theory & Applications, 1988, The Armchair Economist, 1993; contbr. articles to math., philos. and econs. jours. Home: 109 Edgewood Ave Rochester NY 14618-3103 Office: Colo State U Math Dept Fort Collins CO 80525

LAND-WEBER, ELLEN, photography educator; b. Rochester, N.Y., Mar. 16, 1943; d. David and Florence (Miller) Epstein; 1 child, Julia. BA, U. Iowa, 1965, MFA, 1968. Faculty mem. UCLA Extension, 1970-74, Orange Coast Coll., Costa Mesa, Calif., 1973, U. Nebr., Lincoln, 1974; asst. prof. photography Humboldt State U., Arcata, Calif., 1974-79, assoc. prof., 1979-83, prof., 1983—; photographer Seagram's Bicentennial Courthouse Project, 1976-77, Nat. Trust for Hist. Preservation/Soc. Photographic Edn., 1987. Author: The Passionate Collector, 1980; contbr. sects. to books; photographs pub. in numerous books and jours. Nat. Endowment for Arts fellow, 1974, 79, 82; Artist's support grantee Unicolor Corp., 1982, Polaroid 20X24 Artist's support grantee, 1990-92, 83; Fulbright sr. fellow, 1993-94. Mem. Soc. for Photog. Edn. (exec. bd. 1979-82, treas. 1979-81, sec. 1981-83). Office: Humboldt State U Art Dept Arcata CA 95521

LANE, GLORIA JULIAN, foundation administrator; b. Chgo., Oct. 6, 1932; d. Coy Berry and Katherine (McDowell) Julian; m. William Gordon Lane (div. Oct. 1958); 1 child, Julie Kay Rosewood. BS in Edn., Cen. Mo. State U., 1958; MA, Bowling Green State U., 1959; PhD, No. Ill. U., 1972. Cert. tchr. Assoc. prof. William Jewell Coll., Liberty, Mo., 1959-60; chair forensic div. Coral Gables (Fla.) High Sch., 1960-64; assoc. prof. No. Ill. U., DeKalb, 1964-70; prof. Elgin (Ill.) Community Coll., 1970-72; owner, pub. Lane and Assocs, Inc., San Diego, 1972-78; prof. Nat. U., San Diego, 1978-90; pres., chief exec. officer Women's Internat. Ctr., San Diego, 1982—; founder, dir. Living Legacy Awards, San Diego, 1984—. Author: Project Text for Effective Communications, 1972, Project Text for Executive Communication, 1980, Positive Concepts for Success, 1983; editor Who's Who Among San Diego Women, 1984, 85, 86, 90—, Systems and Structure, 1984. Named Woman of Accomplishment, Soroptimist Internat., 1985, Pres.'s Coun. San Diego, 1986, Center City Assn., 1986, Bus. and Profl. Women, San Diego, 1991, Woman of Yr., Girls' Clubs San Diego, 1986, Woman of Vision, Women's Internat. Ctr., 1990, Wonderwoman 2000 Women's Times Newspaper, 1991; recipient Independence award Ctr. for Disabled, 1986. Home and Office: 6202 Friars Rd Apt 311 San Diego CA 92108-1008

LANE, JAMES F., software engineer; b. Jersey City, Nov. 6, 1953; s. Francis Robert and Margaret Ellen Lane. BS in Computer Sci., Worcester Poly. Inst., 1971-75; postgrad., U. Colo., 1978. Software engr. LFE Corp., Waltham, Mass., 1975-76, Martin Maretta, Waterton, Colo., 1976-77; sr. software engr. Digital Group, Denver, 1977; systems analyst Johns-Manville, Littleton, Colo., 1977-78; systems software designer, project leader Microsoft, Redmond, Wash., 1978-85; pres. Elvyn Software, Inc., Redmond, Wash., 1985-87; mgr. PDL group, mgr. software engring. dept. Hanzon Data Inc., Bothell, Wash., 1985-90; owner Novelty Hill Software, Inc., Redmond, 1987—. Editor (newsletter) Madrone Leaf, 1983-84. Vol. Seattle Folklife Fest, 1988-93. Mem. Soc. Creative Anachronism, Ind. Computer Cons. Assn., Pacific N.W. PC Users Group, Seattle Lindyhoppers Performance Dance. Co., Ballos Argentinos Tango Performance Troupe. Home: 22006 NE 114th St Redmond WA 98053-5701 Office: Novelty Hill Software Inc Redmond WA 98053

LANE, JOHN RODGER, art museum director; b. Evanston, Ill., Feb. 28, 1944; s. John Crandall Lane and Jeanne Marie (Rodger) L. Moritz; m. Inge-Lise Eckmann, 1992. B.A., Williams Coll., 1966; M.B.A., U. Chgo., 1971; A.M., Harvard U., 1973, Ph.D., 1976. Asst. dir. Fogg Art Mus., Cambridge, Mass., 1974; exec. asst. to dir., adminstr. curatorial affairs, asst. dir. curatorial affairs Bklyn. Mus., N.Y.C., 1975-80; dir. Carnegie Mus. Art, Pitts., 1980-86, San Francisco Mus. Modern Art, 1987—. Author: Stuart Davis: Art and Art Theory, 1978; co-editor: Abstract Painting and Sculpture in America 1927-1944, 1983, Carnegie International, 1985. Served to lt. USNR, 1966-69. Nat. Endowment Arts Mus. fellow, 1974-75. Mem. Assn. Art Mus. Dirs., Am. Assn. Museums, Internat. Council Museums, Coll. Art Assn. Office: San Francisco Mus Modern Art 401 Van Ness Ave San Francisco CA 94102-4582

LANE, THOMAS ALFRED, laboratory manager; b. Sidney, Mont., July 22, 1947; s. Alfred Ralph and Agnes Lillian (Johnson) L.; m. Shirley Ann Niemuth, June 14, 1970; children: Andrew, Stephanie. BA, Linfield Coll., McMinnville, Oreg., 1969; MS, Oreg. State U., 1976. Chemist Deschutes Valley Sanitation, Terre Bonne, Oreg., 1975-76, Atlantic Richfield Hanford Co., Richland, Wash., 1976-77; chemist Rockwell Hanford Co., Richland, 1977-79, program rep., 1979-82, mgr. plutonium process devel., 1982-86, mgr. applied tech., 1986-87; mgr. applied tech. Westinghouse Hanford Co., Richland, 1987-90, dep. mgr. analytical ops., 1990-92; site mgr. Oak Ridge Rsch. Inst., Richland, 1992—. Loaned exec. United Way, 1990, key person, 1989, 92; leadership officer CAP, 1989—, adminstrv. officer, 1989—, pers. officer, 1989—. Sgt. U.S. Army, 1971-74. Mem. Nat. Mgmt. Assn. (treas. 1984-85, sr. v.p. 1985-86, v.p. 1986-87, pres. 1987-88, dir. 1988-89, Svc. awards 1986, 87, 88), Am. Chem. Soc. (sec. Richland sect. 1984, chair elect 1985, chmn. 1986), Inst. Cert. Profl. Mgrs. (cert. mgr.), Nat. Registry Environ. Profls. (registered). Office: Oak Ridge Rsch Inst 3100 George Washington Way Richland WA 99352

LANE, TIM DENNIS, accounting executive, systems analyst, programmer; b. San Francisco, June 30, 1954; s. Michael Everett and Amanda (Blasig) L.; m. Amy Rose Frankel, Aug. 4, 1984. BA in Bus. Adminstrn. and Acctg., Calif. State U., Fullerton, 1977. Cert. tax preparer, Calif. Mgr. Tastee of Costa Mesa, Calif., 1972-76; zone mgr. Utotem of Calif., Costa Mesa, 1976-79; store mgr. West Coast Convenience Stores, San Diego, 1979-80; sr. payroll auditor Sanford M. Bennett, Acct., San Diego, 1981-87; contr. South Bay Boat Yard, Chula Vista, Calif., 1987-90; dir. fin. and adminstr. San Diego Harbor Excursion, 1990—; cons. in field., San Diego, 1987—. Programmer, author: (software) Inventory Control System, 1989, Lodge Record System, 1990, Contract Log System, 1990. Fin. mgr. Holiday Project, San Diego, 1983-86, chmn., 1987. Mem. Mensa, Beta Alpha Psi (membership chair 1976). Office: San Diego Harbor Excursion PO Box 751 San Diego CA 92112-0751

LANE, WILLIAM KENNETH, physician; b. Butte, Mont., Nov. 5, 1922; s. John Patrick and Elizabeth Marie (Murphy) L.; m. Gilda Antoinette Parision, Aug. 21, 1954; children: William S., Francine Deirdre. Student, U. Mont., 1940-41, Mt. St. Charles Coll., 1941-43; MD, Marquette U., 1946. Intern Queen of Angels Hosp., L.A., 1946-47, resident physician, 1954-56; pvt. practice internal medicine San Francisco, 1947-51; resident in urology VA Hosp., Long Beach, Calif., 1956-58; physician VA Hosp., Long Beach, Oakland and Palo Alto, Calif., 1958—; lectr. on psychology of the elderly Foothill Coll., Los Altos, 1972-74; rschr. in field. Bd. dirs., mem. No. Cheyenne Indian Sch.; mem. Josef Meier's Black Hills Theatrical Group, S.D., 1940. With U.S. Army, 1943-46, ETO, lt. USN, 1951-54, Korea. Mem. AMA, Am. Geriatrics Soc., Nat. Assn. VA Physicians, San Francisco County Med. Soc., Woodrow Wilson Ctr. (assoc.), St. Vincent de Paul Soc., Cupertino Landscape Artists (past pres.), Audubon Soc., Stanford Hist. Soc., San Jose Camera Club. Roman Catholic. Home: 18926 Sara Park Cir Saratoga CA 95070-4164 Office: Stanford VA Med Ctr 3801 Miranda Ave # 171 Palo Alto CA 94304-1207

LANE-OREIRO, LAVERNE TERESA, Indian tribal official; b. Bellingham, Wash., Aug. 29, 1951; d. Vernon Adrian and Nancy Ann (Solomon) Lane; m. David William Cagey Oreiro, Oct. 27, 1979; children: Tyson Hawk, Cody Lane. Student, Grenoble, France, 1972-73; BA in Humanities, Seattle U., 1974. Asst. dir. social svcs. Lummi Indian Tribe, Bellingham, 1974-77, dir. fed. contracts, 1977-78, exec. dir., 1978-81; real estate agt. Ron Bennett & Assocs., Bellingham, 1982-86; Indian edn. coord. Ferndale (Wash.) Pub. Schs., 1984—; vice-chairperson Lummi Indian Nation, 1991-93; pub. speaker and presentor for local confs. and community functions; bd. chairperson Lummi Tribal Enterprises, Bellingham, 1978-80; bd. dirs. minority sci. and engring. adv. bd. U. Wash., Seattle, 1967-91; mem. minority community adv. bd. Western Wash. U., Bellingham, 1989-93; Wash. state del-at-large White House Conf. on Indian Edn., Washington, 1992. Writer eulogies for variety of tribal mems. including tribal leaders, elders, etc. Co-chairperson Nat. Indian Women's Fast Pitch, Lummi Indian Reservation, 1978, co-MC Nat. Indian Edn. Opening Rec., Spokane, Wash., 1985. Mem. Wash. State Indian Edn. Assn. (bd. sec. 1985-86, 1st v.p. 1986-87), Western Wash. Native Am. Edn. Consortium (vice-chairperson 1985-86, chairperson 1986-87). Democrat. Roman Catholic. Home: 2210 Lummi View Dr Bellingham WA 98226-9208 Office: Ferndale Sch Dist #502 PO Box 428 Ferndale WA 98248

LANEY, LEROY OLAN, economist, banker; b. Atlanta, Mar. 20, 1943; s. Lee Edwin and Paula Izlar (Bishop) L.; m. Sandra Elaine Prescott, Sept. 3, 1966; children: Prescott Edwin, Lee Olan III. B Indsl. Engring., Ga. Inst. Tech., 1965; MBA in Fin., Emory U., 1967; MA in Econs., U. Colo., 1974, PhD in Econs., 1976. Budget analyst Martin-Marietta Corp., Denver, 1971-72; economist Coun. Econ. Advisers, Washington, 1974-75; internat. economist U.S. Treasury Dept., Washington, 1975-78; sr. economist Fed. Res. Bank Dallas, 1978-88; prof. econs., chmn. dept. Butler U., Indpls., 1989-90; v.p., chief economist 1st Hawaiian Bank, Honolulu, 1990—; chmn. Fed. Res. Com. on Internat. Rsch., Washington, 1981-83; vis. prof. U. Tex., Arlington and Dallas, 1978-85; adj. prof. So. Meth. U., Dallas, 1982-85. Editor bank periodicals, 1975-88; contbr. articles to profl. jours. Mem. Internat. Fin. Symposium, Dallas, 1982-85, Overland Stage Neighborhood Assn., Arlington, 1983-88, Hawaii Coun. on Revenues. Lt. USN, 1967-71. Scholar Ga. Inst. Tech., 1961; rsch. fellow Emory U., 1965-67, teaching fellow U. Colo., 1972-73; rsch. grantee Butler U., 1989-90. Mem. Am. Econ. Assn., Western Econ. Assn., Indpls. Econ. Forum, Plaza Club, Omicron Delta Epsilon, Kappa Sigma. Office: 1st Hawaiian Bank 165 S King St Honolulu HI 96847-0001

LANG, GEORGE FRANK, insurance executive, consultant, lawyer; b. Orange, N.J., Aug. 21, 1937; s. Frank W. and Hilda I. (Pierson) L.; m. Grace B. Preisler, Jan. 30, 1960; children: Christine, Gregg, Cynthia; m. Valerie J. Hanson, Nov. 24, 1978. BS, Ill. Wesleyan U., 1960; JD, Ill. Inst. Tech., 1968. Account exec. Scarborough & Co., Chgo., 1960-67; dir. fin. inst. George F. Brown & Sons, Chgo., 1967-69; v.p., dir. Fin. Ins. Svc., Schaumburg, Ill., 1969-79; pres. City Ins. Svc., Elizabeth, N.J., 1980-84; mng. dir. Res. Fin. Mgmt., Miami, Fla., 1984-85; v.p. Beneficial Ins. Group, Newport Beach, Calif., 1985-86; v.p. Ask Ins. Svc., Irvine, Calif., 1986-89, cons. product ctr. sales, 1989; cons. Nat. Dealer Ins. Systems, 1989, New Liberty Adminstrn., 1990—, Home Crest Ins., 1991—, Great Western Ins. Agy., 1992—; cons. in field. Bd. dirs. Woodview Civic Assn., Mt. Prospect, Ill., 1964-70, pres., bd. dirs., 1969; bd. dirs. Chippendale Assn., Barrington, Ill., 1972-76, v.p., bd. dirs., 1976. Home: 203 E Ave San Juan San Clemente CA 92672-3212

LANG, MARGO TERZIAN, artist; b. Fresno, Calif.; d. Nishan and Araxie (Kazarosian) Terzian; m. Nov. 29, 1942; children: Sandra J. (Mrs. Ronald L. Carr), Roger Mark, Timothy Scott. Student, Fresno State U., 1939-42, Stanford U., 1948-50, Prado Mus., Madrid, 1957-59, Ariz. State U., 1960-61; workshops with, Dong Kingman, Ed Whitney, Rex Brandt, Millard Sheets, George Post. Maj. exhbns. include, Guadalajara, Mex., Brussels, N.Y.C., San Francisco, Chgo., Phoenix, Corcoran Gallery Art, Washington, internat. watercolor exhbn., Los Angeles, Bicentennial shows, Hammer Galleries, N.Y.C., spl. exhbn. aboard, S.S. France, others, over 50 paintings in various Am. embassies throughout world; represented in permanent collections, Nat. Collection Fine Arts Mus., Smithsonian Instn.; lectr., juror art shows; condr. workshops.; interviews and broadcasts on Radio Liberty, Voice of Am. Bd. dirs. Phoenix Symphony Assn., 1965-69, Phoenix Musical Theater, 1965-69. Recipient award for spl. achievements Symphony Assn., 1966, 67, 68, 72, spl. awards State of Ariz., silver medal of excellence Internat. Platform Assn., 1971; honoree U.S. Dept. State celebration of 25 yrs. of exhbn. of paintings in embassies worldwide, 1989. Mem. Internat. Platform Assn., Ariz. Watercolor Assn., Nat. Soc. Arts and Letters (nat. dir. 1971-72, nat. art chmn. 1974-76), Nat. Soc. Lit. and Arts, Phoenix Art Mus., Friends of Mexican Art, Am. Artists Profl. League, English-Speaking Union, Musical Theater Guild, Ariz. Costume Inst., Phoenix Art Mus., Scottsdale Art Ctr., Ariz. Arts Commn. (fine arts panel 1990-91). Home: 6127 E Calle Del Paisano Scottsdale AZ 85251-4212

LANG, ROBERT JAMES, engineering educator, consultant; b. N.Y.C., Feb. 11, 1952; s. Adam J. and Anna E. (Hofmann) L.; m. Betty Ruiz; children: Alex, Juan. BSCE, U. Calif., Davis, 1978, MSCE, 1982, PhD in Civil Engring., 1989. Registered profl. engr., Calif. Civil engr. U.S. Forest Svc., Porterville, Calif., 1978-80; researcher U. Calif., Davis, 1980-82; civil engr. Imperial (Calif.) Irrigation Dist., 1982-90; assoc. prof. civil engring. Calif. Poly State U., San Luis Obispo, 1991—; cons. in field. Mem. ASCE. Roman Catholic. Home: PO Box 6512 Los Osos CA 93412 Office: Dept Civil Engring Calif Poly State Univ San Luis Obispo CA 93407

LANG, THOMPSON HUGHES, publishing company executive; b. Albuquerque, Dec. 12, 1946; s. Cornelius Thompson and Margaret Miller (Hughes) L. Student, U. N.Mex., 1965-68, U. Americas, Mexico City, 1968-69. Advt. salesman Albuquerque Pub. Co., 1969-70, pres., treas., gen. mgr., dir., 1971—; pub., pres., treas., dir. Jour. Pub. Co., 1971—; pres., dir. Masthead, Internat., 1971—; pres. Magnum Systems, Inc., 1973—; pres., treas., dir. Jour. Ctr. Corp., 1979—; chmn. bd., dir. Starline Printing, Inc., 1985—; chmn. bd. dirs. Corp. Security and Investigation, Inc., 1986—; pres., bd. dirs. Eagle Systems, Inc., 1986—. Mem. HOW Orgn., Sigma Delta Chi. Home: 8643 Rio Grande Blvd NW Albuquerque NM 87114-1301 Office: Albuquerque Pub Co PO Drawer JT(87103) 7777 Jefferson St NE Albuquerque NM 87109-4343

LANG, WILLIAM EDWARD, mathematics educator; b. Salisbury, Md., Oct. 22, 1952; s. Woodrow Wilson and Clara T. L. BA, Carleton Coll., 1974; MS, Yale U., 1975; PhD, Harvard U., 1978. Vis. mem. Inst. for Advanced Study, Princeton, N.J., 1978-79; exch. prof. Universite de Paris, Orsay, 1980; C.L.E. Moore instr. MIT, Cambridge, 1980-82; asst. prof. U. Minn., Mpls., 1982-83, assoc. prof., 1983-89; vis. assoc. prof. Brigham Young U., Provo, Utah, 1988-89, prof., 1989—. Contbr. articles to profl. jours. Fellow NSF 1974-77, 79-80. Mem. Am. Math. Soc., Math. Assn. Am., Math. Scis. Rsch. Inst., Sigma Xi. Republican. Office: Brigham Young Univ Dept Math Provo UT 84602

LANGAGER, JOANNE JACKSON, information systems director; b. Nashville, Mar. 11, 1953; d. Samuel Whatley Jackson and Lois Yvonne (Johnson) Rafferty; m. Robert Maxwell Kelch, June 28, 1975 (div. Apr. 15, 1981); 1 child, Brian Robert Kelch; m. Paul Michael Langager, Jan. 12, 1985. Cert. Completion, U. Poitiers, France, 1973; BA, U. Redlands, 1975; postgrad., U. Nev., 1980-83. V.p. Computer System Concepts, Las Vegas, 1981-86; sr. programmer/analyst Greyhound Exposition Svcs., Las Vegas, 1986-91, dir. info. systems, 1991—. Past pres. Philanthropic Ednl. Ogrn., Las Vegas, 1981-82; bd. dirs. Spanish Trail C.C. Ladies Assn., Las Vegas, 1990-91; den leader, pack leader Boy Scouts of Am., 1986-90. Mem. Assn. for Computer Machinery, Spanish Trail Country Club (club champion 1986), Phi Beta Kappa. Republican. Office: Greyhound Exposition Svcs 1624 S Mojave Las Vegas NV 89104

LANGBERG, BARRY BENSON, lawyer; b. Balt., Nov. 24, 1942; s. Nathan and Marion (Cohen) L.; m. Vickie Williams, Mar. 27, 1978 (div. 1987); children: Mitchell, Marie, Elena. BA, U. San Francisco, 1964, JD, 1968. Bar: Calif. 1971, U.S. Dist. Ct. (cen. dist.) Calif. 1971, U.S. Supreme Ct. 1974, U.S. Tax Ct. 1976. Dep. pub. defender Los Angeles County, 1971-72; assoc. Trope & Trope, L.A., 1972-74, Hayes & Hume, Beverly Hills, Calif., 1974-85; pres. David Jamison Carlyle Corp., L.A., 1979-84; ptnr. Hayes, Hume, Petas & Langberg, L.A., 1985-89; atty. Barry B. Langberg & Assocs., L.A., 1989—; prof. Mid-Valley Coll. Law, L.A., 1972-82; lectr. U. So. Calif., 1980. Mem. ABA. Democrat. Office: 2049 Century Park E Ste 3030 Los Angeles CA 90067

LANGDELL, JOHN IRVING, psychiatrist, retired educator; b. Chino, Calif., Apr. 19, 1922; s. Walter Irving and Florence Delsa (Reichenbach) L.; m. Patricia Louise Waterman, June 9, 1946; children: James Christopher, William Walter. BA, Pomona Coll., 1943, Stanford U., 1944; MD, Stanford U., 1947. Diplomate Am. Bd. Psychiatry and Neurology. (cert. child psychiatry). Rotating intern San Francisco Gen Hosp., 1946-47; resident in psychiatry Langley Inst., San Francisco, 1950-52; resident in child psychiatry U. Calif., San Francisco, 1952-54, from. instr. to assoc. clin. prof., 1956-88; dir. divsn. mental hygiene San Francisco Dept. Pub. Health, 1954-56; pvt. practice psychiatrist San Francisco, 1954—; prin. investigator U. Calif., San Francisco, 1958-67; cons. U.S. Army, San Francisco, 1960-70; cons., surveyor Joint Commn. on Accredation of Hosps., 1974-79. Contbr. articles to profl. jours., chpts. to books. With USNR, 1943-49. Fellow Am. Psychiat. Assn., Am Acad. Child Psychiatry; mem. San Francisco Acad. Hypnosis (bd. dirs., trustee, pres. 1975). Democrat. Home and Office: 1756-14th Ave San Francisco CA 94122

LANGDON, PAUL RUSSELL, retired accountant; b. Columbus, Ohio, Feb. 17, 1914; s. Waren Elmore and Ethel Hulda (Cowgill) L.; m. Marjorie Clark, Nov. 28, 1935; children: Larry R., Robert C. BSc, Ohio State U., 1935; postgrad., Am. U., Northwestern U. CPA, Ohio. Pub. acct. W.E. Langdon & Sons, Columbus, 1935-39, 47-48; dir. fin. U.S. R.R. Retirement Bd., Chgo., 1939-46; procedures analyst Nationwide Ins. Co., Columbus, 1948-49; asst. treas. Battelle Meml. Inst., Columbus, 1949-79. Mem. Columbus Sch. Bd., 1953-83, pres., 1958, 63, 65, 78; pres. Ohio Sch. Bds. Assn., Westerville, 1971; chmn. exec. com. Billy Graham Ctrl. Ohio Crusade, Columbus, 1964; trustee, sec. Malone Coll., Canton, Ohio, 1955-75; trustee mem. Columbus Tech. Inst., 1966-69. Recipient Spl. award for vocat. gidance Columbus Kiwanis, 1983, Emmerling Mgmt. award Adminstrv. Mgmt. Soc., 1960, Bronze Leadership award Jr. Achievement, Columbus, 1983. Mem. Ohio Soc. CPAs (life), PTA (life), Fin. Execs. Inst. (life). Republican. Presbyterian. Home: 4952 Farnham Dr Newark CA 94560

LANGE, GARY DAVID, periodontist; b. Mpls., Dec. 13, 1936; s. Emil and Esther Catherine (Schwartzkopf) L.; m. Donna Lynn Hall, Mar. 23, 1969; 1 child: Christian Elizabeth. BA, Augsburg Coll., Mpls., 1959; BS, U. Minn., 1961, DDS, 1963, MSD, 1971. Lic. periodontist. Dental intern U. S. Army Dental Corps, Tacoma, 1963-64; staff dentist and comdg. officer U. S. Army Dental Sect., Fulda, Fed. Republic of Germany, 1964-67; staff dentist U. S. Army Dental Corps, Ft. Bragg, N.C., 1967-69; periodontal resident U. Minn., Mpls., 1969-71; pvt. practice Rochester, Minn., 1971-74; staff periodontist VA, St. Petersburg, Fla., 1974-83, dir. gen. practice residency, 1983-86; chief dental svc. VA, Columbia, Mo., 1986-92, VA Med. Ctr., Prescott, Ariz., 1992—; asst. prof. Sch. Dentistry U. Minn., 1971-73, Kansas City Dental Sch. div. Grad. Periodontics U. Mo., 1987—. Maj. U.S. Army, 1963-69. Mem. ADA, Am. Acad. Periodontology, Columbia Dental Soc. Republican. Home: 2069 Meadowbrook Rd Prescott AZ 86303

LANGE, HOWARD AARON, non-profit agency administrator; b. Fridley, Minn., Aug. 7, 1964; s. Melvin Howard and Diane Janet L. BA, Grinnell Coll., 1986. Admissions counselor Lake Superior State U., Sault Ste. Marie, Mich., 1987-89; dir. planning, devel. The Community Action Com., Santa Barbara, Calif., 1990—. Recipient Good Citizenship medal SAR, 1982; Sloan Rsch. grantee Grinnell Coll., 1984.

LANGENHEIM, JEAN HARMON, biology educator; b. Homer, La., Sept. 5, 1925; d. Vergil Wilson and Jeanette (Smith) H.; m. Ralph Louis Langenheim, Dec. 1946 (div. Mar. 1961). BS, U. Tulsa, 1946; MS, U. Minn., 1949, PhD, 1953. Rsch. assoc. botany U. Calif., Berkeley, 1954-59, U. Ill., Urbana, 1959-61; rsch. fellow biology Harvard U., Cambridge, Mass., 1962-66; asst. prof. biology U. Calif., Santa Cruz, 1966-68, assoc. prof. biology, 1968-73, prof. biology, 1973—; academic v.p. Orgn. Tropical Studies, San Jose, Costa Rica, 1975-78; mem. sci.adv. bd. EPA, Washington, 1977-81; chmn. com. on humid tropics U.S. Nat. Acad. Nat. Research Council, 1975-77; mem. com. floral inventory Amazon NSF, Washington, 1975-87. Author: Botany-Plant Biology in Relation to Human Affairs.; Contbr. articles to profl. jours. Grantee NSF, 1966-88; recipient Disting. Alumni award U. Tulsa, 1979. Fellow AAAS, AAUW, Calif. Acad. Scis., Calif. Acad. Scis., Bunting Inst.; mem. Bot. Soc. Am., Ecol. Soc. Am. (pres. 1986-87), Internat. Soc. Chem. Ecology (pres. 1986-87), Assn. for Tropical Biology (pres. 1985-86), Soc. for Econ. Btoany (pres. 1993). Home: 191 Palo Verde Ter Santa Cruz CA 95060-3214 Office: U Calif Dept Biology Sinsheimer Labs Santa Cruz CA 95064

LANGER, GLENN ARTHUR, cellular physiologist, educator; b. Nyack, N.Y., May 5, 1928; s. Adolph Arthur and Marie Catherine (Doscher) L.; m. Beverly Joyce Brawley, June 5, 1954 (dec. Nov. 1976); 1 child, Andrea; m. Marianne Phister, Oct. 12, 1977. BA, Colgate U., 1950; MD, Columbia U., N.Y.C., 1954. Diplomate Am. Bd. Internal Medicine. Asst. prof. medicine Columbia U. Coll. Physicians and Surgeons, N.Y.C., 1963-66; assoc. prof. medicine and physiology UCLA Sch. Medicine, 1966-69, prof., 1969—, Castera prof. of cardiology, 1978—, assoc. dean rsch., 1986-91, dir. cardiovascular rsch. lab., 1987—; Griffith vis. prof. Am. Heart Assn., L.A., 1979; cons. Acad. Press, N.Y.C., 1989—. Editor: The Mammalian Myocardium, 1974, Calcium and the Heart, 1990; mem. editorial bd. Circulation Rsch., 1971-76, Am. Jour. Physiology, 1971-76, Jour. Molecular Cell Cardiology, 1974—; contbr. over 170 articles to profl. jours. Capt. U.S. Army, 1955-57. Recipient Disting. Achievement award Am. Heart Assn. Sci. Coun., 1982, Heart of Gold award, 1984, Cybulski medal Polish Physiol. Soc., 1990, award for cardiovascular sci. Pasarow Found., 1993; Macy scholar Josiah Macy Found., 1979-80. Fellow AAAS, Am. Coll. Cardiology; mem. Am. Soc. Clin. Investigation, Am. Assn. Physicians. Office: UCLA Sch Medicine Los Angeles CA 90024

LANGER, JAMES STEPHEN, physicist, educator; b. Pitts., Sept. 21, 1934; s. Bernard F. and Liviette (Roth) L.; m. Elinor Goldmark Aaron, Dec. 21, 1958; children: Ruth, Stephen, David. B.S., Carnegie Inst. Tech., 1955; Ph.D., U. Birmingham, Eng., 1958. Prof. physics Carnegie-Mellon U., Pitts., 1958-82, assoc. dean, 1971-74; prof. physics U. Calif., Santa Barbara, 1982—, dir. Inst. for Theoretical Physics, 1989—; mem. bd. on engring. edn. NRC. Contbr. articles to profl. jours. Vice pres. physics Com. Concerned Scientists, 1979—. Guggenheim fellow, 1974-75; Marshall scholar, 1955-57. Fellow AAAS, Am. Acad. Arts and Scis., Am. Phys. Soc.; mem. NAS, N.Y. Acad. Scis. Democrat. Jewish. Home: 1130 Las Canoas Ln Santa Barbara CA 93105-2331 Office: U Calif Inst Theoretical Physics Santa Barbara CA 93106

LANGER, SIDNEY, physical chemist; b. N.Y.C., Dec. 15, 1925; s. Nathan and Sadie (Shlivek) L.; divorced; 1 child, Gail Margarette. Grad., NYU, 1949; student, U. Calif., Berkeley, 1949-50; PhD, Ill. Inst. Tech., 1955. Chemist Oak Ridge (Tenn.) Nat. Lab., 1954-60; sr. chemist, dept. mgr., sr. scientist Gen. Atomics, San Diego, 1960-83; prin. scientist EG&G, Idaho, Idaho Falls, 1984-89; sr. scientist Sci. Applications Internat. Corp., San Diego, 1989-93, cons., 1993—. Co-author: (booklet) Nuclear Power and the Environment-Questions and Answers, 1975. Fellow Am. Nuclear Soc. (bd. dirs. 1980-83, Meritorious Svc. award 1975, Exceptional Svc. award 1975, Outstanding Svc. award 1983); mem. Am. Chem. Soc., AAAS, Sigma Xi, Phi Beta Kappa. Office: Sci Applications Internat 10210 Campus Point Dr San Diego CA 92121-1598

LANGEREIS-BACA, MARIA, speech-language pathologist; b. Hoorn, Netherlands, Dec. 16, 1930; came to U.S., 1956; d. Jan and Ditje (Schollée) Langereis; m. Stanley H. Skigen (dec.); 1 child, Michelle Arlene; m. Wilhelm Voebel (div.); children: George L., Helene Patimah; m. Gregorio Baca. BS, N.Mex. State U., 1982, MS in Speech, MS in Ednl. Mgmt. Devel., 1985, EdD in Ednl. Mgmt. Devel., 1989. Cert. elem. tchr., ednl. adminstr., speech-lang. pathologist. Asst. personnel mgr. D.M. Read Inc., Bridgeport, Conn., 1960-62; order librarian U. Bridgeport (Conn.), 1962-65; dir. community house Nichols Improvement Assn., Trumbull, Conn., 1960-65; speech-lang. pathologist Las Cruces (N.Mex.) Pub. Schs., 1984-88, Hatch (N.Mex.) Pub. Schs., 1985-89, Albuquerque Pub. Schs., 1989—; cons. Hospice Inc., Las Cruces, 1985-89, Associated Health Service, Las Cruces, 1986-89; ednl. cons., 1988—. Leader Girl Scouts Am., Las Cruces, 1976-77; leader 4H Club, Las

Cruces, 1978-80; vol. Las Cruces Pub. Schs., 1978-79. Mem. Am. Speech Hearing and Lang. Assn., N.Mex. Speech Hearing and Lang. Assn., Assn. Supervision and Curriculum Devel., Phi Kappa Phi, Phi Delta Kappa. Republican. Roman Catholic. Club: Singles Scene (bd. dirs. 1985—). Home: 6309 Loftus Ave NE Albuquerque NM 87109-2717

LANGERMAN, DUANE L., construction executive; b. Ellsworth, Kans., Feb. 4, 1943; s. Dell Miles and Irma Alice Langerman; m. Linda Ruth Wilson, Dec. 27, 1962; children: Scott Miles, Craig James. Student, Brown-Mackie Coll., 1961-62, Morningside Coll., 1976-80. Acct. James & Beckman Constrn., Sylvan Grove, Kans., 1962-63; office mgr. Wells Dept. Store, Salina, Kans., 1963-64; asst. retail mgr. Sch. Splty. Supply, Salina, Kans., 1964-65; project acct. Western Contracting Corp., Sioux City, Iowa, 1965-69, chief acct., 1971-80; acct., internal auditor Univ. Computing, Riverton, Wyo., 1969-71; contr. N.L. Cole Constrn. Co., Lincoln, Nebr., 1980-82; adminstrv. mgr. Green Constrn. Co., Dallas, 1983-89; v.p. adminstrn. Green Alaska, Inc., Anchorage, 1989—; mem. steering com. Green Holdings, Inc., Denver, 1989—. Arctic Nat. Wildlife Refuge Com., The Alliance; chair Pacific N.W. Congl. Del. Subcom.; bd. dirs. Alaska Support Alliance, 1991—; elder, bldg. chair First Presbyn. Ch., 1976-79. Mem. Elks. Office: Green Alaska Inc 125 W 5th Ave Anchorage AK 99501-2521

LANGFORD, ROBERT BRUCE, chemistry educator; b. San Francisco, Mar. 7, 1919; s. Stephen George and Carrie Anna (Williams) L.; m. Wilma Ruth Ostrander, Feb. 1, 1957. BS in Chemistry, UCLA, 1948; MS in Chemistry, U. So. Calif., L.A., 1963, PhD in Pharm. Chemistry, 1972. Registered U.S. Patent Agt. Analytical chemist So. Pacific Co., L.A., 1949-54; rsch. chemist Stauffer Chem. Co., Torrance, Calif., 1954-58; prodn. mgr. Cyclo Chem. Corp., L.A., 1958-61; chemistry educator Marshall High Sch., L.A., 1961-64; prof. chemistry E. L.A. Coll., Monterey Park, Calif., 1964-86; prof. chemistry, emeritus E. L.A. Coll., Monterey Park, 1986—, head chemistry dept., 1968-74. Patentee in field; contbr. articles to profl. jours. Staff sgt. USAF, 1941-45. Mem. Am. Chem. Soc., Masonic Lodge, Elks Lodge, Sigma Xi. Home: 644 Haverkamp Dr Glendale CA 91206-3117

LANGLOIS, LARRY KENT, psychotherapist; b. Salt Lake City, June 20, 1940; s. Charles Vernon and Ruth (Chamberlain) L.; m. Karen Sally Rydman, Dec. 13, 1968 (div. Sept. 1980); m. Amy Gene Fellows, Nov. 23, 1990; children: Daniel Brian, Karalee, Johnathan. BA, U. Utah, 1965; MS, Calif. State U., L.A., 1973; PhD, U. So. Calif., 1984. Lic. Marriage and Family Counselor, Calif. Adminstr. L.A. County, L.A., 1966-77; businessman self-employed, L.A., 1977-80; psychotherapist Taylor Dimont Counseling, Beverly Hills, Calif., 1978-80; mng. dir. Broderick, Langlois Counseling, San Gabriel, Calif., 1980—; assoc. prof. Calif. State U., L.A., 1987—. Contbr. articles to profl. jours. Mem. Am. Assn. Marraige and Family Therapists, Calif. Assn. Marriage and Family Therapists, Assn. Mormon Counselors and Psychotherapists, Employee Assistance Program Assn. Mem. LDS Ch. Office: Broderick Langlois & Assoc 7220 Rosemead Blvd San Gabriel CA 91775

LANGONI, RICHARD ALLEN, civil engineer; b. Trinidad, Colo., Aug. 7, 1945; s. Domenic and Josephine (Maria) L.; A of Applied Sci., Trinidad State Jr. Coll., 1966; BSCE Colo. State U., 1968; MA, U. No. Colo., 1978; m. Pamela Jill Stansberry, Aug. 19, 1972; children: Kristi, Kerri. Civil engr. Dow Chem. Co., Golden, Colo., 1968-71; city engr., dir. public works City of Trinidad, 1971-74; civil engr. Clement Bros. Constrn. Co., 1974-75; instr. Trinidad State Jr. Coll., 1975-78; city engr., dir. public works City of Durango (Colo.), 1978-82; region traffic and safety engr. Colo. Dept. Hwys., Durango, 1982—. Recipient Meritorious Service award City of Durango; registered profl. engr. Colo., N.Mex. Mem. Nat. Soc. Profl. Engrs., ASCE, Am. Public Works Assn., Water Pollution Control Fedn., Profl. Engrs. Colo., Durango C. of C., Nat. Ski Patrol, Phi Theta Kappa, Chi Epsilon. Home: 30 Moenkopi Dr Durango CO 81301-8599

LANGRIDGE, ROBERT, scientist, educator; b. Essex, Eng., Oct. 26, 1933; came to U.S., 1957; naturalized, 1987.; s. Charles and Winifred (Lister) L.; m. Ruth Gottlieb, June 26, 1960; children: Elizabeth, Catherine, Suzanne. B.Sc. in Physics (1st class honours), U. London, Eng., 1954, Ph.D. in Crystallography, 1957. Vis. research fellow biophysics Yale, 1957-59; research assoc. biophysics M.I.T., 1959-61; research assoc. pathology Children's Cancer Research Found., Boston; research assoc. biophysics, lectr. biophysics, also tutor biochem. scis. Harvard, 1961-66; research assoc. Project MAC, Lab. for Computer Sci., M.I.T., 1964-66; prof. biophysics and info. scis. U. Chgo., 1966-68; prof. chemistry and biochem. scis. Princeton, 1968-76; prof. pharm. chemistry, biochemistry and biophysics, dir. Computer Graphics Lab. U. Calif., San Francisco, 1976—; vis. prof. computer sci. Stanford U., 1983-84; mem. computer and biomath. rsch. study sect. NIH, USPHS, 1968-72, chmn., 1975-77, mem. nat. adv. rsch. resources coun., 1992—; mem. vis. com. biology dept. Brookhaven Nat. Lab., 1977-80, mem. adv. com. neutron diffraction, biology dept., 1980-83; mem. sci. and ednl. adv. com. Lawrence Berkeley Labs., 1988-92; chair U. Calif. Berkeley/U. Calif. San Francisco Grad. Group in Bioengring., 1991—; mem. computer sci. and tech. bd. NRC, NAS, 1988-91. Guggenheim fellow, 1983-84. Fellow AAAS; mem. Inst. Medicine of NAS, Am. Soc. Biol. Chemists, Am. Chem. Soc., Am. Cryst. Assn., Biophys. Soc. (editorial bd. 1970-73, council 1971-74), Assn. Computing Machinery. Office: U Calif 926 Med Sci San Francisco CA 94143-0446

LANGSTON, MARK, professional baseball player; b. San Diego, Aug. 20, 1960; m. Michelle Langston; 1 child, Katie. Pitcher Seattle Mariners, 1984-89, Montreal Expos, 1989-90, California Angels, 1990—; mem. Am. League All-Star Team, 1987, 91-93. Office: care Calif Angels Anaheim Stadium 200 State College Blvd Anaheim CA 92806-2911

LANGUINO, LUCIA RAFFAELLA, cell biologist; b. Barletta, Puglia, Italy, Apr. 24, 1958; came to U.S., 1987; d. Domenico and Antonia (Borgia) L. m. Dario C. Altieri, Dec. 23, 1992. PhD, Negti Inst., Milan, 1984. Sr. scientist R.W. Johnson Pharm. Rsch. Inst., La Jolla, Calif., 1991—. Patentee; novel receptors, 1992. Grantee: Am. Heart Assn., 1990. Mem. Am. Soc. Cell Biology. Office: RW Johnson Pharm Rsch Inst 3535 General Atomics Ct San Diego CA 92121

LANIER, MARY SÁNCHEZ, microbiology educator; b. Milw., Sept. 4, 1957; d. Rozier Edmond and Victoria Elizabeth (Wagner) Sánchez; m. Glen Albert Lanier, Jr., July 26, 1980; children: Michael Edmond, Suzanne Marie, Sarah Elizabeth. BS in Biology, U. N.Mex., 1979, PhD in Med. Scis., 1986. Rsch. asst. dept. microbiology U. N.Mex. Sch. Medicine, Albuquerque, 1977-79, 80-86, rsch. technician depts. medicine and pathology, 1979-80, rsch. instr. dept. neurology, 1985-87; rsch. assoc. div. viral diseases Ctrs. for Disease Control, Atlanta, 1987-90; asst. prof. depts. microbiology and basic med. Scis. Wash. State U., Pullman, 1990—; rsch. assoc. NRC, Atlanta, 1987-90; chmn. young scholars rev. panel NSF, Washington, 1990-91, mem. proposal rev. panel rsch. careers for minority scholars, 1991; speaker 20th anniversary minority programs NIH, Washington, 1992. Contbr. articles to sci. jours. Leader youth group St. Mary's Ch., Moscow, Idaho, 1990-91. mem. religious edn. bd., 1991—; asst. sci. club St. Mary's Sch., 1991—; leader Girl Scouts U.S.A., Moscow, 1990—. Rsch. grantee Am. Cancer Soc., 1990-92, also others. Mem. Sigma Xi. Democrat. Home: 132 N Blaine Moscow ID 83843 Office: Dept Microbiology Wash State U Pullman WA 99164-4233

LANING, CHRISTINE BARBARA, editor; b. Boston, Dec. 27, 1949; d. J. Halcombe and Betty Arleen (Kolb) L. BA in Biology, Earlham Coll., 1971; MS in Botany, U. Calif., Davis, 1975, postgrad., 1978. Founding editor Earthlight Mag., Davis, 1989-91; editor Davis Co-op News, 1983—, BeFriending Creation, Chelsea, Mich., 1989—. Coord. Davis Community Gardens, 1990-92. Soc. of Friends.

LANKFORD, DUANE GAIL, investment banker; b. Ft. Collins, Colo., July 18, 1932; s. William Oliver and Mary Martha (Lago) L.; m. Eleanor Polly, June 18, 1955 (div. 1983); children: Scott, Kurt Edwin, Rebecca Ann; m. Jariyaporn Ekkanasing, Nov. 8, 1991. Student, Colo. State Coll. of Edn., 1950-51, Denver U., 1952-55. Lic. stockbroker. Mgr. Dial Fin., Denver, 1953-59; mgr. investment banking Peters Writer & Christianson, Denver, 1959-60, E.I. DuPont De Nemours, Denver, 1960; mgr. mcpl. investment banking Bache & Co., Denver, L.A., N.Y.C., 1961-68; v.p. sales Fin. Programs, Inc., San Francisco, 1968-69; fin. advisor Lankford & Co., Denver, 1969; mgr. muni bonds W.E. Hutton & Co., Denver, 1969-71; owner/operator Lankford & Co., Denver, 1972—, The Wilderness Inst./ Lankford Mountain Guides, Denver, 1978—; chmn. Denver Lenders Exch., 1957-58; cons. advisor numerous cities, towns, states; expert witness, cons. numerous legal firms; cons./advisor numerous fed. agencies. Contbr. articles to profl. jours. Mem. Am. Alpine Club. Republican.

LANNER, RONALD MARTIN, forester, educator; b. Bklyn., Nov. 12, 1930; s. Louis and Esther (Ornstein) L.; m. Harriette A. Flanigan, Nov. 16, 1957; children: Deborah, David. BS, SUNY, Syracuse, 1952; M.Forestry, SUNY, 1958; PhD, U. Minn., 1968. Rsch. forester Pacific S.W. Forest & Range Experiment Sta., USDA Forest Svc, Berkeley, Calif., 1958-64; asst. prof. to prof. forest resources dept. Utah State U., Logan, 1967—; cons. in field. Author: The Pinon Pine, 1981, Trees of the Great Basin, 1984, Autumn Leaves, 1990; editor Western Jour. Applied Forestry, 1986—. 1st lt. U.S. Army, 1952-56. NSF grantee, 1978-81. Home: 1728 E 1500 N Logan UT 84321-2930 Office: Dept Forest Resources Utah State U Logan UT 84322-5215

LANS, CARL GUSTAV, architect, economist; b. Gothenburg, Sweden, Oct. 19, 1907; came to U.S., 1916; s. Carl and Ida Carolina (Schon) L.; m. Gwynne Iris Meyer, Dec. 21, 1935; children: Douglas C., C. Randolph. Student, CCNY, 1925-26, Sch. Architecture, Columbia U., 1926-30. Registered architect, Calif. Architect with Harry T. Lindeberg N.Y.C., 1930-32; architect Borgia Bros. Ecclesiastical Marble, N.Y.C., 1932-34; with architects Paist & Stewart, Miami, Fla., 1934-35; chief engr. insp. Dept. Agr., 1936-38; asst. tech. dir. FHA, 1938-48; tech. dir. Nat. Assn. Home Builders, Washington, 1948-52; with Earl W. Smith Orgn., Berkeley, Calif., 1952-56; architect, economist Huntington Beach, Calif., 1956—; ptnr. John Hans Graham & Assocs. Architects, Washington, 1947-55; spl. adviser Pres. Rhee, Republic of Korea, 1955-56; guest lectr. various univs., 1949-52. Author: Earthquake Construction, 1954. Chmn. bd. edn. adv. com., Arlington, Va., 1948. Recipient Outstanding and Meritorious Svcs. citation Republic of Korea, 1956. Mem. AIA (citation), Nat. Acad. Scis. (bldg. rsch. adv. bd. dirs.), S.W. Rsch. Inst., Seismol. Soc. Am., Prestressed Concrete Inst., Urban Land Inst., Nat. Press Club. Home and Office: 21821 Fairlane Cir Huntington Beach CA 92646-7902

LANSFORD, HENRY HOLLIS, communications consultant, writer; b. Purvis, Miss., Aug. 24, 1929; s. Henry Hollis Sr. and Minnie Coleman (Mobberly) L.; m. Neville Harris, Aug. 26, 1958; children: Tyler, Lewis. BA, Tulane U., 1957; MA, U. So. Miss., 1959. Publs. officer U.S. Dept. of Energy, Oak Ridge, Tenn., 1960-65; info. officer Nat. Ctr. for Atmospheric Rsch., Boulder, Colo., 1965-78; project dir. Accord Assocs., Boulder, 1979-83; writer, editor SUNY-Albany, Boulder, 1986—; cons. editor Weatherwise Mag., Washington, 1978—; cons. Am. Meteorol. Soc., Boston, 1979-90, Nat. Ctr. for Atmospheric Rsch., Boulder, 1988-90, Air Line Pilots Assn., Washington, 1986-87. Co-author: The Climate Mandate, 1978. 1st lt. U.S. Army, 1951-53, Korea. Recipient Disting. Writing on Meteorology award Am. Meteorol. Soc., 1990. Office: Nat Ctr Atmospheric Rsch 3450 Mitchell Ln Boulder CO 80301-2260

LANTER, SEAN KEITH, software engineer; b. Los Alamos, N.Mex., May 8, 1953; s. Robert Jackson and Norma Esther (Jonas) L.; m. Lauri Jane Willand, July 16, 1977; children: Tully Erik, Sarah Elizabeth, Rachel Erin. BA in Physics, U. Utah, 1974, MS in Mech. Engring., 1977. Registered profl. engr. Wash. Sr. engr. Boeing Comml. Airplane Co., Seattle, 1977-82; systems analyst Internat. Submarine Tech. Ltd., Redmond, Wash., 1982-83; engr. software Advanced Tech. Labs., Bellevue, Wash., 1983-84; engr. contract Rho Co., Redmond, 1984-85; sr. mem. tech. staff Cedar Software Inc., Redmond, 1985-87; pres. Connexions Engring. and Software, Woodinville, Wash., 1987-88; pres., chief engr. Connexions Engring., Inc., Woodinville, 1988—; cons. Unison Group, Bothell, Wash., 1990-92; cons., contract programmer, 1992—. Contbr. articles to profl. jours. Mem. Assn. Computing Machinery, NSPE. Lutheran. Office: Connexions Engring PO Box 3007 Woodinville WA 98072-3007

LANTOS, THOMAS PETER, congressman; b. Budapest, Hungary, Feb. 1, 1928; m. Annette Tillemann; children: Annette, Katrina. B.A., U. Washington, 1949, M.A., 1950; Ph.D., U. Calif.-Berkeley, 1953. Mem. faculty U. Wash., San Francisco State U., 1950-83; TV news analyst, commentator, sr. econ. and fgn. policy adviser to several U.S. senators; mem. Presdl. Task Force on Def. and Fgn. Policy, 97th-103rd Congresses from 11th (now 12th) Calif dist. (Mid. East subcom. of fgn. affairs com., employment and housing subcom. govt. ops. com.), 1981—; chmn. subcom. internat. security, internat. orgns. and human rights Fgn. Affairs Com.; founder study abroad program Calif. State U. and Coll. System. Mem. Millbrae Bd. Edn., 1950-66. Democrat. Office: US Ho of Reps 2182 Rayburn Ho Office Bldg Washington DC 20515

LANTZ, GEORGE EVERETT, telecommunications marketing executive; b. Laramie, Wyo., July 11, 1951; s. Everett Delmar and Elizabeth Mary (Stratton) L.; m. Deborah Julia Shama, Aug. 19, 1983; children: John Everett, David Michael. BS in Civil Engring., U. Wyo., 1974, MBA, 1977. Project engr. Texaco Inc., Houston, 1974-77; mktg. rep. IBM, Denver, 1977-83; mktg. mgmt. executive Rolm/IBM, Denver and Santa Clara, Calif., 1983-92; market mgmt. exec. ROLM/Siemens, Denver, 1992—; bd. dirs. A-Enterprises. Author/editor: (video) Complimentary Application Program. Mem. U. Wyo. Found. Mem. Am. Soc. Civil Engrs., Cowboy Joe Club, Sigma Alpha Epsilon, Phi Kappa Phi. Republican. Episcopalian. Home: 5991 S Boston St Englewood CO 80111-5202 Office: Rolm 7900 E Union Ave Denver CO 80237-2735

LANTZ, NORMAN FOSTER, electrical engineer; b. Pekin, Ill., June 8, 1937; s. Norman Gough and Lenore (Elsbury) L.; m. Donnis Maureen Ballinger, Sept. 7, 1958 (div. Aug. 1991); children: Katherine, Deborah, Norman Daniel; m. Judith Eliane Peach, Dec. 7, 1991. BSEE, Purdue U., 1959, MSEE, 1961. System engr. GE Co., Phila., 1961-72; mem. tech. staff The Aerospace Corp., El Segundo, Calif., 1972-75, mgr., 1975-79, dir., 1979-83, prin. dir., 1990, sr. project engr., 1991—; dir. Internat. Found. for Telemetering, Woodland Hills, Calif., 1985—. 2d lt. U.S. Army, 1960-61. Mem. AIAA (sr.), IEEE, Internat. Test and Evaluation Assn., Am. Mgmt. Assn. Office: The Aerospace Corp El Segundo CA 90245-4691

LANYI, JANOS KAROLY, biochemist, educator; b. Budapest, Hungary, June 5, 1937; came to U.S., 1957, naturalized, 1962; s. Istvan and Klara (Rosthy) L.; m. Carol Ann Giblin, Sept. 15, 1962 (div. Dec. , 1984); children: Clara Aileen, Sean Renton, Gabriella; m. Brigitte Schobert, Mar. 27, 1988. Student, Eotvos Lorand U. Scis., Budapest, 1955-56; B.S., Stanford U., 1959; M.A., Harvard U., 1961, Ph.D., 1963. Postdoctoral fellow Stanford U. Sch. Medicine, 1963-65; Nat. Acad. Scis. resident assoc. NASA-Ames Research Ctr., 1965-66; sr. scientist NASA-Ames Research Ctr., Moffett Field, Calif., 1966-80; prof. physiology and biophysics U. Calif.-Irvine, 1980—; vis. fellow Cornell U., 1976. Recipient NASA medal for exceptional sci. achievement, 1977; recipient H. Julian Allen award for best sci. paper Ames Research Ctr., 1978, Alexander von Humboldt award for sr. U.S. Scientists W.Ger., 1979-80. Mem. Am. Soc. Biol. Chemists, Biophys. Soc., Am. Soc. Microbiology, Phi Beta Kappa, Sigma Xi. Office: U Calif Dept Physiology & Biophysics Irvine CA 92717

LAPIC, JEFFREY ROBERT, lawyer; b. Mpls., Dec. 28, 1941. AB, Dartmouth Coll., 1963; JD, Duke U., 1970. Bar: Calif. 1971, U.S. Dist. Ct. (no. dist.) Calif. 1971, U.S. Ct. Appeals (9th cir.) 1971. Assoc. Orrick, Herrington, Rowley & Sutcliffe, San Francisco, 1970-75; counsel Bank Am. NT&SA, San Francisco, 1975-76, sr. counsel, 1976-86, asst. gen. counsel, 1986—; assoc. prof. Armstrong Coll. Sch. Law, Berkeley, Calif., 1975-81. Research editor Duke Law Jour., 1969-70; contbr. articles to legal publs. Lt. USN, 1963-67. Mem. ABA (securities activities of banks and fid. subcom. of fed. regulation securities com. sect. bus. law, fin. and securities subcom. of com. on corp. counsel), Am. Arbitration Assn. (comml. panel 1981—), Order of Coif. Office: Bank Am Legal Dept 555 California St San Francisco CA 94104-1401

LAPIDES, HOWARD, entertainment industry executive/radio personality; b. Buffalo, N.Y., Dec. 2, 1950; s. Harry and Betty (Aroeste) L.; m. Maria T. D'ArcAngelo. BS Speech, Emerson Coll., 1972. Radio announcer Sta. WYSL, Buffalo, 1966-72, Sta. WEIM, Fitchberg, Mass., 1970-72; radio producer Sta. WMEX, Boston, 1970-72; radio announcer, programmer Sta. CFGO, Ottowa, Ont., Can., 1972-77; v.p. Howard Lapides Entertainment Group, Ottawa, Ont., Can., 1977-80; pres. Callex Internat. Inc., Buffalo, 1980-89; pres., TV prodr. Howard Lapides Mgmt. and Prodns., L.A., 1986—; pres. Hiccups, Komedy, Kabaret, Inc., Rochester, N.Y., 1985—; radio personality KFI, L.A., 1992—, Buffalo Bills broadcast team WBEN, 1984-88; director Bass Clef Entertainment, Ottawa, 1972-80, Kayak Pools, Buffalo, 1980-81; prodr. TV spls. Mike MacDonald On Target, 1990 (Gemini award 1991), Mike MacDonald, My House, My Rules, 1991 (Ace award 1992), Mike MacDonald: I'm as Happy as I Can Be!, 1993. Office: Howard Lapides Mgmt Co 355 N Genesee Los Angeles CA 90036 Other: Howard Lapides Prodns of, Can Inc, 10-99 Fifth Ave, Ottawa KIS 5K4, ON Canada

LAPIDUS, MICHEL LAURENT, mathematics educator; b. Casablanca, Morocco, July 4, 1956; came to U.S., 1979; s. Serge and Myriam Gisele (Benathar) L.; m. Odile Ioos, July 5, 1980. BS in Math., Lycee Louis le Grand, Paris, 1976; M in Math., U. Paris (Pierre et Marie Curie), 1977, diploma of advanced studies in Math., 1978, PhD in Math. summa cum laude, 1980, Doctorat D'Etat es Sciences summa cum laude, 1986. Rsch. assoc. dept. math. U. Paris (Pierre et Marie Curie), 1978-80, fellow Gen. Del. to Sci. Rsch., 1979-80; asst. prof. math. U. So. Calif., L.A., 1980-85; vis. asst. prof. U. Iowa, Iowa City, 1985-86; assoc. prof. math. U. Ga., Athens, 1986-90; prof. math. U. Calif., Riverside, 1990—; vis. prof. Instituto de Matematica Pura e Aplicada, Rio de Janeiro, 1986, Yale U., New Haven, Conn., 1990-91; mem. Inst. Math. Scis. Rsch. Inst., Berkeley, Calif., 1984-85. George Lurcy Trust fellow, 1978-80; U. Calif.-Berkeley Math. Dept. fellow, 1979-80. Mem. Am. Math. Soc., Société Mathematique de France, Math. Assn. Am., Internat. Assn. Math. Physicists, N.Y. Acad. Scis., Am. Phys. Soc., AAUP, AAAS, Com. Concerned Scientists. Office: U Calif Dept Math Sproul Hall Riverside CA 92521-0135

LAPLANTE, PEGGY LYNN, controller; b. Glencoe, Minn., Feb. 23, 1960; d. Kenneth L. and Joann L. (Selchow) LaPlante; m. Joel Scott Johnson, Nov. 18, 1989. BS in Acctg., U. S.D., 1982; MBA, U. Wyo., 1986. Adminstrv. analyst Amoco Prodn. Co., Casper, Wyo., 1982-86; acctg. supr. Amoco Corp., Tulsa, 1986-88; gen. acctg. mgr. The Federated Group, Sunnyvale, Calif., 1988-89; account mgr. Domain Tech., Milpitas, Calif., 1989-90; controller Psi Star, Fremont, Calif., 1990, Rancho Santa Fe Assn., Rancho Santa Fe, Calif., 1990—. Yankton Savs. & Loan Fin. scholar, U. S.D., 1981. Home: 3748 Brand Crest Encinitas CA 92024 Office: 3748 Brand Crest Encinitas CA 92024

LA POINTE, LEONARD LYELL, speech, hearing educator; b. Iron Mountain, Mich., June 28, 1939; s. Alexander Lyell and Eileen Margaret (Osborne) La P.; m. Corinne A. Abraham, June 15, 1963; children: Christopher Mark, Adrienne Beth. BA, Mich. State U., 1961; MA, U. Colo., 1966, PhD, 1969. Speech clinician Pub. Sch. System, Menasha, Wis., 1961-64; coord. of instrn. VA Med. Ctr., Gainesville, Fla., 1969-84; chair dept. speech and hearing sci. Ariz. State U., Tempe, 1984-92, prof. dept. speech and hearing sci., 1992—; cons. VA Med. Outpatient Clinic, L.A., 1984-90, VA Med. Ctr., Phoenix, 1984—; lectr. in field; host bi-weekly radio show for blind: Sun Sounds Radio. Editor-in-chief Jour. Med. Speech-Lang. Pathology, San Diego, 1991—; co-author, editor: Apraxia of Speech, 1984, Aphasia: A Clinical Approach, 1989, Aphasia and Related Disorders, 1991; contbr. over 50 articles to profl. jours. Pres. Gainesville Little Theatre, 1973; dir. Melrose (Fla.) Music Theater, 1977-84. Fellow Am. Speech-Lang.-Hearing Assn.; mem. Acad. Neurogenic Comm. Disorders and Scis., Acad. of Aphasia, Nat. Aphasia Assn. (adv. bd.), Internat. Neuropsychol. Soc., Nat. Stroke Assn. Home: 1318 E Bayview Dr Tempe AZ 85283 Office: Ariz State Univ Dept Speech/Hearing Scis Tempe AZ 85287

LAPORTE, KATHLEEN DARKEN, venture capitalist; b. N.Y.C., Sept. 23, 1961; d. John Edward and Sheila Anne (Keane) Darken; m. Brian Edward LaPorte, July 30, 1988. BS in Biology summa cum laude, Yale U., 1983; MBA, Stanford U., 1987. Fin. analyst The First Boston Corp., N.Y.C., 1983-84; fin. analyst The First Boston Corp., San Francisco, 1984-85; assoc. Asset Mgmt. Co., Palo Alto, Calif., 1987-90; prin. Asset Mgmt. Co., Palo Alto, 1990-92; v.p. The Sprout Group, Menlo Park, Calif., 1993—; bd. dirs. Onyx Pharms., Richmond, Calif., Telor Ophthalmic Pharms., Boston, 1988-91, Trancel Corp., Santa Ana, Calif., 1989-91, Metra Biosystems, Inc., Palo Alto, 1990-91, Kinetek Systems, Inc., St. Louis, 1990-91. Founder The Phil Larson Fund, Stanford U., 1988; mem. Community Impact Vol. Group, Palo Alto, 1988—. Recipient Eleanor Dawson award Yale U., 1982, MacLeish Meml. trophy Yale U., 1983. Mem. Nat. Venture Capital Assn., Western Assn. Venture Capitalists, Bay Area Bioscience Women's Group (founding), Phi Beta Kappa. Office: The Sprout Group 3000 Sand Hill Rd Menlo Park CA 94025

LARDY, NICHOLAS RICHARD, economics educator; b. Madison, Wis., Apr. 8, 1946; s. Henry Arnold and Annrita (Dresselhuys) L.; m. Barbara Jean Dawe, Aug. 29, 1970; children: Elizabeth Brooke, Lillian Henry. BA, U. Wis., 1968; MA, U. Mich., 1972, PhD, 1975. Asst. prof. Yale U., New Haven, 1975-79, assoc. prof., 1979-83, asst. dir. econ. growth ctr., 1979-82; assoc. prof. U. Wash., Seattle, 1983-85, chair China program, 1984-89, prof., 1985—, dir. The Henry M. Jackson Sch. Internat. Studies, 1991—; bd. dirs. Nat. Com. on U.S.-China Rels., N.Y.C., 1987—; chmn. Com. on Advanced Study in China; vice chmn. com. on scholarly comm. with China, NAS, Washington, 1991—; bd. dirs. Com. on Internat. Rels. Studies with People's Republic China, 1989-92, Program for Internat. Studies in Asia, 1993—. Author: Economic Growth and Distribution in China, 1978, Agriculture in China's Modern Economic Development, 1983, China's Entry into the World Economy, 1987, Foreign Trade and Economic Reform in China, 1978-90, 1992, (policy study) Economcic Policy Toward China in the Post-Reagan Era, 1989; mem. editorial bd. The China Quar. (London). Rsch. fellow Am. Coun. Learned Socs., 1976, 78-79, 89-90, Henry Luce Found., Inc., 1980-82; faculty rsch. grantee Yale U., 1976, 78. Mem. Am. Econ. Assn., Assn. for Asian Studies (nominating com. 1986-87), Assn. for Comparative Econ. Studies (exec. com. 1986-88). Home: 3802 110th Pl NE Bellevue WA 98004-7760 Office: U Wash Sch of Internat Studies Seattle WA 98195

LAREDO, DAVID CARY, lawyer; b. N.Y.C., Feb. 1, 1950; s. Joseph A. and Ruth (Mautner) L.; m. Virginia Smith, Sept. 23, 1972; children: Christina, Josef, Michael, Matthew. BA, UCLA, 1972; JD, Southwestern U., L.A., 1975. Bar: Calif. 1975, U.S. Ct. Mil. Appeals, 1976, U.S. Supreme Ct. 1979, U.S. Dist. Ct. (no. dist.) Calif. 1981, U.S. Ct. Appeals (9th cir.) 1986. Dep. county counsel Monterey County, Salinas, Calif., 1979-81; ptnr. De Lay & Laredo, Pacific Grove, Calif., 1981—; of counsel Lozano, Smith, Smith, Woliver & Behrens; chmn., bd. dirs. Monterey (Calif.) Fed. Credit Union, 1984—; staff judge adv. U.S. Naval Postgrad. Sch., Monterey, 1976-79; mem. faculty Monterey Coll. Law, 1980-82; instr. Calif. Community Colls.; gen. counsel Monterey Peninsula Water Mgmt. Dist., 1979—, Pajaro Valley Water Mgmt. Agy., 1986—. Contbr. articles to profl. jours. Bd. dirs. Children's Svcs. Ctr., Pacific Grove, 1982—. Lt. JAGC, USNR, 1972-79. Office: 606 Forest Ave Pacific Grove CA 93950-4221

LARGENT, STEVE, former professional football player; b. Tulsa, Sept. 28, 1954; m. Terry Largent; children: Kyle, Kelly, Kramer, Casie. BS in biology, U. Tulsa, 1976. Wide receiver Seattle Seahawks, NFL, Kirkland, Wash., 1976—; player Pro Bowl, 1979, 80, 82, 85-88. Holder NFL record for passes caught in consecutive games, also for career receiving yardage, receptions. Office: Seattle Seahawks 11220 NE 53d St Kirkland WA 98033

LARIMER, THORNTON MICHAEL, JR., petroleum engineer; b. Charlotte, N.C., Nov. 11, 1964; s. T. Michael and Lynn L.; m. Dawn A. Gesell, June 1, 1985; children: Joy Elizabeth, Hope Angela, Grace Virginia. BS in Petroleum Engring., U. Tulsa, 1986. Registered petroleum engr., N.Mex., 1992. Prodn. engr. Phillips Petroleum, Houston, 1986-87, El Dorado, Ark., 1987-89; staff resevoir engr. Phillips Petroleum, El Dorado, 1989-91; assoc. reservoir engr. Phillips Petroleum, Farmington, N.Mex., 1991—. Chmn. Ark. So. Region Reps., El Dorado, 1989-91, El Dorado County Reps., 1990-91, Young Reps. San Juan (N.Mex.) County, 1992-93..

Named Outstanding Regional Chmn. Rep. Party of Ark., Little Rock, 1990. Mem. Soc. Profl. Engrs. Presbyterian. Home and Office: PO Box 2073 Farmington NM 87499

LARIZADEH, M(OHAMMED) R(EZA), business educator; b. Tehran, Iran, Apr. 14, 1947; came to U.S., 1966; s. Hassan and Nosrat (Saremi) L.; m. Dianne Ellen Pincus, Mar. 25, 1973; children: Dariush, Darya Anna. BA in Econs., Bus., UCLA, 1972, cert. in acctg., 1974. Cert. colls. teaching credential, Calif. (life); lic. real estate agent, Calif. Auditor Peat, Marwick & Mitchell, Los Angeles, 1972-74; controller Petromain Constrn. Co., Tehran, 1975-77; v.p. fin. Pilary Marine Shipping Co., Tehran, 1977-79; prof. Iranian Inst. Banking, Tehran, 1975-78; pres. Audicount Acctg. and Auditing Group, L.A., 1984—; prof. bus. and acctg. East L.A. Coll., 1980-87, vice-chmn. dept. bus. and acctg., 1987—, chmn. dept. bus. adminstrn., 1988—; prof. acctg. Santa Monica (Calif.) Coll., 1987—; mgmt. cons. L.P. Assocs. Mfg. Co., Los Angeles, 1981—; mng. dir. Barrington Enterprises, Los Angeles; prof. Santa Monica (Calif.) Coll., 1987. Author/translator: Accounting/Auditing, 1975. Mem. Internat. Fedn. Bus. Edn., Am. Mgmt. Assn., Am. Acctg. Assn., Faculty Assn. Calif. Community Colls., NEA, Am. Fedn. Tchrs., Calif. Tchrs. Assn., Am. Entrepreneur Assn., Nat. Assn. Realtors, Am. Assn. Pub. Accts., Calif. Assn. Bus. Educators, Calif. Assn. Realtors, Iranian Student Assn. (pres. UCLA chpt. 1969-70), Nat. Soc. Pub. Accts., Calif. Bus. Edn. Assn., Internat. Fedn. Bus. Edn., Nat. Trust for Hist. Preservation, Smithsonian Assn., Inst. Mgmt. Accts., UCLA Alumni Assoc. (life), Alpha Kappa Psi.

LARK, DAVID LEE, physician, researcher, entrepreneur; b. Chgo., Aug. 7, 1947; s. Stanley LeRoy and Rosalie (Phillips) L. BA in Chemistry with honors, San Diego State U., 1970; MD, Northwestern U., 1974; PhD in Med. Microscopy, Stanford (Calif.) U., 1987. Resident in surgery to chief resident in urology Standford U., 1975-80, postdoctoral fellow in urology, 1980-83, fellow in med. microbiology, 1982-84; co-founder, vice chmn., pres. Syn-Tek, A.B., Umea, Sweden, 1984-86; dir. emergency rm. John C. Fremont Hosp., Mariposa, Calif., 1987-88, Corcoran (Calif.) Dist. Hosp., 1988-90; regional dir. Valley Emergency Physicians, 1988-90, sec., 1989; ptnr. Corcoran Community Med. Group, Inc., 1990—; chief med. staff Corcoran Dist. Hosp., 1991; med. dir. East Valley Youth Clinic, San Jose, Calif., 1978-81; founder CST, 1984; mem. at large exec. bd. Soc. for Basic Urologic Rsch., 1988-89; cons. Invest Urology Jour.; cons. urinary tract infections com. NIH, 1983; sec. meeting Fedn. of European Microbiol. Soc., Lula, Sweden, 1985. Editor: Protein-Carbohydrate Interactions in Biological Systems, 1986. NSF grantee, 1965, Wyland Leadbetter scholar, 1980-82; Nat. Kidney Found. fellow, 1977, Johnson and Johnson fellow, 1983. Mem. AMA, AAAS, Am. Chem. Soc., Am. Inst. Chemists, Am. Soc. for Microbiology, N.Y. Acad. Sci., Soc. for Basic Urologic Rsch., Am. Mgmt. Assn., King County Med. Rsch., CMA. Home: PO Box 957 Corcoran CA 93212-0957 Office: 1310 Hanna Ave Ste 3 Corcoran CA 93212-2314

LARK, M. ANN, management consultant, strategic planner; b. Denver, Feb. 28, 1952; d. Carl Eugene and Arlena Elizabeth (Bashor) Epperson; m. Larry S. Lark, Apr. 1, 1972 (div. 1979). Asst. corp. sec., savs. dir. Imperial Corp. dba Silver State Savs. & Loan, Denver, 1972-75; client svcs. mgr. 1st Fin. Mgmt. Corp., Englewood, Colo., 1977-81; regional account mgr. Ericsson Info. Systems, Chatsworth, Calif., 1981-82; ind. cons. Denver, 1982-84; regional account mgr. InnerLine/Am. Banker, Chgo., 1984-85; chief info. officer Security Pacific Credit Corp., San Diego, 1985-88; prin. The Genessee Group, Thousand Oaks, Calif., 1988—. Home and Office: 1144 El Monte Dr Thousand Oaks CA 91362-2117

LARKIN, NELLE JEAN, computer programmer, analyst; b. Ralston, Okla., July 4, 1925; d. Charles Eugene and Jennieva Pearl (Lane) Reed; m. Burr Oakley Larkin, Dec. 28, 1948 (div. Aug. 1969); children: John Timothy, Kenneth James, Donald Jerome, Valerie Jean Larkin Rouse. Student, UCLA, 1944, El Camino Jr. Coll., 1946-49, San Jose (Calif.) City Coll., 1961-62. Sr. programmer, analyst III Santa Clara County, San Jose, Calif., 1963-69; sr. analyst, programmer Blue Cross of No. Calif., Oakland, 1971-73; sr. programmer, analyst Optimum Systems, Inc., Santa Clara, Calif., 1973-75, Crocker Bank, San Francisco, 1975-77, Greyhound Fin. Service, San Francisco, 1977-78; analyst, programmer TRW, Mountain View, Calif., 1978-79; sr. programer analyst Memorex, Santa Clara, 1979-80; staff mgmt. cons. Am. Mgmt. System, Foster City, Calif., 1980-82; sr. programmer, analyst, project leader Tymeshare, Cupertino, Calif., 1982-83; sr. programmer, analyst Beckman Instruments, Palo Alto, Calif., 1983-89; analyst, programmer U.S. Postal Svc., San Mateo, Calif., 1989—. Mem. Calif. Scholarship Fedn. (life mem. 1943), Alpha Sigma Gamma. Home: 3493 Londonderry Dr Santa Clara CA 95050-6632 Office: US Postal Svc 2700 Campus Dr San Mateo CA 94497-0001

LAROCCO, LARRY, congressman; b. Aug. 25, 1946; m. Chris Bideganeta; 2 children. BA, U. Portland; MA, Boston U. Stockbroker; mem. 102nd-103rd Congresses from 1st Idaho Dist., 1991—. Capt. U.S. Army, 1969-72. Democrat. Roman Catholic. Office: US House Reps Washington DC 20515*

LAROCHELLE, DENIS ALPHONSE, cell biologist; b. Manchester, N.H., Jan. 8, 1961; s. Roger Bertrand and Jeanne Helen (Lussier) L.; m. Eunice Lee Kwak, Sept. 28, 1991. Student, U. R.I., 1979-81; BA, U. N.H., 1983, MS, 1985; PhD, Stanford U., 1991. Lab. technician U. N.H., Durham, 1982-84; bio-aide N.H. Fish and Game, Greenland, N.H., 1983-85; postdoctoral fellow in cancer biology Stanford U., 1991-92, postdoctoral fellow oncology div., 1992—. Contbr. articles to profl. jours. Wagner-Hosser scholar, 1979-82; Myers grantee, 1988; Nat. Cancer Ctr. grantee, 1991. Mem. Am. Soc. for Cell Biology, Phi Beta Kappa, Sigma Xi. Democrat. Home: 1929 Crisanto Ave # 304 Mountain View CA 94040 Office: VA Med Ctr 154-N 3801 Miranda Ave Palo Alto CA 94304

LAROCK, BRUCE EDWARD, civil engineering educator; b. Berkeley, Calif., Dec. 24, 1940; s. Ralph W. and Hazel M. (Lambert) L.; m. Susan E. Gardener, June 17, 1968; children: Lynne M., Jean E. BS in Civil Engring., Stanford U., 1962, MS in Civil Engring., 1963, PhD, 1966. Registered profl. civl. engr., Calif. Asst. prof. U. Calif., Davis, 1966-72, assoc. prof., 1972-79, prof., 1979—; sr. vis. fellow U. Wales, Swansea, Wales, U.K., 1972-73; U.S. sr. scientist Tech. U., Aachen., Germany, 1986-87. Author: (with D. Newnan) Engineer-in-Training Examination Review, 3d edit., 1991; contbr. over 70 tech. articles to profl. jours. Mem. Am. Soc. Civil Engring., Tau Beta Pi, Sigma Xi. Lutheran. Office: U Calif Davis Dept Civil & Eviron Engring Davis CA 95616-5294

LAROCQUE, MARILYN ROSS ONDERDONK, public relations executive; b. Weehawken, N.J., Oct. 14, 1934; d. Chester Douglas and Marion (Ross) Onderdonk; B.A. cum laude, Mt. Holyoke Coll., 1956; postgrad. N.Y. U., 1956-57; M. Journalism, U. Calif. at Berkeley, 1965; m. Bernard Dean Benz, Oct. 5, 1957 (div. Sept. 1971); children: Mark Douglas, Dean Griffith; m. 2d, Rodney C. LaRocque, Feb. 10, 1973. Jr. exec. Bonwit Teller, N.Y.C., 1956; personnel asst. Warner-Lambert Pharm. Co., Morris Plains, N.J., 1957; editorial asst. Silver Burdett Co., Morristown, 1958; self-employed as pub. rels. cons., Moraga, Calif., 1963-71, 73-77; pub. relations mgr. Shaklee Corp., Hayward, 1971-73; pub. rels. dir. Fidelity Savs., 1977-78; exec. dir. No. Calif. chpt. Nat. Multiple Sclerosis Soc., 1978-80; v.p. pub. rels. Cambridge Plan Internat., Monterey, Calif., 1980-81; sr. account exec. Hoefer-Amidei Assocs., San Francisco, 1981-82; dir. corp. communications, dir. spl. projects, asst. to chmn. Cambridge Plan Internat., Monterey, Calif., 1982-84; dir. communications Buena Vista Winery, Sonoma, Calif., 1984-86, asst. v.p. communications and market support, 1986-87; dir. communications Rutherford Hill Winery, St. Helena, Calif., 1987-88; pres. LaRocque/Hanaford Pub. Rels. and Pub. Affairs, Napa, Calif., 1988-91; pres. Larocque Profl. Svcs., Inc., 1991—; instr. pub. rels. U. Calif. Extension, San Francisco, 1977-79. Mem. exec. bd., rep-at-large Oakland (Calif.) Symphony Guild, 1968-69, Napa County Landmarks, Inc.; co-chmn. pub. rels. com. Oakland Mus. Assn., 1974-75; cabinet mem. Lincoln Child Ctr., Oakland, 1967-71, pres. membership cabinet, 1970-71, 2d v.p. bd. dirs., 1970-71; bd. dirs. Calif. Spring Garden and Home Show, 1971-77, 1st Agrl. Dist., 1971-77, Dunsmuir House and Gardens, 1976-77; mem. Calif. State Rep. Cen. Com., 1964-66; v.p. Piedmont coun. Boy Scouts Am., 1977. Mem. U. Calif. Alumni Assn., Pub. Rels. Soc. Am. (chpt. dir. 1980-82; accredited), Sonoma Valley Vintners Assn. (dir. 1984-87), Internat. Wine and Food Soc. (Marin chpt.), San Francisco Mus. Soc., Smithsonian Assocs., Sonoma Valley C. of C. (bd. dirs. 1984-87), Knights of the Vine (master lady 1985-90), Mount Holyoke Coll. Alumnae Club, Silverado Country Club, Kiwanis Club of Napa. Office: LaRocque Profl Svcs Inc 1804 Soscol Ave Ste 200 Napa CA 94559-1346

LARRIMORE, DAVID ROBERTS, company executive; b. Grove Hill, Ala., Mar. 1, 1952; s. Dennis Lamar and Theda Genevieve (Roberts) L. BChemE, Georgia Tech. U., 1975; MBA, Stanford U., 1985. Process intern ITT Rayonier, Jesup, Ga., 1970-75; engr. Dow Chem. Co., Midland, Mich., 1975-77, rsch. engr., 1977-79; sr. rsch. engr. Dow Chem. Co., Granville, Ohio, 1979-81; mktg. mgr. Dow Chem. Co., Midland, 1981-83; stipendiat Robert Bosch Found., Bonn and Munich, 1985-86; cons. McKinsey and Co., Inc., San Francisco, 1986-91; v.p. mktg. Destiny Technology Corp., Milpitas, Calif., 1991—. Author: Germany Through American Eyes, 1987; contbr. articles to profl. jours. Office: Destiny Technology Corp 3255-1 Scott Blvd Ste 201 Santa Clara CA 95054

LARSEN, ASHBY BROOKS, psychotherapist; b. Mt. Pleasant, Utah, Feb. 15, 1940; s. Leo Christian and Relia (Shaw) L.; m. Carolyn McOmber, July 29, 1964 (div. July 1990); children: Brooks M., Kayle E., Anika K., Seth E., Kiasa K., Sean T., Brett T. BS, Brigham Young U., 1965; postgrad., U. Utah, 1965; MSW, U. Wash., 1967. Lic. clin. social worker. Trainee Ea. Wash. State Hosp., Medical Lake, 1966-67; caseworker San Joaquin County Adoption Agy., Stockton, Calif., 1967-69; supr. San Joaquin County Protective Svc., Stockton, 1969-75; program mgr. San Joaquin County Children's Svcs., Stockton, 1975-81; therapist Psychotherapy Assocs., Stockton, 1986-87; owner, counselor Diet Ctr., Lodi, Calif., 1981—; pvt. practice psychotherapy Lodi, 1987—. Mem. Assn. Mormon Counselors and Psychotherapists. Republican. Mem. Ch. of Jesus Christ of Latter-day Saints. Office: 330 S Fairmont # 2 Lodi CA 95240

LARSEN, B. NEIL, investment broker, life insurance broker, financial consultant; b. Seattle, May 31, 1954; s. Blaine B. and Connie (Shulberg) L.; m. Carla Larsen, Apr. 3, 1975; children: Erin K., Jennifer D., Jason C. AA in Fin., Brigham Young U., 1975; BS in Bus. Mktg., Seattle U., 1979; ChFC, Am. Coll., 1990. Sheet metal line mgr. supr. Kenworth Truck Co., Seattle, 1976-78; ops. v.p. AESCO, Inc., Seattle, 1979-80; prin., owner B. Neil Larsen & Assocs., Seattle, 1981—; registered rep., registered investment adv. KMS Fin. Svcs., Inc., Seattle, 1981—. Scoutmaster Boy Scouts Am., Des Moines, Wash., 1980—; mem. Highline Community Coun., v.p. 1980-85. Mem. Nat. Assn. Securities Dealers, Nat. Life Underwriters Assn., Million Dollar Round Table (life). Office: B Neil Larsen & Assocs 2200 6th Ave # 1125 Seattle WA 98121-1866

LARSEN, CHARLES MARTIN, state education official; b. L.A., Dec. 17, 1948; s. Lief Martin and June Lorraine (Scott-Mitchel) L.; m. Janet Louise Dougherty, Jan. 30, 1970; children: Tara Lyn June, Kathleen Ann. AA, Green River Community Coll., 1973; BA in Edn., U. Puget Sound, 1974; P.B. Edn., U. Wash., 1978; MPA, Pacific Luth. U., 1990. Cert. tchr., ednl. adminstrn.-prin. Tchr., curriculum devel. specialist Tacoma Schs. Dist. 10 Title IV Indian Edn. Program, 1974-80, program lead tchr., 1980-82; classroom tchr. social studies Tacoma Schs. Dist. 10, 1982-85, high sch. adminstrv. asst., 1985-86, classroom tchr. art, social studies, English, 1986-89; supr. for Indian edn. Office of Supt. Pub. Instrn., State of Wash., Olympia, 1989—; adj. faculty art U. Puget Sound, Tacoma, 1981-88; cons.-tchr. trainer, Puyallup, Wash., 1978-93, Tacoma Schs. Star Ctr., 1990—. Contbr. articles to profl. jours., pubs. Indian edn., hist., arts, culture. Bd. dirs. Tacoma Indian Ctr., 1978-80, Bert Peters Meml. Indian Scholarship Found., Tacoma, 1978-85; adv. bd., sr. docent Ft. Nisqually Mus., Tacoma, 1980-93; bd. dirs., v.p., past pres. Rainier Legacy Pub. Benefit Corp. (formerly D.O.V.E. Ctr. Found., Eatonville, 1980-92; mem. ch. coun., tchr. Mountain View Luth. Ch., Puyallup, 1985—. D'Arcy McNickle Rsch. fellow Newberry Libr., Chgo., 1981. Mem. Wash. Assn. Sch. Adminstrs., Nat. Assn. Secondary Sch. Prins., Nat. Indian Edn. Assn., Seneca Tribe, Iroquois Six Nations Reserve, Ont., Can. Home: 2111 7th St SE Puyallup WA 98372-4632

LARSEN, DALE LEVERNE, parks and recreation administrator; b. Beloit, Wis., Nov. 10, 1950; s. Leverne and Millicent (Leadholm) L.; m. Christine Lee Paschke, Aug. 21, 1971; children: Beth, Drew, Kate. BS cum laude, U. Wis., LaCrosse, 1972; MS, U. Wis., Milw., 1978. Cert. leisure profl. Nat. Recreation & Parks Assn. Asst. dir. Wauwatosa (Wis.) Bd. Edn., 1972-73; dir. Wauwatosa Recreation Dept., 1973-77; asst. dir. Milw. County Parks, 1977-79, dir., 1979-82, pub. svcs. mgr., 1982-84; asst. dir. City of Phoenix Parks and Recreation Dept., 1984—; congress co-chair Nat. Recreation & Park Assn., Phoenix, 1990. Co-chair Goals 2000, Milw., 1982; com. mem. United Way, Milw., 1980-84, Futures Forum, Phoenix, 1991-92; lectr. Phoenix Supervisory Acad., 1986-92. Recipient commendations Park People, 1984, Milw. County Bd., 1984. Mem. Ariz. Parks & Recreation Assn. (chmn. 1989, 91, pres.-elect 1992). Home: 2502 W Gelding Dr Phoenix AZ 85023

LARSEN, DONNA KAY, public relations executive, writer, consultant; b. Anniston, Ala., Feb. 14; d. James Murray and Lucy B. Bible. BA, U. Ala., 1970; cert. in pub. rels., UCLA Extension. Feature writer L.A. Times, 1970-73; pres. Larsen Promotions, L.A., 1975—; pub. rels. cons., L.A., 1987—. Contbr. feature articles to various newspapers and mags. Mem. NOW, People for Ethical Treatment of Animals, Hollywood Women's Press Club, L.A. World Affairs Coun. Office: Donna Larsen Pub Rels 720 S Plymouth Blvd Los Angeles CA 90005-3776

LARSEN, KENNETH DAVID, medical researcher, physician; b. Woodburn, Oreg., Oct. 10, 1947; s. Carl Sherman and Doris Lorraine (Lewis) L.; m. Nora Cheng, June 13, 1980; children: Kaarina C., Erik Z. BA, Oreg. State U., 1970; MS, U. N.D., 1973; PhD, Emory U., 1976; MD, U. Miami, Fla., 1983. Diplomate Am. Bd. Anesthesiology. Asst. prof. neurophysiology Rockefeller U., N.Y.C., 1977-80; asst. prof. physiology U. Pitts., 1980-81; clin. asst. prof. U. Rochester, 1988-89; intern, residency Hosp. U. Pa., 1983-86; staff anesthesiologist Sunnyside Hosp., Clackamas, Oreg., 1990—. Contbr. articles to profl. jours. NIH fellow, 1977. Mem. AMA, Internat. Anesthesia Rsch. Soc.

LARSEN, RICHARD LEE, former city manager, business, municipal and labor relations consultant, arbitrator; b. Jackson, Miss., Apr. 16, 1934; s. Homer Thorsten and Mae Cordelia (Amidon) L.; m. Virginia Fay Alley, June 25, 1955; children: Karla, Daniel, Thomas (dec.), Krista, Lisa. B.S. in Econs. and Bus. Adminstrn, Westminster Coll., Fulton, Mo., 1959; postgrad., U. Kans., 1959-61. Fin. dir. Village of Northbrook, Ill., 1961-63; city mgr. Munising, Mich., 1963-66, Sault Ste. Marie, Mich., 1966-72, Ogden, Utah, 1972-77, Billings, Mont., 1977-79; mcpl. cons., 1979—, pub./pvt. sector labor relations cons., arbitrator, 1979—; elected mayor City of Billings, 1989—; dep. gen. chmn. Greater Mich. Found., 1968. Bd. dirs. Central Weber Sewer Dist., 1972-77; chmn. labor com. Utah League Cities and Towns, 1973-77, Mont. League Cities and Towns, 1977-79; bd. dirs., coach Ogden Hockey Assn., 1972-77, Weber Sheltered Workshop, 1974-77, Billings YMCA, 1980-86, Rimrock Found., 1980-86; chmn. community relations council Weber Basin Job Corps Center, 1973-77. Served with USCG, 1953-57. Recipient Community Devel. Disting. Achievement awards Munising, 1964, Community Devel. Disting. Achievement awards Sault Ste. Marie, 1966-70, Citizen award Dept. of Interior, 1977, Alumni Achievement award Westminster Coll., 1990; named Utah Adminstr. of the Yr., 1976. Mem. Internat. City Mgmt. ASsn. (L.P. Cookingham career devel. award 1974, Clarence Ridley in-service tng. award 1979), Utah City Mgrs. Assn. (pres. 1972-74), Greater Ogden C. of C. (dir.), Phi Gamma Delta. Mem. LDS Ch. Club: Rotary. Home and Office: 1733 Parkhill Dr Billings MT 59102-2358

LARSEN, SAMUEL HARRY, pastor-educator, minister; b. Sterling, Kans., Feb. 3, 1947; s. Harold Julius and Edna Marguerite (Wasson) L.; m. Natalie Louise Mahlow, June 21, 1969; children: Samuel Eric, Kristen Joy, Hans Joseph. BS, U.S. Naval Acad., 1969; MDiv, Covenant Theol. Sem., 1979; D of Ministry, Reformed Theol. Sem., 1989. Ordained to ministry Presbyn. Ch., 1981. Various assignments USN, Norfolk, Va., 1969-72; instr. U.S. Naval Acad., Annapolis, Md., 1972-75; pastoral intern Community Presbyn. Ch., Nairobi, Kenya, Africa, 1977-78; officer-in-charge Naval Res. Shipboard Simulator Lab. and Sch., New Orleans, 1979-81; church planter Mission to the World, Brisbane, Australia, 1982-84; team coord. Mission to the World, Queensland, Australia, 1984-86; regional dir. Mission to the World, Australia, 1986-89; squadron chaplain Destroyer Squadron Five, San Diego, 1989-92; chaplain Naval Air Sta. Whidbey Island, Oak Harbor, Wash., 1992—; dean Westminster Theol. Coll., Brisbane, 1986-88; del. La. Congress on World Evangelism, Manila, 1989. Pres. Covenant Sem. Student Assn., St. Louis, 1976-77; chaplain Chs. Soccer Assn., Sunshine Coast, Australia, 1984-86; tutor Logan Elem. Sch., San Diego, 1991-92; adv. bd. YMCA, Oak Harbor, 1992—. Recipient Meritorious Svc. medal Sec. of Navy, 1981. Mem. Res. Officers Assn. Home: 1208 Cascade Dr Oak Harbor WA 98277 Office: Chapel NAS Whidbey Island Oak Harbor WA 98278

LARSEN, THOMAS EVERETT, biotechnology executive; b. American Falls, Idaho, Nov. 10, 1947; s. Anker Everett and Mona Dean (Thomas) L.; m. Marilyn Joy Handly, Sept. 2, 1970; children: Melissa Joy, Deborah Jane, Lesley Anne. BS in Agronomy, Brigham Young U., 1975; MS in Agronomy, U. Minn., 1977; PhD in Crop Sci., N.C. State U., 1985. Product specialist Monsanto Co., St. Louis, 1977-79, product devel. rep., 1979-82, product devel. assoc., 1982-84, tech. supr., 1984-85, tech. mgr., 1985-88, planning mgr., 1988-89; comml. devel. dir. Mycogen Corp., San Diego, 1989-92, bus. unit dir., 1992—; mem. forestry adv. com. Va. Divsn. of Forestry, Charlottesville, 1981-83; pest control advisor Calif. Dept. Food and Agr. Inventor fatty acids for blossom thinning; author: (with others) Innovative Sprayer Technology, 1983. Bishop LDS Ch., Carey, N.C., 1982-84, St. Charles, Mo., 1985-89; explorer advisor Boy Scouts Am., Vista, Calif., 1989-92; charter mem. N.C. Weed Sci. Soc., Raleigh, 1982. Mem. Weed Sci. Soc. Am., So. Weed Sci. Soc., N.C. Weed Control Conf. Home: 5151 Silver Bluff Dr Oceanside CA 92057 Office: Mycogen Corp 4980 Carroll Canyon Rd San Diego CA 92121

LARSON, BRENT T., broadcasting executive; b. Ogden, Utah, Sept. 23, 1942; s. George Theodore and Doris (Peterson) L.; m. Tracy Ann Taylor; children: Michelle, Brent Todd. Student, pub. schs., Los Angeles; diploma in radio operational engring., Burbank, Calif., 1962. Owner, mgr. Sta. KAIN, Boise, Idaho, 1969-77; owner, operator Sta. KXA Radio, Seattle, 1975-83, Sta. KYYX Radio, Seattle, 1980-83, Sta. KGA Radio, Spokane, Wash., 1978-84, Sta. KUUZ Radio, Boise, 1976-82, Sta. KOOS Radio, North Bend, Oreg., 1980-81, Sta. KODL Radio, The Dalles, Oreg., 1974-80, Sta. KKWZ Radio, Richfield, Utah, 1980—, Sta. KSVC Radio, Richfield, 1980—, Sta. KSOS-FM, Sta. KNKK-Am, Salt Lake City, 1984—; v.p. Casey Larson Fast Food Co., Oreg. and Idaho, 1976—, Imperial Broadcasting Corp., Idaho, 1970—, Sta. KSOS-FM and KNKK-AM, 1983—; pres. First Nat. Broadcasting Corp., 1970—; v.p. Larson-Wynn Corp., 1974—, Brentwood Properties, Ogden, 1977—; pres. Sta. KSIT Broadcasting, Rock Springs, Wyo., 1980—, Gold Coast Communications Corp., Oreg., 1980-81, Sevier Valley Broadcasting Co., Inc., Utah, 1980—, Brent Larson Group Stas., Western U.S., 1969—; v.p. mktg. Internat. Foods Corp., Boise, 1983—; ptnr. Larson Tours and Travel, Burley, Idaho, 1977-87; founder 1st Nat. TV Div., 1990; bd. dirs. Casey-Larson Foods Co., La Grande, Oreg. Bd. dirs. Met. Sch., 1981—. Served with U.S. Army, 1961-63. Mem. Am. Advt. Fedn., Nat. Assn. Broadcasters, Nat. Radio Broadcasters Assn., Wash. Broadcasters Assn., Oreg. Broadcasters Assn., Idaho Broadcasters Assn., Utah Broadcasters Assn., Citizens for Responsible Broadcasting (bd. dirs.). Republican. Mormon. Home: 4014 Beus Dr Ogden UT 84403-3208 Office: First Nat Broadcasting Corp PO Box 2129 Salt Lake City UT 84110-2129

LARSON, CHARLES LESTER, television writer, producer, author; b. Portland, Oreg., Oct. 23, 1922; s. Charles Oscar and Ina May (Couture) L.; m. Alice Mae Dovey, Aug. 25, 1966; 1 stepson, Wyn Donavan Malotte. Student, U. Oreg., 1940. Contract writer MGM Studios, Culver City, Calif., 1943-46; freelance mag. writer, 1941-51. Assoc. producer: TV program Twelve O'Clock High, 1964; producer: TV program The FBI, 1965-68, The Interns, 1970-71, Cades County, 1971-72; exec. producer: TV program Nakia, 1974; producer: TV movie Crime Club, 1973; co-creator: TV series Hagen, 1979-80; author: The Chinese Game, 1969, Someone's Death, 1973, Matthew's Hand, 1974, Muir's Blood, 1976, The Portland Murders, 1983. Mem. Writers Guild Am. West, Producers Guild, Mystery Writers Am. (spl. award 1974), Authors League Am. Democrat. Home: 14205 S E 38th St Vancouver WA 98684

LARSON, CHARLES ROBERT, naval officer; b. Sioux Falls, S.D., Nov. 20, 1936; s. Eldred Charles and Gertrude Edythe (Jensen) L.; m. Sarah Elizabeth Craig, Aug. 19, 1961; children: Sigrid Anne, Erica Lynn, Kirsten Elizabeth. B.S. in Marine Engring, U.S. Naval Acad., 1958. Commd. ensign USN, 1958, advanced through grades to adm., 1990; naval aviator, attack pilot, 1958-63, nuclear power, submarine tng., 1963-64, assigned nuclear subs., 1964-76, naval aide to the Pres., 1969-71, comdg. officer USS Halibut, 1973-76, comdr. submarine devel. group one, head operational deep submergence program, 1976-78, chief naval ops. staff Strategic Submarine Programs, 1978-79; dir. long range planning group Washington, 1978-82; comdr. submarines Mediterranean, 1982-83; supt. U.S. Naval Acad. Annapolis, Md., 1983-86; comdr. 2d Fleet, 1986-88; dir. plans, policies and ops. DCNO, 1988-90; comdr. U.S. Pacific Fleet, 1990-91, U.S. Pacific Command, Hawaii, 1991—. Mem. USO Coun., Honolulu, 1990-92; mem. Honolulu area coun. Boy Scouts Am., 1990—. Decorated D.S.M. (6), Legion of Merit (3), Bronze Star medal, others; named Disting. Eagle Scout, Balt. area coun. Boy Scouts Am., 1985; White House fellow, 1968-69. Mem. U.S. Naval Inst. (bd. control 1981—). Home: Qtrs A 6 Halealii Rd Honolulu HI 96818-5008 Office: US CINCPAC Camp H M Smith Pearl Harbor HI 96861

LARSON, CHERIE KAY, organization executive; b. Bismarck, N.D., Aug. 5, 1963. AA with high honors, Skagit Valley Coll., Oak Harbor, Wash., 1985; BA in Psychology/Anthropology with hons., Western Wash. U., 1988. Asst. dir. Lesbian Resource Ctr., Seattle, 1989, co-dir., 1989-90, exec. dir., 1990—. Vol. No on 35 Campaign, Seattle, 1990, Sherry Harris for City Coun. Campaign, Seattle, 1991; mem. Freedom Day Com., Seattle, 1991; mem., speaker Anti-Homophobia Tng. Network, Seattle, 1992; Grand Marshall Gay and Lesbian Pride Parade of Seattle, 1992. Fellow Western Wash. U., 1986-88. Mem. Nat. Lesbian and Gay Task Force. Office: Lesbian Resource Ctr 1208 E Pine St Seattle WA 98122

LARSON, CHRISTOPHER BRACE, human resources professional; b. Denver, Dec. 31, 1952; s. Kenneth Frank and Juanita Jane (Sivey) L.; m. Kathleen Inez Simmons, Aug. 6, 1988. BS, Regis U., 1976; BA, Met. State Coll., 1982; M in Social Sci., U. Colo., 1985. Teaching asst. Regis U., Coll., Denver, 1971-76; youth worker State of Colo., Denver, 1973-76; exploring exec. Boy Scouts Am., Wood River, Ill., 1974; dist. exec. Boy Scouts Am., Grand Island, Nebr., 1976-79; dir. tng. Denver Burglar Alarm, 1979—. Mem. exec. bd. Boy Scouts Am., Denver, 1976; exec. bd. Regis Coll. 1982. Recipient Vigil Honor Boy Scouts Am., Denver, 1976. Mem. Tahosa Alumni Assn. Inc. (pres. 1983-84, chmn. 1984-85, sec. 1986-87, treas. 1987-92). Democrat. Lutheran. Home: 3073 W 35th Ave Denver CO 80211

LARSON, DANIEL NORRIS, environmental and resource development company executive, lawyer; b. Oelwein, Iowa, Dec. 3, 1954; s. Norris Norman and Virginia Rose (Meisner) L.; m. Deborah Anne Linneman, May 31, 1986. BA summa cum laude, Drake U., 1976; JD, Yale U., 1980. Bar: Colo. 1981. Law clk. U.S. Ct. Appeals (7th cir.), Chgo., 1980-81; mem. Calkins, Kramer, Grimshaw & Harring, Denver, 1981-85; gen. counsel Kaiser Resources Inc., Denver, 1985-88; exec. v.p. Kaiser Steel Corp., Rancho Cucamonga, Calif., 1988, pres., 1988—; pres. Kaiser Steel Resources, Inc., Rancho Cucamonga, 1988—; dir. Kaiser Resources Inc., 1992—; leader 1992 Am. Mt. Everest Expdn., co-leader 1985 expdn. Bd. dirs. Old Baldy Coun., Boy Scouts Am. Named Up and Coming Bus. Leader of 1990, San Bernardino (Calif.) Sun Newspaper; recipient Entrepreneur of the Yr. award for Turnarounds in the Inland Empire So. Calif. Region, Ernst & Young, Inc. mag. & Merrill Lynch, 1992. Mem. ABA, Colo. Bar Assn., Denver Bar Assn., Turnaround Mgmt. Assn., Young Pres. Orgn., Phi Beta Kappa. Office: 8300 Utica Ave Ste 301 Rancho Cucamonga CA 91730

LARSON, DICK, acupuncturist; b. Glendive, Mont., Mar. 4, 1953; s. Richard Lee and Sarah Ann (Giles) L.; m. Avadhan Bowman, Sept. 16, 1992. PhD, U. Health Sci., 1990; postgrad., N.Am. Acad. Advanced Asian Medicine, 1991—. Diplomate in Acupuncture Nat. Commn. for the Cert. of

Acupuncture; lic. acupuncture, 1984; lic. in massage, 1980. Mgr. Recycling Ctrs. of Mont., Billings, 1974-77; touch for health instr. Billings, 1977-78, Boulder, 1978-79, Missoula, Mont., 1979—; massage therapist Boulder, 1978-79; massage therapist Missoula, 1979-85, Rolfing pracitioner, 1979—, advanced Rolfing practitioner, 1982—, Rolfing movement tchr., 1990—; acupuncturist Acupuncture Clinic of Misssoula, 1985—; delegation leader to Chinese Hosp. Rolf Inst., 1991; presenter 3rd Ann. Conf. Am. Assn. of Sex Educators, Counselors and Therapists, 1981. Contbr. articles to profl. jours. Mem. Acupuncture Assn. of Mont. (co-founder 1988, treas. 1988-89, v.p. 1989-90, treas. 1992-94), Am. Assn. of Acupuncture and Oriental Medicine, Commonwealth Inst. of Acupuncture and Natural Medicine, Internat. Acad. of Scientific Acupuncture (hon. adv. bd. 1990). Home: 201 Westview Dr Missoula MT 59803-1530 Office: Acupuncture Clin Missoula 715 W Kensington #4 Missoula MT 59801

LARSON, DONALD EDWARD, state legislator; b. Thompson Falk, Mont., Oct. 7, 1946; s. Robert L. and Wilma Virginia (Beasley) L. BA, U. Mont., 1973; MA, U. Fla., 1976. Legislator State of Mont. With USN, 1967-71. Mem. Lions Club. Democrat. Congregationalist. Home: PO Box 285 Seeley Lake MT 59868

LARSON, DOROTHY ANN, business educator; b. Nekoosa, Wis., Feb. 27, 1934; d. Edwin E. and Ruby E. (Burch) L.; children: Jean Marie Fitz Harkey, Kenneth Lee Fitz, Cynthia Ann Fitz Whitney. BS with high distinction in Bus. and English, No. Ariz. U., 1969; MA in English, 1971; EdD in Bus., Ariz. State U., 1980. Tchr. English, Cottonwood (Ariz.) Oak Creek Elem. Sch., 1969-70; tchr. bus. and English, Mingus Union High Sch., Cottonwood, 1970-79, dir. vocat. edn., 1976-79; mem. faculty dept. bus. administrn. Yavapai Coll., 1979—, chairperson Bus. div., 1981-86; cons. Ariz. Dept. Edn.; mem. adv. coun. Gov's. Coun. Practitioners. Mem. Ariz. Bus. Edn. Assn. (pres. 1980-81), Nat. Bus. Edn. Assn., Am. Vocat. Assn., Ariz. Edn. Assn., NEA, Pi Omega Pi, Delta Pi Epsilon, Phi Kappa Phi, Alpha Delta Kappa, Phi Delta Kappa. Republican. Editor Ariz. Bus. Edn. Newsletter, 1972-74. Home: 1401 Haisley Ct Prescott AZ 86303-5370 Office: 1100 E Sheldon Prescott AZ 86301

LARSON, EDWARD DUANE, engineering executive; b. Santa Monica, Calif., Oct. 31, 1946; s. Marie (Schulstad) L. BS, U.S. Mil. Acad., 1968; MS in Physics, N.D. State U., 1977. Commd. 2d lt. U.S. Army, 1968, advanced through grades to capt., 1970, ret., 1974; instr. physics dept. N.D. State U., Fargo, 1974-78; program mgr. Hughes Helicopter Co., Culver City, Calif., 1978-82, Hughes Aircraft Co., El Segundo, Calif., 1982-91; sr. v.p. engring. Loral Aeronutronic, Newport Beach, Calif., 1991—. Decorated D.F.C, Bronze Star, Air Medal with 28 Clusters, Vietnamese Cross of Gallantry, 1971. Mem. Nat. Mgmt. Assn., Am. Def. Preparedness Assn., Assn. Grads. of U.S. Mil. Acad., Sigma Pi Sigma. Office: Loral Aeronutronic Ford Rd Bldg 5/G209 Newport Beach CA 92658-8900

LARSON, ERIC VICTOR, policy and systems analyst; b. Buffalo, May 29, 1957; s. Ralph William and Marilyn Ruth (Werner) L. BA with distinction, U. Mich., 1980. Statistician and staff analyst Decision Info. Display System Office of Mgmt. and Budget-EOP, Washington, 1980-82; policy analyst Office of Planning and Evaluation at the White House, Washington, 1982-83; analyst NSC Staff, Washington, 1983-87; mem. research staff Inst. for Def. Analyses, Alexandria, Va., 1988-89; grad. fellow The Rand Corp., Santa Monica, Calif., 1989—. Trustee 1st Presbyn. Ch. Santa Monica, mem. choral choir. Named one of Outstanding Young Men of Am. Mem. AAAS, Assn. Pub. Policy Analysis and Mgmt., Ops. Rsch. Soc. Am., Internat. Soc. for the System Scis. Home: 1216 Brockton Ave # 6 Los Angeles CA 90025

LARSON, GERALD LEE, auditor; b. Billings, Mont., Apr. 18, 1937; s. Phillip Antone and Eunice (LaPoint) L. Student, U. Nev., 1955-59; AS, Western Nev. U., 1975. Mil. pers. mgr. Nev. Air NG, Reno, 1973-81; mgr. employee rels. Nev. Mil. Dept., Carson City, 1981-82, mil. pers. mgr., 1982-88; auditor Nev. State Indsl. Ins., Reno, 1989-92; sr. auditor Nev. State Indsl. Ins., Carson City, 1992—. State pres. Nev. Enlisted NG Assn., Carson City, 1983-87; nat. conf. chmn. Enlisted Assn. NG U.S., Reno, 1989; project chmn. 40th ann. book Nev. Air NG, 1988. CM Sgt. Nev. Air NG, USAF, 1955-88. Named Outstanding Sr. Non-commd. Officer of Yr., USAF, 1979.

LARSON, JAMES LEE, Scandinavian languages educator; b. Newport, Wash., Sept. 17, 1931; s. Lars W. and Norma (Newburn) L. PhD, U. Calif., Berkeley, 1965; PhD honors cause, Uppsala U., Sweden, 1983. Asst. prof. U. Pa., Phila., 1965-67, U. Calif., Berkeley, 1967-72; assoc. prof. U. Calif., 1972-79, prof. Scandinavian lang., 1979—. Author: Reason and Experience, 1971, Songs of Something, 1982; editor/translator: Linnaeus, 1983, Gothic Renaissance, 1991. With U.S. Army, 1953-55. Mem. Am. Soc. 18th Century Studies, Western Soc. 18th Century Studies, History of Sci. Soc., N.Y. Acad. Sci. Home: 2451 Ashby Ave Berkeley CA 94705-2034 Office: Scandinavian Dept U Calif Berkeley CA 94720

LARSON, MAUREEN INEZ, rehabilitation company executive; b. Madison, Minn., Mar. 10, 1955; d. Alvin John and Leona B. (Bornhorst) L.; m. Michael Earl Klemetsrud, July 7, 1979 (div. Sept. 1988). BA in Psychology, BFA, U. Minn., 1977; MA in Counseling, U. N.D., 1978. Cert. rehab. counselor, ins. rehab. specialist. Employment counselor II, coordinator spl. programs Employment Security div. State of Wyo., Rawlins, 1978-80; employment interviewer Employment Security div. State of Wash., Tacoma, 1980; lead counselor Comprehensive Rehab. Counseling, Tacoma, 1980-81; dir. counseling Cascade Rehab. Counseling, Tacoma, 1981-87, dist. mgr., 1987-90; regional mgr. Rainier Case Mgmt., Tacoma, 1991-92; owner Maureen Larson and Assocs.; state capt. legis. div. Provisions Project Am. Personnel and Guidance Assn., 1980. Adv. Grand Forks (N.D.) Rape Crisis Ctr., 1977-78; mem. Pierce County YMCA; bd. dirs. Boys and Girls Clubs of Tacoma, chairperson sustaining drive, 1991, sec., 1992, treas. 1993. State of Minn. scholar, 1973-77; recipient Alice Tweed Tuohy award U. Minn., 1977, Nat. Disting. Svcs. Registry award Libr. of Congress, 1987; named bd. mem. vol. of Yr. Boys and Girls Clubs of Tacoma, 1992. Mem. Nat. Fedn. Bus. and Profl. Women (rec. sec. 1978-80, runner-up Young Careerists' Program 1980), Nat. Rehab. Assn. (bd. dirs. Olympic chpt. 1988—, pres. 1990-91, chairperson state conf. planning com. 1990), Nat. Rehab. Counseling Assn. (State of Wash. Counselor of Yr. 1991, Pacific Region Counselor of Yr. 1992), Nat. Rehab. Adminstrs. Assn., Women in Workers Compensation Orgn., Pvt. Rehab. Orgn. Wash., Nat. Assn. Rehab. Profls. of Pvt. Sector, Wash. Self-Insured Assn., Pi Gamma Mu. Home: 5501-39th St Ct W Tacoma WA 98466 Office: Industrial Rehab Couns 6314 W 19th St Ste # 13 Tacoma WA 98466

LARSON, NEIL EDWIN, accountant; b. Bellingham, Wash., May 10, 1954; s. Theodore Earl and Carolyn (Hawley) L.; m. Kirby Miltenberger, Sept. 6, 1975; children: Tyler Kenton, Quinn Louis. BA, Western Wash. U., 1976; MS in Tax, Golden Gate U., 1987. CPA, Wash. From payroll to fish clk. Alaska Packers Assn., Chignik, 1973-74; credit and sales clk. Sears Roebuck & Co., Bellingham, Wash., 1974-76; intern Larson, Gross & Assoc., Bellingham, 1976; acct. Benson & McLaughlin, Seattle, 1976-78; sr. acct. Bashey & Co., Bellevue, Wash., 1978-80; supr. Peterson Sullivan & Co., Seattle, 1980-84; mgr. Simonson, Moore & Olson, Bellevue, 1984-86; tax ptnr., sec.-treas. Rabern, Larson & North, PS, Seattle, 1986—. Pres. Prince Peace Luth. Ch., Seattle, 1988-89, treas. 1986-88; legis. com. PTA, Bothell, Wash., 1991-92; legis. v.p. Northshore Coun. PTA, 1992-93; outdoor leader Campfire Girls, Bothell, 1992—. Mem. AICPA, Wash. Soc. CPAs (chmn. programs 1978, not for profit com.), Associated Gen. Contractors, Constrn. Fin. Mgmt. Assn. Office: Rabern Larson & North PS 1800 Ninth Ave Ste 1150 Seattle WA 98101

LARSON, RAY REED, educator; b. Fullerton, Calif., Nov. 6, 1951; S. Ray Forrest and Patricia Louise (Inman) L. BA, Calif. State U., 1974, MLS, 1976; PhD, U. Calif., 1986. Rsch. asst. U.-Wide Libr. Automation Program, Berkeley, 1978-80; programmer/analyst Div. of Libr. Automation, Berkeley, 1980-84; asst. prof. U. Calif., Berkeley, 1984-91, assoc. prof., 1991—. Contbr. articles to profl. jours. Faculty rsch. grant OCLC, Inc., 1989. Mem. ALA, Am. Soc. for Info. Scis. (chair spl. interest group/human computers interest sect. 1990-91, spl. interest group cabinet 1991—). Office: U Calif Sch of Info Studies Berkeley CA 94720

LARSON, RICHARD CARL, aerospace engineer; b. Oshkosh, Wis., Sept. 30, 1942; s. Frank Carl and Edith Imogene (Wacker) L.; m. Lois Garroldine Rummel, Nov. 22, 1962; children: Paul, Jane, Scot. Student, Chapman Coll., 1986. Enlisted USAF, 1961, advanced through grades to chief master sgt., hon. discharged, 1983; with logistics planning dept. Rockwell Space Transp. Div., Lompoc, Calif., 1983-84; system planner Lockheed Space Ops. Co., Lompoc, 1984-86; data engr. Rockwell Space Systems Div., Downey, Calif., 1987—. Author, editor: Program Requirements DOC, 1988, File IX Operating Plan, 1990. Instr. in reading Literacy Vols. of Am., Downey, 1989-90; pres. Lompol Marlins Swim Club, 1980-82. Mem. Air Force Assn. (life), Ret. Enlisted Assn. (life), Toastmasters (treas. 1988-89). Office: Rockwell Internat 12214 Lakewood Blvd Downey CA 90242-2693

LARSON, ROBERT WALTER, retired history educator, consultant; b. Denver, Mar. 20, 1927; s. Walter Sigurd and Helen Carolyn (Leafgren) L.; m. Carole B. Lang, 1959 (div. 1972); children: Helen Elizabeth, Matthew Robert;m. Peggy Anne Logan, Aug. 15, 1987. AB, U. Denver, 1950, AM, 1953; PhD, U. N.Mex., 1961. Tchr. Denver Pub. Schs., 1950-56, supervising tchr. info. svcs., 1956-58; prof. history U. No. Colo., Greeley, 1960-90, ret.; trustee Univ. Press Colo., Niwot, 1973-93; editorial cons. Ency. Brit. Jr., 1969-89, N.Mex. Hist. Rev., 1976-86. Author: New Mexico's Quest for Statehood, 1846-1912, 1968, New Mexico Populism: A Study of Radical Protest in a Western Territory, 1974, Populism in the Mountain West, 1986, Shaping Educational Change: The First Century of the University of Northern Colorado at Greeley, 1989. With USN, 1945-46. Grantee Am. Philos. Soc., 1963, 64, 69, NEH, 1982; Newberry fellow Newberry Libr., Chgo., 1977. Mem. Colo. History Group (pres. 1988-91), Orgn. Am. Historians (co-chmn. membership com. 1976-79), Western History Assn., Weld County UN Assn. (pres. 1962). Democrat. Presbyterian. Home: # 204 3022 S Wheeling Way Aurora CO 80014-3631

LA RUSSA, TONY, JR. (ANTHONY LA RUSSA, JR.), professional baseball manager; b. Tampa, Fla., Oct. 4, 1944; m. Elaine Coker, Dec. 31, 1973; 2 daus.: Bianca, Devon. Student, U. Tampa; BA, U. So. Fla., 1969; LLB, Fla. State U., 1978. Bar: Fla., 1979. Player numerous major league and minor league baseball teams, 1962-77; coach St. Louis Cardinals orgn., 1977; mgr. minor league team Knoxville, 1978, Iowa, 1979; coach Chgo. White Sox, 1978, mgr., 1979-86; mgr. Oakland A's, 1986—; mgr. All-Star team, 1988, coach, 1984, 87. Named Maj. League Mgr. of Yr. Baseball Writers' Assn. Am., 1983, 88, AP, 1983, Sporting News, 1983, Am. League Mgr. of Yr., 1988. Office: Oakland A's Oakland-Alameda County Coliseum Oakland CA 94621*

LASAROW, WILLIAM JULIUS, federal judge; b. Jacksonville, Fla., June 30, 1922; s. David Herman and Mary (Hollins) L.; m. Marilyn Doris Powell, Feb. 4, 1951; children: Richard M., Elisabeth H. BA, U. Fla., 1943; JD, Stanford U., 1950. Bar: Calif. 1951. Counsel judiciary com. Calif. Assembly, Sacramento, 1951-52; dep. dist. atty. Stanislaus County, Modesto, Calif., 1952-53; pvt. practice law L.A., 1953-73; bankruptcy judge U.S. Cts., L.A., 1973—; chief judge U.S. Bankruptcy Ct., Central dist., Calif., 1978-90; judge Bankruptcy Appellate Panel 9th Fed. Cir., 1980-82; fed. judge U.S. Bankruptcy Ct., L.A., 1973; faculty Fed. Jud. Ctr. Bankruptcy Seminars, Washington, 1977-82. Contbg. author, editor legal publs.; staff: Stanford U. Law Review, 1949. Mem. ABA, L.A. County Bar Assn., Wilshire Bar Assn., Blue Key, Phi Beta Kappa, Phi Kappa Phi. Democrat. Jewish. Lodge: Masons. Home: 11623 Canton Pl Studio City CA 91604-4164 Office: US Bankruptcy Ct 1534 Roybal Federal Bldg 255 E Temple St Los Angeles CA 90012

LASCH, ROBERT, former journalist; b. Lincoln, Neb., Mar. 26, 1907; s. Theodore Walter and Myrtle (Nelson) L.; m. Zora Schaupp, Aug. 22, 1931 (dec. 1982); children: Christopher, Catherine; m. Iris C. Anderson, Sept. 14, 1986. A.B., U. Nebr., 1928; postgrad. (Rhodes scholar), Oxford, 1928-31; Nieman fellow, Harvard, 1941-42. Reporter, state editor, editorial writer Omaha World-Herald, 1931-41; editorial writer, then chief editorial writer Chgo. Sun and Sun-Times, 1942-50; editorial writer St. Louis Post-Dispatch, 1950-57, editor editorial page, 1957-71, ret. Contbr. to: Newsmen's Holiday, 1942; Author: For a Free Press, 1944 (Atlantic Monthly prize), Breaking The Building Blockade, 1946. Recipient; St. Louis Civil Liberties award, 1966; Pulitzer prize for distinguished editorial writing, 1966. Home: 320 E El Viento Green Valley AZ 85614-2246

LASHLEY, VIRGINIA STEPHENSON HUGHES, retired computer science educator; b. Wichita, Kans., Nov. 12, 1924; d. Herman H. and Edith M. (Wayland) Stephenson; m. Kenneth W. Hughes, June 4, 1946 (dec.); children: Kenneth W. Jr., Linda Hughes Tindall; m. Richard H. Lashley, Aug. 19, 1954; children: Robert H., Lisa Lashley Van Amberg, Diane Lashley Tan. BA, U. Kans., 1945; MA, Occidental Coll., 1966; PhD, U. So. Calif., 1983. Cert. info. processor, tchr. secondary and community coll., Calif. Tchr. math. La Canada (Calif.) High Sch., 1966-69; from instr. to prof. Glendale (Calif.) Coll., 1970—, chmn. bus. div., 1977-81, coord. instructional computing, 1974-84; 88—; sec., treas., dir. Victory Montessori Schs., Inc., Pasadena, Calif., 1980—; pres. The Computer Sch., Pasadena, 1983-92; ret., 1992; pres. San Gabriel Valley Data Processing Mgmt. Assn., 1977-79, San Gabriel Valley Assn. for Systems Mgmt., 1979-80; chmn. Western Ednl. Computing Conf., 1980, 84. Editor Jour. Calif. Ednl. Computing, 1980. Mem. DAR. NSF grantee, 1967-69, EDUCARE scholar U. So. Calif., 1980-82; John Randolph and Dora Haynes fellow, Occidental Coll., 1964-66; student computer ctr. renamed Dr. Virginia S. Lashley computer ctr., 1992. Mem. AAUP, AAUW, Data Processing Mgmt. Assn., Calif. Ednl. Computing Consortium (bd. dir. 1979—, v.p. 1983—, pres. 1985-87, ret. 1992), Orgn. Am. Historians, San Marino Women's Club, Phi Beta Kappa, Pi Mu Epsilon, Phi Alpha Theta, Phi Delta Kappa, Delta Phi Upsilon, Gamma Phi Beta. Republican. Congregationalist. Home: 1240 S San Marino Ave San Marino CA 91108-1227

LASKIN, BARBARA VIRGINIA, legal association administrator; b. Chgo., July 2, 1939; d. Cyril Krieps and Gertrude Katherine (Kujawa) Szymanski; children: Dawn Katherine Kloski, Amy Lynn Anderson. BA, U. Ill., Chgo., 1967; MA, Am. U. Beirut, 1978, Georgetown U., 1985. Asst. buyer Carson, Pirie, Scott & Co., Chgo., 1967-69; fgn. svc. officer Dept. State, Washington, 1969-79; mgr. gift shops Marriott Hotels, Washington, 1979-81; office mgr. Robt Schwinn & Assoc., Bethesda, Md., 1983-85; exec. dir. Internat. Acad. Trial Lawyers, San Jose, Calif., 1985—. Trustee Opera San Jose, 1987—; chmn. YWCA Adv. Com. for Career Action Ctr., San Jose, 1988; bd. dirs. Children's Counseling Ctr., San Jose, 1989—. Fellow Rotary Club San Jose; mem. AAUW (v.p. 1987). Roman Catholic. Office: Internat Acad Trial Lawyers 4 N 2d St Ste 175 San Jose CA 95113

LASKO, ALLEN HOWARD, entrepreneur, pharmacist; b. Chgo., Oct. 27, 1941; s. Sidney P. and Sara (Hoffman) L.; B.S. (James scholar), U. Ill., 1964; m. Janice Marilynn Chess, Dec. 24, 1968; children: Stephanie Paige, Michael Benjamin. Staff pharmacist Michael Reese Hosp. and Med. Center, Chgo., 1964-68; clin. pharmacist City of Hope Med. Center, Duarte, Calif., 1968-73; chief pharmacist Monrovia (Calif.) Community Hosp., 1973-74, Santa Fe Meml. Hosp., Los Angeles, 1974-77; pvt. investor, 1977—. Recipient Roche Hosp. Pharmacy Research award, 1972-73. Mem. Magic Castle, Flying Samaritans, Mensa, Rho Pi Phi. Jewish. Author books: Diabetes Study Guide, 1972; A Clinical Approach to Lipid Abnormalities Study Guide, 1973; Jet Injection Tested As An Aid in Physiologic Delivery of Insulin, 1973. Home and Office: 376 Hill St Monrovia CA 91016-2340

LASMANIS, RAYMOND, geologist, state government executive; b. Riga, Latvia, Apr. 25, 1938; s. Janis Alfreds and Zinaida (Nikiforov) L.; Betty M. Scott; children: Kevin, John H.; m. Josephine A. Blair, Dec. 29, 1969; children: Larrabee, Diana L., Donald A., Darrell D. BS in Geology, U. Mo., Rolla, 1963. Exploration geologist Cominco Am., Salem, Mo., 1961-65; exploration mgr. S.W. dist. Cominco Am., Prescott, Ariz., 1965-67; rsch. geologist Cominco Ltd., Pine Point, N.W. Ter., Can., 1967-68; exploration mgr. N.W. dist. The Superior Oil Co., Spokane, Wash., 1968-73; asst. dir. Canadian Superior Exploration Ltd., Vancouver, B.C., Can., 1974-80, exploration mgr., 1980-82; mgr., state geologist, state oil & gas supr. Wash. Dept. Natural Resources, Olympia, Wash., 1982—; mem. Wash. State Nuclear Waste Bd., Olympia, 1982-89, Mt. St. Helens Sci. Adv. Bd., 1983—; adv. bd. Wash. Mining and Mineral Resources Rsch. Inst., 1985-90. Contbr. articles to profl. jours. Mem. Friends of Mineralogy(pres. 1985-87), Am. Inst. Mining & Metall. Engrs., N.W. Mining Assoc. Home: Ste 155 800 Sleater Kinney Rd SE Lacey WA 98503-1127 Office: Div Geology & Earth Resources Dept Natural Resources Olympia WA 98504

LASORDA, THOMAS CHARLES (TOMMY LASORDA), professional baseball team manager; b. Norristown, Pa., Sept. 22, 1927; s. Sam and Carmella (Covatto) L.; m. Joan Miller, Apr. 14, 1950; children: Laura, Tom Charles. Student pub. schs., Norristown. Pitcher Bklyn. Dodgers, 1954-55, Kansas City A's, 1956; with L.A. Dodgers, 1956—; mgr. minor league clubs L.A. Dodgers, Pocatello, Idaho, Ogden, Utah, Spokane, Albuquerque, 1965-73; coach L.A. Dodgers, 1973-76, mgr., 1976—. Author: (with David Fisher) autobiography The Artful Dodger, 1985. Served with U.S. Army, 1945-47. L.A. Dodgers winner Nat. League pennant, 1977, 78, 81, 88, winner World Championship, 1981, 88; 2d Nat. League mgr. to win pennant first two yrs. as mgr.; named Nat. League Mgr. Yr. UPI, 1977, AP, 1977, 81, Baseball Writers' Assn. Am., 1988, Sporting News, 1988; recipient Milton Richman Meml. award Assn. Profl. Baseball Players Am. Mem. Profl. Baseball Players Am. Roman Catholic. Club: Variety of Calif. (v.p.). Office: care Los Angeles Dodgers 1000 Elysian Park Ave Los Angeles CA 90012-1112*

LASSETTRE, EDWIN RICHIE, data processing executive; b. Anaconda, Mont., Jan. 16, 1934; s. Edwin Nichols and Marjorie (Richie) L.; m. Pauline Anne English, May 6, 1961; children: Paul, Marian, Christopher, Neil. BSc, Ohio State U., 1958, MSc, 1963. Applied sci. rep. IBM Corp., Columbus, 1959-61; rsch. assoc. Aviation Psychology Lab., Ohio State U. Rsch. Found., Columbus, 1961-63; sr. programmer Numerical Computation lab., Ohio State U. Rsch. Found., 1963-67; sys. programmer supr. Instrn. and Rsch. Computer Ctr., Ohio State U., 1967-69; programmer IBM Corp., 1969-81; sr. tech. staff, 1981-87; fellow San Jose, a1987—. Contbr. articles to profl. jours. Bd. dirs. ACLU, Cen. Ohio, 1967. Recipient Bareis prize, Ohio State U., 1953. Mem. ACM, N.Y. Acad. Sci., Am. Math. Soc., Math. Assn. Am., Hon. Order of Ky. Cols., Pi Mu Epsilon. Home: 123 Vineyard Ct Los Gatos CA 95030-1642

LAST, JEROLD ALAN, medicine and biological chemistry educator; b. N.Y.C., June 5, 1940; s. Herbert and Florence Last; m. Elaine Zimelis, June 1, 1975; children: Andrew, Matthew, Michael. BS in Chemistry, U. Wis., 1959, MS in Biochemistry, 1961; PhD in Biochemistry, Ohio State U., 1965. Postdoctoral fellow biochemistry NYU, 1966-67; sr. rsch. scientist Squibb Inst. for Med. Rsch., New Brunswick, N.J., 1968-69; editor Proceedings of NAS, Washington, 1970-73; rsch. assoc. Harvard U., Cambridge, Mass., 1973-76; prof. U. Calif., Davis, 1976—, dir. systemwide toxic substances prog., 1985—; vice-chmn. Dept. Internal Medicine U. Calif. Med. Sch., Davis; mem. rev. panels various granting agys.; Fulbright lectr. Coun. for Internat. Exch. of Scholars/Fulbright Found., Montevideo, Uruguay, 1983. Editor Methods in Molecular Biology series; editorial bds. various sci. jours.; contbr. sci. papers to profl. jours.; patentee antimicrobial agents. Referee Am. Youth Soccer Orgn. Grantee in lung biology and toxicology. Mem. Am. Soc. Biochemistry and Molecular Biology, Soc. of Toxicology (Frank R. Blood award 1979, ICI Travelling Lectureship, Western Europe, 1992), Am. Fedn. for Clin. Rsch., Western Soc. for Clin. Rsch., Am. Thoracic Soc., Calif. Lung Assn. (chair rsch. com. 1984-86). Home: 510 Hubble St Davis CA 95616-2721 Office: U Calif CPRC Davis CA 95616-8542

LASTRA, WILLIAM A., broadcast executive; b. L.A., Nov. 23, 1956; s. A.M. and N.L. Lastra; m. Karen Prescia, Aug. 17, 1986 (div. Aug. 1990); 1 child, Chancellor. BA in Phys. Edn., Calif. State U., L.A., 1979, secondary teaching credentials, 1981; MA in Sociology, U. Nev., Las Vegas, 1984. Asst. basketball coach U. Nev., Las Vegas, 1982-86; pres. Chancellor Broadcasting Co., Las Vegas, 1989—. Mem. Optimist Club. Republican. Roman Catholic.

LATHEN, CALVIN WESLEY, physical education educator; b. Gooding, Idaho, Nov. 25, 1940; s. Wesley Waldo and Mary Lorita (York) L.; m. Sandra Jean Thompson, Aug. 26, 1961; children: Larry, Roy, Judy, Sheri, Wesley, Jeffrey, Sara, Steven. AA, Ricks Coll., Rexburg, Idaho, 1961; BA, Idaho State U., 1963, MPE, 1967; EdD, U. Idaho, 1973. Cert. leisure profl. Teaching asst. Idaho State U., Pocatello, 1966-67; instr. U. Idaho, Moscow, 1967-70, asst. prof., 1970-75, assoc. prof., 1975-83, prof., 1983—; chmn. Men's Phys. Edn. Dept., U. Idaho, 1975-78; Coord. of Recreation, U. Idaho, 1978—; dir. for Health, Phys. Edn., Recreation and Dance, U. Idaho, 1988—. Contbr. articles profl. jours. Capt. USMC, 1963-66, Vietnam. Recipient Citation award 1984, Fellowship award 1989, Idaho Parks and Recreation Soc. Mem. Idaho Alliance for Health, Phys. Edn., Recreation and Dance (pres. 1981-82), Northwest Dist. (pres. 1991-92), Am. Alliance for Leisure and Recreation (dist. rep. 1987-88). Republican. Mormon. Home: 1634 Lemhi Dr Moscow ID 83843-3830 Office: Phys Edn Bldg 101 U Idaho Moscow ID 83843

LATHI, BHAGAWANDAS PANNALAL, electrical engineering educator; b. Bhokar, Maharashtr, India, Dec. 3, 1933; came to U.S., 1956; s. Pannalal Rupchand and Tapi Pannalal (Indani) L.; m. Rajani Damodardas Mundada, July 27, 1962; children: Anjali, Shishir. BEEE, Poona U., 1955; MSEE, U. Ill., 1957; PhD in Elec. Engring., Stanford U., 1961. Research asst. U. Ill., Urbana, 1956-57, Stanford (Calif.) U., 1957-60; research engr. Gen. Electric Co., Syracuse, N.Y., 1960-61; cons. to semicondr. industry India, 1961-62; assoc. prof. elec. engring. Bradley U., Peoria, Ill., 1962-69, U.S. Naval Acad., Annapolis, Md., 1969-72; prof. elec. engring. Campinas (Brazil) State U., 1972-78, Calif. State U., Sacramento, 1979—; vis. prof. U. Iowa, Iowa City, 1979. Author: Signals, Systems and Communication, 1965, Communication Systems, 1968 (transl. into Japanese 1977), Random Signals and Communication Theory, 1968, Teoria Signalow I Ukladow Telekomunikacyjnych, 1970, Sistemy Telekomunikacyjne, 1972, Signals, Systems and Controls, 1974, Sistemas de Comunicacion, 1974, 86, Sistemas de Comunicacão, 1978, Modern Digital and Analog Communication Systems, 1983, 89 (transl. into Japanese 1986, 90), Signals and Systems, 1987, Linear Systems and Signals, 1992; contbr. articles to profl. jours. Mem. IEEE (sr.). Office: Calif State U 6000 J St Sacramento CA 95819-2605

LATHROP, IRVIN TUNIS, retired academic dean, educator; b. Platteville, Wis., Sept. 23, 1927; s. Irvin J. and Marian (Johnson) L.; m. Eleanor M. Kolar, Aug. 18, 1951; 1 son, James I. B.S., Stout State Coll., 1950; M.S., Iowa State U., 1954, Ph.D., 1958. Tchr. Ottumwa (Iowa) High Sch., 1950-55; mem. faculty Iowa State U., 1957-58, Western Mich. U., 1958-59; mem. faculty Calif. State Coll., 1959-88, prof. indsl. arts, 1966-88, chmn. dept. indsl. edn., 1969-88, assoc. dean extended edn., 1978-88, prof. emeritus, 1988—; cons. Naval Ordnance Lab., Corona, Calif., 1961-63. Author: (with Marshall La Cour) Photo Technology, 1966, rev. edit., 1977, Photography, 1979, rev. edit., 1992, The Basic Book of Photography, 1979, Laboratory Manual for Photo Technology, 1973, (with John Lindbeck) General Industry, 1969, rev. edit., 1977, 86, (with Robert Kunst) Photo-Offset, 1979; Editorial cons.: (with Robert Kunst) Am. Tech. Soc; Contbr. (with Robert Kunst) articles to profl. jours. Mem. adv. com. El Camino and Orange Coast Coll.; mem. Orange County Grand Jury, 1989-90, Orange County Juvenile Justice Commn. With USAAF, 1946-47. Mem. Nat. Soc. for Study Edn., Am. Council Indsl. Arts Tchr. Edn., Am. Vocat. Assn., Nat. Assn. Indsl. and Tech. Tchrs., Internat. Tech. Assn., Am. Ednl. Research Assn., Epsilon Pi Tau, Psi Chi, Phi Delta Kappa, Phi Kappa Phi. Home: PO Box 3430 Laguna Beach CA 92654-3430 Office: 1250 N Bellflower Blvd Long Beach CA 90840-0001

LATHROP, LAWRENCE ERWIN, JR., state agency forester, consultant; b. L.A., Dec. 4, 1942; s. Lawrence Erwin and Anna Maxine (Cypert) L.; m. Elaine Dorothy Baudin, May 16, 1964; 1 child, Lawrence Erwin III. AA in Forestry, Lassen Coll., Susanville, Calif., 1968; BA in Pub. Adminstrn., U. San Francisco, 1976. Cert. fire investigator, coll. instr. Forest firefighter Calif. Dept. Forestry and Fire Protection, Santa Clara, 1961; fire apparatus engr. Calif. Dept. Forestry and Fire Protection, Belmont and Yreka, 1962-64; fire capt. Calif. Dept. Forestry and Fire Protection, Riverside County, 1964-73; fire prevention officer Calif. Dept. Forestry and Fire Protection, Clearlake, 1973; state forest ranger I Calif. Dept. Forestry and Fire Protection, Ione, 1973-82; state forest ranger II Calif. Dept. Forestry and Fire Protection, Susanville, 1982-93, retired, 1993; cons. private practice Calif., 1993—; fire investigation and tng. cons. Nev. Dept. Forestry, Carson City, 1985—, U.S. Bur. Land Mgmt., Elko and Winnemuca, Nev., 1985—.

Author, editor: Tailgate Safety Bulletin, 1984—; author of numerous in-service tng. programs, including Helicopter Safety, Air Attack, Powerline Inspections, 1978-82. Advisor Demolay, Amador County, Calif., 1976-78; active PTA, Amador County, 1975-82, Lassen County Arson Task Force, 1985—, State Arson Unit, 1974—. Mem. Am. Mensa Ltd., Masons (master 1977). Republican. Presbyterian. Home: PO Box 717 Janesville CA 96114-0717 Office: Dept Forestry 711045 Center Rd Susanville CA 96130-9115

LATHROP, MITCHELL LEE, lawyer; b. Los Angeles, Dec. 15, 1937; s. Alfred Lee and Barbara (Mitchell) L.; m. Denice Annette Davis; children: Christin Lorraine Newlon, Alexander Mitchell, Timothy Trewin Mitchell. B.Sc., U.S. Naval Acad., 1959; J.D., U. So. Calif., 1966. Bar: D.C., 1966, Calif. 1966, N.Y. 1981, U.S. Supreme Ct. 1969. Dep. counsel Los Angeles County, Calif., 1966-68; with firm Brill, Hunt, DeBuys and Burby, Los Angeles, 1968-71; ptnr. firm Macdonald, Halsted & Laybourne, Los Angeles and San Diego, 1971-80; sr. ptnr. Rogers & Wells, N.Y.C., San Diego, 1980-86; sr. ptnr. Adams, Duque & Hazeltine, L.A., San Francisco, N.Y.C., San Diego, 1986—, exec. com., 1986—, firm chmn., 1992—; presiding referee Calif. Bar Ct., 1984-86, mem. exec. com., 1981-88; lectr. law Calif. Judges Assn., Practicing Law Inst. N.Y., Continuing Edn. of Bar, State Bar Calif., ABA. Author: State Hazardous Waste Regulation, 1991, Environmental Insurance Coverage, 1991, Insurance Coverage for Environmental Claims, 1992. Western Regional chmn. Met. Opera Nat. Coun., 1971-81, v.p., mem. exec. com., 1971—, now chmn.; trustee Honnold Libr. at Claremont Colls., 1972-80; bd. dirs. Music Ctr. Opera Assn., L.A., sec., 1974-80; bd. dirs. San Diego Opera Assn., 1980—, v.p., 1985-89; bd. dirs. Met. Opera Assn., N.Y.C.; mem. nat. steering coun. Nat. Actors Theatre, N.Y. Capt. JAGC, USNR, ret. Mem. ABA, N.Y. Bar Assn., Fed. Bar Assn., Fed. Bar Council, Calif. Bar Assn., D.C. Bar Assn., San Diego County Bar Assn. (chmn. ethics com. 1980-82, bd. dirs. 1982-85, v.p. 1985), Assn. Bus. Trial Lawyers, Assn. So. Calif. Def. Counsel, Los Angeles Opera Assos. (pres. 1970-72), Soc. Colonial Wars in Calif. (gov. 1970-72), Order St. Lazarus of Jerusalem, Friends of Claremont Coll. (dir. 1975-81, pres. 1978-79), Am. Bd. Trial Advocates, Judge Advocates Assn. (dir. Los Angeles chpt. 1974-80, pres. So. Calif. chpt. 1977-78), Internat. Assn. Def. Counsel, Brit. United Services Club (dir. Los Angeles 1973-75), Mensa Internat., Calif. Soc., S.R. (pres. 1977-79), Calif. Club (Los Angeles), Valley Hunt Club (Pasadena, Calif.), Met. Club (N.Y.C.), The Naval Club (London), Phi Delta Phi. Republican. Home: 455 Silvergate Ave San Diego CA 92106-3327 Office: Adams Duque & Hazeltine 401 W A St 26th fl San Diego CA 92101-7910 also: Citicorp Ctr 153 E 53d St 26th fl New York NY 10022

LATIMER, LINDA GAY, small business owner; b. Washington, Oct. 3, 1943; d. Harry Allen and Beverly Elizabeth (Gosman) Latimer; m. 1963 (div. 1980); children: Debra Ann, Troy Christopher. Pers. mgr. Bozell & Jacobs, Palo Alto, Calif., Coakley Heagerty Advt., Santa Clara, Calif., 1982-85; owner The People Advertisers, Milpitas, Calif., 1985—; lectr. in field; resume evaluator job fairs/career fairs; seminar presenter Women in Bus., 1990. Contbr. articles to profl. jours. Mem. Women in Bus., Milpitas C. of C. Republican. Office: The People Advertisers 259 W Calaveras Blvd Milpitas CA 95035

LATINI, HENRY PETER, real estate management executive; b. Portland, Maine; s. Joseph and Mary Rose (Di Santo) L.; m. Betty Shevock, Oct. 20, 1951; children: Mary Celeste, Lisa Ann Kirkendall, Monica Louise King. AB, U. Miami, Coral Gables, Fla., 1951; postgrad., U. Maine, 1980-81, U. Hawaii, 1984. Spl. agt. FBI, Washington, 1951-79; owner, pres. Nat. Bur. Spl. Investigations, Portland, 1979-84; owner, v.p. Data Base Inc., Reston, Va., 1980-84; v.p. Cert. Mgmt. Inc., Honolulu, 1985-92, Latini-Kirkendall: Architecture, Seattle and Honolulu, 1992—; owner Residential Mgmt. Cons., Seattle, Wash., 1992—; managing ptnr. Latini-Kirkendall Architecture, Seattle and Honolulu, 1992—; owner Koapaka Ctr Inc., Honolulu, 1992—; chmn. bd. dir. A.R. Corp., Honolulu, 1987-92, CMI, 1992—; mem. Community Assns. Inst., Honolulu; pres. Common Area Maintenance Co., 1991—; co-owner Koapaka Ctr., Inc. Membership chair Portland Club, 1980-84; mem. Civil Svc. Commn., Cape Elizabeth, Maine, 1981-83; dir. security Mus. of Art, Portland, Maine, 1982-83; vol. Hawaiian Open and Ko'Olina Sr. Invitational Tournament. Mem. Soc. Former Spl. Agts. of the FBI Inc. (Hawaii chpt., sec. 1987-88, v.p. 1988-89, chmn. 1989-90), Inst. Real Estate Mgmt. Am. Soc. for Indsl. Security (Maine chpt., founder 1980, pres. 1980-82), Elks. Republican. Roman Catholic. Office: Cert Mgmt Inc 3179 Koapaka St Honolulu HI 96819-1927

LATNER, BARRY P., pathologist; b. L.A., Oct. 8, 1957; m. Claudia Pinilla, Sept. 3, 1988. BA, UCLA, 1979; MD, Chgo. Med. Sch., 1984. Diplomate Am. Bd. Pathology. Intern/resident Calif. Pacific Med. Ctr., San Francisco, 1984-89; pathologist Mt. Diablo Med. Ctr., Concord, Calif., 1989—; asst. clin. prof. U. Calif., Berkeley, Calif., 1989—. Contbr. articles to profl. jours. Fellow Coll. Am. Pathologists; mem. Am. Soc. Clin. Pathologists, Am. Assn. Clin. Chemists, Calif. Soc. Pathologists, South Bay Pathology Soc. Office: Mt Diablo Med Ctr 2540 East St PO Box 4110 Concord CA 94524

LATORRE, VICTOR ROBERT, electrical engineer; b. Bklyn., Nov. 17, 1931; s. Victor Alfred and Frances Katherine (Thoms) L.; m. Roberta Jean Robinette, Feb. 26, 1956 (div. June 1965); m. Jeanne Anne Cejka, June 6, 1968; chidlren—Lisa Lynn, David Victor. B.S.E.E., U. Ariz., 1956, M.S., 1957, Ph.D., 1960. Instr. elec. engring. U. Ariz., Tucson, 1956-59, asst. prof., 1959-61; research specialist Boeing Co., Seattle, 1961-64; asst. prof. U. Calif., Davis, 1964-67; research engr. U. Calif.-Lawrence Livermore Nat. Lab., 1967—; cons. Frontier Enterprises, Albuquerque, 1969-80. Author: Handbook of RFI, 4 vols., 1961. Contbr. 100 articles on electronics to profl. jours., 1958—. Pres. Soc. Profl. Scientists and Engrs., Livermore, Calif., 1969. Served with USAF, 1951-54, Korea. Fellow U. Calif., Davis, 1966. Mem. IEEE (sr.), AAUP, N.Y. Acad. Sci., Tau Beta Pi, Sigma Pi Sigma, Sigma Xi. Democrat. Methodist. Home: 535 Fiesta Ct Tracy CA 95376-9132 Office: Lawrence Livermore Nat Lab L-156 PO Box 808 Livermore CA 94551-0808

LATTA, WILLIAM ATHERTON, medical group administrator; b. Oakland, Calif., Dec. 20, 1941; s. Lynn Meredith and Irva Louise (Dale) L.; m. Janet Garland Wilson, Aug. 10,. 1963; children: Courtney Lynn, Casey Brooke. BA, Whitman Coll., 1963; MBA, U. Pa., 1965. Asst. adminstr. The Portland (Oreg.) Clinic, 1969-72; adminstr. Meml. Clinic Ltd., P.S., Olympia, Wash., 1972—. Pres. North St. Assn., Olympia, Wash., 1980-82. Capt. USAF, 1966-69. Mem. Med. Group Mgmt. Assn., Wash. Med. Group Mgmt. Assn. (pres. 1979-80), Rotary Club (pres. Olympia, Wash., 1990-91). Episcopalian. Office: Meml Clinic Ltd PS 500 Lilly Rd NE Olympia WA 98506

LATTANZIO, STEPHEN PAUL, astronomy educator; b. Yonkers, N.Y., June 29, 1949; s. Anthony Raymond and Anella Lattanzio; m. Barbara Regina Knisely, Aug. 14, 1976; children: Gregory Paul, Timothy Paul. BA in Astronomy, U. Calif., Berkeley, 1971; MA in Astronomy, UCLA, 1973, postgrad., 1973-75. Planetarium lectr. Griffith Obs., Los Angeles, 1973-75; instr. astronomy El Camino Coll., Torrance, Calif., 1974-75; planetarium lectr. Valley Coll., Los Angeles, 1975; prof. astronomy Orange Coast Coll., Costa Mesa, Calif., 1975—, planetarium dir., 1975—; mem. adv. commn. Natural History Found. Orange County, Calif., 1988-91; scientific advisor instructional TV series Universe: The Infinite Frontier, 1992—. Co-author: Study Guide for Project: Universe, 1978, 2d rev. edition 1981; textbook reviewer, 1978—; co-screenwriter Project: Universe instructional TV series episode, 1979; contbr. articles to profl. jours. Mem. Astron. Soc. Pacific, Nat. Space Soc., The Planetary Soc., Space Studies Inst. Sigma Xi (assoc.), Phi Beta Kappa. Office: Orange Coast Coll 2701 Fairview Rd Costa Mesa CA 92628-0120

LATTER, DANIEL STUART, lawyer; b. Chgo., June 5, 1956; s. Eugene and Evelyn (Weiss) L. BA, U. Ill., 1978; JD, George Washington U., 1981. Bar: Calif. 1981. Lawyer Pillsbury, Madison & Sutro, San Francisco, 1981-83, Rifkind, Sterling & Levin, Beverly Hills, Calif., 1983-85, Finley, Kumble, Wagner et al., L.A., 1985-87, Chrystie & Berle, L.A., 1988-91; pvt. practice, L.A., 1991—. Mem. ABA, L.A. County Bar Assn. (mem. edn. com. barristers div. 1990—), Calif. Bar Assn. Office: Law Offices Ste 480 2029 Century Park E Los Angeles CA 90067

LATTMAN, LAURENCE HAROLD, college president emeritus; b. N.Y.C., Nov. 30, 1923; s. Jacob and Yetta (Schwartz) L.; m. Hanna Renate Cohn, Apr. 12, 1946; children—Martin Jacob, Barbara Diane. B.S. in Chem. Engring, Coll. City N.Y., 1948; M.S. in Geology, U. Cin., 1951, Ph.D. (Fenneman fellow), 1953. Instr. U. Mich., 1952-53; asst. head photogeology sect. Gulf Oil Corp., Pitts., 1953-57; asst. prof. to prof. geomorphology Pa. State U., 1957-70; prof., head dept. geology U. Cin., 1970-75; dean Coll. of Mines U. Utah, 1975-83, dean Coll. Engring., 1978-83; pres. N.Mex. Tech., Socorro, 1983-93, pres. emeritus, 1993—; Cons. U.S. Army Engrs., Vicksburg, Miss., 1965-69, also maj. oil cos. Author: (with R.G. Ray) Aerial Photographs in Field Geology, 1965, (with D. Zillman) Energy Law; Contbr. articles to profl. jours. Served with AUS, 1943-46. Recipient Distinguished Teaching award Pa. State U., 1968. Fellow Geol. Soc. Am.; mem. Am. Assn. Petroleum Geologists, Am. Soc. Photogrammetry (Ford Bartlett award 1968), Soc. Econ. Paleontologists and Mineralogists, AIME (Disting. mem. 1981, Mineral Industries Edn., award 1986—), Assn. Western Univs. (chmn. bd. dirs. 1986-87), Sigma Xi. Home: One Olive Ln 6433 Glen Oak NE Albuquerque NM 87111

LAU, B. PECK, radiation oncologist; b. Singapore, Nov. 27, 1932; came to U.S. 1952; s. T.K. and Lik (Hon) L.; m. Judith Tien, June 1, 1962; children: Laura Ginn, Benjamin Warn, Estelle Lau Simenon. BS, Randolph-Macon Coll., Ashland, Va., 1955; MD, Va. Commonwealth U., 1959. Diplomate Am. Coll. Radiology. Intern Washington Hosp. Ctr., 1959-60, resident in radiology, 1960-62; attending physician U. Calif. Med. Ctr., Sacramento, 1962-64; instr. radiology U. Calif., San Francisco, 1964-65, asst. prof., 1965-66; fellow M.D. Anderson/U. Tex. Med. Ctr., Houston, 1966-67; assoc. prof. radiology Va. Commonwealth U., Richmond, 1967-68; head radiation oncologist Harbor Gen. Hosp./UCLA, 1969-71; pvt. practice specializing in radiation oncology Fresno, Calif., 1971—; head radiation oncologist Valley Med. Ctr., Fresno, 1971—. Contbr. articles to profl. jours. Mem. Am. Soc. of Therapeutic Radiologists, Radiol. Soc. N.Am., Calif. Radiol. Soc., Calif. Med. Assn., Fresno Madera Med. Soc., Phi Beta Kappa. Home: 5331 N Sequoia Dr Fresno CA 93711-2847 Office: Radiation Groups of Cen Cal 1201 E Herndon Ave Ste 101 Fresno CA 93720-3299

LAU, BOBBY WAI-MAN, investment and financial planner; b. Hong Kong, Dec. 24, 1944; s. Nelson and Ruby (Choy) L.; m. Sharon Tsai. BS in Math., U. Calif., Davis, 1969, MA in Math., 1971; postgrad. in math. Calif. Inst. Tech., in math. and computers UCLA, 1972-75. Ins. agt. Equitable Life Assurance Soc. of U.S., Los Angeles, 1975-80, dist. mgr., 1980-90; pres. Bobby Lau & Assocs., Los Angeles, 1976—, Bobby Lau Seminars for Profls., 1979—; chmn. bd. dirs. Success Pension & Ins. Svcs. Corp., USA Loan Corp. Articles to mags. and newspapers. Mem. Nat. Assn. Life Underwriters, Nat. Assn. Fin. Planners, Nat. Assn. Tax Consultors. Office: 2920 Huntington Dr. #220 San Marino CA 91108

LAU, CHERYL, state official. BM, Ind. U.; JD, U. San Francisco. Bar: 1986. Formerly dep. atty. gen. Nev. Motor Vehicles and Pub. Safety Dept., Carson City, Nev.; sec. of state, State of Nev. Carson City, Nev., 1991—. Address: Office of Sec of State Capitol Complex Carson City NV 89710

LAU, EUGENE WING IU, lawyer; b. Canton, China, Sept. 23, 1931; came to U.S., 1939; s. Eugene K. F. and Ann (Leung) L.; m. Dierdre Florence, July 20, 1962; children: Elyse M., Jennifer M. AB, U. Mich., 1953; LLB, Yale U., 1960. Bar: Hawaii 1960, U.S. Supreme Ct. 1965. Dep. Pros. Attys. Office, Honolulu, 1960-63; pvt. practice Honolulu, 1963-67, 73—; v.p. Hawaii Corp., Honolulu, 1967-73; del. People to People Legal Del. to China, 1987; mem. Commn. on Manpower and Full Employment, Honolulu, 1965-67. With U.S. Army, 1954-55. Mem. ABA, Hawaii Bar Assn., Punahou Tennis Club (Honolulu). Home: 3079 La Pietra Cir Honolulu HI 96815-4736 Office: 1188 Bishop St Ste 1912 Honolulu HI 96813-3308

LAUBE, ROGER GUSTAV, retired trust officer, financial consultant; b. Chgo., Aug. 11, 1921; s. William C. and Elsie (Drews) L.; m. Irene Mary Chadbourne, Mar. 30, 1946; children: David Roger, Philip Russell, Steven Richard. BA, Roosevelt U., 1942; postgrad., John Marshall Law Sch., 1942, 48-50; LLB, Northwestern U., 1960; postgrad., U. Wash., 1962-64. Cert. fin. cons. With Chgo. Title & Trust Co., Chgo., 1938-42, 48-50, Nat. Bank Alaska, Anchorage, 1950-72; mgr. mortgage dept. Nat. Bank Alaska, 1950-56, v.p., trust officer, mgr. trust dept., 1956-72; v.p., trust officer, mktg. dir., mgr. estate and fin. planning div. Bishop Trust Co., Ltd., Honolulu, 1972-82; instr. estate planning U. Hawaii, Honolulu, 1978-82; exec. v.p. Design Capital Planning Group, Inc., Tucson, 1982-83; pres., sr. trust officer, registered investment adviser Advanced Capital Advisory, Inc. of Ariz., Tucson, 1983-89; registered rep., pres. Advanced Capital Investments, Inc. of Ariz., Prescott, 1983-89; pres., chief exec. officer Advanced Capital Devel., Inc. of Ariz., Prescott, 1983-89; mng. exec. Integrated Resources Equity Corp., Prescott, 1983-89; pres. Anchorage Estate Planning Coun., 1960-62, Charter mem., 1960-72, Hawaii Estate Planning Coun., 1972-82, v.p., 1979, pres., 1980, bd. dirs., 1981-82; charter mem. Prescott Estate Planning Coun., 1986-90, pres. 1988. Charter mem. Anchorage Community Chorus, 1946, pres., 1950-53, bd. dirs., 1953-72, Alaska Festival of Music, 1960-72; mem. Anchorage camp Gideons Internat., 1946-72, Honolulu camp, 1972-82, mem. Cen. camp, Tucson, 1982-85, Prescott, 1985-90, Port Angeles-Sequim Camp, 1990—; mem. adv. bd. Faith Hosp., Glenallen, Alaska, 1960—, Cen. Alaska Mission of Far Ea. Gospel Crusade, 1960—; sec., treas. Alaska Bapt. Found., 1955-72; bd. dirs. Anchorage Symphony, 1965-72; bd. dirs. Bapt. Found. of Ariz., 1985-90, bd. dirs., mem. investment com. N.W. Bapt. Found., 1991—; mem. mainland adv. coun. Hawaii Bapt. Acad., Honolulu, 1982—; pres. Sabinovista Townhouse Assn., 1983-85; bd. advisers Salvation Army, Alaska , 1961-72, chmn., Anchorage, 1969-72, bd. advisers, Honolulu, 1972-82, chmn. bd. advisers, 1976-78; asst. staff judge adv. Alaskan Command, 1946-48; exec. com. Alaska Conv., 1959-61, dir. music Chgo., 1938-42, 48-50, Alaska, 1950-72, Hawaii, 1972-82, Tucson, 1982-85, 1st So. Bapt. Ch., Prescott Valley, Ariz., 1985-90; 1st Bapt. of Sequim, Wash., 1990—; chmn. bd. trustees Hawaii, 1972-81, Prescott Valley, 1986-89, Sequim, Wash., 1991—; worship leader Waikiki Ch., 1979-82. 1st lt., JAGD, U.S. Army, 1942-48. Recipient Others award Salvation Army, 1972. Mem. Am. Inst. Banking (instr. trust div. 1961-72), Am. Bankers Assn. (legis. com., trust div. 1960-72), Nat. Assn. Life Underwriters (nat. com. for Ariz.), Yavapai County-Prescott Life Underwriters Assn. (charter), Anchorage C. of C. (awards com. 1969-71), Internat. Assn. Fin. Planners (treas. Anchorage chpt. 1969-72, exec. com. Honolulu chpt. 1972-82, Ariz. chpt. 1982-90, del. to World Congress Australia and New Zealand 1987), Am. Assn. Handbell Ringers. Baptist. Home: Sunland Country Club 212 Sunset Pl Sequim WA 98382-8515

LAUBER, IRVING, human care services organization executive; b. Syracuse, N.Y., Nov. 3, 1941; s. Samuel and Eva (Balsam) L.; m. Helenann Stolusky, Aug. 30, 1964; children: David, Joshua. AB, Syracuse U., 1964, MSW, 1969. Planning assoc. Community Welfare Planning Assn. Greater Houston, 1969-71, dep. dir. planning, 1971-73, dir. planning, 1973-74, assoc. exec. dir., 1974-76; dir. planning and allocations United Way Allegheny County, Pitts., 1976-79; planning dir. United Way Svcs., Cleve., 1979-84, v.p. community svcs., 1984-88, v.p. community resources, chief info. officer, 1988-90; pres., chief profl. officer Aloha United Way, Honolulu, 1990—; cons., trainer United Way Am., Alexandria, Va., 1979—. Mem. Hawaii Gov.'s Coun. on Literacy, Honolulu, 1990—, Hawaii Gov.'s Family Policy Acad., 1991—; bd. dirs. Jewish Fedn. Hawaii. 1st lt. U.S. Army, 1964-66. Mem. Nat. Soc. Fund Raising Execs. (bd. dirs., chmn. ethics com. Aloha chpt. 1991—), Rotary. Jewish. Home: 350-A Kaelepulu Dr Kailua HI 96734 Office: Aloha United Way 200 N Vineyard Blvd Honolulu HI 96817

LAUBER, MIGNON DIANE, food processing company executive; b. Detroit, Dec. 21; d. Charles Edmond and Maud Lillian (Foster) Donaker. Student Kelsey Jenny U., 1958, Brigham Young U., 1959; m. Richard Brian Lauber, Sept. 13, 1963; 1 child, Leslie Viane (dec.). Owner, operator Alaska World Travel, Ketchikan, 1964-67; founder, owner, pres. Oosick Soup Co., Juneau, Alaska, 1969—. Treas., Pioneer Alaska Lobbyists Soc., Juneau, 1977—. Mem. Bus. and Profl. Women, Alaska C. of C. Libertarian, Washington Athletic Club. Author: Down at the Water Works with Jesus, 1982; Failure Through Prayer, 1983, We All Want to Go to Heaven But Nobody Wants to Die, 1988. Home: 321 Highland Dr Juneau AK 99801-1442 Office: PO Box 1625 Juneau AK 99802-0078

LAUCHENGCO, JOSE YUJUICO, JR., lawyer; b. Manila, Philippines, Dec. 6, 1936; came to U.S., 1962; s. José Celis Sr. Lauchengco and Angeles (Yujuico) Sapota; m. Elisabeth Schindler, Feb. 22, 1968; children: Birthe, Martina, Duane, Lance. AB, U. Philippines, Quezon City, 1959; MBA, U. So. Calif., 1964; JD, Loyola U., L.A., 1971. Bar: Calif. 1972, U.S. Dist. Ct. (cen. dist.) Calif. 1972, U.S. Ct. Appeals (9th cir.) 1972, U.S. Supreme Ct. 1975. Banker First Western Bank/United Calif. Bank, L.A., 1964-71; assoc. Demler, Perona, Langer & Bergkvist, Long Beach, Calif., 1972-73; ptnr. Demler, Perona, Langer, Bergkvist, Lauchengco & Manzella, Long Beach, 1973-77; sole practice Long Beach and L.A., 1977-83; ptnr. Lauchengco & Mendoza, L.A., 1983-92; pvt. practice L.A., 1993—; mem. commn. on jud. procedures County of L.A., 1979; tchr. Confraternity of Christian Doctrine, 1972-79; counsel Philippine Presdl. Commn. on Good Govt., L.A., 1986. Mem. So. Calif. Asian Dem. Caucus, L.A., 1977; chmn. Filipino-Am. Bi-Partisan Polit. Action Group, L.A., 1978. Recipient Degree of Distinction, Nat. Forensic League, 1955. Mem. Criminal Cts. Bar Assn., Calif. Attys. Criminal Justice, Calif. Pub. Defenders Assn., L.A. County Bar Assn., Assn. Trial Lawyers Am., Calif. Trial Lawyers Assn., L.A. Trial Lawyers Assn., Philippine-Am. Bar Assn. (bd. dirs.), U. Philippines Vanguard Assn. (life), Beta Sigma. Roman Catholic. Lodge: K.C. Office: Ste 1005 1605 W Olympic Blvd Los Angeles CA 90015-3808

LAUDEMAN, SCOTT KING, petroleum engineer; b. Whittier, Calif., Oct. 31, 1958; s. Edwin Dean Britt and Barbara Ann (King) L.; m. Lisa Ann Citron, July 11, 1981. BS in Petroleum Engring., U. So. Calif., 1981; MS in Petroleum Engring., Colo. Sch. Mines, 1989. Reservoir engr. Chevron U.S.A., Denver, 1981-87; rsch. engr. Chevron Oil Field Rsch. Co., La Habra, Calif., 1987-89; dir. applications devel. SoftSearch, Houston, 1989-90; pres. ApTech Assocs., Pasadena, Calif., 1990—. Mem. Soc. Petroleum Engrs. (editor jour. 1989—, mem. prodns. ops. tech. com. 1986-90, computer applications com., 1987-90), U. So. Calif. Alumni Assn. (Rocky Mountain chpt., chmn. alumni interview scholarship program 1985-87). Republican. Roman Catholic. Office: ApTech Assocs 30 N Raymond Ave Ste 806 Pasadena CA 91103-3930

LAUDERDALE, THOMAS CHARLES, paper mill executive; b. Oregon City, Oreg., Dec. 20, 1946; s. Lawrence Allen and Elizabeth Ann (Williams) L.; m. Gloria F. Tabilog, Nov. 28, 1974; children: Robert S., Joseph T. BS in Aerospace Engring., Oreg. State U., 1969. Assoc. engr., scientist McDonnell Douglas Aircraft, Long Beach, Calif., 1969-70; prodn. engr. Crown Zellerbach Corp., Antioch, Calif., 1977-80; converting supt. Crown Zellerbach Corp., Glen Falls, N.Y., 1980-83; devel. engr. dir. Crown Zellerbach Corp., Antioch, 1983-84; plant mgr. Crown Zellerbach Corp., Bogalusa, La., 1984-86; ops. mgr. James River Corp., Old Town, Maine, 1986-88; maintenance and engring. mgr. Boise Cascade Corp., Vancouver, Wash., 1988-90, paper mill mgr., 1990—. Bd. dirs. Clark County Leadership Coun., Vancouver, 1992—, Columbia River Econ. Devel. Coun., 1990—; umpire-in-chief Ridgefield Little League Baseball, 1989-91. Lt. USN, 1970-77. Mem. Greater Vancouver C. of C. (bd. dirs. 1992—). Republican. Home: 619 NE 246th Cir Ridgefield WA 98642 Office: Boise Cascade 907 W 7th St Vancouver WA 98666

LAUER, GEORGE, environmental consultant; b. Vienna, Austria, Feb. 18, 1936; came to U.S., 1943; s. Otto and Alice (Denton) L.; m. Sandra Joy Comp, Oct. 1, 1983; children by previous marriage: Julie Anne, Robert L. BS, UCLA, 1961; PhD, Calif. Inst. Tech., 1967. Mem. tech. staff N.Am. Aviation, Canoga Park, Calif., 1966-69; mgr. Rockwell Internat., Thousand Oaks, Calif., 1969-75; div. mgr. ERT, Inc., Westlake Village, Calif., 1975-78; dir. Rockwell Internat., Newbury Park, Calif., 1978-85; dir. Tetra-Tech Inc., Pasadena, Calif., 1985-86; pres. Environ. Monitoring and Services, Inc., 1986-88; sr. cons. Atlantic Richfield, Inc., Los Angeles, 1988—. Contbr. articles to profl. jours.; patentee in field. Mem. adv. bd. Environment Rsch. and Tech. Served with U.S. Army, 1957-59. Fellow Assn. for Computing Machinery; mem. Am. Chem. Soc., Am. Statistical Soc., Air Pollution Control Assn. Republican. Jewish. Home: 6009 Maury Ave Woodland Hills CA 91367-1052 Office: Atlantic Richfield Inc 515 S Flower St Los Angeles CA 90071-2200

LAUER, ROBERT HAROLD, human behavior educator, minister; b. St. Louis, June 28, 1933; s. Earl Ervin and Frances Pauline (Bushen) L.; m. Jeanette Carol Pentecost, July 2, 1954; children: Jon Robert, Julie Anne, Jeffrey David. BS, Washington U., St. Louis, 1954; BD, So. Sem., Louisville, 1958; MA, So. Ill. U., Edwardsville, 1969; PhD, Washington U., St. Louis, 1970. Ordained to ministry Bapt. Ch., 1956. Min. Salem Bapt. Ch., Florissant, Mo., 1958-68; prof. So. Ill. U., 1968-82; prof. dept. human behavior U.S. Internat. U., San Diego, 1983—, dean, 1983-90; min. Christian edn. La Jolla (Calif.) Presbyn. Ch., 1991—. Author: Temporal Man, 1983, Spirit & The Flesh, 1983, 'Til Death Do Us Part, 1986, Watersheds, 1988, The Quest for Intimacy, 1991. Mem. Am. Sociol. Assn., Nat. Coun. on Family Rels., Nat. Communal Socs. Assn., Pacific Sociol. Assn. Democrat. Presbyterian. Office: La Jolla Presbyn Ch 7715 Draper Ave La Jolla CA 92037

LAUGHLIN, KEVIN MICHAEL, agriculture educator; b. Tacoma, Apr. 14, 1956; s. Robert Emmet and Marvel Joelene (Whipple) L. BS in Agrl. Edn., Wash. State U., 1979; MS in Horticulture, N.D. State U., 1989. Peace Corps vol. Action/Peace Corps, Belize, 1979-81; agt. Toole County Mont. State U. Extension Svc., Bozeman, 1981-90; agt. Bonner County U. Idaho Extension Svc., Moscow, 1990—. Contbr. articles to profl. jours. Mem. Idaho and Nat. Assn. County Agrl. Agts., Idaho Assn. (Achievement in Svc. award 1990), Idaho and Nat. Assn. Extension 4-H Agts. (sec. 1985-90, Achievement in Svc. award 1989), Alpha Tau Alpha, Alpha Zeta, Epsilon Sigma Phi. Office: Bonner County Extension Svc PO Box 1526 Sandpoint ID 83864-0867

LAUMANN, CURT WILLIAM, physicist; b. San Jose, June 13, 1963; s. Carl William and Judy Lee (Klingbiel) L. BA in Physics, Lawrence U., Appleton, Wis., 1985. Supplemental engr. IBM, Rochester, Minn., 1984-85; physicist Lawrence Livermore (Calif.) Nat. Lab., 1986—. Patentee in field; contbr. articles to profl. jours. Office: Lawrence Livermore Lab M/S L-493 Livermore CA 94550

LAURANCE, LEONARD CLARK, tour company executive; b. Perth, Australia, Aug. 20, 1932; came to U.S., 1963; s. Thomas Clark and Lorna Ruby (Spencer) L.; m. Lorraine Joan Harwood, June 10, 1954 (div. 1960); 1 child, Beverley Lorraine; m. Judith Ellen Krickan, Sept. 8, 1962; children: Cynthia Ellen, Amanda Lee. Gen. mgr. Ketchikan & No. Terminal Co. Inc., Ketchikan, Alaska, 1963-65; regional mgr. Alaska Steamship Co., Ketchikan, 1965-68; pres. Alaska World Travel Inc., Ketchikan, 1968-72, Leisure Corp., Ketchikan, 1972-85, AlaskaBound, Inc., Ketchikan, 1985-88, Mariner Inc., Ketchikan, 1988—; faculty mem. U. Alaska SE, Ketchikan, 1987-93; dir. mktg. Taquan Air, Ketchikan, 1991—; bd. dirs. Hist. Ketchikan, Inc. Mem. Alaska Mktg. Coun., Juneau, 1979-84, chair, 1982-84; mem. SE Alaska Tourism Coun., Juneau, 1982-86, chair, 1982-83; mem. mgmt. com. Sheffield Hotels, Anchorage, 1980-85; chair Alaska Marine Hwy. Task Force, Juneau, 1983-84, UAS Coll. Coun., 1982-83; mem. Ketchikan Gen. Hosp. Adv. Bd., 1973-84, chair, 1979; assemblyperson Ketchikan Gateway Borough, 1976-82. Recipient North Star Alaska Visitors Assn., 1977, Gov.'s award State of Alaska, 1984, Presdl. award Ketchikan C. of C., 1970. Mem. Alaska Visitors Assn. (bd. dirs. 1969—, pres. 1972-73), Ketchikan Visitors Bur. (bd. dirs. 1980—, chair 1983-84), UAS Visitor Ind. Program (adv. bd. 1986—). Republican. Episcopalian. Office: Mariner Inc 5716 S Tongass PO Box 8800 Ketchikan AK 99901-3800

LAURANCE, MARK RODNEY, optics instrumentationist; b. Seattle, Nov. 27, 1959; s. Sidney Laurance and Patricia Louise Sadlier. BS in Astronomy, U. Wash., 1984, BS in Physics, 1984, MS in Astronomy, 1992. Computer ops. programmer Seattle Police Dept., Seattle, 1980-85; researcher U. Wash., Seattle, 1984-90; lighting engr. Korry Electronics Co., Seattle, 1990-92; optics instrumentationist Can.-France-Hawaii Telescope Corp., Kamuela, Hawaii, 1992—. Contbr. articles to profl. jours.

LAURE, PHILLIP JOHN, industrial engineer; b. Ann Arbor, Mich., May 9, 1949; s. Daniel Pierre and Elizabeth Ann (Arigan) L.; m. Nelda Jane Griffing, June 8, 1973; children: Michael James Whitham, Steven Duane Whitham, Charles Allen Whitham, Deanna Jane Hainey. BA, Calif. State

U., San Bernardino, 1978. Sr. engring. technician County of San Bernardino, San Bernardino, 1974-80; prodn. planning supr. Lily-Tulip, Inc., Riverside, Calif., 1980-85; mfg. cons. Laure & Assocs., Riverside, 1985-86; indsl. engr. Northrop Corp., Hawthorne, Calif., 1986-88; sr. indsl. engr. Rohr Industries, Riverside, 1988-92; owner Profit Technologies, 1993—. Sponsor Kids Against Drugs, Moreno Valley, Calif., 1988, '89, '90. Mem. Inst. Indsl. Engrs. (bull. editor 1988, '90, chpt. pres. 1991, 92, 93). Riverside C. of C., Elks. Democrat. Roman Catholic.

LAURENSON, CHARLES RAYMOND, quality manager; b. Canton, Ohio, Aug. 19, 1956; s. Charles Philip and Pauline Grace (Beaudry) L. BA in Applied Math. magna cum laude, Claremont McKenna Coll., 1978; MS in Applied Statistics, U. Wis., Madison, 1981. Engr. Martin Marietta Corp., Denver, 1978-79; sr. statistician Hewlett-Packard Co., Santa Rosa, Calif., 1981-89; quality and statis. resources mgr. Komag Material Tech., Santa Rosa, 1989-92; quality mgr. Parker-Compumotor, Rohnert Park, Calif., 1992—; cons. and speaker in field. Author: An Introduction to the Understanding...Control Charts, 1982. Sec. bd. dirs. Vista Del Lago, Santa Rosa, 1982-85; capt. Team Solon bicycling team, 1989-92. Winner 1989 Race Across Am.; transcontinental world record holder, 1989-90. Mem. Am. Soc. Quality Control (chair Redwood Empire sect. 1990-91, Award of Recognition 1985), Am. Statis. Assn., Nat. Soc. Performance and Instruction, Sonoma County Woodworkers Assn. Home: 3005 Lago Vista Way Santa Rosa CA 95405-8605

LAURETA, ALFRED, federal judge; b. Ewa, Oahu, Hawaii, May 21, 1924; s. Laureano and Victoriana (Pascua) L.; m. E. Evelyn Reantillo, Feb. 21, 1953; children: Michael, Gregory, Pamela Ann, Lisa Lani. B.Ed., U. Hawaii, 1947, teaching cert., 1948; LL.B., Fordham U., 1953. Bar: Hawaii. Partner firm Kobayashi, Kono, Laureta & Ariyoshi, Honolulu, 1954-59; adminstr. to U.S. Congressman Inouye, 1959-63; dir. Hawaii Dept. Labor and Indsl. Relations, 1963-67; judge 1st Circuit Ct., Honolulu, 1967-69, 5th Circuit Ct., Kauai, 1969-78, U.S. Dist. Ct. No. Mariana Islands, Saipan, 1978—. Mem. Nat. Council Juvenile Ct. Judges, Am. Judicature Soc., Hawaii Bar Assn., Kauai Bar Assn. Democrat. Office: US Dist Ct PO Box 687 Saipan MP 96950-0687

LAURIDSEN, KAREN, systems analyst; b. Montpelier, Idaho, Apr. 14, 1959; d. Max D. and Ann (Reeves) L. A in Bus., Ricks Coll., Rexburg, Idaho, 1977-79; student, Univ. Utah, 1980-81. Scheduler Skaggs Telecom. Svc., Salt Lake City, 1981-84; adminstrv. sec. history dept. U. Utah, Salt Lake City, 1984; legal sec. Strong & Hanni, Salt Lake City, 1985; adminstrv. asst. U. Utah Med. Ctr., Salt Lake City, 1985-88; sr. implementation analyst GTE Health Systems Inc., Salt Lake City, 1988—. Camp dir. LDS Ch., Bear Lake, Idaho, 1989; mem. women's youth LDS Ch., Idaho and Utah, 1960—. Home: 619 S Harmony Ct Salt Lake City UT 84102 Office: 175 S West Temple Salt Lake City UT 84101

LAUTH, HAROLD VINCENT, corporate affairs executive; b. St. Paul, Jan. 10, 1933; s. Harold Vincent and Kerrie M. (Denevan) L.; m. Mildred Ann Hellmann, Aug. 6, 1955; children: Susan M. Foster, Michael L., Karen P., Stephen C., Jennifer A., Nancy L. BS in Bus., U. Md., 1957. Press rep. Milk Industry Found., Washington, 1957-59; pub. rels. and advt. mgr. Volkswagen Am., Washington, 1959-60; dir. corp. affairs Kaiser Industries Corp., Oakland, Calif. and Washington, 1960-76, instr. pub. affairs George Washington U., 1967-68; dir. corp. affairs Kaiser Resources Ltd., Vancouver, B.C., Can., 1976-78; dir. corp. affairs Kaiser Engrs. Inc., Oakland, 1978-88; pres. Lauth Pacific, Oakland, 1988—. Pres., Oakland-Dalian Friendship City Soc., 1986-90; chmn. mayor's smoking ordinance com., Oakland, 1987-88, mem. mayor's com. on internat. trade & fgn. investment; mem. steering com. U. Calif./Oakland Metro Forum; mem. adv. bd. United Way Alameda County, 1974-76; chmn. pub. rels. com. Mercy Retirement and Care Ctr.; bd. dirs. New Oakland Com.; mem. bus. symposia Holy Names Coll., Oakland, St. Mary's Coll., Moraga, Calif., chmn. 1991—. Mem. Pub. Relations Soc. Am. (pres. Washington chpt. 1968), Nat. Press Club, Soc. Profl. Journalists, Commonwealth Club, Claremont Country Club, Lakeview Club. Home: 5466 Hilltop Cres Oakland CA 94618-2604

LAUTH, ROBERT EDWARD, geologist; b. St. Paul, Feb. 6, 1927; s. Joseph Louis and Gertrude (Stapleton) L.; student St. Thomas Coll., 1944; BA in Geology, U. Minn., 1952; m. Suzanne Janice Holmes, Apr. 21, 1947; children—Barbara Jo, Robert Edward II, Elizabeth Suzanne, Leslie Marie. Wellsite geologist Columbia Carbon Co., Houston, 1951-52; dist. geologist Witco Oil & Gas Corp., Amarillo, Tex., 1952-55; field geologist Reynolds Mining Co., Houston, 1955; cons. geologist, Durango, Colo., 1955—. Appraiser helium res. Lindley area Orange Free State, Republic of South Africa, 1988, remaining helium res. Odolanow Plant area Polish Lowlands, Poland, 1988. With USNR, 1944-45. Mem. N.Mex., Four Corners (treas., v.p., pres., symposium com.) geol. socs., Rocky Mountain Assn. Geologists, Am. Inst. Profl. Geologists, Am. Inst. Mining, Metall. and Petroleum Engrs., Am. Assn. Petroleum Geologists, Helium Soc., N.Y. Acad. Sci. Am. Assn. Petroleum Landman, Soc. Econ. Paleontologists and Mineralogists, The Explorers Club. Republican. Roman Catholic. K.C. Clubs: Durango Petroleum (dir.), Denver Petroleum, Elks. Author: Desert Creek Field, 1958; (with Silas C. Brown) Oil and Gas Potentialities of Northern Arizona, 1958, Northern Arizona Has Good Oil, Gas Prospects, 1960, Northeastern Arizona; Its Oil, Gas and Helium Prospects, 1961; contbr. papers on oil and gas fields to profl. symposia. Home: 2020 Crestview Dr PO Box 776 Durango CO 81302 Office: 555 S Camino Del Rio Durango CO 81301-6826

LAUTZENHEISER, MARVIN WENDELL, computer software engineer; b. Maximo, Ohio, Feb. 19, 1929; s. Milton Leander and Mary Lucetta (Keim) L.; m. Jean Bethene Baker, Oct. 26, 1946 (div. Nov. 1986); children: Constance Kay, Thomas Edward, Jan Stephen; m. Paula Ann Keane, Mar. 10, 1990. BS in Math., Mt. Union Coll., 1953. Spl. agt. FBI, Washington, 1953-59; computer analyst Tech. Ops., Washington, 1959-64; pres. Anagram Corp., Springfield, Va., 1964-83; computer analyst Onyx Corp., McLean, Va., 1983, Inmark, Springfield, 1983-84, Memory Scis., McLean, 1984-85; software scientist Zitel Corp., San Jose, Calif., 1985—. Inventor, designer in field. Mem. Mensa, Am. Iris Soc. Home: 2035 Lockwood Dr San Jose CA 95132 Office: Zitel Corp 47211 Bayside Pkwy Fremont CA 94538

LAVE, ROY ELLIS, transportation executive; b. Homewood, Ill., Sept. 23, 1935; s. Roy Ellis and Marjorie (Kantzler) L.; m. Penelope Ann Reynolds, June 11, 1960; children: Julia, Reynolds. BS, U. Mich., 1958, MBA, 1958, MS, 1960; PhD, Stanford U., 1965. Registered profl. engr., Calif. Asst. to assoc. prof. Stanford U., Stanford, Calif., 1962-72; CEO Systan, Inc., Los Altos, Calif., 1966—; chmn. Paratransit Com. Trans. Rsch. Bd., 1993—. Editor: TECHNOS, Stanford, Calif.; contbr. articles to profl. jours. Councilman, City of Los Altos (Calif.), 1974-82, Mayor, City of Los Altos, 1976-78; commr. Santa Clara County Transp. Commn., 1974-86 (chmn. Fin. Com. 1978-80, Planning Com. 1980), Met. Trans. Commn. (San Francisco Bay Area), 1980-86; founding pres. Los Altos Tomorrow, 1990—; pres. North County Libr. Authority, 1985—; mem. Exec. Com. Paratransit Coordination Coun., Santa Clara County, 1979-85 (chmn. 1980-82); bd. dirs. Outreach & Escort, Inc., San Jose, 1979-83, Palo Alto Area YMCA, 1984-90. Mem. Inst. Indsl. Engrs. (pres. Peninsula chpt. 1966-67, bd. dirs. 1964-68), Am. Soc. for Engring. Edn. (internat. com., Dow Chem. award for outstanding young faculty 1971), Transp. Rsch. Forum, Ops. Rsch. Soc. Am., Inst. Mgmt. Sci., Am. Pub. Transit Assn. (futures symposium planning com.), Assn. for Commuter Transp. (chmn. tech. coun.), Gold Bend Condominium Assn. (bd. dirs. 1988—), Rotary (Los Altos chpt. 1991-92). Home: 690 University Ave Los Altos CA 94022 Office: Systan Inc 343 Second St Los Altos CA 94022

LAVENTHOL, DAVID ABRAM, newspaper editor; b. Phila., July 15, 1933; s. Jesse and Clare (Horwald) L.; m. Esther Coons, Mar. 8, 1958; children: Peter, Sarah. BA, Yale U., 1957; MA, U. Minn., 1960; LittD (hon.), Dowling Coll., 1979; LLD (hon.), Hofstra U., 1986. Reporter, news editor St. Petersburg (Fla.) Times, 1957-62; asst. editor, city editor N.Y. Herald-Tribune, 1963-66; asst. mng. editor Washington Post, 1966-69; assoc. editor Newsday, L.I., N.Y., 1969, exec. editor, 1969, editor, 1970-78, pub., chief exec. officer, 1978-86, chmn., 1986-87; group v.p. newspapers Times Mirror Co., L.A., 1981-86, sr. v.p., 1986-87, pres., 1987—; pub., chief exec. officer L.A. Times, 1989—, pres.; mem. Pulitzer Prize Bd., 1982—, chmn., 1988—; bd. dirs. L.A. Times Post News Svc., Washington, 1988—, Newspaper Advt. Bur., 1989—, Balt. Sun Co., Inc.; vice chmn. Internat. Press Inst., 1985—; mem. Am. Press Inst., 1988—. Bd. dirs. N.Y. Partnership, 1985-87, United Negro Coll. Fund, 1988, Times Mirror Found., 1987, Mus. Contemporary Art, L.A., 1989—; mem. Calif. Mus. Found., 1989—. With Signal Corps AUS, 1953-55. Mem. Am. Soc. Newspaper Editors (chmn. writing awards bd. 1980-83), Council Fgn. Relations. Club: Century. Home: 800 W 1st St Apt 3202 Los Angeles CA 90012-2440 Office: Los Angeles Times Times Mirror Sq Los Angeles CA 90053-3816*

LAVER, MURRAY LANE, chemist, educator; b. Warkworth, Ont., Can., Mar. 7, 1932; s. Oscar Frederick and Clara Gertrude (Lane) L.; m. Mary Margaret Smolska, Feb. 9, 1963; children: Ann Margaret, Elizabeth Clara. BSA, Ont. Agrl. Coll., Guelph, Ont., Can., 1955; PhD, Ohio State U., 1959. Rsch. chemist Westreco Inc. (Nestlé Co.), Marysville, Ohio, 1959-63; rsch. scientist Rayonier Can., Vancouver, B.C., 1963; profl. specialist Weyerhaeuser Co., Seattle, 1964-67; rsch. fellow U. Wash., Seattle, 1968-69; assoc. prof. forest products dept. Oreg. State U., Corvallis, 1969—; rsch. fellow Harvard U., Cambridge, Mass., 1977-78; cons. Tooze Marshall Holloway & Duden, Portland, Oreg., 1988-90, Am. Cemwood, Albany, Oreg., 1991—, Black-Helterline, Portland, Oreg., 1992-93. Contbr. chpt. to Wood Structure and Composition, 1991; contbr. articles to profl. jours. Speaker local high schs., Alsea and Philomath, Oreg., 1988, 90. Grantee USDA, 1985—, 86-88, 92-93, Hill Family Found., 1990. Mem. AAAS, Am. Chem. Soc. (chair Oreg. sect. 1985), N.Y. Acad. Sci., Oreg. Acad. Sci. Home: 1950 SW Whiteside Dr Corvallis OR 97333-1409 Office: Dept Forest Products Oreg State Univ Corvallis OR 97331-5703

LAVERY, VINCENT JOSEPH, educator; b. Dublin, Ireland, Jan. 21, 1936; came to U.S., 1956; s. Philip and Carmel (O'Connor) L. AA, Merced Jr. Coll., 1968; BA, Fresno State U., 1971, teaching credential, 1974. Asst. mgr. Greyhound Bus Co., N.Y.C., 1959-61; substitute tchr. Fresno (Calif.) Unified Sch. Dist., 1973-88, tchr. high sch., 1988—; tech. adviser NBC movie-of-week Children in the Crossfire, Burbank, Calif., 1982-84. Editor: Fundamental Soccer, 1985, Fundamental Goalkeeping, 1986, Fundamental Tactics, 1987; author numerous articles on No. Ireland conflict, 1981—. Dem. candidate for Calif. Congress, 1972, 74, 78, 88; chmn. Children's Com. 10, 1981—. With U.S. Army, 1956-59, USAF, 1961-65. Recipient Friend of Youth award Boys and Girls Club, Fresno, 1985, Samantha Smith Peace award Educators for Social Responsibility, Fresno, 1987. Roman Catholic. Office: Childrens Com 20 PO Box 16133 Fresno CA 93755-6133

LAVIN, LAURENCE MICHAEL, lawyer; b. Upper Darby, Pa., Apr. 27, 1940; s. Michael Joseph and Helen Clair (McGonigle) L. BS, St. Joseph's U., Phila., 1962; JD, Villanova (Pa.) U., 1965. Bar: Pa., S.C. Vol. U.S. Peace Corps, Thika, Kenya, 1966-67; atty. Community Legal Svcs., Phila., 1968-70, exec. dir., 1971-79; exec. dir. Palmetto Legal Svcs., Columbia, S.C., 1981-85; dir. Law Coordination Ctr., Harrisburg, Pa., 1985-88, Nat. Health Law Program, L.A., 1988—; chmn. Orgn. Legal Svc. Backup Ctrs., 1991—; bd. dirs., chmn. civil com. Nat. Legal Aid and Defender, Washington, 1976-78; chmn. bd. dirs. Medicare Advocacy Project of L.A., 1990—. Editor Health Advocate, 1988—. Founding mem. Pa. Coun. to Abolish Death Penalty, Harrisburg, 1986. Mem. ABA, Pa. Bar Assn. (chmn. legal svcs. to pub. com. 1985-88), Legal Assistance Assn. Calif. (bd. dirs.). Democrat. Home: 952 18th St Santa Monica CA 90403-3210 Office: Nat Health Law Program 2639 S La Cienega Blvd Los Angeles CA 90034-2675

LA VINE, RONALD SCOTT, sales executive; b. Encino, Calif., Apr. 12, 1957; s. Mark Leslie and Mona Joan (Moster) La V. BS in Mgmt. Theory & Practice, Calif. State U., Northridge, 1980; Northridge. Life and disablitity lic.; registered rep. gen. securities (series 7 lic.). Pres. La Vine & Jansen Inc. (Frames Co.), Canoga Park, Calif., 1981-87, Ronald S. La Vine & Assocs., Woodland Hills, Calif., 1987-89; sales rsch. dir. Sterling Software Dylakor Div., Chatsworth, Calif., 1989-91, Sterling Software, Chatsworth, Calif., 1991—. Inventor EZ 2 Recycle Cart. Pres. L.A. Community Action Network, 1988; v.p. Inventors Workshop Internat. Edn. Found., San Fernando Valley, 1990, v.p., bd. dirs. Warner Woodlands II Homeowners Assn., 1990; procurement mgr. Internat. Community Svc. Day, 1992. Named one of Outstanding Young Men of Am., U.S. Jaycees, 1977. Mem. Blue Key Nat. Honor Soc. (fund raising chair), Inter-Fraternity Coun. (pres., 2d v.p., rec. sec.), Phi Kappa Psi (Key Man award Northridge chpt. 1977). Office: Sterling Software 9340 Owensmouth Ave Chatsworth CA 91311-6915

LAVINE, STEVEN DAVID, college president; b. Sparta, Wis., June 7, 1947; s. Israel Harry and Harriet Hauda (Rosen) L.; m. Janet M. Sternburg, May 29, 1988. BA, Stanford U., 1969; MA, Harvard U., 1970, PhD, 1976. Asst. prof. U. Mich., Ann Arbor, 1974-81; asst. dir. arts and humanities Rockefeller Found., N.Y.C., 1983-86, assoc. dir. arts and humanities, 1986-88; pres. Calif. Inst. Arts, Valencia, 1988—; adj. assoc. prof. NYU Grad. Sch. Bus., 1984-85; cons. Wexner Found., Columbus, Ohio, 1986-87; selection panelist Input TV Screening Conf., Montreal, Can., and Granda, Spain, 1985-86; cons., panelist Nat. Endowment for Humanities, Washington, 1981-85; faculty chair Salzburg Seminar on Mus., 1989; co-dir. Arts and Govt. Program, The Am. Assembly, 1991. Editor: The Hopwood Anthology, 1981, Exhibiting Cultures, 1991, Museums and Communities, 1992; editor spl. issue Prooftexts jour., 1984. Bd. dirs. Sta. KCRW-FM (NPR), 1989—, J. Paul Getty Mus., 1990—, Inst. for African Humanities, Northwestern U., 1990—, Music Ctr. of L.A. Operating Co., 1991—, Am. Coun. on the Arts, 1991—. Recipient Class of 1923 award, 1979, Faculty Recognition award, 1980 U. Mich.; Charles Dexter traveling fellow Harvard U., 1972, Ford fellow, 1969-74, vis. rsch. fellow Rockefeller Found., N.Y.C., 1981-83. Jewish. Office: Calif Inst Arts Office Pres 24700 Mcbean Pky Santa Clarita CA 91355-2397

LA VOIE, ROGER MICHAEL, state government official; b. Spokane, Wash., May 13, 1947; s. Elmer Isaac and Dorothy Nadine (Hodgen) La V.; m. Susan Marie Voegel, Dec. 31, 1969; children: Joel Michael, Benjamin Peter. BA in Psychology, Gonzaga U., 1969; MSW, U. Denver, 1977. Social worker Mont. Dept. Social & Rehab. Svcs., Great Falls, Mont., 1973-75; protective svcs. supr. Mont. Dept. Social & Rehab. Svcs., Butte, 1977-80; dist. supr. Mont. Dept. Family Svcs., Great Falls, 1980-90; area supr. Mont. Dept. Social & Rehab. Svcs., Helena, 1990-92, admnstr., 1992—; commr. State Bd. Pub. Welfare, Helena, 1992—. Lobbyist Mont. State Legislature, Helena, 1992. Mem. Mont. Pub. Welfare Assn., Mont. Chess Club. Office: Mont Dept Social & Rehab Svcs PO Box 4210 Helena MT 59601

LAW, FLORA ELIZABETH, community health and pediatrics nurse; b. Biddeford, Maine, Sept. 11, 1935; d. Arthur Parker and Flora Alma (Knutti) Butt; m. Robert F. Law, 1961; children : Susan E., Sarah F., Christian A., Martha F.; m. John F. Brown, Jr., 1982. BA, Davis and Elkins (W.Va.) Coll., 1957; postgrad., Cornell U.-N.Y. Hosp., N.Y.C., 1960; BSN, U. Nev., Las Vegas, 1976, MS in Counseling Edn., 1981. RN, Nev.; cert. sch. nurse. Staff nurse So. Nev. Community Hosp. (now Univ. Med. Ctr.), Las Vegas; relief charge nurse Valley Psychiat. Inst., Las Vegas; pub. health nurse Clark County Dist. Health Dept., Las Vegas; sch. nurse Clark County Sch. Dist., Las Vegas. Chair task force on sch. nursing Nev.'s Commn. for Profl. Standards in Edn. Mem. ANA, Nev. Nursing Assn., Nat. Assn. Sch. Nurses (sch. nurse liaison Clark County Tchrs. Assn.-NEA), Clark County Assn. Sch. Nurses (past pres.), Sigma Theta Tau. Home: 3420 Clandara Ave Las Vegas NV 89121

LAW, JAMES GEORGE, corporate real estate executive; b. Tacoma, Apr. 28, 1944; s. James Cummings and Blanche Loraine (McKay) L.; divorced; 1 child, James Jeremy MacDonald. BS, U. Wash., 1966; MBA, Pacific Luth. U., 1969; MSCE, San Jose State U., 1976. Project engr. The Boeing Co., Seattle, 1966-69, Ampex Corp., Redwood City, Calif., 1969-72; mgr. land devel., planning Hewlett-Packard, Palo Alto, Calif., 1972-87; v.p. corp. real estate McKesson Corp., San Francisco, 1987—; mem. adv. com. Ferguson Ptnrs. Ltd.; advisor Bayside Land Investments, San Mateo, Calif., 1985—; guest lectr. Stanford U., U. Calif. at Berkeley, San Francisco State U. Cochmn. Golden Triangle Task Force, San Jose, Calif., 1986-87; mem. econ. devel. coun. Dept. Commerce State of Calif., Sacramento, 1986—; mem. housing and growth task force San Francisco Bay Area Coun., 1988-90. Mem. Nat. Real Estate Adv. Bd., Internat. Real Estate Inst., Indsl. Devel. Rsch. Coun. (cert. master profl., pres. 1988-89), Indsl. Devel. Rsch. Found. (chmn. 1989-90), Comml. Property World (mem. adv. bd. 1988—), Urban Land Inst., Corp. Real Estate Mgmt. Coun., Soc. Indsl. and Office Realtors. Republican. Presbyterian. Home: 9 Isabella Ave Atherton CA 94027 Office: McKesson Corp 1 Post St San Francisco CA 94104-5203

LAWLER, RICK M., publishing executive; b. Watsonville, Calif., June 13, 1949; s. Myrle W. and Mae A. (Summers) L.; m. Alice T. Tang, May 28, 1981; 1 child, Sara. Tech. instr., USAF Tech. Sch., Tex., 1970; career acctg., Heald Bus. Coll., Fresno, Calif., 1973; student, CSU, Fresno, 1974-76. News editor Shafter (Calif.) Press, 1977-82; editor Los Gatos (Calif.) Times-Observer, 1982-83; media rels. mgr. Systems Plus, Inc., Palo Alto, Calif., 1983-84; adminstrv. asst. U. Calif. Davis Dept. Internal Medicine, Sacramento, 1984-88; sr, word processing specialist U.Calif Davis Dept. Math., 1988-90; adminstrv. asst. U. Calif. Davis Office Continuing Med. Edn., Sacramento, 1990—; owner, pub. MinRef Press, Sacramento, 1989—; co-owner, pub. Lawriel-Gabler Publ., Inc., San Jose, 1982-84. Author: Valley Fire, 1991, How To Write to World Leaders, 1992; editor: Abortion Stories, 1992. Sgt. USAF, 1968-72. Mem. Authors Guild, Nat. Writers Club. Mem. Seventh-day Adventists. Home: 8379 Langtree Way Sacramento CA 95823 Office: Univ California Davis Office Continuing Med Edn 2701 Stockton Blvd Sacramento CA 95817

LAWLESS, MICHAEL WILLIAM, strategic management educator; b. N.Y.C., June 20, 1948; s. Harvey Edward and Anne Elizabeth (Hindenlang) L.; m. Margaret Elizabeth Minton, May 24, 1986; 1 child, Blake Minton. BS, St. John's U., 1970; MBA, UCLA, 1974, PhD, 1980. Asst. prof. U. Colo., Boulder, 1982-90, assoc. prof. strategic mgmt., 1990—; dir. High Tech. Mgmt. Rsch. Ctr. Tech. and Innovation Mgmt. Rsch. Ctr., Boulder, 1987—; vis. prof. UCLA, 1986, Dartmouth Coll., 1992; cons. IBM, Wickes, Phillips Petroleum Corp., US West Corp., U.S. Dept. Def., 1980—. Author: Technology and Strategy, 1990; editor, High Tech Mgmt. Rsch. Jour., 1990, Org. Sci. Jour., 1990; contbr. articles to profl. jours. Lt. comdr. USNR. Mem. Acad. Mgmt. (program chmn. 1990, consortium chmn. 1990, div. chmn. 1991, editor Jour. 1993), Ascendant scholar 1990), Am. Econ. Assn., Strategic Mgmt. Soc., Inst. Mgmt. Sci., USN Inst., USNR Assn., Beta Gamma Sigma. Office: U Colo Grad Sch Bus PO Box 419 Boulder CO 80309-0419

LAWRENCE, CHARLES STEPHEN, lawyer; b. Long Branch, N.J., Jan. 13, 1948; s. Paul Marshall and Mary Shepherd (Simpson) L.; m. Diane Beth Goldman, May 16, 1982. BA, U. Maine, Orono, 1972; JD, Catholic U., Washington, 1984. Bar: Va. 1984, D.C. 1985, Calif. 1993. Investigator U.S. FDA, Boston, 1972-76; compliance officer U.S. FDA, Rockville, Md., 1976-82; atty. Loomis, Owen, Fellman & Howe, Washington, 1984-86, Hogan & Hartson, Washington, 1986-90, Pfizer, Inc., Irvine, Calif., 1990—. Contbr. articles to profl. jours. Mem. ABA, Fed. Bar Assn. (co-chmn. food and drug com. 1985-89), D.C. Bar Assn., Va. Bar Assn., Regulatory Affairs Profl. Soc. Democrat. Office: Pfizer Inc 17672-B Cowan Ave Irvine CA 92714

LAWRENCE, DEAN GRAYSON, retired lawyer; b. Oakland, Calif.; d. Henry C. and Myrtle (Grayson) Schmidt; A.B., U. Calif.-Berkeley, 1934, J.D., 1939. Admitted to Calif. bar, 1943, U.S. Dist. Ct., 1944, U.S. Ct. Appeals, 1944, Tax Ct. U.S., 1945, U.S. Treasury Dept., 1945, U.S. Supreme Ct., 1967; asso. Pillsbury, Madison & Sutro, San Francisco, 1944, 45; gen. practice Oakland, 1946-50, San Jose, 1952-60, Grass Valley, 1960-63, 66—; county counsel Nevada County, 1964-65. Nevada County Bd. Suprs., 1969-73, chmn., 1971. Sec. Nev. County Humane Animal Shelter Bd., 1966-86; state humane officer, 1966-82; pres. Nev. County Humane Soc., 1974-86, mem. Humane Soc. U.S., Fund for Animals; pres. Humane Information Svc., 1992—; bd. dirs. Nevada County Health Planning Council, Golden Empire Areawide Health Planning Council, 1974, 75; trustee Grass Valley Pub. Libr., 1962-64. Mem. Bus. and Profl. Women's Club, AAUW, Animal Protection Inst. Am. (Humanitarian of Yr. 1986), Animal Legal Defense Fund, Golden Empire Human Soc. (Lifetime Achievement award 1990), League Unbiased Women, Phi Beta Kappa, Sigma Xi, Kappa Beta Pi, Pi Mu Epsilon, Pi Lambda Theta. Episcopalian. Office: PO Box 66 Grass Valley CA 95945-0066

LAWRENCE, FRANCES ELIZABETH, educator; b. Glendale, Calif., Feb. 26, 1925; d. Felix William and Bessie Marie Powers; m. Vester Blount Lawrence, Apr. 2, 1955 (div.); children: Elizabeth Gail, Mark William, Cynthia Sue Cherry. AA, Pasadena Jr. Coll., 1945; BA, Whittier Coll., 1949. Tchr. Victor Sch. Dist., Victorville, Calif., 1949-56, Adelanto (Calif.) Sch. Dist., 1965-93; mem. planning bd. San Bernardino County Spelling Connection Com., 1985, Adelanto Dist. Curriculum Com., 1985-86; spl. edn. tchr., 2 yrs. Served with USNR, 1945-49. Mem. Nat. Assn. for Edn. Young Children, Calif. Assn. for Edn. Young Children, Early Childhood Caucus Calif. Tchrs. Assn., Adelanto Dist. Tchrs. Assn. (rep.). Democrat. Lodges: Job's Daus. (majority mem.), Order Eastern Star. Home: 18258 Symeron Rd Apple Valley CA 92307-4538

LAWRENCE, HAPPY JAMES, writer, educator; b. Eau Gallie, Fla., Aug. 25, 1944; s. Happy Othel and Mildred (Hunter) L.; m. Eugenia Peacock, Aug. 31, 1968 (div. 1982). BA, Pfeiffer Coll., Misenheimer, N.C., 1966; MDiv, Duke U., 1970; MA, Calif. State U., Northridge, 1984; PhD, Fla. State U., 1988. Legis. aide U.S. Senate, Washington, 1968-69; youth min. 1st United Meth. Ch., Charlotte, N.C., 1969-70; instr. coll. communications U. Tenn., Knoxville, 1970-71; staff filmmaker Family Films, Panorama City, Calif., 1971-76; freelance writer, dir. L.A., 1976-82; instr. Calif. State U., Northridge, 1982-85, assoc. prof., 1990—; instr. Fla. State U., Tallahassee, 1985-88; asst. prof. Mercer U., Atlanta, 1988-90. Prin. works include (TV movies) Missing Children, 1982, The Sky Trap, 1978, Child of Glass, 1977, (film) Truce in the Forest, 1976, The Greater Glory. Active Moorpark (Calif.) Arts Com., 1990-91, various environ. groups. Stoody-West fellow in religious journalism United Meth. Ch., 1970-71; recipient Jack Oakie Meml. award Calif. State U., 1985; named winner drama category Fla. State Screenplay Competition, 1986. Mem. Dirs. Guild Am., Writers Guild Am., Calif. Faculty Assn., Internat. Radio-TV Soc., Broadcast Educators Assn., Dramatists Guild. Democrat. Home: 600 Spring Rd # 38G Moorpark CA 93021-1243 Office: Calif State U Northridge 18111 Nordhoff St Northridge CA 91330-0001

LAWRENCE, JACOB, painter, educator; b. Atlantic City, Sept. 7, 1917; s. Jacob and Rosealee (Armstead) L.; m. Gwendolyn Knight, July 24, 1941. Student, Harlem Art Workshop, N.Y.C., 1932-39; scholar, Am. Artists Sch., N.Y.C., 1938-39; AFD, Denison U., 1970; DFA (hon.), Pratt Inst., 1970, Colby Coll., 1976, Md. Inst. Coll. Art, 1979, Carnegie-Mellon U., 1981, Yale U., 1986, Spelman Coll., 1987, Rutgers U., 1988, Parsons Sch. Design, N.Y.C., 1988; LHD (hon.), Howard U., 1985, Tulane U., 1989. Artist Yaddo Found., Saratoga, 1954-55; instr. Pratt Inst. Art Sch., N.Y.C., 1958-65, Art Students League, N.Y.C., 1967-69, New Sch. Social Rsch., N.Y.C., 1966-71; artist in residence Brandeis U., 1965—; coord. of the arts Pratt Inst., 1970—, prof. art, 1970; prof. art U. Wash., Seattle, 1970-83, prof. emeritus, 1983—; Disting. Faculty lectr. U. Wash., 1978. Exhibits include John Brown Series, under auspices Am. Fedn. Art, 1947, 30 paintings on history U.S., Alan Gallery, 1957, mural GSA, Jamaica, N.Y.; one-man shows include Migration Series, Mus. Modern Art, 1944, Downtown Gallery, N.Y.C., 1941, 43, 45, 47, 50, 53, M'Bari Artists and Writers Club, Nigeria, 1962, Terry Dintenfass Gallery, N.Y.C., 1963, Francine Seders Gallery, Seattle, 1985; works included Johnson Wax Co. World tour group exhbn., 1963, U.S. State Dept. group exhbn. in, Pakistan, 1963, retrospective exhbn., Whitney Mus. Am. Art, 1974, traveling retrospective Exhbn., Seattle Art Mus., 1986-87; commd. for graphic impressions 1977 Inauguration, Washington, mural commd., Kingdome Stadium, Seattle, 1979, Mural Howard U., 1980, 85, U. Wash., 1985, others; represented in, Met. Mus. Art, Mus. Modern Art, Whitney Mus., Phillips Meml. Gallery, Wash., Portland (Oreg.) Mus., Worcester (Mass.) Mus., Balt. Mus. Art, Wichita Art Mus., Albright Art Gallery, Buffalo, AAAL, N.Y.C., Mus. Modern Art, Sao Paulo, Brazil, R.I. Sch. Design, Va. Mus. Fine Arts, Bklyn. Mus., IBM Corp., Container Corp. Am., various univs.; Author: Harriet and the Promised Land, 1968; illustrator: Aesop's Fables, 1970; (book catalogue for retrospective exhbn.: Jacob Lawrence-American Painter, 1986; executed mural Theatre, 1985; executed, installed mural Orlando Fla. Internat. Airport, 1988. Mem. bd. govs. Skowhegan Sch. Painting and Sculpture; mem. Fulbright Art Com., 1966-67, Wash. State Arts Commn., 1976—; elector Hall of Fame for Gt. Americans, 1976—. Rosenwald fellow, 1940, 41, 42, Guggenheim fellow, 1945; recipient purchase prize Artists for Victory, 1942, purchase prize Atlanta U., 1948, Opportunity mag. award, 1948; Norman Wait Harris medal Art Inst. Chgo., 1948; Acad. Arts and Letters grantee, 1953; Chapelbrook Found. grantee, 1955; recipient 1st prize in mural competition for UN Bldg. Nat. Council U.S. Art, Inc., 1955, Retrospective Exhbn. with Definitive Catalogue Ford Found., 1960, Retrospective Exhbn. with Definitive Catalogue Whitney Mus. Modern Art, 1974; works selected as part of exchange exhibit with Soviet Union, 1959; Spingarn medal NAACP, 1970; ann. citation Nat. Assn. Schs. Art, 1973; recipient U.S. Gen. Svcs. Adminstrn. Design award, 1990, Nat. Medal of Arts award Pres. of U.S., 1990, Gold medal Nat. Arts Club N.Y., 1993. Mem. Artist Equity Assn. (past. sec., pres. N.Y. chpt. 1957), Nat. Endowment for Arts, Nat. Inst. Arts and Letters, Nat. Coun. Arts. Address: 4316 37th Ave NE Seattle WA 98105

LAWRENCE, JAMES ALBERT, artist, photographer; b. Burlingame, Calif., May 23, 1910; s. James and Wilhelmina (Schroeder) L.; m. Geraldine Jackson, June 30, 1945; children: James S., Christopher B., Sarah W., Jeffrey C., Bruce F. Student, U.Calif.-Davis, 1933, Art Ctr. Sch. L.A., 1934-36, Choinard Art Sch., L.A., 1937, N.Y. Sch. Modern Photography, 1940. Owner Advt. & Comml. Photography, San Francisco, 1940-49, Art & Photography, Gardnerville, Nev., 1949—. Art and photography for nat. advt. agys. and pubs., 1939-49; exhibited at Riverside Mus., N.Y., Art Inst., Chgo., San Francisco Mus. Art, Seattle Art Mus., Portland Art Mus., others. Mem. Nat. Watercolor Soc., Photographic Soc. Am., Photographers Assn. Am., Nev. Coun. of the Arts, Masons, Rotary. Home and Office: Rock Creek Ranch 1198 Centerville Ln Gardnerville NV 89410-9702

LAWRENCE, JEROME, playwright, director, educator; b. Cleve., July 14, 1915; s. Samuel and Sarah (Rogen) L. BA, Ohio State U., 1937, LHD (hon.), 1963; DLitt, Fairleigh Dickinson U., 1968; DFA (hon.), Villanova U., 1969; LittD, Coll. Wooster, 1983. Dir. various summer theaters Pa. and Mass., 1934-37; reporter, telegraph editor Wilmington (Ohio) News Jour., 1937; editor Lexington Daily News, Ohio, 1937; continuity editor radio Sta. KMPC, Beverly Hills, Calif., 1937-39; sr. staff writer CBS, Hollywood, Calif. and N.Y.C., 1939-42; pres., writer, dir. Lawrence & Lee, Hollywood, N.Y.C. and London, 1945—; vis. prof. Ohio State Univ., 1969, Salzburg Seminar in Am. Studies, 1972, Baylor Univ., 1978; prof. playwriting Univ. So. Calif. Grad. Sch., 1984—; co-founder, judge Margo Jones award, N.Y.C., 1958—; co-founder, pres. Am. Playwrights Theatre, Columbus, Ohio, 1970-85; bd. dirs. Am. Conservatory Theatre, San Francisco, 1970-80, Stella Adler Theatre, L.A., 1987—, Plumstead Playhouse, 1986—; keynote speaker Bicentennial of Bill of Rights, Congress Hall, Phila., 1991. Scenario writer Paramount Studios, 1941; master playwright NYU Inst. Performing Arts, 1967-69; author-dir. for: radio and television UN Broadcasts; Army-Navy programs D-Day, VE-Day, VJ-Day; author: Railroad Hour, Hallmark Playhouse, Columbia Workshop; author: Off Mike, 1944, (biography, later made into PBS-TV spl.) Actor: Life and Times of Paul Muni, 1978 (libretto and lyrics by Lawrence and Lee, music by Billy Goldenberg); co-author, dir.: (album) One God; playwright: Live Spelled Backwards, 1969, Off Mike, (mus. with Robert E. Lee) Look, Ma, I'm Dancin', 1948 (music by Hugh Martin), Shangri-La, 1956 (music by Harry Warren, lyrics by James Hilton, Lawrence and Lee), Mame, 1966 (score by Jerry Herman), Dear World, 1969 (score by Jerry Herman), (non-mus.) Inherit the Wind (translated and performed in 34 langs., named best fgn. play of year London Critics Poll 1960), Auntie Mame, 1956, The Gang's All Here, 1959, Only in America, 1959, A Call on Kuprin (now called Checkmate), 1961, Diamond Orchid (revised as Sparks Fly Upward, 1966), 1965, The Incomparable Max, 1969, The Crocodile Smile, 1970, The Night Thoreau Spent in Jail, 1970, (play and screenplay) First Monday in October, 1978, (written for opening of Thurber Theatre, Columbus) Jabberwock: Improbablilities Lived and Imagined by James Thurber in the Fictional City of Columbus, Ohio, 1974, (with Norman Cousins and Robert E. Lee) Whisper in the Mind, 1990, The Angels Weep, 1992, (novel) A Golden Circle: A Tale of Stage and the Screen and Music of Yesterday and Now and Tomorrow and Maybe the Day After Tomorrow, 1993; Decca Dramatic Albums, Musi-Plays.; contbg. editor Dramatics mag., mem. adv. bd., contbr. Writer's Digest; Lawrence and Lee collections at Libr. and Mus. of the Performing Arts, Lincoln Ctr., N.Y., Harvard's Widener Libr., Cambridge, Mass., Jerome Lawrence & Robert E. Lee Theatre Rsch. Inst. at Ohio State U., Columbus, est. 1986. A founder, overseas corr. Armed Forces Radio Service; mem. Am. Theatre Planning Bd.; bd. dirs. Nat. Repertory Theatre, Plumstead Playhouse; mem. adv. bd. USDAN Center for Creative and Performing Arts, East-West Players, Performing Arts Theatre of Handicapped., Inst. Outdoor Drama; mem. State Dept. Cultural Exchange Drama Panel, 1961-69; del. Chinese-Am. Writers Conf., 1982, 86, Soviet-Am. Writers Conf., 1984, 85; Am. Writers rep. to Hiroshima 40th Anniversary Commemorative, Japan, 1985; mem. U.S. Cultural Exchange visit to theatre communities of Beijing and Shanghai, 1985; adv. coun. Calif. Ednl. Theatre Assn., Calif. State U., Calif. Repertory Co., Long Beach, 1984—. Recipient N.Y. Press Club award, 1942, CCNY award, 1948, Radio-TV Life award, 1948, Mirror awards, 1952, 53, Peabody award, 1949, 52, Variety Showmanship award 1954, Variety Critics poll 1955, Outer-Circle Critics award 1955, Donaldson award, 1955, Ohioana award, 1955, Ohio Press Club award, 1959, Brit. Drama Critics award, 1960, Hart Meml. award, 1967, State Dept. medal, 1968, Pegasus award, 1970, Lifetime Achievement award Am. Theatre Assn., 1979, Nat. Thespian Soc. award, 1980, Pioneer Broadcasters award, 1981, Ohioana Library career medal, Master of Arts award Rocky Mountain Writers Guild, 1982, Centennial Award medal Ohio State U., 1970, William Inge award and lectureship Independence Community Coll., 1983, 86—, Disting. Contbr. award Psychologists for Social Responsibility, 1985, ann. awards San Francisco State U., Pepperdine U., Career award Southeastern Theatre Conf., 1990; named Playwright of Yr. Baldwin-Wallace Coll., 1960; named to Honorable Order of Ky. Colonels, 1965, Tenn. Colonels, 1988; named to Theater Hall of Fame, 1990. Fellow Coll. Am. Theatre, Kennedy Ctr.; mem. Acad. Motion Picture Arts and Scis., Acad. TV Arts and Scis. (2 Emmy awards 1988), Authors League (council), ANTA (dir., v.p.), Ohio State U. Assn. (dir.), Radio Writers' Guild (a founder, pres.), Writers Guild Am. (dir., founding mem. Valentine Davies award), Dramatists Guild (council), ASCAP, Calif. Ednl. Theatre Assn. (Profl. Artist award 1992), Phi Beta Kappa, Sigma Delta Chi.

LAWRENCE, PAUL FREDERIC, educational consultant; b. Paterson, N.J., Mar. 20, 1912; s. Joshua Emanuel and Louise (Hill) L.; m. Vivian Ann Hall, Sept. 21, 1941; children: Katherine Louise, Robin Ann. BS in Edn., Kean Coll., 1935; MA in Edn., Stanford U., 1945, EdD, 1947; DHL, Kean Coll., 1965. Teaching and adminstrn. credentials, N.J., Calif. Tchr., art supr. Princeton (N.J.) Pub. Schs., 1935-41; assoc. prof., asst. dir. Howard U., Washington, 1948-56; supt. of schs. Willowbrook Sch. Dist., L.A., 1956-60; prof. edn., dean counseling State Coll. Alameda County, Hayward, Calif., 1960-63; assoc. state supt. pub. instrn., chief Divsn. Higher Edn. State Calif., 1963-67; regional commr. edn. Region IX Federal Govt., 1967-73; dep. assoc. commr. U.S. Office Edn., Washington, 1973-77; dir. postsecondary liaison U.S. Office of Edn., Washington, 1978-83; owner, dir. Cons. in Edn. Policy and Adminstrn., Sacramento, 1983—; bd. dirs. Scholastic Mag., N.Y.C.; com. mem. Nat. Acad. Sci., Washington, Nat. Conf. Christians and Jews, L.A.; desegregation monitor 9th Dist. Fed. Ct., San Francisco. Coauthor: Negro American Heritage, 1965, Opportunities in Interracial Colleges, 1947; contbr. articles to profl. jours. With USAF, 1942-46, Lt. col. USAFR, 1946-70. Recipient Disting. Svc. award NABSE, New Orleans, Outstanding Svc. awards City of San Bernardino, Calif., U.S. Dept. HEW, Washington, Calif. Senate and Assembly, Sacramento. Mem. Nat. Conf. Parents and Tchrs., USAF Acad. (liason advisor), Calif. State Commn. on Edn., Exploratory Commn. on Edn., Select Com. Study Higher Edn., Phi Delta Kappa. Home: 4837 Crestwood Way Sacramento CA 95822 Office: Cons in Ednl Policy 615 J St Sacramento CA 95814

LAWRENCE, PAULA DENISE, physical therapist; b. Ft. Worth, May 21, 1959; d. Roddy Paul and Kay Frances (Spivey) Gillis; m. Mark Jayson Lawrence, Apr. 20, 1985. BS, Tex. Women's U., 1982. Lic. phys. therapist, Tex., Calif. Sales mgr. R. and K Camping Ctr., Garland, Tex., 1977-82; staff physical therapist Longview (Tex.) Regional Hosp., 1982-83, dir. phys. therapy, 1983-87, dir. rehab. svcs., 1987-88; staff phys. therapist MPH Home Health, Longview, Tex., 1983-84; owner, pres. Phys. Rehabil. Ctr., Hemet, Calif., 1988—; mem. adv. com. div. health occupations Kilgore (Tex.) Coll., 1985-88; mem. profl. adv. bd. Hospice Longview, 1985-88. Mem. NAFE, Am. Phys. Therapy Assn., Calif. Phys. Therapy Assn., Am. Bus. Women's Assn. (v.p. 1987, 89, pres. 1990, Woman of Yr. 1988, 91), Soroptimist (corres. sec. 1992, dir. 1993-94), Psi Chi, Omega Rho Alpha. Home: 899 Kristin Ln Hemet CA 92545-1645 Office: 901 S State St Ste 500 Hemet CA 92543-7127

LAWRENCE, ROBERT DON, pathologist, consultant; b. Oakland, Calif., Jan. 2, 1941; s. Ernest Orlando and Mary (Blumer) L.; m. Eleanor Long Ardery, Apr. 2, 1967; children: Amy, Beth. BS in Chemistry, U. Pacific, 1962; MD, UCLA, 1966. Diplomate Am. Bd. Pathology. Intern UCLA Hosp, 1966-67; resident Mayo Clinic, Rochester, Minn., 1969-72; Ptnr. Delta Pathology Assocs., Stockton, Calif., 1972—; forensic pathologist San Joaquin County Coroner's Office, Stockton, 1972—; lab. dir. SmithKline Beecham Clin. Lab., Stockton, 1972—; med. dir. Found. Health Plan, Sacramento/Stockton, 1980-92. Author: Snap Diagnoses in Pathology, 1976, Forensic Pathology For The Primary Care Physician, 1982; contbr. aarticles to profl. jours. Bd. dirs. San Joaquin County Child Abuse Prevention Coun., Stockton, 1983-89; bd. dirs., v.p. Delta Blood Bank, Stockton, 1975—. Lt. USN, flight surgeon, 1967-69. Pathology fellow Mayo Clinic, Rochester, Minn., 1970-73. Mem. San Joaquin Young Man's Marching and Chowder Soc. Republican. Home: 1811 Monty Ct Stockton CA 95207-2402 Office: Delta Pathology Assocs 2291 W March Ln # 179E Stockton CA 95207-6600

LAWRENCE, SALLY CLARK, educational administrator; b. San Francisco, Dec. 29, 1930; d. George Dickson and Martha Marie Alice (Smith) Clark; m. Henry Clay Judd, July 1, 1950 (div. Dec. 1972); children: Rebecca, David, Nancy; m. John I. Lawrence, Aug. 12, 1976; stepchildren: Maia, Dylan. Docent Portland Art Mus., Oreg., 1958-68; gallery owner, dir., Sally Judd Gallery, Portland, 1968-75; art ins. appraiser, cons. Portland, 1975-81; interim dir. Mus. Art. Sch., Pacific Northwest Coll. Art, Portland, 1981, asst. dir., 1981-82, acting dir., 1982-84, dir., 1984—; bd. dirs. Art Coll. Exch. Nat. Consortium, 1982-91, pres., 1983-84. Bd. dirs. Portland Arts Alliance, 1987—, Alliance Ind. Colls. of Art and Design, 1991—. Mem. Nat. Assn. Schs. Art and Design (bd. dirs. 1984-91), Oreg. Ind. Coll. Assn. (bd. dirs. 1981—, exec. com. 1989—, pres. 1992—). Office: Pacific NW Coll of Art 1219 SW Park Ave Portland OR 97205-2430

LAWRENCE, SANFORD HULL, physician; b. Kokomo, Ind., July 10, 1919; s. Walter Scott and Florence Elizabeth (Hull) L. AB, Ind. U., 1941, MD, 1944. Intern Rochester (N.Y.) Gen. Hosp., 1944-45; resident Halloran Hosp., Staten Island, N.Y., 1946-49; dir. biochemistry research Lab. San Fernando (Calif.) VA Hosp.; asst. prof. UCLA, 1950—; cons. internal medicine and cardiology U.S. Govt., Los Angeles County; lectr. Faculte de Medicine, Paris, various colls. Eng., France, Belgium, Sweden, USSR, India, Japan. Author: Zymogram in Clinical Medicine, 1965; contbr. articles to sci. jours.; author: Threshold of Valhalla, Another Way to Fly, My Last Satyr, and other short stories; traveling editor: Relax Mag. Mem. Whitley Heights Civic Assn., 1952—; pres. Halloran Hosp. Employees Assn., 1947-48. Served to maj. U.S. Army, 1945-46. Recipient Research award TB and Health Assn., 1955-58, Los Angeles County Heart Assn., 1957-59, Pres.' award, Queen's Blue Book award, Am. Men of Sci. award; named one of 2000 Men of Achievement, Leaders of Am. Sci., Ky. Col., named Hon. Mayor of West Point, Ky. Mem. AAAS, AMA, N.Y. Acad. Scis., Am. Fedn. Clin. Research, Am. Assn. Clin. Investigation, Am. Assn. Clin. Pathology, Am. Assn. Clin. Chemistry, Los Angeles County Med. Assn. Republican. Methodist. Home: 2014 Whitley Ave Los Angeles CA 90068-3235 also: 160 rue St Martin, Paris 75003, France

LAWRENCE, ZAN, computer consultant; b. Cedar Rapids, Iowa, Jan. 19, 1945; s. Stanley Alexander and Doris (Cornelius) L. Student, Calif. State-Fullerton, 1973-75. Sales cons. Computerland, Newport Beach, Calif., 1979-80, 85-86; regional sales mgr. Microbyte Electronic, Newport Beach, 1981-85; sr. sales rep. Pac Tel Infosystems, Irvine, Calif., 1986-87, MIS Triple Crown Industries, Santa Ana, Calif., 1987-88; owner Western Computer Systems, Laguna Beach, Calif., 1988—. Author: (tng. manual) Effective Sales of AT&T, 1985. Sponsor Children's Hosp., Orange, Calif., 1988; quartermaster Orange County Marine Inst., Dana Pt., Calif., 1988. Served with USMC, 1963-66. Republican. Office: Western Computer Systems 490 3rd St Unit I Laguna Beach CA 92651-2328

LAWRY, ROGER HARLOW, sales engineer; b. Hancock, Mich., May 24, 1956; s. Gordon Harlow and Beverley (Anderson) L.; m. Janet Parsell, June 27, 1985; children: Bradley Alan, Trevor Gordon, Sean Parsell. BSChemE, N.C. State U., 1979; MS in Bioengring., U. Utah, 1985. Safety, tech. engr. Milliken Chems., Inman, S.C., 1980-83; rsch. asst. U. Utah, Salt Lake City, 1983-85; sr. rsch. assoc. Cox-Uphoff Internat., Carpinteria, Calif., 1986-87; tech. sales rep. Fisher Sci., Tustin, Calif., 1987-89; sales engr. Wilshire Foam Products, Carson, Calif., 1989-90, Alameda Chem. & Sci., Newbury Park, Calif., 1990—. Mem. LDS Ch. Home: 2290 Woodland Ave Ojai CA 92023 Office: Alameda Chem & Sci 1339 Lawrence Dr Newbury Park CA 91320

LAWS, EDWARD ERNEST, III, university administrator; b. Phila., Apr. 7, 1945; s. Edward Ernest and Jeannette (Johnson) L.; m. M. Kay Antal, Sept. 12, 1970. BSBA, Drexel U., 1968; MA in Edn. Adminstrn., U. North Colo., 1977. With Edward Laws Assocs., Lansdowne, Pa., 1968-71; prin., tchr. East Glacier Park (Mont.) Grade Sch., 1971-72; bus driver Pub. Svc. Co. of Colo., Boulder, 1972-73; tchr. West Grand Pub. Schs., Kremmling, Colo., 1973-76; fin. aid adminstr. Colo. State U., Ft. Collins, 1977-80; dir. fin. aid Adams State Coll., Alamosa, Colo., 1980—. Leader Cub Scouts Am., Kremmling, 1973-76; ch. youth leader Alamosa Presbyn. Ch., 1980-84. Mem. ACT Regional Adv. Coun., Nat. Assn. Fin. Aid Adminstrs., Colo. Assn. Fin. Aid Adminstrs. (exec. coun. 1983-87, treas. 1982-85, pres. 1986-87), Rocky Mt. Assn. State Fin. Aid Adminstrs. (bd.d irs. 1986-87, conf. planning com. 1992). Office: Adams State Coll Fin Aid Office Alamosa CO 81102

LAWSON, DANIEL DAVID, chemist, consultant; b. Tucson, Jan. 13, 1929; s. Morris and Virginia (Lawson) Duncan-Lawson; m. Margaret Charlotte Schaeffer, Aug. 18, 1957; children: David Dale, Monica Ann. BA, U. So. Calif., 1957, MS, 1960. Rsch. fellow Hastings Found., Altadena, Calif., 1960-61; chemist jet propulsion lab. Calif. Inst. Tech., Pasadena, 1961-92, ret., 1992; dir. rsch. Spectra Rsch., Arcadia, Calif., 1958—. Contbr. articles to profl. jours.; patentee in field. With U.S. Army, 1948-61, Korea. Fellow Am. Inst. Chemists; mem. AAAS, Am. Chem. Soc., Electro Chem. Soc., So. Calif. Alumni Assn., Royal Chem. Soc. Home: 919 S Golden West Ave Arcadia CA 91007

LAWSON, EVERETT LEROY, academic administrator, minister; b. Tillamook, Oreg., May 17, 1938; s. Elmer LaVerne Lawson and Margery Evelyn (Foltz) Alcott; m. Joy Annette Whitney, June 11, 1960; children: Kimberly Joy Denton, Candace Annette, Lane Whitney. BA, N.W. Christian Coll., 1960; AB, Cascade Coll., 1962; MA in Teaching, Reed Coll., 1965; PhD, Vanderbilt U., 1970. Ordained to ministry Christian Chs. and Chs. of Christ, 1959. Pastor, founder Tigard (Oreg.) Christian Ch., 1959-65; tchr. Tigard Union High Sch., 1962-64; candidate sec. Christian Missionary Fellowship, 1964-68; asst. prof. Milligan (Tenn.) Coll., 1965-73, v.p., 1970-73; sr. pastor East 38th St. Christian Ch., Indpls., 1973-79, Cen. Christian Ch., Mesa, Ariz., 1979—; pres. Pacific Christian Coll., Fullerton, Calif., 1990—; cons. Standard Pub. Co., 1977-90; adj. prof. Ky. Christian Coll., 1984-90; speaker nat. radio broadcast The Christian's Hour, 1987—; dir. Christian Missionary Fellowship, Indpls., 1968-90. Author: Very Sure of God, 1974; co-author: (with Tetsunao Yamamori) Introducing Church Growth, 1975, Church Growth: Everybody's Business, 1976; also 20 other books, commentaries, study books; contbr. articles to profl. jours. Mem. N.Am. Christian Conv. U.S.A. (pres. 1982), Brit.-Am. Fellowship Com. (bd. dirs. 1979—). Office: Cen Christian Ch 933 N Lindsay Rd Mesa AZ 85213-6048 also: Pacific Christian Coll 2500 E Nutwood Ave Fullerton CA 92631

LAWSON, JAMES LEE, health care consultant; b. Alhambra, Calif., Jan. 7, 1949; s. Charles French and Helen Marie (Gregory) L.; m. Ilene Eleanor Sweeney, Apr. 8, 1973 (div. 1983); children: Charles J., Sara C.; m. Marguerite Adams King, Feb. 25, 1984; 1 child, Zachary David. AA in Polit. Sci., Cypress (Calif.) Coll., 1970; AS in Nursing, Victor Valley Coll., Victorville, Calif., 1980; BBA, Calif. We. U., 1976, MBA, 1978; postgrad., Western State U., 1970-71; JD, Kensington U., Glendale, Calif., 1989; BS in Nursing, U. Phoenix, 1990. RN, Calif., Fla., Ky., Idaho, Ill., Ind., Tex. Wis.; cert. inst., Calif.; cert. emergency nurse practitioner, Calif.; cert. profl. continuing edn. provider Calif. Bd. R.N.'s. Head nurse, charge nurse La Palma (Calif.) Intercommunity Hosp. and Pioneer Hosp., 1974-76; from adminstrv. asst. to staff analyst San Bernardino (Calif.) County Med. Ctr., 1976-79; dir. nursing services Barstow (Calif.) Community Hosp., 1979-80; adminstr. Disabled and Vietnam Vets. Outreach Program Vets House, Inc., Madison, 1981; exec. dir. So. Wis. Emergency Med. Services Council, Inc., Madison, 1981-83; charge nurse, acting head nurse West Side Dist. Hosp., Simi Valley (Calif.) Adventist Hosp., 1983-84; dir. ops. Pasadena Children's Tng. Soc., Altadena, Calif., 1984-86; staff asst. Kapner, Wolfberg & Assocs., Inc., Van Nuys, Calif., 1987-88; v.p. Kapner, Wolfberg & Assocs., Inc., Van Nuys, 1988-89; owner, mgr., healthcare mgmt. systems cons. James L. Lawson, R.N., P.C., Canoga Park, Calif., 1989-93; disaster health supr. Am. Red Cross, L.A., 1992—. Contbr. articles to profl. jours. Loaned exec., Arrowhead United Way, San Bernadino, 1979; mem. Calif. State Bd. of Edn. Child Advisory Nutrition Council, 1986—, Selective Service Bd. Local 14, Wis., 1981-83, ARC, Am. Heart Assn.; vol. campaign worker for Repub. Party. With USN, 1966-74. Mem. Am. Mgmt. Assn., Am. Hosp. Assn., Nat. League for Nursing, Am. Nurses Assn., Am. Public Health Assn., Am. Soc. Nursing Svc. Admistrs., Am. Trauma Soc., Calif. Soc. Nursing Svc. Administrs., Hosp. Mgmt. Systems Soc. of So. Calif. (charter), Hosp. Internal Auditors, Med. Auditors Assn. Calif., Nat. Emergency Nurses Assn. (charter), Nat. Assn. for Emergency Paramedics (charter), Pasadena (Calif.) C. of C., Hosp. Fin. Mgmt. Assn. Republican. Home: 136 S Virgil Ave # 241 Canoga Park CA 91306 Office: 2700 Wilshire Blvd Los Angeles CA 90057

LAWSON, NORMAN ROGER, minister; b. Mount Vernon, Wash., June 6, 1931; s. Willard Alfred and Helen Scott (McInturff) L.; m. Lola Margaret Brooke, Aug. 23, 1953; children: Ellen Adair Lawson, Kathleen Brooke Lawson. BA, Willamette U., 1953; MDiv, Garrett Theol. Sem., 1957; MA, Northwestern U., 1957; DMin, San Francisco Theol. Sem., 1975. Pastor 1st United Meth. Ch., Toppenish, Wash., 1957-61, Auburn, Wash., 1961-66, Tacoma, Wash., 1966-75, Wenatchee, Wash., 1980-85; dist. supt. Columbia River Dist., Wenatchee, 1975-80, Seattle Dist., 1985-87; pastor Cen. United Protestant Ch., Richland, Wash., 1987—; del. to jurisdictional and gen. confs. U. Meth. Ch., 1976, 80, 84, 88. Bd. dirs. United Way, Kennewick, 1988—; pres. Cen. Wash. Hosp., Wenatchee, 1981-85. Fellow Acad. Parish Clergy; mem. Richland Rotary Club (bd. dirs. 1991—, Paul Harris fellow 1991). Republican. Home: 1726 Howell Richland WA 99352 Office: Cen United Protestant Ch 1124 Stevens Dr Richland WA 99352

LAWSON, RICHARD BARRY, minister; b. Oakland, Calif., Feb. 6, 1934; s. Theodore Carey and Louise Schropp (Thaeler) L.; m. Phyllis Doster, Aug. 28, 1965; children: Charlotte L., Richard C., Marie C., Paul L. BA in Polit. Sci., Stanford U., 1956; postgrad., Columbia U., 1956-57, U. Brussels, Belgium, 1957-58; MA, U. Catholique de Louvain, Belgium, 1959; MDiv, San Francisco Theol. Sem., 1964. Cert. secondary tchr., Utah, 1980, 88, Wash. 1989. Interim pastor Community Presbyn. Ch., Coolidge, Ariz., 1964-65; pastor First Presbyn. Ch., Salida, Colo., 1965-72, Community Presbyn. Ch., Brigham City, Utah, 1972-88; dir. Internat. Neighbors, Seattle, 1988—. With Calif. Nat. Guard, 1961-66. Mem. Nat. Assn. Fgn. Student Affairs, Assn. Christian Ministry to Internats. Home: 4407 226th St SW Mountlake Terrace WA 98043 Office: Internat Neighbors 1818 NE 50th St Seattle WA 98105

LAWSON, ROBIN ALASTAIR, congressional press secretary; b. Bexleyheath, Kent, Eng., Jan. 24, 1939; came to U.S., 1958; s. Edward and Gwendoline (Nash) L.; m. Pamela Gene Gaudaur, Aug. 30, 1965; children: Christie Rae, Ali Gwen. TV news reporter/editor Sta. KOBI-TV, Medford, Oreg., 1976-79, TV mag. producer, 1981-82; gen. mgr. Sta. KEKA, Eureka, Calif., 1979-81; news dir., mgr. Sta. KHUG, Phoenix, 1982-84; news dir. Sta. KMFR/KTMT, Medford, 1984-86; book narrator Blackstone Audio Inc., Medford, 1990—; dist. press sec. Congressman Bob Smith, Medford, 1986—; instr. So. Oreg. State Coll., Ashland, 1976-80; narrator travel videos, 1987. Developer a 40 minute presentation called The Wit and Genius of Winston Churchill; contbr. articles to profl. jours. With U.S. Army. Mem. Internat. Churchill Soc. Republican. Home: 674 Berry Ln Ashland OR 97520-1485 Office: Congressman Bob Smith 259 Barnett Ste E Medford OR 97501

LAWSON, THOMAS, artist; b. Glasgow, Scotland, July 16, 1951; came to U.S., 1975; s. Edward and Margaret Lawson; m. Susan Morgan. MA (hons), U. St. Andrews, Scotland, 1973; MA, U. Edinburgh, Scotland, 1975; MPhil, CUNY, 1979. Artist various cities worldwide, 1975—; founding editor Real Life Mag., N.Y.C., 1979—; instr. Sch. Visual Arts, N.Y.C., 1981-90; dean Calif. Inst. of the Arts, Valencia, 1990—; N.Y. advisor Alba Mag., Edinburgh, 1984-89; vis. instr. Rhode Island Sch. Design, Providence, N.Y., 1988-89; vis. faculty Calif. Inst. of the Arts, Valencia, 1986-89. Executed mural Manhattan Mcpl. Bldg., 1989-92; contbr. articles to profl. jours. Artist advisor Rotunda Gallery, Bklyn., 1985-90. Nat. Endowment for the Arts artists fellow, 1982-83, 85-86, 89-90; Real Life Ma g. publ. grantee Nat. Endowment for the Arts, 1979—, N.Y. State Coun. Arts, 1980-89. Mem. Coll. Art Assn. Office: Calif Inst of the Arts 24700 McBean Pkwy Valencia CA 91355

LAWSON, THOMAS CHENEY, security, information and credit bureau executive; b. Pasadena, Calif., Sept. 21, 1955; s. William McDonald and Joan Bell (Jaffee) L.; m. Carolyn Marie Cox; children: Christopher, Tiffany, Erin, Brittany. Student, Calif. State U., Sacramento, 1973-77. Cert. internat. investigator, fraud examiner. Pres. Tomatron Co., Pasadena, 1970-88, Tom's Tune Up & Detail, Pasadena, 1971-88, Tom's Pool Svc., Sacramento, 1975-78, Tom Supply Co., 1975—; mgmt. trainee Permoid Process Co., L.A., 1970-75; prof. automechanics Calif. State U., Sacramento, 1973-75; regional sales cons. Hoover Co., Burlingame, 1974-76; mktg. exec. River City Prodns., Sacramento, 1977-78; territorial rep. Globe div. Burlington House Furniture Co., 1978; So. Calif. territorial rep. Marge Carson Furniture, Inc., 1978-80; pres. Ted L. Gunderson & Assos., Inc., Westwood, Calif., 1980-81; pres., CEO Apscreen, Newport Beach, Calif., 1980—; founder Creditbase Co., Newport Beach, Worldata Corp., Newport Beach, Trademark Enforcement Corp., L.A.; pres. Carecheck, Inc., Newport Beach, Calif., 1990—; CEO Badchex, Inc., Newport Beach, Calif., 1992—. Calif. Rehab. scholar, 1974-77. Mem. Christian Businessmen's Com. Internat., Coun. Internat. Investigators, Am. Soc. Indsl. Security (cert., chmn. Orange County chpt. 1990), Nat. Pub. Records Rsch. Assn., Pers. and Indsl. Rels. Assn., World Assn. Detectives, Assn. Cert. Fraud Examiners, Soc. Human Resource Mgmt. Office: 2043 Westcliff Dr Ste 300 Newport Beach CA 92660-5511

LAWTON, MARK THOMAS, contract administrator, property management consultant; b. L.A., Dec. 24, 1956. BBA, U. San Diego, 1979; MBA, Nat. U., 1991. Real estate, insurance lic.; teaching credentials. Author: Procedures, 1991. mem. pres. Boy's and Girl's Club of Am., La Habra, 1991, treas. 1992, sec. 1990; charter mem. Brea Jaycees, 1989. Mem. Elks.

LAWTON, MICHAEL JAMES, entomologist, pest management specialist; b. Balt., Aug. 6, 1953; s. James William and Mary Eileen (O'Connor) L.; m. Barbara Ann Byron, Dec. 19, 1983. BS, U. Md., 1975. Cert. entomologist. Technician, tech. dir. Atlas Exterminating Co., Towson, Md., 1975-78; asst. tech. dir. Western Exterminator Co., Irvine, Calif., 1978-83, tng. and tech. dir., 1984—. Republican. Office: Western Exterminator Co 1732 Kaiser Ave Irvine CA 92714-5739

LAX, FREDRIC, neurosurgeon; b. Bklyn., Apr. 13, 1950; s. Alex and Florette (Ganz) L.; m. Susan J. Schindler, June 15, 1984; children: Jacob R., Zachary C. BS cum laude, Union Coll., Schenectady, 1971; MD, Hahnemann Med. Coll., Phila., 1975. Diplomate Am. Bd. Neurol. Surgeons. Surg. intern Bronx Mcpl. Hosp., 1975-76; neurosurg. resident Albert Einstein Coll. of Medicine, Bronx, 1981; pvt. practice El Paso, Tex., 1981-83; instr. neurosurgery U. Medicine and Dentistry of N.J., Newark, 1983-88; pvt. practice Corvallis, Oreg., 1988—. Mem. Am. Assn. Neurol. Surgeons, Oreg. Med. Assn. Office: 3615 NW Samaritan #203 Corvallis OR 97330

LAX, KATHLEEN THOMPSON, judge. BA, U. Kans., 1967; JD, U. Calif., L.A., 1980. Law clk. U.S. Bankruptcy Ct., L.A., 1980-82; assoc. Gibson, Dunn & Crutcher, L.A., 1982-88; judge U.S. Bankruptcy Ct., L.A., 1988—; bd. dirs. L.A. (Calif.) Bankruptcy Forum, 1988—; bd. govs. Fin. Lawyers Conf., L.A., 1991—. Bd. editors: Calif. Bankruptcy Jour., 1988—. Office: US Bankruptcy Court Rm 1334 255 E Temple St Los Angeles CA 90012

LAYCRAFT, JAMES HERBERT, judge; b. Veteran, Alta., Can., Jan. 5, 1924; s. George Edward and Hattie (Cogswell) L.; m. Helen Elizabeth Bradley, May 1, 1948; children: James B., Anne L. BA, U. Alta., Edmonton, 1950; LLB, U. Alta., 1951; LLD (hon.), U. Calgary, Alta., 1986. Bar: Alta. Barrister Nolan Chambers & Co., Calgary, 1952-75; justice trial div. Supreme Ct. of Alta., Calgary, 1975-79; justice Ct. of Appeal of Alta., Calgary, 1979-85, chief justice of Alta., 1985-91, ret., 1991. Contbr. articles to law jours. Served to lt. Royal Can. Arty., 1941-46, PTO. Mem. United Ch. of Can.

LAYDEN, FRANCIS PATRICK (FRANK LAYDEN), professional basketball team executive, former coach; b. Bklyn., Jan. 5, 1932; m. Barbara Layden; children: Scott, Michael, Katie. Student, Niagara U. High sch. basketball coach L.I., N.Y.; head coach, athletic dir. Adelphi-Suffolk Coll. (now Dowling Coll.); head basketball coach, athletic dir. Niagara U., Niagara Falls, N.Y., 1968-76; asst. coach Atlanta Hawks, 1976-79; gen. mgr. Utah Jazz, Salt Lake City, 1979-88, head coach, 1981-88, v.p. basketball ops., until 1988, pres., 1989—. Bd. dirs. Utah Soc. Prevention Blindness; bd. dirs. Utah chpt. Multiple Sclerosis Soc., Utah Spl. Olympics. Served to 1st lt. Signal Corps, AUS. Office: Utah Jazz 5 Triad Ctr Ste 500 Salt Lake City UT 84180-1105

LAYE, JOHN E(DWARD), contingency planning and disaster recovery consulting executive; b. Santa Monica, Calif., May 26, 1933; s. Theodore Martin and Evelyn Rosalie (Young) L.; m. Jeanne Tutt Curry, Dec. 23, 1955; children: John Russell, Linda Helen. A.A., Los Angeles Community Coll., 1952; B.A., Naval Postgrad. Sch., 1967; M.S., U. So. Calif., 1975. Enlisted U.S. Navy, 1951, advanced through grades to lt. comdr., 1965; naval aviator, project mgr., worldwide, 1955-75; ret., 1975; emergency services exec. Marin County, Calif., 1975-76, Solano County, Calif., 1976-82; cons., pres. Cartingency Mgmt. Cons. (formerly Applied Protection Systems), Moraga, Calif., 1982—; cons. disaster med. com. Calif. Gov.'s Earthquake Task Force, 1981-89 ; mem. faculty Emergency Mgmt. Inst., Nat. Emergency Tng. Ctr., Emmitsburg, Md., 1982—; mem. bus. mgmt. faculty U. Calif. Bus. and Mgmt. extention, 1993—; pres. Calif. Emergency Services Assn., 1988; mem. bus. mgmt. faculty U. Calif. (Brekeley) Extension, 1993—; pres. Calif. Emergency Svcs. Assn., 1988; lectr. internat. contingency planning and disaster recovery, 1976—. Decorated Air medal, Navy Commendation medal, Navy Achievement medal; recipient commendation Gov.'s Office Emergency Svcs., State Fire Marshal, Calif. Emergency Svcs. Assn., City Orinda. Mem. Nat. Coordinating Council Emergency Mgmt. (chmn. bus. and industry com. 1992—), Orinda Assn. (bd. dirs. 1988-90, pres. 1989, Vol. Yr. award 1991), U. So. Calif. Alumni (bd. dirs. 1980-87, pres. east bay club 1984), U. So. Calif. Inst. Safety and Systems Mgmt. Triumvirate (founding bd. mem.). Presbyterian. Office: Contingency Mgnt Cons 346 Rheem Blvd Ste 202 Moraga CA 94556-1588

LAYTON, MYRON J. (MIKE), writer, consultant; b. Sioux county, Nebr., Nov. 24, 1922; s. George W. and Nellie V. (Barger) L.; m. Carole Kay Dickerson, Aug. 9, 1952 (div. Mar. 1993); children: Geoffrey, Gayle, Gavin. BA, U. Denver, 1950. Reporter, editor Seattle Post-Intelligencer, Olympia, Wash., 1970-82; columnist Seattle Post-Intelligencer, Olympia, 1982-90; writer, author Olympia, 1990—. 1st lt. U.S. Army, 1941-45, ETO, 51-55, Korea. Recipients Blethen award Sigma Delta Chi., 1975, Bosch Meml. award Sigma Delta Chi, 1981. Home: 4933 Cooper Point Rd NW Olympia WA 98502

LAZARECK, LESLIE HOWARD, software publisher; b. Devils Lake, N.D., May 22, 1963; s. Isadore Luke and Sybil Marjorie (Marcoe) L. BSME, U. Calif., Santa Barbara, 1985. Systems engr. IBM, Las Vegas, Nev., 1985-90; pres. Blue Sky Software Corp., Las Vegas, 1989-91; owner Source Connection, Las Vegas, 1988—. Mem. B'nai B'rith (sec. Las Vegas chpt. 1992), Jewish Fedn. Las Vegas, Young Leadership. Democrat. Jewish. Home: 5430 La Palomas Ct Las Vegas NV 89120

LAZARUS, IAN RODNEY, marketing professional; b. Detroit, June 22, 1959; s. Morris and Lena (Bradley) L.; m. Virginia Theresa Mayo, May 28, 1989. BS, U. Mich., 1981, Master of Health Svc. Adminstrn., 1984. Asst. to pres. Voluntary Hosps. Am., Dallas, 1984, mgr. membership, 1985-86; dir. bus. devel. Voluntary Hosps. Am., Denver, 1986-87; dir. network devel. Voluntary Hosps. Am., Hartford, Conn., 1987-89; v.p. product mgmt. Nat. Health Enhancement Systems, Phoenix, 1989—; speaker No. Calif. Healthcare Mktg. Assn., San Francisco, 1991, Am. Hosp. Assn. Soc. for Planning and Mktg., Phoenix, 1991, 92, AHA Soc. for Mktg. and Pub. Rels, 1991. Contbr. articles to Healthcare Strategic Management, Computers in Healthcare, Healthcare Financial Management; editor newsletters, 1987-89. Vol. March of Dimes, Ann Arbor, Mich., 1978, 79. Mem. Am. Coll. Healthcare Execs., U. Mich. Alumni Assn. (class rep. 1990—), Health Adminstrs. Forum. Home: 16401 N 50th St Scottsdale AZ 85254-9653 Office: Nat Health Enhancement 3200 N Central Ave Ste 1750 Phoenix AZ 85012-2437

LAZARUS, RICHARD STANLEY, psychology educator; b. N.Y.C., Mar. 3, 1922; s. Abe and Matilda (Marks) L.; m. Bernice H. Newman, Sept. 2, 1945; children—David Alan, Nancy Eve. A.B., City Coll. N.Y., 1942; M.S., U. Pitts., 1947, Ph.D., 1948; Dr. honoris causa, Johannes Gutenberg U., Mainz, Fed. Republic Germany, 1988. Diplomate in clin. psychology Am. Bd. Examiners in Profl. Psychology. Asst. prof. Johns Hopkins, 1948-53; psychol. cons. VA, 1952—; assoc. prof. psychology, dir. clin. tng. program Clark U., Worcester, Mass., 1953-57; assoc. prof. psychology U. Calif. at Berkeley, 1957-59, prof. psychology, 1959-91, prof. emeritus, 1991—; prin. investigator Air Force contracts dealing with psychol. stress, 1951-53, USPHS grant on personality psychol. stress, 1953-70; NIA, NIDA, and NCI grantee on stress, coping and health, 1977-81, MacArthur Found. research grantee, 1981-84; USPHS spl. fellow Waseda U., Japan, 1963-64. Author 17 books, numerous pubs. in profl. jours. Served to 1st lt. AUS, 1943-46. Recipient Disting. Sci. Achievement award Calif. State Psychol. Assn., 1984, Div. 38 Health Psychology, 1989; Guggenheim fellow, 1969-70; Army Rsch. Inst. rsch. grantee, 1973-75. Fellow AAAS, Am. Psychol. Assn. (Disting. Sci. Contbn. award 1989); mem. Western Psychol. Assn., Argentina Med. Assn. (hon.), Fundacion Raquel Guedikian De Estudios Sobre El Estres (acad. council). Home: 1824 Stanley Dollar Dr Apt 3B Walnut Creek CA 94595-2833 Office: Univ Calif Dept Psychology Berkeley CA 94720

LAZOWSKA, EDWARD DELANO, computer science educator; b. Washington, Aug. 3, 1950. AB, Brown U., 1972; MSc, U. Toronto, Can., 1974, PhD, 1977. Asst. prof. U. Wash., Seattle, 1977-82, assoc. prof., 1982-86; prof. dept. computer sci. & engring. U. Wash., 1986—, chair dept. computer sci. & engring., 1993—; chmn. Grad. Record Exam. Computer Sci. Test. Com., 1986-90; mem. tech. adv. bd. Microsoft Rsch. Mem. IEEE, Assn. Computing Machinery (chmn. spl. interest group on measurement and evaluation 1985-89), Computing Rsch. Assn. (bd. dirs.). Office: U Wash Dept Computer Sci & Engring FR 35 Seattle WA 98195

LE, KHANH TUONG, utility executive; b. Saigon, Vietnam, Feb. 25, 1936; parents Huy Bich and Thi Hop; m. Thi Thi Nguyen, Apr. 22, 1961; children: Tuong-Khanh, Tuong-Vi, Khang, Tuong-Van. BS in Mech. Engring., U. Montreal, 1960, MS in Mech. Engring., 1961. Cert. profl. engr. Project mgr. Saigon Met. Water Project Ministry Pub. Works, Saigon, 1961-66; dep. dir. gen. Cen. Logistics Agy. Prime Min. Office, Saigon, 1966-70; asst. dir., chief auditor Nat. Water Supply Agy. Min. Pub. Works, Saigon, 1970-75; mgr. Willows Water Dist., Englewood, Colo., 1975—; dean sch. mgmt. scis., asst. chancellor acad. affairs Hoa-Hao U., Long-Xuyen, Vietnam, 1973-75; bd. dirs. Asian Pacific Devel. Ctr.; adv. bd. Arapahoe County Utility Douglas County Water Resources Authority. Treas. Met. Denver Water Authority, 1989-92; mem. Arapahoe County Adv. Bd., Douglas County Water Resources Authority, 1993—. Recipient Merit medal Pres. Republic Vietnam, 1966, Pub. Health Svc. medal, 1970, Svc. award Asian Edn. Adv. Coun., 1989; named to Top Ten Pub. Works Leaders in Colo., Am. Pub. Works Assn., 1990. Mem. Am. Water Works Assn., Vietnamese Profl. Engrs. Soc. (founder), Amnesty Internat. Buddhist. Office: Willows Water Dist 6970 S Holly Cir Ste 200 Englewood CO 80112-1066

LEA, ROBERT NORMAN, marine biologist, researcher; b. Watsonville, Calif., Feb. 25, 1939; s. Robert Jackson and Martha Josephine (Lindgren) L.; m. Susan Marie Bartley, June 30, 1979; children: Sabrina Anne, Graham Michael Bartley. BS, U. Idaho, 1963; MA, U. Calif., Berkeley, 1968; PhD, U. Miami, Fla., 1980. Jr. aquatic biologist Calif. Dept. Fish and Game, Sacramento, 1967; asst. marine biologist Calif. Dept. Fish and Game, Long Beach, 1967-71; assoc. marine biologist Calif. Dept. Fish and Game, Monterey, 1972-74, 77-87, dir. marine resources lab., 1987-91; Robert E. Maytag fellow U. Miami, 1974-77; rsch. assoc. Natural History Mus. L.A. County, L.A., 1969—; field assoc. Calif. Acad. Scis., San Francisco, 1972-80, rsch. assoc., 1980—; lectr. Moss Landing (Calif.) Marine Labs., 1988. Coauthor: Guide to California Marine Fishes, 1972, List of Names of North American Fishes, 1980, 91; editor Calif. Fish and Game, 1987-90; contbr. articles to profl. jours. Fellow Am. Inst. Fishery Rsch. Biologists; mem. Am. Fisheries Soc. (life, award of excellence Calif.-Nev. chpt. 1990), Am. Elasmobranch Soc. (charter), Am. Soc. Ichthyologists and Herpetologists (various coms. 1978—), Ichthyological Soc. Japan, Am. Fish Soc. (cert. fisheries scientist), Sigma Xi, Phi Sigma. Democrat. Home: 22 Antelope Ln Monterey CA 93940-6301 Office: Calif Dept Fish and Game 20 Lower Ragsdale Dr Monterey CA 93940

LEABHART, THOMAS GLENN, art educator; b. Charleroi, Pa., Oct. 23, 1944; s. Thomas G. and Tresa Rose (Lacher) L.; m. Sally Diane Garfield, Apr. 29, 1972. BA, Rollins Coll., Winter Park, Fla., 1966; MA, U. Ark., 1968; postgrad., Ecole de Mime Decroux, Paris, France, 1968-72. Instr. U. Ark., Fayetteville, 1972-76; artistic dir. Wis. Sch. of Mime, Spring Green, 1976-78; resident artist Grand Valley State Coll., Allendale, Mich., 1978-81; asst. prof. Ohio State U., Columbus, 1981-82; assoc. prof., resident artist Pomona Coll., Claremont, Calif., 1982—. Author: Modern and Post Modern Mime, 1989; editor: Mime Jour., 1974—. Fulbright fellow, 1968-69, Ohio Arts Coun. Choreography fellow, 1982, NEA fellow, 1980, 84, 85; grantee Calif. Arts Coun. for Mime Jour., 1985, 87, 88, Internat. Rsch. Exchs. Bd, 1975. Mem. (founder, pres. 1986, 87) Nat. Movement Theatre Assn., Assn. Theatre in Higher Edn. Office: Pomona Coll Theatre Dept Claremont CA 91711

LEACH, RICHARD MAXWELL, JR. (MAX LEACH, JR.), corporate professional; b. Chillicothe, Tex., June 14, 1934; s. Richard Maxwell and Lelia Booth (Page) L.; m. Wanda Gail Groves, Feb. 4, 1956; children: Richard Clifton, John Christopher, Sandra Gail, Kathy Lynn. BS in Acctg. magna cum laude, Abilene Christian U., 1955. Registered Fin. Planner., CLU. Asst. dir. agys. Am. Founders Ins. Co., Austin, Tex., 1960-62; owner A.F. Ins. Planning Assocs., Temple, Tex., 1962-65; v.p. sales Christian Fidelity Life Ins. Co., Waxahachie, Tex., 1966-67; exec. v.p. Acad. Computer Tech., Inc., Dallas, 1968-69; pres., chief exec. officer Inta-Search Internat., Inc., Dallas, 1969-71; prin., chief exec. officer, fin. cons. Leach and Assocs., Albuquerque, 1971—; pres. The Wright Edge, Inc., 1988-90; pres., CEO Action Mktg. Programs, Inc., 1989-92; CEO Vacation Premiums Internat., Inc., 1990-92; chmn. bd. United Quest Inc., Albuquerque, Hosanna Inc., Albuquerque; real estate broker; commodity futures broker; exec. dir., bd. dirs. New Heart, Inc., Albuquerque, 1975-85; owner Insta-Copy, Albuquerque, 1973-76, Radio Sta. KYLE-FM, Temple, 1963-64. Editor, author Hosanna newspaper, 1973-74. Gen. dir. Here's Life, New Mexico, Albuquerque, 1976; exec. dir. Christians for Cambodia, Albuquerque, 1979-80. Served with U.S. Army, 1955-57. Home: 3308 June St NE Albuquerque NM 87111-5029 Office: 3240-A Juan Tabo Blvd NE Albuquerque NM 87111-5102

LEADER, JEFFERY JAMES, mathematics educator; b. Elmira, N.Y., Oct. 27, 1963; s. Dennis Thomas and Jeanne Diane (Smith) L.; m. Margaret Ellen Nieburg, Aug. 26, 1989; 1 child, Derek James. BS, Syracuse U., 1985, BSEE, 1985; ScM, Brown U., 1987, PhD, 1989. Vis. asst. prof. math. Harvey Mudd Coll., Claremont, Calif., 1989-90; asst. prof. Naval Postgrad. Sch., Monterey, Calif., 1990—. Mem. Am. Math. Soc., Math. Assn. Am., Soc. for Indsl. and Applied Math., Phi Beta Kappa, Tau Beta Pi, Sigma Xi. Office: Naval Postgrad Sch Code MA/LE Monterey CA 93943

LEADER, JEREMY, software engineer; b. New Brunswick, N.J., Oct. 27, 1961; s. Solomon and Elvera Marie (Grutter) L.; m. Christina Marie Mannino, Feb. 25, 1989. BS, Calif. Inst. Tech., 1983. Sr. systems software engr. Unisys Corp., Irvine, Calif., 1983—. Mem. Assn. Computing Machinery. Office: Unisys Corp 19 Morgan Irvine CA 91776

LEADON, DENISE LYNN, human resources specialist, organizational consultant; b. Junction City, Colo., Feb. 11, 1959; d. Anthony Louis and Doris (McQuiller) Jeffries. BA, U. Colo., 1983; MA, Webster U., St. Louis, 1990. Motivational speaker Alliance of Telecommunications, Denver, 1989; test adminstr. AT&T, Denver, 1987-89; chief exec. officer In Depth Design, Denver, 1988—; exec. dir. In Depth Mgmt., Denver, 1993—; cons. in field. Mem. Colo. Women for Polit. Action, Denver, 1988—; vol. Family Focus Ctr. for Abuse of Children, 1989—; tchr. Jr. Devel., Denver, 1985—. Recipient Martin Luther King award for art, 1986, Gold award, Steele Inc., 1989. Mem. Assn. of Black Psychologists (pub. rels. chmn. 1990—), Black Men and Women Investors of Denver (v.p. 1989—). Home: 3934 W Walsh Pl Denver CO 80219-3242

LEAF, DAVID ALLEN, writer, television producer; b. N.Y.C., Apr. 20, 1952; s. Harold and Bernice (Kroll) L.; m. Eva Easton, Sept. 6, 1984. BBA, George Washington U., 1973. Writer The Beach Boys 25th Yr. Spl., 1987, The Creative Arts Emmy Awards, 1990, The New WKRP, 1991, The New Leave it to Beaver, 1988-89, The Making of Beauty and the Beast, 1991, The Party Machine (Paramount), 1990-91; writer, producer Martin & Lewis Golden Age of Comedy, 1992; segment producer Disney's Salute to the American Tchr., 1992-93; liner notes writer Capitol Records/Rhino Records, L.A., 1988-90; writer/producer Salute to the Am. Songwriter, L.A., 1986-88; reporter/producer ESPN, L.A., 1980; writer TV News Sta. WSNL-TV/WPIX-TV, N.Y.C., 1973-75. Author: The Beach Boys and the California Myth, 1978, The Bee Gees, 1979; editor: Producing and Directory Live TV, 1986, The Billboard Awards, 1992-93; mng. editor: A&M Records: The 1st 25 Years, 1987; writer/producer The Unknown Marx Brothers; producer The Beach Boys: Good Vibration, 1993; contbg. editor: Capitol Records 50th Anniversary, 1992. Writer Retinitis Pigmentosa Internat., L.A., 1986-92, Anti-Defamation League, L.A. Recipient Q Mag. Recorded Music award, London, 1990. Mem. Authors Guild, Am. Soc. of Composers and Performers, Writers Guild Am. West, Rock and Roll Hall of Fame, Soc. Profl. Journalists. Home: PO Box 1404 Santa Monica CA 90403

LEAHY, J. MICHAEL, health care administrator; b. N.Y.C., Sept. 14, 1946; s. John Francis and Ann Marie (Mesloh) L.; m. Elizabeth Blanche Dickinson, July 12, 1966; 1 child, Nicole Elizabeth. BA, SUNY, Stony Brook, 1968; MBA, Harvard U., 1974, postgrad., 1979; postgrad., U. Calif., 1981, Stanford U., 1983-84, 89. Asst. adminstr. planning and devel. Children's Hosp., Oakland, Calif., 1976-77; adminstr. hosp. svcs. Children's Hosp., 1977-80; dir. healthcare Alameda County Health Care Agency, Oakland, 1980-83; area adminstr. Kaiser Permanente, Bess Kaiser Hosp., Portland, 1983-86; v.p., mgr. health plan Kaiser Permanente, Portland, 1986-90; v.p. hosps. and planning Kaiser Permanente, Oakland, 1991—; adminstrv. cons. Joint Commn. Accreditation Hosps., Chgo., 1981—; chmn. State Oreg. Health Coun., Salem, 1989-91, vice chmn., 1988, mem. coun., 1986—; adj. faculty mem. masters in health program U. Soc. Calif., Sacramento, 1987—; adj. faculty mem. U. Calif. Sch. Pub. Health, 1976-82; instr. Peralta Coll., 1976-78; lectr. numerous symposiums and confs.; bd. dirs. CAHHS; chmn. Oreg. Risk Pool, 1988-90. Contbr. various articles on hospital svcs. Bd. dirs. Portland Bus. Group on Health, 1986-91, Nat. Assn. Pub. Hosps., Washington, 1980-83. Recipient cert. of merit State Calif. Legislature, 1983; Hays fellow Harvard Bus. Sch., 1973; N.Y. State Regent's scholar N.Y. State Bd. Edn., 1964-68. Home: # 2 Brentwood Pl Oakland CA 94602 Office: Kaiser Permanente 1950 Franklin Oakland CA 94612

LEAHY, T. LIAM, management consultant; b. Camp Legeunne, N.C., Apr. 15, 1952; s. Thomas James and Margaret May (Munnelly) L.; m. Shannon Kelly Brooks, Apr. 21, 1990. BS, St. Louis U., 1974, MA, 1975; postgrad., Hubbard Coll. of Adminstrn., L.A., 1989. Producer/dir. UniMedia, L.A., 1975-78; v.p. sales Cablecom Inc., Chgo., 1978-81, Kaye Advt., N.Y.C., 1981-83; group pubr. Jour. Graphics Pub., N.Y.C., 1983-85; gen. mgr. Generation Dynamics, N.Y.C., 1985-86; pres. Leahy & Assocs., N.Y.C., 1982-86, Tarzana, Calif., 1982—; chief exec. officer Lambda Group, Inc., Glendale, Calif., 1987-91; assoc. Am Coun. of Execs. Assoc., Glendale, 1991—; bd. dirs. Consultants Assn., 1992—. Contbr. articles to profl. jours. Mem. Am. Coun. Execs. (bd. dirs. 1993—), Turnaround Mgmt. Assn., L.A. C. of C. Office: Leahy & Assocs PO Box 57220 19131 Enadia Way Tarzana CA 91357-2200

LEAKE, PHILIP GREGORY, exercise physiologist, consultant; b. L.A., Mar. 1, 1958; s. Philip Matthew and Carroll Rita (Hithe) L.; m. Barbara June Ehrhardt, July 9, 1983; 1 child, Galen Alexander. BA in Phys. Edn., Calif. State U., Northridge, 1983; MA in Phys. Edn., Calif. State U., 1988. Exercise physiologist JMP Ctr. for Sports Medicine, Van Nuys, Calif., 1983-87, Daniel Freeman Meml. Hosp. Ctr. for Heart and Health, Inglewood, Calif., 1988-90; program dir., exercise physiologist Heart Disease Prevention and Test Ctr., Sacramento, 1990—. Contbr. articles to profl. jour. Vol. coord. ann. 10K Daniel Freemen Meml. Hosp., Inglewood and Marina Del Rey, Calif., 1989. Mem. AAHPERD, CAHPERD, Am. COll. Sports Medicine (chair L.A. county clin. and health promotion sect. 1989, No. Calif. sect. 1990), Am. Diabetes Assn., Am. Heart Assn. Democrat. Baptist.

LEAKE, ROSEMARY DOBSON, physician; b. Columbus, Ohio, July 14, 1937; d. Joseph Lawrence and Rosemary Elizabeth (Brockmeyer) Dobson; m. Donald Leake, Aug. 20, 1967; children: John, Elizabeth, Catherine. BA, Ohio State U., 1959, MD, 1962. Diplomate Am. Bd. Neonatal-Perinatal Medicine. Intern, pediatrics Mass. Gen. Hosp., Boston, 1962-63, resident, pediatrics, 1963-64; rsch. fellow Maternal Infant Health Collaborative Study The Boston Lying-In Hosp., Boston, 1965-67; neonatal fellow Stanford U. Hosp., Palo Alto, Calif., 1968-69; co-dir. NIH sponsored perinatal tng. program Harbor-UCLA Med. Ctr., Torrance, 1979, program dir. NIH sponsored perinatal rsch. ctr., 1980—; prof. pediatrics UCLA Sch. of Medicine, L.A., 1982—; dir. regionalized fellowship Harbor-UCLA/King-Drew Med. Ctr., Torrance, 1986—; chair pediatrics Harbor-UCLA Med. Ctr., Torrance, 1992—; dir. perinatal crisis care program Harbor-UCLA Med. Ctr., Torrance, 1972-76, dir. neonatal ICU, 1974-81, assoc. prof. pediatrics, 1976-82, assoc. chief div. neonatology, 1976-77. Named UCLA Woman of Sci., 1985, Outstanding Woman Acadmician of Yr. Nat. Bd. Award of the Med. Coll. of Pa., 1989; recipient Alumni Achievement award Ohio State U. Sch. Medicine, 1987. Mem. Am. Pediatric Soc., Soc. for Pediatric Rsch. Home: 2 Crest Rd West Rolling Hills CA 90274 Office: Harbon-UCLA Med Ctr 1000 W Carson St Torrance CA 90509

LEAL, JOHN ERWIN, computer imaging administrator; b. Tachakowa, Japan, Feb. 19, 1957; came to U.S., 1957; s. Ben and Iva Jean (Stoneman) L.; m. Susan Maria Stello, May 26, 1990. AS in Radiologic Tech., Pasadena City Coll., 1979; BS in Bus. Adminstrn., Calif. Poly., 1989. Radiologic tech. St. Joseph Hosp., Orange, Calif., 1979-92; supr. computer imaging Physician Care, Ltd., Brea, Calif., 1988-92; adminstrv. dir. Advanced Healthcare, Brea, 1991-93; ultrafast computer imaging specialist Physician Care Ltd., Brea, Calif., 1993—; Ultrafast C.T. specialist Pura Labs, Brea, 1990-92; cons. Heart Vision, San Francisco, 1992. Mem. Calif. Poly. Alumni Assn., Eta Sigma Delta. Office: Physicians Healthcare 603 S Valencia Crest Park CA 92326

LEALE, OLIVIA MASON, import marketing company executive; b. Boston, May 5, 1944; d. William Mason and Jane Chapin (Prouty) Smith; m. Euan Harvie-Watt, Mar. ll, 1967 (div. Aug. 1979); children: Katrina, Jennifer; m. Douglas Marshall Leale, Aug. 29, 1980. BA, Vassar Coll., 1966. Sec. to dir. Met. Opera Guild, N.Y.C., 1966; sec. to pres. Friesons Printers, London, 1974-75; guide, trainer Autoguide, London, 1977-79; ptnr. Inmark Internat. Mktg. Inc., Seattle, 1980—. Social case worker Inner London Ednl. Authority, 1975-76. Democrat. Presbyterian. Home and Office: 5427 NE Penrith Rd Seattle WA 98105-2842

LEAMAN, JACK ERVIN, landscape architect, community/regional planner; b. Mason City, Iowa, Jan. 24, 1932; s. Theodore R. and Dorothy M. (Schrum) L.; m. Darlene A. McNary, June 15, 1952; children: Jeffrey A., Danna J., Jay M., Duree K. B.S. in Landscape Architecture and Urban Planning, Iowa State U., 1954, M. Community and Regional Planning, 1982. Registered landscape architect, Calif., Iowa, Minn., N.Mex. Landscape architect Sam L. Huddleston Office, Denver, 1954-55, Phillips Petroleum Co., Bartlesville, Okla., 1955-58; landscape architect for Price Tower and residence with architect Frank Lloyd Wright Bartlesville, Okla., 1957-58; planning technician Santa Barbara County, Calif., 1958-60; planning cons. Engring. Planners, Santa Barbara, 1960-63; planning dir. City of Santa Barbara, 1963-66, City of Mason City, 1966-72; landscape architect, planning cons. Midwest Research Inst., Kansas City, Mo., 1972-74, Hansen, Lind, Meyer, Iowa City, Iowa, 1974-76, Sheffler, Leaman, Rova, Mason City, 1976-78, RCM Assocs., Inc., Hopkins, Minn. and Ames, Iowa, 1978-82; planning dir. City-County Planning, Albuquerque, 1982-86, City of Colorado Springs, Colo., 1986-90; landscape architect, pvt. practice planning cons. Mason City, Iowa, 1990-92; assoc. ptnr., landscape architect, community/regional planner Yaggy Colby Assocs., Mason City, 1992—. Recipient Residential Landscape Design award Calif. Landscape Contractors Assn., 1962, Design Achievement award Coll. of Design Iowa State U., 1988. Fellow Am. Soc. Landscape Architects (chpt. pres. 1967-68, 90-91, trustee Iowa 1980-82, N.Mex. 1982-86, Award of Excellence 1954); mem. Am. Inst. Cert. Planners, Am. Planning Assn. (chpt. pres. Iowa 1969-70), Urban Land Inst., Tau Sigma Delta.

LEAMING, MARJ P(ATRICIA), management and marketing consultant, researcher; b. Denver; d. Taylor J. Sr. and Augie R. Leaming. BA, U. Colo., 1969, MBA, 1970; PhD, Colo. State U., 1979. Cert. cons., trainer. Asst. supr. State Approving Agy. Vets. Edn., Denver, 1973-82; asst. assoc. dir. State Bd. Community Colls. and Occupational Edn., Denver, 1982-85; mgmt. cons. divsn. mgmt. services Colo. Dept. Adminstrn., 1985-86; pres. Edventure Systems, Lakewood, Colo., 1986—; bd. dirs. Colo. Retail Coun., Denver, 1982-85; dir. mgmt. devel. Mng. for Success, Denver, 1985-86; asst. grad. prof. MBA program Regis Coll., Denver, 1982; vis. asst. prof. Bus. Leadership Inst. U. Alaska, Fairbanks, 1986; pres. Nat. Entrepreneurship Consortium, 1984-85; commr. Colo. Productivity-Study Team, 1988-89; sr. assoc. dir. Affiliated Cons. Colo., 1993. Author: (coll. textbook) Administrative Office Management, 1970, (coll. casebook) Administrative Management Cases, 1970, (handbook) Entrepreneurship, 1988; author, editor: Entrepreneurship Models, 1985, Economic Value of Entrepreneurship, 1985; contbr. articles to nat. jours. Active fin. devel. ARC, Jefferson County, 1988, Mile High, 1988; mem. Denver Art Mus., 1983-88; mem. adv. com. Jefferson County Pub. Schs., 1986-88, Jefferson County Small Bus. Ctr.; mem. Gov. apptd. Commn. on Privatization, 1988—. NSF grantee, Denver, 1972. Mem. SBA (bd. dirs. region VIII, 1987-88) Women Bus. Owners Assn., Exec. Women Internat. (nat. del., 1986), U.S. Assn. for Small Bus., Am. Entrepreneurs Assn., Phi Kappa Phi. Office: Edventure Systems PO Box 15767 Lakewood CO 80215-0767

LEAR, NORMAN MILTON, writer, producer, director; b. New Haven, July 27, 1922; s. Herman and Jeanette (Seicol) L.; children: Ellen Lear Reiss, Kate B. Lear LaPook, Maggie B.; m. Lyn Davis; 1 child, Benjamin Davis. Student, Emerson Coll., 1940-42, HHD, 1968. Engaged in pub. relations, 1945-49; founder Act III Comms., 1987—. Comedy writer for TV, 1950-54; writer, dir. for TV and films, 1954-59; producer: films Come Blow Your Horn, 1963, Never Too Late, 1965; prodr., screenwriter: Divorce American Style, 1967, The Night They Raided Minsky's, 1968; writer, producer, dir.: film Cold Turkey, 1971; exec. prodr. film Start the Revolution Without Me, The Princess Bride, Breaking In, Fried Green Tomatoes; creator, dir.: TV shows TV Guide Awards Show, 1962, Henry Fonda and the Family, 1963, Andy Williams Spl., also, Andy Williams Series, 1965, Robert Young and the Family, 1970; exec. prodr., creator-developer: TV shows All in the Family, 1971 (4 Emmy awards 1970-73, Peabody award 1977), Maude, 1972; Sanford and Son, 1972, Good Times, 1974, The Jeffersons, 1975, Hot L Baltimore, 1975, Mary Hartman, Mary Hartman, 1976, One Day At a Time, 1975, All's Fair, 1976, A Year at the Top, 1977, All That Glitters, 1977, Fernwood 2 Night, 1977, The Baxters, 1979, Palmerstown, 1980, I Love Liberty, 1982, Sunday Dinner, 1991, The Powers That Be, 1992; creator a.k.a. Pablo, 1984; exec. producer Heartsounds, 1984. Pres. Am. Civil Liberties Found. So. Calif., 1973—; trustee Mus. Broadcasting; bd. dirs. People for the American Way; founder Bus. Enterprise Trust. Served with USAAF, 1942-45. Decorated Air medal with 4 oak leaf clusters; named One of Top Ten Motion Picture Producers, Motion Picture Exhibitors, 1963, 67, 68, Showman of Yr., Publicists Guild, 1971-77, Assn. Bus. Mgrs., 1972, Broadcaster of Yr., Internat. Radio and TV Soc., 1973; Man of Yr. Hollywood chpt. Nat. Acad. Television Arts and Scis., 1973; recipient Humanitarian award NCCJ, 1976, Mark Twain award Internat. Platform Assn., 1977, William O. Douglas award Pub. Counsel, 1981, 1st Amendment Lectr. Ford Hall Forum, 1981, Gold medal Internat. Radio and TV Soc., 1981. Disting. Am. award, 1984, Mass Media award Am. Jewish Com. Inst. of Human Relations, 1986, Internat. award of Yr., Nat. Assn. TV Program Execs., 1987; inducted into TV Acad. Hall of Fame, 1984. Mem. Writers Guild Am. (Valentine Davies award 1977), Dirs. Guild Am., AFTRA, Caucus Producers, Writers, and Dirs. Office: Act III Communications #500 1999 Ave of the Stars Los Angeles CA 90067

LEASE, JANE ETTA, librarian; b. Kansas City, Kans., Apr. 10, 1924; d. Joy Alva and Emma (Jaggard) Omer; B.S. in Home Econs., U. Ariz., 1957; M.S. in Edn., Ind. U., 1962; M.S. in L.S., U. Denver, 1967; m. Richard J. Lease, Jan. 16, 1960; children—Janet (Mrs. Jacky B. Radifera), Joyce (Mrs. Robert J. Carson), Julia (Mrs. Earle D. Marvin), Cathy (Mrs. Edward F. Warren); stepchildren—Richard Jay II, William Harley. Newspaper reporter Ariz. Daily Star, Tucson, 1937-39; asst. home agt. Dept. Agr., 1957; homemaking tchr., Ft. Huachuca, Ariz., 1957-60; head tchr. Stonebelt Council Retarded Children, Bloomington, Ind., 1960-61; reference clk. Ariz. State U. Library, 1964-66; edn. and psychology librarian N.Mex. State U., 1967-71; Amway distbr., 1973—; cons. solid wastes, distressed land problems reference remedies, 1967; ecology lit. research and cons., 1966—. Ind. observer 1st World Conf. Human Environment, 1972; mem. Las Cruces Community Devel. Priorities Adv. Bd. Mem. ALA, Regional Environ. Edn. Research Info. Orgn., NAFE, P.E.O., D.A.R., Internat. Platform Assn., Las Cruces Antique Car Club, Las Cruces Story League, N.Mex. Library Assn. Methodist (lay leader). Address: 2145 Boise Dr Las Cruces NM 88001

LEASE, RICHARD JAY, former police officer, educator, consultant; b. Cherokee, Ohio, Dec. 10, 1914; s. Harold and Mabelle (Fullerton) L.; m. Marjorie Faye Stoughton, Sept. 2, 1939 (div. Apr. 1957); children: Richard Jay II, William Harley; m. Jane Etta Omer, Jan. 16, 1960; stepchildren: Janet Radifera, Joyce Carson, Julia Marvin, Catherine Warren. Student, Wittenberg U., 1932-33; BA, U. Ariz., 1937, MA, 1961; postgrad., Ind. U., 1950, 60, Ariz. State U., 1956, 63-65, 67—; grad., U. Louisville So. Police Inst., 1955. Grad. asst . U. Ariz., Tucson, 1937-38; with Tucson Police Dept., from 1938; advanced from patrolman to sgt., also served as safety officer Pima County Sheriff's Dept., Tucson, 1953, patrol supr., 1953-55, investigator, 1955-56; tchr. sci. pub. schs. Tucson, 1957-59; lectr. dept. police adminstrn. Ind. U., Bloomington, 1960-65; asst. prof. dept. police sci. N.Mex. State U., Las Cruces, 1965—; cons. law enforcement problems HEW, 1960, Indpls. Police Dept., 1962, Harrisburg Community Coll. Police Sci. Dept., 1967, Phoenix Police Dept., 1968—; advisor police tng. programs several small city police depts., Ind., 1960-63, Indpls., 1962; mem. oral bd. for selection chief in Bateville, Ind., 1962, oral bd. for selection sgts. and lts., Las Cruces Police Dept., 1966—. Author: (with Robert F. Borkenstein) Alcohol and Road Traffic: Problems of Enforcement and Prosecution, 1963, The Dreams, Hopes, Recollections and Thoughts of a Professional Good Samaritan; cons. editor Police, various rsch. publs. on chem. intoxification tests, psychol. errors of witnesses, reading disabilities, delinquency. Participant numerous FBI seminars; active youth work, philanthropy, among Am. Indians in Southwest; founder awards outstanding ROTC cadets N.Mex. State U., 1967—; founder Wiltberger ann. awards Nat. Police Combat Pistol Matches; scoutmaster Yucca council Boy Scouts Am., 1966—. Served to 1st lt. USMCR, 1942-45, PTO. Fellow Am. Acad. Forensic Scis. (sec. gen. sect.); mem. Internat. Assn. Chiefs of Police, Internat. Assn. Police Profs., Brit. Acad. Forensic Scis., Can. Soc. Forensic Sci., Am. Soc. Criminology, Ret. Officers Assn., Assn. U.S. Army (2d v.p. 1969—), NEA, N.Mex. Edn. Assn., N.Mex. Police and Sheriffs Assn., Internat. Crossroads, NRA (benefactor mem.), Marine Corps League (life), Sigma Chi. Lodges: Masons, Elks. Home and Office: 2145 Boise Dr Las Cruces NM 88001-5149

LEAVITT, LOIS HUTCHEON, consumer and homemaker educator; b. Whiterocks, Utah, Nov. 6, 1920; d. Arthur James and Ada E. (Peterson) Hutcheon; m. Jack William Leavitt, June 19, 1943; children—VaLoy, Joyce, LaJean. B.S., Brigham Young U., 1943, postgrad. 1955-83. Cert. vocat. home econs., secondary edn. tchr. Utah. Tchr. consumer and homemaking edn. Spanish Fork (Utah) High Sch., 1943-45, Roosevelt (Utah) High Sch., 1945-47, Union High Sch., Roosevelt, 1954-83; chpt. advisor Future Homemakers Am. Named Outstanding Utah Home Econs. Tchr., Utah Cowbells of Utah Cattlemen's Assn.; Adviser of Yr., Utah chpt. Future Homemakers Am. 1983. Mem. Am. Home Econs. Assn., Utah Home Econs. Assn. (Home Econs. Tchr. of Yr. 1982), Nat. Assn. Vocat. Home Econs. Tchrs. Vocat. Assn., Utah Assn. Vocat. Home Econs. Tchrs. Vocat. Assn., Am. Vocat. Assn., Utah Vocat. Assn., Bus. and Profl. Women (pres., sec.). Mem. LDS Ch. Home: PO Box 235 Neola UT 84053-0235 Office: Union High Sch PO Box 400 Roosevelt UT 84066-0400

LEAVITT, MICHAEL OKERLUND, governor, insurance executive; b. Cedar City, Utah, Feb. 11, 1951; s. Dixie and Anne (Okerlund) L.; m. Jacalyn Smith; children: Michael Smith, Taylor Smith, Anne Marie Smith, Chase Smith, Weston Smith. BA, So. Utah U., 1978. CPCU. Sales rep. Leavitt Group, Cedar City, 1972-74, account exec., 1974-76; mgr. underwriting Salt Lake City, 1976-82; chief operating officer, 1982-84, pres., chief exec. officer, 1984—, gov., state of Utah, 1993—; bd. dirs. Pacificorp, Portland, Oreg., Utah Power and Light Co., Salt Lake City, Great Western Thrift and Loan, Salt Lake City. Utah Bd. Regents, chmn. instl. coun. So. Utah State U., Cedar City, 1985-89; campaign chmn. U.S. Sen. Orrin Hatch, 1982, 88, U.S. Sen. Jake Garn, 1980, 86; cons. campaign Gov. Norman Angerter, 1984; mem. staff Reagan-Bush '84. 2d lt. USNG, 1969-77. Named Disting. Alumni So. Utah State Coll. Sch. Bus., 1986. Mem. Chartered Property Casualty Underwriters. Republican. Mormon. Office: Office of the Governor 210 State Capitol Salt Lake City UT 84114

LEAVY, EDWARD, judge; m. Eileen Leavy; children: Thomas, Patrick, Mary Kay, Paul. AB, U. Portland, 1950, LLB, U. Notre Dame, 1953. Dist. judge Lane County, Eugene, Oreg., 1957-61, cir. judge, 1961-76; magistrate U.S. Dist. Ct. Oreg., Portland, 1976-84, judge, 1984-87, cir. judge U.S. Ct. Appeals (9th cir.), 1987—. Office: US Ct Appeals Pioneer Courthouse 555 SW Yamhill St Rm 216 Portland OR 97204-1494

LEBARON, MELVIN JAY, consulting company executive; b. Barnwell, Alberta, Can., Nov. 14, 1930; s. Hower Neal and Luella (Wight) LeB.; m. Joan M. Mackay, July 16, 1953; children: Wendy Davison, Janeal, Brad, Graydon. BS, Brigham Young U., 1958; MSPA, U. So. Calif., L.A., 1961, EdD, 1970. Prof., adminstr. U. So. Calif. Sch. Pub. Adminstrn., L.A., 1959-77; pres. Humanistic Consulting, Inc., Brea, Calif., 1977—; part time faculty various colls. and univs., 1970-80; chief of party U.S. State Dept., S.E. Asia, 1971-72. Contbr. articles to profl. jours. Mayor, councilman City of Brea, 1978-82. Recipient Adminstrv. medal Govt. So. Vietnam, Saigon, 1972. Mem. LDS Ch. Office: Humanistic Consulting Inc PO Box 9361 Brea CA 92622

LEBARRON, SUZANNE JANE, librarian; b. Tyndall, S.D., May 29, 1945; d. Ford and Eunice (Venne) LeB. BA, Coll. of Great Falls, 1967; MA, U. Minn., 1972. Prin. libr. asst. Stanford (Calif.) U., 1967-68; reference asst. Great Falls (Mont.) Pub. Libr., 1968-70; pre-profl. Mpls. Pub. Libr., 1970-72, community libr. Sumner Community Libr., 1972-74, libr., 1974-78; NEH project dir. Minn. Office Libr. Devel. and Svc., Mpls., 1978-79; assoc. libr. N.Y. State Libr., Albany, 1979-81; div. dir. Ky. Dept. for Librs. and Archives, Frankfort, 1981-86; dep. state libr. Conn. State Libr., Hartford, 1986-89; state libr. Wyo. State Libr., Cheyenne, 1990—; Author: Humanities in Minnesota, 1979; co-author: Serials for Libraries, 1979, Networking in Kentucky, 1981; editor: Directory of Humanities Research People in New York, 1980. Mem. ALA (councilor 1978-80, 84-88, 89—, chair com. on orgn. 1990-92), Wyo. Libr. Assn. Office: Wyo State Libr 2301 Capitol Ave Cheyenne WY 82002

LEBEAU, CHARLES RAY, finance company executive, writer; b. Oklahoma City, Sept. 6, 1938; s. Robert Eugene and Louise Juanita (McCombs) LeB.; m. Patricia Jo Dillard, Jan. 20, 1963; children: Suzanne, Robert. BA in Fin., Calif. State U., Long Beach, 1963. V.p. E.F. Hutton & Co., L.A., 1967-88, Paine Webber Inc., Rolling Hills Estate, Calif., 1988-89; pres. Island View Fin. Group, Inc., Torrance, Calif., 1989—. Co-author: Computer Analysis of the Futures Market, 1992; editor, pub. Tech. Traders Bull., 1989-93. Capt. U.S. Army, 1963-67. Mem. Nat. Futures Assn. (mem. bus. conduct com. 1983—, waiver rev. bd. 1986—), Managed Futures Assn., Bond Club L.A. Office: Island View Fin Group Inc 25550 Hawthorne Blvd # 100 Torrance CA 90505

LEBEAU, CHRISTOPHER JOHN, mechanical engineer, scientist, researcher; b. Phoenix, May 12, 1959; s. Edward Charles and Carolyn Marie (Sanromá) LeB.; m. Jeanne Marie Moriarty, June 15, 1985; children: Christopher John Jr., James Alexander, Mary Elaine, Elizabeth Ann. BSME, U. So. Calif., 1982; MS in Engring., Ariz. State U., 1987. Project engr. Motorola Inc., Phoenix, 1983-86, sr. engr., 1986-88, sr. staff scientist, 1988-91, prin. staff engr., 1991—, worldwide expert, cons., 1983—; presenter ASME Engring. Design Conf., 1992, SEMICON West Machine Vision Conf., 1992. Contbr. articles to profl. jours.; patentee machine vision field. Mem. Soc. Photo-Optical Instrumentation Engrs. (presenter 1990), Soc. Mfg. Engrs., Inst. Indsl. Engrs. (presenter 1990). Home: 136 E Secretariat Dr Tempe AZ 85284 Office: Motorola Inc SPS 2100 E Elliot Rd Tempe AZ 85284-1801

LE BERTHON, ADAM, lawyer; b. L.A., June 12, 1962; s. Edward Lynch and Veronica Rose (Franks) Le B. BA cum laude, U. San Diego, 1985; JD, U. So. Calif., L.A., 1989. Bar: Calif. 1989, U.S. Dist. Ct. (ctrl. dist.) Calif. 1989, U.S. Ct. Appeals (9th cir.) 1989, U.S. Dist. Ct. (so. dist.) Calif. 1990, (no. dist.) Calif. 1990, (ea. dist.) Calif. 1990. Assoc. White & Case, L.A., 1989-91, Straw & Gilmartin, Santa Monica, Calif., 1991—. Editor So. Calif. Law Rev., 1988-89. Recipient Am. Jurisprudence award U. So. Calif., 1987. Mem. ABA, Calif. State Bar Assn., L.A. County Bar Assn., Order of the Coif, Phi Alpha Delta, Omicron Delta Epsilon, Kappa Gamma Pi. Home: 125 Montana Ave #207 Santa Monica CA 90403 Office: Straw & Gilmartin 100 Wilshire Blvd #1325 Santa Monica CA 90401

LEBLON, JEAN MARCEL, retired French language educator, consultant; b. Chimay, Hainaut, Belgium, June 7, 1928; came to U.S., 1947; s. Alfred and Marcelle (Lefèvre) L.; m. Mary Lorraine Hovorka, June 3, 1952; children: Mitzi, Simone. BS in Edn., Emporia State U., 1951; PhD, Yale U., 1960. Instr. Conn. Coll., New London, 1953-59, CCNY, 1959-62; assoc. prof. Hollins (Va.) Coll., 1962-65; prof. French Vanderbilt U., Nashville, 1966-87; teaching assoc. U. Wash., Seattle, 1988-90; vis. prof. U. Maine, Orono, 1962, Emporia (Kans.) State U., 1965, Fairfield (Conn.) U., 1966; cons. Ednl. Testing Svc., Princeton, N.J., 1963-87, Oxford U. Press, London, 1985-86, Champs-Elysees, Inc., Nashville, 1985—, Wash. Acad. Lang., Seattle, 1987—. Co-author: Précis de Civilisation Française, 1966; translator: Zola (Marc Bernard), 1960; editor, terminologist: Les Choses (Georges Perec), 1969; editor Microsoft Corp., 1990—. Mem. MLA (regional del. 1974-76), Am. Assn. Tchrs. French, N.W. Translators & Interpreters Soc. (pres. 1991-93), Am. Translators Assn., Seattle-Nantes Sister City Assn. (bd. dirs. 1990—), Alliance Française (bd. dirs. 1990—). Home: 1130 5th Ave S Apt 104 Edmonds WA 98020-4666

LEBLOND, CHRISTY BENTON, geneticist; b. Seattle, May 8, 1948; d. R. Clarke and Marjorie (Thomas) Benton; children: Jane, Ellen. BA in Sociology, Whitman Coll., 1970; MS in Genetic Counseling, U. Calif., Berkeley, 1980. Diplomate Am. Bd. Med. Genetics. Genetic counselor March of Dimes, Anchorage, 1981-83, Alaska Genetics Clinic, Anchorage, 1983-90, State of Alaska, Anchorage, 1990—; bd. dirs. March of Dimes, Anchorage, 1983; cons. Muscular Dystrophy Assn., Anchorage, 1983-88; Alaska rep. Pacific N.W. Regional Genetics Group, Portland, Oreg., 1987-92. Active VISTA, Bethel, Alaska, 1971-72; vol. March of Dimes, Anchorage, 1983-90. Mem. Am. Soc. Human Genetics, Nat. Soc. Genetic Counselors, Circumpolar Health. Office: State of Alaska Alaska Genetics Clinic 1231 Gambell St Anchorage AK 99501

LEBRA, TAKIE SUGIYAMA, anthropology educator; b. Shizuoka, Japan, Feb. 6, 1930; came to U.S., 1958; m. William P. Lebra (dec. Jan. 1986). BA, Gakushuin U., Tokyo, 1954; MA, U. Pitts., 1960, PhD, 1967. Lectr. U. Hawaii, Honolulu, 1968-71, assoc. prof., 1971-78, prof., 1978—. Author: Japanese Patterns of Behavior, 1976, Japanese Women: Constraint & Fulfillment, 1984, Above the Clouds: Status Culture of the Modern Japanese Nobility, 1993; author, editor Japanese Social Organizaiton, 1992; contbr. numerous articles to profl. jours. NSF grantee, 1976-78, Japan Soc. for Promotion of Sci. grantee, 1978-79, Social Sci. Rsch. Coun. grantee, 1982, 88-89, Japan Found. grantee, 1984-85, Wenner-Gren Found. for Anthropol. Rsch. grantee, 1989, Fulbright grantee, 1993. Office: U Hawaii Dept Anthropology 2424 Maile Way Honolulu HI 96822-2281

LE CLAIR, DOUGLAS MARVIN, lawyer; b. Montreal, Nov. 13, 1955; s. Lawrence M. and Joan B. Le Clair; m. Debra L. Garland, Oct. 12, 1985. BA, Loyola U., 1977; JD, Southwestern U., 1980; peace officer cert., Mesa Community Coll. Law Enforcement Acad., 1985. Bar: Ariz. 1982, U.S. Dist. Ct. Ariz. 1983, U.S. Ct. Appeals (9th cir.) 1983, U.S. Tax. Ct. 1987, U.S. Ct. Claims 1987, U.S. Supreme Ct. 1987. Corp. counsel Great Western Trading Co., Los Angeles, 1982-83; pvt. practice Mesa, Ariz., 1983—; mem. faculty law & acctg. Sterling Sch., Phoenix, Ariz., 1992—; chief exec. officer, gen. counsel DL Industries, Inc., Mesa, 1983—; corp. counsel various corps., Ariz. Author: Le Clair/Morgan Income Tax Organizer, 1982-83; prodn. editor Computer Law Jour., 1979-80; producer TV Advt., 1983. Res. officer Mesa Police Dept., 1984-92. Named One of Outstanding Young Men Of Am., 1979. Mem. ABA, Ariz. Bar Assn., Maricopa County Bar Assn., Internat. Platform Assn., Southwestern Student Bar Assn. (exec. bd. 1978-79), Southwestern U. Tax Law Soc., Mesa C. of C., Delta Theta Phi, Phi Alpha Theta. Home and Office: PO Box 223 Mesa AZ 85211-0223

LECOMPTE, EDWARD HANK, JR., software specialist, preacher; b. Warren, Ohio, Aug. 12, 1958; s. Edward Hank LeCompte and Dorothy Ann (Imlay) LeC.; m. Rothel Adkisson, Oct. 28, 1988; children: Edward III, Seth, Joshua. Grad. high sch., Shelbyville, Ky.; student, Pacific Luth. U. Field svc. tech. Data Copy Supply, Colorado Springs, Colo., 1981-83; assembly line tech. Digital, Colorado Springs, 1983-86, cast response rep., 1987-89, sofware specialist, 1989-92; vax systems mgr. Pacific Luth. U., 1992. With U.S. Army, 1977-81, Korea, Germany. Mem. So. Baptist Ch. Home: 1204 Nez Perce Dr Colorado Springs CO 80915-3221 Office: Digital 305 S Rockrimmon Blvd Colorado Springs CO 80919-2303

LECRON, MARY FRAZER See FOSTER, MARY FRAZER

LEDBETTER, BRENDA LAVERNE, women's health nurse; b. Jeffersonville, Ind., Dec. 28, 1947; d. Governor Hunt and Mary Ruth (Cockerell) Tipton; m. Charles Jackson Ledbetter, Oct., 17, 1967; 1 child, Keith Avery. AA, LA Southwest Coll., 1973; BSN, Calif. State U., L.A., 1981; MA, Calif. State U., 1986. RN, Calif. Staff nurse UCLA Hosp., L.A., 1974-77, asst. head nurse, 1977-79, 82-84, acting head nurse, 1981; with Kaiser Permanente Med. Ctr., L.A., 1982, head nurse, 1982-84, discharge planner, 1984-85, asst. dept. adminstr. home health agy., 1985-88; dept. adminstr. respiratory and orthopaedics units Kaiser Permanente Med. Ctr., Fontana, Calif., 1988, asst. clin. supr., 1988-89; staff nurse nephrology/oncology unit Kaiser Permanente Med. Ctr., Fontana, 1989-90, coord., planner labor and delivery course, 1990—. Named Surgical Nurse of the Quarter, UCLA Hosps. and Clinics, 1981. Mem. NAACOG, Nat. League Nursing, L.A. Southwest Nurses Alumni Assn., Coun. of Black Nurses. Home: 10818 Teakwood Cir Moreno Valley CA 92557-3932

LEDBETTER, CARL SCOTIUS, counselor, educator; b. Pyatt, Ark., Aug. 19, 1910; s. James Oliver and Lillie Belle (Wall) L.; student Phillips U., Enid, Okla., 1930-32; A.B., Ky. Christian Coll., 1937; A.B., Butler U., 1939, M.A., 1940; M.A., U. Redlands, 1967; postgrad. Claremont Grad. Sch., 1961-64, Mankato (Minn.) State Coll., 1970-73, Calif. State Coll., 1974-76; m. Ruth Slocum Weymouth, June 20, 1948; children—Carla Sue Ledbetter Holte, Carl Scotius, Charles Stephen, Craig Slocum, Candace Sybil Ledbetter Heidelberger, Christa Sharyn Ledbetter. Ordained to ministry Christian Ch., 1933; student pastor, Huntington, W.Va., 1935-36, Russell, Ky., 1936-39, Atlanta, Ind., 1939-40; mem. editorial staff Standard Pub. Co., Cin., 1940-41; commd. 1st lt. U.S. Army, 1941; advanced through grades to col., 1961; command chaplain Augsburg (W. Ger.) area, 1950-53; div. chaplain 3d Inf. Div., 1953-55; dep. army chaplain 6th U.S. Army, 1955-58; command chaplain 5th Region Army Air Def. Command, 1959-61; ret., 1961; dean men U. Redlands, 1961-69; dir. counseling, v.p. acad. affairs Lea (Minn.) Coll., 1969-74; rehab. counselor J.O.B. Work Activities Ctr., Hesperia, Calif., 1976-80, dir., 1980-85, dir. emeritus, 1985—; adj. prof. psychology and religion Chapman Coll., 1976-85. Recipient award of merit Boy Scouts Am., 1967, Silver Beaver award, 1969. Mem. Am. Personnel and Guidance Assn., Nat. Vocat. Guidance Assn., Am. Rehab. Counselors Assn., Alpha Phi Gamma, Phi Delta Kappa, Pi Ch, Pi Gamma Mu, Alpha Phi Omega. Democrat. Club: Masons. Home: 611 Juniper Ct Redlands CA 92374-6236

LEDERER, C. MICHAEL, energy researcher, university administrator; b. Chgo., June 6, 1938; s. Philip C. Lederer and Jane (Bernheimer) Newburger; m. Claudette Gloria Evenson, Feb. 26, 1970; children: Laura Jane, Mark Edward. AB in Chemistry, Harvard U., 1960; PhD in Nuclear Chemistry, U. Calif., Berkeley, 1964. Head isotopes project and sr. staff scientist Lawrence Berkeley Lab., 1964-78, dir. info. and data analysis dept., 1978-80; dep. dir. U. Calif. Energy Inst., Berkeley, 1980—; mem. U.S. Nat. Nuclear Data com., Washington, 1970's. Author/editor: Table of Isotopes, 6th edit., 1967, 7th edit. 1978; contbr. over 35 articles to profl. jours. Chmn. bd. Windrush Sch., El Cerrito, Calif., 1990-92. Mem. AAAS, Am. Phys. Soc., Am. Nuclear Soc., Sigma Xi. Home: 3040 Buena Vista Way Berkeley CA 94708-2020 Office: U Calif Calif Energy Inst 2539 Channing Way Berkeley CA 94720

LEDERER, MARION IRVINE, cultural administrator; b. Brampton, Ont., Can., Feb. 10, 1920; d. Oliver Bateman and Eva Jane (MacMurdo) L.; m. Francis Lederer, July 10, 1941. Student, U. Toronto, 1938, UCLA, 1942-45. Owner Canoga Mission Gallery, Canoga Park, Calif., 1967—; cultural heritage monument Canoga Mission Gallery, 1974—; Vice pres. Screen Smart Set women's aux. Motion Picture and TV Fund, 1973—; founder sister city program Canoga Park-Taxco, Mexico, 1963; Mem. mayor's cultural task force San Fernando Valley, 1973—; mem. Los Angeles Cultural Affairs Commn., 1980-85. Mem. Los Angeles Cultural Affairs Commn., 1980-85. Recipient numerous pub. service awards from mayor, city council, C. of C. Mem. Canoga Park C. of C. (cultural chmn. 1973-75, dir. 1973-75). Presbyn. Home: PO Box 32 Canoga Park CA 91305-0032 Office: Canoga Mission Gallery 23130 Sherman Way Canoga Park CA 91307-1402

LEDFORD, GARY ALAN, real estate developer; b. San Diego, Dec. 30, 1946; s. Loren Oscar and Madge Francis (Condon) L.; m. Linda Halbert Barker, Jan. 7, 1979; children: Kelly, Jeanne, Robert, Kevin. BSCE, U.S. Army Engring. Coll., 1967. Pres. Mastercraft Contractors, Colo. Springs, 1969-73; v.p. K.L. Redfern, Inc., Orange, Calif., 1973-75; pres. Watt Jess Ranch, Inc., Apple Valley, Calif., 1975—; chmn. Watt-Jess/Ledford, Apple Valley; pres. LJ&J Investments, Inc., Apple Valley, Ledford-Schaffer/Rogers, Apple Valley. Designer computer software, 1979. Past pres. Cultural Arts Found., 1991-92, Victorville, Calif; bd. trustees Apple Valley Christian Care Ctr., High Desert Questors, Victorville; pres. Victor Valley Mus., Baldy View B.I.A. Capt. C.E., U.S. Army, 1967-69, Vietnam. Mem. Internat. Coun. Shopping Ctrs., Nat. Assn. Home Builders', Nat. Planning Assn., NRA (life), High Desert Constrn. Indsutry Assn., Bldg. Industry Assn., VFW, Sr. Housing Coun. Republican. Home: 11401 Apple Valley Rd Apple Valley CA 92308 Office: Watt-Jess/Ledford 11000 Apple Valley Rd Apple Valley CA 92308-7505

LEDIN, JAMES ALAN, aerospace engineer; b. Clinton, Iowa, July 29, 1961; s. John Ronald and Rosemary Theresa (Dunlavey) L.; m. Lynda Schmidt, Oct. 12, 1991. BS in Aerospace Engring., Iowa State U., 1983. Aerospace/electronics engr. Naval Air Warfare Ctr., Pt. Mugu, Calif., 1983—. Nat. Merit scholar, 1979. Mem. MENSA, Applied Dynamics Internat. User's Soc. (bd. dirs. Ann Arbor, Mich. 1990-92, software libr. 1988—). Office: Naval Air Warfare Ctr Weapons Div Code PO3931 Point Mugu Nas CA 93042-5000

LEE, ALDORA G., social psychologist; b. Schenectady, N.Y.; d. Alois W. and M. Dorothy (Swigert) Graf. AB, Ind. U.; MA, Stanford U.; PhD, U. Colo. Dir. women studies Wash. State U., Pullman, 1976-78, dir. unit on aging, 1976-81; cons. in market research Syva, Palo Alto, Calif., 1982; staff market rsch. analyst Allstate Rsch. and Planning Ctr., Menlo Park, Calif., 1983—; rep. Wash. Assn. Gerontol. Edn., N.W. region rep. Nat. Women's Studies Assn., 1978-81. Contbr. articles to profl. jours. Mem. Menlo Park Libr. Commn., 1984-92, chmn., 1985-87; instr. Career Action Ctr., Palo Alto, 1984-87; Menlo Park rep. system adv. bd. Peninsula Libr. System, 1992—. Mem. Am. Mktg. Assn., Am. Psychol. Soc., Am. Sociol. Assn., Western Psychol. Assn., SRI Organon, Toastmasters (Toastmaster of Yr. 1989, Able Toastmaster, Competent Toastmaster), Phi Beta Kappa, Sigma Xi.

LEE, ANDREW GONG, database director; b. Hanford, Calif., Sept. 28, 1965; s. Fred and Doris (Loo) L. BSME, U. Calif., Berkeley, 1987; MBA, U. Calif., Irvine, 1991. Stock clk. Super-Way, Hanford, Calif., 1979-83, mng. aide, summer 1984, ordering asst., summer 1985, asst. acct., summer 1986, database dir., 1991—; engring. assoc. Collagen/Celtrix, Palo Alto, Calif., 1987-89; mktg. cons. Orange County Bus. Jour., Newport Beach, Calif., fall 1990; publicity dir. Asian Bus. League of Silicon Valley, Berkeley, 1986-87. Hon. scholarship U. Calif., 1983, Fah Yuen scholarship Fah Yuen Assn., 1983, Elem. scholarship Hanford Elem. Tchrs., 1983.

LEE, ARTHUR CARSON, geology educator; b. Newark, Dec. 20, 1962; s. Ying-Kao and Theresa (Tai) L.; m. Jenny Li, Apr. 14, 1988; children: William, Christine. BS, Pa. State U., 1985; MA, Temple U., 1990; postgrad., U. So. Calif., L.A., 1990—. Chem. technician Occidental Petroleum, Burlington, N.J., 1988; teaching asst. Temple U., Phila., 1988-90; teaching asst. U. So. Calif., L.A., 1990—, rsch. asst., 1990—. Contbr. articles to profl. jours. Rsch. grantee U. So. Calif., 1991. Mem. Am. Geophys. Union, Geol. Soc. of Am., Pa. State Alumni Assn., Sigma Xi. Republican. Home: 234 Fair Oaks Ave J South Pasadena CA 91030 Office: U So Calif Geology Dept 209 Science Bldg Los Angeles CA 90007

LEE, CANDIE CHING WAH, retail executive; b. Hong Kong, British Crown Colony, June 17, 1950; came to U.S., 1973:; d. Willard W. and Yuk Ching (Yau) L. Student, Hong Kong Tech. Coll., Kowloon, 1968-70. Office mgr. Crown Enterprises, Ltd., Hong Kong, 1970-73; buyer, mgr. Hawaii Resort Industries, Inc., Honolulu, 1973-76, v.p., 1976-82; pres. Hawaii Resort Shops, Inc., Honolulu, 1983—. Mem. Am. Mgmt. Assn. Republican. Office: Hawaii Resort Shops Inc 2270 Kalakaua Ave Ste 1000 Honolulu HI 96815-2577

LEE, CHARLES DOUGLAS, mining engineering consultant; b. Pocatello, Idaho, Oct. 8, 1945; s. Charles Albert and Gladys Margaret (Thomas) L. BS in Aerospace Engring., Calif. State Poly. U., 1970; BS in Mining Engring., U. Ariz., 1974, MS in Mining Engring., 1983. Engring. asst. George A. Schroter, Geo. Cons., L.A., 1963-70; field engr. Gordon Miles Mn. Co., Dos Cabezas, Ariz., 1970-72; engring. asst. Sacaton unit ASARCO, Casa Grande, Ariz., summer 1973; mining engr. Duval Corp., Sahaurita, Ariz., 1974-76; sr. engr. Fluor Engring., Inc., Mining and Metals, Redwood City, Calif., 1977-84; ind. cons. mining engring. Tucson, 1984—; mem. of agreement U.S. Bur. Mines, Spokane, Wash., 1984-85; assoc. cons. Pincock Allen & Holt Inc., Tucson, 1984-86, Mineral Resources Devel. Inc., San Mateo, Calif., 1989—, Kennecott, Salt Lake City, 1990. Developer mining software; author: (software user manuals) Opt. Dragline Operating Tec., 1982, Opt. Multiple Seam Dragline, 1984, Multiple Dragline Sim., 1987, Program ASSAY, 1991, Program ASY2, 1992. Mem. Soc. Mining, Metallurgy and Exploration, Inc., Internat. Miniature Aerobatic Club (v.p. 1989—), Am. Cons. League. Home and Office: 1145 E Kleindale Rd Tucson AZ 85719-1829

LEE, CHARLES NICHOLAS, foreign language educator; b. Washington, DC, July 27, 1933; s. Charles Foster and Frances Cornelia (McAllister) L.; m. Mollie Kathleen née Boivin, Jan. 11, 1956; children: Alison, Christopher, Jennifer, Bronwyn. BA, U. Md., 1955; student, Ludwig-Maximilians Universitat, Munich, 1953-54; MA, U. Md., 1958; PhD, Harvard U., 1964. Instr. Univ. Md., College Park, 1956-60; asst. prof. Bucknell Univ., Lewisburg, Pa., 1963-65; asst. prof. Univ. Colo., Boulder, 1965-67, assoc. prof., 1967-74, prof., 1974—. Author: The Novels of M.A. Aldanov, 1969; contbr.

articles to scholarly jours. Recipient Fulbright fellow U.S. Govt., Paris, 1955-56, Nat. Defense Foreign Lang. fellows, Cambridge, Mass., Paris, 1960-65; Adenauer scholar Govt. of W. Germany, Munich, 1953-54. Am. Assn. of tchrs. of Slavic & East European Langs., Am. Assn. for the Advancement of Slavic Studies, Western Slavic Assn., Rocky Mountain Langs. Assn. Episc. Home: 1276 Harrison Ct Boulder CO 80303 Office: Univ of Colo Campus Box 276 University Of Colorado CO 80309

LEE, CRISTINA O., journalist; b. Masbate, The Philippines, Aug. 16, 1952; came to U.S., 1984; d. Roberto and Gregoria Licuan. AB in Journalism, U. Santo Tomas, Manila, 1978; M in Internat. Affairs, Columbia U., 1985. Reporter The Jour. of Commerce, N.Y.C., 1987-90, L.A. Times, Costa Mesa, 1990—. Recipient rsch. scholarship Soka U., Hong Kong, 1979-81, rsch. scholarship Sing Tao Found., Hong Kong, 1980. Mem. Asian Am. Journalists Assn., Orange County Press Club. Office: LA Times 1375 Sunflower Ave Costa Mesa CA 92626

LEE, DAVID KEITH, physician, administrator; b. Deadwood, S.D., Jan. 12, 1947; s. Kenneth Marvin and Rebecca Jane (Furze) L.; m. Joan Marie Cowan, Aug. 7, 1970; children: Mark David, Matthew Charles. BA, Johns HopkinsU., 1969; MD, Harvard U., 1973. Diplomate Am. Bd. Internal Medicine. Asst. prof. U. Tex., Dallas, 1976-78; assoc. chief of staff for ambulatory care Dallas VA Med. Ctr., 1978-84, Boise (Idaho) VA Med. Ctr., 1984—. Contbr. articles to various jours. Chmn. Regional Planning Bd., San Francisco, 1986—; pres. Idaho affiliate Am. Heart Assn., 1987-88, Immanuel Luth. Ch., 1990. Mem. ACP, Soc. Gen. Internal Medicine. Office: Boise VA Med Ctr 500 Fort St Boise ID 83702

LEE, DAVID WOON, chemist; b. Hong Kong, July 14, 1949; came to U.S., 1967; s. Kwoon and Sau Yuen Lee; m. Helen Lee, May 23, 1970; children: Victor, Malinda. BS, U. Winnipeg, Can., 1970; BS with honors, U. Waterloo, Can., 1979; JD, Glendale (Calif.) U., 1991. Bar: Calif. 1992, U.S. Dist. Ct. (cen. dist.) Calif. 1992, U.S. Ct. Appeals (9th cir.) 1993, U.S. Patent Office, 1993. Rsch. chemist Atomic Energy of Can., Pinawa, 1970-80; supr. maj. facilities Atomic Energy of Can., Chalk River, 1980-87; indsl. waste specialist County of L.A., 1987-88; chemist City of L.A., 1988—; del. citizen amb. program nuclear waste mgmt. U.S.S.R., 1989. Contbr. articles to Can. Jour. of Chemistry, Jour. of Colloid and Interface Sci., Jour. Electrochem. Soc., Electrochimica Acta 22; contbr. over 20 articles to profl. jours. Br. rep. Atomic Energy of Can. Profl. Employees Assn., Chalk River, 1984-87; judge Pembroke (Can.) Regional Sci. Fair, 1985-86. Mem. Am. Nuclear Soc., People-to-People Internat. Home: 8636 Zerelda St Rosemead CA 91770-1249 Office: City of LA 2002 W Slauson Ave Los Angeles CA 90047-1019

LEE, EDWARD B., financial consultant; b. L.A., Sept. 19, 1962. BA, U. Calif., San Diego, 1985, MS, 1986. Biochemist U. Calif. San Diego Cancer Ctr., 1986-88; asst. dist. mgr. The Equitable Life, San Diego, 1988-92; Asian mktg. mgr. Mutual Life of N.Y., San Diego, 1992—; pres. Le Tip Bus. Networking Group, San Diego, 1992—. Mem. NALU, Nat. Assn. Securities Dealers, San Diego Athletic Club (instr. World Tang Soo Do Karate Assn.). Office: Mutual Life of NY 6048-A Cornerstone Ct W San Diego CA 92121

LEE, ELIZABETH ANNE, marketing executive; b. Carbondale, Ill., Sept. 5, 1952; d. Kenneth O. and Velma Marquerite (Mizner) McGee; m. Steven Robin Lee, Mar. 27,1987; 1 child, Kelsey Erin. BS in Applied Sci., Miami U., 1974; MBA, St. Louis U., 1978. Staff supr. Southwestern Bell, St. Louis, 1978-80; mgr. market rsch. Angelica Uniform Group, St. Louis, 1980-83; sr. analyst consumer rsch. May Dept. Stores Co., St. Louis, 1983-84; v.p. Data Support Svcs., Inc., St. Louis, 1984-87; pres. Concours Rsch., Inc., St. Louis, 1987-89, also bd. dirs.; v.p. corp. devel. The Rsch. Spectrum, San Francisco, 1991—; cons. Project Bus., St. Louis, 1983-84; mem. adj. faculty U. Mo., 1987—, Webster U., 1988—. Editor: Quantitative Models for Bus. Decisions (Kwak), 1978. Bd. dirs. The St. Louis Ballet, 1989-90. Fellow St. Louis U., 1977-78. Mem. Am. Mktg. Assn., San Francisco C. of C. Republican. Congregationalist. Office: The Research Spectrum 182 Second St Burlingame CA 94010

LEE, EUGENE CANFIELD, political science educator, university official; b. Berkeley, Calif., Sept. 19, 1924; s. Edwin Augustus and Edna (Canfield) L.; m. Jane Gale Myers, Apr. 18, 1953; children: Douglas Edwin, Nancy Gale; m. Joanne K. Hurley, July 11, 1980. B.A., UCLA, 1946; M.A., U. Calif., Berkeley, 1950, Ph.D., 1957. Asst. to city mgr. San Leandro, Calif., 1948-50; exec. asst. Democratic gov. candidate, Calif., 1954; faculty U. Calif., Berkeley, 1955—; assoc. prof. U. Calif., 1962-69, prof., 1969-1989, prof. emeritus, 1990—, asst. to chancellor, 1955-57, asst. to pres., 1958-59, 73-76; asst. dir. Inst. Govt. Studies, 1959-63, assoc. dir., 1964-65, dir. inst., 1967-88; research polit. scientist Inst. Pub. Adminstrn., Univ. Coll., Dar es Salaam, Tanganyika, 1963-64; v.p.-exec. asst. U. Calif., 1965-67; adviser to pres. U. P.R., 1976-77; acad. visitor London Sch. Econs. and Chartered Inst. Pub. Fin. and Acctg., 1984-85; cons. UN U., Tokyo, 1976; staff cons. Calif. Congl. del., 1979; cons. on governance Univs. Ala., Ariz., Houston, Md., La. State, Tex., London; bd. dirs. Calif. Jour., 1972-86, chmn., 1972-83; cons. to spl. masters on reapportionment, Calif. Supreme Ct., 1991. Author: The Politics of Nonpartisanship: A Study of California City Elections, 1960; co-author: The Challenge of California, 1970, 2d edit., 1976, The Multicampus University: A Study of Academic Governance, 1971, The University of London: An American Perspective, 1989, Representative Government and the Initiative Process, 1990; contbr. articles to profl. jours. Chmn. Commn. Calif. Govt. Orgn. and Economy, 1961-63; mem. Calif. Fair Campaign Practices Com., 1962-66; tech. adv. com. Carnegie Commn. Higher Edn., 1970-76; Trustee Pub. Adminstrn. Service, 1968-76, Cal-Tax Found., 1981—; ofcl. observer plebiscite Federated States of Micronesia, 1983; bd. dirs. Trust for Public Land, 1979—. Mem. Am. Polit. Sci. Assn., Nat. Acad. Pub. Adminstrn., No. Calif. Polit. Sci. Assn. (pres. 1965-66). Congregationalist. Home: Berkeley CA Office: U Calif 210 Barrows Hall Berkeley CA 94720

LEE, GILBERT BROWNELL, internist; b. Portland, Oreg., Nov. 7, 1950; s. G. Prentiss and Patty (Brownell) L.; m. C. Frost, Aug. 29, 1970; children: Sean Alexander, Shannon Nicole. BA, U. Oreg., 1972; MD, Oreg. Health Sci. Ctr., 1976. Resident Charleston (W.Va.) Area Med. Ctr., 1976-80; pvt. practice Internal Medicine Assocs., Newport, Oreg., 1980—; dir. ICU Pacific Communities Hosp., Newport, 1985-90; chief of staff Pacific Communities Hosp., Newport, 1987. Pres. Oreg. Coast Coun. for the Arts, Newport, 1990-91. Named Outstanding Analytical Chemist, Am. Chem. Soc., 1972. Mem. Oreg. Soc. Internal Medicine (pres. 1991-92), Lincoln County Med. Soc. (pres. 1982), Oreg. Med. Soc. (del. 1989-92), Phi Beta Kappa. Republican. Lutheran. Office: Internal Medicine Assocs Ste 201 1010 SW Coast Hwy Newport OR 97365

LEE, GRACE TZE, controller; b. Taipei, Republic of China, Aug. 11, 1953; came to U.S., 1974; d. Tang Chi and Ming (Shu) L. BA, Nat. Taipei U., 1974; BS, U. Nev., 1977; postgrad., UCLA, 1988. Fgn. currency specialist Deak-Perera Co., L.A., 1977-80; asst. mgr. Universal Supply Co., L.A., 1980; contr. AJR Electronics Inc., L.A., 1981-84; western zone asst. mgr. Samsung Electronics Co., L.A., 1984; contr. Gideon Nol Inc., L.A., 1985-87, James G. Wiley Co., L.A., 1987-91, Jetset Tours Inc. (N.Am.), L.A., 1991—; pres. G.L. Fin. Svc., 1988—, Real Estate Investment Svc., 1988—. Home: 23442 Batey Ave Harbor City CA 90710-1204

LEE, IVY, JR., public relations consultant; b. N.Y.C., July 31, 1909; s. Ivy and Cornelia (Bigelow) L.; m. Marie F. Devin, Oct. 14, 1988; children: Peter Ivy III (dec.), Jean Downey. BA, Princeton U., 1931; MBA, Harvard U., 1933. Ptnr. Ivy Lee & T.J. Ross, N.Y.C., 1933-45; with Pan Am. World Airways, Miami, Fla. and San Francisco, 1942-45; adminstrv. asst. S.D. Bechtel, Bechtel Cos., San Francisco, 1950-54; pres. Ivy Lee Jr. & Assocs., San Francisco, 1945-85; pres., cons. Ivy Lee Jr. & Assocs., Inc., San Francisco, 1985—. Trustee Princeton (N.J.) U., 1965-69; bd. dirs. San Francisco TB Assn., Bay Area Red Cross, San Francisco, Edgewood Childrens Ctr. Mem. Pub. Relations Soc. Am., Internat. Pub. Relations Assn. (pres. 1976-77). Republican. Presbyterian. Clubs: Bohemian, Pacific Union. Home: 1940 Broadway St San Francisco CA 94109-2299 Office: Ste 609 210 Post St San Francisco CA 94108

LEE, JAMES KING, technology corporation executive; b. Nashville, July 31, 1940; s. James Fitzhugh Lee and Lucille (Charlton) McGivney; m. Victoria Marie Marani, Sept. 4, 1971; children: Gina Victoria, Patrick Fitzhugh. BS, Calif. State U., Pomona, 1964; MBA, U. So. Calif., 1966. Prodn. and methods engrng. foreman Gen. Motors Corp., 1963-65; engrng. adminstr. Douglas MSSD, Santa Monica, Calif., 1965-67; mgr. mgmt. systems TRW Systems, Redondo Beach, Calif., 1967-68; v.p. corp. devel. DataStation Corp., L.A., 1968-69; v.p., gen. mgr. Aved Systems Group, L.A., 1969-70; mng. ptnr. Corp. Growth Cons., L.A., 1970-81; chmn., pres. chief exec. officer Fail-Safe Tech. Corp., L.A., 1981-93. Author industry studies, 1973-79. Mem. L.A. Mayor's Community Adv. Com., 1962-72, aerospace task force L.A. County Econ. Devel. Commn., 1990-92; bd. dirs. USO of Greater L.A., 1990-92, v.p. personnel 1990-92, exec. v.p., 1992-93, pres. 1993—; asst. adminstr. SBA, Washington, 1974; vice chmn. Traffic Commn., Rancho Palos Verdes, Calif., 1975-78; chmn. Citizens for Property Tax Relief, Palos Verdes, 1976-80; mem. Town Hall Calif. Recipient Golden Scissors award Calif. Taxpayers' Congress, 1978. Mem. So. Calif. Tech. Execs. Network, Am. Electronics Assn. (chmn. L.A. coun. 1987-88, vice chmn. 1986-87, nat. bd. dirs. 1986-89), Nat. Security Industries Assn. Republican. Baptist. Home: 28874 Crestridge Rd Palos Verdes Peninsula CA 90274-5063 Office: Fail-Safe Tech Corp Ste 318 710 Silver Spur Rd Rolling Hills Estates CA 90274-3695

LEE, JERRY CARLTON, university administrator; b. Roanoke, Va., Nov. 21, 1941; m. Joan Marie Leo; 1 child, Zan. BA, W.Va. Wesleyan Coll., 1963; postgrad., W.Va. U. Grad. Sch. Indsl. Relations, 1963-64, U. Balt. Sch. Law, 1967-69; MA, Va. Poly. Inst., 1975, EdD, 1977; LLD (hon.), Gallaudet U., 1986. Mgmt. trainee Gen. Motors Corp., 1964-65; v.p. adminstrn. Comml. Credit Indsl. Corp., Washington, 1965-71; dir. gen. services Gallaudet Coll., Washington, 1971-77, asst. v.p. bus. affairs, 1978-82, v.p. adminstrn. and bus., 1982-84; pres. Gallaudet U. (formerly Gallaudet Coll.), Washington, 1984-88, Nat. U., San Diego, 1989—. Hon. bd. dirs. D.C. Spl. Olympics; commn. in adminstrn. org. Rehab. Internat.; bd. dirs. People to People, Deafness Research Found.; hon. advocacy bd. Nat. Capital Assn. Coop. Edn.; mem. Personnel Policies Forum Bur. Nat. Affairs. Served with USAR, 1966-72. Recipient Nat. Service award, Hon. Pres. award Council for Better Hearing and Speech, 1986, One-of-a-Kind award People-to-People, 1987, Advancement Human Rights & Fundamental Freedoms award UN, U.S.A., Disting. Alumni award Va. Poly. Inst., 1985, Pres.' award Gallaudet Coll. Alumni Assn., Gallaudet Community Relations award, U.S. Steel Found. Cost Reduction Incentive award Nat. Assn. Coll. and Univ. Bus. Officers, award Am. Athletic Assn. Deaf, 1987. Mem. Am. Assn. Univ. Adminstrs. (Eileen Tosney award 1987), Consortium of Univs. Washington Met. Area (exec. com.), Nat. Collegiate Athletic Assn. (pres.' commn.), Nat. Assn. Coll. Aux. Services (jour. adv. bd., journalism award), Alpha Sigma Pi (Man of Yr. award 1983-84). Lodge: Sertoma (life, found. nat. adv. com.). Office: Nat U Univ Park 4025 Camino del Rio S San Diego CA 92108-4194

LEE, JOHN JIN, lawyer; b. Chgo., Oct. 20, 1948; s. Jim Soon and Fay Yown (Young) L.; m. Jamie Pearl Eng, Apr. 30, 1983. BA magna cum laude, Rice U., 1971; JD, Stanford U., 1975; MBA, 1975. Bar: Calif. 1976. Assoc. atty. Manatt Phelps & Rothenberg, L.A., 1976-77; asst. counsel Wells Fargo Bank N.A., San Francisco, 1977-79, counsel, 1979-80, v.p., sr. counsel, 1980, v.p., mng. sr. counsel, 1981—; mem. governing com. Conf. on Consumer Fin. Law, 1989—. Bd. dirs. Asian Bus. League of San Francisco, 1981—, gen. counsel, 1981. Mem. ABA (chmn. subcom. on housing fin., com. on consumer fin. svcs., bus. law sect. 1983-90), Consumer Bankers Assn. (lawyers com.), Soc. Physics Students, Stanford Asian-Pacific Am. Alumni/ae Club (bd. dirs. 1989-93, v.p. 1989-91). Democrat. Baptist. Office: Wells Fargo Bank NA Legal Dept 111 Sutter St San Francisco CA 94163-0001

LEE, JOHN MARSHALL, mathematics educator; b. Phila., Sept. 2, 1950; s. Warren W. and Virginia (Hull) L.; m. Pm Weizenbaum, May 26, 1984; 1 child, Nathan Lee Weizenbaum. AB, Princeton U., 1972; student, Tufts U., 1977-78; PhD, MIT, 1982. Systems programmer Tex. Instruments, Princeton, N.J., 1972-74; Geophys. Fluid Dynamics Lab., NOAA GFDL/NOAA, Princeton, 1974-75; tchr. math. and physics Wooster Sch., Danbury, Conn., 1975-77; programmer and cons. info. processing svcs. MIT, Cambridge, Mass., 1978-82; asst. prof. math. Harvard U., Cambridge, 1982-87; asst. prof. math. U. Wash., Seattle, 1987-89, assoc. prof. math., 1989—; sr. tutor Harvard U., Cambridge, 1984-87. Contbr. articles to profl. jours. Rsch. fellow NSF, 1982. Mem. Am. Math. Soc. (Centennial fellow 1989). Home: 5637 12th Ave NE Seattle WA 98105-2603 Office: Univ Wash Math Dept GN-50 Seattle WA 98195

LEE, JOLI FAY EATON, educator; b. Holdredge, Nebr., Sept. 24, 1951; d. Ray Lee and Lois Illeen (Willoughby) Larkins; m. James Edward Eaton, Aug. 16, 1969 (div. Jan. 1979); children: Threva, James, Beth; m. Chris Lee, Aug. 13, 1991; stepchildren: Michael Lee, Robyn Lee. BS in Elem. Edn., N.Mex. State U., Las Cruces, 1980, MA in Curriculum and Instruction, 1984. Cert. elem. tchr., N.Mex. Tchr. elem. Alamogordo (N.Mex.) Pub. Schs., 1980—; co-chmn. City Elem. Sci. Fair, Alamogordo, 1989-90, chmn., 1990-92; with Summer Sci. Pilot Program, 1992-93. Contbr. articles to profl. jours. Nat. conv. co-chmn. Nat. Speleological Study, Tularosa, N.Mex., 1986; joint venturer Cave Rsch. Found., 1983—; person. dir., Guadalupe Area Cave Rsch. Found., N.Mex., 1987-90; del. Cave Exploration Del. to People's Republic of China, 1993. Crimson scholar N.Mex. State U., 1980. Mem. NEA, Nat. Speleological Soc. (sec. Southwestern region 1984, 91-92, 93, Southwestern regional chmn. 1985-86). Republican. Episcopalian. Home: 406 Sunrise Ave Alamogordo NM 88310-4141 Office: North Elem Sch 1300 Florida Alamogordo NM 88310-6331

LEE, JONG HYUK, accountant; b. Seoul, Korea, May 6, 1941; came to U.S., 1969, naturalized, 1975; s. Jung Bo and Wol Sun L. B.A., Sonoma State U., Rohnert Park, Calif., 1971; M.B.A. in Taxation, Golden Gate U., San Francisco, 1976. CPA, Calif.; m. Esther Kim, Jan. 24, 1970. Cost acct., internal auditor Foremost-McKesson Co., San Francisco, 1971-74; sr. acct. Clark, Wong, Foulkes & Barbieri, CPAs, Oakland, Calif., 1974-77; pres. J.H. Lee Accountancy Corp., Oakland, 1977-89, Bay Cities Restaurants, Inc. Wendy's Franchise, 1989—; instr. Armstrong Coll., Berkeley, Calif., 1977-78; lectr. acctg., dir. sch. of bus. The U.S.-Korea Bus. Inst., San Francisco State U.; adv. bd. mem. Ctr. for Korean Studies, Inst. of East Asian Studies U. Calif, Berkeley. Bd. dirs. Korean Residents Assn., 1974, Multi-svc. Ctr. for Koreans, 1979, Better Bus. Bur., 1984-87; chmn. caucus Calif.-Nev. ann. conf. United Meth. Ch., 1977; commr. Calif. State Office Econ. Opportunity, 1982-86; pres. Korean-Am. Dem. Network; mem. Dem. Nat. Fin. Coun.; regional chmn. Adv. Coun. on Peaceful Unification Policy, Republic of Korea; commr. Asian Art Mus. San Francisco, 1988-91. With Korean Marine Corps, 1961-64; 1st lt. Calif. State Mil. Res. Mem. Am. Inst. CPAs, Nat. Assn. Asian Am. CPAs (bd. dir.), Am. Acctg. Assn., Nat. Assn. Accts., Internat. Found. Employee Benefit Plans, Calif. Soc. CPAs, Oakland C. of C., Korean Am. C. of C. (pres. Pacific North Coast, Rotary. Democrat. Author tax and bus. column Korea Times, 1980. Home: 180 Firestone Dr Walnut Creek CA 94598 Office: 369 13th St Oakland CA 94612-2636

LEE, KATE LEARY, financial adviser; b. Hastings, Nebr., Dec. 13, 1946; d. Robert Michael and Alyce Rita (Popp) Leary; widowed; children: Modie Alexander Lee, Marni Sue Lee. AA, Mesa Jr. Coll., 1968; BA in Spl. Edn., U. No. Colo., 1970, MA in Learning Disabilities, 1977, MBA, 1982. Lic. tchr., Colo. Speech pathologist, audiologist Unit 13, Scottsbluff, Nebr., 1971-76; tchr. spl. edn. Sch. Dist. 13, Greeley, Colo., 1977-78; master spl. edn. Havern Ctr., Inc., Denver, 1978-80; v.p. R.M. Leary & Co., Inc., Denver, 1980-84, pres., 1984—; sr. arbitrator Better Bus. Bur., 1988—; broker rep. Titan Value Equities Group, Inc., 1983—. Fin. coun. Notre Dame Cath. Parish, Denver, 1989—. Mem. Western Div. Conf. Pensions and Benefits, Colo. Harvard Bus. Sch. Club, Soc. Asset Allocators and Fund Timers, Inc. (dir. 1990-93), Ambassador Club Greater Denver C. of C. Office: RM Leary & Co Inc 3300 E 1st Ave # 290 Denver CO 80206

LEE, LILA JUNE, historical society officer, library director; b. Ukiah, Calif., July 12, 1923; d. Arthur L. and Leila Edna (Rose) Romer; m. Dale R. Laney, May 1, 1944 (div. Sept. 1952); m. Robert James Lee, Apr. 16, 1955; children: Arthur John, Margarett June. Officer Mendocino County Hist. Soc., Ukiah, 1960—; libr. dir. Held Poage Libr., Ukiah, 1970—. Mem. conf. of Calif. Hist. Soc. (regional v.p. 1980—), Mendocino County Hist. Soc. (v.p., treas., fin. sec.). Republican. Presbyterian. Office: Mendocino County Hist Soc 603 W Perkins St Ukiah CA 95482-4726

LEE, LONG CHI, electrical engineering and chemistry educator; b. Kaohsiung, Taiwan, Oct. 19, 1940; came to U.S., 1965; s. Chin Lai Lee and Wen Wang; m. Laura Meichau Cheng, Dec. 1, 1967 (dec. Dec. 1988); children: Gloria, Thomas; m. Masako Suto, Jan. 6, 1990. BS in Physics, Taiwan Normal U., Taiwan, 1964; MA in Physics, U. So. Calif., L.A., 1967, PhD in Physics, 1971. Rsch. staff U. So. Calif., L.A., 1971-77; physicist SRI Internat., Menlo Park, Calif., 1977-79, sr. physicist, 1979-81; prof. elec. engring. San Diego State U., 1982—; adj. asst. prof. U. So. Calif., L.A., 1977; adj. prof. chemistry San Diego State U., 1986—. Contbr. papers to profl. jours. Pres. Taiwanese Cultural Assn. in San Diego, 1983, 93. Rsch. grantee NSF, 1980—, NASA, 1979—, Air Force Office Sci. Rsch., 1980-89, Naval Rsch. Office, 1986-89. Mem. Am. Phys. Soc., IEEE, Am. Geophys. Union, Inter-Am. Photochem. Soc., Formesan Assn. for Pub. Affairs (pres. San Diego chpt. 1990-91). Office: San Diego State U Dept Elec & Computer Engring San Diego CA 92182

LEE, LOU S., printing company executive, developer; b. Liuzhou, Guangsi, Peoples Republic of China, Nov. 5, 1943; came to U.S., 1959; s. So Sat and Yuen Ching (Leung) L.; m. Irene Woo Lee, Apr. 21. 1971; children: Derrick Chin-Chang, Aaron Cin-Hung. AA, Los Angeles City Coll., 1965; BA, San Jose (Calif.) State U., 1968; MBA, Golden Gate U., 1971. Cert. coll. instr., Calif. Mktg. rep. IBM, San Francisco, 1973-75; chief exec. officer VIP Litho, San Francisco, 1976—; assoc. producer Gold Mountain Prodns., San Francisco, 1986. Active Cathedral Sch. for Boys Christmas Boutique, San Francisco, 1981-82, Merola Opera program, San Francisco, 1983-84, Katherine Delmar Burke Sch. Festival, San Francisco, 1985; v.p. and bd. dirs. Marin Chinese Cultural Group, Calif., 1985; mem. fin. com. Kentfield Sch. Found., Calif., 1986-88; dir. Kentfield Sch. Found., 1987-88; hon. com. mem. San Francisco Boys Chorus Bracebridge Feast, 1986, San Francisco Opera Ctr. Shanghai Fund, 1987—; adv. bd. Asian Performing Arts, San Francisco, 1988; mem. Calif. Spl. Olympic spirt Team, San Francisco, 1988. Named Man of the Yr., Univ. High Sch., San Francisco, 1987. Mem. Asian Bus. Assn., Sierra Club Found., Sierra Club. Club: City (San Francisco). Office: VIP Litho 1 Newhall St San Francisco CA 94124

LEE, MARGARET ANNE, social worker, psychotherapist; b. Scribner, Nebr., Nov. 23, 1930; d. William Christian and Caroline Bertha (Benner) Joens; m. Robert Kelly Lee, May 21, 1950 (div. 1972); children: Lawrence Robert, James Kelly, Daniel Richard. AA, Napa Coll., 1949; student, U. Calif., Berkeley, 1949-50; BA, Calif. State Coll., Sonoma, 1975; MSW, Calif. State U., Sacramento, 1977. Diplomate clin. social worker; lic. clin. social worker, Calif.; lic. marriage and family counselor, Calif.; tchr. Columnist, stringer Napa (Calif.) Register, 1946-50; eligibility worker, supr. Napa County Dept. Social Services, 1968-75; instr. Napa Valley Community Coll., 1978-83; practice psychotherapy Napa, 1977—; oral commr. Calif. Dept. Consumer Affairs, Bd. Behavioral Sci., 1984—; bd. dirs. Project Access, 1978-79. trustee Napa Valley C.C., 1983—, v.p. bd., 1984-85, pres. bd., 1986, 90, clk., 1988-89; bd. dirs. Napa County Con. Econ. Opportunity, 1984-85, Napa chpt. March of Dimes, 1957-71, Mental Health Assn. Napa County, 1983-87; vice chmn. edn. com. Calif. C.C. Trustees, 1987-88, chmn. edn. com., 1988-89, legis. com., 1985-87, bd. dirs., 1989—, 2d v.p., 1991, 1st v.p., 1992, pres., 1993; mem. student equity rev. group Calif. C.C. Chancellors, 1992; bd. dirs. C.C. League Calif., 1992—. Recipient Fresh Start award Self mag., award Congl. Caucus on Women's Issues, 1984. Mem. NASW, Mental Health Assn. Napa County, Calif. Assn. Physically and Handicapped, Women's Polit. Caucus, C.C. League Calif. (1st v.p. 1992, bd. dirs. 1992—), Calif. Elected Women's Assn. Edn. and Rsch., Am. Assn. Women in Community and Jr. Colls. Democrat. Lutheran. Office: 1100 Trancas PO Box 2099 Napa CA 94558

LEE, MARTHA, artist, writer; b. Chehalis, Wash., Aug. 23, 1946; d. William Robert and Phyllis Ann (Herzog) L.; m. Peter Reynolds Lockwood, Jan. 25, 1974 (div. 1982). BA in English Lit., U. Wash., 1968; student, Factory of Visual Art, 1980-82. Reporter Seattle Post-Intelligencer, 1970; personnel counselor Theresa Snow Employment, 1971-72; receptionist Northwest Kidney Ctr., 1972-73; proprietress The Reliquary, 1974-77; travel agt. Cathay Express, 1977-79; artist, 1980—; represented by Pulliam Deffenbaugh Nugent Gallery, Portland, Oreg., Artists' Gallery, Nehalem, Oreg., Oak Harbor (Wash.) Art Gallery. Painter various oil paintings; exhibitor group and one-person shows. Home and Studio: 307 Lynn St Seattle WA 98109

LEE, MARTHA EUGENIA, forestry educator; b. Logan, Utah, Jan. 6, 1952; d. Gurney Worth and Eugenia (Dalton) L. AS, Ricks Coll., 1972; BS, Utah State U., 1975; MS, Oreg. State U., 1982, PhD, 1991. Rshc. technician Inst. for Outdoor Recreation & Tourism, Utah State U., Logan, 1973-75; sr. dept. clk. typist dept. forestry and outdoor recreation Utah State U., Logan, 1975-80; rsch. asst. dept. forest resources Oreg. State U., Corvallis, 1982-90; asst. prof. Sch. Forestry, No. Ariz. U., Flagstaff, 1990—. Acad. scholar Utah State U., 1970, Ricks Coll., 1970. Mem. Soc. Am. Foresters, Human Dimensions in Wildlife Study Group, Phi Kappa Phi, Alpha Zeta, Xi Sigma Pi. Office: No Ariz U Sch Forestry Box 4098 Flagstaff AZ 86011-4098

LEE, MIMI, paralegal; b. Portland, Oreg., Oct. 12, 1964; d. Sigman Roe and June Kim; children: Matthew Aaron, Katherine Ann. Grad. high sch., Rancho Palos Verdes, Calif.; cert. legal asst. with honors, U. San Diego, 1989. Paralegal, office mgr. Law Offices Thomas Kagy, L.A., 1983, Law Office Tong S. Suhr, L.A., 1983-84; head litigation sect., paralegal def. litigation Wells Fargo Bank, N.A., L.A., 1984-85; paralegal bankruptcy and fed. litigation Pachulski, Stang & Ziehl, P.C., L.A., 1985-88; paralegal, office mgr. Law Offices Donald H. Glaser, San Diego, 1989—; paralegal probate, computer cons. Village Law Ctr., San Marcos, 1990-91; paralegal, probate, trust adminstrn. Law Offices Arthur S. Brown, Carlsbad, Calif., 1992-93, Higgs, Fletcher & Mack, San Diego, 1993—. Editor newsletter Noteworthy, 1984-85. Sec.-elect Korean Am. Coalition, L.A., 1983-84; counselor Korean Am. Youth Found., 1974-82. Mem. San Diego Assn. Legal Assts., Nat. Notary Assn. (founding co-chair North County com.). Republican. Presbyterian. Home: 1325 Clear Crest Cir Vista CA 92084-3745 Office: Higgs Fletcher & Mack 401 West A St Ste 2000 San Diego CA 92101

LEE, MURLIN E., program manager; b. Crescent City, Calif., Jan. 4, 1957; s. George Lee and Ida Burl (Wilson) M.; m. Jeanine Marie Metcalfe, Apr. 13, 1985; children: Kimberly, Kristen, Gina. BS in Bus. Adminstrn., Calif. Poly. U., Pomona, 1981; MS in Software Engring., Nat. U., San Jose, Calif., 1988. Mgr. George M. Lee Enterprises Inc., Crescent City, Calif., 1979-80, Wells Aviation, Ontario, Calif., 1980-81, Bard Software, San Jose, Calif., 1982-84; software engr. Litton Applied Techology, San Jose, 1984-89; program mgr. Condor Systems, Inc., San Jose, 1989—. Republican. Home: 4081 Will Rogers Dr San Jose CA 95117-2730 Office: Condor Systems Inc 2133 Samaritan Dr San Jose CA 95124-4408

LEE, NORMAN RANDALL, writer, editor; b. Barre, Vt., Mar. 2, 1929; s. Eugene Kenneth Lee and Madeleine Belle Kerr; m. Lillian Mae Pettitt, Aug. 1961 (div.); children: Henry David, Russell Bertrand. BA, Syracuse U., 1958, MA in English and Edn., 1961; postgrad., SUNY, 1965, 66. Cert. secondary tchr., N.Y. English tchr. Mexico (N.Y.) Acad., 1958-60; dir. Reading, Edn. and Devel., Fulton, N.Y., 1960-64; program asst. Syracuse U., 1964-65; asst. prof. Edinboro (Pa.) Coll., 1965-67, SUNY, Oneonta, N.Y., 1967-70; freelance writer Mt. Vision, N.Y., 1967-71; novice monk Found. Am. Yoga, Bovina, N.Y., 1972-75; freelance writer West Oneonta, N.Y., 1975-78; editor, pub. Homesteaders News, Addison, Naples, N.Y., 1978-88; writer, editor, pub. Lee Publs., Sedona, Ariz., 1988—; also bd. dirs. Lee Publs., Sedona; chief exec. Ariz. Writers Network, 1990—; founder, pres. Homesteaders Assn., 1978—; conf. organizer Homesteaders News, 1978-88. Author: Paperbacks for High School, 1961, Annual Manual of Homesteading, 1982, Five Steps to Self-Reliance, 1985, A Stranger And Afraid, 1992; contbr. articles to various nat. mags. V.p. So. Tier Bluegrass Assn., 1977-78; pres. Cen. N.Y. Com. of 100, 1962-64; mem. Concerned Arizonans for Animal Rights, 1988-90. With USAF, 1947-54, Korea. Mem. Ariz. Authors' Assn., Ariz. Writers Network, Ariz. Bluegrass Assn. Office: Lee Publs Homesteaders Assn 8427 W Glendale Ave Lot 117 Glendale AZ 85305-2111

LEE, PALI JAE (POLLY JAE STEAD LEE), retired librarian, writer; b. Nov. 26, 1929; d. Jonathan Everett Wheeler and Ona Katherine (Grunder) Stead; m. Richard H.W. Lee, Apr. 7, 1945 (div. 1978); children: Lani Kay

Lee, Karin Lee Robinson, Ona Lee Yee, Laurie Lee, Robin Louise Lee Halbert; m. John K. Willis, 1979; stepchildren: Stacie K. Paia, Erin K., Johnna A. Willis Thomas. Student, U. Hawaii, 1944-46, Mich. State, 1961-64. Cataloguer and processor U.S. Army Air Force, 1945-46; with U.S. Weather Bur. Film Library, New Orleans, 1948-50, FBI, Wright-Patterson AFB, Dayton, Ohio, 1952, Ohio Wholesale Winedealers, Columbus, Ohio, 1956-58, Coll. Engring., Ohio State U., Columbus, 1959; writer tech. manual Annie Whittenmeyer Home, Davenport, Iowa, 1960; with Grand Rapids (Mich.) Pub. Library, 1961-62; dir. Waterford (Mich.) Twp. Libraries, 1962-64; acquisition librarian Pontiac (Mich.) Pub. Libraries, 1965-71, dir. East Side br., 1971-73; librarian Bishop Mus., Honolulu, 1975-83. Author: Mary Dyer, Child of Light, 1973; Giant: Pictorial History of the Human Colossus, 1973; History of Change: Kaneohe Bay Area, 1976, English edn. 1983; Na Po Makole—Tales of the Night Rainbow, 1981, rev. edit., 88, Mo'olelo O Na Pohu Kaina, 1983; contbr. articles to Aloha and Honolulu mags., other pubs. Chmn. Oakland County br. Multiple Sclerosis Soc., 1972-73, co-chmn. Pontiac com. of Mich. area bd., 1972-73; sec. Ohana o Kokua, 1979-83, Paia-Willis Ohana, 1982-91, Ohana Kame'ekua, 1988-91; bd. dirs. Detroit Multiple Sclerosis Soc., 1971; mem. Mich. area bd. Am. Friends Svc. com., 1961-69; mem. consumer adv. bd. Libr. for Blind and Physically Handicapped, Honolulu, 1991—; pres. consumer 55 plus bd. Honolulu Ctr. for Ind. Living, 1990—; pres. Honolulu chpt. Nat. Fedn. of Blind, 1991—, 1st v.p. # 93 state affiliate, 1991—, editor Na Na Maka Aloha newsletter, 1990—, 1st v.p. # 93 Hawaii affiliate, 1991, 1st v.p. Honolulu chpt., 1991—. Recipient Mother of the Yr. award Quad City Bus. Men, 1960, Bowl of Light award Hawaiian Community of Hawaii, 1989. Mem. Internat. Platform Assn., Soc. Friends. Office: PO Box 10706 4462 Sierra Honolulu HI 96816

LEE, PAMELA ANNE, accountant; b. San Francisco, May 30, 1960; d. Larry D. and Alice Mary (Reece) L. BBA, San Francisco State U., 1981. CPA, Calif. Typist, bookkeeper, tax acct. James G. Woo, CPA, San Francisco, 1979-85; tutor bus. math. and statistics San Francisco State U., 1979-80; teller to ops. officer Gibraltar Savs. and Loan, San Francisco, 1978-81; sr. acct. Price Waterhouse, San Francisco, 1981-86; corp. acctg. mgr. First Nationwide Bank, Daly City, Calif., 1986-89, v.p., 1989-91, v.p., project mgr., 1991-92, sr. conversion and bus. analyst, 1992—; acctg. cons. New Performance Gallery, San Francisco, 1985, San Francisco Chamber Orch., 1986. Founding mem., chair bd. trustees Asian Acctg. Students Career Day, 1988-89. Mem. NAFE, Am. Inst. CPA's, Calif. Soc. CPA's, Nat. Assn. Asian-Am. CPA's (bd. dirs. 1986, news editor 1987, pres. 1988). Republican. Avocations: reading, music, travel, personal computing, needlework. Office: 820 Stillwater Rd Broderick CA 95605

LEE, PETER Y., electrical engineer, consultant; b. Taipei, Taiwan, May 20, 1959; s. Jack T. and Joanna C. (Chen) L. BSEE, U. So. Calif., MSEE. MTS TTI/Citicorp, Santa Monica, Calif., 1981-82; project mgr. Tomy Corp., Carson, Calif., 1982-83; program devel. officer City Net Rsch. and Devel., L.A., 1983-86; system mgr. Hughes Aircraft Co./EDSG, El Segundo, Calif., 1986-87; founder, pres. Hyper Systems, Walnut, Calif., 1985—. Mem. IEEE. Republican. Roman Catholic. Home: 254 Viewpointe Ln Walnut CA 91789-2078 Office: Hyper Systems 1313 N Grand Ave # 453 Walnut CA 91789-1317

LEE, QWIHEE PARK, plant physiologist; b. Republic of Korea, Mar. 1, 1941; came to U.S., 1965; d. Yong-sik and Soon-duk (Paik) Park; m. Ick-whan Lee, May 20, 1965; children: Tina, Amy, Benjamin. MS, Seoul Nat. U., Republic of Korea, 1965; PhD, U. Minn., 1973. Head dept. plant physiology Korea Ginseng and Tobacco Inst., Seoul, 1980-82; instr. Sogang U., Seoul, 1981, Seoul Women's U., 1981; research assoc. U. Wash., Seattle, 1975-79. Exec. dir. Korean Community Counseling Ctr., Seattle, 1983-86. Named one of 20 Prominent Asian Women in Wash. State, Chinese Post Seattle, 1986. Mem. AAAS. Buddhist. Home: 13025 42d Ave NE Seattle WA 98125 Office: U Wash Dept Pharm SJ-30 1959 NE Pacific St Seattle WA 98195-0001

LEE, RALPH KELLY, systems analyst; b. Salt Lake City, Oct. 9, 1951; s. Ralph Hugh and Hattie (Hadlock) L.; m. Jacquelyn Dowdle, Jan. 15, 1974 (div. Sept. 1985); children: Ralph Adam Lee, Daniel Spencer Lee, Linzl Lee, Jayme Lee, Jordan Duke Lee; m. Carol Elaine Redelings, Oct. 24, 1987; 1 child, Annie Rebecca Anderson. Urban Planning Cert., U. Utah, 1979, BS in Polit. Sci., 1979, BS in Geography, 1979; MBA, U. Phoenix, 1987. Assoc. planner CKK Engrs. & Planners, Holiday, Utah, 1978-79; planner I Salt Lake County Planning Dept., 1979-80; planner II West Valley City (Utah) Community Devel., 1980-81; exec. dir. Redevel. Agy. of Murray City, Utah, 1981-83; forward planning dir. PF West, Inc., Dallas, 1983-88, Systems Constrn. Co., Anaheim Hills, Calif., 1989-90; project mgr. The Orange Coast Group, Inc., Seal Beach, Calif., 1990-91; seminary tchr. Ch. Ednl. Svcs., Cypress, Calif., 1990-93; dir. spl. projects Hill Williams Devel. Corp., Anaheim Hills, 1991-93; mem. faculty U. Phoenix, Fountain Valley, Calif., 1991-93; computer programmer, nat. title coord. Stewart Title, L.A., Calif., 1990—; minister LDS Ch., Perth, Australia, 1971-72, Adelaide, Australia, 1972-73. Composer/performer: (albums) City Moods, 1987, Lucky Dreams, 1987. Recipient Duty to God award LDS Ch., Salt Lake City, 1971, Seminary Ch. Ednl. System award, Anaheim Hills, 1991, 92, 93. Mem. Nat. Assn. Home Builders, Bldg. Industry Assn. So. Calif., Bldg. Industry Assn. So. Calif., Bldg. Industry Assn. So. Calif., Inc., Am. Land Title Assn., Calif. Land Title Assn. Republican. Home: 530 South Ranchview Circle # 43 Anaheim Hills CA 92807-4318 Office: Stewart Title Ste 1200 505 N Brand Blvd Glendale CA 92103

LEE, REX E., university president, lawyer; b. Los Angeles, Feb. 27, 1935; s. Rex E. and Mabel (Whiting) L.; m. Janet Griffin, July 7, 1959; children: Diana, Thomas Rex, Wendy, Michael, Stephanie, Melissa, Christie. B.A., Brigham Young U., 1960; J.D., U. Chgo., 1963. Bar: Ariz., D.C., Utah. Law clk. Justice Byron R. White, U.S. Supreme Ct., 1963-64; atty. Jennings, Strouss & Salmon, 1964-72, ptnr., 1967-72; founding dean J. Reuben Clark Law Sch., Brigham Young U., Provo, Utah, 1972-81; solicitor gen. U.S.A., Washington, 1981-85; ptnr. Sidley & Austin, Washington, 1985-89; pres. Brigham Young U., Provo, Utah, 1989—; asst. U.S. atty-gen. in charge civil div. Justice Dept., Washington.; lectr. Am. Inst. Fgn. Trade, 1966-68, U. Ariz. Sch. Law, 1968-72; George Sutherland prof. law Brigham Young U., 1985—. Mem. gen. bd. Young Men's Mut. Improvement Assn., Ch. of Jesus Christ of Latter-day Saints, 1958-60; bd. dirs. Theodore Roosevelt council Boy Scouts Am., 1967-72. Mem. Am. Law Inst. Home: 2840 Iroquois Dr Provo UT 84604-4318 Office: Brigham Young U D346 ASB Provo UT 84602

LEE, RICHARD FRANCIS JAMES, evangelical clergyman, apologist, researcher; b. Yakima, Wash., Sept. 13, 1967; s. Richard Francis and Dorothy Aldean (Blackwell). Diploma, Berean Coll., Springfield, Mo., 1989; BA, U. Wash., Seattle, 1990. Lic. clergyman Gen. Coun. of the Assemblies of God, Seattle, 1989—. Author: Tell Me the Story, 1982. Named Most Likely to be President, Franklin High Sch., Seattle, 1986. Pentecostal. Home: E 2604 Boone Avenue Spokane WA 99202 Office: Evangel Outreach Ministries E 2604 Boone Avenue Spokane WA 99202

LEE, RICHARD HENRY, computational chemist; b. Summit, N.J., Dec. 7, 1954; s. Floyd Henry Jr. and Mary Helen (Bakker) L. BS in Biochemistry, Upsala Coll., 1977; PhD in Biochem. Scis., Princeton U., 1983. Rsch. assoc. The Milton S. Hershey Med. Ctr., Pa. State U., 1981-86; rsch. scientist Kraft, Inc., Glenview, Ill., 1986-88; mgr. Homology Program Biosym Techs. Inc., San Diego, 1988—. NSF grantee, 1990; recipient Nat. Rsch. Svc. award NIH, 1983-85. Mem. AAAS, Am. Chem. Soc. Office: Biosym Techs Inc 9685 Scranton Rd San Diego CA 92121-2777

LEE, ROBERT ANDREW, librarian; b. Washington, Dec. 7, 1923; s. Frederic Edward and Edna (Stewart) L. BA in English, Oberlin Coll., 1947; MLS, U. So. Calif., 1966. Jr. cataloger Columbia U. Law Library, 1950-51; reference librarian N.Y. Daily Mirror, 1952-54; researcher for Dore Schary MGM, Culver City, Calif., 1955; with Universal City Studios, Calif., 1955—, research librarian, 1960-69, head research dept., 1969-89. Contbr. articles to profl. jours. Served with AUS, 1943-46. Decorated Bronze Star with oak leaf cluster. Mem. Acad. Motion Picture Arts and Scis. (gov. 1973-75), Acad. TV Arts and Scis., Am. Film Inst., Am. Cinematheque. Home: 2212 N Cahuenga Blvd Apt 104 Los Angeles CA 90068-2760

LEE, ROBERT C., superintendent; b. Sept. 18, 1945. BS in Biology, U. So. Utah, 1968; M in Biology, U. Miss., 1973. Cert. essential human resource mgmt., pers. mgmt.; cert. adminstrn. postgrad., Calif. Tchr. jr. high sch. Moreno Valley (Calif.) Unified Sch. Dist., 1968-72, tchr. high sch., 1972-73, asst. prin. jr. high sch., 1973-75, prin. jr. high sch., 1975-78, dir. pers., 1978-80, asst. supt. pers., 1980-84, supt., 1984—; vis. faculty Danforth Found., 1991-93; bd. dirs. Riverside County Sch. Employees Credit Union. Mem. facility adv. coun. Little Hoover Commn.; active Moreno Valley Cultural Arts Found., Moreno Valley Youth Fedn.; mem. pres.'s com. gang violence Calif. State U., San Bernardino; mem. Riverside County Dist. Atty's Adv. Bd.; mem. mil. affairs com. Mar. AFB; bd. dirs. United Way Calif. Recipient Visionary Tech. Leadership award Apple Computer, Inc., 1990; named Outstanding Citizen Moreno Valley, 1992, Outstanding Educator, Hispanic Unidos, 1993. Mem. Am. Assn. Sch. Adminstrs., Nat. Assn. Secondary Sch. Adminstrs., Urban Supt.'s Assn. Am., Assn. Calif. Sch. Adminstrs., Calif. Assn. Suburban Sch. Dists., Western Assn. Schs. and Colls., Moreno Valley C. of C. Office: Moreno Valley USD 13911 Perris Blvd Moreno Valley CA 92553*

LEE, ROGER EDWIN MARK, foundation administrator; b. Kellogg, Idaho, Aug. 19, 1940; s. Edwin George and Alrena (Ellerbroek) L.; m. Asha Singh, Mar. 15, 1969; children: Gayatri Anna, Gitanjali Luia, Nandini Marina. BA in English, Calif. State U., San Francisco, 1965; MEd, U. Calif., Santa Barbara, 1977. Prin. Clear Water Ranch Childrens' Home, Santa Rosa, Calif., 1964-65, Rishi Valley Sch., Andhra Pradesh, India, 1965-72, Alpha Tng. Ctr., Santa Barbara, 1972-75; founding dir. Oak Grove Sch., Ojai, Calif., 1975-85; exec. dir., editor newsletter and bull. Krishnamurti Found. Am., Ojai, 1985—; sec. Sunny House, Inc., Santa Barbara, 1990. Editor bulls. and newsletters Krishnamurti Found. Am., 1985—, Collected Works of Jiddu Krishnamurti, 1991. Founding bd. dirs. Spl. Childrens' Found., Ojai, 1981, trustee, 1981—; v.p. Ojai Fund for Environ., 1981-83. Office: Krishnamurti Found Am PO Box 1560 Ojai CA 93024-1560

LEE, ROLF ELMER, retired public school administrator; b. Richardton, N.D., Oct. 22, 1913; s. Neil Nielson and Petra (Siverts) L.; m. Ora Virginia German, Aug. 23, 1936; children: John Bruce, Richard Allen, Margaret Elaine Costa. BA, DSU, 1935; MA, U. Mont., 1946; EdD, Stanford U., Palo Alto, Calif., 1957; postgrad., U. So. Calif., 1966. Cert. elem. educator, Calif., secondary educator, Calif, gen. adminstr., Calif. High sch. tchr. Wilton (N.D.) Sch. Dist., 1935-36, various schs. Mont., 1936-41; engr. Boeing Airplane Co., Seattle, 1941-43; elem. prin. Sylvan Union Sch. Dist., Modesto, Calif., 1946-48, Turlock (Calif.) Sch. Dist., 1948-53; elem. cons. Stanislaus County Schs. Office, Modesto, 1955-58; field rep., sch. plan. Calif. Dept. of Edn., Sacramento, 1958-60; dir. adminstrv. svc. Moreland Sch. Dist., San Jose, 1960-63; asst. supt. adminstr. Simi Valley (Calif.) Unified Sch. Dist., 1963-73, ret., 1973; adviser grad. program Calif. State U., Long Beach, 1974-75. Svc. mem. Cambria's Anonomous Neighbors, Calif., 1978-89; officer Modesto (Calif.) Inst. for Continued Learning, 1989-92; performing mem. San Luis Obispo (Calif.) Vocal Arts Ensemble, 1978-88. Lt. comdr. USN, 1943-45. Mem. Rotary Club of Modesto East (newsletter editor, bull. 1980), Phi Delta Kappa. Democrat. Presbyterian. Home: 3125 Williamsburg Way Modesto CA 95355-4733

LEE, RONALD DEREK, lawyer; b. Seattle, Aug. 10, 1959; s. Frank B. and Mary (Quan) L. AB, Princeton (N.J.) U., 1980; M of Philosophy, Oxford U., 1982; JD, Yale U., 1985. Bar: N.Y. 1986, D.C. 1987, Calif. 1991. Law clk. to Judge Abner J. Mikva U.S. Ct. Appeals (D.C. cir.), Washington, 1985-86; law clk. to Justice John Paul Stevens U.S. Supreme Ct., Washington, 1986-87; assoc. Arnold & Porter, Washington, 1987-91; assoc. Arnold & Porter, L.A., 1991-92, ptnr., 1993—. Rhodes scholarship Rhodes Trust, 1980. Mem. ABA, State Bar of Calif., Am. Soc. Internat. Law, Phi Beta Kappa. Office: Arnold & Porter 777 S Figueroa St 44th Fl Los Angeles CA 90017

LEE, SAMMY, retired physician, surgeon; b. Fresno, Calif., Aug. 1, 1920; s. Soonkee Rhee and Eunkee Chun; m. Rosalind M.K. Wong, Oct. 1, 1950; children: Pamela Alicia, Sammy Lee II. BA, Occidental Coll., 1943; MD, U. So. Calif., 1947, DSc (hon.), 1984. Diplomate Am. Bd. Otorhino-laryngology. Pvt. practice limited to otology Orange, Calif., 1955-90; intern Orange County Hosp., Calif., 1946-47; resident in otolaryngology Letterman Army Hosp., 1949-53; presdl. rep. Melbourne Olympics, 1956, Munich Games, 1972, Seoul Olympics, 1988; coach diving U.S. Olympics, Rome, 1960, Bob Webster, Rome Olympics, 1960, Tokyo Olympics, 1964, Greg Louganis, Montreal Olympics, 1976; cons. Mission Viejo Nadadores Diving Team, Mission Viejo, Calif.; mem. President's Coun. on Phys. Fitness and Sports, 1971-80; adv. U.S. Internat. Olympic Diving Com. Author: (with other) DIVING, 1983, Not Without Honor, 1987; editor: The New Book of Knowledge, Diving, 1986. Commr. Pres. Commn. on White House Fellows, 1981-88; pres. Coun. on Phys. Fitness and Sports, 1991; hon. chmn. Korean Am. Coalition, L.A., 1986-88, Korean Am. Rep., Orange County, Calif., 1986-88; Olympic flag bearer/torch runner, 1984. Maj. U.S. Army, 1943-55, Korea. Recipient Gold high diving and Bronze medal 3 meter springboard diving London Olympics, 1948, Gold high diving medal Helsinki Olympics, 1952, James E. Sullivan award for outstanding amateur athlete in U.S.A., 1953, Excellence 2000 awards, 1990; named Outstanding Am. Korean Ancestry, Am. Korean Soc., 1967, Outstanding Am. Korean Ancestry, League of Korean Ams., 1986, named to U.S. Olympic Hall of Fame, 1990. Republican. Home: 16537 Harbour Ln Huntington Beach CA 92649-2105

LEE, STEVEN GREGORY, state government employee; b. Butte, Mont., Jan. 15, 1952; s. Charles P. and Joyce (Gilham) L. BA, Idaho State U., Pocatello, 1974. Campaign organizer Andrus for Gov. Campaign, Boise, Idaho, 1986, 90; spl. asst. Gov. Cecil D. Andrus, Boise, 1987-90, Idaho Dept. Adminstrn., Boise, 1991—; freelance photographer, 1977-92. Mem. supervisory com. ESA Credit Union, Boise, 1991—; mem. Gov.'s Lewis and Clark Trail Com., chair, 1992. Named Dem. of Yr., Ada County Dems., Boise, 1990, chmn. award Idaho Dem. Party, 1993. Mem. Idaho State U. Bengal Found., Lewis and Clark Trail Heritage Found. (pres. Idaho chpt. 1992—), Oreg.-Calif. Trails Assn. Home: 3701 Morris Hill Rd # 15 Boise ID 83706

LEE, TING DAVID, JR., cardiologist; b. Portland, Oreg., Jan. 5, 1933; s. Ting David Sr. and Mary (Lau) L.; m. Rosemary Lum, June 29, 1958; children: Jennifer Lee Hirsh, David Michael, Jeffrey Alan. AB, Dartmouth Coll., 1954; MD, Harvard U., 1957. Diplomate Am. Bd. Internal Medicine, Am. Bd. Cardiovascular Disease. Intern in medicine Johns Hopkins Hosp., Balt., 1957-58, asst. resident in medicine, 1958-59; asst. resident in medicine Bellevue Hosp. (Cornell Med. Div.), N.Y.C., 1959-60; fellow in cardiology Johns Hopkins Hosp., 1960-62; clin. assoc. Nat. Heart Inst., Balt., 1962-64; pvt. practice Portland, Oreg., 1964—; Pres. Portland Acad. Medicine, 1983-84; pres. med. staff Physicians and Surgeons Hosp., Portland, 1977-78. With USPHS, 1962-64. Dartmouth Coll. scholar, 1950. Fellow ACP, Am. Coll. Cardiology, Am. Heart Assn. Coun. on Clin. Cardiology; mem. Am. Heart Assn. (pres. Oreg. affiliate 1985-86). Republican. Presbyterian. Home: 10200 SW Hawthorne Ln Portland OR 97225-4327 Office: 9155 SW Barnes Rd Portland OR 97225-6625

LEE, VIN JANG THOMAS, financial company executive, physicist; b. Honan Province, China, Feb. 14, 1937; came to U.S., 1958; s. Tsin-Yin and Hwa-Neu (Mar) L.; m. Doris Y. Feng, Apr. 21, 1957; 1 child, Maxwell. Diploma in ChemE, Ordnance Engring. Coll., Taipei, Taiwan, 1958; MSChemE, U. Notre Dame, 1959; PhD, U. Mich., 1963. Assoc. prof. chem. engring. U. Mo., Columbia, 1965-74; pres. Econo Trading Co., Santa Monica, Calif., 1975-80, Cyberdyne Inc., Santa Monica, 1980—; vis. prof. catalysis and physical chemistry UCLA, 1972-73. Contbr. numerous articles to sci. jours. Mem. Sigma Xi. Lodge: Masons. Office: Cyberdyne Inc 1045 Ocean Ave Apt 2 Santa Monica CA 90403-3539

LEE, W. DAVID, language professional, educator; b. Matador, Tex., Aug. 13, 1944; s. C.D. and Ruth (Rushing) L.; m. Jan M., Aug. 13, 1971; children: Jon Dee, Jodee. MA, Idaho State U., 1970; PhD, U. Utah, 1973. Head, dept. lang. and lit. So. Utah U., Cedar City, 1971—; artist Utah and Wyo. Arts Coun., Salt Lake City, 1978—; judge various literary contests. Poetry editor: Weber Studies, Ogden, Utah, 1985—; author numerous published books including Day's Work (Publ. prize 1989). Bd. dirs. Utah Arts Coun., Salt Lake City, 1978—, Valley View Med. Ctr., Cedar City, 1987; mem. So. Utah U. Faculty Senate. Sgt. U.S. Army, 1967-69. Recipient Creative Writing fellowship Nat. Endowment for Arts, Washington, 1985, 1st place Serious Poetry award Utah Arts Coun., 1988, Publ. prize/Gov.'s award, 1989, Elkhorn Rev. Poetry prize, Norfolk, Nebr., 1989; named Outstanding Educator of Yr., So. Utah State Coll., Cedar City, 1990, Poet Laureate of Zion Canyon, 1990, one of 12 outstanding writers in history of State Utah Endowment for the Humanities. Mem. Am. Colls. and Univs. (selected mem. northwest accreditation team), Utah Acad., UTah Arts Coun. (lit. arts panel, peer review panel), Rocky Mountain Modern Lang. Assn. Home: 883 Mckinley Way Saint George UT 84770-8064 Office: So Utah U Dept Lang and Lit Cedar City UT 84720

LEE, WEI WILLIAM, scientist, company executive; b. Changchun, Jilin, China, June 22, 1958; came to U.S., 1980; s. Geng Yao Lee and Ye Fan. BS, SUNY, Oneonta, 1984; MS, Rensselaer Poly. Inst., 1988, PhD, 1991. Teaching asst. Rensselaer Poly. Inst., Troy, N.Y., 1984-86, rsch. asst., 1986-90; project engr. GTE Products, Co. R & D Engring. Ctr., Salem, Mass., 1990-91; scientist IBM Rsch. Divsn.-Almaden Rsch. Ctr., San Jose, Calif., 1991—; v.p., dir. short-class tng. programs TCM Internat., Fremont, Calif., 1992—; invited speaker various Chinese univs. & insts., 1991. Author, co-author numerous pubs. in field. Mem. Materials Rsch. Soc. (pres. RPI chpt. 1988-89), Am. Vacuum Soc. (Thin Film student award 1990), Am. Chem. Soc., Silicon Valley Chinese Engr. Assn. (v.p. 1992—), Sigma Xi, Phi Lambda Upsilon. Home: 5634 Calmor Ave # 4 San Jose CA 95123 Office: IBM Rsch Divsn Almaden Rsch Ctr 650 Harry Rd K93/801 San Jose CA 95120

LEE, YUAN T(SEH), chemistry educator; b. Hsinchu, Taiwan, China, Nov. 29, 1936; came to U.S., 1962, naturalized, 1974; s. Tsefan and Pei (Tasi) L.; m. Bernice Wu, June 28, 1963; children: Ted, Sidney, Charlotte. BS, Nat. Taiwan U., 1959; MS, Nat. Tsinghua U., Taiwan, 1961; PhD, U. Calif., Berkeley, 1965. From asst. prof. to prof. chemistry U. Chgo., 1968-74; prof. U. Calif., Berkeley, 1974—, also prin. investigator Lawrence Berkeley Lab. Contbr. numerous articles on chem. physics to profl. jours. Recipient Nobel Prize in Chemistry, 1986, Ernest O. Lawrence award Dept. Energy, 1981, Nat. Medal of Sci., 1986, Peter Debye award for Phys. Chemistry, 1986; fellow Alfred P. Sloan, 1969-71, John Simon Guggenheim, 1976-77; Camille and Henry Dreyfus Found. Tchr. scholar, 1971-74. Fellow Am. Phys. Soc.; mem. NAS, AAAS, Am. Acad. Arts and Scis., Am. Chem. Soc. Office: U Calif Dept Chemistry Berkeley CA 94720*

LEEB, CHARLES SAMUEL, clinical psychologist; b. San Francisco, July 18, 1945; s. Sidney Herbert and Dorothy Barbara (Fishstrom) L.; m. Storme Lynn Gilkey, Apr. 28, 1984; children: Morgan Evan, Spencer Douglas. BA in Psychology, U. Calif.-Davis, 1967; MS in Counseling and Guidance, San Diego State U., 1970; PhD in Edn. and Psychology, Claremont Grad. Sch., 1973. Assoc. So. Regional Dir. Mental Retardation Ctr., Las Vegas, Nev., 1976-79; pvt. practice, Las Vegas, 1978-79; dir. biofeedback and athletics Menninger Found., Topeka, 1979-82, dir. children's div. biofeedback and psychophysiology ctr. The Menninger Found., 1979-82; pvt. practice, Claremont, Calif., 1982—; dir. of psychol. svcs. Horizon Hosp., 1986-88; dir. adolescent chem. dependency and children's program Charter Oak Hosp., Covina, Calif., 1989-91; founder, chief exec. officer Rsch. and Treatment Inst., Claremont, 1991; lectr. in field. Contbr. articles to profl. jours. Mem. Am. Psychol. Assn., Calif. State Psychol. Assn. Office: 937 W Foothill Blvd Ste D Claremont CA 91711-3358

LEEDS-HORWITZ, SUSAN BETH, school system administrator, speech-language pathology educator; b. L.A., Mar. 14, 1950; d. Henry Herbert and Lee (Weiss) Leeds; m. Stanley Martin Horwitz, Nov. 28, 1975; 1 child, Brian David. BA, Calif. State U., Northridge, 1971; MEd, U. S.C., 1973; adminstrv. credential, U. LaVerne, 1984. Itinerant speech pathologist L.A. City Schs., 1973-74; severe lang. disorders tchr. L.A. County Bd. Edn., Downey, Calif., 1974-88; tchr. on spl. assignment Santa Clarita Valley Spl. Edn. Local Plan Area, Newhall, Calif., 1986-88; coord. spl. programs, testing, evaluation and migrant edn. Castaic (Calif.) Union Sch. Dist., 1988—, adminstr., 1988—. Author: Project Próspero: A Traditional Bilingual Education Program for Grades 2-8, 1991. Active Santa Clarita Valley Spl. Edn. PTA, Newhall, 1984—; grantee Project VISTA ValVerde-Castaic involvement sports, team activities, 1992—. Grantee student enhancement program Kaiser-Permanente Community Svcs., 1992. Mem. Am. Speech, Lang. and Hearing Assn. (cert.), So. Calif. Assn. Alumnae Panhellenic (pres. 1993—), Downs Syndrome Congress, Assn. Calif. Sch. Adminstrs., San Fernando Valley Panhellenic Assn. (reps. 1976—, pres. 1990-92), Santa Clarita Valley C. of C. (edn. com., anti-gang com., tchr. tribute com.), Delta Kappa Gamma, Alpha Xi Delta (Edna Epperson Brinkman award 1985), Phi Delta Kappa. Office: Castaic Union Sch Dist 31616 Ridge Route Rd Castaic CA 91384-3300

LEELAND, STEVEN BRIAN, electronics engineer; b. Tampa, Fla., Dec. 27, 1951; s. N. Stanford and Shirley Mae (Bahner) L.; m. Karen Frances Hayes, Dec. 20, 1980; children: Crystal Mary, April Marie. BSEE, MSEE magna cum laude, U. South Fla., 1976. Registered profl. engr., Ariz. Engr. Bendix Avionics, Ft. Lauderdale, Fla., 1976-77; prin. engr., instr. Sperry Avionics, Phoenix, 1977-84; prin. staff engr. Motorola Govt. Electronics Group, Scottsdale, Ariz., 1984-88; sr. staff engr. Fairchild Data Corp., Scottsdale, 1988—; cons. Motorola Govt. Electronics Group, 1991. Patentee systolic array, 1990; contbr. articles to profl. jours. Mem. IEEE (Phoenix chpt. Computer Soc. treas. 1978-79, sec. 1979-80, chmn. 1980-81, 81-82), Tau Beta Pi, Pi Mu Epsilon, Phi Kappa Phi, Omicron Delta Kappa, Themis. Republican. Adventist. Home: 10351 E Sharon Dr Scottsdale AZ 85260-9000 Office: Fairchild Data Corp 350 N Hayden Rd Scottsdale AZ 85257-4692

LEEN, TODD KEVIN, physicist; b. Glen Ridge, N.J., Dec. 24, 1955; S. Albert and Miriam (Proskauer) L. BS in Physics, Worcester Poly. Inst., 1977; MS in Physics, U. Wis., 1979; PhD in Physics, U. Wis., Milw., 1982. Research and teaching asst. U. Wis., Madison, 1979-82; scientist, engr. IBM, Burlington, Vt., 1982-87; rsch. assoc. Neurol. Scis. Inst. Good Samaritan Hosp., Portland, Oreg., 1987-89; sr. scientist Oreg. Grad. Inst., Beaverton, Oreg., 1989-90; asst. prof. Oreg. Grad. Inst., Beaverton, 1990—. Contbr. articles to profl. jours. Mem. Am. Phys. Soc., Internat. Neural Network Soc., Tau Beta Pi, Sigma Pi Sigma, Phi Kappa Phi. Jewish. Office: Oreg Grad Inst Dept Computer Sci & Engring 19600 NW Von Neumann Dr Beaverton OR 97006-6904

LEES, ALLAN MILNE, publishing manager; b. Awali, Bahrain, Jan. 14, 1959; s. Peter Allan and Wilma June (Brown) L.; m. Anne-Christine Strugnell, Aug. 11, 1988. BA, Oxford U., 1987; MS, Lancaster U., 1988; MBA, Warwick U., 1991. Cons. BDO Binder Hamlyn, London, 1988-89; prin. Orgn. & System Innovations, London, 1989-91; mgr., dir. Krames Comms., Calif., 1991—. Author: (essay) 2010, 1987, (conf. paper) IEE ITAP, 1989. Mem. Assn. MBAs. Office: Krames Comms 1100 Grundy Ln San Bruno CA 94066-3030

LE FAVE, GENE MARION, polymer amd chemical company executive; b. Green Bay, Wis., May 18, 1924; s. Thomas Paul and Marie Agnes (Young) Le F.; m. Rosemary Beatrice Sackinger, Aug. 28, 1948; children: Laura, Deborah, Michele, Mark, Camille, Jacques, Louis. BS, U. Notre Dame, 1948; MS, Butler U., 1950. Staff engr. P.R. Mallory & Co., Indpls., 1953-54; sr. staff engr. Lear, Inc., Santa Monica, Calif., 1954-56; chief engr. G.M. Giannini & Co., Pasadena, Calif., 1956; v.p., dir. Coast Pro Seal & Mfg. Co., Compton, Calif., 1956-64; cons. Input/Output, Whittier, Calif., 1964-67, Diamond Shamrock, Painesville, Ohio, 1967-71; mem. bd. cons. U.S. Army Corps of Engrs., Mariemont, Ohio, 1964-71; cons. Joslyn Mfg. & Supply Co., Chgo., 1964-72, Arco Chem. Co., Phila., 1969-75; pres. Fluid Polymers, Inc., Las Vegas, Nev., 1970—; bd. dirs. Polimeros Flexibles de Monterrey (Mexico), SA, Desert Industries, Inc., Las Vegas. Contbr. articles to profl. jours. Bd. dirs. adv. com. Nat. Bus., Las Vegas, 1990—; mem. regents com. on sci. and tech. U. Nev., Las Vegas, 1990—; mem., chmn. Rep. Party, Whittier, 1965-67. Mem. Am. Inst. Chem. Engrs., Am. Inst. Chemists, Am. Concrete Inst. Byzantine Catholic. Home: 1568 Leatherleaf Dr Las Vegas NV 89123-1942

LEFEVRE, GREG (LOUIS), bureau chief; b. Los Angeles, Jan. 28, 1947; s. Robert Bazille and Anna Marie (Violé) L.; m. Mary Deborah Bottoms, July

10, 1971. AA, Valley Coll., 1970; BS, San Diego State U., 1972, postgrad. Asst. news dir. Sta. KDEO, San Diego, 1971-73; reporter Sta. KFMB-TV, San Diego, 1973-75; sr. reporter Sta. KDFW-TV, Dallas, 1976-81; news dir. Sta. KSEE-TV, Fresno, Calif., 1981-83; corr. Cable News Network, San Francisco, 1983-89, bur. chief, 1990—. Mem. AP Broadcasters (bd. dirs. 1981-90), Soc. Profl. Journalists (pres. 1979-81), Radio and TV News Dirs. Assn. (bd. dirs. 1988-90). Club: Dallas Press (v.p. 1978-81). Office: CNN Am Inc 50 California St Ste 950 San Francisco CA 94111-4624

LEFF, HARVEY SHERWIN, physics educator; b. Chgo., July 24, 1937; s. Jack William and Anne Sharon (Maiman) L.; m. Ellen Janice Wine, Aug. 17, 1958; children: Lisa, Robyn, Jordan, Jeremy. BS in Physics, Ill. Inst. Tech., Chgo., 1959; MS in Physics, Northwestern U., 1960; PhD in Physics, U. Iowa, 1963. Rsch. assoc. Case Inst. Tech., Cleve., 1963-64; asst. to assoc. prof. physics Case Western Res. U., Cleve., 1964-71; vis. prof. physics Harvey Mudd Coll. of Sci. & Engring., Claremont, Calif., 1977-78; prof. and assoc. prof. physics Chgo. State U., 1971-79; scientist Oak Ridge (Tenn.) Assoc. U., 1979-83; prof. physics and chmn. physics dept. Calif. State Poly. U., Pomona, 1983—; physics co-coord. Calif. State U. Inst. for Teaching & Learning, Long Beach, 1989—; insvc. tchr., workshop leader in field; vis. scientist Am. Inst. Physics, 1973-76. Contbr. articles to profl. jours.; co-author/co-editor: (with A.F. Rex) Maxwell's Demon: Entropy, Information, Computing, 1990; assoc. editor Am. Jour. of Physics, 1992—. Calif. State Poly. U. Meritorious Performance & Profl. Promise award, 1987, 88, 90. Mem. Calif. Sci. Tchrs. Assn., Am. Phys. Soc., Assn. Women in Sci., Am. Assn. Physics Tchrs. (v.p. So. Calif. sect. 1989-91, pres. 1991-93), Sigma Xi (chpt. pres. 1990-91). Home: 538 E Bishop Pl Claremont CA 91711-3506 Office: Calif State Poly Univ 3801 W Temple Ave Pomona CA 91768-2557

LEFFLER, ADRIENNE KAREL, political science educator; b. Chgo., Sept. 24, 1934; d. Bernard and Lenore (Siegal) Karel; m. Robert Leffler, Aug. 28, 1960 (dec. 1990); 1 child, Lawrence Steven. BA in Social Sci. with distinction, San Diego State U., 1969, MA in Polit. Sci., 1975. Instr. ESL Converse Sch. Langs., San Diego, 1976-80; adj. faculty, instr. polit. sci. San Diego C.C. Dist., 1976-85, Grossmont Coll., El Cajon, Calif., 1978—. Author: Wine Country (California), 1992; freelance writer for newspapers and jours. Mem. Faculty Assn. Calif. Community Colls., United Faculty Grossmont Coll. Office: 5156 Judson Way San Diego CA 92115-1625

LEFOND, ANNE MAY, real estate broker; b. Ashland, Wis., Apr. 26, 1917; d. Charles and Anna (Erickson) Newman; BA cum laude, Northland Coll., Ashland, 1939; MLS, U. Wis., 1940; m. Stanley J. Lefond, Dec. 26, 1946 (dec. Nov. 1985); children: Dennis C., Robert E.; m. George V. VonVihl, 1986. Reference librarian Colgate U., Hamilton, N.Y., 1945-46, U. Mich., Ann Arbor, 1949-52; librarian Euclid (Ohio) Public Schs., 1953-66; sales assoc. Lloyd C. Helgager Co., Woodland Hills, Calif., 1967-70; broker New Eng. Realty Co., Westport, Conn., 1970-72; broker-mgr. Crown Realty Co., Evergreen, Colo., 1972-75; broker-assoc. Junction Realty Co., Evergreen, 1976-84, Remax-Evergreen, 1984-87; broker, mgr. Old Mine Real Estate, 1987—; v.p. Indsl. Minerals, Inc., Evergreen, 1976-85. Mem. Evergreen Bd. Realtors (dir.), Colo. Assn. Realtors, Nat. Assn. Real Estate Brokers, Nat. Inst. Real Estate Brokers. C. of C., Hiwan Country Club, Swedish Club of Denver. Lutheran. Home: 29983 Canterbury Cir Evergreen CO 80439-8810

LEFTWICH, JAMES STEPHEN, management consultant; b. Stevenage, Eng., Nov. 30, 1956; came to U.S., 1957; s. James Wright and Del Maureen (Thomson) L.; m. Carol Petersen, Nov. 7, 1980 (div. Jan. 1982). AA in Criminal Justice, Butte Coll., Oroville, Calif., 1981; BA, S.W. U., 1993. Lic. internat. accredited safety auditor; cert. hazardous material specialist. Prodn. mgr. Artistic Dyers Inc., El Monte, Calif., 1976-80; mgr. loss control and risk mgmt. Mervyn's Dept. Stores, Hawyard, Calif., 1982-91; dir. risk mgmt. Save Mart Corp., Modesto, Calif., 1991-93; v.p. ops. I.C.S. Corp., Irvine, Calif., 1993—; cons. R.I.M. Assocs., Walnut Creek, Calif., 1989—; instructor Claims Mgmt., 1993; speaker in field. Scriptwriter, tech. advisor 12 safety videos; contbr. articles on safety and risk mgmt. to profl. publs. Res. police officer Cotati (Calif.) Police Dept., 1983-85; fundraiser United Way, Hayward, 1986, Am. Found. for AIDS Rsch., L.A., 1990; bd. dirs. Bay Area Safety Coun., Oakland, Calif., 1987-88; trustee Calif. Safety Ctr., Sacramento, 1990-91, dir., 1991—. Mem. Am. Soc. for Safety Engrs., Nat. Safety Mgmt. Soc., Nat. Fire Protection Assn., Risk and Ins. Mgmt. Soc., Nat. Assn. Chiefs Police, Nat. Environ. Tng. Assn. Office: ICS Corp Irvine CA

LEGARE, HENRI FRANCIS, archbishop; b. Willow-Bunch, Sask., Can., Feb. 20, 1918; s. Phillippe and Amanda (Douville) L. B.A., U. Ottawa, 1940; theol. student, Lebret, Sask., 1940-44; M.A., Laval U., 1946; Dr. Social Sci., Cath. U. Lille, France, 1950; LL.D. (hon.), Carleton U., Ottawa, 1959, Windsor (Ont.) U., 1960, Queens U., Kingston, Ont., 1961, U. Sask., 1963, Waterloo (Ont.) Luth. U., 1965, U. Ottawa, Can., 1984; Doctor of Univ., U. of Ottawa. Ordained priest Roman Cath. Ch., 1943; prof. sociology Laval U., 1947, U. Ottawa, 1951; exec. dir. Cath. Hosp. Assn. Can., 1952-57; dean faculty social scis. U. Ottawa, 1954-58, pres., 1958-64; provincial Oblate Fathers, Winnipeg, Man., 1966-67; bishop of Labrador, 1967-72; archbishop Grouard-McLennan, Alta., 1972—. Contbr. articles to profl. jours. Chmn. Canadian Univs. Found., 1960- 62. Decorated grand cross merit Order Malta, 1964; order merit French Lang. Assn. Ont., 1965. Mem. Assn. Canadian Univs. (pres. 1960-62), Can. Conf. Cath. Bishops (pres. 1981-83), Internat. Assn. Polit. Sci. Address: Archbishop's House, CP 388, McLennan, AB Canada T0H 2L0

LEGER, RICHARD ROUBINE, public relations executive, writer; b. Schenectady, N.Y., Oct. 27, 1935; s. Roubine Joseph and Catherine Bernice (Waikas) L.; m. Lawrence Lowell Putnam, Sept. 14, 1957 (div. 1971); children: Philip Augustus, William Richard, Catherine Lowell; m. Dianne Lee Williams, May 14, 1978. BA, U. Rochester, 1957. Reporter Wall St. Jour., N.Y.C., 1960-63, 69-70, Atlanta, 1963-69, San Francisco, 1972-76; fgn. corr. Wall St. Jour., London, 1976-78; bur. chief Wall St. Jour., Nairobi, Kenya, 1978-80; econ. editor San Francisco Chronicle, San Francisco, 1982-84; owner/pub. Sebastopol Times, Sebastopol, Calif., 1985-86; pres. Leger Networks, Inc., San Francisco, 1988—.

LEGG, DAVID E., entomologist, educator; b. Kansas City, Mo., Sept. 25, 1955; s. William J. and Ruth Ann (Thompson) L.; m. Cynthia Sue Volden, July 20, 1985; children: Sarah Kirsten, Taylor Marie. BS in Agr., U. Mo., 1978, MS in Entomology, 1980; PhD in Entomology, U. Minn., 1983. Postdoctoral fellow U. Ky., Lexington, 1983-84; prin. investigator Ky. State U., Frankfort, 1984-88; asst. prof. integrated pest mgmt. U. Wyo., Laramie, 1988—; cons. FAO, Bangkok, 1986, 87. Contbr. articles to refereed sci. jours. Grantee USDA, 1985, 86, 87. Mem. Colo.-Wyo. Acad. Sci., Ky. Acad. Sci. (governing bd. 1987-88), Entomol. Soc. Am., S.C. Entomol. Soc., Sigma Xi., Gamma Sigma Delta. Office: Univ Wyo PO Box 3354 Laramie WY 82071-3354

LEGGE, CHARLES ALEXANDER, federal judge; b. San Francisco, Aug. 24, 1930; s. Roy Alexander and Wilda (Rampton) L.; m. Janice Meredith Sleeper, June 27, 1952; children: Jeffrey, Nancy, Laura. AB with distinction, Stanford U., 1952, JD, 1954. Bar: Calif. 1955. Assoc. Bronson, Bronson & McKinnin, San Francisco, 1956-64, ptnr., 1964-84, chmn., 1978-84; judge U.S. Dist. Ct. (no. dist.) Calif., San Francisco, 1984—. Served with U.S. Army, 1954-56. Fellow Am. Coll. Trial Lawyers; mem. Calif. Bar Assn. (past chmn. adminstrn. justice com.). Republican. Clubs: Bohemian, World Trade (San Francisco); Orinda (Calif.) Country. Office: US Dist Ct PO Box 36060 450 Golden Gate Ave San Francisco CA 94102

LEGRAND, SHAWN PIERRE, computer systems programmer; b. San Diego, Nov. 27, 1960; s. Roger and Violet Louise (Howe) L. Grad. high sch., El Cajon, Calif.; student, U. Calif., San Diego, 1992—. Cert. computer programmer. Computer operator Grossmont CCD, El Cajon, 1978-79; computer systems programmer ICW, San Diego, 1979—. Recipient Math. Achievement award Bank of Am., 1978. Mem. IEEE, Math. Assn. Am., Assn. Computing Machinery. Republican. Office: ICW 10140 Campus Point Dr San Diego CA 92121-1592

LEHMAN, GARY DOUGLAS, domestic chef; b. Abington, Pa., Feb. 7, 1951; s. Robert Ralston Sr. and Jane Anna (Springer) L. BA in Social Sci., Mich. State U., 1971; postgrad., Calif. Culinary Acad., San Francisco, 1976-77. Exec. chef Holiday Inn, Honolulu, 1979-80; domestic chef Allan Carr, Honolulu, Beverly Hills, Calif., 1980-81, Clare Boothe Luce, Honolulu, 1981-83, Mr. and Mrs. Bernard Cantor, Beverly Hills, 1984-85, Mr. Joseph Ridder, Honolulu, 1985-86, Mr. and Mrs. Sid Bass, Ft. Worth, 1986-87, Mr. and Mrs. John Devine, Tuxedo Park, N.Y., 1987, Mr. and Mrs. Frank Pearl, Washington, 1989; realtor Prudential Hunter Realty, Lompoc, Calif., 1990—; state dir. Calif. Assn. Realtors, 1993—. Democrat. Home: 517 Venus Ave Lompoc CA 93436-1935 Office: Prudential Hunter Realty 531 N H St Lompoc CA 93436-5398

LEHMAN, GODFREY DAVIDSBURG, advertising sales professional, freelance writer; b. South Naples, Maine, June 5, 1916; s. Eugene Heitler and Madeleine Therese (Davidsburg) L.; m. Jay Adele Rose; children: Madeleine Therese Lehman Bucci, Jennifer Margo Lehman. AB, U. Chgo., 1937; postgrad., U. Minn., U. Calif., Berkeley. Reporter Napa Register, Santa Rosa Press Democrat, 1949-51; journalist, freelance writer, 1951-70; advt. sales rep. Brown and Bigelow, St. Paul, Ohio, 1970-80, Shaw-Barton, Coshocton, Ohio, 1980-92. Author: What You Need to Know for Jury Duty, 1969, The Ordeal of Edward Bushell, 1988, So You've Been Called for Jury Duty. Congratulations!, 1972; columnist Justice Times, L.A. Daily Jour., San Francisco Daily Jour.; commentator sta. KQED-FM, San Francisco; contbr. articles to Am. Heritage, Liberty, other mags. 1st lt. U.S. Army, 1942-46, PTO. Mem. Fully Informed Jury Assn., Nat. Coalition to Reform Money and Taxes, Free Enterprise Soc., Freeman Edn. Assn. Office: 333 Kearny St San Francisco CA 94108

LEHMAN, HYLA BEROEN, performing artist, educator; b. Story City, Iowa; d. Lewis Bernard and Helene Louise (Hagen) Beroen; student Waldorf Coll.; BS in Edn., Drake U., 1939; MA, U. Iowa, 1947; postgrad. in classical theatre, Athens, Greece, 1978; m. Fredrick Brackin Lehman, Apr. 30, 1942; children: Rolfe Beroen, Rhea Helene. Tchr. theatre arts and English, LaPorte City, Iowa, Des Moines, Alexandria, Va., Los Angeles; performing artist Theatre Co., L.A., 1942-44; mem. faculty dept. theatre Coe Coll., Cedar Rapids, Iowa, 1974-79; artistic cons. Dance Theatre of the Hemispheres, 1979—, performing artist including Elizabethan Twelfth Night, The Nutcracker, Le Chemin de la Croix, Afternoon in an English Garden, Chidambaram Karanas, Orpheus and Euridice, The Fairie Queen, Dramatist's Choice, A Digit of the Moon, others, 1967—, also bd. dirs.; chmn. bd., 1981-86; bd. regents Waldorf Coll.; judge Am. Coll. Theatre Festival; performer, lectr. at various colls. and univs. Mem. Gov.'s Conf. on Edn.; mem. nat. alumni bd. Drake U.; chmn. Linn County unit Am. Cancer Soc.; mem. Nat. Commn. on Future Drake U.; mem. Public Health Nursing Bd. Recipient Disting. Alumni award Waldorf Coll., 1969. Mem. Am. Theatre Assn., AAUW (state pres. 1952-54, state arts chmn. 1950-52; fellowship named in her honor), Phi Mu Gamma (nat. alumnae dir. 1947-50, nat. pres. 1950-52), Phi Theta Kappa, Kappa Delta Pi. Lutheran. Home: 130 Thompson Dr SE # 110 Cedar Rapids IA 52403

LEHMAN, JOHN ALAN, business educator, consultant, acting dean; b. Wakefield, Nebr., Oct. 9, 1951; s. Alan Daniel and Kathryn (Kennedy) L.; m. Lisa M. Lehman, Oct. 11, 1974. BA, U. Mich., 1972, MA, 1973, MBA, 1977, PhD, 1982. Cert. mgmt. acct. Instr. Taiwan Nat. Normal U., Taipei, 1973-74; asst. prof. U. Minn., Mpls., 1982-87; assoc. prof., acting dean U. Alaska, Fairbanks, 1987-91, prof., 1991—. Author: Object Based 4th Generation Program Design, 1990. Home: PO Box 83837 Fairbanks AK 99708-3837 Office: U Alaska Sch Mgmt 101 Bunnell Fairbanks AK 99775

LEHMAN, RICHARD HENRY, congressman; b. Sanger, Calif., July 20, 1948. AA, Fresno City Coll., 1968; BA, U. Calif., Santa Cruz, 1971. Adminstrv. aide to Assemblyman George N. Zenovich Calif. State Assembly, Sacramento, 1969-76, mem., 1976-82, asst. majority leader, 1980-82; mem. 98th-103rd Congresses from 18th (now 19th) Dist. Calif., 1983—; mem. Energy and Commerce, Natural Resources Comms.; regional whip 99th and 100th Congresses; , whip at large 101st Congress. With Calif. NG, 1970-76. Democrat. Office: US House of Representatives 1226 Longworth House Office Bldg Washington DC 20515-0519*

LEHMAN, ROBERT GEORGE, electrical engineer; b. Geneva, N.Y., Oct. 17, 1953; s. Robert Frederick and Genevieve Victoria (Grodzicki) L.; m. Melanie Lynn Hendershot, Sept. 13, 1981; children: Paul Andrew, Miranda Elizabeth, Bethany Ellen. BSEE, Wilkes U., Wilkes-Barre, Pa., 1975. Sr. engr. Aerospace Svcs. divsn. Pan Am. World Airways, Patrick AB/Cape Canaveral, Fla., 1975-84; prin. engr. Sperry Corp., Glendale, Ariz., 1984-87, Honeywell Inc., Glendale, 1987—; Contbr. articles to profl. jours.; patentee in field. Dean's scholar Wilkes U., 1975. Office: Honeywell Inc MS AZ77 2AA81A3 5353 W Bell Rd Glendale AZ 85308

LEHMANN, RICHARD J., banker; b. Portland, OR, 1944. BA, U. Wash., 1967, MBA, 1969. Trainee European div. Citibank, 1969-70, planning officer, 1970-71, sr. asst. mgr., 1971-72, gen. mgr. German ops., 1972-74, sr. rep., 1974-76, sr. officer ops. European div., 1976; pres., chief exec. officer Citicorp, 1977-85, sr. corp officer Europe, Africa, Mid. East, from 1985; pres. Valley Nat. Bank of Ariz. and Valley Nat. Corp., from 1988, now chmn. bd., chief exec. officer. Office: Valley Nat Corp PO Box 71 Phoenix AZ 85253*

LEHMANN, WERNER HANS, mail order company executive; b. Bronx, N.Y., July 4, 1946; s. William Charles and Grete (Mueller) L.; m. Noreen V. Warren, Aug. 17, 1985. Student, Collegiate Bus. Inst., 1969. Systems adviser IBM, Germany, 1970-75; sales rep. Zeitelhack Steel, Germany, 1976-77; store mgr. Warren Co., Germany, 1977-82; proprietor Euro Posters, N.Y.C., 1982-92, Denver, 1992—. With U.S. Army, 1964-67. Home and Office: 531 Clayton Denver CO 80206

LEHN, JOHN STEVEN, mayor, county official; b. Visalia, Calif., Nov. 4, 1953; s. George John and Mildred Evelyn (Wilson) Taylor; m. Cheryl Lavonne Bertaina, Feb. 5, 1983; children: Aaron Attebery, Chase. BSW, Calif. State U., Fresno, 1976. Advisor, planner Kings County Supt. of Schs., Hanford, Calif., 1976-77; program technician Kings County Job Tng. Office, Hanford, 1977, ops. analyst, 1977-79, sr. ops. analyst, 1979-80, dir., 1980—. Chmn. Big Bros./Big Sisters of Kings County, 1978-81, Community Action Child Care Com., Hanford, 1984—; councilman City of Hanford, 1989—, mayor, 1992—; bd. dirs. Study Team for At-Risk Students, Hanford High Sch., 1988—. Democrat. Roman Catholic. Office: Kings County Job Tng Office 1222 W Lacey Blvd Hanford CA 93230-5900

LEHR, ELLEN, pediatric psychologist; b. St. Louis, Apr. 3, 1946; d. Clarence Henry and Augusta (Stahmer) Kremmel; m. William Lehr, Jan. 29, 1967; children: Aaron Sung, Adam Manop. AB, Boston U., 1971, EdM, 1972; PhD, Boston Coll., 1978. Lic. psychologist, Wash.; cert. sch. psychologist, Wash.; Diplomate Am. Bd. Med. Psychotherapists. Asst. prof. U. Wis., Milw., 1977-79; postdoctoral fellow Georgetown Univ. Hosp., Washington, 1979-81; sr. pediatric psychologist Rehab. Inst. of Chgo., 1981-88; clin. assoc. prof. Univ. of Medicine and Denistry of N.J., New Brunswick, 1988-89; assoc. program dir. New Medico Community Re-entry Svcs. of Wash., Seattle, 1989-90; psychologist pvt. practice Seattle, 1990—; participant U.S. Dept. of Edn. and the Nat. Inst. of Disability and Rehab. Rsch. Author: Psychological Management of Traumatic Brain Inuries in Children and Adolescents, 1990. Mem. APA, Internat. Neuropsychol. Soc., Nat. Acad. of Neuropsychology, Nat. Head Injury Found. Office: 19105 36th Ave W Ste #206 Lynnwood WA 98036

LEHR, JEFFREY MARVIN, immunologist, allergist; b. N.Y.C., Apr. 29, 1942; s. Arthur and Stella (Smellow) L.; m. Suzanne Kozuk, Apr. 4, 1965; children: Elisa, Alexandra, Vanessa, Ryan. BS, City Coll., Bklyn., 1963; MD, NYU, 1967. Resident, fellow Beth Israel Hosp., N.Y.C., 1968-72; resident in allergy/immunology, internal medicine Roosevelt Hosp., N.Y.C., 1968-72; allergist, immunologist Monterey, Calif., 1974—. Chmn. Monterey Bay Air Pollution Hearing Bd., 1982—; v.p. Lyceum of Monterey, 1977-83. Maj. USAF, 1972-74. Fellow Am. Acad. Allergy/Immunology, Am. Coll. Allergy/Immunology, Am. Assn. Cert. Allergists; mem. Am. Lung Assn. (b.p. 1989-91), Monterey County Med. Soc. (pres. 1990-91). Office: 798 Cass St Monterey CA 93940 also: 262 San Jose St Salinas CA 93901

LEHRER, WILLIAM PETER, JR., animal scientist; b. Bklyn., Feb. 6, 1916; s. William Peter and Frances Reif (Muser) L.; m. Lois Lee Meister, Sept. 13, 1945; 1 child, Sharon Elizabeth. BS, Pa. State U., 1941; MS in Agr., MS in Range Mgmt., U. Idaho, 1946, 55; PhD in Animal Nutrition, Wash. State U., 1951; LLB, Blackstone Sch. Law, 1972; JD, U. Chgo., 1974; MBA, Pepperdine U., 1975. Mgmt. trainee Swift & Co., Charleston, W.Va., 1941-42; farm mgr. Maple Springs Farm, Middletown, N.Y., 1944-45; rsch. fellow U. Idaho, Moscow, 1945; asst. prof. to prof. U. Idaho, 1945-60; dir. nutrition Albers Milling Co., L.A., 1960-62; dir. nutrition and rsch. Albers Milling Co., 1962-74, Albers Milling Co. & John W. Eshelman & Sons, L.A., 1974-76, Carnation Co., L.A., 1976-81; ret.; cons. in field; speaker, lectr. more than 40 univs. in U.S. and abroad. Contbr. articles to profl. jours.; co-author: The Livestock Industry, 1950, Dog Nutrition, 1972; author weekly col., Dessert News, Salt Lake City. Mem. rsch. adv. co. U.S. Brewers Assn., 1969-81; mem. com. on dog nutrition, com. animal nutrition Nat. Rsch. Coun. NAS, 1970-76. With U.S. Army Air Corps, 1942-43. Named Disting. Alumnus, Pa. State U., 1963, 1983, Key Alumnus, 1985; named to U. Idaho Alumni Hall of Fame, 1985, others. Fellow AAAS, Am. Soc. Animal Sci.; mem. Am. Inst. Nutrition, Coun. for Agrl. Sci. & Tech., Am. Registry of Profl. Animal Scientists, Am. Inst. Food Technologists, Animal Nutrition Rsch. Coun., Am. Dairy Sci. Assn., Am. Soc. Agrl. Engrs., Am. Feed Mfrs. Assn. (life, nutrition coun. 1962-81, chmn. 1969-70), Calif. State Poly. U. (adv. coun. 1965-81, Meritorious Svc. award), The Nutrition Today Soc., Am. Soc. Animal Sci., Poultry Sci. Assn., Nat. Block & Bridle Club, Hayden Lake Country Club, Alpha Zeta, Sigma Xi, Gamma Sigma Delta (Alumni Award of Merit), Xi Sigma Pi. Republican. Home: Rocking L Ranch 12180 Rimrock Rd Hayden Lake ID 83835

LEHRNER, LAWRENCE MARSHALL, physician; b. Cin., Feb. 9, 1949; s. Harold Nathan and Ruth (Begun) L.; m. Marilyn Jacobs Lehrner, Aug. 23, 1970; children: Stephanie, David. BS, Ind. U., 1971, PhD, 1974, MD, 1975. Diplomate Am. Bd. Internal Medicine, Nephrology. Resident in internal medicine William Beaumont Army Hosp., El Paso, Tex., 1976-79, internist, 1979-80; fellowship in nephrology Southwestern Med. Sch., Dallas, 1980-82; nephrologist U.S. Army Inst. of Surg. Rsch., San Antonio, 1982-85; internist Aspen Med., Las Vegas, 1985-87; nephrologist Nephrology and Endocrine Assocs., Las Vegas, 1987—; chief dept. medicine Humana Hosp. Sunrise, Las Vegas, 1991-92, med. exec. com., 1991-92, chief nephrology, 1989-90, dir. utilization rev., 1989-90. Contbr. numerous articles to profl. jours. Trustee B'nai B'rith Nate Mack Lodge, Las Vegas, 1992—, pres. 1988-89, v.p. membership, 1987-88; vice chmn. Nev. Physicians Caucus, Las Vegas, 1991—. Maj. U.S. Army, 1976-85. Fellow ACP; mem. AMA, Internat. Soc. Nephrology, Am. Soc. Nephrology, Sigma Xi, Phi Eta Sigma. Jewish. Home: 8 Hummingbird Henderson NV 89014 Office: Nephrology & Endocrine Assocs 500 S Rancho #12 Las Vegas NV 89106

LEHTIHALME, LARRY (LAURI) K., financial planner; b. Montreal, Que., Can., Feb. 26, 1937; came to U.S., 1964; s. Lauri Johann and Selma Maire (Piispanen) L.; m. Elizabeth Speed Smith, Sept. 9, 1961; children: Tina Beth, Shauna Lyn. Student, Sir George Williams U., Montreal, 1960-64, Mission Coll., San Fernando, Calif., 1978-80, Pierce Coll., Woodland Hills, Calif., 1990-92. Acct., customer svc. cons. No. Electric, Montreal, 1957-64; salesman Remington Rand Systems, Wilmington, Del., 1964-67; account exec., comm. cons. Pacific Tel. & Telegraph Co., L.A., 1968-84; tech. customer support specialist AT&T, L.A., 1984-85; fin. planner, registered rep. IDS Fin. Svcs., L.A., 1987—; Lic. in variable annuity, life and disability ins., Calif.; lic. securities series 7 SEC. Mem. ctrl. com. Calif. 39th Assembly Dist. Rep. Com., 1976-81; chmn. subcom. L.A. Recreation, Parks and Librs. Dept., 1976-83; pres. North Hills Jaycees, 1969-70; sec.-treas. Com. Ind. Valley City and County Govt., 1978-82; subchmn. allocations United Way, Van Nuys, Calif., 1990; fundraiser North Valley YMCA, 1986—; formerly active numeroeus comm. and polit. orgns. in San Fernando Valley. Named Jaycee of Yr., Newark (Del.) Jaycees, 1966, Granada Hills Jaycees, 1971, cert. of merit U.S. Ho. of Reps., 1973; cert. appreciation City of L.A., 1980, 84, cert. appreciation State of Calif. 2d senate dist., 1983, Community Spirit award, 1990. Mem. L.A. Olympic Organizing Com. Alumni Assn., Jr. Chamber Internat. (life, senator 1973), U.S. Jaycees (life, Jaycee of Yr. 1965, Outstanding Local Jaycee 1965-66, Presdl. award Honor 1967, Jaycee of Month 1966-67, asst. gen. chmn. 1970-71, state dir. N. Hollywood chpt. 1970-71, Cert. Merit 1971, state gen. chmn., 1971-72, 72-73, Outstanding State Chmn. Calif. dist. 22 1973-74), Granada Hills C. of C. (bd. dirs. 1976-83, Man of Yr. award 1973), Granada Hills Jr. C. of C. Episcopalian. Home: 11408 Haskell Ave Granada Hills CA 91344 Office: IDS Fin Svcs 11145 Tampa Ave Ste 20A Northridge CA 91326

LEI, SHAU-PING, biotechnology company executive; b. Taipei, Taiwan, Republic of China, Oct. 7, 1953; came to U.S., 1980; d. Yu Lei and Pei-Chi Hu; m. Hun-Chi Lin, July 6, 1980; children: Victoria, Benita. BS, Nat. Taiwan U., Taipei, 1976, MS, 1980; PhD, UCLA, 1985. Project dir. INGENE, Santa Monica, Calif., 1985-88, TRIGEN, Santa Monica, Calif., 1989-90; dir. XOMA, Santa Monica, 1990—.

LEIBACHER, JOHN WILLIAM, astronomer; b. Chgo., May 28, 1941; s. George W. and Irene (Novotney) L.; m. Lise H. Ouvarard, Dec. 21, 1976. AB, Harvard U., 1963, PhD, 1971. Postdoctoral fellow U. Colo., Boulder, 1970-71; scientist Laboratoire de Physique Stellaire et Planetaire, Paris, 1972-74, Lockheed Rsch. Lab., Palo Alto, Calif., 1975-81; astronomer Nat. Solar Obs., Tucson, 1982—, dir., 1988-93; mem. Space Studies Bd. NRC, 1986-90. Office: Nat Solar Observatory 950 N Cherry Ave Tucson AZ 85719-4933

LEIBERT, RICHARD WILLIAM, producer of public spectacles; b. N.Y.C., Nov. 11, 1948; s. Richard William and Rosemarie Martha (Bruns) L. BS, Boston U., 1966-70; student, Northwestern U., 1971. Producer Sta. WBZ AM/FM, Boston, 1968-70; prodn. dir. Sta. WMMR-FM, Phila., 1970; exec. producer Sta. WIND-AM, Chgo., 1970-72; program dir. Sta. KGB AM-FM, San Diego, 1972-80; pres. Events Mktg., Inc., L.A., 1980—; dir. Nat. Fireworks Ensemble, Los Angeles, Calif., 1985—. Creator (mascot, publicity stunts) Sta. KGB Chicken, 1974; creator, producer (radio fireworks show) Sta. KGB Sky Show, 1976; writer, producer (network radio show) New Music News, 1983; creator, dir. (touring co.) Nat. Fireworks Ensemble, 1985. Recipient Emmy award, 1978; named Program Dir. of Yr. Billboard Mag., 1976, Radio Program of Yr. Billboard Mag., 1976. Office: Events Mktg Inc PO Box 65694 Los Angeles CA 90065-0694

LEIBOW, KENNETH, retired insurance sales professional; b. N.Y.C., Apr. 16, 1928; s. Louis and Sally (Damenstein) L.; m. Jocelyn Juliet Gilberg, Aug. 21, 1948; children: Corey Jay, David Evan. BS, L.I. U., 1952; student, Sampson Coll., 1948-50. Chemist Gold Leaf Pharm. Corp., New Rochelle, N.Y., 1951-52; sales rep., asst. sales mgr. Standard Sci. Supply Corp., N.Y.C., 1952-65; v.p. sales Sircor Sci., Inc., Roslyn, N.Y., 1965-70; sales rep. Bernard Perlman Ins. Agy., Far Rockaway, N.Y., 1970-72; sales mgr. Aetna Life and Casuality Co., N.Y.C., 1972-75; v.p. Levine Ins. Agy., San Francisco, 1975-90; dist. sales mgr. Mut. of Omaha, Concord, Calif., 1990-92; ret., 1992; moderator Life Underwriters Tng. Coun., San Francisco, 1985-86, Concord, 1991-92. Organizer, pres. Center City Homeowners Assn., Dix Hills, N.Y., 1961-62; fund raiser Dix Hills High Sch., 1970-71; area chmn. San Francisco United Way, 1981-82; asst. chmn. bowling Spl. Olympics Com., San Francisco, 1982-84; bd. dirs., del. Del Webb Sun City, Palm Springs, Calif., 1993-94. Mem. Nat. Assn. Life Underwriters, Calif. Assn. Life Underwriters, San Francisco Assn. Life Underwriters (pres. 1982-83), San Francisco Gen. Agts. and Mgrs. Assn. (bd. dirs. 1982-83), Mt. Diablo Assn. Life Underwriters, Mt. Diablo Gen. Agts. and Mgrs. Assn., B'nai Brith (pres. Diablo Valley lodge 1980-81). Home and Office: 78256 Moongold Rd Bermuda Dunes CA 92201

LEIBU, JACQUES DIETER, management company executive; b. Zurich, Jan. 13, 1941; came to U.S., 1966; s. Heinz Joachim Leibu and Sabine Antoinette (Barberini) Heliotis; m. Marianne Kopf, Apr. 16, 1966; children: Daniela, Rebecca. Diploma elec. engring., Swiss Fed. Inst. Tech., 1965; MSE, U. Mich., 1968, MS in Math., 1969, PhD candidate, 1970. Automation engr. Holderbank (Switzerland) Mgmt. & Cons., 1966-67; systems mgr. Dundee (Mich.) Cement Co., 1968-69; exec. v.p. Interautomation, Inc., Ann Arbor, Mich., 1970-73; pres. Interautomation Ltd., Brugg, Switzerland, 1973-80; exec. v.p. XMIT Ltd., Dietikon, Switzerland, 1980-87; v.p., network mgr. AC Automation Ctr. Ltd., Wettingen, Switzerland, 1988-89; pres.

Comlink Ltd., Wettingen, 1988—, Comlink Internat., Honolulu, 1990—; lectr. Swiss Fed. Inst. Tech., Lausanne, 1980-81; network cons. numerous internat. corp., Switzerland and Hawaii, 1988—. Contbr. articles to profl. jours. Capt. Swiss Army, 1960-90. Office: Comlink Internat PO Box 15486 Honolulu HI 96830

LEIFER, WALLACE, telecommunications company real estate executive; b. Bklyn., Nov. 13, 1943; s. Nathan and Lillian (Jacobs) L.; m. Helen Gutgold, June 4, 1966 (div. Aug. 1989); 1 child, Lorin Semone; m. Francesca Muller, May 22, 1993. BS in CE, U. Vt., 1966; MS in Engring. Mgmt., L.I. U., 1971. Engr. Grumman Aircraft, Bethpage, N.Y., 1966-70; sr. engr. bldg. engring. N.Y. Telephone, N.Y.C., 1970-72; staff mgr. real estate and bldgs. So. Bell Telephone Co., Miami, Fla., 1972-83; corp. real estate mgr. AT&T Info. Sytems, Atlanta, 1983-86; real estate devel. dir. GTE Calif. Inc., Thousand Oaks, 1986—. Mem. Indsl. Devel. and Rsch. Coun. (profl. mem.), Nat. Assn. Corp. Real Estate Execs., Internat. Facility Mgmt. Assn., Tech. Corridor Assn. Home: 12844 Short Ave Los Angeles CA 90066 Office: GTE West One GTE Pl CA500-OK Thousand Oaks CA 91362

LEIGH, HOYLE, psychiatrist, educator; b. Seoul, Korea, Mar. 25, 1942; came to U.S., 1965; m. Vincenta Masciandaro, Sept. 16, 1967; 1 child, Alexander Hoyle. MA, Yale U., 1982; MD, Yonsei U., Seoul, 1965. Diplomate Am. Bd. Psychiatry and Neurology. Asst. prof. Yale U., New Haven, 1971-75, assoc. prof., 1975-80, prof., 1980-89, lectr. in psychiatry, 1989—; dir. Behavioral Medicine Clinic, Yale U., 1980-89; dir. psychiat. cons. svc. Yale-New Haven Hosp., 1971-89; chief psychiatry VA Med. Ctr., Fresno, Calif., 1989—; prof., vice chmn. dept. psychiatry U. Calif., San Francisco, 1989—; head dept. psychiatry U. Calif., San Francisco, Fresno, 1989—; cons. Am. Jour. Psychiatry, Archives Internal Medicine. Author: The Patient, 1980, 2d edit., 1985, 3d edit., 1992; editor: Psychiatry in the Practice of Medicine, 1983. Fellow Am. Psychiat. Assn., ACP, Internat. Coll. Psychosomatic Medicine; mem. AMA, AAUP, World Psychiat. Assn. Office: U Calif 12535 Moffatt Ln Fresno CA 93703-2286

LEIGH, ROBERT EDWARD, consulting engineer; b. Omaha, Sept. 26, 1931; s. Edward Ellsworth and Mildred (Stratbucker) L.; m. Elaine Nicholson, Sept. 17, 1955 (div. 1985); children: Thomas, Jeffrey, Craig; m. Elaine Channon, Jan. 16, 1988. BSCE, Northwestern U., 1954, MSCE, 1959. Chief planner Inter-County Regional Planning Commn., Denver, 1959-65; assoc. Wilbur Smith Assocs., New Haven, Conn., 1965-70; dep. v.p. Alan M. Voorhees & Assocs., Denver, 1970-75; prin. Leigh Assocs., Denver, 1975-78; pres. Leigh, Scott & Cleary Inc., Denver, 1978—. Commr. Hamden (Conn.) Planning Commn., 1967—. Lt. (j.g.) USN, 1954-57. Scholarship Northwestern U., 1949-53. Mem. Am. Planning Assn. (pres. Conn. chpt. 1970), Am. Inst. Cert. Planners, Inst. Transp. Engrs., Am. Cons. Engrs. Coun. Democrat. Lutheran. Home: 633 Cook St Denver CO 80206-3950

LEIGHNINGER, DAVID SCOTT, cardiovascular surgeon; b. Youngstown, Ohio, Jan. 16, 1920; s. Jesse Harrison and Marjorie (Lightner) L.; m. Margaret Jane Malony, May 24, 1942; children: David Allan, Jenny. BA, Oberlin Coll., 1942; MD, Case Western Res. U., 1945. Intern Univ. Hosps. of Cleve., 1945-46, resident, 1949-51, asst. surgeon, 1951-68; rsch. fellow in cardiovascular surgery rsch. lab. Case Western Res. U. Sch. Medicine, Cleve., 1948-49, 51-55, 57-67, instr. surgery, 1951-55, sr. instr., 1957-64, asst. prof., 1964-68, asst. clin. prof., 1968-70; resident Cin. Gen. Hosp., 1955-57; practice medicine specializing in cardiovascular surgery, Cleve., 1957-70; pvt. practice medicine specializing in cardiovascular and gen. surgery Edgewater Hosp., Chgo., 1970-82, staff surgeon, also dir. emergency surg. services, 1970-82; staff surgeon, also dir. emergency surg. svcs. Mazel Med. Ctr., Chgo., 1970-82; emergency physician Miner's Hosp., Raton, N.Mex., 1982-83, 84-85, No. Colfax County Hosp., Raton, 1983-84, Mt. San Rafael Hosp., Trinidad, Colo., 1984-85; assoc., courtesy, or cons. staff Marymount Hosp., Cleve., Mt. Sinai Hosp., Cleve., Geauga Community Hosp., Chardon, Ohio, Bedford Community Hosp (Ohio), 1957-70. Tchr. tng. courses in CPR for med. personnel, police, fire and vol. rescue workers, numerous cities, 1950-70. Served to capt., M.C., AUS, 1946-48. Recipient Chris award Columbus Internat. Film Festival, 1964, numerous other award for sci. exhibits from various nat. and state med. socs., 1953-70; USPHS grantee, 1949-68. Fellow Am. Coll. Cardiology, Am. Coll. Chest Physicians; mem. AMA, N.Mex. Med. Assn., Colfax County Med. Assn., Ill. Med. Assn., Chgo. Med. Assn., U. Cin. Grad. Sch. Surg. Soc. Contbr. numerous articles to med. jours., chpts. to med. texts; spl. pioneer research (with Claude S. Beck) in physiopathology of coronary artery disease and CPR; developed surg. treatment of coronary artery disease; achieved 1st successful defibrillation of human heart, 1st successful reversal of fatal heart attack; provided 1st intensive care of coronary patients. Home: HCR-68 Box 77 Fort Garland CO 81133

LEIGHTON, DAVID ANTHONY, computer software engineer; b. N.Y.C., Oct. 6, 1954; s. Richard Eli and Halin (Pryves) L.; m. Beverly Harper, June 4, 1977; children: Joshua Michael, Christopher Jeremiah, Cassandra Lorraine, Corbin Ryan. BS in Math., MIT, 1976; MS in Applied Math., Calif. Inst. Tech., 1978. Mem. tech. staff Systems, Sci. and Software, San Diego, 1978; software engr. Gen. Dynamics, San Diego, 1978-79; systems analyst ARAMCO, Dhahran, Saudi Arabia, 1979-81; engr.-level 3 Aerojet Electronic Systems Divsn. GENCORP, Azusa, Calif., 1981—. Contbr. articles to profl. jours. Named Eagle Scout Boy Scouts Am., 1970. Mem. IEEE, Assn. for Computing Machinery, Soc. for Photo-Optical Instrumentation Engrs., Digital Equipment Corp. User's Soc. Republican. Mem. Ch. LDS. Home: 212 Buena Vista Dr Claremont CA 91711 Office: GENCORP Aerojet Electronic Systems Divsn 1100 W Hollyvale St Azusa CA 91702

LEIGHTON, FRANK CHARLES, consulting civil engineer, province official; b. Norwich, Norfolk, Eng., Dec. 11, 1919; arrived in Can., 1950; s. James Leslie and Charlotte (Darcus) L.; m. Phyllis May Grantham, Apr. 6, 1953; children: John Charles, Barbara Jean. BSc in Engring., U. London, 1949. Project engr. B.C. Ministry Hwys., Victoria, Can., 1949-51; project engr. Swan Wooster Engring. Co. Ltd., Vancouver, B.C., Can., 1951-64, v.p. planning, 1964-78, vice chmn., 1978-84; prin. Frank Leighton, Cons. Engr., Vancouver, 1985—; mem. B.C. Utilities Commn., Vancouver, 1987—; bd. dirs. Pacific Nat. Exhbn., Vancouver, 1972-75, Vancouver Bd. Trade, 1975-79, Ocean Engring. Ctr., Vancouver, 1988—; mem. Marine Transport R & D Bd., Ottawa, Ont., Can., 1979-83. Contbr. numerous articles on coastal engring., ports and marine transport to tech. jours. Mem. Adv. Planning Commn., Dist. North Vancouver, 1963-67. Flying officer RAF, 1939-45, ETO. Mem. Assn. Profl. Engrs. B.C., Assn. Profl. Economists B.C. Office: BC Utilities Commn, 600-900 Howe St, Vancouver, BC Canada V6Z 2N3

LEIGHTON, HENRY ALEXANDER, physician, consultant; b. Manila, Nov. 12, 1929; (parents U.S. citizens).; s. Raymond Harry and Theola Marie (Alexander) L.; m. Helga Maria Hell, Jan. 17, 1970; children: Alan Raymond, Henry Alexander, Michael Ballinger, John, Marni, Tammy Ballinger. BA in History, U. Calif., Berkeley, 1952, MPH, 1971; MD, U. Calif., San Francisco, 1956. Diplomate Am. Bd. Preventive Medicine. Intern So. Pacific Gen. Hosp., San Francisco, 1956-57; resident in surgery Brooke Gen. Hosp., Ft. Sam Houston, Tex., 1960-62; commd. 2d. lt. U.S. Army, 1957, advanced through grades to col., 1971; div. surgeon 8th Inf. div. U.S. Army, Germany, 1964-66; comdr. 15th Med. Bn. U.S. Army, Vietnam, 1966-67; instr. Med. Field Service Sch. U.S. Army, San Antonio, 1968-70; resident preventive medicine U.S. Army, Ft. Ord, Calif., 1971-72, chief preventive medicine, 1973-76; chief preventive medicine U.S. Army-Europe, 1976-79, ret., 1979; chief occupational health MEDDAC U.S. Army, Ft. Ord, 1981-89; pvt. practice Salinas, Calif., 1990—. Neighborhood commr. Boy Scouts Am., 1964-66; bd. dirs. Am. Lung Assn. of Calif., 1982-84, and of affiliate, 1980-86; pres. The Bluffs Homeowners Assn., 1986. Decorated Air medal with oak leaf cluster, Bronze Star, Legion of Merit, Meritorious Service medal. Fellow Am. Coll. Preventive Medicine; mem. Am. Pub. Health Assn., Am. Coll. Occupational Medicine, Assn. Mil. Surgeons, Ret. Officers Assn., Assn. U.S. Army, Theta Xi. Lodges: Masons, Shriners. Office: 14096 Reservation Rd Salinas CA 93908-9208

LEIGHTON, ROBERT LYMAN, veterinarian, educator; b. Boston, Feb. 27, 1917; s. George Albert and Agnes (Robinson) L.; m. Jeanette Ruth Dibble, Sept. 15, 1945; 1 child, Robert Lyman Jr. VMD, U. Pa., 1941. Diplomate Am. Coll. Vet. Surgeons. Resident Angell Meml. Hosp., Boston, 1941-42; staff surgeon Rowley Animal Hosp., Springfield, Mass., 1946-56; head surg. svc. Animal Med. Ctr., N.Y.C., 1956-65; from asst. prof. to prof. U. Calif., Davis, 1965-83, emeritus prof., 1983—. Author: A Compendium of Small Animal Surgery, 1983, Some Orthopedic Surgeries of the Joints of the Dog, 1988, Sgt. U.S. Army, 1943-45. Mem. Am. Animal Hosp. Assn., Am. Vet. Med. Assn., Calif. Vet. Med. Assn., Sacramento Valley Vet. Med. Assn. Republican. Congregationalist. Home: 908 Pine Ln Davis CA 95616 Office: U Calif Sch Vet Medicine MS-I Dept Vet Surgery Davis CA 95616

LEIN, ALLEN, physiology educator emeritus; b. N.Y.C., Apr. 15, 1913; s. Benjamin and Nina (Elinson) L.; m. Teresa LaFratta, Nov. 29, 1941; children: Laura, David. Student, U. Chgo., 1935; B.A., UCLA, 1935, M.A., 1938; Ph.D., 1940; Muellhaupt scholar physiology, Ohio State U., 1940-41. Instr. surg. research Ohio State U., 1941-42; research assoc. aviation medicine War Research Program, 1942-43; asst. prof. physiology Vanderbilt U. Med. Sch., 1946-47; asst. prof. physiology Northwestern U. Sch. Medicine, 1947-52, assoc. prof. physiology, 1952-53, Abbott assoc. prof. physiology, 1953-61, prof., 1961-68, dir. student affairs, 1960-64; asst. dean Sch. Medicine Northwestern U., 1964-68; asst. dean Northwestern U. Grad. Sch. (Grad. Sch.), 1966-68; assoc. dean Sch. Medicine; prof. medicine U. Calif. at San Diego, 1968-73, prof. reproductive medicine, 1973-84, prof. emeritus, 1984—, assoc. dean for grad. studies-health scis., 1974-77, dir. health professions honors program, 1979-80, acting assoc. dean acad. affairs, 1980-81, assoc. dean health scis., 1981-82; vis. prof. chemistry Calif. Inst. Tech., 1954-55; cons. VA Research Hosp., Chgo., 1964-68; adv. com. office sci. personnel Nat. Acad. Scis., 1969-73; Rockefeller Found. vis. scholar Bellagio Study and Conf. Center, 1977; cons. Dept. of Reproductive Med., 1984-93. Author: The Cycling Female: Her Menstrual Rhythm, 1979, Data Analysis in Biomedical Research, 1993; contbr. articles to sci. jours. Served to capt. USAAF, 1943-46; aviation physiologist, chief dept. biophysics Air Force Sch. Aviation Medicine. Guggenheim fellow biochem. research Collége de France, 1958-59. Fellow AAAS; mem. Soc. Exptl. Biology and Medicine (emeritus), Am. Physiol. Soc., Endocrine Soc., Am. Soc. Biol. Scis., Sigma Xi. Home: 8653 Dunaway Dr La Jolla CA 92037-2032

LEINBERGER, CHRISTOPHER BROWN, urban development consultant, writer; b. Charleston, W.Va., Jan. 2, 1951; s. Fredrick Arthur and Helen (Brown) L.; m. Madeleine LeMoyne McDougal, Aug. 25, 1973; children: Christopher Jr., Rebecca. BA in Urban Sociology, Swarthmore Coll., 1972; MBA, Harvard U., 1976. Asst. to pres. ARA Food Svcs., Inc., Phila., 1973-74, 76-77; dir. concept devel. Saga Corp., Menlo Park, Calif., 1977-79; exec. v.p. Robert Charles Lesser & Co., Beverly Hills, Calif., 1979-82, mng. ptnr., co-owner, 1982-92; pres. Met. Futures Group, 1992—; mng. dir., co-owner Lesser & Weitzman, 1993—. Author: Strategic Planning for Real Estate Companies; contbr. articles to profl. jours. and nat. print media including The Wall Street Jour., L.A. Times, The Atlantic Monthly, The Nation. Bd. dirs. Swarthmore (Pa.) Coll., Coll. of Santa Fe, Realen Homes, Phila. Fellow NSF, 1971, NCAA, 1972, Coro Found., 1972-73. Mem. Urban Land Inst. (coun. mem. 1984—), Juan Tomas Hunt. Democrat. Home: Las Urracas PO Box 489 Tesuque NM 87574-0489 Office: Robert Charles Lesser & Co RR 4 Box 48 Santa Fe NM 87501-9804

LEININGER, ROBERT FARNES, author, screenwriter; b. Berkeley, Calif., Sept. 13, 1946; s. Robert Farnes Leininger and Patricia (MacNeil) Geary; m. Patricia Mary Bradbrook. BS in Mech. Engring., U. Nev., 1980. Mech. engr. Northrop Corp., Newbury Park, Calif., 1981-85; author, writer pvt. practice Reno, Nev., 1985—. Author: Killing Suki Flood, 1991, Black Sun, 1991; screenwriter: The Lemonmobile, 1991. With USN, 1964-71. Mem. Pi Mu Epsilon.

LEINO, DEANNA ROSE, educator; b. Leadville, Colo., Dec. 15, 1937; d. Arvo Ensio Leino and Edith Mary (Bonan) Leino Malenck; adopted child, Michael Charles Bonan. BSBA, U. Denver, 1959, MS in Bus. Adminstrn., 1967; postgrad. Community Coll. Denver, U. No. Colo., Colo. State U., U. Colo., Met. State Coll. Cert. tchr., vocat. tchr., Colo. Tchr. Jefferson County Adult Edn., Lakewood, Colo., 1963-67; tchr. bus., coordinator coop. office edn., Jefferson High Sch., Edgewater, Colo., 1959-93; sales assoc. Joslins Dept. Store, Denver, 1978—; mem. ea. team Denver Svc. Ctr. Nat. Park Svc, 1993—; instr. Community Coll. Denver, Red Rocks, 1967-81, U. Colo. Denver, 1976-79, Parks Coll. Bus. (name now Parks Jr. Coll.), 1983—; dist. adviser Future Bus. Leaders Am. Active City of Edgewater Sister City Project Student Exchange Com.; pres. Career Women's Symphony Guild; treas. Phantoms of Opera, 1982—; active Opera Colo. Assocs. & Guild, I Pagliacci; ex-officio trustee Denver Symphony Assn., 1980-82. Recipient Disting. Svc. award Jefferson County Sch. Bd. 1980, Tchr. Who Makes A Difference award Sta. KCNC/Rocky Mountain News, 1990, Youth Leader award Lakewood Optimist Club, 1993; inducted into Jefferson High Sch. Wall of Fame 1981 Mem. NEA (life), Colo. Edn. Assn., Jefferson County Edn. Assn., Colo. Vocat. Assn., Am. Vocat. Assn., Colo. Educators for and about Bus., Profl. Secs. Internat., Career Women's Symphony Guild, Profl. Panhellenic Assn., Colo. Congress Fgn. Lang. Tchrs., Wheat Ridge C. of C. (edn. and scholarship com.), Delta Pi Epsilon, Phi Chi Theta, Beta Gamma Sigma, Alpha Lambda Delta. Republican. Roman Catholic. Club: Tyrolean Soc. Denver. Avocations: decorating wedding cakes, crocheting, sewing, music, world travel. Home: 3712 Allison St Wheat Ridge CO 80033-6124

LEISER, ERIC J., far east sales and applications manager; b. New York, N.Y., Oct. 13, 1960; s. Werner and Laura (Goldschmidt) L. BS, MIT, Cambridge, Mass., 1982. Engr. Motorola, Phoenix, 1982-85; applications mgr. E. Merck, W. Germany, 1985-89; far eastern sales and applications mgr. Allied-Signal, Milpitas, Calif., 1989—. Democrat. Office: Allied-Signal 1090 S Milpitas Blvd Milpitas CA 95035-6307

LEISNER, JAMES WINGE, retired accounting executive, investor; b. Evanston, Ill., Feb. 23, 1924; s. Paul Winge and Florence Mary (Heath) L.; m. Patricia Ann Ryan, Mar. 29, 1947 (div. Feb. 1973); children: 1 child, Kimberley Ann Leisner Ogle; m. Linda J. Daniel, Mar. 30, 1973. BS with honors, Northwestern U., 1950; MA, U. So. Calif., 1977. CPA, Ill., 15 other states. Fin. analyst U.S. Gypsum, Chgo., 1950-52; mgr. mergers & acquisitions Alexander Grant & Co., Chgo., 1952-53; mgr. mgmt. consulting Peat, Marwick, Mitchell & Co., Chgo., 1953-56; ptnr. in charge western MCD Peat, Marwick, Mitchell & Co., L.A., 1956-59, mng. ptnr. L.A. br., 1959-73, mng. ptnr. western region, 1960-73, also bd. dirs., 1960-72; owner Leisner Trust Properties, Irvine, Calif., 1973—. Chmn. bd. dirs. Children's Hosp. L.A., 1978-81; bd. councilors U. So. Calif., L.A., 1970-85; v.p., bd. dirs. United Way L.A., 1967-75; trustee U. Redlands, 1972-74. Capt. inf. U.S. Army, 1943-46, ETO. Recipient Bishop's Award of Merit Episc. Bishop L.A., 1964, Community Svc. award United Way L.A., 1975. Mem. AICPA (bd. of council 1972-74), Calif. Soc. CPAs (bd. dirs. 1966-69), Nat. Watercolor Soc., Calif. Club, Lakes Country Club, Newport Harbor Yacht Club, Phi Beta Kappa, Phi Kappa Phi. Republican. Home and Office: 4872 Basswood Ln Irvine CA 92715-2802

LEISURE, ROBERT GLENN, physics educator; b. Cromwell, Ky., Jan. 29, 1938; s. Roscoe B. and Lova Leisure; m. Jeanine Smith, Aug. 18, 1962. BS, Western Ky. U., 1960; PhD, Wash. U., St. Louis, 1967. Staff scientist Boeing Sci. Rsch. Labs., Seattle, 1967-70; asst. prof. physics Colo. State U., Ft. Collins, 1970-73, assoc. prof. physics, 1973-78, prof. physics, 1978—, chmn. physics dept., 1984-90; vis. scientist U. Paris, 1978-79; collaborator Los Alamos Nat. Lab., 1990—. Contbr. numerous articles to profl. jours. NSF grantee, 1973-85; SERC fellow U.K., 1983, 87. Mem. Am. Phys. Soc., Phi Kappa Phi, Sigma Xi. Home: 926 Cottonwood Dr Fort Collins CO 80524-1521 Office: Colo State U Dept Physics Fort Collins CO 80523

LEISY, DOUGLAS JERALD, molecular biologist; b. Eugene, Oreg., Feb. 18, 1954; s. Jerald Walter and Nancy Jane (Grove) L.; m. Valerie Jean Peterson, Dec. 21, 1981; children: Paul Douglas, Anna Katherine. BS, U. Oreg., 1976; MS, U. Iowa, 1980; PhD, Oreg. State U., 1986. Postdoctoral rsch. fellow Wash. State U., Pullman, 1986-89; sr. scientist Sandoz Agro Inc., Palo Alto, Calif., 1989-92; rsch. assoc. Dept. Agrl. Chem. Oregon State U., Corvallis, Oreg., 1992—. Contbr. articles to profl. jours. Home: 2247 Dixon St Corvallis OR 97330 Office: Oreg State U Dept Agrl Chem Corvallis OR 97331

LEITMANN, GEORGE, mechanical engineering educator; b. Vienna, Austria, May 24, 1925; s. Josef and Stella (Fischer) L.; m. Nancy Lloyd, Jan. 28, 1955; children: Josef Lloyd, Elaine Michèle. BS, Columbia U., 1949, MA, 1950; PhD, U. Calif., Berkeley, 1956; D Engring. honoris causa, Tech. U. Vienna, 1988; D honoris causa, U. Paris, 1989, Tech. U. Darmstadt, 1990. Physicist, head aeroballistics sect. U.S. Naval Ordnance Sta., China Lake, 1950-57; mem. faculty U. Calif., Berkeley, 1957—, prof. engring. sci., 1963—, assoc. dean acad. affairs, 1981-90, assoc. dean rsch., 1990—, acting dean, 1988; cons. to aerospace industry and govt. Author: An Introduction to Optimal Control, 1966, Quantitative and Qualitative Games, 1969, The Calculus of Variations and Optimal Control, 1981, others; contbr. articles to profl. jours. Served with AUS, 1944-46, ETO. Decorated Croix de Guerre France, Fourragere Belgium; recipient Pendray Aerospace Lit. award, 1979, Von Humboldt U.S. sr. scientist award, 1980, Levy medal, 1981, Mechanics and Control of Flight award, 1984, Berkeley citation, 1991, von Humboldt medal, 1991; named Miller Research prof., 1966. Mem. NAE, Acad. Sci. Bologna, Internat. Acad. Astronautics, Argentine Nat. Acad. Engring., Russian Acad. Natural Sci. Office: U Calif Coll Engring Berkeley CA 94720

LEIWEKE, TIMOTHY, sales executive, marketing professional; b. St. Louis, Apr. 21, 1957; s. John Robert and Helen (Caicuey) L.; m. Pamela Leiweke, Nov. 1, 1984. Grad. high sch., St. Louis. Salesperson New Eng. Mut. Life Ins. Co., St. Louis, 1976-79; asst. gen. mgr. St. Louis Steamers/MISL, 1979-80; gen. mgr. Balt. Blast/MISL, 1980-81; v.p., gen. mgr. Kansas City (Mo.) Comets/MISL, 1981-84; v.p. Leiweke and Co., Kansas City, 1984-85; pres. Kansas City Comets/MISL, 1986-88; v.p. sales and mktg. div. Minn. Timberwolves, Mpls., 1988-91; sr. v.p. of bus. ops. Denver Nuggets, Denver, 1991—; pres. Denver Nuggets, Denver, CO, 1992—. Bd. dirs. Kidney Found., Minn., 1989—, Spl. Olympics, Minn., 1989—, Timberwolves Community Found., Minn., 1989—. Named Rookie of the Yr., Mo. Life Underwriters, 1976, Kansas Citian of the Yr., Kansas City Press Club, 1983; recipient William Brownfield award U.S. Jaycees, 1978, William Brownfield award Mo. Jaycees, 1978, Excalibur award Am. Cancer Soc., 1987. Mem. Kansas City Mktg. and Sales Execs., Mpls. Club. Home: 10930 34th Ave N Minneapolis MN 55441-2444

LELAND, DAVID D., timber company executive; b. Austin, Minn., July 26, 1935; s. P.C. and Leona (Christensen) L.; m. Maralee Brown (div.); children: D. Mark, Todd D., Reid H.; m. Leslie S. Gibbs, Aug. 21, 1987. BS in Forestry, U. Wash., 1958. Various positions Simpson Timber Co., Shelton, Wash., 1959-71, v.p. Calif. ops., 1971-76; sr. v.p. S.W. Forest Industries, Phoenix, 1976-77, exec. v.p. bldg. products, 1977-83; pres., chief exec. officer Plum Creek Timber Co., Seattle, 1983—, chmn., pres., CEO, 1993—; bd. dirs. Plum Creek Mgmt. Co., Seattle. Mem. Nat. Forest Products Assn. (bd. dirs., chmn., 1st vice chmn., 2d vice chmn., treas. 1989—), Am. Plywood Assn. (trustee 1986—), World Forestry Ctr. (bd. dirs. 1988—), Rainier Club, Seattle Yacht Club, Seattle Golf Club. Avocations: fishing, sailing. Office: Plum Creek Timber Co LP 999 3rd Ave Ste 2300 Seattle WA 98104-4096

LELAND, JOY HANSON, anthropologist, alcohol research specialist; b. Glendale, Calif., July 29, 1927; d. David Emmett and Florence (Sockerson) Hanson; m. Robert Leland, May 6, 1961 (dec. Oct. 1986); 1 stepson, John. B.A. in English Lit., Pomona Coll., Claremont, Calif., 1949; M.B.A., Stanford U., 1960; M.A. in Anthropology, U. Nev., 1972; Ph.D. in Anthropology, U. Calif., Irvine, 1975. With Desert Research Inst., U. Nev., 1961—, asst. research prof., 1975-77, assoc. research prof., 1977-79, rsch. prof., 1979-89, rsch. prof. emerita, 1990—. Author: monograph Firewater Myths, Frederick West Lander-A Biographical Sketch; contbg. author: Smithsonian Handbook of North American Indians; also articles, book chpts. Bd. dirs. Desert Rsch. Inst. Found. NIMH grantee, 1972-73; Nat. Inst. Alcohol Abuse and Alcoholism grantee, 1974-75, 79-81. Mem. Am. Anthrop. Assn., Southwestern Anthrop. Assn., Soc. Applied Anthropology, Soc. Med. Anthropology, Gt. Basin Anthrop. Conf. Office: Desert Rsch Inst U Nev System PO Box 60220 7010 Dandini Blvd Reno NV 89506

LELEWER, DEBRA ANN, computer science educator; b. Frostburg, Md., June 22, 1951; d. Richard Fremont and Betty Jo (Cook) Evans; m. Steven Arthur Lelewer, Sept. 3, 1972. BS, Mich. State U., 1973; MS, Calif. State Poly. U., 1976, Calif. State Poly. U., 1985; PhD, U. Calif., Irvine, 1991. Tchr., dept. chair Glendora (Calif.) High Sch., 1973-82; lectr. math. and computer sci. Calif. State Poly. U., Pomona, 1982-85, prof. computer sci., 1985-91, dept. chair computer sci., 1991—. Inventor streamlined context model for data compression, efficient decoding of prefix codes, mutation testing system for Ada programs. Doctoral fellow Calif. State U. System, Long Beach, 1986-89, U. Calif. Regents fellow, 1985, Summer Rsch. fellow U. Calif., 1989. Mem. IEEE, IEEE Computer Soc., Assn. for Computing Machinery (spl. interest group of computer sci. edn., spl. interest group on automata and computing theory), Assn. of Women in Sci. Office: Computer Sci Dept Calif State Poly U Pomona CA 91768

LEM, NORA WAN, biochemist; b. Toronto, Ont., Can., Oct. 4, 1953; d. Fred Kew and Fay Hing (Lee) L. BSc, U. Toronto, 1975, MSc, 1977, PhD, 1981, Diploma in Clin. Chemistry, 1988. NATO fellow Purdue U., West Lafayette, Ind., 1981-82, U. Calif., Davis, 1982-83; rsch. asst. prof. U. Waterloo, Ont., Can., 1983-86; rsch. scientist Alcan Internat., Kingston, Ont., 1988-89; rsch. scientist, biochemist Sola/Barnes-Hind, Sunnyvale, Calif., 1989-91; asst. prof. U. B.C., Columbia, Can., 1991—; vis. scientist Instituto de la Grasa y sus Derividados, Seville, Spain, 1993. Contbr. rsch. reports, papers, articles to sci. jours. Vol. Kingston YMCA, 1988-90, San Jose State Sci. Fair for Girls, 1990-91. Fellow Nat. Sci. & Engring. Rsch. Coun. Can., 1977-81. Mem. Am. Chem. Soc., Can. Soc. Clin. Chemistry, N.Y. Acad. Sci., Am. Soc. Clin. Chemists.

LEM, RICHARD DOUGLAS, painter; b. L.A., Nov. 24, 1933; s. Walter Wing and Betty (Wong) L.; B.A., UCLA, 1958; M.A., Calif. State U.-Los Angeles, 1963; m. Patricia Ann Soohoo, May 10, 1958; 1 son, Stephen Vincent. Exhibited in one-man shows at Gallery 818, Los Angeles, 1965; group shows at Lynn Kottler Galleries, N.Y.C., 1973, Palos Verdes Art Gallery, 1968, Galerie Mouffe, Paris, France, 1976, Le Salon des Nations, Paris, 1984, numerous others; represented in permanent collections; writer, illustrator: Mile's Journey, 1983; cover illustrator: The Hermit, 1990, The Hermit's Journey, 1993. Served with AUS, 1958-60. Mem. UCLA Alumni Assn. Address: 1861 Webster Ave Los Angeles CA 90026

LEMAN, LOREN DWIGHT, civil engineer; b. Pomona, Calif., Dec. 2, 1950; s. Nick and Marian (Broady) L.; m. Carolyn Rae Bratvold, June 17, 1978; children: Joseph, Rachel, Nicole. BSCE, Oreg. State U., 1972; MS in Civil, Environ. Engring., Stanford U., 1973. Registered profl. engr., Alaska. Project mgr. CH2M Hill, San Francisco, 1973, Reston, Va., 1973-74, Ketchikan, Alaska, 1974-75, Anchorage, 1975-87; state rep. State of Alaska, 1989-92; owner Loren Leman, P.E., Anchorage, 1987—. Contbr. articles to profl. jours. Mem. Breakthrough Com., Anchorage, 1978; del. to conv. Rep. Party of Alaska, 1976-90; basketball coach Grace Christian Sch., Anchorage, 1985-88; state legis. Ho. of Reps., Juneau and Anchorage, 1989-92. Mem. ASCE, Alaska Water Mgmt. Assn., The Nature Conservancy, Am. Legis. Exchange Coun., Water Pollution Control Fedn., Toastmasters (pres.). Republican. Home: 2699 Nathaniel Ct Anchorage AK 99517-1016 Office: Alaska State Legis 3111 C St #425 Anchorage AK 99503

LEMASURIER, WESLEY ERNEST, geology educator, researcher; b. Washington, May 3, 1934; s. E. Howard and V. May (Van Arnum) LeM.; m. C. Heather Nelson, Sept. 21, 1963; children: Michelle, Susanne, John. Student, St. Andrews U., Fifeshire, Scotland, 1954-55; BS, Union Coll., Schenectady, N.Y., 1956; MS, U. Colo., 1962; PhD, Stanford U., 1965. Geologist U.S. Geol. Survey, Denver, also Menlo Park, Calif., 1956-63; asst. prof. geology Cornell U., Ithaca, N.Y., 1964-68; from assoc. prof. to prof. geology U. Colo., Denver, 1968—; dir. Guilin Coll. (China)-U. Colo. Denver Scholarly Exch. Program, 1986—. Editor, author: Volcanoes of the Antarctic Plate and Southern Oceans, 1990. Pvt. U.S. Army, 1960. NSF grantee, 1968-85; recipient Antarctic Svc. medal, 1971; Mt. LeMasurier named in his honor, 1971. Fellow Geol. Soc. Am.; mem. Am. Geophys. Union, Internat. Assn. Volcanology. Presbyterian. Home: 1333 Mariposa Ave Boulder CO 80302 Office: U Colo at Denver 1200 Larimer St Denver CO 80217-3364

LEMBERSKY, MARK RAPHAEL, computer company executive; b. Pitts., Sept. 30, 1945; s. Herman K. and Alice Lillian (Berger) (dec.) L.; m. Barbara Jean Diemond, June 6, 1965 (div. 1991); 1 child, Carol Sharon. BS, MIT, 1967; MS, Stanford U., 1968, PhD, 1971, grad. exec. program, 1983. Prof.

ops. research Oreg. State U., Corvallis, 1971-76; mgr. merchandising and allocation Weyerhaeuser Co., Tacoma, 1976-79, dir. raw materials research and devel. div., 1979-81, dir. forestry and timber products research and devel. div., 1981-83, dir. group fin. and systems, 1983-85, div. gen. mgr. Engineered Products div., 1985-87; pres. Innovis Interactive Techs., Tacoma, 1987-91; chair Lembersky Chi, Inc., Seattle, 1992—; bd. dirs. Bioscan, Inc.; cons. western U.S. Patentee in field; contbr. articles to profl. jours. Bd. dirs. Nisqually River Interpretative Ctr. Found., 1993—; mem. MIT Edn. Coun., 1983-92, Wash. Coun. for Tech. Advancement, chmn. subcom. edn., 1984-88; bd. dirs. Sci. Affiliates U. Wash., 1983-86; trustee Somerset Community Assn., Bellevue, Wash., 1977-79, corp. coun. for the arts, 1990-91; served Pres. Reagan's task force AIDS epidemology, 1988. Recipient Carter award Oreg. State U., 1975, Franz Edelman Internat. prize 1985, Computer World Smithsonian Inst. award 1989. Mem. Inst. Mgmt. Sci. (gov. coun. 1990-92, pres. elect 1993), Ops. Rsch. Soc. Am. (edn. com. 1976-77, assoc. editor jour. 1984—), Mgmt. Sci. Roundtable (exec. bd. dirs. 1985-87). Office: Lembersky Chi Inc 651 Strander Blvd Seattle WA 98188

LEMERT, JAMES BOLTON, journalist, educator; b. Sangerfield, N.Y., Nov. 5, 1935; s. Jesse Raymond and Caroline Elizabeth (Brown) L.; m. Rosalie Martha Bassett, Mar. 23, 1972. A.B., U. Calif.-Berkeley, 1957, M.J., 1959; Ph.D., Mich. State U., 1964. Newspaper reporter Oakland Tribune, Calif., 1955-56; Newspaper reporter Chico Enterprise-Record, Calif., 1957, 58-60; asst. prof. journalism So. Ill. U., Carbondale, 1964-67, U. Oreg., Eugene, 1967-69; assoc. prof. U. Oreg., 1969-76, prof., 1976—, dir. div. communication rsch., 1967—, dir. grad. program Sch. Journalism, 1983-86, 88-93; chair U. Oreg. Task Force to Revise Faculty Governance, 1983-84; Mem. senate, U. Oreg., 1981-83, 86-88. chmn. Senate Rules Com., 1987-88; chmn. intercollegiate athletics com., U. Oreg., 1986-89, pres.'s adv. coun., 1990-91, chair, 1991—, mem. grad. coun., 1984-86, 89-90; chair Task Force on Rsch. and Grad. Edn., 1990-91. Producer, on-air host: Old Grooves show, KWAX-FM, 1977-80, 82-84; author: Does Mass Communication Change Public Opinion After All? A New Approach to Effects Analysis, 1981, Criticizing the Media: Empirical Approaches, 1989, News Verdicts, the Debates, and Presidential Campaigns, 1991, The Politics of Disenchantment: Busn, Clinton, Perot and the Press, 1993; editor: Daily Californian, 1957; contbr. articles to profl. jours. Mem. Oreg. Alcohol and Drug Edn. Adv. Com., 1968-69; pres. South Hills Neighborhood Assn., 1976-77, bd. dirs., 1982-84, 86-88; bd. dirs. Traditional Jazz Soc. Oreg., 1981-83, 87; v.p. Met. Cable Access Corp., 1983-84. Recipient Outstanding Journalist award Sigma Delta Chi, 1957, Donald M. McGammon Communication Rsch. Ctr. critical rsch. grantee, 1988-89, Allen Family Found. grantee; NSF fellow, 1963, 64; Calif. Newspaper Pubs. fellow, 1957; Butte County Alumni scholar, 1953-54. Mem. AAUP (exec. bd. 1975-76, 91-93), Assn. Edn. Journalism, Am. Assn. Public Opinion Rsch., Internat. Comm. Assn., Assn. Oreg. Faculties (head chpt., mem. state exec. com. 1981-83, 85-87, state v.p. 1987-89, U. Oreg. del. to Oreg. Faculties Polit. Action Com. 1986-89), Phi Beta Kappa (membership chmn. 1985-86, v.p., pres. 1989-91). Home: 10 E 40th Ave Eugene OR 97405-3487

LEMIEUX, LINDA DAILEY, museum director; b. Cleve., Sept. 6, 1953; d. Leslie Leo LeMieux Jr. and Mildred Edna (Dailey) Tutt. BA, Beloit Coll., 1975; MA, U. Mich., 1979; assoc. cert., Mus. Mgmt. Program, Boulder, Colo., 1987. Asst. curator Old Salem, Inc., Winston-Salem, N.C., 1979-82; curator Clarke House, Chgo., 1982-84; curator Western Mus. Mining and Industry, Colorado Springs, Colo., 1985-86, dir., 1987—. Author: Prairie Avenue Guidebook, 1985; editor: The Golden Years--Mines in the Cripple Creek District, 1987; contbr. articles to mags. and newspapers. Fellow Historic Deerfield, Mass., 1974—; active Colorado Springs Jr. League; mem. bd. dirs. Sunnyrest Health Care Facility. Research grantee Early Am. Industries Assn., 1978. Mem. Am. Assn. Mus., Am. Assn. State and Local History, Colo.-Wyo. Mus. Assn., Colo. Mining Assn. (bd. dirs.), Mountain Plains Assn. Mus., Women in Mining. Republican. Presbyterian. Home: 1337 Hermosa Way Colorado Springs CO 80906-3050 Office: Western Mus of Mining & Industry 1025 N Gate Rd Colorado Springs CO 80921-3099

LEMIRE, DAVID STEPHEN, school psychologist, educator; b. Roswell, N.Mex., May 23, 1949; s. Joseph Armon and Jeanne (Longwill) L.; BA, Linfield Coll., 1972, MEd, 1974; EdS, Idaho State U., 1978; postgrad. U. Wyo.; EdS in Ednl. Adminstrn. and Instructional Leadership, U. Wyo., 1988; postgrad. U. Wyo. Cert. sch. counselor, student pers. worker, psychology instr., Calif. Sch. counselor, psychol. technician and tchr. Goshen County Sch. Dist. 1, Torrington, Wyo., counselor Aspen High Sch., Aspen, Colo.; sch. counselor Unita County Sch. Dist., Evanston, Wyo., coord. R&D Lifelong Learning Ctr. 1986-87; dir. spl. svcs. and sch. psychologist Bighorn County Sch. Dist. #4, Basin, Wyo., 1989-90; sch. psychologist Sweetwater County Sch. Dist. #2, Green River, Wyo., 1990-91; dir. housing, residence supr. Pratt (Kans.) Community Coll., 1991-92; pres. David Lemire Software Enterprises, Evanston; dir. Inst. for Advanced Study of Thinkology. Mem. Nat. Assn. Sch. Psychologists (cert.), Am. Psychol. Assn., Am. Assn. for Counseling and Devel. Former editor WACD Jour.; former mng. editor Jour. Humanistic Edn.; contbr. articles to profl. jours. Address: PO Box 763 Moorcroft WY 82721 also: Creative Self Inst Adminstrv Offices 2390 Riviera St Reno NV 89509

LEMOS, ALBERTO SANTOS, editor; b. Rio de Janeiro, Brazil, Sept. 9, 1921; came to U.S., 1955; s. Casimiro Costa and Elvira (Almeida) L.; divorced; children: Henrique A., Monica Amelia L. Student, Laney Coll., 1973-75, Hayward State U., 1975-76. With British Consulate, Lisboa, 1941-45; dept. head British Bank, Lisboa, 1945-55; owner Lusitania Travel, Oakland, Calif., 1956-57; pub., editor Portuguese Jour., Oakland, San Pablo, Calif., 1957—. Named Comendador, Order Infante D. Henrique (Portugal), 1966; recipient Silver Medal of Merit, Dept. Portuguese Communities, 1992. Mem. Am. Edn. Found., Commonwealth Club Calif. Home: 5404 Valley View Rd El Sobrante CA 94803 Office: Portuguese Jour 1912 Church Ln San Pablo CA 94806

LENARD, ERIC SCOTT, executive chef; b. Ithaca, N.Y., Apr. 30, 1962; s. John Lenard and Gloria Cybele (McCracken) Lebon. BA, Rutgers U., 1985; Grande Diplome, La Varenne Ecole de Cuisine, Paris, 1987; cert. completion, M. Kammans Sch. Am. Chefs, St. Helena, Calif., 1990. Cook Charles Hotel-Rarities Restaurant, Cambridge, Mass., 1985-86; apprentice, commis La Cote St. Jacques, Joigny, France, 1987; chef on board Halcyon Yacht, Inc., St. Thomas, V.I., 1987; sous chef BIX Restaurant, Real Restaurants, San Francisco, 1988-91; exec. chef Heritage House, Little River, Calif., 1991—. Office: Heritage House 5200 Hwy 1 Little River CA 95456

LENARD, MICHAEL BARRY, lawyer; b. Chgo., May 20, 1955; s. Henry Madart and Jacqueline Jo Anne (Silver) L.; m. Amy Jeanne Rifenbergh, Oct. 10, 1987; children: Madeline M., Nicholas X. BBA, U. Wis., 1977; student, NYU, 1981-82; JD, U. So. Calif., 1982. Assoc. Whitman & Ransom, N.Y.C., 1982-83, 1984-91; ptnr. Latham & Watkins, L.A., 1992-93, Whitman & Ransom, N.Y.C., 1992-93; assoc. Latham & Watkins, L.A., 1984-91; ptnr. Latham & Watkins, 1991-93; councillor William E. Simon & Sons, L.A., 1993—. With So. Calif. Law Rev. mag., 1980-81. Vice-pres. U.S. Olympic Com., 1989—, exec. com. and bd. dirs., 1985—, athletes' adv. coun. (vice-chmn. 1985-89), 1981-89; bd. dirs. L.A. Sports Coun., 1988—, Atlanta Com. for Olympic Games, 1990—. Named semi-finalist Outstanding Undergrad. Achievement award, 1977; recipient Harry A. Bullis scholarship, 1977; named USA Team Handball Athlete of the Yr., 1985, USOC Olympian Mag. Team Handball SportsMan of the Yr., 1985; mem. 1984 Olympic Team, U.S. Nat. Team, 1977-85 (capt. 1985). Mem. Order of the Coif, Phi Kappa Phi, Beta Gamma Sigma, Beta Alpha Psi, Phi Eta Sigma. Home: 617 Las Casas Ave Pacific Palisades CA 90272-3313 Office: William E Simon & Sons 10990 Wilshire Blvd Ste 1750 Los Angeles CA 90024

LENEAU, THOMAS ERVIN, gas company executive; b. Mpls., Aug. 3, 1950; s. Thomas J. and Evelyn F. (Schwantees) LeN. BS in Math., St. Cloud State U., 1972; MEd, U. Minn., 1977; B in Acctg., U. Minn., Duluth, 1979; MBA, Ariz. State U., 1985. CPA, Ariz., Minn. Math. instr. Duluth Pub. Schs., 1972-78; acctg. instr. U. Minn., Duluth, 1978-79; auditor Deloitte, Haskins & Sells, Mpls., 1979-81; v.p. fin. Rio Verde Devel., Scottsdale, Ariz., 1981-86; pres., CEO Black Mountain Gas Co., Cave Creek, Ariz., 1986—, also bd. dirs. Treas. Foothills Community Found., Carefree, Ariz., 1989—. Mem. AICPA. Office: Black Mountain Gas Co PO Box 427 Cave Creek AZ 85331

LENGYEL, CORNEL ADAM (CORNEL ADAM), author; b. Fairfield, Conn., Jan. 1, 1915; s. Elmer Alexander and Mary Elizabeth (Bismarck) L.; m. Teresa Delaney Murphy, July 10, 1933; children: Jerome Benedict, Paul Joel, Michael Sebastian, Cornelia (Mrs. Charles Burke). LittD (hon.), World Acad. of Arts and Culture, Taiwan, 1991. Editor, supr. Fed. Research Project, San Francisco, 1938-41; music critic The Coast, San Francisco, 1937-41; shipwright, personnel officer Kaiser Shipyard, Richmond, Calif., 1942-44; mgr. Forty-Nine Theatre, Georgetown, Calif., 1946-50; editor W.H. Freeman Co., San Francisco, 1952-54; founder, exec. editor Dragon's Teeth Press, Georgetown, 1969—; vis. prof., lectr. English lit. Sacramento State Coll., 1962-63; writer-in-residence Hamline U., St. Paul, 1968-69; guest lectr. MIT, 1969; transl. from Hungarian; editorial cons. HEW; ednl. dir. ILGWU. Author: (history) American Testament: The Story of the Promised Land, 1956, Four Days in July, 1958, I, Benedict Arnold: The Anatomy of Treason, 1960, Presidents of the U.S.A., 1961, Ethan Allen and the Green Mountain Boys, 1961, Jesus the Galilean, 1966, The Declaration of Independence, 1969; (poetry) Thirty Pieces, 1933, First Psalms, 1950, Fifty Poems, 1965, Four Dozen Songs, 1970, The Lookout's Letter, 1971, El Dorado Forest: Selected Poems, 1986; (plays) The World's My Village, 1935, Jonah Fugitive, 1936, The Case of Benedict Arnold, 1975, Doctor Franklin, 1976, The Master Plan, 1978, Mengele's Passover, 1987; The Giant's Trap, 1938, The Atom Clock, 1951, Eden, Inc., 1954, rev. edit. Omega, 1963, Will of Stratford, 1964, Three Plays, 1964; also Late News From Adam's Acre, 1983, A Clockmaker's Boy: Part One, 1987; (essays) The Creative Self, 1971; contbr. to anthologies The Golden Year, 1960, Interpretation in Our Time, 1966, The Britannica Library of Great American Writing, 1961, The Menorah Treasury, 1964, The Courage to Grow Old, 1988, From These Hills, 1990, Blood to Remember, 1991, Anthology of Contemporary Poets, 1992, World Poetry, 1993, We Speak for Peace, 1993, also Poet Lore, The Coast, The Argonaut, Saturday Rev., Menorah Jour., others. Served with U.S. Merchant Marine, 1944-45. Recipient Albert M. Bender award in lit., 1945; recipient 1st prize Maritime Poetry Awards, 1945, 1st prize Poetry Soc. Va., 1951, Maxwell Anderson award drama, 1950, Di Castagnola award Poetry Soc. Am., 1971, Internat. Who's Who in Poetry award, 1972; Huntington Hartford Found. resident fellow, 1951, 64; MacDowell Colony resident fellow, 1967; Ossabaw Island Found. fellow, 1968; Nat. Endowment for Arts fellow, 1976-77. Mem. MLA, AAUP, PEN, Poetry Soc. Am., Poetry Soc. Eng., Authors Guild. Address: Adam's Acres Georgetown CA 95634

LENHART, JAMES ROBERT, sales manager; b. Detroit, Apr. 29, 1952; s. Robert Bernard and Harriett Frances (Ebert) L.; m. Lauren Michi Fujimoto, Oct. 1, 1983; 1 child, Amanda Mariko. Student, Naval Schs. of Photography, Pensacola, Fla., 1973, U. Hawaii, 1977-79. Beverage mgr. Bobby McGee's, Honolulu, 1978-79, Marriott Hotels, Maui, Hawaii, 1979-81; bartender various restaurants, Maui, 1981-82; owner Plantation Prime Rib Restaurant, Kauai, Hawaii, 1982-85; account exec. Inter Island Distributors, Kauai, 1985-86; sales mgr. Superior Coffee and Foods, Honolulu, 1986—. With USN, 1973-77, PTO. Mem. VFW, Am. Culinary Assn., Internat. Food Svc. Execs., Hawaii Mfrs. Assn., Chefs de Cuisine/Hawaii. Republican. Methodist. Home: 7007 Hawaii Kai Dr Honolulu HI 96825 Office: Superior Coffee and Foods 99-910 Iwaena St Aiea HI 96701

LENHOFF, HOWARD MAER, biological sciences educator, academic administrator, activist; b. North Adams, Mass., Jan. 27, 1929; s. Charles and Goldie Sarah (Rubin) L.; m. Sylvia Grossman, June 20, 1954; children: Gloria, Bernard. B.A., Coe Coll., 1950, D.Sc. (hon.), 1976; Ph.D., Johns Hopkins U., 1955. USPHS fellow Loomis Lab., Greenwich, Conn., 1954-56; vis. lectr. Howard U., Washington, 1957-58; rsch. assoc. George Washington U., Washington, 1957-58; postdoctoral fellow Carnegie Instn., Washington, 1958; investigator Howard Hughes Med. Inst., Miami, 1958-63; prof. biology, dir. Lab. for Quantitative Biology U. Miami, Coral Gables, 1963-69; prof. biol. scis. U. Calif., Irvine, 1969-92, prof. polit. sci., 1986-92, assoc. dean biol. scis., 1969-71, dean grad. div., 1971-73, faculty asst. to vice chancellor of student affairs, 1986-88, 90—, chair faculty senate, 1988-90, prof. emeritus, 1993; vis. scientist, Louis Lipsky fellow Weizmann Inst. Sci., Rehovot, Israel, 1968-69; vis. prof. chem. engring., Rothschild fellow Israel Inst. Tech., 1973-74; vis. prof. Hebrew U., Jerusalem, spring 1970, fall 1971, 77-78; Hubert Humphrey Inst. fellow Ben Gurion U., Beersheva, Israel, 1981; sr. rsch. fellow Jesus Coll., U. Oxford, 1988; dir. Nelson Rsch. & Devel. Co., Irvine, 1971-73; bd. dirs. BioProbe Internat., Inc., Tustin, Calif., 1983-89, chmn. bd., 1983-86. Editor/author: Biology of Hydra, 1961, Hydra, 1969, Experimental Coelenterate Biology, 1972, Coelenterate Biology—Review and Perspectives, 1974, Hydra: Research Methods, 1983, Enzyme Immunoassay, 1985, From Trembley's Polyps to New Directions in Research on Hydra, 1985, Hydra and the Birth of Experimental Biology, 1986, Biology of Nematocysts, Conception to Birth, 1988; mem. editorial bd. Jour. Solid Phase Biochemistry, 1976-80. Vice chmn. So. Calif. div. Am. Assn. Profs. for Peace in Middle East, 1972-80; bd. dirs. Am. Assn. for Ethiopian Jews, 1974—, pres., 1978-82; bd. govs. Israel Bonds Orange County, Calif., 1974-80, Dade County Heart Assn., Miami, 1958-61, So. Calif. Technion Soc., 1976; pres. Hillel Coun. of Orange County, 1976-78; nat. chmn. faculty div. State of Israel Bonds, 1976; mem. sci. adv. bd. Am. Friends of Weizman Inst. Sci., 1980-84; bd. dirs. Hi Hopes Identity Discovery Found., Anaheim, Calif., 1982-87, pres. bd. govs., 1983-85, William Syndrome Found., trustee, 1992, pres., 1993—. 1st lt. USAF, 1956-58. Recipient Career Development award USPHS, 1965-69; Louis Lipsky fellow, 1968-69; Disting. fellow Iowa Acad. Sci., 1986. Fellow AAAS; mem. Soc. Physics and Natural History of Swiss Acad. Scis. (hon.), Am. Chem. Soc., Am. Biophys. Soc., Am. Soc. Zoologists, History of Sci. Soc., Am. Soc. Cell Biologists, Am. Soc. Biol. Chemists, Biophysics Soc., Soc. Gen. Physiologists, Soc. Growth and Devel. Home: 304 Robin Hood Ln Costa Mesa CA 92627-2134 Office: U Calif Sch Biol Scis Irvine CA 92717

LENNEY, JAMES F., biochemist, educator; b. St. Louis, Oct. 11, 1918; s. James P. and Lenore (Roeder) L.; m. Sara Ann Gates, July 20, 1942 (dec. Apr. 1971); children: Ann, Ellen; m. Ruth Kleinfeld, Feb. 9, 1973. AB, Washington U., St. Louis, 1939; PhD, MIT, 1947. Chemist MIT, Cambridge, Mass., 1942-45; biochemist Standard Brands Inc., Stamford, Conn., 1946-56, Union Starch & Refining Co., Granite City, Ill., 1956-63; prof. U. Hawaii, Honolulu, 1964—. Contbr. 50 articles to profl. jours. and chpts. to books. Pres. Pacific Orchid Soc., Honolulu, 1983. Grantee Nat. Insts. Health, 1968-75, Nat. Sci. Found. grantee, 1965-69. Mem. AAAS (fellow 1966), Am. Chem. Soc., Am. Soc. Pharmacology & Exptl. Therapeutics, Phi Beta Kappa, Sigma Xi. Home: 2856 Komaia Pl Honolulu HI 96822-1745

LENNOX, CAROL, computer scientist, consultant; b. Colorado Springs, Colo., Dec. 22, 1938; d. Willian Orin and Elizabeth Edith (Foster) L. BA, Mills Coll., 1961. Systems programmer Control Data Corp., Palo Alto, Calif., 1963-68; co-founder, mgr. Interaccess Interactive, Palo Alto, 1968-70; cons. Polymorphic Corp., Palo Alto, 1970-71; asst. mgr. Stanford U., Palo Alto, 1971-75; with dept. computing and networks Mills Coll., Oakland, Calif., 1975—, lectr., 1975—, instnl. rschr., 1979-84, dir. interdisciplinary grad. program, 1990-92; bd. dirs. Elsinorg, Ft. Stockton, Tex., SAC, Corvallis, Oreg.; trustee EDUCOM, Washington, 1988—, cons., 1982—; steering com. CNI, 1992-95. Contbg. author: Computing Strategies in Liberal Arts Colleges, 1992. Mem. Assn. Computer Machinery, Assn. Instnl. Rsch., Internat. Interactive Computing Soc., Jr. League, Phi Beta Kappa (Zeta chpt.). Home: 400 Irish Ridge Rd Half Moon Bay CA 94019 Office: Mills Coll Oakland CA 94613

LENNOX, GLORIA (GLORIA DEMEREE), real estate executive; b. Baden, Pa., Feb. 14, 1931; d. Gilbert and Marion (Slosson) Whetson; m. William Lennox, June 19, 1954 (div. 1985); children: Cheryl Lennox Watson, Lynda Lennox Huerta, Jim; m. Philip Demeree, July 4, 1985. BS in Edn., Kent State U., 1954; MA in Spl. Edn., Ariz. State U., 1968; grad., Realtor's Inst. Cert. residential specialist, residential broker. Tchr. Maple Leaf Sch., Garfield Heights, Ohio, 1954-55, Madison (Ind.) Dist. Elem. Sch., 1958, Scottsdale (Ariz.) Schs., 1961-68, Devereux Sch., 1968-70, Tri-City Mental Health Sch., Mesa, Ariz., 1970-71; br. mgr. M. Leslie Hansen, Scottsdale, 1972-74; v.p., gen. mgr. John D. Noble and Assocs., Scottsdale, 1974-83; pres., broker Gloria Lennox & Assocs., Inc., Scottsdale, 1983—. Chmn. bd. Interfaith Counseling Svc., 1988, 89; trustee Scottsdale Congl. United Ch. of Christ, 1986-88, 92. Kent State U. scholar, 1950-54. Mem. Nat. Assn. Realtors, Ariz. Assn. Realtors (Realtor Assoc. of Yr. 1975), Women's Coun. Realtors, Realtor Nat. Mktg. Inst., Scottsdale Bd. Realtors (pres. 1981-82, Realtor of Yr. 1982, grad. Realtor Inst., cert. residential specialist, cert. residential broker state and nat.), Ariz. Town Halls, Ariz. Country Club. Republican. Home: 7561 N Via Camello Del Sur Scottsdale AZ 85258-3005 Office: Gloria Lennox and Assocs 4533 N Scottsdale Rd Ste 200 Scottsdale AZ 85251-7618

LENNOX BUCHTHAL, MARGARET AGNES, neurophysiologist; b. Denver, Dec. 28, 1913; d. William Gordon and Emma Stevenson (Buchtel) L.; m Gerald Klastskinrc 1941 (div. 1947); 1 child, Jane Herner; m. Fritz Buchthal, Aug. 19, 1957. BA, Vassar Coll., 1934; MD, Yale Sch. Medicine, 1939; D of Medicine, Copenhagen U., 1972. Intern pediatrics Strong Meml. Hosp., Rochester, N.Y., 1939-40; asst. resident pediatrics N.Y. Hosp., N.Y.C., 1941-42; instr. Yale Sch. Medicine, New Haven, Conn., 1942-44, asst. prof. dept. psychiatry, 1945-51; asst. prof. U. Copenhagen, Inst. Neurophysiology, Denmark, 1957-72; assoc. prof. U. Copenhagen, Inst. Neurophysiology, 1972-81; ret., 1981; head clin. electroencephalography Yale U. Sch. of Medicine, 1942-51, head clinic epileptology, 1942-51; chief editor Epilesia Pub. by Elsevire, 1967-73. Contbr. articles to profl. jours. Republican. Methodist. Home: 289 El Cielito Rd Santa Barbara CA 93105-2306

LENTES, DAVID EUGENE, corporate executive; b. Spokane, Wash., Dec. 14, 1951; s. William Eugene and Ellen Elsie L.; m. Debra Kay White, May 19, 1973 (div. 1984); children: Janette Adele, Damon Arthur; m. Marlene J. Livingston, Sept. 15, 1990. AA, Spokane Falls Community Coll., 1972; BBA, Gonzaga U., 1975. V.p. Dellen Wood Products, Inc., Spokane, 1972—, also bd. dirs.; v.p. Custom Computer Services, Inc., Spokane, 1980-87, also bd. dirs.; mng. ptnr. Com-Lease, 1980-87, Len-Lease, 1980—; v.p., bd. dirs. DWP Trucking, Inc., 1982-85, Sentel Corp., 1983-88, BDR Investment Corp., 1983—; pres., bd. dirs. ASA Mgmt. Corp., 1984—, also Lenmark Corp., Inc., 1985—. Treas. Dishman Hills Natural Area Assn., 1970—; elder Bethany Presbyn. Ch., 1980-83; active Spokane Econ. Devel. Council. Mem. Assn. Wash. Bus., Nat. Fedn. Ind. Businessmen, Am. Fedn. Bus., Better Bus. Bur. (Spokane chpt.), U.S. C. of C., Spokane C. of C., Timber Products Mfrs., Hoo-Hoo Internat. Republican. Office: 3014 N Flora Rd Spokane WA 99216-1818

LENZ, PHILIP JOSEPH, municipal administrator; b. Monterey Park, Calif., Sept. 15, 1940; s. Philip George and Irene Mary (Bowers) L.; m. Mary Lou Antista, July 16, 1966; children: Brian Joseph, Jonathan Thomas. BA, Calif. State U., L.A., 1966; MS, Pepperdine U., 1974. Dir. West Valley div. San Bernardino County (Calif.) Probation Dept., 1977-79, dir. juvenile div., 1979-82, dir. adminstrv. services, 1982-88, dir. dist. services, 1988-90; dep. chief probation officer, 1990—; instr. dept. bus. Calif. State U., San Bernardino; instr. dept. social rels. Loma Linda U., 1988. Sec. bd. trustees Upland (Calif.) Sch. dist., 1985—, pres. sch. bd., 1989-90; mgr., coach Upland Am. Little League, 1981-90, bd. dirs. 1982-90; pres. Fontana (Calif.) Family Svc. Agy., 1972-74; mem. adv. com. corrections Chaffey Coll., Alta Loma, Calif., 1977—; mem. City of Upland Parks and Recreation com., 1986—, chmn., 1989-90, 90-91; mem. bd. dirs. Highlander Ednl. Found., v.p. 1991—; mem. Calif. Youth Authority CADRE of Cons. Recipient Tim Fitzharris award Chief Probation Officers of Calif., 1987. Mem. Calif. Probation, Parole and Correctional Assn. (liaison, regional v.p. 1981-83, 2d v.p. 1985-86, 1st v.p. 1986—, pres. 1987—), Probation Bus. Mgr.'s Assn. (regional chmn. 1984-86, v.p. 1987), Western Correctional Assn., Assn. for Criminal Justice Rsch. (bd. dirs.), Probation Adminstrs. Assn. (regional chair 1992-93). Democrat. Roman Catholic. Home: 1375 Stanford Ave Upland CA 91786-3147 Office: San Bernardino County Dept Probation 175 W 5th St San Bernardino CA 92415-0001

LENZO, THOMAS JOHN, training and development consultant; b. Waterbury, Conn., Nov. 19, 1949; s. John Anthony and Mary Louise (Perezella) L. BA, Fairfield U., 1971; MEd, Calif. State U., L.A., 1980. Media coord. Valley Vocat. Ctr., Industry, Calif., 1977-78; libr. Washington Sch., Pasadena, Calif., 1978-79; tng. specialist Data Electronics Inc., Pasadena, 1979-82; engring. instr. Litton Data Systems, Van Nuys, Calif., 1982-83; cons. B.P.W. Inc., Costa Mesa, Calif., 1983-86; pvt. practice Pasadena, 1986—. Contbr. articles to profl. jours. Instr. ARC, Pasadena, 1983-85; mem. Towards 2000 mayoral com., Pasadena, 1984-85; speaker advisor All Sts. Ch., Pasadena, 1989—; with USAF, 1972-76. Mem. Am. Soc. Tng. & Devel., Nat. Soc. Performance & Instrn., Soc. Tech. Communications, Pasadena IBM PC User Group (bd. dirs.). Roman Catholic. Home: 2473 Oswego St Apt 10 Pasadena CA 91107-4239

LEO, LOUIS J., university administrator; b. Chgo.; m. Karen Ann Leo. BA, U. Mich., 1966, JD, 1969. Dean for adminstrn., dean of students Calif. State U., Stanislaus, 1969-77; vice chancellor student svcs. U. Calif., Riverside, 1977—. Office: U Calif 3108 Hinderker Hall Riverside CA 92521

LEO, MARY GAYE, school administrator; b. Colorado Springs, Colo., Oct. 19, 1951; d. Bernard Johnston and Mary Ellen (Hardy) Lamar; m. Dominick Louis Leo; children: Dominick Christopher, Rachel Gabreilla. BA, U. Colo., 1973, MA, 1978; PhD in Ednl. Adminstrn. Denver U., 1985. Cert. bicultural/bilingual instr. Communications & group dynamics instr., Denver area, 1972-73; with Denver Pub. Sch. System, 1973—, arts mgmt./theater dir., 1973-87; asst. prin. Lake Mid. Sch., 1987-89, Martin Luther King Mid. Sch., Denver Pub. Schs., 1989-91; asst. prin. West High Sch., 1991—. Author: (rock musical) Celebration, 1979, (children's fantasy) Bob, The Magical Unicorn, 1981, (book) The Raven and I-E Locus of Control as Measures of High Ability; dir., designer, producer profl. & ednl. theatrical prodns. including Godspell, 1974, Guys and Dolls, 1975, My Fair Lady, 1976, Carousel, 1977, Music Man, 1978, Celebration!, 1979, Annie Get Your Gun, 1980, Jesus Christ Superstar, 1982, Grease, 1982, Camelot, 1983, Guys and Dolls, 1987; developer Authentic School Project for Drop Out Prevention, Academy Model for Middle Level Education. Lectr., workshop coord. Colo. Arts and Humanities Coun., 1974-75. Gov.'s Creativity grantee, 1990-91. Mem. ASCD, NAFE, Am. Theatre Assn., Women in Theatre, Nat. Council Tchrs. English, Colo. Assn. Sch. Execs., Colo. Partnership. Home: 11224 E Harvard Dr Aurora CO 80014-1711

LEO, ROBERT JOSEPH, association executive, consultant; b. Paterson, N.J., Nov. 24, 1939; s. Dewey J. and Jean (Bianco) L.; m. Margaret Elena Ingafu, Aug. 5, 1962; children—Christopher, Nicholas. B.A. in Speech, Temple U., 1960, M.A., 1962; Ph.D., U. Wash., 1968. Instr. Monmouth Coll., West Long Branch, N.J., 1962-64; spl. asst. to chancellor Dallas County (Tex.) Community Coll. Dist., 1968-71, dir. spl. services and gov. relations, 1971-76; assoc. exec. dir. League for Innovation in the Community Coll., Los Angeles, 1976-80, exec. dir., Dallas, 1980-82; exec. dir. Los Angeles Jr. C. of C., 1982-93, Palm Desert C. of C., 1993—; founding pres. Nat. Council Resource Devel., adj. assoc. prof. East Tex. State U., 1975-76; chmn. Tex. Health Planning Council. Recipient Disting. Service award Oak Cliff Jaycees, 1973; Spl. Recognition award Nat. Council Resource Devel., 1981; named Significant Contbr. to Fair Housing, Greater Dallas Housing Opportunity Ctr., 1973. Mem. Nat. Council Resource Devel., Internat. Soc. for Planning and Strategic Mgmt., Grand People (bd. dirs.), Rotary, Los Angeles Athletic Club; Author articles in field. Home: 4641 Fulton Ave Apt 204 Sherman Oaks CA 91423-3279 Office: Palm Desert C of C 72-990 Hwy 111 Palm Desert CA 92260

LEOFSKY, JOAN CAROLE, business owner; b. Tonawanda, N.Y., Mar. 11, 1938; d. Frances Joseph Leofsky and Rose Marie (Karkoski) Horst; m. Arlen Dale Goodwine, June 27, 1959 (div. June 1971); children: Stirling Lance Goodwine, Andrew Raleigh Goodwine. BS, Ea. Wash. State Coll., 1973; MA, U. Wash., 1979. Rschr. Hunger Action Ctr., Seattle, 1975; nutritionist Rainier Vista Health Clinic & Neighborhood House, Inc., Seattle, 1975-79; project mgr. Rainier Vista Health Clinic, Seattle, 1979-81; owner Leofsky Art Glass, Seattle, 1981-84; bus. broker agt. VR Bus. Brokers, Bellevue, Wash., 1984-87; owner Cheers & Chocolates, Bellevue, 1987—. Weekly columnist Womanspeak, 1978-80. Founder, coord. South Seattle Women's Network, 1979-81, Seattle Women's Craft Fair, 1979-81. Office: PO Box 1087 Bellevue WA 98009

LEONARD, ELIZABETH ADNEY, social worker; b. Lebanon, Ind., Apr. 27, 1917; d. Frank Brown and Ethel Fern (Coons) Adney; m. Alan J. Leonard, Aug. 4, 1949; children: Arthur Alan, Jean Elizabeth. BA, Ind. U.,

1939, MSW, 1947; postgrad., Columbia U., N.Y.C., 1948. Lic. social worker, Calif. With Psychiat. Clinic for Youth, Long Beach, Calif., 1958-74, chief social worker, 1974-82, ret., 1982. Mem. NASW, Am. Orthopsychiat. Assn., AAUW. Home: 2339A Avenida Sevilla Laguna Beach CA 92653-2215

LEONARD, GLEN M., museum administrator; b. Salt Lake City, Nov. 12, 1938; s. Burnham J. and Allene (Green) L.; m. Karen Wright, Mar. 15, 1968; children: Cory, Kyle, Keith. BA, U. Utah, 1964, MA, 1966, PhD, 1970. Mng. editor Utah State Hist. Soc., Salt Lake City, 1970-73; sr. rsch. assoc. history div. Ch. of Jesus Christ of Latter-day Saints, Salt Lake City, 1973-78; dir. Mus. Ch. History and Art, Salt Lake City, 1979—; mem. adv. bd. editors Utah Hist. Quarterly, Salt Lake City, 1973-88; assoc. editor Jour. Mormon History, Provo, Utah, 1974-80; bd. dirs. Western Studies Ctr., Brigham Young U., Provo. Co-author: The Story of the Latter-day Saints, 1976; contbr. articles to profl. publs. Mem. Hist. Preservation Commn., Farmington, Utah, 1986-92; mem. adv. coun. Mormon Pioneer Nat. Hist. Trail, Nat. Park Svc., 1980-86. Recipient Dale Morgan Article award Utah State Hist. Soc., 1973. Mem. Orgn. Am. Historians, Western History Assn., Am. Assn. Mus. (museum assessment program cons.), Assn. Utah Historians (bd. dirs. 1981-83), Utah Mus. Assn. (bd. dirs. 1980-83), Am. Assn. State and Local History. Office: Mus Ch History and Art 45 N West Temple Salt Lake City UT 84150

LEONARD, MARY CHRISTINE, banking consultant; b. Chehalis, Wash., Dec. 15, 1947; d. John Paul and Charlotte Louise (Koschmann) Hoyt; m. Roy Lawrence Short, June 24, 1971 (div. 1977); m. George Edmund Leonard Jr., Sept. 22, 1990; stepchildren: Tracy, Amy, Kristin. BS in Home Econs., Seattle U., 1970. Sales asst. Nordstrom, Seattle, 1970-72; dept. mgr. Joseph Magnin, Reno, Nev., 1972-74; tng. mgr. Weinstocks, Reno, 1974-76; asst. v.p. Nev. Nat. Bank, Reno, 1976-83; dep. commr. Nev. Fin. Instns. Div., Carson City, 1983-86; supt. of banks Ariz. State Banking Dept., Phoenix, 1986-89; dep. dir. Office of Thrift Supervision, Washington, 1989-90; pres. Compliance Dynamics, Phoenix, 1990—; mem. appraisal subcom. Fed. Fin. Instns. Exam. Coun., Washington, 1989-90; chmn. state liaison com. Fed. Fin. Instns. Exam. Coun., Washington, 1988-89; bd. dirs. Am. Coun. State Savs. Suprs., Washington, 1986-89; dist. vice-chmn. Coun. State Bank Suprs., Washington, 1987-89. Mem. nat. bd. advisors U. Ariz. Coll. Bus. and Pub. Adminstrn., Tucson, 1988-89; mem. adv. bd. Internat. Assn. for Fin. Planning, Phoenix, 1987-88; bd. dirs. Esperanca, Phoenix, 1986-89, Friends of the Phoenix Pub. Libr., 1987-88; mem. women's bd. Barrow Neurol. Found. Mem. Am. Acad. State Cert. Appraisers (adv. bd.), Ariz. Coalition for Tomorrow. Democrat. Home: 3064 E Stella Ln Phoenix AZ 85016

LEONARD, WILLIAM CARSON, pediatrician; b. Harrogate, Tenn., Feb. 6, 1934; s. William Dorsey and Elzabeth (Brooks) L.; m. Judith Ann Glenn, July 8, 1989. BS magna cum laude, Lincoln Meml. U., 1953; MD, U. Tenn., 1956. Intern U. Tenn., Memphis, 1957-58, resident, 1961-63; pvt. practice Orange, Calif., 1963—; asst. prof. pediatrics U. Calif., Orange, 1963-70. Fellow Am. Acad. Pediatrics. Office: # 300 27800 Medical Center Rd Mission Viejo CA 92691

LEONE, WILLIAM CHARLES, business executive; b. Pitts., May 3, 1924; s. Joseph and Fortuna (Sammarco) L.; m. Sara Jane Hollenback, Aug. 26, 1950; children: William Charles, David M., Patricia Ann, Mary Jane. B.S., Carnegie Inst. Tech., 1944, M.S., 1948, D.Sc., 1952. Asst. prof. engring. Carnegie Inst. Tech., Pitts., 1946-53; div. mgr. Indsl. Systems div. Hughes Aircraft, Los Angeles, 1953-59; v.p., gen. mgr., dir. Rheem Califone, Los Angeles, 1960, Rheem Electronics, Los Angeles, 1960-68; group v.p. Rheem Mfg. Co., 1968-71; exec. v.p. Rheem Mfg. Co., N.Y.C., 1971-72; pres. Rheem Mfg. Co., 1972-76, also dir.; pres. City Investing Co. Internat., Inc., 1972-76; pres., dir. Farah Mfg. Co., El Paso, Tex., 1976-77; bus. cons., 1977-79; acting vice chmn. McCulloch Oil Corp. (MCO), Los Angeles, 1979-80; also dir. McCulloch Oil Corp. (MCO); pres., dir. MAXXAM Inc. (formerly MCO Holdings, Inc.), 1980-90; vice chmn. MAXXAM Inc., 1990-92; chmn., CEO, dir. Pacific Lumber Co., 1986-90, Horizon Corp., 1984-89. Trustee Carnegie Mellon U., 1986-92. Mem. ASME, IEEE, Am. Inst. Aeros. and Astronautics. Home: 2209 Chelsea Rd Palos Verdes Peninsula CA 90274-2603

LEONG, CAROL JEAN, electrologist; b. Sacramento, Jan. 9, 1942; d. Walter Richard and Edith (Bond) Bloss; m. Oliver Arthur Fisk III, Apr. 12, 1964 (div. 1973); 1 child, Victoria Kay. BA in Sociology, San Jose (Calif.) State Coll., 1963; degree, Western Bus. Coll., 1964; cert. in electrolysis, Bay Area Coll. Electrolysis, 1978. Registered and cert. clin. profl. electrologist, Calif. Model various orgns., Calif., 1951-64; employment counselor Businessmen's Clearinghouse, Cin., 1966-67; dir. personnel Kroger Food Corp., Cin., 1967-68; prin. Carol Leong Electrolysis, San Mateo, Calif., 1978—; prin. Designs by Carol, San Mateo, 1987—; mem. Profl. Women's Forum, 1988—. Contbr. articles to profl. publs. Recipient Cert. of Appreciation San Francisco Lighthouse for the Blind, 1981-82, 83. Mem. Internat. Guild Profl. Electrologists (mem. continuing edn. com.), NAFE, Profl. Women's Forum, Peninsula Humane Soc., San Francisco Zool. Soc., Friends of Filoli, Am. Electrologists Assn., Electrologists Assn. Calif., Internat. Platform Assn, Chi Omega. Republican. Presbyterian. Home: 3339 Glendora Dr San Mateo CA 94403-3704 Office: Carol Leong Electrolysis 36 S El Camino Real Ste 205 San Mateo CA 94401-3826

LEONG, KIRBY HUNG-LOY, musician, educator; b. Honolulu, Nov. 8, 1945; s. William Hung-Loy Leong and Launa (Chun) Hettinger; divorced; children: Byon, Andrea. BA in Music, Calif. State U., Hayward, 1982; adult edn. credential, San Francisco State Coll., 1988. Pers. mgr. Santa Cruz (Calif.) Symphony Orch., 1969-70; orch. libr. Cabrillo Festival, Aptos, Calif., 1969-70; musician various symphony orchs. and jazz bands including Yak-Tones, 1970—; adult edn. tchr. Hayward (Calif.) Unified Sch. Dist., 1981-93, Castro Valley (Calif.) Unified Sch. Dist., 1981-93; pvt. tchr. guitar/bass, 1984-93. Mem. Am. String Teachers Assn., Internat. Soc. Bassists. Home: PO Box 2633 Castro Valley CA 94546

LEON GUERRERO, WILFRED PACELLI, academic administrator; b. Agana, Guam, Feb. 13, 1942; m. Virginia Leon Artero; children: Wilfred Pacelli, Roderick, Myrna, Alysia, Phyliss, Nadine. BA in Math., U. Guam, 1969; MA in Math. Edn., U. No. Colo., 1971, EdD, 1972. Asst. prof., asst. to dean Coll. Bus. and Applied Tech. U. Guam, Mangilao, 1972-73, assoc. dean Coll. Edn., 1973, dean Land Grant Program, 1973-74, dean, dir. Coll. Agr. and Life Scis., 1974-88, tenured assoc. prof., 1984, pres., 1988—; chmn. Goodwill Industries. Chmn. Goodwill Industries; active Guam Young Men's League Assn. Named one of Outstanding Young Men of Am., 1974; John Hay Whitney fellow, 1971; GovGuam Profl. and Vocat. scholar, 1968. Home: PO Box 3537 Agana GU 96910-3537 Office: U of Guam Office of Pres UOG Sta Mangilao GU 96923

LEONTIE, ROGER EUGENE, industrial engineer; b. San Francisco, May 11, 1937; s. Jerry and Alice (Kirichenko) L.; m. Mari Lee Harrington, Jan. 29, 1967; children: Gerald Thomas, Stephen Eugene. BS in Indsl. Engring., U. Calif.-Berkeley, 1960; MBA, San Jose State Coll., 1969. Registered profl. engr., Calif. Indsl. engring. sect. leader Raychem Corp., Menlo Park, Calif., 1963-69; chief indsl. engr. Crown-Zellerbach, San Francisco, 1969-73; mfg. engring. mgr. ISS, Cupertino, Calif., 1973-75; dir. facilities Rolm Corp., Santa Clara, Calif., 1976-81; facilities engring. mgr. Intel Corp., Santa Clara, 1981; dir. facilities Activision, Mountain View, Calif., 1982-84; v.p., dir. facilities Citibank, Oakland, Calif., 1985—. Served with AUS, 1960-63. Mem. Inst. Indsl. Engrs., Internat. Facility Mgmt. Assn., Alpha Pi Mu, Beta Gamma Sigma, Phi Kappa Phi. Republican. Avocations: carpentry, reading. Office: Citibank 180 Grand Ave Oakland CA 94612-3741

LEOPOLD, JOAN SILVERBERG, educational administrator, educator; b. N.Y.C., Mar. 18, 1947; d. Al and Shirley (Zimmerman) Silverberg; m. John William Leopold, June 22, 1969; 1 dau., Ellen. B.A. summa cum laude, Vassar Coll., 1967; cert. in Victorian Studies, U. London, Eng., 1967; M.A., Harvard U., 1968, Ph.D., 1975; postgrad. Oxford U., Eng., 1970-77; JD, UCLA, 1987. Mellon fellow U. Pa., Phila., 1979-80; research assoc. U. Calif.-Berkeley, 1979-82; adminstrv. service officer Calif. Spanish Lang. Data Base, Hayward, 1981-82; asst. prof. Chapman Coll., Alameda and Mare Island, Calif., 1981-82; dean Coll. Arts and Scis. Internat. Coll., Los Angeles, 1982-83; vis. scholar UCLA, 1982-85, dir. Volney Prize Essay Project, 1982—; instr. Rutgers U., Camden, N.J., 1970. Author: Culture in Comparative and Evolutionary Perspective, 1980; The Letter Liveth: The Life, Work and Library of A.F. Pott, 1983. Contbr. articles, revs. to hist. publs. Rhodes fellow, Oxford U., 1972-74, Humboldt fellow, 1976-78, Volkswagen fellow, 1979, Danforth fellow, 1967-75, Woodrow Wilson Found. Fellow, 1967-68; grantee Am. Council Learned Socs., 1981; recipient Univs. Essay Prize Royal Asiatic Soc., 1971. Mem. Grad. History Assn. (founder, Oxford 1970), Intellectual History Seminar (founder, Oxford 1971), Internat. Assn. Ind. Scholars (founder, pres. 1984-85), Am. Hist. Assn., Assn. Univ. Adminstrs., AAUW (hon. fellowship, Germany 1976-77). Office: PO Box 24250 Los Angeles CA 90024-0250

LEOPOLD, LUNA BERGERE, geology educator; b. Albuquerque, Oct. 8, 1915; s. Aldo and Estella (Bergere) L.; m. Barbara Beck Nelson, 1973; children: Bruce Carl, Madelyn Dennette. BS, U. Wis., 1936, DSc (hon.), 1980; M.S., UCLA, 1944; Ph.D., Harvard, 1950; D Geography (hon.), U. Ottawa, 1969; DSc (hon.), Iowa Wesleyan Coll., 1971, St. Andrews U., 1981, U. Murcia, Spain. With Soil Conservation Service, 1938-41, U.S. Engrs. Office, 1941-42, U.S. Bur. Reclamation, 1946; head meteorologist Pineapple Research Inst. of Hawaii, 1946-49; hydraulic engr. U.S. Geol. Survey, 1950-71, chief hydrologist, 1957-66, sr. research hydrologist, 1966-71; prof. geology U. Calif. at Berkeley, 1973—. Author: (with Thomas Maddock, Jr.) The Flood Control Controversy, 1954, Fluvial Processes in Geomorphology, 1964, Water, 1974, (with Thomas Dunne) Water in Environmental Planning, 1978; also tech. papers. Served as capt. air weather service USAAF, 1942-46. Recipient Disting. Svc. award Dept. of Interior, 1958; Veth medal Royal Netherlands Geog. Soc., 1963; Cullum Geog. medal Am. Geog. Soc., 1968; Rockefeller Pub. Service award, 1971; Busk medal Royal Geog. Soc., 1983, Berkeley citation U. Calif., David Linton award British Geomorphol. Research Group, 1986, Linsley Award Am. Inst. Hydrology, 1989, Caulfield medal Am. Water Resources Assn., 1991, Nat. Medal Sci., 1991. Mem. NAS (Warren prize), ASCE (Julian Hinds award), Geol. Soc. Am. (Kirk Bryan award 1958, pres. 1972, Disting. Career award geomorphological group 1991), Am. Geophys. Union (Robert E. Horton medal 1992), Am. Acad. Arts and Scis., Am. Philos. Soc., Sigma Xi, Tau Beta Pi, Phi Kappa Phi, Chi Epsilon. Club: Cosmos (Washington). Home: 400 Vermont Ave Berkeley CA 94707-1722

LEPAGE, GERALD ALVIN, retired biochemist; b. Medicinehat, Alberta, Can., Oct. 9, 1917; came to U.S., 1945; s. Florence Maude (Armstrong) LeP.; m. Marjorie Harriet Smith, Mar. 6, 1944; children: Gary Sproule LePage, Gaylis Jean LePage. BS with honors, U. Alberta, 1940, MS in Biochemistry, 1941; PhD in Biochemistry, U. Wis., 1943. Post-doctoral fellow U. Wis. Med. Sch., Madison, 1943-44; biochemist FDA, Ottawa, Can., 1944-45; instr. to prof. oncology McArdle Meml. Lab., U. Wis. Sch. Medicine, Madison, 1945-58; chmn. dept. of biochem. oncology Stanford Rsch. Inst., Menlo Park, Calif., 1958-69; Harry C. Weiss prof. of pharmacology U. Tex. M.D. Anderson Hosp., Houston, 1969-72; dir. McEachern Lab. Med. Sch. U. Alta., Edmonton, Can., 1972-80; ret. McEachern Lab. Med. Sch. U. Alberta, Edmonton, Can., 1980. Home: 1111 SE NW 103rd Ave Vancouver WA 98664-4155

LEPAPE, HARRY LEONARD, diversified company executive; b. Sonora, Calif., Nov. 26, 1930; s. Harry Lepape and Ruth (Freitas) Lepape Woodhams; m. Marilyn J. Earley, Mar. 21, 1955; children: Linda Gay, Jeanne Carolyn. BS, Stanford U., 1952, JD, 1956. Bar: Calif. 1956. Atty. Honolulu Oil Corp., San Francisco, 1956-61; v.p. U.S. Natural Gas Corp., Beverly Hills, Calif., 1962-64; with Pacific Enterprises, L.A., 1964—, exec. v.p., from 1981; chmn., CEO Pacific Interstate Co., 1973—, chmn., CEO Pacific Enterprises Oil Co., 1983—. Mem. ABA, Pacific Coast Gas Assn., Interstate Natural Gas Assn. Am. (bd. dirs.), Am. Gas Assn., L.A. County Bar Assn., Calif. Club, L.A. Athletic Club. Office: Pacific Enterprises 633 W 5th St Ste 5400 Los Angeles CA 90071-2080

LEPORIERE, RALPH DENNIS, quality engineer; b. Elizabeth, N.J., Nov. 8, 1932; s. Maximo and Christian (Lello) L.; m. Judith Louise Crowhurst, Nov. 19, 1960; children: Bonnie Ann, David Anthony. BS in Chemistry, Rutgers U., 1954. Registered profl. engr., Calif. Chemist N.Y. Quinine & Chemical Works, Newark, 1954-55; asst. to chief quality control C.D. Smith Pharmacal Co., New Brunswick, N.J., 1955-56; asst. supr. quality control White Labs., Kenilworth, N.J., 1958-60; statistician Calif. and Hawaiian Sugar Co., Crockett, Calif., 1960—; instr., chmn. of quality control dept. Laney Community Coll., Oakland, Calif., 1967-87, asst. prof., chmn. quality control dept. John F. Kennedy U., Martinez, Calif., 1967-72; instr., mem. adv. com. annual statis. short course U. Calif., Davis, Calif., 1969—. Pres. PTA Napa Junction Elem. Sch., Napa County, Calif., 1971-73; mem. early childhood com., program adv. com. Napa Valley Unified Sch. Dist., Napa County, 1972-76; v.p. Am. Canyon County Water Dist., American County, Calif., 1971-73, pres., 1973-83, gen. mgr., 1981. Recipient Hon. Service award Calif. State PTA, 1973. Fellow Am. Soc. Quality Control (cert. quality engr., chmn. San Francisco sect., founder East Bay Subsect. 1970-71); mem. Soc. Mfg. Engrs. (sr.), Am. Statis. Soc., Am. Chem. Soc. Republican. Roman Catholic. Home: 618 Kilpatrick St Vallejo CA 94589-1305 Office: Calif & Hawaiian Sugar Co 830 Loring Ave Crockett CA 94525-1171

LEPP, TARA MARIE, physical education educator; b. Corning, Calif., June 26, 1958; d. Heinrich and Ila Jeane (Meents) L. BA, Calif. State U., Chico, 1980; MS, U. Oreg., 1982. Cert. athletic trainer. Student athletic trainer Calif. State U., Chico, 1979-80, U. Oreg., Eugene, 1980-81; exercise dir. Serenity Lane Alcohol Rehab. Ctr., Eugene, 1981-82; assoc. prof. Linfield Coll., McMinnville, Oreg., 1982—, head athletic trainer, 1982—; leader/facilitator Children of Alcoholics, Linfield Coll., 1990; faculty Children's Summer Sports Program, Eugene, 1981. Contbr. articles to profl. jours. Med. coord. Oreg. Spl. Olympics, Eugene, 1981-82; med. trainer Athletes in Action Internat. Team, Scandinavia, 1986-87. Grad. teaching fellow U. Oreg., 1981-82. Mem. Nat. Athletic Trainers' Assn. Inc. (certification examiner 1984—), N.W. Athletic Trainers' Assn., Nat. Assn. Intercollegiate Athletics, Oreg. Athletic Trainers' Soc. (v.p. 1987-89), Oreg. Alliance of Health, Phys. Edn., Recreation and Dance, Fellowship of Chrisitan Athletes (leader 1985—), Sigma Beta Phi, Phi Kappa Phi. Office: Linfield Coll 900 S Baker St Mcminnville OR 97128-6894

LEPPER, MARK ROGER, psychology educator; b. Washington, Dec. 5, 1944; s. Mark H. and Joyce M. (Sullivan) L.; m. Jeanne E. Wallace, Dec. 22, 1966; 1 child, Geoffrey William. BA, Stanford U., 1966; PhD, Yale U., 1970. Asst. prof. psychology Stanford (Calif.) U., 1971-76, assoc. prof., 1976-82, prof., 1982—; chmn., 1990—; fellow Ctr. Advanced Study in Behavioral Scis., 1979-80; chmn. mental health behavioral scis. research rev. com. NIMH, 1982-84, mem. basic sociocultural research rev. com., 1980-82. Co-editor: The Hidden Costs of Reward, 1978; cons. editor Jour. Personality and Social Psychology, 1977-85, Child Devel., 1977-86, Jour. Edl. Computing Research, 1983—, Social Cognition, 1981-84; contbr. articles to profl. jours. Woodrow Wilson fellow, 1966-67; NSF fellow, 1966-69; Sterling fellow, 1969-70; Mellon fellow, 1975, fellow Stanford U., 1988-90; grantee NSF, 1978-82, 86-88, NIMH, 1978-86, 88—, NICHD, 1975-88, 90—, U.S. Office Edn., 1972-73. Fellow Am. Psychol. Assn.; mem. Soc. Exptl. Social Psychology, Am. Ednl. Research Assn., Soc. Personality and Social Psychology, Soc. Research in Child Devel., Soc. Psychol. Study of Social Issues. Home: 1544 Dana Ave Palo Alto CA 94303-2813 Office: Stanford U Dept Psychology Stanford CA 94305-2130

LEQUESNE, JAMES RICHARD, federal employee; b. Burbank, Calif., Mar. 8, 1957; s. James Sangster and Lorraine Yvette (Jean) LeQ. BA, Calif. State U., Northridge, 1980. Pub. rels. asst. Sta. KCSN-FM, Northridge, Calif., 1976-87; program clk. Sepulveda (Calif.) VA Med. Ctr., 1984—; media liaison Vol. Ctr. of San Fernando Valley, Panorama City Calif., 1987—. Named Carnation Corp. Outstanding Vol., 1991, Outstanding Vol. Dirs. Vols. in Agencies, 1989—, Outstanding Fed. Employee, 1985-87, 89, 91. Mem. Sierra Club, Greater L.A. Zoo Assn., Nature Conservancy. Democrat. Roman Catholic. Office: Vol Ctr San Fernando 8134 Van Nuys Blvd # 200 Panorama City CA 91402-4801

LERAAEN, ALLEN KEITH, financial executive; b. Mason City, Iowa, Dec. 4, 1951; s. Myron O. and Clarice A. (Handeland) L.; m. Mary Elena Partheymuller, Apr. 14, 1978. BBA in Data Processing and Acctg., No. Ariz. U., 1975. Data processing supr. Stephenson & Co., Denver, 1978-81, contr., 1981-85, arbitrageur, trader, 1985-88, v.p., 1985-90, exec. v.p., 1990—; v.p., sec. bd. dirs. Circle Corp., Denver, 1985—, level III CFA candidate. Mem. Assn. Investment Mgmt. and Rsch., Denver Soc. Security Analysts. Home: 5692 S Robb St Littleton CO 80127-1942 Office: 100 Garfield St Fl 4 Denver CO 80206-5550

LERMAN, EILEEN R., lawyer; b. N.Y.C., May 6, 1947; d. Alex and Beatrice (Kline) L. BA, Syracuse U., 1969; JD, Rutgers U., 1972; MBA, U. Denver, 1983. Bar: N.Y. 1973, Colo. 1976. atty. FTC, N.Y.C., 1972-74; corp. atty. RCA, N.Y.C., 1974-76; corp. atty. Samsonite Corp. and consumer products div. Beatrice Foods Co., Denver, 1976-78, assoc. gen. counsel, 1978-85, asst. sec., 1979-85; ptnr. Davis, Lerman, & Weinstein, Denver, 1985-92, Eileen R. Lerman & Assocs., 1993—; bd. dir. Legal Aid Soc. of Met. Denver, 1979-80. Bd. dirs., vice chmn. Colo. Postsecondary Ednl. Facilities Authority, 1981-89; bd. dirs., pres. Am. Jewish Com., 1989-92; mem. Leadership Denver, 1983. Mem. ABA, Colo. Women's Bar Assn. (bd. dir. 1980-81), Colo. Bar Assn. (bd. govs.), Denver Bar Assn. (trustee), N.Y. State Bar Assn., Rutgers U. Alumni Assn. Lodge: Soroptimists. Home: 1018 Fillmore St Denver CO 80206-3332 Office: Eileen R Lerman & Assocs 50 S Steele St Ste 420 Denver CO 80209-2809

LERNER, PRESTON, writer, journalist; b. N.Y.C., Mar. 8, 1956; s. Joseph Jerome and Isabel Lee (Isaacs) L. BA, Tufts U., 1978; MS in Journalism, Medill Sch. Journalism, Evanston, Ill., 1980. Reporter Abilene (Tex.) Reporter-News, 1980-83, Ft. Worth Star-Telegram, 1983-86; feature writer The Dallas Morning News, 1986-87; freelance journalist Dallas and L.A., 1987—; novelist Bantam Books, L.A., 1992—. Author: Scarab, 1991, Fools on the Hill, 1993; contbg. editor D Mag., 1988-89, L.A. Style Mag., 1990-92; contbr. articles to profl. jours. Democrat. Jewish.

LERNER, SHELDON, plastic surgeon; b. N.Y.C., Mar. 3, 1939; s. Louis and Lillian L.; AB with honors, Drew U., Madison, N.J., 1961; MD, U. Louisville, 1965. Intern, resident Albert Einstein Coll. Medicine, Bronx-Mcpl. Hosp. Center, 1965-73; practice medicine, specializing in plastic surgery Plastic Cosmetic and Reconstructive Surgery Center, San Diego, 1973—. Served with USPHS, 1968-70. Mem. AMA, Am. Soc. Plastic and Reconstructive Surgeons, Calif. Med. Soc., San Diego County Med. Soc., San Diego Internat. Plastic Surgery Assn. Clubs: Masons, Shriners. Office: 3399 First Ave San Diego CA 92103

LEROY, DAVID HENRY, lawyer, state and federal official; b. Seattle, Aug. 16, 1947; s. Harold David and Lela Fay (Palmer) L.; 2 children. B.S., U. Idaho, 1969, J.D., 1971; LL.M., NYU, 1972; JD (hon.), Lincoln Coll., 1993. Bar: Idaho 1971, N.Y. State 1973, U.S. Supreme Ct. 1976. Law clk. Idaho 4th Dist. Ct., Boise, 1969; legal asst. Boise Cascade Corp., 1970; asso. firm Rothblatt, Rothblatt, Seijas & Peskin, N.Y.C., 1971-73; dep. prosecutor Ada County Prosecutor's Office, Boise, 1973-74; pros. atty. Ada County Prosecutor's Office, 1974-78; atty. gen. State of Idaho, Boise, 1978-82, lt. gov., 1983-87; ptnr. Runft, Leroy Coffin & Matthews, 1983-88, Leroy Law Offices, 1988—; candidate for Gov. of Idaho, 1986; U.S. nuclear waste negotiator, 1990-93; U.S. Presidential elector 1992; lectr., cons. in field. Mem. State Task Force on Child Abuse, 1975; mem. Ada County Council on Alcoholism, 1976; del. Republican Nat. Conv., 1976, 80, 84; chmn. Nat. Rep. Lt. Gov.'s Caucus, 1983-86; bd. dirs. United Fund, 1975-81; del. Am. Council Young Polit. Leaders, USSR, 1979, Am. Council for Free Asia, Taiwan, 1980, U.S./Taiwan Investment Forum, 1983; del. leader Friendship Force Tour USSR, 1984; legal counsel Young Republicans, 1974-81; presdl. elector, 1992. Mem. Nat. Dist. Attys. Assn., Idaho Prosecutors Assn., Am. Trial Lawyers Assn., Idaho Trial Lawyers Assn., Nat. Assn. Attys. Gen. (chmn. energy subcom., exec. com., del to China 1981), Western Attys. Gen. Assn. (vice chmn. 1980-83, chmn. 1981), Nat. Lt. Govs. Assn. (exec. bd. 1983), Idaho Bar Assn., Sigma Alpha Epsilon. Presbyterian. Office: The Leroy Offices PO Box 193 Boise ID 83701-0193 also: US Nuclear Negotiator 1823 Jefferson Pl NW Washington DC 20036

LERUDE, WARREN LESLIE, journalism educator; b. Reno, Oct. 29, 1937; s. Leslie Raymond and Ione (Lundy) L.; m. Janet Lagomarsino, Aug. 24, 1961; children: Eric Warren, Christopher Mario Leslie, Leslie Ann. BA in Journalism, U. Nev., 1961. Reporter, editor, correspondent The AP, Las Vegas, Reno, Nev., 1960-63; reporter, editor, pub., pres. Reno Evening Gazette, Nev. State Jour., 1963-81; prof. journalism U. Nev., Reno, 1981—; bd. dirs. Oakland (Calif.) Tribune; lectr. Am. Press Inst.; cons. ABA, Nat. Broadcasting Co., Nat. Jud. Coll. Co-author: American Commander in Spain, Robert Hale Merriman and the Abraham Lincoln Brigade, 1986; mem. editorial bd. USA Today, 1982—. Trustee U. Nev.-Reno Found.; trustee, mem. community adv. bd. Sta. KNPB-TV, Reno; mem. legis. com. Greater Reno C. of C.; mem. exec. bd. Biggest Little City Com., Reno, 1988—. Served with USNR, 1957-59. Co-recipient Pulitzer prize, 1977. Mem. Nev. State Press Assn. (past pres.), Calif.-Nev. News Execs. Council of the AP, Calif. Newspaper Pub. Assn. (editors conf.), Sigma Delta Chi. Club: Rotary. Home: 3825 N Folsom Dr Reno NV 89509-3015 Office: U Nev Reynolds Sch Journalism Reno NV 89557

LESKO, RONALD MICHAEL, osteopathic physician; b. Homestead, Pa., Mar. 25, 1948; s. Andrew Paul and elizabeth Ann (Tarasovic) L.; m. Elena Alexandra Shalayeva, July 29, 1990. BS, U. Pitts., 1970; DO, Coll. Osteo. Medicine & Surgery, Des Moines, 1973; MPH, Loma Linda U., 1985. Diplomate Am. Osteo. Bd. Gen. Practice, Am. Osteo. Bd. Preventitive Medicine. Famiy physician pvt. practice Port Richey, Fla., 1974-80; flight surgeon USN, NAS Chase Field Beeville, Tex., 1981-83; resident gen. preventive medicine Loma Linda (Calif.) U. Med. Ctr., 1983-85; family preventive medicine physician pvt. practice, Del Mar, Calif., 1988—; flight surgeon, capt. USNR, NAS Miramar, San Diego, 1988—; staff physician Scripps Meml. Hosp., La Jolla, Calif., 1990—; cons. Jour. Am. Osteo. Assn., Chgo., 1987, USN, Physical Readiness Div., Washington, 1988. Med. adviser March of Dimes Suncoast chpt., New Port Richey, 1977-79; bd. dirs. Fla. Gulf Health Systems Agy., Region IV, 1977-79, Price-Pottenger Nutrition Found., San Diego, 1988—. Fellow Am. Osteo. Coll. Preventive Medicine; mem. Am. Osteo. Assn., San Diego Osteo Med. Assn., San Diego County Med. Soc., Osteo. Physicians and surgeons of Claif., Calif. Med. Assn., Am. Coll. Gen. Practitioners OMS, Am. Osteo. Coll. Preventitive Medicine, Soc. U.S. Naval Flight Surgeons. Office: Ronald M Lesko DO MPH AOBGP FAOCPM 13983 Mango Dr Ste 102 Del Mar CA 92014

LESLEY, SERENA SINCLAIR, freelance journalist; b. Santa Barbara, Calif., Mar. 29, 1926; d. Gustav Anton and Margaret Ebenia (Dunn) Kamper; m. Kenneth Cameron Sinclair, Mar. 29, 1952 (div. Sept., 1970); m. Earl Brown Lesley, Nov. 16, 1982. Student, Wellesley Coll., 1943-44, Pomona Coll., 1945, Radcliffe Coll., 1947; BA, Principia Coll., 1947. Columnist Santa Barbara (Calif.) News Press, 1951-52; feature writer The Star, London, 1953-56; fashion editor Daily Herald, London, 1956-59, Woman's Mirror, London, 1956-59; fashion editor and travel writer Daily Telegraph, London, 1960-84; freelance writer, restaurant critic Portland, Oreg., 1984—. Author: (with others) Paris Fashion and Fashion Genius of the World; editor: Island of Rivers; contbr. numerous articles to newspapers and mags. in U.S. and U.K. Recipient 2nd prize Internat. Travel Writer, Province d' Liguria, Italy, 1966; named Fashion Writer of Yr., Textile Inst., Eng., 1978. Mem. Nat. Fedn. Press Women (1st prize reviews 1990), Oregon Press Women (v.p., 1st prize feature writing 1991).

LESLIE, LARRY LEE, education director, consultant, educator; b. Winnebago, Minn., Aug. 26, 1938; s. Allen Edward and Doris (Whitehead) L.; (div.); children: Jeffry, James, Donna. BS in Chemistry, U. Minn., 1960, Ma in Ednl. Adminstrn., 1961; EdD in Higher Edn., U. Calif., Berkeley, 1968. Doctoral fellow U. Calif., 1966-68; dir. student teaching U. Utah, Salt Lake City, 1968-70; rsch. assoc., chmn., prof. higher edn. Pa. State U., State College, 1970-77; prof. U. Ariz., Tucson, 1977—, dir. Ctr. for the Study of Higher Edn., 1980—; vis. prof. U.S. AID, Quito, Ecuador, 1975. Author: The Economic Value of Higher Education, 1988, Higher Education and the Steady State, 1974, Higher Education Opportunity, 1977. County precinct chmn. Rep. Party, Siskiyou County, Calif., 1965-66, congl. campaign chmn., Pa., 1976; bd. govs. Catalina Foothills Sch. Dist., Tucson, 1978-82. NDEA fellow U. Calif., 1966-68, Fulbright fellow, 1991; NSF Rsch. grantee, 1989-90. Mem. Am. Ednl. Rsch. Assn. (v.p. 1974), Assn. for the Study of Higher Edn. (bd. dirs. 1980-82). Home: 1906 E Campbell Ter Tucson AZ 85718-5952 Office: U Ariz 307 College of Education Tucson AZ 85721

LESLIE, MARLENE MARIE, parochial secondary school educator; came to U.S., 1982; d. Eric John and Hervice Olive (Clother) P.; m. Kenrick Royford Leslie, June 25, 1966; children: Sharon, Heather, Ainsworth. BEd, U. W.I., Mona, Jamaica, 1976; BA, Calif. State U., Dominguez Hills, 1988. Profl. clear single subject credential in English, Calif. Elem. tchr. Anglican Diocesan of Belize, Belize, Central America, 1955-59, prin., 1959-64; asst. lectr. geography and edn. Belize Tchrs. Coll., 1965-67; lectr. English, adminstr. Belize Tech. Coll., 1968-76, 78-81; prin. Anglican Diocesan Girls High Sch., Belize, 1976-78; tchr. English and Math. Archdiocese of L.A., Calif., 1982—; sr. program advisor L.A. Angeles Job Corps, 1983—; tchr. ESL Culver City Adult Sch., 1988—. Mem. ASCD, CATE, SCTE, LARA. Democrat. Episcopalian. Home: 516 W Fairview Blvd Inglewood CA 90302 Office: St Gerard Majella Sch 4471 Inglewood Blvd Los Angeles CA 90066

LESLIE, ROBERT LORNE, lawyer; b. Adak, Alaska, Feb. 24, 1947; s. J. Lornie and L. Jean (Conelly) L.; children—Lorna Jean, Elizabeth Allen. B.S., U.S. Mil. Acad., 1969; J.D., Hastings Coll. Law, U. Calif.-San Francisco, 1974. Bar: Calif. 1974, D.C. 1979, U.S. Dist. Ct. (no. dist.) Calif. 1974, U.S. Ct. Claims 1975, U.S. Tax Ct. 1975, U.S. Ct. Appeals (9th and D.C. cirs.), U.S. Ct. Mil. Appeals 1980, U.S. Supreme Ct. 1980. Commd. 2d lt. U.S. Army, 1969, advanced through grades to maj., 1980; govt. trial atty. West Coast Field Office, Contract Appeals, Litigation Div. and Regulatory Law Div., Office JAG, Dept. Army, San Francisco, 1974-77; sr. trial atty. and team chief Office of Chief Trial Atty., Dept. Army, Washington, 1977-80 ; ptnr. McInerney & Dillon, Oakland, Calif., 1980—; lectr. on govt. contracts CSC, Continuing Legal Edn. Program; lectr. in govt. procurement U.S. Army Materiel Command. Col. USAR. Decorated Silver Star, Purple Heart. Mem. ABA, Fed. Bar Assn. Home: 4144 Greenwood Ave Oakland CA 94602-1147 Office: Ordway Bldg 18th Fl Oakland CA 94612

LESLIE, TIM, state legislator; b. Ashland, Oreg., Feb. 4, 1942; s. Robert Tabor Leslie and Virginia (Hall) P.; m. Clydene Ann Fisher, June 15, 1962; children: Debbie, Scott. BA in Political Sci., Calif. State U., Long Beach, 1963; MPA, U. Southern Calif., L.A., 1969. Prin. analyst Sacramento County Exec. Office, Calif., 1965-69; cons. Assm. W. & M. Commn., Sacramento, 1965-72; prin. legislator rep. County Sups. Assn., Sacramento, 1972-80; founder bd. dirs. Comm. Act. Against Drg., Sacramento, 1975-83; v.p. Moss & Thompson, Inc., Sacramento, 1980-84; exec. v.p. Kuhl. Corp., Sacramento, 1984-86; assemblyman Calif. State Legislature, Sacramento, 1986-91, senator, 1991—; campaign chmn. North Calif. Bush Election, Sacramento, 1988; chair Conf. of Pres. on Family. V. chmn. Budget & Fiscal Review Com., Judiciary Com., mem. Health Com., Natural Resources Com. Recipient Hang Tough Award Nat. Tax Limitation Com., Calif., 1987; named Legislator of the Yr. Sacramento City Taxpayers League & Osteopathic Surgeons of Calif., 1990. Republican. Presbyterian. Home: State Capitol Sacramento CA 95814 Office: District Office 1200 Melody Ln # 110 Roseville CA 95678

LESOWITZ, MIKKI LYNN, small business owner; b. Columbus, Ohio, Aug. 23, 1962; d. Sidney Allan Lesowitz and Barbara Ann Stein Beck. BA, U. Mass., Boston, 1985. Office mgr. Dean Tucker Shaw, Inc., Boston, 1986-89; exec. asst. Frank Gehry & Assocs., Santa Monica, Calif., 1990, Mansour Travel Co., Beverly Hills, Calif., 1990-91; owner Divine Order, West Hollywood, Calif., 1991—. Mem. Nat. Assn. Profl. Organizers. Democrat. Jewish. Home and Office: Divine Order 8944 Dicks St West Hollywood CA 90069

LESSER, FREDERICK ALAN, mining and chemical company executive; b. London, June 20, 1934; s. Frederick Adolfo and Maria Isabel (Yriberry) L.; m. Stella Mary Holmes, Sept. 11, 1961; children: Maria Isabel Lesser Orchard, Frederick Alan, Hugo John. MA in Econs., Cambridge (Eng.) U. Mgmt. trainee U.S. Borax & Chem. Corp., L.A., 1957-60, chmn., 1989—; asst. mgr. subcos. dept. Borax Consol. Ltd., London, 1960-62, European sales mgr., 1963-69, chmn., MD, 1984—; asst. to pres. Boroquimica S.A., Buenos Aires, 1962-63; European mktg. dir. Borax Holdings Ltd., London, 1969-74; mktg. dir. RTZ Borax Ltd., London, 1974-84; chief exec. officer RTZ Borax and Minerals Ltd., London, 1984—. Gov. Farleigh Sch., Basingstoke, Eng., 1980—. Lt. Brit. Army, 1953-54. Mem. Royal Automobile Club. Roman Catholic. Home: Hatch House Farm, West Woodhay NR Newbury, Berkshire RG18 0BG, England Office: Borax Consol Ltd, Borax House Carlisle Pl, London SW1P 1HT, England also: US Borax 3075 Wilshire Blvd Los Angeles CA 90010

LESSER, HARVEY LLOYD, systems engineer; b. Bklyn., Oct. 8, 1951; s. David and Morrine (Scharfman) L.; m. Joan Beth Levy, May 11, 1980. BS, Harvey Mudd Coll., Claremont, Calif., 1973; MBA, Golden Gate U., San Francisco, 1980. Sales engr. Non Linear Systems, Solana Beach, Calif., 1973-74; mem. tech. staff Computer Scis. Corp., Moffett Field, Calif., 1974-77; programmer, analyst Tymshare, Cupertino, Calif., 1977-78; programmer IBM Corp., San Jose, Calif., 1978-84, systems analyst, 1984-87; systems engr. IBM Corp., Seattle, 1987—. Precinct del. Wash. State Rep. party, Kent, 1988. Mem. Assn. Systems Mgmt. (treas. 1990-92, pres. 1992—), Green River Wander Gruppe (pres. 1988-91). Office: IBM Corp PO Box 1830 Seattle WA 98111-1830

LESSER, WENDY, literary magazine editor, writer, consultant; b. Santa Monica, Calif., Mar. 20, 1952; d. Murray Leon Lesser and Millicent (Gerson) Dillon; m. Richard Rizzo, Jan. 18, 1985; 1 stepchild, Tony; 1 child, Nicholas. BA, Harvard U., 1973; MA, Cambridge (Eng.) U., 1975; PhD, U. Calif., Berkeley, 1982. Founding ptnr. Lesser & Ogden Assocs., Berkeley, 1977-81; founding editor The Threepenny Rev., Berkeley, 1980—; vis. lectr. U. Calif., Santa Cruz, 1983, 86, 90; Bellagio resident Rockefeller Found., Italy, 1984. Author: The Life Below the Ground, 1987, His Other Half, 1991; editor: Hiding in Plain Sight, 1993. Fellow NEH, 1983, 92, Guggenheim fellow, 1988. Democrat. Office: The Threepenny Rev PO Box 9131 Berkeley CA 94709

LESSIS, GARY PAUL, engineer, sales executive; b. Dayton, Ohio, Apr. 23, 1960; s. George P. and Irene (Sopronyi) L. BS in Engring., U. Cin., 1983; MS in Computer Sci., U. So. Calif., 1986; MBA, Pepperdine U., 1990. Engr. Northrop Corp., Hawthorne, Calif., 1983-85; systems analyst Tektronix Inc., Woodland Hills, Calif., 1985-86, sales engr., 1986-90, sales mgr. Auto-Trol Tech. Corp., Irvine, Calif., 1990—. Home: 92 Lehigh Aisle Irvine CA 92715

LESTER, HENRY BERNARD, investment management executive; b. Oklahoma City, Oct. 17, 1956; m. Peyton Koeppel, Feb. 15, 1986. BA in Biology, Yale U., 1980; MBA in Fin., U. Colo., 1984. Chartered fin. analyst. Asst. mgr. Household Fin., Denver, 1981-82; v.p. Asset Mgmt. Group, Denver, 1984-90; mng. dir., owner Paragon Capital Mgmt., Denver, 1990—. Mem. Assn. for Investment Mgmt. and Rsch., Denver Soc. Security Analysts. Office: Paragon Capital Mgmt 999 18th St Ste 1220 Denver CO 80202

LESTER, JOHN CLAYTON, life insurance company executive; b. Cheyenne, Wyo., Sept. 26, 1940; s. Arthur C. and Harleen E. (Gorman) L.; m. Ruth A. Whatley, Nov. 21, 1959; children: John Clayton, Connie Sue. BBA, Wichita State U., 1965. CLU. Office supr. State Farm Fire & Casualty Co., Greeley, Colo., 1965-69; agt. Equitable Life Assurance Soc., Greeley, 1969-70, from dist. mgr. to agy. mgr., Denver, 1970-78, regional agy. v.p., 1978-84, agy. mgr., Woodland Hills, Calif., 1984-90, assoc. agy. mgr., Denver, 1991—. Served with USN, 1958-61. Mem. Am. Soc. CLU's, San Fernando Valley Life Underwriters, Gen. Agts. and Mgrs. Assn. (past pres. San Fernando Valley chpt.). Republican. Home: 9293 E Arbor Cir # A Englewood CO 80111-5269 Office: Equitable Life Assurance Soc 370 17th St Ste 4950 Denver CO 80202

LESTER, JOHN JAMES NATHANIEL, II (SEAN LESTER), engineer, environmental analyst, human rights activist; b. Houston, May 7, 1952; s. John James Nathaniel Lester and Margaret Louise (Tisdale) Sharp. Student, U. Tex., 1970, Lee Coll., 1971; AS, Grossmont Coll., 1979; BA in Behavioral Sci., Nat. U., 1987; y. Registered profl. stationary engr., Tex. Nuclear power specialist USN, various, 1971-77; microbiology lab. technician VA, San Diego, 1978; prin. engring. asst. San Diego Gas & Electric, 1979-85, engring. environ. analyst, 1985-88; owner Calif. Triad Gem & Mineral Co.; founder Ctr. for Creative Healing. Dir. logistics, mem. regional bd. Gary Hart Presdl. Campaign, San Diego, 1984; fonding mem. Inlet Drug Crisis Ctr., Houston, 1970; vol. dir. Aid for Guatemalan Refugees and Orphans, 1988; vol. for Dali Lama, Tibetan Refugee Rights and Ceremonies, 1989; mem. bldg. com. Tibetan Sch. Medicine, Crestone, Colo.; mem. San Luis Valley Tibetan Project, Crestone; active Clinton Presdl. Campaign, 1992. Mem. ASME, IEEE (interim pres., founding mem. San Diego region Ocean Engring. Soc. 1984-85), Mensa, Assn. Humanistic Psychology, Amnesty Internat., Hunger Project, Earth Stewards, Human Rights Watch, Tibet Watch, Sierra Club. Democrat. Buddhist. Home and Office: PO Box 710 Makawao HI 96768-0710

LETSON, MICHAEL LEE, oil and management executive; b. Atascadero, Calif., Oct. 15, 1942; s. William Alson and Evelyn Morphet (Lee) L.; m. Susan Kay Smith, Aug. 17, 1974 (div. June 1983); children: Alison, Michael Jr.; m. Michone Della Schweig, June 23, 1990. BSBA, U. Denver, 1964; postgrad., Pierce Coll., 1966, U. So. Calif., 1967. Mgr. ILD United Calif. Bank, L.A., 1964-66; v.p. 1st Western Bank, L.A., 1966-71; pres., CEO Pacific Structures Inc., San Ramon, Calif., 1971-77; v.p., dir. Toole County State Bank, Shelby, Mont., 1977-80; pres., CEO Energy Compression & Leasing, Shelby, 1980-84, No. Plains Energy Co., Shelby, 1981-84; cons. Mgmt., Oil & Gas, Shelby, 1984-87; dir. Mont. Dept. Commerce, Helena, 1989-90; pres., CEO Partnership Mgmt. Co., Helena, 1987—; chmn. Mont. State Banking Bd., Helena, 1989-90; sec., dir. Mont. Ambs., Helena, 1989-90; bd. dirs. Firehole Land Corp., N.Y.C.; cons. Western States Water & Power, Denver, 1990—. Treas. Mont. Rep. Party, Helena, 1986-89, bd. dirs., 1983-89; vice chmn. Mont. delegation Rep. Nat. Conv., New Orleans, 1988. Mem. Registered Fin. Planners, Ky. Oil & Gas Assn., No. Mont. Oil & Gas Assn., Registered Fin. Planners, Elks, Lions. Home: 5515 York Rd Helena MT 59601 Office: Partnership Mgmt Co 1040 Helena Ave Helena MT 59601

LETT, PHILLIP DAVID, psychologist; b. Birmingham, Ala., Feb. 15, 1952; s. Aaron Glen and Eleanor (Chappell) L. BA, Jacksonville (Ala.) State U., 1976; MA, U. South Fla., 1984; PhD, Ill. Inst. Tech., 1988. Lic. psychologist, Ariz.; cert. rehab. counselor. Pvt. practice Phoenix, 1988—; cons. Am. Community Svcs., Inc., Michigan City, Ind., 1985—. Mem. APA (clin. neuropsychology and health psychology), Soc. for Personality Assessment, Phi Kappa Phi. Office: 4222 E Camelback Rd Ste 230H Phoenix AZ 85018-2774

LETTS, J. SPENCER, federal judge; b. 1934. BA, Yale U., 1956; LLB, Harvard U., 1960. Commd. U.S. Army, 1956, advanced through grades to capt., resigned, 1965; pvt. practice law Fulbright & Jaworski, Houston, 1960-66, Troy, Malin, Loveland & Letts, L.A., 1973-74, Hedlund, Hunter & Lynch, L.A., 1978-82, Latham & Watkins, L.A., 1982-85; gen. counsel Teledyne, Inc., 1966-73, 75-78, legal cons., 1978-82; judge U.S. Dist. Ct. (cen. dist.) Calif., L.A., 1986—. Contbr. articles to profl. jours. Mem. ABA, Calif. State Bar, Tex. State Bar, L.A. Bar Assn., Houston Bar Assn. Office: US Dist Ct 312 N Spring St Los Angeles CA 90012

LEUBE, KURT RUDOLPH, economics educator; b. Salzburg, Austria, June 27, 1943; came to U.S., 1983; s. G. Werner and Elfriede (Haselhof) L.; m. Elisabeth A. Payer, Dec. 30, 1968; children: Philipp, Michael, Christian, Jakob. BA, Gymnasium, Salzburg, 1963; AJD, U. Salzburg, 1971. Sr. researcher, univ. assoc. to F.A. von Hayek IFN at U. of Salzburg, 1968-77; sr. economist, resident scholar Austrian Enterprize Inst., Vienna, 1977-83; prof. econs. Calif. State U., Hayward, 1984—; rsch scholar Hoover Instn. Stanford (Calif.) U., 1983—; dir. Internat. Inst. for Austrian Econs., Stanford, 1988—; vis. prof. Université d'Aix en Provence, Institut Für Liberalismus, Vienna, 1992; editor-in-chief Internat. Carl Menger Libr., Munich, 1978; leading authority in Austrian economics. Editor: Essence of Hayek, 1985, Essays in Honor of F.A. von Hayek, 1985, The Political Economy of Freedom, Essays in Honor of F.A. von Hayek, 1985, Essence of Friedman, 1987, Essence of Stigler, 1988, Marktwirtschaft Aufsätze F.A. von Hayek zum Gedenken, 1992; contbr. articles and essays to profl. jours. Recipient numerous awards including F. Leroy Hill award Inst. for Humane Studies, George Mason U., 1984. Mem. Libertas Internat. (founding mem. 1983), Inst. Europeum, Ludwig Erhard Stiftung, Wirtschaftsforum der Führungskräfte, Mont Pelerin Soc. (awards). Office: Stanford U Hoover Instn Stanford CA 94305

LEUNG, CHARLES CHEUNG-WAN, executive; b. Hong Kong, June 27, 1946; came to U.S., 1969; s. Mo-Fan and Lai-Ping (Tam) L.; m. Jessica Lan Lee, Sept. 1, 1972; children: Jennifer W., Cheryl E., Albert H. BS with spl. honors, U. Hong Kong, 1969; PhD, U. Chgo., 1976. Sr. staff scientist Corning (N.Y.) Glass Ctrl. Lab., 1975-79; sr. mem. tech. staff Motorola, Mesa, Ariz., 1979-81; engring. mgr. Avantek, Santa Clara, Calif., 1981-88; chmn., pres. Bipolarics Inc., Los Gatos, Calif., 1981—. Mem. IEEE, Am. Phys. Soc., Am. Vacuum Soc., Asian Am. Mfrs. Assn. Office: Bipolarics Inc 108 Albright Way Los Gatos CA 95030

LEUNG, KASON KAI CHING, computer specialist; b. Hong Kong, July 2, 1962; came to U.S., 1963; s. Patrick Kin Man and Esther Mo Chee (Shum) L. BA in Computer Sci., U. Calif., 1984. Microcomputer specialist Coopers & Lybrand, San Francisco, 1985-87; freelance computer specialist San Francisco, 1988-90; computer applications specialist T.Y. Lin Internat., San Francisco, 1990-92; tech. specialist ZD Labs., San Mateo, Calif., 1993—. Mem. Assn. for Computing Machinery. Home: 90 Stanford Heights Ave San Francisco CA 94127 Office: ZD Labs 320B Lakeside Dr San Mateo CA 94404

LEUS MCFARLEN, PATRICIA CHERYL, water chemist; b. San Antonio, Mar. 12, 1954; d. Norman W. and Jacqueline S. (Deason) Leus; m. Randy N. McFarlen, June 28, 1986; 1 child, Kevin Bryant. AA, Highline Community Coll., 1974; BS in Chemistry, Eastern Wash. U., 1980. Cert. operator grade II water treatment & distbn., grade I wastewater & collection operator Ariz. Dept. Environ. Quality. Lab. technician, oil analyst D.A. Lubricant, Vancouver, Wash., 1982-83; plant chemist Navajo Generating Sta., Page, Ariz., 1983-92, chemist, 1992—. Sci. judge Page Schs. Sci. Project Fair, 1985, 91; chemist Navajo Generating Sta./Page Sch. Career Day, 1986, 89, 90; life mem. Girl Scouts Am. Mem. Sigma Kappa (life mem., treas. 1976-78). Methodist. Office: Navajo Generating Sta Environ & Lab Svcs Dept PO Box W Page AZ 86040-1949

LEUTY, GERALD JOHNSTON, osteopathic physician and surgeon; b. Knoxville, Iowa, July 23, 1919; s. John William and Mable Reichard (Johnston) L.; m. Martha L. Weymouth, Jan. 24, 1940 (div. 1957); children: Maxine Joanne, Robert James, Gerald Johnston Jr., Karl Joseph; m. Norma Jean Hindman, Dec. 30, 1969; children: Barbara Jayne, Patrick Jack. AB, Kemper Mil. Sch., Boonville, Mo., 1939; postgrad., Drake U., Des Moines, 1944-45; DO, Des Moines Coll. Osteopathy, 1949; embalmer, Coll. Mortuary Sci., St. Louis, 1941. Mortician/embalmer Cauldwell-McJihon Funeral Home, Des Moines, 1939-40; aero. engr. Boeing Aircraft Co., Wichita, Kans., 1941-42; osteopathic physician and surgeon Knoxville (Iowa) Osteopathic Clinic, 1949-56; dir. Leuty Osteopathic Clinic, Earlham, Iowa, 1957-77; osteopathic physician and surgeon in pvt. practice Santa Rosa, Calif., 1977—; prof. clin. med. Coll. Osteopathic Medicine of the Pacific, Pomona, Calif., 1985—. With U.S. Army, 1942-46. Named Physician of the Yr., 6th Dist. Iowa Osteopathic Soc., 1975, Disting. Leadership award, Am. Biog. Inst., 1988, others. Fellow Internat. Co.. Angiologists; mem. Am. Osteopathic Assn. (ho. of dels., life mem. 1989), Iowa Osteopathic Soc. (pres. 6th dist. 1974), Soc. Osteopathic Physicians, No. Calif. Osteopathic Med. Soc. (pres. 1981), Osteopathic Physicians and Surgeons of Calif. (pres. 1982), Am. Acad. Osteopathy (chmn. component socs. com. 1988, Calif. div. pres. 1987), North Coast Osteopathic Med. Assn. (pres. 1992), Am. Med. Soc. Vienna (life mem.), Am. Legion (6th dist. comdr. 1974-75), Lions (pres. 1946). Republican. Presbyterian. Home: 5835 La Cuesta Dr Santa Rosa CA 95409-3914

LEVADA, WILLIAM JOSEPH, archbishop; b. Long Beach, Calif., June 15, 1936; s. Joseph and Lorraine (Nunez) L. B.A., St. John's Coll., Camarillo, Calif., 1958; S.T.L., Gregorian U., Rome, 1962, S.T.D., 1971. Ordained priest Roman Cath. Ch., 1961, consecrated bishop, 1983. Assoc. pastor Archdiocese of L.A., 1962-67, aux. bishop, vicar for Santa Barbara County, 1983-86; prof. theology St. John's Sem., Camarillo, Calif., 1970-76; ofcl. Doctrinal Congregation, Vatican City, Italy, 1976-82; exec. dir. Calif. Cath. Conf., Sacramento, 1982-84; archbishop Archdiocese of Portland in Oreg., 1986—. Trustee Cath. U. Am.; chmn. bd. dirs. Pope John XXIII Med.-Moral Rsch. and Edn. Ctr. Mem. Nat. Conf. Cath. Bishops (com. on doctrine, com. for pastoral letter on women in ch. and soc.), U.S. Cath. Conf., Cath. Theol. Soc. Am., Canon Law Soc. Am. Office: Archdiocese of Portland 2838 E Burnside St Portland OR 97214-1895

LEVENSON, ALAN IRA, psychiatrist, physician, educator; b. Boston, July 25, 1935; s. Jacob Maurice and Frances Ethel (Biller) L.; m. Myra Beatrice Katzen, June 12, 1960; children: Jonathan, Nancy. A.B., Harvard U., 1957, M.D., 1961, M.P.H., 1965. Diplomate: Am. Bd. Psychiatry and Neurology. Intern U. Hosp., Ann Arbor, Mich., 1961-62; resident psychiatry Mass. Mental Health Center, Boston, 1962-65; staff psychiatrist NIMH, Chevy Chase, Md., 1965-66; dir. div. mental health service programs NIMH, 1967-69; prof. psychiatry U. Ariz. Coll. Medicine, Tucson, 1969—, head dept. psychiatry, 1969-89; chief exec. officer Palo Verde Mental Health Svcs., Tucson, 1971-91; chief med. officer, med. dir. Palo Verde Mental Health Svcs., 1991—; mem. staff Palo Verde Hosp., Tucson Med. Center, U. Hosp., Tucson. Author: The Community Mental Health Center: Strategies and Programs, 1972; Contbr. papers and articles to psychiat. jours. Bd. dirs. Tucson Urban League, 1971-78, Pima Council on Aging, 1976-83. Served with USPHS, 1965-69. Fellow Am. Psychiat. Assn. (treas. 1986-90, chmn., bd. dirs. Psychiatrists' Ins. Purchasing group, 1991—, chmn., bd. dirs. Risk Retention group 1991—), Am. Coll. Psychiatrists (regent 1980-83, v.p. 1983-85, pres. elect 1985-86, pres. 1986-87), Am. Pub. Health Assn., Am. Coll. Mental Health Adminstrn. (v.p. 1980-82, pres. 1982-83); mem. Group for Advancement of Psychiatry, Harvard Alumni Assn. (bd. dirs. 1988-91). Office: Palo Verde Hosp 2695 N Craycroft Rd Tucson AZ 85712-2244

LEVENSON, COREY HOWARD, chemist; b. N.Y.C., Aug. 26, 1954; s. Edgar Alan and Joanne Leah (Schriver) L.; m. Katherine Mary Ovitt, Feb. 14, 1982; children: Lauren Elyse, Maia Katherine. BS, Hampshire Coll., 1976; PhD, U. Calif., San Francisco, 1981. Regents fellow U. Calif., 1976-80; assoc. scientist Cetus Corp., Emeryville, Calif., 1981-84, scientist, mgr. DNA synthesis lab., 1984-88, sr. scientist, assoc. dir. chemistry dir., 1988-90, dir. nucleic acid chemistry, 1990-91; sr. rsch. investigator Roche Molecular Systems, Alameda, Calif., 1991—. Contbr. numerous articles to profl. jours.; patentee in oligonucleotide functionalizing reagents, precursor to nucleic acid probe, others. Mem. AAAS, Am. Chem. Soc., Am. Assn. Clin. Chemistry, N.Y. Acad. Scis.

LEVENSTEIN, ROSLYN M., advertising consultant, writer; b. N.Y.C., Mar. 26, 1920; d. Leo Rapoport and Stella Schimmel Rosenberg; m. Justin Seides, June 7, 1943 (div. 1948); 1 child, Leland Seides.; m. Lawrence Levenstein, June 25, 1961. BA in Advt., NYU, 1940. Sr. v.p., assoc. creative dir. Young and Rubicam, Inc., N.Y.C., 1962-79; cons. Young and Rubicam, Inc., Los Angeles and San Diego, 1979-83; advt. cons., writer mag. articles La Jolla, Calif., 1979—. Creator: Excedrin Headache commls. (Andy awards 1967, 68, 69), I'm Only Here for the Beer (Cannes award 1970, Clio Jury award 1970). Recipient: Silver Lion award Cannes Film Festival, 1968, multiple advt. awards U.S. and Eng.; named one of YWCA Women of Yr., 1978. Mem. Charter 100, Women's Com. Brandeis U., Nat. Pen Women. Home: 5802 Corral Way La Jolla CA 92037-7423

LEVENTHAL, ROBERT STANLEY, academic administrator; b. Cambridge, Mass., Jan. 8, 1927; s. Harold A. and Matilda (Goldwyn) L.; children by previous marriage—Jeffrey Nelson, Daniel Philip. A.B., Harvard U., 1948, M.B.A., 1956. Commd. ensign USN, 1948, advanced through grades to comdr., 1964; supply officer Naval Support Activity, Da Nang, Vietnam, 1965-66; with Office of Sec. of Def., Washington, 1966-68; ret., 1968; exec. asst. to chmn., dir. supply and distbn. Amerada Hess Corp., Woodbridge, N.J., 1968-71; exec. v.p. Engelhard Industries, Murray Hill, N.J.; sr. v.p. Engelhard Minerals and Chems. Corp., N.Y.C., 1971-75, Beker Industries Corp., Greenwich, Conn., 1975-77; pres., chief exec. officer Publicker Industries Inc., Phila., 1977-81; also. dir. Publicker Industries Inc.; pres. Tele-Total, Inc., 1981-83; pres., chief exec. officer Communications Products Corp., 1983-84; chmn., pres. Western Union Corp., Upper Saddle River, N.J., 1984-87, chief exec. officer, 1984-88, chmn., 1987-88; cons. Western Union Corp., Upper Saddle River, 1988-89; dean Sch. Bus. Adminstrn. U. Wash., Seattle, 1989—; dir. Western Union Corp., Western Union Telegraph Co. Decorated Legion of Merit with gold star. Office: Dean of Business Administration University of Washington Seattle WA 98195

LE VEQUE, MATTHEW KURT, public affairs and marketing consultant; b. Los Angeles, May 24, 1958; s. Edward Albert and Vera Eleanora (Behne) LeV. BA in Polit. Sci., UCLA, 1981. Reapportionment cons. Calif. State Legislature, Sacramento, 1981; cons. Berman and D'Agostino Campaigns, Inc., L.A., 1982-91; coord. L.A. Olympic com., 1984; spl. asst. Congressmen H. Waxman and H. Berman, Calif., 1982-85; cons. The Helin Orgn., Newport Beach, Calif., 1984-86; sr. cons. Calif. State Senate, L.A. and Sacramento, 1985-92; campaign fin. coord Levine for U.S. Senate, L.A., 1991; sr. assoc. Pacific West Comms. Group, L.A., 1992—. Active numerous local and nat. Dem. polit. campaigns. Office: 531 24th St Hermosa Beach CA 90254-2618

LEVERENZ, WINIFRED, home economics educator, nutrition consultant, freelance writer; b. Jacksonville, Tex., Nov. 21, 1913; d. William Lloyd and Anna Pearl (Brinson) Jones; m. Roy Martin Leverenz, Aug. 10, 1943; children: Lynda Nell, Maxine Verlita. BS, Tex. Women's U., 1937; postgrad., Oreg. State U., 1958-66. Cert. sch. tchr., cert. nutrition cons. Home demonstration agt. A&M Ext. Svc., Tyler, Tex., 1937-39, Columbus, Tex., 1939-41, Houston, 1941-42; state specialist foods A&M Ext. Svc., College Station, Tex., 1942-45; adult edn. tchr. Ore Voe Edn. Dept., Pendleton and Wallowa, Oreg., 1946-55; ins. agt. Farmers Union, Wallowa County, 1955-57; tchr. home econs. Sch. Dist. 9, Lostine, Oreg., 1957-61, Sch. Dist. 12, Wallowa, 1963-68; liaison caseworker State Walfare Div., Pendleton, 1968-70; nutrition cons. Wallowa Meml. Hosp., Enterprise, Oreg., 1974-83; chair food preservation com. State Nutrition Coun., College Station, 1943-45; ofcl. foods judge county fair, Tex. and Oreg., 1940-70; freelance writer on food perservation. Contbg. editor (monthly column) Progressive Farmer, 1944-48. Winner Pan Am. Exposition contest 4-H, 1938, Outstanding 4-H Leader award Wallowa County, 1976, 2nd pl. state baking contest Oreg. Wheat League, 1977. Mem. Tex. Home Demonstration Agts. Assn. (state pres. 1939-40), Wallowa County PTA (pres. 1957), Nat. PTA (del. 1965), Vocat. Home Econ. Tchrs. Ea. Oreg. (chmn. 1959, Order Ea. Star (worthy matron 1968-69, 83-84, grand com. ESTARL 1970-71, Grand Cross of Color for Rainbow Order 1972). Democat. Methodist.

LEVERNOIS, EARLE MOSE, surgeon; b. Crystal Falls, Mich., Apr. 5, 1934; s. Mose J. and Sophie Christine (Sutter) LeV.; m. Marie Louise Verle, Sept. 11, 1954; children: Glen, Yvonne, Rebecca. BS, No. Mich. Coll.; MD, U. Mich., 1960. Diplomate Am. Bd. Surgery. Intern, resident Akron (Ohio) City Hosp., Akron Children's Hosp., 1960-65; staff mem., chief of surgery, chief of staff, chmn. various coms. Merle West Med. Ctr., Klamath Falls, Oreg., 1965—; pvt. practice surgery Klamath Falls, 1965—; clin. instr. Oreg. Inst. Tech., 1973—; bd. dirs. Merle West Med. Ctr.; mem. Oreg. State Bd. Med. Examiners, 1982-90, chmn., 1987-90; founding mem., bd. dirs. Pacific Health & Life Ins. Co. Bd. dirs. Klamath Med. Svc. Bur., 1968-88, Oreg. Inst. Tech. Devel. Found., 1982—; mem., chmn. Klamath County Bd. Health, 1972-78; mem. Gov.'s Com. on Health Care, 1980; mem. nursing sch. adv. com. Oreg. Inst. Tech.; mem. adv. com. Klamath County Bd. Sr. Citizens; founding mem., bd. dirs. Oreg. Found. for Med. Excellence, 1985—. Mem. ACS (coun. mem. 1970-74, pres. 1974-75), AMA (del. 1979-80), Oreg. Med. Assn. (del. 1969-73, trustee 1973-76, vice speaker 1976-77, speaker of the house 1977-78, pres.-elect 1978-79, pres. 1979-80), Oreg. Thoracic Soc., Klamath County Med. Soc., Fed. State Med. Bds. (bd. dirs. 1988-91, resolutions com. 1985-88), Oreg. Inst. Tech. Pres.'s Club (pres.), Klamath County C. of C., Rotary. Office: Merle West Med Ctr 2100 Fairmount St Klamath Falls OR 97601

LEVI, DAVID F., lawyer; b. 1951. BA, Harvard U., MA, 1973; JD, Stanford U. Bar: Calif. 1983. U.S. atty. ea. dist. State of Calif., Sacramento, 1986-90; judge U.S. Dist. Ct. (ea. dist.) Calif., 1990—. Office: 2504 Fed Bldg 650 Capitol Mall Sacramento CA 95814

LEVI, HERBERT A., deputy city manager; b. Dunkirk, Ind., May 31, 1931; s. Lawrence Warren and Virginia Roselyn (Avery) L.; m. Virginia Elizabeth Webster, Dec. 7, 1950; children: Victor Herbert, Michael David, Demetrius Titus. BA, Ball State U., Muncie, Ind., 1952; MPA, Calif. State U., Long Beach, 1978. Cert. tchr., Calif. Debit mgr. Mammoth Life Ins. Co., Muncie, 1951-53; chemist City of L.A. Pub. Works, 1954-55, sr. indsl. waste inspector, 1959-66, safety engring. asst., 1967-69, sr. personnel analyst, 1969-71, contract compliance officer, 1971-75; adminstrv. analyst III City of Long Beach (Calif.) City Mgr., 1975-78; personnel analyst III City of Long Beach Personnel, 1978-82; adminstrv. officer Long Beach Pub. Libr., 1982-90; dep. city mgr., exec. dir. police complaint commn. City of Long Beach, 1990-91; ret., 1991—, cons. to bus. and govt., 1993—; mem. policy bd. Ctr. for Pub. Policy and Adminstrn., Calif. State U., 1986-90. Author: Equal Opportunity Compliance for Cities, 1978; co-author: Contract Compliance Manual, 1976. Founder Vet. Stadium Citizen's Com., Long Beach, Calif., 1983; mem. Lakewood (Calif.) High Sch. Community Adv. Coun., 1974; chair Hamilton High Sch. Community Adv. Coun., L.A., 1969; mem. KLON-FM 88 Community Adv. Bd., Long Beach, 1985. Recipient Excellence in Performance award City of L.A. Bd. Pub. Works, 1977, Employee of Yr. award City of Long Beach, Personnel, 1981. Mem. Am. Soc. Pub. Adminstrn., Internat. Personnel Mgmt. Assn., Equal Opportunity Compliance Officers Assn. (pres., co-founder 1971-77), So. Calif. Personnel Mgmt. Assn. (v.p. programs 1983-84), Long Beach Mgmt. Club, Pi Alpha Alpha (v.p. 1989-91). Home and Office: 5153 E Hanbury St Long Beach CA 90808-1845

LEVI, STEVEN C(HANNING), freelance writer, historian; b. Chgo., Dec. 9, 1948; s. Mario and Janice (Houghton) L. B.A. in History, U. Calif.-Davis, 1970; M.A. in History, San Jose State U., 1973; Teaching Credential, U. Calif.-Riverside, 1972. Hist. researcher Mus. Comparative Zoology, Harvard U., 1972-73; part-time instr. Chapman Coll., 1974—, various mil. bases, Alaska, 1976-77, instr. Elmendorf AFB, Alaska, 1974—; staff cons. Ernst & Ernst, 1978; research analyst State of Alaska, Alaska Pub. Utilities Commn., 1977-78, Div. Energy and Power Devel., 1978-79; dir. pub. affairs Resource Devel. Council, Anchorage, 1979-80; coordinator Alaska Trade Shows, Inc. and Am. Diabetes Assn., Anchorage, 1980; editor Parsnackle Press, Anchorage, 1981—; legis. aide, Alaska senate and ho. of reps., 1981—; freelance writer, Anchorage, 1984—; part time instr. Victor Valley Coll., Calif., Riverside Unified Sch. Dist.; reading and math. cons. Appleton-Century-Crofts, 1971-73. Author poetry: Alaskan Phantasmagoria, 1978; The Last Raven, 1979; The Phantom Bowhead, 1979; Fish-Fed Maize, 1980; We Alaskans, 1980; author: Sourdough Journalist, 1981, The Committee of Vigilance of 1916: A Case Study in Official Hysteria, 1983, Our National Tapestry, 1986, The Pacific Rim, The Emerging Giants, 1988, Deadwood Dick, 1988, The Alaska Traveler, 1989, Making It, Personal Survival in the Corporate World, 1990, Bush Flying, 1992, A Treasury of Alaskan Humor, 1993; also articles, short stories. Home: 8512 E 4th Ave Anchorage AK 99504-2130

LEVIN, ALAN SCOTT, pathologist, allergist, immunologist; b. Chgo., Jan. 12, 1938; s. John Bernhard and Betty Ruth (Margulis) L.; m. Vera S. Byers, June 15, 1971. BS in Chemistry, U. Ill., Champaign-Urbana, 1960; MS in Biochemistry, U. Ill., Chgo., 1963, MD, 1964. Diplomate Am. Bd. Allergy and Immunology, Am. Bd. Pathology. Intern Children's Hosp. Med. Ctr., Boston, 1964-65; adj. instr. pediatrics U. Calif., San Francisco, 1971-72, asst. prof. immunology dept. dermatology, 1972-78, adj. assoc. prof., 1978-88; dir. lab. immunology U. Calif. & Kaiser Found. Rsch. Inst. Joint Program Project, San Francisco, 1971-74; attending physician dept. medicine Mt. Zion/U. Calif. San Francisco Hosps., 1971—; dir. div. immunology Western Labs., Oakland, Calif., 1974-77; med. dir. MML/Solano Labs. Div. Chemed-W.R. Grace, Inc., Berkeley, Calif., 1977-79; med. dir. Levin Clin. Labs., Inc., San Francisco, 1979-81; pvt. practice San Francisco, 1981—. Contbr. articles to profl. jours., chpts. to books. Lt. USN, 1966-69, Vietnam. Decorated Bronze Star, Silver Star, 4 Air medals; Harvard Med. Sch. traineeship grantee, 1964, USPHS hematology tng. grantee U. Calif., San Francisco Med. Ctr., 1969-71; recipient Faculty Rsch. award Am. Cancer Soc., 1970-74. Fellow Coll. Am. Pathologists, Am. Coll. Emergency Physicians, Am. Soc. Clin. Pathologists; mem. AMA, Am. Acad. Allergy and Immunology, Am. Coll. Allergy and Immunology, Am. Assn. Clin. Chemists, Am. Acad. Environ. Medicine, Calif. Med. Assn., San Francisco Med. Soc. Jewish. Office: Immunology Inc 500 Sutter # 512 San Francisco CA 94102-1114

LEVIN, ALVIN IRVING, educator, composer; b. N.Y.C., Dec. 22, 1921; s. David and Frances (Schloss) L.; B.M. in Edn., U. Miami (Fla.), 1941; M.A., Calif. State U., Los Angeles, 1955; Ed.D. with honors, UCLA, 1968; m. Beatrice Van Loon, June 5, 1976 (div. 1981). Composer, arranger for movies, TV, theater Allied Artists, Eagle-Lion Studios, Los Angeles, 1945-65; tng. and supervising tchr. Los Angeles City Schs., 1957-65, adult edn. instr., 1962-63; research specialist Los Angeles Office Supt. Edn., 1965-67; asst. prof. ednl. research Calif. State U., Los Angeles, 1968; asst. prof. elem. edn. Calif. State U., Northridge, 1969-73; self-employed, Northridge, 1973—; founder, pres. Alvin Irving Levin Philanthropic Found., 1973—; ordained to ministry Ch. of Mind Sci., 1975; founder, pres. Divine Love Ch.-An Internat. Metaphys. Ch., 1977—, Meet Your New Personality, A Mind Expansion Program, 1975-77. Bd. overseers Calif. Sch. Profl. Psychology, 1974—; gen. chmn., producer Fiftieth Anniversary Pageant of North Hollywood Park, 1977. Author: My Ivory Tower, 1950, Symposium: Values in Kaleidoscope, 1973, (TV series) America, America!, 1978-79, (docudrama) One World, 1980; composer: Symphony for Strings, 1984, Tone Poem for Male Chorus and Brass, 1984, Hymn to the United Nations for Chorus and Symphony Orchestra, 1991, (music-drama) Happy Land, 1971, (musical plays) A Tale of Two Planets, 1988, Blueprint for a New World Model, 1991; producer UN Festival Calif. State U., Northridge, 1991; compiler, contbr. U.S. Dept. Edn. reports Adult Counseling and Guidance, 1967, Parent Child Preschool Program, 1967, English Classes for Foreign Speaking Adult Professionals, 1967, Blueprint for New World Order, 1991. Recipient plaque State of Calif., 1977, Golden Merit medal Rep. Presdl. Task Force, 1985. Named to Rep. Task Force Presdl. Commn., 1986. Mem. Nat. Soc. for Study Edn., AAUP, Am. Statis. Assn., Internat. Council Edn. for Teaching, Los Angeles World Affairs Council, Internat. Platform Assn., World Federalist Assn. (pres. San Fernando Valley chpt. 1991—), North Hollywood C. of C. (dir. 1976—), Phi Delta Kappa. Home and Office: 9850 Reseda Blvd Apt 314 Northridge CA 91324-2054

LEVIN, CLIFFORD ELLIS, psychologist; b. Chgo., Mar. 18, 1947; s. Sam S. and Beverly (Imerman) L.; m. Phyllis Jean Saupe, Dec. 27, 1970 (div. June 1983); m. Lois Jean Allen-Byrd, Jan. 11, 1985. BS, U. Ill., 1970; MA, Sangamon State U., 1976; PhD, Western Grad. Sch. Psychology, Palo Alto, Calif., 1989. Pvt. practice Palo Alto, 1986—; rsch. assoc. Mental Rsch. Inst., Palo Alto, 1985—, mem. clinic staff, 1985—, also treas. of bd. dirs.; dir. Eye Movement Desensitization and Reprocessing Ctr., Palo Alto. Mem. APA (assoc.), Calif. Psychol. Assn., Calif. Assn. of Marriage, Family and Child Counselors. Office: 555 Middlefield Rd Palo Alto CA 94301-2197

LEVIN, HOWARD ALAN, fundraising and marketing consultant; b. Roslyn, N.Y., Feb. 12, 1954; s. Melvin Boris and Phyllis Corinne (Levy) L. BA in Bus. and Econs., SUNY, Oneonta, 1976; postgrad., U. Copenhagen, 1975, Colo. Mountain Coll., 1981, 84, 87,. Gen. mgr. Spa World, Denver, 1976; outdoor guide Colo. Adventures, Steamboat Springs, Colo., 1977-79, Sobek, Anchorage, 1980; profl. ski patrol Steamboat Ski Corp., Steamboat Springs, 1979-86; dir. fundraising Jimmie Heuga Ctr., Vail, Colo., 1986-89; pres. Flagwear, Barcelona, Spain, 1992, HAL Corp., Vail, 1990—; pub., editor Abe Lincoln Press, Quotations for Successful Living. Editor, writer newsletter Friends Always, 1989; designer Flag Fashionwear, 1992—. Project coord. Friends of Eagle County Pub. Libr., Avon, Colo., 1990-91; fundraiser U.S. Disabled Ski Team, Park City, Utah, 1990; dir. Jimmie Heuga Express, 1986-89; bd. dirs. Resource Ctr., Vail, 1990—; coach Steamboat Women's Soccer Club, 1979-86; vol. fundraiser Ski Club Vail, 1987-92. Named Best Fundraiser in Ski Industry, Ski mag., 1987, 88. Mem. Colo. Assn. Fundraisers. Office: HAL Corp PO Box 2262 Vail CO 81658

LEVIN, LAWRENCE ADAM, lawyer; b. Washington, Dec. 4, 1953; s. William and Nina (Wender) L. BA, Yale U., 1975; JD, NYU, 1978. Bar: D.C. 1978, Ind. 1986. Staff atty. Pension Benefit Guaranty Corp., Washington, 1978-80; regulatory counsel Chem. Spltys. Mfrs. Assn., Washington, 1980-85; sr. staff atty. Bristol-Myers Co., Warsaw, Ind., 1985-89; assoc. div. counsel Bristol-Myers Squibb Co., Warsaw, 1990; assoc. counsel Bristol-Myers Squibb Pharm. Rsch. Inst., Seattle, 1990—. Mem. D.C. Bar Assn., Ind. Bar Assn.

LEVIN, MARIO, computer consultant; b. Mexico City, July 30, 1953; came to U.S., 1978; s. Sommer and Clara (Desatnik) L.; m. Deborah Feiner, Jan. 16, 1982; children: Jonathan, Daniela, Aliza. BEE, U. Mex., 1976; MS in Engring., Princeton U., 1980. System programmer Nat. Semiconductor Co., Santa Clara, Calif., 1980-81; computer cons. Mexico City, 1981-83; software engr. Norton & Co., Westport, Conn., 1983-84, Cipherlink Corp., L.A., 1984-87; ind. computer cons. L.A., 1987—. Jewish. Home and Office: 3631 Gleneagles Dr Tarzana CA 91356-5620

LEVIN, ROBERT ALAN, job training company executive; b. St. Paul, July 27, 1957; s. George Lloyd and Mary Louise (Aberle) L. BA, Reed Coll., 1979. Fire mgmt. supr. U.S. Forest Svc., Cottage Grove, Oreg., 1978-79; Nordic dir. Cooper Spur Ski Area, Hood River, Oreg., 1979-80; dir. Nordic skiing Timberline Ski Tng. Ctr., Mt. Hood, Oreg., 1980-83; dir. mktg. Timberline Ski Tng. Ctr., 1981-83; nat. dir. Am. Coaching Effectiveness Program, Champaign, Ill., 1983-86; pres. Levin & Co., Champaign, 1986-91, Boulder, Colo., 1989—; clinic faculty for numerous nat. sport orgns., 1983-86; divisional devel. dir. U.S. Nordic Ski Team, Park City, Utah, 1982-83; tng. cons. U.S. Nordic Ski Demonstration Team, Boulder, Colo., 1984-85; approved U. Colo. Boulder Research Park, 1989, mem. employers adv. coun., 1990—, chmn. East Campus Rsch. Assn., 1993—; del. Info. Economy of the West, 1989. Author: Specialized Job Training System Manuals, 1987; author, editor: YMCA of USA Basketball Manual Series, 1984-86; contbr. articles to profl. jours. Bus. coun. Champaign C. of C., 1986-89; mem. MIT Enterprise Forum Colo., 1990—; mem. mid-east fact finding mission Congressman Terry Bruce, 1988, Boulder Devel. Commn., 1990—; selected 1984 Olympic Sci. Congress. Named Nat. Merit Finalist, Nat. Merit Scholars, 1975; named to 50 for Colo. award Colo. Assn. Commerce and Industry, 1990. Mem. Nat. Soc. for Perfomance & Instruction, Profl. Ski Instructors Am. (Nordic chair Pacific NW, 1985-86), U.S. Ski Coaches Assn. (nat. clinic faculty 1982-83). Office: Levin & Co 1526 Spruce St Boulder CO 80302

LEVIN, WILLIAM EDWARD, lawyer; b. Miami, Fla., June 13, 1954; s. Harold A. and Phyllis (Wolfson) L. Student, Conn. Coll., 1972-74; BA, Emory U., Atlanta, 1976; JD, U. Miami, 1979. Bar: Fla. 1979, Calif. 1982; lic. real estate broker, Calif. Distbr. N.Y. Times, Atlanta, 1975-76; legis. intern Congressman William Lehman, Washington, 1974; law clk. Superior Ct. Hillsborough County, Tampa, Fla., 1974; legal asst./law clk. U. Miami Sch. Law, 1977-78; law clk. Shevin, Shapo & Shevin, Miami, 1977-79; assoc. Law Offices of John Cyril Malloy, Miami, 1979-82; assoc./ptnr. Flehr, Hohbach, Test, Albritton & Herbert, San Francisco, 1982-87; ptnr. Cooper, White & Cooper, San Francisco, 1987-88; trademark atty., pvt. practice San Francisco, 1988-92; broker/sole proprietor Levin Realty, San Francisco, 1987-92; counsel Goldstein & Phillips, San Francisco, 1988-91, Hawes & Fischer, Newport Beach, Calif., 1992—; co-chmn. trademark com. San Francisco Patent & Trademark Assn., 1985-86; moot ct. judge Giles Rich Moot Ct. Competition, San Francisco, 1986; ofcl. arbitrator Am. Arbitration Assn., 1987—; lectr. in field. Editorial bd. Trademark World, London, 1987-90, Trademark Reporter, 1987-89, San Francisco Atty., 1986-89; contbr. articles to profl. jours. Adv. bd. Californians for Missing Children, San Francisco, 1989-92, Hebrew Inst. Law, San Francisco, 1986-88; atty's steering com. Jewish Community Fedn., San Francisco, 1987-88; fin. com. Temple Emanu-El, San Francisco, 1985-86. Mem. ABA, U.S. Trademark Assn., Orange County Bar Assn., Commonwealth Club, Golden Gateway Club, San Francisco Bay Club. Democrat. Jewish. Home: 5405 Alton Pky Ste 219 Irvine CA 92714 Office: 660 Newport Ctr Dr, Ste 460 Newport Beach CA 92660

LEVINE, ALAN J., entertainment company executive; b. L.A., Mar. 8, 1947; s. Phil and Shirley Ann (Lauber) L.; m. Judy B. Birnbaum, July 18, 1973; children: Andrea, Jay. BS in Bus., U. So. Calif., L.A., 1968, JD, 1971. Bar: Calif. 1972, U.S. Dist. Ct. (so. dist.) Calif. 1972. Ptnr. Pacht, Ross, Warne, Bernhard & Sears, L.A., 1971-78, Schiff, Hirsch & Schreiber, Beverly Hills, Calif., 1978-80, Armstrong, Hirsch & Levine, L.A., 1980-89; pres., chief oper. officer film entertainment group SONY Pictures Entertainment, Inc., Culver, Calif., 1989—; v.p. cinema circulus dept. cinema and TV, U. So. Calif., L.A., 1988—; bd. dirs. UCLA Entertainment Symposium, L.A., 1986-89. Chmn. cabinet entertainment div. United Jewish Fedn., L.A., 1990—; bd. govs. Cedars Sinai Med. Ctr., L.A., 1989—. Mem. Calif. State Bar Assn., L.A. County Bar Assn., Beverly Hills Bar Assn., Acad. Motion Picture Arts and Scis., Acad. TV Arts and Scis. Democrat. Office: SONY Pictures Entertainment Inc 10202 Washington Blvd Culver City CA 90232-3119

LEVINE, ARNOLD MILTON, retired electrical engineer, documentary filmmaker; b. Preston, Conn., Aug. 15, 1916; s. Samuel and Florence May (Clark) L.; m. Bernice Eleanor Levich, Aug. 31, 1941; children: Mark Jeffrey, Michael Norman, Kevin Lawrence. BS in Radio Engring., Tri-State U., Angola, Ind., 1939, DSc (hon.), 1960; MS, U. Iowa, 1940. Head sound lab. CBS, N.Y.C., 1940-42; asst. engr., div. head ITT, N.Y.C. and Nutley, N.J., 1942-65; lab. head, lab. dir. ITT, San Fernando, Calif., 1965-71; v.p. aerospace, gen. mgr., sr. scientist ITT, Van Nuys, Calif., 1971-86; ret., 1986. Patentee fiber optics, radar, communications and TV fields. Past mem. bd. dirs., v.p., pres. Am. Jewish Congress, L.A. Recipient San Fernando Valley Engr. of Yr. award, 1968; Profl. designation Motion Picture Art & Scis., UCLA, 1983. Fellow IEEE (life), Soc. Motion Picture and TV Engrs., USCG Aux. (vice comdr. 1990-91, flotilla cmdr. 1992-93). Home: 10828 Fullbright Ave Chatsworth CA 91311-1737

LEVINE, GENE NORMAN, sociology educator; b. Medford, Mass., May 15, 1930; s. Joseph Michael and Jennie (Herman) L.; 1 child, John Albert. AB, Boston U., 1952; PhD, Columbia U., 1959. Rsch. assoc. Bur. Applied Social Rsch., Columbia U., N.Y.C., 1954-64; project dir. UN Rsch. Inst. for Social Devel., Geneva, 1964-65, 66-68; prof. sociology UCLA, 1965-91, prof. emeritus, 1991—; adj. prof. U. N.Mex., Albuquerque, 1992—; mem. core faculty Walden U., Mpls., 1986—. Author: Workers Vote, 1962, Inducing Social Change in Developing Communities, 1967, Japanese American Community, 1981. Mem. bd. scholars Japanese Am. Nat. Mus., L.A., 1989—; project dir. Jewish Fedn. Greater Albuquerque, 1991—. Grantee Russell Sage Found., 1959-60, NIMH, 1965-75; rsch. scholar U. Judaism, L.A., 1976-80. Fellow Am. Sociol. Assn. (emeritus); mem. Am. Soc. for Sociol. Study Jewry (v.p. 1976-77), N.Mex. Psychoanalytic Assn., UCLA Alumni Assn. Democrat. Home: 7303 Montgomery Blvd Albuquerque NM 87109 Office: Dept Sociology U NM Albuquerque NM 87131

LEVINE, JEROME LESTER, lawyer; b. Los Angeles, July 20, 1940. m. Maryanne Shields, Sept. 13, 1966; children: Aron Michael, Sara Michelle. BA San Francisco State U., 1962; JD, U. Calif., 1965. Bar: Calif. 1966, U.S. Supreme Ct., 1986. Dir. operational svcs., assoc. dir. Western Ctr. on Law and Poverty, Los Angeles, 1968-72; assoc. Swerdlow, Glikbarg & Shimer, Beverly Hills, Calif., 1972-77; ptnr. Lans Feinberg & Cohen, L.A., 1977-79, Albala & Levine, L.A., 1980-83, Neiman Billet Albala & Levine, L.A., 1983-90, Levine & Assocs., L.A., 1991—; lectr. in law U. So. Calif. Law Ctr., Loyola U. Sch. Law. Mem. ABA, L.A. County Bar Assn., Beverly Hills Bar Assn., Assn. Bus. Trial Lawyers, Fed. Bar Assn., Nat. Indian Gaming Assn. (bd. dirs.), Internat. Assn. Gaming Lawyers (editorial bd. Indian Gaming Mag.). Office: 2029 Century Park E Ste 1700 Los Angeles CA 90067-3034

LEVINE, JOEL SETH, medical school, hospital administrator; b. Key West, Fla., Feb. 22, 1947; s. Carl Michael and Sophie Barbara (Halpern) L.; m. Frieda Zylberberg, Aug. 1, 1970; children: Daniel Ian, Steven Neal, Karyn Ann. BS, Bklyn. Coll., 1967; MD, SUNY, Bklyn., 1971. Asst. prof. medicine U. Colo., Denver, 1978-84; vice chmn. dept. medicine U. Colo., 1984-92, assoc. prof. medicine, 1984—, assoc. dean clin. affairs, 1989—; dir. gastroenterology unit Univ. Hosp., Denver, 1989—; pres. med. staff Univ. Hosp., 1989-92. Editor: Decision Making in Gastroenterology, 1985, 92; contbr. articles to profl. jours. Trustee Kern Rsch. Found., Denver, 1982—. Lt. comdr. USN, 1973-75. NIH grantee, 1977-78, Clin. Investigator awardee, 1978-81; Robert Wood Johnson Found. fellow, 1988-89. Fellow ACP; mem. Am. Gastroenterological Assn., Am. Fedn. Clin. Rsch., Western Soc. Clin. Rsch., N.Y. Acad. Scis. Jewish. Office: Univ of Colo Health Sci Ctr B-158 4200 E 9th Ave Denver CO 80262

LEVINE, KENNETH MARK, film production professional; b. Seattle, Dec. 6, 1946; s. Harry E. and Naomi (Fleishman) L.; m. Ivory Waterworth, July 11, 1985; 1 child, Luna. BA, U. Wash., 1971. Cinematographer, editor Sky River Productions, 1970; freelance cinematographer, editor KING-TV, Seattle, 1973; photographer The Battelle Inst., 1975; film cons. And/Or Gallery, Seattle, 1976-79; tchr. cinema, special effects Inst. of Creative Media, Seattle Community Coll., 1976; designer, special effects cinematographer, editor Northwest Cinema Specialists, 1976-77; proposal reader Corp. for Pub. Broadcasting, 1981; media cons. to v.p. of pub. relations Burlington Northern Inc., 1982-83; ptnr. New Day Films, 1982-92; location mgr. for dir. Lazlo Pal Eagle Island Productions, 1987, location mgr. for dir. of photography Vilmos Zsigmond, 1987; dir. Kauai County Film Commission, Lihue, Hawaii, 1989-92; co-owner Iris Film and Video, 1975-93; location mgr. for Jurassic Park film Steven Spielberg Amblin Entertainment, Kalaheo, Hawaii, 1992. Producer/dir.: Pigs, 1971, Ocean Dance, 1972, Watermark, 1976, Man Swallows Sword, 1977, Northwest Visionaries, 1979, American Contemporary Dance Company, 1980, Becoming American, 1982-83, Between Time: A Tibetan Village in Nepal, 1984; Field Producer/dir.: Smithsonian Institution and Archives of American Art, 1988-89; Asst. dir.: Second Chance to Live, 1971-72; Cinematographer/editor: All About Elmer, 1972; Editor: Our American System of Justice: The Civil Court, 1973; Producer/cinematographer/editor: Whitman College: Seasons of Change, 1983, Between Time: A Tibetan Village in Nepal, 1984, Radio: The Interactive Teacher, 1984-85, A Link to the Future, 1986; Producer/ videographer/ editor: Warren Reading Foundation, 1990; Founder/dir.: Bumbershoot, The Seatle Arts Film Festival, 1976-79; Co-Producer/ Co-dir: Becoming American: Twelve Years Later, 1993. Mem. Gov.'s Film. Com., State of Hawaii, 1989-92. Recipient The Acad. of Motion Picture Arts and Sciences, award Recognition of Special Merit, The Humbolt State Film Festival award for Best Documentary, The Northwest Film and Video Festival award for Winner of the Festival, The Nat. Council on Family Relations Film Festival award First Place, The Nat. Educational Film Festival award for Best of Festival; Grantee Nat. Endowment for the Arts, 1979, WNET/13 NY and Nat. Endowment for the Arts, 1982-83; The Western States Regional Arts fellowship. Home: PO Box 689 Kalaheo HI 96741 Office: 1628 41st Ave East Ste 24 Seattle WA 98112

LEVINE, LARRY, recording engineer; b. Bklyn., May 8, 1928; s. Harry Levine and Frieda (Appelbaum) Gottlieb; m. Marilyn Spivak, Aug. 18, 1955; children: Richard Harris, Robert Alan, Michael Adam. Grad. high sch., L.A. Rec. engr. Gold Star Rec. Studios, Hollywood, Calif., 1952-67; dir. rec. A&M Records, Hollywood, 1967-75; real estate sales, free lance audio various locations, 1976-82; audio mixer Premore Video Post Prodn., North Hollywood, Calif., 1982-88. Sgt. U.S. Army, 1948-52, Korea. Mem. NARAS (trustee, bd. govs. Grammy 1966). Home: 4840 Gaviota Ave Encino CA 91436

LEVINE, MELDON EDISES, congressman, lawyer; b. Los Angeles, June 7, 1943; s. Sid B. and Shirley B. (Blum) L.; m. Jan Greenberg; children: Adam Paul, Jacob Caplan, Cara Emily. AB, U. Calif., Berkeley, 1964; MPA, Princeton U., 1966; JD, Harvard U., 1969. Bar: Calif. 1970, D.C. 1972. Assoc. Wyman, Bautzer, Rothman & Kuchel, 1969-71; legis. asst. U.S. Senate, Washington, 1971-73; ptnr. Levine Krom & Unger, Beverly Hills, Calif., 1973-77; mem. Calif. Assembly, Sacramento, 1977-82, 98th-102d Congresses from 27th Calif. dist., Washington, 1983—. Author: The Private Sector and the Common Market, 1968; contbr. articles to various publs. Mem. governing bd. So. Calif. chpt. Anti-Defamation League, So. Calif. chpt. Am. Jewish Com., So. Calif. chpt. Am. Jewish Congress, So. Calif. chpt. NAACP Legal Def. Fund, U. Judaism, City of Hope, U. Calif. Alumni Council; mem. amateur baseball team Hollywood Stars, 1971—. Mem. Calif. Bar Assn., Los Angeles Bar Assn. Office: US Ho of Reps 2443 Rayburn Washington DC 20515

LEVINE, MICHAEL, public relations executive, author; b. N.Y.C., Apr. 17, 1954; s. Arthur and Virginia (Gaylor) L. Student, Rutgers U., 1972-77. Owner, operator TV News Mag., Los Angeles, 1977-83; owner Michael Levine Pub. Rels. (now Levine/Schnieder Pub. Rels.), Los Angeles, 1982—; mem. Gov.'s adv. bd. State Calif., Sacramento, 1980-82; pres., owner Aurora Pub., L.A., 1986—; moderator Thought Forum; lectr. in field. Author: The Address Book: How to Reach Anyone Who's Anyone, 1984, The New Address Book, 1986, The Corporate Address Book, 1987, The Music Address Book, 1989, Environmental Address Book, 1991, Kid's Address Book, 1991, Guerrilla P.R.; pub., writer For Consideration newsletter. Mem. Ronald Reagan Pres.'s Libr., Rosey Grier's Are You Comitted, L.A., 1986—; founder The Actor's Conf., Aurora Charity, 1987; bd. dirs. Felice Found., Micah Ctr. Mem. TV Acad. Arts and Scis., Entertainemnt Industries Council, West Hollywood C. of C. (bd. dirs. 1980-82). Jewish. Office: 8730 Sunset Blvd Fl 6 West Hollywood CA 90069-2210

LEVINE, MICHAEL JOSEPH, insurance company executive; b. Boston, Mar. 23, 1945; s. Sam and Helen Alice (Michelman) L.; m. Margaret Mary Gutierrez, Aug. 6, 1983; children: Samuel Jacob, Rebecca Lynn. BA, Boston U., 1967; MBA, N.Mex. State U., 1991. Supr. underwriting Comml. Union. Ins., Boston, 1969-73; mgr. Harris-Murtagh Ins., Boston, 1973-75, Cohen-Goldenberg Ins. Agy., Boston, 1975-77; v.p. Southwest Underwriters Ins., Deming, N.Mex., 1977-83, pres., 1983-86; pres. Consol. Ins. Cons., Deming, N.Mex., 1985—; instr. fin. and ins., N.Mex. State U., Las Cruces. V.p. Border Area Mental Health Svcs., So. N.Mex., 1978—; pres. Deming Arts Council, 1979-81; treas. Luna County (N.Mex.) Crimestoppers, Inc., 1979—. Mem. Mensa, Soc. CPCU's (cert.), Soc. Cert. Ins. Counselors (cert.), Ins. Mktg. Assocs., Luna County C. of C. (v.p. 1981-84), Ind. Ins. Agts. N.Mex. (state dir. 1985—), Southwest N.Mex. Ind. Ins. Agts. (treas. 1981-83, pres. 1983-85). Home: 1920 S Silver Ave Deming NM 88030-5931 Office: Consol Ins Cons Inc 318 S Columbus Rd Deming NM 88030-3867

LEVINE, NORMAN GENE, insurance company executive; b. N.Y.C., Sept. 14, 1926; s. Harris J. and Dorothy S. (Podolsky) L.; m. Sandra Leibow, Dec. 11, 1969; children—Linda, Daniel, Donald. Student, U. Wis.-Madison, 1943-48. Agt. Aetna Life Ins. Co., N.Y.C., 1948-56; supr. Aetna Life Ins. Co., 1956-59, gen. agt., 1959-75; mng. gen. agt. Mut. Benefit Life Ins. Co. in No. Calif., San Francisco, 1975-90; br. mgr. Sun Life of Can., 1990—; pres. Levine Fin. Group, 1975—; internat. speaker in field; past div. v.p. Million Dollar Round Table; nat. chmn. Life Underwriters Tng. Council, 1983-84; nat. pres. Gen. Agts. and Mgrs. Conf., 1986-87. Author: How To Build a $100,000,000 Agency in Five Years or Less, Yes You Can, Life Insurance to Diversification; editor: bi-weekly news report Probe; contbr. numerous articles to profl. jours.; author tapes on ins., mgmt., photography, Americanism. Past mem. bd. dirs. Calif. Law Enforcement Needs Com. Served with AUS, 1944-46, ETO. Recipient Julian Myrick award, 1969, John Newton Russell Meml. award, 1986; named to Hall of Fame Gen. Agts. and Mgrs. Conf., 1982. Mem. N.Y.C. Assn. Life Underwriters (pres. 1967-68), N.Y. State Assn. Life Underwriters (pres. 1968-69), Nat. Assn. Life Underwriters (pres. 1974-75, dir. polit. action com. 1967-69), N.Y.C. Life Mgrs. Assn. (pres. 1974-75), Assn. Advanced Life Underwriters, Am. Soc. C.L.U.s, San Francisco Gen. Agts. and Mgrs. Assn. (pres. 1983), Golden Key Soc., Linnaean Soc., San Francisco C. of C., Audubon Soc., Am. Israel Friendship League (trustee). Mem. Order B'nai Zion (pres. 1964-67). Home: 251 Crest Rd Woodside CA 94062-2310 Office: 1 California St San Francisco CA 94111-5401

LEVINE, PHILIP ROBERT, administrative law judge; b. Boston, Dec. 20, 1940; s. Sydney and Lillian (Ackerman) LeV.; m. Ann Whitcomb (div. 1976); children: Adam Daniel, Sara Rachel; m. Sheri E. Ross, Dec. 6, 1984. AB, Boston U., 1962, LLB, 1965; LLM, George Washington U., 1967. Bar: Mass. 1965, Calif. 1978. Supervising atty. NLRB, Washington and L.A., 1967-80; ptnr. Ross & LeVine, Santa Monica, Calif., 1980-82; sr. labor counsel CBS, L.A., 1982-83; adminstrv. law judge various city agys., L.A. area, 1983—; ct. commr. Culver City (Calif.) Mcpl. Ct., 1989-90. Sec., v.p. Mid City Neighbors, Santa Monica, 1986-88. Named Vol. of Yr. County of Los Angeles, 1987; recipient Disting. Svc. award Culver City Mcpl. Ct., 1990, named Pro Tem of Yr., 1992. Mem. Culver Marina Bar Assn. (v.p. 1990-91, trustee 1990-92, pres. 1991—). Office: Office of Philip R LeVine Ste 31 1314 17th St Santa Monica CA 90404

LEVINE, RICHARD NEIL, film company executive; b. Bklyn., Mar. 7, 1937; s. Murry and Mollie Carol (Powell) L. BA, Brown U., 1958. Asst. agt. William Morris Agy., N.Y.C., 1958-60; pers. mgr. Ackerman Assoc., N.Y.C., 1960-61; prodn. asst., casting asst. M. B. Cohen Prodns., N.Y.C., 1961-63; theatrical agt. various agys., N.Y.C., 1963-69; ind. writer L.A. and N.Y.C., 1969-71; travel writer Holland Today, The Hague, The Netherlands, 1973-76; stage dir. Anglo Am. Theatre, The Hague, 1973-76; post prodn./film specialist Creative Film Arts, L.A., 1977-84; post prodn./film exec. B/G/L Post Inc., L.A., 1984—. Author: (novel) Making Out, 1974; co-author play American Nightmare, 1977 (Dramalog award 1978); co-creator ballet Sanctus, 1978; contbr. columns, feature articles to Holland Today, 1973-76; writer, dir. stage benefit Sing Happy, 1990. Democrat. Jewish. Office: B/G/L Post Inc 726 Cahulenga Los Angeles CA 90038

LEVINE, STEPHEN MARK, financial professional; b. Greenbrae, Calif., Mar. 16, 1965; s. Lawrence Mark and Sandra Elizabeth (Hedlund) LeV. BA in Speech Communication, San Diego State U., 1988. Lic. real estate broker, Calif. Sales assoc. Corrigan Comml. Real Estate, San Diego, 1989; broker assoc. Coldwell Banker Real Estate, San Diego, 1989-92; sales mgr., ptnr. Effective Mktg. Co., San Diego, 1991-92; ptnr., real estate sales trainer Personal Success Group, San Diego, 1991-92; broker assoc. Centre City Properties, San Diego, 1992-93; loan rep. Calif. Fed. Bank, San Diego, 1993—. Mem. Univ. Club, San Diego Tennis and Racquet Club, Kearny Mesa Rotary (sgt. at arms). Republican. Jewish. Office: Calif Federal Bank 6310 Greenwich Dr # 100 San Diego CA 92122

LEVINGSTON, JOHN COLVILLE BOWRING, telecommunications executive; b. Rawalpindi, Punjab, Pakistan, Apr. 10, 1929; came to U.S. 1961; s. Thomas Clarke and Kathleen Patricia (Farley) L.; m. Elizabeth Ann Baumer, June 6, 1958 (div. Apr. 1968); m. Paula Angela Eriksen, Feb. 29, 1980; children: Thomas Arthur, Alexandra Jane. Grad., Harrow Sch., Eng.; student, Sandhurst, Eng. Sales mgr. British-Am. Tobacco Co., East Africa, 1952-55, W.L. Mackenzie Co., Vancouver, B.C., Can., 1957-61; v.p. Precipitator Inc., Santa Fe Springs, Calif., 1973-78; cons. Calif. Inst. Tech., Pasadena, 1979; v.p. Kingmont Oil, Pine Knot, Ky., 1980; cons. Sta. KCET-TV, Hollywood, Calif., 1981; founder, chmn. Straightley Films, Hollywood, 1982-86; founder, chmn., chief exec. officer Interactive Telemedia, Sherman Oaks, Calif., 1986-89; chmn. Levingston & Assocs., Beverly Hills, Calif., 1989—. Inventor Straightley automobile, 1969. Lt. Parachute Regt., 1950-52. Mem. Internat. Platform Assn., Acad. Television Arts Scis., SAG, Masons. Office: Levingston & Assocs PO Box 1951 Beverly Hills CA 90213-1951

LEVINSON, ARTHUR DAVID, molecular biologist; b. Seattle, Mar. 31, 1950; s. Sol and Malvina (Lindsay) L.; m. Rita May Liff, Dec. 17, 1978; children: Jesse, Anya. BS, U. Wash., 1972; PhD, Princeton U., 1977. Postdoctoral fellow U. Calif., San Francisco, 1977-80; sr. scientist Genentech, South San Francisco, 1980-84, staff scientist, 1984—, dir. cell genetics dept., 1988-89, v.p. rsch., 1990-93, sr. v.p. rcsh. and devel., 1993—. Mem. editorial bd. Virology, 1984-87, Molecular Biology and Medicine, 1986-90, Molecular and Cellular Biology, 1987—, Jour. of Virology, 1988-91. Mem. Am. Soc. Microbiology, Am. Soc. Biochemistry and Molecular Biology. Office: Genentech Inc 460 Point San Bruno Blvd South San Francisco CA 94080

LEVINSON, KENNETH LEE, lawyer; b. Denver, Jan. 18, 1953; s. Julian Charles and Dorothy (Milzer) L.; m. Shauna Titus, Dec. 21, 1986. BA cum laude, U. Colo.-Boulder, 1974; JD, U. Denver, 1978. Bar: Colo. 1978, U.S. Ct. Appeals (10th cir.) 1978. Assoc. atty. Balaban & Lutz, Denver, 1979-83; shareholder Balaban & Levinson, P.C., 1984—. Contbr. articles to profl. jours. Pres. Dahlia House Condominium Assn., 1983-85, bd. dirs., 1991—; intern Reporters Com. For Freedom of the Press, Washington, 1977; hearing bd. mem. various grievance proceedings, 1988—. J.V. volleyball coach Good Shephard Catholic Sch., 1992— Recipient Am. Jurisprudence award Lawyers Co-op., 1977. Mem. Denver Bar Assn., Colo. Bar Assn. (profl. liability com. 1991—), Am. Arbitration Assn. (arbitrator). Clubs: Denver Law, Denver Athletic.

LEVIT, VICTOR BERT, lawyer, foreign representative, civic worker; b. Singapore, Apr. 21, 1930; s. Bert W. and Thelma (Clumeck) L.; m. Sherry Lynn Chamove, Feb. 25, 1962; children: Carson, Victoria. A.B. in Polit. Sci. with great distinction, Stanford, 1950; LL.B., Stanford U., 1952. Bar: Calif. 1953. Assoc. Long & Levit, San Francisco and Los Angeles, 1953-55, ptnr., 1955-83; mng. ptnr. Long & Levit, San Francisco and L.A., 1971-83; ptnr. Barger & Wolen, San Francisco, L.A. and Newport Beach, 1983—; assoc. and gen. legal counsel U.S. Jaycees, 1959-61; legal counsel for consul gen. Ethiopia for San Francisco, 1964-71; hon. consul for Ethiopia for San Francisco, Ethiopia, 1971-76; guest lectr. Stanford U. Law Sch., 1958—, Haile Selassie I Univ. Law Sch., 1972-76; mem. com. group ins. programs State Bar Calif., 1980—; Mem. Los Angeles Consular Corps, 1971-77; mem. San Francisco Consular Corps, 1971-77, vice dean, 1975-76; Grader Calif. Bar Exam., 1956-61; del. San Francisco Mcpl. Conf., 1955-63, vice chmn., 1960, chmn., 1961-63. Author: Legal Malpractice in California, 1974, Legal Malpractice, 1977, 2d edit., 1983; Note editor: Stanford Law Rev, 1952-53; legal editor: Underwriters' Report, 1963—; Contbr. articles to legal jours. Campaign chmn. San Francisco Aid Retarded Children, 1960; mem. nat. com. Stanford Law Sch. Fund, 1959—; mem. Mayor's Osaka-San Francisco Affiliation Com., 1959-65, Mayor's Com. for Mcpl. Mgmt., 1961-64; mem. San Francisco Rep. Country Cen. Com., 1956-63; assoc. mem. Calif. Rep. Cen. Com., 1956-63, 70-72; campaign chmn. San Francisco Assemblyman John Busterud, 1960; bd. dirs. San Francisco Comml. Club, 1967-70, San Francisco Planning and Urban Renewal Assn., 1959-60, San Francisco Planning and Urban Renewal Assn. Nat. Found. Infantile Paralysis, 1958, Red Shield Youth Assn., Salvation Army, San Francisco, 1960-70, bd. dirs. NCCJ, San Francisco, 1959—, chmn., No. Calif., 1962-64, 68-70; mem. nat. bd. dirs., 1964-75; bd. dirs. San Francisco Tb and Health Assn., 1962-70, treas., 1964, pres., 1965-67; bd. dirs. San Francisco Assn. Mental Health, 1964-73, pres., 1968-71; mem. com. Nat. Assn. Mental Health, 1969-71; trustee United Bay Area Crusade, 1966-74, Ins. Forum San Francisco; bd. visitors Stanford Law Sch., 1969-75; mem. adv. bd. Jr. League San Francisco, 1971-75. Named Outstanding Young Man San Francisco mng. editors San Francisco newspapers, 1960, One of Five Outstanding Young Men Calif., 1961. Fellow ABA (chmn. profl. liability com. for gen. practice sect. 1979-81, council gen. practice sect. 1982-86, sec.-treas. gen. practice sect. 1986-87); mem. San Francisco Bar Assn. (chmn. ins. com. 1962, 73, chmn. charter flight com. 1962-66), State Bar Calif. (com. on group ins. programs 1980—, chmn. gen. practice sect. 1988—), Consular Law Soc., Am. Arbitration Assn. (arbitrator), World Assn. Lawyers (chmn. parliamentary law com. 1976—), Am. Law Inst. (adviser restatement of law governing lawyers 1985—), Internat. Bar Assn., San Francisco Jr. C. of C. (dir. 1959, pres. 1958), U.S. Jaycees (exec. com. 1959-61), Jaycees Internat. (life, senator), Calif. Scholarship Fedn., U.S. C. of C. (labor com. 1974-76), San Francisco C. of C. (dir.), Phi Beta Kappa, Order of Coif, Pi Sigma Alpha. Clubs: Commercial (San Francisco) (dir.); Commonwealth (quar. chmn.), California Tennis; World Trade; Bankers. Home: 45 Beach Rd Belvedere Tiburon CA 94920-2364 Office: Barger & Wolen 101 California St Ste 4725 San Francisco CA 94111-4725

LEVITAN, ROGER STANLEY, lawyer; b. Washington, Jan. 31, 1933; s. Simon Wolfe and Bessie (Abramson) L.; m. Maria Anneli Stennius, May 27, 1975 (div. 1980); 1 child, Mark Howard; m. Laurel Lynn Allen, July 9, 1982; 1 child, Brandon Wolfe. BS in Econs., U. Pa., 1954; JD, Columbia U., 1957. Bar: D.C. 1957, U.S. Ct. Appeals (D.C. cir.) 1957, Ariz. 1976. Tax specialist, reorgn. br. IRS, Washington, 1957-62; atty. McClure & Trotter, Washington, 1962-65; assoc. ptnr. Main Lafrentz, Washington and N.Y.C., 1970-72; dir. taxes U.S. Industries, Inc., N.Y.C., 1972-73; asst. tax counsel Am. Home Products Co., N.Y.C., 1973-75; ptnr., Bilby & Shoenhair, P.C., Tucson, 1976-89; ptnr. Snell & Wilmer, Tucson, 1989-90; ptnr. Molloy, Jones & Donohue P.C., Tucson, 1991-92; of counsel Hecker, Phillips & Zeeb, 1992—; lectr. Am. Law Inst., State Bar Ariz. Trustee, Tucson Community Found., 1981—. Contbr. articles to profl. jours. Mem. ABA (chmn. ann. report com. 1965-67, continuing legal edn. com. 1969-70), Ariz. Bar Found., State Bar Ariz. (chmn. sect. taxation 1987-88, mem. tax specialization adv. bd.), D.C. Bar Assn. Home: 727 E Chula Vista Rd Tucson AZ 85718-1028 Office: 405 W Franklin St Tucson AZ 85701

LEVY, ALAN DAVID, real estate executive; b. St. Louis, July 19, 1938; s. I. Jack and Natalie (Yawitz) L.; grad. Sch. Real Estate, Washington U., 1960; m. Abby Jane Markowitz, May 12, 1968; children: Jennifer Lynn, Jacqueline Claire. Property mgr. Solon Gershman Inc., Realtors, Clayton, Mo., 1958-61; gen. mgr. Kodner Constrn. Co., St. Louis, 1961-63; regional mgr. Tishman Realty & Constrn. Co., Inc., N.Y.C., 1963-69, v.p., Los Angeles, 1969-77; exec. v.p., dir. Tishman West Mgmt. Corp., 1977-88; pres. Tishman West Cos., 1988-92, chmn. Tishman Internat. Property Svcs., 1993—; guest lectr. on real estate mgmt. to various forums. Mem. L.A. County Mus. Art; chmn. Am. Art Coun.; trustee Archives Am. Art, Harvard-Westlake Sch.; bd. govs. W.L.A. coun. Boy Scouts Am. Mem. bldg. owners and mgrs. assns. L.A. (dir.), N.J. (co-founder, hon. dir.), Inst. Real Estate Mgmt. (cert. property mgr.), Urban Land Inst., Internat. Council Shopping Centers. Contbr. articles on property mgmt. to trade jours. Office: 10960 Wilshire Blvd Los Angeles CA 90024-3702

LEVY, AVNER M., business and technology consultant; b. Jerusalem, Israel; s. Mordechai A. and Shoshana (Refaely) L.; m. Elana Vilensky, Apr. 1; children: Ornah, Allonn E. BSEE, U. Calif., Berkeley, 1965; MSEE, Stanford U., 1968. Mgr., magnetic head engring. Ampex Corp., Redwood City, Calif., 1965-74; mgr. magnetic heads and motor operations Bell & Howell-Data Tape Div., Pasadena, Calif., 1974-79; pres., founder Advance Recording Tech., Inc., Anaheim, Calif., 1979-83; v.p. engring., bd. dirs. Pyramid Magnetics Inc., Chatsworth, Calif., 1983-86; acting gen. mgr., cons. Carcool, Westlake Village, Calif., 1986—; dir., bd. dirs., cons. Cherokee Data System, Boulder, Colo., 1984-91; acting dir. engring., cons. Datum, Inc., Anaheim, 1980-83. Contbr. numerous articles to profl. jours.; patentee in field; developer first high density hot pressed ferrite magnetic recording head. Dir., treas. H.M. Owners Assoc., Thousand Oaks, Calif., 1991—; supr. Work Experience Supervision Program, Orange Coast Coll., 1981. Sgt. Israel Army. Mem. IEEE, Am. Mgmt. Assn., Nat. Assn. Corp. Dirs. Republican. Jewish. Office: A Levy & Assocs PO Box 2074 CVS Thousand Oaks CA 91358

LEVY, BARBARA SUSAN, obstetrician/gynecologist; b. Phila., Sept. 29, 1953; d. Hans Ferdinand and Dolores (Harvey) L.; m. George Gilbert Johnston, Sept. 13, 1981; children: Shannon Johnston, Lily Johnston. AB in Psychology magna cum laude, Princeton U., 1974; MD, U. Calif. San Diego, 1979. Diplomate Am. Bd. Ob-Gyn. Intern, then resident in ob-gyn. Oreg. Health Scis. U., Portland, 1979-80; pvt. practice Seattle, 1984—; cons. ob-gyn. devices panel FDA, 1988—; chair dept. ob-gyn. St. Francis Community Hosp., 1990-92, quality assurance com., 1991-93; clin. asst. prof. ob-gyn. sch. medicine U. Wash. Contbr. articles to profl. jours. Dir. local br. Am. Cancer Soc., pres. 1990-92. Fellow Am. Coll. Obstetrics and Gynecology (jr., chair Wash. sect., dist. VIII 1984-85), Am. Coll. Surgeons; mem. AMA, Am. Assn. Gynecologic Laparoscopists (resident prize paper 1984, trustee 1986-88, sec., treas. 1992-93), Am. Fertility Soc. Office: 34509 9th Ave # 300 Federal Way WA 98003

LEVY, DAVID, lawyer, insurance company executive; b. Bridgeport, Conn., Aug. 3, 1932; s. Aaron and Rachel (Goldman) L. BS in Econs., U. Pa., 1954; JD, Yale U., 1957. Bar: Conn. 1958, U.S. Supreme Ct. 1963, D.C. 1964, Mass. 1965, N.Y. 1971, Pa. 1972; CPA, Conn. Acct. Arthur Andersen & Co., N.Y.C., 1957-59; sole practice Bridgeport, 1959-60; specialist tax law IRS, Washington, 1960-64; counsel State Mut. Life Ins. Co., Worcester, Mass., 1964-70; assoc. gen. counsel taxation Penn Mut. Life Ins. Co., Phila., 1971-81; sole practice Washington, 1982-87; v.p., tax counsel Pacific Mut. Life Ins. Co., Newport Beach, Calif., 1987—. Author: (with others) Life Insurance Company Tax Series, Bureau National Affairs Tax Management Income Tax, 1970-71. Mem. adv. bd. Tax Mgmt., Washington, 1975-90, Hartford Inst. on Ins. Taxation, 1990—; bd. dirs. Citizens Plan E Orgn., Worcester, 1966-70. With AUS, 1957. Mem. ABA (vice-chmn. employee benefits com. 1980-86, ins. cos. com. 1984-86, torts and ins. practice sect.), Assn. Life Ins. Counsel, AICPA, Beta Alpha Psi. Jewish.

LEVY, DAVID, broadcasting executive; b. Phila.; s. Benjamin and Lillian (Potash) L.; m. Lucile Alva Wilds, July 25, 1941 (div. 1970); children: Lance, Linda; m. Victoria Robertson, Apr. 23, 1987; 1 stepchild, Kate Jolson. BS in Econs., U. Pa., 1934, MBA, 1935. With Young & Rubicam, Inc., N.Y.C., 1938-59, v.p., assoc. dir. radio-TV dept.; v.p. charge network programs and talent NBC, N.Y.C., 1959-61; exec. producer Filmways, L.A., 1964-68, Goodson-Todman Prodns., West Coast, 1968-69; exec. v.p., dir. Golden Orange Broadcasting Co., Anaheim, Calif., 1969-88, bd. dirs.; exec. v.p. charge TV activities Four Star Internat., Inc., Beverly Hills, Calif., 1970-72; pres. Wilshire Prodns. Inc., Beverly Hills, 1972—; adviser Sandy Frank Cos., 1974-85; mem. faculty Calif. State U., Northridge, 1973-77; TV adviser Citizens for Eisenhower, 1952, 56, Haig for Pres., 1988; dir. radio and TV for Citizens for Eisenhower-Nixon, 1956; prod., writer 3-network program for closing Rep. campaign broadcast Four More Years; writer, co-producer closing program election eve Behalf of Wendell Willkie, 1940; cons. Sec. Treasury, 1944-46; chief radio sect. war fin. div. Treasury Dept. Exec. producer Double Life of Henry Phyffe, 1965; exec. producer, creator TV series Addams Family, 1964-66, The Pruitts of Southampton ABC-TV, 1966-67; producer world premier Sarge, also exec. producer, creator TV series Universal Studios NBC, 1971-72; creator Hollywood Screen Test, Bat Masterson, Appointment with Adventure, Outlaws, The Americans, Real West, The Kate Smith Daytime Hour, others; launched Father Knows Best, Godfrey's Talent Scouts, People's Choice, I Married Joan, Life of Riley, Dr. Kildare, Bonanza, Hitchcock Presents, Thriller, Saturday Night at the Movies, Walt Disney's Wonderful World of Color, Robert Taylor and The Detectives, The Deputy (starring Henry Fonda), Car 54, 1st Bob Newhart Show, 1st Phil Silver's Show, Goodyear TV Playhouse, Peter Pan (starring Mary Martin), What's My Line, Make the Connection, Say When, others; producer Paramount TV, 1972-73, Hanna Barbera Prodns. NBC, 1973-74; creative cons. The Addams Family, Name That Tune, Ralph Edwards Prodns., 1974-81, new series You Asked for It; TV cons. Mark Goodson Prodns., 1989—; co-creator, exec. producer Face the Music TV series, 1980-81; author: (novels) The Chameleons, 1964, The Network Jungle, 1976, The Gods of Foxcroft, 1970, Potomac Jungle, 1990; contbr. short stories to popular mags. Served as lt. USNR, 1944-46. Recipient Treasury medal and disting. svc. citation U.S. Treasury Dept., 1946. Mem. ASCAP, TV Acad., Writers Guild Am., Producers Guild Am. (sec., bd. dirs.), Hollywood Radio-TV Soc. (pres. 1969-70, citation 1970), Caucus for Producers, Writers and Dirs. (sec., steering com., exec. dir. 1974—, Disting. Svc. award 1985). Republican. Jewish. Office: 210 S Spalding Dr Beverly Hills CA 90212

LEVY, DAVID STEVEN, college administrator; b. L.A., Mar. 9, 1955; s. Henry and Gloria Grace (Barouh) L. BA, Occidental Coll., 1977; MA, 1979. Asst. dir. fin. aid Calif. State Coll., San Bernardino, 1978-79; fin. aid counselor Calif. State U.-Northridge, 1979-80; assoc. dir. student fin. aid Calif. State U.-Dominguez Hills, 1980-82; dir. fin. aid Occidental Coll., L.A., 1982-88; dir. fin. aid Calif. Inst. Tech., Pasadena, Calif., 1988—, assoc. dean of students, 1991—; mem. Title IA Adv. Com. Calif., 1977—; negotiator U.S. Dept Edn. Mem. life-long learning com. Calif. Postsecondary Edn. Commn., 1980—, mem. student fin. aid issues com., 1984—. Recipient Pres. award CASFAA, 1986, Meritorious Achievement award NASFAA, 1988, Disting. Svc. award WASFAA, 1990, Creative Leadership award CASFAA, 1990, Segmental Leadership award CASFAA, 1992, Pres. Disting. Svc. award WASFAA, 1992; Richter fellow Princeton U., 1976; Calif. State U. adminstrv. fellow, 1981—. Mem. Nat. Assn. Student Fin. Aid. Adminstrs. (bd. dirs. 1991—), Mortar Board Alumni Assn. (pres. 1977—), Calif. Assn. Student Fin. Aid Adminstrs. (ind. segmental rep. 1984, sec. 1985, treas. 1986-88), Western Assn. Student Fin. Aid Adminstrs., Nat. Assn. Student Fin. Aid Adminstrs., Phi Beta Kappa, Delta Phi Epsilon, Psi Chi, Phi Alpha Theta, Sigma Alpha Epsilon. Jewish. Co-editor Calif. Student Aid Commn. Student Aid Workbook, 1977—. Home: 41 Northwoods Ln La Crescenta CA 91214-4312 Office: CalTech 515 S Wilson Ave Pasadena CA 91125-0001

LEVY, DELORES JANE, artist; b. Superior, Wis., Nov. 15, 1928; d. Henry George and Emma (Guthmiller) Gross; m. Donald Jerome Levy, Apr. 14, 1953; children: Jane, Nancy, Kenneth, Laura. BS, Wis. State U., 1949; postgrad., Art Inst. Chgo., 1950. Tchr. Abner Baker Elem. Sch., Ft. Morgan, Colo., 1949-50; teller Bank Am., L.A., 1950-51; tchr. Lodi (Calif.) High Sch., 1951-54, 77-82, chmn. creative arts dept., 1978-79; instr. art San Joaquin Delta Evening Coll., Stockton, Calif., 1972-78; art reviewer Stockton Record, 1980-82; portrait artist state and county fairs, festivals, cruise ships Island Princess and Stardancer. Represented in permanent collections San Joaquin County Mus., Lodi Meml. Hosp.; continuous group exhibitions include Lodi (Calif.) Art Ctr.; commd. portraits include Comdr. Dorance Ochs, USN; numerous pvt. collections. Past pres. Lodi Art Ctr. Mem. Nat. League Am. Pen Women, Nat. Mus. Women in Arts (charter), San Joaquin County Hist. Mus. Home and Studio: 128 S Fairmont Ave Lodi CA 95240

LEVY, DOROTHEA YVETTE, therapist; b. Long Beach, Calif., Aug. 4, 1948; d. Christopher Columbus Wyatt and Dorothy Leah (Cyr) Doyle; children: Deems D., Robert K., Nisha Diane; m. Barry Tonnis Levy, Mar. 14, 1990. AA in Theatre Arts, Long Beach City Coll., 1980; BA in Dance, Calif. State U., Long Beach, 1985; MA in Dance/ Movement Therapy, UCLA, 1991; postgrad., USIU, 1990—. Registered dance/movement therapist, Calif. Intern dance/movement Met. State Hosp., Norwalk, Calif., 1986-87; dance/movement for battered women YWCA, Long Beach, Calif., 1987-88; dance/movement Royale TRC, Santa Ana, Calif., 1988, Charter Hosp., Long Beach, Calif., 1988-89; ind. cons. dance/movement Long Beach, Calif., 1989—; staff cons. Barbara Sinatra Children's Ctr., Eisenhower Meml. Hosp., Rancho Mirage, Calif., 1992—; instr. Cypress (Calif.) Coll., 1991—, Calif. State U., Long Beach, spring 1992—; owner, cons. Mindset Ednl. Systems, Anaheim, Calif., 1991—; dance, movement and instr. Annenberg Ctr. Eisenhower Meml., Rancho Mirage, Calif., 1991—; therapist dance, movement Bellwood Hosp., Bellflower, Calif., 1989—; cons. ednl. Expressive Psychotherapy Assocs., Lakewood, Calif., 1988—; mem. summer faculty Saddleback Coll. Eating Disorders Program, Calif., 1991, 92. Participant (dance performance) Certificate of Artistry, 1974; choreographer Jesus Christ Superstar, 1975 (Best Choregraphy award 1975), dancer, 1975; author rehearsal, performance protocal, 1985. Vol. dance, movement abused children Sarah Ctr., Long Beach, 1987. Fulbright-Hays fellow, 1985-86. Mem. NOW, AAUW, Am. Dance Therapy Assn., Am. Civil Liberties Union. Democrat. Office: Mindset Ednl Systems # 10 5150 Candlewood Lakewood CA 90712

LEVY, EUGENE HOWARD, planetary sciences educator, researcher; b. N.Y.C., May 6, 1944; s. Isaac Philip and Anita Harriet (Guttman) L.; m. Margaret Lyle Rader, Oct. 13, 1967; children: Roger P., Jonathan S., Benjamin H. AB in Physics with high honors, Rutgers U., 1966; PhD in Physics, U. Chgo., 1971. Teaching asst. dept. physics U. Chgo., 1966-69, rsch. asst. Enrico Fermi Inst., 1969-71; postdoctoral fellow dept. physics and astronomy U. Md., 1971-73; asst. prof. physics and astrophysics Bartol Rsch. Found., Franklin Inst., Swarthmore, Pa., 1973-75; asst., then assoc. prof. U. Ariz., Tucson, 1975-83, prof. planetary scis., 1983—, mem. faculty applied math. program, 1981—, head dept. planetary scis., dir. lunar and planetary lab., 1983—, mem. theoretical astrophysics program, 1985—, dir. NASA-Ariz. Spacegrant Coll. Consortium, 1989—; mem. com. on planetary and lunar exploration of space sci. bd., Nat. Acad. Scis., 1976-79, chmn., 1979-82, co-chair Space Sci. Bd. Study on Exploration Primitive Solar-System Bodies, 1978, mem. Space Sci. Bd., 1979-82, head U.S. del., co-chair Nat. Acad. Scis.-European Sci. Found. Joint Working Group on Cooperation in Planetary Exploration, 1982-84, mem. steering group com. on major directions for space sci. 1995-2015, 1984-86, chair adv. com. on internat. cooperation for Mars sample return, 1986-88; mem. Comet Halley Sci. Working Group, NASA, 1977, mem. spacelab phys. sci. rev. panel space sci. steering com., 1979, mem. rev. panel on origin plasmas in Earth's neighborhood, 1980, mem. solar system exploration com. of Adv. Coun., 1980-83, mem. Ames Rsch. Ctr. Planetary Detection Study, 1983, Solar System Exploration Mgmt. Coun., 1983-87, mem. com. on future space-sta. sci. projects, 1985, mem. Space Sta. Sci. Users' Working Group, 1985-86, Space and Earth Sci. Adv. Com., 1985-88, chair Comet Rendevous and Asteroid Flyby Rev. Panel, 1986, mem. Mars Exploration Strategy Adv. Group, 1986, Mars Rover Sample Return Sci. Working Group, 1987—; sci. cons. Rockwell Internat. Corp., 1980; mem. COSPAR Internat. Tech. Panel on Comets, 1980-82; U.S.-NASA del. to discussions on internat. cooperation investigations of Comet Halley, Padua, Italy, 1981, to U.S.-USSR Joint Working Group on Near-Earth Space, the Moon and Planets, 1981; mem. program adv. bd. Internat. Conf. on Cometary Exploration, Budapest, Hungary, 1982; mem. exec. com. univs.' space sci. working group Assn. Am. Univs., 1982-86; study panel U.S.-Soviet cooperation in space sci. U.S. Cong. Office of Tech. Assessment, 1984; chair planetary exploration panel Pacific Rim Nations Internat. Space Yr. Conf., Kona, Hawaii, 1987; mem. working group planetary systems sci. NASA, 1988—, rev. panel lunar and planetary, 1988-90, rev. panel origins solar systems programs, 1990-91; mem. astronomy and astrophysics survey com., sci. opportunities panel NAS, 1989-90; mem. study panel on robotic exploration of Moon and Mars, U.S. Cong. Office Tech. Assessment, 1991; chmn. coun. of instns., bd. dirs. U.S. Space Rsch. Assn., 1991—; cons. and lectr. in field. Editor: Protostars and Planets III, 1993; contbr.,author articles for gen. pub., adv. reports for Congl. Record, abstracts, book reviews, others. Recipient Disting. Pub. Svc. medal NASA, 1983, Alexander von Humboldt-Stiftung Sr. Scientist award Fed. Republic Germany, 1989; Disting. vis. scientist Jet Propulsion Lab., Calif. Inst. Tech., 1985-91; NASA predoctoral fellow U. Chgo., 1966-69, fellow Ctr. for Theoretical Physics, U. Md., 1971-73; rsch. grantee NASA, NSF. Mem. AAAS, Am. Astron. Soc., Am. Geophys. Union, Am. Phys. Soc., Internat. Astron. Union, Univs. Space Rsch. Assn. (bd. dirs. 1991—), Coun. Instns. (pres.), Phi Beta Kappa, Sigma Xi. Home: 5442 E Burns St Tucson AZ 85711-3126 Office: U Ariz Lunar and Planetary Lab Tucson AZ 85721

LEVY, JANE, librarian; b. Chgo., Jan. 31, 1945; d. Robert William and Betty (Amos) Van Brunt; m. Neil Martin Levy, Oct. 19, 1969; children: Ariel, Shoshana, Amos. BA, U. Calif., Berkeley, 1967, MLS, 1968. Libr./archivist John Steinbeck Libr., Salinas, Calif., 1970-71, Soc. Calif. Pioneers, San Francisco, 1972-73; libr. Blumenthal Rare Book and Manuscript Libr., Berkeley, 1980—. Co-author (catalog) The Jewish Illustrated Book (Builders Book award 1987); contbr. articles to profl. jours. Mem. Am. Mus. Assn., Soc. Am. Archivist, Assn. Jewish Librs., Soc. Calif. Archivist, Latin Am. Jewish Studies Assn. Office: Magnes Mus 2911 Russell St Berkeley CA 94705-2333

LEVY, JAY ROBERT, construction executive, property manager; b. Denver, Aug. 23, 1936; s. Mandell Nathan and Gertrude Sylvia (Mastrosky) L.; m. Harriet Bernice Shaiman, Sept. 5, 1939; children: Mindy Sue, Laurie Ann. BS-BA Bldg. Industry, Real Estate, U. Denver, 1958. Pres. Hallmark Industries, Denver, 1963-69, Cellular Corp. Colo., Denver, 1969-75, Concrete Placers, Denver, 1969-75, J&B Bldg. Co., Denver, 1972—. Bd. dirs. recovery unit Alcohol Unit and Drug Addictions, Rocky Mountain Hosp., Denver, 1983-88; bd. dirs. Yeshiva Toras Chaim, Denver, 1984-86, honor award, 1987; bd. dirs. Jewish Community Ctr., Denver, 1989-91. Recipient honor award Women's Am. ORT, 1989. Office: J&B Bldg Co 8933 E Union Ave # 216 Englewood CO 80111

LEVY, JOSEPH VICTOR, physiology and pharmacology educator; b. L.A., Apr. 7, 1928; s. Victor Marcus and Rachel Lea (Alhadeff) L.; m. Joanne Bernice Presley, Dec. 18, 1954; children: Virginia Rachel, Suzanne Joyce Levy Garrett. BA, Stanford U., 1950; MS, UCLA, 1956; PhD, U. Wash., 1959. Rsch. asst. in pharmacology Stanford (Calif.) U., 1954-56; rsch. asst., NIH predoctoral rsch. fellow U. Wash., Seattle, 1956-58, rsch. fellow in anesthesiology, 1958-59, Am. Heart Assn. advanced rsch. fellow, 1959-60; mem. affiliated staff Calif. Pacific Med. Ctr., San Francisco, 1960—; clin. assoc. prof. physiology and pharmacology U. Pacific, San Francisco, 1972-84, clin. prof., 1985—, prof., chmn. dept. physiology and pharmacology, 1991—; lectr. over 300 confs. and symposia; mem. hypertension task force NIH, 1976-77; mem. rsch. com. Calif. Heart Assn., 1975-77; mem. expert adv. panel on geriatrics U.S. Pharmacopeia, 1985—; mem. hypertension com. San Francisco Heart Assn., 1975-77. Co-author: Vitamins: Their Use and Abuse, 1976; mem. editorial bd. Clin. and Exptl. Hypertension, 1979-82; contbr. over 120 articles to sci. jours., chpt. to books, monographs, proc., handbooks. Recipient rsch. career devel. award Nat. Heart Inst., NIH, 1965-70; scholar Stanford U., 1954-55; rsch. travel fellow Internat. Union Physiol. Scis., 1961, 65, 71, 77, Internat. Union Pharmacol. Scis., 1969, 75, 78, 84. Mem. Am. Soc. Pharmacology and Exptl. Biology and Medicine (editorial bd. Proc. 1980-86), Am. Chem. Soc., Western Pharmacology Soc., Am. Heart Assn. (coun. on basic rsch.), Am. Pharm. Assn. (interactions task force panel 1973-85), Am. Physiol. Soc., Am. Soc. Clin. Pharmacology Therapy, U.S. Pharmacopeia (expert adv. panel on geriatrics). Office: U Pacific 2155 Webster St San Francisco CA 94115-2399

LEVY, LOUIS, chess master; b. N.Y.C., Feb. 10, 1921; s. Victor and Sarah (Caffina) L.; m. Gloria Alice Cressy, Jan. 21, 1972. B.S., N.Y. U., 1941. Engaged in car washing business, 1947-66, chess and bridge player, 1939—; Bd. dirs. N.J. Bridge League, 1969-73. Served with USAAF, 1942-46. Named U.S. Internat. Master Am. Contract Bridge League, 1972. Mem. Marshall, Manhattan chess clubs, Am. Contract Bridge League. Address: 12317 Ridge Circle Los Angeles CA 90049

LEVY, PENELOPE ANN, cultural and business association administrator; b. LaGrange, Ga., Dec. 31, 1942; d. Paul Taylor and Rosalie (Gilpin) Poage; m. Noel J.R. Levy, Feb. 18, 1960; children: John, Monica, Robert. BS in Econs. magna cum laude, Ariz. State U., 1984. Cert. lawyer's asst. Office mgr. Levy Law Offices, Phoenix, 1976-83; gov.'s intern Gov. of Ariz., Phoenix, 1983-84; internat. trad adminstr. State of Ariz., Phoenix, 1984-85; chief exec. officer, pres. Levy Internat. Cons. Svcs., Tempe, Ariz., 1985—; exec. dir. Japan-Am. Soc., Phoenix, 1989—. Contbr. articles to profl. jours. Mem. Ariz.-Mex. Commn., 1984—; bd. dirs. Ariz. World Trade Assn., 1984-88. Mem. Ariz. State Bar Assn. (assoc., environ. law sect.), Ariz. State U. Coll. Liberal Arts Alumni Assn. (bd. dirs. 1989—), Phi Beta Kappa Alumni Assn. (bd. dirs. 1987—, Disting. Svc. award 1989). Republican. Roman Catholic. Home: 542 E Erie Dr Tempe AZ 85282-3713

LEVY, SHEILA ELLEN, catering company executive; b. Cleve., Mar. 18, 1941; d. Samuel Lewis and Freda F. (Rubin) Rubenstein; children: Adam, Meredith. Student, Ohio State U., 1964. Pres. PMC, Cleve., 1966-80; sales exec. Park Ave. Caterers, Orange, Calif., 1980-85; pres. Very Spl. Occasions, Tustin, Calif., 1985—; cons. Party Planners Internat., Cleve., 1970-75. Mem. NAPE, NASE, Tustin City. Office: Very Spl Occasions 2640 Walnut Ave # I Tustin CA 92680-7035

LEW, RONALD S. W., federal judge; b. L.A., 1941; m. Mamie Wong; 4 children. BA in Polit. Sci., Loyola U., L.A., 1964; JD, Southwestern U., 1971. Bar: Calif. 1972. Dep. city atty. L.A. City Atty's. Office, 1972-74; ptnr. Avans & Lew, L.A., 1974-82; commr. fire and police pension City of L.A., 1976-82; mcpl. ct. judge County of L.A., 1982-84, superior ct. judge, 1984-87; judge U.S. Dist. Ct. (cen. dist.) Calif., L.A., 1987—; Bar: Calif. 1971. Mem. World Affairs Council of L.A., 1976—, Christian Businessmen's Com. of L.A., 1982—. 1st lt. U.S. Army, 1967-69. Recipient Vol. award United Way of L.A., 1979, cert. of merit L.A. Human Relations Commn., 1977, 82. Mem. Am. Judicature Soc., Calif. Assn. of Judges, So. Calif. Chinese Lawyer's Assn. (charter mem. 1976, pres. 1979), Chinese Am. Citizens Alliance, San Fernando Valley Chinese Cultural Assn., Delta Theta Phi. Office: US Dist Ct 312 N Spring St Los Angeles CA 90012-4701

LEWEY, SCOT MICHAEL, gastroenterologist; b. Kansas City, Mo., Sept. 10, 1958; s. Hugh Gene and Janice Vivian (Arnold) L.; m. Julie Ann Williams, July 17, 1982; children: Joshua Michael, Aaron Scot, Rachel Anne. BA in Chemistry, William Jewell Coll., 1980; DO, U. Health Scis., 1984. Resident internal medicine and pediatrics William Beaumont Army Med. Ctr., El Paso, Tex., 1985-89; asst. chief pediatric svc. Irwin Army Hosp., Ft. Riley, Kans., 1989-90; asst. chief dept. medicine Irwin Army Hosp., Ft. Riley, 1990, chief emergency med. svcs., 1990; comdr. F co. 701st support bn. 1st inf. Operation Desert Shield Operation Desert Storm U.S. Army, Saudi Arabia, 1990-91; chief dept. pediatrics Munson Army Hosp., Ft. Leavenworth, Kans., 1991-92, chief dept. medicine, 1992-93; fellow gastroenterology svc. Fitzsimons Army Med. Ctr., Aurora, Colo., 1993—. Named Outstanding Young Man Am., 1982; decorated Bronze Star. Fellow ACP, Am. Acad. Pediatrics; mem. AMA (physician recognition award), Am. Osteo. Assn., Am. Soc. Internal Medicine, Assn. Mil. Osteo. Physicians and Surgeons. Republican. Mem. Christian Ch. Office: Fitzsimons Army Med Ctr Gastroenterology Dept Medicine Aurora CO 80045-5001

LEWIN, RALPH ARNOLD, biologist; b. London, Apr. 30, 1921; came to U.S., 1947; s. Maurice and Ethel Lewin; m. Joyce Mary Chismore, June, 1950 (div. 1965); m. Cheng Lanna, June 3, 1969. BA, Cambridge U., Eng., 1942, MA, 1946; PhD, Yale U., 1950; ScD, Cambridge U., Eng., 1973. Instr. Yale U., New Haven, Conn., 1951-52; sci. officer Nat. Research Council, Halifax, N.S., Can., 1952-55; ind. investigator NIH, Woods Hole, Mass., 1956-59; assoc. prof., now prof. U. Calif., La Jolla, 1960—. Editor: Physiology and Biochemistry of Algae, 1962, Genetics of Algae, 1976, Biology of Algae, 1979, Biology of Women, 1981, Origins of Plastids, 1993; coeditor: Prochloron, a microbial enigma, 1989; transl. Winnie-La-Pu (Esperanto), 1972, La Dektri Horlogoj, 1993. Served with British Army, 1943-46. Mem. Phycological Soc. Am. (pres. 1970-71, Darbaker prize 1963). Home: 8481 Paseo Del Ocaso La Jolla CA 92037-3024 Office: U Calif San Diego Scripps Inst Oceanography 0202 La Jolla CA 92093

LEWIS, ALAIN ALEXANDER, mathematics educator; b. Washington, Aug. 15, 1947; s. Albert Oscar and Bernice Louise (Hammond) L.; m. Christine Sun, Mar. 22, 1984 (div. Apr. 1989); 1 child, Michael Anil. PhD, Harvard U., 1979. Assoc. mathematician RAND Corp., Santa Monica, Calif., 1979-82; assoc. prof. Cornell U., Ithaca, N.Y., 1983-87, U. Calif., Irvine, 1987—; vis. lectr. U. Singapore, 1981-83; vis. prof. U. Ill., Urbana, 1984-85. Contbr. articles to profl. jours. Rsch. grantee NSF, 1984-86. Home: 69 Schubert Ct Irvine CA 92715 Office: U Calif Sch of Social Sciences Irvine CA 92717

LEWIS, ALVIN EDWARD, pathology educator; b. N.Y.C., Nov. 21, 1916; s. Herman and Libbie (Levy) L.; m. Oct. 23, 1943, (widowed 1974); children: Joan, Elizabeth; m. July, 1, 1976. BA, U. Calif. L.A., 1938; MA, Stanford U., 1939, MD, 1944. Chief, pathology sect, atomic energy project UCLA, 1949-53; dir. clin. labs. Mount Zion Hosp., San Francisco, 1953-66; pathology prof. Mich. State U., East Lansing, 1966-72; pathology prof., chmn. U. S. Ala., Mobile, 1972-74; pathology prof. U. Calif., Davis, 1974-87, prof. emeritus, 1987—; rev. com. mem. Nat. Libr. Medicine, Bethesda, Md., 1972-75, med. quality rev. com. Dist. 3, Sonoma, Calif., 1989—. Author: Biostatistics, 1966, 1984 (2d ed.), Principles of Hematology, 1970. Lt. (j.g.) USNR, 1945-46. Fellow Coll. Am. Pathologists; mem. Am. Physiol. Soc. Republican. Jewish. Home: 21 Woodgreen St Santa Rosa CA 95409-5921

LEWIS, BARRY MAX, probation officer; b. Oklahoma City, Okla., June 8, 1951; s. Warren C. and Lucille (Griffith) L.; m. Gayle Boettcher, Apr. 1974 (div. 1982); m. Kathleen Mack, Jan. 22, 1983; children: Geoffrey, Caitlin (twins), Matthew. BS, Okla. State U., 1973; MA, Sam Houston State U., 1978; postgrad., U. So. Calif., 1982. Cert. P.O.S.T.; cert. tchr. Calif. Correctional officer Tex. Dept. of Corrections, Huntsville, 1974-75; instr. North Harris County Coll., Houston, 1976-77; dep. sheriff Harris County Sheriff's Dept., Humble, Tex., 1975-78; dist. parole officer Tex. State Bd. of Pardons and Paroles, Houston, 1978-82; dep. probabion officer Corrections Svc. Agy., Ventura, Calif., 1984—. Pres. Adv. Com. for Occupational Investigation, Kingwood, Tex., 1975-80; active United Meth. Ch., Ventura, Calif., 1982—. Mem. Lions Club. Democrat. Home: 247 Bayview Ave Ventura CA 93003 Office: Corrections Svc Agy 1400 Vanguard Dr Oxnard CA 93033

LEWIS, BRENT RENAULT, computer company executive, restaurateur; b. Mpls., May 23, 1958; s. Willard Russell Lewis and Reatha (Landon) Kay Lewis. Student, Brown Inst., 1978. Computer operator Northwestern Hosp., Mpls., 1977-78; programmer, supr. Dakota County, Mendota Heights, Minn., 1979-81; pres. Renault Sound Video, Mpls., 1981-85; system analyst Compucare, Inc., Mpls., 1981-84; mgr. data processing Golden Valley (Minn.) Health Ctr., 1985-86; pres., bd. dirs. Integration Plus, Scottsdale, Ariz., 1986—. Mem. Ariz. Coun. Black Engrs., Data Processing Mgmt. Assn. Office: Integration Plus 5016 Alta Dr Ste 1 Las Vegas NV 89107-3927 Office: Nina l'Italiana Ristorante 3625 East Bell Rd # 5 Phoenix AZ 85032

LEWIS, CRAIG GRAHAM DAVID, public relations executive; b. Dearborn, Mich., Jan. 25, 1930; s. Floyd B. and Elizabeth (Hickey) L. AB, UCLA, 1951; m. Karen Kerns, Oct. 23, 1954; children: Mark, Kern, Arden, Robin. Corr., McGraw-Hill, Inc., Washington, 1952-56; bur. mgr. Aviation Week mag., Dallas, 1957-59, Washington news editor, 1959-61; dept. dir. pub. affairs FAA, Washington, 1961-63; v.p. pub. rels. Air Transport Assn., Washington, 1963-64; dir. pub. rels. Martin Marietta Corp., N.Y.C., 1964-67; assoc. Earl Newsom & Co., N.Y.C., 1967—, dir., 1968—, pres., 1975—, chmn., 1982—; exec. v.p. Adams & Rinehart, Inc., N.Y.C., 1983—, vice chmn., 1986—; vice-chmn. Ogilvy Pub. Rels. Group, 1988—, Ogilvy Adams & Rinehart, 1992—. Mem. Aviation/Space Writers Assn., Am. Inst. Aero-Astro, Nat. Press Club. Home: PO Box 1052 Ojai CA 93024-1052 Office: Ogilvy Adams & Rinehart 6500 Wilshire Blvd Los Angeles CA 90048

LEWIS, DAVID HOWARD, nuclear medicine physician; b. Alexandria, Va., June 3, 1959; s. Frederick Roland and Frances Patricia (Urchak) L.; m. Mary Helen Mayer, Dec. 17, 1983; 1 child, Piper Elizabeth. BA, U. Va., 1981; MD, Med. Coll. Va., 1985. Diplomate Nat. Bd. Med. Examiners, Am. Bd. Internal Medicine, Am. Bd. Nuclear Medicine. Resident internal medicine U. Wash., Seattle, 1985-88, resident nuclear medicine, 1988-90; dir. nuclear medicine Harborview Med. Ctr., Seattle, 1990—; asst. prof. radiology U. Wash., Seattle, 1990—. Author: (epitome) SPECT of Myocardial Perfusion and Hepatic Blood Pool, 1990; author: (with others) Nuclear Medicine in Oraland Maxillofacial Surgery, 1990; contbr. abstracts to profl. jours. Named one of Outstanding Young Men of Am., Jaycees, Richmond, Va., 1984. Mem. Soc. Nuclear Medicine, Alpha Omega Alpha, Phi Beta Kappa, Phi Kappa Phi, Sigma Delta Pi.

LEWIS, DAVID HUGHES, systems engineer; b. Whittier, Calif., Mar. 11, 1950; s. David Hughes II and Marguerite Alberta (Chandler) L.; m. Nancy Lynne Dickson, July 28, 1979; children: Allison Chelsea, Whitney Erin. BS with honors, U. Calif., Berkeley, 1972; SM in Mech. Engring., MIT, 1974, PhD, 1978. Registered profl. engr., Calif. Sr. engr. Jet Propulsion Lab., Pasadena, Calif., 1977-80; sr. systems engr. TRW Space & Tech. Group, Redondo Beach, Calif., 1980—; lectr. Calif. Inst. Tech., Pasadena, 1987-88, Calif. State U., Long Beach, 1980-90, UCLA extension, 1991—. Contbr. numerous articles to profl. jours. Recipient spl. performance award FAA, 1970, 71, Eminent Engr. award Tau Beta Pi, 1986. Mem. AIAA, ASME, Sigma Xi.

LEWIS, EDWARD B., biology educator; b. Wilkes-Barre, Pa., May 20, 1918; s. Edward B. and Laura (Histed) L.; m. Pamela Harrah, Sept. 26, 1946; children: Hugh, Glenn (dec.), Keith. B.A., U. Minn., 1939; Ph.D., Calif. Inst. Tech., 1942; Phil.D., U. Umea, Sweden, 1982. Instr. biology Calif. Inst. Tech., Pasadena, 1946-48, asst. prof., 1949-56, prof., 1956-66, Thomas Hunt Morgan prof., 1966-88, prof. emeritus, 1988—; Rockefeller Found. fellow Sch. Botany, Cambridge U., Eng., 1948-49; mem. Nat. Adv. Com. Radiation, 1958-61; vis. prof. U. Copenhagen, 1975-76, 82; researcher in developmental genetics, somatic effects of radiation. Editor: Genetics and Evolution, 1961. Served to capt. USAAF, 1942-46. Recipient Gairdner Found. Internat. award, 1987, Wolf Found. prize in medicine, 1989, Rosenstiel award, 1990, Nat. medal of sci., 1990, Albert Lasker Basic Med. Rsch. award, 1991, Louisa Gross Horwitz prize, 1992. Fellow AAAS; mem. NAS, Genetics Soc. Am. (sec. 1962-64, pres. 1967-69, Thomas Hunt Morgan medal), Am. Acad. Arts and Scis., Royal Soc. (London) (fgn. mem.), Am. Philos. Soc., Genetical Soc. Great Britian (hon.). Home: 805 Winthrop Rd San Marino CA 91108-1709 Office: Calif Inst Tech Div Biology 1201 E California Blvd Pasadena CA 91125

LEWIS, EDWIN REYNOLDS, biomedical engineering educator; b. Los Angeles, July 14, 1934; s. Edwin McMurtry and Sally Newman (Reynolds) L.; m. Elizabeth Louise McLean, June 11, 1960; children: Edwin McLean, Sarah Elizabeth. AB in Biol. Sci., Stanford U., 1956, MSEE, 1957, Engr., 1959, PhD in Elec. Engring., 1962. With research staff Librascope div. Gen. Precision Inc., Glendale, Calif., 1961-67; mem. faculty dept. elec. engring. and computer sci. U. Calif., Berkeley, 1967—, dir. bioengring. tng. program, 1969-77, prof. elec. engring. and computer sci., 1971—, assoc. dean grad. div., 1977-82, assoc. dean interdisciplinary studies coll. engring., 1988—; chair joint program bioengring. U. Calif., Berkeley and San Francisco, 1988-91. Author: Network Models in Population Biology, 1977, (with others) Neural Modeling, 1977, The Vertebrate Inner Ear, 1985, also numerous articles. Grantee NSF, Nat. Aero. and Space Adminstrn. 1984, 87, Office Naval Rsch., 1990—; Neurosci. Rsch. Program fellow, 1966, 69; recipient Disting. Teaching Citation U. Calif., 1972; Jacob Javits neurosci. investigator, NIH, 1984-91. Fellow IEEE; mem. AAAS, Assn. Research in Otolaryngology, Acoustical Soc. Am., Soc. Neurosci., Sigma Xi. Club: Toastmasters (area lt. gov. 1966-67). Office: U Calif Dept Elec Engring & Computer Scis Berkeley CA 94720

LEWIS, FREDERICK THOMAS, insurance company executive; b. Tacoma, Apr. 1, 1941; s. Arthur Thomas and June Louise (Levenhagen) L.; m. Sarah Carolyn Boyette, Apr. 18, 1971; adopted children: Johanna, Elizabeth, Sarah, Jonathan, Matthew. Student, Concordia Coll., Portland, Oreg., 1959-61, Dominican Coll., San Rafael, Calif., 1967-71. Registered health underwriter. Enroute coord. Trans World Airlines, N.Y.C., 1961-62, 64-66; customer svc. rep. Trans World Airlines, Oakland, Calif., 1966-75; dist. rep. Aid Assn. for Luths., Twin Falls, Idaho, 1975-84, dist. mgr., 1984—. Vocalist Oakland Symphony Chorus, 1972-75; soloist Magic Valley Chorale, Twin Falls, 1979-83. Cantor Immanuel Luth. Ch., Twin Falls, 1984—; organizer Theos of Magic Valley, Filer, Idaho, 1984. Served with U.S. Army, 1962-64. Mem. Nat. Assn. Life Underwriters (tng. coun. fellow 1984, nat. quality award, nat. sales achievement award, health ins. quality award 1978—), So. Idaho Life Underwriters (pres. 1980-81, edn. chmn. 1984-86, nat. local com. mem. 1986-89), So. Idaho Health Underwriters (bd. dirs. 1986-88), Idaho State Assn. Life Underwriters (area v.p. 1988-89, sec. 1989-90, pres.-elect 1990-91, pres. 1991-92, Bill Rankin Life Underwriter of Yr. award 1993), Idaho Fraternal Congress (ins. counselor 1976, bd. dirs. 1976-85, pres. 1981-82), Lions (local v.p. 1979-81, pres. 1982-83, organizer women's aux. 1983, sec. 1986-87, 92-93, treas. 1993-94). Republican. Home: 1120 South View Dr Twin Falls ID 83301-9661 Office: Aid Assn for Luths 1120 S View Dr Twin Falls ID 83301-8163

LEWIS, GEORGE MCCORMICK, mathematics educator; b. L.A., Sept. 14, 1940; s. J.M. Sholl and Vee (McCormick) L.; m. Helen Sherrill Ames, July 5, 1964; children: Melanie, Heather, Alice Gray. AB, Stanford U., 1961; MA, U. So. Calif., 1964, PhD, 1970. Lectr. math. Calif. State U., Northridge, 1966-67; asst. prof. math. Calif. Poly. Sate U., San Luis Obispo, 1967-74; assoc. prof. math. Calif. Poly. Sate U., 1974-79, prof. math., 1979—. Mem. Calif. Faculty Assn. (del.), Am. Math. Soc., Math. Assn. Am., AAUP, ACLU. Office: Calif Poly State U Dept Mathematics San Luis Obispo CA 93407

LEWIS, GERALD JORGENSEN, judge; b. Perth Amboy, N.J., Sept. 9, 1933; s. Norman Francis and Blanche M. (Jorgensen) L.; m. Laura Susan McDonald, Dec. 15, 1973; children by previous marriage: Michael, Marc. AB magna cum laude, Tufts Coll., 1954; JD, Harvard U., 1957. Bar: D.C. 1957, N.J. 1961, Calif. 1962, U.S. Supreme Ct. 1968. Atty. Gen. Atomic, LaJolla, Calif., 1961-63; ptnr. Haskins, Lewis, Nugent & Newnham, San Diego, 1963-77; judge Mcpl. Ct., El Cajon, Calif., 1977-79; judge Superior Ct., San Diego, 1979-84; assoc. justice, Calif. Ct. of Appeal, San Diego, 1984-87; dir. Fisher Scientific Group, Inc., 1987—; Bolsa Chica Corp., 1991—; of counsel Latham & Watkins, 1987—; dir. Wheelabrator Techs., Inc., 1987—, Henley Mfg., Inc., 1987-89; adj. prof. evidence Western State U. Sch. Law, San Diego, 1977-85, exec. bd., 1977-89; faculty San Diego Inn of Ct., 1979—, Am. Inn of Ct., 1984—. Cons. editor: California Civil Jury Instructions, 1984. City atty. Del Mar, Calif., 1963-74, Coronado, Calif., 1972-77; counsel Comprehensive Planning Orgn., San Diego, 1972-73; trustee San Diego Mus. Art., 1986-89; bd. dirs. Air Pollution Control Dist., San Diego County, 1972-76. Served to lt. comdr. USNR, 1957-61. Named Trial Judge of Yr., San Diego Trial Lawyers Assn., 1984. Mem. Am. Judicature Soc., Soc. Inns of Ct. in Calif., La Jolla Wine and Food Soc., Confrerie des Chevaliers du Tastevin, Order of St. Hubert, Friendly Sons of St. Patrick. Republican. Episcopalian. Clubs: Bohemian; LaJolla Country (dir. 1980-83); Venice Island Hunt Club; Prophets. Home: 6505 Caminito Blythefield La Jolla CA 92037-5806 Office: Latham & Watkins 701 B St Ste 2100 San Diego CA 92101-8197

LEWIS, GORDON CARTER, auditor; b. Billings, Mont., June 14, 1960; s. Gene Eskil and Vanda (Carter) L. Student, U. Utah, 1978-79, 81-82; AA, LDS Bus. Coll., 1984; BBA, Nat. Coll., Denver, 1986. Market rsch. interviewer Colo. Market Rsch. Svcs. Inc., Denver, 1984-87, 93; mgmt. trainee Yellow Front Stores, Aurora, Colo., 1987; auditor, 1987—; computer office coord. US EPA, Denver, 1989-81. Ch. leadership, 1979—, bowling league officer. Mem. Assn. Govt. Accts., Am. Bowling Congress, Am. Philatelic Soc. Republican. Mem. LDS Ch.

LEWIS, GREGORY ALLEN, computer programmer and analyst, consultant; b. Ft. Morgan, Colo., Nov. 24, 1961; s. John Marion and Mary Loretta (Dorsey) L.; m. Tina Helena Hofer, Aug. 13, 1983; children: Daniel Gregory, Cynthia Grace, Sarah Ashley, Maria Bethany. BS, Regis Coll., Colorado Springs, Colo., 1989. Operator, jr. programmer Cen. Electric Co., Denver, 1983; tech. leader Logical Systems, Colorado Springs, 1983-86; sr. programmer, analyst Fed. Express Corp., Colorado Springs, 1986—; cons. Colorado Springs. Neurol. Assocs., 1986-88, Rose Rehab., Colorado Springs, 1987. Tchr. World Bible Sch., 1989—. Home: 3315 Glade Ct Colorado Springs CO 80918-4731

LEWIS, HILDA PRESENT, academic administrator, educator; b. Bridgeport, Conn., Mar. 28, 1925; d. Louis D. and Yetta (Elstein) Present; children: Daniel, David, Jonathan, Rachel. BA, U. Calif., Berkeley, 1948, MA, 1956, PhD, 1959. Cert. tchr., Calif. Lectr. Coll. of the Holy Names, Oakland, Calif., 1957-59, U. Calif., Berkeley, 1958-62; from asst. to full prof. San Francisco State U., 1962—, chair dept. elem. edn., 1987-90; researcher in the arts Inst. for the Devel. Ednl. Activities, L.A., 1973-76; rsch. assoc. Inst. Human Devel., U. Calif., Berkeley, 1976-78. Author: Child Art, 1966, Understanding Children's Art, 1973, Art for the Preprimary Child, 1972; editor: Art Education, 1987-90; contbr. numerous articles to profl. jours. NIMH fellow U. Calif., 1964. Fellow Nat. Art Edn. Assn. (disting.); mem. Am. Ednl. Rsch. Assn., U.S. Soc. for Edn. Through Art (v.p. 1983-84), Internat. Soc. for Edn. Through Art. Home: 17749 Chateau Ct Castro Valley CA 94552-1750 Office: San Francisco State U Dept Elementary Education 1600 Holloway Ave San Francisco CA 94132-1722

LEWIS, HILEL, vitreoretinal surgery educator, researcher; b. Mexico City, Aug. 7, 1956; came to U.S., 1982; s. Ignacio and Myriam (Szyfmanowicz) L.; m. Miriam Kershenovich, Aug. 11, 1979; children: Sharon, Ilana Aliza, Nurit Chana. MD, La Salle U., Mexico City, 1980. Diplomate Am. Bd. Ophthalmology. Fellow in vitreoretinal surgery Eye Inst. Med. Coll. Wis., Milw., 1986-87; fellow in med. retina Wilmer Inst., Johns Hopkins Med. Insts., Balt., 1987-88; intern, resident in ophthalmology Jules Stein Eye Inst., UCLA Sch. Medicine, L.A., 1982-86, asst. prof., 1988-92, assoc. prof., dir. Diabetes Eye Ctr., 1992-93; chmn. dept. ophthalmology Cleve. Clinic Found., 1993—. Contbr. numerous articles to med. jours. Grantee Fight for Sight, Inc., 1987-88; Charles Feldman scholar UCLA, 1988—.

LEWIS, JAMES BELIVEN, state government official; b. Roswell, N.Mex., Nov. 30, 1947; m. Armandie Johnson; children: Terri, James Jr., Shedra, LaRon. BS in Edn., Bishop Coll., 1970; MA in Pub. Adminstrn., U. N.Mex., 1977, BS in Bus. Adminstrn., 1981; chief staff cert., Duke U.; student minority leaders program, U. Va. Coord., counselor pub. svcs. careers program N.Mex. State Personnel Office, Albuquerque; adminstr. consumer affairs div., investigator white collar crime sect., then dir. purchasing div. Bernalillo County Dist. Atty.'s Office; adminstr., educator U. Albuquerque; county treas. Bernalillo County, 1982-85; state treas. State of N.Mex., 1985-90; chief of staff Gov. Bruce King, 1991—; mem. State Investment Coun., Coun. Govs. (policy advisor). Mem. adv. bd. Victims of Domestic Violence; past chmn. Dem. precincts and ward, Albuquerque; mem. N.Mex. State Bd. of Fin., Edn. Found. Bd., State Investment Coun., Oil and Gas Ad-Hoc Com., NAACP. With U.S. Army, 1970-72. Recipient Toll Fellowship Coun. State Govt., Lexington, Ky. Mem. Nat. State Treas.'s Assn. (v.p.), Western State Treas.'s Assn. (pres.), Western Gov.'s Assn. Staff Coun., Pub. Employees Retirement Assn., Edn. Retirement Assn., Mortgage Fin. Authority, N.Mex. Assn. of Counties (past pres. treas.'s affiliate), Nat. Assn. County Treas. and Fin. Officers (chmn. membership com., bd. dirs.), Am. Soc. for Pub. Adminstrn. (past treas. N.Mex. chpt., pres. 1989), Am. GI Forum, Am. Legion, Internat. Alumni Assn. Bishop Coll., Taylor Ranch Neighborhood Assn., Western State Treas.'s Assn. (pres.), Kiwanis, Masons, Omega Psi Phi (life), Alpha Beta Psi. Office: Office of Governor State Capitol State Capitol Bldg Santa Fe NM 87503

LEWIS, JANIE CAROL, tax preparer, accounting consultant; b. Hollandale, Miss., Mar. 20, 1957; d. Elijah Elbert and Josephine (Clay) Lewis. BBA, Delta State U., 1978. Data entry supr. II Hughes Aircraft Co., El Segundo, Calif., 1980-89; pvt. practice tax preparer Inglewood, Calif., 1989—; beauty cons. Aloette Cosmetics of Long Beach, Calif. Mem. Alpha Kappa Alpha (charter). Democrat. Mem. Pentecostal Ch. Home: 536 Evergreen St Apt 4 Inglewood CA 90302-1959

LEWIS, JASON ALVERT, JR., communications executive; b. Clarksville, Tex., Aug. 17, 1941; s. Jason Allen and Mary (Dinwiddie) L. Student, Stockton Coll., 1959-60, San Jose Jr. Coll., 1962-63. Field engr. telephone tech. Pacific Bell, San Francisco, 1983-84; systems technician AT&T, San Francisco, 1984—. Patentee in field. With U.S. Army, 1964-66. Mem. Cousteau Soc., Astron. Soc. Pacific, San Francisco Zool. Soc., Planetary Soc. Democrat. Home: 139 Pecks Ln South San Francisco CA 94080-1744

LEWIS, JEFFREY GEORGE, military officer; b. Medford, Oreg., Aug. 4, 1956; s. Fred Alton and Ruth (Hohwiesner) L. BS in Gen. Engring., BS in Naval Sci., Oreg. State U., 1978; MS in Systems Tech., Naval Postgrad. Sch., Monterey, Calif., 1986; degre in nuclear engring., Naval Nuclear Power Sch., Orlando, Fla., 1987. Registered profl. engr., Oreg. Comdr. USN, 1978-93; tng. officer, comdr. Naval Surface Force Atlantic Fleet, Norfolk, Va., 1978; damage control asst. USS Brisco (DD-977), Norfolk, Va., 1978; damage control asst. USS Harry W. Hill (DD-986), San Diego, 1979-81, elec. officer, 1980-81, navigator, 1981-82; exec. officer USS Gallant (MSO-489), San Francisco, 1982-84; ops. officer, combat systems officer USS Niagara Falls (AFS-3), Guam, 1988-89, Combat Logistics Squadron TWO, Leonardo, N.J., 1990-91; exec. officer USS Milwaukee (AOR-2), Norfolk, Va., 1991-93; ret., 1993; pres., CEO Lewis Tech., Inc., 1993—; panel mem. Chem. Engring. Product Rsch. and Evaluation Bd., N.Y.C., 1978-80; battle fleet navigator Comdr. Surface Combatant Force 7th Fleet Asian Pacific Ocean Ops., 1981; test and evaluation officer Undersea Systems div. GE, Syracuse, N.Y., 1985-86, Undersea Warfare br. Naval Surface Weapons Ctr., White Oak, Md., 1985-86; battle fleet logistics comdr. Comdr. Combat Logistics Support Force 7th Fleet Asian Pacific Ocean Ops., 1989; tactical devel. officer Naval Ocean Systems Ctr. San Diego, 1990, battle fleet logistics coord. Comdr. Strike Fleet Atlantic , 1990-91. Author: United States Navy: Its Challenge and Response, 1977, AN/SQQ-89(V) Surface Antisubmarime Warfare Combat System Handbook, 1986. Decorated 3 Navy Commendation medal; recipient Outstanding Acad. Achievement award Res. Officers Assn., 1978, Nat. Soc. Scabbard & Blade, 1978. Mem. NSPE (assoc.), Ops. Rsch. Soc. Am. Home: 2533 N Carson St Ste 560 Carson City NV 89706-0147

LEWIS, JERRY, congressman; b. Oct. 21, 1934. BA, UCLA, 1956. Former underwriter life ins. underwriter; field rep. for former U.S. Rep. Jerry Pettis; mem. Calif. State Assembly, 1968-78; vice chmn. rules com., chmn. subcom. on air quality; mem. 96th-103rd Congresses from 35th (now 40th) Calif. dist., 1979—; mem. appropriation com., ranking minority mem. Va.-HUD subcom., mem. defense subcom., select com. on intelligence. Presbyterian. Office: House of Representatives Washington DC 20515

LEWIS, JOHN CLARK, JR., manufacturing company executive; b. Livingston, Mont., Oct. 15, 1935; s. John Clark and Louise A. (Anderson) L.; m. Carolyn Jean Keesling, Sept. 4, 1960; children: Robert, Anne, James. BS, Fresno (Calif.) State U., 1957. With Service Bur. Corp., El Segundo, Calif., 1960-70, Computer Scis. Corp., 1970; with Xerox Corp., El Segundo, 1970-77, pres. bus. systems div., 1977; pres. Amdahl Corp., Sunnyvale, Calif., 1983-87, chief exec. officer, 1983—, chmn., 1987—. Served with USNR, 1957-60. Roman Catholic. Office: Amdahl Corp PO Box 3470 1250 E Arques Ave Sunnyvale CA 94086-4730*

LEWIS, JOHN GREGG, computer scientist; b. Chgo., Mar. 27, 1945; s. H. Gregg and Julia Catherine (Elliott) L.; m. Frances Irene Marcus, Aug. 31, 1968; children: Steven, David. AB, Harvard Coll., 1966; MA, U. Calif., Berkeley, 1968; PhD, Stanford (Calif.) U., 1977; postdoctoral, MIT, 1986-87. Dir. acad. computing Saint Olaf Coll., Northfield, Minn., 1968-71; asst. prof. John Hopkins U., Balt., 1976-78; math. Nat. Bur. of Standards, Gaithersburg, Md., 1977-78; computer scientist Boeing Computer Svcs., Seattle, 1978-86, 87-89, assoc. tech. fellow, 1990—; Boeing fellow MIT, Cambridge, 1986-87. Contbr. articles to profl. jours. IBM fellowship Stanford U., 1973-74; fellowship NSF, 1966-68; scholarships GM, Harvard, 1962-66. Mem. Assn. for Computing Machinery (newsletter editor Special

Interest Group on Numerical Math.), Soc. for Indsl. and Applied Math. (chair SIAM Activity Group on Linear Algebra 1992—, program dir. 1986-91). Office: Boeing Computer Svcs Mail Stop 7L-21 PO Box 24346 Seattle WA 98124-0346

LEWIS, JOHN OWEN, real estate developer; b. Quanah, Tex., Nov. 20, 1935; s. John O. and Charles Etta (Vestal) L.; m. Mary Jo McPherson, Oct. 22, 1959 (div.); children: John J., Jeanne M.; m. Ashley Wells, Sept. 20, 1985. BA in Econs., U. Calif., Santa Barbara, 1958. Salesman The Seeley Co., Los Angeles, 1959-70, v.p., ptnr., 1970-76; v.p. Cushman and Wakefield, Los Angeles, 1976-77, sr. v.p., 1977-78, exec. v.p., 1978-79; pres., owner The Lewis Co., Los Angeles, 1979-93; pres. The Lewis Co., Woodland Hills, Calif., 1992-93; pres. & dir. Real Estate Task Force. Served to lt. USN, 1959-64. Mem. Malibu Tennis Club. Office: 20969 Ventura Blvd Ste 216 Woodland Hills CA 91364-2349

LEWIS, JOHN S., JR., geochemist, educator; b. Trenton, N.J., June 27, 1941; s. John S. Sr. and Elsie (Vandenbergh) L.; m. Ruth Margaret Adams, Aug. 1, 1964; children: John V., Margaret Lewis Martell, Christopher F., Katherine R., Elizabeth A., Peter M. AB in Chemistry, Princeton U., 1962; MA in Inorganic Chemistry, Dartmouth Coll., 1964; PhD in Geochemistry and Phys. Chemistry, U. Calif., San Diego, 1968. Asst. prof. dept. chemistry, dept. earth and planetary sci. MIT, Cambridge, Mass., 1968-72, assoc. prof. dept. chemistry, dept. earth and planetary sci., 1972-79, prof. earth and planetary sci, 1979-82; prof. planetary sci. U. Ariz., Tucson, 1982—; co-dir. NASA/U. Ariz. Space Engring. Rsch. Ctr., Tucson, 1988—; vis. assoc. prof. geol. and planetary sci., Calif. Inst. Tech., Pasadena, 1974; bd. dirs. Am. Rocket Co., Camarillo, Calif., 1988—, ASPERA, Tucson, 1989—; advisor govtl. agys. Author: (with R. G. Prinn) Planets and Their Atmospheres: Origin and Evolution, 1984, (with Ruth A. Lewis) Space Resources: Breaking the Bonds of Earth, 1987; translator (with Ruth A. Lewis) books in the field; also articles. Recipient Exceptional Sci. Achievement medal, NASA, 1983. Mem. Am. Astron. Soc. (planetary sci. div., hon. lectr. 1974), Am. Geophys. Union (Macelwane award 1976). Republican. Mem. LDS Ch. Home: 5010 W Sweetwater Dr Tucson AZ 85745-9773 Office: U Ariz Lunar and Planetary Lab Tucson AZ 85721

LEWIS, JOHN THOMSON CONDELL, aerospace company executive; b. Castro Valley, Calif., Nov. 18, 1955; s. Ernest Edward John and Catherine Evangeline (Thomson) L. BA, U. Calif., Santa Barbara, 1977; MBA, Santa Clara U., 1980, MBA (Extended Edition), 1990. Systems analyst Gen. Electric Co., Sunnyvale, Calif., 1978-82; mem. tech. staff Applied Research, Inc., Santa Clara, Calif., 1982-83; co-founder, mng. ptnr. The Delphi Group, Fremont, Calif., 1982-83; aerospace planner Loral Space and Range Systems (formerly Ford Aerospace Corp), Sunnyvale, Calif., 1983—. Mem. Commonwealth Club of Calif. (program com. Contra Costa chpt.), World Affairs Coun. No. Calif. Republican. Presbyterian. Home: 7835 Cross Ridge Rd Dublin CA 94568-3710 Office: Loral Space and Range Systems 1260 Crossman Ave Sunnyvale CA 94089-1116

LEWIS, JOHN WILSON, political science educator; b. King County, Wash., Nov. 16, 1930; s. Albert Lloyd and Clara (Lewis) Seeman; m. Jacquelyn Clark, June 19, 1954; children: Cynthia, Stephen, Amy. Student, Deep Springs Coll., 1947-49; A.B. with highest honors, UCLA, 1953, M.A., 1958, Ph.D., 1962; hon. degree, Morningside Coll., 1969, Lawrence U., 1986. Asst. prof. govt. Cornell U., 1961-64, assoc. prof., 1964-68; prof. polit. sci. Stanford U., 1968—, William Haas prof. Chinese politics, 1972—, co-dir. arms control and disarmament program, 1971-83, co-dir. NE Asia U.S. Forum on Internat. Policy, 1980-90, co-dir. Ctr. for Internat. Security and Arms Control, 1983-91, sr. fellow, 1991—, dir. Project on Peace and Cooperation in the Asian-Pacific Region; chmn. Internat. Strategic Inst., 1983-89; chmn. joint com. on contemporary China Social Sci. Rsch. Coun.-Am. Coun. Learned Socs., 1976-79; former vice chmn. and bd. dirs. Nat. Com. on U.S.-China Relations; cons. Senate Select Com. on Intelligence, 1977-81, Lawrence Livermore Nat. Lab.; chmn. com. advanced study in China Com. Scholarly Communication with People's Republic of China, 1979-82; mem. com. on internat. security and arms control Nat. Acad. Scis., 1980-83; organizer first univ. discussion arms control and internat. security matters Chinese People's Inst. Fgn. Affairs, 1978, first academic exchange agreement Dem. People's Rep. of Korea, 1988; negotiator first univ. tng. and exchange agreement People's Rep. of China, 1978. Author: Leadership in Communist China, 1963, Major Doctrines of Communist China, 1964, Policy Networks and the Chinese Policy Process, 1986; co-author: The United States in Vietnam, 1967, Modernization by Design, 1969, China Builds the Bomb, 1988, Uncertain Partners: Stalin, Mao, and the Korean War, 1993; editor: The City in Communist China, 1971, Party Leadership and Revolutionary Power in China, 1970, Peasant Rebellion and Communist Revolution in Asia, 1974, Uncertain Partners: Stalin, Mao and the Korean War, 1993; contbr.: Congress and Arms Control, 1978, China's Quest for Independence, 1979, others.; mem. editorial bd.: Chinese Law and Govt, China Quar., Survey, The Pacific Rev. Served with USN, 1954-57. Mem. Assn. Asian Studies, Am. Polit. Sci. Assn., Coun. Fgn. Rels. Home: 541 San Juan St Palo Alto CA 94305-8432 Office: Stanford U 320 Galvez St Palo Alto CA 94305-6190

LEWIS, JOHNNYE LYNN, neuropharmacologist; b. Canton, Ohio, Dec. 16, 1948; d. John James and Kathryn Marie (Rukavina) L.; m. Verner S. Westerberg, Apr. 1, 1971. BA in Psychology, Miami U., Oxford, Ohio, 1970; MA in Physiol. Psychology, U. Victoria, B.C., Can., 1976; PhD in Pharmacology, U. Man., Can., 1989. Diplomate Am. Bd. Toxicology. Ind. cons. rsch. design and analysis Victoria, 1977-79; rsch. coord. dept. psychology U. Victoria, 1979-85; developer, coord., tchr. Dept. Women's Studies U. Man., 1987-88; post-doctoral fellow Lovelace Inhalation Toxicology Rsch. Inst., Albuquerque, 1989-92; adj. faculty U. N.Mex. Coll. Pharmacy, 1991—; staff scientist Inhalation Toxicology Rsch. Inst., 1992—; prin. scientist Roy F. Weston, Inc./Uranium Mill Tailings Remedial Action, 1992—; state coord. Expanding Your Horizons Conf., N.Mex., 1990-92; external reviewer toxicology study sect. NIH, Washington, 1990, Toxicology and Applied Pharmacology, San Diego., 1990—. Contbr. articles to profl. jours. Co-founder Canadian Art Deco Soc., Victoria, Can., 1984. U. Victoria fellow, 1973-76; grantee Can. Fed. Govt., 1977, Med. Rsch. Coun., Can., 1985-88, NIH 1992—. Mem. Soc. Toxicology, Assn. Chemoreception Scis., N.Y. Acad. Scis., N.Mex. Hazardous Waste Mgmt. Soc., N.Mex. Women's Found. (grant rev. com. 1990-92, grant writer 1990-92), N.Mex. Network Women in Sci. and Engring. (bd. dirs. 1990-92). Office: WESTON/UMTRA Albuquerque NM 87108

LEWIS, JOSEPH HENRY, retired oil executive; b. Bklyn., July 7, 1928; s. Joseph Victor and Mildred Elizabeth (Knaup) L. BME, Poly. Inst., Bklyn., 1948. Founder Lew-Bar Corp., Bklyn., 1945-50; plant engr. N.Y. Telephone Co., Bklyn., 1948-56; ptnr. J. D. Gratiot Co., L.A., 1956-57; supr. engring. dept. Chevron USA, La Habra, Calif., 1957-82; ret., 1982; mgr. Lewis Trust, Buena Park, Calif., 1982—; chief engr. radio/TV broadcast sta., N.Y. and Calif., 1949-70. Inventor in field. Capt. Signal Corps, U.S. Army, 1950-54. Mem. SAR. Republican. Roman Catholic. Office: PO Box 571 Buena Park CA 90621-0571

LEWIS, LINDON L., physicist; b. Abingdon, Ill., Oct. 13, 1950; s. Everett LeRoy and Norma Beth (Famulener) L.; m. Merilee Anne Schultheiss, May 20, 1972 (div. Aug. 1988); 1 child, Kenneth Edward. BA in Physics, Knox Coll., 1972; PhD in Physics, U. Wash., 1979. Staff cons. Ball Comm. Systems Div., Broomfield, Colo., 1984—. Contbr. articles to profl. publs., patentee in field. Mem. IEEE, AAAS, Am. Phys. Soc., Soc. Photo-optical Instrumentation Engrs. Office: Ball Comm Systems 10 Longs Peak Dr Broomfield CO 80038

LEWIS, MALCOLM, engineering and construction executive; b. Glendale, Calif., Feb. 6, 1946; s. Patton and Claire (Pauli) L.; m. Cynthia Carmelite Truitt, Sept. 1, 1984; children: Holly Carmelite, Geoffrey Patton. B.S. in Engring., Harvey Mudd Coll., 1967; D. Engring., Thayer Sch. Engring., Dartmouth Coll., 1971; Diploma in Housing, Bldg. and Planning, Bouwcentrum, Rotterdam, Netherlands, 1970. Registered profl. engr., Calif., Nev., Ariz., Wash., Colo. Mgr. engring. Levitt Bldg. Systems, Inc., Battle Creek, Mich., 1971-72; asst. to pres. Levitt Constrn. Systems, Inc., Fountain Valley, Calif., 1972-74, pres., 1974-76; pres. Malcolm Lewis Assocs. Engrs., Inc., Irvine, Calif., 1976-90; v.p. Robert Bein, William Frost & Assoc., Irvine, 1990—. Cons. Office State Architect, Sacramento, 1976-77, U.S. Dept. Energy, Washington, 1982—, Office Tech. Assessment, U.S. Congress, 1980. Contbr. articles to various publs. Trustee Harvey Mudd Coll., Claremont, Calif., 1974—; bd. overseers Thayer Sch. Engring., Dartmouth Coll., 1972-75; pres. Irvine Temporary Housing Inc., Irvine, 1984-88; bd. govs. Western Manufactured Housing Inst., 1974-76; pres. Industrialized Housing Council Calif., 1973-74. Lockheed Leadership scholar, 1963-67; NDEA Grad. fellow Dartmouth Coll., 1967-71. Mem. ASHRAE (mem. com. 90 1983-89), ASCE. Office: Robert Bein William Frost & Assoc 14725 Alton Pky Irvine CA 92718-2069

LEWIS, MARION ELIZABETH, social worker; b. Los Alamos, Calif., Dec. 7, 1920; d. James Henry and Carolina Sophia (Niemann) Eddy; m. William Ernest Lewis, May 30, 1943 (dec. Oct. 1954); children: Doris Lenita Lewis Terrill, Paul William. Student, Jr. Coll., Santa Maria, Calif., 1939-40, Bus. Coll., Santa Barbara, Calif., 1940-41, Alan Hancock Coll., 1958-61; BA in Sociology cum laude, Westminster Coll., Salt Lake City, 1964. Office clk. Met. Life Ins. Co., Santa Barbara, 1942-43; sales clk. Sprouse Reitz Co., Laguna Beach, Calif., 1943-44; office clk. U.S. Army, Santa Maria AFB, 1944-45; sch. crossing guard Calif. Hwy. Patrol, Los Alamos, 1956-58; office clk. Holaday Children's Ctr., Salt Lake City, 1964; social worker Sonoma County Social Svc., Santa Rosa, Calif., 1964-78, ret., 1978; sales rep. Avon Products, Los Alamos, 1957-61; sales clk. Gen. Store, Los Alamos, 1957-59; office clk. Sonoma County Pub. Health Dept., 1979-80. Deacon Presbyn. Ch., 1956—, moderator Presbyn. Women, 1990-91, vice moderator, 1989-90, sem. rep., 1978-80, 92—. Mem. AAUW, R.I. Geneal. Soc., Sonoma County Geneal. Soc. (hospitality com.), Calif. Automobile Assn., Nat Geographic Soc., Nat. Assn. Ret. Persons, Commonwealth Club Calif., Sequoia Club, Alpha Chi. Republican. Home: 61 Sequoia Cir Santa Rosa CA 95401-4992

LEWIS, MARK EARLDON, city manager; b. Boston, June 27, 1951; s Frederick Cole Lewis and Barbara (Forsyth) Corrigan; m. Kristine Mietzner, May 1, 1983; children: Anna Kristine, Benjamin Mark. BA, Washington State U., 1975. Adminstrv. asst. City and Borough of Juneau, Alaska, 1975-77; city mgr. City of Valdez, Alaska, 1978-82; commr. State of Alaska Dept. of Community and REgional Affairs, Juneau, 1982-83; dep. city mgr. City of South San Francisco, Calif., 1984-87, city mgr., 1987-88; city mgr. City of Monterey Park, Calif., 1988-91, City of Colton, Calif., 1991—. Dir. Monterey Park Boys' and Girls' Club, 1990; vice chmn. allocation team United Way, 1990, area group chmn. 1989-90; exec. com. mem. Calif., colo., Ariz. and Nev. Innovation Group, 1987. Home: 453 Charleston Dr Claremont CA 91711 Office: City of Colton 650 N La Cadena Dr Colton CA 92324-2823

LEWIS, MARY MOUNT, real estate broker; b. Mt. Kisco, N.Y., Dec. 22, 1921; d. William Hall and Mamie Henrietta (Heitzman) Mount; m. Bateman Earle Lewis, Aug. 8, 1941 (div. Dec. 1981); 1 child, Barry B. Cert. in real estate, Manatee Jr. Coll., Bradenton, Fla., 1973. Cert. residential specialist; cert. real estate broker-mgr., Fla. Sec. Reader's Digest Assn., Pleasantville, N.Y., 1948-61, Computer Usage, Mt. Kisco, 1961-62; exec. sec. Palmer Bank, Sarasota, Fla., 1967-68, Hansen Chris Craft, Sarasota, 1968, Bd. County Commrs., Sarasota, 1969, Maas Bros., Sarasota, 1974-77; realtor assoc. Strathmore Realty, Sarasota, 1978; pvt. practice as realtor, broker Sarasota, 1979-87; realtor A&D Edwards & Assocs Realty Inc., Sarasota, 1988—. Mem. Sarasota Choral Soc., Lacey Presbyn. Ch. Choir. Mem. Am. Bus. Women's Assn. (v.p., sec.), Women's Council Realtors (Realtor of Yr. 1982, pres. 1981), Sarasota Bd. Realtors (membership com.), Realtors Inst. (grad.). Republican. Office: Nat Bristol Properties 8621 Martin Way E Olympia WA 98516

LEWIS, MERRILL LAWRENCE, communications executive; b. Cleve., Feb. 14, 1948; s. Samuel David and Evelyne Paulette (Slor) L. BA in Bus., Calif. State U., Northridge, 1973. Sales mgr. Comml. Data Products, North Hollywood, Calif., 1976-84, Thrifty Bus. Systems, Culver City, Calif., 1984-85; pres. M.L. Communications, Marina Del Rey, Calif., 1985—. Mem. Assn. Diving Instrs. (internal open water diver 1984), Am. Water Ski Assn., Acad. Magical Arts, Tau Epsilon Phi (football capt. 1969-73). Republican. Jewish. Home: #309 13930 Northwest Passage Marina Del Rey CA 90292

LEWIS, NANCY PATRICIA, speech and language pathologist; b. Miami, Fla., Sept. 23, 1956; d. James and Sara (Gilman) L. BS, U. Fla., 1978; MS, U. Ariz., 1980. Postgrad. fellow U. Tex. Med. Br., Galveston, 1979-80, speech lang. pathologist, 1980-81; speech lang. pathologist Albuquerque Pub. Schs., 1982-84; child devel. specialist Albuquerque Spl. Presch., 1984—; pvt. practice speech-lang. pathology Albuquerque, 1985—; coord. Project Ta-kos, 1987—; artist Trash Warrior wearable art; speaker in field. Author (diagnostic procedure) Khan-Lewis Phonological Analysis, 1986; (therapeutic materials) Familiar Objects and Actions, 1985. Labor coord. Lama Found., San Cristobal, 1988, fundraiser, 1988-91, speech pathology cons., 1990—, bd. dirs., 1990—; bd. dirs. Vols. for the Outdoors, Albuquerque, 1984—. Fellow U. Tex. Med. Br., Galveston, 1981. Mem. Am. Speech Lang. and Hearing Assn., N.Mex. Speech Lang. and Hearing Assn. Democrat.

LEWIS, NORMAN, English language educator, writer; b. N.Y.C., Dec. 30, 1912; s. Herman and Deborah (Nevins) L.; m. Mary Goldstein, July 28, 1934; children—Margery, Debra. B.A., CUNY, 1939; M.A., Columbia U., 1941. Instr., lectr CUNY, N.Y.C., 1943-52; assoc. prof. English NYU, N.Y.C., 1955-64; instr. Compton Coll., Calif., summers 1962-64, UCLA, 1962-69; prof. English Rio Hondo Coll., Whittier, Calif., 1964-91, chmn. communications dept., 1964-75. Author: (with Wilfred Funk) Thirty Days to a More Powerful Vocabulary, 1942, rev. edit., 1970, Power with Words, 1943, How to Read Better and Faster, 1944, rev. edit., 1978, The Lewis English Refresher and Vocabulary Builder, 1945, Better English, 1948, Word Power Made Easy, 1949, rev. edit., 1978, The Rapid Vocabulary Builder, 1951, rev. edit., 1980, 3d edit., 1988, How to Get More Out of Your Reading, 1951, Twenty Days to Better Spelling, 1953, The New Roget's Thesaurus in Dictionary Form, 1961, rev. edit., 1978, Dictionary of Correct Spelling, 1962, Correct Spelling Made Easy, 1963, rev. edit. 1987, Dictionary of Modern Pronunciation, 1963, New Guide to Word Power, 1963, The New Power with Words, 1964, Thirty Days to Better English, 1964, The Modern Thesaurus of Synonyms, 1965, RSVP-Reading, Spelling, Vocabulary, Pronunciation, elem. texts, I-III, 1966, coll. edit., 1977, See, Say, and Write!, books I and II, 1973, Instant Spelling Power, 1976, R.S.V.P. for College English Power, book II, 1978, book III, 1979, R.S.V.P. with Etymology, book I, 1980, book II, 1981, book III, 1982, R.S.V.P. books I-III, rev. edits., 1982-83, books A-B, 1985-86, Instant Word Power, 1981, Dictionary of Good English, 1987; also numerous articles in nat. mags.

LEWIS, PAUL THOMAS, ultrasonic applications engineer, volunteer church growth consultant; b. Phoenix, Aug. 4, 1960; s. Basil Winthrop and Martha (Lou) L.; m. Paige Elaine Neese, Jan. 14, 1984; children: Joshua, Caleb. BA in Ch. Growth, Pacific Christian Coll., 1986, MA in Ministry, 1992. Cons. Southwest Tech., Fullerton, Calif., 1981-86; assoc. minister Havasu Christian Ch., Lake Havasu City, Ariz., 1986-88; v.p. Am. Prodn. Products, Anaheim, Calif., 1988-89; engr. DuPont NDT Instruments, Huntington Beach, Calif., 1989—; cons. various local churches, Calif. and Ariz., 1988—; mem. site coun. Tynes Elem. Sch., Placentia, Calif., 1991-92. Republican. Home: 3180 E Orangethorpe Ave Anaheim CA 92806

LEWIS, PHILLIP VERNON, management educator; b. Eastland, Tex., Mar. 27, 1942; s. Walter Vernon and Doris Mintie (Nelmns) L.; m. Marilyn Hermann, Dec. 14, 1963; children—P. Brook, Blair E. B.S., Abilene Christian Coll., 1964; M.A., U. Denver, 1966; Ed.D., U. Houston, 1970. Instr., No. Ariz. U., Flagstaff, 1966-68; prof. bus. communication Okla. State U., Stillwater, 1970-82; prof. mgmt., chmn. dept mgmt. scis., dean coll. bus. adminstrn., Abilene Christian U., Tex., 1982-92; dean sch. bus. & mgmt., Azusa Pacific U., L.A., 1992—; mgmt. trainee S & Q Clothiers, Abilene, 1961-64; teller 1st Nat. Bank, Westminster, Colo., 1965-66. Author: Organizational Communication, 1975, 2nd edit., 1980, 3rd edit., 1987; Managing Human Relations, 1983. Fellow The Assn. for Bus. Communications (pres. 1984); mem. Acad. Mgmt. Republican. Mem. Ch. of Christ. Home: 137 S Hacienda Ave Glendora CA 91740 Office: Azusa Pacific U 901 E Alosta Blvd Azusa CA 91702-7000

LEWIS, RALPH JAY, III, management and human resources educator; b. Balt., Sept. 25, 1942; s. Ralph Jay and Ruth Elizabeth (Schmeltz) L. BS in Engring., Northwestern U., 1966; MS in Adminstrn., U. Calif., Irvine, 1968; PhD in Mgmt., UCLA, 1974. Research analyst Chgo. Area Expressway Surveillance Project, 1963-64, Gen. Am. Transp. Co., Chgo., 1965-66; assoc. prof. mgmt. and human resources mgmt. Calif. State U., Long Beach, 1972—; cons. Rand Corp., Santa Monica, Calif., 1966-74, Air Can., Montreal, Que., 1972-73, Los Angeles Times, 1973;. Co-author: Studies in the Quality of LIfe, 1972; author instructional programs, monographs; co-designer freeway traffic control system. Bd. dirs. Project Quest, Los Angeles, 1969-71. Mem. AAAS, Am. Psychol. Assn., Assn. for Humanistic Psychology, The World Future Soc., Soc. of Mayflower Desc., SAR (Ill. soc.), Beta Gamma Sigma. Democrat. Office: Calif State U Dept Human Resources Mgmt Long Beach CA 90840

LEWIS, ROBERT LEE, III, health facility executive; b. San Francisco, Sept. 20, 1949; s. Robert Lee Jr. and Dolores Patricia (Brady) L.; m. Kari B. Hanson, May 1989; 1 child, Paige Caroline. BS, Calif. State U., Fresno, 1971, MBA, 1978; cert. exec. program, Stanford U., 1983. Ops. officer, adminstrv. asst. to v.p. Security Pacific Nat. Bank, Fresno, 1971-74; service chief County Health Dept., Fresno, 1974-79; adminstrv. dir. clin. labs. Stanford (Calif.) U. Hosp., 1979-84; pres. Western Div. Internat. Clin. Labs., Dublin, Calif., 1984-86; v.p. Performance Health Care, Inc., Danville, Calif., 1986-87; adminstr. Good Samaritan Med. Group, San Jose, Calif., 1987-90; chief exec. officer O'Connor Med. Group, San Jose, 1990—; adj. faculty Coll. Profl. Studies U. San Francisco, 1988—. Author: Optimizing Productivity: Capital Equipment Acquisition, 1985; mem. editorial bd. Syva Monitor, 1984. Served with USNG, 1971-76. Mem. Med. Group Mgmt. Assn., Fresno Assn. for Retarded (bd. dirs. (1975-78), Health Care Fin. Assn. Home: 108 Durham St Menlo Park CA 94025-2526

LEWIS, ROBERT STEVE, construction executive; b. Tucson, Sept. 10, 1946; s. Dan Elwood and Bettie (VanCleave) L.; m. Janice Miles, May 11, 1985; children: Casey, Cotter, Courtney, Cayla. BS in Mining Engring., U. Ariz., 1970. Engr. MM Sundt, Tucson, 1973-75; recruiting mgr. MM Sundt, Manila, Philippines, 1975-76; estimator MM Sundt, Tucson, 1976-80; v.p. Sundt Corp., Saudi Arabia, 1980-82; v.p. Sundt Corp., Tucson, 1982-90, sr. v.p., 1990-91, exec. v.p., 1991—; bd. dirs. Sundt Corp., Tucson, Tiena Internat., Manila, Sundt Ltd., Tucson. Mem. Tucson Conquistadores, 1990—; bd. dirs. Ariz. Kidney Found., Tucson, 1979. With U.S. Army, 1970-72. Office: Sundt Corp 4101 E Irvington Rd Tucson AZ 85726

LEWIS, ROBERT TURNER, psychologist; b. Taft, Calif., June 17, 1923; s. D. Arthur and Amy Belle (Turner) L.; m. Jane Badham, Mar. 23, 1946; children: Jane, William, Richard. BA, U. So. Calif., 1947, MA, 1950; PhD, U. Denver, 1952. Lic. psychologist, Calif. Chief psychologist Hollywood Presbyn. Hosp., Los Angeles, 1953-58; dir. psychol. svcs. Salvation Army, Pasadena, Calif., 1958-68; dir. Pasadena Psychol. Ctr., 1964-74; successively asst. prof., assoc. prof. and prof., Calif. State U.-L.A., 1952-83, prof. emeritus, 1984—; assoc. dir Cortical Function Lab., L.A., 1972-84; clin. dir. Diagnostic Clinic, West Covina, Calif., 1983-85; dir. Job Stress Clinic, Santa Ana, Calif., 1985—. Author: Taking Chances, 1979; co-author: Money Madness, 1978; Human Behavior, 1974; The Psychology of Abnormal Behavior, 1961. Served to lt. (j.g.) USNR, 1943-46, PTO. Mem. Am. Bd. Profl. Disability Cons. (diplomate), Am. Psychol. Assn., Calif. State Psychol. Assn., L.A. County Psychol. Assn., Nat. Acad. Neuropsychology, Am. Acad. Forensic Scis. Republican. Office: Job Stress Clinic 2670 N Main St # 280 Santa Ana CA 92701-1224

LEWIS, ROGER ALLEN, biochemistry educator; b. Wellington, Kans., June 1, 1941; s. B. Kenneth and Marjorie (Crockett) L.; m. Kathy Joanne Milldrum, Aug. 26, 1962; children: Carrie Joanne, Christine Joy, Jennifer Dianne. BA, Phillips U., 1963; PhD, Oreg. State U., 1968. Rsch. assoc. Stanford (Calif.) U., 1968-69; asst. prof. biochemistry U. Nev., Reno, 1969-75, assoc. prof. biochemistry, 1975-82, prof. biochemistry, 1982—, assoc. dean coll. agr., 1992—; mem. edn. com. No. Calif. Cancer Program, 1977-80. Contbr. articles to profl. jours. Mem. Gov.'s Cancer Adv. Coun., 1975-77; trustee No. Nev. Cancer Program, 1977-83. Mem. Am. Soc. of Biochemistry and Molecular Biology, Am. Soc. Pharmacology and Exptl. Therapeutics, Am. Chem. Soc. (biol. chemistry sect.), AAAS. Office: U Nev Dept Biochemistry Reno NV 89557

LEWIS, RUBY ANNE, account executive; b. Santa Barbara, Calif., Apr. 18, 1941; d. Cecil Ameare and Elna Elizabeth (Packer) Talmadge; m. Robert Flint Lewis, Jr., Dec. 17, 1960; children: Pamela Row, Sandra Manro. Grad. high sch., Carpinteria, Calif. Account exec. Mgmt. Recruiters, Clovis, Calif., 1992—. Recipient Editor's Choice award The Nat. Libr. of Poetry, Owings Mills, Md., 1990. Republican. Presbyterian. Home: 687 N Ezie Ave Clovis CA 93612-7317 Office: Mgmt Recruiters 150 Clovis Ave Clovis CA 93612

LEWIS, SHIRLEY JEANE, psychology educator; b. Phoenix, Aug. 23, 1937; d. Herman and Leavy (Hutchinson) Smith; AA, Phoenix Community Coll., 1957; BA, Ariz. State U., 1960; MS, San Diego State U., 1975, MA, 1986; MA, Azusa Pacific U., 1982; PhD, U. So. Calif., 1983. Cert. Tchr., Calif.; m. Edgar Anthony Lewis, June 25, 1966 (div. May 1980); children: Edgar Anthony, Roshaun, Lucy Ann. Recreation leader Phoenix Parks and Recreation Dept., 1957-62; columnist Ariz. Tribune, Phoenix, 1958-59; tchr. phys. edn. San Diego Unified Schs., 1962—; adult educator San Diego Community Colls., 1973—, instr. psychology, health, Black studies, 1977—, counselor, 1981—; community counselor S.E. Counseling and Cons. Svcs. and Narcotics Prevention and Edn. Systems, Inc., San Diego, 1973-77; counselor educator, counselor edn. dept. San Diego State U., 1974-77; marriage, family, child counselor Counseling and Cons. Ctr., San Diego, 1977—; inservice educator San Diego Unified and San Diego County Sch. Dists., 1973-77; lectr. in field. Girl Scout phys. fitness cons., Phoenix, 1960-62; vol. community tutor for high sch. students, San Diego, 1963; sponsor Tennis Club for Youth, San Diego, 1964-65; troop leader Girl Scouts U.S., Lemon Grove, Calif., 1972-74; vol. counselor USN Alcohol Rehab. Center, San Diego, 1978; mem. sch. coun.'s adv. bd. San Diego State U. Named Woman of Year, Phoenix, 1957, One of Outstanding Women of San Diego, 1980; recipient Phys. Fitness Sch. award and Demonstration Sch. award Pres.'s Coun. on Phys. Fitness, Taft Jr. High Sch., 1975; Delta Sigma Theta scholar, 1957-60; Alan Korrick scholar, 1956. Mem. NEA, Calif. Tchrs. Assn., San Diego Tchrs. Assn., Assn. Marriage and Family Counselors, Am. Personnel and Guidance Assn., Calif. Assn. Health, Phys. Edn. and Recreation (v.p. health), Am. Alliance of Health, Phys. Edn. and Recreation, Assn. Black Psychologists (corr. sec. 1993), Assn. African-Am. Educators, Delta Sigma Theta (Delta of Yr. 1987). Democrat. Baptist. Contbr. articles to profl. jours. Home: 1226 Armacost Rd San Diego CA 92114-3307 Office: 2630 B St San Diego CA 92102-1022

LEWIS, TODD JAY, orthopedic surgeon; b. Bronx, N.Y., Apr. 24, 1954; s. Samuel Hull and Barbara (Topper) L.; m. Susan Anne Wright, May 26, 1984; children: Katherine, Natalie, Robert. BA, MD summa cum laude, Boston U., 1978. Diplomate Am. Bd. Orthopedic Surgery. Intern Boston U., 1978-79, resident in orthopedics, 1980-84; fellow in trauma Boston City Hosp., 1979-80; ptnr. Corvallis (Oreg.) Orthopedic Surgeons, 1984—; examiner Am. Bd. Orthopedic Surgeons, Chapel Hill, N.C., 1992—; assoc. prof. Oreg. State U., Corvallis, 1988—. Author: Sports Injuries, 1985. Commr. planning commn., Corvallis, 1982—; pres. N.W. Downtown Neighbor Assn., Corvallis, 1989—. Recipient Civic Beautification award Corvallis City Coun., 1989, 92. Fellow Am. Acad. Orthopedic Surgeons; mem. Oreg. Spine Soc., Oreg. Med. Assn., AMA. Office: Corvallis Orthopedic Surgeons 3640 NW Samaritan Dr Corvallis OR 97330

LEWITT, MILES MARTIN, computer engineering company executive; b. N.Y.C., July 14, 1952; s. George Herman and Barbara (Lin) L.; m. Susan Beth Orenstein, June 24, 1973; children: Melissa, Hannah. BS summa cum laude, CCNY Engring., 1973; MS, Ariz. State U., 1976. Software engr. Honeywell, Phoenix, 1973-78; architect iRMX line ops. systems, x86 line microprocessors Intel Corp., Santa Clara, Calif., 1978; engring. mgr. Intel, Hillsboro, Oreg., 1978-80, 1981-89, corp. strategic staff, 1981-82; engring. mgr. Intel, Israel, 1980-81; v.p. engring. Cadre Techs., Inc., Beaverton, Oreg., 1989-91; v.p. rsch. and devel. ADP, Portland, Oreg., 1991—; instr. Maricopa Tech. Coll., Phoenix, 1974-75. Contbr. articles to profl. jours. Recipient Engring. Alumni award CCNY, 1973, Eliza Ford Prize CCNY, 1973, Advanced Engring. Program award, Honeywell, 1976, Product of Yr.

award Electronic Products Mag., 1980. Mem. IEEE (sr.), IEEE Computer Soc. (voting mem.), Assn. Computing Machinery (voting mem.), Am. Electronics Assn. (exec. com. Oreg. Coun.). Democrat. Office: Automatic Data Processing 2525 SW 1st Ave Portland OR 97201-4753

LEWITZKY, BELLA, choreographer; b. Los Angeles, Jan. 13, 1916; d. Joseph and Nina (Ossman) L.; m. Newell Taylor Reynolds, June 22, 1940; 1 child, Nora Elizabeth. Student, San Bernardino Valley (Calif.) Jr. Coll., 1933-34; hon. doctorate, Calif. Inst. Arts, 1981; PhD (hon.), Occidental Coll., 1984, Otis Parsons Coll., 1989; DFA (hon.), Juilliard Sch., 1993. Chmn. dance dept., chmn. adv. panel U. So. Calif., Idyllwild, 1956-74; founder Sch. Dance, Calif. Inst. Arts, 1969, dean, 1969-74; vice chmn. dance adv. panel Nat. Endowment Arts, 1974-77, mem. artists-in-schs. adv. panel, 1974-75; mem. Nat. Adv. Bd. Young Audiences, 1974—, Joint Commn. Dance and Theater Accreditation, 1979; com. mem. Am. chpt. Internat. Dance Coun. of UNESCO, 1974—; bd. dirs. Am. Arts Alliance, 1974-88; trustee Nat. Found. Advancement Arts, 1982-90, 92—, Calif. Arts Coun., 1983-86; trustee Calif. Assn. Dance Cos., 1976—, Idyllwild Sch. music and Arts, 1986—, Dance/USA, 1988—, Calif. State Summer Sch. of Arts, 1988—; cons. the dance project WNET, 1987—. Co-founder, co-dir., Dance Theatre, Los Angeles, 1946-50; founder, dir., Dance Assocs., Los Angeles, 1951-55; founder 1966, since artistic dir., Lewitzky Dance Co., Los Angeles; choreographer, 1948—; founder, former artistic dir. The Dance Gallery, Los Angeles; contbr. articles in field. Mem. adv. com. Actors' Fund of Am., 1986—, Women's Bldg. Adv. Council, 1985-91, Calif. Arts Council, 1983-86, City of Los Angeles Task Force on the Arts, 1986—; mem. artistic adv. bd. Interlochen Ctr. for Arts, 1988—. Recipient ann. award Dance mag., 1978, Dir.'s award Calif. Dance Educators Assn., 1978, Silver Achievement award YWCA, 1982, Disting. Svc. award Western Alliance Arts Adminstrs., 1987, So. Calif. Libr. for Social Studies & Rsch. award, 1990, Am. Soc. Journalists & Authors Open Book award, 1990, Internat. Soc. Performing Arts Adminstrs. Tiffany award, 1990, Burning Bush award U. of Judaism, 1991; 1st recipient Calif. Gov.'s award in arts for individual lifetime achievement; honoree L.A. Arts Coun., 1989, Nat. Dance Assn., 1991, Hugh M. Hefner First Amendment award, 1991, Artistic Excellence award Ctr. Performing Arts U. Calif., 1992, Lester Horton Lifetime Achievement award Dance Resource Ctr. of L.A., 1992, Occidental Coll. Founders' award, 1992; grantee Mellon Found., 1975, 81, 86, Guggenheim Found., 1977-78, NEA, 1969-86. Mem. Am. Arts Alliance (bd. dirs. 1977), Internat. Dance Alliance (adv. council 1984—), Dance/USA (bd. dirs. 1988). Office: Lewitzky Dance Co 1055 Wilshire Blvd Ste 1140 Los Angeles CA 90017

LEWTHWAITE, GORDON ROWLAND, geography educator; b. Oamaru, Otago, N.Z., Aug. 12, 1925; came to U.S., 1959; s. Harry Stanley and Mary Elizabeth (Savage) L.; m. Lydia Luft, Dec. 21, 1953; children: Rebecca, Karen. BA, U. Canterbury, Christchurch, N.Z., 1946, MA, 1948; diploma of honors, U. Auckland, N.Z., 1950; PhD, U. Wis., 1956. Cert. secondary edn. tchr., N.Z. Tchr. Gisborne (N.Z.) High Sch., 1950; instr. U. Okla., Norman, 1953-54; lectr. geography dept. U. Auckland, 1955-59; prof. geography Calif. State U., Northridge, 1959-92, prof. emeritus, 1992—; vis. prof. U. Hawaii, Honolulu, summer 1964, U. B.C., Vancouver, Can., 1966-67, U. Newcastle, N.S.W., Australia, 1973, U. Auckland, 1980, U. Calif., Santa Barbara, winter 1987, L.A., winter 1993. Contbr. numerous articles to profl. jours. Lectr, tchr. in ch. and community groups. Fulbright fellow U. Wis., 1950, Knapp fellow, 1952; Wenner-Gren Found. grantee, 1964, Calif. State U. Rsch. grantee. Fellow Am. Sci. Affiliation; mem. Assn. Am. Geographers, Assn. Pacific Coast Geographers, N.Z. Geographical Soc. (asst. editor 1955-59), N.Z. Archaeol. Assn., Calif. Geographical Soc., Polynesian Soc. (life). Home: 18908 Liggett St Northridge CA 91324-2844

LEWY, ALFRED JONES, psychiatrist, educator; b. Chgo., Oct. 12, 1945; s. Robnert Barnard and Evelyn (Bluestone) L. BS in Biochemistry, U. Chgo., 1967, MD, 1973, PhD in Pharmacology, 1973. Diplomate Am. Bd. Neurology and Psychiatry. Clin. assoc. NIMH, Bethesda, Md., 1975-77; staff fellow NIMH, Bethesda, 1977-80; asst. prof. to prof. psychiatry, ophthalmology, pharmacology Oregon Health Sci. U., Portland, 1981—. Contbr. almost 100 articles to profl. jours. Lt. commdr. USPHS, 1972-75. Recipient several rsch. awards and NIH grants. Home: 4717 SW Fairhaven Dr Portland OR 97221-2513 Office: Oregon Health Scis U 3181 SW Sam Jackson Park Portland OR 97201

LEY, BETH MARIE, health and nutrition writer; b. Rugby, N.D., Apr. 16, 1964; d. Christ G. and Patricia L. (Buttke) L. BS in Sci. and Tech. Writing, N.D. State U., 1987. Asst. editor Swanson Health Products, Fargo, N.D., 1988-92; writer Muscle and Fitness Mag., Woodland Hills, Calif., 1992—; editor The Natural Child Newsletter, 1992—; dir. R&D Healthy Concepts, Santa Ana, Calif., 1992—. Author: Health Talks, 1989, Castor Oil: It's Healing Properties, 1989, Natural Healing Handbook, 1990, Colostrum: Nature's Gift to the Immune System, 1990. Office: BL Publs 1728 Bedford Ln Apt 17 Newport Beach CA 92660

LEYDEN, MICHAEL JOSEPH, II, international trade and marketing sales consultant; b. Wenatchee, Wash., Feb. 26, 1950; s. Lawrence Ignatius and Wilma LaVerne (Eriksen) L.; m. Xu, Zhong Yu (Ivy), Nov. 1, 1991; children: Yu, Qian (Sophia), Soren Nicolas, Sophia Dion. AA in Econs., Wenatchee Valley Coll., 1970, U. V.I., 1971; BA in Philosophy and Psychology, Cen. Wash. U., 1972; postgrad., U. New Brunswick, Fredericton, Can., 1973; MA in Philosophy and Asian History Edn., Wash. State U., 1974; cert. small bus. mgmt., U. Hawaii, 1975; postgrad., Tianjin Fgn. Trade Inst., China, 1991-92. Mgr., tng. dir. Coldwell Bankers Davenport Realtors, Wenatchee, 1977-81; v.p sales and mktg. John's Real Estate & Securities Co., East Wenatchee, 1981-83; founder and pres. Aero Brokers Trading Co. Inc., Honolulu, 1983-87; gen. mgr. Tadashi & Sons Ltd./Mita-Bruton Enterprises, Moen, Chuuk FSM, Micronesia, 1987-88; adminstv. and fin. mgr. Zorro's of Hawaii, Inc., Honolulu, 1988; v.p., gen. mgr. Harder's Co. Ltd., Syrup Manuf/Foodservice-Wholesale Distbn., Honolulu and Guam, 1989; gen. mgr. Coast Enterprises of Hawaii, Inc., Honolulu, 1990; tchr., spl. asst. to commr., computer coord. No. Marianas Pub. Schs. System, Saipan, CNMI, Micronesia, 1990-91; chmn. Hawaiian Philatelic PPPP Enterprises, Honolulu, 1991—; bd. dirs. Aero-Brokers Inc.; cons. Internat. Trade Adminstrn. U.S. Dept. Commerce, 1979-87; mktg. and sales cons. South Seas Merchantile & Trading Co., Hawaii, Samoa, 1992—; mgr. Cert. Mgmt., Inc., Koapaka Ctr, Honolulu; chmn. bd. dirs., pres. Bon Eternity Internat. Devel. Co. (dvsn. Aero Brokers, Inc. , mng. dir.Honolulu and Tianjin, Peoples Republic of China, 1993—; advisor internat. trade and mktg. Personally Yours Co., Wenatchee, 1983-87; corp. troubleshooter ABI Fin. Svcs. Co., Long Beach, Calif., 1984-86; sr. fin. cons. Red Apple Herbs, Inc., Wenatchee, 1985; fgn. trade expert Tianjin Fgn. Trade Inst., China, 1991-92. Author: China JAde, An Empress of Beauty, Passion, and Business !, China Auto Trade; co-author: Fast Start Real Estate Financing/Training, 1978;exhibitor Micronesian Philalelics, CNMI Cultural Arts Ctr., Saipan, 1991; contbr. articles to profl. jours. including Forbes, 1991, International Business, 1993. Chmn. U.S. Senatorial Campaign of Warren Magnuson, Wenatchee, 1980; bd. dirs. W.B.R.-M.L.S., Wenatchee, 1980-81; mem. UNICEF, N.Y.C., 1989—, Nat. Right to Life Campaign, Honolulu, 1987—, Nat. Rep. Com., Washington and Hawaii, 1978—; vol. USO-Waikiki Ctr., 1989-90. Recipient Internat. Mktg. Distinction award Worldwide S.M.I. Inst., Waco, Tex. 1985; named #1 Australian Import Distbr. USA Promo 1986. Mem. World Trade Assn., Nat. Splty. Food Dealers Assn., Am. Mgmt. Assn. (pres. club 1977—), Am. Philatelic Soc., Hawaii Philos. Soc., China Stamp Soc., Washington State U. Alumni Assn. (life, dist. dir. VI 1979-83), 40 plus of Hawaii (life, membership/mktg. com. 1990), Lions Internat., Rotary Internat., Honolulu Club. Office: PO Box 29131 Honolulu HI 96820

LEYDEN, NORMAN, conductor; m. Alice Leyden; 1 child, Connie. Grad., Yale U., 1938; MA, Columbia U., PhD, 1970. Bass clarinetist New Haven Symphony; arranger Glenn Miller Air Force Band, Eng., France; chief arranger Glenn Miller Orch., 1946-49; freelance arranger N.Y.C.; mus. dir. RCA Victor Records, Arthur Godfrey, 1956-59; with Oreg. Symphony, 1970—, assoc. conductor, 1974—; music dir. Seattle Symphony Pops, 1975—; tchr. Columbia U.; conductor over 30 Am. symphony orchs. including Boston Pops, Minn. Orch., Pitts. Symphony, St. Louis Symphony, San Diego Symphony, San Francisco Symphony, Syracuse Symphony, Nat. Symphony, Utah Symphony; conductor Army Air Force. Author: The Big Band Style: A Guide for Performers. Office: Seattle Symphony Seattle Ctr House 305 Harrison St 4th Flr Seattle WA 98109-4645*

LEYDET, FRANÇOIS GUILLAUME, writer; b. Neuilly-sur-Seine, France, Aug. 26, 1927; came to U.S., 1940, naturalized, 1956; s. Bruno and Dorothy (Lindsey) L. AB, Harvard, 1947, postgrad. Bus. Sch., 1952; postgrad. Johns Hopkins Sch. Advanced Internat. Studies, 1952-53; Bachelier-es-lettres-philosophie, U. Paris (France), 1945; m. Patience Abbe, June 17, 1955 (div.); step-children: Catherine Abbe Geissler, Lisa Amanda O'Mahony; m. Roslyn Carney, June 14, 1970; step-children: Walter E. Robb IV, Rachel R. Avery, Holly H. Prunty, Mary-Peck Peters. Bd. advisers Rsch. Ranch, Elgin, Ariz., Am. Wilderness Alliance; past dir. Marin County Planned Parenthood Assn., Planned Parenthood Center Tucson; docent Ariz.-Sonora Desert Mus. 1st lt. French Army, 1947-48. Mem. Nat. Parks Assn., Wilderness Soc., Sierra Club, Nat. Audubon Soc., World Wildlife Fund, Am. Mus. Natural History, Union Concerned Scientists, Environ. Def. Fund, Friends of the Earth, Ariz.-Sonora Desert Mus., Am. Internat., Ariz. Hist. Soc., LWV, Ariz. Opera League, Western Writers Assn., Commonwealth Club. Author: The Last Redwoods, 1963, Time and the River Flowing: Grand Canyon, 1964, The Coyote: Defiant Songdog of the West, 1977; editor: Tomorrow's Wilderness, 1963; contbr. to Nat. Geog. mag. Home: 5165 N Camino Real Tucson AZ 85718-5026

L'HEUREUX, RICHARD B., construction and warehousing contractor; b. Santa Fe, Mar. 20, 1936; s. Leon Camille and Lois (DeBusk) L'H.; m. Betty Jane Rael, Sept. 13, 1958; children: Michelle D., Richard Mark, Edward A., Brian P. BBA, St. Michael's Coll., 1965. Pres. Warehousing Inc., Santa Fe, 1969—, Ponderosa Constrn. Co., Santa Fe, 1970—. Mem. City/County Planning Commn., Santa Fe, 1975-77; mem., past chmn. City of Santa Fe Bd. Adjustment, 1972-80; v.p., pres., nat. rep. Coll. of Santa Fe, 1966-85, trustee, 1989; mem. Santa Fe Fiesta Coun., 1979-81. Staff sgt. U.S. Army, 1955-56. Mem. Bldg. Contractors Assn. Santa Fe (v.p. 1976-77, pres. 1977-78), Nat. Assn. Home Builders (regional v.p. 1978-80, membership chair 1982). Roman Catholic. Office: Ponderosa Constrn 2505 Ponderosa Ln Santa Fe NM 87505

LI, CHARLES N., linguistics and anthropology educator, graduate dean; b. Shanghai, China, Feb. 6, 1940; came to U.S., 1961; s. Sheng-Wu Li and Edith Lee; m. Katherine Saltzman, Apr. 9, 1983; children: Rachel Alexandra, Gabriel Elihu. BA in Math. magna cum laude, Bowdoin Coll., 1963; postgrad. in Math., Stanford (Calif.) U., 1963-66; PhD in Linguistics, U. Calif., Berkeley, 1971. Asst. prof. U. Calif., Santa Barbara, 1970-76, assoc. prof., 1976-80, prof., 1980—, dean grad. div., 1989—. Co-author: Mandarin Chinese: A Reference Grammar, 1981; editor: Subject and Topic, 1976, Mechanism of Sytactic Change, 1977. Rsch. grantee NSF, 1980-86, NEH, 1986-92. Mem. Linguistic Soc. Am., Societas Linguistica Europaea, Phi Beta Kappa. Office: U Calif Dept Linguistics Santa Barbara CA 93016

LI, DAVID WEN-CHUNG, television company executive; b. Yun-Nan, China, Nov. 13, 1929; came to U.S. 1977; s. Tsung-Huang and Jui-Min (Liang) L.; m. Marjorie Chung-Mei Wang, Apr. 23, 1960; 1 child, Terry Tien-Jen. BA, Nat. Taiwan U., 1951. Editor, reporter, dep. city editor Hsin Sheng Daily News, Taipei, Taiwan, 1951-62; news analyst Broadcasting Corp. of China, Taipei, Taiwan, 1959-62; reporter, news anchor, news dept. dir., news commentator Taiwan TV Ent., Taipei, 1962-77; spl. corres. TTV, San Francisco, 1977-85; pres., gen. mgr. Pan Pacific TV, Inc./KPST-TV, San Francisco, 1985—; news commentator BBC London, San francisco, 1992. Author/editor news mag.: This Year, 1971-72; author: News Commentaries, 1974, Viewing the World From San Francisco, 1992; author pamphlet: Ten Great Constructions, 1975. Sec.-gen. Chinese Youth Anti-Communist League, Taipei, 1950-51; founder, dir. Chinese Acupuncture Sci. Rsch. Found., Taipei, 1972—. Recipient Best TV News Program award GIO Taiwan, 1973, Internat. Preceptor award San Francisco State U., 1974. Home: 9 Jasmine Ct Millbrae CA 94030 Office: Pan Pacific Television 475 El Camino Real #308 Millbrae CA 94030

LI, ELDON Y., information systems specialist, educator; b. Keelung, Taiwan, Feb. 18, 1952; came to U.S., 1977; m. Rebecca Li, Dec. 25, 1978; 1 child, Angelica. BC, Nat. Chengchi U., Taipei, Taiwan, 1975; MS, Tex. Tech. U., 1978, PhD, 1982. Cert. data educator, cert. prodn. and inventory mgmt. Instr. Tex. Tech. U., Lubbock, 1980-81; assoc. prof. Calif. Poly. State U., San Luis Obispo, 1982-90, prof., 1990—; software quality cons. Bechtel Corp., San Francisco, 1984; software scientist IBM Corp., San Jose, 1989; mgmt. cons. Small Bus. Inst., San Luis Obispo, 1987; presenter profl. confs. Contbr. numerous articles to sci. jours. and books. Rsch. grantee Calif. State U., Calif. Poly. State U., RGK Found.; recipient Best Article award Quality Data Processing Jour., 1989, Best Paper award ACME Conf., 1991. Mem. Internat. Assn. Computer Info. Systems, Assn. Computing Machinery, Quality Assurance Inst., Inst. Mgmt. Scis., Decision Scis. Inst., Chinese Profl. Assn. (pres. 1984). Office: Calif Poly State U Coll Bus San Luis Obispo CA 93407

LI, JOSEPH KWOK-KWONG, molecular biologist; b. Hong Kong, UK, Jan. 13, 1940; came to U.S. 1963; s. Kan and Wai Ching (Chan) L.; m. Livia Say, June 28, 1970; children: Karen, Brenda. BS, U. Redlands, 1967; MS, State U. Calif., 1970; PhD, UCLA, 1975. Rsch. asst. UCLA, 1970-74; from postdoctoral fellow to med. rsch. assoc. Duke U. Med. Ctr., Durham, N.C., 1975-80; mgr. Becton Dickinson Rsch. Ctr., Rsch. Triangle Pk., N.C., 1980-82; rsch. assoc. prof. U. N.C., Chapel Hill, 1982-83; from assoc. prof. to prof. Utah State U., Logan, 1984-93, dir. program in molecular biology, 1992—; scientist -at-resident N.C. Mus. Arts & Scis., Durham, 1983. Contbr. articles to profl. jours. Named Capt., all-star, conf. NCAA, S. Calif. Soccer Conf., 1964, 1965; recipient grad. rsch. awd. State U. Calif., L.A., 1970. Mem. Am. Soc. Microbiology, Am. Soc. Virologist, Soc. Chinese Bioscientists Am. (regional coord.), N.Y. Acad. Sci., Sigma Xi. Office: Utah State U Biology Dept UMC 5500 Logan UT 84322-5500

LI, PAUL MICHAEL, judicial educator; b. Hong Kong, July 8, 1938; came to U.S. 1947; s. Norman C. and Hazel (Chow) L.; m. Frances Jean Bill, Nov. 24, 1962 (div. 1984); children: Mary Theresa, Mary Pamela, Michael Edward; m. Shu-Ti Hung Li, Aug. 22, 1987. AB, Maryknoll Coll., Glen Ellyn, Ill., 1960; LLB, Duquesne U., Pitts., 1964. Bar: Calif. 1965, Pa. 1964. Law clk. Common Pleas Ct., Pitts., 1964-65; atty. Adminstrv. Office of the Cts., San Francisco, 1965-72; asst. dir. Adminstrv. Office of the Cts., 1972-73; dir. Calif. Ctr. Judicial Edn and Rsch., Emeryville, 1973-93; chmn. bd. Golden Coin Savs. and Loan Assn., San Francisco, 1987—; cons. jud. edn. and ct administrn. Lafayette, Calif., 1993—; judicial cons. The Asian Found., 1982—, Supreme Cts. of Philippines, 1982, 87, 89, Bangladesh, 1985, 89, Nepal, 1985, 91, Sri Lanka, 1985, 90, Thailand, 1986, Pakistan, 1987, Brunei, Malaysia and Singapore, 1988, Costa Rica, 1988, Taiwan, 1987, 89, 90, 91, Canada, 1990, Egypt ,1990, Korea, 1991, Argentina, 1991, Chile, 1991, Morocco, 1991, and numerous states and the Am. Univ.'s Cts. Tech. Assistance Project; bd. dirs. Nat. Judicial Coll., Reno, Nev., 1975-78. Contbr. articles to profl. jours.; author: Attorneys Guide to California Jurisdiction and Process, 1970; co-author: Attorneys Guide to California Family Law Act Practice, 1972. US AID grantee, 1987-92. Mem. State Bar of Calif., Assn. of Continuing Legal Edn. Adminstrs., Asian Am. Bar Assn. (v.p. 1976-77), Nat. Assn. State Judicial educators (pres. 1978-80). Roman Catholic. Home: 3370 Springhill Rd Lafayette CA 94549-2520

LI, PETER WAI-KWONG, mathematics educator; b. Hong Kong, Apr. 18, 1952; came to U.S., 1971; s. Chun Tat and Lai Mui (Sum) L.; m. Glenna Marie Seaver, Oct. 30, 1982; children: Tiana, Natasha, Talia. BA, Calif. State U., 1974; MA, U. Calif., Berkeley, 1977, PhD, 1979. Rsch. mem. Inst. for Advanced Study, Princeton, N.J., 1979-80; asst. prof. Stanford (Calif.) U., 1980-83; assoc. prof. Purdue U., West Lafayette, Ind., 1983-85; prof. U. Utah, Salt Lake City, 1985-89, U. Ariz., Tucson, 1989-91, U. Calif., Irvine, 1991—. Editor Rocky Mountain Jour. Math., 1989-91, Procs. of Am. Math. Soc., 1991—; Editor-in-Chief Comm. in Analysis and Geometry, 1992—. Grantee NSF, 1980—; fellowship Sloan, 1982-83, Guggenheim, 1989-90. Mem. Am. Math. Soc., Phi Beta Kappa. Office: U Calif Irvine Dept Math Irvine CA 92717-3875

LI, TA MEI, mining executive, marketing professional; b. N.Y.C., June 25, 1948; s. Shih Kuei and Rachel (Lee) L.; m. Tu Leung Lee, Dec. 31, 1969; 1 child, Ta Ming. BS in Mining Engring., Columbia U., 1970. Prodn. supr. Kennecott Copper Corp., Bingham Canyon, Utah, 1970-72; assoc. editor Engring. and Mining Jour., N.Y.C., 1972-74; editor in chief Mining Engring. Mag., Littleton, Colo., 1974-80; sr. mining engr. Golder Assocs., Golden, Colo., 1980-82; dir. bus. devel. Thyssen Mining Constrn., Wheat Ridge, Colo., 1982-85; dir. mktg. Pincock Allen & Holt, Inc., Lakewood, Colo., 1985-87; mng. dir. Pincock, Allen & Holt, Inc., Lakewood, Colo., 1990-93, Minex, C.A. (Venezuela), Denver; v.p., gen. mgr. Behre Dolbear-Riverside, Inc., Denver, 1987-89; v.p. mktg. ACZ, Inc., Steamboat Springs, Colo., 1989-90; mng. dir. Geoambiente Mining, Inc. (formerly Minex, C.A.), Denver, 1993—; dir. Tecnoco Internat., Lakewood, Asian X-M Ltd., Loveland, Colo. Editor: Risk Management/Assessment in Mining, 1992, Small Mines Development in Precious Metals, 1987, Mineral Resource Management by Personal Computer, 1987, Mineral Resources of the Pacific Rim, 1982. Organizer, dir. Salt Lake Chinese for Community Action, 1974-78. Named Ky. Col. State of Ky., 1982; recipient Citation of Svc. U.S. Dept. of Commerce, 1979. Mem. Soc. for Mining, Metallurgy and Exploration (disting., chmn. mining and exploration div. 1992—) N.W. Mining Assn. (life, pres. 1989-90, Starters award 1987), Denver Gold Group (bd. dirs. 1989—, pres. 1990-91), Colo. Mining Assn. (dir. 1991—, vice chmn. programs 1992), Mining and Metall. Soc. Am. (councillor 1991—), Sierra Club, Theta Tau. Republican. Lutheran. Home: 7632 Cottonwood Mountain Littleton CO 80127 Office: Minex CA (Venezuela) 410 17th St Ste 1225 Denver CO 80202

LIANG, JASON CHIA, research chemist; b. Beijing, Peoples Republic China, Feb. 24, 1935; came to U.S., 1978, naturalized 1984; s. Tsang Truan and Shulin (Tang) L.; m. Joan Chorng Chen, June 11, 1960; children: Cheryl, Chuck. BS in Pharm. Chemistry, U. Beijing, 1957; postgrad., Pharm. Research Instn., Beijing, 1961; MS in Organic Chemistry, U. Oreg., 1980. Chemist Beijing Chem. Factory, 1961-71; rsch. chemist Beijing Pharm. Factory, 1971-78; rsch. chemist Tektronix Inc., Beaverton, Oreg., 1980-85, sr. rsch. chemist, 1985-88; sr. rsch. chemist Kalama (Wash.) Chem. Inc., 1988—; presenter Internat. Pitts. Conf. on Analytical Chemistry and Applied Spectroscopy, 1988. Contbr. articles to profl. jours.; patentee in field. Fellow Am. Inst. Chemists; mem. Am. Chem. Soc. (organic chemistry divsn., paper presenter 1984-93), Internat. Union Pure and Applied Chemistry (affiliate). Office: Kalama Chem Inc 1296 NW 3D St Kalama WA 98625

LIANG, JEFFREY DER-SHING, retired electrical engineer, civil worker; b. Chungking, China, Oct. 25, 1915; came to U.S., 1944, naturalized, 1971; s. Tze-hsiang and Sou-yi (Wang) L.; m. Eva Yin Hwa Tang, Jan. 2, 1940; 1 child, Shouyu. BA, Nat. Chengchih U., Chungking, 1940; BAS, U. B.C., Vancouver, 1960. Office asst. Ministry of Fgn. Affairs, Chungking, 1940-43; vice consul Chinese consulate Ministry of Fgn. Affairs, Seattle, 1944-50; consulate-gen. Ministry of Fgn. Affairs, San Francisco, 1950-53; consul Chinese consulate-gen. Ministry of Fgn. Affairs, Vancouver, 1953-56; engr.-in-tng. Can. Broadcasting Corp., Vancouver, 1960-65; assoc. engr. Boeing Co., Seattle, 1965-67, rsch. engr., 1967-70, engr., 1970-73, sr. engr., 1973-75, specialist engr., 1975-78; cons. Seattle, 1979-81. Mem. chancelor's cir. Wesbrook Soc. U. B.C., Vancouver, 1986—, Seattle-King County Adv. Coun. on Aging, 1984-88, Gov.'s State Coun. on Aging, Olympia, 1986-88, Pres. Coun., Rep. Nat. Com.; permanent mem. Rep. Nat. Senatorial Com., Washington State Rep. Party, Seattle Art Mus.; life mem. Am. Assn. Individual Investors, Mutual Fund Investors Assn., Rep. Presdl. Task Force; sustaining mem. Rep. Nat. Congl. Com., Rep. Presdl. Adv. Com.,. Mem. IEEE (life), Heritage Found., Hwa Sheng Chinese Music Club (v.p. 1978-79, chmn. nomination com. 1981-88), Pacific West Clubs, Health and Tennis Corp. Am. Republican. Mem. Christian Ch. Home: 2428 158th Ave SE Bellevue WA 98008-5416

LIAO, ERIC NAN-KANG, structural and mechanical engineer; b. Wu-Feng, Taiwan, China, Nov. 29, 1938; came to U.S., 1964; s. Swei-Mu and Ging-Kwan (Chen) L.; m. Fanny Ho-mei Yen, Feb. 10, 1968; children: Willy, Royce. BS, Cheng-Kung U., Taiwan, 1961; MS, Okla. State U., 1966; PhD, U. Wis., 1970. Registered profl. engr., Wis., Pa.; lic. real estate agt. N.J., Calif. Sr. engr. Westinghouse Electric Corp., Pitts., 1970-71; mem. research faculty U. Wis., Madison, 1971-72; research engr. United Engrs. & Constructors Inc., Phila., 1972-74; prin. engr. Stone & Webster Engring. Corp., Cherry Hill, N.J., 1974-80; mem. tech. staff TRW Def. & Space Systems, Redondo Beach, Calif., 1980-81; tech. staff Aerospace Corp., El Segundo, Calif., 1981—; cons. engring., Cherry Hill, 1973-80. Contbr. articles to profl. jours. Fundraiser Park Jr. High, Fullerton, Calif., 1981-82. Served to lt. Taiwan Air Force, 1961-62. NSF scholar, 1966-68; Wis. Alumni Rsch. fellow U. Wis., 1968-70. Mem. ASME (applied mechanics, pressure vessels and piping coms. Phila. sect. 1975-78), Sigma Xi, Pi Mu Epsilon, Chi Epsilon. Republican. Buddhist. Club: Realty Investment (Orange County, Calif.). Home: 1912 Avenida Del Ossa Fullerton CA 92633-1856

LIAW, HANG MING, engineer; b. Taichung, Taiwan, Republic of China, Feb. 1, 1936; came to U.S., 1965; s. Der Wang and Young Tsing L.; m. Chau Yi, Mar. 3, 1939; children: Tsui Ying, Lucy, Sally. BS, Cheng Kung U., Tainan, Taiwan, 1959; MS, Pa. State U., 1967, PhD, 1970. Engr. Taiwan Sugar Corp., 1960-65; postdoctoral fellow U. S.C., Columbia, 1970-71; engr. Airtron. Litton Industry, Morrisplain, N.J., 1971-73; engr. Semiconductor R & D Lab. Motorola, Phoenix, 1973-78, sect. mgr., 1978-90, dept. mgr., 1990—. Contbr. chpts. to books. Mem. IEEE, Electrochemical Soc. Home: 11540 N 104th St Scottsdale AZ 85260-6004 Office: Motorola Inc 5005 E Mcdowell Rd # 170 Phoenix AZ 85008-4295

LIBBIN, JAMES DAVID, agricultural economics educator; b. Urbana, Ill., Oct. 24, 1950; s. David C. and Lois (Maddox) L.; m. Mary Bray, June 6, 1981; children: Zachary, Christina. BS in Agr., U. Ill., Urbana, 1972, MS in Agrl. Econs., 1975; PhD in Econs., Iowa State U., 1982. Rsch. asst. U. Ill., 1972-75; rsch. assoc. Iowa State U., Ames, 1975-79; prof. agrl. econs., extension farm mgmt. specialist N.Mex. State U., Las Cruces, 1979—; adj. prof. Fla. Inst. Tech., White Sands Missile Range, N.Mex., 1985—. Author: Farm & Ranch Financial Records, 1987; contbr. over 300 articles and rsch. reports to profl. jours. Named State Farmer, N.Mex. Future Farmers Am., 1988. Mem. Am. Agrl. Econs. Assn., Western Agrl. Econs. Assn., Nat. Assn. Colls. and Tchrs. Agrl. (teaching award of merit 1989), Am. Soc. Farm Mgrs. and Rural Appraisers (sec.-treas. N.Mex. chpt. 1980—), Nat. Assn. Farm Bus. Analysis Specialists. Home: 1108 Avenida De Quintas Las Cruces NM 88005-3503 Office: NMex State U PO Box 30003 Dept 3169 Las Cruces NM 88003-0003

LIBBY, LAUREN DEAN, foundation president; b. Smith Center, Kans., Jan. 9, 1951; s. Dean L. and Elizabeth V. (Hansen) L.; m. June Ellen Hofer, Apr. 29, 1979; 1 child, Grant Lauren. BS in Agrl. Econs., Kans. State U., 1973; MBA, Regis U., 1988. Radio sta. employee, 1968-72; asst. program dir. info. br. Kans. State Extension Svc., Manhattan, 1969-73; economist Howard Houk Assocs., Chgo., 1973-75; asst. to pres. The Navigators, Colorado Springs, Colo., 1975-78, ministry devel. coord., 1979-86, dir. min. advancement, 1986-90, v.p. devel./comms., 1990—; pres. New Horizons Found., Colorado Springs, 1990—; bd. dirs. Navigators, Colorado Springs, 1993—; founding bd. dirs. Sta. KTLF-FM/Ednl. Comms. of Colorado Springs, 1987—; cons. 6 listener-supported radio stas., 1989—. Contbr. articles to mags. Mem. Nat. Soc. Fundraising Execs. Home: 6166 Del Paz Dr Colorado Springs CO 80918 Office: The Navigators 3820 N 30th St Colorado Springs CO 80934

LIBBY, RICHARD ALLAN, research mathematician; b. Pasadena, Apr. 9, 1958; s. Harold Dean and Ruth Carol (Greerlings) L. BA in Math., U. Calif. San Diego, La Jolla, 1980, MA in Math., 1982; PhD in Math., U. Calif., Santa Cruz, 1990. Cert. Calif. secondary tchr. Teaching asst. U. Calif. San Diego, 1980-82; record broker Glen Canyon Records Co., Santa Cruz, Calif., 1982-84; teaching asst. U. Calif., Santa Cruz, 1984-90; pvt. tutor San Francisco, 1988—; sr. fin. analyst Bank Am., San Francisco; mem. bd. reps. Grad. Student Assn. U. Calif. Santa Cruz, 1986-89. Dem. campaign worker, Santa Cruz, 1986. Recipient Rensselaer Medal Rensselaer Poly. Inst., 1975. Mem. Am. Math. Soc., Math. Assn. Am., Soc. Indsl. and Applied Math. Home: 129 Steiner St San Francisco CA 94117-3126 Office: Bank Am 555 California St 11th Fl San Francisco CA 94104

LIBER, NEVIN JEROME, computer engineer; b. Chgo., Aug. 12, 1965; p. Theodore and Norma L. BS in Computer Engring., U. Ill., 1989. Computer programmer, troubleshooter Travenol Labs., Inc., Deerfield, Ill., 1982-84; asst. computer systems mgr. Triodyne, Inc., Niles, Ill., 1985-87; info. systems developer AT&T Network Systems, Lisle, Ill., 1987-88; mem. tech. staff AT&T Bell Labs., Naperville, Ill., 1988-90; speech recognition engr. Apple Computer, Inc., Cupertino, Calif., 1990-92; reduced instrn. set computing porting specialist/blue meanie Apple Computer, Inc., Cupertino, 1992—. Mem. IEEE, Assn. for Computing Machinery, Math. Assn. Am., Eta Kappa Nu (treas. 1986). Home: 243 Buena Vista Ave #803 Sunnyvale CA 94086-4869 Office: Apple Computer Inc MS: 302-4Q 20525 Mariani Ave Cupertino CA 95014

LIBET, BENJAMIN, neuroscience educator; b. Chgo., Apr. 12, 1916; s. Morris and Anna L.; m. Fay Rosella Evans, July 1, 1939; children: Julian Mayer, Moreen Lea, Ralph Arnold, Gayla Bea. SB, U. Chgo., 1936, PhD, 1939. Instr. physiology Albany (N.Y.) Med. Coll., 1939-40; rsch assoc. Institute Pa. Hosp., Phila., 1940-43; materials engr. personal equipment lab. USAF, Wright Field, Ohio, 1944-45; instr. physiology sch. medicine U. Pa., Phila., 1943-44; instr. biological scis. U. Chgo., 1945-47, asst. prof. physiology, 1947-48; dir. rsch. Kabat-Kaiser Inst., Vallejo, Calif., 1949; from asst. to assoc. prof. physiology U. Calif. San Francisco, 1949-62, prof. physiology, 1962-84, prof. emeritus, 1984—. Author: Neurophysiology of Consciousness, 1993; contbr. 185 articles to profl. jours. Fellow Lalor Found., 1947-48, Commonwealth Found., 1956-57; scholar in residence Rockefeller Ctr. Study, 1977, vis. scholar Japan Soc. Sci., 1979. Fellow AAAS; mem. Soc. Neuroscience, Am. Physiology Soc.

LIBO, LESTER MARTIN, psychologist; b. Chgo., Sept. 18, 1923; s. Leopold and Anita (Pearl) L.; m. Mary Ann Conley, July 28, 1991; children: Gina Libo Feil, Victor, Felicia Libo Wilbert, Lesley C. Student, Ctrl. YMCA Coll., 1941-43, U. Calif., Berkeley, 1946; AM, Stanford U., 1948, PhD, 1951. Lic. psychologist, N.Mex.; diplomate Am. Bd. Med. Psychotherapists; bd. cert. Biofeedback Cert. Inst. Am.; Nat. Register Health Svc. Providers in Psychology. Clin. psychology intern VA, Palo Alto, San Francisco, Calif., 1948-50; rsch. assoc. Rsch. Ctr. for Group Dynamics, Univ. Mich., Ann Arbor, 1950-53; asst. prof., chief psychologist dept. psychiatry U. Md. Med. Sch., Balt., 1953-57; dir. div. mental health N.Mex. Dept. Pub. Health, Santa Fe, 1957-62; assoc. prof. to prof. psychiatry and psychology U. N.Mex. Sch. Medicine, Albuquerque, 1963-83; pvt. practice clin. psychologist Albuquerque, 1983—; cons. NIMH, Bethesda, Md., 1963-66; chief assessment officer Peace Corps Tng. Ctr., U. N.Mex., Albuquerque, 1963-64; vis. prof. psychology U. Bergen, Norway, 1969-70; program coord. Bernalillo County-U. N.Mex. Mental Health Ctr., Albuquerque, 1970-72; vice chmn. N.Mex. Bd. Psychologists Examiners, Albuquerque, 1971-77; dir. Gen. Addictions Treatment Effort, Albuquerque, 1972-73; part time chief psychologist Vista Sandia Hosp., Albuquerque, 1984-86. Author: Measuring Group Cohesiveness, 1951, Is There Life After Group?, 1977; co-author: Mental Health Consultants: Agents of Community Change, 1968; contbr. articles to profl. jours. V.p. Contemporary Art Soc. N.Mex., Albuquerque, 1989—. Sgt. U.S. Army, 1943-46. Recipient Mental Health Project grant, NIMH, Santa Fe, 1959-63, Rsch. fellowship NIMH, Bergen, 1969-70. Fellow APA, Am. Orthopsychiatric Assn. (bd. dirs. 1979-82), Am. Bd. Med. Psychotherapists (profl. adv. coun. 1986—); mem. N.Mex. Psychol. Assn. (pres. 1965-66), N.Mex. Soc. Biofeedback Behavioral Medicine (pres. 1978-79, 87-88, 92—), Assn. Applied Psychophysiology and Biofeedback, Soc. Behavioral Medicine. Office: Ste A-1 2730 San Pedro NE Albuquerque NM 87110

LICENS, LILA LOUISE, adminstrative assistant; b. Puyallup, Wash., Feb. 18, 1949; d. C.L. and Joan L. (Rubert) Vormestrand. Cert., Knapp Bus. Coll., 1968. Cert. Profl. Sec. From clk. bus. systems to exec. sec. export log mktg. Weyerhaeuser Co., Tacoma, 1968-93, exec. sec. bleached paperboard, 1993—. Mem. Profl. sec. Internat. (Wash.-Alaska div. pres. 1990-91, pres.-elect 1989-90, cert. sec. 1987-89, Sea-Tac chpt. pres. 1985-87), Fed. Way Women's Network (sec. 1989, treas. 1988). Home: 771 S 108th St Tacoma WA 98444

LICHT, ALICE VESS (ALICE O'NEILL), publishing executive, journalist; b. Caroleen, N.C., May 28, 1937; d. Troy Cleet Vess and Clara Ella Lee (Johnson) Littleton; m. Gennaro Pietro Di Biase, Nov. 12, 1955 (div. 1971); children: Stephen Eugene, Michael Antonio; m. Raymond Licht, Feb. 11, 1989. BA in English, Theatre, R.I. Coll., 1969, MA in English, 1976; post-grad., Southwestern U., 1984. Cert. secondary sch. English tchr. English tchr. Scituate (R.I.) High Sch., 1969-83; actress films and TV L.A., 1984-86, freelance journalist, 1984-86; pres., journalist L.A. Features Syndicate, 1986—. Author: (children's books) A Boy Named Steven, 1978, Robert and Minnie, 1978, Dear Teacher, 1992; TV comedy writer Murphy Brown, 1992; contbr. columns to publs. Mem. AAUW, NAFE. Home: 650 Winnetka Mews Winnetka IL 60093-1967

LICHTENBERG, LARRY RAY, chemist, consultant, researcher; b. Marceline, Mo., July 25, 1938; s. Kenneth Ray and Evelyn (Lauck) L.; m. Clarice Elaine Dameron, Dec. 23, 1961; children: Julia-Isabel Dameron. BS in Chemistry, Northeast Mo. State U., 1962. Chemist Bell & Howell, Chgo., 1962-62; jr. chem. engr. Magnavox Corp., Urbana, Ill., 1963-64; process engr. Gen. Electric Co., Bloomington, Ill., 1964-70; mfg. engr. Burr-Brown, Tucson, 1970-72; sr. staff engr. Motorola, Scottsdale, Ariz., 1972—; mem. corp. tech. council Motorola, Scottsdale, 1982—. Contbr. articles to profl. jours. Mem. Am. Chem. Soc., Internat. Soc. Hybrid Microelectronics (pres. Phoenix chpt. 1981-82). Republican. Baptist. Home: 13018 N 32nd Ave Phoenix AZ 85029-1206 Office: Motorola GEG 8220 E Roosevelt St Scottsdale AZ 85257-3804

LICHTENSTEIN, DONALD RAY, marketing educator; b. Birmingham, Ala., Dec. 26, 1956; s. Harold and Hazel Maxine (Marlowe) L. BS in Bus., U. Ala., Tuscaloosa, 1978; PhD in Bus., U. S.C., 1984. Distribution services specialist Western Electric, Atlanta, 1978-80; teaching asst. U. S.C., Columbia, 1980-84; asst. prof. mktg. La. State U., Baton Rouge, 1984-88, U. Colo., Boulder, 1988—. Contbr. articles to profl. jours. Mem. Assn. Consumer Research, Am. Mktg. Assn., So. Mktg. Assn., Am. Psychol. Assn., Beta Gamma Sigma. Office: U Colorado at Boulder Coll of Business Campus Box 419 Boulder CO 80309

LICK, FRANK MARTIN, invester; b. Mount Clemens, Mich., Aug. 17, 1939; s. Martin Harold and Elsie Teresa (Leach) L.; m. Ida Elizabeth Dalvecciho, Jan. 23, 1963; children: Beverly Jean, Francis Andrew. Owner Frank's Mobil Svc., Santa Barbara, Calif., 1965-69; salesman McElhanny Levy & Co., Santa Barbara, 1969-76; pres. Dynaton, Inc., Santa Barbara, 1978-81; owner FML Real Estate, Santa Barbara, 1976-86, FML Enterprises, Inc., Santa Barbara, 1978-86, Laze Daze Retirement Community, Santa Maria, Calif., 1980—. Mem. County Grand Jury, Santa Barbara, 1992-93. Mem. Channel City Club. Republican. Baptist. Home and Office: 451 Live Oaks Rd Santa Barbara CA 93108

LIDDICOAT, RICHARD THOMAS, JR., association executive; b. Kearsarge, Mich., Mar. 2, 1918; s. Richard Thomas and Carmen (Williams) L.; m. Mary Imogene Hibbard, Sept. 21, 1939. BS in Geology, U. Mich., 1939, MS in Mineralogy, 1940; grad. gemologist, Gemological Inst. Am., 1941; MS in Meteorology, Calif. Inst. Tech., 1944. With Gemological Inst. Am., Los Angeles, 1940-42, 46—; dir. edn. Gemological Inst. Am., 1942, 46-49, asst. dir., 1950-52, exec. dir., 1952-83, pres., 1970-83, chmn. bd., 1983—, also author courses; editor Gem and Gemology, 1952—; Supr. ednl. sessions ann. conclaves Am. Gem Soc., 1948-83; hon. certified gemologist, 1947; hon. research staff Los Angeles Mus. Natural History, 1968—; U.S. del. Internat. Gem Conf., 1960, 64, 66, 68, 70, 72, 75, 77, 79, 81, 83, 85, 89; del. President's Conf. Small Bus., 1957. Author: Handbook of Gem Identification, 12th edit, 1987, (with others) The Diamond Dictionary, 1960, 2d edit., 1977, (with Copeland) Jewelers Manual, 2d edit, 1967; numerous articles.; contbr. to Ency. Britannica Jr., Ency. Americana, McGraw-Hill Ency. of Sci. and Tech. Trustee Nat. Home Study Coun., 1988-88. Recipient Lifetime Achievement award Modern Jeweler's mag., 1985, Award, Internat. Soc. of Appraisers, 1985, Spl. award Internat. Colored Stone Assn., 1984, Lifetime Achievement award Morris B. Zale, 1987; named Man of Yr., Consol. Jewelers Assn. Greater N.Y., 1984; named to Nat. Home Study Coun. Hall of Fame, 1991; Liddicoatitic species of tourmaline groupnamed in his honor. Fellow Mineral. Soc. Am., Geol. Soc. Am., Gem Assn. Gt. Britain (hon.); mem. AAAS, Am. Gem Soc (Shipley award 1976), Am. Gem Trade Assn. (hon.), Gem Assn. Australia (hon. v.p.), Gem Testing Lab of Great Britain (1st hon. life mem.), Sigma Xi, Sigma Gamma Epsilon. Clubs: Bel Air Country (bd. dirs. 1980-83) (Los Angeles), Twenty-Four Karat (N.Y.C., So. Calif.). Home: 1484 Allenford Ave Los Angeles CA 90049-3614 Office: Gemological Inst Am 1660 Stewart St Santa Monica CA 90404-4020

LIDDY, STEVEN THOMAS, career military officer, educator; b. St. Louis, Jan. 16, 1960; s. Robert James and Rita Marie (Stuesse) L.; m. JoAnn Claire Brinkmann. BS, Harris-Stowe State U., 1984; MBA, U. Mo., 1989. Commd. 2d lt. USAF, 1984, advanced through grades to capt., 1989; missile combat crew 351 Missile Wing USAF, Whiteman AFB, Mo., 1985-86; alt. command post 351 Missile Wing USAF, Whiteman AFB, Mo., 1986-89; instr., commdr. 351 Missile Wing, Whiteman AFB, Mo., 1989; ops. instr. 4315 Combat Crew Tng. USAF, Vandenberg AFB, Calif., 1989-90; acad. instr. 4315 Combat Crew Tng. USAF, Vanderberg AFB, Calif., 1990-92, flight comdr. 4315 Combat Crew Tng., 1992—. Mem. Parish Coun., Vandenberg AFB, 1989—; baptism coord. Our Lady of the Stars Ch., Vandenberg AFB, 1989—; project officer Spl. Olympics, Santa Barbara, 1992. Mem. Air Force Assn. (life), Kappa Delta Pi, Alpha Kappa Psi. Office: USAF Bldg 8231 Rm 205 4315 Combat Crew Tng Squad Vandenberg AFB CA 93437-5000

LIDGATE, DOREEN WANDA, retired librarian; b. Seattle, Jan. 27, 1925; d. Robert Jesse and Doris Ivy (Giffin) L. BA, U. Wash., 1946, M in Librarianship, 1966. Tchr. music St. Nicholas Sch., Seattle, 1948-70, libr., 1950-70, dean of students, 1968-70; reference libr. depts. edn., sociology, psychology Seattle Pub. Libr., 1971-74; libr. in charge Ratti Perbix Clark, Seattle, 1974-90; ret., 1990; cons. libr. rsch., 1990—. Mem. The Mountaineers, Wash. Athletic Club (v.p. 1955, associate women's bd. 1954), Beta Phi Mu, Alpha Chi Omega. Home: 2214 Viewmont Way W Seattle WA 98199

LIDICKER, WILLIAM ZANDER, JR., zoologist, educator; b. Evanston, Ill., Aug. 19, 1932; s. William Zander and Frida (Schroeter) L.; m. Naomi Ishino, Aug. 18, 1956 (div. Oct., 1982); children: Jeffrey Roger, Kenneth Paul; m. Louise N. DeLonzor, June 5, 1989. B.S., Cornell U., 1953; M.S., U. Ill., 1954, Ph.D., 1957. Instr. zoology, asst. curator mammals U. Calif., Berkeley, 1957-59; asst. prof., asst. curator U. Calif., 1959-65, assoc. prof., assoc. curator, 1965-69; assoc. dir. Mus. Vertebrate Zoology, 1968-81, acting dir., 1974-75, prof. zoology, curator mammals, 1969-89, prof. integrative biology, curator of mammals, 1989—. Contbr. articles to profl. jours. Bd. dirs. No. Calif. Com. for Environ. Info., 1971-77; bd. trustees BIOSIS, 1987-92, chmn., 1992; N.Am. rep. steering com., sect. Mammalogy IUBS, UNESCO, 1978-89; chmn. rodent specialist group Species Survival Commn., IUCN, 1980-89; mem. sci. adv. bd. Marine World Found. at Marine World Africa USA, 1987—; pres. Dehnel-Petrusewicz Meml. Fund, 1985—. Fellow AAAS, Calif. Acad. Scis.; mem. Am. Soc. Mammalogists (dir., 2d v.p. 1974-76, pres. 1976-78, C.H. Merriam award 1986), Am. Soc. Naturalists, others. Club: Berkeley Folk Dancers (pres. 1969, tchr. 1984—). Office: U Calif Mus Vertebrate Zoology Berkeley CA 94720

LIDMAN, RUSSELL MARTIN, academic administrator; b. Rochester, N.Y., Mar. 8, 1945; s. Nathan and Nancy (Phillips) L.; m. Raven Clarke, June 10, 1971; children: Shane, Hannah. BSEE, Cornell U., 1966; MPA, Princeton U., 1968; MS, U. Wis., 1970, PhD, 1972. Mem. faculty The Evergreen State Coll., Olympia, Wash., 1974—; dir. Wash. State Inst. Pub. Policy, Olympia, 1985-90. Fulbright prof., Lima, Peru, 1983-84. Office: The Evergreen State Coll Office Provost Olympia WA 98505

LIDSTONE, HERRICK KENLEY, JR., lawyer; b. New Rochelle, N.Y., Sept. 10, 1949; s. Herrick Kenley and Marcia Edith (Drake) L.; m. Mary Lynne O'Toole, Aug. 5, 1978; children: Herrick Kevin, James Patrick, John Francis. AB, Cornell U., 1971; JD, U. Colo., 1978. Bar: Colo. 1978, U.S. Dist. Ct. Colo. 1978. Assoc. Roath & Brega, P.C., Denver, 1978-85, Brenman, Epstein, Raskin & Friedlob, P.C., Denver, 1985-86; shareholder Brenman, Raskin & Friedlob, P.C., Denver, 1986—; adj. prof. U. Denver Coll. Law, 1985—; speaker in field various orgns.; fluent in Spanish. Editor U. Colo. Law Rev., 1977-78; co-author: Federal Income Taxation of Corporations, 6th edit.; contbr. articles to profl. jours. Served with USN, 1971-75, with USNR, 1975-81. Mem. ABA (Am. Law Inst.), Colo. Bar Assn., Denver Bar Assn., Denver Assn. Oil and Gas Title Lawyers. Office: Brenman Raskin & Friedlob PC 1400 Glenarm Pl Denver CO 80202-5030

LIEBAN, ROBERT ALAN, JR., university administrator; b. L.A., Sept. 28, 1959; s. Robert Alan Lieban and Harriet Ann (Salzberg) Bonn; m. Heather Anne Cumming, Nov. 5, 1988. BA in Polit. Sci., UCLA, 1981. CPCU. Underwriter, mktg. rep. Fireman's Fund Ins. Co., L.A., 1981-84; ins. broker Jardine Ins. Brokers, L.A., 1984-86, Johnson & Higgins Ins. Brokers, L.A., 1986-88; risk mgmt. coord. UCLA, 1989—; free lance ind. cons., L.A., 1989—. Mem. adv. bd. Tau Kappa Epsilon Fraternity, L.A., 1985-90; fundraiser U.S. Govt. Internship Assn., L.A., 1986-89. Fellow Soc. CPCU. Republican. Jewish. Home: 7742 Redlands Ave Unit 1028 Playa Del Rey CA 90293

LIEBAU, FREDERIC JACK, JR., securities analyst; b. Palo Alto, Calif., Sept. 30, 1963; s. Frederic Jack and Charlene (Conrad) L. BA, Stanford U., 1985. Press aide Office of V.P., Washington, 1982; intern L.A. Times, 1983; analyst Capital Rsch. Co., L.A., 1984-86; v.p. Primecap Mgmt. Co., Pasadena, Calif., 1986—. Office: Primecap Mgmt Co 225 S Lake Ave Pasadena CA 91101-3005

LIEBERMAN, BRANDON STUART, broadcast executive; b. L.A., July 30, 1961; s. Barry Sherwin L. and Joan Yvonne (Fischer) Drabkin. Music dir. Sta. KBVR-FM Radio, Corvallis, Oreg., 1982-85, sta. mgr., 1983-85; import and ind. buyer Tower Records, Beaverton, Oreg., 1985-87; ind. buyer Music Millennium, Portland, Oreg., 1987—; music dir., band mgr. M99 Sta. KBOO-FM Radio, Portland, 1990—; pvt. practice as concert promoter, Corvallis, Portland, 1983—. Contbr. articles to profl. jours. Office: Sta KBOO-FM Radio 20 SE 8th Portland OR 97214

LIEBERMAN, FREDRIC, ethnomusicologist, educator; b. N.Y.C., Mar. 1, 1940; s. Stanley and Bryna (Mason L.). MusB, U. Rochester, 1962; MA in Ethnomusicology, U. Hawaii, 1965; PhD in Music, UCLA, 1977; diploma in Electronics, Cleve. Inst. Electronics, 1973; cert. Inst. for Ednl. Mgmt., Harvard U., 1984. Asst. prof. music Brown U., Providence, 1968-75; assoc. prof. U. Wash., Seattle, 1975-83, chmn. div. ethnomusicolgy, 1977-80, dir. sch. music, 1981-83; prof. U. Calif., Santa Cruz, 1983—, dir. dept. arts, 1983-85, provost Porter Coll., 1983-85; chmn. Bd. of Studies in Music, 1988-92; fieldworker Taiwan and Japan, 1963-64, Sikkim, winter 1970, Madras, India, winters 1977, 78, 82, 83; mem. folk arts panel Nat. Endowment for Arts, 1977-80, internat. panel, 1979-80; panelist basic rsch. divsn. NEH, 1982-84, Calif. Arts Coun., 1993; fieldworker, presenter Smithsonian Instn. Festival Am. Folklife, 1978-82; reviewer Ctr. for Scholarly Communication with People's Republic China, 1979—; exchange lectr. U. Warsaw, Poland, spring 1980; co-dir. summer seminar for coll. tchrs. NEH, 1977; dir. Am. Musical Heritage Found., 1991—. Author: Chinese Music: An Annotated Bibliography, 1970, 2d edit., 1979, A Chinese Zither Tutor: The Mei-An Ch'in-P'u, 1983, (with Mickey Hart) Drumming at the Edge of Magic, 1990, Planet Drum: A Celebration of Percussion and Rhythm, 1991; editor (with Fritz A Kuttner) Perspectives on Asian Music: Essays in Honor of Lawrence Picken, 1975; gen. editor Garland Bibliographies in Ethnomusicology, 1980-86; mem. editorial bd. Musica Asiatica, 1984—; contbr. numerous articles and revs. to profl. publs.; composer: Suite for Piano, 1964, Sonatina for Piano, 1964, Two Short String Quartets, 1966, Leaves of Brass (for brass quartet), 1967, Psalm 137; By the Rivers of Babylon (for chorus), 1971; records include China I: String Instruments, 1969, China II: Amoy Music, 1971, Music of Sikkim, 1975; ethnomusicology cons., 19 releases 1988-92 on Ryko label, produced by 360 Degrees Productions; filmer, editor (with Michael Moore) Traditional Music and Dance of Sikkim, Parts I and II, 1976; producer, dir., editor videotape Documenting Traditional Performance, 1978. Mem. exec. bd. Pub. Radio Sta. KRAB-FM, Seattle, 1977-78; mem. King County Arts Commn., Seattle, 1977-80. Grantee Nat. Endowment for the Arts, 1978, NEH, 1978, 80.; N.Y. State Regents fellow, 1958-62, East-West Ctr. fellow and travel grantee, 1962-65, UCLA Chancellor's teaching fellow, 1965-69, John D. Rockefeller 3d Fund research fellow, 1970-71. Mem. Soc. for Ethnomusicology (sec.-treas. So. Calif. chpt. 1966-68, bus. mgr., bd. dirs. Ethnomusicology 1969-72, editor 1977-81, nat. council 1970-72, 74-76, 78-81, 83-86), Soc. for Asian Music (editorial bd. Asian Music 1968-77, editor publs. series 1968—), Coll. Music Soc. (nat. council 1973-75, exec. bd. 1974-75, 76-77), Conf. on Chinese Oral and Performing Lit. (exec. bd. 1971-74, 78-80), ASCAP, Nat. Acad. Recording Arts and Sci., Internat. Council Traditional Music, Am. Musical Heritage Found. (treas. 1991—), Phi Mu Alpha Sinfonia. Office: U Calif Porter Coll Santa Cruz CA 95064

LIEBERMAN, SCOTT ALLAN, radiologist; b. Flushing, N.Y., May 25, 1958; s. Paul and Bernice (Morrow) L. BA, Boston U., 1982, MD, 1982. Diplomate Nat. Bd. Med. Examiners, Am. Bd. Radiology. Resident Winthrop-Univ. Hosp., Mineola, N.Y., 1982-86; fellow magnetic resonance imaging San Jose MRI Ctr., San Jose, Calif., 1986-87; radiologist various, Calif., Tex., 1987-88, Valley Radiologists, San Jose, Calif., 1988—. Publicity chmn. Libertarian Party Santa Clara County, Calif., 1987-93. Mem. Radiologic Soc. No. Am., Am. Radio Relay League. Home: 3200 Payne Ave Apt 714 San Jose CA 95117

LIEBIG, PHOEBE STONE, gerontology educator; b. Cambridge, Mass., Dec. 28, 1933; d. Marshall Harvey Stone and Emmy (Portmann) Allen; m. Anthony E. Liebig, June 19, 1954 (div. 1961); 1 child, Steuart Anthony. Student, Radcliffe Coll., 1951-54; BA, UCLA, 1955, MA, 1956; PhD, U. So. Calif., L.A., 1983. Cert. tchr. Dept. asst. classics dept. UCLA, 1956-62; tchr. L.A. Unified Sch. Dist., 1961-70; info. specialist Ancom Systems, L.A., 1970-71; specialist grants gerontology ctr. U. So. Calif., L.A., 1971-75, lectr., sr. adminitrv. analyst and coord. gerontology ctr., 1976-80, dir. planning gerontology ctr., 1980-86, rsch. asst. prof. sch. gerontology, 1983-86, dir. geriatric edn. cen. sch. med., 1984-86; sr. policy analyst Am. Assn. Retired Persons, Washington, 1986-88, asst. prof. gerontology, acting dir. Program of Policy and Svcs. Rsch., 1988-89; Hanson Family asst. prof. gerontology U. So. Calif., L.A., 1990-93; cons. UCLA 1980—. Author: 50 State Teachers Retirement Systems: A Comparative Analysis, 1987; contbr. articles to profl. jours. Subproject dir. Alzheimer's Disease Rsch. Ctr., 1984-86, Nat. Inst. Health, Nat. Eldercare Inst. Housing & Supportive Svcs., Adminstrn. on Aging, Dept. Health and Human Svcs., 1991—; project dir. Geriatric Edn. Cen., Health Resource and Svc. Adminstn., Dept. Health and Human Svcs. 1984-86; founding mem. Gregg Smith Singers, L.A., 1954; mem. Brentwood Dem. Club, L.A., 1954-56; nomination and selection com. Art Mus. Coun., L.A., 1956-60; founding dir. Neo Renaissance Singers, L.A., 1960; active nat. task force Am. Soc. of Allied Health Profl., Washington, 1985-88. Fellow Gerontol. Soc. Am. (exec. com. sec., sect. study group econs. 1986—, sect. commn.); mem. Am. Soc. Aging (sec. 1985-86, bd. dirs. 1985-87), Am. Soc. Pub. Adminstrn., Assn. Pub. Policy and Mgmt. Analysis (reviewer), Internat. Soc. Preretirement Planners (editorial bd. 1986-88, editorial bd. Jour. of Aging and Social Policy 1989—), Calif. Coun. on Gerontology and Geriatrics (bd. dirs. 1989—, program chair 1991-93, pres. 1993—), Western Govtl. Researcher (editorial bd. 1990—), L.A. County Mus. Art, Early Music Ensemble, Cambridge Singers. Democrat. Home: 10963 Citrus Dr Moorpark CA 93021-9718 Office: U So Calif Andrus Gerontology Ctr University Park CA 90089-0191

LIECHTY, CLINTON, lawyer; b. Logan, Utah, Feb. 28, 1949; s. Mada (Hulse) L.; m. Carol Ann Mathews, July 1, 1972; children: Brian, Heidi, Matthew, Heather, Jennifer, Tyler. BS, Utah State U., 1975; JD, Gonzaga Law Sch., 1978. Bar: Ariz. 1979, U.S. Ct. Appeals (9th cir.) 1980, U.S. Supreme Ct. 1982. Pvt. practice Tucson, 1979—; talk show host, You and The Law Radio, Tucson, 1979-92. Century mem. Boy Scouts Am., Tucson, 1988, com. chmn. 1984—, dist. adv. chmn., 1993—; With USAR, 1967-73. Named Most Valuable Com. Chmn., Boy Scouts Am., Tucson, 1989; Rockefeller Found. research grantee, Utah State U., 1973; J. Reuben Clark fellowship Provo, Utah, 1989—. Mem. Pima County Bar Assn. (ed. com. mem. 1979—), Tucson Rod & Gun Club. Mem. LDS Ch. Office: 360 N Court Ave Tucson AZ 35701

LIEN, ERIC JUNG-CHI, pharmacist, educator; b. Kaohsiung, Taiwan, Nov. 30, 1937; came to U.S., 1963, naturalized, 1973; m. Linda L. Chen, Oct. 2, 1965; children: Raymond, Andrew. B.S. in Pharmacy (Frank Shu China Sci. scholar), Nat. Taiwan U., 1960; Ph.D. in Pharm. Chemistry, U. Calif., San Francisco, 1966; postdoctoral fellow in bio-organic chemistry, Pomona Coll., Claremont, Calif., 1967-68. Hosp. pharmacist 862 Hosp. of Republic of China, 1960-61; asst. prof. pharmaceutics and biomedicinal chemistry U. So. Calif., L.A., 1968-72; assoc. prof. U. So. Calif., 1972-76, prof., 1976—, coord. sects. biomedicinal chemistry and pharms., 1975-78, coord. sect. biomedicinal chemistry, 1975-84; cons. Internat. Medication System, Ltd., 1978, NIH, 1971, 82-87, 92, Inst. Drug Design, Inc., Calif., 1971-73, Allergan Pharms., Inc., 1971-72, EPA, 1985, 89, Ariz. Disease Control Rsch. commn., 1986—; sci. adv. nat. labs. Dept. Health, Foods and Drugs, Executive Yuan, China, Dept. Health Taipei Republic China. Mem. editorial bd. Jour. Clin. Pharmacy and Therapeutics, 1979—, Internat. Jour. Oriental Medicine, Med. Chem. Rsch., 1991—, Chinese Pharm. Jour., 1991—; referee Jour. Pharmacokinetics and Biopharmaceutics, Jour. Medicinal Chemistry, Jour. Food Agr. Chemistry, Jour. Pharm. Sci., Pesticide Biochemistry and Physiology, Chem. Revs., Jour. Organic Chem., Pharm. Rsch., Internat. Jour. Oriental Medicine, Am. Jour. Pharm. Edn.; author 3 books; contbr. numerous articles to profl. jours. Grantee Merck, 1970, Abbott, 1971-72, NSF, 1972-74, 1976-77, IMS, 1979, H & L Found., 1989-92. Fellow AAPS, AAAS, Louis Pasteur Found.; mem. Am. Assn. Cancer Rsch., Acad. Pharm. Scis., Am. Chem. Soc., Am. Assn. Pharm. Scientist, Internat. Union Pure and Applied Chemistry, Sigma Xi, Rho Chi, Phi Beta Phi. Office: U So Calif Sch Pharmacy 1985 Zonal Ave Los Angeles CA 90033-1058

LIENAU, PAUL JOHN, college program director; b. Mitchell, S.D., Jan. 20, 1937; s. Walter L. and Mary Ann (Petersen) L.; m. 1958 (div. 1980); children: Michael, David, Jeffrey; m. Colleen Sue Cashen, Aug. 15, 1981. BS, Black Hills State U., 1959; MS, Temple U., 1963. Prof. Willmar (Minn.) State Jr. Coll., 1963-68; prof. Oreg. Inst. Tech., Klamath Falls, 1968-73, dir. Geo-Heat Ctr., 1974—. Editor: Geothermal Direct Use Engineering and Design Guidebook, 1989. NSF scholar Princeton U., Temple U., 1962. Mem. Geothermal Resources Coun., Geothermal Adv. Commn. (chmn. 1984-89). Lutheran. Office: Geo Heat Ctr 3201 Campus Dr Klamath Falls OR 97601

LIETZEN, JOHN HERVY, human resources executive, health agency volunteer; b. Kansas City, Kans., July 17, 1947; s. Walter Edwin and Kathleen Mae (Griffith) L.; m. Nora Rose Massey, June 12, 1966; children: Gwendolyn Therese, Anne Gabrielle, Sarah Kathleen. BS, Mo. Valley Coll., 1974; MS, U. Mo., 1976; postgrad, U. Nebr., 1982-88. With Union Pacific R.R., 1971—; yard condr. Union Pacific R.R., Kansas City, Kans., 1971-77; pers. officer Union Pacific R.R., Omaha, 1977-78; pers. dir. Union Pacific R.R., Cheyenne, Wyo., 1978-79, sr. tng. officer dept. claims, 1979-83, mgr. staffing, 1983-84, mgr. affirmative action, 1984-86; human resources tng. and devel. cons. Union Pacific R.R., Salt Lake City, 1986—. Bd. dirs. Berkshire Village, Kansas City, 1976-77; bd. ministries Valley View Meth. Ch., Overland Pk., Kans., 1976-77; pastor and staff rels. com. Hanscom Pk. United Meth. Ch., 1980-81, lay leader, 1983; asst. leader Wyo. coun. Girl Scouts U.S.A., Cheyenne, 1978-79, asst. leader, Omaha, 1980-89, Salt Lake, 1989—, bd. dirs. Great Plains Girl Scout Coun., 1987-89; exec. bd. Nebr. affiliate Am. Diabetes Assn., 1981-89, pres. Midlands chpt., 1982-84, mem. planning and orgn. com., 1986-87, bd. dirs. Utah affiliate, 1990—, co-founder Omaha Insulin Pump Club, 1986; loaned exec. United Way of Midlands, 1984. Sgt. U.S. Army, 1968-71, Germany. Mem. Am. Soc. Personnel and Guidance Assn., Adult and Continuing Edn. Assn. Nebr. (planning com. 1982-84), Am. Soc. for Tng. and Devel. Republican. Home: 3077 S 2225 E Salt Lake City UT 84109-2418 Office: Union Pacific 320 W 200 S Salt Lake City UT 84101-1210

LIGGETT, THOMAS MILTON, mathematics educator; b. Danville, Ky., Mar. 29, 1944; s. Thomas Jackson and Virginia Corinne (Moore) L.; m. Christina Marie Goodale, Aug. 19, 1972; children: Timothy, Amy. AB, Oberlin Coll., 1965; MS, Stanford U., 1966, PhD, 1969. Asst. prof. UCLA, 1969-73, assoc. prof., 1973-76, prof., 1976—, chmn. math. dept., 1991—. Author: Interacting Particle Systems, 1985; editor Jour. Annals of Probability, 1985-87; contbr. articles to profl. jours. Fellow Sloan Found., 1973. Fellow Inst. Math. Stats.; mem. Am. Math. Soc., Math. Assn. Am., Bernoulli Soc. Office: UCLA Math Dept 405 Hilgard Ave Los Angeles CA 90024-1301

LIGGINS, GEORGE LAWSON, microbiologist-diagnostic company executive; b. Roanoke, Va., June 19, 1937; m. Joyce Preston Liggins, Sept. 3, 1966; 1 child, George Lawson Jr. BA, Hampton U., 1962; cert. med. technician, Meharry Med. Sch., 1963; MPH, U. N.C., 1969; PhD, U. Va., Charlottesville, 1975. Med. technician Vets. Hosp., Hampton, Va., 1963-66; rsch. technician U. N.C. Med. Sch., Chapel Hill, 1966-69; postdoctoral fellow Scripps Clinic, La Jolla, Calif., 1975-76, Salk Inst., La Jolla, 1976-77; rsch. mgr. Hyland div. Baxter, Costa Mesa, Calif., 1977-78; R & D dir. diagnostics div. Baxter, Roundlake, Ill., 1978-83; pres., COO Internat. Immunology, Murrieta, Calif., 1983-86; chmn., CEO Bacton Assay Systems, Inc., San Marcos, Calif., 1986—; cons. Beckman Instruments, Inc., Brea, Calif., 1987-90, Paramax div. Baxter, Irvine, Calif., 1988-90, Scantibodies Lab., Santee, Calif., 1990-92; presenter in field; mem. virology study Cold Spring Harbor Lab., L.I., N.Y., 1974. Contbr. articles to profl. jours. Fellow NIH, 1975, Am. Cancer Soc., 1976. Mem. Am. Soc. Microbiology, Am. Assn. Clin. Chemistry, Van Slyke Soc. of Am. Assn. Clin. Chemistry, Am. Heart Assn., Nat. Hampton Alumni, Inc. (pres. 1991—), Omega Psi Phi. Republican. Methodist. Office: Bacton Assay Systems Inc 772-A N Twin Oaks Valley Rd San Marcos CA 92069

LIGHT, KEN, photojournalist, educator; b. N.Y.C., Mar. 16, 1951; s. Stanley and Dorothea (Gottfried) L.; m. Carmen Lising, June 1976 (div. Aug. 1985); 1 child, Stephen; m. Melanie Hastings, Aug. 1, 1992. BGS, Ohio U., 1973. Instr. Contra. Costa Coll., San Pablo, Calif., 1974-84; photographer Labor Occ. Health Program, Berkeley, Calif., 1975-81; mem. staff Alameda Neighborhood Arts Program, Oakland, Calif., 1975-81; instr. Grad. Sch. Journalism U. Calif., Berkeley, 1986-89; cons. photographer Libr. Congress Folklife Ctr., 1989-90; faculty San Francisco Acad. Art Coll., 1977—; lectr. Berkeley Grad. Sch. Journalism, 1983—; founder Fund Documentary Photog., 1988—. Author: To the Promised Land, 1988, With These Hands, 1986, In The Fields, 1984. Recipient Meritorious Achievement award Media Alliance, 1990, Thomas More Storke Internat. Journalism award World Affairs Coun., 1989; nominnee Pulitzer Prize Feature Photography, 1993; grantee Am. Film Inst., 1979; NEA fellow, 1982, 86, Dorothea Lange fellow. Mem. Soc. Photog. Edn. Home: 3107 Deakin St Berkeley CA 94705-1950

LIGHT-HARRIS, DONALD, production designer; b. Indpls., Aug. 13, 1944; s. Harry Charles and Hannah Leah (Miller) H.; m. Linaia Light, Apr. 12, 1987; children: Travis Lee, Vanessa Hannah. MA, San Francisco State U., 1968. Prodn. designer Warner Bros., Burbank, Calif., 1991—; prodn. designer NBC, Hollywood, Calif., 1991—, Columbia TV, Burbank, 1991—. Recipient Best Lighting Design award L.A. Drama Critics, 1973, CLIO for Best Prodn. Design, 1980. Mem. Acad. TV Arts and Scis., Internat. Alliance of Theatrical Stagehands.

LIGHTNER, MICHAEL R., electrical engineer, educator; b. Gainesville, Fla., Oct. 9, 1950; m. Linda Lunbeck, Sept., 1991. BEE, U. Fla., 1972, MEE, 1974; DEng, Carnegie-Mellon U., 1979. Asst. prof. U. Ill., 1979-81, rsch. asst. prof. coordinated sci. lab., 1981; asst. prof. Colo. U., Boulder, 1981-83, assoc. prof., 1983-89, prof., dir. grad. sch., 1989—; mem. summer faculty IBM Watson Rsch. Ctr., Yorktown, N.Y., 1982. Contbr. articles to profl. jours. Mem. IEEE (editor transactions on CAD 1989-91), IEEE Cirs. and Systems Soc. (v.p. tech. activity 1990—), Am. Soc. Engring. Edn., European Community CAD. Office: U Colo Dept Elec Computer Engring University Of Colorado CO 80309

LIGHTSTONE, RONALD, lawyer; b. N.Y.C., Oct. 4, 1938; s. Charles and Pearl (Weisberg) L.; m. Nancy Lehrer, May 17, 1973; 1 child, Dana. AB, Columbia U., 1959; JD, NYU, 1962. Atty. CBS, N.Y.C., 1967-69; assoc. dir. bus. affairs CBS News, N.Y.C., 1969-70; atty. NBC, N.Y.C., 1970; assoc. gen. counsel Viacom Internat. Inc., N.Y.C., 1970-75; v.p., gen. counsel, sec. Viacom Internat. Inc., 1976-80; v.p. bus. affairs Viacom Entertainment Group Viacom Internat., Inc., 1980-82, v.p. corp. affairs, 1982-84, sr. v.p. corp. and legal affairs, 1984-87; exec. v.p. Aaron Spelling Prodns., Inc., West Hollywood, Calif., 1988—; exec. v.p. Spelling Entertainment Inc., L.A., 1989-92, COO, 1992—; bd. dirs. Starsight Telecast, Inc. Served to lt. USN, 1962-66. Mem. ABA (chmn. TV, cable and radio com.), Assn. Bar City N.Y., Fed. Communications Bar Assn. Office: Spelling Entertainment Inc 5700 Wilshire Blvd Los Angeles CA 90036-3659

LIGHTWOOD, CAROL WILSON, writer; b. Tacoma, Wash., Oct. 2, 1941; d. Harry Edward and Cora H. Wilson; m. Keith G. Lightwood (div. Dec. 1968); children: Miles Francis, Clive Harry. BA, Smith Coll., 1963. Writer various advt. agencies, 1968-82; v.p. Wakeman & DeForrest, Newport Beach, Calif., 1985-86; owner Lightwood & Ptnrs., Long Beach, Calif., 1986—. Author: Malibu, 1984; contbr. articles to profl. jours. Chair mus. coun. Long Beach Mus. Art, 1989; docent William O. Douglas Outdoor Classroom. Mem. Sierra Club, Sisters in Crime. Episcopalian.

LIGRANI, PHILLIP MEREDITH, mechanical engineer, educator, consultant; b. Cheyenne, Wyoming, Feb. 2, 1952; s. Alfred Joseph Ligrani and Marilyn Virginia (Waugh) Whittaker. BS, U. Tex., 1974; MS, Stanford U., 1975, PhD, 1980. Asst. prof. Von Karman Isnt. for Fluid Dynamics, Rhode St. Genese, Belgium, 1979-82; sr. rsch. fellow Imperial Coll. U. London, 1982-84; assoc. prof. mech. engring. Naval Postgrad. Sch., Monterey, Calif., 1984-92, U. Utah, Salt Lake City, 1992—. Author 4 book chpts.; contbr. over 40 articles to profl. jours. Recipient Menneken award for excellence sci. rsch. Menneken Found., 1990. Mem. AIAA, ASME (K-14 heat transfer com. 1986—), Am. Phys. Soc. Office: U Utah Mech Engring MEB 3209 Salt Lake City UT 84112

LIKENS, JAMES DEAN, economics educator; b. Bakersfield, Calif., Sept. 12, 1937; s. Ernest LeRoy and Monnie Jewel (Thomas) L.; m. Janet Sue Pelton, Dec. 18, 1965 (div.); m. Karel Carnohan, June 4, 1988 (div.); children: John David, Janet Elizabeth. BA in Econs., U. Calif., 1960, MBA, 1961; PhD in Econs., U. Minn., 1970. Analyst Del Monte Corp., San Francisco, 1963; economist 3M Co., Mpls., 1968-71; asst. prof. econs. Pomona Coll., 1969-75, assoc. prof. econs., 1975-83, prof. econs., 1983-85, Morris B. Pendleton prof. econs., 1989—; vis. asst. prof. econs. U. Minn., 1970, 71, vis. assoc. prof. econs., 1976-77; dean Western CUNA Mgmt. Sch., Pomona Coll., 1975—; chmn. bd. 1st City Savs. Fed. Credit Union, 1978—; mem. bd. Health Plan Am., 1983-85; coord. So. Calif. Rsch. Coun., L.A., 1980-81, 84-85; cons. in field. Author: (with Joseph LaDou) Medicine and Money, 1976, Mexico and Southern California: Toward A New Partnership, 1981, Financing Quality Education in Southern California, 1985; contbr. articles to profl. jours. Rsch. grantee HUD-DOT, Haynes Found., Filene Rsch. Inst. Mem. ABA, Am. Econ. Assn., Western Econ. Assn. Home: 725 W 10th St Claremont CA 91711-3719 Office: Pomona Coll Dept Econs Claremont CA 91711-6353

LIKENS, SUZANNE ALICIA, physiologist, researcher; b. Chgo., Nov. 12, 1945; d. Harry Ross and Sibyle Lovelett (Butler) L. BS in Biology, U. N.Mex., 1969, MS in Physiology, 1982. Research asst. biology dept. U. N.Mex., Albuquerque, 1969; sr. research technologist Inhalation Toxicology Research Inst., Albuquerque, 1974—. Contbr. sci. papers and articles to profl. jours. Mem. AAAS, Costeau Soc., N.Mex. Zool. Soc., Humane Soc. of U.S., N.Mex. Herpetological Soc. (charter), Women in Sci. and Engring., Ctr. Environ. Edn. Whale Protection Fund, U.S. Dressage Fedn., N.Mex. Dressage and Combined Tng. Assn., S.W. Dressage Assn. (bd. dirs. 1989-93), N.Y. Acad. Scis., Sigma Xi. Republican. Presbyterian. Home: 1311 Dartmouth Dr NE Albuquerque NM 87106-1803 Office: Inhalation Toxicology Rsch Inst PO Box 5890 Albuquerque NM 87185-5890

LILLEGRAVEN, JASON ARTHUR, paleontologist, educator; b. Mankato, Minn., Oct. 11, 1938; s. Arthur Oscar and Agnes Mae (Eaton) L.; m. Bernice Ann Hines, Sept. 5, 1964 (div. Feb. 1983); children: Brita Anna, Ture Andrew; m. Linda Elizabeth Thompson, June 5, 1983. BA, Long Beach State Coll., 1962; MS, S.D. Sch. Mines and Tech., 1964; PhD, U. Kans., 1968. Professional geologist, Wyo. Postdoctoral fellow Dept. Paleontology U. Calif., Berkeley, 1968-69; from asst. prof. to prof. zoology San Diego State U., 1969-75; from assoc. prof. to prof. geology and zoology U. Wyo., Laramie, 1975—; program dir. NSF Systematic Biology, Washington, 1977-78; assoc. dean U. Wyo. Coll. Arts and Scis., 1984-85, temporary joint appointment Dept. Geography, 1986-87; U.S. sr. scientist Inst. for Paleontology Free U., Berlin, 1988-89. Author, editor: Mesozoic Mammals the First Two Thirds of Mammalian History, 1979, Vertebrates, Phylogeny and Philosophy, 1986; editorial bds. of Research and Exploration (Nat. Geographic Soc.), Jour. of Mammalian Evolution, Jour. of Vertebrate Paleontology; contbr. articles to profl. jours. Recipient numerous rsch. grants NSF, 1970-93; Humboldt Prize. Mem. Am. Soc. Mammalogists, Am. Assn. Petroleum Geologists, Paleontol. Soc., Soc. Vertebrate Paleontology (pres. 1985-86), Linnean Soc. London, Sigma Xi. Office: U Wyo Dept Geology and Geophysics Laramie WY 80271-3006

LILLIE, JOHN MITCHELL, transportation company executive; b. Chgo., Feb. 2, 1937; s. Walter Theodore and Mary Ann (Hatch) L.; m. Daryl Lee Harvey, Aug. 23, 1987; children: Alissa Ann, Theodore Perry. BS, Stanford U., 1959, MS, MBA, 1962-64. Various positions including dir. systems devel., also asst. to pres. Boise Cascade Corp., 1964-68; v.p., chief financial officer Arcata Nat. Corp., Menlo Park, Calif., 1968-70; exec. v.p., chief operating officer Arcata Nat. Corp., 1970-72; pres., chief exec. officer Leslie Salt Co., Newark, Calif., 1972-79; exec. v.p. Lucky Stores Inc., Dublin, Calif., 1979-81, pres., 1981-86, chmn., chief exec. officer, 1986-89; gen. ptnr. Sequoia Assocs., Menlo Park, Calif., 1989-90; pres., COO, Am. Pres. Cos., Ltd., Oakland, Calif., 1990-91, chmn., pres., CEO, 1991—; bd. dirs. Am. Pres. Co., Gap Inc. Trustee Stanford (Calif.) U., 1988—; bd. dirs. Am. Pres. Co. Mem. Beta Theta Pi, Tau Beta Pi. Office: Am Pres Cos 1111 Broadway Oakland CA 94607-4021*

LILLIE, MILDRED LOREE, judge; b. Ida Grove, Iowa, Jan. 25, 1915; d. Ottmar August and Florence Elizabeth (Martin) Kluckhohn; m. Cameron Leo Lillie, Mar. 18, 1947 (dec. April 1959); m. A.V. Falcone, Aug. 27, 1966. AB, U. Calif., Berkeley, 1935, JD, 1938; LLD (hon.), Pepperdine U., 1981, Western States U., 1966. Bar: Calif. 1938, U.S. Dist. Ct. 1942, U.S. Supreme Ct. 1961. Sole practice Fresno, Calif., 1938-42; asst. U.S. atty. U.S. Dept. Justice, Los Angeles, 1942-46; practice law with Charles Carr Los Angeles, 1946-47; judge Mcpl. Ct., Los Angeles, 1947-49, County of Los Angeles Superior Ct., Los Angeles, 1949-58; assoc. justice Calif. Ct. of Appeal, Los Angeles, 1958-84, presiding justice, 1984—, adminstrv. presiding justice, 1988—; justice pro tem Calif. Supreme Ct., L.A., 1960, 77, 79, 81-92, mem. Jud. Coun. State of Calif., San Francisco, 1961-63, 87-89. Bd. dirs. NCCJ, L.A., 1985—; mem. Town Hall, L.A., 1985—; mem. bd. visitors Pepperdine U. Sch. Law, Malibu, Calif., 1985—. Recipient award Mademoiselle Mag., 1947, Vol. Activist award, 1976, Cardinal McIntyre award Catholic Press Club, 1981; named Woman of Yr. Los Angeles Times, 1952, Woman of Yr. Mus. of Science and Industry, Los Angeles, 1980. Mem. ABA, Fed. Bar Assn., Los Angeles County Bar Assn., Calif. Judges Assn. (com. chmn.) Women Lawyers Assn. (Ernestine Stahlhut award 1969), L.A. Trial Lawyers Assn. (Appellate Justice of Yr. 1986), L.A. Area C. of C. (bd. dirs. 1975-83), Boalt Hall Alumni Assn. (Citation award 1985), Nat. Assn. Women Judges, Ebell Club, L.A. Athletic Club, Soroptimists. Democrat. Roman Catholic. Office: 300 S Spring St Los Angeles CA 90013-1230

LILLY, JANE ANNE FEELEY, nursing researcher; b. Palo Alto, Calif., May 31, 1947; d. Daniel Morris Sr. and Suzanne (Agnew) Feeley; children: Cary Jane, Laura Blachree, Claire Foale; m. Dennis C. Hersley, Jan. 16, 1993. BS, U. Oreg., 1968; student, U. Hawaii, 1970; BSN, Sacramento City Coll., 1975. Cert. ACLS, BCLS. Staff and charge nurse, acute rehab. Santa Clara Valley Med. Ctr., San Jose, Calif., staff nurse, surg. ICU and trauma unit; clin. project leader dept immunology and infectious diseases Syntex Rsch., Palo Alto. Mem. adv. com. on AIDS edn. Union Sch. Dist. Mem. AACN, NAFE.

LILLY, MICHAEL ALEXANDER, lawyer; b. Honolulu, May 21, 1946; s. Percy Anthony Jr. and Virginia (Craig) L.; m. Kathryn I. Collins, Aug. 10, 1991; children: Cary J., Laura B., Claire F., Winston W. AA, Menlo Coll., Menlo Park, Calif., 1966; BA, U. Calif., Santa Cruz, 1968; JD with honors, U. of Pacific, 1974. Bar: Calif. 1974, U.S. Dist. Ct. (no., so. and ea. dists.) Calif. 1974, U.S. Ct. Appeals (9th cir.) 1974, Hawaii 1975, U.S. Dist. Ct. Hawaii 1975, U.S. Ct. Appeals (D.C. cir.) 1975, U.S. Supreme Ct. 1978, U.S. Ct. Appeals (7th cir.) 1979. Atty. Pacific Legal Found., Sacramento, 1974-75; dep. atty. gen. State of Hawaii, Honolulu, 1975-79, 1st dep. atty. gen., 1981-84, atty. gen., 1984-85; ptnr. Feeley & Lilly, San Jose, Calif., 1979-81, Ning, Lilly & Jones, Honolulu, 1985—; faculty Hastings Litigation Trial Advocacy Sch., San Francisco, 1984. Alumni rep. U. Calif., Santa Cruz, 1982—, Menlo Coll.; leader sustaining membership drive YMCA, Honolulu, 1984—; chmn. 17th senatorial dist. Rep. Party Hawaii, 1987-89. Lt. USN, 1968-71, Vietnam; capt. USNR. Named Hon. Ky. Col.; recipient Meritorious Svc.medal, 1991, Navy Commendation medal, 1988. Mem. Nat. Assn. Attys. Gen., Hawaii Law Enforcement Ofcls. Assn., Naval Res. Assn. (pres. 14th dist. 1986-89), Navy League (nat. dir., contbg. editor Fore 'N Aft mag., dep. judge adv. to bd. Honolulu coun., dir. Diamond Head Theatre), MADD, U. Pacific Alumnae Assn. Hawaii (pres.). Club: Outrigger Canoe. Home: 2769 Laniloa Rd Honolulu HI 96813-1041 Office: Ning Lilly & Jones 707 Richards St Ste 700 Honolulu HI 96813-4623

LILLY, RAYMOND LINDSAY, JR., neurosurgeon; b. Atlanta, Aug. 14, 1949; s. Raymond Lindsay and Martha Marguerite (Barrow) L.; m. Stona Britt Johnson, Sept. 28, 1990. BS, So. Missionary Coll., 1970; MD, Loma Linda U., 1973. Diplomate Am. Bd. Neurol. Surgery. Comdr. Med. Corps USN, 1970-84; neurosurgeon Neurosurg. Assoc., Beckley, W.Va., 1984-91, Madigan Army Med. Ctr., Ft. Lewis, Wash., 1991, So. Colo. Neurosurgery, Pueblo, 1991—. Lt. col. USAR. Fellow ACS; mem. Am. Assn. Neurol. Surgeons, Congress Neurol. Surgeons, Rotary. Office: So Colorado Neurosurgery 400 W 17th St Pueblo CO 81003

LILLY, SHARON LOUISE, university administrator; b. San Rafael, Calif., Sept. 6, 1957; d. Richard Joseph and Sonia Louise (McComber) Lilly; m. Roy Edward Garner, May 15, 1977 (div. 1989); children: Brionna Louise, Terrence Edward. BS, San Francisco State U., 1989. Devel. officer U. Calif., Berkeley, 1990—; cons. Nat. Cen. U., Taiwan, 1990—, Korea Adv. Inst. of Sci. and Tech., 1990—, Berkeley Photonics Inc., Orinda, Calif., 1990—. Bd. dirs. Contra Costa Youth Assn., Calif., 1991. Mem. Space Astrophysics Group, Earth and Planetary Atmospheres Group. Democrat. Office: Univ of Calif 2150 Kittredge St Berkeley CA 94720

LIM, HENRY CHOL, biochemical engineering educator, researcher; b. Seoul, Korea, Oct. 24, 1935; came to U.S., 1953; s. Kwang Un and Chang (Soon) L.; m. Sun Boo Lee, Dec. 11, 1959; children: David, Carol, Michael. BSChE, Okla. State U., 1957; MS in Engring., U. Mich., 1959; PhD, Northwestern U., 1967. R & D engr. Pfizer, Inc., Groton, Conn., 1959-63; asst. prof. chem. engring. Purdue U., West Lafayette, Ind., 1966-70, assoc. prof. chem. engring., 1970-74, prof. chem. engring., 1974-87; prof., chair dept. biochem. engring. U. Calif., Irvine, 1987—; adj. prof. Purdue U., 1987-90; cons. Novo Enzyme Corp., Mamoroneck, N.Y., 1973-77, Eli Lilly and Co., Indpls., 1982-84, Monsanto Co., St. Louis, 1987-90, Lucky Biotech, Emeryville, Calif., 1988-91. Author: (with others) Biological Waste Water Treatment: Theory and Applications, 1980. Mem. AICE, Am. Chem. Soc., Am. Soc. Microbiology, Soc. Indsl. Microbiology, Sigma Xi, Phi Kappa Phi, Phi Lambda Upsilon. Home: 10 Urey Ct Irvine CA 92715-4045

LIM, LARRY KAY, university official; b. Santa Maria, Calif., July 4, 1948; s. Koonwah and Nancy (Yao) L.; m. Louise A. Simon, Aug. 15, 1988. BA, UCLA, 1970, teaching cert., 1971. Asst. engr. Force Ltd., L.A., 1969; teaching asst. UCLA, 1970-71; tchr. L.A. Sch. Dist., 1971-82; dir. minority programs Sch. Engring., U. So. Calif., L.A., 1979—; presenter minority math.-based intervention symposium U. D.C., Washington, 1988. Newsletter editor, 1981-92. Bd. dirs. Developing Ednl. Studies for Hispanics, L.A., 1983-88. Named Dir. of Yr., Math., Engring., Sci. Achievement Ctr. Adv. Bd., 1986, 91, 92. Mem. Nat. Assn. Pre-Coll. Dirs., Nat. Assn. Minority Engring. Program Adminstr., Lotus/West Club (pres. 1977-83). Office: U So Calif Sch Engring OHE 104 Los Angeles CA 90089-1455

LIM, SALLY-JANE, insurance consultant; b. Manila; came to U.S., 1990; d. Teddy and Sonia (Yii) L.; children: Robin Michael, Rodney Jovin, Romelle Gavin Lim Velasco. BA, BS in Commerce magna cum laude, Coll. of Holy Spirit, Manila. CPA, Manila. Treas, contr. Ky. Fried Chicken, Makati, Philippines, 1968-73; ins. broker Insular Life Assurance Co., Makati, 1972-82; project analyst Pvt. Devel. Corp. of Philippines, Makati, 1973-78; account exec. Genbancor Devel. Corp., Makati, 1978-80; risk mgr. Filcapital Devel. Corp., Makati, 1978-82; pres., gen. mgr. Sally-Jane Multiline Insce., Inc., Makati, 1978-90; real estate broker Sally-Jane Realty, Inc., Manila, 1980-90; ins. broker Sun Life of Can./AIU (Philippines) AFIA, 1982-91; rep. Prudential of Am., L.A., Calif., 1990-91; dist. agt. Asian/Pacific district Prudential of Am., Alhambra, Calif., 1992—. Recipient Young Achiever award Young Achiever Found., Quezon City, Philippines, 1988, Golden Scroll award Philippine Ednl. Youth Devel., Inc., Quezon City, 1988, Young Celebrity Mother's award Golden Mother/Father Found., Quezon City, 1990, Recognition of Excellence cert. San Gabriel Valley YWCA, 1992; named Most Outstanding Ins. Exec. of Philippines Consumers' Union of Philippines, Manila, 1988, Ten Outstanding Profl. Svc. award Achievement Rsch. Soc., Manila, 1988, numerous others. Fellow Life Underwriters Tng. Coun.; mem. NAFE, Nat. Assn. Life Underwriters, Am. Internat. Underwriters Assn., Arcadia C. of C., Asian Bus. Assn., Filipino C. of C., Monrovia C. of C., Duarte C. of C., Million Dollar Round Table (life), Foothills Assn. Life Underwriters, Chinese C. of C. (bd. dirs. L.A. 1992—). Home: 341 W Central Ave Apt F Monrovia CA 91016-5212 Office: Prudential of Am 320 S Garfield Ave Ste 322 Alhambra CA 91801

LIM, TOH-BIN, surgeon; b. Xiamen, Fukien, China, Oct. 21, 1934; came to U.S., 1954; s. Si S. Lim and Po Sio Kua; m. Margaret Lim, June 16, 1962; children: Michael, Andrea. BS, Adrian (Mich.) Coll., 1958; MD, Northwestern U., 1962. Diplomate Am. Bd. Surgery. Intern Northwestern Meml. Hosp., Chgo., 1962-63, resident in gen. surgery, 1963-65; resident in gen. surgery U. Toronto, Ont., Canada, 1965-69; staff surgeon Holy Cross Med. Ctr., Mission Hills, Calif., 1970—; mem. facultyof medicine UCLA, Calif., 1978—, asst. clin. prof.sch. medicine, 1991—; mem. adv. bd. Premier Bank, Northridge, Calif., 1991-92. Trustee Holy Cross Med. Ctr., 1985-91. Fellow ACS (credentials com. 1985—, cancer liaison com. 1982—), Royal Coll. Surgeons Can.; mem. Royal Soc. Medicine, Chinese Physician Soc. (pres. 1981-82). Office: 11550 Indian Hills Rd # 391 Mission Hills CA 91345

LIMA, DONALD ALLAN, oil company executive; b. Pasadena, Calif., Nov. 21, 1953; s. John Kenneth and Fay Gwynneth (Strangman) L.; m. Tina Marie Clark, Nov. 23, 1979 (div. May 9, 1984); m. Joyce Close Cirre, Jan. 17, 1985 (div. Oct. 15, 1987). BS, Calif. State U., Long Beach, Calif., 1982. Research technician Union Oil Co. Calif., Brea, Calif., 1979-84; chief chemist Pennzoil Products Co., Vernon, Calif., 1984-86; tech. service engring. Asia Pacific Region Tribol, Woodland Hills, Calif., 1986-88; internat. engring. mgr. ICI Tribol, Woodland Hills, 1988—. Mem. Am. Soc. Lubrication Engrs. (publicity chmn. 1986-87), Soc. Automotive Engrs. Home: 3700 Ketch Ave # 6-101 Oxnard CA 93035 Office: Ste 600 21031 Ventura Blvd Woodland Hills CA 91364

LIMANDRI, CHARLES SALVATORE, lawyer; b. San Diego, Aug. 19, 1955; s. Joseph John and Florence Anne (Dippolito) LiM.; m. Barbara Ann DeBellis, July 11, 1992. BA, U. San Diego, 1977; Diploma in Internat. Law, U. Wales, 1980; JD, Georgetown U., 1983. Bar: Calif. 1983, D.C. 1984. Tchr. St. Augustine High Sch., San Diego, 1978-79; assoc. Adams & Duque, L.A., 1983-85, Lillick, McHose & Charles, San Diego, 1985-87; pvt. practice San Diego, 1987—. Bd. dirs. Head Injury Activity Ctrs., 1991—. Rotary Internat. grad. fellow U. Wales at Aberystwyth, 1980; recipient award Hattie M. Strong Found., Washington, 1983. Mem. ABA, Assn. Trial Lawyers Am., San Diego County Bar Assn., Italian-Am. Lawyers Assn., U. San Diego Alumni Assn. (bd. dirs., pres.), Thomas More Soc. Am. (bd. dirs. 1982-84), Rotary, Sons of Italy. Democrat. Roman Catholic. Office: 2120 San Diego Ave Ste 100 San Diego CA 92110

LIMBAUGH, RONALD HADLEY, history educator, history center director; b. Emmett, Idaho, Jan. 22, 1938; s. John Hadley and Evelyn E. (Mortimore) L.; m. Marilyn Kay Rice, June 16, 1963; 1 child, Sally Ann. BA, Coll. Idaho, 1960; MA, U. Idaho, 1962, PhD, 1967. Hist. libr. Idaho State Hist. Soc., Boise, 1963-66; instr. Boise Coll., 1964-66; asst. prof. history U. of the Pacific, Stockton, Calif., 1966-71; archivist, curator U. of the Pacific, Stockton, 1968-87, prof. history, 1977—; dir. Holt-Atherton Ctr., U. of the Pacific, Stockton, 1984-87; exec. dir. Conf. of Calif. Hist. Socs., Stockton, 1973-76, 77-78, 82-86, 90—; dir. John Muir Ctr. for Regional Studies, U. of Pacific, Stockton, 1989—; cons., evaluator NEH, 1983, 86. Author: Rocky Mountain Carpetbaggers, 1982; co-editor (microform) John Muir Papers, 1986; (book) Guide to Muir Papers, 1986; contbr. articles to profl. jours. With U.S. Army, 1955-56. NDEA fellow, 1960; grantee Calif. Coun. Humanities, 1976, Nat. Hist. Publs. and Records Commn., 1980-82, NEH, 1983, Inst. European Studies, 1989. Mem. AAUP, Western History Assn., Orgn. Am. Historians, Phi Kappa Phi (pres. UOP chpt. 1988), Mining History Assn. Christian Humanist. Office: Univ Pacific 3601 Pacific Ave Stockton CA 95211-0197

LIN, HUN-CHI, molecular biologist; b. Yun-Lin, Taiwan, Republic of China, Nov. 8, 1953; came to U.S., 1980; s. Shun-Tsu and Yu-Hwa (Tsai) L.; m. Shau-Ping Lei, July 6, 1980; 1 child, Victoria Lei. BS, Nat. Taiwan U., Taipei, 1976, MS, 1978; PhD, UCLA, 1984. Teaching asst. UCLA, 1983; rsch. scientist Ingene, Santa Monica, Calif., 1984-85, project dir., 1985-87, prin. investigator, 1985-87; rsch. dir. Sinogen, L.A., 1987; pres., dir. rsch. Trigen Inc., Santa Monica, 1987—. Contbr. articles to profl. jours. Lt. Chinese Army, 1978-80. Mem. AAAS, Am. Soc. Microbiology. Office: Trigen Inc 2211 Michigan Ave Santa Monica CA 90404-3900

LIN, JAMES PEICHENG, mathematics educator; b. N.Y.C., Sept. 30, 1949; s. Tung Hua and Susan (Zsiang) L.; m. Julie Sano, June 24, 1990. BS, U. Calif., Berkeley, 1970; PhD, Princeton U., 1974. Asst. prof. U. Calif., LaJolla, 1974-76, assoc. prof., 1977-81; prof. U. Calif., San Diego, 1982-83, 1985-90, 90—; vis. prof. Princeton (N.J.) U., 1976, Inst. at Hewbrew U., Jersulem, 1981-82, MIT, Cambridge, 1983-84, Neuchatel (Switzerland) U., 1984; prof. Math Sci. Rsch. Inst., Berkeley, 1989; bd. dirs. Asians in Higher Edn. Author: Steenrod Connections, 1988. Sloan fellow; grantee NSF, 1974—; recipient Excellence in Edn., U. Pan Asian Communities, 1986. Mem. Asian Educators, Pan Asian Staff (bd. dirs.), Sierra Club, Am. Math. Soc., Phi Beta Kappa. Office: Dept Math C-012 U Calif San Diego La Jolla CA 92093

LIN, JASON ZSE-CHERNG, engineering manager; b. Hsin-Chu, Taiwan, Republic of China, Apr. 16, 1955; s. Tung-Chuan and Shu-Lien (Chen) L.; m. Shih-Yin Huang, Dec. 27, 1986; children: Edwin, Laura. BSEE, Nat. Taiwan U., 1977, MSEE, 1979; PhD in Elec. Engring., U. Calif., Santa Barbara, 1984. Rsch. engr. U. Calif., Santa Barbara, 1984-85; vis. scientist U. Ill., Urbana-Champaign, 1985-86; rsch. engr. SRI Internat., Menlo Park, Calif., 1986-88; mem. tech. staff KLA Instruments Corp., San Jose, Calif., 1988-89, engring. mgr., 1989—. Mem. IEEE. Home: 19597 Via Monte Dr Saratoga CA 95070 Office: KLA Instruments Corp 160 Rio Robles San Jose CA 95134-1809

LIN, JOSH CHIA HSIN, psychologist; b. Taipei, Taiwan, Republic of China, Jan. 31, 1954; came to U.S., 1982; s. Pang Fang and Chu (Lee) L.; m. Liwen Wang Lin, Feb. 28, 1982. BA in Edn., Nat. Chengchi U., Taipei, 1976, MA in Edn., 1978; PhD in Counseling Psychology, U. Ky., 1987. Lic. psychologist, Calif. Instr. Jr. Coll. of Chinese Municipality, Taipei, 1980-81, Soochow U., Taipei, 1981-82; intern in psychology San Francisco Gen. Hosp., 1986-87, McAuley Neuropsychiat. Inst., San Francisco, 1986, Richmond Maxi-Ctr., San Francisco, 1986-87; clin. psychologist Pacific Clinics, Rosemead, Calif., 1987—; pvt. practice psychologist, Rosemead, 1989—. Author: Encounter Groups and Human Relations Training, 1980, (with others) Psychological Test: Chinese Revised Personal Orientation Inventory, 1978; contbr. articles to profl. jours. Fellow Soc. for Buddhist Renaissance; mem. APA, Asian-Am. Psychol. Assn., World Fedn. for Mental Health, Chinese Am. Mental Health Assn. Office: Asian Pacific Family Ctr 3907 Rosemead Blvd Ste 100 Rosemead CA 91770-1951

LIN, LAWRENCE SHUH LIANG, accountant; b. China, July 5, 1938; s. Wan Chow and Inn Chi Lin; came to U.S., 1967, naturalized, 1979; LLB, Soochow U., 1963; MBA, Pepperdine U., 1970; m. Grace Yu, July 31, 1966; children: Ray, Lester. Spl. project acctg. supr. Motown Records, Hollywood, Calif., 1975; chief acct. Elektra/Asylum/Nonesuch Records, Beverly Hills, Calif., 1976-77, United Artists Music Pub. Group, Hollywood, 1977-80; contr.-adminstr. Pasadena (Calif.) Guidance Clinics (name now Pacific Clinics, 1980-86; v.p. Stew Kettle Corp., L.A., 1986-87; pres. LKL Corp.,

L.A., 1987-89; internat. fin. cons. Pacific Capital Mgmt., Alhambra, Calif., 1989—. Mem. Inst. Mgmt. Accts., Nat. Assn. Security Dealers. Baptist. Office: Pacific Capital Mgmt 29 N Garfield Ave Alhambra CA 91801-3545

LIN, LEI See LAM, LUI

LIN, TAO, electronics engineering manager; b. Shanghai, People's Republic of China, Aug. 6, 1958; came to U.S., 1986; s. Zheng-hui Lin and Wei-jing Wu; m. Ping Kuo, Aug. 18, 1989; children: Jason, Jessie. BS, East China Normal U., Shanghai, 1982; MS, Tohoku U., Sendai, Japan, 1985; PhD, Tohoku U., 1990. Technician Dongtong Electronics Inc., Shanghai, 1977-78; rsch. asst. Electronics Rsch. Lab U. Calif., Berkeley, 1986-87, postgrad. researcher, 1987-88; applications engr. Integrated Device Technology Inc., Santa Clara, Calif., 1988-90; sr. applications engr. Sierra Semiconductor Corp., San Jose, Calif., 1990-91, applications mgr., 1991—. Contbr. articles to profl. jours. Mem. IEEE. Home: 3552 Rockett Dr Fremont CA 94538-3425 Office: Sierra Semiconductor Corp 2075 N Capitol Ave San Jose CA 95132-1000

LIN, THOMAS WEN-SHYOUNG, accounting educator, researcher, consultant; b. Taichung, Republic of China, June 3, 1944; came to U.S., 1970; s. Ju-chin and Shao-chin (Tseng) L.; m. Angela Kuei-fong Hou, May 19, 1969; children: William Margaret. BA in Bus. Adminstrn., Nat. Taiwan U., Taipei, 1966; MBA, Nat. Chengchi U., Taipei, 1970; MS in Acctg. and Info. Systems, UCLA, 1971; PhD in Acctg., Ohio State U., 1975. Cert. mgmt. acct., Calif. Internal auditor Formosa Plastics Group, Taipei, 1967-69, spl. asst. to the pres., 1969-70; asst. prof. U. So. Calif., L.A., 1975-80, assoc. prof., 1980-86, prof. acctg., 1986-90, acctg. cir. prof., 1990—, dir. doctoral studies acctg., 1982-86; cons. Intex Plastics, Inc., Long Beach, Calif., 1979-81, Peat, Marwick, Mitchell, L.A., 1982, City of Chino, Calif., 1982. Author: Planning and Control for Data Processing, 1984, Use of Mathematical Models, 1986, Advanced Auditing, 1988; contbr. numerous articles to acad. and prof. jours.; mem. editorial bd. Issue in Acctg. Edn., Jour. Mgmt. Acctg. Rsch., Quarterly Jour. Bus. and Econs., Am. Jour. Math. and Mgmt. Scis., 1988—. Bd. dirs. U. So. Calif. Acctg. Circle, L.A., 1986-88, Taiwan Benevolent Assn. Am., Washington, 1986; pres, Taiwan Benevolent Assn. Calif., L.A., 1986-88. 2d lt. Republic of China Army, 1966-67. Recipient cert. appreciation L.A. City Mayor Tom Bradley, 1988, Congressman Martinez award for outstanding community svc., 1988; Faculty Rsch. scholar U. So. Calif. Bus. Sch., L.A., 1984-87. Mem. Am. Acctg. Assn. (bd. dirs. 1986-88), Inst. Cert. Mgmt. Accts. (cert. of disting. performance 1978), Inst. Mgmt. Accts. (coord. 1984—, Author's trophy 1978, 79, 81, 87), EDP Auditor Assn., Inst. Mgmt. Scis. Republican. Baptist. Home: 19975 E Carolyn Pl La Puente CA 91748-4925 Office: U So Calif Sch Acctg Univ Park Acctg 109 Los Angeles CA 90089-1421

LIN, WEN CHUN, electrical and computer engineering educator, consultant; b. Kutien, Fukien, China, Feb. 22, 1926; arrived U.S., 1954; s. Bing-Cio and Seu-Dung L.; m. Shung-Ling Chao, June 6, 1956; children—Carol, Grace, Wendy. B.S. in Elec. Engring., Nat. Taiwan U., 1950; M.S. in Elec. Engring., Purdue U., 1956, Ph.D., 1965. Engr., Taiwan Power Co., Taipei, 1950-54, Gen. Electric Co., Pittsfield, Mass., 1956-59; sr. engr. Data Processing div. Honeywell, Boston, 1959-61; instr. Purdue U., 1961-65; prof. elec. and computer engring. Case Western Res. U., Cleve., 1965-78, U. Calif.-Davis, 1978—. Author: Digital System Design Handbook, 1981, 2nd edition, 1990; Computer Organization and Assembly Programming for the PDP-11 and Vax-11, 1985; editor: Microprocessors: Fundamental Application, 1977. Contbr. numerous articles to tech. and sci. jours. Mem. IEEE. Office: Dept Elec and Computer Engring Bainer Hall U Calif Davis CA 95616

LIN, YING, biologist; b. Shanghai, China, Sept. 3, 1944; came to U.S., 1980; d. Zhong Wen Lin and Wei Ying Zhang; m. Zu Han Gu, Dec. 15, 1969; children: Jing Lin Gu, Belinda Gu. BS in Biology, Fu-Dan U., 1966; MD, Shanghai 1st Med. Sch., 1969; MS in Biology, U. Calif., San Diego, 1983. Med. diplomate, China. Physician Clinic of 4th Silk Mill, Shanghai, 1970-76; rsch. scientist Shanghai Cancer Inst., 1977-80, Salk Inst., San Diego, 1980—. Contbr. articles to profl. jours. Recipient P.E.O. scholarship, San Diego, 1983. Mem. Protein Soc. U.S.A. Office: Salk Inst San Diego CA 92138

LIN, YU-CHONG, physiology educator, consultant; b. Republic of China, Apr. 24, 1935; came to U.S., 1962; s. Shing-Chern and Shern Lin; m. Dora D.R. Liaw, Apr. 27, 1960; children: Mimi C.W., Betty L.W. PhD, Rutgers U., 1968. Rsch. assoc. U. Calif., Santa Barbara, 1968-69; asst. prof. physiology U. Hawaii, Honolulu, 1969-74, assoc. prof., 1974-76, prof., 1976—; cons. on environ. physiology Tripler Army Med. Ctr., Honolulu, 1979—, Nat. Def. Med. Ctr., Taipei, Republic of China, 1989—; advisor panel on diving physiology NOAA, Washington, 1986—. Editor: Hyperbaric Medicine and Physiology, 1988, Man in the Sea, Vol. I and 2, 1990; contbr. over 100 articles to profl. jours. Mem. Am. Physiol. Soc., Undersea and Hyperbaric Med. Soc., Honolulu Country Club. Office: U Hawaii Sch Medicine 1960 East-West Rd Honolulu HI 96822

LINAHON, JAMES JOSEPH, music educator, musician; b. Mason City, Iowa, Sept. 6, 1951; s. Robert Eugene and Teresa Darlene (Mulaney) L.; m. Kathryn Anne Tull, Apr. 12, 1987; children: Michael, Katie, Joseph. BA in Music, U. No. Iowa, 1973; M in Music Edn., North Tex. State U., 1975. Assoc. dir. jazz studies Chaffey Coll., Rancho Cucamonga, Calif., 1975-80; prof. music, dir. jazz studies Fullerton (Calif.) Coll., 1980—; cons. U. No. Colo., U. Alaska, U. Calif., U. Ariz., U. Hawaii, DePaul U., Chgo., U. So. Calif., Wash. State U., S.D. State U., 1978—; cons., artist Playboy Jazz Festival, Reno Internat. Jazz Festival, Queen Mary Jazz Festival, Disneyland, All That Jazz; record producer MCA, Warner Bros, ABC, Columbia; performer for Frank Sinatra, Henry Mancini, Beverly Sills, Ella Fitzgerald, Sarah Vaughan, Tony Bennett, Merv Griffin. Artist, producer: (jazz compact disc) Time Tripping, 1984 (Album of Yr. Downbeat Mag., 1987), (classical compact disc) Gradus Ad Parnassum, 1990; composer: (musical composition) Snow Wisp, 1986 (finalist Columbia Artists search). Performer, producer Theatre Palisades, Pacific Palisades, Calif., 1986, Claremont (Calif.) Community Found., 1992; guest soloist Claremont (Calif.) Symphony Orch., 1991. Recipient Major Landers scholarship Iowa Band Master's Assn., Iowa, 1969; named Dee Bee Album of Yr. (5 awards) Downbeat Mag., 1978-87. Mem. NARAS (Oustanding Recordings 1989), Internat. Assn. Jazz Educators (higher edn. rep. 1992-93), Internat. Trumpet Guild, Internat. Assn. Jazz Edn., Am. Soc. Composers, Authors and Publishers, Nat. Assn. Coll. Wind and Percussion Instrs., Am. Fedn. Musicians. Roman Catholic. Home: 560 W Tenth St Claremont CA 91711 Office: Fullerton College 321 E Chapman Ave Fullerton CA 92632

LINCOLN, ALEXANDER, III, financier, lawyer, private investor; b. Boston, Dec. 1, 1943; s. Alexander Jr. and Elizabeth (Kitchel) L.; m. Isabel Fawcett Ross, Dec. 27, 1969. BA, Denver U., 1967; JD, Boston U., 1971. Bar: Colo. 1972, U.S. Ct. Appeals (10th cir.) 1972, U.S. Supreme Ct. 1979. Atty. Dist. Ct. Denver, 1973-78, Colo. Ct. Appeals, Denver, 1978-80; mng. ptnr. Alexander Lincoln & Co., Denver, 1980—. Mem. Colo. Bar Assn. (fin. com. 1975-76), Colo. Soc. Mayflower Descendants (life, bd. dirs. 1975—), Order of Founders and Patriots (life). Republican. Home and Office: 121 S Dexter St Denver CO 80222-1052

LINCOLN, RICHARD LEE, agricultural marketing executive; b. Omaha, Dec. 5, 1946; s. Shirley Clayton and Erma LaVine (Stivers) L.; m. Mary Kay Purkhiser, June 26, 1966; children: Kelly Lynn, Kristen Ann, Jeffrey Todd. BBA, U. Iowa, 1968; postgrad., U. Mich., 1975, U. Wis., 1987. Dist. sales rep. Quaker Oats Co., St. Joseph, Mo., 1968-69, Wayne Feeds-Allied Mills, Inc., Seneca, Kans., 1969-72; regional sales mgr. Wayne Feeds-Allied Mills, Inc., Columbia, Nebr., 1972-74, Indpls., 1974-76; farmer, businessman self employed, Glenwood, Iowa, 1976-80; dist. sales mgr. Supersweet Feeds-Internat. Multifoods, Oskaloosa, Iowa, 1980-85; v.p., dir. of mktg. Carey Salt, Inc., Hutchinson, Kans., 1985-88; sales mgr., feed products Texasgulf, Inc., Weeping Water, Nebr., 1988—; pres. MOAB (Utah) Salt, Inc., 1989—. Mem. Am. Feed Industries Assn., Nat. Agrl. Mktg. Assn., The Omaha Club, Glenwood Golf Club, Masons, Shriners, Delta Sigma Pi. Republican. Mem. Christian Ch. Home: 214 East Florence Ave Glenwood IA 51534 Office: Texasgulf Inc PO Box 201 Weeping Water NE 68463

LINCOLN, SANDRA ELEANOR, chemistry educator; b. Holyoke, Mass., Mar. 11, 1939; d. Edwin Stanley and Evelyn Ida (Mackie) L. BA magna cum laude, Smith Coll., 1960; MSChem, Marquette U., 1970; PhD in Inorganic Chemistry, SUNY, Stony Brook, 1982. Tchr., prin. Oak Knoll Sch., Summit, N.J., 1964-74; tchr. Holy Child High Sch., Waukegan, Ill., 1974-76; lectr. chemistry, dir. fin. aid Rosemont (Pa.) Coll., 1976-78; teaching asst. SUNY, Stony Brook, 1978-82; assoc. prof. chemistry U. Portland, Oreg., 1982—; researcher Oreg. Grad. Ctr., Beaverton, 1982—. Contbr. articles to profl. jours. Cath. sister Soc. Holy Child Jesus, 1963—. Recipient Pres.'s award for Teaching, SUNY, Stony Brook, 1981; Burlington No. Outstanding scholar, 1987. Mem. Am. Chem. Soc., Phi Beta Kappa, Sigma Xi. Democrat. Home: 5431 N Strong St Portland OR 97203-5711 Office: U Portland 5000 N Willamette Blvd Portland OR 97203-5750

LIND, DENNIS BARRY, psychiatrist; b. Perth Amboy, N.J., Sept. 6, 1940; s. Zoltan Harold and Madeline (Lang) L.; m. Judith Anne Earle, June 17, 1962; children: Miriam Anne, Martin Stuart. BA in English, Franklin & Marshall Coll., 1962; MD, Boston U., 1966. Diplomate Am. Bd. Psychiatry and Neurology. Intern Greenwich (Conn.) Hosp., 1966-67; resident in psychiatry Inst. of Living, Hartford, Conn., 1967-70; pvt. practice Honolulu, 1974—; cons. SSA, Honolulu, 1978—, Hina Mauka, Honolulu, 1980-84, Acute Psychiat. Day Hosp. Queens Med. Ctr., Honolulu, 1984-90; clin. assoc. prof. U. Hawaii Sch. Medicine, Honolulu, 1984—. Bd. dirs. Mental Health Assn. Hawaii, Honolulu, 1980-82, Citizens Against Noise, Honolulu, 1986-88, The House, Inc., Honolulu, 1986—. Mem. Hawaii Psychiat. Soc. (sec. 1977-79, v.p., pres. 1979-83), Am. Psychiat. Assn., Hawaii Med. Assn., AMA. Jewish. Office: Ste 1306 1441 Kapiolani Blvd Honolulu HI 96814

LIND, MARSHALL L., academic administrator. Dean Sch. Extended and Grad. Studies U. Alaska, Juneau, until 1987, chancellor, 1987—. Office: U of Alaska Southeast Office of Chancellor 11120 Glacier Hwy Juneau AK 99801-8625

LIND, MAURICE DAVID, research physicist; b. Jamestown, N.Y., July 25, 1934; s. Paul William Frederic and Florence Rosemond (Hedstrom) L.; m. Carol Norma Dickson, Apr. 21, 1962; 1 child, Diana Nadine. BS, Otterbein Coll., 1957; PhD, Cornell U., 1962. Postdoctoral fellow Cornell U., Ithaca, N.Y., 1962-63; research scientist Union Oil Co., Brea, Calif., 1963-66, Rockwell Internat., Thousand Oaks, Calif., 1966—; vis. prof. applied physics Tech. U. Denmark, Lyngby, 1985. Contbr. articles to profl. jours. Recipient Pub. Service award NASA, 1976. Mem. Am. Phys. Soc., Am. Crystallographic Assn., Am. Assn. Crystal Growth, Sigma Xi. Home: 1690 Stoddard Ave Thousand Oaks CA 91360-2058 Office: Rockwell Internat 1049 Camino Dos Rios Thousand Oaks CA 91360-2398

LIND, TERRIE LEE, social services administrator; b. Spokane, Wash., June 5, 1948; d. Clifford and Edna Mae (Allenbach) Presnell; m. Stephen George Lind, Aug. 29, 1970 (div. Mar. 1981); children: Erica Rachel, Reid Christopher. BA cum laude, Wash. State U., 1970, MA, 1971. Cert. tchr., Wash., Ariz.; cert. in Porch Index Communicative Ability. Specialist communication disorders U. Tex., Houston, 1971-73; clin. supr. The Battin Clinic, Houston, 1973-76; specialist communication disorders Spokane Guilds Sch., 1980-82; program coord. Fresno (Calif.) Community Hosp., 1982-87; program adminstr. Advantage 65* sr. access program Health Dimensions, Inc., San Jose, Calif., 1987-90; dir. patient svcs. San Jose Med. Ctr., 1990—; dir. community svcs. Planned Parenthood of Santa Clara and San Benito Counties, San Jose; cons. Adolescent Chem. Dependency Unit, Fresno, 1984-87. Mem. AAUW (officer 1976-82), Am. Speech and Hearing Assn. (cert., Continuing Edn. award 1985-86), Wash. Speech and Hearing Assn. (co-chmn. state conv. program com. 1981-82), Soc. Consumer Affairs Profls. in Bus., Wash. State U. Alumni Assn. Home: 1717 Don Ave San Jose CA 95124 Office: Planned Parenthood 1691 The Alameda San Jose CA 95126

LINDAUER, JOHN HOWARD, II, radio and newspaper executive; b. Montclair, N.J., Nov. 20, 1937; s. John Howard and Louise (Platts) L.; m. Jacqueline Shelly, Sept. 2, 1960 (dec. 1992); children: Susan, John Howard. BS, Ariz. State U., 1960; PhD in Econs., Okla. State U., 1964. Asst. prof. econs. Occidental Coll., L.A., 1964-66; assoc. prof. Claremont (Calif.) Men's Coll. and Grad Sch., 1966-70, prof., chmn. econs., 1970-74; dean Coll. Bus. Murray (Ky.) State U., 1974-76; chancellor U. Alaska, Anchorage, 1976-78; commr. Alaska Pipeline, Anchorage, 1978; pres., chief exec. officer Alaska Industry and Energy Corp., Anchorage, 1978—; mem. Alaska Ho. of Reps., 1983-84; Rep. candidate for gov., 1990; bd. dirs. various cos.; owner various newspapers and radio sta.; cons. econ. policy and devel. U.S. Congress, 1966—; cons. econs. U.S. corps; mem. AF Adv. Bd. Author: Macroeconomics, 1968, 71, 76, Economics: The Modern View, 1977, Land Taxation and the Indian Economic Development, 1979; editor Macroeconomic Readings; contbr. articles to profl. jours. Co-founder, vice chmn. Group against Smog Pollution, 1968; pres. So. Calif. Econ. Assn., 1974. With Army U.S., 1955-57. Fulbright prof., India, 1972; vis. prof. U. Sussex, Eng., 1972-73. Home: 3933 Geneva Pl Anchorage AK 99508-5055

LINDE, HANS ARTHUR, state supreme court justice; b. Berlin, Germany, Apr. 15, 1924; came to U.S., 1939, naturalized, 1943; s. Bruno C. and Luise (Rosenhain) L.; m. Helen Tucker, Aug. 13, 1945; children: Lisa, David Tucker. B.A., Reed Coll., 1947; J.D., U. Calif., Berkeley, 1950. Bar: Oreg. 1951. Law clk. U.S. Supreme Ct. Justice William O. Douglas, 1950-51; atty. Office of Legal Adviser, Dept. State, 1951-53; pvt. practice Portland, Oreg., 1953-54; legis. asst. U.S. Sen. Richard L. Neuberger, 1955-58; asso. prof., prof. U. Oreg. Law Sch., 1959-76; justice Oreg. Supreme Ct., Salem, 1977-90, sr. judge, 1990—; Fulbright lectr. Freiburg U., 1967-68, Hamburg U., 1975-76; cons. U.S. ACDA, Dept. Def., 1962-76; mem. Adminstrv. Conf. U.S., 1978-82. Author: (with George Bunn) Legislative and Administrative Processes, 1976. Mem. Oreg. Constl. Revision Commn., 1961-62, Oreg. Commn. on Pub. Broadcasting, 1990-93. With U.S. Army, 1943-46. Fellow Am. Acad. Arts and Scis.; mem. Am. Law Inst. (council), Order of Coif, Phi Beta Kappa.

LINDE, LUCILLE MAE (JACOBSON), motor-perceptual specialist; b. Greeley, Colo., May 5, 1919; d. John Alfred and Anna Julia (Anderson) Jacobson; m. Ernest Emil Linde, July 5, 1946 (dec. Jan. 1959). BA, U. No. Colo., 1941, MA, 1947, EdD, 1974. Cert. tchr. Calif., Colo., Iowa, N.Y.; cert. ednl. psychologist; guidance counselor. Dean of women, dir. residence C.W. Post Coll. of L.I. Univ., 1965-66; asst. dean of students SUNY, Farmingdale, 1966-67; counselor, tchr. West High Sch., Davenport, Iowa, 1967-68; instr. grad. tchrs. and counselors, univ. counselor, researcher No. Ariz. U., Flagstaff, 1968-69; vocat. edn. and counseling coord. Fed. Exemplary Project, Council Bluffs, Iowa, 1970-71; sch. psychologist, counselor Oakdale Sch. Dist., Calif., 1971-73; sch. psychologist, intern Learning and Counseling Ctr., Stockton, Calif., 1972-74; pvt. practice rsch. in motor-perceptual tng. Greeley, 1975—; researcher ocumeter survey, Lincoln Unified Sch. Dist., Stockton, 1980, 81, 82, Manteca (Calif.) High Sch., 1981; motor perceptual tng. LUSD, 1981, 82, YMCA, Stockton, 1983, 84, others; presenter seminars in field. Author: Psychological Services and Motor Perceptual Training, 1974, Guidebook for Psychological Services and Motor Perceptual Training (How One May Improve In Ten Easy Lessons!), 1992, Manual for the Lucille Linde Ocumeter: Ocular Pursuit Measuring Instrument, 1992, Motor-Perceptual Training and Visual Perceptual Research (How Students Improved in Seven Lessons!), 1992, Effects of Motor-Perceptual Training on Academic Acheivement and Ocular Pursuit Ability, 1992; inventor ocumeter, instrument for measuring ocular tracking ability, 1989, and target for use with ocumeter, 1991. Mem. Rep. Presdl. Task Force, 1990, trustee, 1991. Recipient medallion World Declaration of Excellence, 1989, Pres. Medal of Merit and lapel insignia, 1990, Internat. Cultural Diploma of Honor, Am. Biog. Inst., 1990, Commemorative medal of honor, 1990, Presdl. Order Merit Nat. Rep. Senatorial Com., 1991, Congl. Cert. Appreciation Nat. Rep. Congl. Com., 1991; named to Hall of Fame Internat. Cultural Diploma Honor, 1990; fellow Internat. Biog. Assn., Cambridge, Eng., 1991. Mem. AAUP, NAFE, Nat. Assn. Sch. Psychologists and Psychometrists (speaker at conf. 1976), Nat. Fedn. Rep. Women, The Smithsonian Assocs., Nat. Trust for Hist. Preservation, Am. Pers. and Guidance Assn., Nat. Assn. Student Pers. Adminstrs., Nat. Assn. Women Deans and Counselors, Calif. Tchrs. Assn., Internat. Platform Assn., Independence Inst., Learning Disabilities Assn. (speaker internat. conv. 1976), Rep. Senatorial Inner Circle (senatorial commn. & cert. 1991), Greeley Rep. Women's Club, Pi Omega Pi, Pi Lambda Theta. Home: 1954 18th Ave Greeley CO 80631-5208

LINDEGREN, JACK KENNETH, educator; b. Fresno, Calif., Feb. 9, 1931; s. Henry Jack and Katherine (Metzler) L.; m. Betty Jo Rowland, Dec. 1960 (div. Apr. 1963); m. Elaine Finnegan, Apr. 27, 1963; children: Susan Carol, Karen Ann. BA, Fresno State Coll., 1954; MA, Calif. State U., Fresno, 1976. Educator, adminstr. Fresno County, Firebaugh, Calif., 1954-5; educator Calaveras County Schs., San Andreas, Calif., 1964-66, Kings County Schs., Corcoran, Calif., 1966-80, Kern County Schs., Bakersfield, Calif., 1985-87, L.A. Unified Schs., 1985—; educator L.A. Unified Schs., 1977-92; instr. ARC, Hanford, Calif., 1974-79.; instr. County Sci. Insvc., 1985. Inventor electroanalysis device Chrysler award., 1965. Participant Desert Opera, Palmdale, Calif., 1986-88; bd. mem., chmn. ARC, Hanford, 1973-78. Sgt. U.S. Army, 1955-57. Mem. NAS, AAAS, NEA, Nat. Assn. Legions of Honor, Nat. Space Soc., Tehran Shrine Fresno East/West Game Corcoran Band Club, Santa Clara U. Alumni Assn., N.Y. Acad. Scis., Assn. Calif. Sch. Admin., Calif. State U. of Fresno Alumni Assn. (life), Scottish Rite (life), Corcoran/Tulare Masons (life, Bethel guardian 1978-80, Pin 1980), Odd Fellows (30 yr. mem. award 1991), Mensa (elder, deacon, 10 yr. membership award). Presbyterian.

LINDEMULDER, CAROL ANN, interior designer, artist; b. San Diego, May 2, 1936; d. Franklin Geert and Leone Augusta (Oltman) L. BA in Decorative Arts, U. Calif., Berkeley, 1959; postgrad. in fine arts, San Diego State U., 1965-67. Tchr. interior design and fine arts adult edn. div. San Diego City Schs., 1960-67; with Milo of Calif., Inc. subs. Milo Electronics Corp., 1968-73, corp. staff asst., 1972, asst. to dir. mktg., 1972-73; with Frazee Industries, 1975-77; owner, designer-artist Call Carol, San Diego, 1976—; former instr. U. Calif. Extension, San Diego. One-woman show Point Loma Art Assn., 1967, Scandia Interiors, 1977, Cen. Fed. Savs. & Loan, 1978, John Duncan Interiors, 1979, Villa Montezuma Mus., 1981; exhibited in group shows Calif. Western U., 1963, Jewish Community Ctr., 1963-64, So. Calif. Expn., 1964, San Diego Mus. Art, 1966, 71, 75, San Diego State U., 1974, Spectrum Gallery, 1985, A.R.T. Beasley Gallery, 1985. Coord. Christmas program San Diego Community Vol. Bur., 1961; a founder, treas., bd. dirs. Save Our Heritage Orgn., 1969-71, pres., 1974-75, 79-81; mem. San Diego Hist. Sites Bd., 1985-93, vice chmn., 1985-92; founder, pres. Save the Coaster Com., 1981-83. Named Vol. of Month, San Diego Community Vol. Bur., 1961; recipient President's commendation Save Our Heritage Orgn., 1984. Mem. Jr. League San Diego. Republican. Office: PO Box 81718 San Diego CA 92138

LINDEN, THEODORE ANTHONY, computer science researcher; b. Cleve., June 25, 1938; s. Anton and Frances Mary (Ott) L.; m. Betty J. Gevatoff, Jan. 18, 1969; children: Jennifer Fran, Gregory David. BA, Loyola U., Chgo., 1961; MA, Yeshiva U., 1965, PhD, 1968. Asst. prof. Fordham Univ., Bronx, N.Y., 1967-69; prin. scientist U.S. Dept. of Defense, Washington, 1970-74, Nat. Bur. Standards, Gaithersburg, Md., 1974-78; dept. mgr. Xerox Corp., Palo Alto, Calif., 1978-84; prog. mgr. Advanced Decision Systems, Mountain View, Calif., 1984—. Contbr. articles to profl. jours. Fellow NSF, 1963-68, Kent Fellowship, Danforth Found., St. Louis, 1963. Mem. IEEE, Assn. Computing Machinery, Am. Assn. Artificial Intelligence (prog. com. 1989-90). Office: Advanced Decision Systems Booz-Allen & Hamilton Inc 1500 Plymouth St Mountain View CA 94043-1230

LINDENBERGER, HERBERT SAMUEL, author, literature educator; b. Los Angeles, Apr. 4, 1929; s. Hermann and Celia (Weinkrantz) L.; m. Claire Flaherty, June 14, 1961; children: Michael James, Elizabeth Celia. BA, Antioch Coll., Yellow Springs, Ohio, 1951; PhD, U. Wash., Seattle, 1955. From instr. to prof. English and comparative lit. U. Calif., Riverside, 1954-66; prof. German and English, chmn. program comparative lit. Washington U., St. Louis, 1966-69; Avalon prof. humanities Stanford U., 1969—, chmn. program comparative lit., 1969-82; dir. Stanford Humanities Ctr., 1991-92. Author: On Wordsworth's Prelude, 1963, Georg Büchner, 1964, (play) Lear and Cordelia at Home, 1968, Georg Trakl, 1971, Historical Drama: The Relation of Literature and Reality, 1975, Saul's Fall: A Critical Fiction, 1979, Opera: The Extravagant Art, 1984, The History in Literature: On Value, Genre, Institutions, 1990. Fulbright scholar Austria, 1952-53; Guggenheim fellow, 1968-69; Nat. Endowment Humanities fellow, 1975-76, 82-83; Stanford U. Humanities Center Fellow, 1982-83. Mem. Modern Lang. Assn., Am. Comparative Lit. Assn. Office: Stanford U Dept English Stanford CA 94305-2087

LINDER, RONALD JAY, accountant, lawyer; b. Dayton, Ohio, Aug. 7, 1934; s. Sam C. and Amelia (Diamond) L.; m. Sandra Loving, June 12, 1966; children: Jeffrey Arthur, Carey Anne. BS in Econ., U. Pa., 1958; LLB, U. Mich., 1959; LLM, NYU, 1960. Bar: Calif., Ohio. Mgr. Arthur Young & Co., San Francisco, 1964-67, prin., 1967-69, ptnr., 1969-85; ptnr. Delagnes, Mitchell & Linder, CPA, San Francisco, 1985—, Delagnes, Linder & Zippel, Attys. at Law, San Francisco, 1985—. Author: Tax Strategies in Financial Planning, 1992. Mem. AICPA (exec. com. div. pers. fin. plan 1991—), Calif. CPA Soc. (chmn. pers. fin. plan com. 1991-93), State Bar of Calif., Ohio State Bar Assn. Office: Delagnes Mitchell & Linder 25 Ecker St Ste 650 San Francisco CA 94105

LINDGREN, KARIN JOHANNA, lawyer; b. Princeton, N.J., July 18, 1960; d. William R. and Abigail H. (Sangree) S. BS in Biology, Ursinus Coll., 1982; JD, Southwestern U., 1985. Bar: Pa. 1985, Calif. 1987, U.S. Dist. Ct. (cen., no., so., ea. dists.) Calif. 1987; U.S. Ct. Appeals (9th cir.) 1987. Assoc. Hillsinger & Costanzo, L.A., 1985-89, Sedgwick, Detert, Moran & Arnold, L.A., 1989—. Author: Handbook of Medical Liability, 1988; co-author: Healthcare Liability Deskbook, 1992, 2d edit.,1993. Mem. ABA, Pa. Bar Assn., L.A. County Bar Assn., Wilshire Bar Assn. (bd. govs. 1987-93, pres. 1991-92), Assn. So. Calif. Def. Counsel, Am. Acad. Hosp. Attys., L.A. World Affairs Coun., Sierra Club. Office: Sedgwick Detert Moran & Arnold 3701 Wilshire Blvd Fl 9 Los Angeles CA 90010-2804

LINDGREN, ROBERT KEMPER, securities investor, county tax collector; b. LaPorte, Ind., Sept. 25, 1939; s. Ralph Arthur and Georgia Lillian (Kemper) L.; m. Charmaine Katherine Freeman, Feb. 2, 1963; children: Scott Edward, Amber Louise, Vincent Kemper. Grad., Culver Mil. Acad., 1958; BS, Western Mich. U., 1963. Comml. printing mgr. Livingston (Mont.) Enterprise Comml. Printing, Livingston, 1968-70; prodn. mgr. Mont. Graphic Arts Ctr., div. of Lee Enterprises, Helena, 1970-71; ptnr., sales mgr. Ashton Printing Co., Butte, Mont., 1971-72; ptnr., sales mgr., corp. sec. Thurber Printing Co./Office Supplies, Helena, 1972-86; securities and investments trader Helena, 1968—; ins. agt. Am. Bankers Life Ins. Co., Helena, 1989-91, Surety Life and Continental Gen. Ins. Co., Helena, 1989-91; instr. Officer Candidate Sch., Mont. Mil. Acad., Mont. Army NG, Helena, 1974-75; adv. staff Civil Def. of the Mont. NG, Helena, 1975-76; chmn. Helena Demolition Derby of the annual Rodeo and Stampede, Helena, 1982-87. Water safety instr. ARC, 1959-62; swimming team coach Ft. Leavenworth Post, Kans., 1963-64; scout leader, Webelo Cub Scouts, Boy Scouts Am., Helena, 1973-76; bd. mem. Lewis & Clark County Planning Bd., Helena, 1977-79, Sch. Dist. No. 4 Bd. Trustees, Canyon Creek, Mont., 1981—, bd. chmn., 1984—; mem. Lewis & Clark Sheriff's Res., Helena, 1988—, Nat. High Sch. Rodeo, 1976; supply officer Sheriff's Res., 1990—; mem. coun. for Prevention Child Abuse, 1987; bd. dirs. Friends of Fairgrounds Found., 1990—; water safety instr. ARC 1959-62. Capt. (Signal Corps) U.S. Army, 1963-68. Recipient Certs. of Achievement, Boy Scouts Am., Helena, 1975, 85; Certs. of Service, County Commrs., Helena, 1977, 79. Mem. Toastmasters Internat., Am. Legion, Mont. Sheriff's and Peace Officers Assn., Lions. Republican. Home and Office: 5200 Hidden Valley Dr Helena MT 59601-9433

LINDH, ALLAN GODDARD, seismologist; b. Mason City, Wash., Mar. 18, 1943; s. Quentin Willis and Helma (Beagle) L.; m. Julie Gunda Pulver, Mar. 21, 1971; children: Briana Christine, Quentin William. BA in Geology and Physics, U. Calif., Santa Cruz, 1972; MS, Stanford U., 1974, PhD, 1980. Geophysicist U.S. Geol. Survey, Menlo Park, Calif., 1972—, chief scientist Parkfield prediction experiment, 1986—. Office: US Geol Survey 345 Middlefield Rd MS 977 Menlo Park CA 94025

LINDHOLM, DWIGHT HENRY, lawyer; b. Blackduck, Minn., May 27, 1930; s. Henry Nathanial and Viola Eudora (Gummert) L.; m. Loretta

Catherine Brown, Aug. 29, 1958; children: Douglas Dwight, Dionne Louise, Jeanne Marie, Philip Clayton, Kathleen Anne. Student, Macalester Coll., 1948-49; B.B.A., U. Minn., 1951, LL.B., 1954; postgrad., Mexico City Coll. (now U. of Ams.), 1956-57. Bar: Minn. 1954, Calif. 1958. Sole practice Los Angeles, 1958-65, 72-81, 84—; ptnr. Lindholm & Johnson, Los Angeles, 1965-69, Cotter, Lindholm & Johnson, Los Angeles, 1969-72; sole practice Los Angeles, 1972-81; of counsel Bolton, Dunn & Moore, Los Angeles, 1981-84. Mem. Calif. Republican Central Com., 1962-63, Los Angeles Republican County Central Com., 1962-66; bd. dirs. Family Service Los Angeles, 1964-70, v.p., 1968-70; bd. dirs. Wilshire YMCA, 1976-77; trustee Westlake Girls Sch., 1978-81; hon. presenter Nat. Charity League Coronet Debutante Ball, 1984; bd. dirs. Calif. State U.-Northridge Trust Fund, 1989—; bd. dirs. Queen of Angeles/Hollywood Presbyn. Med. Ctr., 1990—. Served as capt. JAG Corps USAF, 1954-56. Recipient Presdl. award Los Angeles Jr. C. of C., 1959. Mem. ABA, Calif. Bar Assn., L.A. County Bar Assn., Wilshire Bar Assn. (bd. govs. 1989-91), Internat. Genealogy Fellowship of Rotarians (founding pres. 1979-86), Calif. Club, Ocean Cruising Club Eng. (Newport Harbor port officer), Rotary (dir. 1975-78), Delta Sigma Pi, Delta Sigma Rho, Delta Theta Phi (state chancellor 1972-73). Presbyterian. Home: 255 S Rossmore Ave Los Angeles CA 90004-3738 Office: 3580 Wilshire Blvd Fl 17 Los Angeles CA 90010-2501

LINDHOLM, RICHARD THEODORE, university professor; b. Eugene, Oreg., Oct. 5, 1960; s. Richard Wadsworth and Mary Marjorie (Trunko) L. m. Valaya Nivasananda, May 8, 1987. BA, U. Chgo., 1982, MA, 1983. Adj. asst. prof. U. Oreg., Eugene, 1988—; ptnr. Lindholm and Osanka, Eugene, 1986-89, Lindholm Rsch., Eugene, 1989—; guest lectr. Nat. Inst. Devel. Adminstrn., Bangkok, Thailand, 1989; pres. Rubicon Inst., Eugene, 1988—. Co-campaign chmn. Lane Community Coll. Advocates, Eugene, 1988; coord., planner numerous state rep. campaigns, Oreg., 1988; mem. staff Oreg. Senate Rep. Office, 1989-90; precinct committeeperson Oreg. Rep. Party, 1989-93; bd. dirs. Rubicon Soc., Eugene, 1987—, pres. 1993. Republican. Lutheran. Home: 3335 Bardell Ave Eugene OR 97401

LINDLAND, FRANCES KAY, typesetter, designer; b. Sweetwater, Tex., June 7, 1954; d. Troy Waylon and Annie Frances (Stewart) Collins; m. Arild Lindland, Oct. 11, 1984; children: Shahna Patrice, John Wesley. Med. tech. degree, Lafayette U., 1978. Asst. to v.p. Southeastern Surg. Supply, Tallahassee, Fla., 1980-82; trauma technician Hamlin (Tex.) Meml. Hosp., 1982-83, Stamford (Tex.) Meml. Hosp., 1983-84; owner, mgr. Pro-to-Type Svcs., Tacoma, 1984—; newsletter cons. EIS Probe, Tacoma, 1989—. Author: (novel) Memories of the Morning Calm, 1992, (handbook) Success Is In Your Hands, 1992. Newsletter designer and cons. Boy Scouts Am., Tacoma, 1989—; newsletter designer Tahoma Audubon Soc., Tacoma, 1989—; dir. womens ministries Covenant Life Ch.; bd. dirs. Wash. State Family Alliance. Recipient Charter Pres. award NCO Wives in Korea, 1973. Mem. Writers Practice Group (Tacoma, co-dir., co-founder).

LINDLEY, NORMAN DALE, physician; b. Henrietta, Tex., July 18, 1937; s. Hardie Lindley and Hope (Clement) Mourant; m. Luise Ann Moser, May 29, 1964; children: Norman Dale Jr., Roger Paul. BS, N.Mex. Highlands U., 1960; MD, U. Colo., 1964. Diplomate Am. Bd. Ob-Gyn. Rotating intern Kans. City (Mo.) Gen. Hosp., 1964-65; resident in ob-gyn. St. Joseph Hosp., Denver, 1965-68; med. officer USAF, Cheyenne, Wyo., 1968-70; pvt. practice physician Alamogordo, N.M., 1970—; dir. N.M. Found. for Med. Care, Albuquerque, 1985-88, N.M. Med. Review Assn., Albuquerque, 1985-88; physician liaison Am. Assn. Med. Assts., Chgo., 1987—; physician adv. N.M. Soc. Med. Assts., 1984—. Bd. dirs. Otero County Boys and Girls Club, Alamogordo, 1977—, pres., 1979-81; bd. dirs. Otero County Assn. for Retarded Citizens, 1985—, pres., 1989-90; bd. dirs. Otero County chpt. Am. Cancer Soc., 1970-72. Capt. USAF, 1968-70. Rsch. grantee NSF, 1959, 60. Fellow Am. Coll. Ob-Gyn; mem. AMA, Am. Fertility Soc., Am. Inst. Ultrasound in Medicine, Am. Soc. Colposcopists and Cervical Pathologists, N.Mex. Med. Soc. (councilor 1985-88), Otero County Med. Soc. (pres. 1972-73, 83-84), Rotary (pres. White Sands chpt. Alamogordo 1981-82, bd. dirs. 1988—, Svc. Above Self award 1979, Paul Harris fellow 1987). Home: 2323 Union Ave Alamogordo NM 88310-3849 Office: Thunderbird Ob-Gyn 1212 9th St Alamogordo NM 88310-5863

LINDOW, LOUISA ROSE, lawyer; b. San Antonio, Jan. 25, 1922; d. George Edward and Louisa Augusta (Schweizerhof) L.; m. Richard J. Nugent, May 5, 1950 (div. 1953). BA, U. Colo., 1946; JD, Hastings Coll., 1956. Bar: Calif. 1956, Hawaii 1981. Asst. atty to exec. sec. Calif. Law Revision Commn., Stanford, Calif., 1957-61; sr. staff atty. Calif. Ct. Appeal (3d cir.), Sacramento, 1961-78; pvt. practice Honolulu, 1981—. Home: 1707 Alencastre St Honolulu HI 96816

LINDQUIST, LOUIS WILLIAM, artist, writer; b. Boise, Idaho, June 26, 1944; s. Louis William and Bessie (Newman) L.; divorced; children: Jessica Ann Alexandra, Jason Ryan Louis. BS in Anthropology, U. Oreg., 1968; postgrad., Portland State U., 1974-78. Researcher, co-writer with Asher Lee, Portland, Oreg., 1977-80; freelance artist, painter, sculptor Oreg., 1980-91. Sgt. U.S. Army, 1968-71, Vietnam. Mem. AAAS, Internat. Platform Assn., N.Y. Acad. Scis. Democrat. Home and Office: PO Box 991 Bandon OR 97411

LINDQUIST, STANLEY ELMER, retired psychology educator; b. Georgetown, Tex., Nov. 9, 1917; s. Elmer H. and Esther (Nyberg) L.; m. Ingrid Walden, June 15, 1940; children: Douglas, Russell, Brent. BA, Calif. State U., 1940; PhD, U. Chgo., 1950; LittD (hon.), Trinity Coll., Chgo., 1975. Prof. Psychology Trinity Coll., Chgo., 1946-53; prof. Psychology Calif. State U., Fresno, 1953-88, prof. emeritus, 1988—; dir. Bakersfield br. Calif. State U. Fresno, 1956-58; pres., founder Link Care Found., Fresno, 1964-91, pres. emeritus, 1991—. Author: Action Helping Skills, 1975, Reach Out: Become an Encourager, 1984. With U.S. Army, 1944-46, ETO. Decorated Purple Heart with three bronze stars. Fellow Am. Scientific Assn.; mem. Christian Assn. Psychologists (pres. 1977-78), Sigma Zi. Republican. Mem. Evang. Free Ch. of Am. Home: 5142 N College Ave Fresno CA 93704-2610 Office: Link Care Found 1734 W Shaw Ave Fresno CA 93711-3486

LINDSAY, NATHAN JAMES, management consultant, retired career officer; b. Monroe, Wis., May 24, 1936; s. Ralph Allen and Gertrude (Wartenweiler) L.; m. Shirley Rae Montgomery, Feb. 2, 1958; children: Lori E. Lindsay Smith, Anne, Nathan J. Jr., Susan E. BS in Mech. Engring., U.Wis., 1958, MS in Mech. Engring., 1965; MS in Systems Mgmt., U. So. Calif., L.A., 1976. Commd. 2d lt. USAF, 1958, advanced through grades to maj. gen., 1988; munitions officer USAF Weapons Ctr., Tripoli, Libya, 1959-61; weapons logistics officer USAF Europe, Wiesbaden, Germany, 1961-63; Titan III propulsion officer USAF Space Systems Div., L.A., 1965-69; aircraft guns devel. officer Air Force Armament Lab., Fla., 1969-70; grad. Armed Forces Staff Coll., Norfolk, Va., 1970; mgmt. auditor Air Force Systems Command, Andrews AFB, Md., 1971-73; grad. Def. Systems Mgmt. Coll., Ft. Belvoir, Va., 1973; space systems policy officer Air Force Office Special Projects, L.A., 1973-74, launch systems integration mgr., 1974-78; dir. policy and adminstrn. Air Force Office Space Systems, Pentagon, Washington, 1978-80; dir. space ops. support Air Force Space Div., L.A., 1980-82, program mgr. launch and control systems, 1982-84; comdr. Ea. Space and Missile Ctr., Patrick AFB, Fla., 1985-86; dep. comdr. for space launch and control systems Air Force Space Div., L.A., 1986-87; dir. office spl. projects Office Sec. of Air Force, L.A., 1987-92; mem. investigation task force NASA Challenger Accident, Kennedy Space Ctr., 1986. Co-chmn. Brevard County, Fla. Civilian-Mil. Affairs Coun., Cocoa Beach, 1984-86; elder Presbyn. Ch. Decorated D.S.M., Def. Superior Svc. medal, Legion of Merit with one oak leaf cluster, Meritorious Svc. medal with one oak leaf cluster, Joint Svc. Commendation medal, Air Force Commendation medal with one oak leaf cluster, Defense disting. svc. medal, NASA disting. svc. medal, Gen. Thomas D. Wite USAF Space Trophy, 1992, AAS military Astronautics award, 1993. Mem. Air Force Assn. (Bernard A. Shriever Space award 1989), Nat. Space Club (bd. dirs. 1992—), U. Wis. Alumni Assn., Am. Legion. Home & Office: 6450 Surfside Way Malibu CA 90265

LINDSAY, NORMAN ROY, systems consultant; b. Pitts., May 17, 1936; s. Norman Ward and Beverly Mae (Norris) L.; m. Camille Kaye Biddinger, Nov. 29, 1969. BA, Oberlin Coll., 1958; tech. degree, Control Data Inst., San Francisco, 1977. Budget analyst First Ch. Christ Scientist, Boston, 1965-68; office mgr. Christian Sci. Benevolent Assn., San Francisco, 1968-70; instr. Turner Enterprises, Orlando, Fla., 1970-73; various, 1973-77; computer specialist Lawrence Livermore Nat. Lab., Livermore, Calif., 1977-84; assoc. systems analyst Pacific Bell, San Ramon, Calif., 1984-90; cons. Solution Software, Inc., Livermore, Calif., 1990-92; owner RCL Enterprises & Cons. Svcs., Livermore, 1992—. Contbr. articles to profl. jours. Capt. USAF, 1958-65. Mem. USE Inc. (com. chair 1987-90, plaque 1990, 91, treas. 1991—), UNITE (v.p. 1993). Republican. Christian Scientist. Home: 130 El Caminito Livermore CA 94550-4004 Office: Solution Software Inc PO Box 5030 Ste 262 Livermore CA 94551-5030 also: RCL Enterprises & Cons Svcs 977 E Stanley Blvd Ste 262 Livermore CA 94550

LINDSAY, RICHARD PAUL, artist, jewelry designer; b. Aurora, Colo., Nov. 21, 1945; s. Paul Francis and Geraldine Evelyn (Goulet) L.; m. Susan Lynn Greenwood, Dec. 28, 1982; 1 child, Jared Nicholas. BA in Polit. Sci., Colo. State U., 1967. Profl. ski patrol Santa Fe (N.M.) Ski Basin, 1974-80; prin. Richard Lindsay Designs, Santa Fe, 1973—. Copyrighted designs include Walking Trout (R), Happy Critters (R), Roadkill Rabbit (R), Kachina Klan (R); exhibited in numerous galleries, N.Y.C., Colo., N.M., Tex., France, also others. Served to lt. U.S. Army, 1968-71, Vietnam. Recipient Design award Silversmith Santa Fe Film Festival, 1983, Best Ad Yr., Colo. Press Assn., 1972; decorated Bronze Star, Army Commendation medal. Mem. Jewelers Bd. of Trade. Office: Richard Lindsay Designs 1404 Luisa St Ste 4 Santa Fe NM 87501-4012

LINDSAY, S. BRIAN, health care administrator, consultant; b. Colorado Springs, Colo., Oct. 8, 1961; s. Stanley W. and N. Marie (Gibson) L. BS, Brigham Young U., 1987; M of Health Adminstrn., Duke U., 1990. Adminstrv. aide Health Scis. Ctr., U. Utah, Salt Lake City, 1987-88; adminstrv. intern Duke U. Med. Ctr., Durham, N.C., 1988-89; adminstrv. dir. Preferred Family Clinic, Provo, Utah, 1990—; exec. dir. Profl. Clin. Mgmt., Provo, Utah, 1990—; officer, bd. dirs. Preferred Family Clinic, Provo, Profl. Clin. Mgmt., Provo; officer Family Psychol. Ctr., Provo, 1991—. Compiler: A Pioneer's Story, 1986. Preceptor Utah Valley Bus./Edn. Partnership, Provo, 1990—; mem. Govt. Review Coun., Provo, 1992—. Mem. Duke U. Hosp. and Health Adminstrn. Alumni Assn., Am. Coll. Healthcare Execs., Brigham Young U. Mgmt. Soc., Provo/Orem C. of C. Republican. Mem. LDS Ch. Office: Profl Clin Mgmt Inc 3549 N University Ave Ste 300 Provo UT 84604

LINDSAY, WILLIAM NEISH, III, insurance agency executive; b. Hartford, Conn., Aug. 24, 1947; s. William N. Jr. and Margaret A. (Fraser) L.; m. Pamela J. Laine (div.); children: William N., Elizabeth Ruth; m. Camilla M. Falotico, Dec. 16, 1978; children: Katherine Anne, Sarah Fraser. BA, Gettysburg Coll., 1969. CLU. Asst. regional dir. Aetna Life & Casualty, Hartford, Conn., 1972-74; tng. specialist Aetna Life & Casualty, Hartford, 1974-75; dir., sales edn. Aetna Life & Casualty, 1975-78; brokerage gen. agt. Aetna Life & Casualty, Denver, 1978-81, gen. mgr., Rocky Mt. branch, 1981-84; pres. Benefit Mgmt. & Design, Inc., Denver, 1984—; gen. mgr. Aetna Life & Casualty, Hartford, 1983-84; mem. adv. coun. Personal Fin. Security Div.; cons. Robert Wood Johnson Found., Denver, 1985-89; faculty mem. user liaison program agy. health care policy and rsch. HHS, 1991-92; mem. small bus. adv. com. ins. dept. State of Colo., 1990-92; editorial bd. Law Firm Benifits, 1992. Bd. dirs. Jr. Achievement of Colo., 1982-86, Rocky Mountain Heart Planning Consortium, Phi Gamma Delta Ednl. Found., pres. Denver Chpt., 1984, sec., 1989—; chair steering com. Colo. Health Policy Coun., 1992—. Capt. USMC, 1969-72. Mem. Nat. Assn. Life Underwriters, CLU Assn., Colo. Group Ins. Assn. (v.p. 1992—), Greater Denver C. of C. (bd. dirs. 1989—, vice chair health care com. 1991—), Phi Gamma Delta (sec., bd. archons 1992—). Republican. Roman Catholic. Home: 8247 S Jasmine Ct Englewood CO 80112-3049 Office: Benefit Mgmt & Design Inc Ste 514 5660 Greenwood Plaza Blvd Englewood CO 80111-2403

LINDSEY, JOHN CUNNINGHAM, sales executive; b. Aliceville, Ala., July 23, 1953; s. Joe Alvin and Anne (Cunningham) L.; m. Karen Lynn Skaczkowski, May 3, 1980; children: Christina, Alissa, Jenna. BS, U. So. Calif., 1975, MBA, 1976. Sales rep. Jantzen, Inc., Portland, Oreg., 1977-87, western regional sales mgr., 1987-90; western regional sales mgr. OshKosh B'Gosh, L.A., 1990-92; v.p., gen. mgr. men's divsn. Basic Elements, Inc., L.A., 1993—; cons. D&K Enterprises, Moorpark, Calif., 1990—. Co-author, editor manual: Principles of Retail Math Related to Apparel Sales, 1991. Mem. Mayor's Adv. Coun., Moorpark, 1991. Mem. Am. Mgmt. Assn., Jonathan Club (jr. com. 1984, 86), Sigma Alpha Epsilon (v.p. 1975). Presbyterian.

LINDSEY, JOHN HALL, JR., software company executive; b. Malvern, Ark., July 29, 1938; s. John Hall and Jeannette Francis (Stuart) L.; m. Renetta Louise Harms, July 14, 1962; children: Sabra, Lemecia, Lance. Student, Ark. Poly. U., 1956-58, Okla. State U., 1958-60; BS in Bus., U. Utah, 1964; MBA, U. So. Calif., 1968. Data base mgr. NCR corp., Rancho Bernardo, Calif., 1966-75; data base adminstr. Kal Kan Foods, Vernon, Calif., 1975-77; data base supr. Kaiser Steel, Fontana, Calif., 1977-79; mgr. data base and tech. support Western Gear, Lynwood, Calif., 1979-84; mgr., sr. cons. data base Citicorp/TTI, Santa Monica, Calif., 1984-86; prin. Lindsey & Assocs., Eureka, Calif., 1986-88; ptnr. Lazio Family Products, 1990—; ptnr. Lindsey/Milligan Cos., Houston; mem. computer adv. com. Ontario/Montclaire Schs., Calif., 1980-82; mem. industry advisor Cullinet Corp., Westwood, Mass., 1986—; bd. dirs. IDMS User Assn., Westminster, chmn. large users adv. com., 1985-88; bd. dirs. S.W. User Assn., Los Angeles; guest lectr. U. So. Calif., 1975-76. Author: IDMS DB Design Review, 1982. Elder local Presbyn. Ch., 1980-82; vol. Culver City (Calif.) YMCA, 1986, Santa Monica (Calif.) Real Soccer Club, 1985-86; pres. Mt. Baldy Swim Team, Upland, Calif., 1975-80; bd. dirs. Ontario Community Credit Union, 1979-80; pres. Redwood Heritage Found, Inc., 1990—. Served with USNG, 1956-64. Mem. IDMS User Assn., SW Area IDMS User Assn. (chmn. 1982-84), Assn. System Mgmt. (v.p. 1966-68), Soc. for Mgmt. Info. (co-founder), Eureka C. of C., North Coast Fly Fishers, Trout Unltd., Rotary. Home and Office: 327 2d St Ste 201 Eureka CA 95501-0425

LINDSLEY, MICHELLE LABROSSE, aerospace engineer; b. East Hartford, Conn., Feb. 2, 1962; d. Andre Raymond and Louise (Roy) LaBrosse; m. Glenn Hale Lindsley, Nov. 24, 1984; children: Anne Francis, Katherine Louise. BS in Aero. Engring., Syracuse U., 1984; MS in Mech. Engring., U. Dayton, 1986. CEO Engrs. Justin Time, Seattle, 1993—. Contbr. articles to profl. jours. 1st lt. USAF, 1984-87. Recipient DAR award, 1984. Mem. Inst. Environ. Scis., Soc. Auto. Engrs., Am. Soc. Quality Control, Old Crows, Tau Beta Pi, Sigma, Gamma Tau, Eta Pi Upsilon.

LINDSTROM, BARRY LEE, systems consultant; b. Gary, Ind., Dec. 22, 1952; s. Norman W. and Betty L. (Reimers) L.; m. Melinda King, Nov. 5, 1971; children: Tiffany, Ryan, Samantha. BS in Acctg., Ind. U., 1975. Auditor, acct. Inland Steel, East Chicago, Ind., 1975-79; systems mgr. Motorola, Phoenix, 1979-85; ind. cons. LBP Cons., Mesa, Ariz., 1985-87; systems mgr. Sola Opthalmics, Phoenix, 1987-89; cons. Laughing Bear Prodns., Mesa, 1989—. Author: (movie script) The Dread Combination, 1981; author (software) Dr. Bob, 1987, Captrak, 1988, Walden, 1990, Unitrax, 1992, Audio File, 1993. Democrat.

LINDZEY, GARDNER, psychologist, educator; b. Wilmington, Del., Nov. 27, 1920; s. James and Marguerite (Shotwell) L.; m. Andrea Lewis, Nov. 28, 1944; children: Jeffrey, Leslie, Gardner, David, Jonathan. AB, Pa. State U., 1943, MS, 1945; PhD, Harvard U., 1949; LHD (hon.), U. Colo., 1990. Research analyst OSRD, 1944-45; instr. psychology Pa. State U., 1945-46; teaching fellow Harvard U., Cambridge, Mass., 1946-47, research fellow, 1947-49, research assoc., asst. prof., 1949-53, lectr., chmn. psychol. clinic staff, 1953-56, prof., chmn. dept., 1972-73; prof. psychology Syracuse (N.Y.) U., 1956-57, U. Minn., 1957-64; prof. psychology U. Tex., 1964-72, chmn., 1964-68, v.p. acad. affairs, 1968-70, v.p. ad interim, 1971, v.p., dean Grad. Studies, prof. psychology, 1973-75; dir. Ctr. for Advanced Study in Behavioral Scis., Stanford (Calif.) U., 1975—; mem. psychopharmacology study sect. NIMH, 1958-62, mem. program-project com., 1963-67, mem. adv. com. on extramural research, 1968-71; mem. com. faculty research fellowships Social Sci. Research Council, 1960-63, bd. dirs., 1962-76, mem. com. problems and policy, 1963-70, 72-76, chmn., 1965-70, mem. exec. com., 1970-75, chmn., 1971-75, mem. com. genetics and behavior, 1961-67, chmn., 1961-65; mem. com. biol. bases social behavior, 1967—; mem. com. work and personality in middle years, 1972-77; mem. sociology and social psychology panel NSF, 1965-68, mem. spl. commn. social scis., 1968-69, mem. adv. com. research, 1974—, mem. Waterman award com., 1976—; mem. exec. com., assembly behavioral and social sci. Nat. Acad. Sci.-NRC, 1970—, mem. com. life sci. and pub. policy, 1968-74, mem. panel nat. needs for biomed. and behavioral research personnel, 1974—, mem. com. social sci. in NSF, 1975—, mem. Inst. Medicine, 1975—; mem. com. on drug abuse Office Sci. and Tech., 1962-63; mem. Presdl. Com. Nat. Medal Sci., 1966-69; bd. dirs. Found.'s Fund Research in Psychiatry, 1967-70; bd. dirs. Am. Psychol. Found., 1968-76, v.p., 1971-73, pres., 1974-76. Author: (with Hall) Theories of Personality, 1957, 70, 78; (with Allport and Vernon) Study of Values, 1951, 60; Projective Techniques and Cross-Cultural Research, 1961; (with J.C. Loehlin and J.N. Spuhler) Race Differences in Intelligence, 1975; (with C.S. Hall and R.F. Thompson) Psychology, 1975; also articles; editor: Handbook of Social Psychology, Vols. 1 and 2, 1954, Vols. 1-5, 1969, Assessment of Human Motives, 1958, Contemporary Psychology, 1967-73, History of Psychology in Autobiography, Vol. 6, 1974; assoc. editor Psychol. Abstracts, 1960-62, Ency. Social Scis., 1962-67; co-editor Century Psychology Series, 1960-74, Theories of Personality: Primary Sources and Research, 1965, History of Psychology in Autobiography, Vol. V, 1968, Behavioral Genetics: Methods and Research, 1969, Contributions to Behavior-Genetic Analysis, 1970. Fellow Ctr. Advanced Study Behavioral Scis., Stanford, 1955-56, 63-64, 71-72, Inst. Medicine, 1975—. Fellow Am. Psychol. Assn. (bd. dirs. 1962-68, 70-74, mem. publs. bd., 1956-59, 70-73, chmn. 1958-59, mem. council of reps. 1959-67, 68-74, pres. div. social and personality psychology 1963-64, mem. policy and planning 1975, 78, pres. assn. 1966-67, mem. council of editors 1968-73, chmn. com. sci. award 1968-69, pres. div. gen. psychology 1970-71), Am. Acad. Arts and Scis., Am. Philos. Soc., Inst. Medicine, NAS, AAAS; mem. Am. Eugenics Soc. (bd. dirs. 1962-70), Soc. Social Biology (bd. dirs. 1972—, pres. 1978—), Am. Psychol. Assn. (dir. ins. trust 1973—), Univs. Research Assn. (bd. dirs. 1973-75). Club: Cosmos. Home: 109 Peter Coutts Cir Palo Alto CA 94305-2517

LINEBERGER, LARRY WATSON, financial executive; b. Columbia, S.C., July 27, 1943; s. Francis Marion and Margaret (Watson) L.; divorced, 1989; children: Barbara Lynn, Steven Todd; m. Shirley Powers, 1991. BSBA, U. S.C., 1966. CPA, S.C. Staff auditor S.D Leidesdorf & Co. (name now Ernst & Young), Greenville, S.C., 1966-71; various positions Daniel Internat. Corp., Greenville, S.C., 1971-87, v.p., corp. contr., treas., 1978-87; v.p., contr. Fluor Daniel, Inc., Irvine, Calif., 1987-91; adv. bd. Sch. Bus. Adminstrn., Winthrop Coll., Rock Hill, S.C., 1984-87. Treas. Boy Scouts Am., Greenville and Irvine; v.p. YMCA, Greenville. Recipient Disting. Alumnus award U. S.C., 1987, Silver Beaver award, Boy Scouts of Am., 1987; named. Acct. of Yr. Beta Alpha Psi, 1977-78. Mem. AICPA, S.C. Assn. CPA's, Associated Gen. Contractors Am. (com.), Fin. Execs. Inst. (pres. chpt.), Constrn. Fin. Mgmt. Assn., Greenville C. of C. Republican.

LINER, RICHARD MARK, information technology executive; b. Boston, Dec. 22, 1953; s. Sydney Myar and Alta (Burwen) L.; m. Jane Allison April, Mar. 19, 1988; 1 child, Andrea. BS cum laude, Union Coll., 1975. Tech. rep. Systems & Programming Resources, Denver, 1978-80, acct. mgr., 1980-82; v.p. western region Leardata Info-Svcs. (now ADIA Info. Techs.), Denver, 1982-88, 90—, pres., 1988-90. Mem. Data Processing Mgmt. Assn. Office: ADIA Info Techs 1050 17th St Ste 1650 Denver CO 80265-1601

LINFORD, LAURANCE DEE, cultural organization administrator; b. Cheyenne, Wyo., Mar. 2, 1951; s. Dee Verl and Helen Grace L.; m. Karen Page Stephens, Nov. 23, 1971; children: Justin, Micah. BA, U. N.Mex., 1973; MA, U. Ariz., 1978. Archaeologist Sch. Am. Research, Santa Fe, 1967-75, Ariz. State Mus., Tucson, 1975-77, Nat. Park Service, Tucson, 1977-78, Navajo Nation, Window Rock, Ariz., 1978-82; exec. dir. Inter-Tribal Indian Ceremonial Assn., Gallup, N.Mex., 1982—; bd. dirs. St. Michaels (Ariz.) Hist. Mus., 1979-86. Author: A Measure of Excellence, 1992; author, editor: The Pinon Project, 1982; editor: The Caremonial Mag., 1986-89, Inter-tribal Am. Mag, 1990-92. Pres. Indian Country Tourism Coun., 1982-86; mem. tourism com. Gallup McKinnley County Chamber, 1985-86; bd. dirs. Gallup Conv. and Visitors Bur., 1987-89, 91—. Mem. N.Mex. Assn. Execs. Democrat. Office: Inter-Tribal Indian Ceremonial Assn PO Box 1 Church Rock NM 87311-0001

LINFORD, RULON KESLER, physicist, program director; b. Cambridge, Mass., Jan. 31, 1943; s. Leon Blood and Imogene (Kesler) L.; m. Cecile Tadje, Apr. 2, 1965; children: Rulon Scott, Laura, Hilary, Philip Leon. BSEE, U. Utah, 1966; MS in ElecE, Mass. Inst. Tech., 1969, PhD in ElecE, 1973. Staff CTR-7 Los Alamos (N.Mex) Nat. Lab., 1973-75, asst. group leader CTR-7, 1975-77, group leader CTR-11, 1977-79, program mgr., group leader compact toroid CTR-11, 1979-80, program mgr., asst. div. leader compact toroid CTR div., 1980-81, assoc. CTR div. leader, 1981-86, program dir. magnetic fusion energy, 1986-89, program dir., div. leader CTR div. office, 1989-91, program dir. nuclear systems, 1991—. Contbr. articles to profl. jours. Recipient E. O. Lawrence award Dept. of Energy, Washington, 1991. Fellow Am. Physical Soc. (exec. com. 1982, 90-91, program com. 1982, 85, award selection com. 1983, 84, fellowship com. 1986); mem. Sigma Xi. Office: Los Alamos Nat Lab P O Box 1663 MS H854 Los Alamos NM 87545

LING, ALAN CAMPBELL, chemistry educator, university dean; b. London, July 28, 1940; came to U.S., 1966; s. Albert William and Winifred Rose (Salt) L.; m. Theresa Marie Webb, May, 22, 1986. BSc with 1st class honours, London U., 1963, PhD, 1966. AEC postdoctoral fellow U. Wis., Madison, 1966-68; prof. chemistry W.Va. U., Morgantown, 1968-75; rsch. prof. Wayne State U., Mich., 1975; prof. San Jose (Calif.) State U., 1975—, chmn. chemistry dept., 1985-88, dean Coll. Sci., 1988—; organizer symposia. Contbr. articles to profl. jours.; patentee in field. Trustee Palmer Chiropractic U. System, Davenport, Iowa, 1989—. Named Outstanding Profl., San Jose State U., 1982, Calif. State Univ. System, 1983; recipient numerous grants. Mem. Royal Soc. Chemistry, Am. Chem. Soc. (councillor 1985—), Sigma Xi. Office: San Jose State U One Washington Sq San Jose CA 95192

LING, ROBERT MALCOLM, banker, publishing executive; b. Akron, Ohio, July 6, 1931; s. Howard George and Catherine Zola (Smith) L.; m. Lois Claire Fisher Ling, Nov. 1, 1992; children: Shelly, Robert Jr., Amy, Beth, Patricia. BA in Journalism, Mich. State U., 1952. Asst. pres. Dike-O-Seal, Inc., Chgo., 1955-56; gen. mgr. Vollwerth Marquette (Mich.) Co., 1956-58, pres., 1958-75; pres. Vandco Incorp., Marquette, 1975-85, Cable American Corp., Rancho Cordova, Calif., 1985-89, Romali Holdings, Inc., Rancho Cordova, Calif., 1989—; chmn. Gold River Bank, Fair Oaks, Calif., 1990-92; publisher Grapevine-Independent newspaper, Rancho Cordova, Calif. Mayor City of Marquette, 1980-83, City of Rancho Cordova, Calif., 1986-87. 1st lt. U.S. Army, 1952-55. Republican. Home: 6032 Puerto Dr Rancho Murieta CA 95683 Office: Romali Holdings Inc 3338 Mather Field Rd Rancho Cordova CA 95670

LINHARDT, MARGARITA AGCAOILI, legal secretary, counselor; b. San Nicolas, The Philippines, Feb. 25, 1947; d. Mariano Edralin and Carmen (Dimaya) Agcaoili; m. Wilbur James Linhardt, Nov. 21, 1979; 1 child, Christi Anna. BS in Med. Tech., U. Santo Tomas, Manila, 1967; postgrad., Divine Word Coll., The Philippines, 1967; student, Sch. Speedwriting, N.Y.C., 1973, Legal Rsch., Paralegal Inst., Phoenix, 1982. Legal sec. Wyman Bautzer Rothman Kuchel & Silbert, L.A., 1979-80, Kindel & Anderson, L.A., 1981-82, Hufstedler, Miller Carlson & Beardsley, L.A., 1985-86, McKenna Conner & Cuneo, L.A., 1987, Pryor & Benson Inc., Torrance, Calif., 1988-89; fin. counselor Jerical Fin., Anaheim, Calif., 1982-83; outside pub. contact Royal Reservations, Las Vegas, Nev., 1983, 1st Am. Travel, Las Vegas, 1984. Mem. NAFE, The Exec. Program, Smithsonian Assocs., Nat. Trust for Hist. Preservation, Nat. Wildlife Fedn., Gene Autry Western Heritage Mus., Oblate Ptnrs. Club. Roman Catholic. Home: 1648 W 218th St Apt 9 Torrance CA 90501-3808

LINK, ANN MCCORMICK, reporter; b. Mt. Pleasant, Iowa, June 17, 1947; d. Donald E. and Mary Louise (Burns) McCormick; m. John A. Link, May 15, 1973; children: Erin Louise, Devin McCormick. BA, Creighton U., 1969. French tchr. Driscoll High Sch., Addison, Ill., 1969-70; elem. tchr.

Blessed Sacrament Sch., Omaha, 1971-73; substitute tchr. Pemberton (N.J.) Twp. Schs., 1973-75; news reporter Idaho County Free Press, Grangeville, 1985—. Mem. AAUW, Grangeville, 1978-80, PTA, Grangeville, 1991—; past pres. Syringa Gen. Hosp. Aux., Grangeville, 1981-84. Mem. LWV. Office: Idaho County Free Press PO Box 690 Grangeville ID 83530

LINK, CHARLES EDWARD, pastor; b. Oakland, Calif., Dec. 13, 1927; s. George and Madeline J. (Gonzalves) L.; m. Carol E. Nipper, July 6, 1950; children: David A., Daniel E., Nancy E. Link McColl. BA cum laude, Calif. Coll. Arts and Crafts, 1950; MDiv., San Francisco Theol. Sem., 1956; Rel. D., Claremont Sch. Theology, 1964. Ordained min. Presbyn. Ch., 1956; lic. marriage and family counselor, Calif. Tchr. art Pub. Secondary Schs., Oakland, Salinas, Calif., 1950-52; organizing pastor St. Andrews Presbyn. Ch., La Puente, Calif., 1956-60; pastor Shadow Hills Presbyn. Ch., Sunland, Calif., 1960-66; assoc. pastor Kirk o' the Valley Presbyn. Ch., Reseda, Calif., 1966-69; pastor Cordova Presbyn. Ch., Ranco Cordova, Calif., 1969-86; interim assoc. pastor Davis (Calif.) Community Presbyn. Ch., 1986-87; interim pastor Northminster Presbyn. Ch., Sacramento, Calif., 1987-88, Grace Presbyn. Ch., Sacramento, 1988-89, Westminster Presbyn. Ch., Roswell, N.Mex., 1989-91, Lincoln Presbyn. Ch., Stockton, Calif., 1991-92, Kelseyville (Calif.) Presbyn. Ch., 1992—; moderator Presbytery Sacramento, 1982; adj. prof. San Francisco Theol. Sem., 1984. Author devotions These Days and The Upper Room Daily Devotional, 1987-92; contbg. author Master Sermon Series, 1982—; contbr. articles to profl. jours. Mem. Sacramento County Mental Health Adv. Com., 1984-85; mem. touring choir River City Chorale, 1990, 1993. With U.S. Army, 1951-53. Named Citizen of Yr. YWCA, Sacramento, 1985; recipient art awards Roswell Art League Ann., 1990, Santa Monica Methodist Ann. Religious Art Show, 1967, Verdugo Hills Art Assn. Ann., 1962. Mem. Presbyn. Writers Guild.

LINK, MARY CATHERINE (MOLLY LINK), financial planner; b. Colorado Springs, Colo., May 19, 1934; d. J. Frederick and Mary Ruth (Smith) Bischof; m. Kirby Vern Anderson, Aug. 29, 1954 (div. Aug. 1969); children: Kirby V. Anderson Jr. (dec.), Molly Kathleen Anderson Pelle, Stephen Christopher, Kevin Andrew, Karen Anderson Iolani Hardy; m. Robert Elwood Link, May 8, 1976. BS in Chemistry, Colo. Coll., 1956; MPA, U. Colo., 1976. Tchr. Home of the Good Shepherd, Denver, 1957-60; owner small bus. Aurora, Colo., 1976-78; sales rep. Acacia Mut. Life Ins. Co., Aurora, 1978-82; sales rep., co-owner Link & Assocs., Inc., Aurora, 1978-90; ind. fin. planner Aurora, 1980-92. Mem. adv. coun. C.C. Aurora, 1984-91, chairperson adv. coun., 1988-90; co-chairperson reunion giving com. Colo. Coll., 1990-91; vice chairperson Colo. divsn. Am. Cancer Soc., 1989-91, chairperson, 1991-92; chairperson free enterprise com. Cherry Creek Rep. Women, 1988-90. Recipient Svc. to Mankind award Gateway Sertoma, Aurora, 1976, Outstanding Svc. award Aurora club Rotary Internat., 1976, Award of Excellence, Colo. divsn. Am. Cancer soc., 1986, Women Helping Women award Aurora chpt. Soroptomist Internat., 1979, St. George medal, Nat. Divsn. award Am. Cancer Soc., 1992, Leadership medal Am. Cancer Soc., 1992, Nat. Field Svcs. Builders award Am. Cancer Soc., 1992. Life Underwriters Assn. (bd. dirs. 1984-90, pres. 1988-89), Life Underwriters Polit. Action Com. Colo. (bd. dirs. 1982-84, 85-91, chairperson 1989-90), PEO (treas. Colo. chpt. 1989-90, vice chairperson 1990-91, publicity chairperson 1988-89). Episcopalian. Home: 12809 E Cornell Ave Aurora CO 80014-3346

LINK, MICHAEL PAUL, pediatrics educator; b. Cleve., Jan. 3, 1949; s. J. Alexander and Betty Irene (Lewis) L.; m. Vicki L. Rumpf, May 30, 1985; 1 child, Alexis Arielle. AB, Columbia Coll., 1970; MD, Stanford U., 1974. Diplomate Am. Bd. Pediatrics, subbd. Pediatric Hematology/Oncology. Prof. pediatrics Stanford (Calif.) U., 1991—. Mem. Phi Beta Kappa, Alpha Omega Alpha. Office: Stanford U Children's Hosp 725 Welch Rd Palo Alto CA 94304

LINK, PETER KARL, geologist; b. Batavia, Java, Indonesia, Nov. 7, 1930; s. Walter Karl Peter L. and Miriam Magdalene (Wollaeger) Wilcox; m. Marilynn Joyce Engel, June 1, 1957 (div. Feb. 1987); children: Bennett Karl, Hillary Leslie; m. Lucille R. Morrell, May 29, 1990. BS, U. Wis., 1953, MS, 1955, PhD, 1965. Field party chief Esso Std. (Libya) Inc., Tripoli, 1957-61; regional geologist Humble Oil and Refining Co., Ardmore, Okla., 1961-63; sr. rsch. geophysicist Atlantic Richfield Co., Dallas, 1965-68, 68-70; sr. rsch. scientist Amoco Prodn. Co., Tulsa, Okla., 1970-73; geol. cons. Tulsa, 1973-90; staff instr. Oil and Gas Cons. Internat., Tulsa, 1979—; geol. cons. Evergreen, Colo., 1990—; adj. prof. structural geology U. Tulsa, 1975-77; cons. Placid Oil, Shell Oil, Petroconsultants, Pogo Producing, 1973—; rsch. petroleum geologist Asia, Europe, U.S., Can., S.A., 1973—; instr. structural petroleum geology, worldwide, 1979—. Author: Basic Petroleum Geology, 1982, 2nd ed. 1987; contbr. articles to prof. jours. 1st lt. U.S. Army, 1955-57, Korea. Fellow Geol. Soc. Am.; mem. Am. Assn. Petroleum Geologists, Rocky Mountain Assn. Geologists, Sigma Xi. Home and Office: 7637 S Centaur Dr Evergreen CO 80439-6434

LINKKILA, LESLIE ELIZABETH, marketing professional, microbiologist; b. Putnam, Conn., Aug. 11, 1959; d. Peter Henry and Eleanor Jean (Csiki) L.; m. Philip Joseph DiNuovo, Oct. 8, 1988. BS, U. Conn., 1980; MS, U. N.H., 1983. Rsch. asst. Dept. Microbiology, Univ. N.H., Durham, 1980-83; rsch. scientist Jackson Estuarine Lab., Univ. N.H., Durham, 1983-84; tech. assoc. Mass. Inst. of Tech., Cambridge, Mass., 1984-85; tech. svcs. filtration and molecular biology mktg. mgr. Schleicher & Schuell, Inc., Keene, N.H., 1985-90; original equipment mfg. accounts mgr., v.p. sales and mktg. OWL Scientific, Cambridge, 1990—. Group leader United Way, Keene, 1987. Mem. AAAS, NAFE, Bus. and Profl. Women (named Young Career Woman 1987), Assn. Women in Sci., Sigma Xi.

LINN, BRIAN JAMES, lawyer; b. Seattle, July 8, 1947; s. Bruce Hugh and Jeanne De V. (Weidman) L.; m. Renee Diane Mousley; children: Kelly, Kareem, Kari. BA in Econs., U. Wash., 1972; JD, Gonzaga Sch. Law, 1975. Bar: Wash. 1975, U.S. Supreme Ct. 1979. Mng. atty. Legal Svcs. for Northwestern Pa., Franklin, 1975-76; staff atty. The Nat. Ctr. for Law and the Handicapped, 1976-78, U. Notre Dame Law Sch., South Bend, Ind., 1976-78; pvt. practice, Seattle, 1978—; lectr. Seattle U., 1980-85. Chmn. civil and legal rights subcom. Gov.'s Com. on Employment of the Handicapped, 1981-87; arbitrator King County Superior Ct., 1981—, judge pro tem, 1989—. Editor Gonzaga Law Rev., 1974-75. Mem. Wash. State Devel. Disabilities Planning Council, 1980-83; trustee Community Service Ctr. for the Deaf and Hard of Hearing, Seattle, 1982-84; chmn. legal rights task force Epilepsy Found. Am., 1979-81. Editor Gonzaga Law Rev., 1973-75. Served with U.S. Army, 1967-69; Vietnam. Mem. Wash. State Bar Assn. (chair world peace through law sect. 1990-91, spl. dist. counsel 1991—), Omicron Delta Epsilon. Democrat. Methodist. Hon. editor DePaul Law Rev., 1978; contbr. articles to profl. jours. Home: 9716 S 204th Ct Kent WA 98031-1400 Office: 245 SW 152d St Seattle WA 98166

LINN, CAROLE ANNE, dietitian; b. Portland, Oreg., Mar. 3, 1945; d. James Leslie and Alice Mae (Thorburn) L. Intern, U. Minn., 1967-68; BS, Oreg. State U., 1963-67. Nutrition cons. licensing and cert. sect. Oreg. State Bd. Health, Portland, 1968-70; chief clin. dietitian Rogue Valley Med. Ctr., Medford, Oreg., 1970—; cons. Hillhaven Health Care Ctr., Medford, 1971-83; lectr. Local Speakers Bur., Medford. Mem. ASPEN, Am. Dietetic Assn., Am. Diabetic Assn., Oreg. Dietetic Assn. (sec. 1973-75, nominating com. 1974-75, Young Dietitian of Yr. 1976), So. Oreg. Dietetic Assn., Alpha Lambda Delta, Omicron Nu. Democrat. Mem. Christ Unity Ch. Office: Rogue Valley Med Ctr 2825 E Barnett Rd Medford OR 97504-8332

LINSTONE, HAROLD ADRIAN, management and systems science educator; b. Hamburg, Fed. Republic Germany, June 15, 1924; came to U.S., 1936; s. Frederic and Ellen (Seligmann) L.; m. Hedy Schubach, June 16, 1946; children: Fred A., Clark R. BS, CCNY, 1944; MA, Columbia U., 1947; PhD, U. So. Calif., 1954. Sr. scientist Hughes Aircraft Co., Culver City, Calif., 1949-61, The Rand Corp., Santa Monica, Calif., 1961-63; assoc. dir. planning Lockheed Corp., Burbank, Calif., 1963-71; prof. Portland (Oreg.) State U., 1970—; pres. Systems Forecasting, Inc., Santa Monica, 1971—; cons. 1973—. Author: Multiple Perspectives, 1984; co-author The Unbounded Mind, 1993; co-editor: The Delphi Method, 1975, Technological Substitution, 1976, Futures Research, 1977; editor-in-chief Technol. Forecasting Social Change, 1969—. NSF grantee, Washington, 1976, 79, 85. Mem. Inst. Mgmt. Scis., Ops. Research Soc., Internat. Soc. Systems Scis. (pres.-elect 1992-93). Office: Portland State U PO Box 751 Portland OR 97207-0751

LINTHICUM, LESLIE JEAN, newspaper reporter; b. Preston, Minn., Mar. 18, 1958; d. Lowndes Paca and Loretta Mae (Denning) Linthicum; m. Michael William Haederle, June 3, 1983; 1 child, Kate Martha. BJ, Northwestern U., 1980. Reporter City News Bur., Chgo., 1980-82, The Albuquerque Tribune, 1982-84, The Houston Post, 1984-88, Albuquerque Jour., 1988—. Recipient Best Investigative Story award Nat. Edn. Writers Assn., 1983, Best Feature Story award, 1984, Barbara Jordan award Tex. Gov.'s Commn. on Employment of Handicapped, 1988, Best Feature Story award Tex. Commn. on Disabled. Office: Albuquerque Jour 7777 Jefferson NE Albuquerque NM 87109

LINTON, MARIGOLD L., psychology educator; b. Morongo Reservation, Banning, Calif.; d. Walter Alexander and Wistaria (Hartmann) L.; m. Robert Ellis Barnhill, Feb. 12, 1983; children: John, Margaret. B.A., U. Calif.-Riverside, 1958; M.A., U. Iowa, 1960; Ph.D., UCLA, 1964. Lectr., prof. San Diego State U., 1964-74; prof. U. Utah, Salt Lake City, 1974-86; dir. edn. svcs. Coll. Edn. Ariz. State U., Tempe, 1986—; vis. prof. U. Calif.-San Diego, 1971-72; vis. scholar Learning Research and Devel. Ctr. U. Pitts., 1980-81; mem. nat. adv. research resources council NIH. Co-author: (with Gallo) The Practical Statistician, 1975. Contbr. articles to profl. jours., chpts. to books. Bd. dirs. Malki Mus., 1971-78; bd. adv. Soc. Adv. Chicanos Native Am. Sci., 1989— (founders metal 1993); trustee Carnegie Found. Advancement Teaching, 1977-85. NIH research grantee, 1980. Fellow Am. Psychol. Assn. (bd. advisors psychol. pub. interest 1993—), Am. Psychol. Soc.; mem. Rocky Mountain Psychol. Assn., Western Psychol. Assn., Am. Psychol. Soc., Nat. Indian Edn. Assn. (Cert. Honor award 1976), Phi Beta Kappa, Phi Kappa Phi. Office: Ariz State U Payne Hall B-10 Tempe AZ 85287-2811

LINTON, RUTH COLEMAN, fine arts consultant; b. Wilmington, Del., Aug. 12, 1955; d. Jack Myers and Elaine Bradford (Webster) Linton; m. Richard Urban Thomas, Oct. 10, 1981. B.A. with highest honors, U. Del., 1976, M.A., 1981. Intern Hagley Mus., Greenville, Del., 1979; spl. asst. Hagley Library, 1978-80; teaching asst. dept. history U. Del., Newark, 1980-81; intern Nemours Mansion, Wilmington, Del., 1980-81; curator The Nemours Found., Wilmington, 1981-87; lectr. Speakers Bur., A.I. duPont Inst., Wilmington, 1984—; cons. Am. Assn. Mus., 1985—; instr. U. Del., 1987, U. Colo., Boulder, 1989—; gallery dir. Mountain Shadow Gallery, 1988—. Contbr. articles to profl. jours. Recipient Louis E. Larsen award, U. Del., 1976; Del. Humanities Forum fellow, 1985. Mem. Discover Brandywine Valley Pub. Rels. Assn. (sec. 1984), Am. Assn. Mus., Am. Assn. for State and Local History. Episcopalian. Avocations: early music; hiking. Home: 275 29th St Boulder CO 80303-3313 Office: Mountain Shadow Gallery 1217 Spruce St Boulder CO 80302-4805

LINTON, WILLIAM HENRY, power industry consultant, engineer; b. Jersey Shore, Pa., Feb. 20, 1925; s. John Henry Linton and Emily Helena (Scouten) Linton Sims; m. Mary Bishop Clarke, Aug. 12, 1949; 1 child, Susan Bishop. BSME, Bucknell U., 1949. Registered profl. engr., Calif. Constrn. engr. Penna Power and Light Co., Allentown, Pa., 1949-53, Grinnell Corp., Portsmouth, Ohio, 1953-54; engring. mgr. Bettis Atomic Power Lab., Pitts., 1954-64, 66-69; resident mgr. Bettis Atomic Power Lab., Newport News, Va., 1964-66; resident mgr. west coast Bettis Atomic Power Lab., L.A., 1970-72; mgr. constrn. Westinghouse Hanford, Richmond, Wash., 1972-74; project mgr. Bechtel Corp., San Francisco, 1974-90; ind. cons. to power industry Sausalito, Calif., 1990—; Patentee naval nuclear field. Grand Juror Marin County Grand Jury, San Rafael, 1991. 2nd lt. U.S. Army, 1943-45, ETO. Mem. ASME (life), Masons, Marin County Dog Tng. Club. Republican. Home: 14 Cypress Pl Sausalito CA 94965-1536

LINXWILER, JAMES DAVID, lawyer; b. Fresno, Calif., Apr. 9, 1949; s. George Edwin and Stella Ruth (Schmidt) L.; m. Robyn Kenning, July 12, 1986; children: Elizabeth Ann, John Edwin, Jeffrey David. BA, U. Calif.-Berkeley, 1971; JD, UCLA, 1974. Bar: D.C. 1976, Alaska 1977, U.S. Ct. Appeals (9th and D.C. cirs.), U.S. Dist. Ct. Alaska. Lawyer, Dept. Interior, Washington, 1974-76; lawyer, Cook Inlet Region Inc., Anchorage, 1976-78; lawyer Sohio Petroleum Co., Anchorage, 1978-81; ptnr. Guess & Rudd, Anchorage, 1981—; speaker seminars on environ. law. Contbr. chpts. to book, articles to profl. jours. Chmn. Alaska Coalition Am. Energy Security, 1986-87, Alliance Active Nat. Wildlife Refuge Com., 1986-87; bd. dirs., Commonwealth N., 1993. Mem. ABA, Alaska Bar Assn. (chmn., exec. com. nat. resources sect. 1988-93), Fed. Bar Assn., D.C. Bar Assn.Democrat. Home: 2407 Loussac Dr Anchorage AK 99517-1230 Office: Guess & Rudd 510 L St Ste 700 Anchorage AK 99501-1959

LINXWILER, LOUIS MAJOR, JR., retired finance company executive; b. Blackwell, Okla., Mar. 7, 1931; s. Louis Major and Flora Mae (Horton) L.; m. Susan Buchanan, July 27, 1963; children: Louis Major III, Robert William. BS, Okla. State U., 1954. Mgr. credit dept. Valley Nat. Bank, Tucson, 1957-60; sales rep. Vega Industries, Syracuse, N.Y., 1960-62; program dir. Am. Cancer Soc., Phoenix, 1962-67; v.p., mgr. credit dept. United Bank Ariz., Phoenix, 1967-76; dean edn. Am. Inst. Banking, Phoenix, 1976-80; cons. Phoenix, 1980-81, United Student Aid Funds Inc., Phoenix, 1981-82; founder, pres., chief exec. officer Ariz. Student Loan Fin. Corp., Phoenix, 1982-88, also bd. dirs.; founder, chmn., chief exec. officer Western Loan Mktg. Assn., Phoenix, 1984-90, also bd. dirs. Editor: Money and Banking, 1978. Pres. City Commn. Sister Cities, Phoenix, 1986-87, Am. Inst. Banking, Phoenix, 1973-74, Phoenix YMCA Bd. Dirs., 1974-75; v.p. North Mountain Behavioral Inst., Phoenix, 1975-77. Served to 1st lt. U.S. Army, 1954-56. Mem. Shriners, Hiram Club, Rotary (bd. dirs. 1982-83, 1993—), Beta Theta Pi. Republican. Presbyterian.

LIONAKIS, GEORGE, architect; b. West Hiawatha, Utah, Sept. 5, 1924; s. Pete and Andriani (Protopapadakis) L.; student Carbon Jr. Coll., 1942-43, 46-47; B. Arch., U. Oreg., 1951; m. Iva Oree Braddock, Dec. 30, 1951; 1 dau., Deborah Jo. With Corps Engrs., Walla Walla, Wash., 1951-54; architect Liske, Lionakis, Beaumont & Engberg, Sacramento, 1954-86, Lionakis-Beaumont Design Group, 1986—. Mem. Sacramento County Bd. Appeals, 1967—, chmn., 1969, 75, 76; pres. Sacramento Builders Exchange, 1976. Served with USAAF, 1943-46. Mem. AIA (pres. Central Valley chpt., 1972—), Constrn. Specifications Inst. (pres. Sacramento chpt., 1962; nat. awards, 1962, 63, 65), Sacramento C. of C. (code com., 1970—). Club: North Ridge Country (pres. 1987). Lodge: Rotarian (pres. East Sacramento 1978-79). Prin. works include Stockton (Calif.) Telephone Bldg., 1968, Chico (Calif.) Main Telephone Bldg., 1970, Mather AFB Exchange Complex Sacramento, 1970, Base Chapel Mather AFB, Sacramento, 1970, Woodridge Elementary Sch., Sacramento, 1970, Pacific Telephone Co. Operating Center Modesto, Calif., 1968, Sacramento, 1969, Marysville, Calif., 1970, Red Bluff, Calif., 1971, Wells Fargo Banks, Sacramento, 1968, Corning, Calif., 1969, Anderson, 1970, Beale AFB Exchange Complex, Marysville, 1971, Cosumnes River Coll., Sacramento, 1971, base exchanges at Bergstrom AFB, Austin, Tex., Sheppard AFB, Wichita Falls, Tex., Chanute AFB, Rantoul, Ill., McChord AFB, Tacoma, Wash., health center Chico State U., Sacramento County Adminstrn. Center, Sacramento Bee Newspaper Plant. Home: 160 Breckenwood Way Sacramento CA 95864-6968 Office: Lionakis Beaumont Design Group 1919 19th St Sacramento CA 95814

LIPCHIK, HAROLD, company executive; b. N.Y.C., Apr. 17, 1928; s. Samuel and Ida (Gutterman) L.; m. Elaine Greenberg, Mar. 23, 1952; children: Alan Scott, Debra Anne. BS in Mech. Engring., Carnegie Mellon U., 1948; postgrad., NYU, 1948-49, 49-50. Project engr. Pub. Svc. Commn. N.Y. State, N.Y.C., 1950-51, Bendix Aviation, South Bend, Ind., 1951-52, Hamilton Standard div. United Aircraft, Windsor Locks, Conn., 1952-66; v.p. AMF Inc., N.Y.C., 1966-71, Chromalloy Am. Corp., Clayton, Mo., 1968-71; pres. Water Treatment Corp., City of Industry, Calif., 1971-82, Halco Industries, Glendale, Calif., 1982—, Halco Assocs., Tarzana, Calif., 1984—; v.p. Nat. Tech. Systems, Calabasas, Calif., 1982—; dir. Halco Assocs., Tarzana. Pres. United Synagogue Am., L.A., 1976-78, L.A. Hebrew High Sch., L.A., 1978-84. Jewish. Home: 4429 Trancas Pl Tarzana CA 91356-5302 Office: Nat Tech Systems 24007 Ventura Blvd Calabasas CA 91302-1458

LIPINSKI, ROBERT HENRY, mechanical engineer; b. Pitts., Mar. 31, 1939; s. Henry Francis and Leona Frances (Lejpras) L.; m. Mary Jo Fandozzi, Dec. 28, 1963; children: Robin Alexandra, Jonathan Brett. BSME, U. Pitts., 1961; MBA with highest distinction, Babson Coll., 1972. Commd. U.S. Army, 1962-90, advanced through grades to col., 1981; div. chief Office of Dep. Chief of Staff, R&D, U.S. Army, Pentagon, 1981-83; comdr. Yuma Proving Ground, Ariz., 1983-85; dir. Nat. Range, U.S. Army, White Sands Missile Range, N.Mex., 1985-90; tech. mgr. engring. and analysis United Internat. Engring., Inc., White Sands Missile Range, N.Mex., 1990—; adj. prof. Fla. Inst. Tech. WSMR campus Dept. Mgmt., 1987—. Decorated Legion of Merit (2), Bronze Star, Army Commendation medal (2). Mem. Assn. of U.S. Army (WSMR chpt. pres. 1992—), Scabbard and Blade, (Pitts. chpt. pres., 1960-61), Beta Gamma Scholarship Soc. Babson Coll., Pi Kappa Alpha (chpt. pres. 1960-61). Home: 162 Lytton Cir Las Cruces NM 88002 Office: United Internat Engring Drawer N White Sands Missile Range NM 88002

LIPINSKY DE ORLOV, LINO S., lawyer; b. N.Y.C., Aug. 5, 1958; s. Lino S. and Leah S. (Penner) L.; m. Diana L. DeGette, Sept. 15, 1984; 1 child, Raphaela Anne Lipinsky DeGette. AB magna cum laude, Brown U., 1979; JD, NYU, 1982. Bar: N.Y. 1983, Colo. 1983, U.S. Dist. Ct. Colo. 1983, U.S. Ct. Appeals (10th cir.) 1983, U.S. Supreme Ct. 1989. Assoc. Willkie Farr & Gallagher, N.Y.C., 1982-83, Holme Roberts & Owen, Denver, 1983-90; assoc. Hawley & VanderWerf, Denver, 1990-92, shareholder, 1992—. Co-editor Colorado Cultural Directory, 1989; contbr. articles to profl. jours. Dir. Hospice Metro Denver, 1990—, vice-chair, 1992—; chair Denver area Nat. Alumni Schs. Program Brown U., Providence, 1988-92; trustee Patten Inst. for Arts, Denver, 1984-90. Mem. ABA, Colo. Bar Assn. (chair Bill of Rights com. 1992—, Pro Bono award 1985, 86), Denver Bar Assn., Rocky Mountain Brown Club (pres. 1992—). Democrat. Home: 290 Elm St Denver CO 80220-5739 Office: Hawley & VanderWerf PC 730-17th St # 730 Denver CO 80202

LIPKIN, MARY CASTLEMAN DAVIS (MRS. ARTHUR BENNETT LIPKIN), retired psychiatric social worker; b. Germantown, Pa., Mar. 4, 1907; d. Henry L. and Willie (Webb) Davis; student Acad. Fine Arts, Pa., 1924-28, grad. sch. social work U. Wash., 1946-48; m. William F. Cavenaugh, Nov. 8, 1930 (div.); children: Molly C. (Mrs. Gary Oberbillig), William A.; m. 2d, Arthur Bennett Lipkin, Sept. 15, 1961 (dec. June 1974). Nursery sch. tchr. Miquon (Pa.) Sch., 1940-45; caseworker Family Soc. Seattle, 1948-49, Jewish Family and Child Service, Seattle, 1951-56; psychiat. social worker Stockton (Calif.) State Hosp., 1957-58; supr. social service Mental Health Research Inst., Fort Steilacoom, Wash., 1958-59; engaged in pvt. practice, Bellevue, Wash., 1959-61. Former mem. Phila. Com. on City Policy. Former diplomate and bd. mem. Conf. Advancement of Pvt. Practice in Social Work; former mem. Chestnut Hill women's com. Phila. Orch; mem. Bellevue Art Mus., Wine Luke Mus. Mem. ACLU, Linus Paul Inst. Sci. and Medicine, Inst. Noetic Scis., Menninger Found., Union Concerned Scientists, Physicians for Social Responsibility, Center for Sci. in Pub. Interest, Asian Art Council, Seattle Art Mus., Nature Conservancy, Wilderness Soc., Sierra Club, Cosmopolitan Club Phila., Women's Univ. Club Seattle, Friday Harbor Yacht Club Washington). Home: 10022 Meydenbauer Way SE Bellevue WA 98004-6041

LIPOMI, MICHAEL JOSEPH, health facility administrator; b. Buffalo, Mar. 9, 1953; s. Dominic Joseph and Betty (Angelo) L.; m. Brenda H. Lipomi, Dec. 23, 1977; children: Jennifer, Barrett. BA, U. Ottawa, 1976. Mktg. dir. Am. Med. Internat. El Cajon Valley Hosp., Calif., 1980-83; dir. corp. devel. Med. Surg. Ctrs. Am., Calif., 1983-85; exec. dir. Stanislaus Surgery Ctr., Modesto, Calif., 1985—. Author: Complete Anatomy of Health Care Marketing, 1988; co-host med. TV talk show Health Talk Modesto. Bd. dirs. Am. Heart Assn., Modesto, 1988-89; pres. Modesto Community Hospice, 1987-88; active local govt.; sec.-treas. Modesto Industry and Edn. Council, 1989. Mem. Calif. Ambulatory Surgery Assn. (pres. 1988-89), No. Calif. Assn. Surgery Ctrs. (pres. 1986-88), Federated Ambulatory Surgery Assn. (govt. rels. com. 1988, bd. dirs. 1989—, chmn. govt. rels. com. 1990), C. of C. (bd. dirs. 1989-92), Rotary. Lodge: Rotary. Office: Stanislaus Surgery Ctr 1421 Oakdale Rd Modesto CA 95355-3359

LIPPE, PHILIPP MARIA, neurosurgeon, educator; b. Vienna, Austria, May 17, 1929; s. Philipp and Maria (Goth) L.; came to U.S., 1938, naturalized, 1945; m. Virginia M. Wiltgen, 1953 (div. 1977); children: Patricia Ann Marie, Philip Eric Andrew, Laura Lynne Elizabeth, Kenneth Anthony Ernst; m. Gail B. Busch, Nov. 26, 1977. Student Loyola U., Chgo., 1947-50; BS in Medicine, U. Ill. Coll. Medicine, 1952, MD with high honors, 1954. Rotating intern St. Francis Hosp., Evanston, Ill., 1954-55; asst. resident gen. surgery VA Hosp., Hines, Ill., 1955, 58-59; asst. resident neurology and neurol. surgery Neuropsychiat. Inst., U. Ill. Rsch. and Ednl. Hosps., Chgo., 1959-60, chief resident, 1962-63, resident neuropathology, 1962, postgrad. trainee in electroencephalography, 1963; resident neurology and neurol. surgery Presbyn.-St. Luke's Hosp., Chgo., 1960-61; practice medicine, specializing in neurol. surgery, San Jose, Calif., 1963—; instr. neurology and neurol. surgery U. Ill., 1962-63; clin. instr. surgery and neurosurgery Stanford U., 1965-69, clin. asst. prof., 1969-74, clin. assoc. prof., 1974—; staff cons. in neurosurgery O'Connor Hosp., Santa Clara Valley Med. Ctr., San Jose Hosp., Los Gatos Community Hosp., El Camino Hosp. (all San Jose area); chmn. div. neurosugery Good Samaritan Hosp, 1989—; founder, exec. dir. Bay Area Pain Rehab. Center, San Jose, 1979—; clin. adviser to Joint Commn. on Accreditation of Hosps.; mem. dist. med. quality rev. com. Calif. Bd. Med. Quality Assurance, 1976-87, chmn., 1976-77. Served to capt. USAF, 1956-58. Diplomate Am. Bd. Neurol. Surgery, Nat. Bd. Med. Examiners. Fellow ACS, Am. Coll. Pain Medicine (pres. 1992, bd. dirs., v.p. 1991—); mem. AMA (Ho. of Dels. 1981—), Calif. Med. Assn. (Ho. of Dels. 1976-80, sci. bd., council 1979-87, sec. 1981-87, Outstanding Svc. award 1987), Santa Clara County Med. Soc. (coun. 1974-81, pres. 1978-79, Outstanding Contbn. award 1984, Benjamin J. Cory award 1987), Chgo. Med. Soc., Congress Neurol. Surgeons, Calif. Assn. Neurol. Surgeons (dir. 1974-82, v.p. 1975-76, pres. 1977-79), San Jose Surg. Soc., Am. Assn. Neurol. Surgeons (chm. sect. on pain 1987-90, dir. 1983-86, 87-90, Disting. Svc. award 1986, 90), Western Neurol. Soc., San Francisco Neurol. Soc., Santa Clara Valley Profl. Standards Rev. Orgn. (dir., v.p., dir. quality assurance 1975-83), Fedn. Western Socs. Neurol. Sci., Internat. Assn. for Study Pain, Am. Pain Soc. (founding mem.), Am. Acad. Pain Medicine (sec. 1983-86, pres. 1987-88), Alpha Omega Alpha, Phi Kappa Phi. Assoc. editor Clin. Jour. of Pain; contbr. articles to profl. jours. Pioneered med. application centrifugal force using flight simulator. Office: 2100 Forest Ave Ste 106 San Jose CA 95128-1496

LIPPITT, ELIZABETH CHARLOTTE, writer; b. San Francisco; d. Sidney Grant and Stella L. Student Mills Coll., U. Calif.-Berkeley. Writer, performer own satirical monologues, nat. and polit. affairs for 85 newspapers including Muncie Star, St. Louis Globe-Dem., Washington Times, Utah Ind., Jackson News, State Dept. Watch. Singer debut album Songs From the Heart; contbr. articles to 85 newspaper including N.Y. Post, L.A. Examiner, Orlando Sentinel, Phoenix Rep. Mem. Commn. for Free China, Conservative Caucus, Jefferson Ednl. Assn., Presdl. Adv. Commn. Recipient Congress of Fredom award, 1959, 71-73. Mem. Amvets, Nat. Trust for Hist. Preservation, Am. Security Coun., Internat. Platform Assn., Am. Conservative Union, Nat. Antivivisection Soc., High Frontier, For Our Children, Childhelp U.S.A., Free Afghanistan Com., Humane Soc. U.S., Young Ams. for Freedom, Coun. for Inter.-Am. Security, Internat. Med. Corps, Assn. Vets for Animal Rights, Met. Club, Olympic Club, Commonwealth Club. Home: 2414 Pacific Ave San Francisco CA 94115-1238

LIPPITT, LOUIS, physical science educator, aerospace engineer; b. N.Y.C., Mar. 19, 1924; s. Louis Sr. and Susan Davie (Anderson) L.; m. Adele Dorothy Wissmann, June 27, 1948; children: Laurie, Craig, Bonnie, Nancie. BS, CUNY, 1947; MA, Columbia U., 1953, PhD, 1959. Registered geologist, geophysicist, Calif. Physicist Columbia U., N.Y.C., 1947-51, NYU, N.Y.C., 1951-53; geophysicist Chevron, Calif., 1954-58; staff engr. Lockheed Missiles and Space Co., Vandenberg AFB, Calif., 1958-87; tchr. part time Hancock Coll., Santa Maria, Calif., 1967—, Chapman Coll., Vandenberg AFB, 1985-86. Project leader, 4H, Calif., 1960-77. Recipient Honorarium, State of N.Y., 1952. Fellow Geol. Soc. Am. (sr.); mem. Am. Geophys. Union. Lutheran. Home: 696 Raymond Ave Santa Maria CA 93455-2760

LIPPMANN, BRUCE ALLAN, rehabilitative services professional; b. Balt., Aug. 29, 1950; s. Allan L. and Phyllis Marie (Bunyea) L.; m. Barbara Jean Wood, May 26, 1973 (div. Aug. 1979); m. Susan K. Shampanier, Feb. 1, 1981 (div. Nov. 1990); m. Frances G. Scruggs, Dec. 31, 1991; children: Joshua, Grant. BA, U. Md., Catonsville, 1972; MS, Loyola U., 1979; cert., San Diego Inst., 1989; postgrad., Calif. Sch. Profl. Pyschology, 1992—. Cert. rehab. counselor, ins. rehab. specialist. Social worker Md. Children's Ctr., Catonsville, 1970-72; vocat. cons. St. Md. Workers Compensation Commn., Balt., 1975-79; sr. counselor McGuinness Assocs., Fresno, Calif., 1980-84; pres., chief exec. officer Sierra Rehab. Svcs. Inc., Fresno, 1984-91; vocat. cons. Fresno, 1991—; cons. Doctors Med. Ctr., Modesto, Calif., 1989-92, Calif. Ctr. Rehab. Svcs., Fresno, 1986-89, U.S Dept. Labor, San Francisco, 1984—; curriculum cons. Microcomputer Tng. Inst., Fresno, 1986-91. Mem. Metro Circle-Fresno Metro Mus., 1986—, Fresno Zool. Soc., 1985—, Fresno Arts Mus., 1984—, Bulldog Found., Fresno State U., 1985-91. With U.S. Army, 1972-75. Mem. APA, Central Calif. Rehab. Assn. (pres. 1984-85), Nat. Assn. Rehab. Profls. (Counselor of Yr. 1987, Pvt. Sector Rehab. Counselor or Yr. 1988), Calif. Nat. Assn.Rehab. Profls. Pvt. Sector (membership com. 1984-85, Meritorious Svc. 1985, Cert. of Recognition 1986), Calif. Assn. Rehab. Profls., Nat. Rehab. Assn., Nat. Rehab Counseling Assn. Democrat. Jewish. Office: 1521 E Shields Ave Fresno CA 93704-5140

LIPPOLD, ROLAND WILL, surgeon; b. Staunton, Ill., May 1, 1916; s. Frank Carl and Ella (Immenroth) L.; m. Margaret Cookson, June 1, 1947; children: Mary Ellen Lippold Elvick, Catherine Anne Lippold Rolf, Carol Sue Lippold Webber. BS, U. Ill., 1940, MD, 1941. Diplomate Am. Bd. Surgery. Intern Grant Hosp., Chgo., 1941-42, resident in surgery, 1942-43, 47-48; resident in surgery St. Francis Hosp., Evanston, Ill., 1946-47; fellow in pathology Cook County Hosp., Chgo., 1947-48, resident in surgery, 1949-50; practice medicine specializing in surgery Chgo., 1950-53; also asst. in anatomy U. Ill., Chgo., 1950-53; practice medicine specializing in surgery Sacramento, 1953-68; chief med. officer No. Reception Ctr.-Clinic, Calif. Youth Authority, Sacramento, 1954-68, chief med. services, 1968-79; cons. in med. care in correctional instns.; cons. Calif. State Personnel Bd. Contbr. articles to med. publs. Chmn. Calif. Expn. Hall of Health, 1971-72. Comdr. M.C., USNR, 1943-73, PTO. Mem. Sacramento Surg. Soc., Sacramento County Med. Soc., Calif. Med. Assn., AMA, Assn. Mil. Surgeons U.S., Sacramento Hist. Soc. (life). Republican. Lutheran. Home: 1811 Eastern Ave Sacramento CA 95864-1788

LIPPS, DOUGLAS JAY, mechanical engineer; b. Lincoln, Nebr., June 13, 1954; s. Robert E. and Ruth L. (Stryson) L.; m. Jan A. Henry, Aug. 12, 1978; children: Erik A., Emily K. BSME, U. Nebr., 1978; MBA, Golden Gate U., 1984. Registered profl. mech. engr. Sr. engr. Bechtel Corp., San Francisco, 1978—. Office: Bechtel Corp 50 Beale St San Francisco CA 94119-3965

LIPPS, JERE HENRY, paleontology educator; b. L.A., Aug. 28, 1939; s. Henry John and Margaret (Rosaltha) L.; m. Karen Elizabeth Loeblich, June 25, 1964 (div. 1971); m. Susannah McClintock, Sept. 28, 1973; children: Jeremy Christian, Jamison William. BA, UCLA, 1962, PhD, 1966. Asst. prof. U. Calif., Davis, Calif., 1967-70; assoc. prof. U. Calif., Davis, 1970-75, prof., 1975-88; prof. U. Calif., Berkeley, 1988—, prof. paleontology, 1988-89, prof. integrative biology, 1989—; dir. Mus. Paleontology, Berkeley, 1989—; dir. Inst. Ecology, U. Calif., Davis, 1972-73, chmn. dept. geology, 1971-72, 78-84, chmn. dept. integrative biology, Berkeley, 1991—. Contbr. articles to sci. publs. Fellow, dir. Cushman Found. Recipient U.S. Antarctic medal NSF, 1975. Fellow Calif. Acad. Scis., Geol. Soc. Am., AAAS. Office: Mus Paleontology U Calif Earth Sci Bldg Berkeley CA 94720

LIPSCOMB, ANNA ROSE FEENY, arts organizer, fundraiser b. Greensboro, N.C., Oct. 29, 1945; d. Nathan and Matilda (Carotenuto) L. Student langs., Alliance Francaise, Paris, 1967-68; BA in English and French summa cum laude, Queens Coll., 1977; diploma advanced Spanish, Forester Instituto Internacional, San Jose, Costa Rica, 1990; postgrad. Inst. Allende San Miguel de Allende, Mex., 1991. Reservations agt. Am. Airlines, St. Louis, 1968-69, ticket agt., 1969-71; coll. rep. CBS, Holt Rinehart Winston, Providence, 1977-79, sr. acquisitions editor Dryden Press, Chgo., 1979-81; owner, mgr. Historic Taos (N.Mex.) Inn, 1981-89, Southwest Moccasin and Drum, Taos; pres. Southwest Products, Ltd., 1991—; fundraiser Taos Arts Celebrations, 1989—; bd. dirs. N.Mex. Hotel and Motel Assn., 1986—; sem. leader Taos Women Together, 1989. Editor: Intermediate Accounting, 1980; Business Law, 1981. Contbr. articles to profl. jours.; patentee in field. Bd. dirs., 1st v.p. Taos Arts Assn., 1982-85; founder, bd. dirs. Taos Spring Arts Celebration, 1983—; founder, dir. Meet-the-Artist Series, 1983—; bd. dirs. and co-founder Spring Arts N.Mex., 1986; founder Yuletide in Taos, 1988, A Taste of Taos, 1988; bd. dirs. Music from Angel Fire, 1988—; founding mem. Assn. Hist. Hotels, Boulder, 1983—; organizer Internat. Symposium on Arts, 1985; bd. dirs. Arts in Taos, 1983, Taoschool, Inc., 1985—; mem. adv. bd. Chamisa Mesa Ednl. Ctr., Taos, 1990—. Recipient Outstanding English Student of Yr. award Queens Coll., 1977; named Single Outstanding Contbr. to the Arts in Taos, 1986. Mem. Millicent Rogers Mus. Assn., Taos Lodgers Assn. (mktg. task force 1989), Taos County C. of C. (1st v.p. 1988-89, bd. dirs. 1987-89, advt. com. 1986-89, chmn. nominating com. 1989), Internat. Platform Assn., Phi Beta Kappa. Democrat. Home: Talpa Rte Taos NM 87571 Office: PO Drawer N Taos NM 87571

LIPSCOMB, SCOTT DAVID, musicologist; b. Lafayette, Ind., Aug. 2, 1959; s. David Milton Lipscomb and Dixie Lea (Johnson) Petrey; 1 child, John David. MusB with highest honors, U. Tenn., 1982; MA with distinction, UCLA, 1990. Contrabassist Knoxville Symphony, 1980-82, Oak Ridge (Tenn.) Symphony, 1981-82; instrumentalist, vocalist The Coupe, 1982-87; instr., rsch. asst. UCLA, 1988-92; class lectr. Webster U., Vienna, Austria, 1990-92; bassist, vocalist cassett tape, 1981. Composer title music for Fin. Talk Show, Jacksonville, 1988; presenter in field. Fellow UCLA, 1987—; Elaine Krown-Klein scholar, 1991-92. Mem. Am. Musicological Soc., Soc. Ethromusicology, Soc. Music Perception and Cognition. Home: 5118 Delongpre Ave Los Angeles CA 90027 Office: UCLA Dept ESM 405 Hilgard Ave Los Angeles CA 90024

LIPSET, SEYMOUR MARTIN, sociologist, political scientist, educator; b. N.Y.C., Mar. 18, 1922; s. Max and Lena (Lippman) L.; m. Elsie Braun, Dec. 26, 1944 (dec. Feb. 1987); children: David, Daniel, Carola; m. Sydnee Guyer, July 29, 1990. BS, CCNY, 1943; PhD, Columbia U., 1949; MA (hon.), Harvard U., 1966; LLD (hon.), Villanova U., 1973, Hebrew U., 1981, U. Buenos Aires, 1987, Free U., Brussels, 1990, U. Judaism, 1991, Hebrew Union Coll., 1993, Boston Hebrew Coll., 1993. Lectr. U. Toronto, 1946-48; asst. prof. U. Calif., Berkeley, 1948-50; asst., then assoc. prof. grad. faculty Columbia U., 1950-56, asst. dir. Bur. Applied Social Research, 1954-56; prof. sociology U. Calif., Berkeley, 1956-66, dir. Inst. Internat. Studies, 1962-66; vis. prof. social rels. and govt. Harvard U., 1965-66, prof. govt. and sociology, exec. com. Ctr. Internat. Affairs, 1966-75, George Markham prof. Ctr. Internat. Affairs, 1974-75; sr. fellow Hoover Inst. Stanford U., 1975—, prof. polit. sci. and sociology, 1975-92, Caroline S.G. Munro prof., 1981-92; Hazel prof. pub. policy George Mason U., Fairfax, Va., 1990—; Henry Ford vis. research prof. Yale U., 1960-61; Paley lectr. Hebrew U., 1973; Fulbright program 40th Anniversary Disting. lectr., 1987; vis. scholar Russell Sage Found., New York, 1988-89. Author: Agrarian Socialism, 1950, (with others) Union Democracy, 1956, (with R. Bendix) Social Mobility in Industrial Society, 1959, expanded edit., 1991, Political Man, 1960, expanded edit., 1981, The First New Nation, 1963, expanded edit., 1979, Revolution and Counter Revolution, 1968, expanded edit., 1988, (with Earl Raab) The Politics of Unreason, 1970, expanded edit., 1978, Rebellion in the University, 1972, (with Everett Ladd) Academics and the 1972 Election, 1973, Professors, Unions and American Higher Education, 1973, The Divided Academy, 1975, (with David Riesman) Education and Politics at Harvard, 1975, (with I.L. Horowitz) Dialogues on American Politics, 1978, (with William Schneider) The Confidence Gap, 1983, expanded edit., 1987, Consensus and Conflict, 1987, Continental Divide: The Institutions and Values of the United States and Canada, 1990; co-editor: Class, Status and Power, 1953, Labor and Trade Unionism, 1960, Sociology: The Progress of a Decade, 1961, Culture and Social Character, 1961, The Berkeley Student Revolt, 1965, Class, Status and Power in Comparative Perspective, 1966, Social Structure, Mobility and Economic Development, 1966, Elites in Latin America, 1967, Party Systems and Voter Alignments, 1967, Students in Revolt, 1969, Issues in Politics and Government, 1970, Failure of a Dream? Essays in the History of American Socialism, 1974, rev. edit., 1984; co-editor: Democracy in Developing Countries, 3 vols., Africa, Asia and Latin America, 1988, 89, Politics in Developing Countries, 1990; co-editor Public Opinion mag., 1977-89, Internat. Jour. Pub. Opinion Rsch., 1989—; editor: Students and Politics, 1967, Politics and Social Science, 1969, Emerging Coalitions in American Politics, 1978, The Third Century, 1979, Party Coalitions in the Eighties, 1981, Unions in Transition, 1986, American Pluralism and the Jewish Community, 1990; adv. editor: various jours. including Sci., Comparative Politics. Mem. Bd. Fgn. Scholarships, 1968-71; bd. dirs. Aurora Found., 1985—; Nat. chmn. B'nai B'rith Hillel Found., 1975-79, chmn. nat. exec. com., 1979-84; assoc. pres. Am. Profs. for Peace in Middle East, 1976-77, nat. pres., 1977-81; co-chmn. exec. com. Internat. Ctr. Peace in Middle East, 1982—; co-chmn. Com. for Effective UNESCO, 1976-81; chmn. Com. for UN Integrity, 1981-83; chmn. nat. faculty cabinet United Jewish Appeal, 1981-84; pres. Progressive Found., 1991—. Fellow Social Sci. Research Council, 1945-46; Center Advanced Study Behavioral Sci. Fellow, 1955-56, 72-73; Gunnar Myrdal prize, 1970; Townsend Harris medal, 1971; Guggenheim Found. fellow, 1971-72; 125th Anniversary Alumni medal Coll. City N.Y., 1973, M.B. Rawson award, 1986, No. Telecom Gold Medal for Can. Studies, 1987. Fellow NAS, Am. Acad. Arts and Scis. (v.p. 1974-78), Nat. Acad. Edn., Am. Sociol. Assn. (coun. 1959-62, MacIver award 1962, pres. 1992-93), Japan Soc.; mem. Sociol. Research Assn. (exec. com. 1981-84, pres. 1985), Am. Polit. Sci. Assn. (coun. 1975-77, pres. 1981-82), Internat. Polit. Sci. Assn. (coun. 1981-88, v.p. 1982-88), Internat. Soc. Polit. Psychology (pres. 1979-80), Internat. Sociol. Assn. (chmn. com. polit. sociology 1959-71), World Assn. Pub. Opinion Research (v.p. and pres.-elect 1982-84, pres. 1984-86), Am. Philos. Soc., Finnish Acad. Sci. (hon.), AAAS (chmn. sect. on econ. and social sci. 1975-76). Office: George Mason U Inst of Policy Studies Pohick Module Fairfax VA 22030 also: Stanford U 213 Herbert Hoover Meml Bldg Stanford CA 94305

LIPSHITZ, HOWARD DAVID, biology educator; b. Durban, Natal, S. Africa, Oct. 30, 1955; came to U.S., 1977; s. Marcus and Annie Zelda (Cohen) L.; m. Susanna Maxwell Lewis, Sept. 13, 1986; 1 child, Sarah Starr Lipshitz-Lewis. BS, U. Natal, Durban, S.Africa, 1975, BS with honors, 1976; MPhil, Yale U., 1980, PhD, 1983. Postdoctoral rsch. fellow Stanford U. Biochemistry Dept., Stanford, Calif., 1983-86; asst. prof. Calif. Inst. Tech. Div. Biology, Pasadena, Calif., 1986-92, assoc. prof., 1992—; mem. eukaryotic genetics panel NSF, 1993—. Assoc. Editor: Zygote, 1993—; contbr. articles to profl. jours., book chpts. in field. Recipient Scholarship Searle Found., Chgo., 1988-91, grant, NIH, Bethesda, 1987—, March of Dimes Birth Defects, N.Y., 1990-92, Am. Cancer Soc, 1992—. Fellow AAAS, mem. Genetics Soc. Am. Office: Calif Inst Tech Divsn Biology 156-29 Pasadena CA 91125

LIPSHUTZ, ROBERT JAY, mathematician; b. Oceanside, N.J., Jan. 9, 1955; s. Ralph Salit and Ellen (Cutler) L.; m. Nancy Linsey Wong, Nov. 2, 1984; 1 child, David. BAmagna cum laude, Harvard U., 1977, MA, 1977; PhD, U. Calif., Berkeley, 1985. V.p. Daniel H. Wagner Assoc., Sunnyvale, Calif., 1981-93; prin. scientist Affymetrix, Inc., Santa Clara, Calif., 1993—. Named fellow NSF, 1977. Mem. AAAS, Am. Math. Soc., Ops. Rsch. Soc. of Am., Soc. Indsl. Applied Math., Phi Beta Kappa (fellow 1977). Office: Affymetrix Inc 3380 Central Expy Santa Clara CA 95051

LIPSKY, IAN DAVID, contracting executive; b. Bklyn., May 26, 1957; s. Eugene Herman and Janet Dorothy (Heller) L. BS in Marine Engring., Maine Maritime Acad., 1979. Third asst. engr. Interlake Steamship Co., Cleve., 1979-81; port engr. Exxon Internat. Co., Florham Park, N.J., 1981-84; prodn. supr. Alfred Conhagen Inc. Calif., Hercules, 1984-87, gen. mgr., 1987-89, v.p., 1989—. Mem. Soc. Naval Architects & Marine Engrs., Marine Port Engrs. N.Y., Inst. Marine Engrs., Port Engrs. San Francisco. Democrat. Jewish. Home: 153 Koch Rd Corte Madera CA 94925-1263 Office: Alfred Conhagen Inc Calif 3900 Oregon St Benicia CA 94510

LIPSON, DAVID, biomedical engineer; b. Staten Island, N.Y., June 12, 1951; m. Karyl Jan Oldenburg. BSEE, Cornell U., 1973; MS, Case-Western Res. U., 1975, PhD, 1979. Project engr. NASA/GE Aerospace, Houston, 1979-82; rsch. engr. Abbott Labs., Chgo., 1982-85; rsch. scientist Eli Lilly & Co., Indpls., 1985-92; engring. mgr. advanced devel. Heart Rhythm Techs., Inc., Temecula, Calif., 1992—. Author: Opposing Central and Peripheral Affects of Atropine, 1977, Microfabrication of Flexible Glucose Sensor, 1990, Drilled Optical Fiber Sensors, 1990.

LIPSTONE, HOWARD HAROLD, television production executive; b. Chgo., Apr. 28, 1928; s. Lewis R. and Ruth B. (Fischer) L.; m. Jane A. Nudelman, Apr. 7, 1957; children—Lewis, Gregory. BS in Cinema, U. So. Calif., 1950. Asst. to gen. mgr. Sta. KTLA, Los Angeles, 1950-54; program dir. Sta. KABC-TV, Los Angeles, 1955-61, film and program dir., 1961-63; exec. asst. to pres., exec. producer Selmur Prodns., Inc. subs. ABC-TV, Los Angeles, 1963-69; exec. v.p. Ivan Tors Films and Studios, Inc., 1969-70; pres. Alan Landsburg Prodns., Inc., Los Angeles, 1970-85; pres., chief oper. officer The Landsburg Co., Los Angeles, 1985—. Mem. NATAS, Soc. Motion Picture and TV Engrs., Motion Picture Acad. Arts and Scis., Radio Club Am. Office: The Landsburg Co 11811 W Olympic Blvd Los Angeles CA 90064-1113

LIPTAK, DENNIS GEORGE, controller; b. Huntington Park, Calif., Nov. 2, 1951; s. George Paul and Virginia Mary (Soltis) L.; m. Nancy Anne Lynch, Aug. 13, 1977; children: Shannon Suzanne, Jason Dennis, Ashlee Marie. BS in Acctg. with honors, Calif. Poly., 1974. Acctg. supr. A&B Transp., L.A., 1977-80; contr. Pub. Storage Mgmt., Glendale, Calif., 1980-88; acctg. mgr. PBS Bldg. Systems, Inc., Anaheim, Calif., 1988-90; contr. Westlam Foods, Chino, Calif., 1990—. Republican. Baptist.

LIQUIDO, NICANOR JAVIER, entomology educator; b. Calamba, Philippines, Jan. 10, 1953; s. Francisco Lajara Liquido and Isidra (Mailom) Javier; m. Susan Heftel, Apr. 14, 1984. BS in Applied Zoology, Entomology and Microbiology, U. Philippines, 1975, MS in Entomology and Genetics, 1978; PhD in Entomology and Biometry, U. Hawaii, 1982. Instr. in biology and Entomology U. Philippines, Los Baños, 1976-77; sr. rsch. asst. The Internat. Rice Rsch. Inst., Los Baños, 1978-79; mem. rsch. faculty U. Ill., Champaign, 1983-85; mem. grad. faculty U. Hawaii-Manoa, Honolulu, 1985—; rsch. entomologist Agrl. Rsch. Svc. USDA, Hilo, Hawaii, 1985—; lectr. Internat. Atomic Energy Agy. Guatemala; cons. Food and Agr. Orgn. U.N., Mex., Venezuela, 1987-89. Editor The Exuviae Quar. newsletter, 1978; corr. The Weekly Notes newsletter U. Philippines, 1977-78; contbr. articles to profl. jours. Fellow Ill. Natural Hist. Survey, Champaign, 1983-85; East-West Ctr. scholar, Honolulu, 1979-82; grantee Kasetsart U., Thailand, U. Hawaii, East-West Ctr., 1981. Mem. AAAS, Entomol. Soc. Am. (chair subsect. Ecology, Bionomics and Behavior), Entomol. Soc. Can., Ecol. Soc. Am., Hawaiian Entomol. Soc. (sec.), Am. Inst. Biol. Scis., Assn. Philippine Entomologists, Pest Control Council of Philippines, Hawaii Acad. Sci., N.Y. Acad. Scis., Sigma Xi (pres. Hilo chpt.), Gamma Sigma Delta, Phi Sigma. Roman Catholic. Club: Yacht (Hilo). Home: 1414A Mele Manu St Hilo HI 96720-1794 Office: USDA Agrl Rsch Svc PO Box 4459 Hilo HI 96720-0459

LISALDA, SYLVIA ANN, primary educator; b. San Diego, Oct. 14, 1949; d. Joseph and Irene (Valdez) Lisalda; m. Robert Holguin Marquez, Sept. 1, 1979 (div. 1986). AA, Valley Coll., Van Nuys, Calif., 1964; BA in English, Calif. State U., Northridge, 1971. Tchr. kindergarten L.A. Unified Schs., 1965—. Democrat. Roman Catholic. Office: Sylmar Elem Sch 13291 Phillippi Ave Sylmar CA 91342

LIST, RAYMOND EDWARD, engineering and construction executive, management consultant; b. Bklyn., Apr. 9, 1944; s. Raymond William and Mildred Patricia (Maroney) L.; m. Susan Gladys McKenna ; children: Raymond McKenna, Julia McKenna. BCE, Union Coll., Schenectady, N.Y., 1966; M in Engring., Manhattan Coll., 1967; MBA with honors, Harvard U., 1977. Registered profl. engr., Calif., Nev., Mass., Pa. Project mgr. Kaiser Engrs., Inc., Oakland, Calif., 1968-74; exec. asst. Perini Corp., San Francisco, 1977-78; v.p. Arthur D. Little Inc., Washington, 1978-80; v.p., gen. mgr. Planning Rsch. Corp., McLean, Va., 1980-82; pres. List and Assocs. Inc., Washington, 1982-86; chmn. Am. Venture Investments Inc., Fairfax, Va., 1986—, also bd. dirs.; chmn. ICF Tech. Inc., Fairfax, 1987-89; pres. Kaiser Engrs. Group Inc., Oakland, 1988-89, ICF Kaiser Engrs. Group Inc., Oakland, 1989—; also bd. dirs. ICF-Kaiser Engrs. Group Inc., Oakland; bd. dirs. ICF Corp. Internat. Inc., Am. Capital and Rsch. Inc. Fellow Pub. Health Svc., 1967. Mem. ASCE, AIME, Am. Mining Congress, Harvard Club of N.Y.C., Harvard Bus. Sch. Club of Washington. Lutheran. Office: ICF Kaiser Engrs Group Inc 1800 Harrison St Oakland CA 94612-3429

LISTER, KEITH FENIMORE, publishing executive; b. Clio, Iowa, Aug. 29, 1917; s. W. Frank and Maude (Fenimore) L.; m. Margaret Boman, Sept. 1, 1941; children: Janet, Priscilla. Student, Drake U., 1936-41. Pres. Lister Investment Co., San Diego, 1955-61, Southcoast Capital Co., San Diego, 1961-65, City Bank San Diego, 1965-69; pub. San Diego Daily Transcript, 1972—. Mem. La Jolla Country Club, San Diego Yacht Club, Univ. Club. Presbyterian. Office: San Diego Daily Transcript 2131 3d Ave San Diego CA 92101

LISTERUD, (LOWELL) BRIAN, choir director, music educator; b. Duluth, Minn., Mar. 20, 1951; s. Lowell Fred Listerud and Carol May (Tuttle) Alseth; m. Christine Joyce Gunvaldson, Aug. 24, 1973; children: L. Jason, Bjorn C., Solveig C. BS, Mankato State U., 1973; MMus, Ariz. State U., 1979, postgrad., 1984—; postgrad., U. Mont., 1985-89. Cert. tchr., Mont.; nat. registered music educator. Dir. Presbyn. Ch. Choir, Wolf Point, Mont., 1974-79; tchr. music Wolf Point High Sch., 1974-79; dir. handbell choir Trinity Luth., Phoenix, 1989-90; dir. choral activities Great Falls (Mont.) High Sch., 1979-80; dir. Random Ringers Handbells, Missoula, Mont., 1986—; dir. choirs Big Sky High Sch., Missoula, 1980—; dir. Aesirian Alumni Choir, Missoula, 1991—; adjudicator Mont. High Sch. Assn., 1979—; clinician, dist. music festivals and honor choirs; clinician N.W. Music Educators Regional Conf., Billings, Mont., 1979, N.W. MENC, Portland, Oreg., 1987, 93, Am. Choral Dirs. Assn., Spokane, 1982, Portland, 1984, Louisville, 1989. Dir. several concerts; contbr. articles to profl. jours. Mem. Mont. Arts Coun., Helena, 1985-89. Recipient scholarships, letters of commendation, awards. Mem. Am. Choral Dirs. Assn. (Mont. pres. 1987-89), Mont. Music Edn. Assn. (bus. mgr. 1980-85), Mont. Edn. Assn. (faculty rep. 1985-87), Internat. Fedn. Choral Music, Am. Guild of English Handbell Ringers (state chmn. 1992—), Nat. Assn. Tchrs. Singing, Mankato State U. Alumni Assn., Ariz. State U. Alumni Assn., Sons of Norway, Good Samaritans, Carpenters for Christ, Phi Mu Alpha Sinfonia (pres. chpt. 1972-73). Presbyterian. Home: 501 E 2d St Stevensville MT 59870 Office: Big Sky Sch 3100 South Ave W Missoula MT 59801

LISTERUD, MARK BOYD, surgeon; b. Wolf Point, Mont., Nov. 19, 1924; s. Morris B. and Grace (Montgomery) L.; m. Sarah C. Mooney, May 26, 1954; children: John, Mathew, Ann, Mark, Sarah, Richard. BA magna cum laude, U. Minn., 1949, BS, 1950, MB, 1952, MD, 1953. Diplomate Am. Bd. Surgery. Intern King County Hosp., Seattle, 1952-53; resident in surgery U. Wash., Seattle, 1953-57; practice medicine specializing in surgery Wolf Point, 1958—; mem. admission com. U. Wash. Med. Sch., Seattle, 1983-88; instr. Dept. Rural and Community Health, U. N.D. Med. Sch., 1991. Contbr. articles to med. jours. Mem. Mont. State Health Coordinating Council, 1983, chmn. 1986—; bd. dirs. Blue Shield, Mont., 1985-87. Served with USN, 1943-46. Fellow Am. Coll. Surgeons; mem. N.E. Mont. Med. Soc. (pres.), Mont. Med. Assn. (pres. 1968-69), AMA (alt. del., del. 1970-84). Club: Montana. Lodge: Elks. Home: Rodeo Rd Wolf Point MT 59201 Office: 100 Main St Wolf Point MT 59201-1530

LISTON, ALBERT MORRIS, administrator, educator, investor; b. Carlinville, Ill., Aug. 6, 1940; s. Joseph Bostick and Hazel Marie (Smalley) L.; AB in Econs., U. Calif., Davis, 1963; MA in Govt., Calif. State U., Sacramento, 1970; postgrad., U. Calif., Santa Barbara, 1980—; m. Phyllis Clayton, Feb. 27, 1967 (div. July 1970). Rsch. analyst Ombudsman Activities Project polit. sci. dept. U. Calif., Santa Barbara, 1970-72; asst. prof. polit. sci. dept. Calif. State U., Fullerton, 1973-79; investor, 1980—. Lt. Supply Corps, USNR, 1963-66. Mem. Am. Polit. Sci. Assn., Commonwealth Club Calif., Kappa Sigma, Phi Kappa Phi. Democrat. Office: PO Box 96 Belvedere Tiburon CA 94920-0096

LISZKA, JAMES J., philosophy educator; b. Pitts., Mar. 18, 1950; s. Joseph and Mary (Dombrowski) L.; m. Cecilia Demidoff, Sept. 05, 1982; children: Zachary, Alexandra. BS, Indiana U. Pa., 1972; MA, U. S.C., 1974; PhD, New Sch. Social Rsch., N.Y., 1978. Philosophy prof. St. Francis Coll., Bklyn., 1977-80, CUNY, 1977-80, U. Alaska, Anchorage, 1980—. Author: The Semiotic of Myth, 1989; editor: Grad. Faculty Philosophy Jour., N.Y., 1975-80, Alaska Quarterly Rev., Anchorage, 1980—. Office: Univ Alaska Dept Philosophy 3221 Providence Dr Anchorage AK 99508-4614

LITMAN, BRIAN DAVID, communications executive; b. Kansas City, Mo., May 9, 1954; s. Marvin Wilbur and Louise Diane (Raskin) L. BJ, U. Mo., 1977. Promotion mgr. Atlanta br. CBS Records, Atlanta, 1977-78; promotion mgr. CBS Records, Cleve., 1978-79; dir. mktg. Am. TV and Communications, Pitts., 1980-81; account mgr. Group W Satellite Communications, Stamford, Conn., 1981-82; sales mgr. Hearst/ABC, N.Y.C., 1982-84; account dir. Hearst/ABC/NBC, N.Y.C., 1984, dir. nat. accounts, 1985-86; dir. nat. accounts, western div. Hearst/ABC/NBC, L.A., 1986-90; pres., CEO Entertainment and Communications Holdings Orgn., West Hollywood, Calif., 1990—. Dir. editorial bd. Emmy mag. Mem. L.A. World Affairs Coun., 1991—. Mem. Acad. TV Arts and Scis. (chmn. cable com. 1989—), Hollywood Radio and TV Soc., L.A. Advt. Club, U.S.-Russia Trade and Econ. Coun. Office: Entertainment Communication Holdings Orgn 950 N Kings Rd Ste 250 West Hollywood CA 90069

LITROWNIK, ALAN JAY, psychologist, educator; b. Los Angeles, June 25, 1945; s. Irving and Mildred Mae (Rosin) L.; m. Hollis Merle, Aug. 20, 1967; children: Allison Brook, Jordan Michael. B.A., UCLA, 1967; M.A., U. Ill., Champaign-Urbana, 1969, Ph.D., 1971. Psychologist Ill. Dept. Mental Health, Decatur, 1970-71; asst. prof. psychology San Diego State U., 1971-75, assoc. prof., 1975-78, prof., 1978—, chmn. dept. psychology, 1981-87, assoc. dean for curriculum and acad. planning, North County Campus, 1987-88; co-dir. Ctr. for Behavioral and Community Health Studies, San Diego, 1989—; cons. San Diego County Dept. Edn. Program Evaluation, 1975-81; project dir. Self-Concept and Self-Regulatory Processes in Developmentally Disabled Children and Adolescents, 1975-78; co-dir. Child Abuse Interdisciplinary Tng. Program, 1987—; project dir. tobacco use prevention in youth orgns., 1989-92. Research, publs. in field. Contbr. chpts. to books. Mem. San Diego County Juvenile Justice Commn., 1989-92; mem. juvenile systems adv. group San Diego County Bd. Suprs., 1989-91. Grantee U.S. Office Edn., 1975-78, 80-81, Nat. Ctr. Child Abuse, 1987—, Calif. Dept. Health, 1989-92; U. Calif. Tobacco-Related Disease Rsch. Program, 1992—. Mem. Am. Psychol. Soc., Assn. Advancement Behavior Therapy. Office: Ctr Behavioral & Comm Hlth Studs 6363 Alvarado Ct San Diego CA 92120-4913

LITSEY, ROY THOMAS, insurance executive; b. Nampa, Idaho; s. Roy Allen and Corleen Joyce (Sporledor) L.; m. Georgia Lee Brediger, Sept. 15, 1967; children: Lisa, Cory, Michelle, Ryan. BS, N.W. Nazarene Coll., 1970. English tchr., head basketball coach Nampa High Sch., 1970-80; field underwriter N.Y. Life Ins. Co., Boise, 1980-82, sales mgr., 1982-87, assoc. gen. mgr., 1987-89; agt. Minn. Mut. Life Ins. Co., Boise, 1989—. Mem. Boise Assn. Life Underwriters. Office: Minn Mut Life Ins 18-12th Ave S Ste 103 Nampa ID 83653

LITTLE, CHARLES GORDON, geophysicist; b. Liuyang, Hunan, China, Nov. 4, 1924; s. Charles Deane and Caroline Joan (Crawford) L.; m. Mary Zughaib, Aug. 21, 1954; children: Deane, Joan, Katherine, Margaret, Patricia. B.Sc. with honors in Physics, U. Manchester, Eng., 1948; Ph.D. in Radio Astronomy, U. Manchester, 1952. Jr. engr. Cosmos Mfg. Co. Ltd., Enfield, Middlesex, Eng., 1944-46; jr. physicist Ferranti Ltd., Manchester, Lancashire, Eng., 1946-47; asst. lectr. U. Manchester, 1952-53; prof. dept. geophysics U. Alaska, 1954-58, dep. dir. Geophys. Inst., 1954-58; cons. Ionosphere Radio Propagation Lab. U.S. Dept. Commerce Nat. Bur. Standards, Boulder, Colo., 1958-60, chief Upper Atmosphere and Space Physics div., 1960-62, dir. Central Radio Propagation Lab., 1962-65; dir. Inst. Telecommunication Sci. and Aeronomy, Environ. Sci. Services Adminstrn., Boulder, Colo., 1965-67; dir. Wave Propagation Lab. NOAA (formerly Environ. Sci. Services Adminstr.), Boulder, Colo., 1967-86; sr. UCAR fellow Naval Environ. Prediction Research Facility, Monterey, Calif.,

1987-89; George J. Haltiner rsch. prof. Naval Postgrad. Sch., Monterey, 1989-90. Author numerous sci. articles. Recipient U.S. Dept. Commerce Gold medal, 1964, mgmt. and sci. research awards NOAA, 1969, 77, Presdl. Meritorious Exec. award, 1980. Fellow IEEE, Am. Meteorol. Soc. (Cleveland Abbe award 1984); mem. NAE, AIAA (R.M. Losey Atmos. Sci. award 1992). Address: 6949 Roaring Fork Trail Boulder CO 80301

LITTLE, JULIA ELIZABETH, medical technologist, educator; b. Canton, Ohio, Aug. 23, 1932; d. Nicholas Charles and Julie Ella (Boldizsar) Psenka; children: Linda Marie, Lori Elizabeth. BS, Mt. Union Coll., 1954. Med. technologist Aultman Hosp., Canton, 1955-56; supr. chemistry Barberton (Ohio) Citizens Hosp., 1956-57; supr. bacteriology Massillon (Ohio) City Hosp., 1957-63; chief technologist Lynwood (Calif.) Clin. Lab., 1964-65; med. technologist Los Altos Hosp., Long Beach, Calif., 1966-70, Newhall (Calif.) Community Hosp., 1973-79; med. technologist, hemotology and urinalysis educator Eisenhower Med. Ctr., Rancho Mirage, Calif., 1980—. Mem. Am. Soc. Clin. Pathology, Calif. Assn. Med. Lab. Technologists (pres. Palms to Pines chpt. 1988-90, treas. 1986-88, state membership com. 1989-90, state conv. com.), VFW (charter, ladies aux. sec. post 10149). Democrat. Home: 34161 Linda Way Cathedral City CA 92234-6302 Office: Eisenhower Med Ctr 39000 Bob Hope Dr Rancho Mirage CA 92270-3221

LITTLE, LOREN EVERTON, musician, ophthalmologist; b. Sioux Falls, S.D., Oct. 28, 1941; s. Everton A. and Maxine V. (Alcorn) L.; m. Christy Gyles; 1 child, Nicole Moses; children from previous marriage: Laurie, Richard. BA, Macalester Coll., 1963; BS, U. S.D., 1965; D. Medicine, U. Wash., 1967. Prin. trumpeter Sioux Falls Mcpl. Band, 1956-65; trumpeter St. Paul Civic Orch., 1960-62; leader, owner Swinging Scots Band, St. Paul, 1960-63; trumpeter Edgewater Inn Show Room, Seattle, 1966-67, Jazztet-Arts Council, Sioux Falls, 1970-71, Lee Maxwell Shows, Washington, 1971-74; residency in ophthalmology Walter Reed Med. Ctr., Washington, 1974; co-leader, trumpeter El Paso (Tex.) All Stars, 1975; freelance trumpeter, soloist various casinos and hotels, Las Vegas, Nev., 1977—. Trumpeter (album) Journey by R. Romero Band, 1983; soloist for numerous entertainers including Tony Bennet, Burt Bacharach, Jack Jones, Sammy Davis Jr., Jerry Lewis Telethon, for video Star Salute to Live Music, 1989. Trustee Nev. Sch. of the Arts, Las Vegas, 1983—. Served to lt. col. U.S. Army, 1968-76, Vietnam. Decorated Silver Star, Purple Heart, Bronze Star, Air medal; fellow Internat. Eye Found., 1974; Dewitt Wallace scholar Readers Digest, 1963-65. Fellow ACS, Am. Acad. Ophthalmology; mem. Am. Fedn. Musicians, Nat. Bd. Med. Examiners. Presbyterian.

LITTLE, THOMAS WARREN, broadcast executive; b. Portland, Oreg., June 24, 1939; s. Hollis R. and Bernice (Lesseg) L.; m. Ruth Brady, Aug. 31, 1958; children—Vincent Thomas, Elizabeth Ann. B.A. and M.A. in Radio-TV, UCLA. Stage mgr. Sta. KPIX-TV, San Francisco, 1969-61; producer, dir. Sta. KVCR-TV, San Bernadino, Calif., 1963-65; telecommunications prof. San Bernadino Valley Coll., 1965-75; gen. mgr. Sta. KVCR-TV, Sta. KVCR-FM, San Bernadino, 1975-77, dir. radio, TV, 1979—; dir. TV Sta. KVZK-TV, Pago Pago, Am. Samoa, 1977-79. Served with U.S. Army, 1961-63. Mem. Assn. Calif. Pub. TV Stations, Calif. Pub. Radio, Pub. Broadcasting Service, Pacific Mountain Network. Democrat. Office: Sta KVCR-TV 701 S Mt Vernon Ave San Bernardino CA 92410-2798

LITTLE, WILLIAM HENRY, oceanographer; b. Balt., May 23, 1948; s. Robert Henry and Ruth Alice (Brehm) L.; m. Sally Jeanne Schoppert, June 13, 1971; children: Rachel, Jessica. BS in Geology and Geol. Oceanography, U. Wash., 1971; MS in Air-Ocean Sci., Naval Postgrad. Sch., Monterey, Calif., 1980. Anti-submarine warfare officer USS Horne, San Diego, 1971-74; ops. officer Naval Facility, Coos Head, Oreg., 1975-78; oceanographer Naval Oceanography Ctr., Guam, 1980-82; oceanographer, instr. Anti-Submarine Warfare Sch., San Diego, 1982-84; oceanographer USS Constellation, San Diego, 1984-86; ops. officer Naval Western Oceanography Ctr., Pearl Harbor, Hawaii, 1986-89; oceanographer Comthirdflt, Pearl Harbor, 1989-91; retired USN, 1991; sr. systems scientist Computer Sci. Corp., 1991—. Mem. Am. Meteorology Soc., Oceanography Soc. Lutheran. Office: Cincpacfit (N3WX) Pearl Harbor HI 96860-7000

LITTMAN, RICHARD ANTON, psychologist, educator; b. N.Y.C., May 8, 1919; s. Joseph and Sarah (Feinberg) L.; m. Isabelle Cohen, Mar. 17, 1941; children—David, Barbara, Daniel, Rebecca. A.B., George Washington U., 1943; postgrad., Ind. U., 1943- 44; Ph.D., Ohio State U., 1948. Faculty U. Oreg., 1948—, prof. psychology, 1959—, chmn. dept., 1963-68, vice provost acad. planning and resources, 1971-73; Vis. scientist Nat. Inst. Mental Health, 1958-59. Contbr. articles to profl. jours. Sr. postdoctoral fellow NSF, U. Paris, 1966-67; sr. fellow Nat. Endowment for Humanities, U. London, 1973-74; Ford Found. fellow, 1952-53; recipient U. Oreg. Charles H. Johnson Meml. award, 1980. Mem. Am., Western, psychol. assns., Soc. Research and Child Devel., Psychonomics Soc., Animal Behavior Soc., Soc. Psychol. Study of Social Issues, Internat. Soc. Developmental Psychobiology, History of Sci. Soc., Am. Philos. Assn., AAUP, Sigma Xi. Home: 3625 Glen Oak Dr Eugene OR 97405-4736 Office: U Oreg Dept Psychology Eugene OR 97403

LIU, ALAN FONG-CHING, mechanical engineer; b. Canton, China, Mar. 25, 1933; came to U.S., 1958; s. Gee Call and Shuk Hing (Chen) L.; m. Iris P. Chan, Sept. 2, 1962; children: Kent, Willy, Henry. BSME, U. Chiba, Japan, 1958; MSME, U. Bridgeport, 1965. Sr. structures engr. Lockheed Calif. Co., Burbank, Calif., 1968-73; sr. tech. specialist/project mgr. Rockwell Internat. Space div., Downey, Calif., 1973-76; sr. tech. specialist Northrop Corp. Aircraft div., Hawthorne, Calif., 1976-88, Rockwell Internat./N.Am. Aircraft, El Segundo, Calif., 1988—. Contbr. articles to Jour. of Aircraft, AIAA Jour., Res Mechanica, Jour. Engrng. Materials and Tech., Engrng. Fracture Mechanics, procs. nat. and internat. confs. and symposia. Fellow AIAA (assoc.); mem. ASTM, Am. Soc. Metals Internat.

LIU, EDWIN CHIAP HENN, biochemical ecologist; b. Honolulu, Apr. 11, 1942; s. Edward F. and Margaret (Yuen) L. AB, Johns Hopkins U., 1964; PhD, Mich. State U., 1971. Asst. prof. U. S.C., Columbia, 1973-81; rsch. prof. Savannah River Ecology Lab., Aiken, S.C., 1981-86; coord. Newport Bay Santa Ana Regional Water Quality Control Bd., Riverside, Calif., 1986-88; monitoring coord. EPA, San Francisco, 1988—; newsletter editor Am. Bot. Soc., Columbia, 1981. Contbr. numerous rsch. papers to profl. publs. Recipient Young Scientist award Am. Soc. Plant Physiologists, 1977, Faculty Recognition award U. S.C., 1977. Mem. Ecol. Soc. of Am., Sigma Xi, Phi Kappa Psi. Home: 1510 Ashby Ave Berkeley CA 94703

LIU, EDWIN K. S., state official; b. Honolulu, Oct. 11, 1941; s. Kong Fui and Yuen Kyau (Ling) L. BEd, U. Hawaii, 1963, MA, 1964, MEd, 1965; postgrad., U. Utah, 1968-69. Cert. elem., secondary tchr., libr., Hawaii. Tchr. Hawaii Dept. Edn., Honolulu, 1965-66, registrar, 1966-67; tchr. St. Louis Chaminade Sch., Honolulu, 1967-68; budget analyst Hawaii Dept. Budget and Fin., Honolulu, 1970; asst. to dir. Hawaii Dept. Regulatory Agy., Honolulu, 1970-74; cable program specialist Hawaii Dept. Commerce and Consumer Affairs, Honolulu, 1974—. Bd. dirs. Chinese Christian Assn. Hawaii, Honolulu, 1990, Hawaii Conf., United Ch., Honolulu, 1992; v.p. Oahu Assn. United Ch. of Christ, Honolulu, 1992; chmn. bd. dirs. First Chinese Ch. Christ, Honolulu, 1990—. Mem. Nat. Assn. Telecom. Officers and Advisors, Hawaii Govt. Employees Assn. (steward 1988—). Congregationalist. Home: 1401 Ohialoke St Honolulu HI 96821 Office: Dept Commerce and Consumer Affairs 1001 Bishop St Ste 1460 Honolulu HI 96813

LIU, JIA-MING, electrical engineering educator, researcher; b. Taichung, Taiwan, Republic of China, July 13, 1953; came to U.S., 1978; s. Min-chih and Hsin (Lin) L.; m. Vida H. Chang, July 8, 1990; 1 child, Janelle Jen-Wu. BS in Electrophysics, Nat. Chiao Tung U., 1975; SM in Applied Physics, Harvard U., 1979, PhD in Applied Physics, 1982. Registered profl. engr., Taiwan. Asst. prof. SUNY, Buffalo, 1982-84; sr. mem. tech. staff GTE Lab., Inc., Waltham, Mass., 1983-86; assoc. prof. elec. engr. UCLA, 1986-93, prof., 1993—; cons. JAYCOR, San Diego, 1987—, Battelle, Rsch. Triangle Park, N.C., 1989-90. Contbr. articles to profl. jours. Patent award GTE Labs., Inc., Waltham, 1986, 87, 88, 89. Fellow Optical Soc. Am.; mem. IEEE Laser and Electro-Optics Soc. (sr.), Am. Physical Soc., Photonics Soc. Chinese Americans (founding), Sigma Xi, Phi Tau Phi. Office: UCLA 56-147 C Engring IV Los Angeles CA 90024-1594

LIU, KATHERINE CHANG, artist, art educator; b. Kiang-si, Peoples Republic of China; came to U.S., 1963; d. Ming-fan and Ying (Yuan) Chang; m. Yet-zen Liu; children: Alan S., Laura Y. MS, U. Calif., Berkeley, 1965. lectr. N.J., Oreg., Tex., Ohio, N.C., S.C., New England, Fla., Okla., Ky. Northwestern and Midwest Watercolor Socs., Rocky Mountain Nat. Watermedia Workshop, U. Va. Ext., Longwood Coll. One-man shows include Harrison Mus., Utah State U., Riverside (Calif.) Art Mus., Ventura (Calif.) Coll., Fla. A&M U., Louis Newman Galleries, L.A., L.A. Artcore, Lung-Men Gallery, Taipei, Republic of China, L.A. Artcore, State of the Arts Invitational Biennial, Parkland Coll. Ill., 1989, 91, Watercolor U.S.A. Hon. soc. Invitational, Springfield Art Mus., 1989, 91; Invitational, U. Brit. Columbia Art Gallery, 1992, U. Sydney Art Mus., 1992, Ruhr-West Art Mus., Wise, 1992, Macau Art Mus., 1992, San Diego Watercolor Internat. Competition, 1993, Tenn. Watercolor Soc., 1993; sole juror Watercolor State Open Competitions, N.J., Oreg., Pa. 1988, Watercolor West Nat., 1992, Hawaii, Utah, N.C. Watercolor State Ann. Competitions, 1992, Northwest, Okla. and Gold Coast Watercolor Competitions, 1991, New Eng., Midwest and Ky. Watercolor Anns., 1990, Fla. and S.C. State Open shows, 1989, San Diego Insternat. Water Media Juried Show, 1990, Tenn. Watercolor Soc. show, 1993; contbr. works to 16 books and 14 periodicals. Recipient Rex Brandt award San Diego Watercolor Internat., 1985, Purchase Selection award Watercolor USA and Springfield (Mo.) Art Mus., 1981, Gold medal, 1986, Mary Lou Fitzgerald meml. award Allied Arts Am. Nat. Arts Club, N.Y.C., 1987, Achievement award of Artists Painting in Acrylic Am. Artists Mag., 1993; NEA grantee, 1979-80. Mem. Nat. Watercolor Soc. (life, chmn. jury 1985, pres. 1983, Top award 1984, cash awards 1979, 87), Watercolor U.S.A. Honor Soc., Nat. Soc. Painters in Casein and Acrylic (2nd award 1985), Rocky Mountain Nat. Watermedia Soc. (juror 1984, awards 1978, 80, 86).

LIU, SAMUEL TZUNG-CHEE, investment banker; b. Berkeley, Calif., Feb. 7, 1968; s. David Cheng and Margaret (Liu) Collins. BS, U. So. Calif., 1989. With Expansion Capital Mgmt., San Francisco, 1992—. Mem. World Affairs Coun., 1988, Chinese-Am. Vol. Registration, San Francisco, 1992, Chinese-Am. Dem. Club, 1992. Mem. Nat. Assn. Individual Investors, PBS Sta. KQED, Icc., Alumni Resources, Chinese Am. Voter Edn. Project. Office: Expansion Capital Mgmt 3 Embarcadero Ctr San Francisco CA 94111

LIU, SHIN-TSE, chemical consultant; b. Taipei, Republic of China, Sept. 27, 1932; s. Teng-mien and Alee (Chen) L. BSChemE, Taiwan Nat. U., Taipei, 1956; Diplom-Chemiker, Technische-Hochschule, Aachen, Fed. Republic Germany, 1962, Dr. rer. nat., 1966. Research chemist ITT Rayonier, Whippany, N.J., 1967-70, UCLA, 1970-72; research engr. Jet Propulsion Lab., Pasadena, Calif., 1972-73; pres. S.T. Liu & Co., Los Angeles, 1974—. Mem. Am. Chem Soc. Office: PO Box 17457 Los Angeles CA 90017-0457

LIU, SHI-YI, research chemist; b. Taipei, Taiwan, Oct. 8, 1960; came to U.S., 1975; d. Chien and Ke-Chang (Lee) L.; m. Steven William Topp, Jan. 1, 1988. BS, U. Wash., 1982; PhD, U. Ill., 1987. Sr. rsch. chemist Allied Signal EMRC, Des Plaines, Ill., 1987-88, CAChe Scientific, Inc., Beaverton, Oreg., 1988—. Editor (newsletter) CAChe Connection, 1991—; editor (tech. manual) A Chemist's Guide to CAChe, 1992. Vol. Tualatin Valley Food Ctr., Hillsboro, Oreg., 1989—. Mem. ACS, Sigma Xi (rsch. award 1985). Office: CAChe Scientific Inc PO Box 500 MS 13-400 Beaverton OR 97077

LIU, TZE SHIU, computer company executive; b. Nanking, Peoples Republic of China, June 24, 1947; came to U.S., 1970; m. Yuh-Yun Marjorie Liu; children: Annie, Anthony. PhD, Carnegie-Mellon U., 1975. Adj. prof. U. Pitts., 1975-77; mem. tech. staff GTE Automatic Electric Lab., Elmhurst, Ill., 1977-78; sr./staff engr. large computer system div. Honeywell, Phoenix, Ariz., 1978-84; rsch. analyst IBM Santa Teresa Lab., San Jose, Calif., 1984—. Mem. Chinese Profl. Engring. Assn. (pres. 1983-84, v.p. 1982-83), Parker Ranch Assn. (bd. dirs. 1986-88). Office: IBM Santa Teresa Lab 555 Bailey Ave San Jose CA 95161

LIU, WINGYUEN TIMOTHY, research scientist; b. Hong Kong, Oct. 14, 1946; s. Ching-Hay and Mui (Wong) L.; m. Chia-Ling Wang, June 13, 1974. B.S., Ohio U., 1971; M.S., U. Wash., 1974, Ph.D., 1978. Research assoc. U. Wash., Seattle, 1978-79; sr. scientist, mem. tech. staff Jet Propulsion Lab., Pasadena, Calif., 1979—. Mem. Am. Meteorol. Soc., Am. Geophys. Union, Sigma Xi.

LIU, XU, research chemist, physicist; b. Huang Mei, China, Nov. 27, 1961; came to U.S., 1985; s. Zhi Zhong Wu and Yajun Liu; m. Feng Chen, June 15, 1985; 1 child, Tina. BS, Wuhan (China) U., 1982, MS, 1985; PhD, U. Denver, 1989. Rsch. chemist U. Denver, 1989—, rsch. physicist, 1990—; cons. United World Trade, Inc., Denver, 1992—. Contbr. articles to profl. jours. Recipient Antarctic Svc. medal NSF, 1992, Dept. Navy, 1992, Zhen Shaolung award Wuhan U., 1986, 2nd Prize Contbn. to Sci. award City Wuhan, 1985. Mem. Am. Chem. Soc., Sigma Xi. Office: Dept Physics U Denver 2112 E Wesley Ave Denver CO 80208

LIVERMORE, DONALD RAYMOND, elementary educator, library media specialist, educational consultant; b. Stockton, Calif., May 14, 1947; s. Harry Guy and Cora Edith (Ambrose) L. AA, Delta Jr. Coll., Stockton, Calif., 1967; BS, BA, Chico State U., 1971. Cert. elem., sec. tchr., Calif. Salesman/mgr. Magor's Mens Wear, Tracy, Calif., 1961-75; tchr., K-6 Monterey (Calif.) Peninsula Unified Sch. Dist., 1971—, mentor tchr., cons., 1984-91; instr. Chapman Coll., Monterey, 1982—; aquarium guide Monterey Bay Aquarium, 1985-93, mentor guide, trainer, 1986-92, VVIP tour guide, 1988—; program quality reviewer State of Calif., Monterey County Office Edn., Salinas, 1982-92; mem. IMEP history and social sci. textbook adoption com. Calif. Bd. Edn., 1990, 93; libr. media specialist Manzanita Elem. Model Tech. Sch. Author: (resource workbook) Hands on History; collaborator (with Randy Reinstedt): More Than Memories, 1985; coord. history project curriculum Memories Shared, 1984—. Pres. bd. dirs. PTA, Olson, 1976-78, Hayes, 1986-88. Recipient award, Kern County Hist., Social Sci. Consortium, Fresno, Calif., 1985; named Tchr. in Marine Research, Monterey County Office of Edn., Salinas, 1988. Mem. Monterey Bay Tchrs. Assn. (faculty rep. 1975-77). Democrat. Lutheran. Office: Manzanita Elem Sch Model Technology Sch Calif 1720 Yosemite St Seaside CA 93955-3999

LIVERMORE, FERN CHRISMAN, artist, retired art educator; b. Wooldridge, Mo., May 20, 1921; d. Thomas Oscar and Lulu Ann (Oerly) Chrisman; m. Claude Robert Livermore, Apr. 24, 1941; children: Thomas Robert, Toma Lee, Rosalie Ann. BS, Western N.Mex. U., 1960, MEd, 1965, BA, 1987. Art tchr. Silver City (N.Mex.) Consol. Sch. System, 1960-77. One-woman shows include Frances McCray Gallery Western N.Mex. U., Silver City, 1962, Pinos Altos (N.Mex.) Ch. Gallery, 1970—, La Azteca Mini-Gallery, Silver City, 1989-90, Home Fed. Savs. and Loan Assn., Silver City, 1990, Sunwest Bank, Silver City, 1989-91; W Gallery, El Paso, Tex., Yankie Creek Gallery, Silver City; group exhbns. include N.Mex. Federated Women's Clubs, Silver City, 1962, El Paso Ceramic Show, 1977, Eros, Love and Will Gallery, Silver City, 1989, Ea. N.Mex. U., Portales, 1989, Yucca Ford Motor Co., Silver City, 1989, Silver City Women's Club, 1989, Hanover Outpost, Hanover, N.Mex., 1989-90, Hillsboro (N.Mex.) Apple Festival, 1989-91, Branigan Cultural Ctr., Las Cruces, N.Mex., 1990, Miller Libr. We. N.Mex. U., 1990, Silver City Pub. Libr., 1991, Deming (N.Mex) Ctr. for Arts, 1991, 13th St. Emporium, Silver City, 1991. Mem. Nat. Mus. Women in Arts, Women's Caucus for Arts, N.Mex. Registry Arts, N.Mex. Ret. Tchrs. Assn., Black Range Artists Assn., Las Cruces Potters Guild, Grant County Arts Guild, Mimbres Regional Arts Coun., San Vicente Artists, Kappa Kappa Iota. Democrat. Methodist. Home: 3712 Hugh McKeen Dr Silver City NM 88061

LIVESAY, THOMAS ANDREW, museum administrator; b. Dallas, Feb. 1, 1945; s. Melvin Ewing Clay and Madge Almeda (Hall) L.; m. Jennifer Clark, 1985; children: Heather Marie, Russell Lee. B.F.A., U. Tex., Austin, 1968, M.F.A., 1972; postgrad., Harvard U. Inst. Arts Adminstrn., 1978. Curator Elisabet Ney Mus., Austin, 1971-73; dir. Longview (Tex.) Mus. and Arts Center, 1973-75; curator of art Amarillo (Tex.) Art Center, 1975-77, dir. center, 1977-80; asst. dir. for adminstrn. Dallas Mus. Fine Arts, 1980-85; dir. Mus. of N.Mex., Santa Fe, 1985—; mem. touring panel Tex. Commn. Arts; mem. panel Nat. Endowment Arts, Inst. Mus. Services; adj. tchr. U. Okla., Coll. Liberal Studies, 1992—, U. N.Mex., 1992—. Author: Young Texas Artists Series, 1978, Made in Texas, 1979; editor: video tape American Images, 1979, Ruth Abrams, Paintings, 1940-85, NYU Press. Served with U.S. Army, 1969-71. Mem. Am. Assn. Museums (council 1986-89, commn. on ethics 1992—), Tex. Assn. Museums (v.p. 1981, pres. 1983), N.Mex. State Records and Archives Commn. (chmn. 1986—). Office: Mus NMex PO Box 2087 Santa Fe NM 87504-2087

LIVINGSTON, DANA ALAN, chemical engineer; b. Sheridan, Wyo., Oct. 18, 1957; s. Harold Jr. and Janet Elenita (Wright) L.; m. Janine Leigh Jorgenson, July 25, 1987. BSChemE, U. Wyo., 1980; MBA, U. Calif., Berkeley, 1990. Registered profl. engr., Calif. Rsch. engr. Dow Chem., Pittsburg, Calif., 1980-84; sr. rsch. engr. Dow Chem., Walnut Creek, Calif., 1984-87; rsch. project leader Dow Chem., Pittsburg, 1987—. Inventee in field. Mem. Am. Inst. Chem. Engrs. (chmn. registration com. San Francisco chpt. 1983), alif. Inst. of Am. Inst. Chem. Engrs. (bd. dirs. Bay Area, Calif. chpt. 1982-84), Profit Investor Assn. (pres. Walnut Creek chpt. 1988-90). Office: Dow Chem Co Pittsburg CA 94565

LIVINGSTON, JON JERALD, physical education educator; b. San Jacinto, Calif., Dec. 20, 1935; s. John Walker and Anita (Stone) Livingstone; m. Mary Frances Livingston, July 22, 1967; children: Anne, Mark, Steven. BS, U. Oreg., 1962; MS, Ithaca Coll., 1967. Instr. Bethel Sch. Dist. #52, Eugene, Oreg., 1962-65, Wash. State U., Pullman, 1968-69; prof. Peninsula Coll., Port Angeles, Wash., 1969—; coord. Tompkins County Hosp. Rehab. Ctr., Ithaca, N.Y., 1966-67; game supr. athletic dept. U. Oreg., Eugene, 1961-66. Bd. dirs. Clallam County Park Bd., Port Angeles, 1976-78, Clallam County Blood Donor Coun., 1981-84, Jump Rope for Heart Am. Heart Assn., Port Angeles, 1980-82, 87, Port Angeles City Tennis Championships, 1976-81; pres. Olympic Jr. Babe Ruth League, Port Angeles, 1988-90. With USAF, 1956-59. Mem. Wash. State Community Coll. Phys. Edn. Assn. (pres. 1991—), AFT (pres. Peninsula Coll. chpt. 1985-89), Wash. Assn. Phys. Edn., Health, Recreation and Dance, AAHPER, Wash. Intramural and Recreational Sports Assn. (pres. 1977-78), Elks (Elk of Yr. 1978), Sigma Phi Epsilon (Mem. of Yr. 1961), Phi Epsilon Kappa. Democrat. Roman Catholic. Home: 1158 Olympus St Port Angeles WA 98362-2735 Office: Peninsula Coll 1502 E Lauridsen Blvd Port Angeles WA 98362-6698

LIVINGSTON, MARIE LEIGH, economics educator, researcher; b. Cedar City, Utah, Nov. 15, 1955; d. Richard Hamblin and Fern (Heaton) Leigh; m. Thomas Clark Livingston, May 22, 1982; children: Richard Cole, Paige Leigh Anna. BS, Utah State U., 1977; MS, U. Ariz., 1979; PhD, Colo. State U., 1984. Rsch. asst. U. Ariz., Tucson, 1978-79; rsch. assoc. Colo. State U., Ft. Collins, 1979-80; economist ERS/U.S. Dept. Agr., Ft. Collins, 1980-85; asst. prof. U. No. Colo., Greeley, 1985-87, assoc. prof., 1988—; vis. prof. U. Minn., St. Paul, 1987-88; cons. Denver Water Dept., 1985-88; assoc. editor Water Resources Rsch., Albuquerque, 1989-91; editor coun. Jour. of Environ. Econs. and Mgmt., 1989-92. Contbr. articles to profl. jours., chpts. to books; author book reviews, 1981—. Rev. com. Visual Arts/Lincoln Ctr., Ft. Collins., 1989-91; bd. dirs. Dance Connection, Ft. Collins, 1991—. Mem. Am. Econ. Assn., Internat. Agr. Econ. Assn., Assn. of Environ. and Resource Economists, Am. Agr. Econ. Assn. (internat. travel grant 1989), Western Social Sci. Assn. (program organizer 1989). Home: 4124 Spring Canyon Ct Fort Collins CO 80525-3270 Office: U No Colo Dept Econs Greeley CO 80639

LIVINGSTON, MYRA COHN, poet, writer, educator; b. Omaha, Aug. 17, 1926; d. Mayer L. and Gertrude (Marks) Cohn; m. Richard Roland Livingston, Apr. 14, 1952 (dec. 1990); children: Joshua, Jonas Cohn, Jennie Marks. BA, Sarah Lawrence Coll., 1948. Profl. horn player, 1941-48; book reviewer Los Angeles Daily News, 1948-49, Los Angeles Mirror, 1949-50; asst. editor Campus Mag., 1949-50; various public relations positions and pvt. sec. to Hollywood (Calif.) personalities, 1950-52; tchr. creative writing Dallas (Tex.) public library and schs., 1958-63; poet-in-residence Beverly Hills (Calif.) Unified Sch. Dist., 1966-84; sr. instr. UCLA Extension, 1973—; cons. to various sch. dists., 1966-84, cons. poetry to publishers children's lit., 1975—. Author: Whispers and Other Poems, 1958, Wide Awake and Other Poems, 1959, I'm Hiding, 1961, See What I Found, 1962, I Talk to Elephants, 1962, I'm Not Me, 1963, Happy Birthday, 1964, The Moon and a Star and Other Poems, 1965, I'm Waiting, 1966, Old Mrs. Twindlytart and Other Rhymes, 1967, A Crazy Flight and Other Poems, 1968, The Malibu and Other Poems, 1972, When You Are Alone/It Keeps You Capone: An Approach to Creative Writing with Children, 1973, Come Away, 1974, The Way Things Are and Other Poems, 1974, 4-Way Stop and Other Poems, 1976, A Lollygag of Limericks, 1978, O Sliver of Liver and Other Poems, 1979, No Way of Knowing: Dallas Poems, 1980, A Circle of Seasons, 1982, How Pleasant to Know Mr. Lear!, 1982, Sky Songs, 1984, A Song I Sang to You, 1984, Monkey Puzzle, 1984, The Child as Poet: Myth or Reality?, 1984, Celebrations, 1985, Worlds I Know and Other Poems, 1985, Sea Songs, 1986, Earth Songs, 1986, 1987, Higgledy-Piggledy, 1986, Space Songs, 1988, There Was a Place and Other Poems, 1988, Up in the Air, 1989, Birthday Poems, 1989, Remembering and Other Poems, 1989, My Head Is Red and Other Riddle Rhymes, 1990, Climb Into the Bell Tower: Essays on Poetry, 1990, Poem-making: Ways to Begin Writing Poetry, 1991, Light and Shadow, 1992, I Never Told and Other Poems, 1992, Let Freedom Ring: A Ballad of Martin Luther King, Jr., 1992, Abraham Lincoln, A Man for All the People, 1993, The Writing of Poetry, film strips; co-editor: The Scott-Foresman Anthology, 1984; editor 33 anthologies of poetry; contbr. articles on children's lit. to ednl. publs., essays on lit. and reading in edn. to various books; mem. editorial adv. bd. The New Advocate. Officer Beverly Hills PTA Council, 1966-75; pres. Friends of Beverly Hills Public Library, 1979-81; bd. dirs. Poetry Therapy Inst., 1975—, Reading is Fundamental of So. Calif., 1981—. Recipient Honor award N.Y. Herald Tribune Spring Book Festival, 1958, Excellence in Poetry award Nat. Council Tchrs. of English, 1980, Commonwealth Club award, 1984, Nat. Jewish Book award, 1987. Mem. Authors Guild, Internat. Reading Assn., Soc. Children's Book Writers (honor award 1975), Tex. Inst. Letters (awards 1961, 80), So. Calif. Council on Lit. for Children and Young People (Comprehensive Contribution award 1968, Notable Book award 1972, Poetry Quartet award 89), PEN. Address: 9308 Readcrest Dr Beverly Hills CA 90210

LIVINGSTON, PATRICIA ANN, marine biologist, researcher; b. Detroit, Dec. 10, 1954. BS, Mich. State U., 1976; MS, U. Wash., 1980, M in Pub. Adminstrn., 1987. Ecosystem modeller Nat. Marine Fish Svc., Seattle, 1977-82, trophic interactions program leader, 1983—; mem. sci. and tech. bd. The Sea Use Council, Seattle, 1986—. Contbr. articles on ecosystem modelling and marine fish trophic interactions to profl. jours. Mem. Am. Fisheries Soc. (officer and regional fish corr. Marine Fish sect., 1982-84), Am. Soc. Pub. Adminstrn., AAAS. Office: NW and Alaska Fisheries Ctr Bldg 15700 7600 Sand Point Way NE Seattle WA 98115-6349

LIVINGSTONE, MICHAEL EDWIN, research and development company executive; b. Kirkland Lake, Ont., Can., Jan. 27, 1953; s. William Thomas and Constance Talmadge (Graham) L.; m. Cheryl Bray (div. Sept. 1983); 1 child, Michael Edwin Jr.; m. Bonnie Fraser, Oct. 12, 1991. BA in Polit. Sci. and History cum laude, Northeastern U., 1974; postgrad. in econs., U. Okla., 1979-82; postgrad. in Arab studies, Georgetown U., 1982-83, postgrad in Polit. Sci., 1991-92. Commd. 2d lt. U.S. Army, 1974, advanced through grades to capt., 1979; tactical intelligence officer U.S. Army, Honolulu, 1974-79, sr. Mid-East analyst Pacific Command, 1979-85; pres. XSTEC Expert Systems Devel., San Diego, 1989—; cons. Mid-East affairs, knowledge engrng. to nat. agys., def. contractors, 1985—; co-dir. Peace Through Law Inst., San Diego, 1989—; lectr. in field. Mem. La Jolla (Calif.) Mus. Contemporary Art, 1990. Mem. Middle East Inst., Middle East Studies Assn., Am. Polit. Sci. Assn., Western Polit. Sci. Assn. Democrat. Baptist. Home: 624 Sea Ln La Jolla CA 92037-5446 Office: XTEC 4353 Trias St San Diego CA 92103-1157

LIVZIEY, JAMES GERALD, secondary school educator; b. Buffalo, July 30, 1927; s. James Ephlyn and Helena Charlote (Kiener) L.; m. June Ellen Andersen, July 25, 1955; children: Naomi Lynn, Patricia Ellen. AA, Southwestern Jr. Coll., 1970; BA, San Diego State U., 1972. Enlisted U.S. Navy, 1945, advanced through grades to lt. comdr., 1967, ret., 1969; high sch. instr. SWHS Dist., Chula Vista, Calif., 1972—. Recipient award Freedoms Found., 1991; fellow Taft Inst., 1977, Pacific Acad. Advanced Studies, 1978. Fellow Alpha Gamma Sigma; mem. Naval Inst. USN,

Masons, K.C. (32d degree). Home: 675 Mariposa Cir Chula Vista CA 91911-2510

LJUBICIC DROZDOWSKI, MILADIN PETER, consulting engineer; b. Zajecar, Yugoslavia, Sept. 28, 1921; came to U.S., 1959; s. Peter Miladin and Martha Jovan (Viktorovic) Ljubicic; m. Dusica Cile Pavic, Sept. 9, 1948. Diploma in engring., U. Belgrade, Yugoslavia, 1951, 52; ancien éleve, Ecole Nationale Superieure de l'Armement, Paris, 1956; MSME, UCLA, 1964, PhD in Mec. Engring., 1971. Design and test engr. Fed. Mogul Bower, El Monte, Calif., 1959-62; chief advanced armament analytical support Hughes Helicopters, Culver City, Calif., 1962-78; engring. supr. Bechtel Power Corp., Norwalk, Calif., 1978-80; engring. adviser Bechtel Espana, Madrid, 1980-87; v.p. Koach Engring., Sun Valley, Calif., 1987; engring. cons. Mission Viejo, Calif., 1987—; asst. to chmn. continuum mechanics, Belgrade, 1955-56; guest lectr. Sch. Engring. and Applied Sci., UCLA, 1971; prof., Loyola Marymount U., L.A., 1978-80. Contbr. to profl. publs. Mem. Am. Soc. Mech. Engrs., Am. Def. Preparedness Assn., Spanish Nuclear Soc. Home and Office: 26426 Lope De Vega Dr Mission Viejo CA 92691

LLEWELLYN, FREDERICK EATON, mortuary executive; b. Mexico, Mo., Mar. 28, 1917; s. Frederick William and Mabel (Eaton) L.; BS, Calif. Inst. Tech., 1938; MBA (Baker scholar), Harvard, 1942; LLD, Pepperdine U., 1976; m. Yvonne Maples, July 18, 1990; children: Richard, John, Ann Marie. Asst. gen. mgr., dir. Forest Lawn Life Ins. Co., Glendale, Calif., 1940-41, pres., 1959-61; asst. to gen. mgr. Forest Lawn Meml. Park, Glendale, 1941-42, exec. v.p., 1946-66, gen. mgr., 1966-89; pres. Forest Lawn Found., 1961—, Forest Lawn Co., 1967-88; chmn. bd. Am. Security & Fidelity Corp., Forest Lawn Co., 1988—, Upstairs Galleries Inc., 1974-91, Met. Computer Center, 1973-81, Calif. Citrus Corp., 1971-80, Forest Lawn Mortgage Corp., 1976-92; dir. IT Corp., Trust Svcs. Am., Inc.(chmn. 1983-91). Mem. Found. for the 21st Century, 1986-91, Orthopaedic Hosp., 1976-82, chmn., 1980; chmn. Glendale Meml. Hosp., 1980, trustee, 1982-85; pres. So. Calif. Visitors Coun., 1976-77; chmn. Coun. of Regents, Meml. Ct. of Honor, 1966-93. Mem. Mayor's Ad Hoc Energy Com., L.A., 1973-74, L.A. County Reorgn. Commn., 1978; bd. dirs. L.A. County Heart Assn., 1957; trustee U. Redlands, 1966-77, chmn. bd., 1969-72; mem. Univ. Bd., Pepperdine Coll. (life), chmn. bd. regents, mem. exec. bd., 1977-86; bd. dirs. Pasadena Found. Med. Rsch., 1967-72, So. Calif. Bldg. Funds, 1975-85, Met. YMCA L.A., 1975—; trustee San Gabriel Valley coun. Boy Scouts Am., 1968-74; trustee Calif. Mus. Sci. and Industry, 1977-89, pres., 1983-85, chmn., 1985-86; bd. govs. Dept. Mus. Natural History, L.A. County, 1968-72; mem. L.A. County Energy Commn., 1974-80; chmn. Mayor's Ad Hoc Water Crisis Commn., 1977. Served with USNR, 1942-45. Decorated knight Order of Merit (Italy). Mem. Nat. Assn. Cemeteries (pres. 1956-57), L.A. Area C. of C. (dir. 1969-78, bd. chmn. 1974, pres. 1973), Calif. C. of C. (dir. 1977-89), Newcomen Soc., Tau Beta Pi. Clubs: California, Lincoln, One Hundred, Twilight. Contbr. articles to profl. jours. Home: 1521 Virginia Rd San Marino CA 91108-1933 Office: 1712 S Glendale Ave Glendale CA 91205-3320

LLEWELLYN, JOHN FREDERICK, cemetery executive; b. L.A., Nov. 16, 1947; s. Frederick Eaton and Jane Elizabeth Llewellyn; m. Linda Garrison, Apr. 15, 1989. BA, U. Redlands, 1970; MBA, U. So. Calif., 1972. Foreman Pacific T&T, Orange, Calif., 1970; underwriter Allstate Ins. Co., Santa Ana, Calif., 1971-72; asst. to controller Forest Lawn Co., Glendale, Calif., 1972-73, v.p., 1973-75, exec. v.p., 1976-88, treas., chief fin. officer, 1978-83, sec., bd. dirs., 1983—, pres., 1988—; various offices, bds. dirs. divs. Forest Lawn Co., Glendale, Calif., 1974—; bd. dirs. Beneficial Standard Life Ins. Co., L.A., 1984-91, Braille Inst., L.A.; trustee Glendale Meml. Hosp., 1985-91. Bd. dirs., pres. Greater L.A. Visitors and Convention Bur., 1988-90; bd. dirs. Glendale Devel. Coun.; vice chmn. L.A. Area coun. Boy Scouts Am., 1987-93, commr., 1990-92, chmn. 1992—. Mem. Am. Cemetery Assn. (bd. dirs. 1977-81, 83-86, 88-91, v.p. 1985-86, pres.-elect 1986-87, pres. 1987-88), Interment Assn. Calif. (bd. dirs 1984—, state v.p. 1987-88, pres. 1988-89), Calif. Mortuary Alliance (bd. dirs.), Western Cemetery Alliance (bd. dirs., v.p. 1987—), Econ. Round Table (sec.-treas. 1983-85), Newcomen Soc. N.Am., Calif. C. of C. (bd. dir. 1991—), M & M Assn. (bd. dir. 1991—), Calif. Club, Lincoln Club. Office: Forest Lawn Meml-Parks & Mortuaries 1712 S Glendale Ave Glendale CA 91205-3320

LLOYD, D(AVID) H(UBERT), writer, publisher, physics technician; b. Marietta, Ohio, June 16, 1948; s. Hubert Fenwick and Mary Agnes (Smith) L.; m. Shelley Verde Hellen, Sept. 6, 1980; children: Jesse Collin, Joseph Hubert. BS in Physics, Calif. State U., Long Beach, 1978. Computer operator Humble Oil Co., Houston, 1966-67; tech. U.S. Navy, 1967-73, Krayco Industries, Compton, Calif., 1974-75, Calif. State U., Long Beach, 1976—; pub. Applezaba Press, Long Beach, 1977—. Author: Mog and Glog, 1978, Dreams, Myth and Other Realities, 1983, Bible Bob Responds to a Jesus Honker, 1986; contbr. numerous poems, stories, reviews and articles to mags., 1975—. Elder Geneva Presbyn. Ch., Long Beach, 1976—; steerming com. mem. Coalition for a Nuclear Free Harbor, Long Beach, 1986; founding com. Westside Free Clinic, Long Beach, 1978; with U.S. Navy, 1967-76. Mem. PEN. Democrat. Presbyterian. Office: Applezaba Press Box 4134 Long Beach CA 90804

LLOYD, DOUGLAS GEORGE, watercolor artist, educator; b. Portsmouth, Hampshire, Eng., Jan. 8, 1918; came to U.S., 1946; s. John Albert and Jessie (Lavender) L.; m. Dorothy May Van Alphen, June 10, 1944 (dec. Apr. 1984); children: Ian Douglas (dec.), Lawrence Merrill, Robert Rodney, Jess Andrew, Robin Lee, Barbara Jeanne; m. Martha Clydesdale Amoia, June 21, 1986. Student, Portsmouth Jr. Tech., 1933-36; cert., Royal Naval Extension Coll., Dartmouth, Eng., 1944. Photography tchr. Boston Coll. Photography, 1946-47; photography editor Harvard Film Svc., Boston, 1947-48; microfilm specialist Hall & McChesney, Syracuse, N.Y., 1948-50; exec. v.p. Dakota So. Microfilm, Miami, Fla., 1950-54; microfilm cons. Miami, 1954-60, Oakland, Calif., 1961-67; microfilm specialist, special courses instr. Datagraphix Inc., San Diego, 1968-78; watercolor artist Las Vegas, Nev., 1978—; cons., Indio, Calif.; microfilm cons. Clk. of Cir. Ct., Deland, Fla., 1950-52, Bahamian Govt., Nassau, Bahamas, 1954. Author: (series of articles) Gremlins in the Computer Output Microfilm System, 1975 (monetary award 1975); artist: (series of ink drawings) The California Scene, 1981 (monetary award 1986). Alderman Hayling Island (Eng.) Coun., 1945; fire commr. City Fire Commn., Lake Helen, Fla., 1950-52; spl. dep. to Clk. of Cir. Ct., Deland, 1950-52; pilot and cadet commandant CAP, Miami, 1952-54; mem. Vols. in Police Program, City of Indio, Calif., 1993—; treas. San Diego Watercolor Soc., 1980. With Royal Navy, 1936-45. Mem. Nev. Watercolor Soc. (signature award 1988), San Diego Watercolor Soc. (treas. 1982), Coast Guard Artist Program, Western Fedn. Watercolor Socs., Cochella Valley Watercolor Soc., Riverside Art Mus., 1993—. Republican. Episcopalian. Home and Office: Douglas Lloyd Arts 81297 Avenida Gaviota Indio CA 92201

LLOYD, JOSEPH WESLEY, researcher; b. N.Mex., Jan. 31, 1914; s. William Washington and Mattie May (Barber) L.; m. Lenora Lucille Hopkins, Jan. 24, 1944 (dec. June 1969); 3 children (dec.); m. Ruth Kathryn Newberry, Nov. 19, 1988; children: Kathryn Ruth Jordan, Mary Evelyn Jordan. Student, Pan Am. Coll., 1942. Plumber Pomona, Calif., 1951-57; plumber, pipefitter Marysville, Calif., 1957-79; retired, 1979; ind. researcher in physics and magnetism, Calif., 1944—. With CAP, 1944-45. Mem. AAAS, N.Y. Acad. Scis. Mem. Ch. of Christ.

LLOYD, MARY ELLEN, state legislator; b. Pocatello, Idaho, 1947; m. Bill Lloyd. Owner Mary Lloyd's Kitchen; mem. Idaho State Ho. Reps. from 27th dist., 1986-90, Idaho State Senate from 27th dist., 1990—. Address: PO Box 2557 Pocatello ID 83206

LO, SANSOM CHI-KWONG, bookstore manager, educator; b. Hong Kong, June 6, 1965; came to U.S., 1984; s. Ting and Kum-Mui (Law) L. AS, Humphreys Coll., 1986, BS, 1987, JD, 1991. Bookstore mgr. Humphreys Coll., Stockton, Calif., 1984-91, instr., 1987-91; law clk. Kuvara & Cohen Law Firm, San Francisco, 1991-93; with Pancisco Internat., 1993—. Home: 523-5th Ave # 6 San Francisco CA 94118

LO, WAITUCK, artist; b. Honolulu, June 9, 1919; s. Wai Tong and Kam T. Lo; m. Agnes Ching, Jan. 4, 1958; children: Edwina, Felix, Lisa Ann. BS, Utopia U., Shanghai, China, 1942; postgrad., Yen Yu Inst. Fine Art, Shanghai, Ind. U. Exhibited in group shows at Assn. Honolulu Artist Jury Art Show, 1956, 57 (Most Decorative award 1956, 57), Assn. Honolulu Artists non-jury show, 1957 (Popular award 1957), Narcissus Festival Art Exhbn., 1960 (Kaiser award 1960, Most Popular award 1960), Maui County Fair Art Exhbn., 1963 (2d prize 1963); commd. silk painting Pepsi-Cola U.S.A., 1987; paintings reproduced by Regency Card Co. Recipient 1st Place Water Color award Assn. Honolulu Artists, 1965, 68, Hayward award Assn. Honolulu Artists, 1968, 1st Place Water Color award Home Builders Assn. Art Show, 1966; Honorable Mention in Oil and Water Color, Assn. Honolulu Artists, 1966, Internat. Assn. Artists, 1979. Club: Toastmasters (Honolulu) (pres. 1986). Home: 6080 Keoki Pl Honolulu HI 96821-2225

LOARIE, THOMAS MERRITT, healthcare executive; b. Deerfield, Ill., June 12, 1946; s. Willard John and Lucile Veronica (Finnegan) L.; m. Stephanie Lane Fitts, Aug. 11, 1968 (div. Nov. 1987); children: Thomas M., Kristin Leigh. BSME, U. Notre Dame, 1968; Student, U. Minn., 1969-70, U. Chgo., 1970-71, Columbia U., 1978. Registered profl. engr., Calif. Prodn. engr. Honeywell, Inc., Evanston, Ill., 1968-70; various positions Am. Hosp. Supply Co., Evanston, Ill., 1970-83, pres. Heyer-Schulte div., 1979-83; pres., chief oper. officer, dir. Novacor Med. Corp., Oakland, Calif., 1984-85; pres. ABA Bio Mgmt., Danville, Calif., 1985-87; chmn., chief exec. officer Keravision, Inc., Santa Clara, Calif., 1987—; asst. prof. surgery Creighton U. Med. Sch., Omaha, 1986—; speaker in field. Bd. dirs. Marymount Sch. Bd., 1981-84; bd. dirs. United Way Santa Barbara, 1981-84, assoc. chairperson, 1982-83, treas., 1983. Named One of 50 Rising Stars: Exec. Leaders for the 80's Industry Week mag., 1983. Mem. Contact Lens Assn. Ophthalmology, Med. Mktg. Assn. Roman Catholic. Office: KeraVision Inc 2334 Walsh Ave Santa Clara CA 95051-1301

LOBDELL, FRANK, artist; b. Kansas City, Mo., 1921; m. Ann Morency, 1952; children: Frank Saxton, Judson Earle. Studied, St. Paul Sch. Art, 1938-39, Calif. Sch. Fine Arts, 1947-50, Academie de la Grande Chaumiere, Paris, France, 1950-51. Tchr. Calif. Sch. Fine Arts, 1957-65; prof. art, Stanford, 1965—. One man shows, Lucien Labaudt Gallery, 1949, Martha Jackson Gallery, 1958, 60, 63, 72, 74, de Young Meml. Mus., San Francisco, 1959, Ferus Gallery, 1962, Pasadena Art Mus., 1961, San Francisco Mus. Art, 1969, Benador Gallerie, Geneva, Switzerland, 1964, Gallerie Anderson-Mayer, Paris, 1965, Smith-Anderson Gallery, San Francisco, 1982, Oscarsson Hood Gallery, N.Y.C., 1983, 84, 85, John Berggruen Gallery, San Francisco, 1987, Charles Campbell Gallery, San Francisco, 1988, 90, 92, Stanford Mus. Art, 1988, retrospective show, Pasadena Art Mus. and Stanford Mus., 1966, San Francisco Mus. Modern Art, 1983, Stanford Mus., 1993; exhibited group Shows, Salon du Mai, Paris, 1950, III Sao Paulo Biennial, 1955, Whitney Mus. Am. Art, 1962-63, 72, Guggenheim Mus., N.Y.C., 1964, Van Abbemuseum, Eindhoven, Holland, 1970, Corcoran Gallery Art, Washington, 1971, U. Ill., 1974; represented in permanent collections, San Francisco Mus. Art, Oakland Mus. Art, L.A. County Mus., Nat. Gallery Washington, others. Served with AUS, 1942-46. Recipient Nealie Sullivan award San Francisco Art Inst., 1960, award of merit AAAL, 1988. Home: 2754 Octavia St San Francisco CA 94123-4304

LOBEL, CHARLES IRVING, physician; b. Phila., Nov. 9, 1921; s. Maurice and Dora (Barnett) L.; m. Julia Valentine Skellchock, June 12, 1955; children: Meredith Anne Lobel-Angel. AA, San Jose State U., 1948; student, Stanford U., 1948-49; MD, U. So. Calif., 1953. Physician Permanente Med. Group, Inc., South San Francisco, 1954-65; physician, courtesy staff Chope Community Hosp., San Mateo, Calif., 1965-89, Sequoia Hosp., Redwood City, Calif., 1965—; physician Permanente Med. Group, Inc., Redwood City, Calif., 1965—; clin. prof. medicine div. rheumatology Stanford U. Sch. Medicine, 1965—; chief profl. edn. Kaiser Found. Hosp., Redwood City, 1968-80, rehab. coord, 1968-80, pres med. staff, 1968-70; mem. Calif. Med. Assn. Staff Survey Com., San Francisco, 1970-90; mem. 4th dist. Bd. Med. Quality Assurance State Calif., 1979-84. 1st Lt. U.S. Army, 1942-46. Decorated Combat Infantry Badge, Bronze Star, Presdl. Unit citation, 3 Battle Stars. Fellow Am. Acad. Family Physicians, Am. Coll. Rheumatology; mem. AMA, AAAS, San Mateo County Med. Soc. (bd. dirs. 1975-78), Calif. Med. Soc. (alt. del. 1979-83), N.Y. Acad. of Sci., Am. Heart Assn., Royal Soc. of Med., Med. Friends of Wine, Arthritis Found. No. Calif., Phi Delta Epsilon. Office: Kaiser Permanente Med Ctr 1150 Veterans Blvd Redwood City CA 94063-2087

LOBITZ, W. CHARLES, III, clinical psychologist; b. Rochester, Minn., Oct. 13, 1943; s. Walter C. Jr. and Caroline E. (Rockwell) L.; m. Gretchen K. Young, Sept. 7, 1969. BA, Dartmouth Coll., 1965; MA, Stanford U., 1970; PhD, Oreg. U., 1974. Lic. psychologist, Colo. Intern Neuro Psychiatric Inst. UCLA, 1973-74; asst. prof. Med. Sch. U. Colo., Denver, 1974-78, assoc. clin. prof., 1978—; pres. Lobitz & Lobitz, P.C., Denver, 1978—; cons. Ctr. Creative Leadership, Colorado Springs, 1989—. Co-author: Skiing From the Head Down, 1977, Skiing Out of Your Mind, 1986. Recipient Pres's. award Am. Heart Assn. Colo., 1988. Mem. APA, Assn. Advancement Behavioral Therapy, Soc. Behavioral Medicine, Colo. Psychol. Assn. (pres. 1987-88, E. Graham Disting. Psychologist award 1985), Am. Assn. Sex Educators, Counselors and Therapists, Soc. for Sex Therapy and Rsch., Colo. Assn. Sex Therapy (pres. 1978-79). Office: Lobitz & Lobitz 950 S Cherry St Ste 420 Denver CO 80222-2664

LOBSINGER, THOMAS, bishop; b. Ayton, Ont., Can., Nov. 17, 1927. Ordained priest Roman Cath. Ch., 1954, bishop, 1987. Bishop Whitehorse, Y.T., Can., 1987—. Home: 5119 5th Ave, Whitehorse, YK Canada Y1A 1L5*

LOBUE, VINCENT EDWARD, computer executive; b. Jersey City, Jan. 3, 1941; s. Joseph Dominick and Elizabeth (DiCorcia) LoB.; m. Barbara Clair Robertson, Aug. 6, 1983; children: Vincent S., Robert. BBA, UCLA, 1962. Pres. U-Tec Data Systems, Melville, N.Y., 1964-76; v.p. sales Data Phaze, Corp., Phoenix, 1984-88; v.p. sales and mktg. Intellipower, Inc., Laguna Hills, Calif., 1988-90; dir. bus. devel. Artisoft, Inc., Tucson, 1990-92; computer networking cons. LoBue and Assocs., Laguna Niguel, Calif., 1992—; pres. Data Processing Mgmt. Assn., Hicksville, 1963-66. Republican.

LOCATELLI, PAUL LEO, university president; b. Santa Cruz, Calif., Sept. 16, 1938; s. Vincent Dino and Marie Josephine (Piccone) L. B.S., Santa Clara U., 1961; M. Div., Jesuit Sch. Theology, 1974; D.B.A., U. So. Calif., 1971. C.P.A., Calif. Ordained priest Roman Cath. Ch., 1974. Acct., Lautze & Lautze, San Jose, Calif., 1960-61, 1973-74; prof. acctg. Santa Clara (Calif.) U., 1974-86, acad. v.p., 1978-86, pres., 1988—; mem. Nat. Cath. Bishops and Pres.' Com., Acctg. Edn. Change Commn.; mem. adv. couns. Tech. Ctr. and Community Found.; past rector Jesuit Community at Loyola Marymount U. Trustee St. Louis U.; past trustee U. San Francisco, Seattle U., Regis Coll. and Loyola Marymount U.; past bd. dirs., mem. Sr. Commn. of Western Assn. Schs. and Colls.; mem. ACE Commn. on Minority Assn. Mem. AICPA, Calif. Soc. CPAs, Am. Acctg. Assn., NCCJ (bd. dirs.), Assn. Jesuit Colls. and Univs. (vice chair), Ind. Colls. Calif. (chair), Am. Leadership Forum (bd. dirs.). Democrat. Address: Santa Clara U Office of Pres Santa Clara CA 95053

LOCH, PATRICIA ANN, software company executive, consultant; b. Omaha, May 2, 1944; d. Frank and Elizabeth (Duffield) Barrick; m. Charles Joseph Loch, Nov. 25, 1967; children: Michelle Kathleen, Justin Randall. BS in Math., Wake Forest U., 1966. Programmer IBM, Raleigh, N.C., 1966-68, Almay Cosmetics, Raleigh, N.C., 1968; contract programmer Kelly Assocs., Mpls., 1969-70, Bre-Mar Systems, N.Y.C., 1971; systems analyst Met. Life Ins. Co., N.Y.C., 1970-71; cons. Bd. Coop. Edn. Svcs., Yorktown, N.Y., 1972-75; pres., cons. P. Loch Assocs., Danville, Calif., 1975—; cons. Target Pub., Pleasanton, Calif., 1976-88. Mem. Assn. Small System Users (dir. membership 1981-82, dir. facilities 1985-87), NAFE, AAUW, Round Hill Country (Alamo, Calif.), Amador Athletic Club (Pleasanton). Home and Office: 181 Emmons Canyon Ln Ste 200 Danville CA 94526-1252

LOCHMILLER, KURTIS L., real estate entrepreneur; b. Sacramento, Dec. 30, 1952; s. Rodney Glen and Mary Margaret (Frauen) L.; m. Mariye Susan Mizuki, Nov. 9, 1951; children: Margaux Sian, Chase Jordan. BA in Econs. and Fin., U. Denver, 1975. Dist. sales mgr. Hertz Truck Div., Denver, 1975-76; drilling foreman Shell Oil, Alaska, Mont., Colo., 1976-79; pres., owner Kurtex Mortgage & Devel. Co., Denver, 1979—, Kurtex Properties Inc., Denver, 1980-86; pres., chief exec. officer Kurtex Inc., Denver, 1981—, Bankers Pacific Mortgage, Denver, 1980—, Bankers Fin. Escrow Corp., Denver, 1984—, Northwest Title & Escrow, Denver, 1984—; pres., chief exec. officer Steamboat Title, Steamboat Springs, Colo., 1985—, First Escrow, Denver, 1986—, Fidelity-Commonwealth-Continental Escrow, Denver, 1984—; pres. Colonnade Ltd., Denver, 1981-88; pres., bd. dirs. Breckridge (Colo.) Brewery. V.p., founder Colfax on the Hill, Denver, 1984; mediator, arbitrator Arbitrator/Mediation Assn., Denver, 1986; mem. Police Athletic League, Denver, 1988. Recipient Pres. Spl. Achievement/Founder award Colfax on the Hill, Denver, 1984, Spl. Mayor's award, City & County of Denver, 1985. Mem. Nat. Assn.of Real Estate Appraisers, Internat. Brotherhood of Teamsters, Colo. Mortgage Bankers Assn., Mortgage Banking Assn., Denver C. of C., Phi Beta Kappa, Omicron Delta Epsilon. Clubs: U.S. Karate Assn. (Phoenix) (3d degree Black Belt), Ferrari (Portland). Lodge: Internat. Supreme Council Order of Demolay. Home: 1 Carriage Ln Littleton CO 80121-2010 Office: Bankers Fin Escrow Corp 1660 S Albion St Ste 518 Denver CO 80222-4021

LOCHNER, JIM WARREN, health and physical education educator; b. Denver, June 17, 1940; s. Kenneth Joseph and Ruth Jean (Hayes) L.; m. Bonnie Carol Leavitt, Dec. 30, 1967; 1 child, Crystal Louise. BA, Colo. State Coll., 1962; MA, Adams State Coll., Alamosa, Colo., 1964; EdD, U. No. Colo., 1969; CHES, Nat. Comm. Health Edn. Cred., N.Y.C., 1989. With C&S/Santa Fe R.R., Denver, 1963; salesman Adolph Coors, Denver; grad. asst. Adams State Coll., 1962-63, U. No. Colo., Greeley, 1965-66; instr. Jefferson County Pub. Schs., Lakewood, Colo., 1962-63, 64-65; instr., coach U. Colo., Boulder, 1966-68; asst. prof., coach U. No. Colo., 1968-70; prof. health and phys. edn. Weber State U., Ogden, Utah, 1970—. Author, coeditor: Pocketguide Physical Activities, 1981; author, co-editor jour. UAAHPERĄ, 1988, Sch. Health Rev., 1972; contbr. articles to profl. jours. Vol. fireman Mt. Green Fire Dept., Utah, 1970—. Mem. AAHPERD, Am. Sch. Health Assn. (chmn. phys. activity com. 1983-86), Utah Assn. Health, Phys. Edn., Recreation and Dance, Nat. Rifle Assn., Nat. Commn. for Health Edn. Credentialing (fellow). Democrat. Christian Ch. Office: Weber State U 3750 Harrison Blvd Ogden UT 84408-0001

LOCKART, BARBETTA, counselor, jeweler, artwear designer, artist; b. Sacramento, Calif., Feb. 28, 1947; d. Bernard Elwood and Naomi Joyce (Wilson) L.; m. Michael Stanley Ray, Dec. 29, 1982 (div). AA in English, Southwestern Coll., Chula Vista, Calif., 1974; BA, San Diego State U., 1975; MA in Edn. Adminstrn., N.Mex. State U., Las Cruces, 1979, MA in Counseling and Guidance, 1981. Sec., interim coord., tchr. Indian Edn. Project, Palm Springs (Calif.) Unified Sch. Dist., 1976-79; outreach counselor Tecumseh House/Boston Indian Coun., 1980-81, asst. dir., 1981; acad. counselor, coord. native Am. affairs Ea. N.Mex. U., Portales, 1981-82; ind. researcher in field of counseling, Albuquerque, 1982-89, Sacramento, Calif., 1989—; pres., Sacramento, 1989—; owner Dearwater Designs, Albuquerque, 1985-88, Sacramento, 1988-90, Barbetta's Beads & Art, Sacramento, 1990—; speaker in field of community edn., alcoholism, urban native Am. women. Rockefeller Found. fellow, 1978-79; Nat. Inst. Edn. fellow, 1979-80. Author: Resolving Discipline Problems for Indian Students: A Preventative Approach, 1981, Auctions and Auction-Going: Make Them Pay Off for You; contbr. articles to profl. jours.

LOCKE, FRANCIS PHILBRICK, retired editorial writer; b. Lincoln, Nebr., May 1, 1912; s. Walter Leonard and Annette Elizabeth (Philbrick) L.; m. Isabel Carroll Day, Dec. 31, 1936; children: Margaret Locke Newhouse, Alice Locke Carey, Walter Day. BA, Harvard Coll., 1933; posgrad., Harvard U., 1946-47. Reporter Miami (Fla.) Daily News, 1934-36, editorial writer, 1936-41; editorial writer St. Louis Post-Dispatch, 1941; editor of editorial page Miami Daily News, 1941-46; Nieman fellow Harvard U., Cambridge, Mass., 1946-47; assoc. editor Dayton (Ohio) Daily News, 1947-63; editorial writer Riverside (Calif.) Press-Enterprise, 1963-72. Author: (chpt.) Public Men In & Out of Office, 1943; contbr. articles to profl. jours. Bd. dirs. Mission Inn Found., Riverside, 1987—; trustee Miami U., Oxford, Ohio, 1954-63; div. chair United Way, Dayton, 1957—; pres. Harvard Club, Dayton, 1961—. Recipient Harvard medal Harvard Alumni Assn., 1983, Nat. Editorial Writing prize Sigma Delta Chi, 1946, Aviation Writing award TWA, 1956. Mem. Nat. Conf. of Editorial Writers, Soc. Profl. Journalists, Harvard-Radcliffe Club So. Calif. (bd. dirs. 1975-92). Democrat. Congregational. Home: 7368 W Westwood Dr Riverside CA 92504-2729

LOCKE, HUBERT GAYLORD, public affairs educator; b. Detroit, Apr. 30, 1934; s. Hubert Howard and Willa Lou (Hayes) L.; m. Sharon Doyle, 1972 (div. 1981); children: Gayle P., Lauren M. AB, Wayne State U., 1955; BD, U. Chgo., 1959; AM, U. Mich., 1961; DD (hon.), Payne Theol. Sem., Wilberforce, Ohio, 1968, Chgo. Theol. Sem., 1971; LHD (hon.), U. Akron, 1971, U. Nebr., Omaha, 1992. Exec. dir. Citizens Com. for Equal Opportunity, Detroit, 1962-65; adminstrv. asst. to commr. police Detroit Police Dept., 1966-67; faculty assoc. Ctr. for Urban Studies Wayne State U., Detroit, 1967-72; dean Coll. Pub. Affairs, U. Nebr., Omaha, 1972-76; assoc. dean Coll. Arts and Scis. U. Wash., Seattle, 1976-77, vice provost acad. affairs, 1977-82, dean Grad. Sch. Pub. Affairs, 1982-88, prof., 1988—; bd. govs. Inst. European Studies, Chgo., 1986—. Author: The Detroit Riot of 1967, 1969, The Care and Feeding of White Liberals, 1970; co-editor: The German Church Struggle and the Holocaust, 1974, Exile in the Fatherland, 1986; assoc. editor Jour. Holocaust and Genocide Studies, 1989—. Bd. dirs. Police Found., Washington, 1970-81. Recipient Liberty Bell award Mich. Bar Assn., 1966, Eternal Flame award Anne Frank Inst., 1987. Fellow Nat. Acad. Pub. Adminstrn. (trustee 1988—), Soc. for Values in Higher Edn., William O. Douglas Inst. Democrat. Mem. Christian Ch. (Disciples of Christ). Home: 7117 57th Ave NE Seattle WA 98115-6228 Office: U Wash Mail Stop DC-13 Seattle WA 98195

LOCKE, JOHN GARDNER, chemical company executive; b. Chgo., Sept. 2, 1926; s. John Gardner and Hildur Marie (Ericsson) L.; m. Janyce B. Hill, June 25, 1960; children: James Walter, John Gardner III. BS, U. So. Calif., L.A., 1950, MBA, 1960. Account rep. Kerr & Bell Investments, L.A., 1950-51; salesman, v.p. mktg. Am. Mineral Spirits Co., Western, L.A., 1951-69; regional mgr. Union Oil Co., Amsco div., L.A., 1969-71; pres. Angeles Chem., Santa Fe Springs, Calif., 1971—; bd. dirs. Angeles Chem., Santa Fe Springs. Mem. Nat. Assn. Chem. Distbrs., Nat. Assn. Paint Mfrs., Balboa Yacht Club. Republican. Home: 20449 E Rancho Los Cerritos Rd Covina CA 91724-3528 Office: Angeles Chem Co Inc 8915 Sorensen Ave Santa Fe Springs CA 90670-2660

LOCKETT, PETER PAUL, accounting educator; b. Berkeley, Calif., Aug. 3, 1932; s. Frank Phillips and Gladys Elizabeth (Buechner) L.; m. Marie Barker Johns, July 8, 1989. BS, U. Calif., Berkeley, 1954; M Acctg., U. So. Calif., 1958, D Bus. Adminstrn., 1973. CPA, Calif. Staff acct. Haskins & Sells, San Francisco, 1958-61; chief fin. officer Fruitvale Canning Co., Oakland, Calif., 1961-66, Fabricated Metals Co., San Leandro, Calif., 1966-68; asst. prof. acctg. Calif. State U., L.A., 1968-73; assoc. prof. Calif. State U., 1973-77, prof. acctg., 1977—. Contbr. articles to profl. jours. 1st lt. fin. corps, U.S. Army, 1954-56. Mem. AICPA, Am. Acctg. Assn. Republican. Home: 1150 Volante Dr Arcadia CA 91007-6054 Office: Calif State U LA 5151 State University Dr Los Angeles CA 90032-4221

LOCKHART, ANDREW GLEN, computer industry professional; b. London, Mar. 8, 1961; came to U.S., 1987; s. Thomas Glen Lockhart and Kay Lenore (Hammarstrom) Wiewel. BEE, U. B.C., Vancouver, Can., 1984; MBA, Stanford U., 1989. Engr. Develcon Electronics, Saskatoon, Can., 1984-85; NASA program mgr. Develcon Electronics, Cape Canaveral, Fla., 1985-86; tech. support mgr. Develcon Electronics, Saskatoon, 1986-87; internat. mktg. mgr. Cisco Systems, Inc., Menlo Park, Calif., 1989-90; Japan country mgr. Cisco Systems, Inc., Tokyo, 1990—. Mem. Stanford U. Alumni Assn. Home: 66 Toledo Way San Francisco CA 94123 Office: Cisco Systems Inc 1525 O'Brien Dr Menlo Park CA 94025

LOCKHART, KENNETH BURTON, architectural company executive; b. Charles City, Iowa, Oct. 2, 1916; s. Louis James and Dorothy Hildred (Hurst) L.; m. Mary Francis Coan, July 10, 1945 (div.): children: Brian, Leslie; m. Susan Jacobs, Sept. 27, 1964. Project adminstr. Fla. So. Coll., Lakeland, 1946-50; farm mgr. Frank Lloyd Wright Found., Spring Green, Wis., 1951-52, mem. staff, 1952-62; dir. quality assurance Taliesin Assoc. Architects, Spring Green and Scottsdale, Ariz., 1963—. Fellow Constrn.

Specifications Inst. (cert. constrn. specifier, chmn. regulatory tech. 1983—, spectext com. 1986-88, bd. dirs. Phoenix chpt. 1985-86, 89, 90, sec. Phoenix chpt. 1986-88, Hon. Mention 1982, 83, 86, 87, 89, 90, 91, Honor award 1984, 89, S.W. region Dir.'s Citation 1986, Outstanding Profl. award 1986, chpt. pres.'s cert. 1987, 88, 89, 90, Tech. Commendation award 1990). Home and Office: Frank Lloyd Wright Found 13201 N 108th St Scottsdale AZ 85259-1100

LOCKWOOD, GEORGE SHELLINGTON, business executive, management consultant; b. Chgo., Apr. 2, 1935; s. George Shellington and Genevieve (Tiffany) L.; m. Marcia Whitney Miller Lockwood, June 21, 1958; children: George Shellington III, Andrew Whitney, Catherine Ann, Susan Elizabeth. BS in Civil Engring., Northwestern U., Evanston, Ill., 1958; MBA, Harvard Grad. Sch. Bus. Admin., Cambridge, Mass., 1960; LHD, Ch. Div. Sch. of Pacific, Berkeley, Calif., 1983. Vp. and gen. mgr. Perini Electronics Corp., San Mateo, Calif., 1960-63; mgr. of spl. projects Global Marine Inc., L.A., 1963-67; pres. and founder Monterey Kelp Corp., Monterey, Calif., 1967-70; land developer pvt. practice, Carmel Valley, Calif., 1970-75; gen. partner and founder Monterey Abalone Farms, Monterey, Calif., 1975-84; founder, pres., and chief exec. officer Ocean Farms of Hawaii, Inc., Kailua-Kona, Hawaii, 1984-90; dir., pres. World Aquaculture Soc.; dir., pres., chmn. Calif. Aquaculture Assn.; mem. Gov. Adv. Com. on Aquaculture, Hawaii; cons., 1967—; agriculturist. Contbr. articles to profl. jours.; Author: Fire in Kealakekua, Some Causes and Consequences of Declining Innovation, 1978; inventor: Aquaculture, Marine Engring., Electronics. Mem. exec. coun. Episc. Ch., N.Y.C.; v.p., dir., fouder Hospice of Kona; trustee, chmn. Ch. Div. Sch. of Pacific; dep. and legis. com. chmn. Gen. Conv. of Episc. Ch., 1976—; mem., com. chmn. Adv. Com. Fed. Policy on Indsl. Innovation U.S. Govt. Recipient Small Bus. Innovation Advocate of Yr. Pres. Jimmy Carter, 1981. Mem. Pacific Club Honolulu, Harvard Bus. Sch. Club San Francisco, Harvard Club N.Y., L.A. Athletic Club, World Aquaculture Soc. Republican. Episcopalian. Home: PO Box 345 Carmel Valley CA 93924-0345

LOCKWOOD, JEFFREY ALAN, entomologist; b. Manchester, Conn., Mar. 9, 1960; s. Grant John and Margaret Mary (Althaus) L.; m. Nancy Kay Fosnaugh, June 12, 1982; children: Erin Kay, Ethan John. BS, N.Mex. Tech., 1982; PhD, La. State U., 1985. Alumni fellow La. State U., Baton Rouge, 1982-85, postdoctoral assoc., 1985-86; asst. prof. U. Wyo., Laramie, 1986-91, assoc. prof., 1991—; senator, mem. U. Wyo. Faculty Senate Exec. Com., Laramie, 1990-92; cons. in field; subject editor Jour. Agrl. Entomology, 1991-92. Contbr. over 100 articles, abstracts and tech. reports to profl. jours.; contbr. 2 chpts. to books. Mem., co-pres. Unit-Univ. Fellowship, Laramie, 1986-92; mem., bd. dirs. Unitarian-Universalist Ch., Baton Rouge, 1982-86. Recipient Brown medal N.Mex. Tech., 1982, P. Schilling/L.D. Newsom award Coll. Agriculture, La. State U., 1986, 87, Ellbogen award U. Wyo., 1993; Alumni fellow La. State U., 1982-85. Mem. Entomol. Soc. of Am., Orthopterists' Soc. (bd. govs.), Ctrl. States Entomol. Soc., Ga. Entomol. Soc., S.C. Entomol. Soc. (subject editor 1991-92), Sigma Xi (pres. 1991-92). Unitarian-Universalist. Office: Univ of Wyoming Dept Plant, Soil & Insects Laramie WY 82071

LODGE, EDWARD J., district judge; b. 1933. BS cum laude, Coll. Idaho, 1957; LLB, U. Idaho, 1961. Mem. firm Smith & Miller, 1962-63; probate judge Canyon County, Idaho, 1963-65; judge Idaho State Dist. Ct., 1965-88; U.S. bankruptcy judge State of Idaho, 1988; dist. judge U.S. Dist. Ct. Idaho, 1989—. Recipient Kramer award for excellence in jud. adminstrn.; named three time All-Am., Disting. Alumnus Coll. Idaho; named to Charter Mem. Hall of Fame Boise State. Mem. ABA, Idaho Trial Lawyer Assn., Idaho State Bar Assn., Idaho Dist. Judges Assn., U.S. Bankruptcy Judges Assn., Boise State Athletic Assn., Elks Club. Office: US Dist Ct PO Box 040 550 W Fort St Boise ID 83724

LOEB, JOYCE LICHTGARN, interior designer, civic worker; b. Portland, Oreg., May 20, 1936; d. Elias Lichtgarn and Sylvia Amy (Margulies) Freedman; m. Stanley Robinson Loeb, Aug. 14, 1960; children: Carl Eli, Eric Adam. Student U. Calif.-Berkeley, 1954-56; BS, Lewis and Clark Coll., 1958; postgrad. art and architecture, Portland State U., 1976. Tchr. art David Douglas Sch. Dist., Portland, 1958-59, 61-64; tchr., chmn. art dept. Grant Union High Sch. Dist., Sacramento, 1959-60; designer, pres. Joyce Loeb Interior Design, Inc., Portland, 1976—; cons. designer to various developers of health care facilities. Chairperson fundraisers for civic orgns. and Jewish orgns.; mem. women's com. Reed Coll.; bd. dirs., mem. exec. com. Inst. Judaic Studies, 1989-92; bd. dirs. Met. Family Svc., Portland, 1968-71, Young Audiences, Inc., Portland, 1970-76, 78-80, Portland Opera Assn., 1978-84, Arts Celebration, Inc., Portland, 1984—, Susan B. Kommer Breast Cancer Rsch. Fedn., 1992—; chmn. Artquake Festival, 1985, Operaball, 1987, Children's Charity Ball Com., 1989, Women's Bd. Jewish Fedn. Portland, 1993—; dir. Oreg. Children's Theatre, 1992—; v.p. Beth Israel Sisterhood, 1981-83; bd. dirs., trustee Congregation Beth Israel, 1986-92, chmn. art interior design com.; trustee Robison Home, 1990—. Mem. Am. Soc. Interior Design (allied, bd. dirs. 1993—), Nat. Coun. Jewish Women, Multnomah Athletic Club. Democrat. Home: 1546 SW Upland Dr Portland OR 97221-2651

LOEB, MARVIN PHILLIP, entrepreneur; b. Chgo., Sept. 20, 1926; s. Jacob M. and Goldie (Schloss) L.; m. Rhoda M. Finck, Aug. 5, 1950; children: Jacqueline A., Marcia H., Wendy J., Alan. E. BS in Chemistry and Math., U. Ill., 1948; DSc, Pacific State U., 1991. Pres. Tello Corp., Chgo., 1948-62, Mayflower Investors Inc., Chgo., 1962-65, Progressive Fin. Corp., Chgo., 1966-68, Medequip Corp., Chgo., 1969-70; chmn. Telemed Corp, Chgo., 1969-70; pres. Mediclinic Corp., Chgo., 1971—, Loeb & Co., Torrance, Calif., 1965—; chmn. Trimedyne Inc., Tustin, Calif., 1978—, Pharmatec Inc., Gainesville, Fla., 1980-92, Gynex Inc., Deerfield, Ill., 1986-92, Automedix Scis. Inc., Torrance, 1986—; vice chmn. Petrogen Inc., Arlington Heights, Ill., 1981-92; chmn. Cardiomedics Inc., Torrance, 1986—, Xtramedics Inc., Deerfield, 1986—, Ultramedics Inc., Irvine, Calif., 1988-92, Contracap Inc., Deerfield, 1988—. Inventor in field. Served with U.S. Navy, 1944-46. Mem. AAAS, N.Y. Acad. Scis., Internat. Soc. for Artificial Organs, Am. Heart Assn., Am. Diabetes Assn. Office: Loeb & Co 2801 Barranca Pky Irvine CA 92714-5143

LOEBL, JAMES DAVID, lawyer; b. Chgo., July 4, 1927; s. Jerrold and Ruth Diana (Weil) L.; m. Joan Dorothy Hirsch, Apr. 8, 1960; children: Jeffrey, Susan Loebl Grasso, Ellen. AB, Princeton U., 1948; postgrad., U. Chgo., 1948-49; LLB, Stanford U., 1952. Bar: Calif. 1953, U.S. Dist. Ct. (no. and cen. dists.) Calif. 1953, U.S. Ct. Appeals (9th cir.) 1953, U.S. Supreme Ct. 1959, U.S. Dist. Ct. (so. dist.) Calif. 1987. Ptnr. Willard & Loebl, 1963-64; dep. atty. gen. Calif. Dept. of Justice, 1953-58; dir. Calif. Dept. Profl. and Vocat. Standards, Ventura, 1961-63; ptnr. Willard & Loebl, Ventura, 1963-64, Loebl, Bringgold & Peck, Ventura, 1964-76, Loebl, Bringgold, Peck & Parker, Ventura, 1976-80, Loebl & Parker, Ventura, Calif., 1993—, Loebl, Parker, Murphy & Nelson, Ventura, Calif., 1981-87, Loebl, Parker & Nelson, Ventura, Calif., 1987-93; of counsel Muegenburg, Norman & Dowler, Ventura, 1993—. Elected mayor City of Ojai, Calif., 1972-75, 86-87, 91-92, elected councilman, 1968—. Lt. comdr. USCGR, 1964-74. Fellow Am. Bar Found.; mem. Fed. Bar Assn., State Bar of Calif., Ill. State Bar Assn., Ventura County Bar Assn. (pres. 1983), L.A. County Bar Assn. Office: Muegenburg Norman & Dowler 840 County Square Dr Ventura CA 93003-5406

LOEFFLER, CARL EUGENE, artist, art administrator; b. Cleve., Nov. 14, 1946; s. Charles B. and Lottie (Kalstrom) L.; m. Nina M. Hoyning, Feb. 3, 1992. BA in Art, Calif. State U., Hayward, 1973. Exec. dir. Artcom, San Francisco, 1975-91; project dir. virtual reality Carnegie Mellon U., Pitts., 1991—. Author: Performance Anthology, 1980, Virtual Realities, 1993; editor Leonardo mag., 1991. Critics fellow NEA, 1980, Artists fellow, 1980. Home: PO Box 193123 Rincon San Francisco CA 94119 Office: Carnegie Mellon U Art Com 70 12th St San Francisco CA 94103

LOEHWING, RUDI CHARLES, JR., radio broadcasting executive; b. Newark, July 26, 1957; s. Rudy Charles Sr. and Joan Marie (Bell) L.; m. Claire Popham, Sept. 4, 1987; children: Aspasia Joyce, Tesia Victoria; children from previous marriage: Rudi Douglas, Anna Marie, Samantha Diane, Ian Ryan. Student, Biscayne U., 1975, Seton Hall U., 1977, Hubbard Acad., 1980. Announcer radio sta. WHBI FM, N.Y.C., 1970-71; producer Am. Culture Entertainment, Belleville, N.J., 1973-74; exec. producer Am. Culture Entertainment, Hollywood, Calif., 1988-90, Broadcaster's Network Internat., Hollywood, U.K., 1989-92; v.p. pub. rels. The Dohering Co., Hollywood, Calif., 1991-93; pub. rels. dir. The Dohring Co.; acct. exec. Michael Baybak & Co., Inc., Beverly Hills Calif., 1989—; dir. 1st Break, Hollywood and Eng., 1988—. Author: Growing Pains, 1970; exec. producer TV documentaries and comml. advertisements, 1983; patentee in field. Devel. dir. Tricentennial Found., Washington, 1989-90; dir. Just Say No to Drugs, L.A., 1983. Named Youngest Comml. Radio Producer and Announcer for State of N.Y., Broadcaster's Network Internat., 1972. Mem. Broadcaster's Network Assn. (bd. dirs. 1977—). Office: Broadcasters' Network Internat Ltd 3250 Wilshire Blvd # 900 Los Angeles CA 90010-1515

LOEN, ERNEST LEON, management consultant; b. Novisad, Yugoslavia, May 1, 1914; s. Leon J. and Celestine (Guszek) L.; m. Elisabeth Frances Gausz, 1936 (div. 1972); 1 child, Claire Frances; m. Carmen Estrella, 1988. Degree, Econs. & Mgmt. Coll., Vienna, Austria, 1933, Econ. Coll., Yugoslav Army, Sarajevo, 1936; postgrad., U. So. Calif., 1939. Underwriter Yugoslavija Fin. & Ins. Corp., 1935-36, branch mgr. co., 1936-37, dir., 1937-38; econ. & mgmt. investigator Yugoslavija Fin. & Ins. Corp., Mexico City, 1939; mgmt. cons. Yugoslavija Fin. & Ins. Corp., 1940; pres. Holcraft Corp., 1943-47; dir. Clary Corp., 1949-50, Wells Ind., 1959-60; pres. Ernest L. Loen & Assoc., 1960—; lectr. UCLA Grad. Sch. of Eng., 1962-83; dir. Claims Mgmt. Corp., 1974-77, Phycon. Internat., 1978-81. mem. com. Pres. Eisenhowers Com. on Tech. & Distbn. Rsch.. Mem. The L.A. Club (Emeritus). Home: 1496 Corte Hacienda Upland CA 91786 Office: Ernest L Loen & Assoc 517 North Mountain Ste 242 Upland CA 91786

LOETE, STEVEN DONALD, pilot; b. Tacoma, Aug. 21, 1959; s. Donald Kenneth and Ida Lorraine (Buck) L.; m. Kimberly Kay Estes, July 19, 1992; 1 child, Samantha. BA, Pacific Luth. U., 1984. Pilot contracting office USAF, Williams AFB, Ariz., 1985; flight instr. Clover Park Tech. Coll., Tacoma, 1986; charter pilot Stellar Exec., Chandler, Ariz., 1986-87; pilot, airline capt. Maui Airlines, Guam, 1987; airline capt. Westair Airlines, Fresno, Calif., 1987—. Contbr. Save the Children, 1988-90; mem. Angel Flight, U. Puget Sound, 1981-83; bd. dirs. aviation adv. com. Clover Park Tech. Coll., 1991—. 1st lt. USAF, 1983-93. Mem. Airline Pilots Assn. (chmn. organizing com. 1989, chmn. coun. 1989-91). Republican. Methodist. Home and Office: 6102 84th Ave Ct W Tacoma WA 98467

LOEW, DAVID N., insurance brokerage executive; b. Santa Monica, Calif., May 20, 1949; s. Marcus and Ethel L.; m. Fran, Aug. 29, 1970; children: Jeremy, Kevin, Sarah, Matthew. BS in Mkgt., San Jose State Coll.; MBA, Calif. State U., San Jose. CLU, Chartered Fin. Cons. Pres. Loew & Assocs., L.A., 1974—; Speaker in field; instr. mktg. Calif. State U., San Jose. Past pres., bd. mem. Bay Cities Jewish Community Ctr.; bd. dirs. Jewish Community Ctrs. Assn.; personnel grievance com., Jewish Fedn., Council of Greater L.A.; vol. Jewish Big Brothers, 1976-81; pres. adv. coun., trustee Jewish Community Found.; cons. Jewish Fedn. Council Personnel benefits subcom., pension adminstrn. subcom., cafeteria benefits com.; bd. dirs. Southern Calif. Golf Assn.; trustee So. Calif. Arthritis Found. Recipient Rabbi Edgar F. Magnin Svc. award, 1988, Outstanding Achievement award, Jewish Big Bros., 1981. Mem. Million Dollar Round Table (life, top of the table com.). Office: Loew & Assocs 3130 Wilshire Blvd 6th Fl Santa Monica CA 90403

LOEWENSTEIN, WALTER BERNARD, nuclear power technologist; b. Gensungen, Hesse, Germany, Dec. 23, 1926; came to U.S., 1938; s. Louis and Johanna ((Katz) L.; m. Lenore C. Pearlman, June 21, 1959; children: Mark Victor, Marcia Beth. BS, U. Puget Sound, 1949; postgrad., U. Wash., 1949-50; PhD, Ohio State U., 1954. Registered profl. engr., Calif. Rsch. asst., fellow Ohio State U., Columbus, 1951-54; rsch. asst. Los Alamos Nat. Lab., 1952-54; sr. physicist, div. dir. Argonne (Ill.) Nat. Lab., 1954-73; dept. dir., dep. div. dir. Electric Power Rsch. Inst., Palo Alto, Calif., 1973-89, profl. cons., 1989—, mem. large aerosol containment experiment project bd., 1983-87; mem. Marviksen project bd. Studsvik Rsch. Ctr., Stockholm, 1978-85; mem. LOFT project bd. Nuclear Energy Agy., Paris, 1982-89; mem. tech. adv. nuclear safety Ontario Hydro Corp., 1990—; mem. nuclear engring. dept. adv. com. Brookhaven Nat. Lab., 1992—. With USNR, 1945-46. Recipient Alumnus Cum Laude award U. Puget Sound, 1976. Fellow Am. Phys. Soc., Am. Nuclear Soc. (v.p., pres. 1988-90); mem. Am. Assn. Engring. Socs. (sec., treas. 1990), Nat. Acad. Engring. Jewish. Home and Office: 515 Jefferson Dr Palo Alto CA 94303

LOEWINSOHN, RON(ALD) WILLIAM, English educator, writer; b. Iloilo, Philippines, Dec. 15, 1937; came to U.S., 1945; s. Louis Loewinsohn and Carmen Pilar (Baugh) Gutierrez; m. Dona Budd, Dec. 14, 1986; children: Joseph, William, Stephen. BA, U. Calif., Berkeley, 1967; AM, Harvard U., 1969, PhD, 1971. Prof. U. Calif., Berkeley, 1970—. Author: (novel) Magnetic Field(s), 1983 (Nat. Book Circle award nomination 1983, Bay Area Book Reviewers award 1984), paperback edit., 1984, Where All Ladders Start, 1987, Magnetfeld(ER), German edit., 1988; author poems. Recipient Poets Found. award, 1963; U. Calif. scholar, 1967; Woodrow Wilson Found. fellow, 1967-68, Danforth Found. fellow, 1967-70, Harvard U. fellow, 1967-70, NEA fellow, 1979, 86, U. Calif. fellow, 1983, Guggenheim fellow, 1984-85. Office: U Calif Dept English Berkeley CA 94720

LOEWUS, MARY WALZ, retired biochemist; b. Duluth, Minn., Feb. 15, 1923; d. Ivan George and Mary Ellen (McLennan) Walz; m. Frank Abel Loewus, Dec. 26, 1947; children: Rebecca Ruth, David Ivan, Daniel. BA, U. Minn., 1945, MSA, 1950, PhD, 1953. Teaching asst. biochemistry U. Minn., St. Paul, 1946-51; jr. rsch. biochemist U. Calif., Berkeley, 1956-58, jr. rsch. biochemist Kearney Found. soils, 1958-63, postgrad. rsch. asst. genetics, 1963-64; rsch. assoc. biology SUNY, Buffalo, 1965-75; rsch. assoc. dept. agrl. chemistry Wash. State U., Pullman, 1975-80; rsch. assoc. Inst. Biol. Chemistry, Wash. State U., Pullman, 1980-81, assoc. scientist, 1981-90; ret.; vis. prof. botany U. Nijmegen, the Netherlands, 1976. Contbr. articles to profl. jours. Pres. Pullman-Moscow Jewish Community, 1978-80, treas., 1986-90. NSF grantee, 1965-67. Mem. Am. Soc. Biol. Chemists, Assn. Faculty Women. Home: 1700 NE Upper Dr Pullman WA 99163-4624

LOEWY, KATHY, social worker, therapist; b. Logan, Utah, Mar. 27, 1948; d. Roy and Donna Cook; m. James Loewy, May 22, 1969; children: Krystal, Steve. BS in Psychology, U. Utah, 1986, MSW, 1988. Lic. and cert. clin. social worker. Adminstrv. asst. U. Utah, Salt Lake City, 1984-88; social work intern Youth Svcs. Ctr., Salt Lake City, 1987; P.A.T. clinician Olympus View Hosp., Salt Lake City, 1988-89; social work intern LDS Social Svcs. Sandy, Sandy, Utah, 1988, contract social worker, 1988-93; svcs. dir., social worker Nat. Multiple Sclerosis Soc., Salt Lake City, 1991—, dir. program svcs., 1991-92. Vol. U. Utah Sch. on Alcohol & Drug Abuse, Salt Lake City, 1985-87; vol. speaker local sch. dist., 1988—; women's conf. speaker LDS Ch., American Fork, Utah, 1988; edn. support group leader various chs., Salt Lake City, 1987-88. Mem. NASW, Assn. Mormon Counselors and Psychotherapists, Golden Key, Phi Kappa Phi, Psi Chi, Phi Eta Sigma. Democrat. Mem. LDS Ch. Office: LDS Social Svcs 625 East 8400 South Sandy UT 84070

LOEWY, MICHAEL I, psychologist; b. L.A., July 24, 1952; s. Bert. M.N. and June F. (Rubenstein) L.; 1 child, Hannah Jean Loewy. BA, U. Nev., 1986; MA, U. Calif., Santa Barbara, 1989, postgrad., 1991—. Intern in psychology Camarillo (Calif.) St. Hosp. and Devel. Ctr., 1991-92; coord. AIDS and sexual health svcs. Student Health Svc. U. Calif., Santa Barbara, 1992—; psychol. asst. Ventura County Mental Health, Oxnard, Calif., 1992. Founder, mem. AIDS Coalition to Unleash Power, Santa Barbara, 1990—; founder, pres. Lesbian & Gay Acad. Union, U. Nev., Las Vegas, 1983-86; bd. dirs. Greater Santa Barbara Community Assn., 1988-91, Desert Mountain States Lesbian & Gay Conf., 1986-87. Mem. APA, Am. Counseling Assn., Calif. Psychol. Assn., Nat. Orgn. Men Against Sexism, Nat. Assn. to Advance Fat Acceptance (founder, coord. mental health profls. group 1992). Democrat. Jewish. Home: 794 Cypress Walk Apt C Goleta CA 93117

LOFGREN, CHARLES AUGUSTIN, legal-constitutional historian; b. Missoula, Mont., Sept. 8, 1939; s. Cornelius Willard and Helen Mary (Augustin) L.; m. Jennifer Jenkins Wood, Aug. 6, 1986. A.B. with great distinction, Stanford U., 1961, A.M., 1962, Ph.D., 1966. Instr. history San Jose State Coll., 1965-66; asst. prof. Claremont McKenna Coll., 1966-71, assoc. prof., 1971-76, prof., 1976—, Roy P. Crocker prof. Am. history and politics, 1976—. Served with USAR, 1957-63. Mem. Am. Soc. Legal History, Orgn. Am. Historians, Am. Hist. Assn. Republican. Roman Catholic. Author: Government from Reflection and Choice, 1986, The Plessy Case, 1988; contbr. articles to profl. jours. Office: Claremont McKenna Coll Dept History 850 Columbia Ave Claremont CA 91711

LOFGREN, HOLLI ANN, human resources specialist; b. Seattle, July 14, 1957. Grad. high sch., Snoqualmie, Wash. Pers./adminstrn. mgr. Roberts & Shefelman (now Foster, Pepper & Shefelman), Seattle, 1978-88; adminstr. Phillips & Wilson, Seattle, 1988-92; human resources dir. Heller Ehrman White & McAuliffe, Seattle, 1992—. Mem. Assn. Women in Computing, Assn. Legal Adminstrn., Puget Sound Assn. Legal Adminstrs. Office: Heller Ehrman White & McAuliffe 701 5th Ave # 6100 Seattle WA 98104

LOFTHOUSE, RUSS WILBERT, school administrator; b. Chgo., Jan. 21, 1945; s. Russell Wilber and Anne Marie (Daker) L.; m. Pamlin I. Axelson, Aug. 7, 1976; one child, James. BA in Elem. Edn., U. Denver, 1971; MA in Elem. Edn., U. Colo., Denver, 1978. Cert. elem tchr., Colo., elem. prin., Colo. Tchr. Cherry Creek Schs., Englewood, Colo., 1971-86, prin., 1986—; mem. adv. bd. Teaching and Computers, N.Y.C., 1986—. Recipient Disting. Tchr. award Cherry Creek Schs., 1985; named Colo. Tchr. of Yr., Colo. Dept. Edn., 1986; runner-up Nat. Tchr. of Yr., 1986. Mem. Assn. Supervision and Curriculum Devel., Am. Acad. and Inst. Human Reason (dir. community leaders and succesful schs.), Fulbrite Tchrs. Alumni Assn., NEA, Nat. State Tchs. of Yr., Phi Delta Kappa. Home and Office: 8505 E Temple Dr # 502 Denver CO 80237-2545

LOFTUS, THOMAS DANIEL, lawyer; b. Seattle, Nov. 8, 1930; s. Glendon Francis and Martha Helen (Wall) L. BA, U. Wash., 1952, JD, 1957. Bar: Wash. 1958, U.S. Ct. Appeals (9th cir.) 1958, U.S. Dist. Ct. Wash. 1958, U.S. Ct. Mil. Appeals 1964, U.S. Supreme Ct. 1964. Trial atty. Northwestern Mut. Ins. Co., Seattle, 1958-62; sr. trial atty. Unigard Security Ins. Co., Seattle, 1962-68, asst. gen. counsel, 1969-83, govt. rels. counsel, 1983-89; of counsel Groshong, LeHet & Thornton, 1990—; mem. Wash. Commn. on Jud. Conduct (formerly Jud. Qualifications Commn.), 1982-88, vice-chmn., 1987-88; judge pro tem Seattle Mcpl. Ct., 1973-81; mem. nat. panel of mediators Arbitration Forums, Inc., 1990—. Sec., treas. Seattle Opera Assn., 1980-91; pres., bd. dirs. Vis. Nurse Svcs., 1979-88; pres., v.p. Salvation Army Adult Rehab. Ctr., 1979-86; nat. committeeman Wash. Young Rep. Fedn., 1961-63, vice chmn., 1963-65; pres. Young Reps. King County, 1962-63; bd. dirs. Seattle Seafair, Inc., 1975; bd. dirs., gen. counsel Wash. Ins. Coun., 1984-86, sec., 1986-88, v.p., 1988-90; bd. dirs. Arson Alarm Found., 1987-90; bd. visitors law sch. U. Wash., 1993—. 1st lt. U.S. Army, 1952-54, col. Res., 1954-85. Fellow Am. Bar Found.; mem. Am. Arbitration Assn. (nat. panel arbitrators 1965—), Am. Arbitration Forums, Inc (nat. panel arbitrators 1992), Wash. Bar Assn. (gov. 1981-84), Seattle King County Bar Assn. (sec., trustee 1977-82), ABA (ho. of dels. 1984-90), Internat. Assn. Ins. Counsel, U.S. People to People (del. Moscow internat. law-econ. conf. 1990), Def. Rsch. Inst., Wash. Def. Trial Lawyers Assn., Wash. State Trial Lawyers Assn., Am. Judicature Soc., Res. Officers Assn., Judge Advocate General's Assn., U. Wash. Alumni Assn., Coll. Club Seattle, Wash. Athletic Club, Masons, Shriners, Pi Sigma Alpha, Delta Sigma Rho, Phi Delta Phi, Theta Delta Chi. Republican. Presbyterian. Home: 3515 Magnolia Blvd W Seattle WA 98199-1841 Office: 2133 3d Ave Seattle WA 98121

LOGAN, CHARLES IRA, pilot; b. Ontario, Oreg., July 24, 1942; s. Harry C. and Nellie Opal (Kenward) L.; m. Diane L. Atkinson, Oct. 12, 1989; 1 child, Astrid Atkinson-Logan. DC-8 capt. Evergreen Internat. Airlines, McManville, Oreg., 1989—; asst. chief flight instr. Ontario Flight Svc., 1990—. Mem. Quiet Birdmen, Stud Buzzard from Far Ridge, Airplane Owners and Pilots Assn. Air Safety Found.

LOGAN, JAMES SCOTT, planner; b. Stanford, Ky., June 18, 1948; s. James M.H. and Lillian Elizabeth (Givens) L.; m. Rose Marie Helm, Aug. 31, 1968; children: James Matthew, Tasha Marie. AA, Columbia (Mo.) Coll., 1990, BS/BA cum laude, 1992; postgrad., U. Colo., 1992—. Unit adminstr. USAR, Lakewood, Colo., 1972-82; continuity of govt. planner Fed. Emergency Mgmt. Agy. Region VIII, Lakewood, 1983-90, tech. hazards program specialist, 1991—; exercise planning co-dir. Fed. Emergency Mgmt. Agy. Region VIII, Denver, 1992—, co-dir. tead exercise, 1992—, CSEPP program mgr. Colo., 1991—, CSEPP program mgr. Utah, 1991—. Mem. NAACP, Denver, 1992; mem. NCOA NCO Assn., Devner, 1979—. With U.S. Army, 1968-71, Vietnam, USAR, 1973—. Decorated Meritorious Svc. medal. Mem. VFW, Am. Legion. Democrat. Baptist. Home: 16952 E Bates Ave Aurora CO 80013-2242 Office: FEMA Region VIII Bldg 710A PO Box 25267 Denver CO 80225-0267

LOGAN, LEE ROBERT, orthodontist; b. Los Angeles, June 24, 1923; s. Melvin Duncan and Margaret (Seltzer) L.; m. Maxine Nadler, June 20, 1975; children: Fritz, Dean, Scott, Gigi, Chad, Casey. BS, UCLA, 1952; DDS, Northwestern U., 1956, MS, 1961. Diplomate Am. Bd. Orthodontics. Gen. practice dentistry, Reseda, Calif., 1958-59; practice dentistry specializing in orthodontics, Northridge, Calif., 1961—; pres. Lee R. Logan DDS Profl. Corp.; mem. med. staff Northridge Hosp., Tarzana Hosp.; owner Maxine's Prodn. Co.; owner Maxine's Talent Agency; guest lectr. UCLA, U. So. Calif., dir dental edn. Northridge Med. Ctr. Contbr. articles to profl. jours. Served to lt. USNR, 1956-58. Named (with wife) Couple of Yr. Autistic Children Assn., 1986; recipient Nat. Philanthropy award, 1987, 1st Pl. winner Austistic Jobathon, 1981-93, 1st Pl. winner Best Treated Orthodontic Cases So. Calif., 1990. Fellow Internat. Acad. Nutrition; mem. Am., San Fernando Valley Dental Assn. (chmn. edn., treas.), Am. Assn. Orthodontists, Pacific Coast Soc. Orthodontists (dir., pres. so. sect. 1974-75, chmn. membership 1981-83), Found. Orthodontic Research (charter mem.), Calif. Soc. Orthodontists (chmn. peer rev. 1982-93), G.V. Black Soc. (charter mem.), Angle Soc. Orthodontists (pres. 1981-82, bd. dirs. 1982-93, nat. pres. 1985-87, dir. 1985—), U. S.C. Century Fraternity, Xi Psi Phi. Home: 4830 Encino Ave Encino CA 91316-3813 Office: 18250 Roscoe Blvd Northridge CA 91325

LOGAN, ROBERT F. B., banker; b. 1932. Formerly pres., chief exec. officer Alexander Hamilton Life Ins. Co. of Am.; sr. exec. v.p. Valley Nat. Bank of Ariz., 1989-90, pres., chief oper. officer, 1990—; pres., chief oper. officer Valley Nat. Corp., Phoenix. Office: Valley Nat Corp PO Box 71 Phoenix AZ 85001-0071*

LOGAN, VICKI LYNNE, electro-mechanical draftsperson; b. Zeeland, Mich., May 30, 1958; d. William Edward and Beverly Jean (Stillson) Ollman; m. Larry Lyn Logan, June 11, 1976; children: Roy Raymond II, Jennifer Lynn. Cert. in Mech. Drafting, Ariz. Automotive Inst., Phoenix, 1983. Electro-mech. checker drafter Collins PHX Corp., Tempe, Ariz., 1984-85; electro-mech. drafter Collins PHX Corp., Tempe, 1987-88; sec., treas. Floor Plans Etc., Inc., Prescott Valley, Ariz., 1992—. Co-author: Finding Your Needle in a Haystack: An Individual's Guide to Researching Securities, 1989. Republican. Office: Floor Plans Etc Inc PO Box 26563 Prescott Valley AZ 86312

LOGE, FRANK JEAN, II, hospital administrator; b. Redlands, Calif., May 28, 1945; s. J. Phillip Loge and Helen M. (Booker) Loge Power; m. Sharon Lee Entrekin, Feb. 11, 1967; children—Frank III, Christopher, Gregory. B.A., Claremont Men's Coll., Long Beach, Calif., 1967; M.B.A., Calif. State U.-Long Beach, 1969; postgrad., UCLA Sch. Pub. Health, 1972-73. Mgr. mgmt. analysis UCLA, 1972-73, asst. dir. fin., 1973-74; dir. fin. U. Calif. Davis Med. Ctr., Sacramento, 1975-79, dep. dir. hosp. and clinics, 1979-84, dir. hosp. and clinics, 1984—. Office: U Calif Davis Med Ctr 2315 Stockton Blvd Sacramento CA 95817-2201

LOGSDON, CHARLES ELDON, consultant; b. Mo., May 8, 1921; s. Millison and Mary Vivian (Reimenschneider) L.; m. Arloine Marie Schmidt, Aug. 20, 1948; children: Charles Louis, Onnalie Marie, John Calvert. BA, U. Kansas City, 1942; PhD, U. Minn., 1954. Rsch. assoc. U. Minn., St. Paul, 1947-50; rsch. aide U.S. Dept. Agrl., St. Paul, 1950-53; rsch. plant pathologist U.S. Dept. Agrl., Palmer, Alaska, 1953-68; prof. plant pathologist U. Alaska, Palmer, 1954-78; assoc. dir. Agrl. Exp. Sta. U. Alaska, Palmer, 1970-78; owner Agresources, Palmer, 1978-85; sec., mgr. Alaska Crop Improvement Assn., Palmer, 1953-79; owner Pleasant Green North, Palmer, 1986—; lobbyist Farmers & Stock Growers Assn., Alaska, 1984; seed analyst State of Alaska, 1987-89. Contbr. articles to profl. jours. Mem. city coun. City of Palmer, 1956-59, mayor, 1959-61; bd. trustees Valley Hosp., Palmer, 1962-70; bd. ethics MAT-SU Borough, Alaska, 1974-75; investment adv. bd. State of Alaska, 1976-78. 1st lt. U.S. Air Corps, 1940-45. Mem. Alaska Pioneers. Independent. Lutheran. Home: Box 387 Palmer AK 99645 Office: Pleasant Green North Box 387 Palmer AK 99645

LOHAFER, DOUGLAS ALLEN, health physicist; b. Cherokee, Iowa, June 7, 1949; s. Walter Jessen and Dorothy Ann (Thies) L. Student, Mankato State U., 1974-75, Mayo Sch. Health-Related Scis., Iowa State U., 1976; AA in Liberal Arts magna cum laude, Waldorf Coll., 1975; BA in Biology, Chemistry, Luther Coll., 1977, St. Olaf Coll., 1977; MS in Radiol. Health Physics, San Jose State U., 1993. Sr. satellite ops. engr. Lockheed Missiles & Space Co., Inc., Sunnyvale, Calif., 1978-87, Lockheed Tech. Ops. Co., Inc., Sunnyvale, Calif., 1987-92. Active Gideons Internat.; mem. Obsessive Compulsive Found. Mem. Calif. Acad. Scis., Nat. Eagle Scout Assn. (eagle scout 1966), Am. Chem. Soc. (assoc. Santa Clara Valley sect. 1979, div. biol. chemistry 1979, div. nuclear chemistry and tech. 1986), Health Physics Soc. (assoc. No. Calif. chpt.), Ctr. for Theology and Natural Scis., Fellowship of Confessional Lutherans, Beer Drinkers of Am., U.S. Parachute Assn., Parachutists Over Phorty Soc., N.Y. C.S. Lewis Soc., Soren Kierkegaard Soc., Phi Theta Kappa. Democrat. Lutheran. Home: 403 Los Encinos Ave San Jose CA 95134-1336

LOHMAN, LORETTA CECELIA, social scientist, consultant; b. Joliet, Ill., Sept. 25, 1944; d. John Thomas and Marjorie Mary (Brennan) L. BA in Polit. Sci., U. Denver, 1966, postgrad., 1985—; MA in Social Sci., U. No. Colo., 1975. Lectr. Ariz. State U., Tempe, 1966-67; survey researcher Merrill-Werthlin Co., Tempe, 1967-68; edn. asst. Am. Humane Assn., Denver, 1969-70; econ. cons. Lohman & Assocs., Littleton, Colo., 1971-75; rsch. assoc. Denver Rsch. Inst., 1976-86; rsch. scientist Milliken Chapman Rsch. Group, Littleton, 1986-89; owner Lohman & Assocs., Littleton, 1989—; affiliate Colo. Water Resources Rsch. Inst., Ft. Collins, Colo., 1989-91; tech. adv. com. Denver Potable Wastewater Demo Plant, 1986-90; cons. Constrn. Engrng. Rsch. Lab., 1984—; peer reviewer NSF, 1985-86, Univs. Coun. Water Resources, 1989—; WERC consortium reviewer N.Mex. Univs.-U.S. Dept. Energy, 1989—; course cons. Regis Coll., Denver, 1992—. Contbr. articles to profl. jours. Vol. Metro Water Conservation Projects, Denver, 1986-90; vol. handicapped fitness So. Suburban Parks and Recreation. Recipient Huffsmith award Denver Rsch. Inst., 1983; Nat. Ctr. for Edn. in Politics grantee, 1964-65. Mem. ASCE (social and environ. objectives com.), Am. Water Works Assn., Am. Water Resources Assn., Am. Hist. Assn., Colo. Water Congress., Water Environ. Fedn., Sigma Xi, Phi Gamma Mu, Phi Alpha Theta. Democrat. Home and Office: 3375 W Aqueduct Ave Littleton CO 80123-2903

LOHMANN, GARY BRENT, air force officer, political science; b. Farmington, N.Mex., May 26, 1951; s. Edgar Herman and Norma Irene (Evans) L.; m. Carolyn Jean Kluball, June 21, 1975; children: Cameron, Kimberly. BA, U. Northern Colo., 1973; MPA, Southwest Tex. State U., 1979; grad., Air Command and Staff Coll., 1983, Air War Coll., 1988. Adminstrn. officer 38th Organizational Maintenance Squadron, Moody AFB, Ga., 1973-76; exec. officer 3285th Sch. Squadron, Lackland AFB, Rex., 1976-78; chief base adminstrn. 6112th Air Base Wing, Misawa AB, Japan, 1978-81; asst. prof. Calif. State U., Fresno, 1983-86; chief internat. security affairs 5th Air Force, Yokota AB, Japan, 1986-89; chief internat. affairs northeast Asia HQS Pacific Air Forces, Hickam AFB, Hawaii, 1989-93. Decorated Meritorious Svc. medals, Commendation medals; recipient LeMay-Ohio award Air Force Assn., 1984, 85, Outstanding Squadron award Arnold Air Soc., 1984. Republican. Lutheran. Home: 46-271 Ikiiki St Kaneohe HI 96744 Office: HQ PACAF/XPXP Kickam AFB HI 96853

LOHR, GEORGE E., state supreme court justice; b. 1931. B.S., S.D. State U.; J.D., U. Mich. Bar: Colo. 1958, Calif. 1969. Former judge Colo. 9th Dist. Ct., Aspen; assoc. justice Colo. Supreme Ct., Denver, 1979—. Office: Supreme Ct Colo State Judicial Bldg 2 E 14th Ave Denver CO 80203

LOKEY, FRANK MARION, JR., broadcast executive, consultant; b. Ft. Worth, Oct. 15, 1924; s. Frank Marion Sr. and Corinne (Whaley) L. Student, Smith-Hughes Evening Coll., 1955-59. Asst. gen. mgr., mgr. sales, news anchor Sta. WLW-A TV (now named WXIA-TV), Atlanta, 1955-66; co-owner, gen. mgr. Sta. WAIA, Atlanta, 1960-62; S.E. news corr., talk show host CBS News N.Y., N.Y.C., 1960-66; asst. to owner, gen. mgr. Sta. WBIE-AM-FM, Atlanta, 1962-64; asst. to pres., gen. mgr. Stas. KXAB-TV, KXJB-TV, KXMB-TV, Aberdeen, Fargo, Bismarck, S.D., N.D., 1966-67; exec. v.p., gen. mgr. Sta. WEMT-TV, Bangor, Maine, 1967-70; pres., gen. mgr. Stas. KMOM-TV, KWAB-TV, Odessa-Midland, Big Spring, Tex., 1970-75; exec. v.p., gen. mgr. Sta. KMUV-TV (now named KRBK-TV), Sacramento, Calif., 1975-77; CEO Lokey Enterprises, Inc., Sacramento, L.A., El Centro, Calif., 1977—, also chmn. bd. dirs.; cons., troubleshooter 16 TV stas. nationwide, 1977—; cons., actor 5 movie prodn. cos., Hollywood, Calif., 1980—; cons., outside dir. Anderson Cons., Manhattan, L.I., N.Y., 1981—; news corr., talk show host 7 news orgns. worldwide, 1984—; bd. dirs. Broadcast Audience Behavior Rsch., Manhattan, 1986—, mem. inner circle, 1986—. Creator, originator approach to real estate mktg. Hon. mem. Imperial County Bd. Suprs., El Centro, 1986—, El Centro City Coun., 1987—. Mem. Am. Legion. Baptist. Home: 196 W McCabe Rd El Centro CA 92243 Office: Lokey Enterprises Inc 626 Main St El Centro CA 92243 also: 196 W McCabe Rd El Centro CA 92243

LOLMAUGH, SCOTT DEVERE, engineering executive; b. Ann Arbor, Mich., Nov. 17, 1955; s. Starr Devere and Marjorie Adella (Anderson) L.; m. Constance Elisa Alamat, Aug. 23, 1975; children: Jacob Scott, Katrina Charity. BS in Indsl. Engring., Ea. Mich. U., 1978. Ordained to ministry, Chrisitan Ch., 1991. Assoc. indsl. engring. Burroughs Corp., Plymouth, Mich., 1979-81; indsl. engr. Universal Elec. Co., Owosso, Mich., 1981-82; staff indsl. engr. Wavetek Ind., Inc., Beech Grove, 1982-87; sr. mfg. engr. United Med. Mfg., Indpls., 1987-90; prin. prodn. engr. Honeywell, Inc. IAC, Phoenix, 1990—; owner, CEO Soft Answers, Indpls., 1982—; tech. cons. IPC Video, Ranchos De Taos, N.Mex., 1982—. Mem. ASTM, Suface Mount Tech. Assn. (chmn. 1988-89), Internat. Soc. for Hybrid Microelectronics, Inst. of Indsl. Engrs., Am. Soc. for Quality Control, Instrument Soc. Am., Soc. of Packaging and Handling Engrs., Wavetek PC Users Group (founder, pres. 1984-87). Republican. Home: 16007 N 25th Dr Phoenix AZ 85023 Office: Honeywell Inc IAC 2222 W Peoria Ave MS D10 Phoenix AZ 85029

LOMBARD, JOHN CUTLER, lawyer; b. Berkeley, Calif., Oct. 9, 1918; s. Norman and Ellen (McKeighan) L.; m. Dorothy Brandt, July 9, 1946; children: Lawrence, John, David, Laurie. BA, Principia U., 1946; JD, Northwestern U., 1949. Assoc. Jones, Birdseye & Grey, Seattle, 1950-60; ptnr. Hamley & Lombard, Seattle, 1960-70, Day, Taylor, Lombard & Kiefer, Seattle, 1970-85; pvt. practice Seattle, 1985—; mem. com. Jud. Counsel, 1980-84. Trustee King County Mcpl. League, 1980-84. With USAF, 1941-45. Decorated D.F.C., 5 Air medals, presdl. citation. Mem. Seattle King County Bar Assn. (chmn. probate com. 1975-76, chmn. lawyer referral com. 1989-90), Rainier Club. Home: 3003 26th Ave W Seattle WA 98199-2821 Office: Lombard Law Firm 3029 One Union Square Seattle WA 98101

LOMBARDI, EUGENE PATSY, orchestra conductor, violinist, educator, recording artist; b. North Braddock, Pa., July 7, 1923; s. Nunzio C. and Mary (Roberto) L.; m. Jacqueline Sue Davis, Mar. 1955; children: Robert, Genanne. B.A., Westminster Coll., 1948; M.A., Columbia U., 1948; Edn. Specialist, George Peabody Coll., 1972; Mus.D., Westminster Coll., 1981. Band dir. Lincoln High Sch., Midland, Pa., 1948-49; orch. dir. Male High Sch., Louisville, 1949-50, Phoenix Union High Sch., 1950-57; orch. dir., prof. Ariz. State U., Tempe, 1957-89. Condr., Phoenix Symphonette, 1954-61, 70-73, Phoenix Symphony Youth Orch., 1956-66, Phoenix Pops Orch., 1971-83, asst. concertmaster, Phoenix Symphony Orch., 1950-62, concertmaster, 1962-69, asst. condr., 1967-69, mem., Newart String Quartet, 1965-89, concertmaster, Flagstaff Festival Symphony, 1967-81, Flagstaff Festival Chamber Orch., 1967-81, Phoenix Chamber Orch., 1970-83, condr., music dir., Sun City (Ariz.) Symphony Orch., 1983-87. Served with USAAF, 1943-46. Decorated Bronze Star; named Outstanding Grad. Westminster Coll., 1948; recipient Alumni Achievement award, 1976, gold medal Nat. Soc. Arts and Letters, 1973, Disting. Tchr. award Ariz. State U. Alumni, 1974, Phoenix Appreciation award, 1983. Mem. Music Educators Nat. Conf., Am. String Tchrs. Assn. (pres. Ariz. unit 1965-67), Am. Fedn. Musicians, Ariz. Music Educators Assn. (pres. higher edn. sect. 1973-75, Excellence in Teaching Music award 1989), Ind. Order Foresters, Phi Delta Kappa, Phi Mu Alpha. Republican. Presbyterian. Home: 920 E Manhatton Dr Tempe AZ 85282-5520

LOMBARDO, NICHOLAS JOHN, mining engineer; b. Pueblo, Colo., Mar. 26, 1953; s. Samuel Phillip and Rose Adeline (Petta) L.; m. Mary Kathleen Cooper, Dec. 22, 1973; 1 child, Shauna Kathleen. BA, Colo. U., Boulder, 1979. Chemist Colo. Div. Hwys., Denver, 1975-80, Hazen Rsch., Golden, Colo., 1980-83; project engr. Hazen Rsch., 1983-86, sr. engr., 1986-89, sr. metallurgist, 1989-90; v.p. ops., pres. Indsl. Compliance Tech., Golden, 1990-91, pres., 1991—. Patentee in field. Recipient Disting. Svc. Environ. award, State of Colo., Denver, 1980. Mem. Colo. Mining Assn., Nev. Mining Assn. Republican. Office: Indsl Compliance Tech 12325 W 52nd Ave Wheat Ridge CO 80033

LOMBERG, JON NORMAN, artist, designer, consultant; b. Phila., Aug. 12, 1948; s. Bernard and Lily (Vernick) L.; m. Sharona Ozery, Nov. 7, 1988; 1 child, Merav Leilani. BA, Trinity Coll., 1969. Illustrator Carl Sagan's books, 1972—; reporter, writer IDEAS Can. Broadcasting Corp., 1975-89; designer Voyager Interstellar Record NASA, 1977; chief artist Cosmos TV series Sta. KCET-TV, 1978-80; project artist Search for Extraterrestrial Intelligence NASA, 1987—, project artist curriculum project, 1991—; art dir., designer, producer Stas. WGBH-Boston, KHET-Honolulu, TBS-Atlanta, 1984—; team artist, designer Nuclear Waste Market Project Sandia Nat. Lab., 1991-92; project mgr. Martian Libr. The Planetary Soc., 1992—, sr. cons., 1981—; bd. advisors Students for the Exploration and Devel. of Space (SEDS), 1983-88. Author: Murmurs of Earth, 1978; artist: Galaxy Mural for the Nat. Air and Space Mus., Smithsonian Inst., 1992; writer, reporter: (radio documentary) Halley's Comet, 1987 (Armstrong award Columbia U. Sch. Journalism 1986); numerous artworks and illustrations for books and mags.; nuclear winter animation for TV and film (1st prize Vt. World Peace Film Festival 1985); exhbns. in maj. mus. in U.S. and Can.; science reporting for mags. and newspapers. Recipient Prime Time Emmy award, 1981. Mem. Internat. Assn. of Astron. Artists (trustee 1987—). Jewish. Home and Office: PO Box 207 Honaunau HI 96726

LOMELI, MARTA, bilingual educator; b. Tijuana, Baja Calif, Mex., Oct. 28, 1952; came to U.S. 1954; d. Jesus and Guadalupe (Ascencio) Lomeli; m. Rudolph Benitez, 1978 (div. 1982); children: Pascual Lomeli Benitez; m. David E. Miller, Aug. 16, 1991. BA, San Diego State U., 1977. With M & N Tree Nursery, Vista, Calif., 1957-70; libr. Vista Boys Club, 1969-70; vol. tutor MECHA U. Calif. San Diego, La Jolla, 1971-73; tchr. aide San Diego City Schs., 1976-77; bilingual educator National City (Calif.) Schs., 1978—; mem. restructuring com. Lincoln Acres Sch., 1991. Author numerous poems. Mem. Lincoln Acres Com. to Advise the Prin., National City, 1986-88, Com. to Advise the Supt., National City, 1986-88; art editor Lincoln Jr. High Sch., Vista, Calif., 1964-65, Third World U. Calif., San Diego, 1970-73; mem. Lincoln Acres Sch. Site Coun., 1988-89; mem. high tech. com. Nat. Sch. Dist., 1993—; vol. tchr. St. Vincent de Paul's Ctr. for Homeless, San Diego, 1991-93, Shaolin Kempo. Karate Black belt, 1st degree. Mem. Calif. Tchrs. Assn. (site rep. Nat. City 1985), Calif. Assn. Bilingual Edn. (sec. 1986), Nat. Assn. Bilingual Edn., La Raza Club (pres., co-founder 1970). Democrat. Home: 6920 Alsacia St San Diego CA 92139-2101

LOMELÍ, REFUGIO (JESSE), athletics educator; b. Aguascalientes, Mex., July 23, 1941; came to U.S., 1954, naturalized, 1965; s. J. Jesus and Maria Guadalupe (Ascencio) L.; m. Barbara L. McMinn, Aug. 24, 1968; children: Lorena, Maya, Marc. Assoc., Palomar Coll., 1962; B, U. of the Americas, Mexico City, 1965; M, San Diego State U., 1972; postgrad., U. Pitts., 1972-74. Firefighter U.S. Forest Service, So. Calif. region, 1962-66; tchr. Santana H.S., Santee, Calif., 1967-73; counselor, tchr., soccer coach Mira Costa Coll., Oceanside, Calif., 1973—. Named Community Coll. Soccer Coach of Yr., Pacific Coast Conf., 1985. Mem. Nat. Assn. Fgn. Student Advisors, Am. G.I. Forum. Lodge: KC. Home: 1250 Vista Colina Dr San Marcos CA 92069-4956 Office: Mira Costa Coll PO Box 586312 Oceanside CA 92056-6312

LONERGAN, MICHAEL HENRY, development administrator, journalist; b. Richland, Wash., Sept. 19, 1949; s. Joseph Thornberg and Gertrude (Foxen) L.; m. Cyndi Lou Kniffin, Jan. 8, 1971 (div. 1981); m. Paula Elizabeth Wallace, Jan. 8, 1983; children: Joseph, Ricardo. Student, U. Chgo., 1967-69; BA in History, U. Wash., 1979. News reporter Sta. WTRC Radio, Sta. WSJV-TV, Elkhart, Ind., 1968-71; gen. mgr. Sta. KURB, Mountlake Terrace, Wash., 1972-73; advt. rep. Enterprise Newspaper, Lynnwood, Wash., 1974-77; news dir. Sta. KBRO-AM-FM, Bremerton, Wash., 1977-78; communications rep. Motorola, Inc., Bellevue, Wash., 1980-81; radio announcer Sta. KTNT/KPMA, Tacoma, 1981-84; dir. mktg. TACCOMM, Tacoma, 1984-85; dir. community rels. The Salvation Army, Tacoma, 1985-92; dir. devel. Tacoma Rescue Mission, 1991-93, exec. dir., 1993—. Rep. candidate 6th dist. U.S. Congress, Wash., 1984. Mem. NAACP, Tacoma N.W. Gideons (pres. 1990—), Tacoma Downtown Kiwanis, Phi Beta Kappa. Mem. Christian Ch. Home: 3715 N 27th St Tacoma WA 98407 Office: Tacoma Rescue Mission PO Box 1912 1001 Pacific Ave Ste 330 Tacoma WA 98401

LONERGAN, THOMAS FRANCIS, III, criminal justice consultant; b. Bklyn., July 28, 1941; s. Thomas Francis and Katherine Josephine (Roth) L.; m. Irene L. Kaucher, Dec. 14, 1963; 1 son, Thomas F. BA, Calif. State U., Long Beach, 1966, MA, 1973; MPA, Pepperdine U., L.A., 1976; postgrad., U. So. Calif., L.A., 1976. Dep. sheriff Los Angeles County Sheriff's Dept., 1963-70; U.S. Govt. program analyst, 1968—; fgn. service officer USIA, Lima, Peru, 1970-71; dep. sheriff to lt. Los Angeles Sheriff's Office, 1971-76, aide lt. to div. chief, 1976-79; dir. Criminal Justice Cons., Downey, Calif., 1977—; cons. Public Adminstrv. Service, Chgo., 1972-75, Nat. Sheriff's Assn., 1978, 79; cons. Nat. Inst. Corrections, Washington, 1977—, coordinator jail ctr., 1981-82 ; tchr. N. Calif. Regional Criminal Justice Acad., 1977-79; lectr. Nat. Corrections Acad., 1980-83; spl. master Chancery Ct. Davidson County, Tenn., 1980-82, U.S. Dist. Ct. (no. dist.) Ohio, 1984-85, Santa Clara Superior Ct. (Calif.), 1983-89, U.S. Dist. Ct. Ga., Atlanta, 1986-87, U. S. Dist. Ct. (no. dist.) Calif., 1982—, U.S. Dist. Ct. (no. dist.) Idaho, 1986, U.S. Dist. Ct. Oreg. 1986, U.S. Dist. Ct. Portland 1987, U.S. Dist. (no. dist.) Calif. 1984-89; also ct. expert. Author: California-Past, Present & Future, 1968; Training-A Corrections Perspective, 1979; AIMS-Correctional Officer; Liability-A Correctional Perspective; Liability Law for Probation Administrators; Liability Reporter; Probation Liability Reporter; Study Guides by Aims Media. Mem. Am. Correctional Assn., Nat. Sheriff's Assn. Roman Catholic.

LONERGAN, WALLACE GUNN, economics educator, management consultant; b. Potlatch, Idaho, Mar. 18, 1928; s. Willis Gerald and Lois (Gunn) L.; m. Joan Laurie Penoyer, June 1, 1952; children: Steven Mark, Kevin James. BA, Coll. Idaho, 1950; MBA, U. Chgo., 1955, PhD, 1960. Asst. dir., asst. prof. bus. Indsl. Relations Ctr. U. Chgo., 1960-70, assoc. dir., assoc. prof., 1970-74, dir., prof., 1974-84; vis. prof. Rikkyo U., Tokyo, 1985; vis. fellow Merton Coll. Oxford (Eng.) U., 1986; chair, prof. bus., econs. divsn. Albertson Coll. Idaho, Caldwell, 1987—; v.p. Human Resources Research Cons., Chgo., 1980-87. Author: Leadership and Morale, 1960, Group Leadership, 1974, Performance Appriasal, 1978, Leadership and Management, 1979. Chmn. Episcopal Commn. on Higher Edn., Chgo., 1970-80, mgmt. com. United Way Chgo., 1982-85. 1st lt. U.S. Army, 1950-53, Korea. Named Disting. Alumni Coll. Idaho, 1962; vis. scholar Internat. Anglican Exchange, N.Y.C., 1976, Tokyo, 1986. Mem. Internat. House Japan, Internat. Indsl. Relations Research Assn., Acad. Mgmt., Rotary. Home: 812 E Linden St Caldwell ID 83605-5335 Office: Albertson Coll Idaho Bus Econs Divsn 2112 Cleveland Blvd Caldwell ID 83605-4494

LONG, AUSTIN, geosciences educator; b. Olney, Tex., Dec. 21, 1936; s. Jesse Lee and Sara Louise (Taylor) L.; m. Virginia Lee Haldeman, 1962 (div. 1976), children: Kirsten, Tonya, Lara; m. Karen Anne Long, 1976; children: Kathy, Stephanie. BA, Midwestern State U., 1957; MA, Columbia U., 1959; PhD, U. Ariz., 1966. Sr. sci. Smithsonian Institution, Washington, 1963-68; prof. U. Ariz., Tucson, 1968—. Editor Radiocarbon, 1987—. Rsch. grantee NSF, Dept. Energy, Am. Chem. Soc. Mem. Am. Geophysical Soc., Geochemical Soc. Home: 2715 E Helen St Tucson AZ 85716 Office: Univ of Arizona Geosciences Dept Tucson AZ 85721

LONG, AUSTIN RICHARD, federal agency administrator, research chemist; b. Akron, Ohio, Sept. 15, 1949; s. Aaron Lawrence and Aiko (Sasaki) L. Student, Kent (Ohio) State U., 1976-78; BS, Ohio State U., 1980, MS, 1983, PhD, 1987. Supr. Ohio Urethane Specialists, Newcomerstown, Ohio, 1972-76; shipping clk. Kroger Co., Columbus, Ohio, 1980-82; rsch. assoc. Ohio State U., Columbus, 1985-87; postdoctoral researcher La. State U., Baton Rouge, 1987-89, sr. fellow, 1989-90; dir. Animal Drug Rsch. Ctr. FDA, Denver, 1990—; Contbr. articles to profl. jours.; inventee in field. With USN, 1968-72. Burgwald fellow Ohio State U., 1982. Mem. AAAS, Am. Chem. Soc., Assn. Ofcl. Analytical Chemists, Inst. Food Technologists, Phi Tau Sigma, Gamma Sigma Delta. Office: FDA PO Box 25087 Denver CO 80225-0087

LONG, DARRELL DON EARL, computer scientist, educator; b. San Diego, Aug. 5, 1962; s. Denver Don Long and Mary Elizabeth (Williams) Coggins; m. Mary Katherine Walstrom, June 9, 1984; 1 child, William John Edgar. BS, San Diego State U., 1984; MS, U. Calif., San Diego, 1986, PhD, 1988. Lectr. math. San Diego State U., 1984-86; researcher U. Calif., San Diego, 1985-88; asst. prof. U. Calif., Santa Cruz, 1988—. Author: Theory of Finite Automata with an Introduction to Formal Languages, 1989; assoc. editor: Internat. Jour. in Computer Simulation, 1990—; contbr. articles to profl. jours. Grantee NSF, 1990-92, Office Naval Rsch., 1992—. Mem. Assn. for Computing Machinery, IEEE (exec. com. tech. com. on operating systems 1990—), Sigma Xi, Upsilon Pi Epsilon. Baptist. Office: U Calif Dept Computer Sci Santa Cruz CA 95064

LONG, DAVID ALEXANDER, small business owner; b. Portland, Oreg., Aug. 29, 1963; m. Kim Maree, Jan. 12, 1990. BS, Oreg. State U., 1985. Founder, owner Stafford Press, Kirkland, Wash., 1990—. Home: 9814 116th Pl NE Kirkland WA 98033

LONG, DONALD EUGENE, library media specialist educator; b. Clayton, Kans., June 23, 1934; s. Andrew Isidore and Regina Marie (Otter) L.; m. Beatrice Marie Hollerich, Sept. 11, 1957; children: Daniel, Mary, Dianne, Paul, Karen. BS in Edn., Kans. State Tchrs. Coll., 1960; MA in Sch. Adminstrn., U. Colo., 1970; MA in Libr. Sci., U. Colo., Denver, 1979. Tchr. Junction City (Kans.) Pub. Schs., 1958-59; elem. tchr. Jefferson County Sch. Dist. R-1, Lakewood, Colo., 1960-65, tchr. reading, 1965-72, libr., tchr., 1965-89; tech. writer, computer software cons. Crestwood Inc., Salina, Kans., 1990—; libr. media specialist tchr. Secrest Elem. Sch., Arvada, Colo., 1960-89. Co-author curriculum guides in Library Science, 1967, Science, 1969, Reading, 1971. With Army N.G., 1952-60. Mem. Phi Delta Kappa. Home and Office: 9607 W 63d Ave Arvada CO 80004

LONG, ELGEN MARION, retired airline pilot, explorer, business executive; b. McMinneville, Oreg., Aug. 12, 1927; s. Harry E. and Berniece Elsie (Tooney) L.; m. Marie Katherine Kurilich, May 12, 1946; children: Donna Marie Weiner, Harry Elgen. Student, U. Calif., L.A., 1946-47; AE, Coll. San Mateo, 1961. Radio operator Flying Tiger Line, Inc., L.A., 1947-48, navigator, 1949-50, pilot, 1951—; ptnr. Woodside Investment Co., Whalebone Music; dir. Auto-Nav., Inc.; air safety coun. FAA, 1972; hon. chmn. Powder Puff Derby, 1972. Served with USNR, 1942-46. Named First Citizen of San Mateo County, 1971; recipient World Gold Air medal Fedn. Aeronautique, 1971, Super Achievement award for practicing navigator Inst. Vav., 1971, Franklin Harris trophy, 1972, commendation Calif. State Assembly, 1971, Key to the City of San Francisco, 1971, Special award and trophy Airline Pilots Assn., 1973, Wright Bros. Meml. award Greater L.A. C. of C., 1972. Mem. Nat. Aero. Assn., Am. Polar Soc., Royal Canadian Airforce Assn., Airline Pilots Assn., Inst. Nav. (awards com.), Aircraft Owners and Pilots Assn., Coronado Cays Yacht Club, Explorer's Club. Democrat. Home: 844 Overlook Ct San Mateo CA 94403

LONG, EMMETT THADDEUS, communication educator; b. Kaufman, Tex., Dec. 31, 1923; s. Emmett Thaddeus Sr. and Ruth Eliza (Jones) L.; m. Marjorie Ruth Harris, Feb. 22, 1946; children: David Alan, Steven Harrison. BA, Pepperdine U., 1945, U. Calif., Berkeley, 1946; MA, U. Calif., Berkeley, 1948; EdD, U. So. Calif., L.A., 1965. Asst. prof. Pepperdine U., L.A., 1948-54, dir. admissions, 1954-57; admissions officer Calif. State Poly. U., Pomona, 1957-59; assoc. dean Calif. State U., Fullerton, Calif., 1959-72; assoc. dean office of chancellor Calif. State U., L.A., 1972-75; prof. Calif. State U., Fullerton, 1975-86, prof. emeritus, 1986—. Author: (legis. report) School Relations in California, 1969; editor: Liberal Studies in Communication. Parliamentarian United Ch. of Christ Conf., 1975-91. Named for Disting. Svc., Pi Kappa Delta, 1958, Articulation Conf., Calif., 1975. Mem. Calif. Faculty Assn., Univ. Club Claremont (bd. dirs. 1990-92), Phi Delta Kappa. Democrat. Home: 653 N California Dr Claremont CA 91711-4141 Office: California State U Fullerton CA 92634

LONG, JAMES HARVEY, JR., electronics executive; b. Johnson City, Tenn., Sept. 14, 1944; s. James H. and Beulah (Anderson) L.; m. Laura Stone, Nov. 25, 1988; children: Robert Michael, Christopher William. BS in Chemistry, U. Tenn., 1965, PhD in Chemistry, 1968. Rsch. chemist Shell Chem. Co., Houston, 1968-73, process mgr., 1973-77, staff engr., 1977-81, venture devel. mgr., 1981-84; supt. Shell Chem. Co., Geismar, La., 1984-86; venture mgr. Shell Chem. Co., Houston, 1986-87; v.p. Supercondr. Techs., Santa Barbara, Calif., 1987—. Mem. Am. Electronics Assn., Assn. Old Crows, Soc. Photo Optical Instrument Engrs. Office: Supercondr Techs 460 Ward Dr Ste F Santa Barbara CA 93111-2310

LONG, JEANINE HUNDLEY, state legislator; b. Provo, Utah, Sept. 21, 1928; d. Ralph Conrad and Hazel Laurine (Snow) Hundley; m. McKay W. Christensen, Oct. 28, 1949 (div. 1967); children: Cathy Schuyler, Julie Schulleri, Kelly M. Christensen, C. Brett Christensen, Harold A. Christensen; m. Kenneth D. Long, Sept. 6, 1968. AA, Shoreline C.C., Seattle, 1975; BA in Psychology, U. Wash., 1977. Mem. Wash. State Ho. of Reps., 1983-87, 93—, mem. legis. evaluation and accountability program, pensions & policies. Mayor protem, mem. city coun. City of Brier, Wash., 1977-80. Mem. Nat. Coun. State Legislators (state fed. assembly, comm. com.). Republican. Home: 14730 24th Ave SE Mill Creek WA 98012 Office: JLOB415 Olympia WA 98504

LONG, LAWLAND WILLIAM, management consultant; b. Oakland, Calif., July 20, 1954; s. William Hamilton and Mildred (Chang) L. BS, Calif. State U., Hayward, 1977; MBA, Boston Coll., 1987; M in Pub. Adminstrn., Harvard U., 1990. Adminstrv. dir. Chinatown Youth Ctr., San Francisco, 1981-85; cons. Brighton, Mass., 1986; exec. dir. Quincy Sch. Community Coun., Boston, 1986-89; asst. to dir. Boston Redevel. Authority, 1989-91; dir. capital planning and devel. Oakland Chinese Community Coun., 1991-92; corp. devel. cons. Alta Bates Med. Ctr., Berkeley, Calif., 1992; project mgr. Ctr. for Bus. & Environ. Studies, Hayward, Calif., 1992—; faculty mgmt. Hayward State, 1993—; guest speaker Boston Coll. Law Sch., Harvard U., Tufts U., Wheelock Coll., Mass., 1988-91. Mem. allocations com., speakers' bur. United Way of the Bay Area, San Francisco, 1983-85; chairperson, bd. dirs. Chinatown Occupational Tng. Ctr., Boston, 1986-89; trustee Boston Neighborhood Housing Trust, 1988-91; grant evaluator Innovations program-Ford Found., Kennedy Sch. Govt., Harvard Univ., 1989-91; dir. Ellis Meml. and Eldredge House, Boston, 1990-91. Kennedy fellow Harvard U. Home: 255 Jayne Ave 101 Oakland CA 94610 Office: Ctr for Bus & Environ Studies Dept Mgmt & Fin Hayward CA 94542

LONG, RANDALL CRAIG, financial advisor; b. Salem, Oreg., Mar. 28, 1958; s. Gerald R. and Dorothy (Larson) L.; m. Mary Fels Long, Sept. 3, 1983; children: Kristina M. Long, Kellie N. Long. BSBA, San Diego State U., 1980. Cons. Scribner, Sciarra & Taylor, Inc., L.A., 1980-81; sr. mktg. advisor Integrated Fin., Irvine, Calif., 1981-89; prin. First Fin. Resources, Mission Viejo, Calif., 1990—. Bd. dirs. ABSC, San Diego, 1979-80. Mem. Orange County Life Underwriters Assn., Internat. Assn. Fin. Planners, Million Dolar Round Table, Delta Sigma Pi (bd. dirs. 1979-80). Republican. Office: First Fin Resources Ste 1200 8001 Irvine Center Dr Irvine CA 92718

LONG, ROBERT MERRILL, retail drug company executive; b. Oakland, Calif., May 19, 1938; s. Joseph Milton and Vera Mai (Skaggs) L.; m. Eliane Quilloux, Dec. 13, 1969. Student, Brown U., 1956-58; B.A., Claremont Men's Coll., 1960. With Longs Drug Stores Inc., Walnut Creek, Calif., 1960—, dist. mgr., 1970-72, exec. v.p., 1972-75, pres., 1975-77, pres., chief exec. officer, 1977-91; chmn., chief exec. officer Longs Drug Stores, Walnut Creek, Calif., 1991—. Mem. Nat. Assn. Chain Drug Stores (dir.). Office: Longs Drug Stores Corp PO Box 5222 141 N Civic Dr Walnut Creek CA 94596-3858

LONG, STEPHEN INGALLS, electrical engineering educator; b. Alameda, Calif., Jan. 11, 1946; s. Stanley Merton and Mabel Claire (Ingalls) L.; m. Molly Sue Hammer, Dec. 17, 1966; children: Christopher Andrew, Betsy Elder. BS, U. Calif., Berkeley, 1967; MS, Cornell U., 1969, PhD, 1974. Sr. engr. Varian Assocs., Palo Alto, Calif., 1974-77; mem. tech. staff Rockwell Internat. Sci. Ctr., Thousand Oaks, Calif., 1978-81; prof. U. Calif., Santa Barbara, 1981—; instr. in field; vis. researcher GEC Hirst Rsch. Centre, Wembley, Eng., 1988. Author: Gallium Arsenide Digital IC Design, 1990; contbr. numerous articles to profl. jours. Mem. Grace Ch. of Santa Barbara. Staff sgt. USAF, 1969-73. Fulbright scholar, 1993. Mem. IEEE (sr., Microwave Applications award 1978), Am. Sci. Affiliation, Santa Barbara Amateur Radio Club, Tau Beta Pi. Home: 895 N Patterson Ave Santa Barbara CA 93111-1107 Office: U Calif ECE Dept Santa Barbara CA 93106

LONG, WILLIAM D., retail company executive; b. Watertown, Wis., Nov. 30, 1937; s. William D. and Olive (Piper) L.; m. Doreen Loveall, Sept. 23, 1967; children—Angela, Scott, Irene, Jeffrey, William, Jennifer. Student U. Wis.-Madison. Store mgr. Safeway, Salt Lake City, 1961-68; pres., chief exec. officer Waremart Inc., Boise, Idaho, 1968—. Served to cpl. U.S. Army, 1957-60. Office: Waremart Inc PO Box 5756 Boise ID 83705-0756

LONG, WILLIAM JOSEPH, software engineer; b. Kokomo, Ind., Feb. 1, 1956; s. George Alexander and Rebecca Bethina (Burgan) L. BA, Harvard U., 1979. Cons. Bechtel Corp., San Francisco, 1982-85; assoc. prof. Dalian (Liaoning, People's Republic of China) Inst. Tech., 1985-86; software engr. Bechtel Corp., San Francisco, 1986—; mem. adv. bd. Synetics, Inc., San Francisco, 1987—; owner SerenSoft Cons., Oakland, Calif., 1990—. Vol. English tutor, Oakland, Calif., 1983—. Rsch. grantee Smithsonian Astrophys. Obs., Cambridge, Mass., 1976. Mem. IEEE, Assn. Computing Machinery, Am. Assn. Artificial Intelligence, Am. Math. Soc., Math. Assn. Am. Home: 2225 7th Ave # 33 Oakland CA 94606 Office: Bechtel Corp 50 Beale St San Francisco CA 94105

LONGACRE, WILLIAM ATLAS, anthropology educator; b. Hancock, Mich., Dec. 16, 1937; s. William A. and Doris L. Longacre. BA, U. Ill., 1959; MA, U. Chgo., 1962, PhD, 1963. Asst. prof. U. Ariz., Tucson, 1964-68, assoc. prof., 1968-74, prof. anthropology, 1974—; fellow Ctr. Advanced Study, Palo Alto, Calif., 1972-73; vis. prof. U. Philippines, Quezon City, 1975-76, 79-80, 87-93, U. Hawaii, Honolulu, 1984-85; panel mem. Coun. Internat. Exch. of Scholars (Fulbright), Washington, 1988-91. Author numerous books, book chpts. and articles. Fellow: AAAS, Am. Anthropol. Assn.; mem. Soc. Am. Archaeology, Ariz. Acad. Sci (sec. anthropology sect. 1965-66), Sigma Xi. Home: 2133 W Window Rock Dr Tucson AZ 85745-1854 Office: U Ariz Dept Anthropology Tucson AZ 85721

LONGMAN, ANNE STRICKLAND, educational consultant; b. Metuchen, N.J., Sept. 17, 1924; d. Charles Hodges and Grace Anna (Moss) Eldridge; m. Henry Richard Strickland, June 22, 1946 (dec. 1960); m. Donald Rufus Longman, Jan. 20, 1979 (dec. 1987); children: James C., Robert H. BA in Bus. Adminstrn., Mich. State U., 1945; teaching credentials, U. Calif., Berkeley, 1959; postgrad., Stanford U., 1959-60; MA in Learning Hand, Santa Clara U., 1974. Lic. educator. Exptl. test engr. Pratt & Whitney Aircraft, East Hartford, Conn., 1945-47; indsl. engr. Marchant Calculators, Emeryville, Calif., 1957-58; with pub. rels. Homesmith, Palo Alto, Calif., 1959-62; cons. Right to Read Program, Calif., 1978-79; monitor, reviewer State of Calif., Sacramento, 1976-79; tchr. diagnosis edn. Cabrillo Coll., Aptos, Calif., 1970-79; lectr. edn. U. Calif., Santa Cruz, 1970-79; cons. Santa Cruz Bd. Edn., 1970-79; reading researcher Gorilla Found., Woodside, Calif., 1982—; bd. mem. Western Inst. Alcoholic Studies, L.A., 1972-73; chmn. Evaluation Com., Tri-County, Calif., 1974; speaker Internat. Congress Learning Disabilities, Seattle, 1974. Author: Word Patterns in English, 1974-92, Cramming 3D Kids, 1975—, 50 books for migrant students, 1970-79; contbr. articles on stress and alcoholism and TV crime prevention for police, 1960-79. Founder Literacy Ctr., Santa Cruz, 1968-092; leader Girl Scouts U.S.A., San Francisco, 1947-50; vol. Thursday's Child, Santa Cruz, 1976-79, Golden Gate Kindergarten, San Francisco, 1947-57. Recipient Fellowships Pratt & Whitney Aircraft, 1944, Stanford U., 1959. Mem. Internat. Reading Assn. (pres. 1975), Santa Clara Valley Watercolor Soc., Los Altos Art Club (v.p. 1992), Eichler Swim and Tennis Club. Republican. Epicsopalian. Home and Office: 193 Walter Hays Dr Palo Alto CA 94303

LONGO, LAWRENCE DANIEL, physiologist, gynecologist; b. Los Angeles, Oct. 11, 1926; s. Frank Albert and Florine Azelia (Hall) L.; m. Betty Jeanne Mundall, Sept. 9, 1948; children: April Celeste, Lawrence Anthony, Elizabeth Lynn, Camilla Giselle. B.A., Pacific Union Coll., 1949; M.D., Coll. Med. Evangelists, Loma Linda, Calif., 1954. Diplomate: Am. Bd. Ob-Gyn. Intern Los Angeles County Gen. Hosp., 1954-55, resident, 1955-58; asst. prof. ob-gyn UCLA, 1962-64; asst. prof. physiology and ob-gyn U. Pa., 1964-68; prof. physiology and ob-gyn Loma Linda U., 1968—; head div. perinatal biology Centre Loma Linda U. Sch. Medicine, 1974—; mem. perinatal biology com. Nat. Inst. Child Health, NIH, 1973-77; chmn. reprodn. scientist devel. program NIH; NATO prof. Consiglio Nat. delle Richerche, Italian Govt. Editor: Respiratory Gas Exchange and Blood Flow in the Placenta, 1972, Fetal and Newborn Cardiovascular Physiology, 1978, Charles White and A Treatise on the Management of Pregnant and Lying-in Women, 1987; co-editor: Landmarks in Perinatology, 1976-75; editor classic pages in ob-gyn. Am. Jour. Ob-Gyn., 1970-80; contbr. articles to profl. jours. Served with AUS, 1945-47. Recipient Research Career Devel. award NIH, 1967; NIH grantee, 1966—. Mem. Am. Assn. History Medicine (coun.), Am. Coll. Obstetricians and Gynecologists, Am. Osler Soc. (bd. govs., sec.-treas., Am. Physiol. Soc., Assn. Profs. Ob-Gyn., Perinatal Rsch. Soc., Soc. Gynecologic Investigation (past pres.), Neurosci. Soc. Adventist. Office: Loma Linda U Sch Medicine Divsn Perinatal Biology Loma Linda CA 92350

LONGSTREET, STEPHEN (CHAUNCEY LONGSTREET), author, painter; b. N.Y.C., Apr. 18, 1907; m. Ethel Joan Godoff, Apr. 22, 1932; children: Joan, Harry. Student, Rutgers Coll., Harvard U.; grad., N.Y. Sch. Fine and Applied Art, 1929; student in Rome, Paris. Ind. artist, writer, 1930—; staff lectr. Los Angeles Art Assn., 1954, UCLA, 1955, 58-59, lectr. Los Angeles County Mus., 1958-59; staff mem. arts and humanities dept. UCLA, 1965—; prof. art, dir. dept. Viewpoints Inst. of Gen. Semantics, Los Angeles, 1965; prof. modern writing U. So. Calif., Los Angeles, 1975-80. Began as painter; contbr. to French, Am. and English mags.; also cartoonist; radio writer for NBC, CBS, and other networks, writer shows for Rudy Vallee, Deems Taylor, John Barrymore, Bob Hope, Ellery Queen; writer popular series detective stories for Lippincott and Morrow under pen name Paul Haggrad, 1936; film critic Saturday Rev., 1941; mem. editorial staff Time mag., 1942, Screenwriters mag., 1947-48; critic L.A. Daily News, Book Pages, 1948; assoc. producer Civil War series The Blue and Gray, NBC, 1959—; author: All or Nothing, 1983, Delilah's Fortune, 1984, Our Father's House, 1985; painting exhibited: L.A., 1946, 48, N.Y., 1946, London, 1947; one-man shows include Padlia Galleries, L.A., 1970, Memphis Mus., 1979, Erie Mus., 1981, Coll. of Libr. of Congress, 1980, Jazz Age Revisited, 1983, Smithsonian Nat. Portrait Gallery, 1983, Sr. Eye Gallery, Long Beach, Calif., 1990, Columbus (Ohio) Mus. Art, 1992; retrospective show Longstreet the Mature Years, L.A., 1983, Jazz-The Chgo. Scene, Regenstein Libr. U. Chgo., 1989; author: The Pedlocks, 1951, The Beach House, 1952, The World Revisited, 1953, A Century of Studebaker on Wheels, 1953, The Lion at Morning, 1954, The Boy in the Model-T, 1956, Real Jazz, 1956, The Promoters, 1957, The Bill Pearson Story, 1957, (in French), Complete Dictionary of Jazz, 1957, Man of Montmartre, 1958, The Burning Man, 1958, The Politician, 1959, The Crime, 1959, Geisha, 1960, Gettysburg, 1960, A Treasury of the World's Great Prints, 1961, Eagles Where I Walk, 1961, The Flesh Peddler, 1962, A Few Painted Feathers, 1963, War In Golden Weather, 1965, Pedlock & Sons, 1965, The Wilder Shore: San Francisco '49 to '06, 1968, A Salute to American Cooking, (with Ethel Longstreet), 1968, War Cries on Horseback, An Indian History, 1970, The Canvas Falcons, 1970, Chicago: 1860-1920; a history, 1973, The General, 1974, (with Ethel Longstreet) World Cookbook, 1973, Win or Lose, 1977, The Queen Bees, 1979, Storm Watch, 1979, Pembroke Colors, 1981, From Storyville to Harlem - 50 years of the Jazz Scene, 1987, Magic Trumpets--The Young Peoples Story of Jazz, 1989, (poems) Jazz Solos, 1990; editor, illustrator: The Memoirs of W.W. Windstaff Lower Than Angels, 1993; writer screen plays including Uncle Harry, 1943, Rider on a Dead Horse, The Imposter, First Travelling Saleslady, Stallion Road, 1946, The Jolson Story, 1947, Helen Morgan Story, 1956, plays including High Button Shoes, 1947, Gauguin, 1948, All Star Cast, Los Angeles, A History, 1977, (TV series) Playhouse 90, TV writer for Readers Digest Theatre, 1955; contbr. dialogue for films Greatest Show on Earth, Duel In the Sun. Pres. Los Angeles Art Assn., 1973-90. Recipient Stafford medal London, 1946, Bowman prize, 1948, Photo-Play mag. Gold medal for The Jolson Story, 1948, Billboard-Donaldson Gold medal for High Button Shoes, 1948. Mem. Motion Picture Acad. Arts and Letters, Writers Guild Am. (bd. dirs. 1948), Phi Sigma (charter mem.). Clubs: Sketch, Daguerreotype Society, Winadu Players.

LONSDALE, HAROLD KENNETH, retired high technology company executive; b. Westfield, N.J., Jan. 19, 1932; s. Harold K. and Julia (Papandrea) L.; children: Karen Anne Trachsel, Harold Kenneth Jr. B.S. in Chemistry, Rutgers U., 1953; Ph.D. in Phys. Chemistry, Pa. State U., 1957. Staff mem. Gen. Atomic Co., San Diego, 1959-70; prin. scientist Alza Corp., Palo Alto, Calif., 1970-72; vis. scientist Max Planck Inst. for Biophysics, Frankfurt, W.Ger., 1973-74, Weizmann Inst. Sci., Rehovot, Israel, 1974; pres. Bend Research, Inc., Oreg., 1975-89; bd. dirs. Oreg. Bus. Coun. 1985-89; chair Gov's Sci. Coun., 1987-88. Editor: Reverse Osmosis Membrane Research, 1972; founder, editor Jour. Membrane Sci.; contbr. articles to profl. jours. Candidate U.S. Senate, 1990-92. Served to 1st lt. USAF, 1957-59. Named Small Bus. Entrepreneur of Yr., Oreg. Bus. Mag., 1982.

LOO, WALTER WEI-TO, hazardous waste management company executive, consultant; b. Shanghai, China, Sept. 4, 1946; came to U.S., 1966; s. Yung Tsung and Cecilia (Jiao) L.; m. Alice Chan, Dec. 14, 1973; children: Quincy Walter, Patrice Alice. BS, Okla. State U., 1970, MS, 1972. Cert. engring. geologist; registered environ. assessor. Staff geohydrologist Dames & Moore, Atlanta, 1972-74; sr. staff geohydrologist Woodward Clude Cons., Oakland, Calif., 1974-76; sr. hydrologist Westinghouse, Denver, 1976-78; dir. So. Calif. ops. McKesson Environ., L.A., 1978-84; dir. geosci. ECOVA, Seattle, 1984-85; prin. geohydrologist McLaren Hart, Alameda, Calif., 1985-88; chmn. remedial tech. AWD Tech/ Dow Chem., San Francisco, 1988-91; pres. Environ. and Tech. Svcs., San Francisco, Calif., 1991—. Author, editor: Biotreatment of Organic Chemicals, 1991, Groundwater Plume Management, 1991, Innovative Remedial Technologies, 1991, On-Site Soil Treatment, 1992, Underground Storage Tank Management, 1992. Pres. Okla. State Chinese Student Assn., Stillwater, Okla., 1971; v.p. Okla. State Geology Club, Stillwater, 1969. Mem. ASCE, Am. Geophys. Union, Nat. Groundwater Assn., Hazardous Material Control Rsch. Inst., Commonwealth Club. Office: Environ and Tech Svcs 2081-15th St San Francisco CA 94114

LOOBY, THOMAS P(ATRICK), state official; b. Saginaw, Mich., Mar. 12, 1950; s. Thomas Conrad and Mary Lavonne (Smith) L.; m. Mary Ann Shepphird, July 3, 1987; 1 child, Thomas Patrick Jr. BSCE in Environ. Engring., Mich. State U., 1973; MPA, U. Colo., Denver, 1985. Mgmt. trainee, foreman U.S. Steel Corp., Gary, Ind., 1973-74; chief engring. and inspection Office Ingham County Drain Commr., Lansing, Mich., 1974-75; dir. environ. programs Tri-County Regional Planning Commn., Lansing, 1975-78; mgr. environ. programs Pueblo (Colo.) Area Coun. Govts., 1978-80; staff mgr. Office Health and Environ. Protection, Colo. Dept. Health, Denver, 1980-85, dir. remedial programs, 1985-86, dir. Office of Environ., 1987—; mem. Nat. Adv. Coun. on Environ. Policy and Tech., Washington, 1988—; mem. ops. com. Colo. EPA. Mem. Nat. Environ. Health Assn., Colo. Environ. Health Assn. Roman Catholic. Office: Colo Dept Health Office of Environ 4300 Cherry Creek Dr S Denver CO 80222

LOOMIS, CHRISTOPHER KNAPP, metallurgical engineer; b. San Francisco, May 6, 1947; s. Richard and Evaline Elsie (Crandal) L.; m. Merril Ellen Purdy, Dec. 8, 1968; 1 child, Nicole Lee; m. Sandra Lee Marsh, Feb. 14, 1993. Profl. Engring. degree, Colo. Sch. Mines, 1969. Cert. quality engr. Process engr. Alcan Aluminum Corp., Riverside, Calif., 1969-73, prodn. supt., 1973-76; process engr. Alcan Aluminum Corp., Oswego, N.Y., 1976-78, maintenance engr., 1978-80; metall. engr. Hazelett Strip-Casting Corp., Colchester, Vt., 1980-81; chief engr. ARCO Metals Co., Chgo., 1981-84; maintenance supt. Cerro Metal Products, Paramount, Calif., 1984-85, mgr. engring. and maintenance, 1985-86; supt. tech. svcs. Golden Aluminum Co., Ft. Lupton, Colo., 1987-88; process devel. engr. Golden Aluminum Co., Lakewood, Colo., 1988-91, corp. environ. and process engr., 1991; engr. IV Coors Brewing Co., Golden, Colo., 1991-93, material engr. V, 1993—. Mem. Am. Soc. for Metals, Metall. Soc., Colo. Sch. Mines Alumni Assn., Am. Soc. for Quality Control, Fedn. Fly Fishers (life), Trout Unltd. (life). Episcopalian. Home: 13285 W 65th Dr Arvada CO 80004-2171 Office: Coors Brewing Co Mail Stop RR816 Golden CO 80401

LOOMIS, DAWN MARIE, video camera operator, librarian; b. Bridgeport, Conn., Aug. 11, 1952; d. Harvey Eugene and Irene Josephine (Tague) L. AS in Edn., York Coll. of Pa., 1972; BS in Ednl. Media, Millersville U., 1974; BA in Cinematography, Columbia Coll., 1984. Video camera operator 1st Foursquare Ch. of Van Nuys, Calif., 1984—; libr. King's Inst., Van Nuys, 1987—. Mem. Assn. Christian Librs. Republican.

LOOMIS, RICHARD FRANK, entertainment company executive; b. Eugene, Oreg., Aug. 24, 1947; s. Frank Clark and Elsie Jane (Allgood) L. BA in Acctg., Ariz. State U., 1975. Owner, founder, pres. Flying Buffalo Computer Conflict Simulation, Inc., Scottsdale, Ariz., 1970—. Author game book: Buffalo Castle, 1976; designer play by mail game: Starweb, 1976 (Best Game 1984, 87), Heroic Fantasy, 1982 (Best Game 1989); developer card game: Nuclear Escalation, 1983 (Best Game 1983). Pres. YMCA Ch. Softball League, Scottsdale, 1981-84. With U.S. Army, 1969-71. Recipient Meritorious Svc. to Gaming award Hobby/Metro Detroit Gamers, 1979. Mem. Play by Mail Assn. (exec. dir. 1985-88, 90—), Game Mfrs. Assn. (bd. dirs. 1986—, 1st pres. 1978-79, treas. 1980-86, Hall of Fame 1989, Honor of Svc. award 1991). Republican. Methodist. Office: Flying Buffalo Inc PO Box 1467 Scottsdale AZ 85252

LOONEY, CLAUDIA ARLENE, academic administrator; b. Fullerton, Calif., June 13, 1946; d. Donald F. and Mildred B. (Gage) Schneider; m. James K. Looney, Oct. 8, 1967; 1 child, Christopher K. BA, Calif. State U., 1969. Dir. youth YWCA No. Orange County, Fullerton, Calif., 1967-70; dir. dist. Camp Fire Girls, San Francisco, 1971-73; asst. exec. dir. Camp Fire Girls, Los Angeles, 1973-77; asst. dir. community resources Childrens Hosp., Los Angeles, 1977-80; dir. community devel. Orthopaedic Hosp., Los Angeles, 1980-82; sr. v.p. Saddleback Meml. Found./Saddleback Meml. Med. Ctr., Laguna Hills, Calif., 1982-92; v.p. planning and advancement Calif. Inst. Arts, Santa Clarita, Calif., 1992—; instr. U. Calif., Irvine, Univ. Irvine; mem. steering com. U. Irvine. Mem. steering com. United Way, Los Angeles, 1984-86. Fellow Assn. Healthcare Philanthropy (nat. chair-elect, chmn. program Nat. Edn. Conf. 1986, chair-elect, regional dir. 1985-89, fin. com. 1988—, pres., com. chmn. 1987—, Give to Life com. chmn. 1987-91, Orange County Fund Raiser of Yr. 1992); mem. Nat. Soc. Fund Raising Execs. Found. (cert., vice chmn. 1985-90, chair-elect 1993), So. Calif. Assn. Hosp. Devel. (past pres., bd. dirs.), Profl. Ptnrs. (chmn. 1986, instr. 1988—), Philanthropic Ednl. Orgn. (past pres.). Office: Calif Inst of the Arts 24700 McBean Pky Valencia CA 91355-9999

LOONEY, RALPH EDWIN, newspaper columnist, editor; b. Lexington, Ky., June 22, 1924; s. Arville Zone and Connie Elizabeth (Boyd) L.; m. Clarabel Richards, Dec. 7, 1944. B.A., U. Ky., 1948. Successively proof reader, photographer, chief photographer, sports writer, reporter Lexington Leader, 1943-52; reporter Albuquerque Tribune, 1953-54; reporter, copy editor, chief copy editor St. Louis Globe-Democrat, 1955-56; city editor Albuquerque Tribune, 1956-68, asst. mng. editor, 1968-73, editor, 1973-80; editor Rocky Mountain News, Denver, 1980-89; columnist Scripps Howard News Svc., 1989—; Tribune, Albuquerque, 1989—. Author: Haunted Highways, the Ghost Towns of New Mexico, 1969; contbr.: articles to mags. including Nat. Observer; others, photographs to mags. Founder, mem. N.Mex. Motion Picture Commn., 1967-76; v.p., bd. dirs. Albuquerque C. of C., 1971-75; bd. dirs. Albuquerque Indsl. Devel. Svc., 1971-80; bd. advisors Lovelace Med. Ctr., Albuquerque, 1976-80; bd. advs. UPI, 1983-86; bd. dirs. Newspaper Features Coun., 1984-89; mem. exec. coun. St. Joseph Hosp., 1986—. Recipient N.Mex. medal of Merit, 1968, Robert F. Kennedy Journalism award, 1970, George Washington Honor medal Freedoms Found., 1969, 19 E.H. Shaffer awards N.Mex. Press Assn., 1965-80; named Colo. Newspaper Person of the Yr., 1988, Newspaper Features Coun. Jester award, 1989. Mem. N.Mex. Press Assn. (state pres. 1976), Colo. Press Assn. (bd. dirs. 1982-85), Sigma Delta Chi (N. Mex. pres. 1960). Methodist. Home: 6101 Casa De Vida Dr NE Albuquerque NM 87111-1140

LOOR, RUEYMING, biochemist; b. Kaohsiung, Taiwan, China, Aug. 16, 1948; came to the U.S., 1973; s. Ho and Kang (Huang) L.; m. Chungpei W. Wang, Aug. 28, 1976; 1 child, Jeffrey. BS, Nat. Chungshing U., 1970; MS, U. Wis., 1974; PhD, SUNY, Buffalo, 1978. Rsch. assoc. U. Chgo., 1978-80; sr. scientist Roswell Park Rsch. Inst., Buffalo, 1980-82; sr. chemist Bio-Rad Lab., Richmond, Calif., 1982; project leader Cetus Corp., Emeryville, Calif., 1982-86; asst. dir. Leeco Diagnostics, Southfield, Mich., 1986-88; mgr. Micrologenics Corp., Concord, Calif., 1988—. Contbr. articles to profl. jours.; patentee in field. Grantee SUNY, 1978, Roswell Park Inst., 1981, Nat. Cancer Inst., 1982; recipient Best Abstract award CLASS Soc., 1991. Mem. Am. Assn. for Cancer Rsch., Am. Assn. for Clin. Chemistry, Am. Soc. for Microbiology. Office: Microgenics Corp 2380 A Bisso Ln Concord CA 94520

LOPACH, JAMES JOSEPH, political science educator; b. Great Falls, Mont., June 23, 1942; s. John Ernest and Alma Marie (Schapman) L.; divorced, Dec. 10, 1991; children: Christine, Paul. AB in Philosophy, Carroll Coll., 1964; MA in Am. Studies, U. Notre Dame, 1967, MAT in English Edn., 1968, PhD in Govt., 1973. Mgr. Pacific Telephone, Palo Alto, Calif., 1968-69; adminstr. City of South Bend, Ind., 1971-73; prof. U. Mont., Missoula, 1973—, chmn. dept. polit. sci., 1977-87, assoc. dean Coll. Arts and Scis., 1987-88, acting dir. Mansfield Ctr., 1984-85, spl. asst. to the univ. pres., 1988-92, acting assoc. provost, 1992—; cons. local govts., state agys., 1973—. Author, editor: We the People of Montana, 1983, Tribal Government Today, 1990, Planning Small Town America, 1990; contbr. articles to profl. jours. Roman Catholic. Office: U Mont Dept Polit Sci Missoula MT 59812

LOPATA, MARTIN BARRY, service executive, retired; b. Bronx, N.Y., Apr. 6, 1939; s. Julius A. and Rose (Silverman) L.; m. Sarah G. Lopata, July 4, 1965 (div. 1978; children: Warren A., Lawrence M.; m. Lynette Wyrick, May 6, 1989 (div. 1991). Grad., High Sch. of Art and Design, N.Y.C.; attended N.Y.C. Community Coll., Bklyn. Sales mgr. H. Natoway Co., Los Angeles, 1961-62; contract mgr. A.S. Aloe Co., Los Angeles, 1962-64; merchandise mgr. S.E. Rykoff Co., Los Angeles, 1964-70; v.p. Kirby Sales, Los Angeles, 1970-71; pres. MBL Industries Inc., Santa Ana, Calif., 1971-87, Unicorn Seminars Inc., Huntington Beach, Calif., 1987-88, Unicorn Investments Internat., Huntington Beach, 1988-91; chmn. Soviet Am. Internat. Co., 1988-92; joint venture Sovaminco Soviet Am. Internat. Co. #104, Moscow; pres. Coastal-West Industries, 1991-92. Patron Am. Mus. Nat. History, N.Y.C., 1984-91; bus. chmn. Ctr. for Soviet-Am. Dialogue, Washington, 1987-91; chmn. Com. on Bus.-A New Way of Thinking in a New Age, Moscow, 1987; bd. dirs. Three Mountain Found., Lone Pine, Calif., 1987-88, Inside Edge, Irvine, Calif., 1987—, found. pres., 1993—; vice chmn. United Ch. Religious Science, Los Angeles, 1986-87, pres. Huntington Beach Ch. Religious Sci., 1985. Mem. Masons (32d degree), Shriners. Home: 16391 Wimbledon Ln Huntington Beach CA 92649-2188

LOPER, JAMES LEADERS, broadcasting executive; b. Phoenix, Sept. 4, 1931; s. John D. and Ellen Helen (Leaders) L.; m. Mary Louise Brion, Sept. 1, 1955; children: Elizabeth Margaret Sehran (Mrs. Michael K. Sehran), James Leaders Jr. BA, Ariz. State U., 1953; MA, U. Denver, 1957; PhD, U. So. Calif., 1967; DHL (hon.), Columbia Coll., 1973; LLD (hon.), Pepperdine U., 1978. Asst. dir. bur. broadcasting Ariz. State U., Tempe, 1953-59; news editor, announcer Sta. KTAR, Phoenix, 1955-56; dir. ednl. TV, Calif. State U., Los Angeles, 1960-64; v.p. Community TV So. Calif., Los Angeles, 1962-63; asst. to pres. Sta. KCET-Pub. TV, Los Angeles, 1963-65, sec., 1965-66, dir. ednl. services, 1964-65, asst. gen. mgr., 1965-66, v.p., gen. mgr., 1966-69, exec. v.p., gen. mgr., 1969-71, pres., gen. mgr., 1971-76, pres., chief exec. officer, 1976-82; exec. dir. Acad. TV Arts and Scis., 1983—; bd. dirs., chmn. audit com. Western Fed. Savs. and Loan Assn., L.A., 1979-83; bd. dirs. Global View, Washington; chmn. bd. Pub. Broadcasting Service, Washington, 1969-72; dir. Calif. Arts Coun., 1991—; adj. prof. Sch. Cinema and TV U. So. Calif., 1984—; sr. lectr. U. So. Calif., Los Angeles, 1969-70; pres. Western Ednl. Network, 1968-70; mem. Gov.'s Ednl. TV and Radio Adv. Com., Calif., 1968-74; U.S. rep. CENTO Conf. Radio and TV, Turkey, 1978, trustee Internat. Council Nat. Acad. TV Arts and Scis., 1988—. Contbr. articles to profl. jours; contbr. to ETV: The Farther Vision, 1967, Broadcasting and Bargaining: Labor Relations in Radio and Television, 1970. Mem. adv. bd. Jr. League of Los Angeles, 1970-76, Jr. League of Pasadena, 1972-75, Los Angeles Jr. Arts Ctr., 1968-72; exec. v.p. Assocs. of Otis Art Inst., 1971-77, pres., 1975-77; chmn., dir. The Performing Tree, Los Angeles; bd. dirs. Los Angeles Civic Light Opera Co., 1974—, v.p., 1975—; bd. dirs. Sears-Roebuck Found., 1976-79; chmn. bd. visitors Annenburg Sch. Communications, U. So. Calif., 1975-80; trustee Poly. Sch., Pasadena; mem. Calif. State Arts Commn., 1991. Recipient Disting. Alumnus award Ariz. State U., 1972; Alumni award of Merit, U. So. Calif., 1975; Gov's. award Hollywood chpt. Nat. Acad. TV Arts and Scis., 1975; Alumni Achievement award Phi Sigma Kappa, 1975; named Centennial Alumnus Nat. Assn. of State Univs. and Land Grant Colls., 1988. Mem. Acad. TV Arts and Scis. (past gov., v.p. Hollywood chpt., trustee nat. acad.), TV Acad. Found., Hollywood Radio and TV Soc. (treas., dir.), Western Ednl. Soc. Telecommunications (past pres.), Assn. Calif. Pub. TV Stas. (past pres.), Young Pres.'s Orgn., Phi Sigma Kappa, Pi Delta Epsilon, Alpha Delta Sigma, Sigma Delta Chi. Presbyterian (chmn. Mass Media Task Force So. Calif. synod 1969-75). Clubs: Valley Hunt (Pasadena), Bel-Air Bay, California, Los Angeles, 100 of Los Angeles, Calif. (Los Angeles). Office: Acad TV Arts and Scis 5220 Lankershim Blvd North Hollywood CA 91601-3109

LOPER, WARREN EDWARD, computer scientist; b. Dallas, Aug. 2, 1929; s. Leon Edward and Belva (Fannin) L.; BS in Physics, U. Tex. at Austin, 1953, BA in Math. with honors, 1953; m. Ruth M. Wetzler, June 17, 1967; 1 child, Mary Katherine. Commd. ensign U.S. Navy, 1953, advanced through grades to lt., 1957; physicist U.S. Naval Ordnance Test Sta., China Lake, Calif., 1956-61; operational programmer U.S. Navy Electronics Lab., San Diego, 1962-64; project leader, systems programming br., digital computer staff U.S. Fleet Missile Systems Analysis and Evaluation Group, Corona, 1964-65, sr. systems analyst digital computer staff U.S. Naval Ordnance Lab., Corona, 1965-69; head systems programming br. Naval Weapons Center, Corona Labs, 1969; computer specialist compiler and operating systems devel., Naval Electronics Lab. Ctr., San Diego, 1969-76; project leader langs., operating systems and graphics Naval Ocean Systems Ctr., San Diego, 1977-90, employee emeritus, 1990—. Navy rep. on tech. subgroup Dept. Def. High Order Lang. Working Group, 1975-80. Recipient Disting. Svc. award Dept. Def., 1983. Democrat. Roman Catholic. Home: 6542 Alcala Knolls Dr San Diego CA 92111-6947

LOPEZ, ANDY, university athletic coach. Head coach NCAA Divsn. 1A baseball champions Pepperdine U. Waves, 1992. Office: Pepperdine U 24255 Pacific Coast Hwy Malibu CA 90263

LOPEZ, BARRY HOLSTUN, writer; b. Port Chester, N.Y., Jan. 6, 1945; s. Adrian Bernard and Mary Frances (Holstun) L.; m. Sandra Jean Landers, June 10, 1967. BA, U. Notre Dame, 1966, MA in Teaching, 1968; postgrad., U. Oreg., 1968-69; LHD (hon.), Whittier Coll., 1988. Free-lance writer, 1970—; assoc. The Freedom Forum Media Studies Ctr., N.Y.C., 1985—. Author: Desert Notes, 1976, Giving Birth to Thunder, 1978, Of Wolves and Men, 1978 (John Burroughs Soc. medal 1979, Christophers of N.Y. medal 1979, Pacific Northwest Booksellers award in nonfiction 1979),

River Notes, 1979, Winter Count, 1981 (Disting. Recognition award Friends Am. Writers in Chgo. 1982), Arctic Dreams, 1986 (Nat. Book award in nonfiction Nat. Book Found. 1986, Christopher medal 1987, Pacific Northwest Booksellers award 1987, Frances Fuller Victor award in nonfiction Oreg. Inst. Literary Arts 1987), Crossing Open Ground, 1988, Crow and Weasel, 1990 (Parents Choice Found. award), The Rediscovery of North America, 1991; also numerous articles, essays and short stories; contbg. editor Harper's mag., 1981-82, 84—, N.Am. Rev., 1977—; works translated into Japanese, Swedish, German, Dutch, Italian, French, Norwegian, Chinese, Finnish, Spanish. Recipient award in Lit., Am. Acad. of Arts and Letters, 1986, Gov.'s award for Arts, 1990, Lannan Found. award, 1990, Antarctic Svc. medal USN/NSF, 1989; John Simon Guggenheim Found. fellow, 1987. Mem. PEN Am. Ctr., Authors Guild, Poets and Writers.

LOPEZ, CARLOS CELERINO, accountant; b. Fresno, Calif., Dec. 2, 1952; s. Napoleon Galan and Emma (Garcia) L.; div. Oct. 1991; 1 child, David Carlos. BA, Pacific Union Coll., Angwin, Calif., 1974; BS, U. San Francisco, 1980. Enrolled agt., 1988. Buyer Payless Stores, Inc., Salinas, Calif., 1979-82; owner Dairy Belle # 60, Fremont, Calif., 1982-84, Lopez Tax Svc., Salinas, 1984—. Radio host pub. radio show Call In IRS Questions, 1989; author tax newsletter Newspaper, 1992. Treas. Republican Nat. Hispanic Assembly, Salinas, 1990—; v.p. Mexican-Am. Polit. Assn., Salinas, 1991—; treas. Cortez Homeowners Assn., Salinas, 1986—; bd. dirs. Ariel Theatrical, Inc., Salinas, 1990—. Recipient Cert. of Appreciation, Dep. Sheriff's Assn., Fremont, 1982, Merchandising award Coyle Assocs., Salinas, 1980. Mem. Nat. Assn. Enrolled Agts., Calif. Soc. Enrolled Agts., Calif. Assn. Accts., Nat. Assn. Notary Pubs., Salinas Hispanic C. of C. Office: Lopez Tax Svc 257 John St Salinas CA 93901

LOPEZ, IGNACIO ALBERTO, geodesist, land surveyor; b. Guadalajara, Mex., May 25, 1953; s. Pedro Lopez Garron and Teresa Ramirez Lopez; m. Marianne Wetzel, Sept. 1, 1991. Student, U. Guadalajara, 1971-76; AS in Surveying, City Coll. San Francisco, 1985; BS in Surveying and Photogrammetry, Fresno (Calif.) State U., 1988. Land surveyor Bur. Land Mgmt., Fresno, 1986-91; geodesist Bur. Land Mgmt., Sacramento, 1991—. Recipient Excellence award Dept. of Interior, 1989, Bur. Land Mgmt., 1991, 92. Office: Bur Land Mgmt 2800 Cottage Way Sacramento CA 95825

LOPEZ, JOSÉ ELDAD, JR., navy medical officer; b. Weslaco, Tex., Sept. 10, 1957; s. José E. Sr. and Nicanora (Acevedo) Chavez; m. Gloria S. Lopez; 1 child, Ginger. BS in Health Care Mgmt., So. Ill. U., 1989; MA in Human Resource Mgmt., Nat. U., San Diego, 1993. Cert. and registered clin. hypnotherapist, total quality mgmt. facilitator; fellow in clin. hypnosis. Commd. USN, 1992, advanced through grades to chief hosp. corpsman, 1992; neuropsychiatry technician psychiatry staff Naval Hosp., Portsmouth, Va., 1977-78; neuropsychiatry technician psychiatry & alcohol rehab. ctr. U.S. Naval Hosp., Okinawa, Japan, 1978-80; mgr. neuropsychiatry tech. psychiatry & alcohol rehab. ctr. Naval Hosp./Naval Air Sta., Corpus Christi, Tex., 1980-83; mgr. neuropsychiatry tech. psychiatry staff Naval Hosp., Long Beach, Calif., 1983-85; mgr. neuropsychiatry tech. psychiatry/ARD staff U.S. Naval Hosp., Guam, Marianas Islands, 1985-88; mgr. neuropsychiatry tech. inpatient psychiatry staff Naval Hosp., San Diego, 1988-90; mgr. neuropsychiatry tech./corpsman med. dept. staff Operation Desert Shield and Operation Desert Storm, USN, USS Nassau, Persian Gulf, 1991; mgr. neuropsychiatry tech. psychology dept. Naval Hosp., San Diego, 1991-92; leading chief dermatology dept. Naval Med. Ctr., San Diego, 1993—; Spanish lang. interpretor/translator for patients Naval hosps., 1977—; mgr., neuropsychiatry technician for implementation of Navy-Air Force Med. Evaluation Team, Naval Tng. Ctr., San Diego, 1991-92; cons. Am. bd. Hypnotherapy, 1983—. Mem. Am. Legion, Fleet Res. Assn., Al Bhar Shriners, Scottish Rite, Masons, U.S. Aikido FEdn., Chief Petty Officer Assn., Am. Assn. Profl. Hypnotherapists. Mem. Soc. of Friends. Office: Naval Med Ctr Florida St Canyon San Diego CA 92134-5000 also: US Naval Hosp PSC 475 Box A FPO AP 96350

LOPEZ, ROY CHARLES, community health nurse; b. Florence, Ariz., July 3, 1948; s. Roy Charles Lopez and Nina Glendene (Staggs) Crisler; m. Judy Ann Rotz, Sept. 1, 1972; children: Glenn David, Daniel Roy. ADN, Cen. Ariz. Coll., 1975; BSN, Ariz. State U., 1979; postgrad., Calif. State U., Dominguez Hills, 1989—. RN, Calif. Staff nurse Ariz. Tng. Program at Coolidge, 1975-77; dir. nursing Ariz. Dept. Corrections, Florence, 1979-81; health adminstr. Ariz. Dept. Corrections, Phoenix and Florence, 1981-83; nursing supr. Indian Hosp USPHS Indian Hosp., Shiprock, N.Mex., 1983-85; pub. health nurse Indian Health Svc. USPHS, Sacaton, Ariz., 1985-88; staff nurse fed. correctional instn. USPHS, Terminal Island, Calif., 1988-90; lt. commdr. USPHS western regional ops. officer INS health care program, Laguna Niguel, Calif., 1990—. Mem. ANA, Commd. Officers Asns. of USPHS, Res. Officers Assn., Assn. Mil. Surgeons of U.S., Nat. League for Nursing, Statewide Nursing Honor Soc., Am. Assembly for Men in Nursing. Democrat. Roman Catholic. Office: INS Health Care Program 6th Fl RODDP PO Box 30080 Laguna Beach CA 92607-0080

LOPEZ, STEVEN RICHARD, small business owner, consultant; b. Flagstaff, Ariz., Dec. 14, 1944; s. John and Trinidad (Rodriquez) L.; (div. 1983); children: David Allen, Laura Marie, Jonel Christina, Steven Christopher. BFA, U. Ariz., 1968; MBA, U. Phoenix, 1992. Art dir. Curran-Morton Advt., Phoenix, 1968-70; owner Steve Lopez Graphic Design, Phoenix, 1970-73; asst. art dir. Ulrich Studios, Phoenix, 1973-78; artist, illustrator Goodyear (Ariz.) Aerospace/Loral Def. Systems, 1978-90; pres. Z-Boz, Inc., Glendale, Ariz., 1990-92; pres. Exigency Alert, Inc., Glendale, 1988-90; owner Lopez & Assocs., Glendale, 1989—, pres., 1991; v.p. South Paw, Inc., Peoria, Ariz., 1990-91; cons. Teddy Bear Factory, Inc., Peoria, 1990-91, Beanies Soft Toy Factory, Phoenix, 1990, Maquiladoras, Mex.; exec. advisor Jr. Achievement, Phoenix, 1979-80; amb. to Mex., U.S. JCI Senate, Tulsa, 1987-88. Patentee eyeglass floatation apparatus. Mem. adv. com. City of Glendale, 1985, City of Glendale Cable TV Task Force, 1987; bd. dirs. All Am. Cities Com., Glendale; bd. trustees Valley of the Sun United Way, Phoenix. Mem. Glendale C. of C., U.S. Jaycees (Excellence award 1977, Upson award 1982), Ariz. Jaycees (life, pres. 1985-86, Excellence award 1986), Glendale Jaycees (pres. 1978-81, Chmn. of the Yr. 1977). Democrat. Roman Catholic. Home: 4927 W Mclellan Rd Glendale AZ 85301-4010

LOPEZ, THOMAS MARSH, entrepreneur; b. Wilmington, Del., Apr. 2, 1943; s. S. Henry and Kate Weston (Hawley) L.; m. Su-Allan Latchum, Aug. 28, 1968 (div. 1972); m. Margaret Judd Jacoby, Aug. 20, 1983. BS in Mktg., U. Del., 1967. Recruiter RCA Corp., Camden, N.J., 1970-72; exec. dir. Am. Heart Assn., N.Y.C., 1972-77, Juvenile Diabetes Found., N.Y.C., 1977-79; v.p. ComputerMaster, Inc., Ft. Lee, N.J., 1979-80; account supr. J. Walter Thompson Co., San Francisco, 1980-81; sr. v.p. Activision, Inc., Mt. View, Calif., 1981-84; pres. Cytation Inc., San Francisco, 1984-86; v.p. Microsoft Inc., Redmond, Wash., 1986-88; chmn. bd. Mammoth MicroProdns., Seattle, 1988-93; pres. Interactive Multimedia Assn., 1993—; cons. Interactive Communications Corp., San Jose, 1984. Inventor CD-ROM software, 1985. Mem. St. Mark's Cathedral. Lt. (j.g.) USCG, 1968-70. Republican. Episcopalian.

LOPINA, ROBERT FERGUSON, aerospace company executive; b. Jamestown, N.Y., May 13, 1936; s. Konrad Stephen and Elizabeth (Ferguson) L.; m. Louise Carol Peterson, June 21, 1958; children: Kimberly, Sandra, Amy. BSME, Purdue U., 1957; SMME, MIT, 1965, Mech. Engr., 1966, PhD, 1967. Commd. 2d lt. USAF, 1957, advanced through grades to col., ret., 1983; comdr., dir. avionics lab. USAF, Aero. Systems Div., Wright Patterson AFB, Ohio, 1978-80, dep. enring., 1980-82, dep. reconnaissance, strike and electronic warfare, 1982-83; v.p. Fairchild Republic Co., Farmingdale, N.Y., 1983-87; dir. advanced devel. Ford Aerospace Corp., Detroit, 1987-89, v.p. advanced programs aeronutronic div., Newport Beach, Calif., 1988-90, v.p. Loral Aernoutronic div., 1990—; cons. W.Va. U. Aerospace/Mech., Morgantown, 1981-83; advisor N.Y. Inst. Tech., Woodbury, 1983-85. Co-author: Introduction to Aeronautics, 1971. Decorated Legion of Merit, Meritorious Service medal. Mem. AIAA (treas., vice-chmn. 1970-72), ASME, Air Force Assn., Assn. Old Crows, Tau Kappa Epsilon. Republican. Presbyterian. Avocations: fishing, boating, running, scubadiving. Home: 7 Calle Agua San Clemente CA 92673-2749

LORANCE, ELMER DONALD, organic chemistry educator; b. Tupelo, Okla., Jan. 18, 1940; s. Elmer Dewey and Imogene (Triplett) L.; m. Phyllis Ilene Miller, Aug. 31, 1969; children: Edward Donald, Jonathan Andrew. BA, Okla. State U., 1962; MS, Kansas State U., 1967; PhD, U. Okla., 1977. NIH research trainee Okla. U., Norman, 1966-70; asst. prof. organic chemistry So. Calif. Coll., Costa Mesa, 1970-73, assoc. prof., 1973-80, prof., 1980—, chmn. div. natural scis. and math., 1985-89, chmn. chemistry dept., 1990-93, chmn. divsn. natural scis. and math., 1993—. Contbr. articles to profl. jours. Mem. AAAS, Am. Chem. Soc., Internat. Union Pure and Applied Chemistry (assoc.), Am. Inst. Chemists, Am. Sci. Affiliation, Phi Lambda Upsilon. Republican. Mem. Ch. Assembly of God. Office: So Calif Coll 55 Fair Dr Costa Mesa CA 92626-6597

LORD, HAROLD WILBUR, electrical engineer, electronics consultant; b. Eureka, Calif., Aug. 20, 1905; s. Charles Wilbur and Rossina Camilla (Hansen) L.; B.S., Calif. Inst. Tech., 1926; m. Doris Shirley Huff, July 25, 1928; children—Joann Shirley (Mrs. Carl Cook Disbrow), Alan Wilbur, Nancy Louise (Mrs. Leslie Crandall), Harold Wayne. With Gen. Electric Co., Schenectady, 1926-66, electronics engr., 1960-66; pvt. cons. engr., Mill Valley, Calif., 1966—. Coffin Found. award Gen. Electric Co., 1933, GE Inventors award, 1966. Fellow IEEE (life, tech. v.p. 1962, Centennial medal 1984, IEEE Magnetics Soc. 1984 Achievement award). Contbr. articles to profl. jours. Patentee in field. Home and Office: 1565 Golf Course Dr Rohnert Park CA 94928-5638

LORD, JACK, actor, director, producer, painter; b. N.Y.C., Dec. 30, 1930; s. William Lawrence and Ellen Josephine (O'Brien) Ryan; m. Marie de Narde, Apr. 1, 1952. BS in Fine Arts, NYU, 1954. pres. Lord and Lady Enterprises, Inc., 1968—. Works exhibited in galleries, museums including Corcoran Gallery, Nat. Acad. Design, Whitney Mus., Bklyn. Mus., Met. Mus. Art, N.Y.C., Library of Congress, Brit. Mus., London, Bibliotheque Nationale, Paris, Mus. Modern Art, N.Y.C., Met. Mus. Art, Brit. Mus., Bklyn. Mus., Bibliotheque Nationale, Paris, Fogg Mus., Harvard U., Santa Barbara (Calif.) Mus. Art, John and Mable Ringling Mus. Art, Sarasota, Fla., Grunwald Graphic Arts Found., UCLA, Brooks Meml. Art Gallery, Memphis, Cin. Art Mus., Atkins Mus. Art, Kansas City, Mo., Fine Arts Gallery, San Diego, Colby Coll. Art Mus., Waterville, Maine, Ga. Mus. Art, U. Ga., Atlanta, DePauw U. Art Mus., Greencastle, Ind., Chouinard Art Inst., Los Angeles, Free Library Phila., Columbia U., N.Y.C., Lycoming Coll., Williamsport, Pa., Rutgers U., New Brunswick, N.J., U. Maine, Orono; represented in permanent collections, Dartmouth Coll., Hanover, N.H., Colgate U. Library, Hamilton, N.Y., Simmons Coll., Boston, Kalamazoo Inst. Arts, U. N.C., Chapel Hill, Evansville (Ind.) Mus. Arts, Massillon (Ohio) Mus., Hebrew Union Coll., Cin., N.Y.C., Los Angeles, Jerusalem, Flint (Mich.) Inst. Arts, Lehigh U. Coll. Arts, Bethlehem, Pa., Birmingham (Ala.) Mus. Art, Case Western Res. U., Cleve., Coll. of Wooster (Ohio), Calif. Inst. Arts; Broadway appearances include Traveling Lady, Cat on a Hot Tin Roof, Flame-Out, The Illegitimist, (TV shows) Stoney Burke (star); producer, star of 280 hours in 12 yrs. of series Hawaii Five-O; creator (TV series) The Hunter; creator, dir., producer: (TV film) M Station: Hawaii, 1980; writer (original screenplay) Melissa, 1968; dir. episodes Hawaii Five-O; appeared in feature films The Court Marshall of Billy Mitchell, Williamsburg, The Story of a Patriot, Tip on a Dead Jockey, God's Little Acre, Man of the West, The Hangman, Walk Like a Dragon, Dr. No, Ride to Hangman's Tree, Doomsday Flight; leading TV roles include Omnibus, Playhouse 90, Goodyear Playhouse, Studio One, U.S. Steel Hour, Have Gun Will Travel, Untouchables, Naked City, Rawhide, Bonanza, Americans, Route 66, Gunsmoke, Stagecoach West, Dr. Kildare, Greatest Show on Earth, Combat, Chrysler Theater, 12 O'Clock High, Loner, Laredo, FBI, Invaders, Fugitive, Virginian, The Man from UNCLE, High Chaparral, Ironside, Alcoa Theatre, Loretta Young Show, The Millionaire, Checkmate, Climax, Kraft, Philco, Danger, Suspense, The Web, You Are There, Lineup, Grand Hotel, Kraft Suspense Theatre. Served as 2d officer U.S. Merchant Marines. Recipient St. Gauden's Artist award, 1948, Fame award, 1963, Spl. Law Enforcement award, Am. Legion, 1973, Adminstr.'s award VA, 1980, Legend in His Own Time award State of Hawaii, 1980; named to Cowboy Hall of Fame, 1963. Mem. SAG, Dirs. Guild Am. Home: 4999 Kahala Ave Honolulu HI 96816-5423

LORD, JACKLYNN JEAN, student services representative; b. Sacramento, Feb. 2, 1940; d. Jasper Jackson and Celia (Moreno) Opdyke; m. Brent Andrew Nielsen, Aug. 6, 1966 (dec. Sept. 1974); 1 child, Taumie Celia; m. Mark William Lord, Mar. 5, 1983; 1 child, Jacklynn Michelle. Student, Sacramento State U., 1958-60, Cabrillo Coll., 1962-66, Sacred Coll. of Jamilian Theology and Div. Sch., Reno, 1976—. Ordained Ch. Internat. Community Christ. Communications cons. Pacific Telephone Co., San Jose, Calif., 1966-74, Nev. Bell Co., Reno, 1974-76; student services rep. for extension program Jamilian U. of Ordained, Reno, 1976—; asst. music dir. Internat. Community Christ, Reno, 1980—; choral instr. Jamilian Parochial Sch., Reno, 1976—; sexton Jamilian Handbell Choir, Reno, 1981—; organist Symphonietta, Reno, 1983—. Mem. Nat. League Concerned Clergywomen. Republican. Home: 1990 Humboldt St Reno NV 89509-3645 Office: Internat Community Christ 643 Ralston St Reno NV 89503-4436

LORD, JOHN ROBERT, computer consultant; b. Vancouver, Wash., Mar. 24, 1954; s. John Gerald Betty Jane (Thompson) Kimpton. AA in Mgmt., U. Md., Iwakuni, Japan, 1979; BS in Mgmt., Pepperdine U., 1986. Programmer analyst Hughes Aifcraft Co., Fullerton, Calif., 1981-82, Allergan Pharms., Irvine, Calif., 1982-83; sr. systems analyst Crocker Nat. Bank, Manhattan Beach, Calif., 1983-85; lead systems analyst Transam. Occidental Ins. Co., L.A., 1985-89; ptnr., cons. Constrn. Fin. Svcs.,, West Bloomfield, Mich., 1989-91; owner, cons. Lord Cons., Ocean Park, Wash., 1991—; cons. computer project El Centro Hosp., L.A., 1985. Founder Torch Tape Ministries, Ocean Park, 1974, Trees for L.A. Internat. Airport, 1985, No Graffiti, Playa del Rey, Calif., 1985; congl. candidate Rep. Party, Wash., 1992. Recipient Community award Pres. Ronald Reagan, 1985, Letter of Appreciation, City of L.A., 1986, Vol. award Vols. of L.A., 1985, 86. Baptist. Home: PO Box 604 Ocean Park CA 98640

LORD, MIA W., peace activist; b. N.Y.C., Dec. 2, 1920; m. Robert P. Lord (dec. Nov. 1977); children: Marcia Louise, Alison Jane. BA in Liberal Arts cum laude, Bklyn. Coll., 1940; postgrad., San Francisco State U., 1984—. Hon. sec. Commonwealth of World Citizens, London; membership sec. Brit. Assn. for World Govt., London; sec. Ams. in Brit. for U.S. Withdrawal from S.E. Asia, Eng.; organizer Vietnam Vigil to End the War, London; pres. Let's Abolish War chpt. World Federalist Assn., San Francisco State U.; appointed hon. sec. Commonwealth of World Citizens, London; officially invited to Vietnam, 1973; organizer Vietnam Vigil to End the War, London. Author: "The Practical Way to End Wars and Other World Crises: the case for World Federal Government: listed in World Peace through World Law, 1984, and in Strengthening the United Nations, 1987, War: The Biggest Con Game in the World, 1980. Hon. sec., nat. exec. mem. Assn. of World Federalists-U.K.; founder, bd. dirs. Crusade to Abolish War and Armaments by World Law. Nominated for the Nobel Peace Prize, 1975, 92; recipient four Merit awards Pres. San Francisco State U. Mem. Secretariat of World Citizens USA (life), Assn. of World Federalists USA, Brit. Assn. for World Govt. (membership sec.), Crusade to Abolish War and Armaments by World Law (founder, dir.), World Govt. Orgn. Coord. Com., World Fed. Authority Com., Campaign for UN Reform, Citizens Global Action, World Constitution and Parliament Assn., World Pub. Forum, Internat. Registry of World Citizens. Home: 174 Majestic Ave San Francisco CA 94112-3022

LORENTSON, HOLLY JEAN, health facility executive; b. Mpls., Nov. 27, 1956; d. Leslie Arnold and Mary Ann Jean (Anderson) L. BA in Nursing, Coll. St. Catherine, St. Paul, 1978; MPH, U. Minn., 1986. RN, Minn.; registered pub. health nurse. Nurse Abbott/Northwestern Hosp., Mpls., 1978-79; acting dir. community nursing services Ebenezer Soc., Mpls., 1979-84; patient services coordinator San Diego Hospice Corp., 1984-85, exec. dir., 1985-88, pres., 1988—; mem. fiscal intermediary provider task force Region X Health Care Financing Adminstrn., 1984-88. Recipient Women of Vision award LWV, 1991. Mem. Nat. Hospice Orgn. (bd. dirs.), Internat. Soc. Pres. Non-Profit Orgns., Calif. Hospice Assn. (v.p. 1985-88), Calif. Assn. Health Svcs. at Home (com. mem.), The Exec. Com., Rotary. Office: San Diego Hospice Corp 4311 3d Ave San Diego CA 92103

LORENZ, MARY LOU, nurse; b. Rockford, Ill., Aug. 23, 1954; d. James E. and Bessie I. (Snoddy) Hall; m. Garrett A. Lorenz, July 26, 1976; children: Megan M., Jon G. ADN, U. Nev., Las Vegas, 1981, BSN, 1993. Nurse pediatric ICU, Univ. Med. Ctr., Las Vegas, 1981-87; pediatrics surg. nurse Pediatric Surg. Assocs. So. Nev., Las Vegas, 1988-90; pediatrics surg. rsch. asst. Stephen G. Jolley Chartered, Las Vegas, 1990—. Mem. ANA, FOND. Roman Catholic. Office: Stephan G Jollet Chartered 3201 S Maryland Pky Las Vegas NV 89107

LORENZ, TIMOTHY CARL, real estate agent; b. Glendale, Calif., June 9, 1947; s. Raymond Jerome and Majorie Nadine (Bevis) L.; m. Jeanann Carrington, Apr. 16, 1966 (div. 1982); children: Julianne, Todd; m. Nadyne Claire Buck, Sept. 11, 1982; stepchildren: Ron, Eve, SeAnn, Dray. BA in Psychology, Calif. State U., Los Angeles, 1969, MA in Psychology, 1972. Lic. real estate agt., Calif. Chief investigator L.A. County Dept. Consumer Affairs, 1976-81; co-owner Newport Holistic Health Clinic, Newport Beach, Calif., 1981-83; chief investigator Orange County Office Consumer Affairs, Santa Ana, Calif., 1983-86; agt. Century 21 Niguel, Laguna Niguel, Calif., 1986—, mgr.; owner The Carousel, San Juan Capistrano, Calif., 1987—, Depot...Pourri Gift Shop, San Juan Capistrano, 1991—; instr. psychology Mt. San Antonio, Walnut, Calif., 1976-83; chmn. bd. dirs. Real Reasons, Laguna Niguel; distbr. Amway, Dana Point, Calif., 1983—; instr. Saddleback Coll., 1992—. Co-author Renter Rights and Responsibilities, 1978; producer T.V. talk show Coping in Today's World, 1982 (Best of Pub. Access award 1982). Pres. Bur. Electronic and Appliance Repair Bd., Sacramento, Calif., 1980, 86, legis. com., 1979; founding mem. Nat. Automobile Dealers Consumer Action Panel, L.A., 1978-81. Recipient Letter Commendation Atty. Gen., L.A., 1980. Mem. Nat. Assn. Realtors, Assn. Foster Parents North Cen. South Orange County (pres. 1986-88), State Calif. Foster Parent Assn., Nat. Assn. Foster Parents, Dana Point C. of C., Newport Beach C. of C. Republican. Home: 33391 Ocean Hill Dr Dana Point CA 92629-1122 Office: Century 21 Niguel Realty 30232 Crown Valley Pky Laguna Beach CA 92677-2366

LORENZEN, KENNETH DEAN, personnel director; b. Portland, Oreg., Oct. 1, 1942; Delbert Martin and Bertha Elaine (Woodke) L.; m. Bonnie Jean Tibbs, Apr. 11, 1970; 1 child, Rebecca Jean. AA, Pasadena City Coll., 1962; BA, Calif. State Poly. Coll., 1969. Compensation analyst Aerojet Gen. Corp., El Monte, Calif., 1969-70; pers. asst. Pabst Brewing Co., L.A., 1970-71; pers. adminstr. Coca-Cola Bottling Co. L.A., 1971-76, mgr. employee rels., 1985-86; pers. rep. Miller Brewing Co., Azusa, Calif., 1976-77; dir. pers. Dr. Pepper Bottling Co. So. Calif., Gardena, 1977-85; regional pers. mgr. Hertz-Penske Truck Leasing, Long Beach, Calif., 1986; dir. pers. svcs. Cerritos Coll., Norwalk, Calif., 1986—. Mem. So. 30 Pers. Info. Exch. (sec. 1992), Sch. Employees Assn. Republican. Presbyterian. Office: Cerritos Coll 11110 Alondra Blvd Norwalk CA 90650

LORENZEN, ROBERT FREDERICK, ophthalmologist; b. Toledo, Ohio, Mar. 20, 1924; s. Martin Robert and Pearl Adeline (Bush) L.; m. Lucy Logsdon, Feb. 14, 1970; children: Roberta Jo, Richard Martin, Elizabeth Anne. BS, Duke, 1948, MD, 1948; MS, Tulane U., 1953. Intern, Presbyn. Hosp., Chgo., 1948-49; resident Duke Med. Center, 1949-51, Tulane U. Grad. Sch., 1951-53; practice medicine specializing in ophthalmology, Phoenix, 1953—; mem. staff St. Joseph's Hosp., St. Luke's Hosp., Good Samaritan Hosp., Surg. Eye Ctr. of Ariz. Pres. Ophthalmic Scis. Found., 1970-73; chmn. bd. trustees Rockefeller and Abbe Prentice Eye Inst. of St. Luke's Hosp., 1975—. Recipient Gold Headed Cane award, 1974; named to Honorable Order of Ky. Cols. Fellow ACS, Internat. Coll. Surgeons, Am. Acad. Ophthalmology and Otolaryngology, Soc. Eye Surgeons; mem. Am. Assn. Ophthalmology (sec. of ho. of dels. 1972-73, trustee 1973-76), Ariz. Ophthal. Soc. (pres. 1966-67), Ariz. Med. Assn. (bd. dirs. 1963-66, 69-70), Royal Soc. Medicine, Rotary (pres. Phoenix 1984-85). Republican. Editor in chief Ariz. Medicine, 1963-66, 69-70. Office: 367 E Virginia Ave Phoenix AZ 85004-1275

LORENZO, ARIEL, agronomist, plant breeder; b. Buenos Aires, Dec. 9, 1956; came to U.S., 1990; s. Andres and Cristina (Garcia) L.; m. Maria Lujan Puglia, May 17, 1982; children: Ana Rosa, Maria Martina, Julian Eduardo, Pedro Agustin. Ingeniero agronomo, U. Buenos Aires, 1981; PhD in Genetics and Breeding, Oreg. State U., 1986. Wheat breeder Jose Buck Seed Co., Necochea, Argentina, 1980-85; sunflower breeder Jose Buck Seed Co., Necochea, 1985-88; gen. mgr. Jose Buck Seed Co., Necocher, 1988-90; internat. mgr. Busch Agrl. Resources, Inc., Ft. Collins, Colo., 1990-92; mgr. internat. ops. Busch Agrl. Resources, Inc., Zaragoza, Spain, 1992—. Contbr. articles to profl. jours. Mem. Am. Soc. Agronomy, Am. Soc. for Horticultural Sci., Phi Kappa Phi, Sigma Xi. Roman Catholic. Home: 3515 E County Rd 52 Fort Collins CO 80524 Office: Busch Agrl Resources Inc, TTE Valenzuela 9, 50004 Zaragoza Spain

LORIA, CHRISTOPHER JOSEPH, marine officer; b. Newton, Mass., July 9, 1960; s. Robert Louis and Joan (Novitski) L.; m. Sandra Lee Sullivan, July 5, 1986; 1 child, Taylor Elizabeth Michelle. BS, U.S. Naval Avad., 1983; in tng., USAF Test Pilot Sch., Edwards AFB, 1993—. Commd. 2d lt. USMC, 1983, advanced through grades to capt., 1989; staff officer Marine Aviation Tng. Support Group USMC, NAS Pensacola, Fla., 1984-86; F/A-18 transition pilot VFA-125 COMSTKFITWGPAC USMC, NAS Lemoore Field, Calif., 1988-89; quality assurance officer VMFA-314 MAG-11 3d MAW USMC, MCAS El Toro, Calif., 1989-91, asst. maintenance officer VMFA-314 MAG-11 3d MAW, 1991-92, F/A-18 instr. pilot VMFAT-101 MAG-11 3d MAW, 1992; cons. Los Alamos (N.Mex.) Nat. Lab./DARPA, 1991. Mem. NRA (life), U.S. Naval Acad. Alumni Assn. (life), Marine Corps Aviation Assn. (life), Ducks Unltd. Republican. Roman Catholic. Home: 35 Sharon Dr Edwards CA 93523 Office: Class 93A USAF TPS 220 S Wolfe Ave Edwards CA 93523

LORIA, SERAFINA TERESA, federal agency administrator; b. Wilkes-Barre, Pa., Mar. 26, 1953; d. Joseph and Mary Teresa (Billings) L. Cert., Scranton State Sch. for Deaf, 1985, Glendale C.C., 1990. Claims devel. clk. Social Security Adminstrn., Dept. HHS, Wilkes-Barre, 1977-81; svc. rep. Social Security Adminstrn., Dept. HHS, Phoenix, 1981-89, tech. asst., 1989—. pres. Assn. Retarded Citizens, Wilkes-Barre, 1968-70; coord. U.S. Savs. Bond Campaign, Phoenix, 1986; keyworker United Way Combined Fed. Campaign, Phoenix, 1987, campaign mgr., 1990. Mem. Fed. Women's Program.

LORIMER, JOHN DOUGLASS, geophysicist; b. Oakland, Calif., Dec. 18, 1953; s. John Wallace and Patricia (Moody) L.; m. Sheila Renae Temple, June 13, 1981; children: Shannon Renae, Suzanne Rachael. BS, Colo. Sch. Mines, 1976. Geophysicist Group Seven, Golden, Colo., 1974-77; mgr. user support Compagnie Gen. de Geophysique, Denver, 1977-87; sr. geophysicist McAdams, Roux & Assocs. (changed to Plains Petroleum 1990), Denver, 1987—; assoc. long range planning Plains Petroleum, Lakewood, Colo., 1991-92. Instr. Colo. Youth Pipe Band, Lakewood, 1990-92; sr. ofcl. U.S. Swimming North Jeffco. Mem. Assn. Computer Machinery, Math. Assn. Am., Soc. Exploration Geophysicists (publ. tech. rev. com. 1991-92), GES User Group (pres. Rocky Mt. chpt. 1992), N.Am. Scottish Drum Majors Assn. (pres. 1992). Republican. Lutheran. Office: Plains Petroleum Oper Co 12596 W Bayaud Ste 400 Lakewood CO 80220

LORING, STEVE MARK, electronics executive; b. Stanford, Calif., Mar. 31, 1956; s. Stephen Joseph and Josephine Goldie (Cieloha) L.; m. Laurie Louise Borton, July 26, 1980; children: Charles Ryan, Stephanie Margaret, John Kenneth. BSEE, U. Calif., Davis, 1978; MBA, Stanford U., 1980. Mktg. mgr. BBN Computer, Cambridge, Mass., 1978-79; account mgr. Digital Equipment Corp., Mainard, Mass., 1979-81; sr. sales engr. No. Telecom., Millton, N.J., 1981-84; mktg. mgr. Automatic Data Processing, Ann Arbor, Mich., 1984-86; nat. sales mgr. Network Equipment Techs., Santa Barbara, Calif., 1986-88; v.p. sales and mktg., also bd. dirs. Netcor, Fremont, Calif., 1988-90; pres. LAN Techs., Westlake Village, Calif., 1990—; officer Tekelec, Calabasas, Calif., 1988-89. Contbr. articles to tech. publs. Mem. IEEE, Sigma Phi Epsilon. Republican. Presbyterian. Office: LAN Techs Ste 196 2899 Agora Rd Westlake Village CA 91361

LORING, THOMAS JOSEPH, forest ecologist; b. Haileybury, Ont., Can., May 27, 1921; s. Ernest Moore and Margaret Evangeline (Bacheller) L.; m. Beth Reyes McLaughlin, Oct. 29, 1966; children: John Francis, Christopher

Thomas. BSc in Forestry, Mich. Tech. U., 1946; M Forestry, N.Y. State Coll. Forestry, 1951. Forester McCormick Estates, Champion, Mich., 1947; cons. Porteous and Co., Seattle, 1948-49; forester Penokee Veneer Co., Mellon, Wis., 1951-53; cons. E.M. Loring Consulting, Noranda, Que., Can., 1954-55; forester USDA Forest Svc., Albuquerque, 1956-81; cons. Tom Loring, Cons., Victoria, B.C., Can., 1986—; mem. Parks and Recreation Commn., Victoria, 1988-92, mem. environment adv. com., 1993—. Editor: Directory of the Timber Industry in Arizona and New Mexico,1 972; co-editor: Ecology, Uses and Management of Pinyon-Juniper Woodlands, 1977. Pres. Shawnigan Lake Residents and Rate Payers Assn., B.C., 1985-86. Mem. Soc. Am. Foresters (sect. chair 1960-62), Ecol. Soc. Am., Forest Products Rsch. Soc. (regional rep. 1980-81), Can. Inst. Forestry, Soc. Ecol. Restoration. Home: 59 Moss St, Victoria, BC Canada V8V 4M1

LORINSKY, LARRY, international trade executive, consultant; b. New Britain, Conn., July 31, 1944; s. Jacob and Bernice Edythe (Horn) L.; BA, U. Conn., 1966, MA, 1968; m. Laurie Clark Griffin, June 9, 1968; children: Michael Bliss, Jennifer Bartlett, Jessica Clark. Ops. mgr., then trading mgr. Norwich Iron & Metal Co. (Conn.), 1965-75; ferrous export mgr. Comml. Metals Co., Dallas, 1975-77, br. mgr., San Francisco, 1977-81, West Coast area mgr., 1980-81; exec. v.p. Technalloy Inc., San Jose, Calif., 1981-83; dir. nonferrous alloys David Joseph Co., 1983-84; pres., chief exec. officer Lornat Metals Trading, Inc., 1984-87; project mgr. Mindseed Corp., 1987-89; gen. mgr. Custom Alloy, 1989-90; div. mgr. Ferromet Resources, Inc., 1990-92, pres. 1992; ltd. dir., rep. METALSASIA Internat., 1983—; mng. dir. Ecos Metall. Inc., 1993—. Mem. Nat. Inst. Scrap Recycling Industry, Seaguard Svcs. Inc. (dir.), Locell Assocs. Ltd. (dir.), Brisbane (Calif.) C. of C. (dir. 1977-81), Chickasaw (Ala.) C. of C., Masons. Democrat. Jewish.

LOTHROP, GLORIA RICCI, historian, educator; b. L.A., Dec. 30, 1934; d. Leo N. and Maria (Angeli) R. AB in English (with honors), Immaculate Heart Coll., 1956, MA in Edn., 1963; student, U. of Pisa, Italy, 1960, U. Mysore, India, 1963; postgrad., U. Calif., L.A., 1964-65; PhD in History, U. So. Calif., 1970. Tchr. English, History Sacred Heart High School, 1956-60; tng. tchr., teaching internship program UCLA, 1964; tchr. History Beverly Hills High School, 1962-64; part time supr. of teaching interns Las Virgenes Unified Sch. Dist., 1964-65, Univ. Calif., Riverside, 1965; coord. of tchr. tng., summer internship program Univ. Calif., L.A., 1965; part time instr., U.S. History L.A. Valley C.C., 1966-67; archivist Southwest Regional Lab. for Ednl. Rsch. and Devel., 1967; lecture series coord., Current Affairs Loyola Marymount Univ, 1969-72; vis. lectr., Western Am. History Univ. Calif., 1969-70; supr. student tchrs., asst. prof., History Calif. State Polytechnic Univ., Pomona, 1970-74, supr. student tchrs., assoc. prof., History, 1974-79; vis. prof. Art Ctr. Coll. of Design, 1978-80; acting chair, Dept. of Liberal Studies Calif. State Polytechnic Univ., 1974, 77; adj. prof., Master in Liberal Arts Program Univ. So. Calif., 1980-86; CSU adminstrv. fellow, Office of the Dean of Sch. of Letters and Sci. Calif. State Univ., L.A., 1981-82; prof. of History Calif. State Polytechnic Univ., 1979—; cons. Ontario Mus. of History and Art, 1992, Rancho Los Cerritos, 1991, Constitutional Rights Found., 1988, USC Sch. of Cinema, 1988-89, CSU Inst. for Teaching and Learning, 1989—, Calif. Heritage Quilt Project, 1987-88, L.A. History Project, Public T.V. Sta. KCET, 1986-88, Calif. Project, 1987-89, Afro-Am. Mus., 1985-88, El Pueblo State Historic Park, 1986—, Cattlekate Productions, 1987, So. Calif. Gas Co. and Radio Sta., 1980-88, Ontario Centennial Celebration, 1980, CBS T.V. "Bicentennial Minutes", 1979-80, and participation in numerous other profl. activities. Author: Recollections of the Flathead Mission: The Memorie of Fr. Gregory Mengarini, S.J., 1977, Chi Siamo: The Italians of L.A., 1981, California Woman, A Historic Profile, 1986, Guide to the Historic Resources of the State of Calif., 1989, Rancho San Jose, A Sesquacentennial Tribute, 1987, Pomona Valley: A Centennial History, 1988, A Guide to Historic Outings in Southern Calif., 1991, Quality of Life at California State Polytechnic University, Pomona, 1991; contbr. articles to numerous profl. jours. bd. govs. Calif. Maritime Acad., 1980-82, 82-85, bd. dirs. Photo Friends, L.A. Public Libr., 1990—, hist. adv. Com. to Save Italian Hall Com., 1990—, mem. State and Local Hist. Day Coms., 1987-89, pres. bd. dirs. El Pueblo Park Assn., 1984-85, bd. dirs., 1986-87, pres. emeritus 1988, mem. L.A. 200 Exec. Com. and acting chair edn. com., 1979-91, mem. citizens Adv. Com. for the 1984 Olympics, 1981-84, bd. dirs. L.A. Internat. Visitors Coun., 1981-87, sec. to the exec. com. L.A. Archdiocesan Archival Ctr., 1982-89, chair publications com. and bd. mem. Calif. Hist. Soc., 1987-88. Recipient Community Enrichment award Hist. Soc. of Southern Calif., 1993, Carl Wheat award, 1990, Woman of Distinction award Today's Women's Forum Citrus Coll., 1987, Outstanding Achievement award Southern Calif. Social Sci. Assn., 1987, Calif. Polytechnic Authors Golden Leaves award, 1986, 87, 89, 90, tchr award Daughters of Colonial Wars award, 1983, Outstanding Italian Am. award Targhe d'Oro, Regione Puglia, Italia, 1982, Dist. Alumnae award, Immaculate Heart Coll. Alumnae Assn., 1981, George Danielson Historical Writing Excellence award Westerners Internat., 1978, Outstanding Feminist of the Pomona Valley award NOW, 1974; Haynes Huntington Rsch. fellow Huntington Library, 1986, 91, Fulbright fellow, 1963, Daniel Murphy Found. grantee, 1987. Mem. Am. Hist. Assn., Am. Italian Hist. Assn., Orgn. of Am. Historians, Nat. Women's Studies Assn., Nat. Coun. for the Social Studies, Western Hist. Assn., Southwest Labor Studies Assn., Coast Assn. for Women Historians, Calif. Hist. Soc., Hist. Soc. of So. Calif., Friends of the Huntington Libr., Friends of the Pomina Libr., Friends of the Scripps Coll. Dennison Libr., Pomona Valley Hist. Soc., L.A. City Hist. Soc., Calif. Coun. for the Social Studies, Friends of Banning Park, Associated Hist. Socs. of L.A. County, Friends of the Italian Hall, Orgn. of Hist. Tchrs., Women's Heritage Mus. Democrat. Roman Catholic. Office: California State Polytechnic Univ 3801 West Temple Pomona CA 91768 Home: 880 Paige Dr Pomona CA 91768

LOTT, DAVIS NEWTON, advertising agency executive, publisher; b. San Antonio, May 8, 1913; s. James and Sissilla (Davis) L.; m. Arlene Marion Peterson, Nov. 1, 1942; children: Vicki Arlene, Christy Sue, Laurie Ann. B.S., Northwestern U., 1935; post-grad. UCLA. With Better Homes and Gardens and Successful Farming, Des Moines, Iowa, 1935-36; with Abbott, Labs., North Chicago, Ill., 1936-37; copywriter J. Walter Thompson, Chgo., 1938-39; owner and pres. Lott Advt. Agy., L.A., 1939-41, 46—; pres. USA Corp., Marina Del Rey, Calif.; pres. Lott Publs., Santa Monica, Calif.; pub. Am. Carwash Rev., Am. Personal Protection Rev., Candy WORLD, Tobacco and Sundries WORLD, Specialty/Fancifoods WORLD, Chocolate and Nut WORLD, SugarFree WORLD, New Inventions WORLD, Organic WORLD, Teen Scene, Bubble 'n' ChewinGum WORLD, Cracker/Snack WORLD, Surfing Illustrated, Smoker's Digest, Books and Authors WORLD, New Products and Mail Order WORLD, The Cosa News; dir. spl. projects Microlert Systems Internat. Past bd. dirs. Los Angeles Library Assn. Comdr. USNR, 1941-46, 1951-52, World War II, Korea. Named Assoc. Dean of Candy Industry, Nat. Candy Wholesalers Assn., 1974. Author: Rules of the Road, 1942, Handbook of the Nautical Road; Emergency Shiphandling Manual, 1943, Collision Prevention, 1947, Treasure Trail, 1944, Star Spangled Broadcast, 1950, Mystery of Midnight Springs, 1954, Dodge City Justice, 1957, The Inaugural Addresses of the American Presidents, 1964, The Presidents Speak, 1965, See How They Ran 1972, The Presidents Illustrated, 1976, Jimmy Carter-And How He Won, 1976; co-author: (with Bruce Greenland) musical comedy The Music Room, 1982. Home: 13222 Admiral Ave Unit B Marina Del Rey CA 90292-7042 Office: PO Box 9669 Marina Del Rey CA 90295-2069

LOUCH, ALFRED RICHARD, philosophy educator; b. Fresno, Calif., Feb. 14, 1927; s. Clarence William and Frances (Gould) L.; m. Brenda Schweig; children—Julia Elizabeth, Martin Edward, Sophia Katherine, Peter Charles, John Owen, Hugh William. B.A., U. Calif. at Berkeley, 1949, M.A., 1951; Ph.D., Cambridge U., 1956. Instr. Oberlin Coll., 1957-59; asst. prof., assoc. prof. Syracuse U., 1959-65; vis. assoc. prof. UCLA, 1963-64; assoc. prof., prof. philosophy Claremont (Calif.) Grad. Sch., 1965—, chmn. dept. philosophy, 1966-89. Author: Explanation and Human Action, 1966; contbr. articles to profl. jours. Office: Claremont Grad Sch Claremont CA 91711

LOUCHHEIM, WILLIAM SANDEL, JR., manufacturing company executive; b. Phila., Oct. 4, 1930; s. William and Jean (Benoliel) L.; m. Marlene Marks, Oct. 1, 1952; children: Terry, Mark, Thomas, Deborah. BS in Indsl. Aminstrn., Yale U., 1952; MS in Mgmt. Engring., Rensselaer Poly. Inst., 1965. Commd. ensign USN, 1952, advanced through grades to lt. comdr., 1962; comdg. officer USS Etlah, 1957-58, USS Edmonds, 1962-64; command and control coord. Naval Ship Engring. Ctr., Washington, 1965-68; transferred to Res. USN, 1968; pres., treas., dir. The Bobrick Corp., North Hollywood, Calif., 1968—; chmn., treas., dir. Bobrick Washroom Equipment Inc., North Hollywood, Bobrick Washroom Equipment of Can. Ltd., Scarbrough, Ont.; chmn. Bobrick AG, Basel, Switzerland. Mem. Am. Soc. Naval Engrs., Am. Inst. Indsl. Engrs., U.S. Naval Inst., Sigma Xi. Office: 11611 Hart St North Hollywood CA 91605-5802

LOUCKS, GORDON CRAIG, business educator, consultant; b. Erie, Pa., Aug. 8, 1947; s. Warren M. and Betty Jean (Anderson) L.; m. June Masters, Dec. 21, 1969 (div. 1977); children: David Eric, Michelle Elaine; m. Judith Allen, Dec. 1, 1979; 1 child, Jessica Allene Law. BS in Bus. Adminstrn., Ariz. State U., 1974, M of Quantitative Systems, 1992. Cert. in prodn. and inventory mgmt.; cert. acad. assoc. Goldratt Inst. Asst. dir. admissions DeVry Inst. Tech., Phoenix, 1974-77; dir. admissions Mo. Inst. Tech., Kansas City, Mo., 1977-79; from asst. prof. to prof. DeVry Inst. Tech., Phoenix, 1981-92, sr. prof. bus. ops., 1992—; cons. in field. Contbr. articles to profl. jours. With U.S. Army, 1970-72. Mem. Am. Prodn. and Inventory Control Soc. (region staff 1991—, chpt. acad. liaison 1988—), Prodn. and Ops. Mgmt. Soc. Democrat. Office: DeVry Inst Tech 2149 W Dunlap Ave Phoenix AZ 85021

LOUD, STEWART NELSON, JR., publisher; b. Detroit, Sept. 13, 1940; s. Stewart Nelson and Martha (Woodruff) L.; m. Susan Wilson Conway, Apr. 6, 1963; children: Heather Loud Creighton, Gordon. BBA, U. Mich., 1963. Sales elec., electronics, appliance, bus. equipment divs. Owens-Corning Fiberglas, Toledo, 1963-67, mktg. mgr., 1967-78, mktg. mgr. aerospace, def. div., 1973-79, program dir. Piedmont Products subs., 1979-81; v.p. subcontract mktg. Teledyne Ryan Aero., San Diego, 1983-84; pres. exec. search S.N. Loud & Assocs., Solana Beach, 1981-87; v.p. Spectrum Cons. affiliate S.N. Loud & Assocs., San Diego, 1984-86, N.W. Gibson Internat. affiliate S.N. Loud & Assocs., L.A., 1986-87, Composite Mkt. Reports, Inc., San Diego, 1987—. Fund raiser Ann. Giving Fund U. Mich., Ann Arbor, 1965. Mem. Soc. Advancement of Materials and Process Engring., Soc. Plastics Engrs., Soc. Mfg. Engrs., ASM Internat., Alumni Assn. U. Mich., U. Mich. Club (San Diego, bd. govs. 1983—). Republican. Presbyterian. Home: 1004 Santa Helena Park Ct Solana Beach CA 92075-1543 Office: Composite Mkt Reports Inc 7670 Opportunity Rd Ste 250 San Diego CA 92111-2222

LOUDERBACK, TRUMAN EUGENE, environmental project manager; b. Sterling, Colo., Jan. 17, 1946; s. George DeWayne and Lillian Louise (Harrach) L.; m. Dena Marie Chambers, June 1, 1985; children: Nicole Marie, Kyle Eugene, Matthew Joseph. BS, Colo. State U., 1968; postgrad., U. Colo., 1974-75. Project investigator and biologist, research inst. Colo. Sch. Mines, Golden, 1972-78; adminstr. quality assurance Cleveland-Cliffs Iron Co., Casper, Wyo., 1979, dir. environ. affairs, 1980-83; dir. environ. affairs Cleveland-Cliffs Iron Co., Rifle, Colo., 1984-88, Cliffs Engring., Inc., Rifle, Colo., 1984-88; pvt. practice cons. Lakewood, Colo., 1978-79, Rifle, 1988-89; sr. project mgr. Roy F. Weston, Inc., Lakewood, Colo., 1989—; chmn. environ. com. Pacific Shale Project, Rifle, 1983-87, also mgr. environ. impact statement, 1983-84. Contbr. articles to profl. jours. Industry rep. Colo. Joint Rev. Process Team, Colo. Dept. Nat. Resources, 1983. Mem. Nat. Assn. Environmental Profls., Rocky Mountain Assn. Environmental Profls. Republican. Methodist. Lodge: Rotary (bd. dirs. Rifle chpt. 1984), Masons. Home: 13736 W Auburn Ave Lakewood CO 80228 Office: Roy F Weston Inc 215 Union Blvd Ste 600 Lakewood CO 80228-1842

LOUGANIS, GREG E., former Olympic athlete, actor; b. San Diego, Jan. 29, 1960; s. Peter E. and Frances I. (Scott) L. Student, U. Miami, Fla., 1978-80; B.A. in Drama, U. Calif., Irvine, 1983. Mem. U.S. Nat. Diving Team, 1976—. Recipient Silver medal Olympic Games, 1976, 2 Olympic Gold medals, 1984, 2 Olympic Gold medals, 1988; James E. Sullivan award, Olympic Games, 1984; inducted into Olympic Hall of Fame, 1985; winner 48 U.S. nat. diving titles; World Diving Champion (platform and springboard) 1986, Jesse Owens award, 1987, Pan Am Gold medal, 1979, 83, 87; Gold medalist (platform and springboard) Seoul Olympics, 1988. Home: PO Box 4130 Malibu CA 90265-1430

LOUIE, CHERYL SUSANNE, high technology company executive; b. Gettysburg, Pa., July 14, 1953; d. Floyd James Edward and Verna Kam Lin (Chun) Seiss; m. Wei S. Louie, Aug. 23, 1973; children: Kenna K., Tamara K. BA in Math., U. Md., 1975, MS in Applied Math., 1980. Sci. programmer/analyst Bus. and Tech. Systems, Seabrook, Md., 1975-76; sr. programmer/analyst, then project mgr. Automated Scis. Group, Silver Spring, Md., 1976-80, asst. div. dir., 1980-82; sr. mem. tech. staff Sci. Applications Internat. Corp., McLean, Va., 1982-84; program mgr. SAIC, San Diego, 1984-86, asst. v.p., 1986-89, v.p., 1989-91, corp. v.p., 1991—; mem. Women's Transp. Seminar, Washington, 1976-82. Honoree Tribute to Women in Industry, San Diego YWCA, 1990, Outstanding Young Women Am., 1991. Mem. IEEE, Math. Assn. Am. (selectee sci. and tech. exch. with China 1983), Nat. Security Indsl. Assn., Air Force Com. and Elec. Assn.

LOUIE, LAWRENCE GORDON, real estate company executive; b. San Francisco, Mar. 1, 1954; s. Stanley Kong and Phyllis (Jow) L.; m. Jocelyn Ann Fong, Sept. 9, 1978; children: Daniel Michael, Lindsay Elizabeth. BS summa cum laude, U. Calif., Berkeley, 1976; MBA, Stanford U., 1981. CPA, Calif. Supervising sr. acct. Peat, Marwick, Mitchell & Co., San Francisco, 1976-79; sr. cons. Bain & Co., Palo Alto, Calif., 1981-83; ptnr. Creed & Assocs., San Francisco, 1983-86; exec. v.p., COO, Norris, Beggs & Simpson, San Francisco, 1986—. COGME fellow Stanford U., 1979. Mem. Assn. for Corp. Growth, Phi Beta Kappa. Office: Norris Beggs & Simpson 601 California St Ste 1400 San Francisco CA 94108

LOUIE, STEVEN, multimedia courseware developer, nurse; b. L.A., Jan. 3, 1951; s. Quan Ying and Ngit Seem (Der) L.; m Judith Anne LeFevre, Aug. 16, 1984; children: David Christopher, Linda Danielle, Cameron Quan. Diploma in nursing, U. Ariz., 1977, student, 1984—. RN, Ariz. Mktg. dir. Bus. Computers, Tucson, 1982-84; program coord. Cerebral Palsy Found., Tucson, 1984-85; systems analyst U. Ariz. Coll. Medicine, Tucson, 1987-91; pres. synap TRIX, Tucson, 1992—; dir. Tucson Learning Ctr., 1984-86; interim dir. Children's Mus., Tucson, 1986-87; cons. Burroughs Computer/Cemcorp, Detroit, 1985. Contbr. articles to profl. jours. Bd. dirs. Disability Resources of Tucson, 1988-89, UN Assn., Tucson, 1984-85. Lt. USNR, 1969—. Mem. Apple Programmers and Developers Assn., Naval Res. Officers Assn. Democrat.

LOUNSBURY, GARY DAVID, small business owner, sales representative; b. American Falls, Idaho, May 22, 1953; s. Carlos H. and Louise M. (Liese) L.; m. Rhea Sandra Hofmeister, Aug. 19, 1972; children: Seth Ryan, Chad Aaron. BBA, Idaho State U., 1989. With Electric Svc. Co., Pocatello, Idaho, 1972-74; office mgr. Northwestern Ice and Cold Storage Co., American Falls, 1974-78; with Union Pacific R.R., Pocatello, 1979-83; owner Idaho Golf, American Falls, 1984—; mktg. sales asst. IBM, Pocatello, 1987-89; prodn. supr. Lamb Weston, Inc., American Falls, 1989-91; sales rep. Longview Fibre Co., Twin Falls, Idaho, 1991—. Co-chmn. Southeastern Idaho chpt. Nat. Sudden Infant Death Syndrome Found., Pocatello, 1981-82; bd. dirs. Ken Vanderhoff Meml. Bd., American Falls, 1990—. Mem. Idaho Golf Assn., Golf Clubmakers of Am., American Falls Men's Golf Assn. (bd. dirs. 1987-91). Lutheran. Home: 644 Falls Ave American Falls ID 83211-1414 Office: Idaho Golf 644 Falls Ave American Falls ID 83211-1414

LOUNSBURY, JOHN FREDERICK, geographer, educator; b. Perham, Minn., Oct. 26, 1918; s. Charles Edwin and Maude (Knight) L.; m. Dorothea Frances Eggers, Oct. 3, 1943; children—John Frederick, Craig Lawrence, James Gordon. B.S., U. Ill., 1942, M.S., 1946; Ph.D., Northwestern U., 1951. Asst. dir. rural land classification program Insular Govt., P.R., 1949-52; cons., research analyst Dayton Met. Studies, Inc., Ohio, 1957-60; chmn. dept. earth scis., prof. geography Antioch Coll., 1951-61; prof. geography, head dept. geography and geology Eastern Mich. U., 1961-69; chmn. dept. geography Ariz. State U., 1969-77; dir. Ctr. for Environ. Studies, 1977-80; prof. emeritus Ariz. State U., 1987—; project dir. Geography in Liberal Edn. Project, Assn. Am. Geographers, NSF, 1963-65, project dir. commn. on coll. geography, 1965-74; dir. environment based edn. project US. Office Edn., 1974-75; dir. spatial analysis of land use project NSF, 1975-85. Author articles, workbooks, textbooks. Mem. Yellow Springs Planning Commn., Ohio, dir. research, 1957-60; mem. Ypsilanti Planning Commn., 1961-66; research com. Washtenaw County Planning Commn., 1961-69; mem. cons. Ypsilanti Indsl. Devel. Corp., 1961-63. Served with AUS, 1942-46, ETO. Named Man of Yr., Yellow Springs C. of C., 1956-57. Fellow Ariz.-Nev. Acad. Sci.; mem. Assn. Am. Geographers (chmn. East Lakes div. 1959-61, mem. nat. exec. council 1961-64, chmn. liberal edn. com. 1961-65), Nat. Council Geog. Edn. (chmn. earth sci. com. 1961-68, regional coord. 1961-63, mem. exec. bd. 1968-71, 77-83, v.p. 1977-78, pres. 1979-80, Disting. Svc. award 1988, Disting. Mentor award 1990), Mich. Acad. Sci. Arts and Letters (chmn. pub. relations com. 1964-69, past chmn. geography sect.), Ohio Acad. Sci. (past exec. v.p.), Mich. Acad. Sci., Ariz. Acad. Sci., Am. Geog. Soc., AAAS, Sigma Xi, Delta Kappa Epsilon, Gamma Theta Upsilon. Home: 7850 E Vista Dr Scottsdale AZ 85250-7641 Office: Ariz State U Dept Geography Tempe AZ 85281

LOUTH, EDWIN VERNON, economist, educator; b. Akron, Ohio, Aug. 15, 1920; s. Roland Lawrence and Stella Marie (Mouser) L.; m. Ruth Louise Paul, Aug. 11, 1956; children: Kevin, Gary, Kathy, Bryan, Jacquelyn, Mary. BS in Fin., U. Akron, 1948, postgrad., 1950-51; MS in Mktg., Ohio State U., 1950; cert., Alexander Hamilton Inst., South Bend, Ind., 1960. Economist Studebaker-Packard, Inc., South Bend, 1955-57; asst. to pres. Mercedes-Benz Sales, Inc., South Bend, 1956-65; dir. mktg. rsch. Mercedes-Benz, N.A., Montvale, N.J., 1965-71; gen. mgr. imports & distbn. Nissan Motors, L.A., 1971-75; gen. sales mgr. Downtown L.A. Motors, 1975-83; cons. to automobile industry L.A., 1983—. Ensign USN, 1942-46, World War II. Mem. Am. Mgmt. Assn., Am. Acad. Polit. & Social Scis., Nat. Indsl. Conf. Bd., Pepperdine Assocs., Tau Kappa Epsilon (chmn. local bd.). Roman Catholic. Home: 1208 E California Ave Glendale CA 91206

LOUVAU, GORDON ERNEST, management consultant, educator; b. Oakland, Calif., May 29, 1928; s. Ernest and Ella Meta (Meins) L.; m. Lois Louvau Peterson, June 9, 1984; children: John Pierre, Tanya Lissette, Charles Frederic. Student U. Calif., 1946-49; postgrad. Calif. State U., Hayward, 1975-77; MBA, John F. Kennedy U., 1980. Cert. mgmt. acct., 1975. Accountant, Oakland, 1950-59; asst. controller U.S. Leasing, Inc., San Francisco, 1960-61; pres. Louvau Systems Co., Oakland, 1962-66; v.p., gen. mgr. Prescolite div. U.S. Industries Co., San Leandro, Calif., 1966-68; cons. acctg. systems, 1969—; vis. prof. acctg. U. S.Africa, 1970-71; dir. Inst. Research and Bus. Devel., asst. prof. acctg. Calif. State U. at Hayward, 1972-80; asst. dean., asso. prof. mgmt., dir. acctg. programs J.F. Kennedy U., 1969-85; adj. prof. Golden Gate U., San Francisco, 1985—; instr. U. Calif. Continuing Edn., 1973—. Mem. Inst. Mgmt. Accts. (dir. 1972-74), Am. Acctg. Assn. Republican. Author: Financial Management of the Clinical Laboratory, 1974; Management and Cost Control Techniques for the Clinical Laboratory, 1977; Computers in Accountant's Offices, 1981. Office: PO Box 5808 Carmel CA 93921-5808

LOUX, GORDON DALE, organization executive; b. Souderton, Pa., June 21, 1938; s. Curtis L. and Ruth (Derstine) L.; m. Elizabeth Ann Nordland, June 18, 1960; children: Mark, Alan, Jonathan. Diploma, Moody Bible Inst., Chgo., 1960; BA, Gordon Coll., Wenham, Mass., 1962; BD, No. Bapt. Sem., Oak Brook, Ill., 1965, MDiv, 1971; MS, Nat. Coll. Edn., Evanston,Ill., 1984; LHD (hon.), Sioux Falls Coll., 1985. Ordained to ministry, Bapt. Ch., 1965. Assoc. pastor Forest Park (Ill.) Bapt. Ch., 1962-65; alumni field dir. Moody Bible Inst., Chgo., 1965-66, dir. pub. rels., 1972-76; dir. devel. Phila. Coll. Bible, 1966-69; pres. Stewardship Svcs., Wheaton, Ill., 1969-72; exec. v.p. Prison Fellowship Ministries, Washington, 1976-84, pres., chief exec. officer, 1984-88; pres., chief exec. officer Prison Fellowship Internat., Washington, 1979-87; pres., CEO Internat. Students, Inc., Colorado Springs, Colo., 1988—. Author: Uncommon Courage, 1987, You Can Be a Point of Light, 1991; contbg. author: Money for Ministries, 1989, Dictionary of Christianity in America, 1989. Bd. dirs. Evang. Coun. for Fin. Accountability, Washington, 1979-92, vice chmn., 1981-84, 86-87, chmn., 1987-89; vice chmn. Billy Graham Greater Washington Crusade, 1985-85; bd. dirs. Evang. Fellowship of Mission Agys., 1991—. Named Alumnus of Yr., Gordon Coll., 1986. Republican. Home: 740 Bear Paw Ln Colorado Springs CO 80906-3215 Office: Internat Students Inc Box C Colorado Springs CO 80901

LOUX, ROBERT RICHARD, state agency administrator; b. Owatonna, Minn., Sept. 22, 1949; s. Robert Raymond and Gladys Lucille (Hickerson) L.; m. Donny L. Loux, Nov. 24, 1979. BS in Edn., U. Nev., 1972, postgrad., 1972—. Adminstr. energy program Community Svcs. Agy., Reno, 1974-76; asst. adminstr. for conservation Nev. Dept. Energy, Carson City, 1976-78, adminstr. for R & D, 1978-83; nuclear waste cons. to Office of Gov., State of Nev., Carson City, 1983-84; dir. Nev. Nuclear Waste Project Office, Carson City, 1984-85; exec. dir. Nev. Agy. for Nuclear Projects, Carson City, 1985—; chmn. high level nuclear waste com. Western Govs. Assn., Denver, 1988—, Western Interstate Energy Bd., Denver, 1988—; Nev. solar rep. Western Solar Utilization Network, Portland, Oreg., 1976-78, bd. dirs., 1978-83; mem. Interstate Solar Coordinating Coun., Washington, 1977. Contbr. numerous articles to various mags., jours. and newspapers. Various appointments by Nev. govs. Recipient merit award for environ. leadership, 1989; grantee NSF, 1975. Mem. Nev. Solar Energy Assn. (founder, bd. dirs. 1974). Democrat. Home: PO Box 894 Dayton NV 89403 Office: Nev Agy for Nuclear Projects Capitol Complex Carson City NV 89710

LOVATT, ARTHUR KINGSBURY, JR., manufacturing company executive; b. Ventura, Calif., Mar. 12, 1920; s. Arthur Kingsbury and Flora (Mercedes) L.; B.S., U. So. Calif., 1941; M.B.A., Queens U., 1943; m. Juanita Gray, Feb. 1, 1946; children—Sherry Lynn, Tim Arthur. Leaseman, Shell Oil Co., Los Angeles, 1946-51; dir. indsl. relations Willys-Overland Motors, Inc., Los Angeles, 1952-55; asst. to pres. and gen. mgr. Pastushin Aviation Corp., Los Angeles, 1955-57; pres. Lovatt Assos., Los Angeles, 1957-66; chemn. bd., pres., gen. mgr. Lovatt Tech. Corp., Santa Fe Springs, Calif., 1966—, also dir.; chmn. bd. Lovatt Sci. Corp., Santa Fe Springs, Metal Ore Processes, Inc., Santa Fe Springs; dir. Lovatt Industries, Inc., others. Mem. Calif. Rep. State Central Com., 1964—; chartered mem. Rep. Pres. Task Force, citizens adv. commn.; state adviser U.S. Congl. Adv. Bd. With U.S. Army, 1943-45. Mem. Am. Legion (post comdr. 1946), AAAS, Nat. Space Inst., Am. Soc. Metals, Los Angeles C. of C., U. So. Calif. Alumni Assn. (life), Nat. Hist. Soc. (founding assoc.), N.Y. Acad. Scis., Internat. Oceanographic Found., Smithsonian Assos., Am. Ordnance Assn., Disabled Am. Vets., U.S. Senatorial Club, Nat. Rifle Assn. Club: Masons (past master, Shriner). Inventor, developer tech. processes. Office: Lovatt Tech Corp 10106 Romandel Ave Santa Fe Springs CA 90670-3433

LOVE, LAURIE MILLER, science editor; b. Fed. Republic Germany, May 7, 1960; came to U.S., 1961; d. Thomas Walter and Jacquelyn (Jolley) Miller; m. Raymond Lee Love. Student, U. Minn., 1979-80; BA in Psychology, Scripps Coll., 1983; postgrad., UCLA. Programmer specialist Control Data Corp., San Diego, 1982, asst. mgr. software retail store, 1983-84; support technician Ashton-Tate, Torrance, Calif., 1984, editor-in-chief, 1985-87; mgr. tech. pub. Ashton-Tate, Torrance, 1986-87; product mgr. Apple Products, Nantucket Corp., Los Angeles, 1987-88; sr. mktg. cons. Macintosh Market Launch Systems, Rancho Palos Verdes, Calif., 1988; pres. Miller Tech. Pub., Santa Cruz, 1987—; contractor, writer, editor Claris Corp., Santa Clara, Calif. Tech. and devel. editor Addison-Wesley, Osborne/McGraw Hill, TAB books; author Using ClarisWorks, 1992, Using ClarisWorks for Windows, 1993; contbr. feature articles to monthly mag., 1985—, computer product manuals, 1987—. Mem. Software Pubs. Assn., Soc. Tech. Communication (Silicon Valley chpt.), Santa Cruz Performing Arts Alliance, Pi Beta Phi (asst. treas. 1980). Democrat. Methodist.

LOVE, SANDRA RAE, information specialist; b. San Francisco, Feb. 20, 1947; d. Benjamin Raymond and Charlotte C. Martin; B.A. in English, Calif. State U., Hayward, 1968; M.S. in L.S., U. So. Calif., 1969; m. Michael D. Love, Feb. 14, 1971. Tech. info. specialist Lawrence Livermore (Calif.) Nat. Lab., 1969—. Mem. Spl. Libraries Assn. (sec. nuclear sci. div. 1980-82, chmn. 1983-84, bull. editor 1987-89), Beta Sigma Phi. Democrat. Episcopalian. Office: Lawrence Livermore Nat Lab L-387 PO Box 808 Livermore CA 94551-0808

LOVEJOY, ALAN KENT, human and organizational systems consultant; b. Boston, Feb. 12, 1939; s. Ralph Francis L.; m. Debra Ann Benton, May 10, 1981 (div. Oct. 87); children: Kim, Alan, Robin, Allison, Erica. BSBA, U. Conn., 1961; postgrad., U. Pa. Wharton Sch., 1961-64, Fielding Inst., Santa Barbara, Calif., 1991—. Cert. Profl. Mgmt. Cons. Advt. asst. INA, Phila.,

1964-66; brand asst. Dow Chem. Co., Midland, Mich., 1966-67; account exec. Harold Cabot & Co., Boston, 1967-69; communications mgr. ELBA Systems, Denver, 1969-70; prin. The Lovejoy Group, Denver, 1971-73; v.p. William B. Arnold & Assocs., Denver, 1973-76; pres. Lovejoy & Lovejoy Inc., Denver, 1976—; mem. Nat. Bur. of Profl. Mgmt. Cons., 1991—, 50 for Colo., 1991-93; exec. dir. Nat. Assn. Bus. and Indsl. Saleswomen, Denver, 1984—. Editor (newsletter) Picking Winners, 1983—. Mem. Orgn. Devel. Network, Jung Soc., Multi-Lingual Internat. Soc. (pres. 1989-90). Episcopalian. Office: Lovejoy & Lovejoy Ste 1407 90 Corona St Denver CO 80218-3852

LOVEJOY, ANN ATWATER, author, magazine writer, garden designer; b. Boston, Nov. 19, 1951; d. Thomas Van Valkenburgh and Jean (Langston) A.; m. Mark Timothy Lovejoy, July 5, 1976; children: Peter Langston, Andrew Atwater. BA, Wilmington Coll., 1974. Columnist Seattle Weekly Newsmag., 1985-91; contrb. editor Horticulture Mag., Boston, 1988-91; freelance author Organic Gardening, Emaus, Pa., 1988, 90, N.Y. Times, N.Y.C., 1989, 90, House and Garden, N.Y.C., 1989, 90, Harrowsmith Country Living, Charlotte, Vt., 1988—, Horticulture Mag., 1991—; columnist Eastside Weekly, Bellevue, Wash., 1991—, Seattle Post-Intelligence, 1993—; bd. dirs. Aboretum Found., Seattle, N.W. Horticulture Soc., Seattle. Author: The Year in Bloom, 1986 (Gov.'s book award 1987), The Border in Bloom, 1990; author: (with others) Gardens of the World, 1991 (Quill and Trowel award); editor: Perennials, 1991, American Mixed Borders, 1993. Bd. dirs. Country Dr. Clinic., Seattle, 1980-86; officer Boy Scouts Am., Bainbridge Island, Wash., 1988—; active Bainbridge Island Grange, 1990—. Recipient Quill and Trowel Comm. award Garden Writers Am., 1988, cert. merit award Seattle Garden Club, 1991. Home: 13045 Madison NE Bainbridge Island WA 98110

LOVELAND, PATRICIA MARIE, chemist; b. Seattle, May 10, 1941; d. James Tilgman and Adele Ruth (Schunke) Rice; m. Walter David Loveland, Sept. 7, 1963. BS, U. Wash., 1964. Analyst Am. Potash & Chem., West Chgo., 1966-67; chemist III Oreg. State U., Corvallis, Oreg., 1967-68, rsch. asst., 1968-84, sr. rsch. asst., 1984—. Contbr. articles to profl. jours. Mem. Am. Chem. Soc., Pacific N.W. Assn. Toxicologists, Nat. Audubon Soc., Oreg. Natural Resources Coun., Santiam Wilderness Com., Sigma Xi. Office: Oreg State U Dept Food Wiegand Hall Rm 100 Corvallis OR 97331-6602

LOVELAND, WALTER DAVID, chemist, chemistry educator; b. Chgo., Dec. 23, 1939; s. Walter Hubert and Anna Emelia (Reese) L.; m. Patricia Marie Rice, Sept. 7, 1962. SB, MIT, 1961; PhD, U. Wash., Seattle, 1965. Postdoctoral fellow Argonne (Ill.) Nat. Lab., 1966-67; rsch. asst. prof. Oreg. State U., Corvallis, 1967-68, from asst. to prof., 1968—; vis. scientist Argonne (Ill.) Nat. Lab., 1968, 76, Lawrence Berkeley (Calif.) Lab., 1976-77, 83-84. Author: Radiotracer Methods, 1975, Nuclear Chemistry, 1982, Elements Beyond Uranium, 1990; contbr. numerous articles to profl. jours. NSF fellow, 1962, Tartar fellow Oreg. State U., 1977. Mem. Am. Chem. Soc., Am. Phys. Soc., AAAS, MIT Alumni Assn., Sigma Xi. Democrat. Office: Oreg State U Radiation Ctr Corvallis OR 97331

LOVELESS, EDNA MAYE, English language educator; b. Keene, Tex., Jan. 15, 1929; d. Luther Ray and May (Willhelm) Alexander; m. William Alfred Loveless, Aug. 17, 1952; children: Marti Sue Loveless Olson, Marilynn Kaye Loveless Stepniak. BA, Walla Walla Coll., 1950; PhD, U. Md., 1969. Instr. English Walla Walla Coll., College Place, Wash., 1950-52, Columbia Union Coll., Takoma Park, Md., 1952-53; prof. English Columbia Union Coll., Takoma Park, 1980-90; textbook writer, editor Review Publishers, Hagerstown, Md., 1970-80; prof. English La Sierra U., Riverside, Calif., 1990—; advisor student newspaper Columbia Union Coll. Takoma Park, 1980-90, dir. writers' conf., 1988, 89; lectr. Profl. Writers' Conf., Review Publs. Hagerstown, 1989; dir. freshman English program, La Sierra U., Riverside, 1991—; participant and presenter Internat. Conf. on Critical Thinking, 1991; presenter Nat. Conf. on Critical Thinking, 1992. Author: (book and tchr's manual) What Shall I Live For?, 1976, What Is of Most Worth?, 1978; author: (with others) Penn's Example to the Nations, 1987, Masterplots II, Juvenile and Adult Fiction, 1991. Recipient NDEA fellowship U. Md., 1964-68, 2nd prize Scholastic Mag. Writing Contest for High Sch. Tchrs., 1967. Office: La Sierra U 4700 Pierce St Riverside CA 92515-8247

LOVELL, CHARLES C., federal judge; b. 1929; m. Ariliah Carter. BS, U. Mont., 1952, JD, 1959. Assoc. Church, Harris, Johnson & Williams, Great Falls, Mont., 1959-85; judge U.S. Dist. Ct. Mont., Helena, 1985—; chief counsel Mont. Atty Gen.'s Office, Helena, 1969-72. Served to capt. USAF, 1952-54. Mem. ABA, Am. Judicature Soc., Assn. Trial Lawyers Am. Office: US Dist Ct PO Drawer 10112 301 S Park Helena MT 59626

LOVELL, JEFFREY DALE, investment banker; b. N.Y.C., Apr. 21, 1952; s. Lewis Frederick and Pauline (Dailey) L.; m. Elaine Worley, Apr. 26, 1980; children: McKenzie Brooke, Alexander S. L. BS cum laude, U. Colo., 1974; postgrad., U. So. Calif. Regent's Coll., London, 1986-87. Fin. analyst Gen. Dynamics, San Diego, 1974-75; account exec. SEI Corp., Wayne, Pa., 1976-79; v.p. SEI Corp., L.A. and Wayne, 1980-82, sr. v.p., 1982-88; mng. dir. SEI Fin. Svcs. (U.K.), London, 1985-88; co-founder, pres. Putnam Lovell Inc., Manhattan Beach, Calif., 1988—; registered securities prin. NASD, 1983; trustee PIC Investment Trust Mutual Fund, Pasadena, Calif., 1992; dir. Eagle Mgmt. and Trust Co., Houston, Tex., 1992. Mem. Manhattan Beach Friends of the Arts, Rep. Nat. Com., Washington, 1985, St. Andrews Presbyn. Ch. Mem. U. So. Calif. Assocs., U. Colo. Alumni Assn., Manhattan Country Club, Beta Gamma Sigma, Sigma Nu. Office: Putnam Lovell Inc 317 Rosecrans Ave Manhattan Beach CA 90266-3241 and: Putnam Lovell Inc 19 Fulton St New York NY 10038

LOVELL, TOM, artist; b. N.Y.C., Feb. 5, 1909; s. Henry Saunders and Edith Scott (Russell) L.; m. Gloyd S. Lovell, Aug. 9, 1934 (dec.); children: David, Deborah. BFA, Syracuse U., 1931. Free lance illustrator N.Y., 1930-68; gallery painter N.Mex., 1968—. Sgt. USMC, 1944-46. Named to Cowboy Hall of Fame. Mem. Nat. Acad. Western Art, Cowboy Artists Am., Soc. Illustrators. Republican.

LOVEN, CHARLES JOHN, advertising executive; b. N.Y.C., Feb. 17, 1937; s. John and June Emma (Custer) Azzaro. BA, Occidental Coll., 1962; MA, Calif. State U., L.A., 1967. Group scheduler Douglas Space Systems, Huntington Beach, Calif., 1963-65; personnel rep. Shell Oil Co., L.A., 1965-71; dir. indsl. rels. Calif. Computer Products, Anaheim, 1971-80; sr. v.p., dir. personnel dept. Thompson Recruitment Advt., L.A., 1980-92. With USCG, 1954-58. Mem. Employment Mgrs. Assn., Personnel and Indsl. Rels. Assn., Am. Soc. Personnel Adminstrs., Exec. Human Resources Round Table. Office: Thompson Recruitment Advt 6500 Wilshire Blvd Fl 21 Los Angeles CA 90048-4920

LOVENTHAL, MILTON, writer, playwright, lyricist; b. Atlantic City, Jan. 19, 1923; s. Harry and Clara (Feldman) L.; m. Jennifer McDowell, July 2, 1973. BA, U. Calif., Berkeley, 1950, MLS, 1958; MA in Sociology, San Jose State U., 1969. Researcher Hoover Instn., Stanford, Calif., 1952-53; librarian San Diego Pub. Library, 1957-59; librarian, bibliographer San Jose (Calif.) State U., 1959-92; tchr. writing workshops, poetry readings, 1969-73; co-producer lit. and culture radio show Sta. KALX, Berkeley, 1971-72; editor, pub. Merlin Press, San Jose, 1973—. Author: Books on the USSR, 1951-57, 57, Black Politics, 1971 (featured at Smithsonian Inst. special event, 1992), A Bibliography of Material Relating to the Chicano, 1971, Autobiographies of Women, 1946-70, 72, Blacks in America, 1972, The Survivors, 1972, Contemporary Women Poets an Anthology, 1977, Ronnie Goose Rhymes for Grown-Ups, 1984; co-author: (Off-Off-Broadway plays) The Estrogen Party to End War, 1986, Mack the Knife, Your Friendly Dentist, 1986, Betsy & Phyllis, 1986, The Oatmeal Party Comes to Order, 1986, (play) Betsy Meets the Wacky Iraqi, 1991; co-writer (mus. comedy) Russia's Secret Plot to Take Back Alaska, 1988. Recipient Bill Casey award in Letters, 1980; grantee San Jose State U., 1962-63, 84. Mem. Assn. Calif. State Profs., Calif. Alumni Assn., Calif. Theatre Coun. Office: PO Box 5602 San Jose CA 95150-5602

LOVIN, HUGH TAYLOR, history educator; b. Pocatello, Idaho, Dec. 10, 1928; s. Robert Scott and Hazel Viora (Gleim) L.; m. Ida Carolyn Edwards, June 3, 1956; 1 child, Jeffrey Douglas. BA, Idaho State Coll., 1950; MA, Wash. State U., 1956; PhD, U. Wash., 1963. Instr. history U. Alaska Mil. Br., Elmendorf AFB, 1957-61; asst. prof. history Southwestern Oreg. Coll., North Bend, 1963-64, Kearney (Nebr.) State Coll., 1964-65; assoc. prof. history Boise (Idaho) State U., 1965-68, prof. history, 1968-93, emeritus prof. history, 1993—; abstracter pub. hist. materials Am. Bibiog. Ctr., CLIO Press, Santa Barbara, Calif., 1970—; book reviewer in profl. history jours., 1969—. Editor: Labor in the West, 1986; contbr. numerous articles to profl. jours. including Pacific N.W. Quarterly, Jour. of the West, The Old Northwest. Fellow Nat. Endowment for Humanities, 1982. Home: 1310 Gourley St Boise ID 83705-6042 Office: Boise State U Dept History Boise ID 83725

LOVING, JEAN FRANKLIN, retired elementary school administrator, consultant; b. Kansas City, Kans., Sept. 28, 1925; d. James Wesley and Nine Jane (McMullen) L.; m. Betty Lou Pearsall, May 30, 1947; children: Janet Kay, Donald Franklin. BS in Edn., Ariz. State Coll., 1950, MA in Sch. Adminstrn., 1958; EdS in Sch. Adminstrn., No. Ariz. U., 1966. Cert. elem. tchr., Ariz. Tchr. Prescott (Ariz.) Pub. Schs., 1950-65; asst. supt. bus. Prescott Pub. Schs., 1972-74, elem. prin., 1974-85; adminstrv. asst. No. Ariz. U., 1965-66; asst. prin. Prescott Jr. High, 1966-72; cons. reading programs, Prescott, 1983; speaker Nat. Elem. Sch. Prins. Conv., Denver, 1985; creator edn. computer program, 1984; creator reading program Million Minutes of Reading, 1983. Scoutmaster Boy Scouts of Am., Prescott, 1950-60; active fund drives Big Brothers Big Sisters, Prescott, 1982-84; elder Church of Christ, Prescott, 1985. Served to staff sgt. U.S. Army Air Force 1943-45. No. Ariz. U. fellow, 1965-66. Mem. Ariz. Sch. Admins. (prof. growth com. 1985-86, speaker workshops, Ariz Disting. Elem. Prin. 1985), Nat. Elem. Sch. Adminstrs. (Nat. Disting. Elem. Prin. 1985). Republican. Church of Christ. Clubs: Smoki, Am. Bowling Congress (Prescott). Address: 519 Highland Ave Prescott AZ 86303

LOVINS, AMORY BLOCH, physicist, energy consultant; b. Washington, Nov. 13, 1947; s. Gerald Hershel and Miriam (Bloch) L.; m. L. Hunter Sheldon, Sept. 6, 1979. Student, Harvard U., 1964-65, 66-67, Magdalen Coll., Oxford, Eng., 1967-69; MA, Oxon Coll., Oxford, 1971; DSc (hon.), Bates Coll., 1979, Williams Coll., 1981, Kalamazoo Coll., 1983, U. Maine, 1985; LLD (hon.), Ball State U., 1983; D of Environ. Sci. (hon.), Unity Coll., 1992. Jr. research fellow Merton Coll., 1969-71; Brit. rep., policy advisor Friends of the Earth, San Francisco, 1971-84; regent's lectr. U. Calif., Berkeley and Riverside, 1978, 81; v.p., dir. research Rocky Mountain Inst., Old Snowmass, Colo., 1982—; govt. and indsl. energy cons., 1971—; vis. prof. Dartmouth Coll., 1982; disting. vis. prof. U. Colo., 1982; prin. tech. cons. E Source, 1989—. Author: (also layout artist and co-photographer) Eryri, The Mountains of Longing, 1971, The Stockholm Conference: Only One Earth, 1972, Openpit Mining, 1973, World Energy Strategies: Facts, Issues, and Options, 1975, Soft Energy Paths: Toward a Durable Peace, 1977; co-author: (with J. Price) Non-Nuclear Futures: The Case for an Ethical Energy Strategy, 1975, (with L.H. Lovins) Energy/War: Breaking the Nuclear Link, 1980, Brittle Power: Energy Strategy for National Security, 1982, (with L.H. Lovins, F. Krause, and W. Bach) Least-Cost Energy: Solving the CO2 Problem, 1982, 89, (with P. O'Heffernan, sr. author, and L.H. Lovins) The First Nuclear World War, 1983, (with L.H. Lovins, sr. author, and S. Zuckerman) Energy Unbound: A Fable for America's Future, 1986, (hardware reports) The State of the Art: Lighting, 1988, The State of the Art: Drivepower, 1989, The State of the Art: Appliances, 1990, The State of the Art: Water Heating, 1991, The State of the Art: Space Cooling and Air Handling, 1992; co-photographer (book) At Home in the Wild: New England's White Mountains, 1978; author numerous poems; contbr. articles to profl. jours., reports to tech. jours.; patentee in field. Recipient Right Livelihood award Right Livelihood Found., 1983, Sprout award Internat. Studies Assn., 1977, Pub. Edn. award Nat. Energy Resources Orgn., 1978, Pub. Service award Nat. Assn. Environ. Edn., 1980, Mitchell prize Mitchell Energy Found., 1982, Delphi Prize Onassis Found., 1989. Fellow AAAS, World Acad. Art and Sci., Lindisfarne Assn.; mem. Fedn. Am. Scientists. Home and Office: 1739 Snowmass Creek Rd Snowmass CO 81654-9199

LOVINS, L. HUNTER, public policy institute executive; b. Middlebury, Vt., Feb. 26, 1950; d. Paul Millard and Farley (Hunter) Sheldon; m. Amory Bloch Lovins, Dept. 6, 1979; 1 child, Nanuq. BA in Sociology, Pitzer Coll., 1972, BA in Polit. Sci., 1972; JD, Loyola U., L.A., 1975; LHD, U. Maine, 1982. Bar: Calif. 1975. Asst. dir. Calif. Conservation Project, L.A., 1973-79; exec. dir., co-founder Rocky Mountain Inst., Snowmass, Colo., 1982—; vis. prof. U. Colo., Boulder, 1982; Henry R. Luce vis. prof. Dartmouth Coll., Hanover, N.H., 1982; cons. in field. Co-author: Brittle Power, 1982, Energy Unbound, 1986, Least-Cost Energy Solving the CO2 Problem, 2d edit., 1989. Bd. dirs. Renew Am., The Other Econ. Summit, Basalt and Rural Fire Protection Dist.; vol. firefighter. Recipient Mitchell prize Woodlands Inst., 1982, Right Livelihood Found. award, 1983, Best of the New Generation award Esquire Mag., 1984. Mem. Colo. Profl. Rodeo Assn. Office: Rocky Mountain Inst 1739 Snowmass Creek Rd Snowmass CO 81654-9199

LOVVIK, DARYL VAUGHN, consulting geologist; b. Eau Claire, Wis., July 26, 1941; s. Oscar W. and Pearl B. (Johnson) L.; m. Sherly Birog; children: Alexander Wilhelm, Sheila Najivi. B.S. in Geology, W. Tex. State U., 1975; MBA, U. of Phoenix. Cert. profl. geologist; registered profl. geologist, Alaska, Ariz., Ark. Cons. geologist, Golden, Colo., 1975-77; exploration geologist Cotter Corp., Moab, Utah, 1977-79; pres. Southwestern Geol. Survey, Mesa, Ariz., 1979-86; water resource dir. Tohono O'Odham Nation, Sells, Ariz., 1986-89, Ariz. Dept. Water Resources, 1990—; pres. Southwestern Geol., Tempe, Ariz. Contbr. articles to profl. jours. With USAF, 1960-64. Mem. Am. Inst. Profl. Geologists, Geol. Soc. Am., Am. Assn. Petroleum Geologists, Soc. Mining Engrs. Republican. Episcopalian. Home: 410 E Beatrice St Tempe AZ 85281-1004

LOW, MERRY COOK, civic worker; b. Uniontown, Pa., Sept. 3, 1925; d. Howard Vance and Eleanora (Lynch) Mullan; m. William R. Cook, 1947 (div. 1979); m. John Wayland Low, July 8, 1979; children: Karen, Cindy, Bob, Jan. Diploma in nursing, Allegheny Gen. Hosp., Pitts., 1946; BS summa cum laude, Colo. Women's Coll., 1976. RN, Colo. Dir. patient edn. Med. Care and Rsch. Found., Denver, 1976-78. Contbr. chpt. to Pattern for Distribution of Patient Education, 1981. Bd. dirs. Women's Libr. Assn., U. Denver, 1982—, vice chmn., 1985-86, chmn., 1986-87, co-chmn. spl. event, 1992; docent Denver Art Mus., 1979—, mem. vol. exec. bd., 1988—, mem. nat. docent symposium com., 1991, chmn. collector's choice benefits, 1988, pres. vols., trustee, 1988-90; v.p. bd. dirs. Lamont Sch. Music assocs., 1990—, U. Denver; mem. search com. for dir. Penrose Libr., 1991-92; trustee ch. coun., chmn. invitational art show 1st Plymouth Congl. Ch., Englewood, Colo., 1981-84; co-chmn. art auction Colo. Alliance Bus., 1992, 93. Recipient Disting. Svc. award U. Denver Coll. Law, 1988, King Soopers Vol. of Week award, 1989, Citizen of Arts award Fine Arts Found., 1993. Mem. Am. Assn. Mus. (vol. meeting coord. 1990-91), Colo. Symphony Guild (bd. dirs. 1992—), Opera Colo. Guild, P.E.O. (pres. Colo. chpt. DX 1982-84). Republican. Congregationalist. Home: 2552 E Alameda Ave Apt 11 Denver CO 80209-3324

LOWDERMILK, DALE, retired air traffic controller; b. Alameda, Calif., Jan. 8, 1948; s. Clyde Myron and Florence Ruth (Nelson) L.; m. Pierina Ann Guadagnini, Aug. 21, 1971; children—Dalina Beth, Michael Dale. A.A., Santa Barbara City Coll., 1970; student Gemological Inst. Am., 1980. Air traffic contr. FAA, Santa Barbara Tower/Radar Approach, 1971—. Contbr. articles to profl. jours. Pres., Santa Barbara Apt. Owners Assn., 1983. Served with USAF, 1968-71. Fellow Murphy Ctr. for Codification of Human and Orgnl. Law; mem. Tenn. Squires, Internat. Platform Assn. Libertarian. Club: NOTSAFE (founder, exec. dir.). Office: NOT-SAFE PO Box 5743 Santa Barbara CA 93150

LOWE, AL, entertainment software designer; b. St. Louis, July 24, 1946; s. Albert and Addie (Kesselring) L.; m. Margaret Paul Lowe, Aug. 3, 1968; children: Brian, Megan. BS in Edn., U. Mo., 1967, MS in Edn., 1968. Music coord. Clovis (Calif.) Unified Schs., 1973-83; pres. Al Lowe Assocs., Inc., Fresno, Calif., 1983—; outside designer/cons. Sierra Online Inc., Coarsegold, Calif., 1987—. Designer/programmer entertainment software: The Black Cauldron, 1984, Leisure Suit Larry in the Land of the Lounge Lizards, 1987, Freddy Pharkas, Frontier Pharmacist, 1993, others. Mem. Computer Game Designers Assn., Clovis Exch. Club (pres. 1985), World Saxophone Congress. Office: Al Lowe Assocs Inc 459 E Ascot Pl Fresno CA 93720-0885

LOWE, OARIONA, dentist; b. San Francisco, June 17, 1948; d. Van Lowe and Jenny Lowe-Silva; m. Evangelos Rossopoulos, Dec. 18, 1985; 1 child, Thanos G. BS, U. Nev., Las Vegas, 1971; MA, George Washington U., 1977; DDS, Howard U., 1981; pediatric dental cert., UCLA, 1984. Instr. Coll. Allied Health Scis. Howard U., Washington, 1974-76, asst. prof., 1976-77; research asst. Howard U. Dental Sch., Washington, 1977-81; resident gen. practice Eastman Dental Ctr., Rochester, N.Y., 1981-82; dir. dental services City of Hope Med. Ctr., Duarte, Calif., 1984-86; vis. lectr. pediatric dentistry UCLA; mem. oral cancer task force Am. Cancer Soc., Pasadena, Calif., 1985—. Contbr. articles to profl. jours. Del. People to People Internat. Mem. ADA, Am. Soc. Dentistry for Children (v.p.), Nat. Soc. Autistic Children, Calif. Dental Assn., Am. Acad. Pediatric Dentistry, Sigma Xi, Alpha Omega. Republican. Presbyterian. Office: 11822 Floral Dr Ste D Whittier CA 90601-2917

LOWE, RICHARD GERALD, JR., computer programmer manager; b. Travis AFB, Calif., Nov. 8, 1960; s. Richard Gerald and Valerie Jean (Hoeffer) L. Student, San Bernardino Valley Coll., 1978-80. Tech. specialist Software Techniques Inc., Los Alamitos, Calif., 1980-82, sr. tech. specialist, 1982-84, mgr. tech. services, 1984-85; mgr. cons. services Software Techniques Inc., Cypress, Calif., 1985-86; sr. programmer BIF Accutel, Camarillo, Calif., 1986-87; systems analyst BIF Accutel, Camarillo, 1987-88; mgr. project Beck Computer Systems, Long Beach, Calif., 1986-91, v.p. devel., 1991—. Author: The Autobiography of Richard G. Lowe, Jr., 1991, The Lowe Family and Their Relatives, 1992; contbr. articles to profl. jours. Mem. Assn. Computing Machinery, Digital Equipment Corp. Users Group. Office: Beck Computer Systems 5372 N Long Beach Blvd Long Beach CA 90805-5858

LOWE, ROBERT AUGUSTUS, emergency medicine physician; b. San Francisco, June 24, 1952; s. Gustav Emanuel and Elizabeth (Lowenhaupt) L.; m. Michelle Berlin-Lowe, Aug. 6, 1989. BA in Sociology, U. Calif., Santa Cruz, 1972; MD, U. Calif., Davis, 1977; MPH, U. Calif., Berkeley, 1991. Resident in internal medicine U. Mich., Ann Arbor, 1977-80, clin. instr., 1980-82; resident in emergency medicine U. Cin., 1982-84; asst. chief emergency medicine Valley Med. Ctr., Fresno, Calif., 1984-89; asst. clin. prof. U. Calif., San Francisco, 1989—, postdoctoral scholar, 1991—. Contbr. articles to profl. jours. Fellow Am. Coll. Emergency Physicians, ACP; mem. Soc. for Acad. Emergency Medicine (chair govt. affairs com. 1990-93), Alpha Omega Alpha, Phi Kappa Phi.

LOWE, ROBERT STANLEY, lawyer; b. Herman, Nebr., Apr. 23, 1923; s. Stanley Robert and Ann Marguerite (Feese) L.; m. Anne Kirtland Selden, Dec. 19, 1959; children—Robert James, Margaret Anne. A.B., U. Nebr., 1947, J.D., 1949. Bar: Wyo. 1949. Ptnr. McAvoy & Lowe, Newcastle, 1949-51, Hickey & Lowe, Rawlins, 1951-55; county and pros. atty. Rawlins, 1955-59, individual practice law, 1959-67; asst. dir. Am. Judicature Soc., Chgo., 1967-68; assoc. dir., dir. programs and services Am. Judicature Soc., 1968-74; counsel True Oil and affiliated cos., Casper, Wyo., 1974—; bd. dirs. Mountain Plaza Nat. Bank, Hilltop Nat. Bank, Casper.; mem. Nat. Ski Patrol System div. legal adv., 1975-78 (Yellow merit award 1982, 85, 87, 88); pres., bd. dirs. Snowy Range Ski Corp., 1963-66; city atty., Rawlins, 1963-65. Co-editor: Selected Readings on the Adminstration of Justice and its Improvement, 1969, 71, 73, Current Issues on the Judiciary, 1971, Judicial Disability and Removal Commissions, Courts and Procedures, 1969, 70, 72, 73, others; Contbr. articles to legal jours. mem. Wyo. Ho. of Reps., 1952-54; del. Dem. Nat. Conv., 1952, alt. del., 1956; mem. exec. com. Wyo. Dem. Central Com., 1953-55; bd. dirs. Vols. in Probation, 1969-82; leader People to People legal del. People's Republic of China, 1986. Served to lt. (j.g.) in U.S. Maritime Svc., U.S. Mcht. Marine, 1943-46. Recipient Dedicated Community Worker award Rawlins Jr. C. of C., 1967. Fellow Am. Bar Found. (life); mem. VFW (post advocate 1991—), Am. Judicature Soc. (dir. 1961-67, 85-89, bd. editors 1975-77, Herbert Harley award 1974), ABA (sec. jud. adminstrn. div. Lawyers Conf., exec. com. 1975-76, chmn. 1977-78, chmn. judicial qualification and selection com. 1986—, coun. jud. adminstrn. div. 1977-78, mem. com. to implement Jud. Adminstrn. Standards 1978-82, Ho. of Dels. state bar del. 1978-80, 86-87, state del. 1987—, Assembly del. 1980-83), Wyo. State Bar (chmn. com. on cts. 1961-67, 77-87), Nebr. State Bar Assn., Ill. State Bar Assn., D.C. Bar, Inter-Am. Bar Assn., Inst. Jud. Adminstrn., Rocky Mountain Oil and Gas Assn. (legal com. 1976—, chmn. 1979-82, 90-91), Rocky Mountain Mineral Law Found. (trustee 1980—), Am. Law Inst., Order of Coif, Delta Theta Phi (dist. chancellor 1982-83, chief justice 1983—; Percy J. Power Meml. award 1983, Gold Medallion award 1990). Mem. Ch. Christ, Scientist. Lodges: Masons, Shriners, Elks, Odd Fellows, Rotary (club pres. 1985-86, dist. 5440 exec. comm. 1987-89). Home: 97 Primrose St Casper WY 82604-4018 Office: 895 W River Cross Rd Casper WY 82601-1758

LOWE, SUE ESTHER, optometrist; b. Scottsburg, Ind., July 22, 1954; d. Donald and Etta (Helton) L.; m. Eric Stephen Lundell, May 24, 1953; 1 child, Sven Olaf Lundell. BA, U. Wyoming, 1976; OD, Pacific U., Forest Grove, Oreg., 1980. Rsch. asst. Pacific U. Coll. of Optometry, Forest Grove, Oreg., 1976-77; pvt. practice optometrist, 1980—; assoc. Snowy Range Vision Ctr., Laramie, Wyo., 1980-82, ptnr. Trustee Albany County Hosp. Dist., 1985-88, mem. Episcopal Ch., 1983—, bd. dirs. LWV, 1981—, Wyoming Infant Stimulation, 1982—, Precinct Com. Woman, 1983-84; interviewer Albany County Oral History Project, 1983-86. Named One of the Outstanding Young Women of Am, 1976, 1978, Outstanding Greek Woman, 1976. Fellow Acad. of Optometry, Coll. Optometrists in Vision Devel.; mem. Am. Optometric Assn., Wyoming Optometric Assn., Calif. Optometric Assn., Colo. Optometric Assn., Am. Pub. Health Assn., Infant Stimulation Edn. Assn., Am. Optometric Found., Zontas Internat. Lioness, Omega Epsilon Phi, Alpha Epsilon Delta, Alpha Chi Omega Alumna Club. Democrat. Home: 1704 Skyline Dr Laramie WY 82070-8913 Office: Snowy Range Vision Ctr 301 S 8th St Laramie WY 82070-3914

LOWENSTAM, STEVEN, classica educator; b. Springfield, Ill., Dec. 14, 1945; s. Heinz and Ilse (Weil) L. BA, U. Chgo., 1967; MA, Harvard U., 1969, PhD, 1975. Asst. prof. Classics U. Oreg., Eugene, 1975-81, assoc. prof. Classics, 1981-93, prof., 1993—; chmn. Classics U. Oreg., 1982-83, 85-87; dir. humanities program U. Oreg., Eugene, 1980-83, 84-87. Author: Death of Patroklos, 1981, The Scepter and the Spear, 1993, (with others) Cyrene: Final Report III, 1987; contbr. articles to profl. jours. First Prize Acad. Am. Poets, 1965. Mem. Am. Philol. Assn., Classical Assn. of Pacific N.W. (pres. 1985-86), Archaeol. Inst. (pres. Eugene chpt. 1979-80, 86-87, 92-93), Philol. Assn. of Pacific Coast. Home: 2015 Sunrise Blvd Eugene OR 97405-5524 Office: U Oreg Dept Classics Eugene OR 97405

LOWENTHAL, TINA MARIE, contract negotiator; b. Wyandotte, Mich., Dec. 8, 1961; d. Donald Allen and Namiko (Endo) Pocock; m. Marc Allan Lowenthal, Oct. 27, 1985. BA, Mich. State U., 1984; cert. in govt. contract adminstrn., UCLA, 1989; MBA, U. La Verne, 1991. Asst. mgr. Bakers Square Restaurant, La Verne, Calif., 1985-86; contract negotiator Jet Propulsion Lab., Pasadena, Calif., 1986—. Mem. Nat. Contract Mgmt. Assn., Mich. State U. Alumni Assn. Democrat. Home: 1124 W Juanita Ave San Dimas CA 91773 Office: Jet Propulsion Lab 4800 Oak Grove Dr Pasadena CA 91109

LOWI, ALVIN, JR., mechanical engineer, consultant; b. Gadsden, Ala., July 21, 1929; s. Alvin R. and Janice (Haas) L.; m. Guillermina Gerardo Alverez, May 9, 1953; children: David Arthur, Rosamina, Edna Vivian, Alvin III. BME, Ga. Inst. Tech., 1951, MSME, 1955; PhD in Engring., UCLA, 1956-61. Registered prof. engr., Calif. Design engr. Garrett Corp., Los Angeles, 1956-58; mem. tech. staff TRW, El Segundo, Calif., 1958-60, Aerospace Corp., El Segundo, 1960-66; prin. Alvin Lowi and Assocs., San Pedro, 1966—; pres. Terraqua Inc., San Pedro, Calif., 1968-76; v.p. Daeco Fuels and Engring. Co., Wilmington, Calif., 1978—; also bd. dirs. Daeco Fuels and Engring. Co.; vis. research prof. U. Pa., Phila., 1972-74; sr. lectr. Free Enterprise Inst., Monterey Park, Calif., 1961-71; bd. dirs. So. Calif. Tissue Bank; research fellow Heather Found., San Pedro, 1966--. Contbr. articles to profl. jours.; patentee in field. Served to lt. USN, 1951-54, Korea. Fellow Inst. Humane Studies; mem. ASME, NSPE, Soc. Automotive Engrs., Soc. Am. Inventors, So. Bay Chamber Music Soc., Scabbard and Blade, Pi

Tau Sigma. Jewish. Home and Office: 2146 W Toscanini Dr San Pedro CA 90732-1420

LOWIG, HENRY FRANCIS JOSEPH, former mathematics educator, researcher; b. Prague, Austria/Hungry, Oct. 29, 1904; came to Can., 1957; s. Henry and Catherine (Chwojka) L.; m. Libby Barbara Otta, Sept. 7, 1949; children: Ingrid Henriette, Evan Henry Francis. D. Rerum Naturalium, German U., Prague, 1928; DSc, U. Tasmania, Hobart, Australia, 1951. Faculty, German U., Prague, 1935-38; lectr. math. U. Tasmania, 1948-51, sr. lectr., 1951-57; assoc. prof. U. Alta., Edmonton, Can., 1957-67, prof., 1967-70, prof. math. emeritus, 1970—; reviewer Math. Revs., Ann Arbor, Mich., 1962-91, Zentralblatt für Mathematik und ihre Grenzgebiete, Berlin, 1968-78. Contbr. articles to profl. jours. Vis. fellow Australian Nat. U., 1966-67. Mem. Am. Math. Soc., Can. Math. Soc., Can. Assn. Univ. Tchrs., Czechoslovak Soc. Arts and Scis. Home: 15212 81st Ave, Edmonton, AB Canada T5R 3P1 Office: Univ Alta, Dept Math, Edmonton, AB Canada T6G 2G1

LOWINGER, PAUL LUDWIG, psychiatrist, educator, consultant; b. Chgo., Nov. 14, 1923; m. Margaret Fisher, July 31, 1948; children: Leslie Ann, Wendy Lee, Lawrence Paul. BS, Northwestern U., Evanston, Ill., 1945; MD, Iowa State U., 1949, MS in Psychiat. Rsch., 1953. Diplomate Am. Bd. Psychiatry and Neurology. Intern Marine Hosp., Staten Island, N.Y., 1949-50; resident in psychiatry Marine Hosp. and Psychopathic Hosp. of U. Iowa, 1950-53; dep. chief psychiat. svcs. USPHS Hosp., New Orleans, 1953-55; organizer-dir., cons. adult outpatient svc. Lafayette Clinic Wayne State U. Sch. Medicine, Detroit, 1955-70, assoc. prof. psychiatry, 1965-74; med. dir. Inst. for Labor and Mental Health, Oakland, Calif., 1974—; pvt. practice San Francisco, 1974—; clin. prof. psychiatry and community medicine U. Calif., San Francisco, 1974—; mem. numerous hosp. staffs including Contra Costa County Hosp., Martinez, Calif., chief psychiatry, 1982; instr. Tulane U. Med. Sch., 1953-55; vis. lectr. various Mich. state hosps.; organizer, chief psychiat. svcs. Detroit Meml. Hosp., 1959-70, cons. 1970-74; dir. NIMH grant Wayne State U., 1959-71; med. dir. Detroit Model Neighborhood Drug Abuse Program, 1970-74; lectr. Sch. Pub. Health, U. Calif., Berkeley; med. adminstr. Prisoners' Health Project, San Francisco, 1974-76; mem. advisory and legis. coms. numerous city, state and fed. agys.; cons., internat. lectr. in field. Author: (with Martha Livingston) The Minds of the Chinese People, 1983; contbr. articles to med. jours., chpts. to books. Former bd. dirs. Fund for Equal Justice, ACLU, Metro Jail Ministry, Ams. for Democratic Action, NOW, Metro E. Drug Treatment Ctr., Mich., The Farm, San Francisco. With U.S. Army, World War II. Fellow Am. Psychiat. Assn., Am. Orthopsychiat. Assn., Am. Acad. Psychoanalysis (sci. assoc.), Royal Coll. Psychiatrists, Mich. Assn. Neuropsychiat. Hosp. and Clinic Physicians (past pres.); mem. APHA (past nat. chmn. med. com. for human rights), Coun. Health Orgns. (founding nat. bd. responsibility and med. aid for Indochina com.).

LOWMAN, LARRY LOYD, sales executive; b. Billings, Mont.; s. Loyd Sylvester and Myrtle Sylvia (Linnell) L.; m. Dorothy Eleanor Matthaes, Sept. 27, 1954; children: Randy Grant, Linda Lynette. AA, U. Idaho, 1960. Store supt. Firestone T & R Co., Akron, Ohio, 1955-68; controller No. Mobat, Black Eagle, Mont., 1968-69; dist. mgr. Dayton (Ohio) Tire, 1969-70; v.p., gen. mgr. BL & M Tire Inc., Billings, Mont., 1970-77; owner, mgr. Action Career/Gallery of Rental, Billings, 1977-80; br. mgr. Brad Ragan Inc., Billings, 1980—; cons. in field. Author: (newspaper) TRACKS, 1972-74, (employee manual) Rules & Policy, 1971. Pres. Pvt. Employment Assn. of Mont., Billings, 1979; dir. Nat. Tire Dealers Assn., Billings, 1974, Little League Baseball, Great Falls, Mont., 1966, Labor Arbitration Bd., Helena, Mont., 1978, Mont. Assn. Credit Mgmt., Billings, 1989. Named #1 Store of the Yr., Firestone Tire & Rubber, 1965, #1 Profit Achiever, Brad Ragan Inc., 1990. Office: Brad Ragan Inc 3004 1st Ave S Billings MT 59101-4003

LOWNDES, DAVID ALAN, systems analyst; b. Schenectady, N.Y., Oct. 28, 1947; s. John and Iris Anne (Hepburn) L.; m. Peggy Welco, May 3, 1970; children: Diana Justine, Julie Suzanne. AB, U. Calif., Berkeley, 1969, postgrad., 1972-73. Acct., credit mgr. The Daily Californian, Berkeley, 1973-75; bus. mgr. The Daily Californian, 1975-76; acct. Pacific Union Assurance Co., San Francisco, 1976-77, acctg. mgr., 1977-78; sr. acct. U. Calif., San Francisco, 1978-88, sr. systems analyst, 1988—. Home: 1829 Gaspar Dr Oakland CA 94611-2350 Office: U Calif 250 Executive Park Blvd Ste 2000 San Francisco CA 94143-0976

LOWNEY, BRUCE STARK, artist; b. Los Angeles, Oct. 16, 1937; s. Franklin and Thelma (Poirier) L. B.A., North Tex. State U., 1959; M.A., San Francisco State U., 1966. printer-fellow Tamarind Lithography Workshop Inc., Los Angeles, 1967; printmaking supr. Mpls. Coll. Art and Design, 1971; vis. artist Chgo. Art Inst., 1972, 77, Western Ill. State U., 1973. One man shows, Elaine Horwitch Galleries, Santa Fe, 1975, 80, Louise Allrich Gallery, San Francisco, 1975, Martha Jackson Gallery, N.Y.C., 1975, Hill's Gallery, Santa Fe, 1978, Elaine Horwitz, Santa Fe, 1982, Rettie y Martinez, Santa Fe, 1986; group shows include, Library of Congress, 1975, U. N.D., 1978, Allrich Gallery, 1977, Mus. of Albuquerque, 1980; represented in permanent collections, Chgo. Art Inst., Yale U., Mus. Fine Arts, Santa Fe, Mpls. Mus. Art, No. Ill. U. Served with U.S. Army, 1962-64. Nat. Endowment for Arts grantee, 1974; Western States Art Found grantee, 1979; recipient Louis Comport Tiffany award, 1974. Home and Studio: 800 Oso Ridge Rt El Morro Grants NM 87020

LOWRY, CANDACE ELIZABETH, human resource administrator, consultant; b. Miles City, Mont., Sept. 27, 1950; d. James A. and Nathlee (Azar) Zadick; m. Michael Roy Lowry, June 7, 1980; 1 child, Natalie. BSW with high honors, U. Mont., 1971; MSW with high honors, U. Iowa, 1975; DSW, U. Utah, 1984. Clin. social worker, Utah; cert. marriage and family therapist and supr.; diplomate clin. social work, 1987—. Inpatient social worker II U. Iowa Psychiat. Hosps., Iowa City, 1975-76, inpatient social worker III, 1976-79, coordinator, Iowa Autism Program, 1979-80; coordinator, social work specialist U. Utah Counseling Ctr., Salt Lake City, 1980-86, assoc. dir., 1986; prog. dir. adult unit Wasatch Canyons Hosp., Salt Lake City, 1986—; dir. all adult svcs. Wasatch Canyons Hosp., 1990—; clin. instr. U. Utah, Salt Lake City, 1981—. Co-author: Meeting the Needs of Autistic Children, 1980; contbr. articles to profl. jours. Grantee NIMH, 1986—. Mem. Nat. Assn. Social Workers, Acad. Cert. Social Workers (cert.), Nat. Register Clin. Social Workers, Am. Group Psychotherapy Assn., Salt Lake City C. of C. Home: 2705 Eagle Way Salt Lake City UT 84108 Office: Wasatch Canyons Hosp 5770 S 1500 W Salt Lake City UT 84123-5200

LOWRY, EDWARD FRANCIS, JR., lawyer; b. Los Angeles, Aug. 13, 1930; s. Edward Francis and Mary Anita (Woodcock) L.; m. Patricia Ann Palmer, Feb. 16, 1963; children: Edward Palmer, Rachael Louise. Student, Ohio State U., 1948-50; A.B., Stanford, 1952, J.D., 1954. Bar: Ariz. 1955, D.C. 1970, U.S. Supreme Ct. 1969. Camp dir. Quarter Circle V Bar Ranch, 1954; tchr. Orme Sch., Mayer, Ariz., 1954-56; trust rep. Valley Nat. Bank Ariz., 1958-60; pvt. practice, Phoenix, 1960—; assoc. atty. Cunningham, Carson & Messinger, 1960-64; ptnr. Carson, Messinger, Elliott, Laughlin & Ragan, 1964-69, 70-80, Gray, Plant, Mooty, Mooty & Bennett, 1981-84, Eaton, Lazarus, Dodge & Lowry Ltd., 1985-86; exec. v.p., gen. counsel Bus. Realty Ariz., 1986—; pvt. practice, Scottsdale, Ariz., 1986-88; ptnr. Lowry & Froeb, Scottsdale, 1988-89, Lowry, Froeb & Clements, P.C., Scottsdale, 1989-90, Lowry & Clements P.C., Scottsdale, 1990, Lowry, Clements & Powell, P.C., Scottsdale, 1991—; asst. legis. counsel Dept. Interior, Washington, 1969-70; mem. Ariz. Commn. Uniform Laws, 1972—, chmn., 1976-88; judge pro tem Ariz. State Ct. Appeals, 1986, 92-93. Chmn. Council of Stanford Law Socs., 1968; vice chmn. bd. trustees Orme Sch., 1972-74, treas., 1981-83; bd. trustees Heard Mus., 1965-91, life trustee, 1991—, pres., 1974-75; bd. visitors Stanford Sch. Law; magistrate Town of Paradise Valley, Ariz., 1976-83; juvenile ct. referee Maricopa County, 1978-83. Served to capt. USAF, 1956-58. Fellow Ariz. Bar Found. (founder); mem. ABA, Maricopa County Bar Assn., D.C. Bar Assn., State Bar Ariz. (chmn. com. uniform laws 1979-85), Stanford Law Soc. Ariz. (past pres.), Scottsdale Bar Assn. (bd. dirs. 1991—, v.p. 1991, pres. 1992—), Ariz. State U. Law Soc. (bd. dirs.), Nat. Conf. Commrs. Uniform State Laws, Delta Sigma Rho, Alpha Tau Omega, Phi Delta Phi. Home: 7600 N Moonlight Ln Paradise Valley AZ 85253-2938 Office: Lowry Clements & Powell PC 6900 E Camelback Rd Ste 1040 Scottsdale AZ 85251-2444

LOWRY, LARRY KENNETH, small business owner; b. Denver, July 12, 1949; s. Kenneth Floyd and Maxine Jean (Hill) L.; m. Debra Lynn King, Aug. 8, 1970;l 1 child, Kristi Lynn. Student, Foot Hill Jr. Coll., Los Altos, Calif., 1967-69. Cert. journeyman plumber. Supr. Roto-Rooter Sewer Svc., Mountain View, Calif., 1971-82; gen. mgr. Roto-Rooter Sewer Svc., Kennewick, Wash., 1982—. Mem. Richland Rotary (dir. 1989-91, v.p. 1992-93, pres. 1993—, Paul Harris fellow 1989). Republican. Office: Roto-Rooter Sewer Svc Rt 4 Box 4000-D Kennewick WA 99336

LOWRY, LARRY LORN, management consulting company executive; b. Lima, Ohio, Apr. 12, 1947; s. Frank William and Viola Marie L.; m. Jean Carroll Greenbaum, June 23, 1973; 1 child, Alexandra Kristin. BSEE, MIT, 1969, MSEE, 1970; MBA, Harvard U., 1972. Mgr. Boston Consulting Group, Menlo Park, Calif., 1972-80; sr. v.p., mng. ptnr. Booz, Allen & Hamilton Inc, San Francisco, 1980—; pres. Booz, Allen Capital Inc., San Francisco, 1987—. Western Electric fellow, 1969, NASA fellow, 1970. Mem. Sigma Xi, Tau Beta Pi, Eta Kappa Nu. Presbyterian. Home: 137 Stockbridge Ave Atherton CA 94027-3942

LOWRY, MIKE, governor, former congressman; b. St. John, Wash., Mar. 8, 1939; s. Robert M. and Helen (White) L.; m. Mary Carlson, Apr. 6, 1968; 1 child, Diane. B.A., Wash. State U., Pullman, 1962. Chief fiscal analyst, staff dir. ways and means com. Wash. State Senate, 1969-73; govtl. affairs dir. Group Health Coop. Puget Sound, 1974-75; mem. council King County Govt., 1975-78, chmn., 1977; mem. 96th-100th congresses from 7th dist. Wash., 1979-1989; governor State of Wash., 1993—. Chmn. King County Housing and Community Devel. Block Grant Program, 1977; pres. Wash. Assn. Counties, 1978. Democrat. Address: PO Box 4256 Seattle WA 98104*

LOWRY, ROBERT RONALD, chemist; b. San Francisco, Feb. 23, 1932; s. Herbert Mattern and Ann (Bruegmann) L.; m. Darlene Nelda Peacock, Apr. 18, 1957; children: Janette Eileen, Karen Diane, Cathleen Yvonne. BA, Chico State Coll., 1953. Lab. technician U. Calif., Davis, 1957-61; chemist Oreg. State U., Corvallis, 1962—; reseacher, tour guide Horner Mus., Oreg. State U. Contbr. articles to profl. jours. Chmn. Citizen's Adv. Com. on Transit, Corvallis, 1987—, Linn-Benton Loop Transit Commn., Albany, 1987-90; mem. Transit Levy coms., 1983, 86, 89, 92, Corvallis, Transp. Adv. com., Salem, 1988; Mem. Oreg. Hist. Soc., Benton County Mus. With U.S. Army, 1954-57. Named Outstanding Transit Advocate Oreg. Transit Assn., 1990. Mem. Am. Oil Chemist's Soc., Nat. Assn. Ry. Passengers (bd. dirs. 1985-86), 1000 Friends of Oreg., Sigma Xi. Republican. Mem. Reorganized LDS Ch. Home: 2720 NW Mulkey Ave Corvallis OR 97330-2437 Office: Oreg State U Agrl Chem Dept ALS 1007 Corvallis OR 97331-7301

LOZANO, IGNACIO EUGENIO, JR., newspaper editor; b. San Antonio, Jan. 15, 1927; s. Ignacio E. and Alicia E. de Lozano; m. Marta Navarro, Feb. 24, 1951; children: Leticia Eugenia, José Ignacio, Monica Cecilia, Francisco Antonio. A.B. in Journalism, U. Notre Dame, 1947. Asst. pub. La Opinion, Los Angeles, 1947-53, pub., editor, 1953-76, 77-83, 84-86; pub. La Opinion, 1983-84, editor-in-chief, 1986—; ambassador El Salvador, 1976-77; Am. ambassador to El Salvador, 1976-77; bd. dirs. BankAmerica Corp., Bank of Am. NT & SA, Pacific Enterprises., The Walt Disney Co., Calif. Econ. Devel. Corp. Bd. dirs. Nat. Pub. Radio, Los Angeles World Affairs Council, Santa Anita Found., Youth Opportunity Found., Orange County Performing Arts Ctr.; mem. Council on Fgn. Relations, Council of Am. Ambassadors; trustee U. Notre Dame, Occidental Coll., South Coast Repertory Company; overseer The Rand Corp. Inst. for Civil Justice; bd. govs. Calif. Community Found. Mem. Calif. Newspaper Pubs. Assn. (bd. dirs.), Calif. Press Assn., Cath. Prss Council of So. Calif., Greater Los Angeles Press Club, Inter Am. Press Assn. (pres.), Sigma Delta Chi. Office: La Opinion PO Box 15093 1436 S Main St Los Angeles CA 90015

LU, PAUL HAIHSING, geotechnical engineer; b. Hsinchu, Taiwan, Apr. 6, 1921; came to U.S., 1962; m. Sylvia Chin-Pi, May 5, 1951; children: Emily, Flora. BS in Mining Engring., Hokkaido U., Sapporo, Japan, 1945; PhD in Mining Engring., U. Ill., 1967. Sr. mining engr., br. chief Mining Dept. Taiwan Provincial Govt., Taipei, 1946-56; sr. indsl. specialist mining and geology U.S. State Dept./Agy. for Internat. Devel., Taipei, 1956-62; rsch. mining engr. Denver Rsch. Ctr. Bur. of Mines, U.S. Dept. Interior, 1967-90; geotech. cons. Lakewood, Colo., 1991—. Contbr. over 60 articles to profl. jours. Rsch. fellow Hokkaido U., 1945-46, Ill. Mining Inst., 1966-67. Mem. Internat. Soc. for Rock Mechanics, Soc. for Mining, Metallurgy, and Exploration (AIME), Mining and Materials Processing Inst. Japan, Chinese Inst. of Mining and Metall. Engrs. (dir., mining com. chair 1960-62, Tech. Achievement award 1962). Home and Office: 1001 S Foothill Dr Lakewood CO 80228-3404

LU, PENGZHE, botanist; b. Xi'an, Shaanxi, China, Oct. 1, 1957; came to U.S., 1989; s. Zhonghe and Guofang (Du) L.; m. Liying, Mar. 8, 1986. BA, Beijing Normal U., 1982; MS, Beijing U., 1985; postgrad., U. Calif., Davis, 1990—. Lectr. Liaoning Normal U., Dalian, China, 1985-89; rsch. scholar U. Calif., Davis, 1989-90; student cons. Liaoning Normal U., 1985-89; tech. in field. Jastro-Shields Rsch. scholar U. Calif., 1990-92; Nonresident Tuition Fee fellow U. Calif., 1990-92; recipient Excellent Student award, Beijing Normal U., 1981, Henry A. Jastro Fellowship U. Calif., 1993-94. Mem. Botanical Soc. Am., Sigma Xi. Office: U Calif Dept Agronomy and Range Sci Davis CA 95616

LU, WUAN-TSUN, microbiologist, immunologist; b. Taichung, Taiwan, July 8, 1939; came to U.S., 1964; s. Yueh and Jinmien Lu; m. Rita Man Rom, July 25, 1970; children: Dorcia, Loretta. BS in Agrl. Econs., Nat. Taiwan U., 1960; MS in Microbiology, Brigham Young U., 1968; PhD, U. Okla., 1978. Microbiologist, chemist Murray Biol. Co., L.A., 1969-71; microbiologist Reference Lab., North Hollywood, Calif., 1971-73; rsch. assoc. U. Okla., Okla. City, 1973-78; lab. supr. Reference Med. Lab., San Jose, Calif., 1980; mng. dir. Anakem Labs., Los Gatos, Calif., 1981-85; toxicologist SmithKline Labs., San Jose, 1981; founder, pres. United Biotech, Inc., Mountain View, Calif., 1983—, dir., chmn., mng. dir., 1987—; bd. dirs. Sino-U.S. Hunan Bioengring. Co. Ltd., Internat. Biopharm. Inc., Sacramento. Mem. N.Y. Acad. Sci., Am. Soc. Clin. Pathologists, Am. Soc. Clin. Chemists, Delta Group. Office: United Biotech Inc 110 Pioneer Way # C Mountain View CA 94041-1517

LUBECK, MARVIN JAY, ophthalmologist; b. Cleve., Mar. 20, 1929; s. Charles D. and Lillian (Jay) L. A.B., U. Mich., 1951, M.D., 1955, M.S., 1959. Diplomate Am. Bd. Opthamology; m. Arlene Sue Bitman, Dec. 28, 1955; children: David Mark, Daniel Jay, Robert Charles. Intern, U. Mich. Med. Ctr., 1955-56, resident ophthalmology, 1956-58, jr. clin. instr. ophthalmology, 1958-59; pvt. practice medicine, specializing in ophthalmology, Denver, 1961—; mem. staff Rose Hosp., Porter Hosp., Presbyn. Hosp., St. Luke's Hosp.; assoc. clin. prof. U. Colo. Med. Ctr.; cons. ophthalmologist State of Colo. With U.S. Army, 1959-61. Fellow ACS; mem. Am. Acad. Ophthalmology, Denver Med. Soc., Colo. Ophthalmol. Soc., Am. Soc. Cataract & Refractive Surgery. Home: 590 S Harrison Ln Denver CO 80209-3517 Office: 3865 Cherry Crk North Dr Denver CO 80209-3803

LUBIN, STANLEY, lawyer; b. Bklyn., May 7, 1941; children: David Christopher, Jessica Nicole; m. Barbara Ann Lubin. AB, U. Mich., 1963, JD with honors, 1966. Bar: D.C. 1967, Mich. 1968, U.S. Ct. Appeals (D.C. cir.) 1967, U.S. Ct. Appeals (6th cir.) 1968, U.S. Supreme Ct. 1970, Ariz. 1972, U.S. Ct. Appeals (9th cir.) 1976. Atty. NLRB, Washington, 1966-68; asst. gen. counsel UAW, Detroit, 1968-72; assoc. Harrison, Myers & Singer, Phoenix, 1972-74, McKendree & Tountas, Phoenix, 1975; ptnr. McKendree & Lubin, Phoenix and Denver, 1975-84; shareholder Treon, Warnicke & Roush, P.A., 1984-86; pvt. practice, Law Offices Stanley Lubin, Phoenix, 1986—; mem. Ariz. Employment Security Adv. Council, 1975-77. Active ACLU, dir. Ariz. chpt. 1974-81; mem. Ariz. State Cen. Com. Dem. Party, 1973-78, 84—; vice-chmn. Ariz. State Dem. Party, 1986-91, 1993—, sec., 1991-92, mem. state exec. com., 1986—, Ariz. Dem. Coun., 1987—, chmn., 1988-93, Thomas Jefferson Forum, 1987—, chmn. 1988-93. Mem. ABA, State Bar Ariz., Maricopa County Bar Assn., Indsl. Rels. Rsch. Assn., Ariz. Indsl. Rels. Assn. (exec. bd. 1973—, pres. 1979-80, 84). Club: University. Co-author: Union Fines and Union Discipline Under the National Labor Relations Act, 1971. Home: 719 E Orangewood Ave Phoenix AZ 85020-5033 Office: Ste 875 2700 N Central Ave Phoenix AZ 85004-1147

LUBMAN, DAVID, aerospace engineer, acoustical consultant; b. Chgo., Aug. 3, 1934; s. Abraham and Jeanette (Kluber) L.; m. Beverly Doris Gleekel, Dec. 23, 1956 (dec. 1974); 1 son, Stephen Carl. BSEE, Ill. Inst. Tech., 1960; MSEE, U. So. Calif., 1962. Staff engr. Hughes Aircraft Co., Fullerton, Calif., 1960-67, sr. staff engr., 1976—; sr. scientist LTV Rsch. Ctr., Anaheim, Calif., 1967-68, Bolt Beranek & Newman, Inc., Van Nuys, Calif., 1968-69; dir., cons. D. Lubman & Assocs., Woodland Hills, Calif., 1969-76; cons. Office Naval Rsch., Washington, 1968-76, Nat. Bur. Standards, Washington, 1972-73, Gen. Electric Co., Evendale, Ohio, 1970-73, Krieger Steel Products, 1980—, Gen. Motors, 1989—; dir. Inst. Noise Control Engring., N.Y.C., 1976-79, 90-93; vis. prof. math. Calif. State U., Fullerton, 1982-83, Chapman Coll., Orange, Calif., 1963-68; vis. scientist Nat. Rsch. Coun. Can., Ottawa, 1976; organizer spl. sessions sci. meetings, 1972—. Author sci. publs., 1968—; inventor high speed rotating diffuser. Bd. dirs. Laguna Beach Chamber Music Soc., 1984-88. Served with USAF, 1953. Howard Hughes Masters fellow, 1960-62. Fellow Acoustical Soc. Am. (chmn. tech. com. archtl. acoustics 1980-83, chmn. Orange County Regional chpt. 1988—); mem. Nat. Coun. Acoustical Cons. Inst. Noise Control Engrs., IEEE, AAAS, Sigma Xi. Home: 14301 Middletown Ln Westminster CA 92683-4514 Office: Hughes Aircraft Co PO Box 3310 Bldg 676 MS NI23B Fullerton CA 92631

LUCAS, DONALD LEO, entrepreneur; b. Upland, Calif., Mar. 18, 1930; s. Leo J. and Mary G. (Schwamm) L.; BA, Stanford U., 1951, MBA, 1953; m. Lygia de Soto Harrison, July 15, 1961; children: Nancy Maria, Alexandra Maria, Donald Alexander. Assoc. corp. fin. dept. Smith, Barney & Co., N.Y.C., 1956-59; gen., ltd. ptnr. Draper, Gaither & Anderson, Palo Alto, Calif., 1959-66; pvt. investor, Menlo Park, Calif., 1966—; bd. dirs. Cadence Design Systems, San Jose, Calif., Delphi Info. Systems, Inc., Westlake Village, Calif., ICOT Corp., San Jose, Kahler Corp., Rochester, Minn., Oracle Systems, Redwood Shores, Calif., Quantum Health Resources Inc., Orange, Calif., TriCord Systems, Inc., Plymouth, Minn., Tri-Care, Inc., Santa Ana, Calif.; Mem. bd. regents Bellarmine Coll. Prep., 1977—; regent emeritus U. Santa Clara, 1980—. 1st lt. AUS, 1953-55. Mem. Am. Coun. for Capital Formation, Stanford U. Alumni Assn., Stanford Grad. Sch. Bus. Alumni Assn., Order of Malta, Stanford Buck Club, Vintage Club (Indian Wells, Calif.), Menlo Country Club (Woodside, Calif.), Menlo Circus Club (Atherton, Calif.), Jackson Hole Golf and Tennis Club, Teton Pines Club, Zeta Psi. Home: 224 Park Ln Menlo Park CA 94027-5411 Office: 3000 Sandhill Rd # 3-210 Menlo Park CA 94025-7166

LUCAS, GEORGE W., JR., film director, producer, screenwriter; b. Modesto, Calif., May 14, 1944. Student, Modesto Jr. Coll.; BA, U. So. Calif., 1966. Chmn. Lucasfilm Ltd., San Rafael, Calif. Creator short film THX-1138 (Grand prize Nat. Student Film Festival, 1967); asst. to Francis Ford Coppola on The Rain People; dir. Filmmaker (documentary on making of The Rain People); dir., co-writer THX-1138, 1970, American Graffiti, 1973; dir., author screenplay Star Wars, 1977; exec. producer More American Graffiti, 1979, The Empire Strikes Back, 1980, Raiders of the Lost Ark, 1981, Indiana Jones and the Temple of Doom, 1984, Labyrinth, 1986, Howard the Duck, 1986, Willow, 1988, Tucker, 1988; exec. producer, co-author screenplay Return of the Jedi, 1983; co-exec. producer Mishima, 1985; co-author, co-exec. producer Indiana Jones and the Last Crusade, 1989; exec. producer (TV series) The Young Indiana Jones Chronicles, 1992-93. Office: Lucasfilm Ltd PO Box 2009 San Rafael CA 94912-2009

LUCAS, MALCOLM MILLAR, state supreme court chief justice; b. Berkeley, Calif., Apr. 19, 1927; s. Robert and Georgina (Campbell) L.; m. Joan Fisher, June 23, 1956; children: Gregory, Lisa Georgina. B.A., U. So. Calif., 1950, LL.B., 1953. Bar: Calif. 1954. Ptnr. firm Lucas, Deukmejian and Lucas, Long Beach, Calif., 1955-67; judge Superior Ct., L.A., 1967-71, U.S. Dist. Ct. (cen. dist.) Calif., 1971-84; assoc. justice Calif. Supreme Ct., 1984-87, chief justice, 1987—. Office: Calif Supreme Ct 303 2nd St # 8023S San Francisco CA 94107-1366*

LUCAS, PETER MICHAEL, anesthesiologist; b. Boston, Nov. 6, 1954; s. Robert Michael and Joan Anne (Emery) L.; m. Jeanne A. Harrington, Sept. 6, 1986. BS in Chemistry, Northeastern U., 1980; MD, U. Pa., 1985. Diplomate Am. Bd. Anesthesiology. Intern in internal medicine Crozer-Chester-Med. Ctr., Chester, Pa., 1985-86; resident in anesthesiology Tufts-New Eng. Med. Ctr., Boston, 1986-89; anesthesiologist Bay Group Anesthesia Svc., P.C., North Bend, Oreg., 1989—, pres., 1992—. Mem. AMA, Am. Soc. Anesthesiology, Oreg. Soc. Anesthesiology, Oreg. Med. Assn. Office: Bay Group Anesthesia Svc PC 1860 Virginia Ave North Bend OR 97459

LUCAS, RHETT ROY, painter, lawyer; b. Columbia, S.C., Nov. 27, 1941; s. Spurgeon LeRoy and Elizabeth (Wells) L.; m. Uta Henkel, Apr. 12, 1967 (div. 1973). BSChemE, U. S.C., 1963; JD, NYU, 1967; postgrad., U. Glasgow, Scotland, 1965-66. Bar: U.S. Supreme Ct., Calif., D.C. Rsch. assoc. Twentieth Century Fund, N.Y.C., 1968-69; gen. counsel James Madison Inst., N.Y.C., 1969-72, Population Law Ctr., San Francisco, 1972-75; prin. Lucas & Assocs., Washington, 1972-84; artist The Rhett Lucas Collection, Santa Fe, and Scottsdale, Ariz., 1988—. Prin. author U.S. Supreme Ct. briefs in Roe v. Wade, 1972, U.S. vs. Vuitch, 1971, Doe vs. Bolton, 1972, others; contbr. articles to profl jours.; painter approx. 200 nat. and state parks; exhbns. include Oxford U., 1988, Banff Ctr., 1989, Grand Canyon Nat. Park, Ariz., 1991, Capital Reef Nat. Park, Canyonlands Nat. Park, Cumberland Gap Hist. Nat. Park, Death Valley Nat. Monument, John Wesley Powell Meml. Mus., 1992, Powell River History Mus., 1992-93, O'Laurie (Canyonlands) Mus.; also exhbns. in Santa Fe, Masters Gallery, Taos, N.M., Scottsdale, La Jolla, Calif., Aix-en-Provence, France, Vancouver, B.C. Co-founder NARAL, N.Y.C., 1969. Root-Tilden scholar NYU Law Sch., 1963-67; Rotary Found. fellow U. Glasgow, 1965-66; population rsch. grantee Rockefeller Found., 1972-74. Mem. Scottsdale Artist's League, Rockport (Mass.) Art Assn. (life), Can. Alpine Club, Zero Population Growth, Sierra Club (life), Nat. Geog. Soc. (life), Rotary, Order of Coif, Phi Beta Kappa, Tau Beta Pi, Blue Key (pres.).

LUCAS, ROBERT ANTHONY, academic consultant; b. Chgo., Aug. 11, 1939; s. John Jerome and Bernice Beatrice (Ludwig) L.; m. Nancy Beissner, Nov. 18, 1966 (div. 1978); children: Michael Steven, Daniel Edward; m. Wendy Carol Wayland, Jan. 15, 1989; children: Rachel Anna, Rebecca Kate. BA, John Carroll U., 1961; MA, U. Ill., 1963, PhD, 1970. Asst. prof. English dept. U. Mich., Ann Arbor, 1968-71, program rep. R & D adminstrn., 1971-75; dir. res. dev. Calif. Poly. State U., San Luis Obispo, 1975-86, assoc. v.p. grad. studies, rsch. and faculty developer, 1986-92; dir. Inst. for Scholarly Productivity, San Luis Obispo, 1992—. Contbr. articles to profl. jours. Mem. Nat. Coun. Univ. Rsch. Adminstrs. (mem. exec. com. 1990-91), Soc. Rsch. Adminstrs. Democrat. Roman Catholic.

LUCAS, SUZANNE, statistician, educational consultant; b. Baxter Springs, Kans., Jan. 16, 1939; d. Ralph Beaver and Marguerite (Sansocie) L.; BA in Math., Calif. State U., Fresno, 1967, MA in Ednl. Theory, 1969; MS in Stats., U. So. Calif., 1979; children: Patricia Sue Jennings, Neil Patric Jennings. Asst. to dir. NSF Inst., Calif. State U., Fresno, 1968; Tchr. secondary math. Fresno city schs., 1968-78; statistician corp. indsl. relations Hughes Aircraft Co., Los Angeles, 1979-80; personnel adminstr. Hughes Aircraft Co. Space and Communications Group, Los Angeles, 1981-82, mem. tech. staff in math., 1982-85, staff engr., 1986-87; mem. tech. staff cost analysis The Aerospace Corp., 1987-90; sr. staff engr. Hughes Aircraft Co. Electro Optical Systems, 1990-93, scientist, engr., 1993—; owner, math. cons. Lucas Ednl. Consultants, Manhattan Beach, Calif., 1989—; lectr. in biostats. U. So. Calif., 1979. Kiwanis scholar, 1958. Mem. Internat. Soc. Parametric Analysts (pres. So. Calif. chpt. 1991-92), Soc. Cost Estimating and Analysis (cert.), Am. Psychol. Assn., Nat. Coun. Tchrs. of Math., Am. Statis. Assn., U. So. Calif. Alumni Assn. (life), Kappa Mu Epsilon. Office: Hughes Aircraft Co EOS PO Box 902 EO/E1/D104 El Segundo CA 90245-0902 also: Lucas Ednl Cons PO Box 3868 Manhattan Beach CA 90266

LUCE, R(OBERT) DUNCAN, psychology educator; b. Scranton, Pa., May 16, 1925; s. Robert Rennselaer and Ruth Lillian (Downer) L.; m. Gay Gaer, June 6, 1950 (div.); m. Cynthia Newby, Oct. 5, 1968 (div.); m. Carolyn A. Scheer, Feb. 27, 1988; 1 child, Aurora Newby. BS, MIT, 1945, PhD, 1950; MA (hon.), Harvard U., 1976. Mem. staff research lab electronics MIT, 1950-53; asst. prof. Columbia U., 1953-57; lectr. social relations Harvard U.,

1957-59; prof. psychology U. Pa., Phila., 1959-69; vis. prof. Inst. Advanced Study, Princeton, 1969-72; prof. Sch. Social Scis., U. Calif., Irvine, 1972-75; Alfred North Whitehead prof. psychology Harvard U., Cambridge, Mass., 1976-81, prof., 1981-83, Victor S. Thomas prof. psychology, 1983-88, Victor S. Thomas prof. emeritus, 1988; chmn. Harvard U., 1981-84; disting. prof. cognitive sci., dir. Irvine Research Unit in math. behavioral sci. U. Calif., Irvine, 1988-92; dir. Inst. for Math. Behavioral Sci., 1992—; chmn. assembly behavioral and social scis. NRC, 1976-79. Author: (with H. Raiffa) Games and Decisions, 1957, Individual Choice Behavior, 1959, (with others) Foundations of Measurement, I, 1971, II, 1989, III, 1990, Response Times, 1986, (with others) Stevens Handbook of Experimental Psychology, I and II, 1988, Sound & Hearing, 1993. Served with USNR, 1943-46. Ctr. Advanced Study in Behavioral Scis. fellow, 1954-55, 1966-67, 87-88, NSF sr. postdoctoral fellow, 1966-67, Guggenheim fellow, 1980-81. Fellow AAAS, Am. Psychol. Assn. (disting. sci. contbn. award 1970, bd. sci. affairs 1993—); mem. Am. Acad. Arts Scis., Nat. Acad. Scis. (chmn. sect. psychology 1980-83, class behavioral and social scis. 1983-86), Am. Math. Soc., Math. Assn. Am., Fedn. Behavorial Psychol. and Cognitive Scis. (pres. 1988-90), Psychometric Soc. (pres. 1976-77), Psychonomic Soc., Soc. Math. Psychology (pres. 1979), Am. Psychol. Soc. (bd. dirs. 1989-91), Sigma Xi, Phi Beta Kappa, Tau Beta Pi. Home: 20 Whitman Ct Irvine CA 92715-4057 Office: U Calif Social Sci Tower Irvine CA 92717

LUCENTE, ROSEMARY DOLORES, educational administrator; b. Renton, Wash., Jan. 11, 1935; d. Joseph Anthony and Erminia Antoinette (Argano) Lucente; B.A., Mt. St. Mary's Coll., 1956, M.S., 1963. Tchr. pub. schs., Los Angeles, 1956-65, supr. tchr., 1958-65, asst. prin., 1965-69, prin. elem. sch., 1969-85, 86—, dir. instrn., 1985-86, 1986—; nat. cons., lectr. Dr. William Glasser's Educator Tng. Ctr., 1968—; nat. workshop leader Nat. Acad. for Sch. Execs.-Am. Assn. Sch. Adminstrs., 1980; L.A. Unified Sch. Dist. rep. for nat. pilot of Getty Inst. for Visual Arts, 1983-85, 92—, site coord., 1983-86, team leader, mem. supt.'s adv. cabinet, 1987—. Recipient Golden Apple award Stanford Ave. Sch. PTA, Faculty and Community Adv. Council, 1976, resolution for outstanding service South Gate City Council, 1976. Mem. Nat. Assn. Elem. Sch. Prins., L.A. Elem. Prins. Orgn. (v.p. 1979-80), Assn. Calif. Sch. Adminstrs. (charter mem.), Assn. Elem. Sch. Adminstrs. (vice-chmn. chpt. 1972-75, city-wide exec. bd., steering com. 1972-75, 79-80), Asso. Adminstrs. Los Angeles (charter), Pi Theta Mu, Kappa Delta Pi (v.p. 1982-84), Delta Kappa Gamma. Democrat. Roman Catholic. Home: 6501 Lindenhurst Ave Los Angeles CA 90048-4733 Office: Roscomare Rd Sch 2425 Roscomare Rd Los Angeles CA 90077-1812

LUCERO, SCOTT ALAN, special education educator; b. Denver, Mar. 23, 1968; s. Raymond Lucero and Barbara Jean (McElliott) Gonzales; m. Deborah Ann Cole, Nov. 24, 1989; children: Lori Lynn, Kimberly Ann. Cert. welding, Warren Occupational, Golden, Colo., 1986; student, Arapahoe C.C., Littleton, Colo., 1992—. Cert. nurse, Colo. Self-employed welder Denver, 1986-88; care mgr. for developmentally disabled Arvada, Colo., 1988—. Vol. Polit.-Wyo. Gov., 1985. Mem. Honors Inst., Phi Theta Kappa (officer). Democrat. Home: 9135 W Maplewood Littleton CO 80123

LUCEY, JACK, artist, instructor; b. San Francisco, Feb. 11, 1929; s. John D. and Julia C. (Casey) L.; m. Charlotte M. Wyckoff, July 28, 1956; children: John, Robert, Michael. BA in Vocat. Edn., San Francisco State U., 1982; AA, Indian Valley Coll.; postgrad, U. Calif., 1980; BA, Acad. Art Coll., San Francisco, 1979. Art dir. Ind. Jour. Newspaper, San Rafael, Calif., 1956—; illustrator Lucey Studio & Gallery, San Rafael, Calif., 1956—; instr. Coll. of Marin, Kentfield, Calif., 1975—, Acad. of Art, San Francisco, 1976-77, speaker Internat. Newspaper Internat. Graphics Inst., San Jose, Calif., 1977; mem. adv. bd. Marin Community Colls., Contra Costa Regional Occupational Program. Sgt. USMC, 1950-52. Mem. Marin County Substitute Tchr. Assn., Soc. Western Artists, Art Dir. Club of San Francisco. Home and Studio: 84 Crestwood Dr San Rafael CA 94901

LUCHTERHAND, RALPH EDWARD, financial planner; b. Portland, Oreg., Feb. 9, 1952; s. Otto Charles II and Evelyn Alice (Isaac) L.; m. JoAnn Denise Adams, Aug. 13, 1983; children: Anne Michelle, Eric Alexander, Nicholas Andrew. BS, Portland State U., 1974, MBA, 1986. Registered profl. engr., Oreg.; gen. securities broker NYSE/NASD, CFP. Mech. engr. Hyster Co., Portland, 1971-75, svc. engr., 1975-76; project engr. Lumber Systems Inc., Portland, 1976-79; prin. engr. Moore Internat., Portland, 1979-81, chief product engr., 1981-83; project engr. Irvington-Moore, Portland, 1983, chief engr., 1983-86; ind. cons. engr., 1986; engring. program mgr. Precision Castparts Corp., Portland, 1986-87; personal, bus. fin. planner, reg. rep. IDS Fin. Svcs., Clackamas, Oreg., 1987—, apptd. to Silver Team, 1991. Treas. Village Bapt. Ch., Beaverton, Oreg., 1988-91; bd. dirs. Large Carus Community Planning Orgn., Clackamas, Oreg., 1993—. Republican. Home: 24440 S Eldorado Rd Mulino OR 97042 Office: IDS Fin Svcs Inc 8800 SE Sunnyside Rd Ste 300 Clackamas OR 97015-9786

LUCIANO, MARK JOSEPH, clinical psychologist; b. Boston, July 18, 1959; s. Joseph Henry Luciano and Eleanor (Lipani) Minsky; m. Shelley Ann Luciano, Jan. 3, 1986; children: Claire Ellen, Alexander Mark. BA, U. San Diego, 1979; MA, Profl. Sch. Psycholog. Studies, San Diego, 1982, PhD, 1984. Cert. clin. psychologist, marriage, family, and child therapist. Intern, counselor MITE, Inc., El Cajon, Calif., 1981-82; intern psycholog. Southwood, Chula Vista, Calif., 1982-83; postdoctoral intern Co. Mental Health, San Diego, 1983-84; psychologist Mission Valley Counseling Assocs., San Diego, 1985—. Office: Mission Valley Counseling Assocs 3638 Camino Del Rio N # 200 San Diego CA 92108

LUCIER, GREGORY THOMAS, manufacturing executive; b. Plainfield, N.J., May 9, 1964; s. Thomas Edward and Ann (Rivinius) L.; m. Marilena Cieri, June 4, 1988; 1 child, Ross Edward. BS in Indsl. Engring., Pa. State U., 1986; MBA, Harvard U., 1990. Product mgr. Internat. Paper Co., Memphis, 1986-88; asst. to the pres. Morrison Knudsen Corp., Boise, Idaho, 1990-91, mfg. mgr., 1991-92, dir. ops., 1992—; cons. Chrysler Corp., Highland Park, Mich., 1989, Am. Robotics Corp., Pitts., 1990. Fundraising organizer Arthritis Found., Boise, 1992; instr. Jr. Achievement, Memphis, 1986-88; vol. Project Outreach, Boston, 1989-90. Mem. Inst. Indsl. Engrs., Railway Suppliers Assn., Idaho Total Quality Mgmt. Inst., Harvard Club of Idaho, Tau Beta Pi. Republican. Roman Catholic. Home: 3403 S Ashbury Pl Boise ID 83706 Office: Morrison Knudsen Corp 4600 Apple St Boise ID 83705

LUCKE, LOU, data processing executive; b. Havre, Mont., May 21, 1931; s. Alvin Jack and Jeanette Cronky (Shephard) L.; m. JoAnne (Cloninger), Apr. 2, 1954; children: Louis Alvin, Jean Elaine, Larry Lee. BS in Physics, Mont. State U., 1954, BS in Geology, 1975. Systems engr. IBM, Helena, Mont., 1960-62; programming supr. North Am. Aviation, Downey, Calif., 1962-66; exec. advisor McDonnell-Douglass, Huntington Beach, Calif., 1966-69; dir. computing services Mont. State U., Bozeman, 1969-81, No. Mont. Coll., Havre, 1981—. Contbr. articles to profl. jours. Chmn. bd. Clack Mus. Found., 1992. Recipient Spl. Achievement award, McDonnell Douglas-Astro', 1969, Supervisory Mgmt. award North Am. Aviation, 1965. Mem. Assn. for Computing Machinery (regional sec. 1959), Data Processing Mgmt. Assn. (indsl. rep. 1972-75), Mont. Data Processing Assn. (pres. 1979-81, exec. sec. 1982—), Mont. Land and Mineral Owners Assn. (bd. dirs. 1988—).. Club: Mont. State U. Flying Bobcats (Bozeman) (v.p. 1979). Lodge: Elks. Home: 900 3D Ave Havre MT 59501 Office: No Mont Coll Havre MT 59501

LUCKETT, BYRON EDWARD, JR., air force chaplain; b. Mineral Wells, Tex., Feb. 2, 1951; s. Byron Edward and Helen Alma (Hart) L.; m. Kathryn Louise Lambertson, Dec. 30, 1979; children: Florence Louise, Byron Edward III, Barbara Elizabeth, Stephanie Hart. BS, U.S. Mil. Acad., 1973; MDiv, Princeton U., 1982; MA, Claremont Grad. Sch., 1987. Commd. 2d lt. U.S. Army, 1973, advanced through grades to maj.; stationed at Camp Edwards, Korea, 1974-75; bn. supply officer 563rd Engr. Bn., Kornwestheim, Germany, 1975-76; platoon leader, exec. officer 275th Engr. Co., Ludwigsburg, Germany, 1976-77; boy scout project officer Hdqrs., VII Corps, Stuttgart, Germany, 1977-78; student intern Moshannon Valley Larger Parish, Winburne, Penn., 1980-81; Protestant chaplain Philmont Scout Ranch, Cimarron, N.Mex., 1982; asst. pastor Immanuel Presbyn. Ch., Albuquerque, 1982-83, assoc. pastor, 1983-84; tchr. Claremont High Sch., 1985-86; Protestant chaplain 92nd Combat Support Group, Fairchild AFB, Wash., 1986-90; installation staff chaplain Pirinclik Air Station, 1990-91; protestant chaplain Davis-Monthan AFB, Ariz., 1991; mem. intern program coun. Claremont (Calif.) Grad. Sch. Contbr. articles to profl. jours. Bd. dirs. Parentcraft, Inc., Albuquerque, 1984, United Campus Ministries, Albuquerque, 1984, Proclaim Liberty, Inc., Spokane, 1987-90; bd. dirs. western region Nat. Assn. Presbyn. Scouters, Irving, Tex., 1986-89, chaplain, 1991-93; mem. N.Mex. Employer Co, in Support of the Guard and Reserve, Albuquerque, 1984, Old Baldy coun. Boy Scouts Am., 1986; chmn. Fairchild Parent Coop., Fairchild AFB, 1986-87; pres. Co. Grade Officers Coun., Fairchild AFB, 1987-88. Capt. U.S. Army Reserve; chaplain USAF Reserve 1983-90, maj. 1990—. Recipient Dist. Award of Merit for Disting. Svc. Boy Scouts Am., 1977. Mem. Soc. Cincinnati Md. Presbyterian. Home: 7901 E Garland Rd Tucson AZ 85715-2829 Office: 355 W6/HC 5385 E Ironwood St Davis Monthan A F B AZ 85707-5000

LUCKOW, LYNN D. W., publishing executive; b. Hettinger, N.D., 1949. Grad., U. N.D., 1971, Ind. U., 1974. Pres., chief exec. officer, pub. Jossey-Bass Inc. Pub., San Francisco. Home: 666 Post St San Francisco CA 94109 Office: Jossey-Bass Inc Pub 350 Sansome St San Francisco CA 94104

LUDEMAN, KATE, human resources executive; b. San Antonio, Aug. 14, 1946; d. Ben and Annette (Martin) L.; 1 child from previous marriage, Catherine. BS in Engring., Tex. Tech U., 1967, MA in Psychology, 1972; postgrad., U. Tex., 1974-76; PhD in Psychology, Saybrook Inst., 1979. Project leader Control Data, Saigon, Socialist Republic of Vietnam, 1970-71; cons. Dallas, 1972-79; interviewer morning news ABC Sta. WFAA-TV, Dallas, 1976-77; mgr. tng. and devel. Shaklee Corp., San Francisco, 1979-81; mgr. human resources Impell Corp., San Francisco, 1981-83; corp. v.p. human resources KLA Instruments, Santa Clara, Calif., 1984-88; pres. Worth Ethic Tng. Co., 1988—; developer profl. stress mgmt. conf. for use in Dallas, Albuquerque, and Atlanta. Author: Worth Ethic: How to Profit from changing Values of the New Work Force, 1989; contbr. articles to profl. jours. Chemstrand & Am. Dyers scholar Tex. Tech U., 1965-67. Mem. Am. Soc. Personnel Adminstrs., Am. Soc. Tng. and Devel., Tau Beta Phi. Office: Worth Ethic Tng Co 240 La Cuesta Dr Menlo Park CA 94028

LUDIN, ROGER LOUIS, physics educator; b. Jersey City, June 13, 1944; s. Fredric E. and Gwendolyn C. (Rogers) L.; m. Diane E. Wilson, Aug. 26, 1966; children: Stephen L., Joyce E. BS in Physics, Brown U., 1966; MS in Physics, Worcester Polytech. Inst., 1968, PhD in Physics, 1969. Postdoctoral fellow Worcester (Mass.) Polytech. Inst., 1969-70; prof. Burlington County Coll., Pemberton, N.J., 1970-85; lectr. Calif. Poly. State U., San Luis Obispo, 1984—. Author lab. manuals for introductory physics; author computer assisted instrn. for gen. physics. Active Medford Lakes (N.J.) Bd. Edn., 1976-84, pres. 1978-84; bd. dirs. Medford Lakes Athletic Assn., 1974-84; soccer coach Morro Bay (Calif.) High Sch., 1985—. Named Tchr. of Yr. Burlington County Coll., 1982, 83. Mem. Am. Assn. Physics Tchrs. (sec., treas. N.J. sect. 1976-84, named Outstanding Contbr. to Physics Edn. 1984, editor So. Calif. sect. 1985-87, v.p. 1987-89, pres. 1989-92), Am. Phys. Soc., AAAS, Lions, Sigma Xi. Home: 2691 Koa St Morro Bay CA 93442-1709 Office: Calif Poly State U Physics Dept San Luis Obispo CA 93407

LUDLUM, ANDREW GRAY, broadcast news executive; b. Trenton, N.J., Dec. 11, 1954; s. Charles Henry and Isabel (Pindar) L.; m. Roseanne Marie Shemeta, Feb. 11, 1978; children: Sarah Gray, Mariel Rose. BA in Journalism, San Jose State U., 1976. Lic. FCC Gen. Radiotelephone Operator. Asst. news dir. Sta. KXRX-AM, San Jose, 1975-79; mng. editor Sta. KIRO-AM, Seattle, 1979-84; program dir. Sta. KMBR-FM, Kansas City, Mo., 1985-86; dir. news and programming Sta. KMBZ-AM, Kansas City, Mo., 1984-87; v.p. news and programming Sta. KIRO-AM, Seattle, 1987-92; v.p. news Stas. KIRO-TV, AM, FM, Seattle, 1992—. Adv. bd. Edward R. Murrow Sch. of Communications, Wash. State U., Pullman, 1990—. Mem. Radio and TV News Dirs. Assn. (bd. dirs., region I dir. 1991—). Office: KIRO Inc 2807 3rd Ave Seattle WA 98121

LUDVIGSEN, RICHARD E., entertainment executive; b. Fremont, Nebr., Nov. 3, 1950; s. E.H. and Lois (Dahl) L.; m. Lynda Jannings, Nov. 25, 1972; children: Brian, Megan. Grad. Archtl. Engring., Western Tech. Coll., Denver, 1972. Past exec., v.p. and dir. World Wide Bingo, Inc.; pres. LeisureNet Entertainment, Inc., Denver; ptnr. MAPS Group, Ltd., Denver. Creater, producer TV game shows and promotions, 1986—. Bd. advisers Nat. AIDS Awareness Found. Office: LeisureNet Entertainment Inc PO Box 3443 Littleton CO 80161-3443

LUDVIGSON, DAVID LEE, utility company executive; b. Grand Meadow, Minn., Sept. 28, 1938; s. Harold and Helen Lucille (Betz) L.; children: Brent Aaron, Eric Nordahl, Adam Scott. BA, U. Iowa, 1960, LLB, 1963. Bar: Calif. 1964, U.S. Dist. Ct. (no. dist.) Calif. 1964, U.S. Ct. Appeals (9th cir.) 1964. Assoc. Pillsbury, Madison & Sutro, San Francisco, 1963-70; v.p., gen. counsel, sec. Natomas Co., San Francisco, 1970-75; pvt. practice law, San Francisco, 1975-79; atty. Pacific Gas & Electric, San Francisco, 1979-84; sr. v.p./chief legal officer Calif. Energy Co., Inc., San Francisco and Santa Rosa, Calif., 1984—. Mem. Order of Coif. Home: 160 Seminary Dr Mill Valley CA 94941-3162 Office: Conner Peripherals 3081 Zanker Rd San Jose CA 95134

LUDWIG, ROLF MARTIN, internist; b. Bautzen, Germany, June 3, 1924; came to U.S., 1953; s. Martin Max and Doris (Metz) L.; m. Shirley Jean Ray, Oct. 26, 1956 (div. June 1983); 1 child, Mark Stephen. M.D., Eberhard Karls U. Tuebingen, Germany, 1953. Intern, Mary's Help Hosp., San Francisco, 1953-54, then resident in internal medicine; resident in internal medicine Franklin Hosp., San Francisco, Huntington Meml. Hosp., Pasadena, Calif., Wadsworth VA Gen. Hosp., Los Angeles, 1959-60. Internist, Kaiser/Permanente, Fontana, Calif., 1960-63, 73-87; practice medicine specializing in internal medicine, Yucaipa, Calif., 1963-72; retired, 1987. Served to capt. M.C., U.S. Army, 1956-59. Mem. Am. Soc. Internal Medicine, Calif. Soc. Internal Medicine, Inland Soc. Internal Medicine. Republican. Lutheran. Home: 11711 Holmes St Yucaipa CA 92399-4014

LUEDERS, BETH JOY, magazine editor; b. Pawnee City, Nebr., Sept. 1, 1959; d. Myron Glenn and Bernice Lorraine (Becker) L. BS in Agr., Journalism, U. Nebr., Lincoln, 1981. Editorial asst. Worldwide Challenge Campus Crusade for Christ, San Bernardino, Calif., 1981-82, sr. copywriter Creative Group, 1982-84, copy dir. Creative Group, 1984-89, asst. creative dir. Creative Group, 1987-89, writer Worldwide Challenge, 1989-90, assoc. editor Worldwide Challenge mag., 1990-93; comm. dir. The Commn. Campus Crusade for Christ, Colorado Springs, Colo., 1993—. Counselor Faith Bible Ch., San Bernardino, 1991-92. Office: Campus Crusade for Christ 421 Woodmen Rd Colorado Springs CO 80919

LUEGGE, WILLARD ARTHUR, chemist, consultant; b. Oak Park, Ill., Mar. 19, 1931; s. Theodore Wilhelm and Irma Minnie (Schoepfer) L.; m. Joanna Carleen Wechter, Sept. 1, 1951; children: Sherylene, Lynette. BA, Ind. U., 1953; postgrad., Ind. U., U. Louisville, UCLA, 1954-64. Rsch. chemist Louisville Cement Co., Speed, Ind., 1956-60; quality control chemist Cal Portland Cement Co., Mojave, Calif., 1960-61; chemistry tchr. Palmdale (Calif.) High Sch., 1961-90; owner-dir. PM Labs, Lancaster, Calif., 1968-89; cons. extractive metallurgical chemistry Lancaster, 1989—; sci. dept. chmn. Palmdale High Sch., 1964-79; mem. Calif. Assn. Chemistry Tchrs., 1963-89; rsch. chemist USAF Rocket Propulsion Lab., Edwards AFB, summers, 1966, '67, '68; bd. dirs. Bryman Refining Co., Inc. Inventor assay kit, 1970. Recipient Tchr. of the Yr. award Am. Chem. Soc., 1967; NSF grantee, 1963, 64. Mem. Western Mining Coun., Western States Pub. Lands Coalition. Presbyterian. Home and Office: 560 East Ave J-1 Lancaster CA 93535-9696

LUENBERGER, DAVID GILBERT, electrical engineer, educator; b. Los Angeles, Sept. 16, 1937; s. Frederick Otto and Marion (Crumly) L.; m. Nancy Ann Iversen, Jan. 7, 1962; children: Susan Ann, Robert Alden, Jill Alison, Jenna Emmy. B.S.E.E., Calif. Inst. Tech., 1959; M.S.E.E., Stanford U., 1961, Ph.D. in Elec. Engring., 1963. Asst. prof. elec. engring. Stanford (Calif.) U., 1963-67, assoc. prof. engring.-econ. systems, 1967-71, prof., 1971—, dept. chmn., 1980-91; tech. asst. dir. U.S. Office Sci. and Tech., Exec. Office of Pres., Washington, 1971-72; vis. prof. MIT, Cambridge, 1976; guest prof. Tech. U. of Denmark, Lyngby, 1986. Author: Optimization by Vector Space Methods, 1969, Linear and Nonlinear Programming, 1973, 2d edit., 1984, Introduction to Dynamic Systems, 1979; contbr. articles to tech. jours. Recipient Hendrik W. Bode Lecture prize Control Systems Soc., 1990. Fellow IEEE; mem. Econometric Soc., Soc. for Advancement Econ. Theory, Soc. for Promotion of Econ. Theory, Inst. Mgmt. Sci., Soc. Econ. Dynamics and Control (pres. 1987-88), Math Programming Soc., Palo Alto Camera Club, Sigma Xi, Tau Beta Pi. Lutheran. Office: Stanford U Dept Engring-Econ Systems Terman Ctr 314 Stanford CA 94305-4025

LUEVANO, FRED, JR., computer systems executive; b. Alamogordo, N.Mex., June 21, 1943; s. Fred Macias and Margaret (Baca) L.; m. Lupe Olmos, July 11, 1964; children: Michael, James Paul. AA in bus., Fullerton Coll., 1975; BA in Mgmt., U. Redlands, 1979, MA in Mgmt., 1985. Cert. data processing mgr., disaster recovery planner. Mgr. computer ops. Hoffman Electronics, El Monte, Calif., 1971-76; mgr. computer ops. and tech. services City of Anaheim, Calif., 1976-79; mgr. data processing Wyle Data Services, Huntington Beach, Calif., 1979-83; mgr. corp. computer ops. Northrop Corp., Pico Rivera, Calif., 1983, mgr. corp. computing, 1985—, dir. disaster revovery program, 1983—; dir. disaster recovery and security Pico Rivera, 1988-90, mgr. systems mgmt., 1990—; cons. on info. systems, La Habra, Calif., 1971—; mem. cert. bd. dirs. Disaster Recovery Inst., speaker, 1991-92. Cub master Boy Scouts Am., La Habra, 1979-84, chmn. com. 1975-79; councilman candidate City of La Habra Heights, Calif., 1982; pres. Red Coach Club, 1979-80, 86-88; pres. La Habra Parents for Swimming Inc., 1986-88. Served with USN, 1961-65. Mem. Am. Mgmt. Assn., Telecommunications Assn., Assn. Computer Ops. Mgrs. (speaker 1983-86), Northrop Mgmt. Club. Republican. Roman Catholic. Office: Northrop Corp MS 770/XG 8900 E Washington Blvd Pico Rivera CA 90660

LUFT, HERBERT, dean; b. Frankfurt, Germany, Aug. 17, 1942; came to U.S., 1961; s. Theodor and Hedwig (Theismann) L.; married, Mar. 25, 1965; children: Sebastian, Rebecca. BA, Pepperdine U., 1965, MA, 1966; PhD, U. So. Calif., 1976. Asst. prof. History Pepperdine U., L.A., 1967-72, assoc. prof. History, 1972-81, prof. history, 1982—; exec. v.p. Pepperdine U., Malibu, Calif., 1981-83; dean European Programs Pepperdine U., Malibu, London, Heidelberg (Germany) and Florence (Italy), 1983—. Mem. Kiwanis Club, Phi Alpha Theta. Mem. Ch. of Christ. Home: 24 155 PCH Malibu CA 90253 Office: care Pepperdine U, Graimbergweg 10, 69117 Heidelberg Germany

LUFT, RENE WILFRED, civil engineer; b. Santiago, Chile, Sept. 21, 1943; came to U.S., 1968; s. David and Malwina (Kelmy) L.; m. Monica Acevedo, Aug. 24, 1970; children: Deborah Elaine, Daniel Eduardo. CE, U. Chile, 1967; MS, MIT, 1969, DSc, 1971. Registered profl. engr., Alaska, Calif., Wash., Mass., N.H., R.I., Republic of Chile; registered structural engr., Vt. Asst. prof. civil engring. U. Chile, 1967-68; research asst. MIT, Cambridge, Mass., 1969-71, vis. lectr., 1983-84; staff engr. Simpson, Gumpertz & Heger Inc., Arlington, Mass., 1971-74, sr. staff engr., 1975-78, assoc., 1978-83, sr. assoc., 1984-90; prin. Simpson, Gumpertz & Heger Inc., San Francisco, 1990-91; head design div. Simpson, Gumpertz & Heger Inc., 1991—; sec. seismic adv. com. Mass. Bldg. Code Commn., 1978-80, chmn., 1981-82; mem. Boston seismic instrumentation com. U.S. Geol. Survey. Contbr. articles to profl. jours. Mem. design overview com., bldg. seismic safety coun. Earthquake Hazards Reduction Program, 1983-91, chmn. rsch. com. 1987-88. Mem. ASCE, Boston Soc. Civil Engrs. (chmn. seismic design adv. com. 1981-86, Clemens Herschel award for tech. paper 1980, pres.'s award for leadership in earthquake engring. 1984), Am. Concrete Inst., Earthquake Engring. Research Inst., Structural Engrs. Assn. Calif., NSPE (Young Engr. of Yr., 1979), Sigma Xi, Chi Epsilon. Home: 109 Ardith Dr Orinda CA 94563-4201 Office: 221 Main St Ste 1500 San Francisco CA 94105-1934

LUGER, GEORGE FLETCHER, computer science and psychology educator, consultant; b. Spokane, Wash., Dec. 1, 1940; s. George F. and Loretta C. (Maloney) L.; m. Kathleen Kelly, Aug. 25, 1969; children: Sarah, David, Peter. BS, Gonzaga U., 1963, MS, 1965; MS, Notre Dame U., 1969; PhD, U. Pa., 1973. Rsch. fellow dept. of artificial intelligence U. Edinburgh, Eng., 1974-79; prof. computer sci. and psychology U. N.Mex., Albuquerque, 1979—; cons. in field., U.S. and Europe, 1983—. Author: Artificial Intelligence & Design of Expert Systems, 1989, Artificial Intellegence: Structures and Strategies for Complex Problem Solving, 1993. NSF grantee, U.S. Dept. Edn. grantee, U.S. Dept. of Def. grantee. Mem. IEEE, Assn. for Computing Machinery, Am. Assn. for Artificial Intelligence, Cognitive Sci. Soc. Office: U NMex Dept of Computer Sci Albuquerque NM 87131

LUHN, ROBERT KENT, writer, magazine editor; b. Oakland, Calif., Nov. 23, 1953; s. Joel Adrian and Norma Jeanne (Arnold) L.; m. Marla Mieko Miyashiro, Sept. 14, 1992; 1 child, Pudge. Student, U. Calif., Davis, 1972-76. Freelance writer, 1968—; broadcaster, 1979-80; sr. editor PC World mag., San Francisco, 1983-90, contbg. editor, 1990—; contbg. editor Calif. Republic mag., San Francisco, 1990—. Author: The Swedish Catfish & Other Tales, 1979, Collected Works, Vol. 3, 1985, Going West, 1988, The Wit is Out, 1993; contbr. fiction, features and poetry to numerous publs., including Harper's, Mother Jones, Omni, Am. Film, Hudson Rev., Nantucket Rev., Christian Sci. Monitor, San Francisco Chronicle, Chgo. Tribune, Phila. Inquirer, PC mag., Computerworld, The Oregonian, Exec. Update, Grapevine Weekly; columnist Computer Currents, 1993—. Dir. MIS, Baykeeper, San Francisco, 1990-92; journalism coach San Francisco State U., 1988-92. Mem. ACLU, Amnesty Internat., Greenpeace, Environ. Defense Fund.

LUIZZI, RONALD, wholesale distribution executive; b. Neptune, N.J., Apr. 7, 1953; s. Alfredo Luizzi and Mary Kay (Mumford) Figart; m. Myrna E. Lizama, Feb. 14, 1987 (div. Sept. 1990). BA in Psychology, Trenton State Coll., 1975. Pres., chief exec. officer Profl. Divers, Inc., Neptune, 1975-78; nat. dir. projects Nat. Assn. Scuba Diving Schs., Long Beach, Calif., 1978-81; sales mgr. TW Systems, Inc., Honolulu, 1981-85; gen. mgr. TW Systems, Ltd.-Kona, Kailua-Kona, Hawaii, 1985—; East coast regional dir. Nat. Assn. Scuba Diving Schs., Neptune, 1977-78. Contbg. author: (tng. manual) Gold Book, 1977, Safe Scuba, 1977. Scuba advisor YMCA-Kona, Kailua-Kona, 1985—. Mem. Nat. Assn. Instnl. Laundry Mgrs. (cert.), Hawaii Assn. Instnl. Laundry Mgrs. (allied), Nat. Exec. House Keepers Assn. (allied), Hawaii Hotel Assn. (allied), Rotary (sec. 1988-89, v.p. 1989-90, pres. 1990-91), Kona-Kohala C. of C. Home: 73-1025 Ahikawa St Kailua-Kona HI 96740 Office: TW Systems Ltd-Kona 74-5622 Alapa St Kailua Kona HI 96740

LUJAN, EDWARD L., insurance executive; b. Santa Fe, N.Mex., Aug. 11, 1932; m. Virginia Quintana; children: LouAnne Byrd, Larry, Jerry, Joe. BS, N.Mex. State U., MEd. Tchr. Stanley, N.Mex., 1958-60; with Manuel Lujan Agencies, Santa Fe, 1960-68; chmn. bd., chief exec. officer Manuel Lujan Agencies, Albuquerque, 1968—; bd. dirs. United N.Mex. Bank, Albuquerque, U.S. West Communications, Albuquerque; past bd. dirs. First Bank, Santa Fe; chmn. region V adv. bd. Resolution Trust Corp. Active Albuquerque Econ. Forum, Assn. Commerce and Industry, Albuquerque Econ. Devel. Corp.; past chmn. Rep. Cen. Com. N.Mex.; past chmn. Rep. Nat. Hispanic Assembly; past pres. Young Reps. N.Mex.; past bd. dirs. United Fund, Santa Fe, St. Joseph Hosp. Found.; bd. dirs. U. N.Mex. Found., DARE, Presbyn. Heart Inst. Found., Hispanic Cultural Found. Mem. Albuquerque C. of C. (bd. dirs.), Elks, KC. Address: 2001 San Mateo Blvd NE Albuquerque NM 87110

LUJAN, HERMAN D., university president; m. Carla Lujan; 3 children. B in Polit. Sci., St. Mary's Coll. Calif.; M in Polit. Sci., U. Calif., Berkeley; PhD in Polit. Sci., U. Idaho. Faculty mem., adminstr. U. Kans., dir. inst. social and environ. studies, 1972-78; dir. divsn. state planning and rsch. Gov. of Kans., 1974-75; prof. polit. sci. dept. U. Wash., lectr. Japanese exec. mgmt. program, sch. bus., v.p. minority affairs, 1978-88, vice provost, 1988-91; pres. U. No. Colo., 1991—; bd. dirs. Affiliated Nat. Bank. Author several books; contbr. articles to profl. jours. Bd. dirs. Boy Scouts Am., Latin Am. Ednl. Found. Mem. Rotary (Greeley). Office: Univ of Northern Colorado President Office Univ Of No Colo CO 80639*

LUKE, CLYDE ELLIOT, music educator; b. Burley, Idaho, May 16, 1942; s. Harold Vivian and Sybil (Wilson) L.; m. Janet Peterson, June 7, 1967; children: Laura Kaye, Robert Elliot, Michelle Cherie. B in Music Edn., Brigham Young U., 1967; M in Music Edn., U. Idaho, 1977. Dir. vocal music Madison Sch. Dist., Rexburg, Idaho, 1967-70; med. rep. Burroughs

Wellcome Co., Research Triangle Park, N.C., 1970-71; mem. music faculty, dir. voice and choral activities Ricks Coll., Rexburg, 1971—. Mem. Am. Choral Dirs. Assn. (Idaho state pres. 1979-81, N.W. Div. jr. coll. repertoire and standards chair 1992—), Idaho Music Educators Assn. (state choral chair 1980-82, state higher edn. chair 1986-90), Nat. Assn. Tchrs. Singing. Republican. LDS. Office: Ricks Coll Rexburg ID 83460-1210

LUKE, LANCE LAWTON, real estate and construction consultant; b. Wahiawa, Hawaii, Dec. 27, 1955; s. Samuel C. and Florence (Ng) L.; m. Leilani M. Reelitz, Aug. 12, 1979; children: Samuel E., Solomon L., Spencer L. AA, Windward Community Coll., Hawaii, 1975; student, U. Hawaii; grad. in bldg. constrn., NRI, 1989. Investor, contractor pvt. practice, Honolulu, 1975-79; pres. Lance L. Luke & Assocs., Honolulu, 1979—; constrn. cons. Contbr. articles to profl. jours. Com. chmn. Boy Scouts Am., Kailu Cub Scout Pack 311, 1989—; reviewer Fed. Emergency Mgmt. Agy., 1989—, Nat. Inst. of Bldg. Scis., 1990—; sch. inspector State Sch. Inspection Team, Kailua, Kaneohe, Hawaii, 1990—. Mem. Numerous profl. and related orgns. including: Am. Concrete Inst., Internat. Coun. Bldg. Ofcls., Bldg. Ofcls. and Code Adminstrs., Concrete Reinforcing Steel Inst., Constrn. Specifications Inst., Hawaii Assn. Realtors, Honolulu Bd. of Realtors, Nat. Assn. Home Inspectors, Inc., Project Mgmt. Inst., Real Estate Educators Assn. Republican. Roman Catholic. Office: Lance L Luke & Assocs Inc 470 N Nimitz Hwy Ste 216 Honolulu HI 96817-5028

LUKE, ROBERT A., physics educator; b. Rigby, Idaho, Jan. 5, 1938; s. Lowell M. and Merle (Archibald) L.; m. DeVona Alice Dean, July 8, 1964; children: David, James, Jeffrey, Deborah, Catherine, Matthew. BS, Utah State U., 1962, MS, 1966, PhD, 1968. Asst. prof. Physics Dept. Boise (Idaho) State U., 1968-73, assoc. prof. Physics Dept., 1973-77, prof., 1977—, chmn. physics depts., 1983—. Mem. Am. Assn. Physics Tchrs. (Idaho-Utah sect. pres. 1985-86), Sigma Xi, Sigma Pi Sigma, Phi Kappa Phi, Pi Mu Epsilon. Republican. Mem. LDS Ch. Office: Boise State U Physics Dept Boise ID 83725-1570

LUKEHART, MICHAEL CARTER, public defender; b. El Paso, Tex., Oct. 9, 1953; s. Barron Gust and Patricia Viola (Reichard) L.; m. Alexis Luane Schulte, June 27, 1981; children: Paul Edward, Michael Alexander, Anne Courtney. JD, Southwestern U., L.A., 1979. Bar: Calif. 1992, U.S. Dist. Ct. (ctl. dist.) Calif. 1984. Pvt. practice law Encino, Calif., 1980-82; prin. atty. Kern County Pub. Defender, Bakersfield, Calif., 1982—. Mem. Calif. Pub. Defender's Assn., Kern County Pub. Employee's Assn. (dir. 1989—). Republican. Roman Catholic. Office: Kern County Pub Defender 1315 Truxtun Ave Bakersfield CA 93301

LUKOS, GLENN CHARLES, environmental biologist; b. Ypsilanti, Mich., Nov. 9, 1946; s. Alex Charles and Esther Exilda (Smith) L.; m. Judith Merrylin Hon, June 2, 1985; 1 child, Cameron Hon. Student, Wayne State U., 1964-67; BS, SUNY, Brockport, 1968, MS, 1974; postgrad., U. South Fla., 1974-77. Vol. Peace Corps, Dominican Republic, 1967-69; tchr. Vershire (Vt.) Sch., 1969-71, Rochester (N.Y.) City Sch. Dist., 1971-72; instr. SUNY, 1973-74; environ. specialist Fla. Dept. Environ. Regulation, Tallahassee, 1977-79, U.S. Army C.E., New Orleans, 1979-83; chief South Coast sect. U.S. Army C.E., L.A., 1983-87; dir. regulatory svcs. Michael Brandman Assocs., Santa Ana, Calif., 1987-89; pres. Glenn Lukos Assocs., Inc., Laguna Hills, Calif., 1989—. Vol. pub. TV, Tallahassee, 1977-79, New Orleans, 1979-83. Mem. Soc. Wetland Scientists, Assn. State Wetland Mgrs., Calif. Native Plant Soc. Office: 23441 S Pointe Dr Ste 150 Laguna Hills CA 92653

LUM, HERMAN TSUI FAI, state supreme court chief justice; b. Honolulu, Nov. 5, 1926; s. K.P. and Helen (Tom) L.; m. Almira Ahn, June 17, 1949; children: Forrest K.K., Jonathan K.K. Student, U. Hawaii, 1945-46; LL.B., U. Mo., 1950. Bar: Hawaii 1950. Asst. public prosecutor City and County Honolulu, 1950-52; chief atty. Hawaii Ho. of Reps., 1955, chief clk., 1956-61; partner Suyenaga, Sakamoto & Lum, Honolulu, from 1956; atty. U.S Dist. Ct. Hawaii, 1961-67; judge Cir. Ct. Honolulu, 1967-76, sr. judge Family Ct., 1977-80; assoc. justice Supreme Ct. Hawaii, 1980-83, chief justice, 1983—; Pres. Jr. Bar Assn. Hawaii, 1957. Mem. ABA, Bar Assn. Hawaii, Fed. Bar Assn. Hawaii (pres. 1963), Phi Delta Phi, Lambda Chi Alpha. Home: 2508 Makiki Heights Dr Honolulu HI 96822-2548 Office: Hawaii Supreme Ct PO Box 2560 Honolulu HI 96804-2560*

LUM, JODY MAE KAM QUON, real property appraiser; b. Honolulu, Sept. 15, 1961; d. Joseph Tai and Alice Moi (Lau) L. BA, U. Hawaii, 1983. Cert. residential appraiser. Asst. appraiser Hanamura Appraisal Co., Honolulu, 1986-87; real estate staff appraiser Am. Savs. Bank, Honolulu, 1987-89; real property appraiser III City and County of Honolulu, Hawaii, 1989-90; real property appraiser IV City and County of Honolulu, 1990—. Named Outstanding Woman of Yr., 1991. Mem. Nat. Assn. Rev. Appraisers, Honolulu Chinese Jaycees (rec. sec. 1989-90, mem. devel. v.p. 1990-91, community devel. v.p. 1991-92, Woman of Yr. 1989-90, Outstanding mem. 1990-91, Outstanding Community Devel. v.p. 1991-92). Office: City and County Honolulu 842 Bethel St Honolulu HI 96813

LUM, KWONG-YEN, psychiatrist; b. Honolulu, Nov. 14, 1926; s. Ko Fong and Florence (Chong) L.; m. Dorothy Wells, Feb. 20, 1955; children: Mark K., Nancy Lum Fisher, Steven W., David B. BA, Colgate U., 1951; MD, Columbia U., 1955. Diplomate Am. Bd. Psychiatry and Neurology. Internship U. Wash., Seattle, 1955-56; residency in psychiatry VA Hosp. and Menniga Sch. Psychiatry, Topeka, 1956-59; staff psychiatrist Dept. Health/State of Hawaii, Honolulu, 1959-61, med. dir., state mental health plan, 1962-64; pvt. practice psychiatry Honolulu, 1962—; clin. profl. psychiatry John A. Burns Sch. Medicine U. Hawaii, 1967—; trustee Queen's Med. Ctr., Honolulu, 1984—, Queen's Health Systems, Honolulu, 1984—. With AUS, 1945-47, PTO. Mem. AMA, Hawaii Med. Soc., Hawaii Psychiat. Med. Assn., Pacific Club. Office: 1380 Lusitana St Ste 909 Honolulu HI 96813-2485

LUMMIS, CYNTHIA MARIE, lawyer, rancher; b. Cheyenne, Wyo., Sept. 10, 1954; d. Doran Arp and Enid (Bennett) L.; m. Alvin L. Wiederspahn, May 28, 1983; children: Annaliese Alex. BS, U. Wyo., 1976, U. Wyo., 1978; JD, U. Wyo., 1985. Bar: Wyo. 1985. Rancher Lummis Livestock Co., Cheyenne, 1972—; law clk. Wyo. Supreme Ct., Cheyenne, 1985-86; assoc. Wiederspahn, Lummis & Liepas, Cheyenne, 1986—; mem. Wyo. Ho. Judiciary Com., 1979-86, Ho. Agriculture, Pub. Lands & Water Resources Com., 1985-86; chmn. Ho. Rev. Com., 1987-88; chmn. Joint Revenue Interim Com., 1988-89; chmn. County Ct. Planning Com., Wyo., 1986-88. Sec. Meals on Wheels, Cheyenne, 1985-87; mem. Agrl. Crisis Support Group, Laramie County, Wyo., 1985-87; mem. adv. com. U. Wyo. Sch. Nursing, 1988-90; mem. steering com. Wyo. Heritage Soc., 1986-89. Republican. Lutheran. Club: Rep. Women's (Cheyenne) (legis. chmn. 1982). Office: Wiederspahn Lummis & Liepas Ste 704 2020 Carey Ave Cheyenne WY 82001-3646

LUMSDEN, IAN GORDON, art gallery director; b. Montreal, Que., Can., June 8, 1945; s. Andrew Mark and Isobel Dallas (Wilson) L.; m. Katherine Elizabeth Carson, July 28, 1979; 1 child, Craig Ian. B.A., McGill U., 1968; postgrad., Mus. Mgmt. Inst., U. Calif., Berkeley, 1991. Curator art dept. N.B. Mus., Saint John, 1969; curator Beaverbrook Art Gallery, Fredericton, N.B., 1969-83, dir., 1983—; bd. dirs. ArtsAtlantic; mem. Cultural Property Export Rev. Bd., 1982-85; mem. program com. 49th Parallel Ctr. for Contemporary Can. Art., 1990-92. Author exhbn. catalogues; contbr. numerous articles to Can. art periodicals. Mem. Can. Museums Assn. (sec.-treas. 1973-75), Can. Art Mus. Dirs. Orgn. (1st v.p. 1977-83, pres. 1983-85), Atlantic Provinces Art Gallery Assn. (chmn. 1970-72), Am. Assn. Museums, Union Club (St. John, N.B.). Mem. Anglican Ch. of Can. Home: Fernholme, 725 George St, Fredericton, NB Canada E3B 1K6

LUNA, CARMEN ENCINAS, banker; b. L.A., Feb. 11, 1959; d. Roberto C. and Gloria (Encinas) L. BA in Psychology, U. Redlands, Calif., 1981; MPA, U. So. Calif., L.A., 1983. Field rep. assemblywoman Gloria Molina State of Calif., L.A., 1982-84; budget analyst City of L.A., 1984-87, asst. chief of staff lt. gov. Leo McCarthy, 1987-89; asst. v.p., community outreach coord. Am. Savs. Bank, L.A., 1989—. Vice chair Chicano caucus Calif. Dem. Cen. Com., L.A., 1988; bd. dirs. Angeles Girl Scouts Coun., 1984-90. Mem. Commn. Femenil Mexicana Nacional (pres. 1987-90, Outstanding Svc. award 1990), L.A. County Commn. on Self Esteem (commr. 1988-89), New Econs. for Women (treas. 1990—), Calif. State U. Hispanic Support NEtwork (v.p. 1988-90, pres. 1990-92), Latin Bus. Assocs. (bd. trustees 1991-92). Roman Catholic. Home: 5418 Percy St Los Angeles CA 90022-3306 Office: Am Savs Bank 5726 Whittier Blvd Los Angeles CA 90022-4262

LUNA, CASEY, state official; b. Canon de Jemez, N. Mex., May 26, 1931; m. Beverly Fulton; 6 children. Pres. Casey Luna Ford & Mercury Co., Belen, N. Mex.; now lt. gov.of N. Mex.; mem. Albuquerque Hispano C. of C. With U.S. Army, 1948-51. Office: Office of the Lt Gov Pera Bldg 5th Fl Santa Fe NM 87503*

LUNA-KEENAN, BARBARA, bookstore owner, publisher; b. Nacogdoches, Tex., July 22, 1941; d. Joseph Matthew and Katherine Mary (Lazarine) Luna; m. Rodney Joseph Keenan; Jan. 8, 1965; children: Jay Author, Lee Desmond. Student, Ohlona Jr. Coll., Fremont, Calif., 1970-72. Sec. A. L. Lowery Atty., Nacogdoches, Tex., 1962; mgr. BookMart, Fremont, 1976-81; pub., owner Affaire de Coeur Mag., Fremont, 1980—; owner East Bay Books, Inc., San Leandro, Calif., 1984—; owner, pub. Brandywine Books, Fremont, 1984—; ptnr. BBB Lit. Agy.; promotional dir. numerous confs., 1980—; host TV prgram People, People, People, Fremont, 1986—; lectr. numerous colls. Organizer East Bay Relief Ctr., 1989. With USN, 1962-65. Recipient Persephone award WIN/WIN Wirters Internat. Network, 1991. Mem. Am. Book Sellers Assn., No. Calif. Books Assn., Nat. Bus. Women, Women Writers of Colors, Nat. RWA Am. Roman Catholic. Home: 5660 Roosevelt Pl Fremont CA 94538-1029 Office: Affaire de Coeur 1555 Washington Blvd Fremont CA 94539-5116

LUND, GEORGE ELLSWORTH, protective services official; b. Miles City, Mont., July 24, 1941; s. George A. andd Mary M. (Ellithorp) L.; m. Judy Beth Lautenschlager, June 30, 1962; children: Richard George, Sheryl Denise Lund Swaffar. AA in Fire Sci., Vetura Coll., 1970. Carpenter Lautenschlager & Butte Inc., Culver City, Calif., 1960-66; firefighter Ventura County Fire Protection Dist., Ventura, Calif., 1967-69, fire engr., 1969-70, fire capt., 1970-76, fire bn. chief, 1976-88, asst. fire chief, 1988-89, dep. fire chief, 1989-90, county fire chief, 1990—; mem. task force Firescope Program So. Calif., 1977-80; advisor, instr. Incident Command System Implementation So. Calif., 1980-82. Mem. Nat. Fire Protection Assn., Calif. Fire Chiefs Assn., Fire Chiefs Assn. Ventura County (coord. 1990—). Office: Ventura County Fire Protection Dist 165 Durley Ave Camarillo CA 93010

LUND, VICTOR L., retail food company executive; b. Salt Lake City, 1947; married. BA, U. Utah, 1969, MBA, 1972. Audit mgr. Ernst and Whinney, Salt Lake City, 1972-77; sr. v.p. Skaggs Cos. Inc., from 1977; v.p., contr. Am. Stores Co., 1980-83, sr. v.p., contr., from 1983, exec. v.p., co-chief exec. officer, vice-chmn., chief fin. and adminstrv. officer, now pres., CEO, 1992—. Office: Am Stores Co PO Box 27447 Salt Lake City UT 84127-0447 also: Am Stores Co 709 East South Temple Salt Lake City UT 84102

LUNDAHL, CRAIG RAYMOND, sociology educator; b. Logan, Utah, June 19, 1943; s. Raymond Eugene and Geraldine (Morgan) L.; m. Rafaela Manriquez Dominguez, Sept. 19, 1981. AS, Ricks Coll., Rexburg, Idaho, 1964; BS, Brigham Young U., 1966; MS, Utah State U., 1968, PhD, 1973. Lectr. sociology Western N.Mex. U., Silver City, 1971, asst. prof., 1972-77, rsch. dir., 1976-83, assoc. prof., 1978-86, prof., 1987—, prof. sociology & bus. adminstrn., 1990—, chmn. dept. social scis., 1990—, office dir., 1972-76, univ. records officer and archivist, 1976-83; rsch. cons., Silver City. Author: A Collection of Near-Death Reaearch Readings, 1982; contbr. articles to profl. jours. Mem. Am. Sociol. Assn., Internat Assn. for Near-Death Studies, Alpha Kappa Delta, Pi Gamma Mu. Republican. Mem. LDS Ch. Office: Western NMex U PO Box 680 Silver City NM 88062-0680

LUNDBERG, DOUGLAS TAYLOR, biology educator; b. Atlanta, Nov. 7, 1947; widowed Dec. 1988; 1 child, Claire Jeanette; m. Christa Reichert, Dec. 21, 1991. BS, Wayne State U., Detroit, 1970; MA, Adams (Colo) State Coll., 1985. Instr. Northwestern Jr. High Sch., Battle Creek, Mich., 1970-72, Upwey (Victoria, Australia) High Sch., 1972-75, Air Acad. High Sch., U.S. Air Force Acad., Colo., 1975—; rschr. Agrigenetics Corp., Boulder, Colo., 1986-87, Lawrence Livermore (Calif.) Nat. Lab., 1990; cons. Coll. Bd., Princeton, N.J., 1986—. Contbr. articles to profl. jours. Mem. Pikes Peak Edn. Assn. (pres. Colorado Springs, Colo. chpt. 1986-88), Acad. Edn. Assn. (pres. Colorado Springs chpt. 1982-85). Home: 15270 Pleasant View Dr Colorado Springs CO 80921-2226 Office: Air Acad High Sch USAF Academy CO 80840

LUNDE, DOLORES BENITEZ, educator; b. Honolulu, Apr. 12, 1929; d. Frank Molero and Matilda (Francisco) Benitez; m. Nuell Carlton Lunde, July 6, 1957; 1 child, Laurelle. BA, U. Oreg., 1951, postgrad., 1951-52; postgrad., U. So. Calif., L.A., 1953-54, Colo. State U., 1957-58, Calif. State U., Fullerton, 1967-68. Cert. gen. secondary tchr., Calif.; cert. lang. devel. specialist. Tchr. Brawley (Calif.) Union High Sch., 1952-55; tchr. Fullerton (Calif.) Union High Sch. Dist., 1955-73; tchrs. aide Placentia (Calif.) Unified Sch. Dist., 1983-85; tchr. continuing edn. Fullerton Union High Sch. Dist., 1985-91; tchr. Fullerton Sch. Dist., 1988, Fullerton Union High Sch. Dist., 1989—; presenter regional and state convs., so. Calif., 1986-88. Innovator tests, teaching tools, audio-visual aids. Vol. Luth. Social Svcs., Fullerton, 1981-82, Messiah Luth., Yorba Linda, Calif., 1981-88. Recipient Tchr. of Yr. award Fullerton Union High Sch. Dist., 1989. Mem. NEA, AAUW (life, bull. editor 1979-80, corr. sec. 1981-83, program v.p. 1983-84, gift honoree Fullerton br. 1985), Calif. State Tchrs. Assn., Fullerton Secondary Tchrs. Assn., Internat. Club/Spanish Club (advisor La Habra, Calif. 1965-72), Tchrs. English to Speakers Other Langs., Calif. Assn. Tchrs. English to Speakers Other Langs. Home: 4872 Ohio St Yorba Linda CA 92686-2713 Office: Buena Park High Sch 8833 Academy Dr Buena Park CA 90621-3799

LUNDE, DONALD THEODORE, physician; b. Milw., Mar. 2, 1937; m. Marilynn Krick; children: Montgomery, Christopher, Glenn, Evan, Bret. BA with distinction, Stanford U., 1958, MA in Psychology, 1964, MD, 1966. Diplomate Nat. Bd. Med. Examiners. Ward psychologist Palo Alto (Calif.) VA Hosp., 1965-66, chief resident in psychiatry, 1969-70, assoc. chief tng. and research sect., 1970-72, acting chief tng. and research sect., 1971-72; intern in internal medicine Palo Alto/Stanford Hosp., 1966-67; resident in psychiatry Stanford (Calif.) U. Sch. Medicine, 1967-69, instr. psychiatry, 1969-70, asst. prof. psychiatry, 1970-75, dir. med. sch. edn. in psychiatry, 1971-74, clin. assoc. prof. psychiatry, 1978-89, clin. prof. psychiatry, 1989—; staff physician Atascadero (Calif.) State Hosp., 1968. Author books and articles in field. Served with USN, 1958-61. Fellow Am. Psychiat. Assn., Am. Coll. Forensic Psychiatry; mem. Am. Psychiat. Assn., No. Calif. Psychiat. Soc., Phi Beta Kappa, Alpha Omega Alpha. Office: Stanford U 900 Welch Rd Ste 400 Palo Alto CA 94304-1892

LUNDE, KAREN TAMM, real estate broker; b. Chgo., Feb. 21, 1944; d. George Lewis and Margaret D. (Kiesewetter) Tamm; m. Delmar R. Lunde, Dec. 29, 1984. Diploma, Evanston Hosp., 1965; PhB, Northwestern U., 1976; postgrad., Anthony Schs., 1987, 90. Staff, head nurse labor, delivery Evanston (Ill.) Hosp., 1965-67; staff nurse surgery St. Mary's Hosp., Wausau, Wis., 1967-68; staff, head nurse Adams County Meml. Hosp., Friendship, Wis., 1968-70; head nurse surg. unit, asst., nursing coord. Evanston (Ill.) Hosp., 1970-72; supr. maternal child nursing Ill. Masonic Med. Ctr., Chgo., 1972-74; adminstr. NAACOG, Chgo., 1974-79; asst. dir. nursing/nursery, asst. dir. nursing Children's Hosp. Med. Ctr., Oakland, Calif., 1979-84; dir. svcs. Palo Alto Med. Found. Fremont (Calif.) Ctr., 1984-86; cons. Grass Valley, Calif., 1986—; realtor, assoc. ERA Consol. Brokers, Grass Valley, 1987-91, broker assoc., 1991—. Contbr. articles to profl. jours. Mem. Chgo. area chpt. March of Dimes, 1975-79, ARC, 1975-79, Nev. County Health Planning Coun., 1990—; mem., sec. bd. dirs. Tri Cities Children's Ctr., 1985-87; bd. dirs. Sierra Nev. Community Svcs. Coun., 1988—; mem. Nev. County Health Planning Coun. Mem. NAACOG (Ill. sect., chmn. conf. 1972, fin. chmn. conf. 1972, sec. treas. 1972-74, certification corp. item writer neonatal nurses certification exam. 1982-83, Calif. sect., chmn. conf. 1983, mem. nat. com. on devel. 1984-86, Palo Alto chpt., sec.-treas. 1986-87, others), Nat. Osteoporosis Found., Nat. Assn. Realtors, Calif. Assn. Realtors, Northwestern U. Alumnae Club, Evanston Hosp. NursingAlumnae Assn., Nevada County Bd. Realtors (active), Alpha Sigma Lambda. Office: ERA Network Real Estate 167 S Auburn St Grass Valley CA 95945-6531

LUNDERVILLE, GERALD PAUL, bilingual education educator; b. Springfield, Mass., Feb. 22, 1941; s. Leon Albert and Florence Marion (Jolivette) L.; m. Martha Ann Sumner, Mar. 26, 1966 (div. Aug. 1971); m. Bony Lek, June 30, 1984. BA cum laude, U. N.H., 1963; MA, Middlebury Coll., 1969, U. Rochester, 1973; postgrad., Calif. State U., Long Beach, 1981-84, 86—. Instr. Spanish Berwick Acad., South Berwick, Maine, 1963-64; tchr. French, Spanish Barnstable High Sch., Hyannis, Mass., 1967-68; instr. Spanish Cape Cod Community Coll., West Barnstable, Mass., 1968-71; tchr. French, Spanish Stevens High Sch. Annex, Claremont, N.H., 1973-74; tchr. English Centro de Estudios Norteamericanos, Valencia, Spain, 1974-75; dept. head fgn. langs. Merrimack (N.H.) High Sch., 1975-80; tchr. Spanish El Camino Coll., Torrance, Calif., 1980-85; tchr. ESL Wilson High Sch., Long Beach, Calif., 1980—, dept. head ESL, 1987-88, tchr. bilingual edn./Spanish, 1992—. Author: 20th Century Baseball Trivia, 1992; contbr. articles to Am. Atheist Mag. Active Long Beach Area Citizens Peace, 1982—, Animal Protection Inst. Am., Sacramento., 1983—. Served with U.S. Army, 1964-67, Vietnam. Mem. NEA, ACLU, NOW, Nat. Assn. Tchrs. Spanish and Portuguese, Modern and Classical Lang. Assn. of So. Calif., Tchrs. of English as 2d Lang., Merrimack Tchrs. Assn. (sec. 1977-80), Lambda Pi. Home: 1740 E Washington St Long Beach CA 90805-5535

LUNDGREN, DAVID RUSSELL, lawyer; b. Pocatello, Idaho, Dec. 4, 1955; s. Russell James Lundgren and Billinell Pool; m. Judy Lea Geier, June 6, 1981. BA, Idaho State U., Pocatello, 1981; JD, Antioch Coll., 1987. Bar: Idaho, Wash., D.C. Pvt. practice atty., cons. Washington, 1987-88; tribal atty. Nisqually Indian Tribe, Olympia, Wash., 1988—. With U.S. Army, 1974-77. Office: Nisqually Indian Tribe 4820 She Nah Num Dr SE Olympia WA 98503-9199

LUNDGREN, SUSAN ELAINE, counselor, educator; b. Martinez, Calif., May 31, 1949; d. Elmer Alfred and Shirley (Bright) L.; 1 child, Alicia Hadiya. AA, Diablo Valley Coll., 1969; BA in English, San Francisco State U., 1971, MA in Counseling, 1975; EdD, U. San Francisco, 1983; cert. in gen. mgmt., John F. Kennedy U., 1988. Instr., counselor Diablo Valley Coll., Pleasant Hill, Calif., 1976—, coordinator, 1986-90, women's ctr. faculty dir., 1983-85; lectr. dept. grad. career devel. John F. Kennedy U., Orinda, Calif., 1982—. Sec., bd. dirs. Rape Crisis Ctr., Concord, Calif., 1985. Named participant in leadership devel. inst. AAUW and Nat. Assn. Community Colls., 1985. Mem. NOW (pres. East Bay chpt. 1982-84, bd. dirs. Calif. chpt.), I-Pride, Eureka Consortium (conf. speaker 1984, 86). Home: 3738 Victor Ave Oakland CA 94619-1533 Office: Diablo Valley Coll 321 Golf Club Rd Pleasant Hill CA 94523-1576

LUNDIN, ANN FRANCES, chemist, medical technologist; b. Dallas, Pa., Sept. 22, 1941; d. Walter Stanley and Frances Evelyn (Sholes) Black; m. Lars Norman Lundin, June 10, 1967; children: Lori, Terri, Wendy. BS in Chemistry, Coll. Misericordia, 1963; MS in Chemistry, Villanova U., 1967. Chem. asst. Worcester Found. for Exptl. Biology, Shrewsbury, Mass., 1963-67; research chemist Dow Chem. Co., Wayland, Mass., 1967-71; chem. technologist Children's Hosp., Boston, 1975-80, VA Med. Ctr., San Francisco, 1980-83; quality control chemist Nobel Sci., Alexandria, Va., 1983-84; chemist Nat. Health Labs., Englewood, Colo., 1984-91, chemistry supr., 1991—; cons. sci. projects Randolph Mass., 1975-80,. Sec. Jr. League of Swedish Charitable Soc., Boston, 1970-72. Grantee NSF, 1959. Mem. Am. Chem. Soc. Democrat. Roman Catholic. Club: Gen. Fedn. Womens. Lodge: Order of Eastern Star, Ind. Order Vikings. Home: 11442 E Adriatic Pl Aurora CO 80014-1181 Office: Nat Health Labs 6665 S Kenton St Englewood CO 80111-6822

LUNDRING, L(YNN) KARSTEN, financial planner; b. L.A., Oct. 19, 1942; s. Axel Cornelius and Hazel Luella (Lilland) L.; m. Kirsten Minette Bodding, June 12, 1965; children: Sherith Kirsten Lundring Squires, Erik Karsten. BA, Calif. Luth. U., 1965. CLU; ChFC; CFP. Dist. rep. Luth. Brotherhood Fin. Svcs., Thousand Oaks, Calif., 1961-73, gen. agt., 1973—. Bd. regents Calif. Luth. U., Thousand Oaks, 1980—. 1st lt. U.S. Army, 1966-68. Recipient Outstanding Alumni award Calif. Luth. U., 1980, Disting. Svc. award, 1982. Mem. Gen. Agts. and Mgrs. Assn. (bd. dirs. 1980—, Nat. Mgmt. award 1975—). Republican. Home: 1336 Lamont Thousand Oaks CA 91362-2024 Office: Luth Brotherhood Life 22110 Clarendon St # 103 Woodland Hills CA 91367-6310

LUNDSTROM, MARY MEYER, museum curator, educator; b. Hollywood, Calif., June 23, 1948; d. Archibald deNorville and Ivy Kate (Whitworth) Meyer; m. Eric Arthur Lundstrom, June 26, 1971; 1 child, Tara Carina. BA in Art, San Diego State U., 1971. Lic. real estate salesperson, Calif. Draftsman Genge Industries, Ridgecrest, Calif., 1967-68; draftsman Naval Weapons Ctr., China Lake, Calif., 1969, illustrator, 1970; substitute tchr. Albuquerque Pub. Schs., 1971-72, Kern County High Sch. Dist., China Lake, 1972-74; real estate salesperson Coldwell Banker Best Realty, Ridgecrest, 1974-86; art instr. Cerro Coso C.C., Ridgecrest, 1986-91; art curator Maturango Mus., Ridgecrest, 1986—; freelance artist, 1970—. Juror Lancaster Art Mus. Mixed Media Show, 1990. Mem. AAUW (past pres., name grant award 1987), High Desert Coun. of Arts, Kern Arts Coun., Am. Assn. Museums, Enamel Guild West, San Diego Enamel Guild, Enamelist Soc., Calif. Assn. Museums, Inst. Museum Svcs. (grant reviewer), Desert Art League. Home: 731 W Howell Ave Ridgecrest CA 93555-3445 Office: Maturango Mus PO Box 1776 Ridgecrest CA 93556-1776

LUNDY, GILBERT MOULTON, JR., computer science educator; b. New Orleans, Sept. 29, 1954; s. Gilbert Moulton and Loretta Maureen (Taylor) L.; m. Yong Ae Yi, Feb. 18, 1978 (div. 1988); children: Benjamin Lee, Miriam Yong. BA in Math., Tex. A&M U., 1976; MS in Computer Sci., U. Tex., Dallas, 1983; PhD in Computer Sci., Ga. Inst. Tech., 1988. Software engr. E-Systems, Inc., Dallas, 1981-84; rsch. asst. Ga. Inst. Tech., Atlanta, 1984-88; asst. prof. computer sci. U.S. Naval Postgrad. Sch., Monterey, Calif., 1988—. Contbr. articles on computer and telecom. networks to sci. jours. 1st lt. U.S. Army, 1977-81. Mem. IEEE, Assn. for Computing Machinery. Office: US Naval Postgrad Sch Dept Computer Sci Code CS Monterey CA 93943

LUNDY, JOHN KENT, anthropology educator, consultant; b. Vancouver, Wash., Jan. 21, 1946; s. Olaf and Lola Irene (Fox) L.; m. Sylvia Jean Trevino, Jan. 15, 1968; 1 child, Eric Kristian. AA, Everett (Wash.) Community Coll, 1974; BA, Western Wash. U., 1976, MA, 1977; PhD, U. of the Witwatersrand, Johannesburg, South Africa, 1984. Diplomate Am. Bd. Forensic Anthropology. Dep. sheriff County of Snomomish, Everett, 1972-77; asst. lectr. U. of the Witwatersrand, 1980; dep. med. examiner Multnomah County Med. Examiner, Portland, Oreg., 1982-86; anthropologist U.S. Army Cen. ID Lab., Honolulu, 1986-88; prof. anthropology Clark Coll., Vancouver, 1988—; Fulbright scholar, vis. fellow U. Sheffield, Eng., 1991; cons. Clark County Coroner, Vancouver, 1981—, Oreg. State Med. Examiner, Portland, 1982—; mem. adj. faculty Portland State U., 1983—. Co-editor: Variation, Culture and Evolution in African Populations, 1986; contbr. articles to profl. jours. Fellow Am. Acad. Forensic Scis.; mem. Am. Assn. Phys. Anthropologists. Office: Clark Coll Dept Anthropology 1800 E Mcloughlin Blvd Vancouver WA 98663-3509

LUNGREN, DANIEL EDWARD, lawyer; b. Long Beach, Calif., Sept. 22, 1946; s. John Charles and Lorain Kathleen (Youngberg) L.; m. Barbara Kolls, Aug. 2, 1969; children: Jeffrey Edward, Kelly Christine, Kathleen Marie. A.B. cum laude, Notre Dame U., 1968; postgrad., U. So. Calif. Law Sch., 1968-69; J.D., Georgetown U., 1971. Bar: Calif. 1972. Staff asst. Sen. George Murphy, Sen. William Brock, 1969-71; spl. asst. to co-chmn. Rep. Nat. Com., dir. spl. programs, 1971-72; assoc. Ball, Hunt, Hart, Brown & Baerwitz, Long Beach, 1971-78; mem. 96th-97th Congresses from 34th, 98th-100th Congresses from 42d Calif. Dist., 1979-1989, Rep. State Cen. Com. Calif., 1974-89; ptnr. Diepenbrock, Wulff, Plant & Hannegan, Sacramento, 1989-91; state atty. Office of the Atty. Gen., Sacramento, 1991—. Committeeman Rep. Nat. Com., Calif., 1989; bd. dirs. Long Beach chpt. ARC, Boy's Club, 1976-88. Recipient Good Samaritan award Los Angeles Council Mormon Chs., 1976. Republican. Roman Catholic. Office: Office of the Atty Gen 1515 K St Sacramento CA 95814-4017

LUNGREN, RICHARD WILLHELM, retired minister; b. Moline, Ill., May 3, 1910; s. Oscar E. and Anna J. (Johnson) L.; m. Grace A. Atkinson, Aug. 24, 1935; children: Elaine, David. AB, Nebr. Wesleyan U., 1933; BD, Drew

U., 1937; STM, Union Theol. Sem., N.Y.C., 1938. Pastor M.E. Ch., Rock Springs, Wyo., 1938-42, Meth. Ch., Shelby, Mont., 1942-48, Mountain View Meth. Ch., Butte, Mont., 1948-52, Canon City (Colo.) Meth. Ch., 1952-54, Ft. Lupton (Colo.) Meth. Ch., 1954-58, Lakewood (Colo.) Meth. Ch., 1958-60; min. edn. St. Mark's Meth. Ch., Sacramento, 1960-66, 1st Meth. Ch., Concord, Calif., 1966-69; pastor Lindsey (Calif.) Meth. Ch., 1969-72; ret., 1972; min. edn. 1st United Meth. Ch., Lodi, Calif., 1972-78, Delta Dist. United Meth. Ch., Sacramento, 1978-80; chmn. bd. edn. Mont. Conf. Meth. Ch., Butte, 1949-52; dir. adult work Colo. Conf. Meth. Ch., Denver, 1956-60. Mem. Lodi Arts Commn., 1973-80. Democrat. Home: 135 Woodland Ave # 69 Woodland CA 95695

LUNIEWSKI, ALLEN WILLIAM, computer scientist; b. Pitts., Aug. 5, 1952; s. Alphonse and Helen (Ruszkowski) L.; m. Patsy Ann Fenerin, Nov. 19, 1983; 1 child, Catherine Ann. BS in Math., Carnegie-Mellon U., 1974; SM in Computer Sci., Elect. Engring., MIT, 1977, PhD in Computer Sci., 1979. Devel. mgr. Xerox Corp., Palo Alto, Calif., 1979-86; research staff mem. IBM, San Jose, Calif., 1986-91, mgr. object oriented systems, 1991—. Mem. IEEE, Assn. Computing Machinery. Roman Catholic. Home: 7624 De Foe Dr Cupertino CA 95014-4307 Office: IBM 650 Harry Rd San Jose CA 95120-6099

LUPASH, LAWRENCE OVIDIU, computer analyst, researcher; b. Bucharest, Romania, May 29, 1942; came to U.S., 1980; s. Ovidiu Dumitru and Stefania Maria (Lebu) L. BS, Polytechnic Inst. of Bucharest, 1964; MS, Polytechnic Inst. Bucharest, Romania, 1965, PhD, 1972. Sr. engr., researcher Inst. Automation, Bucharest, 1971-72; sr. analyst, researcher, computing ctr. U. Bucharest, 1972-79; sr. analyst Intermetrics, Inc., Huntington Beach, Calif., 1980—; asst. prof. Polytechnic Inst. Bucharest, 1966-67, 67-68, 71-72; lectr. U. Bucharest, 1973-78; vis. prof. U. Tirana, Albania, 1973. Co-author: Numerical Methods in Systems Theory, 1974; contbr. numerous articles to profile pubs. Recipient Rep. award Polytechnic Inst. Bucharest, 1962; grantee Case Western Reserve U., 1968, Romanian Acad. Scis., 1968. Mem. IEEE, Soc. Indsl. and Applied Math., Assn. Computing Machinery, Am. Philatelic Soc., Orange County Philatelic Soc. Mem. Greek Orthodox Ch. Office: Intermetrics Inc 5312 Bolsa Ave Huntington Beach CA 92649-1090

LUPE, RONNIE, chairman of Apache tribe; b. Cibecue, Ariz., 1930. Student in Bus. and Acctg., Ariz. State Univ. From councilman to chmn. White Mountain Apache Tribe, Ft. Apache Indian Reservation, Ariz., 1964—. Office: White Mountain Apache Tribe Office of Chmn PO Box 1150 Whiteriver AZ 85941-1150

LURVEY, IRA HAROLD, lawyer; b. Chgo., Apr. 6, 1935; s. Louis and Faye (Grey) L.; m. Barbara Ann Sirvint, June 24, 1962; children: Nathana, Lawrence, Jennifer, Jonathan, David, Robert. BS, U. Ill., 1956; MS, Northwestern U., 1961; JD, U. Calif., Berkeley, 1965. Bar: Calif. 1965, Nev. 1966, U.S. Dist. Ct. (cen. dist.) Calif. 1966, U.S. Tax Ct. 1966, U.S. Ct. Appeals (9th cir.) 1966, U.S. Supreme Ct. 1975. Law clk. to hon. justices Nev. Supreme Ct., Carson City, 1965-66; from assoc. to ptnr. Pacht, Ross, Warne, Bernhard & Sears, Inc., 1966-84; predecessor firm Shea & Gould, Los Angeles; founding ptnr. Lurvey & Shapiro, Los Angeles, 1984—; lectr. legal edn. programs; mem. Chief Justice's Commns. on Ct. Reform, Weighted Caseloads. Editor Community Property Jour., 1979-80; contbr. articles to profl. jours. Former chmn. Los Angeles Jr. Arts Ctr.; past pres. Cheviot Hills Homeowners Assn.; exec. v.p., counsel gen. studies com. Hillel Acad. Sch., Beverly Hills, Calif., 1977—. Served with U.S. Army, 1957-58. Fellow Am. Acad. Matrimonial Lawyers (pres. So. Calif. chpt. 1991—, pres. elect 1990-91, v.p. 1988-89, ct. liaison chair 1989-90), Internat. Acad. Matrimonial Lawyers; mem. ABA (governing coun. family law sect. 1986—, fin. officer 1991—, chmn. support com.; chmn. continuing legal edn.; chmn. policy and issues com.; vice chmn. com. arbitration and mediation, bd. of editors Family Adv. mag.), Calif. Bar Assn. (editor jour. 1982-85, chmn. family law sect. 1986-87, exec. com. family law sect. 1982-88, specialization adv. bd. family law 1979-82), L.A. County Bar Assn. (chmn. family law sect. 1981-82, exec. com. family law 1989—), Beverly Hills Bar Assn. (chmn. family law sect. 1976-77). Home: 2729 Motor Ave Los Angeles CA 90064-3441 Office: Lurvey & Shapiro Ste 1550 2121 Avenue Of The Stars Los Angeles CA 90067-5010

LUSH, PAMELA GRACE, international publishing company executive; b. Wellsboro, Pa., Apr. 1, 1961; d. Stanley Gale and Karen (Kohler) L. BA, Colo. State U., 1983. Traffic coord. Leo Burnett Advt., Chgo., 1983-85; sr. account exec. Cardiff Pub., Englewood, Colo., 1985-88; pres. PGL Assocs., Denver, 1988-90; v.p. Interfax-US, Denver, 1991-92; pres. DGL Internat. Pub., Denver, 1990—, DGL Publs., Denver, 1990—. Editor, pub.: The Child Care Directory, 1991; pub.: The Family Resource Guide, 1992, The Petroleum Tech. Resource Guide, 1992, The Agricultural Technical Resource Guide, 1992, The Mining/Environmental Technical Resource Guide, 1992. Mem. Soviet Task Force Under Gov. Roy Romer, Denver, 1990—, Internat. Gateway Com., Denver, 1990—. Named nominee for Pulitzer Prize for Internat. Reporting, 1991, Pulitzer Prize for Meritorious Pub. Svc., 1991. Presbyterian.

LUST, PETER, JR., microwave engineer, consultant; b. Montreal, Que., Can., Apr. 21, 1960; came to U.S., 1975, naturalized, 1987; s. Peter Clark and Evelyn (Heymanson) L.; Gloria Ruth Bingle, Apr. 5, 1985; children: Peter Alexander III, Elizabeth Ann, Matthew Eric. Student, Lowry Tech. Tng. Ctr., Community Coll. A.F., Albuquerque, USAF Acad.; BSEE, Pacific Western U., 1990. Computer meterologist Electro Rent, Burbank, Calif., 1982-84; microwave engr., program mgr. satellite and space shuttle communications systems Transco Products, Camarillo, Calif., 1984-90, internat. tech. mktg. mgr., 1990-93; prin. Electronic Note Co., Port Hueneme, Calif., 1984—; cons. in field, Port Hueneme, 1984—; rep. ANT, Teldix, Germany. With USAF, 1979-82. Recipient Technol. award USAF, 1980, Discovery award NASA, 1987, Internat. Leaders in Achievement award, Cambridge. Mem. Assn. Old Crows, Channel Islands Health Club. Office: Electronic Note Co 300 Esplanade Dr Oxnard CA 93030

LUSTICA, KATHERINE GRACE, publisher, artist, marketing consultant; b. Bristol, Pa., Nov. 20, 1958; d. Thomas Lustica and Elizabeth Delores (Moyer) De Groat. Student, Hussian Sch. Art, Phila., 1976-78, Rider Coll., 1980-82. Comml. artist, illustrator Bucks County Courier Times Newspapers, Levittown, Pa., 1978-82; account exec. Trenton (N.J.) Times Newspapers, 1982-84; promotions and account exec. Diversified Suburban Newspapers, Murray (Utah) Printing, 1984-88; pub. Barclays Ltd. Salt Lake City, 1988—; cover artist, illustrator Accent mag., Bristol, 1978-82; freelance artist, 1978—; advt. and creative cons. Everett & Winthrop Products Group, Salt Lake City, 1988—, Multi Techs. Internat., Salt Lake City, 1990—. Newcombe scholar, 1981=82. Mem. Art Dirs. Salt Lake City. Presbyterian. Office: 4640 S Stratton Dr Salt Lake City UT 84117

LUTALI, A. P., governor of American Samoa; b. Aunu'u, American Samoa, Dec. 24, 1919; married. Gov. AS, 1985-89; former v.p. Senate, AS, from 1988; gov. Am. Samoa, 1993—. Office: Office of Gov Pago Pago AS 96799

LUTE, JACK ANTON, sales executive; b. Portland, Oreg., Feb. 7, 1935; s. Claron A. Lute and Ann (Wald) Moore; m. Sondra L. Parker, May 11, 1953; children: Pam Harrington, Kandy Parks, Darla Weekley, Kevin. Grad., high sch. Sales mgr. KWIL and KHPE Radio, Albany, Oreg., 1963—. Sunday sch. tchr., deacon Bapt. Ch., North Albany, Oreg., 25 yrs. Republican. Office: KWIL AM PO Box 278 Albany OR 97321-0082

LUTER, JOHN, news correspondent, educator; b. Knoxville, Tenn., Jan. 17, 1919; s. John Thomas and Bertha Mae (Carver) L.; m. Mary Hickey, 1948 (dec.); 1 child, Linda; m. Yvonne Spiegelberg, 1966 (div. 1971); m. Nan Hoyt Lawrence, 1974. BA, St. Mary's U., Tex., 1939, postgrad., 1939-42; fellow Time Inc., Sch. Advanced Internat. Studies, Washington, 1945. Reporter San Antonio Light, 1939-42, Washington Star, 1942-44; Wash. corr. Time mag., 1944-45; war corr. Time mag., Pacific, 1945; fgn. corr. Time and Life mags., Southeast Asia, 1945-46, Japan, 1946-47, Israel, 1948-49, Italy, 1949-54; asst. editor internat. edit. Life mag., 1954-56; reporter, writer CBS News, 1957-58; asso. editor Newsweek mag., 1958-61; radio news commentator Stas. WQXR and QXR-FM Network, 1960-61; coord. advanced internat. reporting program Columbia Grad. Sch. Journalism, 1961-72; dir. Maria Moors Cabot Prize Program, 1961-74; mem. profl. staff Bank St. Coll. Edn., 1973-74; prof., dir. journalism U. Hawaii, Honolulu, from 1974, prof. and chmn. journalism dept., 1982-92, prof. journalism, 1992—. Adv. editor: Columbia Journalism Rev., 1961-72. Chmn. internat. rels. com. N.Y.C. Protestant Coun., 1968-71; chmn. adv. screening com. communications Sr. Fulbright Program, 1970-73; trustee Overseas Press Club Found., 1962-72, chmn., 1964-65; bd. dirs. UN Assn. N.Y.C., 1973-74; chmn. Honolulu Community Media Coun., 1982-84. Mem. Assn. Edn. Journalism and Mass Communications, Assn. Schs. Journalism and Mass Communications, Honolulu Com. Fgn. Rels., Pacific and Asian Affairs Coun., Soc. Profl. Journalists (mem. chpt. exec. coun. 1966-69, 89-90), Japan Am. Soc., Overseas Press Club (pres. N.Y.C. 1960-62), Outrigger Canoe Club. Home: 340 Alta Ave San Antonio TX 78209 Office: U Hawaii 208 Crawford Hall 2550 Campus Rd Honolulu HI 96822-2217

LUTI, WILLIAM JOSEPH, U.S. naval officer; b. Boston, Nov. 13, 1953; s. William Vincent and Marjorie Louise (Barnes) L.; m. Donna Margaret King, Dec. 13, 1990; 1 child, Lauren Marie. BA in History, The Citadel, 1975; MA in Nat. Security Affairs, U.S. Naval War Coll., 1986; MA in Internat. Rels., Salve Regina Coll., 1986; MA in Law and Diplomacy, PhD in Internat. Rels., Tufts U., 1990. Commd. USN, 1975, advanced through grades to comdr., 1990; flight student Naval Air Station, Pensacola, Fla., 1975-76; div. officer VQ-1 (EA-3B aircraft), Agana, Guam, 1976-79; asst. dept. head VAQ-131 (EA-6B aircraft), Oak Harbor, Wash., 1979-82; dept. head VAQ-135 (EA-6B), Oak Harbor, 1986-88; commanding officer VAQ-130 (EA-6B squadron) USN, Oak Harbor, 1991-93; admiral's aide U.S. Naval Acad., Annapolis, Md., 1982-85; dep. dir. CNO Exec. Panel, Alexandria, Va., 1993—; panelist Persian Gulf War Symposium, Naval Inst., Pensacola, 1992. Tchr.'s aide Hillcrest Elem. Sch., Oak Harbor, 1991-92. Decorated with Air medal U.S. Navy, Iraq, 1991. Mem. U.S. Naval Inst., Assn. of Naval Aviation, Phi Alpha Theta. Republican. Roman Catholic. Office: CNO Exec Panel 4401 Ford Ave Alexandria VA 22302-0268

LUTIN, DAVID LOUIS, real estate development and finance consultant; b. East Hartford, Conn., Apr. 18, 1919; s. Solomon and Esther (Newman) L.; A.B., Ohio No. U., 1946; M.B.A., Syracuse U., 1949; m. Dorothy Marmor, Dec. 3, 1944; children—Gary, Marnie (Mrs. George Wittig). Housing economist and field rep. HHFA, Washington, 1950-57; dir. urban renewal City of Brookline, Mass., 1957-58; cons. on urban renewal and housing Com. for Econ. Devel., N.Y.C., 1958-59; propr. David L. Lutin Assocs., real estate devel. and fin. cons., Rye, N.Y., 1959-73, Phoenix, 75—; v.p. real estate and mortgages Am. Bank and Trust Co., N.Y.C., 1973-75. Research assoc. Albert Farwell Bemis Found., M.I.T., 1951-52. Served to capt. AUS, 1942-46. Decorated Purple Heart. Mem. Am. Econ. Assn., Nat. Planning Assn., Mortgage Bankers Assn., Urban Land Inst., Am. Planning Assn., Am. Statis. Assn., Nat. Assn. Home Builders. Contbr. articles and reports on econs., housing and urban devel. to profl. jours. Home and Office: 11419 N Century Ln Scottsdale AZ 85254-4827

LUTTRELL, DAN CURTIS, savings and loan company executive; b. Tucson, Dec. 20, 1952; s. Lonnie Calvin and Lois Ann (Jaesche) L.; m. Kathy Lou Sword, Aug. 30, 1975; children: Jason Matthew, Ryan David. Student, Boise State U., 1970-75. Packer, loader Compton Mayflower, Boise, Idaho, 1970-72; billing clk. St. Alphonsus Hosp., Boise, 1972-75; br. mgr. Assocs. Fin. Svcs., Boise, 1975-80; v.p. Farmers & Mchts. State Bank, Meridian, Idaho, 1980-87; asst. v.p. Wash. Fed. Svgs., Nampa, Idaho, 1987—. Chmn. United Way of Ada County, Meridian, 1984-85; judge Am. Cancer Soc. Jail & Bail, Nampa, 1987-88; treas. Soap Box Derby Boise, 1991-93; exec. bd. United Way Canyon area, 1991-95; bd. dirs. Nampa Downtown Econ. Devel. com. 1992. Mem. Consumer Credit Counseling Svc. (pres. 1986—), Inst. Fin. Edn. (sec.-treas. 1988—), Snake River Valley Bldg. Contractors (sec.-treas. 1988-90), Better Bus. Bur. (bd. dirs. 1984-87), Optimist Club (pres. 1979), Sunrise Exch. Club (v.p. 1976), Kiwanis Club Nampa. Republican. Episcopalian. Home: 11491 W Arlen St Boise ID 83704-1512 Office: Washington Fed Svgs & Loan 223 11th Ave S Nampa ID 83651-3920

LUTVAK, MARK ALLEN, computer company executive; b. Chgo., Feb. 9, 1939; s. Joseph Issac and Jeanette Nettie (Pollock) L.; B.S. in Elec. Engring., U. Mich., 1962; M.B.A., Wayne State U., Detroit, 1969; m. Gayle Helene Rotofsky, May 24, 1964; children—Jeffrey, Eric. Sales rep. IBM Corp., 1962-64; successively sales rep., product mktg. mgr., corp. product mgr. Burroughs Corp., Detroit, 1964-76; mgr. product mktg. Memorex Corp., Santa Clara, Calif., 1976-80, product program gen. mgr., 1980-81; dir. product mktg. Personal Computer div. Atari, Inc., Sunnyvale, Calif., 1981-83; dir. mktg., v.p. Durango Systems, San Jose, Calif., 1983-85; dir. mktg. ITTQUME Corp., San Jose, 1985-87; v.p. mktg. Optimem, Mountain View, Calif., 1987-88; dir. mktg. Priam Corp., San Jose, 1988—; prof. Applied Mgmt. Center, Wayne State U., 1967-72, Walsh U., Troy, Mich., 1974-76, West Valley Coll., Saratoga, Calif., 1977-78. Trustee, pres. brotherhood Temple Emanuel, San Jose, Calif., 1979-80. Mem. IEEE, Soc. Applied Math., Alpha Epsilon Pi. Home: 1364 Box Canyon Rd San Jose CA 95120-5627

LUTZ, JOHN SHAFROTH, lawyer; b. San Francisco, Sept. 10, 1943; s. Frederick Henry and Helena Morrison (Shafroth) L.; m. Elizabeth Boschen, Dec. 14, 1968; children: John Shafroth, Victoria. BA, Brown U., 1965; JD, U. Denver, 1971. Bar: Colo. 1971, U.S. Dist. Ct. Colo. 1971, U.S. Ct. Appeals (2d cir.) 1975, D.C. 1976, U.S. Supreme Ct. 1976, U.S. Dist. Ct. (so. dist.) N.Y. 1977, U.S. Tax Ct. 1977, U.S. Ct. Appeals (10th cir.) 1979, N.Y. 1984, U.S. Ct. Appeals (9th cir.) 1990, U.S. Dist. Ct. (no. dist.) Calif. 1993. Trial atty. Denver regional office U.S. SEC, 1971-74; spl. atty. organized crime, racketeering sect. U.S. Dept. Justice, So. Dist. N.Y., 1974-77; atty. Kelly, Stansfield and O'Donnell, Denver, 1977-78; gen. counsel Boettcher & Co., Denver, 1978-87, Kelly, Stansfield and O'Donnel, Denver, 1987; spl. counsel, 1987-88, ptnr., 1988—; allied mem. N.Y. Stock Exch., 1978-87; speaker on broker, dealer, securities law and arbitration issues to various profl. orgns. Contbr. articles to profl. jours. Bd. dirs. Cherry Creek Improvement Assn., 1980-84, Spalding Rehab. Hosp., 1986-89; chmn., vice-chmn. securities sub sect. Bus. Law Sect. of Colo. Bar, 1990, chmn., 1990-91. Lt. (j.g.), USNR, 1965-67. Mem. ABA, Colo. Bar Assn., Denver Bar Assn., Am. Law Inst., Securities Industry Assn. (state regulations com. 1982-86), Nat. Assn. Securities Dealers, Inc. (nat. arbitration com. 1987-91), St. Nicholas Soc. N.Y.C., Denver Law Club, Denver Country Club, Denver Athletic Club (dir. 1990—), Rocky Mountain Brown Club (founder, past pres.), Racquet and Tennis Club. Republican. Episcopalian. Office: Kelly Stansfield & O'Donnell 1225 17th St Ste 2600 Denver CO 80202-4256

LUTZ, WILLIAM RALPH, entertainment industry executive; b. Butler, Pa., Oct. 16, 1963; s. Wilbert Ralph and Eda June (Kuttie) L. BS in Elec. Engring. summa cum laude, Boston U., 1985, MS, 1986; MBA, U. Pa., 1990. Sr. cons. Booz Allen & Hamilton, Inc., Bethesda, Md., 1986-89; sr. assoc. Frank S. Kilpatrick & Assocs., Manhattan Beach, Calif., 1989-90; mgr. bus. devel. Rank Video Svcs. Am., Inc., L.A., 1990—. Mem. Fin. and Adminstrv. Mgrs. in Entertainment, Am. Film Inst., Boston U. Alumni Club. So. Calif., U. Pa. Alumni Assn. So. Calif., Wharton Club So. Calif., Scarlet Key, Lambda Chi Alpha, Tau Beta Pi. Libertarian. Lutheran. Home: 14010 Captains Row # 129 Marina del Rey CA 90292 Office: Rank Video Svcs Am Inc Ste 700 11150 Santa Monica Blvd Los Angeles CA 90025

LUXENBERG, MICHAEL DON, computer services company executive; b. Detroit, June 26, 1945; s. Jack Sam and Beth (Cohen) L.; m. Barbara Ann Bird, Apr. 26, 1968; children: Toni Marie, David Joseph. BA, U. Mich., 1967, MPA, 1968. Contracting officer USN dept. Naval Ordnance Systems Command, Washington, 1968-72; contract mgr. Computer Svc. div. Boeing Co., Vienna, Va., 1972-86; bus. practices mgr. Computer Svc. div. Boeing Co., Seattle, 1986-87, dir. contracts, 1987-92; dir. computing asset mgt. Boeing Co., Seattle, 1992—. Bd. dirs. Children's Mus. Mem. Nat. Contract Mgmt. Assn., Am. Arbitration Assn. Office: Boeing Computer Svcs PO Box 24346 Seattle WA 98124-0346

LUZOVICH, STEVEN ALBERT, computer engineer; b. San Jose, Calif., Mar. 2, 1960; s. Albert and Betty (Compton) L. BSECE, U. Calif., Santa Barbara, 1982. Test engr. Tandem Computers, Watsonville, Calif., 1983-84; electronics engr. MCT/Synerception, Santa Cruz, Calif., 1984-89; systems engr. Meridian Data, Scotts Valley, Calif., 1989-90; sr. electronics engr. Worthington Data Solutions, Santa Cruz, 1990—. Home: 750 Edwardo Ave Ben Lomond CA 95005-9408 Office: Worthington Data Solutions Ste 220 3004 Mission St Santa Cruz CA 95060

LYBARGER, JOHN STEVEN, medical educator; b. Yuba City, Calif., June 13, 1956; s. Rodger Lee and Phyllis Ruth (Roseman) L.; m. Marjorie Kathryn Den Uyl, Aug. 22, 1981; children: Ashley Ann, Ryan Christopher. AA, Yuba Community Coll., 1977; BS in Christian Edn., Biola U., La Mirada, Calif., 1980; MS in Counseling, Calif. State U., Fullerton, 1984; PhD in Psychology, Calif. Coast U., 1985. Lic. marriage, family and child counselor. Assoc. dir. Concept 7 Family Svcs., Tustin, Calif., 1981-85; exec. dir. Family Life Ctr., Tustin, 1984-86; pres. Marriage & Family Counseling, La Habra, Calif., 1985-89; clin. dir. New Life Treatment Ctrs., Inc., Laguna Beach, Calif., 1988-89; faculty Loma Linda (Calif.) U. Sch. Medicine, 1990—; dir. partial hospitalization programs CPC Brea Canyon Hosp., 1991-93; dir. Oasis Counseling Ctr., Denver; pres., CEO Nat. Coun. on Sexual Addiction, Wickenburg, Ariz., 1990—. Mem. Am. Assn. for Marriage and Family Therapy (clin.). Republican. Home: 7391 W Kentucky Dr #E Lakewood CO 80226-4948 Office: PO Box 18871 Denver CO 80218

LYBARGER, MARJORIE KATHRYN, nurse; b. Holland, Mich., Apr. 23, 1956; d. Richard Simon and Mary Kathryn (Homan) Denuyl; m. John Steven Lybarger, Aug. 22, 1981; children: Ashley Ann, Ryan Christopher. BA in Psychology, Biola U., Calif., 1979, BS in Nursing, 1984. RN, Calif. Staff nurse Presbyn. Intercommunity Hosp., Whittier, Calif, 1985-86, Healthcare Med. Ctr., Tustin, Calif., 1986-88; staff nurse med.-telemetry unit Friendly Hills Regional Med. Ctr., La Habra, Calif., 1988-90; staff nurse telemetry unit Riverside (Calif.) Community Hosp., 1990-93; staff nurse med. telemetry unit St. Anthony's Ctrl. Hosp., Denver, 1993—. Mem. Gamma Phi Beta. Republican. Home: 7391 W Kentucky Dr #E Lakewood CO 80226-4948

LYDICK, LAWRENCE TUPPER, federal judge; b. San Diego, June 22, 1916; s. Roy Telling and Geneva (Lydick) L.; m. Gretta Grant, Aug. 7, 1938; children: Gretta Grant, Lawrence Tupper; m. Martha Martinez, Oct. 1969; 1 child, Chip. A.B., Stanford U., 1938, LL.B. (Crothers law scholar), 1942; Sigma Nu exchange scholar, U. Freiburg, Germany, 1938-39; postgrad., Harvard U., 1943, Mass. Inst. Tech., 1943-44. Bar: Calif. 1946. Since practiced in L.A.; dir. disputes div. 10th region Nat. War Labor Bd., San Francisco, 1942-43; asst. to pres., gen. counsel U.S. Grant Export-Import, Ltd., L.A., 1946-48; assoc. Adams, Duque & Hazeltine, L.A., 1948-53, ptnr., 1953-71; U.S. dist. ct. judge Central Dist. Calif., 1971—. Bd. vis. Stanford Law Sch. Lt. USNR, 1943-46. Mem. Am. Law Inst. Republican. Office: US Dist Ct 34 Civic Center Plz Santa Ana CA 92701-4025

LYE, WILLIAM FRANK, history educator; b. Kimberley, B.C., Can., Feb. 19, 1930; came to U.S., 1955, naturalized, 1981; s. Arthur Percy and Jessie Loretta (Prince) L.; m. Velda Campbell, Oct. 16, 1953; children: William Mark, Matthew Campbell, David Arthur, Victoria, Regina. Student Ricks Coll., 1953-55, Duke U., 1963; BS, Utah State U., 1959; MA, U. Calif.-Berkeley, 1959; PhD, UCLA, 1969. Instr. polit. sci. Ricks Coll., Rexburg, Idaho, 1959-63, 67-68, head dept. polit. sci., 1959-63; teaching asst. dept. history UCLA, 1964-65; asst. prof. Utah State U., Logan, 1968-69, acting head dept. history and geography, 1969-70, assoc. prof., head dept. history and geography, 1970-73, prof., head dept. history and geography, 1973-76, dean Coll. Humanities, Arts and Social Scis., 1976-83, v.p. for univ. relations, prof. dept. history and geography, 1983-91, prof. history, 1991—; vis. lectr. dept. history Brigham Young U., Provo, Utah, 1970; temporary lectr. dept. history U. Cape Town, Republic of South Africa, 1974; social cons. for project design teams in land conservation, U.S. Agy. for Internat. Devel. Khartoum, Sudan, 1978, Maseru, Lesotho, 1979; mem. higher edn. taskforce on telecommunications, Utah, 1977-82; chmn. State of Utah Telecommunications Coop., 1987, Regents' Com. on Credit by Exam., Utah, 1976; mem. adv. com. Sta. KULC-TV, State Ednl. Telecommunications Operating Ctr., 1986-90; bd. dirs., exec. com. Children's Aid Soc. Utah, 1985-88, pres., 1990—; mem. Utah Statehood Centennial Commn., Utah Christopher Columbus Quincentenary Commn., 1990—. Author: (with Colin Murray) Transformations on the Highveld: The Tswana and Southern Sotho, 1980, paperback edit., 1985; editor: Andrew Smith's Journal of His Expedition into the Interior of South Africa, 1834-36, 1975. Producer (TV series) Out of Africa, 1977, The God Seekers, 1978; contbr. articles and book revs. to profl. pubs. Chmn. State Day celebration, Logan, Utah, 1973, univ. drive for new Logan Regional Hosp. Recipient Leadership award Standard of Calif., 1957, Idea of Yr. award Utah State U., 1971, Faculty Service award Associated Students, Utah State U., 1977-78; Woodrow Wilson Nat. fellow 1958, Foreign Area fellow Social Sci. Research Council, Republic of South Africa, England, 1966-67, 67-68; faculty devel. grantee Utah State U., 1972, Human Sci. Research Council of South Africa publ. grantee, 1975, Mauerberger Trust grantee, 1976, 79. Mem. African Studies Assn., Royal African Soc., Western Assn. Africanists (program chmn. 1972-74, pres. 1974-76), Am. Soc. Landscape Architects (accreditation bd. 1967-91), Phi Kappa Phi, Phi Alpha Theta. Mormon. Lodge: Rotary. Home: 696 E 400 N Logan UT 84321-4218 Office: Utah State U Dept History 650 N 1100 E Logan UT 84322-0710

LYKINS, JAY ARNOLD, economic development director; b. Shattuck, Okla., Feb. 13, 1947; s. George Eldridge and Lucy Lee (Croom) L.; m. (Mary) Lynn Turner, Jan. 3, 1970; children: Mary Lee and Amy Lynn (twins), Jason. BA, Covenant Coll., 1973; MBA in 3rd World Econ. Devel., Kennedy-Western U., 1987, PhD in Internat. Bus., 1988. Credit specialist Gen. Electric Supply Co., Nashville, 1974-75; owner, mgr. Environment Control Co., Nashville, 1975-78; bus. adminstr. Youth for Christ, Atlanta, 1978-81; controller Young Life, Colorado Springs, Colo., 1981-82, internat. adminstr., 1982-86; exec. dir. Global Reach, Pleasanton, Calif., 1982—; cons. Royal Donuts, Lima, Peru, Barnabas Group, Vancouver. B.C, Manna Corp., Bulawayo, Zimbabwe, Denver Bridge Corp.; started more than 80 businesses in 21 countries, serving 35 chs., missions. Author: Values in the Marketplace, 1985, Development and Technology: Economics for the Third World, 1987, Islamic Business: Philosophy and Methods, 1988. Served with USN, 1966-68. Mem. Internat. Council for Small Bus., Am. Cons. League, Assn. MBA Execs., Ctr. Entrepreneurial Mgmt. Club: Nob Hill Country (Snellville, Ga.) (pres. 1980). Office: Global Reach Ste 203 39 California Ave Pleasanton CA 94566-6577

LYNCH, CHARLES ALLEN, investment executive, corporate director; b. Denver, Sept. 7, 1927; s. Laurence J. and Louanna (Robertson) L; div.; children: Charles A., Tara O'Hara, Casey Alexander; m. Justine Bailey, Dec. 27, 1992. BS, Yale U., 1950. With E.I. duPont de Nemours & Co., Inc., Wilmington, Del., 1950-69, dir. mktg., 1965-69; corp. v.p. SCOA Industries, Columbus, Ohio, 1969-72; corp. exec. v.p., also mem. rotating bd. W.R. Grace & Co., N.Y.C., 1972-78; chmn. bd., chief exec. officer Saga Corp., Menlo Park, Calif., 1978-86, also dir.; chmn., chief exec. officer DHL Airways, Inc., Redwood City, Calif., 1986-88; also dir.; pres., chief exec. officer Levolor Corp., 1988-89, also bd. dir., chmn. exec. com. of bd., 1989-90; chmn. Market Value Ptnrs. Co., Menlo Park, Calif., 1990—; chmn. bd. Greyhound Lines, Inc.; bd. dirs. Pacific Mut. Life Ins. Co., Nordstrom, Inc., SRI Internat., Palo Alto Med. Found., Syntex Corp., Fresh Choice Restaurants, Mid-Peninsula Bank, Age Wave Inc.; chmn. BJ Holdings, Inc., La Salsa Franchise, Inc. Bd. dirs. United Way, 1990-92, past chmn. Bay Area campaign, 1987; chmn., dir. Bay Area Coun.; past chmn. Calif. Bus. Roundtable; mem. adv. bd. U. Calif.-Berkeley Bus. Sch., Governance Bd., Coll. Notre Dame, Belmont, Calif. Mem. Yale Club (N.Y.C.), Internat. Lawn Tennis Club, Menlo Country Club (Calif.), Pacific Union Club (San Francisco), Coral Beach and Tennis Club (Bermuda), Vintage Club (Indian Wells, Calif.), Menlo Circus Club. Republican. Home: 96 Ridgeview Dr Atherton CA 94027 Office: 3000 Sandhill Rd #1-125 Menlo Park CA 94025-7116

LYNCH, CHARLES THOMAS, radio, television and film educator; b. Waterbury, Conn., Oct. 10, 1918; s. Charles Thomas and Sara (Carroll) L.; m. Helen Victoria Kaliss, Aug. 4, 1941; children: Charles Thomas III, Jean, Christopher. Student, U. Ala., 1935-37, Mich. State U., 1960; B.A., Western Mich. U., 1963, M.A., 1966; Ph.D., So. Ill. U., 1972. Announcer, producer, writer various radio stas. Conn., Pa., Fla. and Mich., 1938-49; program dir., exec. producer Fetzer Broadcasting Co., Kalamazoo, 1949-67; asst. prof. radio-TV, sta. mgr. Sta. WSIU, So. Ill. U., 1967-74, assoc. prof., chmn. dept.

radio-TV, 1974-79; chmn. dept. radio-TV-film Calif. State U., Northridge, 1979-87, prof., 1979—. Author various documentaries, spl. broadcast programs; contbr. articles profl. jours. Pres. Kalamazoo Area PTA Council, 1960-61, Kalamazoo Civic Players, 1962-64, Community Theatre Assn. Mich., 1963-65, Am. Cancer Soc., Kalamazoo, 1965-67. Recipient Broadcast Preceptor award Broadcast Industry Conf., 1976. Mem. Hollywood Chpt. Acad. TV Arts and Scis., St. Louis Chpt. Nat. Acad. TV Arts and Scis., Am. Film Inst., Broadcast Edn. Assn., Soc. Profl. Journalists, Ill. News Broadcasters Assn., Hollywood Radio and TV Soc., Am. Women in Radio and TV (bd. dirs. So. Calif. chpt. 1985—), Broadcast Pioneers, Pacific Pioneer Broadcasters (bd. dirs. 1983-86), Sierra Club, Alpha Epsilon Rho, Phi Kappa Phi. Office: Calif State U Dept Radio-TV-Film Northridge CA 91330

LYNCH, EUGENE F., federal judge; b. 1931. B.S., U. Santa Clara, 1953; LL.B., U. Calif., 1958. Assoc. O'Connor, Moran, Cohn & Lynch, San Francisco, 1959-64, ptnr., 1964-71; judge Mcpl. Ct., San Francisco, 1971-74; justice Superior Ct. City and County San Francisco, 1974-82; judge U.S. Dist. Ct. (no. dist.) Calif., San Francisco, 1982—. Office: US Dist Ct PO Box 36060 450 Golden Gate Ave San Francisco CA 94102

LYNCH, GARY LEE, environmental engineer, educator; b. Rogers, Ark., Aug. 29, 1946; s. Glenn Lee and Willa Mae (Johnston) L.; m. Camille Casale, Jan. 14, 1976. BA in Biology, Chaminade U., Honolulu, 1976; MS in Pub. Health, U. Hawaii, 1977; postgrad., UCLA, 1991—. Air pollution officer, environ. health officerr Plumas County, Quincy, Calif., 1977-79; sr. environ. health officer Mendocino County, Ft. Bragg, Calif., 1979-85; rsch. asst. UCLA, 1986-87; mgr. toxics program City of San Jose, Calif., 1987-89, mgr. environ. protection program, 1989—; lectr. San Jose State U., 1989—; co-founder, expert witness Stratospheric Protection Accord Litigation, 1989—. Co-author: Groundwater in California, 1986. Guest speaker various orgns.; mem. various civic coms. and task forces. With USN, 1964-67. Grad. fellow Hewlitt Found., UCLA, 1986. Mem. Am. Water Works Assn., Soc. for Risk Analysis, Assn. Environ. Profls., Water Pollution Control Assn., Assn. Groundwater Scientists and Engrs., Nat. Water Well Assn., Calif. Hazardous Waste Assn. Office: City of San Jose Office Environ Protection 777 N 1st St Ste 450 San Jose CA 95110

LYNCH, JOHN DANIEL, educator; b. Butte, Mont., Sept. 17, 1947; s. Leo and Queenie Veronica Lynch; m. Shannon Christine Crawford, May 7, 1983; 2 children: Kaitlin, Jennifer. B.S., West Mont. Coll.; M.S. No. Mont. Coll. Tchr. Butte High Sch., Mont., 1970-78, Butte Vo-Tech, 1978-89, ABE, 1989—; mem. Mont. State Legis., Helena, 1971-79, state senator, 1982—. Democrat. Roman Catholic. Lodge: Elks, KC.

LYNCH, JOHN PATRICK, classics educator, university official; b. Great Barrington, Mass., Aug. 30, 1943; s. John Joseph and Sophia (Pruhenski) L.; m. Sheilah Eileen Fulbright, Sept. 21, 1973; children—Bernadette, Brendan. B.A. with high honors, Harvard U., 1965; M.A., Yale U., 1968, M.Phil., 1969, Ph.D., 1970. Cert. in archaeology, Am. Sch. Classical Studies, Athens, Greece, 1967. Asst. prof. classics U. Calif., Santa Cruz, 1970-73, assoc. prof., 1974-85, prof., 1985—, provost Cowell Coll., 1983-89, assoc. dir. Edn. Abroad Program, U. Calif. Study Ctr. in London, 1979-81; jr. fellow Harvard U. Ctr. Hellenic Studies, Washington, 1976-77; mem. Inst. Advanced Study Princeton U., 1989-90. Author: Aristotle's School, 1972; editor: Second World and Green World, 1989. Fellow NEH, summer 1973, U. Calif. Humanities Inst., summer 1972, NDEA Title IV, 1967-70, Rotary Internat., 1966-67, Woodrow Wilson, 1965-66; Harvard Coll. scholar, 1961-65. Mem. Am. Philol. Assn. (Excellence in Teaching Classics award 1992), Calif. Classical Assn., Hellenic Soc. (U.K.), Petronian Soc., Virgilian Soc. Democrat. Roman Catholic. Home: 204 King St Santa Cruz CA 95060-3408 Office: U Calif Cowell College Santa Cruz CA 95064

LYNCH, ROBERT BERGER, lawyer; b. LaCrosse, Wis., June 10, 1931; s. Jan P. and Eve (Berger) L.; B.S., U.S. Merchant Marine Acad., 1955; J.D., U. of the Pacific, 1967; m. Ann Godfrey, May 30, 1980; children: Jan Fredrick Lynch, Jerry Wayne Coggins. Sr. engr. Aerojet Gen. Corp., Sacramento, Calif., 1955-61, proposal mgr., 1961-63, asst. contract adminstrn. mgr., 1963-66, contract adminstrn. mgr., 1967-70; admitted to Calif. bar, 1969, U.S. Supreme Ct. bar, 1972; individual practice law. Rancho Cordova, Calif., 1969—; instr. bus. law Solano Community Coll., 1977-79, San Joaquin Delta Coll., 1978-79. Active various charity fund-raising campaigns in Sacramento Calif., 1966-68; mem. mission com. St. Clements Episcopal Ch., Rancho Cordova, Calif., 1967-68; trustee Los Rios Community Coll. Dist., Calif., 1971-79. With USCG, 1949-51, USNR 1951-80, Nat. Guard 1988-91, Maj. AUS, ret. Mem. IEEE, Calif. Wildlife Fedn., Internat. Turtle Club, Marines Meml. Assn., Am. Legion, Mensa. Home: 93 Lexington Dr Chico CA 95926 Office: 10615 Coloma Rd Rancho Cordova CA 95670-3939

LYNCH, ROBERT MICHAEL, university administrator; b. N.Y.C., May 30, 1944; s. John Patrick and Emily Maria (Matson) L.; m. Terry Lynn Bell, Dec. 13, 1969; children: Christopher, Cary. BS, SUNY, Brockport, 1966; postgrad., U. Rochester, 1967-68; PhD, U. No. Colo., 1971. Prof. Coll. of Bus. U. No. Colo., Greeley, 1973—, assoc. dean Coll. of Bus., 1984—; Fulbright prof. Thammasat U., Bangkok, Thailand, 1978-79, cons., researcher Oakridge (Tenn.) Assoc. U., 1982-83; vis. prof. U. Virgin Islands, St. Thomas, 1982-83, Edith Cowen U., Perth, Australia, 1986-87; asst. to v.p. U. No. Colo.. 1987 (summer); researcher cons., State of Wyo. Health Dept., Cheyenne, 1990—. Editor of books on research methods and information systems; contbr. articles to profl. jours.; editor Internat. Bus. Sch. Computing Quarterly. Fellow Royal Stats. Soc.; mem. Intenat. Assn. for Computer Info. Systems (sec. 1990-92, v.p. 1992-94), Internat. Bus. Schs. Computing Assn. (bd. dirs.). Home: 401 Wyndham Greeley CO 80634 Office: U No Colo Coll of Bus Greeley CO 80639

LYNCH, ROBERT PAUL, general surgeon; b. Dunkirk, N.Y., June 29, 1955; s. James Francis Sr. and Catherine Elizabeth (Dolan) L.; m. Barbara Louise Quallen, Dec. 26, 1987; children: Alyssa Anne, Lauren Elizabeth. BS, Xavier U., 1977; MD, Ohio State U., 1982. Diplomate Am. Coll. Surgeons, Nat. Bd. Med. Examiners. Resident in surgery Good Samaritan Hosp., Cin., 1982-86, chief resident in surgery, 1986-87; pvt. practice Renton, Wash., 1991—; acting dept. head Dept. Surgery Naval Hosp., Camp Pendelton, Calif., 1990. Lt. comdr. USN, 1987-91. Fellow ACS (assoc.); mem. AMA, Wash. State Med. Assn., King County Med. Soc. Democrat. Roman Catholic. Home: 13925 SE 61st Pl Bellevue WA 98006 Office: Associated Cons Surgeons 4033 Talbot Rd S # 530 Renton WA 98055

LYNCH, SUSAN H., state legislator; b. Mpls., July 5, 1943; d. Lewis Mifflin and Helen Hayes; m. Thomas Vincent Lynch, June 14, 1969; children: Brian, Robin, Karen. BA in Biology, Cedar Crest Coll., 1965. Genetic rsch. technician NIH, Bethesda, Md., 1965-67, Children's Hosp., L.A., 1967-69; dir. summer arts and crafts City of Prescott, Ariz., 1976-78, dir. preschool, 1978-82, mem. council, 1983-87; mem. Ariz. Ho. Reps., Phoenix, 1993—. Bd. dirs. Prescott Fine Arts, Phippen Mus. Western Art; mem. adv. bd. Anytown U.S.A., 1990-93. Mem. AAUW (br. pres. 1990-92), Ariz. Women's End. and Employment, Rep. Women Prescott (treas. 1991). Methodist. Home: Prescott AZ 86303 Office: Ariz State Legislature 1700 W Washington Phoenix AZ 85007

LYND, GRANT ALBERT, lawyer; b. L.A., Aug. 21, 1949; s. John Joseph Lynd and Janet Grant; m. Amy F. Suehiro, May 9, 1985; children: Shenandoah Grant, Amy Janet Suehiro. AA in Police Sci., Mt. San Antonio Coll., 1969; BA, Calif. State U., Fullerton, 1971, MA in History, 1978, MPA, 1980; JD, Loyola U., L.A., 1983. Bar: Calif. 1984, U.S. Dist. Ct. (cen. dist.) Calif. 1984, U.S. Ct. Apppeals (9th cir.) 1984. Rep. employee rels. Calif. State Employees Assn., 1975-79; dir. acad. rights div. Calif. Faculty Assn., 1979-84; ptnr. Lynd & Suehiro, Westminster, Calif., 1984-89; prin. Law Offices of Grant A. Lynd, Westminster, 1989—. Grantee Dept. Justice, 1970-71. Mem. ABA, Calif. Trial Lawyers Assn., L.A. and Orange County Bar Assn., Phi Alpha Theta. Home: 3745 Prestwick Dr Los Angeles CA 90027-1321 Office: Law Offices Grant A Lynd 14340 Bolsa Chica Rd Ste B Westminster CA 92683-4811

LYNN, FREDRIC MICHAEL, professional baseball player; b. Chgo., Feb. 3, 1952; s. Fredric Elwood and Marie Elizabeth (Marshall) L.; m. Natalie Brenda Cole, Oct. 7, 1986; children from previous marriage: Jason Andrew, Jennifer Andrea. Student, U. So. Calif., 1971-73. Center fielder Boston Red Sox, 1973-81, Calif. Angels, 1981-84; mem. Balt. Orioles, 1985-88, Detroit Tigers, 1988-89; San Diego Padres, 1990—; sportscaster ESPN Network, 1993. Named Am. League Batting Champion, 1979; mem. Am. League All-star Team, 1975-79; named Most Valuable Player and Rookie of Year Am. League, 1975, Most Valuable Player (Play-Offs) Am. League, 1982; recipient Rawlings Gold Glove award, 1975, 78, 79; Seagrams Seven Crowns of Sports award, 1979; named Centerfielder of the 70's; mem. All-Star Team, 1975-83; Rawlings Gold Glove award, 1980; Most Valuable Player, 1983 All Star Game. Mem. Maj. League Baseball Players Assn., Rep. Club. Lutheran. Home: 7336 El Fuerte St Carlsbad CA 92009

LYNN, KATHERINE LYN, engineer, chemist; b. Nagoya, Japan, June 25, 1954; (parents Am. citizens); d. Jimmie Frank and Barbara Sue (Whiteside) Sutton; m. Richard Shelly Lynn, Feb. 28, 1981. BS in Chemistry cum laude, Calif. State U., Fullerton, 1979. Technician U.S. Borax Corp., Anaheim, Calif., 1974-79; chemist Armstrong World Industries, Southgate, Calif., 1979-82; project engr. Hydril Co., Whittier, Calif., 1982-84; staff engr. So. Calif. Gas Co., Los Angeles, 1984—. Patentee fluorspar flotation. Bd. dirs. East Side Christian Ch., 1987-89. Mem. So. Calif. Thermal Analysis Group (chair 1988, sec. 1985-87), Soc. Plastic Engrs., Am. Soc. for Quality Control, Am. Chem. Soc., Sierra Club. Mem. Christian Ch. Home: 5120 Faust Ave Lakewood CA 90713-1924 Office: So Calif Gas Co Box 3249 Terminal Annex ML 723B Los Angeles CA 90051

LYNN, MITCHELL GORDON, retail company executive; b. Los Angeles, Nov. 22, 1948. BA in Econs., UCLA, 1970, MSBA, 1971. CPA, Calif. Acct. Kenneth Leventhal & Co., Los Angeles, 1971-76; controller Sunset Pools, San Diego, 1977-78; controller The Price Co., San Diego, 1979-83, v.p. fin., treas., 1984-87; exec. v.p. Price Club Industries (subs. Price Co.), 1987-89, pres., 1989-90; exec. v.p. The Price Co., 1989-90, pres., 1990—, also bd. dirs. Bd. dirs. Kensington Social and Athletic Club, San Diego. Mem. Am. Inst. CPA's, Calif. Soc. CPA's. Office: The Price Co PO Box 85466 San Diego CA 92186-5466

LYNN, PATRICIA ANNE, sales and service executive; b. Newton, Iowa, Sept. 9, 1950; d. Harold Clifford and Alice Marie (Uhlig) Johnson; divorced. AA in Psychology, Trinidad (Colo.) Jr. Coll., 1970; BS in Psychology, Ft. Lewis Coll., Durango, Colo., 1972; AA in Vet. Tech., Internat. Sch., Scranton, Pa., 1980. Customer svc. agt. Waco Scaffolding & Equipment, Denver, 1980-83; leasing agt. Look Ltd. Realty, Federal Heights, Colo., 1983-84; sales assoc. Lynn & Assocs., Aurora, Colo., 1991—; customer svc. team leader EBSCO Industries, Golden, Colo., 1984—. Author: A Star for Sandra, 1976. Political aide Dem. Party, Denver; docent Denver Zoo; vol. ARC, Aurora. Mem. Rocky Mountain Midget Racing Assn., Vintage Motor Racing Assn. Jehovah's Witness. Home: 19013 E Carmel Cir Aurora CO 80011 Office: EBSCO Industries 2801 Youngfield Golden CO 80401

LYON, FRANK ORVILLE BARFETT, sculptor, artist; b. Bklyn., Jan. 12, 1924; s. Frank A. and Audry (Barfette) L.; m. Shivley Lee Lyon, ug. 2, 1974 (div. June 1986); children: Michelle D., Laurance C. Student, Whitney Sch. Art, New Haven, 1946, Chouinard Art Inst., L.A., 1947-50. Design engr. Cons. & Designers, N.Y.C., 1954-65; R & D engr. Bell Helicopter Corp., Ft. Worth, 1965-67; owner, mgr. Taos (N.Mex.) Art Bronze Foundry, 1967-79; tchr. Lyon Studio, Taos, 1967—; sondr. seminars in wood sculpture, bronze casting, mold making; numerous TV guest appearances, Tex., Calif. Editor, author: Carving Museum Quality Wood Sculpture, 1975; over 100 one-man shows, including Tex. Ranger Mus., Waco, Tex., 1970, Concord, Calif., 1972, Fountain Hills, Ariz., 1973; 2-man show Navajo Gallery, Taos, 1975; 4-man show Empire (Colo.) Art Gallery, 1976; exhibited in group show Heath and Brown Galleries, Houston, 1972; bronze sculptures include Chuck Wagon, Roostered; wood sculptures include Sgt. Major G. Co. Sgt. AUS, 1943-45, ETO. Decorated Purple Heart. Mem. Nat. Wood Carvers Assn., Colo. Nat. Carvers Mus. (life), Am. Foundrymens Soc., Internat. Wood Carvers Assn., VFW (life). Studio: North of Blinking Light Taos NM 87571

LYON, IRVING, biochemist, researcher, consultant; b. L.A., May 10, 1921; s. Charles and Belle (Kvitky) L.; m. Harriette Goodman, Oct. 16, 1948; children: David, Charles, Lawrence. AB in Zoology, UCLA, 1942, MA in Physiology, 1949; postgrad., U. So. Calif., 1946-47; PhD in Physiology, U. Calif., Berkeley, 1952. Rsch. gen. lab. asst. U. Calif., Berkeley, 1947-52; rsch. biochemist med. dept. The Toni Co., Chgo., 1954-58; asst. prof. biol. chemistry U. Ill. Coll. Medicine, Chgo., 1958-62; assoc. prof. biochemistry The Chgo. Med. Sch., 1962-67; prof. biology Bennington (Vt.) Coll., 1967-72; spl. cons. State Energy Resources Conservation & Devel. Commn., L.A., 1975; cons. environ. health and nutrition L.A., 1975—; asst. rsch. physiologist UCLA Med. Sch., 1979-89; rsch. biochemist U.S. V.A. Wadsworth Hosp. Ctr., L.A., 1979-89; cons. New England Coalition vs. Nuclear Pollution, Bennington and Brattleboro, Vt., 1968-72, Another Mother for Peace, Beverly Hills, Calif., 1974-79, Psychemedics Corp., Santa Monica, Calif., 1988-89; invited lectr. various univs. and rsch. insts. Contbr. articles to profl. jours.; patentee in field. Capt. U.S. Army, 1942-46. Fellow Rockefeller Found., 1952-54. Fellow AAAS; mem. Am. Physiol. Soc., N.Y. Acad. Scis., Sigma Xi (pres. 1967-68). Home and Office: Unit C 708 Grant St Santa Monica CA 90405-1221

LYON, JOHN PAUL, financial services company executive, accountant; b. St. Paul, Mar. 4, 1954; s. John P. and Gloria Edith May (Austin) L.; m. Mary Kim Sheridan, June 30, 1979; children: Brendan Sheridan, Heather Marie. BSBA, U. No. Colo., 1978; postgrad., Golden Gate U., 1982-83. CPA, Wash. Tax adminstr. The Boeing Co., Seattle, 1979-84; tax mgr. Ideal Basic Industries, Inc., Denver, 1984-86; tax cons. Arthur D. Little Valuation, Inc., Woodland Hills, Calif., 1986-88; sr. v.p., CFO Arthur Cons. Group, Woodland Hills, 1989—. Soccer referee Am. Youth Soccer Orgn., Agoura, 1990—; vol. Cub Scouts, Agoura, 1989—; mem. PTA, Agoura, 1988—. Mem. AICPA, Wash. Soc. CPAs, Inst. Property Taxation. Republican. Lutheran. Office: Arthur Cons Group Inc 21110 Oxnard St Woodland Hills CA 91367

LYON, MARK ANDREW, dentist; b. Bethesda, Md., Apr. 8, 1953; s. Harvey William and Margaret (Siggelkow) L.; m. Patti Lynn Wagner, Aug. 8, 1988; children: Gunnar Andrew, Kelly Lynn. BS in Chemistry, Colo. State U., 1975; DDS, Northwestern U., 1979. Chemistry research asst. Colo. State U., Ft. Collins, 1974-75; dental research asst. ADA, Chgo., 1975-79; pvt. practice Santa Fe, N.Mex., 1979--. Recipient Cert. of Exemplary Performance, State N.Mex. Corrections Dept., Santa Fe, 1987. Mem. ADA, Santa Fe Dental Soc. (pres. 1987-88), Santa Fe Rugby Club (pres., capt. 1985-87), Sante Fe Sailboard Fleet (commodore 1987). Republican. Lutheran. Home: 14 Mariposa Rd Santa Fe NM 87505-8729 Office: 1418 Luisa St Ste 5A Santa Fe NM 87501-4041

LYON, MAURICE CLEVERLY, school administrator, real estate entrepreneur; b. Woods Cross, Utah, June 14, 1926; s. George Budd and Annie Ellen (Cleverly) L.; m. Pearl Darlene Osguthorpe, Mar. 29, 1948; children: Paul, Rodney, Marcia, Roger, Mark, Michael. BS, U. Utah, 1949; MS, Claremont U., 1957. Cert. tchr. elem. and secondary sch., cert. adminstr., Utah, Calif. Tchr., prin. Richfield (Utah) Sch. Dist., 1949-50; tchr. Provo (Utah) Unified Sch. Dist., 1950-53, Pomona (Calif.) Unified Sch. Dist., 1954-60; sch. prin. Muroc Unified Sch. Dist., Edwards AFB, Calif., 1961, Escondido (Calif.) Unifed Elem. Sch. Dist., 1961-85; missionary Ch. LDS, Peru, 1986-87; investor, entrepreneur MPL Global Investments, Inc., Escondido, 1988—; dir. libr. LDS Ch. Family History Ctr., Escondido, 1990—; pres. MPL Global Investments, Inc., Carson City, Nev., 1991—. Contbr. articles on Peru to pubs. Chmn. Republican Orgn. Escondido area, 1962-63. Named Life Member, Louisa May Alcott PTA, Pomona, Calif., 1960. Mem. Escondido Geneal. Soc. Office: MPL Global Investments Ltd 2533 N Carson Carson City NV 89706

LYON, RICHARD, mayor, retired naval officer; b. Pasadena, Calif., July 14, 1923; s. Norman Morais and Ruth (Hollis) L.; m. Cynthia Gisslin, Aug. 8, 1975; children—Patricia, Michael, Sean; children by previous marriage—Mary, Edward, Sally, Kathryn, Patrick (dec.), Susan. B.E., Yale U., 1944; M.B.A., Stanford U., 1953. Commd. ensign USN, 1944, advanced through grades to rear adm., 1974; served in Pacific and China, World War II; with Underwater Demolition Team Korea; recalled to active duty as dep. chief Naval Res. New Orleans, 1978-81; mayor City of Oceanside, Calif.; mem. Chief Naval Ops. Res. Affairs Adv. Bd., 1978-81; exec. v.p. Nat. Assn. Employee Benefits, Newport Beach, Calif., 1981-90; mem. Bd. Control, U.S. Naval Inst., 1978-81; pres. Civil Svc. Commn., San Diego County, 1990, Oceanside Unified Sch. Bd., 1991. Pres. bd. trustees Childrens Hosp. Orange County, 1965, 72. Decorated Legion of Merit. Mem. Nat. Assn. Securities Dealers (registered prin.). Republican. Episcopalian. Clubs: Newport Harbor Yacht; Rotary (Anaheim, Calif.) (pres. 1966). Home: 4464 Inverness Dr Oceanside CA 92057-5052

LYONS, ARTHUR EDWARD, neurosurgeon; b. Vienna, Austria, Apr. 23, 1931; s. Alfred Labori and Evelyn Belle (Joseph) L.; children: Michael D., Alan J. BA, Columbia Coll., 1952; MD, Vanderbilt U., 1955. Diplomate Am. Bd. Neurol. Surgery. Intern U. Minn., Mpls., 1955-56; resident neurol. surgery U. Calif., San francisco, 1956-64; assoc. clin. prof. dept. neurol. surgery U. Calif., San Francisco, 1964—; chief neurosci. Mt. Zion Hosp., San Francisco, 1986-93. Founder, Bay Area History Medicine Club, San Francisco, 1970. Lt. comdr. USN, 1960-61. Fellow Internat. Pain Soc.; mem. Calif. Med. Assn. (del. 1980—), San Francisco Med. Soc. (pres. 1989-90), San Francisco Neurol. Soc. (pres. 1988-89), Am. Assn. History Medicine, Roxburghe Club San Francisco, Book Club Calif. Office: 2320 Sutter St San Francisco CA 94115-3023

LYTTLE, ROSS ORVILLE, university official; b. Scarborough, Ont., Can., Oct. 1, 1932; s. James Andrew and Marguerite Christina (Brown) L.; m. Joy Aldine MacKenzie, Aug. 22, 1959; children: Bethany, Jackson. BA, Queen's U., Kingston, Ont., 1957; MA, Wheaton (Ill.) Coll., 1958; diploma in edn., U. Toronto, Ont., 1966; MA in Edn., Cen. Mich. U., 1978. Cert. specialist in guidance, Can., instr. Vancouver Sch. Bd. Secondary tchr. Dept. Edn., Quebec City, Que., Can., 1958-65, Ministry Edn., Toronto, 1965-80; registrar Trinity Western U., Langley, B.C., Can., 1982—; cons. Food for Hungry, Vancouver, B.C., 1983-86, Hope Internat. Devel. Agy., New Westminster, B.C., 1986-87, Regent Coll., Vancouver, 1990, Wheaton (Ill.) Coll., 1982—; cons. U. Entrance Rsch. Project Dept. of State, Govt. Can., 1992; presenter in field, leader pilot project Advanced Rsch. and Devel. Can., 1978, Can. Svc. Bur., 1981; active NACAD Advising as a Profession, 1987. Author: Images of Truth, 1983; co-author: Academic Advising as a Comprehensive Campus Process, 1993; contbr. articles to profl. jours. Community counselor Telecare, Sudbury, Ont., 1969-80; presenter Spl. Joint Com. on Senate Reform, Ottawa, Ont., 1984, Senate Com. on Youth, Vancouver, 1985; bd. dirs. World Concern Can., Richmond, B.C., 1986-88; mem. Corp. Inter-Varsity Christian Fellowship, 1975-81, B.C.-Wash. Liaison Com., 1982—; respondent Royal Commn. on Edn., Vancouver, 1988. Scholar Wheaton Coll., 1958. Mem. Can. Internat. DX Assn., Nat. Assn. Acad. Affairs Adminstrs., Assn. Registrars Univs. and Colls. Can., Nat. Assn. Acad. Advisors, Western Assn. Registrars Univs. and Colls. Can. (treas. 1991), B.C. Registrars Assn. (sec.-treas. 1990-92, pres. 192—), Am. Coll. Pers. Assn. (mem. commn.), Am. Assn. Collegiate Registrars and Admissions Officers. Mennonite. Office: Trinity Western U, 7600 Glover Rd, Langley, BC Canada V3A 6H4

MA, FENGCHOW CLARENCE, consulting agricultural engineer; b. Kaifeng, Honan, China, Sept. 4, 1919; came to U.S., 1972; s. Chao-Hsiang and Wen-Chieh (Yang) Ma; m. Fanny Luisa Corvera-Achá, Jan. 20, 1963; 1 child, Fernando. BS in Agr., Nat. Chekiang U., Maytan, Kweichow, China, 1942; postgrad., Iowa State U., 1945-46. Cert. profl. agronomist, Republic of China, 1944; registered profl. agrl. engr., Calif. Chief dept. ops. Agrl. Machinery Operation and Mgmt. Office, Shanghai, China, 1946-49; sr. farm machinery specialist Sino-Am. Joint Commn. on Rural Reconstrn., Taipei, Taiwan, Republic of China, 1950-62; agrl. engring. adviser in Bolivia, Peru, Chile, Ecuador, Liberia, Honduras, Grenada, Bangladesh FAO, Rome, 1962-80; consulting agrl. engr. to USAID projects in Guyana & Peru IRI Rsch. Inst., Inc., Stamford, Conn., 1981-82, 83, 85; chief adviser Com. Internat. Tech. Coop., Taipei, 1984-85; prin., cons. agrl. engr. Fengchow C. Ma and Assocs., Inc., Sunnyvale, Calif., 1962—; short consulting missions to Paraguay, Saudi Arabia, Indonesia, Malawi, Swaziland, Barbados, Dominica, Ivory Coast, Vietnam, Philippines and others. Author papers, studies; contbr. articles to profl. publs. Mem. Am. Soc. Agrl. Engrs. Home: 1004 Azalea Dr Sunnyvale CA 94086-6747 Office: PO Box 70096 Sunnyvale CA 94086-0096

MABEE, SANDRA IVONNE, timpanist, percussionist, educator, clergyman; b. Hato Rey, P.R., Jan. 13, 1955; d. Nelson Custudio Noriega and Norma Ruth (Eiseman) Lee; m. Carl David Mabee, Aug. 2, 1980; 1 child, Rebecca Lee. BA in Bibl. Studies summa cum laude, Patten Coll., 1977; BM magna cum laude, San Francisco Conservatory, 1983; MA in Music cum laude, Calif. State U., Hayward, 1985, postgrad., 1989-90. ordained min. Evang. Ch. Alliance, 1991; cert. Evangelical Tchr.'s Tng. Assn. With Bay Area Women's Philharm., San Francisco, 1980—; prof. music Patten Coll., Oakland, Calif., 1983-89, chairperson prof. studies div., 1986-88; with accounts receivable Western Bookstore, Oakland, 1985-87; min. of music El Cerrito (Calif.) Christian Ctr., 1988-91; prof. music Hayward Christian Sch., 1988-91; intern pastor, dir. music ministry Trinity Ch., Oakland, Calif., 1991-92; pastor, dir. music ministries Unveiled Christ Ministries, Castro Valley, Calif., 1992—; tympanist, percussionist various orchs., Bay Area, Calif., 1977—; pvt. tchr. music lessons, Bay Area, 1977—; percussion ensemble Patten Coll., Oakland, 1983-84; producer sing-it-yourself Messiah Patten Coll., Oakland, 1986; guest dir. choral Landmark Ministries, Oakland, 1990; seminar instr., Landmark Sch. Ministries, Oakland, 1990. Prison ministry vol. Alameda County Jail, Oakland, 1990, Vacaville Fed. Prison; vol. rest home, Oakland, 1985—, Assn. of Christian Schs. Inc./Song Shop; mem. Evang. Ch. Alliance, Follow-up Ministries. San Francisco Conservatory scholar, 1980-83; named Outstanding Young Woman of Am., 1986, 87, winner concerto soloist Redwood Symphony, 1988, for Outstanding Svc. to Teaching Profession A.B.I.; recipient Cert. of Merit World Bibl. Commentary. Mem. Percussive Arts Soc., Hymn Soc. of Am. Home: 2153 Santa Clara Ave Alameda CA 94501-2832

MACALA, GERALD STEPHEN, environmental administrator; b. Youngstown, Ohio, June 14, 1968; s. Gerald Stephen and Susanne Helen (Kish) M. BS in Chemistry, UCLA, 1991. Quality control chemist Lever Bros. Corp., Commerce, Calif., 1989; rschr. dept. chemistry UCLA, 1990-91; environ. mgr. The Norac Co., Inc., Azusa, Calif., 1992—. Mem. Am. Homebrewers Assn., Phi Beta Kappa, Sigma Xi. Byzantine Catholic. Home: 6102 Amethyst Ave Alta Loma CA 91737 Office: The Norac Co Inc 405 S Motor Ave Azusa CA 91702

MACALISTER, ROBERT STUART, oil company executive; b. L.A., May 22, 1924; s. Robert Stuart and Iris Grace (Doman) MacA.; m. Catherine Vera Willby, Nov. 15, 1947; children: Rodney James, Sara Marjorie Pfirrmann. Student, Brighton Coll., Sussex, Eng., 1945; BSME, Calif. Inst. Tech., 1947. Registered profl. engr., Tex. Petroleum engr. Shell Oil Co., 1947-56; mgmt. trainee Royal Dutch Shell, The Hague, Netherlands, 1956-57; with exec. staff, mgr. Shell Oil Co., U.S.A., 1957-68; v.p., ops. mgr. Occidental Petroleum Corp., Tripoli, Libya, 1968-71; mng. dir.various subs. London, 1971-76; mng. dir., pres. Occidental Internat. Oil, Inc., London, 1976-78; pres., chmn. bd. Can. Occidental Petroleum Ltd., Calgary Alberta, 1978-81; mng. dir. Australian Occidental Petroleum Ltd., Sydney, 1982-83, Hamilton Bros. Oil & Gas Ltd., London, 1983-86; petroleum cons. Camarillo, Calif., 1986—; exec. U.K. Offshore Operators, London, 1972-78, 83-86. Cubmaster Boy Scouts Am., Larchmont, N.Y., 1964-65, scoutmaster, Houston, 1965-68. Sgt. U.S. Army, 1944-45, ETO. Mem. Am. Assn. Petroleum Geologists, Soc. Petroleum Engrs.,Las Posas Country Club, Gold Coast Srs. Republican. Episcopalian. Home and Office: 78 Lopaco Ct Camarillo CA 93010-8846

MACALUSO, RALPH TERRY, contracts administration manager; b. Kaiserslautern, Germany, Mar. 25, 1963; came to U.S., 1981; s. Joseph and Aneliese (Bang) M. BA in Philosophy, U. Calif., Santa Barbara, 1985; MBA in Mktg., U. San Francisco, 1992. Asst. sales mgr. The Waverly Group, Kaiserslautern, Germany, 1981-86; computer analyst, supr. Goldberg Securities/L.I.T. Am., San Francisco, 1986-88; ops. mgr. Suslow, Sparks, and Brookshire/First Options of Chgo., San Francisco, 1988-89; options floor mgr. Group One/Wagner Stodt/Merrill Lynch, San Francisco, 1989-90; mgr. contracts adminstrn. Synon Corp., Larkspur, Calif., 1992—. Democrat. Lutheran. Home: 101 Lombard #304E San Francisco CA 94111 Office: Synom Inc 1100 Larkspur Landing Cir Larkspur CA 94939

MACARTHUR, JAMES, actor; b. L.A., Dec. 8, 1937; adopted s. Charles MacArthur and Helen Hayes; children—Charles, Mary. Acting debut in The Corn is Green in summer stock, Olney, Md., 1945; appeared on Broadway in Invitation to a March, 1960; films include: Broadway in The Young Stranger, 1957, The Light in the Forest, 1958, The Third Man on the Mountain, 1959, Kidnapped, 1960, The Swiss Family Robinson, 1960, The Interns, 1962, Spencer's Mountain, 1963, The Truth About Spring, 1965, The Bedford Incident, 1965, Ride Beyond Vengeance, 1966, The Love-Ins, 1967, Hang 'Em High, 1968, The Angry Breed, 1968, Alcatraz, 1980, The Night the Bridge Fell Down, 1983; regular on TV series Hawaii Five-O, 1968-79; numerous other TV appearances. Office: PO Box 230 Crested Butte CO 81224-0230

MACAULEY, CHARLES CAMERON, media appraiser, consultant; b. Grand Rapids, Mich., Oct. 20, 1923; s. George William and Emma Ann (Hobart) M.; m. Marianne Shirley Johanson, June, 1951; children: Gavin Keith, Alison Jean. BA, Kenyon Coll., Gambier, Ohio, 1949; MS, U. Wis., 1958. Ptnr. Cameron-King Photographers, Gambier, 1946-49; film producer U. Wis., Madison, 1951-58; film producer U. Calif., Berkeley, 1959-63, dir. statewide media ctr., 1964-83; pres. CCM Assocs., El Cerrito, Calif., 1984—; prof. U. Wis., Calif., 1951-83; sr. founding cons. Media Appraisal Cons., El Cerrito, 1986—; instr. film seminar San Francisco Art Inst., 1959-60; awards juror numerous nat. and internat. film and video festivals, 1953—. West coast corr. The Appraiser; producer over 50 motion pictures; contbr. numerous articles, essays and fictional works to publs. With USN, 1943-46. NSF grantee, 1959-64, NEA grantee, 1974, 76, Maurice Falk Med. Fund grantee, 1970; recipient Gold Ribbon award Am. Film and Video Festival, 1991. Mem. Appraisers Assn. Am., Edn. Film Libr. Assn. (pres. 1973-74), Am. Film and Video Assn. (life), Consortium Coll. and Univ. Media Ctrs. (life), Fossils, Inc., History of Photography Group, Square Riggers Club (historian 1989—, hon. 1989—). Office: CCM Assocs Studio A 731 Seaview Dr El Cerrito CA 94530-3311

MACBRIDE, THOMAS JAMISON, federal judge; b. Sacramento, Mar. 25, 1914; s. Frank and Lotta Kirtley (Little) MacB.; m. Martha Harrold, Nov. 7, 1947; children—Peter, Thomas Jamison, David, Laurie. A.B., U. Calif. at Berkeley, 1936, J.D., 1940. Bar: Calif. 1940. Dep. atty. gen. Calif., 1941-42; pvt. practice Sacramento, 1946-61; U.S. dist. judge Eastern Dist. Calif., Sacramento, 1961-67; chief judge Eastern Dist. Calif., 1967-79, sr. judge, 1979—; mem. U.S. Temporary Emergency Ct. Appeals, 1982-87; mem. Criminal Justice Act Com., U.S. Jud. Conf., 1969-88; mem. U.S. Jud. Conf., 1975-78; chmn. Criminal Justice Act Com. of U.S. Jud. Conf., 1979-88; mem. U.S. Fgn. Intelligence Surveillance Ct., 1979-80. Pres. Town Hall, Sacramento, 1952, N.E. area YMCA, 1960; mem. Calif. Legislature from Sacramento County, 1955-60 mem. Nat. Commn. on Reform Fed. Criminal Laws, 1967-71; bd. dirs. Sacramento YMCA; trustee U. Calif., San Francisco Found., 1982—; bd. dirs. Sacramento Regional Found., 1988—; founding dir. League to Save Lake Tahoe, 1965. Lt. USNR., 1942-46. Mem. ABA, U. Calif. Alumni Assn. (v.p. 1955, 60), Mason (33 deg., Shriner, Jester), Rotarian (pres. 1966-67), Sutter Club, Univ. (pres. 1951-52), Comstock (pres. 1975-76), Senator Outing (sec.-treas.), Kappa Sigma, Phi Delta Phi. Democrat. Office: US Dist Ct US Courthouse 650 Capitol Mall Sacramento CA 95814-4708

MACCALLUM, (EDYTHE) LORENE, pharmacist; b. Monte Vista, Colo., Nov. 29, 1928; d. Francis Whittier and Berniece Viola (Martin) Scott; m. David Robertson MacCallum, June 12, 1952; children: Suzanne Rae MacCallum Barslund and Roxanne Kay MacCallum Batezel (twins), Tracy Scott, Tamara Lee MacCallum Johnson, Shauna Marie MacCallum Bost. BS in Pharmacy U. Colo., 1950. Registered pharmacist, Colo. Pharmacist Presbyn. Hosp., Denver, 1950, Corner Pharmacy, Lamar, Colo., 1950-53; rsch. pharmacist Nat. Chlorophyll Co., Lamar, 1953; relief pharmacist, various stores, Delta, Colo., 1957-59, Farmington, N.Mex., 1960-62, 71-79, Aztec, N.Mex., 1971-79; mgr. Med. Arts Pharmacy, Farmington, 1966-67; cons. pharmacist Navajo Hosp., Brethren in Christ Mission, Farmington, 1967-77; sales agt. Norris Realty, Farmington, 1977-78; pharmacist, owner, mgr. Lorene's Pharmacy, Farmington, 1979-88; tax cons. H&R Block, Farmington, 1968; cons. Pub. Svc. Co., N.Mex. Intermediate Clinic, Planned Parenthood, Farmington. Author numerous poems for mag. Advisor Order Rainbow for Girls, Farmington, 1975-78. Mem. Nat. Assn. Bds. Pharmacy (com. on internship tng., com. edn., sec., treas. dist. 8, mem. impaired pharmacists adv. com., chmn. impaired pharmacists program N.Mex., 1987—, mem. law enforcement legis. com., chmn. nominating com. 1992), Nat. Assn. Retail Druggists, N.Mex. Pharm. Assn. (mem. exec. coun. 1977-81), Order Eastern Star (Farmington). Methodist. Home and Office: 1301 Camino Sol Farmington NM 87401-8075

MACCARTHY, DOUGLAS EDWARD, financial planner; b. Orange, N.J., Oct. 30, 1945; s. Alan Wallace and Matilda (Wharton) MacC.; m. Joyce Ann Johnson, July 21, 1973; children: Stephanie, Matthew. BA, U. Mich., 1967, MBA, 1968. With IBM, 1971—; planning mgr. IBM, White Plains, N.Y., 1985-87, Mpls., 1987-91; mgr. fin., planning and adminstrn. Rocky Mountain Trading Area IBM, Denver, 1991—. V.p. Friends of the Candlewood, New Fairfield, Conn., 1986-87; event chmn. United Cerebral Palsy Minn., 1989-90; trustee Denver Chamber Orch., 1991—.

MACCAULEY, HUGH BOURNONVILLE, banker; b. Mt. Vernon, N.Y., Mar. 12, 1922; s. Morris Baker and Alma (Gardiner) MacC.; m. Rachael Gleaton, Aug. 30, 1943 (div. May 1980); m. Felice Cooper, Dec. 2, 1980. Student, Rutgers U., 1939-41, Tex. Christian U., 1948-50, U. Omaha, 1957-59. Commd. 2d lt. U.S. Army, 1943; advanced through grades to col. U.S. Army, USAF, Washington, 1943-73; v.p. Great Am. Securities, San Bernardino, Calif., 1979—; chmn. bd. Desert Community Bank, Victorville, Calif., 1980—. bd. dirs. Air Force Village West, 1986-88; chmn. bd. Gen. and Mrs. Curtis E. Lemay Found., 1987—. Decorated Air medal, Legion of Merit. Mem. Daedalian Soc., Rotary. Republican. Presbyterian. Home: 1630 Monroe St Riverside CA 92504-5539 Office: Great Am Securities Inc 325 W Hospitality Ln Ste 106 San Bernardino CA 92408-3210

MACCLINCHIE, ROBERT CLANAHAN, retired federal official; b. Springfield, Ill., Mar. 6, 1910; s. Robert and Myrtle (Clanahan) MacC.; m. Kathryn E. Schaeffer, Jan. 29, 1934. BS, U. Ill., 1932. Elec. officer Grace Line, 1933; operator Commonwealth Edison Co., Chgo., 1933-35; engr. Rural Electrification Adminstrn., U.S. Dept. Agr., Washington, 1935-42, mgmt. engr., budget officer, 1946-50; budget officer, asst. dir. budget Office Asst. Sec. Def., Washington, 1950-61; attaché adminstrv. officer Am. Embassy, Paris, France, 1962-63; pres., mgr. Beardstown (Ill.) C. of C., 1964-65; tchr. Olivet (Mich.) High Sch., 1967-73; faculty Olivet Coll., 1973-74. Commr. Olivet City Park, 1970; pres. PTA, 1972. Lt. comdr. USNR, 1942-45, capt. USNR, ret. Mem. Lions Club (pres. 1971). Home: 10626 W Emerald Pt Sun City AZ 85351-2742

MACCORKLE, EMMETT WALLACE, III, insurance agent; b. Portsmouth, Va., Feb. 10, 1942; s. Emmett Wallace and Nelda (Reymann) MacC.; m. Carol Britton, Dec. 27, 1964; children: Jeffrey W., Steven M. BA, Cornell U., 1964. CLU. Agt. Northwestern Mut. Life, San Francisco, 1967-72; dist. agt. Northwestern Mut. Life, San Mateo, 1972-80; pres. MacCorkle Ins. Svcs., San Mateo, 1980—. Mem. Cornell U. Coun., Ithaca, N.Y., 1986-89; mem. Bellarmine Coll. Prep. Bd. Regents, San Jose, Calif., 1988-91; mem. devel. com. Cartoon Art Mus., San Francisco, 1989-90. With USMC, 1964-67, Vietnam. Named Man of Yr., Peninsula Assn. Life Underwriters, San Mateo, 1980. Mem. Bohemian Club (San Francisco), Menlo Circus Club (Menlo Park, Calif.), Cornell Club No. Calif. (pres. 1974). Democrat. Home: 1060 Continental Dr Menlo Park CA 94025-6652 Office: MacCorkle Ins Svcs 1777 Borel Pl Ste 500 San Mateo CA 94402-3514

MACDONALD, A. EWAN, food products executive. MA, U. Edinburgh, Scotland, 1964. With Leo Burnett, 1966-81, McCann-Erickson, 1981-85; pres., COO, CEO Del Monte Corp., 1985—. Office: Del Monte Corp 1 Market Plz San Francisco CA 94105-1019

MACDONALD, GORDON JAMES FRASER, geophysicist; b. Mexico City, July 30, 1929; s. Gordon and Josephine (Bennett) MacD.; m. Marcelline Kuglen (dec.); children: Gordon James, Maureen, Michael; m. Betty Ann Kipniss; 1 son, Bruce; m. 3d, Margaret Stone Jennings. A.B. summa cum laude, Harvard U., 1950, A.M., 1952, Ph.D., 1954. Asst. prof. geology, geophysics Mass. Inst. Tech., 1954-55, assoc. prof. geology, geophysics, 1955-58; staff assoc. geophysics lab. Carnegie Inst. Washington, 1955-58; cons. U.S. Geol. Survey, 1955-60; prof. geophysics UCLA, 1958-68; dir. atmospheric rsch. lab., 1960-66, assoc. dir. UCLA (Inst. Geophysics and Planetary Physics), 1960-68; v.p. rsch. Inst. for Def. Analyses, 1966-67, exec. v.p., 1967-68, trustee, 1966-70; vice chancellor for rsch. and grad. affairs U. Calif. at Santa Barbara, 1968-70, prof. physics and geophysics, 1968-70; mem. coun. on Environ. Quality Washington, 1970-72; Henry R. Luce prof. environ. studies and policy, dir. environ. studies program Dartmouth Coll., 1972-79; trustee The MITRE Corp., McLean, Va., 1968-70, 72-77, exec. com., 1972-77; disting. vis. scholar The MITRE Corp., 1977-79, chief scientist, 1979-83, v.p., chief scientist, 1983-90; prof. internat. rels., rsch. dir. U. Calif., San Diego, 1990—; cons. NASA, 1960-70, mem. lunar and planetary missions bd., 1967; mem. Def. Sci. Bd., Dept. Def., 1966-70; cons. Dept. State, 1967-70; mem. Pres.'s Sci. Adv. Com., 1965-69; adv. panel on nuclear effects Office Tech. Assessment, 1975-77. Author: The Rotation of the Earth, 1960; co-author: Sound and Light Phenomena: A Study of Historical and Modern Occurrences, 1978, The Long-Term Impacts of Increasing Atmospheric Carbon Dioxide Levels, 1982, Global Climate and Ecosystem Change, 1990; contbr. articles to sci., tech. jours. Fellow AAAS, Am. Mineral. Soc., Am. Meteorol. Soc., Geol. Soc. Am., Am. Geophys. Union, Am. Acad. Arts and Scis., Am. Philos. Soc.; mem. Am. Math. Soc., Nat. Acad. Scis. (chmn. environ. studies bd. 1970, 72-73, chmn. commn. on natural resources 1973-77), Royal Astron. Soc. (fgn. assoc.), Geochem. Soc. Am., Seismol. Soc. Am., Soc. Indsl. and Applied Math., Coun. Fgn. Rels., Cosmos Club, Sigma Xi. Office: U Calif San Diego Inst Global Conflict Coop 9500 Gilman Dr La Jolla CA 92093-0518

MACDONALD, JAMES ELLIS, law educator; b. Henderson, Ky., Sept. 30, 1950; s. Martin Edward and Ruth Elizabeth (Rhoades) M.; m. Nancy Lee Lowe, Dec. 20, 1975; children: Elspeth Ainslee, Ian Fletcher. BS, Ea. Ill. U., 1972; MA, Ind. U., 1974, PhD, 1980; JD, MBA, Ind. U., Indpls., 1981. Bar: Ind. 1981, Utah 1988. Teaching asst. Ind. U., Bloomington, 1972-76; assoc. faculty Ind. U.-Purdue U., Indpls., 1976-81; staff atty. Legal Aid Soc. Ind., Indpls., 1981; asst. prof. law Weber State U., Ogden, Utah, 1982-86, assoc. prof., 1986-90, prof., 1990—, univ. rep., 1989. Contbr. articles to profl. jours. Mem. Am. Bus. Law Assn., Rocky Mt. Bus. Law Assn. (pres. 1986). Republican. Roman Catholic. Office: Weber State U 3750 Harrison Blvd Ogden UT 84408-3802

MACDONALD, KENNETH RICHARD, writer; b. Flint, Mich., June 2, 1912; s. Frederic Vinton and Cora (Muma) MacD.; m. Katherine Fisher; children: Carol, Kenneth Vinton. Reporter Detroit Free Press, Detroit Times, Internat. News Svc., Detroit, UPI, Detroit; freelance writer bus. news, 33 yrs. Democrat. Home: 24 White St San Francisco CA 94109

MACDONALD, NORVAL (WOODROW), safety engineer; b. Medford, Oreg., Dec. 8, 1913; s. Orion and Edith (Anderson) MacD.; m. Elizabeth Ann Clifford, Dec. 8, 1937; children: Linda (Mrs. Bob Comings), Peggy (Mrs. Don Lake), Kathleen (Mrs. Michael Nissenberg). Student, U. So. Calif., 1932-34. Registered profl. safety engr., Calif. Safety engr. Todd Shipyards, San Pedro, Calif., 1942-44, Pacific Indemnity Ins. Co., San Francisco, 1944-50; area safety engring. chief safety engr. Indsl. Ind., San Francisco, 1950-76; v.p. loss control Beaver Ins. Co., 1982-88; tchr. adult evening classes U. San Francisco, 1960-63, Golden Gate U., 1969—. Contbr. articles to profl. jours.; producer safety training films. Mem. ASME, Am. Soc. Safety Engrs. (pres. 1958, 59), Las Posas Country Club, Masons, Shriners. Methodist. Home: 1710 Shoreline Dr Camarillo CA 93010-6018

MACDONALD, RANDAL STUART, university official; b. Oakland, Calif., Aug. 30, 1959; s. James Daniel and Charlotte (Fleming) MacD.; m. Susan S. Horning, Dec. 15, 1984. BA in Polit. Sci. summa cum laude with honors, U. Oreg., 1990. Maintenance mgr. Highway Missionary Soc., Grants Pass, Oreg., 1981-85; legis. asst. Oreg. Legis. Assembly, Salem, 1987-91; dir. legis. and community rels. U. Oreg., Eugene, 1991—; bd. dirs. League Oreg. Cities, Salem, 1991—. Pres. Commn. on Rights of Minorities, Eugene, 1987-88; councilor City of Eugene, 1991—. Mem. Phi Beta Kappa. Democrat.

MACDONALD, VIRGINIA BROOKS, architect; b. Denver, July 17, 1918; d. Emmet Earl and Lulu (Gatchel) Stoffel; widowed; m. Russell A. Apple, Oct. 18, 1981; children: Philip Brooks, Anne Brooks Hormann, Bill Brooks, Mike Brooks. BArch, Case Western Res. U., 1946. Registered architect, Hawaii. Dir. Timberline Camp., Honolulu, 1962-67; planner State of Hawaii, Honolulu, 1967-77; pvt. practice architecture Volcano, Hawaii, 1977—. Author: West Hawaii, 1972; (book/report) Na Ala Hele, 1973. Active Volcano Community Assn., 1980—. Recipient Innovative Energy award U.S. Dept. Energy, 1984, Energy Saving award State of Hawaii, 1984. Mem. AIA (past pres. local sect. 1988, dir. state coun.), Sierra Club (past state bd. dirs), Hawaii Conservation Council (past state pres.).

MACDONOUGH, ROBERT HOWARD, consulting engineer; b. Chgo., Jan. 24, 1941; s. John Haaf and Helen Margaret (McWilliams) MacD.; m. Joan Carol Rosecrants, Dec. 28, 1963 (div. Nov. 1975); children: John Haaf, Thomas William, Mark Peter. BS in Engring. Ops., Iowa State U., 1962; MA in Econ., Drake U., 1966. Registered profl. engr., Iowa. Assoc. Mgmt. Sci. Am., Palo Alto, Calif., 1969; mng. assoc. Theo. Barry & Assoc., Los Angeles, 1970-72; mgr. indsl. engring. Advanced Memory Systems, Sunnyvale, Calif., 1972-73; mgr. planning and engring. Signetics, Sunnyvale, 1973-75; pres. Facilities Cons., Mountain View, Calif., 1976—. Mem. Inst. Indsl. Engrs. (sr.), Am. Inst. Plant Engrs., Am. Contract Bridge League, Phi Gamma Delta. Republican.

MACE, JOHN WELDON, pediatrician; b. Buena Vista, Va., July 9, 1938; s. John Henry and Gladys Elizabeth (Edwards) M.; m. Janice Mace, Jan. 28, 1962; children—Karin E., John E., James E. B.A., Columbia Union Coll., 1960; M.D., Loma Linda U., 1964. Diplomate: Am. Bd. Pediatrics, Sub-bd. Pediatric Endocrinology. Intern U.S. Naval Hosp., San Diego, 1964-65, resident in pediatrics, 1966-68; fellow in endocrinology and metabolism U. Colo., 1970-72; asst. prof. pediatrics Loma Linda (Calif.) U. Med. Center, 1972-75, prof., chmn. dept., 1975—; med. dir. Loma Linda U. Children's Hosp., 1990-92, physician-in-chief, 1992—. Contbr. articles to profl. jours. Treas. Found. for Med. Care, San Bernardino County, 1979-80, pres., 1980-82; mem. Congl. Adv. Bd., 1984-87; pres. So. Calif. affiliate Am. Diabetes Assn., 1985-86, dir., 1987-89; chmn. adv. bd. State Calif. Children's Svcs., 1986—. With USN, 1962-70. Mem. AAAS, N.Y. Acad. Sci., Calif. Med. Soc. (adv. panel genetic diseases State Calif., 1975—), Western Soc. Pediatric Rsch., Lawson Wilkens Pediatric Endocrine Soc., Assn. Med. Pediatric Dept. Chairmen, Sigma Xi, Alpha Omega Alpha. Office: Loma Linda U Sch Medicine Barton & Anderson Sts Loma Linda CA 92350

MACER, GEORGE ARMEN, JR., orthopedic hand surgeon; b. Pasadena, Calif., Oct. 17, 1948; s. George A. and Nevart Akullian M.; m. Celeste Angelle Lyons, Mar. 26, 1983; children: Christiana Marilu, Marina Lynn, Emily Sue. BA, U. So. Calif., 1971, MD, 1976. Diplomate Am. Bd. Med. Examiners, Am. Bd. Orthopaedic Surgery; cert. surgery of hand. Intern Meml. Hosp. Med. Ctr., Long Beach, Calif., 1976; resident Orthopaedic Hosp./U. So. Calif., 1977-81; pvt. practice hand surgery Long Beach, 1983—; asst. clin. prof. orthopaedics U. So. Calif., Long Beach, 1983-89, 1990—; cons. hand surgery svc. Rancho Los Amigos Hosp. Downey, 1990—; cons. Harbor UCLA Med. Ctr., Torrance, 1983—. Joseph Boyes Hand fellow, 1982; mem. AMA, Calif. Med. Assn., L.A. County Med. Assn., Western Orthopaedic Assn., Am. Soc. for Surgery of Hand, Am. Acad. Orthopaedic Surgery. Republican. Office: 701 E 28th St Ste 418 Long Beach CA 90806-2767

MACFARLAND, CRAIG GEORGE, natural resource management professional; b. Great Falls, Mont., July 17, 1943; s. Paul Stanley and Jean Elizabeth (Graham) MacF.; m. Janice Lee Bennett, Dec. 23, 1963 (div. 1987); children: Bennett, Francisco; m. Marilyn Ann Swanson, Mar. 19, 1988; stepchildren: Alyssa, Krista, Sara. BA magna cum laude, Austin Coll., 1965; MA, U. Wis., Madison, 1969; DSc (hon.), Austin Coll., 1978. Dir. Charles Darwin Rsch. Sta., Galapagos Islands, Ecuador, 1974-78; head Wildlands and watershed mgmt. program Cen. Am. Centro Agronomico Tropical de Investigacion Enseñanza, Turrialba, Costa Rica, 1978-85; pres. Charles Darwin Found. for Galapagos Islands, Ecuador, 1985—; cons. natural resources and sustainable devel. in Latin Am. Moscow, Idaho, 1985—; affiliate faculty dept. Resource, Recreation and Tourism, U. Idaho, Moscow, 1988—. Contbr. to numerous profl. publs. Recipient Internat. Conservation medal Zool. Soc. San Diego, 1978, Order of Golden Ark for internat. conservation, Prince Bernhard of Netherlands, 1984. Mem. Ecol. Soc. Am., Internat. Soc. Tropical Foresters, Assn. Tropical Biology, Soc. Conservation Biology, Nature Conservancy, World Wildlife Fund, Greenpeace. Office: Charles Darwin Rsch Sta Charles Darwin Foundation 836 Mabelle Moscow ID 83843-3553

MACFARLANE, GORDON FREDERICK, telephone company executive; b. Victoria, B.C., Canada, Sept. 21, 1925; s. Frederick Randolph and Nora Margaret (La Fortune) MacF.; m. Hazel Louise Major, June 1946; children: Michael Gordon, Ann L. MacFarlane Patterson, Katherine M. MacFarlane Bernard. BSEE, U. B.C., 1950, hon. law degree, 1991. Chief engr., dir. plant services B.C. Telephone Co., Vancouver, 1966-67, v.p. ops., 1967-70, v.p. corp. devel., 1970-76, v.p. adminstr., 1976; pres., chief executive officer GTE Automatic Elec., Brockville, Ont., Can., 1976-77; chmn., chief exec. officer B.C. Telephone Co., Burnaby, 1977-90; chmn. B.C. Telephone Co.; bd. dirs. Air Can., The Bank of Nova Scotia, Fletcher Challenge Can. Ltd., B.C. Gas Inc., Trans Mountain Pipe Line Co., Ltd., MPR Teltech Ltd. Trustee B.C. Advanced Systems Found., Advanced Systems Inst.; mem. U. B.C. Campaign Leadership Com.; mem. Premier's Econ. Adv. Coun., Sci. Coun. Award Com. Served with RCAF, 1943-46. Recipient First Communications Can. award, 1988, Engring. Alumni award of distinction Engring. Alumni div. U. B.C., 1989, United Way's Pres.'s award of distinction, 1990. Mem. Assn. Profl. Engrs. of B.C. (R.A. McLachlan Meml. award 1989), Telephone Pioneers Am. Office: BC Telephone Co, 3777 Kingsway, Burnaby, BC Canada V5H 3Z7

MACGINITIE, WALTER HAROLD, psychologist; b. Carmel, Calif., Aug. 14, 1928; s. George Eber and Nettie Lorene (Murray) MacG.; m. Ruth Olive Kilpatrick, Sept. 2, 1950; children: Mary Catherine, Laura Anne. B.A., UCLA, 1949; A.M., Stanford U., 1950; Ph.D., Columbia U., 1960. Tchr. Long Beach (Calif.) Unified Sch. Dist., 1950, 1955-56; mem. faculty Columbia U. Tchrs. Coll., 1959-80, prof. psychology and edn., 1970-80; Lansdowne scholar, prof. edn. U. Victoria, B.C., Can., 1980-84; research assoc. Lexington Sch. Deaf, N.Y.C., 1963-69; mem. sci. adv. bd. Ctr. for Study of Reading, 1977-80, chmn. 1979-80. Co-author: Gates-MacGinitie Reading Tests, 1965, 78, 89, Psychological Foundations of Education, 1968; Editor: Assessment Problems in Reading, 1972; co-editor: Verbal Behavior of the Deaf Child, 1969. Life mem. Calif. PTA. Served with USAF, 1950-54. Fellow APA, AAAS, Am. Psychol. Soc., Nat. Conf. Research English, N.Y. Acad. Scis.; mem. Internat. Reading Assn. (pres. 1976-77, Spl. Svc. award 1981), Reading Hall of Fame (pres. 1989-90). Home and Office: PO Box 1789 Friday Harbor WA 98250-1789

MAC GOWAN, MARY EUGENIA, lawyer; b. Turlock, Calif., Aug. 4, 1928; d. William Ray and Mary Bolling (Gilbert) Kern; m. Gordon Scott Millar, Jan. 2, 1970; 1 dau., Heather Mary. A.B., U. Calif., Berkeley, 1950; J.D., U. Calif., San Francisco, 1953. Bar: Calif. 1953; cert. family law specialist Calif. State Bar Bd. Legal Specialization. Research atty. Supreme Ct. Calif., 1954, Calif. Ct. Appeals, 1955; partner firm MacGowan & MacGowan, Calif., 1956-68; individual practice law San Francisco, 1968—. Bd. dirs. San Francisco Speech and Hearing Center, San Francisco Legal Aid Soc., J.A.C.K.I.E. Mem. Am., Calif., San Francisco bar assns., Queen's Bench. Clubs: San Francisco Lawyers, Forest Hill Garden. Office: 685 Market St San Francisco CA 94105-4212

MACH, MARTIN HENRY, chemist; b. N.Y.C., Feb. 10, 1940; s. William Leon and Marcia (Cohen) M.; m. Nada L. Mach, June, 1965 (div. 1974); 1 child, Alissa L. BS, CCNY, 1961; MA, Clark U., 1965; PhD, U. Calif., Santa Cruz, 1973. Assoc. chemist Polaroid Corp., Cambridge, Mass., 1965-69; mem. tech. staff Aerospace Corp., El Segundo, Calif., 1973-81; chief scientist TRW Systems, Redondo Beach, Calif., 1981—. Mem. JANNAF Safety and Environ. Protection Subcom., Laurel, Md., 1977—. N.Y. State Regents scholar, 1957. Mem. Calif. Assn. Criminalists (assoc.), Sigma Xi. Office: TRW Bldg 01/2030 1 Space Park Dr Redondo Beach CA 90278-1071

MACINTOSH, SUSAN CARYL, biochemist; b. Watertown, Wis., June 11, 1953; d. Donald James and Cynthia Ann (Stone) MacI.; m. Daniel Lee Hale, Aug. 10, 1974 (div. Dec. 1982); children: Katharine MacIntosh, Laura MacIntosh. BA, U. Iowa, 1974. Research technician St. Mary's Health Ctr., St. Louis, 1975-77; research asst. U. Iowa, Iowa City, 1979-83; chemist Sigma Chem. Co., St. Louis, 1983-87; research biologist II Monsanto Co., St. Louis, 1987-90; sr. staff researcher Protein Chemistry Entotech, Inc., Davis, Calif., 1990—. Contbr. articles to profl. jours. Episcopalian. Office: Entotech Inc Davis CA 95616

MACINTYRE, NORMAN LAW, manufacturing executive, management consultant; b. Barnstable, Mass., Nov. 23, 1940; s. David Stuart and Madeleine Wade (Cote) MacI.; m. Karen Elizabeth Holmes, June 10, 1964 (div. 1987); children: Jennifer Ann, Rebecca Elizabeth; m. Judith Ann Riggs, Dec. 5, 1987; children: Kerry Michael, Kevin Mathew. BS, U.S. Naval Acad., 1964; MBA, So. Ill. U., 1981. Marine project engr. Turbo Power & Marine Systems, Inc., Farmington, Conn., 1969-74; mgr. marine contracts Fairbanks Morse Engine Div., Beloit, Wisc., 1975-76; v.p. Seaworthy Engine Systems, Essex, Conn., 1974-75, 76-78; mktg. mgr. Solar Turbines Inc., San Diego, 1978-88; pres., chief exec. officer Advanced Coatings Techs. and Applications, Inc., San Diego, 1988—; cons. Small Bus. Devel. Ctr., San Diego, 1989—. Trustee Encinitas (Calif.) Union Sch. Dist., 1979-83. Lt. USN, 1964-69. Mem. ASME, Am. Soc. Quality Control, Navy League of U.S., Deming Users Group of So. Calif., San Diego C. of C. (chief exec. officer roundtable). Office: Advanced Coatings Techs and Applications Inc 3554 Kettner Blvd San Diego CA 92101

MACK, BRENDA LEE, sociologist, public relations consulting company executive; b. Peoria, Ill., Mar. 24; d. William James and Virginia Julia (Pickett) Palmer; m. Rozene Mack, Jan. 13 (div.); 1 child, Kevin Anthony. AA, L.A. City Coll.; BA in Sociology, Calif. State U., L.A., 1980. Ct. clk. City of Blythe, Calif.; partner Mack Trucking Co., Blythe; ombudsman, sec. bus facilities So. Calif. Rapid Transit Dist., L.A., 1974-81; owner Brenda Mack Enterprises, L.A., 1981—; lectr., writer, radio and TV personality; cons. European community; co-originator advt. concept View/Door Project; pub. News from the United States newsletter through U.S. and Europe. Past bd. dirs. Narcotic Symposium, L.A. With WAC, U.S. Army. Mem. Women For, Calif. State U. L.A. Alumni Assn., World Affairs Coun., German-Am. C. of C., European Community Studies Assn. Home: 8749 Cattaraugus Ave Los Angeles CA 90034-2558 Office: Brenda Mack Enterprises/Mack Media Presents PO Box 5942 Los Angeles CA 90055-0942

MACK, CHARLES DANIEL, III, labor union executive; b. Oakland, Calif., Apr. 16, 1942; s. Charles Daniel and Bernadine Zoe (Ferguson) M.; m. Marlene Helen Fagundes, Oct. 15, 1960; children—Tammy, Kelly, Kerry, Shannon. B.A., San Francisco State Coll., 1964. Truck driver Garrett Freight Lines, Emeryville, Calif., 1962-66; bus. agt. Teamsters Local No. 70, Oakland, 1966-70, sec.-treas., 1972—; legis. rep. Calif. Teamsters Pub. Affairs Council, Sacramento, 1970-71; trustee Western Conf. Teamsters Pension Trust Fund, 1980—, mem. policy com., 1980-82, pres. Teamsters' Joint Council 7, San Francisco, 1982—; rep. Internat. Brotherhood Teamsters, Chauffeurs, Warehousemen & Helpers of Am., 1984—. Bd. dirs. Econ. Devel. Corp. of Oakland, 1980—, Pvt. Industry Council, Oakland, 1983-84, Children's Hosp. of East Bay, 1981-83, Calif. Compensation Ins. Fund, San Francisco, 1980-86, Alameda County Easter Seals, 1983-85, United Way, 1978-82. Democrat. Roman Catholic. Office: Teamsters' Joint Counc 7 Executive Park Blvd San Francisco CA 94134-3301

MACK, JAMES CARL, oil service company executive; b. Mauston, Wis., Sept. 1, 1948; s. Corwin Cecil and Mildred (Benson) M.; m. Mary Anne Greene, May 12, 1973; children: Kiley, Lauren. BSCHE, U. Wis., 1971; MBA, Colo. State U., 1976. Registered profl. engr., Colo. Analytical engr.

ARCO, Denver, 1971; process engr. Stearns-Roger, Denver, 1971-77; sales engr. Betz, Denver, 1977; v.p. Tiorco Inc., Denver, 1977-83, pres., 1983—; bd. dirs. Pole Duc Mfg., Gillette, Wyo., 1983—. Cons. Jr. Achievement, Denver, 1989-90; big brother Big Bros., Denver, 1975-85. Mem. Soc. Petroleum Engr. (chmn., bd. dirs., Denver Svc. award 1989, Regional Svc. award 1990), Denver C. of C., Japan Am. Soc., Skyline Swim & Tennis Club (bd. dirs. 1986-89), Toastmasters (club pres. 1980-85, Competent Toastmaster 1984), Rotary. Home: 3990 S Hudson Way Englewood CO 80110-5136 Office: Tiorco Inc 1795 W Warren Ave Englewood CO 80110

MACK, SHAEN CASE HOSIE, human resources professional; b. Stockton, Calif., June 13, 1964; d. William Carlton Hosie and Sherryl (Frick) Rasmussen; m. Albert Larry Mack III, Jan. 7, 1990. BA in Comm., U. San Francisco, 1986. Nat. field rep. Delta Zeta Sorority, Oxford, Ohio, 1986-87; cosmetic cons. Clinique Cosmetics, N.Y., 1987-88; benefits adminstr. Macys Calif., Stanford, 1988-89; human resources asst. MIC Telecomm., San Francisco, 1990, benefits adminstr., 1991-92, employment/recruitment coord., 1992, employee rels. specialist, 1992—. Mem. Loyola Guild, U. San Francisco, 1992. Mem. No. Calif. Human Resources Coun., Delta Zeta (chpt. dir. 1990—, nat. alumnae chmn. 1992). Republican.

MACKAY, ALEXANDER RUSSELL, surgeon; b. Bottineau, N.D., Oct. 8, 1911; s. Alexander Russell and Eleanor (Watson) M.; BS, Northwestern U., 1932, MD, 1936; MS in Surgery, U. Minn., 1940; m. Marjorie Andres, July 16, 1941; children: Andrea, Alexander Russell. Intern, Med. Center, Jersey City, 1935-37; fellow in surgery Mayo Clinic, Rochester, Minn. 1937-41; practiced medicine specializing in gen. surgery, Spokane, Wash., 1941-82, now ret.; former staff Deaconess, Sacred Heart hosps., Spokane. Capt., M.C., AUS, 1942-45. Diplomate Am. Bd. Surgery. Fellow ACS; mem. Spokane Surg. Soc., North Pacific Surg. Assn., Alpha Omega Alpha, Phi Delta Theta, Nu Sigma Nu, Phi Beta Kappa. Home: 540 E Rockwood Blvd Spokane WA 99202-1143

MACKEL, MARILYN HORTENSE, law educator; b. Natchez, Miss., July 15, 1945; d. Audley Maurice and Rosetta Libian (Lloyd) M. BA, Bennett Coll., Greensboro, N.C., 1965; MA in Criminal Justice, CUNY, 1972; JD, Georgetown U., 1976. Bar: D.C. 1977, Calif. 1988. Assoc. prof. dept. criminal justice U. D.C., Washington, 1971-87; pvt. practice Washington, 1977-88; assoc. Feldsott and Lee, Newport Beach, Calif., 1988-89; of counsel Feldsott and Lee, Newport Beach, 1989—; assoc. prof. Western State U. Coll. Law, Fullerton, Calif., 1989—; referee Juvenile depts. L.A. Superior Ct., 1991—; researcher equal opportunity/affirmative action Dept. Army, Harry Diamond Labs., Adelphi, Md., 1982; cons. Assessment Ctr. for Fire Lts. Promotion Exam., N.Y.C., Office Personnel, 1982; co-owner Mackel-Middleton, Inc., Export Mgmt. Co., Balt., 1977-81; probation officer, social worker City of N.Y., 1965-71. Mem. State Bar Calif., D.C. Bar, Black Women Lawyers L.A. Office: Western State U Coll Law 1111 N State College Blvd Fullerton CA 92631-3000

MACKENROTH, JOYCE ELLEN, secondary school educator; b. Portland, Oreg., June 22, 1946; d. Ferrel Adelbert and Ellen Ellenora (Setala) McKinney; m. Glen MacKenroth, Sept. 21, 1968; 1 child, Tonia Lynn. BS, Western Oreg. State Coll., 1968; postgrad, U. Oreg., 1980, 81, 83, 85, Portland State U., 1984. Cert. elem. tchr., Oreg. Tchr. Lincoln County Sch. Dist., Newport, Oreg., 1970—; bd. dirs. Curriculum Coordinating Coun., Newport; computer instr. and coordinator Lincoln County Sch. Dist., 1984-87; mem. various lang. arts and writing coms., 1981—; rep. Avon Co., Toledo, 1974-78; piano, organ tutor, Toledo, 1974-78. Sec. State Assn. Pageant Bds., Seaside, Oreg., 1984-85; active Miss Lincoln County Scholarship Pageant, Toledo, Oreg., 1979-87; founder, pres. Youth Activities Council, 1988. Mem. Internat. Reading Assn., Oreg. Reading Assn., Seacoast Reading Assn., Oreg. Edn. Assn. (uniserv treas. 1979-81, bd. dirs. 1981-82), Lincoln County Edn. Assn. (sec. 1974, v.p. 1975, pres. 1976, 81), NEA, Bus. and Profl. Women, Beta Sigma Phi (sec. 1983-84, v.p. 1985-86, pres. 1986-88). Democrat. Home: 264 NE 1st St Toledo OR 97391-1505 Office: Toledo Mid Sch 600 SE Sturdevant Rd Toledo OR 97391-2405

MACKENZIE, PETER SEAN, editor, journalist; b. L.A., Aug. 25, 1954; s. William Duncan and Patricia Ann (Kronschnabel) MacK.; m. Carin Willette, Dec. 28, 1983. BA, Western Wash. U., 1976. Bus. editor Skagit Valley Herald, Mount Vernon, Wash., 1976-79; mng. editor Stanwood (Wash.)-Camano News, 1979-84; graphic artist Pacific Media Group, Seattle, 1985-90, editor, 1990-93; instr. U. Wash. Exptl. Coll., Seattle, 1990-91. Author: Jumper, 1989; rec. artist LP KEZX Album Project, 1987, Victory Music Vol. # 2, 1988; speaker Viacom Cable Pub. Access TV, Seattle, 1990. V.p. Stanwood, Wash. C. of C., 1983. Recipient 1st pl. newswritintg award Wash. Newspaper Pub. Assn., 1981, 82. Mem. Soc. Profl. Journalists (2d pl. investigative journalism award, 1982), Greenpeace. Home: 316 NW 86th St Seattle WA 98117-3125 Office: Piast Mor Systems PO Box 82034 Seattle WA 98028

MACKENZIE, S. THOMPSON, air force officer; b. Abington, Pa., July 31, 1954; s. Sidney Thompson Mackenzie and Patricia (Robertson) Arnold; m. Nancy Pingree, Oct. 6, 1977; children: Cara J., Brooke A. BSBA, New Eng. Coll., Henniker, N.H., 1976; MBA, Golden Gate U., 1988. Patrolman Bedford (N.H.) Police Dept., 1976-81; commd. 2d lt. USAF, 1981, advanced through grades to capt., 1986; navigator, instr. navigator USAF, K.I. Sawyer AFB, Mich., 1983-85; instr. navigator USAF, Mather AFB, Calif., 1985-87, mgr. core program, 1987-89; instr. radar navigator USAF, Fairchild AFB, Wash., 1989-91, flight comdr., 1991, chief scheduling br., 1991—. Mem. Nat. Ski Patrol System, Henniker, 1975-80; post advisor Explorer Scouts, Boy Scouts Am., Bedford, 1977-78, coun. advisor, Spokane, Wash., 1990-91. Mem. Air Force Assn. Office: 92d OSS/DOTB Fairchild AFB WA 99011

MACKEY, KEVIN JAMES, software engineer; b. El Cerrito, Calif., Mar. 6, 1958; s. Howard James and Barbara (Stone) M. BA in Computer Sci., U. Calif., Berkeley, 1982. Software engr. Xerox, Palo Alto, Calif., 1982-89; sr. software engr. Logitech, Inc., Fremont, Calif., 1989—. Co-inventor PC Emulation, 1990. Explainer Tech Museum of Innovation, San Jose, Calif., 1990—. Recipient Scholarship, Achievement Rewards for Coll. Scientists, San Francisco, 1980. Mem. Assn. Computing Machinery. Office: Logitech Inc 6505 Kaiser Dr Fremont CA 94555

MACKEY, SEAN CHARLES, electrical engineering consultant; b. Oceanside, Calif., Mar. 29, 1963; s. Ronald James and Susan (Fuller) M.; m. Lisa Ann Gordon, Nov. 26, 1990. BSE, U. Pa., 1986, MSE, 1986; postgrad., U. Ariz. Waiter Moshulu Restaurant, Phila., 1983-84; engring. tech. LaJolla (Calif.) Tech., 1985; rsch. assoc./biomed. engr. VA Med. Ctr., Phila., 1985-86; rsch. assoc. Univ. Med. Ctr./Anesthesiology, Tucson, 1986-88; owner Altech Cons., Tucson, 1987—; cons. Univ. Med. Ctr. Anesthesiology, 1988—. GTE scholar, 1987, others. Mem. IEEE, Bioengring. Soc., Am. Med. Students Assn. Home: 1514 E Hampton St Tucson AZ 85719

MACKEY, WAYNE ALLISON, electrical engineer; b. Pitts., Sept. 22, 1955; s. George Allison and Dorothy Jayne (Ross) M.; m. Mary Lou Herbers, Nov. 16, 1984; children: Benjamin Paul, Craig Thomas. BSEE and Econs., Carnegie Mellon U., 1977; MS in Engring., Loyola Marymount U., L.A., 1982. Engr. space and info. systems Raytheon Co., Sudbury, Mass., 1977-78; mem. tech. staff Hughes Aircraft Co., El Segundo, Calif., 1978-84, head tech. sect., 1984-87, sr. scientist, engr., 1987-90, div. sr. scientist, 1990—, team leader event based concurrent engring., 1991—, team leader estimating process improvement, 1992, team leader customer focused quality, 1993. Inventor automated environ. tester, universal FLIR tester, automatic bid/spread sheet. Fellow Hughes Corp. Edn. Coun., 1980. Mem. Assn. Proposal Mgmt. Profls., Tau Beta Pi. Home: 1315 10th St Manhattan Beach CA 90266 Office: Hughes Aircraft Co PO Box 902 M103 El Segundo CA 90245

MACKIE, RICHARD JOHN, biology educator; b. Foster City, Mich., July 6, 1933; s. Arvid Axel and Ruth Hildegard (Rein) M.; m. Barbara Ann Rye, June 22, 1957; children: Bryan, Alan, Leann, Lorelyn. BS, Mich. State U., East Lansing, 1958; MS, Wash. State U., Pullman, 1960; PhD, Mont. State U., Bozeman, 1965. Rsch. biologist Mont. Fish & Game Dept., Lewistown, 1960-65; rsch. coord. Mont. Fish & Game Dept., Bozeman, 1965-66; from asst. to assoc. prof. wildlife mgmt. U. Minn., St. Paul, 1966-70; from assoc. to prof. wildlife mgmt. Mont. State U., Bozeman, 1970—; Author chpts. in books; contbr. numerous articles to profl. jours. With U.S. Army, 1953. Recipient O. C. Wallmo Mule and Blacktail Deer award Western Deer Group, 1989. Mem. Wildlife Soc. (pres. N.W. sect. 1976-77, rep. on coun. 1980-86, pres. elect 1989-90, pres. 1990-92, past pres. 1992-93, Disting. Svc. award 1987, pres. Mont. chpt. 1973-74), Phi Sigma (Biologist of Yr. 1965). Presbyterian. Home: 3680 Honeysuckle Rd Belgrade MT 59714 Office: Mont State U Dept Biology Bozeman MT 59717

MACKIN, ROBERT JAMES, JR., physicist; b. Little Rock, Dec. 4, 1925; s. Robert James and Gladys Beverly (Robinson) M.; m. Jeannette Allen, Dec. 27, 1947 (div. 1968); children: Robert James III, Elizabeth Randolph; m. Ruth Estelle Noonan, July 12, 1969; children: Linda Flournoy, Carol Flournoy Lakey, Suzanne Flournoy Frazier, Dana Ruth. BE, Yale U., 1949; MS, Calif. Inst. Tech., 1951, PhD in Physics, 1953. Postdoctoral fellow Calif. Inst. Tech., Pasadena, 1953-54; tech. mgr. U.S. Office Naval Rsch., 1954-56; rsch. scientist Oak Ridge Nat. Lab., Tenn., 1956-62; sec. mgr. physics, planetary scis. Jet Propulsion Lab./Calif. Inst. Tech., Pasadena, 1962-68; mgr. space sci. div. Jet Propulsion Lab./Calif. Inst. Tech., 1969-78, mgr. energy tech. dept., 1978-83, dep. mgr. Army Policy Analysis Ctr., 1983-85, dep. mgr., mgr. Army progs., 1985-88, prog. dir. for tech., 1988—; bd. dirs. Huntington Med. Rsch. Inst., Pasadena, 1974—. Author: Current Knowledge of the Moon and Planets, 1967; co-editor: The Solar Wind, 1964. With U.S. Army, 1944-46; ETO. Decorated Bronze Star, Purple Heart. Mem. Am. Phys. Soc., AAAS, Sigma Xi. Office: Jet Propulsion Lab 4800 Oak Grove Dr Pasadena CA 91109-8099

MACKINNON, ALLAN DONALD, corporate business executive; b. Covina, Calif., Apr. 29, 1958; s. Donald Mathison MacKinnon and Cecile Marie (Desilets) Leavenworth; m. Kathy Jolene Cherry, Apr. 26, 1980 (div. Feb. 1986); m. Victoria ann Carlson, July 3, 1988; children: Jason, Dustin, Denise, Maggie. Student, Mt. San Antonio Coll., Walnut, Calif., 1977-78. Sales rep. Bancker Nicholls Brokerage, Denver, 1979-82; sr. v.p. sales CRI Fin. Systems, Englewood, Colo., 1982-88; regional mgr. Citicorp, Denver, 1989-91; mgr. we. regional sales FISERV, Inc., Englewood, 1991-93, sr. v.p. corp. bus. devel., 1993—. Named Salesperson of Yr., FIserv, Inc., 1991; recipient Successful Selling award FIserv, Inc., 1991, Cert. of Accomplishment, 1990. Republican. Roman Catholic. Office: FIserv Inc 15th Fl 8400 E Prentice Ave Englewood CO 80111

MACKINNON, BARRY ATHOL, physicist, engineer; b. Auckland, New Zealand, Oct. 18, 1940; came to U.S., 1978; s. Kenneth William Charles and Irene (Haddon) MacK.; m. Lola May Nix, Dec. 4, 1960 (div. 1980); children: Blair William, Toni; m. Carolyn Davis, Apr. 16, 1980. BSc, U. New Zealand, 1963; MSc, U. Auckland, 1966. Lectr. in physics U. Auckland, Auckland, New Zealand, 1966-68; gen. mgr. ANAC Ltd., Auckland, New Zealand, 1968-73, engring. mgr., 1974-78, pres., bd. dirs., 1978-82; rsch. assoc. Stanford U., Stanford, Calif., 1973-74; v.p. Resonex Inc., Sunnyvale, Calif., 1984-90; pvt. practice Santa Clara, Calif., 1990—. Contbn. articles to profl. jours. Mem. IEEE, AAAS, Royal Inst. Navagation, Inst. Physics. Home: 927 Lorne Way Sunnyvale CA 94087

MACKINNON, STEPHEN R., Asian studies administrator, educator; b. Columbus, Nebr., Dec. 2, 1940; s. Cyrus Leland and Helen (Wigglesworth) MacK.; m. Janice Carolyn Rachie, July 15, 1967; children: Rebecca, Cyrus R. BA, Yale U., 1963, MA, 1964; PhD, U. Calif., Davis, 1971. Acting instr. Chinese U., Hong Kong, 1968-69; dir. Asian Studies, prof. History Ariz. State U., Tempe, 1971—; vis. assoc. Chinese Acad. Social Sci., Beijing, 1979-81, 85; mem. U.S. State Dept. Selection Bd., Washington, 1991, Nat. Com. on U.S.-China Rels., N.Y.C., 1991—; cons. PBS film documentary "Dragon and Eagle" on U.S.-China rels., San Francisco, 1986—. Author: (book) Power/Politics China, 1980; co-author: (books) Agnes Smedley, 1988, China Reporting, 1987; co-editor: (book) Chinese Women Revolution, 1976 (ALA notable book 1976); lectr. on China to local orgns. and TV, 1981—. Commr. Phoenix Sister Cities, 1986-91; treas. Com. on Fgn. Rels., Phoenix, 1988—. Rsch. fellow Am. Coun. Learned Scholars, Hong Kong, 1978, Fulbright Found., India, 1977-78; rsch. sr. Com. on Scholarly Com. People's Republic China, Washington-Beijing, 1992. Mem. Assn. Asian Studies (bd. dirs. 1990-91), Am. Hist. Assn. (program com. 1990-91). Office: Ariz State U Ctr for Asian Studies Tempe AZ 85287-1702

MACKINTOSH, FREDERICK ROY, oncologist; b. Miami, Fla., Oct. 4, 1943; s. John Harris and Mary Carlotta (King) MacK.; m. Judith Jane Parnell, Oct. 2, 1961 (div. Aug. 1977); children: Lisa Lynn, Wendy Sue; m. Claudia Lizanne Flournoy, Jan. 7, 1984; 1 child, Gregory Warren. BS, MIT, 1964, PhD, 1968; MD, U. Miami, 1976. Intern then resident in gen. medicine Stanford (Calif.) U., 1976-78, fellow in oncology, 1978-81; asst. prof. med. U. Nev., Reno, 1981-85, assoc. prof., 1985-92, prof. medicine, 1992—. Contbr. articles to profl. jours. Fellow ACP; mem. Am. Soc. Clin. Oncology, Am. Cancer Soc. (pres. Nev. chpt. 1987-89, Washoe chpt. 1988-90), No. Nev. Cancer Coun. (bd. dirs. 1981—), No. Calif. Cancer Program (bd. dirs. alt. 1983-87, bd. dirs. 1987-91). Office: Nev Med Group 781 Mill St Reno NV 89502-1320

MACLAREN, WALTER ROGERS, allergist, educator; b. Yokohama, Japan, Dec. 7, 1910; s. Walter Wallace and Zaidee (Rogers) McL.; m. Dorothy Agnes Goodwin, June 1942 (div. 1970); children: Walter Jr., Jean, Anne, Elizabeth, Catherine; m. Dorothy Hamblen, July 7, 1971. BA, Queens U., 1933; MD, Harvard U., 1938. Diplomate Am. Bd. Allergy and Immunology (bd. dirs., sec. 1978-83). Practice medicine specializing in asthma, allergy and immunology Pasadena, Calif., 1947—; clin. prof. medicine U. So. Calif. Sch. Med., L.A., 1948—; dir. Allergy and Immunology Cons. Labs., Inc., Pasadena, 1978-88. Contbr. over 30 articles to profl. jours. Bd. dirs. Pasadena Symphony Orch., 1976-82, Pasadena Chamber Orch., 1984-86. Fellow Am. Acad. Allergy and Immunology, Am. Coll. Allergists, Am. Thoracic Soc., Asthma and Allergy Found. Am., Assn. Clin. Immunology and Allergy (pres.), Pasadena C. of C. (health svcs. com. 1990—), Sigma Xi. Republican. Club: Valley Hunt (Pasadena). Office: 94 N Madison Ave Pasadena CA 91101-1786

MACLAUCHLIN, ROBERT KERWIN, communications artist, educator; b. Framingham, Mass., Oct. 8, 1931; s. Charles Lewis and Elinor Frances (Kerwin) MacL.; m. Elizabeth D'Ann Willson, June 13, 1964. BA in Sociology, U. Mass., Amherst, 1954; MEd, Bridgewater State Coll., 1958; MS in Radio and TV, Syracuse U., 1959; PhD in Speech, Radio, TV, Mich. State U., 1969. Personnel trainee Nat. Security Agy., Washington, 1954-55; elem. sch. tchr. Mattapoisett (Mass.) Pub. Schs., 1957-58; asst. prof., dir. programming Maine Ednl. TV Network, Orono, 1959-66; assoc. prof. speech communications, dir. TV-Radio instrn. Colo. State U., Ft. Collins, 1969-76, prof., dir. TV-Radio instrn., 1976—; cons. U. Maine, Orono, 1968, Ft. Collins Presbyn. Ch., 1976-78, Sta. KCOL-AM-FM, Ft. Collins, 1978, Pub. Health Assn., Ft. Collins, 1985; archives program guest Maine Pub. Broadcast, Orono, 1983. Served with inf. U.S. Army, 1955-57. Recipient Excellence in Teaching award Mich. State U., 1969, Friend of Broadcasting award Colo. Broadcasters Assn., 1985; named Disting. Vis. Prof. U. Vt., Burlington, 1983, A Teacher Who Makes A Difference Denver's Rocky Mountain News, KCNC-TV, 1987. Mem. NATAS (panel Colo. chpt. 1989—), Broadcast Edn. Assn. (Industry State chmn. 1981-86, panel 1991—, chmn. faculty internship com. 1991—), Colo. Broadcasters Assn. (edn. com. 1972—, Hall of Fame com. 1980—, human resources com. 1991, Friends of Broadcast awrd 1985), We. Speech Comm. Assn., Speech Comm. Assn., Kiwanis (Disting. past pres. 1979-80). Republican. Home: 1407 Country Club Rd Fort Collins CO 80524-1907 Office: Colo State U Dept Speech Communication Fort Collins CO 80523

MACLEAN, EILEEN PANIGEO, state legislator; b. Barrow, Alaska, June 12, 1949; d. Henry and May (Ahmaogak) Panigeo; m. Bryan MacLean, 1969 (div.); children: Tara, Apayang. BA in Edn., U. Alaska, 1975; MEd, U. Alaska/U. Copenhagen, 1984. Tchr. North Slope Borough Sch. Dist., Wainwright, Alaska, 1975-77, curriculum developer, 1977-80; coord. Inupiat hist., culture and lang. North Slope Borough, Barrow, Alaska, 1980-82; pers. officer North Slope Borough, Barrow, 1985-86; dir. Alaska Eskimo Whaling Commn., Barrow, 1982-83, coord. media, 1988-89; liaison Inuit circumpolar conf. Alaska Native Commn., Anchorage, 1984-85; mem. Alaska Ho. Reps., Juneau, 1989—; bd. dirs. Artic Slope Regional Corp; co-chair finance com. Alaska Ho. Reps., Juneau, 1991—, chair econ. task force, 1992—; pres. Inuit Circumpolar Conf., Alaska, Can., Greenland, Russia, 1992—. Co-author: Inupiat Curriculumm 1977-80. Bd. dirs. North Slope Borough Sch. Dist., 1980-83; mem. assembly North Slope Borough, 1987-90. Recipient Shareholder of Yr. award Ukpeagvik Village Corp., Barrow, 1990, Appreciation award Alaska Fedn. Natives for Youth, Anchoragem 1992. Democrat. Presbyterian. Home: 4490 North Star St Barrow AK 99723 Office: State of Alaska Ho Reps State Capital #507 Juneau AK 99801

MACLEAN, STEPHANIE MARIA, psychotherapist; b. Cirencester, Wiltshire, Eng., Jan. 13, 1954; came to U.S. 1961; d. Bronislaus Michael Cecelia (Coogan) S.; m. Kurt Alan Maclean, Apr. 3, 1976. Student, U. Sweden, Uppsala, summer 1974; BA, Calif. State U., Long Beach, 1978; MA, Chapman U., Orange, Calif., 1990. Resource tchr. Norwalk/La Mirada (Calif.) Sch. Dist., 1980-84; travel cons. Apollo Travel, San Pedro, Calif., 1984-85; sr. cons. Jet Propulsion Lab., Pasadena, Calif., 1985-87; fundraising coord. Chapman Clinic, Orange, 1990-92, adminstrv. asst., 1990-92; psychotherapist intern Cervantes Inst., Orange, 1992-93; intern Anguino, Brown and Assocs., Placentia, Calif., 1993—; rsch. asst. Chapman U., Orange, 1991—. Contbr. articles to profl. jours. Mem. Orange County Assn. Marriage and Family Therapists, Behavioral Sci. Soc., Western Psychol. Assn., Psi Chi (chpt. pres. 1989), Alpha Lambda Delta. Democrat. Roman Catholic. Office: Anguino Brown and Assocs 101 S Kramer Blvd Ste 234 Placentia CA 92670

MACLEOD, HUGH ANGUS MCINTOSH, optical science educator, physicist, consultant; b. Glasgow, Scotland, June 20, 1933; came to U.S., 1979; s. John and Agnes (Maclure) M.; m. Ann Turner, May 25, 1957; children: Hugh, Ivor, Charles, Eleanor, Alexander. BSc with honors, U. Glasgow, 1954; D of Tech., Coun. for Nat. Acad. Awards, 1979. Chartered physicist. Grad. apprentice Sperry Gyroscope Co. Ltd., Brentford, Eng., 1954-56, engr., 1956-60; chief engr. Williamson Mfg. Co. Ltd., London, 1961-62; sr. physicist Mervyn Instruments Ltd., Woking, Eng., 1963; tech. mgr. Sir Howard Grubb Parsons & Co. Ltd., Newcastle upon Tyne, Eng., 1964-70; reader in thin-film physics Newcastle upon Tyne Poly., 1971-79; assoc. prof. U. Aix-Marseille III, France, 1979; prof. optical scis. U. Ariz., Tucson, 1979—; pres. Thin Film Ctr., Inc., Tucson, 1992—. Author: Thin-Film Optical Filters, 1986; editor Jour. Modern Optics, London, 1988—; contbr. over 100 articles to profl. jours., chpts. to books. Fellow Inst. Physics (London), Optical Soc. Am. (dir.-at-large 1987-89), SPIE-Internat. Soc. Optical Engring. (Gold medal 1987), Am. Vacuum Soc., Soc. Vacuum Coaters, French Vacuum Soc. Anglican. Home: 2745 E Via Rotunda Tucson AZ 85716-5227 Office: U Ariz Optical Scis Ctr Tucson AZ 85721

MACLEOD, KATHLEEN BROMLEY, internist; b. Oakland, Calif., Mar. 25, 1953; d. LeRoy Alton and Bernice (Doyle) Bromley; m. Glen Earl MacLeod, Dec. 22, 1973. BA in Bacteriology with high honors, U. Calif., Berkeley, 1975; MD, UCLA, 1984. Diplomate Am. Bd. Internal Medicine and Infectious Disease. Staff rsch. assoc. dept. genetics U. Calif., Berkeley, 1976-77; microbiologist bacterial zoonoses br. Bur. Epidemiology, Ctrs. for Disease Control, Atlanta, 1978-80; resident in internal medicine Wadsworth VA Med. Ctr., L.A., 1984-87; fellow in infectious diseases U. Calif.-Irvine Sch. Medicine, Orange, 1987-89; pvt. practice infectious diseases Los Alamitos, Calif., 1989—. Mem. ACP, AMA, Infectious Disease Soc. Am., Am. Soc. Microbiology, Calif. Med. Assn. Home: 6310 E Bay Shore Walk Long Beach CA 90803-5637

MACLEOD, RICHARD PATRICK, foundation administrator; b. Boston, Apr. 2, 1937; s. Thomas Everett and Margaret Gertrude (Fay) MacL.; m. Sarah Frances Mancari, Sept. 7, 1963; children: Kimberly Margaret Hamelin, Richard Alexander MacLeod. BA in Govt., U. Mass., 1960; MA in Internat. Rels., U. So. Calif., 1968. Commd. 2d lt. USAF, 1960, advanced through grades to col., 1981; sr. rsch. fellow The Nat. Def. U., Washington, 1978-79; chief Space Policy Br., dep. chief Plans USAF Aerospace Def. Command, 1979-80; exec. officer to the comdr. in chief USAF Aerospace Def. Command, NORAD, 1980-81; chief of staff NORAD, 1981-84, USAF Space Command, 1982-84; ret. U.S. Space Found., 1985; exec. dir. U.S. Space Found., Colorado Springs, Colo., 1985-88; pres. U.S. Space Found., Colorado Springs, 1988—; bd. dirs. Analytical Surveys, Inc., Colorado Springs, 1985—. Author: Peoples War in Thailand, Insurgency in the Modern World, 1980. Mem. White House Space Policy Adv. Bd.; bd. dirs. Pike's Peak Coun. Boy Scouts Am., Colorado Springs; past pres. Colorado Springs Symphony Coun.; past dir. World Affairs Coun., Colorado Springs. Named Outstanding Young Man Am., 1969; disting. grad. Indsl. Coll. Armed Forces. Fellow Brit. Interplanetary Soc.; mem. AIAA, Air Force Acad. Found. (bd. dirs., trustee), U.S. Space Found. (founding). Office: U S Space Found 2800 S Circle Dr # 2301 Colorado Springs CO 80906

MACLEOD, ROBERT FREDRIC, editor, publisher; b. Chgo., Oct. 15, 1917; s. Ernest F. and Martha W. (Ruzicka) MacL.; children—Merrill, Robert Fredric, E. Jay, Ian. B.A., Dartmouth Coll., 1939. Advt. mgr. Town & Country mag., N.Y.C., 1949; v.p., pub. Harper's Bazaar, N.Y.C., 1950-55, 55-60; v.p., advt. dir. Hearst Mags., N.Y.C., 1960-62; pub. Seventeen mag., N.Y.C., 1962-63; v.p., dir. mktg. Subscription TV Inc., Santa Monica, Calif., 1963-64; editor, pub. 'Teen Mag., Los Angeles, 1965—, now editorial dir., exec. pub.; sr. v.p. Petersen Pub. Co., L.A., 1976—. Served to maj. USMC, 1941-46. Named to Football Hall of Fame, 1977. Club: Bel Air Country. Home: 110 Colony Dr Malibu CA 90265-4814 Office: Teen Mag 8831 W Sunset Blvd West Hollywood CA 90069-2109

MACMILLAN, LOGAN T., JR., petroleum geologist; b. St. Louis, June 18, 1949; s. Logan T. and Suzanne (Medart) MacM.; m. Randa Grisham, Sept. 12, 1975; children: Lauren Anne, Katherine Suzanne. BS in Geol. Engring., Colo. Sch. Mines, 1972, MS in Geology, 1974; MBA, U. Colo., Denver, 1988. Ind. cons. geologist Denver, 1988—. Contbr. tech. and sci. articles to profl. publs. Mem. Colo. Oil and Gas Conservation Commn., Denver, 1992—. Mem. Am. Assn. Petroleum Geologists (cert.), Am. Inst. Profl. Geologists (cert., Disting. Svc. award 1991), Rocky Mountain Assn. Geologists (sec. 1980, 2d v.p. 1992), Geol. Soc. Am., Soc. Petroleum Engrs. Office: 518 17th St Ste 740 Denver CO 80202

MACMILLAN, ROBERT SMITH, electronics engineer; b. L.A., Aug. 28, 1924; s. Andrew James and Moneta (Smith) M.; BS in Physics, Calif. Inst. Tech., 1948, MS in Elec. Engring., 1949, PhD in Elec. Engring. and Physics cum laude, 1954; m. Barbara Macmillan, Aug. 18, 1962; 1 son, Robert G. Rsch. engr. Jet Propulsion lab. Calif. Inst. Tech., Pasadena, 1951-55, asst. prof. elec. engring., 1955-58; assoc. prof. elec. engring. U. So. Calif., L.A., 1958-70; mem. sr. tech. staff Litton Systems, Inc., Van Nuys, Calif., 1969-79; dir. systems engring. Litton Data Command Systems, Agoura Hills, Calif., 1979-89; pres. The Macmillan Group, Tarzana, Calif., 1989—; treas., v.p. Video Color Corp., Inglewood, 1965-66. Cons. fgn. tech. div. USAF, Wright-Patterson AFB, Ohio, 1957-74, Space Tech. Labs., Inglewood, Calif., 1956-60, Space Gen. Corp., El Monte, Calif., 1960-63. With USAAF, 1943-46. Mem. IEEE, Am. Inst. Physics, Am. Phys. Soc., Sigma Xi, Tau Beta Pi, Eta Kappa Nu. Research in ionospheric, radio-wave, propagation; very low frequency radio-transmitting antennas; optical coherence and statist. optics. Home: 350 Starlight Crest Dr La Canada Flintridge CA 91011-2839 Office: The Macmillan Group 5700 Etiwanda Ave Unit 260 Tarzana CA 91356-2546

MACMULLEN, DOUGLAS BURGOYNE, writer, editor, retired army officer, publisher; b. Berkeley, Calif., Dec. 26, 1919; s. T. Douglas and Florence (Burgoyne) MacM.; ed. San Francisco State U., 1937-41, Stanford U., U. Calif., Fgn. Service Inst., Indsl. Coll. of the Armed Forces, Air War Coll., Army Mgmt. Sch.; m. Sherry Bernice Auerbach, Mar. 11, 1942; 1 child, Douglas Burgoyne Jr. Commd. 2d lt. F.A. Res. U.S. Army, 1941; advanced through grades to col. M.I., 1967; Army gen. staff Psychol. Ops. Fgn. Svc., PTO; ret., 1972; exec. editor Am. Rsch. Assoc., Sherman Oaks, Calif.; cons. in communication; accredited corr. Def. Dept. Bd. govs. Monte Vista Grove Homes, Pasadena, Calif., Shriners Hosps. for Crippled Children, L.A.; pres. Clan MacMillan Soc. N.Am., 1973-77, trustee, 1975—; mem. L.A. Olympics Citizens Adv. Commn., 1982-84; mem. L.A. Philanthropic Found.; bd. dirs. Masonic Press Club, Los Angeles, 1975, 84-88; mem. steering com. Mayor Los Angeles Council Internat. Visitors and Sister Cities, 1969; chmn. Los Angeles-Glasgow Sister Cities Ad Hoc Com.; former mem. San Francisco Mayor's Mil. and Naval Affairs Com.; mem. wills and gifts com. Shriners Hosp. Crippled Children, Al Malaikah Temple, Los Angeles, 1974-80; cons.

com. on pub. info. Masons Grand Lodge of Calif., 1985-86. Decorated Legion of Merit, Army Commendation medal (U.S.), Knight Comdr. Order of Polonia Restituta (Free Poland), Red Cross of Constantine; Royal Order Scotland. Mem. Internat. Inst. Strategic Studies, Nat. Mil. Intelligence Assn., Assn. Former Intelligence Officers (pres. L.A. County chpt.), U.S. Naval Inst., Assn. U.S. Army, Company Mil. Historians, Am. Def. Preparedness Assn., St. Andrew's Soc. Los Angeles (past pres., trustee), Air Force Assn., Stanford U. Alumni Assn., Calif. Newspaper Pubs. Assn., Nat. Def. Exec. Res., Sigma Delta Chi. Republican. Presbyterian. Clubs: Press, Caledonian (London); Army & Navy Club (Washington), San Francisco Press. Lodges: Masons (32 deg.), K.T., Shriners (editor, pub. The Al Malaikahan, former imperial news editor Shrine of N.Am.), Quatuor Coronati C.C. Co-author: Psychological Profile of Cambodia, 1971; author-editor: A Sentimental Journey--The History of the First Hundred Years, 1988; numerous other publs. and articles; radio commentator and newspaper columnist on mil., polit. and internat. affairs. Address: PO Box 5201 Sherman Oaks CA 91413

MACNAUGHTON, ANGUS ATHOLE, finance company executive; b. Montreal, Que., Can., July 15, 1931; s. Athole Austin and Emily Kidder (MacLean) MacN.; children: Gillian Heather, Angus Andrew. Student, Lakefield Coll. Sch., 1941-47, McGill U., 1949-54. Auditor Coopers & Lybrand, Montreal, 1949-55; acct. Genstar Ltd., Montreal, 1955; asst. treas. Genstar Ltd., 1956-61, treas., 1961-64, v.p., 1964-70, exec. v.p., 1970-73, pres., 1973-76, vice chmn., chief exec. officer, 1976-81, chmn. or pres., chief exec. officer, 1981-86; pres. Genstar Investment Corp., 1987—; bd. dirs. Can. Pacific Ltd., Sun Life Assurance Co. Can. Ltd., Am. Barrick Resources Corp., Stelco Inc., Varian Assocs. Inc.; past pres. Montreal chpt. Tax Exec. Inst. Bd. govs. Lakefield Coll. Sch.; past chmn. San Francisco Bay Area coun. Boy Scouts Am. Mem. Pacific Union Club, World Trade Club, Villa Taverna (San Francisco), Mt. Royal Club (Montreal), Toronto Club. Office: Genstar Investment Corp Ste 1170 950 Tower Ln Foster City CA 94404-2121 also: Am Barrick Resources Corp, 24 Hazelton Ave, Toronto, ON Canada M5R 2E2

MAC NEIL, JOSEPH NEIL, archbishop; b. Sydney, N.S., Can., Apr. 15, 1924; s. John Martin and Kate (Mac Lean) Mac N. BA, St. Francis Xavier U., Antigonish, N.S., 1944; postgrad., Holy Heart Sem., Halifax, N.S., 1944-48, U. Perugia, 1956, U. Chgo., 1964; JCD, U. St. Thomas, Rome, 1958. Ordained priest Roman Cath. Ch., 1948. Pastor parishes in N.S., 1948-55; officialis Chancery Office, Antigonish, 1958-59; adminstrn. Diocese of Antigonish, 1959-60; rector Cathedral Antigonish, 1961; dir. extension dept. St. Francis Xavier U., Antigonish, 1961-69, v.p., 1962-69; bishop St. John, N.B., Can., 1969-73; chancellor U. St. Thomas, Fredericton, N.B., 1969-73; archbishop of Edmonton, Alta., 1973—; chmn. Alta. Bishops' Conf., 1973—; chmn. bd. Newman Theol. Coll., Edmonton, 1973—, St. Joseph's Coll. U. Alta., Edmonton, 1973—. Vice chmn. N.S. Voluntary Econ. Planning Bd., 1965-69; bd. dirs. Program and Planning Agy., Govt. of N.S., 1969; exec. Atlantic Provinces Econ. Coun., 1968-73, Can. Coun. Rural Devel., 1965-75; bd. dirs. Futures Secretariat, 1981, Ctr. for Human Devel., Toronto, Ont., Can., 1985—; mem. bd. mgmt. Edmonton Gen. Hosp., 1983—; mem. Nat. Com. for Can. Participation in Habitat, 1976. Mem. Canadian Assn. Adult Edn. (past pres. N.S.), Canadian Assn. Dirs. Univ. Extension and Summer Schs. (past pres.), Inst. Research on Public Policy (founding mem.), Can. Conf. Cath. Bishops (pres. 1979-81, mem. com. on ecumenism 1985-91, com. on missions 1991—). Address: Archbishop of Edmonton, 8421 101st Ave, Edmonton, AB Canada T6A 0L1

MAC-NOYE, SHIRLEY, public trust executive; b. Sunland, Calif., Aug. 2, 1940; d. Raymond Leonard Smith and Evelyn Shirley (Lawrence) Maldonado; m. Edward Makraczyk, July 26, 1959 (div. 1966); children: Victoria Ann., Edward Ray; m. Harry Robert Noye, Oct. 7, 1978. Owner, mgr. Playmates Pre-Sch., Lake Havasu City, Ariz., 1964-69; broker Lake Havasu City, Ariz., 1969—; founder, exec. sec. Individuals for Havasu Inc., 1984—; tax agt. Advantage 2000, 1990—; pres., chmn. bd. Citizens Island Bridge Co., Ltd., Lake Havasu City, 1992—. Contbr. newsletter The Havasu Citizen, 1992. Pres. Lake Havasu Bd. Realtors, 1978, chmn, 1982; mem. Mohave County Indsl. Devel. Authority, 1990—, Lake Havasu Comprehensive Plan Com., 1985, Ariz. Town Hall, 1983—; dist. II dir. Mohave County Rep. Ctrl. Com., 1991-92; chmn. Lake Havasu Rep. Women. 1990-91. Named Rep. Woman of Yr., 1991. Office: Citizens Island Bridge Co. Ltd 2178 McCulloch Blvd #9 Lake Havasu City AZ 86403

MACON, JERRY LYN, software company owner; b. Okla., Jan. 10, 1941; s. James Westwood and Mary Isabelle (Hankins) M.; m. Carol Ann Gloeckler, Aug. 28, 1981; children: Heather, Scott, Karla. BS in Physics magna cum laude, Colo. Coll., 1963; MS in Physics, MIT, 1966; MBA in Fin., U. Colo., 1980. Physics instr. U.S. Naval Acad., Annapolis, Md., 1966-69; stockbroker Merrill Lynch, Colorado Springs, 1969-71; dir. systems analysis and programming Colorado Springs Pub. Schs., 1971-80; co-founder, pres. Alpine Software, Inc., Colorado Springs, 1980-82, Macon Systems Inc., Colorado Springs, 1981—. Author software: DB Master, 1980, Advanced DB Master, 1981. Mem. Colorado Springs Fine Arts Ctr., 1982—, Colorado Springs Symphony Coun., 1985—, Colorado Springs Better Bus. Bur., 1990—. Cmdr. USN, 1966-69, USNR, 1959-63, 69-82. Boettcher Found. scholar, 1959; Woodrow Wilson fellow, 1963; MIT rsch. assistantship, 1964. Mem. Colorado Springs Rose Soc., Nat. Fedn. Ind. Bus., Colo. Mountain Club, YMCA of the Pikes Peak Region, Phi Beta Kappa. Office: Macon Systems Inc 724 S Tejon St Colorado Springs CO 80903

MACOVSKI, ALBERT, engineering educator; b. N.Y.C., May 2, 1929; s. Philip and Rose (Winogr) M.; m. Adelaide Paris, Aug. 5, 1950; children—Michael, Nancy. B.E.E., City Coll. N.Y., 1950; M.E.E., Poly. Inst. Bklyn., 1953; Ph.D., Stanford U., 1968. Mem. tech. staff RCA Labs., Princeton, N.J., 1950-57; asst. prof., then asso. prof. Poly. Inst. Bklyn., 1957-60; staff scientist Stanford Research Inst., Menlo Park, Calif., 1960-71; fellow U. Calif. Med. Center San Francisco, 1971-72; prof. elec. engring. and radiology Stanford U., 1972—, endowed chair, Canon USA prof. engring., 1991—; dir. Magnetic Resonance Systems Research Lab.; cons. to industry. Author. Recipient Achievement award RCA Labs., 1952, 54; award for color TV circuits Inst. Radio Engrs., 1958; NIH spl. fellow, 1971. Fellow IEEE (Zworykin award 1973), Am. Inst. Med. Biol. Engring., Optical Soc. Am.; mem. NAE, Inst. of Medicine, Am. Assn. Physicists in Medicine, Soc. Magnetic Resonance in Medicine (trustee), Sigma Xi, Eta Kappa Nu. Jewish. Home: 2505 Alpine Rd Menlo Park CA 94025-6314 Office: Stanford U Dept Elec Engring Stanford CA 94305

MACQUEEN, ROBERT MOFFAT, solar physicist; b. Memphis, Mar. 28, 1938; s. Marion Leigh and Grace (Gilfillan) MacQ.; m. Caroline Gibbs, June 25, 1960; children: Andrew, Marjorie. BS, Rhodes Coll., 1960; PhD, Johns Hopkins U., 1968. Asst. prof. physics Rhodes Coll., 1961-63; instr. physics and astronomy Goucher Coll., Towson, Md., 1964-66; sr. research scientist Nat. Ctr. for Atmospheric Research, Boulder, Colo., 1967-90, dir. High Altitude Obs., 1979-86, asst. dir., 1986-87, assoc. dir., 1987-89; prof. physics Rhodes Coll., Memphis, 1990—; prin. investigator NASA Apollo program, 1971-75, NASA Skylab program, 1970-76, NASA Solar Maximum Mission, 1976-79, NASA/ESA Internat. Solar Polar Mission, 1978-83; lectr. U. Colo., 1968-79, adj. prof., 1979-90; mem. com. on space astronomy Nat. Acad. Scis., 1973-76, mem. com. on space physics, 1977-79; mem. Space Sci. Bd., 1983-86. Recipient Exceptional Sci. Achievement medal NASA, 1974. Fellow Optical Soc. Am.; mem. Am. Astron. Soc. (chmn. solar physics div. 1976-78), Assn. Univ. Research Astronomy (dir.-at-large 1984-93, chmn. bd. 1989-92), Am. Assn. Physics Tchrs., Sigma Xi.

MACUMBER, JOHN PAUL, insurance company executive; b. Macon, Mo., Jan. 21, 1940; s. Rolland Deardorf and Althea Villa (Cason) M.; BA, Cen. Meth. Coll., Fayette, Mo., 1962; Asso. in Risk Mgmt., Ins. Inst. Am., 1978; m. Marilyn Sue Ashe, Nov. 10, 1962; children—Leanne, Cheryl. Casualty underwriter U.S. Fidelity & Guaranty Co., St. Louis, 1962-66; automobile underwriter Am. Indemnity Co., Galveston, Tex., 1966-69; auto casualty underwriter St. Paul Cos., New Orleans, 1969-73; sr. comml. casualty underwriter Chubb/Pacific Indemnity, Portland, Oreg., 1973-75; casualty underwriter Interstate Nat. Corp., L.A., 1975-76, underwriting supr., 1976-78, v.p., br. mgr., Mpls., 1978-82, also v.p. subs. Chgo. Ins. Co.; umbrella/spl. risk supr. Guaranty Nat. Ins. Co., Englewood, Colo., 1982-85; br. mgr. Burns & Wilcox, Ltd.-West, Salt Lake City, 1985—. With USAF, 1962-68. Nat. Methodist scholar, 1958; named Co. Person of Yr. Profl. Ins. Agts Utah, 1991. Mem. Ins. Assn. Utah (sec.-treas. 1992-93), Profl. Ins. Agts. Utah, Ind. Ins. Agts. Utah, Surplus Line Assn. Utah, Nat. Assn. Profl. Surplus Lines Offices. Republican. Mem. Unity Ch. of Salt Lake City (v.p., bd. dirs. 1988). Lodges: Optimists (charter pres. 1968) (Friendswood, Tex.); Kiwanis (charter pres. 1979) (Bloomington, Minn.). Clubs: Insurance, Blue Goose (Salt Lake City). Home: 9683 Buttonwood Dr Sandy UT 84092-3245 Office: 420 E South Temple Ste 330 Salt Lake City UT 84111-1314

MACY, JONATHAN ISAAC, ophthalmologist, educator; b. N.Y.C., Sept. 28, 1950; s. Isaac Glass and Florence Goodblatt; m. Jeannette Meerovich, Nov. 28, 1976; children: Alexandra, Adam. BA magna cum laude, Boston U., 1972, MD, 1976. Diplomate Am. Bd. Ophthalmology, Am. Coll. Surgeons., Nat. Bd. Med. Examiners. Intern LAC-U. So. Calif. Med. Ctr., L.A., 1976-77, resident ophthalmology, 1978-81; rsch. fellow Estelle Doheny Eye Found., L.A., 1977-78; clin. instr. Jules Stein Eye Inst. U. So. Calif., L.A., 1981-84, clin. instr. dept. ophthalmology, 1982-85, asst. clin. prof. Jules Stein Eye Inst., 1984—, asst. clin. prof. dept. ophthalmology, 1985—; chief dept. ophthalmology Midway Hosp. Med. Ctr., L.A., 1986-87, vice chief of staff, 1988-89, chief of staff, 1990-91; Bd. dirs. Midway Hosp. Med. Ctr., 1987—, Myasthenia Gravis Found., 1981—; med. adv. bd. Lions Doheny Eye Bank, 1990—, Myasthenia Gravis Found., 1986—; rsch. assoc. Discovery Fund for Eye Rsch., 1986—. Contbr. articles to numerous profl. jours. Exec. bd. Physicians Who Care, 1986-87; bd. dirs. Found. for the Jr. Blind, 1986—. Fellow Am. Physicians, Am. Acad. Ophthalmology, Am. Coll. Surgeons; mem. Am. Soc. Cataract and Refractory Surgery, Nat. MarfanFound., Calif. Assn. Ophthalmology, Calif. Med. Assn., Internat. Clin. Contact Lenses Soc., Internat., Cornea Soc., Internat. Soc. Refractory Keratoplasty, Lions Eye Found., L.A. County Med. Assn., L.A. Soc. Ophthalmology (Merit award for original rsch.), Pan-Am. Assn. Ophthalmology, World Med. Assn., UCLS Alumni Assn., UCLA Dept. Ophthalmology Assn., U. So. Calif./Doheny Residents Assn., U. So. Calif. Profl. Practice Assn., Sjogrens Found. L.A., Phi Beta Kappa, Psi Chi. Office: Am Eye Inst 8635 W Third St # 390W Los Angeles CA 90048

MACY, MICHAEL GAYLORD, financial management consultant; b. Paris, Jan. 29, 1957; s. Homer E. and Arlita M. (Lowis) M.; m. Patricia Jean Beeman, May 10, 1989. BA in Bus., Wash. State U., 1980, MBA, 1981. Supr. receivable finance examiners 1st Interstate Bank of Oreg., Portland, 1981-82, sr. cons. cash. mgmt., 1982-84; br. mgr. 1st Independent Bank, Vancouver, Wash., 1985-87; finance mgr. Clark County, Vancouver, 1987-91; fiscal svcs. mgr. Human Svcs. Coun., Vancouver, 1991—; pres. Macy & Co., Vancouver, 1990—. Author: Banking Services, 1989. Bd. dirs. Human Svc. Coun., Vancouver, 1990-91, Clark Care and Devel. Ctr., Vancouver, 1988-91; bd. dirs., treas. Evergreen Bus. Assn., Vancouver, 1988-89; bd. dirs., pres. Wesley Found. Corp., Pullman, 1980. Named Achievement Winner Nat. Assn. Counties, 1989. Mem. Portland Treas. Mgmt. Assn., Treas. Mgmt. Assn. (cert. cash mgr.). Home and Office: PO Box 6161 Vancouver WA 98668-6161

MACY, RICHARD J., state judge; b. Saranac Lake, N.Y., June 2, 1930; m. Emily Ann Macy; children: Anne, Patty, Mark. BS in Bus., U. Wyo., 1955, JD, 1958. Pvt. practice Sundance, Wyo., 1958-85; judge Wyo. Supreme Ct., Cheyenne, 1985—; Crook County atty., 1970-85; mem. Nat. Conf. Commrs. on Uniform State Laws, 1982—. Mem. Sigma Chi (Nat. Outstanding Sig award 1986). Office: Wyo Supreme Ct Supreme Ct Bldg Cheyenne WY 82002*

MADABHUSHI, GOVINDACHARI VENKATA, civil engineer; b. Guntur, India, Oct. 13, 1933; came to U.S., 1974; s. Narasimhachari Vedantam and Venkatamma M. MSCE, W.Va. U., 1966; PhD, Utah State U., 1985. Registered profl. engr., Calif. Asst. engr. Bhubaneswar Dept. Pub. Works, Orissa, India, 1957-61; instr. Coll. Engring. Duke U., Durham, N.C., 1961-63; rsch. scholar Indian Inst. Tech., Bombay, 1967-69; lectr. in civil engring. Victoria Jubilee Tech. Inst., Bombay, 1969-74; water resources engr. Ark. Soil and Water Conservation, Little Rock, 1977-80; rsch. asst. Utah Water Rsch. Lab., Logan, 1980-83, Assn. Western Univs., Salt Lake City, 1983-84; water resources control engr. Regional Water Quality Control Bd., Riverside, Calif., 1985-86; assoc. waste mgmt. engr. Dept. Toxic Substances Ctrl., Calif. EPA (formerly Berkeley Dept. Health Svcs.), 1986—; mem. shallow founds. cod of practice Indian Standards Inst., New Delhi, 1969. Author profl. conf. procs. Mem. ASCE (ground water sect., mem. earthquake lifeline). Home: 2856 Fruitvale Ave Apt 41 Oakland CA 94601-2043 Office: Dept Toxic Substances Ctrl CA EPA 700 Heinz Ave Bldg F Berkeley CA 94710-2721

MADDEN, GEORGE GRAHAM, orthotist, prosthetist; b. Orange, N.J., Dec. 19, 1947; s. George Graham and Evelyn (Marsh) M.; m. Kathleen Lina Vernell, May, 1970 (div. Nov. 1976); m. Audrey Christine Cutler, July 2, 1978. BBA, U. Mo., 1970; MA in Exercise Physiology, U. No. Colo., 1974; BS in Prosthetics, U. Wash., 1982. Cert. orthotist, prosthetist, U.S., Can. Prosthetist, orthotist Orthotic/Prosthetic Corp., Loveland, Colo., 1983-84; prosthetist, orthotist Fredrickson Orthopedics, Bismarck, N.D., 1984-85; asst. dir. orthotics, prosthetics Sharp Meml. Hosp., San Diego, 1985-88; dir. orthotics, prosthetics Alberta Children's Hosp., Calgary, 1988-90; dir. orthotics dept. Loma Linda (Calif.) U. Med. Ctr., 1990-91, dir. prothetics, 1990-93; pres. Summit Prosthetics, Orthotics & Rehab. Tech., Missoula, Mont., 1993—; cons. Orthotics/Prosthetics Assn., Crestline, Calif., 1990-91. Contbr. articles to profl. jours. Inventor in field. Mem. Am. Acad. of Orthotists/Prosthetists, Can. Assn. Prosthetists/Orthotists, Alberta Assn. Orthotists/Prosthetists.

MADDEN, J. PATRICK, agricultural economics educator; b. Merrill, Oreg., July 20, 1937; s. John Joseph and Ruth Elizabeth (Lommasson) M.; children: Kathryn, Lenia, Theresa, John, Jennifer. B.S., Oreg. State U., 1959; Ph.D., Iowa State U., 1962. Economist, U. P.R., Rio Piedras, 1962-63; agrl. economist Econ. Research Service, U.S. Dept. Agr., Washington, 1963-66; economist, Nat. Adv. Com. on Rural Poverty, Washington, 1966-67; prof. agrl. econs. Pa. State U., University Park, 1967-75, 76-88; founding dir. Nat. Sustainable Agrl. Rsch. and Edn. Program, 1988; assoc. dir. office of pres. U. Calif., 1989—; founder, exec. v.p. World Sustainable Agriculture Assn., 1991—; sr. social scientist Abt Assocs., Inc., Cambridge, Mass., 1975-76; cons. project on alt. agriculture Nat. Acad. of Scis., 1986-87; mgr. fed. research and edn. program on alternative farming systems, 1988—. Editor: Beyond Pesticides, 1992, Alternative Agriculture, 1989, Sustainable Agricultural Rsch and Edn. in the Field, 1991; contbr. 17 articles to profl. jours. Minister, Ann Ree Colton Found. of Niscience, Glendale, Calif., 1978—. NSF fellow, 1960; Iowa State Alumni Achievement Fund fellow, 1959; Alpha Zeta fellow, 1959. Mem. Am. Econ. Assn., Inst. for Alternative Agr., Am. Agrl. Econ. Assn., Ecol. Econs. Assn. Avocations: woodworking, composing music; writing poetry. Home: 1153 Melrose Ave Glendale CA 91202-2872 Office: PO Box 10338 Glendale CA 91209

MADDEN, PALMER BROWN, lawyer; b. Milw., Sept. 19, 1945; m. Susan L. Paulus, Mar. 31, 1984. BA, Stanford U., 1968; JD, U. Calif., Berkeley, 1973. Bar: Calif. 1973, U.S. Dist. Ct. (no. dist.) Calif. 1973, U.S. Supreme Ct. 1982. Ptnr. McCutchen, Doyle Brown & Enersen, Walnut Creek, 1985—. Judge pro term Contra Costa Superior Ct., 1991—. Mem. Contra Costa County Bar Assn. (bd. dirs. 1987—, pres. 1993—). Democrat. Episcopalian. Office: McCutchen Doyle Brown 1331 N California St Walnut Creek CA 94596-5028

MADDEN, PAUL DANIEL, engineering company executive; b. Mansfield, Ohio, June 19, 1948; s. Paul Carl and Jean Ann (Crager) M.; m. Shirley Jean Boreman, June 21, 1970; children: Paul Andrew, Jennifer Renee. BSEE, Ohio U., 1970; postgrad., W. Va. U., 1970-76. Registered profl. engr. Staff engr. energy systems Union Carbide Corp., South Charleston, W.Va., 1970-81; tech. adviser Esso Inter Am., Aruba, Netherlands Antilles, 1981-84; engring. dir. ITT, Galion, Ohio, 1984-88; owner, mgr. Retail Bus., Mansfield, 1981—; v.p. engring., R & D EPE Technologies, Inc., Costa Mesa, Calif., 1988-91; pres. Energy Techs., Mansfield, Ohio, 1991—; mgr. Intelec Internat. Telecommunications Energy Conf., 1987—; instr. W.Va. State Coll., 1971-74, W.Va. Coll. Grad. Studies, 1974-81, both in Nitro. Author: Uninterruptible Power, 1989; inventor advanced control system; contbr. tech. papers to profl. publs. Solicitor Charleston United Way, 1973-75; Cubmaster Aruba area Boy Scouts Am., 1981-84; bd. dirs. Seroe Colo. Ch., Aruba, 1981-84. Mem. IEEE, Nat. Soc. Profl. Engrs., Tustin Tennis Club. Republican. Presbyterian.

MADDEN, PAUL ROBERT, lawyer; b. St. Paul, Nov. 13, 1926; s. Ray Joseph and Margaret (Meyer) M.; m. Rosemary R. Sorel, Aug. 7, 1974; children: Margaret Jane, William, James Patrick, Derek R. Sorel, Lisa T. Sorel. Student, St. Thomas Coll., 1944; AB, U. Minn., 1948; JD, Georgetown U., 1951. Bar: Ariz. 1957, Minn. 1951, D.C. 1951. Assoc. Hamilton & Hamilton, Washington, 1951-55; legal asst. to commr. SEC, Washington, 1955-56; assoc. Lewis and Roca, Phoenix, Ariz., 1957-59, ptnr., 1959-90; ptnr. Beus, Gilbert & Morrill, Phoenix, 1991—. Sec. Minn. Fedn. Coll. Rep. Clubs, 1947-48; chmn. 4th dist. Minn. Young Rep. Club, 1948; nat. co-chmn. Youth for Eisenhower, 1951-52; mem. Ariz. Rep. Com., 1960-62; past chmn., bd. dirs. Camelback Behavioral Health Svcs., Scottsdale, Ariz.; bd. dirs. Found. Jr. Achievement Ctrl. Ariz., Cath. Community Found., Phoenix, Heritage Hills Homeowners Assn.; The Samaritan Found., Phoenix; past bd. dirs. Camelback Charitable Trust; past bd. dirs., past. pres. Ariz. Club, Phoenix, 1990-93; bd. dirs., past chmn. Found. for Sr. Living, Phoenix; bd. dirs., vice chmn., Cen. Ariz. chpt. ARC; past bd. dirs., past pres. Jr. Achievement Cen. Ariz., Inc. With USNR, 1946-48. Mem. ABA, Ariz. Bar Assn., Maricopa County Bar Assn., Fed. Bar Assn., Fedn. Ins. Counsel, Nat. Health Lawyers Assn., Am. Soc. Hosp. Attys., Nat. Assn. Bond Lawyers, Ariz. Assn. for Indsl. Devel., East Valley Partnership, Phi Delta Phi. Clubs: The Barristers (Washington), Arizona. Home: 5847 N 46th St Phoenix AZ 85018-1234 Office: 3200 N Central Ave Ste 1000 Phoenix AZ 85012-2430

MADDEN, RICHARD BLAINE, forest products educator; b. Short Hills, N.J., Apr. 27, 1929; s. James L. and Irma (Twining) M.; m. Joan Fairbairn, May 24, 1958; children: John Richard, Lynn Marie, Kathryn Ann, Andrew Twining. B.S., Princeton U., 1951; J.D., U. Mich., 1956; M.B.A., NYU, 1959. Bar: Mich. 1956, N.Y. 1958. Gen. asst. treas.'s dept. Socony Mobil Oil Corp., N.Y.C., 1956-57; spl. asst. Socony Mobil Oil Corp., 1958-59, fin. rep., 1960; asst. to pres. Mobil Chem. Co.; also dir. Mobil Chems. Ltd. of Eng., 1960-63; exec. v.p., gen. mgr. Kordite Corp.; also v.p. Mobil Plastics, 1963-66; v.p. Mobil Chem. Co., N.Y.C., 1966-68; group v.p. Mobil Chem. Co., 1968-70; asst. treas. Mobil Oil Corp., 1970-71; chmn. Mobil Oil Estates Ltd., 1970-71; pres., chief exec. to chmn., chief exec. officer Potlatch Corp., San Francisco, 1971—; bd. dirs. Pacific Gas and Electric Co., Consolidated Freightways, Inc., URS Corp., Del Monte Corp., AMFAC Inc., Bank Calif. N.A. and BankCal Tri-State Corp.; from lectr. to adj. assoc. prof. fin. NYU, 1960-63. Bd. dirs. Am. Forest and Paper Assn., Nat. Park Found., Smith-Kettlewell Eye Rsch. Inst.; trustee emeritus Am. Enterprise Inst.; bd. govs., mem. exec. com. San Francisco Symphony; trustee Fine Arts Mus. San Francisco; bd. mem. exec. com. Bay Area Coun.; mem. Bus.-Higher Edn. Forum. Lt. (j.g.) USNR, 1951-54. Mem. N.Y. Bar Assn., Mich. Bar Assn. Roman Catholic. Clubs: University (N.Y.C.); Pacific Union (San Francisco), Bohemian (San Francisco); Lagunitas (Ross, Calif.); Metropolitan (Washington). *

MADDEN, WANDA LOIS, gerontology nurse; b. Augusta, Kans., Apr. 26, 1929; d. George W. and Lillian B. (Dobyns) Provost; m. Laurence R. Madden, June 3, 1947 (div. 1961); children: Matthew, Mark, Luke, John, Michele. ADN, Pasadena City Coll., 1970; postgrad., Calif. State U. Consortium, 1986. RN, Calif. CCU nurse Huntington Meml. Hosp., Pasadena, Calif., 1970-71; ICU Community Hosp., Pico Rivera, Calif., 1971-72; CCU nurse Queen of the Valley Hosp., West Covina, Calif., 1973-74; ICU supr. Visalia (Calif.) Community Hosp., 1974-77, 89-90, ICU nurse, 1978; ICU nurse San Miguel Hosp. Assn., San Diego, 1978-79; supr. Casa Blanca Corp., San Diego, 1979-80; dir. nursing Visalia Convalescence Hosp., 1981-89, Westgate Gardens Convalescent Ctr., Visalia, 1990; psychiat. staff nurse Mill Creek Hosp., Visalia, 1990-91. Home: 2725 N Canary Dr Visalia CA 93291-1719

MADDOX, ROBERT ALLEN, clergyman; b. Tooele, Utah, Dec. 19, 1953; s. Ernest Clyde Maddox and Shirley (Kinnee) Wedekind; m. Judith Ann Kennedy, Apr. 6, 1974; children: Ranae, Ben, Laura, Tiffany, Emilie. BS in Criminology, Calif. State U., Fresno, 1975; postgrad., Internat. Christian Grad. U., 1980. Area dir. Campus Crusade for Christ, Portland, Oreg., 1982-91; pastor Good Shepherd Community Ch., Portland, 1991—; adj. faculty Multnomah Sch. of Bible, Portland, 1986—; motivational speaker. Oreg. dir. Network nat. orgn. for youth workers, 1986-89. Republican. Home: 3903 SE Douglass Ct Troutdale OR 97060 Office: Good Shepherd Community Ch 28986 SE Haley Rd Boring OR 97009

MADDY, DONALD LEE, computer company executive, programming consultant; b. Whittier, Calif., Aug. 27, 1949; s. Keith Thomas and Colleen Joanne (Barlow) M.; m. Lynne Louise Juhnke, June 29, 1985; children: Crystal Lynne, Michael Donald. Nuclear weapons, electronics student, Sandia AFB, 1970; BS in Computer Sci., Calif. State U., Sacramento, 1976. Cert. Data Processor. Nuclear weapons electronics specialist U.S. Army, Istanbul, Turkey, 1970-71; programmer Water Resources Control Bd. Div. Water Quality, Sacramento, 1974-75, Calif. State Coll., Bakersfield, 1976-78; programmer, analyst Sierra Pacific Power Co., Reno, Nev., 1979-80; sr. programmer, analyst State of Idaho Transp. Dept., Boise, 1980-81, United Grocers Warehouse, Oakland, Calif., 1981-84; sr. programming cons. Farmers Savings & Loan, Davis, Calif., 1984-87, Pacific Gas & Electric Co., Avila Beach, Calif., 1987—. Co-author: Computer Software Security System for Plant Info. Mgmt. System, 1992. With U.S. Army, 1969-72. Mem. Am. Nuclear Soc. Republican. Office: The Maddy Corp 1220 16th St Los Osos CA 93402-1422

MADDY, PENELOPE JO, philosophy educator; b. Tulsa, July 4, 1950; d. Richard and Suzanne (Lorimer) Parsons. BA in Math., U. Calif., Berkeley, 1972; PhD in Philosophy, Princeton U., 1979. Asst. prof. U. Notre Dame (Ind.), 1978-83; assoc. prof. U. Ill., Chgo., 1983-87; assoc. prof. U. Calif., Irvine, 1987-89, prof., 1989—, dept. chair, 1991—; mem. editorial bd. Jour. Philos. Logic, 1985—. Author: Realism in Mathematics, 1990; editor Notre Dame Jour. Formal Logic, 1979-84, editorial bd., 1984—. Fellow AAUW, 1982-83, U. Calif., 1988-89; NSF grantee, 1986, 88-89, 90-91; Marshall scholar, 1982-83, Westinghouse Sci. scholar, 1968-72. Mem. Assn. for Symbolic Logic (mem. exec. com. 1993—), Am. Philos. Assn. Office: U Calif Dept Philosophy Irvine CA 92717

MADER, CHARLES LAVERN, chemist; b. Dewey, Okla., Aug. 8, 1930; s. George Edgar and Naomia Jane (Harer) M.; m. Emma Jean Sinclair, June 12, 1960; 1 child, Charles L. II. BS, Okla. State U., 1952, MS, 1954; PhD, Pacific Western U., 1980. Fellow Los Alamos (N.Mex.) Nat. Lab., 1950—; sr. fellow JIMR, U. Hawaii, Honolulu, 1985—; pres. Mader Consulting Co., Honolulu, 1985—. Author: Numerical Modeling of Detonation, 1979, Numerical Modeling of Water Waves, 1988, LASL Data Volumes, 1980-82; contbr. 52 articles to profl. jours.; author 70 reports. Scoutmaster Boys Scouts Am., Los Alamos, 1971-85. Fellow Am. Inst. Chemists; mem. Am. Chem. Soc., Am. Phys. Soc., Combustion Inst., Tsumanmi Soc. (editor 1985—), Marine Tech. Soc., Sigma Xi, Pi Mu Epsilon, Phi Lambda Upsilon. Democrat. Methodist. Home: 1049 Kamehame Dr Honolulu HI 96825-2860 Office: Mader Cons Co Honolulu HI 96825

MADER, KELLY FORBES, public policy executive, senator; b. Sheridan, Wyo., Jan. 21, 1952; s. Richard August and Ena Cora (Forbes) M.; m. Nancy Gay Murray, Nov. 16, 1975; children: Amy, Angie, Ian. Student, Bob Jones U., 1970-71, Grace Coll., 1971-72, Tex. A&M U. Owner, pres. Kelly F. Mader & Assocs., Gillette, Wyo., 1973—; rep. Wyo. State Legis., Cheyenne, 1982-84, senator, 1984-91; chmn. senate appropriations com., 1989-91; co-chmn. joint appropriations com.; chmn. Senate Rep. Conf., 1988-90. Officer Campbell County Sheriffs Res., Gillette, 1981-91, Campbell County Search and Rescue Team, Gillette 1981-91. Named one of Outstanding Young Men of Am., 1982, 85, 89. Mem. Am. Legis. Exch. Coun. (state chmn. 1984-91, nat. bd. dirs. 1991-92, Outstanding Legis. Leader award 1989), NRA. Republican.

MADISON, KENNETH EDWARD, career officer; b. Pensacola, Fla., Oct. 3, 1957; s. Willie James and Mary Francis (Tate) M.; m. Bonny Lou Ard, Apr. 10, 1984; children: Temeka S., Christopher M., Jazzlyn N. Assocs., C.C. of the Air Force, 1991; student, Colo. Christian U. Enlisted USAF, 1975, advanced through grades to Master Sgt., 1990; adminstrv. specialist U.S. Mil. Tng. Mission, Riyadh, Saudi Arabia, 1981-82; mgr. unsatisfactory reports Def. Nuclear Agy. Kirtland AFB, Albuquerque, 1982-85; info. mgr. USAF Spl. Activity Squadron, Naples, Italy, 1985-87, chief info. mgmt., 1987-88; air def. ops. info. mgr. Peterson AFB, Colorado Springs, Colo., 1988-89; chief info. mgmt., vice dir. Cheyenne Mountain AFB, Colorado Springs, 1991-92; supt. personnel info. mgmt. Peterson AFB, Colorado Springs, 1992—. Sec. King Solomon Bapt. Ch. Brotherhood, Colorado Springs, 1991-92, Peterson AFB Gospel Svc. Brotherhood, Peterson AFB, Colo., 1991-92. Mem. Protective Order of Elks (asst. sec. 1991), Prince Hall Free and Accepted Masons, Noncommd. Officers Assn., Air Force Sgts. Assn., Sr. Noncommd. Officers Orgn. (mem. chair 1992), Protestant Men of the Chapel. Democrat. Home: USAF Acad Quarters 6303E E Elderberry Dr Colorado Springs CO 80840 Office: HQ/NORAD/J3E Stop 3240 Peterson AFB CO 80914-3240

MADISON, MILES, periodontist, educator; b. Tehran, Iran, May 12, 1965; came to U.S., 1979; s. Mahmoud and Sharifeh (Kashani) Mehdizadeh. AA, Santa Monica Coll., 1983; BS, U. So. Calif., 1985; DDS, UCLA, 1989; cert. in peridontology, U. Calif., San Francisco, 1991. Pvt. practice L.A., 1991—; vis. lectr. Sch. Dentistry, UCLA, 1991—. Recipient UCLA Alumni award, 1989. Mem. ADA, Am. Acad. Periodontology, Am. Acad. Gen. Dentistry, Calif. Dental Assn., Calif. Soc. Periodontists, Omicron Kappa Upsilon. Republican. Jewish.

MADIX, ROBERT JAMES, chemical engineer, educator; b. Beach Grove, Ind., June 22, 1938; s. James L. and Marjorie A. (Strohl) M.; children: Bradley Alan, David Eric, Michella, Evan Scott. BS, U. Ill., 1961; PhD, U. Calif., 1964. NSF post doctoral fellow Max Planck Inst., Gottingen, Fed. Republic of Germany, 1964-65; asst. prof. chem. engr. Stanford (Calif.) U., 1965-72, assoc. prof., chem. engr., 1972-77; prof. chem. engring. Stanford U., 1977—, chmn., chem. engr., 1983-87, prof. chemistry, 1981—; cons. Monsanto Chem., St. Louis, 1975-84, Shell Oil Co., Houston, 1985-86; Peter Debye lectorship Cornell U., 1985; Eyring lectr. chemistry Ariz. State U., 1990. Contbr. articles to profl. jours. Recipient Alpha Chi Sigma award Am. Inst. Chem. Engrs., 1990, Paul Emmett award Catalysis Soc. N.Am., 1984, Humboldt U.S. Sr. Scientist prize, 1978; For Found. fellow, 1969-72. Mem. Am. Chem. Soc., Am. Vacuum Soc., Calif. Catalysis Soc. (assoc. editor catalysis revs. 1986—). Office: Stanford Univ Dept Chemical Engring Stanford CA 94305

MADNI, ASAD MOHAMED, engineering executive; b. Bombay, Sept. 8, 1947; came to U.S., 1966; s. Mohamed Taher and Sara Taher (Wadiwalla) M.; Gowhartaj Shahnawaz, Nov. 11, 1976; 1 child, Jamal Asad. Gen. cert. edn., U. Cambridge, Bombay, 1964; AAS in Electronics, RCA Insts., Inc., 1968; BS in Engring., UCLA, 1969, MS in Engring., 1972; postgrad. exec. inst., Stanford U., 1984; cert. in engring. mgmt., Calif. Inst. Tech., 1987; PhD in Engring., Calif. Coast U., 1987; sr. exec. program, MIT, 1990. Sr. instr. Pacific States U., L.A., 1969-71; electronics auditor Pertec Corp., Chatsworth, Calif., 1973-75; project engr., sr. engr., program mgr, dir. advanced program Microwave div. Systron Donner, Van Nuys, Calif., 1975-82, dir. engring., 1982-92; gen. mgr. Microwave and Instrument div. Systron Donner, Van Nuys, Calif., 1985-90; chmn., pres., chief exec. officer Systron Donner Corp., 1990-92; pres., CEO Sensors and Controls Group BEI Electronics, Inc., 1992—; vice chmn. IEEE-MTTS, San Fernando Valley chpt., 1991-92, chmn., 1992—; tech. advisor Test and Measurement World, Boston, 1986. Mem. editorial rev. bd., West coast chmn. Microwave Systems News and Communications Tech., 1982-90; contbr. more than 50 articles to numerous tech. publs.; patentee in field. Mem. IEEE (sr.), Assn. Old Crows (life, Gold Cert. Merit 1992), NRA (life), Calif. Rifle and Pistol Assn. (life), MIT Soc. Sr. Execs. (life). Home: 3281 Woodbine St Los Angeles CA 90064-4836 Office: Systron Donner Corp 13100 Telfair Ave Sylmar CA 91342

MADRID, LEASHER DENNIS, psychology educator; b. Trinidad, Colo., Apr. 27, 1949; s. Leasher and Helen Febe (Sandoval) M.; m. Mary Celeste Pacheco, Dec. 11, 1971; children: Derrick Kevin, Valerie Beth. BA in Psychology, U. So. Colo., 1972; MS in Psychology, Highlands U., 1976; PhD in Psychology, U. Calif., Santa Barbara, 1981; postgrad., U. Kans., 1986. Counselor Colo. State Hosp., Pueblo, 1975-76; asst. prof. mental health U. So. Colo., Pueblo, 1976-82; assoc. prof. psychology U. So. Colo., 1982-90, prof. psychology, 1990—; project rsch. cons. Kansas City Sch. Dist. 500, 1985-86; chair evaluation panel behavioral and social scis. Ford Found./NRC, Georgetown, Wash. and Washington, 1989-91. Author chpts. in books; contbr. articles to profl. jours. Mentor Sch. Dist. 60, Pueblo, 1987-89. U. Calif. fellow, 1978-81, U. Kans. fellow, 1985-86. Mem. N.Y. Acad. Scis., Assn. for Behavior Analysis, Colo. Assn. for Bilingual Edn. Office: U So Colo 2200 Bonforte Blvd Pueblo CO 81001-4990

MADRIL, LEE ANN, writer; b. Burbank, Calif., Sept. 16, 1944; d. George Mathew McDougall; 1 child, Francis Michael. Student, Granada Hills (Calif.) Coll., 1962. Freelance writer, 1986-90; shoot out artist Bad Co., Auburn, Calif., 1990—; cons. in authenticity, Calif. State Horsemen, Santa Rosa, 1988-90, Bad Co., 1990; staff writer Just Horses, Idaho State Mag. Contbr. articles to jours. Vol. Red Cross, Soques, Calif., 1982, Salinas (Calif.) Valley Meml. Hosp., 1979, Indian Valley Fire Dept. Ladies Aux., Humane Soc. U.S. Recipient Kodak KINSA award, 1989. Mem. Calif. State Horseman's Assn. (state champion 1989-90), Silver Spurs. Republican. Roman Catholic.

MADSEN, ARCH LEONARD, broadcasting company executive; b. Provo, Utah, Dec. 4, 1913; s. Parley William and Christina Little (Nuttall) M.; m. Margaret Dee Higginbotham, Mar. 30, 1938; children: Erik Higginbotham, Margaret Francis Madsen, Alan Leonard, Maren Christina Madsen Williams, Anita Maude Madsen Bennett. Student, Brigham Young U., 1932-33, 34-35, U. Mont., 1934, U. Utah, 1936; hon. doctorate, U. Utah, 1984. Dir. mem. svcs. Radio Advt. Bur., N.Y.C., 1953-57; asst. gen. mgr. Sponsor mag., N.Y.C., 1957-58; asst. mgr. Sta. WLS, Chgo., 1958-59; assoc. dir. Assn. Maximum Svc. Telecasters, Washington, 1959-61, bd. dirs., 1968-81; pres. Radio Svc. Corp. of Utah, Salt Lake City, 1961-64; pres. Bonneville Internat. Corp., Salt Lake City, 1964-85, pres. emeritus, 1985—; chmn. Broadcast adv. bd. UPI, N.Y.C., 1976-81; mem. U.S. Bd. for Internat. Broadcasting, 1983-87, 88-90. Chmn. Utah Exec. Reorgn. Com., Salt Lake City, 1977-82; bd. visitors John S. Knight Fellowship Program, Stanford U., 1980-87; Japan-U.S. Friendship Commn. 1978-84. Recipient Disting. Svc. to State Govt. award Nat. Govs. Assn., 1980, Minuteman award Utah N.G., 1983; named Businessman of Yr. Utah Mfrs. Assn., 1973. Mem. Nat. Assn. Broadcasters (chmn. internat. com. 1979-85, Disting. Svc. award 1981), World Press Freedom Com. (co-vice chmn. 1980—). Mem. LDS Ch. Lodge: Rotary. Home: 1510 Canterbury Dr Salt Lake City UT 84108-2833 Office: Bonneville Internat Corp Broadcast House 5 Triad Ctr PO Box 1160 Salt Lake City UT 84110-1160

MADSEN, WILLIAM WALLACE, mechanical engineer, business executive; b. Rolla, Mo., May 7, 1962; s. Robert Ashley and Caroline (Stewart) M.; m. Stacee Lin Stanley, Oct. 15, 1988; 1 child, Kyle William. BS in ME, U. Utah, 1985; MS in ME, Brigham Young U., 1988; MBA, U. Pa., 1990. Mech. engr. Parker Packing, West Valley, Utah, 1985-86, sr. test engr., 1986; mgmt. assoc. TRW Corp. Offices, Lyndhurst, Ohio, 1990-91, TRW Space & Def. Internat., Redondo Beach, Calif., 1991, TRW Space & Tech. Group, Redondo Beach, 1991, TRW Electronic Systems Group, Redondo Beach, 1991-92, TRW Fuji Valve, Seiverville, Tenn., 1992; mfg. team leader Electronics Divsn. TRW Transp., Marshall, Ill., 1992. Asst. scoutmaster Boy Scouts Am., Mayfield Heights, Ohio, 1990, Knoxville, Tenn., 1992, scoutmaster, Redondo Beach, 1991. Mem. Pi Tau Sigma. Mormon. Home: 1490 Federal Heights Dr Salt Lake City UT 84103

MAEDA, J. A., data processing executive; b. Mansfield, Ohio, Aug. 24, 1940; d. James Shunso and Doris Lucille (Moore) M.; m. Robert Lee Hayes (div. May 1970); 1 child, Brian Sentaro Hayes. BS in Math., Purdue U., 1962, postgrad., 1962-63; postgrad., Calif. State U., Northridge, 1968-75; cert. profl. designation in tech. of computer operating systems and tech. of info. processing, UCLA, 1971. Cons., rsch. asst. computer ctr. Purdue U., West Lafayette, Ind., 1962-63; computer operator, sr. tab operator, mem. faculty Calif. State U., Northridge, 1969, programmer cons., tech. asst. II, 1969-70, supr. acad. applicatons, EDP supr. II, 1970-72, project tech. support coord. programmer II, office of the chancellor, 1972-73, tech. support coord. statewide timesharing tech. support, programmer II, 1973-74, acad. coord., tech. support coord. instrn., computer cons. III, 1974-83; coord. user svcs. info. ctr., mem. tech. staff IV CADAM INC subs. Lockheed Corp., Burbank, Calif., 1983-86, coord. end user svcs., tech. specialist computing dept., 1986-87; v.p., bd. dirs. Rainbow Computing Inc., Northridge, 1976-85; bd. dirs. Aki Tech/Design Cons., Northridge; mktg. mgr. thaumaturge Taro Quipu Cons., Northridge, 1987—; tech. cons. Digital Computer Cons., Chatsworth, Calif., 1988; cons. computer tech., fin. and bus. mgmt., systems integration, 1988-90; tech. customer s/w support Collection Data Systems, Westlake, Calif., 1991; tech. writer Sterling Software Dylakor Div., 1992—. Author over 200 user publs., 98 computer user publs., basic computer programming language, reference manuals, user guides; contbr. articles, papers, photos to profl. jours. Mem. IEEE, SHARE, Digital Equipment Computer Users Soc. (author papers and presentations 1977-81, ednl. spl. interest group 1977-83, steering com. Resource Sharing Timesharing System/Extended (RSTS/E), 1979-82). Office: Sterling Software Dylakor Divsn 9340 Owensmouth Ave Chatsworth CA 91311

MAEHL, WILLIAM HARVEY, historian, educator; b. Bklyn., May 28, 1915; s. William Henry and Antoinette Rose (Salamone) M.; m. Josephine Scholl McAllister, Dec. 29, 1941; children: Madeleine, Kathleen. BSc, Northwestern U., 1937, MA, 1939; PhD, U. Chgo., 1946. Asst. prof. history St. Louis U., 1941-42, Tex. A&M U., College Sta., 1943, De Paul U., Chgo., 1944-49; historian Dept. of Def., Karlsruhe, Stuttgart, Fed. Rep. Germany, 1950-52; chief briefing office U.S. hdqrs. EUCOM, Frankfurt, Fed. Rep. Germany, 1952-53; chief historian Artillery Sch. Ft. Sill, Okla., 1954, war plans office Hdqrs. NAMAE, USAF, Burtonwood, Eng., 1954-55; assoc. prof. European history Nebr. Wesleyan U., Lincoln, 1955-57, prof., 1958-62, 65-68; prof. German history Auburn (Ala.) U., 1968-81, prof. emeritus, 1981—; vis. prof. U. Nebr., 1962, U. Auckland, New Zealand, 1963-64, Midwestern U., Wichita Falls, Tex., 1965. Author: German Militarism and Socialism, 1968, History of Germany in Western Civilization, 1979, A World History Syllabus, 3 vols., 1980, August Bebel, Shadow Emperor of the German Workers, 1980, The German Socialist Party: Champion of the First Republic, 1918-33, 1986, monographs, chpts. to books, atomic, biol. and emergency war plans for NAMAE, USAF, classified studies for hist. div. USAREUR; contbr. articles to profl. jours. Grantee Nebr. Wesleyan U., 1959, Auburn U., 1969-73, 79-80, Am. Philosophical Soc., 1973-74, Deutscher Akademischer Austauschdienst, 1978. Mem. Am. Hist. Assn., Phi Kappa Phi, Phi Alpha Theta.

MAESTRINI, EMILIO, industrial projects contracts manager; b. São Paulo, Brazil, Jan. 15, 1939; came to U.S., 1963; s. Mario and Trieste Yolanda (Sgueglia) M.; m. Virginia Wasson, Feb. 1969 (div. Oct. 1970); 1 child, Tracy; m. Noemia S.M. Pereira Da Silva, May 29, 1971; children: Andrew, Alessandra. AA, L.A. Harbor Coll., 1968; student, Long Beach State U., 1969-70, Escola Superior Adminstrn., Campinas, Brazil, 1976. Asst. gen. mgr. Inds. Texteis Barbero S.A., Sorocaba, Brazil, 1958-63; engring. adminstr. AiRearch Mfg. Co., Torrance, Calif., 1965-72; ptnr. bus. venture Textiles and Gas Stations, Sorocaba, 1972-75; contracts mgr. Kaiser Engrs. Internat. Inc., Oakland, Calif., 1975-89; sr. contracts mgr. Fluor Daniel Inc., Redwood City, Calif., 1989—. Home: Av Grecia 680 Dep 301, Antogagasta Chile Office: Fluor Daniel Inc 10 Twin Dolphin Dr Redwood City CA 94065-1568

MAFNAS, ISABEL IGLESIAS, computer lab specialist, computer consultant; b. Austin, Tex., Sept. 21, 1965; d. Juan Crisostomo and Isabel (Iglesias) M. BA in Statistics, U. Calif., Berkeley, 1987; postgrad., Chabot Coll., 1989-91, Merrit Coll., 1991-92. Statistics tutor, statistics reader U. Calif., Berkeley, 1986-87; statistics reader U. Calif. Extension, Berkeley, 1987-89; instrnl. asst. II Chabot Coll., Hayward, 1988-92, computer lab. specialist, 1992—. Author: (software user's guide) Academic Session Time Keeper, 1990, 91, 92, Eureka!, Girls Inc., 1993. Recipient Newspaper Carrier scholarship Gannett Found., Inc., Guam, 1983, Gannett Spl. scholarship Gannett Found., Inc., Guam, 1983. Office: Chabot College 25555 Hesperian Blvd Hayward CA 94545

MAGADIA, FARLEY LUNA, commercial illustrator; b. Manila, Philippines, Nov. 5, 1965; s. Florencio and Minerva (Luna) M. BA in Graphic Design, Calif. State U., Northridge, 1990. Hosp. transporter Holy Cross Hosp., Mission Hills, Calif., 1985-87; airbrush teaching asst. Calif. State U., Northridge, 1988-90; freelance comml. illustrator L.A., 1988—; airbrush instr. Learning Tree U., Chatsworth, Calif., 1988—; art dir. ASATSU/BBDO, L.A., 1990—. Recipient 1st pl. award 5th Ann. Airbrush Competition Airbrush Action Mag., 1991. Mem. Soc. Illustrators L.A. (Silver medal 1990). Roman Catholic.

MAGALNICK, ELLIOTT BEN, retail medical supply company executive; b. Cleve., Aug. 19, 1945; s. Joseph Hyman and Ann (Resnick) M.; m. Diane Kerner, May 26, 1968 (div. Feb. 1988); children: Joel A., David A.; m. Judy Banjavic, June 9, 1991; stepchildren: Daniel Banjavic, David Banjavic. BS in Bus. Mgmt., Temple U., 1968. Cert. orthopedic fitter Health Industries Dealer Assn. Retail mgr. Milner Surg. Supply Co., Phila., 1970-72, Colo. Surg. Supply Co., Denver, 1972-73; mgr. non wheelchair retail Wheelchairs, Inc., Englewood, Colo., 1973-77; asst. mgr. ops. Denver Surg. Supply Co., 1977-78; owner, founder The Get Well Shop, Inc., Aurora, Colo., 1978—. Mem. Legion of Merit, Republican Party, Denver, 1992; mem. chorus Colo. Symphony Orch., Denver, 1986-92; vol. Allied Fedn. Denver, 1984-87; mem. chorus Shir Ami Singers, Denver, 1978-88; active Cantor Temple Micah, Denver. Named Disting. Pres., Optimist Internat., 1987. Mem. Colo. Assn. Med. Equipment Suppliers (dealer mem.), Health Industries Dealer Assn. (cert. orthopedic fitter), Luncheon Optimist Club Windsor Gardens (prs. 1986), Masons (master mason Columbine lodge), Colo. Consistory, El Jebel Temple. Jewish. Office: The Get Well Shop Inc 12028 E Mississippi Ave Aurora CO 80012

MAGAÑA, MARIA DE LOURDES, actress; b. Dallas. BA, Stanford U., 1981; studied acting with Frank Corsaro, Elaine Aiken, Vivian Nathan, N.Y.C. Costume designer Allenberry Playhouse, Boiling Springs, Pa., 1986; mem. Wooden Horse Theatre Co., N.Y.C., 1986-88, Vertical River Theatre Ensemble, 1992—; artistic dir. Atlantic Sirens' Posse, 1993—. Appeared in plays Tales of the Vienna Woods, 1981, Much Ado About Nothing, 1981, Twelfth Night, 1982, The Comedy of Errors, 1983, Faust, 1983, Measure For Measure, 1984, Tail of the Tiger, 1985, Rustic Chivalry, 1985, Roof, 1986, Sister Mary Ignatius..., 1987, Open Your Golden Gate, 1988, Purblind, 1988, Family Life, 1989, A Soldier's Tale, 1990, numerous others; dir. plays Momentum, 1985, Rocking Chair Dreamer, 1987. Mem. SAG, Actors Equity Assn., The Actors Studio, Stanford Profl. Women.

MAGENTA, MURIEL, artist; b. N.Y.C., Dec. 4, 1932; d. James E. and Sara (Wallman) Gellert; m. Gerald Zimmerman; children: Jean, Eric Vermilion. BA, Queens Coll., 1953; MA in Art History, Ariz. State U., 1962, MFA in Painting, 1965, PhD, 1970. Prof. art Ariz. State U., 1969—. One woman shows include Ariz. State U., 1976, Phoenix Art Mus., 1977, U. So. Calif., 1978, Marian Locks Gallery, Phila., 1979, Rutgers U., 1981, Yares Gallery, Scottsdale, Ariz., 1981, CitiBank, N.Y.C., 1984, U. Ark., 1984, L.A. Contemporary Exhibs., 1985, Scottsdale Ctr. for the Arts, 1990, 93, Kansas City (Mo.) Art Inst., 1991, Gallery 10, Washington, 1991, Scottsdale Ctr. for the Arts, 1993; group shows include L.A. Inst. Contemporary Art, 1978, Rutgers U., 1981, Ariz. State U. Art Mus., The Print Club Phila., 1983, Tweed Gallery, Plainfield, N.J., 1984, Tucson Art Mus., Ariz., 1988, Lawndale Art and Performance Ctr., Mus. of Fine Art, Santa Fe, N.Mex., 1990, Ctr. Simone De Beauvoir, Paris, 1992, Medien Operative Berlin, 1992, 8th Cadiz (Spain) Internat. Video Festival, 1992, South Bend (Ind.) Art Ctr., 1992, John Michael Kohler Art Ctr., Sheboygan, Wis., 1992, CAGE, Cin., 1993, Ctr. Simone DeBeauvoir, Paris, 1993, Drexel U., Phila., 1993; represented in permanent collections Ariz. State U., Valley Nat. Bank, Phoneix, Prudential Life, Scottsdale. Phoenix Art Mus. grantee, 1975-77; Ariz. State U. grantee, 1981-82, 92-93. Mem. NOW, Women's Caucus for Art (nat. pres. 1982-84, Mid-career achievement award 1991), Coll. Art Assn. Am., Mid-Am. Coll. Art Assn., Nat. Women's Polit. Caucus. Home: 8322 E Virginia Ave Scottsdale AZ 85257-1741 Office: Ariz State U Sch Art Tempe AZ 85287 also: Ariz State U Inst Studies in Arts Tempe AZ 85287 Studio: 900 S Mitchell #A 185 Tempe AZ 85281

MAGGAL, MOSHE MORRIS, rabbi; b. Nagyecsed, Hungary, Mar. 16, 1908; came to U.S., 1950, naturalized, 1960; s. David and Ester (Fulop) Gelberman; m. Rachel Delia Diamond, July 8, 1951; children: Davida Elizabeth DeMonte, Michelle Judith Weinstein, Elana Ilene. BA, Nat. Rabbinical Sem., Budapest, Hungary, 1933, Rabbinical degree, 1934; postgrad., U. Zurich, Switzerland, 1935, Hebrew U., Jerusalem, 1936; PhD (hon.), Ben Franklin Acad., Washington, 1979; DDW (hon.), The New Sem., N.Y.C., 1988. Rabbi Temple Meyer-David, Claremont, N.H., 1951-52, Temple Beth Aaron, Billings, Mont., 1952-54, Alhambra (Calif.) Jewish Center, 1955-57, Temple Beth Kodesh, Canoga Park, Calif., 1959-61, Congregation Ahavath Israel, Hollywood, Calif., 1966-70, Temple Emanu-El, Las Vegas, Nev., 1988—; civilian chaplain USAAF Base, Great Falls, Mont., 1952-54; Editor Hebrew weekly Iton Meyuhad, Tel Aviv, 1940-47; asso. editor Heritage newspaper, Los Angeles, 1958-60; lectr. Free Enterprise Speakers Bur., Coast Fed. Savs. & Loan Assn., 1971-76; instr. adult edn. class Temple Beth Sholom, Las Vegas, 1990—; mem. U.S. Congl. Adv. Bd. Author: Acres of Happiness, 1968, The Secret of Israel's Victories: Past, Present and Future, 1983; editor Voice of Judaism, 1960—. Pres. Beverly Hills Zionist Orgn., 1973-77; exec. v.p. So. Pacific Region, 1973—; mem. Los Angeles-Eilat Sister City Com.; Mem. Speakers Bur. of Com. for Re-election of Pres., 1972; hon. lt. col. New Spirit of 76 Found.; mem. nat. adv. bd. Ben Franklin Acad., Inst. Advanced Studies.; Calif. chmn. Spirit of '76 Found. Served with Israel Def. Army, 1948-49. Recipient Nat. Sermon Contest award Spiritual Moblzn., 1952, citation Crusade for Freedom, 1952, Am. Patriot award Ben Franklin Soc., 1981; named to Los Angeles Bicentennial Com. Speakers Bur. for Am. Revolution Bicentennial Adminstrn., 1975; Hon. sheriff Yellowstone County Mont., 1954; hon. adviser to Cecil B. DeMille for film The Ten Commandments, 1954. Mem. Nat. Jewish Info. Service (founder, pres. 1960—), Town Hall of Calif., World Affairs Council, Internat. Visitors Program. Democrat. Club: Greater Los Angeles Press. Home: 3761 Decade St Las Vegas NV 89121

MAGID, GAIL AVRUM, neurosurgery educator; b. Chgo., Oct. 15, 1934; s. Harry M. and Henrietta (Busch) M.; m. Janet Louise Reinhardt, June 15, 1962 (div.); children: Allison Drew, Jonathan Alward; m. Roseanne Cipra Muirhead, Sept. 4, 1982. BSc, U. Ill., 1954; MD, Chgo. Med. Sch., 1958. Diplomate Am. Bd. Neurol. Surgery. Intern Cook County Hosp., Chgo., 1958-59; resident, then fellow neurol. surgery Mayo Clinic, Rochester, Minn., 1959-61, 63-65; clin. instr. neurosurgery U. Calif., San Francisco, 1965-70, asst. clin. prof., 1970-79, assoc. prof., 1979—; chmn. Dominican Neurol. Inst., Santa Cruz, Calif., 1975—, bd. dirs. Dominican Found.; sr. v.p. Frank Magid Assocs., Cedar Rapids, Iowa; cons. neurosurgery U.S. Army; cons. neurosurgeon San Francisco Gen. Hosp. Assoc. editor: Clinical Neurosurgery, 1974. Bd. dirs. Santa Cruz Symphony Assn., 1983-85, U. Calif. Friends of Arts, Santa Cruz, 1985-86. Served to lt. comdr. USN, 1961-63. Fellow ACS, Internat. Coll. Surgeons; mem. AMA, Calif. Med. Assn., Internat. Soc. Pediatric Neurosurgeons, Am. Assn. Neurol. Surgeons, Western Neurosurg. Soc., Cong. Neurol. Surgeons, San Francisco Neurol. Soc. (pres.-elect 1991, pres. 1992), St. Francis Yacht Club (San Francisco). Republican. Home: 241 4th Ave Santa Cruz CA 95062-3815 Office: 1661 Soquel Dr Santa Cruz CA 95065-1709

MAGILL, DAVID W., oil company executive; b. Flemington, N.J., Jan. 18, 1955; s. Donald G. and Elisabeth (Weir) M.; m. Margaret Mondesky, May 8, 1982; children: Laura, Alice. BA in Econs., Middlebury Coll., 1977; MS in Acctg., NYU, 1978. CPA. Sr. acct. Arthur Andersen & Co., N.Y.C., 1977-80; from mgr. E&P econs. to v.p. corp. devel. Am. Ultramar Ltd., Mt. Kisco, Tarrytown, N.Y., 1980-90; retail oper. mgr. Ultramar Inc., Hanford, Calif., 1991—. Home: 449 N Fontana Ct Visalia CA 93291

MAGNESS, BOB JOHN, telecommunications executive; b. Clinton, Okla., 1924; married. Grad., South Western State Coll., 1949. Chmn. Tele-Communications, Inc., Denver; chmn. Community Tele-Communications, Inc.; bd. dirs. Republic Pictures Corp., WestMarc Communications, United Artists Communications, Inc. Office: Tele-Communications Inc PO Box 5630 5619 BTC Pkwy Denver CO 80217*

MAGNESS, RHONDA ANN, microbiologist; b. Stockton, Calif., Jan. 30, 1946; d. John Pershing and Dorothy Waneta (Kelley) Wetter; m. Barney LeRoy Bender, Aug. 25, 1965 (div. 1977); m. Gary D. Magness, Mar. 5, 1977; children: Jay D. (dec.), Troy D. BS, Calif. State U., 1977. Lic. clin. lab. technologist, Calif., med. technologist; cert. clin. lab. scientist. Med. asst. C. Fred Wilcox, MD, Stockton, 1965-66; clk. typist Dept. of U.S. Army, Ft. Eustis, Va., 1967, Def. Supply Agy., New Orleans, 1967-68; med. asst. James G. Cross, MD, Lodi, Calif., 1969, Arthur A. Kemalyan, MD, Lodi, 1969-71, 72-77; med. sec. Lodi Meml. Hosp., 1972; lab. aide Calif. State U., Sacramento, 1977; phlebotomist St. Joseph's Hosp., Stockton, 1978-79; supr. microbiology Dameron Hosp. Assn., Stockton, 1980—. Active Concerned Women Am., Washington, 1987—. Mem. AAUW, Calif. Assn. Clin. Lab. Technologists, San Joaquin County Med. Assts. Assn., Nat. Geog. Soc., Nat. Audubon Soc. Baptist. Lodge: Jobs Daus. (chaplain 1962-63). Home: 9627 Knight Ln Stockton CA 95209-1961 Office: Dameron Hosp Lab 525 W Acacia St Stockton CA 95203-2484

MAGNUSON, ALAN DOUGLAS, banking executive; b. Valparaiso, Ind., Jan. 22, 1942; s. Douglas Harold and Alice Elizabeth (Burch) M.; m. Rose Becerra, Apr. 25, 1971; children: Lori, Kathi, Juli. Diploma, South Bend Coll. Commerce, 1962. Officer trainee Crocker-Citizens Bank, Los Angeles, 1967-70, ops. officer, 1967-70; ops. officer So. Calif. 1st Nat. Bank, San Diego, 1970-73; loan officer 1st Nat. Bank Nev., Las Vegas, 1973-80; br. mgr. 1st Interstate Nev., Las Vegas, 1980-82, v.p., 1984—; instr. Clark County Community Coll., Las Vegas; speaker SBA, Las Vegas.; mem. speakers bur. First Interstate Bank Nev., Las Vegas. Active First Interstate Bank, Nev. Speakers Bur., Nev. Child Seekers. Served as sgt. U.S. Army, 1960-63. Mem. Am. Inst. Banking (gov. So. Nev. chpt. 1971-77, plaque 1977), Bank Adminstrn. Inst. (pres. So. Nev. chpt. 1982-83, plaque 1983), Henderson C. of C., Boulder City C. of C. (v.p. 1980-81), North Las Vegas C. of C. (comml. com., chmn. audit com., chmn. fairshow, chmn. funds appropriation subcom., import-export com., chmn. fin. subcom., pub. relations com.). Republican. Lodge: Lions (chmn. Nev. zone 1982-83, sec. Nev. cabinet 1983-84, gov. Nev. dist. 1985-86, chmn. council govs. Calif./Nev. 1985-86). Office: 1st Interstate Nev PO Box 98588 Las Vegas NV 89193-8588

MAGNUSON, DONALD RICHARD (BLAINE NELLINGTON), motion picture and television screenwriter, producer, director; b. Chgo., Apr. 23, 1951; s. Donald Orville and Olive June (O'Keefe) M.; m. Debra Michelle Ruzek, June 9, 1973; children: Jennifer Jean, Erick Richard. Diploma, No. Ill. U., summer 1968; student, Coll. of Du Page, 1971. Tchr. pro-tennis Westside Racquet Club, Oakbrook Terr., Ill., 1971-73; founder, co-chmn. Chicagoland Pictures Ltd.; founder, pres. Magnuson Entertainment Group, Malibu Magnuson Ltd., 1987—; founder, co-chmn. Chicagoland Picture Ltd. Screenwriter: The Taiwan Factor, Another Autumn, Reunion, Black & White, Harry's Harem, Best Medicine, Midnight Internment, Dancer, The Long & Short of It, Retro Warrior, (with Christina Cardan) An Aspen Affair. Mem. Porsche Club Am., Ferrari Club Am. Roman Catholic. Office: 19866 Ridge Manor Way Yorba Linda CA 92686-6537

MAGNUSSEN, MAX GENE, psychologist; b. Roland, Iowa, Sept. 12, 1927; s. Arthur Christian and Mary E. (Rakard) M.; m. Margaret Anne Hahn, Feb. 2, 1952 (div. Apr. 1985); 1 child, Anne H. BA, U. Iowa, 1952, MA, 1953; PhD, U. Ky., 1958. Lic. psychologist, Pa., N.Mex.; registered health svc. provider in psychology. Staff psychologist VA Hosp., Cin., 1958-59; clin. psychologist, asst. dir., psychol. cons. aircraft nuclear propulsion dept. GE Co., Cin., 1959-60; chief psychologist to dir. Lincoln-Lancaster Child Guidance Ctr., Lincoln, Nebr., 1960-68; chief psychologist to acting dir. Pitts. Child Guidance Ctr., 1968-80; dir. to attending sr. psychologist Programs for Children/U. N.Mex. Med. Ctr., Albuquerque, 1980—; instr. to asst. prof. U. Cin., 1958-60; asst. prof. U. Nebr., 1961-68; assoc. to full prof. U. Pitts., 1968-80; prof. of psychiatry and psychology U. N.Mex., 1980—; vis. prof. Inst. of Psychiatry, London, 1988-89; site vis. Am. Psychol. Assn, Washington, 1972—; field specialist site vis. HEW, 1977—. Contbg. author various books including Individual Versus Family Therapy, 1982, Multiple Impact Therapy, 1982, Development of a Minimal Clinical Data System, 1982, others; author: Pittsburgh Child Guidance Center Data System, 1974, others; contbr. articles to profl. jours. Mem. Health Systems Agy., Southwest Pa., Pitts., 1977-80, monitor, 1977-80. Sgt. U.S. Army, 1946-48. Recipient commendation Calif. Psychol. Assn., 1986—. Fellow Am.

Orthopscyhiat. Assn., Soc. for Personality Assessment, Pa. Psychol. Assn. (ins. chmn. 1979); mem. APA (site visitor), Can. Psychol. Assn. (site visitor, accreditation panel), Nebr. Psychol. Assn. (sec./treas. 1963-66, pres. 1966-67), Am. Psychol. Assn. (recipient overseas grant 1973, vis. psychologist, 1974). Office: U NMex Sch Medicine 2600 Marble Ave NE Albuquerque NM 87106-2797

MAGOWAN, PETER ALDEN, professional baseball team executive, grocery chain executive; b. N.Y.C., Apr. 5, 1942; s. Robert Anderson and Doris (Merrill) M.; m. Jill Tarlau (div. July 1982; children—Kimberley, Margot, Hilary; m. Deborah Johnston, Aug. 14, 1982. B.A., Stanford U.; M.A., Oxford U., Eng.; postgrad., Johns Hopkins U. Store mgr. Safeway Stores Inc., Washington, 1968-70; dist. mgr. Safeway Stores Inc., Houston, 1970-71; retail ops. mgr. Safeway Stores Inc., Phoenix, 1971-72; div. mgr. Safeway Stores Inc., Tulsa, 1973-76; mgr. internat. div. Safeway Stores Inc., Toronto, Ont., Can., 1976-78; mgr. western region Safeway Stores Inc., San Francisco, 1978-79; chmn. bd., chief exec. officer Safeway Stores Inc., Oakland, Calif., 1980—; pres., mng. gen. ptnr. San Francisco Giants, 1993—; bd. dirs. Chrysler Corp., Vons Cos. Inc. Mem. Food Mktg. Inst. (bd. dirs.). Office: Safeway Inc 201 4th St Oakland CA 94660-0001*

MAGRUDER, THOMAS MALONE, marriage and family therapist; b. Columbus, Ohio, Apr. 26, 1930; s. Thomas Malone and Elizabeth (McCarroll) M.; m. Carol Ann Schnitzer, Aug. 16, 1958; children: Scott D., John T., Ellen L. Bargainer. BA, Coll. Wooster, 1952; MDiv, Ch. Div. Sch. of Pacific, Berkeley, Calif., 1956; PhD, U.S. Internat. U., 1969. Lic. marriage and family therapist; ordained Episcopalian priest. Priest, vicar Holy Trinity Episcopal Ch., Fallon, Nev., 1956-60; adminstrv. asst. to bishop Episcopal Diocese of Nev., Reno, 1960-64; asst. priest St. David's Episcopal Ch., N. Hollywood, Calif., 1969-71; dir. People, Inc., Reno, 1971—; bd. dirs. Crisis Call Ctr., Reno. Columnist Gannett News Svc., 1978-85. Vol. counselor Nev. Women's Prison, Carson City, 1983-90, ct. appointed spl. adv., 1992—. With USN, 1948-49. Mem. Am. Assn. Marriage and Family Therapy-Nev. Div. (Therapist of Yr. 1990). Democrat. Home: 3160 Achilles Dr Reno NV 89512-1334 Office: People Inc 275 Hill St Ste 260 Reno NV 89501-1825

MAGUIRE, ALAN EDWARD, public policy consultant; b. Paterson, N.J., Aug. 27, 1954; s. Edward Lawrence and Severna (Arens) M. BS in Econs., Ariz. State U., 1978. Legis. rsch. economist Ariz. State Senate, Phoenix, 1977-80, econ. advisor, 1980-83; chief dep. state treas. Ariz. State Treasury, Phoenix, 1983-87; 1st v.p. Rauscher Pierce Refsnes, Inc., Phoenix, 1987-91; pres. The Maguire Co., Phoenix, 1991—; forecaster Ariz. Blue Chip Econ. Forecast, Tempe, 1985—, Western Blue Chip Econ. Forecast, Tempe, 1988—. Bd. dirs. Ariz. Rep. Caucus, Phoenix, 1988—, Ariz. State Bd. of Deposit, Phoenix, 1988—, Ariz. State Retirement System bd., 1987; active Ariz. Property Tax Oversight Commn., Phoenix, 1987—, Project SLIM Steering Com., 1991-92. Mem. Ariz. Econ. Forum (bd. dirs., v.p. 1983—), Ariz. Town Hall, Phoenix Econ. Club. Office: The Maguire Co PO Box 64382 Phoenix AZ 85082

MAGUIRE, JAMES HENRY, English language educator; b. Denver, Apr. 2, 1944; s. Joseph Cornelius Jr. and Margaret Louise (Monson) M.; m. Betty Joan Keller, Sept. 8, 1967; children: Emily Ann, Stephen Joseph. BA, U. Colo., 1966; AM, Ind. U., 1969, PhD, 1970. Teaching assoc. Ind. U., Bloomington, 1967-69; asst. prof. Boise (Idaho) State U., 1970-75, assoc. prof., 1975-87, prof. English, 1987—. Author: (booklet) Mary Hallock Foote, 1972; author, editor (anthology) Literature of Idaho, 1986 (Idaho Libr. Assn. award 1987); sect. editor: A Literary History of the American West, 1987; contbr. chpt. to The Columbia History of the American Novel, 1991; co-editor Boise State U. Western Writer Series, 1971—. Mem. Zero Population Growth, Washington, 1970—, ACLU, Snake River Alliance, Boise, 1979—. Mem. Western Lit. Assn. (pres. 1981), MLA, Am. Studies Assn., The Mark Twain Circle, The Hemingway Soc., The Henry James Soc., Sierra Club. Democrat. Home: 933 Pierce Ct Boise ID 83712-7448 Office: Boise State U English Dept 1910 University Dr Boise ID 83725-0001

MAGUIRE, JOHN DAVID, university president, educator, writer; b. Montgomery, Ala., Aug. 7, 1932; s. John Henry and Clyde (Merrill) M.; m. Lillian Louise Parrish, Aug. 29, 1953; children—Catherine Merrill, Mary Elizabeth, Anne King. A.B. magna cum laude, Washington and Lee U., 1953, Litt.D. (hon.), 1979; Fulbright scholar, Edinburgh (Scotland) U., 1953-54; B.D. summa cum laude, Yale, 1956, Ph.D., 1960; postdoctoral research, Yale U. and U. Tübingen, Germany, 1964-65, U. Calif., Berkeley, 1968-69, Silliman U., Philippines, 1976-77; HLD (hon.), Transylvania U., 1990. Dir. Internat. Student Ctr., New Haven, 1956-58; mem. faculty Wesleyan U., Middletown, Conn., 1960-70; asso. provost Wesleyan U., 1967-68; vis. lectr. Pacific Sch. Religion and Grad. Theol. Union, Berkeley, 1968-69; pres. SUNY Coll. at Old Westbury, 1970-81, Claremont (Calif.) U. Ctr. and Grad. Sch., 1981—. Author: The Dance of the Pilgrim: A Christian Style of Life for Today, 1967; also numerous articles. Mem. Conn. adv. com. U.S. Commn. Civil Rights, 1961-70; participant White House Conf. on Civil Rights, 1966; advisor, permanent trustee and 1st chmn. bd. dirs. Martin Luther King Ctr. for Social Change, Atlanta, 1968—; bd. dirs. Nassau County Health and Welfare Coun., 1971-81, pres., 1974-76; trustee United Bd. Christian Higher Edn. in Asia, 1975-81, Inst. Internat. Edn., 1980-86, The Tomás Rivera Ctr., Claremont, Calif., 1984—, vice chmn., 1987—, Assn. Ind. Calif. Colls. and Univs., 1985—, chmn. 1990-92, mem. exec. com., 1992—, The Calif. Achievement Coun., 1985—, chmn. 1990—, Transylvania U. Bingham Trust, 1987—, Lincoln Found., Lincoln Inst. of Land Policy, Inc., The JL Found., 1988—, The Bus. Enterprise Trust, 1989—, Ednl. Found. for Black Ams., 1991—; bd. dirs. Assn. Am. Colls., 1981-86, chmn., 1984-85; bd. dirs. Legal Def. and Edn. Fund. NAACP, 1991—, west coast div., 1981—, Thacher Sch., Ojai, Calif., 1982—, vice chmn., 1986—, Salzburg Seminar, 1992—; mem. Am. Com. on U.S.-Soviet Rels., 1981—, Blue Ribbon Calif. Commn. on Teaching Profession, 1984-86; mem. governing coun. Aspen Inst. Wye Faculty Seminar, 1984—, mem. Coun. on Fgn. Rels., 1983—, Adv. Com. to Skirball Inst. Am. Values, 1988—; mem. Pres.'s Adv. Coun. to Commn. on Calif. Master Plan for Higher Edn., 1986-87, L.A. Ednl. Alliance for Restructuring Now, 1992—. Recipient Julia A. Archibald High Scholarship award Yale Div. Sch., 1956; Day fellow Yale Grad. Sch., 1956-57; Kent fellow, 1957-60; Howard Found. postdoctoral fellow Brown U. Grad. Sch., 1964-65; Fenn lectr., 7 Asian countries, 1976-77; recipient Conn. Prince Hall Masons' award outstanding contbns. human rights in Conn., 1965; E. Harris Harbison Gt. Tchr. prize Danforth Found., 1968. Fellow Soc. Values Higher Edn. (pres. 1974-81, bd. dirs. 1972-88); mem. Phi Beta Kappa, Omicron Delta Kappa. Democrat. Office: Claremont U Ctr & Grad Sch Office of Pres 160 E 10th St Claremont CA 91711-6165

MAGUIRE, THOMAS ELDON, accountant; b. Piqua, Ohio, Mar. 7, 1952; s. Fredrick Edward and Lois (Englert) M.; m. Laura Marie Grew, Oct. 18, 1975; children: Steven, David. BBA, U. Notre Dame, 1974; chartered fin. cons., Am. Coll., Bryn Mawr, Pa., 1986. CPA, Ariz., Ill. Agt. IRS, Chgo., 1974-77; tax specialist Bolan Vassar & Barrows, CPA, Phoenix, 1977-78; mem. tax staff, tax mgr. KMG Main Hurdman CPA, Phoenix, 1978-82, tax ptnr., 1982-87; tax ptnr. KMPG Peat Marwick CPAs, Phoenix, 1987—. Bd. dirs. Silent Witness, Phoenix, 1984; active Cen. Ariz. Estate Planning Coun., 1980; treas., exec. com. mem. Valley Forward Assn., 1980—. Mem. AICPA, Ariz. Soc. CPAs, Ariz. Club. Republican. Roman Catholic. Home: 1311 E Le Marche Ave Phoenix AZ 85022-3246 Office: KMPG Peat Marwick CPAs 2020 N Central Ave Ste 1200 Phoenix AZ 85004-4594

MAHABIR, VALERIE INDRANI, ballet dancer, choreographer, actress, model, educator; b. San Fernando, West Indies, Aug. 12, 1951; came to U.S., 1988; d. Winston Jules and Joan (Graham) M.; m. Jerry Douglas MacKenzie, Oct. 4, 1944 (div. 1981); children: Alexander Winston MacKenzie, Charisse Valerie MacKenzie. Cert. ballet tchr., Royal Acad. Dancing, London. Artisitic dir. Valerie Mahabir Acad. Ballet and Jazz, Vancouver, B.C., Can., 1969-88, Palm Springs, Calif., 1990—; founder, artistic dir. West Coast Youth Ballet and Jazz Soc., Palm Springs, Calif., 1985-87. Recipient Woman of Distinction award Vancouver, B.C. YMCA, 1986, 87. Mem. ACTRA, SAG, AEA. Home: 764 E Mesquite Ave Palm Springs CA 92264

MAHADEV, RAJESH, business turnaround specialist; b. Madras, India, Apr. 17, 1966; came to U.S., 1988; s. R.K. and Padma (Alwa) M.; m. Ana Elisa Mendes De Oliveira, Jan. 23, 1992. B. Commerce in Acctg., U. Bangalore (India), 1987; MBA in Mktg. and Fin., U. Denver, 1990. Sr. account exec. Communication Workshop, Bangalore, 1987—; turnaround specialist Corriere & Assocs., Inc., Englewood, Colo., 1992—; cons. Corriere & Assocs., Inc., Englewood, 1990-92. Educator Jr. Achievement of Denver, 1992; amb. Greater Denver Chamber, 1992—. Mem. Am. Mensa Ltd. Office: Corriere & Assocs Inc Ste 101 5650 DTC Pkwy Englewood CO 80111

MAHAFFEY, MARCIA JEANNE HIXSON, secondary school administrator; b. Scobey, Mont.; d. Edward Goodell and Olga Marie (Frederickson) Hixson; m. Donald Harry Mahaffey (div. Aug. 1976); 1 child, Marcia Anne. BA in English, U. Wash.; MA in Secondary Edn., U. Hawaii, 1967. Cert. secondary and elem. tchr. and adminstr. Tchr. San Lorenzo (Calif.) Sch. Dist., 1958-59; tchr. Castro Valley (Calif.) Sch. Dist., 1959-63, vice prin., 1963-67; vice prin. Sequoia Union High Sch. Dist., Redwood City, Calif., 1967-77, asst. prin., 1977-91, ret., 1991; tchr. trainer Project Impact Sequoia Union Sch. Dist., Redwood City, 1986-91; mem. supr.'s task force for dropout prevention, 1987—, Sequoia Dist. Goals Commn. (chair subcom. staff devel. 1988); mentor tchr. selection com., 1987-91; mem. Stanford Program Devel. Ctr. Com., 1987-91; chairperson gifted and talented Castro Valley Sch. Dist.; mem. family services bd., San Leandro, Calif. Vol. Am. Cancer Soc., San Mateo, Calif., 1967, Castro Valley, 1965; Sunday sch. tchr. Hope Luth. Ch., San Mateo, 1970-76; chair Carlmont High Sch. Site Council, Belmont, Calif., 1977-91. Recipient Life Mem. award Parent, Tchr., Student Assn., Belmont, 1984, Svc. award, 1989, Exemplary Svc award Carlmont High Sch., 1989; named Woman of the Week, Castro Valley, 1967, Outstanding Task Force Chair Adopt A Sch. Program San Mateo (Calif.) County, 1990. Mem. AAUW, DAR, Assn. Calif. Sch. Adminstrs. (Project Leadership plaque 1985), Sequoia Dist. Mgmt. Assn. (pres. 1975, treas. 1984, 85), Assn. for Supervision and Curriculum Devel., Met. Mus. Art, Smithsonian Inst., Internat. Platform Assn., Animal Welfare Advocacy, Commonwealth Club of Calif., Delta Kappa Gamma, Alpha Xi Delta.

MAHAK, FRANCINE TIMOTHY, communications consultant; b. Paris, Sept. 28, 1950; d. James Simmons and Francine (Evans) Timothy; m. Vali Mahak, Aug. 3, 1976; children: Nima, Soroosh, Cameron. Baccalauréat Philosophie, Cours Victor Hugo, Paris, 1968; BA in Russian, Wellesley Coll., 1972; MA in Linguistics, U. Tehran, Iran, 1976; PhD in Mid. East and Persian Studies, U. Utah, 1986. Instr. Coll. Jeanne D'Arc, Tehran, 1974-75; translator Scetiran Cons. Co., Tehran, 1976-77; vis. instr. Persian U. Utah, Salt Lake City, 1978-81; translator French Found. for Evolutionary Research, N.Y.C., 1982-84; sr. cons., mgr. facilitated tng. programs Shipley Assocs., Bountiful, Utah, 1985-91; ind. cons., personal coach, 1991—; editor, translator Internat. Inst. for Adult Literacy Methods div. UNESCO, Tehran, 1974-77; instr. ESL U. Utah, Salt Lake City, 1982-83; designer vol. tng. programs Internat. Union Against Cancer, Geneva. Panel mem. United Way, Salt Lake City, 1980-85. Mem. Nat. Assn. for Female Execs. Club: Wellesley. Home: 1326 Harrison Ave Salt Lake City UT 84105-2610

MAHANEY, JOHN GAGE, retired surgeon, councilman; b. Owosso, Mich., Mar. 6, 1927; s. Reynolds Cornelius and Rachel (Preston) M.; m. Billie Kathleen Benzie, Oct. 28, 1956; children: John H., Mark, Michael, Erin. BS, Mich. State U., 1949; MD, George Washington U., 1954. Diplomate Am. Bd. Orthopedic Surgeons. Intern USPHS, San Francisco, 1954-55, resident, 1957-58, 59-60; resident USPHS Hosp., Staten Island, N.Y., 1956-57, Shriners Hosp. for Crippled Children, Salt Lake City, 1958-59; pvt. practice Santa Cruz (Calif.) Med. Clinic, 1960-92; retired, 1992. Councilman City of Santa Cruz, 1973-83, 1988-92; mayor, 1976. 79; pres. Monterey Div. League of Calif. Cities, 1979. With USPHS, 1954-60. Fellow ACS; mem. Am. Acad. Orthopedic Surgeons, Western Orthopedic Assn., Calif. Med. Soc., Am. Orthopedic Soc. for Sports Medicine (emeritus), Rotary (dir.). Republican.

MAHANT, VIJAY KUMAR, medical supplies company executive, consultant; b. Amritsar, India, June 22, 1953; came to U.S., 1985; s. Ram Kumar and Chander Lata (Bawa) M.; m. Camille Mahant, July 1, 1987. BS, U. Salford, Eng., 1978; MS, Loughsborough (Eng.) U., 1979, PhD, 1983. Scientist London Diagnostics, Eden Prairie, Minn., 1986-88; group leader IGEN, Rockville, Md., 1988-89; mgr. Nichols Inst., San Juan Capistrano, Calif., 1989-90; dir. R&D Pantex, Santa Monica, Calif., 1990-92; pres. Innovative Diagnostics, Norwalk, Calif., 1992—; cons. to diagnostic cos. in Calif., 1992. Author immunodiagnostics. Am. Heart Assn. fellow, 1985. Mem. Am. Assn. Clin. Chemistry, Clin. Ligand Assay Soc. Office: Innovative Diagnostics 11645 Firestone Blvd Norwalk CA 90650

MAHER, JOHN FRANCIS, financial executive; b. Berkeley, Calif., Apr. 25, 1943; s. Edward John and Emilia A. (Radovan) M.; m. Ann Elizabeth Breeden (div. 1975); children: Edward John II, Elizabeth Ann; m. Helen Lee Stillman, Mar. 20, 1976; children: Michael Stillman, Helen Cathline. BS, Menlo Coll., 1965; MBA, U. Pa., 1967. Gen. ptnr. Eastman Dillon, N.Y., 1971; 1st v.p. Blyth Eastman Dillon, N.Y., 1972; exec. v.p. Blyth Eastman Dillon, Los Angeles, 1976-79; exec. v.p., chief fin. officer Gt. Western Fin., Beverly Hills, Calif., 1973-76, also bd. dirs.; mng. dir. Lehman Bros. Kuhn Loeb, Los Angeles, 1979-86; pres., chief operating officer Great Western Fin. Corp., Chatsworth, 1986—; bd. dirs. Gt. Western Fin. Corp., Chatsworth, Baker Hughes Inc., Gt. Western Bank. Bd. dirs. L.A. Big Bros., Inc.; nat. bd. trustees Boys and Girls Clubs Am. Joseph Wharton fellow U. Pa., 1965-67. Mem. Calif. Bus. Roundtable Group. Office: Gt Western Fin Corp 9200 Oakdale Ave Chatsworth CA 91311-9999

MAHLER, DAVID, chemical company executive; b. San Francisco; s. John and Jennie (Morgan) M.; PhC, U. So. Calif., 1932; children: Darrell, Glenn. Pres., United Drug Co., Glendale, Calif., 1934-37, Blue Cross Labs., Inc., Saugus, Calif., 1937—. Active Fund for Animals, Friends of Animals, Com. for Humane Legislations; patron Huntington Hartford Theatre, Hollywood, Calif. Mem. Packaging and Rsch. Devel. Inst. (hon.), Anti-Defamation League, Skull and Daggar, Rho Pi Phi. Office: 26411 Golden Valley Rd Santa Clarita CA 91350-2988

MAHLER, RICHARD MARK, journalist, author; b. San Antonio, Feb. 12, 1951; s. Donald and Mary Vencill (Curnutte) M. BA in Liberal Studies, Sonoma State U., Rohnert Park, Calif., 1975; MA in Journalism and Mass Communications, U. Wis., 1978. Freelance writer and broadcaster Calif., 1969-73; news dir. KBBF-FM Radio, Santa Rosa, Calif., 1973-75; reporter WHA-AM/WERN-FM Radio, Madison, Wis., 1975-78; news dir. KPFK-FM RAdio, l.A., 1979-80; bur. chief Broadcasting mag., Hollywood, Calif., 1980-86, Electronic Media mag., L.A., 1986-88; ind. journalist and author Santa Fe, 1988—; bd. dirs. Santa Fe Translators, 1992—; cons. Pacific Found., L.A., 1984-89. Author: Belize: A Natural Destination, 1991, Guatemala: A Natural Destination, 1993; contbr. numerous articles to jours. and mags.; producer numerous radio programs. Vol. Greenpeace, Santa Fe, 1988-92, Amnesty Internat., Santa Fe, 1988-91, Salvation Army, Santa Fe, 1988—, Food Brigade, Santa Fe, 1991—. Recipient awards for radio writing. Mem. Assn. Inds. in Radio (bd. dirs. 1990-93), PEN N.Mex., RadioWest (pres. 1980-88). Home and Office: 2049 Hopi Rd Santa Fe NM 87501-3201

MAHLER, ROBERT LOUIS, soil scientist, educator; b. Huntington Park, Calif., Jan. 7, 1954; s. Robert Alfred and Emily Chonita (Ortega) M.; 1 child, Claudia. BS, Wash. State U., 1976, MS, 1978; PhD, N.C. State U., 1980. Asst. prof., assoc. prof., now prof. soil sci. U. Idaho, Moscow, 1980—, soil fertility researcher, 1980—, extension soil scientist, 1989—, water quality coord., 1990—. Contbr. to profl. publs. Mem. Am. Soc. Agronomy, Soil Sci. Soc. Am., Western Soc. Soil Sci., Rotary, Gamma Sigma Delta (pres. 1989-90). Roman Catholic. Office: Soil Sci Div Univ Idaho Moscow ID 83843

MAHMOUD, EUGENE LEO, physician; b. Newark, May 6, 1951; s. Leo and Ethel Mae (Smith) Milton; m. Quida Deborah Draine, Apr. 12, 1978; children: Eugene Leo Draine, Jasmine Jamillah. BA, Washington U., 1973; MD, State U. N.J., 1980. Diplomate Am. Bd. Pediatrics. Intern family practice U. Kans. Med. Ctr., 1981, resident pediatrics, 1984; staff neonatologist Mercy Hosp. Med. Ctr., Des Moines, 1986-87; asst. clin. prof., cons. U. Calif. Irvine Med. Ctr., Orange, 1987-89, 91—; staff neonatologist FHP Hosp., Fountain Valley, Calif., 1989-91. Contbr. Mothers and Others Against Child Abuse, Huntington Beach, Calif., 1989—. William F. Grupe Found. scholar, 1978-79. Fellow Am. Acad. Pediatrics; mem. AMA, Orange Coutny Med. Assn. Democrat. Islam. Home: 58 Canyon Ridge Irvine CA 92715 Office: U Calif Irvine Med Ctr 101 The City Dr S Rt 81 Irvine CA 92715

MAHMOUDI, KOOROS MOHIT, sociology educator; b. Mashhad, Iran, June 15, 1945; came to U.S., 1960; s. Jalal and Maryam Mahmoudi; m. Nellie Raye, Sept. 6, 1969 (div. 1985); children: Jalal, Roya; m. Natalie Harlan, Mar. 15, 1987; children: Maya, Darius. BS in Sociology, Utah State U., 1968, MS in Sociology, 1969, PhD in Sociology, 1973. Instr. sociology Stephen F. Austin State U., Nacogdoches, Tex., 1969-70; teaching asst. Utah State U., Logan, 1970-71; lectr. Ind. U., Ft. Wayne, 1971-73, asst. prof., 1973-77; lectr. San Diego State U., 1978-81; prof., chmn. dept. sociology No. Ariz. U., Flagstaff, 1981—. Author: Sociological Inquiry, 1973, 5th edit., 1991; cons. editor Western Sociol. Rev., 1977-79; also numerous articles. Bd. dirs. Flagstaff Housing Corp., 1986—; mem. Victim Witness Compensation Bd., Flagstaff, 1988—; founder, dir. Ariz. Conservation Law Enforcement Assn, 1989—. Fulbright grantee, India, 1980. Mem. Am. Sociol. Assn., Population Assn. Am. (cons. editor Demography 1975-76), Soc. for Intercultural Edn., Tng. and Rsch., Pacific Sociol. Assn., Western Social Sci. Assn., Alpha Kappa Delta. Democrat. Home: 797 N Forest View Dr Flagstaff AZ 86001 Office: No Ariz U Dept Sociology Box 15300 Flagstaff AZ 86011

MAHONEY, DAVID L., pharmaceutical wholesale and prescription benefits management company executive; b. Brighton, Mass., June 24, 1954; s. Thomas H.D. and K. Phyllis (Norton) M.; m. Winn Canning Ellis, Sept. 26, 1992. AB in English, Princeton U., 1975; MBA, Harvard U., 1981. Asst. gen. Ogden Food Svc. Corp., L.A., 1975-76; concessions mgr. Ogden Food Svc. Corp., East Boston, Mass., 1976-77, gen. mgr., 1977-78, ops. analyst, 1978-79; assoc. McKinsey & Co., San Francisco, 1981-86, prin., 1986-90; v.p. strategic planning McKesson Corp., San Francisco, 1990—; bd. dirs. Armor All Products Corp.; mem. planning execs. coun. Conf. Bd., N.Y.C., 1990-92. Mem. City Club of San Francisco. Office: McKesson Corp 1 Post St San Francisco CA 94104-5203

MAHONEY, JAMES LYLE, small business owner; b. Reardan, Wash., Nov. 13, 1934; s. Anthony James and Effie Kathryn (Kerwin) M.; m. Frances Edith Castle, Nov. 21, 1956; children: Michael James, Colleen Frances. Student, Ea. Wash. U., 1956-58. Salesman Armour & Co., Inc., Spokane, Wash., 1961-65; mgr. smoked meats Armour & Co., Inc., Spokane, 1965-68; co-owner Covered Wagon Tavern, Spokane, 1965-70; salesman W.H. Rorer, inc., Spokane, 1970-74; owner Lucky's Tavern, Medical Lake, Wash., 1971-73; regional sales mgr. Pierce Packing Co., Spokane, 1975-76; sales mgr. Mahoney Ford Sales, Inc., Coeur d'Alene, Idaho, 1976-80, v.p., 1980-82; owner, mgr. Dirty Shame Tavern, Medical Lake, 1983—. Fundraiser Medical Lake Fire Dept., 1985—, Medical Lake Foodbank, 1989—. Named Outstanding Fundraiser, Medical Lake Fire Dept., 1988-92. Mem. Wash. State Lic. Beverage Assn., Spokane County Tavern Owners Assn. Roman Catholic. Home: 43 E 17th Ave Spokane WA 99203 Office: Dirty Shame Tavern 114 E Lake St Medical Lake WA 99022

MAHONEY, JAMES P., bishop; b. Saskatoon, Sask., Can., Dec. 7, 1927. Ordained priest Roman Cath. Ch., 1952; bishop Saskatoon, 1967—. Office: Chancery Office, 106 5th Ave N, Saskatoon, SK Canada S7K 2N7

MAHONEY, MICHAEL JAMES, investment executive; b. Spokane, Wash., July 18, 1960; s. James Lyle and Frances Edith (Castle) M.; m. Ann Dickinson, May 29, 1993. BA in History cum laude, Whitman Coll., 1982; MBA, Stanford U., 1991. Analyst corp. fin. dept. E.F. Hutton & Co., Inc., N.Y.C., 1982-85; assoc. cons. Bain & Co., Inc., Boston, 1985-87, cons., 1987-89; investment analyst G.T. Capital Mgmt., San Francisco, 1991-93, portfolio manager, 1993—. Pres. Spokane County Young Reps., 1976-78; campaign mgr. Malone for U.S. Senate, Boston, 1988. Mem. Sigma Chi (com. chmn. 1979-80), Phi Beta Kappa. Home: 15 Hoffman Ave San Francisco CA 94114 Office: GT Capital Mgmt Co Inc 27th Fl 50 California St San Francisco CA 94111

MAHONEY, RICHARD, state official; b. Phoenix, Ariz.. AB magna cum laude, Princeton Univ., 1973; MA, Johns Hopkins Univ., 1975, Ph.D., 1980; JD, Ariz. State Univ., 1980. Sec. of state, Ariz., 1991—. Author: JFK: Ordeal in Africa, 1983. Office: Office of the Sec of State State Capital W Wing 1700 W Washington #700 Phoenix AZ 85007

MAHONEY, TIMOTHY JOHN, government relations consultant; b. Rochester, N.Y., Aug. 17, 1952; s. William F. and Phyllis M.; m. Myra A Sullivan, Jan. 21, 1978; children: Mark Timothy, Kevin Michael. AA, Santa Barbara City Coll., 1974; BA, U. Calif., Santa Barbara, 1977. Dir. govt. affairs Santa Barbara C. of C., Santa Barbara, 1981-86; dir. pub. rels. and devel. Santa Barbara Med. Found. Clinic, Santa Barbara, 1986-89; mgr. Nat. Elec. Contractors Assn., Santa Barbara, 1989-90; exec. dir. United Against Crime, Santa Barbara, 1991—; mgmt. cons. Santa Barbara Indsl. Assn., 1983—, Cachuma Resource Conservation Dist., 1987, Tax Payers Assn. Editor (jour.) Security News, 1991. Chmn. bd. dirs. YMCA, Santa Barbara, 1984. Recipient 1st pl. award Soc. Arts & Letters, Santa Barbara, 1975. Mem. Santa Barbara C. of C., Handball Club, Cathedral Oaks Tennis Club, Nat. Soc. Fundraising Execs. Office: United Against Crime 203 Chapala St Santa Barbara CA 93101

MAHONY, ROGER CARDINAL, archbishop; b. Hollywood, Calif., Feb. 27, 1936; s. Victor James and Loretta Marie (Baron) M. A.A., Our Lady Queen of Angels Sem., 1956; B.A., St. John's Sem. Coll., 1958, B.S.T., 1962; M.S.W., Catholic U. Am., 1964. Ordained priest Roman Cath. Ch., 1962, ordained bishop, 1975, created cardinal priest, 1991. Asst. pastor St. John's Cathedral, Fresno, Calif., 1962, 68-73, rector, 1973-80; residence St. Genevieve's Parish, Fresno, Calif., 1964—, adminstr., 1964-67, pastor, 1967-68; titular bishop of Tamascani, aux. bishop of Fresno, 1975-80; chancellor Diocese of Fresno, 1970-77, vicar gen., 1975-80; bishop Diocese of Stockton (Calif.), 1980-85; archbishop Archdiocese of L.A., 1985-91, cardinal priest, 1991—; diocesan dir. Cath. Charities and Social Svc. Fresno, 1964-70, exec. dir. Cath. Welfare Bur., 1964-70; exec. dir. Cath. Welfare Bur. Infant of Prague Adoption Service, 1964-70; chaplain St. Vincent de Paul Soc., Fresno, 1964-70; named chaplain to Pope Paul VI, 1967; mem. faculty extension div. Fresno State U., 1965-67; sec. U.S. Cath. bishops ad hoc com. on farm labor Nat. Conf. Bishops, 1970-75; chmn. com. on pub. welfare and income maintenance Nat. Conf. Cath. Charities, 1969-70; bd. dirs. West Coast Regional Office Bishops Com. for Spanish-Speaking, 1967-70; chmn. Calif. Assn. Cath. Charities Dirs., 1965-69; trustee St. Patrick's Sem., Archdiocese of San Francisco, 1974-75; mem. adminstrv. com. Nat. conf. Cath. Bishops, 1976-79, 82-85, 87-90, com. migration and refugees, 1976—, chmn. com. farm labor, 1981—, com. moral evaluation of deterrence, 1986-88; cons. com. for ProLife Activities, 1990—; mem. com. social devel. and world peace U.S. Cath. Conf., 1985, chmn. internat. policy sect., 1987-90; com. justice and peace, Pontifical Couns., 1984-89, 90—, pastoral care of migrants and itinerant people, 1986—, social communications, 1989—. Mem. Urban Coalition of Fresno, 1968-72, Fresno County Econ. Opportunities Commn., 1964-65, Fresno County Alcoholic Rehab. Com., 1966-67, Fresno City Charter Rev. Com., 1968-70, Mexican-Am. Council for Better Housing, 1968-72, Fresno Redevel. Agy., 1970-75, L.A. 2000 Com., 1985-88, Fed. Commn. Agrl. Workers, 1987—, Blue Ribbon Com. Affordable Housing City of L.A., 1988; mem. commn. to Draft an Ethics Code for L.A. City Govt., 1989-90; bd. dirs. Fresno Community Workshop, 1965-67; trustee St. Agnes Hosp., Fresno. Named Young Man of Yr. Fresno Jr. C. of C., 1967. Mem. Canon Law Soc. Am., Nat. Assn. Social Workers. Home: 114 E 2d St Los Angeles CA 90012 Office: Archdiocese of LA PO Box 15052 Los Angeles CA 90015-0052

MAHRE, PHIL, alpine ski racer, race car driver; b. Yakima, Wash., May 10, 1957; s. David Robert and Mary Ellen (Chotl) M.; m. Holly Mahre; 3 children. Student, pub. schs. Mem. U.S. Men's Pro Tour, 1989. Olympic Silver medalist in slalom Lake Placid, N.Y., 1980, Olympic Gold medalist, Sarajevo, Yugoslavia, 1984, winner World Cup, 1981, 82, 83, First Interstate Bank Cup slalom, 1989. Office: US Ski Team PO Box 100 Park City UT 84060-0100

MAHUTTE, CORNELIS KEES, internist, educator; b. Rotterdam, Holland, May 10, 1944; came to the U.S., 1979; s. Nicolaas Henri and Margareta (Kieboom) M.; m. Gabriele Katherina Pantel, July 13, 1968; 1 child, Neal Gregory. BS, U. Toronto, 1966; MS, U. Waterloo, Ontario, Canada, 1968, PhD, 1971; MD, McMaster U., 1974. Internal med. resident McMaster U., 1974-76, pulmonary fellow, 1977-79; resident Rsch. U. Toronto, 1976-77; asst. prof. medicine U. Calif., Irvine, 1979-86; chief MICU Long Beach (Calif.) VA Med. Ctr., 1979—, chief pulmonary & critical care sect., 1989—; assoc. prof. medicine U. Calif., Irvine, 1986—. Contbr. numerous articles to profl. jours.; patentee for method for continuous cardiac input. Fellow Royal Coll. Physicians, Coll. Chest Physicians. Home: 1371 Gwen Santa Ana CA 92705 Office: Long Beach VA Med Ctr Pulmonary Critical Care 5901 E 7th St Long Beach CA 90822

MAI, HAROLD LEVERNE, federal judge; b. Casper, Wyo., Apr. 5, 1928. B.A., U. Wyo., 1950, J.D., 1952. Bar: Wyo. 1952, U.S. Supreme Ct. 1963. Sole practice, Cheyenne, Wyo., 1953-62, 67-71; judge Juvenile Ct., Cheyenne, 1962-67; U.S. bankruptcy judge, Cheyenne, 1971—. Mem. adv. bd. Salvation Army. Wyo. Mem. ABA, Wyo. Bar Assn., Laramie County Bar Assn., Nat. Conf. Bankruptcy Judges. Office: US Bankruptcy Ct PO Box 763 Cheyenne WY 82003-0763

MAI, JAMES LAWRENCE, art educator, artist; b. Cheyenne, Wyo., Mar. 8, 1957; s. Harold Laverne and Margaret Katherine (Rhodes) M.; m. Laura Kay Brinkman, July 12, 1980. BFA, U. Wyo., 1982, MFA, 1985. Registrar, curatorial asst. art mus. U. Wyo., Laramie, 1980-85, dir. art gallery, 1985-86, vis. lectr. dept. art, 1986-87; prof., chair dept. Wenatchee (Wash.) Valley Coll., 1987—; cons. exhibit designer U. Wyo. Centennial Commn., Laramie, 1987, Wash. Mut. Savs. Corp., Wenatchee, 1988-89; designated book reviewer Collegiate Press, Alta Loma, Calif., 1991-92. Exhibited in group shows at Oreg.-Wash. Biennial Exhbn., 1989, Alcoa Nat. Juried Exhbn., 1990 (juror's award), Mus. Without Walls Internat., Bemus Point, N.Y., 1992, Charlotte (N.C.) Internat. Exhbn., 1993, 57th Cooperstown (N.Y.) Ann., 1992, Acad. of Fine Arts, Easton, Md., 1992; one-man shows include Adam East Art Mus., 1991. Bd. dirs., com. chair Gallery '76, Wenatchee, 1987—. Mem. NEA, Coll. Art Assn., Founds. in Art: Theory and Edn., Phi Beta Kappa, Phi Kappa Phi. Home: 415-A Huber Ct East Wenatchee WA 98802 Office: Wenatchee Valley Coll Dept Art 1300 Fifth St Wenatchee WA 98801

MAIBACH, HOWARD I., dermatologist; b. N.Y.C., July 18, 1929; s. Jack Louis and Sidonia (Fink) M.; m. Siesel Wile, July 8, 1953; children—Lisa, Ed, Todd. A.B., Tulane U., 1950, M.D., 1955. Diplomate: Am. Bd. Dermatology. Intern William Beaumont Army Hosp., El Paso, Tex., 1955-56; resident, fellow in dermatology USPHS, Hosp. of U. Pa., 1959-61; asst. instr. U. Pa., 1958-61, lectr., 1960-61; practice medicine specializing in dermatology U. Calif. Hosps., San Francisco, 1961—; asst. prof. dermatology U. Calif. Sch. Medicine, San Francisco, 1961-63; asso. prof. U. Calif. Sch. Medicine, 1967-73; research asso. Cancer Research Inst., 1967—; mem. staff U. Calif.-H.C. Moffitt Hosps., 1961—; cons. Laguna Honda Hosp., 1962-66, chief dermatology service, 1963-67; cons. Letterman Gen. Hosp., Calif. Med. Facility, Vacaville, San Francisco Gen. Hosp., Sonoma State Hosp., Eldridge, Calif., Stanford Research Inst., Menlo Park, Calif., Calif. Dept. Public Health, Berkeley, VA Hosp., Research Inst. Fragrance Materials, Inc., David Grant USAF Hosp. of Travis AFB, Naval Hosp., San Diego, Wilford Hall AFB, Tex., Army Environ. Health Agy., Md.; mem. Internat. Contact Dermatitis Research Com. Editor: Animal Models in Dermatology, 1965; co-editor: Dermatotoxicology and Pharmacology, 1977, Skin Microbiology, 1981; bd. editors: Internat. Jour. Dermatology, 1974—; editorial bd.: Contact Dermatitis: Environ. Dermatology, 1974—, Clin. Toxicology, 1976—; internat. editorial bd.: Excerpta Media, 1976—; author, coauthor, editor of over 30 books and 750 publs. Served to capt. M.C. U.S. Army, 1955-58. Recipient awards Soc. Cosmetic Chemists, 1970, 71, 73. Fellow A.C.P.; mem. Am. Acad. Dermatology (award for essay 1961), San Francisco Dermatol. Soc. (pres. 1970-71), Pacific Dermatol. Assn., Soc. Investigative Dermatology, N.Y. Acad. Scis., Calif. Med. Assn., Am. Fedn. Clin. Research, AMA, San Francisco Med. Soc., Am. Dermatol. Assn., Internat. Soc. Tropical Dermatology, Am. Soc. Clin. Pharmacology and Therapeutics, Am. Coll. Toxicology; hon. mem. Swedish Dermatol. Soc., Am. Vet. Dermatol. Assn., Am. Acad. Vet. Dermatology, Danish Dermatol. Soc., German Dermatol. Soc. Office: Univ of Calif Hosp San Francisco CA 94143

MAIBACH, MICHAEL CHARLES, government affairs director; b. Peoria, Ill., May 14, 1951. BA in Polit. Sci. cum laude, No. Ill. U., 1973; BA in Am., Latin Am. History cum laude, Calif. State U., 1983; BS in Bus. and Internat. Affairs, Am. Univ., 1989. Govt. affairs mgr., machine shop foreman Caterpillar Inc., Peoria, Ill., 1976-83; asst. to vice chmn. Intel Corp., Washington, 1983-86, dir. govt. affairs, 1983—; staff asst. Pres. Bush's Nat. Adv. Commn. on Semiconductors, Washington, 1991, Pres. Reagan's Commn. on Indsl. Competitiveness, Washington, 1983-85; staff Ill. State Senate, Springfield, 1975-76; mem. Ill. Humanities Coun., 1973-75. Mem. Bd. of Zoning Adjustment, Menlo Park, Calif., 1985; bd. dirs. Dekalb County (1st person elected to pub. office under 21 yrs. of age in Ill. History), 1972-75. Holmes Grad. fellow, 1980; recipient Gov.'s fellowship Ill. Dept. Local Govt., summers 1970, 71, fellowship Ctr. for Study of Presidency, 1977-78. Mem. Nat. Adv. Coun. Home: 1047 Noel Dr Menlo Park CA 94025-3328

MAIENSCHEIN, JANE ANN, historian, philosopher; b. Oak Ridge, Tenn., Sept. 23, 1950; d. Fred Conrad and Joyce Evelyn (Kylander) M.; m. J. Richard Creath, Mar. 13, 1982. BA, Yale U., 1972; MA, Ind. U., 1975, PhD, 1978. Asst. prof. Dickinson Coll., Carlisle, Pa., 1978-80; vis. scholar Harvard U., Cambridge, Mass., 1983-84; vis. assoc. prof. Stanford (Calif.) U., 1987; asst. prof. Ariz. State U., Tempe, 1981-86, assoc. prof. philosophy, 1986-90, prof. philosophy and zoology, 1990—. Author: Transforming Traditions, 1991, 100 Years Exploring Life, 1989; editor: Defining Biology, 1986; co-editor: American Expansion of Biology, 1991. Recipient various grants NSF; fellowship Josiah Macy Jr. Found., 1974-78. Mem. AAAS (various coms.), History of Sci. Soc. (various coms.), Internat. Soc. for History, Philosophy and Social Studies of Sci. (pres. 1989-91), Am. Soc. of Zoologists, Sigma Xi. Office: Ariz State U Philosophy Dept Tempe AZ 85287-2004

MAIER, GERALD JAMES, natural gas transmission and marketing company executive; b. Regina, Sask., Can., Sept. 22, 1928; s. John Joseph and Mary (Passler) M. Student, Notre Dame Coll. (Wilcox), U. Man., U. Alta., U. Western Ont. With petroleum and mining industries Can., U.S., Australia, U.K.; responsible for petroleum ops. Africa, United Arab Emirates, S.E. Asia; chmn., CEO TransCan. PipeLines, Toronto, 1985—, also bd. dirs., chmn., pres., ceo; bd. dirs. BCE Inc., Bank of N.S., TransAlta Utilities Corp., Du Pont Can. Inc., Great Lakes Gas Transmission Co.; chmn. Can. Nat. com. for World Petroleum Congresses, Van Horne Inst. for Internat. Transp.; bd. govs. Bus. Coun. on Nat. Issues; chmn. bd. dirs. Western Gas Mktg. Ltd. Named Hon. Col. King's Own Calgary Regt., Resource Man of Yr. Alta. Chamber of Resources, 1990; recipient Can. Engr.'s Gold medal Can. Coun. Profl. Engrs., 1990, Disting. Alumni award U. Alberta, 1992, Mgmt. award McGill U., 1993. Fellow Can. Acad. Engring.; mem. Am. Gas Assn. (bd. govs.), Can. Petroleum Assn. (bd. govs.), Assn. Profl. Engrs., Geologists and Geophysicists Alta (past pres.), Can. Inst. Mining and Metallurgy (Past President's Meml. medal 1971), Interstate Natural Gas Assn. Am. (bd. govs.). Office: TransCan PipeLines Ltd, PO Box 1000 Sta M, Calgary, AB Canada T2P 4K5

MAIER, MARK DANIEL, news director; b. Burley, Idaho, Sept. 4, 1968; s. Dennis Fred and Judith (Tjaden) M.; m. Nicole Bailey, Oct. 6, 1990; children: Kit Carson, Zackory D. Student, N.D. State U., 1986-88. Disc jockey Sta. KBTO, Bottineau, N.D., 1987-88; news dir. Sta. KBAR/KZDX, Burley, Idaho, 1988—; pub. address announcer Idaho Regatta, Burley, 1992. Mem. Idaho Associated Press (v.p. 1991-92, pres. 1992-93, Best Spot News 1991, 92, Best Pub. Affairs 1991, 92, Best Spl. and Pub. Affairs 1992), Burley Area C. of C. (membership com. 1988—). Republican. Lutheran. Home: 1233 Grandview Sp D-3 Burley ID 83318 Office: Sta KBAR/KZDX Radio 1841 W Main Burley ID 83318

MAIER, PETER KLAUS, law educator, investment adviser; b. Wurzburg, Germany, Nov. 20, 1929; came to U.S., 1939, naturalized, 1945; s. Bernard and Joan (Sonder) M.; m. Melanie L. Stoff, Dec. 15, 1963; children: Michele Margaret, Diana Lynn. BA cum laude, Claremont McKenna Coll., 1949; JD, U. Calif., Berkeley, 1952; LLM in Taxation, NYU, 1953. Bar: Calif. 1953, U.S. Supreme Ct. 1957; cert. specialist in taxation law, Calif. Atty. tax div. U.S. Dept Justice, Washington, 1956-59; mem. firm Bacigalupi, Elkus, Salinger & Rosenberg, San Francisco, 1959-69, Brookes & Maier, San Francisco, 1970-73, Winokur, Maier & Zang, San Francisco, 1974-81; of counsel Crosby, Heafy, Roach & May, Oakland, Calif., 1986—; prof. law Hastings Coll. Law, U. Calif., San Francisco, 1967—; vis. prof. U. Calif. Boalt Sch. Law, Berkeley, 1988-89; pres. Maier & Siebel, Inc., Larkspur, Calif., 1981—; prin. Wood Island Investment Counsel, Inc., Larkspur, 1981—. Author books on taxation; contbr. articles to profl. jours. Chmn. bd. profl. advisors Buck Ctr. for Rsch. on Aging, Calif., 1989—; chmn. Property Resources Inc., San Jose, Calif., 1968-77; pres. Calif. Property Devel. Corp., San Francisco, 1974-81. Capt. USAF, 1953-56. Mem. San Francisco Bar Assn. (chmn. sect. taxation 1970-71), Order of Coif. Home: PO Box 391 Belvedere Tiburon CA 94920-0391 Office: Hastings Coll Law 200 Mcallister St San Francisco CA 94102-4976

MAIERHAUSER, JOSEPH GEORGE, entrepreneur; b. Yankton, S.D., Mar. 23, 1927; s. Joseph and Angela M. (Jung) M.; m. Reta Mae Brockelsby, Nov. 25, 1948 (div. 1965); 1 child, Joe; m. Martha Helen Kuehn, Dec. 10, 1965. Student, U. S.D., Vermillion, 1946, S.D. Sch. Mines and Tech., Rapid City, 1947. Sales mgr. Black Hills Reptile Gardens, Rapid City, S.D., 1949-54; operator Colossal Cave Park, Vail, Ariz., 1956—; ptnr. Sta. KRNR, Roseburg, Oreg., 1961—. Mem. adv. bd. Salvation Army, Tucson, 1979-86; govs. appointee San Pedro Rparian Nat. Cons. Area Adv. Com., 1989—; past pres. So. Ariz. Internat. Livestock Assn., 1987-88; bd. dirs. Friends of Western Art., Tucson; co-founder Pima County Parklands Found.. With U.S. Navy Air Corps., 1944-45. Mem. Mountain Oyster Club (pres. 1989-91, bd. dirs. 1980-83). Republican. Home: Bear Paw Vail AZ 85641 Office: Colossal Cave Mountain Park Box D70 Vail AZ 85641

MAILLOT, PATRICK GILLES, computer scientist; b. Paris, France, June 27, 1958; came to U.S., 1988; s. Marcel and Renee (Pechet) M.; m. Patricia Violette Maurin, May 28, 1983; children: Audrey, Claire. M, U. Lyon, 1982, PhD, 1986. Software engr. Secapa, Dardilly, France, 1983-86; mgr. Thomson Csp., Colombes, France, 1986-88; software engr./project lead Sun Microsystems, Mountain View, Calif., 1988-91, engring. mgr. XGL project, 1991—; reviewer ACM, N.Y.C., 1988—; reviewer IEEE. Patentee in field; contbr. articles to profl. jours. Sgt. AF, 1982-83. Mem. Assn. Computing Machinery. Home: 810 Peach Ave Sunnyvale CA 94087-1148 Office: Sun Microsystems Inc MTV 23-205 2550 Garcia Ave Mountain View CA 94043-1100

MAIN, DOUGLAS CAMERON, provincial cabinet minister; b. Willow Bunch, Sask., Can., July 18, 1946; s. Claude Bruce and Lillian Marie (Bellefleur) M.; m. Judith Marie Sumner, Apr. 25, 1970; children: Joshua David, Jeremy Scott. Student, U. Winnipeg (Man., Can.), 1967, Athabasca (Alta., Can.), 1986. Mutual fund sales exec. Investors Group, Winnipeg, 1969-70; photo sales and prodn. exec. Martin Photo, Winnipeg, 1970; radio newscaster CTOB Radio, Winnipeg, 1970-72; radio and TV newscaster CFTR-CHFI FM, Toronto, Ont., Can., 1972-73, CKY AM-FM TV, Winnipeg, 1973-75; TV newscaster, producer CITV, Edmonton, Alta., 1975-88; minister of culture and multiculturalism Govt. of Alta., Edmonton, 1989—; freelance TV producer, 1980-89; instr. in journalism Grant MacElwan Community Coll., Edmonton, 1980-89; v.p. CJIL Broadcasting Ltd., Edmonton, 1980-82. Candidate Reform Party of Can., Edmonton, 1988, MLA, Progressive Conservative Assn. Alta., Edmonton, 1989. Mem. Royal Glenora Club (chmn. squash com. 1987-88). Home: 1511 Bearspaw Dr E, Edmonton, AB Canada T6J 5E2 Office: Minister of Culture, Legislature Bldg Rm 418, Edmonton, AB Canada T5K 2B6

MAIN, ROBERT GAIL, communications and training consultant, television and film producer, educator, former army officer; b. Bucklin, Mo., Sept. 30, 1932; s. Raymond M. and Inez L. (Olinger) M.; m. Anita Sue Thoroughman, Jan. 31, 1955; children: Robert Bruce, David Keith, Leslie Lorraine. BS magna cum laude, U. Mo., 1954; grad. with honors, Army Command and Gen. Staff Coll., 1967; MA magna cum laude in Communications, Stanford U., 1968; PhD, U. Md., 1978. Commd. 2d lt. U.S. Army, 1954, advanced through grades to lt. col., 1968; various command and staff assignments field arty., 1954-64; sr. instr. and div. chief Pershing missile div. U.S. Army Arty. and Missile Sch., Ft. Sill, Okla., 1964-66; mem. faculty U.S. Army Command and Gen. Staff Coll., 1968-70; chief speechwriting and info. materials div. U.S. Army Info. Office, 1971, chief broadcast and film div., 1972-73; dir. def. audiovisual activities Office of Info. for Armed Forces, 1973-76, ret., 1976; prof., grad. adv. Coll. Communications, Calif. State U., Chico, 1976-87; pres. Grant & Main, Inc., corp. communications and tng. cons. Author: Rogues, Saints and Ordinary People, 1988; contbr. articles on audiovisual communications to profl. pubs.; producer: Walking Wounded, TV documentary, 1983; producer army info. films, army radio series, 1972-73; creating family heritage videos. Decorated Legion of Merit, Meritorious Service medal, Commendation medal with oak leaf cluster, combat Inf. Badge; Vietnamese Cross of Gallantry; recipient Freedom Found. awards, 1972, 73, 74; Bronze medal Atlanta Film Festival, 1972; Best of Show award Balt. Film Festival, 1973; Creativity award Chgo. Indsl. Film Festival, 1973; Cine gold award Internat. Film Producers Assn., 1974; named an Outstanding Prof. Calif State U., 1987-88. Mem. Assn. for Ednl. Communications Tech., Am. Soc. of Curriculum Developers, Nat. Assn. Edni. Broadcasters, Phi Eta Sigma, Alpha Zeta, Phi Delta Gamma, Omicron Delta Kappa, Alpha Gamma Rho. Mem. Christian Ch.

MAINWARING, WILLIAM LEWIS, publishing company executive, author; b. Portland, Oreg., Jan. 17, 1935; s. Bernard and Jennie (Lewis) M.; m. Mary E. Bell, Aug. 18, 1962; children: Anne Marie, Julia Kathleen, Douglas Bernard. B.S., U. Oreg., 1957; postgrad., Stanford U., 1957-58. With Salem (Oreg.) Capital Jour., 1958-76, editor, pub., 1962-76; pub. Oreg. Statesman, 1974-76; pres. Statesman-Jour. Co., Inc., Salem, 1974-76, Westridge Press, Ltd., 1977—; pres., CEO Medi Am., Inc., Portland, 1981—. Author: Exploring the Oregon Coast, 1977, Exploring Oregon's Central and Southern Cascades, 1979, Exploring the Mount Hood Loop, 1992. Pres. Salem Beautification Coun., 1968, Marion-Polk County United Good Neighbors, 1970, Salem Social Svcs. Commn., 1978-79, Salem Hosp. Found., 1978-81. 2d lt. AUS, 1958; capt. Res. Ret. Mem. Salem Area C. of C. (pres. 1972-73), Oreg. Symphony Soc. Salem (pres. 1973-75), Salem City Club (pres. 1977-78), Sigma Chi. Republican. Presbyterian (ruling elder). Home: 1090 Southridge Pl S Salem OR 97302-5947 Office: Oreg Bus Mag 921 SW Morrison St Ste 407 Portland OR 97205-2722

MAIRA, JANET, university relations administrator; b. Detroit, Oct. 21, 1942; d. Maurice Donald and Adeline (Quatro) Worthington; m. Octavio Maira (div.). BA in English, U. Calif., Berkeley, 1964; secondary teaching credential, UCLA, 1965. Producer Cascade Pictures, Hollywood, Calif., 1970-72; ednl. writer Insgroup, Inc., Orange, Calif., 1972; editor The Tolucan, North Hollywood, Calif., 1972; analyst John S. Pennish & Assocs., L.A., 1973; asst. evaluator Alum Rock Union Elem. Sch. Dist., San Jose, 1974-76; editorial dir. KPIX-TV, San Francisco, 1976-78; pub. info. dir. The Insts. of Med. Scis., San Francisco, 1978-81; pub. affairs officer Napa Valley Coll., Napa, Calif., 1981-86; dir. Univ. News Svcs.-Calif. State U., Sacramento, 1986-92; asst. dir. univ. rels. U. of the Pacific, 1992—. Mem. Calif. Press Women (pres. 1980-81).

MAIROSE, PAUL TIMOTHY, mechanical engineer, consultant; b. Mitchell, S.D., Aug. 4, 1956; s. Joseph E. and Phyllis R. (Glissendorf) M.; m. Connie L. Nickell, Apr. 1, 1989 (dec. June 8, 1992). BSME, S.D. Sch. Mines and Tech., 1978; postgrad., Tulane U., 1986. Registered profl. engr., Wash. Mech. engr. UNC Nuclear Industries, Richland, Wash., 1979-80, Wash. Pub. Power Supply System, Richland, 1980-85, 89; cons. La. Power & Light Co., New Orleans, 1985-86, Erin Engring. & Rsch. Inc., Walnut Creek, Calif., 1986-87, Sacramento Mcpl. Utility Dist., 1987-89; mech. engr. GE, Portland, Oreg., 1989-90; sr. cons. Rocky Flats Project Cygna Energy Svcs., 1990-91; v.p. mktg. Data Max, 1991—; pvt. practice cons. engr. Vancouver, Wash., 1991—; project engr. MatTec, Inc., Richland, Wash., 1990-91; pres. Project Tech. Mgmt., 1990—; chief engr. S.W. Air Pollution Control Authority, Vancouver, Wash., 1992—. Co-author: Topical Report on Extreme Erosion at Yucca Mountain, Nevada, 1993. Mem. polit. action com. Sacramento Mcpl. Utility Dist., 1988. Mem. ASME (assoc.), ASHRAE (assoc.), Aircraft Owners and Pilots Assn., Profl. Assn. Diving Instrs., Air & Water Mgmt. Assn., Sierra Club, Bards of Bohemia. Republican. Roman Catholic. Home: 1610 NW 137th St Vancouver WA 98685-1513

MAJERLE, DANIEL LEWIS, professional basketball player, olympic athlete; b. Traverse City, Mich., Sept. 9, 1965. Student, Ctrl. Mich. Forward Phoenix Suns, 1988—. Mem. Bronze Medal Winning Olympic Team, Seoul, Korea, 1988; mem. NBA All-Defensive second team, 1991; mem. NBA All-Star team, 1992, 93. Office: Phoenix Suns PO Box 1369 Phoenix AZ 85001

MAJESTY, MELVIN SIDNEY, psychologist, consultant; b. New Orleans, June 6, 1928; s. Sidney Joseph and Marcella Cecilia (Kieffer) M.; m. Bettye Newanda Gordon, Dec. 18, 1955; 1 child, Diana Sue. BA, La. State U., 1949; MS, Western Res. U., 1951; PhD (USAF Inst. Tech. fellow), Case-Western Res. U., 1967. Commd. 2d lt. USAF, 1951, advanced through grades to lt. col., 1968; program mgr., ast. dir. tng. rsch. Air Force Human Resources Lab., 1967-69; dir. faculty and profl. ednl. rsch. USAF Acad., 1969-72; dir. plot tng. candidate selection program Officer Tng. Sch., Air Tng.Command, 1972-76; ret. USAF, 1976; personnel selection cons. to Calif. State Pers. Bd., Sacramento, 1976—. Patentee listening center; founded pers. testing for ballistic missile and space systems; directed largest study of fighter pilot selection since World War II; pioneered use of phys. testing as replacement for the maximum age requirment in law enformenct jobs; developed phys. fitness tests and established pscyhol. screening standards for state highway patrol officer and police officers; contbr. numerous articles to profl. publs. Decorated Commendation medal (2), Meritorious Svc. medal (2). Mem. Am. Psychol. Assn., Internat. Pers. Mgmt. Assn., Calif. Psychol. Assn., Western Psychol. Assn., Soc. Indsl. and Orgnl. Psychology, Personnel Testing Coun., VFW, DAV, Am. Legion, Amvets. Home: 216 Gifford Way Sacramento CA 95864-6910 Office: 801 Capitol Mall Sacramento CA 95814

MAJOR, MARGUERITE LOUISE, retired magazine editor; b. Kansas City, Mo., Jan. 26, 1929; d. Ray Clark and Celia Marguerite (Fowler) M. AB in Journalism, San Jose State U., 1950. Editorial asst. Greeting Cards, Inc., N.Y.C., 1950-51; reporter, editor Sunnyvale (Calif.) Standard, 1951-52; alumni dir. San Jose State U., 1953-57; pubs. dir. Santa Clara (Calif.) U., 1957-60, news dir., 1960-78, pub. affairs dir., 1978-83; editor Santa Clara Today, Santa Clara U., 1983-86, Santa Clara mag., Santa Clara U., 1986-91. Mem. Am. Coll. Pub. Rels. (regional dir. 1974-75), Pub. Rels. Soc. Am. (accredited), Coun. Advancement & Support Edn. (trustee 1975-77). Republican. Episcopalian. Office: 912 Cypress Point Loop Ashland OR 97520-3754

MAJUMDAR, DEBAPRASAD (DEBU), physicist, nuclear engineer; b. Calcutta, West Bengal, India, Dec. 10, 1941; came to U.S. 1964; s. Hem Chandra and Amala Bala (Roy) M.; m. Marie Catherine Heery, May 30, 1971; children: Rajeev David, Nikhil Daniel. BSc in Physics, MSc in Physics, Calcutta U., 1961, 63; MS in Physics, U. Pa., 1966; MS in Nuclear Engring., U. Mich., 1973; PhD in Physics, SUNY, Stony Brook, 1969. Registered profl. engr., Idaho. Postdoctoral fellow Syracuse (N.Y.) U., 1969-71; assoc. rsch. scientist and postdoctoral fellow U. Mich., Ann Arbor, 1971-74; nuclear engr. Brookhaven Nat. Lab., Upton, N.Y., 1974-80; program mgr. U.S. Dept. Energy, Idaho Falls, 1980—. Co-editor: Anticipated and Abnormal Plant Transients in Light Water Reactors, 1984, Artificial Intelligence and Other Innovative Computer Applications in Nuclear Industry, 1988; contbr. articles to profl. jours. Active Boy Scouts Am., 1989—. Recipient Gold medals, U. Calcutta, 1961, 63; All India Merit scholar, 1957-63; named Outstanding Vol., Idaho Falls Mayor's Office, 1987. Mem. Am. Nuclear Soc. (sec., chmn. nuclear reactor safety div. program com. 1987-90, chmn. and fellow Idaho sect.), Am. Phys. Soc. Home: 1749 Delmar Dr Idaho Falls ID 83404-7461 Office: US Dept Energy 785 Doe Pl Idaho Falls ID 83401-1562

MAKE, BARRY JAY, physician; b. Phila., July 2, 1947; s. Sydney and Beatrice (Hoffman) M.; m. Isabel Elise Rose, June 13, 1970; children: Jonathan David, Jeremy Simon. BS cum laude, Pa. State U., 1968; MD, Jefferson Med. Coll., 1970. Diplomate Am. Bd. Internal Medicine; cert. critical care medicine. Intern Thomas Jefferson U. Hosp., Phila., 1970-71; resident Med. Ctr. U. Mich., Ann Arbor, 1971-73; pulmonary fellow W.Va. U., 1973-74; asst. prof. Sch. Medicine U. W.Va., Morgantown, 1974-75; pulmonary fellow Boston U., 1975-76, asst. prof., 1976-83, assoc. prof., 1983-88; dir. respiratory care ctr. University Hosp., Boston, 1980-88; dir. pulmonary rehab. Nat. Jewish Ctr. for Immunology and Respiratory Medicine, Denver, 1988—; assoc. prof. U. Colo., Denver, 1988—; lectr. in field; mem. ad hoc com. on pulmonary function testing, Am. Occupational Medicine Assn., 1977-79; co-chmn. pulmonary acad. awardee steering com. Nat. Heart, Lung and Blood Inst., 1978-80, mem. sci. rev. com., 1981, ad hoc com. on future of pulmonary acad. award lung div., 1985; mem. pulmonary subspeciality rev. panel. Accreditation Coun. Grad. Med. Edn., 1988—; dir. Nat. Ctr. for Analysis of Home Mech. Ventilation. Author: (with others) Internal Medicine, 3d edit., 1990, Pulmonary Medicine: Problems in Primary Care, 1989, others; mem. edit. bd. Am. Rev. Respiratory Disease, 1989—; contbr. articles to profl. jours. Surgeon USPHS, 1973-75. Fellow ACP, Am. Coll. Chest Physicians (steering com. environ. health forum 1978-80, sec. environ. health forum 1981-83, steering com. sect. on clin. problems assembly, ad hoc com. on mech. ventilation in home 1985-86); mem. Am. Assn. Cardiovascular and Pulmonary Rehab., Am. Assn. Respiratory Care, Am. Fedn. Clin. Rsch., Colo. Pulmonary Physicians, Colo. Thoracic Soc., Am. Thoracic Soc., Am. Heart Assn., Colo. Trudeau Soc. Office: Nat Jewish Ctr Immunology and Respiratory Medicine 1400 Jackson St Denver CO 80206-2761

MAKI, KAZUMI, physicist, educator; b. Takamatsu, Japan, Jan. 27, 1936; s. Toshio and Hideko M.; m. Masako Tanaka, Sept. 21, 1969. B.S., Kyoto U., 1959, Ph.D., 1964. Research asso. Inst. for Math. Scis., Kyoto U., 1964; research asso. Fermi Inst., U. Chgo., 1964-65; asst. prof. physics U. Calif., San Diego, 1965-67; prof. Tohoku U., Sendai, Japan, 1967-74; vis. prof. Universite Paris-Sud, Orsay, France, 1969-70; prof. physics U. So. Calif., Los Angeles, 1974—; vis. prof. Inst. Laue-Langevin, U. Paris-Sud, France, 1979-80, Max-Planck Inst. für Festkörper Forschung, Stuttgart, Fed. Republic Germany, 1986-87, U. Paris-7, 1990. Assoc. editor Jour. Low Temperature Physics, 1969-91; contbr. articles to profl. jours. Recipient Nishina prize, 1972, Alexander von Humboldt award, 1986-87; Fulbright scholar, 1964-65; Guggenheim fellow, 1979-80. Fellow Am. Phys. Soc.; mem. Phys. Soc. Japan, AAAS. Office: U So Calif Dept Physics Los Angeles CA 90089-0484

MAKKER, SUDESH PAUL, physician; b. Sargodha, Punjab, India, June 8, 1941; came to U.S., 1966; s. Manohar Lal and Daya Wati (Kharbanda) M.; m. Donna Mae Stohs, Feb. 15, 1969; children: Vishal, Kirin. Fellow of Sci., Panjab U., 1959; MD, All India Inst. med. Scis., New Dehli, 1964. Bd. cert. Am. Bd. Pediatrics, Am. Bd. Pediatric Nephrology. Intern in internal medicine All India Inst. of Med. Scis., New Dehli, 1965, resident in internal medicine, 1966; rotating intern Queens Gen. Hosp., N.Y.C., 1966-67; resident in pediatrics U. Chgo. (Ill.) Hosps., 1967-69; rsch. fellowship in pediatric nephrology Case Western Res. U., 1969-71; fellowship in pediatric nephrology U. Calif., San Francisco, 1971; instr. to asst. prof. pediatrics Case Western Res. U., Sch. Medicine, Cleve., 1971-76, assoc. prof., div. head pediatric nephrology, 1976-83; prof., div. head pediatric nephrology U. Tex. Health Sci. Ctr., San Antonio, 1983-91; prof., sect. chief pediatric nephrology U. Calif., Davis Sch. Medicine, Davis, 1991—; mem. ad hoc com. on nat. standards for dialysis and transplantation in children Am. Soc. Pediatric Nephrology; ad hoc com. on hypertension in the young Am. Heart Assn., N.E. Ohio Chpt.; mem. end stage renal disease program Crippled Children Svcs. State of Ohio; mem. rsch. grants com. and pub. edn. com. Kidney Found. of Ohio; vis. prof. U. Pa. Children's Hosp., Phila., 1981, U. So. Calif., L.A., 1981, U. Calif. Sch. Medicine, San Francisco, 1982, U. Mich., Ann Arbor, 1990, and many others. Editor: (textbook) Pediatric Nephrology, 1992; editorial bd.: Internat. Jour. Pediatric Nephrology, Indian Jour. Pediatrics; contbr. over 80 articles to profl. jours. Mem. AAAS, Am. Acad. Pediatrics, Am. Soc. Nephrology, The Soc. for Exptl. Biology and Medicine, Am. Assn. Immunologists, Soc. for Pediatric Rsch., Am. Pediatric

Soc., Sigma Chi, Sigma Xi. Office: Univ Calif Davis Med Ctr Pediatric Nephrology 2516 Stockton Blvd Sacramento CA 95817

MAKSYMOWICZ, JOHN, electrical engineer; b. Bklyn., Feb. 3, 1956; s. Theodore John and Helen Mary (Kisinski) M. BEE with highest honors, Pratt Inst., Bklyn., 1983. Elec. engr. RF and digital automated test equipment IBM, Poughkeepsie, N.Y., 1983; elec. engr. AWACS airborne early warning radar Grumman Aerospace Corp., Bethpage, N.Y., 1983-87; elec. engr. radar and spread spectrum comm. Plessey Electronics, Totowa, N.J., 1987-88; sr. mem. tech. staff, radar designer The Aerospace Corp., L.A., 1989—. Recipient Cook-Marsh scholarship Pratt Inst., 1979-83, Samuel Brown scholarship, 1979-83. Mem. IEEE, U.S. Space Found., Old Crows Assn., Tau Beta Pi (coll. chpt. pres. 1981-82), Eta Kappa Nu (coll. chpt. pres, 1981-82). Roman Catholic. Office: The Aerospace Corp M4-900 PO Box 92957 Los Angeles CA 90009-2957

MAKUS, ERIC JOHN, research company executive, speech writer; b. Seattle, May 11, 1962; s. John Eric Makus and Sharon Joy (Price) Bennett. BA in Polit. Sci., Whitman Coll., 1984; M in Planning, U. So. Calif., 1987. Spl. asst. U.S. Rep. Thomas S. Foley, Walla Walla, Wash., 1983-84; prin. Eureka Assocs., L.A., 1986—. Office: Eureka Assocs Ste 2302 255 S Grand Ave Los Angeles CA 90012-6020

MALA, THEODORE ANTHONY, physician, state official; b. Santa Monica, Calif., Feb. 3, 1946; s. Ray and Galina (Liss) M.; children: Theodore S., Galina T. BA in Philosophy, DePaul U., 1972; MD, Autonomous U., Guadalajara, Mex., 1976; MPH, Harvard U., 1980. Spl. asst. for health affairs Alaska Fedn. Natives, Anchorage, 1977-78; chief health svcs. Alaska State Div. of Corrections, Anchorage, 1978-79; assoc. prof., founder, dir. Inst. for Circumpolar Health Studies, U. Alaska, Anchorage, 1982-90; founder Siberian med. rsch. program U. Alaska, Anchorage, 1982, founder Magadan (USSR) med. rsch. program, 1988; commr. Health and Social Svcs. State of Alaska, Juneau, 1990—; mem. Alaska rsch. and publs. com. Indian Health Svc., USPHS, 1987-90; advisor Nordic Coun. Meeting, WHO, Greenland, 1985; mem. Internat. Organizing Com., Circumpolar Health Congress, Iceland, 1992-93; chmn. bd. govs. Alaska Psychiat. Inst., Anchorage, 1990—; cabinet mem. Gov. Walter J. Hickel, Juneau, 1990—; advisor humanitarian aid to Russian Far East U.S. Dept. State, 1992—. Former columnist Tundra Times; contbr. articles to profl. jours. Trustee United Way Anchorage, 1978-79. Recipient Gov.'s award, 1988, Outstanding Svc. award Alaska Commr. Health, 1979, Ministry of Health citiation USSR Govt., 1989; Citation award Alaska State Legislature, 1989, 90, Commendation award State of Alaska, 1990, Honor Kempton Svc. to Humanity award, 1989, citation Med. Community of Magadan region, USSR, 1989; Nat. Indian fellow U.S. Dept. Edn., 1979. Mem. Assn. Am. Indian Physicians, Am. Assn. University Profs., N.Y. Acad. Scis., Internat. Union for Circumpolar Health (permanent sec.-gen. 1987-90, mem. organizing com. 8th Internat. Congress on Circumpolar Health 1987-90), Am. Pub. Health Assn., Alaska Pub. Health Assn. Home: PO Box 232228 Anchorage AK 99523-2228 Office: Alaska Dept Health and Social Svcs Office of Commr PO Box 110601 Juneau AK 99811

MALACHOWSKI, MITCHELL RAYMOND, university administrator; b. Providence, July 31, 1955; s. Mitchell A. and Margaret (O'Connell) M.; m. Elizabeth J. Melaragno, June 8, 1986. BA, R.I. Coll., 1977; PhD, U. N.C., 1983. Lectr. R.I. Coll., Providence, 1977-78; teaching asst. U. N.C., Chapel Hill, 1978-81, rsch. assoc., 1980-83; asst. prof. Gettysburg (Pa.) Coll., 1983-84; from asst. prof. to assoc. prof. chemistry U. San Diego, 1984—, assoc. dean arts and scis., 1989—; cons. Clorox, Pleasanton, Calif., 1986—, Lincoln Ency., San Diego, 1986-87; mentor Rsch. Corp., Tucson, 1990—. Contbr. articles to profl. jours. Pres. San Diego Alliance for Chem. Edn., 1988—; bd. dirs. Circumnavigators Club, San Diego. Recipient Outstanding Alumni award R.I. Coll., Providence, 1990; grantee Petroleum Rsch. Fund, 1984-87, Rsch. Corp. 1990—, Bristol-Myers Co., 1990—, Kresge Found. Mem. AAAS, Am. Chem. Soc. (bd. dirs., mentor project Seed, 1985), Am. Assn. Colls., Nat. Assn. Coll. Tchrs., Nat. Assn. Acad. Advisors, Nat. Sci. Tchrs. Assn. (coun. undergrad. rsch.). Office: U San Diego Alcala Pk San Diego CA 92110

MALAKOFF, JAMES LEONARD, management information executive; b. Phila., June 20, 1933; s. John and Ida Vera (Partman) M.; m. Anne Bronstein Frisch, June 26, 1955; children: Randi Ellen, John Seymour. B in Aerospace Engring., Rensselaer Poly. Inst., 1954, MS, 1955. Structural methods specialist Grumman Aircraft, Bethpage, N.Y., 1955-62; mem. tech. staff Northrop Corp., Hawthorne, Calif., 1962-65; chief, math. analyst Beckman Instruments, Inc., Fullerton, Calif., 1965-68; dir. data processing Beckman Instruments, Inc., Fullerton, 1968-82, v.p. data processing, 1982-85, v.p., mgmt. info., 1985—; bd. dirs. Little Co. Mary Health Svcs., Little Co. Mary Hosp., San Pedro (Calif.) Peninsula Hosp.; vis. prof. computer sci. Calif. State U., Fullerton, 1981-82, mem. indsl. adv. coun. Sch. Engring. and Computer Sci. Fellow AIAA (assoc.); mem. IEEE (computer group), U.S. Council Internat. Bus. (bus. and industry adv. com., West Coast com. Internat. Info. and Telecommunications Policy), Assn. Computing Machinery, Data Processing Mgmt. Assn. Office: Beckman Instruments Inc 2500 N Harbor Blvd Fullerton CA 92635-2600

MALCOLM, RICHARD WARD, college administrator, consultant; b. Columbus, Ohio, July 27, 1933; s. Ralph James and Beatrice (Ward) M.; m. Julie A. A'Hearn, Feb. 6, 1982 (div. Sept. 1986); 1 child, Gwynn Malcolm Socolich. BS, U. Findlay (Ohio), 1956; MA, Ariz. State U., 1960; MEd, U. So. Calif., 1965, EdD, 1966. Acad. dean Martin Coll., Pulaski, Tenn., 1965-67; dean instruction Arapahoe Community Coll., Littleton, Colo., 1967-71; chair edn. div. Chapman Coll., Orange, Calif., 1971-80; assoc. prof. U. So. Calif., 1976-77; dean instruction Mesa (Ariz.) Community Coll., 1980-91; asst. to provost Chandler (Ariz.)/Gilbert Community Coll., 1991-92, chair divsn. social and behavioral scis., 1993—. Author: Mental Measurement Yearbook, 1972. Pres. Ariz. Rail Pasenger Assn., Phoenix, 1984-93. Mem. Am. Assn. Higher Edn., Ariz. Acad. Adminstrv. Assn. (treas. 1991—), Rotary. Methodist. Office: Chandler/Gilbert Community Coll 2626 E Pecos Rd Chandler AZ 85225-2499

MALCZEWSKI, PATRICIA ELWELL, real estate broker; b. Newburgh, N.Y., May 17, 1940; d. John Clement King and Ruth Culver Ahernsdorf-Booth; m. Floyd Allen Elwell, Apr. 4, 1959 (div. Jan., 1972); children: Lori Ann Schwefel, Floyd Allen Jr., Robert Jay; m. John Malczewski, Mar. 14, 1988. Grad. high sch., Santa Fe Springs, Calif.; student, Mohave Community Coll. Sec. Autonetics N.A.A., Anaheim, Calif., 1959-61; sales assoc. King Realty, Bullhead City, Ariz., 1973-80; broker King Realty, Ft. Mohave, Ariz., 1980-85; owner King Realty & Land, Inc., Ft. Mohave, 1985—; sales coord. ind. distributorship Nat. Safety Assocs. Chmn. Ft. Mojave Mesa Fire Dist. Bd., 1985-93; mem. Mohave County Bond Adv. Com., 1986. Mem. NAFE, Nat. Fed. Ind. Businessmen, Worldwide Properties. Libertarian. Episcopalian. Office: King Realty & Land Inc 5635 Hwy 95 PO Box 8549 Fort Mohave AZ 86427

MALDE, HAROLD EDWIN, retired federal government geologist; b. Reedsport, Oreg., July 9, 1923; s. Emil and Bessie May (Alspaugh) M.; m. Caroline Elizabeth Rose, Dec. 21, 1954; children: Margaret Jean, Melissa Ruth. AB, Willamette U., 1947; postgrad. Harvard U., 1947-48, U. Colo., 1948-51. Geologist, U.S. Geol. Survey, Denver, 1951-87, emeritus, 1987—; mem. Colo. com. for Nat. Register Hist. Places, 1972-80; vol. photographer Nature Conservancy, 1987—; mem. paleoanthropology del. to Peoples Republic China, Nat. Acad. Scis., 1975, mem. various coms. for study surface mining; mem. oil shale environ. adv. panel U.S. Dept. Interior, 1976-80. Contbr. numerous sci. papers to profl. lit. Served to ensign USNR, 1942-44. Recipient Meritorious Service award U.S. Dept. Interior, 1979. Fellow Geol. Soc. Am. (Kirk Bryan award 1970, assoc. editor 1982-88), AAAS, Ariz.-Nev. Acad. Sci.; mem. Am. Quaternary Assn., Explorers Club. Democrat. Unitarian. Home: 842 Grant Pl Boulder CO 80302-7415

MALDON, LAWRENCE EARL, law firm office coordinator; b. Detroit, Apr. 4, 1952; s. John and Katie (McCorvey) M. MBA, Wayne State U., 1970. Office coord. Jones Hall Hill & White, San Francisco, 1983-90, Moffatt Thomas, Boise, Idaho, 1990—. With USAF, 1970-82, Vietnam. Decorated Air Force Merit award; named Instr. of Yr., Sim Moo Hapkido Karate U.S. Tae Kwon Do Union, San Francisco, 1983, 3d degree black belt karate. Home: 1796 Annett # 101 Boise ID 83705

MALDONADO, JOSE FRANK, cable television company executive; b. Albuquerque, Apr. 20, 1948; s. Eduardo and Francisca (Mendoza) M.; children: Ian Matthew, Roman Melquides; m. Martha Graciela Aguilar, Mar. 16, 1991. BS in BA, National Coll., Albuquerque, 1979. Installer/technician CableCom Gen., Colorado Springs, Colo., 1970-74; lead technician United Cable TV, Albuquerque, 1974-76; purchasing agt. Universal Constructors, Inc., Albuquerque, 1976-78; tech. mgr. Tribune Comm., Albuquerque, 1978-82, Rogers Cablesystems, Inc., Downey, Calif., 1982-84; dir. engring. Falcon Comm., Pasadena, 1984-86; tech. mgr. Group W/Paragon Cable, Torrance, Calif., 1986-87; dir. ops. United Artists Cable, City of Industry, Calif., 1987-90; tech. ops. mgr. Comcast Cablevision, Santa Ana, Calif., 1990—. Fundraiser DAV, San Bernardino County, Calif., 1982—, VFW, 1982—. With U.S. Army, 1967-70. Decorated Purple Heart, Army Commendation Medal. Mem. Soc. Cable TV Engrs. (founder, 1st pres. So. Calif. chpt., dir. at large 1987—, pres. 1987-89), So. Calif. Cable Assn. (dir. 1986-89), Latinos in Cable (pres. 1989-90), Nat. Assn. of Minorities in Cable. Roman Catholic. Home: 1429 Norwood Ct Upland CA 91786 Office: Comcast Cablevision 1000 E Santa Ana Blvd Santa Ana CA 92701

MALERSTEIN, ABRAHAM JOSEPH, psychiatrist, researcher; b. Cin., Nov. 2, 1924; s. Leo and Rhea (Goldstein) M.; m. Evelyn Mae Cohen (div. 1958); m. Jean Elizabeth Hayward, Dec. 6, 1958; children: Barbara, Sarah, Julia, David. AB, U. Calif., Berkeley, 1949; MD, Chgo. Med. Sch., 1954. Diplomate Am. Bd. Psychiatry. Intern Cook County, Chgo., 1954-55; resident Langley Porter Clinic, San Francisco, 1955-58; assoc. clin. prof. U. Calif., San Francisco, 1967-73; assoc. clin. prof. Davis Med. Ctr. U. Calif., Sacramento, 1987-88; pvt. practice San Francisco, 1958-86; staff psychiatrist Atascadero (Calif.) State Hosp., 1985-87; pvt. rschr. San Francisco, 1988—. Author: The Conscious Mind, 1986; co-author: A Piagetian Model of Character Structure, 1982, Psychotherapy and Character Structures, 1989; contbr. articles to profl. jours. Pfc. U.S. Army, 1943-46. Fellow Am. Psychiatric Assn. (life).

MALEWSKI, EDWARD, health care administrator; b. Pitts., July 11, 1943; s. Roberta Lorraine Pate, July 18, 1964; children: Rachel Malewski Del Rio, Edward Jason, Jennifer Alexi. AA, San Antonio Coll., 1965; BA, Our Lady of the Lake U., 1968; M. Health Adminstrn., Baylor U., 1979. Enlisted U.S. Army, 1963, commd. 2d lt., 1968, advanced through grades to major, 1979, various exec. & commdg. officer positions, 1968-74; chief manpower div. U.S. Army Med. Rsch. & Devel. Command, Washington, 1974-77; chief clin. support Ft. Carson (Colo.) Community Hosp., 1978-80; investigator Office of Inspector Gen., U.S. Army Health Svcs. Command, Ft. Sam Houston, Tex., 1980-83; exec. officer Dunham Clinic, Carlisle, Pa., 1983-84; ret. U.S. Army, 1984; adminstr., chief exec. officer Hubbard (Tex.) Hosp., 1984-86; adminstr., CEO Sitka (Alaska) Community Hosp., 1986-90; CEO Malewski Consulting, Boise, Idaho, 1990—; cons. in field. Chmn. Sitka Emergency Preparedness Com., 1987-89; bd. dirs., treas. Rural Alaska Health Professions Found., Fairbanks, 1988-92. Decorated Bronze Star. Mem. Am. Hosp. Assn., Am. Coll. Healthcare Execs., Healthcare Forum (del. 1987-89), Alaska State Hosp. and Nursing Home Assn. (treas. 1988-89, v.p. 1989-90), Greater Sitka C. of C. (bd. dirs., pres. 1991), VFW, Am. Legion, Elks, Moose. Office: Malewski Consulting PO Box 16246 Boise ID 83715-0246

MALHOTRA, VIJAY KUMAR, mathematics educator; b. Punjab, India, Sept. 23, 1946; came to U.S., 1969; s. Anand K. and Swarn Kanta (Chadha) M.; m. Madhu Chadha, Aug. 18, 1973; children: Jaishri, Vaishali, Vivek.. BA, Delhi (India) U., 1965; MA, Meerut U., India, 1968, Pepperdine U., 1970. Cert. instr. community colls., Calif. Head math. dept. Le Lycee de L.A., 1971-78; instr. math. L.A. Trade Tech. Coll., 1978-84; prof. El Camino Coll., Torrance, Calif., 1984—. Mem. Am. Fedn. Tchrs. Office: El Camino Coll 16007 Crenshaw Blvd Torrance CA 90506-0001

MALICK, PETER BENSON, accountant; b. L.A., July 13, 1957; s. David and Barbara Lynn (Schulman) M.; m. Linda Cherry, Aug. 19, 1989. BA in Econ., UCLA, 1980; MS in Tax, Golden Gate U., 1985. CPA, Calif. Para profl. tax dept. Touche Ross & Co., L.A., 1977-78; staff acct. Cohen & Weir, Encino, Calif., 1978-80; sr. staff acct. Ernst & Whinney, Century City, Calif., 1980-82; mgr. tax dept. Nigro, Karlin & Segal, Century City, 1982-89; pvt. practice Woodland Hills, Calif., 1989—. Mem. AICPA, Calif. Soc. CPAs, Phi Eta Sigma, Omicron Delta Epsilon. Office: Peter Benson Malick CPA 21051 Warner Center Ln #103 Woodland Hills CA 91367

MALIK, SOHAIL, chemistry educator, researcher, consultant; b. Karachi, Pakistan, Nov. 7, 1958; came to U.S., 1986; s. Bakhtiar Malik and Amna Begum; m. Rubina Sial, Jan. 1, 1990. BSc with honors, U. Karachi, 1980, MS, 1982, PhD, 1986; postgrad., Stanford U., 1986-88. Instr. div. chemistry and nephrology, depts. lab. medicine and medicine U. Wash., Seattle, 1988-89, asst. prof. depts. lab. medicine and medicine, 1989—, co-dir. div. chemistry, dept. lab. medicine, 1991—; postdoctoral rsch. assoc. dept. chemistry Stanford (Calif.) U., 1986-88; rsch. cons. SpaceLabs Inc., Redmond, Wash., 1986—, Incyte Techs., Seattle, 1992—. Contbr. articles to profl. jours.; patentee in field. Active UN Assn., Seattle, 1989—. Fellow Am. Inst. Chemists, Stanford U. scholar, 1986-88. Mem. Am. Assn. Advancement Sci., Am. Chem. Soc., Am. Soc. Pharmacognosy, Am. Assn. for Clin. Chemistry, N.Y. Acad. Scis., Internat. Isotope Soc., Acad. Clin. and Lab. Physicians and Scientists. Office: U Wash Div Chemistry Dept Lab Medicine SB-10 Seattle WA 98195

MALINOW, MANUEL RENE, cardiologist; b. Buenos Aires, Feb. 27, 1920; s. Roberto and Beatrix (Shore) M.; m. Marta A Malinow, May 16, 1951; children: Ana Maria Rajkovic, Roberto, Juan Sebastian. MD, Buenos Aires Med. Sch., 1945. Chief electrocardiography Hosp. Ramos Mejia, Buenos Aires, 1946-53; chief rsch. Buenos Aires Med. Sch., 1953-63; chief lab. cardiovascul physiology Oreg. Reg. Primate Ctr., Beaverton, 1963—; assoc. prof. medicine Oreg. Health Scis. Ctr., Portland, 1963-70; prof. medicine Oreg. Health Scis. Univ., 1970—; dir. Cardiac Rehab., St. V Hosp., Beaverton; dir. Advanced Sci. Inst., NATO, 1983; co-dir. YM Cardiac Rehab. Program, YMCA, Portland, 1974-80. Editor: Regression of Athero. Lesions, 1984;; patentee in field. Recipient Paul D. White prize, Argentine Soc. Cardiology, 1954, Rafael M. Bullrich prize, Nat. Acad. Medicine, 1959, Gold medal, 6th Interam. Congress of Cardiology, 1960, Gold medal, Soc. Argentine, 1960, Discovery award, Med. Rsch. Found. Oreg., 1992. Mem. Royal Soc. Medicine, Internat. Primatol. Soc., N.Y. Acad. Sci., Am. Heart Assn., Oreg. Heart Assn., Fedn. Am. Soc. Exptl. Biology. Office: Oregon Reg Primate Rsch Ctr 505 NW 185th Ave Beaverton OR 97006-3499

MALKARY, GREGG HARRIS, product marketing manager; b. Manhasset, N.Y., Jan. 29, 1963; s. Joseph Warren and Barbara (Dix) M. BA in Computer Sci., Brown U., 1985, MS in Computer Sci., 1987. Rsch. scientist Meta Software Corp., Cambridge, Mass., 1987-88; v.p. for R & D Simulogics, Inc., Cambridge, 1988-89; tech. cons. Apollo/HP, Burlington, Mass., 1989-91; product mktg. mgr. Silicon Graphics Computer Systems, Mountain View, Calif., 1991—. N.Am. Philips fellow, 1986. Mem. IEEE, Assn. for Computing Machinery, Sigma Xi. Democrat. Home: 3935 Crow Canyon Rd San Ramon CA 94583 Office: Silicon Graphics 2011 N Shoreline Blvd Mountain View CA 94039

MALKY, ROBERT DREW, personnel executive; b. North Hollywood, Calif., Mar. 6, 1958; s. Norman N. and Bebe B. (Fields) M. BSBA, U. Denver, 1980; MBA, U. Colo., Denver, 1984. Food and beverage mgr. Fairmont Hotels, Denver, 1979-81; catering dir. Kiandra Lodge, Vail, Colo., 1981-82; restaurant mgr. El Torito Restaurants, Aurora, Colo., 1982-83; corp. unit trainer Gregory's Restaurants, Denver, 1983-86; tng. mgr. Turn of the Century Club, Denver, 1984-86; hospitality dir. TOPS Interim Pers. Svcs., Denver, 1984-90; owner, dir. Hospitality Pers. Svcs., Denver, 1990—. Mem. Internat. Food Svc. Exec. Assn. (cert., pres. Colo. chpt. 1989-90, chmn. Colo. chpt. 1990-91, cert. bd. 1991-92, Merit citation 1988, Disting. Svc. award 1989), Greater Denver C. of C., Colo. Restaurant Assn., Denver U. Alumni Assn.. Democrat. Office: Hospitality Pers Svcs 655 Broadway Ste 425 Denver CO 80203-3420

MALLARD, ALBERT KNIGHT, marketing company executive, small business owner; b. Dallas, July 28, 1937; s. Andrew Knight Jr. and Rosalee (Farley) M.; m. Jaqueline Carlann Schooley, Mar. 17, 1968 (dec. Nov. 1980); 1 child, Andrea Carlene; m. Sheryl Lynn Woods, Dec. 4, 1982; children: Angela Marie, Elizabeth Anne. BBA in Mktg. Adminstrn., U. Tex., 1959; postgrad., U. Kans., 1963. Asst. buyer Jones Store Co., Kansas City, Mo., 1959-61; sr. merchandiser Montgomery Ward & Co., Kansas City, 1962-67; nat. buyer Montgomery Ward & Co., Chgo., 1967-82; mgr. mdse. Ambassador Internat., Phoenix, 1983-84; pres. Mallard Mktg. Group, Mesa, Ariz., 1984—. Treas., bd. dirs. Prairie Village (Kans.) Jaycees, 1966-67; lay mem. No. Ill. Conf. Bd. of Missions, Chgo., 1972-80; chair adminstrv. bd. Olympia Fields (Ill.) United Meth. Ch., 1973-75, pres. bd. trustees, 1977-78; chair coun. on ministries St. Matthew United Meth. Ch., Mesa, 1989-90, chair adminstrv. bd., 1993—; mem. corp. bd. dirs. United Meth. Outreach Ministries, Inc., Phoenix, 1985-88, treas., chair fin. com., mem. exec. bd., 1988-93. With USAF 1961-62. Mem. Assn. Am. Weather Observers, U. Tex. Ex-Students Assn. (life), Ariz. Tex. Exes. Home and Office: 904 W Natal Ave Mesa AZ 85210-7652

MALLEK, DALE, information services specialist, consultant; b. Milw., July 2, 1951; s. Benedict Louis and Violet Lucille (Uciechowski) M.; m. Debra Sue Marshall, Apr. 25, 1981; 1 child, Dana Kristine. BS, U. Wis., Milw., 1975. Systems rep. Honeywell, Chatham, N.J., 1973-76; sr. tech. advisor, mgr. prodn. procurement, mgr. tech support Honeywell, Phoenix, 1978-89; tech. advisor Gen. Host Corp., Phoenix, 1976-78; pres. Mallek Computing Svc., Phoenix, 1982—; dir. info. svcs. Meyer, Hendricks, Victor, Osborn & Mapledon, Phoenix, 1989—. Mem. Phoenix Novell Users Group, IBM User Group. Home: 12238 N 45th Dr Glendale AZ 85304 Office: Meyer Hendricks Victor Osborn & Maledon 2929 N Central Ave Phoenix AZ 85012

MALLEN, BRUCE, real estate developer, educator, producer, economist, consultant; b. Montreal, Que., Can., Sept. 4, 1937; Came to the U.S., 1978; s. Mitchell and Mary Mallen; m. Carol Klein; children: Howard Eliot, Jay Leslie, Reesa Lynn. BA in Philosophy, B of Commerce, Sir George Williams U., Montreal, 1958; MS, Columbia U., 1959; MBA, U. Mich., 1960; PhD, NYU, 1963. Registered fin. planner; cert. realtor; lic. real estate broker, Calif. Sr. cons., dir. econ. and market rsch. P.S. Ross & Ptnrs., Montreal, 1961-64; pres. Bruce Mallen & Assocs., Inc., Montreal, 1964-79; assoc. prof. Concordia U., Montreal, 1964-67, chmn. dept. mktg., 1964-71, prof. mktg., 1967-79, founding chmn. grad. studies commerce, 1968-73, acting dean faculty of commerce and adminstrn., 1970-71; pres. Filmcorp Entertainment Fins., Inc., Montreal, L.A., 1979—; econ. cons. Consolate Gen. Japan, Montreal, 1966-78; vis. prof. mktg. Laval U., 1968-70; vis. scholar Grad. Sch. Mgmt., UCLA, 1978-79; vis. prof. U. So. Calif., 1979-81. Author: The Costs and Benefits of Evening Shopping to the Canadian Economy, 1969, Principles of Marketing Channel Management, 1977; co-author: Marketing Canada, 1968 (2d edit.), Marketing in the Canadian Environment, 1973, Principles of Marketing in Canada, 1979, Distribution of Canadian Feature Films in the U.S. Market, 1979, and others; founder, 1st editor-in-chief The Can. Marketer; mem. editorial rev. bd. The Jour. of Mktg.; mem. editorial bd. Internat. Jour. of Phys. Distbn.; contbr. articles to profl. jours.; developer Filmland Corp. Ctr., Culver City, Calif.; prodr. sev. feature films. Ford Found. fellow, 1961-62; recipient Founders Day award, 1963, Alumni Achievement award for distinction in the entertainment industry, 1990. Mem. Am. Mktg. Assn. (past internat. dir., past pres. Montreal chpt.), Prodrs. Guild Am., Acad. Can. Cinema, Assn. of Indsl. Marketers and Advertisers (past pres. Montreal chpt.), Mktg. and Sales Execs. (past dir.), L.A. Arts Coun.(past dir.), Advt. and Sales Execs., Montreal Club (past dir.), Culver City C. of C. (past dir. entertainment industry coun.), Beverly Hills Bd. Realtors.

MALLENDER, WILLIAM HARRY, lawyer; b. Detroit, May 21, 1935; s. Milton F. and Eleanor M. (Rainey) M.; m. Carole Miller, Aug. 8, 1964; children: W. Drew, Gregory. B.A., Yale U., 1957; L.L.B., U. Mich., 1960. Bar: Mich. 1960, N.Y. 1962, Fla. 1970. Assoc. Donovan Leisure, Newton, Irvine, N.Y.C., 1960-69; atty. Ritter & Co., Gibralter Mgmt. Co., GAC Corp., Fort Lauderdale, Fla., 1969-71; v.p., gen. counsel Talley Industries, Inc., Mesa, Ariz., 1971-78, exec. v.p., gen. counsel, sec., 1978-81, dir., 1975—; pres., chief exec. officer Talley Industries, Inc., Phoenix, 1981-83, chmn. bd., chief exec. officer, 1983—; bd. dirs. MicroAge, Inc. Bd. regents Brophy Coll. Preparatory; v.p. Internat. Heart Inst. Found., Phoenix, 1983; bd. dirs. Ariz. Zool. Soc., Phoenix Econ. Growth. Corp., Combined Phoenix Arts and Scis., Phoenix Art Mus.; bd. dirs., pres. Ariz. Mus. for Youth Friends. Mem. ABA, Mich. State Bar, Fla. State Bar, N.Y. State Bar. Office: Talley Industries Inc 2800 N 44th St Phoenix AZ 85008-1500

MALLINSON, JOHN CHARLES, electronics executive, consultant, educator; b. Bradford, U.K., Jan. 30, 1932; came to U.S., 1957; s. Charles Hildred and Elaine (Staeger) M.; m. Suzanne Trevena, Mar. 15, 1953 (div. 1976); children: Caroline, Elizabeth; m. Phebe Cohen, Jan. 5, 1991. BA and MA in Physics., U. Coll., Oxford, Eng., 1953. Physicist AMP Inc., Harrisburg, Pa., 1957-61; mem. rsch. staff Ampex Crop., Redwood City, Calif., 1961-84; dir. Ctr. for Magnetic Recording Rsch. U. Calif., LaJolla, 1984-90; pres. Mallinson Magnetics, Inc., Carlsbad, Calif., 1990—. Author: Fundamentals of Magnetic Recording, Vol. I, 1987, Vol. II, 1993; contbr. articles to profl. jours. Capt. RAF, 1953-56. A. M. Poniatoff award, 1983. Fellow IEEE. Home and Office: 7618 Redosada Dr Carlsbad CA 92009

MALLON, PETER, bishop; b. Prince Rupert, B.C., Dec. 5, 1929; s. Joseph P. and Sheila M. (Keenan) D. Grad., Seminary Christ the King, Burnaby and Mission, B.C. Asst. Holy Rosary Cath., Vancouver, B.C., 1956-64, rector, 1966-82; chancellor Archdiocese Vancouver, 1964-65, dir. religious edn., 1971-73; adminstr. Guardian Angels Parish, Vancouver, 1965-66; pastor St. Anthony's, West Vancouver, 1982-89; bishop Nelson, B.C., 1989—. Prelate of Honor, 1977. Address: 813 Ward St, Nelson, BC Canada V1L 1T4*

MALLORY, MARILYN MAY, lay worker; b. Tulsa; d. John Scott and Mildred (Dennis) M. BA, Stanford U., 1965; BD, Cath. U., Nijmegen, The Netherlands, 1970, licentiate in theology, 1972, PhD, STD, 1977. Lay worker The Netherlands, 1970—; asst. to dir. of devel. YWCA, San Francisco, 1990-91; founder, dir. Challah Caths., Inc. (formerly Calif. Pro-Choice Caths.), 1991—. Author: Christian Mysticism, 1977 (Dutch award 1977); contbr. articles to Revista de Espiritualidad. Canfield Found. scholar, 1961; Nijmegen U. Student Fund rsch. grantee, 1973; recipient Dutch ZWO award, 1977. Mem. Cath. Theol. Soc. Am., Am. Acad. Religion, NOW (chair polit. action com. East Bay chpt. 1989-90). Democrat. Roman Catholic. Home: 3375 Alma St Apt 165 Palo Alto CA 94306-3516

MALMGREN, RENÉ LOUISE, educational theater director, arts administrator; b. Mpls., Nov. 14, 1938; d. Albert William and Hildegarde Ann (Topel) Erickson; m. Donald Elwin Malmgren, Dec. 27, 1958; D. Gustaf, Ericka Susan, Tavus Val, Beret Kristina. BA in Theatre, Speech and English, Colo. Women's Coll., 1966; MA in Ednl. Adminstrn and Curriculum Devel., U. Colo., 1981. Cert. supt., Ariz.; cert. type D adminstr., Colo. Cons. creative drama cultural arts program Denver Pub. Schs., 1970-72; tchr. APS Crawford Elem. Sch., Aurora, Colo., 1972-78; instr. Colo. Women's Coll., Denver, 1974-75; ednl. dir. Colo. Children's Theatre Co., Denver, 1977-86; adminstrv. intern Aurora Pub. Schs., 1981-82, coord. curriculum, 1982-85; asst. dir. instrn. fine arts Tucson Unified Sch. Dist., 1985-90; mng. dir. Ariz. Children's Theatre Co., Tucson, 1990—; adminstr. svcs. Tucson Ctr. for Performing Arts, 1992—; editor dramatic arts curriculum Ariz. Dept. Edn., Phoenix, 1989, mem. essential skills cadre, 1989—; rev. panelist Ariz. Commn. on Arts, Phoenix, 1986-87. Co-author satellite TV curriculum, 1987; appeared in premier of play The Only Woman Awake, 1984. Del. Colo. Dem. Conv., Denver, 1980; peacekeeper Take Back the Night March, Rape Assistance and Awareness Program, Denver, 1982-84; mem. policy com. Tucson Cable Arts Channel, 1986-87; mem. edn. com. Tucson Symphony Orch., 1988-92; mem. So. Ariz. Opera Guild, 1988—; bd. dirs. Arts and Creative Early Childhood, 1990-93, Arts Genesis, 1990-92. Colo. Council on Arts and Humanities grantee, 1978. Mem. ASCD, Nat. Art Edn. Assn., Ariz. Arts Supervisory Coalition, Ariz. Theatre Educators Assn. (bd. dirs. 1985-89, pres. 1988-89), Phi Delta Kappa. Home: 2612 E La Cienega Dr Tucson AZ 85716-1546

MALMUTH, NORMAN DAVID, program manager; b. Brooklyn, N.Y., Jan. 22, 1931; s. Jacob and Selma Malmuth; m. Constance Nelson, 1970; children: Kenneth, Jill. AE, U. Cin., 1953; MA in Aero. Engring., Polytech. Inst. of N.Y., 1956; PhD in Aeronautics, Calif. Inst. Tech., 1962. Rsch. engr. Grumman Aircraft Engring. Corp., 1953-56; preliminary design engr. N.A. Aviation Div., L.A., 1956-68; teaching asst. Calif. Inst. Tech., L.A., 1961; mem. maths. sci. group Rockwell Internat. Sci. Ctr., 1968-75, project mgr. fluid dynamics rsch., 1975-80, mgr. fluid dynamics group, 1980-82, program mgr. spl. projects, 1982—; cons. Aerojet Gen., 1986-89; lectr. UCLA, 1971-72. Referee AIAA Jour.; bd. editors Jour. Aircraft; contbr. articles to Jour. of Heat Transfer, Internat. Jour. Heat Mass Transfer, and others. Named Calif. Inst. Tech. fellow; recipient Outstanding Alumnus award Univ. Cin., 1990. Fellow AIAA (assoc., Aerodynamics award 1991, editorial adv. bd. AIAA Jour. Aircraft); mem. Am. Acad. Mechanics, Am. Inst. Physics (fluid dynamics div.), Soc. Indsl. and Applied Maths. Home: 182 Maple Rd Newbury Park CA 91320-4718 Office: Rockwell Sci Ctr PO Box 1085 Thousand Oaks CA 91358-0085

MALOFF, STEPHEN MARTIN, plastic surgeon; b. Phila., Dec. 21, 1941; s. Abraham and Ruth (Skolkin) M.; m. Joan Fayette Baker; children: Erin, Kerstin. BA, Emory U., 1963; MD, U. Tenn., Knoxville, 1967; degree, U. N.Mex., 1976; student, Grady Meml. Hosp., Atlanta, 1967-68, U. Louisville, 1973-74. Diplomate Am. Bd. Plastic Surgery. Intern Grady Meml. Hosp., Atlanta, 1967-68; resident gen. surgery U. N.Mex. Sch. Medicine, Albuquerque, 1971-72, resident plastic surgery, 1974-76; fellow hand surgery U. Louisville, 1973-74; pvt. practice Pocatello, Idaho, 1976—; adj. staff mem. Idaho State U., Pocatello, 1990—. Maj. USAF, 1969-71, Vietnam. Mem. Am. Soc. Plastic and Reconstructive Surgeons, Rocky Mountain Assn. Plastic Surgeons, Skyline Med. Assn. Office: PO Box 4171 1950 E Clark Ste A Pocatello ID 83205-4171

MALOHN, DONALD A., manufacturing executive; b. South Bend, Ind., Mar. 26, 1928; s. Harry A. and Opal (Baker) M.; m Myla Claire Lockwood, Feb. 9, 1948; 1 child, Chris. BSEE, Tri-State U., Angola, Ind., 1952. Engr. jet engine div. Studebaker Corp., South Bend, Ind., 1952-54; prodn. rsch. engr. Ford Motor Co., Dearborn, Mich., 1954-61; sr. analytical engr. Solar, San Diego, 1961-62; dept. mgr. Sundstrand Aviation, Denver, 1962-66; asst. dir. engring. Ai Rsch. Mfg. Co., Phoenix, 1966-78; exec. v.p. Tiernay Turbines, Phoenix, 1978—. Inventor: Vaporizing Igniter, 1963; contbr. tech. jours. Mem. ASME., Am. Soc. Metals, Soc. Automotive Engrs. Republican. Home: 7848 E Sage Dr Scottsdale AZ 85250-7648 Office: Tiernay Turbines Inc PO Box 21252 Phoenix AZ 85036-1252

MALONE, DEBORAH FRANK, environmental health specialist, state official; b. Grand Forks, N.D., Sept. 4, 1964; d. Roger Joel Frank and Judith Kay (Berg) Moreland; m. John B. Thompson, Mar. 12, 1988 (div. May 1990); m. Michael Wade Malone, Oct. 31, 1990. BS in Microbiology, Ariz. State U., 1986; postgrad., Phoenix Coll., 1989—. Pub. health chemist Ariz. Dept. Health Svcs., Phoenix, 1987-88; environ. health specialist I, Ariz. Dept. Environ. Quality, Phoenix, 1988-90, environ. health specialist II, 1990—. Campaign worker various Dem. polit. campaigns, Phoenix, 1981-82. Mem. NAFE, Nature Conservancy, Phoenix Zoo-Ariz. Zool. Soc. (Keepers Club). Lutheran. Office: Ariz Dept Environ Quality 2655 E Magnolia St Ste 2 Phoenix AZ 85034

MALONE, JAMES ROLAND, counselor; b. Alameda, Calif., June 25, 1955; s. Roland Curtin and Doris Helen (Durgan) M.; m. Jeanne Gay Staats, Sept. 13, 1975; children: James Patrick, Kristle Michelle. BA, Calif. State U., Hayward, 1976; MA, Biola U., 1978. Lic. marriage, family and child counselor, Calif. Exec. dir. Gardenview Counseling Svcs., Hayward, 1980-86; counseling supr. Genesis Counseling Svcs., Manteca and Hayward, Calif., 1983-92; dir., counselor Calvary Counseling Svcs., Manteca, 1992—; speaker in field. Author, presenter: (workshop/workbook) Defusing Anger, 1980, Building Self-Esteem, 1984, (treatment program) Treatment Regarding Abuse of Children Sexually, 1989. Conf. speaker Head Start, Stockton, Calif., 1991, 92, 93. Mem. Am. Assn. Marriage and Family Therapists (clin.), Calif. Assn. Marriage and Family Therapists (clin.), Am. Assn. Christian Counselors (clin.), Christian Assn. for Psychol. Studies (clin.). Republican. Home: 734 Kingery Dr Ripon CA 95366-3211 Office: Calvary Counseling Svcs 602 E Yosemite Ave Manteca CA 95336

MALONE, JOHN C., telecommunications executive; b. 1941; m. Leslie. Attended Yale U., Johns Hopkins U. Formerly pres. Jerrold Electronics Corp.; pres., chief exec. officer Tele-Communications, Inc., Denver; chmn., dir. Liberty Media Corp., Denver. Office: Tele-Communications Inc PO Box 5630 5619 DTC Pky Englewood CO 80111*

MALONE, KARL, professional basketball player; b. Summerfield, La., July 24, 1963. Student, La. Tech. U., 1981-85. Basketball player Utah Jazz, 1985—; mem. U.S. Olympic Basketball Team (received Gold medal), 1992. Mem. NBA All-Star team, 1988-93; recipient NBA All-Star Game Most Valuable Player award, 1989; mem. All-NBA first team, 1989-92; mem. All-NBA second team, 1988; mem. NBA All-Defensive second team, 1988; mem. NBA All-Rookie Team, 1986. Office: Utah Jazz 5 Triad Ctr Ste 500 Salt Lake City UT 84180-1105*

MALONE, MARVIN HERBERT, pharmacology and toxicology educator, editor; b. Fairbury, Nebr., Apr. 2, 1930; s. Herbert August Frederick and Elizabeth Florinda (Torrey) M.; m. Shirley Ruth Cane, Dec. 21, 1952; children: Carla Margaret, Gayla Christa. BS in Pharmacy, U. Nebr., 1951, MS in Physiology and Pharmacology, 1953; postgrad., Rutgers U., 1954-55; PhD in Pharmacology, U. Nebr., 1958. Rsch. asst. Squibb Inst. Med. Rsch., New Brunswick, N.J., 1953-56; asst. prof. U. N.Mex., Albuquerque, 1958-60; assoc. prof. U. Conn., Storrs, 1960-69; prof. pharmacology and toxicology U. of the Pacific, Stockton, Calif., 1969-84, disting. prof., 1984-90, prof. emeritus, 1990—; head Wormwood Assocs., Stockton, Calif., 1990—; cons. U. Wash. Drug Plant Labs., Seattle, 1960-64, Amazon Natural Drug Co., Somerville, N.J., 1967-70, Atlas Chem. Industries, Inc., Wilmington, Del., 1968-78; expert cons. task force on plants for fertility regulation WHO, Geneva, 1982-88, Emprise Inc., Washington, 1990-92, Herb Rsch. Found., Boulder, Colo., 1990—. Author: Experiments in the Pharmaceutical Biological Sciences, 1973; editor The Wormwood Rev., 1961—, Am. Jour. Pharm. Edn., 1974-79, Jour. Ethnopharmacology, 1985-91, Pacific Info. Svc. on Street Drugs, Stockton, Calif., 1971-78; editorial bd. Jour. Natural Products, 1971—, Jour. Ethnpharmacology 1978-86, 91—, Internat. Jour. Pharmacognosy, 1992—. Gov.'s appointee State of Calif. Med. Therapeutics and Drug Adv. Com., Sacramento, 1985-90. Fellow Am. Found. for Pharm. Edn., 1956-58, AAAS, 1981. Mem. Am. Soc. for Pharmacology and Exptl. Therapeutics, Am. Soc. Pharmacognosy. Republican. Home: 722 Bedford Rd Stockton CA 95204-5214

MALONE, MICHAEL PETER, academic administrator, historian; b. Pomeroy, Wash., Apr. 18, 1940; s. John Albert and Dolores Frances (Cheyne) M.; m. Kathleen Malone, Apr. 17, 1983; children: John Thomas, Molly Christine. BA in History, Gonzaga U., 1962; PhD in Am. Studies, Wash. State U., Pullman, 1966. Asst. prof. history Tex. A&M U., College Station, 1966-67; asst. prof., prof. history Mont. State U., Bozeman, 1967—, dean grad. studies, 1979-89, v.p. acad. affairs, 1989-90; pres. Mont. State U., 1991—; bd. dirs. Bultrey Food & Drug. Author: The Battle for Butte, 1981 (Sick award 1981), Historians and The American West, 1983, (with others) Montana: A History of Two Centuries, 1976, 2d edit., 1991, The American West: A 20th Century History, 1989. Mem. Western History Assn. Home: 2310 Spring Creek Dr Bozeman MT 59715-6191 Office: Mont State U Bozeman MT 59717

MALONE, MICHAEL WILLIAM, electronics executive, software engineer; b. Belmore L.I., N.Y., Mar. 31, 1956; s. Daniel Joseph Malone and Frances Ann (Reilly) Coppersmith; m. Jane Pauline Raese, Aug. 20, 1988. BS in Elec. Engring. and Computer Sci., U. Colo., 1986. Test engr. Catalina Controls, Longmont, Colo., 1984-86; design engr. Inlab, Inc., Broomfield, Colo., 1986-87, mgr. engring., 1987-89; software engr. UMG, Inc., Golden, Colo., 1989-90, sr. software engr., 1990-91, v.p., 1991—. Developer software. With USN, 1975-79. Office: UMG Inc 538 Commons Dr Genesse Golden CO 80401

MALONE, MIKE, state senator, police officer; b. Saginaw, Mich., Jan. 13, 1932; s. Ralph Archie and Helen Marie (Johnson) M.; m. Theresa Nancy Tankavich, Jan. 1, 1982. Grad., Las Vegas (Nev.) Metro. Police Acad., 1968. With USN, 1948-68, ret., 1968; police officer Las Vegas Metro. Police Dept., 1968-90; ret., 1990, state senator of Nev., 1986-90. Mem. Nev. Legis., 1978-90; counsellor, Boulder Dam Area Boy Scouts Am., 1983-88. Mem. Sons of Erin. Republican. Home: 3660 Thom Blvd Las Vegas NV 89130-3015

MALONE, ROBERT JOSEPH, bank executive; b. Sept. 3, 1944. With Bank of Am., 1969-81; chmn., pres., CEO First Interstate Bank Boise, Idaho, 1981-84; pres., CEO First Interstate Bank Denver, 1984-90; chmn., pres., CEO Western Capital Investment Corp. (now First Bank System, Inc.), Denver, 1990-92; chmn., CEO First Bank System, Inc., 1992—; chmn., CEO Ctrl. Banks, Denver. Office: Ctrl Banks/Bank Western Nat Assn 1515 Arapahoe St Denver CO 80202

MALONEY, DOUGLAS JAMES, lawyer; b. San Francisco, May 26, 1933; s. James Douglas and Loretta (O'Donnell) M.; m. Elenore Hill, Dec. 31, 1976 (div. 1986); children: Lynn, Karen, Douglas Jr., Susan, Pamela; m. Ellen Caulfield, May 14, 1988. BS, Calif. Maritime Acad., 1954; JD, U. San Francisco, 1958. Bar: Calif. 1959, U.S. Dist. Ct. (no. dist.) Calif. 1959, U.S. Ct. Appeals (9th cir.) 1959, U.S. Supreme Ct. 1970. Dep. county counsel Sonoma County, Santa Rosa, Calif., 1959-60, Marin County, San Rafael, Calif., 1960-62; county counsel Marin County, San Rafael, 1962—; ptnr. Nossaman, Guthner, Knox & Elliott, San Francisco, 1993—. Author (musical satires) Pigmailion, 1979, Electric Politician, 1981, Blazing Ballots, 1983, Scandals of 1933, 1986, Damn Yuppies, 1989. Bd. dirs. Living History Ctr., San Rafael, 1983-86, Buck Ctr. for Rsch. in Aging, San Rafael, 1987—. With U.S. Merchant Marine, 1955-56. Named Citizen of Yr., City of San Rafael, 1986. Mem. ABA, County Counsels Assn., Nat. Assn. County Civic Attys., Irish Am. Bar Assn. Democrat. Roman Catholic. Home: 204 Forbes Ave San Rafael CA 94901-1745 Office: County of Marin Civic Ctr Rm 342 San Rafael CA 94903

MALONEY, JAMES JOHN, librarian; b. Chgo., July 20, 1949; s. James Frederick and Raphael Ann (Stachowiak) M. BA in History, Bradley U., 1971; MA in History, No. Ill. U., 1976; MSLS, U. Ill., 1979. Head info. retrieval svcs. dept. Biblio. Ctr. for Rsch., Denver, 1981-83; sr. mktg. rep., project mgr. Dialog Info. Svcs., Palo Alto, Calif., 1983-87; automation cons. Kepler's Books and Mags., Menlo Park, Calif., 1987-88; mktg. cons. Computer Advanced Software Products, Cupertino, Calif., 1988-89; dir. sales Computer Advanced Software Products, Sunnyvale, Calif., 1992—; libr. automated systems mgr. Contra Costa County Libr., Pleasant Hill, Calif., 1989-92; libr. automation cons. Mission San Antonio Libr. and Archives, Jolon, Calif., 1988—; registered rschr. Hoover Instn. Libr. and Archives, 1990—; mem. Bibliographic Retrieval Svcs. User Adv. Bd., 1981-83. Editor: Online Searching Technique and Management, 1983; contbr. articles to profl. jours. Mem. Peninsula Open Space Trust, 1986. Mem. ALA (mem. and chair machine-assisted ref. sect. 1980—), Libr. and Info. Tech. Assn., Friends of San Francisco Symphony, Phi Alpha Theta. Home: 172 Del Vale Ave San Francisco CA 94127 Office: CASPR Inc 635 Vaqueros Ave Sunnyvale CA 94086

MALONEY, PATSY LORETTA, nursing educator; b. Murfreesboro, Tenn., Feb. 19, 1952; d. Buford Leon Browning and Ina (Bush) Dubose; m. Richard J. Maloney, July 26, 1975; children: Katherine Nalani, Nathaniel A., Elizabeth Maureen. BS in Nursing, U. Md., 1974; MA, Cath. U., 1984, MS in Nursing, 1984; postgrad., U. So. Calif. Commd. 2d lt. U.S. Army, 1974, advanced through grades to lt. col., 1989; asst. chief nurse evenings and nights DeWitt Army Hosp., Fort Belvoir, Va.; chief nurse, tng. officer 85th EVAC Hosp., Ft. Lee, Va.; clin. head nurse emergency rm./PCU Tripler Army Med. Ctr., Honolulu, chief nursing edn.; chief surg. nursing sect. Madigan Army Med. Ctr., Tacoma. Mem. Emergency Nurses Assn., Nat. Nursing Staff Devel. Orgn., Assn. of Mil. Surgeons, Sigma Theta Tau. Home: 7002 53rd St W Tacoma WA 98467-2214

MALONEY, THOMAS J., anthropologist, educator, writer; b. Arlington, Mass., Nov. 16, 1922; s. Thomas Joseph and Doris Eleanor (Edwards) M.; m. Elizabeth Gartner, Feb. 7, 1948; children: Susan, Margaretha, Elizabeth, Thomas Jefferson. BSChemE, Northeastern U., 1948; STB, Harvard U., 1952; AM in Sociology, Wash. U., St. Louis, 1956; PhD in Anthropology, Wash. U., 1966. Chem. engr. Gen. Aniline & Film Corp., Easton, Pa., 1948, U. Colo. Experiment Sta., Boulder, Colo., 1948-49, Aircraft Gas Turbine divsn. GE, Boston, 1950-52; min. Unitarian Ch., Davenport, Iowa, 1952-53, Quincy, Ill., 1953-56; tech. pers. assoc. Bettis Atomic Power divsn. Westinghouse Electric Corp., Pitts., 1956-57; part-time instr. dept. anthropology U. Colo., Boulder, 1957-59; min. Unitarian Ch., Boulder, 1957-62; asst. prof. N.Mex. Highlands U., Las Vegas, 1962-67; assoc. prof. anthropology and sociology Ripon (Wis.) Coll., 1967-69; prof. anthropology So. Ill. U., Edwardsville, 1969-87, prof. emeritus, 1987—. Fellow AAAS, Am. Anthrop. Assn. Address: 1309 City Park Ave Fort Collins CO 80521

MALONEY, THOMAS MARTIN, director materials laboratory, educator; b. Raymond, Wash., Feb. 18, 1931; s. Peter and May (Jacobsen) MaL.; m. Donna Jean MacCallum, Dec. 10, 1960; children: William, Carol, Joseph. BA in Indsl. Arts, Wash. State U., 1956. Sr. wood technologist Wash. State U., Pullman, 1956-61, asst. wood technologist, 1961-69, assoc. prof., sect. head, 1970-77, prof., sect. head, 1977-86, dir., prof., 1986—; cons. in field. Author: Modern Particle Board of Dry Process Manufacturing Processes, 1993. Sec., treas. Kiwanis, Pullman, 1965-67; chmn. Whitman County Dem. Cen. Com., Wash., 1965-72. Recipient Forest Industries Excellence award for leadership in the industry, 1988. Mem. Soc. Wood Sci. and Tech. (pres. 1976-77), Forest Products Rsch. Soc. (pres. 1981-82). Home: SW 830 Fountain Pullman WA 99163 Office: Wash State U Wood Materials & Engring Lab Pullman WA 99164-1806

MALOOF, GILES WILSON, academic administrator, educator; b. San Bernardino, Calif., Jan. 4, 1932; s. Joseph Peters and Georgia (Wilson) M.; m. Mary Anne Ziniker, Sept. 5, 1958 (dec. Oct. 1976); children: Mary Jane, Margery Jo. BA, U. Calif. at Berkeley, 1953; MA, U. Oreg., 1958; PhD, Oreg. State U., 1962. Petroleum reservoir engr. Creole Petroleum Corp., Venezuela, 1953-54; mathematician electronics div. research dept. U.S. Naval Ordnance Rsch. Lab., Corona, Calif., 1958-59; asst. prof. math. Oreg. State U., Corvallis, 1962-68, rsch. assoc. dept. oceanography, 1963-68, vis. prof. math., 1977-78; prof. math. Boise (Idaho) State U., 1968—, head dept., 1968-75, dean grad. sch., 1970-75; project dir. Dept. Energy Citizens' Workshop Energy Environment Simulator for Eastern Oreg., No. Nev. and Idaho, 1976—. Served with Ordnance Corps, AUS, 1950, 54-56. Author, reviewer of coll. textbooks; contbr. to profl. jours. Recipient Carter award, 1963, Mosser prize, 1966, Oreg. State U. Mem. Math. Assn. Am., Am. Math. Soc., Soc. Indsl. and Applied Math., Northwest Coll. and Univ. Assn. for Sci. (dir. 1973—, pres. 1990-92), Northwest Sci. Assn. (trustee 1977-80), Sigma Xi, Pi Mu Epsilon, Phi Kappa Phi. Home: 1400 Longmont Ave Boise ID 83706-3730

MALOTT, ADELE RENEE, editor; b. St. Paul, July 19, 1935; d. Clarence R. and Julia Anne (Christensen) Lindgren; m. Gene E. Malott, Oct. 24, 1957. B.S., Northwestern U., 1957. Coordinator news KGB Radio, San Diego, 1958-60; asst. pub. relations dir. St. Paul C. of C., 1961-63; night editor Daily Local News, West Chester, Pa., 1963-65; editor, co-pub. Boutique and Villager, Burlingame, Calif., 1966-76; sr. editor mag. The Webb Co., St. Paul, 1978-84; editor GEM Pub. Group, Reno, 1985—; co-pub. The Mature Traveler, 1987—; mem. faculty Reader's Digest Writers' Workshops. Co-author: Get Up and Go: A Guide for the Mature Traveler, 1989. Recipient numerous awards Nat. Fedn. Press Women, Calif. Newspaper Pubs. Assn., San Francisco Press Club, Calif. Taxpayers Assn., White House Citations. Mem. Internat. Assn. Bus. Communicators (Merit award 1984), Press Women Minn. (numerous awards), Press Women Nev.

MALOTT, DWIGHT RALPH, accountant; b. Medford, Oreg., Mar. 24, 1947; s. Ralph Joseph and Eugenia (Romanchuk) M.; m. Janet Gail Born, June 28, 1975; children: Jennifer, Paul, Michelle. A.Tech. Arts, Everett Jr. Coll., 1967; BBA, U. Wash., 1969. CPA, Wash. Acct. Main Hurdman, Everett, Wash., 1973-81; controller Shaffer Crane, Inc., Everett, 1981-83; prin. acct. Dwight Malott & Co., P.S., Arlington, Wash., 1983-88; ptnr. Wintch Tobiason & Co. PS CPA, Everett, Wash., 1988—. Loaned exec. United Way of Snohomish County, Everett, 1977, mem. allocations panel, 1980, 81, 82; bd. dirs. Lions Sight and Hearing Found. of Snohomish County, Everett, 1979-84; mem. acctg. adv. com. Everett Community Coll., 1979—; bd. dirs. North Puget Sound Ops. Improvement, 1991—, treas., 1992, 93. With USAF, 1969-73. Mem. AICPA, Wash. Soc. CPAs (sec.-treas. Snohomish chpt. 1991-93), U. Wash. Alumni Assn. (life), Lions (local pres. 1981-82), Beta Alpha Psi. Democrat. Office: Wintch Tobiason & Co PS CPA 3802 Colby Ave Everett WA 98201-4940

MALOTT, JAMES SPENCER, architect; b. Palo Alto, Calif., June 3, 1940; s. James Raymond Malott and Carol Neal Hover Nantker; m. Constance Biaggini (div. 1976); children: Tanya, Lara; m. Susan Ballard, Oct. 18, 1980; children: Danielle, Marc, Morgan. BA, Stanford U., 1962; MFA, Sculpture U. of Del., 1966; MArch, Harvard U, 1969. Draftsman, job capt. Sert Jackson & Assocs., Cambridge, Mass., 1969-70; job capt. Hertzka & Knowles, San Francisco, 1970; prin. Internat. Mod Core, San Francisco, 1971, James Malott Architects, San Francisco, 1971-87; pres. Malott Devel. Internat., San Francisco, 1982—; prin. Malott Architects, Mill Valley, Calif., 1987—; cons. San Francisco Planning Dept., 1970. Sculptor bronze, marble, steel; painter oils, pastels; jeweler in cast gold, colored stones. Chmn. Design Rev. Bd., Tiburon, Calif., 1978-82, mem. Planning Commn., 1982; mem. San Francisco Planning and Urban Rsch., 1970—. Lt. USN, 1962-66. Mem. San Francisco Heritage, Bohemian Club. Republican. Home: 987 Tiburon Blvd Tiburon CA 94920 Office: Malott Architects 1058 Redwood Hwy Mill Valley CA 94941

MALOUF, FREDERICK LEROY, composer, software engineer; b. Ft. Worth, Oct. 7, 1954; s. LeRoy Gabriel and Antoinette Alice (Antoine) M.; m. Bonnie Elizabeth Johanson, Aug. 21, 1977; children: Eric Kyung, Vanita Sara. MusB, Berklee Coll. Music, Boston, 1979; MusM, Bowling Green State U., 1981; ArtsD, Ball State U., 1985. Tech. support mgr. Quintus Computer Systems Inc., Palo Alto, Calif., 1985-87; software engr. Sequential Circuits Inc., San Jose, Calif., 1987, Digideck Inc., Mountain View, Calif., 1987-88, Apple Computer Inc., Cupertino, Calif., 1988-92, Kaleida Labs., Inc., Mountain View, 1992—; concert producer Chromatonal Prodns., Mountain View, 1987—. Compositions include Piano Sonata No. 1, 1979, Avatar, 1981, Chromatonal, 1985, Sacrifice, 1988, Variations on Goodbye Pork Pie Hat, 1989, Bali Jam, 1991, Imijimi, 1992, Miles, 1992; performances throughout U.S., some concerts in Europe; performer with mus. ensemble Tonus Finalis. Recipient Richard Levy Composition award Berklee Coll. Music, 1979, Composer-in-Residence grant Rockefeller/Stanford U., 1984, travel grant for music festival in Poland Arts Internat., 1990. Mem. IEEE, ASCAP (Standard award 1990), Computer Music Assn. Home: 379 Palo Alto Ave Mountain View CA 94041-1117 Office: Kaleida Labs Inc 1945 Charleston Rd Mountain View CA 94043

MALPHURS, ROGER EDWARD, insurance company executive, chiropractor, biomedical technologist; b. Lake Worth, Fla., Dec. 15, 1933; s. Cecil Edward and Muriel Thelma (Ward) M.; m. Carolyn Sue Calapp, Feb. 2, 1963(div. 1993); children: Steven, Brian, Darren, Regina, Victoria. BS, U. Utah, 1961; D of Chiropractic, Palmer Coll. Chiropractic West, 1990. Cert. med. technologist; lic. chiropractor, Calif., Ariz. Supr. spl. chemistry Cen. Pathology Lab., Santa Rosa, Calif., 1968-73; mgr. lab. Community Hosp., Santa Rosa, 1973-76; supr. chem., staff asst. Meml. Hosp., Santa Rosa, 1976-85; pres., chief exec. officer R.E. Malphurs Co., Sunnyvale, Calif., 1972—; dept. mgr. immunochemistry Spectra Labs., Fremont, Calif., 1990—; owner, developer REMCO Mktg. Assocs., Santa Rosa, 1970-71; owner Better Bus. Forms and Typeset, Santa Rosa, 1977-81. Author: A New, Simple Way to Win at Blackjack, 1972. Served as squadron commdr. CAP USAF Aux., 1982-84. Mem. Am. Chiropractic Assn., Calif. Chiropractic Assn., Optimists Internat. (youth awards chmn. 1969-74), Am. Pub. Health Assn., Toastmasters (sec./treas. 1988-89). Republican.

MALSON, REX RICHARD, drug and health care corporation executive; b. Stanberry, Mo., Nov. 26, 1931; s. Albert J. Curtis and Nellie E. Coburn (Bussey) M.; m. Jimmie S., May 25, 1956 (dec. 1980); children: Richard Gary, Gregory Neil; m. Vicki L., Feb. 10, 1983 (div. Aug. 1984). B.B.A., Ga. State U., 1961; postgrad. grad. exec. program, U. Chgo., 1967; postgrad. exec. program hon., Stanford U., 1983; LHD (hon.), L.I. U., 1989. Gen. transp. mgr. John Sexton & Co., Chgo., 1964-68; dir. distbn. system Keebler Co., Chgo., 1968-73; with drug and health care group McKesson Corp., San Francisco, 1973-92, vice pres., 1984-86, exec. v.p. ops., 1986-89, pres. & chief operating officer, 1989-92, also vice chmn.,bd. dirs.; ret., 1992; bd. dirs. Sunbelt Beverage Co., Balt., Stationers Distbg. Co., Ft. Worth; chmn. bd. dirs. Armor All Products Corp. Served with U.S. Navy, 1951-55, Korea. Mem. Am. Soc. Traffic and Transp. Republican. Office: McKesson Corp 1 Post St San Francisco CA 94104-5203

MALTIN, FREDA, retired university administrator; b. Calgary, Alta., Can., June 4, 1923; came to the U.S., 1958; d. Meyers Wolfe and Ida (Kohn) Rosen; m. Manny Maltin, Aug. 25, 1950; 1 child, Richard Allan. Diploma Garbutt's Bus. Coll., Calgary, 1942. Various secretarial and bookkeeping positions, 1951; mem. adminstrv. staff U. So. Calif., 1960-92, asst. to exec. dir. Davidson Conf. Ctr., 1987-92, Grad. Sch. Bus. Adminstrn., 1981-92. Recipient staff achievement award U. So. Calif., 1991. Mem. Exec. Women Internat., U. So. Calif. Staff Club (charter), U. So. Calif. Skull and Dagger (hon.), U. So. Calif. Town and Gown.

MALTIN, LEONARD, television commentator, writer; b. N.Y.C., Dec. 18, 1950; s. Aaron Isaac and Jacqueline (Gould) M.; m. Alice Tlusty, Mar. 15, 1975; 1 child, Jessica Bennett. BA, NYU, 1972. Mem. faculty New Sch. for Social Rsch., N.Y.C., 1973-81; curator Am. Acad. Humor, N.Y.C., 1975-76; guest curator dept. film Mus. Modern Art, N.Y.C., 1976; film corr. Entertainment Tonight, Hollywood, Calif., 1982—. Author: Movie Comedy Teams, 1970, rev. edit., 1985, Behind the Camera (reprinted as The Art of the Cinematographer), 1971, The Great Movie Shorts (reprinted as Selected Short Subjects), 1971, The Disney Films, 1973, rev. edit., 1984, The Great Movie Comedians, 1978, Of Mice and Magic: A History of American Animated Cartoons, 1980, rev. edit., 1987; co-author: Our Gang: The Life and Times of the Little Rascals, 1977; editor: Leonard Maltin's Movie & Video Guide, 1969, rev. annually; producer, writer, host (video) Cartoons for Big Kids, 1989; writer (TV spl.) Fantasia: The Making of a Disney Classic, 1990. Mem. steering com. Hollywood Entertainment Mus., 1989—. Mem. Authors Guild, Soc. for Cinephiles (pres. 1990-91, Man of Yr. 1973). Office: care Entertainment Tonight Paramount TV 5555 Melrose Ave Los Angeles CA 90038-3197

MALTZ, ANDREW HAL, engineering executive; b. Mineola, N.Y., Feb. 27, 1960; s. Joseph A. and Marilyn (Rothchild) M.; m. Leslie Ann Stewart, May 24, 1987. BS in Elec. Engring., SUNY, Buffalo, 1982. Programmer Dubner Computer Systems, Ft. Lee, N.J., 1981; research and devel. engr. Ruxton, Ltd., Burbank, Calif., 1981-84; cons. Andrew H. Maltz Consulting, Burbank, 1984—; v.p. engring. Cinedco, Inc., Glendale, Calif., 1985-91; v.p. engring. and ops. Ediflex Systems, Inc., Glendale, 1991—. Recipient Emmy award Acad. TV Arts and Scis., 1986. Mem. Soc. Motion Picture and TV Engrs., Motion Picture and TV Industry (tech. coun.). Home: 15106 Weddington St Van Nuys CA 91411-3943 Office: Ediflex Systems Inc 1225 Grand Central Ave Glendale CA 91201-2425

MALTZ, JEROME PAUL, broadcasting executive; b. Chgo., June 3, 1935; s. Benjamin Nathan and Bess (Packer) M.; m. Margaret Magda Hoffmann, Mar. 27, 1959 (div. Jan. 1978); children: Jason, Bess; m. Margi Orly Kaufman, Apr. 20, 1986. BA, UCLA, 1956; MBA, NYU, 1967. Pvt. practice oil lease broker Los Angeles, 1969-73, pvt. practice real estate broker, developer, 1973—; broadcasting exec. Gen. Broadcasting Corp., Los Angeles, 1984—; chmn. Gen. Broadcasting Corp., Los Angeles, 1984—. Served with USAR, 1957-63. Named Man of Yr., Gendel chpt. City of Hope, Los Angeles, 1987. Mem. Calif. Broadcasters Assn. (bd. dirs. 1986—). Democrat. Jewish. Club: Friars (Beverly Hills, Calif.). Office: Gen Broadcasting Corp 11685 Magnolia Blvd # A North Hollywood CA 91601-3065

MALUGEN, LOUISE DECARL, bankruptcy judge; b. 1945. BA, Pa. Coll. Women, Pitts.; JD, Loyola U., Chgo. Admitted to bar, 1970. Bankruptcy judge U.S. Bankruptcy Ct. (so. dist.) Calif., San Diego, 1984—. Office: US Dist Ct 940 Front St San Diego CA 92189-0010

MALZBENDER, THOMAS, electrical engineer; b. Munich, Federal Republic of Germany, Sept. 4, 1959; came to U.S., 1965; s. Henry and Irmgard (Müller) M. BSEE, Cornell U., 1981. Devel. engr. Hewlett Packard, Sunnyvale, Calif., 1982-86; rsch. engr. Hewlett Packard Labs, Palo Alto, Calif., 1986—; prin. organizer, editor Hewlett Packard's first Internat. Conf. on Neural Networks, Palo Alto, 1988. Contbr. articles to profl. jours.; patentee in field. Mem. Assn. for Computing Machinery. Office: Hewlett Packard Labs 1501 Page Mill Rd Palo Alto CA 94304-1100

MANAGAN, ROBERT ALAN, physicist; b. Glen Ellyn, Ill., Sept. 22, 1955; s. William Warren and Dorothy Johanna (Tonjes) M.; m. Elizabeth Jayne West, July 31, 1982; children: Julie Elizabeth, Laura Frances, Claire Michelle. BA, Rice U., 1977; MS, U. Chgo., 1979, PhD, 1985. Rsch. asst. U. Chgo., 1977-81, U. Fla., Gainesville, 1981-84; postdoctoral fellow U. Toronto, Ont., Can., 1985-86; physicist Lawrence Livermore Nat. Lab., Livermore, Calif., 1986—. Contbr. articles to profl. jours. Fellow Robert R. McCormick Found. 1977-80. Mem. Am. Astronomical Soc., Nat. Eagle Scout Assn., Phi Beta Kappa, Sigma Pi Sigma. Republican. Baptist. Home: 2115 Westbrook Ln Livermore CA 94550 Office: Lawrence Livermore Nat Lab 7000 East Ave L84 Livermore CA 94550

MANAHAN, MARK STEVEN, computer manufacturing company executive; b. Milw., July 22, 1955; s. Michael Larry and Ruth Virginia (Crosby) M.; m. Terri Ann Reddin, Feb. 14, 1974 (div. 1978); m. Lisa Kay Welch, Jan. 19, 1980; children: Jamie Lin, Sarah Jessica, Jason Scott. Student, Orange Coast Coll., Costa Mesa, Calif., 1974-75, Riverside Community Coll., 1986. Mgr. customer svc. Warmington Homes, Irvine, Calif., 1976-81; mgr. customer svc. Alpha Microsystems, Santa Ana, Calif., 1982-88, dir. customer satisfaction, 1988-89, dir. svc. mktg., 1990, dir. bus. devel., 1990—. Mem. Assn. Field Svc. Mgrs., Alpha Micro Users Soc., Network Dealer Assn., Internat. Alpha Micro Dealers Assn. Republican. Christian Ch. Office: Alpha Microsystems 3501 Sunflower Santa Ana CA 92508

MANARA, JAMES ANTHONY, software executive; b. Westfield, Mass., Sept. 17, 1945; s. James Anthony and Genevieve Sophia (Chlastawa) M.; m. Sheila Aileen Barry, Sept. 6, 1970; children: Gregory James, Beth Ann. BA, Rutgers U., 1973; MBA, Fairleigh Dickenson U., 1977. Programmer AT&T, Bedminster, N.J., 1973-80; v.p. Security Pacific Nat. Bank, Glendale, Calif., 1980-86; mgr. Candle Corp., L.A., 1985—; sr. instr. UCLA, 1980—; cons. Sigma Delta Group, Thousand Oaks, Calif., 1986—; speaker in field. Bd. dirs. Hart Pony League Baseball, 1986-89. Sgt. USMC, 1966-70, Vietnam. Republican. Roman Catholic. Office: Candle Corp 2425 Olympic Blvd Santa Monica CA 90404-9999

MANARY, RICHARD DEANE, manufacturing executive; b. Des Moines, Nov. 11, 1944; s. Robert Claude and Veronica (Cornwell) M.; m. Eileen Cecile, Aug. 16, 1986; children: Erica (dec.), Matthew, Stephen, Lauren. AA in Indsl. Engring., Southwestern Coll., 1976; BA in History, Calif. State U., San Diego, 1967, BS in Edn., 1973; grad., Stanford U. Bus. Ext., 1991. Registered profl. engr., Calif.; cert. elem. tchr., Calif. Mfg. engr. Rohr Industries, San Diego, 1967-78; chief R&D divsn. Rohr Industries, Riverside, Calif., 1978-80, project mfg. mgr., 1980-84; dep. program mgr. Rohr Industries, Wichita, Kans., 1984-87; mgr. Titan 3d, Titan IV missile programs Rohr Industries, Riverside, 1987-89; program mgr. MD-11 Rohr Industries, 1989-91; gen. program mgr. Boing mil. programs Rohr Industries, Chula Vista, Calif., 1991—. Contbr. articles to profl. jours. Chmn. employee and community assistance program Rohr Industries, Riverside, 1981-85; adv. Riverside chpt. Jr. Achievement, 1978-79. Mem. Soc. Mfg. Engrs. (sr., assoc., chmn. 1978-79), Soc. Automotive Engrs., Soc. Material and Process Engrs., Am. Soc. Metals, Nat. Mgmt. Assn. (chmn. 1980-81), Air Force Assn., KC. Democrat. Roman Catholic. Home: 4098 Martin Canyon Ct Bonita CA 91902-2562 Office: PO Box 878 Chula Vista CA 91912-0878

MANASSE, ROGER, physicist, consultant; b. N.Y.C., Apr. 9, 1930; s. Maurice Maxamillian and Claire Catherine (Klotz) M.; m. Jane Carroll Mason, June 12, 1952; children: Michael Edward, Carol Ann. BS in Physics, MIT, 1950, PhD in Physics, 1955. Mem. tech. staff Draper Lab. MIT, Cambridge, 1950-52; mem. tech. staff Lincoln Lab. MIT, Lexington, 1954-59; head radar dept. Mitre Corp., Bedford, Mass., 1959-67; mem. tech. staff Gen. Rsch. Corp., Santa Barbara, Calif., 1967-70; v.p., chief scientist SRS Technologies, Irvine, Calif., 1972-73; pres., chief exec. officer Swerling, Manasse and Smith, Inc., Woodland Hills, Calif., 1983-85; pvt. practice Santa Barbara, 1974-83, 86—; mem. Air Force Sci. Adv. Bd., 1969-78. Contbr. papers to profl. jours. Mem. IEEE, Am. Phys. Soc., Sigma Xi. Home and Office: 234 Canon Dr Santa Barbara CA 93105-2658

MANCINI, ROBERT KARL, computer analyst, consultant; b. Burbank, Calif., May 13, 1954; s. Alfred Robert and Phyllis Elaine (Pflugel) ; m. Barbara Diane Bacon, Aug. 4, 1979; children: Benjamin Robert, Bonnie Kathryn, Brandon Mancini. BA in Econs., UCLA, 1976; cert. in bibl. studies, Multonmah Sch. of the Bible, 1981; MBA, Santa Clara (Calif.) U., 1987. Process clk. Am. Funds Svc. Co., L.A., 1976-77; exec. asst. Sierra Thrift & Loan Co., San Mateo, Calif., 1977-78; sci. programming specialist Lockheed Missiles & Space Co., Sunnyvale, Calif., 1978-90; product mgr. Diversified Software Systems Inc., Morgan Hill, Calif., 1990—; cons. Mancini Computer Svcs., San Jose and Morgan Hill, 1985—; instr. Heald Coll., San Jose, Calif., 1990. Mem. fin. coun. Hillside Ch., 1990-91; mem. blue ribbon budget rev. com. City of Morgan Hill, 1992. Mem. Phi Kappa Sigma (expansion com. 1976-78). Republican. Home: PO Box 1602 Morgan Hill CA 95038-1602

MANCINI, WILLIAM F., international relations executive; b. Downey, Calif., Jan. 16, 1959. BA in Polit. Sci., Calif. State U., 1980. Parts lister and scheduling analyst Rockwell Internat. Corp., Downey, Calif., 1976-78; prodn. asst. Winner/Wagner and Assocs., Los Angeles, 1978-83; protocol officer U.S. Dept. of State, Washington, 1983-84; advance rep. for the Pres. The White House, Washington, 1984-85; asst. to the chmn. Com. for the 50th Am. Presdl. Inaugural Galas, Washington, 1984-85; confidential asst. to the dir. Pub. Affairs Agy. U.S. Dept. of Commerce, Washington, 1985-86; pres. Mancini Internat., Newport Beach, Calif., 1986—; cons. Embassy of Oman, Paramount Pictures, Niles Internat., Burbank, Calif., The Greater Alarm Co., Inc., Huntington Beach, Calif., The Challenger Ctr. for Space Sci. Edn., Washington, Realty Bus. Group, Newport Beach; advance rep. White Ho., 1989—; hon. consul for the Sultanate of Oman, L.A., 1991-92. Patentee in field. Mem. The Big Bros. of Greater Los Angeles and Washington. Mem. Profl. Ski Instrs. Am., Aircraft Owners and Pilots Assn. Office: Mancini Internat 10940 Wilshire Blvd Fl 16 Los Angeles CA 90024-3915

MAND, RANJIT SINGH, device physicist, educator; b. Nairobi, Kenya, Sept. 28, 1956; came to U.S., 1989; s. Naranjan Singh and Gurdev Kaur (Dhanova) M.; 1 child, Anreet Kaur. BS in Solid State Electronics, U. Bradford, Eng., 1981, PhD, 1985; MS, U. Wales, Bangor, 1983. Cons. AT&T Bell Labs., Murray Hill, N.J., 1982-85; Toshiba fellow Toshiba R&D Centre, Kawasaki, Japan, 1985-86; mem. sci. staff Bell Northern Rsch., Ottawa, Ont., Can., 1987-89; lectr. U. Carlton, Ottowa, 1988-89; mgr. optoelectronics Furukawa Electric Techs., Santa Clara, Calif., 1990—; lectr. U. Santa Clara, Calif., 1990—; bd. dirs. Optical Communications Products, Inc., Chatsworth, Calif. Contbr. articles to Electronic Letters, Applied Physics Letters, Jour. Applied Physics, Electron Device Letters, 1985-89, noew assoc. editor; referee IEE Electronic Letters, 1987—. Toshiba R & D Ctr. fellow, 1985; recipient City & Guilds of London Insigna award, 1989. Mem. IEEE (sr.), Inst. Elec. Engrs. (corp.), Inst. Physics (corp.), Engring. Coun. of Eng. (charterd), Am. Phys. Soc. Office: Furukawa Electric Techs 900 Lafayette St Ste 401 Santa Clara CA 95050-4966

MANDEL, DOMINIC ROBERT, educator, education specialist; b. Chgo., May 31, 1956; s. Vincent DePaul and Antionette M.; m. Rose Dolora Villas, Dec. 26, 1982; 1 child, Nikaela. BS in Psychology and Anthropology, Ill. State U., 1978. Asst. mgr. K-Mart Orgn., Denver and Santa Fe, 1975-80; probation and parole officer N.Mex. Dept. of Corrections, Santa Fe, 1981-82, classification officer, 1982-88; correctional adminstr. N.Mex. Youth Authority, Santa Fe, 1988-89, pub. info. officer, adminstrv. asst., 1993, tng. specialist, staff devel. specialist for children, youth and families. Columnist Round the Round House, State Employees Newsletter, Meded-Tng. Rev. Publ. Mem. N.Mex. First, Santa Fe and Albuquerque, 1990—, Chappannal Sch. Site Based Mgmt. Team; mem. criminal justice adv. com. Santa Fe Community Coll. Home: 2335 Camino Pintores Santa Fe NM 87505-5290 Office: Children Youth & Family Dept PO Drawer 5160 Santa Fe NM 87502-5160

MANDEL, JEFF, writer, director, composer; b. L.A., May 27, 1952; s. Sheldon Charles and Renee Babette (Donatt) M. BA, U. Calif., L.A., 1973. V.p. Warren Lockhart Productions, L.A., 1980-82; exec. script cons. Ohara/Warner Bros. TV, L.A., 1987-88; supervising producer Superforce (Viacom), L.A., 1990—; advisor Slavko Vorkapich, L.A., 1974-76. Writer and co-writer for TV and cable; writer, co-writer, producer, directed various films; composed musical material for film and TV, 1975—; co-exec. producer Firehead (the series); contbr. articles to profl. jours. Mem. Libertarian Cen. Com., L.A., 1982, 83; patron Museum of Neon Arts, L.A., 1983—. Recipient 4 Crystal Reel awards Fla. Film Commn., 1991-92. Mem. Writers Guild Am., Am Soc. Composers, Authors and Pubs.

MANDEL, MARTIN LOUIS, lawyer; b. L.A., May 17, 1944; s. Maurice S. and Florence (Byer) M.; m. Duree Dunn, Oct. 16, 1982; 1 child, Max Andrew. BA, U. So. Calif., 1965, JD, 1968; LLM, George Washington U., 1971. Bar: Calif. 1969, U.S. Dist. Ct. (cen. dist.) Calif. 1972, U.S. Ct. Claims, 1971, U.S. Tax Ct. 1971, U.S. Supreme Ct. 1972. With office of gen. csl. IRS, Washington, 1968-72; ptnr. Stephens, Jones, LaFever & Smith, L.A., 1972-77, Stephens, Martin & Mandel, 1977-79, Fields, Fehn, Feinstein & Mandel, 1979-83; sr. v.p., gen. counsel Investment Mortgage Internat., Inc., 1983-84; ptnr. Feinstein, Gourley & Mandel, 1984-85, Mandel & Handin, San Francisco, 1985—; gen. counsel L.A. Express Football Club, 1983-85; instr. corps. U. West L.A., 1973-83. Mem. ABA, L.A. County Bar Assn., L.A. Athletic Club, Phi Delta Phi. Office: 131 Steuart St Ste 700 San Francisco CA 94105

MANDEL, OSCAR, literature educator, writer; b. Antwerp, Belgium, Aug. 24, 1926; came to U.S., 1940; m. Adrienne Schizzano. BA, NYU, 1947; MA, Columbia U., 1948; PhD, Ohio State U., 1951. Asst. prof. English U. Nebr., 1955-60; Fulbright lectr. U. Amsterdam, 1960-61; vis. assoc. prof. English Calif. Inst. Tech., 1961-62, assoc. prof. English, 1962-68, prof. Lit., 1968—. Author: Collected Lyrics & Epigrams, 1981, Three Classic Don Juan Plays, 1981, Philoctetes and the Fall of Troy, 1981, Annotations to Vanity Fair, 1981, Ariadne, 1982, The Book of Elaborations, 1985, The Kukkurrik Fables, 1987, Sigismund, Prince of Poland, 1989, August Von Kotzebue: The Comedy, The Man, 1990, numerous others; contbr. articles to profl. jours. Office: Calif Inst Tech Humanities Divsn Pasadena CA 91125

MANDEL, ROBERT MICHAEL, international affairs educator; b. Washington; s. Philip and Alice Grace M.; m. Annette Kelley, Aug. 1, 1981; 1 child, Travis Scott. BA in Internat. Rels., Brown U., 1972; MA in Internat. Rels., Yale U., 1974, MPhil in Polit. Sci., 1975, PhD in Polit. Sci., 1976. Intern Office of Polit. Rsch. CIA, Washington, 1974-75; asst. prof. internat. affairs Lewis and Clark Coll., Portland, Oreg., 1976-82, assoc. prof. internat. affairs, 1982-88, prof. internat. affairs, 1988—; dean, social sci. div. Lewis and Clark Coll., Portland, 1990-92; cons. and rsch. in field. Contbr. numerous articles to profl. jours. Yale fellow, 1972-76; Lewis and Clark Coll. grantee, 1976-91. Mem. Internat. Studies Assn. (exec. com. environ. studies sect. 1985-86), Internat. Affairs Coordinating Coun. Greater Portland, Am. Polit. Sci. Assn., Atlantic Coun. (academic assoc.). Office: Lewis and Clark Coll 615 SW Palatine Hill Rd Portland OR 97219-7899

MANDEL, SIEGFRIED, English language educator; b. Berlin, Germany, Dec. 20, 1922; came to U.S., 1933, naturalized, 1938; s. Nathan and Pauline (Scheinmann) M.; m. Dorothy Isaacs, Feb. 3, 1946; children: Elise Judith, Theodore Scott. B.A., Bklyn. Coll., 1946; M.A., Columbia U., 1947; Ph.D., U. Denver, 1967. Part-time instr. Poly. U. N.Y., 1948-55; sr. editor Inst. Econ. Affairs, N.Y.C., 1952-53; writer, editor Asso. Transp., Inc., 1954-55; book rev. columnist Newsday, 1954-55; lectr. N.Y.U., 1955; from instr. to assoc. prof. Poly. Inst. Bklyn., 1955-62; mem. faculty U. Colo., Boulder, 1962—, prof. English and comparative lit., 1965-91, chmn. dept. English in engring., 1969-70, dir. grad. studies, dept. English, 1977-79, dir. comparative lit. program, 1988-91, prof. emeritus, 1991—; vis. prof. Am. studies U. Hawaii at Manoa, Honolulu, 1981-82; indsl. lectr. writing workshops Internat. Tel. & Tel Corp., 1959-60. Editor, contbg. author: Writing in Industry, 1959, (with D.L. Caldwell) Proposal and Inquiry Writing, 1962, Modern Journalism, 1962, Rainer Maria Rilke: The Poetic Instinct, 1965, (with Aaron Kramer) Rainer Maria Rilke: Visions of Christ, 1967, Contemporary European Novelists, 1968, Dictionary of Science, 1969, Writing for Science and Technology, 1970, Group 47: The Reflected Intellect, 1973; editor, translator: Lou Andreas-Salomé: Nietzche in His Works, 1988, Ibsen's Heroines, 1985, Karl Kerényi: Excursions of a Hellenist, Homer, Nietzsche, and Kazantzakis; contbr. articles and book revs. to profl. jours.and ency. yearbooks. Served with AUS, 1943-46. Faculty fellow lit. research U. Colo., 1968-69, 75-76; recipient Eugene M. Kayden nat. translation prize, 1983. Mem. MLA, Am. Comparative Lit. Assn., Georg-Groddeck Soc., Rilke-Gesellschaft, N.Am. Nietzsche Assn. Home: 1500 Harrison Ave Boulder CO 80303 Office: U Colo Dept English Hellems 101 Campus Box 226 Boulder CO 80309-0226

MANDER, ANTHONY MICHAEL, psychologist; b. East Orange, N.J., May 7, 1946; s. James Peter and Jean (Richel) M.; m. Sandra Lynn Flowers, Jan. 21, 1970; children: Quinn Michael, Bryce Anthony. BA, Lycoming Coll., 1968; MA, U. N.C., 1975, PhD, 1976. Lic. psychologist, Alaska. Recreational therapist Greystone State Park Mental Instn., Morris Plains, N.J., 1969; cottage parent Guilford Dept. Social Svcs., High Point, N.C., 1972-74; rsch. analyst Alaska State Office of Alcoholism, Juneau, 1974; intern in psychology U. N.C., Greensboro, 1975-76; psychologist Davidson County Mental Health Ctr., Thomasville, N.C., 1976, dir. psychol. svcs., 1976-78; pvt. practice Juneau, 1978—; cons. Youth and Family Counseling Svcs., Lexington, N.C., 1976-78, Juneau Receiving Home, 1979-86, Tongass Community Counseling Ctr., 1989-90. Contbr. articles to profl. jours. Mem. Johnson Youth Ctr. Task Force, Juneau, 1989-90; bd. dirs. sex offender treatment program Dept. Corrections State of Alaska, Juneau, 1979-83, statewide coord., 1992-93. Mem. APA. Home: 14295 Otter Way Juneau AK 99801-8422 Office: 8800 Glacier Hwy Ste 216 Juneau AK 99801-8080

MANDOLINI, DAVID JAMES, financial consultant, commercial pilot; b. Memphis, June 28, 1953; s. Guy Anthony and Mary (Gho) M. BBA, Memphis State U., 1976; MBA, U. Tulsa, 1983. CPA; cert. data processor; cert. flight instr.; cert. info. systems auditor. Internal auditor Phillips Petroleum Co., Bartlesville, Okla., 1977-79; info. systems auditor The Williams Co., Tulsa, 1979-81; mgr. budgets and spl. projects Crane Carrier Co., Tulsa, 1981-82; cons. mgr. Price Waterhouse, Denver, 1983-89; dir. cons. svcs. The Solutions Group, Inc., Denver, 1989—; comml. pilot. Mem. CAP, Denver, 1990—. Named to Outstanding Young Men of Am., 1986. Mem. AICPA, Colo. Soc. CPAs (pub. rels. com. 1987-90), Assn. for Inst. for Cert. of Computing Profls., Nat. Assn. Flight Instrs., Inst. Internal Auditors. Home: 1099 S Fairplay Way # 101 Aurora CO 80012

MANEA-MANOLIU, MARIA, linguist; b. Galatz, Romania, Mar. 12, 1934; came to U.S., 1978, naturalized, 1987; d. Ion T. and Ana S. (Codescu) Manoliu; m. Ion S. Manea, Nov. 26, 1968. BA, French Coll., Galatz, 1951; MA, U. Bucharest, Romania, 1955, PhD, 1966. Asst. prof. Romance linguistics U. Bucharest, 1957-61, assoc. prof., 1961-68, prof., 1968-77; prof. linguistics U. Calif., Davis, 1978—; vis. prof. U. Chgo., 1972-74; cons. NEH, 1980—; mem. adv. bd. Romance Philology, Berkeley, Calif., 1984—, Philologica Canariense, Spain, 1992—. Author: Sistematica Substitutelor, 1968 (Ministry of Edn. award 1968), Gramatica Comparatǎ a limbilor romanice, 1971, El Estructuralismo Lingüistico, 1979, Tipologia e Historia, 1985; editor-in-chief Bull. de la S.R.L.R., Bucharest, 1975-78; corresponding editor Revue Romane, Copenhagen, 1972—; contbr. articles to profl. jours. Grantee Internat. Com. Linguists, 1972, Fulbright, 1972-74, 91-92, U. Calif., 1979—; recipient Evenimentul award for Outstanding Contbn. to Romanian Culture, 1991. Mem. Am. Romanian Acad. (pres. 1982—), Soc. de Linguistique Romane, Soc. Romaine de Linguistique Romane (v.p. 1974-78), Internat. Assn. Hist. Linguistics, MLA, Lingyustics Soc. Am., Internat. Assn. Pragamtics, Romanian Studies Assn. Am. (pres. 1986-88). Office: U Calif Dept French and Italian 509 Sproul Hall Davis CA 95616

MANEATIS, GEORGE A., retired utility company executive; b. 1926. BSEE, Stanford U., 1949, MSEE, 1950. With GE, 1950-53; with Pacific Gas & Elec. Co., San Francisco, 1953—, v.p., 1979-81, sr. v.p., 1981-82, exec. v.p., 1982-86, pres., 1986-91, also bd. dirs. Office: Pacific Gas & Electric Co PO Box 770000 1 California St Ste F31 San Francisco CA 94177

MANES, FRITZ, feature film producer, writer/director; b. Oakland, Calif., Apr. 22, 1936; s. Elmer Frederick and Dorothy Valentine (Short) M.; m. Audrey Louise Jindra, Feb. 14, 1958. Student, U. Calif., Berkeley, 1949-51; BA, UCLA, 1956. Sales exec., on-air personality, writer, dir. NBC, ABC and CBS radio and TV, L.A. and San Francisco, 1957-74; producer, exec. producer 12 Clint Eastwood feature films Malpaso Prodns., Burbank, Calif., 1974-87; producer Sundancer Prodns., L.A., 1987—; commr. Calif. Film Commn., L.A., 1986-89. Producer feature film Any Which Way You Can, 1981 (Best Picture award Acad. Country Music 1981). With USMC 1951-54, Korea. Decorated Purple Heart. Mem. Dir.'s Guild Am., Screen Actors Guild, U.S. Marine Corps Corrs. Assn., 1st Marine Div. Assn., Sausalito Yacht Club, Calif. Yacht Club, The Olympic Club. Republican. Roman Catholic.

MANGAN, TERENCE JOSEPH, police chief; b. Utica, N.Y., Feb. 17, 1938; s. Lawrence and Eloise (Roth) M.; m. Charlotte Mauss, June 19, 1971; children: Sean, Megan. B.A., St. Mary's Coll., Norwalk, Conn., 1961; M.A., St. Albert's Coll., 1965; postgrad. in Pub. Adminstrn., Adminstrn. Justice, U. So. Calif., 1972-76; Grad. FBI Nat. Acad. Cert. Wash. State Criminal Justice Tng. Commn., Calif. Peace Officers Standards and Tng. Commn.; grad. Northwest Law Enforcement Exec. Command Coll., 1986; cert. Gov.'s Rev. Tean Child Abuse Services, 1986. With Seaside (Calif.) Police Dept., 1968-72; with Lakewood (Calif.) Police Dept., 1972-76, chief, dir. community safety, to 1976; chief Bellingham (Wash.) Police Dept., 1976-87; chief Spokane (Wash.) Police Dept., 1987—; chmn. Wash. State Criminal Justice Tng. Commn.; mem. Mgmt. Adv. Group Organized Crime and Narcotics Enforcement; appointed to Death Investigations Coun., Spl. Task Force on Child Abuse, Gov's Criminal Justice Adv. Bd.; master mentor Waspc's Exec. Leadership Inst., coord. Northwest Law Enforcement Exec. Command Coll. Program; lectr. FBI Acad. Mem. archdiocesan steering com. Ann. Catholic Appeal, 1982; chair fund-raising drives Am. Cancer Soc., Am. Heart Assn., Salvation Army, Easter Seal Soc., Assn. for Retarded Citizens; bd. advs. Holy Names Ctr.; exec. bd. Boy Scouts of Am., Inland Empire Coun.; bd. dirs. Spokane Goodwill Industries, United Way, Whatcom County, Calif. Recipient citation U.S. Secret Service, 1969, Congressional Com. Internal Security, 1971, Svc. award City of Seaside, 1972, Disting. Svc. award City of Lakewood, also Wash. Assn. Sheriffs and Police Chiefs, 1978-81, Police Officer of Yr. award Nat. Exchange Club, 1979, Lawman of Yr. award Vets. of Foreign Wars, 1980, Law Enforcement Officer of Yr. award Wash. VFW, 1980, Community Service award Wash. Toastmasters Internat., 1980, Pres. award Pacific Lutheran U., 1981, Paul Harris fellow Rotary Internat., 1986. Mem. Internat. Assn. Chiefs Police, Nat. Council Crime and Delinquency, Wash. Assn. Sheriffs and Police Chiefs (past pres.), Internat. Peace Arch Law Enforcement Council. Roman Catholic. Office: Spokane Police Dept Office of the Chief 1100 W Mallon Ave Spokane WA 99260-0001*

MANGANO, ELIZABETH, cartoonist; b. San Francisco, Jan. 1, 1967; d. Scully and Jennifer (Sultz) Baugh; m. Thomas Mangano, August 3, 1990; 1 child, Scully Thomas. BA, Oberlin Coll., 1989. Cartoonist Oberlin (Ohio) Daily News, 1989-90; freelance artist Oberlin, 1990-91; polit. cartoonist Bakersfield (Calif.) Daily, 1991—. Contbr. cartoons to pop. mags. including Newsweek, Time, Rolling Stone. Vol. Oberlin SPCA, 1990-91, Bakersfield Homeless Shelter, 1993—; treas. Californians for Choice, 1991—; active Calif. for Clinton Campaign, 1992. Mem. Polit. Cartoonists Assn. Am., Calif. Cartoonists Assn. (pres. 1993—). Office: Werik Pk 721 18th St Bakersfield CA 93301-4821

MANGEL, LEROY DWIGHT, information systems professional; b. Westby, Mont., Oct. 18, 1945; s. Ervin LeRoy and Phyllis Delphine (Hereim) M.; m. Jane Irene Wisness, Dec. 27, 1969; children: Lisa Jane, Lori Jo. AS in Data Processing, N.D. State Sch. of Sci., 1969; BS in Computer Mgmt. Sci., Met. State Coll., Denver, 1985; postgrad., U. Denver. Cert. systems profl., data processor. Programmer Blue Cross/Blue Shield, Fargo, N.D., 1969-72; programmer analyst Northwestern Nat. Ins. Corp., Milw., 1972-74; systems analyst Green Giant Co., Le Sueur, Minn., 1974-79; systems and programming mgr. Homestake Mining Co., Golden, Colo., 1979-81, system planning and support mgr., 1982-85, computer systems mgr., 1985-90; tech. svcs. mgr. The Alert Ctr., Englewood, Colo., 1990-91; data processing mgr. Meml. Hosp. Sweetwater County, 1991. Served with USAF, 1963-67. Mem. Data Processing Mgmt. Assn., Golden Key Nat. Hon. Soc. (life). Lutheran. Office: The Alert Ctr 5800 S Quebec St Englewood CO 80111-2007

MANGHAM, JOHN RANDALL, computer programmer, analyst; b. Oklahoma City, July 19, 1957; s. Clarence Madison and Ola B. (Hodges) M. Student, Okla. State U., 1975-77, 80-81. Night ops. mgr. Citizens State Bank, Liberal, Kans., 1982-83; contract programmer M. David Lowe, Inc., Houston, 1983-84; programmer/analyst Thorpe Corp., Houston, 1984-87, Dairy div. Borden, Inc., Houston, 1987-88, Battle Mountain Gold Co., Houston, 1988-89; sr. programmer/analyst Primeco, Inc., Houston, 1989-90, Auto Parts Club, Inc., San Diego, 1990—. Contbr. articles to profl. jours. missionary Ch. Jesus Christ LDS, Italy, 1978-80; bishop, bd. dirs. Restoration Fellowship in Jesus Christ, San Diego, 1990—; v.p. Houston Interfaith Alliance, 1987. Mem. Application Systems Group (bd. dirs. 1992—, treas. 1993—). Libertarian. Mormon. Home: PO Box 371728 San Diego CA 92137-1728 Office: Auto Parts Club Inc 1040 Sherman St San Diego CA 92110

MANGHIRMALANI, MONA, business executive; b. New Delhi, Nov. 1, 1968; d. Ashok and Prabha (Sinha) Gour. BA, J. Nehru U., New Delhi, 1987; cert. in computers, Berkeley U., 1989. Pres. Marco Polo Ltd., Danville, Calif., 1988—; bd. dirs. Maya Found. Asst. pres. Sahara Found., Danville, 1988; mem. ARC, 1989. Mem. Internat. C. of C., Commonwealth Club (London), Congress-I Party (India), Delhi Golf Club. Republican. Hindu. Office: Marco Polo Ltd 230 Powhattan Ct Danville CA 94526

MANGIR, TULIN ERDIM, science educator, consultant; b. Ankara, Turkey, May 3, 1950; d. Ali Riza and Sabahat Erdim; m. Metin S. Mangir, Sept. 19, 1970; children: Alan-Cem, David-Emre. BSEE, UCLA, 1971; attended, U So. Calif., 1973-75, MSEE in Semiconductor Device Physics, 1974, MSEE in Computer Architecture, 1975; PhD in Engring., UCLA, 1981. Engr. Burroughs Western Divsn., Pasadena, Calif., 1974-76; rsch. engr., teaching assoc. UCLA, 1975-81; from sr. staff dir. to v.p. XEROX Microelectronics Ctr., El Segundo, Calif., 1978-81; prof. Computer Engring. UCLA, 1981-86; prin. cons. Advanced Tech. Consulting, West L.A., Calif., 1981-86; tech. acqusition mgr., chief sci., project mgr. TRW, Inc., Redondo Beach, Calif., 1986-92; founding exec. ptnr. The Sci. Alliance, Santa Monica, Calif., 1992—; pres. TM Assocs., Santa Monica, Calif., 1992—; cons. numerous orgns. including European Econ. Commn., Swedish Govt. Microelectronics Program, Nokia, Thompson C.S.F., Aerospace co., NASA, private and pub. co., venture firms, 1981—; lectr. NATO Spl. Studies Inst., 1987-90; rep. U.S. aerospace industry, Japan, 1991-92. contbr. articles to profl. jours., chpts. to books. fund raiser, vol. Westside Dem. Campaign (including Clinton & Gore, Boxer, Feinstein), 1992; vol. sci. instr. Santa Monica Sch. Dist., 1990—; fundraiser Westside Foodbank, City of Hope, AIDS Project, 1988—; chair child devel. com., Santa Monica Sch. Dist., 1991—; reg. v.p. ATAA, 1982-85. Recipient Young Investigator award Internat. Fedn. Info. Processing 1984-86, Service award, 1984-86, Recognition award Swedish Govt., 1984-87, Vol. award Community Action Teams, 1990-92; rsch. grantee, IBM, 1983-86, travel grantee Electronics Rsch. and Sci. Inst., Taiwan, 1985-86. Mem. IEEE (organizing coms. 1980—, referee NSF pubs., proposals 1980—, travel grantee 1984-85, lectr.), Women in Tech. Internat. Office: TM Assocs 536 16th St Santa Monica CA 90402

MANKOFF, ALBERT WILLIAM, cultural organization administrator, consultant; b. Newark, Aug. 24, 1926; s. Albert and Dorothy (Klein) M; Apr. 4, 1959 (div.); 1 child, Robert Morgan; m. Audrey Emery, Mar. 18,

1972. BLS, U. Okla., 1967. With Am. Airlines, Inc., 1947-69, regional mgr. mgmt.tng. and devel., 1957-67; mgr. orgn. devel. Am. Airlines, Inc., Tulsa, 1968-69; dir. personnel Peat, Marwick, Mitchell & Co., Chgo., 1969-72; ptnr. Lexicon, Inc. Cons., Raleigh, N.C., 1972-77; Pacific area mgr. safety and tng. dept. Trailways, Inc., L.A., 1978-80; tng. cons. State of Calif., Sacramento, 1980-91; pres. Inst. Am. Hist. Tech., Ojai, Calif., 1987—. Author: Trolley Treasures, 4 vols., 1986-87, The Glory Days, 1989, Tracks of Triumph, 1993; contbr. articles to profl. jours. Bd. dirs., v.p. OASIS: Midwest Centre for Human Potential, Chgo., 1970-72, Tulsa Urban League, 1962-69; bd. dirs. Meditation Groups Inc., Ojai, Calif., Psychosynthesis Internat., Ojai. With A.C., U.S. Army, 1945-46. Home and Office: PO Box 494 Ojai CA 93024

MANLEY, JOAN A(DELE) DANIELS, retired publisher; b. San Luis Obispo, Calif., Sept. 23, 1932; d. Carl and Della (Weinmann) Daniels; m. Jeremy C. Lanning, Mar. 17, 1956 (div. Sept. 1963); m. Donald H. Manley, Sept. 12, 1964 (div. 1985); m. William G. Houlton, May 31, 1991. BA, U. Calif., Berkeley, 1954; DBA (hon.), U. New Haven, 1974; LLD (hon.), Babson Coll., 1978. Sec. Doubleday & Co., Inc., N.Y.C., 1954-60; sales exec. Time Inc., 1960-66, v.p., 1971-75, group v.p., 1975-84, also bd. dir.; circulation dir. Time-Life Books, 1966-68, dir. sales, 1968-70, pub., 1970-76; chmn. bd. Time-Life Books Inc., 1976-80; vice chmn. bd. Book-of-the-Month Club, Inc., N.Y.C., until 1984; supervising dir. Time-Life Internat. (Nederland) B.V., Amsterdam, until 1984; bd. dirs. Scholastic Inc., Viking Office Products Inc., AON Corp., Sara Lee Corp. Past trustee Mayo Found., Rochester Minn., Nat. Repertory Orch.; trustee Vail Valley Inst., Keystone Ctr., William Benton Found.; former mem. adv. coun. Stanford U. Bus. Sch., Harvard Div. Sch.; mem. adv. coun. Haas Sch. Bus., U. Calif. U. Calif.-Berkeley fellow, 1989. Mem. Assn. Am. Pubs. (past chmn.).

MANLEY, RICHARD WALTER, insurance executive; b. Malone, N.Y., Dec. 26, 1934; s. Walter E. and Ruth (St. Mary) M.; m. Linda Kimberlin, Dec. 18, 1965; children: Stephanie, Christopher. BS in Bus., U. So. Miss., 1960. Cert. real estate broker. Account exec. Colonial Life and Accident, Hattiesburg, Miss., 1960-63; dist. mgr. Colonial Life and Accident, Oklahoma City, 1963-66; regional dir. Colonial Life and Accident, Denver, 1966-76, zone dir., 1976-82; pres. Commonwealth Gen. Group, Denver, 1982-92, Manley Properties Inc., Denver, 1982-90, Richard W. Manley Commonwealth Gen. Grps., Inc., Denver, 1982—; cons. Capitol Am. Life Ins. Co., Cleve., 1987-92; bd. dirs. (merco) Mercy Hosp., Denver, 1982-87. With USAF, 1956-59. Mem. Nat. Life Underwriters, Sertoma, Cherry Hills C. of C., Rotary, Elks, Alpha Tau Omega. Roman Catholic. Home: 6510 E Lake Pl Englewood CO 80111-4411 Office: Commonwealth Gen Group Inc 5000 S Quebec St Ste 430 Denver CO 80237-2701

MANLOVE, ROBERT FLETCHER, college dean; b. St. Louis, June 25, 1937; s. Robert Fletcher and Mary (Coulter) M.; m. Ruth Hull, Sept. 19, 1969; children: Melissa Hull, Amelia Hull. BS in Geology, MIT, 1959; MS in Engring. Geosci., U. Calif., Berkeley, 1964; AB, U. Calif., 1972; MA, U. Calif., Berkeley, 1974, PhD in Anthropology, 1990. Vol. Peace Corps, Philippines, 1964-66; tchr. chemistry Canyon High Sch., Castro Valley, Calif., 1966-68; instr. anthropology City Coll. San Francisco, 1968-91, chair dept. behavioral scis., 1980-88, dean of instrn., 1991—. Fulbright scholar, Philippines, 1975-76. Office: City Coll San Francisco 50 Phelan San Francisco CA 94112

MANLOWE, JAMES STEWART, lawyer; b. San Diego, Mar. 23, 1963; s. James Stewart and Nancy Jean (Dale) M. Student, Monash U., Melbourne, Australia, 1985; BA, UCLA, 1986; JD, Northwestern Sch. Law, Portland, Oreg., 1990. Bar: Oreg. 1990, Ariz. 1991, Hawaii 1991, Hopi 1991, Navajo Nat. 1991. Mng. atty. Hopi Legal Svcs., Keams Canyon, Ariz., 1991-92; atty. DNA-People's Legal Svcs., Inc., Tuba City, Ariz., 1991—; chmn. Environ. Law Caucus, Portland, 1988-89. Dean's fellow Northwestern Sch. Law, 1987-90. Mem. Oreg. State Bar, Hawaii State Bar, Ariz. State Bar, Hopi Bar, Navajo Nation Bar, Golden Key, Phi Beta Kappa. Office: PO Box 765 Tuba City AZ 86045

MANN, CLAUD PRENTISS, JR., retired television journalist, real estate agent; b. Galveston, Tex., June 30, 1925; s. Claud Prentiss and Henrietta Anno (Cline) M.; m. Loris Lea Padgett, Sept. 18, 1948; children: Beatrice Anno, Claudea Padgett, Claud Prentiss III. BS, U. Houston, 1949. Cert. tchr., Calif.; lic. real estate agt., Wash. Fellow Fund for Adult Edn. Mass Media U. Calif., Berkeley, 1958-59; anchor, reporter, writer, prodr., commentator Sta. KTVU-TV, San Francisco, Oakland, Calif., 1962-87; news dir., anchor, prodr. Sta. KTIE-TV, Oxnard, Santa Barbara, Calif., 1987-88; freelance writer, producer, pub. info. specialist, 1988—; journalism instr. Highline and South Seattle Community Colls., 1990-92. Bd. dirs., performer Dramadock Community Theater, Vashon Island, Wash. Recipient No. Calif. Emmy awards for reporting and anchor work, 1975, 76, 77, 79, 81, John Swett award for Edn. Reporting; commendations U.S. State Dept., City of Oakland, City of San Francisco, Calif. State Legis. Mem. Am. Fedn. Radio and TV Artists, Vashon Allied Arts (dir. 1989-91), Nat. Acad. TV Arts and Scis. (Silver Circle), Soc. Profl. Journalists. Home: 25115 122d Ave SW Vashon WA 98070

MANN, DONALD ROBERT See VALA, ROBERT

MANN, FRITZ ALAN, visual artist, photographer; b. Anchorage, Alaska, May 2, 1953; s. William Latimer and Marian Louise (Leffel) M.; m. Mahnaz Fallahi, Mar. 18, 1978; children: Heather Leila, Vincent Mehran. Student, U. So. Colo., 1976-80, Ft. Lewis Coll., 1981-82, U. Colo., Colorado Springs, 1986, 90-91, Pikes Peak C.C., Colorado Springs, 1987. Freelance artist Cromar's Audio-Visual Ctr., Denver, 1974-75; ind. artist, 1976—. Illustrator (children's mag.) Brilliant Star, 1985—; author, illustrator (mag.) Herald of the South, 1987—, (book) The Creative Circle, 1989; artist Amnesty Internat. greeting card, 1992; one-man show, Sangre de Cristo Arts and Conf. Ctr., Pueblo, Colo., 1991. Talent scholar Thatcher Found., Pueblo, 1976-81; recipient Best of Show award Colo. State Fair-Art Gallery, 1990. Mem. The Baha'i Faith. Office: Globetown Art Comm PO Box 6568 Colorado Springs CO 80934

MANN, JOHN KEVIN, management consultant; b. Stanford, Calif., June 22, 1956; s. John Keith and Virginia (McKinnon) M.; m. Christine Suzanna Downs, Dec. 28, 1984. BS, MIT, 1978; MBA, U. Chgo., 1983. Planner Bechtel, San Francisco, 1977, Congl. Budget Office, Washington, 1978-79, Sun Designs Architects, Glenwood Springs, Colo., 1979-80, Hopi Indian Tribe, Oraibi, Ariz., 1980-81; mktg. rep. IBM, Chgo., 1983-86, Balt., 1986-89; market strategy specialist IBM, San Francisco, 1989-91; mgmt. cons. IBM, 1992—. Office: IBM Corp 425 Market St Fl 32 San Francisco CA 94105-2406

MANN, LAURA JOY, banker; b. Milw., Mar. 20, 1966; d. Jerome S. Mann and Philippa Falkner Mahr. Student, Oxford U., 1986; BA, Trinity Coll., 1988. Cert. in pers. fin. planning. Credit analyst Chem. Bank, N.Y.C., 1988-89; pers. banking officer First Interstate Bank Calif., San Diego, 1990-92; credit analyst CDC Small Bus. Fin. Corp., 1992—; treas. San Diego Mus. Art Contemporaries, 1992—. Vol. Sharp Hosp., San Deigo, 1989-90, Hillcrest Receiving Home, San Diego, 1990-91, Fresh Start Surg. Gifts, Encinitas, Calif., 1991—. Mem. Trinity Coll. Club San Diego (v.p. 1990-92). Jewish. Home: 2657 Jefferson St # 101 Carlsbad CA 92008

MANN, MICHAEL MARTIN, electronics company executive; b. N.Y.C., Nov. 28, 1939; s. Herbert and Rosalind (Kaplan) M.; m. Mariel Joy Steinberg, Apr. 25, 1965. BSEE, Calif. Inst. Tech., 1960, MSEE, 1961; PhD in Elec. Engring. and Physics, U. So. Calif., 1969; MBA, UCLA, 1984. Cert. bus. appraiser, profl. cons., mgmt. cons., lic. real estate broker, Calif. Mgr. high power laser programs office Northrop Corp., Hawthorne, Calif., 1969-76; mgr. high energy laser systems lab. Hughes Aircraft Co., El Segundo, Calif., 1976-78; mgr. E-0 control systems labs. Hughes Aircraft Co., El Segundo, 1978-83, asst. to v.p., space & strategic, 1983-84; exec. v.p. Helionetics Inc., Irvine, Calif., 1984-85, pres., chief exec. officer, 1985-86, also bd. dirs.; ptnr. Mann Kavanaugh Chernove, 1986-87; sr. cons. Arthur D. Little, Inc., 1987-88; chmn. bd., pres., chief exec. officer Blue Marble Devel. Group, Inc., 1988—; exec. assoc. Ctr. Internat. Cooperation and Trade, 1989—; sr. assoc. Corp. Fin. Assocs., 1990—; exec. assoc. Reece and Assocs., 1991—; dir. Reece & Assocs., 1991—; mng. dir. Blue Marble Ptnrs. Ltd, 1991—; chmn. bd. dirs., CEO Blue Marble Ptnrs., 1992—; mem. Army Sci. Bd., Dept. Army, Washington, 1986-91; chmn. Ballistic Missile Def. Panel, Directed Energy Weapon Panel, Rsch. and New Initiatives Panel; cons. Office of Sec. of Army, Washington, 1986—, Inst. of Def. Analysis, Washington, 1978—, Dept. Energy, 1988—, Nat. Riverside Rsch. Inst., 1990—; bd. dirs. Datum, Inc.,1988—, Fail-Safe Tech., Corp., 1989-90, Safeguard Health Enterprises, Inc., 1988—, Am. Video Communications, Inc., Meck Industries, Inc., 1987-88, Decade Optical Systems, Inc., 1990—, Forum Mil. Application Directed Energy, 1992—, Am. Bus. Consultants, Inc., 1993—; chmn. bd. Mgmt. Tech., Inc. 1991—; bd. dirs., mem. adv. bd. Micro-Frame, Inc., 1988-91; chmn. bd. HLX Laser, Inc., 1984-86; bd. dirs. Cons's. Roundtable, 1992—, Am. Bus. Cons., Inc., 1993—; rsch. assoc., mem. extension teaching staff U. So. Calif., L.A., 1964-70; chmn. Ballistic Missile Def. Subgroup, 1989-90, Tactical Directed Energy Weapons Subgroup, 1988-90; chmn., chief exec. officer Mgmt. Tech., Inc., 1991—; dir. Am. Bus. Cons., Inc., 1993—. Contbg. editor, mem. adv. bd. Calif. High-Tech Funding Jour., 1989-90; contbr. over 50 tech. articles to profl. jours.; patentee in field. Adv. com. to Engring. Sch., Calif. State U., Long Beach, 1985—; chmn. polit. affairs Am. Electronics Assn., Orange County Coun., 1986-87, mem. exec. com., 1986-88; adv. com. several Calif. congressmen, 1985—; mem. dean's coun. UCLA Grad. Sch. Mgmt., 1984-85; bd. dirs. Archimedes Circle U. Soc. Calif., 1983-85, Ctr. for Innovation and Entrepreneurship, 1986-90, Caltech/MIT Venture Forum, 1987-91. Hicks fellow in Indsl. Rels. Calif. Inst. Tech., 1961, Hewlett Packard fellow. Mem. So. Calif. Tech. Execs. Network, IEEE (sr.), Orange County CEO's Roundtable, Pres.' Roundtable, Nat. Assn. Corp. Dirs., Aerospace/Def. CEO's Roundtable, Am. Def. Preparedness Assn., Security Affairs Support Assn., Acad. Profl. Cons. and Advisors, Internat. Platform Assn., Inst. of Mgmt. Cons's., Pres. Assn., Nat. Assn. Corp. Dirs., Cons's. Roundtable, Pres. Assn., King Harbor Yacht Club. Republican. Home: 4248 Via Alondra Palos Verdes Peninsula CA 90274-1545 Office: Blue Marble Partners 406 Amapola Ave Ste 200 Torrance CA 90501-1475

MANN, NANCY LOUISE (NANCY LOUISE ROBBINS), entrepreneur; b. Chillicothe, Ohio, May 6, 1925; d. Everett Chaney and Pauline Elizabeth R.; m. Kenneth Douglas Mann, June 19, 1949 (div. June 1979); children: Bryan Wilkinson, Laura Elizabeth. BA in Math., UCLA, 1948, MA in Math., 1949, PhD in Biostatistics, 1965. Sr. scientist Rocketdyne Div. of Rockwell Internat., Canoga Park, Calif., 1962-75; mem. tech. staff Rockwell Sci. Ctr., Thousand Oaks, Calif., 1975-78; rsch. prof. UCLA Biomath., L.A., 1978-87; pres., CEO, owner Quality Enhancement Seminars, Inc., L.A., 1982—; pres., CEO Quality and Productivity, Inc., L.A., 1987—; curriculum adv. UCLA Ext. Dept. of Bus. and Mgmt., L.A., 1991—; mem. com. on Nat. Statistics, Nat. Acad. Scis., Washington, 1978-82; mem adv. bd. to supt. U.S. Naval Posgrad. Sch., Monterey, Calif., 1979-82. Co-author: Methods for Analysis of Reliability and Life Data, 1974; author: Keys to Excellence, 1985, The Story of the Deming Philosophy, 2d edit., 1987, 3d edit., 1989; contbr. articles to profl. jours. Recipient award IEEE Reliability Soc., 1982, ASQC Reliability Divsn., 1986. Fellow Am. Statis. Assn. (v.p. 1982-84); mem. Internat. Statis. Inst. Office: Quality and Productivity Inc 1081 Westwood Blvd #217 Los Angeles CA 90024

MANN, ROBERT SAMUEL, video producer; b. Pitts., Feb. 5, 1936; s. Albert Samuel and Hilda Clara (Kalson) M.; children: Curtis, Kelly, Gary. Student, U. Fla., 1973-78. Pvt. practice as real estate developer Daytona Beach, Fla., 1962-68; golf. profl., mfr. Bomman Golf, Daytona Beach, 1968-73; pvt. practice as golf profl. Daytona Beach, 1979-82; pvt. practice as video producer and author Santa Monica, Calif., 1982—. Author: Automatic Golf, 1986, Bob Mann's Proven Golf, 1988, Automatic Golf Complete, 1991; produced and performed in numerous videos including Fitness Testing, 1987, Automatic Golf, 1982-83, Instant Karate, 1986, Isometric Stretch, 1986, Weight Training, 1987. Served with U.S. Army, 1961. Recipient 16 Gold and Platinum Viedo awards Internat. Tape Assn., Recording Industry Assn. Am. Office: 124 S Halcyon Arroyo Grande CA 93420

MANN, THOMAS WILLIAM, JR., management executive; b. Aug. 6, 1949; s. Thomas William and Loris (Mapes) M. BA, U. Ill., 1971, MA, 1972, MS, 1975. Asst. prof. Fla. Atlantic U., Boca Raton, 1974-76; dir., prof. Calif. State U., Long Beach, 1976-84; sr. mgr. KPMG Peat Marwick, L.A., 1984-91; special vice chancellor Univ. Calif., L.A., 1991—; bd. dirs. Internat. Conf. on Librs., U. Wis., 1980, Internat. Conf. on Acad. Librarianship U. Colo., 1984. Author several books; contbr. articles to profl. jours. City commr., Long Beach, 1980-83. Mem. Univ. Club. Home: 3717 Monon St Los Angeles CA 90027-3013 Office: UCLA 405 Hilgard Ave Los Angeles CA 90024

MANNE, ALAN S., economist; b. N.Y.C., May 1, 1925; s. Isidor and Ruth (Liberman) M.; m. Jacqueline Copp, July 2, 1954; children: Edward, Henry, Elizabeth. AB, Harvard U., 1943, MA, 1948, PhD, 1950. Instr. Harvard U., 1950-52; economist RAND Corp., 1952-56; assoc. prof. Yale U., 1956-61; prof. econs. and ops. rsch. Stanford U., 1961-74, 76—; prof. polit. economy Harvard U., 1974-76; econ. advisor U.S. AID Mission to India, 1966-67. Author: Scheduling of Petroleum Refinery Operations, 1956, Economic Analysis for Business Decisions, 1961, Studies in Process Analysis, 1963, Investments for Capacity Expansion, 1967, Multi-Level Planning: Case Studies in Mexico, 1973, Buying Greenhouse Insurance, 1992. Lt. (j.g.) USNR, 1944-46. Recipient Lanchester prize ORSA; fellow Ctr. for Advanced Study in Behavioral Scis., 1970-71. Fellow Econometric Soc.; mem. AAAS, NAE, Phi Beta Kappa. Office: Stanford U Dept Ops Rsch Stanford CA 94305

MANNERS, NANCY, mayor; b. Catania, Sicily, Italy; d. Gioacchino Jack and Maria Providenza (Virzi) Marasa; m. George Manners, Dec. 20, 1941; children: Gene David, Nancy Ellen Manners Sieh, Joan Alice. BA in Pub. Adminstrn., U. La Verne, 1979. Asst. city mgr. City of Covina, 1963-74; mcpl. mgmt. cons., 1975-85; mem. city coun. City of West Covina, Calif., 1984—; pres. Ind. Cities Risk Mgmt. Authority, West Covina, 1988; mayor City of West Covina, 1988-89, 92-93; pres. Ind. Cities Assn., 1989-90. Pres. San Gabriel Valley Planning Com., 1986; chmn. L.A. County Solid Waste Mgmt. Com., 1986-89; pres. Mid-Valley Mental Health Coun., 1988; foremen pro tem, L.A. County Grand Jury, 1980-81; trustee Covina-Valley Unified Sch. Dist., 1973-77; pres. East San Gabriel Valley Regional Occupation Program, 1974-76, pres. Altrusa Club of Covina-West, 1971-72; regional chmn. San Gabriel Valley Lung Assn. 1971-73; pres. Covina Coordinating Council 1970-71; treas., bd. dirs. San Gabriel Valley Commerce and Cities Consortium, 1991, policy and steering com. Nat. League of Cities, 1991, 93; bd. dirs. L.A. County Sanitation Dist.; vice chmn. Policy Com. League Calif. Cities. Named Covina Citizen Yr., 1977, West Covina Citizen Yr., 1983, Woman Yr., Calif. State Legislature, 1990; recipient Woman of Distinction award Today's Woman Forum, 1988, Woman of Achievement award YWCA, 1987, 88, Community Svc. award West Covina C. of C., 1989, and others. Mem. LWV (pres. San Gabriel Valley 1978), Queen of the Valley Hosp. 2100 Club (bd. dirs. 1991—), Ind. Cities Assn. (v.p. 1988, pres. 1989), West Covina Rotary Club. Home: 734 N Eileen Ave West Covina CA 91791-1042

MANNERS, TYLER PAUL, English language educator, radio announcer; b. Anchorage, Alaska, June 17, 1960; s. Paul Lyn and Sheryl Gail (Meyst) M. BA, Pt. Loma Coll., San Diego, 1982; MA, Calif. State U., 1990. Peer counselor, co-leader Multiple Sclerosis Soc., Riverside, Calif., 1982-84; nat. spokesperson Multiple Sclerosis Soc., Riverside, 1993—; missionary, Polish dir. Inner-Court Ministries, Poland, 1984-86; on-air announcer Sta. KUOR Radio, Redlands, Calif., 1989-91; English instr. Riverside Community Coll., 1990—, Pt. Loma Coll., San Diego, 1988-92; speaker Multiple Schlerosis Soc., So. Calif., 1989-90. Editor publ. Driftwood, 1982; writer publ. Pacific Rev., 1989. Mem. Modern Lang. Assn., Nat. English Tchrs. Assn. Republican. Home: 7431 Magnolia Ave Apt 101 Riverside CA 92504-3820 Office: Riverside CC 4800 Magnolia Ave Riverside CA 92501

MANNING, DARRELL V., national guard officer; b. Preston, Idaho, July 17, 1932; s. Virgil and Olive Ann (Jenks) M.; m. Rochelle Manning, June 4, 1954; children: David Scott, Michael Alan. BS, Utah State U., 1955; postgrad., Idaho State U., 1969. Enlisted USAF, 1955, pilot, 1955-60, advanced through grades to maj. gen.; v.p. Manning Inc., Pocatello, Idaho, 1960-71; dir. Idaho Dept. Aeronautics, Boise, 1971-74, Idaho Dept. Transp., Boise, 1974-85; adjutant-gen., chief Idaho N.G., Boise, 1985—; chmn. Trans Research Bd. Nat. Acad. Scis., 1982. State rep., Boise, 1960-63; Idaho sen., 1970-71. Mem. Am. Assn. State Hwy. and Transp. Officials (nat. pres. 1978, Disting. Service award 1985, MacDonald Meml. award 1985), Western Assn. State Hwy. and Transp. Officials, Adjutant-Gens. Assn. U.S., N.G. Assn. U.S., Air Force Assn., Assn. U.S. Army, VFW, Rotary. Home: 8260 Golse Cir Boise ID 83704-4455 Office: Mil Dept Gowen Field PO Box 45 Boise ID 83707-4530

MANNING, DONALD O., protective services official. Fire chief L.A. Office: Los Angeles Fire Dept Office of the Fire Chief 200 N Main St Los Angeles CA 90012-4110*

MANNING, ERIC, computer science and engineering educator, university dean, researcher; b. Windsor, Ont., Can., Aug. 4, 1940; g. George Gorman and Eleanor Katherine (Koehler) M.; m. Betty Goldring, Sept. 16, 1961; children: David, Paula. BSc, U. Waterloo, Ont., 1961, MSc, 1962; PhD, U. Ill., 1965. Registered profl. engr., B.C. Various positions MIT and Bell Telephone Labs., 1965-68; prof. computer sci. U. Waterloo, 1968-86, dir. computer communication networks group, 1973-82, dir. Inst. for Computer Rsch., 1982-86; prof., dean U. Victoria, B.C., Can., 1986-92, prof. computer sci., elec. engring., 1993—; trustee B.C. Advanced Systems Found., 1986—; dir. Sci. Coun. B.C., 1988-91; bd. dirs. Can. Microelectric Corp.; mem. adv. com. on artificial intelligence Nat. Rsch. Coun., 1987-91; IBM vis. prof. computer sci., Keio U., Yokohama, 1992-93. Author: Fault Diagnosis of Digital Systems, 1970; also numerous articles. Fellow IEEE, Engring. Inst. Can.; mem. Assn. Profl. Engrs. B.C., Soc. for Computer Simulation, Can. Inst. for Advanced Rsch. (adv. com. on artificial intelligence and robotics 1986), Can. Soc. for Fifth Generation Rsch. (trustee 1987-88), B.C. Microelectronics Soc. (bd. dirs. 1986-87). Home: 2909 Phyllis St, Victoria, BC Canada V8N 1Y8 Office: U Victoria Faculty Engring, PO Box 3055, Victoria, BC Canada V8W 3P6

MANNING, FRANK THOMAS, dentist; b. Denver, May 5, 1931; s. Francis Patrick and Inga (Brakke) M.; m. Jacqueline E. Coman, June 13, 1955; children: Beth, Douglas, David, Brenda. DDS, Northwestern U., Chgo., 1957. Pvt. practice dentistry Thermopolis, Wyo., 1957—; dir. 1st State Bank, Thermopolis. With U.S. Army, 1950-52, Korea. Fellow Am. Coll. Dentists; mem. ADA (coun. dental practice 1986-90), , Wyo. Dental Assn. (pres. 1975-76), Pierre Fauchard Acad., Thermopolis C. of C. (pres. 1974-75, Man of Yr. 1976), Rotary Internat. Republican. Lutheran. Home: 806 Amoretti Thermopolis WY 82443 Office: Manning Dental Office 316 Broadway Thermopolis WY 82443

MANNING, PATRICIA KAMARAS, biochemist, process engineer, research scientist; b. Harlingen, Tex., May 26, 1953; d. Henry Julius and Audrey Marie (Klimas) Kamaras. BS, U. Ariz., 1975, MS, 1978, PhD, 1987. Grad. rsch. asst. U. Ariz., Tucson, 1976-78, sponsor grad.rsch., 1986-88; rsch. scientist Armour Dial, Inc., Scottsdale, Ariz., 1978-79; sr. chemist Armour Rsch. Ctr., Armour Food Co., Scottsdale, Ariz., 1979-86; exec. v.p., tech. dir. Manning, Batson & Assocs., Inc., Seattle, 1986-90; pres. Manning & Assocs., Gilbert, Ariz., 1989—; v.p. Quality Assurance and Rsch. Oceantrawl, Inc., Seattle, 1990—. Inventor in field. Vol. Humane Soc Ariz., 1986—, Humane Soc. Am., 1987—. Mem. Inst. Food Technologists (profl.), Nat. Fisheries Inst. (tech. subcom. 1988—, govt. rels. com. 1988—, com. chmn. Surimi tech. and scientific subcommittee 1992—), Assn. Ofcl. Analytical Chemists, Am. Oil Chemists Soc., Alaska Fisheries Devel. Found. (voting cons. 1986—, rsch & devel. grantee 1986-89), N.Y. Acad. Scis., So. Ariz. Runners Club. Roman Catholic. Office: Oceantrawl Inc 1200 Market Place Tower 2025 1st Ave Seattle WA 98121

MANNINO, J. DAVIS, psychotherapist; b. Patchoque, N.Y., Sept. 27, 1949; s. Joseph I. and Adrienne Adele (Davis) M. BA magna cum laude, SUNY, Stony Brook, 1971; MSW summa cum laude, San Francisco State U., 1974; EdD in Counseling and Ednl. Psychology, U. San Francisco, 1989. Lic. psychotherapist, Calif.; lic. clin. social worker, Calif., marriage, family and child counselor. Instr. U. Malaysia, 1974-76; dir. refugee programs City San Francisco, 1979-82; instr. U. San Francisco, 1979-85; pvt. practice specializing in psychology San Francisc, Sonoma Counties, 1979—; cons. foster care Calif. State Legis., 1980, community rels., San Francisco Police Dept., 1982-87, Hospice Sonoma County, 1990, Sonoma County Mental Health; forensic task force on A.I.D.S., San Francisco Pub. Health Dept., 1984-85; child abuse investigation supr. City of San Francisco, 1985-88; supr. Reasonable Efforts to Families Unit, 1988-90; project coord. Edna McConnell Clark Found. Family Mediation Demonstration Grant; instr. child growth and devel., death and dying, Intro. to Psychology Santa Rosa Jr. Coll., 1990—; commr. Calif. Bd. Behavioral Sci. Examiners, 1990. Contbr. articles to profl. jours.; local psychology columnist, 1986—. Mem. Am. Psychol. Assn., Nat. Assn. Social Workers (diplomate clin. social work), Orthopsychiat. Assn., Am. Assn. Counseling and Devel., Calif. Assn. Marriage Family and Child Therapists, Golden Gate Bus. Assn. (ethics com. 1986, Disting. Svc. award, 1985), Am. Assn. Marriage and Family Therapists, Nat. Register Clin. Social Workers, Lions (Helen Keller Humanitarian award, bd. dirs. San Francisco chpt. 1986). Office: PO Box 14031 San Francisco CA 94114-0031

MANNIX, KEVIN LEESE, lawyer; b. Queens, N.Y., Nov. 26, 1949; s. John Warren Sr. and Editta Gorrell M.; m. Susanna Bernadette Chiocca, June 1, 1974; children: Nicholas Chiocca, Gabriel Leese, Emily Kemper. BA, U. Va., 1971, JD, 1974. Bar: Oreg. 1974, U.S. Ct. Appeals (9th cir.) 1976, U.S. Supreme Ct. 1978, Guam 1979. Law clk. to judge Oreg. Ct. Appeals, Salem, 1974-75; asst. atty. gen. Oreg. Dept. Justice, Salem, 1975-77, Govt. of Guam, Agana, 1977-79; judge adminstrv. law Oreg. Workers' Compensation Bd., Salem, 1980-83; assoc. Lindsay, Hart, Neil & Weigler, Portland, Oreg., 1983-86; pres. Kevin L. Mannix Profl. Corp., Salem, 1986—. Chmn. St. Joseph Sch. Bd., Salem, 1981-86; pres. Salem Cath. Schs. Corp., 1985; v.p. Salem Cath. Schs. Found., 1985-88, pres., 1988-90, 91—, state rep., 1989—. Mem. ABA, Inter-Am. Bar Assn., Marion Bar Assn., Rotary (bd. dirs. East Salem 1985-89, pres. 1987-88), KC. Democrat. Home: 375 18th St NE Salem OR 97301-4307 Office: 2003 State St Salem OR 97301-4349

MANOLAKAS, STANTON PETER, watercolor artist; b. Detroit, July 25, 1946; s. Constantine Stamatios and Angela (Kaloyerpolous) M.; m. Barbara Soldathos, July 25, 1971. Student, Eastman Sch. of Music, 1964-65; BA in Psychology, U. So. Calif., L.A., 1969; postgrad., Calif. State U., 1969-70. Artist Art Angle's Gallery, Orange, Calif., 1985—, Art At the Power House, Cleve., 1992, Lorentzen Galleries, Glendale, Calif., 1990—, New Masters Gallery, Carmel, Calif., 1991—, Pierside Gallery, Harbor Springs, Mich., 1992—. Exhibited in group show at Zantman Galleries, Carmel, Calif., 1989; represented in permanent collections Bechtel Industries, San Francisco, Marriott Hotel Corp., Newton, Mass., Datum Inc., Anaheim, Calif., Tarbell Realty Inc., Costa Mesa, Calif. Active AFL-CIO County Fedn. of Labor, L.A., 1982-92; mem. Saint Sophia Cathedral Choir, L.A., 1970-82, Burbank Symphony Orch., 1973-76, Glendale (Calif.) Symphony Orch., 1975-77. Mem. Am. Fedn. of Musicians (local 47). Republican. Eastern Orthodox. Home: 2500 Las Flores Dr Los Angeles CA 90041

MANOS, CHRISTOPHER ALEXANDER, protective services official; b. Bklyn., Sept. 16, 1956; s. Alexander Christopher and Eleanore H. (Marx) M. AAS in Police Sci., Community Coll. of USAF, 1980; BS in Criminal Justice, Mercy Coll., 1982; MA in Mgmt., Webster U., 1985. Asst. leasing dir. Am. Can Co., Greenwich, Conn., 1980-82; sr. crime prevention officer Arapahoe County Sheriff's Dept, Littleton, Colo., 1982—. Author: Using Magic in Drug and Alcohol Prevention Presentations, 1991 (Sutherland award 1991). Mem. Cherry Creek Community Task Force, Englewood, Colo., 1988-92; mem. CAP, Maxwell AFB, 1968—; adviser Boy Scouts Am., Dallas, 1984-90. With USAF, 1975-79. Mem. Colo. Crime Prevention Assn. (v.p. 1984-92, Practitioner of Yr. 1984, 88, Pres.'s award 1989), Internat. Soc. Crime Prevention Practitioners (com. mem. 1988—, George B. Sunderland Lifetime Achievement award 1991, bd. dirs. and regional dir. 1988—), Am. Soc. for Indsl. Security (com. mem. 1989-90, Officer of Yr. 1990), Mile High Magicians Soc. (pres. 1988-91). Home: PO Box 714 Littleton CO 80160 Office: Arapahoe Co Sheriffs Dept 5686 S Court Pl Littleton CO 80120

MANOS, PETER NICHOLAS, II, engineering manager; b. Erie, Pa., Mar. 24, 1958; s. Nicholas Peter and Pauline E. (Karicas) M.; m. Kathleen Ann Wuenschel, Sept. 22, 1984; 1 child, Nicholas Peter II. BA in Physics, Cornell U., 1980, M of Engring., 1981; postgrad., Stanford U., 1982-83. Sr. process devel. engr. Advanced Micro Devices, Sunnyvale, Calif., 1981-86; device engring. sect. mgr. Motorola, Austin, Tex., 1986-90; prin. process integration engr. United Technologies Microelectronics Ctr., Colorado Springs, 1990-91; process integration mgr. Zilog, Inc., Nampa, Idaho, 1991—. Patentee in field; contbr. articles to profl. jours. Mem. IEEE. Republican. Baptist. Home: 2253 Ridge Point Way Boise ID 83712

MANOUGIAN, EDWARD, physician; b. Highland Park, Mich., Apr. 11, 1929; s. George Krikor and Vera Varsen (Jernukian) M. BS, Wayne U., 1951; MD, U. Mich., 1955. Intern San Bernardino County (Calif.) Charity Hosp., 1955-56; house physician Patton (Calif.) State Hosp., 1956-60; NIH postdoctoral fellow in biophysics U. Calif., 1960-62; rsch. assoc. Lawrence Berkeley (Calif.) Lab., 1962-77; house physician Peralta Hosp., Oakland, Calif., 1979-81; assoc. med. dir. Hospice Contra Costa, Pleasant Hill, Calif., 1982-90, med. dir., 1991-92; rschr. Ocular Hazards Divsn. U.S. Army. Contbr. articles to profl. jours. Capt. M.C. U.S. Army, 1957-59, Persian Gulf War, USAR, LTC, MC, 1990-91. Mem. AAAS, Acad. Hospice Physicians, Am. Math. Soc., N.Y. Acad. Sci., Am. Med. Soc., Alameda Contra Costa County Med. Soc., Calif. Med. Soc. Home and Office: 1517 Summit Rd Berkeley CA 94708

MANOUKIAN, RITA CHAKE, sales executive; b. Manhasset, N.Y., Feb. 14, 1964; d. Aram Manoukian and Astrid Tchalekian Torosian. BS, St. John's U., 1985. Sales system analyst Bristol-Myers Products, N.Y.C., 1987-88, sales devel. asst., 1988-89; sales and promotion devel. mgr. Bristol-Myers Products, Bridgewater, N.J., 1989-90; div. sales devel. mgr. Bristol-Myers Products, Irvine, Calif., 1990, mgr. category devel., 1990-92; dir. key account sales Intactix Internat., Manhattan Beach, Calif., 1992—. Home: 28192B Newport Way Laguna Niguel CA 92656

MANSFIELD, ROGER LEO, astronomy and space publisher; b. Boston, Feb. 18, 1944; s. Roy D. Sr. and Nellie E. (Venzlowski) M.; m. Alice Lee Waring, Nov. 1, 1969 (div. Mar. 1983); 1 child, Jason Benjamin; m. Karen June Sprout, June 27, 1987. BS in Chemistry with high honors., U. Cin., 1965; MA in Math., U. Nebr., 1972. Chemist Lockheed Missiles & Space Co., Palo Alto, Calif., 1967; orbital analyst USAF, Offutt AFB, Nebr., 1967-73; instr. Dept. of Math. USAF Acad., Colorado Springs, Colo., 1973-74; aerospace engr. Philco-Ford Corp., Palo Alto, 1974-75, Data Dynamics Inc., Mountain View, Calif., 1975-76; aerospace engr. Ford Aerospace & Communications Corp., Colorado Springs, 1976-78, team leader, 1978-84, prin. engr., 1984-86; supr. Ford Aerospace Corp., Colorado Springs, 1986-88; owner Astron. Data Svc., 1976—. Pub. Skywatcher's Almanac, Local Planet Visibility Report, Photographer's Almanac, Comparative Ephemeris, Space Birds; contbr. articles to profl. jours. Mem. Am. Astron. Soc., Math. Assn. Am., Internat. Planetarium Soc., Rocky Mountain Planetarium Assn. Home and Office: 3922 Leisure Ln Colorado Springs CO 80917-3502

MANSFIELD, WILLIAM AMOS, lawyer; b. Redmond, Oreg., Oct. 23, 1929; s. Ellithorpe Garrett and Constance G. (Loney) M.; children—Johathan E., Frederick W., Paul F. B.S., U. Oreg., 1951, J.D., 1953. Bar: Oreg. 1953, U.S. Supreme Ct. 1960, U.S. Dist. Ct. Oreg. 1966, U.S. Ct. Appeals (9th cir.) 1982. Asst. atty. gen. State of Oreg., Salem, 1955-60; staff atty., gen. counsel U.S. Bur. Pub. Roads, Washington, 1961; city atty. City of Medford (Oreg.), 1962-64; sole practice, Medford, 1965—. Bd. dirs. Peter Britt Festival, 1963-65, Planned Parenthood, Jackson County, Oreg., 1978; bd. dirs. Rogue Valley Transp. Dist., 1976-81, chmn., 1977-78; trustee Children's Farm Home, 1970-76; bd. dirs. ACLU, 1971-77; mem. city council, City of Medford, 1985—; bd. dirs. Jackson-Josephine County Headstart, 1989-91, chmn. 1991. Served as 1st lt. USAF, 1953-55. Democrat. Congregationalist. Office: 313 S Ivy St PO Box 1721 Medford OR 97501

MANSINGHKA, SURENDRA KUMAR, finance educator; b. Kanpur, India, Aug. 3, 1944; came to U.S., 1966; s. Badri Prasad and Parmeshwari (Devi) M.; m. Asha Goel, Dec. 30, 1976; 1 child, Vikash. B. Commerce, U. Calcutta, 1973; MS, UCLA, 1968, PhD, 1971. Asst. prof. U. Calif., Riverside, 1970-75; asst. prof. San Francisco State U., 1975-76, assoc. prof., 1976-80, prof., 1980—; cons. several profit and non-profit corps., 1975—. Contbg. author: Readings in Mergers and Acquisitions. Mem. Am. Fin. Assn., Western Fin. Assn., Fin. Mgmt. Assn. Office: San Francisco State U 1600 Holloway Ave San Francisco CA 94132-1722

MANSON, MALCOLM HOOD, educational administrator; b. Melton Mowbray, Leicester, Eng., May 31, 1938; s. James Milne and Williamina (Hood) M.; m. Snowden Sandra Johnston,. BA, Oxford U., Eng., 1961, MA, 1964. Tchr. The Choate Sch., Wallingford, Conn., 1961-63, adminstr., 1963-69; headmaster Marin Country Day Sch., Corte Madera, Calif., 1969-82, Ore. Episcopal Sch., Portland, Oreg., 1982-90; canon headmaster Cathedral Sch. for Boys, San Francisco, 1990—. Mem. Calif. Assn. Ind. Schs. (bd. dirs., v.p. 1976-80), Pacific N.W. Assn. Ind. Schs. (pres. 1985-86). Episcopal. Office: Cathedral Sch for Boys 1275 Sacramento St San Francisco CA 94108

MANSOURI, LOTFOLLAH, opera stage director; b. Tehran, June 15, 1929; arrived in Can., 1976; s. Hassan and Mehri (Jalili) M.; m. Marjorie Anne Thompson, Sept. 18, 1954; 1 child, Shireen Melinda. AB, UCLA, 1953. Asst. prof. UCLA, 1957-60; resident stage dir. Zurich Opera, 1960-65; chief stage dir. Geneva Opera, 1965-75; gen. dir. Can. Opera Co., Toronto, Ont., 1976-88, San Francisco Opera, 1988—; dramatic coach Music Acad. West, Santa Barbara, Calif., 1959; dir. dramatics Zurich Internat. Opera Studio, 1961-65, Centre Lyrique, Geneva, 1967-72; artistic adviser Tehran Opera, 1973-75; opera adviser Nat. Arts Centre, Ottawa, Ont., 1977; v.p. Opera America, 1979—; operatic cons. dir. Yes, Giorgio, MGM, 1981; dir. opera sequence for film Moonstruck (Norman Jewison), 1987. Guest dir. opera cos. including Met. Opera, San Francisco Opera, N.Y.C. Opera, Lyric Opera of Chgo., Houston Grand Opera, La Scala, Covent Garden, Australian Opera, Vienna Staatsoper, Vienna Volksoper, Salzburg Festival, Amsterdam Opera, Holland Festival, Nice (France) Opera, Festival D'Orange, France; co-author: An Operatic Life, 1982 (initiated above-stage projection of Surtitles (a simultaneous transl. of opera) 1983). Mem. Am. Guild Mus. Artists, Can. Actors Equity Assn. •

MANTLE, LARRY EDWARD, radio director; b. L.A., Jan. 12, 1959; s. John Randall Mantle and Carole Jean (Hubka) Morse; m. Kristen Hernandez, Aug. 8, 1993. BA, So. Calif. Coll., 1979. Program and news dir. Sta. KPCC-FM, Pasadena, L.A., Calif., 1984—; host Larry Mantle's AirTalk Sta. KPCC-FM, 1985—; moderator, host Sta. KPAS-TV, Pasadena, 1986—; prof. Pasadena City Coll., 1986—; moderator UN Assn., Pasadena, 1987—, Calif. Inst. Tech., Pasadena, 1986—; advisor Radio West, L.A., 1992—. Recipient Award of Excellence, Greater L.A. Press Club, 1982, Gold Medal award Coun. Advancement & Support Edn., 1989, Diamond award So. Calif. Cable Assn., 1990. Mem. Radio & TV News Assn. So. Calif. (dir. 1987—, v.p. 1993—, sec. 1987-89, Cut-In newsletter editor 1989—, Golden Mike awards 1986, 87, 88), Soc. Profl. Journalists, AP Calif. and Nev. (Excellence awards 1981, 82, 87), Radio-TV News Dirs. Assn. Office: Sta KPCC-FM 1570 E Colorado Blvd Pasadena CA 91106

MANUS, REX LEO, property development executive; b. Newman, Calif., Nov. 21, 1950; s. Leo F. and Beatrice Marie (Assali) Menuz; 1 child, Austin Leonard. Student, Menlo Coll., 1969; BA summa cum laude, Santa Clara U., 1972; MA in Anthropology, U. Mich., 1974; MBA, Calif. State U.-Stanislaus, Turlock, 1981. Gen. ptnr. Sunstates, Inc., Turlock, 1979-83; owner Manus Real Estate, Modesto, Calif., 1983-92, Health Rsch., Mokelumne Hill, Calif., 1992—, Mokelumne Hill Pub., 1992—; also gen ptnr. real estate devel., pres. Manus Enterprises, Turlock. Author: Origins of Christianity, 1986. NSF fellow, 1971. Mem. Am. Mensa, Atlantis Soc. (founder, pres. 1985), Alpha Nu Gamma, Alpha Gamma Sigma. Republican. Roman Catholic. Office: Manus Enterprises PO Box 1548 Modesto CA 95353

MANYGOATS, JOANNE AUSTIN, jewelry executive; b. Black Mesa, Ariz., July 2, 1953; d. Buck and Lillie (Lake) Austin; m. Al Manygoats, July 4, 1973; children: Shawn Alden, Aaron Sheldon, Tawny Alicia. Bilingual cert., Navajo C.C., 1974; BEd, U. N.Mex, 1978; postgrad., U. Phoenix, 1989-90, U. N.Mex., Gallup, 1992—. instr. Navajo C.C., Crownpoint, N.Mex.; cons. Navajo lang. and culture. Tchr. Kayenta (Ariz.) Pub. Schs., 1972-73, Ramah (N.Mex.) Navajo Sch. Bd., Inc., 1975-78; nat. resource specialist, agrl. rsch. coord., mgr. superfund Navajo Nation-Indian Govt., Window Rock, Ariz., 1979-92; mgr. trainee Zales Jewelry, Gallup, N.Mex., 1992—; ind. contractor Environ. & Agrl. Resources Cons., Holbrook, Ariz.; cons. Navajo studies and land mgmt. Co-author, translator Range Management Handbook, 1983; mem. cast video Distant Drum, 1985. Bd. dirs. Resource Mgmt.-N.Mex. Br., 1983-89; commr. Soil and Water Conservation in N.Mex., 1982-84; environmentalist Navajo Nation, Window Rock, 1990—, conservationalsit, 1980—, pub. edn. and awareness specialist, 1980—, educator HRM teaching, 1986-90. Recipient Spl. Navajo Enfiron. Achievement award Pres. U.S., 1991. Home: PO Box 2256 Gallup NM 87305

MANZINI, ALDO, entertainment company executive; b. Istanbul, Turkey, Feb. 9, 1964; came to U.S., 1986; s. Guido and Anny (Eiselt) M.; m. Robyn Lynne Ratcliffe, July 30, 1988. BA, Oxford (Eng.) U., 1984; MBA, U. Chgo., 1988. Asst. brand mgr. Nestle, Croydon, Eng., 1985, Barcelona, Spain, 1986; cons. Bain & Co., Boston, 1988-90; mgr. strategic planning The Walt Disney Co., Burbank, Calif., 1990—. Office: The Walt Disney Co 500 S Buena Vista Burbank CA 91521

MANZO, ANTHONY JOSEPH, painter; b. Saddle Brook, N.J., Apr. 25, 1928; s. Michael and Jennie (Spinneli) M.; m. Ruth Hendricks, Jan. 27, 1956; children—Kathleen, Joanne. Student NAD, N.Y.C., 1946-49, Phoenix Sch. Design, N.Y.C., 1955-58; studied privately with Salvatore Lascari N.A., 1945-65. Freelance comml. illustrator, 1956-59; painter and sculptor, 1958—; instr. pvt. art classes Renaissance Sch. Art, N.J. Served with U.S. Army, 1950-52. Recipient Ray A. Jones award N.J. Painters and Sculptors Soc., 1976. Roman Catholic. Address: Box 2708 Taos NM 87571

MAO, KENT KEQIANG, consulting civil engineer; b. Beijing, People's Republic of China, July 11, 1956; came to U.S., 1984; s. Zhicheng and Shuqing (Dai) M.; m. Yue Zhang, Aug. 20, 1983; 1 child, Jennifer May. BCE, Tsinghua U., Beijing, 1982; MS, Colo. State U., 1985, PhD, 1990. Cert. profl. engr., Colo., Wash. High sch. physics tchr. Beijing #32 High Sch., 1975-78; rsch. engr. Inst. Water Conservancy and Hydroelectric Power Rsch., Beijing, 1982-84; water resources engr. Water and Wastewater Utilities, Ft. Collins, Colo., 1986-91; sr. project water resources engr. HDR Engring., Inc., Bellevue, Wash., 1991-93; sr. water resources engr. KCM, Inc., Seattle, 1993—. Contbr. articles to profl. jours. Pres. Chinese Student Assn., Colo. State U., 1985-86; pres. Tsinghua Alumni Assn. in Am., 1991. Named Outstanding Tchr. of Beijing Dept. Edn. of Beijing, 1976; recipient Rsch. Scholarship award Inst. Water Conservancy and Hydroelectric Power Rsch., Beijing, 1984. Mem. ASCE (co-chmn. internat. Asian affairs com. 1992—), Am. Water Resources Assn. (vice chair internat. affairs com.). Home: 17014 NE 38th Pl Bellevue WA 98008-6120 Office: KCM Inc 1917 First Ave Seattle WA 98101-1027

MAO, NAI-HSIEN, research geophysicist; b. Chungking, Szechuan, China, Apr. 27, 1934; came to U.S., 1960; s. Yi-po and Yi-pyng (Kao) M.; m. Isabelle P. Hou, Dec. 27, 1960 (div. Nov. 1983); children: Annie M., Jeffrey T.; m. Isabel Chung, Apr. 3, 1985. BS, Nat. Taiwan U., Taipei, 1956; MS, Boston Coll., Chestnut Hill, Mass., 1961; PhD, Harvard U., 1971. Rsch. fellow Harvard U., Cambridge, Mass., 1971-74, Smithsonian Astrophys. Obs., Cambridge, 1974-76, U. Calif., Berkeley, 1978-79; cons., Newton, Mass., 1976-78; physicist Lawrence Livermore (Calif.) Nat. Lab., 1979—; cons. Sci. Applications Internat. Corp., McLean, Va., 1991-92. Author: (monograph) Chinese Research on Shock Physics, 1992; patentee on stress in borehole from shear wave. Prin. Newton Chinese Lang. Sch. 1977; chmn. Chinese Ethnic Heritage Studies Com., Newton, 1977; pres. Harmong Singers, Bay Area, Calif., 1980, 91, Dragon Singers, El Cerrito, Calif., 1990. Mem. Am. Geophys. Union. Home: 5605 Greenridge Rd Castro Valley CA 94552 Office: Lawrence Livermore Nat Lab PO Box 808 L-208 Livermore CA 94550

MAPELLI, ROLAND LAWRENCE, food company executive; b. Denver, June 10, 1922; s. Herman M. and Della (Borelli); m. Neoma Robinson, Apr. 1942; children: Terralyn Mapelli DeMoney, Geraldine Mapelli Gustafson. Student, Regis Coll., 1959-61. Owner, operator Mapelli Farms and Ranches, Eaton, Colo., 1960-90; chmn. bd., sr. v.p. Monfort of Colo., Inc., Greeley, 1971-89, pres. energy div., 1983-90, also bd. dirs.; sr. v.p. ConAgra Red Meat Cos., Greeley, 1990—; bd. dirs. Norwest Banks Colo., Norwest Bank Greeley; bd. dirs., exec. com., 2d v.p. Nat. Western Stock Show; mem. Colo. Agrl. Adv. Com., 1966-73. Chmn. Denver Off-Street Parking Commn., 1960-72; mem. Denver City Coun., 1955-59, Colo. Ho. of Reps., 1961-62, Colo. State Senate, 1962-66; mem. adv. bd. Ft. Logan Mental Health Ctr., 1961-64, St. Anthony's Hosp., 1960-65; bd. dirs. N. Denver Civic Assn., 1955-65, Better Bus. Bur., 1966-69; mem. bd. Ambassadors Loretto Heights Coll., 1960-65; bd. dirs., exec. com. Nat. Western Stock Show, 1966—; dir. land coun. Colo. State U., 1984—; mem. Colo. Bus. HIgher Edn. Consortium. 2d lt. USAF, 1942-46, ETO; with USAFR, 1946-55. Recipient Knute Rockne award, 1961, Water for Colo. Conservation award, 1985, Man of Yr. award Colo. Meat Dealers Assn., 1975. Mem. Nat. Cattlemens Assn., Mountain/Plains Meat Assn. (founder, pres. 1968-69), Colo. Cattle Feeders Assn., Cherry Hills Country Club, Greeley Country Club, Thunderbird Country Club, Denver Athletic Club, Rotary. Roman Catholic. Home: Apt 5 1357 43d Ave Greeley CO 80634 Office: Con Agra Red Meat Cos PO Box G Greeley CO 80632-0350

MAPHIS, SAM WELLINGTON, IV, landscape architect; b. Boulder, Colo., Dec. 31, 1954; s. Sam Wellington III and Coila Joy (Goodin) M.; m. Theresa Ann Sullivan, Sept. 8, 1990. B in Lanscape Architecture and Environ. Planning, Utah State U., 1978. Lic. landscape architect, Calif. Field engr. Briscoe Maphis, Boulder, Colo., 1974-78; draftsman Design Worshop, Aspen, Colo., 1978-79; assoc. Richard Taylor, Santa Barbara, Calif., 1979-80; owner, pres. Earthform Design, Santa Barbara, 1980—, Am. Post and Beam Homes, Santa Barbara, 1985—; assoc. v.p. Maphis Internat. Ltd., Boulder, 1990—. Recipient City of Santa Barbara Beautiful award, 1991, City of Goleta (Calif.) Beautiful award, 1991. Mem. Am. Soc. Landscape Architects, Hope Ranch Assn. (archtl. rev. com.). Office: Earthform Design 1129 State St # 21 Santa Barbara CA 93101

MAPP, MITCHELL JEROME, company executive; b. Boise, Idaho, Dec. 19, 1947; s. Mitchell Lee and Midred Junita M.; m. Mabel Lynn Mapp, Aug. 25, 1973; children: Adam, Russell, Andrew. Student, S.E. Jr. Coll., Chgo., 1969, Idaho State U., 1975. Deputy dir. planning and rsch. dept. City of Pocatello, Idaho, 1973-80; chief architecture, space planner dept. adminstrn. State of Idaho, Boise, 1980-82; assoc. planner City of Boise, 1982-85; facility planner Calif. State U., Long Beach, 1985-86; prin., owner Planning and Facility Mgmt., Boise, 1986—; exec. dir. steering com. Elmore County Impact, Mountain Home, Idaho, 1990-91; community devel. specialist IDA-ORE Planning & Devel. Assn., 1992—. Author: Basque Neighborhood Marketplace, 1987. Exec. bd. dirs. Boise Elmore County Community Housing Resource Bd., 1990, pres., 1990—; bd. dirs. East End Neighborhood Com., Boise, 1985—; coun. mem. Boise City, 1993; cub master Boy Scouts of Am., Boise, 1989; assessment com. United Way, Boise, 1989-90; com. mem. Boise Visions, 1991. Baptist. Home and Office: Planning and Facility Mgmt 1855 Danmore Dr Boise ID 83712

MAQUIPOUR, IRAJ, consulting company executive; b. Tehran, Iran, Mar. 17, 1942; came to U.S., 1963; s. Abbas and Maman (Mahdavi) M.;m. Shirin Baygan (div. 1982); m. Giti Maquipour, Mar. 11, 1991; stepchildren: Ali Amir Khosravi, Delara Amir Khosravi. BA, San Diego State U., 1965, MA in Internat. Rels. and Geopolitics, 1971. Sales mgr. and trainer J.C. Penney Dept. Store, San Diego, 1969-72; dep. credit mgr. Iranian Bank, Tehran, 1973-75; dep. mng. dir., sales mgr. Meli Shoes, Tehran, 1975-76; mng. dir. Ardel Trading Co., Tehran, 1976-77; v.p., mktg. and credit officer Crocker Nat. Bank, Beverly Hills, Calif., 1978-84; v.p., mgr. internat. private banking Security Pacific Nat. Bank, Beverly Hills, 1984-91; pres. Maquipour Cons. E&A Inc., Brentwood, Calif., 1991—; bd. dirs. Commerce Internat. Inc., London, Petro-Indelcom, II Unocal Middle East, L.A.; cons. Iran Consumer Coop. Union, Tehran, 1992, Pederson Mgmt. Inc., L.A., 1990. Author: Pre-Conditions and Political Consequences of Land Reform in Iran, 1971. Mem. Phi Sigma Alpha, Delta Sigma Phi, Rotary. Moslem. Home: 451 S Barrington # 303 Los Angeles CA 90049

MARA, THOMAS E., public radio station executive; b. Landstuhl, Germany, Apr. 1, 1964; (parents Am. citizens); s. William James and Brigitte (Manzow) M.; m. Mary Beth Manger, Aug. 21, 1987; 1 child, Caitland Johanna. BA in Comm., U. Wash., 1988. Dir. devel. Sta. KCMU-FM, Seattle, 1989—. Mem. West Coast Pub. Radio Assn. (treas. 1992—).

MARAFINO, VINCENT NORMAN, aerospace company executive; b. Boston, June 8, 1930; m. Doris Marilyn Vernall, June 15, 1958; children: Marli Ann, Sheri Louise, Wendi Joan. A.B. in Acctg. and Econs., San Jose State Coll., 1951; M.B.A., Santa Clara U., 1964. Chief acct. Am. Standard Advance Tech. Lab., Mountain View, Calif., 1956-59; with Lockheed Missiles & Space Co., Sunnyvale, Calif., 1959-70, asst. dir. fin. ops., 1968-70; asst. controller Lockheed Corp., Burbank, Calif., 1970-71, v.p., controller, 1971-77, sr. v.p. fin., 1977-83, exec. v.p., chief fin. and adminstrv. officer, 1983-88, vice chmn. bd., chief fin. and adminstrv. officer, 1988—, also dir.; bd. dirs. Lockheed Missiles & Space Co., Inc.; chmn. bd. dirs. Lockheed Fin. Corp. Served with USAF, 1953-55. Mem. Fin. Execs. Inst., Am. Inst. CPAs, Jonathan Club, North Ranch Country Club. Office: Lockheed Corp 4500 Park Granada Blvd Calabasas CA 91399-0105

MARALDO, USHANNA, multimedia artist, environmental designer; b. Osnabruck, Fed. Republic of Germany; m. Michael Maraldo. BFA, Mich. State U.; MA, U. Osnabruck, Fed. Republic Germany; postgrad., U. Mexico. Owner, pub. Luma Arts Pubs., Woodland Hills, Calif., 1982-87; owner, dir. Sunstar Prodns., Santa Barbara, Calif., 1981—. Artist, photographer for 2029 MAGAZIN (internat. edit.), Humana, Cities of Light, Cosmic Calculus series; published in Printworld Directory of Contemporary Prints, 1988. Recipient Excellence award in Painting, Art Horizons, 1988, Excellence award in Photography, Internat. Art Competition, 1988, Excellence award Photographer's Forum Magazine, 1992. Studio: 535 Barker Pass Rd Santa Barbara CA 93108

MARANDAS, SUSAN MARGARET, secondary education educator; b. Portland, Oreg., Sept. 11, 1942; d. Phil Huth and Sue Louise (Pringle) Bushnell; children: Stephanie, John J., Jason. BA in Liberal Arts, Willamette U., 1964; MA in Polit. Sci., Portland State U., 1987. Cert. secondary edn. tchr. Tchr. Twality Jr. High., Tigard, Oreg., 1964-68, Franklin High Sch., Portland, 1969, Lakeridge High Sch., Lake Oswego, Oreg., 1986, St. Mary's Acad., Portland, 1986—. NEH fellow, 1992. Mem. ASCD, Nat. Coun. Social Studies, Oreg. Coun. Social Studies (tchr. of yr. 1992, sec./jour. editor, 1993). Office: St Mary's Acad 1615 SW 5th Ave Portland OR 97201

MARASCH, MILTON R., electronic systems engineer, consultant; b. New London, Wis., Apr. 15, 1937; s. Bernard William and Cecelia Elizabeth (Smith) M.; m. Nancy Anne Vanevenhoven, Aug. 5, 1961; children: Milton J., Maria, Michelle, Mark, Matthew, Marek. BSEE, U. Wis., 1962, MSEE, 1964. Assoc. electrical engr. IBM, Endicott, N.Y., 1964-67; sr. assoc. staff, adv. engr. IBM, East Fishkill, 1967-75; adv. systems engr. IBM, Rochester, Minn., 1975-85; adv. engr. site tech. IBM, Boulder, Colo., 1985-87, adv. engr., tech. strategist, 1987-90, adv. systems engr., 1990—; fed. systems div. advisor FSD Tech. Adv. Bd., Boulder, 1990-91; mem. IBM Corp. Advanced Tech. Liaison, N.Y.C., 1980-90, IBM Low End Packaging, Tech ITL, N.Y.C., 1980-90; sect. mgr. Path Finder Symposium, San Juan, P.R., 1985. Contbr. articles to profl. jours. Internal v.p. Jaycees, Apalachin, N.Y., 1966. Mem. Internat. Soc. for Hybrid Microelectronics. Roman Catholic. Home: 144 Sentinel Rock Ln Boulder CO 80302-9425 Office: TK7 003D FSD KG9 003K FSC PO Box 1900 Boulder CO 80328-0001

MARAVICH, MARY LOUISE, realtor; b. Fort Knox, Ky., Jan. 4, 1951; d. John and Bonnie (Balandzic) M. AA in Office Adminstrn., U. Nev., Las Vegas, 1970; BA in Sociology and Psychology, U. So. Calif., 1972; grad. Realtors Inst. Cert. residential specialist. Adminstrv. asst. dept. history U. So. Calif., L.A., 1972-73; asst. pers. supr. Corral Coin Co., Las Vegas, 1973-80; realtor, Americana Group div. Better Homes and Gardens, Las Vegas, 1980-85, Jack Matthews and Co., 1985-93, Realty Execs., Las Vegas, 1993—. Mem. Nev. Assn. Realtors (cert. realtors inst.), Las Vegas Bd. Realtors, Nat. Assn. Realtors, Women's Council of Realtors, Am. Bus. Women's Assn., NAFE, Million Dollar Club, Pres.'s Club. Office: Realty Execs #100 2280 S Jones Blvd Las Vegas NV 89102

MARC, DAVID, American studies educator; b. Bklyn. Apr. 27, 1951; s. Benjamin Cohen and Jeanette (Pistiner) Cohen Nissenbaum. BA in English, SUNY-Binghamton, 1972, MA in English, 1976; PhD in Am. Studies, U. Iowa, 1982. Jr. research asst. NBC-TV, N.Y.C., 1976-77; adj. English faculty mem. Wells Coll., Aurora, N.Y., 1980; adj. mem. writing faculty Cornell U., Ithaca, N.Y., 1981; lectr. Am. civilization Brown U., Providence, 1982-85; asst. prof. Am. studies Brandeis U., Waltham, Mass., 1985-89; vis. prof. Annenberg Sch. Communications, U. So. Calif., 1988-93; assoc. prof. Film and Television, Univ. Calif. L.A., 1993—. Author: Demographic Vistas, 1984, Comic Visions, 1989, Prime Time, Prime Movers, 1992; TV appearances include: 60 Minutes, Today and CBC Jour.; radio commentator Performance Today; contbr. articles to profl. jours.; frequent contbr. Atlantic Monthly, Village Voice. Author's Guild, Phi Beta Kappa. Home: 840 Larrabee St # 2-318 Los Angeles CA 90069 Office: UCLA Dept Film & TV 405 Hilgard Ave Los Angeles CA 90024

MARCELYNAS, RICHARD CHADWICK, industrial relations executive; b. New London, Conn., Aug. 21, 1937; s. Anthony F. and Elizabeth A. (Chadwick) M.; m. Betty A. Forray, July 1, 1961; children: Michael R., Thomas R. B.A. in Bus. Adminstrn., U. Wash., 1961; postgrad. Seattle U., 1971-72. Mgmt. trainee, installation foreman Pacific Bell, Fullerton, Calif., 1964-65; cost acct. Scott Paper Co., Everett, Wash., 1965-68; asst. v.p. personnel and adminstrn. Nat. Pub. Service Ins. Co., Seattle, 1968-77; mgr. indsl. relations Heath Tecna Precision Structures Inc., Kent, Wash., 1978-85; mgmt. con. Pilon Mgmt. Co., Seattle, 1985-90; pers. adminstr. Peninsula Group Olympia, Wash., 1990—; cons., lectr. Served to maj. USMCR, 1961-77. Decorated commendations for bravery and tech. expertise, 1962, 63, 64; recipient Seattle Pacific N.W. Personnel Mgrs. Assn. Bd. Dirs. award, 1975. Mem. Am. Soc. Personnel Adminstrs., Pacific N.W. Personnel Mgrs. Assn. (past pres. Tacoma chpt.), Am. Soc. Safety Engrs. Republican. Roman Catholic. Office: 7515 Terminal St Olympia WA 98501

MARCH, GEORGE PATRICK, retired naval officer; b. Corvallis, Oreg., Jan. 16, 1924; s. George Clayton and Margaret Isobel (Motley) M.; m. Betty Eileen Saum, Dec. 20, 1946; children: Maureen, Terese, Margaret. B.S., U.S. Naval Acad., 1946; M.A., Georgetown U., 1952, Ph.D., 1965; now postdoctoral studies, U. Hawaii. Commd. ensign U.S. Navy, 1946, advanced through grades to rear adm., 1973; staff and command assignments (Atlantic and Pacific fleets); shore duty in Morocco, Cyprus, Germany, Eng. and Japan, 1946-73; asst. dir. (Nat. Security Agy.), Washington, 1973-74; comdr. (Naval Security Group Command), dir. electronic warfare and cryptology div. on staff of chief of naval ops., 1974-78, ret. 1978. Author: Cossacks of the Brotherhood. Decorated Legion of Merit (2). Mem. U.S. Naval Inst., Am. Hist. Assn., Am. Assn. for the Advancement of Slavic Studies, Phi Gamma Delta, Phi Alpha Theta. Address: 98-1434 Onikiniki Pl Aiea HI 96701

MARCH, JAMES GARDNER, social scientist, educator; b. Cleve., Jan. 15, 1928; s. James Herbert and Mildred (MacCorkle) M.; m. Jayne Mary Dohr, Sept. 23, 1947; children: Kathryn Sue, Gary Clifton, James Christopher, Roderic Gunn. BA, U. Wis., 1949; MA, Yale U., 1950, PhD, 1953; hon. doctorate, Copenhagen Sch. Econs., 1978, Swedish Sch. Econs., 1979, U. Wis., Milw., 1980, U. Bergen, 1980, Uppsala U., 1987, Helsinki Sch. Econs., 1991. From asst. prof. to prof. Carnegie Inst. Tech., 1953-64; prof., dean Sch. Social Scis., U. Calif.-Irvine, 1964-70; prof. mgmt., higher edn., polit. sci. and sociology Stanford U., 1970—; adj. prof. U. Bergen, 1989-92; cons. in field, 1954—; Mem. Nat. Council Ednl. Research, 1975-78; mem. Nat. Sci. Bd., 1968-74; mem. sociol.-social psychology panel NSF, 1964-66; social sci. tng. com. NIMH, 1967-68; mem. math. social sci. com. Social Sci. Research Council, 1958-60; mem. Assembly Behavioral and Social Sci., NRC, 1973-79, chmn. com. on aging, 1977-82, chmn. com. on math., sci., tech. edn., 1984-

86. Author: (with H.A. Simon) Organizations, 1958, 2nd edit., 1993, (with R.M. Cyert) A Behavioral Theory of the Firm, 1963, 2nd edit., 1992, Handbook of Organizations, 1965, (with B.R. Gelbaum) Mathematics for the Social and Behavioral Sciences, 1969, (with M.D. Cohen) Leadership and Ambiguity, 1974, 2nd edit., 1986, Academic Notes, 1974, (with C.E. Lave) An Introduction to Models in the Social Sciences, 1975, (with J.P. Olsen) Ambiguity and Choice in Organizations, 1976, Aged Wisconsin, 1977, Autonomy as a Factor in Group Organization, 1980, Pleasures of the Process, 1980, Slow Learner, 1985, (with R. Weissinger-Baylon) Ambiguity and Command, 1986, Decisions and Organizations, 1988, (with J.P. Olsen) Rediscovering Institutions, 1989, Minor Memos, 1990; contbr. articles to profl. jour. Fellow Center Advanced Study in Behavioral Scis., 1955-56, 73-74; recipient Wilbur Lucius Cross medal Yale U., 1968. Mem. NAS, Nat. Acad. Edn., Accademia Italiana di Economia Aziendale, Royal Swedish Acad. Scis., Am. Acad. Arts and Scis., Am. Econ. Assn., Am. Polit. Sci. Assn. (v.p. 1983-84), Am. Psychol. Assn., Am. Sociol. Assn., Acad. Mgmt., Russell Sage Found. (trustee 1985—, chmn. 1990—), Finnish Soc. Scis. and Letters, Phi Beta Kappa, Sigma Xi. Home: 837 Tolman Dr Palo Alto CA 94305-1025 Office: Stanford Univ Grad School of Business Stanford CA 94305

MARCH, KATHLEEN PATRICIA, judge; b. May 18, 1949; married; 2 children. BA, Colo. Coll., 1971; JD, Yale U., 1974. Bar: N.Y. 1975, Calif. 1978. Law clk. to hon. judge Thomas J. Griesa U.S. Dist. Ct. (so. dist.) N.Y., 1974-75; assoc. Cahill, Gordon & Reindel, N.Y.C., 1975-77; asst. U.S. atty. criminal div. Office of U.S. Atty. Cen. Dist. Calif., L.A., 1978-82; assoc. Adams, Duque & Hazeltine, L.A., 1982-85; ptnr. Demetriou, Del Guercio & Lovejoy, L.A., 1985-88; judge U.S. Bankruptcy Ct. Cen. Dist. Calif., L.A., Calif., 1988—. Bd. editors Yale U. Law Jour. Mem. ABA, Fed. Bar Assn., L.A. County Bar Assn., Women Lawyers Assn., , Nat. Assn. Women Judges, Phi Beta Kappa. Office: Roybal Fed Ct Bldg 255 E Temple St Ste 1460 Los Angeles CA 90012

MARCH, KENNETH ALFRED, cemetery sales executive; b. St. Paul, Oct. 8, 1956; s. James Alan and Evelyn Hope (Shadick) M.; m. Jami Diane Sheppard, Oct. 7, 1989. AA, Southwestern Jr. Coll., 1976; BS, San Diego State U., 1980. Cemetery sales rep. Greenwood Meml. Park, San Diego, 1973-75; cemetery sales rep. Rest Haven Cemetery, Wichita, Kans., 1982, sales mgr., 1982-83; sales mgr. Cahpel Hill/East Lawn Cemetery, Lansing, Mich., 1983-84, Mount Emblem Cemetery, Chgo., 1984-85; asst. v.p. sales Svc. Corp. Internat., Northeast Region, 1985-89; sales dir. Oak Hill Meml. Park/Oak Hill Devel. Co., San Jose, Calif., 1989-92; v.p. regional sales Svc. Corp. Internat., Western Region, 1992—; faciliator, bd. dirs. Sales Mgr. Cert. Course, Houston; sales cons., Western region, Calif., Nev., 1991—. Contbr. articles to profl. jours. Mem. Calif. Interment Assn. (speaker). Republican. Home: 1421 Mercer Ave San Jose CA 95125 Office: Oak Hill Meml Park 300 Curtner Ave San Jose CA 95125

MARCHESE, LAMAR VINCENT, broadcasting executive; b. Tampa, Fla., Dec. 11, 1943; s. Thomas and Catherine (Palmer) M.; m. Patricia Davis, June 23, 1966; children: Peter, Julia. BA, U. So. Fla., 1964; MA, U. Fla., 1972. Media specialist Morehead (Ky). State U., 1969-72; program coordinator Clark County Library Dist., Las Vegas, Nev., 1972-78; pres., gen. mgr. Sta. KNPR-FM, Las Vegas, 1979—; mem. adv. com. Legis. Subcom. on Pub. Broadcasting, Carson City, Nev., 1983-85; bd. dirs. Sta. KUNV, Las Vegas; chmn. Nev. Pub. Broadcasting Assn., 1986-90; pres. Rocky Mountain Pub. Radio, 1988-90. Pres. Nev. Alliance for the Arts, Las Vegas, 1983-86; chmn. Citizens Against 12, Las Vegas, 1984; mem. steering com. Library Bond Election, Las Vegas, 1985; mem. Las Vegas Hist. Preservation Commn., 1991—. Recipient Gov.'s Arts award Nev. State Council on Arts, 1985; named Outstanding Fundraising Exec., Nat. Soc. Fund Raising Execs., Las Vegas, 1985. Mem. Clark County Cable Comms. Adv. Bd. (chmn.), Las Vegas C. of C., Las Vegas Blues Soc. (pres., founder 1988-89), Las Vegas Women in Comms. (Radio Mgr. of Yr. 1988), Nat. Pub. Radio (bd. dirs. 1990-93, chmn. NPR distbn./interconnection com. 1993), Las. Vegas Hist. Preservation Commn. Democrat. Office: Sta KNPR-FM 5151 Boulder Hwy Las Vegas NV 89122-6088

MARCHETTI, DONALD MERRILL, banker; b. Pawtucket, R.I., Sept. 10, 1932; s. Arthur John and Mary Jane (Perron) M.; m. Maureen Christine Corcoran, Apr. 30, 1955; children: Donald M. Jr., Dawn Marie Martin. BS in Acctg. and Fin., Bryant Coll., Smithfield, R.I., 1958. Dist. supr. Household Fin. Corp., Orange, Calif., 1957-76; regional mgr. Calif. Thrift & Loan Assn., Santa Ana, 1976-79; v.p. mktg. Anvil Ins. Co., Irvine, Calif., 1979-90; v.p. asset mgmt. First Fidelity Thrift & Loan Assn., San Diego, 1990—. Pres. Bella Vista Homeowners Assn., San Clemente, Calif., 1989-90. Mem. Elks. Republican. Roman Catholic. Home: 920 Camino Ibiza San Clemente CA 92672 Office: First Fidelity Thrift & Loan Assn 12750 High Bluff Dr San Diego CA 92130

MARCHI, JON, cattle rancher, exporter, former investment brokerage executive; b. Ann Arbor, Mich., Aug. 6, 1946; s. John Robert and Joan Trimble (Toole) M.; m. Mary Stewart Sale, Aug. 12, 1972; children: Aphia Jessica, Jon Jacob. Student Claremont Men's Coll., 1964-65; BS, U. Mont., 1968, MS, 1972. Sec., treas. Marchi, Marchi & Marchi, Inc., Morris, Ill., 1968-69; account exec. D. A. Davidson & Co., Billings, Mont., 1972-75, asst. v.p., office mgr., 1976-77, v.p. mktg. and adminstrn., Great Falls, Mont., 1977—; sec., dir., v.p. fin. svcs. and exec. devel., D. A. Davidson Realty Corp., Great Falls, 1978-85, chmn. rsch. com., 1980; cattle rancher, Polson, Mont., 1985—; bd. dirs. Big Sky Airlines, Billings, Mont., Energy Overthrust Found., Mansfield Found., Mont. Beverages, Mont. Venture Capital Network, Direct Advantage, Inc., Hamilton, Mont., Mont. Naturals Internat., Inc., Eclipse Techs., Inc., Mont. Small Bus. Investment Corp. Chmn. Mont. Gov.'s Subcom. for Venture Capital Devel., Mont. Community Fin. Corp., Helena; chmn. investment com., State of Mont. Sci. and Tech. Alliance, 1985—; chmn. seed capital com. State of Mont., bd. dirs. job svc. com.; mem. Mont. Peoples Action; sec.-treas. Valley View Assn., 1987—; elected trustee sch. dist. #35, Polson, Mont., 1990—, chmn., 1991—; bd. dirs. Mont. Entrenpreunship Ctr., Missoula, Mont., 1990—; pres., dir., sec./treas. Mont. Pvt. Capital Network, Bozeman, Mont., 1990—, pres., 1992—; chmn., dir. Mont. Naturals Internat., Inc., 1991; dir. Mont. State Rural Devel. Coun., 1992, Mont. SBA Adv. Coun., 1992. With U.S. Army, 1969-71. Mem. Nat. Cattlemen's Assn. (fgn. trade com.), Polson C. of C. (bd. dirs.), Valley View Assn. (bd. dirs.), Mont. Cattle Feeders Assn., Montana Angus Assn., Am. Angus Assn., Western Mont. Stockgrowers Assn., Securities Industry Assn., Mont. Stock Growers Assn., Mont. Ambassadors, Polson C. of C. (dir.), Leadership Great Falls Club, Ski Club, Mont. Club, Helena Wilderness Riders Club, Rotary. Episcopalian. Home: 7783 Valley View Rd Polson MT 59860-9302 Office: Marchi Angus Ranches 7783 Valley View Rd Polson MT 59860-9302

MARCHICK, RICHARD, gynecologist; b. Cheyenne, Wyo., Mar. 18, 1934; s. Benjamin and Rose (Rabinowitz) M.; m. Gloria Ann Becker, Dec. 18, 1960; children: Patricia Sue, David Matthew, Sarah Lynn. AB, Harvard U., 1956; MD, Washington U., St. Louis, 1961. Diplomate Am. Bd. Ob-Gyn. Intern Jewish Hosp., Sch. Medicine Washington U., St. Louis, 1961-62; resident Barnes Hosp. Group, Sch. Medicine Washington U., St. Louis, 1962-66; clin. instr. dept. ob-gyn. Sch. Medicine U. Calif., San Francisco, 1966-72, asst. clin. prof. dept. ob-gyn. Sch. Medicine, 1973-84, assoc. clin. prof. dept. ob-gyn. Sch. Medicine, 1984—; pvt. practice Berkeley, Calif., 1966—; chmn. dept. ob-gyn. and high risk obstetrics program Alta Bates Hosp., Berkeley, 1982-83, mem. med. exec. bd., 1981-83; chmn. ob-gyn. com. Qual-Med HMO Inst. Co., 1986-87; bd. dirs. Alta Bates Med. Group; med. assoc. LeLeche League. Med. cons. Jour. Childbirth Edn., 1970-71; assoc. editor Birth and Family Jour., 1973-80. Mem. interview com. for freshman applicants Harvard U., 1975-82; sec. Jewish Communtiy Rels. Coun., Alameda Contra Costa County, 1972-74; bd. dirs. Congregation Beth Israel, Berkeley, 1970-71; chmn. physicians fund dr. Jewish Welfare Fedn. Harvard U. scholar, 1952-56, Sch. Medicine scholar Washington U., 1957-61. Fellow Am. Coll. Ob-Gyn. (vice chmn. Calif. sect. 1985-88, chmn. 1988-91); mem. AMA, Am. Soc. for Psycho-prophylaxis in Obstetrics (chmn. div. physicians Bay Area chpt. 1971-72, nat. bd. dirs. 1972-73, med. adv. bd. jour. 1971-72), Am. Assn. Gynecologic Laparoscopists, Am. Fertility Soc., Pacific Coast Ob-Gyn. Soc., Calif. Med. Assn., Alameda-Contra Coste Med. Assn. (bd. dirs. retirement investment program 1988—), San Francisco Gynecol. Soc. (sec./treas. 1993—), East Bay Gynecol. Soc. (sec.-treas. 1974-77, pres. 1977-78), Alameda Contra Costa Med. Assn., Sierra Club (life). Home: 516 The Glade Orinda CA 94563 Office: Ob-Gyn and Fertility Specialists 2915 Telegraph Ave Berkeley CA 94705

MARCKWARDT, HAROLD THOMAS, association executive; b. Chgo., May 4, 1920; s. Herman and Carrie (Polachek) M.; AB, U. So. Calif., 1949, AM, 1953; MS, U. Calif., 1970, postgrad., 1970—; m. Patricia Ann Hoffman, Apr. 7, 1945; children: Craig, Diana, Brad, Glenn. Tool and machinery designer Douglas Aircraft, Santa Monica, Cal., 1939-43; playground leader County Los Angeles, 1946-47; community program dir. Hollywood (Calif.) YMCA, 1947-51, dir. community program and bldg., 1952-55; exec. dir. Westchester YMCA, Los Angeles, 1955-63; area dir. Nat. Council YMCA, 1963-66, pres. Western Center Assocs., Los Angeles, 1966—; internat. mgmt. cons., Indonesia, 1985-91, Sri Lanka, 1989; field assoc. Internat. Exec. Service Corps, 1987-93. Exec. dir. Calif. Youth and Govt. Statewide Com., 1965, del. seminar UN, 1959. Colliver lectr. U. Pacific, 1965. Trainer, Leadership Devel. Camp, Los Angeles, 1959; mem. Mayor's Steering Com., 1973-75, chmn. Mayor's Facilitators com. Conf. Children, Youth and Sr. Citizens, 1974; mem. employment and tng. subcom. Los Angeles County Task Force, 1977; mem. Task Force on Equity for Women in Employment, 1976-77. Served to 1st lt., USAAF, 1943-46, USAF (SAC), 1950-52. Recipient One of Hollywood's Top Ten Young Men award, 1954. Mem. Am. Soc. Tool Engrs. (charter mem.), Pacific S.W. Area YMCA Assn. Profl. Dirs. (pres. 1963-66), Orgn. Devel. Network, Airplane Owner's and Pilots Assn., Am. Soc. Tng. and Devel. (v.p. 1979, pres. 1980), Internat. Fedn. Tng. and Devel. Orgns., Pacific Area Travel Assn., Indonesian Bus. Soc., Am. Soc. Travel Agts., Indonesian Trade Mission, World Span-One Club (v.p. 1991-93). Democrat. Author: The Leader Makes The Difference, 1968; Leading Discussion Groups, 1972; How to Make Executive Decisions About Training, 1976; 16 Steps to the Job You Want, 1979; The Quality Circles Kit, 1982. Home: 4216 Colbath Ave Sherman Oaks CA 91423-4210 Office: 8382 Topanga Canyon Blvd Canoga Park CA 91304-2344

MARCO, ANTON NICHOLAS, creative consultant, fund raiser, advocate; b. N.Y.C., May 6, 1943; s. Joseph Anton and Mourine Rose (Heege) M.; m. Siena Gillanne Porta, July 7, 1969 (div. 1975); m. Joyce Lorraine Slater, Oct. 10, 1976; children: Leanne, LeRoy, Annette, Jennifer, Vanessa. MA in Creative Writing, Johns Hopkins U., 1971. Sr. writer, copy chief Christian Broadcasting Network, Virginia Beach, Va., 1984-87; sr. writer Russ Reid Co., Pasadena, Calif., 1987-89; founder, pres. WordWright, Colorado Springs, Colo., 1989—; artist-in-residence Regent U., Va. Beach, 1985, scholar-in-residence, 1986; founder Colo. for Family Values; founder, exec. dir. Am. for Family Values; v.p., dir. of communications Dovetail Ministries; cons. to fund raising agys. Domaine Group, Seattle, Russ Reid, Killion McCabe, Dallas, Finn & Assocs., Redondo Beach, Calif., Epsilon, Burlington, Mass. Author: Fallen Angel, 1982 (Two Hollywood Options 1982-83), Devotions for Busy People, Rites of Passage to the 21st Century, 1991; writer numerous poems and articles. Named Teaching fellow Johns Hopkins U., 1970-71. Mem. Assn. of Non-profit Execs. Republican. Presbyterian. Office: WordWright 5110 Golden Hills Ct Colorado Springs CO 80919-8156

MARCO, DAVID DUANE, biomedical engineer; b. Apollo, Pa., Feb. 3, 1951; s. Peter M. and Jean M. (Merlo) M.; m. Nancy Elizabeth Bierman, Nov. 16, 1985; 1 child, Phoebe Elizabeth. BS in Biomed. Engring., Rensselaer Polytechnic Inst., 1973. Operating engr. Shock & Trauma Unit Albany (N.Y.) Med. Ctr., 1973-75; research technician Abcor Inc., Boston, 1975-76; clin. engr. Boston U. Med. Ctr. Hosp., 1975-77; field clin. engr. Arco/Med. Products, San Francisco, 1977-81; sales rep. Siemens-Elema, Oakland, Calif., 1981-85; field clin. engr. Siemens-Pacesetter, Oakland, 1985—. Contbr. articles to profl. jours. Mem. Shiloh Christian Fellowship, Oakland, 1983, dist. dir., 1991—. Mem. N.Am. Soc. Pacing & Electrophysiology. Republican. Office: Pacesetter Systems 3470 Mt Diablo Blvd Ste 150A Lafayette CA 94549-3996

MARCOTTE, MICHAEL VINCENT, public radio administrator; b. La Crosse, Wis., July 18, 1956; s. Henry Joseph and Ardis Joy (Denton) M.; m. Valerie Ann Prebo, June 28, 1980; children: Nicholas, Aaron, Trevor. BA, U. Ga., 1982, MA, 1984. Radio producer WUOG, Athens, Ga., 1979-83; radio newscaster WGAU/WNGC, Athens, 1982-84; broadcast producer WOSU, Columbus, Ohio, 1984-87; radio instr. Ohio State U., Columbus, 1984-87; news dir. KPLU, Tacoma, 1987-92, asst. program dir./news, 1992—; panelist Voice of Democracy, Columbus, 1985-87. Creator, dir. Theater of Sound, 1982; producer radio features for Nat. Pub. Radio, 1987—; author radio plays. Vis. lectr. Bethel and Franklin Pierce Schs., Wash., 1988-92; mem. communication arts adv. bd. Pacific Luth. U., 1992—. With U.S. Army, 1974-77. Recipient 25 awards for documentaries, series, spots, features. Mem. Pub. Radio News Dirs. Assn. (award 1989), Soc. Profl. Journalists. Home: 310 190th St E Spanaway WA 98387 Office: KPLU-FM 121st and Park Tacoma WA 98447

MARCOU, CONSTANTIN GEORGE, lawyer; b. Athens, Greece, May 28, 1954; came to U.S., 1958; s. George Constantin and Maria Georgia (Michou) M. BA, Pomona Coll., 1975; JD, Southwestern U., 1982. Bar: Calif. Account exec. Direct Mktg. Corp. Am., L.A., 1977-81; ind. cons. L.A., 1982-89; prin. Law Offices C. Marcou, L.A., 1989—. Mem. Greater L.A. Area Mensa (membership dir. 1987-92), Musical Chairs Chamber Music Soc. Greek Orthodox.

MARCOUX, ELIZABETH LOUISE, librarian; b. St. Louis, June 16, 1952; d. Lyman Robert and Ruth Emily (Sides) Amburgey; m. Douglas Ray Marcoux, Feb. 13, 1953; children: Douglas Randall, Jeffrey Paul. BA in Secondary Edn., U. Ariz., 1973, MLS, 1979. Tchr. English as second lang. Colombo Americano, Bogota, Colombia, 1970-71; catalog asst. U. Ariz. Med. Sch. Libr., Tucson, 1971-75; tchr./librarian Pueblo High Sch., Tucson, 1974-80; librarian Sahuaro High Sch., Tucson, 1980-86; head librarian Rincon/Univ. High Sch., Tucson, 1986—; grad. instr. U. Ariz. Grad. Libr. Sch., Tucson, 1989—; evaluator North Cen. Assn. Ariz., 1986—; reviewer ABC-Clio Video Rev. Source, 1989—; exec. bd. Univ. High Sch. Site Based Mgmt. Team, Tucson, 1989—. Vol., bd. dirs. So. Ariz. Rescue Assn., Tucson, 1974—; mem. Ariz. Sonora Desert Mus., 1980—; coord. Am. Field Svc., 1976-79. Fellow ind. study NEH, 1991. Mem. So. Ariz. Rescue Assn., Ariz. State Libr. Assn. (div. pres. 1988-90), ALA, Am. Assn. Sch. Librarians (chair continuing edn./profl. devel. com. 1991—), Phi Delta Kappa, Delta Kappa Gamma. Presbyterian. Home: 6337 E Paseo San Andres Tucson AZ 85710-2120 Office: Rincon/University High Sch 422 N Arcadia Ave Tucson AZ 85711-3097

MARCOVITZ, LEONARD EDWARD, retail executive; b. Bismarck, N.D., Sept. 6, 1934; s. Jacob and Frieda M. Asst. mgr. Greengard's Clothing, Mandan, N.D., 1955-58; mgr. K-G Men's Stores, Inc., Bismarck, 1958-61, Billings, Mont., 1961-69; v.p. store ops. K-G Men's Stores, Inc., 1969-73; pres. Leonard's Men's Stores, Yakima, Wash. and Billings, Mont., 1973-77; chief exec. officer K-G Retail div. Chromalloy Am. Corp., Englewood, Colo., 1977-81; pres. DeMarcos Men's Clothing, Casper, Wyo., 1982—, Idaho Falls, Idaho, 1984—, Billings, Mont., 1986—. Mem. Menswear Retailers Am. (past dir.), Billings Petroleum Club, Order of Demolay (Degree of Chevalier 1952, Internat. Master Councilor 1953, Demolay Dad 1959), Elks. Home: PO Box 23344 Billings MT 59104-3344

MARCUS, FRANK ISADORE, physician, educator; b. Haverstraw, N.Y., Mar. 23, 1928; s. Samuel and Edith (Sattler) M.; m. Janet Geller, June 30, 1957; children: Ann, Steve, Lynn. BA, Columbia U., 1948; MS, Tufts U., 1951; MD cum laude, Boston U., 1953. Diplomate Am. Bd. Internal Medicine, subspecialty cardiovascular diseases. Intern Peter Bent Brigham Hosp., Boston, 1953-54; asst. resident Peter Bent Brigham Hosp., 1956-57, research fellow in cardiology, 1957-58; clin. fellow in cardiology Georgetown U. Hosp., 1958-59, chief med. resident, 1959-60; chief of cardiology Georgetown U. Med. Service, D.C. Gen. Hosp., Washington, 1960-68; instr. medicine Georgetown U. Sch. Medicine, 1960-63, asst. prof., 1963-68, assoc. prof., 1968; prof. medicine, chief cardiology sect. U. Ariz. Coll. Medicine, Tucson, 1969-82, disting. prof. internal medicine (cardiology), 1982—, dir. electrophysiology, 1982—; cons. cardiology VA Hosp., Tucson, 1969, USAF Regional Hosp., Davis-Monthan AFB, Tucson, 1969; mem. courtesy staffs Tucson Med. Ctr., St. Mary's Hosp., Tucson.; mem. panel drug efficacy study, panel on cardiovascular drugs Nat. Acad. Scis.-NRC, 1967-68; chmn. undergrad. cardiovascular tng. grant com. HEW-NIH, 1970. Editor Modern Concepts of Cardiovascular Disease, 1982-84; mem. editorial bd. Circulation, 1976-81, Current Problems in Cardiology, 1976-80, Cardiovascular Drugs and Therapy, 1986—, New Trends in Arrythmias, 1984—, Jour. Am. Coll. Cardiology, 1984-87, Am. Jour. Cardiology, 1984—; contbr. numerous articles to med. jours. Chmn. Washington Heart Assn. High Sch. Heart Program, 1966-68. Served to capt. USAF, 1954-56. Recipient Career Devel. award NIH, 1965, Student AMA Golden Apple award Georgetown U. Sch. Medicine, 1968; Mass. Heart Assn. fellow, 1957-58; John and Mary Markle scholar, 1960-65. Fellow Coun. on Clin. Cardiology Am. Heart Assn., ACP (Ariz. laureate award 1987), Am. Coll. Cardiology (bd. govs. Ariz. 1984-87, asst. sec. 1987-89, trustee); mem. Am. Fedn. Clin. Rsch., Am. Soc. Pharm. and Exptl. Therapeutics, Assn. Univ. Cardiologists, Inc. (v.p. 1989-90, pres. 1990-91), Ariz. Heart Assn. (dir. 1970, v.p. 1972-73, chmn. rsch. com. 1970-72), So. Ariz. Heart Assn. (dir. 1969), N.Am. Soc. for Pacing and Electrophysiology, Alpha Omega Alpha. Home: 4949 E Glenn St Tucson AZ 85712-1212 Office: U Ariz U Med Ctr 1501 N Campbell Ave Tucson AZ 85724-0001

MARCUS, JEFFREY HOWARD, electronic security system company executive; b. Albany, N.Y., June 4, 1950; s. Paul and Phyllis (Zippert) M. BS in Elec. Engring. and Computer Sci., U. Colo., Denver, 1977; MBA, U. Phoenix, Denver, 1985. Specialist counter intelligence U.S. Army, Washington, 1971-73; v.p. engring. Securus, Inc. (formerly Photo-Scan of Colo.), Denver, 1977-81, pres., 1981—; also bd. dirs. Securus (formerly Photo-Scan of Colo.), Denver; Bd. dirs. PSA Fin. Services, Inc., Westminster; vice chmn. bd., tech. com. chmn. PSA Security Network, Westminster. Democrat. Office: Securus Inc 12411 E 37th Ave Denver CO 80239-3404

MARCUS, MELVIN GERALD, geography educator, researcher, consultant; b. Seattle, Apr. 13, 1929; s. Albert Joseph Marcus and Lucille (Plumm) Fitch; m. Mary Ann Allen, June 6, 1953; children: W. Andrew, Annette A., Alison L., Benjamin L. Student, Yale U., 1947-50; BA, U. Miami, 1956; MA, U. Colo., 1957; PhD, U. Chgo., 1963. From instr. to asst. prof. Rutgers U., New Brunswick, N.J., 1960-64; from asst. prof. to prof. U. Mich., Ann Arbor, 1964-74; prof. Ariz. State U., Tempe, 1974—; vis. prof. U. Canterbury, Christchurch, New Zealand, 1972, 81, U.S. Mil. Acad., West Point, N.Y., 1985-86; bd. dirs. Yosemite Nat. Inst., Sausalito, Calif., 1979—; councillor Internat. Mountain Soc., Davis, Calif., 1980—. Contbr. numerous articles to profl. jours., books and monographs. Member Gov.'s Commn. on Ariz. Environment, 1974-80, State Climate Com., Ariz., 1982—. 1st lt. USAF, 1951-55, Korea. Fulbright-Hayes Found. fellow New Zealand, 1972, Erskine fellow, 1985, 93. Fellow Ariz.-Nev. Acad. Sci., Nev. Acad. Sci.; mem. Assn. Am. Geographers (pres. 1978-79), Am. Geog. Soc. (v.p.), Internat. Glaciological Soc., Phi Beta Kappa, Sigma Xi. Office: Ariz State U Dept of Geography Tempe AZ 85287

MARCUS, ROBERT, aluminum company executive; b. Arlington, Mass., Feb. 24, 1925; s. Hymen David and Etta (Arbetter) M.; m. Emily Patricia Ulrich, 1988; children: Lawrence Brian, Janie Sue, Clifford Scott, Emily. AB, Harvard U., 1947; MBA, U. Mich., 1949; MEd, Tufts U., 1950. Market analyst Govt. Commodity Exch., N.Y.C., 1952-54; market rsch. analyst Gen. Electric Co., 1954-55; corp. market analyst Amax Inc., N.Y.C., 1955-62, staff market mgr. aluminum group, 1962-65, pres. internat. aluminum div., 1965-70, v.p., 1970-71; exec. v.p. Amax Pacific Corp., San Mateo, Calif., 1971-72; exec. v.p., dir. Alumax Inc., San Mateo, 1973-82, pres., chief exec. officer, dir., 1982-86; ptnr. Am. Indsl. Ptnrs., San Francisco, 1987-92; dir. Saybrook Inst., 1992—; dir. Domtar, Montreal, 1984-90, Kaiser Aluminum Corp., 1990—. Trustee Mex. Mus., 1988—. With USN, 1943-46. Mem. Japan Soc. (bd. dirs.). Clubs: Harvard (N.Y.C.); University, Commonwealth, (San Francisco). Home: 2700 Scott St San Francisco CA 94123-4637

MARCUS, RUDOLPH ARTHUR, chemist; b. Montreal, Quebec, Canada, July 21, 1923; came to U.S., 1949, naturalized, 1958; s. Myer and Esther (Cohen) M.; m. Laura Hearne, Aug. 27, 1949; children: Alan Rudolph, Kenneth Hearne, Raymond Arthur. BSc, chemistry, McGill U., 1943, PhD, chemistry, 1946, DSc (hon.), 1988; DSc (hon.), U. Chgo., 1983, Poly. U., 1986, U. Göteborg, Sweden, 1987, McGill U., 1988, U. New Brunswick, Can., 1993, Queen's U., Can., 1993. Research staff mem. RDX Project, Montreal, Quebec, 1944-46; Postdoctoral research assoc. NRC of Can., Ottawa, Ont., 1946-49, U. N.C., 1949-51; asst. prof. Poly. Inst. Bklyn., 1951-54, assoc. prof., 1954-58, prof., 1958-64; prof. U. Ill., Urbana, 1964-78; Arthur Amos Noyes prof. chemistry Calif. Inst. Tech., Pasadena, 1978—; temp. mem. Courant Inst. Math. Scis., N.Y. U., 1960-61; trustee Gordon Research Confs., 1966-69, chmn. bd., 1968-69, mem. council, 1965-68; mem. rev. panel Argonne Nat. Lab., 1966-72, chmn., 1967-68; mem. rev. panel Brookhaven Nat. Lab., 1971-74; mem. rev. com. Radiation Lab., U. Notre Dame, 1975-80; mem. panel on atmospheric chemistry climatic impact com. Nat. Acad. Scis.-NRC, 1975-78, mem. com. kinetics of chem. reactions, 1973-77, chmn., 1975-77, mem. com. chem. scis., 1977-79, mem. com. to survey opportunities in chem. scis., 1982-86; adv. com. for chemistry NSF, 1977-80; vis. prof. theoretical chemistry U. Oxford, Eng., IBM, 1975-76; also professorial fellow Univ. Coll. Former mem. editorial bd. Jour. Chem. Physics, Ann. Rev. Phys. Chemistry, Jour. Phys. Chemistry, Accounts Chem. Rsch., Internat. Jour. Chem. Kinetics Molecular Physics, Theoretica Chimica Acta, Chem. Physics Letters; mem. editorial bd. Laser Chemistry, 1982—, Advances in Chem. Physics, 1984—, World Sci. Pub., 1987—, Internat. Revs. in Phys. Chemistry, 1988—, Faraday Trans., Jour. Chem. Soc., 1990—, Progress in Physics, Chemistry and Mechanics (China), 1989—, Perkins Transactions 2, Jour. Chem. Soc., 1992—, Chem. Physics Rsch. (India), 1992—, Trends in Chem. Physics Rsch. (India), 1992—. Recipient sr. U.S. Scientist award Alexander von Humboldt-Stiftung, 1976, Electrochemical Soc. Lecture award Electrochemical Soc., 1979, Robinson medal Faraday div. Royal Soc. Chemistry, 1982, Centenary medal Faraday div., 1988, Chandler medal Columbia U., 1983, Wolf Prize in chemistry, 1985, Nat. Medal of Sci., 1989, Evans award Ohio State U., 1990, Nobel prize in chem., 1992, Hirschfelder prize in theoretical chem. U. Wis., 1993, Golden Plate award Am. Acad. Achievement, 1993; Alfred P. Sloan fellow, 1960-61; NSF sr. postdoctoral fellow, 1960-61; sr. Fulbright-Hays scholar, 1972. Fellow Am. Acad. Arts and Scis. (exec. com. We. sect., co-chmn. 1981-84, rsch. and planning com. 1989-91), Royal Soc. Chemistry (hon.), Royal Soc. Can. (fgn.); mem. NAS, Am. Philos. Soc., Am. Chem. Soc. (past div. chmn., mem. exec. com., mem. adv. bd. petroleum rsch. fund, Irving Langmuir award Chem. Physics 1978, Peter Debye award Phys. Chemistry 1988, Willard Gibbs medal Chgo. sect. 1988, S.C. Lind Lecture, East Tenn. sect. 1988, Theodore William Richards medal Northeastern sect. 1990, Edgar Fahs Smith award Phila. sect. 1991, Ira Remsen Meml. award Md. sect. 1991, Pauling medal Portland, Oreg. and Puget Sound sect. 1991), Royal Soc. London (fgn. mem.), Internat. Acad. Quantum Molecular Sci. Home: 331 S Hill Ave Pasadena CA 91106-3405

MARCY, WILLARD, chemist, chemical engineer, retired; b. Newton, Mass., Sept. 27, 1916; s. Willard Adna and Jane (Locke) M.; m. Helen Butler, Oct. 8, 1938; children: Martha Ann Marcy Simoneau, Ellen Louise. BSChemE, MIT, 1937, PhD in Organic Chemistry, 1949. Refinery asst. supt. Am. Sugar Co., Bklyn., 1937-42; rsch. asst. chemistry MIT, Cambridge, 1946-49; head dept. refinery process devel. Am. Sugar Co., Bklyn., 1946-64; v.p. Rsch. Corp., N.Y.C., 1964-82; pres. ARDUS, Inc., Charleston, S.C., 1983-85; mem. com. on patent matters Am. Chem. Soc., Washington, 1969-83, chmn., 1977-83; chmn. bd. editors Indsl. Rsch. Inst., N.Y.C., 1973-78. Editor: Patent Policy, 1978; contbr. articles to profl. jours. Maj. U.S. Chem. Corps, 1942-46. Recipient grant NSF, 1980. Fellow AAAS, Am. Inst. Chemist (pres. 1984-85), N.Y. Acad. Sci.; mem. AICE, N.Mex. Acad. Scis. , Newcomen Soc., Chemists' Club N.Y. (trustee 1981-83, chmn. libr. com. 1982-86), Sigma Xi, Alpha Chi Sigma. Republican. Home: 621 Caminito del Sol Santa Fe NM 87505

MARDIAN, DANIEL, construction company director; b. Pasadena, Calif., Apr. 10, 1917; s. Samuel and Akabe (Lekerian) M.; m. Katherine Evkhanian, Jan. 30, 1942; children: Daniel Jr., Tom, John, Paul, Scott. Student, Pasadena City Coll., 1937; diploma, U.S. Army Engring. Sch., Ft. Belvoir, Va., 1944, U.S. Army Command and Gen. Staff Coll., 1961. Commd. U.S. Army, 1942, advances through grades to lt. col., 1962, ret., 1970; ptnr. Mardian Constrn. Co., Phoenix, 1945-47, exec. v.p., 1947-66, pres., 1966-78, also bd. dirs.; past chmn., mem. Nat. Joint Apprenticeship/Tng. Commn.

Oper. Engrs., Washington, 1975-78; mem. adv. bd. constrn. programs Ariz. State U., Tempe, 1957—, mem. adv. bd. coll. engring., 1957—; bd. dirs. Citibank, Phoenix, 1962-87. Pres. Am. Coun. Constrn. Edn., Monroe, La., 1991-93; past pres., bd. dirs. Fiesta Bowl, Tempe, 1986-92; gen. campaign chmn. United Way, Phoenix, 1967; pres. Met. Phoenix C. of C., 1967-68. Capt. C.E., U.S. Army, 1942-46, PTO, 1970—. Recipient Hall of Fame Award Ariz. State U., 1990, Excellence in Constrn. Award Am. Subcontractors Assn., 1988, Hall of Fame Award Nat. Football Found., 1987, Brotherhood Award Ariz. chpt. Nat. Conf. Christians and Jews, 1981. Mem. Associated Gen. Contractors Am. (life bd. dirs., chmn. yr. award 1970, mem. manpower tng. com., laborers tng. com., 1969—), Sun Angel Found. (chmn. 1989-91), Ariz. Acad., Phoenix Country Club (bd. dirs., pres. 1985-86), Phoenix Kiwanis Club (past dir.). Republican. Mem. United Ch. Christ. Home: 7215 N 3rd St Phoenix AZ 85020-4904 Office: Perini Building Co 360 E Coronado Rd Phoenix AZ 85004-1524

MARDIAN, ROBERT CHARLES, JR., restauranteur; b. Orange, Calif., Feb. 1, 1947; s. Robert Charles Sr. and Dorothy Driscilla (Denniss) M.; m. Jayne Marie Garvin, June 21, 1970 (div. 1977); 1 child, Robert Charles III; m. Kathleen Frances Dixon, Oct. 13, 1984 (div. 1991); children: Alexandra Quinn, Ashley Michele. BA, Stanford U., 1969; MBA, Pepperdine U., 1986. Gen. mgr. Loft Restaurant, San Jose, Calif., 1969-71; chief exec. officer/chmn. bd. Wind & Sea Restaurants, Inc., Dana Point, Calif., 1971—; bd. dirs. Dana Niguel Bank, cons. U.S. Olympic Com., Colorado Springs, 1984-88. Commr. Dana Point Econ. Devel. Mem. Young Pres. Orgn. Republican. Home: 34699 Golden Lantern Dana Point CA 92629-2870 Office: Wind & Sea Restaurants Inc 34699 Golden Lantern St Dana Point CA 92629-2989

MAREE, WENDY, painter, sculptor; b. Windsor, Eng., Feb. 10, 1938. Student, Windsor & Maidenhead Coll., 1959; studied with Vasco Lazzlo, London, 1959-62. Exhibited at Windsor Arts Festival, San Bernardino (Calif.) Mus.; exhibited in one woman show Lake Arrowhead (Calif.) Libr., 1989, Phyllis Morris Gallery, Many Horses Gallery, L.A., 1990, Nelson Rockefeller, Palm Springs, Calif., 1992, numerous others; represented in pvt. collections His Royal Highness Prince Faisal, Saudi Arabia, Gena Rowlands, L.A., John Cassavetes, L.A., Nicky Blairs, L.A., Guilford Glazer, Beverly Hills, Calif. Recipient award San Bernardino County Mus., Redlands, Calif., 1988. Mem. Artist Guild of Lake Arrowhead. Address: 246 Saturmino Dr Palm Springs CA 92262

MAREI, IBRAHIM, medical technologist; b. Marowe, Sudan, Dec. 6, 1939; s. Hassan and Shafika (Mohamed) M. BS in Chemistry, U. Cairo, 1966; MS in Med. Tech., Calif. State U., 1980. Lic. clinical chemist tech., Calif., clinical lab. tech., Calif. Clinical chemist SmithKline-Beecham, Van Nuys, Calif., 1969-71; supr. ctr. critically ill lab. Hollywood Presbyn. Med. Ctr., L.A., 1971-75; sr. toxicologist, clin. chemist spl. chemistry dept., instr. on the job tng. and edn. new students, tech. staff Reference Labs., Newbury Park, Calif., 1975-88; clin. chemist endochronology dept., med. technologist Smith Kline Biosci. Labs., Van Nuys, Calif., 1988—. Mem. Am. Soc. Clinical Pathologists (cert.), Am. Chem. Soc., Am. Assn. Clinical Chemists (cert.), Am. Pub. Health Assn. Calif. Assn. for Med. Lab. Tech. Home: 7441 Hazeltine Ave Apt 107 Van Nuys CA 91405-1486 Office: Smith Kline Biosci Labs 7600 Tyrone Ave Van Nuys CA 91405-1495

MAREK, DANA, small business owner; b. Perth, Australia, Nov. 21, 1952; came to U.S., 1959; d. Jaromir Franta and Zdena (Liska) M.; m. Glenn Kristopher Miller, 1973 (div. 1980); 1 child, Shahn Kristopher. BS, U. of Pacific, Stockton, Calif., 1980. Gen. mgr. Alpine Design Co., Stockton, 1972-79; rsch. asst. U. of Pacific, Stockton, 1973-80; v.p., gen. mgr. Exec. Boat Club, Golden West Boat Rentals, Stockton, 1979-86; gen. mgr. Am. Internat. Trading Co., San Francisco, 1985—; ptnr. Silken Sheath, San Francisco, 1991—; owner, ptnr. Daly Hustle, San Francisco, 1990—. Rsch. asst.: California Policy Decision Making, 1981. Named Goodwill Ambassador U. of Pacific, Stockton, 1979-86, Stockton C. of C., 1980-81. Mem. Am. Mgmt. Assn. (registrar San Francisco 1992—), Internat. Trade Coun. (pres.). Office: Silken Sheath PO Box 881284 San Francisco CA 94188-1284

MARGALITH, ETHAN HAROLD, moving company executive; b. Bucks County, Pa., Sept. 17, 1955; s. Sanford Harold and Elizabeth Ruth (Eisen) M.; m. Linda Cukler, Aug. 10, 1981 (div.); 1 child, Alexa Pearl; m. Lisa Khonsary, Apr. 17, 1993. BA, UCLA, 1979; JD, Loyola U., 1984. Chief exec. officer, chmn. bd. Starving Students, Inc., L.A., 1973—. Contbr. articles to industry publs. Mem. Calif. Moving and Storage Assn. (bd. dirs.), Nat. Moving and Storage Assn., Am. Movers Conf., Young Pres. Orgn. Office: PO Box 351206 Los Angeles CA 90035-9606

MARGOL, IRVING, consultant; b. St. Louis, May 28, 1930; s. William and Dora (Karsh) M.; m. Myrna Levy, Dec., 1959; children—Bradley, Lisa, Cynthia. B.A., Washington U., St. Louis, 1951, M.A., 1952. Employment mgr. Am. Car & Foundry div. ACF, St. Louis, 1955-59; asst. personnel dir. Vickers Inc. div. Sperry-Rand, St. Louis, 1959-60; instr. personnel mgmt. Washington U. (St. Louis), 1960-62; personnel dir. Energy Controls div. Bendix Corp., South Bend, Ind., 1962-69; exec. v.p. community/employee affairs group, community rels. dept., employee assistance program Security Pacific Nat. Bank, L.A., 1969-92; mng. dir. Southern Calif. Jannotta, Bray & Assocs., Inc., 1992—; pres. Security Pacific Found., L.A., 1989-92; mng. dir. Jannotta Bray & Assocs., L.A., 1992—; instr. UCLA Extension Div., Los Angeles; Grad. Sch. Banking, Rutgers U., Notre Dame U. Bd. dirs. L.A. chpt. ARC, Am. Heart Assn., Am. Cancer Soc., Nat. Conf. Christians & Jews, Braille Inst.; bd. overseers Southwestern U. Law. Mem. Am. Bankers Assn. (exec. com. 1979—), Am. Soc. Tng. and Devel., Am. Soc. Personnel Adminstrs., Am. Inst. Banking, Washington U. Alumni Assn. Democrat. Jewish. Office: Jannotta Bray & Assocs 5320 Pacific Councourse Dr Los Angeles CA 90045

MARGOLIN, ELIAS LEOPOLD, engineering educator; b. N.Y.C., Aug. 13, 1921; s. Irving and Dora (Weinberg) M.; m. Frances Mongin, Mar. 12, 1944; children: Janice, John, Carolyn, Paul. B Chem. Engring., CUNY, 1942; MSME, U. Pa., Phila., 1948; MA, San Diego State U., 1983; degree in novice sci., Technion, Haifa, Israel, 1991. Registered profl. engr., Ohio. Marine engr. Bur. Ships, USN, Phila., 1942-43; stress analyst Budd Aircraft Co., Phila., 1943-44; propulsion engr. USAF, Wright Field, Ohio, 1948-53; project engr. United Aircraft Products, Dayton, Ohio, 1953-55; sr. thermodynamics engr. Convair, San Diego, 1955-61; design specialist Ryan Aircraft, San Diego, 1961-62; rsch. specialist N.Am. Aviation, Downey, Calif., 1962-66; prof. San Diego City Coll., 1967-89, prof. emeritus, 1989—; adj. prof. U. Dayton, 1950-55; dir. Acad. for Edn., Family, Group and Individual Therapy. Leader troop 4 Boy Scouts Am., LaJolla, Calif., 1975-78; bd. dirs. Reps. of LaJolla, 1980-84. With U.S. Army, 1944-46. Recipient Kay Yuhan Lodge Meml. Scholarship San Diego State U., 1982. Mem. AIAA, Am. Inst. Chem. Engrs., Am. Assn. Individual Investors. Home: 887 LaJolla Rancho Rd La Jolla CA 92037

MARGOLIN, WILLIAM, molecular biologist, researcher; b. Englewood, N.J., Sept. 21, 1959; s. Arthur Alvin and Elaine Ida (Schultz) M.; m. Sarah M. Slemmons, May 16, 1993. SB, MIT, 1981; PhD, U. Wis., 1989. Tech. rsch. asst. MIT, Cambridge, 1980-82; grad. rsch. asst. U. Wis., Madison, 1982-86, U. Tenn., Memphis, 1986-89; NSF postdoctoral fellow Stanford U., Palo Alto, Calif., 1989—. Contbr. articles to profl. jours. Home: 811 Channing Ave Palo Alto CA 94301 Office: Stanford U Dept Biol Scis Stanford CA 94305-5020

MARGOLIS, BERNARD ALLEN, library administrator, antique book merchant and appraiser; b. Greenwich, Conn., Oct. 2, 1948; s. Sidney S. and Rose (Birkenfeld) M.; m. Amanda Batey, Nov. 2, 1973. BA in Polit. Sci., U. Denver, 1970, MLS, 1973. Cert. libr., Mich. Libr. asst. Denver Pub. Libr., 1970-72; br. head Virginia Village Libr., Denver Pub. Libr., 1972-73; dep. dir. Monroe County Libr. System, Mich., 1973-75; dir. Raisin Valley Libr. System, Monroe, 1976-78, S.E. Mich. Regional Film Libr., Monroe, 1976-88, Monroe County Libr. System, 1976-88, Pikes Peak Libr. Dist., Colorado Springs, Colo., 1988—; pres. Colo. Ctr. for Books, 1989-92, Colo. Ctr. for the Book, 1993—; cons. in libr. pub. rels., 1976—; chmn. Colo. Gov.'s Conf. on Libr. and Info. Svcs., 1990; lectr. Western Mich. U., Kalamazoo, 1978-81; appraiser rare books, Monroe, Colorado Springs, 1970—. Contbr. articles to profl. jours; mem. editorial bd. Bottom Line Mag. Fin. Mgmt. for Libr., 1986—. Bd. dirs. Monroe Sen. Citizens Ctr., 1976-80, Monroe Fine Arts Coun., 1978-81, Am. the Beautiful Centennial Celebration, Inc., 1993; chmn. Blue Cross-Blue Shield Consumer Coun., Detroit, 1984-88; mem. adv. bd. Access Colo. Libr. and Info. Network (ACLIN), mem. adv. bd. Mercy Meml. Hosp., Monroe, 1984-86; Dem. candidate for Mich. Senate, 1986; mem. allocations com. Pikes Peak United Way, 1988-91, chmn., 1990-91, bd. dirs., 1990-91; chmn. Great Pikes Peak Cowboy Poetry Gathering, 1990, 91, 92; del White House Conf. on Libr. and Info. Scis., 1991; mem. adv. com. Access Colo. Libr. and Info. Network, 1991—, Fifth Congressional Art Competition Com., 1992—. Recipient Mayoral Cert. Commendation award Denver, 1972, 73; named Mich. Libr. of Yr., 1985, Colo. Libr. of Yr., 1990; commendation John F. Kennedy Ctr. for Performing Arts, 1993. Mem. ALA (governing coun. 1986—, endowment trustee 1989—, chmn. resolutions com. 1991-92, exec. com. Am. the Beautiful Centennial Celebration, 1992-93, cons. annual swap and shop 1979-84, John Cotton Dana award 1977, 91, Libr. Awareness Idea Search award Washington 1982), J.F. Kennedy Ctr. for the Performing Arts, 1993, Colo. Libr. Assn. (legis. com.), Libr. Adminstrv. Mgmt. Assn., Pub. Libr. Assn., Libr. Pub. Rels. Coun. Democrat. Jewish. Home: 10640 Hungate Rd Colorado Springs CO 80908-4312 Office: Pikes Peak Libr Dist PO Box 1579 Colorado Springs CO 80901-1579

MARGOLIS, DONALD L., mechanical engineering educator, consultant; b. Washington, Nov. 13, 1945; s. Joel and Jeanette (Lowenwirth) M.; children: Scott, David. BSME, Va. Poly. and State U., 1967; MSME, MIT, 1969, PhD, 1972. Instr. dept. mech. engring. MIT, Cambridge, Mass., 1969-72; prof. dept. mech. engring. U. Calif., Davis, 1972—; cons. various industries, nat. labs., U.S., Japan. Author (textbook) System Dynamics: A Unified Approach, 1990; also over 85 articles. Fellow ASME (Outstanding Teaching award 1980); mem. Soc. Automotive Engrs. (Ralph R. Teeter Ednl. award 1986). Office: U Calif Davis Dept Mech Engring Davis CA 95616

MARGULIS, MICHAEL HOWARD, transportation executive; b. N.Y.C., Jan. 22, 1952; s. Gustave and Aileen Emily Margulis; m. Deborah Ann Braidic, Oct. 3, 1981. BS, Ariz. State U., 1974. Traffic assoc. J.C. Penney Co., Forest Park, Ga., 1977-78; spl. transit supr. J.C. Penney Co., Reno, Nev., 1978-80; traffic supr. Meldisco, Compton, Calif., 1980-81; traffic mgr. Meldisco, Rancho Cucamonga, Calif., 1981—. Panel mem. L.A. Truck Adv. Task Force, 1990—; chmn. Nat. Transp. Week, Calif., 1987. Mem. Western Traffic Conf. (past pres. 1989-90, past chmn. 1990-91, meeting planner 1990—), Traffic Mgrs. Conf. Calif. (past pres. 1987, chmn. 1988), Southern Calif. Assn. Govts./Air Quality Mgmt. Dist. Truck Task Force. Democrat. Jewish. Home: 1088 San Antonio Ave Fullerton CA 92635 Office: Meldisco divsn Melville Corp 9282 Pittsburg Ave Rancho Cucamonga CA 91730

MARHOEFER, GORDON JOSEPH, life underwriter, lawyer; b. Detroit, Aug. 25, 1932; s. Edwin Louis and Lucy Cecilia (Kavenaugh) M.; m. Priscilla Ann Nacozy, Nov. 25, 1953 (div. 1973); children: George, Clifford, Thomas, Robert; m. Patricia Joan Black, Dec. 27, 1977; 1 stepchild, Darci. BA, Loyola-Marymount U., 1954; JD, Loyola U., L.A., 1972. Bar: Calif. 1973; CLU, ChFC. Adminstrv. trainee Pacific Mut. Life Ins. Co., L.A., 1955-57; agt. Pacific Mut. Life Ins. Co., Sherman Oaks, Calif., 1957-59; adminstrv. asst. Pacific Mut. Life Ins. Co., L.A., 1959-61, mgr. conservation, 1961-64, mgr. advanced underwriting, 1964-67, dir. estate and bus. plans, 1967-72; CLU Mass. Mut. Life Ins., Newport Beach, Calif., 1972—; pvt. practice law, 1972—; inst. CLU and Life Mgmt. Assn., L.A., 1960-70. Contbr. articles to profl. mags. Active Costa Mesa Civic Playhouse, Newport Theatre Arts Ctr.; bd. dirs. Wellness Community of Orange County (Calif.), 1992-93, Newport Theatre Arts Ctr., Newport Beach, 1988-90, Burbank (Calif.) Parochial Baseball League, 1968-71; vice chair Alano Club of Costa Mesa (Calif.), 1975-76; charter pres. Burbank Young Republicans, 1962-63. Mem. Nat. Assn. Life Underwriters, Am. Soc. CLU and ChFC, Orange Coast Estate Planning Coun. (pres. 1986-87, bd. dirs. 1982-87, founding dir. 1977), Calif. Bar Assn., Orange County Bar Assn. Home: 342 Sydney Ln Costa Mesa CA 92627 Office: Mass Mut PO Box 1434 Newport Beach CA 92663

MARIANI, ALBERT JOSEPH, surgeon, urologist; b. Springfield, Mass., Mar. 10, 1949; s. Albert Ceasar and Mary Cecelia (Cavanaugh) M.; m. Aurora Cunanan, Feb. 24, 1990; 1 child, Joy. BS in Biology, Fairfield U., 1970; MD, N.Y. Med. Coll., 1975. Diplomate Am. Bd. Urology, Nat. Bd. Med. Examiners. Intern Mayo Clinic, Rochester, Minn., 1975-76, resident in urology, 1976-80; pres. hosp. staff Kaiser Med. Ctr., Honolulu, 1985-86; med. dir. of quality assurance Kaiser Health Plan: Hawaii Region, Honolulu, 1986-90; exec. v.p. Hawaii Permanent Med. Group, Honolulu, 1987; chief surg. svcs. Kaiser Health Plan: Hawaii Region, Honolulu, 1983—. Contbr. articles to profl. jours. Pres. student govt. Fairfield (Conn.) U., 1969-70. Mem. Am. Urologic Assn. (diplomate), Hawaii Urologic Assn. (pres. 1985), Minn. Med. Assn. (del. 1977-80), AMA (Minn. del. 1977-80). Roman Catholic. Home: 3630 Nihipali Pl Honolulu HI 96816 Office: Kaiser Med Ctr 3288 Moanalua Rd Honolulu HI 96816

MARICS, MONICA ANN, human factors engineer; b. Wooster, Ohio, Sept. 3, 1962; d. George Ellis and Elizabeth Louise (Mnich) Merva; m. Frank Louis Marics, Aug. 22, 1987. BS in Indsl. Engring., U. Mich., 1984; MS in Indsl. Engring., Va. Poly. Inst. and State U., 1987. Cert. engr. in tng. Human factors engr., cons. AT&T Consumer Products, Bell Labs., Indpls., 1987-88; human factors engr. Southwestern Bell Tech. Resources, St. Louis, 1989-91, US West Advanced Techs., Boulder, Colo., 1991—. Contbr. articles to profl. jours. Eastman Kodak scholar Eastman Kodak Co., 1981-84; Pratt fellow Va. Poly. Inst. and State U., 1985-87. Mem. Am. Voice Input-Output Soc., Human Factors Soc. (sec.-treas. Communications Tech. Group 1989-91, program chair 1992), Assn. for Computing Machinery, Tau Beta Pi, Alpha Pi Mu. Home: 916 12th St Boulder CO 80302 Office: US West AT 4001 Discovery Dr Boulder CO 80303

MARINAK, JEANNE LEEANN, English language educator; b. Detroit, July 18, 1951; d. Archibald Mackay and Grace Francis (Stickley) Tedesco; m. James Michael Marinak, Dec. 29, 1976; children: Jamie Amanda, Jedediah Strong. BA magna cum laude, Calif. State U., Sacramento, 1984; MA, Sonoma State U., 1991. Cert. tchr., Alaska, Calif. Tchr. trainer Rural CAP, Anchorage, 1985-86; instr. N. Bay Secondary Sch., Mill Valley, Calif., 1986-89, Nova Ednl. Ctr., Novato, Calif., 1989-92; lectr. Sonoma State U., Rohnert Pk., Calif., 1989-90; ednl. cons. Novato, Calif., 1986—, instr. San Marin High Sch., Novato, 1992—. Mem. League Conservation Voters, Marin County, 1986—, Marin County Human Rights Commn., 1990—. Fellow Phi Kappa Phi; mem. Nat. Coun. Tchrs. English, Calif. Coun. Tchrs. English, MLA. Home: 2 Nogales Ct Novato CA 94947-2903

MARINER, WILLIAM MARTIN, chiropractor; b. Balt., Jan. 2, 1949; s. William Joseph and Ellen (Dexter) M. AA, Phoenix Coll., 1976; BS in Biology, L.A. Coll. of Chiropractic, 1980, D Chiropractic summa cum laude, 1980; DD (hon.), Universal Life Ch., Modesto, Calif., 1986. Health food restaurant mgr. Golden Temple of Conscious Cookery, Tempe, Ariz., 1974-75; health food store mgr. Guru's Grainery, Phoenix, 1975; physical therapist A.R.E. Clinic, Phoenix, 1975-76; research dir., founder G.R.D. Healing Arts Ctr., Phoenix, 1974-77; aminstrv. asst., acad. dean L.A. Coll. Chiropractic, Whittier, Calif., 1977-80; faculty Calif. Acupuncture Coll., L.A., 1978-80; ednl. cons. Avanti Inst., San Francisco, 1985—; found, dir., head clinician Pacific Healing Arts Ctr., Del Mar, Calif., 1980—. Patentee in field. Co-dir. "We Care We Share" Charitable Orgn., San Diego, 1985-86. Named Outstanding Sr., L.A. Coll. Chiropractic, 1980. Mem. San Diego Chiropractic Soc., Calif. Chiropractic Assn., Am. Chiropractic Assn., Internat. Coll. Applied Kinesiology, Holistic Dental Assn., Brit. Homopathic Assn., Del Mar C. of C., Rotary. Office: Pacific Healing Arts Ctr PO Box 5000 Del Mar CA 92014-1250

MARION, KATHY, lawyer; b. Cheyenne, Wyo., Apr. 5, 1961; d. H.D. and D. Caryl (Hatch) M. BS in Gen. Bus. Mgmt., U. Wyo., 1983, JD, 1991. Adminstrv. asst. to assoc. dir. Presdl. Pers. The White House, Washington, 1983-85; staff asst. to undersec. U.S. Dept. Energy, Washington, 1985-86; exec. asst. to commr. U.S. Bur. Reclamation, Washington, 1986-88; legal intern Office Gen. Counsel, Fed. Energy Regulatory Commn., Washington, 1989; summer assoc. Hathaway, Speight, Kunz, Trautwein & Barrett, Cheyenne, Wyo., 1990; atty. Office Pub. Defender, Cheyenne, Wyo., 1991-92; acting pub. defender 8th Jud. Dist., Cheyenne, Wyo., 1992; staff atty. office of solicitor, water & power divsn. U.S. Dept. Interior, Cheyenne, Wyo., 1993—. Mem. sr. staff Land and Water Law Rev., 1990-91; contbr. articles to profl. jours. Dep. dir. corp. affairs Presdl. Inaugural Com., Washington, 1988-89; housing coord. Rep. Nat. Conv., New Orleans, summer 1988; mem. Wyo. Heritage Found. Recipient Outstanding Performance award U.S. Dept. Interior and U.S. Dept. Justice, 1984, 85, 86, 87, Spl. Achievement award U.S. Bur. Reclamation, 1988, Superior Svc. award U.S. Dept. Interior, 1988. Mem. ABA (nat. student liaison sect. natural resources, energy and environ. law 1989-91, asst. editor water resources publ., 1993—), Colo. Bar, Wyo. Bar, Laramie County Bar Assn., Larimer County Bar Assn., Natural Resources Law Forum, Delta Theta Pi, Chi Omega (pledge advisor 1989-91). Republican. Episcopalian. Home: 3695 Dover Rd Cheyenne WY 82001 Office: US Dept Interior Solicitors Office 18th and C St NW Washington DC 20240

MARISCAL, GREGORY LEE, manufacturing company executive; b. L.A., Dec. 3, 1965; s. Daniel Joseph and Jane (McClanahan) M. Student, Duke U., 1983-84; BA cum laude, UCLA, 1988. Writer/instr. Britron, Inc., Tokyo, 1989-90; export mgr. Hirsch Pipe & Supply Co., L.A., 1991—. Mem. L.A. World Trade Ctr. Assn., Japan-Am. Soc., L.A. World Affairs Coun., L.A. Jr. C. of C. Republican. Presbyterian. Home: 3450 Vista Haven Rd Sherman Oaks CA 91403 Office: Hirsch Pipe & Supply Co 3317 W Jefferson Blvd Los Angeles CA 90018

MARK, ARTHUR, information systems specialist; b. San Francisco, Aug. 1, 1948; s. Bo You and Chew Lin (Oyoung) M.; m. Alice Look, Sept. 1, 1975 (div. Oct. 1987); children: Jennifer, Brandon. BS, Calif. State U., 1971, MS, 1977. Cert. data processing, info. systems auditor, internal auditor. Lectr. info. systems Calif. State U., Sacramento, 1978—; with State of Calif., Sacramento, 1977-85, 88—. Active United Way. Maj. USMC, 1985-88. Mem. MENSA, Inst. Internal Auditors. Republican. Home: 8985 Laguna Pl Way Elk Grove CA 95758

MARK, WALTER RALPH, university administrator; b. Sioux City, Iowa, Apr. 18, 1946; s. Walter Roy and Wanda Eloise (Zerbe) M.; 1 child, Chris. BS in Forest Mgmt., Utah State U., 1968; MS in Forest Sci., Colo. State U., 1970, PhD in Plant Pathology, 1972. Registered profl. forester, Calif. Forest technician Teton Nat. Forest, Jackson, Wyo., 1965-67; grad. asst. Colo. State U., Ft. Collins, 1968-72; rsch. assoc. Rocky Mountain Forest and Range Exptl. Sta., Ft. Collins, 1972, rsch. forester, 1975; prof. forestry Calif. Poly. State U., San Luis Obispo, 1972—, acad. specialist, 1981-82, acad. program planner, 1982-85, interim vice provost, 1985-86, dir. inst. studies, 1986-92; interim, assoc. dean Coll. Agr., 1992—; cons. County of San Luis Obispo, 1992—, Armstrong Farms, Morro Bay, Calif., 1982—; dir. equipment grant NSF, 1975-77. Contbr. articles to profl. jours. Vice chair So. Forest Dist. Tech. Adv. Com., Fresno, Calif., 1980-86. Grantee U.S. Forest Svc., 1976-78, Calif. Dept. Forestry, 1979-81, 82, development grantee Apple Computer, 1988—. Mem. Soc. Am. Foresters (sec. 1976-79), Student Info. Users, Assn. Instnl. Researchers, Calif. Assn. Instnl. Researchers, Am. Forestry Assn. Office: Calif Poly State U Coll of Agr San Luis Obispo CA 93407

MARKEE, DAVID JAMES, university official, education educator; b. Madison, Wis., Oct. 26, 1942; s. Richard L. and Cathrine Ann (Whalen) M.; m. Lou Ann Markee, Aug. 14, 1965; children: Jeffrey, Gregory. BS in English and Geography, U. Wis., Platteville, 1964, MEd in Counseling and Guidance, 1968; PhD in Counseling Psychology, U. Mo., 1974. Tchr. English, Platteville High Sch., 1964-67; asst. dir. residence halls U. Wis., 1967-69; asst. dir. student life U. Mo., Columbia, 1970-71, assoc. dir., 1971-72, dir., 1972-75; prof. edn. U. Wis., Whitewater, 1973-80, asst. chancellor student affairs, 1975-80; prof., v.p. for student svcs. No. Ariz. U., Flagstaff, 1980—. Contbr. articles to profl. jours. Pres., bd. dirs. Cath. Social Svcs., Flagstaff, 1983—; bd. dirs. Citizens Against Drug Abuse, Flagstaff, 1987-89, Flagstaff Arboretum, 1988—; chmn. Flagstaff Beautification Commn., 1988—; co-chair Flagstaff United Way. Recipient Person of Yr. award U. Wis.-Whitewater Student Govt., 1975, Chief Manueleto award Navajo Nation, 1990. Mem. Nat. Assn. Student Pers. Adminstrs. (bd. dirs. 1989-90), Ariz. Assn. Student Pers. Adminstrs. (pres. 1986-87), Kiwanis (Outstanding Mem. award Flagstaff 1983-85), Kappaa Delta Pi. Democrat. Office: No Ariz U PO Box 4093 Flagstaff AZ 86011

MARKEN, GIDEON ANDREW, III, advertising and public relations executive; b. Hampton, Iowa, June 24, 1940; s. Gideon Andrew Jr. and Cleone (Marie Riss) M.; m. Jeannine Gay Hill, Dec. 28, 1963; children: Tracy Lynn, Gideon Andrew. BS, Iowa State U., 1962; MBA, Hamilton Inst., 1967. Pub. relations mgr. Fairchild Instrumentation, Mountain View, Calif., 1967-68; pub. relations dir. Barnes-Hind Pharms., Sunnyvale, Calif., 1968-69; v.p. acct. supr. Hal Lawrence, Inc., Palo Alto, Calif., 1969-74, Bozell-Jacobs, Palo Alto, 1974-77; pres. Marken Communications, Sunnyvale, Calif., 1977—. Contbr. articles to profl. jours. Served as sgt. USAF, 1963-67. Mem. Pub. Relations Soc. of Am., Peninsula Mktg. Assn., Bus. Publishing Advt. Assn., Am. Mgmt. Assn., Am. Electronics Assn., Am. Med. Writers Assn. (pres. 1968-70, 72-74). Republican. Methodist. Club: San Rafael Yacht. Home: 1428 Bellingham Ave Sunnyvale CA 94087-3811 Office: Marken Communications 3600 Pruneridge Ave Santa Clara CA 95051-5958

MARKEN, PAUL RICHARD, oilfield chemist; b. Wichita, Kans., Sept. 5, 1954; s. Darrell Howard and Shirley Ellen (Wohlgemuth) M.; m. Jennifer Kay Willingham, June 14, 1980; children: Ashley Nichole, Anne Elizabeth. BA in Chemistry and Physics, We. State Coll., Gunnison, Colo., 1982. Prodn. supr. Integrity Oil & Gas, Gillette, Wyo., 1982-86; chem. sales Amoco Chems. (Welchem), Riverton and Casper, Wyo., 1986-89; ops. technician Giant Exploration & Prodn., Farmington, N.Mex., 1990-91; plant operator Meridian Oil, Farmington, 1992—; substitute tchr. Farmington Pub. Schs., 1992—. Republican. Presbyterian. Home: 3003 Northwood Circle Farmington NM 87401

MARKER, MARC LINTHACUM, lawyer, investor; b. Los Angeles, July 19, 1941; s. Clifford Harry and Voris (Linthacum) M.; m. Sandra Yocom, Aug. 29, 1965; children: Victor, Gwendolyn. BA in Econs. and Geography, U. Calif.-Riverside, 1964; JD, U. So. Calif., 1967. Asst. v.p., asst. sec. Security Pacific Nat. Bank, L.A., 1970-73; sr. v.p., chief counsel, sec. Security Pacific Leasing Corp., San Francisco, 1973-92; pres. Security Pacific Leasing Svcs. Corp., San Francisco, 1977-85, dir., 1977-92; bd. dirs., sec. Voris, Inc., 1973-86; bd. dirs. Refiners Petroleum Corp., 1977-81, Security Pacific Leasing Singapore Ltd., 1983-85, Security Pacific Leasing Can. Ltd., 1989-92; lectr. in field. Served to comdr. USCGR. Mem. ABA, Calif. Bar Assn., D.C. Bar Assn., Am. Assn. Equipment Lessors. Republican. Lutheran. Club: Univ. (L.A.). Office: 471 B Magnolia Ave Larkspur CA 94939

MARKEY, THOMAS ADAM, school business manager; b. Dayton, Ohio, June 12, 1956; s. Paul Robert Markey and Cathleen Wilgus; m. Mari Granieri, July 22, 1979. BA, Ariz. State U., 1980, MBA, 1992. CPA. Fin. analyst Maricopa County Sch. Supt., Phoenix, 1982-84; EDP acct. Maricopa County Fin. Dept., Phoenix, 1984-88, sr. fin. acct., 1988-90, sr. budget analyst, 1990-92; dir. bus. East Valley Inst. Tech., Mesa, Ariz., 1992—. Sustaining mem. SW Assn. Indian Affairs, Santa Fe, N.Mex., 1990; active mem. Intertribal Indian Ceremonial Assn., Gallup, N.Mex., 1990. Mem. AICPA, Ariz. Soc. CPA's, Assn. Govt. Accts. (exec. com. Phoenix chpt. 1992—), Ariz. Assn. Sch. Bus. Ofcls., Western Govtl. Rsch. Assn., Am. Acad. Religion, Beta Gamma Sigma. Democrat. Home: 3421 N 26 Pl Phoenix AZ 85016-7435 Office: East Valley Inst Tech 200 S Center St Mesa AZ 85210

MARKHAM, CLARENCE MATTHEW, III, city administrator; b. Toledo, Apr. 26, 1937; s. Clarence Matthew Jr. and Olga Frances (Hughes) M.; m. Katherine Kirwan, Nov. 26, 1960; children: Juliet Kristina, Christopher Matthew, Allan Kirwan. BS, No. Ill. U., 1960; postgrad., Calif. State U., 1962-66, Claremont U., 1969-71, Yale U., 1970; MA in Urban Studies, Occidental Coll., 1972. V.p. Safety Savs. & Loan Assn., L.A., 1966-67; auditor, contr. Pasadena Commn. on Human Needs and Opportunity, 1967-68; exec. dir. Claremont (Calif.) U. Ctr., 1968-69, asst. dir. admissions, 1969-70; exec. dir. Job Resources & Educational Ctr., Monrovia, Calif., 1971-73; adminstr. human svcs. City of West Covina, Calif., 1973—; ptnr. Wilson-Markham & Assocs., L.A., 1986-92; owner C.M. Markham & Assocs., Irwindale, Calif., 1989—. Active YMCA Indian Guides, 1970-74; bd. dirs. La Verne-San Dimas Reachout, 1973-76, East San Gabriel Valley Hotline,

Glendora, 1973-76; spl. olympics Del Haven Community Ctr., 1986-92. Mem. Nat. Assn. Housing and Devel. Ofcls. and Regional Bd. (v.p. 1980-81, pres. 1981-82, bd. dirs., 1982-83), West Covina Kiwanis (treas. 1988-89, v.p. 1989-91, pres. 1991-92). Roman Catholic. Office: City of West Covina 1444 W Garvey Ave West Covina CA 91790

MARKHAM, REED B., education educator, consultant; b. Alhambra, Calif., Feb. 14, 1957; s. John F. and Reeda (Bjarason) M. BA, Brigham Young U., 1982, MA, 1982; BS, Regents Coll., 1981, MA, 1982; MPA, U. So. Calif., 1983; MA, UCLA, 1989; PhD, Columbia Pacific U., 1991. Mem. faculty Brigham Young U., Provo, Utah, 1984; mem. faculty Calif. State U., Fullerton and Long Beach, 1984, Northridge, 1985; mem. faculty El Camino Coll., Torrance, Calif., 1986, Orange Coast Coll., Costa Mesa, Calif., 1986, Pasadena (Calif.) Coll., 1986, Fullerton (Calif.) Community Coll., 1986; instr., mem. pub. rels. com. Chaffey (Calif.) Coll., 1986-87; prof., CARES dir. Calif. State Poly. U., Pomona, 1987—; adj. prof. Calif. State U., L.A., 1992-93; rsch. asst. to pres. Ctr. for the Study of Community Coll., 1985; mem. faculty Riverside (Calif.) Coll., 1989-90, Rio Hondo (Calif.) Coll., 1989-90; speechwriter U.S. Supreme Ct., Washington, 1980; cons. gifted childrens program Johns Hopkins U./Scripps Coll., Claremont, Calif., 1987-88. Editor Trojan in Govt., U. So. Calif., 1983; editorial bd. Edn. Digest, Speaker and Gavel, Innovative Higher Edn., Pub. Rels. Rev., nat. Forensic Jour., The Forensic Educator, Clearinghouse for the Contemporary Educator, Hispanic Am. Family Mag.; writer for N.Y. Times, Christian Sci. Monitor; ednl. columnist San Bernadino (Calif.) Sun., 1992-93. Pres. bd. trustees Regents Coll., 1986. Mem. Doctorate Assn. N.Y. Scholars, Nat. Assn. Private Nontraditional Colls. (accrediting com. 1989—), Pub. Rels. Soc. Am. (dir.-at-large inland empire 1992-93). Republican. LDS. Home: Apt 62 8832 19th St Alta Loma CA 91701-4658 Office: Calif Polytech U Communications Dept 3801 W Temple Ave Pomona CA 91768-2557

MARKHAM, RICHARD GLOVER, research executive; b. Pasadena, Calif., June 18, 1925; s. Fred Smith and Maziebelle (Glover) M.; m. Jonne Louise Pearson, Apr. 29, 1950; children: Janet B., Fred S., Charles R., Richard G., Marilyn A. Student, Stanford U., 1943; BS, Calif. Inst. Tech., Pasadena, 1945; MS, Stanford U., 1947. Pres., owner Aquarium Pump Supply, Prescott, Ariz., 1957-78; 1st v.p., dir. Bank of Prescott, 1981-87; v.p. Oxycal Labs., Prescott, 1981—. Mem. Ariz. Dept. Econ. Planning and Devel., 1967-72; treas. Ariz. State Rep. Com., 1970-72; active Ariz. Acad., 1974—; trustee Orme Sch., Mayer, Ariz., 1970-83, Prescott Coll., 1979-83. Office: Oxycal Labs 533 Madison Ave Prescott AZ 86301

MARKIN, ROM J., college dean, marketing educator, academic administrator; b. Ironton, Ohio, Mar. 16, 1932; m. Marcia M. Coppes, Nov. 2, 1956; children: Rom Jeffrey, Jay Odell, Melinda Maria Lynch. BS, Marshall U., Huntington, W.Va., 1955; MBA, Ind. U., 1957, D Bus. Adminstrn., 1961. Instr. U. Montana, Missoula, 1957-59; asst. prof. Washington State U., Pullman, 1961-65, assoc. prof., 1965-69, prof., 1969—, chair mktg. dept., 1969-72, dir. bur. econ. and bus. research, 1972-75, dean Coll. Bus. and Econs., 1980—; bd. dirs. NW Life Assurance Co., Bellevue, Wash.; cons. Texaco, Inc., White Plains, N.Y., 1984-85, Bovay Engrs., Inc., Houston, 1985-86, Cloudy & Britton, Mountlake Terrace, Wash., 1987—. Author: The Psychology of Consumer Behavior, 1969, Retailing Management, 1971, revised edit., 1977, Russian edit., 1981, Retailing: Concepts, Institutions, and Management, 1971, Consumer Behavior: A Cognitive Orientation, 1974, Marketing, 1979, revised edit. 1982. Named Faculty Mem. Yr., Wash. State U., Pullman, 1980. Mem. Am. Mktg. Assn., Assn. Consumer Research, Acad. Mktg. Sci., Pullman (Wash.) C. of C. (sr. council). Republican. Club: Spokane. Lodge: Rotary. Office: Wash State U Coll Bus and Economics Office of the Dean Pullman WA 99164-4750

MARKOE, M. ALLEN, leasing company executive; b. St. Paul, Feb. 23, 1927; s. Julius and Bernice (Jacobson) M.; student Drake, 1947-48; BS U. Wis., 1950; m. Joan B. Lewensohn, Aug. 7, 1949; children: Guy Leigh, Sara Lynne, Robin Dawn. Owner, Diversified Bus., Milw., 1950-54; dir. mgmt. adv. svcs. Profit Counselors, Inc., Chgo., N.Y.C., 1954-60; pres. Pacific Am. Leasing Corp., Phoenix, 1961-80; ret., 1980; founder, pres. Markoe Fin. Group, Markoe Leasing; pres. AM Leasing Ltd., Phoenix; chmn., chief oper. officer Shillelagh Ventures, Chartered Pub. Co., Phoenix; ret.; owner Animal Arts Dog Grooming Studio, Phoenix, Mark O'Gold Kennels A.K.C.; bd. dirs. Sunsounds, Rio Salade Community Coll. System. With AUS, 1945-46. Mem. Am. Indsl. Devel. Coun., Ariz. Assn. Mfrs., Am. Mgmt. Assn., Soc. for Advancement Mgmt., N.Am. Soc. Sci. Mgmt., Assn. Equipment Lessors, Western Assn. Lessors, Phoenix C. of C., Am. Legion, Frat. Order Police (assoc.). Republican. Jewish. Clubs: Ariz. Aikido Kai, Lions. Home: Westbrook Village Peoria AZ 85382 Office: Animal Arts 717 W Union Hills Dr # 12B Phoenix AZ 85027-5580

MARKOS, DONALD WILLIAM, English language educator; b. LaCrosse, Wis., July 1, 1933; m. Carol I. Theisen, Feb. 23, 1957. BA, Wis. State U., 1959; MA, Mankato (Minn.) State Coll., 1961; PhD, U. Ill., 1966. Prof. Calif. State U., Hayward, 1966—. Author: Ideas in Things: The Poems of W.C. Williams, 1993; contbr. articles on Bellow, Dickey, Styron and W.C. Williams to profl. jours. Home: 5483 Greenridge Rd Castro Valley CA 94552-2621

MARKOVICH-TREECE, PATRICIA, economist; b. Oakland, Calif.; d. Patrick Joseph and Helen Emily (Prydz) Markovich; BA in Econs., MS in Econs., U. Calif.-Berkeley; postgrad. (Lilly Found. grantee) Stanford U., (NSF grantee) Oreg. Grad. Rsch. Ctr.; children: Michael Sean, Bryan Jeffry, Tiffany Helene. With pub. rels. dept. Pettler Advt., Inc.; pvt. practice polit. and econs. cons.; aide to majority whip Oreg. Ho. of Reps.; lectr., instr., various Calif. instns., Chemeketa (Oreg.) Coll., Portland (Oreg.) State U.; commr. City of Oakland (Calif.), 1970-74; chairperson, bd. dirs. Cable Sta. KCOM, Piedmont; coord. City of Piedmont, Calif. Gen. Planning Commn.; mem. Piedmont Civic Assn., Oakland Mus. Archives of Calif. Artists.; commr. Core Adv. Com. City of Oakland, Calif. Mem. Internat. Soc. Philos. Enquiry, Mensa (officer San Francisco region), Bay Area Artists Assn. (coord., founding mem.), Berkeley Art Ctr. Assn., San Francisco Arts Commn. File, Calif. Index for Contemporary Arts, Pro Arts, No. Calif. Pub. Ednl. and Govt. Access Cable TV Com. (founding), Triple Nine Soc.

MARKOWITZ, SAMUEL SOLOMON, chemistry educator; b. Bklyn., Oct. 31, 1931; s. Max and Florence Ethel (Goldman) M.; children: Michael, Daniel, Jonah. B.S. in Chemistry, Rensselaer Poly. Inst., 1953; M.A., Princeton U., 1955, Ph.D., 1957; postgrad. Brookhaven Nat. Lab., 1955-57. Asst. prof. chemistry U. Calif.-Berkeley, 1958-64, assoc. prof., 1964-72, prof., 1972—; faculty sr. scientist Lawrence Berkeley Lab., 1958—; vis. prof. nuclear physics Weizmann Inst. Sci., Rehovot, Israel, 1973-74. Mem. Bd. Edn. of Berkeley Unified Sch. Dist., 1969-73, pres. bd., 1971-72. Recipient Elizabeth McFeely D'Urso Meml. Pub. Ofcl. award Alameda County Edn. Assn., 1973; LeRoy McKay fellow Princeton U., 1955; Charlotte Elizabeth Proctor fellow Princeton U., 1956; NSF postdoctoral fellow U. Birmingham, Eng., 1957-58; NSF sr. postdoctoral fellow Faculte des Scis. de L'Universite de Paris a Orsay, Laboratoire Joliot-Curie de Physique Nucleaire, 1964-65. Fellow AAAS; mem. Am. Chem. Soc. (bd. dirs. Calif. sect., chmn. 1991, 93-94), Am. Phys. Soc., Am. Inst. Chemists, N.Y. Acad. Scis., Calif. Inst. Chemists, Sigma Xi. Home: 317 Tideway Dr Alameda CA 94501-3540 Office: U Calif Dept Chemistry Berkeley CA 94720

MARKS, ARNOLD, journalist; b. Phila., Aug. 4, 1912; s. Morris M. and Esther (Joel) M.; m. Isabelle Ruppert, Oct. 3, 1942 (dec.); 1 son, Rupert William Joel (dec.); m. Emi Seligman Simon. B.A., U. Wash., 1935; M.S., Columbia U., 1939. Editor Pasco (Wash.) Herald, 1946; with Oreg. Jour., Portland, 1946-78; drama, TV, entertainment editor Oreg. Jour., 1948-58, entertainment editor, 1958-78, ret., 1978, freelance writer. Served with AUS, 1942-46. Mem. Sigma Delta Chi, Sigma Alpha Mu. Club: University (Portland). Lodge: Pacific Sea Lions of Depoe Bay. Home: 339 Salishan Dr Box 590 Gleneden Beach OR 97388 also: 2393 SW Park Pl Portland OR 97205

MARKS, MERLE BYRON, education educator; b. Cleve., Feb. 2, 1925; s. Jack and Rose (Davis) M.; m. Patricia Frances Slensky, Dec. 24, 1947; children: Steven, Dale, Thomas. BA, Case Western Reserve U., 1948; MA, Case Western Res. U., 1949; EdD, U. So. Calif., 1960. Elem. tchr. Lennox Sch. Dist., L.A. County, Calif., 1949-52; secondary tchr. L.A. City Schs., 1952-67; tchr. tng. coord., program dir. U. So. Calif., L.A. City Schs., 1960-67; assoc. prof. edn. U. So. Calif., L.A., 1967-76, assoc. dean grad. studies, 1971-81, prof., 1976-90, prof. emeritus, 1990—; v.p. Calif. Coun. Edn. Tchrs., 1974-76, del., 1962-90. Editor-in-chief Ednl. Rsch. Quar., 1978-84, manuscript evaluator, 1984-91; contbr. articles to profl. jours. Ensign USN, 1943-46, PTO. Mem. Am. Assn. Colls. of Tchr. Edn. (Calif. chpt. exec. bd. dirs. 1979-81), Calif. Coun. Edn. of Tchrs. (v.p., bd. dirs.), Am. Ednl. Rsch. Assn., Assn. Tchr. Educators, Phi Delta Kappa (AE chpt. Leadership award 1978, Svc. award 1974, Rsch. award 1983). Office: 5227 Shenandoah Ave Los Angeles CA 90056

MARKS, MERTON ELEAZER, lawyer; b. Chgo., Oct. 16, 1932; s. Alfred Tobias and Helene Fannie (Rosner) M.; m. Radee Maiden Feiler, May 20, 1966; children: Sheldon, Elise Marks Vazelakis, Alan, Elaine Marks Ianchiou. BS, Northwestern U., 1954, JD, 1956. Bar: Ill. 1956, U.S. Ct. Mil. Appeals 1957, Ariz. 1958, U.S. Dist. Ct. Ariz. 1960, U.S. Ct. Appeals (9th cir.) 1962, U.S. Supreme Ct. 1970. Assoc. Moser, Compere & Emerson, Chgo., 1956-57; ptnr. Morgan, Marks & Rogers, Tucson, 1960-62; asst. atty. gen. State of Ariz., Phoenix, 1962-64, counsel indsl. commn., 1964-65; from assoc. to ptnr. Shimmel, Hill, Bishop & Greunder, Phoenix, 1965-74; ptnr. Lewis & Roca, Phoenix, 1974—; lectr. on pharm., health care, product liability, ins. and employers' liability subjects. Contbr. more than 30 articles to various tort and ins. sbujs. to profl. jours. Capt. JAGC, USAR, 1957-64. Mem. ABA (tort and ins. practice sect., chmn. spl. com. on fed. asbestos legislation 1987-89, chmn. workers' compensation and employers liability law com. 1983-84), Am. Bd. Trial Advocates, Am. Coll. Legal Medicine, Internat. Bar Assn., Am. Soc. Pharmacy Law, State Bar Ariz. (chmn. workers' compensation sect. 1969-73), Nat. Coun. Self Insurers, Ariz. Self Insurers Assn., Fedn. Ins. and Corp. Counsel (chmn. pharm. litigation sect. 1989-91, mem. workers' compensation sect. 1977-79, chmn., 1977-79, v.p. 1978-79, 81, bd. dirs. 1981-89), Internat. Assn. Defense Counsel, Ariz. Assn. Defense Counsel (pres. 1976-77), Maricopa County Bar Assn., Defense Rsch. Inst. (mem. drug and device com., chmn. workers' compensation com. 1977-78). Office: Lewis & Roca 40 N Central Ave Phoenix AZ 85004-4424

MARKS, MILTON, state senator; b. San Francisco, July 22, 1920; s. Milton and Olita M. (Meyer) M.; B.A., Stanford U., 1940; LL.B., San Francisco Law Sch., 1949; m. Carolene Wachenheimer, Aug. 14, 1955; children—Carol, Milton, Edward David. Mem. Calif. Assembly, from 1959; judge mcpl. ct., San Francisco, 1966-67; mem. Calif. Senate, 1967—, chmn. election coms., select com. on maritime industry, com. on disabled. Bd. dirs. Nat. Council on Alcoholism, Calif. League for Handicapped, St. Anthony's Dining Room, Mex. Am. Polit. Assn., Chinese-Am. Citizens Alliance. Served with U.S. Army, World War II. Recipient numerous awards including: Bronze Key award Nat. Council on Alcoholism; Man of Yr. award Council for Civic Unity of San Francisco Bay Area, 1973; Legislator of Yr. award Calif. Assn. Physically Handicapped, 1973; Consumer Legislator of Yr. award, 1981; Calif. Preservation award, 1982; Legislator of Yr. award Students of Calif. State Univ. System; Legislator of Yr. award Planning and Conservation League Calif., 1984. Mem. Am. Legion, VFW. Democrat. Jewish. Club: Press Club (San Francisco). Lodge: Lions. Office: 711 Van Ness Ave Ste 310 San Francisco CA 94102

MARKS, PETER AMASA, technical company administrator; b. Passaic, N.J., Dec. 5, 1948; s. Amasa A. and Eunice L. (Irwin) M.; BS in Design Engrng., U. Cin., 1972, MA in Media Communications, 1973, postgrad. in human factors engrng. Rsch. asst. dept. mech. engrng. U. Cin., 1972; sr. engr. Ford Motor Co., Sharonville, Ohio, 1972-75; prin. Design Insight Cin., 1976—; mng. dir. SDRC TEC Services, Milford, Ohio, 1978-84, dir. product planning and devel., SDRC, Inc., Milford, 1981-84; sr. v.p. ops. Automation Tech., Campbell, Calif., 1985-88; lectr., cons. on product design tech. implementation, U.S., Asia, Europe, also for Am. Mgmt. Assns. Grad. fellow; Gen. Motors grantee in design, 1970; winner nat., internat. competitions for tech. programs. Mem. ASME, IEEE Computer Soc., Soc. Mfg. Engrs., Nat. Computer Graphics Assn., Computer and Automated Systems Assn. (bd. dirs.), Mensa. Author books, articles and films in field. Home: 55 Church St Los Gatos CA 95032-6920 Office: Design Insight PO Box 37 Los Gatos CA 95031-0037

MARKS, ROBERT ARTHUR, lawyer; b. Dayton, Ohio, Oct. 9, 1952; s. Arthur Kenneth and Patricia (Wolf) M.; m. Victoria S. Curlock, Oct. 21, 1978; two sons. BA, U. Wis., 1974; JD, U. Cin., 1977. Bar: Ohio 1977, Hawaii 1978, U.S. Ct. Appeals (6th cir.) Ohio 1977, U.S. Ct. Appeals (9th cir.) Hawaii 1978, U.S. Supreme Ct. 1992. Pvt. practice Honolulu, 1978-84; dep. atty. gen. State of Hawaii, Honolulu, 1984-87, supervisory dept. atty. gen., 1987-92, 1st dep. atty. gen., 1992, atty. gen., 1992—. Office: Hawaii Dept Atty Gen 425 Queen St Honolulu HI 96813

MARKS, ROBERT WILLIAM, engineering manager, lawyer; b. Frankfort, Ind., Nov. 14, 1952; s. R. Adrian and Elta F. M.; m. Cynthia Heath, July 9, 1982; children: Ethan, Ruth. BS in Land Survey Engrng., Purdue U., 1975; JD, U. Wash., 1978. Bar: Wash. 1978. Engineering mgr. Custom Iron Co., Pacific, Wash., 1981—. Facility com. mem. S. Cen. Sch. Dist., Tukwila, Wash., 1981—. Home: 14455 58th S Tukwila WA 98168 Office: Custom Iron Co 102 Frontage Rd S Pacific WA 98047

MARKS, SHARON LEA, nurse; b. Arroyo Grande, Calif., June 12, 1942; d. Donald Elmore and Gertrude (Grieb) Shaffer; m. George Conrad Schmidt, June 23, 1963 (div. 1975); children: Kerrilynn, Robert, Marianne; m. Keith Dalton Marks, June 4, 1978; children: Joseph, Erik, Alice. Diploma, Sch. Nursing Samuel Merritt Hosp., 1963; BS in Nursing, Lewis and Clark State Coll., 1984, BS in Mgmt., 1986. RN, Calif., Wash. Staff nurse Vesper Meml. Hosp., San Leandro, Calif., 1968-74; night nurse supr. Tuolumne Gen. Hosp., Sonora, Calif., 1975; nurse Orleans (Calif.) Search and Rescue Team, 1975-78; instr. nursing Pasadena (Calif.) City Coll., 1978-79; resource coord. learning ctr. div. health sci. Spokane (Wash.) Community Coll., 1979-84; staff nurse Kootenai Med. Ctr., 1979-85; instr. North Idaho Coll., Coeur d'Alene, 1984-85; staff nurse North Idaho Home Health, Coeur d'Alene, 1985-86; coord. br. office Family Home Care, Spokane, 1986-87; devel., dir. Good Samaritan Home Health Plummer, Idaho and Fairfield, Washington, 1987-88; mgr. patient svcs. VNS Seattle-King County, Tukwila, Wash., 1988-89; co-owner, v.p. The Wooden Boat Shop, Seattle, 1989—; instr. in emergency med. tech. Orleans campus Coll. Redwoods, Eureka, Calif., 1977-78; book reviewer Brady Co.; film reviewer Olympia Media Info. Mem. Nat. Head Injury Found., Wash. State Head Injury Found. Office: Wooden Boat Shop 1007 NE Boat St Seattle WA 98105-6708

MARKS, WILLIAM J., cable television owner; b. Akron, Ohio, May 24, 1944; s. Richard D. and B. Katherine (Duell) M.; m. Patricia Ann Marks (div. 1985); children: William J., Lanetta; m. Donna Morgan, Apr. 25, 1985. BSME, Akron U., 1966; Hon. PhD, Heed U., Hollywood, Fla., 1980. Exec. v.p., owner Am. Video Corp., Ft. Lauderdale, Fla., 1968-75; founder Coral Springs Cablevision, Inc., West Boca CableVision, Inc., Marks Cablevision of Ohio; owner, pres. Planned Cable Systems, Inc., San Francisco, 1975—; owner, operator The Marks Group; bd. dirs. Insight Comm., Ltd., U.K., 1990— Equitable Banks of Dallas; owner The Marks Group. Mem. Shriners, Masons, Pioneers Club. Home: 2755 Fillmore St San Francisco CA 94123-4700 also: 4639 O'Connor Ct Irving TX 75062

MARLANTES, LEO, academic administrator, educator; b. Seaside, Oreg., Nov. 9, 1916; s. Konstantinos Elias and Sophia Marlantes; m. Elna Elizabeth Erickson, Aug. 7, 1941; children: Lorian Louis, Karl Arthur. BS, U. Oreg., 1940, MEd, 1952; EdD, U. Fla., 1966. Tchr. Seaside High Sch., 1948-56, prin., 1956-62; acad. dean Clatsop Community Coll., Astoria, Oreg., 1962-64, Mt. Hood Community Coll., Gresham, Oreg., 1966-78; cons. Oreg. State Dept. Edn., Salem, 1978-80, ret., 1980. Lt. U.S. Army, 1941-46, maj. USNG. Mem. Am. Legion, Rotary (program chmn. 1986-90), Masons, Shriners.

MARLER, LARRY JOHN, total quality leadership consultant; b. Chgo., Sept. 22, 1940; s. Walter William and Lena Inez (Killen) M.; m. Katy Jo Hibbits, Oct. 17, 1962 (div. Apr. 1971); 1 child, Preston Scott; m. Linda Lee Sorg, Sept. 2, 1982. BA, Christian Coll. Am., 1987; MA, Houston Grad. Sch. Theology, 1988; PhD, U.S. Internat. U., San Deigo, 1992. Acct. Shell Oil Co., New Orleans and Houston, 1964-73; acctg. supr. We. Geophys. Co. Am., Houston, 1974; payroll supr. Olsen Inc., Houston, 1975-77; corp. credit mgr. Grant Corps., Houston, 1977-82; rschr., student contractor Navy Pers. R&D Ctr., San Deigo, 1990-92; pres. Creditmart, Inc., Denver, 1993—. Served with USCG, 1959-62. Mem. Am. Psychol. Soc., Am. Soc. Quality Control, Toastmasters Internat. Republican. Protestant.

MARLETT, DE OTIS LORING, retired management consultant; b. Indpls., Apr. 19, 1911; s. Peter Loring and Edna Grace (Lombard) M.; m. Ruth Irene Pillar, Apr. 10, 1932 (dec. Feb. 1969); children: De Otis Neal, Marilynn Ruth; m. Marie Manning Ostrander, May 1, 1970 (dec. Apr. 1982); m. Peggie P. Whittlesey, Jan. 15, 1983. B.A., M.A., U. Wis., 1934; postgrad., Northwestern U., (part time), 1934-39, Harvard U.; postgrad. (Littauer fellow in econs. and govt.), 1946-47. C.P.A., Wis., 1935. Staff mem. Ill. Commerce Commn., 1934-39; lectr. in econs. and pub. utilities Northwestern U., (part time), 1936-39; staff mem. Bonneville Power Adminstrn., U.S. Dept. Interior, 1939-45, asst. adminstr., 1945-52; acting adminstr. Def. Electric Power Adminstrn., 1950-51; asst. to v.p., gen. mgr. Dicalite and Perlite divs. Gt. Lakes Carbon Corp., 1952-53, v.p., also gen. mgr. Dicalite, Perlite, Mining and Minerals divs., 1953-62, v.p. property investment dept., 1962-81; pres., chief exec. officer Great Lakes Properties, Inc., 1981-83, ret., 1983; past pres., dir. Rancho Palos Verdes Corp., G.L.C. Bldg. Corp., Del Amo Energy Co., Torrance Energy Co.; former mem. L.A. arbitration panel N.Y. Stock Exch. Contbr. articles and reports on public utility regulation, operation and mgmt. to profl. jours. Past bd. dirs. United Cerebral Palsy Assn. Los Angeles County; bd. dirs., past co-chmn. So. Calif. region NCCJ, mem. nat. trustee, mem. nat. exec. bd., nat. protestant co-chmn., 1987-90; past mem. Orthopaedic Hosp. Adv. Coun.; past trustee City of Hope; past pres., dir. Los Angeles area coun., past chmn. relationships com., past pres. Sunshine area, pres. Western region Boy Scouts Am., 1978-81, nat. exec. bd., 1978-88, past mem. nat. exec. com., past chmn. properties com., chmn. logistics for world jamboree delegation to Australia, 1987-88; past trustee Nat. Scouting Mus.; mem. internat. com. Baden Powell fellow World Scouting Found., 1984; past mem. Western Govs. Mining Adv. Coun., Calif. State Mining Bd.; bd. govs. Western div. Am. Mining Congress, chmn., 1962-63; incorporator, past pres., bd. dirs. Torrance Meml. Med. Center Health Care Found.; region III dir., mem. corp. adminstrn. and fin. com., Los Angeles United Way. Recipient Disting. Service medal U.S. Dept. Interior, 1952; named knight Order of Crown Belgium; commd. Ky. Col.; recipient Silver Beaver, Silver Antelope, Silver Buffalo awards Boy Scouts Am., 1984. Mem. AIME, AICPA, Fin. Execs. Inst., L.A. World Affairs Coun., Wis. Alumni Assn., Perlit Inst. (past pres., dir.), L.A. C. of C. (past dir., chmn. mining com.), Mining Assn. So. Calif. (past pres., dir.), Calif. Mine Operators Assn. (past dir.), Bldg. Industry Assn. So. Calif., Calif. Club, Portuguese Bend Club (past pres.), Palos Verdes Bay Club (past v.p.), Phi Kappa Phi, Beta Gamma Sigma, Phi Beta Kappa, Beta Alpha Psi, Lambda Alpha Internat. Democrat. Home: 32759 Seagate Dr Apt 204 Rancho Palos Verdes CA 90274

MARMADUKE, ARTHUR SANDFORD, educational administrator; b. Long Beach, Calif., May 29, 1926; s. William Sandford and Nina Belle (Romberger) M.; m. Carolyn Ann Tilden, Aug. 21, 1949; children: Jennifer, Stephen, Scott. AB, Occidental Coll., 1950; MPA, U. Mich., 1952; DPA (hon.), U. Pacific, 1970. Adminstrv. analyst Office Legis. Analyst Calif. State Legis., Sacramento, 1951-55; dir. admissions Occidental Coll., L.A., 1955-60; dir. Calif. Student Aid Commn., Sacramento, 1960-85; exec. dir. Eureka Project, Sacramento, 1986-90; dir. Independent Solution Project, 1989-91; cons. Weingart Found., 1987, Bush Found., 1985; vice chmn. nat. task force on student aid programs KEppel Com., 1974-75; chmn. Coll. Scholarship Svc., Coll. Entrance Examination Bd., 1967-69; mem. planning com., dir. Calif. Higher Edn. Policy Ctr., 1991—. Contbr. author several student aid books. Trustee Sacramento Country Day Sch. Recipient Disting. Service award Calif. Student Fin. Aid Adminstrs., 1982, Raol Wallenberg New Traditional High Sch., San Francisco, 1985, Coll. Bd. Scholarship Service, N.Y.C., 1985. Home: 1516 Del Dayo Dr Carmichael CA 95608-6011 Office: 564 La Sierra Dr # 122 Sacramento CA 95864

MARONDE, ROBERT FRANCIS, internist, clinical pharmacologist, educator; b. Monterey Park, Calif., Jan. 13, 1920; s. John August and Emma Florence (Palmer) M.; m. Yolanda Cerda, Apr. 15, 1970; children—Robert George, Donna F. Maronde Varnau, James Augustus, Craig DeWald. B.A., U. So. Calif., 1941, M.D., 1944. Diplomate: Am. Bd. Internal Medicine. Intern L.A. County-U. So. Calif. Med. Ctr., 1943-44, resident, 1944-45, 47-48; asst. prof. physiology U. So. Calif., L.A., 1948-49, asst. clin. prof. medicine, 1949-60, assoc. clin. prof. medicine, 1960-65, assoc. prof. medicine and pharmacology, 1965-67, prof. medicine and pharmacology, 1968-90, emeritus, 1990—, prof. emeritus, 1990—; spl. asst. v.p. for health affairs, 1990—; cons. FDA, 1973, Med. Co. Containment, Inc., 1991—. Served to lt. (j.g.) USNR, 1945-47. Fellow ACP; mem. Am. Soc. Clin. Pharmacology and Therapeutics, Alpha Omega Alpha. Home: 785 Ridgecrest St Monterey Park CA 91754-3759 Office: U So Calif 2025 Zonal Ave Los Angeles CA 90033-4526

MAROTTA, GEORGE RAYMOND, money manager, research institute fellow; b. Scotia, N.Y., Oct. 6, 1926; s. Giuseppi and Rosa (Fasulo) M.; m. June Alison Mortlock, Aug. 29, 1948; children: Raymond, Paul, David. AB, Syracuse U., 1950, MPA, 1951; cert. fin. planner. Mgmt. officer Dept. State, Washington, 1951-53; planner, coordinator Nat. Security Council, Washington, 1953-61; Univ. relations officer Peace Corps, Washington, 1961-62; internat. security planner Dept. Defense, Washington, 1962-67; foreign service reserve officer Agency Internat. Devel., Washington, 1967-75; pub. affairs coordinator Hoover Instn., Stanford, Calif., 1975-84, research fellow, 1977—; investment portfolio mgr. Marotta Money Mgmt., Inc. Recipient Meritorious Honor award Agency Internat. Devel., 1968, Honorable Achievement award Pub. Relations Soc. Am., 1980. Mem. Registry Fin. Planning Practitioners, Internat. Assn. Fin. Planners, Inst. Cert. Fin. Planners, Pub. Relations Soc. Am. (accredited mem.). Office: Stanford U Hoover Instn Stanford CA 94305

MARQUARD, PAUL JOSEPH, astronomy and physics educator; b. Cleve., Sept. 1, 1958; s. Conrad and Agnes (Bergantino) M.; m. Anne Elizabeth Schafer, Nov. 29, 1986; children: Jana Katharine, Samantha Laura. BS in Physics, Creighton U., 1979; MSEE, U. So. Calif., L.A., 1981; MS, U. Nebr., 1986. Instr. Casper (Wyo.) Coll., 1986—. Republican. Roman Catholic. Home: 1624 Begonia St Casper WY 82604-3764 Office: Casper Coll 125 College Dr Casper WY 82601-4699

MARQUARDT, LLOYD B., electrical engineer; b. Volga, S.D., Oct. 24, 1952; s. Lloyd B. and Alice (Bundy) M.; m. Cheryl Marquardt (dec. 1990), m. Marilynn Lani Moore, Oct. 30, 1991; 1 child, Allison. BSEE, S.D. Sch. of Mines & Tech., 1975. Divsn. engr. Northwestern Pub. Svc. Co., Huron, S.D., 1975-79, relay engr., 1979-83; city elec. engr. City of Pierre, S.D., 1983-86; sr. hardware engr. ESCA Corp., Bellevue, Wash., 1986-91; prin. engr. R. W. Beck & Assocs., Seattle, 1991—. Patent grounding device, 1978. Mem. IEEE. Home: 721 218th Ave Redmond WA 98053

MARQUESS, LAWRENCE WADE, lawyer; b. Bloomington, Ind., Mar. 2, 1950; s. Earl Lawrence and Mary Louise (Coberly) M.; m. Barbara Ann Bailey, June 17, 1978; children: Alexander Lawrence, Michael Wade. BS in Elec. Engrng., Purdue U., 1973; JD, W.Va. U., 1977. Bar: W.Va. 1977, Tex. 1977, U.S. Dist. Ct. (so. dist.) W.Va. 1977, U.S. Dist. Ct. (no. dist.) Tex. 1977, Colo. 1980, U.S. Dist. Ct. Colo. 1980, U.S. Ct. Appeals (10th cir.) 1980, U.S. Supreme Ct. 1984, U.S. Dist. Ct. (no. dist.) Ohio 1988. Assoc. Johnson, Bromberg, Leeds & Riggs, Dallas, 1977-79, Bradley, Campbell & Carney, Golden, Colo., 1979-82, ptnr., 1983-84; assoc. Stettner, Miller & Cohn P.C., Denver, 1984-85, ptnr., 1985-87; of counsel Nelson & Harding, Denver, 1987-88, Heron, Burchette, Ruckert & Rothwell, 1989-90, Harding & Ogborn, 1990—. Mem. faculty Am. Law Inst.-ABA Advanced Labor and Employment Law Course, 1986, 87. Mem. ABA (labor and litigation sects.), Colo. Bar Assn. (co-chmn. labor law com. 1989-92), Denver Bar Assn., 1st Jud. Dist. Bar Assn., Sierra Club, Nat. Ry. Hist. Soc., ACLU. Democrat. Methodist. Home: 11883 W 27th Dr Lakewood CO 80215-7003 Office: Harding & Ogborn 1200 17th St Ste 1000 Denver CO 80202-5810

MARQUEZ, ALFREDO C., federal judge; b. 1922; m. Linda Nowobilsky. B.S., U. Ariz., 1948, J.D., 1950. Bar: Ariz. Practice law Mesch Marquez & Rothschild, 1957-80; asst. atty. gen. State of Ariz., 1951-52; asst. county atty. Pima County, Ariz., 1953-54; adminstrv. asst. to Congressman

Stewart Udall, 1955; judge U.S. Dist. Ct. Ariz., Tucson, 1980—. Served with USN, 1942-45. Office: US Dist Ct US Courthouse Rm 327 55 E Broadway Blvd Tucson AZ 85701-1719

MARQUEZ, ANTHONY PHILIP, lawyer; b. L.A., Oct. 10, 1950; s. Tony Marquez and Helen (Ruiz) Frescas. BA, Columbia U., 1972; JD, Harvard U., 1975. Bar: N.Mex. 1976, Calif. 1978, Tex. 1986. Mng. atty. Legal Aid Soc., Albuquerque, 1975-77; legal counsel Legis. Counsel, Sacramento, Calif., 1977-78; asst. atty gen. Atty. Gen. Office, Santa Fe, N.Mex., 1978-82; chief counsel Transp. Dept., Santa Fe, 1982-83, deputy sec., 1983-84; adminstrv. asst. N.Mex. Supreme Ct., Santa Fe, 1984-86; ptnr. Diamond & Marquez, El Paso, Tex., 1986-88; dep. counsel Legis Counsel, Sacramento, 1988-89; chief counsel Joint Legis. Ethics Com., Sacramento, 1989—; contracts com. mem. Nat. Transp. Bd., Washington, 1979-84; supreme ct. liaison, N.Mex. Compilation Commn., Santa Fe., 1984-86; pro tem judge Superior Ct., Sacramento, 1989—. Editor Harvard Civil Rights-Civil Liberties Law Rev., 1974; staff mem. Harvard Civil Liberties Law Rev., 1973-74. Del. Dem. Cen. Com., Albuquerque, 1984; mem. Santa Fe City Arts Bd., 1983-86; mem. adv. bd. Hidden Gallery, 1989, Bridge Gallery, El Paso, Tex., 1986-87; mem. Sacramento Met. Arts Commn., 1991, chair, 1992—; bd. dirs. Calif. Confedn. of Arts, 1991—, sec., 1992—; mem. NEA Local Arts Agys. Panel, 1992-93, State-Local Partnership Panel, 1992; active NEA Guidelines, Pres.' Initiative on Rural Am., 1992-93. Recipient Outstanding Service award, N.Mex. Supreme Ct., Santa Fe, 1985, Outstanding Young Man award, Jaycees, 1978, Outstanding Service award, Legal Assts. of N.Mex., Albuquerque, 1986. Mem. ABA (task force on undocumented workers 1978-81), Capitol Latino Staff Assn., La Raza Lawyers Assn., Ferrari Club Am., Sports Car Club Am., Inc. Democrat. Roman Catholic. Office: Joint Legis Ethics Com Sacramento CA 95814

MARQUEZ, MARTINA ZENAIDA, reading educator; b. Santa Rosa, N.Mex., Nov. 5, 1935; d. Jose Zenon and Adelina (Romero) Sanchez; m. George J. Marquez, June 17, 1972. Student, Mt. St. Scholastica Coll., 1954-56, Regis Coll., 1956-59; BA, Coll. Santa Fe, 1963; MA, U. N.Mex., 1968. Cert. tchr., N.Mex. Elem. tchr. St. Rose Lima Sch., Santa Rosa, 1959-67, Cristo Rey Sch., Santa Fe, 1967-68, Los Lunas (N,Mex.) Consol. Schs., 1975-78, head tchr. adults operation; SER Manpower Devel. Tng. Act, Albuquerque, 1968-71, 73-75; tchr., cons. Regional Resource Ctr., N.Mex. State U., Las Cruces, 1971-72; counselor, coord. Taos (N.Mex.) Career Edn. Program, 1972-73; chpt. I reading tchr. Grants (N.Mex.) & Cibola County Schs., 1978—; chmn. ethics com. Profl. Standards Commn., N.Mex. Dept. Edn., 1986-88. Dir. choir St. Vivian's Ch., Milan, N.Mex., 1978—; del. Dem. Women's Club, Grants, N.Mex., 1981—; v.p. Literacy Vols. Am. of Cibola County. Selected as 1991 Cibola County Woman of Achievement 3rd Ann. Women's Resource Conf. Mem. AAUW (bylaws chmn. 1984—, Grants Woman of Yr. award 1988), Internat. Reading Assn. (1st v.p. Malpais coun.1988-89. pres. 1989-90, state pres, 1992-93, Local Literacy award 1986, State Literacy award 1987, state pres. N.Mex. 1992-93), Delta Kappa Gamma (pres. Psi chpt. 1986-88). Democrat. Roman Catholic. Home: PO Box 11 Bluewater NM 87005-0011 Office: Grants-Cibola County Schs Jemez and Del Norte Sts Grants NM 87020

MARRA, P(ETER) GERALD, manufacturers' representative distributor firm executive; b. Cranbrook, B.C., Can., June 29, 1940; came to U.S., 1964, naturalized, 1973; s. John and Angela Rose Marra; BSc, U. B.C., 1963, postgrad., 1963-64; divorced; children: Amber Eileen, Anne-Marie Geraldine. Computer engr. Canadair Ltd., Montreal, Que., 1962-63; rsch. engr. Boeing Corp., Seattle, 1964-68; hardware specialist Computer Sci. Corp., Toronto, Ont., Can., 1969; pres., gen. mgr. D.I.S.C., Seattle, 1970-74; sales mgr. Hayes Tech. Co., Seattle, 1975; owner, pres. Marra & Assocs., Bellevue, Wash., 1976—; cons. small bus., 1970—. Republican party platform chmn. King County, 1976-78, legis. dist. chmn., 1978; pres., dir. fundraising for U. B.C., Friends of U. B.C., 1975—; asst. chmn. archery com. Wash. State Sportsmen's Council, 1980, chmn., 1981-83, chmn. big game com. 1981-83; mem. Mt. Rainier Wildlife Com., 1981—. IBM scholar, 1964. Mem. Can. Soc. of Northwest (exec. com. 1985-88), U. B.C. Alumni (pres. Seattle, Pacific N.W. chpt. 1974-90). Clubs: Cedar River, Bowman Archery, Bellevue Athletic. Home: 1739 172d Pl NE Bellevue WA 98008

MARRINGTON, BERNARD HARVEY, retired automotive company executive; b. Vancouver, B.C., Can., Nov. 9, 1928; s. Fredrick George and Constance Marie (Hall) M.; m. Patricia Grace Hall, Sept. 3, 1953; children: Jodie Lynn, Stacey Lee. Student, U. Pitts., 1982, Bethany Coll., W.Va., 1983; BS in Mktg. Mgmt., Pacific Western U., 1985. V.p., sales mgr. W & L of La Mesa, Calif., 1960-66; pres., gen. mgr. W & L of La Mesa, 1966-68; regional sales mgr. PPG Industries, Inc., L.A., 1977-88, regional mgr. profit ctr., 1988-91; cons. L.A. Unified Sch. Dist., 1972, South Coast Air Quality Mgmt. Dist., El Monte, Calif., 1987-91; adv. com. So. Calif. Regional Occupational Ctr., Torrance, 1978-91. Contbr. articles to profl. jours. Sustaining sponsor Ronald Reagan Presdl. Found., Simi, 1987; sustaining mem. Rep. Nat. Com., L.A., 1985-92; del. Rep. Platform Planning Com., L.A., 1992; charter mem. Nat. Tax Limitation Com., Washington, 1988, Jarvis Gann Taxpayers Assn., L.A., 1979-92; sponsor Regan Presdl. Libr., 1989-92. Recipient Award for Outstanding Community Support, So. Calif. Regional Occupational Ctr., 1986. Episcopalian.

MARROW, MARVA JAN, photographer, author; b. Denver, Apr. 22, 1948; d. Sydney and Helen Berniece (Garber) M. Student, Carnegie-Mellon U., 1965-67. Singer, songwriter RCA Records, Italy, 1972-77; pvt. practice photography Italy and U.S., 1976—; dir. acquisitions RAI TV, L.A., 1990-91; mgn. agt. Thomas Angel Prodns., L.A., 1991—; represented by Shooting Star Photo Agy., Agenzia Marka, Agenzia Masi, Italy, Uniphoto Press Internat., Japan; corr., photographer Italian TV Guide, Milan, 1979—; collaborator, photographer for other U.S. and European publs., radio and TV; TV news and documentary prodr. RAI TV, 1990—. Author numerous songs for Italian pop artists, including: Lucio Battisti, Battiato, Premiata Forneria Marconi (PFM), Patty Pravo, 1972—; author: (photobook) Inside the L.A. Artist, 1988; contbr. photographs for covers and articles to nat. and internat. mags. Mem. Motion Picture Assn. of Am., Fgn. Press Assn. Democrat. Home and Studio: 2080 N Garfield Ave Altadena CA 91001 Office: Shooting Star Agy PO Box 93368 Los Angeles CA 90093-0368

MARRS, LEO RICHARD, JR., corporate executive, educator; b. Birmingham, Ala., June 29, 1949; s. Leo Richard Sr. and Oma Lee (Stone) M.; m. Penny Ann Boals, Dec. 26, 1971; children: Hilary Anne, Thomas Richard. BA, U. So. Ala., 1974; MBA, U. Phoenix, 1985. Lab. asst. U. So. Ala., Mobile, 1973-75; rep. Marrs Electric Co., Tarrant, Ala., 1975-79; buyer Magma Copper Co., San Manuel, Ariz., 1979-81; sr. buyer Magma Copper Co., San Manuel, 1981-85, materials control supr., 1985-86, chief warehouse supr., 1986, warehousing mgr., 1986-89, bus. devel. analyst, 1989-91, dir. corp. devel., 1991; mem. faculty U. Phoenix, 1987—. Mem. Nat. Assn. Purchasing Mgmt., Purchasing Mgmt. Assn. So. Ariz., Am. Prodn. and Inventory Control Soc. Methodist. Home: 12431 N Wayfarer Way Tucson AZ 85737-8966 Office: Magma Copper Co 7400 N Oracle Rd Ste 200 Tucson AZ 85704-6357

MARS, ROBERT, lawyer, real estate associate, financial planner; b. Willimantic, Conn., May 11, 1955; s. David and Marien (Weisser) M. BS, U. So. Calif., L.A., 1977, MPA, JD, 1980. Bar: Calif. 1980, U.S. Dist. Ct. (cen. dist.) Calif. 1984, U.S. Ct. Appeals (9th cir.) 1984, U.S. Supreme Ct. 1989. Pvt. practice Torrance, Calif., 1980—. Named One of Top Ten Environ. Attys. U.S. Mem. Calif. Trial Lawyers Assn., L.A. Trial Lawyers Assn. Home and Office: 3838 W Carson St 3d Flr Torrance CA 90503-6703

MARSH, FRANK RAYMOND, engineering technical writer; b. Waterville, Maine, Aug. 5, 1938; s. Gerald Raymond and Dorothy Marion (Haines) M. B of Gen. Studies, Chaminade U., Honolulu, 1968; BFA, Otis Art Inst., 1971, MFA, 1973; BS in Computer Sci., West Coast U., 1984, MS in Computer Sci., 1986, MIBA, 1987, MMIS, 1988, MSMIS, 1990, BS in Elec. Engring., 1993. Editor, cartographer Thomas Bros. Maps, L.A., 1974-80; engring. writer Singer Co., Glendale, Calif., 1983-87; sr. tech. writer Amperpif Corp., Chatsworth, Calif., 1987-89; prin. engring. writer Litton Data Systems, Van Nuys, Calif., 1990—. One-man shows includes Westwood (Calif.) Art Assn., 1973, Westwood Ctr. of the Arts, 1975, Villa Montalvo, Saratoga, Calif., 1975, Sr. Eye Gallery, Long Beach, Calif., 1979, 81, Studio 1617 Gallery, L.A., 1984; numerous group exhbns. and juried invitationals; permanent collections include Detroit Mortgage Co., Gulf and Western, Homes Savs. and Loan Bank, Otis Art Inst., Palmcrest Ho., United Calif. Bank. Mem. L.A. Art Mus. Graphics Coun., 1976—. With USAF, 1961-69. Mem. AIAA, IEEE, Artists Equity, L.A. Printmaking Soc., Soc. for Tech. Comm., Ann. for Computing Machinery, Math. Assn. of Am., Litton Mgmt. Club. Home: 2800 Lambert Dr Los Angeles CA 90068

MARSH, JAMES ROBERT, federal law enforcement official; b. Grosse Pointe Farms, Mich., June 26, 1947; s. Robert George and Mary Elizabeth (McDonald) M.; m. Nancy Lynn Beaty, Feb. 26, 1982; children: Jason Robert, Matthew James. BS in Police Adminstrn., Mich. State U., 1969; MA in Sociology, U. Detroit, 1974. Supr. Mich. Bell Telephone Co., Lansing, 1968-70; probation officer Oakland County Circuit Ct., Pontiac, Mich., 1970-76; probation officer ea. dist. Mich. U.S. Dist. Ct., Detroit, 1976-82; probation officer no. dist. Tex. U.S. Dist. Ct., Dallas, 1982-84; chief pretrial svcs. officer dist. Nev. U.S. Dist. Ct., Las Vegas, 1984—; regional rep. Chiefs' Mgmt. Coun., Washington, 1990-93; chmn. Pretrial Svcs. Com., Washington, 1990-93; co-chmn. Pretrial Svcs. Supervision Task Force, Washington, 1991—. Pres. Oakland County Corrections Assn., Pontiac, 1975; chmn., bd. dirs. Help Ctr. Drug Program, Highland, Mich., 1978. Methodist. Office: US Pretrial Svcs 330 S 3d St Ste 820 Las Vegas NV 89101

MARSH, JOHN HARRISON, environmental planner, lawyer; b. Auburn, Wash., June 25, 1954; s. F. A. Buzz and Margery Ann (Greene) M.; m. Debra Rose Raniere, June 18, 1977; children: Jenna Rose, Christian John. BS in Fisheries Scis., Oreg. State U., 1977; JD, Lewis & Clark Coll., 1985, cert. natural resources and environ. law, 1985. Bar: Oreg. 1986. Rsch. asst. EPA, Corvallis, Oreg., 1975-77; fisheries biologist Nat. Marine Fisheries Svc., Portland, Oreg., 1977-78, Oreg. Dept. Fish and Wildlife, Astoria, 1978; pub. info. officer Columbia River Inter-Tribal Fish Commn., Portland, 1978-79, fisheries biologist, 1979-85; system planning coord. N.W. Power Planning Coun., Portland, 1985—; speaker, expert witness in field; guest lectr. Lewis and Clark Coll., 1984. Contbr. articles to profl. publs. Organizer food drive Friends of Seasonal Workers, 1987; chair ann. NPPC food drive Sunshine Div., 1987-91; bd. dirs. Panavista Park Homeowners Assn., 1991, mem. archtl. rev. com., 1990—, chair, 1991—; Leader, Sunday sch. instr. grades 4-6 Riverwest Ch., 1992—; asst. scoutmaster Boy Scouts Am., 1972-73. Mem. Am. Fisheries Soc. (cert. profl. fisheries scientist, exec. com. Portland chpt. 1981-84, v.p. 1981-82, pres. 1982-83, chair legis. com. Oreg. chpt. 1988-89, program com. 1980-81, riparian com. Western div. 1982-83, convenor various sessions, mem. various nat. coms.), Oreg. State Bar Assn., Native Am. Fish and Wildlife Assn., Knights of the Vine, Great Lovers of Wine Soc. Oreg. (pres. 1988). Office: NW Power Planning Coun 851 SW 6th Ave Ste 1100 Portland OR 97204

MARSH, KENNETH LEE, chemist; b. St. Petersburg, Fla., May 30, 1952; s. Stan and Estelle Juliet (Milch) M.; m. Sharon Leslie Weekes, July 1, 1983 (div. July 1990). BS, U. South Fla., 1980, PhD, 1983. Assoc. scientist Solar Energy Rsch. Inst., Golden, Colo., 1983-85; rsch. scientist KMS Fusion, Inc., Ann Arbor, Mich., 1985-89, Lawrence Livermore (Calif.) Nat. Lab., 1989—. Contbr. articles to profl. jours. Mem. Am. Chem. Soc., Am. Inst. Chemists, Internat. Union Pure and Applied Chemistry, Inter-Am. Photochem. Soc., Soc. Photo-Optical Instrumentation Engrs. Office: Lawrence Livermore Nat Lab PO Box 808 Livermore CA 94551-0808

MARSH, MALCOLM F., judge; b. 1928. BS, U. Oreg., 1952, LLB, 1954, JD, 1971. Ptnr. Clark & Marsh, Lindauer & McClinton (and predecessors), Salem, Oreg., 1958-87; judge U.S. Dist. Ct. Oreg., Portland, 1987—. With U.S. Army, 1946-47. Fellow Am. Coll. Trial Lawyers; mem. ABA. Office: US Dist Ct 114 US Courthouse 620 SW Main St Portland OR 97205-3023*

MARSH, NOEL R, management consultant; b. San Francisco, Dec. 30, 1931; s. Reginald A. and Lilian (Wolldridge) M.; m. Yin-Chin Marsh, Sept. 14, 1949; children: Rex, Nicole. BA, U. Calif. Berkeley, 1957, MA, 1958; student in Pub. Adminstrn., Harvard U., 1967. Econ. analyst Fed. Reserve Bank, San Francisco, 1958-59; fgn. svc. officer AID Dept. State, Washington, 1959-83; free-lance cons. Berkeley, 1983-90; sr. assoc. E. Petrich & Assoc. Inc., San Luis Obispo, 1990—. Asst. dir. Met. Transp. Commn., Berkeley, 1972-76, Health Mgmt. supr. various ministries of health in Africa, 1983-90, mgmt. systems dir. Nat. Population Coun., Cairo, Egypt, 1990—. With USAF Res., 1956-64. Mem. World Affairs Coun. San Francisco, Fgn. Svc. Assn., Washington. Democrat.

MARSH, RICHARD ALAN, lawyer; b. Grand Island, Nebr., Nov. 27, 1952; s. M. Robert and A. Yvonne (Nitzel) M.; m. Kay Palmer, Aug. 21, 1982; children: Alexa K., Madelyn B. BA, Northwestern U., 1975; JD with honors, Ill. Inst. Tech.-Chgo. Kent, 1979. Bar: Ill. 1979, Colo. 1985. Assoc. law Schumacher Jones Kelly Olson & Pusch, Chgo., 1979-84; ptnr. Grant McHendrie Haines & Crouse, Denver, 1984-90, Marsh & Kolko, Denver, 1990-91, Massey Showalter & Marsh, Denver, 1991—. Bd. dirs. Keep the Lites Found., Denver, 1989—; precinct chair Jefferson County Republican Party, Littleton, Colo.; dir. South Metro Denver Bus. Polit. Action Com., Littleton. Mem. ABA, Colo. Bar Assn., Denver Bar Assn., South Metro Denver C. of C. (bd. dirs. 1988-92). Methodist. Office: Massey Showalter & Marsh PC 518 17th St # 1100 Denver CO 80202

MARSH, SCOTT CLYDE, financial consultant, writer, lecturer; b. Salt Lake City, Aug. 2, 1953; s. Mearle C. and Virginia (Welch) M.; m. Mary Louise Bunker, June 9, 1983; children: Landon David, Christopher Scott, Clayton Bunker, Jordan William. BS in Econs. magna cum laude, U. Utah, 1977, BS in Acctg. magna cum laude, 1978, MBA, 1979; MS in Fin. Svcs., Am. Coll., 1989. ChFC, CLU. Prin. Profl. Edn. Inst., Salt Lake City, 1980—, Marsh Fin. Group, Salt Lake City, 1982—; lic. rep. Richards Investments, Salt Lake City, 1982—; owner, mgr. Wasatch Yamaha Sch. Music, Salt Lake City, 1987—; lic. agt. Marsh Realtors, Salt Lake City, 1974—; ind. ins. agt., Salt Lake City, 1983—; cert. course monitor Life Underwriters Tng. Coun., Salt Lake City, 1992—; cert. ins. instr. Utah State Ins. Dept., Salt Lake City, 1987—, Nev. State Ins. Dept., Carson City, 1986—, Calif. State Ins. Dept., Sacramento, 1993; mem. faculty Brigham Young U. Edn. Week, Provo, Utah, 1992. Author: Investments and Securities Markets, 1983, Risk Management and Insurance Planning, 1985, 1986 Tax Reform Act and Tax Law Since Then, 1986, Retirement...The Payoff!, 1991, Making the Moneymakers Make You Money, 1992. Exec. cabinet Associated Students U. Utah, 1977; active Nat. Com. Planned Giving, bd. dirs. Greater Salt Lake coun. Boy Scouts Am., 1981, chmn., coord., 1992; bd. dirs., chmn. planned giving Granite Edn. Found., 1991. Mem. Utah Planned Giving Roundtable, Sigma Gamma Chi (pres. 1976), Phi Kappa Phi, Beta Gamma Sigma. Mem. LDS Ch. Home and Office: 1313 E 4170 S Salt Lake City UT 84124-1456

MARSH, STUART EMMET, education educator; b. Newark, Apr. 21, 1951; s. Irving J. and Florence Marsh; m. Lori J. Schwarz, May 29, 1984; children: Elise B., Alec S. BS, George Washington U., 1973; MS, Stanford (Calif.) U., 1975, PhD, 1979. Geologist U.S. Geol. Survey, Washington, 1974-78; NRC rsch. assoc. Jet Propulsion Lab., Pasadena, Calif., 1979-80; rsch. geologist Gulf Oil Corp., Pitts., 1980-81; mgr. remote sensing Sun Exploration and Prodn. Co., Dallas, 1981-86, mgr. computer svc., 1986-88; assoc. dir., prof. Ariz. Remote Sensing Ctr. U. Ariz., Tucson, 1989—. Author: (chpt.) Manual of Remote Sensing, 1983; contbr. articles to profl. jours. HEW fellow Stanford U., 1976, NRC fellow, 1980; recipient Cert. of Recognition, NASA, 1983; UN Rsch. grantee, 1990. Mem. Am. Water Resources Assn., Am. Soc. Photogrammetry and Remote Sensing, Assn. Am. Geographers, Ariz.-Nev. Acad. Scis. (bd. dirs. So. Ariz. chpt. 1990—). Office: U Ariz 845 N Park Ave Tucson AZ 85719-4816

MARSH, THOMAS ARCHIE, sculptor, anatomy educator; b. Cherokee, Iowa, May 7, 1951; s. Archie Glen and Florence Margaret (Weber) M. Student, Med. Coll. Wis., 1973-74; BFA in Painting, Layton Sch. Art, Milw., 1974; postgrad., U. So. Calif., 1975-76; MFA in Sculpture, Calif. State U., Long Beach, 1977. Instr. figure sculpture Calif. State U., 1975-77, lectr., 1978-79; instr. drawing Saddleback Coll., Mission Viejo, Calif., 1976-77; instr. anatomy Acad. Art Coll., San Francisco, 1981—; studio asst. Stephen Werlick, Long Beach, 1976-77, Milton Hebald, Rome, 1977-78; instr. sculpture and bronzecasting San Francisco State U., 1979, 80; supervising sculptor San Francisco Goddess of Democracy Project, 1989—; bd. dirs. Acad. Art Coll. Prin. works include lifesize bronze figure Calif. State U., 1977, bronze portrait bust Minor Hall, U. Calif., Berkeley, 1984, bronze relief panel 343 Sansome St., San Francisco, 1990, 20 bronze relief panels facade 235 Pine St., San Francisco, 1990, 18 foot bronze figurative monument Santa Cruz, Calif., 1991, bronze portrait bust Richard M. Lucas Ctr., Stanford U. Med. Sch., Palo Alto, Calif., 1992. Bd. dirs. The New Shakespeare Co., San Francisco, 1982—, Found. for Chinese Democracy, San Francisco, 1991—. Recipient award Elizabeth Greenshields Meml. Found., Montreal, Que., Can., 1978. Mem. Phi Kappa Phi. Libertarian. Lutheran. Studio: 2377 San Jose Ave San Francisco CA 94112

MARSH, TIMOTHY JOHN, academic administrator; b. Rapid City, S.D., Feb. 19, 1948; s. Robert Earley and Marjorie Emily (East) M.; m. Diane Mary Richardson, Apr. 8, 1978; 1 child, Emily Mae. BA in Journalism, Linfield Coll., 1970. Reporter Oreg. Statesman daily newspaper, Salem, Oreg., 1970-71; sports writer Albany (Oreg.) Dem.-Herald daily newspaper, 1972; news and sports editor, sports writer The Observer daily newspaper, La Grande, Oreg., 1971-73; news. svc. dir., sports info. dir. Whitman Coll., Walla Walla, Wash., 1973-75; asst. media rels. officer Oreg. Health Scis. U., Portland, Oreg., 1975-79; asst. press sec. to gov. State of Oreg., Salem, 1979-82; info. dir. system of higher edn. Oreg., Eugene, 1982-85; asst. for university communication Wash. State U., Pullman, 1985—; sports cons. Ea. Oreg. Review weekly newspaper, La Grande, 1973-78. Editor (newsletter) Comets Track Club of Pullman, 1992—. Bd. dirs. United Way of Pullman, Wash., 1990-92; mem. Pullman Sch. Dist. comm. task force, 1991, centennial com., 1992, Inland Empire Lost Eagle Boy Scout Com., Pullman, 1990-91, dist. VIII Coun. for Advancement & Support of Edn. Bd., 1988—, Pullman High Greyhound Booster Bd., 1991—. Recipient Award of Excellence Oreg. Columbia Internat. Assn. of Bus. Communicators, 1987. Mem. Soc. Profl. Journalists (sec. Willamette Valley chpt. 1976-77, bd. dirs. 1977-79), Palouse Asian Am. Assn. Methodist. Home: CS 2354 Pullman WA 99165 Office: Wash State U #1040 Pullman WA 99164

MARSHAL, KIT, restaurateur; b. L.A.; s. Alan Marshal and Mary (Grace) Borel. Student, Menlo Coll. Pres. Au Petit Cafe, Hollywood, Calif., 1963-82; chmn. bd. Cruvinet, L.A., 1980-85; sec., dir. Langan's Brasserie, L.A., 1986-88; ptnr., mgr., distbr. Cruvinet Wine Preserving and Dispensing System, 1981, pres., chmn., 1982-86; dir. Marshal's Guides, Singapore; wine cons. to numerous restaurants. Publ., wine critic: Goodlife Newsletter, 1982-85.

MARSHALL, ARTHUR K., lawyer, judge, arbitrator, educator, writer; b. N.Y.C., Oct. 7, 1911. BS, CUNY, 1933; LLB, St. John's U., N.Y.C., 1936; LL.M., U. So. Calif., 1952. Bar: N.Y. State 1937, Calif. 1947. Practice law N.Y.C., 1937-43, Los Angeles, 1947-50; atty. VA, Los Angeles, 1947-50; tax counsel Calif. Bd. Equalization, Sacramento, 1950-51; inheritance tax atty. State Controller, Los Angeles, 1951-53; commr. Superior Ct. Los Angeles County, 1953-62; judge Municipal Ct., Los Angeles jud. dist., 1962-63, Superior Ct., Los Angeles, 1963-81; supervising judge probate dept. Superior Ct., 1968-69, appellate dept., 1973-77; presiding judge Appellate Dept., 1976-77; pvt. practice, 1981—, arbitrator, referee, judge pro tem, 1981—; acting asst. prof. law UCLA, 1954-59; grad. faculty U. So. Calif., 1955-75; lectr. Continuing Edn. of Bar; chmn. Calif. Law Revision Commn., 1986-87, 92-93, mem., 1984—; past chmn. com. on efficiency and econ. Conf. Calif. Judges, past chmn. spl. action com. on ct. improvement; past chmn. probate law cons. group Calif. Bd. Legal Specialization. Author: Joint Tenancy Taxwise and Otherwise, 1953, Branch Courts, 1959, California State and Local Taxation Text, 2 vols., 1962, rev. edit., 1969, supplement, 1979, 2d edit., 1981, Triple Choice Method, 1964, California State and Local Taxation Forms, 2 vols., 1961-75, rev. edit., 1979, California Probate Procedure, 1961, 5th rev. edit., 1992, Guide to Procedure Before Trial, 1975; contbr. articles to profl. jours. Mem. Town Hall; mem. Com. on Fgn. Affairs. With AUS, 1943-46; lt. col. JAGC Res. (ret.). Named Judge of Yr. Lawyers Club L.A. County, 1975; first recipient Arthur K. Marshall award established by estate planning, trust and probate sect. L.A. Bar Assn., 1981, Disting. Jud. Career award L.A. Lawyers Club, award L.A. County Bd. Suprs., 1981. Fellow Am. Bar Found.; mem. Internat. Acad. Estate and Trust Law (academician, founder, 1st pres., now chancellor), ABA (probate litigation com. real property, probate and trust sect.), Calif. State Bar (advisor to exec. com. real property, probate and trust sect. 1970-83), Santa Monica Bar Assn. (pres. 1960), Westwood Bar Assn. (pres. 1959, bd. govts. 1987—), L.A. Bar Assn., Am. Legion (comdr. 1971-72), U. So. Calif. Law Alumni Assn. (pres. 1969-70), Phi Alpha Delta (1st justice alumni chpt.). Office: 28th Fl 300 S Grand Ave Los Angeles CA 90071

MARSHALL, BILL, protective services official. Chief constable Vancouver (B.C.) Police Svc., Can. Office: Office of the Chief Constable, 453 W 12th St, Vancouver, BC Canada V5Y 1V4*

MARSHALL, CHARLES BOWKER, restaurant executive, consultant; b. Somers Point, N.J., May 1, 1936; s. Elmer Wilbur and Florence (Bowker) M.; m. Phyllis Ann Yates, Sept. 6, 1958 (div. 1984); children: Scott Bradford, Dion Langley, Cara Fleming; m. Susan Brewer, Sept. 1, 1986. BA in Hotel Adminstrn., Cornell U., 1959. Gen. mgr. Gorsuch House Restaurant, Balt., 1962-65, Eastwins Catering, Balt., 1965-69; exec. v.p. Davenport Enterprizes, Lemoyne, Pa., 1969-72; v.p., gen. mgr. Lawry's Associated Restaurants, L.A., 1972-77; gen. mgr. Lawry's Calif. Ctr., L.A., 1989-92; chmn. bd. dirs. Marshall Hosts, Inc., Anaheim, Calif., 1977—; chmn. Anaheim Visitors and Conv. Bur., 1983; mem. wine steering com. Orange County Fair, Irvine, 1980-89; sales com. L.A. Visitors and Conv. Bur., 1990-92. Pres. Anaheim YMCA, 1985, Anaheim East Rotary, 1981, 82; bd. dirs. Anaheim C. of C., 1980-89. Lt. USN, 1959-62. Mem. Soc. Wine Educators, Le Grand Crew, Joie de Vin, Chaine de Rotisseurs, Calif. Restaurant Assn. (bd. dirs. 1984—). Office: Marshall Hosts Inc 1105 E Katella Ave Anaheim CA 92631

MARSHALL, CONRAD JOSEPH, entrepreneur; b. Detroit, Dec. 23, 1934; s. Edward Louis Fedak and Maria Magdalena Berzsenyi; m. Dorothy Genieve Karnafil, Dec. 1, 1956 (div. 1963); children: Conrad Joseph Jr., Kevin Conrad, Lisa Marie; m. Beryle Elizabeth Callahan, June 15, 1965 (div. 1972); 1 child, Farah Elizabeth. Diploma, Naval Air Tech. Tng. Ctr., Norman, Okla., 1952; student, Wayne State U., 1956-59; Diploma, L.A. Police Acad., 1961. Dir. mktg. Gulf Devel., Torrance, Calif., 1980-83; sales mgr. Baldwin Piano Co., Santa Monica, Calif., 1977-80; dir. mktg., v.p. Western Hose, Inc., L.A., 1971-76; city letter carrier U.S. Post Office, L.A., 1969-71; writer freelance L.A., 1966—; police officer L.A. Police Dept., 1961-66; asst. sales mgr. Wesson Oil Co., Detroit, 1958-60; agt. Life Ins. Co. of Va., Wayne, Mich., 1956-58; pres. Am. Vision Mktg., L.A., 1990—, Con-Mar Prodns., L.A., 1983—; sr. v.p. Pacific Acquisition Group, 1992—, Invest. Admin. HealthCom., Int., 1993—; tech. advisor Lion's Gate Films, Westwood, Calif., 1970-74, Medicine Wheel Prodns., Hollywood, Calif., 1965-75. Author: (series) "Dial Hot Line", 1967, (screenplay) "Heads Across the Border", 1968, "The Fool Card", 1970, "Probable Cause", 1972; albums include Song Shark, 1992, Conrad Marshall Quintet, 1991. Campaign vol. Dem. Party, L.A., 1976; vol. Amanda Found., Beverly Hills, Calif., 1992. With USN, 1952-56. Mem. Screen Actors Guild. Home: 11853 Kling #16 N Hollywood CA 91607 Office: Con-Mar Prodns 2026 Holly Hill Terr Hollywood CA 90068

MARSHALL, CONSUELO BLAND, federal judge; b. Knoxville, Tenn., Sept. 28, 1936; d. Clyde Theodore and Annie (Brown) Arnold; m. George Edward Marshall, Aug. 30, 1959; children: Michael Edward, Laurie Ann. A.A., Los Angeles City Coll., 1956; B.A., Howard U., 1958, LL.B., 1961. Bar: Calif. 1962. Dep. atty. City of L.A., 1962-67; assoc. Cochran & Atkins, L.A., 1968-70; commr. L.A. Superior Ct., 1971-76; judge Inglewood Mcpl. Ct., 1976-77, L.A. Superior Ct., 1977-80, U.S. Dist. Ct. Central Dist. Calif., L.A., 1980—; lectr. U.S. Information Agy. in Yugoslavia, Greece and Italy, 1984, in Nigera and Ghana, 1991, in Ghana, 1992. Contbr. articles to profl. jours.; notes editor Law Jour. Howard U. Mem. adv. bd. Richstone Child Abuse Center. Recipient Judicial Excellence award Criminal Cts. Bar Assn., 1992; research fellow Howard U. Law Sch., 1959-60;. Mem. State Bar Calif., Calif. Women Lawyers Assn., Calif. Assn. Black Lawyers, Calif. Judges Assn., Black Women Lawyers Assn., Los Angeles County Bar Assn., Nat. Assn. Women Judges, NAACP, Urban League, Beta Phi Sigma. Office: US Dist Ct 312 N Spring St Los Angeles CA 90012-4701

MARSHALL, DAVID LAWRENCE, freight forwarding, mining company executive; b. Orange, N.J., Mar. 10, 1939; s. Lawrence Clark and Sylvia (Hitch) M.; m. Lucy Smith, June 17, 1961; children: Lucy, Jennifer, Christopher, Stephen. B.A., Princeton U., 1961; M.S., Pa. State U., 1962. Vice pres. Freeport of Australia, Melbourne, 1969-71, pres., 1971-73; v.p. Freeport Minerals Co., N.Y.C., 1973-79, sr. v.p., 1979-81, exec. v.p., 1981-84; with Pittston Co., 1984—; chief fin. officer, exec. v.p. Pittston Co., until 1990, now vice-chmn. bd., CEO; chmn. bd. Burlington Air Express, Irvine, Calif. Republican. Episcopalian. Clubs: Wee Burn (Darien, Conn.); Sky.

MARSHALL, GRAYSON WILLIAM, JR., biomaterials scientist, educator; b. Balt., Feb. 12, 1943; s. Grayson William and Muriel Marie M.; BS in Metall. Engring., Va. Poly. Inst., 1965; PhD in Materials Sci., Northwestern U., 1972, DDS, 1986; MPH, U. Calif., Berkeley, 1992; m. Sally Jean Rimkus, July 4, 1970; children: Grayson W. III, Jonathan Charles. Rsch. assoc., design and devel. ctr. Northwestern U., Evanston, Ill., 1972-73, NIH fellow, 1973, instr. Dental and Med. schs., Chgo., 1973-74, asst. prof. Dental Sch., 1974-78, assoc. prof. Dental Sch. and Grad. Sch., 1978-87; prof. restorative dentistry U. Calif., San Francisco, 1987—, chief biomaterials sect., 1988-92, chmn. biomaterials divsn., 1992—; with bioengring. program U. Calif., San Francisco and Berkeley, 1988—; guest scientist Lawrence Livermore Nat. Lab., 1989—, Lawrence Berkeley Lab., 1989—; cons. oral biology and medicine study section NIH, 1988-92. Contbr. articles to profl. jours. Vis. fellow U. Melbourne (Australia), 1981. Recipient Spl. dental research award Nat. Inst. Dental Rsch., 1975. Fellow AAAS, Acad. Dental Materials (exec. sec. 1983-85, chmn. credentials 1984-91, bd. dirs. 1985—, sec. 1988-91, pres. 1991-93, mem. editorial bd. Scanning Microscopy 1987—, Cells and Materials 1992—, sect. editor 1993—); mem. Am. Assn. Dental Schs. (sect. officer 1981-83), Soc. Biomaterials, Internat. Assn. Dental Rsch. (Chgo. sect. officer 1978-80, councelor dental materials 1990—), Am. Coll. Sports Med., Am. Soc. Metals, Electron Microscopy Soc. Am., AIME, N.Y. Acad. Scis., ADA, Acad. Gen. Dentistry, Calif. Acad. Scis., U.S. Naval Inst., Inst. Nav., U.S. Power Squadrons, Alpha Sigma Mu, Sigma Xi, Sigma Gamma Epsilon, Omicron Kappa Upsilon. Office: U Calif Dept Restorative Dentistry San Francisco CA 94143-0758

MARSHALL, JAMES FREDERICK, semiconductor capital equipment executive; b. St. Louis, June 15, 1949; s. Donald and Jeanne (Cawley) M.; m. Terry Small, Sept. 6, 1969 (div. 1978); m. Gail Parker, May 5, 1979; children: Gretchen, Alexander, Jessica. BSME, MSME, Stanford U., 1972. Project mgr. Hewlett-Packard Labs., Palo Alto, Calif., 1972-79; engring. mgr. Kasper Instruments/Eaton, Sunnyvale, Calif., 1979-81; dir., bus. mgr. Applied Materials, Inc., Santa Clara, Calif., 1981-83; exec. v.p., co-founder Mesa Tech., Moutain View, Calif., 1983-85; dir. ops., engr. Applied Materials, Inc., Santa Clara, 1985-88; pres., chief oper. officer A.S.E.T., Inc., Woodland Hills, Calif., 1988-90; chief oper. officer S.V.G. Inc./Thermco Systems, Orange, Calif., 1991-92; sr. v.p. ops. Plasma and Materials Tech., Chatsworth, Calif., 1992—. Contbr. articles to profl. jours. Chmn. Dept. Commerce-Semiconductor Tech. Adv. Com., Washington, 1987-91; bd. dirs. Mountain View/Los Altos YMCA, 1984-86, Mountain View Schs. Fund, 1985-86. Democrat. Presbyterian. Office: Plasma and Materials Techs 9255 Deering Ave Chatsworth CA 91311

MARSHALL, JAMES KENNETH, consulting services executive; b. Providence, Dec. 25, 1952; s. James William and Eileen Frances (O'Connell) M.; m. Mary H. Jackson, Mar. 17, 1987. BA in Chemistry, SUNY, Plattsburgh, 1974; MBA in Fin., U. R.I., 1977; postgrad., U. Wash., 1978-79. Fin. instr. U. R.I., Kingston, 1978; teaching assoc. U. Wash., Seattle, 1978-79; asst. dir. facilities mgmt. U. Colo., Boulder, 1979-86, dir. buying and contracting, 1986-90; transp. mgr. Town of Vail, Colo., 1991-92;, 1981-85; v.p. Women at the Wheel Automotive Cons. and Consumer Edn. Svc., Avon, Colo., 1990—; honorarium instr. U. Colo., Denver, 1981-85; bd. dirs. Minority Enterprises, Inc., 1988-90. Contbr. chpt. to book on plant administration. Recipient Job Well Done award U. Colo. Boulder Dept. Facilities Mgmt., 1983. Mem. Beta Gamma Sigma, Phi Kappa Phi. Office: Women at the Wheel PO Box 2829 Avon CO 81620-2829

MARSHALL, JOHN MURRAY, minister; b. Toronto, Ont., Can., Apr. 27, 1930; came to U.S., 1948; s. John Ramage and Martha Lilian (Veall) M.; m. Nancy Orne Hodges, June 23, 1956; children: J. Douglas, J. Scott; 1 adopted child, Kimberlee Anne. BA, Wheaton Coll., 1951; MDiv, Fuller Theol. Sem., 1954; DD (hon.), Whitworth Coll., 1976. Ordained to ministry, Congl. Ch., 1955. Asst. pastor Park St. Ch., Boston, 1954-61; pastor 1st Presbyn. Ch., Flushing, N.Y., 1961-72, Seattle, 1972—; founding pres. Presbyns. for Renewal, Louisville, 1989-90; pres. Presbyns. United for Biblican Concerns, Phila., 1974-82. Trustee emeritus Whitworth Coll., Spokane, 1974—; chmn. bd. trustees Latin Am. Mission, Miami, Fla., 1984-92. Mem. Wash. Athletic Club, Rotary. Office: First Presbyn Ch 1013 8th Ave Seattle WA 98104

MARSHALL, L. B., medical technologist; b. Chgo., Feb. 10; s. Gillman and Ethel (Robinson) M.; m. Esther Wood, Sept. 28, 1961; 1 child, Lelani. Student, San Francisco State U., 1950; AA, City Coll. San Francisco, 1957; BS in Pediatric Medicine, U. Puget Sound, 1961; ScD, London Inst., Eng., 1972. Pres., Med. Offices Health Services Group Inc., San Francisco, 1964—. Mem. NAACP. With U.S. Army, 1947-53. Decorated Bronze Star, Med. Combat Badge; recipient cert. Appreciation Pres. Nixon, 1973, Urban League, 1973, Calif. Dept. Human Resources, 1973. Mem. Am. Calif. Assns. Med. Technologists, Calif. State Sheriff's Assn. (assoc.), Oyster Point Yacht Club, Press Club, Commonwealth Club (San Francisco).

MARSHALL, PAUL (PAUL MARSHALL SOLOMON), songwriter, musician; b. L.A., Sept. 13, 1949; s. Sidney Jerome and Jean (Sukernek) Solomon; m. Mary Colleen Driscoll, June 25, 1978; children: Scott Driscoll, Stefanie Driscoll, Patricia Jean. Student, U. Calif., Santa Barbara, 1967-69, UCLA, 1969, San Fernando Valley State Coll, 1971. Recording artist, writer Mustang Records, L.A., 1965-67; band mem., lead vocalist Strawberry Alarm Clock, L.A., 1969-71; freelance recording artist L.A., 1971-73, 80-88; bassist Frank Fara/Comstock Records, 1974-77, Mary Kay Place Band, L.A., 1978-80, George Highfill, L.A., 1988-91, Karen Tobin, L.A., 1991—; accompanist Hank Thompson, West Coast, 1988-91, Johnny Rodriguez, Ventura, 1991. Songwriter: Someone Believed, 1987 (Gold album 1990); singer, songwriter: Beyond the Valley of the Dolls, 1968; singer: Silhouette, 1991. Mem. N.O.R.M.L., 1991; vol. Apperson Elem. Sch., Tujunga, Calif., 1989—. Mem. NRA, SAG, Am. Fedn. Musicians, Calif. Country Music Assn. (Bass Player of Yr. L.A. chpt. 1991). Libertarian. Home: 7534 Thousand Oaks Dr Tujunga CA 91042

MARSHALL, RICHARD LEE, data processing analyst; b. Trenton, Mo., Jan. 1, 1950; s. Robert Stephen and Doris Lee (Hopkins) M.; m. Mary Angela Bolton, Nov. 30,. 1985; children: Daniel S., Bethanie M., Michael R. Diploma in data processing, Punch Card Machine Tng. Sch., 1968; basic cert., A.I.B., 1978. Programmer analyst United Mo. Bank, Kansas City, 1969-79; data processing prodn. analyst Valley Nat. Bank, Phoenix, 1979—; mem. standard subcom. Valley Nat. Bank, Phoenix, 1980, mem. employee's coun., 1989. Mem. Cen. Ariz. Tall Soc. (v.p. 1980-81, social dir. 1984-85). Home: 6809 W Georgia Ave Glendale AZ 85303-5923 Office: Valley Nat Bank 3625 N 27th Ave # 549Q Phoenix AZ 85017-4701

MARSHALL, ROBERT HERMAN, economics educator; b. Harrisburg, Pa., Dec. 6, 1929; s. Mathias and Mary (Bubich) M.; m. Billie Marie Sullivan, May 31, 1958; children: Mellisa Frances, Howard Hylton, Robert Charles. A.B. magna cum laude, Franklin and Marshall Coll., 1951; M.A., Ohio State U., 1952, Ph.D., 1957. Teaching asst. Ohio State U., 1952-57; mem. faculty, then prof. econs. U. Ariz., Tucson, 1957—, head dept., 1967-69; dir. Internat. Bus. Studies Project, 1969-71; research observer Sci.-Industry Program, Hughes Aircraft Co., Tucson, summer 1959. Author: Commercial Banking in Arizona: Structure and Performance Since World War II, 1966, (with others) The Monetary Process, 2d edit, 1980. Bd. dirs. Com. for Econ. Opportunity, Tucson, 1968-69. Faculty fellow Pacific Coast Banking Sch., summer 1974. Mem. Am. Econ. Assn., Phi Beta Kappa, Beta Gamma Sigma, Pi Gamma Mu, Phi Kappa Phi, Delta Sigma Pi. Democrat. Roman Catholic. Home: 6700 N Abington Rd Tucson AZ 85743-9795

MARSHALL, THOMAS DAVID, judge; b. Wainfleet, Ont., Can., Feb. 23, 1939; s. Albert Haydow Marshall and Ora Colback; m. Jill Smith, 1961; children: Jillian, Julie, Albert, Tom, David Jr. MD, U. Toronto, 1963; LLB, Osgoode Hall, Toronto, 1970. Cert. LMCC barrister and solicitor, judge. Prof. law U. Windsor, Ont., 1981-82; justice Supreme Ct. N.T., 1983-88; dir. Nat. Judicial Inst., Ottawa, 1988-92; hon. prof. law Ottawa U., 1988; justice Ont. Ct. Justice, Hamilton, 1992—; chmn. com. ethics medical reserve coun. of Can., Ottawa, 1984-93. Author: Canadian Law of Inquests, 1988, Canadian Physician and the Law. Lt. col. Can. Armed Forces Reserve, 1988-93. Mem. Can. Bar Assn., Can. Medieval Assn. Office: Court House, 50 Main St, Hamilton, ON Canada

MARSHALL, WILLIAM EUGENE, real estate appraiser, builder, designer; b. Alliance, Ohio, June 13, 1932; s. William Jacob Marshall and Mary Louise (Sucaciu) Mazanti; m. Delores Cashero, Feb. 6, 1965 (div. Sept. 1966); 1 child, Tina; m. Sharon Michele Scott, July 30, 1980. Student, San Francisco City Coll., 1968, Merritt Coll., 1968-69; cert. appraiser I, Am. Savs. Inst., L.A., 1973. Lic. gen. contractor, N.Mex., S.C. Plastering gen. contractor Marshall Plastering & Bldg., Alliance, Ohio, 1955-62, Carmel, Calif., 1962-66; bldg. ofcl. Redevel. Agys., San Francisco and Fresno, Calif., 1966-70; appraiser, cons. Calif. Fed. Bank, L.A., 1970-74; constrn. supr. State of Fla. HRS, Tallahassee, 1977-78; builder, designer Marshall Plastering & Bldg., Tijeras, N.Mex., 1980-92; appraiser II Tax. and Revenue N.Mex., Tijeras, N.Mex., 1992—; Mem. region VI HUD-Nat. Assn. Housing and Redevel. Officials Rehab. Com., San Francisco, 1969-70. Pres., producer Carnation City Players, Alliance, 1960-62. Mem. Calif. Lathing & Plastering Contractors Assn. (sec., treas. Monterey chpt., 1965-66). Mem. Jehovah's Witnesses. Office: Tax and Rev Dept State NM PO Box 1689 Tijeras NM 87059

MARSHALL, WILLIAM STUART, biochemist; b. Sheboygan, Wis., Nov. 21, 1963; s. Judson Earl and Claire Elaine (Schenkenberg) M.; m. Michele Marie Nemecek, Aug. 7, 1987. BS in Biochemistry, U. Wis., 1986; PhD in Chemistry, U. Colo., 1991. Rsch. assoc. U. Wis., Madison, 1984-86; teaching asst. U. Colo., Boulder, 1986-87, rsch. asst., 1987-91, postdoctoral rsch. assoc., 1991-92; rsch. scientist Amgen, Inc., Boulder, 1992—. Contbr. articles to profl. jours.; patentee in field. Mary Shine Peterson scholar U. Wis., 1986. Mem. Am. Chem. Soc., Golden Key, Sigma Xi, Phi Kappa Phi. Home: 495 Mohawk Dr Boulder CO 80303 Office: Amgen Inc 4765 Walnut St Boulder CO 80301

MARSTON, MICHAEL, urban economist, asset management executive; b. Oakland, Calif., Dec. 4, 1936; s. Lester Woodbury and Josephine (Janovic) M.; m. Alexandra Lynn Geyer, Apr. 30, 1966; children: John, Elizabeth. BA, U. Calif., Berkeley, 1959; postgrad. London Sch. Econs., 1961-63. V.p. Larry Smith & Co., San Francisco, 1969-72, exec. v.p. urban econ. div., 1969-72; chmn. bd. Keyser Marston Assocs., Inc., San Francisco, 1973-87; gen. ptnr. The Sequoia Partnership, 1979-91; pres. Marston Vineyards and Winery, 1982—, Marston Assocs., Inc., 1982—. Cert. rev. appraiser Nat. Assn. Rev. Appraisers and Mortgage Underwriters, 1984—. Chmn., San Francisco Waterfront Com., 1969-86; chmn. fin. com., bd. dirs., mem. exec. com., treas. San Francisco Planning and Urban Rsch. Assn., 1976-87, Napa Valley Vintners, 1986—, mem. gov. affairs com.; trustee Cathedral Sch. for Boys, 1981-82, Marin Country Day Sch., 1984-90; v.p. St. Luke's Sch., 1986-91; pres. Presidio Heights Assn. of Neighbors, 1983-84; chmn. Presidio Com. 1991—; v.p., bd. dirs., mem. exec. com. People for Open Space, 1972-87, chmn. adv. com., 1988—; mem. Gov.'s Issue Analysis Com. and Speakers Bur., 1966; mem. speakers bur. Am. embassy, London, 1961-63; v.p., bd. dirs. Dem. Forum, 1968-72; v.p., trustee Youth for Service. Served to lt. USNR. Mem. Napa Valley Vintners, Napa Grape Growers, Urban Land Inst., World Congress Land Policy (paper in field), Order of Golden Bear, Chevalier du Tastevin, Commanderie de Bordeaux, Bohemian Club, Pacific Union Club, Lambda Alpha. Contbr. articles to profl. jours. Home: 3375 Jackson St San Francisco CA 94118-2018

MARTENS, CRAIG COLWELL, chemist, educator; b. Washington, Aug. 29, 1958; s. Harvey Arthur and Barbara (Colwell) M.; m. Rebecca Rae Booth, Dec. 24, 1982; 1 child, Richard Andrew. BS in Chemistry, U. Nebr., Lincoln, 1981; MS in Chemistry, Cornell U., 1985, PhD in Chemistry, 1987. Postdoctoral assoc. U. Pa., Phila., 1987-89; asst. prof. chemistry U. Calif., Irvine, 1989—. Contbr. articles to profl. jours. Mem. Am. Chem. Soc., Am. Phys. Soc., Sigma Xi. Office: Univ Calif Irvine Dept Chemistry Irvine CA 92717-2025

MARTI, OSCAR R., philosophy educator; b. Havana, Cuba, Oct. 24, 1942; came to U.S., 1955; s. Oscar H. and Victoria M.; m. Judith K. Ettinger, Nov. 2, 1969; children: Frances Alethea, George Edward. BA, CCNY, 1964, postgrad., 1964-67, PhD, 1978. Instr. philosophy dept. CCNY, N.Y.C., 1970-73, fellow philosophy dept., 1973-76; asst. prof. philosophy SDSU, San Diego State U., 1976-79; assoc. prof. philosophy UCLA, 1979-82, dir. publs. Chicano Studies Rsch. Ctr., 1982-85; instr. Calif. State U., Northridge, 1983—; assoc. dir. 1789-1989: The French Revolution: A UCLA Bicentennial, 1985-91. Author: (essays) Cuadernos Americanos, 1989; editor, author: La Revolucion Francesca Y El Mundo Iberico, 1989; editor jour. Aztlan, 1982-85, editor, writer, 1983; editor Prometeo, 1986-92. CUNY fellow, 1973-76; Inst. for Am. Cultures postdoctoral fellow UCLA, 1979-82; Fulbright scholar, 1986-88. Mem. LASA, Am. Philos. Assn., Philosophy Sci. Assn., Soc. Iberian and Latin Am. Thought (v.p. 1980-82, pres. 1982-84). Office: Calif State U Philosophy Dept Northridge CA 91330

MARTIN, BARNEY, investment executive; b. St. Louis, Oct. 30, 1925; s. John Cunningham and Margaret Burrage (Bills) M.; m. Virginia Ann Wheeler, Oct. 2, 1954. BS in Marine Engring., U.S. Naval Acad., 1946. Lic. naval aviator. Commd. ensign USN, 1946, advanced through grades to capt., 1976; commdr. Task Force 157 Washington, 1967-71; dir. U.S. Naval Investigative Svc., 1973-76; pres. LBCA Investments Inc., Long Beach, Calif., 1976—; gen. ptnr. Delta Devel. I, San Diego, 1976—. Chmn. Pub. Interest Com., Rancho Sante Fe, Calif., 1989—; co-chmn. Pres.'s Assocs. Planning Com., Zool. Soc. San Diego, 1991—. Recipient (2) Legions of Merit awards. Mem. Rancho Sante Fe Golf Club, Univ. Club (San Diego). Republican. Home: PO Box 2589 Rancho Santa Fe CA 92067-2589

MARTIN, BOYD ARCHER, emeritus political science educator; b. Cottonwood, Idaho, Mar. 3, 1911; s. Archer Olmstead and Norah Claudine (Imbler) M.; m. Grace Charlotte Swingler, Dec. 29, 1933; children: Michael Archer, William Archer. Student, U. Idaho, 1929-30, 35-36, B.S., 1936; student, Pasadena Jr. Coll., 1931-32, U. Calif. at Los Angeles, summer 1934; A.M., Stanford, 1937, Ph.D., 1943. Rsch. asst. Stanford U., 1936-37, teaching asst., 1937-38; instr. polit. sci. U. Idaho, 1938-39; acting instr. polit. sci. Stanford U., 1939-40; John M. Switzer fellow, summer 1939-40; chief personnel officer Walter Butler Constrn. Co., Farragut Naval Tng. Center, summer 1942; instr. polit. sci. U. Idaho, 1940-43, asst. prof. polit. sci., 1943-44, asso. prof. polit. sci., 1944-47; prof., head dept. social sci., asst. dean coll. letters and sci. U. Idaho, 1947-55, dean, 1955-70, Borah Distinguished prof. polit. sci., 1970-73, prof., dean emeritus, 1973—; vis. prof. Stanford U., summer 1946, spring 1952, U. Calif., 1962-63; affiliate Center for Study Higher Edn., Berkeley, 1962-63; mem. steering com. N.W. Conf. on Higher Edn., 1960-67, pres. conf., 1966-67; mem. bd. Am. Assn. of Partners of Alliance for Progress; chmn. Idaho Adv. Coun. on Higher Edn.; del. Gt. Plains UNESCO Conf., Denver, 1947; chmn. bd. William E. Borah Found. on Causes of War and Conditions of Peace, 1947-55; mem. Commn. to Study Orgn. Peace; dir. Bur. Pub. Affair Rsch., 1959-73, dir. emeritus, 1973—; dir. Martin Peace Inst., 1970—. Author: The Direct Primary in Idaho, 1947, (with others) Introduction to Political Science, 1950, (with other) Western Politics, 1968, Politics in the American West, 1969, (with Sydney Duncombe) Recent Elections in Idaho (1964-70), 1972, Idaho Voting Trends: Party Realignment and Percentage of Voters for Candidates, Parties and Elections, 1890-1974, 1975, In Search of Peace: Starting From October 19, 1980, 1980, Why the Democrats Lost in 1980, 1980, On Understanding the Soviet Union, 1987; editor: The Responsibilities of Colleges and Universities, 1967; contbr. to: Ency. Britannica, 1990, 91; also articles. Mem. Am. Polit. Sci. Assn. (exec. council 1952-53), Nat. Municipal League, Am. Soc. Pub. Adminstrn., Fgn. Policy Assn., UN Assn., AAUP, Western Polit. Sci. Assn. (pres. 1950), Phi Beta Kappa, Pi Gamma Mu, Kappa Delta Pi, Pi Sigma Alpha. Home: 516 N Eisenhower St Moscow ID 83843-9559

MARTIN, BRYAN LESLIE, allergist, immunologist; b. Macomb, Ill., June 25, 1954; s. George Albert and Vernal Louise (Stutsman) M.; m. Deborah Ann Schettig, June 22, 1979; children: Emily, Stephanie, Scott. BA, St. Vincent Coll., 1976; postgrad., Ohio U., 1976-79; DO, U. Osteopathic Medicine, 1984. Diplomate Am. Bd. Osteo. Medicine, Am. Bd. Internal Medicine. Commd. 2d lt. U.S. Army, 1980, advanced through grades to maj., 1990—; resident in internal medicine William Beaumont Army Med. Ctr., 1987-90, chief med. resident, 1990-91. Student body pres. U. Osteopathic Medicine and Health Scis., Des Moines, 1981-82. Allergy/immunology fellow Fitzsimons Army Med. Ctr., Aurora, Colo., 1991-93; Health Professions scholar U.S. Army, 1980-84; decorated Bronze star. Mem. AMA (del. resident physicians sect. 1992-93), Am. Coll. Allergy & Immunology (fellow-in-tng. rep. to Bd. Regents 1991-93, co-chmn. fellow-in-tng. sect. 1991-92, chmn. fellow-in-tng. sect. 1992-93), Am. Acad. Allergy & Immunology, ACP, Am. Osteo. Assn. (del. 1981-83), Dustoff Assn., Sigma Sigma Phi. Office: Fitzsimons Army Med Ctr Allergy.Immunology Svc Aurora CO 80045

MARTIN, CLYDE VERNE, psychiatrist; b. Coffeyville, Kans., Apr. 7, 1933; s. Howard Verne and Elfrieda Louise (Moehn) M.; m. Barbara Jean McNeilly, June 24, 1956; children: Kent Clyde, Kristin Claire, Kerry Constance, Kyle Curtis. Student Coffeyville Coll., 1951-52; AB, U. Kans., 1955; MD, 1958; MA, Webster Coll., St. Louis, 1977; JD, Thomas Jefferson Coll. Law, Los Angeles, 1985. Diplomate Am. Bd. Psychiatry and Neurology. Intern, Lewis Gale Hosp., Roanoke, Va., 1958-59; resident in psychiatry U. Kans. Med. Ctr., Kansas City, 1959-62, Fresno br. U. Calif.-San Francisco, 1978; staff psychiatrist Neurol. Hosp., Kansas City, 1962; practice medicine specializing in psychiatry, Kansas City, Mo., 1964-84; founder, med. dir., pres. bd. dirs. Mid-Continent Psychiat. Hosp., Olathe, Kans., 1972-84; adj. prof. psychology Baker U., Baldwin City, Kans., 1969-84; staff psychiatrist Atascadero State Hosp., Calif., 1984-85; clin. prof. psychiatry U. Calif., San Francisco, 1985—; chief psychiatrist Calif. Med. Facility, Vacaville, 1985-87; pres., editor Corrective and Social Psychiatry, Olathe, 1970-84, Atascadero, 1984-85, Fairfield, 1985—. Contbr. articles to profl. jours. Bd. dirs. Meth. Youthville, Newton, Kans. 1965-75, Spofford Home, Kansas City, 1974-78. Served to capt. USAF, 1962-64, ret. col. USAFR. Fellow Am. Psychiat. Assn., Royal Soc. Health, Am. Assn. Mental Health Profls. in Corrections, World Assn. Social Psychiatry, Am. Orthopsychiat. Assn.; mem. AMA, Assn. for Advancement Psychotherapy, Am. Assn. Sex Educators, Counselors and Therapists (cert.), Assn. Mental Health Adminstrs. (cert.), Kansas City Club, Masons, Phi Beta Pi, Pi Kappa Alpha. Methodist (del. Kans. East Conf. 1972-80, bd. global ministries 1974-80). Office: PO Box 3365 Fairfield CA 94533-0587

MARTIN, CONNIE RUTH, lawyer; b. Clovis, N.Mex., Sept. 9, 1955; d. Lynn Latimer and Marian Ruth (Pierce) M.; m. Daniel A. Patterson, Nov. 21, 1987; step-children: David Patterson, Dana Patterson. B in Univ. Studies, Ea. N.Mex. U., 1976, MEd, 1977; JD, U. Mo., Kansas City, 1981. Bar: N.Mex. 1981, U.S. Dist. Ct. N.Mex. 1981. Asst. dist. atty. State of N.Mex., Farmington, 1981-84; ptnr. Tansey, Rosebrough, Gerding & Strother, P.C., Farmington, 1984-93; pvt. practice Connie R. Martin, P.C., Farmington, 1993—; dep. med. investigator State of N.Mex., Farmington, 1981-84; part-time instr. San Juan Coll., 1987, chmn. paralegal program adv. com., 1988; bd. Bar Examiners State of N.Mex., 1989—; mem. 4 Corners Estate and Fin. Planning Coun.; asst. bar counsel Disciplinary Bd. Bd. dirs., exec. com. San Juan County Econ. Opportunity Council, Farmington, 1982-83; bd. dirs. Four Corners Substance Abuse Council, Farmington, 1984; chmn. Community Corrections-Intensive Supervision Panel, Farmington, 1987-88. Recipient Distinguished Svcs. award for Outstanding Young Woman San Juan County Jaycees, 1984. Mem. ABA, San Juan County Bar Assn. (treas. 1985-87, v.p. 1987, pres. 1988), N.Mex. Bar Assn. (asst. to new lawyers com. 1986-87, local bar com. 1988, bd. dirs. young lawyers div. 1989-91), N.Mex. Sch. Bd. Atty. Assn., N.Mex. Bd. Bar Examiners, Farmington C. of C. (bd. dirs. 1991—). Republican. Baptist.

MARTIN, DANIEL TUNNIE, academic surgeon; b. Nagpur, Maharastra, India, Nov. 28, 1953; came to U.S. 1972; s. Tunnie and Eloise Madrid (Butler) M.; m. Carolyn S. Campbell, Apr. 2, 1988; children: Joshua Daniel, Caitlyn Campbell. BA, Anderson Coll., 1976; MD, Ohio State U., 1980. Diplomate Am. Bd. Surgery. Clin. instr. surgery (intern and resident) Ohio State U. Hosps., Columbus, 1980-87, rsch. fellow, 1981-83, adminstr. surg. rsch., 1982-88; chmn. dept. surgery Meml. Hosp., Fremont, Ohio, 1988-91; clin. asst. prof. surgery Med. Coll. of Ohio, Toledo, 1988-92; assoc. dir. surg. endoscopy and asst. prof. surgery U. N.Mex., Albuquerque, 1992—. Contbr. articles to profl. jours., chpts. to books. Fellow ACS. Home: 5500 Estrellita Del Norte Albuquerque NM 87111 Office: Univ N Mex Dept Surgery 2211 Lomas Blvd NE Albuquerque NM 87131-5341

MARTIN, DAVID LOUIS, financial systems analyst; b. Oak Park, Ill., Dec. 20, 1950; s. Donald Maxwell and Marian Sylvia (Goers) M.; m. Norma Kay Allen, June 7, 1975. BA, Calif. State U., Fullerton, 1972. Mgr. programming Mortgage Systems, Anaheim, Calif., 1974-79; sr. programmer McDonnell Douglas, Huntington Beach, Calif., 1979-80; systems analyst Downey Savs., Costa Mesa, Calif., 1980-83; sr. project mgr. Columbia Savs., Irvine, Calif., 1983-89; free lance data processing cons., 1989-92; sr. corp. analyst Director's Mortgage, Riverside, Calif., 1993—; cons. La Mesa, Calif., 1989. Lutheran. Home and Office: 4267 Calavo Dr La Mesa CA 91941-7069

MARTIN, DERIC KRISTON, securities broker; b. Abilene, Tex., June 30, 1959; s. Hollis Deon and Patsy Janelle (Morrow) M.; married. BSBA in Fin. summa cum laude, U. Denver, 1981. Account exec. Dean Witter, Denver, 1981-86, assoc. v.p., 1986—; mut. fund coord. Dean Witter, Denver, 1984—, investment lectr., 1984—; pre-retirement planning cons. Allstate Pre-Retirees, Rocky Mountain Region, 1988—. Charter mem. Second Century Found., Denver, 1985—, Citizens Against Govt. Waste, 1986—. Recipient Wall Street Jour. award, 1981. Mem. Lakewood Bus. Network, U. Denver 1864 Club, South Met. Denver C. of C., Beta Gamma Sigma. Republican. Methodist. Office: Dean Witter 4582 S Ulster St Ste 300 Denver CO 80237-2662

MARTIN, DOM, writer, artist, foundation director; b. Moshi, Tanzania, Aug. 4, 1950; s. Vincent Xavier Verediano and Teodora Effrezina (D'Souza) M.; m. Patricia Ann Maier, June 4, 1982. Student, St. Anthony's Coll., Gauhati, Assam, India, 1968; DSc (hon.), U. Danzig, 1977; ThD (hon.), Coll. and Sem. the Holy Spirit, 1978; D in Comparative Religions (hon.), Sacred Heart Coll., 1978; LHD (hon.), World Acad. Langs. and Lit., 1976; PhD (hon.), Acad. Philosophy, 1976. Founder, dir. Dominus, Goa, India, 1973-80; founder, pres. Project Door, Goa, 1974-78; founder, editor Verbum Mundi, Goa, 1976-79, Trans-Galactic Publs., Mill Valley, Calif., 1985—; founder, dir. Vincent Xavier Verediano Found., Mill Valley, 1989—. Author: (poems) The Day Before the Day After, 1986, (econs.) The Principles of Zerometrics, 1989. Recipient Diploma of Merit award U. Delle Arte, 1982, Artist of Mankind award Acad. Antero Quental, 1978, Knighthood of the Royal Order of Piast award World Acad. Scis., 1977; named Outstanding Young Person in India, Jaycees, 1979, Internat. Man of Yr. Internat. Biog. Centre, Cambridge, Eng., 1992-93. Office: 20 Sunnyside Ave Ste 134A Mill Valley CA 94941-1928

MARTIN, DONALD WALTER, author, publisher; b. Grants Pass, Oreg., Apr. 22, 1934; s. George E. and Irma Ann (Dallas) M.; m. Kathleen Elizabeth Murphy, July, 1970 (div. May 1979); children: Daniel Clayton, Kimberly Ann; m. Betty Woo, Mar. 18, 1985. Enlisted USMC, 1952; advanced through grades to staff sgt. USMC, Japan, Republic of Korea, Republic of China, 1956-61; reporter Blade-Tribune, Oceanside, Calif., 1961-65; entertainment editor Press-Courier, Oxnard, Calif., 1965-69; mng. editor Argus-Courier, Petaluma, Calif., 1969-70; assoc. editor Motorland mag., San Francisco, 1970-88; founder, prin. Pine Cone Press, Columbia, Calif., 1988—. Author: Best of San Francisco, 1986, 90, Best of the Gold Country, 1987, 92, San Francisco's Ultimate Dining Guide, 1988, Best of Arizona, 1990, 93, Inside San Francisco, 1991, Coming to Arizona, 1991, Best of the Wine Country, 1991, Best of Nevada, 1992, Oregon Discovery Guide, 1993, No. California Discovery Guide, 1993, The Ultimate Wine Book, 1993; contbr. articles on travel to various publs. Recipient Diane Seely award Ventura County Theatre Council, 1968. Mem. Soc. Am. Travel Writers. Republican. Home and Office: 11362 Yankee Hill Rd Box 1494 Columbia CA 95310

MARTIN, DORIS ELLEN, publisher, management consultant; b. Chgo., Oct. 26, 1927; d. John L. and Marie (Miller) Martin; m. Morton Rosenberg,

Dec. 15, 1963 (div. 1964). BS, NYU, 1952; MS, Boston U., 1958; EdD, Columbia U., 1964. Instr. Colby Coll., Waterville, Maine, 1952-54; dir. edn. dept. YWCA, Honolulu, 1954-59; dir. The Conf. Ctr., U. Hawaii, Honolulu, 1960-65; dir. spl. projects and assoc. prof. NYU, N.Y.C., 1965-66; dir. state plan Dept. Planning/Econ. Devel., State of Hawaii, Honolulu, 1966-69; spl. asst. George Washington U., Washington, 1970; mgmt. cons. Dr. D. Martin Assocs., Wailuku, Hawaii, 1980—; pres., pubr. Martin Mgmt. Books, Wailuku, Hawaii, 1985—. Author 7 books. Mem. Rep. Nat. Com., 1975—. Mem. Pubrs. Mktg. Assn. Home and Office: Martin Mgmt Books Box 119 RR 1 Wailuku HI 96793

MARTIN, GARY DEWAYNE, clergyman; b. Hemet, Calif., Jan. 16, 1954; s. James Robert and Jewell Ilene (Rogers) M.; m. Nancy Elizabeth Young, Aug. 11, 1973; children: Anna Louise, Erin Elizabeth. BA, Calif. Bapt. Coll., 1976; M. Religious Edn., Golden Gate Sem., 1982; MDiv., Luther Rice Sem., 1993. Ordained minister in Bapt. Ch., 1976. Assoc. pastor Valle Vista Bapt. Ch., Hemet, 1972-76; pastor First Bapt. Ch., Gustine, Calif., 1976-77; assoc. pastor Calvary Bapt. Ch., Modesto, Calif., 1977-80; pastor Santa Cruz Ave. Bapt. Ch., Modesto, Calif., 1981-86, First Bapt. Ch., Winton, Calif., 1986—; instr. Calvary Bible Inst., Modesto, 1984-86, Cen. Valley Sem. Extension, Turlock, Calif., 1987—, dir. 1988—. Vice-moderator Cen. Valley Bapt. Assn., Turlock, 1986-87; asst. dir. Bapt. Dist. Children's Camps, Jenness Park, Sonora, Calif., 1986-92. Named Outstanding Young man in Am., U.S. Jaycees, Montgomery, Ala., 1986. Democrat. Home: 7289 Anne Cir Winton CA 95388-9382 Office: First Southern Baptist Ch 7264 Myrtle Ave Winton CA 95388-9711

MARTIN, GEORGE, psychologist, educator; b. L.A., May 8, 1940; s. George Leonard and Margaret (Padigamus) M.; m. Penny Harrell, July 18, 1963 (div. 1984); children: Jeni, Kimberle. BA, UCLA, 1965; MA, Calif. State U., L.A., 1967; MS, Calif. State U., Fullerton, 1988. Systems analyst L.A. Dept. Water & Power, 1965-67; project coord. L.A. Police Dept., 1967-70, edn. cons., 1980-83; alcohol researcher Pomona (Calif.) Coll., 1970-73; tng. systems researcher Lanterman State Hosp., Pomona, 1973-77; prof. psychology Mt. San Antonio Coll., Walnut, Calif., 1970—, dir. rsch., 1986—. Contbr. articles to profl. jours. Rsch. dir. Orange County Dem. Party, 1985-86. With U.S. Army, 1959-61. Grantee Nat. Inst. Law Enforcement, 1967-70, Nat. Inst. Alcohol, 1970-74. Mem. Am. Psychol. Assn., Nat. Sci. Assn., Lions. Home: 1313 N Grand Ave Ste 326 Walnut CA 91789-1317 Office: Mt San Antonio Coll 1100 N Grand Ave Walnut CA 91789-1341

MARTIN, GEORGE M., pathologist, gerontologist; b. N.Y.C., June 30, 1927; s. Barnett J. and Estelle (Weiss) M.; m. Julaine Ruth Miller, Dec. 2, 1952; children: Peter C., Kelsey C., Thomas M., Andrew C. BS, U. Wash., 1949, MD, 1953. Diplomate Am. Bd. Pathology, Am. Bd. Med. Genetics. Intern Montreal Gen. Hosp., Quebec, Can., 1953-54; resident-instr. U. Chgo., 1954-57; instr.-prof. U. Wash., Seattle, 1957—; vis. scientist Dept. Genetics Albert Einstein Coll., N.Y.C., 1964; chmn. Gordon Confs. Molecular Pathology, Biology of Aging, 1974-79; chmn., nat. res. Plan on Aging Nat. Inst. on Aging, Bethesda, Md., 1985-89; dir. Alzheimer's Disease Rsch. Ctr. U. Wash., 1985—. Editor Werner's Syndrome and Human Aging, 1985; contbr. articles in field to profl jours. Active Fedn. Am. Scientists. With USN, 1945-46. Recipient Allied Signal award in Aging, 1991; named Disting. alumnus U. Wash. Sch. Medicine, 1987; USPHS rsch. fellow dept. genetics Glasgow U., 1961-62; Eleanor Roosevelt Inst. Cancer Rsch. fellow Inst. de Biologie, Physiologie, Chimie, Paris, 1968-69; Josiah Macy faculty scholar Sir William Din Sch. Pathology, Oxford (Eng.) U., 1978-79; Humboldt Disting. scientist dept. genetics U. Wurzburg, Germany, 1991. Fellow AAAS, Gerontological Soc. Am. (chmn. Biol. Sci. 1979, Brookdale award 1981), Tissue Culture Assn. (pres. 1986-88); mem. Inst. Medicine, Am. Assn. Univ. Pathologists (emeritus), Am. Soc. Human Genetics, Am. Assn. Pathologists. Democrat. Home: 2223 E Howe Seattle WA 98112 Office: U Wash Sch Medicine Dept Pathology SM 30 Seattle WA 98195

MARTIN, GEORGE RAYMOND RICHARD, author; b. Bayonne, N.J., Sept. 20, 1948; s. Raymond and Margaret (Brady) M.; m. Gale Burnick, Nov. 15, 1975 (div. Dec. 1979). B.S. summa cum laude, Northwestern U., 1970; M.S. cum laude, 1971. Journalism intern Medill News Service, Washington, 1971; sportswriter, pub. relations officer N.J. Dept. Parks, Bayonne, 1971; coordinator communications and edn. Cook County (Ill.) Legal Assistance Found., Chgo., 1972-74; instr. journalism Clarke Coll., Dubuque, Iowa, 1976-78; writer-in-residence Clarke Coll., 1978-79; founder, chmn. Windy City Sci. Fiction Writers' Workshop, Chgo., 1972-76. Author sci. fiction: A Song for Lya, 1976, Songs of Stars and Shadows, 1977, Sandkings, 1981, Dying of the Light, 1977, Windhaven, 1981, Fevre Dream, 1982, The Armageddon Rag, 1983, Songs the Deadmen Sing, 1983, Portraits of His Children, 1987; editor: New Voices I, 1977, New Voices II, 1979, New Voices III, 1980, New Voices IV, 1981, John W. Campbell Awards vol. 5, 1984, Nightflyers, 1985, TUF Voyaging, 1986, Night Visions 3, 1987, Wild Cards, 1987, Aces High, 1987, Jokers Wild, 1987, Aces Abroad, 1988, Down & Dirty, 1988, Ace in the Hole, 1990, Dead Man's Hand, 1990, One-Eyed Jacks, 1991, Jokertown Shuffle, 1991, Double Solitaire, 1992, Dealer's Choice, 1992, Turn of the Cards, 1993, Card Sharks, 1993; story editor The Twilight Zone, CBS-TV, 1987; producer Beauty and the Beast, CBS-TV, 1987-88; contbr. short stories to mags. Mem. Sci. Fiction Writers Am. (dir. Central region 1977-79), Horror Writers Am., Writers Guild Am. West. Home: 102 San Salvador Ln Santa Fe NM 87501-1740

MARTIN, GORDON EUGENE, electrical engineer; b. San Diego, Aug. 22, 1925; s. Carl Amos and Ruth Marie (Fountain) M.; m. Tricia Jane Totten, June 10, 1949; children: Gloria, Theodore, Kathryn, Susan. BSEE, U. Calif., Berkeley, 1947; MS in Engring., UCLA, 1951; MA in Physics, S.D. State U., 1961; PhD in Elec. Engring., U. Tex., 1966. Elec. engr. Convar (Gen. Dynamics), San Diego, 1947; rsch. physicist Navy Electronics Lab., San Diego, 1947-52, Naval Ocean Systems Ctr., San Diego, 1954-80; acoustics dept. head Systems Exploration Inc., San Diego, 1980-82; pres. Martin Analysis Software Tech., Inc., San Diego, 1982—; cons. USN Hdqrs., Washington, 1954-80, piezoelectric bd. USN, Washington, 1960-80. Patentee of sonar and radio system. Lt. USNR, 1943-45, 52-54. Fellow Acoustical Soc. Am. (chpt. pres.); mem. N.Y. Acad. Scis., Inst. Electronics & Elec. Engring. (com. mem.), Sigma Xi, Sigma Pi Sigma. Office: Martin Analysis Software Tech Inc 3675 Syracuse Ave San Diego CA 92122-3322

MARTIN, JAMES FRANKLIN, physician, lawyer; b. Chattanooga, Feb. 22, 1929; s. Delbert Chester and Doshia (Locke) M.; m. Mary Edna Connelly, June 5, 1950; children: Samuel Franklin, Mary Karen, John Delbert, Molly Frances. MD, U. Tenn., Memphis, 1960; LLB, U. Tenn., Knoxville, 1952. Bar: Tenn. 1952, U.S. Ct. Mil. Appeals 1953. Engring. draftsman Combustion Engring. Co., Chattanooga, 1947-48; engr. mech. Combustion Engring. Co., Chattanooga, 1952; lawyer Harold Stone Law Firm, Knoxville, 1955-60; atty. Tenn. Valley Authority, Knoxville, 1955-56; intern James Walker Meml. Hosp., Wilmington, N.C., 1960-61, attending staff mem., 1962-66; pvt. practice in family practice Wilmington, N.C., 1961-66, Yuma, Ariz., 1968—; med. dir. Provident Life Accident Ins. Co., Chattanooga, 1966-68; instr. medicine James Walker Meml. Hosp., 1962-64; bd. dirs. Yuma Regional Med. Ctr., Mutual Ins. Co. of Ariz., Phoenix. Editor Tenn. Law Rev., 1951-52; author: Principal Security Devices in Tennessee, 1952. Capt. U.S. Army, 1952-55. Fellow Am. Acad. Family Practice, Am. Coll. Legal Medicine; mem. AMA, Ariz. Med. Assn., Am. Coll. Legal Medicine. Democrat. Home: 1733 Arcadia Ln Yuma AZ 85364 Office: Ste 4 2451 Ave A Yuma AZ 85364

MARTIN, JAMES PATRICK, florist; b. Seattle, May 25, 1946; s. John Dennis and Catherine (Kirley) M.; m. Denise Marie Widen, Apr. 24, 1982; children: Michele, David, Nicholas, Patrick, Christopher. BA in Humanities, Gonzaga U., 1968, BS in Philosophy, 1968; MBA in Bus., U. Seoul, Seoul, Korea, 1969. Capt. U.S. Army 7th Infantry Div., Korea, 1968-70; retail sales mgr. Pacific Coast Comml., Los Angeles, 1970-71; v.p. Ballard Blossom Inc., Seattle, 1971—; fin. com. mem. Florists Transworld Delivery, Southfield, Mich., 1983-86, Am. Floral Mktg. Coun., Washington, 1986-88. V.p. Seattle Allied Florists, Seattle, 1974-78; asst. soccer coach Seattle Pacific U., 1980—; bd. dirs. N.W. Soccer Found.; mem. selected pres.'s coun. Gonzaga U.; mayoral appointment to King County Bd. of Alcohol and Drug Abuse, 1991; appointed to FTD Pres.'s Coun. on Govt. Affairs, Washington, 1991—; chmn. sch. commn. Christ the King, 1991—. Named Bus. Person of the Yr. Seattle C. of C.; recipient Small Bus. award Washington Gov., 1985, Florists Transworld Delivery Top 100 award, 1977—; elected fellow Seattle Pacific U., 1986; Seattle Pacific U. Nat. Champions, 1978, 83, 85, 86. Mem. FTD, Seattle Allied Florists (v.p. 1974-78, com. on govt. affairs 1991), Am. Acad. Floraculture (elected). Republican. Roman Catholic. Home: 11931 Stendall Dr N Seattle WA 98133-8333 Office: Ballard Blossom Inc PO Box 70587 Seattle WA 98107-0587

MARTIN, JEFFRY RAY, financial executive; b. Anchorage, Alaska, Mar. 3, 1954; s. George Robert and Nayse Kathleen (Becker) M.; m. Lynne Elise Hassell, July 30, 1978; children: Nicholas Adam, Timothy Eric, Camille Aislinn. BS, Oreg. State U., 1976. Cert. mgmt. acct. Staff auditor Laventhol & Horwath, Portland, Oreg., 1976-77; cost acctg. supr. Hewlett Packard, Corvallis, Oreg., 1977-82; v.p. fin., chief fin. officer Intelledex, Corvallis, 1982—; cons. Electron Sci. Industries, Corvallis, 1991, Oreg. Digital Systems, Corvallis, 1987-89. Exec. planning com. United Way, Corvallis, 1986-90.

MARTIN, JOHN E., fast food resturant executive; b. 1945. BS, Middlebury Coll., 1967. Food svcs. mgr. Canteen Corp., 1971; food svcs. dir. ARA Svcs., Phila., 1972; with Burger King Corp., Edison, N.J., 1973-78; regional mgr. Burger Chef Systems, Inc., N.Y., 1979-82, pres., chief exec. officer; pres., chief exec. officer Hardees Food Systems, Inc., Rocky Mt., N.C., 1983, La Petite Boulangerie; with Taco Bell Corp., 1983—; now pres., chief exec. officer Taco Bell Corp., Irvine, Calif., also bd. dirs. 1st lt. U.S. Army, 1968-70. Office: Taco Bell 17901 Von Karman Ave Irvine CA 92714-6212

MARTIN, J(OHN) EDWARD, architectural engineer; b. L.A., Oct. 23, 1916; s. Albert C. and Carolyn Elizabeth (Borchard) M.; m. Elizabeth Jane Hines, May 27, 1944; children: Nicolas Edward, Peter Hines, Sara Jane McKinley Reed, Christopher Carey, Elizabeth Margaret Ferguson. Student, U. So. Calif., 1934-36; BS in Archtl. Engring., U. Ill., 1939. Registered profl. engr., Calif., Ill. Structural engr. Albert C. Martin & Assocs., L.A., 1939-42, ptnr., 1945-75, mng. ptnr., 1975-86. Founding mem. bd. trustees Thomas Aquinas Coll., Santa Paula, Calif., 1971—. Lt. USNR, 1942-45. Fellow ASCE; mem. Structural Engrs. Assn. Calif., Cons. Engrs. Assn. Calif., Jonathan Club (bd. dirs. 1978-81), Calif. Club (Ranchero Visitadores), Valley Hunt Club, Flintridge Riding Club, West Hills Hunt Club (Master of Fox Hounds 1975-88). Republican. Roman Catholic. Office: Albert C Martin & Assocs 811 W 7th St Los Angeles CA 90017-3408

MARTIN, JOSEPH, JR., lawyer, diplomat; b. San Francisco, May 21, 1915; m. Ellen Chamberlain Martin, July 5, 1946; children: Luther Greene, Ellen Myers. AB, Yale U., 1936, LLB, 1939. Assoc. Cadwalader, Wickersham & Taft, N.Y.C., 1939-41; ptnr. Wallace, Garrison, Norton & Ray, San Francisco, 1946-55, Pettit & Martin, San Francisco, 1955-70, 73—; gen. counsel FTC, Washington, 1970-71; ambassador, U.S. rep. Disarmament Conf., Geneva, 1971-76; mem. Pres.'s Adv. Com. for Arms Control and Disarmament, 1974-78; bd. dirs. Arcata Corp., Astec Industries, Inc. Pres. Pub. Utilities Commn., San Francisco, 1956-60; Rep. nat. committeeman for Calif., 1960-64; treas. Rep. Party Calif., 1956-58; bd. dirs. Patrons of Art and Music, Calif. Palace of Legion of Honor, 1958-70, pres., 1963-68; bd. dirs. Arms Control Assn., 1977-84; pres. Friends of Legal Assistance to Elderly, 1983-87. Lt. comdr. USNR, 1941-46. Recipient Ofcl. commendation for Outstanding Service as Gen. Counsel FTC, 1973, Distinguished Honor award U.S. ACDA, 1973, Lifetime Achievement award Legal Assistance to the Elderly, 1981. Fellow Am. Bar Found. Clubs: Burlingame Country, Pacific Union. Home: 1177 California St Apt 1514 San Francisco CA 94108-2224 Office: Pettit & Martin 101 California St Fl 35 San Francisco CA 94111-5802

MARTIN, JOSEPH BOYD, neurologist, educator; b. Bassano, Alta., Can., Oct. 20, 1938; s. Joseph Bruce and Ruth Elizabeth (Ramer) M.; m. Rachel Ann Wenger, June 18, 1960; children: Bradley, Melanie, Douglas, Neil. B.Sc., Eastern Mennonite Coll., Harrisonburg, Va., 1959; M.D., U. Alta., 1962; Ph.D., U. Rochester, N.Y., 1971; M.A. (hon.), Harvard U., 1978. Resident in internal medicine Univ. Hosp., Edmonton, Alta., 1962-64; resident in neurology Case-Western Res. U. Hosps., 1964-67; rsch. fellow U. Rochester, N.Y., 1967-70; mem. faculty McGill U. Faculty Medicine, Montreal, Que., Can., 1970-78; prof. medicine and neurology, neurologist-in-chief Montreal Neurol. Inst., 1976-78; chmn. dept. neurology Mass. Gen. Hosp., Boston, also Dorn prof. neurology Harvard U. Med. Sch., 1978-89; dean Sch. Medicine U. Calif., San Francisco, 1989-93; chancellor U. Calif., San Francisco, 1993—; mem. med. adv. bd. Gairdner Found., Toronto, 1978-83; adv. council neurol. disorders program Nat. Inst. Neurol., Communicative Disorders and Stroke, 1979-82. Co-author: Clinical Neuroendocrinology, 1977, The Hypothalmamus, 1978, Clinical Neuroendocrinology: A Pathophysiological Approach, 1979, Neurosecretion and Brain Peptides: Implications for Brain Functions and Neurological Disease, 1981, Brain Peptides, 1983; editor Harrison's Principles of Internal Medicine, Clin. Neuroendocrinology 2d edit., 1987. Recipient Moshier Meml. gold medal U. Alta. Faculty Medicine, 1962, John W. Scott gold med. award, 1962; Med. Research Council Can. scholar, 1970-75. Mem. Internat. Soc. Neuroendocrinology (council 1980—), Am. Neurol. Assn., Am. Physiol. Soc. (Bowditch lectr. 1978), Royal Coll. Phys. and Surg. Can., Endocrine Soc., Soc. Neurosci., Am. Soc. Clin. Investigation, Assn. Am. Physicians, Am. Acad. Arts and Scis., Inst. of Medicine, Nat. Acad. Scis., Nat. Adv. Coun., Nat. Inst. Aging. Office: U Calif Sch Medicine 513 Parnassus Ave Ste 126 San Francisco CA 94143-0001

MARTIN, JUNE JOHNSON CALDWELL, journalist; b. Toledo, Oct. 6; d. John Franklin and Eunice Imogene (Fish) Johnson; A.A., Phoenix Jr. Coll., 1939-41; B.A., U. Ariz., 1941-43, 53-59; student Ariz. State U., 1939, 40; m. Erskine Caldwell, Dec. 21, 1942 (div. Dec. 1955); 1 son, Jay Erskine; m. 2d, Keith Martin, May 5, 1966. Free-lance writer, 1944—; columnist Ariz. Daily Star, 1956-59; editor Ariz. Alumnus mag., Tucson, 1959-70; book editor, gen. feature writer, tape audio rev. columnist Ariz. Daily Star, Tucson, 1970—; panelist, co-producer TV news show Tucson Press Club, 1954-55, pres., 1958; co-founder Ariz. Daily Star Ann. Book & Author Event. Contbg. author: Rocky Mountain Cities, 1949; contbr. articles to World Book Ency., and various mags. Mem. Tucson CD Com., 1961; vol. campaigns of Samuel Goddard, U.S. Rep. Morris Udall, U.S. ambassador and Ariz. gov. Raul Castro. Recipient award Nat. Headliners Club, 1959, Ariz. Press Club award, 1957-59, Am. Alumni Council, 1966, 70. Mem. Nat. Book Critics Circle, Jr. League of Tucson, Tucson Urban League, P.E.N. U.S.A. West, Pi Beta Phi. Democrat. Methodist. Club: Tucson Press. Home: Desert Foothills Sta PO Box 65388 Tucson AZ 85728 Office: PO Box 26807 Tucson AZ 85726

MARTIN, KATHRYN LEE, chemical dependency counselor, educator; b. Bellevue, Pa., July 1, 1935; d. Stanley Alfred and Mary Lee (Starr) Orr; m. Joan Ian Martin, June 20, 1957 (div. Oct. 1982); children: Kristie Lee Peters, Mark Edward, Valerie Lynn Larson, Jennifer Ellice. BA, So. Ill. U., 1973; MA, Pacific Luth. U., 1974. Cert. chem. dependency counselor. Counselor, sr. counselor Puget Sound Hosp. Tx. Ctr., Tacoma, 1975-78; counselor, treatment dir. Naval Hosp. Alcohol Rehab. Svc., Bremerton, Wash., 1978-87; pvt. practice Olympic Mental Health Assocs., Bremerton, 1986-90; founder, exec. dir. Advantages Counseling Svcs., Bremerton, 1990—; instr. Ft. Steilacoom Community Coll., Tacoma, 1981-84, Olympic Coll., Bremerton, 1985, O'Leary Clinic, Bremerton, 1985; cons. North, Cen., South Kitsap Sch. Dists., Bremerton, 1984—; mem. Wash. State Counselor Cert. Bd., 1982-87, 13th Naval Dist. Admiral's Drug and Alcohol Adv. Bd., Seattle, 1982-86, Wash. State Bur. of Alcohol and Substance Abuse Ednl. Approval Com., Seattle, 1985-87, Kitsap Mental Health Multidisciplinary Adv. Team, Bremerton, 1990—; others. Appointee chair, County Commr. Substance Abuse Adv. Bd., Bremerton, 1990—; mem. bd. dirs. Awareness Express (adolescent treatment program), Port Orchard, Wash., 1982-83, Kitsap County Coun. on Alcoholism, Bremerton, 1982-83; task force mem. Wash. State Chem. Dependency Training Coalition on Treatment Outcomes. With USAF, 1956-58. Mem. Chem. Dependency Profls. of Wash. State (chair ethics com. 1986-93, pres. 1993—), Wash. State Coun. on Alcoholism, Nat. Assn. Alcoholism and Drug Abuse Counselors, County Assn. Substance Abuse Providers, Wash. State Assn. Ind. Outpatient Programs (ethics com. 1991—). Home: 2965 Spartacus St NE Bremerton WA 98310-9553 Office: Advantages Counseling Svcs 400 Washington Ave Ste 3 Bremerton WA 98310

MARTIN, KENNETH DAVID, manufacturing executive; b. Salt Lake City, May 15, 1952; s. David Owen and Virginia Marie (Hedlund) M.; m. Sandra Ellen Christensen, May 5, 1978; children: David, Kenneth Jr., Brandon, Sharee, Nathan, Jonathan. BS, U. Utah, 1976. Employee Martin Door Mfg. Inc., Salt Lake City, 1960-76, v.p., 1976-86, pres., 1986—. Recipient Regional award, SBA, U.S., 1976. Mem. Nat. Assn. Garage Door Mfrs. (dir., v.p. 1987—, pres. 1990, 91), South Salt Lake C. of C., Skull & Bones Honor Soc., Owl & Key Honor Soc., Phi Kappa Phi, Beta Gamma Sigma. Republican. LDS Church. Office: Martin Door Mfg Inc PO Box 27437 2828 S 900 W Salt Lake City UT 84119

MARTIN, LEONARD AUSTIN, II, music educator; b. McCook, Nebr., July 18, 1949; s. Austin Berwell and Marie Elizabeth (Kimbro) M.; m. Sandra Lou Lindley, June 11, 1988; 1 stepchild, Heather Betz. BA summa cum laude, Metro State Coll., 1971; MA, Denver U., 1972, PhD, 1984. Cert. Type B profl. tchr., Type D adminstr., Colo. Music instr. Peetz (Colo.) Elem. & Secondary Schs., 1972, Denver Sch. Dists., 1973, Martin's Studio, Denver, 1965-81; music instr., master scheduler Adams County 5-Star Schs., Northglenn, Colo., 1974—; adj. prof. music Colo. U. at Denver, 1990-93; youth choir dir. Faith Evang. Presbyn. Ch., Aurora, 1973-75, adult substitute dir. for choir, 1987-90; worship team mem., substitute choir dir. Cornerstone Community Ch., Denver, 1991—. Author: High School Music Theory, 1978, Basic Music Theory, 1989. Cornet player Colo. All-State Band, Greeley, 1967, Aurora Summer Community Band, 1967-71. Mem. Colo. Music Educators Assn., Music Educators Nat. Conf., NEA, Colo. Edn. Assn., Dist. 12 Edn. Assn., Nat. Geog. Soc., Smithsonian Assocs. Republican. Mem. of Evangelical Presbyterian Ch. Home and Office: 1357 Hanover St Aurora CO 80010-3334 Office: Fed Heights Elem Sch 2500 W 96th Ave Denver CO 80221-5701

MARTIN, LEONARD GILMAN, university official; b. Hanover, Pa., May 24, 1937; s. Leonard B. and Lucile (Gilman) M.; m. Madeline Johnson, Aug. 24, 1968 (div. Aug. 1980); 1 child, Elizabeth Anne. BS, Trinity U., San Antonio, 1959. Dept. mgr. bookstore U. Utah, Salt Lake City, 1959-60, U. Wash., Seattle, 1960-61, Tex. Tech U., Lubbock, 1961-65; dept. mgr. bookstore U. Idaho, Moscow, 1965-66, mgr., 1981-93, asst. mgr., 1966-81, 93—. Mem. Lions (pres. Moscow Paradise club 1977-78, zone chmn. multiple dist. 19 1978-79, dist. gov. 1980, 100% Pres. award 1978, 100% Zone Chmn. award 1979, 100% Gov. award 1980). Episcopalian. Home: 403 N Monroe St Moscow ID 83843 Office: U Idaho Bookstore Moscow ID 83843

MARTIN, MARK WILLIAM, computer programmer and designer; b. West Covina, Calif., Aug. 14, 1969; s. William and Elizabeth (Murphy) M. AA in Liberal Arts, Mt. San Antonio Coll., Walnut, Calif., 1987, AS in Computer Info. Sci., 1989. Ptnr., cons. Gigabytes Cons., Covina, Calif., 1989-90; floor mgr. Inacomp Computers, Covina, 1990-91; mus. guide Griffith Obs., L.A., 1991-92, instr. travelling telescope, 1992—. Author computer program Desert Trader, 1988. Mem. Greater L.A. Zoo Assn. Democrat. Home: 15913 Three Palms Dr Hacienda Heights CA 91745 Office: Griffith Obs 2800 E Observatory Rd Los Angeles CA 90027

MARTIN, MELISSA CAROL, radiological physicist; b. Muskogee, Okla., Feb. 7, 1951; d. Carl Leroy and Helen Shirley (Hicks) Paden; m. Donald Ray Martin, Feb. 14, 1970; 1 child, Christina Gail. BS, Okla. State U., 1971; MS, UCLA, 1975. Cert. radiol. physicist, Am. Bd. Radiology, radiation oncology, Am. Bd. Med. Physics. Asst. radiation physicist Hosp. of the Good Samaritan, L.A., 1975-80; radiol. physicist Meml. Med. Ctr., Long Beach, Calif., 1980-83, St. Joseph Hosp., Orange, Calif., 1983-92, Therapy Physics, Inc., Bellflower, Calif., 1993—; cons. in field. Editor: (book) Current Regulatory Issues in Medical Physics, 1992. Fund raising campaign div. mgr. YMCA, Torrance, Calif., 1988-92; dir. AWANA Youth Club-Guards Group, Manhattan Beach, Calif., 1984-92. Named Dir. of Symposium, Am. Coll. Med. Physics, 1992. Mem. Am. Assn. Physicists in Medicine (profl. coun. 1990-95), Am. Coll. Radiology (econs. com. 1992-94), Calif. Med. Physics Soc. (treas. 1991-93), Am. Coll. Med. Physics (chancellor western region 1992-95), Am. Soc. for Therapeutic Radiology and Oncology, Health Physics Soc. (pres. So. Calif. chpt. 1992-93), Am. Endocurietherapy Soc. Baptist. Home: 507 Susana Ave Redondo Beach CA 90277 Office: Therapy Physics Inc 9156 Rose St Bellflower CA 90706

MARTIN, MICHAEL DAVID, science data systems technologist; b. Portland, Oreg., Sept. 13, 1946; s. Clifford Alvin and Rachel Ann (McLarty) M.; m. Jancis Mathews, Oct. 14, 1978; children: Dusty Ann, Kelly Diana. BA in Mktg., U. Wash., 1968. Data analyst Jet Propulsion Lab., Pasadena, Calif., 1971-73; team leader Jet Propulsion Lab., Pasadena, 1973-78, group supr., 1978-82, project engr., 1982—; editorial advisor CD-Rom Profl. jour., 1991—. Author: (computer program) IMDISP, 1990 (NASA Tech. award 1990); contbr. chpts. to books, articles to profl. jours. With U.S. Army, 1968-70, Vietnam. Recipient NASA Exceptional Svc. award, Pasadena, 1990. Mem. Assn. for Computing Machinery, Spl. Interest Group for CD-Rom Applications and Tech., JPL Golf Club (pres. 1984). Republican. Office: Sci Data Systems 4800 Oak Grove Dr Pasadena CA 91109

MARTIN, MICHAEL ROBERT AKERS, information systems specialist; b. Panorama City, Calif., Jan. 10, 1964; s. Robert Akers and Linda Eileen (Edgerton) M.; m. Carol Lynn Vilter, Oct. 13, 1990. BA, UCLA, 1987. LAN adminstr. Magnetic Transit of Am., Century City, Calif., 1987-90; info. systems mgr. Grobstein and Co., Sherman Oaks, Calif., 1990-91, Fox Broadcasting Co., L.A., 1991—; authorized reseller Novell Netware, L.A., 1989—, 386 cert., 1991—. Sole programmer: (computer program) IBM Quick Scan, part of the IBM ProPlan Dealer Tng. Series, 1988. Vol. Students with Gary Hart, UCLA, 1984; svc., hon. guest Dem. Nat. Conf., San Francisco, 1984. Mem. Delta Tau Delta. Roman Catholic. Home: 1115 5th St # 217 Santa Monica CA 90403 Office: Fox Broadcasting Co PO Box 900 Beverly Hills CA 90213

MARTIN, NANCY L., communications exective; b. Phoenix, Dec. 6, 1931; d. Donald Mackenzie and Mary (Wilson) M. BA, U. Calif., 1954. Reporter Phoenix Gazette, 1951-52; creative dir. Modern Advtg., Santa Monica, Calif., 1954-60; publicist Los Angeles, 1960-63; exec. v.p. Ad Mktg., Beverly Hills, Calif., 1963-68; pres. Martin Ptnrs., Inc., Beverly Hills, 1968-75; supr. Sitmar Cruises, Los Angeles, 1975-86, nat. tng. cons., 1986-90; v.p. mktg. and sales Uniglobe Hi Desert Travel, Victorville, Calif., 1990—. Recipient Design Excellence award Type Dirs. Club, 1963. Mem. ASTD. Democrat. Roman Catholic. Home: 31350 157th St E Llano CA 93544-9742

MARTIN, PERRY CLYDE, electronic specialist, soil scientist; b. Orem, Utah, Aug. 10, 1950; s. Albert Clyde and Wanda Burneta (Atchison) M.; m. Sunmieng Poomduong, Jue 5, 1988; children: T.S., Terradi Burneta. B in Biophysics Rsch., Westminster Coll., 1983; student, Utah State U., 1986. Expeditor Western Div. EDO Corp., Salt Lake City, 1980-83; electronics specialist Hill Air Force Base, Clearfield, Utah, 1983—; creator, owner Thai-Berry Park, Clearfield, 1988—. Chmn. bd. dirs. Western Youth Clearfield, 1989—. Home: 458 East 450 South Clearfield UT 84015

MARTIN, PRESTON, merchant bank executive; b. L.A., Dec. 5, 1923; s. Oscar and Gaynell (Horne) M.; 1 child, Pier Preston. BS in Fin., U. So. Calif., 1947, MBA, 1948; PhD in Monetary Econs., U. Ind., 1952. Prof. fin. Grad. Sch. Bus. Adminstrn. U. So. Calif., 1950-60; prin. in housebldg. firm, 1952-56; with mortgage fin. and consumer fin. instns., 1954-57; developer, adminstr. Pakistan Project for Grad. Bus. Edn., 1960-63; commr. savs. and loan State of Calif., 1967-69; chmn. Fed. Home Loan Bank Bd., Washington, 1969-72; founder, CEO PMI Mortgage Ins. Co., 1972-80; chmn., CEO Seraco Group subs. Sears, Roebuck & Co., 1980-81, also bd. dirs. parent co.; chmn., CEO Westfed Holdings Inc., L.A., 1986-92, SoCal Holdings, Inc., L.A., 1987—, H.F. Holdings, Inc., San Francisco, 1986-92; chmn. So. Calif. Savs. and Loan Assn., Beverly Hills, 1987—, Western Fed. Savs. and Loan Assn., Marina Del Rey, Calif., 1992—, So. Calif. Savs., Beverly Hills, Calif., 1987—; vice-chmn. Fed. Res. Bd., Washington, 1982-86; mem. adv. com. Fed. Home Loan Mortgage Corp.; prof. fin. Pakistan (AID) Project; prof. bus. econ. and fin. IPSOA, Italy; mem. TIAC Fed. Res. Bd., mem. USA/ROC Econ. Coun.; mem. bd. overseers Hoover Instn. War, Revolution and

Peace Stanford U. Author: Principles and Practices of Real Estate, 1959. Mem. President's Commn. on Housing, 1980-81; prin. Coun. Excellence in Govt., Washington. Recipient House and Home award, 1969, award Engring. News Record, 1971, NAHB Turntable award, 1973. Mem. Lambda Chi Alpha. Presbyterian.

MARTIN, RAY, banker; b. Nogales, AZ, 1936. With Coast Savs. and Loan Assn. (now Coast Fed. Bank), L.A., 1959—, pres., 1980-84, pres., chief exec. officer, from 1984, now chmn. bd., chief exec. officer, also bd. dirs. Office: Coast Fed Bank 1000 Wilshire Blvd Los Angeles CA 90017-2457*

MARTIN, ROBERT BURTON, consultant; b. Takoma Park, Md., Mar. 17, 1935; s. Herbert Lester and Lenora Marie (Sponseller) M.; m. Mary Lou Rushworth, Sept. 7, 1959 (div. Dec. 1982); children: Laurajean, Kenneth, Donna Beth. BEE, Cornell U., 1958; MS, Northwestern U., 1966, PhD, 1967. Dir. mgmt. systems Denver and Rio Grande Western R.R., 1967-71; v.p. Mgmt. Design Assoc., Denver, 1971-79; owner Martin & Assoc., Denver, 1979—; treas. Rocky Mountain Chpt., Inst. of Mgmt. Sci., Denver, 1968-70; opening speaker Am. Inst. CPA's, Las Vegas, Nev., 1988. Author and Pub. Martin Reports, newsletter, 1981—. Served to lt. USN, 1958-63. Mem. Inst. of Mgmt. Cons., Alpha Pi Mu, Sigma Xi. Home and Office: 180 Cook St Ste 110 Denver CO 80206-5331

MARTIN, ROBERT GREGORY, chemist; b. Denver, Apr. 24, 1959; s. Harold Gregory and Margaret C. (Mayer) M. BS, U. Denver, 1982. Computer distbr. Tronics Sales Corp., Ft. Worth, 1983; lab. technician Hager Labs., Denver, 1983-84, chem. analyst I, 1984-85, chem. analyst II, 1985-86, chem. analyst III, 1986-87, operator GC/MS, 1987-88; chemist IV, operator GC/MS Rocky Mountain Analyyical Labs, Environ. Svc. Co., Arvada, Colo., 1988-91; chemist V Rocky Mountain Analytical Labs, Environ. Svc. Co., 1991-92; chemist U.S. geol. survey Nat. Water Quality Lab., Arvada, Colo., 1992—. Recipient Hornbeck award U. Denver, 1982; scholar U. Denver, 1982. Mem. AAAS, Am. Chem. Soc., N.Y. Acad. Sci., Am. Inst. Chemists, The Planetary Soc., Gold Key, Alpha Lambda Delta, Alpha Epsilon Delta. Roman Catholic. Home: 7911 Otis Cir Arvada CO 80003-2309 Office: US Geol Survey Nat Water Quality Labs 5293 B Ward Rd Arvada CO 80002

MARTIN, ROBERT MICHAEL, prosecutor; b. N.Y.C., Nov. 28, 1922; s. Charles Augustus and Mary Corcoran (Shannon) M.; m. Monica Maria Schmid, Jan. 22, 1951; children: Tara J., C. Brian, Stacy D. BA, Amherst Coll., 1949; grad. cert., Trinity Coll., Dublin, Ireland, 1950; JD, U. So. Calif., 1965; diploma in law, Nat. D.A. Coll., 1973. Bar: Calif. 1966. Mem. faculty Chadwick Sch., Rolling Hills, Calif., 1952-56; mgmt. Servo-Mechanisms, Torrance, Calif., 1956-58, Systems Devel.Corp., Santa Monica, Calif., 1958-62, Douglas Missile & Space, Santa Monica, Calif., 1962-63; v.p. Automation Svc. Co., Beverly Hills, 1963-65; dep. pub. defender L.A. County, 1965-67, spl. asst. dist. atty., dept. dist atty., 1971—; chief counsel, exec. officer Calif. Alcohol Beverage Control Bd., 1967-69; state dir. Calif. Dept. of Social Welfare, Sacramento, 1969-71; instr. travel law West L.A. Coll. Author: Automation in Medicine. Sgt. U.S. Army Air Corp., 1942-45. Mem. Calif. Bar Assn., Calif. Dist. Atty. Assn., Irish-Am. Bar Assn., Asia-Pacific Lawyers Assn., Internat. Forum of Travel and Tourism Advisors, Air Force Assn., 454th Bombardment Group Assn., Amherst Coll. Alumni Assn., U. So. Calif. Alumni Assn. Republican. Office: Dist Atty 825 Maple Ave Torrance CA 90503

MARTIN, RUDY, lawyer; b. Dixon, N.Mex., Oct. 17, 1951; s. Severiano and Maria (Barela) M.; m. Carolina Martinez, Oct. 16, 1971 (div. Oct. 1987); children: Antonio D., Carlos R. BS in Bus. Adminstrn., U. Albuquerque, 1979, BA in Spanish, 1980; JD, U. N.Mex., 1983. Bar: N.Mex, U.S. Dist. Ct. N.Mex. Investigator, paralegal Josephine Rohr, Atty., Albuquerque, 1983-85; atty. Indian Pueblo Legal Svcs., Laguna, N.Mex., 1985-88, City of Albuquerque, 1988, Rudy Martin & Assocs., Aubuquerque, 1988—. Active DARE, 1990—, Lawyers with Class, 1991. With U.S. Army, 1970. Mem. Am. Trial Lawyers Assn., Hispanic Bar Assn., Laguna/Acoma Tribal Bar Assns., Chicano Police Officers Assn., Latino Peace Officers Assn. (Meritorious Svc. award 1991). Democrat. Home: 1219 Del Mastro SW Albuquerque NM 87120 Office: Rudy Martin & Assoc PA 303 San Mateo NE Ste 204 Albuquerque NM 87108

MARTIN, SCOTT GRADDY, mechanical engineer; b. Pueblo, Colo., July 23, 1947; s. James Marvin and Beverly Jean (Graddy) M.; m. Josephine Karen Riccillo (div. 1981); children: Michael Scott, Tracy Lynn, Patrick James; m. Karen V. Christensen, Sept. 2, 1989. BSME, Colo. State U., 1971; MS in Sci. and Engring. Mgmt., West Coast U., 1985. Mechanical engr. Gen. Dynamics, Pomona, Calif., 1975-79; sr. mechanical engr. Gen. Dynamics, Pomona, 1979-81, group engr., 1981-82, project engr., 1982-85, engr. advanced devel. project, 1987—; sr. staff engr. Lockheed Aircraft Svcs., Ontario, Calif., 1985-87. Patentee in field. With U.S. Army 1971-74. Home: 10350 Baseline Rd Trlr 31 Alta Loma CA 91701-6027 Office: Hughes Missile Systems Co 1675 W Mission Blvd Pomona CA 91769

MARTIN, SUNNY, accountant; b. Ft. Bragg, Calif., Mar. 10, 1913; d. John William and Magdalena Wilhelmina (Giesler) Meyer; m. Arthur L. Smith, June 21, 1941 (div. 1951); m. Alphonso Martin, June 28, 1958 (dec. Oct. 1981). Student, Heald Bus. Coll., Oakland, Calif., 1931-33. Acct., office mgr. various cos., 1933-75; founder, sec./treas. Am. Bashkir Curly Register, Ely, Nev., 1971—. Author various cowboy poems, western street skits; editor newsletter, historical photos for Ely Daily Times. Founder Ely Riding Club, 1951, Ely Jr. Riding Club and Gymkhana, 1951; book com. editor Friends of Nev. Northern Railway, 1985-91; del. State Rep. Conv., 1965; active Ret. Sr. Vol. Program (recipient numerous awards). Recipient Golden Rule award for saving Curly Horse breed from extinction in the U.S., J.C. Penney, 1992; named to White Pine High Sch. Hall of Fame, Ely, Nev., 1992. Mem. White Pine Hist. Soc. (past pres., 1979-81, historian 1973-91, editor slide show, 1980, 4-H Club (horsemanship leader). Methodist. Home: PO Box 453 Ely NV 89301-0453 Office: Am Bashkir Curly Registry Valley View Hwy 50 Ely NV 89301

MARTIN, SUSAN FRY, lawyer; b. Coronado, Calif., Mar. 17, 1952; d. Leonard Henry and Verden Frances (Korth) Fry; m. Richard Lee Martin, May 17, 1986. BA in Econs., U. Calif., San Diego, 1974; JD, U. Calif., Berkeley, 1977, MBA, 1979. Bar: Calif. 1978, N.Mex. 1986. Counsel energy and commerce com. U.S. Ho. Reps., Washington, 1978-81; sr. project atty. Nat. Resources Def. Coun., Washington, 1981-83; rsch. dir. Western Network, Santa Fe, 1983-85; policy analyst N.Mex. Environ. Improvement Div., Santa Fe, 1985-88, planner dir., 1988-93; staff mem. health and safety divsn. Los Alamos (N.Mex.) Nat. Lab., 1993—. Author: Western Water Flows to the Cities, 1985. Bd. dirs. Youth Shelters and Family Svcs., Santa Fe, 1984-88, Santa Fe chpt. Am. Cancer Soc., 1992—; mem. Santa Fe Met. Water Bd., 1990—. Mem. Nat. Assn. Environ. Profls., State Bar Calif., N.Mex. Bar Assn., N.Mex. Water Resources Rsch. Inst. (water conf. adv. com.), Environ. Law inst. Democrat. Roman Catholic. Home: 20 E Wildflower Dr Santa Fe NM 87501-8502 Office: Los Alamos Nat Lab Health and Safety Divsn Mail Stop K499 Los Alamos NM 87545

MARTIN, SUSAN MELINDA (LINDA), city manager; b. Longview, Tex., Sept. 26, 1954; d. Thomas Allen and Dorothy Jane (Schell) Martin; m. William Carl Jorgensen, Aug. 18, 1979; children: Rebecca Jane Jorgensen, Stephanie Lynn Jorgensen. BS, U. Colo., 1975, MPA, 1979. Salesperson Life Ins. Co., Boulder, Colo., 1975; engring. technician City of Lakewood, Colo., 1975-78, project mgr., 1979-80; asst. dir. transp. City of Boulder, Colo., 1978-79; transp. planner Denver Regional Coun. of Govts., 1980-81; circuit rider city mgr. Towns of Superior, Erie, Columbine Valley, Nederland, City of Black Hawk, Colo., 1982-85; adminstrv. officer State of Colo., Denver, 1986-89; dep. city mgr. City of Englewood, Colo., 1989-92; city mgr. City of Black Hawk, 1992—; mem. exec. bd. Sr. Transp. Systems, Boulder, 1984; com. mem. Colo. Mcpl. League, Denver, 1985—. Mem. Gov.'s Bd. Non-Rated Securities, Denver, 1991-92. Named Outstanding Supporter, Colorado County Treasurers' Assn., 1988, 89; named to Outstanding Young Women of Am., 1988. Mem. Internat. City Mgmt. Assn., Colo. City/County Mgrs. Assn., Colo. Mcpl. Mgmt. Assts. Assn. (entertainment chair 1991, pres.-elect 1992), Women in Mcpl. Govt. (treas. 1991-92). Democrat. Episcopalian. Home: 5283 E Euclid Boulder CO 80303 Office: City of Black Hawk P O Box 17 Black Hawk CO 80422

MARTIN, VINCENT FRANCIS, JR., real estate investment executive; b. Waterbury, Conn., Oct. 20, 1941; s. Vincent Francis and Mary Elizabeth (Fugilese) M.; m. Kathy Sue Plummer, May 26, 1979; children—Christopher, Paige, Vincent Francis III. B.S., Boston Coll., 1963; M.B.A., Harvard U., 1968. Auditor, Peat Marwick Mitchell, Waterbury, 1964-65; exec. v.p. EFM, Inc., Boston, 1968-70, Coldwell Banker, Los Angeles, 1970-82; mng. ptnr. TCW Realty Advisors, Los Angeles, 1982—. Bd. dirs. Nat. Realty com., Los Angelses Entrepreneur Acad. Author articles in fin. jours. Active Lowman Club, Los Angeles. Mem. Urban Land Inst., Soc. Rev. Appraisers (sr.), Internat. Found. Employee Benefit Plans, Pension Real Estate Assn. (bd. dirs.), Nat. Realty Com. Roman Catholic. Clubs: Jonathan, Los Angeles Athletic. Home: 1551 Sorrento Dr Pacific Palisades CA 90272-2746 Office: TCW Realty Advisors 400 S Hope St Los Angeles CA 90071-2801

MARTIN, WARREN HOWARD, lawyer; b. Pasadena, Calif., Mar. 26, 1964; s. Warren Leicster and Laura Paez (Reed) M. Student, U. So. Calif., L.A., 1983-85; BA, Georgetown U., Washington, 1987; JD, U. Calif., Davis, 1990. Bar: Calif. 1991, U.S. Dist. Ct. (cen. dist.) Calif. 1992. Staff aide L.A. County Supr. Peter Schabarum, 1984-85; paralegal McDermot, Will & Emory, Washington, 1986-87; assoc. O'Melveny & Myers, L.A., 1990—. Mem. Calif. Bar Assn., County Bar Assn., Bruin Athletic Club UCLA. Republican. Home: 731 LaPorte Dr LaCanada CA 91011 Office: O'Melveny & Myers 400 S Hope St Ste 1500 Los Angeles CA 90071

MARTIN, WILFRED WESLEY, psychologist, property manager; b. Rock Lake, N.D., Dec. 3, 1917; s. William Isaac and Anna Liisa (Hendrickson-Juntunen) M.; m. Stella Helland, Sept. 25, 1943; children: Sydney Wayne, William Allan. BA, Jamestown Coll., 1940; army specialized tng. program, Hamilton Coll., 1944; MS, EdD, U. So. Calif., 1956. Highsch. prin., coach pub. sch., Nekoma, N.D., 1940-42; contact rep., psychologist VA, L.A., 1946-49, psychologist, chief rehab., 1972-77; from intern to resident Fargo (N.D.) VA Hosp., 1953-58; guidance dir., instr. Concordia Coll., Moorhead, Minn., 1951-53; psychologist VA, Fargo, N.D., 1953-57; assoc. Sci. Rsch. Assoc./IBM, Boulder, Colo., 1957-65; regional dir. Sci. Rsch. Assoc./IBM, L.A., 1966-72; owner, mgr. Martin Investements, Huntington Beach, Calif., 1977—; adjutant U. Miss., Oxford, 1942; trustee Wilfred W. and Stella Martin Trust, Huntington Beach, 1991. Author: Veterans Administration Work Simplification, 1948, 57. Charter mem. Rep. Presdl. Task Force, 1980; adv. sr. ptnrs. bd. dirs. U. Calif. Med. Sch., Irvine, 1990; donor Dr. and Mrs. W.W. Martin Endowment, Jamestown Coll., N.D., 1985. With U.S. Army, 1942-45. Mem. Am. Psychol. Assn., Cardinal & Gold U. So. Calif., Jamestown Coll. Heritage Circle (charter), Suomi Coll. Second Century Soc., Elks. Republican. Lutheran. Home: 9695 Verde Mar Dr Huntington Beach CA 92646

MARTIN, WILLIAM BLAIN, clergyman; b. L.A., Dec. 1, 1953; s. William Blaine Sr. and Ruth Lee (Gosey) M.; m. Deborah V. Martin, Dec. 11, 1976; children: William Blaine III, Laquenta V., Christina J. BA in Ethnic Studies and Religion, Pepperdine U., 1974, MA in Religion, 1976; MA, Calif. Grad. Sch. Theology, Glendale, 1988; PhD, Assoc. Christian Theol. Sch., 1990. Asst. pastor Met. Missionary Bapt. Ch., L.A., 1972-76, L.A. Christian Ctr., L.A., 1977-79; corp. pres. Inner City Christian Ctr., L.A., 1978—, sr. pastor, min. of music, choir dir., 1979—; pianist, mus. dir. Met. chpt. Full Gospel Businessmen's Fellowship Internat., L.A. Christian Ctr. Praise Team and Choir, 1976-78; organizer, dir. Keyboards, Instruments and Vocalist for Jesus Christ, 1975-78; ch. pianist, organist Met. Bapt. Ch. Sch., Heavenly Angels, Celestial and Inspirational Choirs, 1972-76; tchr. Believer's Faith Ctr. Sch. of Ministry, Victory Bible Ch., Crenshaw Christian Ctr. Sch. of Ministry; council officer Police Clergy, 1984-92; mem. bd. Fellowship Inner City Word Faith Chs; pres., owner, tchr., pastor Inner City Christian Ctr. Ch., 1980—. Mem. So. Calif. Minister's Fellowship (dir. 1986-93, Met. Ministers Coalition, Internat. Convention of Faith (area dir.). Democrat. Home and Office: Inner City Christian Ctr 6075 S Normandie Los Angeles CA 90044

MARTINES, KAREN LOUISE, hospital administrator, nurse; b. Paris, Ont., Can., July 24, 1952; d. Norman Walter and Shirley Lorraine (Ford) Watts; m. Lawrence James Martines, Feb. 23, 1980; 1 child, Maria Nicole. BSN, U. Western Ont., London, Can., 1976; MS, Chapman U., 1983. RN Centinela Hosp., Inglewood, Calif., 1976-77, gastroenterology RN III, 1977-83; med./surg. mgr. Flagstaff (Ariz.) Med. Ctr., 1983-87, cluster mgr. med./surg., 1987-89; dir. managed care McKenzie-Willamette Hosp., Springfield, Oreg., 1989—. Mem. NAFE, Profl. Women's Network, Calif. Soc. Gastrointestinal Assts. (v.p. 1981-82, pres. 1982-83), Soc. Gastrointestinal Assts (by-laws com. 1982-83), Nat. Assn. Quality Assurance Profls. Office: McKenzie Willamette Hosp 1460 G St Springfield OR 97477

MARTINETTI, RONALD ANTHONY, lawyer; b. N.Y.C., Aug. 13, 1945; s. Alfred Joseph and Frances Ann (Battipaglia) M. Student, U. Chgo., 1981-82; JD, U. So. Calif., 1982. Bar: Calif. 1982; U.S. Dist. Ct. (cen. and no. dists.) Calif. 1982, U.S. Dist. Ct. Ariz., 1992; U.S. Ct. Appeals (9th cir.) 1982. Ptnr. Kazanjian & Martinetti, Glendale, Calif., 1986—. Author: James Dean Story, 1975; editorial bd. The Advocate, 1991—; contbr. articles to profl. jours. Vol. trial lawyer Bet Tzedek Legal Svcs., 1987—. Mem. Calif. Bar Assn. Roman Catholic. Office: Kazanjian & Martinetti 520 E Wilson Ave Glendale CA 91206-4374

MARTINEZ, ARTURO DAVID, marketing representative, social activist; b. Lynwood, Calif., Feb. 6, 1966; s. Ernest Altamirano and Alma (Licano) M. BA in Internat. Econs., Boston U., 1988, BS in Journalism, 1988. Founder, mgr. Arts Mailing Svc., L.A., 1982-84; journalist Boston U. Today, 1984-86, advt. mgr., 1985-87; econ. analyst Compass Internat., Inc., Boston, 1987-88; mkgt. rep. IBM 100% Club 1990, L.A., 1988-91; account mgr. Lexmark Internat., Inc., Santa Monica, Calif., 1991—; advt. cons. Bostonia Mag., 1985-87, compensation cons. Pfizer Internat., Inc., Boston, 1987-88, Texaco, Boston, 1987-88. Dir.'s asst. Friends Without Barriers, Baja, Calif. and Mex., 1980-87; project coord. L.A. Homeless, 1988—. Scholar Boston U., 1984-88. Home: 17012 N Almont Dr Beverly Hills CA 90211-1814 Office: Lexmark Internat Inc 2450 Broadway St Fl 3D Santa Monica CA 90404-3036

MARTINEZ, CAMILLA MARIA, lawyer; b. Santa Fe, Feb. 26, 1954; d. Eloy A. and Frances (Roybal) M. BS, U. N.Mex., 1975, MA with honors, 1978; JD, U. Denver, 1985. Classroom tchr. Albuquerque Pub. Schs., 1975-82; with staff Martinez Bail Bond Co., Santa Fe, 1975-82; with legal staff Willis A. Belford, Jr. Law Offices, Colorado Springs, Colo., 1985-92; children's coord. Adult Learning Source Family Lit., Denver, Colo., 1988-91; mem. master tchr. lab. Metro State Coll. of Denver Early Childhood Devel. Ctr. Reader Mother of God Catholic Ch., Denver, 1983—, eucharistic minister, 1985—. Named one of Outstanding Young Women Am., 1985. Mem. Am. Trial Lawyers Assn., Colo. Trial Lawyers Assn., Student Am. Bar Assn., Mexican-Am. Law Students Assn., Phi Alpha Delta. Democrat. Home: PO Box 26327 Colorado Springs CO 80936-6327 Office: 1751 E Girard Pl # 716 Englewood CO 80110

MARTINEZ, EDGAR, professional baseball player; b. N.Y.C., Jan. 2, 1963. Student, Am. Coll., Puerto Rico. Third baseman Seattle Mariners, 1987—. Office: Seattle Mariners PO Box 4100 411 1st Ave S Seattle WA 98104

MARTINEZ, ELIZABETH, librarian. City libr. City of L.A. Office: Los Angeles Library Dept 548 S Spring St Los Angeles CA 90013*

MARTINEZ, JOHN STANLEY, aerospace engineer; b. Phila., Apr. 14, 1930; s. Joseph Vincent and Helen Leeds (Simpson) M.; m. Britta K. Ponder, Dec. 29, 1987; children: John Jr., Joseph G., Mary Lynn. BChemE, Rensselaer Poly. Inst., 1951; diploma, Oak Ridge Sch. Reactor Tech., 1957; PhD, U. Calif., Berkeley, 1962. Rsch. engr. N.Am. Aviation Co., Santa Susanna, Calif., 1954-55, Jet Propulsion Lab., Calif. Inst. Tech., Pasadena, Calif., 1955-61; rsch. assoc. Livermore (Calif.) Nat. Lab., 1959-61; with TRW Systems Group, Redondo Beach, Calif., 1961-76, mgr. high energy laser bus. area, 1970-76; pres. Physics Internat. Co., San Leandro, Calif., 1976-84, Jamar Enterprises, Moraga, Calif., 1970—, HLX Laser Inc., San Diego, 1986-87, Air-Sea Comm. Corp., San Diego, 1988-89; pres., CEO Jamar Tech. Co., San Diego, 1987-89, Calif. Jamar, Inc., 1989-92; chmn. Surgilase, Inc., Warwick, R.I., 1991—, Benchmark Industries, Goffstown, N.H., 1991—; CEO JMAR Industries, San Diego, 1993—; chmn. Texcel Inc., Westfield, Mass.; supervisory dir. Pisces Internat., Netherlands, 1982-84; pres., chmn. Hermosa Entertainment Corp., Hermosa Beach, Calif., 1969-72. Contbr. articles to profl. publs.; patentee in field. Chmn. Hermosa Beach City Improvement Commn., 1968-70. Capt. USMC, 1951-54, Korea. AEC fellow, 1958, Ford Found. fellow, 1960. Mem. IEEE, Sigma Xi, Tau Beta Pi. Home: PO Box 1030 Del Mar CA 92014-1030 Office: 3956 Sorrento Valley Blvd San Diego CA 92121-1403

MARTINEZ, JOSE BENITO, JR., radio and television broadcasting executive; b. Reedley, Calif., Aug. 10, 1964; s. Jose Benito and Maria de Los Angeles (Robledo) M. AA, Kings River Coll., 1987; BA, Calif. State U., Fresno, 1991. Asst. mgr. ops. Sta. KYNO, Fresno, 1990—; on line editor Sta. KMPH-TV, Fresno, 1990—. Translator (book) Comanja, 1980. Big brother Kinship, Reedley, 1985-87. Mem. NATAS, NARAS, Audio Engring. Soc., Soc. Broadcast Engrs., Inst. Elec. and Engring. Soc., Cinema Audio Soc., Illuminating Engring. Soc. North Am., Radio Club Am. Democrat. Protestant. Home: 4092 N Chestnut # 163 Fresno CA 93726-4712 Office: Sta KYNO AM 1300 2125 N Barton Ave Fresno CA 93703

MARTINEZ, MARLO RAY, small business owner, consultant; b. Espanola, N.Mex., Sept. 12, 1957; s. Jose Celso and Corina (Abeyta) M. Student, U. N.Mex., 1974-77, Dale Carnegie, 1977. Owner Marlos Athletics, Espanola, 1977—, Espanola T/W Svc. N.Mex. Office Product Co., 1979—, Total Look Hair Salon, Espanola, 1987—; exec. com. mem. Balance State/Pvt. Industry Coun., Santa Fe, 1983-86; co-exec. com. mem. Los Alamos Nat. lab. Com. Coun., 1985—; mem. SBA Region VI Adv. Coun., Albuquerque, 1989-90; chmn. Small Bus. Devel. Ctrs. State Adv. Coun., Santa Fe, 1990-91. Good will amb. People to People Internat., N.Mex., 1985; bd. mem. Citizen Rev. Bd. State of N.Mex., Espanola, 1988-89; adminstrv. asst., reader N.Mex. State Senate, Santa Fe, 1989-93; coord. for N.Mex. Sec. of State Campaign, 1990. Recipient Los Alamos (N.Mex.) Nat. Lab. Small Bus. of Yr. award, 1985, 86, Administrn. award for excellence SBA, Washington, 1987. Mem. Jaycees, Image, Espanala C. of C. (pres. 1985). Democrat. Roman Catholic. Home and Office: 216 N Riverside Dr Espanola NM 87532

MARTINEZ, MATTHEW GILBERT, congressman; b. Walsenburg, Colo., Feb. 14, 1929; children: Matthew, Diane, Susan, Michael, Carol Ann. Cert of competence, Los Angeles Trade Tech. Sch., 1959. Small businessman and bldg. contractor; mem. 97th-103rd Congresses from 30th (now 31st) Calif. dist., 1982—; mem. edn. and labor com., fgn. affairs com. Mem. Monterey Park Planning Commn., 1971-74; mayor City of Monterey Park, 1974-75; mem. Monterey Park City Council, 1974-80, Calif. State Assembly, 1980-82; bd. dirs. San Gabriel Valley YMCA. Served with USMC, 1947-50. Mem. Congl. Hispanic Caucus, Hispanic Am. Democrats, Nat. Assn. Latino Elected and Apptd. Ofcls., Communications Workers Am., VFW, Am. Legion, Latin Bus. Assn., Monterey Park C. of C., Navy League (dir.). Democrat. Lodge: Rotary. Office: US Ho of Reps 2231 Rayburn House Office Washington DC 20515-0531*

MARTINEZ, RUBEN MARTIN, logistics engineer; b. L.A., Mar. 12, 1948; s. Elias and Emma Louise (Jurado) M.; m. Deanna Jean Rein, May 1969 (div. 1976); children: Ruben Jr., Victor; m. Linn Ann Hampton, Apr. 5, 1980; children: Michael, Martin, Linnita, Loretta. AA in Bus., Rio Hondo Coll., 1973; AA in Logistics, BA in Computer System, Nat. U., 1989, Cert. in Exec. Computer Mgmt., 1990, MBA in Mgmt. Info. Systems, 1991. Registered engr., Calif. Sr. data analyst Continental Data Graphics, Culver City, Calif., 1972-79; provisioning engr. Hughes Aircraft, Ground Systems, Fullerton, Calif., 1979-83; sr. logistics engr. Rockwell Internat., Anaheim, Calif., 1983-87; sr. tech. writer B-2 div. Northrop Corp., Pico-Rivera, Calif., 1987—. Officer Civil Air Patrol, Compton, Calif., 1984. Mem. Soc. Logistics Engr., Am. Defense Preparedness Assn., Nat. Mgmt. Assn., KC. Republican. Roman Catholic. Home: 9605 Armley Ave Whittier CA 90604 Office: Northrop Corp B-2 Div L581/XY 8900 E Washington Blvd Pico Rivera CA 90660-3737

MARTINEZ, RUBÉN ORLANDO, sociology educator, researcher, consultant; b. Pueblo, Colo., Aug. 20, 1952; s. Eloy B. and Elvira (Martinez) M.; m. Peggy Lea Bean, Aug. 12, 1990. BS, U. So. Colo., 1976; MA, Ariz. State U., 1978; PhD, U. Calif., Riverside, 1984. Assoc. prof. U. Colo., Colorado Springs, 1984—; with Tomas Rivera Rsch. Ctr., 1989—; chair Sociology Dept. U. Colo., Colorado Springs, 1992—, pres. faculty assembly, 1993—; cons. Chicano Unity Coun., Colorado Springs, 1988—, Asociación Naciónal Pro Personas Mayores, L.A., 1980; rsch. asst. Ariz. Task Force on Organized Crime, Phoenix, 1977. Contbr. articles to profl. jours. Chair Human Rels. Commn., Colorado Springs, 1986-88, Chicano Unity Coun., 1988—; mem. Colorado Springs Minority Coalition, 1992—; mem. Pvt. Industry Coun., Colorado Springs, 1989-90, Immigration Svcs. Bd., Cath. Diocese, Colorado Springs, 1987. With U.S. Army, 1971-73. Recipient Community Svc. award Latino Forum, Pomona, Calif., 1991, Pres.'s Svc. award U. Colo., Boulder, 1988, Community Svc. awards NAACP, 1987, Latin Am. Edn. Fund, 1986; named Hispanic of Yr. Cinco de Mayo Coun., Colorado Springs, 1990. Mem. Western Social Sci. Assn. (exec. coun. 1992—), Am. Sociol. Assn., Nat. Assn. for Chicano Studies, Pacific Sociol. Assn., Colo. Assn. Chicanos in Higher Edn., Hispanic Rsch. and Arts Network (Ariz. State U.). Home: 2 Crownbridge Ct Pueblo CO 81001-9999 Office: U Colo at Colo Springs Austin Bluff Pky Colorado Springs CO 80933

MARTINEZ SMITH, ELIZABETH, librarian. BS in Latin Am. Studies, UCLA, 1965; MS in Libr. Sci., U. So. Calif., 1966. County libr. Orange County Pub. Libr., Orange, Calif.; dir. L.A. Pub. Libr. Systems, 1990—. Contbr. articles to profl. jours. Named Woman of Achievement Orange County, 1988, Hispanic Libr. of Yr., Hispanic Book Distributers, 1990; recipient Woman's Alert Award Orange County, 1990. Office: LA Pub Libr System Office of Dir 630 W 5th St Los Angeles CA 90071-2002

MARTINI, ARTHUR PETE, manufacturing company executive; b. El Paso, Sept. 19, 1943; s. Arthur Peter and Beatrice Martini; m. Linda Louise Fowler, July 11, 1968 (div. 1983); children: Russell Robert, James Dale, Bradwell Peter. BS in Anthropology, U. Oreg., 1972, postgrad., 1975-76. With Harold Club, Reno, 1966-68; salesman Cougill & Hansen Realtors, Eugene, Oreg., 1972-76; v.p. Duco-Lam, Inc., Drain, Oreg., 1976-77, pres., chief exec. officer, 1977-81; pres., chief exec. officer Am. Laminators, Inc., Eugene, 1982—; Bd. dirs. Douglas Nat. Bank, 1993—. Mem. exec. bd. Boy Scouts Am., Eugene, 1980—, coun. City Coun. of Yoncalla, Oreg., 1980-81; active Rep. Party, Portland, Oreg. With U.S. Army, 1962-65. Mem. Am. Inst. Timber Constrn. (bd. dirs. 1979-86, pres. 1984-85), Pres's. Assn. N.Y., Eugene Athletic Club, Rotary (community svc. chmn. 1984-92), Elks. Home: PO Box 336 Yoncalla OR 97499-0336 Office: Am Laminators Inc 1839 Garden Ave Eugene OR 97403-1927

MARTINO, DIANNE MARIE, financial consultant, jeweler; b. Norristown, Pa., July 21, 1954; d. James Martin and Nancy Jane (Heyser) M.; m. Lloyd Jerald Campbell, July 4, 1980 (div. June 1984), Richard Joseph Scafuto, July 21, 1984. B.S., Calif. State Poly. U., 1976; MBA, Pepperdine U., Malibu, Calif., 1989. Cert. netware engr.; registered fin. cons. Documentation coordinator Mitsubishi Internat., Los Angeles, 1976-78; material coordinator McDonnell Douglas Corp., Long Beach, Calif., 1978-81; system coordinator C.F. Braun, Alhambra, Calif., 1981-82; subcontract adminstr. Rockwell Internat., El Segundo, Calif., 1982-84; procurement adminstr. Northrop Corp., Pico Rivera, Calif., 1984-86; major subcontract administrator, 1986-92; fin. cons. Independent Capital Mgmt., Irvine, Calif., 1992—; owner Scatuto Jewelry; owner InfoServ (formerly Campbell News & Info. Svcs.). Author: The PLain English Guide to Starting your own Business. Republican. Club: Mensa. Avocations: reading, horseback riding, skiing, computers. Home: 11123 Arroyo Dr Whittier CA 90604-1921 Office: Independent Captial Mgmt 8001 Irvine Ctr Dr Ste 1100 Irvine CA 92718

MARTINS, EVELYN MAE, theatre owner; b. Salinas, Calif., June 12, 1929; d. Earl Baldwin and Esther Martine (Harding) Andersen; m. Nolan Anthony Martins, Aug. 20, 1946 (dec. June 1982); children: Dennis, Noelyn, Antonette, Darrin. Owner Skyview Drive-In Theatres, Salinas, 1948—. Mem. Nat. Assn. Theatre Owners, Showest (Calif. Woman Exhibitor of Yr. 1976), Variety Club, Jr. Women's Club (publicity dir. 1965-67), Optimist

Youth Found. (treas. 1966-68). Republican. Roman Catholic. Home and Office: Skyview Drive-In Theatres 201 Harrison Rd Salinas CA 93907-1612

MARTINS-GREEN, MANUELA, cell biologist; b. Luso, Moxico, Angola, Dec. 30, 1947; came to U.S., 1973; d. Joaquim P. and Maria Alice (Marques) Martins; m. Harry W. Green, II, May 15, 1975; children: Alice, Harry, Maria Green. BS, U. Lisbon, 1970; MS, U. Calif., Riverside, 1975; PhD, U. Calif., Davis, 1987. Chief scientist EM lab Agronomical Sta., Oeiras, Portugal, 1970-73; electron microscopist, dept. ophthalmology U. Calif., Davis, 1975-82; postdoctoral researcher Lawrence Berkeley Lab., U. Calif., 1987-88, postdoctoral fellow, 1988-91, staff rsch. scientist, 1992-93; adj. asst. prof. Rockefeller U., 1991-92; asst. prof. biology U. Calif., Riverside, 1993—; vis. lectr. U. Wuhan, China, 1988. Contbr. articles to profl. jours., books. Recipient Fulbright Travel grant Internat. Exch. Scholars, Riverside, 1973, dept. fellowship U. Calif., Riverside, 1973-75, Regents fellowship, 1985, NIH traineeship, 1986-87, Nat. Rsch. Svc. award, 1988-91; NIH grantee, 1992—. Mem. Am. Cancer Soc., Am. Soc. for Cell Biology, Am. Soc. Devel. Biology, Elec. Microscopy Soc. of Am., Women for Cell Biology, Wound Healing Soc., Phi Kappa Phi. Office: U Calif Dept Biology Riverside CA 92521

MARTINSON, CONSTANCE FRYE, television program hostess, producer; b. Boston, Apr. 11, 1932; d. Edward and Rosalind Helen (Sperber) Frye; m. Leslie Herbert Martinson, Sept. 24, 1955; 1 child, Julianna Martinson Carner. BA in English Lit., Wellesley Coll., 1953. Dir. pub. relations Coro Found., Los Angeles, 1974-79; producer/host KHJ Dimensions, Los Angeles, 1979-81, Connie Martinson Talks Books, Los Angeles, 1981—; instr. dept. humanities UCLA, 1981—; moderator, instr. Univ. Judaism; celebrity advisor Book Fair-Music Ctr., L.A., 1986; bd. dirs. Friends of English UCLA. Author Dramatization of Wellesley After Images, 1974; book editor, columnist Calif. Press Bur. Syndicate, 1986—. Pres. Mayor's adv. council on volunteerism, Los Angeles, 1981-82; chmn. community affairs dept. Town Hall of Calif., Los Angeles, 1981-85; bd. dirs. legal def. fund NAACP, Los Angeles, 1981-84. Mem. Women in Cable, Am. Film Inst., Jewish TV Network (bd. dirs. 1985-87), PEN, Nat. Book Critics Assn., Wellesley Coll. Club (pres. 1979-81), Mulholland Tennis Club. Democrat. Jewish. Home and Office: 2288 Coldwater Canyon Dr Beverly Hills CA 90210-1756

MARTINSON, JOHN ROBERT, investment banker; b. Chgo., Sept. 9, 1935; s. Warren Charles Martinson and Jane (Martin) Finlayson; m. Kathryn Hellyer, June 14, 1958 (div. Dec. 1970); children: Kate, John Robert Jr., Johanna; m. Patricia Richardson, Nov. 17, 1973 (div. Sept. 1981); children: Erik, Torgen; m. Jacyln Norwood, Aug. 30, 1986; 1 stepchild, Jack Thomas. BSE, Princeton U., 1957; MBA, Northwestern U., Chgo., 1959. Planning assoc. Mobil Oil Corp., N.Y.C., 1959-62, 65-66, London, 1967-69; stockbroker Kidder Peabody & Co., N.Y.C., 1962-65, Oppenheimer & Co., N.Y.C., 1969-73; owner Hawthorne Exploration Co., N.Y.C., 1973—; Ketchum, Idaho, 1984—; owner MVP, Ketchum, Idaho, 1984-88, also bd. dirs.; owner, mng. dir. Wood Roberts, Inc., Ketchum, 1988—; bd. dirs., v.p. Parker Tech., Houston, 1988—. Inventor radio controlled electric load mgmt. Bd. dirs. Boise (Idaho) Philharmonic Assn., 1988—. Mem. Vikings of Scandia. Republican. Presbyterian. Home: 161 Laurel Ln Ketchum ID 83340 Office: Wood Roberts Inc 220 1st Ave N Ste E Box 1017 Ketchum ID 83340

MARTINSON, JULIA ELLENOR, health science administrator; b. Paso Robles, Calif., May 1, 1951; d. John Elwyn and Betty Jeanne (Fruehling) M. BA in Journalism, U. Nev., 1973, BA in Phys. Edn., 1976. Store mgr. S. S. White, Reno, 1979, Kelly Dental Supply Co., Reno, 1979-81; office mgr. Fine Arts Dental Studio, Reno, 1981-88; sec., treas. Superior Dental Lab. Inc., Reno, 1988—. Mgr. Reno Royals, 1979—; active Campus Christian Assn. (treas. 1986-92), Reno Urban Forestry Commn., 1992—, Reno Park and Recreation Commn., 1993—. Mem. Women's Softball Alumni Assn. (treas. U. Nev.-Reno chpt. 1983-88, publicity dir. 1993), U. Nev. Boosters (v.p. 1986-88). Democrat. Episcopalian. Home: 1200 Casa Loma Dr Reno NV 89503-3132 Office: Superior Dental Lab Inc 300 Brinkby Ave # 201 Reno NV 89509-4349

MARTO, PAUL JAMES, mechanical engineering educator, researcher; b. Flushing, N.Y., Aug. 15, 1938; s. Peter Joseph and Natalie Janet (Verrinoldi) M.; m. Mary Virginia Indence, June 10, 1961; children: Terese V. Marto Sanders, Paul J. Jr., Wayne T., Laura C. BS, U. Notre Dame, 1960; SM, MIT, 1962, ScD, 1965. Asst. prof. Naval Postgrad. Sch., Monterey, Calif., 1965-69, assoc. prof., 1969-77, prof., 1977-85, Disting. prof., 1985—, chmn. dept. mech. engring., 1978-86, dean of rsch., 1990—; cons. Modine Mfg. Co., Racine, Wis., 1986—. Editor: Power Condenser Heat, 1981; contbr. articles to profl. jours. Lt. USN, 1965-67. Recipient Rear Adm. John J. Schieffelin award Naval Postgrad. Sch., 1976, Alexander von Humboldt U.S. Sr. Scientist award Humboldt Stiftung, Fed. Republic Germany, 1989-90. Fellow ASME (assoc. tech. editor Jour. of Heat Transfer 1984-90); mem. Am. Soc. Naval Engrs., Am. Soc. for Engring. Edn., Sigma Xi. Office: Naval Postgrad Sch Dept Mechanical Engring Code ME/MX Monterey CA 93943

MARTONE, FREDRICK J., judge; b. Fall River, Mass., Nov. 8, 1943. BS, Coll. Holy Cross, 1965; JD, U. Notre Dame, 1972; LLM, Harvard U., 1975. Bar: Mass. 1972, Ariz. 1974, U.S. Dist. Ct. Mass. 1977, U.S. Dist. Ct. Ariz. 1977, U.S. Ct. Appeals (1st and 9th cirs.) 1977, U.S. Supreme Ct. 1977. Law clk. to Hon. Edward F. Hennessey Mass. Supreme Judicial Ct., 1972-73; pvt. practice Phoenix, 1973-85; assoc. presiding judge Superior Ct. Ariz., Maricopa County; judge Superior Ct. Ariz., Maricopa County, Phoenix, 1985—. Editor notes and comments Notre Dame Lawyer, 1970-72; contbr. articles to profl. jours. Capt. USAF, 1965-69. Mem. ABA, Ariz. Judges Assn., Maricopa County Bar Assn. Office: Central Court Bldg 201 W Jefferson St Phoenix AZ 85003*

MARTY, LAWRENCE A., magistrate, lawyer; b. Leigh, Nebr., June 17, 1926. Student Wayne State U., 1944-46, Creighton Sch. Law, 1946-48; J.D., U.Wyo., 1954. Bar: Wyo. 1954. Sole practice, Green River, Wyo., 1954-67; ptnr. Mart & Clark, Green River, 1967-74; ptnr. Marty & Ragsdale, Green River, 1975—; judge Green River Mcpl. Ct., 1956-58; U.S. Magistrate Dist. Wyo., 1958—. Alt. del. Rep. Nat. Conv., 1964. Mem. ABA, Wyo. Bar Assn., Sweetwater County Bar Assn., Wyo. State Bar Commrs. Office: 20 E Flaming Gorge Way Green River WY 82935-4210

MARTZ, JOHN ROGER, lawyer; b. Buffalo, June 13, 1937; s. George Albert and Dorothy (Dinsbier) M.; m. Charlotte Gail Lemberes, July 22, 1966; children: Teresa Gail, Nicole Jackie. BS, U.S. Mil. Acad., 1960; MS in Engring., Purdue U., 1964; JD, U. San Francisco, 1980. Bar: Nev. 1980. Commd. 2d lt. U.S. Army, 1960; nuclear engr. Army Nuclear Power Program, 1964-66; with Spl. Forces in Okinawa, Vietnam, Thailand, Korea, Taiwan,, Philippines, 1966-72; elec. engr. Armed Forces Radiobiology Rsch. Inst. and Def. Nuclear Agy., 1972-75; advisor N.G., Calif. and Nev., 1975-80; ret. U.S. Army, 1980; atty. Henderson & Nelson, Reno, 1980-85; pvt. practice Reno, 1985—. Decorated Bronze Star, Combat Inf. badge; recipient Joint Svc. Commendation medal U.S. Dept. Def., 1975. Mem. Nev. State Bar Assn., Washoe County Bar Assn. Office: 440 Ridge St Reno NV 89501

MARTZ, SANDRA KAY, publishing executive, editor; b. Lubbock, Tex., Sept. 21, 1944; d. George Monroe and Jo (White) Gregory; m. John Van Dyke, Sept. 25, 1961 (div.); children: John, James; m. Roger Martz, Feb. 15, 1968 (div.). MBA, Calif. State U., Dominguez Hills, 1978; cert. in exec. mgmt., UCLA, 1987. Mgr., adminstr. TRW, Redondo Beach, Calif., 1969-88; owner Papier-Mache Press, Watsonville, Calif., 1984—; ind. cons., Watsonville, 1988—. Editor: When I Am an Old Woman I Shall Wear Purple, 1987 (Ben Franklin award 1988, 92, Abby Honors award 1991), If I Had My Life to Live Over I Would Pick More Daisies, 1992. Named Outstanding Bus. Woman, Am. Bus. Women, 1989. Mem. NAFE, NOW. Democrat. Office: Papier-Mache Press 135 Aviation Way # 14 Watsonville CA 95076

MARUMOTO, BARBARA CHIZUKO, state legislator; b. San Francisco, July 21, 1939; d. Takeo and Kathleen (Tsuchiya) Okamoto; B.A., U. Hawaii, 1971; student U. Calif., 1957-60, UCLA, 1957; children—Marshall, Jay, Wendy, Megan. Legis. aide, researcher, Honolulu, 1972-78; mem. Hawaii Ho. of Reps., 1978—, minority floor leader, 1981; elected del. to Constl. Conv., 1978; real estate agt., 1979—. Mem. exec. bd. Hist. Hawaii Found.; bd. dirs. Pacific council Girl Scouts U.S.A.; active Rep. Party, Common Cause, LWV, PTA, Ripon Soc. Clubs: Honolulu, Jr. League Honolulu. Contbr. various news columns to publs. Office: Ho of Reps Rm 420 State Capitol Honolulu HI 96813

MARX, ADAM NEAL, technology company executive; b. N.Y.C., Oct. 20, 1961; s. Alan Stephen and Joanne Beth (Trupin) M.; m. Robyn Lauri Jozefowski, May 28, 1989; 1 child, Eric Jozef. BA, Cornell U., 1983; MA, Boston U., 1987. Software engr. Agfa-Compugraphic, Wilmington, Mass., 1983-85; staff scientist Bolt, Beranek and Newman, Cambridge, Mass., 1985-86; rsch. engr. Price-Waterhouse, Waltham, 1987-89; user interface rschr. US West Advanced Technologies, Boulder, Colo., 1989—. Mem. Toastmasters. Office: US West Advanced Tech Ste 280 4001 Discovery Dr Boulder CO 80303

MARX, JOSEPH JACOB, benefits administrator; b. Burlington, Colo., Jan. 13, 1956; s. Harold William and Virginia Katherine (Jacobs) M. AA, NE Jr. Coll., Sterling, Colo., 1976; BS, Colo. State U., 1978. Loan officer/field rep. Sterling Prodn. Credit Assn., Ft. Morgan, Colo., 1979-81, Farmers State Bank, Ft. Morgan, 1981-87; detached field agt. N.Y. Life Ins. Co., Denver, Ft. Morgan, 1987-88; multi-line agt. Shelter Ins. Co., Longmont, Colo., 1988-89; benefits adminstr. Morgan County Rural Elec. Assn., Ft. Morgan, 1989—. Recipient Outstanding Young Men of Am. award, 1984. Mem. Ft. Morgan Evening Optimists, Ft. Morgan Jaycees (pres. 1981-82, bd. dirs. 1980-81, Gold Keyman 1980). Home: 625 Prospect Fort Morgan CO 80701 Office: Morgan County Rur Elec Assn PO Box 738 20169 Hwy 34 Fort Morgan CO 80701

MARX, SUZANNE, finance executive; b. L.A.; d. Rose Erbsen; m. Joseph Marx, Mar. 19, 1955; children: Craig J., Gary J., Eric J., Jason J. Student, U. Ariz. Chmn. fundraising So. Calif. Princeton U., L.A., 1977-89; exec. com. John F. Kennedy Sch. Govt., Boston, 1989—; bd. mem. Nat. Vol. Ctr., Washington, 1990—; comm. mem. Statue Liberty - Ellis Island Centennial Commn., Washington, 1985-88; bd. dirs. DARE, L.A. Police Dept., 1986—; nat. campaign chmn. Nancy Reagan Ctr., L.A., 1987-89; jury mem. L.A. County Grand Jury, 1985-86; dep. dir. fin. Ronald Reagan Presdl. Libr., L.A., 1989-93 —, dir. fin., 1993—. Bd. Regents Loyola Marymount U., L.A.; bd. dirs. Constl. Rights Found., L.A.; founders bd. L.A. Music Ctr., 1987; benefit chmn. Harvard U., Boston, 1985. Republican. Home: 2102 Century Park Ln Los Angeles CA 90067 Office: Ronald Reagan Pres Found 2121 Ave of Stars Ste 3400 Los Angeles CA 90067

MARXMAN, GERALD ALBERT, venture capital executive; b. Rochelle, Ill., Apr. 10, 1933; s. Albert Edward and Helen Margaret (Allaben) M. BA, Monmouth Coll., 1956; BS, Case Western U., 1956, MS, 1959; PhD, Calif. Inst. Tech., 1962. Sr. staff scientist United Technologies Ctr., Sunnyvale, Calif., 1961-65; dir. phys. scis. Stanford Rsch. Inst., Menlo Park, Calif., 1965-71; sr. v.p. Envirodyne Industries, L.A., 1971-79; co-founder, pres. Nepenthe Group, San Francisco, 1979—; co-founder, pres., dir. CommTech Internat., Menlo Park, Calif., 1982—; co-founder, dir Digideck, Inc., Mountain View, Calif., Coloray Display Corp., Fremont, Calif., Amati Comms. Corp., Palo Alto, Calif. Contbr. articles to profl. jours. Ramo Wooldridge fellow Calif. Tech., Pasadena, 1959-61. Office: Commtech Internat 545 Middlefield Rd Menlo Park CA 94025-3400

MARZKE, MARY WALPOLE, physical anthropologist; b. Oakland, Calif., May 29, 1937; d. Ronald Noel and Doris (Hoyt) Walpole; m. Robert Franklin Marzke, June 23, 1962; children: Carolyn, Ronald, Sarah. AB, U. Calif., Berkeley, 1959, PhD, 1964; MA, Columbia U., 1961. From lectr. to instr. Hunter Coll., N.Y.C., 1963-65; lectr. U. N.C., Chapel Hill, 1967-69; acting asst. prof. step II U. Calif., L.A., 1976-77; adj. vis. prof. Ariz. State U., Tempe, 1978-82, part-time asst. prof., 1982-89, full time asst. prof., 1989-92, assoc. prof., 1992—; project anatomist Primate Found. Ariz., Mesa. Author book chpts.; contbr. aticles to profl. jours. Fellow AAAS, Am. Anthrop. Assn.; mem. Am. Assn. Phys. Anthopologists, Am. Soc. Primatologists, Am. Soc. for Surgery of the Hand (hon.), Internat. Primatological Soc., Sigma Xi. Office: Dept Anthropology Ariz State U Tempe AZ 85287-2402

MASAGATANI, ERNESTA, school superintendent; b. Sept. 24, 1937; d. Louis Keahiuaokalani Sr. and Lei Lincoln Collins; children: Jason T.K., Jesse L.K., Jobie M.K. BE, U. Hawaii, 1960, M of Ednl. Adminstrn., 1983. Cert. tchr., Hawaii. Tchr. Aiea High Sch., Kailua High Sch., 1962-66; beginning tchr. supr. Windward Dist. Office, 1966-69, dist. resource tchr., 1971-75; tchr. Kainalu Elem. Sch., 1969-71; vice prin. Kalaheo High Sch., Kailua High Sch., Palisades Elem. Sch., 1975-79; prin. Robert Louis Stevenson Intermediate Sch., 1979-87; dep. dist. supt. Honolulu Dist., 1987-93, dist. supt., 1993—. Mem. Liliuokalani Trust Adv. Coun., Pihana Na Mano Adv. Coun., Alii Pauahi Civic Club. Mem. Daus. Hawaii. Mem. Kawaiahao Ch. Address: 3137 Hinano St Honolulu HI 96815*

MASCIALE, DIANE MARIE, television executive; b. Richmond Hill, N.Y., Mar. 12, 1956; d. Mauro and Rose Gloria (Rossiello) M.; m. James Edward Paymar, June 24, 1990; 1 child, William Maxwell. BJ, U. Mo., 1978. Reporter/anchor KRNT-KRNQ Radio, Des Moines, 1978-79; producer/reporter WLOS-TV, Asheville, N.C., 1979-80, KNTV-TV, San Jose, 1980-81; producer Cable News Network, Atlanta, 1981-82; producer KRON-TV, San Francisco, 1982-86, exec. producer, 1986-88; field producer Fox TV "America's Most Wanted", Washington, 1991—; sr. field producer Fox TV "The Reporters", N.Y.C., 1988-91; asst. gen. mgr., dir. programming KCNS-TV-38, San Francisco, 1991—. Producer news special: Women and AIDS, 1990 (Am. Women Radio and TV award); producer: News Series, 1981. Scripps Howard Found. scholar U. Mo., 1977. Mem. Am. Women in Radio and TV, Internat. Women's Media Found. Office: KCNS-TV 1550 Bryant St #850 San Francisco CA 94103

MASER, CLARK WALTON, lawyer; b. Chgo., Sept. 30, 1925; s. Lewis Clark and Helen (Thorp) M.; m. Nancy Carter Thomas, Nov. 9, 1955 (dec. Mar., 1981); children: Hill Carter, Minot Clark; m. Margaret Phillips Burgwyn, Feb. 14, 1982. AB, U. Calif., 1948; JD, Harvard U., 1951. Assoc. Athearn, Chandler & Hoffman, San Francisco, 1951-56, ptnr., 1956-83; ptnr. Law Offices of Clark W. Maser, San Francisco, 1983—. Pres. San Francisco Symphony Found., 1960-62, Mechanic's Inst. and Libr., San Francisco, 1980-82, World Affairs Coun. No. Calif., San Francisco, 1977-79; acting exec. dir., 1986; chmn. San Francisco Com. of Coun. on Fgn. Rels., 1975-77. With U.S. Army, 1943-45. Foreign Policy Conf. grantee Ford Found., Wilton Park, Sussex, Eng., 1965. Mem. Univ. Club, Calif. Tennis Club, Lagunitas Country Club. Republican. Episcopalian. Home: PO Box 666 Ross CA 94957 Office: Law Offices Clark W Maser Ste 2220 425 California St San Francisco CA 94104

MASI, EDWARD A., computer company executive; b. Medford, Mass., May 7, 1947; s. Joseph Carl and Rita Olivine (Metras) M.; m. Kristine Ann Lauderbach Masi, Jan. 24, 1970. BSME, Tufts U., 1969. Mktg. sales IBM, Boston, 1969-76; commercial analysis IBM, Westchester, N.Y., 1976-78; mktg. mgr. IBM, Bethesda, Md., 1978-80; region mgr. mktg. sales Cray Rsch., Calverton, Md., 1980-87; exec. v.p. mktg. Mpls., 1988-92; corp. v.p. and pres. Intel Corp., Beaverton, Minn., 1992. Mem. Am. Electronics Assn. (vice chair 1991-92). Office: Intel Supercomputers 5200 NE Elam Young Pkwy Beaverton OR 97124

MASKELL, DONALD ANDREW, contracts administrator; b. San Bernadino, Calif., June 22, 1963; s. Howard Andrew Maskell and Gloria Evelyn (Iglesias) White. BA, U. Puget Sound, 1985. Adminstrv. asst. State of Wash., Kent, 1986-87; data analyst Boeing Co., Seattle, 1987-93, engring. contract requirements coord., 1993—. Mem. Elks. Republican. Presbyterian.

MASLAND, LYNNE S., public relations administrator; b. Boston, Nov. 18, 1940; d. Keith Arnold and Camilla (Puleston) Shangraw; m. Edwin Grant Masland, Sept. 19, 1960 (div. 1975); children: Mary Conklin, Molly Allison. Student, Mt. Holyoke Coll., South Hadley, Mass., 1958-60; BA, U. Calif., Riverside, 1970; MA, U. Calif., 1971; postgrad., U. B.C., Vancouver, Can., 1990—. Asst. pub. rels. dir. Inter-Am. U., San German, P.R., 1963-64; asst. to dir. elem. edn. Govt. of Am. Samoa, Pago Pago, 1966-68; project dir., cons. Wash. Commn. for Humanities, Seattle, 1976-80; exec. editor N.W. Happenings Mag., Greenbank, Wash., 1980-84; media specialist Western Wash. U., Bellingham, 1984-88; dir. pub. info. Western Wash. U., 1988—; cons. William O. Douglas Inst., Seattle, 1984, Whatcom Mus. History and Art, Bellingham, 1977; instr. U. Nebr., Omaha, 1972-86, Western Wash. U., 1972-86. Editor: The Human Touch: Folklore of the Northwest Corner, 1979, Proceedings: The Art in Living, 1980, Reports to the Mayor on the State of the Arts in Bellingham, 1980-81; contbr. numerous articles to profl. jours. Pres. LWV, Whatcom County, Bellingham, 1977-79; bd. dirs. N.W. Concert Assn., 1981-83, Wash. State Folklife Coun., 1985-90; docent Nat. Gallery, Washington, 1969; bd. dirs. Sta. KZAZ Nat. Pub. Radio, Bellingham, 1992—. Univ. grad. fellow U. B.C., Vancouver, Can., 1990—. Mem. Am. Comparative Literature Assn., Nat. Assn. Presswomen, Wash. Press Assn. (pres. 4th Corner chpt. 1987-88, Superior Performance award 1986), Can. Comparative Literature Assn., Philological Assn. of Pacific Coast, Coun. for Advancement and Support Edn. (Case Dist. VIII Gold award for Media Rels.), Rotary Club (bd. dirs. 1992—). Episcopalian. Office: Western Wash U High St Bellingham WA 98225-5942

MASLIN, HARRY, music business executive; b. Phila., Apr. 4, 1948; s. Philip and Sarah (Jacobs) M. Rec. engr. Regent Sound, N.Y.C., 1969-71; chief engr. Hit Factory Studios, N.Y.C., 1971-73, 74-75; rec. engr. Record Plant Studios, N.Y.C., 1973-74; record producer HRM Prodns., Hollywood, Calif., 1975—; co-owner, pres. Image Rec. Studios, Hollywood, 1983—. Recipient 20 gold and platinum records Rec. Industry Assn. of Am. Mem. Nat. Acad. Rec. Arts and Scis., ASCAP, Audio Engring. Soc. Office: Image Rec Studios 1020 N Sycamore Ave Los Angeles CA 90038-2308

MASLIN, HARVEY LAWRENCE, temporary service company executive; b. Chgo., Oct. 22, 1939; s. Jack and Shirley Maslin; m. Marcia Silberman, Aug. 21, 1960; children: Elaine, Shelley, Bonnie. BS, U. Ariz., 1961, JD, 1964. Bar: Ariz., 1964, Calif., 1966, U.S. Dist. Ct., 1964, 66. Ptnr. Maslin, Rotundo & Maslin, Sherman Oaks, Calif., 1966-67; gen. counsel Western Temporary Svcs., Inc., San Francisco, 1967-71, v.p., 1972-78, sr. v.p., sec., 1979-84; pres., chief oper. officer Western Temporary Svcs., Inc., Walnut Creek, Calif., 1985—; dir. Western Staff Svcs., U.K. Ltd., London, Western Personnel Svcs. Pty Ltd., Sydney, Australia, Western Staff Svcs. (N.Z.) Ltd., Auckland, Western Svc. A/S, Copenhagen, Denmark, Western Svc./Kontorsvc. A/S Oslo, Western Svc., Inc., Zurich, Western Video Images, Inc., San Francisco. Mem. Rep. Presidential Task Force, Washington, 1981. Mem. Nat. Assn. Temporary Svcs., Calif. Bar Assn., Ariz. Bar Assn., World Trade Club, Phi Alpha Delta. Home: 2300 Deer Valley Ln Walnut Creek CA 94598-5005 Office: Western Temporary Svcs Inc Exec Offices 301 Lennon Ln Walnut Creek CA 94598

MASLOW, PHYLLIS F., retired educator; b. Cleve., May 6, 1927; d. Joseph C. and Avis Ethel (Leggett) Findley; m. William C. Maslow (dec. Mar. 1987); children: Mark J., Carolyn J., Leslie A. PhB, U. Chgo., 1946, MA, 1951; PhD, U. So. Calif., L.A., 1975. Adminstrv. sec. Ctr. for Study Am.-Fgn. and Mil. Power U. Chgo., 1951-52; rsch. coord. Marianne Frostig Ctr. Ednl. Therapy, L.A., 1961-69, 70-74, asst. to dir., 1969-70; dir. spl. edn. programs Mt. St. Mary's Coll. and Frostig Ctr., L.A., 1974; asst. prof. ednl. psychology Calif. State U., Long Beach, 1977-81, assoc. prof. ednl. psychology, 1981-86, prof. ednl. psychology, 1986-90, acting assoc. dean, 1988-90, prof. emerita, 1990—; sec. exec. bd. Multidisciplinary Acad. Clin. Educators, 1988—. Author: (with others) Learning Problems in the Classroom, 1973; cons. mem. editorial bd. Jour. Learning Disabilities, 1979—. Calif. State U. Disting. scholar, 1982. Fellow Assn. Ednl. Therapists; mem. Am. Ednl. Rsch. Assn., Coun. for Exceptional Children, Learning Disabilities Assn., Phi Beta Kappa. Home: 765 Calderwood Ln Pasadena CA 91107-2135

MASLOW, RICHARD EMANUEL, psychology educator; b. Bklyn., Dec. 20, 1929; s. Louis William and Helen Lillian (Danziger) M.; m. Karen Mae Olson, May 11, 1956; children: Troy Mae, Darcy Sue. BS, Western N.Mex. U., 1952, MS, 1957. Tchr., coach Eddyville High Sch., Nebr., 1955-57; tchr., coach, counselor Quincy High Sch., Calif., 1957-62; psychology instr. San Joaquin Delta Coll., Stockton, Calif., 1963-91; student tchr. supr. Calif. State U., Stanislaus, 1993—; text book cons. Harper & Row, McGraw Hill, Houghton-Mifflin; basketball ofcl. No. Calif. Coll. Basketball Ofcls., 1979-90. Contbr. articles to profl. jours. Mem. Sch. Bd., Lincoln Unified Sch. Dist., Stockton, Calif., 1978—, pres. bd., 1980, 85, 88, 91. Served with U.S. Army, 1952-55. Mem. Am. Psychol. Assn., Am. Psychol. Soc., Western Psychol. Assn., San Joaquin County Psychol. Assn. (pres. 1977-78), Calif. Sch. Bd. Assn., Nat. Sch. Bd. Assn. Home: 3788 W Benj Holt Dr Stockton CA 95219

MASON, ANTHONY HALSTEAD, lawyer; b. N.Y.C., Dec. 23, 1938; s. Anthony Taylor and Margaret Adams (Halstead) M.; children: Linda Gaye, David Anthony. BA, U. Denver, 1961, JD, 1965. Bar: Colo. 1965, Ariz. 1966. Atty. Ariz. Atty. Gen.'s Office, Phoenix, 1966-67, Maricopa County Atty.'s Office, Phoenix, 1967-69; ptnr. McCall & Mason, Phoenix, 1969-71, Mason, McCall & Ross, Phoenix, 1971-74, Mason & Ross, Phoenix, 1974-77, Carmichael, McClue, Stephens, Mason & Toles, Phoenix, 1977-78, Levy, Mason, Spector & Sherwood, Phoenix, 1978-84, Deltacor, Phoenix, 1984-91, Morrison and Hecker, Phoenix, 1991—; guest lectr., moot ct. judge Ariz. State U., Tempe; lectr. continuing legal edn. State Bar Ariz., 1978, Crittenden Real Estate Conf., 1984—. Chmn. City of Phoenix Planning Commn., 1974-76, Mayor's Task Force on Drug Abuse, Phoenix, 1987-88; pres. bd. dirs. Phoenix Symphony Assn., 1981-84; mem. steering com. Phoenix 40, 1988-90; candidate for Gov. Ariz., 1986; co-chmn. Ariz. Bus. Leadership for Edn., Inc., 1989-90. Named Best Land Use Planner in U.S. Am. Soc. Planning Ofcls., 1975, Valley Leadership Visionary of the Yr., 1992. Mem. Ariz. Bar Assn., Maricopa County Bar Assn. (pres. 1975-76), Valley Leadership (Visionary Leadership award 1992), Plaza Club, Univ. Club, Ariz. Club. Democrat. Office: Morrison & Hecker 2800 N Central Ave Ste 1600 Phoenix AZ 85004

MASON, DEAN TOWLE, cardiologist; b. Berkeley, Calif., Sept. 20, 1932; s. Ira Jenckes and Florence Mabel (Towle) M.; m. Maureen O'Brien, June 22, 1957; children: Kathleen, Alison. B.A. in Chemistry, Duke U., 1954, M.D., 1958. Diplomate: Nat. Bd. Med. Examiners, Am. Bd. Internal Medicine (cardiovascular diseases). Intern, then resident in medicine Johns Hopkins Hosp., 1958-61; clin. assoc. cardiology br., sr. asst. surgeon USPHS, Nat. Heart Inst., NIH, 1961-63, asst. sect. dir. cardiovascular diagnosis, attending physician, sr. investigator cardiology br., 1963-68; prof. medicine, prof. physiology, chief cardiovascular medicine U. Calif. Med. Sch., Davis-Sacramento Med. Center, 1968-82; dir. cardiac ctr. Cedars Med. Ctr., Miami, Fla., 1982-83; physician-in chief Western Heart Inst., San Francisco, 1983—; chmn. dept. cardiovascular medicine St. Mary's Med. Ctr., San Francisco, 1986—; co-chmn. cardiovascular-renal drugs U.S. Pharmacopeia Com. Revision, 1970-75; mem. life scis. com. NASA; med. rsch. rev. bd. VA, NIH; vis. prof. numerous univs., cons. in field; mem. Am. Cardiovascular Splty. Cert. Bd., 1970-78. Contbr. numerous articles to profl. publs. Recipient Research award Am. Therapeutic Soc., 1965; Theodore and Susan B. Cummings Humanitarian award State Dept.-Am. Coll. Cardiology, 1972, 73, 75, 78; Skylab Achievement award NASA, 1974; U. Calif. Faculty Research award, 1978; named Outstanding Prof. U. Calif. Med. Sch., Davis, 1972. Fellow Am. Coll. Cardiology (pres. 1977-78), A.C.P., Am. Heart Assn., Am. Coll. Chest Physicians, Royal Soc. Medicine; mem. Am. Soc. Clin. Investigation, Am. Physiol. Soc., Am. Soc. Pharmacology and Exptl. Therapeutics (Exptl. Therapeutics award 1973), Am. Fedn. Clin. Research, N.Y. Acad. Scis., Am. Assn. U. Cardiologists, Am. Soc. Clin. Pharmacology and Therapeutics, Western Assn. Physicians, AAUP, Western Soc. Clin. Research (past pres.), Phi Beta Kappa, Alpha Omega Alpha. Republican. Methodist. Club: El Marcero Country. Home: 44725 Country Club Dr El Macero CA 95618-1047 Office: Western Heart Inst St Mary's Med Ctr 450 Stanyan St San Francisco CA 94117-1079

MASON, JAMES ALBERT, university dean; b. Eureka, Utah, 1929; married, 1956; 3 children. BA, Brigham Young U., 1955, MA, 1957; EdD, Ariz. State U., 1970. Cons., clinician in fine arts, 1955—; former chmn. dept. music Brigham Young U., Provo, now dean Coll. Fine Arts and Communications; vis. prof., lectr. Ind. U., Northwestern U., Cin. Coll.-Conservatory, U. Tex., Central Conservatory, Beijing, Internat. Soc. Music Edn., Warsaw; chmn. nat. symposium Applications of Psychology to the Teaching and

Learning of Music; chmn., bd. dirs. The Barlow Endowment for Music Composition; co-founder, 1st pres. Utah Valley Symphony Orch.; past condr. Utah Valley Youth Orch. Editor: The Instrumentalist, Orch. News, Utah Music Educator, Research News column, Jour. Research in Music Edn. Bd. dirs. Presser Found. Mem. Music Educators Nat. Conf. (past nat. pres., council), Nat. Music Council (past bd. dirs.), Am. Music Conf. (past bd. dirs.). Office: Brigham Young U Coll Fine Arts and Communications A-410 Harris Fine Arts Ctr Provo UT 84602

MASON, JOE BEN, prison mission executive; b. Texhoma, Tex., Oct. 24, 1910; s. Lloyd Elliot and Lillie Mae Mason; m. Helen Sutton, May 1936 (dec. 1971); 1 child, Joe Lawrence; m. Ada Giebelhaus, Mar. 25, 1972. 2-yr. cert., Amarillo Coll., 1932; student, U. Tex., 1933, Biola U., L.A., 1954; ThD (hon.), Faith Bible Coll. and Sem., Lagos, Nigeria, 1988. Ins. adjuster Md. Casualty Co., El Paso, Tex., 1935-36, FCAB Co., El Paso and Lubbock, Tex., 1937-41; owner, mgr. Mason Claim Svc., Phoenix, 1945-54; founder, dir. Prison Mission Assn., Inc., Weatherford, Tex., 1955-90; dir. emeritus Prison Mission Assn. Inc., Weatherford, Tex., 1990—. With USN, 1943-45. Mem. Marketplace Ministries. Republican. Home: 3993 10th St Apt 513 Riverside CA 92501-3540

MASON, JOSEPH WAYNE, microelectronics company executive, educator; b. Tremonton, Utah, June 22, 1949; s. Reese B. and Martha Christine (Blossom) M.; m. Cherie Lee Johanson, Sept. 7, 1971; children: Christy, Candise, Valerie, Matthew, Gregory, Nathan, Jeremy, Stephanie, Karen. BS in Acctg., Brigham Young U., 1973; MA in Human Rels., U. Okla., 1977. Cert. info. systems auditor. Supr. mfg. cost. acctgs. Digital Equipment Corp., Colorado Springs, Colo., 1979-80, sr. fin. analyst, 1980-81; cost acctg. and budget mgr. United Techs. Microelectronics Ctr., Colorado Springs, 1982-84, mgr. planning and measurement systems, 1984-85; mgr. fin. and acctg. svcs. Ford Microelectronics, Inc., Colorado Springs, 1985-88, mgr. systems and contract compliance, 1988-89, team leader fin. planning and analysis, 1990—; adj. prof. Webster U., Colorado Springs, 1983—; assoc. prof. U. Phoenix, Aurora, Colo., 1990—, area chmn., 1991—; chmn. Ross Systems Internat. Users Group, Palo Alto, Calif., 1986-88. Author books. Asst. dist. commr. Pikes Peak coun. Boy Scouts Am., 1991—; mem. student enrollment Sch. Dist. 11, Colorado Springs, 1984—, mem. budget com., 1985—, candidate for Bd. Edn., 1985, 87. Capt. USAF, 1973-79. Recipient Dist. award of merit Boy Scouts Am., 1990. Mem. EDP Audit Found., Nat. Contract Mgmt. Assn., Inst. Mgmt. Accts., Internat. Soc. for Planning and Strategic Mgmt. Mormon. Office: Ford Microelectronics Inc 9965 Federal Way Colorado Springs CO 80921

MASON, KEN DONALD, aerospace engineering company executive, consultant; b. Cleve., July 7, 1955; s. Donald Anthony and Marian Rose (Konte) M.; m. Roxanna J. Wells, Mar. 20, 1990. Grad. high sch., Placer, Calif. Chief propulsion engr. Truax Engring., Inc., Saratoga, Calif., 1979-81; propulsion coord., cons. GCH, Inc., Sunnyvale, Calif., 1981-82; tech. specialist Chem. Systems div. UTC, San Jose, Calif., 1982-87; rsch. lab. mechanic Air Force Astroutics Lab., Edwards AFB, Calif., 1987-89; propulsion test mgr. Truax Engring., Inc., Carlsbad, Calif., 1989—; dept. head test Truax Engring., Inc., Saratoga and Carlsbad, Calif., 1978—; dept. head liquid rocket propulsion Rocket Rsch. Inst., Inc. Home: 90 Pinecrest Dr Applegate CA 95703 Office: Truax Engring Inc 5925 Farnsworth Ct Carlsbad CA 92008

MASON, LORNA COGSWELL, author, editor, consultant; b. Del Norte, Colo., Oct. 15, 1937; d. John and Marjorie (Means) C.; m. Curtis E. Mason, June 22, 1963; children: Carolyn, Eliot. BA cum laude, U. Colo., 1959; MA, U. Calif., 1962. Cert. tchr., adminstr., Calif. Tchr. Bishop's Sch., La Jolla, Calif., 1960-61, Antioch (Calif.) High Sch., 1962-64, Merritt Coll., Oakland, Calif., 1965-66; editor Harcourt Brace Jovanovich, San Francisco, 1980-83; editor, writer pvt. practice, Castro Valley, Calif., 1983—; author Houghton Mifflin, Boston, 1989—; cons. Curriculum Concepts, Inc., N.Y.C., 1988, The Galef Inst., L.A., Calif., 1992—. Editor: Voice of the Plains, 1987, But What, My Dear, Do You Know About Hotels?, 1992; author (with others): History of the United States, 1991, 93, History of the United States, Vol. I, 1992. vol. Castro Valley Unified Sch. Dist., 1970-78; participant U.S.-U.S.S.R. Textbook Study Project, Moscow, 1989. Mem. Nat. Coun. for Social Studies, Orgn. for Am. Historians. Home: 5869 Greenridge Rd. Castro Valley CA 94552

MASON-FEILDER, CLIVE LEE, scriptwriter; b. Brentford, Middlesex, U.K., Jan. 10, 1938; came to U.S., 1968; s. Arthur Leonard and Dorothy Florance (Packer) F.; m. Kathleen McQuillan, Oct. 4, 1972 (div. 1976); 1 child, Rachel; m. Florence Elizabeth Thorsteinson, Sept. 7, 1991. BA, Richmond Royal Arts, 1957; MA, St. Thomas U., V.I., 1967. 2d asst. Nat. Geog. Films, Washington, 1985-86; 2d asst. dir. Barry & Enright CBS Films, Hollywood, Calif., 1986; prodn. design Molesworth Films, Hong Kong, 1986-87; art dir. New Gold Pictures, Hollywood, Calif., 1987-88, TransBay Pictures, Hollywood, 1988-89, Penn Ante Films, Hollywood, 1989, Artistic License Films, Sacramento, Calif., 1989-90; writer, producer Anchandio Video Prodns., Chgo., 1990-91, MovieTime Prodns., Los Gatos, Calif., 1991—. Author: (screen play) It's A Wrap, 1991, (novel) How Far To Neptunas, 1987, (radio play series) High Wire Radio Choir, 1976; co-author: (TV series) Chicken Little Comedy Hour, 1976. Flight lt. R.A.F., 1958-61. Recipient Best Design FIlm Set, No. Calif. Film Bd., 1989, Best Sci. Fiction Set, Molesworth Films, 1987. Mem. Writers Union (local 7). Home and Office: PO Box 67145 Scotts Valley CA 95067-7145

MASOUREDIS, SERAFEIM PANAGIOTIS, pathologist, educator; b. Detroit, Nov. 14, 1922; s. Panagiotis and Lemonia (Moniodis) M.; m. Marion Helen Mykytew, Oct. 1943; children: Claudia, Linus. AB, U. Mich., 1944, MD, 1948; PhD in Med. Physics, U. Calif., Berkeley, 1952. Diplomate Am. Bd. Pathology. Intern U. Calif. Svc./San Francisco Gen. Hosp., 1952-53, asst. resident in medicine, 1954-55; fellow Clinic Hematology/Donner Lab./Univ. Calif., Berkeley, 1953-54; asst. prof., then assoc. prof. pathology U. Pitts. Med. Sch., 1955-59; asst. dir. Cen. Blood Bank Pitts., 1955-59; assoc. prof. preventive medicine U. Calif., San Francisco, 1959-62, assoc. prof. medicine, 1962-67, assoc. prof. clin. pathology, 1966-67; prof. medicine Marquette U., Milw., 1967-69; exec. dir. Milw. Blood Ctr., 1967-69; prof. pathology U. Calif., San Diego, 1969-90, prof. emeritus, 1990—; cons. WHO, Geneva, 1965-67; bd. dirs. Am. Assn. Blood Banks, Washington,1 981-83. Assoc. editor Jour. Transfusion, Washington, 1981-90; contbr. sci. articles and rsch. papers to various publs. Emily Cooley Meml. lectr. Am. Assn. Blood Banks, 1973, recipient Karl Landsteiner Meml. award, 1979. Mem. Am. Assn. Immunologists, Am. Soc. Clin. Investigation, Am. Soc. Hematology, Brit. Soc. Immunology, Am. Assn. Cancer Rsch., Internat. Soc. Blood Transfusion, Western Assn. Physicians. Office: U Calif San Diego Dept Pathology Sch Medicine La Jolla CA 92093-0612

MASRI, MERLE SID, biochemist, consultant; b. Jerusalem, Palestine, (Israel), Sept. 12, 1927; came to U.S., 1947; s. Said Rajab and Fatima (Muneimné) M.; m. Maryjean Loretta Anderson, June 28, 1952 (div. 1974); children: Kristin Corinne, Allan Eric, Wendy Joan, Heather Anderson. BA in Physiology, U. Calif., Berkeley, 1950; PhD in Mammalian Physiology and Biochemistry, U. Calif., 1953. Rsch. asst. Dept. Physiology, Univ. Calif., Berkeley, 1950-53; predoctoral fellow Baxter Labs., Berkeley, 1952-53; rsch. assoc. hematology Med. Rsch. Inst., Michael Reese Hosp., Chgo., 1954-56; sr. rsch. biochemist Agrl. Rsch. Svc., USDA, Berkeley, 1956-87; supervisory rsch. scientist Agrl. Rsch. Svc., USDA, N.D. State U. Sta., Fargo, N.D., 1987-89; pvt. practice as cons. Emeryville, Calif., 1989—; lectr. numerous confs. Contbr. more than 120 articles to profl. jours. Fellow Am. Inst. Chemists; mem. AAAS, Am. Chem. Soc., Am. Oil Chemists Soc., Am. Assn. Cereal Chemists, N.Y. Acad. Scis., Sigma Xi. Home: 9 Commodore Dr Emeryville CA 94608

MASSEY, DOUGLAS GORDON, physician, educator; b. Clinton, Ont., Can., Oct. 14, 1926; came to U.S., 1973; s. Douglas and Zeralda (Churchill) M.; m. Gisele Fournier, Aug. 27, 1967; children: Anne, Nicole, Jennifer. MD, U. Toronto, 1951; MSc, McGill U., 1964. Intern St. Michaels Hosp., Toronto, 1951-52; resident Sunnybrooke Hosp., Toronto, 1952-53, Leahi Hosp., Honolulu, 1953-55; assoc. prof. U. Sherbrooke (Que., Can.), 1964-73; prof. U. Hawaii, Honolulu, 1973—; dir. inst. rsch. Francis Med. Ctr., 1991—. Editor: Asthma Bulletin, 1990—. Mem. Alliance Francaise of Hawaii (pres. 1986-92). Home: 4523 Aukai Ave Honolulu HI 96816-4922 Office: John A Burns Sch Medicine Leahi Hosp 3675 Kilauea Ave Honolulu HI 96816

MASSEY, MARILYN CHAPIN, college president. BA in English and Philosophy, Marquette U., 1963, MA in History of Religion, 1965; MA in Interdisciplinary Religious Studies, U. Chgo., 1969, PhD Philosophy Religion with distinction, 1973. Instr. and asst. prof. religious studies Mundelein Coll., 1966-73, chair dept. religious studies, 1972-73; adj. prof. religion and women's studies U. Louisville, 1974-77; adj. prof. history Christianity Louisville Presbyn. Seminary, 1974-76; asst. prof. dept. religion Duke U., 1977-81, dir. undergrad studies dept. religion, 1980-81; assoc. prof. history Christianity Sch. Div. Harvard U., 1981-84, co chair dept. ch. history Sch. Div., 1982-84; prof. divsn. history, philosophy, and religion, dean sch. arts and scis. Coll. New Rochelle, 1984-87; prof. divsn. humanities, v.p. acad. affairs, dean faculty Marymount Manhattan Coll., 1987-92; pres. Pitzer Coll., Claremont, Calif., 1992—; mem. community edn. study group sch. edn. Harvard U., 1985-87; rep. nat. identification program Am. Coun. on Edn., N.Y.C., 1989-92, mem. commn. on govtl. rels., 1993—. Author: Christ Unmasked: The Meaning of "The Life of Jesus" in German Politics, 1983 (Outstanding book Choice, 1983), The Feminine Soul: The Fate of an Ideal, 1985.; contbng. author Beyond Androcentrism: New Essays of Women and Religion, 1977; translator: In Defense of My "Life of Jesus" Against the Hegelians, 1983; contbr. articles to profl and religious jours.; lectr. in field. Carnegie Faculty fellow Bunting Inst. Radcliffe Coll., 1983; named alumna of yr. Trinity High Sch., 1989, U. Chgo. Div. Sch., 1989. Mem. Am. Acad. Religion (sec. So. region. 1980-84). Office: Pitzer Coll Office of Pres 1050 N Mills Ave Claremont CA 91711*

MASSICK, JAMES WILLIAM, heavy equipment manufacturing company executive; b. Seattle, Jan. 19, 1932; s. Peter James and Annetta Jean (Dormier) M.; m. Joyce Allair Puckey, Apr. 7, 1973; children—Scott, Christopher, Kit, Timothy, Nina, Sally, John, Jill. BS, U. Wash., 1954; MBA, U. Calif. at Los Angeles, 1966. Constrn. engr. Kaiser Engrs., Oakland, Calif., 1957-60; project mgr. Ralph M. Parsons Co., Los Angeles, 1960-65; engring. mgr. Weyerhauser Co., Tacoma, 1965-68; ops. mgr. Western Gear Corp., Everett, Wash., 1968-70; pres. Truckweld Equipment Co., Seattle, 1970—; dir. Truckweld Corp., Truckweld Utilities, Inc., Puget Sound Lease Co., Pacific N.W. Utility & Supply Co. Served to capt. USNR, 1950, 54-57. Decorated Navy Cross, Silver Star, Legion of Merit, Purple Heart. Mem. ASCE, Soc. Am. Mil. Engrs., Seattle C. of C., Mcpl. League, Chosen Few, Theta Delta Chi. Episcopalian. Club: Overlake Golf and Country, The Harbor Club, The Lakes Club. Patentee in field. Home: 2760 76th Ave SE # 601 Mercer Island WA 98040

MASSIMINO, ROLAND V., university basketball coach; b. Hillside, N.J., Nov. 13, 1934; s. Salvatore and Grace (Alberti) M.; m. Mary Jane Reid, Aug. 13, 1958; children—Thomas, Lee Ann, Michele, R.C., Andrew. Degree in Bus., U. Vt., 1956; M.P.E., Rutgers U., 1959; guidance cert., Tufts U., 1969. Asst. coach Cranford High Sch., N.J., 1956-59; coach Hillside High Sch., N.J., 1959-63, Lexington High Sch., Mass., 1963-69; head coach SUNY-Stony Brook, 1969-71; asst. coach U. Pa., 1971-73; head coach Villanova U., Pa., 1973-92, U. Nev., Las Vegas, 1992—. Winning coach NCAA Nat. Basketball Championship, 1985; named Coach of Yr., Phila. Big 5, 1975-76, 77-78, 81-82, 82-83, 84-85, Eastern Athletic Assn., 1976-77, Eastern 8 Conf., 1978-79, 79-80, Widmer Cup Eastern Coach of Yr., 1981-82, Coach of Yr., Big East Conf., 1981-82, Eastern Basketball Eastern Coach of Yr., 1984-85, Harry Latwick/Herb Good Phila. Mem. Nat. Assn. Basketball Coaches. Office: Univ Nevada Las Vegas Basketball Office Las Vegas NV 89154

MASSMAN, BRIAN VINCENT, actor; b. Helena, Mont., Jan. 15, 1958; s. Hubert J. Massman and Evalyn Doranell (Guth) Stoner; m. Denise Lora Reimers, June 16, 1978; children: Tambre Rose, Alexis Violet. BA with honors, U. Mont., 1992. Cert. engring. technician. Engring. technician Mont. Dept. Transp., Helena, 1978-89; lab. supr. Mont. Dept. Transp., Missoula, 1989-91; actor Mt. Shakespeare in the Parks, Bozeman, 1991-92, Vigilante Theatre Co., Bozeman, 1992—. Recipient recognition Grandstreet Theatre, Helena, 1990. Mem. Baha'i Faith. Office: Vigilante Theatre Co PO Box 507 Bozeman MT 59771-0507

MASSOLETTI, DEXTER JAMES, SR., science and engineering specialist; b. San Francisco, Feb. 8, 1941; s. James Michael and Stella Massoletti; m. Cynthia Diane Kirby, Sept. 13, 1981; children: Jessica, Dexter Jr. Ops. supr. Magnetic Fusion Energy Group Lawrence Berkeley Lab., Berkeley, Calif., 1975-83; sr. sci. assoc. RTNS-II and E-Div. Lawrence Livermore Lab., Livermore, Calif., 1983-89; sr. sci. engring. assoc. Advanced Light Source Lawrence Berkeley Lab., 1989—. With U.S. Army, 1963-65. Mem. AAAS, Am. Phys. Soc., Instrument Soc. Am. Office: ALS-AFRD MS 80-101 LBL One Cyclotron Rd Berkeley CA 94720

MASSY, WILLIAM FRANCIS, university educator, higher education consultant; b. Milw., Mar. 26, 1934; s. Willard Francis and Ardys Dorothy (Digman) M.; m. Sally Vaughn Miller, July 21, 1984; children by previous marriage: Willard Francis, Elizabeth. BS, Yale U., 1956; SM, MIT, 1958, PhD in Indsl. Econs., 1960. Asst. prof. indsl. mgmt. MIT, Cambridge, 1960-62; from asst. prof. to prof. bus. adminstrn. Stanford U., Calif., 1962—, assoc. dean Grad. Sch. Bus., 1971, vice provost for research, 1971-77, v.p. for bus. and fin., 1977-88, v.p. fin., 1988-91; prof. edn., dir. Stanford Inst. Higher Edn. Research, Calif., 1988—; bd. dirs. Stanford Mgmt. Co., Diebold, Inc., Bijur Lubricating Corp., grants com. Hong Kong U. and Poly., Yale U. Coun.; mgmt. cons. Author: Stochastic Models of Buying Behavior, 1970, Marketing Management, 1972, Market Segmentation, 1972, Planning Models for Colleges and Universities, 1981, Endowment, 1991; mem. editorial bd. Jour. Mktg. Research, 1964-70, Harcourt, Brace Jovanovich, 1965-71; contbr. articles to profl. jours. Bd. dirs. Palo Alto-Stanford chpt. United Way, 1978-80, Stanford U. Hosp., 1980-91, MAC, Inc., 1969-84. Ford Found. faculty research fellow, 1966-67. Mem. Am. Mktg. Assn. (bd. dirs. 1971-73, v.p. edn. 1976-77), Inst. Mgmt. Scis., Fin. Execs. Inst. Republican. Episcopalian. Club: Yale N.Y. Office: Stanford U 508 Ceras Bldg Stanford CA 94305-3084

MASTERS, RICK DAVID, film producer; b. Ithaca, N.Y., June 13, 1950; s. Arthur Earl and Jean (Tyler) M.; m. Nancy Jane Bright, June 17, 1978; 1 child, Rosemary Star. Student, Calif. Poly. State U., 1982. Owner Rick Masters' Prodns., Independence, Calif., 1982—. Producer of documentary films including Aoli, Comet Clones and Pod People, 1982 (U.S. Gray prize 1982); cartoonist including series Pterosoars, 1982-86; contbr. articles to profl. jours. Meet dir. Don Partridge Meml. Open and George Worthington Meml. Classic, Owens Valley, Calif., 1985; organizer Cross Country World Championships, Owens Valley, 1984; mem. Rep. Ctrl. Com. Home: PO Box 478 Independence CA 93526-0478

MASTIN, GARY ARTHUR, research engineer; b. Wichita, Kans., Mar. 6, 1954; s. Arthur Ward and Mary Helen (Case) M.; m. Jeanette Lee Johnson, June 19, 1981; children: Dana Andrew, Alisa Mae. BA in Physics summa cum laude, Ottawa (Kans.) U., 1976; MSEE, U. Mo., 1977; PhD in Engring. Sci., La. State U., 1983. Rsch. engr. Environ. Rsch. Inst. of Mich., Ann Arbor, 1977-79; sr. mem. tech. staff Sandia Nat. Labs., Albuquerque, 1983—. Active Asbury United Meth. Ch., Albuquerque, 1984—; chair com. Troop 392 Boy Scouts Am., Albuquerque, 1984-86; tchr. math. and computer sci. Sandia Summer Sci. Acad., Bernalillo, N.Mex., 1986-90. Mem. Sigma Xi.

MASTRINI, JANE REED, social worker, consultant; b. Lincoln, Nebr., July 23, 1948; d. William Scott and Ellen (Daly) Cromwell; m. Charles James Mastrini, July 19, 1969. BA, Western State Coll., Gunnison, Colo., 1970; MSW, U. Denver, 1980. Lic. social worker Colo.; cert. alcohol counselor Colo. and nat. Tchr. Flandreau (S.D.) Indian Sch., 1970; social worker S.D. Dept. Welfare, Pierre, 1970-75; child care worker Sacred Heart Home, Pueblo, Colo., 1975-76; counselor Fisher Peak Alcohol Treatment Ctr., Trinidad, Colo., 1976-77; family therapist West Nebr. Gen. Hosp., Scottsbluff, 1980-81; adolescent coord. St. Luke's Hosp., Denver, 1981-86; exec. dir. New Beginnings At Denver, Lakewood, Colo., 1986-90; pres. Counseling Dimensions of Colo., Denver, 1990-92; trainer Mile High Inst., 1987—; managed care mgr. Arapahoe House, 1992—; cons. Colo. Counseling Consortium, Denver, 1984—; field work supr. U. Denver, 1983—. Lectr., group leader Colo. Teen Inst., Denver, 1984-85. Mem. NASE (cert.), P.E.O. (pres. 1984-87) Colo. Assn. Addiction Treatment Programs (v.p. 1991-92). Democrat. Episcopalian. Home: 11785 W 66th Pl #D Arvada CO 80004 Office: Arapahoe House 8801 Lipan Denver CO 80221

MASUDA, YOSHINORI, systems analyst; b. Kasai, Hyogo, Japan, Apr. 6, 1953; came to U.S., 1977; s. Saburo and Mitsuyo (Masuda) M. BL, Kobe U., Japan, 1977; MBA, U. San Francisco, 1981. Gen. mgr. Kotobuki Trading Co., San Francisco, 1981-85; distbn. analyst Kikkoman Internat. Inc., San Francisco, 1986-87; mgr. mgmt. info. system Kokkoman Internat. Inc., San Francisco, 1987-88, mgr. electronic data interchange, 1988—. Mem. Beta Gamma Sigma. Home: 480 Wellesley Ave Mill Valley CA 94941 Office: Kikkoman Internat Inc 50 California St Ste 3600 San Francisco CA 94111

MATA, DAVID JOSEPH, physician, hospital administrator; b. Houston, Feb. 3, 1956; s. José and Josephine M.; m. Judith Symons, Sept. 9, 1978; children: Daniel José, Timothy John. BA in Biology, Point Loma Coll., 1978; postgrad., Calif. State U., L.A., 1978-80; MD, U. Minn., 1987. Diplomate Am. Bd. Family Practice, Nat. Bd. Med. Examiners. Resident in family medicine San Bernardino (Calif.) County Med. Ctr., 1987-90; med. dir. Salud Med. Ctr., Woodburn, Oreg., 1990—; adj. asst. prof. Oreg. Health Scis. U. Sch. Medicine, Portland, 1991—; active staff mem. Salem Hosp., Oreg., 1992—; active staff mem. Silverton Hosp., Oreg., 1992—; cons., steering com. mem. Am. Lung Assn., Salem, 1992—. Expert witness to U.S. Congress, Oreg. Supreme Ct., 1992; counselor East L.A. Task Force, 1979-80. Geriatric Medicine fellow U. Minn., 1985, Med. Student Rsch. Tng. grantee Nat. Inst. Health, 1985, scholar Nat. Hispanic Scholarship Found., 1987; named one of 10 Outstanding Young Americans, U.S. Jr. C. of C., 1993; recipient Golden Aztec award Oreg. Human Devel. Corp., 1993, Citation of Merit award Oreg./Pacific Dist. Ch. of Nazarene, 1993, Mentorship award Dept. Family Medicine Oreg. Health Scis. U., 1993. Mem. Nazarene Health Care Felloship, Am. Acad. Family Physicians, Northwest Regional Primary Care Assn. (clinicians com. 1990-93), Marion-Polk County Med. Soc., Oreg. Med. Assn. Democrat. Mem. Ch. of the Nazarene. Office: Salud Med Ctr 347 N Front St PO Box 66 Woodburn OR 97071

MATARAZZO, JOSEPH DOMINIC, psychologist; b. Caiazzo, Italy, Nov. 12, 1925; (parents Am. citizens); s. Nicholas and Adeline (Mastroianni) M.; m. Ruth Wood Gadbois, Mar. 26, 1949; children: Harris, Elizabeth, Sara. Student, Columbia U., 1944; BA, Brown U., 1946; MS, Northwestern U., 1950, PhD, 1952. Fellow in med. psychology Washington U. Sch. Medicine, 1950-51; instr. Washington U., 1951-53, asst. prof., 1953-55; research assoc. Harvard Med. Sch., assoc. psychologist Mass. Gen. Hosp., 1955-57; prof., head med. psychol. dept. Oreg. Health Scis. U., Portland, 1957—; mem. nursing research and patient care study sect., behavioral medicine study sect. NIH, nat. mental health adv. bd. NIMH; mem. bd. regents Uniformed Services U. Health Scis., 1974-80. Author: Wechsler's Measurement and Appraisal of Adult Intelligence, 5th edit., 1972, (with A.N. Wiens) The Interview: Research on its Anatomy and Structure, 1972, (with Harper and Wiens) Nonverbal Communication, 1978; editor: Behavioral Health: A Handbook of Health Enhancement and Disease Prevention, 1984; editorial bd.: Jour. Clin. Psychology, 1962—; cons. editor: Contemporary Psychology, 1962-70, 80—, Jour. Community Psychology, 1974-81, Behavior Modification, 1976-91, Intelligence: An Interdisciplinary Jour, 1976-90, Jour. Behavioral Medicine, 1977—, Profl. Psychology, 1978—, Jour. Cons. and Clin. Psychology, 1978-85; editor: Psychology series Aldine Pub. Co, 1964-74; psychology editor: Williams & Wilkins Co, 1974-77; contbr. articles to psychol. jours. Ensign USNR, 1943-47; capt. Res. Recipient Hofheimer prize Am. Psychiat. Assn., 1962. Fellow AAAS, APA (pres. divsn. health psychology 1991-92, mem. Coun. of Reps. 1982-91, bd. dirs. 1986-90, pres. 1989-90); mem. Western Psychol. Assn., Oreg. Psychol. Assn., Am. Assn. State Psychology Bds. (pres. 1963-64, 86-87), Nat. Assn. Mental Health (bd. dirs.), Oreg. Mental Health Assn. (bd. dirs., pres. 1962-63), Internat. Coun. Psychologists (bd. dirs. 1972-74, pres. 1976-77), Assn. Advancement of Psychology (trustee 1980-84, chmn. bd. trustees 1983-85). Home: 1934 SW Vista Ave Portland OR 97201-2455 Office: Oreg Health Scis U Sch of Medicine 3181 SW Sam Jackson Park Rd Portland OR 97201-3011

MATARÉ, HERBERT F., physicist, consultant; b. Aachen, Germany, Sept. 22, 1912; came to U.S., 1953; s. Josef P. and Paula (Broicher) M.; m. Ursula Krenzien, Dec. 1939; children: Felicitas, Vitus; m. Elise Walbert, Dec. 1983; 1 child, Victor B. BS in Physics, Chemistry and Math., Aachen U. Geneva, 1933; MS in Tech. Physics, U. Aachen, 1939; PhD in Electronics, Tech. U. Berlin, 1942; PhD in Solid State Physics summa cum laude, Ecole Normale Supérieure, Paris, 1950. Asst. prof. physics & electronics Tech. U. Aachen, 1936-45; head of microwave receiver lab. Telefunken, A.G., Berlin, 1939-46; mgr. semicondr. lab. Westinghouse, Paris, 1946-52; founder, pres. Intermetall Corp., Düsseldorf, Fed. Republic Germany, 1952-56; head semincondr. R & D, corp. rsch. labs. Gen. Telephone & Electronics Co., N.Y.C., 1956-59; dir. rsch. semicondr. dept. Tekade, Nürnberg, Fed. Republic Germany, 1959-61; head quantum physics dept. rsch. labs. Bendix Corp., Southfield, Mich., 1961-64; tech. dir., acting mgr. hybrid microelectronics rsch. labs. Lear Siegler, Santa Monica, Calif., 1963-64; asst. chief engr. advance electronics dept. Douglas Aircraft Co., Santa Monica, 1964-66; tech. dir. McDonnell Douglas Missile Div., 1964-69; sci. advisor to solid state electronics group Autonetics (Rockwell Internat.), Anaheim, Calif., 1966-69; pres. Internat. Solid State Electronics Cons., L.A., 1973—; prof. electronics U. Buenos Aires, 1953-54; vis. prof. UCLA, 1968-69, Calif. State U., Fullerton, 1969-70; dir. Compound Crystals Ltd., London, 1989—. Author: Receiver Sensitivity in the UHF, 1951, Defect Electronics in Semiconductors, 1971, Conscientious Evolution, 1978, Energy, Facts and Future, 1989, (with P. Faber) Renewable Energies, 1993; patentee first European transistor, vacuum crystal growth, solid state oscillators, grain boundary transistor, unipolar tunnel transistor, light detection with grain-boundaries; contbr. over 100 articles to profl. jours. Fellow IEEE (life); mem. AAAS, IEEE Nuclear Plasma Scis. Soc., IEEE Power Engring. Soc., Inst. for Advancement of Man (hon.), Am. Phys. Soc. (solid state div.), Electrochem. Soc., Am. Vacuum Soc. (thin film div.), Materials Rsch. Soc., N.Y. Acad. Scis. (emeritus). Home: 23901 Civic Ctr Way #130 Malibu CA 90265 Office: ISSEC PO Box 2661 Malibu CA 90265

MATAS, MYRA DOROTHEA, interior architect, kitchen and bath designer; b. San Francisco, Mar. 21, 1938; d. Arthur Joseph and Marjorie Dorothy (Johnson) Anderson; m. Michael Richard Matas Jr., Mar. 15, 1958; children: Michael Richard III, Kenneth Scott. Cert. interior design, Canada Coll.; cert. interior design, Calif. Owner, operator Miquel's Antiques Co., Millbrae, Caifl., 1969-70, Miguel's Antiques & Interiors Co., Burlingame, Calif., 1970-79, Country Elegance Antiques & Interiors Co., Menlo Park, Calif., 1979-84, La France Boutique Co., 1979-84, Myra D. Matas Interior Design, San Francisco, 1984—; mgr. La France Imports, Inc., 1982-92; pres., gen. contractor Artisans 3 Inc., Burlingame, 1988-92; gen. contractor Matas Constr., Millbrae, 1993—; instr. interior design dept. Canada Coll. Mem. Nat. Home Fashion League, Am. Soc. Interior Designers (assoc.). Contbr. articles in field to profl. jours. Office: 331 Potrero Ave San Francisco CA 94103-4816

MATEO, JULIO, JR., prosecutor; b. N.Y.C., Nov. 8, 1959; s. Julio and Sylvia (Laracuente) M. BA, U. Chgo., 1981; JD, U. Minn., 1985. Bar: Calif. 1986, U.S. Dist. Ct. (no., ea., cen. and so. dists.) Calif., U.S. Ct. Appeals (9th cir.). Assoc. Pillsbury, Madison & Sutro, San Francisco, 1985-86, Baker & McKenzie, San Francisco, 1987-90; dep. dist. atty. San Mateo (Calif.) County Dist. Atty.'s Office, 1990—. Contbr. articles to profl. publs. Mem. San Mateo County Young Reps.; mem. com. bar examiners State Bar of Calif., 1991—. Mem. Hispanic Nat. Bar Anns. (chmn. inter-bar relations com. conf. 1993), San Mateo County La Raza Lawyers Assn. (founder, first pres.), Bar Assn. of San Francisco (ex-officio bd. dirs. 1988-91), Calif. LaRaza Lawyers, Barristers Club San Francisco (chmn. 1986-87, bd. dirs. 1987-92, pres. 1991-92, award of recognition 1987, 88, 89, 90). Roman Catholic. Office: San Mateo Dist Atty 603 Hamilton St Redwood City CA 14063

MATERN, STEPHEN EDGAR, power system technician; b. Henderson, Nev., Feb. 25, 1943; s. Raymond M. and Willis M. (Taylor) M.; m. Elizabeth A. Dinsmore, Sept. 24, 1964; children: Stephanie M., Philip D. AAS, Big

Bend C.C., Moses Lake, Wash., 1991. Substation operator So. Calif. Edison Co., L.A., 1965-69; sr. substation operator Bonneville Power Adminstrn., Madras, Oreg., 1969-72; power system control craftsman Bonneville Power Adminstrn., Longview, Wash., 1972-76, Moses Lake, Wash., 1976—; part time instr. Big Bend C.C., 1981—. Pres. Nova/honors Parent Adv. Com., Moses Lake, 1985-91. Cpl. USMC, 1960-65. Mem. Wash. Air Nat. Guard, 1984—. Mem. Elks, Phi Theta Kappa. Republican. Home: PO Box 485 Moses Lake WA 98837

MATHAUDHU, SUKHDEV SINGH, mechanical engineer; b. Dhamtan Sahib, Haryana, India, Sept. 11, 1946; came to U.S., 1965; s. Kesho Ram and Channo Devi (Dhiman) M.; m. Veena Chand, Aug. 20, 1972; children: Suveen Nigel, Suneel Adrian. BSME, Walla Walla (Wash.) Coll., 1970. Registered profl. engr., Calif., Pa. Mech. engr. McGinnis Engring., Inc., Portland, Oreg., 1970-71, Can. Union Coll., LaCombe, Alta., Can., 1971-72, H.D. Nottingham & Assocs., McLean, Va., 1972; project engr. Shefferman & Bigelson Co., Silver Spring, Md., 1973-77; mech. engr. Buchart Assocs., York, Pa., 1977-78; sr. mech. engr. Gannett Fleming, Harrisburg, Pa., 1978-80; chief mech. engr. Popov Engrs., Newport Beach, Calif., 1981-83; pres. Mathaudhu Engring., Inc., Riverside, Calif., 1983—. Vice chmn. LaSierra Acad. of SDA, Riverside, 1988-92; law adv. counselor SE Conf. SDA, 1987-92. Mem. ASHRAE (chpt. pres. 1988-90, regional vice-chmn. 1990-92, jour. com. 1992-93, bd. dirs., region chmn. 1993—), NSPE, Am. Soc. Plumbing Engrs., Soc. Am. Mil. Engrs., Am. Cons. Engrs. Coun. Calif. Soc. Profl. Egnrs. (pres. 1985-86, state dir. 1986-87), Cons. Engrs. Assn. Calif. Republican. Seventh-Day Adventist. Home: 5394 College Ave Riverside CA 92505-3123 Office: 3903 Brockton Ave Ste 5 Riverside CA 92501-3212

MATHENY, JAMES HARNLY, computer scientist; b. Oak Park, Ill., Oct. 16, 1924; s. Willard Reynolds Matheny and Betty (Harnly) Martin; m. Coralie Era Schrader, June 15, 1947 (dec. Apr. 1955); children: Penelope Sue Matheny, Winifred Era Gill; m. Dania Elizabeth Cross, Apr. 7, 1956; children: Charles Kysor Matheny, Mabel Ann Fanrguy. Student, Ind. U., 1943-44, Knox Coll., 1942-43, 46-47; BS, Mich. State Coll., 1949, MS, 1950. Sr. project math. Texaco, Beacon, N.Y., Houston, 1950-62; sr. computer scientist Computer Scis. Corp., El Segundo, Calif., 1962-87, ret., 1987; mem. tech. subcom. X3J3, Am. Nat. Standards Inst., 1972-89. Contbr. articles to profl. publs. Capt. USAR, 1949-57. Mem. Assn. for Computing Machinery (exec. bd., sec. 1989-90). Episcopalian. Home: 41 Silver Spring Dr Rolling Hills Estates CA 90274

MATHENY, ROBERT LAVESCO, history educator, former university president; b. Lubbock, Tex., Jan. 15, 1933; s. Samuel Worth and Elsie Jane (Jones) M.; m. Sandra Hansen, July 6, 1973; children: Nelda, Monica, Cali. B.A., Eastern N.Mex. U., 1961, M.A., 1962; Ph.D., U. Ariz., 1975. Asst. prof. Eastern N.Mex. U., Portales, 1968-72, assoc. prof., 1972-76, v.p. Clovis campus, 1977-80, exec. v.p., 1981-83, pres., 1983-89, prof. dept. history, 1989—; dean continuing edn. Ft. Hays State U., Hays, Kans., 1980-81. Rockfellow Found. fellow, 1967-68. Mem. Western History Assn. Club: N.Mex. Amigos. Lodge: Rotary (Portales). Office: Eastern New Mexico U Office of Devel Portales NM 88130

MATHER, CHARLES E., JR., staff educator, consultant; b. St. Louis, Apr. 24, 1948; s. Charles E. and Doris M. (Boyd) M.; m. Veronica L. Vogt, May 3, 1969; children: Eric J., Jason C. BS in Indsl. Vocat. Edn., U. So. Miss., 1983; MA in Human Resource Devel., Webster U., St. Louis, 1992. Commd. USAF, 1968, advanced through grades to msgt., 1992; with tactical air control party USAF, Vietnam, 1970-71; administrator USAF, Topeka, 1971-73; sr. radio operator USAF, Osan AFB, Korea, 1973-74; dir. adminstrn. USAF, Scott AFB, Miss., 1974-75; acad. instr. USAF, Keesler AFB, Miss., 1975-80, chief enlisted adminstrn. tng., 1980-85; ops. coord. U.S. Def. Attache Office, Kinshasa, Zaire, 1985-88; human resource dir. Phillips Lab., Albuquerque, 1988-91; sr. facilitator United Nuclear Corp. Analytical Svcs., Albuquerque, 1991-92; sr. engr. Stone & Webster Engring. Corp., Albuquerque, 1992—. Author: Continuous Improvement Tool Kit, 1992. Mem. ASTD, Am. Soc. Quality Control (edn. and tng. com. energy and environ. divsn.), Albuquerque Quality Network, Air Force Sgts. Assn. (trustee 1988—), Vietnam Vets. Am. Roman Catholic. Home: 12533 Tomlinson Dr SE Albuquerque NM 87123

MATHER, E. COTTON, geography educator; b. West Branch, IA, Jan. 3, 1918; s. Anders Vetti and Alleda (Zwickey) M.; m. Julia Marie Eiler, Dec. 23, 1944; children: Cotton Vetti, J'Lee Alleda. AB, U. Ill., Champaign, 1940, MS, 1941; PhD, U. Wis., Madison, 1950. Geographer Army Map Svc., Washington, 1941; rsch. analyst Office of Strategic Svcs., Washington, 1942-44; instr. U. Wis., Madison, Wis., 1945-46; assoc. to full prof., dept. chmn. U. Minn., Mpls., 1957-85; pres. N.Mex. Geog. Soc., Mesilla, N.Mex., 1985-90; vis. prof. numerous univs. U.S., Can., overseas, 1959-88. Co-editor: Atlas of Kentucky, 1977, (14) International Geographical Guidebooks of North America, 1992; co-author: India, Cultural Patterns and Processes, 1982, Prairie Border Country, 1980, Upper Coulee Country, 1975, St. Croix Border Country, 1968. Recipient research award, Assn. of Am. Geographers, 1954, Ford Found., 1964, 65. Mem. Assn. Am. Geographers, Pierce County Geog. Soc., Internat. Geog. Union, N.Mex. Geog. Soc., Ctr. Am. Places (dir.), Explorers Club. Home: PO Box 1184 Mesilla NM 88046-1184 Office: N Mexico Geographical Soc PO Box 1201 Mesilla NM 88046-1201

MATHER, ROBERT LAURANCE, physicist; b. Clarksville, Iowa, Oct. 1, 1921; s. Milo Ghion and Lillie Mabel (Lister) M.; m. F. Isabel Brown, Sept. 29, 1956; children: Anne, David. BS in Physics, Iowa State U., 1942; MA in Physics, Columbia U., 1947; PhD in Physics, U. Calif., Berkeley, 1951. Physicist U.S. Naval Ordnance Lab., Washington, 1942-44; electronic engr. Radio Corp. Am., Harrison, N.J., 1944-46; physicist N.Am. Aviation, Berkeley, Calif., 1950-52, U.S. Naval Radiol. Def. Lab., San Francisco, 1952-69; electronic engr. U.S. Naval Ocean Systems Ctr., San Diego, 1969-85, Computer Scis. Corp., San Diego, 1985-87; retired, 1987; vis. scholar U. Calif., Berkeley, 1991—; mem. physics astronomy coun. Iowa State U., Ames, 1992—. Fellow Am. Physical Soc.; mem. IEEE, AAAS, Sigma Xi. Home: 100 Bay Pl #2110 Oakland CA 94610

MATHERON, MICHAEL EARL, plant pathologist; b. Pitts., Jan. 2, 1947; s. Earl Francis and Clelia (Fabbris) M.; m. Phyllis Diane Wells, June 29, 1971; children: David, Daniel. BS, U. Calif., Davis, 1968; MS, Oreg. State U., 1973; PhD, U. Calif., Davis, 1984. Staff rsch. assoc. U. Calif., Davis, 1973-84; asst. ext. plant pathologist U. Ariz., Yuma, 1984-88, assoc. ext. plant pathologist, 1988—. Contbr. articles to profl. jours. With U.S. Army, 1969-71, Vietnam. Mem. Am. Pathol. Soc., Sigma Xi. Office: Yuma Agrl Ctr 6425 W 8th St Yuma AZ 85364-9737

MATHEWS, BARBARA EDITH, gynecologist; b. Santa Barbara, Calif., Oct. 5, 1946; d. Joseph Chesley and Pearl (Cieri) Mathews; AB, U. Calif., 1969; MD, Tufts U., 1972. Intern, Cottage Hosp., Santa Barbara, 1972-73, Santa Barbara Gen. Hosp., 1972-73; resident in ob-gyn Beth Israel Hosp., Boston, 1973-77; clin. fellow in ob-gyn Harvard U., 1973-76, instr., 1976-77; gynecologist Sansum Med. Clinic, Santa Barbara, 1977—. faculty mem. ann. postgrad. course Harvard Med. Sch.; bd. dirs. Sansum Med. Clinic; dir. ann. postgrad course UCLA Med. Sch. Bd. dirs. Meml. Rehab. Found., Santa Barbara, Channel City Club, Santa Barbara, Music Acad. of the West, Santa Barbara; mem. citizen's continuing edn. adv. council Santa Barbara Community Coll. Diplomate Am. Bd. Ob-Gyn. Fellow ACS, Am. Coll. Obstetricians and Gynecologists; mem. AMA, Am. Soc. Colposcopy and Cervical Pathology (dir. 1982-84), Harvard U. Alumni Assn., Tri-counties Obstet. and Gynecol. Soc. (pres. 1981-82), Phi Beta Kappa. Clubs: Birnam Wood Golf (Santa Barbara). Author: (with L. Burke) Colposcopy in Clinical Practice, 1977; contbg. author Manual of Ambulatory Surgery, 1982. Home: 2105 Anacapa St Santa Barbara CA 93105-3503 Office: 317 W Pueblo St Santa Barbara CA 93105-4365

MATHEWS, KENNETH PINE, physician, educator; b. Schenectady, N.Y., Apr. 1, 1921; s. Raymond and Marguerite Elizabeth (Pine) M.; m. Alice Jean Elliott, Jan. 26, 1952 (dec.); children: Susan Kay, Ronald Elliott, Robert Pine; m. Winona Beatrice Rosenburg, Nov. 8, 1975. A.B., U. Mich., 1941, M.D., 1943. Diplomate Am. Bd. Internal Medicine, Am. Bd. Allergy and Immunology (past. sec.). Intern, asst. resident, resident in medicine Univ. Hosp., Ann Arbor, Mich., 1943-45, 48-50; mem. faculty dept. medicine med. sch. U. Mich., 1950—, assoc. prof. internal medicine, 1956-61, prof., 1961-86, prof. emeritus, 1986—, head div. allergy, 1967-83; adj. mem. Scripps Clinic and Research Found., La Jolla, Calif., 1986—; past chmn. residency rev. com. for allergy and immunology, past chmn. allergy and immunology rsch. com. NIH. Co-author: A Manual of Clinical Allergy, 2d edit, 1967; editor: Jour. Allergy and Clin. Immunology, 1968-72; contbr. numerous articles in field to profl. jours. Served to capt. M.C. AUS, 1946-48. Recipient Disting. Service award Am. Acad. Allergy, 1976; Faculty Disting. Achievement award U. Mich., 1984. Fellow Am. Acad. Allergy (past pres.), A.C.P. (emeritus); mem. Am. Assn. Immunologists (emeritus), Ctrl. Soc. Clin. Rsch. (emeritus), Am. Fedn. Clin. Rsch., Alpha Omega Alpha, Phi Beta Kappa. Home: 7080 Caminito Estrada La Jolla CA 92037-5714 Office: Scripps Clinic & Rsch Found Dept Molecular & Exptl Medicine 10666 N Torrey Pines Rd La Jolla CA 92037-1027

MATHEWS, THOMAS JOHN, Spanish educator; b. Santa Monica, Calif., July 14, 1956; s. Robert L. Mathews and Joanne Walt Kennedy. BA, Weber State Coll., 1981; MA, Middlebury Coll., 1984; PhD, U. Del., 1992. Spanish tchr. Wahlquist Jr. High Sch., Weber County, Utah, 1981-82; instr., teaching asst. U. Del., Newark, 1985-89; lectr. Spanish Ill. State U., Normal, 1989-90; asst. instr. U. Utah, Salt Lake City, 1990-91; asst. prof. Spanish Brigham Young U., Provo, Utah, 1991—. Contbr. articles to profl. jours. Mem. MLA, Utah Fgn. Lang. Assn. (bd. dirs. 1991—), Rocky Mountain MLA, Linguistic Soc. Am., Am. Assn. Tchrs. of Spanish and Portuguese. Republican. LDS. Office: Brigham Young Univ Dept Spanish/Portuguese Provo UT 84602

MATHEWS, WILLIAM EDWARD, neurological surgeon, educator; b. Indpls., July 12, 1934; s. Ples Leo and Roxie Elizabeth (Allen) M.; m. Eleanor Jayne Comer, Aug. 24, 1956 (div. 1976); children: Valerie, Clarissa, Marie, Blair; m. Carol Ann. Koza, Sept. 12, 1987; 1 child, William Kyle. BS, Ball State U., 1958; DO, Kriksville Coll. Osteopathic Medicine, 1961; MD, U. Calif., L.A., 1962; student, Armed Forces Trauma Sch., Ft. Sam Houston, Tex., 1967-68. Diplomate Am. Bd. Neurol. and Orthopedic Surgery, Am. Bd. Pain Mgmt., Am. Bd. Indsl. Medicine, Am. Bd. Spinal Surgeons (v.p. 1990-92). Intern Kirksville (Mo.) Osteopathic Hosp., 1961-62; resident neurosurgery Los Angeles County Gen. Hosp., 1962-67; with Brookes Army Hosp., Ft. Sam Houston, 1967-68; with 8th field hosp. U.S. Army Neurosurgeon C.O. & 933 Med. Corp, Vietnam, 1968-69; chief neurosurgery Kaiser Med. Group, Walnut Creek, Calif., 1969-77; staff neurosurgeon Mt. Diablo Med. Ctr., Concord, Calif., 1977—; chief resident neurosurgery Los Angeles County Gen. Hosp., 1962-67; chief neurosurgery Kaiser Permanente Med. Group, Walnut Creek, 1969-77; comdg. officer 933d Med. Detachment Vietnam R.V.N., 1968-69; asst. prof. Kriksvelle Coll. Osteopathic Medicine, 1958-62; asst. lecturing prof. Neuroanatomy U. Calif. Coll. of Medicine, 1962-65. Author: (jour./book) Intracerebral Missile Injuries, 1972. Mem. adv. com. Rep. Presdl. Selection Com.Maj. U.S. Army, 1967-69, Vietnam. Recipient Disting. Svc. award Internat. Biography, 1987; scholar Psi Sigma Alpha, 1989. Fellow Congress Neurol. Surgeons (joint sect. on neurotrauma), Royal Coll. Medicine, Am. Acad. Neurologic and Orthopedic Surgeons (pres. 1981-82); mem. AMA, Calif. Med. Assn., San Francisco Neurologic, Contra Costa County Med. Soc. Roman Catholic.

MATHEWSON, CHARLES NORMAN, manufacturing company executive; b. Huntington Park, Calif., June 12, 1928; s. Alfred C. and Mildred (Niquette) M.; m. Lucille Linkowitz (div. June 1975); children: Gail P., Robert A., Curtis N., Christina Easter, Miles Carlton; m. Barbara Martin (div. June 1982); m. Ann Ballinger. BS in Fin., U. So. Calif., 1953; postgrad., UCLA, 1961. Office mgr., v.p. Hill Richards & Co., L.A., 1953-59; pres. Fradelis Frozen Foods, L.A., 1959-61; account exec. Morgan & Co., L.A., 1961-62; sales mgr. R.J. Henderson & Co., L.A., 1962-63; sr. v.p. Jefferies & Co., L.A., 1963-71; chmn. Arden-Mayfair, Inc., L.A., 1971-75, Wagenseller & Durst, L.A., 1979-80; ind. mgr. pvt. investments Laguna Beach, Calif., 1980-86; chmn. Internat. Game Tech., Reno, 1986—; bd. dirs. Baron Asset Fund, N.Y.C. With U.S. Army, 1946-48. Named Exec. of Yr., Internat. Gaming Bus. Expn., 1990. Mem. Prospectors Club. Republican. Roman Catholic. Office: Internat Game Tech 520 S Rock Blvd Reno NV 89502-4169

MATHIAS, BETTY JANE, communications and community affairs consultant, writer, editor, lecturer; b. East Ely, Nev., Oct. 22, 1923; d. Royal F. and Dollie B. (Bowman) M.; student Merritt Bus. Sch., 1941, 42, San Francisco State U., 1941-42; 1 child, Dena. Asst. publicity dir. Oakland (Calif.) Area War Chest and Community Chest, 1943-46; pub. rels. Am. Legion, Oakland, 1946-47; asst. to pub. rels. dir. Cen. Bank of Oakland, 1947-49; pub. rels. dir. East Bay chpt. of Nat. Safety Council, 1949-51; propr., mgr. Mathias Pub. Rels. Agy., Oakland, 1951-60; gen. assignment reporter and teen news editor Daily Rev., Hayward, Calif., 1960-62; freelance pub. rels. and writing, Oakland, 1962-66, 67-69; dir. corp. communications Systech Fin. Corp., Walnut Creek, Calif., 1969-71; v.p. corp. communications Consol. Capital companies, Oakland, 1972-79, v.p. community affairs, Emeryville, Calif., 1981-84, v.p. spl. projects, 1984-85; v.p., dir. Consol. Capital Realty Svcs., Inc., Oakland, 1973-77; v.p., dir. Centennial Adv. Corp., Oakland, 1976-77; communications cons., 1979—; cons. Mountainair Realty, Cameron Park, Calif., 1986-87; pub. rels. coord. Tuolumne County Visitors Bur., 1989-90; lectr. in field; bd. dirs. Oakland YWCA, 1944-45, ARC, Oakland, So. Alameda County chpt., 1967-69, Family Ctr., Children's Hosp. Med. Ctr. No. Calif., 1982-85, March of Dimes, 1983-85, Equestrian Ctr. of Walnut Creek, Calif., 1983-84, also sec.; adult and publs. adv. Internat. Order of the Rainbow for Girls, 1953-78; communications arts adv. com. Ohlone (Calif.) Coll., 1979-85, chmn., 1982-84; mem. adv. bd. dept. mass communications Calif. State U.-Hayward, 1985; pres. San Francisco Bay Area chpt. Nat. Reyes Syndrome Found., 1981-86; vol. staff Columbia Actors' Repertory, Columbia, Calif., 1986-87, 89; mem. exec. bd., editor newsletter Tuolumne County Dem. Club, 1987; publicity chmn. 4th of July celebration Tuolumne County C. of C., 1988. Recipient Grand Cross of Color award Internat. Order of Rainbow for Girls, 1955. Order Eastern Star (publicity chmn. Calif. state 1955). Editor East Bay Mag., 1966-67, TIA Traveler, 1969, Concepts, 1979-83. Home: 20575 Gopher Dr Sonora CA 95370-9034

MATHIAS, HARRY MICHAEL, cinematographer, consultant, author; b. London, Aug. 15, 1945; came to U.S., 1949.; s. Eric Manfred and Elsa (Herbst) M.; m. Ann C. Johnston, Oct. 4, 1987; 1 child, Morgan A. AA, San Francisco City Coll., 1965; BA, Calif. State U., 1968, MA, 1974. Dir. photography numerous motion pictures, 1969-88; sr. cons. Panavision Inc., Tarzana, Calif., 1981—; cons. Eastman Kodak Co., Rochester, N.Y., 1982-84; pres. Image Tech. Inc., Santa Monica, Calif., 1986—; mem. faculty UCLA, 1984—; lectr. Swedish Film Inst., Am. Film Inst., Stanford U. Author: Electronic Cinematography, 1985; author (with others) Image Quality, 1984, The American Cinematographers Handbook, 1986, HDTV: The Politics, Policies and Economics of Tommorows Television, 1990; contbr. articles to profl. jours.; dir. photography Solly's Dinner, 1980 (Oscar nomination). Mem. Mus. Contemporary Art, Los Angeles, 1988, Los Angeles County Mus. Art, 1987, 88. Mem. Soc. Motion Picture and T.V. Engrs., Working Group on High Definition Electronic Prodn. Standards (chmn. film splty. com.). Democrat. Clubs: Pacific Mariners (Marina Del Rey), Yacht. Office: PO Box 11083 Marina Del Rey CA 90295-8837

MATHIAS, LESLIE MICHAEL, electronic manufacturing company executive; b. Bombay, Dec. 17, 1935; came to U.S., 1957; s. Paschal Lawrence and Dulcine (D'Souza) M.; m. Vivian Mae Doolittle, Dec. 16, 1962. BSc, U. Bombay, 1957; BS, San Jose (Calif.) State U., 1961. Elec. engr. Indian Standard Metal, Bombay, 1957; sales engr. Bleisch Engring. and Tool, Mt. View, Calif., 1958-60; gen. mgr. Meadows Terminal Bds., Cupertino, Calif., 1961-63; prodn. mgr. Sharidon Corp., Menlo Park, Calif., 1963-67, Videx Corp., Sunnyvale, Calif., 1967-68, Data Tech. Corp., Mt. View, 1968-69; pres. L.G.M. Mfg., Inc., Mt. View, 1969-83; pvt. practice plating cons. Los Altos, Calif., 1983-87; materials mgr. Excel Cirs., Santa Clara, Calif., 1987-91, acct. mgr., 1991—. Social chmn. Internat. Students, San Jose, 1958-59. Mem. Nat. Fedn. Ind. Bus., Calif. Cirs. Assn., Better Bus. Bur., Purchasing Assn., U.S. C. of C. Roman Catholic. Home: 20664 Mapletree Pl Cupertino CA 95014-0449

MATHIES, ALLEN WRAY, JR., physician, hospital administrator; b. Colorado Springs, Colo., Sept. 23, 1930; s. Allen W. and Esther S. (Norton) M.; m. Lewise Austin, Aug. 23, 1956; children: William A., John N. BA, Colo. Coll., 1952; MS, Columbia U., 1956, PhD., 1958; MD, U. Vt., 1961. Rsch. assoc. U. Vt., Burlington, 1957-61; intern L.A. County Hosp., 1961-62; resident in pediatrics L.A. Gen. Hosp., 1962-64; asst. prof. pediatrics U. So. Calif., L.A., 1964-68, assoc. prof., 1968-71, prof., 1971—, assoc. dean, 1969-74, interim dean, 1974-75, dean, 1975-85; head physician Communicable Disease Svc. U. So. Calif., Los Angeles, 1964-75; pres., chief exec. officer Huntingtom Meml. Hosp., Pasadena, Calif., 1985—; bd. dirs. Pacific Mut. Contbr. articles to med. jours. Bd. dirs. Occidental Coll. With U.S. Army, 1953-55. Mem. Am. Acad. Pediatrics, Infectious Disease Soc. Am., Am. Pediatric Soc., Soc. Pediatric Rsch. Republican. Episcopalian. Home: 314 Arroyo Dr South Pasadena CA 91030-1623 Office: Huntington Meml Hosp 100 W California Blvd Pasadena CA 91105-3027

MATHUR, ASHOK, telecommunications engineer, educator, researcher; b. Gorakhpur, Uttar Pradesh, India; came to U.S., 1979; s. Raj Swarup and Savitri Mathur; m. Jayanti Srivastava, May 31, 1978; children: Menka, Puja. BS, U. Agra, India, 1963, MS, 1965; PhD, U. Southampton, Hampshire, Eng., 1974. Cert. telecommunications engr., Calif.; teaching credential, Calif. Lectr. upper atmospheric physics Kanpur, India, 1965-68; doctoral researcher U. Southampton, 1968-73; postdoctoral research fellow U. Poitiers, Vienne, France, 1973-74; assoc. prof., research supr U. Kanpur, 1974-79; mem. tech. staff telecomms. sci. and engring. divsn. Jet Propulsion Lab. Calif. Inst. Tech., Pasadena, 1979-92; prin. systems engr. applied tech. divsn. Computer Scis. Corp., Pasadena, 1992—. Contbr. numerous publs. to profl. jours.; mem. editorial bd. Acta Ciencia Indica Jour., 1975-78. Recipient 10-Yr. Svc. award Jet Propulsion Lab. Calif. Inst. Tech., 1990, Overseas Students award Brit. Coun., London, 1968, Délégation Générale a la Recherche Scientifique et Technique award, Paris, 1973, cert. of merit for disting. svcs. Internat. Biographical Ctr., Cambridge, Eng., 1988, Group Achievement award NASA, 1991. Mem. IEEE (sr.), AIAA (vice chmn. pub. policy San Gabriel Valley, sec. L.A. 1987-92), The European Phys. Soc., Calif. Inst. Tech. Mgmt. Club, Armed Forces Comms. and Electronics Assn. Home: 1923B Huntington Dr Duarte CA 91010-2659 Office: Jet Propulsion Lab 4800 Oak Grove Dr MS 264-805 Pasadena CA 91109-8099

MATIN, ABDUL, microbiology educator, consultant; b. Delhi, India, May 8, 1941; came to U.S., 1964, naturalized, 1983; s. Mohammed and Zohra (Begum) Said; m. Mimi Keyhan, June 21, 1968. BS, U. Karachi, Pakistan, 1960, MS, 1962; PhD, UCLA, 1969. Lectr. St. Joseph's Coll., Karachi, 1962-64; research assoc. UCLA, 1964-71; sci. officer U. Groningen, Kerklaan, The Netherlands, 1971-75; from asst. to assoc. prof. microbiology Stanford U., Calif., 1975—; cons. Engenics, 1982-84, Monsanto, 1984—; chmn. Stanford Recombinant DNA panel; lectr. ASM Found.; convener of microbiological workshop and confs. Mem. editorial bd. Jour. of Bacteriology; bd. dirs. Ann. Rev. Microbiol., Rev. of NSF and other Grants; contbr. numerous publs. to sci. jours. Fellow Fulbright Found., 1964, NSF, 1981—, Ctr. for Biotech. Research, 1981-85, EPA, 1981-84, NIH, Coll. Biotech., U.N. Tokten, 1987. Mem. AAAS, AAUP, Am Soc. for Microbiology (Found. lectr. 1991-92), Soc. Gen. Microbiology, Soc. Indsl. Microbiology, No. Soc. Indsl. Microbiology (bd. dirs.), Biophys. Soc. Home: 690 Coronado Ave Palo Alto CA 94305-1039 Office: Stanford U Dept Microbiology & Immunology Fairchild Sci Bldg Stanford CA 94305-5402

MATLEY, BENVENUTO GILBERT, computer engineer, educator, consultant; b. Monroe, La., Sept. 8, 1930; s. Welcome Gilbert and Lucette Marie (Renaud) M.; m. Patricia Jean McWilliams, JUne 21, 1959; children: Elizabeth, Katherine, John, Stephen, Richard, David. AB, San Diego State U., 1960; MBA, U. So. Calif., 1964; EdD, Nova U., 1980. Cert. data processor. Mathematician, engr. various data processing and computing firms, San Diego and L.A., 1956-64; sr. computer systems engr. Nortronics div. Northrop Corp., Hawthorne, Calif., 1964-69; prof. data processing and math. Ventura (Calif.) Coll., 1969—; lectr. in mgmt. and computer sci. West Coast U., L.A., 1982—; software cons, ednl. cons., Ventura, 1972—. Author: Principles of Elementary Algebra: A Language and Equations Approach, 1991; sr. author: National Computer Policies, 1988; contbr. chpts. to books, articles to profl. jours. Active Ventura County coun. Boy Scouts Am., 1979-82; cons. Calif. Luth. U., Thousand Oaks, Calif., 1989. Lt. (j.g.) USNR, 1952-55, Europe. Mem. IEEE Computer Soc. (Disting. Visitor 1988-91), Assn. for Computing Machinery, Spl. Interest Group-the Ada Lang. Office: Ventura Coll 4667 Telegraph Rd Ventura CA 93003

MATLOCK, STEPHEN J., business owner, consultant; b. Lewiston, Idaho, May 26, 1949; s. John H. and Alice (Alford) M.; children: Stephanie, Christopher. BS, U. Idaho, 1971. Editor Potlatch Corp., Lewiston, 1971-74; pub. Valley News, Meridian, Idaho, 1974-80; owner, operator Matlock Communications, Eagle, Idaho, 1980-85; pres. M Capital Corp., Eagle, 1983—. Councilman City of Eagle, Idaho, 1985-89. Capt. USNG, 1971-77. Office: M Capital Corp PO Box 328 Eagle ID 83616-0328

MATOSSIAN, JESSE NERSES, scientist; b. L.A., Feb. 2, 1952; s. Hagop Sarkis and Alice Elizabeth (Barsoomian) M. BS in Physics, U. So. Calif., L.A., 1975; MS in Physics, Stevens Inst. Tech., Hoboken, N.J., 1976; PhD in Physics, Stevens Inst. Tech., 1983. Mem. tech. staff Hughes Rsch. Labs., Plasma Physics Lab., Malibu, Calif., 1983-91, sr. mem. tech. staff, sr. staff physicist, 1992—. Reviewer Jour. Propulsion and Power, 1987-91; contbr. articles to profl. jours.; 6 patents in field. Patron mem. Los Angeles County Mus. of Art, sustaining mem. graphic arts coun. Recipient Superior Performance award Hughes Rsch. Labs., 1992, also 33 div. invention awards. Mem. AIAA, IEEE, Am. Phys. Soc. (life), N.Y. Acad. Scis., Sigma Xi.

MATOVICH, MITCHEL JOSEPH, JR., motion picture producer, executive; b. Watsonville, Calif., Dec. 16, 1927; s. Mitchel Joseph and Mildred Florence (Ingrom) M.; widowed, 1968; divorced, 1983; children: Wayne, Mark, Laura; m. Patte Dee Matovich, 1989. Student, San Jose State U., 1946-49. Mechanical designer Stanford Rsch. Inst., Menlo Park, Calif., 1955-59; rsch. specialist Lockheed Missiles & Space Co., Sunnyvale, Calif., 1959-70; mgr. NASA and Dept. of Def. bus. sect. Engineered Systems Div. FMC Corp., San Jose, Calif., 1970-77; pres. and chief exec. officer Morton Co. Div. of Haycor Corp., Hayward, Calif., 1977-82; pres. Concept Devel. Co., Newark, Calif., 1982-89, Matovich Prodns., Hollywood, Calif., 1987—, Stereotronics Inc., Beverly Hills, Calif., 1988—; co-owner Vagabond Theatre, L.A., 1990-91. Author: The Image Machine, feature length screenplays, stories for screenplays, short stories; producer (feature films) Lightning in a Bottle, 1993, I Don't Buy Kisses Anymore, 1992; co-producer: Social Suicide; co-inventor: Stereotronics 3-D Video System; patentee in field. With USN, 1945-46, 51-52, Korea. Mem. Soc. Motion Picture and TV Engrs., Producers' Guild, Mensa, Intertel. Home: 26544 Cardwick Ct Newhall CA 91321-1319 Office: Matovich Prodns Inc PO Box 5744 Beverly Hills CA 90210

MATSCH, LEE ALLAN, aerospace company executive; b. Chgo., Feb. 21, 1935; s. L. W. and Agnes (Swanson) M.; m. Diane Mary Noon, June 8, 1957; children: Sally Matsch Bernsten, Pamela, Gary. Student, Iowa State U., 1953-55; BSME, U. Ariz., 1957; MSME, U. Pitts., 1961; PhD, Ariz. State U., 1967. Assoc. engr. Westinghouse Electric Corp., Pitts., 1957-61; engr., sr. supr. Garrett Corp., Phoenix, 1961-70; mem. rsch. staff Ampex Corp., Redwood City, Calif., 1970-71; engring. mgr. Ampex Corp., Opelica, Ala., 1971-76; sr. supr., v.p. engring. Allied Signal Aerospace Co., Phoenix, 1976—. Co-author: Fluid Film Lubrication, 1981. Fellow ASME (com. chmn. 1991-93), Soc. Automotive Engrs.

MATSCH, RICHARD P., federal judge; b. 1930. A.B., U. Mich., 1951, J.D., 1953. Bar: Colo. Asst. U.S. atty. Colo., 1959-61; dep. city atty. City and County of Denver, 1961-63; judge U.S. Bankruptcy Ct., Colo., 1965-74, U.S. Dist. Ct. for Colo., 1974—. Served with U.S. Army, 1953-55. Mem. ABA, Am. Judicature Soc. Office: US Dist Ct 1929 Stout St Denver CO 80294-2900

MATSEN, JOHN MARTIN, pathology educator, microbiologist; b. Salt Lake City, Feb. 7, 1933; s. John M. and Bessie (Jackson) M.; m. Joneen Johnson, June 6, 1959; children: Marilee, Sharon, Coleen, Sally, John H., Martin K., Maureen, Catherine, Carl, Jeri. BA, Brigham Young U., 1958; MD, UCLA, 1963. Diplomate Am. Bd. Pediatrics, Am. Bd. Pathology, Spl. Competence in Med. Microbiology. Intern UCLA, L.A., 1963-64; resident L.A. County Harbor/UCLA, Torrance, Calif., 1964-66; USPHS fellow U.

Minn., Mpls., 1966-68, asst. prof., 1968-70, assoc. prof., 1971-74, prof., 1974; prof. U. Utah, Salt Lake City, 1974—, assoc. dean, 1979-81, chmn. Dept. of Pathology, 1981-93, v.p. health scis., 1993—; pres. Associated Regional and Univ. Pathologists, Inc., Salt Lake City, 1983-93, chmn. bd. dirs., 1993—. Author over 200 publs. in field. Mem. Acad. Clin. Lab. Physicians and Scientists (pres. 1978-79), Assn. of Pathology Chmn. (pres. 1990-92). Mem. LDS Church. Home: 2845 St Marys Way Salt Lake City UT 84108-2041 Office: U Utah Dept Pathology 50 N Medical Dr Salt Lake City UT 84132

MATSON, MERWYN DEAN, educational consultant; b. Forest City, Iowa, Aug. 6, 1937; s. Archie Alvin and Henrietta (Wittgreve) M.; m. Audrey Christine Gaydos, Apr. 9, 1988; children: Candace, Kevin, Shaunna, Dan, Cathy, Mindy, Lisa, Matthew. AB, Northwest Nazarene Coll., 1959; MEd, Oreg. State U., 1963; EdM, U. Oreg., 1962. Cert. tchr., sch. counselor, sch. psychologist, Iowa. Elem. sch. guidance coord. Pottawattami County Schs., Council Bluffs, Iowa, 1969-70; sch. psychologist Hancock County Schs., Garner, Iowa, 1970-71; dir. career edn. Mason City (Iowa) Pub. Schs., 1971-73; regional dir. Am. Coll. Testing Program, Springfield, Mo., 1973-84; Midwest regional dir. career planning svcs. Am. Coll. Testing Program, Lincolnshire, Ill., 1984-86; Mountains/Plains regional dir. career planning svcs. Am. Coll. Testing Program, Aurora, Colo., 1986—. Mem. AARP, Am. Counseling Assn., Rotary Club of Univ. Hills (Denver). Presbyterian. Home: 831 E Phillips Ln Littleton CO 80122-2982 Office: Am Coll Testing Program 3131 S Vaughn Way Ste 218 Aurora CO 80014-3507

MATSUDA, FUJIO, academic research administrator; b. Honolulu, Oct. 18, 1924; s. Yoshio and Shimo (Iwasaki) M.; m. Amy M. Saiki, June 11, 1949; children: Bailey Koki, Thomas Junji, Sherry Noriko, Joan Yuuko, Ann Mitsuyo, Richard Hideo. B.S. in Civil Engring., Rose Poly. Inst., 1949; D.Sc., Mass. Inst. Tech., 1952; D. Engring. (hon.), Rose Hulman Inst. Tech., 1975. Rsch. engr. MIT, 1952-54; rsch. asst. prof. engring. U. Ill., Urbana, 1954-55; asst. prof. engring. U. Hawaii, Honolulu, 1955-57; assoc. prof. U. Hawaii, 1957-62, chmn. dept. civil engring., 1960-63, prof., 1962-65, 74-84, dir. engring. expt. sta., 1962-63, v.p. bus. affairs, 1973-74, pres., 1974-84; exec. dir. Research Corp. U. Hawaii, 1984—; dir. Hawaii Dept. Transp., Honolulu, 1963-73; v.p. Park & Yee, Ltd., Honolulu, 1956-58; pres. SMS & Assos., Inc., 1960-63; pvt. practice as structural engr., 1958-60; dir. C. Brewer & Co., Ltd., UAL Corp., First Hawaiian Bank, First Hawaiian Inc., Pacific Internat. Ctr. for High Tech. Research, Rehab. Hosp. of Pacific, Maui Econ. Devel. Bd., Kuakini Health System, Japanese Cultural Ctr. of Hawaii, Hawaii Community Found., Japan-Am. Inst. Mgmt. Sci., Tampa Bay Lighting, Nat. Ocean Resources Tech. Corp.; mem. bd. Water Supply, Honolulu, 1963-73; mem. Airport Ops. Council Internat., 1968-73; pres. Pacific Coast Assn. Port Authorities, 1969; mem. sci. bd. Dept. Army, 1978-80; mem. U.S. Army Civilian Adv. Group, 1978—; mem. exec. com. transp. rsch. bd. NRC, 1982-86; mem. vis. com. on sponsored rsch. MIT, 1991—; mem. Rose-Hulman Inst. Tech. Com. on the Future, 1992—. Bd. dirs. Aloha United Way, 1973-76, Kuakini Med. Ctr., 1987-89; trustee Kuakini Health Systems, 1984-86, bd. dirs., 1986-89; trustee Nature Conservancy, 1984-89. Recipient Honor Alumnus award Rose Poly. Inst., 1971; recipient Disting. Svc. award Airport Ops. Coun. Internat., 1973, Disting. Alumnus award U. Hawaii, 1974 87, 91; named Hawaii Engr. of Yr., 1972. Mem. NAE, NSPE, ASCE (Parcel-Sverdrup Engring. Mgmt. award 1986), Social Sci. Assn., Western Coll. Assn. (exec. com. 1977-84, pres. 1980-82), Japan-Am. Soc. Honolulu (trustee 1976-84, adv. council 1984—), Japan-Hawaii Econ. Coun., World Sustainable Agr. Assn., Beta Gamma Sigma, Sigma Xi, Tau Beta Pi. Office: U Hawaii Rsch Corp 2800 Woodlawn Dr Ste 200 Honolulu HI 96822

MATSUI, JIRO, importer, wholesaler, small business owner; b. Honolulu, Hawaii, Apr. 5, 1919; s. Juro and Tsuta (Murai) M.; m. Barbara Toshiko Tanji; children: Kenneth Jiro, Alan Kiyoshi, Carol Ritsu. BA, U. Hawaii, 1949. Owner Honolulu Aquarium and Pet Supply, Honolulu, 1946-77, Bird House, Honolulu, 1957-61; owner, pres., chmn. Petland, Inc., Honolulu, 1961—, Pets Pacifica, Inc., Honolulu, 1977—, Global Pet Industries, Honolulu, 1975—; organizer, coord. first Pet Consumer Show in U.S., 1979, pres. 1979-82; first Internat. Pet Show; cons. Japan Pet Product Mfr. Assn. Fair, Japan, 1981-92. Pres. Waikiki Vets. Club, Kapahulu, Oahu, Hawaii, 1948-66, Waiawa (Oahu) Farmers, 1948-88. Sgt. U.S. Army, 1941-46. Decorated with Bronze Star, U.S. Army, 1947. Mem. Am. Pet Soc. (pres. 1979-82, chmn. 1989-92), Western World Pet Supply Assn. (bd. dirs. 1974—, pres. 1989-90, Edward B. Price award 1982), Honolulu C. of C. (bd. dirs. 1974—). Office: Pets Pacifica Inc 94-486 Ukee St Waipahu HI 96797

MATSUI, ROBERT TAKEO, congressman; b. Sacramento, Sept. 17, 1941; s. Yasuji and Alice (Nagata) M.; m. Doris Kazue Okada, Sept. 17, 1966; 1 child, Brian Robert. A.B. in Polit. Sci, U. Calif.-Berkeley, 1963; J.D., Hastings Coll. Law, U. Calif., San Francisco, 1966. Bar: Calif. 1967. Practiced law Sacramento, 1967-78; mem. Sacramento City Council, 1971-78, vice mayor, 1977; mem. 96th-103d Congresses from 3d Calif. dist., 1979—; mem. budget com. 96th-102d Congresses from 3d Calif. dist.; mem. ways and means com. 96th-103d Congresses from 5th Calif. dist., 1979—; chmn. profl. bus. forum Dem. Congl. Campaign Com.; congl. liaison nat. fin. council Dem. Nat. Com.; mem. adv. council on fiscal policy Am. Enterprise Inst. chmn. Profl. Bus. Forum of the Dem. Congl. Co. and Com.; congl. liaison Nat. Fin. Council, Dem. Nat. Com.; mem. Am. Enterprise Inst. Adv. Council on Fiscal Policy. Named Young Man of Yr. Jr. C. of C., 1973; recipient Disting. Service award, 1973. Mem. Sacramento Japanese Am. Citizens League (pres. 1969), Sacramento Met. C. of C. (dir. 1976). Democrat. Clubs: 20-30 (Sacramento) (pres. 1972), Rotary (Sacramento). Office: US Ho of Reps 2311 Rayburn House Office Washington DC 20515-0505*

MATSUMOTO, KEITH TADAO, diversified company executive; b. Honolulu, Dec. 30, 1957; s. Albert Yoshio and Edith Tomiko (Nomura) M.; m. Sherrie Akiko Sakamoto, July 23, 1988. BS in Civil and Urban Engrings., U. Pa., 1979; MBA, U. Mich., 1984. Jr. engr. Community Planning, Inc., Honolulu, 1979-82; cons. intern Ernst and Whinney, Honolulu, 1983, staff cons., 1984; project engr. Hawaiian Dredging and Constrn., Honolulu, 1985-86; mgmr. cons. Grant Thornton, Honolulu, 1986; pricing adminstr. GTE Hawaiian Telephone, Honolulu, 1986-87, internat. pricing and bus. analysis adminstr., 1987-88; mgr. mktg. and planning svcs. Gasco, Inc., Honolulu, 1988-90, mgr. bus. devel., 1990-91; mgr. investment analysis Alexander & Baldwin Inc., Honolulu, 1992—. Active Dem. Ctrl. Com. Hawaii, Honolulu, 1980—; wrestling coach McKinley High Sch., Honolulu, 1979-81, 85-88, PAC-5, Honolulu, 1990—; coun. Nuuanu Congl. Ch., Honolulu, 1985-88. Mem. ASCE (assoc.), Nat. Contract Mgrs. Assn., Hawaii Soc. Corp. Planners, Assn. Demand-Side Mgmt. Profls., U. Mich. Alumni Assn., U. Pa. Alumni Assn. (chairperson secondary sch. com. 1989-90). Mem. Christian Ch. Home: 45-573 Pilipaa St Kaneohe HI 96744

MATSUNAGA, GEOFFREY DEAN, lawyer; b. L.A., Sept. 30, 1949; s. Hideo Arthur and Yuri (Yamazaki) M.; m. Masako Inoue, Aug. 20, 1981; children: Ayako, Hideko, Lisa Fumi. BS, USAF Acad., 1971; MBA, U. Calif., Los Angeles, 1972; postgrad., Inter U. Ctr. Japanese Lang. Studies, 1979-80; JD, U. Calif., Berkeley, 1982. Bar: Calif. 1982, U.S. Dist. Ct. (cen. dist.) Calif. 1982, N.Y. 1983, U.S. Dist. Ct. (so. dist.) N.Y. 1983. Jud. extern U.S. Dist. Ct. (cen. dist.), L.A., 1981; atty. Milbank, Tweed, Hadley & McCloy, N.Y.C., 1982-84, Tokyo, 1984-87; atty. Sidley & Austin, Tokyo, 1987-88, L.A., 1988-91; assoc. Sheppard, Mullin, Richter & Hampton, L.A., 1991—. Founding bd. dirs. Futures Industry Assn., Japan, 1987; counsel East West Players, 1992—. Lt. USN, 1972-78. Japan Found. fellow, Tokyo, 1979-80. Mem. Am.-Japan Soc. (coun. Tokyo 1986-92), Japan Am. Soc. So. Calif. (adv. bd. South Bay 1992—). Episcopalian. Office: Sheppard Mullin Richter & Hampton 333 S Hope St Los Angeles CA 90071-1406

MATSUNAGA, MATTHEW MASAO, lawyer, accountant; b. Honolulu, Nov. 22, 1958; s. Spark Masayuki and Helene (Tokunaga) M.; m. Loretta Ann Sheehan, Apr. 20, 1986. BS, Bucknell U., 1980; JD, Georgetown U., 1985. Bar: Hawaii 1985, U.S. Ct. Appeals (9th cir.); CPA, Hawaii. Assoc. Carlsmith, Ball, Wichman, Murray & Case, Honolulu, 1985—. Bd. dirs. Moiliili Community Ctr., Honolulu, 1987—. Mem. ABA, Hawaii Bar Assn., Am. Judicature Soc., Hawaii Soc. CPAs. Home: 2207 Kuahea Pl Honolulu HI 96816-3415 Office: Carlsmith Ball Wichman Murray & Case PO Box 656 Honolulu HI 96809-0656

MATSUOKA, ERIC TAKAO, mathematics educator; b. Honolulu, May 9, 1967; s. Kenneth Tamotsu and Hilda Sumie (Hino) M. BA in Math. with distinction, U. Hawaii, 1987. Acctg. clk. Wayne Choo, CPA, Honolulu, 1987-88; lab. instr. in math. Leeward Community Coll., Pearl City, Hawaii, 1988—, lectr. in math., 1989—; contr. Computronics, Honolulu, 1989-93. Mem. Math. Assn. Am. (Instnl. award 1987). Office: PO Box 1857 Aiea HI 96701

MATSUSHIMA, MISLYN TERUKO, human resources specialist; b. Honolulu, Dec. 14, 1958; d. Tasuku and Kazue (Kimura) M.; m. Rodney T. Alensonorin, June 2, 1991. BA, U. Hawaii, 1980. Personnel clk. dept. Edn. State of Hawaii, Honolulu, 1981-83; personnel/payroll clk. Times Super Mkt. Ltd., Honolulu, 1983-86; v.p., treas. Personnel Office Mgmt. Systems Inc., Waipahu, Hawaii, 1986—. Bd. dirs. Am. Cancer Soc. ctrl. Leeward unit, Aiea, Hawaii, 1990—. Named Protegee of Yr. Small Bus. Adminstrn., Honlulu, 1991. Mem. Waipahu Bus. Assn., Soc. for Human Resource Mgmt., Honolulu Downtown Jaycees (chpt. pres. 1989, 90), Hawaii Jaycees (dist. dir. 1990, 91); Jr. Chamber Internat. Office: Personnel Office Mgmt Sys Inc 94-1036 Waipio Uka 104B Waipahu HI 96797

MATSUURA, GEORGE A., controller; b. Honolulu, Aug. 22, 1960; s. Michael I. and Elaine S. (Yamada) M. BS in Acctg., U. Denver, 1982, MBA, 1983. CPA, Calif. Audit staff Arthur Andersen, Denver, 1984-85; audit mgr. Pannell Kerr Forster, L.A., 1986-90; controller McCann's Engring. and Mfg. Co., L.A., 1990—. Mem. AICPA, Calif. Soc. CPAs. Office: McCann's Engring & Mfg Co 4570 W Colorado Blvd Los Angeles CA 90039

MATTATHIL, GEORGE PAUL, communications specialist, consultant; b. Kottayam, India, May 12, 1957; came to U.S., 1985; s. Paul and Annamma M. Bs, U. Kerala (India), 1973-78; MS, Indian Inst. Tech., 1978-82. Project engr. Tekelec, Calabasas, Calif., 1986-89; sr. systems analyst Security Pacific Automation, L.A., 1989-90; sr. design. engr. Telenova, Camarillo, Calif., 1990-91; founder Silicom, Inc., Mountain View, Calif., 1991—; cons. Raynet, Menlo Park, Calif., 1991, Larse, Santa Clar, Calif., 1991—. Nat. Sci. Talent scholar, India, 1975-80. Mem. IEEE, Assn. Computing Machinery, Software Entrepreneurs Forum, Soc. Telecom. Cons. Office: Silicom Inc PO Box 2264 Cupertino CA 95015-2264

MATTEOLI, RALPH, JR., nursing educator; b. Yreka, Calif., Jan. 30, 1938; s. Ralph Francis and Hazel Grace (McNeal) M. BS, U. Calif., San Francisco, 1962, MS, 1964; EdD, U. San Francisco, 1989. RN; cert. marriage, family and child counselor. Staff nurse Santa Rosa (Calif.) Gen. Hosp., 1962-63; psychiat. nurse Napa (Calif.) State Hosp., 1963-66; asst. prof. Chico (Calif.) State Coll., 1966-70; assoc. prof., coord. psychiat./mental health nursing San Francisco State U., 1970—; cons. U.S.-Asia Nurse Recruitment Co., Sonoma County Alliance for Mentally Ill, Santa Rosa, Sonoma County AIDS Project, Santa Rosa. Author: (with others) Nursing Assessment, 1969. Vol. AIDS Network, Santa Rosa. Recipient French Medal of Honor, French Consulate, San Francisco, 1957, Cert. of Recognition, Calif. State Senate, 1991; named Outstanding Individual Calif. Human Devel. Corp., 1991. Mem. Am. Psychiat. Nurses Assn. (Native Son Trailblazer award 1992), Nat. Alliance for Mentally Ill, Bay Area Psychiat. Nurse Educators (sec. 1985—), Assn. Am. Indian and Alaskan Native Profs. Democrat. Roman Catholic. Office: San Francisco State U Dept Nursing 1600 Holloway Ave San Francisco CA 94132-1722

MATTERSDORFF, GUENTER HANS, economics and public administration educator; b. Dresden, Germany, Nov. 11, 1926; came to U.S., 1939; s. Hans and Hertha (Sluzewski) M.; m. Eleanor Anne MacLean, Sept. 10, 1960; children: Donald Ward Mattersdorff, Peter Weld Mattersdorff. BA, Harvard U., 1948, MPA, 1951, PhD, 1958. Jr. economist Econ. Coop. Adminstrn., Washington, 1948-50; econs. instr. Yale U., New Haven, Conn., 1952-54, U. Mass., Amherst, Mass., 1954-56, Conn. Coll., New London, 1956-59; sr. economist McGraw-Hill Pub. Co., N.Y.C., 1959-63; assoc. prof. Econs. Lewis and Clark Coll., Portland, Oreg., 1963-68; prof. Econs. and Pub. Adminstrn. Lewis and Clark Coll., Portland, 1968—; vis. prof. econs. U. British Columbia, Vancouver, 1965, Haverford (Pa.) Coll., 1982, Carleton Coll., Northfield, Minn., 1986-87; exec. sec. Pacific N.W. Regional Econ. Conf., 1989—, bd. dirs., 1966—. Mem. Gov.'s Blue Ribbon Comm. on State Liquor Control Comm., Portland, Salem, Oreg., 1977-78, Tri-County Local Govt. Comm., Portland, 1976-77. With U.S. Army, 1945-46. Recipient NSF fellowship, W.Va. U., 1973, Sci. Faculty Rsch. fellowship, NSF, London Sch. Econs., 1971-72, NSF fellowship, Urban Studies Inst., Stanford, Calif., 1971, Faculty Rsch. fellowship, Ford Found., MIT, 1959. Mem. City Club of Portland (bd. govs. 1974-76, mem. rsch. com. on Oreg.'s tax structure 1983), Soc. Oreg. Economists, Am. Econ. Assn. Home: 930 Bullock St Lake Oswego OR 97034-4914 Office: Lewis and Clark Coll Dept Econs Portland OR 97219

MATTESON, J. HARROLD, medical educator; b. Miami, Fla., Mar. 31, 1947; s. J. Harrold Sr. and Mary Marjorie (Fitzell) M.; m. Karen Lee, Nov. 13, 1946; children: Scott, Jennifer. BS, Fla. State U., 1969, MS, 1971, PhD, 1982. Tchr. Dade County Schs., Miami, 1972-74; ednl. trainer USN, San Diego, 1974-76; ednl. cons. Human and Health Resources, Tallahassee, Fla., 1976-77; educator San Diego C.C., 1982; pres. Internat. Health Scis., Santa Fe, N.Mex., 1982—; inventor Algologics Corp., Santa Fe, 1992. Author: Medical Robotics, 1992. Fellow Am. Acad. Pain Mgmt. (diplomate), Am. Back Soc. (founding mem.). Republican. Office: Internat Health Scis 747 W Manhattan Ave Santa Fe NM 87501

MATTESON, SANDRA ANNE, audit manager; b. Eau Claire, Wis., May 12, 1956; d. Ivan Arthur and Benita Arlene (Draeger) Duerkop; m. Steven Lowell Matteson, Apr. 1, 1977; children: Christopher Lee, Wayne Aaron. BA, Evergreen State Coll., 1982, MPA, 1985. CPA, Wash. Accounts payable clk. ARC, Portland, 1978-79; acctg. asst. 2 Wash. State Dept. Social and Health Svcs., Olympia, 1980-81; employer auditor 2 Wash. State Dept. Labor and Industries, Olympia, 1982-84; acct. 2 Wash. State Gambling Commn., Olympia, 1984-86, investigative auditor, 1986-89; audit mgr. Wash. State Gambling Commn., Seattle, 1989—. With U.S. Army, 1974-78. Mem. AICPA, NAFE, Wash. Soc. CPA, Am. Soc. Women Accts. Republican. United Methodist.

MATTEUCCI, DOMINICK VINCENT, real estate developer; b. Trenton, N.J., Oct. 19, 1924; s. Vincent Joseph and Anna Marie (Zoda) M.; BS, Coll. of William and Mary, 1948; BS, Mass. Inst. Tech., 1950. Registered profl. engr., Calif.; lic. gen. bldg. contractor, real estate broker; m. Emma Irene DeGuia, Mar. 2, 1968; children: Felisa Anna, Vincent Eriberto. Owner, Matteucci Devel. Co., Newport Beach, Calif.; pres. Nat. Investment Brokerage Co., Newport Beach. Home: 2104 Felipe Newport Beach CA 92660-4040 Office: PO Box 8328 Newport Beach CA 92660

MATTHAU, CHARLES MARCUS, film director; b. N.Y.C., Dec. 10, 1964; s. Walter and Carol M. BA, U. So. Calif., 1986. Pres. The Matthau Co., L.A., 1986—. Dir. motion picture; Doin' Time on Planet Earth, 1988 (Saturn award Coun. Film Orgns., Silver Scroll award Acad. Sci. Fiction); dir., producer TV show Mrs. Lambert Remembers Love, 1991 (Golden Angel award Best TV spl. 1991, Golden Medal award Best Drama Prodn. 1991, Grand award The Houston Internat. Film Festival); dir. over 50 feature shorts. Nat. spokesperson Am. Lung Assn., L.A., 1989—; active Action on Smoking and Health, Washington, 1986—. Recipient Cine award, Coun. Non-Theatrical Events, Washington, 1985, Golden Seal award, London Amateur Film Festival, 1986. Mem. Dirs. Guild Am., Acad. Sci.-Fiction, Fantasy and Horror Films, Am. Film Inst.

MATTHEW, KATHRYN KAHRS, museum director; b. Charleston, S.C.. BA, Mt. Holyoke Coll., 1976; PhD, U. Pa., 1981; MBA, U. Minn., 1988. Collection asst., mgr. Acad. Natural Scis., Phila., 1979-82; curator sci. Cranbrook Inst. of Sci., Bloomfield Hills, Mich., 1983-85; asst. dir. Santa Barbara (Calif.) Mus. Natural History, 1988-89; dep. dir. Va. Mus. Natural History, Martinsville, 1989-91; dir. N.Mex. Mus. Natural History, Albuquerque, 1991—; prin. sci. adviser Omnimax film Sci. Mus. Minn., Mpls., 1988-92. Bd. dirs. Albuquerque Conv. and Visitors Bur., 1992—; mem. steering com. Magnifico Arts Festival, 1992; mem. govs. coun. Advance Math and Sci. Edn., 1992—; mem. rsch. com. N.Mex. First, 1992—. Mem. N.Mex. Women's Forum. Office: NMex Mus Natural History 1801 Mountain Rd NW Albuquerque NM 87104-1375

MATTHEW, LYN, art marketing consultant, educator; b. Long Beach, Calif., Dec. 15, 1936; d. Harold G. and Beatrice (Hunt) M.; m. Wayne Thomas Castleberry, Aug. 12, 1961 (div. Jan. 1976); children: Melanie, Cheryl, Nicole, Matthew. BS, U. Calif.-Davis, 1958; MA, Ariz. State U., 1979. Cert. hotel sales exec., 1988, meeting profl. Pres., Davlyn Cons. Found., Scottsdale, Ariz., 1979-82; cons., vis. prof. The Art Bus., Scottsdale, 1982—; pres., dir. sales and mktg. Embassy Stes., Scottsdale, 1987—, bd. trustees Hotel Sales and Mktg. Assn. Internat. Found., 1988—, chmn., 1991-93; vis. prof. Maricopa Community Coll., Phoenix, 1979—, Ariz. State U., Tempe, 1980-83; cons. Women's Caucus for Art, Phoenix, 1983-88. Bd. dirs. Rossom House and Heritage Square Found., Phoenix, 1987-88. Author: The Business Aspects of Art, Book I, 1979, Book II, 1979; Marketing Strategies for the Creative Artist, 1985. Mem. Women Image Now (Achievement and Contbn. in Visual Arts award 1983), Women in Higher Edn., Nat. Women's Caucus for Art (v.p. 1981-83), Ariz. Women's Caucus for Art (pres. 1980-82, hon. advisor 1986-87), Ariz. Vocat. Edn. Assn. (sec. 1978-80), Ariz. Visionary Artists (treas. 1987-89), Hotel Sales and Mktg. Assn. Internat. (pres. Great Phoenix chpt. 1988-89, regional dir. 1989-90, bd. dirs. 1985-90), Meeting Planners Internat. (v.p. Ariz. Sunbelt chpt. 1989-91, pres. 1991-92, Supplier of Yr. award 1988), Soc. Govt. Meeting Planners (charter bd. dirs. 1987, Sam Gilmer award 1992), Ariz. Visionary Artists (treas. 1987-88), Ariz. Acad. Performing Arts (v.p. bd. dirs. 1987-88, pres. 1988-89).

MATTHEW, WARREN BODY, non-profit foundation president; b. Clinton, Iowa, Nov. 26, 1922; s. Albert David and Etta (Body) M.; ;m. Jeannine Davis-Kimball, Dec. 27, 1987. BA with honors, U. Calif., Berkeley, 1950. Staff civil engr. U. Calif., Berkeley, 1965-88; pres. Kazakh/Am. Rsch., Berkeley, 1989—. Lt. USNR, 1942-46, 50-53. Decorated Air medal with gold star. Democrat. Office: Kazakh/Am Rsch Project Inc 1607 Walnut St Berkeley CA 94709

MATTHEWS, EUGENE EDWARD, artist; b. Davenport, Iowa, Mar. 22, 1931; s. Nickolas Arthur and Velma (Schroeder) M.; m. Wanda Lee Miller, Sept. 14, 1952; children: Anthony Lee, Daniel Nickolas. Student, Bradley U., 1948-51; BFA, U. Iowa, 1953, MFA, 1957. Prof. fine arts grad. faculty U. Colo., Boulder, 1961—, dir. vis. artists program, 1985—; vis. artist Am. Acad. Rome, 1989. Exhibited in one-man shows U. Wis., Milw., 1960, Brena Gallery, Denver, 1963, 65, 67, 70, 74, 76, 78, 80, 83, 88, Colorado Springs Fine Arts Ctr., 1967, Sheldon Art Gallery, U. Nebr., 1968, Denver Art Mus., 1972, James Yu Gallery, N.Y.C., 1973, 77, Dubins Gallery, L.A., 1981, Galeria Rysunku, Poznan, 1983; exhibited numerous group shows U.S., Europe, Africa, Asia, internat. watercolor exhbn. New Orleans, 1983, Louvre, Paris, Met. Mus. of Art, N.Y.C., Internat. Art Ctr., Kyoto, Japan, Mus. of Modern Art, Rijeka, Yugoslavia, Taipei Fine Arts Mus., Taiwan, Republic of China; represented in permanent collections Nat. Mus. Am. Art, Washington, Denver Art Mus., Butler Inst. Am. Art, Chrysler Art Mus., others. Recipient Penello d'Argento award Acitrezza Internazionale, 1958, S.P.Q.R. Cup of Rome, Roma Olimpionica Internazionale, 1959, Gold medal of honor Nat. Arts Club, N.Y.C., 1969, Bicentennial award Rocky Mountain Nat. Watercolor Exhbn., 1976, Am. Drawings IV Purchase award, 1982, others; fellow in painting Am. Acad. Rome, 1957-60, U. Colo. Creative Rsch. fellow, 1966-67. Mem. Watercolor U.S.A. Honor Soc. (charter). Home: 3066 7th St Boulder CO 80304-2510

MATTHEWS, FRED LEWIS, management consultant, medical sales executive; b. Santa Fe, June 11, 1948; s. Edwin H. and Dorothy (Ferguson) M.; m. Carol Anne Krings, Feb. 12, 1972; children: Kimberly, Katie. BS in Life Scis., U.S. Air Force Acad., 1971. Dispatch and resv. patrol Buckly (Washington) Police Dept., 1978-80; owner, mgr. Rainier County Cabins, Ashford, Wash., 1980-87; mktg. dir. Adventure N.W. Mag., Tacoma, 1984-86; v.p. sales and mktg. Travel Wash. Mag., Seattle, 1986-87; exec. dir. Dove Ctr. Pioneer Mus., Eatonville, Wash., 1987-90, bd. dir.; nat. sales mgr. Orthopedic Sports Medicine Dist., Valencia, Calif., 1990—; bd. dir. Knapp Coll. Travel Adv., Tacoma, 1985-86. Mem. Rainier and St. Helens Tourism Bd., Ashford, Wash., 1984-85, Comprehesive Planning Bd., Ashford, 1985-86. Combat control officer USAF, 1972-78. Mem. St. Rainier Bus. Assn. (pres. 1983-84). Home: PO Box 631 249 Mashell Eatonville WA 98328

MATTHEWS, GENE LEROY, liaison engineer; b. Chenalis, Wash., June 17, 1945; s. Rolla Roy and Frances Alvina (Plog) M.; m. Jodelle Eileen Fischer, May 9, 1981. BSME, U. Wash., 1968. Supt. of utilities City of Winlock, Wash., 1971-74; city engr. City of Castle Rock, Wash., 1974-75; asst. supt. water-sewer utilities City of Olympia, Wash., 1976; liaison engr. The Boeing Co., Seattle, 1968, 70, 78—. Commr. Kittitas County Sewer Dist., Snoqualmie Pass, Wash., 1977-82; del. state conv. Dem. Party, Spokane, 1970, Olympia, 1988. Home: 15308 111th Ave NE Bothell WA 98011 Office: US Hang Gliding Assn PO Box 8300 Colorado Springs CO 80933

MATTHEWS, JOHN LOUIS, military officer, educator; b. Copperton, Utah, June 27, 1932; m. Darlene Davis, 1956 (dec.); 3 children; m. Janice Holbrook, June 27, 1990. BS in Geology, Brigham Young U., 1955, MEd in Ednl. Adminstrn., 1967; Air War Coll. Grad., 1976. Commd. 2d lt. USAF, 1954; advanced through grades to instr. pilot, Laredo, Tex., 1955-58; mem. Utah Air N.G., 1959—, Colo. Air N.G., 1961-62, commdr. 151st Air Refueling Group, adj. gen. State of Utah, 1982—; prin. Dixon Jr. High Sch., Provo, Utah, 1967-73; prin. Timpview High Sch., Provo, 1976-79. Mem. Steering Com. Pres. Sixth Quadrennial Rev. of Mil. Compensation, Washington; former chmn. air Res. Forces Policy com.; mem. pers. com. Res. Forces Policy Bd. Sec. of Def., Washington. Decorated Legion of Merit, Vietnam Svc. medal, Nat. Def. Svc. medal, others. Mem. N.G. Assn. of U.S. (pres. 1992—), Adjs. Gen. Assn. of U.S. (past pres.), Air Force Assn., Assn. U.S. Army, Rotary.

MATTHEWS, NELSON ROSS, JR., banker; b. Spring Lake, N.J., Oct. 1, 1929; s. Nelson Ross and Louis (Kingsley) M.; m. Rosemary E. Reinhard, Jan. 1, 1955; children: Ross E., Gregory J., Richard D., Susan L. BS in Bus., Rutgers U., 1951, MA in Econs., 1952. Sr. v.p. Morgan Guaranty Trust Co., N.Y.C., 1954-89, mng. dir., 1987-89; mng. dir. J. P. Morgan Securities, Inc., San Francisco, 1989—; bd. dirs. J. P. Morgan Calif. With U.S. Army, 1952-54, Korea. Republican. Presbyterian. Home: 1655 Chestnut St # 301 San Francisco CA 94123

MATTHEWS, NORMAN SHERWOOD, JR., insurance company executive; b. San Antonio, Tex., Apr. 23, 1944; s. Norman Sherwood and Alice Ann (Hathaway) M.; student Middle Tenn. State U., 1962-64, Ventura Coll., 1965, Calif. State U., 1965-66, U. Md., 1968-70; BBA, U. Tex., 1972; postgrad. U. Hawaii, 1977-79; m. Masayo Nakamura, Sept. 1, 1970; children: Debbie Ann, Scott Tsuyoshi. Research asst. State Farm Ins. Co., Murfreesboro, Tenn., 1963-64; inventory control analyst Minn. Mining & Mfg. Co., Camarillo, Calif., 1964-65; sr. acct. Peat, Marwick, Mitchell & Co., Honolulu, 1973-75; dir. mgmt. analysis Hawaii Med. Service Assn., Honolulu, 1975-89; asst. v.p. mgmt. analysis and security Hawaii Med. Svc. Assn., 1989—. With USAF, 1966-70. Decorated Air medal with 8 oak leaf clusters. CPA, Hawaii; cert. internal auditor. Mem. AICPA, Hawaii Soc. CPAs, Nat. Assn. Accts., Am. Acctg. Assn., Inst. Internal Auditors, EDP Auditors Assn., Am. Mgmt. Assn. Home: 2724 Kahoaloha Ln Apt 1903 Honolulu HI 96826-3338 Office: Hawaii Med Svc Assn 818 Keeaumoku St Honolulu HI 96814-2365

MATTHEWS, SHAW HALL, III, reliability engineer; b. Washington, May 29, 1942; s. Shaw Hall Matthews Jr. and Helen Louise (Evans) Floyd; m. Judith Arlene Jones, Aug. 2, 1976; children: Louise Anna, Alyson Ross. BS in Math., U. Ill., Chgo., 1972; MS in Ops. Rsch., Ill. Inst. Tech., 1979. Reliability engr. Zenith Corp., Chgo., 1967-73, reliability engring. mgr., 1973-76; component engring. mgr. Zenith Corp., Glenview, Ill., 1976-79; reliability and quality assurance mgr. Burr-Brown Corp., Tucson, 1979-82; systms reliability mgr. Storage Tech. Corp., Louisville, 1982—; mem. Joint Electron Devices Engring. Coun., 1980-82; chmn., mem. Electronics Adv. Group, State Bd. Community Colls. and Occupational Edn., Colo., 1984-86. Contbr. articles to profl. jours. Mem. Longmont (Colo.) Symphony Orch., 1988—, Mahler Fest Orch., Boulder, Colo., 1988—. Sgt. USAF, 1963-67.

Mem. Soc. Applied and Indsl. Math., IEEE (treas. 1974-75). Office: Storage Tech Corp 2270 S 88th St Louisville CO 80028-5207

MATTHEWS, WARREN WAYNE, state supreme court justice; b. Santa Cruz, Calif., Apr. 5, 1939; s. Warren Wayne and Ruth Ann (Maginnis) M.; m. Donna Stearns, Aug. 17, 1963; children: Holly Maginnis, Meredith Sample. A.B., Stanford U., 1961; LL.B., Harvard U., 1964. Bar: Alaska 1965. Assoc. firm Burr, Boney & Pease, Anchorage, 1964-69, Matthews & Dunn, Matthews, Dunn and Baily, Anchorage, 1969-77; justice Alaska Supreme Ct., Anchorage, 1977—, former chief justice, from 1987. Bd. dirs. Alaska Legal Services Corp., 1969-70. Mem. Alaska Bar Assn. (bd. govs. 1974-77), ABA, Anchorage Bar Assn. *

MATTHIAS, JUDSON STILLMAN, civil engineering educator, consultant; b. Scofield Barracks, Hawaii, Oct. 6, 1931; s. Norman Arthur and Charlotte Aleta (Stillman) M.; m. Georgia Stewart, June 9, 1956; children: Mary, Elizabeth, Judson Jr., Anne. BS, grad. U.S. Mil. Acad., 1954; MSCE, Oreg. State U., 1963; PhD, Purdue U., 1967. Commd. 2d lt. U.S. Army, 1954, resigned, 1961; instr. Oreg. State U., Corvallis, 1962-64, Purdue U., West Lafayette, Ind., 1964-67; prof. civil engring. Ariz. State U., Tempe, 1967—. Contbr. articles to profl. jours. Mem. Traffic Accident Reduction Program, Phoenix, 1982-85, Valley Forward, Phoenix, 1972-84. Grantee Fed. Hwy. Administrn., Evanston, Ill., 1980, Washington, D.C., 1982; elected Outstanding Engr. of Yr., Ariz. Soc. Profl. Engrs., 1986. Fellow Inst. Transp. Engrs.; mem. ASCE (hwy. and traffic safety), Am. Rd. and Transp. Builders Assn. (pres. ednl. div. 1984-185, bd. dirs. 1984-85), Transp. Research Bd. of Nat. Acad. of Scis. (univ. rep. 1971—). Home: 2032 E Laguna Dr Tempe AZ 85282-5915 Office: Ariz State U Dept Civil Engring Tempe AZ 85287

MATTIONI, THOMAS A., physician, electrophysiologist; b. Chgo., Aug. 5, 1955; s. Adelio and Diana Mattioni; m. Michele S. West, May 18, 1985; 1 child, Lauren Nicole. BS, U. Ill., Chgo., 1977; MD, Northwestern U., Chgo., 1981. Diplomate Am. Bd. Internal Medicine and Cardiovascular Diseases. Instr. of medicine Northwestern U., Chgo., 1987-89; asst. prof. medicine U. Md., Balt., 1989-91; dir. electrophysiology Ariz. Heart Inst., Phoenix, 1991—. Contbr. book chpts. and articles to profl. jours. Fellow ACP, Am. Coll. Cardiology, Am. Coll. of Chest Physicians; mem. Coun. of Clin. Cardiology of Am. Heart Assn., N.Am. Soc. of Pacing and Electrophysiology. Office: Ariz Heart Inst 2632 N 20th St Phoenix AZ 85006

MATTISON, ELISA SHERI, industrial psychologist; b. Grand Rapids, Mich., Apr. 24, 1952; d. Andrew and Loraine R. Wierenga; m. John Mattison, Sept. 29, 1978. BS cum laude, Western Mich. U., 1974, MA, 1979; postgrad., Fielding Inst., 1990. Trainer No. Inst., Anchorage, 1980; mgmt. cons., trainer Alaska Assocs. Human Devel. Inc., Anchorage, 1980-82; job devel. specialist Collins, Weed and Assocs., Anchorage, 1982-83; owner Mattison & Assocs., Anchorage, Mattison Assocs., 1993—; mem. adj. faculty Anchorage Community Coll., 1981-82; work environment and design coord. ARCO Alaska Inc., 1983-86; cons. Employee Assts. Cons. Alaska, Anchorage, 1982; v.p. Human Resource Mgmt. and Mktg. Alaskan Fed. Credit Union, 1986-90; asst. dir. degree completeion program, adult and continuing edn., Alaska Pacific U., 1990-92, adj. faculty, 1990—. Mem. Am. Soc. Tng. and Devel., Am. Soc. Personnel Adminstrs. Soc. Contbr. articles to profl. publs. Office: 4101 University Dr Anchorage AK 99508-4672

MATTOON, SARA HALSEY (SALLY MATTOON), consultant, educator; b. Bronxville, N.Y., July 8, 1947; Henry Amasa Jr. and Dorothy Ann (Teeter) M. AAS in Edn., Bennett Coll., 1967; BS in Edn. and Scis., So. Conn. State U., 1969; MA in Edn. and Humanistic Psychology, Calif. State U., Chico, 1976. Cert. tchr., Calif. Tchr. San Diego Unified Sch. Dist., 1969-72, Montgomery Creek Sch. Dist., Round Mountain, Calif., 1972-73; founder, tchr., dir. Chico Youth Devel. Ctr., Inc., 1973-80; pres. Exec. Excellence/ 6unrise Comm., San Diego and Weston, Conn., 1973-93, EarthStar Alliance, San Diego, 1992—; chmn. bd. dirs. Chico Youth Devel. Ctr., Inc., 1980—. Mem. Am. Assn. Profls. Practicing Transcendental Mediation Program (pres. San Diego chpt. 1985—), MIT Enterprise Forum (founding mem. San Diego chpt. 1985—), World Plan Exec. Coun. (bd. govs. 1978—, Info. and Inspiration award 1985). Office: EarthStar Alliance 625 Law St San Diego CA 92109-2433

MATTSON, JAMES ALLEN, clinical psychologist; b. Seattle, July 4, 1949; s. Glenn Arthur and Lillian B. (Schnaidt) M.; m. Charyl B. Thurber, July 22, 1972; children: Robert Charles, David James. BS in Psychology, U. Wash., 1971; PhD in Clin. Psychology, U. Tex., Austin, 1975. Lic. psychologist, Wash. Assoc. dir. planning and evaluation N. Cen. Community Mental Health Ctr., Columbus, 1975-78; exec. dir. Drug Abuse Coun., Everett, Wash., 1978—; co-founder Substance Abuse Treatment Assn.; mgr. Creative Investments. Pres. Wash. Assn. TASC programs. Mem. Am. Psychol. Assn. Unitarian. Office: Pacific Treatment Alternatives 1114 Pacific Ave Everett WA 98201-4247

MATTSON, MICHAEL DANE, optometrist; b. Oregon City, Oreg., Dec. 30, 1953; s. Chester Richard and Margaret Jean (Watkins) M.; m. Rilla Mae McCrorie, July 6, 1991; children: Mark Beardsley, Hannah Jean. BS in Biology cum laude, Pacific U., 1975, D of Optometry, 1980. Pvt. practice Tacoma, Wash., 1981-85; with Cole Nat.-Sears, Fed. Way, Wash., 1985-89, 92-93, Pearle Express, Puyallup, Wash., 1989-92. Active Kiwanis Internat., Puyallup, 1989-92. Christian Missionary Alliance. Home: 816 4th St NE Puyallup WA 98372-2922 Office: Sears Optical 1701 S 320th St Federal Way WA 98003

MATTSON, ROY HENRY, engineering educator; b. Chisholm, Minn., Dec. 26, 1927; s. Gust and Hilma (Appel) M.; m. June Eileen Lindstrom, June 14, 1948; children—Kristi Lynn, Lisa Kay, Greta Lee, Linnea Jean, Marla Jo, Brent Anders, Brian Alan. B.Elec. Engring., U. Minn., 1951, M.S. in Elec. Engring, 1952; Ph.D., Iowa State U., 1959. Registered profl. engr. Mem. tech. staff Bell Telephone Labs., Inc., 1952-56; asst. prof., then asso. prof. Iowa State U., 1956-61; asso. prof. U. Minn., 1961-66; prof. elec. engring., head dept. U. Ariz., 1966-86, prof. elect, comp. engring., 1986-88; acad. v.p. Nat. Technol. U., Ft. Collins, Colo., 1988—; Del. to A.S. Popov Congress, Moscow, USSR, 1972; non-govt. observer to UN Conf. on Human Environment, Stockholm, 1972; chmn. grad. faculty, acad. exec. com. Nat. Tech. U., 1986-88. Author: Basic Junction Devices and Circuits, 1963, Electronics, 1966, also articles; patentee in field. Mem. Amphitheater Bd. Sch. Trustees, 1971-76, pres., 1976. Served with USNR, 1946-47. Fellow IEEE (editor Transactions on Edn. 1970-73, chmn. validation of ednl. achievement program 1976-82), AAAS; mem. Am. Soc. Engring. Edn., Sigma Xi, Theta Tau, Eta Kappa Nu, Tau Beta Pi. Home: PO Box 369 Bellvue CO 80512-0097 Office: Nat Technol U 700 Centre Ave Fort Collins CO 80526-1842

MATZDORFF, JAMES ARTHUR, investment banker; b. Kansas City, Mo., Jan. 3, 1956. BS, U. So. Calif., 1978; MBA, Loyola U., Los Angeles, 1980. Comml. loan officer Bank of Am., Los Angeles, 1976-78; mng. dir. James A. Matzdorff & Co., Beverly Hills, Calif., 1978—. Mem. Rep. Nat. Com., 1980—. Mem. NRA, Am. Fin. Assn., Porsche Car Club, Corvette Collectors Club, Harley Davidson Club, Phi Delta Theta. Office: 9903 Santa Monica Blvd Ste 374 Beverly Hills CA 90212-1671

MATZER, JOHN WAYNE (JACK MATZER), janitorial services company executive; b. Chgo., Apr. 25, 1945; s. C. John and Lillian D. (Wirth) M. BS, U. Ill., 1968; MBA, Northwestern U., 1973. Lic. real estate salesperson, Ill.; cert. mgmt. cons. Salesman Inland Steel Co., Chgo., 1968-72; prin. Hayes/Hill Inc., Chgo., 1973-80; group mktg. mgr., gen. mgr. Automated Mktg. Systems, Inc., Chgo., 1980-84; bus. mgr., cons. Lakeview Renovations, Inc., GJC, Inc., Chgo., 1984-88; pres., chief exec. officer Contract Cleaning Inc., Denver, 1989—; lectr. seminars various Am. Mgmt. Assn., 1978-80. Mem. Greater Denver C. of C., Rockies Venture Club. Office: Contract Cleaning Inc 1560 Broadway Ste 665 Denver CO 80202-5139

MATZNER, BRUCE, mechanical and nuclear engineer; b. Bklyn., July 16, 1933; s. Hugo Victor and Ruth Gloria (Phillips) M.; m. Phyllis Barbara Brambir, May 30, 1957; children: David Marc, Lee Susan. BS, Queens Coll., 1955; BSME, Columbia U., 1955, MSME, 1962; postgrad., Oak Ridge Sch. Reactor Tech., 1958. Registered profl. engr., N.Y. Assoc. to sr. engr. Ford Instrument Co., Div. Speery Rand Corp., L.I. City, 1955-59; project engr. Columbia U. Chem. Engr. Rsch. Lab., N.Y.C., 1959-64, rsch. assoc. lab., 1965-69; prin. engr. GE Nuclear Energy, San Jose, 1969-72, mgr. thermal hydraulic test engring., 1972-82, mgr. thermal hydraulic devel., 1983-85, sr. program mgr., 1986—. Patentee in field; contbr. articles to profl. jours. Mem. ASME, U.S. Chess Fedn. (life mem.). Office: GE Nuclear Energy MC 151 175 Curtner Ave San Jose CA 95125

MAUER, RICHARD DAVID, journalist; b. Bronx, N.Y., May 29, 1949; s. Arnold F. and Rosalyn (Bederson) M.; m. Barbara Jacobs, June 3, 1979; children: Jessica, Michael. BS in Journalism, U. Colo., 1973. Reporter Grand Junction (Colo.) Daily Sentinel, 1976, Idaho Statesman, Boise, Idaho, 1977-80; stringer Gannett News Svc., Jerusalem, 1980-82; reporter Miami (Fla.) News, 1982-83; reporter Anchorage Daily News, 1983-91, project editor, 1991-93, city editor, 1993—; stringer N.Y. Times, 1988—. Recipient Pulitzer Prize for Pub. Svc., 1989. Mem. Investigative Reporters and Editors (outstanding investigative reporting awards, 1986, 1989, 1990), Soc. Environ. Journalists, Reporters' Com. Freedom Press, Alaska Press Club. Office: Anchorage Daily News 1001 Northway Dr Anchorage AK 99508

MAUERMAN, MARY DRAKE, professional association administrator; b. Seattle, Jan. 2, 1939; d. Lee Joyner and E. Arline (Keys) Drake; m. Derald L. Mauerman, Jan. 16, 1959 (div. Sept. 1980); children: Julia Mauerman Davidson, Lisa, Michael. BS, Evergreen State Coll., 1977. Membership dir. Assn. Wash. Bus., Olympia, 1977-80; legis. coord. Seattle Master Builders, Seattle, 1980-83; dir. governmental affairs Wash. Assn. Realtors, Olympia, 1983-87; exec. dir. AIA Wash. Coun., Olympia, 1987—; lobbyist Home Builders Assn. Wash., Olympia, 1983. Chmn. Transp. Policy Bd., Olympia, 1991; councilman Federal Way (Wash.) Community Coun., 1970-74; bd. dirs. LWV, Federal Way, 1963-67. Mem. Wash. Soc. Assn. Execs. (bd. dirs. 1993—), Rotary, The Mountaineers (sec. 1984), Olympia C. of C. (trustee 1991-93). Republican. Office: AIA Wash Coun 1110 Capitol Way S Olympia WA 98501

MAUGHAN, O(WEN) EUGENE, fishery biologist; b. Preston, Idaho, Jan. 3, 1943; s. Owen Weston and Ione (Stocks) M.; m. LuDean Lewis, Aug. 30, 1962; children: Terry Lynn, Cindy Jean, Kimberly Dene, James Benjamin, Robert Samuel, Summer Nicole. BS, Utah State U., 1966; MA, U. Kans., 1968; PhD, Wash. State U., 1972. Fishery biologist, comprehensive planner U.S. Fish and Wildlife Svc., Spokane, 1971-72; asst. leader Va. coop. fishery rsch. unit U.S. Fish and Wildlife Svc., Blacksburg, 1972-77; leader Okla. coop. fishery rsch. unit U.S. Fish and Wildlife Svc., Stillwater, 1977-84, leader Okla. coop. fsh and wildlife rsch. unit, 1984-87; leader Ariz. coop. fish and wildlife rsch. unit U.S. Fish and Wildlife Svc., Tucson, 1987—. Contbr. articles to profl. jours. Mem. Am. Fisheries Soc. (Most Significan Paper 1982), Am. Soc. of Ichthyologists and Herpetologists, Southwestern Assn. of Naturalists, Sigma Xi. Mem. Ch. LDS. Office: U Ariz Ariz Coop Fish & Wildlife Unit U 210 Biosciences E Tucson AZ 85721

MAUGHAN, WILLARD ZINN, dermatologist; b. Riverside, Calif., Apr. 21, 1944; s. Franklin David and Martha Charlotte (Zinn) M.; m. Rona Lee Wilcox, Aug. 20, 1968; children: Julie Anne, Kathryn Anita, Willard Wilcox, Christopher Keith. Student, Johns Hopkins U., Balt., 1962-64; BS, U. Utah, 1968, MD, 1972. Diplomate Am. Bd. Dermatology. Intern Walter Reed Army Med. Ctr., Washington, 1972-73; fellow Mayo Clinic, Rochester, Minn., 1976-79; pvt. practice Ogden, Utah, 1979—. Contbr. articles to profl. jours. Commr. Boy Scouts Am., Weber County, Utah, 1980-84, dist. chmn.; pres. Am. Cancer Soc., Weber County, 1985-86. Maj. U.S. Army, 1971-76. Recipient Dist. award of merit Boy Scouts Am., 1985. Fellow ACP, Am. Acad. Dermatology; mem. Royal Soc. Medicine (London), N.Y. Acad. Scis., Kiwanis Club. Republican. Mormon. Home: 2486 W 4550 S Roy UT 84067-1944 Office: 3860 Jackson Ave Ogden UT 84403-1956

MAUK, PAMELA ANNE, marketing and development consultant; b. L.A., Apr. 25, 1953; d. Frederick Henry and Marion (Morris) M.; m. Mark Randolph Cross, Mar. 24, 1990. BA, U. Calif., Long Beach, 1976; MA, U. Washington, 1980. Ins. processor St. Mary Med. Ctr., Long Beach, 1973-77; teaching asst. U. Washington, Seattle, 1977-79; slide libr. Seattle Art Mus., 1978-79, writer, 1980; summer staff lectr. Nat. Gallery Art, Washington, 1979; freelance newsletter editor Seattle, 1981; asst. to dir. Childhaven, Seattle, 1981; pub. rels. and devel. mgr. Ryther Child Ctr., Seattle, 1982-87; dir. mktg. and devel. Snoqualmie (Wash.) Valley Hosp., 1987-90; dir. devel. and community rels. Marianwood, Issaquah, Washington, 1987-89; pres. Pamela Mauk Communications, Redmond, Wash., 1990—; trustee Pub. Rels. Round Table, Seattle, 1983-86, pres. 1985. Commr. Issaquah (Wash.) Arts Commn., 1988-91, chair, 1991; creator, sr. editorial adv. Issaquah Arts, 1989-91; adv. Children's Svcs. of Sno-Valley, Snoqualmie, 1989-90, Citizen's for Better Sch., Snoqualmie, 1989-90; coun. mem. Eastside Ops. Coun. United Way of King County Bellevue, Wash., 1990-92; svc. panel mem. United Way King County, 1990-92. Recipient Award in Art Bank of Am., 1971, two 1st prizes Washington Press Assn., 1984, Commendation Issaquah Sch. Dist., 1989, Pacesetter award Internat. Assn. Bus. Communicators, 1986. Mem. Internat. Assn. Bus. Communicators, Puget Sound Grant Writers Assn., N.W. Devel. Officers Assn. Office: 247 208th Ave NE Redmond WA 98053-6937

MAUL, TERRY LEE, psychologist, educator; b. San Francisco, May 6, 1946; s. Chester Lloyd and Clella Lucille (Hobbs) M.; AB, U. Calif., Berkeley, 1967, MA, 1968, PhD, 1970; student Coll. San Mateo, 1964-65; m. Gail Ann Retallick, June 27, 1970 (div. Dec. 1986); 1 son, Andrew Eliot. Prof. psychology San Bernardino Valley Coll., San Bernardino, Calif., 1970—, chmn. dept., 1979-82; researcher self-actualization. Mem. AAUP (chpt. pres. 1971-73), Am. Psychol. Assn., Audubon Soc., Mensa, Nature Conservancy, Rachel Carson Council, Wilderness Soc., Sierra Club. Democrat. Author: (with Eva Conrad) Introduction to Experimental Psychology, 1981; (with Gail Maul) Beyond Limit: Ways to Growth and Freedom, 1983; contbg. author other psychol. texts. Home: 6155 Bluffwood Dr Riverside CA 92506-4605 Office: San Bernardino Valley Coll 701 S Mt Vernon Ave San Bernardino CA 92410-2798

MAULDIN, JEAN HUMPHRIES, aviation company executive; b. Gordonville, Tex., Aug. 16, 1923; d. James Wiley and Lena Leota (Noel-Crain) Humphries; B.S., Hardin Simmons U., 1943; M.S., U. So. Calif., 1961; postgrad. Westfield Coll., U. London, 1977-78, Warnborough Coll., Oxford, Eng., 1977-78; m. William Henry Mauldin, Feb. 28, 1942; children—Bruce Patrick, William Timothy III. Psychol. counselor social services 1st Baptist Ch., 1953-57; pres. Mauldin and Staff, public relations, Los Angeles, 1957-78; pres. Stardust Aviation, Inc., Santa Ana, Calif., 1962—. Mem. Calif. Democratic Council, 1953-83; rep. 69th Assembly Dist. Caucus to Calif. Dem. State Central com. exec. bd., 1957—, Orange County Dem. Central Com., 1960—; mem. U.S. Congl. Peace Adv. Bd., 1981—; del. Dem. Nat. Conv., 1974, 78, Dem. Mid-Term Conv., 1976, 78, 82, 86, Dem. Nat. Issues Conf.; mem. nat. advisor U.S. Congl. Adv. Bd. Am. Security Council; pres. Santa Ana Friends of Public Library, 1973-76, McFadden Friends of Library, Santa Ana, 1976-80; chmn. cancer crusade Am. Cancer Soc., Orange County, 1974; mem. exec. bd. Lisa Hist. Preservation Soc., 1970—; lay leader Protestant Episcopal Ch. Am., Trinity Ch., Tustin, Calif. Named Woman of Yr., Key Woman in Politics, Calif. Dem. Party, 1960-80. Am. Mgmt. Assn. (pres.'s club), Bus. and Profl. Women Am., Exptl. Aircraft and Pilots Assn., Nat. Women's Polit. Caucus, Dem. Coalition Central Coms., Calif. Friends of Library (life), Women's Missionary Soc. (chmn.), LWV, Nat. Fedn. Dem. Women, Calif. Fedn. County Central Com. Mems., Internat. Platform Assn., Peace Through Strength, Oceanic Soc., Nat. Audubon Soc., Sierra Club, Nat. Wildlife Fedn., Internat. Amnesty Assn., Am. Security Council, Nat. Women's Pilot. Club: U. So. Calif. Ski, Town Hall of Calif. Author: Cliff Winters, The Pilot, The Man, 1961; The consummate Barnstormer, 1962; The Daredevil Clown, 1965. Home: 1013 S Elliott Pl Santa Ana CA 92704-2224 also: 102 E 45th St Savannah GA 31405 Office: 16542 Mount Kibby St Fountain Valley CA 92708

MAURATH, GARRY CALDWELL, hydrogeologist; b. Cleve., July 24, 1952; s. George Anthony and Iona May (Caldwell) M.; m. Lesa Maria, Aug. 28, 1977. BS, Lehigh U., 1974; MS, Kent State U., 1980, PhD, 1989. Lic. geologist, N.C.; registered environ. assessor, Calif. Sr. geologist O'Brien Resources, Grass Valley, Calif., 1980-82; prin. hydrogeologist Ebasco Svcs., Sacramento, Calif., 1979—. Contbr. over 41 articles to profl. jours. Staff sgt. U.S. Army, 1974-77. Mem. AAAS, Geol. Soc. Am., Groundwater Rsch. Assn. Calif., Assn. Ground Water Scientists and Engrs., Sigma Xi. Roman Catholic. Office: Ebasco Svcs Ste 250 2525 Natomas Park Dr Sacramento CA 95833

MAURER, ADAH ELECTRA, psychologist; b. Chgo., Oct. 26, 1905; d. Frank Ulysses and Mary Louise (Meng) Bass; m. Harry Andrew Maurer, June 14, 1937 (div. 1947); children: Douglas, Helen. BS, U. Wis., 1927; MA, U. Chgo., 1957; PhD, Union Inst., 1976. Lic. sch. psychologist, Calif. Tchr. pub. schs. Chgo., 1927-61; psychologist pub. schs. Calif., 1962-71; pvt. practice marriage, family and child counselor Berkeley, Calif., 1965-75; organizer, chief exec. officer End Violence Against the Next Generation, Inc., Berkeley, 1972—; lectr. U. Calif., Davis, 1965-68; bd. dirs. Nat. Ctr. for Study Cpl. Punishment & Alternatives in Schs., Phila.; liaison People Opposed to Paddling Students, Houston, 1981—; vice chair Nat. Coalition to Abolish Cpl. Punishment in Schs., Columbus, Ohio, 1987—; cons. Calif. State Dept. Social Svcs., 1988. Author: Paddles Away, 1981, 1001 Alternatives, 1984, (with others) The Bible and the Rod, 1983, Think Twice, 1985; editor: (newsletter) The Last? Resort, 1972—; contbr. numerous articles to profl. jours. Recipient Disting. Humanitarian award Calif. State Psychol. Assn., Presdl. award Nat. Assn. Sch. Psychologists, 1988, Donna Stone award Nat. Commn. for Prevention of Child Abuse, 1988, commendation Giraffe Project, 1988. Mem. Am. Psychol. Assn., Hemlock Soc. Home and Office: 977 Keeler Ave Berkeley CA 94708-1498

MAURER, HANS ANDREAS, aerospace consultant; b. Frankfurt, West Germany, May 7, 1913; came to U.S., 1951; s. Alfred Hyppolithe and Louise Anna (Abt) M.; m. Daisy Alice Poppel, June 25, 1941; 1 child, Michael Alfred. BS, 1932; MS, U. Munich, 1934; PhD, J.W.V. Goethe U., Frankfurt, 1937. Registered profl. engr. Mass. Project leader Manning Maxwell Moore, Danbury and Conner, Conn., 1953-55; chief engr. Miss. Systems div. Raytheon, Lexington and Bedford, Mass., 1957-65; group v.p. tech. Hughes Aircraft/Missile Systems Group, Canoga Park, Calif., 1965-85; aerospace cons. Teledyne Electronics, Newbury Park, Calif., 1985—. Fellow IEEE (life). Home: 4447 Conchita Way Tarzana CA 91356-4901 Office: Teledyne 649 Lawrence Dr Newbury Park CA 91320-2298

MAURER, JOHN EDWARD, retired chemistry educator; b. Matherville, Ill., Apr. 3, 1923; s. Casper Edward and Alvera (Carlson) M.; m. Gladys Marie Barman, Nov. 27, 1946; children: John E. II, Bruce A., Mardell L., Diane K. AB, Augustana Coll., 1947; MS in Organic Chemistry, State U. Iowa, 1948, PhD, 1950. Postdoctorate Northwestern U., Evanston, Ill., 1950-52; chemist Rock Island (Ill.) Arsenal, 1952-53; from assoc. prof. to prof. Chemistry U. Wyo., Laramie, 1953-88; dept. head, 1977-80; prof. emeritus U. Wyo., Laramie, 1988—. Contbr. articles to profl. jours. With USN, 1944-46. Fellow AAAS; mem. Am. Chem. Soc. (councilor 1988-91), Sigma Xi, Gamma Sigma Epsilon, Alpha Chi Sigma. Home: 601 S 12th St Laramie WY 82070-4023

MAURICE, DON, personal care industry executive; b. Peoria, Ill., Aug. 29, 1932; s. Imajean (Webster) Crayton; m. CindLu Jackson, Aug. 31, 1990. Student, Loma Linda U., 1984-86, Calif. State U., San Bernardino, 1992—. Lic. hair stylist, skin therapist. Owner 2 schs. in advanced hair designs, San Diego, 1962-64; dist. mgr. AqRo Matic Co. Water Purification Systems, San Diego, 1972-75; profl. sales educator Staypower Industries, San Diego, 1972-76, 3d v.p., 1975-76; regional bus. cons. Estheticians Pharmacology Rsch., Garden Grove, Calif., 1975-81; owner, operator Don Maurice Hair Designs, Hemet, Calif., 1980-83; dir., operator Hair Sytles by Maurice, Loma Linda, Calif., 1984-88; owner, pres. Grooming Dynamics, Redlands, Calif., 1988—; bus. cons. Yogurt Place, Paradise Valley, Ariz., 1978-79, and others; regular guest Channel 6/Channel 8, San Diego, 1968-78. Author: The New Look For Men, 1967, The Art of Men's Hair Styling, 1968 (accepted by Library of Congress), Baldness, To Be or Not To Be, 1989. Promoter Spl. Olympics, Hemet, 1981. Sgt. U.S. Army, 1950-53, Korea. Decorated Purple Heart, 1952; named Leading Businessman in His Profession, Union and Evening Tribune, 1969. Mem. Christian Businessmen's Assn. Office: Grooming Dynamics PO Box 1279 Loma Linda CA 92354

MAURO, JACK ANTHONY, physicist; b. Bklyn., Feb. 21, 1916; s. Francis and Lucia (Buono) M.; m. Camille Dolores Montaperto, June 19, 1937; children: Richard F., George E., Barbara L. Student, NYU, 1936-42; BS in Physics, Columbia U., 1947; D Optometry, Phila. Optical Coll., 1951. Optician, mgr. Equitable Optical Co., N.Y.C., 1934-43; chief instr. theoretical optics N.Y. Inst. Optics, 1947-53; dir. engring. Saratoga (N.Y.) div. Espey Mfg. Co., 1950-55; cons. optics engr. Gen. Elec. Co., 1955-70, dir. rsch. and devel., 1970-74, cons., sub-contractor fo U.S. Army Missile Command, 1974-75; cons. high energy lasers U. Dayton Rsch. Inst./Teledyne Brown Engring. Co., 1975-78; cons. New England Laser Inc., Waltham, Mass., 1978—, Nat. Aperture Inc., Windham, N.H., 1978—; mem. Polaris missile design team; optical cons. on 1st 151-inch diameter quartz primary mirror for Kitts Peak Obs. telescope, 1965; bd. dirs. Columbia U.; trustee N.Y. Inst. Optics. Editor, co-author: Optical Engineering Handbook, 1957, optical sect. Industrial Electronics Handbook, 1958; patentee in optics and electronics field. Fellow Am. Acad. Optometry; mem. Am. Phys. soc., Mohawk Assn. Scientists and Engrs., Soc. Photog. Instrumentation Engrs., Am. Inst. Physics, Optical Soc. Am., Omega Epsilon Phi. Home and Office: 2581 SE Lema Dr Rio Rancho NM 87124

MAURO, RICHARD FRANK, lawyer, investment manager; b. Hawthorne, Nev., July 21, 1945; s. Frank Joseph and Dolores D. (Kreimeyer) M.; m. LaVonne M. Madden, Aug. 28, 1965; 1 child, Lindsay Anne. AB, Brown U., 1967; JD summa cum laude, U. Denver, 1970. Bar: Colo. 1970. Assoc. Dawson, Nagel, Sherman & Howard, Denver, 1970-72; assoc. Van Cise, Freeman, Tooley & McClearn, Denver, 1972-73, ptnr., 1973-74; ptnr. Hall & Evans, Denver, 1974-81, Morrison & Forester, Denver, 1981-84; of counsel Parcel, Mauro, Hultin & Spaanstra, P.C., Denver, 1984—, pres., 1988-90, of counsel, 1992—; pres. Sundance Oil Exploration Co., 1985-88; exec. v.p. Castle Group, Inc., 1992—; adj. prof. U. Denver Coll. Law, 1981-84. Symposium editor: Denver Law Jour., 1969-70; editor: Colorado Corporation Manual; contbr. articles to legal jours. Pres. Colo. Open Space Coun., 1974; mem. law alumni coun. U. Denver Coll. Law, 1988-91. Francis Wayland scholar, 1967; recipient various Am. jurisprudence awards. Mem. ABA, Colo. Bar Assn., Denver Bar Assn., Colo. Assn. Corp. Counsel. (pres. 1974-75), Am. Arbitration Assn. (comml. arbitrator), Order St. Ives, Denver Athletic Club (bd. dirs. 1986-89). Home: 2552 E Alameda Ave Denver CO 80209-3325 Office: 475 17th St Ste 750 Denver CO 80202

MAUS, CONNIE, nursing administrator; b. Nampa, Idaho, Apr. 10, 1945; d. Raymond Vera and Connie (Acevez) Serratos; m. James McMurtrey, Aug. 12, 1967 (div. 1974); 1 child, James Jason; m. Errol R. Maus, Dec. 28, 1976; 1 child, Martha. Diploma in nursing, St. Alphonsus Sch. Nursing, 1966; BS, Boise State U., 1976; MS, Idaho State U. RN, Idaho. Staff nurse Mercy Med. Ctr., Nampa, 1964-67, head nurse, 1967-68, dir. insvc., 1968-72; instr. staff devel. St. Alphonsus Med. Ctr., Boise, Idaho, 1972-73, asst. dir., 1973-76, nurse mgr., 1976-81, oncology cons./supportive care, 1981-83, mgr. home health, 1983-86, asst. dir. utilization/discharge mgmt., 1986—; mem. quality improvement coun. St. Alphonsus Med. Ctr., Boise; bd. dirs. Ronald McDonald House, Idaho; presenter, participant ednl. programs on ethics. Mem. Mujeres Unidos De Idaho, Image. Contbr. poems to profl. publs. (Golden award 1987, 89, Silver award 1990). Mem. Asns. Christian Therapists, Am. Soc. Quality Control (chmn. transcultural com., past. chmn. hosp. ethics com.), Sigma Theta Tau (provider continuing edn. in transcultural issues). Roman Catholic. Home: 2066 Varian Pl Boise ID 83709-2459 Office: St Alphonsus Med Ctr 1055 N Curtis Rd Boise ID 83706-1370

MAUS, JOHN ANDREW, computer systems engineer; b. Whittier, Calif., July 13, 1945; s. Kenneth Waring and Bertha Estella (Eckman) M.; M. Diana Barba, April 16, 1977 (div. May 1, 1983); m. Colette An Moschelle, Nov. 23, 1985; stepchildren: BreAnn, Adam; children: Steven Andrew, Terra An. BA in Physics, U. Calif., Riverside, 1963-67; MS in Physics, San Diego State U., 1967-70. Cert. data processor, 1983. Programmer, analyst San Diego State Found., 1970-72; instr. bus. San Diego State U., 1971-73; systems programmer San Diego State U., San Diego, 1971-74; data processing mgr. M.H. Golden Co., San Diego, 1974-79; computer systems engr. Hewlett-Packard Co., Spokane, Wash., 1979-84, sr. systems engr., 1984-86, network systems engr., 1986-89, sr. tech. cons., 1989—; physics lab. asst. USDA Salinity Lab., Riverside, Calif., 1965-67; underwater acoustics programmer Naval Undersea Ctr., San Diego, 1967-70; programmer San Diego Inst. Pathology, 1972-76; mem. adv. com. Computer Sci. Bus. Applications North Idaho Coll, 1989—; mem. career network U. Calif., Riverside, 1990—. Author: INTEREX Conference Proceedings, 1989; co-author: Chemical Physics Letters, 1971, Electronic and Atomic Collisions, 1971. Merit badge counselor Spokane chpt. Boy Scouts Am., 1983—. Mem. Assn. Computing Machinery (founder Spokane chpt., chpt. chmn. 1980-82, service award 1981). Home: 12417 W Sunridge Dr Nine Mile Falls WA 99026-9311 Office: Hewlett-Packard Co 1121 N Argonne Rd Ste 121 Spokane WA 99212-2657

MAVROS, JOHN NICHOLAS, hotel executive; b. Milw., Mar. 28, 1950; s. Alexander and Evangeline (Mackris) M.; m. Kathy Haeseley, June 7, 1971 (div. Jan. 1980); children: Angela Nicole, Alexander Charles; m. Melanie Emily Bernardez, Feb. 23, 1980; children: John Alexander, Michelle Katherine. Cert. hotel adminstr. Front office mgr. Westin Century Plz. Hotel, L.A., 1968-75; sr. asst. mgr. Westin So. Coast Plz., Costa Mesa, Calif., 1975-76, Westin Philippine Plz., Manila, 1976-79; gen. mgr. Hotel Grande Bretagne, Athens, 1979-81, Tulsa Excelsior Hotel, 1981-83, Provo (Utah) Excelsior Hotel, 1983-84; mng. dir. Loews Ventana Canyon Resort, Tucson, 1984-86; v.p., gen. mgr. Registry Hotel, Irvine, Calif., 1986-88, Universal City, L.A., 1989-91; sr. v.p. Calif. Hotels Corp., Irvine, 1992—; gen. mgr. Embassy Suites, L.A., 1990-91, Orange County Santa Ana, Calif., 1991-92. Chmn. bd. Am. Cancer Soc., Utah County, 1983-84; bd. mem. Irvine Youth Basketball, 1991—. Mem. Am. Hotel Motel Assn. (instr.), Calif. Hotel Motel Assn., Rotary Internat. (Paul Harris fellow). Greek Orthodox. Office: Calif Hotels Corp 2152 Dupont Dr Irvine CA 92715

MAXCY, LAWRENCE STAHL, education administrator; b. Rochester, N.Y., May 28, 1935; s. William Frank and Gertrude (Stahl) M.; m. Carol Marie Silvernail, June 1, 1957; children: Ann, Lee, Frank, Paul, Mark. AB, Syracuse U., 1958, MPA, 1960. Administr. NIH, Bethesda, Md., 1960-62; administrv. officer NIH Latin Am. Office, Rio de Janeiro, 1962-66; administr. NIH, Bethesda, Md., 1966-68; asst. to dean U. Calif. Div. Natural Scis., Santa Cruz, Calif., 1968-91. Contbr. articles to popular mags. Pres. Santa Cruz Schs. Pers. Commn., 1975-81; active Santa Cruz Vol. Ctr., 1981-91 (pres. 1987-89), Santa Cruz County Grand Jury, 1988-89. Democrat. Home: 221 Dick George Rd Cave Junction OR 97523

MAXEY, DIANE MEADOWS, artist; b. Lufkin, Tex., Feb. 26, 1943; d. Warren Gaston and Jackie (Keen) Meadows; m. William Brant Maxey, Sept. 5, 1964; children: Dananne, Robert Warren. BA in Art and Edn., North Tex. State U., 1965; postgrad., U. Tex., Arlington, Tex. Tech U., Lubbock; studied with Al Brouilette, Bud Biggs, Edgar Whitney, Dick Phillips, Robert E. Wood, Rex. Brandt, Milford Zornes. Art tchr. Dallas Pub. Schs., 1965-66; substitute tchr. Arlington Pub. Schs., 1969-72; pvt. classes San Angelo, Tex., 1973-77, Scottsdale, Ariz., 1978-92; owner Maxi Watercolor Studio, Paradise Valley, 1978—, Bandanna Tours, Scottsdale, 1988—; mem. staff Scottsdale Artist Sch., Lighthouse Art Ctr., Dillman's Art Found.: Exhibited works at Four Seasons Gallery, Jackson, Wyo., The Frame and Design, Nacogdoches, Tex., The Gold Nuggett Art Gallery, Wickenburg, Ariz., Pinehurst (N.C.) Gallery. Dir. visual ministry First So. Bapt. Ch., Scottsdale, 1988—. Recipient Merit award Ariz. Artist Guild Show, 1988, Disting. Merit award, 1986, Claude Howison award Nat. League Am. Pen Women Nat. Exhbn., 1984, Award of Excellence, 1983, Best of Show award Ariz. Watercolor Assn., Spring. Exhbn., 1981. Mem. Western Fedn. Watercolor Soc. (gen. chmn. 1981-82), Southwestern Watercolor Assn., Ariz. Artist Guild (pres. 1982-83), Ariz. Watercolor Assn., Tex. Watercolor Assn., 22 x 30 Profl. Critique Group. Home and Office: Maxi Watercolor Studio 7540 N Lakeside Ln Paradise Valley AZ 85253-2857

MAXFIELD, PETER C., law educator, university dean, lawyer; b. 1941. AB, Regis Coll., 1963; JD, U. Denver, 1966; LLM, Harvard U., 1968. Bar: Colo. 1966, Wyo. 1969. Trial atty. Dept. Justice, 1966-67; assoc. Hindry, Erickson & Meyer, Denver, 1968-69; asst. prof. U. Wyo. Coll. Law, 1969-72, assoc. prof., 1972-76, prof., 1976—, dean, 1979-87; vis. assoc. prof. U. N.Mex., 1972-73; Raymond F. Rice Disting. prof. U. Kans., fall, 1984, Chapman vis. Disting. prof., U. Tulsa, spring, 1987; vis. prof. U. Utah, 1992. Coord. Wyo. State Planning, 1988-89; spl. asst. Gov. Wyo. 1989-90; Dem. nominee U.S. Ho. Reps., 1990; mem. Wyo. Environ. Quality Coun., 1991-93, Wyo. Senate 1993—. Mem. Order St. Ives, Omicron Delta Kappa, Pi Delta Phi. Author: (with Bloomenthal) Cases and Materials on the Federal Income Taxation of Natural Resources, 1971, 72, 77; (with Houghton) Taxation of Mining Operations, 1973, 76; (with Trelease and Dietrich) Natural Resources Law on American Indian Lands, 1977. Office: U Wyo Coll Law PO Box 3035 Laramie WY 82071-3035 Home: 1059 Frontera Laramie WY 82070

MAXMIN, JODY LEWIS, educator; b. Phila.; d. Henry Wertheimer and Louise Olga (Strousse) M. BA, Oberlin (Ohio) Coll., 1971; diploma with distinction, Oxford (Eng.) U., 1973, PhD, 1979. Acting asst. prof. Stanford (Calif.) U., 1979-80, asst. prof., 1980-88, assoc. prof., 1988—; undergrad. advisor, chair honors com. art dept. Stanford U., 1989—. Author poems; contbr. articles to profl. jours. Woodrow Wilson Found. fellow, 1971; Danforth Found. fellow, 1971; Leonard and Katherine Woolley fellow Somerville Coll, Oxford U., 1973; Jr. Rsch. fellow Wolfson Coll., Oxford U., 1975-79. Mem. Archaeol. Inst. Am., Coll. Art Assn. (Millard Meiss award 1982), Soc. for Promotion Hellenic Studies, Soc. for Preservation of Greek Heritage, Phi Beta Kappa (Excellence in Teaching award 1991, Excellence in Undergrad. Teaching award 1992). Jewish. Office: Stanford U Dept Art Stanford CA 94305-2018

MAXSON, ROBERT C., university president. Former sr. v.p. acad. affairs U. Houston Systems, Houston; pres. U. Nev., Las Vegas, 1984—. Office: U Nev-Las Vegas Office of Pres 4505 S Maryland Pky Las Vegas NV 89154-0002

MAXWELL, DAVID E., academic executive, educator; b. N.Y.C., Dec. 2, 1944; s. James Kendrick and Gertrude Sarah (Bernstein) M.; children: Justin Kendrick, Stephen Edward. BA, Grinnell Coll., 1966; MA, Brown U., 1968, PhD, 1974. Instr. Tufts U., Medford, Mass., 1971-74, asst. prof., 1974-78, assoc. prof. Russian lang. and lit., 1978-89, dean undergrad. studies, 1981-89; pres. Whitman Coll., Walla Walla, Wash., 1989-93; dir. Nat. Fgn. Lang. Ctr., Washington, 1993—; chmn. steering com. Coop. Russian Lang. Program, Leningrad, USSR, 1981-86, chmn. 1986-90; cons. Coun. Internat. Ednl. Exchange, 1974—, bd. dirs., 1988-92, vice chair, 1991-92, cons. Internat. Rsch. Exchanges, 1976—; assoc. Pacific Sci. Ctr. Contbr. articles to scholarly jours. Fulbright fellow, 1970-71, Brown U., 1966-67, NDEA Title IV, 1967-70; recipient Lillian Leibner award Tufts U., 1979; citation Grad. Sch. Arts & Scis., Brown U., 1991. Mem. MLA, Am. Coun. Edn. (commn. on internat. edn., pres.'s coun. on internat. edn.), Am. Assn. Advancement of Slavic Studies, Am. Assn. Tchrs. Slavic and E. European Langs., Assn. Am. Colls., Am. Assn. Higher Edn., Brown U. Alumni Assn. Democrat. Avocations: tennis, running, music. Office: Nat Fgn Lang Ctr 1619 Massachusetts Ave NW Ste 400 Washington DC 20036

MAXWELL, DAVID KEITH, finance executive; b. Jackson, Tenn., Aug. 6, 1965; s. Cephus E. and Gwendolyn (Maxwell) Williams; m. Darcie Deanne Olson, Aug. 23, 1985; 1 child, Taylor Ann. BBA, U. Wash., 1986. CPA, Wash. Gen. ledger acct. Cone-Heiden Corp., Seattle, 1984-86; acct. Carter Subaru, Seattle, 1986; personal banking officer SeaFirst, Seattle, 1986-89, asst. v.p., sr. fin. devel. officer, 1989—, mng. ptnr., in-balance acctg., 1990—; instr. Am. Inst. of Banking, Seattle, 1989—. Bd. treas. Operational Emergency Ctr., Seattle, 1991—; bd. treas. Thalia Symphony Orch., Seattle. Mem. NAACP, AICPA, Nat. Assn. Black Accts., Wash. Soc. CPAs.

MAXWELL, DONALD STANLEY, publishing executive; b. L.A., May 30, 1930; s. Harold Stanley and Margaret (Trenam) M.; m. Martha Helen Winn, Dec. 5, 1952; children: Sylvia Louise, Cynthia Lynn, Bruce Stanley, Bradley Erl, Walter James, Wesley Richard, Amy Bernice. Student, Long Beach City Coll., 1948-50; BBA, Woodbury Coll., 1956; D of Bus. Adminstrn. (hon.), Woodbury U., 1991. CPA. Ptnr. Robert McDavid & Co. (CPAs), L.A., 1955-61; controller Petersen Pub. Co., L.A., 1961-68; v.p. fin. Petersen Pub. Co., 1969; controller L.A. Times, 1969-79; v.p. Los Angeles Times, 1977-79, v.p. fin., 1979-81; asst. treas. Times Mirror Co., 1971-82, v.p., controller, 1982-87, v.p., chief acctg. officer, 1987—. Trustee Woodbury U., 1981—, chmn. bd. trustees, 1984-87. Served with AUS, 1950-52. Mem. Fin. Execs. Inst. (dir. 1979-82, pres. L.A. chpt. 1973-74), Internat. Newspaper Fin. Execs. (dir. 1978-82, pres. 1980-81), Am. Inst. CPAs, Calif. Soc. CPAs, Am. Horse Council, Internat. Arabian Horse Assn., Arabian Horse Assn. So. Calif., Friendly Hills Country Club. Republican. Baptist. Home: 2160 Le Flore Dr La Habra Heights CA 90631-8020 Office: Times Mirror Co Times Mirror Sq Los Angeles CA 90012-3816

MAXWELL, NEAL A., church official; m. Colleen Hinckley; four children. B in Polit. Sci., M in Polit. Sci., U. Utah, LLD (hon.); LLD (hon.), Brigham Young U.; LittD (hon.), Westminster Coll.; HHD (hon.), Utah State U., Ricks Coll. Legis. asst. U.S. sen. Wallace F. Bennett, Utah; exec. v.p. U. Utah, Salt Lake City; various ch. positions including bishop Salt Lake City's Univ. Sixth Ward, mem. gen. bd. youth orgn., adult correlation com. and one of first Regional Reps. of the Twelve; elder Ch. Jesus Christ Latter Day Sts., Asst. to the Council of Twelve, 1974-76, mem. of Presidency of First Quorum of the Seventy, 1976-81, mem. of Council of Twelve Apostles, 1981—; bd. dirs. Quester Corp., Deseret News Pub. Co. Mem. Quorum of the Twelve Ch. of Jesus Christ of Latter-Day Saints, Salt Lake City. Recipient Liberty Bell award Utah State Bar, 1967; named Pub. Adminstr. of Yr. Inst. Govt. Service Brigham Young U., 1973. Office: LDS Church Quorum of the Twelve 47 E South Temple Salt Lake City UT 84150

MAXWELL, RAYMOND ROGER, accountant; b. Parmer County, Tex., Jan. 7, 1918; s. Frederick W. and Hazel Belle (Rogers) M.; m. Jeanne Hollarn, June 16, 1945 (dec. Dec. 1987); children: Donald R., Bruce Edward, Sabrina G. Spiering Warren. Ed.B., Western Ill. State Tchrs Coll., 1941; MBA in Acctg., U. Fla., 1949; postgrad., UCLA, 1965-68. CPA, Fla., Calif. Asst. to bus. mgr. Western Ill. State Tchrs. Coll., Macomb, 1939-41; apprentice acct. Charles H. Lindfors, CPA, Ft. Lauderdale, Fla., 1946-48; acct./auditor Frederic Dunn-Rankin & Co. CPA, Miami, Fla., 1948-49; CPA staff Charles Costar, CPA, Miami, 1951; resident auditor/CPA prin. Raymond R. Maxwell CPA, Ft. Lauderdale, 1951-56; supt. pub. instrn. Broward County, Ft. Lauderdale, 1956-61; staff asst. in fin. North Am. Aviation, Inc., El Segundo, Calif., 1961-65; acctg. prin. Raymond R. Maxwell, CPA, Whittier, Calif., 1968—; owner Maxwells Homelink Learning Center, Whittier, Calif., 1993—. Active precinct election bds., Whittier, L.A. County, 1989; 1st reader First Ch. of Christ, Scientist, Whittier, 1990-92, exec. bd., 1989, participant Bible Explorations, 1991-92. 1st lt. USAAF, 1942-46. Republican. Office: Unit # C 13217 E Whittier Blvd Whittier CA 90602

MAXWELL-BROGDON, FLORENCE MORENCY, school administrator, educational adviser; b. Spring Park, Minn., Nov. 11, 1929; d. William Frederick and Florence Ruth (LaBrie) Maxwell; m. John Carl Brogdon, Mar. 13, 1957; children: Carole Alexandra, Cecily Ann, Daphne Diana. B.A., Calif. State U., L.A., 1955; MS, U. So. Calif., 1957; postgrad. Columbia Pacific U., San Rafael, Calif., 1982-86. Cert. tchr., Calif. Dir. Rodeo Sch., L.A., 1961-64; lectr. Media Features, Culver City, Calif., 1964—; dir. La Playa Sch., Culver City, 1968-75; founding dir. Venture Sch., Culver City, 1974—, also chmn. bd.; bd. dirs., v.p. Parent Coop. Preschools, Baie d'Urfe Que., Can., 1964—; del. to Ednl. Symposium, Moscow-St. Petersburg, 1992; del. to U.S./China Joint Conf. on Edn., Beijing, 1992; del. to Internat. Confederation of Prins., Geneva, 1993. Author: Let Me Tell You, 1973; Wet 'n Squishy; 1973; Balancing Act, 1977; (as Morency Maxwell) Framed in Silver, 1985; (column) What Parents Want to Know, 1961—; editor: Calif. Preschooler, 1961-74; contbr. articles to profl. jours. Treas. Democrat Congl. Primary, Culver City, 1972. Mem. Calif. Council Parent Schs. (bd. dirs. 1961-74), Parent Coop. Preschools Internat. (advisor 1975—), Pen Ctr. USA West, Mystery Writers of Am. (affiliate), Internat. Platform Assn., Nat. Assn. Secondary Sch. Prins., Libertarian. Home: 10814 Molony Rd Culver City CA 90230-5451 Office: Venture Sch 5333 Sepulveda Blvd Culver City CA 90230-5233

MAXWORTHY, TONY, mechanical and aerospace engineering educator; b. London, May 21, 1933; came to U.S., 1954, naturalized, 1961; s. Ernest Charles and Gladys May (Butson) M.; m. Emily Jean Parkinson, June 20, 1956 (div. 1974); children: Kirsten, Kara; m. Anna Barbara Parks, May 21, 1979. BS in Engring., U. London, 1954; MSE, Princeton U., 1955; PhD, Harvard U., 1959. Research asst. Harvard U., Cambridge, Mass., 1955-59; sr. scientist, group supr. Jet Propulsion Lab., Pasadena, Calif., 1960-67, cons., 1968—; assoc. prof. U. So. Calif., Los Angeles, 1967-70, prof., 1970—, Smith Internat. prof. mech. and aero. engring., 1988—, chmn. dept. mech. engring., 1979-89; cons. BBC Rsch. Ctr., Baden, Switzerland, 1972—, J.P.L., Pasadena, Calif., 1968—; lectr. Woods Hole Oceanographic Inst., Mass., summers 1965, 70, 72, 83; Forman vis. prof. in aeronautics Tech. Haifa, 1986; vis. prof. U. Poly, Madrid, 1988, Inst. Sop. Tech., Lisbon, 1988, E.T.H., Zürich, 1989, E.P.F., Lausanne, 1989—. Mem. editorial bd. Geophys. Fluid Dynamics, 1973-79, 88—, Dynamic Atmospheric Oceans, 1976-83, Phys. Fluids, 1978-81, Zeitschrift fuer Angewandte Mathematik und Physik, 1987—; contbr. articles to profl. jours. Recipient Humboldt Sr. Scientist award, 1981-83; fellow Cambridge U., 1974, Australian Nat. U., 1978, Nat. Ctr. Atmospheric Research, 1976, Glennon fellow U. Western Australia, 1990, Sr. Queen's fellow in Marine Scis., Commonwealth of Australia, 1984; recipient Halliburton award U. So. Calif., 1980, Otto Laporte award Am. Physics Soc., 1990. Fellow Am. Phys. Soc. (chmn. exec. com. fluid dynamics div. 1974-79); mem. NAE, Am. Meteorol. Soc., Am. Geophys. Union, ASME (fluid mechs. com.), European Geophys. Soc., Acad. Applied Mechanics. Office: U So Calif Dept Mech Engring Exposition Park Los Angeles CA 90089-1453

MAXX, DAVE FRANK, mechanical design engineer, consultant; b. Des Moines, Iowa, Aug. 29, 1955; s. Wilbur John and Velma Ann (Miller) M.; m. Michiyo Jamie Hirase, June 9, 1979. AAS, Des Moines Community Coll., 1979; CDA, Instn. Touraine, Tours, France, 1981; BA, BS, Iowa State U., 1982; DCH, Am. Inst. Hypnotherapy, 1988. With security div. N.W. Bell Telephone, Des Moines, 1974-77; design engr. Dack Engring., Des Moines, 1977-82; project quality coord. Quail Corp., Rancho Mirage, Calif., 1982-83; produce analysis statis. Riverside (Calif.) County, 1983-85; systems designer Riverside-Coachella RCD, Indio, Calif., 1985-87; project mgr. MIS Corp., Anaheim, Calif., 1987-91; materials engr. City of L.A., 1991—. Contbr. articles to profl. jours. Councilman City of Thousand Palms, Calif., 1986-87. With USMC, 1975-81. Iowa State U. grantee, 1970-74, State of Calif. grantee, 1987. Mem. Am. Assn. Mining Engrs., Internat. Assn. Mining Engrs., NRA, Am. Bd. Hypnotherapists, Sapeurs & Pompiers du Tarn, Sierra.

MAY, ADOLF DARLINGTON, civil engineering educator; b. Little Rock, Mar. 25, 1927; s. Adolf Darlington and Inez (Shelton) M.; m. Margaret Folsom, Dec. 23, 1948; children—Dolf, Barbara, David, Larry. B.Sc. in Civil Engring, So. Meth. U., 1949; M.Sc., Iowa State U., 1950; Ph.D., Purdue U., 1955. Asst. prof., then assoc. prof. Clarkson Coll. Tech., 1952-56; assoc. prof. Mich. State U., 1956-59; research engr. Thompson-Ramo Wooldridge, 1959-62; project dir. Ill. Div. Hwys., 1962-65; mem. faculty U. Calif., Berkeley, 1965—, prof. civil engring., 1965—; guest prof. numerous univs., 1965—, cons. to industry, 1965—. Contbr. to profl. jours., books. Served with USNR, 1944-47. Recipient Disting. Engring. Alumnus award Purdue U., 1978; Fulbright scholar to Netherlands, 1977; German Humboldt Scholarship awardee, 1980. Mem. Transp. Rsch. Bd., Nat. Acad. Engring. (Matson Transp. Rsch. award 1992), AAm. Soc. Engring. Edn., Inst. Traffic Engrs., Sigma Xi, Tau Beta Pi. Home: 1645 Julian Dr El Cerrito CA 94530-2011 Office: U Calif Dept of Civil Engring 114 McLaughlin Hall Berkeley CA 94720

MAY, DONALD FRANCIS, state official; b. Boston, Dec. 8, 1946; s. Daniel Harry and Anna Denise (MacArthur) M.; m. Lin Irene Janusua, Dec. 21, 1969; children: Justin, Christina. BA, Fordham U., 1968; MA, U. Wash., 1974, Yale U., 1975; MPPM, Yale U., 1981. CPA, Alaska; CMA. Acct. Coopers & Lybrand, CPA's, Anchorage, 1981-83; cons. Honchen & Uhlenhott, Inc., Anchorage, 1983-89; contr. Anchorage Tel. Utility, 1989-90; mem. Alaska Pub. Utilities Commn., Anchorage, 1990—. Lt. (j.g.) USCG, 1968-72. Mem. AICPA. Office: Alaska Pub Utilities Commn 1016 W 6th Ave Anchorage AK 99501

MAY, DOUGLAS HUTTON, aerospace company executive; b. Tacoma, June 28, 1941; s. Raymond William and Carol Mary (Hutton) M.; m. Euritha Anne Headrick, Aug. 6, 1967; 1 child, Damon Hutton. BSME, Wash. State U., 1963; MSAE, Air Force Inst. Tech., 1974. Registered profl. engr., Calif., Ohio. Assoc. engr. Lockheed Missiles and Space Co., Sunnyvale, Calif., 1963-65; engr. Boeing, Seattle, 1965-66; commd. 2d lt. USAF, 1966, advanced through grades to lt. col., 1985; pilot USAF Tactical Air Command, 1966-73; mgr. USAF Systems Command, 1973-85, USAF Readiness Command, Tampa, Fla., 1985-87; retired USAF, 1987; mgr. Thiokol Corp., Brigham City, Utah, 1987—; adj. faculty Fla. Inst. Tech., Melbourne, Fla., 1981-85, Weber State U., Ogden, Utah, 1988-89. Advisor Ctr. for Aerospace Tech., Weber State U., Ogden, 1988. Decorated DFC, Def. Meritorious Svc. medal; recipient NASA Group Achievement award, 1992. Mem. AIAA (sect. chmn. Utah 1992-93), ASME.

MAY, GERALD WILLIAM, university administrator, educator, civil engineering consultant; b. Kenya, Jan. 2, 1941; s. William and Ruth (Koch) M.; m. Mary Joyce Pool, July 27, 1963; children: Erica Ruth, Christian William, Heidi Clara. B.S., Bradley U., 1962; M.S., U. Colo., 1964, Ph.D., 1967. Registered profl. engr., N.Mex. Civil engr. Ill. Hwy. Dept., Peoria, summer 1959-63; instr. U. Colo., Boulder, 1964-67; from asst. to prof. engring. U. N.Mex., Albuquerque, 1967-77, prof. of civil engring, 1977—; dean Coll. Engring., U. N.Mex., Albuquerque, 1980-86; pres. U. N.Mex., Albuquerque, 1986-90; dir. accident study program, Albuquerque, 1970-75, cons. to corps., govtl. agys. Contbr. articles to profl. jours., chpts. to books. Recipient Borden Freshman award Bradley U., 1958. Mem. ASCE (pres. N.Mex. sect. 1982-83), Am. Soc. Engring. Edn. (Outstanding Young Faculty award 1973), Nat. Soc. Profl. Engrs., Sigma Xi, Chi Epsilon, Tau Beta Pi, Phi Eta Sigma. Office: Univ N Mex Civil Engring Dept Albuquerque NM 87131

MAY, MICHAEL WAYNE, technical school executive; b. Springhill, La., Mar. 31, 1949; s. Willie Wilmer and Ethel Florene (Sigler) M. Student So. Ark. U., 1968-70, La. Tech. U., 1970-71. Prodn. dir. Sta. KKAM, Pueblo, Colo., 1973-75; quality control dir. Sta. KBOZ, Bozeman, Mont., 1975-78; music dir., dir. rsch., disk jockey Sta. KOOK, Billings, Mont., 1978-80; founder, operator May Tech. Coll., Billings, Great Falls, 1980—; owner Sta. KMAY, Billings, Mont. Mem. Career Coll. Assn. (Key mem. for Mont.). Author: Building with the Basics: Radio Personality Development, 1979, Radio Personality Basics, 1992. Home: 80 Skyline Dr Billings MT 59105-3038 Office: PO Box 127 Billings MT 59103

MAY, RICHARD PAUL, data processing professional; b. Milw., Oct. 19, 1946; s. Gorden Elliot and Marie Karen (Leidgen) M.; m. Amy Yamashiro, Mar. 5, 1982. BBA, U. Hawaii, 1972; Cert. in Owners/Pres's. Mgmt., Harvard U., 1989; MBA, U. Hawaii, 1990. Customer engr. IBM, Honolulu, 1968; co-founder, chief exec. officer Aloha Tax Svc., Honolulu, 1972-88; founder, pres., chief exec. officer Honolulu Bar Supply Ltd./May Foodsvc., 1972-90; co-founder Indtl. Distbrs., Kahului, Hawaii, 1976-88; mng. ptnr. Data Capture Systems, Kaneohe, Hawaii, 1990—; pres. Rick May, Inc., Honolulu, 1989—. With U.S. Army, 1968-70, Vietnam. Decorated Bronze Star medal, Air medal, 2 Purple Heart medals. Mem. Harvard Bus. Sch. Club, C. of C., Hawaii Visitors Bur., Beta Gamma Sigma. Republican. Roman Catholic. Office: Data Capture Systems 46-001 Kamehameha Hwy Ste 317 Kaneohe HI 96744

MAY, ROLLO, psychoanalyst; b. Ada, Ohio, Apr. 21, 1909; s. Earl Tittle and Matie (Boughton) M.; m. Florence DeFrees, June 5, 1938 (div. 1968); children: Robert Rollo, Allegra Anne, Carolyn Jane; m. Ingrid Schöll, 1971 (div. 1978). AB, Oberlin Coll., 1930, HHD (hon.), 1980; BD cum laude, Union Theol. Sem., N.Y.C., 1938; PhD summa cum laude, Columbia U., 1949; DHL (hon.), U. Okla., 1970; LLD (hon.), Regis Coll., 1971; LHD (hon.), St. Vincent Coll., 1972, Mich. State U., 1976, Rockford Coll., 1977, Ohio No. U., 1978, Oberlin Coll., 1980, Sacred Heart U., 1982, Calif. Sch. Profl. Psychology, 1983, Rivera Coll., 1986, Gonzaga U., 1986, Saybrook Inst., 1987; 5 other hon. degrees. Tchr. Am. Coll., Saloniki, Greece, 1930-33; student adviser Mich. State Coll., 1934-36; student counselor CCNY, 1943-44; mem. faculty William Alanson White Inst. Psychiatry, Psychology and Psychoanalysis, 1958-75; lectr. New Sch. Social Research, N.Y.C., 1955-76; tng. fellow supervisory analyst Williams Alanson White Inst. Psychiatry, 1958—; co-chmn. Conf. on Psychotherapy and Counseling, N.Y. Acad. Scis., 1953-54; vis. prof. Harvard U., summer 1964, Princeton U., 1967, Yale U., 1972; Dean's scholar N.Y. U., 1971; Regents' prof. U. Calif., Santa Cruz, 1973; disting. vis. prof. Bklyn. Coll., 1974-75. Author: Art of Counseling, 1939, Meaning of Anxiety, 1950, rev. edit., 1977, Man's Search for Himself, 1953, Psychology and the Human Dilemma, 1966, Existence: A New Dimension in Psychiatry and Psychology, 1958, Love and Will, 1969, Power and Innocence, 1972, Paulus-Reminiscences of a Friendship, 1973, The Courage to Create, 1975, Freedom and Destiny, 1981, The Discovery of Being, 1983; Editor: Existence: A New Dimension in Psychiatry and Psychology, 1958, Existential Psychology, 2d edit, 1961, Symbolism in Religion and Literature, 1960, My Quest for Beauty, 1985. Trustee Am. Found. Mental Health; bd. dirs. Soc. Arts, Religion and Culture. Recipient award for disting. contbn. to profession and sci. of psychology N.Y. Soc. Clin. Psychology, 1955; Ralph Waldo Emerson award for Love and Will Phi Beta Kappa, 1970; Disting. Contbns. award N.Y. U., 1971; Centennial Medallion St. Peter's Coll., 1972; ann. citation Merrill-Palmer Inst., Detroit, 1973; spl. Dr. Martin Luther King, Jr. award N.Y. Soc. Clin. Psychologists, 1974; Disting. Grad. award Columbia U. Tchrs. Coll., 1975; fellow Branford Coll. Yale U., 1960—; Whole Life Humanitarian award Whole Life Expn., 1986. Fellow Am. Psychol. Assn. (award for disting. contbn. to sci. and profession of clin. psychology 1971, Gold medal for Disting. Career 1987), Nat. Council Religion Higher Edn., William Alanson White Psychoanalytic Soc. (past pres.); mem. N.Y. State Psychol. Assn. (past pres.).

MAY, RONNY JOE (RON MAY), computer scientist, state legislator; b. Sherman, Tex., Sept. 16, 1934; s. Joe Danover and Athie (Fennell) M.; m. Onilla Essary, Sept. 2, 1956; children: Mark D., Marisa May Rogers. B of Gen. Studies, U. Nebr., Omaha, 1972. Commd. sgt. U.S. Signal Corp; advanced through grades to lt. col. USAF, 1954; ret., 1974; computer scientist Sci. Applications, Inc., Colorado Springs, Colo.; pres., broker Pikes Peak Realty, Inc., Colorado Springs, Colo.; pres., owner May Corp., Colorado Springs, Colo.; mem. Colo. Ho. of Reps., 1993—. City councilman City of Colo. Springs, 1981-85; chmn. Colo. Springs Internat. Airport, 1985-91; bd. dirs. Colo. Springs Mcpl. Utilities, 1981-85. Decorated Air medal with three bronze oak leaf clusters. Mem. Colo. Springs Exec. Assn., Retired Officers Assn., Sertoma Internat. (life, pres. 1978-79, gold coat disting. pres. 1979). Republican. Presbyterian. Home: 4980 Daybreak Circle N Colorado Springs CO 80917 Office: May Corp 730 Citadel Dr S-201 Colorado Springs CO 80909

MAY, TERRENCE ANTHONY, county administrator; b. San Jose, Calif., Oct. 18, 1956; s. Earl Edward and Claire Louise (Molloy) M. BA in Polit. Sci., UCLA, 1979; postgrad. in Pub. Adminstrn., U. So. Calif., 1979-80; postgrad. in Politics and Strategy, U. Coll. Galway, Ireland, 1984-85. Local govt. specialist State of Alaska, Dept. Community and Regional Affairs, Juneau, Alaska, 1980-84; adminstrv. svc. officer U. Calif. San Francisco, Sch. Medicine, 1985-86; adminstrv. analyst City of Lemoore, Calif., 1986-87; asst. to county adminstrv. officer Couny of San Benito, Hollister, Calif., 1987-89; dep. county adminstrv. officer County of San Benito, Hollister, 1990—; sr. adminstrv. analyst County of Yolo, Woodland, Calif., 1989-90. Calif. County Personnel Adminstrs. Assn., Internat. Personnel Mgmt. Assn. Home: 808 Helen Dr Hollister CA 95023 Office: County San Benito Adminstrv Office 498 5th St 2nd Flr Hollister CA 95023

MAYA, WALTER, chemistry educator; b. N.Y.C., Oct. 25, 1929; s. Walter and Harriet (Kaplan) M.; m. Karen Greenbaum, June 30, 1985; children: Lynn Maya Fenstermaker, Leslie Maya-Charles, Susan H., Theodore W. Student, Pasadena (Calif.) C.C., 1948-50; BS with honors, UCLA, 1954, PhD, 1958. Rsch. chemist E.I. Du Pont de Nemours & Co., Wilmington, Del., 1958-59, Rocketdyne, Canoga Park, Calif., 1959-70; prof. chemistry Calif. Poly. U., Pomona, 1971—. Contbr. articles to profl. jours.; co-patentee on preparation chlorine pentafluoride. With U.S. Army, 1951-52, Korea. DuPont predoctoral fellow UCLA, 1957, Pfizer postdoctoral fellow U. Ill., 1958. Mem. AAAS, Am. Chem. Soc., Sigma Xi. Democrat. Home:

1845 Antioch Rd Claremont CA 91711 Office: Chemistry Dept Calif Poly U Pomona CA 91768

MAYBERRY, PATRICIA ANN TINTHOFF, artist, educator, interior designer; b. Urbana, Ill., Oct. 19, 1940; d. Fred S. and Alyce L. (Tyler) Tinthoff; m. William Thomas Mayberry, July 16, 1962; children: Michael, Karrin. BA, DePauw U., 1962. Cert. K-12 art tchr., Ariz. Tchr. Maplewood Elem. Sch., Rantoul, Ill., 1962-65; artist, propr. Custom Welded Jewelry and Sculpture, Scottsdale, 1970-78; tchr. art Pueblo Elem. Community Sch., Scottsdale, 1973-74; propr. Panache Interior Design, Scottsdale, 1979-87, Artforms, Paradise Valley, Ariz., 1987—; tchr., propr. Children's Art Sch., Paradise Valley, 1975—; juror South Mountain Magnet Sch. for Arts, Phoenix, 1990, 91, 92, Horizons Show, Shemer Art Ctr., Phoenix, 1991, 92. Exhibited at Western Fedn. Watercolor Show, Corpus Christi, Tex., 1991, El Paso (Tex.) Mus. Art, 1992; two woman show Ch. of Beatitudes, Phoenix, Ariz., 1991-92; three person show Citibank Bldg. Lobby, Phoenix, 1993; permanent collections include Maricopa County C.C., Baker, Livermore & Quinn Pvt. Collections. Recipient purchase award Maricopa County C.C.'s, 1987. Mem. Am. Watercolor Soc. (assoc.), Ariz. Artists Guild (3rd v.p. 1988-90, pres. 1990-92), Ariz. Watercolor Assn. (2d v.p. 1989-90, Best of Show award 1989, Disting. Merit award 1991, 92), Contemporary Watercolor Assn. (sec. 1991-92, Merit award 1991), Alpha Omicron Pi (pres. alumni chpt. 1974-75). Republican. Home and Studio: 8818 N 66th Pl Paradise Valley AZ 85253

MAYENKAR, KRISHNA VAMAN, environmental engineer, consultant; b. Bombay, Nov. 16, 1943; came to U.S., 1969; s. Vaman Krishna and Tara Vaman (Deshpande) M.; m. Shobhana Krishna Karnik, Feb. 12, 1967; children: Kiefer, Neelan. BChemE, Indian Inst. Tech., Bombay, 1966; M in Chem. Engring., U. Louisville, 1970. Registered profl. engr., environ. assessor, Calif. Devel. engr. West Coast Paper Mill, India, 1966-69, 71-72; project engr. Roy F. Weston, Inc., Wilmette, Ill., 1973-75; with Harza Engring. Co., Chgo., 1975-85, engr. VI, 1979-81, sect. head, 1982-85; sr. project mgr. EMCON Assocs., San Jose, Calif., 1986-87, exec. mgr., 1987-89, dir. tech. svcs. div., 1990-91, v.p., bd. dirs., 1991-93; bd. dirs. EMCON Associates, 1993; v.p. Harza Environ. Svcs., Chgo. Inventor toxic metal removal process from water and wastewater; contbr. articles to profl. jours. Mem. Rep. Party, Washington, 1980—, mem. presdl. task force, 1988—. mem. Am. Inst. Chem. Engrs., Nat. Soc. Profl. Engrs., Calif. Soc. Profl. Engrs. Home: 12311 Saraglen Dr Saratoga CA 95070-3224 Office: EMCON Assocs 1921 Ringwood Ave San Jose CA 95131-1788

MAYER, FRANK ANTHONY, history educator, legal assistant; b. Santa Cruz, Calif., Sept. 22, 1942; s. Milton Joseph and Sally Nel (Utley) M.; m. Maria Eugenia Saez, Sept. 3, 1983; 1 child, Teresa. BA, Calif. State U., San Francisco, 1964, MA, 1969; cert. legal asst., UCLA, 1976; PhD, U. So. Calif., 1987. Legal asst. Lewis, D'Amato, Brisbois, Bisgaard, L.A., 1979—; prof. history Calif. State U., L.A., 1990—; mem. Calif. State Adv. Com. U.S. Civil Rights Commn., 1993. Author: Churchill and Conservative Party, 1992; contbr. articles to profl. jours. Recipient John Kennedy Presidential Libr. Found. grant, Columbia Point, Mass., 1988. Fellow Consortium for Atlantic Studies; mem. ABA (assoc., cert. legal asst.), Am. Coun. on Germany. Roman Catholic. Office: Calif State U LA 5151 State University Dr Los Angeles CA 90032

MAYER, HERBERT CARLETON, JR., computer consultant; b. Newton, Mass., Aug. 2, 1922; s. Herbert Carleton and Elsie Marie (Hauser) M.; m. Maryetta Brodkord, Aug. 21, 1948; children: Judith Marie, Christine Louise. BS, Parsons Coll., 1943; MS, U. Iowa, 1947; PhD, U. So. Calif., 1975. Instr. math. U. Idaho, Moscow, 1947-48, U. Utah, Salt Lake City, 1949-51; edn. adminstr. Gen. Electric co., Richland, Wash., 1951-59; systems engr., univ. industry specialist IBM, Chgo., 1959-81; assoc. prof. mgmt. info. systems Wash. State U., Pullman, 1980-82; assoc. prof. U. Wis.-Parkside, Kenosha, 1982-85, Eastern Wash. U., Cheney, 1985-90; adj. prof. mgmt. U. Tex., El Paso, 1976-78. Pres. Tri-City Heights Assn., Kennewick, Wash., 1956-58, PTA, Kennewick, 1957-58; v.p. Kennewick Sch. Bd., 1958, pres., 1959. Mem. Math. Assn. Am, Internat. Assn. Computing in Edn., Am. Soc. Engring. Edn., Data Processing Mgmt. Assn. (bd. dirs., sec. Spokane chpt. 1988, v.p. edn. Spokane chpt. 1989, v.p. student chpt. 1990), Phi Delta Kappa (found. chmn. Spokane chpt. 1992-93). Home: 3334 S Bernard St Spokane WA 99203-1636

MAYER, PATRICIA JAYNE, financial officer, management accountant; b. Chgo., Apr. 27, 1950; d. Arthur and Ruth (Greenberger) Hersh; m. William A. Mayer Jr., Apr. 30, 1971. AA, Diablo Valley Coll., 1970; BSBA, Calif. State U., Hayward, 1975. Cert. mgmt. acct. Staff acct., auditor Elmer Fox Westheimer and Co., Oakland, Calif., 1976; supervising auditor Auditor's Office County of Alameda, Oakland, 1976-78; asst. acctg. mgr. CBS Retail Stores doing bus. as Pacific Stereo, Emeryville, Calif., 1978-79; contr. Oakland Unified Sch. Dist., 1979-84; v.p. fin., chief fin. officer YMCA, San Francisco, 1984—; instr. acctg. to staff YMCA, San Francisco, 1984—, CBS Retail Stores, 1978-79. Draft counselor Mt. Diablo Peace Ctr., Walnut Creek, Calif., 1970-72; dep. registrar of voters Contra Costa County Registrar's Office, Martinez, Calif., 1972-77. Mem. Fin. Execs. Inst. (San Francisco chpt.), Inst. Mgmt. Accts., Dalmatian Club No. Calif., Dalmatian Club Am. Democrat. Jewish. Home: 2395 Lake Meadow Cir Martinez CA 94553-5475 Office: YMCA of San Francisco Ste 770 44 Montgomery St San Francisco CA 94104

MAYER, ROBERT FABIAN, sales engineer; b. Cleve., Sept. 30, 1946; s. Ludwig Theodore and Amelia (Fabian) M.; m. Elizabeth Mayer, Jan. 12, 1949; children: Jeremy, Brent, Laura. BS in Aero. Engring., Tri State U., Angola, Ind., 1968; MBA, Pepperdine U., 1985. Sales engr. Hartwell Corp., Placentia, Calif., 1970-76; tech. sales engr. Cherry Aerospace Fastener, Santa Ana, Calif., 1976-78; sr. sales rep. Huck Mfg., Carson, Calif., 1978-83; sr. sales engr. Litton Fastening Systems, Lakewood, Calif., 1983-85; regional sales mgr. Monogram Aerospace, L.A., 1985-86; sr. tech. sales engr. Fairchild Aerospace Fastener, Carson, 1986-92; sr. engr., scientist McDonnell Douglas Space Systems, Huntington Beach, Calif., 1992—. Mem. Soc. for Advancement of Materials and Process Engring., Soc. Mfg. Engrs. Home: 8911 Ann Cross St Garden Grove CA 92641

MAYER, THOMAS, economics educator; b. Vienna, Austria, Jan. 18, 1927; s. Felix and Helen (Pollatschek) M.; m. Dorothy JoAnne Harmison, Apr. 7, 1963. BA, Queens Coll., 1948; MA, Columbia U., 1949, PhD, 1953. Economist Treasury Dept., 1951-52, Office of Price Stabilization, 1952, Bur. of Mines, 1953; asst. prof. U. Notre Dame, 1954-56; from asst. to assoc. prof. Mich. State U., 1956-61; vis. assoc. prof. U. Calif., Berkeley, 1961-62; prof. U. Calif., Davis, 1962-93, prof. emeritus, 1993—; vis. ast. prof. W.Va. U., 1953-54. Author: Monetary Policy in the United States, 1968, Permanent Income, Wealth and Consumption, 1972; (with D.C. Rowan) Intermediate Macroeconomics, 1972; (with others) The Structure of Monetarism, 1978; (with others) Money, Banking and the Economy, 1981, 2d edit., 1984, 3d edit., 1987, 4th edit., 1990, 5th edit., 1993, Chineses edit., 1988; Revealing Monetary Policy, 1987, Monetarism and Macroeconomic Policy, 1990; editor: The Political Economy of American Monetary Policy, 1990, Monetary Theory, 1990, (with F. Spinelli) Studies in Macroeconomics and Monetary Policy Issues, 1991; mem. editorial bd. Jour. of Econ. Lit., 1985—, others. Mem. Am. Econ. Assn., Am. fin. Assn., Internat. Network Econ. Method (chmn. 1993—), Western Econ. Assn. (v.p. 1976-77, pres. 1978-79), Royal Econ. Soc. Home: 3054 Buena Vista Way Berkeley CA 94708

MAYES, DAVID LEE, computer marketing executive; b. Long Beach, Calif., June 15, 1947; s. Ollie Lee and Dorothy Roberta (Faure) M.; m. Teresa Ann Linda Gayard, Sept. 11, 1982 (div. 1989); 1 child, Matthew. BA, San Jose State U., 1971, MA, 1975; postgrad., Oxford U., Eng., 1971-72. Mfg. mgr. Intel Corp., Santa Clara, Calif., 1975-78; internat. mktg. mgr. Intel Corp., Hillsboro, Oreg., 1978-82; northern European mktg. mgr. Intel Internat., Swindon, U.K., 1982-83; strategic bus. devel. mgr. Intel Internat., 1983; mng. dir. 01 Computers Group (UK) Ltd., London, 1984-86; dir. mktg. Mobile Data Internat., Vancouver, B.C., Can., 1986-87; dir. OEM and subsys. progs. Silicon Graphics Inc., Mountain View, Calif., 1987-90; OEM mktg. The Santa Cruz Operation, 1991—. Recipient IBM Quality award, London, 1985. Home: 633 Townsend Dr PO Box 2302 El Granada CA 94018-2302

MAYEUX, JERRY VINCENT, biotechnology executive, microbiologist; b. Mamou, La., Apr. 22, 1937; s. Avie and Ida (Fontenot) M.; m. Sally Louise Brown, June 13, 1981; children by previous marriage: Anne Claire, Peter John. B.S., La. State U., 1960, M.Sc., 1961; Ph.D., Oreg. State U., 1965. Nat. Acad. Sci. research fellow NASA, 1965-66; asst. prof. Colo. State U., Ft. Collins, 1966-70; chief life scis. sect. Martin Marietta Aerospace Corp., Denver, 1970-74; dir. research Ferma Gro Corp., Storm Lake, Iowa, 1974-75; chmn. bd., pres. Dawn Corp., Denison, Iowa, 1976-80; founder Burst AgriTech, Inc., Overland Park, Kans., 1980, chmn. bd., 1982-86, pres., 1987—; pres., chief exec. officer Plant Bioregulator Techs., Inc., Corrales, N.Mex. Adv. com. Kans. Tech. Enterprise Corp., 1987, chmn. Biotechnology Steering Com. Silicon Prarie Technology Assn., 1990-92. Served to 1st lt. M.S.C., U.S. Army, 1965. Mem. Am. Soc. Microbiology, Am. Chem. Soc., AAAS, Plant Growth Regulator Soc., Soc. Indsl. Microbiology.

MAYLAND, HENRY FREDRICK, research soil scientist; b. Greybull, Wyo., Dec. 31, 1935; s. Christian F. and Molly Mayland; m. Vesta Catherine Muenster, Aug. 4, 1957; children: Mark Ross, Michelle Rene. BS, U. Wyo., 1960, MS, 1961; PhD, U. Ariz., 1965. Rsch. soil scientist USDA/Agrl. Rsch. Svc., Kimberly, Idaho, 1964—. Contbr. articles to profl. jours. Office: USDA Agrl Rsch Svc 3793N 3600E Kimberly ID 83341

MAYNARD, ARTHUR HOMER, religious studies educator; b. Centerville, Mich., Aug. 28, 1915; s. Floyd Ray and Harriet (Crumb) M.; m. Pauline E. Schroeder, Sept. 13, 1941; children: Paulette Ann Grinager, Kent Arthur. BA, Cornell Coll., Mt. Vernon, Iowa, 1936; MA, Boston U., 1938, STB, 1939; PhD, U. So. Calif., 1950. Ordained to ministry Meth. Ch. as deacon, 1938, as elder, 1940. Pastor The Meth. Ch., Iowa, Wis., Calif., 1935-50; asst. prof. religion Willamette U., Salem, Oreg., 1950-52; assoc. prof. religion, chmn. dept. U. Miami, Coral Gables, Fla., 1952-56, prof. religion, chmn. dept., 1956-58; prof. Bible U. of Pacific, Stockton, Calif., 1958-85, chair dept. religious studies, 1962-75, acting chair dept., 1979, 84, prof. emeritus, 1985—. Author: The Enduring Word, 1964, revised edit., 1968, Understanding the Gospel of John, 1991; author numerous book revs. and papers for profl. meetings. Mem. Soc. Bibl. Lit. (v.p. West Coast sect. 1972-73, pres. 1973-74), Phi Beta Kappa, Phi Kappa Phi (pres.). Democrat. Home: 2009 Meadow Ave Stockton CA 95207

MAYNARD, HARRY LEE, bank executive; b. DeWitt, Iowa, Nov. 5, 1927; s. Hosea Joseph and Mildred Alta (Bourne) M.; m. Carolyn Joyce Messersmith, June 22, 1952; 1 child, Linda Lea. BA, U. No. Iowa, 1950. Tchr. Stuart (Iowa) High Sch., 1950-52; mgr. Beneficial Fin. Co., Ventura, Calif., 1952-59, Security Pacific Nat. Bank, Ventura, 1959-63; exec. v.p. Channel Islands State Bank, Ventura, 1963-69; v.p., mgr. Wells Fargo Bank, Ventura, 1969-76; pres., chief exec. officer Am. Comml. Bank, Ventura, 1976—. Bd. trustees Community Meml. Hosp., 1978—, treas. 1979—, fin. com., chmn. 1979—, spl. hosp. task force 1960-63, publicity chmn. fund dr. 1969 team capt.; hon. bd. mem. Ventura Unified Sch. Dist. Found.; trustee Found. for Preservation of Ventura County Parks, 1979, friend 4-H; county adv. bd. pres. Salvation Army, 1976-77, treas. 1972-75, co-chmn bldg. fund, 1976-77; coach Little League; founding dir. Ventura Boys' Club; coach, founding dir. Ventura Youth Basketball Assn.; and others. Mem. Am. Legion, Ventura Downtown Lions Club (bd. dirs., pres. 1971-72), U. No. Iowa Alumni Assn. (life), Am. Bankers Assn. (community bankers adv. coun. 1984-88), Calif. Bankers Assn. (bd. dirs. 1968-80, 1st v.p. 1972, pres. 1973), Calif. Bankers Assn. (Wash. legis. team 1987), Ind. Bankers Assn., Ventura County Farm Bur., Masons (numerous offices), Shriners, Knight Masons of Ireland (Brian Born Coun. 1990), Order of Eastern Star (Ventura chpt. #79), Order of Golden Poppy. Home: 5448 N Bryn Mawr St Ventura CA 93003-2252 Office: Am Comml Bank 300 S Mills Rd Ventura CA 93003-3478

MAYOL, RICHARD THOMAS, advertising executive, political consultant; b. Springfield, Ill., Oct. 30, 1949; s. Richard McFaren and Marjorie (Maddex) M. AA, Springfield Coll., 1969; BS, U. Tulsa, 1972. Co-owner First Tuesday Inc., Phoenix, 1976-85; pres. Mayol and Assocs., Phoenix, 1985—; cons. Dem. candidates, Western U.S., Mo. Udall for Congress, Tucson, Mayor Terry Goddard, Phoenix, Senator John Melcher, Mont. Mem. Phoenix Film Commn., 1985—. Mem. Am. Assn. Polit. Cons., Phoenix Grand Prix Commn. Home and Office: Mayol and Assocs 2329 N 57th Pl Scottsdale AZ 85257-1907

MAYRON, LEWIS WALTER, clinical ecology consultant; b. Chgo., Sept. 20, 1932; s. Max and Florence Minette (Brody) M.; divorced; children: Leslie Hope Mayron Coff, Eric Brian. BS in Chemistry, Roosevelt U., 1954; MS in Biochemistry, U. Ill., 1955, PhD in Biochemistry, 1959. Rsch. assoc. Dept. Biochemistry and Nutrition U. So. Calif., L.A., 1959-61; asst. biochemist Dept. Biochemistry Presby.-St. Luke's Hosp., Chgo., 1961-62; instr. Dept. Biological Chemistry U. Ill., Chgo., 1961-62; biochemistry group leader Tardanbek Labs., Chgo., 1962-63; sr. devel. chemist Abbott Labs., Chgo., 1963-64; asst. attending physician, mem. spl. staff Michael Reese Hosp. and Med. Ctr., Chgo., 1964-66, rsch. assoc. Dept. Allergy Rsch., 1964-66; asst. prof. in biochemistry and physiology Sch. Dentistry Loyola U., Chgo., 1968-71; guest investigator Argonne (Ill.) Nat. Lab., 1973-79; rsch. chemist V.A. Hosp., Hines, Ill., 1968-79; chief clin. radiobiochemist nuclear medicine svc. V.A. Wadsworth Hosp. Ctr., L.A., 1979-83; cons. in clin. ecology, 1980—. Contbr. articles to profl. jours. Mem. Am. Assn. Clin. Chemists, Am. Assn. for the Advancement of Sci., Soc. for Experimental Biology and Medicine, Sigma Xi. Home: 1779 Summer Cloud Dr Thousand Oaks CA 91362-1217

MAYS, WILLIAM BERNARD, computer company official; b. Anchorage, Feb. 28, 1957; s. Fred L. and S. Viola (Martinez) M.; m. Carol A. Pesch, April 5, 1986; children: Clint, Wendy, Melissa. BS in Mgmt., USAF Acad., 1979; MS in Ops. Rsch., U. So. Calif., 1982; BS in Aero. Engring., U. Ariz., 1984. Commd. 2d lt. USAF, 1979, advanced through grades to capt., resigned,, 1987; maj. USAFR, 1993—; program mgr. Evans & Sutherland Computer Corp., Salt Lake City, Utah, 1990—. Advisor CAP, Salt Lake City, 1990—. Recipient achievement award CAP, 1989. Home: 1982 E Everleigh Circle Sandy UT 84093

MAYS, WILLIE HOWARD, JR., former professional baseball player; b. Westfield, Ala., May 6, 1931; s. William Howard and Ann M.; m. Mae Louise Allen, Nov. 27, 1971; 1 adopted son, Michael. Mem. Birmingham Black Barons Baseball Team, 1948-50; joined N.Y. (now San Francisco) Giants system, 1950; mem. Trenton team, 1950-51, Mpls. Millers, 1951; mem. San Francisco Giants, 1951-72, capt.; mem. N.Y. Mets, 1972-73; with Bally's Park Place, Atlantic City, 1980—, San Francisco Giants, 1986—. Author: Willie Mays: My Life In and Out of Baseball, 1966, Say Hey: The Autobiography of Willie Mays, 1988. Served with AUS, 1952-54. Named Most Valuable Player Nat. League, 1954, 65; named Player of Yr. Sporting News, 1954, Baseball Player of Decade Sporting News, 1970, Male Athlete of Yr. AP, 1954; recipient Hickok belt, 1954, Golden Bat award to commemorate 600 home runs, 1st Commissioner's award, 1970, Golden Plate awarded to America's Captians of Achievement by Am. Acad. Achievement, 1976, Spirit of Life award CIty of Hope, 1988, Sportsman of Decade, Cong. Racial Equality, 1991, Legendary Star award HBO Video; inducted into Ala. Sports Hall of Fame, Baseball Hall of Fame, 1979, Black Hall of Fame, 1973, Calif. Sports Hall of Fame. Office: care San Francisco Giants Candlestick Park San Francisco CA 94124

MAYTUM, HARRY RODELL, retired physician; b. Alexandria, S.D., Jan. 25, 1913; s. Wellington James and Lillian May (Syferd) M.; m. Louetta Susanna Stoltz, Apr. 27, 1937; children: James, Nancy, Joan. BS magna cum laude, U. Wis., 1936, MD, 1938. Intern Alameda County Hosp., Oakland, Calif., 1938-39, resident in surgery, 1946-47; resident in surgery Merced County Hosp., Merced, Calif., 1939-41; pvt. practice, Merced, 1947—; chief staff Mercy Hosp., Merced, Merced County Hosp. Bd. dirs. Merced County Mosquito Abatement Dist., 1954-64. Lt col. M.C., USAAF, 1941-47, ETO. Fellow Am. Geriatric Soc., Am. Acad. Family Practice (charter); mem. AMA, Calif. Med. Assn. (Plessner Meml. award 1992), Merced-Mariposa County Med. Soc. (pres. 1955), Merced C. of C. (bd. dirs. 1973-77, former chmn. health affairs com., Merced Citizen of Yr. award 1989), Kiwanis (pres. Merced 1953), Elks, Phi Beta Kappa, Alpha Omega Alpha. Republican. Home: 2887 Forist Ln Merced CA 95340

MAZARAKIS, MICHAEL GERASSIMOS, physicist, researcher; b. Volos, Greece; came to U.S., 1966, naturalized, 1980; s. Gerassimos Nikolaos and Anthie Gerassimos (Kappatos) M.; m. Carolyn Seidel, June 30, 1990. BS in Physics, U. Athens, Greece, 1960; MS in Physics, U. Sorbonne, Paris, 1963, PhD in Physics, 1965; PhD in Physics, Princeton U. and U. Pa., 1971; cert. in mgmt., MIT, 1976. Mem. faculty Rutgers U., New Brunswick, N.J., 1971-74; v.p. and dir. exptl. program Fusion Energy Corp., Princeton, N.J., 1974-77, also exec. v.p., 1975-77; research physicist Argonne Nat. Lab., U. Chgo., 1978-81; research physicist Sandia Nat. Lab. Div. 1242, Albuquerque, 1981—. Contbr. articles to profl. jours. Patentee in field. Bd. dirs. Orthodox Ch., Albuquerque, 1981—; Served to maj. Greek Army, 1960-62. Recipient award Italian. Govt., 1956, Greek Govt., 1956-60, French Govt., 1962-65; Yale U. grantee, 1966. Mem. Am. Phys. Soc., IEEE, Alliance Francaise, N. Mex. Mountain Club, N.Y. Acad. Sci., Sigma Xi. Current work: Particle beam physics, accelerator research and development, inertial fusion, pulse power technology, plasma physics. Subspecialty: Nuclear fusion, particle beam physics.

MAZELIS, MENDEL, plant biochemist, educator, researcher; b. Chgo., Aug. 31, 1922; s. Jacob and Anna (Brvarnick) M.; m. Noreen Beimer, Mar. 24, 1969; 1 son, Jacob Russell. B.S., U. Calif.-Berkeley, 1943, Ph.D., 1954. Jr. research biochemist U. Calif.-Berkeley, 1954-55; research assoc., instr. U. Chgo., 1955-57; assoc. chemist Western Regional Research Lab., Albany, Calif., 1957-61; asst. prof. U. Calif.-Davis, 1961-64, assoc. prof., 1964-73, prof., 1973-91, prof. emeritus, 1991—. Served to lt. (j.g.) USN, 1943-46. Mem. Am. Soc. Plant Physiologists, Am. Soc. Biochemists and Molecular Biologists, Biochem. Soc. London, Phytochem. Soc. N.Am., Phytochem. Soc. Europe, Inst. Food Technologists. Office: U Calif Dept Food Sci/Tech 109 FS and T Bldg Davis CA 95616-0207

MAZENKO, DONALD MICHAEL, aerospace engineering consultant, educator; b. Benld, Ill., July 11, 1925; s. Mike George and Anna Agnes (Kozak) M.; m. Joyce Christine Patrick, Apr. 22, 1950; children: Donna Nijmeh, Joyce Ann, Martha Jane Nishimura. Student, Mont. Sch. Mineral Sci. and Tech., 1944, U. Wash., 1945-46; BSME, U. Ill., 1949; MBA, U. Santa Clara, 1965. Tech. supt. Reynolds Metals Co., Listerhill, Ala., 1949-62; sr. staff engr. Lockheed Missiles and Space Co., Sunnyvale, Calif., 1962-89; cons. Reno, Nev., 1976—; instr. De Anza Community Coll., Cupertino, Calif. 1973—. Contbr. articles to profl. jours. Adv. bd. exec. com. South Reno Neighborhood; Lt. USNR, 1943-47. Fellow Soc. Advanced Material and Process Engring. (various offices); mem. Soc. Automotive Engrs., Aero. Material Specifications, Ascension Men's Club, KC (dep. grand knight 1958-62, grand knight Nev. coun. 1978, 90-91, controller 612 assembly 1992-93, navigator 612 assembly 1993-94), Delta Upsilon. Republican. Roman Catholic. Home: 13510 South Hills Dr Reno NV 89511

MAZO, ROBERT MARC, chemistry educator; b. Bklyn., Oct. 3, 1930; s. Nathan and Rose Marion (Mazo) M.; m. Joan Ruth Spector, Sept. 5, 1954; children: Ruth, Jeffrey, Daniel. B.A., Harvard U., 1952; M.S., Yale U., 1953, Ph.D., 1955. Research assoc. U. Chgo., 1956-58; asst. prof. Calif. Inst. Tech., 1958-62; assoc. prof. U. Oreg., Eugene, 1962-65; prof. chemistry U. Oreg., 1965—, head chemistry dept., 1978-81, dir. Inst. Theoretical Sci., 1964-67, 84-87, assoc. dean Grad. Sch., 1967-71; program dir NSF, 1977-78; Alfred P. Sloan fellow, NSF Sr. Postdoctoral fellow, vis. prof. U. Libre de Bruxelles, Belgium, 1968-69; vis. prof. Technische Hochschule Aachen, Weizmann Inst., Rehovoth, Israel, 1981-82, U. New South Wales, Australia, 1989. Author: Statistical Mechanical Theories of Transport Processes, 1967; also research articles. NSF Postdoctoral fellow U. Amsterdam, Netherlands, 1955-56. Mem. Am. Chem. Soc., Am. Phys. Soc., AAAS, AAUP. Home: 2460 Charnelton St Eugene OR 97405-3214 Office: U Oreg Inst Theoretical Sci Eugene OR 97403

MAZUR, MEREDITH MARGIE HANDLEY, reading educator; b. Tulsa, Mar. 27, 1941; d. Joyce Samuel and MaryPaul (Ellsworth) Handley; m. Don Leroy Mazur, Aug. 31, 1962 (div. Nov. 1974); children: Susan Diane, Michael. BA in Art, U. Tulsa, 1962, M of Teaching Arts in Spl. Edn., 1967; postgrad., Calif. State U., L.A., UCLA, Purdue U., Calumet, Ind., San Jose State U. Accredited tchr., reading specialist, adminstr., Calif. Classroom tchr. Tulsa Pub. Schs., 1963-65; fellow, clinician, diagnostician, instr. Mabee Reading Clinic, U. Tulsa, 1965-67; instr. So. Meth. U. Reading Clinic, Dallas, fall 1969; classroom tchr. L.A. Unified Sch. Dist., 1975-76; reading specialist Sierramont Middle Sch., Berryessa Union Sch. Dist., San Jose, Calif., 1976-87; tchr. Laneview Elem. Sch., 1989—; pvt. tutor, San Jose, 1976—; owner, operator Eastside Learning Ctr. and Reading Clinic, San Jose, 1978-82; Calif. lang. devel. tng. specialist, 1991. Cons., activist in women's and children's rights in child-support enforcement; chmn. child-support enforcement task force San Jose-South Bay chpt. NOW, 1984-85; mem. child support div. rev. ad-hoc. com. Santa Clara County Bd. Suprs. Entrance Exam. scholar U. Tulsa, 1959; John Mabee grad. fellow, 1966; recipient 1st place Bronze award Am. Waltz, Palo Alto, Calif., 1987, 1st Place Silver award Am. Fox Trot and Silver Viennese Waltz, Palo Alto, 1989. Mem. Women Leaders in Edn., Mortar Bd., Alpha Delta Kappa, Kappa Alpha Theta (chpt. pres. 1961-62). Mem. Bahai Faith Ch. Avocations: ballroom dancing, sailing, reading. Home: PO Box 32744 San Jose CA 95152-2744

MAZUREK, JOSEPH P., lawyer, state senator; b. San Diego, July 27, 1948; B.A., U. Mont., 1970, J.D., 1975; m. Patty Mazurek; 3 children. Bar: Mont. 1975; atty. Gough, Shanahan, Johnson, and Waterman, Helena, Mont.; mem. Mont. Senate from 23d Dist., 1981-92; atty. gen., State of Mont., 1993—; mem. Revenue Oversight Com., 1983-92; chmn. Senate Judiciary Com.; assoc. editor Mont. Law Rev., 1974-75. Served with U.S. Army, 1970-72. Mem. ABA, Beta Gamma Sigma, Phi Delta Phi, Phi Delta Theta. Office: Justice Bldg PO Box 201401 215 N Sanders 3rd Fl Helena MT 59620

MAZZA, JOHN GAMBLE, financial company executive; b. Trona, Calif., Nov. 8, 1945; s. Harold and Edith (Gamble) M.; m. Toni Swords Ferring, Dec. 31, 1981 (div. Aug. 1985); m. Robby Bertheau Fulton, Aug. 25, 1990. BA, Claremont McKenna Coll., 1967; MBA, U. So. Calif., 1969. Sec., treas., dir., chief fin. officer William O'Neil & Co. Inc., L.A., 1969-84; pres., dir. Drake Holding Co., Santa Monica, Calif., 1984—. Mem. Fin. Analysis Soc., Lincoln Club. Republican. Home: 6613 Zumirez Dr Malibu CA 90265-4312 Office: Drake Capital Inc 1250 4th St Santa Monica CA 90401-1353

MCALISTER, MAURICE L., savings and loan association executive; b. 1925; married. Pres., dir. Downey Savs. and Loan, Newport Beach, Calif., 1957—, chmn. bd. Office: Downey Savs & Loan Assn PO Box 6000 3501 Jamboree Rd Newport Beach CA 92660*

MCALLISTER, BYRON LEON, mathematics educator; b. Midvale, Utah, Apr. 29, 1929; s. Donald Leon and Julia Vilate (Roundy) McA.; m. Kay Marie Keithley, Nov. 29, 1957; children: Marie Elizabeth, Galen Arthur, Tamara Ann. BA, U. Utah, 1951, MA, 1955; PhD, U. Wis., 1966. Asst. prof. to assoc. prof. S.D. Sch. of Mines and Tech., Rapid City, 1958-67; assoc. prof. to prof. Mont. State U., Bozeman, 1967-91, prof. emeritus, 1991—; instr. U. Wis., Menasha, 1961-62. Contbr. articles to profl. jours. With U.S. Army, 1952-54. Mem. Am. Math. Soc., Math. Assn. of Am. Office: Mont State U Dept Math Scis Bozeman MT 59717

MCALLISTER, CHASE JUDSON, human resource director; b. Idaho Falls, Idaho, Apr. 23, 1942; s. Charles Thane and Margaret Frances (Witherspoon) McA.; children: Branden Jason, Frances Paige. Student, Idaho State U., 1960-63. Laborer Basic Am. Foods, Blackfoot, Idaho, 1965-66; mechanic Basic Am. Foods, Blackfoot, 1966-67, electrician, 1967-72, personnel mgr., 1972-77, mgr. labor rels., 1977-88, mgr. labor rels., safety and security, 1989, mgr. div. human resources, 1989-90, dir. human resources, 1990—; pension com. mem. Basic Am. Foods, Blackfoot, 1979—. Chmn. Blackfoot United Fund, 1977-78, Bingham County Personnel Adv. Coun., Blackfoot, 1981-83, Bingham Meml. Hosp. Bd. Dirs., 1989-91; pres. Eastern Idaho Am. Soc. for Pers. Adminstrn., Pocatello, 1978-79. Recipient Idaho State Outstanding Personnel Adminstr., 1977. Mem. Rotary, Soc. for Human Resource Adminstrn. (sr. profl. 1992). Episcopalian. Office: Basic Am Foods PO Box 592 Blackfoot ID 83221-0592

MCALLISTER, PETER MICHAEL, healthcare executive; b. Glendale, Calif., Mar. 27, 1938; s. Paul Blanchard and Blanche Isabell (Kirkpatrick) McA.; m. Diane Marie Williams, Feb. 4, 1961; children: Kevin Michael, Paul Scott, Kim Marie, Jeannie Isabella. BS in Indsl. Mgmt., U. So. Calif., 1961. Asst. plant dir. Krasne div. Royal Industries, L.A., 1968-69; dir. mgmt. engring. Am. Medicorp, Inc., L.A., 1970-73; chief oper. officer Sunrise Hosp., Las Vegas, Nev., 1973-82; adminstr. Huntington Park Community Hosp., L.A., 1982-83; cons. McAllister & Assocs., Las Vegas, 1983-84; salesman Americana Group Realtors, Las Vegas, 1984-85, Real Corp., Las Vegas, 1985-86; cons. Adelman & Assocs., Las Vegas, 1986-88; dir. mgmt. svcs. U. Med. Ctr., Las Vegas, 1988—. Capt. USMC, 1961-66, Vietnam. Decorated Air medal, Purple Heart. Mem. Nev. Hosp. Assn. (chmn. so. coun. 1975-76, pres. 1981-82). Home: 7435 Rogers St Las Vegas NV 89118-5750 Office: U Med Ctr 1800 W Charleston Blvd Las Vegas NV 89102-2329

MCALPINE, STEPHEN A., former lieutenant governor of Alaska, lawyer; b. Yakima, Wash., May 23, 1949; s. Robert Eugene and Myrtle B. (Loomis) McA.; m. Dana Sue Hill, Jan. 15, 1982; 1 child, Sean Michael. B.A., U. Wash., 1972; J.D., U. Puget Sound, 1976. Bar: Alaska. With Alaska Dept. Health and Social Svcs., Valdez, 1972-73; contracts adminstr. Fluor Alaska, Valdez, 1974-75; assoc. Law Offices James Ginotti, Valdez, 1977-80; pres. Ginotti & McAlpine, Valdez, 1980-82; lt. gov. State of Alaska, Juneau, 1982-91; of counsel Jermain, Dunnagan & Owens, Anchorage, 1991; bd. dirs. Enstar Nat. Gas, Commonwealth North; mem. Alaska Resource Devel. Coun., 1978—, exec. com. Council of State Govts., Nat. Conf. Lt. Govs., 1988. Mem. Valdez City Coun., 1979-82; mayor City of Valdez, 1980-82; bd. dirs. Alaska Mcpl. League, 1979-82; chmn. Westrends Bd. Dirs., 1989-90, Nat. Conf. Lt. Govs., 1988; del. Alaska Dem. Party Nat. Conv., 1980, 88. With USAR, 1968-71. Named Young Alaskan of Yr., Anchorage Jaycees, 1982; Toll fellow Council of State Govts., Lexington, 1988. Mem. Alaska Bar Assn., ABA, Assn. Trial Lawyers Am., Valdez Fisheries Devel. Assn., Nat. Assn. Secs. of States, Alaska Native Brotherhood, Am. Legion, Elks, Moose. Democrat. Roman Catholic. Office: Law Office Stephen McAlpine 605 W 2d Ave Ste 200 Anchorage AK 99501

MCANDREW, ELIZABETH PEET, electric utility executive; b. Ann Arbor, Mich., Feb. 9, 1953; d. Atwood Richardon Jr. and Martha Eunice Ann (Peet) McA. BS, U. Utah, 1977, MS, 1981. Cert. residential energy auditor, light comml. energy auditor. Engring. clk. Mountain Fuel Supply Co., Salt Lake City, 1978-79; rsch. specialist Utah Dept Natural Resources, Salt Lake City, 1981; pvt. contractor U.S. Rockwool Co., Salt Lake City, 1981-83; dir., gen. contractor Energy Works, Inc., Salt Lake City, 1982-86; mgr. energy conservation power dept. Murray (Utah) City Corp., 1986—, mem. recycling com., 1989—. Project coord. Mill Creek Canyon Clean-up, Wasatch Forest, Utah, 1979; mem. solar adv. com. Salt Lake Neighborhood Housing Svcs., 1980-84; leader bike trek Am. Lung Assn., Salt Lake City, 1989—. Recipient hist. preservation award Utah Hist. Soc., 1982, energy innovation award State of Utah, 1986, environ. achievement award Nat. Environ. Awards Coun., 1990; grantee U.S. Dept. Energy, 1981, Utah Energy Office, 1988. Mem. Nat. Assn. Women in Constrn. Office: Murray City Power Dept 171 West 4800 South Murray UT 84107

MCARTHUR, ELDON DURANT, geneticist, researcher; b. Hurricane, Utah, Mar. 12, 1941; s. Eldon and Denise (Dalton) McA.; m. Virginia Johnson, Dec. 20, 1963; children: Curtis D., Monica McArthur Bennion, Denise, Ted O. AS with high honors, Dixie Coll., 1963; BS cum laude, U. Utah, 1965, MS, 1967, PhD, 1970. Postdoctoral rsch. fellow, dept. demonstrator Agrl. Rsch. Coun. Gt. Britain, Leeds, Eng., 1970-71; rsch. geneticist Intermountain Rsch. Sta. USDA Forest Svc., Ephraim, Utah, 1972-75; rsch. geneticist Shrub Scis. Lab., Intermountain Rsch. Sta. USDA Forest Svc., Provo, Utah, 1975-83, project leader, chief rsch. geneticist, 1983—; adj. prof. dept. botany and range sci. Brigham Young U., Provo, 1976—. Author over 220 rsch. papers; contbr. chpts. to books; editor symposium procs. Grantee Sigma Xi, 1970, NSF, 1981, 85, USDA Coop. State Rsch. Svc., 1986, 91. Mem. Soc. Range Mgmt. (pres. Utah sect. 1987), Botan. Soc. Am., Soc. Study Evolution, Am. Genetic Assn., Shrub Rsch. Consortium (chmn. 1983—), Intermountain Consortium for Aridlands Rsch. (pres. 1991—). Mormon. Home: 555 N 1200 E Orem UT 84057-4350 Office: USDA Forest Svc Shrub Scis Lab 735 N 500 E Provo UT 84606-1899

MCARTHUR, JAMES DUNCAN, equipment leasing executive; b. Seattle, May 25, 1937; s. William Duncan and Madge Marie (Stutzman) McA.; m. Susan Wheeler, June 15, 1962 (div. 1972); children: Michael, Patrick; m. Vivian Stein, June 21, 1974 (div. 1984); children: Max, Peter; m. Michele Monteleone, Nov. 15, 1986; children: Jennifer, Jamie. BA in Econs. and Indsl. Engring., Stanford U., 1959. Mktg. rep. IBM, San Francisco and L.A., 1959-68; pres. Forsythe/McArthur Assocs., Inc., Chgo., 1970-84; mktg. exec. El Camino Resources, Inc., L.A., 1985-87; western regional mgr. Gen. Electric Capital Corp., L.A., 1987-89, Atlantic Computer Corp., L.A., 1989-90; pres. Classic Leasing Corp., L.A., 1990—; gen. ptnr. Pacific Access Captial, Sacramento, 1991—. 1st lt. infantry, U.S. Army, 1959-61. Mem. Computer Dealers and Lessors Assn. (bd. dirs. 1970-78), Fairbanks Ranch Country Club, Riviera Tennis Club, Zeta Psi. Home: 1638 San Remo Dr Pacific Palisades CA 90272-2741 Office: Classic Leasing Corp 1638 San Remo Dr Pacific Palisades CA 90272-2741

MCATEER, JAMES FRANCIS, lawyer; b. Seattle, Feb. 23, 1931; s. George Henry and Irene Mary (Ethier) McA.; m. Joan Francis Fitzpatrick, July 31, 1954 (div. Aug. 1977); children: Maryjeanne, Anne, Patricia, Margaret, Kathleen, Suzanne, Heidi; m. Judith Ann Gautsch, Jan. 24, 1978. Student, Santa Clara U., 1948-51; BS, U. Wash., 1953, JD, 1954. Bar: Wash. 1954, U.S. Supreme Ct. 1976. Asst. U.S. atty. for western dist. Wash., Seattle, 1959-62; ptnr. Lenihan, Ivers & McAteer, 1962-86, Schwabe, Williamson, Ferguson & Burdell, Seattle, 1986—. Mem. Law Rev., U. Wash., 1953-54. Capt. JAGC, U.S. Army, 1954-58. Mem. Wash. State Bar Assn., Seattle-King County Bar Assn., Wash. Athletic Club, Central Park Tennis Club, Order of Coif. Roman Catholic. Home: 2109 E Crescent Dr Seattle WA 98112 Office: Schwabe Williamson Ferguson & Burdell 1420 5th Ave Ste 3400 Seattle WA 98101

MCBEATH, GERALD ALAN, political science educator, researcher; b. Mpls., Sept. 13, 1942; s. Gordon Stanley and Astrid Elvira (Hjelmeir) McB.; m. Jenifer Huang, June 7, 1970; children: Bowen, Rowena. BA, U. Chgo., 1963, MA, 1964; PhD, U. Calif., Berkeley, 1970. Vis. asst. prof. polit. sci. Rutgers Coll., New Brunswick, N.J., 1970-72; asst. prof. John Jay Coll., CUNY, N.Y.C., 1972-74, 75-76; assoc. prof. Nat. Chengchi U., Mucha, Taipei, Taiwan, 1974-75; prof., dir. faculty devel. U. Alaska, Fairbanks, 1976—, acting dean coll. liberal arts, 1991-93; cons. Inst. Social and Econ. Research, Anchorage, 1976-77; contract researcher Alaska Dept. Natural Resources, Alaska Dept. Edn., Nat. Inst. Edn., others; staff dir. task force on internat. trade policy Rep. Conf., U.S. Senate. Sr. author: Dynamics of Alaska Native Self-Government, 1980; author monograph: North Slope Borough Government and Policymaking, 1981; jr. author: Alaska's Urban and Rural Governments, 1984; sr. editor Alaska State Government and Politics, 1987; editor: Alaska's Rural Development, 1982. Mem. bd. edn. Fairbanks North Star Borough, 1986—, pres. 1989-90, treas., 1991-93. Recipient Emil Usibelli Disting. Svc. award 1993; named Outstanding Faculty Mem., Assn. Students U. Alaska, Fairbanks, 1979, Alumni Assn. U. Alaska, Fairbanks, 1981; grantee Nat. Inst. Edn., 1980-83, Alaska Council on Sci. and Tech., 1982-84, Spencer Found., 1987-88. Mem. Asian Studies on Pacific Coast (program chmn. 1983, bd. dirs. 1982-83), Assn. Asian Studies, Western Polit. Sci. Assn. (mem. editorial bd. Western Govtl. Researcher), Am. Polit. Sci. Assn., Am. Soc. Pub. Adminstrn. (v.p. Alaskachpt.), Fairbanks N. Star Borough Bd. Edn. Democrat. Home: 1777 Red Fox Dr Fairbanks AK 99709-6625 Office: U Alaska Dept Polit Sci Fairbanks AK 99775

MCBEE, JERRY BURTON, academic program director; b. Wenatchee, Wash., Apr. 18, 1939; s. Virgil William and Lorna Angela (Grover) McB.; m. Helen Louise Cox, Aug. 29, 1963; children: Janet Louise, Keith Allen. BA in Speech, Pepperdine Coll., 1964; MEd in Counseling, U. Idaho, 1976. Dir. admissions Magic Valley Christian Coll., Albion, Idaho, 1967-69; counselor Dept. of Employment, Burley, Idaho, 1969-77; dean of students Columbia Christian Coll., Portland, Oreg., 1977-84; adminstr. Calif. Christian Sch., Sepulveda, 1984-87; dir. career ctr. Pepperdine U., Malibu, Calif., 1987—. Mem. Ch. of Christ. Office: Pepperdine U Career Ctr Malibu CA 90263-4184

MCBRIDE, CRIS DON, radiological technologist; b. Provo, Utah, Aug. 7, 1962; s. William Don and Eva Carol (Monson) McB. Student, Weber State U., Ogden, Utah, 1992. Lic. radiology technologist, Utah. Radiol. technologist St. Benedict's Hosp., Ogden, 1992—. Mem. Am. Assn. Radiol. Technologists, Utah Soc. Radiol. Technologists. Home: 1549 South 720 West Woods Cross UT 84087

MCBRIDE, FRANCIS DESALES, II, accountant; b. Chgo., May 9, 1962; s. Robert Joseph and Elaine Virginia (Ambagis) McB. BA in Liberal Arts, U. San Diego, 1986. Account exec. Baldoni Entertainment, L.A., 1987-88; dir. ops. WD&O/Silver State Commn., Washington, Las Vegas, 1988; sr. mktg. assoc. Am. Express IPS, Englewood, Colo., 1989-91; nat. sales mgr. Am. Express IPS, Englewood, 1991—; guest speaker U. Colo., Boulder, 1991—. Republican. Office: Amer Express 181 Inverness Dr W Englewood CO 80112

MCBRIDE, JOAN GREATRAKE, fundraising executive; b. Inglewood, Calif., Oct. 16, 1962; d. Edwin Arthur and Ruth Corinna (Scott) G.; m. James William McBride, Jan. 11, 1992. BA, U. Calif., 1983; MBA, Calif. State U., Long Beach, 1993. Cert. fundraising exec. Asst. dir. devel. St. Francis Med. Ctr., Lynwood, Calif., 1983-84, Downey (Calif.) Community Hosp., 1984-87; dir. spl. projects Hoag Hosp., Newport Beach, Calif., 1987-93; dir. fund devel. Corona (Calif.) Regional Med. Ctr., 1993—. 1st v.p. Soroptimist Internat., Newport Beach, 1990-92. Mem. Nat. Assn. Hosp. Devel., Southern Calif. Assn. Hosp. Devel. (sec. 1991, treas. 1992), Assn. Healthcare Philanthropy (region X sec. 1989). Home: 2776 Monza Tustin CA 92680 Office: Corona Regional Med Ctr 800 S Main Corona CA 91720

MC BRIDE, JOHN ALEXANDER, retired chemical engineer; b. Altoona, Pa., Mar. 29, 1918; s. Raymond E. and Carolyn (Tinker) McB.; m. Elizabeth Anne Vogel, Aug. 28, 1942; children: Katherine M. Harris, Susan McBride Malick, Carolyn McBride Nafziger. A.B., Miami U., Oxford, Ohio, 1940; M.Sc., Ohio State U., 1941; Ph.D., U. Ill., 1944. Registered profl. engr., Calif. Various positions in research and devel. dept. Phillips Petroleum Co., 1944-58, 59-65; dir. chem. tech. Phillips Petroleum Co. (Atomic energy div.), 1963-65; chief applications engring. Astrodyne, Inc., 1958-59; dir. div. materials licensing AEC, 1965-70; v.p. E.R. Johnson Assocs., Inc., Oakton, Va., 1970-92; asst. gen. mgr. Nuclear Chems. & Metals Corp., 1970-71; Adviser U.S. del. 3d Internat. Conf. Peaceful Uses Atomic Energy, 1964. Author articles. Mem. Am. Chem. Soc., Am. Inst. Chem. Engrs. (chmn. nuclear engring. div. 1966, Robert E. Wilson award 1991), Am. Nuclear Soc., Alpha Chi Sigma, Phi Kappa Tau. Home: 1727 Sherman Ave Canon City CO 81212-4354 Address: PO Box 1482 Canon City CO 81215-1482

MCBRIDE, LAURIE, lobbyist; b. L.A., June 8, 1949; m. Donna Yutzy, May 17, 1985. BA, U. of the Pacific, 1971. Exec. dir. LIFE AIDS Lobby (Lobby for Individual Freedom & Equality), Sacramento, 1990—; co-chair Mobilization Against AIDS, 1988-90; v.p. polit. action Stonewall Gay Dem. Club, 1990-91, v.p. membership, 1989-90, treas., 1988-89; co-chair No on 69/No on 64 Grassroots Organizing/CAN, 1986-87; chair Community Partnership on AIDS, 1984-86; sec. Golden Gate Bus. Assn., 1982-83, pres., 1984-86; prs. GGBA Found./now Horizons, 1983-84. Talk show host Rubyfruit Terr, KITS FM 105.3, 1989-90. Mem. Bay Area Career Women (chair community rels. 1988-89), Statewide Lobby Assn. on AIDS and Gay/Lesbian Issues. Office: Lobby for Indiv Freedom & Equality 926 J St # 1020 Sacramento CA 95814

MCBRIDE, SHERRY LOUEEN (SHARON MCBRIDE), magazine editor; b. Eureka, Kans., Aug. 1, 1937; d. Marvin Chester and Vera Minnie Shaw; m. William Thomas McBride Jr., Sept. 12, 1959 (div. Apr. 1972); children: Erin, Sean. BA, UCLA, 1964. Mng. editor Hi-Way Herald TL Enterprises, Agoura, Calif., 1979-81, editor Hi-Way Herald, 1981-83, mng. editor MotorHome mag., 1983-84, sr. editor MotorHome and Trailer Life mags., 1984-90; mng. editor Trailer Life mag., 1990—; sr. editor Trailer Life's Campground & RV Svcs. Directory, 1989-91. Mem. Western Publs. Assn. Democrat.

MCBRIDE, WILLIAM, legal consultant, transportation company executive; b. Pitts., June 21, 1928; s. Albert Sr. and Mabelle (Danhart) McB.; m. Jennie Francis Pelloni, Sept. 30, 1960; children: Blair A. Weaver, Dale W. Weaver, Scott R. Weaver, Lorraine D. BA, U. Pitts., 1953; JD, Dickinson Sch. Law, 1956. Safety inspector U.S. Steel Corp., Ellwood City, Pa., 1957-60; tng. rep. N. Am. Aviation, Anaheim, Calif., 1960-65; mgr. personnel services Food Giant Markets, Santa Fe Springs, Calif., 1965-66; adminstr. employee relations Auto Club So. Calif., Los Angeles, 1967-71, asst. mgr. safety and security, 1971-83, adminstr. safety, 1983-88, staff cons., mem. legal svcs., 1988-93; ret.; instr. N. Orange County Jr. Coll. Dist., Anaheim, Calif., 1965-70, Cerritos Coll., Norwalk, Calif., 1968. Dist. chmn. Boy Scouts Am., Ellwood City, 1957-59; petitioner Various Civic Causes, Los Angeles, 1975—; communicator State and Fed. Reps., Sacramento and Washington, 1975—; mem. bus. adv. com. Rep. Assemblyman Frank Hill, 1986-91; donor Heritage Found., Washington, 1983—, Rep. Presdl. Task Force, Washington, 1980—. Served to sgt. USAF, 1946-53, PTO. Mem. Am. Soc. Safety Engrs. Lodges: Masons, Shriners (life). Office: Auto Club So Calif 2601 S Figueroa St Los Angeles CA 90007-3294

MCBURNETT, ROBERT KEITH, child and adolescent psychology educator, researcher; b. Brunswick, Ga., Feb. 10, 1953; s. Kenneth Stewart and Betty Jean (Pilgrim) McB. BA, U. Ga., 1976, MS, 1985, PhD with honors, 1989. Lic. psychologist, Calif. Juvenile svc. staff Clarke County Youth Dept. Ct., Athens, Ga., 1974-76; rsch. asst. psychology dept. U. Ga., Athens, 1977-78, 85-87; behavior specialist Elbert County Mental Retardation Ctr., Elberton, Ga., 1979-81, Barrow County Mental Retardation Ctr., Winder, Ga., 1980-87; mental health profl. WPIC ADD program U. Pitts., 1987; psychology intern Rusk Inst., Bellevue Hosp./NYU Med. Ctr., N.Y.C., 1987-88; psychologist Child Devel. Ctr., U. Calif., Irvine, 1989-90; asst. prof. dept. pediatrics U. Calif., Irvine, 1990—, dir. rsch. and clin. tng. div. child devel. pediatrics dept., 1992—; reviewer Leon Lowenstein Found., 1992. Contbr. articles to profl. jours., book chpts. to publs. in field. NIMH grantee, 1991-93; recipient NIMH Rsch. Scientist Devel. award 1993-98. Mem. Am. Psychol. Assn., Am. Psychol. Soc., Assn. for Advancement Behavior Therapy, Soc. Rsch. in Child and Adolescent Psychopathology, Profl. Group for Attention and Related Disorders, Phi Beta Kappa. Office: Univ Calif Child Devel Ctr 19262 Jamboree Blvd Irvine CA 92715

MCBURNEY, GEORGE WILLIAM, lawyer; b. Ames, Iowa, Feb. 17, 1926; s. James William and Elfie Hazel (Jones) McB.; m. Georgianna Edwards, Aug. 28, 1949; children: Hollis Lynn, Jana Lee McBurney-Lin, John Edwards. B.A., State U. Iowa, 1950, J.D. with distinction, 1953. Bar: Iowa 1953, Ill. 1954, Calif. 1985. With Sidley & Austin and predecessor, Chgo., 1953—, ptnr., 1964—; resident ptnr. Singapore, 1982-84. Editor-in-chief: Iowa Law Rev., 1952-53. Mem. Chgo. Crime Commn., 1966-84; trustee Iowa Law Sch. Found., 1988—, Old People's Home of City of Chgo., 1968-83, sec., 1967-69, exec. v.p., 1969-74, pres., 1974-82, hon. life trustee, 1983—; hon. life trustee Georgian, Evanston, Ill., trustee, counsel, 1976-82, v.p., 1980-82. Served with inf. AUS, 1944-46. Fellow Am. Coll. Trial Lawyers, Am. Bar Found.; mem. ABA, State Bar of Calif., Los Angeles County Bar Assn., Fed. Bar Assn., Am. Judicature Soc., Bar Assn. 7th Fed. Circuit, Am. Arbitration Assn. (panelist large complex dispute resolution program), Assn. Bus. Trial Lawyers, The Ctr. for Internat. Comml. Arbitration L.A. (bd. dirs., exec. v.p.), Nat. Coll. Edn. (bd. assocs. 1967-84), U.S. C. of C. (govt. and regulatory affairs com. of council on antitrust policy 1980-82), L.A. Complex Litigation Inn of Ct., Law Soc. Singapore (hon.), Western Ctr. on Law and Poverty (bd. dirs. 1992—), L.A. Union League Club (vet.), Law Club (life), Legal Club, Mid-Day Club Chgo., Am. Club, Cricket Club, Town Club Singapore, Phi Kappa Psi, Omicron Delta Kappa, Delta Sigma Rho, Phi Delta Phi. Republican. Presbyterian. Home: Malibu Pacifica 13 3601 Vista Pacifica Malibu CA 90265-4830 Office: Sidley and Austin Ste 4000 555 W 5th St Los Angeles CA 90013-1010

MCCABE, RICHARD LEE, real estate developer; b. Cheyenne, Wyo., June 9, 1943; s. Thomas Junior and Alice May (Vernon) McC.; m. Janet Ann Lefkow (div.); children: Bradley Samuel, Kevin Ira; m. Julianne Clements, Dec. 22, 1979; children: Thomas Durant, Claire Angela Kim. BArch., U. Colo., 1967. V.p., sec. McSan Enterprises, Inc., Boulder, 1968-72; pres. Boulder (Colo.) Design & Tool Group, Inc., 1972-74; pvt. practice R.L. McCabe & Assocs., Boulder, 1974-77; pres. R.L.M. Inc., Boulder, 1977-80, Cubit Corp., Boulder, 1980-84, Centermark Corp., Boulder, 1984-87, Cubit Constrn. Corp., Boulder, 1987-88, Core Corp., Boulder, 1988—; dir. Boulder (Colo.) Builders Group, 1988-89, Nat. Fastpitch Assn., Boulder, 1990—; pres. Boulder County Builders Assn., 1990-91. Co-author: (mcpl. legislation) Community Housing Assistance Plan, 1991. Mem. Affordable Housing Task Force, Boulder, 1989, Thistle Community Housing Corp., Boulder, 1991. Recipient Svc. award Assn. Student Chpts. of AIA, 1966, award of appreciation City Boulder Housing Authority, 1989, cert. award Dept. Housing and Human Svcs., Boulder, 1990, cert. appreciation Boulder County Safehouse, 1991. Mem. Boulder County Chpt. of the Met. Denver Home Builders Assn. (pres. 1991-92). Home: 526 Arapahoe Ave Boulder CO 80302 Office: Core Corp 4845 Pearl East Cir #302 Boulder CO 80301

MC CAFFREY, STANLEY EUGENE, university president; b. Taft, Calif., Feb. 26, 1917; s. Joseph Cormack and Dorothy (Bunyard) McC.; m. Beth Conolley, July 6, 1941 (div. Jan. 1991); children: Stephen Conolley, Nancy (dec.); m. Sue Richardson Heapes, Apr. 26, 1992. A.B., U. Calif., 1938; LL.D. (hon.), Golden Gate U., 1972, Pepperdine U., 1978, Korea U., 1981. Personnel work Standard Oil Co., Calif., 1939-40; coordinator vets. affairs U. Calif. at Berkeley, 1946, v.p., exec. asst., 1957-60; exec. mgr. Alumni Assn., 1948-56; advt. mgr. Kaiser Aluminum, Oakland, Calif., 1946-48; exec. asst. to Vice Pres. U.S., 1960; pres., exec. officer San Francisco Bay Area Council, 1960-71; pres. U. Pacific, Stockton, Calif., 1971-87. Mem. Vets. Bd. Calif., chmn., 1956; del. Gov's Conf. on Children and Youth, 1956; mem. Berkeley Recreation Commn., v.p., 1957; mem. Oakland Manpower Commn., 1965-67, State Commn. on Government Orgn. and Economy, 1966-68; Dir. Berkeley Community Chest, 1952-55, Berkeley YMCA, 1953-54, Internat. House; pres. Berkeley Service Club Council, 1954-55; Trustee Peralta Jr. Coll. Dist., 1962-68, pres., 1964-66; trustee U. Calif. Alumni Found., Pacific Med. Center, San Francisco, Golden Gate U.; governing mem. San Francisco YMCA, 1960-66; bd. advisers Nat. Indsl. Coll. of U.S. Armed Forces, 1964-66. Served from ensign to lt. comdr. USNR, 1940-45; capt. Res. Decorated Silver Star, Legion of Merit. Mem. Am. Alumni Council (treas. 1952-54), Am. Legion, Big C Soc. of U. Calif. (dir. 1948-57), Internat. House-Assn. (nat. exec. com. 1955-60), Assn. Ind. Cal. Colls. and Univs. (v.p. 1975-76, pres. 1976-78), Western Coll. Assn. (exec. com., pres. 1979-80), Ind. Colls. No. Calif. (dir.), Navy League (v.p. San Francisco council 1966), Order of Golden Bear, Phi Beta Kappa, Pi Sigma Alpha. Conglist. Clubs: Rotary (pres. Berkeley 1954-55, dist. gov. 1964-65, chmn. internat. youth com. 1966-67, internat. dir. 1969-71, 1st v.p. 1970-71, research com. 1976, nominating com. 1976, 79, internat. pres. 1981-82); Tennis (Berkeley) (dir. 1952-55); Berkeley Fellows (U. Calif.), Family (San Francisco), Commonwealth of Calif. (San Francisco) (quar. chmn. 1955, gov.), Bohemian (San Francisco), St. Francis Yacht (San Francisco), Moraga Country, Rotary (chmn. found trustees 84-85). Address: 557 Augusta Dr Moraga CA 94556

MCCAFFRY, BARBARA LESCH, academic administrator, English educator; b. Bklyn., June 14, 1947; d. Samuel and Anne (Rappaport) Lesch; m. Michael J. McCaffry, May 20, 1984. BA, Bklyn. Coll., 1968; MA, U. Maryland, 1970; PhD, U. Wis.-Madison, 1979. Instr. dept. liberal studies U. Wis.-Ctr. System, Madison, 1975-80; coord. affirmative action and minority/disadvantaged programs U. Wis., Madison, 1978-80; dir. affirmative action Sonoma State U., Rohnert Park, Calif., 1980—, vis. lectr.dept. English, 1982—; cons. Sonoma State U. Enterprises, Inc., Acad. Found., Sonoma State, Rohnart Park, Calif., 1980—, City of Santa Rosa, Calif., 1988, Calif. Maritime Acad., Vallejo, 1992—. Author: Basil Bunting Dictionary of Lit. Biography, 1983; contbr. articles to profl. jours.; presenter in field. Founding mem. Community Affirmative Action Forum of Sonoma County, Santa Rosa, Calif., 1981. Administrv. Fellow Calif. State U., San Jose State U., 1984-85; recipient affirmative action program award, Community Affirmative Action Forum, Sonoma County, Calif., 1989. Mem. MLA, Nat. Poetry Found., Nat. Women's Studies Assn., Women's Coun. of the Sate Univ. (treas. 1990-92, corres. sec. 1992—). Home: 18 Frederick Dr Rohnert Park CA 94928-1382 Office: Sonoma State U 1801 E Cotati Ave Rohnert Park CA 94928

MCCAHAN, JOSEPH BRUCE, certified public accountant; b. Riverside, N.J., Dec. 23, 1931; s. Joseph and Miriam (Carter) McC.; m. Sandra Keeney, Mar. 19, 1954 (div. 1964); m. Roselyn A. Brewer, Dec. 12, 1964; children: Lori Lynn Brickley, Randal Bruce, Jeffrey Scott, Jennifer Megan. AA, San Jose City Coll., 1956; BA, San Jose State U., 1958. CPA, Calif. Staff acct. Hood, Worley & Gre CPAs, San Jose, Calif., 1957; staff acct. T.C. Worley & Co. CPAs, San Jose, Calif., 1957-61, partner, 1961-65; partner Worley, McCahan, Farman & Co. CPAs, San Jose, Calif., 1966-67; prin. J. Bruce McCahan & Co. CPAs, San Jose, Calif., 1967-72, J. Bruce McCahan Accountancy Corp., San Jose, Calif., 1973-78; CEO McCahan, Helfrick Thiercof & Butera Accountancy Corp., San Jose, Calif., 1979—; speaker various orgns. Mem. AICPA, Calif. Soc. CPAs, Alpha Eta Sigma, Beta Gamma Sigma, Phi Kappa Phi. Republican. Office: McCahan et al CPAs 1655 Willow St San Jose CA 95125

MCCAIN, JOHN SIDNEY, III, senator; b. Panama Canal Zone, Aug. 29, 1936; s. John Sidney and Roberta (Wright) McC.; m. Cindy Hensley, May 17, 1980; children: Doug., Andy, Sidney, Meghan, Jack, Jim. Grad. U.S. Naval Acad., 1958; grad., Nat. War Coll., 1973-74. Commd. ensign U.S. Navy, 1958, capt., navy pilot, 1977; prisoner of war Hanoi, Vietnam, 1967-73; dir. Navy Senate Liaison Office, Washington, 1977-81; mem. 98th-99th Congress from 1st Ariz. Dist.; U.S. senator from Ariz., 1987—. Bd. dirs. Community Assistance League, Phoenix, 1981-82. Decorated Legion of Merit; decorated Silver Star, Bronze Star, Purple Heart, D.F.C., Vietnamese Legion of Honor. Mem. Soc. of the Cin., Am. Legion, VFW. Republican. Episcopalian. Office: US Senate 111 Russell Senate Office Bldg Washington DC 20510-0303*

MCCALL, STEPHEN SHAWN, philanthropist; b. Balt., July 29, 1950; s. Henry David and Olivia Genevieve (Gunkel) McC.; m. Irene Takeko Kitagawa, Feb. 24, 1985; children: Emily Teiko, Stephen Hideo. BS, Towson State U., 1972. Educator Balt. City Pub. Sch. System, 1972-79; trainer, tech. writer Hawaii Med. Svcs. Assn., Honolulu, 1990—; founder, pres. Johanna Hawkins Meml. Inst. for the Humanities, Inc., Honolulu, 1984—. Mem. Am. Mensa Ltd. Democrat. Home: 3249 Hoolulu St Honolulu HI 96815-3840 Office: Johanna Hawkins Meml Inst Humanities Inc 3249 Honolulu St Honolulu HI 96815-3840

MCCALL, WILLIAM CALDER, oil and chemical company executive; b. Hoquiam, Wash., Feb. 1, 1906; s. Dougall Hugh and Hughena (Calder) McC.; m. Marian Hall, Mar. 22, 1946; children—Ernest, Robert. Student U. Oreg., 1924-28; LHD Lewis & Clark Coll., 1992. Asst. sales mgr. Anaconda Sales Co., Chgo., 1932-39; chmn. McCall Oil & Chem. Corp., Portland, Oreg., 1939—, Gt. Western Chem. Co., Portland, 1955—, Chemax, Inc., Portland, 1975—; dir. Oreg. Bank, Portland, King Broadcasting Co., Seattle. Pres. Oreg. Art Mus., Portland; trustee Lewis and Clark Coll., Portland; exec. v.p. Oreg. Symphony Soc.; dir. Med. Research Found., Good Samaritan Hosp. Found., Portland. Republican. Episcopalian. Clubs: Eldorado Country (Indian Wells, Calif.) (pres. 1978-79); Arlington (Portland); Pacific-Union (San Francisco); Los Angeles Country, Vintage (Palm Desert, Calif.), Waverley Country, Rainier (Seattle). Office: McCall Oil and Chem Corp 808 SW 15th Ave Portland OR 97205-1907

MCCALLISTER, WREN VANCE, building services company executive; b. Seattle, Aug. 14, 1969; s. Warren Vance and Sanora Jean (Hansen) McC. AA, Shoreline C.C., 1992. Founder Titan Maint. Co., Seattle, 1988-90; chmn., chief exec. officer Eastlake Bldg. Maint., Inc., Seattle, 1990—. Mem. Bldg. Svc. Contrs. Assn. Internat. (selected to svc. on 1991 membership com., candidate for registered bldg. svc. mgr.), Cleaning Mgmt. Inst. Republican. Office: Eastlake Bldg Maint Inc 19924 Aurora Ave N # 152 Seattle WA 98133-3526

MCCAMMAN, JOHN WILLIAM, county administrator; b. Ventura, Calif., May 26, 1953; s. Kenneth Taylor and Gertrude Mary (Wachob) McC.; m. Joan Rae Guissi, May 1, 1982; children: Meaghan Anne, Sarah kathleen, Michael John. BA, U. Calif., Santa Barbara, 1975; MA in Pub. Adminstrn., Sonoma State U., 1982. Adminstrv. analyst County of Sonoma, Santa Rosa, Calif., 1979-87; county adminstr. County of Mariposa, Calif., 1987-92, County of Shasta, Calif., 1993—. Sec. bd. United Way Mariposa-Yosemite, 1990-92. Mem. County Adminstrsv. Officers Assn., Internat. City/County Mgrs. Assn. Office: County of Shasta 1815 Yuba St Redding CA 96001

MCCANCE, THOMAS LAWRENCE, airline pilot; b. Munich, Apr. 26, 1952; came to the U.S., 1953; s. Donovan Low and Dorothy Lee (Endom) M.; m. Cindy Lou Garrettson, Feb. 4, 1976 (div. Jan. 1978); 1 child, Michelle; m. Shell Lynn Stott, April 20, 1991; 1 stepdaughter, Gina Kizerian. BS in Chem., USAF Acad., 1974; MA in Bus., Ctrl. Mich. U., 1976. Cert. airline transport pilot. Capt. USAF, N.C., Nev., Calif., Ariz., 1974-81; KC-135 copilot 911 Air Refueling SQ, Goldsboro, N.C., 1975-77; T-39 instr. pilot DET 1, 1401 MAJ, Omaha, Neb., 1977-81; transp. analyst 1401st MAS, Las Vegas, 1981-85; BAE 146 first officer Pacific Southwest Airlines, San Francisco, Calif., 1985-87; MD80 1st officer USAIR, L.A., 1987-89; F28 capt. USAIR, Charlotte, N.C., 1989-90; 737-300 1st officer USAIR, L.A., 1990-93; owner, mgr. Mack's Aircrew Shop, Las Vegas, Nev., 1993—. Mem. Nat. Assn. of Realtors, Airline Pilots Assn. Office: Mack's Aircrew Shop PO Box 93056 Las Vegas NV 89193

MC CANDLESS, ALFRED A. (AL MC CANDLESS), congressman; b. Brawley, Calif., July 23, 1927; s. Max T. and Fleta (Beaty) Mc C.; m. Gail W. Glass, Nov. 26, 1982; children: Cristina, Alfred A., Craig, Blaine, Ward. B.A. in Polit. Sci. and Pub. Adminstrn., UCLA, 1951. Mem. Riverside County Bd. Supvrs., Calif., 1971-82, chmn. bd., 1971-72, 80-81; founder McCandless Motors, Indio, Calif., 1953-75; mem. 98th-103rd Congresses from 37th (now 44th) dist. Calif., 1983—. Founding mem. South Coast Air Quality Mgmt. Dist.; founding mem. Sunline Transit Agy.; founder Coachella Valley Assn. Govts.; exec. com., dir. County Suprs. Assn. Calif.; bd. dirs. Coachelle Valley Housing Coaltion. Served to capt. USMC, 1945-46, 50-52. Mem. Indio Co. of C. (hon. life), Greater Riverside C. of C. Lodge: Indio Rotary (past pres.). Office: US Ho of Reps 2422 Rayburn House Office Bldg Washington DC 20515

MCCANN, DEAN MERTON, lawyer, former pharmaceutical company executive; b. Ontario, Calif., Mar. 13, 1927; s. James Arthur and Alma Anis (Hawes) McC.; m. Carol Joan Geissler, Mar. 23, 1957. AA, Chaffey Coll., 1948; BS in Pharmacy, U. So. Calif., 1951; JD, U. Calif., San Francisco, 1954; LLM, NYU, 1955. Bar: Calif. 1955; lic. pharmacist, Calif. Pharmacist San Francisco and Ontario, 1951-54; sole practice law Los Angeles, 1955-60; ptnr. MacBeth, Ford & Brady, Los Angeles, 1960-65, McCann & Berger, Los Angeles, 1965-68; v.p., sec. and gen. counsel Allergan Pharms., Inc., Irvine, Calif., 1968-78; sr. v.p., sec., gen. counsel Allergan, Inc., Irvine, 1978-89; pvt. practice Irvine, 1989—; instr. pharmacy law U. So. Calif., Los Angeles, 1956-68; exec. v.p. Pharm. Wholesaler Assn., Los Angeles, 1956-68. Mem., past. chmn. bd. counsellors Sch. Pharmacy U. So. Calif., Los Angeles, 1975—, mem., past chmn. QSAD centurion, 1963—. Served with USNR, 1945-46. Fellow Food and Drug Law Inst., 1954-55; recipient Outstanding Alumni Award Sch. Pharmacy U. So. Calif., 1973. Mem. ABA, Calif. Bar Assn., Orange County Bar Assn., Am. Pharm. Assn., Calif. Pharm. Assn., Orange County Pharm. Assn., U. So. Calif. Pharmacy Alumni Assn. (past pres., oustanding alumni award, 1973), Newport Beach Country Club, Balboa Bay Club, Skull and Dagger Club, Phi Delta Chi. Republican. Home: 21 Rockingham Dr Newport Beach CA 92660-4219 Office: 2525 Dupont Dr Irvine CA 92715-1599

MCCANN, JACK ARLAND, former construction and mining equipment company executive, consultant; b. Chestnut, Ill., Apr. 16, 1926; s. Keith Ogden and Miriam Imogene McC.; m. Marian Adele Gordon, Mar. 31, 1956; 1 son, Christopher John. A.B., Bradley U., 1950. Mgr. Washington Office, R.G. LeTourneau Inc., 1950-53; mgr. def. and spl. products Westinghouse Air Brake Co., 1958-64, mgr. nat. accounts, 1964-67, mng. dir. Belgian plant and European mktg., 1967-70; gen. sales mgr. WABCO div. Am. Standard Inc., Peoria, Ill., 1970-73, v.p. mktg., 1973-80, v.p. staff, 1980-82; ret., 1982; now cons. With USNR, 1944-46. Decorated chevalier Ordre de la Couronne (Belgium). Mem. Nat. Def. Transp. Assn. (life), U.S. C. of C., Am. Legion, Bradley Chiefs Club, Country Club Green Valley (v.p., dir.), Green Valley Rep. Club (bd. dirs.), Shriners, Masons.

MCCANN, WILLIAM VERN, JR., lawyer; b. Lewiston, Idaho, June 10, 1943; s. William V. and Anna Gertrude (Hoss) McC.; children: Malinda Ann, William Vern III. BS in Bus., U. Idaho, 1966, JD, 1969. Bar: Idaho 1969, U.S. Dist. Ct. Idaho 1969, U.S. Supreme Ct. 1974. Pvt. practice law Lewiston, 1969—. Pres. Lewiston Roundup Assn., 1977, 86; chmn. Lewiston Airport Commn., 1987-93; master of ceremonies Lewiston Jr. Miss Pageant, 1985-93, Idaho Jr. Miss Pageant, 1987; sec. Lewis & Clark Air Festival Inc., 1988-90; pres. Lewis Clark Am. festival, 1990-92; v.p. Port City Action Corp., Inc., 1988-89, pres., 1989-90. Mem. Idaho Bar Assn. (commr. 1983-86, pres. 1985-86, Dues Evaluation com. 1987-88, Lead Team 1989—), Clearwater Bar Assn. (v.p. 1980, pres. 1981-83, chmn. of Clearwater Bar Bench-Bar Liaison Com. 1986-89), Lawyer-Pilot Bar Assn., Internat. Platform Assn., U.S. Jaycees (v.p. 1974-75, legal counsel 1975-76, amb. 1974, pres. Found. 1984, trustee 1980-83, Hall of Leadership 1984, War Meml. bd. dirs. 1988—). Lodge: Elks. Office: 1027 Bryden Ave Lewiston ID 83501-5352

MCCARDELL, HARRIETT WYNN See STAMBAUGH, HARRIETT MCCARDELL

MC CARDLE, RANDALL RAYMOND, real estate developer; b. Phila., Sept. 2, 1931; s. Russell Henry and Ruth Hertha (Snyder) McC.; m. Yong Suk; 1 child, Mark. AA, Orange Coast Coll., 1956; BA, Chapman Coll., 1958, MA, 1966; PhD, Western Colo. U., 1974; Real estate broker, Newport Beach, Calif., 1953-61; founder, pres. The Real Estaters, Orange County, Calif., 1961—, Treeco Escrow Co., Inc., Costa Mesa, Calif., 1971—; founder Bank of Costa Mesa, 1972, dir. bus. devel., 1973—; also newspaper columnist, lectr., investment counselor. Fund-raising chmn. Boys' Club of Am., Harbor area, 1979-80; bd. dirs. Boys Club Harbor Area; mem. adv. com. Orange Coast Coll., 1964—, Golden West Coll., 1969—; dir. Harbor Ridge Masters, 1990. With USNR, 1950-53. Recipient Appreciation award Bd. Realtors, 1967, 68, 70, 76, 80, UN citation; inducted into Orange Coast Coll. Hall of Fame, 1983; named Realtor of Yr., 1989. Mem. Calif. Assn. Realtors (state dir. 1963-67), Calif. Assn. Real Estate Tchrs. (state dir. 1966-80), Orange County Coast Assn. (dir. 1974—), C. of C., Nat. Assn. Real Estate Appraisers, Bd. Realtors (pres. 1966-67 long-range planning com. 1981), U. So. Calif. Faculty Assn., Red Baron Flying Club, Mason, Shriner. Contbr. articles to profl. jours. Home: 12 Geneve Newport Beach CA 92660-6813 Office: 1000 Quail St Ste 260 Newport Beach CA 92660-2721

MCCARTHY, BEA, state legislator; b. Great Falls, Mont., Apr. 17, 1935; d. Robert Joseph and Rose Mary (Krier) McKenna; m. Edward Joseph McCarthy, June 27, 1959; children: Colleen, Mary, Edward Jr., Patrick, John. BS in Elem Edn., Mont. State U., 1957. Tchr. 1st grade Anaconda, Mont.; rep. dist. 66 Mont. State Legis., 1991—. Mem. Mont. Bd. Regents, 1983-90, Mont. Bd. Edn., 1983-90. Mem. Am. Legion Aux., Ladies Ancient Order Hibernians (past pres.), Phi Beta Phi, Delta Kappa Gamma. Democrat. Roman Catholic. Home: 1906 Ogden Anaconda MT 59711

MCCARTHY, BETTY LYNNE GRUE, rancher; b. Miles City, Mont., Aug. 7, 1959; d. Charles M. and Helen M. (Warner) Grue; m. Sean M. McCarthy, June 2, 1990. BS, Ea. Wyo. Coll., 1979. Vdt. technician Circle (Mont.) Vet. Clinic, 1979-80; treas. Grue Ranch, Inc., Terry, Mont., 1980—; poet state and regional cowboy poetry gatherings, Mont., Nev., Oreg., Nebr., Wyo., Ariz., N.D., S.D., Alta. Author: Frost on the Fork Handle, 1987, Charmin Fourbuckles, 1990; co-author cassette tape You Want Me To Do What??!!!, 1988; contbr. articles to Western Horseman. Vice chmn. Prairie County Planning Bd., Terry, 1992—. Mem. Am. Quarter Horse Assn.

MCCARTHY, BEVERLY FITCH, retired civic leader, educator; b. St. Louis, Aug. 10, 1933; d. Clyde and Elsie (Graf) Fitch; m. Carl M. Bosque, Sept. 13, 1958 (div. 1973); children: Charles, Elizabeth; m. John Linley McCarthy, Mar. 17, 1973. AA, L.A. City Coll., 1953; BA in Social Scis., U. Calif., Berkeley, 1955; MA in Edn., Stanford U., 1957; adminstrv. credential, U. Pacific, 1980. Mem. faculty Monterey (Calif.) Peninsula Coll., 1957-58, Santa Barbara (Calif.) City Coll., 1958-59, San Jose (Calif.) City Coll., 1959-60; tchr. Bret Harte High Sch., Angels Camp, Calif., 1960-62; instr. psychology San Joaquin Delta Coll., Stockton, Calif., 1962-85, dir. reentry program for women and men, 1974-85; mem. Stockton City Coun., Calif., 1990-92; ret., 1992. Pres. Assistance League Stockton, 1969-71, Dem. Women's Club San Joaquin County, 1987, San Joaquin chpt. Nat. Women's Polit. Caucus, 1982, Stockton Symphony Assn., 1973-77, Stockton Opera Guild, 1977-78, 87-89, Stockton Civic Theatre League, 1981-82, San Joaquin County Child Abuse Prevention Coun. Aux., 1989-90; chmn. Stockton Redevel. Commn., 1986, San Joaquin County Commn. on Status Women, 1974-82, San Joaquin Family Resource and Referral Employer-Assisted Child Care Coalition, 1986-89; elected Jr. Aid Stockton, 1993. Recipient Woman of Yr. award Soroptimist Club, Stockton, 1970, 74, arts recognition award Stockton Arts Commn., 1978, Women of Achievement award San Joaquin County Commn. on Status Women, 1983; Rosalie M. Stern award U. Calif.-Berkeley Alumni Assn., 1976, Alumni citation, 1985. Mem. AAUW (named gift Ednl. Found. 1977-78), Women Execs. Stockton (founder), Cal Club San Joaquin County (founder, pres. 1981-82), Stanford Women's Club San Joaquin County (founder, pres. 1974-76), Mortar Bd., Prytanean Soc., Gavel and Quill, Nu Sigma Psi, Delta Psi Omega, Pi Lambda Theta, Phi Delta Kappa. Democrat. Home: 215 W Stadium Dr Stockton CA 95204

MCCARTHY, BRIAN NELSON, marketing and distribution company executive; b. Detroit, May 24, 1945; s. Andrew Nelson and Ruth Elizabeth (Hill) McC.; married, 1974; children: Amanda Lang, Kelly Elizabeth, Meghan Virginia; m. Shannon Headley, Sept. 7, 1991; 1 child, Conner Michael. BS in Engring. Sci., Oakland U., Rochester, Mich., 1966; MBA, Harvard U., 1972. Engr. Gen. Motors Corp., Pontiac, Mich., 1965-67; co-owner Sound Wave Systems, Costa Mesa, Calif., 1971-78; chief fin. officer, controller A&W Gershenson Co., Farmington, Mich., 1972-75; chief op. officer Devel. Group, Southfield, Mich., 1975-81; chief exec. officer Brichard & Co., San Francisco, 1982-87; pres., chief exec. officer Watermark Corp., Sausalito, Calif., 1987-89; chief exec. officer Indian Wells Water Co., Inc., 1989—. Lt. USNR, 1967-70, Rear Adm.S.C. USNR. Recipient Navy Commendation medal with gold star, Meritorious Svc. medal with two gold stars. Mem. Navy Supply Corps Assn. (bd. dirs. 1987—), Internat. Bottle Water Assn., Calif. Bottle Water Assn., Harvard Bus. No. Calif. Club, Commonwealth Club. Republican. Office: Indian Wells Water Co 1120 Mar West St Belvedere Tiburon CA 94920-1854

MCCARTHY, J. HOWARD, JR., geochemist, researcher; b. Denver, Jan. 28, 1927; s. J. Howard and Helen (O'Neill) McC.; m. Henriette Neubuerger, Jan. 27, 1949 (dec. 1969); children: Thomas O., Jennifer A., David W., Steven J.; m. Lucy Zareckis, Aug. 3, 1970, (div. Oct., 1985); children:Laura M., Michelle A. B.A., U. Denver, 1946-50; postgrad. U. Colo., 1952-56. Research chemist, U.S. Geol. Survey, Denver, 1951-88, Reno, 1988—. Contbr. articles to profl. publs. Served with USN, 1945-46, ETO. Mem. Soc. Econ. Geologists, AAAS, Geochem. Soc., Assn. Exploration Geochemists (pres. 1981, counselor 1980-84). Democrat. Unitarian. Home: 310 Lorraine Ct Reno NV 89509-5418 Office: U Nev US Geol Survey Mackay Sch of Mines Reno NV 89557

MCCARTHY, JOANNE HAFTLE, English language educator; b. Missoula, Mont., Mar. 18, 1935; d. Charles and Helen (Frischke) Haftle; m. Thomas O. McCarthy, June 4, 1955 (div. Apr. 23, 1973); children: Michael, Thomas, John, Matthew, Kate, Claire. BA, U. Mont., 1955; MA, U. Puget Sound, Tacoma, Wash., 1969. Teaching fellow U. Puget Sound., 1965-68; mem. faculty, dept. English Tacoma Community Coll., 1969—; Fulbright exch. fellow Berufsaufbauschule, Nuernberg, Fed. Republic Germany, 1984-85; mem. humanities edn. del. People to People, People's Rep. China, 1993. Author: (poetry book) Shadowlight, 1989; contbr. articles to profl. publs., poetry to lit. mags. and anthologies. Named Writer's Omnibus winner Allied Arts, Tacoma, 1980. Mem. Am. Fedn. Tchrs., Artist Trust, Phi Kappa Phi. Home: 1322 N Cascade Ave Tacoma WA 98406-1113 Office: Tacoma Community Coll 5900 S 12th St Tacoma WA 98465-1950

MCCARTHY, LAURENCE JAMES, physician, pathologist; b. Boston, Aug. 11, 1934; s. Theodore Clifford and Mary Barrett (Moran) McC.; m. Cynthia Marion DeRoch, Aug. 28, 1978; children: Laurence J. Jr., Jeffrey A., Karen E., Patrick K., Ryan N. BA, Yale U., 1956; student, Georgetown U. Sch. Med., 1956-58; MD, Harvard U., 1960; MS, U. Minn., 1965. Cert. Am. Bd. Pathology, 1965. Intern Boston City Hosp., 1960-61; resident in pathology Mayo Clinic, Rochester, Minn., 1961-65; pathologist Honolulu Heart Program, 1965-67; chief pathology Kelsey-Seybold Clinic, Houston, 1967-68; clin. asst. pathologist M.D. Anderson Hosp., Houston, 1967-68; chief pathology Straub Clinic, Honolulu, 1968-72; assoc. pathologist Wilcox Hosp., Lihue, Hawaii, 1972-74; chief pathology A.R. Gould Hosp., Presque Isle, Maine, 1975-78; assoc. pathologist Kuakini Med. Ctr., Honolulu, 1978—. Med. dir. USPHS, 1965-67. Fellow Coll. Am. Pathologists, Am. Soc. Clin. Pathologists; mem. AMA, Hawaii Soc. Pathologists (pres. 1970), Am. Acad. Forensic Sci., Hawaii Med. Assn., Honolulu County Med. Soc. (del. 1982-83). Roman Catholic. Home: 249 Kaelepulu Dr Kailua HI 96734-3311 Office: Kuakini Med Ctr 347 N Kuakini St Honolulu HI 96817-2372

MCCARTHY, LEO TARCISIUS, state lieutenant governor; b. Auckland, N.Z., Aug. 15, 1930; came to U.S., 1934, naturalized, 1942; s. Daniel and Nora Teresa (Roche) McC.; m. Jacqueline Lee Burke, Dec. 17, 1955; children: Sharon, Conna, Adam, Niall. BS, U. San Francisco, 1955; JD, San Francisco Law Sch., 1961. Bar: Calif. 1963. Supr. Bd. of Supr., San Francisco, 1964-68; assemblyman Calif. State Legislature, Sacramento, 1969-82, assembly speaker, 1974-80; lt. gov. State of Calif., Sacramento, 1983—; Democratic nominee U.S. Senate, 1988. Chmn. Econ. Devel. Commn. of Calif., 1983—; chmn. State Lands Commn., 1989—; regent U. Calif., 1983—; trustee State Coll. and Univ. System, Calif., 1983—; mem. Dem. State Cen. Com., 1969—. With USAF, 1951-52. Roman Catholic. Office: Office of Lt Gov 5777 W Century Blvd #1650 Los Angeles CA 90045

MCCARTHY, MARY ANN BARTLEY, electrical engineer; b. Drummond, Okla., Nov. 27, 1923; d. William Clifford and Estella Florence (Williams) Bartley; m. Joseph Manderfield McCarthy, Aug. 23, 1946 (dec. 1983); 1 child, Mary Ann McCarthy Morales. BEE, B of Material Sci., U. Calif., Berkeley, 1976. Aircraft radio technician U.S. Civil Svc., San Antonio and Honolulu, 1942-46; salesperson Sears Roebuck & Co., Enid, Okla., 1954-56; specialist reliability engring. Lockheed Corp., Sunnyvale, Calif., 1977-82, program responsible parts engr., 1986—; rsch. engr. Lockheed Corp., Austin, Tex., 1982-86; presenter 9th Internat. Conf. Women Engrs. and Scientists U. Warwick, Eng., 1991. Contbr. articles to profl. jours. Vol. coord. 4-H Series Excel Program. Fellow Soc. Women Engrs. (sr. life mem., pres. S.W. Tex. chpt. 1984, counsel reps. sec. 1985, pres. Santa Clara Valley chpt. 1986-87, nat. v.p. 1987-88, 88-89, chmn. nat. career guidance 1988-89, coord. 1990-91, counsel sect. rep 1991-92, coord. Resnik Challenger medal 1990-91, 91-92, 92-93); mem. AAUW (com. chmn. 1984, co-chmn. literacy com. 1984), Toastmasters (Vanderhoof award 1992, vol. coord. 4-H series, Excel program 1992-93), Advanced Toastmaster Silver. Republican. Roman Catholic. Home: 6103 Edenhall Dr San Jose CA 95129-3006

MC CARTHY, PATRICIA MARGARET, retreat house administrator, social worker; b. L.A., Mar. 2, 1943; d. Alphonsus Martin and Margaret (Kroutil) Mc C. BA, Dominican Coll., San Rafael, Calif., 1964; MSW, U. So. Calif., 1967. Lic. clin. social worker, Calif. Community organizer Holy Name Parish Archdiocese L.A., 1980-82; social worker St. Anne's Maternity Home, L.A., 1967-73, Holy Family Adoption Svc., L.A., 1973-78, Stanford Home, Sacramento, 1982-84; info. specialist Info. & Referral Svc. L.A. County, El Monte, Calif., 1984-87; exec. dir. Holy Spirit Retreat Ctr., Encino, Calif., 1987—. Mem. Jericho, L.A., 1988; inc. mem. Sisters of Social Svc. L.A., 1978—. Named Outstanding Citizen L.A. City Coun., 1982. Mem. Retreats Internat. (so. Calif. area rep.). Democrat. Roman Catholic. Office: Holy Spirit Retreat Ctr 4316 Lanai Rd Encino CA 91436-3698

MC CARTY, PAUL JAMES, JR., architect; b. L.A., Feb. 6, 1925; s. Paul James and Camilla (Tabor) McC.; m. Lucille Romant, Sept., 1947; children: Karen, Dale Joan, Paul, Delwyn. Assoc. architect City of L.A., 1956-60, architect, 1960-67, sr. architect, 1967-69, prin. architect, 1969—; commr. Calif. Bd. Architect Examiners. Flotilla cmmdr. U.S. Coast Guard Aux., L.a., 1977. Mem. AIA (chpt. sec.), Internat. Facility Mgmt. Assn. (chpt. treas.), Nat. Fire Protection Assn., Internat. Conf. of Bldg. Officials, Am. Arbitration Assn., Radia Amateurs Soc. Home: PO Box 3 FEB Sta Los Angeles CA 90053

MCCARTY, W(ILLARD) DUANE, obstetrician-gynecologist, physician executive; b. Alliance, Ohio, Dec. 15, 1930; s. Willard Raymond and Louise L. (Allmon) McC.; m. Frances Ann Rings, Dec. 5, 1959; children: Susan L., James A., Rebecca Ann, Sharon L. BS in Chemistry, Biology, Mt. Union Coll., 1952; MD, Ohio State U., 1956, MMS, 1961. Diplomate Am. Bd. Ob-Gyn. Intern, Univ. Hosps. Ohio State Univ., 1956-57; resident in ob-gyn. Ohio State U. Hosps., Columbus, 1957-61, instr. ob-gyn., 1960-61; assoc. ob-gyn. Lovelace Clinic, Albuquerque, 1963-86; chmn. ob-gyn. Lovelace-Bathan Hosp., Albuquerque, 1967-70; clin. assoc. prof. dept. ob-gyn., Sch. Medicine Univ. New Mex., Albuquerque, 1970-86; v.p., med. dir. Lovelace Health Plan, Albuquerque, 1972-84; clin. dir. Vista Pathways-Vista Scandia Hosp., Albuquerque, 1986-87; field rep., cons. Joint Commn. Accreditation of Hosps.-Ambulatory Care, Chgo., 1975-86; cur. rep. group practice Med. Group Mgmt. Assn., Denver, 1975-80; cur. quality assurance com. Am. Group Practice Assn., Chgo., 1978-82; v.p. bd. trustees Lovelace Health Plan-Lovelace FDN., Albuquerque, 1980-85. Author, rschr.: Recurrent Abortion, 1963 (MMS award). Founding dir. Profl. Stds. Rev. Orgn., Albuquerque, 1974; counselor Alcoholics Anonymous, Albuquerque, 1988—. Capt. USAF, 1961-63. Recipient Tchr.-Leader award N.Mex. Ob-Gyn. Soc., 1981. Fellow Am. Coll. Ob-Gyn., Am. Fertility Soc., Am. Coll. Physician Execs.; mem. AMA, Am. Acad. Med. Dirs. (founding trustee 1975—), Am. Soc. Addiction Medicine (cert.), S.W. Ob-Gyn. Soc. (pres. 1981-82), Presbyn. Men (John Knox fellow, exec. com., v.p. for missions 1992—). Republican. Home: 610 Graceland Dr SE Albuquerque NM 87108

MCCARTY, WILLIAM BRITT, natural resource company executive, educator; b. Shawnee, Okla., Apr. 6, 1953; s. William B. and Georgia M. (Lindsay) McC.; m. Jennifer Serio, Apr. 10, 1976; children: Patrick, Sara. BS in Computer Sci., Calif. State U., Fullerton, 1979; MBA in Fin., Claremont Grad. Sch., 1983, postgrad., 1990—. Chief fin. officer Republic Geothermal, Inc., Santa Fe Springs, Calif., 1980-88; v.p. CRM, Fullerton, Calif., 1988-89; mgr. corp. planning Republic Cos., Santa Fe Springs, 1989—; asst. prof. computer sci. Azusa (Calif.) Pacific U., 1990—. Bd. dirs. Eternal Truth Ministry, Huntington Beach, Calif., 1986-90. Republican. Office: Republic Cos 11823 Slauson Ave Santa Fe Springs CA 90670-2236

MCCASLIN, TERESA EVE, management executive; b. Jersey City, Nov. 22, 1949; d. Felix F. and Ann E. (Golaszewski) Hrynkiewicz; m. Thomas W. McCaslin, Jan. 22, 1972. BA, Marymount Coll., 1971; MBA, L.I. U., 1981. Adminstrv. officer Civil Service Commn., Fed. Republic Germany, 1972-76; personnel dir. Oceanroutes, Inc., Palo Alto, Calif., 1976-78; mgr., coll. relations Continental Grain Co., N.Y.C., 1978-79, corp. personnel mgr., 1979-81, dir. productivity, internal cons., 1981-84; dir., human resources Grow Group, Inc., N.Y.C., 1984-85, v.p. human resources, 1985-86, v.p. adminstrn., 1986-89; v.p. human resources Avery Dennison Corp., Pasadena, Calif., 1989—. Career counselor Marymount Coll. Career Ctr., Tarrytown. Recipient Sustained Superior Performance award U.S. Civil Service Commn., Fed. Republic Germany. Mem. Conf. Bd., Am. Mgmt. Assn., Human Resources Coun. Roman Catholic. Office: Avery Dennison Corp 150 N Orange Grove Blvd Pasadena CA 91103

MCCASLIN, THOMAS WILBERT, real estate developer; b. Scottsbluff, Nebr., Mar. 28, 1947; s. Robert Orr and Martha Mae (Cratty) McC.; m. Teresa Eve Hrynkiewicz, Jan. 22, 1972. BS, U.S. Mil. Acad., 1969; MS, Stanford U., 1978; MBA, L.I. U., 1981. Registered profl. engr., Va. Commd. 2d lt. U.S. Army, 1969, advanced through grades to major, 1979, resigned, 1982; v.p. Tishman Realty and Constrn. Corp., N.Y.C., 1982-89; v.p. constrn. mgmt. Tishman Realty and Constrn. Corp., L.A., 1989-92, sr. v.p., 1992—; bus. adv. coun. Loyola Marymount U.; bd. mem. Five Acres Children's Home. Mem. ASCE, Soc. Am. Mil. Engrs. Republican. Presbyterian.

MCCAULEY, GEORGE, federal agency administrator; b. Bklyn., May 9, 1945; s. Thomas Francis and Anne (Chupko) McC.; m. Marianne Janice O'Connor, May 25, 1980; children: Daniel Thomas, Kathleen Claire. BA, Belmont Abbey Coll., 1967. U.S. Marshal U.S. Dept. Justice, N.Y.C., 1971-78, Honolulu, 1978-79; spl. agt. U.S. Dept. State, N.Y.C., 1979-81, U.S. Mission to U.N., N.Y.C., 1981-83, U.S. Dept. State, L.A., 1983-85; counter intelligence U.S. Dept. State, Washington, 1985-87; attache U.S. Embassy, Canberra, Australia, 1987-89; adviser U.S. Mission to. U.N., N.Y.C., 1989-91; spl. agt. in charge U.S. Dept. State, L.A., 1992—. Capt. U.S. Army, 1967-71, Vietnam. Mem. Fed. Law Enforcement Officers Assn., Am. Fgn. Svc. Assn. Roman Catholic. Office: US Dept State Edward R Roybal Fed Bldg 255 East Temple St Rm 1273 Los Angeles CA 90053

MCCAW, CRAIG O., communications executive; b. Centralia, Wash., 1949. Grad., Stanford U., 1971. Pilot; chmn., CEO McCaw Cellular Comm., Inc., 1968-88; chmn. bd. dirs., CEO McCaw Cellular Comm., Inc., Kirkland, Wash., 1982—; chmn., CEO Lin Broadcasting Co., 1990—. Office: McCaw Cellular Comm Inc 5400 Carillon Pt Kirkland WA 98033-7356*

MCCLAIN, RICHARD STAN, cinematographer; b. Los Angeles, Oct. 7, 1951; m. Kim Girard, Nov. 7, 1987. Pres. Pasadena Camera Systems, Inc. Aerial cameraman: (feature films) Cops and Roberson, Falling Down, Heart & Soul, So, I Married an Axe Murderer, The Good Son, Made In America, This Boy's Life, Fearless, Hoffa, Jennifer Eight, Passenger 57, Wind, At Play in the Fields of the Lord, The Right Stuff, The Iceman, Rambo, Firebirds, Wind, Basic Instinct, Innerspace, Buster, U2 Rattle and Hum, Karate Kid III, Crazy People, The Hunt for Red October, The Doors, Flatliners; (TV shows) Magnum P.I., Airwolf. Recipient Best Cinematography award 1992 London Internat. Advt. Awards, 1993. Mem. Internat. Photographers, Screen Actors Guild, Dirs. Guild Am.

MCCLAIN, RONALD THEODORE, health care executive; b. Boulder, Colo., Feb. 6, 1948; s. Lew Everette and Vivian Frances (Reddin) McC.; m. Barbara Whitney White, Dec. 30, 1971 (div. May 1986); 1 child, William Thomas; m. Nancy C. Sleater, Mar. 30, 1991. BA in Chemistry magna cum laude, Colo. Coll., 1969; MS in Biochemistry, U. Colo., 1974, MBA in Fin., 1973. Rsch. chemist Great Western Sugar Co., Denver, 1969-70; strategic planning analyst Pfizer Inc., N.Y.C., 1974-77; dir. bus. planning and devel. Pfizer Hosp. Products Group, N.Y.C., 1977-80, v.p. bus. planning and devel., 1981-84; dir. planning Pfizer Diagnostics, N.Y.C., 1980-81; v.p. fin. and adminstrn. Shiley Europe Div. Pfizer Inc., London, 1984-86, v.p. ops., 1986-88; v.p. planning and devel. Valleylab Inc., Boulder, 1988—. NSF fellow, 1970-71. Mem. Phi Beta Kappa, Phi Delta Theta.

MC CLANAHAN, MOLLY, city council member, former mayor; b. San Jose, Calif., 1937; children: Patricia, David, Cynthia. Student, U. Redlands, 1955-57; AA in Bus. Mgmt., Fullerton Coll., 1982. Farmer San Luis Obispo County, Calif.; dir. YWCA Youth Employment Svc., Anaheim, Calif., 1982—; mem. Fullerton (Calif.) City Coun., 1982—; mayor City of Fullerton, 1988—. Pres. Fullerton Beautiful; trustee Fullerton Coll. Found.; Fullerton City Coun. rep., pact chmn. Tri-City Park Authority; past chmn. Fullerton Human Rels. Commn., Orange County Housing Authority Adv. Com., Arbor Day Com.; mem. Sr. Citizens Task Force, Fullerton Arboretum Commn., Fullerton Hist. Bldg. Survey, Fullerton Sch. Dist. Master Plan Task Force, Wilshire Jr. High Sch. Bd., Fullrton-Morelea sister City Assn., Fullerton Mus. Ctr., Muckenthaler Cultural Ctr., Friends of the Library, Friends of the Arboretum, Fullerton Friends of Music, Calif. State U.-Fullerton Art Alliance, CSUF Music Assocs. Named Fullerton Coll. Woman of Distinction, 1982, YWCA Vol. of Yr., 1981. Mem. LWV, Anaheim C. of C. (women's div., Woman of Yr. 1977). Office: City Hall 303 W Commonwealth Ave Fullerton CA 92632-1710

MCCLANE, GEORGE EDDINGTON, emergency physician; b. Londrina, Parana, Brazil, June 22, 1958; s. George Eddington and Margaret Gertrude (Williams) McC. BA, Taylor U., 1980; MD, Mich. State U., 1985. Diplomate Am. Bd. Emergency Medicine. Intern Carney Hosp., Dorchester,

Mass., 1985-86; resident in emergency medicine Boston City Hosp., 1986-90, chief resident in emergency medicine, 1989-90; emergency physician Redlands Community Hosp., Redlands, Calif.; paramedic instr. Crafton Hills Coll., Yucaipa, Calif., 1990—. Mem. Christian Med. and Dental Soc. (student advisor 1986—), Calif. Med. Assn., San Bernardino County Med. Assn. Republican. Presbyterian. Office: Redlands Community Hosp 350 Terracina Blvd Redlands CA 92373

MCCLATCHY, JAMES B., editor, newspaper publisher; b. Sacramento; s. Carlos K. and Phebe (Briggs) McC.; m. Susan Brewster; children: Carlos F., William B. B.A., Stanford U.; M.S., Columbia U. Reporter Sacramento Bee; reporter, editor Fresno Bee, Calif.; pub., chmn. McClatchy Newspapers, Sacramento.; pres., bd. dirs. InterAm. Press Assn.; bd. dirs. Calif. Nature Conservancy. Pres., bd. dirs. French Am. Bilingual Sch. Maj. USAFR, 1945-57. Mem. Am. Press Inst. (bd. dirs.). Office: McClatchy Newspapers 21st & Q Sts Sacramento CA 95813

MCCLAVE, DONALD SILSBEE, association executive; b. Cleve., May 7, 1941; s. Charles Green and Anne Elizabeth (Oakley) McC.; m. Christine Phyllis Mary Tomkins, Feb. 19, 1966; children: Andrew Green, Susan Elizabeth (dec.). BA, Denison U., 1963. Mktg. research officer Bank of Calif., San Francisco, 1968-70; v.p. Cen. Nat. Bank, Chgo., 1970-75; v.p. First Interstate Bank, Portland, Oreg., 1975-77, sr. v.p., 1977-79, exec. v.p., 1979-86; pres., chief exec. officer Portland Met. C. of C., 1987—; instr. Grad. Sch. Mktg. and Strategic Planning, Athens, 1982-84, Pacific Coast Sch. Banking, Seattle, 1976-78. Pres. Oreg. Episc. Sch. Bd., Portland, 1983-84; pres. Assn. Oreg. Industries Found., Salem, 1984-85; pres., co-chmn. Japan-Am. Conf. Mayors and C. of C., Portland, 1985, trustee, 1991—, exec. com., 1992—; trustee YMCA of Columbia-Willamette, 1990-92, Portland Student Svcs. Corp., 1992—; mem. METRO Urban Growth Mgmt. Adv. Com., 1989-92; mem. adv. com. Downtown Housing Preservation Partnership Adv. Com., 1989—; mem. City of Portland Mayoral Transition Team, 1992, Mayor's Bus. Roundtable, 1993—. Office: Portland Met C of C 221 NW 2d Ave Portland OR 97209-3999

MCCLEAR, RICHARD VANCE, public radio station executive; b. Jersey City, Nov. 21, 1946; s. Vance Albert and Margaret (Brew) McC.; m. Susan A. McClear, June 10, 1968; children: Brian Boru Michael, Kevin Seamus Padraic. BA in Polit. Sci. magna cum laude, St. Olaf Coll., Northfield, Minn., 1968; postgrad., Soochow U., Taipei, Taiwan, 1969; MA in Speech and Comm., U. Minn., 1975. Announcer, engr. Sta. WCAL-AM-FM, Northfield, Minn., 1965-72; pres. No. Community Radio, Grand Rapids, Minn., 1970-80; mgr. Sta. KTOO-FM, Juneau, Alaska, 1980; CEO, gen. mgr. Sta. KCAW-FM, Raven Radio Found., Sitka, Alaska, 1980—; grad. teaching assoc. U. Minn., Mpls., 1968-70; bd. dirs. Alaska Pub. Radio Network, Anchorage, 1984—, chmn. bd., 1991—; mem. long range planning com. Alaska Pub. Broadcasting Commn., Juneau, 1991—; an owner Sta. KLEF-FM, Anchorage, 1987—; cons. on strategic planning, fund raising, grant writing, and gen. mgmt. Native Broadcast Ctr., Anchorage, Superior Radio Network, Duluth, Minn., pub. radio stats., also others; former instr. U. Alaska S.E., Sitka, St. Cloud (Minn.) State U. Contbr. articles to profl. publs. Chmn. Sitka Econ. Devel. Commn., 1986—; mem. Russian com. Sitka Hist. Soc., 1991—; chmn. Sitka Unitarian-Universalist Fellow, 1985; mem. Alaska grants rev. panel Grotto Found., St. Paul, 1983-85. Recipient Best Use of Medium award Alaska Press Club, 1983, best radio feature award, 1992; Founders award Raven Radio Found., 1992. Mwm. Nat. Fedn. Community Broadcasters (nat. bd. dirs. 1986-90, treas. 1989-90), Sitka C. of C., Sitka World Affairs Coun., Phi Beta Kappa. Democrat. Office: Raven Radio Found 2B Lincoln St Sitka AK 99835

MCCLEERY, RICHARD GRIMES, retired pathologist; b. Washington, Iowa, May 7, 1928; s. Richard Hamilton and Sara Lois (Grimes) McC.; m. Patsy Ruth Hollister, Aug. 11, 1950 (div. Apr. 1964); children: Mark, Michael, Scott; m. Patricia Lee Foreman, Aug. 7, 1965; 1 child, Andrew. BA, The Colo. Coll., 1950; MD, U. Iowa, 1954. Diplomate Am. Bd. Pathology. Pathologist Meml. Hosp. of Laramie County, Cheyenne, Wyo., 1960-85, D. Paul Hosp., Cheyenne, 1960-85; con. pathologist VA Hosp., Cheyenne, 1960-85; officer, trustee Clin. Lab., Cheyenne, 1970-85, ret., 1985. Bd. dirs. Cheyenne Family YMCA, 1962-63; allocations com. United Way, Cheyenne, 1963. Capt. USAF, 1957-59. Rsch. fellowship Am. Cancer Soc., 1959. Fellow Coll. Am. Pathologists (emeritus); mem. Wyo. State Med. Soc. (pres. 1981), Am. Soc. of Clin. Pathologists (emeritus), Cheyenne Young Men's Lit. Club (pres. 1990). Presbyterian.

MCCLELLAN, BENNETT E., producer; b. Sedalia, Mo., Nov. 20, 1952; s. G. Earl and Ruth E. (McQueen) McC.; m. Gail Jones, Sept. 5, 1952; children: Ian Michael, Elizabeth Gayle. MBA, Harvard U., 1981; MFA in Film and TV, UCLA, 1989. Writer, dir. Old Globe Theater, San Diego, 1973-76; artistic dir. Genesis Theater, San Diego, 1977-79; cons. McKinsey & Co., L.A., 1981-87; producer McClellan Entertainment, L.A., 1987—; cons. Arthur D. Little Media & Entertainment Group, Cambridge, Mass., 1987—. Producer (TV series) Good News, Bad News, 1988; author (play) Kitty Makes it Home, 1987. Paramount Fellow Paramount Pictures, 1989, Recipient Medica award L.A. C. of C., 1986, HRTS IBA award Hollywood Radio and TV Assn., 1989; named Outstanding Grad. student UCLA Alumni Assn., 1990. Mem. Am. Film Inst., Hollywood Radio and TV Assn.

MCCLELLAN, CRAIG RENE, lawyer; b. Portland, Oreg., June 28, 1947; s. Charles Russell and Annette Irene (Benedict) McC.; m. Susan Armistead Nash, June 7, 1975; children: Ryan Alexander, Shannon Lea. BS in Econs., U. Oreg., 1969; JD magna cum laude, Calif. We. U., 1976. Bar: Calif. 1976, U.S. Dist. Ct. (so. dist.) Calif. 1976, U.S. Dist. Ct. (ea., ctrl., no. dists.) Calif. 1991, U.S. Supreme Ct. 1991. Compliance specialist Cost of Living Coun. and Price Commn., Washington, 1972-73, dir. Oil Policy subcom., 1973; ptnr. Luce, Forward, Hamilton & Scripps, San Diego, 1976-87; owner McClellan & Assocs., San Diego, 1987—. Chmn. annual fundraising auction KPBS, 1984. Capt. USMC, 1969-72. Mem. Assn. Trial Lawyers Am., Am. Bd. Trial Advocates, Am. Inns of Ct. (master), Calif. State Bar Assn., San Diego County Bar Assn., Calif. Trial Lawyers Assn. (bd. govs. 1985-87), San Diego Trial Lawyers Assn. (bd. dirs. 1983-90), Nat. Forensics League, Phi Gamma Delta, Phi Alpha Delta. Presbyterian. Office: McClellan & Assocs 1144 State St San Diego CA 92101-3590

MCCLELLAN, MARK HOWELL, oil industry executive, geologist; b. Roswell, N.Mex., Feb. 5, 1957; s. Jack Love and Barbara Ann (Walden) McC.; m. Paula Sue Dilldine, Aug. 29, 1981; children: Sara, Jill, Ross. BS in Geology, Tex. Tech U., 1980. Well site geologist W. S. Wallace and Assocs., Wichita Falls, Tex., 1980-81; geologist McClellan Oil Corp., Roswell, 1981-84, exploration mgr., 1984-88, v.p., 1989-93, pres., 1993—. Bd. dirs. Roswell Girls Club, 1987-89, Boy Scouts Am., Roswell, 1991—; co-chmn. operators div. campaign United Way, Roswell, 1990. Mem. Am. Assn. Petroleum Geologists, Ind. Petroleum Assn. of Am. (bd. dirs. Washington 1987-89), Ind. Petroleum Assn. N.Mex. (bd. dirs. Santa Fe chpt. 1990—), N.Mex. Landman's Assn., Roswell Geol. Soc. Republican. Methodist. Office: McClellan Oil Corp PO Box 730 Roswell NM 88202-0730

MCCLELLAND, JOHN MORRIS, retired publishing executive; b. Rogers, Ark., May 31, 1915; s. John Morgan and Adlyn (Morris) McC.; m. Burdette Craig, June 24, 1939; children: John M. III, Genevieve Sue. BA, Stanford U., 1937. Editor, pub. Daily News, Longview, Wash., 1950-77; founder, editor, pub. Jour.-Am., Bellevue, Wash., 1976-86; pres. Evergreen Pub. Co., Seattle, 1984-86. Author: R.A. Long's Planned City-Longview, 1971, Cowlitz Corridor, 1964, Wobbly War, The Centralia Story, 1987. Chmn. State Parks and Recreation Commn., Washington, 1952-56; mem. Wash. Bd. Geographic Names, 1978-89; bd. dirs. Health and Hosp. Svcs., Bellevue, 1977-92, N.W. Kidney Ctr., Seattle, 1976-89, Annie Wright Sch., Tacoma, 1986-92. Lt. USNR, 1942-45. Named Internat. Boss of Yr., Nat. Secs. Assn., 1968; named to Wash. Newspaper Hall of Honor, Wash. State U., 1984. Fellow Soc. Profl. Journalists; mem. Am. Soc. Newspaper Editors, Am. Antiquarian Soc., Wash. State Hist. Soc. (pres. 1982-88), AP (bd. dirs. 1968-71, 72-81), Am. Legion, Golf Collectors Soc., Royal and Ancient Golf of St. Andrews Club (Scotland), Broadmoor Golf Club, U. Seattle Golf Club, Elks, Sigma Delta Chi, Kappa Sigma. Office: 206 E Madison St Seattle WA 98112

MCCLENDON, IRVIN LEE, SR., technical writer and editor; b. Waco, Tex., June 12, 1945; s. Irvin Nicholas and Evelyn Lucile (Maycumber) McC.; divorced; children: Michael Boyd, Irvin Lee Jr., Laura Ann, Paul Nicholas, Richard Lester. Student El Camino Coll., 1961-63, U. So. Calif., 1962-66; BA in Math., Calif. State U.-Fullerton, 1970, postgrad. in bus. adminstrn., 1971-76; cert. nat. security mgmt. Indsl. Coll. Armed Forces, 1974; postgrad. in religion Summit Sch. Theology, 1982-84. Engring. lab. asst. Rockwell Internat. Corp., Anaheim, Calif., 1967-68, test data analyst, 1968, assoc. computer programmer, 1968-70, mem. tech. staff, 1970-82; systems programmer A-Auto-trol Tech. Corp., Denver, 1982-84, sr. tech. writer, 1984-86; sr. tech. writer, editor Colo. Data Systems, Inc., Englewood, Colo., 1986-87; engring. writer III CalComp subs. Lockheed Co., Hudson, N.H., 1987; sr. tech. writer CDI Corp., Arvada, Colo., 1987-88; staff cons. CAP GEMINI AM., Englewood, 1989; sr. tech./instrnl. writer & editor Tech. Tng. Systems, Inc., Aurora, Colo., 1990—. Sec. of governing bd. Yorba Linda Libr. Dist., 1972-77; trustee Ch. of God (Seventh Day), Bloomington, Calif., 1979-81, treas., 1980-81, mem. Calif. State U. and Coll. Statewide Alumni Coun., 1976-77; 2d v.p. Orange County chpt. Calif. Spl. Dists. Assn., 1976, pres., 1977; mem. Adams County Rep. Cen. Com., 1984-90, mem. Denver County Republican Ctrl. Com., 1992—; charter mem. Harmony: A Colo. Chorale, 1991— (treas., bd. dirs. 1992—). With USAFR, 1967-71. USAF Nat. Merit scholar, 1963-67. Mem. Calif. Assn. Libr. Trustees and Commrs. (exec. bd., So. Calif. rep. 1976-77), Nat. Eagle Scout Assn. (life), Scottish-Am. Mil. Soc., St. Andrew Soc. Colo., Am. Coll. Heraldry, Calif. State U.-Fullerton Alumni Assn. (dir. 1975-77). Republican. Home: 13870 Albrook Dr Apt C-106 Denver CO 80239-4736 Office: 3131 S Vaughn Way Ste 300 Aurora CO 80014

MCCLENDON, JOHN HADDAWAY, retired botanist, biology educator; b. Mpls., Jan. 17, 1921; s. Jesse Francis and Margaret (Stewart) McC.; m. Betty Morgan, June 27, 1947; children: Susan, Lise, Natalie. BA, U. Minn., 1942; PhD, U. Pa., 1951. Asst. prof. agrl. biochemistry U. Del., Newark, 1953-64; assoc. prof. botany U. Nebr., Lincoln, 1965-86, prof. biol. sci., 1987-89, ret., 1989. Contbr. articles to profl. jours. 1st lt. M.I., U.S. Army, 1942-45, CBI. NSF grantee, 1960, 65. Mem. Am. Soc. Plant Physiologists, Native Plant Soc. Oreg., Zero Population Growth, Bot. Soc. Am., Audubon Soc., Wilderness Soc., Sigma Xi. Democrat. Home: 105 Bush St Ashland OR 97520-2607

MCCLENNEN, MIRIAM J., former state official; b. Seattle, Sept. 16, 1923; d. Phillip and Frieda (Golub) Jacobs; m. Louis McClennen, Apr. 25, 1969; stepchildren: Peter Adams, James C.A., Helen, Persis, Crane, Emery. BA, U. Wash., 1945; MBA, Northwestern U., 1947. Exec. trainee Marshall Field & Co., Chgo., 1945-47; asst. buyer Frederick & Nelson (subs. of Marshall Field), Seattle, 1947-49; buyer Frederick & Nelson (subs. of Marshall Field), 1949-57; fashion coordinator, buyer Levy Bros., Burlingame/San Mateo, Calif., 1957-63; buyer Goldwaters, Phoenix, 1963-67; adminstrv. asst. to pres. Ariz. State Senate, Phoenix, 1973-76; dir. publs. Office of Sec. of State, Phoenix, 1976-87; chairwoman legis. subcom. adminstrv. procedure Ariz. State Legislature, Phoenix, 1984-85. Original compiler, codifier, editor publ. Ariz. Adminstrv. Code, 1973-87, Ariz. Adminstrv. Register, 1976-87. Bd. dirs., mem. Phoenix Art Mus. League, 1972-90, Phoenix Symphony Guild, 1970-88; bd. dirs., sec. Combined Metro. Phoenix Arts and Scis., 1974-90, mem. adv. bd., 1990—; bd. dirs. Phoenix Arts Coun., Master Apprentice Programs, 1980-83; bd. dirs., mem. exec. com. Heard Mus., 1982-88, 90—, chmn. publs. com., 1982-88, chmn. exhibit and edn. com., 1990-93; mem. Ariz. State Hist. Records Adv. Bd., 1987-90, Ariz. Commn. on Arts, 1989—, Phoenix Art Mus., 1972-92. Recipient Disting. Svc. award Atty. Gen. Ariz., 1987, Outstanding Svc. to People, Ariz. State Senate, 1987, Nat. Assn. Secs. of State award, 1987. Mem. English Speaking Union, Nat. Soc. Arts and Letters, Charter 100 (bd. dirs. 1981-85), Phoenix County Club, Ariz. Club. Home: 5311 N La Plaza Cir Phoenix AZ 85012-1415

MCCLOSKEY, RICHARD JOHN, biology educator; b. Mt. Vernon, N.Y., Mar. 4, 1944; s. Hugh A. and Alice Mary (Barber) McC.; m. Linda Louise Ciccone, Feb. 24, 1968; children: Richard-Paul, Erin Bridget. BA, Franklin (Ind.) Coll., 1965; MS, Iowa State U., 1968, PhD, 1975. Instr., teaching asst. Iowa State U., Ames, 1965-72; asst. prof. Carlow Coll., Pitts., 1972-76; prof. biology Boise (Idaho) State U., 1976—; rsch. biologist Iowa Conservation Commn., Boone, 1965-68; lectr. NSF, Pitts., 1972-74; workshop dir. U.S. Forest Svc., Idaho, Wyo., Utah, Nev., 1979—, Idaho State U., Pocatello, 1979—; facilitator environ. issues Coll. of Idaho, Caldwell, 1983; vis. prof., workshop dir. U. Nev., Reno and Las Vegas, 1985—; co-dir. Intermountain Environ. Edn. Tng. Team, Idaho, Utah, Nev., Wyo., 1983—; mem. environ. adv. bd. Idaho Dept. Edn., Boise, 1982—; bd. dirs. Idaho Natural Resources Legal Found., 1986—. Author: Fire in the Forest: Influence on Landscape and Management Decisions, 1989; contbr. articles to profl. jours. Mem. Ada County Planning Commn., Boise, 1981-83; mem. Idaho steering com. Project Learning Tree, 1988—; state outreach chmn. Idaho Spl. Olympics, Boise, 1987-92. Recipient Disting. Citizen award Idaho Statesman, Gannet Press, 1988, Environ. Edn. Leadership award U.S. Forest Svc., 1989, Disting. Svc. award Boise State U., 1991; scholar Prudential Group Am., 1989; Eisenhower Math., Sci. and Edn. Act grantee, 1988-91, grantee Fed. Ctrs. for Disease Control, 1990-91, Nat. Environ. Edn. and Tng. Found., 1992-93, Nat. Resources Conservation Edn. Program, 1992-94, EPA, 1993-94. Mem. Idaho Soc. for Energy and Environ. Edn. (bd. dirs. 1985—), Nat. Wildlife Fedn. (edn. dir. 1980—, Conservation award 1986, 88, 89), Idaho Acad. Scis., Population Inst. (population action coun. 1983—, Merit award 1984, 88), Idaho Wildlife Fedn. (bd. dirs. 1979—), Idaho Fedn. Tchrs. (treas. 1980-84), Ptnrs. in Edn. (Recognition award 1990), Sigma Xi, Phi Delta Kappa, Alpha Kappa Delta, Kappa Delta Pi. Democrat. Roman Catholic. Home: 326 Santa Fe Eagle ID 83616-5346 Office: Boise State U 1910 University Dr Boise ID 83725-0001

MCCLUNG, J(AMES) DAVID, corporate executive, lawyer; b. Lamesa, Tex., July 16, 1943; s. Jack Weldon Sr. and Ruby (Brown) McC.; m. Linda Nelson, Feb. 12, 1966; children: LeEtta McClung Felter, Dennis, Pamela, Jennifer. Student, N.E. La. State Coll., 1961-62, McNeese State Coll., 1963; BSBA cum laude, Bethany Nazarene Coll., 1965; postgrad., U. Okla., 1967-68; JD cum laude, Baylor U., 1973. Bar: Tex. 1973, U.S. Dist. Ct. (no. dist.) Tex. 1975, U.S. Ct. Appeals (5th cir.) 1974. Assoc. Jackson & Walker, Dallas, 1973-76; exec. v.p. Austin Industries, Inc., Dallas, 1976-88; pres., chief exec. officer, chmn. bd. Green Internat., Inc., Denver, 1988—; arbitrator Am. Arbitration Assn., 1978—; bd. dirs. Green Holdings, Inc., Denver; chmn. bd. Green Construction Co., Green Mining, Inc., Green Alaska, Inc., GEM Investors, Inc., Green Overseas Corp., Northland Maintenance Co., Northland Alaska, Inc., Green Investments, Inc., Denver, 1988—. Contbr. articles to profl. jours. Trustee So. Nazarene U., Bethany, Okla., 1978-86; mem. gen. bd. Ch. of the Nazarene, Kansas City, 1985-89, sec. Commn. Report, 1989. Capt. USAF, 1965-71, Vietnam. Decorated 6 Air medals; recipient Young Grads. award of merit Baylor U., 1983, Outstanding Alumni award So. Nazarene U., 1989, Disting. Svc. award Ch. of the Nazarene, 1989. Mem. ABA, Tex. Bar Assn., The Beavers. Republican. Home: 3551 S Franklin St Cherry Hills Village CO 80110-4005 Office: Green Internat Inc 8055 E Tufts Ave Ste 700 Denver CO 80237-2879

MCCLURE, ALLAN HOWARD, space contamination specialist, space materials consultant; b. Phila., Mar. 29, 1925; s. C. Howard and Edda Cherry (Speirs) McC.; m. Jean Florence Hall, May 31, 1947; children: Joyce Ann, Allan Hall. BS, Widener U., 1949; postgrad., Command & Gen. Staff Coll., 1972. Chemist Am. Cyanamid, Pitts., 1950-52; materials engr. Piasecki/Vertol Helicopter Co., Morton, Pa., 1952-59; lead engr. Boeing Aerospace Co., Seattle, 1959-71; sr. specialist engr. Boeing Aerospace Co., Kent, Wash., 1974-85; tech. cons. Adhesive Engring. Co., San Carlos, Calif., 1971-74. Author, investigator spacecraft contamination control documents and govt. reports. Pres. Seattle Crime Prevention League, 1974-84. Served to maj. U.S. Army, 1943-46, ETO, PTO; sec. Boeing Employees Amateur Radio Soc., 1984; membership chmn. Amateur Radio Emergency Services, 1984-85. Recipient Silver Beaver award and William H. Spurgeon III award Boy Scouts Am., Seattle, 1964. Mem. Am. Chem. Soc., Soc. for Advancement of Material and Process Engring. (nat. dir., pres. Seattle chpt.), Rainier C. of C., Res. Officers Assn. (life). Republican. Home: 12026 SE 216th St Kent WA 98031-2272

MCCLURE, DAVID ROBERT, psychologist; b. Englewood, Calif., Apr. 20, 1963; s. Robert Eugene and Nellie (DelMar) McC.; m. Martina Ann Fava, Apr. 18, 1992. BA in Psychology, BS in Natural Sci., Pepperdine U., 1987. Cert. in neuro-associative conditioning. Commun. coord. Pepperdine U., Malibu, Calif., 1986-87; unit svc. coord. neurosurgery trauma ICU UCLA Med. Ctr., Westwood, 1987-88; office mgr. Anaheim (Calif.) Med., 1989-90; pres. real estate Roberts & Assocs., Yorba Linda, Calif., 1990—; area mgr. Canyon Crest Mortgage, Tustin, Calif., 1992—. Home: 5052 Grandview Yorba Linda CA 92686

MCCLURE, DONALD EDWIN, electrical construction executive, consultant; b. Pasadena, Calif., Mar. 13, 1934; s. Robert Wirt and Edna Buela (Williamson) McC.; m. Diana Lee Myrick, Feb. 9, 1958; children: Scott Patrick, Christopher Daniel. BS in Bus. Adminstrn., San Diego State U., 1957. Lic. gen. engring., bldg., elec. Elec. estimator Calif. Electric Works, San Diego, 1953-57; v.p. JCS Elec., San Diego, 1958-61; owner, proprietor McClure Electric, San Diego, 1961-63; chief estimator Am. Electric Contracting Corp., La Mesa, Calif., 1963-65; pres. Cal Pacific Electric Inc., San Diego, 1965-69; v.p., sec., dir. Am. Elec. Contracting, La Mesa, 1969-79; v.p. Steiny and Co., Inc., San Diego, 1979—; cons. constrn., expert witness Don E. McClure, San Diego, 1987—. Active Nat. Rep. Com., Washington, 1984—. Mem. Am. Subcontractors Assn., Singing Hills Tennis Club, Big Bear Tennis Ranch, Friendly Sons' of St. Patrick, Kappa Sigma Alumni Assn. Presbyterian. Office: Steiny and Co Inc 1083 Cuyamaca St El Cajon CA 92022

MCCLURE, HOWE ELLIOTT, ornithologist, entomologist; b. Chgo., Apr. 29, 1910; s. Howe Alexander and Clara (Phillips) McC.; m. Lucy Esther Lou Fairchild, Oct. 1, 1933; children: Lucy Jeannette, Clara Ann. BS, U. Ill., 1933, MS, 1936; PhD, Iowa State Coll., 1941. Wildlife biologist Game Forestation & Parks Commn., Ord, Nebr., 1941-46; entomologist Mare Island, Vallejo, Calif., 1946-47; ornithologist Hooper Med. Found., U. Calif., San Fransico, 1947-50, U. Pitts., 1950, Walter Reed Army Inst. Rsch., Washington, 1951-75. Author: Migration and Survival of the Birds of Asia, 1974, Bird Banding, 1984, Whistling Wings, 1991; co-author: Haematozoa in the Birds of Eastern and Southern Asia, 1978, Inago-Children of Rice, 1993. Bd. dirs. Defenders of Wildlife, Washington, 1978-89; scoutmaster Boy Scouts Am., various locations, 1933-57. Lt. (j.g.) USN, 1945-46. Recipient Silver Beaver award Boy Scouts Am., 1956. Mem. Conejo Audubon Club (conservation chair 1976-93), Sigma Xi (sci. com. 1987-91). Home: 69 E Loop Dr Camarillo CA 93010-2327

MCCLURE, JAMES A., retired U.S. senator; b. Payette, Idaho, Dec. 27, 1924; s. W. R. and Marie McC.; m. Louise Miller; children: Marilyn, Kenneth, David. JD, U. Idaho, 1950; DL (hon.), Coll. Idaho, 1986. Mem. Idaho State Senate, 1961-66; asst. majority leader, 1965-66; city atty. City of Payette, Idaho; pros. atty. Payette County, Idaho; mem. 90th-92nd Congresses 1st Idaho Dist., 1967-73; U.S. Senator from Idaho, 1973-90; with Energy and Natural Resources Com.; mem. Com. on Rules and Adminstrn., Com. on Appropriations; pres. McClure, Gerard & Neuenschwander, Inc., Washington, 1990—; ptnr. Givens, Parsley, & Huntley, Boise, Idaho, 1990—. Trustee Kennedy Ctr., Meth. Ch. Mem. Elks, Masons, Kiwanis, Phi Alpha Delta. Methodist. Office: McClure Gerard & Neuenschwander Inc 801 Pennsylvania Ave NW Washington DC 20004-2615 also: Givens Parsley & Huntley Ste 200 Park Pl 277 N 6th St Boise ID 83701

MCCLURE, THOMAS FULTON, artist, retired educator; b. Pawnee City, Nebr., Apr. 17, 1920; s. Clate Ray and Virginia Ann (Carden) McC.; m. Roberta Lucille Estey, Mar. 14, 1942; children: Colleen Elaine Kotila, James Ray. BFA, U. Nebr., 1941; postgrad., Wash. State Coll., 1941; MFA, Cranbrook Acad. of Art, 1947. Tech. illustrator Boeing Aircraft Co., Seattle, 1942-45, Pontiac (Mich.) Motor Co., 1946; instr. Sch. for Am. Craftsmen, Alfred (N.Y.) Univ., 1947-48; asst. prof. art Univ. Okla., Norman, 1948-49; prof. of art Univ. Mich., Ann Arbor, 1949-81. Exhibited in Pa. Acad. of Fine Arts, 1958, Neon & Kinetic Art Mus. of Neon Art, L.A., 1987, and others; represented in many pub. collections including, Seattle Art Mus., Detroit Inst. Arts, Syracuse Mus. Fine Arts; work illustrated in books, Sculpture Casting, Plastics in Sculpture, Public Art-New Directions, American Artists, An Illustrated Survey. Recipient many commissions for works and many prizes in sculpture and drawing. Home: 2406 Pine Cove Rd Prescott AZ 86301-4054

MCCLURE, WILLIAM OWEN, biologist; b. Yakima, Wash., Sept. 29, 1937; s. Rexford Delmont and Ruth Josephine (Owen) McC.; m. Pamela Preston Harris, Mar. 9, 1968 (div. 1979); children: Heather Harris, Rexford Owen; m. Sara Joan Rorke, July 27, 1980. BSc, Calif. Inst. Tech., 1959; PhD, U. Wash., 1964. Postdoctoral fellow Rockefeller U., N.Y.C., 1964-65; rsch. assoc. Rockefeller U., 1965-68; asst. prof. U. Ill., Urbana, 1968-75; assoc. prof. U. So. Calif., L.A., 1975-79; prof. biology, prof. neurology U. So. Calif., 1979—; v.p. sci. affairs Nelson Rsch. & Devel. Co., Irvine, Calif., 1981-82; acting v.p. rsch. & devel. Nelson Rsch. & Devel. Co., 1985-86; dir. programs info. scis. U. So. Calif., 1982—; dir. cellular biology U. So. Calif., 1979-81, dir. neurobiology, 1982-88; cons. in field; dir. Marine & Freshwater Biomed. Ctr., U. So. Calif., 1982-83; co-dir. Baja Calif. Expedition of the R/V Alpha Helix, 1974, others; chmn. Winter Conf. on Brain Rsch., 1979, 80, others; lectr. in field; sci. adv. bd. Nelson R & D, 1972-91; mem. bd. commentators Brain and Behavioral Scis., 1978—. Editor or author 3 books; co-editor: Wednesday Night at the Lab; patentee in field; mem. editorial bd. Neurochem. Rsch., 1975-81, Jour. Neurochemistry, 1977-84, Jour. Neurosci. Rsch., 1980-86; contbr. over 100 articles to profl. jours. Bd. dirs. San Pedro & Peninsula Hosp. Found., 1989—, Faculty Ctr., U. So. Calif., 1991—, San Pedro Helath Svcs., 1992—. Scripps Inst. fellow, 1958, NIH fellow, 1959-64, 64-65, Alfred P. Sloan fellow, 1972-76, others; recipient rsch. grants, various sources, 1968—; Intersci. Rsch. Inst. fellow, 1989. Mem. AAAS, Am. Soc. Neurochemistry, Soc. for Neurosci., Am. Soc. Biol. Chemistry and Molecular Biology, Internat. Soc. Neurochemistry, Assn. Neurosci. Depts. and Programs, Univ. Park Investment Group, N.Y. Acad. Scis., Univ. Club L.A. Republican. Presbyterian. Home: 30533 Rhone Dr Palos Verdes Peninsula CA 90274-5742 Office: U So Calif Dept Biol Scis Los Angeles CA 90089-2520

MCCLUSKEY, MATTHEW CLAIR, physical chemist; b. New Kensington, Pa., Jan. 2, 1957; s. John J. and Carole Sue (Hilliard) McC.; m. Cornelia Mary Sanders, Sept. 26, 1981. BS, Ohio State U., 1985; PhD, U. Va., 1990. Post-doctoral fellow in chemistry Dept. Energy Lawrence Berkeley Lab., Berkeley, 1990-92; cons. Annapolis Rsch. Assocs., Fontana, Calif., 1991—; historic ho. preservationist The Ridge, Manchester, Ohio, 1992—. Contbr. articles to profl. jours. Pres. Manchester Parks Bd. Mem. Ohio Archeol. Soc., Manchester Hist. Soc. Home: 503 E 8th St Manchester OH 45144

MCCOLLUM, ALVIN AUGUST, real estate company executive; b. L.A., Jan. 20, 1920; s. Nile Clarkson and Ida Martha (Kuhlman) McC.; m. Maxine Eleanor Seeberg, July 29, 1944; children: Robert Michael, James Alan, Patricia Kathleen. BA, UCLA, 1941; postgrad., U.S. Naval Acad., 1946, Southwestern U., 1949-50. Exec. v.p., dir. Strout Realty, N.Y.C., 1948-61, Del E. Webb Corp., Phoenix, 1961-67; pres., dir. Sahara Nev. Corp., Las Vegas, 1964-67, Devel. Svcs., Inc., Scottsdale, Ariz., 1967-69; pres., chmn. Recreation Leisure Land, Inc., Scottsdale, 1969-71; asst. pres., dir. A.J. Industries, Inc., L.A., 1971-74; pres., dir. Carefree (Ariz.) Ranch, Inc., 1974-76; pres., bd. dir. Cons. Internat., Scottsdale, 1976—; chmn. CEO Greenway Environmental Svs., Inc., Gilbert, Ariz., 1992—; pres., bd. dirs. Combined Assets, Inc., Westlake Village, Calif., First Realty Fin., Inc., L.A., Corp. Capital Resources, Inc., Westlake Village. Bd. dirs. Admiral Nimitz Found., Fredericksburg, Tex., 1970—, Boys Club Las Vegas, 1964-68, United Fund, Las Vegas, 1966; co-chmn. Nat. Conf. Christians and Jews, Las Vegas, 1966; elder Presbyn. Ch. USA, 1954—. Lt. USN, 1943-48, PTO. Mem. Masons, Shriners, Am. Legion, Mt. Shadows Country Club (bd. dirs. 1962-64). Republican. Home: 4118 N 87th Way Scottsdale AZ 85251-2940 Office: Greenway Environmental Svs Inc 1400 N Gilbert Rd Ste C Gilbert AZ 85234

MCCOMAS, BRUCE JAMES, production manager pulp and paper company; b. Anacortes, Wash., Feb. 11, 1950; s. Robert Laverne and Barbara Louise (Barker) McC; m. Teresa Linnea Valentine, Oct. 3, 1970; children: Aaron James, Alicia Linnea. BS in Chem. Engring., U. Wash., 1972, MBA, 1992. Cert. waste water treatment operator, Wash. Asst. brewmaster Rainier Brewing Co., Seattle, 1972-74; process engr. Alaska Lumber & Pulp Co., Sitka, 1974-76; process engr., ops. supr. Crown Zellerbach, Wauna,

Oreg., 1976-78; asst. supt. recovery and utilities Crown Zellerbach, Port Townsend, Wash., 1981-84; supt. power and recovery Port Townsend Paper Corp., 1984; prodn. mgr. Port Townsend Paper Co., 1984—. Advisor Port Townsend Watershed Advisory, 1989-92, Slade Gorton Jeffco adv. com. Port Townsend 1990-92; bd. dirs. Jefferson County Edn. Found., Port Townsend, 1990—; mem. fin. adv. com. Jefferson Gen. Hosp., 1988—; ruling elder Presbyn. Ch., Port Townsend. Mem. Paper Industry Mgmt. Assn., Tech. Assn. Pulp and Paper Industry, Kiwanis (v.p. 1990-91, pres. elect 1991-92). Office: Port Townsend Paper Corp 100 Paper Mill Hill Rd Port Townsend WA 98368

MCCONKIE, JAMES WILSON, lawyer; b. Salt Lake City, Jan. 21, 1946; s. James Wilson McConkie and Gwendoly (Wirthlin) Cannon; m. Judith Evlyn Miller, Aug. 11, 1967; children: James Wilson III, Bryant Joseph, Kelly Ann. BA, Brigham Young U., 1970; JD, U. Utah, 1973. Bar: Utah 1973, U.S. Ct. Appeals (9th and 10th cirs.) 1978, U.S. Supreme Ct. 1979. Adminstrv. asst. Ho. of Reps., Washington, 1973—; asst. U.S. atty. U.S. Dept. Justice, Salt Lake City, 1977-88; ptnr. Parker, McKeown, McConkie, Salt Lake City, 1988—; adj. faculty Westminster Coll., Salt Lake City, 1990—. Mem. Am. Trial Lawyers Assn., Utah State Bar Assn. (chmn. com. on advt. and specialization 1981-82). Democrat. LDS. Office: Parker McKeown McConkie 4001 7th E Salt Lake City UT 84124

MCCONKIE, LAVONNE MAY, business owner, executive; b. Bellville, Ohio, June 30, 1937; d. Kenneth Ralph and Gladys Elizabeth (Stevens) McC. BA, John Brown U., 1959; Med. Technologist, Confederate Meml. Med. Ctr., 1961. Med. technologist Confederate Meml. Hosp., Shreveport, La., 1961-72; sales rep. Hycel, Inc., Denver, 1972-77, Waters Assocs., San Francisco, 1977-84; mfr. rep. Instruc Spec Assoc., San Francisco, 1985-86; sales rep. BPL Toxicology Lab., San Francisco, 1986-87; owner, pres. Leadership Resources, San Francisco, 1987—. Pub. speaker Toastmasters Speakers Bur., San Francisco, 1990-92, Calif. Transplant Donor Network, San Francisco, 1992. Mem. ASTD, Assn. for Quality and Participation, Bay Area Quality Improvement Network, Cable Car Toastmasters (pres. 1990, area E-4 gov. 1990-91, div. E gov. 1991-92). Home and Office: Leadership Resources 3650 Fillmore Ste 205 San Francisco CA 94123

MCCONNEL, RICHARD APPLETON, aerospace company official; b. Rochester, Pa., May 29, 1933; s. Richard Appleton and Dorothy (Merriman) McC.; m. Mary Francis McInnis, 1964 (div. 1984); children: Amy Ellen, Sarah Catherine; m. Penny Kendzie, 1993. BS in Naval Engring., U.S. Naval Acad., 1957; MS in Aerospace Engring., USN Postgrad. Sch., 1966. Commd. ensign USN, 1957; naval aviator Operation ASW, 1959-63, 68-71, 75-79; asst. prof. math. U.S. Naval Acad., 1966-68; program mgr. P3C update Naval Air Devel. Ctr., 1971-75; range program mgr. Pacific Missile Test Ctr., 1979-82; ret. USN, 1982; program mgr. Electromagnetic Systems div. Raytheon Co., Goleta, Calif., 1982-87; sr. engr. SRS Techs., Inc., Camarillo, Calif., 1987-92, High Tech. Solutions, Inc., Camarillo, Calif., 1992—; Please give your home address (not for publication if desired). Mem. Internat. Test and Evaluation Assn., Assn. Old Crows. Republican. Office: High Tech Solutions 80 Wood Rd Camarillo CA 93010

MCCONNELL, CALVIN DALE, clergyman; b. Monte Vista, Colo., Dec. 3, 1928; s. Roy and Leota Fern (Taylor) McC.; m. Mary Caroline Bamberg, Sept. 2, 1952 (dec. Apr. 1986); children: David William, Mark Andrew; m. Velma Duell, Dec. 17, 1988. B.A., U. Denver, 1951; M.Div., Iliff Sch. Theology, 1954; S.T.M., Andover Newton Theol. Sem., 1967. Ordained to ministry United Meth. Ch.; pastor Meth. Ch., Williams, Calif., 1955-58, 1st United Meth. Ch., Palo Alto, Calif. and Stanford U. Wesley Found., 1958-61; chaplain and asst. prof. religion Willamette U., Salem, Oreg., 1961-67; pastor Christ United Meth. Ch., Denver, 1968-72; pastor 1st United Meth. Ch., Boulder, Colo., 1972-79, Colorado Springs, Colo., 1979-80; bishop United Meth. Ch., Portland Area, 1980-88, Seattle Area, 1988—. Trustee U. Puget Sound, Iliff Sch. Theology; pres. United Meth. Ch. Bd. Higher Edn. and Ministry. Office: 2112 3d Ave Ste 301 Seattle WA 98121

MCCONNELL, RANDALL (MICHAEL) SCOTT, investment company executive; b. Chgo., Sept. 20, 1945; s. Michael Joseph Sypien and Estelle Louise (Scott) Boden; m. Linda Faye Ormand, Oct. 3, 1973 (div. Oct. 1976); 1 child, Megan Elizabeth Louise; m. Nancy Lee Morphew, July 25, 1987; 1 child, Seana Leighan Morphew. Student, U. So. Calif., 1962-63, U. Nev., Reno, 1970-72, U. Colo., 1981-82, Colo. State U., 1989, 92. Clk. 1st Nat. Bank Chgo., 1963-64; asst. mgr. Bancwest, Las Vegas, Nev., 1964-65; supr. savs. Coast Savs. Bank, L.A., 1965-69; asst. mgr. loan svc. 1st Fed. Wis., Milw., 1969-70; supr. U.S. Dept. Edn., Denver, 1978-81; v.p. Dean Witter, Inc., Denver, 1982-85; CEO Colo. RMS Holdigs Corp., Ft. Collins, 1989—; dir. AMS, Inc., Denver; mng. dir. RMC Corp. Hawaii, Kihei, 1985—; cons. Americorp., Inc., Denver, 1986-87. Actor (stage) Andersonville Trial, 1962 (2d pl. award 1962). Mgr. Wilshire dist. Nixon for Gov., L.A., 1962; dir. Exptl. Coll., U. Nev., Reno, 1971-72; dir. So. Calif. Young Reps., L.A., 1962; dir. Native Am. Coun., Denver, 1984-86. Mem. Wailea Rotary. Episcopalian/Budhist. Office: Colo RMS Holdings Corp PO Box 8059 Fort Collins CO 80526

MCCONNELL, STEVEN CHARLES, software engineer; b. Moses Lake, Wash., Sept. 3, 1962; s. Paul William and Betty Vene (Du Mond) McC. BA, Whitman Coll., 1985; MSE, Seattle U., 1991. Systems mgr. NW Consulting Inc., Bellevue, Wash., 1984-86; sr. software engr. Sygenex, Inc., Redmond, Wash., 1986-89; sr. consulting engr. pvt. practice Bellevue, 1989—. Author: Code Complete, 1993; contbr. articles to profl. jours.; architect (software product) Criterium; inventor Compu-Flog. Nat. Merit scholar, 1981; recipient merit award Soc. for Tech. Comms., 1989. Mem. Computer Soc. of the IEEE, Assn. for Computing Machinery.

MCCONNER, STANLEY JAY, SR., academic administrator; b. Detroit, Dec. 7, 1929; s. Walter Richard and Norma Louise (Hafford) McC.; m. Peggy Miller, June 1951(div.); children: Michele Jay, Stanley Jay; m. Dorothy Hamilton, Apr. 5, 1974. BS in Spl. Edn., Ea. Mich. U., 1953; MS in Reading, U. Conn., 1956; MS in Psychology, Cen. Conn. State U., 1967; PhD in Adminstrn., U. Sarasota, 1973; PhD in Adminstrn. and Policy Studies, Northwestern U., 1986. Tchr. Hartford (Conn.) Pub. Schs., 1953-67; asst. prof., asst. dir. U. Conn., Storrs, 1967-70; exec. dir. Balt. Pub. Schs., 1970-74; dean arts and scis. Kennedy, King Coll., Chgo., 1974-76; dean continuing edn. Chgo. State U., 1976-77, exec. dir. found., 1977-85; asst. prin. Pritzker-Grinker Sch., Chgo., 1985-86; coord. Body Awareness Resource Network Chgo. Health Info. Ctr., 1986-91; staff devel. specialist, reading specialist African Am. Studies Dept. Tucson Unified Sch. Dist., 1991—. Author: Famous Black Americans, 1972, Senate Bill 730: A Report Card, 1985. Bd. dirs. Girl Scouts U.S., Chgo., 1983, Roseland Community Hosp., Chgo., 1986; mem. Chgo. Urban League, Operation People United to Save Humanity, Chgo., Planned Giving Roundtable, Chgo., 1982-86. Named Community Ambassador-Norway Hartford Conn. Bus. Group, 1958; fellow Nat. Counselor Educator, Washington 1976; recipient achievement award, Nat. Assn. Pub. Continuing Adult Edn., Washington 1978; named to Hall of Fame Ea. Mich. U.,1988. Mem. Nat. Soc. Fundraising Execs., Chgo, 1982-86, Chgo. Urban League, 1988—, Operation PUSH, Chgo. 1988—, Phi Delta Kappa, Storrs, Conn., Am. Ednl. Research Assoc., Kiwanis of Chgo. Democrat. Episcopalian.

MCCOOL, STEPHEN FORD, wildland recreation management educator; b. Phila., Aug. 10, 1943; s. William Douglas and Ruth Ann (Stentz) McC.; m. Ann Elin Magnuson, June 8, 1968; children: Tera, Heather, Shauna, Amy, Saundra. BS in Forestry, U. Idaho, 1965; MS, U. Minn., 1967, PhD, 1970. Asst. prof. U. Wis., River Falls, 1970-72, Utah State U., Logan, 1973-76; asst. prof. U. Mont., Missoula, 1977-79, assoc. prof., 1979-83, prof., 1983—, dir. Inst. for Tourism and Recreation Rsch., 1987—. Office: Univ Mont Missoula MT 59812

MCCOPPIN, PETER, symphony orchestra conductor; b. Toronto, Ont., Can.; m. Roswitha McCoppin, 1975. BMus in Performance Art, U. Toronto; studied conducting with, Erich Leinsdorf, Prof. Hans Swarosky, Lovro von Maticic, Seriu Celibidache. Formed chamber choir Toronto, 1970-75; condr. orchestral program, prof. conducting Cleve. Inst. Music, 1975-78; guest condr. Alta. Ballet Co., Nat. Ballet Can., major orchs. Can.; music. advisor, condr. Vancouver (B.C.) Symphony Orch., 1988-89, now guest condr.; music dir. Victoria (B.C.) Symphony Orch., 1989—, Charlotte (N.C.) Symphony Orch., 1993—. Guest condr. Thunder Bay (Ont.) Symphony, Syracuse (N.Y.) Symphony; condr. Shanghai Symphony, Ctrl. Philharmonic, Beijing, Tokyo Symphony, Osaka Philharmonic, Gunma Symphony, Sapporo Symphony, Nat. Symphony Mex., Rochester Philharmonic, Buffalo Philharmonic, Tucson Symphony, most major orchs. in Can.; concerts with KBS Symphony, Korea; host B.C. TV Knowledge Network Classic Theatre, TV spls., radio programs. Office: Victoria Symphony Orch, 846 Broughton St lower level, Victoria, BC Canada V8W 1E4

MCCORKLE, ROBERT ELLSWORTH, agribusiness educator; b. Salinas, Calif., Apr. 3, 1938; s. Stanley Harold and Muriel Eugenia (Vosti) McC.; m. Mary E. McCorkle, June 26, 1965; children: Bonnie Kathleen, Robyn Krystyna. BSc in Farm Mgmt., Calif. Poly. State U., San Luis Obispo, 1960; MSc in Agrl. Econs., U. Calif., Davis, 1962; postgrad., U. Wis., 1969, Oreg. State U., 1966. Rsch. statistician U. Calif., Davis, 1960-62; asst. prof. agrl. bus. Calif. Poly. State U., San Luis Obispo, 1962-66, dir. internat. edn., 1970-74, asst. prof. agrl. mgmt., 1969-76, prof. agribus., 1976—; chief farm mgmt. officer Ministry Agr., Lusaka, Zambia, 1967-69; dir., owner McCorkle Farms, Inc., Willows, Calif., 1970—; vis. prof. Mich. State U., U.S. AID, Washington, 1984-85; dir., owner McCorkle Trucking, Glenn, Calif., 1988—; agrl. economist U.S. AID-Redso ESA, Nairobi, Kenya, 1984-85. Author: Guide for Farming in Zambia, 1968. Pres. Cabrillo Property Owners Assn., Los Osos, Calif., 1976-78; vol. Atty. Gen.'s Adv. Com., Calif., 1972-74. U.S. Peace Corps strategy grantee, Washington, 1976—. Mem. Am. Agrl. Econs. Assn., Western Agrl. Econs. Assn., Calif. Poly. Farm Mgmt. Club, Calif. Poly. Alumni Assn., Blue Key, Alpha Zeta (sr. advisor). Republican. Episcopalian. Office: Calif Poly State U San Luis Obispo CA 93407

MC CORMAC, WESTON ARTHUR, retired educator and army officer; b. Tacoma, Mar. 5, 1911; s. Jesse Carney and Jessie (Myron) McC.; B.A., Golden Gate U., M.B.A., 1968; diploma Nat. War Coll., 1956; M.P.A., U. So. Calif., 1972; M.A., Calif. Poly. State U., 1975. m. Mary Jeanne Rapp, Sept. 5, 1940. Account exec. Merrill, Lynch, Pierce, Fenner & Beane, Tacoma, Seattle, 1929-40; commd. lt. U.S. Army, 1940, advanced through grades to col., 1946; asst. chief of staff 7th Army G 1, 1952-54; comdg. officer 35th F.A. Group, Germany, 1956-58; dep. chief of staff V Corps, 1958-60, asst. chief of staff G 1, Pacific, 1962-65; ret., 1966; prof. bus., dept. chmn. Calif. Poly. State U., San Luis Obispo, 1968-80, ret., 1980. Decorated Legion of Merit with 2 oak leaf clusters, Silver Star, Bronze Star medal, Commendation medal with oak leaf cluster. Fellow Fin. Analysts Fedn.; mem. Los Angeles Soc. Fin. Analysts. Club: San Luis Obispo Golf and Country. Home: 176 Country Club Dr San Luis Obispo CA 93401-8917

MCCORMACK, DENNIS K., clinical psychologist; m. Nancy K. McCormack; children: Kelly, Karen. BA in Math., Calif. Western U., 1969; MA, U.S. Internat. U., 1971, PhD in Leadership and Human Behavior, PhD in Psychology, 1974, 78. Diplomate Internat. Council Profl. Counseling and Psychotherapy, Am. Inst. Counseling and Psychotherapy, Internat. Acad. Health Care Profls. Pvt. practice family therapist Coronado, Calif.; guest speaker at numerous clubs, lodges and local orgns. Contbr. articles to profl. jours. Mem. Sr. Citizen Adv. Com., 1982—, Land Use Adv. Com., Coronado, 1979-80; chmn. Coronado Planning Commn., 1978-83, St. Paul's United Meth. Ch., 1978-81, personnel com., 1978-81, mem. adminstrv. bd., 1983—; pres. Coronado Coordinating Council, 1983—; mem. adv. bd. Mil. Affairs Com., 1984—; bd. dirs. Vietnam Vets. Leadership Program, 1984—, Coronado Hosp. Found., 1988—; mem. Southbay Chember Exec. Com., 1986—, Coronado Visitor Promotion Bd., 1986—. Fellow Internat. Council of Sex Edn. and Parenthood of Am. U., Am. Bd. Med. Psychotherapists (clin. assoc.), S.D. Acad. Psychologists (chmn. membership com. 1988—), Coronado C. of C. (pres. 1986—). Office: PO Box 577 Richmond Hill GA 31324

MCCORMACK, RANDOLPH WAYNE, metals company administrator; b. Jacksonville, Fla., Nov. 21, 1945; s. James and Margie Lee (Hamilton) McC.; m. Sue M. Whipple, Feb. 8, 1969; children: Robin Sue, Timothy James. BS in Bus. Adminstrn., Fla. State U., 1967; MBA, U. Mont., 1973. Commd. lt. USAF, 1967, advanced through grades to lt. col., 1981, ret., 1988; program mgr. Exotic Metals Forming Co., Kent, Wash., 1988-89, prodn. control mgr., 1990-91, materiel mgr., 1991—. Chmn. Simi Valley First Bapt. Ch., 1982, Edgewood Bapt. Ch., Edmonds, Wash., 1992; bd. dirs. Beavercreek (Ohio) Ch. of the Nazarene, 1984. Named to Outstanding Young Men of Am., 1979. Mem. Am. Prodn. and Inventory Control Soc. Republican. Baptist. Home: 528 6th Ave S Edmonds WA 98020 Office: Exotic Metals Forming Co 5411 S 226th St Kent WA 98032

MCCORMICK, CARROLL CHARLES, physics and chemistry educator; b. Spokane, Wash., Feb. 25, 1933; s. Charles Cummings and Alice Margery (Stockwell) McC.; m. Betty Ann Mulalley, June 13, 1958; children: John Charles, Robert Alan, William Terrance. BS, Whitworth Coll., 1959, MEd, 1984. Tchr. Mt. Selinda (Zimbabwe) Secondary Sch., 1960-65, Park Jr. High Sch., Spokane, 1965-72, Micronesian Occupational Ctr., Palau, Micronesian Islands, 1972-74, Havermale Jr. High Sch., Spokane, 1976-78, N. Cen. High Sch., Spokane, 1978-92; with Peace Corps, Panama, 1993—. Baseball and basketball coach, Spokane, 1960-90. With U.S. Army, 1953-55, Korea. Democrat. Congregationalist.

MCCORMICK, FLOYD GUY, JR., agricultural educator; b. Center, Colo., July 3, 1927; s. Floyd Guy and Gladys (Weir) McC.; m. Constance P. Slane, Sept. 18, 1965; children: Angela Lynn, Craig Alan, Kim Ann, Robert Guy. BS, Colo. State U., 1950, MEd, 1959; PhD, Ohio State U., 1964. Tchr. vocat. agr. State Colo., 1956-62; asst. prof. agrl. edn. Ohio State U., 1964-67; mem. com. agr. edn. Commn. Edn. in Agr. and Natural Resources, Nat. Acad. Sci., 1967-69; prof. agrl. edn., head dept. U. Ariz., 1967-89, prof. emeritus, dept. head emeritus, 1990—; cons. in-svc. edn., div. vocat. edn. Ohio Dept. Edn., 1963-64; vis. prof. Colo. State U., 1973, U. Sierra Leone, Njala Univ. Coll., 1989; external examiner U. Sierra Leone, 1984, 85, 87; adv. trustee Am. Inst. Cooperatives, Washington, 1985-88; mem. Nat. Coun. Vocat. and Tech. Edn. in Agr., Washington, 1985-88. Author: (with others) Teacher Education in Agriculture, 1982, Supervised Occupational Experience Handbook, 1982; Author instructional units, tech. bulls., articles in profl. jours.; Spl. editor: Agrl. Edn. mag, 1970-74. Trustee Nat. FFA Found. Served with USNR, 1945-46. Named hon. state farmer Colo., 1958, Ariz., 1968, Am. farmer, 1972; recipient Centennial award Ohio State U., 1970, E.B. Knight award NACTA Jour., 1980, Regional Outstanding Tchr. award Nat. Assn. Coll. Tchrs. Agr., 1989, also fellow, 1988, VIP citation Nat. FFA Assn., 1990, Diamond Anniversary award Ohio State U., 1992. Mem. Am. Vocat. Assn. (mem. policy com. agrl. edn. div. 1976-79, v.p. div. 1985-88, chmn. membership com. 1980-83, sec. agrl. edn. div. 1983-86, pres. 1985-88, outstanding svc. award 1989), Nat. Vocat. Agr. Tchrs. Assn. (life, Outstanding Svc. award Region I 1974, 83), Am. Assn. Tchr. Educators in Agr. (disting. lectr. 1984, editor newsletter 1975-76, pres. 1976-77, Disting. Svc. award 1978, 88, Rsch. award western region rsch. 1988), Alpha Zeta, Alpha Tau Alpha (hon.), Gamma Sigma Delta, Phi Delta Kappa, Epsilon Pi Tau. Home: 6933 E Paseo San Andres Tucson AZ 85710-2203

MCCORMICK, NANCY LOUISE, councilwoman; b. Billings, Mont.; d. Walter William and Mary Louise (Hanson) Mauritson; m. Robert E. McCormick, Dec. 29, 1966; children: Jeffrey Scott, Ryan Walter. BS, Mont. State U., 1966. Tchr. Three Forks (Mont.) High Sch., 1966-67, Bellevue (Wash.) Sch. Dist., 1967-70; council mem. City of Redmond, Wash., 1986—; bd. dirs. Regional Water Assn., Redmond. Mem. State Legis. Task Force, Olympia, Wash., 1986; chair Overlake Transp. Task Force, Redmond, 1984-86, Redmond Planning Commn., 1984-85; bd. dirs. Eastide Transp. Com., Redmond, 1988-89; pres. Redmond City Coun., 1988-90; bd. dirs. centennial project Redmond History Book, 1989. Named Citizen of the Yr., City of Redmond, 1984. Mem. Assn. Wash. Cities (legis. com.), Eastside Human Svcs. Coun., Suburban Cities Legis. Com., Redmond C. of C. (transp. and econ. devel. coms.). Office: City of Redmond 15670 NE 85th St Redmond WA 98052-3584

MCCORMICK, RICHARD DAVID, telecommunications company executive; b. Fort Dodge, Iowa, July 4, 1940; s. Elmo Eugene and Virgilla (Lawler) McC.; m. Mary Patricia Smola, June 29, 1963; children: John Richard, Matthew David, Megan Ann, Katherine Maura. B.S. in Elec. Engring., Iowa State U., 1961. With Bell Telephone Co., 1961-85; N.D. v.p., chief exec. officer Northwestern Bell Telephone Co., Fargo, 1974-77; asst. v.p. human resources AT&T, Basking Ridge, N.J., 1977-78; sr. v.p. Northwestern Bell, Omaha, 1978-82, pres., chief exec. officer, 1982-85; exec. v.p. U.S. West Inc., Englewood, Colo., 1985-86, pres., chief oper. officer, 1986-90, pres., chief exec. officer, 1990-91, chmn., pres., chief exec. officer, 1992—; bd. dirs. Super Valu Stores, Norwest Corp. Mem. Phi Gamma Delta. Office: US West Inc 7800 E Orchard Rd Englewood CO 80111-2533

MCCORMICK, ROBERT MATTHEW, III, newspaper executive; b. N.Y.C., Dec. 31, 1938; s. Robert Matthew Jr. and Rita Patricia (McGuinness) McC.; m. Janet Severin Ahrens, Apr. 27, 1957; children: Susan Anne Heisler, Mary Teresa Berrier, Robert M. IV, Mark P. BA, Georgetown U., 1960; grad. advanced mgmt. program, Harvard U., 1978. Mktg. rep. Gen. Foods, Washington, 1960-62; various sales and mktg. positions The Washington Post, 1962-76, v.p. sales, 1976-82; exec. v.p. Chgo. Sun-Times, 1982-83; sr. v.p., sales and mktg. San Francisco News Agy., 1984-86, pres., chief exec. officer, 1987—; dir. Met. Sunday Newspapers, N.Y.C., 1987—. Bd. dirs. Conv. and Visitors Bur., San Francisco, 1987—, mem. exec. com., 1990—; mem. Mayor's Fiscal Adv. Com., San Francisco, 1987—; sector chair United Way Bay Area, San Francisco, 1989-91. Mem. Newspaper Assn. Am. (circulation and readership com.), Blackhawk Country Club, Burning Tree Club. Home: 2945 Deer Meadow Dr Danville CA 94506-2188 Office: San Francisco Newspaper Agy 925 Mission St San Francisco CA 94103-2905

MCCORMICK, SHARON SMITH, social worker; b. Galveston, Tex., Sept. 19, 1943; d. Laurence K. Jean (McFarland) Smith; m. Richard G. Schubert, Jul. 4, 1979 (div. 1985); m. Thomas J. McCormick, Dec. 20, 1986;. BA, Coll. Wooster, 1965; MSW, U. Kans., 1970; PhD, U. Denver, 1984. Clin. supr. Drug Rehab. Ctr., Ft. Carson, Colo., 1972-74; therapist Sopris Mental Health Clinic, Glenwood Springs, Colo., 1974-76; dir. Battered Women Svcs., Colorado Springs, Colo., 1977; therapist N.W. Colo. Mental Health Svcs., Craig, 1978; therapist, supr. Marriage & Family Counseling Ctr., Grand Junction, Colo., 1980-82; officer Grand Valley Devel. Corp., Grand Junction, Colo., 1980-83; clin. supr. Mesa Sch., Colorado Springs, Colo., 1984-86; pvt. prac. Woodland Park, Colo., 1986—; sch. social worker Harrison Sch. Dist., Colorado Springs, Colo., 1986—; rsch. Neurolpsychological Rsch. Ctr. Colorado Springs, 1989—; cons. High Winds Child Placment Agy., Woodland Park, Colo., 1990-92. Commr. Town Planning Comm., Green Mountain Falls, Colo. 1985-87; mem. Child Protection Team, Woodland Park, 1987-89. NIMH fellow, 1978-79, VA fellow, 1968-70. Mem. NASW, Am. Bd. Examiners Clin. Social Work (diplomate). Democrat. Home: PO Box 327 Green Mountain Falls CO 80819-0327

MCCORMICK, TIMOTHY BRIAN BEER, lawyer; b. Northampton, Mass., May 16, 1959; s. Brian Beer and Margaret Ann McCormick; m. Lee Hillary Kadis, Sept. 2, 1979 (div. June 1991); m. Virginia Lee Kostner, June 30, 1991; 1 child, Cameron A. BA, U. Calif., Berkeley, 1984; JD, Am. U., 1987. Bar: Calif. 1987, U.S. Dist. Ct. (no. dist.) Calif. 1987, U.S. Ct. Appeals (9th cir.) 1987, U.S. Dist. Ct. (ea. dist.) Calif., 1991. Staff asst. Office of Lt. Gov., Sacramento, 1982-83; cons. Calif. Rep. Party, Sacramento, 1984; rsch. asst. Nat. Right to Work Found., Springfield, Va., 1985-86; assoc. Graham & James, San Francisco, 1987-93, McPharlin & Mahl, San Jose, Calif., 1993—. Comments editor Adminstrv. Law Jour., 1986-87. Patron mem. Crocker Art Mus. Assn., Sacramento; mem. Rep. State Cen. Com. of Calif., 1983-85, assoc. mem., 1985—, mem. exec. com., 1983-84; gen. coun. Asian Am.Polit. Edn. Found., 1992—. Mem. ABA (litigation sect., forum com. on the constrn. industry, tort and ins. practice sect.), Bar Assn. San Francisco, Engring. and Utility Contractors Assn. (legis. com. 1991—). Home: 5441 Broadway Oakland CA 94618-1753 Office: McPharlin & Mahl 50 W San Fernando Ste 810 San Jose CA 95113

MCCORMICK, WILLIAM CHARLES, manufacturing company executive; b. Glendale, Ohio, Oct. 24, 1933; s. Warren Starling and Helen Catherine (Haering) McC.; children—William Charles II, Timothy L., Anthony R. B.S. in Math., U. Cin., 1968. Mfg. engring. mgr. Gen. Electric Co., Evendale, Ohio, 1972-74; plant mgr. Gen. Electric Co., Lynn, Mass., 1974-76; mfg. mgr. Gen. Electric Co., Detroit, 1976-80; gen. mgr. Gen. Electric Co., Plainville, Conn., 1980-85; pres. Precision Castparts Corp., Portland, Oreg., 1985—. Served to sgt. U.S. Army, 1952-54; Korea. Office: Precision Castparts Corp 4600 SE Harney Dr Portland OR 97206-0898*

MCCORQUODALE, DAN A., state senator; b. Longville, La., Dec. 17, 1934; s. Dan A. and Lallah Mae (Thornton) McC.; m. Jean A. Botsford; children—Mike, Sharon, Dan. B.Edn., San Diego State U., 1962. Mem. Chula Vista City Council, Calif., 1960-64, mayor, 1964-68; tchr. elem. sch., National City and San Jose, Calif., 1962-72; rep. Santa Clara County Bd. Suprs., Calif., 1972-82; mem. Calif. Senate, 1982—, chmn. agr. and water com. Founder, pres. Santa Clara County Consumers Protection and Edn. Council; chmn. Santa Clara County Consumer Protection Conf.; sec. adv. bd. Napa State Hosp.; chmn. Area VII Planning Bd. for Developmentally Disabled; rep. Statewide Homeowners Assn., others. Served to sgt. USMC, 1953-57; Pacific. Democrat.

MCCOTTER, JAMES RAWSON, lawyer; b. Denver, May 19, 1943; s. Charles R. and Jane M. (Ballantine) McC.; m. Carole Lee Hand, Sept. 5, 1965; children: Heidi M., Sage B. BA, Stanford U., 1965; JD, U. Colo., 1969. Bar: Colo. 1969, D.C. 1970, U.S. Dist. Ct. Colo. 1969, U.S. Ct. Appeals (10th and D.C. cirs.) 1970, U.S. Ct. Appeals (5th cir.) 1972, U.S. Supreme Ct. 1974. Law clk. U.S. Ct. Appeals (10th cir.), Denver, 1969-70; assoc. Covington & Burling, Washington, 1970-75; assoc. Kelly, Stansfield & O'Donnell, Denver, 1975-76, ptnr., 1977-86; assoc. gen. counsel Pub. Svc. Co. Colo., 1986-88; sr. v.p., gen. counsel, corp. sec., 1988—. Editor in chief U. Colo. Law Rev., 1968-69 (Outstanding Achievement award 1969). Dem. precinct committeeman, Denver, 1983-84; bd. dirs. Sewall Rehab. Ctr., Denver, 1979-84, Opera Colo., 1987—; dir., vice chmn. Denver Civic Ventures, Inc.; mem. law alumni bd. U. Colo., 1988-91; bd. dirs. Colo. Coun. on Econ. Edn., Found. for Denver Ctr. for Performing Arts Complex. Recipient Disting. Achievement award U. Colo. Law Sch., 1989; named to Outstanding Young Men Am., U.S. Jaycees, 1971; Storke scholar U. Colo., Boulder, 1967. Mem. ABA, Colo. Bar Assn. (adminstrv. law com. 1979-84), Fed. Energy Bar Assn. (chmn. com. on environment 1982-83), Law Club, Univ. Club, Denver Country Club, Order of Coif. Episcopalian. Home: 345 Lafayette St Denver CO 80218-3924 Office: Pub Svc Co Colo Ste 900 1225 17th St Denver CO 80202-4256

MC COVEY, WILLIE LEE, former professional baseball player; b. Mobile, Ala., Jan. 10, 1938; s. Frank and Ester (Jones) McC. Mem. minor league profl. baseball teams, 1955-59; mem. San Francisco Giants Profl. Baseball Team, 1959-73, 77-80, active in pub. rels., 1981-86, spl. asst. to the pres., 1986—; with San Diego Padres, 1974-76; coach Oakland (Calif.) A's, 1976-81. Named Nat. League Rookie of Year, 1959, Most Valuable Player, 1969; Home Run Champion, 1963, 68, 69; Runs Batted In Leader, 1968, 69; Comeback Player of Year, 1977; 8th on All-Time Major League List of Career Home Runs; All-Time Nat. League leader in grand slam home runs; mem. Nat. League All-Star Team, 1963, 66, 68-71; inducted into Baseball Hall of Fame, 1986. Office: care San Francisco Giants Candlestick Park San Francisco CA 94124-3998

MCCOWN, LINDA JEAN, medical technology educator; b. Pitts., Mar. 18, 1953; d. William Earnest and Mary Elizabeth McC. BS, Pa. State U., 1975; MS, U. Pitts., 1979. Cert. med. technologist, clin. lab. scientist. Microbiology aide Pa. State U., University Park, 1973-74; med. technologist, asst. supr., rsch. technologist Children's Hosp. of Pitts., 1975-80; asst. prof. med. tech., assoc. program dir. Ctrl. Wash. U., Ellensburg, 1980—; critiquer, insp. Nat. Accreditation Agy. for Clin. Lab. Scis., Chgo., 1984—; test item writer Nat. Cert. Agy., Washington, 1989—; recruiter Am. Soc. Clin. Pathologists, Chgo., 1988—. Contbr. articles to profl. jours. Stephen ministry, deacon First Presbyn. Ch., Yakima, Wash., 1992—; bd. dirs. The Campbell Farm, Wapato, Wash., 1990—; rally chmn. Heifer Project Internat., Wapato, 1991, 93. Mem. Am. Soc. for Med. Tech. (mem. commn. on accreditation 1988-91), Wash. State Soc. for Med. Tech. (conv. chair 1992, edn. chair 1996—, Pres.'s award 1992), Columbia Basin Soc. Clin. Lab. Sci. (pres.-elect 1993—), Omicron Sigma. Home: 1305 Jefferson Ave Yakima WA 98902 Office: Ctrl Wash U Ctr for Med Tech 1114 W Spruce Ste 34 Yakima WA 98902

MCCOY, EUGENE LYNN, civil engineer; b. Ridgefield, Wash., Apr. 9, 1926; s. Eugene Victor McCoy and Thelma Lucinda (Ayres) Martin; m. Marcia Helen Schear, Sept. 14, 1955 (div. 1974); children: Thomas Edwin, Susan Lynn, Molly Kay (dec.). AS, Lower Columbia Coll., 1948; BS, Wash. State U., 1950; MS, U. Wash., 1955. Registered profl. engr., Wash. Successively civil engr. soils, chief soils engr. sect., chief geotech. br. Portland (Oreg.) dist., chief geotech. br. North Pacific div. U.S. Army Corps. Engrs., 1955-85; staff cons. Shannon and Wilson, Portland, 1985-88, Cornforth Cons. Inc., Tigard, Oreg., 1988—; tech. specialist delegation for design of Longtan Dam, U.S. Army Corps. Engrs., Beijing, 1981, People to People's delegation Dams and Tunnels, 1987. Contbr. articles to profl jours. Active camp com. Campfire Girls, 4-H Clubs, Oregon City; vol. Loaves and Fishes, Oreg. State U. Ext., AARP Tax Aid. Cpl. U.S. Army, 1950-52. Mem. ASCE, U.S. Com. Large Dams, Oreg. Master Gardener. Democrat. Unitarian. Home: 20551 S Fischers Mill Rd Oregon City OR 97045-9646 Office: Cornforth Cons Inc Ste 111 10250 SW Greenburg Rd Portland OR 97223-8243

MC COY, FRANK MILTON, concert pianist, educator, lecturer; b. El Centro, Calif., s. Henderson C. and Annie (Lee) McC.; A.B. (Rotary scholar), San Francisco State Coll., 1949, M.A., 1960; postgrad. U. Wash., 1952-53, U. Calif. at Santa Barbara, 1957-58, U. So. Calif., 1961-65, U. Valencia (Spain), summer 1967, Walden U.; studied piano under Jean Le Duc, 1947-49, Madame Berthe Poncy-Jacobsen, 1952-53, Amparo Iturbi, 1960-62. Grad. asst. Sch. Music, U. Wash., Seattle, 1952-53; tchr. music edn. San Diego City Schs., 1953-54, El Centro Pub. Schs., 1954-57, Los Angeles City Schs.; counselor Social Service Center, Calexico, Calif., 1955-59; prof. piano and English Compton Coll., 1971-73; chmn. dept. music Portola Jr. High Sch., Los Angeles. Piano, soloist All Am. Chorus tour 1956; 1st Am. to concertize on islands of St. Pierre and Miguelon, 1960; regional rep. Robert S. Gregg Concert Assns., 1963-65; made concert tours Europe, Can., Latin Am., U.S., North Africa, Caribbean, Middle East, USSR; TV appearance CBC, 1965; adjudicator piano div. Southwestern Youth Music Festival, 1964; mem. bd. adjudicators Nat. Piano Playing Auditions, 1965; music-drama critic Post-Press Newspapers; founder, chmn. Annie Lee McCoy-Chopin Meml. Piano Award, 1975—; master tchr. in music Los Angeles City Schs., 1983-84. Bd. dirs. El Centro Community Concert Assn. Recipient Leona M. Hickman award U. Wash., 1953. Mem. Music Educators Nat. Conf., Nat. Guild Piano Tchrs., Am. Guild Mus. Artists, Nat. Music Tchrs. Assn., Souteast Symphony Assn. (bd. dirs.), Internat. Platform Assn., Nat. Negro Musicians, Nat. Council Tchrs. English. Author: Black Tomorrow: A Portrait of Afro-American Culture, 1976; Playlet: Music Masters, Old and New, 1966; Our American Heritage; We, Too, Are Americans, 1977; also articles. Home: 234 S Figueroa St Apt 431 Los Angeles CA 90012-2509 Office: 18720 Linnet St Tarzana CA 91356-3392

MCCOY, GERALD EDWARD, consultant, project manager; b. Casper, Wyo., July 11, 1944; s. William James McCoy and Marie (Reese) Burgess; m. Frieda Ann Noell, Oct. 12, 1968. AS, Casper Coll., 1966; student, U. Wyo., 1966-67; B in Architecture, U. Utah, 1971. Registered profl. architect, Alaska. Project rep. HUD, Salt Lake City, 1972-75; mgr. and contractor QC contracts compliance TMW, Milw., 1975; sr. contracts engr. Alyeska Pipeline, Anchorage, 1975-78; contracts mgr. Eaton-Kenway, Salt Lake City, 1975-78; mgr. project mgmt. TCS, Salt Lake City, 1983-84; v.p. tenant coordination Triad Am., Salt Lake City, 1984-85; owner project and contracts mgmt. G.E. McCoy & Assocs., Salt Lake City, 1986—.

MCCOY, JAMES M., data processing, computer company executive; b. Cheyenne, Wyo., 1946. Grad., San Jose St. U., 1969. With Internat. Bus. Machines Corp., 1968-73; v.p. mktg. Verbatim Corp., 1973-78; with Shugart Assocs., 1978-80; v.p. Quantum Corp., 1980-81; pres., CEO Maxtor Corp., 1982—. chmn. bd., 1986—; Bd. dirs. Centigram Corp., Exabyte Corp. Office: Maxtor Corp 211 River Oaks Pky San Jose CA 95134-1913*

MC COY, LOIS CLARK, social services executive, retired county official, magazine editor; b. New Haven, Oct. 1, 1920; d. William Patrick and Lois Rosilla (Dailey) Clark; m. Herbert Irving McCoy, Oct. 17, 1943; children: Whitney, Kevin, Marianne, Tori, Debra, Sally, Daniel. BS, Skidmore Coll., 1942; student Nat. Search and Rescue Sch., 1974. Asst. buyer R.H. Macy & Co., N.Y.C., 1942-44, assoc. buyer, 1944-48; instr. Mountain Medicine & Survival, U. Calif. at San Diego, 1973-74; cons. editor Search & Rescue Mag., 1975, Rescue mag., 1988-89; coord. San Diego Mountain Rescue Team, La Jolla, Calif., 1973-75; exec. sec. Nat. Assn. for Search and Rescue, Inc., Nashville and La Jolla, 1975-80, comptr., 1980-82; disaster officer San Diego County, 1980-86, Santa Barbara County, 1986-91, ret. Contbr. editor Rescue Mag., 1989—, editor-in-chief Response! mag., 1982-86; mem. adv. bd. Hazard Montly, 1991—; cons. law enforcement div.; Calif. Office Emergency Svcs., 1976-77; pres. San Diego Com. for Los Angeles Philharmonic Orch., 1957-58. Bd. dirs. Search and Rescue of the Californias, 1976-77, Nat. Assn. for Search and Rescue, Inc., 1980-87, pres., 1985-87, trustee, 1987-90, mem. Calif. OES strategic com., 1992—; pres., CEO Nat. Inst. For Urban Search & Rescue, 1989—; mem. Gov.'s Task Force on Earthquakes, 1981-82, Earthquake Preparedness Task Force, Seismic Safety Commn., 1982-85. Recipient Hal Foss award for outstanding service to search and rescue, 1982. Mem. AIAA, IEEE, Armed Forces Comm. and Electronics Assoc., Soc. for Computer Simulation, Nat. Assn. for Search & Rescue (Svc. award 1985), Mountain Rescue Assn., San Diego Mountain Rescue Team, Santa Barbara Amateur Radio Club, Sierra Club. Episcopalian. Author: Search and Rescue Glossary, 1974; contbr. to profl. jours. Office: PO Box 91648 Santa Barbara CA 93190

MCCOY, NORMA LOUISE, psychologist, educator, researcher, consultant; b. Galveston, Tex., Aug. 6, 1934; d. George Jr. and Nell Louise (Samuel) McC.; m. R. Bruce Irons III, Aug. 17, 1967 (div. Apr. 1974); children: Robert B. IV, Juliet McCoy. BA in Psychology, Stanford U., 1956; MA in Child Devel. and Psychology, U. Minn., 1960, PhD in Child Psychology, 1963. Rsch. assoc. Yale U., New Haven, 1962-63; asst. prof. dept. psychology San Francisco State U., 1963-67, assoc. prof., 1967-71, 73-76, prof., 1976—; vis. assoc. prof. Amherst (Mass.) Coll., 1971-73; cons. Health Outcomes Group, Palo Alto, Calif., 1990—. Contbr. chpts. to books, numerous articles to profl. jours. Bd. dirs. Hamilton Family Ctr., San Francisco, 1988-91. NIMH grantee, 1969-71. Mem. AAAS, APA, Am. Psychol. Soc., Internat. Menopause Soc., N.Am. Menopause Soc., Internat. Acad. Sex. Rsch., Soc. for Sci. Study of Sex (pres.-elect Western Region 1992—). Office: San Francisco State U Dept Psychology 1600 Holloway Ave San Francisco CA 94132

MC COY, ROBERT BAKER, publisher; b. Arrowsmith, Ill., Mar. 26, 1916; s. Robert Benton and Charlotte (Miller) McC. B.S., Northwestern U., 1950; M.S., 1951; postgrad., U. Ill. extension. Various positions with branches U.S. Govt., 1939-51; mng. editor book dept. Popular Mechanics Mag. Co., Chgo., 1951-60; mng. editor high sch. textbook div. J.B. Lippincott Co., Chgo., 1960-62; owner, pres., chmn. bd. Rio Grande Press Inc. (pubs. nonfiction Western Americana books), Chgo., 1962—; chmn. bd., pres. Rio Grande Press of N.Mex., Inc. Lectr., author articles on Am. Indian, ornithology, travel. Served with AUS, 1941-45. Office: The Rio Grande Press Inc La Casa Escuela Glorieta NM 87535

MCCOY, SUSAN DOUGLAS, gerontologist; b. Cleve., Mar. 7, 1944; d. Douglas Dallam and Jane Bixby. BS in Elem. Edn., Mount Union Coll., Alliance, Ohio, 1966; MS in Counseling, Calif. State U., Long Beach, 1989. Primary tchr. Noble Road Elem. Sch., Cleveland Heights, Ohio, 1966-67; primary and intermediate tchr. Spurgeon Elem. Sch., Santa Ana, Calif., 1967-72; med. asst. John R. Evans, M.D., Orange, Calif., 1975-78; restorative nursing asst. Wilshire Convalescent Hosp., Fullerton, Calif., 1979-83; long-term care ombudsman Orange County Coun. on Aging, 1983-85; liaison, gerontologist Lakeview Med. Group, Orange, 1985-91, program dir. gerontology svcs., 1991—; cons. South County Srs., San Clemente, 1986; counselor, rsch. asst. Adult Learning Disability Program, Long Beach, 1986-88; therapist Santa Ana Med. Ctr. Eating Disorder Unit, 1988-89; dir. Advanced Geopsychiatric Edn., 1991—. Co-author, editor: Counselor Handbook for the College Learning Disabled Adult, 1986. Dir. community edn. Orange County Coun. on Aging, 1985; liaison devel. instr./counselor svcs. to learning disabled students English dept. Calif. State U., Long Beach, 1986-87. Mem. Calif. Assn. Marriage and Family Therapists, Gerontology Rsch. and Study Program, Interfaith Action for Aging (vice chmn., pres. bd. dirs. 1990-91), Soroptimist Internat. (Garden Grove chpt. 1991), Kappa Delta Pi, Phi Kappa Phi, Chi Sigma Iota. Office: Lakeview Med Group 928 W Town And Country Rd Orange CA 92668-4714

MCCOY, WALLY WARREN, tax consultant; b. Weston, Oreg., Feb. 28, 1936; s. Ashby W. and Mildred (Knechtley) McC.; m. Jeanne August, Feb. 20, 1964 (div. 1973); children: Timothy, Shaun, Geoffrey. BSBA, Portland State U., 1965. Lic. tax cons. Ins. salesman Standard Ins., Portland, Oreg., 1965-66; fin. cons. Internat. Securities, Portland, 1966-68; tax. cons. Portland, 1967—, real estate salesman, 1970-82. Editor, pub. newsletter The Enlightened Investor, 1991—. With U.S.Army, 1959-61. Mem. Computer Users Group of Am. Assn. Ind. Investors, Oreg. Assn. Tax Cons., Oreg. Soc. Tax Cons., Alpha Kappa Psi (pres. 1964-65). Republican. Home and Office: 2515 SE Division Portland OR 97202

MCCRACKEN, EDWARD R., electronics executive; b. Fairfield, Iowa, 1943. BSEE, Iowa State U., 1966; MBA, Stanford U., 1968. With Hewlett Packard Co.; pres., CEO Silicon Graphics, Inc., 1984—; dir. Digital Rsch., Inc. Home: 11 Angela Dr Los Altos CA 94022 Office: Silicon Graphics Inc PO Box 7311 2011 N Shoreline Blvd Mountain View CA 94043-1389*

MCCRACKEN, HORACE W(ILLIAM), solar company executive; b. Ft. Benton, Mich., Mar. 5, 1922; s. (Albert) Ray and Blanche (Spear) McC.; m. Opal Olive Erickson, Sept. 21, 1947 (div. 1967); children: Carol, Wayne, Keith; m. Joyce Stoddard, Feb. 15, 1981. Grad., Glad Tidings Bible Inst., San Francisco, 1941; BSc in Edn., U. Tenn., 1949; postgrad., Vanderbilt U., 1950-51. Adminstrv. asst. dir. rsch. Consol. Paper Corp., Ltd., Grand'Mere, Que., Can., 1955-58; technician Sea Water Conversion Lab., U. Calif., Berkeley, 1958-61; various positions in solar energy and desalination, 1961-83; founder, owner, mgr. McCracken Solar Co., solar stills, Alturas, Calif., 1959—. Author: History of Church of God Missions, 1942. With Signal Corps, AUS, 1942-45, PTO. Named to Solar Hall of Fame, 1984. Home and Office: 329 W Carlos St Alturas CA 96101

MC CRACKEN, PHILIP TRAFTON, sculptor; b. Bellingham, Wash., Nov. 14, 1928; s. William Franklin and Maude (Trafton) McC.; m. Anne MacFetridge, Aug. 14, 1954; children—Timothy, Robert, Daniel. B.A. in Sculpture, U. Wash., 1954. Asst. to Henry Moore Eng., 1954. One-man shows: Willard Gallery, N.Y.C., 1960, 65, 68, 70, Seattle Art Mus., 1961, Wash. State Capitol Mus., Olympia, 1964, Art Gallery of Greater Victoria, B.C., 1964, LaJolla (Calif.) Mus. Art, 1970, Anchorage Hist. and Fine Arts Mus., 1970, Tacoma Art Mus., 1980, Kennedy Galleries, N.Y.C., 1985, Lynn McAllister Gallery, Seattle, 1986, 89, others; group shows include: Mus. Art, Ogunquit, Maine, 1957, Chgo. Art Inst., 1958, Detroit Inst. Arts, 1958, Pa. Acad. Fine Arts, 1958, Contemporary Art Gallery, Houston, 1958, DeYoung Meml. Mus., San Francisco, 1960, Los Angeles Mcpl. Art Mus., 1960, Galerie Claude Bernard, Paris, 1960, Phillips Gallery, Washington, 1966, Corcoran Gallery, 1966, Mus. Art, Akron, 1967, Finch Coll., N.Y.C., 1968, Rutgers U., 1968, Whitney Mus. Art, 1978, Portland Art Mus., 1976, Mont. State U., Bozeman, 1979, Brigham Young U., 1980, Bellvue (Wash.) Art Mus., 1986, Lynn McAllister Gallery, 1986, Am. Acad. Arts and Letters, N.Y.C., 1986, Schmidt Bingham Gallery, N.Y.C., 1987, Wash. State Capital Mus., 1987, 89, Cheney-Cowles Mus., Spokane, Wash., 1988, Smithsonian Instn., 1991—, Nat. Mus., Ottawa, Can., 1991-92, others; sculptures represented: Norton Bldg., Seattle, Kankakee (Ill.) State Hosp., Swinomish Indian Tribal Center, LaConner, UN Assn., N.Y.C., King County King Dome, Seattle, City Hall, Everett, Wash., others. (Recipient numerous prizes, awards). Address: 401 B Guemes Island Anacortes WA 98221

MCCRACKEN, SHIRLEY ANN ROSS, educational consultant; b. Rochester, N.Y., Aug. 15, 1937; d. Bernard Anthony Ross and Marian Elizabeth (Taliento) Heimann; m. Paul Arthur McCracken, June 25, 1971; children: Donna Ann, Glenn Allan. BA in Math., Nazareth Coll., 1959; MS in Math., Marquette U., Milw., 1968; PhD in Human Behavior, LaJolla U., 1980. Cert. math., Eng. tchr., Calif. Tchr., dept. chair Mount Carmel High Sch., Auburn, N.Y., 1959-68; asst. workshop supr. Jewish Vocat. Svc., Milw., 1968; rehab. counselor Curative Workshop, Milw., 1968-69; tchr. Anaheim (Calif.) Union High Sch. Dist., 1969-72; cons. Anaheim Hills, Calif., 1980-87; dir. religious edn. San Antonio Ch., Anaheim Hills, 1987-90; instr. Orange (Calif.) Catechetical Inst., 1989—; cons. Cath. parishes, Orange County, 1990—. Author: Take Off to a New You, 1979, Creative Leadership; poem: The Creative Women, 1977 (award winner 1977); editor: Planning Model for Leadership, Decision Making, Management Training; staff handbook com. Orange Catechetical Inst., 1989—. Treas. Broadmoor Northridge Community Assn., Anaheim Hills, 1976; corr. sec. Anaheim Hills Friends of Libr., 1980; bd. dirs. Friends of Libr. Found., Orange County; mem. Anaheim Mus., 1985-91; mem. elem./jr. high religious edn. adv. bd. Diocese of Orange, Calif., 1990—; commr. Budget Adv. Commn., City of Anaheim, 1991—, chmn., 1992-93. Mem. AAUW (officer Anaheim br., Calif. State divsn., Anaheim Hills br.), Nat. Coun. Tchrs. Math., Ebell Club (sec. 1977-78, 91-92, 4th v.p. 1978-79, pres. 1992-93). Home: 6553 E Calle Del Norte Anaheim CA 92807-4205

MCCRAVEN, CARL CLARKE, health services administrator; b. Des Moines, May 27, 1926; s. Marcus Henry and Buena Vista (Rollins) McC.; BS in Elec. Engring., Howard U., 1950; MS in Health Svcs. Adminstrn., Calif. State U.-Northridge, 1976; m. Eva Louise Stewart, Mar. 18, 1978; 1 child, Carl B. Radiation physicist Nat. Bur. Standards, 1951-55; rsch. engr. Lockheed Calif. Co., 1955-63; mem. tech. staff TRW Systems, 1963-72; assoc. adminstr. Pacoima Meml. Hosp., Lake View Terrace, Calif., 1972-74; founder, chief exec. officer Hillview Mental Health Ctr., Inc., Lake View Terrace, 1974—; asst. prof. Calif. State U., Northridge, 1976-78. Regent Casa Loma Coll.; bd. dirs. San Fernando Valley Girl Scout Council, Pledgerville Sr. Citizens Villa, ARC; treas. San Fernando Valley Mental Health Assn. Recipient citation Calif. Senate, 1971, 88, Resolution of commendation, 1988, Calif. Assembly, 1971, 88, commendation, 1989, City of Los Angeles, 1971, 78, 88, commendation, 1989, County of Los Angeles, 1988, commendation, 1989, Mayor of L.A. commendation, 1989; developer, mgr. Hillview Village Housing Project. Fellow Assn. Mental Health Adminstrs.; mem. Am. Pub. Health Assn., Am. Mgmt. Assn., Nat. Assn. Health Svcs. Execs., NAACP (pres. so. area Calif. conf. 1967-71, nat. dir. 1970-76), North San Fernando Valley Rotary (pres. 1983), Sigma Pi Phi. Home: 17109 Nanette St Granada Hills CA 91344-1410

MCCRAVEN, EVA STEWART MAPES, health service administrator; b. L.A., Sept. 26, 1936; d. Paul Melvin and Wilma Zech (Ziegler) Stewart; m. Carl Clarke McCraven, Mar. 18, 1978; children: David Anthony, Lawrence James, Maria Lynn Mapes. ABS magna cum laude, Calif. State U., Northridge, 1974, MS, Cambridge Grad. Sch. Psychology, 1987; PhD, 1991. Dir. spl. projects Pacoima Meml. Hosp., 1969-71, dir. health edn., 1971-74; asst. exec. dir. Hillview Community Mental Health Center, Lakeview Terrace, Calif., 1974—; past dir. dept. consultation and edn. Hillview Ctr., developer, mgr. long-term residential program, 1986-90; former program mgr. Crisis Residential Program, Transitional Residential Program and Day Treatment Program for mentally ill offenders, dir. mentally ill offenders svcs.; former program dir. Valley Homeless Shelter Mental Health Counseling Program; dir. Integrated Services Agy., Hillview Mental Health Ctr., Inc., 1993—; Former pres. San Fernando Valley Coordinating Coun. Area Assn., Sunland-Jujunga Coordinating Coun.; bd. dirs. N.E. Valley Health Corp., 1970-73, Golden State Community Mental Health Ctr., 1970-73. Recipient Resolution of Commendation award State of Calif., 1988, Commendation award, 1988, Spl. Mayor's plaque, 1988, Commendation awards for community svcs. City of L.A., 1989, County of L.A., 1989, Calif. State Assembly, 1989, Calif. State Senate, 1989, award Sunland-Tujunga Police Support Coun., 1989, Woman of Achievement award Sunland-Tujunga BPW, 1990. Fellow Assn. Mental Health Adminstrs.; mem. Am. Pub. Health Assn., Women in Health Adminstrn., Health Services Adminstrn. Alumni Assn. (former v.p.), Sunland-Jujunga Bus. and Profl. Women, LWV. Office: Hillview Community Mental Health Ctr 11500 Eldridge Ave San Fernando CA 91342-6523

MCCRAW, LES, engineering and construction company executive; b. Sandy Springs, S.C., Nov. 3, 1934; s. Leslie Gladstone and Cornelia (Milam) McC.; m. Mary Earle Brown; children: Leslie Gladstone III, James B., John. BSCE, Clemson U., 1956. Registered profl. engr., Del. Design engr. Gulf Oil Corp., Phila., 1956-57; various engring. and constrn. positions E.I. DuPont Co., Wilmington, Del., 1960-75; v.p., mgr. div. Daniel Constrn. Co., Greenville, S.C., 1975-82, pres., 1982-84; pres., chief exec. officer Daniel Internat., Greenville, 1984-86, Fluor Daniel, Greenville and Irvine, Calif., 1986-88; pres. Fluor Corp., Irvine, 1988-90, vice chmn., chief exec. officer, 1990-91, chief exec. officer, chmn. bd. dirs., 1991. Bd. dirs. Allergan and Multimedia Inc., Orange County Performing Arts Ctr.; trustee Columbia Coll., S.C. and Hampden-Sydney Coll., Va.; mem. adv. bd. rsch. found., mem. pres.'s adv. coun. Clemson U. Mem. Bus. Roundtable, Constrn. Industry's Pres.'s Forum, Nat. Assn. Mfrs. (bd. dirs.), Calif. Bus. Roundtable Palmetto Bus. Forum. Republican. Presbyterian. Office: Fluor Corp Inc 3333 Michelson Dr Irvine CA 92730-0001

MCCRAY, CURTIS LEE, university president; b. Wheatland, Ind., Jan. 29, 1938; s. Bert and Susan McCray; m. Mary Joyce Macdonald, Sept. 10, 1960; children: Leslie, Jennifer, Meredith. B.A., Knox Coll., Galesburg, Ill., 1960; postgrad. U. Pa., 1960-61; Ph.D., U. Nebr., 1968. Chmn. dept. English, Saginaw Valley Coll., University Center, Mich., 1972-73, dean arts and scis., 1973-75, v.p. acad. affairs, 1975-77; provost, v.p. acad. affairs Govs. State U., Chgo., 1977-82; pres. U. North Fla., Jacksonville, 1982-88, Calif. State U., Long Beach, 1988—. Bd. dirs., 1982-88, campaign chmn. Jacksonville United Way, 1987; bd. dirs. Sta. WJCT Channel 7 and Stereo 90, Jacksonville, 1982-88, Jacksonville Art Mus., 1983-88, Meml. Med. Ctr., Jacksonville, 1983-88, Jacksonville Community Council, Inc., 1982-88, Arts Assembly Jacksonville, 1984-88, Jacksonville Urban League, 1985-88; hon. dir. Jacksonville Symphony Assn., 1983; mem. Dame Point Bridge Commn., Jacksonville, 1982; mem. Jacksonville High Tech Task Force, 1982; chmn. SUS High Tech. and Industry Council, 1986-88; mem. state relations and undergrad. edn. com. Am. Assn. State Colls. and Univs., 1985-88. Woodrow Wilson fellow, 1960; Johnson fellow, 1966; George F. Baker scholar, 1956; Ford Found. grantee, 1969; recipient Landee award for excellence in teaching Saginaw State Coll., 1972. Mem. AAUP. Club: Torch. Office: Calif State U-Long Beach Office of Pres 1250 N Bellflower Blvd Long Beach CA 90840-0001*

MCCREA, STEPHEN BRIAN, lawyer; b. Washington, Oct. 29, 1949; s. William Sherborne and Edith (Rivera) McC.; m. Theresa A. Porcarelli, Feb. 21, 1981; children: Christopher, Brian. BA in Polit. Sci., UCLA, 1971; JD, U. Idaho, 1974. Bar: Idaho 1974, U.S. Dist. Ct. Idaho 1974, U.S. Ct. Appeals (9th cir.) 1991, U.S. Supreme Ct. 1980. Staff atty. Idaho Legal Aid Svcs., Inc., Caldwell, 1974-75, pres. bd., 1977-81; ptnr. Powers & McCrea, Post Falls, Idaho, 1975-77; staff atty. Kootenai County Pub. Defender, Coeur d 'Alene, Idaho, 1977-78, mng. atty., 1979-80; pvt. practice Coeur d'Alene, 1980—; hearing officer Idaho Transp. Dept., Coeur d'Alene, 1982—. Chmn. Pub. Works Com., Coeur d'Alene, 1990—; city councilman, City of Coeur d'Alene, 1982—. Mem. Rotary. Presbyterian. Home: 807 W Lakeshore Dr Coeur D Alene ID 83814-2131 Office: 111 N 2d St Ste 200 Coeur D Alene ID 83814

MCCREADY, KENNETH FRANK, electric utility executive; b. Edmonton, Alta., Can., Oct. 9, 1939; s. Ralph and Lillian McCready; m. Margaret E. Randall, Sept. 2, 1961; children: John, Brian, Janet. BSc, U. Alta., 1963. Supr. data processing and systems Calgary (Alta.) Power Ltd., 1965-67, supr. rates and contracts, 1967-68, adminstrv. asst. to exec. v.p., 1968-72, v.p. adminstrn., 1976-80; asst. mgr. mgmt. cons. div. Montreal Engring. Co., Calgary, 1972-75, mgr. mgmt. systems dept., 1975-76; gen. mgr. Morenco Computing Svcs. Ltd.; sr. v.p. ops. TransAlta Utilities, Calgary, 1980-85, pres., chief operating officer, 1985—, also bd. dirs., 1988—; pres., chief exec. officer TransAlta Utilities, 1989—; pres., CEO TransAlta Utilities and TransAlta Energy, 1990; bd. dirs. Keyword Office Techs. Ltd., Maloney Steel Ltd., PanCan. Petroleum Ltd., Hewlett Packard (Can.) Ltd., Conf. Bd. Can.; chmn. bd. Advanced Computing Techs., Inc. Past dep. chmn. bd. govs. So. Alta. Inst. of Tech; chair Alberta Round Table on Environment and Econ.; v.p. Northwest Electric Light and Power Assoc.; bd. dirs. Marigold Found. Ltd.; dir. Calgary Internat. Organ Festival. Mem. Assn. Profl. Engrs., Geologists and Geophysicists of Alta, ASEA, ABB (Brown Boveri), Bus. Coun. on Nat. Issues, Can. Elec. Assn., Bus. Coun. for Sustainable Devel., CESO (adv. coun.), Can. West Found. Coun., Constrn. Owners' Assn. Alta (past pres.), Calgary C. of C., Men's Can. Club Calgary (past pres.), Ranchmen's Club. Office: TransAlta Utilities Corp, 110 12th Ave SW Box 1900, Calgary, AB Canada T2P 2M1

MCCREADY, WILLIAM FLOYD, venture capitalist, entrepreneur; b. Tillamook, Oreg., Mar. 29, 1944; s. William S. and Eleanor L. (Wildfong) McC. BS in Engring. Physics and Math., Oreg. State U., 1966. Lic. real estate salesman, Hawaii. Chief nuclear test engr. Pearl Harbor Naval Shipyard, Honolulu, 1971-73; supt. Mauna Kea Astron. Obs., U. Hawaii, Hilo, 1973-76; gen. ptnr. Venture Planning Assocs., Honolulu, 1976—; bus. cons. UN Devel. Program, Bhutan; prin., bd. dirs. Sanchez Communication Sta. KQNG-AM-FM, Lihue, Kauai, Hawaii, Studebakers of Australia, Sydney, Group (4) Logistics, Ltd.; prin., cons. Kula Bay Tropical Clothes Co., Honolulu, 1988—; gen. ptnr. Venture Investment Ptnrs., Honolulu, 1992; key note speaker Hawaii Gov.'s Symposium on Software Devel., 1991; co-coord. Hawaii Gov.'s Symposium on High Tech. Devel. 1992. Mem. Gov.'s Hawaii 2000 Commn., Hilo, 1973-76; course marshall Honolulu Marathon, 1986-89; telethon panelist Hawaii Easter Seals Soc. for Handicapped, 1985-92; spl. instr. applied econs. Jr. Achievement, 1988-89; mem. Better Bus. Bur. Hawaii. Officr USN, 1966-71, Vietnam. Mem. Inst. Mgmt. Cons. (cert.), Acad. Profl. Cons. and Advisors (cert. profl. cons.), Hawaii Venture Capital Assn. (co-founder, past pres.), Nat. Fedn. Ind. Bus., Small Bus. Hawaii, Rotary (dir. community sect. Pearl Harbor 1990). Office: Venture Planning Assocs Inc 1188 Bishop St Ste 1508 Honolulu HI 96813

MCCREERY, GLENN ERNEST, research scientist; b. Palo Alto, Calif., June 18, 1943; s. John Harold and Marguerite (Hannah) McC.; m. Ann Adele Henry, Mar. 19, 1987; children: James, Anita. BS in Mech. Engring., San Jose State U., 1966, MS in Mech. Engring., 1968; PhD in Chem. Engring., U. Calif., Santa Barbara, 1987. Mech. engr. Applied Tech. Inc., Sunnyvale, Calif., 1968-69, Lawrence Livermore (Calif.) Nat. Lab., 1969-71; scientist Lockheed Rsch. Lab., Palto Alto, 1971-73; sr. scientific specialist Idaho Nat. Engring. Lab., Idaho Falls, 1973—; cons. Ontario Hydro Can., 1986-87. contbr. articles to Fluid Dynamics, Nuclear Reactor Safety; reviewer jours. Ski patrollman Nat. Ski Patrol, Grand Targhee Resort, 1975—. Dean's scholar San Jose State U., 1967, 68. Mem. Am. Nuclear Soc., Tau Beta Pi. Home: 2290 Briarcliff Ave Idaho Falls ID 83404-6363

MCCRELESS, THOMAS GRISWOLD, nuclear engineer; b. San Antonio, Aug. 20, 1927; s. Thomas G. Sr. and Laura (Sparks) McC.; m. Nancy Ament, June 1, 1951; children: Cynthia M. Tate, Nancy M. Klein. BS in Engring., U.S. Naval Acad., 1951; MS in Nuclear Engring., U. Md., 1965, PhD in Nuclear Engring., 1977. Staff engr. AEC, Bethesda, Md., 1960-75; br. chief Adv. Com. Reactor Safeguards U.S. Nuclear Regulatory Commn., Washington, 1975-80, asst. exec. dir., 1980-88; pres. Cyprus Cove Community Assn., San Clemente, Calif., 1989-92, also bd. dirs. Author: Nuclear Interactions, 1965. Capt. USMC, 1951-60, Korea. Mem. Am. Nuclear Soc. (emeritus), Sigma Xi. Republican. Methodist. Home: 3817 Calle De Las Focas San Clemente CA 92672-4538 Office: Transcontinental Mgmt 944 Calle Amanecer Ste D San Clemente CA 92672-6219

MCCROCKLIN, WILLIAM MAURICE, JR., medical cost containment company executive; b. Louisville, Mar. 19, 1946; s. William Maurice and Katheryn Lucille (Swearingen) McC.; m. Maria Sophia Nemeth, June 5, 1971 (div. 1977); m. Judith Mae Brown, June 3, 1978; 1 adopted child, Leah Lynn. BA in Sociology and Polit. Sci., U. Conn., 1972; MPH, U. Pa., 1976. Dep. dir. emergency medicine State of Conn. Dept. Health, Hartford, 1970-76; coord. emergency svc. Pitkin County Sheriff's Office, Aspen, Colo., 1976-81; exec. dir. Cen. Calif. Emergency Med. Svc., Visalia, Calif., 1985-87; cons. Med. Crisis Cons., San Francisco, 1981-85; area. mgr. for western U.S., Med Plus-In-Med Ltd., Anaheim, Calif., 1987-91; cost containment specialist Colo. Compensation Ins. Authority, Denver, 1991-92; pres. Medically Creative Concepts, Denver, 1992—; cons. contract mgr. Med View Svcs., Inc., Monument, Colo., 1992—; instr. med. rescue Colo. Mountain Coll., Aspen, 1978-80; cons. Broker Svcs., Boulder, Colo., 1989-91; cons. grant reviewer HEW, 1976. Rescue coord. Hampton (Conn.) Vol. Fire Dept., 1972-76, Pitkin County Sheriff Res., 1976-81; fire rescue responder Sugarloaf Fire Protection Dist., Boulder, 1988-91. With USN, 1966-70; sec. Regional Emergency Med. Svcs. Adv. Bd., New Eng., 1976; sr. first aid examiner Nat. Ski Patrol, 1974; instr., trainer CPR, Am. Heart Assn., Conn., 1975; mem.

allocations com. United Way, 1988; mem. adv. bd. New Eng. Heart Assn., 1974-75, sec., 1974; chmn. bd. Hampton-Chaplin Ambulance, 1973-75. Mem. Women in Workers' Compensation, Ky. Soc. Mayflower Descs. Home: 4505 Red Forest Rd Monument CO 80132 Office: Med View Svcs Inc 1850 Woodmoor Dr Ste 201 Monument CO 80132

MC CRONE, ALISTAIR WILLIAM, university president; b. Regina, Sask., Can., Oct. 7, 1931; came to U.S., 1953, naturalized, 1963; s. Hugh McMillan and Kathleen Maude Tallent (Forth) McCrone; m. Judith Ann Saari, May 8, 1958; children: Bruce, Craig, Mary. B.A., U. Sask., 1953; M.S. (Shell fellow), U. Nebr., 1955; Ph.D., U. Kans., 1961. Instr. geology NYU, 1959-61, asst. prof., 1961-64, assoc. prof., 1964-69, prof., 1969-70; chmn. dept. geology N.Y. U., 1966-69; assoc. dean NYU Grad. Sch. Arts and Scis., 1969-70; acad. v.p. U. of Pacific, Stockton, Calif., 1970-74; prof. geology U. of Pacific, 1970-74; pres., prof. geology Humboldt State U., Arcata, Calif., 1974—; lectr. geology CBS-TV network, 1969-70. Contbr. articles to profl. jours. Trustee Pacific Med. Center, San Francisco, 1971-74; mem. Calif. Council for Humanities., 1978-82. Recipient Erasmus Haworth Honors award U. Kans., 1957; named Danforth Assos. convenor N.Y. U., 1966-68, Outstanding Educator of Am., 1975. Fellow AAAS, Geol. Soc. Am., Calif. Acad. Sci.; mem. Am. Assn. Univ. Adminstrs. (bd. dirs. 1986-89), Am. Auto Assn. (bd. dirs. 1990-93), Calif. State Auto Assn. (bd. dirs. 1988—), Assn. Am. Colls. (bd. dirs. 1989, chair 1991), St. Andrews Soc. of N.Y., Sigma Xi. Lodge: Rotary. Office: Humboldt State U Univ Campus Arcata CA 95521

MCCUE, DENNIS MICHAEL, management consultant; b. Pitts., July 28, 1952; s. Stephen J. and Mary (Maddalon) McC.; m. Cynthia Anne Roberts, Oct. 22, 1988. BA, U. Dayton, 1974. Dist. exec. Allegheny Trails Coun., Boy Scouts Am., Pitts., 1974-77; area mgr. The Nestle Co., Pitts., 1977-79; account mgr. So. Pacific Communications, Pitts., 1979-82; dir. sales and mktg. Amertel Co., Pitts., 1982-84, ITT Bu. Communications, Newport Beach, Calif., 1985-86; dir. mktg. Damac Products, Santa Fe Springs, Calif., 1986-87; ptnr. Hunter-McCue Mgmt. Cons., Newport Beach, Calif., 1987-89; pres. McCue Assocs., Newport Beach, 1989—. Contbr. articles to profl. jours. Grad. Leadership Tomorrow, 1988, program chmn., bd. dirs., 1993—. Mem. Nat. Assn. Corp. Dirs., Nat. Bur. Profl. Mgmt. Cons. (recieved CPCM, 1992), Lew Epstein Men's Club (mgr. 1986-90). Office: 4570 Campus Dr Newport Beach CA 92660-1835

MCCUE, THOMAS ALBERT, housing developer, urban planner, consultant; b. San Francisco, July 16, 1950; s. Thomas Decklan and Lorraine Marie (Arata) McC.; m. Noreen Winkler, July 7, 1974 (div. Dec. 1983); children: Erin Margaret Winkler-McCue, Benjamin Thomas Winkler-McCue. BA with honors, U. Calif., Santa Cruz, 1972; M Urban Planning, CUNY, Hunter Coll., 1976. Lic. real estate salesman, Calif. Coord. housing and community devel. City of Campbell, Calif., 1976-79; assoc. planner Santa Cruz County, Santa Cruz, 1979-82, sr. planner, 1982-87; dir. housing devel. Housing for Ind. People, Inc., San Jose, Calif., 1987-91; program coord. Pub./Pvt. Leadership Com. on Housing Issues, Santa Cruz, 1992—; acting asst. dir. Community Housing Developers, Inc., San Jose, 1992—; cons. on housing devel. and urban planning, Aromas, Calif., 1991—. N.Y.C. urban fellow, 1972. Democrat. Mem. Soc. of Friends. Office: 240 Snyder Ave Aromas CA 95004

MCCULLISS, PAUL LEONARD, resource company executive; b. Phila., Nov. 8, 1957; s. Leonard Joseph and Katherine Cecilia (Allen) McC.; m. Debora L. Light; children: Brian Paul, Emily Clair. BS in Petroleum Engring., Colo. Sch. Mines, 1984. Engr. Trend Exploration Ltd., Denver, 1984-86; pres. McCulliss Resources Co., Inc., Denver, 1986—. Capt. U.S. Army, 1977-80. Mem. Soc. Petroleum Engrs. Republican. Roman Catholic. Office: 621 17th St Ste 1320 Denver CO 80293

MCCULLOCH, WILLIAM HENRY, mechanical engineer; b. Lamesa, Tex., Mar. 28, 1941; s. W.H. and Mable Endora (Trice) McC.; m. Katie V. Neill, July 5, 1963; children: Katie Lyn, William Neil, Carrie Leigh. BS in Engring. Physics, Tex. Tech. U., Lubbock, 1963; MS in ME, Tex. Tech. U., 1964, PhD in ME, 1968. Registered profl. engr., N.Mex. Mem. tech. staff Sandia Nat. Labs., Albuquerque, 1967—. Contbr. articles to profl. jours. Coach, Young Am. Football League, Albuquerque, 1976-83. Baptist. Home: 9008 Lona Ln NE Albuquerque NM 87111-1660

MCCULLOUGH, JOHN MARTIN, anthropology educator, forensic consultant; b. Chgo., Mar. 9, 1940; s. Donald James and Carla (Jørgensen) McC.; m. Yoshiko Tsutsui, Jan. 25, 1967 (div. Oct. 1971); 1 child, Lily Hana; m. Christine Schwab, Oct. 12, 1971; children: Jonathan James, Evan Padruig. BA, Pa. State U., 1962; PhD, U. Ill., 1972. Forensic anthropologist Office of the Med. Examiner, State of Utah, Salt Lake City, 1969—; asst. prof. anthropology U. Utah, Salt Lake City, 1969-75, assoc. prof., 1975-91, chmn. anthropology dept., 1978-84, prof., 1991—; vis. fellow human genetics U. Newcastle-upon-Tyne, Eng., 1984-85; ind. forensic anthropologist, Salt Lake City, 1969—; chmn. acad. senate U. Utah., 1993—. Ward counselor Dem. Party, Salt Lake City, 1988—. Fellow Am. Assn. Phys. Anthropology (nomination com. 1991—), Human Biol. Coun. (nominations com.), Soc. for the Study of Human Biology, Sigma Xi; mem. Soc. for Med. Anthropology. Lutheran. Home: 1352 Emigration St Salt Lake City UT 84108 Office: U Utah Dept Anthropology 102 Stewart Bldg Salt Lake City UT 84112

MCCUNE, ELLIS E., retired university system chief administrator, higher education consultant; b. Houston, July 17, 1921; s. Ellis E. and Ruth (Mason) McC.; m. Hilda May Whiteman, Feb. 8, 1946; 1 son, James Donald. Student, Sam Houston State U., 1940-42; B.A., UCLA, 1948, Ph.D., 1957. Teaching asst. UCLA, 1949-51; from instr. to assoc. prof. polit. sci. Occidental Coll., Los Angeles, 1951-59; chmn. applied politics and econs. curriculum Occidental Coll., 1951-56; asst. prof. Calif. State U., Northridge, 1959-61, assoc. prof., chmn. dept. polit. sci., 1961-63, prof., 1963, dean letters and sci., 1963; dean acad. planning Calif. State Univs. and Colls., 1963-67; pres. Calif. State U., Hayward, 1967-90, pres. emeritus, 1991—; acting chancellor The Calif. State U. System, 1990-91, ret., 1991; cons. govtl. units and agys.; lectr., panelist; mem. Calif. State Scholarship and Loan Commn., 1964-68, chmn., 1967-68; pres. Govtl. Adminstrn. Group Los Angeles, 1959. Chmn. univs. and colls. div. United Bay Area Crusade, 1969-70, 73-74; bd. dirs. Oakland (Calif.) Museum Assn., 1974-77, 86-88; vice chmn. higher edn. div., East Bay United Way, 1989-90; mem. arts adv. council, 1986-87, devel. com., 1988-89, Bay Area Urban League, bd. trust Calif. Coun. Econ. Edn. No. sect., Emergency Shelter Program Adv. Coun., Hayward Area Hist. Assn., NAACP Hayward chpt.; trustee Calif. Council Econ. Edn.; sec. bd. dirs. Eden Community Found., 1978-79; rsch. fellow Haynes Found, 1957. With USAAF, 1942-46. Mem. Am. Coun. Edn. (adv. com. 1970-72, inst. coll. & univ. adminstrs. 1973-74, bd. dirs. 1985-86), Western Assn. Schs. and Colls. (accrediting commn. sr. colls. and univs. 1974-78, chmn., 1978-82, pres. 1979-81), N.W. Assn. Schs. and Colls. (commn. colls. 1974-80), Assn. Am. Colls. (bd. dirs. 1972-75, vice chmn. 1975-76), Assn. Western Univs. (bd. dirs.), Coun. Postsecondary Accreditation (bd. dirs. 1977-88, exec. com. 1979-88, chmn. 1985-87, immediate past chmn., 1988-89, chmn. com. recognition 1982-84), Am. Assn. State Colls. and Univs. (chmn. accreditation com. 1983-86, com. acad. pers. and acad. freedom 1987-88, com. on acad. affairs 1988-91), Calif. Coun. Edn. (trustee), Western Polit. Sci. Assn. (exec. coun. 1958-61), Hayward C. of C. (dir. 1968-71, 73-76, 77-80, 82-85, 86-90), Regional Assn. East Bay Colls. and Univs. (exec. com. 1974-90, sec. 1975-76, 87-88, vice chmn. 1976-77, 84-85, chmn. 1977-79, 85-86), Rotary, Phi Beta Kappa, Pi Gamma Mu, Pi Sigma Alpha. Club: Bohemian (San Francisco). Home: 17577 Parker Rd Castro Valley CA 94546-1227 Office: Calif State U Hayward CA 94542-3052

MCCURDY, JOHN ANDREW, JR., cosmetic surgeon; b. Kingsville, Tex., July 17, 1945; s. John Andrew and Elizabeth (Smith) McC.; AB in Chemistry, Duke U., 1967; MD, Wake Forest U., Winston-Salem, N.C., 1971; divorced; children: John Andrew, Elizabeth Anne; m. Maria Victoria McCurdy. Intern, Letterman Gen. Hosp., San Francisco, 1971-72; resident Madigan Army Med. Ctr., Tacoma, 1972-76; practice medicine specializing in cosmetic surgery, Wailuku, Hawaii, 1979—; mem. staff Tripler Army Med. Ctr., Maui Meml. Hosp., Castle Meml. Hosp.; asst. clin. prof. surgery U. Hawaii Med. Sch. Lt. col. M.C., USAR, 1971-79. Decorated Army Commendation medal; diplomate Am. Bd. Otolaryngology, Am. Bd. Cosmetic Surgery. Fellow ACS, Am. Acad. Facial Plastic and Reconstructive Surgery, Am. Acad. Head and Neck Surgery. Author: The Complete Guide to Cosmetic Facial Surgery, 1981, Beautiful Eyes, 1984, Sculpturing Your Body: Diet, Exercise and Lipo Suction, 1987, Cosmetic Surgery of the Asian Face, 1990. Home: 3126 Mapu Pl Kihei HI 96753-9451 Office: 1063 E Main St Ste 225 Wailuku HI 96793-2008 also: 1188 Bishop St Ste 2402 Honolulu HI 96813

MCCUSKEY, ROBERT SCOTT, anatomy educator, researcher; b. Cleve., Sept. 8, 1938; s. Sidney Wilcox and Jeannette M. (Scott) M.; m. Rebecca Woodworth, July 19, 1958 (div.); children: Geofrey, Gregory, Michael; m. Margaret A. Krasovich, Apr. 17, 1993. A.B., Western Res. U., 1960, Ph.D., 1965. Instr. anatomy U. Cin., 1965-67, asst. prof., 1967-71, assoc. prof., 1971-75, prof., 1975-78; prof., chmn. anatomy W.Va. U., Morgantown, 1978-86; prof., head dept. anatomy U. Ariz., Tucson, 1986—, prof. physiology, 1987—; vis. prof. U. Heidelberg, Fed. Republic Germany, 1981-83, 87-88, 93—; cons. Hoffmann-La Rouche, N.J., 1972-75, Procter & Gamble Co., Cin. 1966-86. Recipient NIH Rsch. Career Devel. award, 1969-74; Humboldt Sr. U.S. Scientist prize, Fed. Republic Germany, 1982, Nishimaru award Japan Microcirculatory Soc., 1987; grantee NIH, NSF, 1966—. Mem. AAAS, Microcirculatory Soc., Am. Assn. Anatomists, Am. Assn. Study Liver Diseases, Rsch. Soc. on Alcoholism, Internat. Soc. Exptl. Hematology. Mem. editorial bd. Microvascular Rsch., 1974-84; contbr. numerous articles to profl. jours. Office: Ariz Health Scis Ctr Dept Anatomy 1501 N Campbell Ave Tucson AZ 85724-0001

MCCUTCHEN, EDNA ELIZABETH, counselor; b. Washington, Iowa, Sept. 6, 1914; d. Charles Sanford and Gertrude Josephine (Swift) Ragan; m. Carl Richard McC., July 3, 1938; children: Evelyn Hitchcock, Carl Richard III, Charles. BA cum laude, Calif. State U., Long Beach, 1971. Researcher State Univ. System, Iowa, 1953-62, Gallup Poll, Palos Verdes (Calif.) Estates, and Iowa, 1954-68, Palos Verdes Estates, 1960-69; counselor for family svc. Long Beach, 1971-73; social worker L.A. County, 1973-83; pvt. practice in counseling Long Beach, 1983—; vol. Gov.'s Study of Aged State of Iowa, 1960-69; lectr. St. Bartholomew's, Long Beach. Insp. election bds., Los Angeles County, Long Beach, 1964—; crew leader U.S. Census, Washington County, Iowa, 1950; Eucharistic min. St. Bartholomew's Ch. Recipient Commendation Community Svc. award Family Svc., Long Beach, 1972. Mem. LWV, AAUW, Nat. Social Workers, Consumer's Union-Consumer's Rsch., DAR (sec. 1948-49), Dau. Am. Colonists, Friends of Library, Phi Kappa Phi. Home: 3435 E 1st St Long Beach CA 90803-2658

MCCUTCHEON, JAMES MILLER, history and American studies educator; b. N.Y.C., Oct. 31, 1932; s. James Cochrane and Katharine (Miller) McC.; m. Elizabeth Douglas North, Apr. 4, 1959; children: Ian North, Eric James. BA summa cum laude, Hobart Coll., Geneva, N.Y., 1954; MS, U. Wis., 1955, PhD, 1959. Grad. asst. U. Wis., Madison, 1954-59; Fulbright fellow U. London, 1959-60; asst. prof. history Simpson Coll., Indianola, Iowa, 1960-61; asst. prof. history and Am. studies U. Hawaii Manoa, Honolulu, 1961-66, assoc. prof., 1966-72, prof., 1972—, chair Am. studies, 1984-88; sr. Fulbright fellow Beijing Fgn. Studies U., 1981-82; spl. asst. pres. U. Hawaii Manoa, Honolulu, 1979, program coord. coll. opportunity, 1971-72; mem. selection com. Community Scholarships, Honolulu, 1973-85; prin. scholar Hawaii Commn. for Humanities, Honolulu, 1973—. Author: China and America: Bibliography, 1972. Recipient Clopton Community Svc. award U. Hawaii Manoa, Honolulu, 1978. Mem. Am. Hist. Assn., Orgn. Am. Historians, Am. Studies Assn., Urban Studies Assn., World History Assn., Phi Beta Kappa. Episcopalian. Home: 3618 Woodlawn Terr Pl Honolulu HI 96822 Office: U Hawaii Manoa Am Studies Dept 1890 East West Rd Honolulu HI 96822

MCCUTCHEON, RANDALL JAMES, educator; b. Salem, Oreg., Mar. 4, 1949; s. James Vale and Delores (Bertholsen) McC. BS in Secondary Edn., U. Nebr., 1971. Announcer KRFS Radio, Superior, Nebr., 1966-67, KFMQ Radio, Lincoln, Nebr., 1968-75; grad. teaching asst. U. Nebr., Lincoln, 1971-73; tchr. East High Sch., Lincoln, 1975-85, Milton (Mass.) Acad., 1985-88, Valley High Sch., West Des Moines, Iowa, 1988-89, Albuquerque Acad., 1989—. Author: Get Off My Brain, 1985, Can You Find It?, 1989 (Ben Franklin Book of Yr. 1990); co-author: Communication Matters, 1993. Named Dale E. Black Outstanding Young Speech Tchr. of Yr. Nebr. Speech Communication Assn., 1979, Nebr. Tchr. of Yr. Dept. Edn., 1985. Mem. Speech Communication Assn., Nat. Forensic League (Nat. Coach of Yr. 1987), Cath. Forensic League (diocesan dir. 1990—). Office: Albuquerque Acad 6400 Wyoming NE Albuquerque NM 87109

MCDANIEL, BRUCE ALAN, economist, educator; b. Warsaw, Ind., June 12, 1946; s. Maurice M. and Hattie M. (Stidham) McD.; m. Darcy L. Stouder, Dec. 29, 1972; children: Rachel L., Nathan A., Jordan J. BS, Manchester Coll., 1968; MA, Ball State U., 1972; PhD, Colo. State U., 1979. Instr. Colo. State U., Fort Collins, 1975-79; asst. prof. Ind. U., Indpls., 1979-82, Marquette U., Milw., 1982-85; pres., owner Prairieland, Atwood, Ind., 1985—; asst. prof. U. No. Colo., Greeley, 1992—. Contbr. articles to profl. jours. Mem. Assn. for Social Econs. (midwest regional dir. 1986-92, exec. coun. 1983-92, Helen Potter award 1983), Phi Kappa Phi, Omicron Delta Epsilon. Office: U No Colo Dept Econs Greeley CO 80639

MCDANIEL, CHARLOTTE SUE, public relations consultant, fundraiser; b. Loveland, Colo., Sept. 5, 1943; d. Luther Jr. and Doris Nelle (Dillard) Crenshaw; m. James Ellis McDaniel, Aug. 16, 1969; children: Jonathan, Douglas. BA, U. Colo., 1965. Pub. rels. asst. Children's Hosp., Denver, 1965-67; dir. women's coms. Nat. Jewish Hosp., Denver, 1967-68; asst. dir. pub. rels. Great Western Sugar Co., Denver, 1968-69, 70-71; publs. cons. Thompson Sch. Dist., Loveland, 1991—; devel. dir. Colo. Dem. Party, 1993—; mem. pub. rels. adv. com. Thompson Sch. Dist., 1991—. Merit badge counselor Boy Scouts Am., 1988—; publicity, legislature chair Loveland-Berthoud Jane Jefferson Club, 1988—; Larimer County Dem. County Chair, 1989—; mem. oversight com. Colo. Dem. Party Coordinated Campaign, 1991—; coord. Colo. Dem. Party County Chmn. Assn., 1991—; co-chair Colo. 2000 Citizens Edn. Initiative, 1991—; program presenter, mem. Agenda for Nineties Citizen Initiative, 1991—; mem. adv. com. Colo. Inst. Leadership Tng., 1992—; organizer, mem. steering com. Moderate Voters Project, 1992—; active Denver Zool. Found.; bd. dirs. Thompson Edn. Found., chair, 1992—. Named Colo. Outstanding Young Career Woman, Bus. and Profl. Women, 1969, Outstanding Nat. Sch. Vol., Nat. Assn. Ptnrs. Edn., Inc., 1992; recipient Spark Plug award Boy Scouts Am., 1988. Mem. Century Club Colo. Dem. Party. Presbyterian. Office: 770 Grant St Ste 200 Denver CO 80203

MCDANIEL, JOSEPH CHANDLER, lawyer; b. Covington, Va., Mar. 24, 1950; s. Everts Hardin and Betty (Chandler) McD.; m. Sandra Lee Bonds, Dec. 27, 1976; children: Sean Kenneth, Caitlin Bonds. BA in Philosophy, Ariz. State U., 1974, JD, 1980. Bar: Ariz. 1980, U.S. Dist. Ct. Ariz. 1981. Law clk. U.S. Bankruptcy Ct., Phoenix, 1980-82; pvt. practice Phoenix, 1982-84; ptnr. McDaniel and Jaburg, P.C., Phoenix, 1984-89, McDaniel and Lee, Phoenix, 1989-91, McDaniel & Gan, P.C., 1991—; mem. Scriveners Com. Local Rules of Ct. for Dist. of Ariz. Bankruptcy Cts., Phoenix, 1980. Author: A Guide to Researching Bankruptcy Law, 1980; editor: (with others) Arizona Civil Remedies, 1982. Bd. dirs. St. Patrick's Day Parade, 1988-89, Irish Cultural Assn. Phoenix, 1988-89. Mem. ABA (gen. practice sect. bankruptcy com., chmn.), Ariz. Bar Assn. (lectr., co-chmn. continuing legal edn. com., bankruptcy sect. 1987-88, chmn. 1988-89, co-chmn. jud. rels. com. 1990-92), Maricopa County Bankruptcy Practitioners (chmn.), Ariz. Bankruptcy Coalition (bd. dirs. 1986—), Maricopa County Bar Assn., Am. Bankruptcy Inst. Democrat. Roman Catholic. Office: McDaniel & Gan PC Ste 990 3636 N Central Ave Phoenix AZ 85012-1941

MCDANIEL, PAUL WILLIAM, physicist, researcher; b. Robards, Ky., Jan. 1, 1916; s. Leslie Elbert and Lillie (Ligon) McD.; m. Loreen Webb, June 4, 1937 (div. Aug. 1975); m. Kathryn Mitchell, Aug. 16, 1975. BS, Western Ky. U., 1936; MA, Ind. U., 1938, PhD, 1941. Dep. dir. rsch. AEC, Washington, 1950-60, dir. rsch., 1960-72; pres. Argonne U. Assn., Washington and Argonne, Ill., 1973-75, ret., 1975. Maj. U.S. Army, 1942-45. Home: 4295 Warren Way Reno NV 89509-5245

MCDANIEL, WILLIAM J., career military officer; b. Muskogee, Okla., Feb. 26, 1943; s. L.B. Allen and Vera Juanita (Purdom) McD.; m. Judy Siebert, May 30, 1964 (div. Apr. 1969); m. Shirely Blair, Dec. 13, 1969; children: Valerie Park, Natalie Park, Tara. MD, U. Okla., 1968. Commd. ensign USN, advanced through grades to rear adm., 1989; orthopedic resident Oakland Naval Hosp., Calif., 1973-77; chief of orthopedics Naval Hosp., Rota, Spain, 1977-80; orthopedics dept. Naval Acad., Annapolis, Md., 1980-83, Nat. War Coll., Washington, 1983-84; fleet surgeon Seventh Fleet, Yokosuka, Japan, 1984-86; commanding officer Naval Hosp., Oak Harbor, Wash., 1986-88, Charleston, S.C., 1988-90, Portmouth, Va., 1992—. Team Physician U.S. Olympic Team, L.A., 1984, cons., Colorado Springs, Colo., 1981—. Mem. Am. Acad. Orthopedic Surgery. Republican. Office: Naval Hosp Portsmouth VA 23708

MCDAVID, DOUGLAS WARREN, systems consultant; b. San Francisco, Feb. 25, 1947; s. James Etheridge and Elizabeth Rae (Warren) McD.; m. Nancy Kathleen Somers, June 1968 (div. 1982); 1 child, Amy Kemp; m. Carleen Ann Richmond, Feb. 14, 1987; ! child, Amanda Claire. BA in Sociology, U. Calif., Santa Cruz, 1969; MA in Libr. Sci., San Jose State U., 1972. Libr. Palo Alto (Calif.) City Libr., 1969-81; systems analyst Tymnet (Tymshare), Cupertino, Calif., 1981-84; mgr. systems architecture Tymnet McDonnell Douglas, San Jose, Calif., 1984-86; data modeling cons. Fireman's Fund Ins., Terra Linda, Calif., 1986-87, Bank of Calif., San Francisco, 1988; systems cons. Pacific Bell, San Ramon, Calif., 1989—; speaker Entity/Relationship Conf. Internat., Burlingame, Calif., 1991. Mem. IEEE, Assn. for Computing Machinery, Data Adminstrn. Mgmt. Assn. (San Francisco bd. dirs. 1987-91, Sacramento bd. dirs. 1992, speaker 1991, 92), Data Processing Mgmt. Assn. (speaker 1992). Home: 8611 Kingslynn Ct Elk Grove CA 95624 Office: Pacific Bell 2600 CAmino Ramon San Ramon CA 94583

MCDERMOTT, DAVID JOHN, artist, consultant; b. Wrangell, Alaska, Apr. 8, 1958; s. A.W. and Margaret (Price) McD.; m. Rebeca Reyna, Dec. 29, 1978; children: Amy, Rachel, Kelly. Student, U. Alaska, Ketchikan, 1974-75, Seattle Pacific Coll., 1976-77. Nat. registered and cert. emergency med. technician; cert. instr. NRA. Pres., owner Mut. Devel. Co., Ketchikan, 1980—; fireman, emergency med. technician Ketchikan Vol. Fire Dept., 1989-91; contbg. cons. bodybldg. books and mags., 1986—. Artist ltd. edit. art print series, 1977. Recipient Expert Rifleman award U.S. Govt., 1973. Mem. NEA (exec. bd. 1992—, del. state, nat. assemblies). Home: 626 Anderson Dr Ketchikan AK 99901 Office: Mut Devel Co 627 Carlanna Ketchikan AK 99901

MCDERMOTT, JAMES A., congressman, psychiatrist; b. Chicago, Ill., Dec. 28, 1936; children: Katherine, James. BS, Wheaton Coll., 1958; MD, U. Ill., 1963. Intern Buffalo Gen. Hosp., 1963-64; resident in adult psychiatry U. Ill. Hosps., Chgo., 1964-66; resident in child psychiatry U. Wash. Hosps., Seattle, 1966-68; asst. clin. prof. dept. psychiatry U. Wash., Seattle, 1970-83; mem. Wash. Ho. of Reps., 1971-72, Wash. Senate, 1975-87; regional med. officer U.S. Fgn. Svc., 1987-88; mem. 101st-103rd Congresses from 7th Wash. dist., Washington, D.C., 1989—; mem. ways and means com., standard of official conduct com.; chair D.C. com.; mem. ways and means com., com. on D.C., com. on Standards of Official Conduct, exec. and edn. com. Nat. Conf. State Legislatures. Mem. Wash. State Arts Commn., Wash. Coun. for Prevention Child Abuse and Neglect; Dem. nominee for gov., 1980. Lt. comdr. M.C., USN, 1968-70,. Mem. Am. Psychiat. Assn., Wash. State Med. Assn., King County Med. Soc. Democrat. Episcopalian. Office: US Ho of Reps 1707 Longworth Washington DC 20515-4707*

MCDERMOTT, KELLIE MARIE, elementary school educator, reading specialist; b. Denver, Mar. 1, 1958; d. William James and Carolyn Ann (Kreutzer) McD. BS in Edn., U. So. Calif., 1980; MA in Edn., Calif. State U., L.A., 1984. Tchr. Downey (Calif.) Unified Sch. Dist., 1980-81, St. James Episcopal Sch., L.A., 1981-85; tchr. New Temple Elem. Sch., South El Monte, Calif., 1985—, mentor tchr., 1990-94, reading specialist, 1991—. Classrm. Tchr. Instrl. Improvement grantee Valle Lindo Sch. Bd., 1986. Mem. Internat. Reading Assn., Valle Lindo Edn. Assn. (sec. 1989-90, treas. 1990—), Valle Lindo PTA (auditor 1989-91). Home: 5436 Warman Ln Temple City CA 91780 Office: New Temple Elem Sch 11033 E Central South El Monte CA 91733

MCDEVITT, CHARLES FRANCIS, state supreme court justice; b. Pocatello, Idaho, Jan. 5, 1932; s. Bernard A. and Margaret (Hermann) McD.; m. Virginia L. Heller, Aug. 14, 1954; children: Eileen A., Kathryn A., Brian A., Sheila A., Terrence A., Neil A., Kendal A. BS, U. Idaho, 1955, LLB, 1956. Bar: 1956. Ptnr. Richards, Haga & Eberle, Boise, 1956-62; gen. counsel, asst. sec. Boise Cascade Corp., 1962-65; mem. Idaho State Legislature, 1963-66; sec., gen. counsel Boise Cascade Corp., 1965-67, v.p. sec., 1967-68; pres. Beck Industries, 1968-70; group v.p. Singer Co., N.Y.C., 1971-72, exec. v.p., 1973-76; pub. defender Ada County, Boise, 1976-78; co-founder Givens, McDevitt, Pursley & Webb, Boise, 1978-89; justice Idaho Supreme Ct., Boise, 1989—, chief justice, 1993—; served on Gov.'s Select Com. on Taxation, Boise, 1988-89. Home: 4940 Boise River Ln Boise ID 83706 Office: Idaho Supreme Ct 451 West State St Boise ID 83720

MCDONALD, ALAN ANGUS, federal judge; b. Harrah, Wash., Dec. 13, 1927; s. Angus and Nell (Britt) McD.; m. Ruby K., Aug. 22, 1949; children: Janelle Jo, Saralee Sue, Stacy. BS, U. Wash., 1950, LLB, 1952. Dep. pros. atty. Yakima County, Wash., 1952-54; assoc. Halverson & Applegate, Yakima, 1954-56; ptnr. Halverson, Applegate & McDonald, Yakima, 1956-85; judge U.S. Dist. Ct. (ea. dist.) Wash., Spokane, 1985—. Fellow Am. Coll. Trial Lawyers; Yakima C. of C. (bd. dirs.). Clubs: Yakima Country, Royal Duck (Yakima). Office: US Dist Ct PO Box 2186 Spokane WA 99210-2186

MCDONALD, DANIEL ROBERT, senator; b. Seattle, Feb. 4, 1944; s. Robert William and Josephine Dorothy (Quigley) McD.; m. Norah Jane Cornwall, Dec. 28, 1966; children: Tod Robert, Evan Daniel. BSME, U. Wash., 1965, MA in Econs., 1975. Registered profl. engr., Calif., Wash. Mem. Wash. Ho. of Reps., Olympia, 1979-83, floor leader, 1983; mem. Wash. Senate, Olympia, 1983—, floor leader, 1985-86, chmn. Ways and Means Com., 1988—; mem. revenue forecast council, Olympia, 1984—, chmn. 1984-85; mem. legis. evaluation and accountability program, Olympia, 1983—; commr. exec. bd. Western Interstate Com. on Higher Edn., 1983-87; mem. State Investment Bd. Mem. Seattle/King County Drug Commn., 1978-79, Mcpl. League, Seattle, 1979—. Served to lt. (j.g.) USN, 1966-69, Vietnam. Mem. Am. Pub. Works Assn., Am. Waterworks Assn., Bellevue (Wash.) C. of C. Republican. Presbyterian. Lodge: Rotary. Home: 4650 92nd Ave NE Bellevue WA 98004-1397 Office: Wash State Senate 105 JAC Bldg Olympia WA 98504

MCDONALD, IAN MACLAREN, college dean, psychiatrist, educator; b. Regina, Sask., Can., May 20, 1928; s. George and Alexandrina Sutherland (MacLaren) McD.; m. Margaret Anne McGavin, Nov. 21, 1953; children: David, Bruce, Catherine, Susan, Shelagh. M.D., U. Man., Can., 1953. Intern Vancouver Gen. Hosp., B.C., 1952-53; resident Crease Clinic, Essondale, B.C., Can., 1953-54, Munroe Wing, Regina Gen. Hosp., Can., 1954-55; fellow in neurology U. Hosp. Saskatoon, Can., 1956; resident Colo. Psychopathic Hosp., Denver, 1956-57; lectr. U. Colo., Denver, 1957-58; asst. prof. U. Sask., Saskatoon, Sask., Can., 1958-62, assoc. prof., 1962-68, prof. coll. medicine, 1968—, dean of medicine, 1983-93; vis. prof. Harvard U., 1992. Fellow U. Edinburgh, 1967-68; recipient Spl. Recognition award Can. Mental Health Assn., 1983. fellow Royal Coll. Physicians Can., Am. Psychiat. Assn. (life); mem. Can. Med. Assn., Can. Psychiat. Assn. Presbyterian. Club: Saskatoon. Office: Royal U Hosp, Dept Psychiatry, Saskatoon, SK Canada S7N 0W0

MCDONALD, JAMES BOTT, economics educator; b. Logan, Utah, Apr. 16, 1942; s. Leonard Webb and Arola (Bott) McD.; m. Kathleen Thomas, Dec. 28, 1966; children: Jan, Michael, Jonathan, Robert. BS, Utah State U., 1964, MS, 1967; PhD, Purdue U., 1970. Asst. prof. Utah State U., Logan, 1970-72; asst. prof. Brigham Young U., Provo, Utah, 1972-73, assoc. prof., 1974-79, prof., 1980—. Contbr. articles to profl. jours; referee for profl. jours. Recipient rsch. award NSF, 1986-87. Mem. Econometric Soc., Am. Statis. Assn., Am. Econ. Assn., Am. Fin. Assn. Home: 4058 Quail Run Provo UT 84604-5219 Office: Brigham Young U Provo UT 84602

MCDONALD, JEANNE GRAY (MRS. JOHN B. MCDONALD), television producer; b. Seattle, Sept. 10, 1917; d. George Patrick and Mary Edna

(Gray) Murphy; m. John B. Mc Donald, June 30, 1951; children: Gregory Roland Stoner, Jeanne Eve. Student, Columbia U., 1940, Art Students League, 1940-43, Nat. Acad. Dramatic Art, 1945. Radio producer, commentator The Woman's Voice Sta. KMPC, L.A., 1947-50; TV producer, commentator, writer The Woman's Voice Sta. KTTV-CBS, L.A., 1950-51; TV producer, commentator The Jeanne Gray Show Sta. KNXT-TV CBS, L.A., 1951-53; West Coast editor Home Show NBC, L.A., 1955-56; TV film producer documentaries and travelogues Virgonian Prodns., L.A., 1953—. Author: The Power of Belonging, 1978. Women's chmn. Los Angeles Beautiful, 1971; mem. Women's Aux. St. John's Hosp.; trustee Freedoms Found. at Valley Forge, 1966—, founder, pres. women's chpt., Los Angeles County chpt., 1965-66, Western dir. women's chpt., 1967-68, nat. chmn. 1968-71, nat. chmn. women vols., 1973-75, hon life mem. Recipient Francis Holmes Outstanding Achievement award, 1949, Silver Mike award, 1948, Emmy award Acad. TV Arts and Scis., 1951, Lulu award Los Angeles Advt. Women, 1952, Genii award Radio and TV Women, 1956, George Washington Honor award Freedoms Found. Valley Forge, 1967, honor cert., 1972, Morale award Christians and Jews for Law and Morality, 1968, Exceptional Service award Freedoms Found., 1975, Liberty Belle award Rep. Women's Club, 1975, Leadership award Los Angeles City Schs., 1976, Theodore Roosevelt award USN League, 1986. Mem. Am. Women in Radio and TV, Radio and TV Women So. Calif. (hon., life, founder, 1st pres. 1952), Footlighters (v.p. 1958-59), Los Angeles C. of C. (bd. dirs. women's div. 1948-54, exec. bd., women's div. 1954-66, pres. women's div. 1963-64, hon. past pres. women's div. 1979), L.A. Orphanage Guild, DAR, Les Dames de Champagne, Bel Air Garden Club, Calif. Yacht Club. Home: 910 Stradella Rd Bel Air Los Angeles CA 90077

MCDONALD, JOSEPH LEE, insurance broker; b. Bremerton, Wash., Aug. 15, 1931; s. Joseph Okane and Ida Elizabeth (Finholm) McD.; m. Glorietta Maness, Jan. 22, 1954 (dec. 1984); children: Holly Ann Chaffin, Andrew Lee McDonald; m. Beverly Mae Falkner, June 22, 1986. BS, U. Wash., 1954. Various mgmt. positions AT&T, 1956-62; broker, ptnr. McDonald & McGarry Co., Seattle, 1962-84; ptnr., exec. McDonald Ins. Group, Kirkland, Wash., 1984—; v.p., bd. dirs. Chimayo Inc., Seattle, 1990—, Santa Fe Food Corp., Seattle, 1991—. City councilman City of Bellevue, 1971-75; commr. Water Dist. #97, Bellevue, 1967-71, Lake Hills Sewer Dist., Bellevue, 1965-71; pres. Wash. State Assn. of Sewer Dists., Seattle, 1969. With U.S. Army, 1954-56. Mem. Coll. Club of Seattle, Overlake Golf and Country Club, Western Assn. of Ins. Brokers, Ind. Ins. Agts. Assn., Seattle Master Builders Assn., Apt. Assn. of Seattle and King County, Roche Harbor Yacht Club. Home: 7235 91st Pl SE Mercer Island WA 98040 Office: McDonald Ins Group 416-6th St South Kirkland WA 98033

MCDONALD, KEITH LEON, theoretical physicist, research consultant; b. Murray City, UT, Apr. 20, 1923; s. Thomas Francis and Ada Pearl (Russell) McD. BS, U. UT, Salt Lake City, 1950, MS, 1951, PhD, 1956. Staff mem. U. Calif. Scientific Lab., Los Alamos, N.Mex., 1956-57; theoretical hydrodynamist U.S. Naval Ordnance Test Station, Pasadena, Calif., 1957; math physics rsch. U.S. Army Chemical Corps Proving Ground, Dugway, UT, 1957-60; asst. prof. physics Brigham Young U., Provo, UT, 1960-62; theoretical physics rsch. Nat. Bur. of Standards, Boulder, Colo., 1963-64; visiting assoc. prof. ID State U., Pocatello, ID, 1965; theoretical geophysicist U.S. dept. of Commerce, ESSA, Environmental Rsch. Labs., Boulder, Colo., 1966-68; cons. U.S. Dept. of Commerce, NOAA, ERL, Boulder, Colo., 1969-71; pvt. rsch. U. Utah, Salt Lake City, 1971—; vis. asst. prof. physics, U. Utah, Salt Lake City, 1962-63. Contbr. articles to profl. jours.; author: numerous abstracts published in Bulletin, American Physical Society. Corporal, USAF, 1942-46. Grantee U. UT Engring. Expt. Station, Salt Lake City, 1962, 63. Mem. Am. Astron. Soc., Am. Phys. Soc., Sigma Xi., Sigma Pi Sigma, Am. Assn. of Physics Tchrs., Am. Geophys. Union, Phi Beta Kappa. Republican. Mem LDS Ch. Office: PO Box 2433 Salt Lake City UT 84110-2433

MCDONALD, MALCOLM GIDEON, education educator; b. Boise, Idaho, Mar. 22, 1932; s. Gideon L. and Annette (Connell) McD.; m. Glenda S. Yarbrough, Nov. 23, 1962; children: Ronald, Steven, Michael. AA, Boise Jr. Coll., 1951; BA, Wash. State U., 1954, MA, 1972; EdD, U. Idaho, 1991. Prof. North Idaho Coll., Coeur d'Alene, Idaho, 1977-78; exec. dir. Spokane Higher Edn. Office, 1978-84; dir. CAREERS, Eastern Wash. U., 1984-86; dir. continuing edn. Eastern Wash. U., Cheney, Wash., 1986-89, asst. prof. dept. comm. studies, 1989—. Ret. lt. col. U.S. Army. Recipient Legion of Merit award, Bronze stars (2), Air medals (11), Meritorious Svc. medal, Commendation medal (5), Vietnam medal of Gallantry, 1954-76. Presbyterian. Home: 2841 Spelding Dr Las Vegas NV 89134

MCDONALD, MARIANNE, classicist; b. Chgo., Jan. 2, 1937; d. Eugene Francis and Inez (Riddle) McD.; children: Eugene, Conrad, Bryan, Bridget, Kirstie (dec.), Hiroshi. BA magna cum laude, Bryn Mawr Coll., 1958; MA, U. Chgo., 1960; PhD, U. Calif., Irvine, 1975, doctorate (hon.) Am. Coll. Greece, 1988, hon. diploma Am. Archaeological Assn. Teaching asst. classics U. Calif., Irvine, 1972-74, instr. Greek, Latin and English, mythology, modern cinema, 1975-79, founder, rsch. fellow Thesaurus Linguae Graecae Project, 1975—; bd. dir. Centrum. Bd. dirs. Am. Coll. of Greece, 1981—, Scripps Hosp., 1981; Am. Sch. Classical Studies, 1986—; mem. bd. overseers U. Calif. San Diego, 1985—; nat. bd. advisors Am. Biog. Inst., 1982—; founder Hajime Mori Chair for Japanese Studies, U. Calif., San Diego, 1985, McDonald Ctr. for Alcohol and Substance Abuse, 1984, Thesaurus Linguarum Hiberniae, 1991—; adj. prof. theatre U. Calif., San Diego, 1990. Recipient Ellen Browning Scripps Humanitarian award, 1975; Disting. Svc. award U. Calif.-Irvine, 1982, Irvine Medal, 1987, 3rd Prize Midwest Poetry Ctr. Contest, 1987, Civis Universitatis award U. Calif. San Diego, 1993, Hypatia award Hellenic U. Women, 1993; named one of the Community Leaders Am., 1979-80, Philanthropist of Yr., 1985, Headliner San Diego Press Club, 1985, Philanthropist of Yr. Honorary Nat. Conf. Christians and Jews, 1986, Woman of Distinction Salvation Army, 1986, Eleventh Woman Living Legacy, 1986, Woman of Yr. AHEPA, 1988, San Diego Woman of Distinction, 1990, Woman of Yr. AXIOS, 1991; recipient Bravissimo gold medal San Diego Opera, 1990, Gold Medal Soc. Internationalization of Greek Lang, 1990, Athens medal, 1991, Piraeus medal, 1991, hon. diploma Am. Archeol. Assn., 1991, award Desmoi, 1992, award Hellenic Assn of Univ. Women, 1992, Academy of Achievement award AHEPA, 1992, Woman of Delphi award European Cultural Ctr. Delphi, 1992. Mem. MLA, AAUP, Am. Philol. Assn., Soc. for the Preservation of the Greek Heritage (pres.), Libr. of Am., Am. Classical League, Philol. Assn. Pacific Coast, Am. Comparative Lit. Assn., Modern and Classical Lang. Assn. So. Calif., Hellenic Soc., Calif. Fgn. Lang. Tchrs. Assn., Internat. Platform Assn., Greek Language Found. (pres.), Olbos Enterprises (pres.), KPBS Producers Club, Hellenic Univ. Club (bd. dir.). Author: Terms for Happiness in Euripides, 1978, Semilemmatized Concordances to Euripides' Alcestis, 1977, Cyclops, Andromache, Medea, 1978, Heraclidae, Hippolytus, 1979, Hecuba, 1984, Hercules Furens, 1984, Electra, 1984, Ion, 1985, Trojan Women, 1988, Iphigenia in Taurus, 1988, Euripides in Cinema: The Heart Made Visible, 1983; translator: The Cost of Kindness and Other Fabulous Tales (Shinichi Hoshi), 1986, (chpt.) Views of Clytemnestra, Ancient and Modern, 1990, Classics and Cinema, 1990; writer: Ancient Sun/Modern Light: Greek Drama on the Modern Stage, 1990; contbr. numerous articles to profl. jours. Avocations: karate, harp (medieval), skiing, diving. Home: PO Box 929 Rancho Santa Fe CA 92067-0929 Office: U Calif at San Diego Dept Classics La Jolla CA 92093

MCDONALD, MARY ANN MELODY, investment management executive; b. Sandwich, Ill., Apr. 30, 1944; d. Theodore Harvey and Sarah Elizabeth (Irving) Larson; m. John G. McDonald, June 19, 1973. BS, No. Ill. U., 1966; MusM, New England Conservatory, 1970; studies with Nadia Boulanger, Paris, 1971; MusD, Stanford U., 1975; MBA, Harvard U., 1986. Credit analyst Wells Fargo Bank, San Francisco, 1976-77; loan officer, 1977-79, asst. v.p., 1979-80; chmn. bd. dirs. Cornwall Corp., Stanford, Calif., 1980-84; dir. client svcs. RCM Capital Mgmt., San Francisco, 1986-88, ptnr., 1989—. Active Ill. Youth Commn., 1963-66. Recipient Rockefeller grantee Oberlin (Ohio) Coll. 1967; winner Miss Boston-Miss Am. Pageant, 1968. Mem. Stanford Alumni Assn., Harvard Alumni Assn., Sigma Alpha Iota, Kappa Delta (Telford Cup). Republican. Lutheran. Home: 1098 Vernier Pl Stanford CA 94305 Office: RCM Capital Mgmt 4 Embarcadero Ctr Ste 2900 San Francisco CA 94111-4189

MCDONALD, MICHAEL BRIAN, economist, consultant; b. Tulsa, Jan. 1, 1948; s. William Gerald and Agnes Gertrude (Sellman) McD.; m. Jane Anne Fahey, Aug. 25, 1969; children: Kelly, Anne. BA in Econs. cum laude, Georgetown U., 1969; PhD in Econs., U. Pa., 1978. Teaching fellow U. Pa., Phila., 1976-77; rsch. fellow Logistics Mgmt. Inst., Washington, 1977-78; assoc. dir. Bur. Bus. and Econ. Rsch. U. N.Mex., Albuquerque, 1978-82, dir. Bur. Bus. and Econ. Rsch., 1982—; dir. Kirtland Fed. Credit Union, Albuquerque, 1982—. Contbr. articles to profl. jours. Lt-Col. USAFR, 1978—. Capt. USAF, 1972-76. NDEA Title IV fellow U. Pa., 1969-72. Mem. Phi Beta Kappa. Office: U NMex Bur Bus and Econ Rsch Albuquerque NM 87131

MCDONALD, ROBERT, art museum curator, director; b. Phila., Jan. 13, 1933; s. William Anthony and Dorothy Elizabeth (Herwick) McD. BA, U. Calif., Berkeley, 1954, MA, 1959. Cert. Mus. Mgmt. Inst., 1983. Dir. Daniel Weinberg Gallery, San Francisco, 1974-76; adminstrv. asst. to dir. U. Calif. Art Mus., Berkeley, 1977-79; chief curator La Jolla (Calif.) Mus. Contemporary Art, 1979-82; dir. The Art Mus. of Santa Cruz County, Calif., 1982-84; chief curator Laguna Beach (Calif.) Art Mus., 1984-85; art critic L.A Times San Diego Edit., 1985-87; syndicated columnist Copley News Svc., San Diego, Calif., 1985-86; lectr. U. San Diego, 1986-87; dir. de Saisset Mus. Santa Clara (Calif.) U., 1987-91. Author (exhibition catalog): Craig Kauffman, 1981, Terry Allen, 1983, D.J. Hall, 1986; contbr. articles to profl. publs.; contbg. editor: Artweek, 1973-88, Zyzzyva, 1987-92. Visual arts panelist, Calif. Arts Coun., Sacramento, 1981-83; bd. dirs. Bay Area Consortium for the Visual Arts, 1990-92, New Langton Arts, San Francisco, 1977-79; mem. grants com. VISUAL AID, San Francisco, 1992—. With U.S. Army, 1954-56. Recipient scholarship U. Calif., 1953, J. Paul Getty Trust, 1983. Mem. Coll. Art Assn., Am. Assn. Mus., Internat. Assn. Art Critics, U. Calif. Alumni Assn., Phi Beta Kappa. Home and Office: 281 Chestnut St San Francisco CA 94133-2406

MCDONALD, ROBERT GARLAND, county official; b. Burlington, Iowa, Oct. 12, 1942; s. Robert Franklin and Lorraine Ione (Foster) McD.; m. Judith Ann McDonald, Mar. 25, 1967 (div. Dec. 1977); children: Kristin, Jeffrey. AA, San Bernardino Valley Coll., 1963; BS, Calif. Poly. U., 1967; MBA, So. Ill. U., Edwardsville, 1974. Med. adminstr. Kaiser Found. Health Care, L.A., 1967-69; adminstrv. analyst San Bernardino County, San Bernardino, 1969-74, health care clinic adminstr., 1974-78, assoc. dir. Pub. Social Svcs., 1978—; instr. San Bernardino Valley Coll., 1976—; chmn. bd. dirs. San Bernardino County Credit Union, 1976—; dir. San Bernardino Job Tng. Partnership, 1990—. Mem. Family Svc. Assn., San Bernardino, 1991. Sgt. USAF, 1963-65. Mem. Masons. Republican. Office: County of San Bernardino 468 W 5th St San Bernardino CA 92415-0001

MCDONALD, SLOAN MEBANE, oral-maxillofacial surgeon; b. N.Y.C., Aug. 6, 1952; d. Edward Charles and Randy (Mebane) McD. BS, U. So. Calif., L.A., 1975; DDS, U. Pacific, San Francisco, 1982; Cert. Oral-Maxillofacial Surgery, La. State U., 1986. Diplomate Am. Bd. Oral and Maxillofacial Surgery; ACLS, BLS; lic. dentist Calif., La., Oreg. Dental hygienist Dr. Charles Decker, Portland, Oreg., 1975-79; oral-maxillofacial surgeon Dr. Larry V. Franz, Oakland, Calif., 1986-88; pvt. practice Antioch, Calif., 1988—; adj. asst. prof. oral and maxillofacial surgery U. Pacific, 1989; chief resident oral and maxillofacial surgery La. State U., Charity Hosp. of New Orleans, 1986; active staff Sierra Surgicenter, Walnut Creek, Calif., 1990—, Delta Meml. Hosp., Antioch, 1987—; courtesty staff John Muir Med. Ctr., Walnut Creek, 1987—; active staff The Surgery Ctr., Oakland, 1986—; rsch. assoc. Bristol Myers Co., 1985-87, Pfizer, Inc., 1985-86, Merck, Sharp & Dohme. Contbr. articles to profl. jours. Sponsor Antioch Community Scholarship Fund, 1992, Antioch Recreation Dept., 1989, Regional Occupation Program, Los Medanos Community Coll. Fellow Internat. Coll. Dentists; mem. Western Soc. Oral and Maxillofacial Surgeons, East Bay Orthognathic Surg. Panel, East Bay Cleft Palate Panel, Contra Costa County Dental Soc. (nomination com. 1990, community awareness com. chmn. 1989-90), Am. Dental Soc. of Anesthesiology, Calif. Soc. Oral Maxillofacial Surgeons (bd. dirs. 1990—), No. Calif. Soc. Oral Maxillofacial Surgeons (sec.-treas. 1992—, bd. dirs. 1990—, pres.-elect 1992-93), Calif. Dental Assn., Am. Assn. Oral Maxillofacial Surgeons (Achievement Award 1982, com. pub. information), Tau Kappa Omega, Rotary. Office: 3725 Lone Tree Way Fl Antioch CA 94509-6038

MCDONALD, THOMAS EDWIN, JR., electrical engineer; b. Wapanucka, Okla., June 19, 1939; s. Thomas Edwin and Rosamond Bell (Enoch) McD.; m. Myrna Kay Booth, Sept. 10, 1961; children: Stephen Thomas, Jennifer Kay, Sarah Lynn. BSEE, U. Okla., 1962, MSEE, 1963; PhDEE, U. Colo., 1969. Asst. prof. elec. engring. U. Okla., Norman, 1969-70; planning engr. Okla. Gas and Electric Co., Oklahoma City, 1970-72; staff mem. Los Alamos (N.Mex.) Nat. Lab., 1972—, group leader, 1974-80, program mgr., 1980—; program mgr. Centurion program Los Alamos (N.Mex.) Nat. Lab., Los Alamos, 1986-90; dep. program dir. inertial confinement fusion program Los Alamos (N.Mex.) Nat. Lab., 1990-92, program coord. mine detection and laser tech., 1992—; adj. prof. elec. engring. U. Okla., 1970-72; cons. Los Alamos Tech. Assocs., 1980—, mgr. design sect., 1980-81. Researcher: Inertial Confinement Fusion; Contbr. articles to profl. jours. Bd. dirs., mem. United Ch. Los Alamos, 1987—, chmn. bd. elders, 1992. Served to capt. U.S. Army, 1963-67. Mem. IEEE (chmn. Los Alamos sect.), AAAS, Los Alamos Gymnastics Club (treas., bd. dirs. 1980-88), Rotary (sec. Los Alamos club, v.p.), Sigma Xi, Etta Kappa Nu. Republican. Home: 4200 Ridgeway Dr Los Alamos NM 87544-1956 Office: Los Alamos Nat Lab PO Box 1663 Los Alamos NM 87544-0010

MCDONALD, TIM, professional football player; b. Fresno, Calif., Jan. 6, 1965. Student, U. So. Calif. With St. Louis Cardinals, 1987; safety Phoenix Cardinals (formerly St. Louis Cardinals), 1988-92; with S.F. 49ers, 1993—. Office: San Francisco 49ers 4949 Centennial Blvd Santa Clara CA 95054-1229

MCDONNEL, WILLIAM GEORGE, chemical instrumentation executive; b. Rabat, French Morocco, May 10, 1952; came to U.S., 1953; s. Harold Albert and Anna (Yoos) McD.; BS in Chemistry/Biochemistry, Calif. State U., Fullerton, 1974, MBA Pepperdine U., 1987; m. Nancy Ann Hopwood, Aug. 27, 1977; children: Melissa, Allison Roe. Product specialist Process Instruments div. Beckman Instruments, Inc., Fullerton, 1974; sr. tech. specialist ion selective electrodes Lab. Products div. Orion Research Inc., Cambridge, Mass., 1975-87; region mgr. Milton Roy Inc., 1988-91; gen. mgr. Southwest Sci., Inc., 1991—; speaker in field. Mem. Am. Chem. Soc., Am. Electroplaters Spc., Phi Kappa Tau. Republican. Home: 27412 Cenajo Mission Viejo CA 92691

MCDONOUGH, PATRICK KEVIN, engineer; b. Denver, Feb. 21, 1949; s. Michael Joseph and Patricia (Watson) McD.; m. Julia C. Stricker, June 13, 1970; children: Ryan Patrick, Caitlin Michaela, Kim Michael, Kerry Leigh. BSBA, U. Phoenix, Denver, 1988. System tech. Pueblo TV Power, Colo., 1970-73; sr. tech. Teleprompter Los Gatos, Calif., 1973-75; chief tech. Teleprompter Newport Beach, Calif., 1975-78, Teleprompter Newark, Calif., 1978-79; corp. chief engr. United Cabel TV Corp., Denver, 1979-89; dir. of engring. United Artists Cabel TV, Denver, 1989; v.p. of engring. United Internat. Holdings Inc., Denver, 1989—. Contbr. articles to profl. jours. Mem. Soc. Cable TV Engrs. (tuition assistance com.). Home: 8413 E Otero Cir Englewood CO 80112-3312 Office: United Internat Holdings 4643 S Ulster Ste 1300 Denver CO 80237-2754

MCDONOUGH, RUSSELL CHARLES, state supreme court justice; b. Glendive, Mont., Dec. 7, 1924; s. Roy James and Elsie Marie (Johnson) McD.; m. Dora Jean Bidwell, Mar. 17, 1946; children: Ann Remmich, Michael, Kay Jensen, Kevin, Daniel, Mary Garfield. JD, George Washington U., 1949. Bar: Mont. 1950. Pvt. practice Glendive, Mont., 1950-83; judge Gen. Jurisdiction State of Montana, Glendive, 1983-87; justice Mont. Supreme Ct., Helena, 1987-93. City atty. City of Glendive, Mont., 1953-57; county atty. County of Dawson, Mont., 1957-63; del. Mont. Constl. Conv., Helena, 1972. 1st lt. AC, U.S. Army. 1943-45, ETO. Recipient Disting. Flying Cross, U.S. Army, 1944. Mem. Mont. Bar Assn. Roman Catholic. Home: 516 S Sanders St Helena MT 59601-5437 Office: US Supreme Ct Mont Justice Bldg Rm 323 215 N Sanders St Helena MT 59601-4522

MCDOUGAL, DENNIS EDWARD, journalist, writer; b. Pasadena, Calif., Nov. 25, 1947; s. Carl Albert and Lola (Irvin) McD.; m. Diane Benbenek, June 13, 1970 (div. June 1989); children: Jennifer Erin, Amy Suzanne, Kate Michelle; m. Sharon Murphy, Feb. 24, 1990. BA, UCLA, 1972, M in Journalism, 1973. Staff writer Riverside (Calif.) Press-Enterprise, 1973-77, Long Beach (Calif.) Press-Telegram, 1977-83, L.A. Times, 1983—; contbg. writer FAME mag., N.Y.C., 1989-90. Author: Angel of Darkness, 1991, (with Pierce O'Donnell) Fatal Subtraction, 1992. Recipient various journalism awards AP News Execs. Calif.; Knight fellow Stanford U., 1981-82. Mem. Atlantic City Press Club, Greater L.A. Press Club, Orange County Press Club, Twin Counties Press Club, Pacific Coast Press Club. Office: PO Box 7725 Long Beach CA 90807-7725

MCDOUGALL, I. ROSS, nuclear medicine educator; b. Glasgow, Scotland, Dec. 18, 1943; came to U.S., 1976; s. Archibald McDougall and Jean Cairns; m. Elizabeth Wilson, Sept. 6, 1968; children: Shona, Stewart. MBChB, U. Glasgow, 1967, PhD, 1973. Diplomate Am. Bd. Nuclear Medicine (chmn. 1985-87), Am. Bd. Internal Medicine (gov. 1984-86). Lectr. in medicine U. Glasgow, 1969-76; assoc. prof. radiology and medicine Stanford (Calif.) U., 1976-84, prof. radiology and medicine, 1985—. Contbr. numerous articles to sci. jours. Fellow Royal Coll. Physicians (Glasgow), Am. Coll. Physicians; mem. Am. Thyroid Assn., Soc. Nuclear Medicine, Western Assn. for Clin. Research. Office: Stanford U Med Ctr Div Nuclear Medicine Stanford CA 94305

MCDOUGALL, JACQUELYN MARIE HORAN, therapist; b. Wenatchee, Wash., Sept. 24, 1924; d. John Rankin and Helen Frampton (Vandivort) Horan; m. Robert Duncan McDougall, Jan. 24, 1947 (div. July 1976); children: Douglas, Stuart, Scott. BA, Wash. State U., 1946. Lic. therapist, Wash.; cert. nat. addiction counselor II. Pres. oper. bd. Ctr. for Alcohol/Drug Treatment, Wenatchee, 1983-85; sec. Wash. State Coun. on Alcoholism, 1988-89, supr. out-patient svcs., 1989-90; case mgmt. counselor Lakeside Treatment Ctr., East Wenatchee, Wash., 1991—. Treas. Allied Arts, Wenatchee, 1984; pres. Rep. Women, Wash., 1969-70.

MCDOWELL, CARLY SHAW (CLAUDIA MCDOWELL), public relations executive; b. Schenectady, N.Y., Aug. 13, 1957; d. Stanley Dick and Joanne (Hubbard) Gimbel; m. Michael Merrideth McDowell, Oct. 29, 1988. Student, U. Puget Sound, 1976-77, U. Wash., 1977-81. Spl. events mgr. Children's Hosp. and Med. Ctr., Seattle, 1986-87; community rels. dir. Ballard Community Hosp., Seattle, 1988-91; prin. Carly McDowell Comm., 1992—. Contbr. articles to profl. jours. Recipient Silver Advt. award Healthcare Mktg. Report, 1990, Internat. award, 1991. Mem. Pub. Rels. Soc. Am.

MCDOWELL, DAVID E., pharmaceutical executive; b. 1942. AA, Orange Coast Jr. Coll., 1962; MS, Stamford U., 1978. V.p., gen. mgr. quality control Internat. Bus. Machines, Armonk, N.Y., 1962-91; pres., COO McKesson Corp., 1991—. Office: McKesson Corp 1 Post St San Francisco CA 94101*

MCDOWELL, JEFFREY STEVEN, corporate information executive; b. Eugene, Oreg., Oct. 30, 1954; s. Howard G. and Jean B. McDowell. BA, U. Mont., 1979, postgrad., 1984-85. Reporter Tobacco Valley News, Eureka, Mont., 1979-80, asst. editor, 1980-82; sports editor Lewistown (Mont.) News-Argus, 1982-84; sr. editor Mont. Kaimin, Missoula, 1984; legis. corr. Mont. Kaimin, Helena, 1985; night editor Ravalli Rep., Hamilton, Mont., 1985; corp. info. mgr. Ribi ImmunoChem Rsch., Inc., Hamilton, 1986—. Asst. scoutmaster Boy Scouts Am., Missoula, 1972-76. Mem. Soc. Profl. Journalists (bd. dirs. 1983-85, v.p. 1985-86, pres. 1986-87), Mont. Press Women (bd. dirs. 1983-84), Bitterroot Valley C. of C. (bd. dirs. 1989-92). Office: Ribi ImmunoChem Rsch Inc 533 Old Corvallis Rd Hamilton MT 59840-3131

MCDOWELL, JENNIFER, sociologist, composer, playwright, publisher; b. Albuquerque, May 19, 1936; d. Willard A. and Margaret Frances (Garrison) McD.; m. Milton Loventhal, July 2, 1973. BA, U. Calif., 1957; MA, San Diego State U., 1958; postgrad., Sorbonne, Paris, 1959; MLS, U. Calif., 1963; PhD, U. Oreg., 1973. Tchr. English Abraham Lincoln High Sch., San Jose, Calif., 1960-61; free-lance editor Soviet field, Berkeley, Calif., 1961-63; rsch. asst. sociology U. Oreg., Eugene, 1964-66; editor, pub. Merlin Papers, San Jose, 1969—, Merlin Press, San Jose, 1973—; rsch. cons. sociology San Jose, 1973—; music pub. Lipstick and Toy Balloons Pub. Co., San Jose, 1978—; composer Paramount Pictures, 1982-88; tchr. writing workshops; poetry readings, 1969-73; co-producer radio show lit. and culture Sta. KALX, Berkeley, 1971-72. Author: (with Milton Loventhal) Black Politics: A Study and Annotated Bibliography of the Mississippi Freedom Democratic Party, 1971 (featured at Smithsonian Instn. spl. event 1992), Contemporary Women Poets: An Anthology of California Poets, 1977, Ronnie Goose Rhymes for Grown-ups, 1984; co-author: (plays off-off Broadway) Betsy and Phyllis, 1986, Mack the Knife Your Friendly Dentist, 1986, The Estrogen Party to End War, 1986, The Oatmeal Party Comes to Order, 1986, (play Burgess Theatre) Betsy Meets the Wacky Iraqi, 1991; contbr. poems, plays, essays, articles, short stories, book revs. to lit. mags., news mags. and anthologies; researcher women's autobiog. writings, contemporary writing in poetry, Soviet studies, civil rights movement and George Orwell, 1962—; writer: (songs) Money Makes a Woman Free, 1976, 3 songs featured in Parade of Am. Music; co-creator: (mus. comedy) Russia's Secret Plot to Take Back Alaska, 1988. Recipient 8 awards Am. Song Festival, 1976-79, Bill Casey award in Letters, 1980; AAUW doctoral fellow, 1971-73; grantee Calif. Arts Council, 1976-77. Mem. Am. Sociol. Assn., Soc. Sci. Study of Religion, Poetry Orgn. for Women, Dramatists Guild, Phi Beta Kappa, Sigma Alpha Iota, Beta Phi Mu, Kappa Kappa Gamma. Democrat. Office: care Merlin Press PO Box 5602 San Jose CA 95150-5602

MCDOWELL, ROBIN SCOTT, physical chemist; b. Greenwich, Conn., Nov. 14, 1934; s. James Duffil and Aimee Marguerite (Lavers) McD.; m. Arlene R. Egertsen, Nov. 23, 1963; children: Jennifer Ellen, Allison Elizabeth. BA, Haverford Coll., 1956; PhD, MIT, 1960. Mem. staff Los Alamos (N.Mex.) Nat. Lab., 1960-81, asst. group leader, 1981-82, fellow, 1983-91; sr. chief scientist and chem. structure & dynamics program Battelle Pacific N.W. Labs, Richland, Wash., 1991—. Contbr. articles to profl. jours. and encyclopaedias. Chmn. Los Alamos County Library Bd., 1981-82. Mem. AAAS, Am. Chem. Soc., Optical Soc. Am., Coblentz Soc. Inc. (pres. 1987-89), Am. Chem. Soc., Soc. Applied Spectroscopy, Sigma Xi. Office: Battelle Pacific NW Labs Richland WA 99352

MCEACHEN, JAMES ALLEN, cardiologist; b. Mar. 14, 1925; s. James A. and Edna Charlotte (Pegler) McE.; m. Eileen Joyce, June 16, 1956; children: James Allen, Brian Pail, Gregory Elwood. BA, U. Nebr., 1946; MD, Western Res. U., 1950. Intern Univ. Hosp., Cleve., 1950-51, asst. resident in medicine, 1951-52; resident Wadsworth VA Hosp., L.A., 1952-54; dir. cardiology St. Johns Hosp., Santa Monica, Calif., 1955-78; dir. coronary care St. Johns Hosp., Santa Monica, 1968-83, staff cardiologist, 1978-88, hon. staff, 1988—. Recipient Disting. Svc. award Holy Family Adoption Svc., L.A., 1967. Fellow Am. Coll. Cardiology, Soc. for Cardiac Angiography and Intervention. Republican.

MCEACHERN, ALLAN, Canadian justice; b. Vancouver, B.C., Can., May 20, 1926; s. John A. and Blanche L. (Roadhouse) McE.; m. Gloria, July 17, 1953; children: Jean Williams, Joanne Evans. BA, U. B.C., Vancouver, 1949; LLB, U. B.C., 1950. Assoc., sr. ptnr., barrister, solicitor Messrs. Russell & DuMoulin, Vancouver, B.C., 1950-78; chief justice Supreme Ct. B.C., Vancouver, 1979-88, Ct. Appeals B.C., Vancouver, 1988—. Pres. Kats Rugby Club, Vancouver, 1953-64, B.C. Lions Football Club, Vancouver, 1967, 68, 69. We. Football Conf., 1964, Can. Football League, 1967-68, commr. 1967-68. Mem. Can. Bar Assn. (bd. dirs.), Vancouver Bar Assn. (bd. dirs.), Legal Aid Soc. (pres. 1977-78), Law Soc. B.C. (bencher 1971-79). Home: 1414 W King Edward Ave, Vancouver, BC Canada V6H 2A2 Office: Law Cts, 800 Smithe St, Vancouver, BC Canada V6Z 2E1

MCELIGOT, DONALD MARINUS, thermal scientist, engineering educator; b. Passaic, N.J.; s. Maurice Joseph Benedict and Shirley Irene (Gambling) McE.; m. Julimae Albright; children: Kim, Kyle, Sean. BS in Mech. Engring., Yale U.; MS in Engring., U. Wash., postgrad.; PhD,

Stanford U. Registered profl. engr., N.J. Assoc. prof. U. Ariz., Tuscon, 1963-68; prof. U. Ariz., Tucson, 1968-85, prof. emeritus, 1985—; thermohydromechanics scientist, mgr. Gould Ocean Systems Divsn. (name changed to Westinghouse Naval Systems Divsn.), Middletown, R.I., 1984-91; prin. thermal scientist, Idaho Nat. Engring. Lab. EG&G Idaho, Idaho Falls, 1991—; vis. staff Imperial Coll. Sci. and Tech., London, 1969-70; guest prof. U. Karlsruhe, Germany, 1975-76, 79, Max Planck Institut fuer Stoemungsforschung, Goettingen, Germany, 1982-84; adj. prof. mechanical engring. U. R.I., West Kingston, 1986-91. Lt. (j.g.) USN; Capt. USNR-Ret. Recipient Gold badge for soaring Fedn. Aeronautique Internat. 1971, Calif. State Altitude Gain record (15m sailplane) 1978, Abzeichen fuer Truppendienst in Silber Bundeswehr Germany 1976, 83, Charles H. Jennings Meml. award Am. Welding Soc. 1992; Yuba Consolidated Industries fellow Stanford U., AEC Sci. and Engring. Fellow U. Wash., Stanford U.; Sr. Fulbright Rsch. scholar U.S.-Deutschland Fulbright Commn., 1982-83; U. Ariz. Outstanding Prof. award for Excellence in teaching, 1983; grantee NSF. Fellow ASME (chmn. heat transfer gen. papers com. 1981-82, assoc. tech. editor J. Heat Transfer 1986-92, gas turbine heat transfer com., Cert. Appreciation award 1992), Am. Phys. Soc., U.S. Naval Institute, Tucson Soaring Club (treas. 1972-73), Yale Club of Tucson (sec.-treas. 1967-69), Idaho Falls Ski Club, Sigma Xi, Tau Beta Pi.

MCELLIGOTT, ANN THERESA, accounting manager; b. Portland, Oreg., Nov. 15, 1942; d. Frank J. and Florence L. (Swanson) McE.; m. Forrest G. Hawkins, Sept. 9, 1961 (div. Sept. 1982); children: Michelle, Brenda, Sandra. Student, Portland Community Coll., 1971-72; BS, Portland State U., 1974; postgrad., U. Oreg., 1988-91. CPA, Oreg. Staff acct. Coopers & Lybrand, Portland, 1974-76, in-charge acct., 1976-78, audit mgr., 1978-83; reporting and gen. ledger mgr. Tektronix, Beaverton, Oreg., 1983-86, group acctg. mgr., 1986—; instr. in acctg. Linfield Coll., Beaverton, 1985-86. Director Campfire Girls, Portland, 1979-81, treas., 1988-91, now v.p. Recipient Guleck award Campfire Girls, 1986. Mem. AICPAs, Oreg. Soc. CPAs, City Club. Office: Tektronix PO Box 500 Mail Sta 55-850 Beaverton OR 97077

MCELROY, CHARLOTTE ANN, principal; b. Dimmitt, Tex., Oct. 24, 1939; d. William Robert and Mary Ilene (Cooper) McE. BA, West Tex. State U., 1962, MEd, 1964; postgrad., Calif. State U., Santa Barbara, 1966-68. Tchr. Amarillo (Tex.) Schs., 1962-65; 1st and 2d grade tchr. Ventura (Calif.) Schs., 1965-66, 4th, 5th and 6th grade tchr., 1966-74, elem. counselor, 1974-76, spl. edn. tchr., 1976-77, counselor, phys. edn. tchr., 1977-78; asst. prin. Cabrillo Jr. High Sch., Ventura Unified Schs., 1978-80; prin. E. P. Foster Elem. Sch., Ventura Unified Schs., 1980-84, Anacapa Middle Sch., Ventura Unified Schs., 1984—; presenter in field. Recipient Nat. Blue Ribbon Sch. award Nat. Edn. Dept., 1990-91, Calif. Disting. Sch. award, 1989-90; named one of Outstanding Principals, State Calif. Mem. Ventura Adminstrs. Assn., Calif. League Middle Schs., Assn. Calif. Sch. Adminstrs., Kappa Kappa Gamma. Democrat. Home: 2250 Los Encinos Rd Ojai CA 93023-9709 Office: Anacapa Middle Sch 100 S Mills Rd Ventura CA 93003-3487

MCELROY, LEO FRANCIS, communications consultant, journalist; b. Los Angeles, Oct. 12, 1932; s. Leo Francis and Helen Evelyn (Silliman) McE.; m. Dorothy Frances Montgomery, Nov. 3, 1956 (div. 1981); children: James, Maureen, Michael, Kathleen; m. Judith Marie Lewis, May 30, 1992. BS in English, Loyola U., L.A. 1953. News dir. KFI, KRLA, KABC Radio, L.A., 1964-72; pub. affairs host Sta. KCET, Pub. TV, L.A., 1967-74; v.p. Sta. KROQ AM/FM, L.A., 1972-74; polit. editor Sta. KABC-TV, L.A., 1974-81; pres. McElroy Communications, L.A. and Sacramento, 1981—; pres. sec. Lt. Gov.'s Office, Sacramento, 1983-84; chmn. Calif. AP Broadcasters, 1972-74; cons. State Office Migrant Edn., Sacramento, 1974, Californians for Water, L.A. , 1982, Calif. Water Protection Coun., Sacramento, 1982, Planning and Conservation League, Sacramento, 1984—, Common Cause, Sacramento, 1988—. Author: Uneasy Partners, 1984; author plays: Mermaid Tavern, 1956, To Bury Caesar (Christopher award 1952), 1952. State del. Western Am. Assembly on Prison Reform, Berkeley, Calif., 1973; chmn. State Disaster Info. Task Force; Calif., 1973-74; campaign media cons. statewide issues, various candidates, Sacramento, L.A., 1981—; bd. dirs. Vols. in Victim Assistance, Sacramento, 1984, Rescue Alliance, Sacramento, 1987—, Mental Health Assn., Sacramento, 1985-89, Leukemia Soc., 1992—. Recipient Gabriel award Cath. Archdiocese, L.A., 1972, Golden Mike award Radio-TV News Assn., L.A., 1973; Hon. Resolution, Calif. State Assembly, Sacramento, 1981. Mem. ASCAP, AFTRA, Screen Actors Guild, Am. Assn. Polit. Cons. Republican. Roman Catholic. Office: McElroy Communications 2410 K St Ste C Sacramento CA 95816-5002 also: 6363 Wilshire Blvd Ste 129 Los Angeles CA 90048

MC ELWAIN, JOSEPH ARTHUR, retired power company executive; b. Deer Lodge, Mont., Nov. 13, 1919; s. Lee Chaffee and Johanna (Petersen) McE.; m. Mary Cleaver Witt, Mar. 8, 1945 (dec. June 1992); children—Lee William and Lori Louise (twins). B.A., U. Mont., 1943, LL.B., 1947. Bar: Mont. 1947. Individual practice law Deer Lodge, 1947-63; Washington legis. counsel Mont. Power Co., Butte, 1954-63, counsel, 1963-65, asst. to pres., 1965-67, v.p., 1967-70, exec. v.p., dir., 1970, then chmn., chief exec. officer, now ret.; dir. Mont. Power Co., First Bank System 1975-84, Devel. Credit Corp. Mont.; MHD Devel. Corp. 1986—; mem. U.S. nat. com. World Energy Conf.; Mont. dir. for U.S. Savs. Bonds, 1980-81; cons. in field. Mem. Mont. Pub. Land Law Rev. Adv. Com. City atty. Deer Lodge, 1950-57, 60-63; mem. Mont. Ho. of Reps., 1949-55, majority floor leader, 1951; mem. Mont. State Senate, 1962-64; state chmn. Republican Central Com., Mont., 1952-54; mem. adv. com. Edison Electric Inst., U. Mont. Found., Missoula, Rocky Mountain Coll., Billings; bd. dirs. Mont. Internat. Trade Commn. Served with AUS, World War II and Korea. Recipient Judstin Miller award, 1947. Mem. Mont., Am. bar assns. Episcopalian. Clubs: Masons, Shriners, Kiwanis. Home: 1500 Carolina Ave Butte MT 59701-5557 Office: 40 E Broadway St Butte MT 59701-9394

MCELYEA, ULYSSES, JR., veterinarian; b. Ft. Collins, Colo., Oct. 29, 1941; s. Ulysses and Hazel (Hall) McE.; m. Rexanna Bell, Dec. 29, 1975 (div. 1980). BS in Pharmacy, U. N.Mex., 1963; DVM, Colorado State U., 1967, MS, 1968. Diplomate Am. Bd. Vet. Practicioners; cert. in companion animals. Owner Alta Vista Animal Clinic, Las Cruces, N.Mex., 1970—; bd. dirs. N.Mex. Acad. Vet. Practice, Albuquerque, bd. dirs. state of N.Mex. Bd. Vet. Examiners, v.p., 1989-92, vice chair, 1992, chair, 1992—, Bank of the Rio Grande. Pres. Las Cruces Community Theater, 1974; founder, bd. dirs. Dona Ann Arts Coun., Las Cruces, 1976-80. Capt. U.S. Army, 1968-70. Mem. AVMA, Am. Pharm. Assn., Am. Assn. Feline Practitioners, Am. Soc. Vet. Ophthalmologists, N.Mex. Vet. Med. Assn. (bd. dirs. 1976-82), So. N.Mex. Vet. Assn. (pres. 1974, 84), N.Mex. State U. Athletic Assn. (bd. dirs. 1976—, pres. elect 1992-93), N.Mex. State U. Pres.'s Assn. (bd. dirs. 1988-91), U. N.Mex. Alumni Assn. (bd. dirs. 1976-80). Republican. Home: 2635 Fairway Dr Las Cruces NM 88001-5044 Office: Alta Vista Animal Clinic 725 S Solano Dr Las Cruces NM 88001-3244

MCENTIRE, MALETA MAE, real estate manager; b. L.A., Sept. 22, 1957; d. Floyd Steven and Joan Marie (Kioskli) Odessa; m. Robert James Ornellas, Aug. 25, 1980 (div. 1982); m. Jack Walton McEntire, Jr., Oct. 25, 1986; children: Jason, Jeremy. Student, Delta Jr. Coll., Stockton, Calif., 1977. Lic. real estate ins. Personnel adminstrv. aide World Airways, Oakland, Calif., 1975-77; flight attendant World Airways, 1977-81; with sales Winner Chevrolet, Tracy, Calif., 1981-88; dir. San Joaquin County Food Bank, Tracy, 1981-85; commr. San Joaquin County, Stockton, Calif., 1981-84, Brown Bag, State of Calif., Sacramento, 1982, Food Bank, State of Calif., Sacramento, 1985; regional mgr. Sutter Office Ctr., Stockton, 1985—; bd. dirs. Downtown Devel. and Planning, Stockton; student instr. Jr. Achievement, Stockton, 1988—; bd. dirs., advisor Stockton Redevel. Dist. IB, 1987—. Author: Brown Bag Manual, 1982 (Govt. of Calif. award 1982), State of California Distribution, 1983 (Calif. Sec. of State award 1983). Advisor Stockton Rep. Com., 1976—, 4-H Club Am.; bd. dirs. McHenry Shelter, Tracy, 1987—; mem. Calif. Food Bank and Commodity Commn., Sacramento, 1983-85. Recipient Outstanding Sales cert. Winner Cheu, Tracy, 1984, Rescue Mission Baby Lifts cert. Govt. of Calif., 1979; named Miss Tracy-Talent, Tracy C. of C., 1975. Mem. Nat. Assn. Notaries, Stockton C. of C. (Vol. of Yr. award 1981), Lyons Club (Outstanding Citizen award 1985), Tracy Exch. Health and Safety. Republican. Baptist. Office: Sutter Office Ctr 242 N Sutter St Ste 700 Stockton CA 95202-2402

MC EVILLY, THOMAS VINCENT, seismologist; b. East Saint Louis, Ill., Sept. 2, 1934; s. Robert John and Frances Nathalie (Earnshaw) McE.; m. Dorothy K. Hopfinger, Oct. 23, 1970; children: Mary, Susan, Ann, Steven, Joseph, Adrian. B.S., St. Louis U., 1956, Ph.D., 1964. Geophysicist California Co., New Orleans, 1957-60; engring. v.p. Sprengnether Instrument Co., St. Louis, 1962-67; asst. prof. seismology U. Calif., Berkeley, 1964-68, assoc. prof., 1968-74, prof., 1974—, chmn. dept. geology and geophysics, 1976-80, asst. dir. seismographic sta., 1968-90; dir. earth sci. div. Lawrence Berkeley Lab., 1982-93; chmn. bd. dirs. Inc. Research Instns. for Seismology, 1984-86; cons. numerous govt. agys., geotech. cos. Contbr. numerous articles to profl. jours. Mem. Am. Geophys. Union, Royal Astron. Soc., Seismol. Soc. Am. (editor bull. 1976-85), Soc. Exploration Geophysicists, AAAS, Phi Beta Kappa. Office: U Calif Dept Geology and Geophysics 1 Cyclotron Rd Berkeley CA 94720

MCEVOY, RICHARD FRANKLIN, composites executive; b. Litchfield, Ill., Dec. 27, 1946; s. John William McEvoy and Genevieve Ann (McCarthy) Shirk; m. Carol Lee Franz, Mar. 22, 1941; 1 child, Andrea Lynn. BA, Lehigh U., 1968. Retail rep. Shall Oil Co., Clifton, N.J., 1968-72; mktg. mgr. Sunset Life Ins., Olympia, Wash., 1972-73; quality audit supr. Weyerhaeuser Co., Springfield, Oreg., 1973-77; gen. mgr. Stimson Lumber Co., Portland, Ore., 1977-85, WTD Industries, Sedro Woolley, Wash., 1985, Danlo Mfg., Portland, 1986-88; v.p. McKenzie Products, Eugene, Oreg., 1988-90; gen. mgr. Skyline Products, Harrisburg, Oreg., 1992—; bd. dirs. Simpson Timber Co., Shelton, Wash., Sierra-Pacific Industries, Redding, Calif. Mem. Oreg. Govs. Coun. of Econ. Advisors, Salem, 1982-90. Republican. Presbyterian. Home: 28100 Ferguson Rd Junction City OR 97448 Office: Skyline Products 495 Territorial Rd Harrisburg OR 97446

MCEWAN, WILLARD WINFIELD, JR., lawyer, judge; b. Evanston, Ill., Dec. 26, 1934; s. Willard Winfield Sr. and Esther (Sprenger) McE.; children: Michael, Elizabeth, Allison. BS, Claremont Men's Coll., 1956; JD, U. Calif., San Francisco, 1960. Bar: Calif. 1960, U.S. Dist. Ct. (no. and so. dists.) Calif. 1960, U.S. Supreme Ct. 1974. Commd. U.S. Army, 1956, advanced through grades to capt., 1965, resigned, 1968; dep. legis. counsel. City of Sacramento, Calif., 1960-61; asst. city atty. City of Santa Barbara, Calif., 1961-62; pvt. practice atty. Santa Barbara, 1962—; judge U.S. Magistrate Ct., Santa Barbara County, 1973—; atty. Goleta Water Dist., 1986-87; lectr. Santa Barbara Adult Edn. Program. Founder, bd. dirs., officer, gen legal coun. Santa Barbara Coun. for Retarded, 1962-72; active WORK Workshop for Handicapped, Assn. Retarded Citizens, Santa Barbara City Landmarks Adv. Com., 1967-73; v.p. Santa Barbara Harbor Pageants and Exhibits Com., 1964; chmn. Citizens Save our Shoreline Com., 1964, Citizens Community Master Plan Com., 1964, YMCA Membership Drive, 1964, Citizens Adv. Com. on Sch. Dist. Tax Needs, 1965; commr. Santa Barbara City Water Commn., 1965, City of Santa Barbara Recreation Commn., 1970-73. Recipient Disting Svc. award Jr. C. of C., 1965; named Santa Barbara's Young Man of Yr. 1965. Mem. Am. Heart Assn. (pres. Santa Barbara County chpt. 1981-82), Santa Barbara Heart Assn. (bd. dirs., pres. bd. dirs. 1981-82, chmn. Heart Sunday 1973, 75), Santa Barbara Malacological Soc., Santa Barbara Kiwanis (pres. 1967), C. of C. (com. on local govt., state legisaltion com., bd. dirs., past v.p. bd. dirs., pres. bd. dirs. 1981-82, chmn. several coms.). Republican. Roman Catholic. Office: US Courthouse 8 E Figueroa St Ste 210 Santa Barbara CA 93101

MCFADDEN, BRUCE ALDEN, biochemistry educator; b. La Grande, Oreg., Sept. 23, 1930; s. Eugene Field and Mary Elizabeth (McMaster) McF.; m. Roberta Ray Wilson, June 14, 1958; children: Paul, David, John. AB in Chemistry with honors, Whitman Coll., 1952, DSc (hon.), 1978; PhD in Biochemistry, UCLA, 1956. From instr. to prof. chemistry Wash. State U., Pullman, 1956-66, prof. biochemistry, 1974—, dir. sci. devel., 1974-78, chmn. dept. biochemistry, 1978-84; vis. prof. U. Leicester, Eng., 1972-73, U. Florence, Italy, 1980, Tech. U., Munich, 1980-81; vis. scientist Minority Instns. (FASEB), 1988; mem. study sect. NIH, Bethesda, Md., 1978-79, 82; panelist rsch. grants U.D. Dept. Energy, 1983, 91; panelist Frasch grants Am. Chem. Soc., 1982-87; cons. to numerous jours. and agys., Pullman, 1966—. Editor Archives Microbiology, 1977-83; contbr. articles to profl. jours.; patentee in field. Pres. Sunnyside Sch. PTA, Pullman, 1972; chmn 1984 and Beyond Citizens' com., Pullman Sch. Bd., 1983-84. Recipient Disting. Sr. U.S. Scientist award Humboldt Found. Tech. U. Munich, 1980-81; fellow Guggenheim Found., 1972-73, NIH, 1963-69,73; numerous others. Fellow AAAS; mem. Am. Chem. Soc. (pres. Wash.-Idaho Border sect. 1963-64), Am. Soc. Biol. Chem. & Molecular Biol., Am. Soc. Microbiologists, Pacific Slope Biochem. Soc. (pres. 1973-74), Am. Soc. Plant Physiologists, Sigma Xi, Phi Kappa Phi, Phi Lambda Upsilon (pres. 1955). Democrat. Home: 1465 SW Wadleigh Dr Pullman WA 99163-2048 Office: Wash State U Biochemistry Dept Pullman WA 99164

MCFADDEN, JO BETH, oil company executive; b. Tucumcari, N.Mex., Oct. 26, 1938; d. Ernest and Oveta (Barnes) Hogan; m. Gerald B. McFadden, Oct. 15, 1965. BS, Regis U., Denver, 1983. Adminstrv. asst. Gov. State N.Mex., Santa Fe, 1967-71; com. coord. Taxation and Revenue State N.Mex., Santa Fe, 1971-78; budget adminstr. Canterra Petroleum, Denver, 1979-84; corp. sec.-treas. Sharon Resources, Inc., Englewood, Colo., 1984—; also dir. Named Good Citizen of Yr., DAR, Tucumcari, 1955. Mem. Am. Assn. Retired Persons, Rocky Mountain Mineral Law Found., 40 Plus of Colo., Nat. Writer's Club. Home: 7233 S Vine St Littleton CO 80122-1626

MCFADDEN, LEON LAMBERT, artist, inventor; b. St. Paul, Apr. 19, 1920; s. Frank Grover and Irene Manilla Lambert (Deane) McF.; m. Karyn Flannery, Nov. 6, 1986. Student, several colls., univs., art insts. Prin. McFadden Commercial Studios, 1946-50; with McFadden-Kaump Art Service, 1952-54; pres. McFadden Advt. (merger with Sundial Services, Inc.), 1954-70; mktg. dir. Kinelogic Corp., Mountain View, Calif., 1965-70; mktg. dir. rsch. and devel. proprietary patents Sundial Systems div. Sundial Services, Inc., 1968-70; art instr. various Calif. community colls., 1972-74; minority bus. cons. VISTA/ACTION, 1974-75; pres., CEO Prometheus Project, Inc., Yreka, Calif., 1975—. Inventor, patentee 17 mechanical tools and devices; prin. artistic works include large assemblage painting of Liberty, found image works (represented in White House spl. collection). Served with USN, 1942-46, PTO. Mem. IEEE, AIAA, AAAS, N.Mex. Solar Energy Assn., Mensa, Artists Equity Assn. Inc., Artists Equity Assn. of N.Y., Siskiyou Artists Assn., , Sierra Club (life). Home: 418 3D St Yreka CA 96097 Studio: Liberty Painting Corp 6725 Old Hwy 99 Yreka CA 96097-9725

MCFADDEN, TERRY TED, arctic engineering educator, consultant; b. Dillon, Mont., June 28, 1936; s. Everett Kuhle and Eleanor Mae (Baril) McF.; m. Ruth Finlayson; children: Sharon Aleta, Lori Scott; m. Loretta Stejer, Dec. 29, 1955 (div. 1966); children: Tammy Roben, Ronn Kevin, Toni Lynn, Kary Scott. B in Engring. Sci., Brigham Young U., 1960; MS, Stanford U., 1965; PhD, U. Alaska, Fairbanks, 1974. Registered profl. engr., Alaska. Engr. R & D Hewlett Packard Co., Palo Alto, Calif., 1960-68; rsch. engr. Arctic Health Rsch. Ctr., Fairbanks, 1968-73; rsch. engr. Cold Regions Rsch. & Engring. Lab., Fairbanks, 1973-74, regional dir., 1974-82; dir. rsch. Shannon & Wilson Co., Fairbanks, 1982-83; prof. engr. U. Alaska, Fairbanks, 1983—; prin., owner McFadden Engring. Consul, Fairbanks, 1986—; exch. prof. Valtion Tek. Tutkimuskeskus, Helsinki, Finland, 1988-89; dir. Permafrost Tech. Found., Fairbanks. Author: Construction in Cold Regions, 1991; contbr. articles to profl. jours.; mem. adv. bd. Daily News Miner, 1986-87. Mem. CAP, Fairbanks, 1972-90, Maverick Ski Patrol, Cleary Summit, Alaska, 1970-90, Alaska Housing Task Force, Fairbanks, 1989-90, adv. com. Arctic Rsch. Commn., 1992—. With N.G., 1964-68. Mem. ASCE (pres. Alaska chpt. 1983, tech. coun. for Cold Regions Engring. exec. com. 1981-87, chmn. 1985-86, pres. Fairbanks chpt. 1986, pres. 1986-87), ASME, Nat. Soc. Profl. Engrs., Quiet Birdmen. Republican. Home: 3400 Sandvik St Fairbanks AK 99709-3903

MCFADDEN, THOMAS, academic administrator; b. N.Y.C., Nov. 12, 1935; m. Monica A. Dowdall; children—Monica, David. B.A., Cathedral Coll., 1957; S.T.L., Gregorian U., 1961; S.T.D., Cath. U., 1963. Asst. prof. St. Joseph's Coll., Bklyn., 1963-66; chmn. theology dept. Cathedral Coll., Douglaston, N.Y., 1966-68; asst. prof. Loyola Coll., Balt., 1968-69; prof. St. Joseph's U., Phila., 1970-82, dean Coll. Arts and Scis., 1982-87; acad. v.p. St. John Fisher Coll., Rochester, N.Y., 1987-92; pres. Marymount Coll., Calif., 1992—; vis. prof. Cath. U., Washington, 1967-68, LaSalle U., Phila., summer 1974-79. Author, editor: New Cath. Ency., 1974, 79. Editor, Dictionary of Religion, 3 vols., 1979; editor: Liberation, Revolution and Freedom, 1975, America in Theological Perspective, 1976. Recipient Disting. Teaching award Lindback, 1978, N.Y. State Excelsior award Bd. Examiners, 1991; HEW grantee, 1972; CAPHE grantee, 1985. Mem. AAUP, Coll. Theology Soc. (chmn. pubs. com. 1973-77). Democrat. Roman Catholic. Office: Marymount Coll 30800 Palos Verdes Dr E Rancho Palos Verdes CA 90274

MCFARLAND, EDWARD MELVIN, educator; b. Colorado Springs, Colo., Nov. 24, 1944; ss. Wilbur Melvin and Rosemary Margaret (McArthur) McF. BS, U. So. Colo., 1971, MA, 1977. Tchr. history Rapid City (S.D.) Pub. Schs., 1971-75, Fountain (Colo.)-Ft. Carson Pub. Schs., 1975—. Author: Midland Route, 1980, Cripple Creek Road, 1984; co-author: Rocketing to the Rockies, 1989, Phantom Canyon, 1990. Editor, bd. dirs. Colo. Midland Hist. Soc., Colorado Springs, 1980—; pres. Pikes Peak Hist. R.R. Mus., Manitou Springs, Colo., 1977-78; dir. photog. collections Ute Pass Hist. Soc. and Mus., Cascade, Colo., 1984-91. Sgt. USAF, 1965-68. Mem. Nat. Ry. Hist. Soc. (pres. Colo. Midland chpt. 1986), Hist. Soc. Pikes Peak Region (pres. 1982), Westerners Internat. (pres. Pikes Peak posse 1986). Home: 1731 Cooper Ave Colorado Springs CO 80907-7240 Office: 211 S Main St Fountain CO 80817-2305

MCFARLAND, JAMES DORSEY, manufacturing executive; b. Pueblo, Colo., Mar. 2, 1946; s. Lloyd and Margaret (Smith) McF.; m. Rene Ellen Rehm, July 17, 1971; children: Candice Ann, Melissa Erin. BS in Bus. Mgmt., U. Redlands. Indsl. engr. GM, Van Nuys, Calif., 1967-82; sr. corp. indsl. engr. I.M.E.D., San Diego, 1982-83; from mgr. indsl. engring. to sr. mgr. prodn. and indsl. engring. Advanced Cardiovascular Systems, Temecula, Calif., 1983—; cons., owner Pacific Datagraphics, Carlsbad, Calif. Bd. dirs. Am. Heart Assn., Temecula Valley Br., 1991-92. Sgt. U.S. Army, 1965-67, Vietnam. Mem. Inst. Indsl. Engrs. (sr.), Intertel, Mensa.

MCFARLAND, JON WELDON, county commissioner; b. Wenatchee, Wash., Aug. 23, 1938; s. Charles Edward and Maud Elizabeth (Brennan) McF.; m. Kay Annette Erbes, Apr. 5, 1956; children: Colleen, Michael, Heather. BS in Edn., Eastern Wash. State U., 1961; MS in Personnel Adminstrn., George Washington U., 1966; Grad., Command and Gen. Staff Coll., Fort Leavenworth, Kans., 1970, U.S. Army War Coll., Carlisle Barracks, Pa., 1980. Commd. U.S. Army, 1961, advanced through grades to col., 1981, retired, 1988; ops. officer European Hdqtrs. U.S. Army, Heidelberg, Fed. Republic Germany, 1980-83; commdr. 16th mil. police brigade U.S. Army, Fort Bragg, N.C., 1983-85, provost marshal 18th Airborne Corps, 1983-85; asst. commandant, commdr. of troops U.S. Army Mil. Police Sch., Fort McClellan, Ala., 1985-88; county commr. Columbia County, Wash., 1989—; dir., owner Mr. Mc's Direct Mktg. Svcs., 1992—; vice-chmn. Southeastern Emergency Med. and Trauma Coun., Wash., 1990—, chmn. Columbia County Bd. Commrs., 1990, 93; bd. dirs. Emergency Mgmt. Svcs., Columbia County. Author: History of Civil Disturbance 1960-68, 1969. Bd. dirs. Columbia County Pub. Health Dist., Dayton, 1989—, Project Timothy Pub. Svcs. Decorated Legion of Merit, Bronze Star, numerous others. Mem. Assn. of the U.S. Army, Columbia County Health Found. (bd. dirs. 1989—), Palouse Econ. Devel. Corp. (vice-chmn. 1990—, chmn. 1993—), Wash. State Assn. of Counties, U.S. Army War Coll. Found., Kiwanis (bd. dirs. 1990—). Democrat. Roman Catholic. Home: RR 3 Box 248 Dayton WA 99328-9792 Office: Columbia County 341 E Main Dayton WA 99328

MCFARLAND, JOSEPH EDWARD, counselor, consultant, educational kinesiologist; b. St. Louis, June 12, 1945; s. Joseph Francis and Alveva Clara Henrietta Marie (Detert) McF. AB in Psychology, St. Louis U., 1968; MA in Creative Edn., Sangamon State U., Springfield, Ill., 1978, MA in Human Devel. Counseling, 1981. Nat. cert. counselor, edn.-Kinesthetics Instr., ednl. therapist, religious instr., St. Louis Archdiocese and Springfield (Ill.) diocese. Math, sci. tchr. St. Louis Archdiocese, 1966-70; tchr. therapist Edgewood Children's Ctr., St. Louis County, 1970-72; math tchr., rel. edn. coord. St. Mary's, Taylorville, Ill., 1972-74; work adj. counselor placement supr. Christian County Mental Health, Springfield, Ill., 1975-76; counselor Sacred Heart-Griffin High Sch., Springfield, Ill., 1976-90; child devel. spec. Portland (Oreg.) Pub. Schs., 1990—; adminstr. Triad, Kwen Family Inst., Springfield, 1984-86; asst. dir. Office for Ministry with Persons with Disabilities, Springfield, 1986-87; ; counselor Catholic Charities, 1986-87, Personal Cons., 1988-89; chaplain St. John's Hosp., 1982-90. Creative Designer: Huff and Puff, 1982; trainer: Ill. Teen Inst, 1983-85; com. mem. Counselor's Audit, Am. Sch. Coun. Assn., 1988. Pres. Ill. Sch. Counselor's Assn., 1984-87; gov. Ill. Assn. for Coun. and Devel., 1987-90; mem. Ill. Coalition for Disabled Citizens, 1988-90; hosp. rep. Share, 1987-90; founding mem. Ctr. Health and Well Being, Portland; dir. Mind and Body Works, Portland. Mem. Am. Sch. Coun. Assn., Am. Assn. for Coun. & Devel., Nat. Assn. of Catholic Chaplains, Oreg. State Grange, Victorious Missionaries, Ill. Sch. Coun. Assn., SSU Alumni Assn. Home: 10806 E Burnside St Portland OR 97216-3140 Office: Faubion Elementary 3039 NE Portland Blvd Portland OR 97211-6699

MCFARLAND, KEVIN JOHN, foundation administrator; b. Mt. Clement, Mich., Mar. 18, 1958; s. Chuck Paul and Myrna (Bell) McF.; m. Betty Ann Bolton, Nov. 26, 1976; children: Michelle, Michael, Melinda. BS in Bibl. Studies magna cum laude, Abilene Christian U., Tex., 1980; postgrad., Tex. Tech. U., 1980-81, Stanford U., 1982-83. Resident asst. Abilene (Tex.) State Sch., 1976-78; pvt. landscaping bus. Abilene, 1978-80; research assoc., home and family life dept. Tex. Tech. U., Lubbock, 1980-81; youth and family minister Redwood City (Calif.) Ch. of Christ, 1981-84; pres. Manna Internat. Relief and Devel. Corp., Redwood City, 1984—. Bd. dirs. Am. Coun. Voluntary Internat. Action; dir. Inst. Cooperation Internat. Devel.; mem. Amnesty Internat., Bread for the World. Mem. Nat. Honor Soc., Cultural Survival, Soc. Internat. Devel. Global Affairs Coun., Inst. Cooperation Internat. Devel. (bd. dirs., founder, exec. dir.), Inst. Cultural Affairs, Acad. Polit. Sci., Evang. for Social Action, ALpha Chi. Democrat. Home: 227 E St Redwood City CA 94063-1033 Office: Manna Internat PO Box 3507 Redwood City CA 94064-3507

MC FARLAND, NORMAN FRANCIS, bishop; b. Martinez, Calif., Feb. 21, 1922; student St. Patrick's Sem., Menlo Park, Calif.; J.C.D., Cath. U. Am. Ordained priest Roman Catholic Ch., 1946, consecrated bishop, 1970; titular bishop of Bida and aux. bishop of San Francisco, 1970-74; apostolic adminstr. Diocese of Reno, 1974-76; bishop Diocese of Reno-Las Vegas, 1976-87, Diocese of Orange, Calif., 1987—. Office: Marywook Ctr 2811 E Villa Real Dr Orange CA 92667-1999

MCFARLAND, ROBERT DONALD, mechanical engineer; b. East St. Louis, Ill., Aug. 16, 1934; s. Donald George and Kathryn Louise (Snyder) McF.; m. Laura Alice Johnson, May 25, 1957; children: Eric Robert, Julia Kathryn. BS in Aero. Engring., U. Cin., 1957; MSME, U. N.Mex., Los Alamos, 1972. Rsch. engr. Rocketdyne div. Rockwell Internat., Canoga Park, Calif., 1957-67; staff mem. Los Alamos Nat. Lab., 1967—. Co-author: Sunspace Primer, 1984. Mem. ASHRAE. Democrat. Home: 32260 Walnut Los Alamos NM 87544 Office: MS J576 Los Alamos Nat Lab Los Alamos NM 87545

MCFEELEY, MARK B., federal judge; b. Orlando, Fla., May 5, 1944; s. William Joseph and Belle (Levy) M.; m. Patricia Anne Josephson, June 10, 1972; children—Matthew Randolph, Morgan Diana. B.S., U.S. Mcht. Marine Acad., 1966; J.D. cum laude, U. N.Mex., 1972. Bar: N.Mex. 1972, U.S. Dist. Ct. N.Mex. 1972, U.S. Ct. Appeals (10th cir.) 1972. Law clk. presiding judge U.S. Ct. Appeals, 10th Cir., 1972-73; ptnr. Felker & McFeeley, 1974-77, officer, dir. Felker, McFeeley & Ish, 1977-83; judge U.S. Bankruptcy Ct. Dist. N.Mex., Albuquerque, 1981-83, 83—. Mem. editorial bd. N.Mex. Law Rev., 1971-72. Contbr. articles to profl. jours. Served with USNR, 1966-78. Mem. ABA, Nat. Conf. Bankruptcy Judges, Comml. Law League Am., N.Mex. Bar Assn., Albuquerque Bar Assn. Office: US Dist Ct PO Box 546 Albuquerque NM 87103-0546

MCGAHA, MICHAEL DENNIS, Spanish educator; b. Dallas, Tex., Dec. 31, 1941; s. William N. and Helen Charlotte (Fields) McG.; m. Agnes Anne Mycue, Aug. 7, 1964; children: Joseph P., John M. BA, U. Dallas, 1965; PhD, U. Tex., 1970. Prof. of Spanish Pomona Coll., Claremont, Calif.,

1970—. Editor: Cervantes and the Renaissance, 1980, Approaches to Theater, 1982, Lope's Fábula de Perseo, 1985; translator: Acting Is Believing, 1986. Fulbright Found. grantee, 1965-66; NEH fellow, 1980-81. Mem. MLA (assembly del. 1990—), Soc. for Spanish and Portuguese Hist. Studies (assoc. editor Hispania 1986—), Cervantes Soc. Am. (editor Cervantes 1987—), Assn. for Hispanic Theater (bd. dirs. 1987-89). Democrat. Jewish. Office: Pomona Coll 333 College Way Claremont CA 91711 Home: 424 W Harrison Ave Claremont CA 91711-4631

MCGANN, JOHN MILTON, real estate executive; b. Omaha, Mar. 18, 1948; s. John Byron and Donna M. (Rehnquist) McG.; m. Barbara June Scott, June 2, 1978. BSBA, cert. real estate, U. Nebr., Omaha, 1971. Property mgr. Boetel & Co., Omaha, 1971-73; asst. office bldg. mgr. The Irvine Co., Newport Beach, Calif., 1973-74; property mgr. Harbor Investment Co., Corona Del Mar, Calif., 1974-76, Robert A. McNeil Corp., Santa Ana, Calif., 1976-78; gen. mgr. Daon Mgmt., Newport Beach, 1978-80; v.p. August Mgmt. Inc., Long Beach, Calif., 1980-82, Calif. Fed. Asst. Mgmt., L.A., 1982-83; pres. Wespac Mgmt. Realty Corp., Newport Beach, 1983-87; v.p., dir. asset mgmt., pres. CalFed Asset Mgmt. Co., L.A., 1987-90; v.p. com. ops. Sovereign/Ring, Santa Monica, 1990—. Mem. Inst. Real Estate Mgmt. (L.A. chpt., cert. property mgr.), Internat. Coun. Shopping Ctrs. (cert. shopping ctr. mgr.), Lambda Chi Alpha, Delta Sigma Pi, Rho Epsilon (pres.). Republican. Mem. Christian Sci. Ch. Home: 1009 4th St Hermosa Beach CA 90254 Office: Sovereign/Ring 501 Santa Monica Blvd # 610 Santa Monica CA 90401-2411

MCGARRY, REGIS KANE, software engineer; b. Oakland, Calif., Mar. 11, 1966; s. Howard Kenneth and Lois Ann (Kane) McG.; m. Tracy Lee Weatherton, Oct. 3, 1992. BS in Computer Sci., Calif. State Poly. U., 1990. Warehouse worker Target Western Distbn. Ctr., Fontana, Calif., 1984-88; engrs. aide Hughes Tng. and Control Systems, West Covina, Calif., 1989-90; project mgr. Rockwell Internat., Lakewood, Calif., 1990; tech. programmer Loral Librascope, Glendale, Calif., 1990—. Mem. Assn. for Computing Machinery (voting). Roman Catholic.

MCGARVEY, JOHN JAMES, computer systems company executive; b. Yonkers, N.Y., Dec. 26, 1931; s. John Joseph and Elizabeth Marie (Flanagan) McG.; m. Patricia Ann Marsteller, May 18, 1957; children: Daniel, Sheila, Michael, John Timothy. BS in Acctg., Pa. State U., 1956; MS in Computer Systems Mgmt., Naval Postgrad. Sch., Monterey, Calif., 1966; PhD candidate, Golden Gate U. Cert. data processor, cert. systems profl. Commd. ensign USN, 1956, advanced through grades to comdr., 1969; dir. data systems Naval Air Systems Command, Washington, 1969-73; head logistics dept. USS Coral Sea, 1973-75; dir. EDP auditing Dept. Navy, Washington, 1975-77; ret. USN, 1977; sr. systems designer Bay Area Rapid Transit, Oakland, Calif., 1977-78; tech. systems mgr. Am. Pres. Lines, Ltd., Oakland, 1978-79; nat. dir. profl. svcs. Optimum Systems, Inc., Santa Clara, Calif., 1979-80; v.p. Info. Systems Group, Inc., San Leandro, Calif., 1979-83; pres. Applied Systems Assocs., San Leandro, 1980—; lectr. U. Md., College Park, 1976-77, Calif. State U., Hayward, 1978-83, Golden Gate U., 1983—, U. Calif., Berkeley, 1987—; cons. in field. Mem. Assn. Computing Machinery, Assn. Systems Mgmt., Naval Inst. Republican. Roman Catholic. Home and Office: 8111 Phaeton Dr Oakland CA 94605

MCGATH, MICHAEL RAY, mining company official; b. Grand Junction, Colo., May 17, 1947; s. Raymond Lloyd and Wilma Lucille (Million) McG.; m. Mary E. Heidlebaugh, Feb. 14, 1969; 1 child, Michael René. BA, Coll. of Ozarks, Point Lookout, Mo., 1970; BSChemE, U. Mo., Rolla, 1970; postgrad., W.Va. Coll. Grad. Studies, 1976-78. Jr. engr. NL Industries, St. Louis, 1971-72; project engr. NL Industries, Charleston, W.Va., 1972-74, supt. Bentone Plant, 1974-78; plant mgr. Rheox Inc. div. NL Industries, Newberry Springs, Calif., 1978—; mem. adv. com. Mojave Desert Mining, Barstow, Calif., 1987—, lower basin adv. com. Mojave Water Agy., 1986-87. Mem. Calif. Mining Assn. (exec. com. 1989—, chmn. membership com. 1991—), Alpha Chi Sigma (profl.). Republican. Home: 13676 Coachella Rd Apple Valley CA 92308 Office: Rheox Inc 31763 Mountain View Rd Newberry Springs CA 92365

MC GAUGH, JAMES LAFAYETTE, psychobiologist; b. Long Beach, Calif., Dec. 17, 1931; s. William Rufus and Daphne (Hermes) McG.; m. Carol J. Becker, Mar. 15, 1952; children: Douglas, Janice, Linda. BA, San Jose State U., 1953; PhD (Abraham Rosenberg fellow), U. Calif. - Berkeley, 1959; sr. postdoctoral fellow, NAS-NRC, Istituto Superiore di Sanità, Rome, 1961-62; DSc (hon.), So. Ill. U., 1991. Asst. prof., assoc. prof. psychology San Jose State U., 1957-61; assoc. prof. psychology U. Oreg., 1961-64; assoc. prof. U. Calif., Irvine, 1964-66, founding chmn. dept. psychobiology, 1964-67, 71-74, 86-89, prof., 1966—, dean sch. Biol. Sci., 1967-70, vice chancellor acad. affairs, 1975-77, exec. vice chancellor, 1978-82, founding dir. Ctr. Neurobiology of Learning and Memory, 1983—; Mem. adv. coms. NIMH, 1965-78, Mental Health Coun. NIMH, 1992—. Author: (with J.B. Cooper) Integrating Principles of Social Psychology, 1963, (with H.F. Harlow, R.F. Thompson) Psychology, 1971, (with M.J. Herz) Memory Consolidation, 1972, Learning and Memory: An Introduction, 1973, (with R.F. Thompson and T. Nelson) Psychology I, 1977, (with C. Cotman) Behavioral Neuroscience, 1980; editor: (with N.M. Weinberger, R.E. Whalen) Psychobiology, 1966, Psychobiology-Behavior from a Biological Perspective, 1971, The Chemistry of Mood, Motivation and Memory, 1972, (with M. Fink, S.S. Kety, T.A. Williams) Psychobiology of Convulsive Therapy, 1974, (with L.F. Petrinovich) Knowing, Thinking, and Believing, 1976, (with R.R. Drucker-Colín) Neurobiology of Sleep and Memory, 1977, (with S.B. Kiesler) Aging, Biology and Behavior, 1981, (with G. Lynch and N. M. Weinberger) Neurobiology of Learning and Memory, 1984, (with N.M. Weinberger and G. Lynch) Memory Systems of the Brain, 1985, Contemporary Psychology, 1985, (with C.D. Woody and D.L. Alkon) Cellular Mechanisms of Conditioning and Behavioral Plasticity, 1988, (with N.M. Weinberger and G. Lynch) Brain Organization and Memory: Cells, Systems and Circuits, 1990, (with R.C.A. Frederickson and D.L. Felten) Peripheral Signaling of the Brain, 1991, (with L. Squire, G. Lynch and N.M. Weinberger) Memory: Organization and Locus of Change, 1991; founding editor Behavioral Biology, 1972-78, Behavioral and Neural Biology, 1979—; contbr. over 300 papers to sci. jours. Recipient medal U. Calif., Irvine, 1992. Fellow AAAS, Am. Acad. Arts and Scis., Soc. Exptl. Psychologists, APA (chief sci. advisor 1986-88, APA Sci. Contbn. award 1981); mem. NAS (chmn. Psychol. sect. 1992-95), Am. Psychol. Soc. (William James fellow 1989, pres. 1989-91), Western Psychol. Assn. (pres. 1992-93), Internat. Brain Rsch. Orgn., Soc. Neurosci., Am. Coll. Neuropsychopharmacology, Psychonomic Soc., European Behavioral Pharmacology Soc., Phi Beta Kappa, Sigma Xi. Office: U Calif Ctr Neurobiol Learning & Memory Irvine CA 92717

MCGAULEY, JACQUELYNE SUE, social welfare administrator; b. L.A., Aug. 23, 1951; d. Richard Courtney and Marion Lucia (Otto) May; children: Julie Anna, Jonathan Daniel. Instr. Gen. Tel. Co., Downey, Calif., 1971-82; rschr. Ted Gunderson and Assocs., Santa Monica, Calif., 1989—; speaker U. So. Calif., 1991, UCLA, 1992, Fresno Christian Growth Ctr., 1993, Ventura County Pub. Social Svcs. Foster Parents Conf., 1993, others. Contbr. articles to profl. and popular newspapers and jours. Recognized for outstanding service to children Enough. Mem. Affirming Children's Truths (pres.), Believe the Children (exec. bd.), Childrens' Civil Rights Fund (founder), Nat. Coalition for Children's Justice, C.O.V.E.R. (founder). Office: PO Box 417 Redondo Beach CA 90277-0417

MCGAVIN, JOCK CAMPBELL, airframe design engineer; b. L.A., Sept. 14, 1917; s. Campbell and Irene (LeMarr) McG.; m. Catherine Marcelle Glew, Jan. 12, 1952; 1 child, James Campbell. AA, L.A. City Coll., 1950; AB, U. So. Calif., 1970, MS, 1975; PhD, Calif. Coast U., 1989. Airframe design engr. Rockwell Internat. Corp., L.A., 1946-82; ret., 1982; sr. design engr. X-15 airplane, Apollo Command Module, space shuttle, others. Vol. mem. pub. involvement subcom. Puget Sound Water Quality Authority, Seattle, 1987-89. Capt. C.E., U.S. Army, 1940-46, ETO. Recipient Apollo Achievement award NASA, 1969. Mem. Soc. for History Astronomy, Izaak Walton League Am. (pres. Greater Seattle chpt. 1991-93, vol. worker environ. projects 1985—), U. So. Calif. N.W. Alumni Club (pres. 1987-89). Home: 12939 NE 146th Pl Woodinville WA 98072

MCGEAN, KELLY KENNISON, corporate executive; b. N.Y.C., Jan. 11, 1946; s. Douglas Fredwill Winnek and Jean (Phillips) McG.; m. Lois Jeanne Hutto, May 27, 1967 (wid. Nov. 1971); children: Kendra Lois (dec.), Michael Christopher (dec.); m. Annick Mireille Todd-Le Douarec, June 16, 1989. MA, Stanford U., 1972; MSM, Fla. Internat. U., 1976; MBA, Wesleyan U., 1974, PhD, 1978. Regional dir. of sales Bestline Pharms., Inc., Miami, 1971-73; v.p. of mktg. Hansen Music & Books, Inc., Miami, 1973-76; exec. dir. Kern County Profl. Standards Rev. Orgn., Bakersfield, Calif., 1976-78; pres., CEO Vantage Mgmt., Inc., Palo Alto, Calif., 1978-82; lead instr. Sml. Bus. Devel. Ctr./Lane C.C., Eugene, Oreg., 1984-91; pres., CEO Camarata Group, Inc., Eugene, 1982—; adj. prof. U. Miami, 1972-74, U. Oreg., 1983-84, 90-92, Linfield Coll., McMinnville, Oreg., 1991—; cons. U.S. Dept. HEW, Washington, 1976-81; co-founder, bd. dirs. Am. Gramophone, inc., L.A. Composer: (musical composition) Symphony #1 Heritage, 1966, Requiem and Gloria, 1981 (Best New Work 1988), various choral works, 1964—, (opera) Calico, 1971; author: Book Management in An International Context, 1976, 1989; contbr. articles to profl. jours. Chmn. Found. for the Performing Arts, San Francisco, 1980-83; comm. mem. Comm. for Health-care Reform, State Dept. of Health Svcs., Sacramento, 1978-80; v.p. Young Reps. Orgn., Palo Alto, Calif., 1977; bus. advisor Bus. Assistance Team, Eugene, 1984-91; bd. dirs. Goodwill Industries, Eugene, 1988-91, Am. Founds. for Med. Care, Sacramento, 1976-88. Lt. USN, 1967-71, Vietnam. Recipient Outstanding Svc. award U.S. Dept. HEW, Washington, 1978; named Composer of Yr., Phi Mu Alpha Sinfonia, Chgo., 1967. Mem. Internat. Assn. Composers and Dirs. (pres. 1975-77, Composer of Yr. 1989), Am. Mktg. Assn., Lane C.C. Edn. Assn. (v.p. 1990-91), Oreg. Edn. Assn. (bd. dirs. 1987-90), NEA, Am. Assn. Health Care Execs. (pres. 1978-79, Man of Yr. 1980). Republican. Methodist. Office: Camarata Group Inc 1176 Monroe St Eugene OR 97402

MCGEE, CHARLES EDWARD, resort industry executive; b. Phila., Dec. 16, 1935; s. Charles E. and Julia R. (Doyle) McG.; m. Marianne E. Merman, June 29, 1957 (div. 1973); children: Charles E. III, Marianne, Catherine, Patricia; m. Candace E. Kerr, Aug. 21, 1992. BA in Physics/Math., LaSalle U., 1957; postgrad., MIT, 1958. Dept. mgr. Western Electric Co., Cambridge, Mass., 1957-60; cons. MIT, Cambridge, Mass., 1960-62; regional mgr. IBM, Honolulu, 1962-68; pres. Digital Systems Svcs. Corp., Honolulu, 1968-75; sr. v.p. First Ins. Co. of Hawaii Ltd., Honolulu, 1975-92; exec. v.p. Castle Group Ltd., Honolulu, 1992—. Home: 4300 Waialae Ave Apt 2002A Honolulu HI 95816-5746 Office: The Castle Group Ltd 745 Fort St Ste 2110 Honolulu HI 96813

MCGEE, JAMES SEARS, history educator; b. Houston, July 12, 1942; s. William Sears and Mary Elizabeth (Peterson) McG.; m. Mary Arnall Broach, Aug. 20, 1966; children: Elizabeth, Claude. BA, Rice U., 1964; MA, Yale U., 1966, M in Philosophy, 1968, PhD, 1971. Asst. prof. Ga. So. Coll., Statesboro, 1969-71; asst. prof. U. Calif., Santa Barbara, 1971-78, assoc. prof., 1978-84, prof., 1984—, chair, 1990—. Author: The Godly Man in Stuart England, 1976; editor: The Miscellaneous Works of John Bunyan, Vol. 3, 1987. Named Disting. Tchr. in Soc. Scis., U. Calif., Santa Barbara, 1989; fellow Abraham Found., 1962-63; Woodrow Wilson fellow, 1964-65; recipient summer stipend NEH, 1975. Mem. Am. Soc. Ch. History, Am. Hist. Assn., N.Am. Conf. on Brit. Studies. Democrat. Episcopalian. Office: U Calif Dept History Santa Barbara CA 93106

MCGEE, JOHN B., pilot, retired; b. Reno, Feb. 26, 1922; s. Charles Bartton and Clara Belle (Henley) M.; m. Carol Anna, Feb. 14, 1946; children: Jack Bart, Diana Lee, Holly Ann. Grad. high sch., Reno. Capt. Am. Airlines, San Francisco, 1956-82. Maj. USMCR, 1944-54. Republican. Home: 935 Foothill Rd Reno NV 89511-9413

MCGEE, MICHAEL JAY, fire marshal, educator; b. Ft. Worth, June 9, 1952; s. Cecil Carl McGee and Helen Ruth (Peeples) McGee-Furrh; m. Carol Lee Garbarino, Sept. 18, 1982; children: Megan Rose, John Michael, Molly Caitlin. Student, U. Tex., 1970-73, Western Oreg. State U., 1983; AAS in Fire Protection Tech., Colo. Mountain Coll., 1990. Lic. fire suppression systems insp., Colo., vocat. educator, Colo.; cert. hazardous materials technician, Colo., 1992, EMT, Colo. Driver Massengale Co., Austin, Tex., 1970-73; gen. mgr. Sundae Palace, Austin, 1973-74; staff mem. Young Life, Colorado Springs, Colo., 1970-75; mgr. Broadmoor Mgmt. Co., Vail, Colo., 1974-76; technician Vail Cable Communications, 1976-77; fire marshal Vail Fire Dept., 1977—; instr. Colo. Mountain Coll., 1980—; dist. rep. Joint Coun. Fire Dist. Colo., 1983-85; co-chmn. Eagle County Hazardous Materials, 1984-85, mem. planning com., 1987-90; mem. accountibility com. Eagle Couty Sch. Dist., 1991—, vice chair accountibility com. 1992-93; chmn. adv. com. Eagle County Sch. Dist., 1993—. Chmn. Eagle County chpt. ARC, 1980-83, disaster chmn., 1977-80; tng. officer Eagle Vol. Fire Dept., 1988-90; mem. parish coun. St. Mary's Parish, Eagle County, 1989-90; mem. citizen's adv. com. Colo. Mountain Coll., 1990-91, bd. dirs. 1990. Mem. Internat. Assn. Arson Investigators (Colo. chpt.), Internat. Platform Assn., Nat. Fire Protection Assn., Colo. State Fire Marshals Assn., Colo. State Fire Chiefs Assn. Office: Vail Fire Dept 42 W Meadow Dr Vail CO 81657-5704

MCGEE, MIKE JAMES, gallery director, writer; b. Ft. Lee, Va., Mar. 2, 1955; s. Lloyd James and Sylvia L. (Mounts) McG. BA, Calif. State U., Fullerton, 1978; MFA, U. Calif.-Irvine, 1980. Dir. The Edge Gallery, Fullerton, 1982-85; programs coord. Laguna Art Mus., Laguna Beach, Calif., 1986-88; writer, educator various instns., 1988—; art gallery dir. Orange Coast Coll., Costa Mesa, Calif., 1989-91; art forum lecture series head Rancho Santiago Jr. Coll., Santa Ana, 1991—; art gallery dir., asst. prof. Calif. State U., Fullerton, 1992—. Pres. bd. trustees Orange County Ctr. for Contemporary Art, Santa Ana, 1990—; arts com. chair Orange County Arts Alliance, Santa Ana, 1982. Mem. Am. Assn. Museums. Home: 27683 Aquamarine Mission Viejo CA 92691 Office: Calif State U Fullerton Fullerton CA 92634-9480

MCGEE, SAM, laser scientist; b. Louisville, Mar. 4, 1943; s. Walter R. and Sue (Burchett) McG. BA, Vanderbilt U., 1965. Mktg. dir. Brown-Forman Corp., Louisville, 1966-73; pres. FYI Corp., L.A., 1973-75; sr. v.p., gen. mgr. Brady Enterprises, East Weymouth, Mass., 1979-82; pres. Laser Images, Inc., L.A., 1982-85; pres., owner Starlasers, L.A., 1985—; mgmt. cons. L.A., 1976-78; cons. in field; bd. dirs. various cos. Mem. Hon. Order Ky. Cols. Office: Starlasers 13156 Leadwell St North Hollywood CA 91605-4117

MCGEE, WILLIE, professional baseball player; b. San Francisco, Nov. 2, 1958. Student, Diablo Valley Coll., Pleasant Hill, Calif. Profl. baseball player St. Louis Cardinals, 1982-90, Oakland A's, 1990, San Francisco Giants, 1990—. Mem. Nat. League All-Star Team, 1983, 85, 87-88; recipient Gold Glove Award, 1983, 85-86; named Nat. League Most Valuable Player, Basball Writers Assoc. of Am., 1985; Sporting News Nat. League Player of the Year, 1985; recipient Silver Slugger award, 1985; Nat. League Batting Champion, 1985, 90; mem. World Series Champions, 1982. Office: San Francisco Giants Candlestick Park San Francisco CA 94124-3998

MCGEER, PATRICK CHARLES, computer scientist; b. Vancouver, B.C., Can., Mar. 6, 1957; came to U.S., 1983; s. Patrick Lucey and Edith Ann (Graef) McG.; m. Karen Louise Whiteley, Aug. 23, 1981; 1 child, Sean. BSc, Simon Fraser U., Burnaby, B.C., 1980; M of Math., Waterloo (Ont., Can.) U., 1982; PhD, U. Calif., Berkeley, 1989. Asst. prof. U. B.C., Vancouver, 1989-91; asst. rsch. engr. U. Calif., Berkeley, 1991—; gen. chair Tau-90, Vancouver, 1990, IWLS '93, Lake Tahoe, 1993; cons. Distinctive Software, Burnaby, 1990. Author: Integrating Functional and Temporal Domains in Logic Design, 1991; contbr. articles to profl. jours. Recipient Best Paper award Hawaii Internat. Conf. on System Scis., 1990, Internat. Conf. VLSI, 1993. Mem. IEEE, Assn. for Computing Machinery. Republican. Episcopalian. Office: U Calif Berkeley EECS Dept 563 Cory Hall Berkeley CA 94720

MCGEHAN, FREDERICK PARSONS, JR., public affairs professional; b. Hartford, Conn., Oct. 20, 1941; s. Frederick Parsons and Doris Gertrude (Clough) McG.; m. Barbara Joan Beckley, Nov. 11, 1967; children: John, Matthew, Anne. BS, Coll. of Holy Cross, Worcester, Mass., 1963; MS, Columbia U., 1964. Reporter Providence Jour., 1964-65, Newhouse News Svc., Washington, 1965-68; sci. reporter Balt. Sun, 1968-74; pub. affairs specialist Nat. Bur. Standards, Gaithersburg, Md., 1974-77, Boulder, Colo., 1977-85; dir. pub. affairs Nat. Inst. Standards and Tech., Boulder, 1985—. Sgt. U.S. Army N.G., 1964-68. Recipient award of excellence Soc. for Tech. Comm., 1980, award of distinction, 1981, award of merit, 1982. Mem. Denver Pub. Affairs Coun. (com. chmn.), Boulder Press Club (pres. 1990-91). Office: Nat Inst Standards and Tech 325 Broadway Boulder CO 80303

MCGIFFIN, ROBERT FLOYD, JR., museum official; b. Glendale, Calif., Oct. 2, 1942; s. Robert F. and Jane E. (Poor) McG.; m. Barbara Mary Rice, May 19, 1973; 1 child, Kimberly Ann. AA, Orange Coast Coll., Costa Mesa, Calif., 1971; BA, Syracuse U., 1973; MA, cert. adv. study, SUNY, Oneonta, 1976. Conservator Balboa Art Conservation Ctr., San Diego, 1976-77; futniture conservator N.Y. State Conservation Collections Care Ctr., Waterford, N.Y., 1977-82; chief mus. conservator, adminstr. Kans. Mus. History, Topeka, 1982-86; chief mus. conservator Gene Autry Western Heritage Mus., L.A., 1986—. Author: Furniture Care and Conservation, 1983, 3d edit., 1992; also articles. Bd. dirs. Balboa Art Conservation Ctr., 1988-89. With U.S. Army, 1965-67. Fellow Internat. Inst. for Conservation Hist. and Artistic Works, Am. Inst. for Conservation Hist. and Artistic Works; mem. Western Assn. Art Conservators. Office: Gene Autry Western Heritage Mus 4700 Western Heritage Way Los Angeles CA 90027-1462

MCGILL, LAWRENCE DAVID, veterinary pathologist; b. Waverly, Nebr., Mar. 24, 1944; s. Stanley Raymond and Phyllis Roylene (Quick) McG.; m. Cheryl Lynn Nelson, 1966 (div. Jan. 1974); m. Marilyn Sue Nyren, June 15, 1975; children: Marchelle Elizabeth, Mark Stanley-John. Student, U. Nebr., 1962-64; BS, Okla. State U., 1966, DVM, 1968; PhD, Tex. A&M U., College Station, 1972. Diplomate Coll. Vet. Pathologists. Asst. prof. U. Minn., St. Paul, 1971-72, U. Nebr., Lincoln, 1972-77; vet. pathologist Vet. Reference Lab., Salt Lake City, 1977-81, chief pathologist, 1981-85; med. dir. Vet. Reference Lab., San Leandro, Calif., 1985-88; dir. contract rsch. Animal Reference Pathology, Salt Lake City, 1988-91, asst. v.p., 1991-93; v.p., 1993—. Contbr. articles to profl. jours. Singer, bd. dirs. Utah Symphony Chorus, Salt Lake City, 1979—; bd. dirs. Iron Blosum Lodge, Snowbird, Utah. NIH postdoctoral fellow, 1968-71; named Veterinarian of Yr., Utah, 1990. Mem. Am. Vet. Med. Assn., Utah Vet. Med. Assn. (chair pub. rels. 1988-90), Salt Lake Vet. Med. Assn. (pres. elect 1992, pres. 1993), Masons, Order Eastern Star. Republican. Methodist. Home: 8288 Top of the World Dr Salt Lake City UT 84121-6032 Office: Animal Reference Pathology 500 Chipeta Way Salt Lake City UT 84108-1221

MCGILLICUDDY, JOAN MARIE, psychotherapist, consultant; b. Chgo., June 23, 1952; d. James Neal and Muriel (Joy) McG. BA, U. Ariz., 1974, MS, 1976. Cert. nat. counselor. Counselor ACTION, Tucson, 1976; counselor, clin. supr. Behavioral Health Agy. Cen. Ariz., Casa Grande, 1976-81; instr. psychology Cen. Ariz. Coll., Casa Grande, 1978-83; therapist, co-dir. Helping Assocs., Inc., Casa Grande, 1982—, v.p., sec., 1982—; cert. instr. Silva Method Mind Devel., Tucson, 1986—; presenter Silver Mind Control Internat., 1988-91. Mem. Mayor's Com. for Handicapped, Casa Grande, 1989-90, Human Svcs. Planning, Casa Grande, 1985-90. Named Outstanding Am. Lectr. Silva Mind Internat., 1988-91. Mem. AACD. Office: Helping Assocs Inc 1901 N Trekell Rd Casa Grande AZ 85222-4119

MCGINLEY, EDWARD STILLMAN, II, naval officer; b. Allentown, Pa., June 9, 1939; s. Edward Stillman and Dorothy Mae (Kandle) McG.; m. Connie Lee Mayo, July 1, 1962; children: Amanda Lee, Edward Stillman III. BS, U.S. Naval Acad., 1961; SM in Naval Engring., MIT, 1970; MSA, George Washington U., 1972; cert. exec. program, U. Va., 1981. Commd. ensign USN, 1961, advanced through grades to rear adm., 1990, various positions in submarine engring., 1962-76; repair officer USN, Rota (Spain) and Charleston, S.C., 1976-83; ops. mgr. Mare Island Naval Shipyard, Vallejo, Calif., 1983-87; comdr. Norfolk Naval Shipyard, Portsmouth, Va., 1987-90; maintenance officer U.S. Pacific Fleet, Honolulu, 1990-93; comdr. Naval Surface Warfare Ctr., Washington, 1993—. Contbr. articles to profl. jours. Recipient Environ. award Sec. of Navy, 1987, Productivity Improvement award Inst. Indsl. Engrs., 1988, Quality Improvement award Office Mgmt. and Budget, 1989, Productivity award U.S. Senate, 1990. Mem. Am. Soc. Naval Engrs. (sect. chmn. 1980-81), Soc. Naval Architects and Marine Engrs., U.S. Naval Inst., Am. Soc. for Quality Control, Rotary, Sigma Xi, Tau Beta Pi. Republican. mem. United Church of Christ. Office: Naval Surface Warfare Ctr Navy Dept NAVSEASYSCOM Washington DC 20362-5160

MCGINN, SUSAN FRANCES, musician; b. Detroit, May 26, 1961; d. Michael Thomas and Bernice Frances (DePollo) McG. MusB, U. Mich., 1983; MusM, U. Ill., 1985; postgrad., Ind. U., 1985-89. Co-prin. flute L.A. Philharm. Inst., 1985, Nat. Repertory Orch., Keystone, Colo., 1987, Nat. Orchestral Inst., College Park, Md., 1989, Schleswig-Holstein Musik Festival, Salzau, Germany, 1988, 89; prin. flute, flutist wind quintet Canton (Ohio) Symphony Orch., 1989-90, Honolulu Symphony Orch., 1990—; grad. teaching asst. U. Ill., Urbana, 1983-85; assoc. instr. Ind. U., Bloomington, 1986-89; flutist spring wind quinted Chamber Music Hawaii, Honolulu, 1990—. Scholar U. Ill., 1983-85; fellow Ind. U., 1985-86, scholar, 1986-89. Mem. Nat. Flute Assn., People for Ethical Treatment Animals, Doris Day Animal League. Roman Catholic. Office: Honolulu Symphony Orch 1441 Kapiolani Blvd Ste 1515 Honolulu HI 96814-4495

MCGINNIS, MICHAEL PATRICK, psychotherapist; b. Madison, Wis., Oct. 4, 1950; s. James and Patricia Jane (Cole) McG.; m. Carol Ann Bailey, Aug. 8, 1982; children: Arielle Dominque, Chandra Eden. Student, U. Wis., 1968-69, U. Maine, 1971-73; BA, Sonoma State U., 1980, MA, 1984. Cert. marriage, family and child counselor, Calif. Offset printer Portland (Maine) Printing Co., 1970-71, Pronto Prints, Madison, 1972-74; mental health specialist Sheltered Workshop, Madison, 1975-77; mental health worker social svc. dept. Treatment Alternatives to Street Crimes, Santa Rosa, Calif., 1977-79; counselor Nat. Coun. on Alcoholism, Santa Rosa, 1978-79, exec. dir. Sonoma County, 1979-81; counselor, trainer Sonoma County Family Svc. Agy., Santa Rosa, 1981-86; pvt. practice, Healdsburg, Calif., 1985—; trainer, cons. domestic violence treatment Calif. Dept. Mental Health, 1979-84, YWCA Women's Emergency Shelter, Santa Rosa, 1980-86. Mem. Calif. Assn. Marriage and Family Therapists (clin.), Am. Profl. Soc. on Abuse on Children (clin.), Calif. Profl. Soc. on Abuse of Children (clin.). Democrat. Home and Office: 610 Alta Vista Dr Healdsburg CA 95448-4651

MCGINNIS, ROBERT WILLIAM, electronics company executive; b. Modesto, Calif., Oct. 31, 1936; s. George Crawford and Lola May (Provis) McG.; B.S. in Elec. Engring. with highest honors, U. Calif., Berkeley, 1962; postgrad. N.Y. U., 1962-63; m. Sondra Elaine Hurley, Mar. 1, 1964; children—Michael Fredrick, Traci Anne, Patrick William. Mem. tech. staff Bell Telephone Labs, Murray Hill, N.J., 1961-63; devel. engr., engring. mgr., product mgr., ops. mgr. Motorola Semiconductor Group, Phoenix, 1963-73, ops. mgr. for hybrid circuits group, communications div., Fort Lauderdale, Fla., 1973-76, solar ops. mgr., 1976-79; v.p., gen. mgr. Photowatt Internat., Inc., Tempe, Ariz., 1979-83; gen. mgr. SAFT Electronic Systems Div., 1983-85, pres., Safe Power Systems, Inc., Tempe, 1985-88; gen. mgr. Advanced Energy Systems Acme Electric Corp., 1988—. Mem. Ariz. Solar Energy Commn., 1977-83; chmn. photovoltaic subcom. Am. Nat. Standards Inst., 1978-83; mem. coordinating council Solar Energy Research Inst. Standards, 1977-82. Served with USNR, 1955-58. Mem. IEEE, Phi Beta Kappa, Tau Beta Pi, Eta Kappa Nu. Republican. Methodist. Contbr. articles in field to profl. jours. Home: 7887 E Via Bonita Scottsdale AZ 85258-2809 Office: Acme Electric Corp Advanced Energy Systems Divsn 528 W 21st St Tempe AZ 85282-2038

MCGLASSON, JAMES DEAN, publishing executive; b. Roswell, N.Mex., Mar. 22, 1944; s. Dean A. and Nadean (McPherson) McG.; m. Christine Gail Dawson, Feb. 17, 1966 (div. Jan. 1980); m. Linda Renee Horn, Sept. 1, 1981; children: Kimberly Ann, Patrick Dean. Student, Mira Costa Coll. Dir. advt. Daily Tribune, Greeley, Colo., 1977-81; v.p. sales and mktg. Tahoe Tribune, South Lake Tahoe, Calif., 1981-82; v.p., pub. Press-Courier Pub. Co., Vista, Calif., 1982-85; v.p., gen. mgr. Newhall (Calif.) Signal, 1985—; pres. Newhall (Calif.) Printing, 1985—. Bd. dirs. Boys Club of Vista, 1983—; bd. dirs. YMCA, Vista, 1984-85. Served with USN, 1966-68. Mem. Calif. Newspaper Advt. Execs. Assn., Calif. Newspaper Pubs. Assn. Club: Civitan (Vista). Lodges: Rotary, Masons. Home: PO Box 4815 Las Vegas NV 89127-0815 Office: Newhall Signal/Newhall Printing 24000 Creekside Rd PO Box 877 Valencia CA 91355

MCGLAUGHLIN, THOMAS HOWARD, publisher, retired naval officer; b. Cin., Jan. 12, 1928; s. George Godden and Cordelia (Herrlinger) McG.; m.

Moana Maharam-Stone, Jan. 4, 1984. BS in Elec. Engring., U.S. Naval Acad., 1950. Lic. master mariner. Commd. ensign U.S. Navy, 1950, advanced through grades to capt., 1970; White House aide to Pres. John F. Kennedy, Washington, 1960-63; exec. officer USS Prichett, Long Beach, Calif., 1963-65; comdg. officer USS Maddox, Long Beach, 1965-67; exec. officer USS Boston, Boston, 1967-70; chief naval ops. Comdr.-in-Chief, Pacific, Honolulu, 1970-74; chief of staff Mil. Sealift Command, N.Y.C., 1974-79; ret. U.S. Navy, 1979; pres. Falmouth Press, Honolulu, 1983—; marine surveyor R.W. Dickieson Internat., Inc., Honolulu, 1982—; master M.V. Rella Mae, Honolulu, 1981-90, Royal Taipan, Cebu, Philippines, 1990. Hon. police chief Boston Police Dept., 1969. Decorated Bronze Star; recipient medal for Outstanding Svc., Am. Legion, Pitts., 1942. Mem. Nat. Def. Transp. Assn., VFW (life), U.S. Naval Acad. Alumni Assn. (life), The Retired Officers Assn. Republican. Presbyterian. Home: 581 Kamoku St The Royal Iolani # 1702 Honolulu HI 96826 Office: RW Dickieson Internat Inc 46-208 Kahuhipa St Kaneohe HI 96744

MCGLYNN, BETTY HOAG, art historian; b. Deer Lodge, Mont., Apr. 28, 1914; d. Arthur James and Elizabeth Tangye (Davey) Lochrie; m. Paul Sterling Hoag, Dec. 28, 1936 (div. 1967); children: Peter Lochrie Hoag, Jane Hoag Brown, Robert Doane Hoag; m. Thomas Arnold McGlynn, July 28, 1973. BA, Stanford U., 1936; MA, U. So. Calif., 1967. Cert. secondary tchr., Calif. Rsch. dir. So. Calif. Archives of Am. Art, L.A., 1964-67, Carmel (Calif.) Mus. Art, 1967-69; dir. Triton Mus. Art, Santa Clara, Calif., 1970; archivist, libr. San Mateo County (Calif.) Hist. Soc. Mus., 1971-74; cons. Monterey Peninsula Mus. Art, Calif., 1964—; tchr. art extension Monterey Peninsula Coll., Calif., 1970, San Jose City Coll., 1971; lectr. in field. Author: The World of Mary DeNeale Morgan, 1970, Carmel Art Association: A History, 1987; contbg. author: Plein Air Painters of California, The North, 1986, Orchid Art of the Orchid Isle, 1982, Hawaiian Island Artists and Friends of the Arts, 1990; editor, author of jours. La. Peninsula, 1971-75, Noticias, 1983-88; author of booklets; contbr. articles to profl. jours. Appraiser art work City of Carmel, 1967, City of Monterey, 1981. Mem. Butte (Mont.) Arts Chateau, Carmel Art Assn. (hon.), Carmel Heritage Soc., (preservation com.), Carmel Found., Chinese Hist. Soc., Friends of Bancroft Libr., Monterey History and Art Assn. (art cons.), Monterey Peninsula Mus. Art (acquisitions bd., steering com. bd.), Nat. Trust for Hist. Preservation, Stanford Alumni Assn., Robinson Jeffers Tor House Found. (art cons.), Hawaiian Hist. Soc., Nat. Mus. of Women in the Arts, The Westerners, P.E.O., Book Club of Calif. Republican. Home and Office: PO Box 5034 Carmel CA 93921-5034

MCGONIGLE, THOMAS PATRICK, chemical plant executive; b. San Lorenzo, Calif., Apr. 12, 1960; s. John Leo and Mary Francis (McInerney) McG.; m. Patricia Jackomis, June 20, 1987; 1 child, Thomas Shane. BSME, Pa. State U., 1982; MBA, Case Western Res. U., 1991. Career devel. program Air Products Chem. Inc., Allentown, Pa., 1982-83; maintenance engr. Air Products Chem. Inc., Pensacola, Fla., 1983-85; plant engr. Air Products Chem. Inc., 1985-87; plant production engr. Air Products Chem. Inc., Cleve., 1987-88, plant mgr., 1988-91, product mgr., 1991-92; dir. ops. Gen. Chems. Co., San Francisco, 1992—. Big Bro., Little Bro. Allentown, 1982-83; instr. Jr. Achievement Allentown, 1982-83; jr. scout master Boy Scouts Am., 1977. Mem. ASME, Kiwanis (Young Leader award 1978). Republican. Roman Catholic. Home: 561 Mt Olivet Pl Clayton CA 94517 Office: 501 Nichols Rd Pittsburg CA 94565

MCGOURTY, GLENN THOMAS, plant science farm advisor; b. Freeport, N.Y., Dec. 3, 1952; s. Thomas Kevin and Julia (Florek) McG.; m. Janice Lee Wright, Dec. 28, 1974; children: Catherine, Carolyn, Kevin. AB in Botany, Humboldt State U., Arcata, Calif., 1974; MS in Agrl., U. Nev., 1978. Urban horticulturist U. Nev. Coop. Extension, Las Vegas, 1979-81; lectr. ornamental hort. Calif. Poly., San Luis Obispo, 1983-85; farm advisor U. Calif. Coop. Extension, Ukiah, Calif., 1987—; chair Parks and Recreation Commn., City of Ukiah, 1989—; chair design com. Mendocino Coast Bot. Gardens, Ft. Bragg, Calif., 1988-91; lectr. in field. Mem. Growth Mgmt. Steering Com., City of Ukiah, 1991-92; bd. dirs. San Luis Obispo County Farm Bur., 1982-86. Named Horticulturist of Yr. Nev. Nurserymen's Assn., 1979. Mem. Am. Soc. of Enology and Viticulture (profl.), Mendocino Bounty Agrl. Mktg. Assn. (exec. com. 1991—). Office: UCCE Mendocino County Co Ag Ctr Courthouse Ukiah CA 95482-6310

MCGOVERN, RICKY JAMES, architect, educator; b. Tacoma, June 16, 1948; s. James Patrick and Betty Irene (Baxter) McG.; m. Kathleen Joy Kerrone, June 14, 1968; children—Jamie Francis, Brandon James. B.Arch., Wash. State U., 1973, B.S., 1973. Registered architect, Wash. Architect Burr Assocs., Tacoma, 1973-79, Erickson-Hogenson Architects, Tacoma, 1979-81; ptnr. Erickson-McGovern Architects, Tacoma, 1981—; instr. Tacoma Community Coll., 1979-85; vocat. advisor Bethel Sch. Dist., Spanaway, Wash., 1981—; sec. Avitar Inc., Tacoma, 1980—; bd. dirs. Sound Ventures, Inc., Plaza Hall. Co-chmn. Clearwood Community Assn., Pierce County, Wash., 1976-82; designer Bethel Community Daffodil Float, Spanaway, 1983-84. Recipient appreciation award Clearwood Community Assn., 1982; named Citizen of Yr., 1988. Mem. AIA, Council Ednl. Facilities Planning, Soc. Am. Value Engrs. (bd. dirs. 1982-83), Shelter Industry Coalition (vice chmn. 1983-90), Parkland-Spanaway C. of C. (chmn. Community Days 1984, 90, 91, 92, pres. 1987-88, citizen of yr. award 1985, 86, 91), Winner's Circle (v.p. 1983-90). Clubs: Plaza Hall (bd. dirs. 1985—) City. Lodge: Kiwanis (pres. 1984-85, Kiwanian of Yr. award 1982, 83, 84, Citizen of Yr. 1988). Office: Erickson-McGovern Architects 120 131st St S Tacoma WA 98444-4804

MC GOVERN, WALTER T., federal judge; b. Seattle, May 24, 1922; s. C. Arthur and Anne Marie (Thies) McG.; m. Rita Marie Olsen, June 29, 1946; children: Katrina M., Shawn E., A. Renee. B.A., U. Wash., 1949, LL.B., 1950. Bar: Wash. 1950. Practiced law in Seattle, 1950-59; mem. firm Kerr, McCord, Greenleaf & Moen; judge Municipal Ct., Seattle, 1959-65, Superior Ct., Wash., 1965-68, Wash. Supreme Ct., 1968-71, U.S. Dist. Ct. (we. dist.) Wash., 1971—; chief judge, 1975-87; mem. subcom. on supporting personnel Jud. Conf. U.S., 1981-87, chmn. subcom., 1983, mem. adminstrn. com., 1983-87, chmn. jud. resources com., 1987-91. Mem. Am. Judicature Soc., Wash. State Superior Ct. Judges Assn., Seattle King County Bar Assn. (treas.), Phi Delta Phi. Club: Seattle Tennis (pres. 1968). Office: US Dist Ct US Courthouse 5th Fl 1010 5th Ave Seattle WA 98104-1130

MCGOWAN, JEFFREY OWEN, marketing professional; b. Camden, N.J., June 12, 1962; s. Owen Francis and JoAnn (Majkszak) McG.; m. Anna Marie Andersen, Nov. 22, 1992. BA in Mktg., Calif. State U., Fullerton, 1985; MBA, Chapman U., 1991. Sr. sales corr. Cherry Textron, Santa Ana, Calif., 1983-85, project coord. prodn., 1985-86, project coord. fin., 1986-87, mktg. analyst, 1987-91, mktg. mgr., 1991—. Asst. scoutmaster Boy Scouts Am., Buena Park, Calif., 1980; pres. youth ministry San Antonio Cath. Ch., Anaheim, Calif., 1979-81. Named Eagle Scout Boy Scouts Am., 1980. Republican. Office: Cherry Textron 1224 E Warner Ave Santa Ana CA 92707

MCGOWAN, JOHN FRANK, insurance agent, land developer; b. Yerington, Nev., Apr. 15, 1934; s. Jack H. and Margaret Lucille (McKinney) McG.; m. Myrna J. Crouse, Dec. 28, 1957; children: Darrell, Michael, Patrick, Mary, Kelly, Ann, Robert, Lucille. Student, U. Nev., Reno, 1952-54; AS (hon.), We. Nev. C.C., 1989. CLU. Chmn. Mason Valley Econ. Devel. Coun., Yerington, 1984-90. With USAF, 1954-58. Named Man of Yr., Community of Yerington, 1986. Mem. Mason Valley C. of C. (pres. 1973), Toastmasters (pres. Yerington 1968), 20-30 Svc. Club (pres. Yerington 1962), Kiwanis (pres. Yerington 1981). Republican. Roman Catholic. Home: 324 Modesto St Yerington NV 89447 Office: 215 W Bridge St PO Box 999 Yerington NV 89447

MCGRATH, MICHAEL WILLIAM, lawyer; b. Phoenix, Aug. 18, 1953; s. Gerald William and Patricia Lee (Springer) McG.; m. Eileen Frances Romer; 1 child, Katlin Lee. BA, U. Ariz., 1975, JD, 1979. Bar: Ariz. Supreme Ct., 1979, U.S. Dist. Ct. Az., 1979,. Jud. law clk. U.S. Bankruptcy Judge, Phoenix, 1979-80, U.S. Dist. Judge, Phoenix, 1980-82; assoc. Stompoly & Sproud, P.C., Tucson, 1982-86, ptnr., 1986-88, mng. ptnr., 1988-90; ptnr. Mesch, Clark & Rothschild, P.C., Tucson, 1990—. Editor: Arizona Civil Remedies, 1990; author: Reporter's Guide to Arizona Law, 1991; writer seminar Ariz. Continuing Legal Edn., 1987-92. Mem. Ariz. Right to Choose, Tucson, 1992, United Way of Tucson, 1992. Mem. ABA (specialist, cert. in bankruptcy law 1992), Ariz. Bar Assn., Pima County Bar Assn. Democrat. Roman Catholic. Home: 937 N 5th Ave Tucson AZ 85705 Office: Mesch Clark & Rothschild 259 N Meyer Tucson AZ 85701

MCGRATH, PATRICK JOSEPH, bishop; b. Dublin, Ireland, July 11, 1945; came to U.S., 1970; Grad., St. John's Coll. Sem., Waterford, Ireland; student, Lateran U., Rome. Ordained priest Roman Cath. Ch., 1970, titular bishop of Allegheny. Aux. bishop Archdiocese San Francisco, 1989—. Office: Archdiocese San Francisco Chancery Office 445 Church St San Francisco CA 94114*

MCGREGOR, QUENTIN JOHN, aerospace studies educator, air force officer; b. Weehauken, N.J., June 24, 1946; s. Quentin Paul and Magdalen Marcella (Power) McG.; m. Leslie Anne Fiumara (div. June 1989); children: Lisa C., Julie K., Jenny A.; m. Virginia Moira McClory, Dec. 18, 1989. AB in Govt., Georgetown U., 1968; MS in Internat. Rels., Troy (Ala.) State U., 1981; MS in Bus. Adminstrn., Boston U., 1988. Commd. 2d lt. U.S. Air Force, 1968, advanced through grades to col., 1990; fighter pilot, instr. pilot, flight examiner U.S. Air Force, various locations, 1968-79; asst. ops. officer 86 Tactical Fighter Wing, Ramstein AB, Germany, 1979-82; staff officer Hdqrs. USAF, Pentagon, Washington, 1982-86; exch. officer RAF War Coll., Cranwell, U.K., 1986-87; strike ops. officer Allied Air Forces Ctrl. Europe, Ramstein AB, 1987-91; prof. aerospace studies Air Force ROTC, U. Portland, Oreg., 1991—. Nat. advisor Arnold Air Soc., U. Portland, 1992—. Mem. Air Force Assn. Roman Catholic. Office: U Portland Det 695 AFROTC 5000 N Willamette Portland OR 97203

MCGREGOR, SCOTT LEE, applications software designer; b. Topeka, Aug. 10, 1956; s. James L. and Nancy (Vaughn) McG.; m. Mary Lou Sutz, May 12, 1978; children: Taylor Elise, James Theodore. BA, Haverford Coll., 1978; MS in Indsl. Adminstrn., Carnegie-Mellon U., 1980. Programmer Haskins & Sells, N.Y.C., 1975-76; programmer analyst Fin. Computer Systems, Stanford, Conn., 1977; software cons. Neoterics, Pitts., 1978; with Corning (N.Y.) Glass Works, 1979; productivity mgr. Hewlett-Packard, Palo Alto, Calif., 1980-87; R&D project mgr. Hewlett-Packard, Cupertino, Calif., 1987-90; mgr. of applications Atherton Tech., Sunnyvale, Calif., 1990-91, divsn. gen. mgr., 1992; founder, pres. Prescient Software, Inc., San Jose, Calif., 1992—; founder, pres. Graphic Magic, Haverford, Pa., 1977-78, Prescient, San Jose, 1990-92. Contbr. tech. articles to profl. jours.; inventor Prescient Agts. software tech., SWIFT software devel. methology; chief designer Merge Ahead software application. Mem. IEEE Computer Soc., Assn. for Computing Machinery (spl. interest group in computer human interaction), Bay Area Spl. Interest Group in Computer Human Interaction.

MCGREW, MELINDA LOUISE, interior designer; b. Long Beach, Calif., Oct. 13, 1960; d. Charles Thompson and Florence Gayle (Baughman) McG. Student in archtl. studies, Copenhagen, 1983-84; BArch, Calif. Poly. State U., San Luis Obispo, 1984. Intern Irwin & Assocs., Huntington Beach, Calif., 1984-85; project mgr. Rengel & Co., Tustin, Calif., 1985-88, Gilbert Aja Assocs., Irvine, Calif., 1988-90; job capt. SGPA Architecture & Planning, Irvine, 1990-92. administr. Bowers Mus., Santa Ana, Calif. Democrat. Presbyterian. Home: 1323 N Spurgeon 2d Santa Ana CA 92701

MCGROGAN, MICHAEL PATRICK, molecular and cell biologist; b. San Francisco, Apr. 4, 1947; s. John Thomas and Veneta Almeta (Wideman) McG.; m. Sharol Kay Hudson, Sept. 13, 1969; 1 child, Melissa Catherine. Student, U. Mo., St. Louis, 1965-67; BA in Microbiology, U. Mo., Columbia, 1969; student, St. Louis U., 1971-73; PhD in Molecular and Cell Biology, Wash. U., St. Louis, 1977. Postdoctoral rschr. Wash. U. Med. Sch., St. Louis, 1977-78; NCI postdoctoral fellow dept. bio. scis. Stanford (Calif.) U., 1978-81; scientist, rsch. group leader molecular biology dept. Cetus Corp., Emeryville, Calif., 1981-85; sr. scientist, rsch. group leader molecular biology dept. InVitron Corp., Redwood City, Calif., 1985-90; dir., sr. staff scientist Dept. of Gene Expression, Berlex Biosci., Alameda, Calif., 1990-93; chief scientific officer Sierra BioSource, Gilroy, Calif., 1993—; project leader Interleukin 2 (IL-2) Cetus Corp., 1982-84; primary investigator Protease Nexin, InVitron Corp., Redwood City, 1986-88; rsch. leader for granulocyte proteins project, 1988-90. Contbr. articles to profl. jours.; patentee in field. Fellow NDEA, St. Louis U., 1971; rsch. grantee NIH, Wash. U., 1973. Mem. AAAS, Am. Soc. of Microbiology. Office: Sierra BioSource 1180-C Day Rd Gilroy CA 95020

MCGRUDER, JAMES PATRICK, lawyer; b. L.A., Mar. 11, 1926; s. James S. and Margaret T. (McHugh) McG.; m. Patricia M. Harrison, June 28, 1952; children: Eileen, Coleen, Mark. JD, Denver U., 1953. Bar: Colo. 1954. Asst. city atty. City of Denver, 1954-61; asst. U.S. atty. U.S. Dept. Justice, Denver, 1961-64; regional counsel Prudential Ins. Co., L.A., Denver, 1964-75; div. counsel Prudential Ins. Co., L.A., 1975—. With USMC, 1943-46. Mem. Calif. Bar Assn., Colo. Bar Assn., Am. Land Title Assn. (assoc.). Democrat. Office: Prudential Ins Co 2029 Century Park E Bldg 3700 Los Angeles CA 90067-3023

MC GUANE, THOMAS FRANCIS, III, author, screenwriter; b. Wyandotte, Mich., Dec. 11, 1939; s. Thomas Francis and Alice Rita (Torphy) McG.; m. Portia Crockett, Sept. 8, 1962; children: Thomas Francis, Maggie; m. Laurie Buffett, Sept. 19, 1977; 1 child, Anne Buffett; 1 stepchild, Heather. BA, Mich. State U., 1962; MFA, Yale U., 1965; Wallace Stegner fellow, Stanford U., 1966; PhD (hon.), Mont. State U., 1993. Author: The Sporting Club, 1969, The Bushwacked Piano, 1971, Ninety-Two in the Shade, 1973, Panama, 1978, An Outside Chance: Essays on Sport, 1980, Nobody's Angel, 1981, Something to be Desired, 1983, To Skin a Cat, 1986, Keep the Change, 1989, Outside Chance, 1990, Nothing But Blueskies, 1992; (screenplays) Rancho Deluxe, 1975, Ninety-Two in the Shade, 1975, Missouri Breaks, 1974, Tom Horn, 1980; contbr. to Sports Illustrated mag., 1969-73. Recipient Richard and Hinda Rosenthal Found. fiction award Nat. Inst. Arts and Letters, 1972, Mont. Gov.'s award 1988, N.W. Bookseller's award 1992, Golden Plate award, Am. Acad. Achievement, 1993. Mem. Tale Club of N.Y. Address: PO Box 25 Mc Leod MT 59052

MC GUIGAN, FRANK JOSEPH, psychologist, educator; b. Oklahoma City, Dec. 7, 1924. BA, UCLA, 1945, MA, 1949; PhD, U. So. Calif., 1950. Instr. Pepperdine Coll., 1949-50; asst. prof. U. Nev., 1950-51; rsch. assoc. Psychol. Corp., 1950-51; rsch. scientist, sr. rsch. scientist, acting dir. rsch. Human Resources Rsch. Office, George Washington U., 1951-55; prof. psychology (Hollins Coll.), Roanoke, Va., 1955-76; chmn. dept. (Hollins Coll.), 1955-76; rsch. prof. (Grad. Sch.); prof. dept. psychology, dep. psychiatry and behavioral scis. (Sch. Medicine); dir. Performance Rsch. Lab., Inst. Advanced Study, U. Louisville, 1976-83; prof. psychology, dir. Inst. Stress Mgmt. U.S. Internat. U., San Diego, 1983—; vis. prof. U. Calif., Santa Barbara, 1966; adj. rsch. prof. N.C. State U., 1970-72; vis. prof. U. Hawaii, summer 1965; Nat. Acad. Scis. vis. scientist, Hungary, 1975, Bulgaria, 1987. Author: numerous books in field including The Biological Basis of Behavior, 1963, Contemporary Studies in Psychology, 1972, Cognitive Psychophysiology - Principles of Covert Behavior, 1978, Experimental Psychology: Methods of Research, 6th edit., 1990, Psychophysiological Measurement of Covert Behavior—A Guide for the Laboratory, 1979, Calm Down—A Guide for Stress and Tension Control, 2d edit., 1992, Stress and Tension Control: Procs. of Internat., Interdisciplinary Conf. on Stress and Tension Control, 1980, vol. 2, 1984, vol. 3, 1989; (with Edmund Jacobson) cassettes Self-Directed Progressive Relaxation Training Instructions, 1981, Critical Issues in Psychology, Psychiatry and Physiology, 1986; editor numerous works in field.; editor, Internat. Jour. Stress Mgmt.; contbr. articles to profl. jours.; mem. editorial bd. Archiv fur Arzneitherapie, Biofeedback and Self-regulation, Activitas Nervosae Superioris. Served with USNR, 1942-46. Recipient award for outstanding contributions to edn. in psychology Am. Psychol. Found., 1973, Blue medal of honor Union Scientists Bulgaria, 1980, medal of Sechenov USSR Acad. Med. Scis., 1982, medal of Anohkin, 1984, Pres.'s medal U. Hiroshima-Shudo, 1982, medal Okayama U., 1987, medal Tbilisi (USSR) Inst. Physiology, 1989. Fellow APA, Internat. Soc. Rsch. on Aggression; mem. Am. Assn. Advancement of Tension Control (now Internat. Stress Mgmt. Assn.) (exec. dir. 1973-82, pres. 1985-89, exec. dir. 1992—, chmn. bd. dirs.), Pavlovian Soc. (mem. exec. bd. 1973—, pres. 1975-86, editor, chmn. publ. bd. Pavlovian Jour. Biol. Sci.), Am. Physiol. Soc., Biofeedback Soc. Am., Internam. Soc. Psychology, Internat. Congress of Applied Psychology, Psychonomic Soc., Soc. Psychophysiol. Rsch., Bulgarian Soc. for Psychiatry (hon.), Sigma Xi. Office: US Internat U Inst for Stress Mgmt 10455 Pomerado Rd San Diego CA 92131-1799

MCGUIRE, JAMES CHARLES, aircraft company executive; b. St. Louis, Aug. 8, 1917; s. John Patrick and Anna Beulah (Erbar) McG.; A.B., Washington U., St. Louis, 1949, M.A. (Univ. fellow), 1953, Ph.D., 1954; m. Ingrid Elisabeth Getreu, Sept. 16, 1954. Research assoc. Ohio State U., 1953-56; rsch. psychologist Aeromed. Lab., Wright-Patterson AFB, Ohio, 1956-59; group supr. Boeing Airplane Co., Seattle, 1959-61; dept. mgr. Internat. Electric Corp., Paramus, N.J., 1961-62; sr. human factors scientist System Devel. Corp., Santa Monica, Calif., 1962-67; v.p. Booz-Allen Applied Rsch., Saigon, Vietnam, 1967-72; v.p. Assoc. Cons. Internat., Saigon, 1972-75, Bethesda, Md., 1975-78; br. chief Human Factors, System Tech. Devel., 1978-82; prin. staff engr. tech. modernization methodology Douglas Aircraft Co., Long Beach, Calif., 1982-85; program mgr. cockpit automation tech. program, Northrop Aircraft div., Hawthorne, Calif., 1985-87; sect. mgr. aircraft programs human factors engring. dept. Douglas Aircraft Co., Long Beach, 1987—, sr. staff engr. Crew Systems Tech., 1990—; lectr. Nat. Def. Coll., Vietnamese Armed Forces, Saigon, 1971. Served with AUS, 1940-46. Decorated Bronze Star medal with oak leaf cluster; recipient Tech. Svc. First Class medal Republic South Vietnam Armed Forces, 1968. Mem. Am. Psychol. Assn., IEEE, Computer Soc. of IEEE, Human Factors Soc., Am. Assn. Artificial Intelligence, Phi Beta Kappa, Sigma Xi. Democrat. Home: 23201 Mindanao Circle Monarch Beach CA 92629 Office: Douglas Aircraft Co 78-73 3855 Lakewood Blvd Long Beach CA 90846

MCGUIRE, JOSEPH SMITH, physician; b. Logan, W.Va., Apr. 19, 1931; s. Joseph Smith and Ruby Kellogg (Rose) McG.; m. Margaret Michael, June 5, 1954 (div. 1966); children: Mary Elizabeth, Joseph Smith III, Alison Litz, D. Thompson; m. Mary Lake Polan, 1979, Joshua Lake, Lindsay Kellogg, Scott Hunter. AB, W.Va. U., 1952; MD, Yale U., 1955. Clin. assoc. NIH, Bethesda, Md., 1956-59; asst. to assoc. prof. dermatology Yale U., New Haven, Conn., 1961-64, prof., 1964-72;, 1972-90; Carl Herzog prof. dermatology, pediatrics Stanford (Calif.) U., 1990—. sr. asst. surgeon USPHS, 1956-59. Mem. Am Soc. Clin. Investigation, Am. Soc. Cell Biology, Soc. Investigative Dermatology (pres. 1988-89), Am. Dermatol. Assn., Am. Acad. Dermatology, Pacific Dermatology Assn. Office: Stanford U Dept Dermatology MSLS P-204 Stanford CA 94305-5486

MCGUIRE, KEVIN ROBERT, jewelry consultant; b. Garden Grove, Calif., May 8, 1957; s. Robert Eugene and Margery Laurale (Beasley) McG. AS, Weber State U., 1986. Lic. realtor, Utah. Realtor assoc. Gregory Realty, Ogden, 1977-80; weld inspector Wallace-Superior, Elma, Wash., 1980-81; fine jewelry cons. Ogden, 1981—. Vol. Weber Mental Health, Ogden, 1992. Mem. Planetary Soc. Republican. Mem. LDS Ch. Home: PO Box 324 Roy UT 84067

MC GUIRE, MICHAEL JOHN, environmental engineer; b. San Antonio, June 29, 1947; s. James Brendan and Opal Mary (Brady) McG.; BS in Civil Engring., U. Pa., 1969; MS in Environ Engring., Drexel U., 1972, PhD in Environ. Engring., 1977; diplomate Am. Acad. Environ. Engring.; m. Deborah Marrow, June 19, 1971; children: David, Anna. San. engr. Phila. Water Dept., 1969-73; rsch. assoc. Drexel U., Phila., 1976-77; prin. engr. Brown & Caldwell Cons. Engrs., Pasadena, Calif., 1977-79; water quality engr. Met. Water Dist. of So. Calif., L.A., 1979-84, water quality mgr., 1984-86, dir. water quality, 1986-90, asst. gen. mgr., 1990-92; pres. McGuire Environ. Cons., Inc., Santa Monica, Calif., 1992—; cons. to subcom. on adsorbents, safe drinking water com. Nat. Acad. Scis., 1978-79; cons. mem. Techs. Workgroup USEPA, DBP Reg Neg, 1992-93. Registered profl. engr., Pa., N.J., Calif. Mem. Am. Water Works Assn. (Acad. Achievement award 1978, edn. div. chmn. 1982-83, chair taste and odor com. 1993—, Calif.-Nev. sect., chmn. water quality and resources div. 1982-83, governing bd. 1984-87, 89—, exec. com. 1989—, chmn. 1991-92, nat. dir. 1993—, trustee Research Found. 1983-86), Am. Chem. Soc., ASCE, Internat. Water Supply Assn., Internat. Assn. on Water Quality (specialist group on taste and odor control 1982—, chmn. organizing com. 1991, off-flavor symposium 1987-91), Internat. Ozone Assn. (internat. bd. dirs. 1992—), Sigma Xi, Sigma Nu, Sigma Tau. Editor: (with I.H. Suffet) Activated Carbon Adsorption of Organics From the Aqueous Phase, 2 vols., 1980; Treatment of Water by Granular Activated Carbon, 1983; contbr. articles to profl. jours. Office: McGuire Environ Cons Inc 469 25th St Santa Monica CA 90402-3103

MCGUIRE, MICHAEL WILLIAM, communications executive; b. Pomona, Calif., Aug. 1, 1960; s. Frederick L. and Anna Belle (Crum) McG.; m. Victoria Jean Von Tobel; children: Gordon, Michael Jr. BA in Polit. Sci., U. San Diego, 1984. Account exec. Ken Rietz & Co., San Diego, 1984-85; spokesman, dir. Congl. affairs Voice of Am., Washington, 1986-88; owner, chief exec. officer McGuire Rsch. Svcs., Reno, 1988—. Cons., Microsoft Corp, D'arcy, Masius, Benton & Bowles, Nat. Rep. Campaign Com., Nat. Rep. Senatorial Com., various candidates for pub. office, 1988; exec. dir. Nev. Rep. Party. Mem. Jefferson Ale Club. Republican. Office: 708 N Center St 2d Flr Reno NV 89501

MCGULPIN, ELIZABETH JANE, nurse; b. Toledo, Oct. 18, 1932; d. James Orville and Leah Fayne (Helton) Welden; m. Daivd Nelson Buster, Apr. 9, 1956 (div. Nov. 1960); children: David Hugh, James Ray, Mark Stephen; m. Fredrick Gordon McGulpin, Oct. 7, 1973. AA in Nursing, Pasadena City Coll., 1968. RN, Wash. Lic. nurse Las Encinas Hosp., Pasadena, Calif.; nurse Hopi Indian Reservation HEW, Keams Canyon, Ariz., 1969-70; nurse, enterostomal therapist Pasadena Vis. Nurse Assn., 1972-74; nurse Seattle King County Pub. Health, 1977-81; home care nurse Victorville, Calif., 1983-85; nurse Adult Family Home, Woodinville, Wash., 1986—; vol. nurse, counselor Child Protective Svcs., Victorville, 1984; realtor Century 21, Lynden, Wash., 1993—. Vol. nurse Am. Cancer Soc., Pasadena, 1973-75, United Ostomy Assn., Los Angeles, Victorville, 1973-84. Am. Cancer Soc. grantee. Mem. Nat. Assn. Realtors, Wash. Assn. Realtors, Whatcom County Assn. Realtors, Vis. Nurse Assn. (Enterostomal Therpay grantee 1973). Home: 106 Kale St Everson WA 98247

MCGWIRE, MARK, professional baseball player; b. Pomona, Calif., Oct. 1, 1963; s. John and Ginger McGwire; m. Kathy McGwire; 1 child, Matthew. Student, U. So. Calif. With Oakland A's, 1986—. Named Am. League Rookie of Yr. Baseball Writers' Assn. Am., 1987, Sporting News, 1987; recipient Gold Glove award, 1990; named to All-Star team, 1987-92; recipient Silver Slugger Award, 1992; Am. League Home Run Leader, 1987; mem. U.S. Olympic Baseball Team, 1984. Office: Oakland A's Oakland-Alameda County Coliseum 7000 Coliseum Way Oakland CA 94621-1918

MCHARDY, LOUIS WILLIAM, professional association executive, educator; b. Baton Rouge, Oct. 31, 1930; s. Colin Andrew and Julia Clara (Zoeller) McH.; m. Ann Evelyn Carter, May 30, 1951; children: Colin Andrew (dec.), Louis William, Hugh Carter, Julie Ann. BA, La. State U., 1951, cert. in social work, 1955, MSW, 1956; LLD (hon.), U. Nev., 1987. Probation officer, casework supr., then chief probation officer Family Ct., Baton Rouge, 1955-64; dir. ct. svcs. juvenile div. Cir. Ct. City of St Louis, 1965-72; dean Nat. Coll. Juvenile and Family Law, Reno, 1972—; exec. dir. Nat. Coun. Juvenile and Family Ct. Judges, Reno, 1972—; sec., treas. Nat. Coun. Juvenile and Family Ct. Judges Fund, Inc., Reno, 1989—; adj. prof. U. Nev. Reno, 1972—; exec. dir. Nat. Juvenile Ct. Found., Inc., 1972—; bd. dirs. Cystems, Washington; past v.p. So. States Probation and Parole Conf.; former chmn. So. Council on Tng. for Prevention Crime and Deliquency; past spl. instr. Juvenile Officer's Inst. and Peace Officer's In-Service Program, La. State U.; past spl. cons. probation and detention, La. Youth Commn.; past pres. La. Conf. Juvenile Correctional Workers, Mo. Correction Assn., Mo. Juvenile Officers Assn., Greater St. Louis Probation and Parole Assn.; del. White Ho. Confs. on Children and Youth, 1960, 70; past chmn. Nat. Inst. on Crime and Delinquency; bd. dirs. Correctional Services Council S.W. Regional Lab. Ednl. Research and Devel., 1960-81. Pub., mem. edit. adv. com. Juvenile and Family Ct. Jour., Juvenile and Family Law Digest, Juvenile and Family Ct. Newsletter, Juvenile Justice Textbook Series, 1972—; cons. author UN Soc. Def. Research Inst., Rome. Sec.-treas John Shaw Field Found., 1980—; mem. nat. grant adv. bd. Women's Crusade Against Crime, St. Louis; cons. secretariat UN Crime Prevention Br., Vienna, Austria; Post Gault Expert Adv. Panel Nat. Ctr. for State Cts.; past mem. exec. bd. Nev. Area Council Boy Scouts Am.; past mem. Mo. Joint Task Force on Cts. Improvement, Nat. Action for Foster Care Children

Com.; former bd. dirs. Nev. Cath. Welfare. With U.S. Army, 1951-53, Korea, lt. col. Res. ret. Recipient UN Peace medal, 1979, 1st Annual Pres.'s award NAt. Coun. Juvenile and Family Ct. Judges, 1992. Mem. Acad. Cert. Social Workers, Nat. Assn. Social Workers, Am. Correctional Assn., Am. Soc. Assn. Execs., Internat. Juvenile Officers' Assn., Internat. Assn. Juvenile and Family Ct. Magistrates (hon. v.p., Pres. medal 1992), Nev. Crime Prevention Assn. (adv. com.), Am. Family Soc. (nat. adv. bd.), Mo. Juvenile Police Officers Assn. (adv. com.), No. Nev. Soc. Scottish Clans, United Comml. Travelers, Sierra Club (Reno chpt.), Elks, KC. Republican. Office: U Nevada Nat Coun Juvenile & Family Ct Judges 1041 N Virginia St Reno NV 89557-0001

MCHENRY, PATRICIA ROSE, state agency administrator; b. Burbank, Calif., Mar. 24, 1950; d. Clarence U. and Neota Etta (Common) Benton. BA with distinction, U. N.Mex., 1977. Office mgr. S.W. Cable TV, Espanola, N.Mex., 1978-79; exec. asst. Baha'i' Internat. Ctr., Haifa, Israel, 1980-83; exec. mgmt. analyst N.Mex. Dept. Fin. and Adminstrn., Santa Fe, 1979, exec. budget analyst, 1983-85; sr. fiscal analyst N.Mex. Legis. Fin. Com., Santa Fe, 1985-88; dep. dir. adminstrv. svcs. div. N.Mex. Dept. Corrections, Santa Fe, 1988-89; adminstr. data processing N.Mex. Human Svc. Dept., Santa Fe, 1990-92; dep. dir. property control div. N.Mex. Gen. Svc. Dept., Santa Fe, 1992—. Mem. Baha'i' Faith. Office: NMex Gen Svc Dept Property Control Divsn 1100 Saint Francis Dr Santa Fe NM 87502

MCHUGH, JAMES JOSEPH, associate dean; b. Phila., Aug. 12, 1930; s. James Joseph and Patience Mary (McGowan) McH.; m. Rita Marie Huber, May 21, 1960; children: Margaret Marie, James Joseph IV. B.A. (with honors), U. Pa., 1951, LL.B., 1954; M.S. in Internat. Relations, George Washington U., 1972. Bar: Pa. 1955. Commd. ensign U.S. Navy, 1955, advanced through grades to rear adm., 1980; legal officer Naval Air Station, Point Mugu, Calif., 1955-58; staff officer Office Judge Adv. Gen., Washington, 1959-63; staff instr. U.S. Naval Justice Sch., Newport, R.I., 1963-65; counsel Bur. Naval Personnel, Washington, 1965-68; asst. fleet judge adv. to comdr. in chief U.S. Pacific Fleet, 1968-71; spl. counsel to chief naval ops. Washington, 1972-76; comdg. officer Naval Legal Service Office, San Francisco, 1976-78; asst. judge adv. gen. Washington, 1978-80; dep. judge adv. gen. Alexandria, Va., 1980-82, judge adv. gen., 1982-84; asst. dean McGeorge Sch. Law, Sacramento, 1984-86, assoc. dean, 1987—. Decorated D.S.M., Legion of Merit (2), Meritorious Svc. medal (2), Navy Commendation medal. Mem. ABA, Order of Coif (hon.), Phi Beta Kappa. Republican. Roman Catholic. Home: 4704 Olive Oak Way Carmichael CA 95608-5663 Office: 3200 5th Ave Sacramento CA 95817-2705

MC HUGH, MARGARET ANN GLOE, psychologist; b. Salt Lake City, Nov. 8, 1920; d. Harold Henry and Olive (Warenski) Gloe; BA, U. Utah, 1942; MA in Counseling and Guidance, Idaho State U., 1964; PhD in Counseling Psychology, U. Oreg., 1970. Lic. psychologist; nat. cert. counselor; m. William T. McHugh, Oct. 1, 1943; children: Mary Margaret McHugh-Shuford, William Michael, Michelle. Tchr. kindergarten, Idaho Falls, Idaho, 1951-62, tchr. high sch. English, 1962-63; counselor Counseling Center, Idaho State U., Pocatello, 1964-67; instr. U. Oreg., Eugene, 1967-70; asst. prof. U. Victoria, B.C., Can., 1970-76; therapist Peninsula Counseling Center, Port Angeles and Sequim, Wash., 1976-81, McHugh & Assocs. Counseling Center, 1981—. Served with WAVES, 1943-44. Mem. Am. Psychol. Assn., Am. Counseling Assn., Am. Assn. Marriage and Family Therapy, Wash. Psychol. Assn. (rsch. women issues, rels's., depression and women, sexual abuse, ritual abuse). Home: 1175 Cameron Rd Sequim WA 98382-9437

MCINERNEY, JOHN GERARD, research physicist, engineering educator; b. Cork, Ireland, May 9, 1959; came to U.S., 1986; s. David John and Mary Margaret (Scott) McI.; m. Alison Kay Ford, Dec. 12, 1987. BSc, Nat. U. of Ireland, Cork, 1980; PhD, Trinity Coll., 1985; MA (h.c.), Cambridge U., Eng., 1986. Lab. instr. Univ. Coll., Cork, 1978-80; rsch. engr. Standard Telecommunications Rsch. Labs., Harlow, Eng., 1981; rsch. asst. Trinity Coll., Dublin, Ireland, 1982-84; rsch. fellow Cambridge U., 1984-86; prof. physics and elec. engring. U. N.Mex., Albuquerque, 1986—, chmn. optolectronics program, 1988—; cons. USAF, Kodak Corp., IBM, Alcoa Inc., McDonnel-Douglas Corp., Mission Rsch. Corp., RDA Logicon. Univ. Coll. scholar, 1976. Mem. IEEE, London Inst. of Physics, Optical Soc. Am., Cambridge Philos. Soc. Home: PO Box 848 Cedar Crest NM 87008-0848 Office: U NMex Ctr for High Tech Materials Albuquerque NM 87331-6081

MCINNIS, SCOTT STEVE, congressman, lawyer; b. Glenwood Springs, Colo., May 9, 1953; s. Kohler McInnis and Carol Kreir; m. Lori McInnis; children: Daxon, Tessa, Andrea. BA, Ft. Lewis Coll., 1975; JD, St. Mary's Law Sch., 1980. Atty. Delaney & Balcomb P.C., Glenwood Springs, Colo., 1981—; mem. Colo. Ho. of Reps. from 57th Dist., 1984-93; majority leader, 1990-93; mem. 103d Congress from 3d Colo. Dist., 1993—; chmn. Agrl., Livestock, and Nat. Resources com., 1986-90; mem. Judiciary, Appropriations and Local Govt. coms. Recipient Florence Sabin award, 1984, Guardian of Small Bus. award Nat. Fed. Ind. Bus., 1990, Lee Atwater Leadership award, 1991, and various awards from United Vets. Commn.; named Legislator of Decade and Legislator of Yr by Colo. Ski Country and Colo. Wildlife Found. Mem. Elks, Rotary, Phi Delta Phi. Republican. Roman Catholic. Office: US Ho of Reps Office House Members Washington DC 20515

MCINNIS, SUSAN MUSÉ, corporate communications specialist; b. Seattle, July 22, 1955; d. Emmett Emory Jr. and Florence Howardine (McAteer) McI. BSBA, U. Denver, 1977; cert. in environ. design, UCLA, 1985; MA in Journalism, Calif. State U., Fullerton, 1992. Researcher Denver Gen. Hosp., summer 1973; mktg. coord. 3M Bus. Products, Emeryville, Calif., 1978-79; spl. libr. Reel Grobman & Assocs., L.A., 1981-83; tchr. Mayfield Sr. Sch., Pasadena, Calif., 1985-87; community and employee rels. mgr. Calif.-Am. Water Co. (coop. co. Am. Water Works), San Marino, Calif., 1988—. Mem. Am. Water Works Assn. (cert. water distbn.), Pub. Rels. Soc. Am., Kiwanis (v.p.).

MCINTOSH, DOUGLAS LLOYD, screenwriter, director; b. South Charleston, W.Va., July 6, 1947; s. Charles Leamon and Charlotte Juanita (Higginbotham) McI. AB, U. Miami, 1970; MFA, NYU, 1972. Screenwriter Warner Bros., Burbank, Calif., 1982-83, Twentieth Century Fox, L.A., 1984, Universal TV, Universal City, Calif., 1984-85, Glenray Prodns., Pasadena, Calif., 1986, Paramount Pictures Corp., Hollywood, Calif., 1987-88, Stephen J. Cannell Prodns., Hollywood, 1989, Envoy Prodns., Hollywood, 1990, ABC Prodns., L.A., 1990—. Screenwriter film: Waiting for the Wind, 1991, TV movies: Notorious, 1992, Disaster at Silo Seven, 1988; Miami Vice episode, 1985, Amazing Stories episode, 1985. Press dir. Sang Kormon for Congress Com., Ventura County, Calif., 1988. Woodrow Wilson fellow, 1970; NYU Class Filmmaking scholar, 1971. Mem. Writers Guild of Am. West, Inc. (sect. leader strike com. 1984, credits arbitration com. 1985—). Republican. Evangelical Covenant. Office: Morning Star Prodns PO Box 2703 Beverly Hills CA 90213

MCINTURFF, KIM, design engineer, mathematician; b. Spokane, Wash., June 13, 1948; s. Don R. and Mae (Lancaster) McI.; m. Denise E. Lockhart, July 17, 1976; children: Ian, Margo. BS in Math., Stanford U., 1971; MA in Math., U. Calif., Santa Barbara, 1976, MSEE, 1986. Software engr. Raytheon ESD, Goleta, Calif., 1978-82, design engr., 1983—. Contbr. articles on antenna design and analysis to profl. jours.; co-patentee multibeam antenna system. Mem. Math. Assn. Am. Home: 5433 Thames Ct Santa Barbara CA 93111 Office: Raytheon ESD 6380 Hollister Ave Goleta CA 93117

MCINTYRE, ADELBERT, geophysicist, environmental scientist; b. Providence, Jan. 1, 1929; s. Adelbert Sr. and Lucy Forbes (MacKay) McI.; divorced; children: Carole M. Schiessel, Marguerite, David E. (dec.), Sheryle M. Davis, Mark L. Student, Ind. U., 1952; BS in Physics, U. R.I., 1958, postgrad., 1958-60. Instr. physics U. R.I., Kingston, 1958-60; scientist Office of Aerospace Rsch., Washington, 1961-63; phys. scientist Air Force Cambridge Rsch. Labs., Hanscom AFB, Mass., 1963-73, tech. dir. Air Force Geophysics Lab., 1973-83; chief atmospheric backgrounds br., dep. infrared tech. Air Force Geophysics Lab., Hanscom AFB, 1983-86; pres., chief scientist Infratech, Inc., Wayland, Mass., 1986-88; scientist Aerojet Electronics System Div., Azusa, Calif., 1988—; cons. Fletcher (Star Wars) Com., Washington, 1983, Air Force Geophysics Lab., 1986-87. Contbr. numerous articles to profl. jours. Maj. USAF, 1951-53, 61-66. Bulova Watch Found. fellow, 1953-57; Grad. fellow U. R.I., 1958; recipient Sci. Achievement award Air Force, 1980, 82, 83,87. Mem. AIAA, Internat. Platform Assn., Reserve Officers Assn., Sigma Xi. Home: 1729 Orangewood Ave Upland CA 91786

MCINTYRE, CAROLYN, college student affairs administrator, counselor; b. East Chicago, Ind., Mar. 23, 1939; d. Chester R. and Alma (Ockomon) Crisler; m. John G. McIntyre, Aug. 31, 1981; children: Dawn M., Dana L. Navarre. BA in Communications, Purdue U., Hammond, Ind., 1971; postgrad., U. Wyo., 1972-82; MA in Counseling/Psychology, Lesley Coll., Cambridge, Mass., 1987. Social worker Fremont County DPASS, Lander, Wyo., 1971-72; mktg./copywriter KCHY AM Radio, Cheyenne, Wyo., 1973; tchr./counselor Arapaho Sch., Wind River Reservation, Wyo., 1973-78; tutor coord. St. Michael's Mission, Ethete, Wyo., 1977-78; social worker Wyo. State Tng. Sch., Lander, 1978-81; counselor SEO-Univ. Wyo., Laramie, 1982-84; rehab. counselor div. vocat. rehab. State of Wyo., Cheyenne and Cody, 1984-88; dir. adult svcs. Northwest Coll., Powell, Wyo., 1988—; advisor Native Ways student orgn. Mem. Welfare Reform Com., Park County, Wyo., 1990—; mem. string sect. N.W. Civic Orch. Mem. Am. Counseling Assn., Wyo. Assn. Counseling & Devel. Office: Northwest Coll 231 W 6th St Powell WY 82435-1898

MCINTYRE, COLIN F., software manager; b. Gainesville, Fla., Sept. 14, 1957; s. Calvin F. and Verna Mae (Leader) McI.; m. Linda L. French, July 5, 1983. BSEE Tech., DeVry Inst. Tech., Phoenix, 1978; MBA, Nat. U., San Jose, Calif., 1992. Test engr. Burroughs Corp., San Diego, 1978-81; cons. Prog-Gen Inc., San Diego, 1981-83; engr. LTX/Trillium, San Jose, 1983-88, software supr., 1988-90, software mgr., 1990—. Mem. IEEE. Home: PO Box 23274 San Jose CA 95153

MCINTYRE, GARY ALLEN, plant pathology educator; b. Portland, Oreg., July 16, 1938; s. John H. and Onie Marie (Meihoff) McI.; m. Loene Beneva, Sept. 1, 1963; children: Paula Lynn, Laura Ann. BS, Oreg. State U., 1960, PhD, 1964. Asst. prof. botany and plant pathology U. Maine, Orono, 1963-68, assoc prof., 1968-73, prof., 1973-75, chmn. botany, plant pathology dept., 1969-75; prof., chmn. botany, plant pathology Colo. State U., Ft. Collins, 1975-84, prof., head plant pathology and weed sci. dept., 1984—; Coordinator Western Regional Integrated Pest Mgmt. program, 1979—. Mem. Am. Phytopathol. Soc., Potato Assn., Phi Kappa Phi, Phi Sigma Soc., Soc. Sigma Xi, Gamma Sigma Delta. Office: Colo State U Dept Plant Pathology/Weed Sci Fort Collins CO 80523

MCINTYRE, GUY MAURICE, professional football player; b. Thomasville, Ga., Feb. 17, 1961. Student, Ga. State U. Offensive guard San Francisco 49ers, 1984—. Office: San Francisco 49ers 4949 Centennial Blvd Santa Clara CA 95054

MCINTYRE, HUGH BAXTER, neurology educator; b. Jacksonville, Fla., June 26, 1935; s. Hugh Baxter and Helen (Watson) McI.; m. Patricia Ann Bowne, July 11, 1959; children: Anne Louise, Hugh Cameron. BS, U. Fla., 1957, MD, 1962; PhD, UCLA, 1972. Diplomate Am. Bd. Psychiatry and Neurology, Am. Bd. Qualification in Electroencephalography; lic. med. examiner, Calif., Fla. Intern straight medicine UCLA Med. Ctr., 1962-63, resident I medicine, 1963-64, resident I neurology, 1964-65, resident II neurology, 1965-66, sr. resident neurology, 1966-67; spl. rsch. fellow Nat. Inst. Nervous Disorders Harbor-UCLA Med. Ctr., 1969-72, staff physician, chief div. neurophysiology, 1972—; asst. prof. neurology in residence UCLA Sch. Medicine, 1972-74, adj. assoc. prof. neurology, adj. prof. neurology, 1972—; adj. prof. biomed. scis. U. Calif., Riverside, 1983—; assoc. chair dept. neurology Harbor-UCLA Med. Ctr., 1990—; bd. dirs. Harbor/UCLA Med. Found., Inc., 1986—; assoc. examiner Am. Bd. Psychiatry and Neurology, 1974—, Am. Bd. Clin. Neuophysiology, 1975—; civilian cons., lectr. neurology U.S. Naval Hosp., Long Beach, Calif., 1970-85; acad. cons. St. Mary Med. Ctr., Long Beach, 1982—, Long Beach Meml. Hosp., 1973—; co-chmn. Orange Coast Coll. Electro-Diagnostic Technician Adv. Com., 1973—; site visit team mem. Joint Rev. Com. on Edn. in EEG Tech. and Div. Allied Health and Accreditaiton of AMA, 1976—. Editor-in-chief Bull. Clin. Neuroscis., 1976—; author: The Primary Care of Seizure Disorders, 1982, Primary Care: Symposium on Clinical Neurology, Vol. II, 1984; contbr. articles to profl. jours. Lt. comdr., M.C., USNR, 1967-69. Recipient Certs. of Appreciation, San Deigo County Epilepsy Soc., 1968, Orange Coast Coll., 1989. Fellow ACP, Am. Acad. Neurology, Am. EEG Soc. (com. on guidelines in EEG); mem. Am. Acad. Neurology, Los Angeles Soc. Neurology and Psychiatry (pres. 1979), Fedn. Western Socs. Neurol. Sci., L.A. County Med. Assn., Western Electroencephalographic Soc., Internat. Soc. Neuroendocrinology, Am. Epilepsy Soc., Calif. Epilepsy Soc. (bd. dirs., 2d v.p. 1982-86, svc. award 1985). Republican. Presbyterian. Office: Harbor UCLA Med Ctr 1000 W Carson St Torrance CA 90509-2004

MC INTYRE, JAMES A., diversified financial services executive; b. 1932. BS, U. So. Calif., 1954. With Ernst & Ernst, L.A., 1958-63; pres. Fremont Indemnity Co., 1963-80; pres., CEO Fremont Gen. Corp., Santa Monica, Calif., 1980—. Office: Fremont Gen Corp 2020 Santa Monica Blvd Santa Monica CA 90404-2023*

MCINTYRE, NORMAN F., petroleum industry executive; b. Pangman, Sask., Can., Oct. 21, 1945; s. Donald and Jean (Cruickshank) McI.; m. Lana Jean McIntyre, June 10, 1967; children: Jason Lee and Spencer James. BSc in Petroleum Engring., U. Wyo., 1971; MS in Mgmt., MIT, 1991. Various positions with Mobil Oil, U.S., Can., to 1982; group mgr. engring. offshore divsn. Petro-Can., 1982-83, gen. mgr. frontier devel. offshore divsn., 1983, v.p. frontier devel., 1983-85, v.p. prodn. devel., 1985-86; sr. v.p. prodn. Petro-Can. Resources, 1986-89; sr. v.p. western region Petro-Can. Products, 1989-90; pres. Petro-Can. Resources, Calgary, Alta., Can., 1990—; dir. Panarctic Oils Ltd., Panarctic Transmission Co. Office: Petro-Canada, 150-6th Ave SW PO Box 2844, Calgary, AB Canada T2P 3E3

MCINTYRE, ROBERT FRANCIS, naval officer; b. Trenton, N.J., Sept. 7, 1954; s. John Henry and Margaret (McIntyre) McI; m. Marla June Wolfe, June 28, 1980; 1 child, Matthew Robert. BA in Polit. Sci., Waynesburg (Pa.) Coll., 1976; M Pub. Internat. Affairs, U. Pitts., 1983; postgrad., U. Denver, 1984—. Commd. ensign USN, 1978, advanced through grades to lt. comdr., 1988; squadron intelligence officer Naval Air Sta., Whidbey Island, Wash., 1979-81; operational intelligence analyst Naval Operational Intelligence Ctr., Suitland, Md., 1982-83; analyst, briefer Office Chief Naval Ops., Washington, 1983-84; instr. Navy Marine Corps Intelligence Tng. Ctr., Damneck, Va., 1984-87; battle group staff intelligence officer Cruiser-Destroyer Group 8, Norfolk, Va., 1987-89; ops. officer Fleet Ocean Surveillance Info. Ctr., Pearl Harbor, Hawaii, 1989-91; intelligence data systems and dissemination officer, comdr. in chief U.S. Pacific Fleet, 1991—. Home: 22 McGrew Loop Honolulu HI 96860 Office: US Pacific Fleet (21) PO Box 2 Pearl Harbor HI 96860-0001

MCINTYRE, ROBERT MALCOLM, utility company executive; b. Portland, Oreg., Dec. 18, 1923; s. Daniel A. and Bessie W. (Earsley) McI.; m. Marilyn Westcott, Aug. 27, 1949; 1 child, Julie. BA, UCLA, 1950; postgrad., UCLA, U. So. Calif., Columbia U. With So. Calif. Gas Co. (subs. Pacific Enterprises), L.A., 1952-67, gen. sales mgr., 1967-70, v.p., 1970-74, sr. v.p., 1974-80, pres., 1980-85, chmn., chief exec. officer, 1985-88; also bd. dirs. So. Calif. Gas Co. (subs. Pacific Enterprises); regent's prof. U. Calif., Irvine. Mem. Korean Am. Centennial Commn., Huntington Libr. Soc. Fellows, L.A. Olympic Citizens Adv. Commn.; mem. bus. coun. Newport Harbor Art Mus.; mem. steering com. Orange County Bus. Com. for Arts; mem. ad hoc com. on city fin., L.A.; bd. dirs. NCCJ, Calif. Coun. Environ. and Econ. Balance, Calif. Found. Environment and Economy, L.A. United Way, Hoag Meml. Hosp.; trustee UCLA Found., L.A. Orthopaedic Hosp., mem. exec. com.; pres. Hoag Hosp. Found., L.A. Chamber Assocs. Lt. USN, 1942-46. Decorated Order of the Rising Sun with Gold Rays and Ribbon (Japan); recipient Outstanding Svc. award Mex. Am. Legal Def. Fund, 1981, Humanitarian award NCCJ, Roy Wilkins award L.A. chpt. NAACP, others. Mem. Pacific Coast Gas Assn. (past dir., 49er Club award 1979), Am. Gas Assn., Inst. Gas Tech. (trustee), U.S.-Mex. C. of C., L.A. C. of C. (past chmn. Medici award), Calif. Club, 100 Club, Big Canyon Country Club, Center Club, Pacific Club, The Lakes Country Club, Phi Kappa Psi. Republican. Presbyterian. Office: So Calif Gas Co 555 W 5th St Los Angeles CA 90013-1010

MCINTYRE, ROBERT WHEELER, conservation organization executive; b. Chgo., Aug. 26, 1936; s. Henry Langenberg and Winifred (Wheeler) McI.; m. Emily Beardsley Taylor, Oct. 12, 1961 (div. 1985); children: W. Burley, Nancy T., Oliver W., Shanna L., Amanda K.; m. Miriam de Jesus Zarate, June 23, 1990. AB in Sociology, Stanford U., 1959; MBA, Harvard U., 1964. Loan analyst Wells Fargo Bank, San Francisco, 1964-65; supr. budget analysis Ford Aerospace, Palo Alto, Calif., 1965-69; controller Allied Life Scis., San Leandro, Calif., 1969-70; ptnr. Diplomat Mfg. Co., Palo Alto, 1970-71; staff cons. Opportunity Through Ownership, San Francisco, 1971-72; gen. mgr. Quality Metal Finishers, San Francisco, 1972-73; sr. v.p., chief fin. officer The Trust for Pub. Land, San Francisco, 1973—. Adv. bd. Peninsula Open Space Trust, Menlo Park, 1978—, Resource Renewal Inst., Sausalito, 1988—, Wter Heritage Trust, Sausalito, 1988—, Dorothy Erskine Open Space Fund, San Francisco, 1978—; bd. dirs. Environ. Vols., Palo Alto, 1980—; bd. dirs., treas. Robert C. Wheeler Found., Palo Alto, 1965—. Lt. (j.g.) USNR, 1959-62. Recipient Presdl. Citation award, The Trust for Pub. Land, 1988, Spl. Svc. award, Environ. Vols., 1989. Mem. Harvard Club of N.Y., Harvard Club of Boston, Bankers Club San Francisco, Pacific Athletic Club (San Carlos), Sundown Tennis Club (San Mateo). Office: The Trust for Public Land 116 New Montgomery St Fl 4 San Francisco CA 94105-3607

MCJIMSEY, ROBERT DUNCAN, English and European history educator; b. Dallas, Mar. 9, 1936; s. Joseph Bailey and Harriet (Tilden) McJ.; m. Marianna Presler, June 24, 1961; children: Elizabeth, George, Katharine. BA, Grinnell Coll., 1958; MA, U. Wis., 1961, PhD, 1968. Instr. Oberlin (Ohio) Coll., 1965-66; asst. prof. Ohio Wesleyan U., Delaware, 1966-68; prof. history Colo. Coll., Colorado Springs, 1968—, chair history dept. Contbr. articles to profl. jours. Sr. warden, vestry mem. Grace Episcopal Ch., Colorado Springs, 1972—. Fulbright fellow, Eng., 1963-64, Benezet fellow Colo. Coll., Eng., 1980-81. Mem. Western Conf. Brit. Studies (treas.). Home: 119 E San Miguel Colorado Springs CO 80903 Office: Colo Coll 14 E Cache La Poudre Colorado Springs CO 80903

MCJONES, ROBERT WAYNE, consulting aeronautical engineer; b. Dodge City, Kans., Aug. 19, 1922; s. John William and Emma Eudora (Fowler) McJ.; m. Norma Jeane Prater, Aug. 25, 1946; children: Paul R., Bruce P., Justin F., Stephen F. BS in Aero. Engring., U. Kans., 1947, Aero. Engr., 1957; MS in Aero., Calif. Tech., Pasadena, 1948. Registered mech. engr., Calif. Aerodynamicist Douglas Aircraft, El Segundo, Calif., 1948-50, Marquardt Corp., Van Nuys, Calif., 1950-52; chief power plant engr. Am. Helicopter, Manhattan Beach, Calif., 1952-54; cons. engr. Palos Verdes, Calif., 1955—. Contbr. articles to profl. jours.; patentee in field. 1st lt. USAAF, 1943-45, PTO. Mem. ASME, Soc. Automotive Engrs., Palos Verdes Yacht Club (commodore). Home: 1 Limetree Ln Rancho Palos Verdes CA 90274

MCKARNS, JAMES STEPHEN, industrial hygiene engineer; b. Bryan, Ohio, June 25, 1938; s. James Russell and Florence Bernice (Werder) McK. BME, Ohio State U., 1961; SM in Engring., Harvard U., 1963. Cert. indsl. hygienist, safety profl. Mech. engr. Texaco Rsch. Ctr., Beacon, N.Y., 1961-62; indsl. hygienist Exxon Rsch. & Engring. Co., Linden, N.J., 1963-65, Reynolds Elec. and Engring. Co., Mercury, Nev., 1965-66; bioenviron. specialist Gen. Dynamics/Convair Aerospace, Ft. Worth, 1966-72; indsl. hygiene engr. Bethlehem Steel Corp., San Francisco, 1972-81; indsl. hygienist Pacific Gas and Electric Co., San Francisco, 1981-89; safety and environ. specialist Lockheed Missiles and Space Co., Sunnyvale, Calif., 1989—. Coauthor tech. papers. Spl. Health Phys. fellow U.S. AEC, 1962. Mem. MENSA, Am. Indsl. Hygiene Assn., Soc. Automotive Engrs., Am. Nuclear Soc., Human Factors and Ergonomics Soc., Rolls-Royce Owners' Club (bd. dirs. 1988-90), Bentley Drivers' Club, Mercedes-Benz Club Am., Mid Peninsula Old Time Auto Club (treas. 1988-93). Libertarian. Methodist. Home: Condo 504 833 N Humboldt St San Mateo CA 94401-1484 Office: Lockheed Missiles & Space Co 47-20/106 1111 Lockheed Way Sunnyvale CA 94089-3504

MC KAUGHAN, HOWARD PAUL, linguistics educator; b. Canoga Park, Calif., July 5, 1922; s. Paul and Edith (Barton) McK.; A.B., UCLA, 1945; M.Th., Dallas Theol. Sem., 1946; M.A., Cornell U., 1952, Ph.D., 1957; m. Barbara Jean Budroe, Dec. 25, 1943; children: Edith (Mrs. Daniel Skene Santoro), Charlotte (Mrs. Charlotte Barnhart), Patricia (Mrs. Stephen B. Pike), Barbara (Mrs. Ronald Chester Bell), Judith (Mrs. Frank L. Achilles III). Mem. linguistic research team Summer Inst. Linguistics, Mexico, 1946-52; asso. dir. Summer Inst. Linguistics, Philippines, also assoc. dir. summer sessions U. N.D., 1952-57, dir. Philippine br., 1957-61; research asst. prof. anthropology U. Wash., 1961-62; research assoc. prof., 1962-63; assoc. prof. linguistics U. Hawaii, 1963-64, prof. linguistics, 1964-88, prof. emeritus, 1988—, chmn. dept., 1963-66, dir. Pacific and Asian Linguistics Inst., 1964, 1966-69, assoc. dean grad. div., 1965-72, dean grad. div., dir. research, 1972-79, acting chancellor, 1979, interim vice chancellor acad. affairs, 1981-82, acting dir research, 1982-84, acting dean grad. div., 1982-83, dean, 1984-87, dir. research relations, 1987-88; lectr. linguistics U. Philippines, summers, 1954, 60; Fulbright vis. prof. Philippine Normal Coll.-Ateneo De La Salle Consortium, Philippines, 1977, De La Salle U., Philippines, 1992, Bakidnon State Coll., Philippines, 1993; prin. Wycliffe Sch. Linguistics, summers 1953, 61; vis. prof. Australian Nat. U., Canberra, 1970; adj. prof. linguistics U. Okla., summers 1984, 85, 86; vis. prof., head dept. linguistics Payap U., Chiang Mai, Thailand, 1989-90. Sr. scholar East-West Ctr., Honolulu, 1964; NDEA Maranao-Philippines research grantee, 1963-65; Office of Edn. Hawaii English grantee, 1965-66; NSF Jeh Language of South Vietnam grantee, 1969-70, Maranao Linguistic Studies, 1971-72, numerous other research grants. Mem. linguistic socs. Am., Philippines, Western Assn. Grad. Schs. (pres. 1978), Hawaii, Linguistic Circle N.Y., Philippine Assn. Lang. Tchrs., Hawaii Govt. Employees Assn., Phi Beta Kappa, Phi Kappa Phi. Author (with B. McKaughan): Chatino Dictionary, 1951; (with J. Forster) Ilocano: An Intensive Language Course, 1952; The Inflection and Syntax of Maranao Verbs, 1959; (with B. Macaraya): A Maranao Dictionary, 1967. Editor: Pali Language Texts: Philippines, 21 vols., 1971; The Languages of the Eastern Family of the East New Guinea Highlands Stock, 1973. Contbr. articles, chpts. to books, sci. jours. Home: 420 S Hill Rd Mcminnville OR 97128

MCKAY, ALICE VITALICH, school system administrator; b. Seattle, Sept. 6, 1947; d. Jack S. and Phyllis (Bourne) Vitalich; m. Larry W. McKay, Aug. 14, 1973 (div. Jan. 1983). BA, Wash. State U., 1969; MEd, U. Nev., Las Vegas, 1975; EdD, U. Nev., Reno, 1986. High sch. tchr. Clark County Sch. Dist., Las Vegas, 1972-77, specialist women's sports, 1977-80, high sch. counselor, 1980-84, high sch. asst. prin., 1984—; pres. Lotus Profit, Inc., Las Vegas, 1985-86. Mem. Am. Assn. Counseling and Devel. (committee on women 1985—), Nev. State Counseling and Devel. (pres. 1985-86), Nat. Assn. Female Execs., AAUW, Phi Delta Kappa (exec. bd. 1980-82). Office: Washoe County Sch Dist 425 E 9th St Reno NV 89520-0106

MCKAY, D. BRIAN, lawyer; b. Billings, Mont., Jan. 18, 1945. A.B., Colgate U., 1971; J.D., Albany Law Sch., 1974. Bar: Nev., U.S. Dist. Ct. Nev., N.Y., U.S. Dist. Ct. (no. dist.) N.Y., U.S. Ct. Appeals (9th cir.) 1978, U.S. Supreme Ct. Former mem. Sully, McKay & Lenhard, Las Vegas, Nev.; atty. gen. State of Nev., Carson City, 1983-90; with Lionel, Sawyer & Collins, Reno, 1990—; mem. adv. policy bd. Nat. Crime Info. Ctr., 1986—; chmn. Conf. of Western Attys.-Gen., 1987. With USAF, 1966-69. Mem. ABA, State Bar Nev., N.Y. State Bar Assn., Nat. Assn. Attys. Gen. Office: Lionel Sawyer & Collins 50 W Liberty St Ste 1100 Reno NV 89501-1990*

MCKAY, FLOYD JOHN, journalist, educator; b. Bottineau, N.D., Oct. 18, 1935; s. Harold S. and Maude (Steinmeier) McK.; m. Dixie Ann Johnson, Mar. 29, 1957; children: Karen LeAnn McKay Wolf, David Scott. BA, Linfield Coll., 1957; MA, U. Md., 1990. Reporter Springfield (Oreg.) News, 1958-60, The Oreg. Statesman, Salem, 1960-70; news analyst Sta. KGW-TV, Portland, Oreg., 1970-86; adminstv. asst. to gov. State of Oreg., Salem, 1987-89; sr. fellow The East-West Ctr., Honolulu, 1989; asst. prof. journalism Western Wash. U., Bellingham, 1990—; mem. steering com. Reporters' Com. for Freedom of the Press, Washington, 1980-87; cons. Ctr. for Fgn. Journalists, Washington, 1989-90. Trustee Linfield Coll., McMinnville, Oreg., 1972-

78, The Catlin Gabel Sch., Portland, 1976-81. Nieman fellow Harvard U., 1967-68; recipient DuPont-Columbia Broadcast award Columbia U., 1977. Mem. Sigma Delta Chi. Office: Western Wash U Dept Journalism Bellingham WA 98225-9101

MCKAY, JANET HOLMGREN, college president; b. Chgo., Dec. 1, 1948; d. Kenneth William and Virginia Ann (Rensink) H.; m. Gordon A. McKay, Sept. 7, 1968 (div. 1990); children: Elizabeth Jane, Ellen Katherine. BA in English summa cum laude, Oakland U., Rochester, Mich., 1968; MA in Linguistics, Princeton U., 1971, PhD in Linguistics, 1974. Asst. prof. English studies Federal City Coll. (now U. D.C.), Washington, 1972-76; asst. prof. English U. Md., College Park, 1976-82, asst. to chancellor, 1982-88; assoc. provost Princeton (N.J.) U., 1988-90, vice-provost, 1990-91; pres. Mills Coll., Oakland, Calif., 1991—; state coord. Md. regional planning coun. nat. identification program for women Am. Coun. on Edn., 1988-89, also bd. dirs.; mem. external adv. bd. English dept. Princeton U. Bay Area Biosci. Ctr. Author: (with Spencer Cosmos) The Story of English: Study Guide and Reader, 1986, Narration and Discourse in American Realistic Fiction, 1982; contbr. articles to profl. jours. Faculty rsch. grantee U. Md., 1978; fellow NEH, 1978, Princeton U., 1968-69, 70-72, NSF, 1969-70; recipient summer study aid Linguistic Soc. Am., Ohio State U., 1970. Mem. Assn. Ind. Calif. Colls. and Univs. (exec. com.), Calif. Acad. Sci. (coun.). Democrat. Episcopal. Office: Mills Coll Office Pres 5000 MacArthur Blvd Oakland CA 94613-1301

MCKAY, JOHN, lawyer; b. Seattle, June 19, 1956; s. John Larkin and Kathleen (Tierney) M. BA, U. Wash., 1978; JD, Creighton U., 1982. Bar: Wash. 1982, U.S. Dist. Ct. (we. dist.) Wash. 1982, U.S. Supreme Ct. 1990, U.S. Ct. Appeals (9th cir.) 1990. Ptnr. Lane Powell Spears Lubersky, Seattle, 1982-92, Cairncross & Hempelmann, Seattle, 1992—. Recipient White House fellowship, Washington, 1989-90. Mem. ABA (bd. govs. 1991—), Wash. State Bar Assn. (pres. young lawyers div. 1988-89). Republican. Roman Catholic. Office: Cairncross & Hempelmann 701 Fifth Ave Ste 7000 Seattle WA 98104-7016

MCKAY, MONROE GUNN, federal judge; b. Huntsville, Utah, May 30, 1928; s. James Gunn and Elizabeth (Peterson) McK.; m. Lucile A. Kinnison, Aug. 6, 1954; children: Michele, Valanne, Margaret, James, Melanie, Nathan, Bruce, Lisa, Monroe. B.S., Brigham Young U., 1957; J.D., U. Chgo., 1960. Bar: Ariz. 1961. Law clk. Ariz. Supreme Ct., 1960-61; assoc. firm Lewis & Roca, Phoenix, 1961-66; ptnr. Lewis & Roca, 1968-74; assoc. prof. Brigham Young U., 1974-76, prof., 1976-77; judge U.S. Ct. of Appeals (10th cir.), Denver, 1977—, chief judge, 1991—. Mem. Phoenix Community Council Juvenile Problems, 1968-74; pres. Ariz. Assn. for Health and Welfare, 1970-72; dir. Peace Corps, Malawi, Africa, 1966-68; bd. dirs., pres. Maricopa county Legal Aid Soc., 1972-74. Served with USMCR, 1946-48. Mem. ABA, Ariz. Bar Assn., Maricopa County Bar Assn., Am. Law Inst., Am. Judicature Soc., Order of Coif, Blue Key, Phi Kappa Phi. Mem. Ch. Jesus Christ of Latter-day Saints. Office: US Ct Appeals 6012 Fed Bldg 125 S State St Salt Lake City UT 84138-1102

MCKEAN, THOMAS ARTHUR, physiologist, educator; b. Boise, Idaho, Jan. 27, 1941; s. Robert S. and Gwendolyn (Lyons) McK.; m. Cynthia Fanshawe, May 17, 1963 (div. 1978); m. Corinne K. Ostroot, Jan. 4, 1980; children: Jeffrey, Leslie. AB in Math., Whitman Coll., 1963; PhD in Physiology, U. Oreg., Portland, 1968. Rsch. asst. U. Oreg. Med. Sch., Portland, 1963-64; postdoctoral fellow U. Minn., Mpls., 1968-69; asst. dir. mktg. Hoechst Pharm., Cinn., 1969-70; asst. prof. U. Wyo., Laramie, 1970-74; assoc. prof. U. Idaho, Moscow, 1974-82, acting dir. Wash., Alaska, Mont., Idaho med. program, 1977-78, 87-88, prof., 1982—; affiliate prof. U. Wash., Seattle, 1984—; vis. scientist Oregon Health Scis. U., Portland, 1980-81. Hon. editor Comparative Biochemistry and Physiology; contbr. articles to profl. jours. Reviewer Clearwater Econ. Devel. Corp., Moscow, Idaho, 1977-80, NIH, NSF, Nat. Sci. and Engring. Rsch. Coun. (Can.); pres. Latah County Humane Soc., Moscow, 1977-80; bd. dirs. Am. Heart Assn., Idaho chpt., Boise, 1986—, pres., 1991; chmn. west peer rev., Dallas, 1988-90. Grantee NIH, 1972, 92, Am. Heart Assn., 1974-93. Mem. AAAS, Am. Physiol. Soc. Office: Univ Idaho Dept Biol Sci Moscow ID 83843

MCKEE, FREDERICK A., planning and development director, photography educator; b. Buffalo, Jan. 10, 1945; s. Frederick A. and Helen (Clees) McK.; m. Caroline Gittings, July 29, 1972; children: Brendan Hunter, Adam Clees. BFA, Rochester (N.Y.) Inst., 1967; MFA, Utah State U., 1977. Edn. cons. Indian Devel. and Edn. Alliance, Miles City, Mont., 1977-78; impact planner Custer County, Miles City, 1978-79; instr. photography Miles Community Coll., 1974—, fed. programs officer, 1979—, dir. planning and devel., 1983—; exec. sec. Miles Community Coll. Endowment, 1982—. Photographer show catalog Native Am. Visual Art in Mont., 1986, Images of an Idyllic Past, 1988. Commr. Zoning Commn., Miles City/Custer County, 1980—, City of Miles Arts Coun., 1989—. Mem. Nat. Coun. Resource Devel. (bd. dirs./region 8 dir. 1986-88, 92-93). Presbyterian. Office: Miles Community Coll 2715 Dickinson St Miles City MT 59301-4799

MCKEE, JOHN CAROTHERS, management consultant; b. San Diego, Apr. 25, 1912; s. John Joseph and Margaret (Giesman) McK.; BA, U. So. Calif., 1935, MA, 1937; PhD, Tulane U., 1947; m. Gladys Irene Michel, Jan. 10, 1941 (Dec. Feb. 1968); children—John Michael, Hillary Barbara; m. Sara Forman, June 25, 1968; 1 child, Evan. Gen. mgr. Hotel Royal, La Ceiba, Honduras, 1932-33; mgmt. cons. Douglas Aircraft Co., Long Beach, Calif., 1942-67, exec. adviser, dir. ops. control, 1967—, also pres. mgmt. assn. Douglas Space Systems Center; exec. adviser fin. mgmt. McDonnell Douglas Astronautics, v.p. Santa Monica Health Spot Shoe Corp., 1949—; pres. McKee Mgmt. Ctr., Volumetrics, Inc., Mentron Corp.; exec. v.p. Consearch Inc.; pres. McKee Mgmt. Ctr., Stanton, Calif., Quantek Internat. Inc.; ptnr. McKee & Wright and Assn., Stanton; v.p. Advion Corp.; lectr. Acad. of Justice, Riverside, Calif.; cons. Space Systems Ctr., Huntington Beach, Calif., 1964—; cons. Hanford, Orange, Cypress police depts. (all Calif.), Saanich Police Dept., Victoria, B.C., Can., 1988; mem. Fed. Res. Fin. Bd., Washington; bd. dir. Consultron, Inc.; mem. Fed. Res. Bd., 1990-91. Author: Law Enforcement Manager's Handbook, Antique Arms Appraisal Handbook. Pres. sports coun. YMCA. Bd. dirs. Long Beach YMCA. Assoc. dir. mgmt. ctr. Chapman Coll., bd. dirs. mgmt. ctr. McKee Wright La Verne Coll., Cavaliers Fencing Schs., 1935—, Law Enforcement Mgmt. Ctr., Calif.; mgr. Stanton Bd. Trade, 1978—; Olympic fencing coach, 1984; pres. Ctr. for Strategic Planning, Orange County, Calif.; mem. fed. res. adv. bd. Recipient Personagraph Speaker of Yr. award Indsl Mgmt. Assn, Outstanding Law Enforcement Work award Calif. Atty. Gen., 1984; named to Am. Police Hall of Fame, 1984; recipient Charles R. Able citation for co. mgmt., Cert. of Merit Amateur Fencers League Am., Citizen of Yr. award Calif. Office Atty. Gen., 1984,Civilian of Yr. award Calif. Atty. Gen. Office; resolution of thanks for work with police City of Hartford; resolution of Excellence Hartford City Coun.; Calif. Gov.'s award for civilian svc. to law enforcement, honored by Can. Police Commn.; named Cavalier Fencing Coach of Yr., 1982; named to Pub. Hall of Fame, 1985; Nat. Police Hall of Fame, 1985; cert. instr. Calif. Dept. Justice POST program. Mem. Internat. Platform Assn., Am. Statis. Assn. (past pres., mem. nat. coun.). Nat. Mgmt. Assn. (recipient Silver Knight of Mgmt., 1961, v.p. area coun.), Nat. Assn. Chiefs of Police, Internat. Assn. Chiefs Police, Calif. Assn. Police Tng. Officers, Fedn. Internationale D'Esgrime, (hon.) Can. Mounted Police, Amateur Fencers League Am., Internat. Fencing Commn., AAAS, C. of C. (mem. rsch. com. of L.A.), Inst. Mgmt. Scis., Am. Assn. Indsl. Editors, Internat. Coun. Indsl. Editors, So. Calif. Indsl. Editors Assn., Nat. Assn. Bus. Economists, Orange County Econ. Roundtable (Exec. of Yr. award, pres.), Am. Soc. Quality Control (chmn. criminal justice sect.), Calif. Adminstrn. Justice Educators, Calif. Assn. Peace Officers, Can. N.W. Mounted Police, Coll. of Heraldry (London), Phi Beta Kappa. Author: Learning Curves, Quantity-Cost Curves, Estimating Engineering Costs, Systems Analysis, Cost and Budgeting Analysis and Statistics for Non-Mathematical Managers; Zero Base Budgeting, The Fencer's Work Book, Fiscal Management, The Police Chief's Financial Handbook. Home: 8361 Westminster Blvd Westminster CA 92683-3376 Office: PO Box 273 Stanton CA 90680-0273

MCKEE, MELISSA MARIE, artist; b. Santa Rosa, Calif., Nov. 25, 1964; d. Rodney Park McKee and Marian Esther (Taylor) McKee-Roberts; children: Misty Marie, Michael David Christopher. Student, Hartnell Coll., Salinas, Calif., 1985-87, Colo. Inst. Art, Denver, 1987, Front Range C.C., 1992-93. Artist Good Decal, Denver, 1987-90, Sachs Lawlor, Denver, 1991, Exec. Design, Denver, 1991; owner Graphic Connection, Denver; mem. Hanes Group Microenterprizing, Denver, 1991—. Bd. dirs. Child Opportunity Program, Head Start, 1992—; bd. dirs. Colo. State Parent Tchr. Assn., Parent Edn. Commn., 1991-94. Mem. Colo. State Parents Assn. (pres., bd. dirs. region VIII 1992-93), People for Children Coun. (treas. 1988-91, Top Vol. 1992).

MCKEE, PENELOPE MELNA, library director; b. New Liskeard, Ont., Can., Dec. 31, 1938; d. Melvin Hugh and Violet Mary (Hooton) Olimer; m. Arthur Donald McKee, Mar. 5, 1960 (div. 1985); children: Suzanne, Carolyn, Stephen. BA with honors, U. Toronto, Can., 1960, BLS, 1961, MLS, 1980. Fine arts libr. North York Pub. Libr., Ont., Can., 1961-63, reference libr., 1969-74; reference libr. Toronto Montessori Schs., Thornhill, Ont., 1974-76; cons. Grolier Pub., Toronto, 1976; libr. supr. Toronto Pub. Libr., 1977-80; dir. Aurora Pub. Libr., Ont., Can., 1980-86, Peterborough Pub. Libr., Ont., Can., 1986-90, Edmonton Pub. Libr., Alta., Can., 1990—; adj. assoc. prof. U. Alta., Edmonton, 1992—; cons. Edmonton Cath. Sch. Bd., 1992. Contbr. articles to profl. jours. Vice chmn. Project Hostel, Aurora, 1986-89; bd. dirs. Friends of Trent Severn Waterway, Peterborough, 1990; active Edmonton Centennial Celebrations Com., 1992. Russell scholar U. Toronto, 1956. Mem. Canadian Libr. Assn., Ontario Libr. Assn. (pres.), Libr. Assn. Alta., Alta. Pub. Libr. Dirs. Coun. (chair), Rotary Club of Downtown Edmonton (pub. rels. chmn.). Office: Edmonton Public Libr, 7 Sir Winston Churchill Sq, Edmonton, AB Canada T5J 2V4

MC KEE, RAYMOND WALTER, accountant; b. Joplin, Mo., Dec. 24, 1899; s. Charles Edward and Sarah Ellen (Epperson) McK.; student pub. schs., Joplin; m. Frances Ida Howe, Nov. 1, 1947; children: Michael, David, Roderick, Duncan, Malcolm, Brude. Acct., Price, Waterhouse & Co., 1923-25, Haskins & Sells, 1925-26; pvt. practice acctg., La Puente, Calif., 1964—; lectr. St. Louis U., 1923-24; v.p. Richfield Oil Corp., Pan Am. Petroleum Corp., 1928-30; sec. West Coast Air Transport, 1926-30; sec.-treas. West Coast div. Anchor Hocking Corp.; gen. mgr., dir. Maywood Mut. Water Co. # 3; pres. Cross Water Co. Co-founder Nat. Paraplegia Found. (name now Nat. Spinal Cord Found.), 1927. C.P.A., Calif. Mem. Petroleum Accts. Soc. (co-founder, life). Club: Lions. Author: Accounting for Petroleum Industry, 1925; Petroleum Accounting, 1938; Saludos California, 1947; Book of McKee, 1959. Home and Office: 738 S 3d Ave La Puente CA 91746

MCKEE, ROGER CURTIS, judge, educator; b. Waterloo, Iowa, Feb. 11, 1931; s. James A. and Leonace (Burrell) McK.; m. Roberta Jeanne Orvis, Sept. 3, 1954; children: Andrea Jane, Brian Curtis, Paul Robert. BA, State Coll. of Iowa, 1955; MA, U. Ill., 1960; JD, U. San Diego, 1968. Bar: Calif. 1970, U.S. Dist. Ct. (so. dist.) Calif. 1969, U.S. Ct. Appeals (9th cir.) 1971. Telegrapher, agt. Ill. Cen. R.R., 1950-55; tng. asst. No. Ill. Gas Co., Aurora, 1959-60; with indsl. rels. dept. Convair div. Gen. Dynamics Corp., San Diego, 1960-68; contract adminstr. and supr. Datagraphix div. Gen. Dynamics Corp., San Diego, 1968-69, asst. counsel, 1969-70; ptnr. Powell & McKee, San Diego, 1970-75, Millsberg, Dickstein & McKee, San Diego, 1975-83; judge U.S. Dist. Ct. for So. Dist. Calif., San Diego, 1983—. Bd. trustees So. Calif. Presbyn. Homes, L.A., 1979-81; moderator Presbytery of San Diego, 1980. Capt. USNR, 1949-85. Mem. Calif. Bar Assn., Fed. Magistrate Judges Assn., Navy League U.S., Naval Res. Officers Assn., Res. Officers Assn., Dixieland Jazz Soc. (bd. dirs. San Diego chpt. 1984—). Republican. Office: US Cts Bldg 940 Front St San Diego CA 92189-0010

MCKEEVER, PAMELA SUE, engineer; b. El Paso, Tex., Apr. 3, 1958; d. Harold R. and Carol S. (Boone) McK. BSCE, U. N.Mex., 1980; MBA, U. Phoenix, 1988. Registered profl. engr., N.Mex., Colo.; lic. gen. contractor. Energy conservation engr. Pub. Svc. Co. of N.Mex., Albuquerque, 1980-83, comml.-indsl. engr., 1983-85, supr. comml. indsl. accounts, 1985-90; project mgr. Sandia Nat. Labs., Albuquerque, 1990—. Bd. dirs. Campfire Boys and Girls, Albuquerque, 1990—; mem. City's Energy Conservation Coun., Albuquerque, 1991-94; class adminstr. Bible Study fellowship, Albuquerque, 1991-92; mentor for high sch. students Albuquerque Bus. Edn. Compact, 1988-92. Named Young Engr. of Yr. N.Mex. Soc. of Profl. Engr., 1989, Woman on the Move in Sci. and Engring. YWCA, 1988. Fellow N.Mex. Engring. Found.; mem. Project Mgmt. Inst., N.Mex. Soc. of Profl. Engrs. (state pres. 1991-92, state pres. elect, v.p., treas. 1988-91, pres. Albuquerque chpt. 1982-86, elect. v.p. treas., state dir. 1986-88). Republican. Southern Baptist.

MCKELL, CYRUS M., college dean, plant physiologist; b. Payson, Utah, Mar. 19, 1926; s. Robert D. and Mary C. (Ellsworth) McK.; m. Betty Johnson; children: Meredith Sue, Brian Marcus, John Cyrus. BS, U. Utah, 1949, MS, 1950; PhD, Oreg. State U., 1956; postgrad., U. Calif., Davis, 1957. Instr. botany Oreg. State U., Corvallis, 1955-56; research plant physiologist U. Calif. USDA-Agrl. Research Service, Davis, 1956-60; prof., dept. chmn. U. Calif., Riverside, 1960-69; prof. dept. head., dir. Utah State U., Logan, 1969-80; v.p. research NPI, Salt Lake City, 1980-88; dean Coll. of Sci. Weber State U., Ogden, Utah, 1988—; cons. Ford Found. 1968-72, Rockefeller Found., 1964-70, 89, UN, 1978, 90, NAS, 1980, 89, 91, 92, 93, USAID, 1972, UN Devel. Program, 1989. Editor Grass Biology and Utilization, 1971, Useful Wildland Shrubs, 1972, Rehabilitation of Western Wildlife Habitat, 1978, Paradoxes of Western Energy Development, 1984, Resource Inventory and Baseline Study Methods for Developing Countries, 1983, Shrub Biology and Utilization, 1989, Wilderness Issues, Arid Lands of the Western United States, 1992; contbr. numerous articles to profl. jours. Chmn. Cache County Planning Commn., Logan, 1974-79; mem. Utah Energy Conservation and Devel. Coun., 1976-79, Gov.'s Sci. Adv. Coun., 1988—, chmn. 1990-91; active Commn. of the Californias, Riverside, 1965-68. 1st lt. USAF, 1951-53. Recipient Utah Gov.'s Sci. and Tech. medal, 1990; Fulbright scholar Spain, 1967-68; World Travel grantee Rockefeller Found., 1964. Fellow AAAS (com. chmn. 1979-89, sci. exchange to China grantee 1984-85, 89, sci. panel U.S.-Chile 1987); mem. Am. Soc. Agronomy, Soc. Range Mgmt. (pres. Calif. sect. 1965, pres. Utah sect. 1982). Mem. LDS Ch. Home: 2248 E 4000 S Salt Lake City UT 84124-1864 Office: Weber State U Coll of Sci Ogden UT 84408-2501

MCKELL, LYNN J., information systems educator; b. Payson, Utah, May 25, 1943; s. Frank Joseph and Mary LaFaye (Hansen) McK.; m. Katherine Joyce Slocum, Sept. 1, 1967; children: Sean, Robert, Kenneth, J. D. B Engring. Sci., Brigham Young U., 1968; MSEE, Purdue U., 1970, MS in Ind. Mgmt., 1972, MS in Computer Sci., 1973, PhD in mgt. sci., 1973. Data base devel. staff Hill Air Force Base, Clearfield, Utah, 1966; mem. engring. design staff US Steel Geneva Works, Orem, Utah, 1967; elec. engr. Bell Telephone Labs., Indpls., 1968-70; bus. systems specialist Bell Telephone Labs., Piscataway, N.J., 1971; instr. in computer sci. Purdue U., West Lafayette, Ind., 1971-72; vis. prof. U. Minn., Mpls., 1973-74; prof. acctg. and info. systems Brigham Young U., Provo, Utah, 1974—; faculty resident Arthur Young & Co., Reston, Va., 1978-79; cons. IBM, Armonk, N.Y., 1981—, U.S. Dept. Transp., Washington, 1972-76. Co-developer software PLANMAN, 1983; patentee signal generator. Bishop Mormon Ch., Provo, 1987-92; scout master Boy Scouts Am., Provo, 1982-87; soccer coach Provo Youth Soccer League, 1990-91. With Utah NG, 1960-65. Mem. AICPA (edn./profl. devel. subcom. 1980-83), Am. Acctg. Assn., Utah Acad. Sci. Arts and Letters (div. chmn. 1989—), Decision Scis. Inst., Am. Acctg. Assn. (organizing chmn. MAS div. 1975-76). Republican. Office: Brigham Young U 536 TNRB Provo UT 84602

MCKELLIPS, GORDON WAYNE, JR., lawyer, land developer; b. Phoenix, Feb. 6, 1941; s. Gordon Wayne and Eunice J. (Fife) McK.; m. Joslyn M. Guerin, Aug. 4, 1964; children: Briant W., Eric G. BA, Duke U., 1962; JD, U. Ariz., 1965. Bar: Ariz. 1965. Officer, dir. McKellips Land Corp., Phoenix, 1966—, Gem Land Co., Phoenix, 1982—, Willow Valley Water Co., Inc., Mohave Valley, Ariz., 1966—, Granite Reef Farms, Inc., Mohave Valley, Ariz., 1966—; assoc. Carson Messinger Elliott Laughlin and Ragan, Phoenix, 1965-70, ptnr., 1971—. Editorial bd. Ariz. Law Rev., 1965. Com. mem. North Phoenix Young Life, 1989—. Fellow Ariz. Bar Found.; mem. Plaza Club. Republican. Office: Carson Messinger Elliott Laughlin Ragan 3300 N Central Ave Ste 1900 Phoenix AZ 85012-2577

MC KENNA, MARIAN CECILIA, historian; b. Scarsdale, N.Y., July 3, 1926; d. John Francis and Marguerite (Hanfling) McK. BS, Columbia U., 1949, MA, 1950, PHD in History (Am. Philos. Soc. Penrose award 1952-53, Erb fellow), 1953. Instr. Hunter Coll., CUNY, 1953-59; assoc. prof. Manhattanville Coll., Purchase, N.Y., 1959-66; prof. Am . history U. Calgary, Alta., Can., 1966—; cons. Nat. Endowment for Humanities. Author: Borah, 1960, Pictorial History of Catholicism, 1961, Myra Hess: a Portrait, 1976, Tapping Reeve and the Litchfield Law School, 1986, Canadian and American Constitutions in Comparative Perspectives, 1993. Recipient Can. Coun. award, 1967, 68, 69, 72, 76, Social Scis. and Humanities Rsch. Coun. Can. award, 1989, Faculty of Social Sci. Disting. Tchr. award U. Calgary, 1993; Danforth fellow, 1965. Mem. Orgn. Am. Historians, Am. Hist. Assn., Am. Soc. Legal History. Roman Catholic. Home: 3343 Upton Pl NW, Calgary, AB Canada T2N 4G9 Office: U Calgary, History Dept, 2500 University Dr NW, Calgary, AB Canada T2N 1N4

MCKENZIE, ALLAN DEAN, art historian, consultant; b. Pendleton, Oreg., Aug. 17, 1930; s. Hugh Samuel and Helen Josephine (Raymond) McK.; m. Mary Joyce Matson, June 30, 1955 (div. 1961); children—Donald, Kathleen; m. Lucile Irene Johnston, Dec. 21, 1982. B.A., San Jose State U., 1952; M.A., U. Calif.-Berkeley, 1955; Ph.D., NYU, 1965. Instr., NYU, N.Y.C., 1957-59, 60-64; asst. prof. U. Wis.-Milw., 1964-66; assoc. prof. medieval art U. Oreg., Eugene, 1966-74, prof., 1974-90; prof. emeritus, 1990—. Author: Greek and Russian Icons, 1965; Russian Art: Old and New, 1968; Russian Icons in the Santa Barbara Museum of Art, 1982; Windows to Heaven: Icons of Russia, 1982, Mystical Mirrors: Russian Icons in the Maryhill Museum of Art, 1986; Sacred Images and The Millennium: Christianity and Russia, 1988. Served with U.S. Army, 1954-56. Recipient Founders' Day Scholastic award NYU, 1966, Samuel H. Kress grant, 1986; Fulbright scholar, 1959; Internat. Rsch. Exch. Bd. ad hoc grantee, 1973. Mem. Internat. Ctr. Medieval Art, Archaeol. Inst. Am. (chpt. pres. 1969-71, 73-75, 76-77, 87-88, 90-92). Office: Dept Art History U Oreg Eugene OR 97403

MCKENZIE, JAMES MILTON, excavating company executive; b. Fairbury, Nebr., Mar. 10, 1945; s. Donald Eugene and Elizabeth June (Green) McK.; m. Alice Jay Unrath, July 31, 1971; children: Matthew James, Sabrina Alice. Student, Colo. State U., Ft. Collins, 1965-66. Heavy equipment operator Valley Excavating, Inc., Boulder, Colo., 1968-73, owner, pres., 1973—; cons. bldg. trades dept. Boulder Valley Dist. Vocat. Tech. Sch., 1985—. Adviser Boulder area Boy Scouts Am., 1983—. Sgt. U.S. Army, 1966-68, Vietnam. Mem. Boulder C. of C. (Small Bus. of Yr. 1991), Am. Legion, Elks. Republican. Presbyterian. Office: Valley Excavating Inc 1726 N 63d St Boulder CO 80301

MCKENZIE, NEIL ROBIN, computer scientist, researcher; b. Watsonville, Calif., Mar. 13, 1961; s. Keith Sylvio and Della Marie (Christopherson) McK.; m. Angela Rose Thalls, July 6, 1991. BSEE, U. Calif., Berkeley, 1983; MS in Computer Sci., U. Wash., 1989. Engr. Imagic, Los Gatos, Calif., 1982-84; pvt. practice cons. Cupertino, Calif., 1984-85, 86-87; engr. Via Video, Santa Clara, Calif., 1985-86, Wyse Tech., San Jose, Calif., 1986; rsch. asst. Univ. Wash., Seattle, 1987-89, 91—; engr. Laseraccess Corp., Bothell, Wash., 1990-91; cons. Magnetic Peripherals, Inc., Santa Clara, 1984-85, Aurora Systems, Inc., San Francisco, 1987. Recipient Tektronix fellowship Tektronix, Inc., Beaverton, Oreg., 1991. Mem. IEEE, Assn. for Computing Machinery, Tau Beta Pi, Eta Kappa Nu. Home: 3022 NW 66th St Seattle WA 98117 Office: Univ Wash Dept CSE FR-35 Seattle WA 98195

MCKEON, HOWARD P. (BUCK), congressman, mayor; b. Los Angeles; m. Patricia; 6 children. BS, Brigham Young U. Mem. Coun. City of Santa Clarita, Calif., 1987-92, mayor, 1987-88; mem. 103rd Congress from 25th Calif. dist., 1993—; founding dir., chmn. Valencia Nat. Bank; co-owner Howard & Phil's Western Wear, Inc. Hon. chmn. Leukemia Soc. Celebrity program, 1990, Red Cross Community Support Campaign, 1992; active Dist. Com. Boy Scouts Am.; chmn., trustee William S. Hart Sch. Dist., 1979-87; chmn., dir. Henry Mayo Newhall Meml. Hosp., 1983-87; mem. Calif. Rep. State Ctrl. Com., 1988-92; bd. dirs. Santa Clarita Valley Small Bus. Devel. Ctr., 1990-92, Canyon Country C. of C., 1988-92. Office: US Ho of Reps 307 Cannon Ho Office Bldg Washington DC 20515

MCKERRACHER, DAVID MICHAEL, educator; b. Pasadena, Calif., Sept. 11, 1949; s. William Findlayson and Sylvia (Cramer) McK.; m. Llyn Carol Fritz, Jan. 6, 1969; children: Rebbecca, Sarah, Joshuah. BA, So. Calif. Coll., 1981; postgrad., Calif. State U., Long Beach, 1982; MRE, So. Calif. Theol. Sem., 1983, ThD, 1985. Cert. tchr., Wash. Evangelist, radio speaker Ch. of God, 1972-75; missionary overseer Ch. of God, Scotland, Ireland, 1975-81; sr. pastor Fairwood Assembly of God, Seattle, 1984-86; archtl. designer Mercer II Wash, Seattle, 1986-88; prof. West Coast Coll., Fresno, Calif., 1988-90; tchr. high sch. Federal Way Sch. Dist., Seattle, 1991-92; tchr. spl. request Renton and Kent Sch. Dists., 1992-93; pioneer of over 20 ministries, Hollywood, Germany, Scotland, 1969-81; sr. pastor Assemblies of God, Renton, Wash., 1984-86; pres., ceo Thelamon Inc., Renton, 1986-92. Author: Greek Grammar, 1985, History of the World, 1991; author stress mgmt. booklet; creator various seminars, including Growing in Love (1st, 2d,3d place European Art Contest 1972). Counsellor Good Neighbor Ctr., Renton, 1985-88, West Coast Coll. Counseling Ctr., Fresno, 1988-90; teen camp supr. Assembly of God, Calif., 1980-91. With U.S. Army, 1970-73. Mem. NEA, Wash. Edn. Assn., Kent Edn. Assn., Communicators Club Am. (Speaker of Yr. 1973).

MCKEVITT, GERALD LAWRENCE, priest, historian; b. Longview, Wash., July 3, 1939; s. Edward Henry and Evelyn (Acock) McK. BA, U. San Francisco, 1961; MA, U. So. Calif., L.A., 1964; PhD, UCLA, 1972; BST, Gregorian U., Rome, 1975. Ordained priest Roman Cath. Ch., 1975. Univ. archivist Santa Clara (Calif.) U., 1975-85, chmn. history dept., 1984-88, prof. history, 1975—, univ. historian, 1985—. Author: Univ. of Santa Clara, A History, 1851-1977; contbr. articles to profl. jours. Trustee Gonzaga U., Spokane, 1988, Santa Clara U., 1993—; mem. Nat. Seminar on Jesuit Higher Edn., 1990—. Fellow NSF, 1985-87, U.S. Dept. Health, Edn. and Welfare, 1961-63; recipient Oscar O. Winther award, 1991. Mem. Am. Hist. Assn., Am. Cath. Hist. Assn., Am. Italian Hist. Assn., Am. Soc. Ch. History, Western History Assn., Calif. Hist. Soc. Roman Catholic. Home: Univ Santa Clara Nobili Hall Santa Clara CA 95053 Office: Santa Clara Univ History Dept Santa Clara CA 95053

MCKEWON, KAREN LEE, accountant; b. Stillwater, Okla., Aug. 25, 1952; d. Kerry Duane Jackson and Mickey Lee (Wright) Conklin; m. John Dean McKewon, June 9, 1978; children: Jenny Lee, Jackie Rae. BS, Northeastern State U., 1974. Field rep. Sigma Sigma Sigma, Inc., Woodstock, Va., 1975-76; store mgr. Pizza Hut, Inc., Tulsa, 1976-77, Long John Silvers, Inc., Tulsa, 1977-78; accts. payable supr. Mini Mart, Inc., Casper, Wyo., 1979-81; asst. banking, cashflow analyst Energy Distributing/Convience Plus, Inc., Casper, 1991—. Vol. Spl. Olympics, Casper, 1989; directory chmn. Verda James Parent Tchr. Orgn., Casper, 1990-92, enrichment chmn., 1991-92; youth volleyball coach YMCA, Casper, 1991, 92. Mem. Youth Sports Coaches Assn. Home: 951 Waterford Casper WY 82609

MCKIBBEN, HOWARD D., federal judge; b. Apr. 1, 1940; s. James D. and Bernice McKibben; m. Mary Ann McKibben, July 2, 1966; children: Mark, Susan. B.S., Bradley U., 1962; M.P.A., U. Pitts., 1964; J.D., U. Mich., 1967. Assoc. George W. Abbott Law Office, 1967-71; dep. dist. atty. Douglas County, Nev., 1969-71, dist. atty., 1971-77; dist. ct. judge State of Nev., 1977-84; judge U.S. Dist. Ct. Nev., Reno, 1984—. Mem. ABA, Nev. Bar Assn., Am. Inns of Ct. (pres. Nev. chpt. 1986-88). Methodist. Home: PO Box 588 Verdi NV 89439-0588 Office: US Dist Ct 300 Booth St Rm 5137 Reno NV 89509-1384

MCKIM, HARRIET MEGCHELSEN, education educator; b. Keokuk, Iowa, Oct. 17, 1919; d. Herbert John and Florence Josephine (Ottowa) Megchelsen; m. Lanier McClure, Nov. 1, 1944 (div. 1948); 1 child, Janet Gray; m. L.A. McKim, July 28, 1950 (div. 1968). BA, Calif. State U., Sacramento, 1952; MA, U. So. Calif., 1963, EdD, 1979. Tchr., prin. Cumberland County Schs., Crossville, Tenn., 1939-42; sec. Tenn. Valley Authority, Oak Ridge Def. Plant, Mare Island Naval Shipyard and Cal-West Ins., 1942-52; tchr., vice-prin., reading specialist, dir. ESEA I various pub. schs., Oxnard, Orcutt, Sacramento, Edwards AFB, Calif. and Spokane, Wash., 1950-64; coord. Yuba City and Yuba County Schs., 1964-70; cons.

Calif. Dept. Edn., 1970-83; part-time instr. Alan Hancock Community Coll., Santa Maria, Calif., Polytech. U., San Luis Obispo, Calif., U. Calif., Davis, Santa Barbara, 1960-70; supr. student tchrs. Calif. State U., Sacramento, 1984; adj. prof. edn. Nat. U., Sacramento, 1986-88. Vol. tchr. ARC parenting classes, Sacramento, 1984-85; docent, speaker Crocker Art Mus.; vol. Loaves and Fishes; bd. dirs. Sacramento Internat. Students' coun., Friends of Libr. Calif. State U., Elderhostel Calif. State U.; docent Sacramento History Ctr.; deacon Fremont Presbyn. Ch. Mem. AAUW, Nat. Assn. Edn. Young Children, Calif. Retired Tchrs., Am. Assn. Retired Persons Assn., Profs. of Early Childhood Edn., Sacramento Affiliates, Amnesty Internat., Sierra Club, Delta Kappa Gamma, Phi Delta Kappa. Address: 5332 State Ave Sacramento CA 95819

MCKINLEY, JOSEPH WARNER, health science facility executive; b. Champaign, Ill., Jan. 9, 1943; s. Lyle Warner and Eloise M. (Coleman) McK. BS, Georgetown U., 1968; MBA, George Washington U., 1973. Asst. adminstr. Weiss Meml. Hosp., Chgo., 1973-75; assoc. v.p. Rockford (Ill.) Meml. Hosp., 1975-78; v.p. ops. Phoenix Meml. Hosp., 1978-84, exec. v.p., chief exec. officer, 1984-88; exec. v.p. St. Francis Med. Ctr., Lynwood, Calif., 1988-90; chief exec. officer Meridian Point Rehab. Hosp., Scottsdale, Ariz., 1990—. Capt. U.S. Army, 1968-71, Vietnam. Mem. Am. Coll. of Healthcare Execs., Am. Hosp. Assn., Ariz. Club, Plaza Club. Republican. Episcopalian. Home: 6 Colonia Miramonte Paradise Valley AZ 85253 Office: Meridian Point Rehab Hosp 11250 N 92nd St Scottsdale AZ 85250

MCKINNEY, BETTY JO, publisher; b. Maryville, Mo., July 16; d. Joseph Glenn and Virginia Joy (Schubert) Thomas; student N.W. Mo. State U., 1959, Tarkio (Mo.) Coll., 1960-62, Colo. State U., 1967-69; m. George Wendell McKinney, Jan. 29, 1966. Asst. dir. office public relations, Tarkio Coll., 1963-65; publ. specialist office univ. communications, Colo. State U., Ft. Collins, 1966-81; founder, pres., partner Alpine Publs., Loveland, Colo., 1975-80, pub., 1980—. Mem. Dog Writers Assn. Am., Am. Kennel Club. Am. Shetland Sheepdog Club, Com. Small Mag. Editors and Pubs., Rocky Mountain Pubs. Assn. Author: Sheltie Talk, 1976, rev., 1985; Beardie Basics, 1978. Address: 1901 S Garfield St Loveland CO 80537 Office: Alpine Publications 225 S Madison Loveland CO 80537

MC KINNEY, ROBERT MOODY, newspaper editor and publisher; b. Shattuck, Okla., Aug. 28, 1910; s. Edwin S. and Eva (Moody) McK.; married, 1943; 1 child, Mrs. Meade Martin; m. Marie-Louise de Montmollin, May 7, 1970. AB, U. Okla., 1932; LLD, U. N.Mex., 1964. Investment analyst Standard Stats. Co., Inc. (now Standard and Poor's Co.), 1932-34; ptnr. Young-Kolbe & Co., 1934-38, Robert R. Young & Co., 1938-42; exec. v.p., treas. Pathe Film Co., 1934-39, Allegheny Corp., 1936-42, Pittston Corp. and subs., 1936-42; v.p. Fremkir Corp., 1937-50, Allan Corp., 1937-50; exec. v.p., treas. Mo. Pacific R.R., 1938-42; ptnr. Scheffmeyer, McKinney & Co., 1945-50; editor, pub. Santa Fe New Mexican, 1949—; chmn. bd. The New Mexican, Inc., 1949—; profl. corp. dir. 10 N.Y.S.E. cos., 1934-86; chmn. Robert Moody Found.; chmn. N.Mex. Econ. Devel. Commn. and Water Resources Devel. Bd., 1949-51; asst. sec. U.S. Dept. Interior, 1951-52; chmn. panel to report to Congress on impact of Peaceful Uses of Atomic Energy, 1955-56; permanent U.S. rep. to Internat. Atomic Energy Agy., Vienna, 1957-58; U.S. rep. Internat. Conf. Peaceful Uses Atomic Energy, Geneva, 1958; U.S. ambassador to Switzerland, 1961-63; exec. officer Presdl. Task Force on Internat. Investments, 1963-64; chmn. Presdl. Commn. on Travel, 1968; chmn. bd. visitors U. Okla., 1968-72; U.S. rep. Internat. Centre Settlement Investment Disputes, Washington, 1967-74. Author: Hymn to Wreckage: A Picaresque Interpretation of History, 1947, The Scientific Foundation for European Integration, 1959, On Increasing Effectiveness of Western Science and Technology, 1959, The Red Challenge to Technological Renewal, 1960, Review of the International Policies and Programs of the United States, 1960, The Toad and the Water Witch, 1985, Variations on a Marxist Interpretation of Culture, 1986. Served from lt. (j.g.) to lt. USNR, 1942-45. Recipient Disting. Service medal U.S. Dept. Treasury, 1968, Disting. Service medal U. Okla., 1972. Mem. Am. Soc. Newspaper Editors, Coun. Fgn. Rels., Newspaper Assn. of Am., Phi Beta Kappa, Phi Gamma Delta. Democrat. Episcopalian. Clubs: Chevy Chase (Md.); F Street, Metropolitan (Washington); University, Brook, Century, Links, Knickerbocker, River (N.Y.C.). Home: Wind Fields RR 1 Box 64 Middleburg VA 22117-9411 Office: PO Box 1705 Santa Fe NM 87504-1705

MC KINNON, CLINTON D., editor, former congressman; b. Dallas, Feb. 5, 1906; s. John C. and Tennie Clifdell (Hawkins) McK.; m. Lucille Virginia McVey, Oct. 15, 1932; children—Clinton Dan, Michael, Connie. A.B., U. Redlands, Calif., 1930, L.H.D. (hon.), 1967; postgrad., U. Geneva, Switzerland, 1930. Reporter, editor, advt. mgr. on various So. Calif. newspapers, 1931-35; pres., gen. mgr. Valley News Corp., North Hollywood, Calif., 1935-43; established San Fernando Valley Times, 1935, Los Angeles Aircraft Times, 1940, Long Beach Shipyard Times, 1941; established San Diego Daily Jour., 1944, editor, pub. and owner, 1944-48; co-owner Coronado Jour., 1953-72; owner Radio Sta. KSDJ (Columbia affiliate), San Diego, 1945-48; pres., editor and pub. Los Angeles Daily News, 1954; pres., gen. mgr. Alvarado Television Co., Inc., KVOA-TV, Tucson and KOAT-TV, Albuquerque, 1955-63; chmn. San Diego North Shores Pub. Co., San Diego, 1953-72, Sentinel Savs. and Loan Assn., 1963-69, San Diego Transit Co., 1966-71; sec. South Tex. Telecasting Co. Inc., 1963-79; Chmn. Indsl. Devel. Commn., San Diego, 1964-66, Econ. Devel. Corp., San Diego County, 1966-67, San Diego Urban Coalition, 1967-69; mem. Gov.'s Bus. Adv. Council, Calif. Bd. dirs. U. Calif., San Diego Sch. Medicine, 1979—; bd. dirs. Cancer Center Research Bd., U. Calif., San Diego, 1981—; Mem. 81st-82d Congresses from Calif.; vice chmn. Democratic State Central Com. of Calif., 1952-54. Recipient San Diego Golden Man and Boy award, 1968; San Diego Mayor's award of merit, 1971; named to San Diego Transit Hall Fame, 1987. Clubs: Rotarian, San Diego Yacht. Home: 1125 Pacific Beach Dr Apt 401 San Diego CA 92109-5155 Office: 4425 Cass St San Diego CA 92109-4015

MCKINNON, JAMES BUCKNER, real estate sales executive, writer, researcher; b. Tacoma, Dec. 5, 1916; s. James Mitchell and Rochelle Lenore (Buckner) McK.; m. Mary C. Corbitt, Dec. 1961 (div. June 1963); 1 child, James H.C.; m. Marylyn Adelle Coote, Mar. 12, 1967 (div. May 1977); 1 child, Michelyn; m. Martha Sackmann, June 12, 1977. BA in Internat. Studies, U. Wash., 1983, H.M. Jackson Sch. Police detective Los Angeles Police Dept., 1946-50; bn. security officer 1st med. bn. 1st Marine div. Fleet Marine Force, 1950-53; owner, operator, mgr., dir. promotional sales The Saucy Dog Drive-In, Venice, Calif., 1953-63; salesman new car sales and leasing Burien Mercury, Seattle, 1963-66; real estate salesman and appraiser various firms Seattle, 1966—; instr., lectr. U.S. Naval Support Activity, Sandpoint, Wash., 1964-74; mem., lectr. NRC 11-8, Naval Postgrad. Sch., Monterey, Calif., 1975-76; Burien Mercury announcer KOMO TV. Author: (poetry) On the Threshold of a Dream, Vol. III, 1992, Best Poems of the 90's, 1992; published poetry in anthologies; contbr. articles to various newspapers and mil. jours. Mem. br. adv. com. Wash. State YMCA, Seattle, treas., 1988-93, mem. so. dist. fin. bd., 1989-93. With USN, 1939-53, PTO, Korea. Recipient Wilmer Culver Meml. award Culver Alumni Fictioneers, Seattle, 1979, Silver Poet award World of Poetry Press, 1986, Golden Poet award, 1987-92, Best Poet of the 90's Nat. Libr. of Poetry, 1992; Occidental Coll. scholar, 1935; named to Honorable Order Ky. Cols., 1976; named One of Best New Poets, Am. Poetry Assn. Anthology, 1988. Mem. Internat. Platform Assn., U.S. Naval Inst., N.W. Writers Conf., Ret. Officers Assn. (life), Mensa, KP, Masons, Internat. Soc. Poets. Republican. Home: 2312 41st Ave SW Seattle WA 98116-2060

MCKINNON, JOHN KENNETH, commissioner; b. Winnipeg, Man., Can., Apr. 20, 1936; m. Judy Steven; children: Craig, Alexia. Student, St. Paul's Coll., Winnipeg; BA in Polit. Scis., U. Man. Commr. of the Yukon Whitehorse, 1986—; mgr., shareholder, dir. No. TV Systems Ltd., apptd. v.p., gen. mgr., 1984; shareholder, dir. Klondike Broadcasting Co. Ltd., Whitehorse Motors Ltd.; mem. Yukon Legis. Assembly, 1961, 67, 70, 74; mem. fin. adv. com. Yukon Territorial Govt., 1962-64, chmn. fin. adv. com., 1968-70; minister local govt., 1974; minister hwys. and pub. works, 1976; co-chmn. Alaska Hwy. Gas Pipeline hearings, 1979; Yukon adminstr. No. Pipeline Agy., 1979-84. 1st v.p. Porter Creek Citizens' Assn.; 1st bd. dirs. Skookum Jim Friendship Ctr.; pres. 1st Arctic Winter Games Corp.; mem. Yukon Basketball team Can. Winter Games, Arctic Winter Games; hon. chief Yukon Native Brotherhood; mem. task force No. Conservation, 1983-84; chmn. No. Resources Scholarship Com.; hon. chmn. Yukon Anniversaries Commn.; hon. mem. Yukon Arts Coun. Recipient Internat. Travel bursary to study in Japan, Rotary Club, 1970, Gov. Gen.'s Centennial medal, 1967, Queen's Silver Jubilee medal, 1977, Gov. Gen.'s Can. 125 medal. Mem. Arctic Inst. of No. Am. (bd. dirs. 1987), Coun. for Can. Unity (Yukon pres. 1987), Yukon C. of C. (hon.), Whitehorse C. of C. (hon.), Whitehorse Rotary Club (hon.). Office: Office of the Commr, 211 Hawkins St, Whitehorse, YK Canada Y1A 1X3*

MCKINNON, PAUL DAMIEN, chiropractor; b. Marville, France, Apr. 7, 1961; came to U.S., 1963; s. John David and Joan Mary (McGrath) McK. BA in Biology, Colgate U., 1986; D Chiropractic, L.A. Coll. Chiropractic, 1990. Ptnr. Huntington Chiro Care, 1992—; part-time faculty mem. L.A. Coll. Chiropractic, Whittier, Calif., 1991. Mem. Health Svcs. Com., Fountain Valley, 1992. Mem. Am. Chiropractic Assoc., Calif. Chiropractic Assoc., Am. Acad. Indsl. Cons., Fountain Valley C. of C. Home: 205 15th St # 11 Huntington Beach CA 92648

MCKINNON, SUSAN, artist, educator; b. Portland, Oreg., Nov. 16, 1949; d. John William and Eleanor Jean (Tice) McKinnon; m. Donald Morris Rasmussen, Jr., Aug. 7, 1971 (div. Nov. 1989); m. Bernard Ross Kliks, Sept. 12, 1992. BA in Humanities and Social Sci., Oreg. State U., 1971. Mgr. Clair's, Hillsboro, Oreg., 1971-72; mgr., buyer The Clothes Tree, Portland, 1972-78; artist, educator, Portland, 1978—; condr. workshops in field; exhibited in numerous group shows, 1982—, including. Numerous one-woman shows, 1979—; exhibited in numerous group shows, 1982—, including Midwest Watercolor Soc., West Bend, Wis., 1982, 85, Nat. Watercolor Soc., 1983, 87, La. Watercolor Soc., New Orleans, 1984, 85, 86, Catharine Lorillard Wolfe Art Club, 1983, 85, 86, Audubon Artists, N.Y.C., 1984, 86, 87. Watercolor USA, Springfield, Mo., 1987, 91, 92, Fedn. Can. Artists, Vancouver, B.C., 1989, N.W. Watercolor Soc., Kirkland, Wash., 1992; works represented in various publs. Mem. activities coun. Oreg. Art Inst., Portland, 1987-89. Mem. Nat. Watercolor Soc. (regional rep.), Westcoast Watercolor Soc., N.W. Watercolor Soc., Watercolor West, Audubon Artists, Midwest Watercolor Soc. (assoc., bd. dirs. 1983-85), Am. Watercolor Soc. (assoc.), Oreg. Soc. Artists, Watercolor Critique Group, Watercolor Soc. Oreg. (v.p. 1983-85, pres. 1985-87, bd. dirs. 1987-89, bronze merit award 1984, gold and silver merit awards 1985, platinum award 1986, diamond award 1992), Catharine Lorillard Wolfe Art Club. Republican. Home and Studio: 2225 SW Winchester Portland OR 97225

MCKINSTRY, RONALD EUGENE, lawyer; b. Bakersfield, Calif., Aug. 11, 1926; s. Melville Jack and Lillian Agatha (Saner) McK.; m. Shirley Danner, June 19, 1948; children: Michael R., Jill I. McKinstry Epperson, Jeffrey A., Carol A. McKinstry Sundquist. BS, U. Wash., 1950, JD, 1951. Bar: Wash. 1951, U.S. Ct. Claims 1970, U.S. Ct. Appeals (D.C. cir.) 1981, U.S. Supreme Ct. 1982. Assoc. Evans, McLaren, Lane, Powell & Beeks, Seattle, 1951-55, Bogle, Bogle & Gates, Seattle, 1955-61; ptnr., chmn. litigation dept. Bogle & Gates, Seattle, 1962-91, chmn. litigation dept., 1970-91, ptnr., 1970-91; sr. trial ptnr. Ellis Li & McKinstry, Seattle, 1992—; apptd. spl. master by U.S. Dist. Ct. (we. dist.) Wash., 1976-81, apptd. settlement mediator, 1980—. Editor-in-chief Washington Civil Procedure Before Trial Deskbook, 1981, Supplement to Deskbook, 1986; contbr. articles to profl. jours. With USN, 1944-46, PTO. Recipient Svc. award Western Ctr. for Law and Religious Freedom, 1990. Fellow Am. Coll. Trial Lawyers (regent 1978-82); mem. ABA, Internat. Assn. Def. Counsel (mem. exec. com. 1974-78), AAA Club Wash. (mem. exec. com. 1983—), Seattle Tennis Club. Republican. Mem. Mercer Island Covenant Ch. Office: Ellis Li & McKinstry 3700 First Interstate Ctr 999 Third Ave Seattle WA 98104-4001

MCKNIGHT, LENORE RAVIN, child psychiatrist; b. Denver, May 15, 1943; d. Abe and Rose (Steed) Ravin; m. Robert Lee McKnight, July 22, 1967; children: Richard Rex, Janet Rose. Student, Occidental Coll., 1961-63; BA, U. Colo., 1965, postgrad. in medicine, 1965-67; MD, U. Calif., San Francisco, 1969. Diplomate Am. Bd. Psychiatry and Neurology. Cert. adult and child psychiatrist Am. Bd. Psychiatry. Intern pediatrics Children's Hosp., San Francisco, 1969-70; resident in gen. psychiatry Langley Porter Neuropsychiat. Inst., 1970-73, fellow child psychiatry, 1972-74; child psychiatrist Youth Guidance Center, San Francisco, 1974-74; pvt. practice medicine specializing in child psychiatry, Walnut Creek, Calif., 1974—; asst. clin. prof. Langley Porter Neuropsychiat. Inst., 1974—; clin. assoc. in psychiatry, U. Calif. at Davis Med. Sch; asst. clin. prof. psychiatry U. Calif. San Francisco Med. Ctr. Internat.; med. dir. CPC Walnut Creek (Calif.) Hosp., 1990—. Insts. Edn. fellow U. Edinburgh, 1964; NIH grantee to study childhood nutrition, 1966. Mem. Am. Acad. Child Psychiatry, Am. Psychiat. Assn., Am. Coll. Physician Execs., Psychiat. Assn. No. Calif., Am. Med. Women's Assn., Internat. Arabian Horse Assn., Diablo Arabian Horse Assn. Avocation: breeding Arabian Horses. Office: 130 La Casa Via Walnut Creek CA 94598-3008

MC KNIGHT, WILLIAM WARREN, JR., publisher; b. Normal, Ill., June 9, 1913; s. William Warren and Isabel Alida (Travis) McK.; m. Alice McGuire, Oct. 30, 1937; children: William Warren, III, Michael Joe, John James. B.S. in Bus. Adminstrn., Northwestern U., 1938. With McKnight Pub. Co., Bloomington, Ill., 1938-83; sec.-treas. McKnight Pub. Co., 1949-56, pres., 1956-67, chmn. bd., 1968-79; bd. dirs. Gen. Telephone Co. Ill., Champion Fed. Savs. & Loan Assn., chmn. bd. Pres. Bloomington Rotary Club, 1952, Bloomington C. of C., 1954; mem. Ill. Commn. Higher Edn., 1956-60; chmn. Bloomington-Normal Airport Authority, 1965-70, CETA Pvt. Industry Council Ill. Balance of State, 1979-81. Served with USNR, 1942-46. Recipient Disting. Service award Bloomington Kiwanis Club, 1963, Disting. Service award Normal C. of C., 1973; Good Govt. award Bloomington Jaycees, 1970; Edn. Constrn. award Edn. Council Graphic Arts Industry, 1974; Disting. Alumni award Ill. State U., 1978; Disting. Service award Spirit of McLean County, 1982; Disting. Service citation Epsilon Pi Tau, 1983; award of Merit Am. Vocat. Assn., 1990. Mem. Graphic Arts Edn. Assn., Internat. Tech. Edn. Assn., Nat. Assn. Indsl. and Tech. Tchrs. Educators, Ill. C. of C. (dir. 1964-69), Ill. Mfrs. Assn. (dir. 1954-62). Republican. Presbyterian. Clubs: Coll. Alumni, Bloomington Country. Home: 401 W Vernon Normal IL 61761 Home (winter): 7788 Stallion Rd Scottsdale AZ 85258

MCKOWN, JANNA LYN, pharmacist; b. Ulysses, Kans., Mar. 22, 1955; d. Harold Virgil and Lillian Blanche (Everett) Farmer; m. David Ross McKown, May 10, 1986; 1 child, Jenna Leilani. Student, Otero Jr. Coll., 1973-74; AA, Barton County C.C., 1974-75; BS in Pharmacy, U. Kans., 1978. Registered pharmacist, Tex., Kans., Hawaii. Mgr. pharmacy Eckerd Drugs, Dallas, 1978-80, 82-85, Preston Forest Pharmacy, Dallas., 1980-81; computer sales staff Radix Comp Corp., Dallas., 1981-82; staff pharmacist Dillons Pharmacy, Great Bend, Kans., 1985-86; staff pharmacist Longs Drugs, Lahaina, Hawaii, 1986-89, Kahului, Hawaii, 1989-91; over the counter mgr. and pharmacy mgr. Longs Drugs, Kihei, Hawaii, 1991—; pres. Over The Rainbow, Inc., Kihei, 1986—. Bd. dirs. Maui Childbirth Edn., Wailuku, Hawaii, 1991. Mem. Hawaii Pharmacy Assn. Republican. Home: 186 Mehani Cir Kihei HI 96753

MCKUSICK, MARSHALL KIRK, computer scientist; b. Wilmington, Del., Jan. 19, 1954; s. Blaine Chase and Marjorie Jane (Kirk) McK. BSEE with distinction, Cornell U., 1976; MS in Bus. Adminstrn., U. Calif., Berkeley, 1979, MS in Computer Sci., 1980, PhD in Computer Sci., 1984. System designer Hughes Aircraft Co., 1977-79; software cons., 1982—; rsch. computer scientist U. Calif., Berkeley, 1984-93. Author: The Design and Implementation of the 4.3BSD UNIX Operating System, 1989, translated into German, 1990, Japanese, 1991, The Design and Implementation of the 4.3BSD UNIX Operating System Answer Book, 1991, translated into Japanese, 1992; contbr. to profl. publs. Mem. IEEE, Usenix Assn., Assn. Computing Machinery. Democrat. Office: 1614 Oxford St Berkeley CA 94709-1608

MCLAIN, JOHN LOWELL, resource specialist, consultant; b. Havre, Mont., Jan. 23, 1942; s. Woodrow B. and Ann Teresa (Bolta) McL.; m. Carolyn Louise Peterson, June 27, 1964; children: Nicole Rachelle, Tanya Lynn. BS in Range Mgmt., Mont. State U., 1969. Cert. range mgmt. cons.; cert. soil erosion & sediment control specialist. Soil conservationist USDA Soil Conservation Svc., Miles City, Mont., 1969-71; range conservationist USDA Soil Conservation Svc., Glendive, Mont., 1971-74; area range conservationist USDA Soil Conservation Svc., Minden, Nev., 1974-76, dist. conservationist, 1976-78; prin. resource specialist Resource Concepts Inc., Carson City, Nev., 1978—; bd. dirs. Range Mag., Carson City. Mem. citizens adv. bd. U. Nev.-Reno, 1981-92; Nev. del. Coun. for Agrl. Rsch. Ext. & Teaching, Washington, 1983—. Recipient Outstanding Achievement award Carson Valley Conservation Dist., 1978; named Man of 1980s Carson City Appeal newspaper, 1980. Mem. Soc. for Range Mgmt. (pres. Nev. sect. 1980, Rangeman of Yr. Nev. sect. 1981), Soil Conservation Soc. (pres. Nev. sect. 1980), Soc. Range Mgmt (dir. 1993—), Resource Restoration Internat. (mem. adv. com. 1992—). Roman Catholic. Home: 2424 Manhattan Dr Carson City NV 89703 Office: Resource Concepts Inc 340 N Minnesota St Carson City NV 89703

MCLANE, BETSY ANN, association administrator; b. Erie, Pa.; d. Robert R. and Phyllis C. (Zaun) McL. BSc, Ithaca (N.Y.) Coll., 1974; MA, U. So. Calif., L.A., 1978, PhD, 1983. Asst. prof. U. Vt., Burlington; v.p. mktg. Direct Cinema Ltd., Santa Monica, Calif.; exec. dir. Internat. Documentary Assn., L.A.; adj. prof. L.A. program Emerson Coll.; alternate adv. panel on classic Am. films Libr. of Congress. contbr. articles to profl. jours. Mem. U. Film Video Assn. (pres. 1986-88). Office: Internat Documentary Assn 1551 S Robertson Blvd #201 Los Angeles CA 90035

MCLAREN, ARCHIE CAMPBELL, JR, marketing executive; b. Atlanta, Sept. 25, 1942; s. Archie Campbell and Virginia Lynn (Sides) McL.; m. Georgia Mae Blunt, 1969 (div. 1971); 1 child, Leslie Michelle. BA, Vanderbilt U., 1964; JD, Memphis State U., 1968. Clk. FBI, Memphis, 1965-66; tchr., tennis coach Memphis U. Sch., 1966-68; tchr. Hunt High Sch., Columbus, Miss., 1968-69; tennis coach Miss. State U., Starkville, Miss., 1968-69; concierge The Roosevelt Hotel, New Orleans, 1969-70; sales rep. West Pub. Co., St. Paul, 1970-84, adminstr. internat. mktg. The Orient, 1985-90; freelance wine cons., 1985—; cons. Calif. Ctrl. Coast Wine Growers Assn., Santa MAria, 1987-91; lectr. advanced wine appreciation Calif. Poly. U. Extended Edn., San Luis Obispo, 1986-90; dir. KCBX Ctrl. Coast Wine Classic, San Luis Obispo, 1985—, KHPR Wine Calssic, Honolulu, 1987-91, Winesong, Ft. Bragg, Calif., 1987—, WETA Washington Wine Classic, 1989-90, KCRW Summerday, 1991. Dir. Avila Beach County Water Dist., 1992—; bd. dirs. San Luis Obispo Calif. Mozart Festival, 1988-92, pres., 1991, 92, dir. Internat. festival of Champagne and Sparkling Wine, 1992—, Santa Barbara Wine Auction, 1992—; mem. Avila Valley adv. coun., 1993—. Mem. Calif. Cen. Coast Wine Soc. (pres. 1985), Am. Soc. Wine Educators, German Wine Soc. Honolulu, Vintners Club San Francisco, Avila Bay Wine Soc., Cen. Coast Chaine des Rotisseurs (chpt. pres. 1987, 88, 89), Marin County Food and Wine Soc., Internat. Food, Wine & Travel Writers' Assn., Austrian Wine Brotherhood, Ferrari Owners Club, Avila Bay Club, Pismo Beach Athletic Club. Office: PO Box 790 Avila Beach CA 93424-0790

MCLARNAN, DONALD EDWARD, banker, corporation executive; b. Nashua, Iowa, Dec. 19, 1906; s. Samuel and Grace (Prudhon) McL.; m. Virginia Rickard, May 5, 1939; children: Marilyn, Marcia, Roxane. A.B., U. So. Calif., 1930; grad., Southwestern U. Law Sch., 1933; postgrad., Cambridge U. Trust appraiser, property mgr. Security-Pacific Nat. Bank, Los Angeles, 1935-54; regional dir. SBA for, So. Calif., Ariz., Nev., 1954-61; area adminstr. SBA for, Alaska, Western U.S., Hawaii, Guam, Samoa, U.S. Trust Terr., 1969-73; pres. Am. MARC, Inc. (offshore oil drillers and mfr. diesel engines), 1961-63, Terminal Drilling & Prodn. Co., Haney & Williams Drilling Co., Western Offshore, 1961-63; v.p., dir. Edgemar Dairy, Santa Monica Dairy Co., 1954-70; founder, pres., chmn. bd. Mission Nat. Bank, 1963-67; pres. Demco Trading Co., Mut. Trading Co.; dir. Coast Fed. Savs. & Loan; cons. numerous corps.; guest lectr. various univs. Contbr. articles on mgmt. and fin. to profl. jours. Chmn. fed. agys. div. Community Chest, 1956; nat. pres. Teachers Day, 1956; bd. councillors U. So. Calif.; founder, chmn., pres. Soc. Care and Protection Injured Innocent; adv. bd. Los Angeles City Coll.; bd. dirs. Calif. Easter Seal Soc.; nat. chmn. U. So. Calif. Drug Abuse Program. Recipient Los Angeles City and County Civic Leadership award, 1959. Mem. Nat. Assn. People with Disabilities (pres.); Mem. Skull and Dagger, Delta Chi. Clubs: Mason (Los Angeles) (K.T., Shriner), Los Angeles (Los Angeles), Jonathan (Los Angeles). Home: 135 S Norton Ave Los Angeles CA 90004-3916 Office: 1111 Crenshaw Blvd Los Angeles CA 90019-3112

MCLAUGHIN, THOMAS FORD, education educator; b. Spokane, Wash., Mar. 30, 1944; s. Thomas Marsten and Johanna (Hove) McL.; m. Rosemary L. Young, Feb. 10, 1976; children: Sean Thomas, Sarah Louise. B in Edn., Ea. Wash. U., 1966, MS in Psychology, 1972; PhD, U. Kans., 1975. Classroom tchr. Med. Lake (Wash.) Sch. Dist., 1966-69; classroom tchr. Spokane Sch. Dist., 1969-72, tchr., 1975-78; from assoc. prof. to prof. Gonzaga U., Spokane, 1978—; cons. div. devel. disabilities Dept. Social and Health Svcs., Spokane, 1988—. Editor: Behavior Analysis in Education, 1976; contbr. numerous articles to profl. jours. Recipient Meritorious award for rsch. Project Innovation, 1979, Excellence in Leaderhip award, 1983. Mem. Assn. for Behavior Analysis, Coun. for Learning Disabilities, Am. Ednl. Rsch. Assn., N.Y. Acad. Scis., Kappa Delta Pi. Democrat. Home: E 720 34th Spokane WA 99203 Office: Gonzaga U Spokane WA 99203

MCLAUGHLIN, BARBARA JEANETTE, counselor, educator, consultant; b. Cleburne, Tex., Sept. 9, 1939; d. Willard Hughes Fry and Dorothy Merle (Williams); m. Raymond Vester, May 12, 1957 (div. Jan. 1977); children: David Wayne, Lewis Edward, Minda Kaye, Cinda Raye. Cert., Durham Bus. Sch., 1971-72, Addiction Counselor Tng., 1980-81. Cert. Alcohol and Drug Counselor, Nat. Cert. Addiction Counselor. Adminstrn. Tex. House of Reps., Austin, 1973-77, Stacey and Assocs., Dallas, 1977-82; office mgr. St. Paul Hosp., Dallas, 1982-84; community outreach Wastgate Dallas Challenge, Dallas, 1984-85; family program dir. Parkside Lodge, Dallas, 1985-87; instr. Addiction Counselor Tng., Dallas, 1985-89; pvt. practice counselor Dallas, 1986—; designer, owner Calif. Addiction Counselors, San Pedro, Calif., 1988—; instr. Tng. Inst., San Pedro, 1988—; ethics instr., cons. U. Calif., L.A., 1992—; instr., cons. Cypress (Calif.) Coll., 1991—, scriptwriter, 1992—; cons. Nat. Coun. on Alcoholism, Long Beach, Calif., 1992—. Author profl. newsletter 1991. Campaign worker, Austin, 1973-77; officer Bus. and Profl. Women, Austin, 1973-77; precint judge Hays County, Tex., 1977. Mem. Nat. Assn. Alcoholism and Drug Abuse Counselors, Nat. Coun. on Alcoholism and Drug Dependencies, Calif. Assn. Alcoholism and Drug Abuse Counselors/Calif. Alcoholism and Drug Counsleors Edn. Program (presenter), Calif. Women's Commn. on Alcohol and Drug Dependencies, Calif. Cert. Bd. of Alcohol and Drug Counselors. Home and Office: 1621 W 25th St Ste 282 San Pedro CA 90732-4301

MCLAUGHLIN, DOROTHY CLAIRE, sociologist, consultant; b. Kansas City, Mo.; d. Earl H. and Hazel Loucille (Allen) Klopfenstine; m. Patrick M. McLaughlin, Feb. 24, 1968; children by previous marriage: Michael L. Gant (dec.), Margaret C. Gant. BA in Sociology, Calif. State U., Los Angeles, 1976; postgrad. Eastern Mont. Coll., 1977; MBA Columbia Pacific U., 1987. Student governance coord. Calif. State U., L.A., 1974-76; dir. Am. Assn. Ret. Persons Sr. Community Service Employment Program, Billings, Mont. 1977-81, Dallas, 1981-87; sociologist, Dallas, 1987-88, Billings, 1988—; exec. bd. mem. TV-Seven; prodr./host (TV show) Wisdom of the Ages, 1992—; cons., lectr., speaker in field. Co-founder Gray Panthers Dallas, 1985; rep. pub. sector Employment Security Council, Helena, Mont., 1979-81; mem. aging com. Mental Health Aging Program, Dallas, 1981-82; co-founder Senior Helping Hands, Inc., 1977, bd. dirs., 1991—; bd. dirs. Eastern Mont. Radio Reading Svc., 1991-92. Recipient Superior Achievement honors Pasadena City Coll., 1974, Pres.'s Club award Avon Products, Inc., 1973, Rosalyn Carter Community Service award Assn. Women Entrepreneurs Dallas Speaker's Bur., 1987. Mem. AAUW (chmn. women's issues 1979, v.p. Billings br. 1989-91, pres. Billings br. 1991—), Assn. Bus. Profl. Women, Am. Sociol. Assn., Nat. Assn. Accts., Am. Personnel Guidance Assn., Mont. Assn. for Female Execs. (co-founder 1980). Home: PO Box 1314 Billings MT 59103-1314 Office: 2423 Pine St Billings MT 59101-0534

MCLAUGHLIN, FRANK E., nursing educator; b. Bklyn., Mar. 27, 1935; s. Edward Patrick and Anna (Barr) McL. BS, Adelphi U., 1959; MA, NYU, 1961; PhD, U. Calif., Berkeley, 1968. Lecturer U. Calif., San Francisco, 1968-69, asst. prof., 1969-70, coord. rsch. grad. programs, 1970-72, chief rsch. in clin. nursing, 1972-81, assoc. clin. prof., 1975—; asst. clin. prof. U. Calif., Davis, 1972-84; assoc. prof. San Francisco State U., 1981-84, vice chmn. dept. nursing, 1984-87, prof., 1984—, grad. coord. Sch. Edn., 1990—. Author: Advanced Nursing and Health Care Research, 1990 (Book of Yr.

award Am. Jour. Nursing 1990). V.p. bd. trustees Cen. City Hospitality House, San Francisco, 1975-78; chmn. Mental Health Adv. Bd. San Francisco, 1979-85; bd. dirs. San Francisco Mental Health Assn., 1985-88. Recipient Outstanding Nurse Leadership award Golden Gate Nurses Assn., 1986. Fellow Am. Acad. of Nursing; mem. ANA, Sigma Theta Tau.

MCLAUGHLIN, JAMES DANIEL, architect; b. Spokane, Wash., Oct. 2, 1947; s. Robert Francis and Patricia (O'Connel) McL.; B.Arch., U. Idaho, 1971; m. Willa Kay Pace, Aug. 19, 1972; children: Jamie Marie, Robert James. Project architect Neil M. Wright, Architect, AIA, Sun Valley, Idaho, 1971-74, McMillan & Hayes, Architects, Sun Valley, 1974-75; now pres., prin. McLaughlin Architects Chartered, Sun Valley. Prin. works include Oakridge Apts., Moscow, Idaho (Excellence in Design award AIA), Walnut Ave. Mall, Ketchum, Idaho (Excellence in Design award AIA, 1987), McMahan Residence, Sun Valley (Excellence in Design award AIA, 1987). Chmn., Ketchum Planning and Zoning Commn., Ketchum Planning Commn., Ketchum Zoning Commn.; chmn. Sun Valley Planning and Zoning Commn.; vice-chmn. Idaho Archtl. Licensing Bd. Served to 1st lt. U.S. Army. Registered architect, 10 states including Idaho. Mem. AIA , Nat. Coun. Archtl. Registration Bds., Nat. Home Builders Assn., Ketchum-Sun Valley C. of C. (dir.). Roman Catholic. Club: Rotary. Prin. archtl. works include James West Residence, First Fed. Savs., Fox Bldg. Rehab., Walnut Ave. Mall, First St. Office Bldg. Home: PO Box 6 Lot # 5 Red Cliffs Subdivsn Ketchum ID 83340-0006 Office: McLaughlin Architects Chartered PO Box 479 Sun Valley ID 83353-0479

MCLAUGHLIN, LINDA HODGE, judge; b. 1942. BA, Stanford U., 1963; LLB, U. Calif., Berkeley, 1966. With Keatinge & Sterling, L.A., 1966-70, Richards, Martin & McLaughlin, Beverly Hills and Newport Beach, Calif., 1970-73, Bergland, Martin & McLaughlin, Newport Beach, 1973-76, Bergland & McLaughlin, Costa Mesa, Calif., 1976-80; judge North Orange County Mcpl. Ct., Fullerton, Calif., 1980-82, Orange County Superior Ct., Santa Ana, Calif., 1982-92, U.S. Dist. Ct. (ctrl. dist.) Calif., Santa Ana, 1992—; mem. adv. com. jud. forms Jud. Coun., 1978—, mem. adv. com. gender bias in cts., 1987-90. Active Edgewood Sch. Parents Assn., Cate Sch. Parents Aux.; mem. governing bd. Victim-Witness Assistance Program Orange County. Mem. Nat. Assn. Women Judges, Calif. State Bar Assn. (mem. com. profl. ethics 1976-80, disciplinary referee dist. 8 1978-80), Calif. Women Lawyers (gov. dist. 8 1978-80), Calif. Judges Assn. (chair civil law and procedure com. 1985-86), Orange County Bar Assn. (mem. com. adminstrn. justice 1975-78, client rels. com. 1978-80, com. jud. appointments 1979-80), Orange County Women Lawyers, Boalt Hall Alumni Assn., Stanford U. Alumni Assn., Cap and Gown Hon. Soc. Office: US District Court Rm 101 751 W Santa Ana Blvd Alta Loma CA 91701-4599*

MCLAUGHLIN, MARGUERITE P., state senator, logging company executive; b. Matchwood, Mich., Oct. 15, 1928; d. Harvey Martin and Luella Margaret (Livingston) Miller; m. George Bruce McLaughlin, 1947; children: Pamela, Bruce Jr., Cynthia. Owner, operator contract logging firm, Orofino, Idaho; mem. Idaho Ho. of Reps., 1978-80; now mem. Idaho Senate, 6th term., asst. Dem. leader, 1990, 91, 92—; mem. Senate Fin. Com., 1987—. Trustee Joint Sch. Dist. 171, 1976-80; pres. Orofino Celebration, Inc. Democrat. Roman Catholic. Office: Idaho State Senate State Capitol Boise ID 83720

MCLAUGHLIN, THOMAS FORD, special education educator; b. Spokane, Wash., Mar. 30, 1944; s. Thomas and Johana A. (Hove) M.; m. Tamara Louise Ochs (div. Sept. 1972); children: Thomas T. Weeks, Ted A. Weeks; m. Rosemary Louise, Feb. 1973; children: Sean T., Sarah Louise. BEd, E. Wash. U., Cheney, 1966, MS in Psychology, 1972; PhD in Devel. and Child Psychology, U. Kans., Lawrence, 1975. Tchr. Med. Lake Sch. Dist., Medical Lake, Wash., 1966-69, Spokane Sch. Dist., Spokane, Wash., 1969-73; rsch. assoc. U. Kans., Lawrence, Kans., 1973-75; spl. edn. Spokane Sch. Dist., 1975-78; adj. prof. East Wash. U., Cheney, 1976-78; adj. prof. Gonzaga U., Spokane, 1976-78, prof. and chair dept. spl. edn., 1978—. Editor: Behavior Analysis in Education, 1976; author: Handbook of Behavior Therapy in Education, Human Behavior in Today's World, Contemporary Psychology. Recipient Project Innovations, Award in Rsch. in Spl. Edn., Leadership Award. Mem. Coun. for Exceptional Children, Am. Edn. Rsch. Assn., Assn. for Behavior Analysis, Coun. for Learning Disabilities, N.Y. Acad. of Sci., Phi Delta Kappa, Kapa Delta Pi, Am. Assn. for Coll. of Tchr. Edn. Democrat. Office: Gonzaga U E 502 Boone Spokane WA 99258-0001

MCLEAN, GORDON CHARLES, hospital administrator; b. Walla Walla, Wash., Oct. 5, 1944; s. Gordon Spurgeon and Ethylene Margery (Lamb) McL.; m. Tresa Louise Pounders, July 8, 1967; children: Gordon Scott, William John. BS in Agrl. Econs., Wash. State U., 1967, MA in Speech, 1973. Head resident Wash. State U., Pullman, 1971-73; news bur. mgr., instr. Cen. Mo. State U., Warrensburg, 1973-75; dir. pub. rels. St. Mary's Med. Ctr., Evansville, Ind., 1975-77, Cen. Wash. Hosp., Wenatchee, Wash., 1977-82; editor Valley Herald Newspaper, Milton-Freewater, Oreg., 1983—; adminstr. North Valley Hosp. & Nursing Home, Tonasket, Wash., 1984-87, Whitman Community Hosp., Colfax, Wash., 1987—; bd. dirs. Home Health and Hospice, Pullman, 1987—. Editor Wash. Rural Health Assn. Newsletter, 1989—. Bd. dirs. Ea. Wash. Area Health Edn. Ctr., Spokane, 1988—. With USAF, 1967-71. Named Citizen of Yr. Tonasket (Wash.) C. of C., 1987, Businessman of Yr., Oroville (Wash.) C. of C., 1986, one of Outstanding Young Men of Am., 1970; recipient Outstanding Contbn. Rural Health award, 1992. Mem. Wash. Assn. Pub. Hosp. Dists. (bd. dirs. 1988—), Rural Hosps. Wash. State Hosp. Assn. (bd. dirs. 1988—), Soc. Profl. Journalists, Colfax C. of C., Rotary (pres. Colfax chpt.), Sigma Delta Chi, Phi Gamma Delta (alumni advisor, Excellence Trophy 1990), Pi Sigma Alpha. Office: Whitman Hosp and Med Ctr 1200 W Almota St Colfax WA 99111-9579

MCLEAN, HUGH ANGUS, management consultant; b. Salt Lake City, Feb. 19, 1925; s. George Mark and Rose (Powell) McL.; m. Martha Lane Green, Nov. 23, 1949; children: Michael Hugh, Merrie Smithson. Student, U. Kans., 1943-44; BSME, Iowa State U., 1946; postgrad., U. Utah, 1946, 61-66. Registered profl. engr., Utah. With Utah Oil Refining Co., Boise, Idaho, Twin Falls, Idaho and Salt Lake City, 1953-61, Am. Oil Co., Salt Lake City and 11 western states, 1961-66; cons. Standard Oil (Ind.), Chgo., 1966-69; v.p. Mahler Assocs., Midland Park, N.J., 1969-76; pres. McLean Mgmt. Systems, Wyckoff, N.J., 1976-84, Heber City, Utah, 1984—. Author: There Is a Better Way to Manage, 1982, Developmental Dialogues, 1972, Career Planning Program, 1975; creator, host (TV) live shows and commls., 1956-57; creator stewardship mgmt. system, 1987. Rep. election judge, Salt Lake City, 1964, Operation Eagle Eye, Chgo., 1968; pub. communications dir. Ch. Jesus Christ Latter-Day Saints, N.Y. metro area, 1981-84; introduced SAFE HOMES in county and state, 1987; chmn. bd. dirs. Town Hall Playhouse, 1990; served to lt. (j.g.) USNR, 1943-46. Recipient Silver award Am. Petroleum Inst., 1957. Mem. Am. Soc. Tng. Devel. (chmn. N.Y. metro chpt. field trips 1972-74). Home: 3384 S Mill Rd Heber City UT 84032-3519 Office: McLean Mgmt Systems PO Box 251 Heber City UT 84032-0251

MCLEAN, IAN SMALL, astronomer, physics educator; b. Johnstone, Scotland, U.K., Aug. 21, 1949; s. Ian and Mary (Small) McL.; (div.); 1 child, Jennifer Ann; m. Janet Wheelans Yourston, Mar. 4, 1983; children: Joanna, David Richard, Graham Robert. BS with hons., U. Glasgow, 1971, PhD, 1974. Rsch. fellow Dept. Astronomy U. Glasgow, Scotland, 1974-78; rsch. assoc. Steward Observatory U. Ariz., Tucson, 1978-80; sr. rsch. fellow Royal Observatory U. Edinburgh, Scotland, 1980-81, sr. scientific officer Royal Observatory, 1981-86; prin. scientific officer Joint Astronomy Ctr., Hilo, Hawaii, 1986-89; prof. Dept. Physics and Astronomy UCLA, 1989—. Author: Electronic and Computer-Aided Astronomy: From Eyes To Electronic Sensors, 1989; contbr. articles to profl. jours. Recipient Exceptional Merit award U.K. Serc, Edinburgh, 1989; NSF grantee, 1991. Fellow Royal Astron. Soc.; mem. Internat. Astron. Union (pres. com. Paris chpt. 1988-91, v.p. 1985-88), Inst. Physics, Am. Astron. Soc. Office: UCLA Dept Astronomy 405 Hilgard Ave Los Angeles CA 90024-1301

MCLEAN, KIRK, professional hockey player; b. Willowdale, Ont., Can., June 26, 1966. Goalie Vancouver (Can.) Canucks. Named to NHL All-Star 2nd Team, 1991-92. Office: Vancouver Canucks, 100 N Renfrew St, Vancouver, BC Canada V5K 3N7

MCLEAN, ROBIN JENNIFER, marketing, advertising professional; b. Denver, Dec. 15, 1960; d. Robert Earl and Marjorie Lee (Worland) McL. BA, U. Denver, 1983, postgrad., 1986—. Prodn. asst. Sta. KOA, Denver; advt. intern Colle & McVoy, Englewood, Colo.; advt. sales rep. Dow Jones & Co., Inc., Englewood, 1983-85; acct. exec. Univ. Graphics, Inc., Englewood, 1985-86; v.p. Columbine Mktg., Denver, 1986-90; acct. exec. Century Media, 1990-91; dir. advertising, mktg. Cherry Creek Locale, Denver, 1992—; advisor U. Denver, 1985—; mktg. and pub. rels. cons. U.S. West, Inc. Mem. Internat. Assn. Bus. Communicators, Bus./Profl. Advt. Assn., Denver Art Mus., Nat. Hist. Preservation Soc. Republican. Roman Catholic. Home and Office: 270 Glencoe St Denver CO 80220-5716

MCLELLAN, STEVEN JAMES, governmental affairs specialist; b. North Chicago, Ill., Sept. 19, 1957; s. James Robert and Marian Louise (Rader) McL.; m. Deborah Ann Vincent, June 21, 1980; children: Daniel, Matthew. BA summa cum laude, U. Puget Sound, 1979; MPA, JD with honors, U. Wash., 1983. Bar: Wash. 1983. Staff counsel Wash. State Legislature, Olympia, 1983-85; adminstr., spl. asst. to chmn., sr. policy specialist Wash. Utilities and Transp. Commn., Olympia, 1985-92; asst. to dir. legis. and intergovtl. affairs Wash. State Energy Office, Olympia, 1992—; pres. Serious Fun Corp., Olympia, 1990-93; mem. telecommuting steering com. Wash. State Energy Office, Olympia, 1990-92; staff subcom. Nat. Assn. Regional Utilities Commn., Washington, 1991-92; presenter at profl. confs.; tchr. course on legis. process Evergreen State Coll., 1991. Contbr. articles on telecommunications to various publs. Bd. dirs. Olympia Food Coop., 1984-85; bd. dirs. Unity of Olympia, 1993—; mem. Stars Devel. Com., Olympia, 1991—. Pub. policy fellow Washington Ctr., 1982. Mem. Wash. State Bar Assn., Phi Kappa Phi. Mem. Unity Ch. Office: WSEO PO Box 43165 Olympia WA 98504

MCLEMORE, VIRGINIA TERESA, economic geologist; b. Balt., June 11, 1955; d. Robert C. Hedrich and Annette B. (Somers) Mellor; m. James V. McLemore, May 29, 1976; children: Jennifer, Christine. BS in Geology, BS in Geophysics, N.Mex. Inst. Mining and Tech., 1977, MS in Geology, 1980. Geologist Natural Gas Pipeline Co. Am., Houston, 1975; teaching asst. N.Mex. Inst. Mining and Tech., Socorro, 1976; field geologist Urangelsellshaft, U.S.A., Denver, 1977; student asst. N.Mex. Bur. Mines, Socorro, 1977-79, rsch. asst., 1979-80, geologist N.Mex. Bur. Mines and Mineral Resources, 1980—; mem. N.Mex. State Highpower Service Rifle Team, 1986-88, 90. Compiler: (with M. R. Bowie) Guidebook to the Socorro Area, 1987; author (with W.L. Chenoweth) Uranium Resources in New Mexico, 1989, contbr. articles to profl. publs. With N.Mex. Mounted Patrol, 1983-90, mem. scholarship com., 1984-88; orgn. leader 4-H N.Mex., Socorro, 1984—. Mem. AIME, Clay Minerals Soc. Meeting (field trip chmn., spouse's trip chmn. 1987), N.Mex. Geol. Soc., Assn. Exploration Geochemists, Am. Assn. Petroleum Geologists, Geol. Soc. Am., Soc. Econ. Paleontologists and Mineraologists, Soc. Econ. Geologists, Soc. Mining, Metallurgy & Exploration (com. on publs. 1991—), Nat. Rifle Assn. Am. (instr. basic markmanship 1983—, class B rifle coach 1987—, hunters safety), N.Mex. Shooting Sports Assn. Inc. (various coms. including exec. com., Pres.'s award 1988), Socorro Gun Club (treas. 1980-86), N.Mex. Tech. Gun Club (faculty sponsor 1980—), Sigma Xi. Home: 701 Caine St Socorro NM 87801-4609 Office: N Mex Bur Mines & Mineral Resources Campus Sta Socorro NM 87801

MCLEOD, ALAN, school superintendent. Supt. Vancouver (B.C.) Sch. Dist. 39, Can. Office: Vancouver Sch Dist 39, 1595 West 10 Ave, Vancouver, BC Canada V6J 1Z8*

MCLEOD, JAMES RICHARD, English language educator; b. Spokane, Wash., Jan. 8, 1942; s. Richard Leland and Bernice Lola (Smith) McL.; m. Judith Ann Osterberg Sylte, June 11, 1982; children: Anne, Brock, Rory, John. BA in English, U. Wash., 1966; MA in English, Ea. Wash. U., 1969. Cert. tchr., Wash. Psychiat. group worker Ryther Child Ctr., Seattle, 1961-63; tchr. Cen. Valley Sch. Dist., Spokane, 1966-69; prof. English North Idaho Coll., Coeur d'Alene, 1970—, dir. Scottish studies program, 1982—; coord. two-yr. coll. programs, mem. exec. com. Associated Writing Programs, 1974-75. Author: Theodore Roethke: A Manuscript Checklist, 1971, Theodore Roethke: A Bibliography, 1973, Mysterious Lake Pend Oreille and its Monster, 1987; contbr. to scholarly publs. Bd. dirs., Kootenai County Coun. Alcoholism, Coeur d'Alene, 1977-80; mem.-at-large, United Ministries in Higher Edn., Seattle, 1979-85; cubmaster, Kootenai County coun. Boy Scouts Am., 1983-84; coord., Kootenai County Centennial Com., Ft. Sherman Day, Coeur d'Alene, 1988—. Named honored author, Wash. State Arts Commn., 1972, Idaho State Library, Boise, 1976. Mem. An Comunn Gaidhealach, Internat. Soc. Cryptozoology, P.E.I. Heritage Found., Community Coll. Humanities Assn., Nat. Trust Scotland, Clan MacLeod Soc. USA (nat. v.p. 1982-86), Wash. Poets Assn. (bd. dirs. 1973-76), Spokane Piobaireachd Soc. (treas. 1983-91), North Idaho Coll. Rowing Club, North Idaho Coll. Cryptozoology Club. Democrat. Episcopalian. Home: 701 S 12th St Coeur D Alene ID 83814-3815 Office: North Idaho Coll 1000W Garden Ave Coeur D Alene ID 83814-9506

MCLEOD, JOHN, psychologist, educator; b. Blackburn, Lancashire, Eng., Feb. 26, 1925; s. Norman and Betsy (Duckworth) McL.; m. Maureen Rickard, Mar. 17, 1955 (dec. Aug. 1984); children: Maire Jane, Andrew Norman, Maureen Anne, Joan, Marian, Pat Michelle; m. Rita Kloudová, Apr. 30, 1987. B.S., Manchester U., 1944; Ed.B., St. Andrews U., Scotland, 1950, M.Ed., 1968; Ph.D. Queensland U., Australia, 1965; Ph.D., U. Sask., Can., 1973. Physics master March Grammar Sch., Eng., 1945-47; ednl. psychologist Wallasey Ednl. Authority, Eng., 1950-59; dep. dir. Schonell Ednl. Research Centre, Brisbane, Australia, 1959-68; head dept. edn. exceptional children U. Sask., Saskatoon, Can., 1968-78, dir. Inst. Child Guidance and Devel., 1968-92; cons. Australian Rsch. Grants Coun., Australia, 1960—; chmn. adjudication com. Social Scis. and Humanities Rsch. Coun., Ottawa, Ont., Can., 1979-82, 1984. Author: (with Schonell and Cochrane) The Slow Learner: Integration or Segregation, 1962; The GAP Reading Comprehension Tests and Manual, 1965; The Slow Learner in the Primary School, 1969; Dyslexia Schedule and Manual, 1969; Standards for Educators of Exceptional Children in Canada, 1971; McLeod Phonic Workshop and Manual, 1972; (with Cropley) Begabung und Begabungsforderung, 1988; Fostering Academic Excellence, 1989; NewGap Tests of Reading Comprehension, 1990. Editor Jour. Slow Learning Child, 1959-68, Jour. Thalamus, 1980-82. Contbr. articles to profl. jours. Chmn. Queensland Subnormal Childrens Welfare Orgn., Australia, 1966-68; pres. Sask. Coordinating Council Social Planning, 1973-75. Recipient Ednl. Research Services award Can. Edn. Assn., 1985, Mona Tobias Nat. award Australian Remedial Edn. Assn., 1983, Can. 125 medal, 1993; sr. Fulbright travel fellow Australian/Am. Friendship Soc., 1966; research grantee IBM, 1974-76; Social Scis. and Humanities Can., 1971-87. Fellow Brit. Psychol. Soc., Royal Soc. Arts; mem. Nat. Soc. Study Edn., Internat. Council Psychologists, Fulbright Assn. (Australia). Anglican. Club: University Faculty (Saskatoon). Home: 2325 Taylor St, Saskatoon, SK Canada S7H 1W8

MCLEOD, JOHN HUGH, JR., mechanical and electrical engineer; b. Hattiesburg, Miss., Feb. 27, 1911; s. John Hugh and Martha (Caldwell) McL.; m. Suzette Boutell, June 23, 1951; children: John Hugh III, Robert Boutell. BS, Tulane U., 1933. Registered profl. engr., Calif. Engr. various firms, 1933-39; field engr. Taylor Instrument Co., Rochester, N.Y., 1940-42; rsch. and devel. engr. Leeds & Northrup Co., Phila., 1943-47; sect. head guidance systems and guided missiles U.S. Naval Air Missile Test Ctr., Point Mugu, Calif., 1947-56; design specialist Gen. Dynamics/Astronautics, San Diego, 1956-63, cons., 1963-64; pvt. practice mech. and elec. engring. cons., La Jolla, Calif., 1964—; disting. vis. prof. Calif. State U. Chico, 1975; mem. exec. com. Fall Joint Computer Conf. Am. Fedn. Info. Processing Socs., 1965. Co-founder San Diego Symposium for Biomed. Engring., 1961. Author: Simulation: The Dynamic Modeling of Ideas and Systems with Computers, 1968, Computer Modeling and Simulation: Principles of Good Practice, 1982; editor, pub.: Simulation Council Newsletter, 1952-55; editor: Simulation, 1963-74; assoc. editor Instruments & Control Systems, 1955-63, Behavioral Sci., 1973—; tech. editor Simulation in the Service of Soc., 1971—; co-author: Large-Scale Models for Policy Evaluation, 1977. With USN, 1942-43. Recipient Sr. Sci. Simulation award Electronic Assocs., Inc., 1965, TIMS award Inst. Mgmt. Scis., 1986; NEH, NSF grantee, 1983. Mem. IEEE, AAAS, Soc. Computer Simulation (chmn. com. on profl. ethics, publs. advisor, John McLeod award 1987). Home: 8484 La Jolla Shores Dr La Jolla CA 92037-3019 Office: Soc Computer Simulation PO Box 17900 San Diego CA 92177-7900

MCLESKEY, CHARLES HAMILTON, anesthesiology educator; b. Phila., Nov. 8, 1946; s. W. Hamilton and Marion A. (Butts) McL.; m. Nanci S. Simmons, June 3, 1972; children: Travis, Heather. BA, Susquehanna U., 1968; MD, Wake Forest U., 1972. Diplomate Am. Bd. Anesthesiology. Intern Maine Med. Ctr., Portland, 1972-73; resident in anesthesiology U. Wash. Sch. Medicine, Seattle, 1973-76, NIH rsch. trainee, 1974-75; clin. teaching assoc. dept. anesthesiology U. Calif., San Francisco, 1976-78; asst. prof. anesthesiology Wake Forest U. Bowman Gray Sch. Medicine, Winston-Salem, N.C., 1978-83, assoc. prof., 1983-84; assoc. prof. U. Tex. Med. Br., Galveston, 1985-87; assoc. prof. anesthesiology U. Colo. Health Sci. Ctr., Denver, 1987-91, prof., 1991-93, dir. acad. affairs, 1987-93; prof., chmn. dept. anesthesiology Tex. A&M U., 1993—; chmn. dept. anesthesiology Scott and White Clinic, Temple, Tex., 1993; cons., lectr. Janssen Pharmaceutica, Piscataway, N.J., 1980—, Alza Corp., Palo Alto, Calif., 1986—; cons. Burrough Welkome Co., Research Triangle Park, N.C., Abbott Labs., Chgo., Marion Merrill Dow, Kansas City, Kans.; lectr. to over 250 nat. and state med. orgns., 1982—; examiner Am. Bd. Anesthesiology. Assoc. editor Anesthesiology Rev.; editor Geriatric Anesthesiology, 1989; contbr. numerous articles to med. jours. Mem. choir Friendswood (Tex.) Meth. Ch., 1985-87; mem. Friendswood Fine Arts Commn., 1985-87. Lt. comdr. M.C., USN, 1976-78. Woodruff-Fisher scholar, 1964-68. Mem. Internat. Platform Assn., Assn. U. Anesthetists, Am. Soc. Anesthesiologists (del. 1983-85, 88—), Soc. for Edn. in Anesthesia (v.p.), Colo. Soc. Anesthesiologists (pres.), Oenophile Soc., Nat. Speakers Assn., Evergreen Newcomers, Alpha Omega Alpha. Republican. Presbyterian.

MCLEVIE, JOHN GILWELL, education consultant; b. Masterton, Wairarapa, N.Z., Nov. 2, 1929; came to U.S., 1968.; s. Edward Mitchell and Gwendoline Mary (Faire) McL.; m. Elaine Marianne Foote, May 7, 1955; children: Anne, Karen, Lynne. BA in History, Victoria U., Wellington, N.Z., 1955, MA in Edn., 1957; PhD in Edn., Mich. State U., 1970. Tchr. Rongotai Coll., Wellington, 1953-57; tchr., housemaster Alexandra Grammar Sch, Singapore, 1958-63; lectr. U. Hong Kong, 1963-68; chief of party Calif. Brazil Project, Brasilia, 1973-76; prof. edn. San Diego State U., 1970-84, chmn. dept., 1978-84; assoc. dean U. Houston-Clear Lake, 1984-89; cons. Calif. Commn. on Tchr. Credentialing, Sacramento, 1989—; integration analyst San Diego Unified Sch. Dist., 1980-81. Contbr. articles to profl. jours. Mem. Assn. for Tchr. Educators, Phi Delta Kappa (Leadership award 1981, Educator of Yr. award 1988). Episcopalian. Home: 823 W El Dorado Dr Woodland CA 95695-5011 Office: Calif Commn on Tchr 1812 9th St Sacramento CA 95814-7000

MCLIN, JAMES CURTIS, accountant; b. Saginaw, Mich., Mar. 8, 1947; s. Charles Curtis and Marion Claire (Paddock) McL.; m. Kathleen M. Carter, Oct. 31, 1990; 1 child, Colleen Marie. BBA, Western Mich. U., 1969. CPA, Colo., Ill. Acct. Alexander Grant & Co., Chgo., 1969-72; mgr. internal audit Seded Power Corp., Muskegon, Mich., 1979-81; acct. Rodriguez, Roach & Assoc., Denver, 1982-87, Roger Nittler & Co., Inc., Denver, 1988—; chmn. Wildwood Resources, Inc., Denver,; bd. dirs. Elder Excavating, Denver, Gen. Engine, Inc.; sec., treas. AHM Mktg. Co., Denver, 1992—. Chair Wildwood Food Program, Denver, 1987—; vol. Sta. KCFR Pub. Radio, Denver, 1981—, Denver Mus. Nat. History, Denver, 1988—. Fellow AICPA, Colo. Soc. CPA, Mich. Soc. CPA. Office: Roger Nittler & Co Inc 7935 E Prentice Ave Ste 111 Englewood CO 80111

MCLURKIN, THOMAS CORNELIUS, JR., lawyer; b. L.A., July 28, 1954; s. Thomas Cornelius and Willie Mae (O'Connor) McL. BA, U. So. Calif., 1976, MPA, 1980, PhD in Pub. Adminstrn., 1993; JD, U. LaVerne, 1982. Bar: Calif. 1984, U.S. Dist. Ct. (cen. dist.) Calif. 1984, U.S. Dist. Ct. Hawaii 1984, U.S. Ct. Appeals (9th cir.) 1984, U.S. Dist. Ct. (ea. and no. and so. dists.) Calif. 1985, U.S. Tax Ct. 1988, U.S. Ct. Mil. Appeals 1989. Law clk. Dept. Water and Power City of L.A., 1979-82; jud. clk. U.S. Dist. Ct. (cen. dist.) Calif., L.A., 1982-83; law clk. Office City Atty., L.A., 1983-84, Dep. City Atty., 1984—. Author (with others): Facts in American History, 1968, 2nd edit. 1989, Eagle Scout, 1970. Mem. L.A. World Affairs Coun., 1980—, Smithsonian Assocs.; bd. dirs. L.A. area coun. Boy Scouts Am., Hillsides Homes for Children. Mem. ABA, ALA, L.A. County Bar Assn., Assn. Trial Lawyers Am., Langston Law Assn. L.A., Am. Soc. Pub. Adminstrs., U. So. Calif. Gen. Alumni Assn. (bd. govs. exec. bd. 1986-90), U. So. Calif. Black Alumni Assn.-Ebonics (pres. 1988-89), U. So. Calif. Pres.'s Cir., Elks, Phi Alpha Delta, Kappa Alpha Psi. Republican. Methodist. Office: LA City Atty Office, Water and Power Div 1848 Beaudry PO Box 111 Los Angeles CA 90051

MCMAHON, FRED, speech communications educator; b. Springfield, Mo., Aug. 13, 1920; s. Fred and Ethel (Arno) McM.; m. Katherine Garbee; children: Marina Fedrid, Kreg. B.A., U. Iowa, 1942; M.A., U. So. Calif., 1954, Ph.D., 1957. Lectr. theatre arts U. Ariz., Tucson, 1942, Glendale Coll., Calif., 1949, 52-57; emeritus prof. dept. comm. Calif. State U.-Northridge, 1957-90, prof. emeritus, 1990—; cons. in field. Editor: Western Communication, 1967-71, Exetasis, 1977-85. Capt. U.S. Army, 1942-46, 50-52. Mem. Speech Communication Assn., Western Communication Assn. (Disting. Service award 1984). Democrat. Jewish. Office: Calif State Univ Northridge CA 91330

MCMAHON, PATRICIA ANNE, mayor; b. Feb. 2, 1945; m. Murray Joseph McMahon; children: Shawn, Lorena. Student, Shaws Bus. Sch., 1964, U. Toronto, 1966, Simon Fraser U., 1983, NGWT, 1984. News broadcaster Cable TV Yellowknife (N.W.T., Can.), 1976; fin. officer YK Hardware, Yellowknife, 1977-81; dir. Travel Industry N.W.T., Yellowknife, 1981, v.p., 1982, pres., 1982-83, 2d v.p., 1984-85; real estate sales assoc. NRS, Yellowknife, 1986-87; mayor City of Yellowknife, 1988—; v.p. MCM Cons., Yellowknife, 1986—. Mem. Fed. Bd. Nat. Parks Cen. Citizens, 1983-85; mem. City of Yellowknife Recration Bd., 1978, City of Yellowknife Tax Revision Bd., 1978; chmn. Miss Yellowknife Pageant, 1976, Can. Week Celebration, N.W.T., 1976; mem. women's liberation com. Liberal Party of Can., Ottawa; bd. dirs. Foothill's Postal Svc. Com., Edmonton, Alta., 1989—. Mem. Fedn. of Can. Municipalities (bd. dirs. 1988—), N.W.T. Assn. Municipalities (pres. 1988—), Daus. of Midnight Sun (pres. 1978). Office: City of Yellowknife, PO Box 580, Yellowknife, NT Canada X1A 2N4

MCMAHON-HOLDEN KINGSMORE, BRANDIE KATHLEEN, state official; b. St. Louis, Mar. 12, 1970; d. Tommy Lee and Mary Ann (McMahon) Holden; m. James Monroe Kingsmore, Mar. 31, 1964. Student, Glendale (Ariz.) C.C., 1988—; AA in Liberal Arts, Phoenix Coll., 1992. Shift mgr. Pizza Hut Corp., Buckeye, Ariz., 1988-90; pub. assistance eligibility interviewer State of Ariz., Avondale, 1990—; co-chairperson Buckeye chpt. Ariz. Transitional Team, Buckeye, 1992—. Vol. St. Vincent de Paul Soc., St. Henry's Parish, Buckeye, 1988-90; mem. Buckeye Planning and Zoning Commn., 1989-90. Mem. Greenpeace. Democrat.

MCMANAMY, DAVID KENNETH, software company executive; b. Washington, July 28, 1943. BS in Computer Sci., Fla. Technol. U., 1971; MA in Computer Resource Mgmt. and Mgmt., Webster U., 1993. Sr. computer operator Lockheed, Cape Kennedy, Fla., 1968-70; sr. analyst Computer Micro Svcs., St. Louis, 1972-74; project leader First City Svcs., Houston, 1974-76; cons. EBASCO Svcs., N.Y.C., 1977-79; sr. system programmer Fed. Express Corp., Colo. Springs, 1979-86; sr. cons. self-employed Colo. Springs, 1986-89; sr. systems programmer HFSI, Phoenix, 1989-91; under contract as sr. cons. Computer Assistance, Denver, 1992; dir. Computer Scis. & Systems Engring. Consultants, Colo. Springs, 1991—. Contbr. articles to profl. jours. Mem. Nat. Assn. System Programmers, Assn. Computing Machinery, Ind. Computer Cons. Assn. Home: 4160 Autumn Hgts Dr Unit B Colorado Springs CO 80906

MCMANUS, DANIEL ALBERT, paper company manager; b. Walla Walla, Wash., Jan. 1, 1954; s. Albert Matthew and Mary Joyce (DeVaney) McM.; m. Valerie Jean Leigh, July 29, 1980; children: Matthew, Simon, Alexander, Joanie. BS, U.S. Mil. Acad., 1976. Sr. mech. engr. Crown Zellerbach Corp., West Linn, Oreg., 1981-82, tech. asst. stock, 1982-84; supt. James River Corp., West Linn, 1984-90; materials mgr. Simpson Paper Co., West Linn, 1990-93, mill mgr., 1993—. Bd. dirs. Keep Oreg. Green, 1993. Capt. U.S. Army, 1976-81. Mem. Assn. Oreg. Recyclers, Tech. Assn. of the Pulp and

Paper Industry (project officer 1990-92), West Linn C. of C. (bd. dirs. 1993). Home: 1950 Furlong West Linn OR 97068

MCMASTER, GRACE ISABEL, artist; b. San Francisco, July 13, 1923; d. Howard Andrew Bradley and Gladys (Zier) Breeding; m. Chas Wilbur McMaster, Apr. 3, 1943 (div. July 1971); children: Howard Edward, Leland Andrew, Bippy Eileen. BA, San Francisco State U., 1966, life elem. credential, 1967. Pvt. piano tchr. San Bruno, Calif., 1962-64; long term substitute tchr. San Bruno (Calif.) Park Elem. Schs., 1969-70; mgr. Lisle Ramsey Portrait Studio, Daly City, Calif., 1970; substitute tchr. So. San Francisco (Calif.) Unified Sch. Dist., 1970-72; sales rep. Lifesavers, Inc., Daly City, 1973; car salesperson Dick Bullis Chevrolet, Burlingame, Calif., 1973-74; tv. and stereo sales J.C. Penney Co., San Bruno, 1974-81; pvt. artist San Bruno, 1981-93; pvt. artist, watercolorist Gualala, Calif., 1993—. One-woman shows include Garden Cafe, Burlingame, 1986, Studio Showings, Gualala, 1987, 88, 89, Kennedy & Assoc., Gualala, 1992, Dolphin Gallery, Gualala, 1993; exhibited in group shows at North San Mateo County Ctr. for the Arts, 1985, San Mateo County Arts Coun., 1986, Peninsula Hosp. Aux., 1987, Skyline Coll., San Bruno, 1989, Barnegat Light (N.J) Gallery, 1992, Art in the Redwoods, Gualala, 1992; represented in pvt. and corp. collections. Pres. Crestmoor High Sch. PTA, 1965. Mem. Gualala (Calif.) Arts. Democrat. Home: PO Box 1087 Gualala CA 95445

MCMASTER, JULIET SYLVIA, English language educator; b. Kisumu, Kenya, Aug. 2, 1937; emigrated to Can., 1961, naturalized, 1976; d. Sydney Herbert and Sylvia (Hook) Fazan; m. Rowland McMaster, May 10, 1968; children: Rawdon, Lindsey. B.A. with honors, Oxford U., 1959; M.A., U. Alta., 1963, Ph.D., 1965. Asst. prof. English U. Alta., Edmonton, Can., 1965-70; assoc. prof. U. Alta., 1970-76, prof. English, 1976-86, Univ. prof., 1986—. Author: Thackeray: The Major Novels, 1971, (ed.) Jane Austen's Achievement, 1976, Jane Austen on Love, 1978, Trollope's Palliser Novels, 1978, (with R.D. McMaster) The Novel from Sterne to James, 1981, Dickens the Designer, 1987; contbr. articles to profl. jours. Can. Council fellow, 1969-70; Guggenheim fellow, 1976-77; Killam fellow, 1987-89. Fellow Royal Soc. Can.; mem. Victorian Studies Assn. Western Can. (founding pres. 1972), Assn. Can. Univ. Tchrs. English (pres. 1976-78), MLA, Jane Austen Soc. N.Am. (dir. 1980-91). Office: U Alta, Dept English, Edmonton, AB Canada T6G 2E5

MCMATH, CARROLL BARTON, JR., past college administrator, retired army officer; b. Godfrey, Wash., Sept. 18, 1910; s. Carroll Barton and Grace Jenness (Matthews) McM.; BS, Oreg. State U., 1932; MS (A. Olson Research scholar), N.Y. U., 1936; m. Betty Ruth Thompson, Nov. 26, 1937; children: Robert Thompson, Carol. With Sacramento Bee Newspaper, 1932-35; jr. exec. Lord & Taylor, N.Y.C., 1936-39; head dept. bus. Boise (Ida.) Jr. Coll., 1939-40; Res. officer on active duty U.S. Army, 1940-46, assigned gen. staff War Dept., 1943-45; commd. capt. regular U.S. Army 1947, advanced through grades to lt. col., assigned Joint Chiefs of Staff, 1951-53, Office Sec. of Army, 1953-55, ret., 1963; campaigns include Okinawa, Korea, Vietnam; mem. faculty U. Hawaii, Honolulu, 1964-77, asst. to dir. research, profl. adviser to faculty on rsch., 1964-77; faculty Indsl. Coll. of Armed Forces, Washington, 1945-46; asst. prof. retailing N.Y. U., N.Y.C., 1946-47. Mem. Assn. U.S. Army, AAAS, AAUP, Ret. Officers Assn., Honolulu Acad. Arts, Hawaiian Hist. Soc., Am. Theatre Organ Soc., Hawaii Found. History and Humanities, Scabbard and Blade, Alpha Delta Sigma, Alpha Kappa Psi, Eta Mu Pi, Elk, Koa Anuenue. Democrat. Home: 1624 Kanunu St Honolulu HI 96814-2718

MCMILLAN, JOHN A., retail executive; b. 1931. BA, U. Wash., 1957. With Nordstrom Inc., Seattle, 1957—, exec. v.p., 1975—, pres., 1989—. Office: Nordstrom Inc 1501 5th Ave Seattle WA 98101-1603

MCMILLIN, MARILYNN PATRICIA, secretary; b. Evanston, Ill., Sept. 15, 1947; d. Eldon and Eleanor Mary (Camomile) Martin; m. Clarence Russell McMillin, Jan. 5, 1983. Exec. sec. Medicus Systems & Mktg., Chgo., 1976-77; mktg. sec. Northcare, Inc., Evanston, Ill., 1978; intermediate typist Elcajon (Calif.) Social Svcs., 1981-84; office mgr., sec. Heartland Fire Facility, 1986; sec. U. Puget Sound, Tacoma, Wash., 1989—. Poetry included in: The Poetry of Life: A Treasury of Moments, 1991, American Poetry Anthology 1987, 1990. Bd. sec. relief soc. LDS, Tacoma, 1990. Republican. Home: 1515 N Verde St Tacoma WA 98406

MC MILLION, JOHN MACON, retired newspaper publisher; b. Coffeyville, Kans., Dec. 25, 1929; s. John Dibrell and Mattie Anna (Macon) McM.; m. Melanie Ann McMillion; children: John Thomas, Johanna, Jennifer, Amanda. Student, Vanderbilt U., 1947-49; B.S. in Journalism, U. Kans., 1956. Police reporter Amarillo (Tex.) Globe-News, 1956; sports editor, telegraph editor Grand Junction (Colo.) Daily Sentinel, 1956-58; mng. editor Alliance (Nebr.) Times-Herald, 1958-59, Clovis (N.Mex.) Jour., 1959-62; gen. mgr. Pasadena (Tex.) Citizen, 1962; bur. mgr. UPI, 1962-66; exec. editor Albuquerque Jour., 1966-69; bus. mgr. Albuquerque Pub. Co., 1971-75; pub. Herald and News-Tribune, Duluth, Minn., 1975-86, Akron (Ohio) Beacon Jour., 1986-90, ret.; campaign mgr. gubernatorial campaign, 1969-71. Served with USN, 1950-54. Address: 12404 Royal Oak Ct NE Albuquerque NM 87111

MCNALL, BRUCE, professional sports executive, numismatist; m. Jane Cody; children: Katie, Bruce. Student, UCLA. Founder, chmn. bd. Numismatic Fine Arts, Inc., L.A.; owner, chmn. bd. Summa Stable, Inc.; chmn. bd. Gladden Entertainment Corp.; former ptnr. Dallas Mavericks NBA; co-owner L.A. Kings, 1986-87, sole owner, 1988—; also gov., pres.; owner Toronto Argonauts, 1991—. Office: Los Angeles Kings 3900 W Manchester Blvd Inglewood CA 90305*

MCNALL, LESTER RAY, chemist, horticultural specialist; b. Gaylord, Kans., Oct. 28, 1927; s. Webster and Bertha Katherine (Heide) McN. BS in Chemistry, U. Wis., 1950; PhD in Chemistry, UCLA, 1955. Rsch. chemist Esso Rsch. & Engring. Co., Linden, N.J., 1955-56; head chem. rsch. PaperMate Mfg. Co. div. Gillette Co., Santa Monica, Calif., 1956-65; tech. dir. Leffingwell Chem. Co., Brea, Calif., 1965-76; gen. mgr. Leffingwell div. Thompson-Hayward Chem. Co., Brea, 1976-84; pres. Nutrient Techs., Inc., La Habra, Calif., 1984—. Mem. Am. Chem. Soc., Am. Soc. for Hort. Sci. Home: 311 E Country Hills Dr La Habra CA 90631 Office: Nutrient Techs Inc PO Box 2961 La Habra CA 90631

MCNALLY, JAMES HENRY, physicist; b. Orange, N.J., Dec. 18, 1936; s. James Osborne and Edith Maude (Jones) McN.; m. Nancy Lee Eudaley, July 4, 1976. B. in Engring. Physics, Cornell U., 1959; PhD in Physics, Calif. Inst. Tech., 1966. Staff mem. program mgr. Los Alamos (N.Mex.) Nat. Lab., 1965-74; asst. dir for laser and isotope separation tech. AEC/ERDA, Washington, 1974-75; assoc. div. leader, dep. for inertial fusion, asst. for nat. sec. issues Los Alamos Nat. Lab., 1975-86; dep. asst. dir. Arms Control and Disarmament Agy., Washington, 1986-88; dir. office staff Los Alamos Nat. Lab., 1988-90, Washington Inst., 1990—; cons., 1990—; U.S. del. Geneva Conf. on Disarmament, 1969, 73, 74, Threshold Test Ban Treaty, Moscow, 1974, Nuclear Testing Talks, Geneva, 1986-88. Bd. dirs. Wilson Mesa Met. Water Dist., 1976-88. Mem. Am. Phys. Soc., AAAS, Internat. Inst. Strategic Studies. Home and Office: 550 Rim Rd Los Alamos NM 87544-2931

MC NAMARA, JOSEPH DONALD, researcher, retired police chief, novelist; b. N.Y.C., Dec. 16, 1934; s. Michael and Eleanor (Shepherd) McN.; divorced; children: Donald, Laura, Karen. BS, John Jay Coll., 1968; fellow, Harvard Law Sch., 1970; DPA (Littauer fellow), Harvard U., 1973. Served to dep. insp. Police Dept., N.Y.C., 1956-73; police chief Kansas City, Mo., 1973-76, San Jose, Calif., 1976-91; rsch. fellow Hoover Instn., Stanford U., 1991—; adj. instr. Northeastern U., 1972, John Jay Coll., 1973, Rockhurst Coll., 1975-76, San Jose State U., 1980; cons. U.S. Civil Rights Commn., 1978; lectr., appearances on nat. TV; apptd. nat. adv. bd. U.S. Bur. Justice Stats., 1980; commentator Pub. Broadcasting Radio. Author: (non-fiction) Safe and Sane, 1984, (novel) The First Directive Crown, 1985, Fatal Command, 1987, The Blue Mirage, 1990; contbr. articles to profl. publs. Active NCCJ. Served with U.S. Army, 1958-60. Named one of 200 Young Am. Leaders Time mag., 1975; recipient disting. alumni award John Jay Coll., 1979, Pres.'s award Western Soc. Criminology1979, Morrison Gitchoff awrd Western Soc. Criminology, 1992, H.B. Spear award Drug Policy Found., 1992; Kansas City police named Best in Country by Nat. Newspaper Enterprises, 1974, San Jose Police Dept. named Nat. Model U.S. Civil Rights Commn., 1980; named Law Enforcement Officer of Yr., Calif. Trial Lawyers Assn., 1991. Mem. Internat. Assn. Chiefs of Police, Calif. Police Chiefs Assn., Calif. Peace Officers Assn., Major Cities Police Chiefs Assn., Police Exec. Research Forum (dir.). Office: Hoover Instn Stanford CA 94305

MCNAMARA, ROBERT JAMES, English language educator, poet; b. N.Y.C., Mar. 28, 1950; s. James Joseph and Doris Agnes (Maier) McN.; m. Bridget Culligan (div. 1985); 1 child, Catlin. BA, Amherst Coll., 1972; MA, Colo. State U., 1975; PhD, U. Wash., 1985. Lectr. English U. Wash., Seattle, 1985—. Author: Second Messengers, 1990; editor L'Epervier Press, Ft. Collins, Colo., Seattle, 1977—; contbr. articles and poems to profl. jours. Fellow Nat. Endowment for the Arts, 1987-88. Mem. Acad. of Am. Poets, Nat. Coun. Tchrs. English. Office: Dept English GN-30 U Wash Seattle WA 98195

MCNAMEE, EVELYN HAYNES, civilian military employee; b. Monticello, Miss., Dec. 10, 1947; d. Leroy and Leslie (Hammond) Haynes; m. George Allen McNamee Jr., Aug. 23, 1970; children: Leonard, George Allen, Paula Elizabeth, Candace Renee. BS, Alcorn State U., Lorman, Miss., 1969; MS, Tuskegee Inst., 1971. Indsl. hygienist U.S. Army, White Sands Missile Range, N.Mex., 1985-88; sr. indsl. hygienist USN Naval Hosp., San Diego, 1988-90; indsl. hygienist, command staff Naval Aviation Depot Naval Air Sta. North Island, San Diego, 1990-91; sr. indsl. hygienist David Taylor Model Basin Carderock Divsn. Naval Surface Warfare Ctr., Bethesda, Md., 1991—. Mem. Sidwell Friends' Parent Group, Washington, Sidwell Friends' Resource Bank, 1991-93. Mem. Am. Conf. Govt. Indsl. Hygienists, Am. Indsl. Hygiene Assn., Navy Indsl. Hygiene Assn., NAFE, Toastmasters (past pres. local chpt.). Democrat. Roman Catholic. Home: 13009 Flack St Silver Spring MD 20906 Office: Nat Navy Med Ctr Bldg 22 Br Med Clinic Carderock DTMB CDNSWC Code 0231 1H Bethesda MD 20084

MCNAMEE, STEPHEN N., lawyer. U.S. atty. State of Ariz., Phoenix. Office: 1400 US Courthouse 230 N 1st Ave Phoenix AZ 85025-0230

MC NEALY, SCOTT, computer company executive; b. 1954. BA, Harvard U., 1976; MBA, Stanford U., 1980. Chmn., pres., chief exec. officer Sun Microsystems Inc., Mountain View, Calif.; with Rockwell Internat. Corp., Troy, Mich., 1976-78, sales engr.; staff engr. FMC Corp., Chgo., 1980-81; dir. ops. Onyx Systems, San Jose, Calif., 1981-82; with Sun Microsystems Inc., Mountain View, Calif., 1982—, now chmn. bd., pres., chief exec. officer. Office: Sun Microsystems Inc 2550 Garcia Ave Mountain View CA 94043-1100*

MCNEES, CARYL, English language educator, researcher; b. Sewickley, Pa., Nov. 5, 1938; d. Floyd Raymond and Ione (Earl) McN. BA in English, Grove City (Pa.) Coll., 1960; MEd in English Edn., U. Pitts., 1968; PhD in English Edn., U. Va., 1972; MS in Marriage, Family and Child Therapy, LaVerne (Calif.) U., 1992. Assoc. prof. English Calif. State U., Pomona, 1972-82, full prof. English, 1982—; edn. cons. Claremont (Calif.) Unified Sch. Dist., 1977-78; researcher in children's lit. Contbr. articles to profl. jours. and books. Mem. MLA, Nat. Coun. Tchrs. English, Golden Key Soc., Kappa Delta Pi, Sigma Tau Delta, Psi Chi. Presbyterian. Home: 870 W Harrison Ave Claremont CA 91711-4128 Office: Calif State U Temple Ave Pomona CA 91768-3240

MCNEIL, ALLYSON, trainer, consultant; b. Albuquerque, Apr. 23, 1962; d. Warren Q and Darlene Esther (Kmetzsch) McN. BS in Elem. Edn., Brigham Young U., 1983, M Orgnl. Behavior, 1992. Cert. tchr., Utah. Optometric asst. Sunnyvale (Calif.) Eye Care Ctr., 1979-80; word processor Brigham Young U., Provo, Utah, 1980-83; microsystems analyst 1st Nat. Mortgage Co., San Jose, Calif., 1983-85; missionary for LDS ch. Spain Madrid Mission, 1985-87; ind. cons. Sunnyvale, 1987-89, Orem, Utah, 1990-92; computer instr. Tek/Link Corp., Santa Clara, Calif., 1989-90, The Dublin Group Inc., Santa Clara, 1993—; mgmt. facilitator, contractor, tech. instr. various firms in Utah and Calif., 1987—. Author, editor tng. manuals. Mem. ASTD. Republican. Mem. LDS Ch.

MCNEIL, JOHN STUART, publisher; b. L.A., Oct. 17, 1935; s. Murray Charles and Helen Katherine (Curtis) McN.; divorced; children: Elizabeth Ann, Kenneth John, Karen Lynn. BS, San Jose State U., 1962. Asst. dean for fiscal affairs U. Hawaii Sch. Medicine, Honolulu, 1968-72; fiscal officer Postgrad. Med. Edn. Program for Ryukyus, Honolulu, 1968-72; bus. mgr. Ann. Revs., Inc., Palo Alto, Calif., 1962-68, chief exec. officer, 1973-81; sec.-treas. Ann. Revs., Inc., Palo Alto, 1973—, pub., 1981—; lectr. on econs. sci. book pub., 1973—; mem. adv. coun. Astron. Soc. Pacific, 1991—; trustee Soc. for Promotion Sci. and Scholarship, 1982—. Vol. United Way Santa Clara County, San Jose, 1988—. With USN, 1954-56. Mem. Internat. Group Sci., Tech. and Med. Pubs., Bookbuilders West. Democrat. Office: Ann Revs Inc PO Box 10139 Palo Alto CA 94303

MCNEIL, ROBERT DUELL, family businesses consultant; b. Chehalis, Wash., Sept. 16, 1935; s. Robert Maxwell Donahoe and Alice Julia (Duell) McN.; m. Lila G. Davis, Sept. 5, 1958 (div. 1961); children: Katrina, Kathleen; m. Virginia Allen, June 1964 (div. 1966); children: Mark, Marceline; m. Rita Camille Grove, June 29, 1972. Student, U. Oreg., 1954. Mgr. retail sales Standard Oil Calif., Santa Monica, 1956-63; dist. mgr. Questor Corp., 1963-65; regional sales mgr. Perfection Gear Co., L.A., 1965-66; gen. mgr. San Diego Tool Co., 1966-68; pres. F. Mohling Co., San Diego, 1968-70; with Midas Internat., Inc., L.A., Chgo., 1970-72; pres. Muffco, Inc., Lakewood, Colo., 1972-78; v.p. devel. Glassrock Med. Co., Atlanta, 1978-80; prin. R.D. McNeil & Assocs., Scottsdale, Ariz., 1981-86; mng. ptnr. Vaughn-McNeil & Assocs., Denver, 1986-89; prin. R.D. McNeil & Assocs., Littleton, Colo., 1990—. Home and Office: 7040 W Fairview Dr Littleton CO 80123-5416

MCNEILL, DOUGLAS ARTHUR, priest; b. Bklyn., Mar. 6, 1942; s. Daniel Patrick and Elizabeth (Gallagher) McN. Student, Sacred Heart Sem., 1965, MTh, 1968; MS in Edn., Fordham U., 1973. Founder, CEO St. Bonaventure Indian Missions, Thoreau, N.Mex., 1974—; chmn. Diocesan Pers. Bd., Gallup, N.Mex., 1975-81, Greater Thoreau (N.Mex.) Found., 1986—; founder Blessed Kateri Tekakwitha Acad., Thoreau, 1980; Episcopal vicar McKinley Vicariate, Gallup, 1985—. Candidate N.Y. State Assembly, Bklyn., 1972, Gallup-McKinley Sch. Bd., Gallup, 1976; mem. N.W. N.Mex. Drug Coun., Gallup, 1990—; exec. bd. dirs. S.W. Indian Found., Gallup, 1976-82; mem. Thoreau Water & Sanitation Bd., 1976-86. Mem. Diocesan Pastoral Coun., Diocesan Presbyteral Coun., Nat. Cath. Devel. Conf., Diocesan Religious Edn. (bd. dirs. Gallup chpt. 1973-86), Propagation of the Faith Soc. (bd. dirs. Gallup chpt. 1980—), K.C. (chaplain 1987—). Republican. Roman Catholic. Home: PO Box 1120 9 1st Ave Thoreau NM 87323-1120 Office: St Bonaventure Indian Missions 25 W Navarre Blvd Thoreau NM 87323

MCNEILL, KEVIN MICHAEL, software research specialist; b. Tucson, Sept. 19, 1956; s. George Charles and Ana Laura (Celaya) McN.; divorced; 1 child, Katheryn Amalthea. BA in Math., U. Ariz., 1983, MS in Computer Sci., 1987. Systems analyst Dept. Radiology U. Ariz., Tucson, 1977-85, rsch. specialist, 1985—; cons. BAZIS-IMAGIS Acad. Hosp., Leiden, The Netherlands, 1987, 89, Toshiba Corp., Tokyo, 1983—. Inventor parallel searching system, 1989; co-inventor an image viewing sta. for PACS, 1989. Mem. IEEE. Am. Coll. Radiology, Nat. Elec. Mfrs. Assn. (standards com. working group VI), Assn. Computing Machinery, Soc. Photo-optical Instrumentation Engrs. Republican. Office: Ariz Health Sci Ctr Dept Radiology Tucson AZ 85724

MCNUTT, DOUGLAS PAGE, space physics consultant; b. Rome, Ga., Apr. 24, 1935; s. Homer E. and Catherine (Page) McN.; children: Jill, Lynn, Ross, Todd. BA, Wesleyan U., 1956; MS, PhD in Physics, Math., U. Wis., 1963. Lic. comml. pilot. Postdoctoral rschr. U. Wis., Madison, 1962-63; rschr. U.S. Naval Rsch. Lab., Washington, 1963-83; with Profl. Flight Svc., Pomonkey, Md., 1980—; instr. aircraft electricity U. D.C., Washington, 1983-84; cons. U.S. Naval Rsch. Lab., Space Sci. Div. Univs. Sapce Rsch. Assocs., Washington, 1983-86; cert. developer Apple Computer, Inc., Cupertino, Calif., 1987—; founder The MacNauchtan Lab., Colorado Springs, Colo., 1987—; cons. Sachs Freeman Assocs., 1986—. Patentee in field; contbr. articles to profl. jours. Mem. IEEE, Optical Soc. Am. Office: The MacNauchtan Lab 7255 Suntide Pl Colorado Springs CO 80919-1060

MCNUTT, STEPHEN RUSSELL, volcanologist, geophysical scientist; b. Hartford, Conn., Dec. 21, 1954; s. Elmer Ellsworth and Leona (LaPointe) McN. BA, Wesleyan U., Middletown, Conn., 1977; MA, Columbia U., 1982, MPhil, 1984, PhD, 1985. Sr. seismologist Calif. Div. Mines and Geology, Sacramento, 1984-91; cons. U. Costa Rica, San José, 1982-83. Contbr. articles to profl. jours. Mem. Seismol. Soc. Am., Am. Geophys. Union, Internat. Assn. Volcanology and Chemistry of Earth's Interior, Buffalo Chips Running Club (Sacramento, bd. dirs. 1986-90). Democrat. Roman Catholic. Office: U Alaska Fairbanks Geophysical Inst Alaska Volcano Observatory Fairbanks AK 99775-0800

MCPHEE, RODERICK FULTON, school administrator; b. Eau Claire, Wis., Jan. 30, 1929; s. Eugene Roderick and Frances (Fulton) McP.; m. Sharon Sullivan, Aug. 29, 1948; 1 child, Dennis Roderick. BS, U. Wis., 1950, MS, 1953; PhD, U. Chgo., 1959. Secondary sch. tchr. Kohler (Wis.) Pub. Schs., 1950-52; instr. extension div. U. Wis., Madison, 1952-55; field rep. White House Conf. Edn., Washington, 1955-56; staff assoc. Midwest Adminstrn. Ctr., Chgo., 1956-60; assoc. sec. Am. Assn. Sch. Adminstrs., Washington, 1960-61; asst. prof. Grad. Sch. Edn. Harvard U., Cambridge, Mass., 1961-65; supt. of schs. Town of Glencoe, Ill., 1965-68; pres. Punahou Sch., Honolulu, 1968—; cons. Arthur D. Little Co., Cambridge, 1967-68; bd. dirs. First Hawaiian Bank, Honolulu; chmn. Barstow Found., Honolulu; active Armed Forces YMCA, Community Fedn. Hawaii. Co-author: The Organization and Control of American Schools, 1968; contbr. articles to profl. jours. Named Scot of Yr. Caledonian Soc., Honolulu, 1991, Hawaii Bus. Hall of Fame Laureate, 1993. Mem. Hawaii Assn. Ind. Schs. (pres. 1972, 81, 82), Social Sci. Assn. Honolulu, Oahu Country Club, Waialae Country Club, Rotary (pres. 1975-76), The 200 Club (sec., pres. 1983-84). Home: 25 Pipers Pali St Honolulu HI 96822-3387 Office: Punahou Sch 1601 Punahou St Honolulu HI 96822-3399

MCPHERSON, CHRISTOPHER GEOFFREY, theater critic, documentary producer; b. Phoenix, July 27, 1959; s. James Earl and Merlie (Martinez) McP. Lic. operator, FCC. Various journalism positions, Phoenix, 1976—; columnist The Observer, Phoenix, 1984-92; mng. editor Ariz. Living mag., Phoenix, 1987-89; art writer Scottsdale (Ariz.) Progress, 1989, fashion writer, 1989-92; theater critic Phoenix Gazette, 1989—; owner, documentary prodr. Documentaire, Phoenix, 1990—. Contbr. articles on archaeology, art and Hollywood history to various publs.; writer, prodr. radio documentary Lost Youth: Children in Crisis, 1991 (award Scripps Howard and AP 1992), TV documentary Bad Boys?, 1992, also various documentaries on theater, bus. and environ. Mem. minority adv. bd. Sta. KPNX, 1984-91, chmn., 1990; mem. Foster Care Rev. Bd., 1991-92; judge Zony awards Valley Theater Assn., 1990—. Recipient George Washington honor medal Freedoms Found., 1992, Disting. Health Journalism award Am. Chiropractic Assn., 1992, Maggie award for health journalism Planned Parenthood, 1992, U.S. Senate Certificate of Recognition in Broadcast Journalism, 1992. Mem. Ariz. Press Club. (award for 1st place radio documentary 1992). Office: PO Box 37214 Phoenix AZ 85069-7214

MCPHERSON, JAMES WILLIS, III, health care public affairs director; b. Canton, Ohio, Aug. 9, 1956; s. James Willis Jr. and Bea (Shaheen) McP. BA in Pub. Adminstrn., Miami U., Oxford, Ohio, 1978; MA in Pub. Adminstrn., Ohio State U., 1981. Transp. planner Mid-Ohio Regional Planning Commn., Columbus, 1979-81; asst. project dir. Triad Am. Corp., Salt Lake City, 1983-86; mktg. coord. FHP Health Care, Salt Lake City, 1987, pub. affairs dir., 1987—; pres., mem. FHP Health Care PAC, 1987—. Author: History of Hartville, Ohio, 1976. Healthcare reform chmn. Ariz. Assn. Managed Care Plans, 1992—; dir. Ariz. Partnership for Infant Immunization, 1992—, Ariz. Preservation Found., 1992—; active Ariz. Affordable Healthcare Found., 1991—. Named Outstanding Vol., Utah Heritage Found., 1988. Mem. Pub. Rels. Soc. Am., Miami U. Alumni Assn. (pres. Utah chpt. 1988-91), Ohio State U. Alumni Assn., Alpha Tau Omega, Pi Sigma Alpha.

MCPHERSON, MICHAEL C., oil industry specialist, freelance writer; b. Ottawa, Ont., Can., Feb. 23, 1949; s. Joseph Ellwood and Norma Bernice (Langill) McP.; m. Linda Jane Gale, Dec. 22, 1953; children: James Michael, Natalie Marie. Grad. high sch., Ottawa. Gen. foreman Catalytic Enterprises, Ft. McMurray, Can., 1980-86; planner Syncrude Can. Ltd., Ft. McMurray, 1986—. Author short stories; contbr. articles to profl. jours. Fellow Writer's Guild of Alta., Small press and Artists Orgn. of fla. Roman Catholic. Office: PO Box 5693, Fort McMurray, AB Canada T9H 4V9

MCPHERSON, MICHAEL DALE, chemist; b. Roswell, N.M., Dec. 23, 1952; s. Dale Roy and Irene Claire (Poisson) McP.; m. Susan Helen Martin, Apr. 20, 1979. AA in Math and Sci., Am. River Coll., 1976; BA in Chemistry, Cal. State U., Sacramento, 1980, MS in Chemistry, 1986. Chemistry specialist Aerojet Propulsion Div., Sacramento, 1979—. Tchg. asst. Aerojet's "Adventures in Aerospace," Sacramento area elem. schs., 1985—. With USN, 1970-74; exec. officer USNR, 1976—. Recipient Delaney award, USNR, 1989. Mem. USNR Assn., Sacramento Personal Computer User's Group. Republican. Roman Catholic. Home: 945 Spyglass Ct Lincoln CA 95648-9575 Office: Aerojet Propulsion Div Hwy 50 and Hazel Ave PO Box 13222 Sacramento CA 95813-6000

MCPHERSON, WILLIAM DEAN, public affairs director; b. Enid, Okla., May 2, 1947; s. Norman Lewis and Jean Earline (Ziegler) McP. BA, Phillips U., 1969; BJ, U. Tex., 1975. News bur. dir. Phillips U., Enid, 1969; asst. editor Pearl Mag., U. Tex., Austin, 1974; asst. to dir. of advt. Army Western Recruiting Brigade, Sausalito, Calif., 1975-76; pub. affairs dir. 516th Signal Brigade, Honolulu, 1976—. Editor-in-chief: (entertainment mag.) Sunbums, 1977-79, (army newsletter) Pacific News, 1982-91; exec. editor: (army newspaper) Pacific Voice, 1992—. Sec. Hawaii Fed. Health and Safety Coun., Honolulu, 1983-86. With U.S. Army, 1970-72. Recipient Keith L. Ware award Dept. of the Army, Washington, 1984; named one of Outstanding Young Men of Am., 1984. Mem. Armed Forces Communications-Electronics Assn. (Hawaii chpt.), Hawaii Signal Corps. Regimental Assn. Republican. Methodist. Home: 1524 Pensacola St Apt 008 Honolulu HI 96822 Office: 516th Signal Brigade Palm Circle T-128 Ft Shafter HI 96858-5410

MCQUAID, SALLI LOU, writer, educator, artist; b. Eugene, Oreg., May 17, 1943; d. William D. Randall and Mary Lou (Robertson) Duwell; m. Patrick C. Wiley, July 15, 1962 (div. Oct. 1972); children: James W., Colleen L., Darren P.; m. Michael James McQuaid, June 27, 1987. BA, San Jose State U., 1975; MA in Art, 1983; grad., Nikon Sch. Photography, 1978. Freelance writer numerous newspapers and mags., San Francisco and others, 1975-78, 84—, Eugene and Springfield, Oreg., 1978-81; prof. San Jose State U., 1973-75, San Francisco State U., 1975; prof. of English Calif. State U., Hayward, 1987-92; writer, lectr. panelist Triton Mus. Art, Santa Clara, 1988; instr. fiction writing Las Positas Coll., Livermore, Calif., 1992; editor, pub. Artist Writer, Pleasanton, Calif., 1992—. Author: (poetry) I Looked Into Narcissus and Discovered a Mirror, 1977, (novella) In Oregon the Rain Is Gray, 1987, (screenplay) Death Quest, 1988, Omega Cop, 1990, Swords of Venus, 1991. Vol. Am. Cancer Soc., Pleasanton, Oreg., 1988, Aerobics for AIDS, 1992, Aerobics for Hearts, 1992. Named Foremost Art Critic, San Jose Art League, 1988. Mem. San Jose State U. Art Alumni Assn. (bd. dirs. 1984-86), Calif. Faculty Assn., World Kuk Sool Won Assn., Nat. Assn. Underwater Instrs., Nat. Writers Union. Democrat. Roman Catholic.

MCQUARRIE, TERRY SCOTT, technical director, executive; b. Springville, Utah, Dec. 27, 1942; s. Evan Dain and Fay (Torkeldsen) McQ.; m. Judith Lynn Lewellen, June 20, 1970; children: Devin Daniel, Melanie Fay. BA, U. Oreg., 1966; MA, San Jose State U., 1977. Production mgr. Lunastran Co., San Jose, Calif., 1974-76; group leader Koppers Co., Inc., Pitts., 1978-79, industry mgr., 1980-87; v.p., tech. dir. Glasforms, Inc., San Jose, Calif., 1987—; Chmn. Pultrusion Industry Coun. of SPI, N.Y.C., 1988-90; vice-chmn. Panel Coun. of SPI, 1986-87. Contbr. articles to profl. publs. Mem. ASTM, Composites Inst. of Soc. of Plastics Industry (bd. dirs. 1991—), Nat. Assn. Corrosion Engrs. Republican. Mem. LDS Ch.

MCQUEEN, STANLEY EUGENE, systems engineer; b. Lindsay, Calif., Aug. 24, 1946; s. Eugene Boggs and Mildred Louise (Knick) McQ.; m. Sue Jane Cupples, Sept. 2, 1967; children: Laura Melinda, Keith Eugene. BS in Physics, Tex. Christian U., Ft. Worth, 1968; MS in Space Physics, Air Force Inst. Tech., 1970. Engr. Martin Marietta Aerospace, Denver, 1977-80; mem. tech. staff Charles Stark Draper Lab., Cambridge, Mass., 1980-87; group ldr. The Mitre Corp., Bedford, Mass., 1987—; adj. prof. computer sci. Colo. Tech. Coll., 1990—. Dist. capt. Rep. Party, Colo., 1979; scoutmaster Boy Scouts Am., Lynnfield, Mass., 1982-84, scouting coord., Oxford, Mass., 1989. Capt. USAF, 1968-77. Mem. IEEE (participant in devel. software quality audit standard), ACM, NRA, Nat. Speleological Soc., Soc. for Computer Simulation, Sigma Pi Sigma. Republican. Mormon. Home: 2145 Sather Dr Colorado Springs CO 80915-4433 Office: The Mitre Corp 1259 Lake Plaza Dr Colorado Springs CO 80906-3568

MCQUERN, MARCIA ALICE, newspaper publishing executive; b. Riverside, Calif., Sept. 3, 1942; d. Arthur Carlyle and Dorothy Louise (Krupke) Knopf; m. Lynn Morris McQuern, June 7, 1969. BA in Polit. Sci., U. Calif., Santa Barbara, 1964; MS in Journalism, Northwestern U., 1966. Reporter The Press-Enterprise, Riverside, 1966-72, city editor, 1972-74, capitol corrs., 1975-78, dep. mng. editor news, 1984-85, mng. editor news, 1985-87, exec. editor, 1988—; pres., 1992—; asst. metro editor The Sacramento Bee, 1974-75; editor state and polit. news The San Diego Union, 1978-84, city editor, 1979-84; juror Pulitzer Prize in Journalism, 1982, 83, 92, 93. Mem. editorial bd. Calif. Lawyer mag., San Francisco, 1983-88. Bd. advisors U. Calif.-Berkeley Grad. Sch. Journalism, 1991—. Recipient Journalism award Calif. State Bar Assn., 1967, Sweepstakes award Twin Counties Press Club, Riverside and San Bernardino, 1972. Mem. Am. Soc. Newspaper Editors (bd. dirs. 1992—), Calif. Soc. Newspaper Editors (bd. dirs. 1988—), Calif. Newspaper Pubs. Assn. (bd. dirs. 1992—), Soc. Profl. Journalists, U. Calif.-Santa Barbara Alumni Assn. (bd. dirs. 1983-89). Home: 5717 Bedford Dr Riverside CA 92506-3404 Office: Press-Enterprise Co 3512 14th St Riverside CA 92501-3878

MCQUERRY, WAYNE HARRISON, aerospace engineer; b. St. Joseph, Mo., Sept. 28, 1922; s. James Madison and Anna Lois (Harrison) McQ.; m. Ruth Verle Collins, Dec. 21, 1945; children: Thomas Owen, Patricia Ann, Samuel Allen, Bruce Dean. BA, Northwest Mo. State U., 1949; postgrad., U. Kans., 1949-50, U. So. Calif., L.A., 1954-58, 58-59, UCLA, Irvine, 1978-80. Supt. schs. Hurdland (Mo.) Pub. Schs., 1950-51; physicist CAA Tech. Devel. & Evaluation Ctr., Indpls., 1951; engr. N.Am. Aviation, Inc., L.A., 1953-60; head antenna sect. Bendix Systems Div., Ann Arbor, Mich., 1960-62; rsch. specialist Calif. Tech. Jet Propulsion Lab., Pasadena, 1962-63; mem. tech. staff Rockwell Internat., Downey, Calif., 1963-90, ret., 1990. Mem. com. Boy Scouts Am., L.A., 1955-59, chmn. com., Ann Arbor, 1961-62; numerous offices St. Paul's United Meth. Ch., Orange, Calif., 1965—. Comdr. USN, WWII, Korea. Recipient numerous awards NASA. Republican. Home: 2938 E Roberta Dr Orange CA 92669-4757

MCQUILLEN-SHELTON, PAMELA JEAN, law library clerk, legal assistant; b. Youngstown, Ohio, Dec. 4, 1959; d. Arthur and Rosemary (Felitti) Humphries; m. John A. McQuillen, July 8, 1979 (dec. 1981); m. Donald William Shelton, Oct. 17, 1990. AA, Rio Salado Coll., 1986, A. of G.S., 1986, cert. couns., 1987; legal asst. degree, Internat. Corr. Sch., Scranton, Pa., 1990. Cert. paralegal. Merchandiser sales K-Mart Corp., Tucson, 1979-81; sales merchandiser La Canasta Distributors, Phoenix, 1982-83; law libr. clk. Ariz. State Prison-PV/SM, Goodyear, 1986-88, Ariz. State Prison-WP, Florence, 1989—. Home: Box 8000 Florence AZ 85232

MCQUILLIN, CYNTHIA ANN, songwriter, singer, owner; b. Santa Monica, Calif., July 25, 1953; d. John and Betty McQ. AA, City Coll. State U., Long Beach, Calif., 1976. Singer Calif., 1972—; rsch. asst. Richard C. Spurney, Long Beach, Calif., 1974-77; drafter R.E. Pearsalls, Long Beach, Calif., 1978-79; asst. office mgr. Compex, Inc., Culver City, Calif., 1981-84; shift supr. Etak, Inc., Menlo Pk., Calif., 1984-86; head of client liaison Compex, Inc., San Francisco, 1987-88; recording artist, producer Off Centaur Publs., El Cerrito, Calif., 1980-89; geographic tech. Etak, Inc., Menlo Pk., 1989-90; owner, operator Unlikely Publs., Berkeley, Calif., 1985—; Ind. recording artist, co-producer with Flowinglass Studios, Berkeley, Calif., 1991—, Wail Songs, Oakland, Calif., 1992—, Dag Prodns., L.A., 1991—, Thor Records, L.A., 1992—. Contbr. stories and poetry to profl. publs.; composer of over 200 recorded songs. Mem. BMI, Sci. Fiction and Fantasy Writers of Am. Office: Unlikely Publs PO Box 8542 Berkeley CA 94707

MCQUILLIN, RICHARD ROSS, management consultant; b. Elyria, Ohio, Oct. 15, 1956; s. Wayne Rupp and Frana Rose (Romp) McQ. BS, Ohio State U., 1979; MS, U. So. Calif., L.A., 1983; MBA, UCLA, 1990. Sr. staff mem. TRW Inc., Redondo Beach, Calif., 1979-88; sr. cons. Deloitte & Touche, L.A., 1990—. Treas., controller Patio Creek Homeowners Assn., Torrance, Calif., 1986-91, pres. 1991—; pres. TRW Investment Club, Redondo Beach, 1984-87. UCLA fellow, 1989. Mem. IEEE, Beta Gamma Sigma. Home: 19028 Entradero Ave Torrance CA 90503-1360 Office: Deloitte & Touche 333 S Grand Ave Wells Fargo Ctr Los Angeles CA 90071-3190

MCRAE, HAMILTON EUGENE, III, lawyer; b. Midland, Tex., Oct. 29, 1937; s. Hamilton Eugene and Adrian (Hagaman) McR.; m. Betty Hawkins, Aug. 27, 1960; children: Elizabeth Ann, Stephanie Adrian, Scott Hawkins. BSEE, U. Ariz., 1961; student, USAF Electronics Sch., 1961-62; postgrad., U. Redlands, Calif., 1962-63; JD with honors and distinction, U. Ariz., 1967; LHD (hon.), Sterling Coll., 1992; vis. fellow, Darwin Coll., Cambridge (Eng.) U. Bar: Ariz. 1967, U.S. Supreme Ct. 1979. Elec. engr. Salt River Project, Phoenix, 1961; assoc. Jennings, Strouss & Salmon, Phoenix, 1967-71, ptnr., 1971-85, chmn. real estate dept., 1980-85, mem. policy com., 1982-85, mem. fin. com., 1981-85, chmn. bus. devel. com., 1982-85; ptnr. and co-founder Stuckey & McRae, Phoenix, 1985—; co-founder, chmn. bd. Republic Cos., Phoenix, 1985—; magistrate Paradise Valley, Ariz., 1983-85; juvenile referee Superior Ct., 1983-85; pres., dir. Phoenix Realty & Trust Co., 1970—; officer Indsl. Devel. Corp. Maricopa County, 1972-86; instr. and lectr. in real estate; officer, bd. dirs. other corps.; adj. prof. Frank Lloyd Wright Sch. Architectute, Scottsdale, Ariz., 1989—; instr. Ariz. State U. Coll. Architecture and Environ. Design; lead instr. ten-state-bar seminar on Advanced Real Estate Transactions, 1992; freelance writer. Contbr. articles to profl. jours. Elder Valley Presbyn. Ch., Scottsdale, Ariz., 1973-75, 82-85, chair evangelism com. 1973-74, corp. pres., 1974-75, 84-85, trustee, 1973-75, 82-85, chmn. exec. com., 1984, mem. mission com. 1993; trustee Upward Found., Phoenix, 1977-80, Valley Presbyn. Found., 1982-83, Ariz. Acad., 1971—; trustee, mem. exec. com. Phi Gamma Delta Ednl. Found., Washington, 1974-84; trustee Phi Gamma Delta Internat., 1984-86; bd. dirs. Archon, 1986-87; founder, trustee, pres. McRae Found., 1980—; bd. dirs. Food for Hungry Inc. (Internat. Relief), 1985—, exec. com., 1986—, chmn. bd. dirs., 1987-92, Food for Hungry Internat., 1993—; trustee, mem. exec. com. Ariz. Mus. Sci. and Tech., 1984—, 1st v.p., 1985-86, pres., 1986-88, chmn. bd. dirs., 1988-90; Lambda Alpha Internat. Hon. Land Econs. Soc, 1988—; sec.-treas. Ariz. State U. Coun. for Design Excellence, 1989-90, bd. dirs. 1988—, pres. 1990-91; mem. Crisis Nursery Office of the Chair, 1988-89, Maricopa Community Colls. Found., 1988—, sec. 1990-91, 2d v.p. 1993—, Phoenix Community Alliance, 1988-90, Interchurch Ctr. Corp., 1987-90, Western Art Assocs., bd. dirs., 1989-91, Phoenix Com. on Fgn. Rels., 1988—, U. Ariz. Pres.'s Club, 1984—, chmn., 1991-92; bd. dirs. Econ. Club of Phoenix, 1987—, sec.-treas., 1991-92, v.p., 1992-93, pres. 1993—; mem. adv. bd. Help Wanted USA, 1990—; vol. fund raiser YMCA, Salvation Army, others; bd. dirs. Frank Lloyd Wright Found., 1992—; mem. Taliesin Coun., 1985—; founding mem. Frank Lloyd Wright Soc., 1993—, bd. dirs., 1992—; mem. fin. com. Kyl for Congress, 1985—, Symington for Gov. '90, 1989—, mem. gubernatorial adv. bd., 1990—; mem. Gov.'s Selection Com. for State Revenue Dir., 1993; mem. bond com. City of Phoenix, 1987-88; mem. Ariz. State U. Coun. of 100, 1985-89, investment com., 1985-89; bd. govs. Twelve Who Care Hon Kachina, 1991; mem. adv. coun. Maricopa County Sports Authority, 1989—; mem. Ariz. Coalition for Tomorrow, 1990—; bd. dirs. Waste Not Inc., 1990—, pres., 1990-92, chmn., 1990—. With USAF, 1961-64,. Recipient various mil. award. Mem. ABA, AIME, Ariz. Bar Assn., Maricopa County Bar Assn., U. Ariz. Alumni Assn., Nat. Soc. Fund Raising Execs., Clan McRae Soc. N.Am., Phoenix Exec. Club, Jackson Hole Racquet Club, Teton Pines Country Club, Tau Beta Pi. Republican. Home: 8101 N 47th St Paradise Vly AZ 85253-2907 Office: Republic Cos 2425 E Camelback Rd Ste 900 Phoenix AZ 85016-4215

MCRAE, JACK ARDON, sheep rancher; b. Miles City, Mont., Jan. 13, 1953; s. Charles William and Hazel Lavonne (Schultz) McR.; m. Kathryn Adams Hagstrom, Oct. 27, 1974; children: Cora Kathryn, Ian Charles, Kristin Emery, Malcolm Scott. Vice pres. Big Dry Angus Co., Jordan, Mont., 1974—; wool purchaser Ctr. of the National Wool, Belle Fourche, S.D., 1986-90; coring agt. Yokom McColl Testing Labs., Denver, 1982-86. Editor newsletter, Targhee News & Notes, 1986-90; contbr. articles to profl. jours. Mem. Mont. Targhee Sheep Assn. (sec.-treas. 1984-86), U.S. Targhee Sheep Assn. (exec. sec. 1986-90), Mont. Wool Growers Assn. (chmn. prodn. mktg. and health com. 1989-90), Nat. Wool Growers Assn. (breed improvement com. 1989), Am. Sheep Industry Assn. (rsch. edn. com. 1990), Am. Sheep Ind. Assn. (seedstock forum 1990—), World Sheep Breeders Coun. (dir. 1989—, v.p. 1992—).

MCREYNOLDS, BARBARA, artist; b. Omaha, May 5, 1956; d. Zachariah Aycock and Mary Barbara (McCulloh) McR.; m. Stephen Dale Dent, Mar. 12, 1983 (div. Dec. 30, 1992); children: Madeleine Barbara, Matthew Stephen. Student, U. N.Mex., 1979, MA in Community and Regional Planning, 1984. Artist, 1986-92; lectr. U. N.Mex. Sch. of Architecture, Albuquerque, 1979-82, 91—; assoc. planner, urban designer City of Albuquerque Planning Div., 1982-84; city planner, urban designer City of Albuquerque, N.Mex. Redevel. Div., 1984-88; cons. City of Albuquerque Redevel. Dept., 1987-88; urban design cons. Southwest Land Rsch., Albuquerque, 1991. Contbr. articles to profl. jours.; columnist for "Kids and Art", 1990-92; author: Coors Corridor Plan (The Albuquerque Conservation Assn. urban design award 1984), Electric Facilities Plan, Downtown Core Revitalization Strategy and Sector Development Plan. Vol. art tchr. Chaparral Elem. Sch., Albuquerque, 1989-92. Recipient First Pl. for Pastels, 20th Ann. Nat. Small Painting Exhibition, N.Mex. Art League, 1991, Best of Show awards Pastel Soc. of N.Mex., 1990, Award of Merit, Pastel Soc. of S.W., 1989, TACA award for Urban Design, 1984. Mem. Pastel Soc. of Am., Pastel Soc. N.Mex. (pres. 1991-92). Democrat. Episcopalian. Office: University of New Mexico Univ Of New Mexico NM 87131

MCREYNOLDS, GLENNA JEAN, writer; b. Lewiston, Idaho, Mar. 25, 1953; d. Richard Lloyd and Lois (Wilson) Gillis; m. Stanley Ryan McReynolds, Sept. 21, 1974; children: Kathleen Kleir, Chase Ryan. Author novels: Shameless, 1992, A Piece of Heaven, 1992, Outlaw Carson, 1991, Dateline: Kidd & Rios, 1990, 8 others. Mem. Colo. Romance Writers Assn., Colo. Authors League, Romance Writers of Am., Rocky Mountain Fiction Writers.

MCREYNOLDS, PAUL WYATT, psychologist, educator; b. Adrian, Mo., June 18, 1919; s. William Wilson and Edith Ella (McCune) McR.; m. Billie Bert Huffsmith, Aug. 14, 1955; 1 child, David Paul. BS, Ctrl. Mo. State U., 1940; MA, U. Mo., 1946; PhD, Stanford U., 1949. Clin. psychologist VA Med. Ctr., Palo Alto, Calif., 1947-51, chief psychol. rsch., 1952-59, chief Behavioral Rsch. Lab., 1960-68; prof. psychology U. Nev., Reno, 1969-87, prof. psychology emeritus, 1987—; lectr. dept. psychology San Francisco State U., 1956-57, U. Calif., Berkeley, 1961-65; cons. assoc. prof. Stanford U., 1956-68; vis. prof. psychology U. Oreg., Eugene, summer 1961. Editor: Advances in Psychological Assessment, vols. 1-8, 1968-92. Sgt. USAAF, 1942-45. Fellow APA, AAAS, Soc. for Personality Assessment. Office: U Nev Dept Psychology Reno NV 89557

MCRITCHIE, BRUCE DEAN, advertising agency executive; b. Buffalo, Apr. 12, 1938; s. D.R. and Augusta Louise (Schmidt) McR.; m. Barbara A. Baske, Dec. 8, 1962; children: Marilyn, Scott, John. AB, U. Mich., 1960, MBA, 1961. Media buyer Leo Burnett Inc., Chgo., 1962-64; acct. exec. Leo Burnett Inc., 1964-71; v.p., account supr. Grey Advt., Detroit, 1971-75; sr. v.p., mgmt. supr. Marschalk Co., Cleve., 1975-78, Kenyon & Eckhardt, Detroit, 1979-81; sr. v.p., gen. mgr. Grey Advt., Detroit, 1981-85; sr. v.p., gen. mgr. Grey Advt., Orange County, Calif., 1986-88, exec. v.p., gen. mgr., 1988—. Bd. dirs. Opera Pacific. Mem. Adcraft Club Detroit, Orange County Ad Club, L.A. Ad Club. Office: Grey Advt Inc One Pacific Plz 7711 Center Ave Ste 400 Huntington Beach CA 92647

MCROBERT, MARC KELLY, systems analyst; b. Carmel, Calif., May 22, 1954; s. Chester and Norma McRobert; m. Donna Sue West, Aug. 25, 1979. AA, Linn Benton C.C., Albany, Oreg., 1988; BA, Linfield Coll., 1990. Systems analyst CH2M Hill Inc., Corvallis, Oreg., 1979-91, BMC West Corp., Boise, Idaho, 1992—. Mem Data Processing Mmgt. Assn. (bd. dirs.). Office: BMC West Corp 1475 Tyrell Ln Boise ID 83707

MCROBERTS, JOYCE, state legislator; b. Salmon, Idaho, July 31, 1941; m. Darrell S. McRoberts; children: Walter, Angela, Douglas. Ed., Twin Falls Bus. Coll. Mem. Idaho State Senate. Republican. Home: 342 Monroe Pl Twin Falls ID 83301-3855

MCSORLEY, CISCO, lawyer; b. Albuquerque, July 8, 1950; s. Frank N. and Virginia E. (Norton) McS. BA, U. N.Mex., 1974, JD, 1979; postdoctoral sch. govt., Harvard U., 1986. Bar: N.Mex. 1980, U.S. Dist. Ct. N.Mex. 1980. Tchr. Academia Cotopaxi, Quito, Ecuador, S. Am., 1973-76; sole practice Albuquerque, 1980—. State rep. N.Mex. Ho. Reps., Albuquerque, 1984—. Mem. ABA, N. Mex. Bar. Assn., N. Mex. Trial Lawyers Assn., Assn. Trial Lawyers Am. Democrat. Mem. Soc. of Friends.

MCSWAIN, MARC DANIELL, electrical engineer; b. Bryan, Tex., Apr. 9, 1965; s. C.V. and Mary Cathryn (Ohmes) McS. BSEE, Tex. A&M U., 1985; MSEE, La. State U., 1988; engr. degree, U. So. Calif., 1992. Teaching asst. dept. elec. engring. La. State U., Baton Rouge, 1988; teaching asst. dept. elec. engring. U. So. Calif., L.A., 1988-91, rsch. asst. dept. elec. engring., 1989-90; asst. devel. engr. EEsof, Inc., Westlake Village, Calif., 1990, consulting devel. engr., 1990-91, devel. engr., 1991—. Mem. IEEE, NRA, CRPA. Home: 1642 E Hillcrest Dr Apt 201 Thousand Oaks CA 91362-2615 Office: EESOF Inc 5601 Lindero Canyon Rd Thousand Oaks CA 91362-4020

MCTERNAN, MYLES JAMES, retired air force officer, correctional officer; b. Cambridge, Mass., Mar. 9, 1948; s. Myles James and Margaret Josephine (Connors) McT.; m. Caren Marie Koons, July 21, 1979; children: Jason M. Purdy, Sabrina D. McTernan. BBA, U. Mass., 1969; MBA, Golden Gate U., 1978. Commd. 2d lt. USAF, 1969, advanced through grades to lt. col., 1985; chief tng. and ops. officer USAF Nav. Tng., Mather AFB, Calif., 1985-91; ret. USAF, 1992; correctional officer Folsom (Calif.) Return to Custody Inc., 1991-92; retail mgr. Izod, Folsom, 1993—; chmn. supervisory com. Mather Fed. Credit Union, Mather AFB, Calif., 1987-90. Vol., Folsom C. of C., 1986—. Named Vol. of Yr., Folsom C. of C., 1991. Mem. The Ret. Officers Assn., DAV, Mil. Order Purple Hearts. Home: 256 Randall Dr Folsom CA 95630

MCTIERNAN, MIRIAM, government executive; b. Limerick, Ireland, May 2, 1952; arrived in Can., 1973; d. Michael and Marjorie (Woulfe) Lynch; m. Timothy Patrick McTiernan, Oct. 31, 1972; 1 child, Leah Rhiannon. BA with honors, Nat. U. Ireland, U. Coll. Dublin, 1972, diploma in archival studies, 1973; diploma in pub. sector mgmt. U. Victoria, 1985. Coll. archivist Douglas Coll., New Westminster, B.C., 1973-76; univ. archivist U. B.C., Vancouver, 1975; credit union archivist B.C. Cen. Credit Union, Vancouver, 1976-79; govt. records archivist Govt. of Yukon, Whitehorse, Yukon Ter., 1979-80, territorial archivist, 1980-84, dir. librs. and archives, 1984-90; asst. dep. min. policy planning and adminstrn. Dept. of Govt. Svcs., 1990-91; asst. dep. min. econ. programs Bus. Dept. of Econ. Devel., 1991-92; acting dep. minister Dept Econ. Devel., 1993; dep. minister Econ. Devel. Contbr. articles to profl. jours. Mem. Assn. Can. Archivists (bus. archives com. 1976-79, treas. 1981-83, v.p. 1983-84, pres. 1984-85, chmn. nominations and elections com. 1985-87), Bur. Can. Archivists, Assn. B.C. Archivists (sec.-treas. 1976-78, pres. 1978-80), Can. Council of Archives (Yukon rep. 1985-90, bd. dirs. 1987-90, chair planning and priorities com. 1987-90), Yukon Geog. Names Bd., Yukon Hist. and Mus. Assn. (treas. 1981), Yukon Women's Bus. Network (bd. dirs. 1990-92), Soc. Am. Archivists, Assn. Records Mgr. and Adminstrs., Inst. Pub. Adminstrn. Can.

MCVAY, JOHN EDWARD, professional football club executive; b. Bellaire, Ohio, Jan. 5, 1931; s. John A. and Helen (Andrews) McV.; m. Eva Lee; children: John R., James P., Timothy G. B.S. in Edn., Miami U., Oxford, Ohio, 1953; M.A. in Sch. Adminstrn., Kent (Ohio) State U., 1963. Asst. football coach, instr. phys. edn. Mich. State U., 1962-65; head coach, dir. athletics U. Dayton, Ohio, 1965-74; head coach, gen. mgr. Memphis in World Football League, 1974-76; head football coach New York Giants, Nat. Football League, 1976-78; dir. player personnel San Francisco 49ers, Nat. Football League, 1979-80, dir. football ops., 1980-81, v.p. adminstrn., 1981-83, gen. mgr., v.p., 1983-89; v.p. FB ops., 1990—. Exec. dir. Catholic Youth Council, Canton, Ohio, 1959-62. Named to Miami U. Athletic Hall of Fame, named NFL exec. of the year, 1989. Mem. Sigma Chi, (significant Sig award), Phi Epsilon Kappa, Phi Delta Kappa. Office: care San Francisco 49ers 4949 Centennial Blvd Santa Clara CA 95054-1254

MCVEIGH, BYRON JOSEPH, economist; b. Cheyenne, Wyo., May 14, 1956; s. William Patrick and Carolyn Irene (Hoover) McV.; m. Lucy Ann Freeman, Oct. 29, 1987; children: Hayden Michael, Myles Taylor. AA, Laramie County C.C., Cheyenne, 1974-76; BS, U. Wyo., 1979. Agrl. statistician Dept. Agr., State of Wyo., Cheyenne, 1980-85; economist Dept. Adminstrn., State of Wyo., Cheyenne, 1985-88, sr. economist, 1988—; economist Consensus Revenue Estimating Group, Cheyenne, 1985—; chair Socio-Econ. Rsch. Coordinating Com., Cheyenne, 1991-92; mem. Community Assessment Team-Econ. Devel., Cheyenne, 1989-91. Author: Wyoming Gross State Product Report, 1988, 91, Wyoming Sales and Use Tax Revenue Report, 1986-91; editor: Wyoming Data Handbook, 1985, 87, 89, 91. Bd. dirs. Laramie County C.C. Golden Eagles Club, Cheyenne, 1986-87; mem. adv. bd. DePaul Health and Fitness Inst., Cheyenne, 1990-91. Named to Outstanding Young Men of Am., 1980. Mem. Sigma Chi (life). Republican. Roman Catholic. Home: 2319 Van Lennen Ave Cheyenne WY 82001 Office: State of Wyo Div Econ Analysis 327 E Emerson Bldg Cheyenne WY 82002-0060

MCVEIGH-PETTIGREW, SHARON CHRISTINE, communications consultant; b. San Francisco, Feb. 6, 1949; d. Martin Allen and Frances (Roddy) McVeigh; m. John Wallace Pettigrew, Mar. 27, 1971; children: Benjamin Thomas, Margaret Mary. B.A. with honors, U. Calif.-Berkeley, 1971; diploma of edn. Monash U., Australia, 1975; M.B.A., Golden Gate U., 1985. Tchr., adminstr. Victorian Edn. Dept., Victoria, Australia, 1972-79; supr. Network Control Ctr., GTE Sprint Communications, Burlingame, Calif., 1979-81, mgr. customer assistance, 1981-84, mgr. state legis. ops., 1984-85, dir. revenue programs, 1986-87; communications cons. Flores, Pettigrew & Co., San Mateo, Calif., 1987-89; mgr. telemarketing Apple Computer, Inc., Cupertino, Calif., 1989—; telecommunications speaker Dept. Consumer Affairs, Sacramento, 1984. Panelist Wash. Gov.'s Citizens Council, 1984; founding mem. Maroondah Women's Shelter, Victoria, 1978; organizer nat. conf. Bus. Women and the Polit. Process, New Orleans, 1986; mem. sch. bd. Boronia Tech. Sch., Victoria, 1979. Recipient Tchr. Spl. Responsibilities award Victoria Edn. Dept., 1979. Mem. Women in Telecommunications (panel moderator San Francisco 1984), Am. Mgmt. Assn., Peninsula Profl. Women's Network, Am. Telemktg. Assn. (bd. dirs. 1992), Women's Econ. Action League. Democrat. Roman Catholic. Office: 333 W San Carlos St Ste 700 San Jose CA 95110-2721

MCVICAR, MARK ALBERT, sports broadcaster; b. Independence, Mo., Feb. 11, 1961; s. Thomas Henry and Janice Marie (Lampe) McV.; m. Susan Emery Jenkins, June 18, 1988. BA, Syracuse U., 1983. Baseball announcer Syracuse Chiefs Baseball Team, 1982-83; sport dir., asst. news dir. Sta. KFKA Radio, Greeley, Colo., 1983-88; TV sports reporter Columbine Cablevision, Ft. Collins, Colo., 1988-89; sports dir. Sta. KIIX Radio, Ft. Collins, 1988-89; news reporter, radio talk host Sta. KNUS Radio, Denver, 1989-90; play-by-play announcer Denver Zephyrs Baseball Club, 1991-92; TV sports host United Artists Cable, Greeley, 1990—; program dir., sports dir. Sta. KFKA, Greeley, 1990—. Recipient numerous sportscasting awards AP, 1992, Best Sports Spl. award AP, 1993, Best Sportscast 2d Pl. award AP, 1993. Home: 4208 Redbird Pl Loveland CO 80537 Office: KFKA Radio 820 11th Ave Greeley CO 80631

MC VIE, CHRISTINE PERFECT, musician; b. Eng., July 12, 1943; m. John McVie (div.); m. Eddy Quintela. Student art sch., pvt. student sculpture. Singer, keyboardist, Fleetwood Mac, from 1970; albums with Fleetwood Mac include: Bare Trees, 1972, Penguin, Mystery To Me, Heroes Are Hard to Find, 1975, Fleetwood Mac, 1976, Rumours, 1977, Tusk, 1979, Mirage, 1982, Tango in the Night, 1987, Greatest Hits, 1988, Behind the Mask, 1990; solo albums include Christine Perfect, 1969, Christine McVie, 1984; composer: songs including Spare Me a Little of Your Love, Don't Stop, You Make Loving Fun, Over and Over, Hold Me, Songbird, Got a Hold on Me, Heroes Are Hard to Find, Little Lies, As Long as You Follow, Save Me., Skies the Limit. Office: care Warner Bros Records 3300 W Warner Blvd Burbank CA 91505-4694

MCWHIRTER, JAMES JEFFRIES, psychologist, educator; b. Big Spring, Tex., Jan. 31, 1938; s. James Davidson and Hazel Barbara (Jeffries) McW.; m. Mary Clare Plasker, Aug. 27, 1960; children: Robert, Benedict, Anna, Mark, Paula. BA, St. Martin's Coll., Olympia, Wash., 1961; MEd, U. Oreg., 1964, Oreg. State U., 1965; PhD, U. Oreg., 1969. Psychologist, Ariz.; diploamte Am. Bd. Profl. Psychology. Tchr./counselor Cen. Cath. High Sch., Portland, 1961-63, Centenniel High Sch., Portland, 1963-67; psychology resident VA Hosp./U. Oreg. Med. Sch., Portland, 1969-70; prof. counseling psychology Ariz. State U., Tempe, 1970—; vis. summer prof. various instns., U.S.A., Can., Europe; Fulbright prof. Hacettepe U., Ankara, Turkey, 1977-78, Australia, 1984-85; psychologist in pvt. practice, Tempe, 1970—; cons. in field. Author: Learning Disabled Children, 1977, 88, Problem Solving in Families, 1983, At-Risk Youth: A Comprehensive Response, 1993; editor various books; contbr. numerous articles to profl. jours. Fulbright scholar, 1977-78, 84-85; recipient Disting. Tchr. award, Ariz. State U. Alumni Assn., 1989, Profl. Advancement award, Assn. of Specialists in Group Wk., 1985-86. Fellow APS, APA, Div. 17 of Counseling Psychology; mem. ACA. Democrat. Roman Catholic. Office: Arizona State U Psychology in Edn Payne 425 Tempe AZ 85287-0611

MCWILLIAMS, ROBERT HUGH, judge; b. Salina, Kans., Apr. 27, 1916; s. Robert Hugh and Laura (Nicholson) McW.; m. Catherine Ann Cooper, Nov. 4, 1942 (dec.); 1 son, Edward Cooper; m. Joan Harcourt, Mar. 8, 1986. A.B., U. Denver, 1938, LL.B., 1941. Bar: Colo. bar 1941. Colo. dist. judge Denver, 1952-60; justice Colo. Supreme Ct., 1961-68, chief justice, 1969-70; judge U.S. Ct. Appeals (10th cir.), Denver, 1970—. Served with AUS, World War II. Mem. Phi Beta Kappa, Omicron Delta Kappa, Phi Delta Phi, Kappa Sigma. Republican. Episcopalian. Home: 137 Jersey St Denver CO 80220-5918 Office: US Ct Appeals 10th Circuit C-402 US Courthouse 1929 Stout St Denver CO 80294-2900

MCWILLIAMS, ROGER DEAN, physicist, educator; b. Ames, Iowa, Aug. 18, 1954; s. Donald Arthur and Margaret Ann (Edgar) McW.; m. Carol Lee Carter, Sept. 7, 1985; 1 child, Alice Louise. BA, U. Calif., Irvine, 1975; PhD, Princeton U., 1980. Rsch. asst. Princeton (N.J.) U., 1975-80; asst. prof. in physics U. Calif., Irvine, 1980-87, assoc. prof., 1987-91, prof., 1991—, cons., expert witness for physics and law, 1983—, cons., expert witness for physics in sports, 1988—. Mem. Am. Phys. Soc., Am. Geophys. Union, Phi Beta Kappa. Office: U Calif Physics Irvine CA 92717

MEACHAM, CHARLES P., fish and game commissioner, biologist; b. Susanville, Calif., Apr. 29, 1947; m. Charlene D. Heriot, 1969; 3 children. BS, Humboldt State U., 1969, MS in Fisheries, 1971. Comml. fisherman Bristol Bay, Alaska, 1963-66; with Bumble Bee Seafoods, Bristol Bay, S.E. Alaska, 1967-69; fisheries cons. Winzler & Kelly Engring., Eureka, Calif., 1970; seafood insp. U.S. Army Med. Dept., Ft. Richardson, Alaska, 1971-74; staff biologist Alaska Dept. of Fish and Game, Juneau, Alaska, 1974-75; rsch. biologist Artic Char investigations Alaska Dept. of Fish and Game, Dillingham, Alaska, 1975-77; Bristol Bay rsch. project leader Alaska Dept. of Fish and Game, Anchorage, 1978-81, regional rsch. supr., 1981-89, mgr. fishery program divsn. of oil spill impact assessment and restoration, 1990-91; dep. commr. Alaska Dept. of Fish and Game, Juneau, 1991—; affiliate faculty U. Alaska, 1983-87; mem. Bering Sea/Aleutians plan team N. Pacific Fisheries Mgmt. Council, 1989, Alaska Regional Marine Rsch. Bd., 1992-93, Pacific Fisheries Mgmt. Coun., 1991-93; commr. Pacific States

Marine Fisheries Commn., 1991-93, Pacific Salmon Commn., 1991-93. Mem. Mayor's Task Force on Fisheries, Anchorage, 1988-89, Alaska Tourism Coordinating Commn., 1992-93; mem. review team Alaska Sci. & Tech. Found., 1989; alt. mem. Exxon Valdez Oil Spill Trustee Coun., 1992-93. Mem. NAS, OSB (fisheries com., 1992, 93), Am. Fisheries Soc. (life, v.p. Alaska chpt. 1975, pres. elect 1977, pres. 1978), Am. Inst. of Fishery Rsch. Biologists. Home: 533 Main St Juneau AK 99801

MEAD, SEDGWICK, physician; b. Guymon, Okla., July 2, 1911; s. Redmond Boyd and Bertha Mabel (Hunter) Corbett; m. Marjorie Frances Chick, Sept. 22, 1940 (dec.); children: Sedgwick Jr., Marshall. Student, U. Ariz., 1930-31; SB cum laude, Harvard U., 1934, MD, 1938. Diplomate Am. Bd. Phys. Medicine and Rehab. Baruch fellow Harvard Med. Sch., Boston, 1946-47; assoc. prof. Sch. of Medicine Washington U., St. Louis, 1948-54; med. dir. Kaiser Found. Rehab. Ctr., Vallejo, Calif., 1954-69; ast. clin. prof. Sch. of Medicine Stanford (Calif.) U., 1955-60; clin. prof. U. Calif., Davis, 1969-72; chief neurology Kaiser-Permanente Med. Ctr., Vallejo, 1969-77; med. dir. Easter Seal Rehab. Ctr., Oakland, Calif., 1983-93; intern Mass. Gen. Hosp., 1938-40, resident pathology, 1940-41, resident neurology, 1941-42; cons. coun. on med. physics AMA, Chgo., 1950-54; pres. Assn. Rehab. Ctrs., 1953, Am. Acad. Cerebral Palsy, Richmond, Va., 1967. Chmn. governing bd. Retired Physicians Assn. Perm Med. Group, Oakland, 1989-90; trustee Costra Costa County Mosquito Abatement Dist., Concord, Calif., 1970-73; mem. White House Conf. on Health, Washington, 1953. With AUS, 1942-45, col. USAR, ret. 1971. Scholar Harvard Coll., 1932. Mem. AMA, World Med. Assn., Mass. Med. Soc., Am. Acad. Neurology, Am. Acad. Cerebral Palsy (pres. 1967), Faculty Club U. Calif. Berkeley, Harvard Club San Francisco, Commonwealth Club San Francisco. Unitarian.

MEAD, TERRY EILEEN, hospital administration consultant, physician practice consultant; b. Portland, Oreg., Mar. 14, 1950; d. Everett L. and Jean (Nonken) Richardson; divorced; 1 child, Sean Wade Adcock. AA, Seattle U., 1972; postgrad., U. Wash., 1971. Project mgr. Assoc. Univ. Physician, Seattle, 1971-74; pathology supr. Swedish Hosp., Seattle, 1974-77; svcs. supr. Transamerica, Seattle, 1977-78; various mgmt. positions Providence Hosp., Seattle, 1978-83; adminstr. Evergreen Surg. Ctr., Kirkland, Wash., 1983-86; bus. mgr. Ketchikan (Alaska) Gen. Hosp., 1986—; instr. U. Alaska, Ketchikan, 1990; sec. SE adv. bd. U. Alaska, Ketchikan, 1987—; cons. hosps. and physicians, Wash., Alaska, 1980-89; mgr. Practice Mgmt. Cons., Seattle, 1982-83. Mem. City Charter Rev. Com., Ketchikan, 1990, High Sch. Facilities Com, Ketchikan, 1990; S.E. dir. search com U. Alaska, Ketchikan, 1990; treas. Calvary Bible Ch., Ketchikan, 1989-91; bd. dirs. S.E. Alaska Symphony, 1992—, Jr. Achievement, 1992-93. Mem. Rotary Internat. Home: PO Box 8096 Ketchikan AK 99901-3096 Office: 3100 Tongass Ave Ketchikan AK 99901-5794

MEADE, JODEEN VONNE, real estate executive; b. Covina, Calif., July 9, 1962; d. Glenn Atwood and Norma Jean (Leech) M. BA in Biology and Chemistry, Calif. State U., Northridge, 1985. Gen. mgr. Nat. Redevel. Co., Beverly Hills, Calif., 1985-88; v.p. Comml. Properties Divsn. Rescor, Inc., Beverly Hills, 1988-91; dir. property mgmt. retail divsn. Shea Bus. Properties, Walnut, Calif., 1991—. Mem. Women in Comml. Real Estate (bd. dirs., chmn. program com. 1993, mem. program com. 1991-92), Internat. Coun. Shopping Ctrs., Bldg. Owners Mgmt. Assn. Republican. Presbyterian. Office: Shea Bus Properties 655 Brea Canyon Rd Walnut CA 91789

MEADE, KENNETH JOHN, realty company owner, broker; b. N.Y.C., Nov. 25, 1925; s. John Joseph and Blanche (Woodworth) M.; m. Alice Elizabeth (Steinmann), Nov. 8, 1952; children: Steven, Janet, Patricia. Student, N.Y. Inst. Fin., 1960-62. Cert. real estate residential broker. Sales broker Del Webb Devel., Sun City, Ariz., 1974-82; mgr. Mull Realty Inc., Sun City, Ariz., 1982-83; broker, owner 4 offices Ken Meade Realty Inc., Sun City, Ariz., 1983—; dir., treas. Sun City Bd. Realtors, 1988—. Bd. dirs., v.p. Sun City Ambs., 1988—. With USN, 1942-45. Mem. Nat. Assn. Realtors, Ariz. Assn. Realtors, Dale Carnegie Club (past instr. sales course, Outstanding Achievment 1964). Republican. Lutheran. Home: 13306 W Meeker Blvd Sun City West AZ 85375-3815 Office: Ken Meade Realty Inc 17001 N Del Webb Blvd Sun City AZ 85373

MEADE, ROBERT DALE, psychology educator; b. Washington, Ind., Apr. 9, 1927; s. Jesse Lee and Martha Mildred (Ball) M. BA, Ind. U., 1950; AM, U. Pa., 1952, PhD, 1956. Instr. U. Pa., Phila., 1952-55; asst. prof. Trinity Coll., Hartford, Conn., 1955-60, assoc. prof., 1960-65; assoc. prof. psychology Western Wash. U., Bellingham, 1965-66, prof., 1966-93, prof. emeritus, 1993—, founder, dir. Ctr. for Cross-Cultural Rsch., 1969-89; Fulbright prof., India, 1964-65; rsch. assoc. Chinese U., Hong Kong, 1968-69, U. Rhodesia, 1965-66, U. Calif., Berkeley, 1985-86; rsch. assoc. Meerut (India) U., 1971-72, fellow Inst. Advanced Study, 1971—; sci. faculty fellow NSF, 1972-79; bd. dirs. Le Grand Cuisinier, Bellingham. Co-founder Jour. of Cross-Cultural Psychology, 1969. Sci. faculty fellow NSF, 1971-73. Mem. Internat. Soc. Tchr. Edn., Chevaliers du Tastevin, Chaine des Rotisseurs, Knights of Vine (master knight, master chef). Office: Western Wash U High St Bellingham WA 98225-5942

MEADER, WILLARD L., health foundation executive; b. LaPorte, Ind., Nov. 23, 1933; s. Robert Paul and Julia Louise (Lingel) M.; m. Sharon Sue Inman, Jan. 21, 1961; children: Richard P., Dana L. Albion Coll., 1954, MD; Temple U. Sch. Med., Phila., 1958; MPH, U. Calif., 1965; postgrad., Indsl. Coll. Armed Forces, Ft. McNair, DC, 1975. Commd. USAF, 1959, advanced through grades to brig. gen.; various med. positions to comdr. 377th Dispensary USAF, Tan Son Nhut Airfield, Vietnam, 1967-68; comdr. USAF, Clinic RAF, Wethersfield, Great Britain, 1968-70; dir. of aero med. & deputy surgeon Hdqrs. 2d Air Force, Barksdale AFB, La., 1970-71; cmmdr. USAF, Clinic RAF, Bentwaters, Great Britain, 1971-74; dir. of biotech. & dep. surgeon hdqrs. Air Force Systems Command USAF, Andrews AFB, Md., 1975-78; hosp. cmmdr. USAF, Nellis AFB, Nev., 1978-80; command surgeon hdqrs. Pacific Air Forces USAF, Hickam AFB, Hawaii, 1980-83; command surgeon hdqrs. Air Force Logistics Command USAF, Wright-Patterson AFB, Ohio, 1983-89; retired USAF, 1989; pres. Hanford Environ. Health Found., Richland, Wash., 1989—; preceptor aerospace med. HQ 2nd Air Force Barksdale, 1971-72, assoc. clinical prof. Wright State U. Sch. of Med. Dayton, 1984—, Sch. Pub. Health and Community Medicine U. Wash., 1989—. Fellow Am. Coll. Preventive Med., Am. Coll. Physician Execs., Am. Coll. Occupational Medicine, Aerospace Med. Assn.; mem. AMA, Am. Mgmt. Assn., Soc. USAF Flight Surgeons (pres. 1980-81),. Republican. Methodist. Home: 2013 Greenview Dr Richland WA 99352-9698 Office: 3070 George Washington Way Richland WA 99352-1658

MEADE-TOLLIN, LINDA CELIDA, biochemist, educator, researcher; b. London, W.Va., Aug. 16, 1944; d. Robert Alfred and Virginia May (Daniels) Meade; m. Gordon Tollin, Aug. 5, 1978; 1 child, Amina Rebecca. BS, W.Va. State Coll., 1964; MA, Hunter Coll., 1969; PhD, CUNY, 1972. Asst. prof. SUNY, Old Westbury, 1972-75; NIH rsch. fellow biochemistry U. Ariz., Tucson, 1975-77, rsch. assoc. microbiology, 1977-79, coord. Women in Sci. and Engring. Office, 1980-82, vis. asst. prof. chemistry, 1982-85, rsch. asst. prof. anatomy, sr. lectr. biochemistry, 1987-92, rsch. asst. prof. radiation oncology, 1990—; vis. asst. prof. Rockefeller U., N.Y.C., 1973-75; faculty devel. fellow Morehouse U. Sch. Medicine, Atlanta, 1985-86; cons., workshop facilitator Am. Med. Women's Assn. Profl. Resources Rsch. Ctr., Tucson, 1977-85. Contbg. author: What People Eat, 1974; also articles and abstracts. Bd. dirs. Ododo Theatre Found., Tucson. Recipient Minority Special Investigator award Nat. Cancer Inst., 1987-89, 90-93. Mem. Am. Assn. Cancer Rsch., Nat. Orgn. for Profl. Advancement Black Chemists and Chem. Engrs. (chmn. exec. bd. 1981-82). Democrat. Office: U Ariz Ariz Cancer Ctr Dept Radiation Oncology 1515 N Campbell Ave Tucson AZ 85724

MEADOWS, GARY GLENN, pharmacy science educator, researcher; b. American Falls, Idaho, June 6, 1945; s. Melvin Glenn and Wilmetta (Hartley) M.; m. Kathleen Michelle Smith, June 8, 1968; children: Sarah Agnes, Philip Glenn. BS, Idaho State U., 1968, MS, 1972; PhD, U. Wash., 1976. Lic. pharmacist, Idaho, Wash. Asst. prof. Wash. State U., Pullman, 1976-82, assoc. prof., 1982-89, chmn. dept. pharmacy sci., 1990—, prof., 1989—; mem. panel grant review Am. Inst. for Cancer Rsch., Washington, 1985—; mem. alcohol biomed. review com. NIAAA, Bethesda, Md., 1987-91. Author: (chpt.) Alcohol, Immunity, Cancer, 1992; contbr. articles to profl. jours. Mem. Pullman Community Band, 1990. Recipient Rsch. Scientist Devel. award Nat. Inst. Alcohol Abuse and Alcoholism, 1991-96, rsch. grant, 1992—. Mem. Am. Assn. for Cancer Rsch., Rsch. Soc. on Alcoholism, Metastasis Rsch. Soc., Am. Assn. Colls. of Pharmacy, Am. Soc. for Pharmacology and Exptl. Therapeutics. Office: Wash State Univ Coll Pharmacy Pullman WA 99164-6510

MEAGHER, CYNTHIA NASH, journalist; b. Detroit, Dec. 24, 1947; d. Frederick Copp and Carolyn (Coffin) Nash; 1 child, Lydia Anne. BA, U. Mich., 1969. Reporter, Detroit News, 1970-75, sports columnist, 1975-77, Life Style columnist, 1977-79, Life Style editor, 1979-82; news features editor Seattle Times, 1983, asst. mng. editor Sunday Seattle Times, 1983-86, assoc. mng. editor, 1986—. Mem. City Club, Harbor Sq. Club. Office: Seattle Times PO Box 70 Fairview Ave N & John St Seattle WA 98111-0070

MEAGHER, MICHAEL, radiologist; b. New Rochelle, N.Y., Oct. 24, 1942; s. Joseph Aloysius and Elizabeth (Ahern) M.; m. Martha Batten Mitchell, 1968; children: Kelly, Courtney. Student, Rensselaer Poly. Inst., 1960-62; AB with distinction, U. Rochester, 1964; MD, Stanford U., 1969. Diplomate Am. Bd. Radiology, Nat. Bd. Med. Examiners. Intern in medicine Cornell U., N.Y. Hosp., 1969-70; jr. asst. resident in diagnostic radiology U. Wash., Seattle, 1970-71, sr. asst. resident diagnostic radiology, 1973-74, resident diagnostic radiology, 1974-75; active staff mem. dept. radiology Queen's Med. Ctr., Honolulu, 1975—, Leahi Hosp., Honolulu, 1981—, Kahuku (Hawaii) Hosp., 1988—; pres. Radiology Assocs., Inc., 1978, 81-84, 90; chmn. dept. radiology Queen's Med. Ctr., 1979-80, 82-86, 88-90, dir. dept. radiology, 1985-91, dir. magnetic resonance imaging, 1991—, chmn. cancer com., 1980-82; mem. med. staff Hawaii Health Tech. Magnetic Resonance Imaging Facility, Honolulu, 1986—, chief of staff, 1978; clin. instr. dept. radiology U. Hawaii Sch. Medicine, 1983-89, clin. assoc. prof., 1989-93, clin. prof., 1993—, asst. rsch. prof. Cancer Rsch. Ctr. Hawaii, 1989—; clin. asst. prof. dept. radiology U. Wash. Sch. Medicine, 1980-88; presenter in fld. Contbr. articles to profl. publs. Chmn. high tech. adv. com. State Health Planning and Devel. Agy., 1983—; bd. dirs. Friends of Hawaii Pub. TV, 1979-81; pres., CEO Queen's Health Care Plan, Honolulu, 1985-89, chmn. bd. dirs., 1989-91; bd. dirs. Managed Care Mgmt., Inc., Honolulu, 1990; v.p. bd. dirs. Hawaii Opera Theatre, 1990-91, treas., 1991—. Lt. comdr. USN, 1971-73. NIH fellow, 1966; Kaiser Found. grantee, 1967. Fellow Am. Coll. Radiology; mem. AMA, Hawaii State Radiol. Soc. (sec.-treas. 1978-79, v.p. 1979-80, pres. 1980-81), Radiol. Soc. N.Am., Soc. Computer Applications in Radiology (charter), Am. Roentgen Ray Soc. Home: 1234 Maunawili Rd Kailua HI 96734 Office: Queen's Med Ctr Dept Radiology Honolulu HI 96813

MEANS, JAMES ANDREW, engineer; b. Heavener, Okla., Oct. 11, 1937; s. Edward Andrew and Lorena (Nobles) M.; Therese Louise Zimmerman, Feb. 21, 1959; children: James A. Jr., William R., Charles E., Vicky M. Locken. BSEE, U. Ariz., 1962, MSEE, 1966; PhD, U. Calif., Santa Barbara, 1972; MS in Computer Sci., Chapman Coll., Orange, Calif., 1988. Engr. Pacific Missile Test Ctr., Pt Mugu, Calif., 1962-72; engr. mgr. Pacific Missile Test Ctr., 1972-79; tech. dir. Space & Missile Test Orgn., Vandenberg AFB, Calif., 1979-89; sr. tech. advisor SRI Internat., Menlo Park, Calif., 1990—; cons. Agri-Craft, Camarillo, Calif., 1968-70, Astro-Geo-Marine, Ventura, Calif., 1972-74. Patentee in field. Mem. Internat. Found. for Telemetering (pres. 1988—), Internat. Test and Evaluation Assn. Democrat. Baptist. Home: 284 St Andrews Way Lompoc CA 93436-1355 Office: SRI Internat 333 Ravenswood Ave Menlo Park CA 94025-3493

MEANS, PAUL RICHARD, management consultant; b. Tulsa, Aug. 19, 1943; s. Paul Willard and Marie Louise (Conkey) M.; m. Joan Mary Stein, Aug. 12, 1972; children: Emily, Paul. BA, U. Tulsa, 1965; MPA, Syracuse U., 1972. Lic. real estate broker, Calif. Adminstrv. asst. to city mgr. City of Naperville, Ill., 1972-75; resident community mgr. Ygnacio Gardens Homeowners Assn., Walnut Creek, Calif., 1976; community mgr. Promex Community Mgmt., San Francisco, 1977-81; pres. Metro Community Mgmt., Inc., Walnut Creek, Calif., 1982-92; owner Community Assn. Realty, Walnut Creek, Calif., 1981—; v.p. mgmt. svcs. Hudson Mgmt. Co., Pleasant Hill, Calif., 1992—. Author: Selling in Homeowners Associations, 1984; contbr. articles to profl. jours. Vol. U.S. Peace Corps, Kerala, India, 1965-67, Boy Scouts Am., Pleasant Hill, Calif., 1990—, Pleasant Hill Martinez Soccer, 1987-89; sponsor Pleasant Hill-Martinez Baseball Assn., 1985-90. With U.S. Army, 1967-69. Decorated Bronze Star medal. Mem. Bldg. Industry Assn., Calif. Assn. Realtors, Am. Assn. Pub. Adminstrs., Community Assns. Inst. (Bay area chpt. pres. 1984-85), Lions.

MEARS, RICHARD RILEY, music publishing executive; b. Orange, N.J., June 19, 1951; s. George Wood Mears and Ruth Mears (Riley) Gates; m. Marilyn Ruth Covington, Oct. 25, 1986; children: James Covington, Davis Riley. Student, Moravian Coll., 1974, Columbia U., 1974; BA in Music, Lehigh U., 1974. Cert. sound engr. Songwriter Curb Music Co., Burbank, Calif., 1986—, music pub., 1991—. Songwriter: Dreamin's the Best Thing, 1988. Bd. mem. Thirteenth Ch. of Christ Scientist, Calif., 1992. Republican. Home: 1315 Shirley Jean St Glendale CA 91208 Office: 3907 W Alameda Burbank CA 91805

MEARS, RICK RAVON, professional race car driver; b. Wichita, Kans., Dec. 3, 1951; s. Bill Ravon and Mae Louise (Simpson) M.; m. Christyn Bowen, Nov. 28, 1986; children—Clint Ravon, Cole Ray. Student public schs. Profl. race car driver, 1973—; mem. Roger Penske Racing Team (with Danny Sullivan)and Emerson Fittipaldi Racing Team, 1978—. Named Rookie of Yr. championship div. U.S. Auto Club, 1976; nat. driving champion Championship Auto Racing Teams, 1979; Am. Auto Racing Writers and Broadcasters Assn. Auto Racing All American, 1979; Jerry Titus Meml. Trophy as U.S. Driver of Yr., 1981. Address: PO Box 40565 Bakersfield CA 93384

MEAUX, ALAN DOUGLAS, facilities technician, sculptor; b. Joliet, Ill., Sept. 10, 1951; s. Berry Lee and Luella Ann (Ferguson) M.; m. Letta Sue Nygaard, Sept. 15, 1984; children: Ashley Nicole, Lacey Marie. Student, Joliet Jr. Coll., 1969-71, Bradley U., 1971-72, U.S. Dept. Agr. Grad. Sch., 1972, Skagit Valley Coll., 1983-85. Photographer J.J.C. Blazer, Joliet Herald News, Joliet, 1969-71; auto mechanic Pohanka Olds and Fiat, Hillcrest Heights, Md., 1972-74, Hoffman Olds and Rolls Royce, Hartford, Conn., 1974-75; carpenter Klappenbach Constrn. Co., Moscow, Idaho, 1975-79; property mgr. Olympic Builders, Oak Harbor, Wash., 1979-86; maintenance technician Troubleshooters Inc., Oak Harbor, 1986-87; facilities technician Island County Govt., Coupeville, Wash., 1987—; bronze sculptor Ronin Art Prodns., Oak Harbor, 1979—; appraiser class A Mid-Am. Appraisers Assn., Springfield, Mo., 1986—; bd. dirs. North West Token Kai, U. Waington, Seattle, 1989—, lectr., 1985; contbr. Nanka Token Kai, L.A., 1985—. Author: Japanese Samurai Weapons, 1989; prin. works exhibited at Mini Guild Children's Orthopedic Show, Ballard, Wash., 1986, Worldfest/Ethnic Heritage Coun., Seattle, 1988, 89, 90, Stanwood (Wash.) Invitational Art Show, 1988. Mem. Japanese Sword Soc. U.S. (life), N.W. Token Kai (charter, bd. dirs. 1989-91), Western Mus. Conf., Wash. Mus. Assn., Ethnic Heritage Coun., Nanka Token Kai, Japan Soc. Inc., Nat. Rifle Assn., Wash. Arms Collectors Assn, North Whidbey Sportmen's Assn., Cen. Whidbey Sportmen's Club. Office: Ronin Art Prodns PO Box 1271 Oak Harbor WA 98277-1271

MECHAM, GLENN JEFFERSON, lawyer; b. Logan, Utah, Dec. 11, 1935; s. Everett H. and Lillie (Dunford) M.; BS, Utah State U., 1957; JD, U. Utah, 1961; m. Mae Parson, June 5, 1957; children: Jeff B., Scott R., Marcia, Suzanne. Admitted to Utah Bar, 1961, Supreme Ct. U.S., U.S. Ct. Appeals 10th Cir., U.S. Dist. Ct. Utah, U.S. Ct. Claims; engaged in gen. practice law, 1961-65; Duchesne County atty., 1962, Duchesne City atty., 1962; city judge Roy City, 1963-66; judge City of Ogden, Utah, 1966-69; lectr. law and govt. Stevens-Henager Coll., Ogden, 1963-75; asst. U.S. atty. Dist. Utah, 1969-72; ptnr. Mecham & Richards, Ogden, Utah, 1972-82; pres. Penn Mountain Mining Co., South Pacific Internat. Bank, Ltd.; mem. Bur. Justice Stats. Adv. Bd., U.S. Dept. Justice. Chmn. Ogden City Housing Authority; chmn. bd. trustees Utah State U., Space Dynamics Lab. Utah State U.; mem. adv. coun. Fed. Home Loan Bank; mayor City of Ogden; pres. Utah League Cities and Towns, 1981-82. Col. USAF, 1957. Mem. ABA, Weber County Bar Assn. (pres. 1966-68), Utah Bar Assn., Am. Judicature Soc., Weber County Bar Legal Svcs. (chmn. bd. trustees 1966-69), U.S. Conf. Mayors, Utah Assn. Mcpl. Judges (sec.), Sigma Chi, Phi Alpha Delta. Home: 1715 Darling St Ogden UT 84403-0556

MECHAM, STEVEN JAMES, police administrator; b. Idaho Falls, Idaho, Dec. 5, 1953; s. Hyrum Mononi and Mildred Vivian (Paskett) M.; m. Darlene Speas, May 6, 1977; children: Jan, Douglas James, Travis Quentin, Daniel Steven, Eric Moroni, Shonnee. A., Ricks Coll., 1976; B., Brigham Young U., 1986; M. Social Sci., Utah State U., 1990. Police officer Ricks Coll. Campus Police, Rexburg, Idaho, 1977-79, investigator, 1979-81; police officer Utah State U. Police Dept., Logan, 1981-82, sgt., 1982-92, chief, 1992—. Republican. Mem. LDS Church. Office: Utah State U Police Dept Logan UT 84322-5800

MECHEM, EDWIN LEARD, judge; b. Alamogordo, N.Mex., July 2, 1912; s. Edwin and Eunice (Leard) M.; Dorothy Heller, Dec. 30, 1932 (dec. 1972); children: Martha M. Vigil, John H., Jesse (dec. 1968), Walter M.; m. Josephine Donavan, May 28, 1976. L.L.B., U. Ark., 1939; L.L.D. (hon.), N.Mex. State U., 1975. Bar: N.Mex. 1939, U.S. Dist. Ct. N.Mex. 1939. Lawyer Las Cruces and Albuquerque, 1939-70; now judge U.S. Dist. Ct. N.Mex., Albuquerque; spl. agt. FBI Dept. Justice, various locations, 1942-45; mem. legislature State of N.Mex., 1947-48, gov., 1951-54, 57-58, 61-62; senator U.S. Govt., Washington, 1963-64. Mem. ABA, N.Mex. Bar Assn., Am. Law Inst. Republican. Methodist. Office: US Dist Ct PO Box 97 Albuquerque NM 87103-0097

MECKEL, PETER TIMOTHY, arts administrator, educator; b. Yankton, S.D., Nov. 28, 1941; s. Myron Eugene and Cynthia Ann (Turnblom) M.; m. Louise Gloria Mudge, Sept. 8, 1962; children: Christina Louise, Christopher Mark; m. Adrienne Dawn Maravich, Dec. 30, 1972; children: Moya Anne, Jon-Peter. Ed. Rockford Coll., Occidental Coll. Founder, gen. dir. Hidden Valley Music Seminars, Carmel Valley, Calif., 1963—, dir. Hidden Valley Opera Ensemble, Masters Festival of Chamber Music, Master Class Series; cons. in field. Mem. Music Educators Nat. Conf. Congregationalist. Office: Hidden Valley Opera Ensemble PO Box 116 Carmel Valley CA 93924-0116

MECKLENBURG, KARL BERNARD, professional football player; b. Seattle, Sept. 1, 1960; s. Fred and Marjory Mecklenberg; m. Kathi Mecklenberg; 1 child, Luke. Student, Augustana Coll.; BS in Biology, U. Minn. Linebacker Denver Broncos, 1983—. Played in Pro Bowl, 1985-87, 91. Office: Denver Broncos 13655 Broncos Pky Englewood CO 80112

MECKLER, MILTON, engineering consultant; b. Long Branch, N.J., Dec. 29, 1932; s. Morris and Irma (Hering) M.; m. Marlys Enid Alpert, Aug. 15, 1959; children: Ilyce Bonnie, Reneé Barbara. BS in Engring. with distinction, Worcester Poly. Inst., 1954; MS in Engring., U. Mich., 1955. Registered profl. engr., Calif., 15 others; lic. gen. bldg. and engring. contractor, Calif., diplomate Nat. Acad. Forensic Engrs. Sr. mech. engr. Daniel, Mann, Johnson & Mendenhall, L.A., 1963-65; ptnr. Silver, Meckler & Assocs., L.A., 1965-69; prin. Hellman, Silver, Lober & Meckler, Hollywood, Calif., 1969-71; pres. Meckler Assocs., L.A., 1971-74, Envirodyne Energy Svcs., Long Beach, Calif., 1974-76, The Energy Group, Century City, Calif., 1976-78; pres., chief exec. officer The Meckler Group, Encino, Calif., 1978—. Author: Energy Conservation in Buildings and Industrial Plants, 1980, Innovative Energy Design for the 90's, 1992; author, editor: Retrofitting of Commercial, Industrial, and Institutional Buildings for Energy Conservation, 1984, Indoor Air Quality Design Guidebook, 1990; co-author: Pumps and Pump Systems, 1983; contbr. over 180 tech. publs. Dir. Bus. Coun. on Indoor Air, 1988—. Fellow Am. Soc. Mech. Engrs., Am. Inst. Chemists, Am. Soc. Heating, Refrigeration and Air Conditioning Engrs. (Crosby Field award 1990, Best Symposium Paper award 1990, Disting. Svc. award 1993), Environ. Engrs. and Mgrs. Inst. (Environ. Profl. of Yr. award 1992), Assn. Energy Engrs., Nat. Acad. Forensic Engrs.; mem. Encino Chamber of Commerce (dir. 1982-83, v.p. 1983), Am. Inst. Constructors, Sigma Xi, Tau Beta Pi. Office: The Meckler Group 17525 Ventura Blvd Encino CA 91316-3843

MEDEARIS, KENNETH GORDON, research consultant, educator; b. Peoria, Ill., Aug. 5, 1930; s. Harold Oscar and Ferol Mae (Rowlett) M.; m. Mary Genevieve Barlow, June 28, 1953; children—Mark Allen, Mary Lynne, Terry Gordon. B.S., U. Ill., 1952, M.S., 1953; Ph.D., Stanford U., 1962. Registered profl. engr., Calif., Colo., N.Mex., Pa. Stress analyst Sandia Corp., Albuquerque, 1957-58; asst. prof. civil engring., U. N.Mex., 1958-62; assoc. prof. engring. Ariz. State U., 1962-63; engr., computer cons., Sunnyvale, Calif., 1963-66; dir. Computer Ctr., prof. civil engring. Colo. State U., Ft. Collins, 1966-69, adj. prof. civil and mech. engring., 1969—; lectr. N.Mex. State U., 1982—; cons. Kenneth Medearis Assocs., Ft. Collins, 1969—; research and vibration engring. cons., Ft. Collins., 1969—; evaluation cons. UN. Author: Numerical-Computer Methods for Engineers and Physical Scientists, 1974. Contbr. articles to profl. jours. Mem. Stanford Regional Cabinet. Served to 1st lt. USAF, 1953-56. Recipient Outstanding Engring. Achievement award No. Colo. Profl. Engrs., 1974, Outstanding Engring. Achievement award Profl. Engrs. Colo., 1974, Disting. Engring. Alumnus award U. Ill., 1988. Mem. Colo. Earthquake Research Soc. (v.p.), Univs. Council for Earthquake Engring., Internat. Orgn. for Standardization, UN Tech. Evaluation Team, ASCE, Seismol. Soc. Am., Larimer County Computer Soc. (chmn. 1974—), Aircraft Owners and Pilots Assn., Sigma Xi, Phi Sigma Kappa, Chi Epsilon, Sigma Tau, Tau Beta Pi. Methodist. Lodge: Rotary. Home: 1901 Seminole Dr Fort Collins CO 80525-1537 Office: 1413 S College Ave Fort Collins CO 80524-4115

MEDEIROS, RUSSELL FRANCIS, language arts educator, administrator; b. Honolulu, Nov. 8, 1952; s. Louis Vincent and Mabel Y. (Chun) M. AA, Leeward C.C., 1980; BA, U. Hawaii at Manoa, Honolulu, 1982, MA, 1987. Lang. arts. para-profl., instr. Kapiolani C.C., Honolulu, 1983-85; lang. lab. monitor Cen. Texas Coll., Honolulu, 1986-87; editor Delta Pub. Co., Honolulu, 1987-88; staff writer Trade Pub. Co., Honolulu, 1988; non-fiction editor Hawaii Rev., Honolulu, 1988-89; editor, researcher C. of C. of Hawaii, Honolulu, 1990-91; proofreader U. Hawaii Press, Honolulu, 1989-92; adminstr. learning ctr. Hawaii Pacific U., Honolulu, 1991—. Author, editor: Manual on Economic Development, 1991; contbr. articles to mags.

MEDINA, DANIEL ANDREW, banker; b. Monterey Park, Calif., Nov. 23, 1957; s. Andrew and Maria (Barboa) M.; m. Laura Martin, July 16, 1983; 1 child, Andrew Martin. AB, Harvard Coll., 1979, MBA, 1983. Assoc. Salomon Bros. Inc., N.Y.C. and L.A., 1983-86; v.p. Bear, Stearns & Co. Inc., L.A., 1986-90; mng. dir. mcht. banking Union Bank, L.A., 1992—. Bd. mem. Plaza de la Raza, L.A., 1990—; fin. task force Rebuild L.A., 1992—. Home: 1825 W Haven Rd San Marino CA 91108-2567 Office: Union Bank Mcht Banking Dept 445 S Figueroa Los Angeles CA 90071

MEDINA, JOSEPH A., protective services official. Fire chief San Francisco Fire Dept. Office: San Francisco Fire Commn 260 Golden Gate Ave San Francisco CA 94102*

MEDINA, SANDRA SELLMAN, social worker, educator; b. Tulsa, Oct. 4, 1947; d. James and Erleen (Austin) Meeks; m. Michael Sellman, 1966 (div. 1979); children: Rhainnie, Morgan; m. Ernest Medina, Aug. 21, 1985; 1 child, Brendyn. Cert., Community Coll. of Denver, 1975; BS summa cum laude, Met. State Coll., Denver, 1981; MSW, U. Denver, 1983. Lic. clin. social worker, Colo. Dir. Lafayette (Colo.) Presch./Playtime, 1973-75, Bennett (Colo.) Non-Denominational Presch., 1975-76; intern. in clin. social work Brighton (Colo.) Schs., 1981-82; adminstrv. social work intern Jefferson County (Colo.) Schs., 1982-83; med. social worker Las Animas County Health Dept., Trinidad, Colo., 1985-85; psychiat. social worker Colo. State Hosp., Pueblo, 1985-89; clin. social worker PsychCare, Greeley, 1990-92; counselor high sch. U. Northern Colo. Lab. Sch.; instr. Trinidad State Jr. Coll., 1984-85; field instr. N.Mex. Highlands U., Las Vegas, 1986-87, U. So. Colo., Pueblo, 1988-89. Mem. exec. com. Gov.'s Task Force on Child Abuse, Denver, 1985; bd. dirs. Adams County Rep. Advs. for Children Today, Denver, 1978-79; chairperson membership com. Met. Child Protection Coun., Denver, 1982-83. Mem. NASW. Democrat. Presbyterian. Office: U Northern Colo Lab Sch Greeley CO 80639

MEDINA, THOMAS JULIAN, information management consultant, educator; b. Denver, July 24, 1928; s. Frank John and Francis Josephine

(Grasmuck) M.; m. Maryem McKell, Apr. 16, 1973; children: Kim Jordan, Vickie Jeanne, Michael McKell. AA, Mira Costa Coll., 1968; BA, San Diego State U., 1969; PhD, Pacific Western U., 1982. Lic. computer scientist, career counselor, Calif. Commd. 2d. lt. USMC, 1953, advanced through grades to maj., 1945-65, computer specialist, 1945-66, ret., 1966; owner, mgr. Medina Fish Finding Co., San Diego, 1970-82; instr. entrepreneurship San Diego County Schs., 1972-82, San Diego Unified Schs., 1984-90; computer scientist Computer Scis. Corp., San Diego, 1982-83, Sci. Applications, Inc., San Diego, 1983-84; cons. entrepreneurship Calif. Dept. Edn., 1985—; owner The Entrepreneur, Livingston, Tex., 1988—; mem. adv. bd. Internat. U. Sch. Info. Mgmt., Santa Barbara, Calif., 1986—, mem. faculty, 1988—; condr. rsch. project on rural entrepreneurs in U.S. and Can., 1990—. Calif. Entrepreneur Ednl. grantee, 1986, 87; recipient award for model program in entrepreneurial edn. U.S. Assn. Small Bus. and Entrepreneurship, 1989, W.S. Curran Disting. svc. award San Diego Internat. Trade, 1989, Leavy award Freedoms Found. Valley Forge, 1990, Mag. award Ernst & Young, 1990. Mem. Am. Assn. Artificial Intelligence, U.S. Assn. for Small Bus. and Entrepreneurship, Calif. Bus. Edn. Assn., Am. Entrepreneur Assn. (dir. acad. rels. 1985-88), Assn. Pvt. Enterprise Edn., World Future Soc. (adv. coun. 1988-90), Southwestern Yacht Club (port capt. 1985-86), Thalians. Republican. Mem. LDS Ch.

MEDINA-PUERTA, ANTONIO, scientist; b. Almeria, Spain, Jan. 20, 1956; s. Antonio and Maria Mar (Puerta) Medina; m. Mary Medina-Puerta, Sept. 20, 1986. MS, U. Politecnica, Madrid, 1979, MIT, 1982; OD, U. Complutense, Madrid, 1979; diploma Electrical Engring., MIT, 1981; PhD, U. Politecnica, Madrid, 1983. Optometrist Centro de Vision Luz, Almeria, 1978-79; engr. Philips, Eindhoven, Holland, 1979-80; rsch. asst. MIT, Cambridge, Mass., 1981-83; sci. assoc. Eye Rsch. Inst., Boston, 1983-88; task mgr. Calif. Inst. Tech., Pasadena, 1988-91; adviser NASA, Washington, 1988—, USN, 1989—. Contbr. articles to profl. publs.; patentee in field. Fellow Christ's Coll., Cambridge Univ., Eng. Fellow Acad. Applied Sci.; mem. IEEE, Optical Soc. Am., Soc. Photo-optical Instrumentation Engrs., Biomed. Soc. Roman Catholic. Home and Office: 281 E Colorado Blvd # 1002 Pasadena CA 91102

MEDITCH, JAMES STEPHEN, electrical engineering educator; b. Indpls., July 30, 1934; s. Vladimir Stephen and Alexandra (Gogeff) M.; m. Theresa Claire Scott, Apr. 4, 1964; children: James Stephen Jr., Sandra Anne. BSEE, Purdue U., 1956, PhD, 1961; SM, MIT, 1957. Staff engr. Aerospace Corp., Los Angeles, 1961-65; assoc. prof. elec. engring. Northwestern U., 1965-67; mem. tech. staff Boeing Sci. Research Labs., Seattle, 1967-70; prof. U. Calif., Irvine, 1970-77; prof. U. Wash., Seattle, 1977—, chmn. dept. elec. engring., 1977-85, assoc. dean engring., 1987-90. Author: Stochastic Optimal Linear Estimation and Control, 1969; co-editor: Computer Communication Networks, 1984. Fellow IEEE (Disting. mem. control systems soc., 1983, editor Proceedings 1983-85, Centennial medal 1984). Office: U Wash Dept Elec Engring FT-10 Seattle WA 98195

MEDLEY, MICHAEL RAYMOND, airline industry executive, training manager; b. Riverside, Calif., Oct. 20, 1946; s. Donald Raymond Medley and Josephine Ruth (Blakely) Cartter; m. Anastatia Ruth Halstead, Aug. 1966 (div. Aug. 1977); children: Edward Raymond, Linda Diane; m. Jamie Ann Lemmons, Sept. 6, 1977. AS in Avionics Tech., Community Coll. of Air Force, 1981; BA in Bus. Adminstrn., U. Phoenix, 1988, MBA, 1990. Enlisted USAF, 1965; aircraft radio technician 60th Military Aircraft Wing USAF, Travis AFB, Calif., 1967-69; aircraft radio technician Southern Command USAF, Howard AFB, Canal Zone, Panama, 1969-72; shift chief avionics maintenance 57 Tactical Fighter Wing USAF, Nellis AFB, Nev., 1972-73; lead tech. U.S. Military Assistance Command Thailand Tng. and Logistics Detachment USAF, Udorn RTAFB, Thailand, 1973-74; mgr. spl. sytems maintenance 6948 Security Squadron (Mobile) USAF, Kelley AFB, Tex., 1974-78; supt.-Electronic Counter Measures maintenance 366 Tactical Fighter Wing USAF, Mountain Home AFB, Idaho, 1978-80, lead instr. project devel. Field Tng. Detachment 513, 1980-82; supr. Field Tng. Detachment 307 USAF, Shaw AFB, S.C., 1982-85; project officer, scheduling mgr. Pacific Power Source Corp., Huntington Beach, Calif., 1986-87; avionics instr. comml. tech. tng. Douglas Aircraft Co., Long Beach, Calif., 1987-88, mgr. bus. adminstrn., quality, media devel. comml. tech. tng., 1988—. Mem. Air Force Assn., Aviation Industry Computer Based Tng. Com., Air Transport Assn., Aviation Industry Assn. Presbyterian.

MEDLEY, STEVEN PAUL, association executive; b. Palo Alto, Calif., July 11, 1949; s. Robert William and Hermie May (Palmer) M.; m. Jane Rowley, Mar. 12, 1976; children: Charles, Joseph, Andrew. Student, Brown U., 1967-69; BA, Stanford U., 1971; MLS, U. Oreg., 1975; JD, U. Calif., Davis, 1981. Bar: Oreg. 1981. Park ranger, then libr., curator Nat. Park Svc., Yosemite Nat. Park, Calif., 1971-78; ptnr. Schultz, Salisbury, Cauble and Medley, Grants Pass, Oreg., 1981-85; pres. Yosemite Assn., Yosemite Nat. Park, 1985—. Author: Complete Guidebook to Yosemite National Park, 1990. Office: Yosemite Assn PO Box 230 El Portal CA 95318-0230

MEDLIN, KING EVERETT, insurance agent; b. Oklahoma City, Apr. 4, 1964; s. Everett Oren Medlin and Nancy Ann (Bostock) Whittall; m. Tamera Ann Waterman, Jan. 19, 1990. BBA, U. Okla., 1986; M of Internat. Mgmt., Am. Grad. Sch. Internat. Mgmt., 1991. Field rep. The Travelers, Hartford, Conn., 1986-87; acct. exec. Drexel Burnham Lambert, Beverly Hills, Calif., 1987-91; agt. Calif. State Auto Assn., Reno, 1992—; internat. export cons., Reno, 1991—. No. Nev. coord. Clinton/Gore Campaign, Reno, 1992; mem. legis. com. Washoe County Dem. Party Ctrl. Com. Home: 3348 Candelaria Sparks NV 89434 Office: Calif State Auto Assn 199 E Moana Ln Reno NV 89502

MEDLOCK, ANN, non-profit organization executive, writer, lecturer; b. Portsmouth, Va., May 6, 1933; d. Frank Wesley and Olive Edna (Litz) M.; m. Thomas Proctor Crawford, Mar. 5, 1955 (div.); 1 child, Philip Courtney; m. John Peasley Miraglia, June 22, 1966 (div.); children: Cynthia Medlock, David Medlock; m. John A. Graham, June 13, 1982. BA magna cum laude, U. Md., 1964. Free-lance writer N.Y.C., Princeton (N.J.) and Saigon, Republic of Vietnam, 1959-65; editor Vietnam Presse, Saigon, 1959-61, Macmillan Pub. Inc., N.Y.C., 1966-69; speechwriter the Aga Khan, N.Y.C., 1979-80; editor in chief Children's Express, N.Y.C., 1978-79; founder, pres. The Giraffe Project, N.Y.C. and Whidbey Island, Wash., 1983—; judge Creative Altruism Awards, Sausalito, Calif., 1988—, Eddie Bauer Heroes for the Earth award, 1990—. Editor The Giraffe Gazette, 1983—; contbr. articles to various publs. Mem. planning bd. City of Langley, Wash., 1986-88; co-founder Citizens for Sensible Devel., Whidbey Island, 1988; bd. advisers Community Action Network, 1986—, Windstar Found., Snowmass, Colo., 1984—, U.S.-Soviet Ptnrs. Project, Seattle, 1989—. Recipient Pub. Svc. award Am. Values, 1989, 1st Pl. award Wash. Press Assn., 1991. Office: The Giraffe Project 197 Second St PO Box 759 Langley WA 98260

MEDLOCK, EUGENE SHIELDS, cell biology researcher; b. Petersburg, Va., Sept. 30, 1954; s. Baskerville Cody and Catherine (White) M.; m. Armecia Spivey, Nov. 4, 1978; children: Ian Christian, Taylor Armecia. BS, Va. Polytechnic Inst., 1976; PhD, Med. Coll. Va., 1980. Post-doctoral fellow Sloan Kettering Cancer Ctr., N.Y.C., 1980-82; rsch. assoc. U. Conn., Farmington, 1982-84, instr., 1984-87; rsch. scientist Amgen, Inc., Thousand Oaks, Calif., 1987—. Contbr. articles to profl. jours. Mem. Am. Assn. Immunologists, Transplantation Soc. Office: Amgen Inc 1840 De Havilland Dr Newbury Park CA 91320-1701

MEDOFF, MARK HOWARD, playwright, screenwriter, novelist; b. Mt. Carmel, Ill., Mar. 18, 1940; s. Lawrence Ray and Thelma Irene (Butt) M.; m. Stephanie Thorne, June 24, 1972; children: Debra, Rachel, Jessica. B.A., U. Miami, Fla., 1962; M.A., Stanford U., 1966; D.H.L., Gallaudet Coll., 1981. Instr. English and drama N.Mex. State U., 1966-79, dramatist in residence, 1974—, head dept. drama, 1978-87, prof. drama, 1979-93, artistic dir., 1982-87; artistic dir. Am. S.W. Theatre Co., 1984-87. Author: (plays) When You Comin' Back, Red Ryder?, 1974, The Wager, 1975, The Kramer, 1975, The Halloween Bandit, 1978, The Conversion of Aaron Weiss, 1978, Firekeeper, 1978, The Last Chance Saloon, 1979, Children of a Lesser God, 1980 (Soc. West Theatres best play award 1982), The Majestic Kid, 1981, The Hands of Its Enemy, 1984, Kringle's Window, 1985, The Heart Outright, 1986 (novel) Dreams of Long Lasting; (films) When You Comin' Back, Red Ryder?, 1979, Off Beat, 1986, Apology, 1986, Children of a Lesser God, 1986, Good Guys Wear Black, 1978, Clara's Heart, 1988, The Majestic Kid, 1988, City of Joy, 1992; works appear in Best Plays, 1973-74, 74-75, 79-80, Best Short Plays, 1975, The Homage that Follows, 1987; plays Stumps, 1989, Stefanie Hero, 1990. Guggenheim fellow, 1974-75; recipient Obie award, Drama Desk award, Outer Critics Circle award, Media award Pres.'s Com. Employment Handicapped, Tony award; Oscar award nominee for Best Screenplay for Children of A Lesser God, 1987. Mem. Dramatists Guild, Writers Guild Am., Actors Equity Assn., Screen Actors Guild. Office: PO Box 3072 Las Cruces NM 88003-3072

MEDUSKI, JERZY WINCENTY, nutritionist, biochemist; b. Kalusz, Poland, Oct. 29, 1918; s. Dobieslaw Antoni and Katarzyna (Barbowska) M.; came to U.S., 1962, naturalized, 1969; M.D., Warsaw (Poland) Med. Sch., 1946; Ph.D. in Biochemistry, U. Lodz (Poland), 1951; 1 son, Jerzy Dobieslaw. Organizer, chief pharmacology labs. Polish Nat. Inst. Hygiene, Warsaw, 1945-52, organizer, head lab. of intermediary metabolism, 1952-59; asso. prof. biochemistry Warsaw Med. Sch., 1955-59; asst. prof. neurology U. So. Calif. Sch. Medicine, Los Angeles, 1973—; pres. Nutritional Cons. Group, Inc. Mem. Los Angeles County Bd. Suprs. Task Force on Nutrition. WHO fellow, Holland, Scotland, 1948-49; research grantee, USSR, 1956. Mem. Polish Acad. Sci. (sci. sec. biochem. com. 1952-59), Polish Med. Assn. (sci. sec. nat. bd. 1958-59), Polish Biochem. Soc. (founding mem.), Biochem. Soc. London, Royal Soc. Chem. London, Internat. Soc. on Toxinology, AMA, Am. Soc. Microbiology, Internat. Soc. on Oxygen Transport to Tissues, Sigma Xi. Author 3 books on biochemistry; contbr. more than 80 articles to internat. jours.; author textbook on nutritional biochemistry, 1977. Home: 1066 S Genesee Ave Los Angeles CA 90019-2448 Office: U So Calif Sch Medicine 2025 Zonal Ave Los Angeles CA 90033-4526

MEDVED, EVA, dietitian, educator; b. Cadiz, Ohio, May 15, 1922; d. Joseph and Lucy (Truly) M. BS, Kent State U., 1943; MS, Ohio State U., 1952, PhD, 1964. Cert. tchr.; lic. dietitian. Tchr. Alliance (Ohio) High Sch., 1943-47, Lincoln High Sch., Canton, Ohio, 1947-62; asst. prof. Ohio U., Athens, 1963-65; prof. Kent (Ohio) State U., 1965-87, Ariz. State U., Sun City, 1988—; cons., speaker Prentice-Hall Pubs., 1987—. Author: World of Food, 1970, 73, 77, 80, 86, 88, 90, Food in Theory and Practice, 1978, Food Preparation and Theory, 1986. Rsch. grantee USDA 1968-70; scholarship Timken Co. 1960, 62. Mem. Am. Home Econs. Assn. (nutrition chair 1965—), Am. Dietetic Assn., Nutrition Today Soc., Ohio Nutrition Coun. (publ. chair 1979—), Ohio Home Econs. Assn. (exec. com. 1965—, Outstanding Home Economist award 1987), Ohio Dietetic Assn., Stark County Home Econs. Assn. (pres. 1965—), Stark County Dietetic Assn. Republican. Roman Catholic. Home: 4885 Pond Dr NW Canton OH 44720-7434

MEDVITZ, JAMES THOMAS, director of symphony operations; b. Cleveland, Calif., Dec. 28, 1936; s. Joseph Thomas and Ann (Emrich) M.; m. Sandra Lee Tierney, Apr. 11, 1964; children: Christopher Anthony, Benjamin Alexander. BA, UCLA, 1959. Prin. trombone Burbank (Calif.) Symphony, 1969-74, orch. libr., 1971-74; prin. trombone Downey (Calif.) Symphony, 1969-74; music copiest, arranger, composer Santa Monica, Calif., 1969-74; orch. libr. Houston Symphony, 1974-85; orchestrator, 1976—; gen. mgr. Pacific Symphony Orch., Santa Ana, Calif., 1987; dir. ops. Pacific Symphony Orch., Irvine, Calif., 1987—. With U.S. Army, 1960-62. Mem. Am. Symphony Orch. League, Assn. Calif. Symphony Orchs., Assn. Composers, Authors and Pubs. Republican. Roman Catholic. Home: 35 Fremont Irvine CA 92720 Office: Pacific Symphony Orch 1231 E Dyer Rd Ste 200 Santa Ana CA 92705

MEECH, SONJA ROSEMARY, interior design studio owner; b. Mpls., Jan. 16, 1950; d. Frank Mike and Elvira Gertrude (Stolzman) Schumm; m. Frank Otis, Feb. 17, 1968 (div. 1975); 1 child, Christopher; m. James W. Bretall, Oct. 16, 1992. Student pub. schs., Robbinsdale, Minn. Non-foods mgr. Red Owl, Mpls., 1968-71; real estate agt. Century 21, Mpls., 1976-79; teller Valley Nat. Bank, Tucson, 1981-85; owner Sonja's, Tucson, 1981—. Telephone solicitor Rep. Party, Tucson, 1982. Mem. Gen. Contractors (spl. events Tucson 1985-86). Office: 4826 N Altos Pl Tucson AZ 85704

MEECHAM, WILLIAM CORYELL, engineering educator; b. Detroit; s. William Edward and Mabel Catherine (Wilcox) M.; m. Barbara Jane Brown, Sept. 4, 1948 (dec. 1965); children: Janice Lynn, William James; m. Della Fern Carson, Sept. 11, 1965. BS, U. Mich., 1948, MS, 1948, PhD in Physics, 1954. Head acoustics lab. Willow Run Labs., Ann Arbor, Mich., 1959-60; asst. prof. U. Mich., Ann Arbor, 1958-60; prof. U. Minn., Mpls., 1960-67; prof. fluid mechanics and acoustics UCLA, 1967—, chmn. dept. mechanics and structures, 1972-73; cons. Aerospace Corp., El Segundo, Calif., 1975-80, Rand Corp., Santa Monica, Calif., 1964-74, Bolt, Beranek and Newman, Cambridge, Mass., 1968-73, Arete Assocs., Encino, Calif., 1976—, CRT Corp., Chatsworth, Calif., 1985—. Author: (with R. Lutomirski) Lasar Systems, 1973; author 120 papers on fluid mechanics and acoustics. Treas. Unitarian Ch., Ann Arbor, Mich., 1958-60; advisor U.S. Congress Com. on Pub. Works, Congl. Record Report N.J., 1972; mem. Calif. Space and Def. Council, U.S. Congress, 1982—. Served with U.S. Army, 1944-46. Mich. Alumni scholar 1942-44, Donovan scholar U. Mich., 1944-45; UCLA senate rsch. grantee, 1968—, NASA rsch. grantee, 1971—, Office Naval Rsch. grantee, 1977-85; recipient Disting. Svc. award U.S. Army. Fellow Acoustical Soc. Am. (gen. chmn. meeting 1973), AIAA (assoc. fellow); mem. com. aeroacoustics 1972-75) mem. Am. Phys. Soc. (fluid dynamics div.), Inst. Noise Control Engring., Sigma Xi, Tau Beta Pi. Home: 927 Glenhaven Dr Pacific Palisades CA 90272-2202 Office: UCLA Sch Engring & Applied Sci Los Angeles CA 90024

MEECHAM, WILLIAM JAMES, ophthalmologist; b. Ann Arbor, Mich., Nov. 30, 1958; s. William Coryell and Barbara (Brown) M. AB in Zoology, U. Calif., Berkeley, 1980, MA in Biophysics, 1983; MD, U. Calif., San Francisco, 1987. Diplomate Nat. Bd. Med. Examiners, Am. Bd. Ophthalmology. Med. intern Cabrini Med. Ctr., N.Y.C., 1987-88; resident in ophthalmology U. Calif., San Francisco, 1988-91, ocular oncology fellow, 1991-92, clin. instr., 1991—, ocular plastics fellow, 1992—; attending physician San Francisco Gen. Hosp., 1991—; career physician Kaiser Permanente, San Rafael, 1993. Contbr. articles to profl. publs.; editor-in-chief U. Calif.-San Francisco Synapse, 1984-85. Mem. Am. Acad. Ophthalmology, Am. Soc. Ophthalmic Plastic and Reconstructive Surgeons. Office: 99 Monticello Rd San Rafael CA 94903

MEEHAN, RICHARD THOMAS, internist, rheumatologist; b. C.Z., Panama, Feb. 16, 1949; s. John Bernard and Violet Ruth M.; children: Gregory Patrick, Mackenzie Leigh; m. Jane Ellen Pope; children: Evan Pope, Addison Pope, Anne Pope. BA with honors, U. Tex., 1971; MD, U. Tex., Houston, 1974. Diplomate Am. Bd. Internal Medicine, Am. Bd. Rheumatology. Resident in internal medicine U. Iowa Hosps. and Clinics, Iowa City, 1974-77; rheumatology fellow U. Iowa Hosps. and Clinics, 1980-84; pvt. practice Salem (Oreg.) Clinic, 1977-80; asst. prof. internal medicine U. Tex. Med. Br., Galveston, 1984-89; asst. prof. internal medicine U. Colo. Health Scis. Ctr., Denver, 1989-92, assoc. prof., 1992—; participant NASA workshops, prin. investigator Shuttle experiments, 1985-92; investigator Johnson Space Ctr., 1986-89. Patentee in field; contbr. articles to profl. jours. Comdr., USNR, 1990—. Recipient Community Svc. award CIBA Found., 1974; A. Blaine Bower Traveling scholar, 1983; Am. Soc. Engring. Edn. fellow, 1984, 85. Fellow ACP, Am. Coll. Rheumatology, Aerospace Med. Assn.; mem. AIAA, Am. Assn. Immunologists, Am. Soc. for Gravitational and Space Biology. Lutheran. Office: Univ of Colo Health Sci Ctr 4200 E 9th Ave # 115B Denver CO 80262-0001

MEEK, GERRY, library director. Dir. Calgary (Alta.) Pub. Libr., Can. Office: Calgary Pub Libr, 616 Macleod Trail SE, Calgary, AB Canada T2G 2M2*

MEEKER, JOHN G., energy systems manager consultant; b. Denver, Feb. 9, 1946; m. Janet S. Elston, June 22, 1968. BS in Tech. Mgmt. magna cum laude, Regis U., 1992. Cert. state energy auditor. Sales technician McCombs Supply Co., Denver, 1966-72; svc. technician A&D Heating Co., Wheat Ridge, Colo., 1972-75; mgr. of engring. svcs. Solaron Corp., Englewood, Colo., 1975-81; regional sales mgr. Ramada Energy Systems, Ltd., Tempe, Ariz., 1982-84; project engr. BHCD Engrs., Inc., Denver, 1984-86; mgr. of product & systems engring. Solaron Corp., Englewood, Colo., 1985-86; mktg. rep. Rains-Flo Mfg., Denver, 1987-91, Dynamic Energy Group, Denver, 1991; tech. mgr. LöF Energy Systems, Inc., Lakewood, Colo., 1992—, gen. & tech. mgr. Editor, Artist: (book) Dwellers of the Mountain Tops, 1989. Instr. Boy Scouts Am. adventure programs, Denver and Ward, Colo., 1985-93; coach Littleton Knights, Bear Creek & Kickers Soccer Clubs, Lakewood United Denver Metro, 1981-91. Recipient Daley Tech. Mgmt. award Regis U., 1992. Mem. ASHRAE (membership chmn. 1975-76), Colo. Solar Energy Industries Assn. (v.p. 1981-83, bd. dirs., 1980-93).

MEGAHAN, WALTER FRANKLIN, research hydrologist; b. Oceanside, N.Y., Jan. 22, 1935; s. Hubert Norman and Ada Irene M.; m. Frances Miriam Dodd, June 3, 1956; children: Mark Howard, John Walter. B.S., SUNY, Syracuse U., 1957, M.S., 1960; Ph.D., Colo. State U., 1967. Registered profl. hydrologist, Am. Inst. Hydrology, 1984—. Regional hydrologist U.S. Forest Svc. Intermountain Region, Ogden, Utah, 1960-66, supervisory rsch. hydrologist, leader project to evaluate effects of forest practices on water pollution in Idaho and Mont., U.S. Forest Service Intermountain Rsch. Sta., Boise, 1967-91; rsch. hydrologist Nat. Coun. of Paper Industry for Air and Stream Improvement (mgr. rsch. and devel. program); affiliate prof. U. Idaho; vis. prof. Fellow Padova U., Italy, 1978; rsch. fellow East-West Environment and Policy Inst., Honolulu, 1983, 85, 90. Assoc. editor Western Jour. Applied Forestry; contbr. articles to profl. jours. Mem. Am. Geophys. Union, Soil Sci. Soc. Am., Western Snow Conf., Sci. Rsch. Soc. Am. Internat., Assn. Sci. Hydrology. Home: 615 W St Port Townsend WA 98368-3543

MEGEATH, JOE D., dean; b. Rock Springs, Wyo., Aug. 21, 1939; s. Samuel Anthony and Isabelle (Thompson) M.; m. Sally Holme, Apr. 26, 1988; children: JoDee, James, Anthony, Joannie, Katy, Mary. MS, U. Wyo., 1963; PhD, Colo. Sch. Mines, 1976. Zone mgr. Ford Motor Co., Louisville, 1963-67; rsch. analyst Gates Rubber Co., Denver, 1967-69; dept. chmn. Met. State Coll., Denver, 1969-91, dean, 1992—. Author: How to Use Statistics, 1971; contbr. articles to profl. jours. Pres. Adult Learning Source, Denver, 1973. Mem. Rocky Mountain Chpt. Inst. Mgmt. Sci. (pres. 1980, 90), Golden Key Honor Soc. Office: Met State Coll Denver Box 173362 Denver CO 80217-3362

MEGRATH, KIMBERLEY LEWIS, physical therapy educator, consultant; b. Hartford, Conn., May 9, 1953; d. Lewis Edwin and Jeanne (MacDermid) Schoonmaker; children: Todd Matthew, Kyle Lewis. BS in Phys. Therapy, NYU, 1975; MBA, U. Colo., Colorado Springs, 1988; postgrad., U. Oreg., 1991—. Lic. phys. therapist, N.Y., Utah, Oreg. Phys. therapist No. Westchester Hosp., Mt. Kisco, N.Y., 1975-76; dir. phys. therapy Richmond Children's Hosp., Yonkers, N.Y., 1976-77; sr. phys. therapist Blythedale Children's Hosp., Valhalla, N.Y., 1977-80; phys. therapist Holy Family Hosp., Spokane, Wash., 1981-82; dir. phys. therapy Nye Gen. Hosp., Tonopah, Nev., 1982-83; adminstrv. dir. St. Mary-Corwin Regional Med. Ctr., Pueblo, Colo., 1983-87; dir. Pediatric Rehab. Ctr., Ogden, Utah, 1988-90; asst. prof. phys. therapy Idaho State U., Pocatello, 1990-91; cons. Pueblo Regional Med. Ctr., 1984-87, State of Idaho Dept. Health and Welfare, 1990; owner, pres. Kids in Motion, 1990—. Mem. Pueblo County Commrs. Adv. Bd., 1985-86, Regional IV Infant and Toddler Adv. Coun., Pocatello, 1990-91; participant Leadership Pueblo, 1987; chmn. dist. 3 Utah Interagy. Coordinating Coun., Ogden, 1990. Mem. Am. Phys. Therapy Assn., Am. Coll. Health Care Execs. (faculty affiliate).

MEHDIZADEH, PARVIZ, insurance company executive; b. Tehran, Iran, Sept. 15, 1934; came to U.S., 1981; s. Alexander and Sedigheh (Siavooshy) M.; m. Manijeh Sadri, Sept. 12, 1961; children: Sheida, Peyman, Pejman. BS, Forestry Sch., Tehran, 1958; MS, N.C. State U., 1963, PhD, 1966. Pres. Research Inst. Natural Resources, Tehran, 1968-73; assoc. prof. U. Tehran, 1973-74; prof. environ. sci. U. Tabriz, Iran, 1974-76; chmn. resolution com. FAO, Rome, 1976-77; chmn. natural resources Cen. Treaty Orgn., Ankars, Turkey, 1977-78; spl. adviser to sec. Ministry of Agr., Tehran, 1978-79; dist. mgr. Am. Family Life Assurance Co., Beverly Hills, Calif., 1981—; v.p. Point Internat. Corp. Inc., Los Angeles, 1986—; cons. Ministry of Sci., Tehran, 1972-75, UN U., Tokyo, 1975-76; chmn. bd. dirs. Active Universal Corp., Inc. Author: Flowering Plants of Semi-Arid Regions, 1976, Economizing of Water Use in Agriculture, 1977; editor Khandamhayeh Hafteh, 1979. Mem. U.S. Senatorial Club, Washington, 1984; charter mem. Rep. Presdl. Task Force, Washington, 1984. Mem. Life Underwriters Assn. (L.A. chpt., Health Ins. Quality award 1985, 88, 89), Rotary (chmn. dist. 5280 1992, Paul Harris Fellow award 1989). Office: Am Family Life Assurance 9301 Wilshire Blvd Ste 508 Beverly Hills CA 90210-5412

MEHL, DOUGLAS WAYNE, finance company executive; b. Wenatchee, Wash., Oct. 21, 1948; s. Ed and Mildred (Rassmussen) M.; m. Cheryl Duncan, May 16, 1970; children: Mehgan, Kiera. BA, Eastern Wash. State U., 1973. Underwriter Allstate Ins. Co., Seattle, 1974-75, with mgmt. devel. rotation, 1975, account underwriter, 1975-76, underwriter div. supr., underwriting departmental tng. coord., 1976-77; mktg. rep. SAFECO Credit Co., Inc., Seattle, 1977-79; area mgr. SAFECO Credit Co., Inc., Phoenix, 1979-80; asst. v.p., div. mgr. SAFECO Credit Co., Inc., Denver, 1980—. With USN, 1974. Mem. Nat. Assn. Credit Mgmt. Office: SAFECO Credit Co Inc 165 S Union Blvd Ste 610 Lakewood CO 80228-2212

MEHLIG, DONALD HOMER, insurance broker; b. Torrance, Calif., Feb. 3, 1935; s. John Homer Mehlig and Melita Evelyn (Hawkins) Wolford; m. Patricia Ann Nield, Mar. 19, 1954; children: Steven, Sharon, Susan. BA, UCLA, 1957. CLU, ChFC. Ins. agt. Provident Mut., L.A., 1957-62; pres. Cal-Surance Benefits Plans, Inc., Torrance, 1962—; adv. bd. mem. M Life Ins. Co, 1993; nat. speaker CLU Inst., U.S., 1992—. Bd. dirs. Little Co. Mary Hosp., Torrance, 1987—; bd. trustees Am. Coll., Bryn Mawr, Pa., 1989—. Named Outstanding Life Ins. Man, Leader's Mag., 1978, 88; recipient William G. Farrell award L.A. Life Underwriting Assn., 1985. Mem. Life Ins. and Trust Coun., Am. Soc. CLUS (bd. dirs., past pres.), Christian Businessmen's Com. (bd. dirs. 1987—), Million Dollar Round Table (life), Palos Verdes Golf Club, Del Amo Rotary Club. Republican. Office: Cal Surance Benefit Plans PO Box 3459 Torrance CA 90510-3459

MEHLMAN, LON DOUGLAS, information systems specialist; b. Los Angeles, Apr. 29, 1959; s. Anton and Diane Mehlman. BA, UCLA, 1981; MBA, Pepperdine U., 1983. Systems programmer Ticom Systems Inc., Century City, Calif., 1978-81; systems analyst NCR Corp., Century City, 1981-83; sr. systems analyst Tandem Computers Inc., L.A., 1983-91; info. systems specialist Computer Scis. Corp., El Segundo, Calif., 1991—. Mem. Am. Mgmt. Assn., Assn. for Info. and Image Mgmt., Armed Forces Communications and Electronics Assn., Sierra Club, Phi Delta Theta. Office: Computer Scis Corp 2100 E Grand Ave El Segundo CA 90245

MEHLSCHAU, ROBERT EUGENE, software engineer, small business owner; b. Nipomo, Calif., June 27, 1960; s. Peter Eugene and Nancy (Ballenge) M. BS in Fruit Industries, Calif. Poly., Pomona, 1986; student, Massey U, Palmerston North, New Zealand, 1983. Combine operator Santa Maria, Calif., 1980-84; prodn. mgr., pest control advisor Sunwest, Nipomo, 1985-89; software engr., owner The Corp. Originality Workshop, Nipomo, 1987—; quality control rep. Silicon Beach Software, San Diego, 1990—; pest control advisor Calif. State Pest Control Advisors, 1989—. Mem. Calif. Farm Bur. Republican. Methodist. Office: The COW 530 Mehlschau Rd Nipomo CA 93444-9705

MEHLUM, DAVID L., otolaryngologist; b. Phoenix, Sept. 10, 1950; s. Charles J. and Jessaline (V.) M.; m. Mary Jo Mills, June 17, 1972; children: N. Eric, Kristen M. AA, Phoenix Coll., 1970; BS, U. Ariz., 1972; MD, U. Tex., Dallas, 1976. Diplomate Am. Bd. Otolaryngology. Intern U. Tex. Southwestern Affiliated Hosp., Dallas, 1976-77, resident, 1977-80; med. staff mem. Group Health Coop., Seattle, 1983—; cons. Indian Health Svc., Ariz., Nev., 1981-83; clin. asst. prof. otolaryngology U. Calif., San Francisco, 1981-83; clin. instr. otolaryngology U. Wash. Med. Sch., Seattle, 1984—; chief of otolaryngology Group Health-Cen., Seattle, 1987-90. Contbr. articles to profl. jours. Lt. comdr. USNR, 1980-83. Recipient Medallion of Merit, Ariz. State U., 1970. Mem. Am. Acad. Otolaryngology, ACS, Am. Assn. Facial Plastic and Reconstructive Surgery, Nat. Ski Patrol (bd. dirs. ski access patrol 1989—, nat. appointment 1992, asst. patrol dir. 1992—). Lutheran. Office: Group Health Coop Dept Otolaryngolgy 125 16th Ave E Seattle WA 98112

MEHRA, RAJNISH, finance educator; b. New Delhi, Jan. 15, 1950; came to U.S., 1972; s. Mohan Dev and Raj-Mohini (Vadera) M.; m. Neeru Narula, Jan. 4, 1977; 1 child, Chaitanya. BTech. in elec. engring., Indian Inst. Tech., Kanpur, 1972; MS in computer sci., Rice U., 1974; MS in indsl. adminstrn., Carnegie-Mellon U., 1975, PhD, 1978. Instr. adminstrn. and mgmt. sci. Carnegie-Mellon U., Pitts., 1974-76; asst. prof. Queens U., Kingston, Ont., Can., 1976-77; asst. prof., then assoc. prof. fin. Columbia U. Grad. Sch. Bus., 1977-85; assoc. prof., then prof. fin. U. Calif., Santa Barbara, 1985—, dir. Masters of Business Economics program, 1992—; vis. asst. prof. UCLA, 1980; vis. prof. fin. U. Laussane, Switzerland, 1981, Sloan Sch. Mgmt., MIT, 1987-89; vis. scholar U. Chgo., 1979, Norwegian Sch. of Econs. and Bus. Adminstrn., 1982, Stockholm Sch. Econs., 1988, Wharton Sch., U. Pa., 1990; vis. assoc. Oxford U., 1986; cons. Internat. Monetary Fund, 1989-90, 92, 93. Assoc. editor Jour. Econ. Dynamics and Control; contbr. Growth Theory, Vol. 10, Internat. Library of Critical Writings in Economics, 1991; contbr. articles to profl. jours.; referee maj. jours. in field. William Larimer Mellon fellow, 1974-76; NSF grantee, 1980—. Mem. IEEE (sr.), Am. Econ. Assn., Am. Fin. Assn., Econometric Soc., Tau Beta Pi. Home: 938 W Campus Ln Santa Barbara CA 93117-4344 Office: U Calif Santa Barbara CA 93106

MEHRABIAN, ALBERT, psychology educator, author, researcher; b. Tabriz, Iran, Nov. 17, 1939; came to U.S., 1957; s. Vartan and Victoria Mehrabian; m. Linda Sanfilippo, Jan. 14, 1986. BS, MS, MIT, 1961; PhD, Clark U., Worcester, Mass., 1964. Asst. prof. psychology UCLA, 1964-70, assoc. prof., 1970-76, prof., 1976—; researcher in field. Cons. editor Jour. Personality and Social Psychology, 1973-76, Sociometry, 1974-77; mem. editorial bd. Jour. Nonverbal Behavior, 1975-86, Jour. Psycholinguistic Rsch., 1971—; author: An Analysis of Personality Theories, 1968, Tactics of Social Influence, 1970, Silent Messages, 1971, Nonverbal Communication, 1972, A Theory of Affiliation, 1974, An Approach to Environmental Psychology, 1974, Public Places and Private Spaces: The Psychology of Work, Play, and Living Environments, 1976, Basic Dimensions for a General Psychological Theory: Implications for Personality, Social, Environmental, and Developmental Studies, 1980, Eating Characteristics and temperament: General Measures and Interrelationships, 1987, The Name Game: The Decision That Lasts a Lifetime, 1990, Your Inner Path to Investment Success, 1991, numerous others. Libertarian. Home: 1130 Alta Mesa Rd Monterey CA 93940-4603

MEHRING, CLINTON WARREN, engineering executive; b. New Haven, Ind., Feb. 14, 1924; s. Fred Emmett and Florence Edith (Hutson) M.; m. Carol Jane Adams, Mar. 9, 1946; children—James Warren, Charles David, John Steven (dec.), Martha Jane. B.S., Case Inst. Tech., 1950; M.S., U. Colo., 1956. Registered profl. engr., Wyo., Colo., Nev. Design engr. U. S. Bur Reclamation, Denver, 1950-56; design engr. Tipton & Kalmbach, Denver, 1956-58; asst. resident engr. Tipton & Kalmbach, Quito, Equador, 1959-61; asst. chief design engr. Tipton & Kalmbach, Lahore, Pakistan, 1962-65; v.p. Tipton & Kalmbach, Denver, 1966-73, exec. v.p., 1973-79, pres., 1979—, also bd. dirs. Served with AUS, 1943-45. Recipient Theta Tau award as outstanding grad. Case Inst. Tech., 1950. Fellow ASCE (life); mem. Am. Cons. Engrs. Council, Colo. Soc. Engrs., U.S. Com. on Large Dams, Am. Concrete Inst., U.S. Com. Irrigation and Drainage (life), Sigma Xi, Tau Beta Pi, Theta Tau, Sigma Chi, Blue Key. Methodist. Club: Denver Athletic. Home: 1821 Mt Zion Dr Golden CO 80401-1733 Office: 1331 17th St Denver CO 80202-1566

MEHTA, RAHUL CHANDRAKANT, radiologist; b. Bombay, Sept. 22, 1959; came to U.S., 1984; s. Chandrakant J. and Devila H. (Shah) M.; m. Nita P. Trivedi, July 14, 1991. MB BS, U. Bombay, 1982, DMRD, 1984. Diplomate Am. Bd. Radiology, Am. Bd. Nuclear Medicine. Resident in radiology U. Wis. Hosp., Madison, 1985-91; fellow in neuroradiology Stanford (Calif.) U. Med. Sch., 1991-93. Mem. Am. Coll. Radiology, Radiol. Soc. N.Am. (magna cum laude 1989), Am. Soc. Neuroradiology (summa cum laude 1989), Am. Roentgen Ray Soc. Home: 350 Sharon Park Dr Apt I-2 Menlo Park CA 94025 Office: Stanford U Med Ctr Rm H1307 300 Pasteur Dr Stanford CA 94305

MEHTA MALANI, HINA, biostatistician, educator; b. Songad, Gujrat, India, June 24, 1958; came to U.S. 1978.; d. Jashwantlal and Usha (Modi) Mehta; m. Narendra Malani, Jan. 17, 1982; 1 child, Neil-Kanth. MA, SUNY, Buffalo, 1979; PhD, Columbia U., 1986. Statistician Merck and Co., Rahway, N.J., 1980-82, sr. statistician, 1982-86, biometrician, 1986-87; asst. prof. biostatistics U. Calif., Berkeley, 1987—. Contbr. articles to profl. jours. Mem. Am. Statis. Assn., Biometrics Soc., Sigma Xi.

MEIER, THOMAS JOSEPH, geologist, consultant, engineering firm executive; b. Superior, Nebr., June 16, 1948; s. Hugh Milton and Stella Bella (Dugas) M.; student U. Kans., 1966-69, U.S. Army Engr. Sch., 1969, Met. State Coll., 1976-78; BA in Geology, U. Colo., 1980; m. Jo Ann Weeks, June 4, 1968; 1 child, Nicole Victoria. Office mgr. Testing & Engring. Services, Inc., Colorado Springs, Colo., 1972-74; v.p. Thomas E. Summerlee & Assos., Inc., Vail, Colo., 1974-76; mktg. exec. Fox & Assocs., Inc., Phoenix, Denver, 1976-84, v.p. mktg. corp. hdqrs., Denver, 1984—, dir., 1982—; tech. services rep., geologist, Phoenix, 1981-84; dir. Thomas E. Summerlee & Assos., 1975-76. Rep. Dist. Committeeman, Jefferson County, Colo., 1980. Served with C.E., U.S. Army, 1969-72. Decorated Bronze Star; recipient Meritorious Service award Lai Kae Orphanage, Lai Kae, S.Vietnam, 1970. Mem. Soc. Mktg. Profl. Services, Denver Info. Network, Industries for Jeffco, Soc. Am. Mil. Engrs. (past pres. Phoenix), Am. Mgmt. Assn., U. Kans. Alumni Assn., U. Colo. Alumni Assn., Denver C. of C., Colo. Assn. Commerce and Industry, Metro North C. of C., Nat. Assn. Indsl. and Office Parks, Colo. Mining Assn., Cons. Engrs. Council. Roman Catholic. Contbr. articles to profl. publs. Author: Environmental Geology Digest, 2 vols. Home: 7535 S Jasmine Ct Englewood CO 80112-2464 Office: 4765 Independence St Wheat Ridge CO 80033-2999

MEIERAN, EUGENE STUART, material scientist; b. Cleve., Dec. 23, 1937; s. Elias and Rae (Linetsky) M.; m. Rosalind Berson, Mar. 25, 1962; children—Sharon Elizabeth, Andrew Marc. B.S. in Metallurgy, Purdue U., 1959; M.S. in Metallurgy, MIT, 1961, Sc.D. in Material Sci., 1963. Sr. mem. tech. staff Fairchild R & D., Palo Alto, Calif., 1963-73; engring. mgr. Intel Corp., Santa Clara, Calif., 1973-77, sr. mgr. quality assurance, 1977-84, Intel fellow, 1984—, mgr. AI lab., 1989—; vis. lectr. Technion, Haifa, Israel, 1970-71, H.H. Wills Physics Lab., Bristol, Eng., 1970-71. Contbr. articles to profl. jours. Mem. adv. bd. Lawrence Berkeley Lab., 1984—. AEC fellow, 1960; recipient Internat. Reliability awards, 1970, 79, 85.; appt. Disting. Engring. Alumnus Purdue U., 1988. Mem. AIME (chmn. electronic material symposium 1973—), Electron Microscope Soc. U.S.A., Tau Beta Pi, Phi Lambda Upsilon. Democrat. Jewish. Home: 5421 E Camello Rd Phoenix AZ 85018-1910 Office: Intel Corp 5000 W Chandler Blvd Chandler AZ 85226-3699

MEIERDING, LOREN E., systems engineer; b. Missoula, Mont., Jan. 16, 1946; s. Leslie Esra and Mae Gwendolyn (Christianson) M. BA, Yale U., 1967; MA, U. Tex., 1975, PhD, 1978. Actuarial asst. Nat. Assocs., L.A., 1980-82; staff engr. Hughes Aircraft Co., Fullerton, Calif., 1982—. Contbr. articles to profl. jours. With U.S. Army, 1968-70. Mem. IEEE, Am. Philos. Assn., U.S. Chess Fedn. Home: 1113 S Paula Dr Fullerton CA 92633 Office: Hughes Aircraft Co Bldg 618 M/S L311 1901 W Malvern Fullerton CA 92634

MEIGEL, DAVID WALTER, musician, military officer; b. Chgo., Feb. 27, 1957; s. Thomas Arent and Annie Elizabeth (Thomas) M. Diploma, USAF NCO Leadership Sch., Chanute AFB, Ill., 1981, USAF/CAP SQD Officer Sch., 1987, USAF NCO Acad., Norton AFB, Calif., 1991. Enlisted USAF, 1976; commd. staff sgt. to 2d lt. CAP, Travis AFB, Calif., 1986; advanced through grades to tech. sgt. USAF, 1989; percussionist 724th USAF Band, McChord AFB, Wash., 1976-78, 752d USAF Band, Elmendorf AFB, Alaska, 1978-80, 505th USAF Band, Chanute AFB, Ill., 1980-84, 504th USAF Band, Travis AFB, 1984-90; prin. percussionist, chief of adminstrn. Am.'s Band in Blue, USAF, Travis AFB, 1990-92. Prin. percussionist San Diego (Calif.) Civic Orch., 1973-76, Poway (Calif.) High Sch. Band, 1974-75; percussionist Anchorage (Alaska) Civic Opera, 1979-80, Anchorage (Alaska) Scottish Soc., 1979-80, Fairfield Civic Theatre, Fairfield, Calif., 1984—; communications officer USAF Civil Air Patrol, Travis AFB, 1986—. Recipient Gov.'s medal Youkon Internat. Invitational Scottish Games, Whitehorse City Coun., B.C., 1980; decorated Achievement medal, Comdrs. Commendation medal; named one of Outstanding Young Men Am., 1988, 92. Mem. Percussive Arts Soc., CAP USAF Aux. Home: PSC # 3 PO Box 6013 Travis AFB CA 94535 Office: Americas Band in Blue 271 Dixon Ave Travis AFB CA 94535-2867

MEIGHAN, STUART SPENCE, hospital consultant, internist, writer; b. Glasgow, Scotland, Jan. 30, 1923; came to U.S., 1962; s. Stuart Spence and Annie Louise (Brown) M; m. Anne Stewart Henderson, Nov. 4, 1952 (div. 1968); children: Jane Spence, Stuart Spence; m. Louise Rhys McGregor, July 7, 1985. MB, U. Glasgow, 1945. Registrar, sr. registrar Nat. Health Svc., U.K., 1948-57; sr. staff mem. Allan Blair Meml. Clinic, Regina, Sask., Can., 1957-62; internist Cleland Clinic, Oregon City, Oreg., 1962-64; dir. med. affairs Good Samaritan Hosp., Portland, Oreg., 1964-78; pres. Spence Meighan and Assocs., Portland, 1978—; cons. several hosps. and orgns. Contbr. over 100 articles to profl. jours. Lt. Royal Navy, 1946-48. Recipient Disting. Svc. award Am. Soc. Internal Medicine. Fellow Am. Coll. Physicians, Royal Coll. Physicians. Home and Office: 619 NW Alpine Terr Portland OR 97210

MEIKLEJOHN, ALVIN J., JR., state senator, lawyer, accountant.; b. Omaha, June 18, 1923; B.S., J.D., U. Denver, 1951; m. Lorraine J. Meiklejohn; children: Pamela Ann, Shelley Lou, Bruce Ian, Scott Alvin. Mem. Colo. Senate from 19th dist., 1976—, chmn. com.; edn.; mem. Edn. Commn. of States, 1981—, v. chmn., Colo. Commn. on Ach. in Edn., 1993; chmn., 1993—. Mem. Jefferson Sch. Dist. No. R-1 Bd. Edn., 1971-77, pres., 1973-77; commr. Commn. on Uniform State Laws, 1988—. Served to capt. U.S. Army, 1940-46; to maj. USAF, 1947-51. Mem. Colo. Bar Assn. (bd. govs. 1989—), Denver Bar Assn., Colo. Soc. CPA's, Arvada C. of C. Republican. Clubs: Masons, Shriners. Home: 7540 Kline Dr Arvada CO 80005-3732 Office: Jones & Keller PC 1600 DeKalb Energy Bldg 1625 Broadway Denver CO 80202-4731

MEILY, PAMELA JEANNE, writer, motion picture studio official; b. Bellefonte, Pa., July 28, 1965; d. Richard Hershey and Ruth Elizabeth (Reese) M. BS in Comm. and Broadcasting, Millersville (Pa.) U., 1987. News assignment editor Sta. WGAL-TV, Lancaster, Pa., 1986-88; news anchor Stas. WLPA and WNCE, Lancaster, 1987-90; pub. rels. asst. Jr. Achievement, L.A., 1991; internat. exec. asst. 20th Century Fox Film Corp., L.A., 1991, asst. to co-exec. producer, 1991-92, asst. to co-exec. producer LA Law, 1992—; guest announcer Wilmington (Del.) Tennis Classic, 1987; news corr. Lancaster newspapers, 1988-89; pub. rels. cons. S. June Smith Ctr., Lancaster, 1987-90. Recipient awards for pub. affairs, documentary, spot news, feature Pa. Assn. Broadcasting, 1987, 88, 89, media excellence award Travelers Protective Assn., 1990, S. June Smith Ctr., 1990. Office: 20th Century Fox 10201 W Pico Blvd Los Angeles CA 90035

MEINDL, ROBERT JAMES, English language educator; b. Wausau, Wis., Sept. 17, 1936; s. George Martin and Adeline Emilie (Goetsch) M.; m. Victoria Lynn Chavez; children: Karin Rose, George Andrew, Damian Kurt, Erika Wittmer, Christopher Smith, Gabrielle Remelia. BS, U. Wis., 1958; MA, U. Conn., 1960; PhD, Tulane U., 1965. Teaching asst. U. Conn., Storrs, 1958-60; teaching fellow Tulane U., 1960-62; lectr. U. Wis., Green Bay, 1963-65; from asst. to full prof. English Calif. State U., Sacramento, 1965—. Translator: Studies in John Gower, 1981; book rev. editor: Studia Mystica Jour., 1984-89; contbr. numerous articles to profl. jours. With USNR, 1953-61, 79—, PTO, ETO. Mem. Medieval Acad. Am., Modern Lang. Assn., Sacramento Turn Verein (v.p. 1976-77, sec. 1977-79), Medieval Assn. of the Pacific, Early English Text Soc. Home: 3320 M St Sacramento CA 95816-5336 Office: Calif State U 6000 J St Sacramento CA 95819-2605

MEINEL, MARJORIE PETTIT, optical engineer; b. Pasadena, Calif., May 13, 1922; d. Edison and Hannah (Steele) Pettit; m. Aden Baker Meinel, Sept. 5, 1944; children: Carolyn, Walter, Barbara, Elaine, Edward, Mary, David. BA, Pomona Coll., Claremont, Calif., 1943; MA, Claremont Coll., 1944. Rsch. assoc. Calif. Inst. Tech., Pasadena, 1944-45, U. Ariz., Tucson, 1974-85; mem. tech. staff Jet Propulsion Lab., Pasadena, 1985—; vis. faculty Nat. Cen. U., Chung-Li, Taiwan, 1978-80; commr. Ariz. Solar Energy Commn., Phoenix, 1975-81; mem. office tech. assessment U.S. Congress, Washington, 1974-79. Author: Applied Solar Energy, 1977, Sunsets, Twilights and Evening Skies, 1983; patentee in field. Recipient Exceptional Svc. medal Nat. Aeronautics and Space Adminstrn., Kingslake medal. Fellow Internat. Soc. Optical Engring. Lutheran. Office: Jet Propulsion Lab 4800 Oak Grove Dr Pasadena CA 91109-8099

MEINERT, LYNLEY SHERYL, clinical psychologist; b. Battle Creek, Mich., Nov. 30, 1964; d. Lewis Sanford and Janis Gayle (Palmiter) M.; m. Mark Alan Ebeling, July 14, 1990. BA, Mich. State U., 1986; MA, Calif. Sch. Profl. Psychology, 1988, PhD, 1990. Lic. psychologist, Ariz. Trainee psychology St. Mary's Rehab. Care, Enid, Okla., 1990-91; assoc. psychologist in pvt. practice Lubbock, Tex., 1991; clin. psychologist Community Rehab. Svcs. Ariz., Scottsdale, 1991—. Mem. APA, Internat. Neuropsychol. Assn., Phi Beta Kappa, Psi Chi, Phi Kappa Phi. Office: Community Rehab Svcs Ariz Ste 260 11000 N Scottsdale Rd Scottsdale AZ 85254

MEISSNER, LOREN PHILLIP, JR., systems analyst; b. Fontana, Calif., May 12, 1953; s. Loren P. and Peggy Louise (Pritchard) M. BA in English, San Francisco State U., 1981, MBA, 1984. Sales asst. IBM Corp., San Francisco, 1983; systems analyst Pacific Bell, San Francisco, 1984; software purchasing agt. ComputerLand USA, Hayward, Calif., 1985; computer analyst/programmer State of Wash., Olympia, 1986-90; sys. analyst/programmer U. Wash., Seattle, 1990—. With USN, 1971-74. Office: Univ Wash Mail Stop XD-04 Seattle WA 98195

MEISTER, JOHN EDWARD, JR., systems analyst; b. Elgin, Ill., Nov. 17, 1956; s. John Edward and Marilyn Barbara (Futter) M.; m. Rebecca Marie Buehner, Nov. 15, 1975; children: Christine Marie, Mark Christopher. AA, Cen. Tex. Coll., 1979, U. Md., 1980; BS cum laude, U. Md., 1981; postgrad., Western Conservative Baptist Sem., 1982-83. Enlisted U.S. Army, 1974, advance through grades to staff sgt., 1980; electronics technician Frankfurt, Fed. Republic of Germany, 1974-77; maintenance supr. Darmstadt, Fed. Republic of Germany, 1978-81; transferred from 232d Signal Co. Telecommunications, 1981; instr. U.S. Army Signal Sch., Ft. Gordon, Ga., 1981-82; resigned U.S. Army, 1982; sr. electronics instr. ITT Tech. Inst., Portland, Oreg., 1982-83; equipment engring. and engring. svcs. technician Intel Corp., Aloha, Oreg., 1983-85; dealer Amsoil, Snohomish, Wash., 1983—; electronic designer Boeing Electronics Co., Everett, Wash., 1985-89; systems analyst Boeing Comml. Airplanes, Everett, 1989—; electronics engr. Innovative Designs and Electronic Systems Techs., Portland, 1982-85. Bd. dirs. Machias Ridge East Homeowner's Assn., 1988-91; fin. advisor Jr. Achievement, Everett High Sch., 1988-89. Mem. Pacific NW Four Wheel Drive Assn. Republican. Baptist. Home: 2111 157th Ave SE Snohomish WA 98290-4710 Office: Boeing Comml Airplane Co M/S OF-FA PO Box 3707 Seattle WA 98124-2207

MEISTER, SHAWN DEE, retail executive; b. Ft. Scott, Kans., Feb. 13, 1962; d. Benny Ralph and Charlotte Ruth (Surrell) Jackson; m. Robert Louis Meister, Aug. 13, 1983; children: Taylor James, Parker Jay. Student, Okla. State U., 1980-82; BS, U. Utah, 1985. Cert. mid. sch. tchr. Elem. tchr. Granite Sch. Dist., Salt Lake City, 1985-86, mid. sch. tchr., 1986-88; retail accounts svc. rep. McKesson Drug Co., Salt Lake City, 1988-90; retails accounts mgr. McKesson Drug Co., San Diego, 1990—. Sunday sch. supt. Hope Meth. Ch., San Diego, 1992. Democrat.

MEISTER, VERLE MARTIN, management recruiter; b. Moville, Iowa, Mar. 16, 1937; s. Otto John Fred and Ruth Louise (Hughes) M.; m. Connie Margaret Sturm, May 11, 1968; 1 child, John Martin. BA in Bus. and Econs., Wartburg Coll., 1964. Employment interviewer J.I. Case Co., Bettendorf, Iowa, 1964-65; employment mgr. J.I. Case Co., Terre Haute, Ind., 1966-68, Am. Air Filter Co., Moline, Ill., 1965-66; adminstrv. asst. to pres. Vindale Corp., Dayton, Ohio, 1968-75; mgr. labor rels. Robbins & Myers, Springfield, Ohio, 1975-78; pres. Mgmt. Recruiters Cheyenne, Wyo., 1978—; del. White House Conf. on Small Bus., 1986. Chmn. spl. events Am. Cancer Soc., Cheyenne, 1979-80. With U.S. Army, 1960-63. Mem. Am. Soc. Pers. Adminstrs. (pres. 1986), Small Bus. Coun. (chmn. 1987-89, bd. dirs. 1989-92), Cheyenne C. of C. (pres. 1991), Kiwanis (pres. 1991, 92, lt. gov. 1993-94). Home: 123 Longs Peak Dr Cheyenne WY 82009-3550 Office: Mgmt Recruiters Cheyenne 1008 E 21st St Cheyenne WY 82001-3910

MEISTRICH, HERBERT ALAN, real estate investment company executive; b. Neptune, N.J., Mar. 28, 1942; s. Sidney Jules and Sylvia (Inselberg) M.; m. Susan Friedman, Aug. 14, 1963 (div. Feb. 1979); 1 child, Lawrence; m. Madeline Gail Aultman, June 23, 1979; 1 child, Jason. BA in History, Rutgers U., 1963; JD, Columbia U., 1966. Assoc. Raphael, Searles & Vischi, N.Y.C., 1966-68, Wien, Lane & Malkin, N.Y.C., 1968-72; prs. HSM Corp., N.Y., San Diego, 1972—; exec. v.p. Exec. Monetary Mgmt. Inc., N.Y.C., 1972-82, Coparco Realty Corp., N.Y.C., 1975-82; pres. Continental Am. Capital Corp., San Diego, 1983-92; chmn. bd. dirs. AspenCrest Hospitality Inc., Englewood, Colo., 1989—; pres. Meistrich Capital Resources Inc., San Diego, 1992—. Mem. devel. com. San Diego Zool. Soc., 1986-88, pres.'s assn. planning com., 1989—; bd. dirs. Ctr. for the Reprodn. of Endangered Species, San Diego, 1988—; mem. corp. sponsorship com. March of Dimes, San Diego, 1991—, Walk Am. Corp. Coun., 1993—. Mem. Urban Land Inst. Office: Meistrich Captial Resources Inc Ste 332 3760 Convoy St San Diego CA 92111

MEJIA, LELIO HERNAN, civil engineer, educator; b. Bogota, Colombia, Feb. 18, 1956; came to U.S., 1977; s. Luis Alfonso and Teresa (Ortiz) M.; m. Sandra Susan Ritter, Mar. 5, 1983; children: Natalia, Daniel. BS, U. Javeriana, Bogota, 1977; MS, U. Calif., Berkeley, 1978, PhD, 1981. Registered profl. engr., Calif. Sr. engr. Harding-Lawson Accocs., San Francisco, 1981-85; sr. project engr. Woodward-Clyde Cons., Oakland, Calif., 1985-91, assoc., 1991—; lectr. U. Calif. Extension, Berkeley, 1987—; speaker in field. Contbr. articles to profl. jours. Fullbright scholar, 1977. Mem. ASCE (editor Jour. Geotech. Engring. 1989—, invited speaker Iowa sect. 1991), U.S. Com. on Large Dams, Structural Engrs. Assn. Calif., Earthquake Engring. Rsch. Inst., Internat. Soc. Soil Mech. and Found. Engring. Office: Woodward-Clyde Cons 500 12th St Oakland CA 94607

MELANSON, LEO MATTHEW, army officer; b. Salem, Mass., Dec. 20, 1941; s. Leo Joseph and Gertrude Frances (Phelan) M.; m. Kathryn Marie Drabin, Mar. 18, 1963 (div.); 1 child, Leo Michael; m. Susan Jeanne Balmat, May 19, 1990; 1 stepchild, Kimberly. BA, Providence Coll., 1963; MEd, U. Mass., 1970; postgrad., U. So. Calif., 1978-81; M Mgmt., U.S. Army War Coll., 1984. Cert. tchr., R.I., Hawaii. Commd. 2d lt. U.S. Army, 1963, advanced through grades to col., 1985; comdr. 371st co., 1st cavalry div. U.S. Army, Vietnam, 1967-68, ops. officer 509th group, 1971-72; dep. dir. Office Tng. Requirements, Intelligence Sch. U.S. Army, Ft. Devens, Mass., 1972-76; signals intelligence comdr. in chief Pacific Hdqrs. U.S. Army, Aiea, Hawaii, 1976-80; dep. comdr. field sta. U.S. Army, Hawaii and Germany, 1980-85; comdr. cryptologic group Europe U.S. Army, Heidelberg, Fed. Republic Germany, 1985-86; dep. commandant Intelligence Sch. U.S. Army, Ft. Devens, 1986-90; chair intelligence, comdr. in chief Pacific Hdqrs. U.S. Army, Aiea, 1990—. Decorated Legion of Merit, Bronze Star with oak leaf cluster. Fellow Rotary. Home: 92-1200 Hookeha St Ewa Beach HI 96707

MELCHER, PIERSON FORT, retired academic headmaster; b. Phila., Mar. 29, 1926; s. Harold Porter and Marjorie Pope (Fort) M.; m. Jean Searle Nelson, 1952 (div. 1976); children: Cynthia Porter, Peter Thorne; m. Margaret Barksdale Nuttle, July 16, 1977. BA, Yale U., 1950, MA, 1953. Cert. secondary sch. prin. Tchr. of English Hopkins Grammar Sch., New Haven, 1950-52, Cate Sch., Carpinteria, Calif., 1953-58; head English dept. St. Stephen's Episcopal Sch., Austin, Tex., 1958-60; asst. headmaster, dir. of studies St. Louis Country Day Sch., 1960-63; headmaster Chadwick Sch., Palos Verdes Peninsula, Calif., 1963-68, St. Margaret's Sch., Waterbury, Conn., 1968-72; founding headmaster The Southborough Sch. (now St. Mark's), Southboro, Mass., 1972-78; headmaster Bartram Sch., Jacksonville, Fla., 1978-82; cons. Ind. Sch. Mgmt., Wilmington, Del., 1982-89; trustee Cisqua Sch., Bedford, N.Y., 1971-72. Author: Year of Wonder: 1968, 1991, The Flame and the Phoenix, 1993. Del. St. Louis White House Conf. on Edn., 1962; cons. Colo. Symphony Orch., Denver, 1991-93. With USAAF, 1944-46, PTO. Mem. New Wizard Oil Combination. Episcopal. Home: 25107 Giant Gulch Rd Evergreen CO 80439

MELDMAN, BURTON ALAN, insurance salesman; b. Milw., Sept. 5, 1933; s. Edward Harry and Rose (Bortin) M.; m. Margery Scholl, June 11, 1955; children: Sharon, Michael, Debra. BBA, U. Wis., 1955; JD, Marquette U., 1958. CLU, Chartered Fin. Cons. Life ins. salesman Mass. Mut. Life, Springfield, Mass., 1956—; registered rep. Integrated Resources Equity Corp., N.Y.C., 1979-87, MML Investors Svcs., Inc., Springfield, Mass., 1988—; pres., chief exec. officer ERISA, Ltd., Phoenix, 1975-85; chief exec. officer Meldman Fin. Svcs., Ltd., 1985—. Mem. Nat. Assn. Life Underwriters, Phoenix Assn. Life Underwriters, Million Dollar Roundtable. Office: Mass Mutual Cos 7600 N 16th St Ste 200 Phoenix AZ 85020-4443

MELDRUM, DANIEL RICHARD, general surgeon resident, researcher; b. Flint, Mich., Sept. 27, 1965; s. Richard Terry and Patricia Ellen (Klug) M. BS, Univ. Mich., 1987; MD, Mich. State Univ., 1992. Teaching asst. dept. biochemistry Univ. Mich., Ann Arbor, 1986, rsch. asst., 1987-88; rsch. student fellow Mich. State Univ., East Lansing, 1989-92; resident surgery Univ. Colo., 1992—; advisor Mich. State Univ. Adv. Com., 1990-92; supr., adv. Biochemistry Teaching Assts, Ann Arbor, 1986; guest speaker 18 internat. and nat. confs. Contbr more than 20 articles to profl. jours. Del. Am. Medical Student Assn.; coord. Mich. State Univ. Red Cross Medical Sch Blood Drives, 1989-90. Recipient Young Investigator award The Shock Soc., 1992, Student Rsch. award Assn Acad. Surgery, 1992, Moorhead Rsch. award Gramec Found., 1991, NIH Biomedical Rsch. grant 1989, 90, Excellence award Mich. State Univ., 1992. Mem. AMA, Am. Assn. Advancement Sci., N.Y. Acad. Scis., Shock Soc., Assn. Acad. Surgery, Am. Medical Student Assn. (pres. 1989-90), Am. Assn. Medical Colls. (rep.), Alpha Omega Alpha. Home: 870 Dexter # 301 Denver CO 80220 Office: Univ Colo Dept Surgery 4200 East Ninth Ave Denver CO 80262

MELENDEZ, JOAQUIN, orthopedic assistant; b. San Gabriel, Calif., Aug. 16, 1929; s. Guadalupe and Gudelia (Maldonado) M.; m. Lola Hester Harris, Sept. 3, 1954. BS, Instituto del Estado, Chihuahua, Mex., 1949; AA, Foothill Coll., Los Altos Hill, Calif., 1973. Enlisted U.S. Army, 1950, advanced through grades to sgt. 1st class, ret., 1971; orthopedic asst. St. Vrain Valley Orthopedics, Longmont, Colo., 1973—. Author: (poems) Saturday Night, 1990, Reflections, 1991, Freedom, 1992. With U.S. Army, 1950-71. Decorated Bronze Star with V, Meritorious Svc. medal with V; recipient marathon awards. Mem. Nat. Assn. Orthopedic Technologists, Colo. Acad. Physician Assts., Nat. Assn. Parlimentarians, Toastmasters Internat. (named Outstanting Div. Gov. 1988-89, recipient speech awards), Internat. Soc. Poets. Republican. Roman Catholic. Home: 3331 Mountain View Ave Longmont CO 80503 Office: St Vrain Valley Orthopedics 1331 Linden St Longmont CO 80501

MELICH, MITCHELL, lawyer; b. Bingham Canyon, Utah, Feb. 1, 1912; s. Joseph and Mary (Kalembar) M.; m. Doris M. Snyder, June 3, 1935; children: Tanya (Mrs. Noel L. Silverman), Michael, Nancy, Robert A. LL.B., U. Utah, 1934. Bar: Utah bar 1934. Pvt. practice Moab, 1934-63, city atty., 1934-55; county atty. Grand County, 1940-42; sec., dir. Utex Exploration Co., Moab, 1953-62; pres., dir. Uranium Reduction Co., Moab, 1954-62; cons. to pres. Atlas Minerals, div. Atlas Corp., 1962-67; dir., treas. New Park Mining Co., 1962-65; assoc. law firm Ray, Quinney & Nebeker, 1973—; solicitor Dept. Interior, Washington, 1969-73;. Mem. of Colorado River Com. of Utah, 1945-47; mem. Utah Water and Power Bd., 1947; chmn. Citizens Adv. Com. on Higher Edn., 1968; mem. nat. adv. council U. Utah, 1976—; Mem. Utah Senate, 1942-50, minority leader, 1949-50; mem. Utah Legislative Council, 1949-54; del. Republican Nat. Conv., 1952-72; mem. Rep. Nat. Com. for Utah, 1961-64; Rep. candidate for gov., 1964; cons. on staff Congressman Sherman P. Lloyd, Utah, 1967-68; bd. dirs. St. Marks Hosp., 1973-87; bd. regents U. Utah, 1961-65, also mem. devel. fund com., mem. nat. adv. council, 1968-73, 76—; mem. Utah Statewide Health Coordinating Coun., 1985; mem. Utah Fusion Energy Coun., 1989—. Recipient Disting. Alumni award U. Utah, 1969, Man of Yr. award, Arthritis Found., 1991. Mem. Am. Bar Assn., Utah State Bar, Utah Mining Assn. (pres. 1962-63), Kappa Sigma. Republican. Club: Alta Salt Lake Country (Salt Lake City). Lodges: Masons; Shriners. Home: 900 Donner Way Apt 708

Salt Lake City UT 84108-2112 Office: 400 Deseret Bldg 79 S Main St Salt Lake City UT 84111-1901

MELICHER, RONALD WILLIAM, finance educator; b. St. Louis, July 4, 1941; s. William and Lorraine Norma (Mohart) M.; m. Sharon Ann Schlarmann, Aug. 19, 1967; children: Michelle Joy, Thor William, Sean Richard. BSBA, Washington U., St. Louis, 1963; MBA, Washington U., 1965, DBA, 1968. Asst. prof. fin. U. Colo., Boulder, 1969-71, assoc. prof., 1971-76, prof. fin., 1976—, chmn. fin. div., 1978-86, 90, MBA/MS programs dir., 1990—; assoc. dir. space law bus. and policy ctr. U. Colo., 1986-87; rsch. cons. FPC, Washington, 1975-76, GAO, Washington, 1981, RCG/Hagler, Bailly, Inc., 1985—, Ariz. Corp. Commn., 1986-87, Conn. Dept. Pub. Utility Control, 1989, U.S. SEC, 1992; cons. tech. edn. IBM Corp., 1985—; dir. ann. Exec. Program for Gas Industry, 1975—; instr. ann. program Nat. Assn. Regulatory Utility Commrs., Mich. State U., 1981—. Co-author: Real Estate Finance, 2d edit., 1984, 3d edit. 1989, Finance: Introduction to Markets, Institutions and Management, 7th edit., 1988, 8th edit., 1992, Financial Management, 5th edit., 1982; assoc. editor The Financial Rev., 1988-91. Recipient News Ctr. 4 TV Teaching award, 1987, MBA/MS Assn. Teaching award 1988; grantee NSF, 1974, NASA, 1986, 87; scholar W.H. Baughn Disting., 1989—, U. Colo. Pres.'s Teaching, 1989—. Mem. Fin. Mgmt. Assn. (membership com. 1974-76, regional dir. 1975-77, assoc. editor 1975-80, v.p. ann. meeting 1985, v.p. program 1987, pres. 1991-92, exec. com. 1992—), Am. Fin. Assn., Western Fin. Assn. (bd. dirs. 1974-76), Fin. Execs. Inst. (acad. mem. 1975—), Eastern Fin. Assn., Southwestern Fin. Assn., Midwest Fin. Assn. (bd. dirs. 1978-80), Alpha Kappa Psi, Beta Gamma Sigma. Presbyterian. Home: 6348 Swallow Ln Boulder CO 80303 Office: U Colo Coll Bus Campus Box 419 Boulder CO 80309

MELIKIAN, ARMEN, small business owner; b. May 3, 1962; came to U.S., 1984; s. Haig and Takouhi M.; m. Irina Serghiyan, Oct. 19, 1990; children: Natalie, Arthur. MA, Am. U., 1988. Rsch. asst. Am. Enterprise Inst., Washington, 1986-87; in charge Armenian sect. Libr. of Congress, Washington, 1987-88; exec. dir. Am. Friends of Armenia, Century City, Calif., 1988-90; pres. Hexagon Enterprises, Inc., 1991—, chmn. Founder Am. Friends of Armenia, Century City, 1988. Office: 431 N Brand Blvd Ste 201 Glendale CA 91203

MELLO, DONALD R., state senator; b. Owensboro, Ky., June 22, 1934; s. Jack and Gladys (Jasper) M.; student U. Nev.; grad. B.F. Goodrich Co. Mgmt. Sch., Sacramento; m. Barbara Jane Woodhall; children—Donald, David. Condr., S.P. Transp. Co.; mem. Nev. Assembly from 30th Dist., 1963-82, chmn. Interim Finance com., 1975-77, chmn. Legis. Commn., 1973-74, chmn. Ways and Means com., 1973-80, sr. Democratic assemblyman, 1973-82, sr. assemblyman, 1977-82, Nev. state senator, 1983-89; chmn. com. on transp., 1985, vice chmn. com. on fin., 1985. Mem. adv. com. Title III, Nev. Dept. Edn. Mem. Washoe County Dem. Cen. Com., 1968-89; mem. Pres.'s Club, United Transp. Union, PTA (life). Served with USNR. Recipient Friend of Edn. award Washoe County Tchrs. Assn., 1974, Appreciation award Nev. N.G., 1973-75, Assembly Speaker's award, 1977, Appreciation award Ret. Public Employees Nev., 1979, award Clark County Classroom Tchrs., 1981, appreciation award United Transp. Union, 1981, Pres.' award Nev. State Edn. Assn., 1981, 85, Nev. AFL-CIO, 1981; commd. hon. Ky. col.; named One of 10 Outstanding Legislators in U.S., Assembly State Govtl. Employees, 1976; Don Mello Sports Complex named in his honor City of Sparks (Nev.). Democrat. Lodge: Masons. Home: 2590 Oppio St Sparks NV 89431-1930

MELLO, RENEE LORRAINE, marketing executive; b. San Jose, Dec. 5, 1964; d. Edward Jesse and Mary Edith (Bledsaw) M. BA in English, San Jose State U., 1987, BS in Politics, 1988. Lic. in real estate, Calif. Swim instr. Decathlon Club, Santa Clara, Calif., 1984-88; with Axlon Toy Co., Sunnyvale, Calif., 1986-87; salesperson Nordstroms, San Jose, 1986-88; exec. mktg. asst. Mass Microsys., Sunnyvale, 1988-89; v.p. mktg./communications UIC Internat. Corp., Santa Clara, 1989-93; mktg. exec. worldwide ops. Photon Dynamics Inc., Milpitas, Calif., 1993—. Newsletter editor Internat. Bus. Assn., Japan, 1990—. Active Republicans Abroad., 1990—; bd. dirs. Santa ClaraUnified Sch. Dist. Edn Found. Mem. NAFE, Fgn. Women Execs. (progs. dir. 1990—). Republican. Roman Catholic. Office: Photon Dynamics Inc 1504 McCarthy Blvd Milpitas CA 95035

MELLON, WILLIAM DANIEL, communications executive; b. Darby, Pa., June 22, 1951; s. William and Eleanor M.; m. Nikki Dersin, July 15, 1978; children: William D. III, Logan, Megan. BA, St. Louis U., 1972, MA, 1974. Dir. regional pub. rels. Boeing Co., Seattle, 1978-85; dir. corp. communications Beech Aircraft Corp., Wichita, Kans., 1985-87; dir. news and info. Rockwell Internat., Seal Beach, Calif., 1987-92, dir. pub. rels., 1992—. Capt. USAF, 1973-78; Lt. Col. USAFR, 1978—. Mem. Internat. Assn. Bus. Communicators, Assn. Aero. and Astronautics, Am. Mktg. Assn., Nat. Investor Rels. Inst., Nat. Press Club, Coun. Communications Mgmt., Pub. Rels. Soc. Am., Aviation and Space Writers Assn., L.A. Press Club. Office: Rockwell Internat Corp World Hdqts PO Box 4250 2201 Seal Beach Blvd Seal Beach CA 90740-5727

MELLON, WILLIAM KNOX, foundation executive, consultant; b. Houston, Oct. 20, 1925; s. William Knox and Zelma (Cochran) M.; m. Josselyn Bale, Aug. 6, 1948 (div. 1968); children: Lesley, Andrea, Frederick; m. Carlotta Herman, June 8, 1972. BA, Pomona Coll., 1950; MA, Claremont Grad. Sch., 1952, PhD, 1972. Prof. history Mt. San Antonio Coll., Walnut, Calif., 1955-60, Immaculate Heart Coll., L.A., 1960-75; dir. State Office Hist. Preservation, State of Calif., Sacramento, 1975-83, state hist. preservation officer, 1977-83; dir. Mission Inn Found., Riverside, Calif., 1986—; adj. prof. history, U. Calif., Riverside, 1987—; pres. Mellon & Assocs., hist preservation cons., Riverside, 1986—. Editor: Development of Civilization, 1960, Like It Is, Like It Was: Readings in Western Civilization, 1972. Dem. nominee for U.S. Ho. of Reps., 1962; dir. orgn. Brown for Gov. Campaign, L.A., 1974. Recipient Hist. Preservation award Calif. Hist. Soc., 1978, Calif. Preservation Found., 1984, Annual Historic Preservation award. Home: 4631 Ladera Ln Riverside CA 92501-2013 Office: Mission Inn Found 3739 6th St Riverside CA 92501-2832

MELNICK, MICHAEL B., actuary; b. Phila., Apr. 19, 1948; s. David Melnick and Betsy (Ross) Rothblatt; m. Patricia Beth Givner, Apr. 11, 1968; 1 child, David J. BA in Math., Antioch Coll., 1970. Cons. actuary Alexander & Alexander, San Francisco, 1980-84; regional v.p. Mut. of Am., L.A., 1984-87; prin., chief actuary The Epler Co., Woodland Hills, Calif., 1987—. Mem. Am. Soc. Pension Actuaries (vice chmn. com. 1991—), Am. Acad. Actuaries. Jewish. Home: 5811 Rolling Rd Woodland Hills CA 91367

MELOAN, TAYLOR WELLS, marketing educator; b. St. Louis, July 31, 1919; s. Taylor Wells and Edith (Graham) M.; m. Anna Geraldine Leukering, Dec. 17, 1944 (div. 1974); children: Michael David, Steven Lee; m. Jane Innes Bierlich, Jan. 30, 1975. B.S. cum laude, St. Louis U., 1949; M.B.A., Washington U., St. Louis, 1950; D of Bus. Admin., Ind. U., 1953. Advt. mgr. Herz Corp., St. Louis, 1941-42; sales promotion supr. Liggett & Myers Tobacco Co., St. Louis, 1942-43; asst. prof. mktg. U. Okla., Norman, 1953; asst., then assoc. prof. mktg. Ind. U., Bloomington, 1953-59; prof., chmn. dept. mktg. U. So. Calif., Los Angeles, 1959-69, prof. mktg., 1969-92, Robert E. Brooker prof. mktg., 1970-79, Robert E. Brooker prof. mktg. emeritus, 1991—; dean Sch. Bus. Adminstrn. U. So. Calif., 1969-71, assoc. v.p. acad. adminstrn. and research, 1971-81; prof. bus. adminstrn. U. Karachi, Pakistan, 1962; vis. prof. mktg. Istituto Post U. Per Lo Studio Dell Organizzazione Aziendale, Turin, Italy, 1964; disting. vis. prof. U. Witwatersrand, Johannesburg, 1978; editorial adviser bus. adminstrn. Houghton Mifflin Co., Boston, 1959-73; cons. to industry and govt., 1953—; bd. dirs. Council Better Bus. Burs., Inc., 1978-84, Nat. Advt. Rev. Bd., 1985-89. Author: New Career Opportunities, 1978, Innovation Strategy and Management, 1979, Direct Marketing: Vehicle for Department Store Expansion, 1984, Preparing the Exporting Entrepreneur, 1986, The New Competition: Dilemma of Department Stores in the 1980's, 1987, Franchise Marketing: A Retrospective and Prospective View of a Contractual Vertical Marketing System, 1988; co-author: Managerial Marketing, 1970, Internationalizing the Business Curriculum, 1968, Handbook of Modern Marketing, contbg. author, 1986; bd. editors: Jour. Mktg., 1965-72. Lt. (j.g.)h USNR, 1943-46. Mem. Newcomen Soc. N.Am., Am. Mktg. Assn. (pres. Los Angeles chpt. 1963-64), Order of Artus, Beta Gamma Sigma, Delta Pi Epsilon. Clubs: Calif. Yacht, University (Los Angeles). Lodge: Rotary. Home: 59 Lakefront Irvine CA 92714-4683 Office: U So Calif Los Angeles CA 90089

MELOTT, RONALD K., fire protection engineer, consultant; b. Hillsboro, Oreg., May 8, 1939; s. Quinlin W. and Alma (Doern) M.; m. Marilyn R. Volz, Feb. 3, 1961; children: Pamela S. Heathman, Carla M., Daniel W. BS, Portland State U., 1970. Profl. engr. Oreg., Calif., Wash. Fire fighter Portland (Oreg.) Bur. Fire, 1961-64, fire insp., 1964-68, fire lt., 1968-69, staff lt., 1969-72; chief fire prevention spec. Nat. Fire Protection Assn., Boston, 1972-77; fire protection cons., owner Melott and Assocs., Inc., Beaverton, Oreg., 1977—. Contbr. author, editor: Fire Inspection Manual; co-author: Flammable Liquids Code Handbook; co-developer audio-visual tng. program. Treas. Roth Scholarship Found., Portland. With U.S. Army, 1961-63. Named Fireman of Yr. Internat. Assn. Fire Chiefs, 1965-66. Mem. Soc. Fire Protection Engrs., Nat. Fire Protection Assn. (MAC region vice-chair), Fire Marshals Assn. N.Am. (exec. sec. 1974-77), Internat. Soc. Fire Svc. Instrs., Internat. Assn. Arson Investigators, Am. Soc. Mech. Engrs., Nat. Soc. Profl. Engrs. Republican. Baptist. Office: Melott & Assocs Inc 11650 SW Bel Aire Ln Beaverton OR 97005-5908

MELROSE, BARRY JAMES, professional hockey team coach; b. Kelvington, Sask., Can., July 15, 1956. Player various minor league teams, 1973-77, 82-83, 83-86, 86-87; player Cin. Stingers, 1976-79, Winnipeg Jets, 1979-81, Toronto Maple Leafs, 1981-82, 82-83, Detroit Red Wings, 1983-84, 85-86; former gen. mgr., head coach Adirondack Red Wings; now head coach L.A. Kings, 1992—. Office: LA Kings PO Box 17013 3900 W Manchester Blvd Inglewood CA 90308

MELSHEIMER, HAROLD, obstetrician, gynecologist; b. Legenfeld, Germany, June 11, 1927; came to U.S., 1955; naturalized, 1960; s. Louis and Hella Leonie (Schwehr) Peterman; m. Norma Sykes Sabrina, Nov. 27, 1967; children: Laura, Linda. BS, Marburg U., West Germany, 1951, MD, 1954. Diplomate Am. Bd. Ob-Gyn. Intern Baden County Hosp., West Germany, 1954-55, St. Mary's Hosp. Med. Ctr., Long Beach, Calif., 1955-56; resident Queens Hosp. Med. Ctr., Honolulu, 1956-57, Calif. Hosp. Med. Ctr., L.A., 1957-59; pvt. practice ob-gyn. Encino, Calif., 1959-87; ret.; former dept. chief, now hon. staff mem. Am. Med. Internat. Med. Ctr., Tarzana, Calif., Encino Hosp.; founder Technion Inst. of Tech. Contbr. articles to profl. jours. Operational mem. USCG Aux., 1971. Recipient cert. of honor Wisdom Soc.; named Hon. Citizen, Rep. of Korea, 1966. Fellow ACS (life), Am. Coll. Ob-Gyn., Internat. Coll. Surgeons; mem. Calif. Med. Assn., L.A. County Med. Assn., Am. Physicians Fellowship for Israel Med. Assn., N.Y. Acad. Scis., Braemar Country Club. Home: 25660 Deertrail Dr Tehachapi CA 93561-9140

MELTON, CHERYL ANN, educator, small business owner; b. Bklyn., Jan. 5, 1949; d. Raymond Franklin and Irene Louise (Cotton) Blair; m. Gilbert Edmund Melton, Aug. 26, 1972; children: Byron Adrian, Brandie Alicia. BS in Edn., Ohio State U., 1971; MS in Edn., Nazareth Coll., Rochester, N.Y., 1976. Prof. clear multiple subject teaching credential, Calif. Elem. tchr. N.Y.C. Bd. Edn., Bklyn., 1971-72, Rochester City Sch. Dist., 1973-84; elem. tchr. Long Beach (Calif.) Unified Sch. Dist., 1984-90, lang. arts specialist, 1990—, reading recovery tchr.-in-tng., 1992—; owner franchise Cajun Joe's, Ontario, Calif., 1992—; mem. Sch. Program Improvement Leadership Team, Long Beach, 1990—. Chmn. membership devel. Jr. League Long Beach, 1991-92, mem. by-laws task force, 1992-93, advisory future planning, 1989—, selected mentor, 1991—, chosen delagate Jr. League Dallas,. Scholar Calif. literature project Calif. State U., Dominguez Hills, 1992. Mem. Nat. Coun. Tchrs. English, English Coun. Long Beach, Calif. Tchrs. Assn., Nat. Coun. Negro Women, Links (Orange County chpt. Inc., Rochester, N.Y. chpt.), Delta Sigma Theta (charter, Long Beach alumnae), Jack and Jill of Am. (charter mem. Long Beach chapter). Democrat. Baptist. Home: 4508 Hazelnut Ave Seal Beach CA 90740 Office: Cajun Joe's 3045 A South Archibald Ave Ontario CA 91761

MELTZER, STEVE, photographer; b. Bronx, N.Y., June 30, 1945; s. David and Esther (Pess) M.; m. Diane du Bois, June 6, 1982; 1 child, Alyx. BS in Psychology, CUNY, 1966. Exec. dir. North Greenwood Project Com., Seattle, 1972-75; gallery owner Photo Printworks, Seattle, 1975-77; founder, owner West Stock Photo Agy., Seattle, 1977-81; photographer, writer freelance, Seattle, 1977—. Author: Photographing Your Craftswork, 1986; author monthly feature column. Pres. Second Landing Artist Co-op, Seattle, 1972-74, Madrona Dance Program, Seattle, 1976, Amici del Vino, Seattle, 1989-91; photographer Seattly Symphony Orch., Seattle, 1982—. Recipient Gold medal for Feature Story, 1984, Photography award, 1987, Mag. Photography award, 1989. Office: Steve Meltzer Photography PO Box 99613 Seattle WA 98911

MELTZOFF, ANDREW N., psychologist, educator; b. N.Y.C., Feb. 9, 1950; s. Julian and Judith (Novikoff) M. BA, Harvard U., 1972; PhD, Oxford U., Eng., 1976. Rsch. instr. U. Wash., Seattle, 1977-80, rsch. asst. prof., 1980-84, assoc. prof., 1984-88, prof., 1988—, adj. prof. psychiatry and behavioral scis., 1988—. Contbr. articles to profl. jours.; mem. editorial bd. Infant Behavior and Devel. Grantee NSF, 1983, NIH, 1986; MacArthur Found. grantee, 1984; recipient James McKeen Cattell award, 1990. Fellow AAAS, Am. Psychol. Assn., Am. Psychol. Soc.; mem. Soc. Rsch. and Child Devel., N.Y. Acad. Scis., Western Psychol. Assn., Phi Beta Kappa. Office: U Wash Dept Psychology WJ-10 Seattle WA 98195

MELTZOFF, JULIAN, psychologist; b. N.Y.C., Feb. 16, 1921; s. Nathan G. and Sadie L. (Marcus) M.; m. Judith Novikoff (div. 1975); children: Andrew, Nancy; m. Antonia Ratensky, Oct. 16, 1976. BS, CCNY, 1941; MLitt, U. Pitts., 1946; PhD, U. Pa., 1950. Lic. psychologist, Calif. Clin. psychologist U.S. Army, 1942-46; asst. NYU Testing & Advisement Unit, N.Y.C., 1946; clin. psychology trainee VA Regional Office Mental Hygiene Clinic, Phila., 1946-50, asst. chief psychology, 1950-53; chief psychology sect. VA Hosp., Phila., 1953-54; chief psychology svc. VA Outpatient Clinic, Bklyn., 1954-77; prof., dir. rsch. Calif. Sch. Profl. Psychology, San Diego, 1979—. Author: Day Treatment Center: Principles, Application & Evaluation, 1966, Research in Psychotherapy, 1970; also articles. Staff sgt. U.S. Army, 1942-46, ETO. Fellow APA, Am. Psychol. Soc. Home: 7056 Vista Del Mar La Jolla CA 92037

MENCIN, ALAN JAY, chemical engineer; b. Denver, July 1, 1957; s. Joseph C. and Helen Louise (Kotlar) M.; m. Catherine Ann Opekar, July 19, 1980; children: Pamela Susan, Jennifer Marie. BS in Chem. Engring., Colo. Sch. Mines, 1979; MBA, U. Denver, 1989. Lic. profl. engr., Colo. Engr. Stearns Catalytic Corp., Denver, 1979-84; tech. sales mgr. Colo. Radio Ctr., Denver, 1984-85; sales mgr. Compressor Industries, Golden, 1985; fin. specialist Martin Marietta Corp., Denver, 1985-90, systems engr., 1990-91; product devel. mgr. CCW Products Inc., Arvada, Colo., 1991—. Mem. Colo. Sch. Mines Alumni Assn., Grad. Bus. Alumni Assn. U. Denver (v.p. 1990-91), Ghost Town Club Colo. Inc. Republican. Office: CCW Products Inc 5055 W 58th Ave Arvada CO 80002-7048

MENDAL, GEOFFREY OWEN, computer company executive; b. Chgo., May 25, 1961; s. William Louis and Sandra Ruth (Sol) M. BS in Computer Sci., U. Mich., 1983. Researcher U. Mich. Computing Ctr., Ann Arbor, 1980-84; engr. Lockheed Missiles & Space Co., Sunnyvale, Calif., 1984-85; rscher. Stanford (Calif.) U., 1985-90; v.p. Systems Engring. Rsch. Corp., Mountain View, Calif., 1990—. Co-author: Exploring Ada, 1990, 92; composer Chekmate, 1979. Mem. IEEE (computer soc., jour. referee), ACM SIG Ada (exec. com., tech. editor, program coms.), Assn. for Computing Machinery. Republican. Jewish. Home: 20580 Shady Oak Ln Cupertino CA 95014-0454 Office: Systems Engring Rsch Corp 2555 Charleston Rd Mountain View CA 94043-1610

MENDELSON, RICHARD PAUL, lawyer; b. Jacksonville, Fla., Sept. 14, 1953; s. Max and Naomi (Rosenberg) M.; m. Marilyn Knight Mendelson, Dec. 15, 1979; children: Margot Knight Mendelson, Anthony Knight Mendelson. BA in Govt., Harvard Coll., 1975; MA in Econ. and Polit., Magdalen Coll., Oxford U., 1977; cert., London Wine and Spirits Edn., 1979; JD, Stanford Law Sch., 1982. Specialist in Alcohol Beverage Law. Asst. to export dir. Bouchard Ainé et Fils, Beaune, France, 1977-78; cons. Dornbusch & Co., San Francisco, 1979; legal dept. Wine Inst., San Francisco, 1981, 82; assoc. Jackson, Tufts, Cole & Black, San Francisco, 1982-85; ptnr. Internat. Tech. Mgmt., Los Altos, Calif., 1985-91; dir. Dickenson, Peatman & Fogarty, Napa, Calif., 1986—; vis. prof. Université d'Aix-Marseille Law Faculty, France, 1986, 88, 90; lectr. Université de Bordeaux Law Faculty, France, 1988, 91, 93; mem. steering com. Com. on Alcoholic Beverages Law, ABA, 1992—. Co-author: U.S. Wine Law, 1988. U.S. Delegate Office Internat. du Vin, Paris, 1986—. Mem. Napa Valley Stanford Club, Hospitaliers de Pomerol, Alliance Francaise de Napa. Office: Dickenson Peatman & Fogarty 809 Coombs St Napa CA 94559

MENDEZ, CELESTINO GALO, mathematics educator; b. Havana, Cuba, Oct. 16, 1944; s. Celestino Andres and Georgina (Fernandez) M.; came to U.S., 1962, naturalized, 1970; BA, Benedictine Coll., 1965; MA, U. Colo., 1968, PhD, 1974, MBA, 1979; m. Mary Ann Koplau, Aug. 21, 1971; children: Mark Michael, Matthew Maximilian. Asst. prof. maths. scis. Met. State Coll., Denver, 1971-77, assoc. prof., 1977-82, prof., 1982—, chmn. dept. math. scis., 1980-82; adminstrv. intern office v.p. for acad. affairs Met. State Coll., 1989-90. Mem. advt. rev. bd. Met. Denver, 1973-79; parish outreach rep. S.E. deanery, Denver Cath. Community Svcs., 1976-78; mem. social ministries com. St. Thomas More Cath. Ch., Denver, 1976-78, vice-chmn., 1977-78, mem. parish council, 1977-78; del. Adams County Rep. Conv., 1972, 74, Colo. 4th Congl. Dist. Conv., 1974, Colo. Rep. Conv., 1982, 88, 90, 92, Douglas County Rep. Conv., 1980, 82, 84, 88, 90, 92; alt. del. Colo. Rep. Conv., 1974, 76, 84, 5th Congl. dist. conv., 1976, mem. rules com., 1978, 80, precinct committeeman Douglas County Rep. Com., 1976-78, 89—, mem. cen. com., 1976-78, 89—; dist. 29 Rep. party candidate Colorado State Senate, 1990; Douglas county chmn. Rep. Nat. Hispanic Assembly, 1989—; bd. dirs. Rocky Mountain Better Bus. Bur., 1975-79, Rowley Downs Homeowners Assn., 1976-78, Douglas County Leadership Program, 1990—; mem. Rep. Leadership Program, 1989-90, mem. exec. bd., v.p. Assoc. Faculties of State Inst. Higher Edn. in Colo., 1971-73; trustee Hispanic U. Am., 1975-78; councilman Town of Parker (Colo.), 1981-84, chmn. budget and fin. com. 1981-84; chmn. joint budget com. Town of Parker-Parker Water and Sanitation Dist. Bds., 1982-84. Recipient U. Colo. Grad. Sch. excellence in teaching award, 1965-67; Benedictine Coll. grantee, 1964-65. Mem. Math. Assn. Am. (referee rsch. notes sect. Am. Math. Monthly 1981-82, gov. Rocky Mountain section 1993—), Am. Math. Soc., Nat. Coun. Tchrs. of Math., Colo. Coun. Tchrs. of Maths., Colo. Internat. Edn. Assn., Assoc. Faculties of State Insts. Higher Edn. in Colo. (v.p. 1971-73). Republican. Roman Catholic. Assoc. editor Denver Metro. Jour. Math. and Computer Sci., 1993—; contbr. articles to profl. jours. including Am. Math. Monthly, Procs. Am. Math. Soc., Am. Math. Monthly, Jour. Personalized Instruction, Denver Met. Jour. Math. and Computer Sci., and newspapers. Home: 11482 S Regency Pl Parker CO 80134-7330 Office: 1006 11th St Denver CO 80204

MENDEZ, JANA WELLS, senator; b. Moscow, Idaho, Jan. 18, 1944; d. Earl Dean and Alverta (Dalberg) Hall; m. Richard Albert Mendez, Sept. 16, 1965; children: Amy, Jennifer, Christopher. BS in Journalism, U. Colo., 1981. Community and issue activist Boulder County Housing Authority and Citizens for the Right To Vote, Longmont, Colo., 1975-83; legis. asst. Senate Minority Leader, Denver, 1982-84; Colo. state senator, 1985—; asst. whip minority leader, 1986, caucus chair, 1990—. Author: (with others) Chile From The Ground Up, 1982. Dem. precinct leader, area coordinator, senate dist. chmn. Boulder County, Colo., 1975-84; chair, commr. Boulder County Housing Authority, 1974-83. Regents scholar, 1963, Cervi scholar, 1980; U. Colo. Women's Ctr. grantee, 1980; named Outstanding Freshman Senator Colo. Social Legis. Com., 1985; recipient tax fairness award, 1988, 89, various awards Common Clause, Audibon Soc., Am. Cancer Soc., 1992, Children's Advocacy Network, 1992. Mem. Kappa Tau Alpha. Avocations: gardening, reading, photography, cooking. Office: State Senate PO Box 1126 Boulder CO 80306

MENDIUS, PATRICIA DODD WINTER, editor, educator, writer; b. Davenport, Iowa, July 9, 1924; d. Otho Edward and Helen Rose (Dodd) Winter; m. John Richard Mendius, June 19, 1947; children: Richard, Catherine M. Graber, Louise, Karen M. Chooljian. BA cum laude, UCLA, 1946; MA cum laude, U. N.Mex., 1966. Cert. secondary edn. tchr., Calif., N.Mex. English teaching asst. UCLA, 1946-47; English tchr. Marlborough Sch. for Girls, L.A., 1947-50, Aztec (N.Mex.) High Sch., 1953-55, Farmington (N.Mex.) High Sch., 1955-63; chair English dept. Los Alamos (N.Mex.) High Sch., 1963-86; writer, editor Los Alamos Nat. Lab., 1987—; adj. prof. English, U. N.Mex., Los Alamos, 1970-72, Albuquerque, 1982-85; English cons. S.W. Regional Coll. Bd., Austin, Tex., 1975—; writer, editor, cons. advanced placement English test devel. com. Nat. Coll. Bd., 1982-86, reader, 1982-86, project equality cons., 1985-88; book selection cons. Scholastic mag., 1980-82. Author: Preparing for the Advanced Placement English Exams, 1975; editor Los Alamos Arts Coun. bull., 1986-91. Chair Los Alamos Art in Pub. Pls. Bd., 1987—; chair adv. bd. trustees U. N.Mex., Los Alamos, 1987—; pres. Los Alamos Concert Assn., 1972-73; chair Los Alamos Mesa Pub. Libr. Bd., 1990—. Mem. Soc. Tech. Communicators, AAUW (pres. 1961-63, state bd. dirs. 1959-63, Los Alamos Coordinating Coun. 1992-93, pres. Los Alamos br. 1993-94), DAR, Order of Ea. Star, Mortar Bd., Phi Beta Kappa (pres. Los Alamos chpt. 1969-72), Phi Kappa Phi, Delta Kappa Gamma, Gamma Phi Beta. Home: 124 Rover Blvd Los Alamos NM 87544-3634 Office: Los Alamos Nat Lab Diamond Dr Los Alamos NM 87544

MENDONÇA, MARIA LUISA, video producer, educator; b. Rio de Janeiro, Brazil, Mar. 8, 1962; came to U.S., 1989; d. Aramis Marengo and Suely Rocha (Ferreira) M. Student, Estacio de Sá, Rio de Janeiro, 1983, San Francisco State U., 1990. Tchr. asst. Estacio de Sá U., Rio de Janeiro, 1982-84; prodr. videos Olhar Electronico, São Paulo, Brazil, 1984-89; mem. core faculty New Coll. Calif., San Francisco, 1990—; artist in residency The Banff Ctr. for the Arts, Can., 1992. Prodr. video documentary, exptl. video; prodr., dir. exptl. video, multimedia presentation. Panelist grants program dept. cultural affairs City of L.A., 1990; bd. dirs. Cine Acción, San Francisco, 1991—. Recipient Best Video award Festival Internat. Cinema and Video Rio de Janeiro, 1987, Best Documentary award Rio Cine Festival and Festival Internat. de Havana, 1987, Video Brazil Festival and Festrio, 1988. Fellow Brazil Action Solidarity Exch., Lilith Video Collective (prodr. 1985-88), Olhar Electronico Found.; mem. Bay Area Video Coalition (educator 1991), Film Arts Found. (educator 1991), Alliance for Cultural Democracy. Office: New Coll Calif 766 Valencia St San Francisco CA 94110

MENDOZA, GEORGE JOHN, college administrator, public speaker; b. Governors Island, N.Y., Apr. 1, 1955; s. George John Mendoza and Lucinda Marion Huber; m. Maria Rosario Escobedo, May 14, 1982; children: Michael George, Maria Guadalupe. B in Individualized Studies, N.Mex. State U., 1978. Coord. handicapped svcs. N.Mex. State U., Las Cruces, 1985—; Mem. Govs. Com. Concerns Handicapped, Santa Fe, 1986—; keynote speaker UCLA Upward Bound, 1987, Dallas County Community Coll., 1986, S.W. Assn. Students Assistance Programs, San Antonio, 1989. Author: (screenplay) Blinding Speed, 1988; subject (PBS documentary) The George Mendoza Story, 1989, also numerous mag. articles. Athlete Olympics for Disabled, The Netherlands, 1980, Internat. Games for Disabled, N.Y., 1984. Named One of Outstanding Young Men Am., 1980; recipient Outstanding Blind Athlete Award State N.Mex., 1980, Nat. Trio Achievers Award U.S. Dept. Edn., 1986, N.Mex. Hispanic Heritage Award Las Cruces Fed. Agys., 1983; nat. record holder 1500 meter run, 1979, 800 meter run, 1980; proclaimed George Mendoza Day Gov. Gary Carruthers, 1989. Mem. Assn. Handicapped Student Svc., U.S. Assn. Blind Athletes. Republican. Lutheran. Office: NMex State U Student Devel Office PO Box 3001 Las Cruces NM 88003-3001

MENDOZA, TONY C., insurance company official; b. Roswell, N.Mex., June 1, 1950; s. Dennis and Mary Inez Mendoza; m. Juanita Ann Sosa, June 10, 1972; children: Theresa Renee, Benjamin Anthony, Selina Marie. BBA in Acctg., Ea. N.Mex. U., 1973. Acct. Arthur Andersen & Co., Dallas, 1973-74, North Vista Med. Ctr., Hobbs, N.Mex., 1974-75, Armstrong & Armstrong, Roswell, 1975-78; salesman Duran Floor Coverings, Roswell, 1978-84; agt. Allstate Ins. Co., Roswell, 1984—. Fellow Life Underwriters Tng. Coun.; mem. Nat. Assn. Life Underwriters, Roswell C. of C. (life Red Coats), KC. Roman Catholic. Home: 1905 W Juniper St Roswell NM 88201 Office: Allstate Ins Co 1600 S Main St Roswell NM 88201

MENELL, PETER SETH, law educator; b. Jersey City, Dec. 2, 1958; s. Allan and Carole Janice (Godin) M.; m. Gillian Kereldena Hadfield. SB in Econs., MIT, 1980; MA in Econs., Stanford (Calif.) U., 1982; PhD in Econs, 1986; JD, Harvard U., 1986. Law clk. to presiding judge U.S. Ct. Appeals (2d cir.), Hartford, Conn., 1986-87; assoc. prof. law Georgetown U. Law Ctr., Washington, 1987-90; acting prof. sch. law U. Calif., Berkeley, 1990—; vis. prof. Harvard Law Sch., 1990, Stanford Law Sch., 1992-93. Stanford U. fellow, 1980, Olin fellow Harvard U., 1985, Olin Found. fellow, 1989. Mem. Am. Econs. Assn., Calif. Bar Assn. Jewish. Office: U Calif Boalt Hall Berkeley CA 94720

MENÉNDEZ, JOSÉ, physics educator; b. Tandil, Buenos Aires, Argentina, Feb. 12, 1957; came to U.S., 1985; s. Norberto Atilio and Delia (Cosmen) M.; m. Carmen Urioste, Nov. 29, 1991. Licenciado en fisica, Instituto Balseiro, Bariloche, Argentina, 1980; Dr.rer.nat. physics, U. Stuttgart, Fed. Republic Germany, 1985. Postdoctoral mem. tech. staff AT&T Bell Labs., Murray Hill, N.J., 1985-87; asst. prof. physics Ariz. State U., Tempe, 1987-92, assoc. prof. physics, 1992—; speaker in field. Contbr. articles to profl. jours. Presdl. Young Investigator, NSF, 1990; NSF grantee, 1988. Mem. Am. Phys. Soc. Home: 9635 S 47th Pl Phoenix AZ 85044 Office: Ariz State U Dept Physics and Astronomy Tempe AZ 85287-1504

MENGEL, RAYMOND LOUIS, associate clergyman, church custodian; b. Pottstown, Pa., Oct. 28, 1950; s. Paul Edward Mengel and Mary Jane (Tessitore) Clark; m. Pamela Rose Austrom, July 5, 1986. AA, Multnomah Sch. of Bible, Portland, Oreg., 1984, BS in Bibl. Studies, 1986; MDiv, Western Conservative Bapt. Sem, Portland, 1991. Cert., lic. preacher. Electronics mechanic Naval Undersea Engring. Sta., Keyport, Wash., 1972-81; bus driver Kitsap County Para-Transit, Bremerton, Wash., 1986-87; assoc. pastor, ch. custodian Grant Park Bapt. Ch., Portland, 1991—; chmn. worship commn., sr. adult outreach Grant Park Bapt. Ch., Portland, 1991—. With U.S. Army, 1969-72, Vietnam. Named to Outstanding Young Men of Am., 1985. Mem. Delta Epsilon Chi. Home: 6110 SE 52nd Ave # 6 Portland OR 97206

MENIKOFF, BARRY, English language educator; b. Bklyn., Jan. 2, 1939; s. Frank and Blanche (Goldman) M.; m. Michael Eastus, Aug. 20, 1966 (div. Oct. 1974); children: Carrie, Alec, Aaron. BA, Bklyn. Coll., 1960; MS, U. Wis., 1962, PhD, 1966. Asst. prof. English U. Hawaii, Honolulu, 1965-69; Fulbright lectr. U. Santiago (Spain), 1968-69; assoc. prof. English U. Hawaii, Honolulu, 1969-83, prof. English, 1983—; vis. assoc. prof. U. So. Calif., L.A., 1976-78, vis. prof. English, 1985-86; vis. prof. English U. Victoria, B.C., 1992. Author: R.L. Stevenson & Beach of Falesa, 1984, The Short Story, 1969, 75; contbr. chapts. to books and articles to profl. jours. Rsch. fellow U. Coll. London, 1992; fellow NEH-Huntington Libr., San Marino, Calif., 1984, Newberry Libr., Chgo., 1981, Clark Libr., L.A., 1983; grantee Am. Philos. Soc., 1978, 81. Mem. MLA, AAUP. Home: 2729 Peter St Honolulu HI 96816-2015 Office: U Hawaii Dept English 1733 Donaghho Rd Honolulu HI 96822-2368

MENJO, HIROSHI, management consultant; b. Tokyo, Feb. 11, 1954; came to U.S., 1991; s. Takashi and Toyoko (Watanabe) M.; m. Mikako Tamiya, Feb. 10, 1980. BS in Chemistry, U. Tokyo, 1976, MS Phys. chemistry, 1978; MS in Electronic Materials, MIT, 1985. Rsch. staff Konica Corp., Tokyo, 1978-83, sr. rsch. staff, 1986-87; cons. The Boston Cons. Group, Tokyo, 1988-91; engagement mgr. AZCA, Inc., Redwood City, Calif., 1991—; vis. scientist microsystems tech. lab. MIT, Cambridge, 1985-86, mem. Stanford venture lab. Patentee color phtographic film, 1980-82; contbr. articles to profl. jours. Active Plan Internat., Warwick, R.I., 1988—. Mem. MIT Club No. Calif., Pacific Club, Sigma Xi. Office: AZCA Inc 100 Marine Pky Ste 305 Redwood City CA 94065

MENKIN, CHRISTOPHER (KIT MENKIN), leasing company executive; b. Manhattan, N.Y., Jan. 1, 1942; s. Lawrence and Columbia (Riland) M.; children: Dashiel, Tascha, Ashley. Student, Julliard Sch. of Music, 1960, Santa Monica Coll., 1959-61, UCLA, 1961-64. News editor, dir. Sta. KRFC Radio, San Francisco, 1964-67; adminstrv. asst. to assemblyman Leo J. Ryan South San Francisco, 1967-68; mng. editor Sta. KGO TV News, San Francisco, 1968-69; news producer west coast Sta. ABC TV, Los Angeles, 1969; city mgr. City of San Bruno (Calif.), 1970; owner Menkin & Assocs., Santa Clara, Calif., 1971—; sr. ptnr. Am. Leasing, Santa Clara, 1971—; ptnr. Medallon Leasing, Santa Clara, 1974-80; pres. Monte Sereno Wine Co., Santa Clara, 1978—; dir. Meridian Nat. Bank, 1982-84. Chmn. nominating com. San Jose (Calif.) Symphony, 1988—; sec. Salvation Army, Santa Clara, 1968—, bd. dirs. 1990—, bd. dirs., San Jose, 1990, mem. county adv. bd., 1992; bd. dirs. Community Against Substance Abuse, Los Gatos, Calif., 1988—, Valley Inst. of Theater Arts, Saratoga, Calif., 1987-88, San Jose Trolley, 1988—. Mem. WAEL (regional chmn. 1990), Santa Clara Valley Wine Soc. (pres. 1988), Credit Profls. Santa Clara Valley (pres. 1990-91), Assn. Credit Grantors (past pres.), Credit Women Internat. (first male pres.), Santa Clara C. of C. (past pres. 1973-76), Bay Area Exec. Club (sec.), Confrerie de la Chaine de Rotisseurs (charge da presse 1992), Royal Rose Soc. Gt. Britain (rep. No. Calif. 1990). Democrat. Office: Am Leasing 348 Mathew St Santa Clara CA 95050-3114

MENKIN, HARLAN LEE, demographer, economist; b. Chgo., Apr. 29, 1948; s. Irving J. Menkin and Sylvia R. Levin Handler; m. Velma T. Lucero, Oct. 3, 1980. BA in Econs., U. Calif., Irvine, 1969; MA in Econs., Calif. State U., Fullerton, 1975. Rsch. planner Orange County Planning Dept., Santa Ana, Calif., 1968-71; sr. economist Contra Costa County Planning Dept., Martinez, Calif., 1971-79; pres. Menkin/Lucero & Assocs., Inc., Rocklin, Calif., 1980—. Mem. Hosp. and Long Term Care Data and Pub. Info. Advisory Com. to Calif. Health Policy and Data Advisory Commn., Sacramento, 1991. Mem. Am. Coll. Healthcare Execs., Health Care Execs. of No. Calif. Republican. Home: 4913 Dewey Ct Rocklin CA 95677

MENNELLA, VINCENT ALFRED, automotive manufacturing and airplane company executive; b. Teaneck, N.J., Oct. 7, 1922; s. Francis Anthony and Henrietta Vernard (Dickson) M.; B.A. in Acctg., U. Wash., 1948; m. Madeleine Olson, Aug. 18, 1945; children—Bruce, Cynthia, Mark, Scott, Chris. Sales and bus. mgmt. positions Ford div. Ford Motor Co., 1949-55; founder, pres. Southgate Ford, Seattle, 1955-80; pres. Flightcraft, Inc., Seattle, 1973-86; chmn. bd. Stanley Garage Door Co., 1981-86, Zman Magnetics, 1990—. Former chmn. March of Dimes. Served to capt. USNR, 1942-45. Republican. Roman Catholic. Clubs: Rainier Golf, Seattle Tennis, Rotary (past pres.). Home: 1400 SW 171st Pl Seattle WA 98166-3453

MENNIS, EDMUND ADDI, investment management consultant; b. Allentown, Pa., Aug. 12, 1919; s. William Henry and Grace (Addi) M.; m. Selma Adinoff, Sept. 25, 1945; children: Ardith Grace, Daniel Liam. B.A., CCNY, 1941; M.A., Columbia U., 1946; Ph.D., NYU, 1961. Security analyst Eastman, Dillon & Co., N.Y.C., 1945-46; sr. research asst. Am. Inst. Econ. Research, Great Barrington, Mass., 1946-50; security analyst Wellington Mgmt. Co., Phila., 1950-61; dir. research Wellington Mgmt. Co., 1958-61, v.p., mem. investment com., 1958-66, economist, 1953-66; sr. v.p., chmn. trust investment com. Republic Nat. Bank, Dallas, 1966-72; sr. v.p., chmn. investment policy com. Security Pacific Nat. Bank, Los Angeles, 1973-81; pres., dir. Bunker Hill Income Securities, Inc., 1973-81; chmn. bd. Security Pacific Investment Mgrs., Inc., 1977-81; ind. cons. to investment mgmt. orgns., 1982—; Tech. cons. Bus. Council, Washington, 1962-66, 72-77, 79-81; econ. adviser sec. commerce, 1967-68; mem. investment adv. panel Pension Benefit Guaranty Corp., 1981-83. Assoc. editor: Financial Analysts Jour., 1960-88; editor: C.F.A. Digest, 1971-86, Bus. Econs., 1985—, Bank Funds Mgmt. Report, 1993—; author or editor books, chpts., numerous articles in field of econs. and investments. Trustee Fin. Analysts Research Found., 1981-86. Served to 1st lt. USAAF, 1942-45; to capt. USAF, 1951-53. Fellow Nat. Assn. Bus. Economists (coun. 1967-69), Fin. Analysts Fedn. (dir. 1970-72, Graham and Dodd award 1971, Molodovsky award 1972); mem. Am. Econ. Assn., Am. Fin. Assn., N.Y. Soc. Security Analysts, L.A. Soc. Fin. Analysts, Conf. Bus. Economists (vice chmn. 1977, chmn. 1978), Inst. Chartered Fin. Analysts (pres. 1970-72, trustee 1968-74, C. Stewart Sheppard award 1978). Home: 721 Paseo Del Mar Palos Verdes Estates CA 90274-1222 Office: 405 Via Chico Ste 7 Palos Verdes Estates CA 90274-6818

MENOHER, PAUL EDWIN, JR., army officer; b. West Palm Beach, Fla., July 20, 1939; s. Paul E. and Gladys (Bingaman) M.; m. Kay I. Craddock; 1 child, Scott A.; m. 2d, Bebe Doris Etzler, Aug. 21, 1980. BA in Polit. Sci., U. Calif., Berkeley, 1961; MS in Internat. Rels., George Washington U., 1972. Commd. 2d lt. U.S. Army, 1961, advanced through grades to maj. gen.; student USN Coll. Command and Staff, Newport, R.I., 1971-72, U.S. Army War Coll., Carlisle, Pa., 1977-78; chief plans br. Hdqrs. U.S. Army Forces Command, Ft. McPherson, Ga., 1978-79, chief combat intelligence div., 1979-81; chief collection div. Hdqrs. U.S Army Europe, Heidelberg, Fed. Republic Germany, 1981-82; G2 VII Corps, Stuttgart, Fed. Republic Germany, 1982-84; comdr. 501st Mil. Intelligence Brigade, Seoul, Republic of Korea, 1984-86; dir. U.S. Army Intelligence and Electronic Warfare Master Plan, Washington, 1986-89; comdg. gen. U.S. Army Intelligence Agy., Washington, 1987-89, U.S. Army Intelligence Ctr., Ft. Huachuca, Ariz., 1989—. Mem. Assn. U.S. Army, Armed Forces Communications and Electronics Assn. (bd. dirs. 1990-91), Assn. Old Crows. Home: Quarters 2 Fort Huachuca AZ 85613

MENSH, IVAN NORMAN, medical psychology educator; b. Washington DC, Oct. 30, 1915; s. Shea Jacob and Rose (Clayman) M.; m. Frances Levitas. AB, George Washington U., 1940, AM, 1942; PhD, Northwestern U., 1948. Diplomate Am. Bd. Clin. Psychology; lic. psychologist, Calif. Prof., head med. psychology, dept. psychiatry Washington U., St. Louis, 1948-58; prof., head div. med. psychology, dept. psychiatry UCLA, 1958-86, prof. emeritus, 1986—. Author 2 text books; contbr. chpts. to books and numerous articles to profl. jours. Capt. USNR, 1943—. Recipient Certs. of Appreciation, Office Naval Rsch., Am. Bd. Profl. Psychology, Jour. Med. Edn., NIH. Fellow APA (past pres., past sec.); mem. Calif. Psychol. Assn. (past treas., past bd. chair, Silver Psi award), Assn. Am. Med. Colls., Assn. Am. Profs. Med. Psychology, Assn. Behavioral Scis. and Med. Edn., N.Y. Acad. Scis., Western Psychol. Assn. Office: UCLA Dept Psychiatry & Biobehavioral Scis 760 Westwood Pla Los Angeles CA 90024-1759

MENTLEY, LEE C., special events administrator; b. Erie, Pa., June 2, 1948; s. Laroy Anthony Mentley and Sarah (Bassil) Rodriguez. AAin Theatre and Creative Writing, East L.A. City Coll., 1970; BFAin Theatre and Art History, U. Calif., Long Beach, 1972; MFA in Art Adminstrn., U. Without Walls, 1975. Art organizer San Francisco Neighborhood Arts Commn., 1976-79; owner California Landscapes and Interior Design, L.A., 1980-83; substitute tchr. Hawaii Bd. of Edn., 1984-85; mgr. Waldenbooks Store, Wailua, Hawaii, 1985-88; curator The Hawaiian Art Mus. and Bookstore, Kilauea, Hawaii, 1988-89; asst. dir. collections mgmt. and cultural edn. Kaua'i Mus., Lihue', Hawaii, 1989-90. Pres. Eureka/Noe Valley Artist Coalition, San Francisco, 1974-80; Mem. Mayor's Bicentennial Commn., San Francisco, 1976; vol. San Francisco Arts Commn., 1978-79; mem. reelection com. State Senator Milton Marks, San Francisco, 1978-79; pres. Eureka Valley Promotion Assn., 1979, Garden Island Arts Coun., 1986—; founder END/AIDS Ednl. Network, 1988—; coord. Kaua'i Mokihaha Festival, 1986—; curator Kaua'i Mus., 1989. Home: PO Box 590 Kapaa HI 96745-0590

MENZEL, DANIEL BRUCE, toxicology educator; b. Cin., Sept. 27, 1934; s. Clifford Edward and Frances Lee (Hopkins) M.; m. Sally Fay McDonald, June 23, 1956; children: Robert Daniel, Lynn Margaret Menzel Micol, Carolyn Ann. BS, U. Calif., Berkeley, 1956, PhD, 1961. Registered profl. entomologist-toxicologist. Postdoctoral fellow NIH, Bethesda, Md., 1959; asst. prof. U. Calif., Berkeley, 1961-67; mgr. biology dept. Battelle Meml. Inst., Richland, Wash., 1967-70; dir. clin. rsch. Ross div. Abbott Lab., Columbus, Ohio, 1970-71; assoc. prof. pharmacology and medicine Duke U., Durham, N.C., 1971-73, prof. pharmacology and medicine, 1973-88; prof., chmn. dept. community and environ. medicine U. Calif., Irvine, 1989—; bd. dirs. U.S. EPA Sci. Adv. Bd., Washington, 1972—, NAS Environ. Scis. and Toxicology, Washington, 1972-79, 81-84, Nat. Drinking Water Adv. Coun., Washington, 1985-90, Govs. Task Force on Hazardous and Solid Waste, Raleigh, N.C., 1985, USAF Sci. Adv. Bd., Washington, 1986—; expert witness U.S. Congress Joint Com. on Commerce and the Environment, Washington, 1981-87; cons. Orange County Sheriff's Dept., Hillsborough, N.C., 1985; chmn. Carcinogens Working Group World Health Orgn., Geneva, 1985. Editor: Safe Drinking Water & Health, Vols. IV, V, VI, 1976, 80, 86; co-editor: Extrapolation Modelling, 1984, Toxicity of Organic Solvents, 1988—; founding editor jour. Toxicology Letters, 1975—; contbr. over 200 articles to profl. jours. With U.S. Army, 1957-59. Recipient medal Alexander von Humboldt Found., Bonn, Fed. Republic Germany, 1980, Kauffman medal Ohio Pharm. Soc., 1982; fellow Fogarty Internat., 1980. Fellow Acad. Toxicological Scis.; mem. Am. Inst. Nutrition, Am. Chem. Soc. (keynote speaker 1968), Am. Coll. Toxicology (sec. 1985-87), Am. Soc. for Pharmaceutics and Exptl. Therapy, Sigma Xi. Democrat. Episcopalian. Home: 2 Young Irvine CA 92715-4055 Office: Univ Calif Dept Community and Environ Medicine Irvine CA 92715

MENZIES, LEILA KAY, college official; b. Gary, Ind., Mar. 3, 1947; d. Walter Wayne and Hazel (Annadown) Leonard. BA in History, UCLA, 1969; MBA in Mgmt. and Stats., Calif. State U., Dominguez Hills, 1980. Asst. bus. mgr. housing, conf. dir. U. Calif., Davis, 1976-78; gen. mgr. housing UCLA, 1978-80; dir. budget and ops. for housing U. Cin., 1980-84; sales rep., owner Yurika Foods, Mich., 1983-84; dean fin. and adminstrv. svcs. Coll. Ea. Utah, Price, 1984-88; v.p. L.A. Harbor Coll., Wilmington, Calif., 1988—. Lay del. Calif.-Pacific Ann. Conf., United Meth. Ch., 1990, 91, 92. Mem. Nat. Assn. Coll. and Univ. Bus. Officers (community coll. com. 1990-92), Western Assn. Coll. and Univ. Bus. Officers (chmn. community coll. com. 1991-92, participant Exec. Leadership Inst. 1992), L.A. C.C. Dist. (mgmt. retreat planning com. 1992), Geneal. Soc. Pa., Wilmington Hist. Soc. Office: LA Harbor Coll 1111 Figueroa Pl Wilmington CA 90744

MEO, MICHAEL, educator, translator; b. Marblehead, Mass., Feb. 12, 1947; s. Dominic and Mary (Saviano) M.; m. Elly Rabben, June 10, 1979 (div. 1982); m. Trudy Diane Markiw, July 27, 1990. BS in Astronomy, Calif. Inst. Tech., 1968; MA in European History, U. Calif., Berkeley, 1970; AA in Electronic Tech., Laney Coll., Oakland, Calif., 1982; teaching cert., Calif. State U., Hayward, 1985. Teaching asst. history dept. U. Calif., Berkeley, 1970, 73; lecture demonstrator Northeastern U., Boston, 1974-75; mus. technician Smithsonian Instn., Washington, 1976-78; eligibility technician Alameda County Welfare dept., Oakland, Calif., 1979-82; tchr. Frick Jr. High Sch., Oakland, 1985-86; self-employed tchr., Oakland, 1987-89; longterm substitute tchr. Lincoln High Sch., Portland, Oreg., 1989-90; ESL bldg. liaison Roosevelt High Sch., Portland, 1990—. Translator: Marx's Mathematical Manuscripts, 1983; contbr. biog. articles to Am. Acad. Ency., 1971. Served alt. mil. svc. Fed. Penal Instn., Lompoc, Calif., 1971-72. Scholar Sloan Found., 1966-68. Mem. History of Sci. Soc., Math. Assn. Am., Oreg. Acad. of Scis., Oreg. Multicultural Edn. Assn. Office: Roosevelt High Sch 6941 N Central Portland OR 97203

MERCANT, JON JEFFRY, lawyer, educator, musician; b. San Jose, Calif., Dec. 17, 1950; s. Anthony J. and Margie Vivian (Diaz) M. BA, U. Calif., Berkeley, 1972; JD, U. Calif., L.A., 1975. Bar: Calif. 1975. Atty. Redondo Beach, Calif., 1975—; prof. El Camino Coll., Torrance, Calif. Mem. exec. bd. Calif. Dem. Party, 1986—; mem. exec. bd., COPE chmn. El Camino Coll. Fedn. Tchrs., Torrance, 1991—; Dem. nominee for State Assembly, 1986, Los Angeles County Ctrl. Co., 1986-90; dir. Peninsula Symphony Assn., Consumer Coalition Calif.; dir., founder South Bay Concern, Coastal Environ. Coalition; vice chmn., legal counsel Ret. Sr. Vol. Program. Named one of Outstanding Young Men of Am., 1984. Mem. Rotary North Redondo, Redondo Beach C. of C. (sec.-treas., v.p., bd. dirs. 1990—), Phi Beta Kappa. Office: 707 Torrance Blvd Ste 220 Redondo Beach CA 90277

MERCED, VICTOR, state agency administrator; b. Yabucoa, P.R., Dec. 16, 1956; s. Eleuterio Victor and Anamaria (Jimenez) M.; m. Leticia Maldonado, Nov. 23, 1979; children: Una Victoria, Emiliano Victor. BS, CUNY, 1982; JD, NYU, 1985. Dir. ops. People's Devel. Corp., Bronx, N.Y., 1975-79; summer assoc. N.Y. Atty. Gen., N.Y.C., 1983; summer intern U.S. Atty., Ea. Dist. N.Y., N.Y.C., 1984; legal intern N.Y. State Supreme Ct., N.Y.C., 1984-85; assoc. Cummings and Lockwood, Stanford, Conn., 1985-87; exec. dir. Oreg. Coun. Hispanic Advancement, Portland, Oreg., 1987-90; dep. adminstr. Oreg. Adult and Family Svcs., Salem, 1990—; chmn. bd. dirs. Housing Authority Portland, 1988-92; trustee Oreg. Health Scis. Univ., 1991—; pres. Oreg. Coalition Fund, Portland, 1991—; mem. Portland Leaders Roundtable, 1991—. Contbr. articles to newspapers, profl. jours. Root-Tilden scholar NYU, 1982; W.K. Kellogg Found. fellow, 1988. Fellow Am. Leadership Forum. Office: Oreg Adult/Family Svcs Human Resources Bldg 500 Summer St Salem OR 97310

MERCER, JOSEPH HENRY, lawyer, former state senator; b. Peoria, Ill., Feb. 1, 1937; s. Maurice D. and Dorothy J. M.; children: Stephen, Jennifer, Matthew. BA, U. N. Mex., 1961; JD, Harvard U., 1964. Bar: N. Mex. 1966. With Hanna and Mercer, Mercer and Carpenter, Mercer and McCash, to 1980; ptnr. Mercer, Lock, and Keating, Albuquerque, 1980-86, Mercer Profl. Assn., Albuquerque, 1986—; mem. N.Mex. Ho. of Reps., 1975-76; mem. N. Mex. Senate, 1977-84, minority floor leader, 1980-84. Chmn. Albuquerque Com. on Fgn. Relations, 1975-76, mem., 1967—, jud. council, 1981-84; mem. Gov.'s Organized Crime Prevention Commn., 1986-89, chmn., 1988-89, mem. oversight com., 1981-84. Served to 1st lt. arty U.S. Army, 1955-58. Mem. N. Mex. State Bar (Outstanding Service award 1974), Albuquerque Bar Assn. (dir. 1977-78). Republican. Presbyterian. Office: 4221 Silver Ave SE Albuquerque NM 87108-2720

MERCHANT, ROLAND SAMUEL, SR., hospital administrator, educator; b. N.Y.C., Apr. 18, 1929; s. Samuel and Eleta (McLymont) M.; m. Audrey Bartley, June 6, 1970; children—Orelia Eleta, Roland Samuel, Huey Bartley. B.A., N.Y.U., 1957, M.A., 1960; M.S., Columbia U., 1963, M.S.H.A., 1974. Asst. statistician N.Y.C. Dept. Health, 1957-60, statistician, 1960-63; statistician N.Y. TB and Health Assn., N.Y.C., 1963-65; biostatistician, adminstrv. coord. Inst. Surg. Studies, Montefiore Hosp., Bronx, N.Y., 1965-72; resident in adminstrn. Roosevelt Hosp., N.Y.C., 1973-74; dir. health and hosp. mgmt. Dept. Health, City of N.Y., 1974-76; from asst. adminstr. to adminstr. West Adams Community Hosp., L.A., 1976; spl. asst. to assoc. v.p. for med. affairs Stanford U. Hosp., Calif., 1977-82, dir. office mgmt. and strategic planning, 1982-85, dir. mgmt. planning, 1986-90; v.p. strategic planning Cedars-Sinai Med. Ctr., L.A., 1990—; clin. assoc. prof. dept. family, community and preventive medicine Stanford U., 1986-88, dept. health rsch. and policy Stanford U. Med. Sch., 1988-90. Served with U.S. Army, 1951-53. USPHS fellow. Fellow Am. Coll. Healthcare Execs., Am. Pub. Health Assn.; mem. Am. Hosp. Assn., Nat. Assn. Health Services Execs., N.Y. Acad. Scis. Home: 27335 Park Vista Rd Agoura Hills CA 91301-3639 Office: Cedars-Sinai Med Ctr 8700 Beverly Blvd Los Angeles CA 90048

MERCIER, MICHAEL ANTHONY, advertising executive; b. Inglewood, Calif., Nov. 7, 1959; s. Terrence Joseph and Patricia Marie (Rodriguez) M.; married, Oct. 1, 1989 (div. 1991); 1 child, Scott T. BA in Polit. Sci., Calif. State U., Long Beach, 1982; MBA, U. So. Calif., 1991. Field rep. Assemblyman Chet Wray, Garden Grove, Calif., 1982-83; sr. account exec. Cerrell Assocs., 1983-84; cons. assembly selcect com. Assemblyman Bruce Young, Norwalk, Calif., 1984-85; v.p. Englander/Adler & Droz, Newport Beach, Calif., 1985-88; ptnr. Mercier/Kukurin, Beverly Hills, Calif., 1985-88; dir. non-profit fundraising div. Mailing & Mktg., Orange, Calif., 1988-90; exec. v.p. Pacific Admail, Fountain Valley, Calif., 1991-92, pres., COO, 1992—. Contbr. articles to profl. jours. Chair Youth Commn., Buena Park, Calif., 1979-80; mem. Rent Arbitration bd., Norwalk, Calif., 1983. Recipient Gold Ink award Printing Tech. Mag., 1989, Gold Pioneer award Diret Mktg. Creative Guild, 1990. Mem. Am. Mktg. Assn., Nat. Soc. Fundraising Cons., Direct Mktg. Guild, Acad. for Health Svcs. Mktg., Internat. Assn. Polit. Cons. Office: Pacific Admail 11080 Talbert Fountain Valley CA 92208

MERCURIO, EDWARD PETER, natural science educator; b. Orange, Calif., Dec. 28, 1944; s. Peter Amadeo and Jeanne (Monteleone) M.; m. Jeanne Roussel Gable, Oct. 18, 1980 (div. Dec. 1984); 1 child, Katherine Roussel; m. Patricia Ann Kahler, Apr. 12, 1987; children: Peter Edward and Rose Sierra. BA, UCLA, 1967, MA, 1970, CPhil, 1978. Research asst. UCLA, 1971, teaching asst., 1968-71; instructional assoc. Golden West Coll., Huntington Beach, Calif., 1972-73; cons. Monterey County Planning Dept., Salinas, Calif., 1980; prof. Hartnell Coll., Salinas, Calif., 1973—; photographer in field, Calif., 1961—; lectr. in field, Calif., 1970—; cons. in field, 1980—. Fellow Woodrow Wilson Nat. Fellowship Found., 1967. Mem. AAAS, Sierra Club. Democrat. Home: 647 Wilson St Salinas CA 93901-1346 Office: Hartnell Coll 156 Homestead Ave Salinas CA 93901-1628

MEREDITH, ALLEN KENT, real estate developer; b. Schenectady, Mar. 27, 1949; s. Jack Allen and Georgia (Pulliam) M.; m. Kim Myegaard, Sept. 23, 1978; 1 child, Alexis. BA in Econs., Stanford U., 1972; MBA, Harvard U., 1976. Assoc. Trammell Crow Co., Dallas, 1978-79; ptnr. Trammell Crow Co., Atlanta, 1980-84; div. ptnr. Trammell Crow Co., L.A., 1984-87; area ptnr. Trammell Crow Co., 1987-89, reg. ptnr., 1989—. Mem. Harvard Bus. Sch Assn., Stanford Buck Club, Regency Club of L.A., Capital City Country Club (Atlanta). Republican. Methodist. Home: 44 Tuscaloosa Ave Menlo Park CA 94027-4015 Office: Trammell Crow Co Ste 1900 950 Tower Lane Foster City CA 94404

MEREDITH, D(ARRIS) ROSCOE, financial planning firm owner; b. Paonia, Colo., May 3, 1937; s. Roscoe Marion and Ray Idella (Bell) M.; m. Marlyn Ann Kirkpatrick, Dec. 19, 1958; children: Laurie Rene, Bryan LaVelle. BS in Chemistry, Colo. State U., 1960. CLU, ChFC, CFP. Dir. quality control Keebler Co., Denver, 1960-63, prodn. mgr., 1963-67; dir. quality control Jolly Rancher Candies, Denver, 1967-68; dir. mfg. Archway Cookies, Denver, 1968-70; ptnr. ins. Curtis/Meredith Ins., Denver, 1970-73; career agent life and health Washington Nat., Denver, 1973-78; regional life mgr. Reliance/United Pacific, Denver, 1978-83; regional advanced sales mgr. Fidelity Union Life, Denver, 1983-87; owner, mgr. personal fin. planning firm Denver, 1987—; chmn. bd. dirs., treas. Reach Internat., Inc. Bd. dirs., com. head Colo. Assn. Life Underwriters, Englewood, Colo., 1973-77; precinct com. mem. Adams County (Colo.) Republican Party, 1964-70, dist. capt., 1970-80, 84—; chmn. 2d Congl. State of Colo., Adams, Westminster County, 1984-88. Mem. Nat. Assn. Life Underwriters (sales rep., Nat. Sales Achievement awards 1973-78, Nat. Quality award 1977). Home: 8200 Baylor Ln Westminster CO 80030 Office: Fidelity Planning Svcs 2727 Bryant St # 300 Denver CO 80211

MERICLE, JAMES ROBERT, minister; b. Culver City, Calif., Sept. 9, 1962; s. Robert Charles and Mary Ann (Hoppe) M.; m. Sondra Stickney, June 30, 1984; children: Alison, Kyle. BA, U. Calif., Riverside, 1983; MDiv, Sch. of Theology, Claremont, 1991. Ordained to ministry Luth. Ch., 1993. Tax auditor IRS, Riverside, Calif., 1984-88, tax auditor coord., 1988-91; youth min. First Luth. Ch., Redlands, 1986-91; pvt. practice in tax acctg. Murrieta, Calif., 1991-92; pres. C&J Rentals, Inc., Murrieta, 1991-93, also bd. dirs.; intern pastor Gloria Dei Luth. Ch., Fontana, 1991-92; assoc. min. Hope Luth. Ch., Temecula, Calif., 1992-93, assoc. pastor, 1993—. Fundraising coord. Fontana We Care, 1991. Mem. Am. Acad. of Religion, Soc. of Bibl. Lit., U. Calif. Riverside Alumni Assn. (ext. rels. com.). Democrat. Office: Hope Luth Ch 23985 Rancho California Rd Temecula CA 92591

MERICLE, (JAMES) MARK, radio news director, journalist, playwright; b. Cleve., Nov. 24, 1946; s. James and Dorothy Rebecca (Armpriester) M.; 1 child, Katrina Ann Holmes. Student, Antioch Coll., 1964-66. Pub., editor The Minority Report, Dayton, Ohio, 1968-71; news dir. WYSO-FM, Nat. Pub. Radio, Yellow Springs, Ohio, 1973-77; station mgr. WYSO-FM, Nat. Pub. Radio, Yellow Springs, 1977-81; news dir. KPFA-FM, Pacifica Radio, Berkeley, Calif., 1981—; instr. comm. St. Mary's Coll., Morcsa, Calif., 1983, Antioch Coll., Yellow Springs, 1977-81; trustee Ohio Pub. Radio, Columbus, 1978-81; cons. Sinclair C.C., Dayton, 1979-81. Author: (play) The Homeless, 1991. mem. Dem. Socialists Am., N.Y.C., 1981—; officer New Am. Movement, Chgo., 1973-81. Recipient Radio Programing award Corp. for Pub. Broadcasting, Washington, 1989, Radio Programing award Nat. Fed. Community Broadcasters, Washington, 1989, Radio Achievement award Media Alliance, San Francisco, 1991. Home: 4118 Opal St Oakland CA 94609 Office: KPFA-FM 1929 Martin Luther King Berkeley CA 94704

MERIDITH, LYNNE ANN, addictions counselor, educator; b. Woodland, Calif., Aug. 31, 1946; d. Ray Clark and Marie Helen (Seno) M. AA in Gen. Edn., Merced Coll., 1967; BA in Psychology, Stanislaus State Coll., 1969; AA in Addiction Studies, Merced Coll., 1992. Human svcs. cert. in drug and alcohol counseling. Rsch. asst. State of Calif. Mental Hygiene, San Francisco, 1969-71; supr. Vis. Nurse Assn., Merced, Calif., 1973-75, Vis. Home Svcs., Inc., Merced, Calif., 1975-76; co-owner, dir., supr. San Joaquin Valley Homemakers, Merced, Calif., 1976-78; bookkeeper dept. mktg. Meridith Ranch/Meridith Realty, Merced, Calif., 1981—; owner, wedding, party cons. A Time to Remember, Merced, Calif., 1984-92; instr., counselor Merced Coll. DUI Program, Merced, Calif., 1990—; addictions counselor pvt. practice, Merced, Calif., 1990—. Film columnist Merced County Times, 1990—. Co-facilitator Merced County Drug and Alcohol Svcs., Mental Health, 1989-91, co-chmn. women's alcohol project, 1987-88; com. chmn. Merced County Grand Jury, 1974-75; adult literacy tutor Merced County Libr., 1988-89; mem. adv. bd. Merced Downtown Assn., 1985-86; coord. Single Mother's Day picnic, 1991-92. Recipient Coord.'s award Spl. Merit Merced County Drug and Alcohol Svc., 1990. Democrat. Office: PO Box 1069 Merced CA 95341

MERIFIELD, PAUL M., geologist, consultant; b. Santa Monica, Calif., Mar. 17, 1932; m. Ruth Ann Friend. BA, UCLA, 1954, MA, 1958; PhD, U. Colo., 1963. Rsch. scientist Lockheed Aircraft Corp., Burbank, Calif., 1962-64; cons. geologist L.A., 1964—; adj. prof. UCLA, 1970—. Mem. Assn. Engring. Geologist, Geol. Soc. Am.

MERIGAN, THOMAS CHARLES, JR., physician, medical researcher, educator; b. San Francisco, Jan. 18, 1934; s. Thomas C. and Helen M. (Greeley) M.; m. Joan Mary Freeborn, Oct. 3, 1959; 1 son, Thomas Charles III. B.A. with honors, U. Calif., Berkeley, 1955; M.D., U. Calif., San Francisco, 1958. Diplomate: Am. Bd. Internal Medicine. Intern in medicine 2d and 4th Harvard med. services Boston City Hosp., 1958-59, asst. resident medicine, 1959-60; clin. assoc. Nat. Heart Inst., NIH, Bethesda, Md., 1960-62; asso. Lab. Molecular Biology, Nat. Inst. Arthritis and Metabolic Diseases, NIH, 1962-63; practice medicine specializing in internal medicine and infectious diseases Stanford, Calif., 1963—; asst. prof. medicine Stanford U. Sch. Medicine, 1963-67, assoc. prof. medicine, 1967-72, head div. infectious diseases, 1966-92, prof. medicine, 1972—, George E. and Lucy Becker prof. medicine, 1980—; dir. Diagnostic Microbiology Lab., Univ. Hosp., 1966-72, Diagnostic Virology Lab., 1969—, Ctr. AIDS Rsch. Stanford U., 1988—; hosp. epidemiologist, 1966-88; mem. microbiology rsch. tng. grants com. NIH, 1969-73, virology study sect., 1974-78; cons. antiviral substances program Nat. Inst. Allergy and Infectious Diseases, 1970—, mem. AIDS clin. drug devel. commn., 1986—; mem. Virology Task Force, 1976-78, bd. sci. counselors, 1980-85; mem. U.S. Hepatitis panel U.S. and Japan Coop. Med. Sci. Program, 1979-90, AIDS subcom. Nat. Adv. Allergy and Infectious Diseases Coun., 1988-89; co-chmn. interferon evaluation Group Am. Cancer Soc., 1978-81; mem. vaccines and related biol. products adv. com. Ctr. for Drugs and Biols., FDA, 1984-88; mem. internat. adv. com. on biol. sci. Sci. Council, Singapore, 1985-88; mem. adv. com. J.A. Hartford Found., 1979-84; mem. Albert Lasker awards jury, 1981-84; mem. peer review panel U.S. Army Med. Rsch. and Devel. Com., 1986-88; nat. com. to rev. current procedures for approval New Drugs for Cancer and AIDS, 1989; mem. Com. to Study Use of Coms. within FDA, 1991-92. Contbr. numerous articles on infectious diseases, virology and immunology to sci. jours.; editor: Antivirals with Clinical Potential, 1976, Antivirals and Virus Diseases of Man, 1979, 2d edit., 1984, 3d edit., 1990, Regulatory Functions of Interferon, 1980, Interferons, 1982, Interferons as Cell Growth Inhibitors, 1986; assoc. editor: Virology, 1975-78, Cancer Research, 1987-91; co-editor: monograph series Current Topics in Infectious Diseases, 1975—, Cytomeglovirus Infect and Ganciclovir, 1988, Focus on Didanosine (ddI), 1990, Practical Diagnosis of Viral Infection, Textbook of AIDS Medicine, 1993; editorial bd.: Archives Internal Medicine, 1971-81, Jour. Gen. Virology, 1972-77, Infection and Immunity, 1973-81, Intervirology, 1973-85, Proc. Soc. Exptl. Biology and Medicine, 1978-87, Reviews of Infectious Diseases, 1979-89, Jour. Interferon Research, 1980-89, Antiviral Research, 1980-86, Jour. Antimicrobial Chemotherapy, 1981-91, Molecular and Cellular Biochemistry, 1982-89 , AIDS Research and Human Retroviruses, 1983—, Jour. Virology, 1984-89, Biotechnology Therapeutics, 1988—, Jour. Infectious Diseases, 1989—, Drug Investigation, 1989—, HIV: Advances in Research and Therapy, 1990—, Internat. Jour. Antimicrobial Agts. 1990—, The AIDS Reader, 1991—, AIDS, 1993. Recipient Borden award for Outstanding Rsch., Am. Assn. Med. Colls., 1973, Merit award, Nat. Inst. Allergy and Infectious Diseases, 1988, Maxwell Finland award Infectious Diseases Soc. Am., 1988; Guggenheim Meml. fellow, 1972. Mem. Assn. Am. Physicians, Western Assn. Physicians, Am. Soc. Microbiology, Am. Soc. Clin. Investigation (coun. 1977-80), Am. Assn. Immunologists, Am. Fedn. Clin. Rsch., Western Soc. Clin. Rsch., Soc. Exptl. Biology and Medicine (publ. com. 1985-89), Infectious Diseases Soc. Am., Am. Soc. Virology, Inst. Medicine, Pan Am. Group for Rapid Viral Diagnosis, AMA, Internat. Soc. Interferon Rsch. (coun. 1983-89), Calif. Med. Assn., Santa Clara County Med. Soc., Calif. Acad. Medicine, Royal Soc. Medic AAAS, Alpha Omega Alpha. Home: 148 Goya Rd Menlo Park CA 94028-7307 Office: Stanford U Sch Medicine Div Infectious Diseases Stanford CA 94305

MERIN, ROBERT LYNN, periodontist; b. L.A., Jan. 25, 1946; s. Marcus and Belle Merin; m. Barbara Rosen, June 27, 1971; children: Lori, Kimberly. DDS, UCLA, 1970; MS, Loma Linda U., 1972. Diplomate Am. Bd. Periodontology. Chief periodontal svc. Mather Air Force Hosp., Sacramento, 1972-74; pvt. practice, Woodland Hills, Calif., 1974—; chmn. dental staff Humana-West Hills (Calif.) Hosp., 1982-84; lectr. Sch. Dentistry, UCLA, 1970, 74—, dir. periodontal bd. cert. course, 1993—. Author: (with others) Glickman's Clinical Periodontics, 1978, 84, 90; contbr. articles to profl. jours. Active UCLA Dental Scholarship and Loan Com., 1984—; cons. L.A. Olympic Com., 1984. Mem. ADA, Am. Acad. Periodontics, Calif. Soc. Periodontists, San Fernando Valley Dental Soc. (mem. polit. action com. 1988), UCLA Dental Alumni Assn. (pres. 1979-80, bd. dirs. 1970—), UCLA Apollonians (pres. 1983-86). Office: 6342 Fallbrook Ave Ste 101 Woodland Hills CA 91367-1616

MERKIN, ALBERT CHARLES, pediatrician, allergist; b. Chgo., Sept. 4, 1924; s. Harry A. and Goldie (Lamasky) M.; m. Eunice Aprill, Aug. 22, 1948; children: Audrey, Ellen, Joseph. Student, U. Ill., 1942-44; MD, U. Ill., Chgo., 1949. Diplomate Am. Bd. Allergy and Immunology, Am. Bd. Pediatrics. Intern, resident Cook County Hosp., Chgo.; resident Children's Meml. Hosp., Chgo.; with Valley Pediatric and Allergy Clinic, Las Vegas, Nev. Capt. USAF, 1950-53. Fellow Am. Acad. Pediatrics (state chmn. Nev. 1961-64, sect. allergy and immunology), Am. Coll. Allergy; mem. Am. Acad. Allergy, Allergy Subsplty. Group of Acad. Pediatrics. Office: Valley Pediatric and Allergy Clinic 1820 E Sahara Las Vegas NV 89104

MERKLE, RALPH CHARLES, research scientist; b. Berkeley, Calif., Feb. 2, 1952; s. Theodore Charles and Helene (Suarez) M.; m. Carol Blythe Shaw, Sept. 24, 1983. BS, U. Calif., Berkeley, 1974, MS, 1977; PhD, Stanford U., 1979. Mem. sci. staff Bell No. Rsch., Mountain View, Calif., 1979-80; mgr. compiler devel. Elxsi, San Jose, Calif., 1980-88; mem. rsch. staff Xerox Palo Alto (Calif.) Rsch Ctr., 1988—. Mem. IEEE, Assn. for Computing Machinery. Office: Xerox PARC 3333 Coyote Hill Rd Palo Alto CA 94304

MERLO, HARRY ANGELO, forest products executive; b. Stirling City, Calif., Mar. 5, 1925; s. Joseph Angelo and Clotilde (Camussa) M.; 1 son, Harry A. B.S., U. Calif.-Berkeley, 1949, postgrad., 1949. Vice pres. Rockport Redwood Co., Cloverdale, Calif., 1967; v.p. No. Calif. div. Ga.-Pacific Corp., Samoa, Calif., 1967-69; v.p. Western lumber div. Ga.-Pacific Corp., Portland, Oreg., 1969-71, exec. v.p. Western timber, plywood and lumber operations, 1971-73; pres., chmn. bd. La.-Pacific Corp., Portland, 1973—; mem. adv. bd. Sch. Bus. Adminstrn. U. Calif., Berkeley; bd. dirs. World Forestry Ctr., Whitman Industries. Mem. Pres.'s Coun., Columbia Pacific coun. Boy Scouts Am.; former mem. nat. adv. coun. Salvation Army; trustee Hugh O'Brian Youth Found., Oreg. Mus. Sci. and Industry, Goodwill Industries; past chmn. bd. Am. Acad. Achievement; former western fin. chmn. U.S. Olympic commn.; past chmn., adv. bd. Salvation Army, Oreg.; past bd. dirs. Marshall U. Soc. Yaeger Scholars. Lt. USMCR. Named Man of Year Ga.-Pacific Corp., 1969; recipient Golden Plate award Am. Acad. Achievement, 1974; Horatio Alger award, 1980, Gold award for forest products industry The Wall St. Transcript, 1982, 83, Disting. Service award La. Tech. U., 1984, Aubrey Watzek award Lewis and Clark Coll., 1984, Citizen of Merit award Assoc. Builders and Contractors, 1986, Piemontese Del Munde award, 1986, Merit award Calif. Parks & Recreation Soc., 1988, John J. Mulrooney award N.Am. Wholesale Lumber Assn., 1989. Mem. Calif. Redwood Assn. (past pres., bd. dirs.), Horatio Alger Assn. (pres., chmn.), Founders Club (bd. dirs.), Waverly County Club, Multnomah Athletic Club, Ingomar Club, Knight of the Vine. Office: La-Pacific Corp 111 SW 5th Ave Portland OR 97204-3604*

MERRELL, ROBERT BRUCE, clothing company executive; b. Brigham City, Utah, Dec. 20, 1945; s. Elliott Hepworth and Doris (Jensen) M.; BS in Indsl. Engring., U. Utah, 1969, MEA, 1973; m. Lynne McDermott, Apr. 4, 1968; children: Melissa Ann, Jason Matthew, David Bruce, Jeffrey Todd. Sales rep. Shell Oil Co., Portland, Oreg., Seattle, 1969-70, 72-74, head office rep., Houston, 1974-75; v.p., treas., dir. Lilyblad Petroleum Co., Tacoma, 1975-77, also bd. dirs.; dir. mktg. Pacific No. Oil Corp., Seattle, 1975-77, pres., chief exec. offficer, dir., 1977, chmn. pres., chief exec. officer, 1989-91, Seattle T-Shirt Co., 1993—. Mem. exec. bd. dirs. Chief Seattle council Boy Scouts Am., 1984—; bd. dirs. Seattle Urban League, Sea Fair; chmn. Latter-day Sts. relationship com., 1984-87. Served to capt. USAR, 1970-71. Decorated Bronze Star. Recipient Council Merit award Boy Scouts Am., 1985. Mem. Seattle C. of C. Mormon. Clubs: Washington Athletic, Columbia Tower (Seattle); Mercer Island Country (Wash.).

MERRELL, VICTOR DALLAS, business executive; b. Basalt, Idaho, Jan. 25, 1936; s. Victor Lybbert and Beatrice (Jensen) M.; m. Karen Dixon, June 8, 1959; children: Ann, Kay, Joan, Paul, Mary, Mark, John, Ilene, David. BS, Brigham Young U., 1960, MS, 1964; MPA, PhD, U. So. Calif., L.A., 1970. Instr. Brigham Young U., Provo, Utah, 1959, 60-61, coord. student orgns., 1960-61, chmn. Dept. of Community Edn., 1962-64; dir. Calif. Ctr. Brigham Young U., L.A., 1964-68; fellow Am. soc. for Pub. Adminstrn., Washington, 1968-69; chmn. Leadership Systems, Inc./Merrell Assocs., Washington, 1969-89, Merrell Inc., Salt Lake City, 1989-92; chmn., chief exec. officer Bonneville Found.; chmn. pvt. trust for pub. edn.; cons. Cassidy & Assocs., Washington, 1989-92; cons. Exec. Office of the Pres., fed. depts., fortune 500 cos. and Am. Indian tribes.; advisor Reagan and Bush Presdl. Transition. Author: Family Leadership, 1962, Huddling: Politics of Management, 1979, Merrell Index of Presidential Leadership; contbr. articles in Wall St. Jour., N.Y. Times and others. Pres. United Families of Am., Washington, 1978-80; del. White House Conf. on Families; mem. nat. adv. coun. Marriott Sch. of Mgmt. Brigham Young U., mem. exec. com. alunmi bd.; del. Nat. Conv. of Higher Edn.; pres. LDS Ch., misson pres., 1986-89, regional rep., 1989-92, bishop, 1965-68, mem. of The Seventy, 1992—; candidate U.S. Senate, Md., 1980; pres. PTA, pres. Md. Taxpayers Assn.; bd. dirs. Intermountain Healthcare. Mem. Utah Roundtable (chmn. 1989-92), Alpha Kappa Delta, Alpha Beta Kappa. Republican. Home: 843 Three Fountains Dr Salt Lake City UT 84107-5264

MERRICK, TERRY ALLEN, computer repair company executive; b. Kokomo, Ind., June 21, 1950; s. Frank Edward and Virginia Ruth (Brown) M.; m. Terrie Colleen Terhune, Mar. 11, 1967 (div. June 1988); children: Teresa, Terry Jr., Tina, Todd, Ty; m. Lynn Ann Greivelle, July 4, 1992. BA, Ind. U., Kokomo, 1972; DD, Ch. of God, Houston, 1978. Lic. bldg. constrn., electronics technician, computer repair. Mgr. Shell Oil Corp., Kokomo, Ind., 1968-72; inspector Chrysler Corp., Kokomo, 1972-75; owner Merrick Constrn., Tampa, Fla., 1975-77; mgr. Dairy Queen Stores Inc., Houston, 1977-82, Ky. Fried Chicken, Long Beach, Calif., 1982-86; nursing asst. Kimberley Nurses Registry, Los Alamitos, Calif., 1986-89; owner Merrick Electronics, El Monte, Calif., 1989—. Pastor Ch. of God, 1976—. Sgt. U.S. Army, 1970-72, Vietnam. Decorated 3 Purple Hearts, Bronze Star, Air medal. Mem. VFW (sgt. at arms 1974-75), Am. Legion (Outstanding Citizen 1978), Nat. Rifle Assn. Republican.

MERRIGAN, MARY ELLEN, sales executive; b. Maryville, Mo., July 7, 1951; d. James Robert and Coletta Marie (Seipel) M. BA in Speech, Northwest Mo. State U., 1973. Account exec. Sta. WMKC Radio, Oshkosh, Wis., 1973-74, Sta. KHAK Radio, Cedar Rapids, Iowa, 1974-77; account exec. Sta. KARN Radio, Little Rock, 1977-79, sales mgr., 1979-80; account exec. Sta. KCKN Radio, Kansas City, Kans., 1980-81; account exec. Sta. KMJQ Radio, Houston, 1981-85, sales mgr., 1985-86, gen. sales mgr., 1986-88; broadcast sales cons. Merrigan Enterprises, Houston, 1988-89; v.p., gen. mgr. Sta. KKSS Radio, Albuquerque, 1989—. Bd. dirs. YMCA, 1990—; hostess Leukemia Soc. Celebrity Waiters Luncheon, 1991, 92. Named Vol. of Yr., Met. YMCA Bd., 1992. Mem. NAT, N.Mex. Mus. Natural History, Albuquerque Radio Broadcasters Assn. (chair), N.Mex. Broadcasters Assn.. Office: Sta KKSS Radio 5301 Central Ave NE Ste 1200 Albuquerque NM 87108-1517

MERRILL, CHARLES MERTON, federal judge; b. Honolulu, Dec. 11, 1907; s. Arthur M. and Grace Graydon (Dickey) M.; m. Mary Luita Sherman, Aug. 28, 1931 (dec.); children: Julia Booth Stoddard, Charles McKinney. AB, U. Calif., 1928; LLB, Harvard, 1931. Bar: Calif. 1931, Nev. 1932. Sole practice Reno, 1932-50; judge Nev. Supreme Ct., 1951-59, chief justice, 1955-56, 59; judge U.S. Ct. of Appeals (9th cir.), San Francisco, 1959-74, sr. judge, 1974—. Mem. ABA, State Bar Nev. (gov. 1947-50), Am. Law Inst. (council 1960—). Office: US Ct of Appeals PO Box 193939 San Francisco CA 94119-3939

MERRILL, FRANK HARRISON, data processing executive, consultant; b. Pitts., June 20, 1953; s. Edgar Frank and Harriet Margaret (Gallagher) M.; m. Rita Alice Mae Murray, May 27, 1977; 1 child, Laura Dawn. BSMetE, Colo. Sch. Mines., 1971-76; M of Computer Info. Systems, U. Denver, 1988. Cert. systems profl., computer programmer; cert. PICK profl. Metall. engr. Inspiration Copper Co., Miami, Ariz., 1979-80, Cominco Am., Inc., Bixby, Mo., 1980-81; programmer, analyst M.L. Foss, Inc., Denver, 1981-83, Titsch & Assocs., Denver, 1983; data processing mgr. PBI/BAXA, Inc., Denver, 1983-86; owner (systems cons.) Dynamic Solutions, Denver, 1986—; cons. in field, Denver, 1985—; instr. continuing edn. User's Group, Denver, 1985—; instr. computer info. systems U. Denver, 1990—; mem. grad. computer info. systems faculty Colo. campus, U. Phoenix, 1991—. Adult leader Boy Scouts Am., Denver and Globe, Ariz., 1973-88; mem. Marriage Encounter Interfaith Bd., Denver, 1985-89, chair, 1988-89; mem. coun. Rocky Mtn. Aldersgate Marriage Encounter, 1986—, exec. couple 1990—; mem. Volksmarch Steering Com. Lakewood on Parade, 1990—; mem. St. Andrew's Soc. Colo.; nominating com. Free Meth. Ch., 1989-92, ch. bd. property and fin., 1992—. 2d lt U.S. Army, 1977-79. Named to PICK Industry Accreditation Coun., 1990; recipient God and Svc. award Free Meth. Ch., 1984, Recognition award Assn. for Systems Mgmt., 1991, Merit award, 1993. Mem. SAR, Assn. Systems Mgt. (profl. sec. Mile-Hi chpt. 1989-91, v.p. 1991-92, pres. 1992-93, liason com. mem. internat. cert. 1993—), Colo. Pick Users' Group (edn. chmn. 1984—), Info. systems Security Assn., Scotish-Am. Mil. Soc. (charter, post contr. of Post 100 Colo), Falcon Wanderers Club, Cheyenne High Plains Wanderers Club. Republican. Free Methodist.

MERRILL, JOHN RUSSELL, public affairs officer; b. Hillsboro, Oreg., Mar. 9, 1931; s. Chester Russell and Wilma Etta (Lincoln) M.; m. Barbara Louise Blakley, Sept. 6, 1952 (dec. May 1989); children: Theresa Joan. BS in Natural Resources, Oreg. State U., 1953, MA in Pub. Adminstrn., 1964. Planning dir. Clackamas County, Oregon City, Oreg., 1956-59, City of Vancouver, Wash., 1959-65; interagy. commr. Wash. State Gov.'s Office, Olympia, 1966; asst. regional dir. HUD, Seattle, 1967-78; pub. affairs officer Bonneville Power Adminstrn., Portland, 1979—. Lt. col. USMC, 1951-73. Mem. Am. Inst. Cert. Planners, Toastmasters (pres.). Home: 2883 SW Champlain Dr Portland OR 97201-1833 Office: Bonneville Power Adminstrn PO Box 3621Oalg Portland OR 97208-4000

MERRILL, LYNN LESLIE, technical writer; b. N.Y.C., Mar. 20, 1951; d. F. Bruce and Audrey (Teufel) M. BA, Colo. Coll., 1973; MA, U. Colo., 1975, PhD, 1984. Editorial asst. English Lang. Notes, Boulder, Colo., 1975-77; instr., lectr. U. Colo., Boulder, 1977-84; sr. tech. writer ViTel Internat., Inc., Boulder, 1985-89, NBI, Inc., Boulder, 1989-92; tech. editor XVT Software Inc., Boulder, 1992—; editorial asst. Comm. of the ACM, Boulder, 1983, Frontiers: A Jour. of Women Studies, Boulder, 1978-84. Author: The Romance of Victorian Natural History, 1989; co-editor: A Concordance to the Poetry of George Meredith, 1982; contbr. articles, book revs., poetry to jours. Mem. MLA, Soc. Vertebrate Paleontology, Soc. for Tech. Communication (sr. mem., Disting. award 1992, Merit awards 1991, 92).

MERRILL, ROBERT EDWARD, special machinery manufacturing company executive; b. Columbus, Ohio, Oct. 21, 1933; m. Donna Rae Bernstein, Mar. 19, 1967; children: Robert Edward, Aaron Jay, Jonathan Cyrus, Raquel Naomi. MBA, Pepperdine U.; Pres., PSM Corp., San Jose, Calif., 1974—. Author: The ABC's of Small Business Money. Served with AUS, 1950-51; Korea. Patentee in pneumatic applications for indsl. press machinery. Home: 858 Fieldwood Ct San Jose CA 95120-3311

MERRILL, ROBERT HULL, physicist, consultant; b. Edgar, Nebr., Feb. 7, 1922; s. Bruce Wiltshire and Verdie Emma (Hull) M.; m. Alberta Faye Keith, Feb. 12,1944; children: Sandra Sue, Rick Hull. AB, Nebr. Wesleyan U., 1947; BS, MS, U. Wyo., 1949. Registered profl. engr., Colo. Physicist U.S. Bur. Mines, Rifle, Colo., from 1949; rsch. supr. U.S. Bur. Mines, Denver, 1960-77; ind. cons. Lakewood, Colo., 1977—; speaker in field. Patentee; contbr. articles to tech. publs. Mem. AIME (pres. 1981), Soc. Mining Engrs. (pres. 1973), Am. Assn. Engring. Home: 890 Reed Ct Lakewood CO 80215-6130

MERRILL, RONALD THOMAS, geophysicist, educator; b. Detroit, Feb. 5, 1938; s. Robert Able and Freda (Havens) M.; m. Nancy Joann O'Byrne, Sept. 1, 1962; children: Craig Elliot, Scott Curtis. BS in Math., U. Mich., 1959, MS in Math., 1961; PhD in Geophysics, U. Calif., Berkeley, 1967. Asst. prof. oceanography U. Wash., Seattle, 1967-72, assoc. prof. geophysics and oceanography, 1972-77, prof. geophysics and geol. sci., 1977—, chmn. dept. geophysics, 1985-92. Author: (with M.W. McElhinny) The Earth's Magnetic Field, 1984; contbr. numerous articles to profl. jours. Recipient numerous rsch. grants from NSF, other founds. Fellow Am. Geophys. Union (pres. geomagnetism and paleomagnetism sect. 1988-90); mem. AAAS, Soc. Geomagnetism (Japan). Office: U Wash Dept Geophysics AK-50 Seattle WA 98195

MERRILL, ROY RICHARD, healthcare executive; b. Ft. Worth, Aug. 9, 1946; s. David Ledrick and Alma Celia (Terry) M.; 1 child, Teressa Louise; m. Sandra Claire Roberts, June 27, 1982. BBA, U. Tex., Arlington, 1973. Asst. adminstr. Doctors Community Hosp., Euless, Tex., 1973-75; controller Valley View Hosp., Denver, 1975-77; regional fin. mgr. Humana, Inc., Lousiville, Ky., 1977-79; v.p. fin., treas. St. Anthony Hosp. Systems, Denver, 1979-89; exec. v.p HM Enterprises, Inc., Denver, 1989-91; prin. Managed Care Options, Denver, 1991-92; pres. Imaging Network Corp., Culver City, Calif., 1992—; chmn. bd, dirs., Colo. Hosp. Assn. Workers Compensation Trust, Denver, 1986-87. With U.S. Navy, 1967-70. Mem. Accts. 52 Club, Am. Acad. Med. Adminstrs. (bd. dirs. Colo. 1984-88), Healthcare Fin. Mgmt. Assn. (bd. dirs. Colo. 1986-91, William G. Follmer award, 1985, Reeves Silver Merit award 1991). Republican. Roman Catholic. Home: 2776 E Irish Pl Littleton CO 80122 Office: Imaging Network Corp Ste 515 400 Corporate Pointe Culver City CA 90230

MERRILL, STEVEN WILLIAM, research and development executive; b. Oakland, Calif., Aug. 6, 1944; s. David Howard and Etha Nadine (Wright) M. BA in Chemistry, Calif. State U., 1987. Lic. pyrotechnic, Calif. Apprentice Borgman Sales Co., San Leandro, Calif., 1960-64; assembler Calif. Fireworks Display, Rialto, Calif., 1970; pyrotechnician Hand Chem. Industries, Milton, Ont., Can., 1972-74; dir. R&D Pyrospectaculars, Rialto, 1988—; experimenter in field, 1958—; chief chemist Baron Blakesly Solvents, Newark, Calif., 1987-88; court expert San Francisco Superior Ct., 1971, Victorville (Calif.) Superior Ct. Counselor Xanthos, Inc., Alameda, Calif., 1970. Mem. Am. Chem. Soc. Home: PO Box 676 Crestline CA 92325-0676 Office: Pyrospectaculars 3196 N Locust Ave Rialto CA 92376-1414

MERRILL, THOMAS ST. JOHN, medical photographer; b. Jersey City, N.J., Feb. 21, 1946; s. Willard St. John and Frances Minnie (Havlieck) M.; m. Marie Knoetig, Mar. 19, 1967; children: Monica Marie-Rose, Michelle St. John. Student, Fairleigh Dickenson U., 1963-64, Germain Sch. Photography, 1967-68; AA, Saddleback Coll., 1990; student, Mt. San Antonio Coll., 1990—. Cert. retinal angiographer. Photography asst. VA Hosp., N.Y.C., 1968; dept. head, photography Manhatten Eye, Ear and Throat Hosp., N.Y.C., 1968-69; med. photographer Don Allen Studio, N.Y.C., 1969-71; sr. ophthalmic photographer Mt. Sinai Sch. Medicine, N.Y.C., 1971-76; ophthalmic photographer U. Calif., Irvine, 1976-86; photographer Allergan Inc., Irvine, 1986-89; owner, pres. The Med. Image, Chine, Calif., 1983—; sr. med. photographer St. Joseph Med. Ctr., Burbank, Calif., 1991—. Mem. Luth. Hour Rose Float Com., Pasadena, Calif. With U.S. Army, 1964-67, Vietnam. Mem. Biol. Photographic Assn. (fellow 1991, chmn. so. Calif. chpt. 1990-92), Ophthalmic Photographers' Soc., VFW (life), AMVETS. Home: 4395 Goldenrod Ct Chino CA 91710 Office: St Joseph Med Ctr 501 S Buena Vista Burbank CA 91505

MERRITT, BRUCE GORDON, lawyer; b. Iowa City, Iowa, Oct 4, 1946; s. William Olney and Gretchen Louise (Kuever) M.; m. Valerie Sue Jorgensen, Dec. 28, 1969; children: Benjamin Carlyle, Alicia Marie. AB magna cum laude, Occidental Coll., 1968; JD magna cum laude, Harvard U., 1972. Bar: Calif. 1973. Assoc. Markbys, London, 1972-73; assoc. Nossaman, Krueger & Marsh, L.A., 1973-79, ptnr., 1979-81; asst. U.S. atty., L.A., 1981-85; ptnr. Hennigan & Mercer, L.A., 1986-88; ptnr. Debevoise & Plimpton, L.A., 1989—. Fellow Am. Coll. Trial Lawyers; mem. Calif. State Bar Assn. (exec. com. litigation sect. 1992—), L.A. County Bar Assn. (del. state bar conf. 1984-86), Phi Beta Kappa. Office: Debevoise & Plimpton Ste 3700 601 S Figueroa St Los Angeles CA 90017-5742

MERRITT, CATHY LYN, health facility administrator; b. Phoenix, Ariz., Dec. 16, 1952; d. Robert Charles and Dixie Marie (McAllister) Melton; m. William Hubert Merritt, July 28, 1974; children: Corey Scott, Brian Thomas. BSN, Ill. Wesleyan U., 1975; M in Nursing Adminstrn., U. Phoenix, 1992. CCRN, ACLS. Staff nurse N.C. Meml. Hosp., Chapel Hill, 1975-79; staff nurse Desert Samaritan Med. Ctr., Mesa, Ariz., 1979-84, asst. dir. intensive care, 1984—. Mem. AACCN, ABWA (Bus. Assoc. of Yr. 1992). Home: 1876 E Auburn Dr Tempe AZ 85283 Office: Desert Samaritan Med Ctr 1400 S Dobson Rd Mesa AZ 85202

MERSEL, MARJORIE KATHRYN PEDERSEN, lawyer; b. Manila, Utah, June 17, 1923; d. Leo Henry and Kathryn Anna (Reed) Pedersen; A.B., U. Calif., 1948; LL.B., U. San Francisco, 1948; m. Jules Mersel, Apr. 12, 1950; 1 son, Jonathan. Admitted to D.C. bar, 1952, Calif. bar, 1955; Marjorie Kathryn Pedersen Mersel, atty., Beverly Hills, Calif., 1961-71; staff counsel Dept. Real Estate State of Calif., Los Angeles, 1971—. Mem. Beverly Hills Bar Assn., L.A. County Bar Assn., Trial Lawyers Assn., So. Calif. Women Lawyers Assn. (treas. 1962-63), Beverly Hills C. of C., World Affairs Council. Clubs: Los Angeles Athletic, Sierra. Home: 13007 Hartsook St Sherman Oaks CA 91423-1616 Office: Dept Real Estate 107 S Broadway Los Angeles CA 90012-3113

MERTA, PAUL JAMES, cartoonist, photographer, engineer, restauranteur, real estate developer; b. Bakersfield, Calif., July 16, 1939; s. Stanley Franklin and Mary Ann (Herman) M.; AA, Bakersfield Jr. Coll., 1962; BS in Engring., San Jose State Coll., 1962. Cartoonist nat. mags., 1959—; civilian electronics engr. Air Force/Missiles, San Bernardino, Calif., 1962-65; electronics countermeasures engr., acquisition program mgr. Air Logistics Command, Sacramento, 1965-90; ret.; TV film, video animator, producer, owner Merge Films, 1965—; photographer, owner The Photo Poster Factory, Sacramento, 1971—; owner restaurant La Rosa Blanca, Sacramento, 1979-91; ptnr. Kolinski and Merta Hawaiian Estates, 1981—; polit. cartoonist Calif. Jour., 1958-59, Sacramento Union Newspaper, 1979—, Sacramento Legal Jour., 1979. Home: 4831 Myrtle Ave Apt 8 Sacramento CA 95841-3621 Office: 1005 12th St Sacramento CA 95814-3920

MERTON, EGON STEPHEN, English literature educator; b. N.Y.C., Nov. 26, 1912; s. Leslie Rudolph and Fanny (Schor) M. BA, Columbia U., 1933, MA, 1935, PhD, 1949. Instr. Colo. Coll., Colorado Springs, Colo., 1939-42; asst. prof. Coll. of William and Mary, Williamsburg, Va., 1943-46; instr. Cornell U., Ithaca, N.Y., 1946-50; prof. CUNY, 1950-75; prof., chmn. English dept. U. Cairo, 1957-58; prof. emeritus CUNY, 1975—. Author: Science and Imagination, 1949, reprint 1969, Skyscrapers and Pyramids, 1965, Mark Rutherford, 1967; contbr. articles to profl. jours. Grantee U.S. govt., Taiwan, 1965.

MERTZ, SUSAN JEANNE, small business owner, writer; b. Toms River, N.J., May 15, 1953; d. Norman Patrick and Jeanne Barbara (Seibel) Trepiccione; m. Kenneth Alexander Mertz, Jr., Aug. 3, 1975; 1 child, Kenneth Alexander III. BS, Hood Coll., Frederick, Md., 1975; MA in Teaching, George Washington U., 1987. Freelance edn. specialist, Washington, Md., Va., 1983-88; dir. Sandy Spring (Md.) Mus., 1987-88; assoc. dir. devel. San Diego Space and Sci. Found., 1988-91; owner, mgr., writer IMPACT! Innovative Mus Programs and Creative Teaching, San Diego, 1991—; cons.

fukutake Pub. Co., Ltd., Torrance, Calif., 1991, Nat. Coun. for History Edn., Ohio, 1992. Author curriculum materials Recycle Team. Officer, v.p. Navy Dental Wives Club, Virginia Beach, Va., 1981-85; v.p. Sunset Hills Sch. PTA, San Diego, 1990-92; mem. Jr. League San Diego, 1990—. Mem. Am. Assn. Mus., Am. Assn. for State and Local History, Mus. Edn. Round Table. Republican. Home: 141 Scalybark Rd Summerville SC 29485 Office: IMPACT! Summerville SC 29485

MERWIN, EDWIN PRESTON, educator; b. Revere, Mass., Oct. 13, 1927; s. George Preston and Edith Charlotte (Miller) M.; m. Marylynn Joy Bicknell, Nov. 3, 1979; 1 son by previous marriage, Ralph Edwin; stepchildren: Charles John Burns, Patrick Edward Burns, Stephen Allen Burns. BS, U. So.Calif., 1955, postgrad. Law Sch., 1955-57; postgrad., San Fernando Valley State Coll., 1965-66; M in Pub. Health (USPHS fellow), U. Calif. at Berkeley, 1970; PhD, Brantridge Forest (Eng.), 1971. Tng. officer Camarillo (Calif.) State Hosp., 1961-66; asst. coordinator Mental Retardation Programs, State of Cal., Sacramento, 1966-67; project dir. Calif. Council Retarded Children, Sacramento, 1967-69; asst. dir. Golden Empire Comprehensive Health Coun., Sacramento, 1970-76, health care cons., 1976-77; gen. ptnr. EDRA Assocs., 1976—; cons. Calif. Dept. Health, 1977-78; cons. Calif. Office Statewide Health Planning and Devel., 1978-79; chief Health Professions Career Opportunity Program State of Calif., Sacramento, 1979-81; chief Health Personnel Info. and Analysis Sect., Office of Statewide Health Planning and Devel., 1981-82, asst. div. chief div. Health Professions Devel., 1982-84, asst. dep. dir., 1984-86; project dir. Alzheimers Disease Insts., Calif., 1986-87; chief Demonstration Project Sect. div. Health Projects and Analysis, 1987-89, chief Policy Analysis and Professsions Devel. Sect., 1989-93; tchr. Ventura (Calif.) Coll., 1962-66, Merritt Coll., Oakland, Calif., 1969; sr. adj. prof. Golden Gate U., 1976—; lectr. continuing edn. program U. Calif. at Berkeley; instr. Los Rios Community Coll. Dist., 1982—; cons. NIMH, HEW, Calif. Assn. Health Facilities. Mem. Health Adv. Council San Juan Sch. Dist., 1972-73; treas. Calif. Camping and Recreation Council, 1972-73. Bd. dirs. Sacramento Rehab. Facility, 1970-86, v.p., 1973-76, bd dirs. Sacramento Vocational Services, 1986-93. Recipient Pres.'s award Golden Gate U., 1982. Mem. Am. Assn. Mental Deficiency, Calif. Pub. Health Assn., Sacramento Mental Health Assn., Sacramento Assn. Retarded (life mem., dir., service award 1984), Nat. Assn. for Retarded Children, DAV (life), Am. Legion, Marines Meml. Assn. (life), AAAS, SCAPA Praetors U. So. Calif., Miles Merwin Assn. Founder, editor: T. Patrick Heck Meml. Case Series, 1982; co-author textbook: (with Dr. Fred Heck) Written Case Analysis, 1982; contbr. articles to profl. lit. Home: 8008 Archer Ave Fair Oaks CA 95628-5907 Office: Golden Gate U 3620 Northgate Blvd Ste 100 Sacramento CA 95834-1619

MERZ, JAMES LOGAN, electrical engineering and materials educator, researcher; b. Jersey City, Apr. 14, 1936; s. Albert Joseph and Anne Elizabeth (Farrell) M.; m. Rose-Marie Weibel, June 30, 1962; children: Kathleen, James, Michael, Kimarie. BS in Physics, U. Notre Dame, 1959; postgrad., U. Göttingen, Fed. Republic Germany, 1959-60; MA, Harvard U., 1961, PhD in Applied Physics, 1967; PhD (hon.), Linghöping U., Sweden, 1993. Mem. tech. staff Bell Labs., Murray Hill, N.J., 1966-78; prof. elec. engring. U. Calif., Santa Barbara, 1978—, prof. materials, 1986—, chmn. dept. elec. and computer engring., 1982-84, assoc. dean for rsch. devel. Coll. Engring., 1984-86, acting assoc. vice chancellor, 1988, dir. semiconductor rsch. corp. core program on GaAs digital ICs, 1984-89, dir. Compound Semiconductor Rsch. Labs., 1986-92, dir. NSF Ctr. for Quantized Electronic Structures, 1989—; NATO Advanced Study Inst. lectr. Internat. Sch. Materials Sci. and Tech., Erice-Sicily, Italy, 1990; mem. exec. com. Calif. Microelectronics Innovation and Computer Rsch. Opportunities Program, 1986-92; mem. NRC com. on Japan, NAS/NAE, 1988-90; mem. internat. adv. com. Internat. Symposium on Physics of Semiconductors and Applications, Seoul, Republic of Korea, 1990, Conf. on Superlattices and Microstructures, Xi'an, China, 1992; participant, mem. coms. other profl. confs. and meetings. Contbr. numerous articles to profl. jours.; patentee in field. Fulbright fellow, Danforth Found. fellow, Woodrow Wilson Found. fellow. Fellow IEEE, Am. Phys. Soc.; mem. IEEE Lasers and Electo-Optics Soc. (program com. annual meeting 1980), Am. Vacuum Soc. (exec. com. electronic materials and processing div. 1988-89), Electrochem. Soc., Materials Rsch. Soc. (editorial bd. jour. 1984-87), Soc. for Values in Higher Edn., Inst. Electronics, Info. and Comm. Engrs. (overseas adv. com.), Sigma Xi, Eta Kappa Nu. Office: U Calif 1413 Phelps Hall Santa Barbara CA 93106

MESA, RICHARD, school superintendent. Supt. schs. Oakland (Calif.) Unified Sch. Dist. Office: Oakland Unified School District 1025 2d Ave Oakland CA 94606*

MESEC, DONALD FRANCIS, psychiatrist; b. Waukegan, Ill., Aug. 29, 1936; s. Joseph Mesec and Johanna (Setnicar) M.; m. Francesca Auditore, June 20, 1964 (div. 1987); 1 child, Steven Francis; m. Patricia Guitteau, Mar. 27, 1988. BS cum laude, U. Notre Dame, 1958; MD, N.Y. Med. Coll., 1963. Diplomate Am. Bd. Psychiatry and Neurology. Resident in psychiatry and neurology N.Y. Med. Coll.-Manhattan State Hosp., N.Y.C., 1964-67; chief of svc. Manhattan Psychiat. Ctr., N.Y.C., 1970-76, dir. psychiat. rsch., 1974-75, dir. Meyer Manhattan Alcohol Rehab. Ctr., 1975; med. dir. Meyer Day Ctr., N.Y.C., 1976-77; staff psychiatrist Asheville VA Hosp., N.C., 1977-78; practice medicine specializing in psychiatry, Phoenix, 1978—; instr. clin. psychiatry Columbia U., N.Y.C., 1972-77; dir. psychiat. edn. St. Joseph's Hosp., Phoenix, 1982—, co-dir. pain program, 1982—, vice chmn. dept. psychiatry, 1984—, chmn. dept. psychiatry, 1987—; chief div. mental health MacDonald Meml. Hosp., Republic Palau, 1991—; with pacific ops. U.S. Dept. Health and Human Svcs., 1991—. Served with USPHS, 1963-64. Mem. New York County Med. Soc., Ariz. Med. Assn., Maricopa County Med. Soc., Ariz. Psychiat. Soc., AMA, Am. Psychiat. Assn., Am. Acad. Clin. Psychiatrists. also: PO Box 3009 Kingman AZ 86402

MESERVE, BRUCE ELWYN, mathematics educator; b. Portland, Maine, Feb. 2, 1917; s. Walter Joseph and Bessie Adelia (Bailey) M.; m. Gertrude Morey Holland, June 7, 1941 (div. 1961); children: Arthur, Virginia, Donald; m. Dorothy Spencer Tucker, Aug. 5, 1961. AB, Bates Coll., Lewiston, Maine, 1938; MA, Duke U., 1941, PhD, 1947. Tchr. Moses Brown Sch., Providence, R.I., 1938-41; from instr. to asst. prof. U. Ill., Champaign, 1946-54; from assoc. prof. to prof., chmn. math. dept. Montclair State Coll., Upper Montclair, N.J., 1954-64; prof. U. Vt., Burlington, 1964-83, prof. emeritus, 1983—; co-chmn. Internat. Study Group on Rels. Between History and Pedagogy of Math., 1980-84. Author: Fundamental Concepts of Algebra, 1951, Fundamental Concepts of Geometry, 1955, and others; contbr. articles to profl. jours.; editor several books. Moderator Town of Fairfax, Vt., 1976-84. Fellow AAAS; mem. Am. Math. Soc., Math. Assn. Am., Nat. Coun. Tchrs. Math. (pres. 1964-66, bd. dirs. 1958-67), Phi Beta Kappa, Sigma Pi Sigma. Home: 521 S Paseo Del Cobre Green Valley AZ 85614-2321

MESHEW, PATRICIA WEBER, graphologist; b. Cheyenne, Wyo., Mar. 10, 1953; d. John Gaylord and Patricia Jean (Ballantyne) Weber; m. Gary Alan Meshew, May 26, 1984. BS, Boston U., 1975. Cert. graphologist. Bus. mgr. Assoc. Internists, P.A., Phoenix, 1978-84; accounts payable staff Tempe (Ariz.) Sch. Dist. #3, 1984-88; owner Mi Casa Day Care, Tempe, 1988—, The Am. Congress of Graphology, Tempe, 1977-91, Southwest Handwriting Resources, 1991—; instr. City of Phoenix Parks and Recreation, 1980-81; conv. speaker Scottsdale C. of C., 1990—. Pres. PTA, Tempe, 1991-92; com. mem., alumni admissions vol. Boston U., 1990—. Mem. Am. Handwriting Analysis Found., Phoenix Area Graphology Ent. (sec. 1991-92), Pi Lambda Theta. Republican. Home and Office: 2083 E Minton Dr Tempe AZ 85282

MESHKE, GEORGE LEWIS, drama and humanities educator; b. Yakima, Wash., Oct. 7, 1930; s. George Joseph and Marye Elizabeth (Lopas) M. BA, U. Wash., 1953, MA, 1959, PhD in Drama, 1972. Cert. tchr., Wash. Tchr. English and drama Zillah High Sch., Wash., 1955-58; tchr. English and drama high sch., Bellevue, Wash., 1958-60, Federal Way, Wash., 1960-70; prof. drama Yakima Valley C.C., Yakima, 1970—; casting dir., dir. summer seminar Laughing Horse Summer Theatre, Ellensburg, Wash., 1989—; lectr. Inquiring Mind series Wash. State Humanities, 1989-91; regional dir. Am. Coll. Theatre Festival, Washington, 1980-86; arts dialogue J.F. Kennedy Ctr., Washington, 1987—. Author, producer Towers of Tomorrow, 1985. Regional bd. dirs. Common Cause, Yakima, 1971-73; active Wash. State Commn. Humanities. With U.S. Army, 1953-55, Austria. Recipient Gold medallion Kennedy Ctr., 1985, Wash. State Humanities medal, 1983, NISAD medallion, 1989. Mem. ACLU, Wash. Edn. Assn., N.W. Drama Assn., Am. Edn. Theatre Assn., Am. Fedn. Tchrs., Phi Delta Kappa. Democrat. Home: 5 N 42d Ave Yakima WA 98908 Office: Yakima Valley CC 16th and Nob Hill Blvd Yakima WA 98907

MESLOH, WARREN HENRY, civil, environmental engineer; b. Deshler, Nebr., Mar. 17, 1949; s. Herbert Frederick and Elna Florence (Petersen) M.; m. Barbara Jane Anderson, Sept. 7, 1969; children: Christopher Troy, Courtney James. BS, U. Kans., 1975; postgrad., Kans. State U., 1976-77. Registered profl. engr. Colo., Kans., Nebr. Project mgr. Wilson & Co. Engrs., Salina, Kans., 1975-80, process design dir., 1980-82; engring. dir. Taranto, Stanton & Tagge, Fort Collins, Colo., 1982-85; pres. The Engring. Co., Fort Collins, Colo., 1985—; mem. civil engring. adv. bd. Kans. U., Lawrence, 1982—. Contbg. author (book) Pumping Station Design, 1989, (water pollution control manual) Manual of Practice No. OM-2, 1991; contbr. articles to profl. jours. Cub master Boy Scouts Am., Salina, 1980-81; active Luth. Ch., 1982—; vol. Paralyzed Vets. Orgn., Fort Collins, 1985—; pres. Foothills Green Pool Assn., Fort Collins, 1987-88. Sgt. U.S. Army, 1971-73, Germany. Named Outstanding Engr.-In-Tng. NSPE, 1978. Mem. Am. Pub. Works Assn., Am. Water Works Assn., Water Pollution Control Fedn., Fort Collins Country Club. Republican. Office: The Engring Co 2310 E Prospect Rd Fort Collins CO 80525-9729

MESQUITA, ROSALYN ESTHER, artist, educator; b. Belen, N.Mex., Aug. 21, 1935; d. Trinidad Jose and Margaret Oliva (Aragon) Anaya; m. Theodore Richard Mesquita, Jan. 14, 1956 (div.); children: John, Richard, Larry, Thresa. BA, Calif. State U., Northridge, 1974; MFA, U. Calif., Irvine, 1976. Cert. community coll. credential, Calif. Curator State of N.Mex., Santa Fe, 1968-72; lectr. L.A. Hist. Soc., 1978—; prof. Pasadena (Calif.) City Coll., 1981—; lectr. Non Govtl. Orgn. UN Planning Com., Nairobi, Kenya, and N.Y., 1985—; curator, participant Am. Women in Art, UN World Conf., Nairobi, 1985; curator Mus. Natural History, Los Angeles, 1978. Lectr. L.A. BiCentennial and 1985 Olympic Com., 1976-84; mem. Santa Monica Art Commn., 1991—. Recipient Col.-Aide-De Camp award Gov. David F. Cargo, 1972; Ford Found. fellow, 1975. Mem. Coll. Art Assn., Nat. Women's Caucus for Art (affirmative action officer 1980-83, honorarium 1983), Hispanic Faculty Assn. (treas. 1980-90), Assn. Latin Am. Artists (pres. 1982-90), L.A. La Raza Faculty Assn. (sec. 1979-85, v.p. 1988-89). Democrat. Roman Catholic. Home: 13426 Vanowen St Van Nuys CA 91405-4329 Office: Santa Monica City Coll 1900 Pico Blvd Santa Monica CA 90405-1628

MESSENGER, GEORGE CLEMENT, engineering consultant; b. Bellows Falls, Vt., July 20, 1930; s. Clement George and Ethel Mildred (Farrar) M.; m. Priscilla Betty Norris, June 19, 1954; children: Michael Todd, Steven Barry, Bonnie Lynn. BS in Physics, Worcester Poly. U., 1951; MSEE, U. Pa., 1957; PhD in Engring., Calif. Coast U., 1986. Rsch. scientist Philco Corp., Phila., 1951-59; engring. mgr. Hughes Semicondr., Newport Beach, Calif., 1959-61; div. mgr. Transitron Corp., Wakefield, Mass., 1961-63; staff scientist Northrop Corp., Hawthorne, Calif., 1963-68; cons. engr., Las Vegas, Nev., 1968—; lectr. UCLA, 1969-75; v.p., dir. Am. Inst. Fin., Grafton, Mass., 1970-78; gen. ptnr. Dargon Fund, Anaheim, Calif., 1983—; v.p., tech. dir. Messenger and Assoc., 1987—, registered investment adviser, 1989—. Co-author: The Effects of Radiation on Electronic Systems, 1986; contbg. author: Fundamentals of Nuclear Hardening, 1972; contbr. numerous articles to tech. jours.; patentee microwave diode, hardened semicondrs. Recipient Naval Rsch. Lab. Alan Berman award, 1982; Best Paper award HEART Conf., 1983, Spl. Merit award HEART Conf., 1983; fellow IEEE, 1976, annual merit award 1986, Pete Haas award. HEART Conf., 1992. Mem. Rsch. Soc. Am., Am. Phys. Soc. Congregationalist. Home and Office: 3111 Bel Air Dr Apt 7F Las Vegas NV 89109-1510

MESSER, DONALD EDWARD, theological school president; b. Kimball, S.D., Mar. 5, 1941; s. George Marcus and Grace E. (Foltz) M.; m. Bonnie Jeanne Nagel, Aug. 30, 1964; children: Christine Marie, Kent Donald. BA cum laude, Dakota Wesleyan U., 1963; M. Divinity magna cum laude, Boston U., 1966, PhD, 1969; LHD (hon.), Dakota Wesleyan U., 1977. Asst. to commr. Mass. Commn. Against Discrimination, Boston, 1968-69; asst. prof. Augustana Coll., Sioux Falls, S.D., 1969-71; assoc. pastor 1st United Meth. Ch., Sioux Falls, 1969-71; pres. Dakota Wesleyan U., Mitchell, S.D., 1971-81, Iliff Sch. Theology, Denver, 1981—. Author: Christian Ethics and Political Action, 1984, Contemporary Images of Christian Ministry, 1989, Send Me? The Itineracy In Crisis, 1991, The Conspiracy of Goodness, 1992; contbr. articles to Face To Face, The Christian Century, The Christian Ministry. Active Edn. Commn. of U.S., 1973-79; co-chmn. Citizens Commn. Corrections, 1975-76; vice chmn. S.D. Commn. on Humanities, 1979-81. Dempster fellow, 1967-68; Rockefeller fellow, 1968-69. Mem. Soc. Christian Ethics, Am. Acad. Religion, Assn. United Meth. Theol. Schs. (v.p. 1986-91, pres. 1991-92). Democrat. Office: Iliff Sch Theology Office Pres 2201 S University Blvd Denver CO 80210-4798

MESSNER, KATHRYN HERTZOG, civic worker; b. Glendale, Calif., May 27, 1915; d. Walter Sylvester and Sadie (Dinger) Hertzog; m. Ernest Lincoln, Jan. 1, 1942; children: Ernest Lincoln, Martha Allison Messner Cloran. BA, UCLA, 1936, MA, 1951. Tchr. social studies L.A. schs., 1937-46; mem. L.A. County Grand Jury, 1961. Mem. exec. bd. L.A. Family Svc., 1959-62; dist. atty.'s adv. com., 1965-71, dist. atty.'s adv. coun., 1971-82; mem. San Marino Community Coun.; chmn. San Marino chpt. Am. Cancer Soc.; bd. dirs. Pasadena Rep. Women's Club, 1960-62, San Marino dist. coun. Girl Scouts U.S.A., 1959-68, Am. Field Svc., San Marino, 1983—; pres. San Marino High Sch. PTA, 1964-65; bd. mem. Pasadena Vol. Placement Bur., 1962-68; mem. adv. bd. Univ. YWCA, 1956—; co-chmn. Dist. Atty.'s Adv. Bd. Young Citizens Coun., 1968-72; mem. San Marino Red Cross Coun., 1966—, chmn., 1969-71, vice chmn., 1971-74; mem. San Marino bd. Am. Field Svc.; mem. atty. gen.'s vol. adv. com., 1971-80; bd. dirs. L.A. Women's Philharm. Com., 1974-89, Beverly Hills-West L.A. YWCA, 1974-85, L.A. YWCA, 1975-84, L.A. Law Affiliates, 1974-89, Pacificulture Art Mus., 1976-80, Reachout Com., Music Center, Vol. Action Center, West L.A., Calif., 1980-85, Stevens House, 1980—, Pasadena Philharm. Com., 1980-85, Friends Outside, 1983—, Internat. Christian Scholarship Found., 1984—; hon. bd. dirs. Pasadena chpt. ARC, 1978-82. Recipient spl. commendation Am. Cancer Soc., 1961; Community Svc. award UCLA, 1981. Contbr. articles to profl. jours. Mem. Pasadena Philharmonic, Las Floristas, Huntington Meml. Clinic Aux., Nat. Charity League, Gold Shield (co-founder), Pi Lambda Theta (sec. 1983-89), Pi Gamma Mu, Mortar Bd., Prytanean Soc. Home: 1786 Kelton Ave Los Angeles CA 90024-5508

MESTER, JORGE, conductor; b. Mexico City, Apr. 10, 1935; came to U.S., 1946, naturalized, 1968; s. Victor and Margarita (Knöpfler) M. B.S., Juilliard Sch. Music, 1957, M.S., 1958; studied conducting with, Jean Morel, Leonard Bernstein., Albert Wolff. Faculty Juilliard Sch. Music, 1956-68, chmn. conducting studies, 1980—. Also condr., Juilliard Theatre Orch., 1961-62, Beaux Arts Trio, 1961-65; mus. dir., Louisville Orch., Greenwich Village Symphony, 1961-62, mus. dir., condr., Louisville Orch., 1967-79, artistic adviser, Kansas City Philharmonic, 1971-72, then music dir., Kansas City Philharmonic, 1973-77, music dir., Aspen Music Festival, 1970—, Festival Casals, 1978-85; music dir. Pasadena Symphony, 1984—; prin. guest condr., St. Paul Chamber Orch., 1978-79, guest condr., Orquesta Sinfonica Nacional de Mexico, Philharmonica Triestina, Spoleto Festival Orch., Japan Philharmonic, Yomiuri Nippon Symphony, Boston Symphony, Pitts. Symphony, New Orleans Philharmonic, Indpls. Symphony, N.Y.C. Opera, Phila. Orch., London Royal Philharmonic, Denver Symphony, Bach Aria Group, Cin. Orch., Rochester Philharmonic, Utah Symphony, Oreg. Symphony, Cin. Symphony, others; condr. dance season, Spoleto Festival, Grant Park, Chgo., Tanglewood, Mass., Harkness Dance Festival, 1964, Cosi Fan Tutte, 1964, L'Elisir D'Amore, rec. with, Columbia, Vanguard, Mercury, Desto, CRI, Cambridge records, also, Louisville 1st Edit. Recs. Named Ky. col., 1967; recipient Naumburg award, 1968, Ditson Condrs. award, 1985. Office: care Aspen Music Festival 250 W 54th St 10th Fl E New York NY 10019 also: PO Box AA Aspen CO 81612

MESZAROS, MURRAY ILLES, education specialist, business consultant; b. Whitewood, Sask., Can., Oct. 30, 1954; came to U.S., 1989; s. Frank and Emily (Papp) M.; m. Melanie Hadfield, Aug. 21, 1979; children: Amanda, Benjamin Illes, Celeste, Daniel Davis-Wells. Student, U. Sask., 1979; BS magna cum laude, Brigham Young U., 1981, MA, 1982. Direct salesman Pa. Life Ins., Saskatoon, Sask., 1976; vol. ch. rep. Ch. of Jesus Christ of Latter Day Saints, Vienna, 1977-79; community sch. coord. A.B. Daley Community Sch., Nanton, Alta., Can., 1982-87; CEO Moose Jaw (Sask) YM/YWCA, 1987-88; owner, CEO Alpha Tng. Group, Kindersley, Sask., 1989; edn. specialist Utah State Office of Edn., Salt Lake City, 1989—; owner, CEO, Internat. Bus. Advisory, Ogden, Utah, 1992—; exec. dir. Utah Community Edn. Svcs. Assn., Salt Lake City, 1981-82. Researcher, author, video producer. Legis. candidate Representative Party of Alta., 1984; chmn., founder Citizens Against Casino Gambling, Moose Jaw, 1988; legis. analyst Community Edn. Assn. Alta., 1984-85; scoutmaster Boy Scouts Am., 1979-91. Mott fellow; rsch. grantee. Mem. Utah Mktg. Assn., Utah Vocat. Assn., Am. Vocat. Info. Assn., Nat. Assn. Industry-Specific Tng. Dirs., Blue Key. Mormon. Office: Utah State Office of Edn 250 E 500 S Salt Lake City UT 84111

METCALF, CHARLES DAVID, military officer, administrator; b. Anamosa, Iowa, June 18, 1933; s. Hubert Charles and Ruth Elora (Young) M.; m. Patricia Ann Sedlacek, June 7, 1955; children: Christon Marie, Karen Louise. BA, Coe Coll., 1955; MBA, Mich. State U., 1964; grad. sr. exec. program, Harvard U., 1985; grad, Air War Coll., Air Univ., 1974. Commd. lt. USAF, 1955, advanced through grades to maj. gen., 1986; chief budget div., 1975-76, Mil. Airlift Command, 1977-78; comptr. Mil. Airlift Command, Scott AFB, Ill., 1978-82; dep. dir. budget Hdqrs. USAF, Washington, 1982-83, chief budget div., 1985-86; comptr. Air Force Logistics Command, Dayton, Ohio, 1983-88; comdr. Air Force Acctg. and Fin. Ctr., Denver, 1988—; dep. dir. Def. Security Assistance Agy., Washington, 1988—. Treas., chief fin. officer Greater Dayton United Way, 1984-88; mem. exec. bd. Boy Scouts Am., Springfield, Ohio, 1984-88; mem. findings and audit com. Denver United Way, 1988-89. Decorated D.S.M., Legion of Merit; recipient Outstanding Alumnus award Mich. State U., 1986, Coe Coll., 1989. Mem. United Ch. of Christ. Republican. Home: 1100 Shafor Blvd Dayton OH 45419 Office: Air Force Acctg & Fin Ctr Office of Comdr Denver CO 80279-5000

METCALF, EUGENE MAX, artist, educator; b. Wellington, Kans., Apr. 22, 1927; s. Lloyd Everett Metcalf and Lenore Marietta Ray Dolven; m. Norma Dean Crouch, Aug. 23, 1953; children: Steven Allen, Kevin Eugene, Jill Stephanie Stafford. Art dir. Melrose Outdoor Advt. Co., Hollywood, Calif., 1954-56, L.A. Outdoor Advt. Co., Baldwin Park, Calif., 1956-66; self employed artist, 1966—. Author: Calligraphy Techniques and Uses. Recipient numerous awards in design, for watercolors, others. Mem. Soc. Calligraphers, L.A. Soc. Illustrators. Home: 1006 E Rosewood Ave Orange CA 92666

METCALF, JACK, retired state senator; b. Marysville, Wash., Nov. 30, 1927; s. John Read and Eunice (Grannis) M.; m. Norma Jean Grant, Oct. 3, 1948; children: Marta Jean, Gayle Marie, Lea Lynn, Beverlee Ann. Student U. Wash., 1944-45, 47; BA, BEd, Pacific Luth. U., 1951. Tchr., Elma (Wash.) pub. schs., 1951-52, Everett (Wash.) pub schs., 1952-81; mem. Wash. Ho. of Reps., 1960-64; mem. Wash. Senate, 1966-74, 80-92; chmn. environment and natural resources com., 1988-92. Chmn. Honest Money for Am. Mem. Council State Govts., Wash. Edn. Assn. (dir. 1959-61), Wash. Assn. Profl. Educators (state v.p. 1979-81, state pres. 1977-79). Mem. Nat. Conf. State Legislatures, Western States Recycling Coalition, South Whidbey Kiwanis, Deer Lagoon Grange. Republican. Home: 3273 E Saratoga Rd Langley WA 98260-9694

METCALF, LYNNETTE CAROL, naval officer, journalist, educator, gemologist; b. Van Nuys, Calif., June 22, 1955; d. William Edward and Carol Annette (Keith) M.; m. Scott Edward Hruska, May 16, 1987. BA in Communications and Media, Our Lady of Lake, 1978; MA in Human Rels., U. Okla., 1980; MA in Mktg. Webster U., 1986; cert. diamond grading, gem identification and colored stone grading Gemology Inst. Am., 1991, diploma, grad. gemologist, 1992. Enlisted USAF, 1973, advanced through grades to sgt., 1975; intelligence analyst, Taiwan, Italy and Tex., 1973-76; historian, journalist, San Antonio, 1976-78; commd. officer USN, 1978, advanced through ranks to lt. comdr., 1988; pub. rels. officer, Rep. of Panama, 1979-81; mgr. system program, London, 1981-82; ops. plans/tng., McMurdo Sta., Antarctica, 1982-84; exec. officer transient pers. unit Naval Tng. Ctr., Great Lakes, Ill., 1984-86, comdg. officer transient pers. unit, 1986-87; asst. prof. naval sci. U. Notre Dame NROTC, 1987-89; nat. curriculum, 1987-89; staff communications plans U.S. Naval Forces Japan, 1989-91, network transp. officer pers. support activity Far East, Japan, 1991-92, adminstrv. mgr., automated Data processing and management review dir. pers. support activity , 1992—; anchorwoman USN-TV CONTACT, 1986-87; adj. prof. Far East div. Chapman U.; founder Profl. Gemological Cons., Japan, 1992, Far East Fed. Sales Group, Inc., 1993. Author: Winter's Summer, 1983; editor Naval Station Anchorline, 1979-81, WOPN Caryatides, 1985-86; contbr. articles to profl. jours. Sec. San Vito Dei Normanni theatre group, Italy, 1975-76; coord. Magic Box Theater, Zion, Ill., 1984-86; dir. Too Bashful for Broadway variety show, Naval Tng. Ctr., 1986-87; treas. Yokosuka Little Theatre Group, 1990-91. Mem. Women Officers' Prof. Network (communications chair 1985-86, programs chair 1986-87), Am. Legion, Nat. Press Photographers Assn., Internat. Soc. Appraisers, Corp. Sponsor Tokyo Internat. Players, JHF Theater Soc. (co-founder 1990-93), McMurdo Club, Soc. of South Pole, Gemological Inst. Am. Alumni. Avocations: golf, mineralogy, gemology, scuba diving, traveling theatre. Home: 647 TsuKui, Yokosuka-shi Honshu 239, Japan Office: Pers Support Activity PSC 473 Box 19 PSA FPO AP 96349-1700

METCALF, VIRGIL ALONZO, economics educator; b. Branch, Ark., Jan. 4, 1936; s. Wallace Lance and Luella J. (Yancey) M.; m. Janice Ann Maples, July 2, 1958; children: Deborah Ann, Robert Alan. BS in Gen. Agr., U. Ark., 1958, MS in Agrl. Econs., 1960; Diploma in Econs., U. Copenhagen, 1960; PhD in Agrl. Econs., U. Mo., 1964. Asst. prof. U. Mo., Columbia, 1964-65, asst. to chancellor, 1964-69, assoc. prof., 1965-69, prof., exec. asst. to the chancellor, 1969-71; prof. econs., v.p. administrn. Ariz. State U., Tempe, 1971-81, prof. Sch. Agribus. and Natural Resources, 1981-88, prof. internat. bus. Coll. of Bus., 1988—; asst. to the chancellor U. Mo., 1964-69, coord. internat. programs and studies, 1965-69, mem. budget com., 1965-71, chmn., co-chmn. several task forces; cons. Ford Found., Bogota, Colombia, 1966-67; mem. negotiating team U.S. Agy. for Internat. Devel., Mauritania, 1982, cons., Cameroon, 1983, agrl. rsch. specialist, India, 1984, agribus. cons., Guatemala, 1987, 88, asst. dir. Reform Coops. Credit Project, El Salvador, 1987-90; co-dir. USIA univ. linkage grant Cath. U., Bolivia, 1984-89; cons. World Vision Internat., Mozambique, 1989. Contbr. numerous articles to profl. jours. Mem. City of Tempe U. Hayden Butte Project Area Com., 1979; bd. commrs. Columbia Redevel. Authority; mem. workable project com. City of Columbia Housing Authority. Econs. officer USAR, 1963, econ. analyst, 1964-66. Fulbright grantee U. Copenhagen, 1959-60, U. Kiril Metodij, Yugoslavia, 1973. Mem. Am. Assn. Agrl. Economists, Soc. for Internat. Devel., Samaritans (chmn. 1976, bd. dirs. 1976, mem. task force of health svc. bd. trustees 1974, health svc. 1974-78, chmn. program subcom. 1975), Kiwanis, Blue Key, Gamma Sigma Delta, Alpha Zeta, Alpha Tau Alpha. Democrat. Home: 8415 S Kachina Dr Tempe AZ 85284-2517 Office: Ariz State U Tempe AZ 85287-4105

METHENY, JOHN STEPHEN, restaurant owner; b. San Francisco, Apr. 1, 1962; s. John A. and Susan (Ulrich) M. Student, U. Calif., Berkeley, 1985. Trader asst. Pacific Stock Exch., San Francisco, 1987-90; bartender Harry's, San Francisco, 1986-90; owner, bartender The Fillmore Grill, San Francisco, 1990—, The Blue Light, San Francisco, 1991—, Johnny Love's, San Francisco, 1992—. Founder Love Found., San Francisco, 1992. Named Hastings Man of Yr. Am. Leukemia Soc., 1991. Mem. Old Blues Rugby Club (social chmn.). Home: 3079 California St San Francisco CA 94115

METOS, THOMAS HARRY, educator; b. Salt Lake City, June 14, 1932; s. Harry George and Grace (Milner) M.; m. Marilyn Oberg, Sept. 3, 1955; children: Jeffery, Melissa. BS, U. Utah, 1954, MS, 1958, PhD, 1963. Tchr. Salt Lake City pub. schs., 1954-62, curriculum supr., 1962-63; asst. prof. U. Utah, Salt Lake City, 1963-64; curriculum coord. San Diego County Dept. Edn., 1964-65; asst. prof. Ariz. State U., Tempe, 1965-67, assoc. prof. edn., 1965-71, prof. edn., 1971—, dir. rsch. svcs. Bur. Edn., Rsch. and Svc., 1965-78, program coord. Coll. Edn., 1987—; cons. U.S. Office Edn., 1965-78, various Ariz. sch. dists. Editorial cons. Prentice Hall, 1985—; author: The Human Mind, 1990; co-author: The University President in Arizona, 1945-1980, 1990; contbr. articles to profl. jours. Recipient award for Outstanding Sci. Book for Children, Children's Book Coun., 1975, 78. Mem. Ariz. Sch. Adminstrs. Office: Ariz State U Coll Edn Tempe AZ 85287-2411

METROPOLIS, NICHOLAS CONSTANTINE, mathematical physicist; b. Chgo., June 11, 1915; s. Constantine Nicholas and Katharine (Ganas) M.; m. Patricia Hendrix, Oct. 15, 1955 (div. 1977); children: Katharine, Penelope, Christopher. B.S., U. Chgo., 1936, Ph.D., 1941. Staff mem. Manhattan Project U. Chgo., 1942, asst. prof., 1946-48, prof., 1957-64; group leader Los Alamos Sci. Lab, Los Alamos, N.Mex., 1943-46, 1948-57, sr. fellow, 1965-85, emeritus, 1985—; cons. nat. labs. U. Ill. at Champaign-Urbana, 1970—; mem. com. for rsch. NSF, Washington, 1974-76; mem. tech. mission UN, Calcutta, India, 1961; mem. US-USSR Exch. State Dept., USSR, 1976; mem. 70th anniversary celebration Internat. Conf. on Quantum, Monte Carlo; J.R. Oppenheimer Meml. Lectr., Los Alamos, 1992; speaker 50th anniversary celebration Los Alamos Nat. Lab., 1993. Editor: J.R. Oppenheimer, 1984, The Los Alamos 40th Anniversary Vol.: New Directions in Physics; editor-author: History of Computing, 1980, Essays in Applied Math., 1976, MIT publ. Daedalus, 1993; mem. editorial bds. profl. jours., 1970—; contbr. articles to profl. jours. Mem. J.R. Oppenheimer Meml. Com., Los Alamos, 1965—; trustee Santa Fe Inst., 1985-88, bd. advisors, 1988—; sec., bd. dirs. Global Pursuits, Inc., 1986—. U. Chgo. fellow, 1938-41; recipient Computer Pioneer medal IEEE, 1984. Fellow Am. Phys. Soc.; mem. AAAS, Am. Math. Soc., Soc. Indsl. and Applied Math., Am. Acad. Arts and Scis. (contbr. to Daedalus 1992 annual speaker). Home: 71 Loma Vista St Los Alamos NM 87544-3090 Office: Los Alamos Nat Lab Mail Stop B210 Los Alamos NM 87545

METROS, MARY TERESA, librarian; b. Denver, Nov. 10, 1951; d. James and Wilma Frances (Hanson) Metros. BA in English, Colo. Women's Coll., 1973; MA in Librarianship, U. Denver, 1974. Adult svcs. libr. Englewood (Colo.) Pub. Libr., 1975-81, adult svcs. mgr., 1983-84; libr. systems cons. Dataphase Systems, Kansas City, Mo., 1981-82; circulation libra. Westminster (Colo.) Pub. Libr. 1983; pub. svcs. supr. Tempe (Ariz.) Pub. Libr., 1984-90, libr. adminstr., 1990—. Mem. ALA, Pub. Libr. Assn., Ariz. Libr. Assn, Libr. Adminstrn. and Mgmt. Assn. Democrat. Home: 1001 N Pasadena St Unit 28 Mesa AZ 85201-3518 Office: Tempe Pub Libr 3500 S Rural Rd Tempe AZ 85282-5482

METZ, MARY SEAWELL, university dean, retired college president; b. Rockhill, S.C., May 7, 1937; d. Columbus Jackson and Mary (Dunlap) Seawell; m. F. Eugene Metz, Dec. 21, 1957; 1 dau., Mary Eugena. B.A. summa cum laude in French and English, Furman U., 1958; postgrad., Institut Phonetique, Paris, 1962-63, Sorbonne, Paris, 1962-63; Ph.D. magna cum laude in French, La. State U., 1966; H.H.D. (hon.), Furman U., 1984; LL.D. (hon.), Chapman Coll., 1985; D.L.T. (hon.), Converse Coll., 1988. Instr. French La. State U., 1965-66, asst. prof., 1966-67, 1968-72, assoc. prof., 1972-76, dir. elem. and intermediate French programs, 1966-74, spl. asst. to chancellor, 1974-75, asst. to chancellor, 1975-76; prof. French Hood Coll., Frederick, Md., 1976-81, provost, dean acad. affairs, 1976-81; pres. Mills Coll., Oakland, Calif., 1981-90; dean of extension U. Calif., Berkeley, 1991—; vis. asst. prof. U. Calif.-Berkeley, 1967-68; mem. commn. on leadership devel. Am. Coun. on Edn., 1981-90, adv. coun. SRI, 1985-90, adv. coun. Grad. Sch. Bus. Stanford U.; assoc. Gannett Ctr. for Media Studies, 1985—; bd. dirs. PG&E, Pacific Telesis, PacTel & PacBell, Rosenberg Found., Union Bank, Longs Drug Stores, S.H. Cowell Found. Author: Reflets du monde francais, 1971, 78, Cahier d'exercices: Reflets du monde francais, 1972, 78, (with Helstrom) Le Francais a decouvrir, 1972, 78, Le Francais a vivre, 1972, 78, Cahier d'exercices: Le Francais a vivre, 1972, 78; standardized tests; mem. editorial bd.: Liberal Edn., 1982—. Trustee Am. Conservatory Theater. NDEA fellow, 1960-62, 1963-64; Fulbright fellow, 1962-63; Am. Council Edn. fellow, 1974-75. Mem. Western Coll. Assn. (v.p. 1982-84, pres. 1984-86), Assn. Ind. Calif. Colls. and Univs. (exec. com. 1982-90), Nat. Assn. Ind. Colls. and Univs. (govt. rels. adv. coun. 1982-85), So. Conf. Lang. Teaching (chmn. 1976-77), World Affairs Coun. No. Calif. (bd. dirs. 1984—), Bus.-Higher Edn. Forum, Women's Forum West, Women's Coll. Coalition (exec. com. 1984-88), Phi Kappa Phi, Phi Beta Kappa. Address: PO Box 686 Stinson Beach CA 94970

METZ, MATT, materials manager; b. Phoenix, Ariz., Jan. 29, 1954; s. E. David and Irene Janet (Bluestone) M.; m. Claudette Evelyn Krontz, June 3, 1984. BS in Math., Ariz. State U., 1976, MBA, 1980. Planner Honeywell Comml. Flight Systems, Phoenix, 1981-82, supr. material planning, 1982-85, supr. prodn. planning, 1985-87, mgr. procurement systems, 1987-88; sr. cons. Deloitte & Touche, Phoenix, 1988-90; materials mgr. Honeywell Optical Storage Systems Operation, Phoenix, 1990—. Mem. Nat. Assn. Purchasing Mgrs., Am. Prodn. and Inventory Control Soc. Office: Honeywell 18401 N 25th Ave Phoenix AZ 85023

METZ, STEVEN WILLIAM, small business owner; b. Inglewood, Calif., Nov. 30, 1946; s. Glenn Ludwig and Kathleen Martha (Peterson) M.; m. Michelle Marie McArthur, Aug. 11, 1989. Student, Fullerton Coll., Calif. Supt. Oahu Interiors, Honolulu, 1969-71, Hackel Bros., Miami, Fla., 1971-73; exec. v.p. Tru-Cut Inc., Brea, Calif., 1974-82; gen. mgr. The Louvre', Grass Valley, Calif., 1983-85; mfg. engring. mgr. Rexnord Aerospace, Torrance, Calif., 1986-87; pres., founder Metz/Calcoa Inc., Torrance, Calif., 1987—. Mfg. rep. consul Alard Machine Products, Gardena, Calif., 1988—, Orange County Spring, Anaheim, 1987—, Cempi Industries, Inc., Orange, 1987—; charter mem. Rep. Presdl. Task Force, 1991—; mem. L.A. Coun. on World Affairs, 1991-92. With U.S. Army, 1966-68. Recipient Appreciation awards DAV, 1968, Soc. Carbide & Tool Engrs., 1981, Soc. Mfg. Engrs., 1991. Fellow Soc. Carbide Engrs.; mem. Soc. Carbide & Tool Engrs. (chpt. pres. 1980-82).

METZGER, DARRYL EUGENE, mechanical and aerospace engineering educator; b. Salinas, Calif., July 11, 1937; s. August and Ruth H. (Anderson) M.; m. Dorothy Marie Castro, Dec. 16, 1956; children: Catherine Ann, Kim Marie, Lauri Marie, John David. BS in Mech. Engring., Stanford U., 1959, MS, 1960, PhD, 1963. Registered profl. engr., Ariz. Asst. prof. mech. engring Ariz. State U., Tempe, 1963-67, assoc. prof., 1967-70, prof., 1970-92, Regents' prof., 1992—, prof., chmn. dept., 1974-88, dir. thermosci. research, 1980-88; cons. Pratt & Whitney Aircraft, East Hartford, Conn., 1977—, Pratt & Whitney Aircraft Can. 1979—, United Techs. Corp., 1989—, Garrett Turbine Engine Corp., Phoenix, 1966-77, NASA Lewis Research Ctr., NASA Office of Aeronautics and Space Tech., USAF Aeropropulsion Lab., Worthington Turbine Internat., Solar Turbine Internat., Allied Chem. Corp., Office of Naval Research, Sundstrand Aviation, AT&T, Bell Labs., Calspan Advanced Tech. Ctr., Rocketdyne div. Rockwell Internat., Ishikawajima-Harima Heavy Industries Co., Ltd., Tokyo, United Tech. Corp.; keynote address NATO Adv. Group for Aerospace Research and Develop., Norway, 1985; U.S. del. U.S./China Binat. Workshop on Heat Transfer, Beijing, Xian, Shanghai, 1983, NSF U.S./China Program Dev. Meeting, Hawaii, 1983, NSF/Consiglio Nazionale delle Ricerche Italy Joint Workshop on Heat Transfer and Combustion, Pisa, Italy, 1982; gen. chmn. Symposium on Heat Transfer in Rotating Machinery, Internat. Centre for Heat and Mass Transfer, Yugoslavia, 1982, 92; mem. U.S. sci. com. Internat. Heat Transfer Conf., 1986; mem. NASA Space Shuttle Main Engine Rev. Team, 1986-87, NASA Space Engring. Program Externat. Task Team, 1987; chair prof. Office of Naval Tech. U.S. Naval Postgrad. Sch., Montery, Calif., 1989. Contbr. articles to profl. jours.; editor: Regenerative and Recuperative Heat Exchangers, 1981, Fundamental Heat Transfer Research, 1980, Heat and Mass Transfer in Rotating Machinery, 1983, Heat Transfer in Gas Turbine Engines, 1987, Compact Heat Exchangers, 1989, A Festschrift for A.L. London, 1990; mem. editorial bd. Internat. Jour. Exptl. Heat Transfer, 1987—. Ford Found. fellow, 1960, NSF fellow, 1981, ASEE/NASA fellow, 1964-65; recipient Alexander von Humboldt sr. rsch. scientist award Fed. Republic of Germany, 1985, 86, 87, Achievement award ASME, Japan Soc. Mech. Engrs., 1985, Faculty Achievement award Ariz. State U. Alumni Assn., 1987, Grad. Coll. Disting. Rsch. award Ark. State U., 1991; Sonderforschungsbereich grantee U. Karlsruhe, 1988, 89, 90. Fellow ASME (mem. gas turbine com., chmn. heat transfer div. 1982-84, mem. com. on faculty quality 1986), AIAA (assoc. fellow); mem. Soaring Soc. Am., Fed. Aero. Inst. (Internat. Diamond award), Phi Beta Kappa, Sigma Xi, Tau Beta Pi, Pi Tau Sigma, Phi Kappa Phi. Home: 8601 N 49th St Paradise Vly AZ 85253-2023 Office: Ariz State U Mech and Aerospace Engring Dept Tempe AZ 85287

METZGER, VERNON ARTHUR, management educator, consultant; b. Baldwin Park, Calif., Aug 13, 1918; s. Vernon and Nellie C. (Ross) M.; B.S., U. Calif., Berkeley, 1947, M.B.A., 1948; m. Beth Arlene Metzger, Feb. 19, 1955; children: Susan, Linda, 1 step-son, David. Estimating engr. C. F. Braun & Co., 1949; prof. mgmt. Calif. State U. at Long Beach, 1949-89, prof. emeritus, 1989—, founder Sch. Bus.; mgmt. cons., 1949-89. Mem. Fire Commn. Fountain Valley, Calif., 1959-60; pres. Orange County Dem. League, 1967-68; mem. State Dept. mgmt. task force to promote modern mgmt. in Yugoslavia, 1977; mem. State of Calif. Fair Polit. Practices Commn., Orange County Transit Com. Served with USNR, 1942-45. Recipient Outstanding Citizens award Orange County (Calif.) Bd. Suprs. Fellow Soc. for Advancement of Mgmt. (life; dir.); mem. Acad. Mgmt., Orange County Indsl. Rels. Rsch. Assn. (v.p.), Beta Gamma Sigma, Alpha Kappa Psi, Tau Kappa Upsilon. Home: 1938 Balearic Dr Costa Mesa CA 92626-3513 Office: 1250 N Bellflower Blvd Long Beach CA 90840-0001

METZLER, YVONNE LEETE, realtor, legal assistant; b. Bishop, Calif., Jan. 25, 1930; d. Ben Ford and Gladys Edna (Johnson) Leete; m. Richard Harvey Metzler, June 2, 1950; children: David Grant, Regan M., Erin E. Student, U. Calif., Berkeley, 1949, JD, Empire Coll., 1992. Lic. realtor, Calif. Vocat. instr. Ukiah (Calif.) Jr. Acad., 1962-63; bookkeeper Sid Beamer Volkswagen, Ukiah, 1963-64; acct. Ukiah Convalescent Hosp., 1964, Walter Woodard P.A., Ukiah, 1964-66; assoc. dir. Fashion Two Twenty, Ukiah, 1966-67, dir., Santa Rosa, Calif., 1967-71; acct. P.K. Marsh, M.D., Ukiah, 1971-72, Walter Woodard P.A. and Clarence White CPA, Ukiah, 1972-74; ptnr., travel agt. Redwood Travel Agy., Ukiah, 1973-76; owner, mgr. A-1 Travel Planners, Ukiah, 1976-90; owner A-1 Travel Planners of Willits, Calif., 1979-88; realtor Mendo Realty, Ukiah, 1989-92; law clk. Family Support div. Sonoma County Dist. Atty., 1990-91; freelance legal asst., 1991—. Commr., Ukiah City Planning Commn., 1979-84, chmn., 1981-83; bd. dirs., rep. Mendocino County Visitors and Conv. Bur., 1988, Pvt. Industry Coun., 1988-90; mem. Rep. County Cen. Com., 1978-80. Mem. Am. Soc. Bus. and Profl. Women, Sonoma County Bar Assn., Sonoma County Young Lawyers Assn., Ukiah C. of C. (1st v.p. 1980, pres. 1981, 82), Mendocino County C. of C. (dir. 1981), Soroptimist (pres. 1977-78, v.p. 1993-94), Ukiah Soc. Bus. and Profl. Women (treas. 1977-78, named Woman of the 80's).

METZNER, RICHARD JOEL, psychiatrist, computer software developer, educator; b. L.A., Feb. 15, 1942; s. Robert Gerson and Esther Rebecca (Groper) M.; BA, Stanford U., 1963; MD, Johns Hopkins U., 1967; children: Jeffrey Anthony, David Jonathan; m. Leila Kirkley, June 26, 1993. Intern, Roosevelt Hosp., N.Y.C., 1967-68; resident in psychiatry Stanford U. Med. Center, 1968-71; staff psychiatrist div. manpower and tng. NIMH-St. Elizabeths Hosp., Washington, 1971-73; chief audiovisual edn. system VA Med. Center Brentwood, L.A., 1973-79, chmn. VA Dist. 26 Ednl. Task Force, 1976-78; asst. prof. psychiatry UCLA Neuropsychiat. Inst., 1973-80, assoc. clin. prof., 1980—, lectr. Sch. Social Welfare, 1975-84; pvt. practice medicine specializing in psychiatry, Bethesda, Md., 1972-73, L.A., 1973—; dir. Western Inst. Psychiatry, L.A., 1977—; pres. Psychiat. Resource Network, Inc., 1984—; Served with USPHS, 1968-71. Recipient 6 awards for film and videotape prodns., 1976-80; diplomate Am. Bd. Psychiatry and Neurology (cons. 1974-78, producer audiovisual exam. programs 1975-77). Fellow Am. Psychiat. Assn.; mem. So. Calif. Psychiat. Soc., Mental Health Careerists Assn. (chmn. 1972-73), AAAS, Am. Film Inst., Phi Beta Kappa. Democrat. Jewish. Contbr. numerous articles to profl. publs., 1963—; producer, writer numerous ednl. films and videotapes, 1970—; developer videoscan treatment technique in psychiatry. Office: 9911 W Pico Blvd Ste 1570 Los Angeles CA 90035-2703

MEUNIER, JOHN CHARLES CHRISTOPHER, architecture educator, university dean; b. Nottingham, Eng., June 17, 1936; came to U.S., 1976; s. Stanislass and Louie (Naylor) M.; m. Dorothy Elizabeth Donnelly, Feb. 6, 1960; children: Matthew John, Elizabeth Ann. BArch with 1st class honours, Liverpool (Eng.) U., 1959; MArch, Harvard U., 1960; MA, Cambridge (Eng.) U., 1962. Registered architect, U.K. Archtl. asst. Buro Fred Angerer, Munich, 1960-62; asst. lectr. Cambridge U., 1962-66, lectr., 1966-76; head architecture dept. U. Cin., 1976-79, dir. Sch. Architecture and Interior Design, 1979-87; prof. architecture, dean Ariz. State U. Coll. Architecture and Environ. Design, Tempe, 1987—; prin. John Meunier Architect, Cambridge, 1962-76, Gasson & Meunier Architects, Cambridge, 1964-74, Cambridge Design Coop., 1974-76. Contbr. numerous articles to profl. jours. in Eng., U.S., Japan, Germany; prin. works include Burrell Mus., Glasgow, Scotland, 1972-83 (1st prize 1972). Mem. Urban Design Rev. Bd., Cin., 1985-87, Cen. City Bd. Archtl. Rev., Phoenix, 1989—, Phoenix Community Alliance, 1988—, Phoenix Little Theatre, 1988-90. Frank Knox fellow Harvard U., 1959. Fellow Royal Soc. Arts; mem. Royal Inst. Brit. Architects (bd. edn. and practice 1970-76), Assn. Collegiate Schs. Architecture (bd. dirs. 1989-92, pres. 1990-91). Home: 6744 N 63d Pl Paradise Valley AZ 85253 Office: Ariz State U Coll Arch-Environ Design Tempe AZ 85287

MEYE, ROBERT PAUL, retired seminary administrator; b. Hubbard, Oreg., Apr. 1, 1929; s. Robert and Eva (Pfau) M.; m. Mary Cover, June 18, 1954; children: Marianne Meye Thompson, Douglas, John. BA, Stanford U., 1951; B.D., Fuller Theol. Sem., 1957, ThM, 1959; D.Theol. magna cum laude, U. Basel, Switzerland, 1962; DD Eastern Bapt. Theol. Sem., 1990. Prof. No. Bapt. Theol. Sem., Lombard, Ill., 1962-77, dean, 1971-77; dean Sch. Theology, Fuller Theol. Sem., Pasadena, Calif., 1977-90, dean emeritus, 1992—, assoc. provost for Ch. Rels. and Christian Community, 1990-92, prof. N.T. interpretation, 1977-92, prof. emeritus, 92—. Author: Jesus and The Twelve; contbr. articles to profl. jours. Served to lt. (j.g.) USN, 1946-47, 51-54, Korea. Am. Assn. Theol. Schs. grantee, 1970-71; 75-76. Mem. Am. Acad. Religion, Assn. Theol. Schs. in U.S. and Can., Studiorum Novi Testamenti Societas, Chgo. Soc. Bibl. Res., Soc. Bibl. Lit., Inst. Bibl. Research, Christianity Today Inst. Republican. Home: 1170 Rubio St Altadena CA 91001-2027 Office: Fuller Theol Sem 135 N Oakland Ave Pasadena CA 91182-0001

MEYER, ALYCE-BELLE (ABBIE MEYER), painter, sculptor; b. Quincy, Calif., Dec. 24, 1916; d. Edmund Emil and Alice (Parkin) M. Student, Sacramento Jr. Coll., 1933-35. Clk. typist various cos., Sacramento, 1936-38; graphic artist State of Calif., Sacramento, 1938-45; draftsman/artist Breuner's Dept. Store, Sacramento, 1945-46; ind. ceramic sculptor Abmeyer Originals, Sacramento, 1946-59; artist, sec. to med. dir. Sacramento County Hosp., 1958-61; ind. painter, sculptor Abmeyer Originals, Sacramento, 1961—. Mem. No. Calif. Arts, Inc., Sacramento Fine Art Ctr. Democrat. Episcopalian. Home: 2525 Portola Way Sacramento CA 95818-3529

MEYER, AUGUST CHRISTOPHER, JR., broadcasting company executive, lawyer; b. Champaign, Ill., Aug. 14, 1937; s. August C. and Clara (Rocke) M.; m. Karen Haugh Hassett, Dec. 28, 1960; children: August Christopher F., Elisabeth Hassett. BA cum laude, Harvard U., 1959, LLB, 1962. Bar: Ill. 1962. Ptr. Meyer, Capel, Hirschfeld, Muncy, Jahn and Aldeen, Champaign, Ill., 1962-77, of counsel, 1977—; owner, dir., officer Midwest TV, Inc., Sta. KFMB-TV-AM-FM, San Diego, Sta. WCIA-TV, Champaign, Ill , Sta. WMBD-TV-AM, WKZW, Peoria, Ill., 1968—; pres. Sta. KFMB-TV-AM-FM, San Diego, Sta. WCIA-TV, Champaign, Ill , Sta. WMBD-TV-AM, WKZW, 1976—; dir. Bank of Ill.; spl. asst. atty. gen. Ill., 1968-76. Chmn. bd. trustees Carle Found. Hosp., Urbana, Ill. Mem. Ill. Bar Assn., Champaign County Bar Assn. Club: Champaign Country. Home: 1408 S Prospect Ave Champaign IL 61820 Office: Midwest TV Inc 509 S Neil Box 777 Champaign IL 61820 also: 7677 Engineer Rd San Diego CA 92111

MEYER, CARL BEAT, chemical consultant, lawyer; b. Zurich, Switzerland, May 5, 1934; came to U.S., 1960; s. Karl and Alice (Wegenstein) M.; m. Elizabeth Anne Cousins, Feb. 26, 1960; 1 child, Birgit Franziska. Matura, Kantonsschule, Zuerich, Switzerland; PhD in Chemistry, U. Zurich, 1960; JD, Calif. Western Sch. Law, 1988. Bar: Nev. 1988, Calif. 1989. Postdoctoral fellow U. Calif., Berkeley, 1961-64; from asst. prof. to prof. chemistry U. Wash., Seattle, 1964-86; cons. San Diego, 1986—, pvt. practice, 1988—; cons. Lawrence Berkeley Lab., U. Calif., Berkeley, 1964-88, U.S. Consumer Product Safety Commn., Washington, 1980-83. Author: Sulfur, Energy and Environment, 1976, Urea-Formaldehyde Resins, 1978, Indoor Air Quality, 1984; contbr. 118 articles to profl. jours. Recipient Nathan Burkan Meml. Competition award ASCAP, 1988. Fellow Am. Inst. Chemistry; mem. ASTM (vice-chair com. D-22.05 1986—), ABA, Am. Chem. Soc., Am. Phys. Soc. Office: Kapsa & Meyer 325 S 3d St # 3 Las Vegas CA 89101

MEYER, DALE THOMAS, architect; b. St. Louis, Aug. 21, 1948; s. Thomas Patrick and Dorothy Ann (Bene) M. Exchange student, London, 1970; B. Arch., U. Nebr., 1971. Owner, architect Dale Meyer Assoc., Redwood City, Calif., 1976-83, Burlingame, Calif., 1984—; ptnr. Meyer Stewart Assoc., San Carlos, Calif., 1983-84. Mem. Bartonville Planning Commn., Tex., 1985, Redwood City Hist. Commn., Calif., 1981-83. Curators scholar U. Nebr.; Rash scholar State of Mo. Mem. AIA (design commn., hist. commn.), AIA (San Mateo chpt.), Nat. Hist. Preservation Soc. Democrat. Roman Catholic. Avocations: art; photography; sports.

MEYER, DANIEL KRAMER, real estate executive; b. Denver, July 15, 1957; s. Milton Edward and Mary (Kramer) M. Student, Met. State Coll., Denver, 1977-78, U. Colo., 1978-80. Ptnr., developer RM & M II (Ltd. Partnership), Englewood, Colo., 1981-87; pres. Centennial Mortgage and Investment, Ltd., Englewood, Colo., 1984-87; prin. Capriole Properties, Greenwood Village, Colo., 1983—. Alumni mem. bd. trustees Kent Denver Country Day Sch., 1981-83; sec. Colo. House Dist. 37 Ctrl. and Vacancy Com., 1991—. Mem. Kent Denver Sch. Alumni Assn. (vice chmn. 1992-93), Greenwood Athletic Club. Republican.

MEYER, IVAH GENE, social worker; b. Decatur, Ill., Nov. 18, 1935; d. Anthony and Nona Alice (Gamble) Viccone; A.A. with distinction, Phoenix Coll., 1964; B.S. with distinction, Ariz. State U., 1966, M.S.W., 1969; post-grad. U.S. Internat. U.; m. Richard Anthony Meyer, Feb. 7, 1954; children—Steven Anthony, Stuart Allen, Scott Arthur. Social worker Florence Crittendon Home, Phoenix, 1969-70; social worker Family Service of Phoenix, 1970-73; faculty asso. Ariz. State U., 1973; field supr. Pitzer Coll., Claremont, Calif., 1977—; social worker Family Service of Pomona Valley, Pomona, Calif., 1975—; field supr. Grad. Sch. Social Services, U. So. Calif., 1978—; pvt. practice Chino (Calif.) Counseling Center. Lic. clin. social worker, Calif. Mem. Nat. Assn. Social Workers, Acad. Cert. Social Workers. Republican. Roman Catholic. Home: 778 W Via Monte Video St Claremont CA 91711-1567 Office: 12632 Central Ave Chino CA 91710

MEYER, JEROME J., diversified technology company executive; b. Caledonia, Minn., Feb. 18, 1938; s. Herbert J. and Edna (Staggemeyer) M.; m. Sandra Ann Beaudoin, June 18, 1960; children—Randall Lee, Lisa Ann, Michelle Lynn. Student, Hamline U., 1956-58; B.A., U. Minn., 1960. Devel. engr. Firestone Tire & Rubber Co., Akron, Ohio, 1960-61; v.p., gen. mgr. Sperry Univac, St. Paul, 1961-79; group v.p. Honeywell, Inc., Mpls., 1979-84; pres., chief operating officer Varian Assocs., Palo Alto, Calif., 1984-86, also bd. dirs.; pres., chief exec. officer Honeywell Inc., 1986-90; chmn. bd., pres., chief exec. officer Tektronix Inc., Beaverton, Oreg., 1990—; dir. Magnetic Data Inc., Mpls., Keycom Electronic Pub. Co., Chgo., Honeywell Erickson Devel. Co., Anaheim, Calif. Bd. dirs. YMCA, West St. Paul, Minn., 1977. Clubs: Southview Country (West St. Paul) Palo Alto Hills Country, Mission Viejo Country. Office: Tektronix Inc PO Box 1000 26600 S W Pky Wilsonville OR 97070*

MEYER, JOSEPH B., state attorney general; b. Casper, Wyo., 1941; m. Mary Orr; children: Vincent, Warren. Student, Colo. Sch. Mines; BA, U. Wyo., 1964, JD, 1967; postgrad., Northwestern U., 1968. Dep. county atty. Fremont County, Wyo., 1967-69; assoc. Smith and Meyer, 1968-71; asst. dir. legis. svc. office State of Wyo., Cheyenne, 1971-87, atty. gen., 1987—; conductor numerous govt. studies on state codes including Wyo. probate, criminal, state adminstrn., banking, domestic rels., game and fish, state instn., employment security, worker's compensation, motor vehicle, others; conductor legis. rev. of adminstrv. rules; negotiator with Office of Surface Mining for Wyo. state preemption; instr. Wyo. Coll. Law, fall 1986; lectr. Rocky Mountain Mineral Law Found., 1977; chmn. Conf. Western Atty. Gen., 1992-93; mem. exec. com. Nat. Assn. Attys. Gen. Bd. dirs. Cheyenne Jr. League, 1982-85, Jessup PTO, 1980-81; instr. Boy Scouts Am. Mem. Rotary. Congregationalist. Office: Office of Atty Gen 123 Capitol Bldg Cheyenne WY 82002

MEYER, KRAIG RANDOLPH, computer scientist; b. Ann Arbor, Mich., Dec. 12, 1966; s. Donald Irwin and Mary Lee (Rogers) M. BS in Computer Engring., U. Mich., 1988; MS in Computer Sci., U. So. Calif., 1991. Systems rsch. programmer Merit Computer Network, Ann Arbor, Mich., 1985-89; lectr., teaching asst. U. So. Calif., L.A., 1989-91; rsch. intern Digital Equipment Corp., Palo Alto, Calif., 1990; computer scientist The Aerospace Corp., El Segundo, Calif., 1991—. Bd. dirs. Christopher St. West Assn., West Hollywood, Calif., 1992. CERFNET Grad. Rsch. fellowship Calif. Edn. and Rsch. Found. Network, 1990. Mem. Assn. for Computing Machinery. Office: The Aerospace Corp PO Box 92957 Los Angeles CA 90009-2957

MEYER, LEE GORDON, attorney, energy company executive; b. Washington, Oct. 22, 1943; s. Edmond Gerald and Betty (Knobloch) M.; children: Veronica, Victoria, David. BS in Chemistry, U. Wyo., 1966, MBA, 1969, JD (hon.), 1973. Bar: Wyo. 1973, Tex. 1973, Ohio 1981, Ky. 1982, Colo. 1985, U.S. Patent Office, U.S. Supreme Ct. Patent atty. Texaco Corp., Austin, Tex., 1974-77; chief patent and trademark counsel Alcan Aluminum Co., Cleve., 1977-79; gen. counsel Donn, Inc., Cleve., 1979-81; asst. gen. counsel Diamond Shamrock Co., Lexington, Ky., 1981-83; v.p. fin. and adminstrn. Fort Union Coal Co., Denver, 1983-84; pres., chief exec. officer Carbon Fuels Corp., Denver, 1984—. Patentee in field. Mem. ABA, Am. Mgmt. Assn., Am. Chem. Soc., Licensing Exec. Soc., Ops. Rsch. Soc., Denver C. of C. Republican. Home: 12706 E Pacific Dr # 201 Aurora CO 80014 Office: Carbon Fuels Corp 5105 Dtc Pky # 317 Englewood CO 80111-2600

MEYER, M. E. JOSEPH, III, small business owner; b. Ft. Campbell, Ky.; s. Milton Edward Jr. and Mary Charlotte (Kramer) M. BA in Humanities, U. Colo., 1974; cert. massage therapy, Boulder Sch. Massage Therapy, 1980; student, Hakomi Inst., Boulder and Munich, 1982-84. Ski instr. Geneva Basin, Squaw Pass, Arapaho Basin, Keystone, Colo., 1967-71; instr. guitar Musikschule Schöneberg, West Berlin, Federal Republic of Germany, 1977-81; instr. guitar (docent) Conservatory in West Berlin, 1978-81; pvt. practice massage therapy, instr. Oslo, Copenhagen, Stockholm, Berlin, Munich, Aspen, Colo., Reykjavik, Iceland, 1981-85; fgn. editor Aspen Daily News, 1986; instr. German Colo. Mountain Coll., Aspen, 1986-87; dir., loan officer Centennial Mortgage Investments, Englewood, Colo., 1986-87; dir., owner Aspen Therapeutic Massage Assocs., Englewood, 1986-92; dir. Massage Therapy at the Internat., Englewood, 1992—; owner Aspen Fitness Assocs., Englewood, 1992—; dir. massage therapy Greenwood Athletic Club, Englewood, 1986-92; massage therapist Aspen Valley Hosp., 1983-86, World Disabled Ski Championship, Winter Park, Colo., 1990; translator World Cup Ski Races, Aspen, 1986-87. Contbr. articles to profl. jours.; scriptor, actor instructional video The Swedish Massage, 1987; exec. producer video Lisa Ericson's Seated Aerobic Workout, 1992. Mem. Clean Air Adv. Bd., Aspen, 1985-87; ski guide Blind outdoor Leadership Devel., Aspen, 1985-87; vol. Monoski & Sitski Tether, Nat. Sports Ctr. for Disabled, Winter Park, Colo., 1990-92. Mem. Am. Massage Therapy Assn. (conf. coord., bd. dirs. Colo. chpt.), Hakomi Inst., II Bass, Opera Colo. (chorus 1992—), Colo. Symphony Orch. (chorus 1991—), Japan Am. Soc. Colo., Alliance Francaise, Mensa, Greenwood Athletic Club, Internat. Wellness Ctr. and Athletic Complex. Republican. Home: 7434 S Cherry Ct Littleton CO 80122-2408 Office: Aspen Fitness Assocs 6006 S Holly St Ste 145 Englewood CO 80111-4200

MEYER, MAX EARL, lawyer; b. Hampton, Va., Oct. 31, 1918; s. Earl Luther and Winifred Katherine (Spacht) M.; m. Betty Maxwell Dodds, Sept. 22, 1945; children—Scott Maxwell, Ann Culliford. A.B., U. Nebr., 1940, J.D., 1942. Bar: Nebr. 1942, Ill. 1946. Assoc. firm Lord, Bissell & Brook, Chgo., 1945-53; ptnr. Lord, Bissell & Brook, 1953-85; chmn. Chgo. Fed. Tax Forum, 1965, U. Chgo. Ann. Fed. Tax Conf., 1972; mem. Adv. Group to Commr. of IRS, 1967; lectr. in field. Chmn. bd. dirs. Music Acad. of the West. Maj. USAAF, 1942-45. Mem. ABA (mem. council tax sec. 1969-72), Ill. Bar Assn. (mem. council tax sect. 1973-76), Nebr. Bar Assn., Chgo. Bar

Assn. (chmn. taxation com. 1959-61), Am. Coll. Tax Counsel. Republican. Presbyterian. Clubs: Legal, Law (Chgo.); Valley Club of Montecito, Birnam Wood Golf. Lodge: Masons.

MEYER, MICHAEL EDWIN, lawyer; b. Chgo., Oct. 23, 1942; s. Leon S. and Janet (Gorden) M.; m. Catherine Dieffenbach, Nov. 21, 1982; children: Linda, Mollie, Patrick, Kellie. B.S., U. Wis., 1964; J.D., U. Chgo., 1967. Bar: Calif. 1968, U.S. Supreme Ct. 1973. Assoc. Lillick & McHose, L.A., 1967-73, ptnr., 1974-90, mng. ptnr., 1986-87; ptnr. Pillsbury Madison Sutro, 1990—, mem. mgmt. com., 1990-92; judge pro tem Beverly Hills Mcpl. Ct., Calif., 1976-79, Los Angeles Mcpl. Ct., 1980-86; lectr. in field. Bd. dirs. Bldg. Owners and Mgrs. Assn. of Greater L.A., L.A. Coun. Boy Scouts Am., United Way Greater L.A. Recipient Good Scout award L.A. coun. Boy Scouts Am., 1992. Mem. Am. Arbitration Assn. (arbitrator), Calif. Bar Assn., Los Angeles Bar Assn., U. Chgo. Alumni Assn. So. Calif. (pres. 1980-82). Jewish. Clubs: Calif., U. Los Angeles (dir. 1979-85, pres. 1984-85). Home: 4407 Roma Ct Marina Dl Rey CA 90292-7702 Office: Pillsbury Madison Sutro 725 S Figueroa Los Angeles CA 90017

MEYER, NATALIE, state official; b. Henderson, N.C., May 20, 1930; d. Ranie Thomas and Mary Osborne (Johnson) Clayton; m. Harold Meyer, June 17, 1951; children—Mary, Becky, Amy. Student, U. No. Iowa, 1951. Tchr. pub. schs. Jefferson County, Colo., 1951-57; tchr. and prin. Ascension Luth. Ch. Midweek Sch., 1966-77; leasing mgr. for office complex, 1973; sec. of state State of Colo., Denver, 1982—; Presdl. appointee to del. observing Philippine election, 1986; leader of State Leadership Initiative del. to USSR.; adv. coun. FEC. Past vice chairperson Arapahoe County Republicans, Colo.; mgr. Senator Bill Armstrong's 1974 Fifth Congl. Campaign; exec. dir. Pres. Reagan's 1976 Colo. Campaign; dir. Ted Strickland's 1978 Gubernatorial Race; mgr. Phil Winn's race for Rep. state chmn., 1980; author, adminstr. Colo. program for Rep. legis. races, 1980, other statewide campaign plans; coordinator Draft Phil Winn effort. Mem. Women in State Govt., Nat. Assn. Secs. of State (pres.), Colo. and Internat. Women's Forum Coun. State Govts. Office: Colo State Dept 1560 Broadway Ste 200 Denver CO 80202-5169

MEYER, RICHARD ERWIN, English language educator; b. Evanston, Ill., Sept. 20, 1939; s. Erwin Conrad and Florence Nettie (Wussow) M.; m. Lotte Norvig Larsen, Sept. 10, 1983; 1 child, Anne Elizabeth. BA summa cum laude, Northwestern U., 1965; MA, U. Wash., 1969; postgrad., U. Oreg., 1974-75. Dir. liberal arts seminars, asst. dean continuing edn. U. Wash., Seattle, 1965-69; prof. English/Folklore Western Oreg. State Coll., Monmouth, 1969—; cons. Office Historic Preservation, State of Hawaii, Honolulu, 1987. Author, editor: Cemeteries and Gravemakers: Voices of American Culture, 1989; (with others) A Sense of Place: Essays in American Regional Culture, 1990, Ethnicity and the American Cemetery, 1993; editor: Markers the Jour. of the Assn. for Gravestone Studies; contbr. articles to profl. jours. Sgt. U.S. Army, 1959-62. Mem. Am. Folklore Soc., Am. Culture Assn. (chmn. cemeteries and gravemarkers sect. 1984—), Pacific N.W. Am. Studies Assn., Oreg. Folklore Soc. (pres. 1975-76), Phi Kappa Phi. Democrat. Episcopalian. Home: 407 19th St NE Salem OR 97301-4304 Office: English Dept/Humanities Div Western Oreg State Coll Monmouth OR 97361

MEYER, ROBERT ALLEN, human resource management educator; b. Wisconsin Rapids, Wis., May 31, 1943; s. Charles Harold and Viola Bertha (Stoeckmann) M.; 1 child, Timothy Charles. BA, Valparaiso (Ind.) U., 1966; MA, Mich. State U., 1967, PhD, 1972, postgrad., 1981. Asst. prof. Muskingum Area Tech. Coll., Zanesville, Ohio, 1972-74; adj. prof. U. Fla., Gainesville, 1974-80; dean acad. affairs Santa Fe Community Coll., Gainesville, 1974-80; asst. prof. Purdue U., W. Lafayette, Ind., 1982-84, Ga. State U., Atlanta, 1985-89; assoc. prof., program coord. U. N. Tex., Denton, 1989-91; Fulbright profl. scholar Fulbright program, Bangkok, Thailand, 1991-92; coord. travel, tourism, hotel, restaurant mgmt. program U. Hawaii, Kapiolani, 1992—; investor, asst. mgr. LaSiene Restaurant, Ann Arbor, Mich., 1970-72; investor, cons. Cafe Brittany St. Thomas, U.S. V.I., 1974-80, owner, operator, Houston, 1980; pres. RTM Cons., Honolulu, Hawaii, 1989—. Contbr. articles to profl. jours. Recipient White House Commendation for Partnerships with Industry and Higher Edn.,1984, George Washington Medal of Honor for innovations in higher edn., Freedoms Found., 1985, 86, Achievement award in hospitality edn. Coun. of Hotel, Restaurant & Instl. Edn., 1987. Mem. Tarrant County Hotel and Motel Assn., Dallas Hotel Assn., Am. Soc. Tng. and Devel., Travel Ind. Assn. Tex., Hotel Sales & Mktg. Assn. (bd. dirs. 1985-89), Coun. of Hotel, Restaurant and Instl. Edn. (grad. com. 1989-90). Home: Apt 1608 2611 Ala Wai Honolulu HI 96815 Office: U Hawaii-Kapiolani 4303 Diamond Head Rd Honolulu HI 96816

MEYER, ROGER DENNIS, academic administrator; b. Parkston, S.D., Oct. 31, 1941; s. Reuben and Cordelia (Hahn) M.; m. Madonna S. Friedman, Apr. 18, 1969; children: Deana R., Jon C. BA in Math. and Psychology, Yankton Coll., 1963; MS in Indsl. Mgmt., U. N.D., 1967. Police officer Yankton Police Dept., 1963-64; commd. 2d lt. USAF, 1964, advanced through grades to capt., 1968; with air police and sec. svc. USAF, Osan Air Base, Korea, 1967-68; with mil. pers. ctr., air staff USAF, San Antonio, 1968-70; space and satellite control facility USAF, L.A., 1970-71; resigned USAF, 1971; ops. officer dean's office Sch. Medicine U. Calif., La Jolla, 1971-74, asst. dean for adminstrn. Sch. Medicine, 1974-81, assoc. dean for adminstrn. Sch. Medicine, 1981—. Mem. Assn. Am. Med. Colls. (group on bus. affairs, chair western region 1985, chair profl. devel. com. 1986, sec. 1987, chairperson elect 1988, nat. chairperson 1989). Office: U Calif 9500 Gilman Dr La Jolla CA 92093-0602

MEYER, ROGER JESS CHRISTIAN, pediatrics educator; b. Olympia, Wash., May 14, 1928; s. Paul Eugene and Martha Bell Rogers Meyer; m. Joyce Langley, Mar. 14, 1959; children: Paul, John, William, Douglas, Nancy, Liz. BS in Chemistry, U. Wash., Seattle, 1951; MD, Washington U., St. Louis, 1955; MPH, Harvard U., 1959. Cert. pediatric bds. eligible rehab., preventive medicine, family practice. Instr. pediatrics Harvard Med. Sch., Boston, 1959-62; asst. prof. U. Vt. Coll. Medicine, Burlington, 1962-65; assoc. prof. U. Va. Sch. Medicine, Charlottesville, 1965-68; assoc. prof. pediatrics Northwestern U., Chgo., 1968-76; asst. dean U. Ill. Sch. Pub. Health, Chgo., 1974-76; prof. pediatrics and pub. health Sch. Medicine U. Wash., Seattle, 1976—; with U.S. Army Res. Med. Corps, 1982; advanced through grades to col. U.S. Army, 1986; chair, bd. dirs. community pediatrics sect. Am. Acad. Pediatrics, Evanston, Ill., 1973-74; pres. Child and Family Health Found., 1976—; bd. dirs. Nat. Com. Prevention Child Abuse, Chgo., 1974-76. Author 130 books; contbr. articles to profl. jours. Bd. dirs. NW orgn. ARC, Rotary, Tacoma; chief pub. health Pacific Rim, U.S. Army Med. Corps 364 Civil Affairs, 1986-93. Shaller scholar U. Wash., 1950-51, NIMH Health scholar U. Rochester, 1957-58; recipient Children's Hosp. Annual award, Boston, 1959, NIMH Social Sci. in Medicine award Harvard U., 1961; decorated Army Achievement medal (2) for disting. svc., 1988-90. Mem. Am. Pub. Health Assn., Am. Acad. Pediatrics, Harvard Washington U. Assn.

MEYER, ROGER PAUL, physician; b. Atlanta, Mar. 30, 1950; s. Leonard Arthur and Janet Elanor (Miller) M.; children: Seth E., Hilary R. BA in Psychology with honors, U. N.C., 1972; MD, Medical Coll. of Ga., 1976; postgrad., U. N.Mex., Albuquerque, 1980. Physician in pvt. practice Carson Medical Group, Carson City, Nev., 1980—; chief of staff Carson Tahoe Hosp., Nev., 1986-87, chmn. dept. obstetrics-gynecology, 1990, 91; v.p. Nev. Physicians Rev. Orgn., 1987. Govtl. affairs commn. Nev. State Med. Assn., Reno, 1984—. Fellow Am. Coll. of Obstetricians and Gynecologists (Nev. legislature liaison 1991); mem. Am. Fertility Soc. Democrat. Jewish. Office: Carson Med Group 1200 N Mountain St Carson City NV 89703-3824

MEYER, SALLY CAVE, personnel director; b. Coulee Dam, Wash., Oct. 20, 1937; d. Verl Edwin and Etha Laree (Moore) Cave; m. Ronald Lee Meyer, July 27, 1957; children: John Lee, Deanna, Michael Ron, Geri Anne, Deborah Sue. BA, Wash. State U., 1959, postgrad., 1986. Cert. tchr., Wash. Tchr. English Colfax (Wash.) High Sch., 1959-60; tchr. Pasco (Wash.) High Sch., 1961-62, Chief Joseph Jr. High Sch., Richland, Wash., 1968-69; instr. Columbia Basin Community Coll., Pasco, 1962-70; mem. staff Wash. State U., Pullman, 1955-61, 71-77, dir. faculty, adminstrv., and profl. personnel, 1977-91, acting dir. affirmative action program, 1986-87, coord. human rels. devel., 1991-92, instr. human rels. mgmt., 1993—; coordinator Nat. Faculty Exchange Wash. State U., 1986-88; dep. chmn. Wash. State Employees Combined Fund Drive, 1987—, state steering commn., 1989—. Sec. Camp Fire Girls Am., Pullman, 1979; mem. Wash. State U. Pres.'s Commn. on Status of Women, 1985-88; mem. Wash. State U. Pres.'s Commn. on Status of Minorities, 1989—, Wash. State U. Pres.'s Child Care Com.; mem. leadership com. Community Mobilization Against Substance Abuse, 1991, Pullman Meml. Hosp. Found. Bd, 1990—, Coll. & Univ. Pers. Assn. Coord. NW Region, 1991—; Wash. State U. Pres'. Commn. on Status of Individuals with Disabilities. Mem. NAFE, NW Women's Studies Assn., Coll. and Univ. Personnel Assn., Lakewood Rsch. Tng. Group, Wash. State U. Alumni Assn., Phi Delta Kappa. Office: Wash State U French Adminstrn 232 Pullman WA 99164-1014

MEYER, STEVEN JOHN, electrical engineer; b. Glendale, Calif., Mar. 17, 1961; s. Albert John and Diane (Whitehead) M.; m. Wendy Dawn Fullmer, Apr. 23, 1988; children: Joshua David, Trevor John. BSEE, Brigham Young U., 1987; MSEE, Calif. State U., Northridge, 1991. Elec. engring. intern Radio Free Europe, Radio Liberty, Lisbon, Portugal, 1984; elec. engr. Weapons divsn. Naval Air Warfare Ctr., China Lake, Calif., 1987—. Contbr. articles to profl. jours. Asst. scoutmaster Boy Scouts Am., Ridgecrest, Calif., 1989—. Mem. Mercury Amateur Radio Assn. Republican. Mem. LDS Ch. Office: Naval Air Warfare Ctr Weapons Divsn Code C3923 (6424) China Lake CA 93555

MEYER, THOMAS ROBERT, television product executive; b. Buffalo, Apr. 20, 1936; s. Amel Robert and Mildred Lucille M.; m. Dawn E. Shaffer, 1985. Student Purdue U., 1953-55, Alexander Hamilton Inst. Bus., 1960-62, West Coast U., 1969-72; B in Math., Thomas Edison State Coll., 1988. Sect. chief wideband systems engring. Ground Elec. Engring. and Installation Agy., Dept. Air Force, 1960-66; product mgr., systems engr. RCA Corp., Burbank, Calif., 1966-71; systems cons. Hubert Wilke, Inc., L.A., 1971-72; product mgr. Telemation, Inc., Salt Lake City, 1972-77; v.p. engring. Dynair Electronics, San Diego, 1977-92; prin. Duir Assocs., San Diego, 1992—. Recipient Bronze Zero Defects award Dept. Air Force, 1966, Tau Beta Pi Eminent Eng. award, 1987. Fellow Soc. Motion Picture and TV Engrs. (mem. task force on TV/computer digital image architecture,); mem. Soc. Broadcast Engrs. (sr.), Computer and Electronics Mktg. Assn. Rsch. and publs. on color TV tech. and optics, TV equipment and systems, application of computer to TV systems. Office: Duir Assocs 1220 Rosecrans St Ste 302 San Diego CA 92106

MEYER, URSULA, library director; b. Free City of Danzig, Nov. 6, 1927; came to U.S., 1941; d. Herman S. and Gertrud (Rosenfeld) M. BA, UCLA, 1949; M.L.S., U. So. Calif., 1953; postgrad., U. Wis., 1969. Librarian Butte County (Calif.) Library, 1961-68; asst. pub. libraries div. library devel. N.Y. State Library, Albany, 1969-72; coordinator Mountain Valley Coop. System, Sacramento, 1972-73; chmn. 49-99 Coop. Library System, Stockton, Calif., 1974-85; dir. library services Stockton-San Joaquin County Pub. Library, 1974—. Higher Edn. Title II fellow, 1968-69. Active Freedom to Read Found. Mem. ALA (council 1979-83, chmn. nominating com. 1982-83, legis. com. 1985-87), Calif. Library Assn. (pres. 1978, council 1974-82), Am. Assn. Pub. Adminstrs., Sierra Club. AAUW, LWV, Common Cause. Lodges: Rotary, Soroptimists. Office: Stockton-San Joaquin County Pub Libr 605 N El Dorado St Stockton CA 95202-1999*

MEYERS, ALBERT IRVING, chemistry educator; b. N.Y.C., Nov. 22, 1932; s. Hyman and Sylvia (Greenberg) M.; m. Joan Shepard, Aug. 10, 1957; children—Harold, Jill, Lisa. B.S., NYU, 1954, Ph.D., 1957. Research chemist Cities Service Oil Co., Cranbury, N.J., 1957-58; asst., assoc. prof., prof. La. State U., New Orleans, 1958-70; prof. Wayne State U., Detroit, 1970-72; prof. Colo. State U., Fort Collins, 1972—, disting. prof., 1986-93, John K. Stille prof. chemistry, 1993—; spl. postdoctoral fellow Harvard U., Cambridge, 1965-66; cons. G. D. Searle Co., Skokie, Ill., 1972-84, Mid-West Research Inst., Kansas City, Mo., 1974-77, Bristol-Myers Squibb Co., 1984—, NIH, Bethesda, Md., 1977-79, 85-89, Syntex Co., 1989—. Editor Jour. Am. Chem. Soc., 1980-85; contbr. over 300 articles to profl. jours. Recipient Alexander von Humboldt award Fed. Republic of Germany, 1984, Disting. Alumni award NYU, 1990; named Man of Yr., New Orleans Jaycees, 1968, Boyd Prof. La. State U., 1969. Fellow AAAS, Japan Chem. Soc.; mem. Am. Chem. Soc. (editorial adv. bd. Jour. Am. Chem. Soc. 1987-90, ACS award 1985, Colo. sect. award 1983, chmn. organic div. 1982, Arthur C. Cope scholar 1986), Royal Soc. Chemistry (silver medalist 1982), Phila. Organic Chemistry Soc. (Allan Day award 1987—). Home: 1500 Hepplewhite Ct Fort Collins CO 80526-3822 Office: Colorado State Univ Dept Chemistry Fort Collins CO 80523

MEYERS, CHARLES D., outdoor writer, newspaper columnist; b. Sicily Island, La., Oct. 30, 1937; s. Simon M. and Doris (Watson) M.; m. Jan Fuqua, Aug. 8, 1958 (div. Feb. 1983); children: Kirk, Lisa, Kara, Kevin. BS, La. State U., 1959. Reporter Am. Press newspaper, Lake Charles, La., 1960-66; writer, editor Colo. mag., Denver, 1969-71; reporter, outdoor writer Denver Post, 1966-69, ouddoor writer, columnist, 1971—. Author: Skiing the Rockies, 1979, Colorado Ski Country, 1986. Bd. dirs. Colo. Ski Mus. and Hall of Fame, Vail, 1985—. Recipient Harold Hirsch award U.S. Ski Writers, 1977, 81, 82, 88, Lowell Thomas award Colo. Ski Country USA, 1986, 90. Mem. Outdoor Writers Assn. Am., Rocky Mountain Spl. Interest Group Media (pres. 1978-80), Trout Unltd. Office: Denver Post 1560 Broadway Denver CO 80202

MEYERS, HERBERT, geophysicist; b. N.Y.C., Nov. 15, 1931; s. Sam and Pauline Meyers; m. Ethel V. Knight; children: David, Greg, Karen, Tiffany. BS in Geology, CCNY, 1958; postgrad., Am. U., 1959-64. Geophysicist Coast and Geodetic Survey, Washington, 1958-63, chief. spl. projects, 1963-66; chief earth scis. Environ. Data Service NOAA, Washington, 1966-72; chief solid earth Nat. Geophysics Data Ctr. NOAA, Boulder, Colo., 1972—; dir. World Data Ctr. for Solid Earth, Boulder, 1979—. Served to capt. USAF, 1952-55. Mem. Am. Geophys. Union, Soc. Exploration Geophysicists, Sigma Xi. Home: 986 Mcintire St Boulder CO 80303-2725 Office: NOAA 325 B'Way Boulder CO 80303

MEYERS, HOWARD CRAIG, lawyer; b. Chgo., Nov. 15, 1951; s. Spencer M. and Joyce L. (Dresdner) M.; m. Sonia Marlow-Marais, Dec. 30, 1980. BA in English, Ariz. State U., 1973, JD, 1977. Bar: Ariz. 1977. Of counsel Burch & Cracchiolo, P.A., Phoenix, Ariz. Mem. ABA, Comml. Law League of Am., Am. Bankruptcy Inst., State Bar Ariz., Maricopa County Bar Assn., Internat. Council of Shopping Ctrs., Plaza Club. Republican. Home: 6711 E Camelback Rd #65 Scottsdale AZ 85251 Office: PO Box 16882 702 E Osborn Rd Ste 200 Phoenix AZ 85011

MEYERS, JAMES WILLIAM, judge; b. Natick, Mass., Sept. 16, 1942. BSA with high honors, Bentley Coll., 1964; JD, Harvard U., 1970. Bar: Mass., Calif. Sr. acct. Ernst & Ernst, Boston, 1964-67; trial atty. criminal div. Dept. Justice, Washington, 1970-72; chief appellate sect. Office U.S. Atty., So. Dist. Calif., 1972-76; judge U.S. bankruptcy Ct. (so. dist.) Calif., San Diego, 1976—; mem. bankruptcy appellate panel Ninth Cir. Ct. of Appeals, 1985—. Mem. ABA. Office: US Bankruptcy Ct 5N9 US Courthouse 940 Front St San Diego CA 92189-0010

MEYERS, PIETER, JR., chemist; b. Oostkapelle, Zeeland, Netherlands, July 10, 1941; came to U.S., 1968; s. Pieter Sr. and Jacomina Cornelia (Daamen) M.; m. Alida Lubertha Van Den Brink, Sept. 24, 1965. Student, U. Amsterdam, Netherlands, Doctorandus, 1965, PhD, 1968. Rsch. assoc. Inst. for Nuclear Physics Rsch., Amsterdam, 1965-68, Brookhaven Nat. Lab., Upton, N.Y., 1968-69; vis. prof. Am. U., Cairo, 1969-70; rsch. collaborator Brookhaven Nat. Lab., 1970-85; rsch. chemist Met. Mus. Art, N.Y.C., 1970-76; sr. rsch. chemist Met. Mus. Art, 1976-81; sr. rsch. chemist L.A. County Mus. of Art, 1981-85, head conservation, 1985—; adj. prof. art history dept. Columbia U., N.Y.C., 1981. Fellow Internat. Inst. for Conservation of Hist. and Artistic Works, Am. Inst. Conservation (pres. 1982-84); mem. Am. Assn. Mus., Internat. Coun. of Mus. Office: LA County Mus of Art Conservation Ctr 5905 Wilshire Blvd Los Angeles CA 90036-4523

MEYERS, RICHARD STUART, college president; b. Chgo., Sept. 6, 1938; m. Yasuko Kamata, Sept. 15, 1965; children—Anne Akiko, Toni Takiko. B.M., DePaul U., 1961; M.S., U. So. Calif., 1963, Ph.D., 1971. With Inglewood Unified Sch. Dist., Calif., 1967-68; with Dept. Def. Overseas Sch. System, Tokyo, 1964-67; jr. and sr. high sch. tchr. Palos Verdes Peninsula Unified Sch. Dist., Palos Verdes, Calif., 1962-64; instr. media coordinator Grossmont Coll., El Cajon, Calif., 1968-72; dean instrn. Cerro Coso Community Coll., Ridgecrest, Calif., 1972-75, pres., 1975-78; sec. to bd. trustees, supt. and pres. Pasadena City Coll., Calif., 1978-83; pres. Western Oreg. State Coll., Monmouth, 1983—; speaker; cons. Contbr. articles to profl. jours. Bd. dirs. United Way, Salem, Oreg., 1984-89; mem. Oreg. Internat. Trade Commn., 1983-86, bd. dirs. Oreg. Symphony Assn., 1985-90, pres., 1909—. Fulbright scholar, Egypt, 1975. Fellow Am. Leadership Forum; mem. Am. Assn. State Colls. and Univs., Pi Gamma Mu , Phi Delta Kappa. Republican. Lodge: Rotary. Home: 395 College St S Monmouth OR 97361-2015 Office: Western Oreg State Coll 345 Monmouth Ave N Monmouth OR 97361-1314*

MEYERS, ROGER JOSEPH, telegram company executive; b. Kansas City, Mo., Feb. 15, 1955; married; 2 children. BFA, NYU, 1977. Founder, chief exec. officer Am. Telegram Corp., Beverly Hills, Calif., 1986—. Address: 270 N Canon # 1167 Beverly Hills CA 90210

MEYERS, THEDA MARIA, textile company executive; b. Bremen, West Germany, Feb. 16; came to U.S. 1957; d. Johann-Friedrich and Christophina E.L.J. (Fentrohs) Ficke; m. Laurence Jay Meyers, Oct. 2, 1960 (div. 1970); 1 child, Jayson Bennett. Dipl., U. Bremen, 1956; student, Fashion Inst. Tech., N.Y.C., 1960. Artist-stylist Rosewood Fabrics, N.Y.C., 1960-62; textile stylist Belding Corticelli, N.Y.C., 1962-65; chief designer Jerry Mann of Calif., L.A., 1969-74; fashion designer Sunbow Ltd., Prisma Corp., L.A., 1974-81, Frig & Frag Inc., L.A., 1981-83, Jonathan Martin, L.A., 1983-85; textile stylist, v.p. design E.M.D.A.Y., Inc., L.A., 1985-92; cons. Theda Meyers Consultancy, L.A., 1993—; part-time tchr. Fashion Inst. of Design & Merchandising, L.A., to 1974; part-time judge Trade Tech. Coll., L.A. to 1981; textile designer extensive nat. and internat. experience in womenswear apparel design and textile design. designer Calif. apparel. Mem. NAFE. Office: 600 W 9th St Ste 1003 Los Angeles CA 90015

MEYYAPPAN, A., research engineer; b. Karaikudi, Tamil Nadu, India, Aug. 12, 1949; came to U.S., 1980; s. S. Alagappan and S. Lakshmi Achi. BTech in Aero. Engring., Indian Inst. Tech., Madras, 1971, MS in Biomed. Engring., 1976; MS in Elec. and Computer Engring., U. Calif., Santa Barbara, 1984, PhD in Elec. and Computer Engring., 1989. Coun. Sci. and Indsl. Rsch. sr. rsch. fellow Indian Inst. Tech., 1976-79; teaching asst. U. Calif., 1980-84, postgrad. rschr., rsch. asst., 1984-90, asst. rsch. engr., 1989—. Contbr. articles to profl. jours. Mem. IEEE, Eta Kappa Nu. Office: U Calif Dept Elec-Computer Engring Santa Barbara CA 93106

MEZEY, ROBERT, poet, educator; b. Phila., Feb. 28, 1935; s. Ralph Abram and Clara (Mandel) M.; m. Olivia Simpson (div.); children: Naomi, Judah, Eve. Student, Kenyon Coll., 1951-53; BA, U. Iowa, 1959; postgrad., Stanford U., 1960-61. Lectr. Western Res. U., Cleve., 1963-64, Franklin & Marshall Coll., Lancaster, Pa., 1965-66; asst. prof. Fresno (Calif.) State U., 1967-68, U. Utah, Salt Lake City, 1973-76; prof., poet-in-residence Pomona Coll., Claremont, Calif., 1976—. Author: (poems) White Blossoms, 1965, The Lovemaker, 1960 (Lamont award), The Door Standing Open, 1970, Selected Translations, 1981, Evening Wind, 1988 (Bassine citation P.E.N. 1989); editor: Naked Poetry, 1968, Collected Poems of Henri Coulette. With U.S. Army, 1953-55. Fellow Ingram Merrill, 1973, 89, Guggenheim Found., 1977, Stanford U., 1960, NEA, 1987; recipient Poetry prize Am. Acad. Arts and Letters, 1982. Home: 1663 N Chattanooga Ct Claremont CA 91711-2935 Office: Pomona Coll Dept English 140 W 6th St Claremont CA 91711

MIANK, DAVID CHARLES, general contracting company executive; b. Flint, Mich., Nov. 26, 1946; s. Harlin C. and Evelyn (Melanson) M.; m. m. Teresa A. Leichtweis, Aug. 15, 1965 (div. July 1977); children: Leslie, Aaron; m. Karen E. Smith, Oct. 20, 1978 (dec. July 1991); children: Edward, Geoffrey. AA in Archtl. Design, Manatee Jr. Coll., Bradenton, Fla., 1976; BA in Psychology cum laude, U. South Fla., 1978, MA in Indsl. and Orgnl. Mgmt., 1978; postgrad., U. Calif., Irvine, 1991. Gen. supt. Harlin Industries, Flushing, Mich., 1964-68; sr. project mgr. McLean Constrn., Flint, 1068-73; pres., chief exec. officer Harlin & Sons, Inc., Sarasota, Fla., 1973-77; v.p., chief operating officer SGS Constrn., Inc., Tampa, Fla., 1977-83; v.p. estimating and bus. devel. Hughes-Townsend, Inc., Newport Beach, Calif., 1984-86; nat. dir. facility devel., architecture, engring., constrn. Taco Bell Corp., Irvine, 1986-87; pres. The Edwards Group, gen. contractors, cons., Newport Beach, 1987—; pres., chmn. bd. The Edwards Devel. Corp., Newport Beach, 1987—; asst. prof. stats. U. South Fla., Tampa, 1978-79; prof. mgmt. Manatee Jr. Coll., 1982-83. Contbr. articles to profl. publs. Mem. Rep. Inner Circle, Washington, 1991—, Constl. Rights Found., Newport Beach, 1991—. Mem. Am. Mgmt. Assn., Urban Land Inst., Nat. Assn. Indsl. and Office Parks, Newport Beach C. of C., Mortar Bd., KC, Psi Chi, Phi Theta Kappa, Omicron Delta Kappa. Office: The Edwards Group 14147 Red Hill Tustin CA 92680

MICHAEL, ERNEST ARTHUR, mathematics educator; b. Zurich, Switzerland, Aug. 26, 1925; came to U.S., 1939; s. Jakob and Erna (Sondheimer) M.; m. Colette Verger Davis, 1956 (div. 1966); children: Alan, David, Gerard; m. Erika Goodman Joseph, Dec. 4, 1966; children: Hillary, Joshua. B.A., Cornell U., 1947; M.A., Harvard U., 1948; Ph.D., U. Chgo., 1951. Mem. faculty dept. math. U. Wash., Seattle, 1953—; asst. prof. U. Wash., 1953-56, assoc. prof., 1956-60, prof., 1960—; mem. Inst. for Advanced Study, Princeton, 1951-52, 56-57, 60-61, 68, Math. Research Inst., E.T.H., Zürich, 1973-74; vis. prof. U. Stuttgart, Ger., 1978-79, U. Munich, Fed. Republic Germany, 1987, 88, 92-93. Editor: Procs. Am. Math. Soc., 1968-71, Topology and Its Applications; contbr. articles to profl. jours. Served with USNR, 1944-46. Grantee AEC; Grantee Office Nav. Research; Grantee NSF; Grantee Guggenheim Found.; Grantee Humboldt Found. Mem. Am. Math. Soc., Math. Assn. Am., ACLU, Amnesty Internat. Jewish. Home: 16751 15th Ave NW Seattle WA 98177-3842

MICHAEL, GARY G., supermarket and drug chain executive; b. 1940; married. B.S. in Bus., U. Idaho, 1962. Staff acct. Ernst & Ernst, C.P.A.s, 1964-66; with Albertson's, Inc., Boise, Idaho, 1966—, acct., 1966-68, asst. controller, 1968-71, controller, 1971-72, v.p., controller, 1972-74, sr. v.p. fin., treas., 1974-76, exec. v.p., 1976-84, vice chmn., chief fin. officer, corp. devel. officer, 1984-91, chmn., chief exec. officer, 1991—; also dir. Albertson's, Inc. Served to 1st lt. U.S. Army, 1962-64. Office: Albertson's Inc PO Box 20 250 Parkcenter Blvd Boise ID 83726

MICHAEL, JAMES DANIEL, computer scientist; b. Peoria, Ill., May 27, 1957; s. Thomas Proctor and Mary Lou (Wagner) M.; m. Judith Ann O'Donnell, June 23, 1979. BS in Psychology, U. Calif., Davis, 1978. Teller Bank of Am., Davis, 1978-79, Fresno, Calif., 1979; computer operator Fresno County Computer Svcs., 1979-81; computer programmer Gesco Corp., Fresno, 1981-83, systems programmer, 1983-89; supr. operating systems support Calif. State U., Fresno, 1989—. Co-author: The Porter Tract - An Historical and Architectural Survey, 1990; contbr. articles to profl. publs. Mem. Fresno City and County Hist. Soc., 1989—; founding mem. Landmarks Preservation Coun., Fresno, 1991—, Tree Fresno, 1987—; mem. Fresno Zool. Soc. Mem. Assn. for Computing Machinery, Nat. Systems Programmer Assn. Democrat. Office: Calif State U CCMS 2225 E San Ramon Ave Fresno CA 93740-0093

MICHAEL, PATRICK DOYLE, insurance company executive; b. Port Arthur, Tex., Sept. 7, 1952; s. Harold D. and Dorothy P. (Stafford) M.; m. Pattie Sue Peyton, Aug. 1, 1970; children: John Bradley, Brandon Keith, Mary Robin. BBA, Methodist Coll., Fayetteville, N.C., 1981. CLU. Enlisted U.S. Army, 1971, advanced through grades to 1st lt., 1979, resigned, 1979; gen. agt., owner Independent Fin. Programming, Fayetteville, 1979-82; new bus. mgr. Am. Nat. Ins. Co., Galveston, Tex., 1982-84; gen. mgr., controller East Bay Enterprises, Crystal Beach, Tex., 1984; asst. v.p. policy adminstrn. Am. Founders Life, Austin, Tex., 1984-86; v.p. ops. Exec. Life Ins. Co., L.A., 1986—. 2d lt. USNG, 1981-84. Methodist Coll. scholar, 1982. Fellow Life Mgmt. Inst. c. (v.p. 1990, pres. 1991). Republican. Home: 3427 Indian Mesa Dr Thousand Oaks CA 91360-1133 Office: Exec Life Ins Co 11444 W Olympic Blvd Los Angeles CA 90064-1507

MICHAELS, MARY BETH, artist; b. Alameda, Calif., Oct. 12, 1949; d. Orrin Howard and Norma (Miller) Harder; m. Sidney W. Michaels, Aug. 1, 1988. BA in Art History, U. Calif., Berkeley, 1971; BFA in Printmaking, U. Alaska, 1984. Lectr. drawing U. Alaska, Fairbanks, 1986, prodr. exhibits Univ. Mus., 1986-89; exhibits designer Noel Wien Libr., Fairbanks, 1986-87; arts corr. All Alaska Weekly, Fairbanks, 1990-91; freelance art reviewer, critic Fairbanks Daily News-Miner, 1984—; juror art shows, 1988, 90, 91; artist-in-sch. Weller Sch., Fairbanks, 1992, Bettles Sch., Fairbanks, 1984, Brown's Sch., Clear, Alaska, 1984, also others. One-woman shows include Stonington Gallery, Anchorage, 1988, 89, Civ. Ctr. Gallery, Fairbanks, 1988, 92; exhibited in group shows at Anchorage Mus. History and Art, 1984, 86, Fine Arts Gallery at U. Alaska, 1987, 89, 90, Civ. Ctr. Gallery, Fairbanks, 1988-91. Recipient purchase award Alaska Art Bank, 1979, 86, 1st place for graphics 2d Ann. Audubon Exhbn., Anchorage, 1980; travel grantee Alaska Coun. on Arts, 1991. Mem. Fairbanks Arts Assn. (visual arts com. 1987—), Visual Arts Ctr. Alaska. Home and Studio: PO Box 40045 Clear AK 99704

MICHAELS, PATRICK FRANCIS, broadcasting company executive; b. Superior, Wis., Nov. 5, 1925; s. Julian and Kathryn Elizabeth (Keating) M.; A.A., U. Melbourne, 1943; B.A., Golden State U., 1954; Ph.D., London U., 1964; m. Paula Naomi Bowen, May 1, 1960; children—Stephanie Michelle, Patricia Erin. War corr. CBS; news editor King Broadcasting, 1945-50; war corr. Mid-East Internat. News Service, 1947-49; war corr. MBS, Korea, 1950-53; news dir. Sta. WSDU-AM-FM-TV, 1953-54; fgn. corr. NBC, S. Am., 1954-56; news dir. Sta. KWIZ, 1956-59; commentator ABC, Los Angeles, 1959-62; fgn. corr. Am. News Services, London, 1962-64; news commentator McFadden Bartell Sta. KCBQ, 1964-68; news commentator ABC, San Francisco, 1968-70; news dir. Sta. KWIZ, Santa Ana, Calif., 1970-74, station mgr., 1974-81; pres. Sta. KWRM, Corona, Calif., Sta. KQLH, San Bernardino, Calif., 1981-88; chmn. Michaels Media, Corona del Mar, Calif., 1988—. Bd. dirs. Econ. Devel. Corp. Mem. Nat. Assn. Broadcasters (bd. dirs.), Calif. Broadcasters Assn. (v.p.), Am. Fedn. TV and Radio Artists, Orange County Broadcasters Assn. (pres.), Sigma Delta Chi (ethics com.). Republican. Clubs: Rotary, Balboa Bay (bd. govs.), South Shore Yacht, Internat. Yachting Fellowship of Rotarians (staff commodore). Home: 816 Gardenia Way Corona Del Mar CA 92625-1544

MICHALIK, EDWARD FRANCIS, construction company executive; b. Hartford, Conn., Apr. 4, 1946; s. Edward S. and Helen A. (Sito) M.; m. Dianne E. Del Cegno, 1967 (div. 1978); children: Marc Edward, Michael Donald; m. Cecilia C. Zoltanski, 1987; children: Alexander Edward, Gabrielle Therese. BBA, Nichols Coll., Dudley, Mass., 1969. Cost auditor Wigton-Abbott Corp., Plainfield, N.J., 1969-70; dir. cost control The John W. Cowper Co., Inc., Buffalo, 1970-73; v.p. Titan Group Inc., Paramus, N.J., 1973-76; exec. v.p. Harrison Western Corp., Denver, 1976-85; pres. The John W. Cowper Co., Inc., Buffalo, 1985-88, Adrian Devel., Inc., Buffalo and Denver, 1988—; pres., chief exec. officer, bd. dirs. Sunburst Excavation, Inc., Denver, 1991—. Member: Soc. Am. Mil. Engrs., Associated Gen. Contractors of Am., The Beavers. Republican.

MICHALIK, JOHN JAMES, law school administrator; b. Bemidji, Minn., Aug. 1, 1945; s. John and Margaret Helen (Pafko) M.; m. Diane Marie Olson, Dec. 21, 1968; children: Matthew John, Nicole, Shane. BA, U. Minn., 1967, JD, 1970. Legal editor Lawyers Coop. Pub. Co., Rochester, N.Y., 1970-75; dir. continuing legal edn. Wash. State Bar Assn., Seattle, 1975-81, exec. dir., 1981-91; asst. dean devel. & community rels. Sch. of Law U. Wash., 1991. Mem. Am. Soc. Assn. Execs., Nat. Assn. Bar Execs., Am. Mgmt. Assn., Am. Judicature Soc. Univ. Faculty Club, Coll. Club Seattle. Lutheran. Office: U Wash Sch of Law 1100 NE Campus Pky Seattle WA 98105-6617

MICHAUD, DAVID L., protective services official. Student, Met. State Coll., U. Denver, FBI Acad., Quantico, Va., Northwestern U., Denver Police Dept. Tng. Acad. Patrol officer Colo. Police Dept., Ft. Lupton; sgt. Colo. Sheriff's Dept., Weld County; with Denver Police Dept., 1967—, detective, 1970-75, sgt., 1975-83, supr. spl. crime attack team, 1975-80, comdr. spl. crimes bur., 1980-86, lt., 1983-87, capt., 1987-91, comdr. internal investigations and inspection bur., 1987-89, comdr. urban st. crime bur., 1989-91, divsn. chief staff svcs. divsn., 1991-92, divsn. chief traffic divsn., 1991-92, chief of police, 1992—; instr. Denver Police Tng. Acad.; cert. instr. Colo. Law Enforcement Tng. Acad.; speaker in field. Author: (with J.M. MacDonald) The Confession: Interrogation and Criminal Profiles for Police Officers, 1987. Active N.E. Denver Community Youth Forum, City Pk. Pavilion Task Force, N.W. Denver Gang Eradication Task Force, Gov.'s Job Tng. Office Task Force, Denver Pub. Schs. Gang Task Force; bd. dirs. N.E. Denver Coalition Against Drugs. Sgt. USMC. Recipient Cert. of Merit, Manual High Sch., Denver Pub. Schs., 1990, Officer of Yr. award Hispanic Pub. Affairs Com., 1990, Cert. of Appreciation, Pk. Hill Community Safe Neighborhoods, 1991, 58 Letters of Commendation various law enforcement sources. Office: Police Dept 1331 Cherokee St Denver CO 80204*

MICHAUD, GERALD FREDRICK, media advocacy nonprofit executive; b. Rochester, N.Y., June 16, 1949; s. Eric Joseph and Dorothy (Daigle) M.; m. Jennifer Italiano, May 1, 1982. BA magna cum laude, U. Detroit, 1971, MA, 1975; postgrad., Loyola U., New Orleans, 1975. Asst. dir., writer Alba House Communications, Canfield, Ohio, 1972-73; dir. Alba House Media, Detroit, 1973-75; pub. rels. Youth for Understanding, Ann Arbor, Mich., 1975-79; editor EDM Digest, Farmington, Mich., 1978-80; creative dir., v.p. Dimon and Assocs. Advt., Burbank, Calif., 1980-87; exec. dir. End Hunger Network, Beverly Hills, Calif., 1987—; bd. dirs., chief exec. officer End Hunger Network, Beverly Hills; mem. exec. com. InterAction, Washington. Graphic designer (TV spl.) End Hunger Televent, 1983, Live Aid, 1985; editor jour. Nutrition, 1985-87. Co-chmn. Prime Time to End Hunger, 1989. Recipient John Vismara award U. Detroit, 1971, Pioneer Gold award Creative Direct Mktg. Guild West, 1993. Democrat. Roman Catholic. Home: 15215 Magnolia Blvd Apt 103 Sherman Oaks CA 91403-1116 Office: End Hunger Network 365 Sycamore Rd Santa Monica CA 90402

MICHEL, DIANE CAROL, missionary; b. Englewood Cliffs, N.J., Jan. 23, 1958; d. Joseph Francis and Patricia Ann (Mattern) Hickey; m. Jeffrey Earl Michel, Mar. 26, 1988; children: Ruth, Matthew, Luke. B in Nursing, U. Fla., 1981. Labor and delivery staff nurse Shands Teaching Hosp., Gainesville, Fla., 1981-83, labor and delivery charge nurse, 1984-86; missionary Wycliffe Bible Translators, Brussels, Belgium, 1989-90, Ivory Coast, Africa, 1990-91; U.S., 1992—. Mem. Sigma Theta Tau. Home: 2525 Old Tavern Rd Apt 19 Lisle IL 60532 Office: Wycliffe Bible Translators PO Box 2727 Huntington Beach CA 92647

MICHEL, MARY ANN KEDZUF, nursing educator; b. Evergreen Park, Ill., June 1, 1939; d. John Roman and Mary (Bassar) Kedzuf; m. Jean Paul Michel, 1974. Diploma in nursing, Little Company of Mary Hosp., Evergreen Park, 1960; B.S. in Nursing, Loyola U., Chgo., 1964; M.S., No. Ill. U., 1968, Ed.D., 1971. Staff nurse Little Co. of Mary Hosp., 1960-64; instr. Little Co. of Mary Hosp. (Sch. Nursing), 1964-67, No. Ill. U., DeKalb, 1968-69; asst. prof. No. Ill. U., 1969-71; chmn. dept. nursing U. Nev., Las Vegas, 1971-73; prof. nursing U. Nev., 1975—, dean Coll. Health Scis., 1973-90; pres. PERC, Inc.; mgmt. cons., 1993—; mgmt. cons. Nev. Donor Network, 1993; mem. So. Nev. Health Manpower Task Force, 1975; mem. manpower com. Plan Devel. Commn., Clark County Health System Agy., 1977-79, mem. governing body, 1981-86; mem. Nev. Health Coordinating Coun.,, Western Inst. Nursing, 1971-85; mem. coordinating com. assembly instnl. adminstrs. dept. allied health edn. and accreditation AMA, 1985-88; mem. bd. advs. So. Nev. Vocat. Tech. Ctr., 1976-80; sec.-treas. Nev. Organ Referral Svcs., 1988-89, bd. dirs., 1988-90. Contbr. articles to profl. jours. Trustee Desert Spring Hosp., Las Vegas, 1976-85; bd. dirs. Nathan Adelson Hospice, 1982-88, Bridge Counseling Assocs., 1982, Everywoman's Ctr., 1984-86; chmn. Nev. Commn. on Nursing Edn., 1972-73, Nursing Articulation Com., 1972-73, Yr. of Nurse Com., 1978; moderator Invitational Conf. Continuing Edn., Asm. Soc. Allied Health Professions, 1978; active Nev. Donor Network, Donor Organ Recovery, S.W. Eye and Tissue Banks. NIMH fellow, 1967-68. Fellow Am. Soc. Allied Health Professions (chmn. nat. resolutions com. 1981-84, treas. 1988-90, sec's. award com. 1982-83, 92-93, nat. by-laws com. 1985, conv. chmn. 1987); mem. AAUP, Am. Nurses Assn., Nev. Nurses Assn. (dir. 1975-77, treas. 1977-79, conv. chmn. 1978), So. Nev. Area Health Edn. Coun., Western Health Deans (co-organizer 1985, chair, 1988-90), Nat. League Nursing, Nev. Heart Assn., So. Nev. Mem. Hosps. (mem. nursing recruitment com. 1981-83, mem. nursing practice com. 1983-85), Las Vegas C. of C., Phi Kappa Phi (chpt. sec. 1981-83, pres.-elect 1983, pres. 1984, v.p. Western region 1989—, editorial bd. jour. Nat. Forum 1989—), Alpha Beta Gamma (hon.), Sigma Theta Tau, Zeta Kappa. Club: Slovak Catholic Sokols. Office: U Nev Las Vegas 4505 S Maryland Pky Las Vegas NV 89154-0002

MICHEL, VICTOR JAMES, JR., retired librarian; b. St. Louis, Feb. 2, 1927; s. Victor James and Bernadette (Fox) M.; student St. Louis U., 1946-48; m. Margaret A. Renaud, Feb. 3, 1951; children: Dennis W., Daniel J., Catherine A., Denise M. Asst. librarian McDonnell Aircraft Corp., St. Louis, 1948-55; mgr. Anaheim (Calif.) Information Center, Electronics Ops., Rockwell Internat. Corp., 1955-84; pres. V.J. Michel Inc., Grass Valley, Calif., 1986—; sec. Placentia Devel. Co., 1964-71. Charter mem. Placentia-Tlaquepaque Sister City Orgn., 1964-84; founder, pres. Placentia chpt. St. Louis Browns Fan Club. Planning commr., Placentia, Calif., 1957-60, city councilman, 1960-70, vice-mayor, 1960-64, mayor, 1964-68. Trustee Placentia Library Dist., 1970-79, pres., 1974-79; city historian, Placentia, 1976-84, city treas., 1980-84; chmn. Placentia Fine Arts Commn., 1978-80. Served from pvt. to staff sgt. AUS, 1945-46. Named Placentia Citizen of Yr., 1979. Mem. Placentia C. of C. (v.p. 1960), Placentia Jaycees (hon. life), Calif., Orange County (pres. 1976) library assns. Democrat. Roman Catholic. Club: West Atwood Yacht (hon. yeoman emeritus with citation 1970, ship's librarian). Author: Pictorial History of the West Atwood Yacht Club, 1966; Placentia—Around the World, 1970; also articles in profl. jours. Home: 107 Bernadine Ct Grass Valley CA 95949-9480

MICHELS, ALAN, financial executive; b. Passaic, N.J., Mar. 4, 1950; s. Emmanuel and Faye (Galonsky) M.; m. Catherine Jayne Mills, Apr. 1, 1978; 1 child, Erin Lynn. BA, Rutgers Coll., 1972; MBA in Fin., Rutgers U., 1974. Exec. fin. programmer RCA Corp., N.Y.C., 1974-75; internat. acct. RCA Solid State Div., Somerville, N.J., 1975-76; fin. analyst RCA Globcom, N.Y.C., 1976-78, mgr. budgets, 1978-80, mgr. fin. analysis, 1980-82; dir. group fin. communications group RCA Corp., N.Y.C., 1982-85; dir. fin. analysis RCA Globcom, Piscataway, N.J., 1985-87; dir. corp. fin. Diversified Cos. U.S. West, Denver, 1987-88; v.p. finance and adminstrn. Applied Communications, Inc. (US West subs.), Omaha, Nebr., 1988-91; v.p. fin., treas., CFO U.S. West Cellular, Bellevue, Wash., 1992—. Advisor Rutgers Undergrad. Alumni Assn., Piscataway, N.J., 1976-79. Home: 14103 216th Way NE Woodinville WA 98072-5815 Office: US West Cellular Bellevue WA 98009-2216

MICHELS, ELIZABETH FRANCES, international economist; b. Fayetteville, N.C., Mar. 16, 1959; d. John Henry and Helen Faye (Kondracki) McMinn; 1 child, Christopher Patrick. BS in Fgn. Svc., Georgetown U., 1979; MA in Internat. Econs., Johns Hopkins U., Washington, 1985. Internat. economist U.S. Internat. Trade Adminstrn., U.S. Dept. Commerce, Washington, 1985-86, U.S. Dept. Treasury, Washington, 1986-87; industry economist IRS, San Francisco, 1988-89; study abroad advisor City Coll. San Francisco, 1990-93; economist Bank of Am., San Francisco, 1993—; admissions interviewer, recruiter Georgetown U., Washington and San Francisco, 1988—; cons. Accent Internat. Edn. Programs Abroad, Ltd., San Francisco, 1991-92. Instr. religion St. Gabriel's Parish, San Francisco, 1990—; career advisor Alumnae Resources, San Francisco, 1992—. Recipient award for sustained superior performance U.S. Civil Svc., Goeppingen, Germany, 1981; scholar Nat. Spanish Contest, 1974; fellow Army Officers Wives Club Greater Washington Area, 1983. Mem. Am. Econ. Assn., Nat. Assn. Bus. Economists, World Affairs Coun. No. Calif., Georgetown U. Alumni Club. Roman Catholic. Home: 1606 Graystone Ln Daly City CA 94014

MICHELSON, HAROLD, production designer; b. N.Y.C., Feb. 15, 1920; s. Max and Gussie (Reichel) M.; m. Lillian Farber, Dec. 14, 1947; children: Alan Bruce, Eric Neil, Dennis Paul. Student, Pratt Inst., 1938, NYU, 1939, Art Students League, N.Y.C., 1945-47, Calif. Sch. Art, L.A., 1947-49. Illustrator Columbia Pictures, L.A., 1949-52; illustrator Paramount Pictures, L.A., 1953-58, art dir., prodn. designer, 1959-89; illustrator Warner Bros., Burbank, Calif., 1959-89; art dir. 20th Century Fox, Beverly Hills, Calif., 1959-89, visual cons., 1990-91; ind. prodn. designer, Hollywood, Calif., 1959-89; visual cons. Metro-Goldwyn-Mayer, Hollywood, 1992—; lectr. U. So. Calif., L.A., 1988-91; instr. UCLA, 1989-90, Maine Photog. Workshop, Rockport, Maine, 1991; mem. faculty Am. Film Inst., L.A., 1992. Exhibited in group show Storyboard-Le Cinema Dessiná, 1992. 1st lt. USAAF, 1941-45, ETO. Decorated Air medal with 7 oak leaf clusters. Mem. Soc. Motion Picture Art Dirs. (exec. bd. 1985—), Acad. Motion Picture Arts and Scis. (membership bd. 1975—, 2 Acad. award nominations 1978, 84).

MICHELSON, SONIA, music educator, author; b. L.A., Feb. 14, 1928; d. Maurice and Elizabeth (Jacobs) Saeta; m. Irving Michelson, Apr. 4, 1954 (div. Aug. 1982); children: Ann Michelson Shoham, Louis E., Hadassah Zelman, Zahava Waldman, Elisheva Levin, Eliyahu Michaeli, Jack. BA, U. Calif., Berkeley, 1949. Instr. in guitar Suzuki Music Acad. of Chgo., 1980-81, Music Arts Sch., Highland Park, Ill., 1973-82; dir. in classical guitar Michelson Classic Guitar Studio, Chgo., 1973-88; dir. Michelson Classic Guitar Studio, L.A., 1988—; cons. Music Educators Nat. Conf., Atlantic City, N.J., 1976; columnist Guitar Found. of Am., L.A., 1984—. Author: Easy Classic Guitar Solos, 1977, Classical Guitar Study, 1982, New Dimensions in Classical Guitar for Children, 1984; contbr. articles to profl. jours. Mem. Am. String Tchrs. Assn. (spl. cons. 1977-85), Chgo. Classical Guitar Soc. (pres. 1978-88), Guitar Found. of Am. (mem. editorial bd. 1972—), Suzuki Assn. Am., Nat. Music Tchrs. Assn., Music Tchrs. Assn. Calif. Democrat. Jewish. Home: 1465 Reeves St Los Angeles CA 90035-2945

MICKELSON, ARLENE JO, artist; b. Seattle, Nov. 29, 1938; d. Hurley Vernon and Jesse Audrey (McLean) Boggess; m. Duane Thomas Mickelson, Sept. 9, 1959 (div. 1992); children: Tamara Ann, Craig Thomas, Bradley Jon. Student, U. Wash., 1957-59, Bellevue (Wash.) C.C., 1978-79, Pratt Sch. Fine Arts, 1979-81, 92; studied with Munemori Makino, Shizuoka, Japan, 1988. Pres. Mickelson Fine Arts, Inc., Issaquah, Wash., 1960—; tchr., cons. Issaquah (Wash.) Sch. Dist., 1978-79, artist in residence, 1980-81. Exhibited in group shows at N N Gallery, Seattle, 1976, 77, Fairtree Gallery, New York, 1978, Yakima (Wash.) Western Arts Show, 1981, Issaquah Gallery, 1981, Annual Nat. Western Art Show and Auction, Ellensburg, Wash., 1982, 83, 84, Museum of Native Am. Culture Nat. Western Art Show, 1983, 84, 85, Spokane, Wash., 1983, Western Americana Art Show and Auction, C.M. Russel Western Art Show , Great Falls, Mont., 1984, 85, the Artique, Ltd., 1989, Nat. Contemporary Exposition of Artists of Achievement, 1989, Friendship Force World Conf., Shizuoka, Japan, 1989, Visual Individualists United show, Stuhr Mus., Grand Island, Nebr., 1989, C.W. Post Coll., Long Island U., N.Y., 1990, 1991, Edmonds (Wash.) Art Festival, 1990, Mercer Island (Wash.) Visual Arts League Show, 1990, Wolf Walker Gallery, Sedona, Ariz., 1990; one woman shows include Issaquah (Wash.) Gallery, 1983, 87, and the Blue Heron Gallery, Portland, Oreg.; represented in permanent collections including the Favell Mus., Klamath Falls, Oreg., Seattle First Nat. Bank, Safeco Ins. Co., Seattle, Western Industrial Supply, Inc., Portland, Oreg., Honeywell Corp., Mukilteo, Wash., Alaska Pacific U., Anchorage, St. Joseph Hosp., Portland, Oreg. Alaska Cruise and Expeditions, Shizuoka City (Japan) Offices, Kanuma Coll., Kanuma-Shi, Tochigi-Ken, Japan. Recipient Best of Show Sculpture for "Sitka Jack" Annual Nat. Western Art Show and Auction, 1983, for "The Eternal Battle" Western Americana Art Show and Auction, 1983, for Raven's Discovery Contemporary Artists of Acheivement, 1992; award for "Beneath Eagles Shadow" NAFE. Unitarian.

MICKELSON, H(ERALD) FRED, electric utility executive; b. Pratt, Kans., Oct. 4, 1938; s. Herald E. and Arvilla (Knight) M.; m. D. Joan Mickelson, Feb. 21, 1958; children: Mikel Tod, Janet Lynn. BS in Mgmt. Sci., Pepperdine U., 1974; postgrad. Mgmt. Policy Inst., U. So. Calif., 1978. Dist. mgr. So. Calif. Edison, Santa Ana, 1982-84; mgr. corp. communications So. Calif. Edison, Rosemead, 1984-85; div. ops. mgr. So. Calif. Edison, Santa Ana, 1985-86, San Bernardino, 1986-87; mgr. mktg. So. Calif. Edison, Rosemead, 1987-91; regional v.p. So. Calif. Edison, Santa Ana, 1992—. Officer, bd. dirs. Calif. div. Am. Cancer Soc.; exec. com., bd. dirs. United Way of Orange County, ARC of Orange County; bd. dirs. St. Joseph's Hosp. of Orange; adv. bd. St. Jude's Hosp. of Fullerton, Sch. Bus. and Econs. Chapman U.; bd. dirs. Nat. Conf. Christians and Jews, Orange County Bus. Com. for the Arts, Orgn. Unified Concerned Homeowners; bd. govs. Orange County Human Rels. Coun.; mem. Indsl. League Orange County, Orange County Transp. Coalition. Recipient Field Svcs. Builder award Am. Cancer Soc., 1992. Mem. Edison Elec. Inst. (customer svc. and mktg. bd. dirs.), Pacific Coast Elec. Assn. (customer svc. and mktg. exec. com.), Orange County C. of C. (bd. dirs.). Republican. Mem. Evangelical Free Ch. Office: So Calif Edison Co 1325 S Grand Ave Santa Ana CA 92705

MICKELSON, SIG, broadcasting executive, educator; b. Clinton, Minn., May 24, 1913; s. Olaf and Harriet (Reinholdson) M.; m. Maybelle Brown, June 8, 1940 (dec. Apr. 1985); children: Karen Ann (Mrs. Christiaan De Brauw), Alan; m. Elena Mier y Teran, June 14, 1986. B.A., Augustana Coll., 1934, LLD, 1987; M.A., U. Minn., 1940. With CBS, N.Y.C., 1943-61; pres. CBS News, 1954-61; v.p., dir. Time-Life Broadcast, Inc., N.Y.C., 1961-70, Ency. Brit. Ednl. Corp., Chgo., 1970-72; prof., chmn. editorial dept. Medill Sch. Journalism, Northwestern U., Evanston, Ill., 1972-75; pres. RFE/RL, Inc., Washington, 1975-78; Disting. vis. prof. San Diego State U., 1978-79, exec. dir. Ctr. for Communications, 1979-82, adj. prof, 1984-90, Van Deerlin prof. communications, 1989-90; pres. San Diego Communications Coun., 1989-90; Manship prof. journalism La. State U., 1991-93; research fellow Hoover Instn., 1981—; advisor Nat. News Council, 1973-80; ex-officio Bd. Internat. Broadcasting, 1975-78; dir. Stauffer Communications Inc. Author: The Electric Mirror, 1972, America's Other Voice, 1983, The First Amendment: The Challenge of New Technology, 1989, From Whistle Stop to Sound Bite, 1989, The Northern Pacific Railroad and the Selling of the West, 1993. Bd. regents Augustana Coll., 1983—. Mem. Radio TV News Dirs. Assn. (founder; v.p. 1946-48, pres. 1948-49), Internat. Inst. for Communications (founder; chmn. 1970-71, chmn. exec. com. 1967-70, 71-73), Council on Fgn. Relations, Soc. Profl. Journalists, Sigma Delta Chi. Clubs: Century Assn. (N.Y.C.); Cosmos (Washington). Home: 6443 Pasatiempo San Diego CA 92120

MIDDLEBROOK, GRACE IRENE, nurse, educator; b. L.A., Mar. 5, 1927; d. Joel P. and Betty (Larson) Soderberg; dip. West Suburban Hosp., 1950; BS in Nursing, Wheaton Coll., 1951; MEdn Ariz. State U., 1965, EdD, 1970; m. Albert William Middlebrook, July 7, 1950; children: Alberta Elizabeth, Jo Anne. Office nurse, Dr. G.A. Hemwall, Chgo., 1950-51; supr. Bates Meml. Hosp., Bentonville, Ark., 1955-58; instr. Sparks Meml. Hosp. Sch. Nursing, Ft. Smith, Ark., 1959-61; instr., coord. med.-surg. nursing Sch. of Nursing, Good Samaritan Hosp., Phoenix, 1961-64, asst. dir. Sch. Nursing, 1964-73, dir. edn. and tng., 1968-80; corp. dir. edn. Samaritan Health Svc., Phoenix, 1969—; adj. prof. Samaritan Coll. Nursing, Grand Canyon U. Mem. speakers bur. Sch. Career Days, 1970—. Recipient award for leadership co-op programs Phoenix Union High Sch., 1980, Sammy award Samaritan Health Svc. and Samaritan Med. Found., 1981. Mem. Am. Hosp. Assn., Nat. League Nursing, Ariz. League for Nursing, Adult Edn. Assn., Ariz. Heart Assn. (instr.), Pi Lambda Theta, Kappa Delta Pi, Sigma Theta Tau. Home: 4242 N 15th Dr Phoenix AZ 85015-4711 Office: Samaritan Health Svc Edn Ctr 1441 N 12th St Phoenix AZ 85006

MIDDLEBROOK, R. DAVID, electrical engineering educator. BA, Cambridge (Eng.) U., 1952, MA, 1956; MS, Stanford U., 1953, PhD, 1955. Sr. tech. instr., mem. trade testing bd. Radio Sch. No. 3, Royal Air Force, Eng., 1947-49; asst. prof. electrical engring. Calif. Inst. Tech., Pasedena, 1955-58, assoc. prof., 1958-65, prof., 1965—; mem. hon. editorial adv. bd. Solid State Electronics, 1960-74; mem. WESCON tech. program com., 1964; lectr. 23 univs. and cos. in Eng., The Netherlands, Germany, 1965-66; mem. rsch. and tech. adv. coun. com. on space propulsion and power, NASA, 1976-77; gen. chmn. Calif. Inst. Tech. Indsl. Assocs. Conf. Power Electronics, 1982; cons. in field. Author: An Introduction to Transistor Theory, 1957, Differential Amplifiers, 1963, (with S. Cuk) Advances in Switched-Mode Power Conversion, Vols. I and II, 1981, 2d edit., 1983, Vol. III, 1983; mem. editorial bd. Internat. Jour. Electronics, 1976-82; presented 77 profl. papers; patentee in field. Recipient I*R 100 award Indsl. Rsch. Mag., 1980, award for the Best Use of Graphics Powercon 7, 1980, Powercon 8, 1981, PCIM award for Leadership in Power Electronics Edn., 1990, Edward Longstreth Medal Franklin Inst., 1991. Fellow IEEE (exec com. San Gabriel Valley section, 1964-65, treas. 1977-78, gen. chmn. poer electronics specialists conf. 1973, AES-S electrical power/energy systems panel 1977-87, William E. Newell Power Electronics award 1982, program chmn. applied electronics conf. 1986, 87), Institution Electrical Engrs.; mem. Inst. Radio Engrs. (Honorable Mention award 1958, subcom. 4.1 1956-62, chmn. L.A. chpt., 1960-61, vice chmn. Pasadena subsect. 1960-61), Sigma Xi. Office: Calif Inst of Tech Engring & Applied Sci 116-81 Pasadena CA 91125

MIDDLETON, ANTHONY WAYNE, JR., urologist, educator; b. Salt Lake City, May 6, 1939; s. Anthony Wayne and Dolores Caravena (Lowry) M.; BS, U. Utah, 1963; MD, Cornell U., 1966; m. Carol Samuelson, Oct. 23, 1970; children: Anthony Wayne, Suzanne, Kathryn, Jane, Michelle. Intern, U. Utah Hosps., Salt Lake City, 1966-67; resident in urology Mass. Gen. Hosp., Boston, 1970-74; practice urology Middleton Urol. Assocs., Salt Lake City, 1974—; mem. staff Primary Children's Hosp., staff pres., 1981-82; mem. staff Latter-Day Saints Hosp., Holy Cross Hosp.; assoc. clin. prof. surgery U. Utah Med. Coll., 1977—; vice chmn. bd. govs. Utah Med. Self-Ins. Assn., 1980-81, chmn. 1985-87. Bd. dirs. Utah chpt. Am. Cancer Soc., 1978-86; bishop, later stake presidency Ch. Jesus Christ Latter-day Saints; vice chmn. Utah Med. Polit. Action Com., 1978-81, chmn., 1981-83; chmn. Utah Physicians for Reagan, 1983-84; mem. U. Utah Coll. Medicine Dean's Search Com., 1983-84; bd. dirs. Utah Symphony, 1985—. Capt. USAF, 1968-70. Mem. ACS, Utah State Med. Assn. (pres. 87-88), Am. Urologic Assn. (socioecons. com. 1987—), AMA (alt. del. to House of Dels. 1989-92), Salt Lake County Med. Assn. (sec. 1965-67, pres. liaison com. 1980-81, pres.-elect 1981-83, pres. 1984), Utah Urol. Assn. (pres. 1976-77), Salt Lake Surg. Soc. (treas. 1977-78), Am. Assn. Clin. Urologists (bd. dirs. 1989-90, nat. pres. elect 1990-91, pres. 1991-92, nat. bd. chmn. urologic polit. action com. 1992—), Phi Beta Kappa, Alpha Omega Alpha, Beta Theta Pi (chpt. pres. Gamma Beta 1962). Republican. Contbr. articles to profl. jours. Home: 2798 Chancellor Pl Salt Lake City UT 84108-2835 Office: 1060 W 1st S Salt Lake City UT 84102-1501

MIDDLETON, BLACKFORD, internist, educator; b. Montclair, N.J., Oct. 11, 1957; s. Elliott Jr. and Elizabeth (Blackford) M.; m. Ursula G. King, Sept. 12, 1987. BA, U. Colo., 1979; MPH, Yale U., 1981; MD, SUNY, Buffalo, 1985; MSc, Stanford U., 1991. Diplomate Am. Bd. Internal Medicine. Student rsch. intern Beth Israel Hosp., Boston, summers 1975-76; resident in internal medicine U. Conn. Health Ctr., Farmington; adminstrv. asst. USPHS Hosp., Norfolk, Va., summer 1980; physican specialist Stanford (Calif.) U. Med. Ctr., 1989—, clin. asst. prof. medicine, 1990—, acting chief internal medicine, 1991; CFO Inst. for Decision Systems Rsch., Palo Alto, Calif., 1991—; med. dir. clin. info. systems Stanford U. Hosp., 1992—; cons. Lexical Tech. Inc., Alameda, Calif., 1989-91, Knowledge Data Systems Inc., Larkspur, Calif., 1991—; speaker in field. Contbr. articles to profl. jours. U. Colo. regent scholar; Glenn H. Leak meml. cancer fellow, 1983; Buffalo Found. student rsch. grantee, 1982. Mem. Am. Coll. Physicians, Am. Med. Infomatics Assn., Am. Fedn. for Clin. Rsch., Soc. for Gen. Internal Medicine, Soc. for Med. Decision Making, Assn. for Health Svcs. Rsch. Office: Stanford U Med Ctr MSOB X214 Stanford CA 94305-5475

MIDDLETON, CHARLES RONALD, educator, academic dean; b. Hays, Kans., Sept. 16, 1944; s. Charles Buster and Dorothy Bryant (Parsons) M.; m. Sandra Leigh Paulson, Dec. 19, 1964 (div. Jan. 1979); children: Charles Christopher, Kevin Andrew, Kathryn Gillian. AB with honors, Fla. State U., 1965; MA, Duke U., 1967, PhD, 1969. Asst. prof. U. Colo., Boulder, 1969-77, assoc. prof., 1977-85, asst. dean, 1979-80, prof. history, 1985—, assoc. dean Coll. Arts and Scis., 1980-88, dean Coll. Arts and Scis., 1988—. Contbr. articles to profl. jours. Bd. dirs. Found. for World Health, Denver and Boulder, 1985-87, Boulder County AIDS project (hon.), 1990—. Recipient Faculty Teaching Excellence award U. Colo., Boulder, 1978; research grantee Am. Philos. Soc., 1977, U. Colo., 1972. Fellow Royal Hist. Soc.; mem. North Am. Conf. on Brit. Studies, Western Conf. on Brit. Studies (pres.-elect 1985-86, pres. 1986-87), Western Humanities Conf. (bd. dirs. 1990—), Am. Hist. Assn., Am. Con. for Irish Studies, Brit. Politics Group, Rotary, Phi Beta Kappa, Phi Eta Sigma. Democrat. Home: 5685 Euclid Pl Boulder CO 80303-2952 Office: U Colo Arts and Scis Adminstrn Old Main I-42 Boulder CO 80309-0001

MIDDLETON, MICHAEL JOHN, civil engineer; b. N.Y.C., May 14, 1953; s. Vincent Aloysius and Mary Hilda (Lehane) M. BS in Civil Engring., U. Calif., Davis, 1975. Registered profl. engr., Calif., Wash., Hawaii. Project mgr. G.A. Fitch & Assoc., Concord, Calif., 1975-78, v.p., 1978-80; project mgr. Santina & Thompson, Inc., Concord, 1980-83, dir. engring., 1983-88, sr. v.p., 1988—. scholar, Calif. Scholarship Fedn., 1971. Mem. ASCE, Nat. Soc. Profl. Engrs., Soc. Am. Mil. Engrs. Roman Catholic. Home: 1409A Bel Air Dr Concord CA 94521 Office: Santina & Thompson Inc 1355 Willow Way Ste 280 Concord CA 94520

MIDDLETON, ROBERT ALLAN, JR., public relations executive; b. San Francisco, Mar. 27, 1948; s. Robert Allan and Eunice Barbara (Kuhlman) M.; m. Amy Rita Kennon, Mar. 24, 1979; 1 child, Robert Allan III. AB in Rhetoric, U. Calif., Berkeley, 1971, MA in Rhetoric, 1973. Teaching asst. U. Calif., Berkeley, 1971-73; asst. adminstrv. analyst Oakland (Calif.) Police Dept., 1973-75, tech. writer, 1975-77; community info. rep. Port of Oakland, 1977-82, media rels. rep., 1982-90, pub. affairs mgr., 1990—; pub. rels. com. Am. Assn. Port Authorities, 1988—. Photo editor: Modern Marine Terminal Operations and Management, 1983. Mayor's Strategic Plan Com., City of Oakland, 1991; advisor transp. program Peralta C.C. Dist., Berkeley, 1978-84; Celebrate Oakland, Oakland C. of C., 1988—; bd. govs. Treasure Island Mus., San Francisco, 1985—. Recipient Merit awards for black and white advt. Am. Assn. Port Authorities, 1986, 87, 88, 1st and 2d place awards Airport Operators Coun. Internat., Washington, 1985. Mem. U. Calif. Bear Backers, Propeller Club of U.S. (bd. govs. 1987—). Episcopalian. Office: Port of Oakland 530 Water St Oakland CA 94607

MIDDLETON, VINCENT FRANCIS, manufacturing company executive; b. N.Y.C., June 24, 1951; s. Vincent Aloysius and Mary Hilda (LeHane) M.; m. Collette Carolyn Peters, July 26, 1986; 1 child, Brendan Austin. BSCE cum laude, So. Meth. U., 1974; MBA in Mgmt. summa cum laude, Golden Gate U., 1986. Registered profl. civil engr., Calif. Sr. structural engr. Bechtel, Inc., San Francisco, 1974-77; project mgr. Fisher Devel., Inc., San Francisco, 1977-80; mgr. projects Ecodyne Corp., Santa Rosa, Calif., 1980-81, dir. constrn., 1981-84; mgr. engring. and constrn. Custodis-Ecodyne, Inc., Santa Rosa, 1984-86; mgr. devel. and constrn. Custodis-Ecodyne Inc., Santa Rosa, 1986-87, v.p., gen. mgr., 1987-89; regional v.p. Cottrell Cos., Inc., 1988-89; exec. v.p., chief operating officer Rsch.-Cottrell Cos., Somerville, N.J., 1989-91; pres., CEO Wahlco, Inc., Santa Ana, Calif., 1991—; sr. v.p. New Venture Devel. Wahlco Environ. Systems, Irvine, Calif., 1992—; pres., CEO Process Systems Group Wahlco Environmental Systems, 1992—. Bd. dirs. Jr. Achievement, Sonoma County, Calif., 1986-89, Inst. Clean Air Cos., Washington, 1993; mem. environ. policy adv. coun. State of Calif., world affairs coun. Orange County. Named Tex. Pub. Works scholar, 1973. Mem. ASCE, Am. Concrete Inst., Nat. Asbestos Coun., Cooling Tower Inst., Environ. Tech. Export Coun. (bus. planning com.), Nat. Soc. Profl. Engrs., Mensa. Republican. Roman Catholic. Home: 27332 Silver Creek Dr San Juan Capistrano CA 92675 Office: Wahlco Inc 3600 W Segerstrom Ave Santa Ana CA 92704

MIDDLEWOOD, MARTIN EUGENE, technical communications specialist, writer, consultant; b. Galesburg, Ill., Mar. 21, 1947; s. Martin and Bernetta Maxine (Henderson) M.; m. Mona Marie Jarmer, Sept. 10, 1971; children: Erin, Martha, Emily, Margaret. BA, Ea. Wash. U., 1973, MA, 1980. Writer tech. manuals Tektronix, Inc., Beaverton, Oreg., 1976-77, tech. writer, 1977-79, sr. tech. writer, 1979-82, supr. pub. rels., 1982-84, mgr. pub. rels., 1984-85; mgr. mktg. communications Tektronix, Inc., Vancouver, Wash., 1985-87; account supr. Waggener Edstrom, Portland, Oreg., 1987—; pub. Cognizer Report, Portland, Oreg., 1990—; chmn. adv. bd. sci. and tech. writing, Clark Coll., Vancouver, 1984—; owner communications cons. firm, Vancouver, 1978—. Author: (ednl. brochure series) Oscilloscope Measurements, 1979 (award of excellence Willamette Valley chpt. Soc. Tech. Communication, 1980); contbr. articles to profl. jours. Served with USMC, 1967-70. Recipient Cert. Recognition Clark Coll., Vancouver, 1984, 86, 89, 92; award of Excellence Pacific N.W. chpt. Internat. Assn. Bus. Communicators, 1985. Mem. Soc. Tech. Communication (sr., pres. Willamette Valley chpt. 1983-85, award of recognition 1986, chpt. pub. achievement award 1985, 2 awards of distinction 1981). Home: 1107 SE 98th Ave Vancouver WA 98664-4119 Office: Waggener Edstrom 6915 SW Macadam Ave Ste 300 Portland OR 97219-2396

MIDKIFF, DONALD WAYNE, program manager; b. Post, Tex., Sept. 26, 1940; s. Colvert Crockett Midkiff and Judy M. (Poss) Hinckley; m. Olga Maria Androvitch, June 21, 1961 (div. 1968); m. Manbeth Jean Crowell, Apr. 29, 1979. BS in Tech. Mgmt., Denver Tech. Coll., 1988, MS in Mgmt., 1993. With USAF, 1960, advances through grades to staff sgt., 1968; electronics supr. Lockheed Aircraft, Jidda, Saudi Arabia, 1969-71; site mgr. Kentron Hawaii, Ltd., Pleiku, South Vietnam, 1971-73; supr. Kentron, Kwajalein, Marshall Islands, 1973-80, range ops. engr., 1980-84; ops. supr. Kentron PRC, Maui, Hawaii, 1984-85; ops. mgr. Kentron PRC, Colorado Springs, Colo., 1985-87; div. security mgr. PRC, Colorado Springs, Colo., 1987-89; program mgr. PRC Inc., Colorado Springs, Colo., 1989—; advisor Denver Tech. Coll., Colorado Springs, 1991—. CPR instr. Am. Red Cross, 1980-86; pres. Kwajalein Dive Club, 1981-83, Kwajalein Tennis Club, 1978-80. Recipient Group Achievement award NASA, 1992. Mem. MENSA, Nat. contract Mgmt. Assn., Profl. Assn. Diving Instrs. (dive master), Rosicrucians. Republican. Office: PRC Inc 985 Space Ctr Dr Ste 200 Colorado Springs CO 80915

MIECH, ALLEN C., financial services company executive; b. 1939. Attended, U. Wis., 1960. With Transamerica Fin. Group. Inc., L.A., 1962—, br. mgr., 1965-68, dist. mgr., 1968-77, area mgr., 1977-79, asst. to pres., gen. mgr. br. Sys Lyon Moving & Storage, 1979-81, regional v.p., 1981-83, chief credit officer, 1983-84; exec. v.p. sales & mktg. ops., then pres. TransAmerica Fin. Svcs. Calif., L.A., 1984—. With USNG, 1960-62. Office: TransAmerica Fin Svcs Calif 1150 S Olive St Los Angeles CA 90015-2211

MIEL, VICKY ANN, municipal government executive; b. South Bend, Ind., June 20, 1951; d. Lawrence Paul Miel and Virginia Ann (Yeagley) Hernandez. BS, Ariz. State U., 1985. Word processing coordinator City of Phoenix, 1977-78, word processing adminstr., 1978-83, chief dep. city clk., 1983-88, city clk. dir., 1988—; assoc. prof. Phoenix Community Coll., 1982-83, Mesa (Ariz.) Community Coll., 1983; speaker in field, Boston, Santa Fe, Los Angeles, N.Y.C. and St. Paul, 1980—. Author: Phoenix Document Request Form, 1985, Developing Successful Systems Users, 1986. Judge Future Bus. Leaders Am. at Ariz. State U., Tempe, 1984; bd. dirs. Fire and Life Safety League, Phoenix, 1984. Recipient Gold Plaque, Word Processing Systems Mag., Mpls., 1980, Green Light Productivity award City of Phoenix, 1981, Honor Soc. Achievement award Internat. Word Processing Assn., 1981, 1st Ann. Grand Prize Records Mgmt. Internat. Inst. Mcpl. Clks., 1990, Olsten Award for Excellence in Records Mgmt., 1991. Mem. Assn. Info. Systems Profls. (internat. dir. 1982-84), Internat. Inst. Mcpl. Clks. (cert.), Am. Records Mgrs. Assn., Assn. Image Mgmt., Am. Soc. Pub. Adminstrs., Am. Mgmt. Assn. Office: City of Phoenix 251 W Washington St Phoenix AZ 85003-2245

MIELKE, CLARENCE HAROLD, JR., hematologist; b. Spokane, Wash., June 18, 1936; s. Clarence Harold and Marie Katherine (Gillespie) M.; m. Marcia Rae, July 5, 1964; children: Elisa, John, Kristina. BS, Wash. State U., 1959; MD, U. Louisville, 1963. Intern, San Francisco Gen. Hosp., 1963-64; resident in medicine Portland VA Hosp., 1964-65, San Francisco Gen. Hosp., 1965-67; fellow in hematology U. So. Calif., 1967-68; teaching fellow, asst. physician, instr. Tufts-New Eng. Med. Ctr. Hosps., Boston, 1968-71; sr. scientist Med. Rsch. Inst., San Francisco, 1971-90; chief hematology Presbyn. Hosp., San Francisco, 1971-82; asst. clin. prof. medicine U. Calif. Sch. Medicine, San Francisco, 1971-80, assoc. clin. prof., 1979-90, bd.92—dirs. Inst. Cancer Rsch.; trustee, bd. dirs. Med. Rsch. Inst. San Francisco. NIH grantee, 1973-88; dir. emeritus Inst. Cancer Rsch.; trustee emeritus, bd. dirs. Med. Rsch. Inst., 1988—; dir. Health Rsch. and Edn. Ctr., Wash. State U., 1989—, prof. pharmocology, 1989—, prof. vet. medicine, 1989—, assoc. dean rsch., 1992—. Fellow ACP, Internat. Soc. Hematology, Am. Coll. Angiology; mem. Am. Soc. Internal Medicine, Internat. Soc. Thrombosis and Hemostasis, Am. Heart Assn., N.Y. Acad. Scis., AMA, San Francisco Med. Soc., Am. Thoracic Soc., AAAS, Internat. Soc. Angiology. Editor emeritus, Jour. Clin. Aphersis, 1981; contbr. chpts. to books, articles to med. jours. Office: Wash State U Health Rsch & Edn Ctr West 601 First Ave Spokane WA 99204-0399

MIELKE, FREDERICK WILLIAM, JR., retired utility company executive; b. N.Y.C., Mar. 19, 1921; s. Frederick William and Cressida (Flynn) M.; m. Lorraine Roberts, 1947; children: Bruce Frederick, Neal Russell. A.B., U. Calif., 1943; J.D., Stanford U., 1949. Bar: Calif. 1950. Law clk. to Assoc. Justice John W. Shenk, Calif. Supreme Ct., 1949-51; with Pacific Gas and Electric Co., San Francisco, 1951-86; exec. v.p. Pacific Gas and Electric Co., 1976-79, chmn. bd., chief exec. officer, 1979-86; bd. dirs. The Bay Area Coun., SRI Internat., Edison Electric Inst., 1979-82. Trustee Stanford U., 1977-87, Golden Gate U., 1977-79; mem. adv. coun. Stanford Grad. Sch. Bus., 1984-90; bd. dirs. Calif. C. of C., 1979-85, San Francisco C. of C., 1977-79, Ind. Colls. No. Calif., 1969-79; chmn. bd. dirs. United Way of Bay Area, 1986-88. With USN, 1943-46. Mem. ABA, Calif. Bar Assn., Pacific Coast Elec. Assn., Pacific Coast Gas Assn. Club: Electric of San Francisco. Office: Pacific Gas and Electric Co PO Box 770000 1 California St F31 San Francisco CA 94177

MIGAKI, JAMES M., education educator; b. Spokane, Wash., Sept. 27, 1931; s. Kametaro and Ichiye (Hashimoto) M.; m. Ruth M.K. Tsai, Aug. 19, 1967 (div. July 1974); children: Grace, Paul. BA, Wash. State Coll., 1954; EdD, Wash. State U., 1978. Cert. elem. and secondary edn. tchr. and prin., Wash. Rsch. mechanic dept. math. Washington State Coll., Pullman, 1950-51; substitute tchr. physics Spokane Sch. Dist. 81, 1953, elem. sch. tchr., 1954-59, acting prin., tchr., 1959, secondary sci. and math. tchr., 1959-65; teaching asst. Wash. State U., 1966-67, from instr. to assoc. prof. elem. and seconary edn., 1967-90, dir. Peace Corp/Master of Edn. Program, 1990—; dir. Masters'-Peace Corp Program Coll. Edn. and Internat. Devel. Office, Wash. State U., 1990—; dir. Saturday Sci. Project, Spokane Tech. and Profl. Coun., 1963-65; vis. faculty sci. and math. Wash. State U., 1965; dir., assoc. dir., acting dir. numerous projects NSF, 1965-92; cons. to numerous sch. dists. Inventor math. model for higher plane curves in rotation, 1950; contbr. numerous articles to profl. jours. Del. Gov.'s Conf. on Health Care, Seattle, 1967; recorder Gov.'s Conf. on Edn., Seattle and Olympia, Wash., 1967-68; cons., mem. evaluation panel NSF, Washington, 1974; del. nat. fgn. policy conf. U.S. Dept. State, 1980. Named Patron of Youth, YMCA, 1978; recipient numerous awards and scholarships. Mem. NEA (life, state rep.), Wash. Sci. Tchrs. Assn. (charter; pres., other offices), YMCA (pres. 1966-81), Nat. Sci. Tchrs. Assn. (life; various coms.), Phi Delta Kappa (life; pres. 1969-83, svc. award 1981), Kappa Delta Pi. Home: 750 SE High St Pullman WA 99163-2321 Office: Wash State U Coll Edn Cleveland 272 Pullman WA 99164-2122

MIHALY, EUGENE BRAMER, consultant, corporate executive, writer, educator; b. The Hague, The Netherlands, Nov. 11, 1934; s. Eddy and Cecile (Bramer) Kahn; stepson of Eugene Mihaly; m. Linda Davis, Oct. 7, 1978; children: Lisa Klee, Jessica; 1 stepson, Russell C. DuBrow. A.B. magna cum laude, Harvard U., 1956; Ph.D., London Sch. Econs. and Polit. Sci., 1964. Aviation/space editor Hartford (Conn.) Courant, 1960-61; internat. economist AID, Washington, 1964-65; dep. dir. Peace Corps, Tanzania, 1966, dir., 1967-68; dep. dir. East Asia/Pacific bur. Peace Corps, Washington, 1969, dir. office program devel., evaluation and rsch., 1969-70; assoc. dir. Inst. Internat. Studies, U. Calif., Berkeley, 1970-72; pres. Mihaly Internat. Corp., 1972—; chmn. bd. Mihaly Internat. Can., Ltd., 1992—; sr. lectr. Haas Sch. Bus. U. Calif., Berkeley, 1991—. Author: Foreign Aid and Politics in Nepal: A Case Study, 1965; contbr.: Political Development in Micronesia, 1974, Management of the Multinationals, 1974; also articles to various publs. Chmn. bd. dirs. Childreach (Plan Internat. U.S.A.) and dir. Plan Internat., Inc.; trustee World Affairs Coun. No. Calif., World Without War Coun.; pres. Calif.-S.E. Asia Bus. Coun.; mem. Dist. Export Coun. No. Calif.; mem. adv. bd. World Resources Inst., Ctr. for Slavic Studies U. Calif., Berkeley; mem. U.S. nat. com. Pacific Econ. Coop. Mem. Coun. on Fgn. Rels., Signet Soc., San Francisco Com. on Fgn. Rels., Harvard Club (N.Y.C.and San Francisco). Home: 18 Manzanita Pl Mill Valley CA 94941-1018 Office: 637 E Blithedale Ave Mill Valley CA 94941

MIHAN, RICHARD, dermatologist; b. L.A., Dec. 20, 1925; s. Arnold and Virginia Catharine (O'Reilly) M.; student U. So. Calif., 1945; M.D., St. Louis U., 1949. Rotating intern Los Angeles County Gen. Hosp., 1949-51, resident in dermatology, 1954-57; practice medicine specializing in dermatology, Los Angeles, 1957—; emeritus clin. prof. dept. medicine, dermatology and syphilology U. So. Calif. Served as lt. (j.g.) M.C., USNR, 1951-53, ret. as lt. comdr. Diplomate Am. Bd. Dermatology. Fellow ACP; mem. Internat. Soc. Tropical Dermatology, Soc. Investigative Dermatology, Pacific Dermatologic Assn. (exec. bd. 1971-74), Calif. Med. Assn. (chmn. dermatologic sect. 1973-74), AMA, Los Angeles Dermatol. Soc. (pres. 1975-76), Am. Acad. Dermatology, L.A. Acad. Medicine (pres. 1988-89). Office: 1245 Wilshire Blvd Los Angeles CA 90017-4810

MIHNEA, TATIANA, mathematics educator; b. Bucharaest, Romania, May 24, 1951; came to U.S, 1984; m. Andrei Mihnea, May 29, 1976; 1 child, Radu. BS, U. Bucharest, 1975, MS, 1976. Community coll. instr. credential, Calif. Tchr. math. high sch., Bucharest, 1976-82, Lawrence Acad., Santa Clara, Calif., 1985-86; lectr. math. San Jose (Calif.) State U., 1986-87; instr. math. West Valley Coll., Saratoga, Calif., 1986—. Contbr. articles to Poetics. Mem. Math. Assn. Am., Am. Math. Soc. Home: 4967 Kenlar Dr San Jose CA 95124-5106 Office: West Valley Coll Dept Math 14000 Fruitvale Ave Saratoga CA 95070-5640

MIKALOW, ALFRED ALEXANDER, II, deep sea diver, marine surveyor, marine diving consultant; b. N.Y.C., Jan. 19, 1921; m. Janice Brenner, Aug. 1, 1960; children: Alfred Alexander, Jon Alfred. Student Rutgers U., 1940; MS, U. Calif., Berkeley, 1948; MA, Rochdale U. (Can.), 1950. Owner Coastal Diving Co., Oakland, Calif., 1950—, Divers Supply, Oakland, 1952—; dir. Coastal Sch. Deep Sea Diving, Oakland, 1950—; capt. and master rsch. vessel Coastal Researcher I; mem. Marine Inspection Bur., Oakland. marine diving contractor, cons. Mem. adv. bd. Medic Alert Found., Turlock, Calif., 1960—. Lt. comdr. USN, 1941-47, 49-50. Decorated Purple Heart, Silver Star. Mem. Divers Assn. Am. (pres. 1970-74), Treasury Recovery, Inc. (pres. 1972-75), Internat. Assn. Profl. Divers, Assn. Diving Contractors, Calif. Assn. Pvt. Edn. (no. v.p. 1971-72), Authors Guild, Internat. Game Fish Assn., U.S. Navy League, U.S. Res. Officers Assn., Tailhook Assn., U.S. Submarine Vets. WWII, Explorer Club (San Francisco), Calif. Assn. Marine Surveyors (pres. 1988—), Masons, Lions. Author: Fell's Guide to Sunken Treasure Ships of the World, 1972; (with H. Rieseberg) The Knight from Maine, 1974. Office: 320 29th Ave Oakland CA 94601

MIKEAL, PATRICIA ANN, airline training professional; b. Hickory, N.C., Dec. 27, 1960; d. J.C. and Rosalyn Mae (Duprey) M. Cert. travel agt., N.Am. Correspondence Sch., 1989. Clk. typist Airline Tng. Ctr., Goodyear, Ariz., 1979, sec., 1979-88, bookkeeper, 1979-87, adminstrv. asst., payroll clk., 1987-91, pers. adminstr., 1992—. Sunday sch. tchr. Temple of Faith Pentecostal Ch., Avondale, Ariz., 1986-92; tutor Literacy Vols., Phoenix, 1987-90; credit union rep. Ariz. Fed. Credit Union, 1989—; notary public State of Ariz., 1989—; missions dir. Bethel Chapel, 1993—. Mem. NAFE, Pentecostal Young Peoples Assn., Pentecostal Ladies Aux. (v.p. 1989), Airline Tng. Ctr. Employees Club (bd. dirs.). Office: Airline Tng Ctr Bld 104 1658 S Litchfield Rd Goodyear AZ 85338-1512

MIKEL, THOMAS KELLY, JR., laboratory administrator; b. East Chicago, Ind., Aug. 27, 1946; s. Thomas Kelly and Anne Katherine (Vrazo) M.; B.A., San Jose State U., 1973; M.A., U. Calif.-Santa Barbara, 1975. Asst. dir. Santa Barbara Underseas Found., 1975-76; marine biologist PJB Labs., Ventura, Calif., 1976-81; lab. dir. CRL Environ., Ventura, 1981-88; lab. dir. ABC Labs, Ventura, 1988—; instr. oceanography Ventura Coll., 1980-81. With U.S. Army, 1968-70. Mem. Assn. Environ. Profls., Soc. Population Ecologists, ASTME (rsch. contbr. 10th ann. symposium 1986). Biol. coord.Anacapa Underwater Natural trail U.S. Nat. Park Svc., 1976; designer ecol. restoration program of upper Newport Bay, Orange County, Calif., 1978; rsch. contbr. 3d Internat. Artificial Reef Conf., Newport Beach, Calif., 1983, Ann. Conf. Am. Petroleum Inst., Houston. Democrat.

MIKHAIL, MARY ATTALLA, computer systems development executive; b. Cairo, Egypt, Apr. 2, 1945; came to U.S., 1980.; d. Attalla Shehata and Soad (Kamel) Abd-El-Malek; m. Ibrahim Fahmy Mikhail, May 1 ,1967; 1 child, Ireny. BS in Math. and Physics, U. Assiut, Egypt, 1965; MS in Math. and Computer Sci., U. Clausthal, Fed. Republic Germany, 1973; PhD in Math., U. Tuebingen, Fed. Republic Germany, 1976. Lectr. Math. Inst., Assiut, Egypt, 1965-67; from instr. to asst. prof. Math. Inst., Tuebingen, Fed. Republic Germany, 1973-78; cons., project mgr. Datel, Fed. Republic Germany, 1978-80; planner, systems analyst C.F. Braun, Alhambra, Calif., 1980-82; optic dept. mgr. Burroughs Corp., City of Industry, Calif., 1982-87; project mgr. continuous transaction processing Unisys Corp., Mission Viejo, Calif., 1987-88, project mgr. systems software devel. Open Systems Interconnectivity, 1988-92, program mgr. Open/OLTP, 1992—. Contbr. articles to profl. jours. Mem. IEEE (standards for software error, faults and failures com., standards for quality metrics com.), Am. Mgmt. Assn. Mem. Coptic Orthodox Ch.

MIKULKA, RONALD TROY, investment banker; b. Bridgeport, Conn., Feb. 17, 1962; s. Ronald Paul and Lynne (Monroe) M. BS in Acctg. cum laude, Ctrl. Conn. U., New Britain, 1988. Systems analyst Travelers Ins. Co., Hartford, Conn., 1986-88; ptnr. in firm co-founder Woodbridge & Assocs., Newport Beach, Calif., 1988—; pres. U.S. Venture Cons., Newport Beach, 1990-92. Newsletter chmn. Cox Congl., Newport Beach, 1991-92. With USMC, 1980-84. Office: Woodbridge & Assocs 5000 Birch St West Tower Ste 6400 Newport Beach CA 92660

MILANDER, HENRY MARTIN, community college president; b. Northampton, Pa., Apr. 17, 1939; s. Martin Edward and Margaret Catherine (Makovetz) M.; children: Martin Henry, Beth Ann. B.S. summa cum laude, Lock Haven U., Pa., 1961; M.A., Bowling Green (Ohio) State U., 1962; Ed.S. (Future Faculty fellow 1964), U. No. Iowa, 1965; Ed.D., Ill. State U., Normal, 1967. Instr. Wartburg Coll., Waverly, Iowa, 1962-64; asst. prof. Ill. State U., 1966-67; dean instrn. Belleville (Ill.) Area Coll., 1967-69; v.p. acad. affairs Lorain County Community Coll., Elyria, Ohio, 1969-72; pres. Olympic Coll., Bremerton, Wash., 1972-87, Northeastern Jr. Coll., Sterling, Colo., 1988—; pres. Bremers, Inc., 1986-87. Contbr. articles to profl. jours. Pres. Kitsap County Comprehensive Health Planning Council, 1975-76; pres. Logan County Colo. United Way, 1992-93. Recipient Faculty Growth award Wartburg Coll., 1963, Community Service award, 1975, Chief Thunderbird award, 1985. Mem. Am. Assn. C.C., Am. Assn. Sch. Adminstrs., N.W. Assn. Community and Jr. Coll., Wash. Assn. C.C. (pres. 1984-85), Wash. C.C. Computing Consortium (chmn. bd. dirs. 1985-87), Puget Sound Naval Bases Assn. (pres. 1982-86), Wash. Assn. C.C. Presidents (pres. 1984-85), Bremerton Area C. of C. (pres. 1977-78), Colo. Assn. of C.C. Pres. (pres. 1993—), Rotary (pres. Sterling club 1992-93), Kappa Delta Pi, Phi Delta Kappa. Lutheran. Home: 302 Delmar St Sterling CO 80751-3904 Office: Northeastern Jr Coll 100 College Dr Sterling CO 80751-2344

MILAVSKY, HAROLD PHILLIP, real estate executive; b. Limerick, Sask., Can., Jan. 25, 1931; s. Jack and Clara Milavsky. B in Commerce, U. Sask., Saskatoon, Can., 1953. Chief acct., treas., controller Loram Internat. Ltd. div. Mannix Co. Ltd., Calgary, Alta., Can., 1956-65; v.p., chief fin. officer Power Corp. Devels. Ltd., Calgary, Alta., Can., 1965-69; exec. v.p., bd. dirs. Great West Internat. Equities Ltd. (name now Trizec Corp. Ltd.), Calgary, Alta., Can., 1969-76; former pres., now chmn. of exec. com., bd. dirs. Trizec Corp. Ltd., Calgary, Alta., Can., 1976—; bd. dirs. Trizec Corp. related cos., Brascan Ltd., Toronto, Can., Carena-Bancorp Inc., Toronto, London Life Ins. Co., London Ins. Group Ltd., Hees Internat., Toronto, Coscan Devel. Corp., Toronto, Saskatchewan Oil & Gas Corp., Regina, Nova Corp. Alberta, Calgary, Amoco Can., Calgary. Past dir. Terry Fox Humanitarian Award Program; past dir. Conf. Bd. Can.; past gov., Acctg. Edn. Found. Alta.; mem. Chancellor's Club, U. Calgary. Fellow Inst. Chartered Accts. Alta.; mem. Inst. Chartered Accts. Sask. and Alta., Can. Inst. Pub. Real Estate Cos. (past pres., bd. dirs.), Can. C. of C. (past chmn.), Internat. Profl. Hockey Alumni (founder). Clubs: Petroleum, Ranchmen's, Glenmore Racquet (Calgary). Office: Trizec Corp Ltd, 1700-855 Second St, Calgary, AB Canada T2P 4J7

MILD, EDWARD EUGENE, marketing professional, consultant; b. Henderson, Nev., May 1, 1943; s. Martin E. and Edna A. (Smith) M.; m. Theresa A. Zirillo, Aug. 25, 1973; children: Andrew D., Christine E. BE, Youngstown (Ohio) State U., 1968; MS, U. Pitts., 1970. Rsch. engr. Nat. Steel, Weirton, W.Va., 1970-73; tech. supr. Youngstown Steel, 1973-76; dir. tech. svc. Metall. Svc. & Supply Inc., Pitts., 1976-80; dir. mktg. RMI Co./Micron Metals, Niles, Ohio, 1980-85; dir. market devel. Timet, Henderson, 1985—; chmn. com. Titanium Devel. Assn., Dayton, Ohio, 1986—. Treas. Brook Park Civic Assn., Pitts., 1987-89; dir. Green Valley Little League, Henderson, pres., 1991. Mem. ASTM (subcom. chmn. 1987—), AIME (chmn. Warren chpt. 1978), ASM Internat., Titanium Devel. Assn. (chmn. 1986-90). Roman Catholic. Office: Timet PO Box 2128 Henderson NV 89009-7009

MILES, DONALD GEOFFREY, economist; b. Melbourne, Victoria, Australia, Aug. 26, 1952; s. Harry Raymond and Marian Edith (Lightfoot) M.; m. Judy E. Roberts, Dec. 14, 1991. B. Bus. with distinction, Curtin U. Tech., Muresk, Australia, 1981; MS in Econs., Iowa State U., 1983. Rsch. asst. Iowa State U., Ames, 1980-84; econs. lectr. Curtin U. Tech., Muresk, 1985-87; rsch. economist PRD Consulting Svcs., Pty., Ltd. & Max Christmas Pty. Ltd., Gold Coast, Australia, 1988-89; pres. Miles Internat., Australia and U.S., 1989—; econometric revenue forecaster State of Wash., 1990—. Inventor environ. wholistic and econ. models, Dept. of Licensing WA/U.S. growth index and transforms, trading day seasonality, copyrights for laws of human ecology, problem shifting analysis, systems econs., wholistic analysis, systems repair, systems improvement, quantifying inefficiency and waste, optimal rates of adjustment, adjustment boxes, events-prices and incomes analysis. Participant World Food Conf., Ames, 1976, Inst. World Affairs, Ames, 1981. Recipient Edwards Prize, Curtin U. Tech., 1987. Mem. World Future Soc. (life). Home and Office: 1015 7th Ave N Tumwater WA 98512-6315

MILES, MARCINE MILLER, lawyer; b. Cheyenne, Wyo., Oct. 24, 1942; d. Daniel Verner and Ellen Ida (Utter) Miller; m. William Leslie Miles II; children: Morgan Daniel, Mason William. BS, U. Wash., 1964; JD, U. Okla., 1971. Bar: Okla. 1971, U.S. Dist. Ct. (we. dist.) Okla. 1971, U.S. Ct. Appeals (10th cir.) 1971, U.S. Dist. Ct. (no. dist.) Okla. 1975, U.S. Dist. Ct. (we. dist.) Wash. 1978, Wash. 1979, U.S. Ct. Appeals (9th cir.) 1983. Youth dir. USAF, Marysville, Calif., 1964; youth dir. USAF, Riverside, Calif., 1967; tchr. Gulfport Sch. Dist., Gulfport, Miss., 1967-68; legal aid dir. S.W. Okla. Legal Aid, Altus, 1971-74, Tulsa Legal Aid Soc., 1974-75; staff atty. U.S. Army Corps Engrs., Tulsa, 1975-77, Portland, Oreg., 1977-79; pvt. practice law, 1979-83; ptnr. Miles & Miles, Vancouver, Wash., 1985—; magistrate Dist. Ct. Clark County, Wash., 1983-85; forfeiture hearing officer City of Vancouver, 1990—; bd. dirs. Heritage Trust Clark County, Wash., Tears of Joy, Vancouver, Wash. State Safety Restraint Coalition, Olympia. Bd. dirs. Clark Coll., Vancouver, 1977-83; organizer Keep Kids Healthy Funday, Vancouver, 1984—; mem. DWI Task Force, Vancouver, 1984—, Traffic Safety Commn., Clark County, 1984— (Traffic Safety award 1985); affirmative action and Clark County Dem. Cen. Com., Vancouver, 1980-83; mem. Health Scis. Ethics Com. U. Oreg., 1980—. Named one of 10 Outstanding Women in Wash. State, Gov. of Wash., 1987; recipient Commendation award Dept. U.S. Army, 1977, Cert. of Honor City of Tulsa, 1977, Gentleman of the Yr. award Clark County, 1982, Certs. of Appreciation, 1988-91. Mem. LWV, Wash. State Bar Assn., Clark County Bar Assn. (treas. 1980). Office: Miles & Miles PS 1220 Main St Ste 545 Vancouver WA 98660-2964

MILES, RALPH FRALEY, JR., systems engineer; b. Phila., May 15, 1933; s. Ralph F. Sr. and Genevieve Marie (Angus) M. BS, Calif. Inst. Tech., 1955, PhD, 1963. Tech. staff mem. Jet Propulsion Lab., Pasadena, Calif., 1963—. Editor: Systems Concepts, John Wiley, 1973; contbr. articles to profl. jours. Lt. USAF, 1955-57. Recipient Outstanding Performance award Mariner Mars, 1969, Exceptional Svc. award Voyager, NASA, 1981, Outstanding Achievement award Am. Inst. for Decision Scis., 1984, Group Achievement award Voyager, NASA, 1986. Mem. Ops. Rsch. Soc. Am., Inst. Mgmt. Sci., N.Y. Acad. Scis., Sigma Xi. Home: 3608 Canon Blvd Altadena CA 91001-4010

MILES, SAMUEL ISRAEL, psychiatrist; b. Munich, Mar. 4, 1949; came to U.S., 1949; s. Henry and Renee (Ringel) M.; m. Denise Marie Robey, June 26, 1977; children: Jonathan David, Justin Alexander. BS, CCNY, 1970; MD, N.Y. Med. Coll., 1974; PhD, So. Calif. Psychoanalytic Inst., 1986. Diplomate Am. Bd. Psychiatry and Neurology. Intern D.C. Gen. Hosp., Washington, 1974-75; resident in psychiatry Cedars-Sinai Med. Ctr., Los Angeles, 1975-78; practice medicine specializing in psychiatry Los Angeles, 1978—; ind. med. examiner Calif. Dept. Indsl. Relations, 1984—, qualified med. examiner, 1991—; asst. clin. prof. psychiatry UCLA Sch. Med., 1978—; attending psychiatrist Cedars-Sinai Med. Ctr., 1978—, co-chmn. util. rev./qual. assurance com. dept. psychiatry, 1984-89, chmn. qual. assurance com. dept. psychiatry, 1990-91, mem. in-patient adv. com., 1983-85, 87-90, psychiatry adv. com., 1984-86; attending psychiatrist Brotman Med. Ctr., Culver City, Calif., 1978—; faculty mem. So. Calif. Psychoanalytic Inst., 1986—; mem. psychiat. panel Superior Ct., L.A. Co., 1990—, Fed. Ct., 1990—. Fellow Am. Acad. Psychoanalysis, Am. Orthopsychiat. Assn.; mem. Acad. Psychiatry and the Law, Calif. Psychiat. Assn. (manage and care com. 1991—), So. Calif. Psychiat. Soc. (coun. rep. 1985-88, 92—, chair pvt. practice com. 1988-92, sec. 1991-92, worker's compensation com. 1992—), Am. Coll. Legal Medicine, So. Calif. Soc. Adolescent Psychiatry (treas. 1980-81), So. Calif. Psychoanalytic Inst. (pres. clin. assocs. orgn. 1981-82, mem. admissions com. 1988—, ethics com. 1991-92, chair 1993). Jewish. Office: 8631 W 3d St # 425E Los Angeles CA 90048

MILES, SHEILA LEE, artist, consultant; b. Indpls., Aug. 10, 1952; d. Robert Evan and Elizabeth Louise (Marcum) Miles; 1 child, Paris Miles-Brenden. BA, Purdue U., 1973, MA, 1974. Dir. Provincetown Art Assn. & Mus., Provincetown, Mass., 1975-77; instr. art Ea. Mont. Coll., Billings, 1980-85; artist-in-the-schs. Mont. Arts Coun./Custer County Art Ctr., Miles City, Mont., 1982-83; gallery dir. Ea. Mont. Coll., 1984-85; gallery dir./instr. Mont. State U., Bozeman, 1985-86; curator Yellowstone Art Ctr., Billings, 1986-90. Panel mem. Mont. arts Coun., Helena, 1986—; cons. Deaconess Hosp., Billings, 1989—, ACLU, 1986—. Mont. arts Coun. fellow, 1984. Home: 1005 N 32d St Billings MT 59101-0745

MILFORD, JOHN WINDSOR, retirement housing company executive; b. Pitts., Mar. 30, 1945; s. John James Jr. and Anna Claire (Snyder) M.; m. Wanda Carolyn Godwin, Aug. 24, 1969; children: John Windsor, Ashlie Caroline, Jeremy Kirk, Allison Claire. BA, U. Richmond, 1967; MHA, Med. Coll. Va., 1969; MDiv, Golden Gate Sem., Mill Valley, Calif., 1977. Adminstr. Terra Linda Convalescent Hosp., San Rafael, Calif., 1978-80, Oakland (Calif.) Hosp., 1981-85; assoc. adminstr. Merritt-Peralta Med. Ctr., Oakland, 1985-90; exec. dir. Sr. Living Communities, Inc., San Francisco, 1991—. Capt. U.S. Army, 1969-74, Vietnam. Decorated Meritorious Svc. medal.; recipient Pres.'s award for excellence Paracelsus Hosp. Corp., Oakland, 1982. Mem. Am. Coll. Healthcare Execs., Healthcare Execs. No. Calif., Am. Soc. on Aging, NRA. Office: The Carlisle 1450 Post St San Francisco CA 94109

MILGRIM, DARROW A., insurance broker, recreation consultant; b. Chgo., Apr. 30, 1945; s. David and Miriam (Glickman) M.; m. Laurie Stevens, Apr. 15, 1984; children: Derick, Jared, Kayla. BA, Calif. State U., San Bernardino, 1968; postgrad., U. So. Calif., 1972. Accredited ins. adv.; cert. ins. counselor; cert. sch. administr. Tchr. Rialto (Calif.) Unified Sch. Dist., 1969-70, Las Virgines Unified Sch. Dist., Westlake Village, Calif., 1970-78; instr. Calif. State U., Northridge, Calif., 1980-84; ins. broker, v.p. Speare Ins. Brokers, Blade Ins. Svcs., Brentwood, Calif., 1984—; dir. Calamigos Star C Ranch Summer Camp, Malibu, Calif., Calamagos Environ. Edn. Ctr., Malibu. Editor: Legislation and Regulations for Organized Camps, 1987. Pres. Calif. Camping Adv. Coun., Long Beach, 1985-87; bd. dirs. Am. Camping Assn., Calif. Collaboration for Youth, Sacramento, 1985—, Ind. Camp Nat. Adv. Commn., Sickle Cell Disease Rsch. Found. Camp, L.A., 1985—, Camp Ronald McDonald for Good Times, 1989—; commr. dept. parks and recreation City of Agoura Hills, Calif., 1987—; cons. So. Calif. Children's Cancer Svcs., L.A., 1986—. Mem. Am. Camping Assn. (bd. dirs. So. Calif. sect., vice-chmn. nat. legis. com. Martinsville, Ind., 1980—, nat. bd. dirs. 1990—, legis. liaison, regional honor 1986). Office: Speare and Co Ins Brokers 11620 Wilshire Blvd Ste 900 Los Angeles CA 90025-6820

MILLAR, RICHARD WILLIAM, JR., lawyer; b. Los Angeles, May 11, 1938. LLB, U. San Francisco, 1966. Bar: Calif. 1967, U.S. Dist. Ct. (cen. dist.) Calif. 1967, U.S. Dist. Ct. (no. dist.) Calif. 1969, U.S. Dist. Ct. (so. dist.) Calif. 1973, U.S. Supreme Ct. Assoc. Iverson & Hogoboom, Los Angeles, 1967-72; ptnr. Eilers, Stewart, Pangman & Millar, Newport Beach, Calif., 1973-75, Millar & Heckman, Newport Beach, 1975-77, Millar, Hodges & Bemis, Newport Beach, 1979—. Mem. ABA (litigation sect., trial practice com., ho. of dels. 1990—), Calif. Bar Assn. (lectr. continuing legal edn.), Orange County Bar Assn. (chmn. bus. litigation sect. 1981, chmn. judiciary com. 1988-90), Am. Judicature Soc., Balboa Bay Club (Newport Beach). Home: 2546 Crestview Dr Newport Beach CA 92663-5625 Office: Millar Hodges Bemis & Mozingo One Newport Pl Ste # 900 Newport Beach CA 92660

MILLARD, ESTHER LOUND, foundation administrator, educator; b. Metaline, Wash., June 10, 1909; d. Peter S. and Emily Christine (Dahlgren) Lound; m. Homer Behne Millard, Apr. 25, 1951 (dec. May 1962). BA, U. Wis., 1933, MA, 1935. Cert. tchr., Oreg., Wis. Instr. U. Hawaii, Honolulu, 1938-43; joined USN, 1943, advanced through ranks to lt. commdr., resigned, 1952; dir. Millard Sch., Bandon, Oreg., 1954-81; pres. Millard Found., Bandon, 1984—. Trustee Falcon Found., Colorado Springs, Colo., 1986—; established scholarship fund for med. sch. students, U. Wis. Mem. Bascom Hill Soc. (U. Wis.), Phi Beta Kappa. Republican. Home: 52 Tom Smith Rd Bandon OR 97411-9311

MILLARD, GEORGE RICHARD, bishop; b. Dunsmuir, Calif., Oct. 2, 1914; s. George Ellis and Constance (Rainsberry) M.; m. Mary Louise Gessling, June 29, 1939; children: George, Martha, Joseph. A.B., U. Calif.-Berkeley, 1936; B.D., Episcopal Theol. Sch., Cambridge, Mass., 1938; S.T.M., Pacific Sch. Religion, 1958; D.D., Ch. Div. Sch. Pacific, 1960; M.A., U. Santa Clara, 1983. Ordained to ministry Episcopal Ch. as priest 1938. Asst. in Episc. Ch., N.Y.C., 1938-39, Waterbury, Conn., 1930-40; rector in Episc. Ch., Danbury, Conn., 1940-50, Alameda, Calif., 1951-59; suffragan bishop Episc. Diocese Calif., 1960-76; bishop of San Jose, 1969-76; exec., venture in mission program, exec. council Episc. Ch., 1977-78; bishop in charge Am. Chs. in Europe, 1978-80, bishop in charge ch. divinity sch. pacific exec. office for alumni/ae affairs, 1978-80; dean Convocation of Oakland, Calif., 1957-60; chmn. dept. missions Diocese Calif., 1958-60; mem. Joint Commn. on Structure, Episc. Ch., 1967-76. Chmn. Maria Kip Orphange; chmn. devel. program U. Calif. at Berkeley Student Coop. Assn., 1966; coord. Ch. Div. Sch. Pacific Alumni Affairs, 1986-88. Mem. The Club of Rome.

MILLARD, MALCOLM STUART, lawyer; b. Highland Park, Ill., Mar. 22, 1914; s. Everett L. and Elizabeth (Boynton) M.; m. Joanne T. Blakeman; 1 child, Anne W. Benjamin. BA, Harvard U., 1936; JD, Northwestern U., 1939. Bar: Ill. 1939, Calif. 1951. Ptnr. Farr & Millard, Carmel, Calif., 1951-55, Millard, Tourangeau, Morris & Staples, P.C., Carmel, 1955-91, Millard, Morris & Staples, Carmel, 1991—; dir. Leslie Salt Co., 1975-81. Trustee Community Hosp. of Monterey Peninsula, 1982-88, Monterey Inst. Fgn. Studies, 1955-76, Community Found. Monterey County, 1988—; pres. Community Chest of Monterey Peninsula, 1958. Served to lt. USN, 1943-46. Mem. Monterey Inst. Internat. Relations (hon. lifetime trustee 1982—, hon. DHL 1991), Ill. State Bar, Calif. State Bar, Monterey County Bar Assn. (pres.), Old Capital Club, Harvard Club. Office: Millard Morris & Staples PO Box 5427 Carmel CA 93921-5427

MILLARD, NEAL STEVEN, lawyer; b. Dallas, June 6, 1947; s. Bernard and Adele (Marks) M. BA cum laude, UCLA, 1969; JD, U. Chgo., 1972. Bar: Calif. 1972, U.S. Dist. Ct. (cen. dist.) Calif. 1973, U.S. Tax Ct. 1973, U.S. Ct. Appeals (9th cir.) 1987, N.Y. 1990. Assoc. Willis, Butler & Schiefly, Los Angeles, 1972-75; ptnr. Morrison & Foerster, Los Angeles, 1975-84, Jones, Day, Reavis & Pogue, Los Angeles, 1984-93, White & Case, L.A., 1993—; instr. Calif. State Coll., San Bernardino, 1975-76; lectr. Practising Law Inst., N.Y.C., 1983-90, Calif. Edn. of Bar, 1987-90. Member citizens adv. com. L.A. Olympics, 1982-84; trustee Altadena (Calif.) Libr. Dist., 1985-86; bd. dirs. Woodcraft Rangers, L.A., 1982-90, pres., 1986-88; bd. dirs. L.A. County Bar Found., 1990—. Capt. U.S. Army, 1970-72. Mem. ABA, Calif. Bar Assn., N.Y. State Bar Assn., L.A. County Bar Assn. (trustee 1985-87), Pub. Counsel (bd. dirs. 1984-87, 90-93), U. Chgo. Law Alumni Assn. (bd. dirs. So. Calif. chpt. 1981—), Calif. Club, Altadena Town and Country Club, Phi Beta Kappa, Pi Gamma Mu, Phi Delta Phi. Office: White & Case 633 W 5th St Ste 1900 Los Angeles CA 90071

MILLER, ANITA HADASSAH, mental health services professional; b. Chgo., Feb. 22, 1938; d. Erwin and Leah (Regensberg) Kornfeld; m. Erwin Sheldon Miller, Apr. 30, 1957; children: Michelle Woodine, Edynn, Elliot. Student, Roosevelt U., Chgo., 1954-57, 61-62; BA, Pacific Oaks Coll., Pasadena, Calif., 1987, MA in Human Devel., 1990. Registered intern marriage, family and child counseling; cert. geriatric mental health. Field mgr. Welcome Wagon Internat., Memphis, 1975-76; moving cons. Calif. Moving & Storage Co., Van Nuys, 1976-78; sales rep. Universal Drapery Fabrics, L.A., 1978-87, sales and mktg. mgr., 1987-89; mktg. rep. Life Plus Treatment Ctr., Panorama City, Calif., 1989-90; community and profl. svcs. coord. Life Plus Mental Health Svcs., Valley Hosp. Med. Ctr., Van Nuys, 1990—; mem. HIV counseling program adv. bd. Community Cons. Ctr., 1991-92. Mem. older adults task force L.A. County Dept. Mental Health, 1991-92; mem. adv. bd. Santa Clarita Sr. Ctr., Newhall, Calif., 1990-92; mem. community com. Bernardi Sr. Multipurpose Ctr., Van Nuys, 1990-92; sec. bd. dirs. Teen-Age Grief, 1990-92; conf. presenter Am. Soc. Aging, 1992; mem. Area Agy. on Aging Hosp. Com., 1992; co-founder San Fernando Valley Aging Network; bd. chair City of Hope, 1981-83. Recipient Presdl. award Nat. Women's League, Midwest region, Chgo., 1966, award Maine Twp. Jewish Congregation Sisterhood, Des Plaines, Ill., 1976. Mem. Calif. Assn. Marriage and Family Therapists (co-chair hosp. com. San Fernando Valley chpt.), Coun. Aging, B'nai B'rith Women (v.p. 1979-80). Office: Valley Hosp Med Ctr Mental Health Adminstrn 14500 Sherman Circle Van Nuys CA 91405-9978

MILLER, ANNE KATHLEEN, training company executive and technical marketing consultant; b. Denver, Sept. 15, 1942; d. John Henry and Kathryn Elizabeth (Doherty) Meyer; m. Edgar Earle Miller, Aug. 20, 1966 (div. Aug. 1976); children: Sheila Anne, Rebecca Elizabeth; m. Warren Ross Landry, Dec. 11, 1982 (dec. Oct. 1990). BS in Chemistry, St. Mary Coll., Leavenworth, Kans., 1964. Cert. jr. coll., secondary tchr., Calif. Lectr. San Jose (Calif.) U., 1978-82; product mgr. Jasco Chem., Mountain View, Calif., 1979-82; v.p., gen. mgr. Micropel, Hayward, Calif., 1982-84; product mgr. Cambridge Instruments, Santa Clara, Calif., 1984-86; product mktg. mgr. KLA Instruments, Santa Clara, 1986-87; pres., owner Meyland Enterprises, Redwood City, Calif., 1987—, Semiconductor Svc. Tng. Orgn., Redwood City, Calif., 1988—. Inventor formation of optical film. Mem. Soc. Photo Optical Instrumentation Engrs., Am. Chem. Soc., Semiconductor Industry Equipment Materials Inst., Am. Electronics Assn. Office: Meyland/Semiconductor Svcs 735 Hillcrest Way Redwood City CA 94062-3428

MILLER, ARJAY, retired university dean; b. Shelby, Nebr., Mar. 4, 1916; s. Rawley John and Mary Gertrude (Schade) M.; m. Frances Marion Fearing, Aug. 18, 1940; children: Kenneth Fearing, Ann Elizabeth (Mrs. James Olstad). B.S. with highest honors, UCLA, 1937; LL.D. (hon.), 1964; postgrad., U. Calif.-Berkeley, 1938-40; LL.D. (hon.), Washington U., St. Louis; LL.D., Whitman Coll., 1965, U. Nebr., 1965, Ripon Coll., 1980. Teaching asst. U. Calif. at Berkeley, 1938-40; research technician Calif. State Planning Bd., 1941; economist Fed. Res. Bank San Francisco, 1941-43; asst. treas. Ford Motor Co., 1946-53, controller, 1953-57, v.p., controller, 1957-61, v.p. finance, 1961-62, v.p. of staff group, 1962-63, pres., 1963-68, vice chmn., 1968-69; dean Grad. Sch. Bus., Stanford U., 1969-79, emeritus, 1979—; former chmn. Automobile Mfrs. Assn., Econ. Devel. Corp. Greater Detroit; councillor The Conf. Bd.; past chmn., life trustee Urban Inst.; mem. Public Adv. Commn. on U.S. Trade Policy, 1968-69, Pres.'s Nat. Commn. on Productivity, 1970-74. Trustee Internat. Exec. Svc. Corps; hon. trustee The Brookings Instn.; bd. dirs. Wm. and Flora Hewlitt Found., S.R.I. Internat.; former pres. Detroit Press Club Found.; former chmn. Bay Area coun. Capt. USAAF, 1943-46. Recipient Alumnus of Year Achievement award UCLA, 1964; Distinguished Nebraskan award, 1968; Nat. Industry Leader award B'nai B'rith, 1968. Fellow Am. Acad. Arts and Scis. Presbyterian. Clubs: Pacific Union, Bohemian.

MILLER, ARNOLD JOSEPH, JR., seminary student; b. Denver, May 24, 1957; s. Arnold Joseph and Betty Lou (Ebbs) M. BS in Microbiology, Colo. State U., Ft. Collins, 1981; postgrad., Mt. Angel Sem., St. Benedict, Oreg., 1993—. Asst. fishery biologist Wyo. Fish and Game Dept., Laramie, Wyo., 1979; laborer Colo. Div. of Wildlife, Montrose, Colo., 1981; sales and design solar and wind energy systems Creative Energy Ctr., Loveland, Colo., 1981-82; biological aide Idaho Fish and Game Dept., Idaho Power, Stanley, Challis, Idaho, 1982-84; asst. fish biologist/roving fish culturist U.S. Army Corps. of Engrs., Pomeroy, Wash., 1984-86; hatchery supt. I Idaho Fish and Game Dept., Idaho Power, Wendell, Idaho, 1986-87, Riggins, Idaho, 1988-90; Hatchery Supt. II Idaho Fish and Game Dept., Grace, Idaho, 1990-93; mem. Am. Fisheries Soc., Fish Culture Section, Fish Health Section, Boise, ID. Author: Hatchery Brood Year Reports, 1985-87, Fish Transportation-Lower Granite Assistant Fishery Biologist, 1985. Speaker Cursillo Movement, Twin Falls, ID, 1986-90. Recipient Eagle Scout, Boy Scouts of Am., Denver, 1969. Mem. 4th Degree Knights of Columbus. Roman Catholic. Home: 386 Fish Hatchery Rd Grace ID 83241-5321 Office: Idaho Fish and Game Dept 390 Fish Hatchery Rd Grace ID 83241-5321

MILLER, ARTHUR DUSTY, molecular biologist; b. Salisbury, Eng., Feb. 14, 1952; came to U.S., 1952; s. Arthur G. and Nancy (Pettersen) M.; m. Sandy Fox Haight, Dec. 23, 1979; children: Shayla, Adrien. BA and BS, Brown U., 1975; PhD, Stanford U., 1982. Postdoctoral fellow The Salk Inst., La Jolla, Calif., 1982-84; asst. mem. Fred Hutchinson Cancer Rsch. Ctr., Seattle, 1984-89, assoc. mem., 1989-93, mem., 1993—; speaker to profl. groups; contbr. to first human gene therapy experiments. Mem. editorial bd. Jour. Somatic Cell and Molecular Genetics, 1985, Molecular Biology and Medicine, 1988-90; mem. editorial bd. Human Gene Therapy, 1989—, assoc. editor, 1991—; contbr. numerous articles to profl. jours. Home: 5524 16th Ave NE Seattle WA 98105-3415 Office: Fred Hutchinson Cancer Rsch Ctr 1124 Columbia St Seattle WA 98104-2092

MILLER, BARBARA DARLENE, art educator; b. Jarbidge, Nev.; d. Herbert Beard and Gerra Vanetten (Carncross) Beard; 2 children. BA, U. Wash., 1955; MEd, U. Hawaii, 1974. Cert. secondary tchr. Occupational therapist N.D. State Hosp. for Mental Illness, Jamestown, 1954-55; art tchr. Dept. Edn. Hilo (Hawaii) High Sch., 1957-58; art specialist Elem. Intermediate Sch., Kahului, Hawaii, 1964-65; art instr. Maui Community Coll., Kahului, 1965—; art dir. Sta. KHVH-TV, Honolulu, 1962-63. One-woman shows include County Bldg., 1985, 87-90, MCC Libr., 1987, 90; exhibited in group shows at Am. Fac Pla., 1980, 91, Hawaii State Libr., 1980, Honolulu Acad. Arts; commd. numerous portraits. Visual Arts chairperson Maui Community Arts Coun., 1972-80; bd. dirs., past pres. Hui Noeau Art Soc., 1966-90; v.p. Maui Weavers Guild, 1976; planning com., bd. dirs. Art Maui '80-'84, 1979-84; bd. dirs. Maui Symphony Orch., 1984-87; mayor's adv. coun. for culture and the arts Archtl. Art Com., 1986-87; Maui rep. on budget com. Hawaii State Found. on Culture and the Arts, 1991. Recipient Certificate of Appreciation for Beautification of Maui County Council of Maui. Mem. NEA, AAUP, Maui Aikido Ki Soc. Office: Maui Community Coll 310 W Kaahumanu Ave Kahului HI 96732-1625

MILLER, BARBARA STALLCUP, medical foundation administrator; b. Montague, Calif., Sept. 4, 1919; d. Joseph Nathaniel and Maybelle (Needham) Stallcup; m. Leland F. Miller, May 16, 1946; children: Paula Kay, Susan Lee, Daniel Joseph, Alison Jean. B.A., U. Oreg., 1942. Women's editor Eugene (Oreg.) Daily News, 1941-43; law clk. to J. Everett Barr, Yreka, Calif., 1943-45; mgr. Yreka C. of C., 1945-46; Northwest supr. Louis Harris and Assocs., Portland, Oreg., 1959-62; dir. pub. relations and fund raising Columbia River council Girl Scouts U.S.A., 1962-67; pvt. practice pub. relations cons., Portland, 1967-72; adviser of student publs., asst. prof. communications U. Portland, 1967-72, dir. pub. relations and info., asst. prof. communications, 1972-78, dir. devel., 1978-79, exec. dir. devel., 1979-83; assoc. dir. St. Vincent Med. Found., 1983-88; dir. planned giving Good Samaritan Found., 1988—. Pres. bd. dirs. Vols. of Am. of Oreg., Inc., 1980-84, pres. regional adv. bd., 1982-84; chmn. bd. dirs. S.E. Mental Health Network, 1984-88; nat. bd. dirs. Vols. of Am., Inc., 1984—; pres., bd. dirs. Vol. Bur. Greater Portland, 1991-93; mem. U. Oreg. Journalism Advancement Coun., 1991—; named Oasis Sr. Role Model, 1992. Recipient Presdl. Citation, Oreg. Communicators Assn., 1973, Matrix award, 1976, 80, Miltner award U. Portland, 1977, Communicator of Achievement award Oreg. Press Women, 1992, Barbara Stallcup Miller Profl. Achievement award, 1992, Willamette Valley Devel. Officers award, 1992. Mem. Nat. Assn. Hosp. Devel., Nat. Soc. Fundraising Execs., Nat. Planned Giving Coun, Women in Communications (NW regional v.p. 1973-75, Offbeat award 1988), Nat. Fedn. Press Women, Oreg. Press Women (dist. dir.), Pub. Rels. Soc. Am. (dir. local chpt., Marsh award 1989), Oreg. Fedn. Womens Clubs (communications chmn. 1978-80), Alpha Xi Delta (found. trustee, editor 1988—). Unitarian. Clubs: Portland Zenith (pres. 1975-76, 81-82). Contbr. articles to profl. jours. Home: 1706 Boca Ratan Dr Lake Oswego OR 97034-1624 Office: 1015 NW 22d Ave Portland OR 97210

MILLER, BILL, management and marketing consultant; b. Jersey City, Mar. 6, 1933; Children: Valerie, Lynn, Lori, Michael, Billy Joe. MBA, La Jolla U., 1980. Cert. (life) coll. level tchr. psychology, bus. mgmt. and mktg., mgmt. orgn. and human relations, Calif. Enlisted USMC, 1948, ret., 1967; instr. karate, judo and mob control N.J. and Calif. Police Depts.; owner, pres. Bill Miller and Assocs., Inc., 1976—, Mgmt. Dynamics; cons. to mgmt. in healthcare, exec. search; presenter mgmt. seminars; instr. psychology, bus. mgmt. and mktg., mgmt. orgn. and human relations U. Calif.-La Jolla and Nat. U., San Diego. Home: 12696 Pacato Cir N San Diego CA 92128-2370

MILLER, BRAD STEVEN, artificial intelligence researcher; b. Phila., Oct. 17, 1953; s. Bennett and Elaine (Goodman) M.; m. Laura Ann Oseran, July 9, 1988; children: Michael, Cora. BA, Wesleyan U., Middletown, Conn., 1975; BSEE, U. Wash., 1978, postgrad., 1984-86. Project engr. Seatronics Inc., Auburn, Wash., 1979-84; artificial intelligence specialist Boeing Co., Seattle, 1986—. Mem. IEEE. Office: Boeing Def & Space Group PO Box 3707 MS 4C-64 Seattle WA 98124-2207

MILLER, BRADLEY LEE, financial planner; b. Lewiston, Idaho, Sept. 8, 1937; s. Paul Clark Miller and Joeene B. (Ackley) Wiles; m. Lora Mae Lunn, Mar. 25, 1959; children: Debra Cherie Miller Biel, Scott Allen, Misti Jo Miller Cleveland. BS, Drury Coll., 1963, MBA, 1967. Engrng. mgr. Spirngday Co., Springfield, Mo., 1960-67, Clow Corp., Conora, Calif., 1979-80, Continental Can Co., Hopewell, Va., 1968-70; div. engr. Continental Can Co., Chgo., 1971-72; corp. engring. mgr. United Can Co., Buena Park, Calif., 1972-74; mgr. Found. Press, Anaheim, Calif., 1975-78; br. mgr. Linsco/Pvt. Ledger, Orange, Calif., 1981—. Pastor Omega Ministries, San Bernardino, Calif., 1977-81; fellowship leader Christian Chapel, Walnut, Calif., 1982-84, Zion Christian Ctr., Orange, 1985—. Mem. Internat. Assn. Fin. Planners. Republican. Avocations: bicycling, photography, fly fishing. Office: Lisco/Pvt Ledger 1835 W Orangewood Ste 323 Orange CA 92668

MILLER, BURTON LEIBSLE, construction project manager; b. L.A., July 17, 1944; s. Kenneth Wilbur and Dorothy (Leibsle) M.; m. April Suydam, Dec. 22, 1969 (div. 1983); children: Brandon, Gregory; m. Linda L. Reynolds, Aug. 11, 1990. BSCE, San Jose State U., 1968; MS in Engring., U. So. Calif., 1977. Civil engr. USN, San Bruno, Calif., 1968-74; cost engr. Bechtel Corp., L.A., 1974-79; supr. Bechtel Corp., Saudi Arabia, 1979-81; project mgr. Bechtel Corp., San Francisco, 1981-84, Bay Area Contractors, San Francisco, 1984—; cons. KMD/Kimco Mgmt. Co., San Francisco, 1989-90. Mem. World Affairs Coun., San Francisco, 1991, C of C., San Francisco, 1986. Recipient Commendation, V.P. Dan Quayle, 1992, Cert. of Appreciation, Pres. George Bush, 1989, Cert. of Appreciation, Congressman Bob Mitchel, 1991. Mem. Commonwealth Club of Calif., Olympic Club, Project Mgmt. Inst. Republican. Home: 1035 Cabrillo San Francisco CA 94118

MILLER, CARL DUANE, transportation company executive; b. Tulare, Calif., Aug. 24, 1941; s. Carl D. and Ida Ferne (Martin) M.; m. Cheryl Rae Henard, Mar. 29, 1961; children: Kelli R. Walker, Lori Leigh Elmore, Craig D. Student, Coll. of Sequoias, 1959-60, Am. Inst. Banking, 1964-69. Ops. supr. Crocker Citizens Nat. Bank., Tulare, 1964-69, Am. Nat. Bank, Tulare, 1969-70; Modesto terminal mgr. Kings County Truck Lines, 1970-75; Fresno outbound supr. Calif. Motor Express, 1975-77; terminal mgr. System 99 Transport, Tulare, 1977-80; pres., CEO Cal-Western Transport, Tulare, 1980-90, Daystar Transp., Tulare, 1990—; dir. Silver Arrow Express, Regency Transport Inc.; cons. Calif. Milk Producers, Artesia, Calif., 1990; transp. cons. Calif. Coop. Creamery, Petaluma, Calif., 1990; speaker world govt. and world monetary system various svc. clubs. Mem. City Coun., City of Tulare, 1979-83, mayor, 1983-87, Bd. Pub. Utilities, 1978; bd. mem. Nat. Coun. for Drugs and Alcohol, Tulare, 1980—; mem. exec. bd. Tulare County Econ. Devel.; transp. com. League of Calif. Cities. With USAF, 1960-64; v.p. Little League Baseball, Babe Ruth Baseball. Louis Pasteur fellow Scripps Clinic Rsch. Coun. Mem. NRA, AMVETS, Am. Legion, Am. Mgmt. Assn., Elks, Lions (v.p.). Republican. Home and Office: Daystar Transp Inc 2511 E Vassar Ct Visalia CA 93277

MILLER, CAROLE ANN LYONS, editor, publisher, advertising specialist; b. Newton, Mass., Aug. 1; d. Markham Harold and Ursula Patricia (Foley) Lyons; m. David Thomas Miller, July 4, 1978. BA, Boston U., 1964; bus. cert., Hickox Sch., Boston, 1964; cert. advt. and mktg. profl. UCLA, 1973; cert. retail mgmt. profl. Ind. U., 1976. Editor Triangle Topics, Pacific Telephone, L.A.; programmer L.A. Cen. Area Speakers' Bur., 1964-66; mng. editor/mktg. dir. Teen mag., L.A. and N.Y.C., 1966-76; advt. dir. L.S. Ayres & Co., Indpls., 1976-78; v.p. mktg. The Denver, 1978-79; founder, editor, pub. Clockwise mag., Ventura, Calif., 1979-85; mktg. mgr., mgr. pub. rels. and spl. events Robinson's Dept. Stores, L.A., 1985-87, exec. v.p., dir. mktg. Harrison Svcs., L.A., 1987—; instr. retail advt. Ind. U., 1977-78. Recipient Pres.'s award Advt. Women of N.Y., 1974; Seklemian award 1977; Pub. Svc. Addy award, 1978. Mem. Advt. Women N.Y., Fashion Group Internat., Bay Area Integrated Mktg., San Francisco Fashion Group, San Francisco Direct Mktg. Assn., San Francisco Ad Club (life), UCLA Alumni Assn. Editor: Sek Says, 1979. Home: 3709 Carson Rd Camino CA 95709-9506

MILLER, CHARLES DALY, business executive; b. Hartford, Conn., 1928; married. Grad., Johns Hopkins U. Sales mgr. Yale & Towne Mfg. Co., 1955-59; assoc. Booz, Allen & Hamilton, 1959-64; with Avery Internat. Corp., Pasadena, Calif., 1964—, group v.p., 1969-72, exec. v.p. ops., 1972-75, pres., 1975-77; chief exec. officer, chmn. bd. dirs. Avery Dennison Corp. (formerly Avery Internat. Corp.), Pasadena, Calif., 1977—. Office: Avery Dennison Corp PO Box 7090 Pasadena CA 91109*

MILLER, CLARA BURR, educator; b. Higganum, Conn., July 19, 1912; d. Eugene Orlando and Mabel (Clark) Burr; m. James Golden Miller, Sept. 19, 1942; children: Clara Elizabeth, Eugenia Manelle. BA, Mt. Holyoke Coll., 1933; MA, Columbia U., 1942. Cert. tchr., Conn., N.Y. Tchr. Suffield (Conn.) Jr. High Sch., 1934-36, Rockville (Conn.) High Sch., 1936-41, Buckeley High Sch., Hartford, Conn., 1941-42, Pitts. Schs., 1952-55, Winchester-Thurston Sch., Pitts., 1955-58, Vail-Deane Sch., Elizabeth, N.J., 1959-69, Kingman (Ariz.) High Sch., 1971-76; mem. res. faculty Mohave Community Coll., Kingman, 1978—; pres. bd. edn., clk. Mohave Union High Sch. Dist. 30, 1983-91, bd. dirs., 1983—; bd. dirs. Mohave Mental Health Clinic, v.p. bd. dirs., 1988, pres. bd. dirs., 1989-90. Author: Trails, Rails and Tales, 1981, (with others) Short Stories, 1984. Bd. dirs. No. Ariz. Comprehensive Guidance Ctr., Flagstaff, 1985-90, Kingman Aid to Abused People; sec. Good Samaritan Assn., Inc., Kingman, 1979—; pres., Ch. Women United, 1972-74, Presbyn. Women, 1987, elected elder session Kingman Presbyn Ch., 1986—; mem. Mohave County Community Action Bd., Western Ariz. Coun. Govts.; coord. League Friendship Indians & Ams., 1981—; co-chmn. Women Making History Com., 1992—. Recipient Nat. Community Svc. award Mohave County Ret. Tchrs. Assn., 1987, Leta Glancy/Cecil Lockhart-Smith award No. Ariz. Comprehensive Guidance Ctr., 1990; named one of Women Making History Kingman Multi-Club Com., 1985. Mem. NEA, AAUW (pres. 1979-81), Ariz. Edn. Assn., Ariz. Sch. Bds. Assn., Soc. Profl. Journalists, Mohave County Ret. Tchrs. Assn. (v.p. 1991-93, pres. 1993—), Footprinters. Democrat. Home: 2629 Mullen Dr Kingman AZ 86401-4264

MILLER, CLIFFORD ALBERT, banker, business consultant; b. Salt Lake City, Aug. 6, 1928; s. Clifford Elmer and LaVeryl (Jensen) M.; m. Judith Auten, Sept. 20, 1976; 1 child, Courtney; children by previous marriage, Clifford, Christin, Stephanie. Student, U. Utah, 1945-50, UCLA, 1956. Staff corp. UP, Salt Lake City, 1949-55; pres. Braun & Co., L.A., 1955-82, chmn., 1982-87; exec. v.p. Gt. Western Fin. Corp., Beverly Hills, Calif., 1987-91; chmn. Clifford Group, Inc., bus. cons., 1992—; bd. dirs. Shamrock Holdings, Inc., Burbank, Calif., L.A. Gear, Inc., Santa Monica, Calif.; cons. to The White House, 1969-74. Chmn. bd. trustees Harvey Mudd Coll., Claremont, Calif.; chmn. emeritus L.A. Master Chorale; mem. chmn.'s coun. Music Ctr. Unified Fund Campaign. Mem. UCLA Chancellor's Assocs., Skull and Bones, Lakes Country Club, Calif. Club, L.A. Tennis Club, Pi Kappa Alpha. Office: Clifford Group Inc 4444 Lakeside Dr Burbank CA 91505

MILLER, CLIFFORD JOEL, lawyer; b. L.A., Oct. 31, 1947; s. Eugene and Marian (Millman) M.; m. Coco Ando, Apr. 9, 1990. BA, U. Calif., Irvine, 1969; JD, Pepperdine U., 1973. Bar: Calif. 1974, Hawaii 1974, U.S. Dist. Ct. Hawaii 1974. Ptnr. Rice, Lee & Wong, Honolulu, 1974-80, Goodsill Anderson Quinn & Stifel, Honolulu, 1980-89, McCorriston Miho & Miller, Honolulu, 1989—. Mem. ABA, Calif. Bar Assn., Hawaii Bar Assn., Am. Coll. Real Estate Lawyers. Office: McCorriston Miho & Miller Five Waterfront Pla Ste 400 500 Ala Moana Blvd Honolulu HI 96813

MILLER, DANIEL JAMES, management consultant; b. Denver, Feb. 21, 1958; s. Martin P. and Edythe (Stern) M.; m. Renee Dupont, Aug. 13, 1983; children: Sarah Danielle, Ryan James. BA, Pomona Coll., 1980; MBA, U. Denver, 1987. Sales mgr. Robert Waxman, Inc., Denver, 1980-83, sr. product mgr., 1983-86, corp. contr., chief fin. officer, 1986-89; pres. The Miller Mgmt. Group, Littleton, Colo., 1987—. Treas., officer, bd. dirs. Cottonwood Presch., Littleton, 1990-92; mem. Gov. Small Bus. Coun., 1991—, exec. com., 1992—. Mem. Pomona Coll. Alumni Assn., Rockies Venture Club (bd. dirs. 1991—). Office: 1901 W Littleton Blvd Littleton CO 80120-2058

MILLER, DAVID FOSTER, college president, educator; b. Cleve., Nov. 2, 1940; s. Thomas Theodore and Mildred D. (Seitz) M.; m. Koyce J. Morgan, Aug. 5, 1961; children: David Scott, Michael Thomas. BA, We. Bapt. Coll., El Cerrito, Calif., 1963; BD, San Francisco Bapt. Sem., 1966, ThM, 1968; ThD, Grace Sem., Winona Lake, Ind., 1977. Ordained to ministry Bapt. Ch., 1966. Prof. Bibl. studies We. Bapt. Coll., Salem, Oreg., 1966—, pres., 1991—; pastor, founder Valley Bapt. Ch., Perrydale, Oreg., 1974-91. Contbr. articles to profl. jours. Bd. dirs. KIDS Inc., Dallas, Oreg., 1979-87. Republican. Home: 5270 Woodscape Dr Salem OR 97306 Office: We Bapt Coll 5000 Deer Park Dr SE Salem OR 97306

MILLER, DAVID W., respiratory care practitioner; b. Petaluma, Calif., Sept. 7, 1956; s. Robert and Wanda L. (Green) M.; m. Barbara A. Fratts, Apr. 1, 1989. AS, Santa Rosa Jr. Coll., 1983; AS in Respiratory Therapy, Napa Valley Coll., 1984. Cert. respiratory therapy technician; registered respiratory therapist; respiratory care practitioner. Biology tutor ctr. ind. learning Santa Rosa (Calif.) Jr. Coll., 1976-77; respiratory therapist Pulmonary Technician Svcs., Concord, Calif., 1984-85, Los Meadanos Hosp., West Pittsburg, Calif., 1985, VA Med. Ctr., San Francisco, 1985—; instr. CPR ARC, Santa Rosa, 1980-81, instr. 1st aide, 1981-83. Vol. hotline cirsis Petaluma (Calif.) People Svcs. Ctr., 1982-84. Mem. Am. Assn. Respiratory Care, Nat. Bd. Respiratory Care, Calif. Soc. Respiratory Care.

MILLER, DAVID WAYNE, construction inspector, coordinator; b. Yuba City, Calif., June 23, 1949; s. Lloyd Wayne and Beverly Lorene (Ryan) M.; children: Quinlan Kenneth, Erin Patricia, Justin Michael Francis. AA in Constrn. Tech., Delta, 1985; BA in Art, Calif. State U., Hayward, 1989. Plumber/fitter local 492 United Assn. Pipe Trades, Stockton, Calif., 1972—; plumber/fitter Lawrence Livermore Nat. Lab., Livermore, Calif., 1983-87, estimator, 1987-90; owner Moon Studios, 1976-80, Moonraker, 1991—. Author: (short story) Morgan's Tide, 1982, (Fremont C. of C. lit.) History of Fremont, 1982—; contbr. articles to CitySports, 1982. Sgt. U.S. Army, 1969-71, Vietnam. Mem. Lawrence Livermore Armed Force Vets. Assn., (founder, pres. 1986), Toastmasters.

MILLER, DIANE WILMARTH, human resources director; b. Clarinda, Iowa, Mar. 12, 1940; d. Donald and Floy Pauline (Madden) W.; m. Robert Nolen Miller, Aug. 21, 1965; children: Robert Wilmarth, Anne Elizabeth. AA, Colo. Women's Coll., 1960; BBA, U. Iowa, 1962; postgrad., U. No. Colo., 1972—. Cert. tchr., Colo.; vocat. credential, Colo. Sec.-counselor U. S.C., Myrtle Beach AFB, 1968-69; instr. U. S.C., Conway, 1967-69; tchr. bus. Poudre Sch. Dist R-1, Ft. Collins, Colo., 1969-71; travel cons. United Bank Travel Svc., Greeley, Colo., 1972-74; dir. human resources Aims Community Coll., Greeley, 1984—; instr. part-time Aims Community Coll., Greeley, 1972—. Active 1st Congl. Ch., Greeley. Mem. Women's Investment Group Soc., Questers, Coll. Univ. Pers. Assn., Colo. Higher Edn. Pers. Adminstrs., No. Colo. Human Resource Assn., Philanthropic Ednl. Orgn. (pres. 1988-89), Women's Panhellenic Assn. (pres. 1983-84), Scroll and Fan Club (pres. 1985-86), WTK Club. Home: 3530 Wagon Trail Pl Greeley CO 80634-3405 Office: Aims Community Coll 5401 W 20th St PO Box 69 Greeley CO 80632-3000

MILLER, DUSTY CAMPBELL, financial planner; b. Glasgow, Scotland, Aug. 7, 1920; came to U.S., 1921; s. David and Annie (Matson) M.; m. Doris Lucile Benninger, Nov. 2, 1946; children: Kathleen Ann, Diane Doris. BA, U. Pacific, 1942, MA, 1952. Coach Folsom (Calif.) High Sch., 1946-49, prin., 1949-53; asst. supt. schs. Folsom Unified Sch. Dist., 1953-54; sales agt. Calif. Western Life Ins. Co., Sacramento, 1954-56, dir. tng. & manpower devel., 1956-71; pvt. practice Sacramento, 1971—; cons. Acacia Fin. Group, Sacramento, 1988—; com. mem. Estate Planning Coun., Sacramento, 1989—. Pres. Camellia Festival Assn., Sacramento, 1979, Am. River Coll. Found., Sacramento, 1980-82, Los Rios Coll. Found., Sacramento, 1983-85, No. Calif. Hall of Fame, Sacramento, 1970-85. Lt. U.S. Army, 1942-46, ETO. Mem. Internat. Assn. Fin. Planners (bd. dirs. Sacramento chpt. 1981-82), Internat. Assn. Cert. Fin. Planners (pres. 1981-82). Office: Acacia Group 2151 River Plaza Dr # 200 Sacramento CA 95833-3505

MILLER, EDDIE LEROY, philosophy and religious studies educator, author; b. L.A., Apr. 6, 1937; s. William Don Miller and Georgia Leota (Davidson) Barrington; m. Yvonne Marie Farrar, July 6, 1956 (div. June 1975); children: Terryl Eddie, Timothy Allen, Tad Stephen; m. Cynthia Lou Carter, Mar. 3, 1979; 1 child, Sean Davidson Miller. BA in Philosophy, U. So. Calif., 1959, MA in Philosophy, 1960, PhD in Philosophy, 1965; ThD, U. Basel (Switzerland), 1981. Jr. mathematician Bendix Computer Co., L.A., 1961-62; inst. philosophy Calif. Luth. Coll., Thousand Oaks, 1962-64; asst. prof. philosophy St. Olaf Coll., Northfield, Minn., 1964-66; asst. prof. philosophy U. Colo., Boulder, 1966-70, dir. theology forum, 1968—, assoc. prof. philosophy/religious studies, 1970-76, prof. philosophy/religious studies, 1976—; book rev. editor Theol. Students Fellowship Bull., Chgo., 1986-87. Author: Salvation-History in the Prologue of John, 1989 (CUSP award 1989), Questions That Matter, 3rd edit., 1992, God and Reason, 1972; editor: (anthologies) Classical Statements of Faith and Reason, 1970, Philosophical and Religious Issues, 1971. Mem. Studiorum Novi Testamentum Societas, Am. Acad. Religion, Soc. Christian Philosophers, Soren Kierkegaard Soc. Democrat. Lutheran. Home: 4220 Corriente Pl Boulder CO 80301-1629 Office: U Colo Philosophy Dept Campus Box 232 Boulder CO 80309

MILLER, EDMUND KENNETH, electrical engineer; b. Milw., Dec. 24, 1935; s. Edmund William and Viola Louise (Ludwig) M.; m. Patricia Ann Denn, Aug. 23, 1958; children: Kerry Ann, Mark Christopher. BSEE, Mich. Tech. U., 1957; MS in Nuclear Engring., U. Mich., 1958, MSEE, 1961, PhD in Elec. Engring., 1965. Rsch. assoc. U. Mich., Ann Arbor, 1965-68; sr. scientist MB Assocs., San Ramon, Calif., 1968-71; group leader engring. rsch. div. Lawrence Livermore Lab., Livermore, Calif., 1971-78, leader engring. rsch. div., 1978-83, leader nuclear energy systems div., 1983-85; regents prof. elect. and computer engring. U. Kans., 1985-87; mgr. electromagnetics Rockwell Sci. Ctr., Thousand Oaks, Calif., 1987-88; dir. electromagnetics rsch. operation Gen. Rsch. Corp., Santa Barbara, Calif., 1988-89; group leader MEE div. Los Alamos (N.Mex.) Nat. Lab., 1989—. Editor: Time Domain Measurements in Electromagnets, 1986; past assoc. editor Radio Sci.; assoc. editor IEEE Potentials, 1985-91, editor, 1992—; assoc. editor IEEE AP-S mag.; co-editor (with L. Medgyesi-Mitschang and E.H. Newman) Computational Electromagnetics, 1991; editorial bd. Internat. Jour. Numerical Modeling, 1990—, Computer Applications in Engring. Edn., 1992—; editor: Jour. Electromagnetic Waves and Applications, 1991—, Jour. of Applied Computational Electromagnetics Soc.; contbr. 100 articles to profl. jours. Singer Lyra Male Chorus, Ann Arbor, Mich., 1966-68, Livermore Civic Chorus, 1969-71. Fellow IEEE (mem. press. bd. 1991—), mem. Am. Phys. Soc., Optical Soc. Am., Acoustical Soc. Am., Am. Soc. Engring. Edn., Electromagnetics Soc. (past bd. dirs.) Internat. Sci. Radio Union (past chmn. U.S. Commn. A), Applied Computational Electromagnetics Soc. (past pres.). Office: Los Alamos Nat Lab MSJ580 Los Alamos NM 87545

MILLER, EMMETT EMMANUEL, physician; m. Nitza Miller (div.); 1 child, Yuval; m. Sandra Miller; children: Emmett Jr., Lauren. BS in Math./Physics, Trinity Coll., Hartford, Conn., 1963; MD, Albert Einstein Coll. Medicine, 1967. Internship Pacific Medical Ctr., San Francisco, 1967-68; pvt. practice Carmel, Calif., 1970-74, Menlo Park, Calif., 1974—; speakers coord. Physicians for Social Responsibility, Palo Alto, Calif., 1985; mem. staff Monterey County Gen. Hosp., Gilroy Migrant Workers Health Clinic, Kaiser Found. Hosps., Monterey Hosp. Lt., Community Hosp. Monterey Peninsula; med. dir. Creighton Health Inst., Menlo Park, Calif.; cons. stress mgmt. and optimal performance to bus., industry, athletes, govt., performing artists, others; instr., lectr. various colls. and univs.; mem. nat. adv. bd. Cancer Counseling Inst., Calif. Task Force on Self Esteem & Personal and Social Responsibility. Author: Selective Awareness, 1975, Self-Imagery: Creating Your Own Good Health, 1986, Software for the Mind, 1988, Opening Your Inner Eye, 1990, Living in Hope, 1991; author and narrator audio cassette programs, 1973-92; contbg. author: Holistic Medicine, A Multidimensional Approach, 1982, Body, Mind and Health: Toward an Integral Medicine, 1979, Holistic Medicine: Harmony of Body Mind Spirit, 1982, Healers on Healing, 1989; media appearances on TV and radio; contbr. articles to profl. jours. Bd. advisors Avanta Network, The Hermes Project, Inc., The Inside Edge; dir. Better & Better, Inc.; medical cons. Cancer Support and Edn. Ctr., Menlo Park, Calif. Capt. U.S. Army, 1968-70. Mem. Am. Soc. Clin. Hypnosis, Am. Soc. Psychoprophylaxis in Obstetrics, Assn. Humanistic Psychology, Calif. Assn. Marriage and Family Therapists, Esalen Inst., Internat. Assn. Cancer Counselors, Wellness Assocs. (bd. dirs.), Western Psychol. Assn., Yung Pres. Orgn., Am. Soc. Clin. Hypnosis, Internat. Soc. Hypnosis. Office: Source Cassette Learning System 945 Evelyn St Menlo Park CA 94025

MILLER, FRANKLIN EMRICK, software engineer, project engineer; b. Greenville, Ohio, Aug. 12, 1946; s. Rollin Linde and E. Evelyn (Emrick) M.; m. Sandra Lewis, Dec. 20, 1969; children: William Rollin, Rose Mary. BS, Otterbein Coll., 1969; MEd in Ednl. Psychology and Counseling, Wayne State U., 1975; PhD, U. Denver, 1984. Lic. pvt. pilot FAA. Commd. U.S. Air Force, 1969, advanced through grades to capt.; space surveillance officer SLBM, Maine, 1970-71, BMEWS Thule, Greenland, 1971-72; chief instr./systems analyst, Correlation Ctr. 440L, McGuire AFB, N.J., 1972-73; site space surveillance officer, Aviano, Italy, 1973-75; chief Defense Support Program support programming unit, Colo., 1975-79; chief applications support programming DSP, South Australia, 1979-81, ret., 1988; software engr. Aerojet Electro Systems Corp., Aurora, Colo., 1981-88. Bd. dirs., Aurora Community Mental Health Ctr., 1976-79; vol. counselor Comitis Crisis Ctr., YMCA, Aurora, 1976-78. Mem. Am. Psychol. Assn. (div. Applied Experimental and Engring. Psychologists), Denver Astron. Soc. (sec.), Phi Delta Kappa. Republican. Author: The Preliminary Online Rorschach Test Manual, 1980; contbr. article to profl. jour. Office: The Aerospace Corp Buckley Ang Base 18300 E Crested Butte Ave Aurora CO 80011-9518

MILLER, GEORGE, congressman; b. Richmond, Calif., May 17, 1945; s. George and Dorothy (Rumsey) M.; m. Cynthia Caccavo, 1964; children: George, Stephen. B.A., San Francisco State Coll., 1968; J.D., U. Calif., Davis, 1972. Legis. counsel Calif. senate majority leader, 1969-73; mem. 94th-102nd Congresses from 7th Calif. dist., 1975—; chmn. subcom. on oversight and investigations, 1985—, mem. subcom., 1993—; chmn. subcom. on labor standards, 1981-84; chmn. select com. on children, youth and families, 1983-91, chmn. com. on natural resources, 1992—; mem. com. on edn. and lab., dep. majority whip, 1989—. Mem. Calif. Bar Assn. Office: House of Representatives House Office Bldg 2205 Rayburn Washington DC 20515

MILLER, GEORGE, mayor; b. Detroit; m. Roslyn Girard; 4 children. BS, U. Ariz., 1947, MEd, 1952. Tchr. high schs., owner, prin. painting contracting co., until 1989; mayor City of Tucson, 1991—. Active mem. Dem. Party So. Ariz., 1960—, treas. Pima County div., state chmn. Presdl. Del. Selection Reform Commn.; bd. dirs. Tucson Jewish Community Ctr., Anti-Defamation League of B'nai Brith; councilman Tucson City Coun., 1977-91, also vice mayor. With USMC, WWII. Decorated Purple Heart; recipient recognition award United Way, Community Svcs. Support award Chicanos Por La Causa (2), cert. appreciation San Ignacio Yaqui Coun., Old Pasqua, Man of Yr. award So. Ariz. Home Builders Assn. Office: Office of Mayor City of Tucson 255 W Alameda Tucson AZ 85701

MILLER, GORDON HOLMAN, chemical, nuclear and environmental engineering consultant; b. Kansas City, Mo., Jan. 12, 1916; s. Mervin Thurmond and Alice Henshaw (Snively) M.; m. Marjorie Jane Trimble, Feb. 14, 1942. AS, Kansas City Jr. Coll., Mo., 1934; BSChemE, U. Kans., Lawrence, 1936; MSChemE, Pa. State U., 1939; PhD in Nuclear Engring., U. Mich., 1962. Chemist, Kansas City Testing Labs., Mo., 1936; chief chemist Certain-Teed Products Corp., Kansas City, 1937; from chemist to supr. Texaco Inc., Port Arthur, Tex., 1939-56, sr. engr. radiation research, Beacon, N.Y., 1956-62, environ. coordinator, Denver, 1974-82; research assoc. Texaco Experiment Inc., Richmond, Va., 1962-74; cons. chem., nuclear and environ. engring. Texaco Inc., Littleton, Colo., 1982-84; pvt. cons. chem., nuclear and environ. engring., Littleton, 1982—. Patentee in field. Recipient Thiokol award Am. Rocket Soc., 1959. Mem. Am. Chem. Soc. (sect. chmn. 1955-56), N.Y. Acad. Scis. (Boris Pregel award 1962), AAAS, Am. Forestry Assn., Research Soc. Am. (sec. chmn. 1962), Sigma Xi, Tau Beta Pi, Sigma Tau, Pi Mu Epsilon. Home and Office: 1321 E Costilla Ave Littleton CO 80122-1346

MILLER, GREGORY M., broadcast engineer; b. Yuba City, Calif., Oct. 20, 1961; s. Larry Ralph M. and Bonnie Lee (Alden) Murphree; m. Cynthia Lynn Atkisson, May 3, 1992. A in Elec. Engring. Tech., Lane Community Coll., 1990. Radar computer tech. USN, various cities, 1980-86; asst. engr. Sta. KSND-FM, Eugene, Oreg., 1988-89, Sta. KLCX-FM, Eugene, 1989-90; chief engr. Sta. KZMG-FM, Boise, Idaho, 1990-92; chief engr. prodn. dept. TCI Cablevision, Eugene, 1992—. Office: TCI Cablevision Oreg 990 Garfield Eugene OR 97402

MILLER, HAROLD WILLIAM, nuclear geochemist; b. Walton, N.Y., Apr. 21, 1920; s. Harold Frank and Vera Leona (Simons) M. BS in Chemistry, U. Mich., 1943; MS in Chemistry, U. Colo., 1948, postgrad. Control chemist Linde Air Products Co., Buffalo, 1943-46; analytical research chemist Gen. Electric Co., Richland, Wash., 1948-51; research chemist Phillips Petroleum Co., Idaho Falls, Idaho, 1953-56; with Anaconda (Mont.) Copper Co., 1956; tech. dir., v.p. U.S. Yttrium Co., Laramie, Wyo., 1956-57; tech. dir. Colo. div. The Wah Chang Co., Boulder, Colo., 1957-58; analytical chemist The Climax (Colo.) Molybdenum Co., 1959; with research and devel. The Colo. Sch. of Mines Research Found., Golden, 1960-62; cons. Boulder, 1960—; sr. research physicist Dow Chem. Co., Golden, 1963-73; bd. dirs. Sweeney Mining and Milling Corp., Boulder; cons. Hendricks Mining and Milling Co., Boulder; instr. nuclear physics and nuclear chemistry Rocky Flats Plant, U. Colo. Contbr. numerous articles to profl. jours. Recipient Lifetime Achievement award Boulder County Metal Mining Assn., 1990. Mem. Sigma Xi. Home and Office: PO Box 1092 Boulder CO 80306-1092

MILLER, HARRIET EVELYN, management consultant; b. Council, Idaho, July 4, 1919; d. Colwell and Vera (Crome) M. B.A. magna cum laude, Whitman Coll., 1941, D.H.L., 1979; M.A., U. Pa., 1949. Chemist Atlantic Refining Co., Phila., 1944-50; student personnel adminstr. U. Mont., Missoula, 1950-54; acting asso. dean students U. Mont., 1954-55, asso. dean students, 1955-56; supt. pub. instrn. Mont., 1956-69; pres. Harriet Miller Assocs. (mgmt. cons.), Helena, Mont., 1969-75; assoc. dir. Am. Assn. Ret. Persons/Nat. Ret. Tchrs. Assn., 1975-76, exec. dir., 1976-77; mgmt. cons., 1977—; pres. HMA, Inc., 1984-88; exec. dir. U.S. Occupational Safety and Health Rev. Commn., Washington, 1979-81. Commr. Santa Barbara County (Calif.) Parole Bd., 1981-84; chmn. City Housing Authority, Santa Barbara, 1984-86; bd. oveerseers Whitman Coll., Walla Walla, Wash., 1983—; mem. city coun. City of Santa Barbara, Cith Housing Authority, 1982-87; bd. dirs. Cen. Coast Congregation Care, Inc., Westside Neighborhood Med. Clinic, Community Action Commn., Santa Barbara County Assn. Govt. Mem. P.E.O., Mont. Congress Parents and Tchrs. (life), AAUW, Phi Beta Kappa, Delta Kappa Gamma, Phi Kappa Phi, Psi Chi, Alpha Chi Omega. Unitarian (former trustee). Address: PO Box 1346 Santa Barbara CA 93102

MILLER, JAMES LYNN, lawyer; b. Fairmont, W.Va., June 1, 1951; s. Robert Ogden Jr. and Dora Alice (Ward) M.; m. Maureen Clancy, Apr. 16, 1983; children: James Clancy, Bailey Ward. BA, Calif. State U., Humboldt, 1973; JD, U. Calif., Berkeley, 1976. Bar: Calif. 1976, Hawaii 1988. From assoc. to ptnr. Brobeck, Phleger & Harrison, San Francisco, 1976—. Republican. Office: Brobeck Phleger & Harrison Spear St Tower 1 Market Pla San Francisco CA 94105

MILLER, JEAN RUTH, librarian; b. St. Helena, Calif., Aug. 4, 1927; d. William Leonard and Jean (Stanton) M. BA, Occidental Coll., 1950; MLS, U. So. Calif., Los Angeles, 1952. Base librarian USAF, Wethersfield, Eng., 1952-55; post librarian USMC Air Sta., El Toro, Calif., 1955-63; data systems librarian Autonetics (Rockwell), Anaheim, Calif., 1963-65; mgr. library services Beckman Instruments, Inc., Fullerton, Calif., 1966—; mem. adv. com. Library Technician Program, Fullerton Coll., 1969—. Author: (bibliography) Field Air Traffic Control, 1965, Electrical Shock Hazards, 1974. Chair Fullerton Are U. So. Calif. Scholarship Alumni Interview Program, Fullerton, 1974—. Mem. IEEE, So. Calif. Assn. Law Libraries, Med. Library Group of So. Calif., Spl. Libraries Assn. (pres. So. Calif. chpt. 1975-76, chair Sci./Tech. Div. 1985-86). Republican. Home: 3139 E Chapman Ave Apt 9C Orange CA 92669-3743

MILLER, JEROME K., retired publisher, copyright law consultant; b. Gt. Bend, Kans., Apr. 18, 1931; s. Walter J. and Kathleen M. (Kliesen) M. BA in History, Emporia State U., 1965; MLS, U. Mich., 1966; MA in History, U. Kans., 1967; EdD, U. Colo., 1976. Bibliographic searcher, cataloger, coord. audiovisual libr. svcs. Boullion Libr., Cen. Wash. U., 1967-74; lectr., then asst. prof. Grad. Sch. Libr. and Info. Sci. U. Ill., Urbana-Champaign, 1975-83, coord. doctoral studies Grad. Sch. Libr. and Info. Sci., 1977-81; pres. Copyright Info. Svcs., 1983-87, Harbor View Publs. Group, Inc., Friday Harbor, Wash., 1988-93. Author: Applying the New Copyright Law: A Guide for Educators and Librarians, 1979, U.S. Copyright Documents: An Annotated Collection for Use by Educators and Librarians, 1980, Using Copyrighted Videocassettes in Classrooms and Libraries, 1984, 2d edit., 1987, The Copyright Directory, 1985, Umbrella Guide to Friday Harbor and San Juan Island, 1988, others; contbr. articles to profl. publs.; producer audio-visual prodns. on copyright. Adv. bd. Ctr. Ecumenical Campus Ministry, Ellensburg, Wash., 1971-73, chmn., 1972-73; lay minister St. Francis parish, Friday harbor, 1985-90, chmn. liturgy com., 1987—, chmn. bldg. com., 1987—, mem. parish coun., 1987—, pres., 1989—; trustee San Juan Island Libr. Dist., 1985—, pres. bd. trustees, 1988—; mem. lay adv. bd. Ellensburg Pub. Schs., 1973-74. Mem. ALA, Libr. and Info. Tech. Assn. (bd. dirs. 1978-81), Am. Assn. Sch. Librs. (editorial com. 1979-82), Assn. Ednl. Communications and Tech. (chmn. copyright taskforce 1974-77, 82-83), Consortium of Univ. Film Ctrs. (charter mem., chmn. copyright com. 1974-76), Wash. Libr. Assn., Wash. Assn. Ednl. Communications and Tech., Ellensburg Kiwanis Club, San Juan Lions Club (bd. dirs. 1986-93, pres. 1991-92, zone chmn. 1992-93), Phi Alpha Theta, Phi Delta Kappa. Office: Harbor View Pub Group Inc PO Box 1460 Friday Harbor WA 98250-1460

MILLER, JERRY A., state agency administrator; b. Wichita, Kans., Oct. 15, 1935; s. Otis Ardell and Dortha Paula (Farmer) M.; m. Marilyn "Kay" Corneil, Feb. 14, 1963; children: Wade Otis, Mark Ward. BS in Phys. Edn. and Health and Recreation, U. N.Mex., 1957, MA in Recreation Adminstrn. and Composite of Bus. Adminstrn., Sociology Rsch. and Conservation, 1965. Gen. supr. recreation City of Wichita, 1962-64; assoc. planner recreation N.Mex. State Planning Office, Santa Fe, 1965-68; dir. pks. and recreation City of Hobbs (N.Mex.) Pks. and Recreations Dept., 1968-72; adminstr. pks. Idaho State Pk. and Recreation Dept., Boise, 1972-76; dir. social svc. N.Mex. Human Resources Dept., Santa Fe, 1976-77; dir. adminstrn. svc. N.Mex. Natural Resources, Santa Fe, 1977-80; dir. Los Alamos City/ County Pks. and Recreation, N.Mex., 1980-84; gen. mgr. The Sports Bag, Santa Fe, 1984-85; dir. Utah State Pks. and Recreation Div., Salt Lake City, 1985—; part-time instr. N.Mex. Jr. Coll., 1972, Coll. S.W., 1970, U. N.Mex., 1964-65; guest lectr. Oreg. State U., 1975. Contbr. articles to profl. jours. Pres. Roadrunner Ski Team; active participation and speaking roles in nat., regional and state confs., 1965—; mem. First Presbyn. Ch. of Santa Fe; coach, mem. Hobbs Am. Legion Baseball; officer, coach Santa Fe Little League, Babe Ruth League, Hobbs United Fund. Lt. USN, 1958-62. Recipient Spl. Recognition award Intermountain Region Nat. Forest Svc., 1988, Santa Fe Simpatico award for Outstanding Community Citizenship KVSF Radio Sta. Mem. Nat. Assn. State Pk. Dirs., Utah Recreation and Pk. Assn. (bd. dir. 1987-89), Nat Soc. Pk. Resources, Nat. Assn. State Liaison Officers, Hobbs Jaycees, Lea Lions Club of Hobbs. Home: 790 Clover Blossom Cir Salt Lake City UT 84123-4505 Office: Utah Pks and Recreation Div 1636 W North Temple Salt Lake City UT 84116-3156

MILLER, JERRY HUBER, university chancellor; b. Salem, Ohio, June 15, 1931; s. Duber Daniel and Ida Claire (Holderieth) M.; m. Margaret A. Setter, 1958; children: Gregory, Joy, Carol, Beth, David. BA, Harvard U., 1953; MDiv., Hamma Sch. Theology, 1957; DD (hon.), Trinity Luth. Sem., 1981. Ordained to ministry Luth. Ch., 1957. Research assoc., intern Cornell U., Ithaca, N.Y., 1955-56; instr. Wittenberg U., Springfield, Ohio, 1956-57; parish pastor Ch. of Good Shepherd, Cin., 1957-62; asst. to pres. Ohio Synod Luth. Ch. Am., 1962-66; sr. campus pastor, dir. campus ministry U. Wis., Madison, 1966-69; regional dir. Nat. Luth. Campus Ministry, Madison, 1969-76; exec. dir. Nat. Luth. Campus Ministry, Chgo., 1977-81; pres. Calif. Luth. U., Thousand Oaks, 1981-92, chancellor, 1992—; mem. exec. com. Council. Ind. Colls., Washington, Assn. Ind. Calif. Colls. and Univs., 1981—, Council Luth. Colls., Luth. Ednl. Conf. N.Am., 1977—. Editor: The Higher Disciplines, 1956; contbr. articles to profl. jours. Bd. dirs. Wittenberg U., Augustana Coll., Rock Island, Ill., United Way, Thousand Oaks, Ventura County chpt. ARC, Thousand Oaks; chmn. Los Robles Hosp. Bd., Thousand Oaks, Bank Bd., Thousand Oaks. Named Man of Yr., Salem, 1975; Siebert Found. fellow, 1975. Mem. Am. Assn. Higher Edn., Council Advancement and Support Edn., Harvard Alumni Assn., Western Coll. Assn. (bd. dirs.), Conejo Valley C. of C. (bd. dirs.), Conejo Symphony Orch. (bd. dirs.). Club: Harvard (Ill., Ohio, Wis., Calif.). Lodge: Rotary. Office: Calif Luth U Office of the Chancellor 60 Olsen Rd Thousand Oaks CA 91360

MILLER, JOHN LAURENCE, professional golfer; b. San Francisco, Apr. 29, 1947; s. Laurence O. and Ida (Meldrum) M.; m. Linda Strouse, Sept. 17, 1969; children: John Strouse, Kelly, Casi, Scott, Brent, Todd. Student, Brigham Young U., 1965-69. Profl. golfer, 1969—; Pres. Johnny Miller Enterprises, Inc. Author: Pure Golf, 1976, Johnny Miller's Golf for Juniors, 1987. Named PGA Player of Yr., 1974. Office: PO Box 2260 Napa CA 94558-0060

MILLER, JOHN NELSON, banker; b. Youngstown, Ohio, Sept. 15, 1948; s. W. Frederic and Julia Elizabeth (Lohman) M.; MusB in Cello, Westminster Coll., 1970; MBA in Fin., Wharton Sch. Fin., U. Pa., 1974; m. Judy Congleton, Aug. 18, 1980. Asst. br. mgr. Mahoning Nat. Bank, Youngstown, 1970-72; asst. dir. fin. services dept. Mellon Bank N. Am., Pitts., 1974-76; v.p., head cash mgmt. div. Md. Nat. Bank, Balt., 1976-78; v.p., mgr. corp. cash mgmt. div. N.Y. Bank of Am., N.Y.C., 1978-80; dir. cash mgmt., strategic planning, product mgmt. and tng. Bank of Am. S.F., 1980-81; v.p., global account officer for utilities/telecommunications S.E. unit Bank of Am., N.Y.C., 1981-84; team leader, chief fin. officer, corp. payment div. large corp. sales, 1984-87; mgr. credit preparation and analysis unit N.

Am. Div., N.Y.C., 1987-88; v.p., eastern region mgr. cash mgmt. div. Wells Fargo Bank N.Y., 1988-90; v.p., div. mgr. Eastern, Midwestern, Rocky Mountain, Pacific and nat. fin. instns., 1990-93; v.p. and group sales mgr., Bank of Am. NT & SA Foreign Currency Svcs., San Francisco, 1993—; lectr. Wharton Grad. Sch., Am. Mgmt. Assn. cash mgmt. seminars, Bank Adminstrn. Inst., others; speaker Payment Systems Inc., Corp. EFT Seminar, Atlanta, Nat. Conv. Treasury Mgmt. Assn.; mem. Corp. Payment Task Force, N.Y.C., Corp. EFT Cost-Benefit Task Force. Chmn. ann. giving program Wharton Grad. Sch., 1977-79. Mem. Wharton Grad. Alumni Assn. (pres., local club, rep., nat. dir., mem. exec. com.), Bank Adminstrn. Inst. (mem. subcom. interindustry commn.), Am. Nat. Standards Inst. (sub com. on interindustry optical scan standards), Cash Mgmt. Inst. (dir.), Omicron Delta Kappa. Clubs: Mchts. (Balt.); University (Pitts.); Rotary (San Francisco). Office: Bank of Am NT & SA Foreign Currency Svcs 3068 Two Embarcadero San Francisco CA 94111

MILLER, JON PHILIP, research institute executive; b. Moline, Ill., Mar. 30, 1944; s. Clyde Sheldon and Alice Mae (Taes) M.; m. Shirley Ann Hymes, Aug. 21, 1965; children: Melissa, Elizabeth. AB, Augustana Coll., 1966; PhD, St. Louis U., 1970; MBA, Pepperdine U., 1983. Rsch. assoc. to sr. biochemist ICN Pharm., Inc., Irvine, Calif., 1970-72, leader molecular pharmacology group, 1972-73, head molecular pharmacology/drug metabolism dept., 1973-76, dir. biology div., 1976-78; dir. SRI-NCI liaison group SRI Internat. (formally Stanford Rsch. Inst.), Menlo Park, Calif., 1976-78, sr. bioorganic chemist, 1978-80, head medicinal biochemistry program, 1980-84, dir. biotech. rsch. dept., 1982-85, dir. biotech. and biomed. rsch. lab., 1985-92, assoc. dir. life scis. div., 1989-92; regional dir. Panlabs, Inc., Bothell, Wash., 1992—. Office: Panlabs West Coast Office 1147 Blythe St Foster City CA 94404-3646

MILLER, JOSEPH ARTHUR, manufacturing engineer, educator, consultant; b. Brattleboro, Vt., Aug. 28, 1933; s. Joseph Maynard and Marjorie Antoinette (Hammerberg) M.; m. Ardene Hedwig Barker, Aug. 19, 1956; children: Stephanie L., Jocelyn A., Shana L., Gregory J. BS in Agrl., Andrews U., Berrien Springs, Mich., 1955; MS in Agrl. Mechs., Mich. State U., 1959; EdD in Vocat. Edn., UCLA, 1973. Constrn. engr. Thornton Bldg. & Supply, Inc., Williamston, Mich., 1959-63, C & B Silo Co., Charlotte, Mich., 1963-64; instr. and dir. retraining Lansing (Mich.) Community Coll., 1964-68; asst. prof./prog. coord./coop coord. San Jose State U., 1968-79; mfg. specialist Lockheed Missiles & Space Co., Sunnyvale, Calif., 1979-81, rsch. specialist, 1981-88, NASA project mgr., 1982-83, staff engr., 1988—, team leader Pursuit of Excellence award winning project, 1990—; agrl. engring. cons. USDA Poultry Expt. Sta., 1960-62; computer numerical control cons. Dynamechtronics, Inc., Sunnyvale, 1987—; machining cons. Lockheed, Space Sys. Div., 1986—; instr. computer numerical control DeAnza Coll., Cupertino, Calif., 1985-88, Labor Employment Tng. Corp., San Jose, Cliaf., 1988—. Author: Student Manual for CNC Lathe, 1990; contbr. articles to profl. jours. Career counselor Pacific Union Coll., Angwin, 1985-92. UCLA fellow, 1969-73. Mem. Soc. Mfg. Engrs. (sr. mem.), Nat. Assn. Indsl. Tech. (pres. industry div. 1987-88, bd. cert. 1991—), Calif. Assn. Indsl. Tech. (pres. 1974-75, 84-85), Am. Soc. Indsl. Tech. (pres. 1980-81). Seventh-day Adventist. Home: 338 Raccoon Rd Berry Creek CA 95916-9518 Office: Lockheed Missiles & Space 1111 Lockheed Way Sunnyvale CA 94089-3504

MILLER, JOSEPH EDWARD, JR., media company executive; b. Seattle, Jan. 4, 1945; s. Joseph Edward and Kathleen Bell (Campbell) M.; m. Ingrid Maria Exner, Mar. 5, 1965 (div. July 1972); 1 child, Nancy Marie; m. Barbara Leigh Gregson, May 25, 1986. AA, Montgomery Coll., 1974; BS, U. Md., 1976, MA, 1978. Mktg. mgr. Inst. Modern Lang., Silver Spring, Md., 1974-75; pres. JEMPRO Films Ltd., Silver Spring, 1975-79; writer/dir. WRAMC Inst. of Rsch., Washington, 1979-81; lobbyist The Am. Legion, Washington, 1981-86; ptnr. Miller-Gregson Prodns., Sherman Oaks, Calif., 1986—; cons. Renaissance Communications, Silver Springs, 1983-88, Loreen Arbus Prodns., L.A., 1988, Boss Film Corp., 1989, Four Point Entertainment, 1989, 90, 91, Varied Directions, Inc., 1990, Group W Prodns., 1990, 91, Blair Entertainment, 1990, CBS Entertainment, 1991, Fox TV, 1991, Barry Weitz Prodns., 1991, Carolco TV, 1991, Multi-Media TV, 1992, Prodrs. Video Inc., 1992, Lewisfilm, Ltd., 1991-93. Author: House on Thayer Hill, 1988. Orgn. fund raiser United Way, Washington, 1984-85; bd. dirs. Vietnam Veterans Inst., Washington, 1981—; With U.S. Army, 1962-72. Decorated Bronze Star, Air medal with oak leaf cluster, Purple Heart with oak leaf cluster; Recipient Honor award Assn. of Mil. Surgeons Internat., 1979, spl. recognition award Walter Reed Army Inst. of Research, 1981. Mem. Ind. Media Producers Assn., Alpha Sigm Lambda, Phi Kappa Phi, Phi Theta Kappa. Republican. Presbyterian.

MILLER, KENNETH A., manufacturing executive; b. Spokane, Wash., Feb. 9, 1944; s. Reuben A. Miller and Frances M. Kirlin; m. Andria J. Wright, May 16, 1964; children: Donald G., Janet E. BBA, Calif. State U., 1975, MS, 1979. Dir. mfg. Photo Rsch., Burbank, 1973-79, v.p. mfg., 1979-80, v.p. mktg., 1980-85, v.p. product line mgr., 1985-87; v.p., gen. mgr. photo rsch. div. Kollmorgen, Chatsworth, Calif., 1987-88, pres., 1988—; standards writer Soc. Automotive Engrs., 1981-87, Electronic INdustries Assn., 1984-87, ASTM, 1985-87; lectr. display engring. UCLA, 1984-86, 89—; guest lectr. various orgns., 1979—. Contbr. articles to profl. jours.; patentee small distance measure. Served as staff sgt. USAF, 1962-70. Mem. Soc. Info. Display, U.S. Nat. Com. Internat. Commn. on Illumination, Internat. Soc. Color Coun., Soc. Photo-Optical Instrumentation Engrs. Republican. Office: Photo Rsch 9330 De Soto Ave Chatsworth CA 91311-4926

MILLER, KENNETH EDWARD, mechanical engineer, consultant; b. Weymouth, Mass., Dec. 24, 1951; s. Edward Francis and Lena Joan (Trotta) M.; m. Florence Gay Wilson, Sept. 18, 1976; children: Nicole Elizabeth, Brent Edward. BSME, Northeastern U., 1974; MS in Systems Mgmt., U. So. Calif., 1982. Registered profl. engr., N.Y., N.H., Ariz., Nev.; registered land surveyor, Ariz. Test engr. Stone & Webster Engring., Boston, 1974-76; plant engr. N.Y. State Power Authority, Buchanan, 1976-80; maintenance engr. Pub. Service Co. of N.H., Seabrook, 1980-82; cons. engr. Helios Engring. Inc., Litchfield Park, Ariz., 1982-87; sr. supervisory service engr. Quadrex Corp., Coraopolis, Penn., 1987-89; cons. engr. Helios Engring., Inc., Litchfield Park, Ariz., 1989—. Republican. Roman Catholic. Office: 360 Ancora Dr S Litchfield Park AZ 85340-4639

MILLER, KENNETH JAMES, political organization administrator, consultant; b. Toledo, Ohio, May 24, 1954; s. Norman John and Nancy Louise (Textor) M. BA, U. Toledo, 1976; MA, San Francisco State U., 1991. Office mgr. Campaign 88, Sacramento, Calif., 1988; cons. various orgns., San Francisco, 1989-90; exec. dir. San Francisco County Dem. Ctrl. Com., San Francisco, 1990-93; direct mail cons. Sunset Community Dems., San Francisco, 1990, 92; prin. Kenneth Miller & Assocs. 1st lt. U.S. Army, 1977-80. Mem. Mechanics Inst., San Francisci State Univ. Alumni Assn. Roman Catholic.

MILLER, KENT DUNKERTON, physics and computer science educator; b. Duluth, Minn., Apr. 17, 1941; s. Paul Theodore and Melba D. (Dunkerton) M.; children: Kendra, Jeffrey. BA in Physics, Ariz. State U., 1964, MA in Physics, 1965. Physics tchr. Claremont (Calif.) Sch. Dist., 1964-79, computer instr., cons., 1979-86; astronomy tchr. Citrus Coll., Glendora, Calif., 1969-88, prof. physics, 1987—; computer edn. and staff devel. cons., So. Calif., 1980—; planetarium presentor Citrus Coll., 1975—. Recipient McLuhan Disting. Educator award Marshall McLuhan Ctr. on Global Communications, 1984. Mem. AAAS, NEA, Am. Assn. Physics Tchrs., Calif. Tchrs. Assn. Democrat. Presbyterian. Home: 1166 Eileen Ct Upland CA 91786-1552 Office: Citrus Coll Foothill Blvd Glendora CA 91740-3335

MILLER, KIMBERLEY JEAN, newspaper editor; b. West Bend, Wis., Oct. 11, 1957; d. Lee H. and Darlene R. (Lehn) M. BS, U. Wis., Milw., 1980, BA, 1981. Reporter, editor Randolph (Wis.) Advance, 1983-85; copy editor Odessa (Tex.) Am., 1985-87, Tampa (Fla.) Tribune, 1987-88, Lesher Communs., Walnut Creek, Calif., 1988-92; asst. city editor Lesher Communs.-Valley Times, Pleasanton, Calif., 1992—. Lutheran. Office: Valley Times 127 Spring St Pleasanton CA 94566

MILLER, LARRY H., automobile dealer, professional sports team executive; b. Salt Lake City; m. Gail Miller; 5 children. Formerly with auto parts bus., Denver and Salt Lake City; now owner auto dealerships, Salt Lake City, Albuquerque, Denver and Phoenix; part-owner Utah Jazz, NBA, Salt Lake City, 1985-86, owner, 1986—. Office: care Utah Jazz 5 Triad Ctr Ste 500 Salt Lake City UT 84180-1105*

MILLER, LESTER LIVINGSTON, JR., librarian, researcher; b. Portland, Oreg., June 5, 1930; s. Lester Livingston Sr. and Alice Jane (Howell) M.; m. Velma Grace Ross, Sept. 1, 1961; 1 child, Michelle Freia-Anne. BS, Portland State U., 1963; MEd, U. Oreg., 1965. Cert. secondary edn. tchr., libr., Wash. With U.S. CIA, 1958-60; sch. libr. Tigard (Oreg.) Pub. Schs., 1964-66; instr. Continuation Ctr. U. Oreg., Portland, 1966; sch. libr. U.S. Naval Sta., Guantanamo Bay, Cuba, 1966-68, Jefferson High Sch., Portland, 1968-70; asst. libr. Acad. Library, Ft. Benjamin Harrison, Ind., 1972-74; reference libr. U.S. Army Field Artillery Sch., Ft. Sill, Okla., 1974-78, adminstrv. libr., 1978-88; chief exec. officer Les Miller Enterprises Rsch. Svcs., Centralia, Wash., 1988—. Bibliographer for numerous periodical articles; editor biographical sketches; indexer mil. periodicals; author numerous poems. Sgt. USAF, 1949-56. Named Boss of Yr., Lawton (Okla.)-Ft. Sill Toastmistress, Inc. Mem. NEA, Assn. for Bibliography of History, VFW (Lewis comdr. 1990—), Masons. Democrat. Episcopalian. Home and Office: 1316 W Main St Centralia WA 98531-1338

MILLER, LYLE G., bishop. Bishop Sierra Pacific dist. Evang. Luth. Ch. in Am., Oakland, Calif. Office: Evang Luth Ch in Am #240 401 Roland Way Oakland CA 94641

MILLER, M. JOY, financial planner, real estate broker; b. Enid, Okla., Dec. 29, 1934; d. H. Lee and M.E. Madge (Hatfield) Miller; m. Richard L.D. Berlemann, July 21, 1957 (div. Nov. 1974); children: Richard Louis, Randolph Lee. BSBA, N.Mex. State U., 1956. Cert. fin. planner; grad. Realtors Inst. Tchr. of bus. and mathematics Alamogordo (N.Mex.), Las Cruces (N. Mex.) and Omaha Pub. Schs., 1956-63; tchr., dir. Evelyn Wood Reading Dynamics Southern N.Mex. Inst., 1967-68; registered rep. Westamerica Fin. Corp., Denver, 1968-76; gen. agt. Chubb Life Am., Concord, N.H., 1969—, Delta Life & Annuity, 1969—; registered rep. Am. Growth Fund Sponsors, Inc., Denver, 1976-90; pres., broker Fin. Design Corp. R.E., Las Cruces, 1977—; br. mgr. Chubb Securities Corp., Concord, N.H., 1990—; official goodwill ambassador of U.S. Treasury, U.S. Savs. Bond Div., Washington, 1968-70. Contbr. articles to profl. jours. Recipient Top Sales Person award Investment Trust and Assurance, 1976-77. Mem. SWNMALU (treas. 1990-91, pres.-elect 1991-92, pres. 1992-93), Nat. Assn. Realtors, Nat. Assn. Life Underwriters, Internat. Bd. Cert. Fin. Planners, Internat. Assn. Registered Fin. Planners, Dona Ana County Fedn. Rep. Women, Las Cruces City Panhellenic, Altrusa Club, Order Eastern Star, Delta Zeta Alumnae. Republican. Presbyterian. Home: 1304 Wolf Trl Las Cruces NM 88001-2357 Office: Fin Design Corp PO Box 577 Las Cruces NM 88004-0577

MILLER, MARION, manufacturing company executive; b. Spokane, Wash., July 7, 1913; s. Herman Gottleib and Maud (Fyke) M.; m. Marylouise Page, July 24, 1942 (div. 1968); children: Michael Afton; m. Doris Marie Dilley, Nov. 29, 1986. Student, U. Wash., 1931-34. Farm mgr. Miller Bros. Farm, Greenacres, Wash., 1933-45; irrigation mgr. Arnold & Jeffer, Spokane, 1946-47; pres. Anderson-Miller Mfg. Co., Spokane, 1947-68; mktg. specialist W.R. Ames, Milpitas, Calif., 1968-71; mfrs. agt., pres. Marion Miller & Assocs., Colorado Springs, Colo., 1971—; pres. Irrigation Industries, Colorado Springs, 1976-86. Inventor irrigation equipment accessories. Named Man of the Year Idaho Irrigation Equipment Assn., 1987. Mem. Irrigation Assn. (bd. dirs. 1949-51, v.p. 1952, pres. 1953, Industry Achievement award 1982, Spl. Assn. Achievement award 1992), Am. Soc. Agrl. Engrs. (v.p. NW chpt. 1947), Ctrl. Plains Irrigation Assn. (Public Service award 1993), Spokane Club, Kiwanis, Lions. Unitarian. Home: 815 Old Dutch Mill Rd Colorado Springs CO 80907-3820 Office: Marion Miller & Assocs PO Box 790 Colorado Springs CO 80901-0790

MILLER, MARTIEY MARIE, sales manager; b. Moline, Ill., Dec. 28, 1954; d. Thomas Garfield and Margaret Agnes (Watters) Maynard; m. George C. Miller II, July 2, 1977 (dec. 1986); m. Steven L. Heller, Oct. 3, 1992; 1 child, Michelle Marie. BS, Utah State U., 1976. Cert. Radio Mktg. Cons., Radio Sales Mgr. Account exec. Sta. KRSV-AM, Afton, Wyo., 1984-86; account exec. Sta. KEKB-FM, Grand Junction, Colo., 1986-87, gen. sales mgr., 1987—; gen. sales mgr. Sta. KOOL-FM, 1993—; cons. M4 Comm., Grand Junction, 1990—; lectr. Leading Edge Program, Grand Junction, 1991—. Pres. Vineyard Homeowners Assn., Grand Junction, 1988-89; dir. C. of C., Grand Junction, 1991-92, exec. v.p., 1993; dir. Chipeta Girl Scout Coun., Grand Junction, 1992. Recipient Spl. Recognition award C. of C., 1992. Mem. Kiwanis. Democrat. Congregationalist. Office: KEKB-FM 315 Kennedy Ave Grand Junction CO 81501

MILLER, MARY ALICE, nursing educator; b. Searcy, Ark., May 21, 1941; d. Victor D. Sr. and Ida G. Wall. BSN, Union Coll., 1963; MS, Loma Linda U., 1964; cert. GNP, U. Colo. Health Scis. Ctr., Denver, 1977; PhD, U. Colo., Boulder, 1987. RN, Colo. Staff nurse, team leader Belinda Hosp., Port Hueneme, Calif., 1964-65, Loveland (Colo.) Meml. Hosp., 1964-65; instr. Union Coll., Denver, 1965-67; prof. nursing and health care mgmt. dept. Met. State Coll., Denver, 1967—, prof., chmn. dept. nursing and health care mgmt., 1987-91, assoc. dean, 1990—. Contbr. articles to profl. publs. Fed. Nurse Practitioner grantee. Mem. Colo. League Nursing (bd. dirs.), Am. Cancer Soc. (bd. dirs. Adams unit), Colo. Nurses Assn. (mem. various coms.).

MILLER, MAYNARD MALCOLM, geologist, educator, research foundation director, explorer, state legislator; b. Seattle, Jan. 23, 1921; s. Joseph Anthony and Juanita Queena (Davison) M.; m. Joan Walsh, Sept. 15, 1951; children: Ross McCord, Lance Davison. BS magna cum laude, Harvard U., 1943; MA, Columbia U., 1948; PhD (Fulbright scholar), St. John's Coll., Cambridge U., Eng., 1957; student, Naval War Coll., Air War Coll., Oak Ridge Inst. Nuclear Sci.; D of Sci. (hon.), U. Alaska, 1990. Registered profl. geologist, Idaho. Asst. prof. naval sci. Princeton (N.J.) U., 1946; geologist Gulf Oil Co., Cuba, 1947; rsch. assoc., coordinator, dir. Office Naval Rsch. project Am. Geog. Soc., N.Y.C., 1948-52; staff scientist Swiss Fed. Inst. for Snow and Avalanche Rsch., Davos, 1952-53; instr. dept. geography Cambridge U., 1953-54, 56; assoc. producer, field unit dir. film Seven Wonders of the World for Cinerama Corp., Europe, Asia, Africa, Middle East, 1954-55; rsch. assoc. Lamont Geol. Obs., N.Y.C., 1955-57; sr. scientist dept. geology Columbia U., N.Y.C., 1957-59; asst. prof. geology Mich. State U., East Lansing, 1959-61, assoc. prof., 1961-63; prof. Mich. State U., Lansing, 1963-75; dean Coll. Mines and Earth Resources U. Idaho, Moscow, 1975-88, prof. geology, dir. Glaciological and Arctic Scis. Inst., 1975—; dir., state geologist Idaho Geol. Survey, 1975-88; elected rep. Legislature of State of Idaho, Boise, 1992—; prin. investigator, geol. cons. sci. contracts and projects for govt. agys., univs., pvt. corps., geographic socs., 1946—; geophys. cons. Nat. Park Svc., NASA, USAF, Nat. Acad. Sci.; organizer leader USAF-Harvard Mt. St. Elias Expdn., 1946; chief geologist Am. Mt. Everest Expdn., Nepal, 1963; dir. Nat. Geographic Soc. Alaskan Glacier Commemorative Project, 1964-74; organizer field leader Nat. Geographic Soc. Joint U.S.-Can. Mt. Kennedy Yukon Meml. Mapping Expdn., 1965, Muséo Argentino de Ciencias Naturales, Patagonian expdn. and glacier study for Inst.. Geologico del Peru & Am. Geog. Soc., 1949-50, participant adv. missions People's Republic of China, 1981, 86, 88, geol. expdns. Himalaya, Nepal, 1963, 84, 87, USAF mission to Ellesmere Land and Polar Sea, 1951; organizer, ops. officer USN-LTA blimp geophysics flight to North Pole area for Office Naval Rsch., 58; prin. investigator U.S. Naval Oceanographic Office Rsch. Ice Island T-3 Polar Sea, 1967-68, 70-73; dir. lunar field sta. simulation program USAF-Boeing Co., 1959-60; co-prin. investigator Nat. Geographic Soc. 30 Yr. Remap of Lemon & Taku Glaciers, Juneau Icefield, 1989-92; exec. dir. Found. for Glacier and Environ. Rsch., Pacific Sci. Ctr., Seattle, 1955—, pres., 1955-85, trustee, 1960—, organizer, dir. Juneau (Alaska) Icefield Rsch. Program (JIRP), 1946—; cons. Dept. Hwys. State of Alaska, 1965; chmn., exec. dir. World Ctr. for Exploration Found., N.Y.C., 1968-71; dir., mem. adv. bd. Idaho Geol. Survey, 1975-88; chmn. nat. coun. JSHS program U.S. Army Rsch. Office and Acad. Applied Sci., 1982-89; sci. dir. U.S. Army Rsch. Office-Nat. Sci. & Humanities Jr. Sci. and Humanities Symposia program, 1991—; disting. guest prof. China U. Geoscis., Wuhan, 1981-88, Changchun U. Earth Scis., People's Republic of China, 1988—. Author: Field Manual of Glaciological and Arctic Sciences; co-author books on Alaskan glaciers and Nepal geology; contbr. over 200 reports, sci. papers to profl. jours., ency. articles, chpts. to books, monographs; producer, lectr. 16 mm. films and videos. Past mem. nat. exploring com., nat. sea exploring com. Boy Scouts Am.; mem. nat. adv. bd. Embry Riddle Aero. U.; bd. dirs. Idaho Rsch. Found.; pres. state divsn. Mich. UN Assn., 1970-73; mem. Centennial and Health Environ. Commns., Moscow, Idaho, 1987-93. With USN, 1943-46, PTO. Decorated 11 battle stars; named Leader of Tomorrow Seattle C. of C. and Time mag., 1953, one of Ten Outstanding Young Men U.S. Jaycees, 1954; recipient commendation for lunar environ. study USAF, 1960, Hubbard medal (co-recipient with Mt. Everxpdn. team) Nat. Geographic Soc., 1963, Elisha Kent Kane Gold medal Geog. So. Phila., 1964, Karo award Soc. Mil. Engrs., 1966, Franklin L. Burr award Nat. Geog. Soc., 1967, Commendation Boy Scouts Am, 1970, Disting. Svc. commendation plaque UN Assn. U.S.A., Disting Svc. commendation State of Mich. Legislature, 1975, Outstanding Civilian Svc. medal U.S. Army Rsch. Office, 1977, Outstanding Leadership in Minerals Edn. commendations Idaho Mining Assn., 1985, 87; recipient numerous grants NSF, Nat. Geographic Soc., others, 1948—. Fellow Geol. Soc. Am., Arctic Inst. N.Am., Royal Geographic Soc., Explorers Club; mem. councilor AAAS (Pacific divsn. 1978-88), AIME, Am. Geophys. Union, Internat. Glaciological Soc. (past councilor), ASME (hon. nat. lectr.), Am. Assn. State Geologists (hon. life), Am. Assn. Amateur Oarsmen (life), Am. Alpine Club (past councilor, life mem.), Alpine Club (London), Appalachian Club (hon. corr.), Brit. Mountaineering Assn. (hon., past v.p.), Himalyan Club (Calcutta), English Speaking Union (nat. lectr.), Naval Res. Assn. (life), Dutch Treat Club, Circumnavigators Club (life), Adventurers Club N.Y. (medalist), Harvard Club (N.Y.C. and Seattle), Sigma Xi, Phi Beta Kappa (pres. Epsilon chpt. Mich. State U. 1969-70), Phi Kappa Phi. Republican. Methodist. Home: 514 E 1st St Moscow ID 83843 Office: U Idaho Coll Mines & Earth Resources Mines Bldg Rm 204 Moscow ID 83843 also: House of Reps Idaho State House Boise ID 83720 also: Found for Glacier & Environ Rsch 4470 N Douglas Hwy Juneau AK 99801

MILLER, MILTON DAVID, agronomist, educator; b. Melmont, Wash., Nov. 27, 1911; s. Milton and Katie Virginia (Manney) M.; m. Mary Eleanor McGraw, July 24, 1932; children: Mary Lee Varone, Judith Marie McCullough. BS, U. Calif., Davis, 1935, MS, 1960. Extension agronomist emeritus U. Calif., Davis, 1936-74; tech. advisor Calif. Rice Research Bd., (disting. service award 1974), Yuba City, Calif., 1970-82; cons. World Bank, Romania, 1975, US Aid, Egypt, 1977. Served to lt. col. Q.M.C., 1941-46. Recipient Legion of Merit award U.S. Army, 1949, award of distinction Coll. Agriculture and Environ. Scis. U. Calif., Davis, 1990. Fellow AAAS, Am. Soc. Agronomy, Am. Crop Sci. Soc.; mem. Commonwealth Club of Calif., Masons, Sigma Xi, Alpha Zeta, Alpha Gamma Rho. Republican. Home: 624 Oak Ave Davis CA 95616-3627

MILLER, PAUL NEIL, psychologist, social science computer consultant; b. N.Y.C., June 29, 1950; s. Arthur Murray and Mollie (Slutsky) M.; m. Mary Jasnoski, June 15, 1969 (div. Sept. 1972). BA in Clin. Psychology, Calif. State U., L.A., 1977, MA in Clin. Psychology, 1979; PhD, Calif. Sch. Profl. Psychology, Berkeley, 1989. Psychology intern The Family Ctr., Pleasanton, Calif., 1979-80; psychology intern USPHS Hosp., San Francisco, 1980-81, Langley-Porter Psychiat. Inst., U. Calif. Med. Ctr., San Francisco, 1981-82; rsch. cons. Calif. Med. Facility, Vacaville, 1982-84; neuropsychology cons. VA Med. Ctr., San Francisco, 1984-85; psychol. asst. Paul Walker PhD, San Francisco, 1981-88; vocat. psychologist Vocat. Rehab. Svcs., Belmont, Calif., 1985-87; psychologist Merrithew Meml. Hosp., Martinez, Richmond, Calif., 1986-90; psychologist psychiat. emergency svcs. Marin Gen. Hosp., Greenbrae, Calif.; clin. psychologist Napa (Calif.) State Hosp., 1990—; computer cons. VA Med. Ctr., San Francisco, 1988, Merritt Hosp., Oakland, Calif., 1989-90, St. Francis Med. Ctr., San Francisco, 1989; psychology cons. Disaster Response Com. (formed after earthquake), Napa, 1990. Mem. Animals Action Network, 1991, Nat. Pub. Radio/Pacifica/Fair, 1985. Mem. APA, Soc. for Personality Assessment, Internat. Rorschach and Projective Techniques Soc. Democrat. Office: Napa State Hosp 2100 Napa Valley Hwy Dept Psychology Napa CA 94558-6293

MILLER, PEGGY SUZANNE, dog trainer; b. Seattle, Dec. 4, 1952; d. Paul Henry and Orba Ruth (Goodwill) Brumbaugh; m. David Allen Brewer, Oct. 10, 1973 (div. 1989). Occupational canine cert., Tacoma (Wash.) C.C., 1983-86; student, U. Wash./Tacoma C.C., 1992—. Trainer Prison Pet Partnership Program, Gig Harbor, Wash., 1982—, instr. asst., 1983-88, instr., 1988—, kennel mgr., 1982-89, tng. mgr., 1990—. Contbr. articles to dog mags. Home: 4214 Harborview Gig Harbor WA 98335 Office: Prison Pet Partnership PO Box 17 Gig Harbor WA 98335

MILLER, RALPH MENNO, minister, religious organization administrator; b. Hubbard, Oreg., Mar. 22, 1925; s. Samuel S. and Catherine (Hooley) M.; m. Evelyn Irene Whitfield, Feb. 23, 1947; children: Judith Karen, Donna Joyce. D of Ministry, Internat. Bible Inst. and Sem., 1985. Owner, operator M & M Logging, Sweet Home, Oreg., 1952-56; support person Children's Farm Home, Palmer, Alaska, 1956-58; pastor North Pole (Alaska) Assembly of God, 1959-68, Sitka (Alaska) Assembly of God, 1968-78; pioneer pastor Sand Lake Assembly of God, Anchorage, 1978-84; sec., treas. Alaska Dist. Assemblies of God, Anchorage, 1978—, presbyter, 1964—; gen. presbyter Gen. Council Assemblies of God, Springfield, Mo.; exec. presbyter Alaska Assemblies of God, Anchorage, 1978—; exec. dir. Alaska Ch. Builders, 1984—, Revolving Loan Fund, Anchorage, 1984—, Little Beaver Camp, Big Lake, Alaska, 1984-90. Pres. PTA, North Pole, 1964-66. Republican. Home: 2111 Tasha Dr Anchorage AK 99502-5466 Office: Alaska Dist Assemblies of God 1048 W Internat Airport Rd # 101 Anchorage AK 99518

MILLER, RHODA EVANGELINE, college director; b. N.Y.C., Oct. 1, 1930; d. Herman Joseph Roy and Rose Ellen (Gwerty) Andersen; m. Frank William Porter, Aug. 23, 1952 (dec. Sept. 1954); m. William Renne Miller, Aug. 29, 1955; children: Steven, Marian. BA in Journalism, Hunter Coll., 1950; MA in Edn., Wagner Coll., 1954; MSc in Ednl. Tech., U. Hawaii, 1975, MLS, 1976, PhD in Am. Studies, 1990. Tchr. Bd. Edn., N.Y.C., 1955-71; libr., tchr. Star of the Sea High Sch., Honolulu, 1976-82; adminstr. St. Andrews Priory, Honolulu, 1982-85; instr. Am. St. Univ. Hawaii, Honolulu, 1985-90, assoc. dir. Spark M. Matsunaga Inst. for Peace, 1990—. Mem. LWV (pres. 1980-82), Phi Kappa Phi, Beta Phi Mu. Home: 664 Keolu Dr Kailua HI 96734

MILLER, RICHARD ALAN, agricultural consultant; b. Everett, Wash., Mar. 16, 1944; s. John Harrison and Katheryn Ada (Nelson) M.; m. Patricia Merz, June 30, 1964 (div. 1972); 1 child, Paula Anne; m. Iona Roberta Orr, May 1, 1981; stepchild: Charis Eastman. BS in Physics, Washington State U., 1966; Degree in Fluidics (hon.), MIT, 1967; MS in Physics, U. Del., 1968; engr. in tng./profl. engr., U. Wash., 1969. Cert. biophysicist, 1972, hypnotherapist. Physicist instruments products div. Dupont, Wilmington, Del., 1966-68; physicist The Boeing Co./MASD, Seattle, 1968-71; biophysicist dept. anesthesiology U. Wash., Seattle, 1971-73; owner, mgr. The Beltane Corp., Inc., Seattle, 1973-80; ltd. ptnr. Western Herb Farms/Country Spice, Seattle, 1980-82; owner, mgr., writer Orgn. Advancement of Knowledge, Grants Pass, Oreg., 1983—; owner, mgr., broker Northwest Bots., Inc., Grants Pass, 1987—; ptnr., sales mgr. Coltsfoot, Inc., Grants Pass, 1986—; advisor Ariz. Herb Growers Assn., Phoenix, 1988—; mem. New Crops Devel. Oreg. Dept. Agriculture; cons. in field; lectr. in field. Author: The Potential of Herbs as a Cash Crop, 1985, The Magical and Ritual Use of Herbs, 1985, The Magical and Ritual Use of Aphrodisiacs, 1987, The Magical and Ritual Use of Perfumes, 1989, Native Plants of Commercial Importance, 1989, Forest Farming, 1990; contbr. articles to profl. jours. Amb. All Am. City, Grants Pass, 1987—. Small Bus. Innovative Rsch. grante USDA, 1986, Neighborhood Devel. grantee SBA, 1977. Mem. Am. Coun. Hypnotist Examiners, Masons. Home: 1305 Vista Dr Grants Pass OR 97527-5262 Office: Northwest Botanicals Inc 1305 Vista Dr Grants Pass OR 97527-5262

MILLER, RICHARD FRANKLIN, educator, researcher, educational administrator; b. San Francisco, Sept. 9, 1927; s. Henry G. and Hulda M. M. AB, San Francisco State U., 1950; MA, U. Calif.-Berkeley, 1964, EdD, 1970. Cert. secondary tchr., gen. supr. Calif. With San Francisco Unified Sch. Dist., 1956-89, tchr. bus. edn., econs. and social studies Mission High Sch., 1967-89, adminstr. career edn. program, 1970-80; ednl. cons., 1989—. Mem. San Francisco Symphony, Fine Arts Mus. Soc. Served to sgt., U.S. Army,

1952-54. Fellow in edn. U. Calif.-Berkeley, 1974-75. Mem. ASCD, United Educators San Francisco, Phi Delta Kappa. Democrat. Unitarian.

MILLER, ROBERT G., retail company executive; b. 1944. With Albertson's Inc., 1961-89, exec. v.p. retail ops., 1989-91; chmn. bd., CEO Fred Meyer Inc., Portland, Oreg., 1991—. Office: Fred Meyer Inc 3800 SE 22d Ave Portland OR 97202-2918*

MILLER, ROBERT JENNINGS, medical board administrator; b. Battle Creek, Mich., Nov. 26, 1949; s. Mary Margaret (Jennings) M.; m. Shereen Ann Lerner, Jan. 16, 1982; children: Alyssa Josephine, Benjamin Jennings. BA, Western Mich. U., 1973, MA summa cum laude, 1976; PhD, Ariz. State U., 1981. Teaching asst. sociology dept. Western Mich. U., Kalamazoo, 1973, teaching asst. anthropology dept., 1973-75, instr., 1975; instr. social sci., anthropology Mesa (Ariz.) Community Coll., 1980-85; assoc. dir. rsch. Ariz. Emergency Med. Systems, Phoenix, 1981-82, dep. dir., 1982-84, exec. dir., 1984-89; pres. Advanced Emergency Med. Svc., Phoenix, 1984-85; v.p. med. svc. S.W. Med. Svcs., Phoenix, 1989-90; exec. dir. Ariz. Bd. Osteo. Med. Examiners, Phoenix, 1990—; faculty Nat. Symposium on Trauma Care, Phoneix, 1984; rsch. asst. Ariz. State U., Tempe, 1977-78, Ariz. State U., U.S. Forest Svc. Nat. Sci. Found., 1979-80, others; project supr. Auckland Mus. Ariz. State U., 1978; cons. Cen. Ariz. Health Systems Agy., Phoneix, 1984, Northland Rsch., Inc., Tempe, 1989-90, Saferide Svcs., Inc., 1990; cons. program devel. evaluation People-to-People Health Found., San Jose, Costa Rica, 1990. Contbr. articles to profl. jours. Chair Design Rev. Bd., Tempe, 1985—; bd. dirs. Tri City Jewish Community Ctr., Tempe, 1988—, treas., 1990-92; mem. Rover Sch. Adv. Com., Tempe, 1992—. John L. and Helen Kellogg Found. scholar, 1968, 69, Bd. dirs. scholar Western Mich. U., 1970, 71, Tuition scholar Ariz. State U., 1976, 77; rsch. grantee U.S. Forest Svc., 1979. Mem. Am. Pub. Health Assn., Am. Osteopathic Assn., Fedn. State Med. Bds., Adminstrs. in Medicine. Office: Ariz Bd Osteo Examiners 1830 W Colter Ste 104 Phoenix AZ 85015

MILLER, ROBERT JOSEPH, governor, lawyer; b. Evanston, Ill., Mar. 30, 1945; s. Ross Wendell and Coletta Jane (Doyle) M.; m. Sandra Ann Searles, Oct. 17, 1949; children: Ross, Corrine, Megan. BA in Polit. Sci., U. Santa Clara, 1967; JD, Loyola U., Los Angeles, 1971. First legal advisor Las Vegas (Nev.) Met. Police Dept., 1973-75; justice of the peace Las Vegas Twp., 1975-78; dep. dist. atty. Clark County, Las Vegas, 1971-73, dist. atty., 1979-86; lt. gov. State of Nev., 1987-89, acting gov., 1989-90, gov., 1991—. Chmn. Nev. Commn. on Econ. Devel., Carson City, 1987-91, Nev. Commn. on Tourism, Carson City, 1987-91; mem. Pres. Reagan's Task Force on Victims of Crime, 1982; chmn. Nev. divsn. Am. Cancer Soc., 1988-90. Mem. Nat. Dist. Atty.'s Assn. (pres. 1984-85), Western Govs. Assn. (chair-elect 1992-93, chmn. 1993—, past chmn. com. on justice and pub. safety, chmn. legal affairs com. 1992—, lead gov. on trasp. 1992—) Nev. Dist. Atty.'s Assn. (pres. 1979, 83). Democrat. Roman Catholic. Home: Gov Mansion 606 N Mountain St Carson City NV 89703 Office: State of Nev Office of Gov Capitol Bldg Carson City NV 89710

MILLER, ROBERT LINDSEY, bishop; b. Eagle Grove, Iowa, June 24, 1933; m. Doris Mandsager; children: Tedd, Darrell, Diane. BA, St. Olaf Coll., 1966. Pastor Luth. congregations, St. Louis Park, Minn., Riverside and Santa Barbara, Calif., First Luth. Ch., Fullerton, Calif.; bishop Pacifica Synod, Evang. Luth. Ch. in Am., Yorba Linda, Calif., 1988—. Office: Evang Luth Ch in Am 23655 Via Del Rio Yorba Linda CA 92687-2718

MILLER, ROBERT MORTON, veterinarian, writer; b. Ariz., Mar. 4, 1927; s. Samuel and Sally (Marks) M.; m. Deborah H. Miller, Sept. 16, 1956; children: Mark Richard, Laurel Kathleen. BS, U. Ariz., 1951; DVM, Colo. State U., 1956. Founder, chief of staff Conejo Valley Vet. Clinic, Thousand Oaks, Calif., 1957-87; cons., researcher for pharm. industry; legal cons., expert witness in many ct. cases; lectr. in field. Mem. editorial staff Vet. Medicine, Modern Vet. Practice, Western Horseman; author: Health Problems of the Horse, 1967, revised edit., 1988, Most of My Patients are Animals, 1985, paperback edit., 1986, Germany and Eng. edits., 1987, The Second Oldest Profession, Imprint Training of the Newborn Foal, Ranchin' Ropin' and Doctorin'; author 6 books of vet. cartoons, 1960—, video films; contbr. chpts. to, illustator for several books; author sci. papers; contbr. over 100 articles to mags. With U.S. Army, 1945-47. Recipient Award of Merit, Calif. Vet. Med. Assn., 1973, Am. Animal Hosp. Assn., 1978, Far West Region award for outstanding svc. Am. Animal Hosp. Assn., 1989. Mem. Ventura County Vet. Med. Assn., So. Calif. Vet. Med. Assn. (life hon. mem.), Am. Assn. Equine Practitioners, Am. Assn. Zoo Veterinarians, Am. Vet. Soc. Animal Behavior, Sierra Vet. Med. Assn., (life hon. mem.). Home and office: RRM Ranch 320 Carlisle Rd Thousand Oaks CA 91361

MILLER, ROBERT RYAL, history educator; b. Lake Andes, S.D., Oct. 3, 1923; s. John Carroll and Hazel C. (Peck) M.; m. Penelope Handsaker, June 12, 1955. AB, U. Calif., Berkeley, 1948, MA, 1951, PhD, 1960. Asst. prof. history U. Southwestern La., Lafayette, 1959-60; asst. to assoc. prof. N.Mex. State U., Las Cruces, 1960-68; prof. history Ind. U. Southeast, New Albany, Ind., 1970; prof. history Calif. State U., Hayward, 1970-80, prof. emeritus, 1980—; vis. prof. San Marcos U., Lima, Peru, 1966. Author: For Science and National Glory, 1968, Mexico: A History, 1985, Shamrock and Sword, 1989; editor: Mexican War Jour., 1991. Sgt. U.S. Army Air Corps, 1942-46, Med. Mem. Conf. on Latin Am. History, Calif. Hist. Soc.

MILLER, ROBERT SCOTT, not-for-profit organization administrator, social worker; b. Seattle, Dec. 12, 1947; s. Bert Lester and Carol Theresa (Gustafson) M.; m. Karen Ann Staake, Nov. 12, 1977; children: Sarah, Megan, Emily. BA in Sociology cum laude, Seattle Pacific U., 1970; AM in Social Work, U. Chgo., 1972; MA in Human Resources Mgmt., Pepperdine U., 1977. Cert. social worker, Wash. Br. supr. Wash. State Dept. Social and Health Svcs., Oak Harbor and Anacortes, 1975-78; supr. casework Wash. State Dept. Social and Health Svcs., Everett, 1973-75; lectr., coord. rural community mental health project U. Wash., Seattle, 1978-83; exec. dir. Armed Svcs. YMCA, Oak Harbor, 1984-86; area dir. United Way of Island County, Oak Harbor, 1986-88, exec. dir., 1988-92; exec. dir. Saratoga Community Mental Health, Coupeville, Wash., 1992—; part-time instr. Chapman U., Orange, Calif., 1988—; adv. bd. Island Family Health Ctr., Oak Harbor, 1990-91. Contbr. articles to profl. jours. Bd. dirs. Puget Sound chpt. Huntington's Disease Soc. Am., 1989-93, pres., 1991, fundraising chmn., 1989-91, v.p., 1990; adv. bd. United Way Washington, 1991-92; chmn. Island County bd. emergency food and shelter program Fed. Emergency Mgmt. Agy.; vice chair Community Resource Network, Oak Harbor, 1991; steering com. Greater Oak Harbor Econ. Summit, 1991; mem. strategic planning com. Whidbey Gen. Hosp., Coupeville, 1992—; exec. com. Mt. Baker Coun. Boys Scouts Am., 1993. Recipient outstanding service award Armed Svcs. YMCA of U.S., Dallas, 1985, two program merit awards, McDonald's Corp., Oak Harbor, 1986; named Alumni of a Growing Vision, Seattle Pacific U., 1991. Mem. NASW (bd. dirs. Wash. chpt. 1982-85), Wash. Assn. Social Welfare (pres. 1975-76), Acad. cert. Social Workers, Bus. and Profl. Women (v.p. Oak Harbor chpt. 1985-86, pres. 1986-87), Internat. Platform Assn., Navy League, Wildlife Haven Water Assn. (pres. 1989—), Greater Oak Harbor C. of C. (diplomat, Diplomat of Yr. 1991), Officer's Club, Naval Air Sta. Whidbey Island, Lions (pres. Whidbey club 1989-90, 100% Pres. award 1990), Masons. Lutheran. Home: 2450 S Rocky Way Coupeville WA 98239-9610 Office: United Way of Island County Navy Family Svc Ctr Seaplane Base Bldg 13 Rm 152 PO Box 798 Oak Harbor WA 98277

MILLER, ROBERT STEVEN, history educator, researcher; b. Van Nuys, Calif., Aug. 9, 1963; s. Frederick Earl and Mary (Brash) M. AA, L.A. Valley Coll., 1984; BSBA, Calif. State U., 1987, MA in History, 1990. Study group leader, study skills researcher Ednl. Opportunity Program Calif. State U., L.A., 1989—, faculty mem. History Dept., lectr., 1990-92; sec., treas. Agate/Amethyst World, Inc., Van Nuys, Calif., 1986-91, v.p., 1992—. Mng. editor (jour.) Perspectives, 1990, editor-in-chief, 1991. Jake Gimbel scholar, 1989. Mem. Am. Historians Assn., The Soc. for Historians of Am. Fgn. Rels., Phi Alpha Theta (v.p. 1990, pres. 1991, Eta Xi chpt., Ledeboer Family scholar 1989), Pi Sigma Epsilon (v.p. 1986-87, pres. 1988 Phi chpt.), Mu Kappa Tau (pres. and founder 1989, Calif State U. LA chpt.). Democrat. Roman Catholic. Home: 13750 Runnymede St Van Nuys CA 91405-1515 Office: Agate Amethyst World Inc 7712 Gloria Ave # 8 Van Nuys CA 91406 also: Calif State U Learning Resource Ctr Spl Svc Project 5151 State U Dr Los Angeles CA 90032-4221

MILLER, ROBERT STEVENS, JR., investment banker; b. Portland, Oreg., Nov. 4, 1941; s. Robert Stevens and Barbara (Weston) M.; m. Margaret Rose Kyger, Nov. 9, 1966; children: Christopher John, Robert Stevens, Alexander Lamont. AB with distinction, Stanford U., 1963; LLB, Harvard U., 1966; MBA, Stanford U., 1968. Bar: Calif. bar 1966. Fin. analyst Ford Motor Co., Dearborn, Mich., 1968-71; spl. studies mgr. Ford Motor Co., Mexico City, 1971-73; dir. fin. Ford Asia-Pacific, Inc., Melbourne, Australia, 1974-77, Ford Motor Co., Caracas, Venezuela, 1977-79; v.p., treas. Chrysler Corp., Detroit, 1980-81, exec. v.p. fin., 1981-90, vice chmn., 1990-92; sr. ptnr. James D. Wolfensohn, Inc., N.Y.C., 1992-93; bd. dirs., treas. Moore Mill & Lumber Co., Bandon, Oreg.

MILLER, ROBERT VICTOR, scientific research administrator; b. Batavia, N.Y., Apr. 30, 1936; s. James Joseph and Josephine (Brunovsky) M.; m. Mildred Rose Canne, June 8, 1956; children: Stephen, Cheryl, Eric, Elizabeth. BS, Cornell U., 1958, PhD, 1964; MS, U. Ark., 1961. Rsch. asst. prof. U. Md., Solomons, 1963-65; systematic zoologist U.S. Bureau Comml. Fisheries, Miami, Fla., 1965-71; leader marine mammal rsch. program U.S. Nat. Marine Fisheries Svc., Washington, 1971-80; dep. dir. NOAA/Nat. Marine Fisheries Svc. Nat. Marine Mammal Lab, Seattle, 1980—; mem. affiliate faculty U. Miami, Fla., 1966-71, Fla. Atlantic U., Miami, 1966-71, U. Wash. Sch. Fisheries, Seattle, 1983—; U.S. chair U.S.-Russia Marine Mammal Project, 1973—. Author nat. reports to internat. orgns., papers in field. Coord. blood donor drives NOAA campus Puget Sound Blood Ctr., Seattle, 1990—. Mem. Am. Soc. Ichthyologists and Herpetologists, Am. Soc. Mammalogists, Am. Inst. Fisheries Rsch. Biologists, Soc. Marine Mammalogists, Soc. for Preservation and Encouragement of Barber Shop Quartet Singing in Am. (sec. 1989—). Office: Nat Marine Mammal Lab 7600 Sand Point Way NE Bldg 4 Seattle WA 98115

MILLER, RODGER DALE, private investigator, intelligence analyst; b. Onnalinda, Pa., July 7, 1945; s. Louis Grant and Anna Eve (Sherman) M.; m. Jeanne Ellen Flinn, Nov. 15, 1969; children: Ginger Louise, Spring Leanne. Cert. in Crime Investigation, Wichita State U., 1967; cert. in Dactaloscopy, U. Calif., Santa Barbara, 1969; AA in Liberal Arts, Allen Hancock Coll., 1971; BA in Ancient History, Calif. State U., Chico, 1974. Lic. pvt. investigator, Calif.; cert. in law enforcement; cert. diplomatic courier; cert. space analyst. Coal miner A.R. Burkett Coal Co., Beaverdale, Pa., 1959-62; police investigator Wichita (Kans.) Police Dept., 1966-69; sheriff, coroner investigator Santa Barbara (Calif.) County Sheriff's Dept., 1969-74; owner heavy equip. Redding, Calif., 1974-82; lead intelligence analyst GTE Govt. Systems/Space, Sunnyvale, Calif., 1986-89; lead planner analyst Martin-Marietta Space Corp., Denver, 1989-91; qualified mgr., owner All Answers Detective Agy., Redding, 1991—; cons. analyst various U.S. agencies, Washington, 1982—; tech. cons. authors/motion picture industry, Calif., 1986—. Author: (text) Orbits of Artificial Bodies, 1983; author rsch. treatise Cave Paintings as Graffiti, 1977; author (fingerprints) Dactaloscopy, 1970. Staff sgt. U.S. Army, 1962-66, 82-86, Vietnam. Decorated Silver Star with V device, 1965, Bronze Star with V device, 1966. Mem. Nat. Rifle Assn., Am. Legion, Greater Redding C. of C. Republican. Southern Baptist. Home: 3336 Meadow Oak Dr Cottonwood CA 96022 Office: All Answers Detective Agy 2750 Eureka Way Ste 112 Redding CA 96001

MILLER, ROYAL DEVERE, JR., mechanical engineer; b. Tucson, June 7, 1938; s. Royal DeVere and Martha Elizabeth (Williams) M.; m. Rita Leone Townsend, May 24, 1980. BSME, U. Ariz., 1959; MSAE, Stanford U., 1963. Project engr. Sperry Flight Sys., Phoenix, 1966-69; sr. devel. engr. AiResearch Mfg. Co., Phoenix, 1969-75; asst. project engr. AiResearch Mfg. Co., 1975-78, project engr., 1978-79; sr. project engr. Garrett Turbine Engine Co., 1979-80, chief project engr., 1980-85; chief engr. Allied Signal Propulsion Engines, Phoenix, 1985—. Inventor in field. Capt. USAF, 1959-66. Fellow AIAA. Home: 4710 E White Dr Paradise Vly AZ 85253-2416 Office: Allied Signal Aerospace 111 S 34th St # 5217 Phoenix AZ 85034-2892

MILLER, RUTH, lawyer; b. Denver, June 2, 1931; d. Charles Albert and Marion (Reinhardt) Rymer; children: Nevin Lane, Stefanie Joan. B.A. with honors, San Francisco State U., 1965; J.D. with highest honors, Golden Gate U., 1970. Bar: Colo. 1971, Calif. 1971. Sole practice, San Mateo, Calif., 1971-74; mem. firm Davidson, Miller and Digiacinto, 1975-79, Davidson & Miller, 1989-93; pvt. practice, San Mateo, Calif., 1993—; chmn. family law adv. commn. Calif. Bd. Legal Specialization, 1977-82. Mem. Queen's Bench (pres. 1976), State Bar Calif. (chmn. exec. com. family law sect. 1978-79), San Mateo County Bar Assn. (chmn. conf. dels. 1979, dir. 1980-82, chmn. family law sect. 1978-79, chmn. women and the law com. 1975), Am. Acad. Matrimonial Lawyers (sec. No. Calif. chpt. 1982-83, pres. 1987). Editor, pub.: Family Law Brief Brief Briefs; author: California Divorce Through the Legal Maze, 1988. Office: 177 Bovet Rd # 600 San Mateo CA 94402

MILLER, STANLEY RAY, sound system consultant; b. Lincoln, Neb., Oct. 25, 1940; s. Maurice Winston and Blanche Fern (Mosier) M.; div.; children: Cordie Lynne, Neil Andrew. BA, Kearney State Coll., 1965. Founder, pres., chief exec. officer Stanal Sound Ltd., Hollywood, Calif., 1962-89; founder, chief exec. officer Sound Mfg. Inc., North Hollywood, 1987—; lectr. in field at numerous colls.; cons., trainer Altec Sound Contractor, JBL SND Contractors. Cons. engr./audio mixer for sound systems and concerts; chief live concert mixing engr. for Neil Diamond, 1969—; designed, manufactured, and toured large sound systems, worldwide 1964—; has toured sound systems for Simon & Garfunkel, Johnny Cash, Christy Minstrels, Young Americans, Bill Cosby, Mac Davis, Dolly Parton, Pink Floyd, Bob Dylan, John Denver, The Osmond Bros., Donnie & Marie Osmond, Tom Jones and Englebert Humperdink, 1964—; dir. sound svcs. at the Universal Amphitheatre, Greek Theatre, Pantages Theatre, and Wilshire Theatre, Henry Fonda Theatre, Fiddler's Green; supplied sound systems for Papal visit L.A., Sept. 1987; sound designer audio systems for Rep. Nat. Conv., 1984, 88; responsible for functional design of more than ten different models of Yamaha Sound Mixing Consoles, and numerous other Yamaha, JBL products for Concert Sound Industry. Mem. Audio Engring Soc. (nat. convs.), Profl. Entertainment Prodn. Soc. (treas.), Elks. Republican. Lutheran. Home: 3336 Primera Ave Los Angeles CA 90068-1550

MILLER, STEVE, musician; b. Dallas. Student, U. Wis., U. Copenhagen. Started group with Boz Scaggs, The Ardells, then with Barry Goldberg, The Goldberg/Miller Blues Band, now the Steve Miller Band; albums include Children of the Future, 1968, Sailor, Brave New World, 1969, Your Saving Grace, 1969, Number Five, 1970, Rock Love, 1971, Journey from Eden, Recall the Beginning, Anthology, The Joker, Fly Like an Eagle, Book of Dreams, Abracadabra, Circle of Love, 1985, Living in the 20th Century, 1986, Born 2 B Blue, 1988, Wide River, 1993. Recipient 5 platinum albums and 4 Number 1 singles. Office: PO Box 4127 Mercer Island WA 98040-9099 also: care Capitol Records 1750 N Vine St Hollywood CA 90028

MILLER, SUSAN WISE, career counselor, consultant; b. Cambridge, Mass., Feb. 1, 1941; d. Joseph and Madeline (Komar) Wise; m. Joseph Monte Miller, Dec. 29, 1963; children: Joanne Wise, Emily Wise. BS, Wheelock Coll., 1963; MA in Counseling Psychology, U. Calif., Berkeley, 1965; postgrad., UCLA, Loyola Marymount U., 1974-76. Nat. cert. career counselor, cert. vocat. evaluator; diplomate Am. Bd. Vocat. Experts. Career couseling, cons. Vocat. Tng. Consulting Svcs., L.A., 1975—; pvt. career counselor, 1977—; cons. Career and Vocat. Unit Calif. State Dept. Edn., Sacramento, 1974-90, assoc. project. dir. TIDE Project Career and Vocat. Unit, 1982-90; cons. UCLA Office Spl. Pers. Programs, 1980, 83, mem. ext., 1979—; speaker Am. Assn. Matrimonial Lawyers, 1989, L.A. Employee Relocation Coun., 1989; workshop leader Conciliation Ct. Conf., 1979—; instr. Mchts. and Mfrs. Assn., 1983—; mem. vocat. edn. div. Nev. State Dept. Edn.; mem. guidance div. Ariz. State Dept. Edn.; adj. prof. U. Judaism, 1983-86, U. San Francisco, 1987—. Area rep. Career Planning and Adult Devel. Network, 1982—; bd. dir. Nat. Network Adv. Bd., catalyst, 1981-85; adv. bd. dir. L.A. County Career Guidance Ctr., 1979-80; commr. L.A. Sch. Dist. Commn. for Sex Equity, 1980-83. Recipient Appreciation award L.A. County Commn. on the Status Women, 1978. Mem. ASTD (Appreciation award 1989), Beverly Hills Bar Assn. (adj. mem. 1983—), San Fernando Valley Bar Assn. (assoc. 1990—), Am. Vocat. Assn., Calif. Assn. Counseling and Devel., Calif. Career Guidance Assn.

MILLER, TERRY DENNIS, aerospace executive; b. Norfolk, Nebr., Mar. 12, 1941; s. Clayton Orval and Dorothy Louise (Reiken) M.; m. Barbara Ann Gembala, Feb. 8, 1964; children: Michelle, Patricia, Teri. BS, U. Nebr., 1964; student, U. No. Colo., 1972-74; MPS, Auburn U., 1975; MS, Salve Regina U., 1986; MA, Naval War Coll., 1986. Commd. 2d lt. USAF, 1964, advanced through grades to col., 1984, ret., 1990; dir. tech. requirements Grumman Aerospace and Electronics Systems Group, Colorado Springs, 1990—. Pres. Arnold Air Soc. Alumni Assn., Colorado Springs, 1967. Mem. U.S. Space Found., Air Force Assn. (officer 1990—, v.p. membership 1990, v.p. chpt. 1991, Medal of Merit 1991), Space Force Assn. (officer 1967-70), Armed Forces Commn. Electronics Assn. (Medal of Merit 1981), Space force Assn., Lions. Republican. Home: 65 Ellsworth St Colorado Springs CO 80906-7955

MILLER, THOMAS CECIL, private investigator, forensic examiner; b. Los Angeles, Jan. 27, 1951; s. Thomas Cecil Miller and Oetta Elizabeth (Buckman) Harrison; m. Michele Marie Austin, Aug. 23, 1986; two children. BA in History and Journalism, Metro State Coll., 1974; BA in Classical Langs., U. Denver, 1985; MA in English, Middlebury Coll., 1985; JD, U. Denver, 1992. Bar: Colo. 1993. Freelance writer, journalist Denver; prin. Investigative Reporting Services, Inc., Denver, 1983—; tchr. creative writing and mag. editing Arapahoe Community Coll., 1985-88, 92—, Met. State Coll., 1987-88, leal investigations Denver Paralegal Inst., 1993—; lectr. in investigation U. Denver, 1991—; founder Pearl St. Press, 1988. Author numerous poems. Mem. Profl. Pvt. Investigators Assn. Colo. (bd. dirs. 1988, 89, 90, pres. 1992-93), World Assn. of Detectives, Colo. Press Assn., Rocky Mountain Graphology Assn., Am. Handwriting Analysis Assn. Roman Catholic. Office: Investigative Reporting Svcs PO Box 10844 Denver CO 80250-0844

MILLER, THOMAS EUGENE, lawyer, writer; b. Bryan, Tex., Jan. 4, 1929; s. Eugene Adam and Ella Lucille (Schroeder) M. BA, Tex. A&M U., 1950; MA, U. Tex., 1956, JD, 1966; postgrad. U. Houston, 1956-58, U Calif., 1983. Bar: Tex. 1966. Rsch. technician M.D. Anderson Hosp., Houston, 1956-58; claims examiner trainee Soc. Security Adminstrn., New Orleans, 1964; trademark examiner U.S. Patent and Trademark Office, Washington, 1966; editor Bancroft-Whitney Co., San Francisco, 1966-92. Author book under pseudonym, 1984. Contbg. mem. Dem. Nat. Com., 1981-93; mem. Common Cause, People for the Am. Way. Decorated Medal of Honor; named World Intellectual, Internat. Biog. Ctr., 1993. Mem. World Lit. Assn., World Inst. of Achievement, United Writers Assn. India; mem. ABA, Nat. Trust for Hist. Preservation, Tex. Bar Assn., African Wildlife Found., World Affairs Coun. No. Calif., Internat. Platform Assn., Golden Gate Nat. Park Assn., Nat. Writers Club, Scribes, Press Club, Commonwealth Club, Phi Kappa Phi, Psi Chi, Phi Eta Sigma. Methodist. Home: 101 N Haswell Dr Bryan TX 77803-4848

MILLER, WARREN EDWARD, political scientist; b. Hawarden, Iowa, Mar. 26, 1924; s. John Carroll and Mildred Ovedia (Lien) M.; m. Ruth S. Jones, May 1981; children by previous marriage: Jeffrey Ralph, Jennifer Louise. B.S., U. Oreg., 1948, M.S., 1950; Ph.D., Maxwell Sch. Citizenship and Public Affairs, Syracuse U., 1954; Ph.D. (hon.), U. Goteborg, Sweden, 1972. Asst. study dir. Survey Research Ctr., Inst. Social Research, U. Mich., 1951-53, study dir., 1953-56, research assoc., 1956-59, program dir., 1959-68, research coordinator polit. behavior program, 1968-70, prin. investigator nat. election studies, 1977—; dir. Ctr. Polit. Studies, Inst. Social Research, 1970-81; program dir. Ctr. Polit. Studies, 1982—; asst. prof. polit. sci. Ctr. Polit. Studies, Inst. Social Research, 1956-58, asso. prof., 1958-63, prof., 1963—, Arthur W. Bromage prof. polit. sci., 1981-82; prof. polit. sci. Ariz. State U., 1981—; fellow Center Advanced Study in Behavioral Scis., 1961-62; exec. dir. Inter-univ. Consortium for Polit. and Social Research, 1962-70, assoc. dir., 1978—; vis. prof. U. Tilburg, Netherlands, 1973, U. Geneva, 1973, European U. Inst., Florence, Italy, 1979; vis. Disting. prof. Ariz. State U., 1981; trustee Inst. Am. Univs., 1970-88; Regents' prof., Ariz. State U., 1988—. Author: (with others) books including The Voter Decides, 1954, American Voter, 1960, Elections and the Political Order, 1966, (with T.E. Levitin) Leadership and Change: Presidential Elections from 1952-1976, 77, (with M.K. Jennings) Parties in Transition, 1986, Without Consent, 1988, (with others) The American National Election Studies Data Sourcebook, 1952-1978, 80, The American National Election Studies Data Sourcebook, 1952-86, 89; contbr. (with others) articles to profl. publs.; editorial bd.: (with others) Am. Polit. Sci. Rev, 1966-71, Computers and the Humanities, 1969-71, Social Science History, 1976-91, Social Science Rev., 1973; editorial adv. bd.: (with others) Sage Electoral Studies Yearbook, 1974. Served with USAAF, 1943-46. Recipient Disting. Alumnus award Maxwell Sch. Citizenship and Public Affairs, Syracuse U., 1974, Disting. Faculty Achievement award U. Mich., 1977. Fellow Am. Acad. Arts and Scis.; mem. Assn. for the Advancement of Scis., Am. Polit. Sci. Assn. (pres. 1979-80), Internat. Polit. Sci. Assn. (coun. 1969-73), M.W. Polit. Sci. Assn., Internat. Soc. Polit. Psychology, So. Polit. Sci. Assn., Social Sci. History Assn. (pres. 1979-80). Office: Ariz State U Dept Polit Sci Tempe AZ 85287-2001

MILLER, WENDELL SMITH, chemist, consultant; b. Columbus, Ohio, Sept. 26, 1925; s. Wendell Pierce and Emma Josephine (Smith) M.; m. Dorothy Marie Pagen, Aug. 18, 1949; children: William Ross, Wendell Roger. BA, Pomona Coll., 1944; MS, UCLA, 1952. Chemist U.S. Rubber Co., Torrance, Calif., 1944; sr. chemist Carbide & Carbon Chemicals Corp., Oak Ridge, 1944-48; ptnr. Kellogg & Miller, Los Angeles, 1949-56; patent coordinator Electro Optical Systems, Inc., Pasadena, Calif., 1956-59; v.p. Intertech. Corp. optical and optoelectronic system devel., North Hollywood, Calif., 1960-66, dir., 1966—; assoc. Ctr. for Study Evolution and Origin of Life, UCLA. Commr. Great Western Council Boy Scouts Am., 1960-65. Served with AUS, 1944-46. Decorated Army Commendation medal. Mem. Los Angeles Patent Law Assn., IEEE, AAAS, 20th Century Round Table, Sigma Xi, Phi Beta Kappa, Pi Mu Epsilon. Numerous patents in field. Home: 1341 Comstock Ave Los Angeles CA 90024-5314

MILLER, WILLIAM CHARLES, lawyer; b. Jacksonville, Fla., Aug. 6, 1937; s. Charles and Mary Elizabeth (Kiger) M.; m. Hadmut Gisela Larsen, June 10, 1961; children: Monica Lee, Charles Andreas. BA, Washington and Lee U., 1958, LLB, 1961; LLM, N.Y. U., 1963; postgrad., Harvard U., 1978. Bar: Fla. 1961, Calif. 1984, Ind. 1987, U.S. Supreme Ct. 1968. Counsel to electrochem., elastomers and internat. depts. E.I. duPont de Nemours & Co., Wilmington, Del., 1963-66; counsel S. Am. ops. Bristol-Myers Co., N.Y.C., 1967-69; internat. counsel Xerox Corp., Stamford, Conn., 1969-79; assoc. gen. counsel Xerox Corp., Stamford, 1979-80; v.p., gen. counsel, sec. Max Factor & Co., Hollywood, Calif., 1981-85, Boehringer Mannheim Corp., Indpls., 1985-92; gen. counsel Collagen Corp., Palo Alto, Calif., 1992—. Bd. dirs. Southwestern Legal Found., 1975-85. Fulbright scholar, 1959-60; Ford Found. fellow, 1961-62; Hague Acad. fellow, 1963; German Govt. grantee, 1962-63; Kappa Sigma scholar, 1959. Mem. Internat. Bar Assn., ABA, Calif. Bar Assn., Fla. Bar Assn., Ind. Bar Assn., Masons, Elks, Phi Beta Kappa, Phi Eta Sigma, Delta Theta Phi. Republican. Mem. Christian Ch. Home: 4931 Monaco Dr Pleasanton CA 94566-7671

MILLER, WILLIAM ELWOOD, mining company executive; b. Bend, Oreg., May 9, 1919; s. Harry Adelbert and Sarah (Heyburn) M.; B.A., Stanford, 1941, M.B.A., 1947; m. Constance Alban Crosby, July 2, 1955; children: William, Constance, Harold, Mary, Sarah Crosby, Charles Crosby, Helen, Harry. Owner and operator Central Oregon Pumice Co., Bend, 1948—; pres. The Miller Lumber Co., Bend, The Miller Ranch Co., Bend, Miller Tree Farm. Commr., City of Bend, 1959-62, mayor, 1960. Bd. dirs. Central Oreg. Coll.; pres. Central Oreg. Coll. Found., 1956-57; dir. Central Oregon Coll. Area Ednl. Dist., 1961-65, chmn., 1964-65; bd. govs. Ore. Dept. Geology and Mineral Industries, 1971-75. Served with A.C., USNR, 1942-45. Decorated D.F.C., Air medal. Mem. Central Oreg. (v.p. 1954), Bend (pres. 1954) C. of C., Bend Golf Club, Rotary (dir. Bend 1955-56), Kappa Sigma. Republican. Episcopalian. Home: 527 NW Congress St Bend OR 97701-2509 Office: 1 NW Greenwood Ave Bend OR 97701-2028

MILLER, WILLIAM FREDERICK, research company executive, educator, business consultant; b. Vincennes, Ind., Nov. 19, 1925; s. William and Elsie M. (Everts) M.; m. Patty J. Smith, June 19, 1949; 1 son, Rodney Wayne. Student, Vincennes U., 1946-47; BS, Purdue U., 1949, MS, 1951, PhD, 1956; D.Sc., 1972. Mem. staff Argonne Nat. Lab., 1955-64, assoc. physicist, 1956-59, dir. applied math. div., 1959-64; prof. computer sci. Stanford U., Palo Alto, Calif., 1965—; Herbert Hoover prof. pub. and pvt.

mgmt. Stanford U., 1979—, assoc. provost for computing, 1968-70, v.p. for research, 1970-71, v.p., provost, 1971-78; mem. Stanford Assocs., 1972—; pres., chief exec. officer SRI Internat., Menlo Park, Calif., 1979-90; chmn. bd., chief exec. officer SRI Devel. Co., Menlo Park, David Sarnoff Research Ctr., Inc., Princeton, N.J.; profl. lectr. applied math. U. Chgo., 1962-64; vis. prof. math. Purdue U., 1962-63; vis. scholar Ctr. for Advanced Study in Behavioral Scis., 1976; bd. dirs. Varian Assocs. Inc., 1st Interstate Bancorp, 1st Interstate Bank Calif., Pacific Gas and Electric Co., Regis McKenna, Inc., Scios-Nova, Inc.; mem. adv. coun. BHP Internat.; mem. computer sci. and engring. bd. Nat. Acad. Sci., 1968-71; mem. Nat. Sci. Bd., 1982-88; mem. corp. com. computers in edn. Brown U., 1972-79; mem. policy bd. EDUCOM Planning Coun. on Computing in Edn., 1974-79, chmn., 1974-76; ednl. adv. bd. Guggenheim Meml. Found., 1976-80; com. postdoctoral and doctoral rsch. staff NRC, 1977-80, mem. computer sci. and telecommunications bd., Nat. Inst. Standards Tech. bd. assessment; mem. internat. adv. panel Nat. Sci. and Tech. Bd., Singapore. Assoc. editor: Pattern Recognition Jour, 1968-72, Jour. Computational Physics, 1970-74. Served to 2d lt. F.A. AUS, 1943-46. Recipient Frederic B. Whitman award United Way Bay Area, 1982. Fellow IEEE, Am. Acad. Arts and Scis., AAAS; mem. Am. Math. Soc., Am. Phys. Soc., Soc. Indsl. and Applied Math., Assn. Computing Machinery, Nat. Acad. Engring., Sigma Xi, Tau Beta Pi. Office: Stanford U Grad Sch Bus Stanford CA 94305-5015

MILLER, WILLIAM HUGHES, theoretical chemist, educator; b. Kosciusko, Miss., Mar. 16, 1941; s. Weldon Howard and Jewel Irene (Hughes) M.; m. Margaret Ann Westbrook, June 4, 1966; children: Alison Leslie, Emily Sinclaire. B.S., Ga. Inst. Tech., 1963; A.M., Harvard U., 1964, Ph.D., 1967. Jr. fellow Harvard U., 1967-69; NATO postdoctoral fellow Freiburg (Germany) U., 1967-68; asst. prof. chemistry U. Calif., Berkeley, 1969-72, assoc. prof., 1972-74, prof., 1974—, dept. chmn., 1989-93; fellow Churchill Coll., Cambridge (Eng.) U., 1975-76. Alfred P. Sloan fellow, 1970-72; Camille and Henry Dreyfus fellow, 1973-78; Guggenheim fellow, 1975-76; recipient Alexander von Humboldt-Stiftung U.S. Sr. Scientist award, 1981-82, Ernest Orlando Lawrence Meml. award, 1985. Fellow AAAS, Am. Acad. Arts and Scis., Am. Phys. Soc. (Irving Langmuir award 1990); mem. NAS, Internat. Acad. Quantum Molecular Sci. (Ann. prize 1974). Office: U Calif Dept Chemistry Berkeley CA 94720

MILLER, WILLIAM J., computer company executive; b. 1946. Exec. v.p., pres. info. svcs. Control Data Corp.; CEO Quantum Corp., 1992—. Office: Quantum Corp 500 McCarthy Bld Milpitas CA 95035*

MILLER, ZOYA DICKINS (MRS. HILLIARD EVE MILLER, JR.), civic worker; b. Washington, July 15, 1923; d. Randolph and Zoya Pavlovna (Klementinovska) Dickins; m. Hilliard Eve Miller, Jr., Dec. 6, 1943; children: Jeffrey Arnot, Hilliard Eve III. Grad. Stuart Sch. Costume Design, Washington, 1942; student Sophie Newcomb Coll., 1944, New Eng. Conservatory Music, 1946, Colo. Coll., 1965; grad. Internat. Sch. Reading, 1969. Instr. Stuart Summer Sch. Costume Design, Washington, 1942; fashion coord. Julius Garfinckel, Washington, 1942-43; fashion coord., cons. Mademoiselle mag., 1942-44; star TV show Cowbelle Kitchen, 1957-58, Flair for Living, 1958-59; model mags. and comml. films, also nat. comml. recs., 1956—; sr. devel. officer Webb-Waring Lung Inst., Denver, 1973—. Contbr. articles, lectures on health care systems and fund raising. Mem. exec. com., bd. dirs. El Paso County chpt. Am. Lung Assn., Colo., 1954-63; mem. exec. com. Am. Lung Assn. Colo., 1965-84, bd. dirs. 1965-87, chmn. radio and TV coun., 1963-70, mem. med. affairs com., 1965-70, pres., 1965-66, procurer found. funds, 1965-70; developer nat. radio ednl. prodns. for internat. use Am. Lung Assn., 1963-70, coord. statewide pulmonary screening programs Colo., other states, 1965-72; chmn. benefit fund raising El Paso County Cancer Soc., 1963; co-founder, coord. Colorado Springs Debutante Ball, 1967—; coord. Nat. Gov.'s Conf. Ball, 1969; mem. exec. com. Colo. Gov.'s Comprehensive Health Planning Coun., 1967-74, chmn., 1971-72; chmn. Colo. Chronic Care Com., 1969-73, chmn. fund raising, 1970-72, chmn. spl. com. congl. studies on nat. health bills, 1971-73; mem. Colo.-Wyo. Regional Med. Program Adv. Coun., 1969-73; mem. Colo. Med. Found. Consumers Adv. Coun., 1972-78; mem. decorative arts com. Colorado Springs Fine Arts Ctr., 1972-75; founder, state coord. Nov. Noel Pediatrics Benefit Am. Lung Assn., 1973-87; founder, state pres. Newborn Hope, Inc., 1987—; mem. adv. bd. Wagon Wheel Girl Scouts, 1991—. Zoya Dickins Miller Vol. of Yr. award established Am. Lung Assn. of Colo., 1979; recipient James J. Waring award Colo. Conf. on Respiratory Disease Workers, 1963, Nat. Pub. Rels. award Am. Lung Assn., 1979, Gold Double Bar Cross award, 1980, 83, Jefferson award Am. Inst. Pub. Svc., 1991; named Humanitarian of Yr., Am. Lung Assn. of Colo., 1987, One of 50 Most Influential Women in Colorado Springs by Gazette Telegraph Newspaper, 1990, One of 6 Leading Ladies Colo. Homes & Lifestyles Mag., 1991. Lic. pvt. pilot. Mem. Nat. Cowbell Assn. (chmn. nat. father of year contest 1956-57, Colo., El Paso County, pres. 1954, TV chmn. 1954-59), Colo. Assn. Fund Raisers, Denver Round Table for Planned Giving, Nat. Soc. Fund Raising Execs., Broadmoor Garden Club. Home: 74 W Cheyenne Mountain Blvd Colorado Springs CO 80906-4336

MILLER CAVANAGH, VIRGINIA LEE, accountant, real estate broker; b. Tucson, Jan. 10, 1952; d. Hugo Searle and Nancy Nolen (Bailey) Miller; m. Kirk Douglas Lashmett, Oct. 3, 1971 (div. Feb. 1983); children: Heather Marie, Amber Rae; m. Gregory Cavanagh, Sept. 30, 1988. BA in Acctg. magna cum laude, Ft. Lewis Coll., Durango, Colo., 1987; MBA, Colo. State U., 1991. CPA, Colo. Teller Ft. Leonard Wood (Mo.) Credit Union, 1972-73; motel mgr. Surf Motel, Eureka, Calif., 1974; accounts payable clk. Colo.-Ute Electric Assn., Montrose, 1975-78; acctg. clk. La Plata County Dept. Social Svcs., Durango, Colo., 1979-80; meter reader La Plata Electric Assn., Durango, 1980-84, customer svc. rep., 1984-85; v.p., broker assoc. Assoc. Real Estate Mgmt., Inc., Durango, 1986—; pres., sr. acct. Accountax Cons., Inc., Durango, 1983-91, Accountax CPAs, P.C., Durango, 1992—; bd. dirs., treas. La Plata Electric Assn., 1990—; bd. dirs. Tri-State Generation & Transmission, Denver. Mem. Leadership La Plata, Durango, 1991-92. Mem. Fin. Women (pres. 1992—), Colo. Soc. CPAs, Durango Rotary (bd. dirs. 1991-93). Democrat. Presbyterian. Office: Accountax CPAs PC 1020 1/2 Main Ave Ste 202 Durango CO 81301

MILLETT, MERLIN LYLE, aerospace consultant, educator; b. East Moline, Ill., Dec. 29, 1923; s. Merlin Lyle Sr. and Erie Lucille (Hyland) m.; m. Glendola Mae Westlic, Feb. 23, 1945 (dec. 1968); 1 child, Debra Sue; m. Esther Lee Dayhuff, Aug. 21, 1970. BS, Iowa State Coll., 1945, MS, 1948, PhD, 1957. Registered profl. engr., Iowa. Draftsman Am. Machine and Metals, East Moline, Ill., 1941-42; instr. Iowa State Coll., Ames, 1946-48, asst. prof. aerospace engring., 1952-57, assoc. prof., 1957-61; prof. Iowa State U., Ames, 1961-75; flight test engr. Douglas Aircraft Co., Santa Monica, Calif., 1948-52; dean of faculty Parks Coll. St. Louis U., Cahokia, Ill., 1975-78; mgr. fighter aircraft Boeing Mil. Airplanes, Wichita, 1978-89; adj. prof. Oklahoma State U., Stillwater, 1979—; design cons. Architects Associated, Des Moines, 1970-72; aeronautical cons. Iowa Aeronautics Commn., Des Moines, 1972-74; co-prin. investigator U.S. Dept. Transp., Ames, 1973-75; power plant engr. Fed. Aviation Agy., Ames., 1971-75; cons. City of Ames., 1973. Patentee low cost drone. Sec. bd. dirs. Suntree East Home Owners Assn., 1991-92. Lt. sr. grade USNR, ret. Mem. AIAA (assoc. fellow, dep. dir. 1986—), Scottsdale Ranch Community Assn. (pres. 1993—, mem. arch. com. 1989—, bd. dirs. 1989—). Home: 10515 E Fanfol Ln Scottsdale AZ 85258-6032

MILLIGAN, GATEWOOD CARLISLE, physician, retired; b. Shannon, Miss., July 23, 1907; s. Martin Gatewood and Johnnie Carlisle (McCown) M.; m. Maxine Louise Redeker, Apr. 1, 1933; children: Jociele Aline Nordwall, Joanna Lee Dilsaver. Student, Park Coll., 1924-26, Hastings Coll., 1927, U. Wyo., 1927-28; MD, U. Colo., 1929-33. Lic. to practice medicine Colo. 1933, Tex., 1935. Pvt. practice Denver, 1934-36; partner C.W. Bixler & G.C. Milligan, Erie, Colo., 1935, Drs. Alldredge & Milligan, Englewood, Colo., 1935-46, Drs. Milligan & Hogan, Englewood, 1946-52, Drs. Milligan & Miner, Englewood, 1952-69, Drs. Milligan, Miner & Langstaff, Englewood, 1957-60; ob.-gyn. pvt. practice Englewood, 1969-84; pres. Arapahoe county Med. Soc., Englewood, 1940-41, Colo. Med. Soc., Denver, 1957-58; pres. med. staff Porter Hosp., Denver, 1944-45, Swedish Hosp., Englewood, 1960-61. Mem. Englewood City Coun., 1954-58, Colo. Commn. on Aging, Denver, 1964-72, Colo. State Bd. Health, Denver, 1977-86, Elsie Malley Sr. Recreation Ctr. Adv. Bd., Englewood, 1975-81; chmn. bd. trustees Malley Trust Fund, Englewood, 1983—. Recipient Outstanding Svc. award Arapahoe Med. Soc., Englewood, 1973-74, Cert. of Svc. award Colo. Med. Soc., Denver, 1957, 66, 78, Excellence award U. Colo. Med. Alumni, Denver, 1986, Humanitarian award Rocky Mt. Conf. United Meth. Ch., Denver, 1990. Mem. AMA (hon.), Arapahoe County Med. Assn. (hon.), Colo. Med. Assn. (hon.), Englewood Rotary (Compassion award dist. 5450 1992), Englewood United Meth. Ch. Democrat. Methodist. Home: 3975 S Fox St Englewood CO 80110

MILLIGAN, NANCY PATRICIA, computer programmer, consultant; b. San Diego, Sept. 4, 1958; d. King Dale and Pauline Mildred (Crego) M. MusB, U. Rochester, 1980; cert. in programming, Coleman Coll., La Mesa, Calif., 1984. Programmer Computer Cognition, San Diego, 1984-87; sr. system adminstr. Telesoft, San Diego, 1987-91; system adminstr. SKF Condition Monitoring, San Diego, 1991; system mgr. Titan Linkabit, San Diego, 1991—; computer consultant, San Diego, 1990—; cons. NCR, San Diego, 1991. Mem. San Diego Computer Soc., San Diego Assn. Secular Humanists (founder, steering com. 1992—), Coalition of Dem. and Ednl. Secular Humanists. Democrat. Office: Titan Linkabit 3033 Science Park Rd San Diego CA 92121

MILLIKEN, JOHN GORDON, research economist; b. Denver, May 12, 1927; s. William Boyd and Margaret Irene (Marsh) M.; m. Marie Violet Machell, June 13, 1953; children: Karen Marie, Douglas Gordon, David Tait, Anne Alain. BS, Yale U., 1949, BEng, 1950; MS, U. Colo., 1966, PhD, 1969. Registered profl. engr., Colo. Engr. U.S. Bur. Reclamation, Denver, 1950-55; asst. to plant mgr. Stanley Aviation Corp., Denver, 1955-56; prin. mgmt. engr., dept. mgr. Martin-Marietta Aerospace Div., Denver, 1956-64; mgmt. engr. Safeway Stores, Inc., Denver, 1964-66; sr. rsch. economist, prof., assoc. div. head U. Denver Rsch. Inst., 1966-86; pres. Univ. Senate, 1980-81; prin. Milliken Chapman Rsch. Group, Inc., Littleton, Colo., 1986-88, Milliken Rsch. Group, Inc., Littleton, 1988—; vis. fellow sci. policy rsch. unit U. Sussex, Eng., 1975-76; bd. dirs. Sci. Mgmt. Corp.; cons. mgmt. engr. Author: Aerospace Management Techniques, 1971, Federal Incentives for Innovation, 1974, Recycling Municipal Wastewater, 1977, Water and Energy in Colorado's Future, 1981, Metropolitan Water Management, 1981, Technological Innovation and Economic Vitality, 1983, Water Management in the Denver, Colorado Urban Area, 1988, Benefits and Costs of Oxygenated Fuels in Colorado, 1990; contbr. articles to profl. jours. Bd. dirs. Southeast Englewood Water Dist., 1963—, South Englewood San. Dist., 1965—; bd. dirs. South Suburban Park and Recreation Dist., 1971—, chmn., 1990-92; chmn. Dem. Com. of Arapahoe County, 1969-71, 5th Congl. Dist. Colo., 1972-73, 74-75; mem. exec. com. Colo. Faculty Adv. Coun., 1981-85; mem. Garrison Diversion Unit Commn., 1984; trustee Colo. Local Govt. Liquid Asset Trust, 1986—, chmn., 1991-93. With M.C. U.S. Army, 1945-46. Recipient Adlai E. Stevenson Meml. award, 1981. Mem. Acad. Mgmt., Nat. Assn. Bus. Economists, Yale Sci. and Engring. Assn., Am. Water Works Assn., Sigma Xi, Tau Beta Pi, Beta Gamma Sigma, Sigma Iota Epsilon. Congregationalist. Home and Office: 6502 S Ogden St Littleton CO 80121-2561

MILLIN, LAURA J., museum director; b. Elgin, Ill., June 11, 1954; d. Douglas Joseph and PAtricia Ruth (Feragen) M. BA in Interdisciplinary Studies, The Evergreen State Coll., 1978. Dir. On The Boards, Seattle, 1979; art dir. City Fair Merocenter YMCA, Seattle, 1980; dir. Ctr. on Contemporary Art, Seattle, 1981; co-owner Art in Form Bookstore, Seattle, 1981-89; co-dir. 3d internat festical of films by women dirs. Seattle Art Mus.. & 911 Contemporary Arts, 1988; auction coord. Allied Arts of Seattle, 1989; dir. Missoula (Mont.) Mus. of the Arts, 1990—; dir. Visual AIDS Missoula Missoula Mus. of the Arts, 1989; curator Radio COCA, Ctr. on Contemporary Art, Seattle, 1986, co-curator, 1981, 83; lectr. in field. Co-editor: AnOther (ind. feminist newspaper), Seattle, 1989, editor: (exhibition catalog) James Turrell: Four Light Installations, 1981. Bd. dirs. Internat. Festival of Films by Women Dirs., SEattle, 1987, 89, Nine One One Comtemporary Arts Ctr., Seattle, 1981-87, bd. chmn. 1981-85; bd. advisors REFLEX (art mag.), Seattle, 1988-89, Ctr. on Contemporary Art, Seattle, 1983-86; state vis. Mont. Arts. Coun., Missoula, 1991, NEA, Mpls., 1988, Chgo., 1987; ; panelist Mont. Arts Coun., Helena, 1990; cons. Seattle Arts Commn., 1989, juror, 1985. Home: 330 Evans St Missoula MT 59801 Office: Missoula Mus of the Arts 335 N Pattee Missoula MT 59802

MILLS, ALAN BENJAMIN, insurance company executive; b. Tacoma, June 1, 1945; s. Benjamin Franklin and Guinevere (Crouch) M.; m. Vickie Lynn, June 26, 1976; adopted children: James Edward, James Wayne, Pamela Jane. BA, U. Calif., Berkeley, 1967. Claims rep. Farmers Ins. Group, Oakland and Concord, Calif., 1970-86; br. claims supr. Farmers Ins. Group, Salinas, Calif., 1986-89, Oakland, 1989-92, Concord, 1992—. Republican. Office: Farmers Ins Group 1660 Challenge Dr Concord CA 94524

MILLS, BARTON ADELBERT, journalist, author; b. N.Y.C., Nov. 20, 1942; s. Adelbert Philo and Martha (McKecknie) M.; m. Nancy Dunhoff, Feb. 19, 1967; children: Bonnie, Kevin. AB, Cornell U., 1964. Copy editor Dow Jones & Co., N.Y.C., London, 1967-72; pvt. practice writer London, L.A., 1972—. Author: Tina, 1986, Mickey Rourke, 1988, Marilyn on Location, 1989, Beverly Hills 90210 Exposed, 1991, Melrose Place Off the Record, 1992. With USMC, 1965-67. Democrat. Home and office: 563 29th St Manhattan Beach CA 90266

MILLS, CAROL MARGARET, business consultant, public relations consultant; b. Salt Lake City, Aug. 31, 1943; d. Samuel Lawrence and Beth (Neilson) M.; BS magna cum laude, U. Utah, 1965. With W.S. Hatch Co., Woods Cross, Utah, 1965-87, corp. sec., 1970-87, traffic mgr., 1969-87, dir. publicity, 1974-87; cons. various orgns., 1988—; dir. Hatch Service Corp., 1972-87, Nat. Tank Truck Carriers, Inc., Washington, 1977-88; bd. dirs. Intermountain Tariff Bur. Inc., 1978-88, chmn., 1981-82, 1986-87; bd. dirs. Mountainwest Venture Group. Fund raiser March of Dimes, Am. Cancer Soc., Am. Heart Assn.; active senatorial campaign, 1976, gubernatorial campaign, 1984, 88, congl. campaign, 1990, 92, vice chair voting dist., 1988-90, chmn. 1990-92, chmn. party caucus legis. dist.; witness transp. com. Utah State Legislature, 1984, 85; apptd. by gov. to bd. trustees Utah Tech. Fin. Corp., 1986—, corp. sec., mem. exec. com., 1988—. Recipient service awards W. S. Hatch Co., 1971, 80; mem. Pioneer Theatre Guild, 1985—; V.I.P. capt. Easter Seal Telethon, 1989, 90, recipient Outstanding Vol. Svc. award Easter Seal Soc. Utah, 1989, 90. Mem. Nat. Tank Truck Carriers, Transp. Club Salt Lake City, Am. Trucking Assn. (public relations council), Utah Motor Transport Assn. (dir. 1982-88), Internat. Platform Assn., Beta Gamma Sigma, Phi Kappa Phi, Phi Chi Theta. Home and Office: 77 Edgecombe Dr Salt Lake City UT 84103-2219

MILLS, DEREK MAITLAND, strategic planning consultant, educator; b. Palos Verdes, Calif., Aug. 7, 1942; s. Ervin E. and Doris (Mitts) M.; m. Judith Warr, Dec. 31, 1962 (div. Oct. 1970); m. Esther B. Ray, Feb. 12, 1972; children: Søren Anselm, Graham Christenson. BA, U. Wash., 1973, MPA, 1976. Chief announcer KSLY and KCJH Radio, San Luis Obispo, Calif., 1959-62; interim dir. Coun. for SANE Nuclear Policy, N.Y.C., 1965-66; regional rep. Ctr. for War/Peace Studies, Seattle, 1966-70; exec. dir. Project Equality, Seattle, 1970-73; mem. grad. faculty Seattle U., 1974—, chair MPA program, 1976-80; prin. Mills Cons. Group Inc., Derek M. Mills Inc., Seattle and Denver, 1984—; faculty mem. U.S. Govt. Western Mgmt. Devel. Ctr., Denver, 1990—; speaker in field; faculty lectr. King Abdul Aziz U., Jeddah, Saudi Arabia, 1982; named Margaret Mead lectr. Internat. Halfway House Assn., 1987. Contbr. articles, revs. on opera to various mags.; author, narrator tng. video Bonneville Power Adminstrn., 1988. Home: 14339 22d Ave NE Seattle WA 98125 Office: 9010 Garland Ct Westminster CO 80021

MILLS, GARY WAYNE, school system administrator; b. Cin., Dec. 8, 1941; s. Raymond Jr. and Helen Rae (Bolender) M.; children: Jennifer Dawn, Jacqueline Amber. AB, Morehead State U., 1965; MA, Xavier U., 1968; postgrad., U. So. Calif., 1984-87. Cert. tchr., Ohio. Tchr., coach New Richmond (Ohio) Sch. Dist., 1965-68; prin. Parkway Local Schs., Rockford, Ohio, 1968-69; supt. Mendon (Ohio)-Union Schs., 1969-71; asst. supt. Finneytown Local Schs., Cin., 1971-80; supt. East Whittier (Calif.) Sch. Dist., 1980-87; interim supt. Wilsona Sch. Dist., Palmdale, Calif., 1987; supt. Sunnyvale (Calif.) Sch. Dist., 1987—; cons. Edn. Rsch. and Devel. Inst., Lincoln, Nebr., 1984. Author taped presentations in field. Named to N.Am.'s 100 Top Sch. Execs., Exec. Educator Mag., 1986; recipient Leadership Excellence award De Anza chpt. Assn. Calif. Sch. Adminstrs., 1992. Office: Sunnyvale Sch Dist 830 McKinley Ave Sunnyvale CA 94086-5918

MILLS, LAWRENCE, lawyer, business and transportation consultant; b. Salt Lake City, Aug. 15, 1932; s. Samuel L. and Beth (Neilson) M. BS, U. Utah, 1955, JD, 1956. Bar: Utah 1956, ICC 1961, U.S. Supreme Ct. 1963. With W.S. Hatch Co. Inc., Woods Cross, Utah, 1947-89, gen. mgr., 1963-89, v.p., 1970-89, also dir.; bd. dirs. Nat. Tank Truck Carriers, Inc., Washington, 1963—, pres., 1974-75, chmn. bd., 1975-76; mem. motor carrier adv. com. Utah State Dept. Transp., 1979—; keynote speaker Rocky Mountain Safety Suprs. Conf., 1976. Contbr. articles to legal publs. Del. to County and State Convs., Utah, 1970-72; v.p. Utah Safety Coun., 1979-82, bd. dirs., 1979—, pres., 1983-84; mem. Utah Gov's Adv. Com. on Small Bus.; capt. Easter Seal Telethon, 1989, 90; state vice chmn. High Frontier, 1987—; mem. adv. com. Utah State Indsl. Commn., 1988—, chmn. com. studying health care cost containment and reporting requirements 1990—. Recipient Disting. Svc. award Utah State Indsl. Commn., 1992, Safety Dir. award Nat. Tank Carriers Co., 1967, Trophy award W.S. Hatch Co., 1975. Mem. Salt Lake County Bar Assn., Utah Motor Transport Assn. (dir. 1967—, pres. 1974-76, Outstanding Achievement Award 1989), Utah Hwy. Users Assn. (dir. 1981—), Indsl. Rels. Coun. (dir. 1974—), Salt Lake City C. of C., U.S. Jaycees (life Senator 1969—, ambassador 1977—, pres. Utah Senate 1979-80, Henry Giessenbier fellow 1989), Nat. Petroleum Coun., Utah Associated Gen. Contractors (assoc. 1975-77, 88—), Silver Tank Club. Home: 77 Edgecombe Dr Salt Lake City UT 84103-2219 Office: 80 S Redwood Rd Ste 212 North Salt Lake UT 84054

MILLS, MICHAEL ALBERT FARLEIGH, building contractor; b. Evanston, Ill., Apr. 30, 1934; s. Alden Brewster and Patsy (Neilan) M.; m. Marjorie Elena Pfitzenmayer, Sept. 11, 1955 (div. 1977); children: Donald, David, Suzanne, Martin, Sandra; m. Opal McAllister, May 25, 1980. BA in Econs., U. Calif., 1959. Lic. bldg. & plumbing contractor. Adminstr., sales mgr. Mut. Fund Assocs./Putnam Fin. Svcs., San Francisco, 1960-70; office mgr. Parallel Planning Assocs., Walnut Creek, Calif., 1970-71; owner Michael Mills, Cons., Orinda, Calif., 1971-74; mgr. Calif. Domes, Inc., Santa Cruz, 1974-76; owner Michael A.F. Mills Constrn., Aptos, Calif., 1976—. Dir., officer Jaycees, San Francisco, 1961-66. With U.S. Army, 1954-56. Mem. Nat. Assn. for Remodeling Industry, Internat. Conf. Bldg. Ofcls., Santa Cruz County Builders Exch., Soc. for Preservation & Encouragement of Barbershop Quartet Singing in Am., Inc. (numerous offices, Man of Yr. 1988). Office: Michael A F Mills Constrn 142 Rancho del Mar Aptos CA 95003

MILLS, THOMAS C. H., lawyer; b. Long Beach, Calif., Dec. 14, 1949; s. William Donald and Roberta Mae (Fogg) M.; m. Jan Walsh, June 21, 1980. Student Brown U., 1968-70; B.A. Stanford U., 1972; J.D., Hastings Coll. of Law, 1976. Bar: Calif., 1977, N.Mex., 1981. Staff atty. Office of San Francisco City Atty., 1977-78, State Bar Calif., San Francisco, 1978-81; gen. counsel N.Mex. Energy and Minerals Dept., Santa Fe, 1981-83; assoc. Stephenson Carpenter, Crout & Olmsted, Santa Fe, 1983-86; ptnr. Potter, Mills & Cassutt, Santa Fe, 1986—; bd. dirs. Sante Fe Econ. Devel. Corp., 1986-89, v.p., 1988-89; bd. dirs. TRADE, Inc., 1986-93, pres., 1989-90. Mem. Santa Fe Planning Commn., 1982-86, chmn., 1984; mem. Los Alamos Nat. Lab. Community Council, 1986—; chmn. Sante Fe Group, 1990-91; mem. N.Mex. First., Inc., 1987—, mem. exec. com., chmn., 1993—; gov. appointee to N.Mex. Fin. Authority, 1992—. Recipient Exceptional Performance award N.Mex. Energy and Minerals Dept., 1982, Gov.'s Cert. Merit, 1984. Mem. Am. Planning Assn., Urban Land Inst., Bar Assn. Sante Fe, Indsl. Devel. Execs. Assn., Leadership Santa Fe Alumni Assn. (named Alumnus of the Yr. 1988, bd. dirs., pres. 1985-88). Democrat. Episcopalian. Club: Stanford of N.Mex. (pres. 1983-85, bd. dirs. 1983-88, 91—) Home: 2943 Plaza Blanca Santa Fe NM 87505 Office: Potter Mills & Cassutt 126 E De Vargas St Santa Fe NM 87501

MILLS, THOMAS COOKE, psychiatrist; b. San Francisco, Nov. 24, 1955; s. Willard Cooke and Billie Dee (Hunt) M. BS, MIT, 1977; MD, U. Ill., Chgo., 1981; MPH, U. Calif., Berkeley, 1991. Diplomate Am. Bd. Psychiatry and Neurology. Resident in psychiatry U. Calif., San Francisco, 1981-85, asst. clin. prof., 1985-91, assoc. clin. prof., 1991—; med. dir. Jail Psychiat. Svcs., San Francisco, 1985-88; pvt. practice San Francisco, 1985-88; staff psychiatrist Dept. Vets. Affairs, San Francisco, 1988—, psychiat. authorizing physician, 1991—; postdoctoral fellow U. Calif., Berkeley, 1990-91. Fellow NIMH, 1990-91. Mem. Am. Psychiat. Assn., No. Calif. Psychiat. Soc. Office: PO Box 460520 San Francisco CA 94146-0520

MILLS, WYMAN FELLERS, purchasing executive; b. Table Rock, Nebr., Apr. 12, 1924; s. Bryan Orman and Dorcas Lewellyn (Fellers) M.; m. Betty Lou Walls, Mar. 2, 1946; children: Michael, Robert, Steve, John, David. BS, Oreg. State U., 1949. Cert. purchasing mgr. Asst. purchasing agt. M&M Wood Working Co., Portland, Oreg., 1950-56; purchasing agt. Oreg. div. Simpson Timber Co., Portland, 1956-64; purchasing agt. Simpson Timber Co., Shelton, Wash., 1964-67; corp. purchasing mgr., fleet mgr. Simpson Timber Co., Seattle, 1967-82; owner Art Pauge/Mills Co., Woodinville, Wash., 1983-91. Mem. Mark E. Reed Scholarship Bd., Shelton, 1959-62; pres. Mt. Sylvania Little League, Portland, 1961, Shelton Little League, 1966, Simpson Employees Recreation Assn., Shelton, 1965. With USN, 1942-46, PTO. Democrat. Methodist. Home: 11203 12th Ave NE Seattle WA 98125

MILMORE, BENNO KARL, epidemiologist, retired; b. Schwerin, Fed. Republic of Germany, Jan. 27, 1914; came to U.S., 1916; s. Alphonse Ernst and Christine Marie (Prûss) M.; m. Marsha Anna Healy, July 31, 1937; children: Marsha U. Milmore Leake, Frank H., Donald E., Maxine A. Milmore Schreiner. BA, U. Calif., Berkeley, 1935; MD, U. Calif., San Francisco, 1939; MPH, Johns Hopkins U., 1942. Diplomate Am. Bd. Preventive Medicine and Pub. Health. Commd. med. officer USPHS, 1938, advanced through grades to col., 1954; med. intern U.S. Marine Hosp., San Francisco, 1938-39; ward surgeon U.S. Marine Hosp., Savannah, Ga., 1939-40; med. officer USPHS Typhus Control Unit, Savannah, Ga., 1940-41, Atlanta, 1942-43; chief med. sect. USPHS Office of Malaria Control in War Areas, Atlanta, 1943-44; med. officer USN Mil. Govt. in Western Pacific, Okinawa, Japan, 1944-45; chief outpatient dept. U.S. Marine Hosp., San Francisco, 1945-48; diabetes cons. Calif. State Dept. Pub. Health, Bur. Chronic Diseases, Berkeley, 1948-53; chronic disease cons. USPHS Region IX, San Francisco, 1953-54; epidemiologist Nat. Cancer Inst., Bethesda, Md., 1954-61; chief bur. chronic diseases Calif. State Dept. Pub. Health, Berkeley, 1961-63, chief epidemiology ctr., 1963-66, asst. chief contract counties health svcs. sect., 1967-77; lectr. Sch. Pub. Health, U. Calif., Berkeley, 1950-54, 61-77; mem. cardiac in industry com. Calif. Heart Assn., San Francisco, 1952-54, statewide case finding com. Calif. Tb and Health Assn., San Francisco, 1953, community adv. bd. East Bay Rehab. Ctr., Berkeley, 1961-66. Assoc. editor Jour. of Nat. Cancer Inst., 1957-59; contbr. articles to profl. jours. Recipient Kraft prize scholarship U. Calif., Berkeley, 1932. Fellow APHA, Am. Coll. Preventive Medicine; mem. AMA, Am. Diabetes Assn., Am. Soc. Tropical Medicine and Hygiene, Calif. Acad. Preventive Medicine, Calif. Pub. Health Assn., Phi Chi, Sierra Club. Unitarian-Universalist. Home: 36 Kenyon Ave Kensington CA 94708-1025

MILNE, BRUCE THOMAS, biology educator; b. Buffalo, Jan. 8, 1957; s. James C. Milne and Arlene M. Fassl; m. Diane L. Marshall, May 15, 1988. BS, SUNY, 1979, MS, 1981; PhD, Rutgers, 1985. Lecturer Harvard U., Cambridge, Mass., 1985-86; assoc. prof. U. New Mex., Albuquerque, 1986—. Contbr. articles to profl. jours. Recipient Pres. Young Investigator award Nat. Sci. Found., Washington, 1990, numerous grants for ecological rsch. Mem. AAAS (best student speaker 1981), N.Am. Chpt. Internat. Assn. Landscape Ecology (treas. 1988-90), Ecological Soc. Am., Sigma Xi. Office: U New Mex Dept Biology Albuquerque NM 87131

MILNER, JOE W., journalism educator; b. Winnsboro, Tex., Jan. 2, 1929; s. O.K. and Annie (Boyd) M.; children: Derek Jeffrey, Brent Martin. BS, East Tex. State U., 1954; MA, U. Okla., 1955; EdD, U. Wyo., 1963. Reporter Commerce (Tex.) Daily Jour., 1947-49; reporter Dallas Times Herald, 1949-51, Greenville (Tex.) Herald, 1953-54; journalism instr. Eastern N.Mex. U., Portales, 1955-57; head journalism dept. Miss. State Coll. for Women,

Columbus, 1957-58; prof. U. Wyo., Laramie, 1960-67; dir. Journalism Sch. Ariz. State U., Tempe, 1970-79, prof., 1967—; vis. prof. Angelo State U., San Angelo, Tex., 1992-93. Editor Wyo. Press, Laramie, 1960-67, Journalism Roundtable, 1965-73. Recipient Disting. Newspaper Advisor award, Nat. Coun. Coll. Advisors, 1965. Mem. Soc. Profl. Journalists. Home: 2095 E Manhatton Dr Tempe AZ 85282-5967 Office: Sch of Journalism Ariz State U Tempe AZ 85287

MILNER, MARTIN, naturopathic cardiologist; b. Bklyn., July 14, 1952; s. Nathan and Lillie (Kamen) M.; m. Mary Anna Carpenter, Oct. 12, 1985; children: Ari, Benjamin. BA in Edn., U. R.I., 1974, MA in Counseling, 1975; degree in naturopathic medicine, Nat. Coll. Naturopathic Medici, Portland, Oreg., 1983. Internship Portland Naturopathic Clin., 1982-84; dir. Ctr. for Natural Medicine, Portland, 1983—; med. dir. Diagnostic Cons., Portland, 1987—; assoc. prof. cardiology Nat. Coll. Naturopathic Medicine, 1988—; past pres. East West Coll. Healing Arts, Portland, 1984-87; cons. for formula design, Bellevue, Wash., 1989—; lectr. on naturopathic cardiovascular and pulmonary medicine, 1992. Author: Concise Homeopathic Repertory, 1982; contbr. articles to profl. jours. Mem. Am. Assn. Naturopathic Physicians (chair ins. com. 1989—, now v.p.), Oreg. Assn. Naturopathic Physicians (chair ins. com., pres. 1985-86), N.Y. Acad. Scis., Am. Holistic Med. Found., Nat. Health Fedn., Lions. Democrat. Home: 22463 S Evergreen Dr Beavercreek OR 97004-9652 Office: Ctr for Natural Medicine 1330 SE 39th Ave Portland OR 97214-4322

MILNER, SUSAN JEANNE, financial services company executive; b. Inglewood, Calif., May 23, 1947; d. Dale Philip and Jeanne (Higburg) Treible; divorced; 1 child, Steven. Mem. office staff D.P. Treible, MD, Van Nuys, Calif., 1963-65; dist. office supr. Pacific Bell, Woodland Hills, Calif., 1966-73; mgr. State Farm Ins., Canoga Park, Calif., 1974-75; v.p. Associated Adminstrs., Van Nuys, 1976-88; pres. Commonwealth Adminstrn., Mission Hills, Calif., 1988-91, Providence Adminstrn., Mission Hills, 1991—; bd. dirs. Providence Trust Co., Houston. Columnist Creative Real Estate newsletter, 1990—; contbr. articles to profl. jours. Office: Providence Adminstrn 10200 Sepulveda Blvd Ste 180 Mission Hills CA 91345-2549

MILONE, ANTHONY M., bishop; b. Omaha, Sept. 24, 1932. Grad., North American Coll. (Rome). Ordained priest Roman Catholic Ch., 1957. Ordained titular bishop of Plestia and aux. bishop Diocese of Omaha, 1982; apptd. bishop Mont. Diocese, Great Falls-Billings, 1987—. Office: PO Box 1399 121 33rd St S Great Falls MT 59405-3322*

MILONE, EUGENE FRANK, astronomer, educator; b. N.Y.C., June 26, 1939; arrived in Can., 1971; s. Frank Louis and Vera Christine (Joeckle) M.; m. Helen Catherine Louise (Ligor), Mar. 1, 1959; children: Bartholomew Vincenzo Llambro, Marie Christina Milone Jack. AB, Columbia U., 1961; MSc, Yale U., 1963, PhD, 1967. Astronomer space sci. div. rocket spectroscopy br. Naval Rsch. Lab., Washington, 1967-84; asst. prof. Gettysburg (Pa.) Coll., 1968-71; asst. prof. dept. physics and astronomy U. Calgary, Alta., Can., 1971-75, assoc. prof., 1976-81, prof., 1981—. Author: Infrared Extinction and Standardization, 1989, Challenges of Astronomy, 1991; contbr. over 150 articles to profl. jours. Elected mem. com. for coll. and univ. svcs. Evang. Luth. Ch. in Can., Synod of Alberta and the Territories, Edmonton, Alta., 1989-93. Operating and Equipment grantee Natural Scis. and Engring. Rsch. Coun. Can., 1972—; Killam Resident fellow Killam Found. U. Calgary, 1982, 88. Mem. Internat. Astron. Union (mem. organizing com., commn. 25 1985-91), Am. Astron. Soc. (chmn. local organizing com. Calgary meeting 1981), Can. Astron. Soc., Sigma Xi (pres. U. Calgary chpt. 1979-80). Democrat. Lutheran. Home: 1031 Edgemont Rd NW, Calgary, AB Canada T3A 2J5 Office: U Calgary Dept Physics and Astronomy, 2500 University Dr NW, Calgary, AB Canada T2N 1N4

MILOSZ, CZESLAW, poet, author, educator; b. Lithuania, June 30, 1911; came to U.S., 1960, naturalized, 1970; s. Aleksander and Weronika (Kunat) M. M Juris, U. Wilno, Lithuania, 1934; LittD (hon.), U. Mich., 1977; honoris causa, Harvard U., 1989, Jaqellonian U., Poland, 1989, U. Rome, Italy, 1992. Programmer Polish Nat. Radio, 1935-39; diplomatic service Polish Fgn. Affairs Ministry, Warsaw, 1945-50; vis. lectr. U. Calif., Berkeley, 1960-61; prof. Slavic langs. and lits. U. Calif., 1961-78, prof. emeritus, 1978—. Author: The Captive Mind, 1953, Native Realm, 1968, Post-War Polish Poetry, 1965, The History of Polish Literature, 1969, Selected Poems, 1972, Bells in Winter, 1978, The Issa Valley, 1981, Separate Notebooks, 1984, The Land of Ulro, 1984, The Unattainable Earth, 1985, Collected Poems, 1988, Provinces, 1991, Beginning With My Streets, 1992. Recipient Prix Littéraire Européen Les Guildes du Livre, Geneva, 1953, Neustadt Internat. prize for lit. U. Okla., 1978, citation U. Calif., Berkeley, 1978, Nobel prize for lit., 1980, Nat. Medal of Arts, 1990; Nat. Culture Fund fellow, 1934-35; Guggenheim fellow, 1976. Mem. AAAS, Am. Acad. Arts and Scis., Am. Acad and Inst. Arts and Letters, Polish Inst. Letters and Scis. in Am., PEN Club in Exile. Office: U Calif Dept Slavic Langs and Lits Berkeley CA 94720

MILROD, JONATHAN CRAIG, chiropractor, administrator civic organization; b. L.A., Calif., Apr. 29, 1957; s. Joe and Elizabeth (Grey) M. MICU Paramedic, Butte Coll., 1979; D in Chiropractic, Palmac West U. of Chiropractic, Sunnyvale, Calif., 1992. Fire fighter, emergency med. technician trainer Los Altos (Calif.) Fire Dept., 1975-77; MICU paramedic Medevac, San Diego, 1980-83, Mobile Life Support, San Mateo, Santa Barbara, Calif., 1984-86; paramedic, H2 So4 officer Life Ctr., Prudhoe Bay, Alaska, 1986-87; flight/rescue medic Alyeska Pipeline Svcs., Anchorage, Alaska, 1987-89; asst. instr. cardio-vascular physiology Palmer Chico Coll., Sunnyvale, Calif., 1989—; founder, dir. Health and Environ. Internat., Los Altos, Calif., 1990—. Named Ambassador of Health La Concepion, Nicaragua Govt., 1990; recipient grant Nicaragua Govt., 1992.

MILROD, LINDA JANE, museum director; b. Saint John, N.B., Can., Mar. 4, 1953; d. Samuel and Joyce (Levine) M. Student, U. London, 1973-74; BFA in Art History, U. Toronto, Ont., Can., 1975. Curatorial asst. Agnes Etherington Art Ctr., Kingston, Ont., 1975-79; dir. Dalhousie Art Gallery, Halifax, N.S., Can., 1979-84, Mendel Art Gallery, Saskatoon, Sask., Can., 1984—. Gallery rep. Meewasin Valley Authority Steering Com. Mendel site plan, Sask., 1984-87; visual arts mem. Can. Games Cultural Events Com., Sask., 1987—; mem. Bd. of Trade, Sask., 1984—. J. Paul Getty Trust scholar, 1986. Mem. Can. Mus. Assn. (councillor 1983-86, chmn. conf. planning com. 1985-86), Sask. Arts Alliance (sec. 1985, v.p. 1986, pres. 1987—), Western Can. Art Assn. (exec. 1985), Can. Art Mus. Dirs. Orgn., Council Assoc. Mus. Dirs., Sask. Mus. Assn. Jewish. Office: Mendel Art Gallery, 950 Spadina Crescent E, Saskatoon, SK Canada S7K 3L6

MILSTEIN, MICHAEL CRAIG, journalist; b. L.A., Oct. 4, 1966; s. Roger Wolfe and Roberta Jean (Cameron) M. BA, Duke U., 1988. Reporter The News and Observer, Raleigh, N.C., 1987-88, L.A. Times, 1988-89, Billings (Mont.) Gazette, 1989—; freelance writer L.A. Times, The Christian Sci. Monitor, Reader's Digest, Nat. Parks, High Country News, Harrowsmith Country Life, 1989—. Recipient Mark of Excellence award Soc. Profl. Journalist, 1989; named Communicator of Yr. Wyoming Wildlife Fedn., 1992. Mem. Soc. Environ. Journalists. Office: Billings Gazette Wyoming Bur PO Box 821 Cody WY 82414

MIMS-RICH, ROBIN ELEANOR, health organization administrator, researcher; b. L.A., Jan. 13, 1965; d. Robert Bradford and Eleanor Veronica (Merseburgh) M.; m. Tony Trent Rich, Oct. 8, 1988. BA in Psychology, UCLA, 1988; M in Pub. Health Adminstrn., Calif. State U., Hayward, 1991—. Owner Ednl. Svc. West, Oakland, Calif., 1988-89; mgr. utilization ops. Heals Health Plan, Oakland, Calif., 1989—; rsch. assoc. Endocrine Metabolic Rsch. Ctr., Santa Rosa, Calif., 1982—. Contbr. articles in endocrinology to profl. jours.

MINAMI, ROBERT YOSHIO, artist, graphic designer; b. Seattle, May 1, 1919; s. Kichitaro and Suma (Fujita) M.; m. Shizu Tashiro, May 30, 1953; 1 child, Ken. Student, Goodman Theatre of Design, Chgo., 1955-56, Art Inst., Chgo., 1957, Acad. Art, Chgo., 1980-81. Graphic artist Filmack Studios, Chgo., 1945-48, S. Taylor & Leavitt Assocs., Chgo., 1949-50; head graphic designer NBC-TV, Chgo., 1950-82; fine artist Robert Minami's Studio, Oceanside, Calif., 1983—. Active Supporters for City Couns., Oceanside, 1984—. Recipient Merit award Artist Guild Chgo., 1956, People's Choice award Carlsbad Oceanside Art League, 1986, Dick Blick award, 1992. Mem. San Diego Watercolor Soc., United Scenic Artists (life).

MINARD, MICHAEL KENT, protective services official; b. Mpls., Feb. 14, 1944; s. Hume Raymond and Phyllis Adele (Larson) M.; m. Gloria Jean Rigsbee, Apr. 3, 1971; children: Blake Michael, Denise Jean. Student, Grinnell Coll., 1962-64; BA, U. Minn., 1966; MPA, U. So. Calif., 1972. Police officer Beverly Hills (Calif.) Police Dept., 1970-76; chief of police Waterford (Calif.) Police Dept., 1976-77, Calif. State U.-Chico Police Dept., 1987—; sgt. Calif. State U.-Sonoma Police Dept., Rohnert Park, 1977-81; lt. Paradise (Calif.) Police Dept., 1981-87. Co-author: POST Records Management Manual, 1987; contbr. articles to profl. publs. Mem. pub. safety adv. bd. 4th Calif. Senate Dist., Sacramento, 1991-92; bd. dirs., past pres. United Way of Butte and Glenn Counties, Chico, 1982-92; mem. governing bd., treas. Paradise Alliance Ch., 1989-92. 1st lt. U.S. Army, 1966-69. Nat. Merit scholar, 1962. Mem. Internat. Assn. Campus Law Enforcement Adminstrs., Butte County Law Enforcement Adminstrs. Home: PO Box 711 Paradise CA 95967 Office: Calif State U Chico Police Dept Chico CA 95929-0133

MINDELL, ARNOLD, psychologist; b. Schenectady, N.Y., Jan. 1, 1940; s. Max and Bianca (Gruenberg) M.; m. Amy Kaplan, Aug. 1986. MA, MIT, 1962; diploma, Jung Inst., Zurich, Switzerland, 1969; PhD, Union Inst., Ohio, 1972. Founder Inst. for Process Oriented Psychology, Zurich, London, Portland, Oreg. Author: Dreambody, 1982, Work with Dreambody, 1983, Coma, 1989, Leader as Martial Artist, 1992, others; appeared on nat. TV and radio. Home and Office: 605 NW 22d Ave Portland OR 97210-3202

MINDELL, EARL LAWRENCE, nutritionist, author; b. St. Boniface, Man., Can., Jan. 20, 1940; s. William and Minerva Sybil (Galsky) M.; came to U.S., 1965, naturalized, 1972; BS in Pharmacy, N.D. State U., 1963; PhD in Nutrition, Pacific We. U., 1985; m. Gail Andrea Jaffe, May 16, 1971; children: Evan Louis-Ashley, Alanna Dayan. Pres. Adanac Mgmt. Inc., 1979—, Compact Disc-Count, Inc.; instr. Dale Carnegie course; lectr. on nutrition, radio and TV. Mem. Beverly Hills, Rancho Park, Western Los Angeles (dir.) regional chambers commerce, Calif., Am. pharm. assns., Am. Acad. Gen. Pharm. Practice, Am. Inst. for History of Pharmacy, Am. Nutrition Soc., Internat. Coll. Applied Nutrition, Nutrition Found., Nat. Health Fedn., Am. Dieticians Assn., Orthomolecular Med. Assn., Internat. Acad. Preventive Medicine. Clubs: City of Hope, Masons, Shriners. Author: Earl Mindell's Vitamin Bible, Parents Nutrition Bible, Earl Mindell's Quick and Easy Guide to Better Health, Earl Mindell's Pill Bible, Earl Mindell's Shaping Up with Vitamins, Earl Mindell's Safe Eating, Earl Mindell's Herb Bible; columnist Let's Live mag., The Vitamin Supplement (Can.), The Vitamin Connection (U.K.), Healthy N' Fit; contbr. articles on nutrition to profl. jours. Home: 244 El Camino Dr Beverly Hills CA 90212 Office: 10739 W Pico Blvd Los Angeles CA 90064-2219

MINDEN, R. DOYLE, university administrator; b. Storm Lake, Iowa, May 7, 1933; s. Clarence and Alma (Sievers) M.; m. Marilyn L. Anderson, Aug. 16, 1953; children: Steven, Sandra, Constance. BJ, U. Mo., 1957. News editor Laurens (Iowa) Sun, 1957-59; assoc. editor Northwestern Banker, Des Moines, 1959-64, Underwriters Rev., Des Moines, 1959-64; dir. pub. rels. Drake U., Des Moines, 1964-68; dir. univ. rels. U. of the Pacific, Stockton, Calif., 1968—. Author, editor: Management by Objectives for Public Relations, 1972. Del. Rep. Party, Des Moines, 1966. Cpl. U.S. Army, 1953-55. Mem. Pub. Rels. Soc. Am. (accredited), Sacramento Pub. Rels. Soc. Am. (pres. 1970-71), Oakland-East Bay Pub. Rels. Soc. Am. (v.p. 1980-81), Rotary Internat. (bd. dirs. 1981-85, Rotarian of Yr. 1984). Home: 3308 Riverton Way Stockton CA 95219 Office: U of the Pacific 3601 Pacific Ave Stockton CA 95211

MINDLING, MARTIN JOHN, automobile dealership executive; b. Chgo., June 12, 1947; s. Walter Herbert and Lillian Gertrude (Schwarz) M.; m. Marilyn Jeannette Schroeder, Nov. 5, 1981; children: Marissa, Miranda, Madeleine, Jonathon. BS in Acctg., No. Ill. U., 1969; MBA, Northwestern U., 1974. V.p. Citicorp, N.Y.C., 1974-83, Corp. Focus, Rolling Meadows, Ill., 1983-86; contbr. John Schroeder Group, Springfield, Ill., 1986-88; chief fin. officer Motor Werks, Ill., 1988-92; owner, pres. Riverside (Calif.) Chevrolet-Geo, 1992—. Mem. Union League Club Chgo. Home: 7128 Hawarden Dr Riverside CA 92506 Office: Riverside Chevrolet 8200 Auto Dr Riverside CA 92504

MINEAR, WILLIAM LORIS, surgeon, educator; b. Bismarck, N.D., Mar. 18, 1910; s. William Harold and Ida Sophia (Iverson) M.; m. Julia Donohue Newton, Nov. 24, 1950 (dec. 1960); children: Lisa Maria, William Harold; m. Charlene Dee Hechtner, Oct. 14, 1976. BS, U. Wash., Seattle, 1932; MD, Northwestern U., Chgo., 1936, PhD, 1937; MS in Orthopaedic Surgery, U. Tenn., 1946. Fellow in anatomy Med. Sch. Northwestern U., 1932-36; med. dir. Carrie Tingley Hosp. for Crippled Children, Hot Springs, N.Mex., 1946-56; pvt. practice orthopaedic surgeon Albuquerque, 1956-75; adj. prof. anthropology U. N.Mex., Albuquerque, 1975—; mem. Pres.'s Com. on Employment of the Physically Handicapped. Recipient Meritorious Svc. award N.Mex. Orthopaedic Assn., 1988, Citation for Oustanding Svc., 1956. Fellow Am. Acad. Orthopaedic Surgeons; mem. AMA, FACS, Am. Bd. Orthopaedic Surgery, N.Mex. Med. Soc., Albuquerque Med. Soc. Home: 1121 Marquette Pl NE Albuquerque NM 87106-4703

MINER, BERT DEAN, non-profit foundation executive; b. Springville, Utah, May 22, 1926; s. Cyrus Grant and Geneva Bernece (Nielsen) M.; m. Dorothy Tranquilia Clark, July 23, 1952; children: Denis Clark, Alan Grant, Jan Kristy Miner Richards, Julie Lynn Miner Frazier. BS, Utah State U., 1953; MS, Mich. State U., 1955; postgrad., U. Md., 1957-60; diploma, Command and Gen. Staff Coll., 1965. Agrl. economist Farmer Coop. Svc., USDA, Washington, 1955-66, br. chief, 1966-67, dir. soybean program, 1971-77; coop. specialist Agy. for Internat. Devel., Brazil, 1967-69, team leader, 1969-71; program specialist Agrl. Stabilization and Conservation, Washington, 1977-80, supr., 1980-82; exec. Family Resources Found., Sandy, Utah, 1984—, also bd. dirs.; bd. dirs. Buffalo Enterprises, Sandy, C.G. Miner, Inc., Springville. Author numerous tech. reports and articles in field. Mem. sch. bd. Am. Sch., Campinas, Brazil, 1968-71; post and troop chmn. Boy Scouts Am., New Carrollton, Md., 1965-67. Lt. U.S. Army, 1944-48. Recipient Industry award Nat. Inst. Locker and Freezer Provisioners, 1967, Nat. Assn. Brazilian Farmer Coops., 1971, Meritorious Svc. medal Pres. of U.S., 1977. Republican. Mem. LDS Ch. Office: Family Resources Found 11458 Willow View Way Sandy UT 84092

MINER, JOHN EDWARD, city manager; b. Wabash, Ind., Feb. 6, 1937; s. Carlos Monroe and Mary Rebecca (Hoover) M.; m. Sharon Rose Craft, Mar. 24, 1961; children: Carla Marie, Heather Lynet. BS, Manchester Coll., North Manchester, Ind., 1962, Ind. U., 1972; MPA, Ind. U., 1978. Reg. adminstr. Ind. Criminal Justice, Lafayette, Ind., 1970-73; chief rsch. Allen County Sheriff's Dept., Ft. Wayne, Ind., 1973-75; city adminstr. City of Wabash, Ind., 1976-79; exec. budget analyst State of Ariz., Phoenix, 1980; prof. pub. adminstrn. Western Internat. U., Phoenix, 1981-83; city mgr. City of Benson, Ariz., 1981-84; pres., chief exec. officer Municipal MegeTrends, 1984—; govt./environ. affairs specialist Laurent Bouillet-Howard, Phoenix, Paris, 1985-90; city mgr. City of Quartzsite, Ariz., 1990—. With USMC, 1957-59. Gov.'s fellow in pub. adminstrn., State of Ind., 1976-78; recipient Award of Excellence in Energy Conservation, Govt., State of Ariz., 1983. Mem. Rotary, Masons, Elks. Home: 2311 W Tuckey Ln Phoenix AZ 85015-1041 Office: City of Quartzsite PO Box 2812 Quartzsite AZ 85346-2812

MINER, JOHN RONALD, agricultural engineer; b. Scottsburg, Ind., July 4, 1938; s. Gerald Lamont and Alice Mae (Murphy) M.; m. Betty Katheron Emery, Aug. 4, 1963; children—Saralena Marie, Katherine Alice, Frederick Gerald. B.S. in Chem. Engring, U. Kans., 1959; M.S.E. in San. Engring, U. Mich., 1960; Ph.D. in Chem. Engring. and Microbiology, Kans. State U., 1967. Lic. profl. engr., Kans., Oreg. San. engr. Kans. Dept. Health, Topeka, 1959-64; grad. research asst. Kans. State U., Manhattan, 1964-67; asst. prof. agrl. engring. Iowa State U., 1967-71, assoc. prof., 1971-72; assoc. prof. agrl. engring. Oreg. State U., 1972-76, prof., 1976—, head dept., 1976-86, acting assoc. dean Coll. Agrl. Sci., 1983-84, assoc. dir. Office Internat. Research and Devel., 1986-90, extension water quality specialist, 1991—; environ. engr. FAO of UN, Singapore, 1980-81; internat. cons.; cons. to livestock feeding ops., agrl. devel. firms. Co-author book on livestock waste mgmt.; author 3 books of children's sermons; contbr. numerous articles on livestock prodn., pollution control, control of odors associated with livestock prodn. to profl. publs. Mem. Am. Soc. Agrl. Engrs. (bd. dirs. 1985-87), Water Pollution Control Fedn., Sigma Xi, Gamma Sigma Delta, Alpha Epsilon, Tau Beta Pi. Presbyterian. Office: Dept Bioresource Engring Oreg State U Bioresource Eng Dept Corvallis OR 97331

MINERBI, LUCIANO MARIO LAURO, urban and regional planning educator, consultant, community volunteer; b. Milan, Italy, Aug. 13, 1941; came to U.S., 1967, permanent resident, 1971; s. Giulio and Beatrice (Tosi) M.; m. Daniela Rocco, June 18, 1975; children: Lahela, Makia, Mareva. D. Arch., Poly. U., Milan, 1966; cert. Harvard U., 1967; M.U.P., U. Wash., 1969; cert. Northwestern U., 1970. Researcher Istituto Lombardo Studi Economici e Sociali, Milan, 1967; asst. prof. urban and regional planning U. Hawaii, Honolulu, 1969-73, assoc. prof., 1973-80, prof., 1980—; vis. prof. Inst. U. Venice, Italy, 1972-74; planning cons., Milan, 1967-69, Honolulu, 1969—; adj. research assoc. East West Ctr., 1984; expert UN Tech. Coop. Roster, 1973—; cons. UN Statis. Office, Govt. of Fiji, 1980-83, UN Ctr. Regional Devel., Nagoya, Japan, 1984-89, Environ. Planning Tng., Solomon Islands and U.S. Aid, 1987, Nat. Coastal Devel. Inst., 1990-91, Greenpeace, 1991-92. Contbr. articles and chpts. on urban and regional planning to nat. and internat. profl. jours. and books; author, editor reports on urban and land devel. and land readjustment, community and indigenous based planning and sustainable devel., environ. mgmt., cultural risk assessment, native Hawaiian sanctuaries and places of refuge, alternative and responsible tourism in Hawaii, S. Pacific and Asia. Chmn. planning com. Moiliili Community Ctr., Honolulu, 1982-83; vice chmn. bd. dirs. Neighborhood Bd. 8, Honolulu, 1977-79; bd. dirs. Moiliili Community Ctr., 1980-83; mem. City and County Adv. Com. on Mixed Uses, Honolulu, 1982, Aloha United Way unit coord., 1986—, Neighborhood Reinvestment Corp., 1986; commr. Housing and Community Devel., City and County Honolulu, 1987—; mem. Hawaii Economical Coalition on Tourism, 1989—, S.M. Matsunaga Inst. for Peace, U. Hawaii, 1988—, exec. com. mem., 1989, 91-92; advisor to several native Hawaiian community groups. Mellon fellow U. Wash., 1967-69; grantee East-West Ctr. and U. Hawaii, 1981, 84-85; research fellow East-West Ctr., 1984; instrnl. research mentioned in various State of Hawaii legis. resolutions, 1979-86. Mem. Am. Inst. Cert. Planners (charter), Soc. Internat. Devel., AIA (assoc.). Roman Catholic. Office: U Hawaii Dept Urban and Regional Planning Porteus Hall 107 Honolulu HI 96822

MINES, MICHAEL, lawyer; b. Seattle, May 4, 1929; s. Henry Walker and Dorothy Elizabeth (Bressler) M.; m. Phyllis Eastham, Aug. 24, 1957; children: Linda Mines Elliott, Sandra, Diane Paull, Michael Lister. Student Whitman Coll., 1947-49; BA, U. Wash., 1951, JD, 1954. Bar: Wash. 1954, U.S. Dist. Ct. (we. dist.) Wash. 1957, U.S. Dist. Ct. Mont. 1970, U.S. Ct. Appeals (9th cir.) 1961, U.S. Supreme Ct. Assoc. Skeel, McKelvy, Henke, Evenson & Uhlman, Seattle, 1956-66, ptnr., 1966-68, Hullin, Roberts, Mines, Fite & Riveland, Seattle, 1968-75, Skeel, McKelvy, Henke, Evenson & Betts, Seattle, 1975-79, Betts, Patterson & Mines, Seattle, 1978—. Moderator Wash.-No. Idaho conf. United Ch. of Christ, 1975-76; trustee U. Wash. Law Sch. Alumni Assn. With U.S. Army, 1954-56. Mem. ABA, Wash. State Bar Assn., Seattle-King Bar Assn., Am. Coll. Trial Lawyers (state chair 1982-83, Internat. Assn. Def. Counsel, Wash. Assn. Def. Counsel (pres. 1971-72), Internat. Acad. Trial Lawyers (bd. dirs. 1991—), Def. Rsch. Inst. Home: 2474 Crestmont Pl W Seattle WA 98199-3714 Office: Betts Patterson Mines PS 800 Financial Ctr 1215 4th Ave Seattle WA 98161-1001

MINETA, NORMAN YOSHIO, congressman; b. San Jose, Calif., Nov. 12, 1931; s. Kay Kunisaku and Kane (Watanabe) M.; m. Danealia; children: David, K., Stuart S. B.S., U. Calif.-Berkeley, 1953; D of Pub. Svc., Santa Clara U., 1989. Agt./broker Mineta Ins. Agy., San Jose, 1956-89; mem. adv. bd. Bank of Tokyo in Calif., 1961-75; mem. San Jose City Council, 1967-71; vice mayor San Jose, 1969-71, mayor, 1971-75; mem. 94th-103rd Congresses from 13th (now 15th) Calif. dist., 1975—, chmn. house com. on pub. works and transp., subcom. surface transp.; mem. sci., space and tech., select com. on intelligence; mem. budget com. 95th-97th Congresses; dep. Dem. whip 94th Congresses; chmn. fin. com. Santa Clara County (Calif.) Council Chs., 1960-62; commr. San Jose Human Relations Commn., 1962-64, San Jose Housing Authority, 1966—. Precinct chmn. Community Theater Bond Issue, 1964; mem. spl. gifts com. Santa Clara County council Boy Scouts Am., 1967; sec. Santa Clara County Grand Jury, 1964; bd. dirs. Wesley Found., San Jose State Coll., 1956-58, Pacific Neighbors, Community Council Cen. Santa Clara County, Japan Soc., San Francisco, Santa Clara County chpt. NCCJ, Mexican-Am. Community Services Agy.; mem. exec. bd. No. Calif.-Western Nev. dist. council Japanese Am. Citizens League, 1960-62, pres. San Jose chpt., 1957-59; bd. regents Smithsonian Instn., 1979—; chmn. Smithsonian vis. com. for Freer Gallery, 1981—; mem. bd. regents Santa Clara U. Served to lt. AUS, 1954-56. Mem. Greater San Jose C. of C., Nat. Assn. Indsl. Ins. Agts., Calif. Assn. Indsl. Ins. Agts., San Jose Assn. Ind. Ins. Agts. (dir. 1960-62), North San Jose Optimists Club (pres. 1956-58), Jackson-Taylor Bus. and Profl. Assn. (dir. 1963). Methodist. Office: House of Representatives 2221 Rayburn House Office Bldg Washington DC 20515-0515*

MINGER, TERRELL JOHN, management company executive; b. Canton, Ohio, Oct. 7, 1942; s. John Wilson and Margaret Rose M.; m. Judith R. Arnold, Aug. 7, 1965; 1 child, Gabriella Sophia. BA, Baker U., 1966; MPA, Kans. U., 1969; Urban Exec. Program, MIT, 1975; Loeb fellow Harvard U., 1976-77; Exec. Devel. Program, Stanford U., 1979; MBA, U. Colo., 1983. Asst. dir. admissions Baker U., 1966-67; asst. city mgr. City of Boulder, Colo., 1968-69; city mgr. City of Vail, Colo., 1969-79; pres., chief exec. officer Whistler Village Land Co., Vancouver, B.C., Can., 1979-81; v.p., gen. mgr. Cumberland S.W. Inc., Denver, 1981-83; exec. asst., dep. chief of staff to Gov. Colo., 1983-87; pres., chief exec. officer Sundance (Utah) Inst. for Resource Mgmt., 1986—; pres., chief exec. officer Sundance Enterprises Ltd., 1988-91; adj. prof. grad. sch. pub. affairs U. Colo., 1983—, Sch. Bus. U. Denver, 1992—; bd. dirs. Colo. Open Lands, Inc., 1986—; participant UN Conf. on Environment and Devel., Rio de Janeiro, 1992. Editor: Greenhouse/Glasnost—The Global Warming Crisis, 1990. Spl. del. UN Habitat Conf. Human Settlements, spl. rep. to UN Environment Program, 1992; founder Vail Symposium; co-founder, bd. dirs. Colo. Park Found., 1985—; founding mem. Greenhouse/Glasnost U.S./USSR Teleconf. with Soviet Acad. Scis., 1989—. Nat. finalist White House Fellowship, 1978; named one of B.C.'s Top Bus. Leaders for the '80's, 1980. Mem. Urban Land Inst., Colo. Acad. Pub. Adminstrn. (charter, founding mem. 1988), Colo. City Mgmt. Assn., Internat. City Mgrs. Assn. (Mgmt. Innovation award 1974-76), Western Gov.'s Assn. (staff coun., chmn. adv. com. 1985-86), Denver Athletic Club. Editor: Vail Symposium Papers, 1970-79; author, editor: Growth Alternatives for Rocky Mountain West, 1976; Future of Human Settlements in the West, 1977. Home: 785 6th St Boulder CO 80302-7416 Office: Ctr for Resource Mgmt 1410 Grant St Ste 307C Denver CO 80203-1846

MINHAS, FAQIR ULLAH, aerospace engineer; b. Shadiwal, Pakistan, Dec. 4, 1924; came to U.S. 1962; s. Ata M. and Sakeena (Khokhar) M.; m. Dolly Patricia Testa, Jan. 4, 1987. BA, Panjab U., Lahore, 1952; MA in Math., Panjab U., 1957; MASc, Laval U., Que., 1965; DSc, Laval U., 1973; MEngr., McGill U., Montreal, Que., 1984. Mechanic Rwy. Workshops, Lahore, 1943-47; instr. Govt. Sch. Engring., Rasul, 1952-53, Govt. Coll., Rawal Kot, 1954-55; devel. engr. John Inglis, Toronto, Ont., 1963-64; head transp. phen. br. Dominion Engring., Montreal, 1966-80; sys. engr. Canadair, Montreal, 1980-83; sys. engr. aerodynamics Reflectone, Tampa, Fla., 1984-85; fellow MIT, Cambridge, 1985-86; researcher U. Toronto, Ont., 1987-89; computer specialist U. Hawaii, Honolulu, 1990—; adj. faculty prof. Pacific Western U., L.A., 1990—. Contbr. articles to profl. jours. Edn. officer Pakistan Air Force, 1958-61. Mem. N.Y. Acad. Scis., AIAA, U.S. Power Squadron (Tampa, Fla.). Home: 2511 Kapiolani Blvd Apt 7 Honolulu HI 96826-4705

MINK, PATSY TAKEMOTO, congresswoman; b. Paia, Maui, Hawaii, Dec. 6, 1927; d. Suematsu and Mitama (Tateyama) Takemoto; m. John Francis Mink, Jan. 27, 1951; 1 child, Gwendolyn. Student, Wilson Coll., 1946, U. Nebr., 1947; BA, U. Hawaii, 1948; LLD, U. Chgo., 1951; DHL (hon.), Chaminade Coll., 1975, Syracuse U., 1976, Whitman Coll., 1981. Bar:

Hawaii. Pvt. practice Honolulu, 1953-65; lectr. U. Hawaii, 1952-56, 59-62, 79-80; atty. Territorial Ho. of Reps., 1955; mem. Ter. Hawaii Ho. of Reps., 1956-58, Ter. Hawaii Senate, 1958-59, State Hawaii Senate, 1962-64, 89-92d Congresses from Hawaii, 93-94th Congresses from 2d dist. Hawaii, 101st-103d Congresses from 2d dist. Hawaii; mem. edn. and labor com., budget com., natural resources com.; mem. U.S. del. to UN Law of Sea, 1975-76, Internat. Woman's Yr., 1975, UN Environ. Program, 1977, Internat. Whaling Commn., 1977; asst. sec. of state U.S. Dept. State, 1977-78. Charter pres. Young Dem. Club Oahu, 1954-56, Ter. Hawaii Young Dems., 1956-58; del. Dem. Nat. Conv., 1960, 72, 80; nat. v.p. Young Dem. Clubs Am., 1957-59; v.p. Ams. for Dem. Action, 1974-76, nat. pres., 1978-81; mem. nat. adv. com. White House Conf. on Families, 1979-80; mem. nat. adv. coun. Federally Employed Women. Recipient Leadership for Freedom award Roosevelt Coll., Chgo., 1968, Alii award 4-H Clubs Hawaii, 1969, Nisei of Biennium award, Freedom award Honolulu chpt. NAACP, 1971, Disting. Humanitarian award YWCA, St. Louis, 1972, Creative Leadership in Women's Rights award NEA, 1977, Human Rights award Am. Fedn. Tchrs., 1975, Feminist of Yr. award Feminist Majority Found., 1991, Margaret Brent award ABA, 1992. Office: US House of Reps 2135 Rayburn House Offices Bldg Washington DC 20515-1102

MINNERLY, ROBERT WARD, educator; b. Yonkers, N.Y., Mar. 21, 1935; s. Richard Warren and Margaret Marion (DeBrocky) M.; m. Sandra Overmire, June 12, 1957; children: Scott Ward, John Robert, Sydney Sue. AB, Brown U., 1957; MAT, U. Tex., Arlington, 1980. Tchr., coach Rumsey Hall Sch., Washington, Conn., 1962-64; tchr., coach Berkshire Sch., Sheffield, Mass., 1964-70, asst. head, 1969-70, headmaster, 1970-76; dir. Salisbury (Conn.) Summer Sch. Reading and English, 1970; prin. upper sch. Ft. Worth Country Day Sch., 1976-86; headmaster Charles Wright Acad., Tacoma, Wash., 1986—; cons. Tarrant County Coalition on Substance Abuse, 1982-84; mem. mayor's task force Tacoma Edn. Summit, 1991-92. Contbr. articles to profl. jours. Bd. dirs. Tacoma/Pierce County Good Will Games Art Coun., 1989; mem. exec. com. Am. Leadership Forum, 1991—, Broadway Ctr. for Performing Arts, Tacoma, 1990—. Lt. USN, 1957-62. Named Adminstr. of Yr. Wash. Journalism Edn. Assn., 1991. Mem. Pacific N.W. Assn. Ind. Schs. (chmn. long-range planning com. 1989-92, exec. com. 1990-92). Republican. Presbyterian. Home: 4214 39th Ave Ct NW Gig Harbor WA 98335 Office: Charles Wright Acad 7723 Chambers Creek Rd Tacoma WA 98467

MINNICH, DIANE KAY, state bar executive director; b. Iowa City, Feb. 17, 1956; d. Ralph Maynard Minnich and Kathryn Jane (Obye) Tompkins. BA in Behavioral Sci., San Jose State U., 1978. Tutorial program coord./instr. Operation SHARE/La Valley Coll., Van Nuys, Calif., 1979-81; field exec. Silver Sage Girl Scout Coun., Boise, Idaho, 1981-85; continuing legal edn. dir. Idaho State Bar/Idaho Law Found. Inc., Boise, 1985-88, dep. dir., 1988-90, exec. dir., 1990—. Mem. Assn. CLE Adminstrs., Chgo., 1985-90; bd. dirs. Silver Sage coun. Girl Scouts, Boise, 1990-93, nominating com. mem., 1990—, chair nominating com., 1991-92. Named one of Outstanding Young Women in Am., 1991. Mem. Nat. Orgn. Bar Execs. (membership com. 1992), Zonta Club Boise (prs. 1991-92, bd. dirs. 1989-93, chair long range planning com.), Rotary Club Boise. Office: Idaho State Bar/Idaho Law Found PO Box 895 204 W State Boise ID 83701

MINNICH, JOSEPH EDWARD, tourist railway consultant; b. Swanton, Ohio, Sept. 13, 1932; s. Charles and Leila (Gaiman) M.; m. Frances Katherine Searcy, Feb. 6, 1977; children: Christopher, Susan, Teresa. Student, U. Toledo, 1956-58, Am. U., 1969. Ins. broker Wright Russell & Bay Co., Toledo, 1961-67; ch. adminstr. St. Paul's Luth. Ch., Toledo, 1968-80; pres. Toledo Lake Erie & Western R.R., 1978-81, Heritage R.R. Co., 1981-83; exec. v.p. Centennial Rail, Ltd., Denver, 1981—; v.p. Airpower West Ltd., 1992—. Author: Steam Locomotives in the United States, 1985, Historic Diesels in the United States, 1988; editor Trainline mag., 1979—. V.p. Airpower West, Ltd., 1992—. Sgt. USAF, 1951-55. Nat. Assn. Ch. Bus. Adminstrs. fellow, 1971. Mem. Tourist Ry. Assn. (bd. dirs. 1984—, Disting. Svc. award 1991), Colo. Ry. Mus. Republican. Lutheran. Home: 3641 S Yampa St Aurora CO 80013-3527 Office: Centennial Rail Ltd PO Box 460393 Aurora CO 80046-0393

MINNIE, MARY VIRGINIA, social worker, educator; b. Eau Claire, Wis., Feb. 16, 1922; d. Herman Joseph and Virginia Martha (Strong) M. BA, U. Wis., 1944; MA, U. Chgo., 1949, Case Western Reserve U., 1956. Lic. clin. social worker, Calif. Supr. day care Wis. Children Youth, Madison, 1949-57; coordinator child study project Child Guidance Clinic, Grand Rapids, Mich., 1957-60; faculty, community services Pacific Oaks Coll., Pasadena, Calif., 1960-70; pvt. practice specializing in social work various cities, Calif., 1970-78; ednl. cons. So. Calif. Health Care, North Hollywood, Calif., 1978—; med. social worker Kaiser Permanente Home Health, Downey, Calif., 1985-87; assoc. Baby Sitters Guild, Inc., 1987—; cons. Home Health, 1987-90; pres. Midwest Assn. Nursery Edn., Grand Rapids, 1958-60; bd. dirs., sec. So. Calif. Health Care, North Hollywood; bd. dirs., v.p. Baby Sitters Guild Inc., South Pasadena; cons. project Head Start Office Econ. Opportunity, Washington, 1965-70. Mem. Soc. Clin. Social Workers, Nat. Assn. Social Workers, Nat. Assn. Edn. Young Children (1960-62). Democrat. Club: Altrusa (Laguna Beach, Calif.) (pres. 1984-87). Home and Office: 1622 Bank St South Pasadena CA 91030-3830

MINOR, JOHN THREECIVELOUS, III, computer science educator; b. Fulton, Mo., Nov. 17, 1950; s. John Threecivelous and Ruth Edna (Neuenswander) M. BA, Rice U., 1973; PhD, U. Tex., 1979. Asst. prof. U. Okla., Norman, 1979-85; assoc. prof. computer sci. U. Nev., Las Vegas, 1985-90, chmn. dept., 1990—; cons. Nev. Gaming Control Bd., Las Vegas, 1990, Parnell and Assocs., Las Vegas, 1991-92. Rsch. fellow Air Force Office Sci. Rsch., 1984; rsch. grantee Army Rsch. Office, 1986-91. Mem. Assn. for Computing Machinery, Am. Assn. for Artificial Intelligence, Assn. for Automated Reasoning, Phi Kappa Phi, Upsilon Pi Epsilon. Office: U Nev Las Vegas Computer Sci Dept 4505 Maryland Pkwy Las Vegas NV 89154

MINOVITCH, MICHAEL A., scientist; b. Yonkers, N.Y., June 7, 1935; s. Michael A. and Viola J. (Gurzdzlovitch) M. AB, UCLA, 1958; PhD, U. Calif., Berkeley, 1970. With tech. computer dept. Douglas Aircraft, El Segundo, Calif., 1956-58; mem. tech. staff Calif. Inst. Tech., Pasadena, 1961-72; pres. Phaser Telepropulsion Inc., L.A., 1972—. Patentee gravity, laser and magnetic propulsion. Recipient Exceptional Svc. medal NASA, 1972. Mem. U.S. Space Found., 1989—. Republican. Office: Phaser Telepropulsion Inc Ste 1900 1888 Century Park E Los Angeles CA 90067

MINSKER, ANDREW CLAUDE, corporation executive, boxing coach; b. Portland, Oreg., Mar. 20, 1962; s. Hugh Godfrey and Vivian Leigh (Parker) M.; m. Caroline Samantha Cox, Apr. 20, 1992. Grad., Milwaukie (Oreg.) High Sch., 1980. Boxing coach Mt. Scott Community Ctr., Portland, 1975—; model Calvin Klein/Versace, 1987-90; corp. pres. Andrew Minsker Ltd., Inc. dba Winners Edge Tobaccoless Chew, Fight Team Enterprises, Positive Impact Unlimited, Milw., 1988—. Patentee in field of tobaccoless chew; copyright fight team logo. Named Nat. Golden Gloves Champion, 1983, Nat. U.S. Amatuer Champion, Am. Boxing Fedn., 1983, U.S. Olympic Trials Champion, 1984, U.S. Nat. Boxing Team Mem., 1980-84. Home: 15160 S Brunner Rd Oregon City OR 97045 Office: Andrew Minsker Ltd Inc Ste G 5699 SE International Way Milwaukie OR 97222

MINTON, THOMAS WAYNE, non-commissioned military officer, executive; b. Nashville, Nov. 15, 1952; s. Larry Wayne and Mary Lou (Anderson) M.; m. Jaci Lynn Hill, Dec. 24, 1972 (div. Nov. 1977); children: Thomas Johnathan Kitch, Heather Joy Kitch; m. Supatra Chaipitaktakul, May 30, 1980; children: Matthew Sumpope, Nathan Satit. AA, U. Md., 1984, C.C. of A.F., Maxwell, Ala., 1989; BA in Liberal Arts, SUNY, Albany, 1990. Enlisted USAF, 1973, advanced through grades to tech. sgt.; linguist various squadrons, 1974-93; vendor stocker, ind. contractor Schofield Brks., Hawaii, 1989—; pres. Giant Enterprises, Wahiawa, Hawaii, 1991—; ind. distbr. Eagle's Nest Homes, Atlanta, 1992, Brentwood Log Homes, Nashville, 1992; ind. credit card broker Eagle Fin. Svcs., Spokane, Wash., 1992. Mem. Save the Children, 1989—, Nat. Wildlife Fedn., 1991—, Windstar Found., 1992—, Nat. Parks Assn., 1991—. Mem. Ind. Real Estate Assn., Inst. Noetic Scis., Smithsonian Inst., Rosicrucian Order. Home and Office: 1341-C Wiliwili Cir Wahiawa HI 96786-4017

MINTON, TORRI, journalist; b. San Rafael, Calif., Oct. 7, 1956; d. John and Mary. BA in Ethnic Studies, U. Calif., Berkeley, 1983; M of Journalism, Columbia U., 1984. Reporter Associated Press, San Francisco, 1984, Bay City News Svc., San Francisco, 1984-86, San Francisco Chronicle, 1986—; vice chmn. San Francisco Chronicle Northern Calif. Newspaper Guild, 1992; rep. assembly del., 1992, 93. Community devel. vol. Oper. Crossroads Africa, Tiriki, Kenya, 1979. Mem. Phi Beta Kappa. Office: San Francisco Chronicle 901 Mission St San Francisco CA 94119

MINTY, KEITH LARRY, medical services corporation executive; b. Roseburg, Oreg., Mar. 1, 1933; s. John Raymond and Vivian Melba (Adams) M.; m. Mary Louise Davis, May 4, 1953; children: Ronald, Karen, Gary. Enlisted airmen USAF, 1952—, advanced to master sgt., ret., 1978; bus. mgr. Nev. MRI Assocs., L.P., Las Vegas, 1987—, Palomino-Tonopah Assocs., Las Vegas, 1987—; ptnr., treas. Nev. MRI Assocs., Inc., Las Vegas, 1986—, also bd. dirs.; ptnr. Nev. MRI Assocs. Ltd. Partnership, Las Vegas, 1987—; COO Taylor Knudson & Lum Profl. Assn., Las Vegas, Nev., 1993—; dir., treas. Nev. MRI Assocs., Inc., Las Vegas, 1987—; mgmt. com., mem. Palomino-Tonopah Assocs., Las Vegas, 1987—. Decorated Air Force Commendation medal with 2 oak leaf clusters, Bronze Star. Republican. So. Baptist. Office: Taylor Knudson & Lum PA 2020 Palomino Ln # 100 Las Vegas NV 89106-4812

MINTZ, LEIGH WAYNE, university official, geological sciences educator; b. Cleve., June 12, 1939; s. William Michael and Laverne (Bulicek) M.; m. Carol Sue Jackson, Aug. 4, 1962; children—Kevin Randall, Susan Carol. B.S. in Geology, U. Mich., 1961, M.S., 1962; postgrad. U. Pacific, Dillon Beach, Calif., 1963; Ph.D. in Paleontology, U. Calif.-Berkeley, 1966. Asst. prof. earth scis. Calif. State U., Hayward, 1966-70, assoc. prof., 1970-75, prof. geol. scis., 1975—, assoc. dean instrn., 1969-70, assoc. dean Sch. Sci., 1971-72, dean undergrad. studies, 1974-79, assoc. v.p. acad. programs, 1979-93, assoc. v.p. admissions and enrollment svcs., 1992-93, assoc. v.p. acad. svcs. and programs, 1993—; judge geology exhibits Alameda County Fair, Pleasanton, Calif., 1968-91. Author: (textbook) Historical Geology, 1972, 3d edit., 1981; (with others) Physical Geology, 1982. Contbr. articles to profl. jours. and ency. Mem. planning com. Joint Hill Area Plan for Hayward, 1969. Morris M. Wells scholar Gen. Biol. Supply House, 1965-66; fellow NSF, 1961-64. Fellow Geol. Soc. Am.; mem. Paleontol. Soc., Sigma Xi. Home: 5940 Highwood Rd Castro Valley CA 94552-1824 Office: Calif State U Office Assoc VP Acad Svcs & Programs Hayward CA 94542-3011

MINTZ, STUART ALAN, insurance company executive, consultant; b. L.A., Jan. 7, 1956; s. Robert Meyer and Sondra Ruth (Handler) M.; m. Joanna Ruth Toombs, May 20, 1977 (div. Jan. 1985); children: Daniel Isaac, Jacob Aaron; m. Paula Mae Nevlin, Nov. 25, 1987. AA, Orange Coast Coll., 1975; BA, U. Calif., Irvine, 1976; A in Claims, Ins. Inst. Am., 1990. Claims mgr. Farmers Ins., L.A., 1979-88, deVries and Co., Glendale, Calif., 1988-91, Blaker, Monk and Elliston, Glendale, 1991—; access control supr. L.A. Olympic Organizing Com., 1984. Mem. Calif. Fraud Investigators, So. Calif. Fraud Investigators, No. Calif. Investigators, L.A. Adjusters Assn., Orange County Adjusters Assn., Villa Sestri Ho (treas. 1990—), Blue Goose Internat, Eagle Scout. Office: Blaker Monk & Elliston 330 N Brand Blvd Ste 1150 Glendale CA 91203

MINUDRI, REGINA URSULA, librarian, consultant; b. San Francisco, May 9, 1937; d. John C. and Molly (Halter) M. B.A., San Francisco Coll. for Women, 1958; M.L.S., U. Calif.-Berkeley, 1959. Reference librarian Menlo Park (Calif.) Pub. Library, 1959-62; regional librarian Santa Clara County (Calif.) Library, 1962-68; project coordinator Fed. Young Adult Library Services Project, Mountain View, Calif., 1968-71; dir. profl. services Alameda County (Calif.) Library, 1971, asst. county librarian, 1972-77; library dir. Berkeley Pub. Library, 1977—; lectr. U. San Francisco, 1970-72, U. Calif., Berkeley, 1977-81, 91—; cons., 1975—; adv. bd. Miles Cutter Ednl., 1992—. Mem. bd. mgrs. cen. br. Berkeley YMCA, 1988-93. Bd. dirs. Community Memory, 1989-91. Recipient proclamation Mayor of Berkeley, 1985, 86; named Woman of Yr. Alameda County North chpt. Nat. Women's Polit. Caucus, 1986, Outstanding Alumna U. Calif. Sch. Library and Info. Scis., Berkeley, 1987. Mem. ALA (pres. 1986-87, exec. bd. 1980-89, council 1979-88, 90—, Grolier award 1974), Calif. Library Assn. (pres. 1981, council 1965-69, 79-82), LWV (dir. Berkeley chpt. 1980-81). Author: Getting It Together, A Young Adult Bibliography, 1970; contbr. articles to pubs. including School Library Jour., Wilson Library Bulletin. Office: Berkeley Pub Libr 2090 Kittredge St Berkeley CA 94704-1491

MINZNER, DEAN FREDERICK, aviation company executive; b. Winchester, Mass., July 20, 1945; s. Frederick Louis and Winifred (Hughes) M.; B.A., Franklin and Marshall Coll., 1967; M.B.A., Columbia U., 1972. Dist. exec. Greater N.Y. councils Boy Scouts Am., N.Y.C., 1972-76; sales exec. Coast Avia, Long Beach, Calif., 1976-78, Performance Aircraft, Inc., Hayward, Calif., 1978; owner, pres. Western Aviation Consultants, Inc., Hayward, 1978-82, Cal-Pacific Assocs., Inc., Hayward, 1979—, Cal-Pacific Enterprises, Hayward, 1982—. Mem. Assn. M.B.A. Execs., Columbia U. Grad. Sch. Bus. Alumni Assn., Aircraft Owners and Pilots Assn. Office: PO Box 6206 Hayward CA 94540

MIRANDA, GLORIA P., company executive; b. L.A., Feb. 15, 1962; d. Jose and Gloria J. (Vickes) Olvera; m. Ralph N. Miranda, Oct. 4, 1986; 1 child, Ryan A. BS, U. So. Calif., 1983. Sr. pers. specialist The Crocker Bank, L.A., 1983-85; human resources specialist Mechanics Nat. Bank, Paramount, Calif., 1985-87, Haight Dickson Brown & Bonesteel, Santa Monica, Calif., 1987; human resources adminstr. ESD Corp., San Jose, Calif., 1987-88; human resource specialist Resonex Inc., Sunnyvale, Calif., 1988-89, prodn. control supr. MIS, 1989—. Mem. Am. Prodn. and Inventory Control Soc.

MIRES, RONALD E., communications executive; b. Port Huron, Mich., July 31, 1930; s. Charles Edical and Ella Etta (Frink) M.; m. Nancy Jane O'Hara, July 12, 1952; children: Geoffrey, Ronald II, Scott. Student, Port Huron Jr. Coll., 1949-50, Mich. State U., 1950, Syracuse U., 1951. Announcer, disc jockey Sta. WTTH Radio, Port Huron, 1948-50, news dir., asst. mgr., 1955-61; accouncer WKAR/WKAR-FM, E. Lansing, Mich., 1950, WILS, Lansing, Mich., 1950; news dir. WHAM, Rochester, N.Y., 1961-63, WBZ, Boston, 1963-65, KYW, Phila., 1965-68, KPIX-TV, San Francisco, 1968-73; news dir. KGTV, San Diego, 1973-83, asst. gen. mgr., 1985-86; v.p. news McGraw-Hill Broadcasting Co., San Diego and N.Y.C., 1983-85; v.p., gen. mgr. KERO-TV, Bakersfield, Calif., 1987—; broadcast judge Hearst Found. Journalism Awards Program, San Francisco. Bd. dirs. Golden Empire Gleaners, Kerv View Found., United Way of Kern County, Meml. Hosp. Found., all in Bakersfield. With USAF, 1951-55. Recipient Disting. Service award in Journalism Sigma Delta Chi, 1982. Mem. Nat. Assn. Broadcasters, Nat. Assn. TV Program Execs., Radio/TV News Dirs. Assn., Soc. Profl. Journalists, Bakersfield Better Bus. Bur. (bd. dirs.), Rotary, Stockdale Country Club. Methodist. Office: Sta KERO-TV 321 21st St Bakersfield CA 93301-4199

MIRICH, DAVID GAGE, secondary education educator; b. Rock Springs, Wyo., June 17, 1956; s. John Jack and Kay Marie (Garvin) M. Student, U. de Filologia, Sevilla, Spain, 1981-82; BA in Psychology, Dakota Western U., 1981; teaching cert., U. Colo., 1989; postgrad., U. de Complutense, Madrid, 1991, U. Colo., 1993. Pvt. practice tchr., interpreter Sevilla, 1981-83; tchr. bilingual Horace Mann Middle Sch., Denver (Colo.) Pub. Schs., 1989-92; tchr. bilingual/ESOL coord. North High Sch., Denver (Colo.) Pub. Schs., 1992—; chmn. design adv. com. Horace Mann Middle Sch., Denver, 1991-92. Founder, chmn. Boulderiety Conv., Boulder, Colo., 1989-92; candidate Boulder Valley Sch. Bd., 1989; founder, pres. Front Range Children's Orthodontic Fund, Denver, 1991-92. With USN, 1974-75. Named Vol. of Week, Vol. Boulder (Colo.) County, 1987. Mem. Nat. Assn. Bilingual Edn. Home: PO Box 203 Jamestown CO 80455 Office: North High Sch 2960 N Speer Denver CO 80211

MIRISOLA, LISA HEINEMANN, air quality engineer; b. Glendale, Calif., Mar. 25, 1963; d. J. Herbert and Betty Jane (Howson) Heinemann; m. Daniel Carl Mirisola, June 27, 1987; 1 child, Ian Cataldo. BS in Engring., UCLA, 1986. Registered engr.-in-tng., Calif. Air quality engr. South Coast Air Quality Mgmt. Dist., Diamond Bar, Calif., 1988—. Chancellor's scholar UCLA, 1981. Mem. ASME, NSPE, Soc. Women Engrs. Office: South Coast Air Quality Mgmt Dist 21865 E Copley Dr Diamond Bar CA 91765

MIRK, JUDY ANN, elementary educator; b. Victorville, Calif., June 10, 1944; d. Richard Nesbit and Corrine (Berghoefer) M. BA in Social Sci., San Jose (Calif.) State U., 1966, cert. in teaching, 1967; MA in Edn., Calif. State U., Chico, 1980. Cert. elem. edn. tchr., Calif. Tchr. Cupertino (Calif.) Union Sch. Dist., 1967—; lead tchr. lang. arts Dilworth Sch., San Jose, 1988-90, mem. supt.'s adv. team, 1986-90, mem. student study team, 1987—; mem. Dilworth Sch. Site Coun., 1981—. Mem. Calif. Tomorrow. Mem. ASCD, Daytime Drama Guild (charter), Calif. Assn. Counseling and Devel., Mary Beth Evans Fan Club, Matthew Ashford Fan Club, Camilla Scott Fan Club, Susan Seaforth Hayes Fan Club, Stephen Nichols News Network, Phi Mu. Republican. Home: 4132 Valerie Dr Campbell CA 95008-3728 Office: Cupertino Union Sch Dist 10301 Vista Dr Cupertino CA 95014-2091

MIRRA, JOSEPH MEREDITH, physician, educator, consultant; b. N.Y.C., Nov. 22, 1937; s. William and Irene (DeNaro) M.; m. Carmen Laundry, May 13, 1937; 1 child, Theodore. BS, Columbia Coll., 1959; MD, Downstate Med. Ctr., 1963. Asst. prof. hosp. spl. surgery Cornell Med. Sch., N.Y.C., 1970-73; asst. to full prof. U. Calif. Med. Ctr., L.A., 1973-91; dir. orthopedic oncology Good Semaritan Hosp., L.A., 1991-93; pathologist-in-chief, dir. orthopaedic pathology Orthopaedic Hosp., L.A., 1993—. Author: Bone Tumors Vols. 1 and 2, 1989 (NIH award 1990), Bone Tumors, 1980. Capt. USAF, 1968-70. Mem. Internat. Skeletal Soc. Office: Orthopaedic Hosp 2400 Flower St Rm 524 Los Angeles CA 90007

MISA, KENNETH FRANKLIN, management consultant; b. Jamaica, N.Y., Sept. 24, 1939; s. Frank J. and Mary M. (Soszka) M.; BS cum laude in Psychology, Fairfield U., 1961; MS in Psychology, Purdue U., 1963; PhD in Psychology (Fellow 1963-66), St. John's U., 1966. Staff psychologist Rohrer, Hibler & Replogle, Los Angeles, 1966-67; assoc. A.T. Kearney, Inc., Los Angeles, 1968-71, sr. assoc., 1972-74, prin., 1975-78, v.p., partner, 1979-86; pres. HR Cons. Group, 1987—. Cert. mgmt. cons.; lic. psychologist, Calif. Mem. Am. Psychol. Assn., Calif. State Psychol. Assn., Los Angeles County Psychol. Assn., Soc. for Human Resources Mgmt., Human Resources Planning Soc., Acad. of Mgmt., Indsl. Rels. Rsch. Assn., Soc. for Indsl. and Organizational Psychology, World Affairs Coun. of L.A., Town Hall of So. Calif., Glendale C. of C., Jonathan Club. Republican. Roman Catholic. Home: 924C S Orange Grove Blvd Pasadena CA 91105-3514 Office: HR Cons Group 100 N Brand Blvd Ste 200 Glendale CA 91203-2614

MISBRENER, JOSEPH MICHAEL, labor union official; b. Crucible, Pa., June 17, 1924; s. Martin and Catherine (Schneider) M.; m. Dorothy Rose Lakatos, Dec. 31, 1963; children: Robert Norman, Michael Frank, Deneen Marie, Patricia Ann. Grad., North High Sch., 1942. Sec., treas. local chpt. Oil Chem. and Atomic Workers Internat. Union AFL-CIO, Lawndale, Calif., 1961-63; internat. rep. Oil Chem. and Atomic Workers Internat. Union AFL-CIO, Denver, 1963-76, asst. to pres., 1976-81, v.p., 1981-83; pres. Oil Chem. and Atomic Workers Internat. Union AFL-CIO, 5, 1983-91; U.S. rep. U.S. Petroleum Worker Internat. Labor Orgn. Conf., Geneva, 1980; v.p. indsl. union dept. AFL-CIO, Washington, 1983-91, food and allied svcs. dept., 1983-91. Civil svc. commr. City of Martinez (Calif.), 1969-70; mem. energy crisis com. City of L.A., 1972-76; mem. Long Beach (Calif.) Manpower Adv. Coun., 1972-76; mem. L.A. County Labor Fedn. Manpower Com., 1972-76. Cpl. U.S. Army, 1942-46. Mem. Export Processing Industry Coalition, Labor-Industry Coalition for Internat. Trade, Workers Inst. Safety and Health (trustee 1983), Nat. Petroleum Coun. Democrat. Roman Catholic. Office: Oil Chem & Atomic Workers Internat Union PO Box 2812 Denver CO 80201-2812 Home: 2650 S Garland St Denver CO 80227-2936

MISHKIN, MARJORIE WONG, aviation and marketing consultant; b. Los Angeles, Oct. 28, 1940; d. Thomas A. and Mayme M. (Moe) Wong; children: Barbara Joanne, Cynthia Anne; m. David Gordon Mishkin, Jan. 6, 1991. BA, Goucher Coll., 1962; MA, U. Calif. at Berkeley, 1965. Research economist Fed. Reserve Bank San Francisco, 1964-65; bus. cons., travel industry, 1968-74; marketing analyst The Flying Tiger Line Inc., Los Angeles, 1974-76, systems analyst, 1976-77, mgr. mgmt. reporting and performance analysis, 1977-78; dir. passenger pricing and fare devel. Continental Airlines, 1978-80, dir. internat. pricing, 1980-83; aviation and mktg. cons. Chen & Assocs., 1983—, dir. practice devel. Greenberg, Glusker, Fields, Claman & Machtinger, 1989-90; fin. cons. Shearson Lehman Hutton; bd. dirs. Continental Fed. Credit Union. Trustee, chmn. devel. Marlborough Sch.; trustee, deacon 1st Congl. Ch. of Los Angeles; mem. evaluation com. Am. Heart Assn. Danforth Found. assoc., 1968-79. Mem. Nat. Mgmt. Assn. (membership chmn.), World Affairs Council L.A., L.A. Libr. Assn. (v.p., treas.), Town Hall Calif., U. Calif. Alumni Assn., Marlborough Alumni Assn. Republican. Home: 640 N June St Los Angeles CA 90004-1012

MISSAL, JOSHUA MORTON, composer, conductor; b. Hartford, Conn., Apr. 12, 1915; s. Joseph I. and Rose R. (Bayer) M.; m. Pegge McComb, July 16, 1944; children: Sonya Anne, Stephen Joseph. MusB, Eastman Sch. of Music, Rochester, N.Y., 1937, MusM, 1938; MusD (hon.), London Coll. of Music, 1972. Violist Rochester Philharmonic Orchestra, 1935-40; conductor Albuquerque Philharmonic, 1940-42; chief warrant officer/band leader 608th AAF Band, Tyndall, Fla., 1942-46; head of instrumental dept. Danfelser Sch. of Music, Albuquerque, 1946-50; lectr. U. N.Mex., Albuquerque, 1946-50; head of music edn. dept. So. Miss. U., Hattiesburg, 1950-52; assoc. prof., chmn. music theory/composition dept. Wichita (Kans.) State U., 1952-70; chmn., music dept. Tunxis Community Coll., Farmington, Conn., 1972-76; assoc. conductor Wichita Symphony, 1954-70; conductor Hartford Civic Orchestra, 1972-76, Scottsdale (Ariz.) Civic Orchestra, 1979-85; co-dir. Missal Art Gallery, Farmington and Scottsdale, 1970-86. Composer pub. compositions for band, orchestra, chorus and small ensembles. Mem. ASCAP, Music Tchrs. Nat. Assn., Music Educators Nat. Conf., Am. String Tchrs. Assn. Home: 1343 E Enrose Cir Mesa AZ 85203-5709

MITCHELL, CRAIG MARTIN, graphic designer, artist; b. Sacramento, May 2, 1962; s. Clifford Martin and Selma Renee (King) M.; m. Lori Susan Gilmour, July 26, 1986. BA, U. Nev., Reno, 1986. Graphic artist The Baker Group, Reno, 1986-87; art dir. Doyle-McKenna-Bayer-Brown, Reno, 1987—. Mem. Nev. Artists Assn. Republican. Office: Doyle McKenna Bayer Brown 1175 Harvard Way Reno NV 89502

MITCHELL, DAVID CAMPBELL, corporate executive; b. Sacramento, Dec. 11, 1957; s. Alan Campbell and Lorraine May (Grant) M.; m. Noreen Peterson, May 8, 1988 (dec.); children: Kendal Raymond (dec.), Brian Jerry, Mark Reid, David Kirk, Joshua Grant (dec.). Student, U. Utah, 1973-74, Brigham Young U. Rsch. dir. Flex Inc., Williston, N.D., 1976-78; with Deseret Industries, Salt Lake City, 1978-81; head R&D Pro Biotiks Labs., Ogden, Utah, 1981—, Melaleuca, Idaho Falls, Idaho, 1987-89; pres., chmn. David C. Mitchell Med. Rsch. Inst., Salt Lake City, 1980—; rsch. cons. U. Utah Rsch. Park, Salt Lake City, 1981—; environ. cons. Hi-Valley Chem., Salt Lake City, 1988—; v.p. Mitchell Products, Orem, Utah, 1989—. Inventor, patentee in biochemistry. Vol. Freeman Inst., Salt Lake City, 1980-87; vol. supr. Granite Bakery (Feed the Poor), Salt Lake City, 1982-87; active rehab. handicapped Deseret Industries, Salt Lake City, 1978-81; pres., young adults rep. Latter-day Saints Ch., Salt Lake City, 1977-78. Scholar NSF, 1973; named one of Outstanding Young Men of Am., 1989. Fellow AAAS. Home and Office: 3131 Deer Hallow Dr Sandy UT 84092

MITCHELL, DAVID T., electronic computing equipment company executive; b. 1942. Prodn. control mgr. Honeywell Inc., Mpls., 1966-69; dir. mfg. planning Memorex Corp., Santa Clara, Calif., 1969-72; dir. materials Fairchild Camera and Instrument Corp., Mountain View, Calif., 1972-75; pres. Castell Inc., Santa Ana, Calif., 1975-77; dir. materials Bendix Corp., San Francisco, 1977-78; gen. mgr. Commodore Bus. Machines Inc., Santa Clara, 1978-80; pres., chief operating officer Seagate Tech., Scotts Valley, Calif., 1980-92, also bd. dirs.; pres., COO Conner Peripherals, San Jose, Calif., 1992—. Capt. USMC, 1963-66. Office: Conner Peripherals 3081 Zanker Rd San Jose CA 95134

MITCHELL, DIANNE, artist; b. Joliet, Ill., June 5. Student, U. Hartford Art Sch., 1982-83. patentee in field. Exhibitions include Pastel Soc. Am.

Nat. Arts Club, N.Y., 1979-82, Smithsonian Instn. Nat. Archives, Washington, 1982, Salmagundi Club, N.Y., 1984, Nat. Midyear exhbn. Butler Inst. of Am. Art, Youngstown, Ohio, 1984, 100 Nat. Finalists Exhbn., Grand Cen. Galleries, N.Y., 1985, Egg Tempera & Watercolor Exhbn., Esther Wells Collection, Laguna Beach, 1986, Am. Watercolor Soc., 1986; one woman show at Lake Tahoe Visitors Ctr., 1988-89; illustrator Handweavers Guild Am. mag., 1985, Lake Tahoe Music Festival ltd. edit. print, 1991, Conn. Transport Mag. cover, 1992, others. Recipient Lo Monaco Studio award, Pastel Soc. Am., 1982, 1st Place Watercolor and 2nd Place Best of Show in Emerald City Classic, Nepenthe Mundi Soc., 1986, George Gray award, USCG, 1990; named official artist USCG. Mem. Pastel Soc. Am. Home and Office: 4269 Bridge St Cambria CA 93428

MITCHELL, EDDIE, aerospace engineer; b. Opportunity, Wash., Jan. 16, 1947; m. JoAnna L. Mitchell. BS in Engring., U.S. Mil. Acad., 1970; MS in Bus. Adminstrn., U.S. Naval Postgrad. Sch., 1980; MS in Space Systems Mgmt., Webster U., 1990; cert. material acquisition mgr., DOD Def. Systems Mgmt. Coll., 1984. Commd. 2d lt. U.S. Army, 1970, advanced through grades to lt. col.; mem. troop duty staff U.S. Army, U.S. and Korea, 1970-79; mem. faculty, instr. Orgnl. Effectiveness U.S. Army, Monterey, Calif., 1980-82; dep. chief USASDC BM/C3 Divsn. U.S. Army, Huntsville, Ala., 1985-88; space systems applications analyst U.S. Space Command, Colorado Springs, Colo., 1989-90; ret. U.S. Army, 1990; concepts and analysis engr. Def. Missile Systems (GBI) Lockheed Missile and Space Command, Sunnyvale, Calif., 1990—. Author: Apogee, Perigee & Recovery: Chronology of Army Exploration of Space, 1989. Fellow Rand Corp., 1988. Mem. Retired Officers Assn. Republican. Home: 70 Carlsen Rd Salinas CA 93907

MITCHELL, ELIZABETH ALLEN, computer scientist, software company executive; b. Washington, Oct. 2, 1957; d. Albert Oswald and Mary Dickinson (Liggett) Allen; m. Steven Wylie Mitchell, Jan. 2, 1988. BS, U. Md., 1979, MS, 1984, PhD, 1990. Computer scientist Naval Surface Weapons Ctr., White Oak, Md., 1975-79; ind. cons. Smart Systems Techs., McLean, Va., 1983-84, Software Architecture and Engring., Rosslyn, Va., 1984-85, Applied Physics Lab., Laurel, Md., 1985-86; sr. prtnr. Coll. Pk. Software, Altadena, Calif., 1987—. Sec. Coalition for Pregnancy Assistance, Washington, 1986-87. Mem. Am. Assn. for Artificial Intelligence, Assn. for Computing Machinery, Cognitive Sci. Soc., Internat. Network of Women in Tech. (L.A. local steering com. 1992), Lisp Industry Coun. Republican.

MITCHELL, GARY DAVID, psychology educator; b. Keene, N.H., May 4, 1940; s. John David and Pauline (Parker) M.; m. Jacqueline A. Germain, Feb. 17, 1960 (div. Aug. 1969); children: Jody Lynn, Lisa Deanna, Gary David Jr.; m. Patricia Ann Jones, Feb. 23, 1986; children: Robert John, Samuel Parker-Jones. MA, U. Wis., 1965, PhD, 1966. Prof. U. Calif., Davis, 1967—. Author: Behavioral Sex Differences, 1979, Human Sex Differences, 1981; editor: comparative Primate Biology, Vol. 2A, Vol. 2B, 1987; assoc. editor Zoo Biology, 1986—. Woodrow Wilson felllowship, 1963; recipient Eldon L. Johnson Creativity award, 1962. Mem. Am. Soc. of Primatologists (founder), Consortium of Aquariums Univs. and Zoos (founder). Democrat. Office: U Calif Davis Dept Psychology A St Davis CA 95616

MITCHELL, GENEVA BROOKE, hypnotherapist; b. Ringgold, Tex., Feb. 15, 1929; d. Roy Banks and Willie Jewel (Lemons) Shaw; m. Roy David Mitchell, Nov. 30, 1947; children: Ronald, Donald, Joel, Pamela, Annette. Cert. master hypnotist Hypnosis Tng. Inst., L.A., 1980, cert. hypnotherapist, 1983; cert. in advanced investigative and forensic hypnosis Tex. A&M U., 1982; D. Clin. Hypnosis, Am. Inst. Hypnotherapy, Calif., 1989. Chiropractic asst. Alamogordo, N.Mex., 1962-79; hypnotherapist Alamogordo Hypnosis and Counseling Ctr., 1980-92; mgr. Shaw Mobile Home Park, 1986—; mng. ptnr. Shaw, Mitchell & Mallory, Albuquerque, 1986, mgr., 1987-88; hypnotherapist M&M Horses Corp., Tularosa, N.Mex., 1985-92; owner A New Image Hypnosis Ctr., Albuquerque, retired, 1992; pres. N.Mex. Chiropractic Aux., 1984-85; mem. Am. Council Hypnotist Examiners, 1980-85; hypnotist for tape series; instr. New Forever Trim Life Loss Program. Author: Take The Power, 1991. Charter pres. La Sertoma, Alamogordo, 1957; pres. Oregon sch. PTA, Alamogordo, 1958, La Luz Sch. Parents Club, N.Mex., 1962; sec. N.Mex. Jr. Rodeo Assn., 1964; co-founder Pre-Sch. La Luz, 1969; mem. N.Mex. Gov.'s Council on Youth, 1969; bd. dirs. Otero County Jr. Rodeo Assn., N.Mex., 1968; dir. self-hypnosis sch.; speaker Am. Bd. Hypnotherapy Conv., 1991. Recipient Speakers award Life Found., 1984. Mem. Am Assn. Profl. Hypnotherapists, Ladies for Life (Appreciation award 1984, 90), N.Mex. Ladies Life Fellowship (pres. 1983, bd. dirs. 1985), S.W. Hypnotherapy Examining Bd., Internat. Chiropractic Assn. Aux. (conv. chmn. 1993), Ladies for Life Chiropractic Orgn. (pres. elect 1993). Avocations: golf, painting, swimming, martial arts, writing.

MITCHELL, HARRY E., mayor, educator; b. Phoenix, July 18, 1940; s. Harry Casey and Irene Gladys (Childres) M.; m. Marianne Prevratil, May 5, 1962; children—Amy, Mark. B.A., Ariz. State U., 1962, M.P.A., 1981. Tchr. Tempe High Sch., Ariz., 1964—; councilman City of Tempe, 1970-76, vice mayor, 1976-78, mayor, 1978—. Bd. dirs. Tempe Sister City; trustee Tempe St. Lukes Hosp., Rio Salado Devel. Dist.; state rep. Sister Cities Internat., Washington; mem. Ariz. State U. Liberal Arts Alumni Adv. Bd., Adv. Council Ctr. Pub. Affairs, Ariz. Commn. Post Secondary Edn.; mem. Nat. League Cities Resolutions Com.; exec. com. League Ariz. Cities; bd. dirs. Ariz. Mcpl. Water Users. Recipient Disting. Service award Tempe Jaycees, Pub. Programs Disting. Achievement award, Ariz. State U. Mem. Ariz. State U. Alumni Bd. (chmn.), Ariz. State U. Advanced Pub. Exec. Program. Democrat. Roman Catholic. Office: Office of Mayor 31 E 5th St Tempe AZ 85281-3680*

MITCHELL, JAMES HERBERT, public relations consultant; b. Tacoma, Wash., May 11, 1946; s. Emmett George and Marvel (Carscadden) M.; m. Catherine Anne Latourette, Mar. 22, 1969; children: Ryan James, Claire Therese, Rose Catherine. BA, U. Portland, 1968; postgrad., U. Wash., 1969-70. Pub. rels. mgr./No. Calif. Div. Georgia-Pacific Corp., Fort Bragg, Calif., 1973-79; ednl. svcs. mgr. Georgia-Pacific Corp., Portland, Oreg., 1979-82; v.p. Bacon & Hunt, Inc., Portland, 1983-86; pres. Mitchell, Hagley, Malek, Inc., Portland, 1986-92; practice devel. dir. Lane Powell Spears Lubersky, Portland, 1992—; instr. pub. rels., Marylhurst Coll. Co-author: The Attorneys' Complete Guide to Practice Development: How to Build Your Practice and Career, 1991; contbr. articles to profl. jours. 1st lt. U.S. Army, 1971-73. Mem. Tualatin Hills Dive Club (bd. dirs. 1987—, pres. 1989-92), Pub. Rels. Soc. Am. (cert., bd. dirs. Columbia River chpt. 1984-89, pres. 1988), Oreg. State Bar (pub. svc. and info. com. 1987—). Republican. Roman Catholic. Home: 15525 NW Oakhills Dr Beaverton OR 97006-5508 Office: Lane Powell Spears Lubersky 520 SW Yamhill Portland OR 97204

MITCHELL, JAMES KENNETH, civil engineer, educator; b. Manchester, N.H., Apr. 19, 1930; s. Richard N. and Henrietta (Moench) M.; m. Virginia D. Williams, Nov. 24, 1951; children: Richard A., Laura K., James W., Donald M., David L. B.C.E., Rensselaer Poly. Inst., 1951; M.S., M.I.T., 1953; D.Sc., 1956. Mem. faculty U. Calif., Berkeley, 1958-93, prof. civil engring., 1968-89, chmn. dept., 1979-84, Edward G. and John R. Cahill prof. civil engring., 1989-92, Edward G. and John R. Cahill prof. civil engring. emeritus, 1993—; Berkeley citation, 1993; geotech. cons., 1960—. Author: Fundamentals of Soil Behavior, 1976, 2d edit., 1993; contbr. articles to profl. jours. Asst. scoutmaster Boy Scouts Am., 1975-82; mem. Moraga (Calif.) Environ. Rev. Com., 1978-80. Served to 1st lt. AUS, 1956-58. Recipient Exceptional Sci. Achievement medal NASA, 1973, Berkeley Citation, 1993. Fellow ASCE (hon., Huber prize 1965, Middlebrooks award 1962, 70, 73, Norman medal 1972, Terzaghi lectr. 1984, Terzaghi award 1985, pres. San Francisco sect. 1986-87); mem. Nat. Acad. Engring., Am. Soc. Engring. Edn. (We. Electric Fund award 1979), Geotech. bd. of NRC (chmn. 1990—), Transp. Rsch. Bd. (exec. com. 1983-87), Internat. Soc. Soil Mechanics and Found. Engring. (v.p. N.Am. 1989—), Earthquake Engring. Rsch. Inst., Brit. Geotech. Soc. (Rankine lectr. 1991), Sigma Xi, Tau Beta Pi, Chi Epsilon. Office: U Calif Dept Civil Engring Berkeley CA 94720

MITCHELL, JOHN HENDERSON, retired army officer, management consultant; b. Atlanta, Sept. 9, 1933; s. William Lloyd and Jessie (Henderson) M.; m. Joan Ann Cameron, Apr. 8, 1961; children—John Cameron, Christopher Lloyd, Colin MacKenzie. BA in Bus. Adminstrn., St. Bonaventure U., 1956, PhD in Sci., 1991; MA in Pub. Adminstrn., Shippensburg State U., 1973. Commd. 2d lt. U.S. Army, 1956, advanced through grades to maj. gen., 1982; comdr. 8th Battallion, 6th Arty., 1st Infantry div. U.S. Army, Vietnam, 1968; chief officer assignments, field arty. br., Officer Personnel Directorate U.S. Army, Washington; chief of staff 8th div. U.S. Army, 1973-75; asst. dept. chief of staff for personnel, Hdqrs. U.S. Army Europe and 7th Army U.S. Army, Heidelberg, Fed. Republic Germany, 1975-77; div. arty. comdr., chief of staff, 1st Inf. Div. U.S. Army, Ft. Riley, Kan., 1977-79; comdr., Field Command, Def. Nuclear Agy. U.S. Army, Kirtland AFB, N.Mex., 1979-81; dir. Human Resources Devel. Office, dept. chief staff for pers. U.S. Army, Washington; U.S. comdr. Berlin, 1984-88; ret., 1989; now spl. asst. chmn., CEO Krone, Inc., Englewood, Colo., 1989—. Bd. dirs. Nat. Safety Council, 1982-84. Decorated D.S.M. with oak leaf cluster, Legion of Merit with oak leaf cluster, D.F.C. with oak leaf cluster, Bronze Star with oak leaf cluster and V., Air medals. Mem. Assn. U.S. Army, VFW, Army Navy Club, Army War Coll. Alumni, Soc. of First Inf. Div. Democrat. Roman Catholic. Home: 375 Hidden Creek Dr Colorado Springs CO 80906-4386

MITCHELL, JOHN NOYES, JR., electrical engineer; b. Pownal, Maine, Dec. 16, 1930; s. John Noyes and Frances (Small) M.; m. Marilyn Jean Michaelis, Sept. 1, 1956; children: Brian John, Cynthia Lynn Mitchell Tumbleson, Stephanie Lee Mitchell Judson. BSEE, Milw. Sch. Engring., 1957. Registered profl. engr., Ohio. Elec. rsch. engr. Nat. Cash Register Co., Dayton, Ohio, 1957-65; sr. engr. Xerox Corp., Rochester, N.Y., 1965-70, area mgr., 1970-73; area mgr. Xerox Corp., Dallas, 1973-76; area mgr. Xerox Corp., El Segundo, Calif., 1976-79, tech. program mgr., 1979-85, competitive benchmarking mgr., 1985—. With USN, 1949-53. Mem. IEEE, Mason. Republican. Episcopalian. Home: 11300 Providencia St Cypress CA 90630-5351 Office: Xerox Corp 701 S Aviation Blvd El Segundo CA 90245-4898

MITCHELL, JOHN WILLIAM, economist; b. New Haven, Conn., July 13, 1944; s. Frank Sprague and Martha Louise (Bridge) M.; m. Susan Catherine Lewis, Aug. 27, 1966 (div. 1983); children: Heather, Kiandra; m. Carol Diane Overlund, Sept. 11, 1988. BA in Econs., Williams Coll., Williamstown, Mass., 1966; MA in Econs., U. Oreg., 1968, PhD in Econs., 1970. Prof. econs. Boise (Idaho) State U., 1970-83; chief econ. U.S. Bancorp, Portland, Oreg., 1983—; prin. M&H Econ. Cons., Boise, 1973-83. Chmn. leadership coun. N.W. Policy Ctr., Seattle, 1990-91; active Emanuel Found. Bd., Portland, 1989—. Mem. Nat. Assn. Bus. Econs. (chmn.), Oreg. Coun. Econs. Advisors, Phi Beta Kappa. Office: US Bancorp 111 SW 5th Ave Portland OR 97204-3604

MITCHELL, JOSEPH PATRICK, architect; b. Bellingham, Wash., Sept. 29, 1939; s. Joseph Henry and Jessie Delila (Smith) M.; student Western Wash. State Coll., 1957-59; BA, U. Wash., 1963, BArch, 1965; m. Marilyn Ruth Jorgenson, June 23, 1962; children: Amy Evangeline, Kirk Patrick, Scott Henry. Asso. designer, draftsman, project architect Beckwith Spangler Davis, Bellevue, Wash., 1965-70; prin. J. Patrick Mitchell, AIA & Assoc./Architects/Planners/Cons., Kirkland, Wash., 1970—. Chmn. long range planning com. Lake Retreat Camp, 1965—; bldg. chmn. Northshore Baptist Ch., 1980—, elder, 1984-90; mem. bd. extension and central com. Columbia Baptist Conf., 1977-83; Northshore Bapt. Ch. del. World Bapt. Alliance Congress, Soul Korea, 1990. Recipient Internat. Architectural Design award St. John Vianney Parish, 1989. Cert. Nat. Council Archtl. Registration Bds. Mem. AIA, Constrn. Specification Inst., Interfaith Forum Religion, Art, and Architecture, Nat. Fedn. Ind. Bus., Christian Camping Internat., Wash. Farm Forestry Assn., Rep. Senatorial Inner Circle, Woodinville C. of C., Kirkland C. of C. Republican. Office: 12620 120th Ave NE Ste 208 Kirkland WA 98034-7511

MITCHELL, KATHLEEN ANN, illustrator, graphic designer; b. Cin., July 27, 1948; d. Gerald Paige and Velma Alice (Bleier) Clary; m. Terence Nigel Mitchell, Feb. 2, 1977; children: Jessica Rose, Alexander Christien. BSc in Design, U. Cin., 1971. Graphic designer Lippincott & Margulies, N.Y.C., 1971, Allied Internat., London, 1972, Moura-George Briggs, London, 1973-75; art dir., photographer Phonograph Record Mag., L.A., 1976-77; ptnr. Walter Morgan Assocs., Santa Monica, Calif., 1977-80; illustrator Artists Internat., L.A. and N.Y.C., 1983—. Illustrator: The Snow Queen, 1982, Jane Eyre, 1983, Once Upon a Cat, 1983, Alice in Wonderland, 1986, The Wizard of Oz, 1986, A Bible Alphabet, 1986, The Secret Garden, 1986, The Christmas Cat, 1988, Timimoto, 1988, The Story of Christmas, 1989, Silent Night, 1989, Santa's Elves, 1991, The First Christmas, 1992, Cinderella, 1992, Aladdin and the Magic Lamp, 1993, Moses, 1993, David, 1993. Democrat. Home: 1040 22d St Santa Monica CA 90403-2041

MITCHELL, KEVIN DARRELL, baseball player; b. San Diego, Jan. 13, 1962. Grad. high sch., San Diego. With N.Y. Mets, 1984, 86, San Diego Padres, 1987, San Francisco Giants, 1987-91, Seattle Mariners, 1992, Cincinnati Reds, 1992—. Named Major League Player Yr. The Sporting News, 1989, recipient Silver Slugger award, 1989; named Most Valuable Player Baseball Writers' Assn. Am., 1989, All-Star team, 1989, 90. Office: Cincinnati Reds 100 Riverfront Stadium Cincinnati OH 45202-0100

MITCHELL, LAURA ELLEN, adult critical care and high-risk/critical care obstetrics nurse; b. Boston, July 5, 1959; d. Milton G. and Bruce (Bowman) Campbell; m. Edward L. Mitchell, Apr. 12, 1987; 1 child, Amy. ADN, Palomar Coll., 1988. CCRN; cert. in perinatal nursing. Staff nurse Nurse Care Plus, Oceanside, Calif., Tri-City Med. Ctr., Oceanside; clin. nurse II U. Calif. Med. Ctr., Irvine; clin. nurse U. Calif. San Diego Med. Ctr. With U.S. Army, 1977-81. Mem. AACN, Soc. Critical Care Medicine, Calif. Nurses Assn. Home: PO Box 4915 Oceanside CA 92052-4915

MITCHELL, LYNN LEE, educator; b. Scottsbluff, Nebr., Feb. 18, 1945; s. Robert A. and Maxine M. (Holm) M.; m. Gertrude W. Wahl, Aug. 27, 1966; children: Anthony M., Robert L. Degree in Metall. Engring., Colo. Sch. Mines, 1968; M in Vocat.-Tech. Edn., Colo. State U., 1972. Metall. engr. Youngstown Steel, East Chgo., Ind., 1968-71; tchr. math. Baker (Oreg.) High Sch., 1972-78; tchr. math. and sci. Seisen Internat. Sch., Tokyo, 1978-83; tchr. sci. Hood River (Oreg.) Valley High Sch., 1983—. Named NSF chem. tchr., U. Wash., Seattle, summer 1988; recipient Presdl. Citation for instrn. & profl. devel. Oreg. Edn. Assn., 1990. Mem. Oreg. Sci. Tchrs. Assn., Oreg. Coun. Tchrs. Math. (tech. writer 1968—), Hood River Edn. Assn. (pres. 1992—). Office: Hood River High Sch 1220 Indian Creek Rd Hood River OR 97031-9624

MITCHELL, MADELEINE ENID, nutritionist, educator; b. Jamaica, W.I., Dec. 14, 1941; came to U.S., 1963, naturalized, 1974; d. William Keith and Doris Christine (Levy) M. B.Sc. in Home Econs., McGill U., Montreal, Que., Can., 1963; M.S., Cornell U., 1965, Ph.D., 1968. Asst. prof. Wash. State U., Pullman, 1969-77, assoc. prof., 1978—, acting chmn. home econs. research ctr., 1981-83, asst. dir. Agri Research Ctr., Coll. Agr. and Home Econs., 1984-86; nutrition scientist U.S. Dept. Agr., Washington, 1980-81. Mem. Am. Dietetics Assn., Am. Soc. Clin. Nutrition, Am. Inst. Nutrition, Assn. Faculty Women, Sigma Xi, Phi Kappa Phi, Omicron Nu. Episcopalian. Avocations: genealogy, music. Office: Wash State U Dept Food Sci/Human Nutrition Pullman WA 99164-6376

MITCHELL, MAURICE EDWARD, business owner, engineer, inventor; b. Taylor County, Ky., Mar. 28, 1921; s. David Weaver and Eve Adeline (Hord) M.; m. Mary Lucille Roth, Sept. 12, 1952; children: Marianne, Kevin. BSME, U. Ky., 1943; MS, U. Calif., Berkeley, 1946. Registered profl. engr., Ohio; CLU. Commd. 2d lt. USAF, 1942, advanced through grades to capt.; chief test unit, equipment lab. Wright Patterson AFB USAF, Dayton, Ohio, 1942-45, spl. asst. to chief guided missiles br., 1951-52; resigned USAF, 1952; prin. Maurice Mitchell & Assocs., Walnut Creek, Calif., 1952—. Patentee scalable massively parallel microcomputer, edn. device; rsch. includes work on oppositely charged twin monopole theory of light, gravity, matter, earth and cosmos. Mem. Engrs. Club Rossmoor (v.p. 1987-88), Rotary Club Rossmoor. Roman Catholic. Home: Apt 4 601 Terra California Dr Walnut Creek CA 94595 Office: Maurice Mitchell & Assocs Ste 110 1875 Olympic Blvd Walnut Creek CA 94596

MITCHELL, MICHAEL CRESWELL, marine corps officer; b. Cleve., Dec. 4, 1950; s. Elbert Harold and Vera M.; m. Betty Bonita Stewart, June 7, 1973; children: Shawn Michael, Melanie Renee. BS in Ocean Engring., U.S. Naval Acad., 1973; MS in Ops. Analysis, Naval Postgrad. Sch., 1981; MA in Govt., Georgetown U., 1984; MA in Nat. Security, Naval War Coll., 1989. Forward observer artillery 1st BN, 10th Marines, 2d Marine Div., Camp Lejeune, N.C., 1974-76; combat cargo officer USS Dubuque, San Diego, 1977-79; logistics readiness officer Hdqrs. Marine Corps, Washington, 1981-84; battalion S-4 officer 2d Battalion, 10th Marines, 2d Marine Div., Camp Lejeune, 1984-86; battalion exec. officer 1st Battalion, 10th Marines, 2d Marine Div., Camp Lejeune, 1986-87, 4th Battalion, 12th Marines, 3d Marine Div., Camp Foster, Okinawa, Japan, 1987-88; marine corps rep. Ctr. for Naval Warfare Studies, Naval War Coll., Newport, R.I., 1989-91; regimental S-3 officer 11th Marines, 1st Marine Div., Camp Pendleton, Calif., 1991-92; commanding officer 1st Battalion, 11th Marines, 1st Marine Div., Camp Pendleton, Calif., 1992—; Contbr. numerous articles to profl. jours. Pres. PTO, John F. Kennedy Sch., 1989-91. Recipient Navy Commendation medal Sec. of Navy, 1984, Meritorious Svc. medal, 1991, W.S. Sims Navy League award, 1989. Republican. Lutheran. Home: 184 Peck Ct San Clemente CA 92672 Office: 1st Battalion 11th Marines 1st Marine Div REIN Camp Pendleton CA 92055

MITCHELL, PETER W., writer, consultant; b. Quincy, Mass., Dec. 9, 1942; s. Everett L. and Helen M. (Dooley) M. AB, Boston U., 1966. Scientist Avco Rsch La., Everett, Mass., 1966-75; owner Mystic Valley Audio, Medford, Mass. and Oceanside, Calif., 1976—. Contbr. approximately 600 articles to mags. and newspapers. Mem. Audio Engring Soc., Boston Audio Soc. (co-founder, pres.). Home and Office: 423 Los Arbolitos Blvd Oceanside CA 92054-1529

MITCHELL, RICHARD LEROY, molecular biologist; b. St. Cloud, Jan. 28, 1954; s. Richard S. and Elinor (Danforth) M.; m. Diane Flagg, Dec. 31, 1988; 1 child, Scott Richard. BA, U. Calif., Santa Cruz, 1976; PhD, U. Minn., 1984. Postdoctoral fellow Salk Inst., La Jolla, Calif., 1984-86; sr. scientist Calif. Biotech., Inc., Mountain View, 1986-90; prin. scientist, project mgr. Panlabs, Inc., Bothell, Wash., 1990—; chmn. biotech. adv. com. Shoreline C.C., Seattle, 1991—. Contbr. articles to profl. publs.; patentee production of vascular andothelial growth factor. Recipient Bacaner Rsch. award Minn. Med. Found., 1985. Mem. Am. Soc. Microbiology, Soc. for Indsl. Microbiology. Home: 15920 177th Ave NE Seattle WA 98072 Office: Panlabs Inc 11804 N Creek Pkwy S Bothell WA 98011

MITCHELL, ROBERT CAMPBELL, nuclear engineering executive; b. West Point, N.Y., Mar. 28, 1940; s. Herbert V. and Beatrice Cheeseman (Campbell) M.; m. Mardeene Burr, Aug. 19, 1963 (div. Dec. 1983); children: Wendolyn, Dawnelle; m. Patricia Johnson, Aug. 17, 1987. B of Engring., Stevens Inst. Tech., 1962; MEE, Rensselaer Poly. Inst., 1965. Registered profl. engr., Calif. Design engr. Knolls Atomic Power Lab., Schenectady, N.Y., 1962-65, sr. reactor operator, 1965-67; prin. tng. engr. Nuclear Energy Div. Gen. Electric Co., San Jose, Calif., 1967-72, project engr., 1972-75, mgr. advanced projects, 1975-77, project mgr., 1977-87, licensing mgr., 1987—. Contbr. articles to profl. jours. Nominee White House fellow Gen. Electric Co., San Jose, 1973. Mem. Elfun Soc. Republican. Episcopalian. Home: 1011 Foothill Dr San Jose CA 95123-5302 Office: Gen Electric Co 175 Curtner Ave San Jose CA 95125-1014

MITCHELL, TERENCE EDWARD, materials scientist; b. Haywards Heath, Sussex, Eng., May 18, 1937; came to U.S., 1963, naturalized, 1978; s. Thomas Frank and Dorothy Elizabeth (Perrin) M.; m. Marion Wyatt, Dec. 5, 1959; children: Robin Norman, Jeremy Neil. B.A. (Coll. Open scholar), St. Catharine's Coll., Cambridge (Eng.) U., 1958, M.A., 1962, Ph.D. in Physics, 1962. Research fellow Cavendish Lab., Cambridge, 1962-63; asst. prof. metallurgy Case Inst. Tech., 1963-66; assoc. prof. Case Western Res. U., 1966-75, prof., 1975-87, adj. prof., 1987—, chmn. dept., 1983-86, dir. high voltage electron microscopy facility, 1970-82, co-dir. materials research lab., 1982-83; vis. scientist NASA at Ames Lab., Stanford U. and Electric Power Research Inst., Palo Alto, Calif., 1975-76; scientist Ctr. Materials Sci. Los Alamos (N.Mex.) Nat. Lab., 1987—, lab fellow, 1991—; chmn. steering com. Electron Microscopy Ctr. Argonne (Ill.) Nat. Lab., 1979-83; cons. in field; mem. vis. com. metals and ceramics div. Oak Ridge Lab., 1987-91; vis. com. solid state scis. div. Ames Lab., 1987-89; sci. adv. com. Sci. and Tech. Ctr. for Superconductivity, 1989—. Materials sci. editor Microscopy Rsch. and Technique, 1986—; contbr. numerous articles, revs. on metallurgy, ceramics, radiation damage, oxidation, electron microscopy, superconductivity, mechanical properties and others to profl. jours. Pres. Cleve. Ethical Soc., 1970-72; bd. dirs. Am. Ethical Union, 1972-74; steward Los Alamos Unitarian Ch., 1992—; mem. policy com. Univ. Materials Coun., 1986-89; mem. policy com. Argonne Electron Microscopy Steering Com., chmn., 1978-82. Electric Power Research Inst. fellow, 1975-76; NSF grantee, 1966-88; Dept. Energy grantee, 1970-86, 87—; NIH grantee, 1969-72; NASA grantee, 1974-77, 81-87; USAF Office Sci. Research grantee, 1974-85; U.S. Army Research Office grantee, 1970-75, 79-83, EPRI grantee, 1986-89. Fellow Am. Soc. Metals, Am. Phys. Soc., Am. Ceramics Soc. (assoc. editor jour.), Los Alamos Nat. Lab.; mem. Metall. Soc. (editorial bd. 1981—), Electron Microscopy Soc. Am. (program chmn. 1981-82, dir. 1984-86), Mterials Rsch. Soc., Soc. Francaise de Microscopie Electronique (sci. com. 1982-90). Office: Los Alamos Nat Lab Ctr Materials Sci MS K-765 Los Alamos NM 87545

MITCHELL, WARREN I., utility company executive; b. 1937. BSAS, Pepperdine U., MBA, 1976. With So. Calif. Gas Co., 1958—, v.p., 1981-90, pres., 1990—; also bd. dirs. Office: So Calif Gas Co 555 W 5th St ML 29AO Los Angeles CA 90013-1011

MITCHELL, WAYNE LEE, social worker, educator; b. Rapid City, S.D., Mar. 25, 1937; s. Albert C. and Elizabeth Isabelle (Nagel) M.; m. Marie Galletti; BA, U. Redlands (Calif.), 1959; MSW, Ariz. State U., 1970, EdD, 1979. Profl. social worker various county, state, and fed. agys., 1962-70, Bur. Indian Affairs, Phoenix, 1970-77, USPHS, 1977-79; asst. prof. Ariz. State U., 1979-84; with USPHS, Phoenix, 1984—. Bd. dirs. Phoenix Indian Community Sch., 1973-75; bd. dirs. Phoenix Indian Ctr., 1974-79, Community Service award, 1977; mem. Phoenix Area Health Adv. Bd., 1975; mem. Community Behavioral Mental Health Bd., 1976-80; lectr. in field. Bd. dirs. Cen. Ariz. Health Systems Agy.; mem. Fgn. Rels. Com. Phoenix. Served with USCG, 1960-62. Recipient Community Service award Ariz. Temple of Islam, 1980. Mem. NASW, UN Assn., Am. Orthopsychiat. Assn., NAACP, Internat. Platform Assn., Asia Soc., U.S.-China Assn., Kappa Delta Pi, Phi Delta Kappa, Chi Sigma Chi, Nucleus Club. Congregationalist. Democrat. Contbr. articles to publs. Home: PO Box 9592 Phoenix AZ 85068-9592 Office: 3738 N 16th St Phoenix AZ 85016-5915

MITCHELL-KERNAN, CLAUDIA, university dean, vice chancellor; b. Gary, Ind., Aug. 29, 1941; d. Joseph Henry Mitchell and Claudia (Whiting) Mitchell Tatum; m. Keith T. Kernan, Dec. 14, 1968; children: Claudia Kernan, Ryan Kernan. BA, Ind. U., 1963, MA, 1965; PhD, U. Calif., Berkeley, 1969. Anthropology lectr. Harvard U., Cambridge, Mass., 1969-70; asst. prof. Harvard U., Cambridge, 1970-73; asst. prof. Anthropology/Joint Psychia UCLA, 1973-77, assoc. dir. Ctr. for Afro-Am. Studies, 1975-76, acting dir. Ctr. for Afro-Am. Studies, 1976-77, assoc. prof. Anthropology/Joint Psychia, 1977-83, dir. CAAS Ctr. for Afro-Am. Studies, 1977-89, prof. Anthropology/Joint Psychia, 1983—, dean/vice chancellor Grad. Div., 1989—; mem. several univ. coms. including U. Calif. Coun. Grad. Deans, U. Calif. Com. for All Univ. Conf. on Affirmative Action, UCLA Chancellor's Cabinet, UCLA Acad. Senate Grad. Coun., UCLA Fin. Aids Policy Commn. Co-editor: (with G. Berry) Television and the Socialization of the Ethnic Minority Child, 1982, (with S.M. Ervin-Tripp) Children's Discourse, 1977; author (monograph) Language Behavior in a Black Urban Community, 1971; contbr. numerous articles to profl. jours. Active in wide range of civic orgns. including bd. dirs. Child Care Referral Svc. of L.A., 1980—, Black Agenda of L.A., 1983-87, Mus. African Am. Art, 1980-84; cons. Brotherhood Crusade of L.A., 1977, Compton Action Ctr. for Youth Devel., 1977-78, Richmond Unified Sch. Dist., 1973, Nat. Urban League Alternative Schs. Project, 1973. Recipient Ford Found. rsch. grant, 1988-91, NIMH rsch. grant, 1986-87, Nat. Inst. Child Health and Devel. rsch. grant, 1985-89. Mem. Am. Anthropological Assn., Caribbean Studies Assn. (exec. com.), Assn. Black Anthropologists, Coun. Grad. Schs., Assn. Grad. Schs. Office: UCLA Grad Div 405 Hilgard Ave Los Angeles CA 90024-1419

MITHUN, ROBERT JAMES, physician; b. Seattle, June 4, 1949; s. Omer Lloyd Mithun and Ruth Eleanor (Trueblood) Klopfer; m. Anne Kimi Fukutome, Apr. 7, 1984; children: Paul, Julie, Lisa. BA, Stanford U., 1971; MD, U. Colo., 1975. Diplomate Am. Bd. Internal Medicine. Owner Mithun Electronics, Denver and San Francisco, 1971-84; intern in medicine Children's Hosp., San Francisco, 1975-76, resident in medicine, 1976-78; rsch. fellow Vets. Hosp., Martinez, Calif., 1978-79; internist French Health Plan, San Francisco, 1979-88, med. dir., 1983-88; internist Permanente Med. Group, San Francisco, 1988—, asst. chief of medicine, 1991—; cons. Biofeedback Inst. of San Francisco, 1976-83, Children's Hosp. Health Plan, San Francisco, 1978-79, Richmond (Calif.) Hosp., 1978-79. Mem. ACP, San Francisco Med. Co., Calif. Med. Assn. Office: Permanente Med Group 2200 Ofarrell St San Francisco CA 94115-3394

MITIO, JOHN, III, state agency administrator; b. Michigan City, Ind., Jan. 15, 1950; s. John Mitio Jr. and Bonnie Gloria (Pearce) Morse; Eugene A. Morse (stepfather); m. Judy Sena, Nov. 25, 1971 (div. 1985); m. Gail Stefl, Sept. 5, 1987; 1 child, Kevin Michael. AA in Liberal Arts, N.Mex. State U., Alamogordo, 1976; BA in Anthropology, N.Mex. State U., Las Cruces, 1979. Engr. aide U.S. Civil Service, Alamogordo, 1974-75, Dynalectron Corp., Alamogordo, 1976; law enforcement campus police N.Mex. State U., Las Cruces, 1977-79; eligibility worker human svcs. dept. State of N. Mex., Albuquerque, 1984-86; medicaid planner human svcs. dept. State of N. Mex., Santa Fe, 1986—. Sgt. USAF, 1969-73, 1st lt., 79-83. Decorated Nat. Def. Svc. medal, Armed Forces Expeditionary medal, Air Force Overseas Svc. medal, Air Force Good Conduct medal. Mem. Planetary Soc., World Future Soc., Nat. Space Soc. Republican. Roman Catholic. Home: 2054 Placita De Quedo Santa Fe NM 87505-5496 Office: Human Svcs Dept Kennedy Bldg 331 Sandoval St Santa Fe NM 87501-2630

MITLER, MERRILL MORRIS, psychologist, researcher; b. Racine, Wis., Jan. 6, 1945; s. Benjamin and Dorothy Ann (Farrell) M.; m. Elizabeth A., Aug. 27, 1976; children: Marc Harold, Morris Henry, Maximillian Edward. BA in Psychology, U. Wis., 1967; MA in Psychology, Mich. State U., 1968, PhD in Psychology, 1970; postdoctoral cert., Stanford U. Med. Sch., 1973. Lic. psychologist, N.Y., Calif. Instr. psychology Stanford (Calif.) U., 1970-78, research assoc. med. sch., 1973-78; research prof. SUNY, Stony Brook, 1978-83; prof. Scripps Clinic and Research Found., La Jolla, Calif., 1983—, U. Calif., San Diego, 1985—; pres. Wakefulness-Sleep Edn. and Rsch. Found., Del Mar, Calif., 1977—, U.S. Congl. Testimony Sleep Disorders and Health Policy, 1985-88; mem. nat. task force NIH Strategic Plan, 1992. Author: 101 Questions About Sleep and Dreams, 1986, 88, 90, 93, (with others) Sleep: A Scientific Perspective, 1988; contbr. articles to profl. jours. NIH research grantee, 1970—. Mem. APA, AAAS, Internat. Soc. Chronobiology, Am. Narcolepsy Assn. (bd. dirs. 1985-93), Sleep Info. Ctr. (adv. bd. 1983—). Jewish. Office: Scripps Clinic & Rsch Found 10666 N Torrey Pines Rd La Jolla CA 92037-1027

MITO, ROBERT KEN, physician; b. Seattle, Dec. 23, 1949; m. Annika C. Mito. AB, Princeton (N.J.) U., 1972; MD, U. Wash., 1976. Diplomate Am. Bd. Internal Medicine and Cardiovascular Diseases. Resident in medicine Baylor Coll. of Medicine, Houston, 1976-79, cardiology fellow, 1979-81; pvt. practice in cardiology Seattle, 1981-88, Edmonds, Wash., 1988—. Fellow Am. Coll. Cardiology; mem. Am. Heart Assn., King County Med. Soc., Sigma Xi. Office: Kruger Clinic #100 21600 Hwy 99 Edmonds WA 98026

MITRA, SANJIT KUMAR, electrical and computer engineering educator; b. Calcutta, West Bengal, India, Nov. 26, 1935; came to U.S., 1958; MS in Tech., U. Calcutta, 1956; MS, U. Calif., Berkeley, 1960, PhD, 1962; D of Tech. (hon.), Tampere (Finland) U., 1987. Asst. engr. Indian Statis. Inst., Calcutta, 1956-58; from teaching asst. to assoc. Univ. Calif., Berkeley, 1958-62; asst. prof. Cornell U., Ithaca, N.Y., 1962-65; mem. tech. staff Bell Telephone Labs., Holmdel, N.J., 1965-67; prof. U. Calif., Davis, 1967-77; prof. elec. and computer engring. U. Calif., Santa Barbara, 1977—, chmn. dept. elec. and computer engring., 1979-82; cons. Lawrence Livermore (Calif.) Nat. Lab., 1974—; cons. editor Van Nostrand Reinhold Co., N.Y.C., 1977-88; mem. adv. bd. Coll. Engring. Rice U., Houston, 1986-89. Author: Analysis and Synthesis of Linear Active Networks, 1969, Digital and Analog Integrated Circuits, 1980; co-editor: Modern Filter Theory and Design, 1973, Two-Dimensional Digital Signal Processing, 1978, Miniaturized and Integrated Filters, 1989, Handbook for Digital Signal Processing, 1993. Named Disting. Fulbright Prof., Coun. for Internat. Exch. of Scholars, 1984, 86, 88, Disting. Sr. Scientist, Humboldt Found., 1989. Fellow AAAS, IEEE (Edn. award Circuits and Systems Soc. 1988), Internat. Soc. Optical Engring.; mem. Am. Soc. for Engring. Edn. (F. E. Terman award 1973, AT&T Found. award 1985), European Assn. for Signal Processing. Office: Univ Calif Dept Elec & Computer Engring Santa Barbara CA 93106

MITROS, LOUIS JEFFREY, taxidermist, farrier; b. Phila., Sept. 27, 1958; s. Louis Francis and Nancy Louise (Gill) M.; m. Eleanore Sarah Mathison, May 27, 1989; m. July 16, 1984 (div.). BS in Earth Sci. and Geology, Pa. State U., 1980. Geologist Exlog, U.S.A., Houston, 1980-81; cons. geologist Aldirita Logging, Denver, 1981-83; environ. geologist Western Water Cons., Laramie, Wyo., 1983, Trihydro Corp., Laramie, 1985-88; pvt. cons. geologist, Laramie, 1983-85, farrier, 1988—, taxidermist, 1990—. Republican. Roman Catholic. Office: 1979 Snowy Range Rd Laramie WY 82070

MITSUHASHI, MASATO, immunology rsearcher, pediatrician, educator; b. Tokyo, Mar. 20, 1954; came to U.S., 1985; m. Takako Matsuguma, May 25, 1980; children: Katsuya, Shuji. MD, Gunma U., Maebashi, Japan, 1978, PhD, 1992. Diplomate Japanese Bd. Pediatrics. Intern dept. pediatrics Gunma U., 1978-79, adj. asst. prof. dept. pharmacology Sch. Medicine, 1992—; sr. resident Saku Cen. Hosp., Usuda, Japan, 1979-80; mem. med. staff dept. pediatrics Gunma U. Hosp., 1980-84; chief dept. Gunma Cancer Hosp., Ohta, 1984-85; postdoctoral fellow U. Calif., San Francisco, 1985-88; assoc. Howar Hughes Med. Inst., San Francisco, 1987-90; sr. scientist Hitachi Chem. Rsch. Ctr., Irvine, Calif., 1990-92, asst. dir., 1992—; adj. clin. mem. Scripps Clinic and Rsch. Found., La Jolla, Calif., 1992—; adj. assoc. prof. dept. pathology U. Calif., Irvine, 1992—. Author: Psychoneuroimmunology, 1990; also articles; patentee immunoglobulin binding substance. Camp counselor Maebashi YMCA, 1972-77; camp dir. Gunma Assn. for Asthmatic Children, 1984-85. Grantee for statis. analysis Japanese Dept. Edn., 1985. Mem. AAAS, Am. Assn. Immunologists, Internat. Soc. for Neuroimmunomodulaton, Japanese Soc. Allergology. Home: 8 Brookmont Irvine CA 92714 Office: Hitachi Chem Rsch Ctr 1003 Health Sciences Rd W Irvine CA 92715

MITTAL, YASHASWINI D., statistician, educator; b. Pune, India, Oct. 1, 1941; came to U.S. 1964; s. Vishwanath Mahadeo and Malati Vishnanath (Pazajape) Deval. BSc, U. Poona, India, 1961; MSc, U. Poona, 1963; MS, U. Ill., 1966; PhD, UCLA, 1972. Asst. prof. Northwestern U., Chgo., 1972-73; vis. mem. Inst. for Advanced Studies, Princeton, N.J., 1973-74; asst. prof. Stanford (Calif.) U., 1974-80; assoc. prof. Va. Tech., Blacksburg, 1981-90; program dir. NSF, Washington, 1986-88; prof. and head dept. statistics U. Ariz., Tucson, 1990—. Fellow Inst. Math. Statistics; mem. Internat. Statis. Inst. Office: Univ of Ariz Dept Statistics Econ Bldg Rm 200 Tucson AZ 85721

MITTELMAN, PHILLIP SIDNEY, business executive; b. N.Y.C., Sept. 28, 1925; s. Joseph F. and Rose (Brooks) M.; m. Myra I. Schoenfeld, Apr. 10, 1948; children: Vicki, David. BS in Physics, Rensselaer Poly. Inst., 1945; PhD in Physics, Rensselaer Poly. Inst., 1953; MA in Physics, Harvard U., 1947. Mgr. physics and math United Nuclear Corp., Elmsford, N.Y., 1953-66; pres., chmn. Math. Application Group, Elmsford, 1966-86; dir. lab. for tech. in art UCLA, 1986-89; pres., chmn. CD-I Systems, Inc., L.A., 1989—. Fellow AAAS; mem. Nat. Computer Graphics Assn. (past pres.). Office: 257 S Barrington Ave Los Angeles CA 90049-3303

MITZE, CLARK HAROLD, retired arts administrator; b. Cedar Falls, Iowa, Mar. 28, 1918; s. George H. and Alace (Brown) M.; m. Verla Marie Diekman, May 20, 1941; children: Thomas, Michael Terry, Robert. BA, No. Iowa U., 1939; MA, U. Iowa, 1947. Asst. prof. Washngton U., St. Louis, 1951-67; dir. Mo. Arts Coun., St. Louis, 1965-68, Calif. Arts Coun., Sacramento, 1976-78; dir. state community Nat. Endowment for Arts, Washington, 1968-76; dir. Ill. Arts Coun., Chgo., 1978-81; ret., 1981; vis. prof. arts adminstrn. San Francisco State U., 1981-84; music reviewer Sacramento Pub. Radio, 1984—. Lt. col. USAAF, 1941-46. Recipient Disting. Alumni award No. Iowa U., 1979. Home: 626 Rivercrest Dr Sacramento CA 98531

MIX, ESTHER, magistrate; b. Warner, Okla., Dec. 21, 1920; d. Burk and Bertie (Hawkins) Markham; children—Sarah, Richard. Student U. Okla., 1937-39; McGeorge Coll. Law, 1948. Bar: Calif. 1951, U.S. Dist. Ct. (ea. dist.) Calif. 1956, U.S. Ct. Appeals (9th cir.) 1956. Practice law, 1951-71; magistrate judge U.S. Dist. (ea. dist.) Calif., Sacramento, 1971—. Mem. Women Lawyers Sacramento, Nat. Council Fed. Magistrates, Sacramento County Bar Assn., Calif. State Bar Assn., Fed. Bar Assn. Office: 1034 US Courthouse 650 Capitol Mall Sacramento CA 95814-4708

MIYAGISHIMA, KENNETH DANIEL, small business owner; b. Biloxi, Miss., May 15, 1963; s. Kazuji and Catalina (Porras-Gallegos) M.; m. Kathryn Sanchez Pacheco, Aug. 8, 1992. AA, N.Mex. State U., 1984, BBA in Real Estate and Fin., 1985. Store supr. TG&Y Stores Co., Las Cruces, N.Mex., 1981-85; agy. owner/agt. Miyagishima & Co., Ins., Las Cruces, N.Mex., 1985—; pres. Miyagishima Inc., Real Estate, Las Cruces, N.Mex., 1992—; instr. Dona Ana Br. Community Coll., Las Cruces, 1989—. County commr. Dona Ana County, N.Mex., 1992—; bd. dirs. High Range Neighborhood Assn., 1989—. Mem. S.W. Assn. Life Underwriters. Democrat. Roman Catholic. Office: Miyagishima & Co Ins 225 E Idaho Ste 3 Las Cruces NM 88001

MIYAMOTO, WAYNE AKIRA, painter, printmaker, educator; b. Honolulu, Sept. 6, 1947; s. James Masato and Thelma Kimiko (Ito) M.; children: Tyler Iolani, Akira Oakaokalani, Yasuo Iomaka. Studied Rensselaer Poly. Inst., Troy, N.Y., 1965-68; BA, BFA, U. Hawaii, 1970, MFA, 1974. Asst. prof. dept. art Fla. Tech. U. (U. Central Fla.), Orlando, 1976-78; asst. prof. art Calif. State U., Sacramento, 1980-81; prof. art dept. U. Hawaii, Hilo, 1981—, chair, 1983-85, 86-92, dir. printmaking seminar, 1982, 84; mem. nat. painting jury Scholastic Mag., Inc., N.Y.C., 1977; guest artist Art Inst. Chgo., 1978; mem. selection com. State Found. for Culture and Arts, Hilo, 1981—; mem. adv. panel, Honolulu; cons. East Hawaii Cultural Ctr., Hilo, 1981-82; artist-in-residence Fellowship 11th Asilah Internat. Festival, Morocco, 1988. One man shows Wailoa Ctr., Hilo, 1982, C.N. Gorman Mus., Davis, Calif., 1983; group shows include Pacific State Regional, 1984 (purchase award), 30th Ann. Ball State Small Sculpture and Drawing Exhibit, Muncie, Ind., 1984, 9th Kans. Nat., 1984 (purchase award), 7th Hawaii Nat., 1984, Boston Printmakers 34th Nat., 1985, 17th Dulin Nat., Knoxville, Tenn., 1985, 19th Dixie Ann., Montgomery, Ala., 1985, Pacific States Regional Juror's award 1985, Art-USA, Grand Junction, Colo., 1986, 1st Internat Bienniel, Somers, N.Y., 1986, Pacific Coastline Drawing Competition, Salem, Oreg., 1986, 58th Ann. Honolulu Printmakers Exhibit, 1986, 14th Boston Printmakers Members Show, 1986., 37th Artists fo Hawaii, 1987, 19th Dulin Nat., Knoxville, 1987, 15th Boston Printmakers, 1987, 13th Kans. Nat., Hays, 1988, 21st Bradley Nat., Peoria, Ill., 1988, 17th Boston Printermakers, Duxbury, Mass., 1989, N.W. Print Coun. Print Biennial, Portland, Oreg., 1989, Art Inst. of the Permian Basin, Odessa, Tex, 1989, Pa. Sch. of Art and Design, Lancaster, 1989, 22nd Bradley Nat., 1989, Print Club of Phila., Princeton, N.J., 1989, 64th Internat. Competition, Phila., 1989, 2nd Internat. Biennial, Somers, N.Y., 1989, 16th Boston Printmakers, 1989, Baylor U., Tex., 1990, Hui No'eau Visual Arts Ctr. Maui, Hawaii, 1990, 3rd Internat., Somer, 1990, 18th Ann. Boston Printmakers, 1990, Wash. State U., Spokane, 1990, Morehead State U., Ky., 1990, N.D. Ann., Grand Forks, 1990, Thirty-Fourth Hunterdon Nat., Clinton, N.J., 1990, 62nd Ann. Honolulu Printmakers, Hawaii, 1990, Silvermine Internat., New Canaan, Conn., 1990, Nat. Mus. of Fine Arts, Veitnam, 1991, 2nd Bharat Bhavan Internat. Biennial of Prints, Bhopal, India, 1991, 23rd Bradley Nat., 1991, U. of Cen. Arks., 1991, Nat. Mus., Hanoi, 1991, 34th N.D. Ann., Grand Forks, 1992, Silvermine Internat. Exhibit, New Canaan, Conn., 1992, N.Am. Print Exhibit, Boston, 1993, 7th Parkside Nat., Kenosha, Wis., 1993. Recipient Regional award Nat. Soc. Arts and Letters, Purchase award State Found. for Culture and the Arts, 1971, 74, 75, 87, 91, 92, Ft. Hays State U., 1984, Knoxville Mus. of Art, 1987, Juror's award Eugene Feldman Meml., 1988, award Hawaiian Graphics Corp., 1990; travel grantee U. Hawaii, 1988, 90, 92; guest artist fellow The Printmaking Workshop, 1990. Mem. N.W. Print Coun., Coll. Art Assn. Am., Soc. Am. Graphic Artists, Boston Printmakers, Print Club Phila., So. Graphics Coun. Office: U Hawaii At Hilo Art Dept Hilo HI 96720

MIYATA, KEIJIRO, culinary arts educator; b. Tokyo, Mar. 8, 1951; came to U.S., 1967; s. Yataro Miyata and Hekkiken (Liu) Choy; m. Connie Joyce Nelson, Mar. 8, 1976; children: Michelle, Kelly, Adam. Assoc. in Occupational Study, Culinary Inst. Am., Hyde Park, N.Y., 1972, cert. of nutrition, 1991; cert., Seattle Wine Sch., 1991. Cert. exec. chef; cert. culinary educator. Garde mgr. Mid-Pacific Country Club, Kailua, Hawaii, 1972; working chef Waikiki Yacht Club, Honolulu, 1972-74, Sagano Japanese Restaurant, New Rochelle, N.Y., 1974-76; asst. pastry chef Rye Town (N.Y.) Hilton Hotel, 1976-77; working chef The Explorer, Everett, Wash., 1977-79; exec. chef Holiday Inn, Everett, 1979-81, Mill Creek (Wash.) Country Club, 1981; culinary art instr. Everett Community Coll., 1981-85, North Seattle (Wash.) Community Coll., 1985-90, Seattle Cen. Community Coll., 1990—; cons. Chalon Corp., Redmond, Wash., Chiang-Mai Restaurant, Mukilteo, Wash., 1988, Holiday Inn Crown Plaza, Seattle. Recipient Gold awards Am. Culinary Fedn., Oreg. State Chef's Assn., Portland, 1983, Gold and Bronze medals World Culinary Olympic, Frankfurt, Germany, 1984, 88, Grand Champion award U.S. Nat. Ice Carving Contest, N.Y.C., 1986, 2d place award All Japan Ice Carving Assn., Asahikawa, 1988, Ednl. Excellence award Oreg. and Wash. Community Coll. Couns. Wash. Fedn. of Tchrs. & Am. Fedn. of Tchrs., AFL-CIO, 1988, 89; ACF Seafood Challenge State finalist, Charlotte, N.C., 1989, New Orleans, 1990; 1st place Pacific Rim Invitational World Ice Sculpting Classic, 1989; 1st place Seymour Ice Sculpting Competition, 1991; 1st place 3d Ann. Internat. Ice Sculpting Competition, Lake Louise, Alta., Can., 1993, Award of Excellence Wash. Fedn. Tchrs./Am. Fedn. Tchrs./AFL-CIO, 1993. Mem. Wash. State Chefs Assn. (bd. dirs. 1982, 83, 86, 87, 88, cert. chmn. 1986-92, Chef of Yr. 1986), Am. Acad. Chefs. Office: Seattle Cen Community Coll 1701 Broadway Seattle WA 98122-2400

MIZE, ROBERT HERBERT, JR., bishop; b. Emporia, Kans., Feb. 4, 1907; s. Robert Herbert and Margaret Talman (Moore) M. B.A., U. Kans., 1928 grad. Gen. Theol. Sem., N.Y.C., 1932, S.T.D., 1960. Vicar ch. missions Episcopal Ch., Hays Kans., 1932-41, Wakeeney, Kans., 1941-45; founder, dir. St. Francis Acad., Ellsworth and Salina, Kans., 1945-60; bishop of Damaraland Anglican Ch., Windhoek, Southwest Africa, 1960-68, asst. bishop, Gaberone, Botswana, 1968-70, 73-76; vicar Trinity Episcopal Ch., Marshall, Mo, 1970-73; assisting bishop Episcopal Ch. Diocese of San Joaquin, Fresno, Calif., 1978-88; dir. Gen. Theol. Seminary's Assoc. Mission, Hays, 1933-41; vicar St. Raphael's Episcopal Ch., Oakhurst, Calif., 1977-81. Mem. Phi Beta Kappa, Sigma Delta Chi, Phi Delta Theta. Office: Episcopal Diocese of San Joaquin 4159 E Dakota Ave Fresno CA 93726-5297

MIZER, RICHARD ANTHONY, technology consultant; b. San Francisco, Jan. 7, 1952; s. Conrad Xavier and Sally Jo (Hagan) M. BA in Bioengring. and Econs., U. Calif., San Diego, 1977. Founding ptnr. Microdoctors, Palo Alto, Calif., 1974—; mgr., ptnr. K-Family Corp. dba Harlow's Night Club, Fremont, Calif., 1977-79, Restaurants Unique Inc., Mountain View, Calif., 1980-83; mgr. engring. Pacific Bell, San Ramon, Calif., 1983-89; tech. cons. advanced techs. Pacific Bell, 1989—; product engr. Advanced Broadcast Video, Advanced Digital Network, Switched Multimegabit Data Svc. Exec. producer Cinema of the Future, 1992. Mem. security staff Republican Task Force, San Francisco, 1984, tech. staff U.S. Olympic Com., Los Angeles, 1984. Mem. IEEE, Soc. Motion Picture and TV Engrs. Roman Catholic. Office: Pacific Bell 2600 Camino Ramon 1S900 San Ramon CA 94583

MIZOKAWA, DONALD TSUNEO, education educator; b. Honolulu, Nov. 12, 1943; s. Motoyasu and Tsuku (Nozawa) M.; m. Lynn Hisako Takemoto, Aug. 1, 1970; children: Stacey Tamie, Jana Kimie. BEd, U. Hawaii, 1965, 5-yr. diploma, 1966, MEd, 1969; PhD, Ind. U., 1974. English tchr. Konawaena High & Intermediate Sch., Kealakekua, Hawaii, 1966, Kauai High Sch., Lihue, Hawaii, 1966-68; lectr. U. Hawaii, Honolulu, 1968-70; teaching assoc. Ind. U., Bloomington, 1970-73; prof. U. Wash., Seattle, 1973—; cons. Seattle Sch. Dist., 1986-89, Northshore Sch. Dist., Bothell, Wash., 1990, Microsoft, Redmond, Wash., 1993; presenter in field. Contbr. articles to profl. jours. Trustee Crisis Clinic, Seattle, 1978-80, chair nominating com., 1979-80. Rsch. grantee Inst. for Ethnic Studies in the U.S., 1983. Mem. Am. Edn. Rsch. Assn. (Spl. Interest Group/Rsch. on Edn. of Asian and Pacific Ams.; pres. 1991—, program chair 1989-91, editor newsletter 1989—). Office: U Wash Coll Edn Seattle WA 98195

MIZUNO, NOBUKO SHIMOTORI, biochemist; b. Oakland, Calif., Apr. 20, 1916; d. Shinichiro and Kii (Niyomura) S.; m. Walter M. Mizuno, Mar. 20, 1942 (dec. 1946). AB, U. Calif.-Berkeley, 1937, MA, 1939; PhD, U. Minn., 1956. Rsch. asst. U. Calif., Berkeley, 1939-41; instr. Macalester Coll., St. Paul, 1943-51; rsch. assoc. U. Minn., St. Paul, 1956-62; rsch. biochemist VA Med. Ctr., Mpls., 1962-79; ret. Contbr. articles to profl. jurs. NSF fellow, 1956. Mem. AAAS, Am. Inst. Nutrition, Am. Soc. Biochemistry and Molecular Biology, Iota Sigma Pi (historian 1970-72). Home: 3628 Loma Way San Diego CA 92106-2034

MLAKAR, ROY A., professional hockey team executive; b. 1953; m. Nancy; children: Tracy, Jill. Student, Cuyahoga Western Coll., 1968-69, Kent State U., 1970-72; grad., U. Akron, 1972. With sales, promotions, pub. rels. Cleve. Barons, 1969-73; merchandising and promotions dir. Cleve. Cavaliers and Cleve. Indians, 1969-73; exec. dir. pub. rels. Providence Reds, 1973-78; from pub. rels. dir. to dir. ops., pres. New Haven Nighthawks, 1978-88; gen. mgr. New Haven Night Hawks, 1983-88; exec. v.p. L.A. Kings., 1988-92, pres., 1992—. Recipient Hendy award as League Exec. of Yr. AHL's Bd. Govs., 1983; named AHL Publicist of Yr., The Hockey News, 1978. Office: Los Angeles Kings PO Box 17013 3900 W Manchester Blvd Inglewood CA 90306

MOBERLY, LINDEN EMERY, educational administrator; b. Laramie, Wyo., Jan. 4, 1923; s. Linden E. and Ruth (Gathercole) M. BS, Coll. Emporia, 1952; MS, Kans. State Tchrs. Coll., 1954; m. Viola F. Mosher, Apr. 29, 1949. Tchr. sci., Florence, Kans., 1952-54, Concordia, Kans., 1954-56, Grand Junction, Colo., 1957-60; asst. prin. Orchard Mesa Jr. High Sch., Grand Junction, 1960-66, prin., 1967-84; field cons. Nat. Assn. Secondary Sch. Prins., 1985—. Sgt. USMC, 1941-46. Recipient Outstanding Secondary Prin. award Colo. Assn. Sch. Execs., 1978. Mem. NEA, VFW, Nat. Assn. Secondary Prins. (bd. dir. 1979-83), Colo. Edn. Assn. (bd.dir. 1968-71), Colo. North Central Assn. Colls. and Secondary Schs., Colo. Assn. Secondary Sch. Prins. (bd. dir. 1974-77), Lions, Sons of the Revolution, Marine Corps League (life), Masons (award of Excellence 1990). Home: 2256 Kingston Rd Grand Junction CO 81503

MOBLEY, CHARLES MURRAY, archaeologist; b. Paulding, Ohio, Feb. 18, 1954; s. Charles Richard and Theresa (Bradley) M.; divorced; 1 child, Charles Ottar Carlson Mobley. BA in Anthropology, Case Western Res. U., 1974; MA in Conservation Archaeology, So. Meth. U., 1978, PhD in Anthropology, 1981. Cert. Soc. Profl. Archeologists. Prof. anthropology Sheldon Jackson Coll., Sitka, Alaska, 1986-88; dir. Exxon Cultural Resource Program, Anchorage, 1989-90; pres. Charles M. Mobley & Assocs., Anchorage, 1982—; adj. prof. U. Alaska, Anchorage, 1982, 83, 85, 91; guest lectr. Crystal Cruises, L.A., 1990. Author: The Campus Site: A Prehistoric Camp, 1991; contbr. articles to profl. jours. Grantee Inst. for Study of Earth and Man, 1978, Alaska Hist. Commn., 1983, 84, Sheldon Jackson Coll., 1986, 87; Geist Fund grantee U. Alaska Mus., 1982. Mem. Soc. for Am. Archaeology, Alaska Anthrop. Assn., Soc. Profl. Archaeologists. Office: Charles M Mobley & Assocs 200 W 34th # 534 Anchorage AK 99503

MOBLEY, JONNIEPAT, director, theatre; b. Detroit, Aug. 1, 1932; d. John Patrick and Charlotte Pauline (Tillman) Moore; m. J. Dwight Mobley; 1 child, Eve Stanlyn Mobley. BA, Mount St. Mary's Coll., 1962; MA, Calif. State U., L.A., 1964; PhD, U. So. Calif., L.A., 1974. Cert. English, speech and theatre tchr., Calif. Instr. Cuesta Coll., San Luis Obispo, Calif., 1985—; lectr. Mount St. Mary's Coll., L.A., 1962-67; prof. West L.A. Coll., 1969-78; dir. Parish Players, 1981-82, Mission Players, 1983. Author: Dictionary of Theatre and Drama, 1992, Play Production Today!, 1993; writer/dir.: (radio plays) Nursery Crimes, 1981, Snug Harbor, 1981 (theatre) Murder At Maywood, 1983, The Orange Grove, 1990; dir. workshop prodn. Two Stars Evenly Placed, for Edward Albee Workshop Summer Arts Festival, 1987. Mem. Right-to-Life (Peta), 1985—. Named to Outstanding Young Women of Am., 1965. Mem. So. Calif. Ednl. Theatre, Alpha Mu Gamma, Lambda Iota Tau. Roman Catholic. Office: Cuesta Coll PO Box 8106 San Luis Obispo CA 93403-8106

MOBLEY, KAREN RUTH, art gallery director; b. Cheyenne, Wyo., Aug. 26, 1961; d. David G. and Marlene G. (Franz) M. BFA, U. Wyo., 1983; MFA, U. Oka., 1987. Sales assoc. Morgan Gallery, Kansas City, Mo., 1984-85; grad. asst. U. Okla. Mus. Art, Norman, 1985-87; dir. Univ. Art Gallery N.Mex. State U., Las Cruces, 1988—; guest artist Okla. City Community Coll., 1986. Paintings exhibited in numerous exhbns. including Phoenix Triennial, 1990, New Am. Talent, Lagua Gloria Art Mus., Austin, Tex., 1992, Adair Margo Gallery, El Paso, 1992. Named Outstanding Young Women Am. Mem. Am. Assn. Mus., Mountain Plains Mus. Assn., N.Mex. Mus Assn., Coll. Art Assn., Phi Beta Kappa, Phi Kappa Phi. Home: PO Box 3817 Las Cruces NM 88003-3817 Office: NMex State U U Art Gallery PO Box 30001 Las Cruces NM 88003-8001

MOBLEY, LUCILLE JOHANNA, real estate broker; b. Albuquerque, Aug. 16, 1944; d. Vernon Theodore Mobley and Esther May Beckstrom; divorced; children: Leah Rae, Sarah Renee, Debrah Rebecca Bonn. AA, Phoenix Coll., 1962. Bldg. mgr. Murdock Mgmt. Co., Phoenix, 1969-81; real estate salesperson Century 21/John Noble Real Estate, Scottsdale, Ariz., 1988-90, Realty Execs., Phoenix, 1990-92, Terra Comml. Property Svcs., Phoenix, 1992—. Vol. St. Luke's Hosp., Phoenix, 1986-88, also various polit. campaigns; fund raiser Tavan Sch., Phoenix, 1987, 88, Easter Seals, Phoenix, 1990. Mem. Phoenix Bd. Realtors (edn. chair 1992, mktg. meeting chair 1991-92), Cen. Ariz. CCIM (sec., bd. dirs. 1992), Optimists, DAR. Republican. Home: 4902 E Osborn Phoenix AZ 85018 Office: Terra Comml Property Svc 2633 E Indian School Rd Phoenix AZ 85016

MOCKARY, PETER ERNEST, clinical laboratory scientist, researcher; b. Zghorta, Lebanon, Jan. 6, 1931; came to U.S., 1953; s. Ernest Peter and Evelyn (Kaddo) M.; m. Yvette Fadlallah, Aug. 27, 1955; children: Ernest, Evelyn, Paula, Vincent, Marguerite. BA in Philosophy, Coll. des Freres, Tripoli, Lebanon, 1948; BA in Medicine, Am. U. Beirut, 1950, postgrad., 1950-52. Cert. clin. lab. technologist, Calif.; cert. clin. lab. scientist Nat. Certification Agy. Chief hematology unit VA Wadsworth Med. Ctr., West Los Angeles, Calif., 1956-81; CEO Phoenicia Trading Co., 1981-88; dir. Coagulation Lab., Orthopaedic Hosp., L.A., 1988—; lab. supr. Westside Hosp., L.A., 1964-79; lectr. hematology UCLA, West Los Angeles, 1970-78. Pres. World Lebanese Cultural Union, L.A., 1978-79. With U.S. Army, 1954-56. Recipient outstanding performance award lab. svc. VA Wadsworth Med. Ctr., 1972-76. Republican. Roman Catholic. Home: 3103 Gilmerton Ave Los Angeles CA 90064 Office: Orthopaedic Hosp 2400 S Flower St Los Angeles CA 90007

MOCKLER, E. JAYNE, research consultant, state legislator; b. Jackson, Wyo., Sept. 21, 1957; d. Franklin and Nancy (Fisher) Mockler. BA in Polit. Sci., Wellesley Coll., 1980. Pvt. practice Cheyenne, Wyo., 1987-93; mem. Wyo. Ho. of Reps., 1993-94. Office: PO Box 1857 Cheyenne WY 82003

MOCKLER, JOHN BARRY, school finance consultant, education advocate; b. Chgo., Oct. 2, 1941; s. William Richard and D. Jane (Cowden) M.; divorced; children: Robert William, Jessica Antonia. AB in Econs., U. Calif., Santa Barbara, 1963; MA in Econs., Calif. State U., Sacramento, 1968. Automobile mechanic, San Francisco, San Diego, 1958-62; cons. edn. com. Calif. Legislature, Sacramento, 1969-70, cons. ways and means com., 1971-74, dep. chief staff to speaker of Assembly,, 1983-84; mgr. sch. econ. project Calif. Dept. Edn., Sacramento, 1974-77; dir. ind. analysis unit L.A. City Unified Sch. Dist., 1977-81; sr. ptnr. Murdoch, Mockler & Assocs., Sacramento, 1981-82, 85-92; cons., mem. panel neutrals Pub. Employee Rels. Bd., Sacramento, 1981-85. Mem. editorial bd. Jour. Sch. Fin., 1980-82; contbr. articles to profl. jours. Fellow Coro Found., 1963-64. Roman Catholic. Home: 1144 7th Ave Sacramento CA 95818 Office: 1130 K St Ste 250 Sacramento CA 95814

MOE, ANDREW IRVING, veterinarian; b. Tacoma, Jan. 2, 1927; s. Ole Andrew and Ingeborg (Gordham) M.; BS in Biology, U. Puget Sound, 1949; BA, Wash. State U., 1953, DVM 1954; m. Dorothy Clara Becker, June 25, 1950; children: Sylvia Moe McGowan, Pamela Moe Barker, Joyce. Meat cutter Art Hansen, Tacoma, 1943-48; gen. practice as veterinarian Baronti Vet. Hosp., Eugene, Oreg., 1956-57; veterinarian, regulatory Calif. Animal Health br. Calif. Dept. Food and Agr. Resident veterinarian II, Modesto, Calif., 1957-64, acting veterinarian-in-charge Modesto Dist. Office (veterinarian III), 1976-77, ret., 1990—. Watersafety instr. ARC, 1958-61. Capt., Vet. Corps., 1954-56, 62; comdr. 417th Med. Svc. Flight Res. (AFRES), 1965-66, 71-73; lt. col. Biomed. Scis. Corps USAF, ret., 1982. Recipient Chief Veterinarian badge, 1975. Mem. Am., Calif., No. San Joaquin (pres. 1979) vet. med. assns., Calif. Acad. Vet. Medicine (charter), Res. Officers Assn. (life), Ret. Officers Assn. (life), Assn. Mil. Surgeons U.S. (life), U.S. Animal Health Assn., Sons of Norway, Masons (Illustrious Master Modesto chpt. 1983, Allied Masonic degrees, pres. Modesto Masonic Luncheon Club 1991, Meritorious Svc. medal 1992), Shriners, Internat. Order of the Rainbow for Girls, Theta Chi. Alpha Psi. Lutheran (del. 102d Synod 1961). Home: 161 Norwegian Ave Modesto CA 95350-3542 Office: Field Vets Emeritus 1620 N Carpenter Rd Ste 48D Modesto CA 95351-1160

MOE, ORVILLE LEROY, racetrack executive; b. Spokane, Wash., Nov. 26, 1936; s. Clarence Orville and Georgia Maria (Lombard) M.; m. Deonne Wesley Schultz, Jan. 11, 1953; children: Susan Marie, Terry Ann. Co-owner Moe's Sudden Svc. Fuel Co., Spokane, Wash., 1956-74; sec. Gold Res. Mining Corp., Spokane, 1973-89, Bonanza Gold Corp., Spokane, 1973-85; pres., founder Spokane Raceway Park, Inc., 1971—; regional v.p. Am. Hot Rod Assn., Kansas, Mo., 1968-84, mktg. dir., 1978-84; co-producer Internat. Car Show Assn., Spokane, 1969-90. Co-producer Spokane Auto Boat Speed Show, 1964—. Mem. Nat. Rep. Senatorial Com., 1984—; mem., trustee Rep. Presdl. Task Force, mem. 1992 Presdl. Trust Rep. Nat. Com. Mem. ISCA, Eagles, Am. Hot Rod Assn. (exec. v.p. Spokane, Wash. 1986—), Internat. Footprint Assn., Am. Auto Racing Assn. (regional v.p.). Republican. Office: Spokane Raceway Park Inc 101 N Hayford Rd Spokane WA 99204-9510

MOE, STANLEY ALLEN, architect, consultant; b. Fargo, N.D., May 28, 1914; s. Ole Arnold and Freda Emily (Pape) M.; m. Doris Lucille Anderson, May 25, 1937; children: Willa Moe Crouse, Myra Moe Parsons. BArch, U. Minn., 1936; D of Engring. (hon.), U. N.D., 1993. lic. architect several states; NCARB cert. Project architect several firms in Midwest, 1936-42; project architect U.S. Army Corps Engrs.., Africa, 1942-43; ptnr. H.S. Starin, Architects & Engrs., Duluth, Minn., 1943-47; sr. ptnr. Moe & Larsen, Architects & Engrs., L.A., 1947-54; ptnr., gen. mgr., exec. v.p. Daniel, Mann, Johnson & Mendenall, L.A., 1954-71, corp. v.p., 1972-79; prin. Stanley A. Moe, AIA, L.A., 1979—; chmn. control com. DMJM & Assocs., 1958-63; project dir. Space Shuttle facilities Kennedy Space Ctr., 1973; project dir. aircraft maintenance complex Iraninan Aircraft Industries, 1978; project mgr. major med. facility program Ministry of Def. and Aviation, Saudi Arabia, 1975-76; project mgr. Boufarik Internat. Airport, Algeria, 1983. Pres. San Fernando Valley Young Reps., 1952, Van Nuys (Calif.) Jaycees, 1949; bd. dirs. Wilshire Ctr. Community Involvement Assn., L.A., 1984-85. Recipient Disting. Svc. award Van Nuys Jaycees, 1949, Sioux award U. N.D. Alumni Assn., 1985. Mem. AIA, Rotary. Republican. Presbyterian. Home: 447 S Plymouth Blvd Los Angeles CA 90020

MOEL, STEVEN ALLEN, ophthalmologist; b. Charleston, W.Va., Sept. 18, 1943; s. Harry and Ruth (Lee) M.; m. Susan Gayle Dill, Aug. 13, 1981; children: Andrew, Erin. AB, U. Miami, Fla., 1965; MD, W.Va. U., 1970. Diplomate Am. Bd. Ophthalmology. Intern Gen. Rose Meml. Hosp., U. Colo., Denver, 1970-71; resident in ophthalmology La. State U., New Orleans, 1971-75; research fellowship in ophthalmology U. Ill. Eye and Ear Infirmary, Chgo., 1973-74; pvt. practice medicine specializing in ophthalmology Monterey Park, Calif., 1980—; v.p. acquisitions and mergers, bd. dirs. Akorn Inc., New Orleans; pres. Redwood Inc., 1986—; pres., chmn. SEN Enterprises, 1986-88; chmn. bd. Grudzen Devel. Corp., 1991—, Paradigm Techs., Inc., 1991—. Contbr. articles to profl. jours. Fellow Am. Acad. Ophthalmology. Office: 500 N Garfield Suite 100 Monterey Park CA 91754

MOELLER, JAMES, state supreme court justice; b. Valley, Nebr., Nov. 14, 1933; s. Hans and Marie Grace (Shumaker) M.; m. Nancy Lee Kiely, Dec. 16, 1961; children: Amy Jo, Linda Anne. BA, Nebr. Wesleyan U., 1954; JD with high distinction, George Washington U., 1959. Bar: Ariz. 1959, U.S. Dist. Ct. Ariz. 1959, U.S. Ct. Appeals (9th cir.) 1961. Assoc. Lewis and Roca, Phoenix, 1959-64, ptnr., 1964-70; ptnr. Moeller Hover Jensen & Henry, Phoenix, 1970-77; judge Maricopa County Superior Ct., Phoenix, 1977-87; justice Ariz. Supreme Ct., Phoenix, 1987—. Editor-in-chief George Washington U. Law Rev., 1958-59. Bd. dirs. Found. for Blind Children, Scottsdale, Ariz., 1964-70, Ariz. Found. Prevention of Blindness, Phoenix, 1966-70; Rep. committeeman, Phoenix and Scottsdale, 1965-69. Served with U.S. Army, 1954-56. Mem. ABA, Am. Judicature Soc., Ariz. Bar Assn., Maricopa County Bar Assn. Methodist. Office: Ariz Supreme Ct 432 Ariz Courts Bldg 1501 W Washington Phoenix AZ 85007

MOERBEEK, STANLEY LEONARD, lawyer; b. Toronto, Ont., Can., Nov. 12, 1951; came to U.S., 1953; s. John Jacob and Mary Emily (Giroux) M.; m. Carol Annette Mordaunt, Apr. 17, 1982; children: Sarah, Noah. BA magna cum laude, Calif. State U., Fullerton, 1974; student, U. San Diego, 1977, Sorbonne, Paris, 1977; JD, Loyola U., 1979. Bar: Calif. 1980; cert. in internat. bus. transactions, U. San Diego, 1977. From law clk. to assoc. McAlpin Doonan & Seese, Covina, Calif., 1977-81; assoc. Robert L. Baker, Pasadena, Calif., 1981-82, Miller Bush & Minnott, Fullerton, 1982-83; prin. Law Office of Stanley L. Moerbeek, Fullerton, 1984—; judge pro tem Orange County Superior Ct., Calif., 1984—; lt. gov. 9th cir. law student divsn. ABA, 1979. Mem. Heritage Found., Washington, 1989—. Calif. Gov.'s Office scholar, 1970; recipient Plaque of Appreciation, Fullerton Kiwanis, 1983. Mem. Calif. Assn. Realtors (referral panel atty. 1985—), Orange County Bar Assn., L.A. Trial Lawyers Assn., Phi Kappa Phi. Roman Catholic. Office: 1370 N Brea Blvd Ste 210 Fullerton CA 92635-4128

MOFFATT, HUGH MCCULLOCH, JR., hospital administrator, physical therapist; b. Steubenville, Ohio, Oct. 11, 1933; s. Hugh McCulloch and Agnes Elizabeth (Bickerstaff) M.; m. Ruth Anne Colvin, Aug. 16, 1958; children: David, Susan. AB, Asbury Coll., 1958; cert. in phys. therapy, Duke U., 1963. Lic. in phys. therapy and health care adminstrn., Alaska. Commd. officer USPHS, 1964, advanced through grades to capt.; therapist USPHS, N.Y.C., 1964-66, Sitka, Alaska, 1970-72; therapist cons. USPHS, Atlanta, 1968-70; clinic adminstr. USPHS, Kayenta, Ariz., 1972-73; hosp. dir. USPHS, Sitka, 1973-78; therapist cons. Idaho Dept. Health, Boise, 1966-68; contract health officer USPHS, Anchorage, 1978-89, ret., 1989; phys. therapy cons. Ocean Beach Hosp., Ilwaco, Wash., 1989—, Harbors Home Health Svcs., Aberdeen, Wash., 1990—; therapist cons. Our Lady of Compassion Care Ctr., Anchorage, 1979—, Alaska Native Med. Ctr., Anchorage, 1988—. With U.S. Army, 1955-57. Mem. Am. Phys. Therapy Assn., Commd. Officers Assn. USPHS, Res. Officers Assn., Ret. Officers Assn., Am. Assn. Individual Investors, Am. Assn. Ret. Persons, Eagles.

MOFFATT, JOYCE ANNE, performing arts executive; b. Grand Rapids, Mich., Jan. 3, 1936; d. John Barnard and Ruth Lillian (Pellow) M. BA in Lit., U. Mich., 1957, MA in Theatre, 1960; HHD (hon.), Sch. Psychology, San Francisco, 1991. Stage mgr., lighting designer Off-Broadway plays, costume, lighting and set designer, stage mgr. stock cos., 1954-62; nat. subscription mgr. Theatre Guild/Am. Theatre Soc., N.Y.C., 1965-67; subscription mgr. Theatre, Inc.-Phoenix Theatre, N.Y.C., 1963-67; cons. N.Y.C. Ballet and N.Y.C. Opera, 1967-70; asst. house mgr. N.Y. State Theater, 1970-72; dir. ticket sales City Ctr. of Music and Drama, Inc., N.Y.C., 1970-72; prodn. mgr. San Antonio's Symphony/Opera, 1973-75; gen. mgr. San Antonio Symphony/Opera, 1975-76, 55th St. Dance Theater Found., Inc., N.Y.C., 1976-77, Ballet Theatre Found., Inc./Am. Ballet Theatre, N.Y.C., 1977-81; v.p. prodn. Radio City Music Hall Prodns., Inc., N.Y.C., 1981-83; artist-in-residence CCNY, 1981—; propr. mgmt. cons. firm for performing arts N.Y.C., 1983—; exec. dir. San Francisco Ballet Assn., 1987-93; mng. dir. Houston Ballet Assoc., 1993—; cons. Ford Found., N.Y. State Coun. on Arts, Kennedy Ctr. for Performing Arts.; mem. dance panels N.Y. State Coun. on Arts, 1979-81; mem. panels for Support to Prominent Orgns. and Dance, Calif. Arts Coun., 1988-92. Appointee San Francisco Cultural Affairs Task Force, 1991; trustee of I.A.T.S.E. Local 16 Pension and Welfare Fund, 1991-94. Mem. Assn. Theatrical Press Agts. and Mgrs., Actors Equity Assn., United Scenic Artists Local 829, San Francisco Visitors and Conv. Bur. (bd. dirs.). Club: Argyle (San Antonio). Office: Houston Ballet 1921 W Bell Houston TX 77219-0487

MOFFATT, ROBERT HENRY, accountant, publisher, writer, consultant; b. Montreal, Que., Can., June 30, 1930; came to U.S., 1968, naturalized, 1973; s. James Bigelow and Edwige Edith M.; m. Hannelore Mann, Jan. 7, 1989. Student Loyola Coll., Montreal, Que., 1948-52, Acadia U., 1962, UCLA, 1970, 72. Lic. in air navigation, Can.; enrolled agt., Dept. Treasury. Mng. editor, pub. Kings-Annapolis Wings, 1961-66; pres., Valley Pubs. Ltd., Kingston, N.S., Can., 1961-67 exec. dir. Maritime Motor Transport Assn. and editor Maritime Truck Transport Rev., Moncton, N.B., Can., 1967-68; dir. spl. products div. Wolf-Brown Inc., Los Angeles, 1968-77; newsletter pub, writer, 1980—; pvt. practice tax acctg., Los Angeles, 1970—; noetic ethicist. Columnist, author editorials in mags. Clk., author constn. Village of Greenwood, N.S., 1961-63; chmn. bd. commrs., 1963-66; publicity chmn. Voluntary Econ. Planning Program, province N.S., 1965-66. Served to lt. Can. Air Force, 1954-60. Mem. Nat. Assn. Enrolled Agts. (newsletter editor, bd. dirs.), Nat. Soc. Pub. Accts (accredited in taxation), Calif. Soc. Enrolled Agts. Home and Office: 7509 W 88th St Los Angeles CA 90045-3408

MOFFEIT, TONY ARCHIE, poet, librarian; b. Claremore, Okla., Mar. 14, 1942; s. Archie and Virginia Ruth (Bell) M.; m. Diana Lee Black, Apr. 28, 1964 (div. 1977); 1 child, Miles. BS in Psychology, Okla. State U., 1964; MLS, U. Okla., 1965. Asst. dir. libr. svcs. U. So. Colo., Pueblo, 1979-87, dept. chair libr. svcs., 1988—, poet in residence, 1987—, honors faculty, 1991—; dir. Pueblo Poetry Project, 1980—; performance poet., 1985—. Author: Pueblo Blues, 1986 (Jack Kerouac award 1986), Luminous Animal, 1989, Dancing With the Ghosts of the Dead, 1992, Neon Peppers, 1992; editor: Prairie Smoke, 1990. Fellow U. So. Colo., 1991, Nat. Endowment for Arts, 1992; Colo. Coun. Arts and Humanities grantee, 1992. Mem. ALA, Colo. Libr. Assn. (div. chmn. 1981-83). Home: 1501 E 7th Pueblo CO 81001 Office: U So Colo 2200 Bonforte Blvd Pueblo CO 81001

MOFFETT, FRANK CARDWELL, architect, civil engineer, real estate developer; b. Houston, Dec. 9, 1931; s. Ferrell Orlando and Jewell Bernice (Williams) M.; BArch, U. Tex., 1958; m. Annie Doris Thorn, Aug. 1, 1952 (div.); children: David Cardwell (dec.), Douglas Howard; m. Darlene Adele Alm Sayan, June 7, 1985 (div.). Architect with archtl. firms, Seattle, Harmon, Pray & Detrich, Arnold G. Gangnes, Ralf E. Decker, Roland Terry & Assocs., 1958-64; ptnr. Heideman & Moffett, AIA, Seattle, 1964-71; chief architect Wash. State Dept. Hwys., Olympia, 1971-77, Wash. State Dept. Transp., 1977-87; owner The Moffett Co., Olympia, 1974—; founder, treas. TAA, Inc., Olympia, 1987-90, pres., 1991—; advisor Wash. State Bldg. Code Council, 1975—; instr. civil engring. tech. Olympia Tech. Community Coll., 1975-77; adv. mem. archtl. barriers subcom. Internat. Conf. Building Ofcls.; archtl. works include hdqrs. Gen. Telephone Directory Co., Everett, Wash., 1964; Edmonds Unitarian Ch., 1966; tenant devel. Seattle Hdqrs. Office, Seattle-First Nat. Bank, 1968-70; Wash. State Dept. Transp. Area Hdqrs. Offices, Mt. Vernon, Selah, Raymond, Colfax and Port Orchard 1973-87; Materials Lab., Spokane, Wash., 1974; Olympic Meml. Gardens, Tumwater, Wash., 1988, City Anacortes emergency power stas., 1989, L. Albert Residence, 1990, F. Gasperetti Residence, 1991; archtl. barriers cons. State of Alaska, 1978, State of Wash., 1992-93. Chmn. Planning Commn. of Mountlake Terr., Wash., 1963, 64, mem., 1961-67; mem. State of Wash. Gov.'s Task Force on Wilderness, 1972-75, Heritage Park Task Force, Olympia, Wash., 1986—; trustee Cascade Symphony Orch., 1971; incorporating pres. United Singles, Olympia, 1978-79; 2d lt. Civil Air Patrol, pub. affairs officer Olympia Squadron. With USN, 1951-54. Registered architect, Alaska, Calif., Wash., profl. engr., Wash.; cert. Nat. Council Archtl. Registration Bds., U.S. Dept. Def., Fallout Shelter Analysis, environ. engring. Mem. AIA (dir. S.W. Wash. chpt. 1980-82, pres.-elect 1985, pres. 1986, dir. Wash. council 1986, architects in govt. nat. com. 1978-87, chmn. N.W. and Pacific region conf. 1991), Am. Public Works Assn., Inst. Bldgs. and Grounds, ASCE, Constrn. Specifications Inst., Am. Arbitration Assn. (invited panelist), Gen. Soc. Mayflower Descs. (gov. Wash. Soc. 1982-83), Nat. Huguenot Soc. (pres. Wash. Soc. 1981-83, 85-87), Olympia Geneal. Soc. (pres. 1978-80), SAR (state treas. 1984-85), SCV, Sons and Daus. of Pilgrims, (gov. Wash. Soc. 1984), Order of Magna Charta, Aircraft Owners' and Pilots' Assn., Rotary (pres. Edmonds, 1969-70), Olympia, Coll. Club of Seattle, Olympia Yacht Club, Olympia Country and Golf Club. Co-author: An Illustrated Handbook for Barrier-Free Design, 2d edit., 1984, 3d edit., 1987, 4th Edit., 1989, Accessibility Design for All, 1992. Republican. Unitarian. Home and Office: PO Box 2422 Olympia WA 98507-2422

MOFFETT, JONATHAN PHILLIP, drummer, musical director, songwriter; b. New Orleans, Nov. 17, 1954; s. Eddie Vernon and Elnora (Dillon) M.; m. Rhonda Catherine Bartholomew, June 26, 1976; children: Tamara Renee, Julian Ryann. Grad. high sch., New Orleans. Drummer, vocalist Patti Austin, Los Angeles, 1982; drummer Cameo Tour, Atlanta, 1982, 83, 86, Lionel Richie, Los Angeles, 1983; drummer, mus. dir. Michael Jackson and the Jacksons' Victory Tour, Los Angeles, 1984; drummer Madonna, Los Angeles, 1985-87, Tina Marie, Los Angeles, 1986; drummer, mus. dir. Jermaine Jackson, Los Angeles, 1986-87; drummer The Jacksons Tour, Los Angeles, 1979, 81, 84, Elton John World Tour, 1988; recorded with Julian Lennon, Peter Cetera, Marilyn Martin, The Jacksons, Kenny Loggins, Chico DeBarge, Nia Peeples, Richard Marx, Jodi Watley; mem. Elton John World Tour, 1989, Madonna World Tour, 1990, George Michael Tour and Rock in Rio Festival. Designer (drum equipment sculpture) Victory Tour Set, 1984; appeared on TV and in videos with Marilyn Martin, Tony Terry, The Kane Gang, Isacc Hayes, Rick James, Cameo, Madonna's Virgin Tour video, Madonna's Ciao Italia Tour video; appeared on TV shows for The O'Jays (Arsenio Hall Show), Jasmine Guy (Arsenio Hall Showú), Linsey Buckingham (Arsenio Hall Show, Jay Leno-Tonight Show), Wilson Phillips (Arsenio Hall Show, Jay Leno-Tonight Show), Go West (Arsenio Hall Show); producer, writer song All Dressed Up for film soundtrack Coming to America; Elton John Album, 1989, Madonna Album, 1989; recordings (albums) Madonna's Like A Prayer, 1989, Brian Eno, 1990, Richard Marks' Rush Street, 1991, Or-N-More, 1991, 10-Inch Men, Anri, 1992; (singles) I'm Breathless; tours include Madonna Blond Ambition, 1990, George Michael Cover to Cover Eng.-Japan-U.S.A., 1990-91; films include Madonna Truth or Dare, 1991; concerts include Rock in Rio festival with George Michael, 1991, videos include George Michael/Elton John's Don't Let the Sun Go Down on Me, 1991, Richard Marks' Keep Coming Back, 1991. Mem. Musician's Union. Democrat. Roman Catholic.

MOFFETT, WILLIAM ANDREW, librarian, educator; b. Charlotte, N.C., Jan. 25, 1933; s. Alfred Nisbet and Mary Elizabeth (McLean) M.; m. Deborah Ellen Hoover, May 9, 1958; children: Pamela, Andrew, Charles, Stephanie. BA, Davidson Coll., 1954; MA, Duke U., 1959, PhD, 1968; MS, Simmons Coll., 1974; LLD (hon.), Davidson Coll., 1992; LittD (hon.), Potsdam Coll., 1993. Chmn. dept. history Charlotte Country Day Sch., N.C., 1959-61; lectr. Alma Coll., Mich., 1964-68; asst. prof. history U. Mass.-Boston, 1968-74; dir. libraries SUNY-Potsdam Coll., 1974-79; prof. history, Azariah Root dir. libraries Oberlin Coll., Ohio, 1979-90; dir. Huntington Libr., San Marino, Calif., 1990—; cons. in field. Contbr. articles to profl. pubs., newspapers. Named Librarian of Yr., Spl. Librs. Assn., 1993, Rsch. Librarian of Yr., Assn. Coll. and Rsch. Librs., 1993; recipient Imroth Meml. award Am. Libr. Assn., 1993. Mem. Assn. Coll. and Rsch. Librs. (exec. bd. 1988-91, pres. 1989-90), Grolier (N.Y.) Club, Rowfant Club (Cleve.). Office: Huntington Libr 1151 Oxford Rd San Marino CA 91108-1299

MOFFIE, ROBERT WAYNE, clinical psychologist; b. L.A., June 22, 1950; s. Marvin Louis Moffie and Dorothy Ruth (Morris) Miller. BA, U. Calif., Riverside, 1972; MA, U. Notre Dame, South Bend, Ind., 1976, PhD, 1978; PhD, Calif. Sch. Prof. Psychology, L.A., 1989. Instr. dept. psychology U. Notre Dame, 1976-78; adj. faculty instr. dept. psychology Ind. U., South Bend, 1978-79; instr. dept. psychology Coll. St. Francis, Joliet, Ill., 1979; assoc. prof. psychology Oglethorpe U., Atlanta, 1979-86; psychology fellow Childrens Hosp., L.A., 1989-91; pvt. practice Studio City, 1991—; cons. United Way of St. Joseph County, South Bend, 1978-79, United Way of Scioto County, Portsmouth, Ohio, 1981, TLY Assocs., Atlanta, 1982-87; mgmt. cons. clin. assessment Michael R. Wagner and Assocs., cons. mgmt. scientist, Calgary, Alta., Can., 1981-83; cons., bd. dirs. Geodetics Ltd., Calgary, 1981-86; area coord. select employee-mgmt. evaluation program Chi-Chi's Inc., Louisville, 1982-84. Reviewer, contbr. The Psychology of Being Human, 4th edit., 1985. Nat. Inst. Child Health and Human Devel. grantee. Mem. Am. Psychol. Assn., Southeastern Psychol. Assn., Mental Health Assn. Ga., Psi Chi. Democrat. Home: 13100 Valleyheart Dr Studio City CA 91604-1959

MOFFITT, DONALD EUGENE, transportation company executive; b. Terre Haute, Ind., May 22, 1932; s. James Robert and Margaret Mary (Long) M.; m. Billie Duffy, Feb. 21, 1989; 1 child, Jaime. BA, Ind. State U., 1954; postgrad., Ind. U., 1956; grad., Advanced Mgmt. Program, Harvard U., 1972. Acct. Foster Freight Lines, Indpls., 1955-56; with Consol. Freightways Inc., San Francisco, 1956-88, v.p. planning, 1961-69; v.p. fin., motor carrier subs. Consol. Freightways Corp. Del., 1969-75; v.p. fin., treas. parent co. Consol. Freightways Inc., San Francisco, 1975-81; exec. v.p. Consol. Freightways Inc., Palo Alto, Calif., 1981-86; vice chmn. parent co. bd. Consol. Freightways, Inc., Palo Alto, Calif., 1986-88; chmn., CEO Circle Express, Indpls., 1988-90; pres., CEO Consol. Freightways, Inc., Palo Alto, Calif., 1990—, also bd. dirs.; chmn. bd. dirs. all subsidiaries Consolidated Freightways, Inc., 1990—. Bd. dirs. Bay Area Coun., Calif. Bus. Roundtable, Conf. Bd., Boy Scouts Am., ARC; bd. dirs., exec. com. Hwy. Users Fedn.; bd. trustees Automotive Safety Found.; bus. adv. coun. Northwestern U. Transp. Ctr. Mem. Nat. C. of C. (Washington) (bd. dirs.). Office: Consolidated Freightways Inc 3240 Hillview Ave Palo Alto CA 94304*

MOFFITT, KEVIN DAVID, food products executive; b. Portland, Oreg., Apr. 23, 1957. BSBA, U. Oreg., 1980. Mgr. new product Dole Food Co., San Francisco, 1981-86; sales mgr. Agrl. Mktg. and Devel., Florence, N.J., 1986-88; internat. mktg. svcs. mgr. Sun Diamond Growers of Calif., Pleasant, Calif., 1988-89; v.p. internat. promotions Oreg.-Wash.-Calif. Pear Bur., Portland, 1989—. Contbr. articles to profl. jours. Mem. Moffat Clan Soc. N.Am., Chi Psi (bd. dirs. undergrad. 1978-79). Office: Oreg-Wash-Calif Pear Bur 813 SW Alder Ste 601 Portland OR 97205

MOFFITT, PHILLIP WILLIAM, magazine editor; b. Kingsport, Tenn., Sept. 11, 1946; s. Wallace and Claire Matilda (Allen) M. BS, U. Tenn., 1968, MS, 1971. Co-founder 13-30 Pub. (now Whittle Communications), Knoxville, Tenn., 1971, editor, 1971-79, pres., 1976—; editor-in-chief 13-30 Publs. Group, Knoxville, Tenn., 1979-86; editor, pres. Esquire Magazine, N.Y.C., 1979-84, editor-in-chief, pres., 1984-86; chmn. Light Source Computer Images, Inc., 1989—. Co-author: The Power to Heal, 1990, Medicine's Great Journey, 1992; contbr. columns to Esquire Mag., 1979-88. Bd. dirs. C.J. Jung Found. Mem. Mag. Pubs. Assn. (bd. dirs. 1984—). Home and Office: 1 Pelican Point Belvedere Tiburon CA 94920-2456

MOGG, DONALD WHITEHEAD, chemist; b. La Grange, Ill., Feb. 11, 1924; s. Harold William and Margaret (Whitehead) M.; B.S., Allegheny Coll., 1944; postgrad. Harvard U., 1946-47. Asst. chemist Gt. Lakes Carbon Corp., Morton Grove, Ill., 1947-48, chemist, 1948-53, research chemist, 1953-56, project supr., 1956-59, sect. head, 1959-63; sect. head Gt. Lakes Research Corp., Elizabethton, Tenn., 1963-66; research and devel. mgr. bldg. products div. Grefco, Inc., Torrance, Calif., 1966-68, corp. research and devel. mgr., 1968-72, group mgr., 1972-81, sr. research assoc., 1981-82. Served with U.S. Army, 1944-46. Mem. Am. Chem. Soc., AAAS, Phi Beta Kappa, Phi Kappa Psi. Presbyterian. U.S. and fgn. patentee in field of bldg. products. Home: Apt B202 3823 Ingraham St San Diego CA 92109-6436

MOGULOF, MELVIN BERNARD, consultant; b. N.Y.C., June 17, 1926; s. Nathan and Ida (Platkin) M.; m. Mildred Edith Goldfarb, June 3, 1956; children: Daniel, Dena. BS, Denver U., 1949; MA, Syracuse U., 1950; MS, U. Conn., 1956; PhD, Brandeis U., 1963. Program officer Pres.'s Commn. on Juvenile Delinquency, Washington, 1963-64; regional mgr. community action program OEO, San Francisco, 1964-66; regional dir. model cities program HUD, San Francisco, 1966-68; assoc. prof. San Francisco State Coll., 1968-69; sr. rsch. assoc. The Urban Inst., Washington, 1969-74; exec. dir. community svcs. Fedn. Jewish Philanthropies, N.Y.C., 1974-76; exec. v.p. Jewish Fedn. East Bay, Oakland, Calif., 1980-86; chief exec. officer Koret Found., San Francisco, 1986-88; dir. task force Pres.'s Adv. Com. on Exec. Orgn., Washington, 1970; cons. Kaiser Found., Packard Found., Osher Found., Bay Vision 20/20 Commn. Author: Governing Metropolitan Areas, 1973, Saving the Coast, 1974; contbr. 35 articles to profl. jours., 10 book chpts. Sgt. U.S. Army, 1944-46. Sr. Fulbright lectr. U.S. Fulbright Commn., London, 1971-72, Jerusalem, Israel, 1976-77. Mem. Mayor's Drug Task Force, Berkeley, 1989; bd. dirs. Berkeley Dispute Resolution Svc., 1989. Jewish.

MOHAN, SUBBURAMAN, biochemist, educator; b. Salem, India, June 15, 1951; came to U.S., 1979; s. Subburama and Pavayee Gounder; m. Shanthi Mohan, Nov. 4, 1985; 1 child, Shilpa. BSc, Bangalore (India) U., 1972, MSc, 1974, PhD, 1978. CSIR rsch. fellow Bangalore U., 1974-78, CSIR postdoctoral fellow, 1978-79; Am. Heart Assn. rsch. fellow U. So. Calif., L.A., 1979-80; lectr., rsch. assoc. Calif. Poly. U., Pomona, 1980-82; asst. rsch. prof. Loma Linda (Calif.) U., 1982-87, assoc. rsch. prof., 1987-91, rsch. prof., 1991—; lectr. in field; presenter symposia. Contbr. numerous articles to sci. publs. Mem. Am. Soc. Biochemistry and Molecular Biology, Am. Soc. Cell Biology, Am. Soc. Clin. Rsch., Am. Soc. Bone and Mineral Rsch., Sigma Xi (Rsch. Merit award Loma Linda chpt. 1990). Office: Pettis Vets Hosp 151 11201 Benton St Loma Linda CA 92357-0002

MOHLER, JAMES WILLIAM, minister; b. Lynwood, Calif., Nov. 8, 1955; s. Lionel Louis and Shelia (Howard) M.; m. Miriam Ruth Moses, Aug. 23, 1980. MusB cum laude, Biola U., 1979, postgrad., 1990; MA in Christian Edn., Talbot Sem., 1984. Ordained to ministry Am. Bapt. Ch., 1986. Min. to jrs., middlers 1st Bapt. Ch., Downey, Calif., 1977-86; min. children and youth 1st Bapt. Ch., Scottsdale, Ariz., 1986—; adj. prof. Biola U., La Mirada, Calif., 1985-86; leader Tonto Rim Am. Bapt. Camp, Payson, Ariz., 1986—. Mem. project area com. City of Downey, 1985-86. Recipient Scholastic REcognition award, nat. Assn. Profs. of Christian Edn. Office: 1st Bapt Ch 7025 E Osborn Rd Scottsdale AZ 85251-6324

MOHR, JOHN LUTHER, biologist, environmental consultant; b. Reading, Pa., Dec. 1, 1911; s. Luther Seth and Anna Elizabeth (Davis) M.; m. Frances Edith Christensen, Nov. 23, 1939; children: Jeremy John, Christopher Charles. A.B. in Biology, Bucknell U., 1933; student, Oberlin Coll., 1933-34; Ph.D. in Zoology, U. Calif. at Berkeley, 1939. Research asso. Pacific Islands Research, Stanford, 1942-44; research asso. Allan Hancock Found., U. So. Calif., 1944-46, asst. prof., 1946-47, asst. prof. dept. biology, 1947-54, asso. prof., 1954-57, prof., 1957-77; chmn. dept., 1960-62, prof. emeritus, 1977—; vis. prof. summers U. Wash. Friday Harbor Labs., 1956, '57; marine borer and pollution surveys harbors So. Calif., 1948-51, arctic marine biol. research, 1952-71; chief marine zool. group U.S. Antarctic research ship Eltanin in Drake Passage, 1962, in South Pacific sector, 1965; research deontology in sci. and academia; researcher on parasitic protozoans of anurans, crustaceans, elephants; analysis of agy. and industry documents, ethics and derelictions of steward agy., sci. and tech. orgns. as they relate to offshore oil activities, environ. effects of oil spill dispersants and offshore oil industry discharges. Active People for the Am. Way; mem. Biol. Stain Commn., 1948-80, trustee, 1971-80, emeritus trustee, 1981—, v.p., 1976-80. Recipient Guggenheim fellowship, 1957-58. Fellow AAAS (coun. 1964-73), So. Calif. Acad. Sci., Sigma Xi (exec. com. 1964-67, 68, 69, chpt. at large bd. 1968-69); mem. Am. Micros. Soc., Marine Biol. Assn. U.K. (life), Am. Soc. Parasitologists, Western Soc. Naturalists (pres. 1960-61), Soc. Protozoologists, Am. Soc. Tropical Medicine and Hygiene, Am. Soc. Zoologists, Ecol. Soc. Am., Planning and Conservation League, Calif. Native Plant Soc., Am. Inst. Biol. Scis., L.A. MacIntosh Group, Save San Francisco Bay Assn., Ecology Ctr. So. Calif., So. Calif. Soc. Toxicologists, So. Calif. Soc. Parasitologists, Common Cause, Huxleyan, Sierra Club, Phi Sigma, Theta Upsilon Omega. Democrat. Home: 3819 Chanson Dr Los Angeles CA 90043-1601

MOHR, SELBY, retired ophthalmologist; b. San Francisco, Mar. 11, 1918; s. Selby and Henrietta (Foorman) M.; AB, Stanford U., 1938, MD, 1942; m. Marian Buckley, June 10, 1950; children—Selby, John Vincent, Adrianne E., Gregory P. Asst. resident in ophthalmology U. Calif. Hosp., 1942-43; pvt. practice ophthalmology, San Francisco, 1947-88; mem. past pres. med. staff

Marshall Hale Meml. Hosp.; mem. staff Mt. Zion Hosp., St Francis Meml. Hosp. Dir. Sweet Water Co., Mound Farms, Inc., Mound Farms Oil & Gas, Inc. Lt. (j.g.) USNR, 1943-46; PTO. Diplomate Am. Bd. Ophthalmology. Fellow Am. Acad. Ophthalmology and Otolarngology; mem. AMA, Calif., San Francisco Med. Socs., Pan-Pacific Surg. Soc., Pan-Am. Assn. Ophthalmology, Pacific Coast Oto-Ophthalmol. Soc., Pan-Am. Med. Soc. Home: 160 Sea Cliff Ave San Francisco CA 94121-1125 Office: 450 Sutter St San Francisco CA 94108-3903

MOHR, SIEGFRIED HEINRICH, mechanical and optical engineer; b. Vöhrenbach, Baden, Fed. Republic Germany, Sept. 20, 1930; came to U.S., 1958.; s. Adolf and Luise (Faller) M.; m. Gloria P. Vauges, Apr. 25, 1959 (div. 1972); children: Michael S., Brigitte M.; m. Jeani Edith Hancock, Mar. 24, 1973; 1 child, Suzanne A. Diplom-Ingenieur, Universität Stuttgart, Fed. Republic Germany, 1957; MS in Optical Engring., SUNY, 1971. Thesis researcher Daimler Benz AG, Stuttgart, 1957; design engr. Russell, Birdsall & Ward B & Nut Co., Port Chester, N.Y., 1958-59; devel. engr. IBM Advanced Systems Devel. div., San Jose, Calif., 1960-64; rsch. engr., inventor Precision Instrument Co., Palo Alto, Calif., 1964-67; prin. engr. RCA Instructional Systems, Palo Alto, 1967-70; rsch. engr., scientist Singer Simulation Products, Sunnyvale, Calif., 1971-73; project leader Dymo Industries Tech. Ctr., Berkeley, Calif., 1973-77; leader, adv. rsch. & devel. NCR Corp. Micrographic Systems Div., Mountain View, Calif., 1977-89; advanced project mgr. electro-optics dept. (U.S.A.) Angénieux, Santa Clara, Calif., 1989—; translator for books in English, French and German; corr., writer for European jazz publs. Patentee, author in field. Bicycle activist League of Am. Wheelmen, Balt., 1975—; del. mem. U.S. Del. ISO Conf., Paris, 1988. Mem. Soc. Photo-Optical Instrumentation Engrs., Assn. Info. and Image Mgmt., Internat. Soc. Optical Engring. Home: 3311 Benton St Santa Clara CA 95051-4420

MOHRDICK, EUNICE MARIE, nurse, health educator; b. Alameda, Calif.; d. Walter William and Eunice Marie (Connors) M. BS in Nursing Edn., U. San Francisco, 1955; MA in Edn. spl interest, San Francisco State Coll., 1967; Pub. Health Cert., U. Calif., San Francisco, 1968; EdD, Western Colo. U., 1977. RN, Calif. Supr. oper. rm. St. John's Hosp., Oxnard, Calif., 1947-50, supr. maternity, delivery and nursery rms., 1950-53; nurse, supr. St. Mary's Hosp., San Francisco, 1943-45, supr., instr., 1955-60, 62-65; asst. dir. nursing, tchr. nursing history St Mary's Coll. of Nursing, San Francisco, 1953-55; tchr. home nursing Mercy High Sch., San Francisco, 1960-61; tchr. Health, Family Life San Francisco Unified Schs., 1968-83; tchr. holistic health Contra Costa Coll., 1981-86; cons. pvt. practice Albany, Calif., 1986—; tchr. El Cerrito (Calif.) Senior Ctr., 1986-88. Author: Elementary Teacher Handbook, How to Teach Sex Education, Grades, 4,5,6, 1977. Mem. Madonna Guild, San Francisco, 1986—, v.p., 1989—; mem. Half Notes' Singing Club to Sick and Spl. Needy, 1970—. Recipient Title I Grant U. Calif. San Francisco, 1968, Workshop Grant for Culture Inter-relationship Study, Singapore, UNESCO, Washington U., St. Louis, 1973. Mem. AAUW, San Francisco State U. Alumna, U. San Francisco Nursing Alumni (charter mem., bd. dirs. 1974-88), Mensa. Republican. Roman Catholic. Home & Office: 555 Pierce St Apt 129 Albany CA 94706-1011

MOHRMAN, KATHRYN, academic administrator. Pres. The Colo. Coll., Colo. Springs. Office: Colo Coll Office of President Colorado Springs CO 80903

MOIRAO, DANIEL R., educator; b. Oakland, Calif., Mar. 31, 1952; s. Manuel Joseph and Anna G. (Zuniga) M.; m. Anita Louise Stakenburg, June 16, 1979; children: Jacqueline Christine, Jennifer Margaret. BA, U. Calif., Davis, 1974; MS, Calif. State U., Hayward, 1980. Cert. tchr. k.- community coll., Calif., 1975; Sch. administrn. credential, Calif., 1979. Tchr. Tracy (Calif.) Pub. Schs., 1975-76; tchr. San Ramon VAlley Unified Sch., Danville, Calif., 1976-80, prin., 1980-86; dir., coordinatior Calif. Sch. Leadership Acad., Hayward, 1986-87; asst. supt. Pittsburg (Calif.) Unified Sch. Dist., 1987--; cons. Riverside (Calif.) County Office of Edn. Co-author: Enhancing Student Success Positive School Climate, 1987. Named Outstanding Tchr., San Ramon Valley Dist., 1977. Mem. Assn. of Calif. Sch. Adminstrs. (pres. 1987), Am. Assn. Sch. Adminstrs., Assn. for Supervision and Curriculum Devel., Nat. Assn. Elementary Sch. Prins., Phi Delta Kappa, Toastmasters (Best Speaker Area 5, 1986). Roman Catholic. Home: 110 Danforth Ct Danville CA 94526-5513 Office: Hayward Unified School District PO Box 5000 Hayward CA 94540

MOLBY, DOUGLAS STEVEN, civil engineer; b. Sandstone, Minn., Jan. 23, 1958; s. Carl Aage and Barbara Louise (Lenway) M.; children: Erik Carlton, Alyssa Ann. AA, Columbia Christian Coll., 1982; BS, U. Alaska, 1986. Registered profl. engr., Calif. Drafting tech. Dept. of Transp., State of Alaska, Anchorage, 1977-80; engring. tech. Lounsbury & Assocs., Anchorage, 1984-85; asst. civil engr. Corwin & Assocs., Inc., Anchorage, 1985-87; assoc. structural engr. County of San Diego, 1987—. Author computer programs: Tile Maker, 1991, Ansi-Zap, 1992, File Infotron, 1992. Mem. County of San Diego Water Conservation Task Force, 1990—.

MOLDANADO, SWARNALATHA ADUSUMILLI, nursing educator, researcher; b. Vijayawada, Andhra, India; came to U.S., 1977; d. Punnaih and Nagaratna (Chintapally) A.; m. Alexander Moldanado, Dec. 23, 1979; 1 child, Arjun. RN, and midwife, Ill. Calif. Lectr. Postgrad. Inst. of Medical Edn. and Research, Chandigarh, India, 1971-77; research assoc., teaching asst. U. Ill. Coll. of Nursing, Chgo., 1977-81; tchr. practice Rush U. Coll of Nursing, Chgo., 1981-82; assoc. prof., chmn. dept. nursing Rockford Coll., Ill., 1982-85; prof., Calif. State U., San Bernardino, 1985-87; prof. San Francisco State U., 1988—. Mem. Voice for Choice Campaign of San Mateo County Planned Parenthood. Mem. Am. Pub. Health Assn., Sigma Xi Research Soc., Sigma Theta Tau Internat. Avocations: music, gardening. Office: San Francisco State Univ 1600 Holloway Ave San Francisco CA 94132-1722

MOLDE, DAVID LAWRENCE, financial service executive; b. Rochester, Minn., Jan. 31, 1959; s. Sherman Melborne and Dorothy Irene (Christenson) M.; m. Maureen Ann St. Martin, June 6, 1981; 1 child, James David. BA in Bus. Mgmt. and Psychology, Luther Coll., Decorah, Iowa, 1981. Asst. div. mgr. F.W. Woolworth/Woolco, Tucson, Ariz., 1981-82; sr. regional mgr. ITT Consumer Fin. Svcs., Phoenix, Ariz. and Misson Viejo, Calif., 1982-88; sr. dist. mgr. Nova Fin. Svcs., Aurora, Colo., 1988-90, Trans. Am. Fin. Svcs., Aurora, 1990—. Rep. precinct commiteeman, Tucson, 1982; chmn. fin. com. Holy Love Luth. Ch., Aurora, 1991. Mem. Colo. Fin. Svcs. Assn. (bd. dirs. 1988—, audit chmn. 1989-91, v.p. 1990-91, pres. 1991—), Wyo. Fin. Svcs. Assn. (bd. dirs. 1990—). Home: 16810 E Crestline Ln Aurora CO 80015-4005

MOLENKAMP, CHARLES RICHARD, physicist; b. San Francisco, Aug. 26, 1941; s. Charles and Sophia Henrietta (Lappinga) M.; m. Margaret Joyce Wattron, Aug. 26, 1967; children: Robin Christine, William Charles. BS, Calvin Coll., 1963; MS, U. Ariz., 1967, PhD, 1972. Physicist Lawrence Livermore (Calif.) Nat. Lab., 1972—. Contbr. articles to profl. jours. Mem. Am. Meteorol. Soc., Am. Sci. Affiliation, Am. Assn. for Aerosol Rsch., Phi Beta Kappa. Office: Lawrence Livermore Nat Lab PO Box 808 Livermore CA 94551-0808

MOLINA, RAFAEL ANTONIO, chief executive officer; b. Sept. 5, 1963; s. Rafael Antonio and Rosa Isabel (Villacorta) M.; m. Maria Asuncion Cornejo, Sept. 28, 1985; children: Elisa Maria, Rafael Augusto, Cristian Adolfo. AA, Sacramento City Coll., 1983; BS, Golden Gate U., 1993. CFO MVM Investments, Sacramento, 1983-85; adminstr. State of Calif., Sacramento, 1985—; CEO, mng. dir. C & T Investments, Dixon, Calif., 1988—; dir. MAM Co., Sacramento, 1985—; CEO, dir. Del Sol Investments, Dixon, 1989—. Mem. Calif. State Employees Assn., Sacramento, 1985, Am. Mgmt. Assn., Sacramento, 1991; pres. St. Peter's Ch., Dixon, 1992. Recipient Outstanding Achievement award Calif. Dept. Health Svcs., 1988, Primary Clinics, 1990. Mem. Am. Mgmt. Assn., Tele-Comms. Assn., Calif. Microcomputers Users. Roman Catholic. Office: C & T Investments Co PO Box 671 Dixon CA 95620

MOLINSKY, BERT, tax consultant; b. Bronx, N.Y., Feb. 25, 1938; s. Joseph and Ida G. (Rosenberg) M.; m. Donna L. Thurman, June 26, 1964; children: Avery, Lucy, Lois, Sarah. Student, U. Ariz., 1956-61, Diablo Valley Coll., 1986-88, Calif. State U., Hayward, 1988-92. CFP; CLU; ChFC; Enrolled Agt. Field supt. INA Life, Phoenix, 1968-72; regional life mgr. Sentry Life Ins. Co., Oklahoma City, 1972-73, Mpls., 1973-75, San Francisco, 1975-78; mgr. Acacia Mutual Life, Oakland, Calif., 1978-80; gen. agt. Am. United Life, Concord, Calif., 1980-82; owner East Bay Triple Check Tax Svcs., Walnut Creek, Calif., 1982—, Triple Check Income Tax Shoppe, Peoria, Ariz., 1993—; instr. Golden Gate U. CPD, San Francisco, 1983-93, Mt. Diablo Sch. Dist., Concord, 1986-93; faculty Coll. for Fin. Planning, Denver, 1983—. Contbr. articles to profl. jours. Nat. dir. U.S. Jaycees, Phoenix, 1967; pres. Bnai Brith Coun. of Lodges, San Francisco, 1986. With USNR, 1955-72. Named Jaycee of Yr. Ariz. Jaycees, 1967. Mem. Enrolled Agts., East Bay Assn. Life Underwriters (pres. 1985-86), Nat. Assn. Enrolled Agts. Office: East Bay Triple Check Tax Svcs 3000 Citrus Circle #110 Walnut Creek CA 94598 also: 8466 W Peoria Ave Peoria AZ 85345

MOLITORIS, BRUCE ALBERT, nephrologist, educator; b. Springfield, Ill., June 26, 1951; s. Edward and Joyce (Tomasko) M.; m. Karen Lynn Wichterman, June 16, 1973; children: Jason, Jared, Julie. BS, U. Ill., 1973, MS in Nutrition, 1975; MD, Wash. U., 1979. Resident Sch. Medicine U. Colo., Denver, 1979-81, nephrology fellow, 1981-84, asst. prof. medicine, 1984-88, assoc. prof. medicine, 1988-93, prof., 1993—; vis. scientist U. Colo., MCDB, Boulder, 1989-90, Max Planck Inst., Federal Republic of Germany, 1984-85; mem. editorial bd. Am. Jour. Physiology, 1989—, Am. Jour. Kidney Disease; NIH reviewer, 1991—; dir. home dialysis Denver VA Med. Ctr., 1984—. Contbr. articles to profl. jours. Pres. Cherry Creek Village South Homeowners Assn., 1989-90; v.p. Our Father Luth. Ch., Denver, 1989-90; coach Cherry Creek Soccer Assn., Greenwood Village, 1988-91, Centennial little league Titans Basketball; bd. dirs. CSSA, 1993. Recipient Upjohn Achievement award, 1979, Liberty Hyde Bailey award, 1973. Mem. ADA, Am. Soc. Nephrology, Internat. Soc. Nephrology, N.Y. Acad. Sci., Am. Soc. Clin. Investigation, Am. Fedn. for Clin. Rsch. (nat. counselor 1991—), Western Assn. Physicians. Office: Denver VA Med Ctr 111C 1055 Clermont St Denver CO 80220-3873

MOLLARD, JOHN DOUGLAS, consulting engineering and geology executive; b. Regina, Sask., Can., Jan. 3, 1924; s. Robert Ashton and Nellie Louisa (McIntosh) M.; m. Mary Jean Lynn, Sept. 18, 1952; children: Catherine Lynn, Jacqueline Lee, Robert Clyde Patrick. BCE, U. Sask., 1945; MSCE, Purdue U., 1947; PhD, Cornell U., 1952. Registered profl. engr., profl. geologist Sask., Alta. and B.C., Can. Resident constrn. engr. Sask. Dept. Hwys and Transp., 1945; grad. asst. Purdue U., West Lafayette, Ind., 1946-47, rsch. engr. Sch. Civil Engring., 1950-52; air surveys engr., soil and water conservation and devel. Prairie Farm Rehab. Adminstrn., Govt. of Can., 1947-50; chief, airphoto analysis and engring. geology div. Prairie Farm Rehab. Adminstrn., Govt. of Can., Regina, 1953-56; pres. J.D. Mollard and Assocs. Ltd., Regina, 1956—; aerial resource mapping surveys tech. adv. Colombo plan, Govts. Ceylon and Pakistan, 1954-56; advisor Shaw Royal Commn. on Nfld. Agr.; disting. lectr. series Ea. Can. Geotech. Soc., 1969; Cross Can. disting. lectr. Can. Geotech Soc., 1993; guest lectr., vis. lectr., instr. over 50 short courses on remote sensing interpretation aerial photos and satellite imagery numerous univs., cities and provinces in Can., also Cornell U., Ithaca, N.Y., Harvard U., Cambridge, Mass., U. Calif., Berkeley, U. Wis., Madison, U. Hawaii, 1952—. Author: Landforms and Surface Materials of Canada, 7 edits.; co-author: Airphoto Interpretation and the Canadian Landscape, 1986; contbr. over 100 articles to profl. pubs. Organizer, canvasser United Appeal campaigns; former bd. dirs. Regina Symphony Orch. Recipient Engring. Achievement award Assn. Profl. Engrs. Sask., 1983, Massey medal Royal Can. Geog. Soc., 1989, R. F. Legget award Can. Geotech. Soc., 1992. Fellow ASCE, Geol. Soc. Can., Geol. Soc. Am., Am. Soc. Photogrammetry and Remote Sensing (award for contbns. airphoto interpretation and remote sensing 1979), Internat. Explorers Club; mem. Engring. Inst. Can. (Keefer medal 1948), Assn. Cons. Engrs. Can., Can. Geotech. Soc. (1st R.M. Hardy Meml. Keynote lectr. 1987, Thomas Roy award with engring. geology div. 1989, R.F. Legget award 1992), Regina Geotech. Soc., Geol. Soc. Sask., Can. Soc. Petroleum Engrs., Regina YMCA (former dir.), Rotary (former dir. Regina club). Mem. United Ch. of Can. Home: 2960 Retallack St, Regina, SK Canada S4S 1S9 Office: JD Mollard/Assoc 810 Avord Tower, 2002 Victoria Ave, Regina, SK Canada S4P 0R7

MOLLMAN, JOHN PETER, book publisher, consultant electronic publishing; b. Belleville, Ill., Feb. 8, 1931; s. Kenneth John and Maurine (Farrow) M.; m. Jane Michael Kendall, Aug. 22, 1953; children—Sarah Chase, Eric Cleburne. B.Arts, Washington U., St. Louis, 1952. Advt. specialist Gen. Electric Co., Schenectady and Boston, 1952-54; mgr. Enterprise Printing Co., Millstadt, Ill., 1956-66; gen. mgr. Monarch Pub. Co., N.Y.C., 1966-67; dir. prodn. Harper & Row Pubs., N.Y.C., 1967-74; pub. Harper's Mag. Press, N.Y.C., 1971-74; v.p. prodn. Random House Inc., N.Y.C., 1974-81; sr. v.p. World Book-Childcraft Inc., Chgo., 1981-88; pres. World Book Pub., 1988-91; pub. cons., 1991-92; dir. intellectual property devel. Multimedia Publishing Microsoft, 1992—. Chmn. graphics standards rsch. com. NEH; mem. vis. com. Washington U., pub. com. Art Inst. of Chgo. With U.S. Army, 1954-56. Mem. Assn. Am. Pubs., Siwanoy Club (Bronxville, N.Y.), Sigma Delta Chi, Omicron Delta Kappa. Unitarian. Home: 4511 103d Ln NE Kirkland WA 98033 Office: Microsoft 1 Microsoft Way Redmond WA 98052

MOLLNER, FREDERICK RICHARD, director publications, graphic designer; b. L.A., Aug. 21, 1946; m. Virginia Donahoo, Jan. 6, 1973. BA, Calif. State U., L.A., 1971, MA, 1972; postgrad., Art Ctr. Coll. Design, L.A. Graphic designer Calif. State U., L.A., 1972-77; art dir. Amb. Coll., Pasadena, Calif., 1977-78; art dir. Pepperdine U., Malibu, Calif., 1978-80, creative dir., 1980-84, dir. pubs., 1984—; tchr. Calif. State U., 1983-84, Pepperdine U., 1988; freelance graphic designer. Mem. Coun. for the Advancement and Support of Edn., Univ. and Coll. Designers Assn. (sec. 1980), Advt. Club Ventura County, Art Dirs. Club L.A., AIGA. Office: Pepperdine U 24255 Pacific Coast Hwy Malibu CA 90263-9999

MOLT, CYNTHIA MARYLEE, author, publisher; b. Sierra Madre, Calif., Nov. 1, 1957; d. Lawrence Edward and Evelyn Mary (Novak) Molt. BA in English Lit., Calif. State U., Long Beach, 1980. Mng. editor Assoc. Graphics, Arts and Letters, Monrovia, Calif., 1981-87, pub., sr. and mng. editor, 1987—, authenticator, 1981—; lectr., speaker, 1992—; author McFarland and Co., Inc., Pubs., Jefferson, N.C., 1988-90, Greenwood Press, Inc., Westport, Conn., 1989-93; author pilot prog. Arcadia Unified Sch. Dist., Calif. 1992—. Author: Gone with the Wind on Film: A Complete Reference, 1990, (bio-bibliography) Vivien Leigh, 1992, Maria Callas, Joan Crawford, Agnes de Mille, Margot Fonteyn, Rita Hayworth, Edith Head, Grace Kelly, Abraham Lincoln, Laurence Olivier, David O. Selznick, Joan Sutherland, Elizabeth Taylor, Spencer Tracy, 1991—; author, editor: The Wind, 1981-89, Calif. Film, 1987-89; spl. corr.: Monrovia News-Post, 1985; corr.: Monrovia Rev., 1975, G.W.T.W. Collector's Club newsletter, 1979-82; editor: Iris Notes, 1992—. Vol. adminstrv. asst. student activities Monrovia High Sch., 1976; mem. Friends of Arcadia Pub. Libr., Friends of Monrovia Pub. Libr. Mem. Am. Biog. Inst. (mem. rsch. bd. advisors 1989—), Am. Iris Soc., Hist. Iris Preservation Soc., So. Calif. Iris Soc. (editor 1991—), Gone with the Wind Soc. (pres. 1985-89), Vivien Leigh Fan Club, Monrovia Garden Club (v.p. publicity programs 1992-93). Home and Office: 364 May Ave Monrovia CA 91016-2264

MOLTER, DANIEL ALAN, investment company executive; b. Pitts., Nov. 6, 1940; s. Daniel W.C. and Helen T. Molter; m. Hester J. V. H. Molter, June 18, 1977; children: Theresa H. E., Anna C. BS, Lehigh U., 1962; MBA, U. Pa., 1968. CPA, N.Y.; registered investment advisor. In-charge acct. Price Waterhouse and Co., N.Y.C., 1962-66; sr. planner analyst Mobil Corp., N.Y.C., 1968-72; mgr. bus. planning and analysis Union Pacific Corp., N.Y.C., 1972-74; dir. corp. fin. planning M. Lowenstein Corp., N.Y.C., 1974-77; exec. v.p. fin. Botany 500 McGregor Sportswear, Phila., 1977-81; v.p., controller INA Corp., Phila., 1981-82; CFO Decision Data Computer Corp., Phila., 1982-83; fin. cons. Molter Investments, Phila. and Tucson, 1983-90; pres., CEO Molter, Brennan and Co., Tucson, 1990—; bd. dirs., fin. cons. Deer Park Baking Co., Hammonton, N.Y., 1986-92. Bd. dirs. Lane Justus Chorale, Tucson, 1989-92. Republican. Home: 6255 Via de la Yerba Tucson AZ 85715 Office: Molter Brennan and Co 55 N. Avenida de la Vista Tucson AZ 85710

MOLTON, PETER MICHAEL, waste conversion researcher, consultant; b. Wolverhampton, Eng., Aug. 21, 1943; came to U.S., 1971; s. Cuthbert Joseph and Fay (Hudson) M.; m. Elizabeth Eirwen Carrington, Nov. 17, 1964 (div. Feb. 1971); m. Marion Elizabeth Glock, Feb. 25, 1971; children: Sharon Elizabeth, Ivan Robert, Kerrin Amy. BSC with honors, U. Manchester, Eng., 1964; PhD in Organic Chemistry, U. London, 1967, MPhil in Microbiology, 1971, Diploma in Space Physics, 1971. NAS postdoctoral fellow NASA-Ames, Moffett Field, Calif., 1971-72; rsch. assoc. U. Md., College Park, 1972-74; sr. rsch. scientist Battelle-N.W. Lab., Richland, Wash., 1975—. Contbr. articles to profl. jours.; inventor sludge to oil reactor system; patentee tritum polymer lights. Ward treas. Chiswick Conservative Party, London, 1969-70. Recipient R & D 100 award R & D mag., 1988, Excellence in Tech. Transfer award Fed. Lab. Consortium, 1988. Fellow Brit. Interplanetary Soc.; mem. Am. Chem. Soc., Internat. Soc. for Study Origin of Life, Alpha Chi Sigma. Republican. Home: 6915 W 6th Ave Kennewick WA 99336 Office: Battelle-Pacific NW Lab Battelle Blvd K6-24 Richland WA 99352

MOMADAY, NAVARRE SCOTT, author, English educator; b. Lawton, Okla., Feb. 27, 1934; s. Alfred Morris and Natachee (Scott) M.; m. Gaye Mangold, Sept. 5, 1959; children: Cael, Jill, Brit; m. Regina Heitzer, July 21, 1978; 1 dau., Lore. A.B., U. N.Mex., 1958; A.M., Stanford U., 1960, Ph.D., 1963. Asst. prof., assoc. prof. English U. Calif., Santa Barbara, 1962-69; prof. English and comparative lit. U. Calif., Berkeley, 1969-72, Stanford U., 1972-80, from 1985; prof. English and comparative lit. U. Ariz., Tucson, 1980-85, now Regents Prof. English; cons. Nat. Endowment for Humanities, Nat. Endowment for Arts, 1970—. Author: The Complete Poems of Frederick Goddard Tuckerman, 1965, House Made of Dawn, 1968, The Way to Rainy Mountain, 1969, Angle of Geese and Other Poems, 1973, The Gourd Dancer, 1976, The Names, 1976, American Indian Authors, 1972, Colorado: Fall, Summer, Winter, Spring, 1973, The Ancient Child, 1989; co-author: American Indian Photographic Images, 1868-1931, 1982. Trustee, Museum of Am. Indian, Heye Found., N.Y.C., 1978—. Guggenheim fellow, 1966; recipient Pulitzer prize for fiction, 1969; Premio Letterario Internazionale Mondello Italy, 1979; Disting. Service award Western Lit. Assn., 1983. Mem. MLA, Am. Studies Assn., PEN. Office: Univ Ariz Dept English Tucson AZ 85721-0001

MOMMAERTS, WILFRIED FRANCIS HENRY MARIA, physiologist, educator; b. Broechem, Belgium, Mar. 4, 1917; came to U.S., 1948, naturalized, 1956; s. Hendrik David and Maria (van Damme) M.; m. Elizabeth Barbara Batyka, July 29, 1944 (dec.); children—Robert Wilfried Anthony, Edina Maria, Quentin Francis. Student, U. Leiden, Netherlands, 1934-39; Ph.D., Kolozsvar, Hungary, 1943; Dr. honoris causa, U. Dijon, 1976. Faculty Am. U., Beirut, 1945-48, Duke U., 1948-53, Western Res. U., 1953-56; coordinator Commonwealth Fund Med. Curriculum Expt., 1955-56; spl. Rockefeller fellow U. Coll., London, 1956; prof. medicine, physiology, dir. L.A. County Heart Assn. Cardiovascular Rsch. Lab. U. Calif., 1956-87; emeritus prof. UCLA, 1987-88, chmn. dept. physiology, 1966-87; mem. Roger Wagner L.A. Master Chorale; Commonwealth Fund fellow Centre des Recherches sur les Macromolecules, Strasbourg, 1963-64; chmn. physiology tng. com. NIH, 1967-71; vis. prof. U. Dijon, 1973-74; mem. Internat. Commn. on Genetic Experimentation, 1980—; researcher Max Planck Inst. for Med. Rsch., Heidelberg, Fed. Rep. Germany; chmn. planning com. European Union Socs. Exptl. Biology, 1987-90. Author: Muscular Contraction, a Topic in Molecular Physiology, 1950; contbr. articles to profl. jours. Recipient award for outstanding contbn. to sci. knowledge Los Angeles County Heart Assn., 1967, award of merit, 1972; Samuel Racz medal, Budapest, 1985, Alexander von Humboldt prize, 1986. Mem. Am. Physiol. Soc., Am. Soc. Biol. Chemists, Biophys. Soc., Am. Acad. Arts and Scis., Royal Belgian Acad. Medicine, Hungarian Physiol. Soc. (hon.), others. Republican. Episcopalian. Home: 969 Hilgard Ave Penthouse 05 Los Angeles CA 90024

MOMMSEN, KATHARINA, German language and literature educator; b. Berlin, Sept. 18, 1925; came to U.S., 1974, naturalized, 1980; d. Hermann and Anna (Johannsen) Zimmer; m. Momme Mommsen, Dec. 23, 1948. Dr.phil., U. Tübingen, 1956; Dr. habil., Berlin Free U., 1962. Collaborator Acad. Scis., Berlin, 1949-61; assoc. prof. Free U., Berlin, 1962-70; prof. German Carleton U., Ottawa, Can., 1970-74; Albert Guerard prof. lit. Stanford U., 1974—; vis. prof. U. Giessen, Tech. U. Berlin, 1965, State U. N.Y., Buffalo, 1966, U. Calif., San Diego, 1973. Author over 150 publs. on 18th-20th century German and comparative lit.; editor: Germanic Studies in America. Mem. Internat. Assn. Germanic Langs. and Lit., Goethe Soc., Schiller Soc. Home: 980 Palo Alto Ave Palo Alto CA 94301-2223 Office: Stanford U Dept German Stanford CA 94305

MONACO, FERDINAND ROGER, mathematics educator; b. Pitts., Oct. 2, 1940; s. Charles Anthony and Bertha Ann (Grove) M.; m. Roberta Denise Karl, Jan. 30, 1987. BA, Calif. State U., Long Beach, 1979, MA, 1982; PhD, Walden U., 1989. Prof. emeritus L.A. Community Coll. Dist., 1982—; cons., prin. Learning Resources Co., McMinnville, Oregon, 1985—. Author: (textbooks) Intro Microwave Technology, 1989, Essential Mathematics for Electronics Technicians, 1990, FCC Licensing, 1990, Resources in Mathematics for Electronics, 1990, Laboratory Activities in Microwave Technology, 1990, Interactive Software: Math for Physics, 1993, Applied Math, 1993. Mem. Am. Math. Assn., Am. Math. Assn. Two Yr. Colls., Phi Kappa Phi, Phi Delta Kappa. Home: 15500 SW Dusty Dr McMinnville OR 97128

MONACO, MICHELLE ANNE, police detective; b. Twenty-Nine Palms, Calif., May 8, 1962; d. Charles Anthony and Verene Christine (Fendo) M. AA, Phoenix Coll., 1983. Police detective City of Phoenix, 1986—. Mem. Phoenix Law Enforcement Assn. (union rep. 1989-88). Roman Catholic.

MONACO, PAUL, department head, educator, artist, writer; b. Niskayuna, N.Y., Sept. 11, 1942; s. Angelo M. and Birdena (O'Melia) M. BS, Columbia U., 1965; MA, U. N.C., 1966; PhD, Brandeis U., 1974. Asst. prof. hist. Brandeis U., Waltham, Mass., 1973-75; prof. arts and humanities U. Tex., Dallas, 1975-85, dir. grad. studies arts and humanities, 1976-80; dept. head, prof. media and theatre arts Mont. State U., Bozeman, 1985—; bd. dirs. U. Film and video Assn.; mem. Hist. Preservation Com., Bozeman, 1988-90, Mont. Com. for Humanities, Missoula, 1989-93. Author: Modern Europe Culture..., 1983, Ribbons in Time, 1988 (ALC 10 best award 1988); prodr., dir.: Montana: 2nd Century, 1990 (Mont. broadcasters award 1991); prodr., dir., co-writer: Home to Montana, 1988. Bd. mem. Mont. Ballet Co., Bozeman, 1986-90. Recipient Fulbright Prof. award U.S., Germany, 1982-83, 92. Mem. Bozeman Film Festival, U. Film and Video Assn. (nat. bd. 1989-92), Acad. Motion Picture Arts and Scis., IAMHIST, Phi Kappa Phi (pub. rels. officer 1989-93). Home: 919 W Koch Bozeman MT 59715

MONAGHAN, JAMES EDWARD, JR., political consultant; b. South Bend, Ind., Mar. 31, 1947; s. James Edward and Marion (Currigan) M.; m. Carol Lynn Foster (dec.); children: James Edward III, Brian Foster. BS, Colo. State U., 1971; cert. in environ. mgmt., Harvard U., 1976. Press sec. Coloradans for Lamm, Denver, 1974; asst. to gov. for natural resources State of Colo., Denver, 1975-78; campaign mgr. Coloradans for Lamm/Dick, Denver, 1978; dir. intergovtl. relations State of Colo., 1979-83; energy dir. Western Govs. Policy Office, Denver, 1979; asst. to the dir. U.S. Synthetic Fuels Corp., Washington, 1980; campaign mgr. Coloradans for Lamm/Dick, Denver, 1982; pres. Monaghan & Assocs., Denver, 1983—; pres., prin. Strategies West, 1984—; bd. dirs. Western Interstate Nuclear Bd., Denver, 1975-80; gov.'s alt. Western Govs. Policy Office, 1977-83; staff chmn. energy and natural resources com. Nat. Govs. Assn., Washington, 1978-79; bd. dirs. Ltd. Term Mcpl. Fund, Santa Fe, 1985—; campaign cons. Gov. Roy Romer, Colo., 1986, 90, Gov. Mike Sullivan, Wyo., 1986, 90, U.S. Senator Tim Wirth, Colo., 1992, Richard D. Lamm for U.S. Senate, Colo., 1992. Democrat. Roman Catholic. Office: Monaghan & Assocs 1625 Broadway Ste 1800 Denver CO 80202

MONAHAN, JOHN FRANCIS, satellite launch engineer; b. Whiteman AFB, Mo., Nov. 9, 1964; s. John Edward and Carol Anne (Nekola) M. BEE, Villanova U., 1986; MBA, U. Houston, 1989. Elec. engr. Sci. Applications Internat. Corp., Arlington, Va., 1985-86; commd. lt. USAF, 1986, advanced through grades to capt., 1990; space shuttle flight contr., systems engr. NASA USAF, Houston, 1986-89; satellite systems engr. USAF, Colorado Springs, 1989-90, satellite launch officer, 1990-92, mgr. satellite launch branch, 1992—. Com. bd. dirs. Spl. Olympics Tex., Houston, 1987-89; vol. Boy Scouts Am., Shelton, 1976—. Named Eagle Scout Boy Scouts Am., 1980. Mem. IEEE (Villanova chpt. 1984-85), Paugessett Lodge (treas. 1980-81), Lambda Chi Alpha. Roman Catholic. Home: 5260 Slickrock Dr Colorado Springs CO 80918-7645 Office: 3SOPS/DOLD Falcon Air Station CO 80912

MONAHAN, RITA SHORT, nursing educator; b. Waterloo, Iowa, Sept. 16, 1954; d. Andrew T. and Lillian R. (Weber) Short; m. W. Gregory Monahan, Jr., June 2, 1976; children: Andrew G., Catherine R. BSN, U. Iowa, 1976; MS in Nursing, Duke U., 1980; EdD, W.Va. U., 1986. Cert. gerontology clin. nurse specialist. From instr. to asst. prof. sch. nursing W.Va. U., Morgantown, 1981-86; assoc. prof. sch. nursing Oreg. Health Scis. U., LaGrande, 1986—. Contbr. articles to profl. jours. Mem. ANA, AAUW, Am. Diabetes Assn., Oreg. Nurses Assn., Sigma Theta Tau. Office: Oreg Health Scis U Sch Nursing 1410 L Ave La Grande OR 97850

MONARCHI, DAVID EDWARD, management scientist, information scientist, educator; b. Miami Beach, Fla., July 31, 1944; s. Joseph Louis and Elizabeth Rose (Muller) M.; BS in Engring. Physics, Colo. Sch. of Mines, 1966; PhD (NDEA fellow), U. Ariz., 1972; 1 son by previous marriage, David Edward. Asst. dir. of Bus. Rsch. Div., U. Colo., Boulder, 1972-75, asst. prof. mgmt. sci./info. systems, 1972-75, assoc. prof. mgmt. sci. and info. systems, 1975—; assoc. dir. Bus. Rsch. Div., 1975-80, dir. Div. Info. Sci. Rsch., 1982-84; prin. investigator of socio-econ. environ. systems for govtl. agys., and local govt. orgns., State of Colo., also info. systems for pvt. firms, 1972-77. Mem. Gov.'s Energy Task Force Com., 1974. Mem. IEEE, Inst. for Mgmt. Sci., Assn. Computing Machinery, Am. Assn. Artificial Intelligence. Contbr. numerous articles on socio-econ. modeling, object-oriented systems and artificial intelligence to profl. jours. Home: 32 Benthaven Pl Boulder CO 80303-6252 Office: U Colo Grad Sch Bus Boulder CO 80309-0419

MONCUS, MARY LYNN, English language educator; b. Clovis, N.Mex., July 23, 1934; d. Claude C. and Sara Carolyn (Clough) M. BA in English, N.Mex. State U., 1955, MA in Counseling and Guidance, 1962, EdS in Counseling and Guidance, 1964; MA in English, U. Tex., El Paso, 1971. Tchr. Forrest (N.Mex.) High Sch., 1955-56, Tucumcari (N.Mex.) High Sch., 1956-62, Las Cruces (N.Mex.) High Sch., 1962-63; grad. asst. N.Mex. State U., Las Cruces, 1963-64, prof. Eng., 1964-89; vol. death and terminal illness counselor, Las Cruces, Tucumcari, N.Mex., 1970—. Columnist weekly newspaper, Quay County Sun, 1970-90; radio commentator KTNM, 1985—. Mem. com. to honor N.Mex. and Spain during Quintessentennial celebration of Columbus' discovery of Am. Smithsonian Inst. NSF scholar, 1961, 63, Theta State scholar Delta Kappa Gamma, 1963. Fellow Internat. Biog. Assn.; mem. Quay Coun. for Arts and Humanities Inc., Tucumcari Hist. Rsch. Inst., N.Mex. State U. Pioneers, N.Mex. Ret. Tchrs. Assn., N.Mex. Alzheimers Assn., DAR. Democrat. Roman Catholic. Home: 1301 S Adams St Tucumcari NM 88401-3439

MONDA, MARILYN, quality improvement consultant; b. Paterson, N.J., Aug. 11, 1956; d. Thomas John and Lydia Mary (Dal Santo) M.; m. Lawrence G. Gifford, Jr., Aug. 25, 1984. BA, San Diego State U., 1980; MA, Baylor U., 1984. Math. statistician Navy Personnel Rsch. and Devel. Ctr., San Diego, 1984-86; quality engr. Info. Magnetics, Inc., San Diego, 1986-87; mgmt. cons. Process Mgmt. Inst., Inc., Mpls., 1987-89; staff assoc. Luftig & Assocs., Inc., Detroit, 1989-92; founder Quality Disciplines, San Diego, 1992—; bd. dirs. Deming Users Group, San Diego, 1985-87; lecturer in the field. Contbr. articles to profl. jours. Mem. San Diego Deming Users Group, Am. Soc. Quality Consultants, Am. Statistical Assn., Phi Beta Kappa.

MONDAVI, ROBERT GERALD, winery executive; b. Virginia, Minn., June 18, 1913; s. Cesare and Rosa (Grassi) M.; m. Marjorie Declusin, 1940 (div.); 3 children: Robert, Timothy, Marcia; m. 2nd, Margrit Biever, 1980. BA, Stanford U., 1936. Dir. Sunny St. Helena Wine Co., St. Helena, Calif., 1937-45; v.p., gen. mgr., Charles Krug Winery, St. Helena, 1943-66; pres. Robert Mondavi Winery, Oakville, Calif., from 1966, ret., now chmn. bd. Office: Robert Mondavi Winery PO Box 106 Oakville CA 94562-0106

MONDAY, JOHN CHRISTIAN, electronics company executive; b. West Bend, Wis., June 29, 1925; s. Leo John and Emilie Suzanne (Klapper) M.; m. Alyce S. Riesch, Aug. 20, 1949 (div. Jan. 1981); children: Linda Lee Monday Orlando, John Scott; m. Virginia M. Clayton, Jan. 29, 1981. BA in Math. and Econs., Ripon Coll., 1949; BSBA, MIT, 1951; MBA, U. Wis., 1954. Dir. research Hevi Duty Elec. Co., 1951-54, div. mgr., 1954-59; v.p., gen. mgr. Hubbard Aluminum Products Co., Pitts. and Abingdon, Va., 1959-65; pres. Am. Vitrified Products Co., Cleve., 1965-69; exec. v.p., bd. dirs. Intermark Inc., La Jolla, Calif., 1969-91; pres., chmn. Specialties Engring. Corp, San Diego, 1991—; pres., bd. dirs. Specon Inc.; pres., chmn. bd. dirs. Spltys. Engring. Corp., 1976—, San Diego; pres. Specon Inc., La Jolla, 1981—. Author: Radiography of Copper Casting, 1951. Mem. Com. of 25, Washington, 1967-69; Trustee Johnston Meml. Hosp., 1963-65, Va. Highlands Found., 1963-65; dir. Street and Hwy. Safety Lighting Bur., 1959-65; regional chmn. ednl. council M.I.T., 1969-82. Served with AUS, 1943-46. Mem. ASTM (mem. D 33 com., subcom. chmn., steel structures painting coun.), Nat. Elec. Mfrs. Assn., Am. Mgmt. Assn., Clay Pipe Assn. (vice chmn. 1965-69), Nat. Assn. Corrosion Engrs., La Jolla Country Club (San Diego), Baillage La Chaine des Rotisseurs (Bailli of La Jolla). Republican. Presbyterian. Home: 5192 Chelsea St La Jolla CA 92037-7908

MONDINI, GREGORY FRANCIS, obstetrician-gynecologist, educator; b. San Jose, Calif., Mar. 11, 1948; s. Emanuel Frederick and Victoria Marie (Soares) M.; m. Karen Nancy Biester, May 29, 1987; children: Alessandro Fredric, Maximo Corradino. BS, Ohio State U., 1970; postgrad., U. Bologna, Italy, 1970-76; MD with honors, Mt. Sinai Sch. Medicine, 1978. Diplomate Nat. Bd. Med. Examiners. Intern and resident St. Vincent Hosp. and Med. Ctr., 1982; admitting physician Manhattan Bowery Project, N.Y.C., 1982; staff physician ob-gyn. Kaiser Permanente, San Jose, 1982-83, Friendly Hills Med. Group, La Habra, Calif., 1983-84; dir. dept. ob-gyn. Universal Care Med. Group, Long Beach, Calif., 1984-89; vice chman. dept. ob-gyn. Garden Grove (Calif.) Hosp. and Med. Ctr., 1989-91; pvt. practice Orange, Calif., 1989—; asst. clin. prof. Irvine Med. Ctr., U. Calif., Orange, 1991—; vice chmn. dept. obstetrics and gynecology Western Med. Ctr. and Regional Hosp., Santa Ana, Calif., 1993—. Pres. Ridgeline Ranch Home Owners Assn., Orange, 1989-91, com. mem., 1993—. Mem. AMA, Calif. Med. Assn., Orange County Med. Assn., Orange County Obstetrics and Gynecologic Soc., Mt. Sinai Alumni Assn. Office: 1920 E Katella Ave Ste I Orange CA 92667

MONINGER, EDWARD GEORGE, JR., naval officer; b. Chgo., Feb. 6, 1943; s. Edward George and Le Nora (Newberger) M.; m. Carol Lynn Leedy, Nov. 27, 1965; children: Edward George III, Thomas P. BS in Engring., U.S. Naval Acad., 1965; MS in Mgmt., U.S. Naval Postgrad. Sch., 1972; MA in Internat. Rels., Boston U., 1985. Commd. ensign USN, 1965, advanced through grades to capt., 1987; ops. officer Helicopter Antisubmarine Squadron Two, San Diego, 1977-78; exec. officer Helicopter Antisubmarine Squadron Eleven, Jacksonville, Fla., 1978-79, commdg. officer, 1979-81; mil. policy advisor U.S. Ambassador to NATO, Brussels, 1982-85; exec. officer U.S.S. Guam, Norfolk, Va., 1985-87; nuclear/arms control advisor Supreme Allied Comdr. Atlantic (NATO), Norfolk, Va., 1987-90; commdg. officer Naval Comm. Sta., Stockton, Calif., 1990-92; dir. fleet ops. U.S. Atlantic Fleet, 1992—. Exec. coun. Boy Scouts Am., 49er Coun., Stockton, 1991, dist. chmn., 1992; chmn. Rough and Ready Island Combined Fgn. Campaign, Stockton, 1990-92. Decorated DFC, Purple Heart, Air Medal (21 citations), Navy Commendation medal, Legion of Merit, Def. Superior Svc. medal. Mem. U.S. Naval Inst., U.S. Naval Acad. Alumni Assn., Stockton Rotary.

MONIZE, ROBERT RAY, labor union official; b. Everett, Wash., July 17, 1942; s. Raymond Alemada and Fairy Ione (Goldthorpe) M.; m. Billye Juninta, Jan. 17, 1984; children: Debbie, Shelley, Robert Ray Jr. AA, Everett C.C., 1972; BA in Pub. Adminstrn., U. Puget Sound, 1974. Notary pub., Wash. Dep. sheriff Snohomish County Sheriff's Dept., Everett, 1969-80; detachment comdr. Kawajalen Missile Range, Marshall Islands, 1980-84; laborer Laborers' Internat. Union N.Am. Local 292, Everett, 1964-69, bus. agt., 1992—, rec. sec., 1992—; cons. TRAG Cons. Inc., Everett, 1980-84; union counselor AFL-CIO, Everett, 1991—. Sec. Snohomish County Dem. Club, 1972-73. With USN, 1960-65. Mem. N.W. Fair Contractors Assn. (del. 1992—), Am. Legion, Eagles. Roman Catholic. Home: 16804 103d St SE Snohomish WA 98290 Office: Laborers Union 292 2810 Lombard Ave Everett WA 98201

MONK, DIANA CHARLA, artist, stable owner; b. Visalia, Calif., Feb. 25, 1927; d. Charles Edward and Viola Genevieve (Shea) Williams; m. James Alfred Monk, Aug. 11, 1951; children: Kiloran, Sydney, Geoffrey, Anne, Eric. Student, U. Pacific, 1946-47, Sacramento Coll., 1947-48, Calif. Coll. Fine Arts, San Francisco, 1948-51, Calif. Coll. Arts & Crafts, Oakland, 1972. Art tchr. Mt. Diablo Sch. Dist., Concord, Calif., 1958-63; pvt. art tchr. Lafayette, Calif., 1963-70; gallery dir. Jason Aver Gallery, San Francisco, 1970-72; owner, mgr. Monk & Lee Assocs., Lafayette, 1973-80; stable owner, mgr. Longacre Tng. Stables, Santa Rosa, Calif., 1989—. One-person shows include John F. Kennedy U., Orinda, Calif., Civic Arts Gallery, Walnut Creek, Calif., Vallery Art Gallery, Walnut Creek, Sea Ranch Gallery, Gualala, Calif., Jason Aver Gallery, San Francisco; exhibited in group shows at Oakland (Calif.) Art Mus., Crocker Nat. Art Gallery, Sacramento, Le Salon des Nations, Paris. Chair bd. dirs. Walnut Creek (Calif.) Civic Arts, 1972-74, advisor to dir., 1968-72; exhibit chmn. Valley Art Gallery, Walnut Creek, 1977-78; juror Women's Art Show, Walnut Creek, 1970, Oakland Calif. Art. Home and Office: Longacre Tng Stables 1702 Willowside Rd Santa Rosa CA 95401

MONK, GREGORY BRITTAIN, artist, business owner; b. San Francisco, Dec. 28, 1942; s. John Clarkson and Barbara (Brittain) M.; m. Yvonne Adele Jones, Mar. 30, 1974 (div. Jan. 1987). AA, City Coll., San Francisco, 1963; BA in Econs., San Francisco State U., 1965. Freelance actor and extra various media Calif. and Hawaii, 1961—; salesman, mgr. San Francisco Luggage Co., 1961-65; computer programmer Western Union, Mahwah, N.J., 1969-72; owner Gregory Monk - Wood and Glass, Sausalito, Calif., 1973-74, G. Brittain M. Co., Haleiwa, Hawaii, 1975-80, Greg Monk Stained Glass, Aiea, Hawaii, 1981—. Artist (stained glass designs) Maka Koa, 1981 (1st prize 1982), Flowing, 1984; glass artist (TV show) Portraits of Paradise, 1988. Sgt. USMC, 1966-68. Mem. SAG, Assn. Hawaii Artists, Stained Glass Assn. Hawaii (co-founder 1979, pres. 1979-81, treas. 1982-83), Glass Art Soc., Arts Coun. Hawaii, Hawaiian Craftsmen, Pacific Handcrafters, Honolulu Acad. Arts, The Contemporary Mus., Profl. Stained Glass Guild, Art Glass Suppliers Assn. Democrat. Office: Greg Monk Stained Glass 98-027 Hekaha St Aiea HI 96701

MONK, JANICE JONES, women's studies researcher, university program administrator; b. Sydney, Australia, Mar. 13, 1937; came to U.S., 1961; d. Harold Frederick and Edith Emily (Collins) J.; m. David Monk, July 31, 1964. BA with honors, U. Sydney, 1958; MA, U. Ill., 1963, PhD, 1972. Instr. geography U. Ill., Urbana, 1967-72, asst. prof., 1972-80; assoc. dir. women's studies U. Ariz., Tucson, 1980-83, exec. dir., 1983—; cons. Nat. Geog. Soc., 1979-81, 86, 87; mem. U.S. Nat. Com. Internat. Geog. Union, Washington, 1980-88, vice chairperson gender study group, 1988-92, Commn. on Gender, 1992—; bd. dirs. Ctr. for Geography in Higher Edn., Oxford, England. Co-editor: Women and the Arizona Economy, 1987, The Desert is No Lady, 1987, Western Women: Their Land, Their Lives, 1988, Full Circles: Geographies of Women over the Life Course, 1993; contbr. articles to various publs. Mem. rsch. com. nat. bd. YWCA, N.Y.C.; bd. dirs. Prescott Coll., 1990—. Mem. Assn. Am. Geographers (councilor 1978-81, meritorious svc. award perspectives on women group 1988, honors award, 1992), Nat. Coun. Geog. Edn. (sec. 1984-86, bd. dirs. 1980-83), Nat. Women's Studies Assn., Soc. Woman Geographers (Washington, nat. councilor 1987-90). Office: U Ariz SW Inst Rsch Women 102 Douglass Bldg Tucson AZ 85721-0001

MONKEWITZ, PETER ALEXIS, mechanical and aerospace engineer, educator; b. Berne, Switzerland, Nov. 9, 1943; came to U.S., 1977; s. Kurt and Marie M. (Krähenbühl) M.; m. Annelise Heidy Sturzenegger, Jan. 15, 1972; children: Serge M., Florence S., Cyril P. Diploma Physics, Fed. Inst. Tech., Zurich, 1967, D of Natural Scis., 1977. Software cons. Sperry Rand UNIVAC, Zurich, 1968; teaching asst. Fed. Inst. Tech., Zurich, 1969-77; rsch. assoc. U. So. Calif., L.A., 1977-80; asst. prof. UCLA, 1980-85, assoc. prof., 1985-91, prof., 1991—. Co-editor Jour. Applied Math. and Physics, 1991—; contbr. articles to Jour. Fluid Mechanics, Physics of Fluids, Ann. Revs. Fluid Mechanics, others. Recipient U.S. Sr. Scientist award Humboldt Found., Germany, 1988. Fellow Am. Phys. Soc.; mem. AIAA. Office: UCLA MANE Dept 405 Hilgard Ave Los Angeles CA 90024-1597

MONLUX, STANTON DEL, sales and marketing executive; b. Longview, Wash., Apr. 29, 1964; s. Jacob Albert and Marie Anne (Oliver) M. BA in Polit. Sci., Wash. State u., Pullman, 1987, BA in Communication, 1987. Pres. Vikos Group Inc., Seattle, 1987-91; dir. sales Vertical Connection, Inc., Seattle, 1991—. Mem. Wash. Software Assn., World Trade Club, Phi Beta Kappa. Office: Vertical Connection 2510 Western Ave Ste 500 Seattle WA 98121

MONROE, ERIC GEORGE, professional association executive; b. Wheeling, W.Va., May 11, 1944; s. Carl A. and Eileen (Carroll) M. BA, Washington & Jefferson Coll., 1966; MA, Duquesne U., 1968; MS, Stetson U., 1972; postgrad., USAF Air War Coll., 1982; MBA, Ariz. State U., 1984; postgrad., Nova U., 1990-91; PhD, Columbia Pacific U., 1993. Systems engr. GE Aerospace, Daytona Beach, Fla., 1972-74; program mgr. Air Force Human Resources Lab., Williams Air Force Base, Ariz., 1974-86; rsch. lab. mgmt. McDonnell Douglas, Mesa, Ariz., 1986-91; pres. IMAGE Soc., Inc., Tempe, Ariz., 1987—; chmn. bd. dirs., founder IMAGE Soc., Inc., Tempe, 1987—. Editor conf. procs. for IMAGE I-IMAGE VI Confs., 1977—; pub. IMAGES newsletter, 1987—. Capt. U.S. Army, 1968-70. Mem. Acad. of Mgmt., Am. Soc. Assn. Execs., IMAGE Soc. Inc., Mensa, Phi Beta Kappa, Beta Delta Gamma, Sigma Iota Epsilon. Office: IMAGE Soc Inc 1308 E Greentree Dr Tempe AZ 85284-4503

MONROE, KEITH, writer, consultant; b. Detroit; s. Donald and Gladys Violet (Wiley) M. Student, Stanford U., 1934-35, UCLA, 1936-38. Suburban corr. N.Y. Times, N.Y.C., 1930-33; mng. editor Teaneck (N.J.) Post, 1933-34; rschr. Foote Cone & Belding, L.A., 1938-39; copy chief Advt. Counselors, Phoenix, 1940-41; asst. dir. pub. rels. Ryan Aero. Co., San Diego, 1942-45; freelance writer and cons., L.A., 1946-58; copywriter Fuller & Smith & Ross, L.A., 1958-61; exec. editor N.Am. Rockwell, El Segundo, Calif., 1963-70; writer, cons., L.A., 1970—; cons. Govt. of Pakistan, Karachi, 1949-50, Govt. of Guatemala, Guatemala City, 1954-55, Bank Am., L.A., 1955-58; editor RAND Corp., Santa Monica, Calif., 1970-71. Author: (book and film) Be Prepared, 1953, (book) How To Succeed in Community Service, 1962, City for Sale—A History of Century City, 1965; contbr. over 150 articles to Fortune, Life, N.Y. Times Mag., Harper's, New Yorker, also others. V.p. Family Svc. Assn., L.A., 1955-58; mem. exec. bd. Adoption Inst., L.A., 1957-60; dist. chmn. Welfare Planning Coun., L.A., 1959-61; mem. health and safety com. Boy Scouts Am., Irvine, Tex., 1978-91. Recipient Silver Beaver award Boy Scouts Am., 1958. Mem. Authors Guild, Am. Soc. Journalists and Authors, Rotary (sec. Santa Monica 1986-87). Home and Office: 11965 Montana Ave Los Angeles CA 90049-5039

MONROE, STANLEY EDWIN, surgeon; b. Bangor, Mich., June 26, 1902; s. Samuel E. and Ella (Monroe) M.; AB, U. Mich., 1925; MD, U. Chgo./Rush Med. Coll., 1936; m. Ruth Williams, June 14, 1932 (dec. 1981); m. 2d, Flora Doss, Aug. 6, 1982. Intern, Evanston (Ill.) Hosp., 1935-36, resident surgeon, 1936-37, asst. surgeon, 1940-41; clin. asst. surgeon Northwestern U., 1938-39, instr. surgery, 1940-41; asst. to Dr. Frederick Christopher, 1937-41; chief surgery VA Hosp., Tucson, 1947-49; surgeon ARAMCO, Saudi Arabia, 1950; pvt. practice, Chula Vista, Calif., 1952-82; former chief of septic and plastic surgery, Thayer Gen. Hosp., Nashville; staff Paradise Valley Hosp., Mercy Hosp. (San Diego); founder Monroe Clinic. Maj. AUS Med. Corps 1942-47, PTO. Diplomate Am. Bd. Surgery. Fellow Soc. for Academic Achievement, Internat. Coll. Surgeons; mem. Soc. Gen. Surgeons of San Diego, Am. Med. Writers Assn., Assn. Mil. Surgeons, Am. Soc. Abdominal Surgeons (founding), Alpha Omega Alpha, Phi Beta Pi. Author: Medical Phrase Book with Vocabulary (also Spanish edit.). Office: 2 Palomar Dr Chula Vista CA 91911-1414

MONROE, SYLVESTER, journalist, writer; b. Leland, Miss., Aug. 5, 1951; s. Kittrel D. Peoples and Hattie M. (Monroe) Kelley; m. Regina A. Johnson, Sept. 20, 1972 (div. Oct., 1989); children: Sherita A., Jason L.; m. Tonju E. François, May 18, 1991. BA, Harvard U., 1973; postgrad., Stanford U., 1979-80. Corr. Newsweek Mag., Boston, 1973-76; corr. Newsweek Mag., Chgo., 1976-78, dep. bur. chief., 1978-83; bur. chief Newsweek Mag., Boston, 1983-85; nat. corr. Newsweek Mag., Washington, 1985-87, White House corr., 1987-88; corr. Time Mag., L.A., 1989—; instr. journalism UCLA Extension, Westwood, Calif., 1990—. Co-author: Brothers, 1988. Trustee St. George's Sch., Newport, R.I., 1984-90. Recipient Page One award Newspaper Guild N.Y., 1987, Gold medal NCCJ, 1988; Profl. Journalism fellow Stanford U., 1979-80. Mem. Nat. Assn. Black Journalists (Frederick Douglass 1st Pl. award 1987), A Better Chance Speakers Bur., Black Journalists Assn. So. Calif. Office: Time Mag 10880 Wilshire Blvd Ste 1700 Los Angeles CA 90024-4193

MONSMAN, GERALD, English literature educator; b. Balt., Mar. 3, 1940; s. Gerald and Diana (DeKryger) M.; m. Nancy Weaver, Mar. 25, 1972; children: Claire Diana, Cecily Grey, Christina Wood. BA, Johns Hopkins U., Balt., 1961, MA, 1963, PhD, 1965. Grad. instr. Johns Hopkins U., Balt., 1962-65; asst. prof. Duke U., Durham, N.C., 1965-70, assoc. prof., 1970-81, prof., 1981-86; prof., head dept. U. Ariz., Tucson, 1986-90, prof. English lit., 1990—. Author: Pater's Portraits, 1967, Walter Pater, 1977, Walter Pater's Art of Autobiography, 1980, Confessions of a Prosaic Dreamer: Charles Lamb's Art of Autobiography, 1984, Olive Schreiner's Fiction: Landscape and Power, 1991. Recipient The Blackwood Prize, Blackwood's Mag., Edinburgh, Scotland, 1967, 69; John Simon Guggenheim Meml. fellow, N.Y.C., 1982-83. Mem. MLA, Pater Soc., Wordsworth-Coleridge Assn. Office: U Ariz Dept English Tucson AZ 85721

MONSON, JAMES EDWARD, electrical engineer; b. Oakland, Calif., June 20, 1932; s. George Edward and Frances Eleanor (Fouche) M.; m. Julie Elizabeth Conzelman, June 25, 1954; children—John, Jamie, Jennifer. B.S.E.E., Stanford U., 1954, M.S.E.E., 1955, Ph.D. in Elec. Engring, 1961. Mem. tech. staff Bell Telephone Labs., Murray Hill, N.J., 1955-56; devel. engr. Hewlett-Packard Co., Palo Alto, Calif., 1956-61; Robert C. Sabini prof. engring. Harvey Mudd Coll., 1961—. Mem. governing bd. Claremont Unified Sch. Dist., 1966-71, pres., 1969-70; pres. Claremont Civic Assn., 1974-75; bd. dirs. Claremont YMCA, 1978-82. NSF fellow, 1954-55; Fulbright research grantee, 1975-76; Fulbright sr. lectr., 1980; Japan Soc. Promotion of Sci. fellow, 1984. Mem. AAUP, IEEE, Magnetics Soc. Japan, Phi Beta Kappa, Sigma Xi, Tau Beta Pi. Home: 353 W 11th St Claremont CA 91711-3806 Office: Harvey Mudd Coll 301 East 12th St Claremont CA 91711

MONSON, THOMAS SPENCER, church official, publishing company executive; b. Salt Lake City, Aug. 21, 1927; s. George Spencer and Gladys (Condie) M.; m. Frances Beverly Johnson, Oct. 7, 1948; children—Thomas L., Ann Frances, Clark Spencer. B.S. with honors in mktg, U. Utah, 1948; M.B.A., Brigham Young U., 1974, LL.D. (hon.), 1981. With Deseret News Press, Salt Lake City, 1948-64; mgr. Deseret News Press, 1962-64; mem. Council Twelve Apostles, Ch. of Jesus Christ of Latter Day Saints, 1963-85, mem. first presidency, 1985—, bishop, 1950-55; pres. Canadian Mission, 1959-62; chmn. bd. Deseret News Pub. Co., 1977—; dir. Deseret Mgmt. Corp.; pres. Printing Industry Utah, 1958; bd. dirs. Printing Industry Am., 1958-64; mem. Utah exec. bd. U.S. West Communications. Mem. Utah Bd. Regents; mem. nat. exec. bd. Boy Scouts Am.; trustee Brigham Young U.. With USNR, 1945-46. Recipient Recognition award, 1964, Disting. Alumnus award U. Utah, 1966; Silver Beaver award Boy Scouts Am., 1971; Silver Buffalo award, 1978. Mem. Utah Assn. Sales Execs., U. Utah Alumni Assn. (dir.), Salt Lake Advt. Club, Alpha Kappa Psi. Club: Exchange (Salt Lake City). Office: LDS Ch 47 E South Temple Salt Lake City UT 84150-0001 also: Deseret News Pub Co PO Box 1257 30 E 1st St Salt Lake City UT 84110

MONTAG, DAVID MOSES, computer company executive; b. Los Angeles, Apr. 30, 1939; s. Gustave and Esther (Kessler) M.; student UCLA, 1957-61; children: Daniel Gershon, Esther Yael, Michael Menachem; m. Olga Volozova, June 18, 1992. Tech. writer L.H. Butcher Co., Los Angeles, 1961; phys. sci. lab. technician East Los Angeles Coll., Monterey Park, 1961—, planetarium lectr., 1963-78; owner EDUCOMP, Monterey Park, Calif., 1980—; ptnr. David M. Montag & Assocs., Monterey Park, 1993—; pres. Aquinas Computer Corp.; ednl. cons. for computer-assisted instrn. pres., dir. Or Chadash, Inc., Monterey Park, 1968—; v.p., bd. dirs. Coll. Religious Conf., 1968-92. Mem. Assn. of Orthodox Jewish Scientists, Laser Inst. Am., AIAA. Home and Office: PO Box 384 Monterey Park CA 91754-0384

MONTAGNE, JOHN, geology educator, consulting geologist; b. White Plains, N.Y., Apr. 17, 1920; s. Henry and Ella Tappey (Spurgeon) de la Montagne; m. Phoebe Morris Corthell, Dec. 23, 1942; children: Clifford, Mathew Hagen. B.A., Dartmouth Coll., 1942; M.A., U. Wyo., 1951, Ph.D., 1955. Cert. profl. geologist. Instr., Colo. Sch. Mines, Golden, 1953-55, asst. prof., 1955-57; asst. prof. Mont. State U., Bozeman, 1957-60, assoc. prof., 1960-63, prof. dept. earth scis., 1963-83, prof. emeritus, 1983—; chmn. Internat. Snow Sci. Workshop, Bozeman, 1981-82. Pres. Mont. Wilderness Assn., 1965; pres. bd. Bridger Bowl Ski Area, Inc., Bozeman, 1973. Served to capt. U.S. Army, 1942-46, MTO. Named Rotarian of Yr., 1989; recipient Gold and Blue award Mont. State U., 1987. Fellow Geol. Soc. Am. (sr., chmn. Rocky Mountain sect. 1982); mem. Am. Assn. Petroleum Geologists, Internat. Glaciol. Soc., Am. Inst. Profl. Geologists, Am. Assn. Avalanche Profls. (pres. 1991-94). Lodge: Rotary (pres. Bozeman 1967-68, dist. gov. 1979). Home: 17 Hodgeman Canyon Dr Bozeman MT 59715-9527 Office: Dept Earth Scis Mont State Univ Bozeman MT 59717

MONTAGUE, GARY LESLIE, newspaper advertising executive; b. Mullan, Idaho, Apr. 4, 1939; s. William Bryan and Gladys Viola (Finkbeiner) M.; m. Dorothy Barclay, Feb. 14, 1959 (div. 1973); children: Teresa Montague Scofield, Douglas; m. Mikael Jones, Mar. 13, 1982. Grad., Am. Press Inst. Columbia U., 1973; postgrad., Cen. Wash. U., 1977. Classified advt. rep. The Wenatchee World, 1957-71, classified advt. mgr., 1971—; sr. ptnr. Leslie/Bryan/Jones, Wenatchee, 1992—; cons., lectr. arts adminstrn. Chmn. Wash. State Arts Commn., Olympia, 1985-88, commr., 1974-78, 82-88; trustee Wash. State Arts Alliance Found., 1981-88, Western States Arts Found., Santa Fe, N.M., 1982-88; pres. Cen. Wash. Hosp. Found., Wenatchee, 1987-88, Wenatchee Area Visitor and Conv. Bur., 1980-81, Allied Arts Coun. of North Cen. Wash., 1973-74, Music Theater of Wenatchee, 1970-71, Wenatchee Valley Dance Found., Gallery '76 art gallery Wenatchee Valley Coll.; commr. City of Wenatchee Arts Commn., 1975-78; exec. com. Wash. State Rep. Cen. Com., 1975-77. Mem. Assn. Newspaper Classified Advt. Mgrs., Western Classified Advt. Assn. (pres. 1990-91), Pacific N.W. Assn. of Newspaper Classified Advt. Mgrs. (pres. 1981-82), Wenatchee Area C. of C. (pres. 1978-79). Mem. Unity Ch. Lodge: Rotary. Home: 2142 Sunrise Cir Wenatchee WA 98801-1047 Office: World Pub Co 14 N Mission Ave Wenatchee WA 98801-2240 also: Leslie/Bryan/Jones PO Box 4644 Wenatchee WA 98807-4644

MONTAGUE, RICHARD MARK, management consultant; b. Mpls., Aug. 31, 1938; s. James Ignatius and Erma Agatha (Dwyer) M.; m. Eleanor Ann Ems, Aug 8, 1962 (div. 1978); children: Lorelei Ann, Scott David; m. Mary Alice Avery, Oct. 6, 1979. BA in Econs., U. Chgo., 1963; MBA, Northwestern U., 1967. Programming project leader Western Electric Co., Chgo., 1963-67; systems analyst Container Corp. Am., Chgo., 1967; spec.-advanced planning systems Gen. Electric Co., San Jose, Calif., 1967-75; policy analyst Regional Transp. Dist., Denver, 1976-79; mgr. corp. planning Frontier Airlines Inc., Denver, 1979-86; cons. Mgmt. Analysis Co., San Diego, 1987-88; pvt. practive Boulder, Colo., 1988-92; owner, mgr. Montague Cons. Svcs., Boulder, Colo., 1992—. Chmn. CommonCause, 13th Congl. dist., San Jose, 1975, issues com. chmn., 1974; air quality chmn. Sierra Club, San Jose, 1970. With USN, 1958-60. Home: 3495 17th St Boulder CO 80304 Office: Montague Cons Svcs 3495 17th St Boulder CO 80304

MONTAGUE, SIDNEY JAMES, real estate developer; b. Denver, Oct. 3, 1950; s. Jerome Edward and Donna Sherrill (Nixon) M.; m. Mary Francis Terry, Dec. 26, 1987; stepchildren: Jonathan Ramsey Shockley, Britt Elizabeth Shockley. BA in Econs., Midland Luth. Coll., Fremont, Nebr., 1972. Loan counselor Am. Nat. Bank, Denver, 1972-74; loan officer First

Nat. Bank Denver, 1974-79; exec. v.p. Buell Devel. Corp., Denver, 1979-84; v.p. The Writer Corp., Denver, 1985-86; pres. Mondevco Inc., Littleton, Colo., 1986-87; devel. mgr. Perini Land & Devel. Co., Phoenix, 1987-91; v.p. Perini Land & Devel. Co., San Francisco, 1991—. Mem. Urban Land Inst., Internat. Coun. Shopping Ctrs. Republican. Office: Perini Land & Devel Co 75 Broadway San Francisco CA 94111

MONTALBANO, WILLIAM DANIEL, foreign correspondent, novelist; b. N.Y.C., Sept. 20, 1940; s. Vincent Francis and Gertrude (Reilly) M.; m. Kathleen Feeney, June 18, 1964 (div. 1977); children: Dennis, Andrea; m. Rosanna Mary Bell-Thomson, Dec. 3, 1977; children: Tiva, Teresa, Daniel. BA, Rutgers U., 1960; MS in Journalism, Columbia U., 1962; Nieman fellow, Harvard U., 1970. Reporter Newark (N.J.) Star-Ledger, 1960-62; editor Patriot Ledger, Quincy, Mass., 1962-63, Buenos Aires Herald, 1964-65, United Press Internat., N.Y.C., 1965-67; corr., editor Miami (Fla.) Herald, 1967-79, chief of corrs., 1981-83; Peking (China) bur. chief Knight Ridder Newspapers, Miami, Fla., 1979-81; El Salvador bur. chief L.A. Times, 1983-84, Buenos Aires bur. chief, 1984-85, Rome bur. chief, 1987—. Author: Powder Burn, 1981, Trap Line, 1983, Death in China, 1984, Sinners of San Ramon, 1989. Recipient Ernie Pyle award Scripps Howard Newspapers, 1974, 75, Maria Moors Cabot prize Columbia U., 1974. Office: L A Times Times Mirror Sq Los Angeles CA 90053

MONTANARI, JOHN RICHARD, strategic management educator, writer; b. Greenville, S.C., Mar. 11, 1944; s. John William and Freda (Foutz) M.; m. Ellen Jean Orton, Mar. 14, 1980. BSME, U. Dayton, 1966; MBA, U. N.Mex., 1973; D in Bus. Adminstrn., U. Colo., 1976. Asst. prof. U. Houston, 1976-79; from assoc. prof. to prof. Ariz. State U., 1980-90, asst. dean grad. programs, 1981-83; prof. Calif. State U., San Marcos, 1991—; disting. vis. prof. USAF Acad., 1987-88; cons. and speaker in field. Author: (with others) Strategic Management: A Choice Approach, 1990, The Advantage Ski Company: A Strategic Simulation, 1990, Strategic Management: A Choice Approach Instructor's Manual, 1990, Cases in Strategic Management, 1991; contbg. author: The Organization and Development of a Medical Group Practice, 1976; contbr. articles to profl. jours.; author numerous nat. procs., monographs, tech. reports, and profl. papers; mem. editorial rev. bd. Jour. Mgmt., The Exec., and others. Strategic planner Sundt Corp., 1992; cons. Johnson Carlier Corp., 1993, and others. Mem. Acad. Mgmt., S.W. Div. of Acad. Mgmt., Decision Scis. Inst., Strategic Mgmt. Soc., Sigma Iota Epsilon. Office: Calif State U Coll Bus Administrn San Marcos CA 92096

MONTANÉ, DAVID, site development coordinator; b. Glendale, Calif., Apr. 25, 1960; s. Ben and Dorothy Ouida (Thompson) M.; m. Deborah Leah Strunk, Aug. 20, 1983 (div. Sept. 1985). BS, Nat. U., 1992. With Topographic Surveyors, Marshall, Tex., 1981-82, Geo-Metrics Surveying & Mapping, Ukiah, Calif., 1985-87, Clifford Ruzicka Engring., Lakeport, Calif., 1988-89; site devel. coord. Mission Engrs., Inc., Santa Clara, Calif., 1990—. Performer rhythm juggling as Saturn Dave. Mem. Nat. Trust Hist. Preservation, Woodrow Wilson Ctr. Internat. Scholars, Foresight Inst. (nanotech. discussion group), Lakeport C. of C., Internat. Jugglers Assn.

MONTEITH, STANLEY KIMBALL, orthopedic surgeon; b. Oakland, Calif., Feb. 17, 1929; s. Clayton and Blanche (Hart) M.; m. Barbara Elizabeth Johnston, Mar. 1974; children: David, Dorothy DeKock, David Culp. BS, U. Calif., Berkeley, 1949; MD, U. Calif., San Francisco, 1952. Diplomate Am. Bd. Orthopedic Surgery. Intern San Francisco Gen. Hosp., 1952-53; resident physician Santa Cruz (Calif.) County Hosp., 1955-56; orthopedic trainee U. Calif., 1956-59; sr. resident orthopedic surgery Alameda (Calif.) County Hosp., 1959-60; pvt. practice orthopedic surgery Santa Cruz, 1960-74, 77—; prin. surgeon orthopedic dept. U. Free Orange State, Bloemfontein, South Africa, 1974-77; mem. faculty Am. Back Soc. Author: AIDS: The Unnecessary Epidemic-America Under Seige, 1991. Co-chmn. com. on health and human svcs. Calif. State Rep. Cen. Co., 1992. 1st lt., M.C., U.S. Army, 1953-55. Mem. Am. Acad. Orthopedic Surgeons, Leroy C. Abbot Orthopedic Soc., Western Orthopedic Soc. Office: 618 Frederick St Santa Cruz CA 95062

MONTERO, DARREL MARTIN, sociologist, social worker, educator; b. Sacramento, Mar. 4, 1946; s. Frank and Ann Naake; m. Tara Kathleen McLaughlin, July 6, 1975; children: David Paul, Lynn Elizabeth, Laura Ann, Emily Kathryn. AB, Calif. State U., 1970; MA, UCLA, 1972, PhD, 1974. Postgrad. researcher Japanese-Am. Research Project UCLA, 1971-73, dir. research, 1973-75; assoc. head Program on Comparative Ethnic Studies, Survey Research Ctr. UCLA, 1973-75; asst. prof. sociology Case Western Res. U., Cleve., 1975-76; asst. prof. urban studies, research sociologist Pub. Opinion Survey, dir. urban ethnic research program U. Md., College Park, 1976-79; assoc. prof. Ariz. State U., Tempe, 1979—; cons. rsch. sect. Viewer Sponsored TV Found., Los Angeles, Berrien E. Moore Law Office, Inc., Gardena, Calif., 1973, Bur. for Social Sci. Research, Inc., Washington, Friends of the Family, Ltd., Nat. Sci. Found. Author: Japanese Americans: Changing Patterns of Ethnic Affiliation Over Three Generations, 1980, Urban Studies, 1978, Vietnamese Americans: Patterns of Resettlement and Socioeconomic Adaptation in the United States, 1979, Social Problems, 1988; mem. editorial bd. Humanity and Society, 1978-80; contbr. articles to profl. jours. Served with U.S. Army, 1966-72. Mem. Am. Sociol. Assn., Am. Assn. Pub. Opinion Research (exec. council, standards com.), Am. Ednl. Research Assn., Council on Social Work Edn., Soc. Study of Social Problems, D.C. Sociol. Soc., Am. Soc. Pub. Adminstrn., Nat. Assn. Social Workers, Pacific Sociol. Assn. Office: Sch Social Work Ariz State U Tempe AZ 85281

MONTERROSA, JOSÉ NAPOLEÓN, bilingual school psychologist; b. San Vicente, El Salvador, Feb. 5, 1953; came to U.S., 1972; s. Napoleon and Elia (Roque) M. BA in Philosophy, Don Bosco Coll., 1978; MA in Counseling & Guidance, Loyola Marymount U., L.A., 1984, MA in Ednl. Psychology, 1985, MA in Sch. Adminstrn., 1990. Tchr. St. John Bosco High Sch., Bellflower, Calif., 1978-81, Daniel Murphy High Sch., L.A., 1982-84; counselor L.A. City Coll., 1983-84; specialist Found. for Jr. Blind, L.A., 1985-86; instr. Don Boaso Tech. Inst., Rosemead, Calif., 1988; bilingual sch. psychologist L.A. Unified Sch. Dist., 1986—, pub. rels. media cons., in-svc. cons., 1988—; college counselor West Los Angeles City Coll., 1992-93; edn. cons. Gestión Y Control de Calidad, Valencia, Spain, 1992-93. Mem. Nat. Assn. Sch. Psychologists, Calif. Assn. Psychologists, Am. Psychol. Assn. (assoc.). Mailing: PO Box 3134 Huntington Park CA 90255 Office: Miles Ave Elem Sch 6720 Miles Ave Huntington Park CA 90255-5099

MONTEVERDE, RONALD PETER, psychiatrist; b. S.I., N.Y., Aug. 11, 1947; s. Paul Eugene and Inez (Bazzuro) M.; m. Valerie Vannessa Valdez, Dec. 8, 1984; children: Dominic, Matthew, Cristina. BS, St. Peters Coll., 1968; MD, George Washington U., 1972. Intern Evanston (Ill.) Hosp. Northwestern U., 1972-73, resident Evanston (Ill.) Hosp., 1973-75; chief cons. liason in psychiatry Cook County Hosp., Chgo., 1976; chief of psychiatry, staff psychiatry, admissions dir. N.Mex. State Hosp., Las Vegas, 1977-84; pvt. practice psychiatry Hobbs, N.Mex., 1985—; cons. Altzheimers unit Hobbs Health Care, 1988—; med. dir. Lea County Mental Health Ctr., Lea County Guidance Ctr., Hobbs, 1987—, adult mental health Lea Regional Hosp., 1989—, adolscent unit, 1989—. Bd. dirs. Leaders Industries, 1990. Mem. AMA, Am. Psychiat. Assn., Nat. Bd. Med. Examiners., Am. Bd. Psychiatry & Neurology. Republican. Roman Catholic. Office: 5419 N Lovington Hwy Ste 6 Hobbs NM 88240-9135

MONTGOMERY, JAMES FISCHER, savings and loan association executive; b. Topeka, Nov. 30, 1934; s. James Maurice and Frieda Ellen (Fischer) M.; m. Diane Dealey; children: Michael James, Jeffrey Allen, Andrew Steven, John Gregory. B.A. in Acctg., UCLA, 1957. With Price, Waterhouse & Co., C.P.A.'s, Los Angeles, 1957-60; controller Conejo Valley Devel. Co., Thousand Oaks, Calif., 1960; asst. to pres. Gt. Western Fin. Corp., Beverly Hills, Calif., 1960-64; fin. v.p., treas. United Fin. Corp., Los Angeles, 1964-69, exec. v.p., 1969-74, pres., 1975; pres. Citizens Savs. & Loan Assn., Los Angeles, 1970-75; chmn., chief exec. officer, dir. Gt. Western Fin. Corp., also Great Western Bank, Beverly Hills, 1975—. Served with AUS, 1958-60. Office: Gt Western Fin Corp 8484 Wilshire Blvd Beverly Hills CA 90211*

MONTGOMERY, JOHN ALAN, surgeon; b. L.A., Jan. 24, 1944; s. Milford Jefferson and Ilah Claudine (Whitely) M.; m. Jean Nishita, Mar. 28, 1970; children: Maggie Mae, Max Alan. BA, UCLA, 1965; MD, U. So. Calif., 1969. Diplomat Am. Bd. Surgery. Intern Los Angeles County-U. So. Calif. Med. Ctr., L.A., 1969-70, resident in surgery, 1970-74; pvt. practice Fortuna, Calif., 1976—; clin. prof. Los Angeles County-U. So. Calif. Med. Ctr.,1 982—; chief of staff Redwood Meml. Hosp., 1990-91. Maj. USAF, 1974-76. Fellow ACS; mem. Calif. Med. Assn., Grad. Soc. Surgeons Los Angeles County Gen. Hosp., Internat. Soc. Philos. Enquiry, Triple 9 Soc., Mensa, Skull and Dagger Honor Soc./U. So. Calif. Home: 4175 Mill St Fortuna CA 95540 Office: 3301 Renner Dr Fortuna CA 95540

MONTGOMERY, ROBERT F., state legislator, retired surgeon, cattle rancher; b. Ogden, Utah, May 13, 1933; s. William Floyd and Adrianna (Van Zweden) M.; m. Jelean Skeen, June 24, 1953; children: Lance, Dana, Kristen, Keri, Tanya. AS, Weber State U., 1953; BS, Brigham Young U., 1957; MD, U. Utah, 1961. Pvt. practice Anaheim, Calif., 1966-88; senator Utah State Senate, 1992—; chief surgery Anaheim Gen. Hosp., 1970, Anaheim Meml. Hosp., 1972-74. Rep. chmn. Weber County, Utah, 1991-93; pres. Am. Cancer Soc., Salt Lake City, 1992—. Sgt. U.S. Army, 1953-55, Korea. Mem. Rotary, Utah Elephant Club, Travelor's Century Club. Mormon. Home: 1825 N Mountain Rd Ogden UT 84414

MONTGOMERY, ROBERT LOUIS, chemical engineer; b. San Francisco, Nov. 20, 1935; s. Louis Clyde and Fay Elythe (Myers) M.; m. Patricia Helen Cook, Mar. 17, 1962; children: Cynthia Elaine, Jeanette Louise, Cecelia Irene, Howard Edwin. BS in Chemistry, U. Calif., Berkeley, 1956; PhD in Phys. Chemistry, Okla. State U., 1975. Registered profl. engr., Kans., Tex., Colo. Phys. chemist U.S. Bur. Mines, Reno, 1956-62; NSF predoctoral fellow Okla. State U., Stillwater, 1963-66; sr. engr. Boeing Co., Wichita, Kans., 1966-75; postdoctoral fellow Rice U., Houston, 1975-77, sr. research assoc., 1982-84; tech. data engr. M.W. Kellogg Co., Houston, 1977-82; staff engr. Martin Marietta, Denver, 1984—. Contbr. articles to profl. jours. Mem. AIAA, Am. Chem. Soc., Am. Soc. for Metals, Profl. Engrs. Colo., Sigma Xi. Home: 9933 Fairwood St Littleton CO 80125-8811 Office: Martin Marietta Astronautics Group PO Box 179 Denver CO 80201-0179

MONTGOMERY, SETH DAVID, justice; b. Santa Fe, Feb. 16, 1937; s. Andrew Kaye and Ruth (Champion) M.; m. Margaret Cook, Oct. 29, 1960; children: Andrew Seth, Charles Hope, David Lewis. AB, Princeton U., 1959; LLB, Stanford U., 1965. Bar: N.M. 1965. Ptnr. Montgomery & Andrews, P.A., Santa Fe, 1965-89; justice N.Mex. Supreme Ct., 1989—; vis. instr. U. N.Mex. Sch. Law, Albuquerque, 1970-71; chmn. N.Mex. adv. coun. Legal Svcs. Corp., Santa Fe, 1976-89. Bd. visitors Stanford U. Sch. Law, 1967-70, 82-85; pres., chmn. Santa Fe Opera, 1981-86; pres. Santa Fe Opera Found., 1986-89; chmn., vice chmn. Sch. Am. Rsch., Santa Fe, 1985-89; bd. dirs. New Vistas, Santa Fe, 1986-89, First Interstate Bank of Santa Fe, 1977-89, Old Cienega Village Mus., 1980-89. Lt. (j.g.) USN, 1959-62. Named Citizen of the Yr., Santa Fe C. of C., 1986; recipient Disting. Community Svc. award Anti-Defamation League, 1991, Western Area Outstanding Achievement award Nat. Multiple Sclerosis Soc., 1992. Fellow Am. Coll. Trial Lawyers, Am. Coll. Probate Counsel, Am. Bar Endowment, N.Mex. Bar Assn. (bd. bar commrs. 1986-89, sec., treas. 1988-89); mem. ABA, Am. Judicature Soc. Democrat.

MONTONE, KENNETH ALAN, art director, creative director, consultant; b. Chgo., Aug. 30, 1938; s. George Joseph and Beatrice Mabel (Calcott) M.; m. Patricia Joan Klapperich, Feb. 1, 1964; children: James Paul, Ian Andrew, Paul Matthew, Anne Elizabeth. BFA with honors, U. Ill., 1963. Graphic designer U. Ill. Press, Champaign, 1962-63; staff graphic designer ABC-TV, Chgo., 1963-65; art dir. McCann-Erickson, Inc., Sydney, Australia, 1965-67; staff graphic designer CBS-TV, Chgo., 1967-69; syndicated cartoonist, "Kiwi" Chgo. Tribune-N.Y. News Syndicate; art dir. McCann-Erickson, Inc., Portland, Oreg., 1969-80; creative dir. Morton Advt., Portland, 1980-84, Ken Montone & Assocs., Portland, 1984—. Art dir.: "Celebrate" series, 1980. With USN, 1956-59. Recipient Reata Howard Trombley award Portland Ad Fedn., 1983, Art Dirs. Club award N.Y. Ad, 1983, Best in West award Am. Advt. Fedn., 1983. Mem. Advt. Industry Emergency Fund (bd. dirs.), Portland Ad Fedn., Advt. Museum. Home and Office: Ken Montone & Assocs 165 NW 95th Ave Portland OR 97229-6303

MONTOYA, DENNIS WILLIAM, lawyer; b. Wichita Falls, Tex., Nov. 12, 1954; s. Ferdinando Florencio and Katherine Elizabeth (Miller) M.; m. Jeanmarie Torres, June 28, 1986. Student, U. Wash. Sch. Medicine, 1975-77; BS, N.Mex. Highlands U., 1981; JD, U. N.Mex. Bar: N.Mex. 1985, U.S. Dist. Ct. N.Mex. 1985, U.S. Ct. Appeals (10th cir.) 1985. Reginald Heber-Smith Fellow Legal Aid Soc. Albuquerque, 1985-86; assoc. staff atty. N.Mex. Ct. Appeals, Santa Fe, 1986-88; asst. pub.. defender N.Mex. Pub. Defender Dept., Albuquerque, 1988; deputy dist. atty. 4th Jud. Dist. Atty., Las Vegas, N.Mex., 1989-90; pro se law clk., staff atty. U.S. Dist. Ct. N.Mex., Albuquerque, 1990-92; cons. in ct. adminstrn. project tech. assistance to Supreme Ct. and Pub. Ministry of Republic of Panama (USAID) Checchi & Co. Consulting, Inc., Miami, Fla., 33102. Mem. Am. Judicature Soc., Assn. Trial Lawyers Am., ABA, N.Mex. Hispanic Bar Assn., N.Mex. Trial Lawyers Assn., N.Mex. State Bar Assn. (chmn. legal svcs. com. 1987-88), 4th Jud. Dist. Bar Assn. Democrat. Home: PO Box 2674 Las Vegas NM 87701-2674

MONTOYA-RAEL, LILLIAN JOSEPHINE, state agency administrator; b. Albuquerque, Nov. 16, 1966; d. Dickie Joe and Carlotta (Flores) Montoya; m. Carlos Donaciano Rael, Aug. 26, 1988; 1 child, Joshua Alan. BA, U. N.Mex., 1988. Exec. analyst Dept. Fin. and Adminstrn., Santa Fe, 1988-91; adminstrv. svcs. dir. N.Mex. State Treas. Office, Santa Fe, 1991, state cash mgr., 1992—. Mem. Mex. Am. Womens Nat. Assn. Office: NMex State Treas Office PO Box 608 Albuquerque NM 87504

MONTROSE, DONALD W., bishop; b. Denver, May 13, 1923. Student, St. John's Sem., Calif. Ordained priest Roman Cath. Ch., 1949. Aux. bishop Roman Cath. Ch., Los Angeles, 1983; bishop Diocese of Stockton, Calif., 1985—. Office: Diocese of Stockton PO Box 4237 1105 N Lincoln St Stockton CA 95204*

MONTROSE, JAMES KARL, communications technologist; b. Denver, Dec. 24, 1954; s. Karl D. and Marjorie (Addison) M. BSEE, U. Colo., 1977; MSEE, Washington U., St. Louis, 1978; MBA, Stanford U., 1989. Jr. engr. Nat. Bur. Standards, Boulder, Colo., 1975-78; rsch. assoc. Biomed. Computer Lab., St. Louis, 1978; sr. engr. Codex Corp. (Motorola), Canton, Mass., 1979-83; founder, dir. product devel. Chipcom Corp., Northboro, Mass., 1983-87; assoc. strategic planning LSI Logic Corp., Milpitas, Calif., 1988-89; dir. internat. ops. Telebit Corp., Sunnyside, Calif., 1989-90; owner, prin. Montrose Assocs., Redwood City, Calif., 1990—; adj. tchr. Northeastern U., Needham, Mass., 1981-83; rsch. asst. Washington U. St. Louis, 1978-79. Mem. IEEE (chmn. 1986-87, cert. of accomplishment 1989), Eta Kappa Nu. Home and Office: 1911 Roosevelt Ave Redwood City CA 94061

MOOD, JOHN, writer; b. Nocona, Tex., July 29, 1932; s. Francis A. and Emily (Jordan) M.; m. Ann Hardin, May 22, 1952 (div. 1971); 5 children; m. Stephanie Lindemann Eble, May 3, 1974. BA, Southwestern U., 1953; MTh, So. Meth. U., 1956; PhD, Drew U., 1969. Asst. min. Chickasha (Okla.) Meth. Ch., 1956-57; dir. Ole Miss. Wesley Found., Oxford, 1957-58; child welfare worker Okla. Dept. of Welfare, Oklahoma City, 1958-60; min. Frenchtown (N.J.) Meth. Ch., 1960-63; instr. liberal arts Trenton (N.J.) Jr. Coll., 1963-66; prof. humanities Ill. Wesleyan U., Bloomington, Ill., 1966-68; prof. English Ball State U., Muncie, Ind., 1968-73. Author: Rilke on Love and Other Difficulties, 1975, The Descent into the Self, 1969; contbr. more than 300 articles to profl. jours.; freelance press credentials to Jet Propulsion Lab., NASA, to Edwards AFB. Vice chair San Diego County Dems. for Gore Vidal for U.S. Senator, 1982. Home: 4812 1/2 Del Mar Ave San Diego CA 92107 Office: PO Box 7905 San Diego CA 92167

MOODY, CHARLES RUSSELL, medical sales and marketing professional; b. Phoenix, Oct. 16, 1956; s. Dean Dalby and Barbara Ann (Peabody) M.; m. Barbie Lynne Gercke, Sept. 21, 1979; children: Nicole, Charles, Chelsea, Alexandria. Student, U.S. Naval Acad., 1974-76, Ariz. State U., 1976-79. Consumer sales Procter & Gamble Dist. Co., Cin., 1979-81; unit mgr. Procter & Gamble Dist. Co., Phoenix, 1981-83; med. sales Johnson & Johnson, Phoenix, 1983—. Pres. Intrafraternity Coun., 1978-79; dep. registrar Maricopa County (Ariz.) Voter Registration, 1987—; precinct capt. Maricopa County Democrats, Phoenix, 1987—; chmn. bd. Children in Need Found., Phoenix, 1988—; big brother Valley Big Bros., Phoenix, 1976-79; mem. Semper Fidelis Soc., Annapolis, 1975-76; mem. Active 20/30 Internat., 1983-89 (Man of Yr. 1987), pres. Phoenix #99, 1986-87 (Regular Man of Yr. 1987); nat. pres. Active 20/30 U.S. & Can., 1987-88 (Best Nat. Pres. 1987-88); Am. regional chmn. World Coun., 1988-89. With USN 1974-76. Mem. Am. Legion, Sigma Phi Epsilon. Democrat. Episcopalian.

MOODY, DAVID EDWARD, toxicologist, educator; b. Oak Lawn, Ill., Mar. 30, 1950; s. John Edward and Marcia May (Lininger) M.; m. Peggy Ann Harmon, May 20, 1972; 1 child, Anna Renee. BA in Chemistry, U. Kans., 1972; PhD in Exptl. Pathology, U. Kans. Med. Ctr., 1977. Postdoctoral fellow dept. pathology U. Calif. Sch. Medicine, San Francisco, 1977-80, rsch. asst. scientist, 1980-82; rsch. asst. scientist depts. entomology, environ. toxicology U. Calif., Davis, 1982-86; assoc. dir. U. Utah, Ctr. Human Toxicology, Salt Lake City, 1986—; rsch. asst. prof. dept. pharmacology and toxicology U. Utah, Salt Lake City, 1986-89, rsch. assoc. prof., 1989—. Contbr. articles to profl. jours. Patroller Nat. Ski Patrol Assn., Heavenly Valley, Calif., 1979-86. Gianini Fund fellow Bank of Am., 1977-78; Monsanto Fund fellow in toxicology, San Francisco, 1978-80; grantee Nat. Inst. Drug Abuse, 1988—. Mem. Am. Assn. Pathologists, Soc. Toxicology, Soc. Forensic Toxicology, Calif. Assn. Toxicologists. Office: U Utah Ctr Human Toxicology 417 Wakara Way Rm 290 Salt Lake City UT 84108-1255

MOODY, MICHAEL JAY, investment counselor, stock market analyst; b. Billings, Mont., May 22, 1958; s. William James and Marlene Adeline (Amdor) M.; m. Jennifer Lenore Hinman, Sept. 7, 1985; 1 child, Neil William. BA in Psychology and English, Pitzer Coll., Claremont, Calif., 1980. Investment exec. Merrill Lynch, N.Y.C., 1984-86, Smith Barney, Harris Upham & Co., L.A., 1987—. Contbr. articles to profl. jours. Team mem. YMCA Ptnrs. Campaign, L.A., 1989. Recipient 5th pl. U.S. Trading Championship futures div. Fin. Traders Assn., L.A., 1989; Bishop John Fletcher Hurst doctoral fellow Am. U., Washington, 1982-83. Mem. Am. Mensa, Market Technicians Assn. (chartered, bd. dirs. 1990—, chmn. libr. com., editor jour.), Tech. Analysts So. Calif. (bd. dirs. 1989—, pres. 1990). Home: 617 Purdue Dr Claremont CA 91711 Office: Smith Barney Harris Upham & Co 333 S Grand Ave Bldg 5200 Los Angeles CA 90071

MOOERS, DOUGLAS FRANCIS, mathematics educator; b. L.A., Jan. 15, 1949; s. Douglas Francis and Viola M. AA in Math., Santa Monica (Calif.) Coll., 1969; BA in Pub. Svc./Polit. Sci., UCLA, 1971; BA in Math., San Diego State U., 1975; MA in Curriculum & Instrn., U. Calif.-Davis, 1986. Cert. tchr., Calif., Iowa, Wash. Tchr. San Diego Unified Sch. Dist., 1975-76, Sweetwater Sch. Dist., Chula Vista, Calif., 1975-76; dept. chmn. math and computer programming Bishop Garcia Diego High Sch., Santa Barbara, 1976-81; instr., teaching asst. math. U. Calif.-Davis, 1981-83; math. and microcomputer instr. Kirkwood Community Coll., Cedar Rapids, Iowa, 1983-85; math. instr. Iowa City (Iowa) pub. schs., 1984-85; math. substitute Bellingham and Ferndale (Wash.) Schs., 1985-86; math. instr., math. lab. coord. Whatcom Community Coll., Bellingham, 1986—; co-coord. math tour England, Skagit Valley Coll. and Whatcom C.C., 1988—; instr. Whatcom C.C., designer math history honors seminar; lectr. in field. Producer 200 math videos. Active Ret. Sr. Vol. Prog., 1986—, Soviet visitation, 1988-90, others. Recipient award of excellence, 1993, Am. Fedn. of Tchrs. AFL-CIO, 1993, Wash. Fedn. of Tchrs, 1993; IDEA grantee, 1986-88. Mem. Am. Math. Assn. of 2 Yr. Colls., Math. Assn. Am., Nat. Coun. Tchrs. Math., Wash. Math. Assn. of 2 Yr. Colls., Wash. State Math. Coun. Home: 1320 Lakeway Dr Apt 104 Bellingham WA 98226-2004 Office: Whatcom Community Coll 237 W Kellogg Rd Bellingham WA 98226-8003

MOON, DANNY RAY, wholesale/retail business owner; b. Lakeview, Oreg., Oct. 1, 1947; s. Glen Everett Moon and Rose Marie (Clemens) Beneski; m. Hazel Marie Skaggs, Oct. 10, 1967. Diploma, Centennial High Sch., Gresham, Oreg., 1965. Security patrolman Bay Area Pvt. Police, St. Petersburg, Fla., 1980-81; capt. patrol div. Chaparral Security Police, Phoenix, 1981-83; telemktg. mgr. Comml. Comms., Inc., Oklahoma City, 1983-85, Am. Frozen Foods, Clearwater, Fla., 1986-87, Export Financing Svcs., Vancouver, Wash., 1988-89; corp. telemktg. dir. N.Mex. Telephone Exch., Albuquerque, 1985-86; sales mgr. Media Mktg. Group, Clearwater, 1987; promotions dir. N.W. Lustrecraft, Portland, Oreg., 1989-90; owner, pres. Gold Star Mktg. Group, Portland, 1990—; promotions dir. Nat. Missing Children's Locate Ctr., Portland, 1992—. Phone bank vol. M.D.A., Portland, 1991; fundraiser Fraternal Order Police, Oklahoma City, 1984, Jr. C. of C., Phoenix, 1982. Home and Office: 1020 SE 190th Portland OR 97233-5938

MOON, JOHN SCAFA, religious organization executive, evangelist; b. Kennewick, Wash., June 8, 1960; s. Lantha Scafa and Terry (Lee) Moon; m. Shari Lynn Schoessler, Aug. 18, 1984; children: Jonathan Christopher, Stephanie Grace. BA in Econs., Wash. State U., 1984. Sales assoc. Kinney's Stores, Moscow, Idaho, 1984-85, Coldwell Banker Beasley Realty, Pullman, Wash., 1985-87; campus evangelist Maranatha Campus Ministries, Pullman, 1987-90; pres., evangelist Lord of All Ministries, Woodinville, Wash., 1990—; Apostolic cons. Vashon (Wash.) Christian Fellowship, 1990. Missionary evangelist Maranatha Campus Ministries, N.Z., 1989, Lord of All Ministries, Poland, 1990, Scotland, 1990, 91, Denmark, 1991, 92, 99, France, 1991, 92, USA, 1991, Can., 1991, Nethrlands, 1992, Germany, 1992, Guatemala, 1992. Mem. Ministerial Fellowship of U.S.A. Republican. Office: Lord of All Ministries PO Box 3003 Woodinville WA 98072-3003

MOON, JOHN WESLEY, mathematics educator; b. Hornel, N.Y., Mar. 27, 1940; s. Wesley G. and Blanche R. (Gage) M. BA, Bethany Nazarene Coll., 1959; MA, Mich. State U., 1960; PhD, U. Alberta, Edmonton, Can., 1962. Postdoctoral fellow U. Coll., London, 1962-64; asst. prof. U. Alta., 1964-66, assoc. prof., 1966-69, prof., 1970—. Author: Topics on Tournaments, 1968, Counting Labelled Trees, 1970. Mem. Am. Math. Soc., Can. Math. Soc. (treas. 1975-77, 80-82). Office: U Alberta, Dept Math, Edmonton, AB Canada T6G 2G1

MOON, RONALD T. Y., chief justice; b. Sept. 4, 1940; m. Stella H. Moon. B in Psychology and Sociology, Coe Coll., 1962; JD, U. Iowa, 1965. Bailiff, law clk. to Chief Judge Martin Pence U.S. Dist. Ct., 1965-66; dep. prosecutor City and County of Honolulu, 1966-68; assoc. Libkuman, Ventura, Ayabe, Chong & Nishimoto (predecessor firm Libkuman, Ventura, Moon & Ayabe), Honolulu, 1968-72, ptnr., 1972-82; judge 9th div. 1st cir., Cir. Ct., State of Hawaii, Honolulu, 1982-90; assoc. justice Supreme Ct., State of Hawaii, Honolulu, 1990-93; chief justice, 1993—; adj. prof. U. Hawaii. 1986, 87, 88; mem. cir. ct. rules com., 1983-89, supreme ct. com. on jud. administration, 1987, com. to study and report on lawyer professionalism in Hawaii, 1988; apptd. to ct. annexed arbitration program com., 1985-90; apptd. chairperson of study for judiciary's automation application transfer team, 1985; apptd. arbitration judge 1st cir. cir. ct., 1986-90; apptd. to bd. advisors Ctr. for Alternative Dispute Resolution, 1989; chairperson jud. arbitration commn., 1986-90; co-chairperson exec. com. on tech./info. mgmt., 1988—; source person jud. selection commn., 1989; lectr. and guest speaker numerous events. Mem. ABA, Hawaii Bar Assn., Assn. Trial Lawyers Am., Am. Bd. Trial Advocates (pres. 1986—, nat. sec. 1989—), Am. Inn of Cts. IV (bencher 1983—), Am. Judicature Soc., Hawaii State Trial Judges' Assn. (mem. seminar orgn. com. 1987, exec. com. 1985-90, liaison supreme ct. 1990—). Office: Supreme Ct Hawaii PO Box 2560 Honolulu HI 96813

MOONEY, HAROLD ALFRED, plant ecologist; b. Santa Rosa, Calif., June 1, 1932; s. Harold Walter and Sylvia Anita Stefany; m. Sherry Lynn Gulmon, Aug. 15, 1974; children—Adria, Alyssa, Arica. A.B., U. Calif., Santa Barbara, 1957; M.A., Duke U., 1958, Ph.D., 1960. From instr. to assoc. prof. UCLA, 1960-68; asso. prof. Stanford U., 1968-73, prof. biology, 1975—, Paul S. Achilles prof. environ. biology, 1976—; adviser NRC, Dept. Energy, NSF, Electric Power Research Inst., Ford Found. Author: Mediterranean-type Ecosystems, 1973, Convergent Evolution in Chile and California, 1977, Components of Productivity of Mediterranean Climate Regions, 1981; Disturbance in Ecosystems, 1983, Physiological of Plants in the Wet Tropics, 1984, Physiological Ecology of North American Plant Communities, 1985, Ecology of Biological Invasions of North America and Hawaii, 1986, Biological Invasions, A Global Perspective, 1989. Served with

AUS, 1953-55. Recipient Humboldt award, 1989; Guggenheim fellow, 1974; Nat. Acad. Scis. fellow, 1982. Fellow AAAS; mem. Ecol. Soc. Am. (Mercer award 1961), Brit. Ecol. Soc. Home: 2625 Ramona St Palo Alto CA 94306-2315 Office: Stanford U Dept of Biol Sci 459 Herrin Lab Stanford CA 94305

MOONEY, JEROME HENRI, lawyer; b. Salt Lake City, Aug. 7, 1944; s. Jerome Henri and Bonnie (Shepherd) M.; m. Carolyn Lasrich, Aug. 10, 1965 (div. Dec. 1978); 1 child, Dierdre Nicole; m. Catherine Lee, May 3, 1986. BS, U. Utah, 1966, JD, 1972. Bar: Utah 1972, U.S. Ct. Appeals (10th cir.) 1974, U.S. Supreme 1984. Sole practice Salt Lake City, 1972-75, 79-83; sr. ptnr. Mooney, Jorgenson & Nakamura, Salt Lake City, 1975-78, Mooney & Smith, Salt Lake City, 1983-87, Mooney & Assocs., Salt Lake City, 1987—; bd. dirs. Mooney Real Estate, Salt Lake City. Mem. Gov.'s Council on Vet. Affairs, Salt Lake City, 1982-89; trustee Project Realty, Salt Lake City, 1976—. Served to capt. U.S. Army, 1966-69, Vietnam, col. Utah NG, 1969—. Mem. ABA (criminal justice sect. U.S. Sentencing Commn. com.), Utah Bar Assn. (chmn. criminal bar sect. 1987-88), Utah NG Assn. (trustee 1976), 1st Amendment Lawyers Assn. (v.p. 1986-88, pres. 1988-89), Nat. Assn. Criminal Def. Lawyers, VFW. Democrat. Jewish. Home: 128 I St Salt Lake City UT 84103-3418 Office: Mooney & Assocs 236 S 300 E Salt Lake City UT 84111-2502

MOONEY, PATRICIA KATHRYN, business owner; b. Galesburg, Ill., July 1, 1955; d. Joseph Edmond and Magi (Richard) M.; m. Mark Levon Schulze, July 23, 1987. Student, Mich. State U., 1973-75, Mueller Coll. of Massage, San Diego, 1980. Cert. massage therapist. Office mgr. REGAIN, San Diego, 1977-81; pvt. practice massage therapy San Diego, 1981-82; owner, pres. A-Action Profl. Typing, San Diego, 1983-86; co-owner, v.p. Crystal Pyramid Prodns., San Diego, 1982—, New and Unique Videos, San Diego, 1985—; office coord. Svc. Employees Internat. Union Local 535, San Diego, 1987—. Author (video script) Ultimate Mountain Biking, 1989, Great Mountain Biking, Battle at Durango, Massage for Relaxation; co-author (video script) John Howard's Lessons in Cycling, 1991. Treas. Evonne Schulze for Coll. Bd., San Diego, 1988—, Coalition of Labor Union Women, San Diego, 1990-92; vol. Lynn Schenk for Congress, San Diego, 1992. Recipient 1st place San Diego Reader, 1978, 1st place poetry Calif. Press Women, 1979, N.Y. Film and TV Festival, 1990, 92, Silver Telly, 1990, 92, Silver medal Houston Internat. Film and TV, 1993. Mem. Mountain Bike Patrol Unit-Cuyamaca Rancho State Park, Nat. Off-Road Bicycle Assn., Planned Parenthood, Cousteau Soc., ACLU. Democrat. Home: 2336 Sumac Dr San Diego CA 92105

MOONEY, WALTER DOHERTY, geophysicist, educator; b. Floral Park, N.Y., Nov. 17, 1951; s. Vincent John and Martha Bowers (Doherty) M.; m. Josephine Anne Gandolfi, Nov. 2, 1977. BS, Cornell U., 1973; PhD, U. Wis., 1979. Rsch. geophysicist, project chief crustal studies U.S. Geological Survey, Menlo Park, Calif., 1978—; consulting prof. Stanford (Calif.) U., 1984—; bd. dirs. and standing com. Incorp. Rsch. Insts. for Seismology, Arlington, Va., 1985-89; vis. prof. U. Kiel, Germany, 1988; bd. dirs. Lithoprobe Can., Vancouver, B.C., 1991—. Editor: Geophysical Framework U.S.A., 1989; contbr. numerous articles to profl. jours. Fellow Geol. Soc. Am.; mem. Am. Geophys. Union, Seismol. Soc. Am., Sigma Xi. Office: US Geol Survey 345 Middlefield Rd MS 977 Menlo Park CA 94025

MOOR, WILLIAM CHATTLE, industrial engineering educator; b. St. Louis, Jan. 17, 1941; s. William A. and M. Carmen (Cross) M.; m. Marilyn E. Nichols, Sept. 19, 1964; children: Kathryn E., William E. BS in Indsl. Engring., Washington U., St. Louis, 1963, MS, 1965; PhD, Northwestern U., 1969. Indsl. engr. GSA, St. Louis, 1963-64; assoc. prof. Ariz. State U., Tempe, 1968—. Contbr. articles to profl. jours. Bd. dirs. Mesa (Ariz.) Bowling Assn., 1977-80, 89—. Mem. Inst. Indsl. Engrs. (sr. dir. for R&D Atlanta 1973-75), Am. Soc. for Engring. Mgmt. (charter) Am. Soc. for Engring. Edn. Methodist. Office: Ariz State U Dept Indsl Engring Tempe AZ 85287-5906

MOORE, BENJAMIN, theatrical producer; b. Boston, Oct. 25, 1945; s. Charles Frederick and Adeline Reeves (Nichols) M.; m. Mary Bradford Paine, May 31, 1969 (div. Jan. 1982); children: Alexandra Paine, Brendan Adams; m. Barbara Ann Dirickson, June 25, 1983; children: Lillian, Richard Braden. BA, Dartmouth U., 1967; MFA, Yale U., 1970. Asst. mng. dir. Yale Repertory Theatre, New Haven, 1969-70; gen. mgr. Westport (Conn.) Country Playhouse, 1970; prodn. dir. Am. Conservatory Theatre, San Francisco, 1970-79, gen. mgr., 1979-81, mng. dir., 1981-85; mng. dir., bd. dirs. Seattle Repertory Theatre, 1985—. Active Seattle Arts Commn., 1986-90, chair, 1989. Mem. Wash. State Arts Alliance (bd. dirs. 1985—), League Resident Theatres (mem. exec. com. 1986—), Rainier Club. Office: Seattle Repertory Theatre 155 Mercer St Seattle WA 98109-4639

MOORE, BEVERLY ANN, librarian; b. Evanston, Wyo., Mar. 17, 1934; d. James H. and Louise M. (Miller) Barrett; m. James O. Moore, Oct. 6, 1957 (div. 1966); children: Louis Barrett, Ann Louise Cushman. AA, Hutchinson (Kans.) Jr. Coll., 1954; BA, U. No. Colo., 1957; MA in Libr. Sci., Denver U., 1970. Br. libr. Pueblo (Colo.) Libr. Dist., 1966-70; documents libr. U. So. Colo., Pueblo, 1970-74, head cataloger, 1974-76, libr. dir., 1976—. Editor: Colo. Academic Libr. Master Plan, 1988. Mem. ALA, Pueblo AAUW, Colo. AAUW (coll. and univ. rep.), Colo. Libr. Assn. (pres. 1985), Colo. Acad. Libr. Com., Pueblo LWV, Colo. Women in Higher Edn. Adminstrn. (state coord. 1990-92), Beta Phi Mu. Democrat. Congregationalist. Office: U So Colo 2200 Bonforte Blvd Pueblo CO 81001-4901

MOORE, C. BRADLEY, chemistry educator; b. Boston, Dec. 7, 1939; s. Charles Walden and Dorothy (Lutz) M.; m. Penelope Williamson Percival, Aug. 27, 1960; children—Megan Bradley, Scott Woodward. B.A. magna cum laude, Harvard U., 1960; Ph.D., U. Calif., Berkeley, 1963. Asst. prof. chemistry U. Calif., Berkeley, 1963-68, assoc. prof., 1968-72, prof., 1972—, vice chmn. dept., 1971-75, chmn. dept. chemistry, 1982-86, dean Coll. of Chemistry, 1988—; professeur associé Faculté des Scis., Paris, 1970, 75; vis. prof. Inst. for Molecular Sci., Okazaki, Japan, 1979; adv. prof. Fudan U., Shanghai, 1988—, Peoples Republic China, 1979; vis. fellow Joint Inst. for Lab. Astrophysics, U. Colo., Boulder, 1981-82; adv. prof. Fudan U., Shanghai, 1988—; mem. editorial bd. Jour. Chemical Physics, 1973-75, Chemical Physics Letters, 1980-85, Jour. Physical Chem., 1981-87, Laser Chemistry, 1982—. Editor: Chemical and Biochemical Applications of Lasers; assoc. editor Annual Review of Physical Chemistry, 1985-90; contbr. articles to profl. jours. Fellow Alfred P. Sloan Found., 1968, Guggenheim Found., 1969; Harvard Nat. scholar, 1958-60; recipient Coblentz award, 1973, E.O. Lawrence Meml. award, U.S. Dept. of Energy, 1986, Lippincott award, 1987, 1st Inter-Am. Photochem. Soc. award., 1988. Fellow Am. Phys. Soc., AAAS; mem. NAS (chmn. com Undergraduate Sci. Edn.), Am. Chem. Soc. (past chmn. div. phys. chemistry, Calif. sect. award 1977), Coun. for Chem. Rsch. (gov. bd.), Indsl. rsch. Inst. (acad. adv. coun.). Home: 936 Oxford St Berkeley CA 94707-2435 Office: U Calif Dept Chemistry 211 Lewis Hall Berkeley CA 94720

MOORE, CARLETON BRYANT, geochemistry educator; b. N.Y.C., Sept. 1, 1932; s. Eldridge Carleton and Mabel Florence (Drake) M.; m. Jane Elizabeth Strouse, July 25, 1959; children—Barbara Jeanne, Robert Carleton. B.S., Alfred U., 1954, D.Sc. (hon.), 1977; Ph.D., Cal. Inst. Tech., 1960. Asst. prof. geology Wesleyan U., Middletown, Conn., 1959-61; mem. faculty Ariz. State U., Tempe, 1961—; prof., dir. Ctr. for Meteorite Studies Ariz. State U., Regents' prof., 1988—; vis. prof. Stanford U., 1974; Prin. investigator Apollo 11-17; preliminary exam. team Lunar Receiving Lab., Apollo, 12-17. Author: Cosmic Debris, 1969, Meteorites, 1971, Principles of Geochemistry, 1982, Grundzügeder Geochemie, 1985; editor: Researches on Meteorites, 1961, Jour. Meteoritical Soc.; contbr. articles to profl. jours. Fellow Ariz.-Nev. Acad. Sci. (pres. 1979-80), Meteoritical Soc. (life hon., pres. 1966-68), Geol. Soc. Am., Mineral. Soc. Am., AAAS (council 1967-70); mem. Geochem. Soc., Am. Chem. Soc., Am. Ceramic Soc., Sigma Xi. Home: 507 E Del Rio Dr Tempe AZ 85282-3764 Office: Ariz State U Ctr for Meteorite Studies Tempe AZ 85287

MOORE, CHARLES AUGUST, JR., psychologist; b. Medford, Oreg., Feb. 22, 1944; s. Charles August and Bernadine (Newlun) M. BS, Lewis and Clark Coll., 1965; MA, U. Colo., 1967, PhD, 1972. Lic. psychologist, Calif., Oreg. Teaching asst. U. Colo., Boulder, 1965-66, 70-71, rsch. asst., counselor, practicum supr., 1966-67, 71-72; asst. psychologist State Home and Tng. Sch., Grand Junction, Colo., 1967; intern in psychology Camarillo (Calif.) State Hosp., 1968-69; psychology assoc., program psychologist Camarillo Drug Abuse Program (The Family), 1969-70; intern in psychology Oxnard (Calif.) Mental Health Ctr., 1969; clin. psychologist, dir. intern tng. Rural Clinics, Reno, 1972; clin. psychologist Kern County Mental Health Svcs., Bakersfield, Calif., 1972-74; clin., cons. psychologist San Diego County Mental Health Svcs., 1974-88; pvt. practice La Jolla (Calif.) Clinic, 1976-78; August Ctr., Chula Vista, Calif., 1978-85; staff psychologist Dept. Vet.'s Affairs Domiciliary, White City, Oreg., 1988—; guest lectr. Calif. State Coll., Bakersfield, 1973-74; mem. Health Systems Agy. Mental Health Task Force, 1979; mem. doctoral dissertation com. U.S. Internat. U., 1975-76; mem. mental health task force San Diego County Bd. Suprs., 1979. Contbr. articles to profl. jours. Mem. Univ. City Community Coun., San Diego, 1976-78; bd. dirs. Pub. Employees Assn., 1976-77. Recipient Experiment in Internat. Living European Study award Lewis and Clark Coll., 1962; USPHS fellow, 1967-68; U. Colo. Grad. Sch. Rsch. grantee, 1971; recipient Hands and Heart award Dept. Vets. Affairs, 1989-90, Domiciliary Spl. Contbn. and Outstanding Performance awards, 1990, 91. Mem. APA, Am. Psychology and Law Soc., Calif. Psychol. Assn., Western Psychol. Assn., San Diego County Psychol. Assn., Assn. County Clin. Psychologists San Diego, San Diego Psychology and Law Soc., San Diego Soc. Clin. Psychologists. Office: Dept VA Domiciliary Psychology Svc 8495 Crater Lake Hwy White City OR 97503

MOORE, DAN STERLING, insurance executive, sales trainer; b. Lincoln, Nebr., June 27, 1956; s. Jack Leroy and Carolyn Marie (Bachman) M.; m. Marla Janine Collister, June 2, 1979; children: Tyler David, Anna Rose. Student, Red Rocks Coll., 1977. Lic. ins. exec. Asst. mgr. European Health Spa, Englewood, Colo., 1975-78; sales mgr. Colo. Nat. Homes, Westminster, 1979-80; sales assoc. Dale Carnegie, Denver, 1981; sales mgr. Paramount Fabrics, Denver, 1981-84; sales assoc. Mighty Distbg., Arvada, Colo., 1984-87; regional dir. Nat. Assn. for Self Employed/United Group Assn., Englewood, Colo., 1987—. Leader, trainer Alpine Rescue Team, Evergreen, Colo., 1971-74; minister Jehovah's Witnesses, 1972—. Home: 892 Nob Hill Dr Franktown CO 80116 Office: Nat Assn Self Employed/United Group 6855 S Havana St Ste # 300 Englewood CO 80112

MOORE, DANIEL ALTON, JR., state supreme court justice; b. 1933. BBA, U. Notre Dame, 1955; JD, U. Denver, 1961. Dist. ct. magistrate judge Alaska, 1961-62; pvt. practice law, 1962-80; judge 3d Jud. Dist. Superior Ct., 1980-83; justice Alaska Supreme Ct., Anchorage, 1983-92, chief justice, 1992—. Office: Alaska Supreme Ct 303 K St Anchorage AK 99501-2013

MOORE, DAVID AUSTIN, pharmaceutical company executive, consultant; b. Phoenix, May 8, 1935; s. Harry Theodore and Helen Ann (Newport) M.; m. Emily J. McConnell, Jan. 26, 1991; children by previous marriage: Austin Newport, Cornelia Christina, Christopher Robinson. Grad. high sch., Glendale, Ariz.; study opera and voice with Joseph Lazzarini, 1954, 55, 57-64; studies with Joseph Lazzarini, U.S., 1954-55, 57-64; studied opera and voice, Italy, 1955-56; study with Clarence Loomis, 1958-60. Pres., owner David A. Moore, Inc., Phoenix, 1969-71, Biol. Labs. Ltd., Phoenix, 1972-78; pres., co-owner Am. Trace Mineral Rsch. Corp., Phoenix, 1979-83; pres., owner Biol. Mineral Scis., Ltd., Phoenix, 1979-82; rsch. dir., pres., owner Nutritional Biols. Inc., Phoenix, 1979-83; nutritional dir.-owner Nutritional Biol. Rsch. Co., Phoenix, 1984-85; rsch. dir., product formulator, owner Nutrition and Med. Rsch., Scottsdale, Ariz., 1986—; biochem. cons. Nutripathic Formulas, Scottsdale, 1975-88; introduced di Calcium Phosphate free concept and 100 percent label disclosure, 1979-83. Pub. NMR Newsletter. Inventor first computerized comprehensive hair analysis interpretation, 1976. Recipient Plaque Am. Soc. Med. Techs., 1982, Mineralab Inc., 1976. Home and Office: PO Box 98 Barnesboro PA 15714

MOORE, DAVID LEWIS, trade association executive; b. Arvin, Calif., Aug. 22, 1931; s. John Chessher and Bonnie (Carter) M.; m. Priscella Jane Martin, Aug. 1, 1953; children: John, Leslie, David, Elizabeth, Andrew. BS, U. So. Calif., 1954. Owner, operator White Wolf Potato Co., 1956-87; chmn. Western Growers Assn., Irvine, Calif., 1984-87, pres., chief exec. officer, 1987—; appointed Fed. Res. Bd., 1992; mem. Coun. on Calif. Competitiveness, 1992, Sweet Potato Whitefly Adv. Panel, 1991, Eximbank Adv. Com., 1990—, Agrl. Policy Adv. Com. for Trade, 1987—, Calif. Econ. Devel. Corp., 1987—, Calif. Fgn. Market Devel. Export Incentive Com., 1986-87, Kern County Water Resources Bd., 1978-87; pres. Arvin Co-op Gin, 1968-75, Arvin-Edison Water Storage Dist., 1971-87; vice chmn. Cal-Cot, 1971-76; mem. exec. com. Ranchers Cotton Oil, 1971-76. Former vestryman St. Paul's Episc. Ch., Bakersfield, Calif.; trustee Bakersfield Coll. Found., 1986-87; founder presdl. assocs. U. So. Calif., L.A. Capt. USAF, 1954-56. Republican. Home: 4507 Roxbury Rd Corona Del Mar CA 92625 Office: Western Growers Assn 17620 Fitch St Irvine CA 92714

MOORE, DAVID MARKLEY, software company executive; b. Seattle, Sept. 13, 1954; s. John Westley and Helen Ramona (Blanton) M.; m. Jacquelyn Theresa, Jan. 17, 1980; children: Michelle Marie, Michael Thomas. Student, U. Wash., 1976. Group lead Boeing, Seattle, 1979-81; software design engr. Microsoft, Redmond, Wash., 1981-82, devel. lead, 1982-83, assoc. dir. devel., 1984-87, dir. devel., 1988—; testing mgr. Microsoft, Redmond, 1985-87, dir. testing, 1990—; bd. dirs. Baycrest Industries, Woodinville, Wash. Developer (PC software) Multiplan; devel. mgr. (PC software) MS Word, MS Chart, MS Works. Mem. Am. Soc. for Quality Control, Aircraft Owners and Pilot Assn. Office: Microsoft 1 Microsoft Way Redmond CA 98052-6399

MOORE, DERRITH RACHELLE, environmental specialist; b. Flagstaff, Ariz., Feb. 5, 1964; d. Leo Chester Sr. and Pauline Mae (Yellowhair) Watchman; m. Henry Kee Moore, June 12, 1992; children: Chantal, Callan, Cheyenne. BS in Animal Sci., Colo. State U., 1986. Extension agt. The Navajo Nation Dept. Agrl., Window Rock, Ariz., 1988; environ. specialist The Navajo Nation, EPA, Window Rock, 1988-92; asst. dir., site assessment mgr. all Indian Pueblo coun. Pueblo Office Environ. Protection, Albuquerque, 1992—. Recipient scholarship Am. Indian Sci. and Engring. Soc., Boulder, Colo., 1984; named Outstanding Young Women of Am., 1988. Democrat. Roman Catholic. Home: PO Box 207 Navajo NM 87328 Office: Pueblo Office Environ Protection Po Box 3256 Albuquerque NM 87190

MOORE, DIANNE LEA, recording studio owner; b. North Tonawanda, N.Y., Jan. 30, 1949; d. Donald Robert and Dorothy (Ghise) Wilke; m. William Lewis Tremont, Aug. 21, 1966 (div. Apr. 1973); children: Eric, Michelle; m. Allen Charles Moore, July 11, 1981. AA, Scottsdale Community Coll., 1978; student, Ariz. State U., 1978-81. Powder paint troubleshooter McGraw Edison, Phoenix, 1980-81; v.p., mgr. Cereus Recording, Tempe, Ariz., 1981—; adminstrv. asst. McKesson, Phoenix, 1982-83; owner, mgr. Cereus Letter Processing, Tempe, 1983-93. Mem. Soc. Profl. Audio Recording Svcs., Nat. Fedn. Ind. Businessmen, Better Bus. Bur., Ariz. Road Racers. Democrat. Office: Cereus Letter Processing 1733 E McKellips Ste 107 Tempe AZ 85281

MOORE, DONALD WALTER, educator; b. Culver City, Calif., June 9, 1942; s. Raymond Owen amd Jewel Elizabeth (Young) M.; m. Dagmar Ulbrich, Mar. 28, 1968; 1 child, Michael. AA, L.A. Valley Coll., 1967; BA in History, Calif. State U., Northridge, 1970; MA in Learning Disability, Calif. State U., 1973; MLS, U. So. Calif., 1974. Part time librarian L.A. Pierce Coll., Woodland Hills, Calif., 1974—; instr. vocat. edn. act program L.A. Trade Tech. Coll., 1978-80, pres.'s staff asst., 1983-87; instr. learning skills L.A. City Coll., 1987-88, dir. amnesty edn., 1988—. Author: Cavalrymen, 1983; contbr. fiction, articles, revs. to various publs. Mem. Ednl. Writers Am., Co. Mil. Historians, Nat. Indian Wars Assn., Little Big Horn Assn. Republican. Roman Catholic. Office: Amnesty Program LA City Coll 855 N Vermont Ave Los Angeles CA 90029-3500

MOORE, DONALD WILLARD, metal products company executive, researcher; b. Keansburg, N.J., Nov. 20, 1928; s. Percy L. and Mildred M. (Webster) M.; m. Gloria Kril; children: Craig W., Dale A., Kathy Moore Arnao. Student in bus. adminstrn., Syracuse U., 1945-48. Leadman Lee Mar Wood Products, Red Bank, N.J., 1948-50; owner, operator D.W. Moore Co., Red Bank, 1950-60; plant mgr. Rebco Inc., L.A., 1960-61; dist. mgr. Rigid Metal Products, L.A., 1961-62, Borg-Warner, L.A., 1962-66; constrn. specialist Conwed Corp., St. Paul, 1966-74; mgr. western region Chgo. Metallic Corp., L.A., 1974—; seismic tester new non-structural components, 1983-90. Author: Seismic Guidelines, 1990; co-author: Uniform Building Code, 1991. Chmn. State Ski Champion Jr. C. of C., Red Bank, 1950-60. Home: 10611 Horley Ave Downey CA 90241-2105

MOORE, ELIZABETH JANE, banker; b. Long Branch, N.J., Dec. 14, 1940; d. Robert William and Ruth Elizabeth (Dunphy) Marton; m. Gerard George Moore, Mar. 3, 1962; children: Christine Marie, Stephanie Ann, Gerard Marton, Paul Henry George, Barbara Jean. BBA, U. Phoenix, 1987. Charge card specialist Valley Nat. Bank, Phoenix, 1971-74, corp. trust specialist, 1974-80; trust specialist Valley Nat. Bank, Prescott, Ariz., 1980-84, 84-86, trust adminstr., trust officer, 1986, asst. v.p., 1989-93; v.p. Bank One, Ariz., 1993—. Bd. dirs. Ctrl. Yavapai County (Ariz.) Fire Dist., 1988-89, clk., 1989—, chmn. bd., 1990-91; bd. dirs. Yavapai Humane Soc., 1989-91, 1st v.p., treas., 1990-91; bd. dirs. Vol. Firefighters Relief and Pension Fund, 1989-91; chmn. bd. dirs. Ctrl. Yavapai Pub. Safety Pers., 1991. Recipient 1st Place Photo COntest award Parade mag., 1992. Mem. Fin. Women Internat., Ariz. Assn. Legal Secs. (conv. chmn. 1986, nominations chmn. 1985-86), Yavapai County Legal Secs. Assn. (treas. 1983-85, gov. 1985-86, Legal Sec. of Yr. 1984), U. Phoenix Network for Profl. Devel. (chartered), Soroptimists. Office: Bank One Ariz Nat Advantage Trust PO Box 71 Phoenix AZ 85001-0071

MOORE, GORDON E., electronics company executive; b. San Francisco, Jan. 3, 1929; s. Walter Harold and Florence Almira (Williamson) M.; m. Betty I. Whittaker, Sept. 9, 1950; children: Kenneth, Steven. B.S. in Chemistry, U. Calif., 1950; Ph.D. in Chemistry and Physics, Calif. Inst. Tech., 1954. Mem. tech. staff Shockley Semicondr. Lab., 1956-57; mgr. engring. Fairchild Camera & Instrument Corp., 1957-59, dir. research and devel., 1959-68; exec. v.p. Intel Corp., Santa Clara, Calif., 1968-75; pres., chief exec. officer Intel Corp., 1975-79, chmn., chief exec. officer, 1979-87, chmn., 1987—; bd. dirs. Varian Assocs. Inc., Transamerica Corp. Fellow IEEE; mem. Nat. Acad. Engring., Am. Phys. Soc. Office: Intel Corp RN 2-01 2200 Mission College Blvd Santa Clara CA 95052-8119

MOORE, HAL G., mathematician, educator; b. Vernal, Utah, Aug. 14, 1929; s. Lewis Henry and Nora (Gillman) M.; m. D'On Empey, July 20, 1956; children: David, Nora, Alison. B.S., U. Utah, 1952, M.S., 1957; Ph.D., U. Calif., Santa Barbara, 1967. Tchr. Salt Lake City Public Schs., 1952-53; instr. math. Carbon Jr. Coll., also Carbon High Sch., Price, Utah, 1953-55, Purdue U., Lafayette, Ind., 1957-61; adminstrv. asst. dept. math Purdue U., 1960-61; from asst. prof. math. to assoc. prof. math. Brigham Young U., Provo, 1961-71; prof. Brigham Young U., 1971—, assoc. chmn. dept. Math., 1986-89. Author: Precalculus Mathematics, 2d edit, 1977, (with Adil Yaqub) Elementary Linear Algebra With Applications, 1980, College Algebra and Trigonometry, 1983, A First Course in Linear Algebra, 1992; contbr. articles to profl. jours. Mem. High Coun., Ch. of Jesus Christ of Latter Day Saints, 1985-91, MTC br. pres., 1991—, Bishop, 1958-61, 78-82. NSF faculty fellow U. Calif., Santa Barbara, 1964-66. Mem. Am. Math Soc., Math Assn. Am. (bd. govs. 1989-92), Utah State Math. Coalition (planning dir. 1990, bd. dirs. 1991-92), Sigma Xi (dir. 1974-80, 82-85, com. chmn. 1982-90), Phi Kappa Phi. Home: 631 W 650 S Orem UT 84058-6027 Office: 316 TMCB Brigham Young U Provo UT 84602

MOORE, JAMES COLLINS, museum director; b. Topeka, Kans., Oct. 12, 1941; s. Albert Ora and Alice Winifred (Collins) M.; m. Margaret Ruth Vasquez, Jan. 30, 1965; children—Daniela Ruth, Evan Albert. B.F.A., U. N.Mex., 1966; M.A., Ind. U., 1968, Ph.D., 1974. Asst. prof. art history Wichita State U., Kans., 1970-77; chmn. dept. art history Wichita State U., 1975-77; coordinator art history Toledo Mus. Art, Ohio, 1977-79; dir. Albuquerque Mus., 1979—; adj. curator Wichita Art Mus., Kans., 1970-77, trustee, 1975-77; adj. assoc. prof. U. Toledo, Ohio, 1977-79, U. N.Mex., Albuquerque, 1980—. Author: Harry Sternberg, 1975; also articles in field. Bd. dirs. The Albuquerque Conservation Assn., 1979-81, Albuquerque Arts Alliance, 1985. Served to sgt. Air N.G., 1963-69. Woodrow Wilson Found. fellow, 1966-67; Samuel H. Kress Found. fellow, 1968-69, 1969-70, grantee, 1971. Mem. Am. Assn. Mus. Lodge: Rotary. Office: Albuquerque Mus PO Box 458 Albuquerque NM 87103-1293

MOORE, JAMES RICHARD, manufacturing engineer; b. Flint, Mich., Apr. 7, 1955; s. Richard and Cathrine (Paulen) M.; children: Sarah, Amy, Timothy. AAS, Spartan Sch. Aeronautics, Tulsa, 1983; BS in Mgmt., Western Internat. U., 1988, MBA, 1990. Mfg. methods engr. McDonnell Douglas, Tulsa, 1981-84; mfg. engr. McDonnell Douglas Helicopter Co., Mesa, Ariz., 1984-87, mfg. R&D engr., 1987-91, mfg. engr., 1991—; pres. Moore Comm. Co., Tempe, 1992—; mem. adj. faculty Embry-Riddle Aero. U., Phoenix, 1992—. Democrat. Home: 1816 E Velvet Dr Tempe AZ 85284

MOORE, JEFFREY CLYDE, construction company owner; b. Roseville, Calif., Jan. 21, 1962; s. Roy Malcolm and Ethel (Stricker) M.; m. Sherry Lyn Dripps, June 1983 (div. Dec. 1985); m. Jamie Danielle McGuire, Aug. 13, 1988; 1 child, Sean Steven. Student, Am. River Coll., 1985-87. Piece carpenter various constrn. cos., Calif., 1985-86; trencher operator Moore Bros. Trenching, Lincoln, Calif., 1986-88; owner, operator Jeff Moore Trenching, Elverta, Calif., 1988-91, Rocklin, Calif., 1991—. Home and Office: Jeff Moore Trenching 5431 Paragon Ct Rocklin CA 95677

MOORE, JERRY LUKE, regional manager; b. Nashville, Oct. 21, 1959; s. William E. Moore and Joan F. (Henshaw) Young; m. Terri Ann Ramsey, Nov. 17, 1990 (div. 1993). BBA, Murfreesboro Tenn. State U., 1984. Class A profl. golfer. Golf profl. Ormond Country Club, New Orleans, 1984-86, Stonebridge Country Club, New Orleans, 1986-87, The Olympic Cub, San Francisco, 1987-89; gen. mgr. Indian Hills Country Club, Bowling Green, Ky., 1989; mgr. Golf Corp., Dallas, 1989-90, regional mgr., 1990—; pres. PGA Apprentice Assn., New Orleans, 1981. Author: Food and Beverage Manual for Golf Corp., 1992. Mem. Nat. Golf Day Com., Anaheim, Calif., 1991, 92, C. of C., Diamond Bar, Ventura, Calif., 1991, 92. Republican. Presbyterian. Home: 236 Backs Ln Placentia CA 92670

MOORE, JOHN D., consultant; b. Mt. Pleasant, Iowa, Apr. 7, 1937; s. Burris P. and Esther I. (Copenhaver) M.; m. Karen K. Kriegel, June 19, 1957; children: Charles A., Michael J., Susan K., David J. AB, Muscatine Community Coll., 1961; BBA, Augustana Coll., 1966; postgrad. U. Iowa, 1966-68. Office mgr. Stanley Engring., Muscatine, Iowa, 1956-64; pers. mgr. Oscar Mayer & Co., Davenport and Perry, Iowa, 1964-68; Midwest regional mgr. A. S. Hansen, Lake Bluff, Ill., 1968-73; legal adminstr. Gardner, Carton & Douglas, Chgo., 1973-78, Heller Ehrman White & McAuliffe, San Francisco, 1978-84; v.p. and dir. Hildebrandt, Inc., Walnut Creek, Calif., 1984-90; pres. Moore Cons. Inc., 1990—. Pres., Libertyville (Ill.) High Sch. Bd., 1974, Libertyville Ecumenical Council, 1975; bd. dirs. Libertyville YMCA, 1969-71. Recipient Muscatine Disting. Service award, 1963; named Outstanding State V.P., Iowa Jaycees, 1964; Outstanding Nat. Dir., U.S. Jaycees, 1965. Mem. Assn. of Legal Adminstrs. (regional v.p. 1977-78, nat. v.p. 1979-81, nat. pres. 1982-83), Found. Assn. of Legal Adminstrs. (pres. 1986-88), Golden Gate Assn. Legal Adminstrs. Republican. Methodist. Home: 2632 Quiet Place Dr Walnut Creek CA 94598-4440 Office: 2632 Quiet Place Dr Walnut Creek CA 94598-4440

MOORE, JOHN PORFILIO, federal judge; b. Denver, Oct. 14, 1934; s. Edward Alphonso Porfilio and Caroline (Carbone) Moore; m. Joan West, Aug. 1, 1959 (div. 1983); children—Edward Miles, Joseph Arthur, Jeanne Kathrine; m. Theresa Louise Berger, Dec. 28, 1983; 1 stepchild, Katrina Ann Smith. Student, Stanford U., 1952-54; BA, U. Denver, 1956, LLB, 1959. Bar: Colo. 1959, U.S. Supreme Ct. 1965. Asst. atty. gen. State of Colo., Denver, 1962-68, dep. atty. gen., 1968-72, atty. gen., 1972-74; U.S. bankruptcy judge Dist. of Colo., Denver, 1975-82; judge U.S. Dist. Ct. Colo., Denver, 1982-85, U.S. Ct. Appeals (10th cir.), Denver, 1985—; instr. Colo. Law Enforcement Acad., Denver, 1965-70, State Patrol Acad., Denver, 1968-70; guest lectr. U. Denver Coll. Law, 1978. Committeeman Arapahoe County Republican Com., Aurora, Colo., 1968; mgr. Dunbar for Atty. Gen., Denver, 1970. Mem. ABA. Roman Catholic. Office: US Ct Appeals C-438 US Courthouse 1929 Stout St Denver CO 80294-2900

MOORE, JOHN SEABROOK, III, technical consultant; b. Memphis, Aug. 15, 1949; s. John Seabrook Jr. and Anita (Terazzas) M. BA in Econ. and Fin., U. Ariz., 1977; MBA, U. So. Calif., 1980; postgrad. computer sci., Calif. State U., 1990—. Avionics tech. USAF, Tex., S.E. Asia, Ariz., 1970-74; sales mgr. Coldwell Banker, L.A., 1980-82; customer svc. technician Host Internat., Santa Monica, Calif., 1983-86; JCL-COBOL programmer Lockheed ACFT, Burbank, Calif., 1986-87, Unix "C" programmer, 1987-89; freelance programmer Z0L Tech Corp., Van Nuys, Calif., 1989-90; tech. cons. O.S.I. Retix Corp., Santa Monica, 1990-93. Rep. candidate for Ariz. state senate, Dist. 10, Tucson, 1976. Sgt. USAF, 1970-74, Southeast Asia. Republican. Roman Catholic. Home: 2110 4th St # 3 Santa Monica CA 90405

MOORE, JOSEPH LAVON, city official; b. Bingham Canyon, Utah, Aug. 19, 1944; s. Lester Irvin Moore and Gladys Isabelle Pumphrey Brown; (stepfather) John P. Brown; m. Dawna Lee Schauerhamer, Aug. 20, 1969; children: Brett Joseph, Carter Jay, Travis Clark, Davis Scott, Jessica Jo, Taylor John, Tiffany Dawn. BS, U. Utah, 1969, MS, 1972. Econ. devel. planner Salt Lake Model Cities Agy., 1970-71; dir. land use econs. Wasatch Front Regional Coun., Bountiful, Utah, 1971-74; dir. planning Davis County, Farmington, Utah, 1974-80; dir. community devel. City of West Valley City, Utah, 1980—; cons. North Salt Lake City, 1977-80; teaching asst. U. Utah, 1969—. Editor: Mitigating Earthquake Hazards, 1982; co-author: Planning and Zoning Administration in Utah, 1989; contbr. articles to profl. jours. Com. mem. Utah State Legis., Salt Lake City, 1978, 80, 91; scoutmaster Boy Scouts Am., Bountiful, 1982-83, varsity team leader, 1983-89. Lt. col., dep. inspector general USAR, 1970—. U. Utah rsch. fellow, 1968-69; recipient Meritorious Svc. medal with two oak leaf clusters, Army Reserve Commendation medal with 3 oak leaf clusters. Mem. Am. Inst. Cert. Planners, Inst. Traffic Engrs., Am. Planning Assn. (Utah chpt. pres. 1979-81), , Urban Land Inst., Gamma Theta Upsilon (chpt. pres. 1969-70), Phi Kappa Phi. Republican. LDS. Home: 421 W 3300 S Bountiful UT 84010 Office: West Valley City 3600 Constitution Blvd West Valley City UT 84119-3720

MOORE, JOYCE WEST, social worker, psychotherapist; b. Anadarko, Okla., Nov. 18, 1936; d. Carl Edwin and Alma (Hunter) West; children: Richard Britain, Cynthia Jane. BS, Okla. U., 1958; MSW, U. Tex., Arlington, 1973. Diplomate in Clin. Social Work; cert. social worker; lic. clin. social worker, Calif. Clin. social worker Baylor U. Med. Ctr., Dallas, 1973-76; psychiat. social worker Tex. Tech. U. Health Scis. Ctr., Lubbock, 1976-78; clinician, supr. Mental Health Svcs. So. Okla., Ada, 1978-83; exec. dir. Area Youth Shelter, Ada, 1983-84; program evaluator, dir. satellite svcs. Taliaferro Ctr., Lawton, Okla., 1984-88; forensic social worker State of Calif. Patton State Hosp., 1988-93; psychotherapist Family Svcs. Agy., San Bernardino, Calif., 1989-91; supervising social worker R.J. Donovan Correction Facility, San Diego, 1993—; mem. adv. bd. East Cen. Univ., Ada, 1980-83; coord. The Chem. People Project, Ada, 1983; adj. asst. prof. U. Okla., Norman, 1982-83; social work cons. Harmon County Hosp., Hollis, Okla., 1984-88; treas. Okla. State Bd. Lic. Social Workers, 1982-84. V.p. Ada Community Svcs. Coun., 1984; mem. Child Abuse Prevention Task Force, Altus, Okla., 1985, Inland Empire Symphony Assn., San Bernardino, 1990; mem. chancel choir First Congl. Ch., San Bernardino, 1989-90. Mem. Nat. Assn. Social Workers (bd. dirs. 1981-84, Social Worker of Yr. 1986, pres. Okla. chpt. 1981-84, bd. trustees legal def. fund 1985-87, mem. polit. action com. 1981-88), Forensic Mental Health Assn. Calif. Office: Dept Corrections State of Calif F.J. Donovan Correctional Facility 480 Alta Rd San Diego CA 92179

MOORE, JULIE LOUISE, bibliographer, librarian; b. Sioux City, Iowa, Sept. 11, 1941; d. Mabel (DeRaad) Rude. BA, U. Denver, 1962, MS, 1963. Indexer Conservation Libr., Denver, 1965-67; head libr. Gerontology Libr., U. So. Calif., L.A., 1968-85; owner, mgr. Wildlife Info. Svc., Las Cruces, N.Mex., 1971—. Compiler: Thesaurus of Sport-Fish and Wildlife, 1968, Bibliography of Wildlife Theses, 1969, Wildlife Literature in Wildlife Techniques Manual, 1980, Bibliography of Reported Biological Phenomena...Attributed to Microwave and Radio-Frequency Radiation, 1984; indexer: Updata Index to U.S. Dept. Agriculture Handbooks, 1980; editor: Abstracts in Social Gerontology, 1989—.

MOORE, JUSTIN EDWARD, data processing executive; b. West Hartford, Conn., June 17, 1952; s. Walter Joseph and Victoria Mary (Calcagni) M. BS in Mgmt. Sci., Fla. Inst. Tech., 1974. Systems assoc. Travelers Ins., Hartford, Conn., 1974-77; data processing programmer R.J. Reynolds Inc., Winston-Salem, N.C., 1977-78; programmer/analyst Sea-Land Svc., Elizabeth, N.J., 1978-79; mgr. market analysis Sea-Land Svc., Oakland, Calif., 1979-82; asst. v.p., dir. application systems Fox Capital Mgmt. Corp., Foster City, Calif., 1982-86; mgr. bus. svcs. dept mktg. and pricing Am. Pres. Cos., Ltd., Oakland, 1987-88, dir. mktg. and pricing systems, 1988-89; dir. systems devel. The Office Club, Concord, Calif., 1989-91; dir. MIS Revo, Inc., Mountain View, Calif., 1992-93; account mgr. Imrex Computer Systems, Inc., South San Francisco, 1993. Democrat. Roman Catholic. Home: 5214 Jomar Dr Concord CA 94521-2343

MOORE, MARY FRENCH (MUFFY MOORE), potter, community activist; b. N.Y.C., Feb. 25, 1938; d. John and Rhoda (Teagle) Walker French. B.A. cum laude, Colo. U., 1964; m. Alan Baird Minier, Oct. 9, 1982; children: Jonathan Corbet, Jennifer Corbet, Michael Corbet. Ceramics mfr., Wilson, Wyo., 1969-82, Cheyenne, Wyo., 1982—; commr. County of Teton (Wyo.), 1976-83, chmn. bd. commrs., 1981, 83, mem. dept. pub. assistance and social svc., 1976-82, mem. recreation bd., 1978-81, water quality adv. bd., 1976-82. Bd. dirs. Teton Sci. Sch., 1968-83, vice chmn., 1979-81, chmn., 1982; bd. dirs. Teton Energy Coun., 1978-83; mem. water quality adv. bd. Wyo. Dept. Environ. Quality, 1979-83; Dem. precinct committeewoman, 1978-81; mem. Wyo. Dem. Cen. Com., 1981-83; vice chmn. Laramie County Dem. Cen. Com., 1983-84, Wyo. Dem. nat. committeewoman, 1984-87; chmn. Wyo. Dem. Party, 1987-89; del. Dem. Nat. Conv., 1984, 88, mem. fairness commn. Dem. Nat. Com., 1985, vice-chairwoman western caucus, 1986-89; chmn. platform com. Wyo. Dem. Conv., 1982; mem. Wyo. Dept. Environ. Quality Land Quality Adv. Bd., 1983-86; mem. Gov.'s Steering Com. on Troubled Youth, 1982, dem. nat. com. Compliance Assistance Commn., 1986-87; exec. com. Assn. of State Dem. Chairs, 1989; mem. Wyo. Coun. on the Arts, 1989—, Dem. Nat. Com. Jud. Coun., 1989—; legis. aide for Gov. Wyo., 1985, 86; project coord. Gov.'s Com. on Childrens' Svcs., 1985-86; bd. dirs. Wyo. Outdoor Coun., 1984-85. Recipient Woman of Yr. award Jackson Hole Bus. and Profl. Women, 1981, Dem. of Yr. Nellie Tayloe Ross award, Wyo. Dems., 1990. Mem. Alden Kindred of Am., Jackson Hole Art Assn. (bd. dirs., vice chmn. 1981, chmn. 1982), Assn. State Dem. Chairs, Pi Sigma Alpha. Home: 8907 Cowpoke Rd Cheyenne WY 82009-1234

MOORE, MATTHEW EMERSON, environmental and planning consultant; b. Tuscaloosa, Ala., Aug. 5, 1964; s. Charles Thomas Moore Sr. and Annabel (Owens) Moore Allen; m. Anne Goldthwaite Dorr, March 20, 1993. BS, No. Ariz. U., 1987; MA, Claremont Grad. Sch., 1989. Mem. policy clinic team Ctr. for Politics and Policy, Claremont (Calif.) Grad. Sch., 1987-89; rsch. asst. Rose Inst. State and Local Govt., Claremont, 1989; analyst, asst. planner LSA Assocs., Inc., Irvine, Calif., 1989-90; project mgr. Urban Vision, Irvine, 1991-93. Founding pres. Explorer Post 477, Boy Scouts Am., Tempe, Ariz., 1980-82; interpretive specialist Walnut Canyon Nat. Monument, Flagstaff, Ariz., 1987; mem. drought planning adv. bd. City of Claremont, 1988-89. Mem. Am. Planning Assn., Nat. Assn. Environ. Profls., Internat. Assn. Impact Assessment. Methodist.

MOORE, OMAR KHAYYAM, experimental sociologist; b. Helper, Utah, Feb. 11, 1920; s. John Gustav and Mary Jo (Crowley) M.; m. Ruth Garnand, Nov. 19, 1942; 1 child, Venn. BA, Doane Coll., 1942; MA, Washington U., St. Louis, 1946, PhD, 1949. Instr. Washington U., St. Louis, 1949-52; teaching assoc. Northwestern U., Evanston, Ill., 1950-51; rsch. asst., prof. sociology Tufts Coll., Medford, Mass., 1952-53; researcher Naval Rsch. Lab., Washington, 1953-54; asst. prof. sociology Yale U., New Haven, 1954-57, assoc. prof. sociology, 1957-63; prof. psychology Rutgers U., New Brunswick, N.J., 1963-65; prof. social psychology, sociology U. Pitts., 1965-71, prof. sociology, 1971-89, prof. emeritus, 1989—; scholar-in-residence Nat. Learning Ctr.'s Capital Children's Mus., Washington, 1989-90; pres. Responsive Environ. Found., Inc., Estes Park, Colo., 1962—; assessor of rsch. projects The Social Scis. and Humanities Rsch. Coun. Can., 1982—; adj. prof. U. Colo., Boulder, 1992—. Contbg. editor Educational Technology; contbr. numerous articles to profl. jours.; patentee in field; motion picture producer and director. Recipient Award The Nat. Soc. for Programmed Instruction, 1965, Award Doane Coll Builder Award, 1967, Ednl. Award Urban Youth Action, Inc., 1969, Award House of Culture, 1975, Cert. of Appreciation, 1986, Cert. of Appreciation D.C. Pub. Schs., 1987, da Vinci Award Inst. for the Achievement of Human Potential, 1988, Cert. of Appreciation Capital Children's Museum, 1988, award Jack & Jill of America Found., 1988, Cert. of Appreciation U.S. Dept. of Edn., 1988, Cert. of Appreciation D.C. Pub. Schs., 1990, Person of Yr. in Ednl. Tech. award Ednl. Tech. mag., 1990. Mem. AAAS, Am. Math. Soc., Am. Psychol. Assn., Internat. Sociol. Assn., Am. Sociol. Assn., Assn. for Symbolic Logic, Assn. for Anthrop. Study of Play, Philosophy Sci. Assn., Psychonomics Soc., Soc. for Applied Sociology, Soc. for Exact Philosophy, Math. Assn. Am. Republican. Home and Office: 2341 Upper High Dr PO Box 1673 Estes Park CO 80517

MOORE, RICHARD, physicist, educator; b. Hollywood, Calif., Jan. 19, 1927; s. Dennis Albert and Marjorie Jane (Kahn) M.; m. Irene McManus, Apr. 1, 1956 (div. 1965); m. Lillian Elizabeth Karska, Apr. 5, 1969; children: Don Andrew, Ann Marie. Student, Deep Springs Coll., 1944-46; BS in Engring., U. Mo., 1949; PhD in Biophysics, U. Rochester, 1955; DSc in Bioengineering, George Washington U., 1970. Engr. USPHS, Washington, 1955-57; scientist NIH, Bethesda, Md., 1957-60; rsch. scientist Am. Nat. Red Cross Labs., Bethesda, 1960-69; assoc. prof. U. Minn., Mpls., 1969-82; prof., dept. chair U. Witwatersrand, Johannesburg, Republic of South Africa, 1982-87; health physicist U.S. Dept. of Energy, Idaho Falls, Idaho, 1987—; rsch. assoc. U. Rochester, N.Y., 1950-55; radiol. safety officer Johannesburg Hosp., 1982-87; pres. Svc. and Rsch. Co., Chubbuck, Idaho, 1987—; software coord. Pocatello (Idaho) MacIntosh Users Group, 1988—; consulting physicist Intermountain Cancer Ctr., Bannock Regional Med. Ctr., Pocatello. Editor (jour.) Pattern Recognition, 1968—, Computers in Biology and Medicine, 1968—; contbr. chpts. to 6 books, articles to profl. jours. Mem. spl. study sect. NIH, Bethesda, 1976; mem. cancer com. Minn. Dept. Health, Mpls., 1976; mem. neutron therapy com. Coun. Sci. and Indsl. Rsch., Johannesburg, 1986. Recipient internat. rsch. fellowship Internat. Exchange Com., Prague, Czechoslovakia, 1977, pres.'s award Soc. Radiol. Engring, Chgo., 1977, fellowship German Acad. Exchange Svc., Berlin, 1980, sr. scientist fellowship NATO, Berlin, 1980, study grant U. Witwatersrand, 1987. Fellow AAAS, Soc. Advanced Med. Systems; mem. Am. Heart Assn. (fellow coun. on cardiovascular radiology 1980), Royal Soc. (Republic South Africa), Am. Coll. Med. Physics, Am. Soc. Therapeutic Radiology and Oncology, Health Physics Soc. (nominating com. 1989), Am. Acad. Health Physics, Am. Bd. Health Examiners (panel of examiners). Democrat. Unitarian. Home: 812 Garden Dr Pocatello ID 83202-1602 Office: US Dept Energy 785 Doe Pl Idaho Falls ID 83401-1562

MOORE, RONALD CLARK, mechanical designer; b. Springfield, Ohio, Dec. 18, 1949; s. Harry Alva and Virginia Kay (Clark) M.; m. Rebecca Jane Culp, Apr. 17, 1971 (div. July 1974); m. Emperatriz Seretti, June 21, 1986. Student, San Jose City Coll., 1979. With systems test-mfg. Coherent Radiation Inc., Palo Alto, Calif., 1976-78; researcher Stanford Rsch. Inst., Menlo Park, Calif., 1978-79; with satellite systems test Santa Barbara Rsch. Ctr., Gleta, Calif., 1979-80; with optical storage rsch. Omex Inc., Santa Clara, Calif., 1980-82; sr. lab. specialist IBM Rsch. Lab, San Jose, Calif., 1982—. Contbr. articles to profl. jours.; inventor serial EP printer. Home: 912 Chelan Dr Sunnyvale CA 94087-4006 Office: IBM Almaden Rsch Ctr 650 Harry Rd San Jose CA 95120-6099

MOORE, SHEILA FRANCES, technical writer; b. San Francisco, Sept. 25, 1956; d. Richard Lecompte and Frances (von Geldern) M. BA, U. Calif., Berkeley, 1979. Mem. tech. staff Hewlett-Packard, Cupertino, Calif., 1979-82, tech. writer, 1982-89; tech. writer Tandem Computers, Cupertino, 1989—. Democrat.

MOORE, SIDNEY DWAYNE, inventor, product designer, entrepreneur, consultant; b. Monahans, Tex., June 2, 1938; s. Sidney Augusta and Florence Elizabeth (Van Loh) M.; m. Peggy Caffey, June 11, 1959; 1 child, Adam C. Student, Pratt Inst., 1956-57; BFA, U. Tex., 1963; MFA, R.I. Sch. of Design, Providence, 1965. Pvt. practice artist N.Y.C., 1965-69; asst. prof. Drexel U., Phila., 1969-74; owner, operator Camera Craft Photo-Tech Ctr., Prescott, Ariz., 1974-86; engring. mgr. Bushnell Div., Bausch & Lomb, San Dimas, Calif., 1986-90; product designer Bausch & Lomb, Bushnell Div., 1990-92; teaching fellow R.I. Sch. Design, Providence, 1963-65. Inventor: electronically controlled rangefinders, microcomputer-controlled rangefinding and aiming-compensating devices for projectile firing apparatuses, microcontroller-controlled active reticle for microscopes, locking device for binocular focusing mechanism, keyless chucking device for electric drills, automatic power change mechanism for variable power riflescopes; patentee in field. With U.S. Army, 1958-60. Mem. Soc. Advancement Materials & Process Engring., Internat. Soc. for Optical Engring., Am. Soc. Design Engrs., Indsl. Designers Soc. Am.

MOORE, TERRY WAYNE, engineering executive; b. North Kingston, R.I., Feb. 26, 1957; s. Robert Wendell and Marilyn (Rose) M. BS in Engring., U. Fla., 1981; MBA, U. San Diego, 1993. Sr. materials engr. U.S. Dept. Def., Alameda, Calif., 1981-85, program mgr., 1985-87; staff engr., scientist Gen. Atomics, La Jolla, Calif., 1987-89, project mgr., 1989—; entrepreneur Venture Mgmt., San Diego, 1990—. Judge San Diego Sci. Fair, 1989—; rep. Neighborhood Watch, La Costa, Calif., 1989—; vol. fund raiser Am. Cancer Soc., San Diego, 1989—. Mem. Am. Soc. for Materials (sec.-treas. 1990-92, bd. dirs. 1989—, nat. chpt. ops. com., computer subcom. chmn. 1991—), Venture Mgmt. Group, MIT Enterprise Forum, San Diego Yacht Club. Republican. Presbyterian. Home: 905 Orchid Way Carlsbad CA 92009 Office: Gen Atomics 3550 Gen Atomics Ct San Diego CA 92186

MOORE, TILLMAN MARION, medical facility administrator, surgeon; b. Amarillo, Tex., July 18, 1927; s. Tillman Marion and Velma Eva Moore; m. Shirley Louise Mayer, Dec. 22, 1950; children: Paul Truett, Anne Louise Moore Wicknick, Shannon Yvette Moore-Ferraro, Elizabeth Lynne. BS, Iowa State U., 1949; MD, Washington U., St. Louis, 1953. Diplomate Am. Bd. Surgery, Am. Bd. Orthopaedic Surgery; ordained priest Episcopal Ch., 1968. Surg. intern Barnes Hosp., St. Louis, 1953-54, resident, 1954-58; resident and fellow in orthopedic surgery Los Angeles County-U. So. Calif. Med. Ctr. Orthopedic Hosp., Rancho Los Amigos, 1967-70; pvt. practice, Sitka, Alaska, 1958-67; asst. prof. dept. orthopaedic surgery U. So. Calif. Sch. Medicine, L.A., 1967-86, prof. emeritus clin. orthopaedic surgery, 1986—, chmn. site orient sarcoma Comprehensive Cancer Ctr., 1974-80, chmn. tumor cons. svc., 1979-87; chief tumor clinic Los Angeles County-U. So. Calif. Med. Ctr., 1971-89; chief tumor cons. svc. Orthopaedic Hosp. L.A., 1979-87, dir. tumor clinic, 1980-87; chief orthopaedic surgery Norris Cancer Hosp.-U. So. Calif., 1983-87; v.p., med. dir. Pacific Coast Tissue Bank, L.A., 1987—; cons. in kinesiology Rancho Los Amigos Hosp., Downey, Calif., 1970-72. Editor: Musculoskeletal Tumors, 1977, Injuries of the Leg, 1981; mem. editorial bd. Contemporary Orthopaedics, 1980-90; also over 50 articles, chpts. to books. Chmn. bd. dirs. Sta. KSEW, Sitka, 1962-67; mem. Sitka Common Coun., 1962-66; v.p. Assembly of Tongass Borough, Alaska, 1966-67; trustee Hosp. of Good Samaritan, L.A., 1985-90. Ensign USNR, 1945-54. Recipient Nicolas-Andrey award Assn. Bone and Joint Surgeons, 1980; Carl Berg fellow Orthopaedic Rsch. and Edn. Found., 1971; grantee HEW, 1967-70, 71-76. Fellow ACS, Am. Acad. Orthopaedic Surgeons, Am. Orthopaedic Assn.; mem. numerous surg. and orthopaedic assns., Phi Beta Pi, Sigma Alpha Epsilon. Republican. Home: 2316 Via Carrillo Palos Verdes CA 90274-2717

MOORE, TOM LOYD, foundation executive; b. Laurel, Nebr., June 22, 1926; s. Thomas Loyd and Ruth Ellen (Flisram) M.; m. Diane Borders, May 16, 1949; children: Terry Ellen Boothman, Tom L. III. Student, U. Wyo., 1946-49, NYU, 1952. Sec., treas. Moore's, Inc., Santa Fe, 1949-53, pres., 1953-80; exec. dir. Menswear Retailers of Am., Washington, 1980-83; pvt. practice Santa Fe, 1983-89; exec. dir. St. Vincent Hosp. Found., Santa Fe, 1989-92; pres. Menswear Retailers of Am., 1973-74, Nat. Clothier Svc., Chgo., 1973-80; bd. dirs. 1st Interstate Bank, N.A., Santa Fe. Mem. Santa Fe City Libr. Bd., 1974-80; pres. Coll. of Santa Fe Libr. Friends, 1984-89; chmn. City of Santa Fe Parking Authority, 1961-80. With USN, 1944-46, PTO. Mem. Santa Fe Opera Assn., Quail Run, Montezuma, Shriners. Presbyterian. Home: 320 Calle Estado Santa Fe NM 87501-1020

MOORE, WALTER DENGEL, rapid transit system professional; b. Chgo., Sept. 16, 1936; s. Walter D. and Velma Louise (Rhode) M.; m. Sandra M. Stetzel, Jan. 23, 1965 (div. 1980); children: Thomas, Timothy. BA in Liberal Arts and Scis., U. Ill., 1958; BSEE, Ill. Inst. Tech., 1972. Supt. maintenance of way Chgo. Transit Authority, 1963-89; supt. of rail facilities activation and tech. support Met. Transp. Assn. Los Angeles County, L.A., 1989—. Mem. L.A. County Transit Commn.'s Rail Constrn. Corp. Users Group, 1990—. With U.S. Army, 1958-60. Mem. am. Pub. Tranp. Assn. (vice chmn. power com. 1974-75), Am. Ry. Engring. Assn. (vice chmn. subcom. on power signals and comm. 1990—), Underwater Soc. Am. (N.Am. record in spear-fishing 1988), Calif. Pub. Utilites Commn. (gen. order 95). Home: 12741 Andy St Cerritos CA 90701-6044 Office: Met Transp Assn L A County 320 Santa Fe Ave Los Angeles CA 90012

MOORE, WILLIAM HOWARD, history educator, writer; b. Harriman, Tenn., June 26, 1942; s. Lonnie Henry and Goldie Myrtle (Williams) M.; m. Mary Elizabeth Galvan, Sept. 27, 1969 (div. 1980); 1 child, Adam William; m. June Uvalda Vialpando, Mar. 8, 1986. BS, U. Tenn., 1964, MA, 1965; PhD, U. Tex., 1971. Instr. Southwest Tex. State U., San Marcos, 1971-72; asst. prof. Ohio U., Athens, 1972-73; from asst. prof. to prof. U. Wyo., Laramie, 1973—, chair dept. history, 1992—; cons. Harper Collins Pubs., N.Y.C., 1991-92, McGraw Hill Pubs., N.Y.C., 1992. Author: Kefauver Committee, 1974, Company Town, 1989; article referee Jour. American History, Bloomington, Ind., 1989; mem. editorial adv. bd. Annals of Wyoming, Cheyenne, 1990—; contbr. articles to profl. jours. Cons. Albany County Sch. Bd., Laramie, 1989, 91. Grantee Nat. Endowment Humanities, 1977, 90, Eisenhower World Affairs Inst., 1990, Hoover Pres. Libr. Assn., 1992. Mem. Orgn. Am. Historians, Ctr. Study Presidency. Home: 802 University Ave Laramie WY 82070 Office: U Wyo Dept History Box 3198 Laramie WY 82071

MOORE, WILLIAM JAMES, newspaper editor; b. Corpus Christi, Tex., Oct. 7, 1943; s. Edwin R. and Mary Wilson (Clokey) Ross M.; m. Ann Sarae Bancroft, May 2, 1976 (div. Dec. 1990); 1 child, Matthew. BA in Comm. and Polit. Sci., Stanford U., 1965, MA in Comm., 1966. Reporter Ariz. Daily Star, Tucson, Ariz., 1962; editor Stanford (Calif.) Daily, 1964; reporter San Francisco Chronicle, 1967-79; news editor Oakland (Calif.) Tribune-Eastbay Today, 1979-81; met. editor Sacramento Bee McClatchy Newspapers, 1982, editor Forum, 1982—. Press asst., vol. Robert F. Kennedy Presdl. campaign, San Francisco, 1968; vol. VISTA, San Juan, P.R., 1966-67. Served with USCGR, 1967-73. Democrat. Office: Sacramento Bee PO Box 15779 Sacramento CA 95852-0779

MOORE, WILLIS HENRY ALLPHIN, educator; b. N.Y.C., Dec. 14, 1940; s. Carl Allphin and Mary Catherine (Moody) M.; children: Patrick Kakela, Michael Kirby, Catherine Malia. BA Letters, U. Okla., 1962; MEd in Adminstrn., U. Hawaii, 1971. Teaching asst. dept. history U. Hawaii, 1962-64; dir. edn. Bernice P. Bishop Mus., Honolulu, 1967-76; pres. Hawaii Geog. Soc., Honolulu, 1976-78, exec. sec., editor, 1978—; mem. Hawaii Com. for Humanities, 1976-78; producer, narrator film-lecture programs Nat. Audubon Soc. and travelogue forums; instr. in history and geography Chaminade U. of Honolulu, 1987—; lectr. elderhostel U. Hawaii, Hawaii Pacific U.. Co-author/co-editor: Hawaii Parklands, Sociological History of Honolulu, Total Solar Eclipse over Hawaii, 1991; contbr. articles to Honolulu Advertiser, Pacific Daily News, Guam, Pacific Mag., Honolulu Star-Bull. Escort USIS East-West Ctr.; lay reader St. Andrew's Cathedral. Mem. N.Am. Cartographic Info. Soc., Am. Assn. State & Local History, Am. Museums Assn., Pacific Sci. Assn., Hawaii Mus. Assn. (pres. 1972-74), Pacific Asia Travel Assn., Hawaii Pub. Radio, Am. Guild Organists, Sierra Club (chmn. Hawaii chpt. 1973-75), Hawaiian Hist. Soc., Nat. Soc. of Arts and Letters. Office: PO Box 1698 Honolulu HI 96806-1698

MOORHEAD, CARLOS J., congressman; b. Long Beach, Calif., May 6, 1922; s. Carlos Arthur and Florence (Gravers) M.; m. Valery Joan Tyler, July 19, 1969; children: Theresa, Catharine, Steven, Teri, Paul. B.A., UCLA, 1943; J.D., U. So. Calif., 1949. Bar: Calif. 1949, U.S. Supreme Ct. 1973. Pvt. practice law Glendale, Calif., 1949-72; dir. Lawyers Reference Service, Glendale, 1950-66; mem. 93rd-103rd Congresses from 22nd (now 27th) Dist. Calif., 1973—, Judiciary Com.; ranking Rep. Energy and Commerce Com.; dean Calif. Congl. Rep. Delegation; apptd. to Fed. Cts. Study Com. Pres. Glendale Hi-Twelve Club; mem. Verdugo Hills council Boy Scouts Am.; mem. Calif. Assembly, 1967-72; mem. Calif. Law Revision Commn., 1971-72; pres. 43d Dist. Republican Assembly, Glendale Young Republicans; mem. Los Angeles County Rep. Central Com., Calif. Rep. Central Com.; pres. Glendale La Crescenta Camp Fire Girls, Inc. Served to lt. col. AUS, 1942-46. Recipient Man of Yr. award USO, 1979. Mem. Calif. Bar Assn. L.A. County Bar Assn., Glendale Bar Assn. (past pres.), Glendale C. of C., Masons, Shriners, Lions, Moose, VFW. Presbyterian. Office: US House of Representatives 2346 Rayburn House Office Bldg Washington DC 20515

MOORHEAD, JOHN COUPER, emergency physician; b. Toronto, Ont., Can., Nov. 4, 1949; came to U.S., 1978; s. David Earle and Elizabeth Cook (Couper) M.; married, 1 child, Couper John. BA, Queens Coll., Kingston, Ont., 1971; MD, Queens U., Kingston, Ont., 1975; MS, NYU, 1989. Emergency physician Oreg. Health Svcs. U., Portland, 1978—, chief emergency svcs., 1986—, chair dept. emergency medicine, 1991—; mem. State Trauma Adv. Bd., Oreg., Residency Rev. Com. for Emergency Medicine. Editorial bd. three med. jours.; contbr. articles to profl. jours. Mem. AMA, SAEM, Am. Coll. Emergency Physicians. Office: Oregon Health Sciences Univ 3181 SW Sam Jackson Park Rd Portland OR 97201-3011

MOORHEAD, MICHAEL JOHN, police captain; b. Tacoma, Wash., Oct. 2, 1943; s. Frank Ira and Helen Jane (Hermsen) M. AA, Tacoma C.C., 1976, AS, 1977; BA in Police Sci., Pacific Western U., 1988, D of Pub. Adminstrn., 1990. Patrol officer Tacoma (Wash.) Police Dept., 1966-73, detective, 1973-77, sgt., 1977-87, lt., 1987-90, capt., 1990—; EEO officer Tacoma Police Dept., 1989—; N/A #147 Fed. Bur. of Investigation, Quentico, Va., 1986, bd. dirs.; affirmative action com. Tacoma Pub. Schs., 1984; bd. dirs. Pierce County Law and Justice Com., Tacoma, 1975; mem. FBI Nat. Acad. Assocs., Quantico, 1986—. Author (manual) Special Investigations, 1987, Traffic Division, 1986, Tacoma Police Manual, 1975. Recipient Lifetime Master award NRA, 1968, Wa. State Indoor Pistol champion, 1968. Mem. Internat. Assn. of Chiefs of Police, Nat. Acad. of Assocs. FBI, Amateur Radio Svc. (examiner), Maple Valley Wireless Assn., Internat. Assn. of Chiefs of Police (adv. com. for police adminstrn. 1985-92). Home: 2404-199th Ave Ct East Sumner WA 98390 Office: Tacoma Police Dept 930 Tacoma Ave South Tacoma WA 98402

MOORHOUSE, DOUGLAS CECIL, engineering consulting company executive; b. Oakland, Calif., Feb. 24, 1926; s. Cecil and Lynda (Roe) M.; BS in Civil Engring., U. Calif., Berkeley, 1950, postgrad., 1961; student Advanced Mgmt. Program, Harvard U., 1973; m. Dorothy Johnson; children: Scott, Jan. Research and resident engr. State of Calif. Div. Hwys., 1950-59; dir. San Diego office Woodward-Clyde & Assos., 1959-62; pres. Woodward-Moorhouse & Assos., 1962-73; pres., chief exec. officer Woodward-Clyde Cons., San Francisco, 1973-87; chief exec. officer, chmn. bd. dirs. Woodward-Clyde Group Inc., 1988—. mem. adv. com., dept. engring. U. Calif. Berkeley. Pres. Hazardous Waste Action Coalition, 1988-89. Served with inf. U.S. Army. Mem. Nat. Acad. Engring., ASCE (Wesley W. Horner award 1979). Office: Woodward-Clyde Group Inc 4582 S Ulster Pkwy Ste 600 Denver CO 80237

MOOS, CHRISTOPHER ROBIN, social science analyst; b. Ft. Collins, Colo., Jan. 22, 1954; s. John G. and Madeline (Evans) M. BA summa cum laude, U. Denver, 1981, MA, 1987; PhD, U. Kans., 1991. Instr. U. Kans., Lawrence, 1987-91; social sci. analyst U.S. Gen. Acctg. Office, Denver, 1991—. Author: (book) Crime Over the Life Course: The Effects of Under- and Over-Engagement, 1992. With U.S. Army, 1972-75. Fellow U. Denver, 1986, NIH fellow U. Kans., 1988. Mem. Midwest Coun. Social Rsch. on Aging (fellow 1988-91), Am. Sociol. Assn., Gerontol. Assn. Am., Alpha

Kappa Delta. Office: US Gen Acctg Office Ste 800 1244 Speer Blvd Denver CO 80204

MOOSE, CHARLES A., state official; b. Aug. 11, 1953. BA in U.S. History, U. N.C., 1975; MA in Pub. Adminstrn., Portland State U., 1984, student, 1984—; student, FBI Nat. Acad. Patrol officer Portland Police Dept., 1975-81, sergeant, 1981-84, lieutenant, 1984-91, capt. of No. Precinct, 1991-92, dep. chief of Ops. Branch, 1992-93, chief of police, 1993—. Mem. Am. Soc. Criminology, Nat. Orgn. of Black Law Enforcement Execs., Comprehensive Options for Drug Abusers (mem. bd. dirs.), Black United Fund of Oreg. (mem. funding allocation com.), Portland House of Umoja (mem. adv. bd.), Boys and Girls Club of Portland (mem. bd. dirs.), Regional Drug Initiative (mem. new programs and planning com.), Mainstream Youth Program, Inc. (mem. bd. dirs.), Multnomah County Community Action Commn., Soc. of Police Futurists Internat. Address: 1111 SW 2d Ave Portland OR 97204*

MORAIN, MARY STONE DEWING, volunteer association executive; b. Boston, Mar. 18, 1911; d. Arthur S. and Frances (Hall Rousmaniere) Dewing; student Radcliffe Coll., 1930-33; BS, Simmons Sch. Social Work, 1934; MA, U. Chgo., 1937; cert. social work U. So. Calif., 1941; m. Lloyd L. Morain, July 6, 1946. Social worker, Calif., N.Y.C., 1941-45; tchr. social scis. Keuka Coll., N.Y., 1945-46; v.p. LWV, Boston, 1946-53; bd. dirs., v.p. Planned Parenthood League Mass., 1948-52; bd. dirs., pres. Planned Parenthood Assn. San Francisco, 1953-60; bd. dirs. Internat. Humanist and Ethical Union, 1953-65; bd. dirs., v.p. Assn. Vol. Sterilization, 1963-77, 79—, UNESCO Assn. U.S.A., 1977—, Monterey YWCA, 1975-80, UN Assn. San Francisco, 1961-69; pres. Internat. Soc. Gen. Semantics, 1976-85, bd. dirs. Inst. Gen Semantics, 1992—, v.p. mem. 1985—; bd. dir. Tor House Found., 1984—. . Fellow World Acad. Art and Sci.; mem. Am. Assn. Social Workers. Club: Altrusa. Author: (with Lloyd Morain) Humanism as the Next Step, 1954; contbr. articles to profl. jours. Editor: Teaching General Semantics, 1969; Classroom Exercises in General Semantics, 1980; Bridging Worlds through General Semantics, 1984; Enriching Professional Skills Through General Semantics, 1986. Home and Office: PO Box 7190 Carmel CA 93921-7190

MORALES, ARMANDO, psychotherapist, educator; b. Los Angeles, Sept. 18, 1932; m. Rebecca Gonzales, Aug. 27, 1955 (div. Apr. 1980); children: Roland Victor, Gary Vincent; m. Cynthia Torres, June 30, 1989. AA, East Los Angeles Jr. Coll., 1955; BA, Los Angeles State Coll., 1957; MSW, U. So. Calif. Sch. Social Work, 1963, DSW, 1971. Diplomate Am. Bd. Clin. Social Work. Gang group worker Los Angeles Times Boys Club, 1954-57; sr. dep. probation officer Los Angeles County Probation Dept., 1957-63, Las Palmas Sch. for Girls, Los Angeles County Probation Dept., 1963-66; supervising psychiat. social worker, mental health cons. Los Angeles County Dept. Mental Health, 1966-71; prof., chief clin. social work dept., dir. Spanish speaking psychosocial clinic, dir. intern tng. program Neuropsychiat. Inst. UCLA Sch. Medicine, 1971—; cons. Calif. Youth Authority, East Los Angeles, 1977—; speaker in field. Author: Ando Sangrando: A Study of Mexican American-Police Conflict, 1973, Social Work: A Profession of Many Faces, 1977, 80, 83, 86, 89, 92; co-editor: The Psychosocial Development of Minority Group Children, 1983; composer ethnic songs. pres. Western Ctr. on Law and Poverty, Inc., Los Angeles, 1975-77, bd. dirs., 1968-78; vice chmn. Citizens Adv. Council, Calif. Dept. Mental Health, 1977-82. Served as sgt. USAF, 1951-54. Appointed to Pres.' Commn. on Mental Health Task Panel on Legal and Ethical Issues, 1977-78; fellow NIMH, 1962, 69, 77; named Far East Air Force Bantamweight Champion, 1952, 53. Mem. Nat. Assn. Social Workers (cert., bd. dirs. 1989-92), Trabajadores de la Raza, Council on Mental Health Western Interstate Commn. for Higher Edn. (chmn. 1976-78), Commn. Human Relations (commr., v.p. 1975-78). Democrat. Roman Catholic. Office: UCLA Sch Medicine Neuropsychiatric Inst 760 Westwood Pla Los Angeles CA 90024

MORALES, MARGO MELINDA, government analyst; b. Pomona, Calif., Nov. 2, 1958; d. Roman Montes and Nancy Ruth (Sloan) M. BA in Polit. Sci., Calif. State Poly. U., Pomona, 1982. Loan processor Crocker Nat. Bank, El Segundo, Calif., 1983-86; rehab. specialist Los Angeles County Community Devel. Commn., Monterey Park, Calif., 1986-87, mktg. specialist, 1987-88, environ. specialist, 1988-89; mgmt. analyst Los Angeles County Community Devel. Commn., L.A., 1989—; mem. L.A. Means Bus. Task Force, 1992-93; chair Drug Diversion Task Force, L.A., 1991; mem. Calif. Perservation Found., San Francisco, 1988-89. Editor newsletter Calif. State U. Alumni Coun. News and Notes, 1991-92. Team handball support svcs. coord. Olympic Festival, L.A., 1988-91; mem. Calif. State U. Alumni Coun., 1991—; vol. various local, state and fed. campaigns, Los Angeles County, 1980—; bd. dirs. Fair Housing Found., Long Beach, Calif., 1993—. Named to Outstanding Young Women of Am., 1983. Mem. Calif. State Poly. U. Pomona Alumni (hon. life, bd. dirs. 1989—, v.p. 1989). Democrat. Roman Catholic. Office: Los Angeles County Chief Adminstrv Office 500 W Temple Rm 723 Los Angeles CA 90012

MORAN, MARY ANNE, health association program director; b. Dallas, Mar. 13, 1947; d. Patrick Charles and Minnie Morson (Hemphill) Moran; children: Edward L. IV, Cathleen Lorraine, Charles Andrew, Anthony Patrick. BS in Nursing, Loretto Heights Coll., Denver, 1969. Med. dir. Western Med. Svcs., Colorado Springs, Colo., 1976-77; office mgr. Callaway Senatorial Campaign, Colorado Springs, Colo., 1980, Kramer Congl. Campaign, Colorado Springs, Colo., 1982; dir. El Paso div. Am. Heart Assn., Colorado Springs, Colo., 1984-87; dir. programs and rsch. Am. Heart Assn., Denver, 1987-92; projects coord. Merck Ctr. Tech., Edn. & Info., Denver, 1992-93; with Feiger PsychMed Ctr., Wheat Ridge, Colo., 1993—; projects coord. Merck Ctr. Tech., Edn. & Info., Denver, 1992-93. Mem. Colorado Springs Health Edn. Coun., 1986-87, Coloradans for Clean Indoor Air, Colorado Springs, 1985-87; v.p. The Downtowners, Colorado Springs, 1981-85; pres. El Paso Rep. Women, Colorado Springs, 1979-84; chmn. community svcs. Cherry Creek Rep. Women, 1989—; mem. Colo. Biomed. Rsch. Found., Colo. Cardiovascular Coalition. Named an Outstanding Young Woman of Am., 1979-80, Young Rep. Woman of Colo., 1977. Roman Catholic. Home: 1415 E 9th Ave Apt 4 Denver CO 80218 Office: Feiger PsychMed Ctr 3555 Lutheran Pky Ste 320 Wheat Ridge CO 80033

MORAN, RACHEL, lawyer, educator; b. Kansas City, Mo., June 27, 1956; d. Thomas Albert and Josephine (Portillo) M. AB, Stanford U., 1978; JD, Yale U., 1981. Bar: Calif. 1984. Assoc Heller, Ehrman, White & McAuliffe, San Francisco, 1982-83; prof. law U. Calif., Berkeley, 1984—; vis. prof. UCLA Sch. Law, 1988, Stanford (Calif.) U. Law Sch., 1989; ann. civil rights lectr. Creighton U. Sch. Law, Omaha, 1989; Pirsig lectr. William Mitchell Coll. St. Paul, 1989, others; mem. steering com. Nat. Resource Ctr., Berkeley, 1988-89. Contbr. numerous articles to profl. jours. Grantee Joseph and Polly Harris Trust Inst. Govtl. Studies, Berkeley, 1987-89, Faculty Devel. U. Calif. Berkeley, 1985-86. Mem. ABA, AAUP, Calif. Bar Assn., Phi Beta Kappa. Democrat. Unitarian. Office: U Calif Sch Law Boalt Hall Berkeley CA 94720

MORAN, THOMAS FRANCIS, writer; b. Phila., Dec. 5, 1943; s. George Francis and Alice (Foulk) M.; m. Marilyn Groch, June 24, 1978; children: Rachel Louise, Michael Thomas. BSME, Calif. State Poly. Inst., San Luis Obispo, Calif., 1965; MSME, Calif. State U., Long Beach, 1968. Engr. Jet Propulsion Lab., Pasadena, 1966-71; coun. aide City of L.A., 1975-79; editor Ocean Front Weekly, Marina del Rey, Calif., 1979-80; tech. writer Xerox Electro-Optical, Pasadena, 1982-83; specialist Rockwell Internat., Lakewood, Calif., 1983-92, G&H Tech., Santa Monica, Calif., 1992—; instr. tech. writing Calif. State U., Dominguez Hills, Calif., 1990—; instr. writing L.A. Harbor Coll., Wilmington, 1989—. Author: The U.S. Army, 1990, Bicycle Motocross Racing, 1986, Fantasy by the Sea,1979, The Photo Essay, 1974. Bd. dirs. Venice Hist. Soc., 1988-89; bd. advisors Beyond Baroque Found., Venice, 1980-83. Named Citizen of the Yr., Bd. Realtors, Marina del Rey; Apollo Achievement awardee, NASA. Mem. Soc. Tech. Communication. Office: 218 Howland Canal Venice CA 90291-4511

MORAN, THOMAS HARRY, university administrator; b. Milw., Oct. 21, 1937; s. Harry Edward and Edna Agnes Moran; BS, U. Wis., 1964, MA, 1972, PhD, 1974; m. Barbara Ellen Saklad, June 10, 1969; children: David Thomas, Karen Ellen. Dir. capital budgeting Wis. Dept. Adminstrn., 1962-64; exec. dir. Wis. Higher Ednl. Aids Bd., 1964-69; spl. cons. tax policy Wis. Dept. Revenue, 1973-74; dep. dir. Wis. Manpower Coun., Office of Gov., 1974-76; v.p. bus. and fin., treas. U. Detroit, 1976-78; exec. assoc. v.p. health affairs U. So. Calif., L.A., 1979-87; v.p. bus. affairs, 1988—. USN fellow, 1957-59; U.S. Office Edn. rsch. fellow, 1973. Mem. Am. Assn. Higher Edn., Phi Kappa Phi. Office: U So Calif 102 Owens Hall University Park Los Angeles CA 90007

MORAND, BLAISE E., bishop; b. Tecumseh, Ont., Can., Sept. 12, 1932. Ordained priest Roman Cath. Ch., 1958. Ordained coadjutor bishop Diocese of Prince Albert, Sask., Can., 1981, bishop, 1983—. Office: Diocese of Prince Albert, 1415 4th Ave W, Prince Albert, SK Canada S6V 5H1*

MORAVCSIK, JULIUS MATTHEW, philosophy educator; b. Budapest, Hungary, Apr. 26, 1931; came to U.S., 1949; s. Julius and Edith (Fleissig) M.; m. Marguerite Germain Truninger, Sept. 14, 1954; children: Adrian Clay, Peter Matthew. BA, Harvard U., 1953, PhD, 1959. Asst. prof. U. Mich., Ann Arbor, 1960-66, assoc. prof., 1966-68; prof. Stanford (Calif.) U., 1968—. Author: Understanding Language, 1975, Thought and Language, 1990, Plato and Platonism, 1992. Recipient Sr. Humanist prize Humboldt Found., 1983; fellow Ctr. Advanced Studies Behavioral Scis., 1986-87, Inst. Advanced Studies, 1988. Mem. Am. Philos. Assn. (pres. Pacific divsn. 1987-88), Am. Soc. Aesthetics (trustee 1988-92), Soc. Ancient Greek Philosophy (pres. 1989-91). Office: Stanford U Dept of Philosophy Stanford CA 94305-2155

MORAVEC, MILAN, management and organization consultant; b. Apr. 16, 1940; m. Margaret Doris Moravec; children: Darrin Trevor, Todd Andrew. MBA, U. Western Ont., London, 1963; postgrad., UCLA, 1972. With Corning (N.Y.) Co., 1972-74, Bechtel, San Francisco, 1975-87, Nat. Semiconductor, Santa Clara, Calif., 1987-90; mgr. Brit. Petroleum, dir., v.p. human resources Moravec & Assocs., Walnut Creek, Calif., 1990—. Contbr. articles to profl. jours. Mem. Inst. Mgmt. Cons., Bay Area Human Resource Exec. Coun., Soc. Human Resources Mgmt. Office: Moravec & Assocs 2453 Providence Ct Walnut Creek CA 94596-6454

MOREHART, THOMAS BERTON, associate dean; b. Henderson, Tex., Nov. 17, 1942; s. William Franklin and Marian Louise (Pugh) M.; m. Kaaren Lee Forkner, Mar. 21, 1964; children: Jennifer Lee Morehart Hartin, Jeffrey William Morehart. BS in Math., N.Mex. State U., 1964; MS in Computer Info. Systems, Colo. State U., 1971; PhD in Bus. Adm., Ga. State U., 1976. Mathematician White Sands (N.Mex.) Missile Range, 1966, 1968-70; grad. asst. Colo. State U., Ft. Collins, 1970-71; instr. Western Ill. U., Macomb, 1971-72; asst. to the dean Ga. State U., Atlanta, 1972-74, instr., 1974-75; asst. prof. Ariz. State U., Tempe, 1975-80, assoc. prof., 1980-86; assoc. dean N.Mex. State U., Las Cruces, 1986—; cons. Tempe, Ariz., 1976-86, Las Cruces, N.Mex., 1986—; bd. dirs. Bd. of Pensions PC USA, Phila., 1982-89. Author: Personal Financial Management, 1980; contbr. articles profl. jours. 1st lt. U.S. Army, 1966-68. Mem. Am. Risk and Ins. Assn., Am. Soc. CLUs and Chartered Fin. Cons., Am. Soc. CPCUs, Phi Kappa Phi, Beta Gamma Sigma. Presbyterian. Home: 2420 Desert Dr Las Cruces NM 88001-1609 Office: N Mex State U Coll Bus Adminstrn & Econs PO Box 30001 Dept 3AD Las Cruces NM 88003

MOREHEAD, ANNETTE MARIE, disabled children's facility administrator; b. San Diego; d. Michael Peter and Katherine Helen (Keegan) Russomondo; m. Peter James Morehead; children: Bradley Michael Caloca, Katherine Dana. Student, Southwestern Coll., Grossmont Coll. Dir. Rayito Day Care Ctr., San Diego, 1981-85; instrnl. asst. for children with disabilities San Diego City Schools, 1985-88; owner, operator Scripps Ranch Childcare Ctr. for Disabled Children, San Diego, 1990—; spkr. San Diego Bd. Edn., 1986, News Eight Local TV News, 1989, Miramar Coll., 1991, Scottish Rite Charities, 1992, Exceptional Parents Found., 1993. vol. Schweitzer Ctr. for Disabled Children, San Diego, 1985, Stein Edn. Ctr. fof Autistic Children, San Diego, 1987-88. Mem. Autism Soc. Am. (bd. dirs.), Mensa. Democrat.

MOREHOUSE, CARL EDWARD, land use planner; b. Louisville, Aug. 9, 1951; s. Alan L. and Marjorie Ellen (Holt) M.; m. Felicia C. Tiritilli, Aug. 17, 1977 (div. Dec. 1979). BA, Purdue U., 1973; MPA, Ind. U., 1980. Asst. dir. City-County Planning Commn., Henderson, Ky., 1975-77; housing rsch. asst. Dept. Met. Devel., Indpls., 1980; hist. preservation planner City Planning Dept., Paso Robles, Calif., 1984; asst. planner Community Devel. Dept., Santa Barbara, Calif., 1985-86; from planner I to planner III Resource Mgmt. Agy., Ventura County, Calif., 1986-89, planner IV, 1989—. Mem. Am. Planning Assn., Calif. chpt. Am. Planning Assn., Am. Inst. Cert. Planners.

MORELLI, JOSEPH GABRIEL, JR., chiropractor; b. Phila., Sept. 28, 1953; s. Joseph Gabriel and Anna Marie Louise (Cetrone) M. Cert. Latin Am. Studies, U. Ibero Am., Mexico City, 1974; BS in Pre Medicine, St. Joseph's U., Phila., 1975; cert. Med. Sociology, St. Joseph's U., 1975; D of Chiropractic, Palmer Coll. Chiropractic, Davenport, Iowa, 1978. Cert. chiropractor, physical therapist, impairment disability evaluator,, chiropractic orthopedics, radiology and dignostic imaging. Assoc. chiropractic Rathjen Clinic, Honolulu, 1978-81; owner, clinic dir. Morelli Clinic, Honolulu, 1981—; clinic dir. Morelli Clinic-Molokai, Kaunakakai, Molokai, Hawaii, 1983-88; pres., clinic dir. Mililani Chiropractic Clinic, Mililani, Hawaii, 1988—; exec. dir., exec. sec. Back in Action Rehab. Ctr. Hawaii, Honolulu, 1988-92. Active Hawaii Assn. Blind, 1978—; marathon physician Honolulu Marathon Assn., 1983-87. Mem. Am. Chiropractic Assn. (coun. on dianostic imaging, coun. on sports injuries, alt. del. from Hawaii), Am. Coll. Chiropractic Orthopedists (assoc.), Hawaii State Chiropractic Assn. (conv. chmn. 1987—, ethics com. 1989—, chmn. seminar com. 1987—, peer review com. 1989, cert. appreciation 1989, v.p. 1990-91, pres. 1991-92). Republican. Roman Catholic. Home: Apt 3801 1330 Ala Moana Blvd Honolulu HI 96814-4242 Office: Morelli Clinic 1150 S King St Ste 905 Honolulu HI 96814-1922 also: Mililani Chiropractic Clinic Inc 95-119 Kamehameha Hwy Ste D Mililani HI 96789-3393

MOREL-SEYTOUX, HUBERT JEAN, civil engineer, educator; b. Calais, Artois, France, Oct. 6, 1932; came to U.S., 1956; s. Aimé and Suzanne Claire (Rousseau) M.-S.; m. Margery K. Keyes, Apr. 16, 1960; children: Aimée, Claire, Sylvie, Marie-Jeanne. BS, Ecole St. Genevieve, Versailles, France, 1953; MS, Ecole Nationale des Ponts et Chaussées, Paris, 1956; PhD, Stanford U., 1962. Research engr. Chevron Oil Field Research Co., La Habra, Calif., 1962-66; prof. Colo. State U., Ft. Collins, 1966-91, prof. emeritus, 1991—; chargé de recherches U. Grenoble, France, 1972-73; maitre de recherches Ecole des Mines de Paris, Fontainebleau, France, 1982; directeur de recherches ORSTOM, Montpellier, France, 1991—; cons. hydrology Atherton, Calif., 1992—; cons. AID, Dakar, Senegal, 1985-86, Ministry of Agriculture and Water, Riyadh, Saudi Arabia, 1978-83, City of Thornton, Colo., 1986-88, King Abdulaziz U., Jeddah, Saudi Arabia, 1987, 89—, Ford Found., India, 1976, 79, South Fla. Water Mgmt. Dist., West Palm Beach, 1991—, Battelle Pacific Northwest Labs., Richland, Wash., 1991—, City of Paris, France, 1992—, Agence de l'Eau Seine-Normandie, 1992—; vis. prof. Ecole Polytechnique Federale de Lausanne, 1987; vis. scholar Stanford U., 1992—; adj. prof. U. Colo., Boulder, 1992—; lectr. U. Calif., Berkley, 1993—. Editor: Hydrology Days, 1981—, 3d Internat. Hydrology Symposium, 1977, Unsaturated Flow in Hydrologic Modeling, 1989. Pres. Internat. Ctr., Ft. Collins, 1984-86. Served to lt. French Army Marine Corps Engrs., 1959-62. Sr. Fulbright scholar, France, 1972-73; recipient Abell Faculty Rsch. award Colo. State U. Coll. Engring., 1985. Mem. Am. Geophys. Union, ASCE, Soc. Petroleum Engrs., Am. Meteorol. Soc., Am. Soc. Agrl. Engrs. Home: 57 Selby Ln Atherton CA 94027-3926 Office: Hydrology Days Publs 57 Selby Ln Atherton CA 94027-3926

MORENO, ANTHONY ERNEST, finance executive, controller; b. L.A., May 15, 1954; s. Gregory Gomez and Socorro Maria (Mendoza) M.; m. Karen Eithne Connolly, Aug. 9, 1975; children: Rebecca Noelle, Anthony Michael. BS in Bus., U. Calif., Long Beach, 1978. Internal auditor L.A. County Auditor-Controller, 1979-81; internal auditor Centinela Hosp. Med. Ctr., L.A., 1981-83, acctg. mgr., 1984-85, controller, asst. adminstr., 1985-86; corp. controller Am. Healthcare Systems, San Diego, 1986-90, v.p. fin., controller, 1990-92, v.p. fin., CFO, 1992—. Mem. Nat. Assn. Accts. Democrat. Roman Catholic. Office: Am Healthcare Systems 12730 High Bluff Dr Ste 300 San Diego CA 92130-2099

MORENO, ARMANDO, organization executive; b. Vienna, Austria, June 21, 1920; came to U.S., 1985; s. Julius and Sabina (Silberman) M.; m. Angelia Kostic, June 17, 1921 (div. Nov. 1984); children: Dolores, Mario; m. Hilde Kula, Nov. 9, 1987. Prof., U. Sarajevo, Yugoslavia, 1967. Sec. Diplomatic Sch., Belgarde, Yugoslavia, 1945-50; chief staff UNICEF Misssion, Belgarde, 1950-53; mgr. Tourist Offices in Scandinavia, Stockholm, Copenhagen, 1953-57, Tourist Offices Dalmatia, Split, Yugoslavia, 1957-75; prof. English, French, German langs. and letters U. Split, 1967-80; sec.-gen. Internat. Fedn. Festival Orgns., L.A., 1967—; chief press Mediterranean Games, Split, 1979; mem., advisor UNESCO, 1971—. Author: Tourism--The Passport to Peace, 1967, About Information Service and Publicity in Tourism, 1976; contbr. numerous articles to tourism, arts and show bus. mags. Recipient medal for merit Pres. Republic of Yugoslavia. Home and Office: Internat Fedn Festival Orgn 4230 Stansbury Ave Apt 105 Sherman Oaks CA 91423

MORENO, FRANK JAVIER, communications executive; b. Nogales, Ariz., Aug. 9, 1961; s. Frank B. and Margarita (Urbina) M. BSBA, No. Ariz. U., Flagstaff, 1989. Supr. Payless Cashways Bldg. Materials, Tucson, Ariz., 1985-86; account svc. rep. MCI Telecommunications, Phoenix, 1986-87, communications specialist commercial accounts, 1987, communications specialist major accounts, 1987-89, communications specialist strategic accounts, 1989-90, customer svc. exec. nat. accounts, 1991—. Big Bro. Phoenix Valley Big Bros., 1987—. Mem. Kappa Sigma (pres. 1983). Office: MCI Telecommunications Corp 2525 E Camelback Rd # 400 Phoenix AZ 85016-4219

MORENO, MANUEL D., bishop; Educator U. of Calif., L.A., St. John's Sem., Camarillo, Calif. Ordained priest Roman Cath. church, 1961. Ordained aux. bishop of Los Angeles, titular bishop of Tanagra, 1977; installed as bishop of Tucson, 1982—. Office: PO Box 31 192 S Stone Ave Tucson AZ 85702

MORENO, RICHARD MILLS, fire chief; b. Tucson, June 30, 1938; s. Fred Elias and Lupe (Mills) M.; m. Yolanda Bertha Rodriquez, Sept. 3, 1960; children—Richard, Robert, Sonya, Rene. B.A, U. Ariz., 1976. With Tucson Fire Dept., 1959—, fire chief, 1982—; mem. adj. faculty Nat. Fire Acad. Md., 1978-79. Contbr. articles to profl. jours. Tng. chmn. Tucson Boy Scouts. Served with USMC, 1956-59. Mem. Internat. Fire Chiefs Assn., Nat. Fire Protection Assn., Ariz. Fire Chiefs Assn. Democrat. Roman Catholic. Club: Centurions. Office: Tucson Fire Dept 265 S Church Ave Tucson AZ 85701-1648*

MOREY, ROBERT HARDY, communications executive; b. Milw., Sept. 5, 1956; s. Lloyd W. and Ruby C. (McElhaney) M. AA, Ricks Coll., 1978; BA, Brigham Young U., 1983. Program dir. Sta. KABE-FM, Orem, Utah, 1982-83, sales mgr., 1983; nat. mgr. ops. Tiffany Prodns. Internat., Salt Lake City, 1983-84; account exec. Osmond Media Corp., Orem, 1984; corp. sec., bd. dirs. Positive Communications, Inc., Orem, 1984—, chief exec. officer, 1987—; gen. mgr. Sta. KSRR, Orem, 1985—; pres. K-Star Satellite Network, Orem, 1986—, Broadcast Media Svcs., Orem, 1989-93; gen. mgr. Sta. KMGR, Salt Lake City, 1993; guest lectr. various colls. and univs., 1981—. Chmn. Rep. voting dist., Orem, 1984. Recipient Community Service award Utah Valley Community Coll., 1983; named one of Outstanding Young Men in Am. U.S. Jaycees, 1983. Mem. Rotary. Mormon. Home: PO Box 828 Orem UT 84059 Office: Sta KSRR Ventura Media Ctr 1240 E 800 N Orem UT 84057-4318

MOREY, WILLIAM CALVIN, credit industry executive; b. Missoula, Mont., Mar. 25, 1949; s. Ross Harold and Harriet Rose (Hagler) M.; m. Beth Louise Weeks, May 1, 1976; children: Stacey Lee, Carrie Denise. BS in Fin., Mont. State U., 1974. Credit mgr. Allied Stores Corp., Missoula, Mont., 1974-76; collection mgr. Allied Stores Corp., Boise, Idaho, 1976-77; new accts. mgr. Allied Stores Corp., Seattle, 1977-79; gen. credit mgr. Emporium, Inc., Eugene, Oreg., 1979—. Officer, bd. dirs., mem. exec. com. Consumer Credit Counseling, Eugene, 1987—; officer Toastmasters, Eugene, 1989—. With USN, 1967-74. Mem. Internat. Customer Svc. Assn., Nat. Retail Fedn., Internat. Credit Assn., Oreg. Retail Coun. (com. mem. credit and checks 1992, officer), Lane County Credit Assn. Office: Emporium Inc 86776 McVay Eugene OR 97405

MORGAN, ALAN D., state education official. State supt of education New Mexico. Office: N Mex Edn Dept Edn Bldg 300 Don Gaspar Ave Santa Fe NM 87501-2786

MORGAN, AUDREY, architect; b. Neenah, Wis., Oct. 19, 1931; d. Andrew John Charles Hopfensperger and Melda Lily (Radtke) Anderson; m. Earl Adrian Morgan (div); children: Michael A., Susan Lynn Heiner, Nancy Lee, Diana Morgan Lucio. B.A., U. Wash., 1955. Registered architect, Wash., Oreg.; cert. NCARB. Project mgr. The Austin Co., Renton, Wash., 1972-75; med. facilities architect The NBBJ Group, Seattle, 1975-79; architect constrn. rev. unit Wash. State Divsn. Health, Olympia, 1979-81; project dir., med. planner John Graham & Co., Seattle, 1981-83; pvt. practice architecture, Ocean Shores, Wash., 1983—, also health care facility cons., code analyst. Contbg. author: Guidelines for Construction and Equipment of Hospitals and Medical Facilities; co-editor Design Considerations for Mental Health Facilities; co-editor: Design Considerations for Mental Health Facilities; contbr. articles to profl. jours. and govt. papers; prin. works include quality assurance coord. for design phase Madigan Army Med. Ctr., Ft. Lewis, Wash.; med. planner and code analyst Rockwood Clinic, Spokane, Wash., Comprehensive Health Care Clinic for Yakima Indian Nation, Toppenish, Wash.; code analyst S.W. Wash. Hosps., Vancouver; med. planner facilities for child, adult, juvenile and forensic psychiatric patients., States of Wash. and Oreg. Cons. on property mgmt. Totem council Girl Scouts U.S.A., Seattle, 1969-84, troop leader, cons., trainer, 1961-74; mem. Wash. State Bldg. Code Coun. Barier Free Committed Tech. adv. group for Ams. with Disabilties Act; assoc. mem. Wash State Fire Marshals Tech. Adv. Group. Mem. AIA (nat. com. on architecture for health 1980—, subcoms. codes and standards, health planning, chair mental health com., 1989-92, and numerous other coms., founding mem. Wash. council AIA architecture for health panel 1981—, recorder 1981-84, vice chmn., 1987, chmn. 1988, bd. dirs. S.W. Wash. chpt. 1983-84), Nat. Fire Protection Assn., Soc. Am. Value Engrs., Am. Hosp. Assn., Assn. Western Hosps., Wash. State Hosp. Assn., Wash. State Soc. Hosp. Engrs. (hon.), Seattle Womens Sailing Assn., Audubon Soc., Alpha Omicron Pi. Lutheran. Clubs: Coronado 25 Fleet 13 (Seattle) (past sec., bull. editor); GSA 25 Plus. Home and Office: PO Box 1990 Ocean Shores WA 98569-1990 also: 904 Falls of Clyde SE Ocean Shores WA 98569-1990

MORGAN, CHARLES EDWARD PHILLIP, bank executive; b. Wichita, Kans., Nov. 3, 1916; s. Wells C. Morgan and Mary E. (Brown) Allredge; m. Elizabeth Ann Brown, Oct. 14, 1943 (div. Dec. 1972); children—Valerie Donahue, Renee Tompkins. Student U. Wichita, 1935; student bus. adminstrn., U. Calif.-Berkeley, 1963. Teller First Nat. Bank, Santa Fe, 1938-42; safety officer Libby-McNeil-Libby, Sacramento, 1946-48; from teller to v.p./br. mgr. Wells Fargo Bank, Sacramento, 1948-76; sr. v.p. Capitol Bank of Commerce, Sacramento, 1976-86. Served to 1st lt. USAF, 1942-45. Democrat. Mem. Christian Ch. Lodges: Masons, Shriners, Elks. Home: 6371 Grangers Dairy Dr Sacramento CA 95831-1039

MORGAN, DAVID ALLEN, electronic engineer; b. Sidney, Nebr., June 1, 1962; s. Richard Denis and Gerda Dorene (Foged) M.; m. Ann Marie Zollman, June 7, 1987. BS in Elec. Engring., Colo. State U., 1984; MSEE, U. Colo., 1992. Engr. NCR VLSI Processor Products, Colo. Springs, Colo., 1984-85, NCR Digital Signal Processing, Fort Collins, Colo., 1985-87; engr., project leader NCR Computer Aided Design, Fort Collins, 1987—. Mem. IEEE, Assn. for Computing Machinery, NCR Golf Club (organizer 1987-90). Office: NCR Microelectronics Div 2001 Danfield Ct Fort Collins CO 80525-2998

MORGAN, DAVID FORBES, minister; b. Toronto, Ont., Can., Aug. 3, 1930; came to U.S., 1954; s. Forbes Alexander and Ruth (Bamford) M.; m. Delores Mae Storhaug, Sept. 7, 1956; children—Roxanne Ruth, David Forbes II. BA, Rocky Mt. Coll.; ThB, Coll. of the Rockies, M.Div.; postgrad. Bishop's Sch. Theology; LittD (hon.), Temple Coll., 1956, D.C. Nat.

Coll. Ordained priest. Pres., Coll. of the Rockies, Denver, 1960-73; founder and rector Prior Order of Christ Centered Ministries, Denver, 1973—; canon pastor St. John's Cathedral, Denver, 1982—; bd. dir. Alpha Inc., Denver, 1981—. Author: Christ Centered Ministries, A Response to God's Call, 1973; Songs with A Message, 1956. Clubs: Oxford, Denver Botanic Garden. Home: 740 Clarkson St Denver CO 80218-3204 Office: St Johns Cathedral 1313 Clarkson St Denver CO 80218-1806

MORGAN, ELLIOTT WAYNE, insurance company executive; b. Hartford, Conn., May 7, 1957; s. Earl William Sr. and Eleanor (Kruse) M. AS, Manchester C.C., 1979; BS, Met. State Coll. Denver, 1986. Ins. rater Western Ins. Co., Denver, 1979-80, systems coord., 1980-81; personal lines supr. Western Ins. Co., Aurora, Colo., 1981-87; personal ins. mgr. Denver divsn. Am. States Ins. Co., Aurora, Colo., 1987—; mem. CPCU spl. project on cost containment measures, 1992-93; chmn. employee devel. com. Denver divsn. Am. States Ins. Co., 1989-91. Chairperson Denver divsn. Am. States Ins. Co. campaign United Way, 1988, sect. chairperson Denver campaign, 1992, 93, Employee Devel. Com., 1989-91. Mem. Colo./Wyo. Ins. Assn. (sec. 1993), Cen. Conn. Legal Assn. Republican. Roman Catholic. Home: 18905 E Ida Dr Aurora CO 80015-3179 Office: Am States Ins Co 14485 E Evans Dr Aurora CO 80014-1473

MORGAN, GARY B., journalism educator; b. San Diego, Nov. 5, 1943; s. Howard Wilson and Loyola Elizabeth (Heiberger) M.; m. Sharon Kay Traylor, June 16, 1965 (div. 1974); children: Stephen William Laurence, David Nathan Robert. BA, N.Mex. Highlands U., Las Vegas, 1966; MA, Colo. State U., 1968; DA, U. No. Colo., 1990. So. Calif. prep sports editor L.A. Examiner, 1959-61; sports editor Star-News, National City, Calif., 1960-61; announcer KFUN Radio, Las Vegas, N.Mex., 1963-66; sports info. dir. New Mex. Highlands U., 1964-66; grad. teaching asst. dept. English Colo. State U., 1966-68; info. dir. Mt. Plains Intercollegiate Athletic Assn., 1968-71, 74-76; asst. dir. info. svc. U. No. Colo., 1968-77; asst. prof. journalism Met. State Coll., Denver, 1977-84; prof. journalism Oxnard Coll., Calif., 1984—. Author: Yes You Can, 1990, The Georgetown Loop, 1976, Sugar Tramp, 1975, Three Foot Rails, 1970, There Was So Much Laughter, 1984; contbr. articles to profl. jours. Recipient Mark Dever award for excellence in teaching, Oxnard Coll., 1985-86. Mem. Nat. Collegiate Baseball Writers Assn. (pres. 1976), Coll. Sports Info. Dirs. Am. (bd. dirs.), Journalism Assn. Community Colls. (state pres. 1989-90, So. Calif. pres. 1988-89), Community Coll. Journalism Assn. (nat. pres. 1992, pres.-elect 1991), Assn. for Edn. in Journalism and Mass Communication, Calif. Newspaper Pubs. Assn. Office: Oxnard College 4000 S Rose Ave Oxnard CA 93033-6699

MORGAN, GEORGE DOUGLAS, rocket society administrator; b. Van Nuys, Calif., Sept. 30, 1953; s. G. Richard and Mary S. (Sherman) M.; m. Lisa Jane Mensing, Feb. 12, 1984; children: Jarom, Averie, Justin, Carley, Kristin, Annie. BS, So. Calif. U., 1976. Lic. Rockets 2d class Calif. State Fire Marshall, 1986—. Pres. Pacific Rocket Soc., Ventura, Calif., 1980-92. Author: Design and Testing of a Nitric Acid/Furfuryl Alcohol Liquid Fuel Rocket, 1987. Office: Pacific Rocket Soc 1825 N Oxnard Blvd Ste 24 Oxnard CA 93030

MORGAN, JACK M., lawyer; b. Portales, N.Mex., Jan. 15, 1924; s. George Albert and Mary Rosana (Baker) M.; BBA, U. Tex., 1948; LLB, 1950; m. Peggy Flynn Cummings, 1947; children: Marilyn, Rebecca, Claudia, Jack. Admitted to N.Mex. bar, 1950; sole practice law, Farmington, N.Mex., 1956—; mem. N.Mex. State Senate, 1973-88 . Served with USN, 1942-46. Mem. Am. Bar Assn., N.Mex. Bar Assn., S.W. Regional Energy Council (past chmn.), Kiwanis, Elks. Republican. Office: PO Box 2151 Farmington NM 87499-2151

MORGAN, JAMES C., electronics executive; b. 1938. BSME, Cornell U., MBA. With Textron Inc., 1963-72, West Ven Mgmt., San Francisco, 1972-76; chmn. bd., pres., CEO Applied Materials, Inc., Santa Clara, Calif., 1976-87, chmn. bd., CEO, 1987—. Office: Applied Materials Inc 3050 Bowers Ave Santa Clara CA 95054-3201

MORGAN, JIM LEE, retired business educator; b. Little Rock, Apr. 14, 1943; s. James Charles and Lois Marie (McPherson) M.; BS/BA, U. Ark., 1961, MEd, 1968. Asst. city mgr. City of Beverly Hills, Calif., 1972-74; dir. Human Service Planning, Simi Valley, Calif., 1975-76; prof. bus. and mgmt. West Los Angeles Coll., 1975-91, prof. emeritus, 1991—, pres. acad. senate, 1975—, Internat. Ednl. Found., 1992—; lectr. in field. Bd. advisors U. So. Calif. Traffic Safety Center, 1974-75; bd. dirs. Beverly Hills Chamber Orch., 1973-75, West Los Angeles chpt. ARC, 1972-75; founder, hon. chmn. Ann. Festival of Arts, City of Beverly Hills, 1972-75; founding mem. Research Coordinating Forum of Ventura County, 1976—; v.p. dist. senate Los Angeles Community Coll., 1978-80; treas. Acad. Senate, Calif. Community Colls., 1980-81, fin. task force commn. Chancellor's Office, 1980—. Served to capt. USAF, 1967-72. Decorated Air Force medals; honored by Jim Lee Morgan Day, City of Beverly Hills, Apr. 14, 1974; named Air Force Systems Command Personnel Officer of the Yr., 1970. Mem. Internat. City Mgrs. Assn., So. Calif. Assn. Human Resources Dirs., Am. Soc. Planning Ofcls., Am. Mgmt. Assn., Phi Delta Kappa, Blue Key, Beta Gamma Sigma. Author: Social Planning for the City, 1975; Business of Management, 1982; Study Guide to Management, 1982; editor Community Services Newsletter, 1974-75, Customer Relations: Policy and Procedures, 1975, Human Services Directory, City of Simi Valley, 1976, Rev. mag., 1972-74. Office: 7820 W Capitol # 1305 Little Rock AR 72205

MORGAN, JOE LEONARD, former professional baseball player, investment company executive; b. Bonham, Tex., Sept. 19, 1943. Student, Oakland City (Ind.) Coll., Calif. State U.-Hayward. Infielder Houston Astros, 1964-71, 2d baseman, 1980-81; 2d baseman Cin. Reds, 1971-80, San Francisco Giants, 1981-82, Phila. Phillies, 1982-83, Oakland A's, 1983-84; pres. Joe Morgan Investments Inc., Oakland, 1984—. Named Most Valuable Player Tex. League, 1964; Rookie of Yr. in Nat. League Sporting News, 1965; Most Valuable Player Nat. League, 1975, 76; Maj. League Player of Year. Sporting News, 1975, 76; named to Nat. League All-Star Team, 1970, 72-79; elected to Baseball Hall of Fame, 1990. Office: Joe Morgan Investments Inc 3650 Hayman St Hayward CA 94544-7124

MORGAN, JOHN ADRIAN, physicist; b. Louisville, Feb. 18, 1952; s. John Tramble and Lois Meredith (Hodgson) M.; m. Ann Elizabeth Wehrle, June 26, 1983; 1 child, Eileen. BS, Calif. Tech., 1974; MS, Rice U., 1977, PhD, 1979. Rsch. fellow Astronomy Ctr., Sussex U., Falmer, U.K., 1979-82; staff scientist solar physics Calif. Tech., Pasadena, 1982-84; mem. tech. staff Aerospace Corp., El Segundo, Calif., 1984-89, engrng. specialist, 1989—. Original rsch. pub. in Nucleosynthesis Theory and Physics of the Early Universe, 1977-83; contbr. tech. reports, monographs on space-based remote sensing to sci. publs. Fellow Royal Astron. Soc.; mem. Am. Phys. Soc., Am. Astron. Soc., Internat. Astron. Union. Office: Aerospace Corp MS M4/041 PO Box 92957 Los Angeles CA 90009

MORGAN, JOHN DERALD, electrical engineer; b. Hays, Kans., Mar. 15, 1939; s. John Baber and Avis Ruth (Wolf) M.; m. Elizabeth June McKneely, June 23, 1962; children: Laura Elizabeth, Kimberly Ann, Rebecca Ruth, John Derald. BSEE, La. Tech. U., 1962; MS, U. Mo., Rolla, 1965, Degree in Elec. Engring. (hon.), 1987; PhD, Ariz. State U., 1968. Registered profl. engr., forensic engr., Mo., N.Mex. Elec. engr. Tex. Eastman div. Eastman Kodak Co., 1962-63; instr. U. Mo., Rolla, 1963-65, Ariz. State U., 1965-68; asso. prof. elec. engring. U. Mo., Rolla, 1968-72; Alcoa Found. prof. elec. engring. U. Mo., 1972-75, chmn. elec. engring., 1978-85, assoc. dir. Ctr. Internat. Programs, 1970-78, Emerson Electric prof., 1975-85; dean engring. N.Mex. State U., 1985—; cons. to industry. Author: Power Apparatus Testing Techniques, 1969, Computer Monitoring and Control of Electric Utility Systems, 1972, Control and Distribution of Megawatts Through Man-Machine Interaction, 1973, Electromechanical and Electromagnetic Machines and Devices, 1986; also articles. Pres. bd. trustees First Meth. Ch., Rolla, 1971-73; pres. adminstrv. bd. First United Meth. Ch. Rolla, 1978-79; v.p., mem. bd. adminstrn. People to People, 1976; bd. dirs., cubmaster Ozarks dist. Boy Scouts Am., 1968-79, asst. dist. commr., 1971-73, cubmaster Yucca coun., 1986-90, coun. commr., 1989-90, asst. scout master, 1990—, dist. com. Sushine Dist.; dist. chmn. Meramec dist., 1978-80; bd. dirs. Mo. Partners of the Americas. Recipient Scouters Key award Ozarks council Boy Scouts Am., 1971, District award of merit Ozarks council Boy Scouts Am., 1977, Silver Beaver award Ozarks council Boy Scouts Am., 1982; T.H. Harris scholar, 1959-61; John H. Horton scholar, 1961-62. Fellow IEEE (chmn. internat. practices subcom. 1972-79, sec. PSE com., vice chmn., chmn. 1979-85, chmn. ednl. resources subcom. 1973-78, selected award of Merit St. Louis sect., Educators award St. Louis sect., honor award St. Louis sect., Centennial award 1984), Nat. Acad. Forensic Engrs.; mem. ASTM, NSPE (bd. govs., nat. dir., vice chmn., S.W. chmn. Profl. Engrs. in Edn.. v.p.), N.Mex. Soc. Profl. Engrs., Am. Soc. Engring. Edn., Sigma Xi, Tau Beta Pi, Eta Kappa Nu, Omicron Delta Kappa, Phi Kappa Phi, Kappa Sigma (faculty advisor), Epsilon Gamma (grand master, grand procurator). Home: 2425 Janet Ann Ln Las Cruces NM 88005-5177 Office: NMex State U Main Campus Coll Engring PO Box 30001 Las Cruces NM 88003-8001

MORGAN, KAREN SUE, association executive, management consultant; b. L.A., Aug. 1, 1944; d. Emery Leroy Morgan and Jayne Elizabeth (Musser) Heller; m. James David Westwood, July 26, 1962 (div. 1965); children: James David Jr., Joel Warner; m. Robert Clayton Wagoner, July 31 1990. Student, San Diego State U., 1963-68. Adminstrv. asst. San Diego State U., 1966-70; adminstrv. U. Calif., San Diego, 1970-79; pres. Unconventional, Inc., San Diego, 1979-90, Aligned Mgmt. Assocs., San Diego, 1990—; exec. dir. Outpatient Ophthalmic Surgery Soc., San Diego, 1986—. Sec. Plastic Surgery Rsch. Found., San Diego, 1976; bd. dirs. Cardiothoracic Rsch. and Edn. Found., San Diego, 1981, Global Energy Network Internat., San Diego, 1986; pres. We Are Coaches, Inc., San Diego, 1990. Mem. Soc. Applied Learning Tech., Am. Inst. Wine and Food, Charter 100 (bd. dirs. 1985-87). Office: Aligned Mgmt Assocs PO Box 23220 San Diego CA 92193

MORGAN, MARILYN, federal judge; b. 1947; 1 child, Terrence M. Adamson. BA, Emory U., 1969, JD, 1976. Bar: Ga. 1976, Calif. 1977. Ptnr. Morgan & Towery, San Jose, Calif., 1979-88; bankruptcy judge U.S. Bankruptcy Ct. (no. dist.) Calif., 1988—. Mem. Santa Clara County Bar Assn. (pres. 1985-86), Rotary Club San Jose (bd. dirs. 1992—), Nat. Assn. Bankruptcy Trustees (founder). Office: US Bankruptcy Ct 280 S 1st St Rm 3035 San Jose CA 95113-3099

MORGAN, MARK ALLEN, obstetrician-gynecologist; b. Enid, Okla., June 17, 1957; s. Wayne Thomas and Della Mae (Goodhue) M.; m. Sharyl Jaleen Scharn, June 7, 1980; children: Robert Wayne, Jamie Lynn. BS, So. Nazarene U., 1979; MD, Okla. U., 1983. Diplomate Am. Bd. Obstetrics and Gynecology. Intern, then resident obstetrics & gynecology, chief adminstrv. resident Okla. U. Health Scis. Ctr., Oklahoma City, 1983-87, fellow maternal fetal medicine, 1987-89, asst. prof., dir. primate colony, 1989-91; asst. prof. obstetrics-gynecology Irvine Med. Ctr. U. Calif., Orange, 1991—; med. cons. Emerson Teen Parent Program, Oklahoma City, 1987-91, adv. bd., 1988-91. Reviewer Am. Jour. Obstetrics and Gynecology, 1991—. Jr. fellow Am. Coll. Obstetricians and Gynecologists; mem. AMA, So. Med. Assn., Soc. Perinatal Obstetricians (assoc.), Phi Delta Lambda. Republican. Nazarene. Office: U Calif Irvine Med Ctr 101 The City Dr Bldg 25 Orange CA 92668

MORGAN, MARK QUENTEN, astronomer, astrophysics educator; b. Topeka, Dec. 27, 1950; s. Walter Quenten and Barbara Gene (Haynes) M. BA in Astronomy, San Diego State U., 1972; PhD in Astronomy, U. Addison, Ont., Can., 1976. Jet engine and power plant engr. N.Am. Aviation, Palmdale, Calif., 1966-68; astron. observer San Diego State U., 1970-74; engr., solar observer U. Md.-Clark Lake Radio Obs., Borrego Springs, Calif., 1978-82; engr., lectr. Sci. Atlanta, San Diego, 1979—. Inventor continuous wave laser, 1965, high intensity sound acoustic screening system, 1979. Mem. Inst. Environ. Scis., Acoustic Soc. Am., Astrophys. Soc. Am., Union Concerned Scientists, Planetary Soc. Office: Sci Atlanta PO Box 4254 San Diego CA 92164-4254

MORGAN, MEREDITH WALTER, optometrist, retired educator; b. Kingman, Ariz., Mar. 22, 1912; s. Meredith Walter and Florence (Forsyth) M.; m. Ida Marcia Engelking, Mar., 7, 1937 (dec. Nov. 1990); 1 child, Linda Morgan-Outhisack. AB, U. Calif., Berkeley, 1934, MA, 1939, PhD, 1942; DOS (hon.), Ill. Coll. Optometry, 1968; DSc, So. Calif. Coll. Optometry, 1974, Pa. Coll. Optometry, 1976, SUNY, 1989. Pvt. practice optometry Richmond, Calif., 1934-60; from instr. to prof. U. Calif., 1942-75, dean Sch. Optometry, 1960-73, prof. and dean emeritus, 1975—; vis. prof. U. Waterloo, Ont., 1974, U. Ala., Birmingham, 1977; mem. const. rev. com. USPHS, Washington, 1964-65, Nat. Adv. Coun. on Med., Dental, Optometric and Podiatric Edn., 1966-67; mem. adv. coun. Nat. Eye Inst., NIH, Washington, 1969-71; adminstrv. cons. SUNY, 1976. Author: Optics of Ophthamic Lenses, 1978; co-editor: Vision and Aging, 1986, Pediatric Optometry, 1990; contbr. sci. articles to profl. jours. Pres., mem. West Contra Costa County YMCA, Richmond, Calif., 1940-70, Meml. Youth Ctr. Bd., Richmond, 1950-68, Union High Sch. Bd., Richmond, 1950-55, Bd. Edn., Richmond, 1954-61. Fellow Am. Acad. Optometry (life, awards com., pres. 1953-54, Prentice medal 1967); mem. Am. Optometric Assn. (Apollo medal 1975), Sons in Retirement, Rotary. Democrat. Presbyterian. Home: 1217 Skycrest Dr # 4 Walnut Creek CA 94595 Office: U Calif Sch Optometry Berkeley CA 94720

MORGAN, MICHAEL BREWSTER, publishing company executive; b. L.A., Dec. 30, 1953; s. Brewster Bowen and Eleanor (Boysen) M.; m. Debra Hunter, July 20, 1986. BA, Conn. Coll., 1975. Coll. sales rep. Addison Wesley Pub. Co., Chapel Hill, N.C., 1977-81; sponsoring editor Addison Wesley Pub. Co., Reading, Mass., 1981-84; chief exec. officer Morgan Kaufmann Pubs., San Mateo, Calif., 1984—. Mem. Am. Assn. for Artificial Intelligence, Assn. for Computing Machinery. Office: Morgan Kaufmann Pubs 2929 Campus Dr Ste 260 San Mateo CA 94403-2534

MORGAN, NEIL, author, newspaper editor, lecturer, columnist; b. Smithfield, N.C., Feb. 27, 1924; s. Samuel Lewis and Isabelle (Robeson) M.; m. Caryl Lawrence, 1945 (div. 1954); m. Katharine Starkey, 1955 (div. 1962); m. Judith Blakely, 1964; 1 child, Jill. A.B., Wake Forest Coll., 1943. Columnist San Diego Daily Jour., 1946-50; columnist San Diego Evening Tribune, 1950-92, assoc. editor, 1977-81, editor, 1981-92; assoc. editor, sr. columnist San Diego Union-Tribune, 1992—; syndicated columnist Morgan Jour., Copley News Service, 1958—; lectr.; cons. on Calif. affairs Bank of Am., Sunset mag. Author: My San Diego, 1951, It Began With a Roar, 1953, Know Your Doctor, 1954, Crosstown, 1955, My San Diego 1960, 1959, Westward Tilt, 1963, Neil Morgan's San Diego, 1964, The Pacific States, 1967, The California Syndrome, 1969, (with Robert Witty) Marines of the Margarita, 1970, The Unconventional City, 1972, (with Tom Blair) Yesterday's San Diego, 1976, This Great Land, 1983, Above San Diego, 1990; contbr. non-fiction articles to Nat. Geog., Esquire, Redbook, Reader's Digest, Holiday, Harper's, Travel and Leisure, Ency. Brittanica. Served to lt. USNR, 1943-46. Recipient Ernie Pyle Meml. award, 1957, Bill Corum Meml. award, 1961, Disting. Svc. citation Wake Forest U., 1966, grand award for travel writing Pacific Area Travel Assn., 1972, 78, Fourth Estate award San Diego State U., 1988, The Morgan award Leadership Edn. Awareness Devel. San Diego, 1993; co-recipient Ellen and Roger Revelle award, 1986; named Outstanding Young Man of Yr. San Diego, 1959. Mem. Authors Guild, Am. Soc. Newspaper Editors, Soc. Profl. Journalists, Explorers Club, Soc. of Am. Travel Writers, Bohemian Club, Phi Beta Kappa, Omicron Delta Kappa. Home: 7930 Prospect Pl La Jolla CA 92037-3721 Office: PO Box 191 San Diego CA 92112-4106

MORGAN, PATRICK MICHAEL, political science educator; b. Syracuse, N.Y., Dec. 6, 1940; s. George Amos and Mary Kathleen (Cartin) M.; m. Marilyn Adele Kelly, Aug. 24, 1963; children: Kelly Sue, Christopher, Kimberly. BA, Harpur Coll., 1962; MA, Yale U., 1964, PhD, 1967. Asst. prof. Wash. State U., Pullman, 1967-72, assoc. prof., 1972-76, prof., 1976-91; vis. prof. U. Wash., 1980-82, Coll. of Europe, Bruges, Belgium, 1985, 87-88, 1989-91; vis. prof. Katholieke Universiteit Leuven, Belgium, 1992-93; Tierney prof., chair Peace Rsch. U. Calif., Irvine, 1991—; cons. Sloan Found., 1977, Am. Coun. on Edn., Washington, 1979. Author: Deterrence: A Conceptual Analysis, 2d edit., 1983, Theories and Approaches to International Politics, 4th edit., 1987; co-author: Strategic Military Surprise, 1983; co-editor: Security and Arms Control, 2 vols., 1989. Fulbright fellowship U.S. Govt., 1985; fellowship Am. Coun. on Edn., U. Calif., 1976-77, Woodrow Wilson Ctr., 1973-74. Mem. Internat. Studies Assn. (v.p. 1988-89), Am. Polit. Sci. Assn., Coun. on U.S.-Korean Security Studies (co-coord. 1984—). Democrat. Home: 5 Whitman Ct Irvine CA 92715 Office: Univ Calif Irvine CA 92717

MORGAN, REBECCA QUINN, state senator; b. Hanover, N.H., Dec. 4, 1938; d. Forrest Arthur and Rachel (Lewis) Quinn; m. James C. Morgan, June 10, 1960; children: J. Jeffrey, Mary Frances. BS, Cornell U., 1960; MBA, Stanford U., 1978. Trustee Palo Alto (Calif.) Bd. Edn., 1973-78; asst. v.p. Bank of Am., Sunnyvale, Calif., 1978-80; county supr. Santa Clara County, San Jose, Calif., 1980-84; state senator State of Calif., Sacramento, 1984—; bd. dirs. Calif. Leadership, Tech. Ctr. of Silicon Valley. Mem. adv. bd. YWCA, Palo Alto, 1983—, Palo Alto Adolescent Svcs., 1975—, Stanford Bus. Sch., 1989—. Named Calif. Legislator of Yr, Sch. Bd. Assn. of Sacramento, 1987, Calif. Probation Parole and Correctional Assn., 1987-88, Calif. Sch. Age Consortium, 1989, Calif. NOW, 1990, Woman of Achievement Santa Clara County, 1983. Mem. Calif. Elected Women's Assn. Republican. Office: Office of State Senate State Capitol Rm 5066 Los Altos CA 94022

MORGAN, RIC, broadcast executive; b. Grand Forks, N.D., Jan. 21, 1949; s. George E. and Ruth G. (Chaplin) Peabody; m. DiAnn A. Decker, Aug. 22, 1970; children: Kelly M., Kerry L. Grad., Vocat.-Tech. Inst., Thief River Falls, Minn., 1969. Announcer KVOX radio, Moorhead, Minn., 1970-76, WEBC radio, Duluth, Minn., 1976-81, KKPL radio, Spokane, Wash., 1981-84; program dir. KIZZ radio, Minot, N.D., 1984-87, KVUU/KSSS radio, Colorado Springs, Colo., 1988—. Home: 7060 Churchwood Circle Colorado Springs CO 80918 Office: KVUU 2864 S Circle Dr #150 Colorado Springs CO 80906

MORGAN, RONALD WILLIAM, sales executive; b. Redlands, Calif., May 9, 1951; s. Liberty W. and Eleanor L. (Creech) M.; m. Debra Ann Lein, Nov. 30, 1991. AA in Machine Shop, Valley Coll., 1973; BA in Bus., Calif. State U., San Bernardino, 1977. Sales mgr. Combined Ins., Redlands, 1976-77; ter. sales mgr. Bullard Safety, L.A., 1977-79; sales engr. H.E.S. Machine Tool, Whittier, Calif., 1979-81, Machinery Sales, L.A., 1981-89; regional mgr. Ingersoll Rand Water Jet, Yorba Linda, Calif., 1989-91; ter. sales mgr. Machinery Sales, L.A., 1991-93; dist. mgr. Ellison Machinery, L.A., 1993—. With USCGR. Mem. Soc. Mfg. Engrs., Sons Am. Revolution.

MORGAN, SHANNON THOMAS, accountant; b. Okarche, Okla., Mar. 29, 1950; s. Bernard Earl Morgan and Maxine Susan Earp Robichad; m. Kalanda Flynn, Dept. 7, 1974 (div. 1988); children: Conor, Teryl. BS, Western State Coll., 1972; MS, Colo. State U., 1973. CPA, Colo. Staff acct. Van Schooneveld & Co. CPAs, Englewood, Colo., 1973-76; asst. prof. Mesa State Coll., Grand Junction, Colo., 1976-79; ptnr. Toft, Morgan & Co. CPAs, Grand Junction, 1979—. Bd. dirs. Grand Junction Downtown Devel. Authority, 1985-88, Sta. KPRN Pub. Radio, Grand Junction, 1987-91, Grand Junction Downtown Assn., 1982-85, Community Ctr. Bd. for Retarded, Grand Junction, 1979-82; chmn. loan com. Mesa County Revolving Loan Fund, Grand Junction, 1991—, mem. loan com., 1988-91; treas. Western Colo. coun. Boy Scouts Am., Grand Junction, 1990—. Mem. AIPCA, Colo. Soc. CPAs. Republican. Roman Catholic. Office: Toft Morgan & Co 326 Main St Ste 201 Grand Junction CO 81501

MORGAN, STEPHEN CHARLES, university president; b. Upland, Calif., June 2, 1946; s. Thomas Andrew and Ruth Elizabeth (Miller) M.; m. Ann Marie McMurray, Sept. 6, 1969; 1 child, Kesley Suzanne. BA, U. La Verne, 1968; MS, U. So. Calif., 1971; EdD, U. No. Colo., 1979. Devel. officer U. La Verne, Calif., 1968-71, asst. to pres., 1971-73, dir. devel., 1973-75, v.p. devel., 1975-76, pres., 1985—; dir. devel. U. So. Calif., L.A., 1976-79; exec. dir. Ind. Colls. No. Calif., San Francisco, 1979-85; dir. Ind. Colls. So. Calif., L.A., 1985—. Bd. dirs. Mt. Baldy United Way, Ontario, Calif., 1988—, McKinley Home for Boys, San Dimas, Calif., 1989—; chair nat. com. on higher edn. Ch. of Brethren, Elgin, Ill., 1988-90; dir. Pomona Valley Hosp. Med. Ctr., Inter Valley Health Plan, 1992—. Mem. Assn. Ind. Calif. Colls. and Univs. (exec. com. 1989—), L.A. County Fair Assn., Western Coll. Assn. (exec. com. 1992—), University Club of L.A., Pi Gamma Mu. Home: 2518 N Mountain Ave Claremont CA 91711-1579 Office: U of La Verne Office of Pres 1950 3D St La Verne CA 91750

MORGAN, THOMAS MICHAEL, computer software engineer; b. Pasadena, Calif., Mar. 10, 1953; s. Robert Lester and Janet Mary (Jewett) M. BS, U. So. Calif., 1975; PhD, U. Calif., Berkeley, 1982. Engr. Jet Propulsion Lab., Pasadena, Calif., 1975; software designer Rational, Santa Clara, Calif., 1982—. Mem. IEEE, Assn. for Computing Machinery. Home: 445 Mountain Laurel Ct Mountain View CA 94043 Office: Rational 3320 Scott Blvd Santa Clara CA 95054

MORGAN, THOMAS OLIVER, bishop; b. Jan. 20, 1944; s. Charles Edwin and Amy Amelia (Hoyes) M.; m. Lillian Marie Textor, 1963; three children. BA, U. Sask., Can., 1962; BD, King's Coll., London, Ont., 1965; DD (hon.), Coll. of Emmanuel and St. Chad, Sask., 1986. Curate Ch. of the Saviour, Blackburn, Lancashire, Can., 1966-69; rector Ch. of the Saviour, Porcupine Plain, Sask., 1969-73, Kinistino, 1973-77, Shellbrook, 1977-83; archdeacon Indian Missions Sask., 1983-85; bishop Diocese of Sask., Prince Albert, 1985-93, Diocese of Saskatoon, Sask., 1993—. Office: Diocese of Saskatoon, PO Box 1965, Saskatoon, SK Canada S7K 3S5

MORGAN-FADNESS, CORRINA MAY, staff-charge nurse; b. Longview, Wash., Jan. 12, 1963; d. Arthur Dallas and Dorothy Irene (Ellis) Miller; 1 child, Michael Patrick. AA, Lower Columbia Coll., 1982; BSN, U. Portland, 1987. RN, Wash. Staff nurse Centralia (Wash.) Gen. Hosp., 1987; charge nurse Walker Care Ctr., Centralia, 1987-89, Park Royal Med. Ctr., Longview, Wash., 1987, 89; house supr. WHCC Riverside, Centralia, 1989-92; staff nurse Auburn (Wash.) Gen. Hosp., 1992—; IV cons. on-call Evergreen Pharms., Inc., 1990—; unit mgr. Oakhurst Convalescent Ctr., Elma, Wash., 1992-93; patient care coord. Rehab. Sharon Care Ctr., Centralia, Wash., 1993—. Home: 403 2D Ave NE Napavine WA 98565-9999

MORGANTHALER, JOHN RICHARD, retired newsman; b. Stockton, Calif., Aug. 6, 1921; s. Joseph L. and Edna Viola (Arrington) M. BA, Chapman Coll., 1942; MA, Stanford U., 1947. Reporter Modesto (Calif.) Bee, 1947-51; newsman AP, Columbus, Ohio, 1951-54, Cleve., 1954-57, Sacramento, 1957-63, 75-87, N.Y.C., 1963-75; ret. AP, 1987. Sgt. U.S. Army, 1943-45, ETO. Democrat. Mem. Christian Ch. (Disciples of Christ). Home: 1049 55th St Sacramento CA 95819

MORGENROTH, EARL EUGENE, entrepreneur; b. Sidney, Mont., May 7, 1936; s. Frank and Leona (Ellison) M.; m. Noella Nichols, Aug. 2, 1958; children: Dolores Roxanna, David Jonathan, Denise Christine. BS, U. Mont., 1961. From salesman to gen. mgr. Sta. KGVO-AM Radio, Missoula, Mont., 1958-65; sales mgr. Stas. KGVO-TV, KTVM-TV and KCFW-TV, Missoula, Butte, Kalispell, Mont., 1965-66, gen. mgr., 1966-68; gen. mgr. Sta. KCOY-TV, Santa Maria, Calif., 1968-69; v.p., gen. mgr. Western Broadcasting Co., Missoula, 1966-69, gen. mgr., pres., 1969-81; gen. mgr., pres. numerous cos., Mont., Calif. Idaho, P.R., Ga., 1966-84; pres., chmn. Western Broadcasting Co., Missoula, 1981-84, Western Communications, Inc., Reno, 1984—; chmn. Western Fin., Inc., Morgenroth Music Ctrs., Inc., Mont. and Wash., Mont. Band Instruments, Inc.; prin. Western Investments, Reno, 1984—. Mem. bank bd. State of Mont., Helena; trustee U. Mont., 1985—, commencement speaker, 1988; bd. dirs. U. Mont. Found. With U.S. Army, 1954-57. Named Boss of Yr. Santa Maria Valley J.C.s, 1968. Mem. U. Mont. Century Club (pres.), Missoula C. of C. (pres.), Rocky Mountain Broadcasters Assn. (pres.), Craighad Wildlife-Wildlands Inst. (bd. dirs.), Boone and Crockett Club. Republican. Methodist. Home: 3525 Brighton Way Reno NV 59806

MORGENSEN, JERRY LYNN, construction company executive; b. Lubbock, Tex., July 9, 1942; s. J.J. and Zelline (Butler) M.; m. Linda Dee Austin, Apr. 17, 1965; children: Angela, Nicole. BCE, Tex. Tech U., 1965. Area engr. E.I. Dupont Co., Orange, Tex., 1965-67; div. engr. E.I. Dupont Co., La Place, La., 1967-73; project mgr. Hensel Phelps Constrn. Co., Greeley, Colo., 1973-78, area mgr., 1978-80, v.p., 1980-85, pres., 1985—. Office: Hensel Phelps Constrn Co 420 Sixth Ave PO Box O Greeley CO 80632

MORGENSTERN, NORBERT RUBIN, civil engineering educator; b. Toronto, Ont., Can., May 25, 1935; s. Joel and Bella (Skornik) M.; m. Patricia Elizabeth Gooderham, Dec. 28, 1960; children: Sarah Alexandra, Katherine Victoria, David Michael Gooderham. BASc, U. Toronto, 1956, DEng h.c., 1983; DIC, Imperial Coll. Sci., 1964; PhD, U. London, 1964; DSc h.c., Queen's U., 1989. Research asst., lectr. civil engring. Imperial Coll. Sci. and Tech., London, 1958-68; prof. civil engring. U. Alta., Edmonton, Can., 1968-83, Univ. prof., 1983—; cons. engr., 1961—. Contbr. articles to profl. jours. Bd. dirs. Young Naturalists Found., 1977-82, Edmonton Symphony Soc., 1978-85. Athlone fellow, 1956; recipient prize Brit. Geotech. Soc., 1961, 66, Huber prize ASCE, 1971, Legget award Can. Geotech. Soc., 1979, Alta. order of Excellence, 1991. Fellow Royal soc. Can., Can. Acad. Engring.; mem. U.S. Nat. Acad. Engring. (fgn. assoc.), Cancian Geosci. Coun. (pres. 1983), Can. Geotechnical Soc. (pres. 1989-91), Internat. Soc. for Soil Mechanics and Found. Engring. (pres. 1989—), Royal Glenora Club, Athenaeum (London), various other profl. assns. Home: 106 Laurier Dr, Edmonton, AB Canada T5R 5P6 Office: U Alta, Edmonton, AB Canada T6G 2G7

MORGENTHALER, JOHN HERBERT, chemical engineer; b. Cleve., Jan. 5, 1929; s. Frederick Herman and Anna Margarethe (Welke) M.; m. Kathleen Ann Merriman, June 23, 1956 (dec. Oct. 1986); children: John David, Jennifer Ann, Jeffrey Paul; m. Susan Kay Braaten, Dec. 27, 1988. SB, MIT, 1951, SM, 1952; PhD, U. Md., 1965. Group leader Procter & Gamble Co., Cin., 1954-58; project mgr. Atlantic Rsch. Corp., Alexandria, Va., 1958-62; sr. staff engr. Applied Physics Lab. Johns Hopkins U., Silver Spring, Md., 1962-65; project scientist Marquardt's Gen. Applied Sci. Labs., Westbury, N.Y., 1965-67; rsch. dir. Textron's Bell Aerospace Co., Buffalo, 1967-74; sect. mgr. Stauffer Chem. Co., Richmond, Calif., 1974-77; mgr. comml. ventures Bechtel Corp., San Francisco, 1977-78; pres. JHM Assocs., Tacoma, Wash., 1978—; cons. Moore Rsch. Labs., Inc., Bethesda, Md., 1959-65; mem. adv. bd. U. Tenn. Space Inst., Tullahoma, 1967-68, Assn. Bay Area Govts., Oakland, Calif., 1976-77; chmn. membership com. Nat. Capitol sect. Am. Inst. Chem. Engrs., 1959-61; treas. Buffalo sect. AIAA, 1974. Contbr. articles to Internat. Jour. Heat and Mass Transfer, Jour. Fluids Engring., Jour. Spacecraft and Rockets. Chmn. Joe Berg Sci. Soc., Niagara Falls, N.Y., 1967-71, com. chair Lewiston (N.Y.) Cub Scouts., 1970-71, Walnut Creek (Calif.) Boy Scouts, 1980-82; v.p. Homeowners Assn., Walnut Creek, 1983-85. 1st lt. chem. corps U.S. Army, 1952-54. Scholar Westinghouse Corp., 1947, MIT, 1947-51. Mem. AAAS, Elks, Sigma Xi, Kappa Kappa Sigma (hon.). Republican. Unitarian. Home and Office: 46 Bonney St Steilacoom WA 98388-1502

MORGESE, JAMES N., broadcast executive; b. Bronx, N.Y., Jan. 5, 1951; s. George N. and Tina C. (Papa) M.; m. Zoe A. Larsen, July 11, 1976; children: Mila, Lane. BA in Mass Comm., U. Denver, 1973, MA in Pub. Comm., 1979. Prodn. asst. NBC, N.Y.C., 1971-74; mem. creative staff Prodns. Unltd., Denver, 1974-75; prodn. asst. Sta. KOA-TV, Denver, 1975-79; prodn. mgr. WKYU-TV, Bowling Green, Ky., 1980-82; mgr. prodn. ops. Sta. KUID-TV, Moscow, Idaho, 1982-85; local program mgr. Sta. WUFT-TV, Gainsville, Fla., 1985-86, sta. mgr., 1986-90; sta. mgr. KRMA-TV, Denver, 1990-93, pres., gen. mgr., 1993—; exec. prodr. Borah Symposium, Moscow, 1980; adv. bd. Alachua County Cable T.V. , Fla., 1989-90; exec. in charge prodn. And Learning For All, Denver, 1992-93, A Place to Call Home, Denver, 1992-93. Mem. adv. commn. U. Denver Alumni, 1991-92. Mem. NATAS, Colo. Hispanic Media Assn., Denver Advertising Fedn., Urban League Met. Denver. Office: Station KRMA-TV 1089 Bannock St Denver CO 80204

MORI, ALLEN ANTHONY, university dean, consultant, researcher; b. Hazleton, Pa., Nov. 1, 1947; s. Primo Philip and Carmella (DeNoia) M.; m. Barbara Epoca, June 26, 1971; 1 child, Kirsten Lynn. BA, Franklin and Marshall Coll., Lancaster, Pa., 1969; MEd, Bloomsburg U. Pa., 1971; PhD, U. Pitts., 1975. Spl. edn. tchr. White Haven (Pa.) State Sch. and Hosp., 1969-70, Hazleton Area Sch. Dist., 1970-71, Pitts. Pub. Schs., 1971-74; supr. student tchrs. U. Pitts., 1974-75; prof. spl. edn. U. Nev., Las Vegas, 1975-84; dean coll edn. Marshall U., Huntington, W.Va., 1984-87; dean sch. edn. Calif. State U., L.A., 1987—; hearing officer pub. law 94-142 Nev. Dept. Edn., Carson City, 1978—; mem. Nev. Gov.'s Com. on Mental Health and Mental Retardation, 1983-84; cons. Ministry Edn., Manitoba, Can., 1980-82; pres. Tchr. Edn. Coun. State Colls. & Univs., 1993—. Author: Families of Children with Special Needs, 1983; co-author: Teaching the Severely Retarded, 1980, Handbook of Preschool, Special Education, 1980, Adapted Physical Education, 1983, A Vocational Training Continuum for the Mentally and Physically Disabled, 1985, Teaching Secondary Students with Mild Learning and Behavior Problems, 1986, 93; contbr. numerous articles, book revs. and monographs to profl. jours. Bd. dirs. Assn. Retarded Citizens San Gabriel Valley, ElMonte, 1989—. Recipient grants U.S. Dept. Edn., 1976-91, Nev. Dept. Edn., W.Va. Dept. Edn., Calif. State U. Chancellor's Office. Mem. Assn. Tchr. Educators, Coun. for Exceptional Children (div. on Career Devel. exec. com. 1981-83), Nat. Soc. for Study of Edn., Kiwanis, Phi Beta Delta, Phi Delta Kappa, Pi Lambda Theta. Office: Calif State U 5151 State University Dr Los Angeles CA 90032-4221

MORI, JOSEPH HIDENOBU, electrical engineer, consultant; b. Tojomachi, Hibagun, Japan, Dec. 12, 1922; came to U.S., 1924; s. Tanekichi Tom and Chiyo (Seo) M.; m. Emma Yukawa, July 9, 1949; children: Christine, David. BSEE, U. Dayton, 1947; MBA, San Jose State U., 1976; postgrad., Santa Clara U., 1977-82. Registered profl. engr. Chief elec. engr. Lesco Mfg. Co. Inc., Dayton, Ohio, 1950-54, Chgo. Elevator and Machine Co., 1954-61; chief design engr. C.J. Anderson & Co., Chgo., 1961-63; coord. control designers Dover Elevator Co. Ltd., L.A., 1963-65; project engr. F&M Automation, Montebello, Calif., 1965-67; sr. staff engr. F.M.C., Santa Clara, Calif., 1967-84; sr. elec. engr. Ground Systems Div. F.M.C., San Jose, Calif., 1984-88; elec. engr. cons. Saratoga, Calif., 1988—. co-inventor: Elevator signal machine drive spl. self correcting drive, 1959 (patent). Mem. IEEE, Profl. and Tech. Cons. Assn. (bd. dirs. 1991—). Home and Office: 18973 Sara Park Cir Saratoga CA 95070-4169

MORI, KOICHI, physiologist, researcher; b. Himeji, Hyogo, Japan, Sept. 26, 1956; came to U.S., 1989; s. Yoshimi and Tomoko (Nakatani) M.; m. Mami Haeno, Dec. 16, 1990. MD, U. Tokyo, 1981, PhD, 1988. Cert. otolaryngologist. Resident U. Tokyo Hosp., 1981, 82, asst., 1982-83, 88-89; resident Jichi Med. Sch. Hosp., Minamikawachi, Tochigi, Japan, 1981-82; rsch. fellow Calif. Inst. Tech., Pasadena, 1989—. Mem. Amnesty Internat., N.Y., 1991—. Japan Ikueikai fellow, 1983-88, Del E. Webb Found. fellow, 1989-90, Human Frontier Sci. Orgn. long-term fellow (France), 1991-92. Mem. Physiol. Soc. Japan, Otology Soc. Japan, Audiology Soc. Japan, Japanese Soc. for Otorhinolaryngology, Internat. Soc. for Neuroethology, Soc. for Neurosci. Home: 4-8-3-409 Yushima, Bunkyo-ku Tokyo 113, Japan Office: Div Biology M/S 216-76 Calif Inst Tech Pasadena CA 91125 also: U Tokyo Fac of Med Inst Logo & Phon, 7-3-1 Hongbo, Bunkyo-ku Tokyo 113, Japan

MORIARTY, DONALD PETER, II, engineering executive, military officer; b. Alexandria, La., Jan. 26, 1935; s. Donald P. and Catherine G. (Stafford) M.; children by previous marriage: Erin, Donald P. III; m. Diana Mary Blackburn, Feb. 4, 1984. BS, La. State U., 1957; MA, Fla. Atlantic U., 1973; diploma, U.S Army Comdr. and Gen. Staff Coll., 1977. Commd. 2d lt. U.S. Army, 1957, advanced through grades to lt. col., 1978; artillery officer U.S. Army, various, 1957-74; head tactical plans sect. Army Air Def. Command, Darmstadt, Federal Republic of Germany, 1975-77; dir. C3I div. Army Air Def. Ctr., Ft. Bliss, Tex., 1977-80; retired Army Air Def. Ctr., 1980; sr. system engr. Hughes Aircraft Co., Fullerton, Calif., 1980-82, mgr. engr. design dept., 1982-84, project mgr., 1984-90; mgr. advanced systems programs, 1990--; U.S. Army Rep. to Tactical Airpower Com. NATO hdqrs., Brussels, 1977-79, Tri-Service Group on Air Def., NATO, 1978-80, Air Def. Electronic Equipment Com., NATO, 1978-80; lead systems engr. Hughes Aircraft Co., Fullerton, 1980-83; Strategic Def. Initiative Program Coordinator Systems Div. Hughes Aircraft Co., 1985-87; mgr. Tac Def. and Tac Command Control Program, Systems Div., GSG, Hughes Aircraft Co., 1987—. Author: The U.S. Army Officer as Military Statesman, 1973; author genealogical articles. Parade chmn. South Fla. Fair Assn., West Palm Beach, 1971; staff commr. Boy Scouts Am., Kaiserslautern, Federal Republic of Germany, 1974-76; sr. warden Episcopal Ch., Kaiserslautern, 1975, Wiesbaden, Federal Republic of Germany, 1977, Placentia, Calif., 1985-88; pres. Episcopal Synod of Am., 1993—. Decorated Vietnamese Cross of Gallantry with Palm, Air medal with two oak leaf clusters, Bronze Star with one oak leaf cluster, Legion of Merit; recipient Wood Badge award Boy Scouts Am., Newburgh, N.Y., 1969. Fellow Am. Coll. Genealogists; mem. AIAA, Assn. U.S. Army, Armed Forces Com.-Elect Assn., Am. Electronics Assn., SAR, Gen. Soc. Mayflower Descendants, Phi Alpha Theta, Acacia. Republican. Home: 626 E Riverview Ave Orange CA 92865-1336 Office: Hughes Aircraft Co 1901 W Malvern Ave Fullerton CA 92633-2100

MORIARTY, JOHN, opera administrator, artistic director; b. Fall River, Mass., Sept. 30, 1930; s. John J. and Fabiola Marie (Ripeau) M. MusB summa cum laude, New Eng. Conservatory, 1952; D.M. New England Conservatory, 1992. Artistic adminstr. Opera Soc. of Washington, 1960-62, Santa Fe Opera, N.Mex., 1962-65; dir. Wolf Trap Co., Vienna, Va., 1972-77; chmn. opera dept. Boston Conservatory , 1973-89; chmn. opera dept. New Eng. Conservatory, 1989—; prin. condr. Central City Opera, Denver, 1978—, artistic dir., 1982—; panelist Nat. Inst. Music Theater, 1985, 86, 87, Conn. Arts Council, 1982, 84; adjudicator various contests including Met. Opera auditions, 1965—. Author: Diction, 1975. Trustee Boston Concert Opera. Recipient Frank Huntington Beebe award, Boston, 1954, Disting. Alumni award New Eng. Conservatory Alumni Assn., 1982, Gold Chair award Cen. City Opera House Assn., 1988. Mem. Nat. Opera Assn., Sigma Alpha Iota, Delta Omicron, Pi Kappa Lambda. Office: New Eng Conservatory 290 Huntington Ave Boston MA 02115-5000 also: Cen City Opera House Assn 621 17th St Ste 1601 Denver CO 80293-1601

MORIMOTO, CARL NOBORU, computer system engineer, crystallographer; b. Hiroshima, Japan, Mar. 31, 1942; came to U.S., 1957, naturalized, 1965; s. Toshiyuki and Teruko (Hirano) M.; m. Helen Kiyomi Yoshizaki, June 28, 1969; children: Matthew Ken, Justin Ray. B.A., U. Hawaii, 1965; Ph.D., U. Wash., 1970. Research assoc. dept. chemistry Mich. State U., East Lansing, 1970-72; postdoctoral fellow dept. biochemistry and biophysics Tex. A&M U., College Station, 1972-75; sr. sci. programmer Syntex Analytical Instruments Inc., Cupertino, Calif., 1975-78; prin. programmer analyst, software engring. mgr. Control Data Corp., Sunnyvale, Calif., 1978-83; mem. profl. staff GE Aerospace, San Jose, Calif., 1983-93; prin. engr. GE Nuclear Energy, San Jose, 1993—. Mem. Am. Crytallographic Assn., Assn. Computing Machinery, Am. Chem. Soc., Sigma Xi. Am. Baptist. Home: 4003 Hamilton Park Dr San Jose CA 95130-1223

MORIOKA, SHARON EMI, social services planner; b. Honolulu, June 15, 1959; d. Paul Tsugio and Mae Sachiko (Hirano) M. BA, Western Wash. U., 1981; MSW, U. Wash., 1983. Rsch. asst. U. Wash. Sch. Social Work, Seattle, 1981-83; planning and allocations assoc. United Way Pierce County, Tacoma, 1983-84, sr. planning and allocations assoc., 1984-85; planning cons. United Way San Diego County, San Diego, 1986, planning and allocations assoc. II, 1986-90, sr. planning and allocations assoc., 1990-93; human svcs. coord. City of Chula Vista, Calif., 1993—. Author, editor: Future Scan, 1989, Latino Future Scan, 1991, Children's Future Scan, 1993. Sec. bd. dirs. Pioneer Pony League, San Diego, 1990—. Mem. Altrusa (newsletter editor San Diego 1990—, yearbook editor 1991—, corr. sec. 1991-92, bd. dirs. 1992-94). Democrat. Home: 7084-247 Camino Degrazia San Diego CA 92111 Office: Norman Park Sr Ctr 270 F St Chula Vista CA 91910

MORIS, LAMBERTO GIULIANO, architect; b. Siena, Tuscany, Italy, Mar. 29, 1944; came to U.S., 1972; s. Gualtiero Luigi and Giovanna (Avanzati) M.; m. Tracy P. Schilling, 1970 (div. 1985); children: Giacomo, Stefano; m. Beverly Chiang, Mar. 28, 1986; 1 child, Christopher. MA in Arch., U. Florence, Italy, 1970. Assoc. Marquis Assocs., San Francisco, 1972-78, prin., 1978-85; prin. Simon Martin-Vegue Winkelstein Moris, San Francisco, 1985—; tchr. San Francisco City Coll.; juror DuPont Antron Design Awards, 1989; mem. adv. com. Acad. of Art-Coll., San Francisco, 1991—. Mem. San Francisco Opera Guild. Mem. AIA, Interior Architecture AIA, The Engrs. Club, Il Cenacolo Club. Roman Catholic. Office: Simon Martin-Vegue Winkelstein & Moris 501 2d St San Francisco CA 94107

MORISON, JACK, international adventure travel company owner; b. Santa Monica, Calif., Dec. 17, 1954; s. James Sanford and Helene (Walker) M.; m. Julie Margaret Ogawa, Sept. 9, 1989; 1 child, Walker Martin. AA, Cabrillo Coll., 1978; student, Golden Gate U., 1986-87, Coll. of Marin, 1988. Mgr. and guide river trips in West and Southwest O.A.R.S. Inc., Angles Camp, Calif., 1971-85; mgr. internat. ops., participant expeditions 27 countries Sobek Expeditions, Angels Camp, Calif., 1979-84; coord. for internat. adventure travel trips, asst. Esprit De Corp, San Francisco, 1983-87; project coord. Project Russians and Ams. for Teamwork, 1987—; owner Adventure Travel Co. affiliate White Magic Unlimited, Mill Valley, Calif., 1983—; cons. mktg. and sales Wilderness Travel, Berkeley, Calif., 1987; advisor ops. White Magic Nepal; leader first Albanian Black Drini Expedition, 1992. Producer film documentaries Bill Burrud Prodns., LA.., 1979, Richard Kidd Prodns., Dallas, 1981, Wingstar Film Prodns., N.Y., 1982, Stan Boor Prodns., 1983, 2 films Pakistani TV, 1985, 86. Pres. Episcopal Youth Coun., 1972. Office: White Magic Unlimited 317 Miller Ave Mill Valley CA 94941-2818

MORONEY, MICHAEL JOHN, lawyer; b. Jamaica, N.Y., Nov. 8, 1940; s. Everard Vincent and Margaret Olga (Olson) M.; children: Sean, Megan, Matthew. BS in Polit. Sci., Villanova U., 1962; JD, Fordham U., 1965; Police Sci. (hon.), U. Guam, 1976. Bar: Hawaii 1974, U.S. Dist. Ct. Hawaii 1974, U.S. Ct. Appeals (9th cir.) 1974, Guam 1976, U.S. Dist. Ct. (Guam dist.) 1976, U.S. Ct. Claims 1976, U.S. Tax Ct. 1976, U.S. Ct. Mil. Appeals 1977, U.S. Supreme Ct. 1977, High Ct. Trust Ters. 1977, U.S. Dist. Ct. (No. Mariana Islands) 1983. Spl. agt. FBI, Memphis and Nashville, 1965-67, Cleve. and Elyria, Ohio, 1967-71; spl. agt., prin. legal advisor FBI, U.S. Dept. Justice, Honolulu, 1971—; bar examiner and applications rev. com. Supreme Ct. Hawaii, 1980—; pres. Hawaii State Law Enforcement Adminstrn., 1985-86; mem. and del. to congress Gov.'s Task Force on Hawaii's Internat. Role, 1988. Mem. gov.'s task force, del. gov.'s congress on Hawaii's Internat. Role, 1988—; trustee, v.p. Takatani Found., Honolulu, 1992—. Recipient Govs. Award for Outstanding Contbns. to Law Enforcement, Gov. of Guam, 1974, 76, cert. of appreciation Supreme Ct. Hawaii, 1981, cert. of appreciation Honolulu Police Commn., 1984, 86; named Fed. Law Enforcement Officer of Yr., State of Hawaii, 1992. Mem. ABA, Fed. Bar Assn., Hawaii Bar Assn., Guam Bar Assn., Assn. Trial Lawyers Am., Inst. Jud. Adminstrn., Hawaii State Law Enforcement Ofcls. Assn. (law enforcement officer of yr. 1992), Internat. Assn. Chiefs of Police, Hilo Yacht Club. Office: US Dept Justice PO Box 50164 Honolulu HI 96850-0001

MORONEY, MICHAEL VINCENT, national and international shipping manager; b. Negritos, Peru, Dec. 18, 1930; came to U.S., 1943; s. Vincent John and Helen Streeter (LaGorce) M.; m. Sousan Reddin, Aug. 25, 1956; children: Vincent, Elizabeth, Caroline, Stephen. Student, U. Mo. Cert. engring tech., Alberta, Can. Various entry level and middle mgmt. positions various petroleum corps., 1950-51; mgr. Moraine Construction Co., 1956-60; various assignments pvt. practice, 1960-70; ops. mgr. Deminex Can. Ltd., Can., 1970-75; pres. Measurement Systems Corp. Internat., Calif., 1975-85; shipping mgr., export control BIO 101 Inc., Vista, Calif., 1985—. Corps. of Engrs., U.S. Army, 1951-53.

MOROYE, LESTER YOSHIO, foundation executive; b. Pueblo, Colo., Sept. 8, 1947; m. Julianne Daveline, Sept. 2, 1967; children: Leslie Michele, Jennifer Lynn, Eric Scott. BS in Behavioral Scis., U. So. Colo., 1972; MA in Mgmt., U. Phoenix, Denver, 1988. Div. adminstr. Colo. State Jud. Dept., Denver, 1973-87; exec. dir. Career Dimensions Found., Denver, 1987—; parttime faculty Regis U., 1987—, Arapahoe Community Coll., 1987—, Aurora Community Coll., 1987—. Vol. Colo. Easter Seals, denver, 1987-91, Aurora (Colo.) Youth League, 1985-89. Mem. Colo. Assn. Probation Officers (past pres.), Colo. Correctional Assn. (bd. dirs. 1975-87), Am. Correctional Assn. (del. assy. 1979-82), Colo. Trainers Assn. (bd. dirs. 1987-91). Office: Career Dimensions Found Ste C-208 16000 Centretech Pky Aurora CO 80011

MORRELL, PATTY LOU, daycare administrator/owner; b. L.A., June 21, 1951; d. Clayton Ralph and Anne Marie (Fritzie) Bedford; m. Ben E. Franklin III, Feb. 12, 1972 (div. Sept. 1979); children: Dana Sue Orms, Jodi Lynn; m. Terry Floyd Morrell, June 14, 1980; 1 child, Bradford James. AA, Pierce Jr. Coll., 1972. Cert. early childhood devel. Exec. sec. Phi Alpha Delta Law Fraternity, Granada Hills, Calif., 1970-76; personnel coun. B&B Personnel, Inc., Denver, 1976-78; pvt. practice Kolor Korner Paint-n-Paper, Douglas, Wyo., 1978-82, Child Day Care, Douglas, Wyo., 1982—. Recipient Henry Giessenbier, Founders, Silver and Blue Chip awards Jaycees 1991. Mem. U.S. Jaycees (amb., consul gen. 1992—). Republican. Roman Catholic. Home: 1322 Sweetwater Douglas WY 82633

MORREY, JOHN ROLPH, scientist; b. Joseph, Utah, May 30, 1930; s. John E. and Vera (Mortensen) M.; m. Barbara Mortensen, Mar. 14, 1952; children: John D., Stephen R., Dianna, Eugene V., Stacie K. BA, BS, Brigham Young U., 1954; PhD, U. Utah, 1958. Scientist GE, Richland, Wash., 1958-65; staff scientist Battelle N.W., Richland, 1965—; mem. adv. com. Joint Ctr. for Grad. Study, Richland, 1984-90; mem. adv. coun. Wash. State U. TriCity Br., Richland, 1990—; adj. assoc. prof. Wash. State U., 1965—. Author 100 publs. Mem. exec. bd. Blue Mountain Coun. Boy Scouts of Am., Richland, 1980-91; stake pres. LDS Ch., 1980-89. Mem. AAAS, Am. Chem. Soc. (alt. counselor 1972), Sigma Xi. Home: 1408 Westwood Ct Richland WA 99352-2447 Office: Battelle NW PO Box 999 Richland WA 99352-0999

MORRILL, RALPH ALFRED, computer company executive; b. Denver, Oct. 24, 1930; s. Ralph A. and Winifred Elizabeth (Dorsey) M.; m. Nancy Anne Adams, Apr. 12, 1953; children: Deanne Elizabeth, Ralph Danial, Alice Lynn. AAS, City Coll., 1952; BSEE, Calif. State U., 1958; postgrad., U. Santa Clara, 1960-62. Project mgr. Sylvania Electronics West, Mountain View, Calif., 1958-64; mgr. rsch. Arinc Rsch. Corp., Santa Anna, Calif., 1964-66; rsch. project mgr. Philco-Ford Corp., Newport Beach, Calif., 1966-67; with project mgmt./staff Rockwell Internat. Co., L.A., 1967-69; pres., owner RAMA Corp., Denver, 1974—; v.p. systems R&D RAMA Corp., Mercer Island, Wash., 1969—; program mgr. U.S. Dept. Interior, Denver, 1970-76, U. Chgo./Argonne (Ill.) Lab., 1980-81; founder, bd. chair RAMA Corp., 1974—; sr. cons. Boeing Computer Svcs., Seattle, 1987-90; bd. dirs. Humanities Rsch. Inst., Santa Anna, Calif., 1966-71; chmn. several govt. coms., Denver, 1970—; lectr. and pub. speaker in field. Contbr. articles to profl. jours.; patentee in field. Chmn. Children and Family Svcs. Adv. Com., Santa Ana, 1967-70; founder several bus. and community svc. orgns. With U.S. Army, 1952-54. Mem. Assn. of Computing Machinery (sr.), Artificial Intelligence Assn. Am. (founder), Digital Computer User Soc./Am. (sr.). Home: 7314 Island Crest Way Mercer Island WA 98040 Office: RAMA Corp PO Box 214 Mercer Island WA 98040

MORRIN, THOMAS HARVEY, engineering research company executive; b. Woodland, Calif., Nov. 24, 1914; s. Thomas E. and Florence J. (Hill) M.; m. Frances M. Von Ahn, Feb. 1, 1941; children: Thomas H., Diane, Linda, Denise. B.S., U. Calif., 1937; grad., U.S. Navy Grad. Sch., Annapolis, Md., 1941. Student engr. Westinghouse Electric Mfg. Co., Emeryville, Calif., 1937; elec. engr. Pacific Gas & Electric Co., 1938-41; head microwave engring. div. Raytheon Mfg. Co., Waltham, Mass., 1947-48; chmn. elec. engring. dept. Stanford Research Inst., 1948-52, dir. engring., research, 1952-60, gen. mgr. engring., 1960-64, vice pres. engring., sci., 1964-68; pres. University City Sci. Inst., Phila., 1968-69; pres., chmn. bd. Morrin Assos., Inc., Wenatchee, Wash., 1968-72. Trustee Am. Acad. Transp. Served as officer USNR, 1938-58, comdr. USN, 1945-48. Decorated Bronze Star; recipient Bank Am. award for automation of banking during 1950's, 1992. Fellow IEEE, AAAS; mem. Sci. Research Soc. Am., U.S. Naval Inst., Navy League, Marine Meml. Club (San Francisco). Address: 654 23d Ave San Francisco CA 94121

MORRIN, VIRGINIA WHITE, educator; b. Escondido, Calif., May 16, 1913; d. Harry Parmalee and Ethel Norine (Nutting) Rising; B.S., Oreg. State Coll., 1952; M.Ed., Oreg. State U., 1957; m. Raymond Bennett White, 1933 (dec. 1953); children: Katherine Anne, Marjorie Virginia, William Raymond; m. 2d, Laurence Morrin, 1959 (dec. 1972). Social caseworker Los Angeles County, Los Angeles, 1934-40, 61-64; acctg. clk. War Dept., Ft. MacArthur, Calif., 1940-42; prin. clk. USAAF, Las Vegas, Nev., 1942-44; high sch. tchr., North Bend-Coos Bay, Oreg., 1952-56, Mojave, Calif., 1957-60; instr. Antelope Valley Coll., Lancaster, Calif., 1961-73; ret., 1974. Treas., Humane Soc. Antelope Valley, Inc., 1968—. Mem. Nat. Aero. Assn., Calif. State Sheriffs' Assn. (charter assoc.), Oreg. State U. Alumni Assn. (life). Address: 3153 Milton Dr Mojave CA 93501-1329

MORRIS, ALVIN LEE, retired consulting corporation executive, meteorologist; b. Kim, Colo., June 7, 1920; s. Roy E. and Eva Edna (James) M.; BS in Meteorology (U.S. Weather Bur. fellow), U. Chgo., 1942; MS, U.S. Navy Postgrad. Sch., 1954; m. Nadean Davidson, Jan. 16, 1979; children: Andrew N., Nancy L., Mildred M., Ann E., Jane C. Meteorologist Pacific Gas and Electric Co., San Francisco, 1947-50; commd. U.S. Navy, 1942, advanced through grades to capt., USNR, 1962, assignments including staff, comdr. 7th Fleet; dir. rsch. Navy Weather Research Facility, Norfolk, Va., 1958-62; facilities coord., mgr. sci. balloon facility, Nat. Ctr. for Atmospheric Rsch. Boulder, Colo., 1963-75; pres. Ambient Analysis Inc., Internat. Cons., Boulder, 1975-86. Treas. Home Hospitality for Fgn. Students Program, U. Colo., 1969-70; del. People to People Del. on Environment; Peoples Republic of China, 1984. Served with USN, 1942-46, 50-58. Mem. Am. Meteorol. Soc. (cert. cons. meteorologist), Am. Geophys. Union, ASTM, Ret. Officers Assn., N.Y. Acad. Scis., Boulder County Knife and Fork Club. Editor Handbook of Scientific Ballooning, 1975; assoc. editor Jour. Oceanic and Atmospheric Tech., 1984-88; contbr. articles to profl. jours.; convenor, editor proceedings ASTM conf. Home: 880 Sunshine Canyon Dr Boulder CO 80302-9727

MORRIS, BYRON FREDERICK, biological oceanographer; b. Montevideo, Minn., July 29, 1943; s. Byron Mahon and Louella Rebecca (Eckhart) M.; m. Mary Ruth Donica, Aug. 15, 1981 (div.); children: Robert Byron, Christopher Robin; m. Carla Jan Briske, June 21, 1987. BSc, Calif. State U., Long Beach, 1966; MA, Calif. State U., 1968; PhD, Dalhousie U., Halifax, Nova Scotia, 1975. Rsch. assoc. Bermuda Biol. Sta., St. Georges, Bermuda, 1971-75, asst. dir., 1975-77; environ. studies coord. Bur. of Land Mgmt., Anchorage, 1977-80; outer continental shelf coord. Nat. Marine Fisheries Svc., Anchorage, 1980-89; chief oil spill damage assessment office Nat. Marine Fisheries Svc., Juneau, Alaska, 1989—; rep. Oil Spill Mgmt. Team, Juneau, 1989-91, Oil Spill Restoration Team, Juneau, 1992—. Coauthor: Pelagic Tar, 1976, Bermuda Inshore Environment, 1977, Studies of Sargassum, 1978. Grantee NSF, 1971-75, fellowship, 1968. Mem. AAAS, Bermuda Biol. Sta. (assoc.). Home: Mendenhall Peninsula Rd Juneau AK 99801 Office: Nat Marine Fisheries Svc PO Box 210029 Auke Bay AK 99821

MORRIS, DALE L., broadcast executive; b. Artesia, Calif.; s. William G. and Mary Lou (Graves) M. Prodn. dir. Sta. KVCV, Redding, Sta. KSXO, Redding, Sta. KHSL-AM-TV, Chico, Calif., Sta. KWSA, Klamath Falls, Oreg.; program dir. Sta. KRIJ, Paradise, Calif.; exec. producer World of Collector Cars, Chico, 1991—. Author: How to Break Into Radio Broadcasting, 1983; writer, entertainer comedy records; columnist newspaper Pottshots. Office: World of Collector Cars PO Box 8808 Chico CA 95926

MORRIS, DAVID JOHN, mining engineer, consultant, mining executive; b. Seattle, May 6, 1945; s. Jack Abraham and Alice Jean (Hanson) M.; m. Melania F. Kearney, July 28, 1978; children: Whitney Elizabeth, Benton James, Sienna Elise. BA in Math. and Physics, Whitman Coll., 1968; BS in Mining Engring., Columbia U., 1968. Registered profl. engr., Colo., Utah, Wash. Mining engr. Union Oil of Calif., Los Angeles, 1968-69; mining engr. John T. Boyd Co., Denver, 1974-76, sr. mining engr., 1976-78, v.p., mgr., 1978-87; mng. ptnr. Palmer Coaking Coal Co., Black Diamond, Wash., 1976-82, 1990—; pres. Pacific Coast Coal Co., Black Diamond, 1982—. Mem. Bd. Overseers Whitman Coll., Walla Walla, Wash., 1986—, vice chair, 1993—, chmn. Rep. camapign for Whitman, Denver, 1985. Served as lt. USN, 1969-74, Vietnam. Henry Krumb scholar Columbia U., N.Y.C., 1967-68. Mem. NSPE, Soc. Mining Engrs. (admissions com. 1985-88, Howard Eavenson award com. 1984-87, Woomer award com. 1990-93, chair 1993—), Nat. Coal Assn. (bd. dirs. 1990-93, exec. com. 1993—), Nat. Coal Coun. (appointed by sec. of energy 1992), Seattle C. of C. (chmn. energy com. 1991—), Western Rugby Football Union (sec. 1980), Denver Country Club, Broadmoor Golf Club, Rotary. Republican. Home: 3711 E Madison St Seattle WA 98112-3838 Office: Pacific Coast Coal Co Inc 900 4th Ave Ste 3625 Seattle WA 98164-1095

MORRIS, DONALD CHARLES, real estate developer; b. Iowa City, Nov. 15, 1951; s. Lucien Ellis and Jean (Pinder) M.; m. Barbara Louise Small, Apr. 28, 1973 (div. Apr. 1980); m. Jana Susan Moyer, Aug. 28, 1982; children: Alexander Charles, Elisa Jean. Student, Cantab Coll., Toronto, Can., 1970-71; BSC, U. Guelph, Can., 1974; MSC, U. Guelph, 1975; PhD, U. B.C., Vancouver, 1978. Instr. U. B.C., Vancouver, 1975-77; pres. Morley Internat., Inc., Seattle, 1976-81; self-employed Comml. Investment Real Estate, Seattle, 1981-83; v.p., regional mgr. DKB Corp., Seattle, 1983-86; pres. Morris Devel. Svcs., Inc., Seattle, 1986—, Washington Group, Inc., Seattle, 1986—; bd. dirs. Preservation Action, Washington. Dir. Preservation Action, Washington, 1985—; mem. Nat. Trust for Hist. Preservation. Mem. Seattle King County Bd. Realtors (legis. com.), Wash. Assn. Realtors, Nat. Assn. Realtors, Pioneer Square Assn. Seattle, Pioneer Square Property Owners Assn. Seattle, Meydenbauer Yacht Club. Office: Wash Group Morris Devel PO Box 4584 Rollingbay WA 98061-0584

MORRIS, DONALD JAMES, banker; b. Phoenix, July 6, 1933; s. Hillman Errol and Alice Katherine (Ryan) M.; m. Mary Kathleen Hartnett, Aug. 23, 1952; children: Dawn Marie, Stephen, Jaimie, Andrea, Donald James. Grad., Pacific Sch. Banking, U. Wash., 1980; BA, St. Mary's Coll. of Calif., Moraga, 1982. Br. mgr. Valley Nat. Bank, Phoenix, 1952-67; v.p. Union Bank, L.A., 1967-77; sr. v.p. Bank of Sonoma County, Santa Rosa, Calif., 1977-82, Plaza Bank of Commerce, San Jose, Calif., 1982-83; pres. Morris Fin. Cons., San Jose, 1983-84; sr. v.p. Comml. Bank of Fremont, Calif., 1984-87; exec. v.p., chief adminstrv. officer Bank of Petaluma, Calif., 1987—; pres. employers adv. group Employment Devel. Dept. Calif., 1990-92. V.p. Petaluma Boys and Girls Club, 1991-93. Named Boss of Yr., Bus. and Profl. Women, Flagstaff, Ariz., 1961. Mem. Bank Adminstrn. Inst. (pres. Golden Gate chpt. 1990-92), Calif. Banking Assn. (ops. com. 1990-92), Western Ind. Bankers (strategic task force 1991-92), Kiwanis Club (pres. club 1955), Rotary Club (Paul Harris fellow 1990), Grand Canyon Ariz. Club (pres. 1967), Petaluma Valley Club (pres. 1993-94). Office: Bank of Petaluma 100 Petaluma Blvd S Petaluma CA 94952

MORRIS, DORIS CALDWELL, horse breeder, office administrator; b. Hollis, Okla., Apr. 12, 1933; d. Robert Young and Era (Abernethy) Darnell; m. Charles E. Caldwell, Mar. 25, 1949 (div. July 1982); children: Cheri Caldwell Cunningham, Chris Darnell Caldwell, C.D. Caldwell; m. Richard Trent Morris, Nov. 18, 1989. Co-owner, operator Caldwell Appaloosa Ranch, Washington, Okla., 1959-81; advt. rep. The Appaloosa Jour., Oklahoma City, 1984-85; mgr. designer sportswear Rothschilds, Oklahoma City, 1985-89; co-owner, operator Morris 2 Mile High Ranch, Cripple Creek, Colo., 1989—; mgr. office Gold Rush newspaper, Cripple Creek, 1992—. Breeder numerous World and National Championship-class horses; contbr. articles to profl. jours. Republican. Methodist. Address: Morris 2 Mile High Ranch 12658 Hwy 67 Cripple Creek CO 80813

MORRIS, EDWARD J(AMES), JR., business owner, insurance agent; b. Jersey City, Jan. 9, 1936; s. Edward James Sr. and Mary Alice (Carr) M.; m. Joan M. O'Keefe, Sept. 17, 1955; children: Edward James III, Glenn D., Gary J. Student, Drakes Bus. Coll., 1953; cert. ins. broker, Vale Tech. Inst., 1962. CLU, Chartered Fin. Cons. Part-time salesperson Stanley Home Products, Jersey City, 1958-60; selector Am. Stores, South Kearny, N.J., 1957-62; owner Ed Morris State Farm Agy., Jersey City, 1962-72; owner, mgr., restauranteur E&J Morris Enterprises, Inc., New Bern, N.C., 1972-79; owner, mgr. Morris Ins. Agy., Jackson, N.J., 1979-82; spl. agt., reg. rep. Morris Fin. and Ins. Agy., Matawan, N.J., 1982-92; owner, mgr. Sunset Selections, Scottsdale, Ariz., 1992--. Contbr. articles to profl. jours. Mem. com. Boy Scouts Am., Jersey City, 1966-72; basketball coach Our Lady of Mercy Ch., Jersey City, 1967-69; treas., basketball coach Coll. Little League, Jersey City, 1966-71; mcpl. chmn. Citizens for Goldwater, Jersey City, 1963-64. Sgt. USMC, 1954-57.

MORRIS, ELIZABETH TREAT, physical therapist; b. Hartford, Conn., Feb. 20, 1936; d. Charles Wells and Marion Louise (Case) Treat; BS in Phys. Therapy, U. Conn., 1960; m. David Breck Morris, July 10, 1961; children: Russell Charles, Jeffrey David. Phys. therapist Crippled Children's Clinic No. Va., Arlington, 1960-62, Shriners Hosp. Crippled Children, Salt Lake City, 1967-69, Holy Cross Hosp., Salt Lake City, 1970-74; pvt. practice phys. therapy, Salt Lake City, 1975—. Mem. nominating com. YWCA, Salt Lake City. Mem. Am. Phys. Therapy Assn., Am. Congress Rehab. Medicine, Nat. Speakers Assn., Utah Speakers Assn., Salt Lake Area C. of C., Friendship Force Utah, U.S. Figure Skating Assn., Toastmasters Internat., Internat. Assn. for the Study Pain, Internat. Platform Assn., World Confederation Phys. Therapy, Medart Internat. Home: 4177 Mathews Way Salt Lake City UT 84124-4021 Office: PO Box 526186 Salt Lake City UT 84152-6186

MORRIS, GEORGE ALLEN, III, small business owner; b. Norman, Okla., Aug. 2, 1958; s. George Allen Jr. and Freda Grace (Addison) M.; children: Addison Wesleigh, Zachary Alexander. Engring. cons. Spectra Data, Inc., Northridge, Calif., 1976-81; adminstr. Hypnosis Clearing House, Oakland, Calif., 1982-86; owner Soft Gam's Software, Ft. Bragg, Calif., 1986—. Author: (computer program) Disk Organizer, 1986. Mem. IEEE (assoc.), League of Am. Wheelman (life), Assn. Computing Machinery, Assn. Shareware Profls. Office: Soft Gam's Software PO Box 1311 Mendocino CA 95460

MORRIS, HAROLD LEON, corporation executive, publisher; b. Hazleton, Pa., Nov. 8, 1929; s. Sam and Fannie E. (Smulyan) M.; m. Barbara Dorothy Gray, Mar. 3, 1957; children: John David, Robert Allen. BS in Econs., U. Pa., 1951. Exec. trainee Morris Jewelers, N.Y.C., 1951-53, Emporium-Capwell Corp., San Francisco, 1953-57; mdse. mgr. Yosemite (Calif.) Park and Curry Co., 1958-63; pres. Morris and Morris, Inc., Santa Cruz, Calif., 1963—; pub. Western Tanager Press, Santa Cruz, Calif., 1979—; pres. Blacks Beach Cafe, Inc., Santa Cruz, Calif., 1992—. Chmn. City/County Libr. Trustees, Santa Cruz, 1985-87, City Mus. Assn., Santa Cruz, 1979-80; co-chmn. Com. to Elect Leon Panetta, Santa Cruz, 1976; mem. Yosemite Conversation Club, 1961-63. Democrat. Office: Morris and Morris Inc 1111 Pacific Ave Santa Cruz CA 95060

MORRIS, HENRY ARTHUR, JR., export company executive, consultant; b. Phila., May 26, 1923; s. Henry A. Sr. and Eleanor (Samuel) M.; widowed; 1 child, Henry A. III; m. Farideh R. Ranjandish, Feb. 9, 1991. BA, Lycoming Coll., 1952; LLB, Cath. U., 1954. Pres., chief exec. officer Am. Funding Int., Inc., Beverly Hills, Calif., 1956—; bd. dirs. McLean Agro-Indsl., Arlington, Va., Am. Housing Internat., Inc., Fairfax, Va.; chief exec. officer Export Cons., Inc., West L.A., 1983—. With U.S. Army, 1943-45, Europe. Democrat. Roman Catholic. Office: Am Funding Internat Inc PO Box 2085 Beverly Hills CA 90213-2085

MORRIS, HENRY MADISON, III, software manufacturing executive, minister; b. El Paso, Tex., May 15, 1942; s. Henry Madison and Mary Louise (Beach) M.; m. Janet Deckman, July 25, 1964; children: Henry M., Scotta Marie. BA summa cum laude, Christian Heritage Coll., 1976; MDiv, Luther Rice Sem., 1977, DMin, 1978; MBA Pepperdine U., 1989. Regional mgr. Integon Ins. Co., Greenville, S.C., 1969-75; ordained to ministry Bapt. Ch., 1968; pastor Hallmark Bapt. Ch., Greenville, 1969-75; assoc. prof. Bible, Christian Heritage Coll., El Cajon, Calif., 1977-78, adminstrv. v.p., 1978-80; pastor First Bapt. Ch., Canoga Park, Calif., 1980-86; chief adminstrv. officer, chief fin. officer SunGard Fin. Systems Inc., Canoga Park, 1986—; lectr. in field. Served with U.S. Army, 1959-66. Republican. Author: Baptism: What is It?, 1977; Explore the Word, 1978; Churches: History and Doctrine, 1980. Office: SunGard Fin Svcs Inc 22134 Sherman Way Canoga Park CA 91303-1126

MORRIS, JAMES GRANT, educator; b. Brisbane, Queensland, Australia, Aug. 30, 1930; came to U.S., 1969; s. Fredrick Grant and Mary (Wadley) M.; m. Jocelyn Morris, June 15, 1959; children: Elizabeth Anne, Julie Ione, James Peter Grant. B in Agrl. Sci., U. Queensland, 1952, B in Agrl. Sci. honors 1st class, 1954, M in Agrl. Sci., 1958; PhD, Utah State U., 1961. Asst. husbandry officer Primary Industries, Australia, 1954-58; husbandry officer Primary Industries, 1958-62, sr. husbandry officer, 1962-65; dir. Primary Industries, Brisbane, 1965-69; assoc. prof. U. Calif., Davis, 1969-75; prof. U. Calif., 1975—. Recipient FA Brodie Meml. prize Australian Meat Bd., 1968, Small Animal Nutrition award, Ralston Purina Am. Vet. Med. Assn., 1986; Fulbright scholar, 1958-61. Home: 38344 Larue Way Davis CA 95616-9422 Office: U Calif Sch Veterinary Medicine Davis CA 95616

MORRIS, JOHN NICKERSON, educator; b. N.Y.C., Mar. 30, 1942; s. Robert John and Doris Elizabeth (Nickerson) M.; foster children: Lee J. Kearnes, Brian W. Loehn, Jimmy O. Rodriguez. BS, SUNY, New Paltz, 1966; MS, SUNY, 1970, CAS, 1974. Tchr. Marlboro (N.Y.) Cen. Schs., 1966-74; fgn. svc. officer U.S. Dept. State, Washington, 1974-75; asst. prin. Lewis Cen. Community Schs., Council Bluffs, Iowa, 1975-76; prin. Winnebago (Nebr.) pub. schs., 1977-78; pres. Summers Co., Council Bluffs, 1978-84, Mountainland Liquors, Idaho Springs, Colo., 1981-84; tchr. L.A. Unified Sch. Dist., 1985-93; adminstrv. asst. Juniper Mid. Sch., Palmdale, Calif., 1993—; bd. dirs. Newburgh Tchrs. Credit Union, 1971-74. Mem. Assn. of Calif. Sch. Adminstrs. Home: 3155 Rodney St Rosamond CA 93560 Office: Juniper Mid Sch 39066 Palm Tree Way Palmdale CA 93551

MORRIS, JOHN THEODORE, planning official; b. Denver, Jan. 18, 1929; s. Theodore Ora and Daisy Allison (McDonald) M.; BFA, Denver U., 1955; m. Dolores Irene Seaman, June 21, 1951; children: Holly Lee, Heather Ann, Heidi Jo, Douglas Fraser. Apprentice landscape architect S.R. DeBoer & Co., Denver, summer 1949, planning technician (part-time), 1954-55; sr. planner and assoc. Trafton Bean & Assocs., Boulder, Colo., 1955-62; prin. Land Planning Assocs., planning cons., Boulder, 1962-65; planning dir. and park coord. Boulder County, 1965-67; sch. planner Boulder Valley Sch. Dist., 1967-84, also dir. planning and engring., 1967-84, supr. facility improvement program, 1969-84; pvt. sch. planning cons., 1984—; cons. U. Colo. Bur. Ednl. Field Svcs., 1974. Bd. dirs. Historic Boulder, 1974-76; mem. parks and recreation adv. com. Denver Regional Coun. Govts., 1975-84. Served with USCG, 1950-53. Mem. Am. Inst. Cert. Planners, Am. Planning Assn., Coun. of Ednl. Facility Planners Internat., Longmont Artist Guild. Home and Office: 7647 N 32d St Boulder CO 80302

MORRIS, LEANNE ALLEN, social service administrator; b. Logan, Utah, July 21, 1949; d. Norman C. and Olga (Price) Allen; m. Scott Warburton Morris, June 21, 1968; 1 child, Alan Scott. BS, Utah State U., 1971, M Social Sci., 1983. Cert. geronologist. Recreation aide Brigham City (Utah) Sr.Ctr., 1979-84, dir., 1984—. Vol. Arthritis Found., Brigham City, 1985—, United Way, No. Utah, 1986—, Adult Literacy Program Brigham, 1987-89. Recipient Community Svc. award Am. Assn. Retired Persons, 1987, cert. of Recognition Adminstrn. on Aging Region VIII, 1991. Mem. Nat. Assn. Meal Programs, Nat. Assn. Nutrition and Aging Svcs. Programs, Women in Bus. (publicity chair 1990), Nat. Coun. Aging, Utah Assn. Sr. Ctrs. and Nutrition Programs (1st v.p. 1992, tech. assistance team 1992), Am. Legion Aux., DAV Aux., Interagy. Coun. Transp. Com., 1992, Nat. Eldercare Inst. on Multipurpose Sr. Ctrs. speakers bur., Phi Upsilon Omicron. Mormon. Office: Brigham City Sr Ctr 24 N 300 W Box 1005 Brigham City UT 84302

MORRIS, LEONARD LESLIE, horticulturist, plant physiologist, educator; b. Terre Haute, Ind., Aug. 5, 1914; s. Ivan Leslie and Anna Eleanor (Huster) M.; m. Marsaille Crandall, Aug. 24, 1940. BS in Agr., Purdue U., 1937; MS, Cornell U., 1939, PhD, 1941. From lectr. to prof. vegetable crops U. Calif., Davis, 1941-82, prof. emeritus, 1982—. Contbr. articles to profl. jours., chpts. to books. Recipient C.W. Hauck award Produce Packaging Assn., 1956. Fellow AAAS, Am. Soc. Horticultural Sci. (L.H. Vaugn award 1957); mem. Sigma Xi, Phi Kappa Phi. Republican. Presbyterian. Home: 27485 Willowbank Rd Davis CA 95616 Office: Univ Calif Davis Mann Lab Davis CA 95616

MORRIS, MARIA ANTONIA, controller; b. Bucaramanga, Colombia, Mar. 11, 1940; came to U.S., 1966; d. Jesus A. and Elisa (Caycedo) Moreno; m. Todd S. Morris, Feb. 12, 1971; 1 child, John Edward. AA in Acctg., Trade Tech. Coll., 1972; BSBA, Calif. State U., Long Beach, 1985. Payroll mgr. U.S. Mags.-Art Hale Inc., Long Beach, 1973-79, pers. mgr., 1980-84; corp. asst. contr. Am. Racing Equipment, Compton, Calif., 1984—. Republican. Mem. Christian Ch. Office: Am Racing Equipment 19067 S Reyes Ave Compton CA 90221-5818

MORRIS, RALPH ODELL, physician; b. Gray, Okla., Dec. 20, 1917; s. Jay Thomas and Tessa (Clark) M.; m. Manuela Frasquella, Aug. 28, 1990; children: Aurora Morris Coppola, Jean Morris Roberts, Marrian Morris De Leon, Magale, Wanda Morris Lent, Thomas, Linda Morris Hargrove, Fred, Ketty Morris Arrazote (dec.). BA, Whittier Coll.; DO, Coll. Osteopathic Medicine; MD, Calif. Coll. Medicine. Pvt. practice med. hypnosis, 1966—. Home: 18340 Falda Ave Torrance CA 90504-5016

MORRIS, RICHARD STRATTON, financial services executive; b. Denver, Apr. 18, 1937; s. Cecil Hathaway and Margaret (Stratton) M.; m. Joan Beyer, Aug. 20, 1964 (div. Dec. 1985); children: Julie A., Todd R., Robin S. BBA, U. Wis., 1960, MBA, 1964. CLU; ChFC. Instr. U. Wis., Sch. Bus., 1962-64; dir. tng. Mutual Benefit Life Ins. Co., 1964-65; founder, pres. Fin. Planning Svcs., Inc., Colorado Springs, Colo., 1966-86; prin. Pvt. Capital Corp., 1986-88; v.p. Hawaii ops. Benefit Capital Fin. Svcs., Inc., Honolulu, 1988-91, pres. Hawaii ops., 1991—; vice chmn. State of Hawaii Employee Stock Ownership and Participation Adv. Com.; bd. dirs. Hawaii Estate Planning Coun., 1991—; speaker in field. Vol. Heart Fund; past pres., bd. chmn. USO Coun.; past exec. bd. mem. YW-YMCA-USO Coun.; active Young Reps.; organizer, past chmn. Colorado Springs (Colo.) Symphony Coun.; bd. mem. Colorado Springs (Colo.) Symphony Assn.; steering com. mem. Citizen's for a Theater-Auditorium; task force mem. Citizen's Goals for Colorado Springs; chancellor's adv. coun. Univ. Colo., Colorado Springs. gen. chmn. excellence fund campaign, 1983, pres. exec. club, 1983-86; bd. dirs. U. Colo. Found., 1984-90, others. Mem. ESOP Assn. (bd. dirs. Hawaii chpt.), Am. Risk and Ins. Assn., Nat. Assn. Security Dealers, Assn. for Advanced Life Underwriting, Colo. Assn. Life Underwriters, Nat. Assn. Life Underwriters, Nat. Assoc. Mutual Benefit Life (life mem., exec. com. 1983-85), Am. Soc. CLU and ChFC (bd. dirs.), Estate Planning Coun. Colorado Springs (founder, original trustee 1968, pres. 1975-76), Colorado Springs Assn. Life Underwriters (legis. chmn. 1969-72, bd. mem. 1970-77, pres., v.p., sec.-treas. 1973-76, immediate past pres. 1976-77, Disting. Svc. award 1985), Hawaii C. of C. (various coms.) Pacific Club, Honolulu Club. Republican. Congregational. Home: 920 Ward Ave Apt 11B Honolulu HI 96814 Office: Benefit Capital Fin Svcs Pauahi Tower 840 1001 Bishop St Honolulu HI 96813

MORRIS, RICHARD WARD, nonprofit organization administrator, author; b. Milw., June 16, 1939; s. Alvin Harry and Dorothy Lydia (Wissmueller) M. BS, U. Nev., 1962, PhD, 1968; MS, U. N.Mex., 1964. Exec. dir. COSMEP, Inc., San Francisco, 1968—. Author: Poetry Is a Kind of Writing, 1975, Light, 1979, The End of the World, 1980, The Fate of the Universe, 1982, Evolution and Human Nature, 1983, Dismantling the Universe, 1983, Time's Arrows, 1985, The Nature of Reality, 1987, The Edges of Science, 1990, Assyrians, 1991, (with others) The Word and Beyond, 1982, Cosmic Questions, 1993. Office: COSMEP Inc PO Box 420703 San Francisco CA 94142-0703

MORRIS, STEVEN LYNN, career officer, aeronautical engineering educator; b. Dallas, Dec. 7, 1952; s. William Ira and Alta Faye (McCarley) M.; m. Jacqueline Ann Fenter, July 30, 1977; children: Steven Sean, Michael Wayne. BS in Engring. Scis., USAF Acad., 1975; MS in Aero. Engring, Air Force Inst. Tech., 1980; PhD in Aerospace Engring., Tex. A&M U., 1989. Commd. 2d lt. USAF, 1975, advanced through grades to lt. col.; assoc. prof., dep. head for ops. dept. aeronautics USAF Acad., Colo., 1989—. Named Outstanding Young Man Am., Jaycees, 1981. Mem. AIAA (sr. flight mechanics tech. com. 1991—, dep. dir. for edn. region V 1992—), USAF Acad. Assn. Grads., Am. Soc. for Engring. Edn., Tex. A&M U. Assn. Former Students. Baptist. Home: 6935 Snowbird Dr Colorado Springs CO 80918 Office: Hdqs USAF Acad-DFAN USAF Academy CO 80840

MORRISON, BRADFORD CARY, oil and gas industry executive; b. Fergus Falls, Minn., Feb. 5, 1944; s. Clifford Byron and Bessie Caroline (Danielson) M.; m. Brenda Kay Perry, Nov. 15, 1969; children: Ashley Marie, Devon Lane. BA, Augustana Coll., 1966; MA, U. Wis., 1968. Geologist Shell Oil, New Orleans, 1968-74, Sherwood Exploration, Denver, 1974-75, Fluor Oil & Gas, Denver, 1975-78, Patrick Petroleum, Denver, 1978-80; v.p. United Resources, Denver, 1980-83; ptnr., geologist Banner Oil & Gas, Denver, 1983-85; geologist Ultramar Oil & Gas, Denver, Houston, 1985-88; v.p. Chuska Energy Co., Denver, 1988-91; owner Terrafocus, Ltd., Denver, 1991—. Mem. Am. Assn. Petroleum Geologists (cert., del.), Rocky Mountain Assn. Geologists (v.p. 1991), Houston Geological Soc., New Orleans Geological Soc. Home: 9728 S Ashleigh Ln Highlands Ranch CO 80126

MORRISON, GEORGE THORNTON, pharmacist; b. Oakdale, Calif., Mar. 13, 1924; s. George Thornton and Eva Caroline (Holton) M.; m. Shirley Adele Murdock, June 25, 1945; children: Kevin Murdock, Pamela Ann. BS in Pharmacy, U. Calif., San Francisco, 1950. Pharmacist Kerstens Pharmacy, Oakdale, Calif., 1950-55; pharmacist/ptnr. Seeber-Morrison Pharmacy, Oakdale, 1955-63; owner Morrison's Pharmacy, Oakdale, 1963-79; pharmacist/ptnr. Round Hill Pharmacy, Zephyr Cove, Nev., 1964-74, Riverbank Pharmacy, Riverbank, Calif., 1964-75, Med. Ctr. Pharmacy, Oakdale, Calif., 1974-79; staff pharmacist Oak Valley Dist. Hosp., Oakdale, 1974—; gen. oper. mgr. Oakdale Profl. Ctr., 1974—. Bd. dirs. Comprehensive Health Planning Com., Calif.; pres. Oak Valley Dist. Hosp. Found., 1981-82, bd. dirs., 1983—; pres., trustee Stanislaus County Bd. Edn., 1969—, vice chmn., 1992-94. With USN, 1942-45; PTO. Recipient Outstanding Vol. award, Oak Valley Hosp. Found., 1986. Mem. Calif. Soc. Hosp. Pharmacists, Tri-Valley Pharm. Assn., Calif. Pharm. Assn., Am. Pharm. Assn., Nat. Assn. Retail Druggists, Oakdale C. of C. (bd. dirs. 1951), Oakdale Golf and Country Club (dir. 1972). Republican. Methodist. Home: 131 W G St Oakdale CA 95361-3822 Office: Oak Valley District Hosp 350 S Oak Ave Oakdale CA 95361-3581

MORRISON, JAMES IAN, research institute executive; b. Irvine, Scotland, Dec. 22, 1952; came to U.S., 1985; s. James Morrison and Janet Miller (McCondach) Munro; m. Nora Cadham, Dec. 6, 1980; children: David, Caitlin. BPhil, U. Newcastle-upon-Tyne, Eng., 1976; MA, U. Edinburgh, Scotland, 1974; PhD, U. B.C., Can., 1985. Isntr. B.C. Inst. Tech., Vancouver, 1980-85; rsch. assoc. U. B.C., Vancouver, 1980-85; rsch. fellow Inst. for the Future, Menlo Park, Calif., 1985-86, dir. health care rsch. program, 1986—, pres., 1990—; bd. dirs. Interim Svcs., Ft. Lauderdale, Fla.; mem. corp. adv. bd. Bristol-Myers Squibb, Princeton, N.J., 1992—; mem. UNIS Press Adv. Bd., 1990—. Co-author: Looking Ahead at American Health Care, 1988, Directing the Clinical Laboratory, 1990, System in Crisis: The Case for Health Care Reform, 1991, Reforming the System: Containing Health Care Costs in an Era of Universal Coverage, 1992; contbr. articles to profl. jours. Mem. environ. scanning com. United Way of Am., 1990—. Social Sci. Rsch. Coun. scholar U. Newcastle-upon-Tyne, 1974-76. Office: Inst for the Future 2744 Sand Hill Rd Menlo Park CA 94025-7020

MORRISON, JOHN STUART, technology company executive; b. St. Louis, Jan. 21, 1947; s. John Gracie and Annebelle (Gordon) M.; m. Patricia Ann Myers, Dec. 3, 1971; children: James, Thomas, Geoffrey. BA in Psychology, Wash. U., St. Louis, 1969; MS, Naval Postgrad. Sch., Monterey, Calif., 1980. Commd. 2d lt. USAF, 1969, advanced through grades to lt. col., 1986; intelligence officer 388 TFW, Korat, Thailand, 1970-71, HW, Strategic Air Command, Omaha, 1971-73; dir. air intelligence RAF Alconbury, U.K., 1974-77; command control and coms. mgr. Tactical Air Forces Interoperability Group, Hampton, Va., 1980-83; joint C3 advisor U.S. Mil. Tng. Mission, Riyadh, Saudi Arabia, 1983-85; dir. plans Nat. Test Bed, Boston, 1985-88; dir. systems engring. and devel. Nat. Test Bed, Colorado Springs, 1988-91; ret. USAF, 1991; pres. Transnat. Techs. Inc., Colorado Springs, Colo., 1991—; cons. Boeing, Martin Marietta, SofTech, USAF, Rockwel Internat., NCR, 1991-92. Co-author: Tactical C3 for the Ground Forces, 1984; contbr. articles to profl. jours. Mem. IEEE, Assn. of Computer Mfrs. Office: Transnational Techs Inc 6736 War Eagle Pl Colorado Springs CO 80919-1634

MORRISON, MARTHA KAYE, photolithography engineer; b. San Jose, Calif., Oct. 5, 1955; d. Myrle K. and Arthena R. Morrison; 1 child, Katherine A. AA, West Valley Coll., Saratoga, Calif., 1978. Prodn. worker Signetics Co., Sunnyvale, Calif., 1973-75, equipment engr., 1976-78, 79-80, prodn. supr., 1978-79; expediter Monolithic Memories, Sunnyvale, 1975-76; photolithography engr. KTI Chems., *5, 1980-81; founder, chief engr., CEO Optalign, Inc., Livermore, Forest Ranch, Calif., 1981—; tennis prof., 1983-86. Mem. USPTA (cert.). Office: PO Box 718 Forest Ranch CA 95942

MORRISON, MICHELLE WILLIAMS, nursing administrator, writer; b. Reno, Nev., Feb. 12, 1947; d. Robert James and Dolores Jane (Barnard) Williams; m. Harrison Russell Morrison, Dec. 29, 1974. BSN, U. Nev., Reno, 1973; M Health Svc., U. Calif., Davis, 1977. RN, Oreg.; cert. family nurse practitioner. Staff nurse VA Hosp., Reno, 1973-77; family nurse practitioner Tri-County Indian Health Svc., Bishop, Calif., 1977-78; instr. of nursing Roque Community Coll., Grants Pass, Oreg., 1978-82; psychiat. nurse VA Hosp., Roseburg, Oreg., 1982; dir. edn. Josephine Meml. Hosp., Grants Pass, 1983-84; geriatric nurse practitioner Hearthstone Manor, Medford, Oreg., 1984-86; chmn. nursing dept. Roque Community Coll., Grants Pass, 1986-89; prin. Health and Ednl. Cons., Grants Pass, 1989—; dir. nursing Highland House Nursing Ctr., Grants Pass, 1990; bd. dirs. Tri-County Indian Health Svc. Author Professional Skills for Leadership. Mem. Josephine County Coalition for AIDS, Grants Pass, 1990. With USN, 1965-69. Mem. NAFE, Nat. League Nursing, Oreg. Long Term Care Nurses Assn., Oreg. Ednl. Assn., Oreg. State Bd. Nursing (re-entry nursing com. 1992—). Office: PO Box 89 Williams OR 97544-0089

MORRISON, MURDO DONALD, architect; b. Detroit, Feb. 21, 1919; s. Alexander and Johanna (Macaulay) M.; B.Arch., Lawrence Inst. Tech., 1943; m. Judy D. Morrison; children from previous marriage—Paula L., Reed A., Anne H. Individual practice architecture, Detroit, 1949, Klamath Falls, Oreg., 1949-65, Oakland, Calif., 1965-78; ptnr. Morrison Assocs., San Francisco, 1978-85, Burlingame, Calif., 1985-89, Redwood City, Calif., 1989—; v.p. Lakeridge Corp., 1968—; chmn. Oreg. Bd. Archtl. Examiners, 1961-65, chmn., 1964. Mem. Town Council Klamath Falls, 1955-57; co-chmn. Oakland Pride Com., 1968-77; mem. Redwood City Gen. Plan Com., 1986, Redwood City Design REv. Com., 1991—, Emerald Hills Design Rev. Bd., 1990—. Served with USN, 1943-46. Recipient Progressive Architecture award, 1955, Alumni of Yr. award Lawrence Inst., 1965. Mem. AIA (treas. East Bay, chmn. Oakland chpt.). Presbyterian. Architect: Gilliam County Courthouse (Progressive Architecture design award), 1955, Chiloquin (Oreg.) Elem. Sch., 1963, Lakeridge Office Bldg., Reno, 1984, Provident Cen. Credit Union Bldg., Monterey, Calif., 1986, Embarcadero Fed. Credit Union, San Francisco, 1991, others. Home and Office: 3645 Jefferson Ave Redwood City CA 94062-3137

MORRISON, RICHARD PEARCE, microbiologist; b. Great Falls, Mont., Aug. 17, 1954. BS, Mont. State U., 1976, MS, 1978; PhD, U. Okla., 1982. Staff fellow NIH, NIAID, Rocky Mountain Labs., Hamilton, Mont., 1982-86, sr. staff fellow, 1986-90, rsch. microbiologist, 1990—. Contbr. articles and revs. to profl. jours.; patentee in field. Grantee Edna McConnell Clark Found., 1986, 88. Mem. Am. Soc. for Microbiology, Am. Soc. Clin. Pathologists, Sigma Xi. Office: NIH NIAID Rocky Mountain La 903 S 4th St Hamilton MT 54840

MORRISON, ROGER BARRON, geologist; b. Madison, Wis., Mar. 26, 1914; s. Frank Barron and Elsie Rhea (Bullard) M.; BA, Cornell U., 1933, MS, 1934; postgrad. U. Calif., Berkeley, 1934-35, Stanford U., 1935-38; PhD, U. Nev., 1964; m. Harriet Louise Williams, Apr. 7, 1941 (deceased Feb. 1991); children: John Christopher, Peter Hallock and Craig Brewster (twins). Registered profl. geologist, Wyo. Geologist U.S. Geol. Survey, 1939-76; vis. adj. prof. dept. geoscis. U. Ariz., 1976-81, Mackay Sch. Mines, U. Nev., Reno, 1984-86; cons. geologist; pres. Morrison and Assocs., 1978—; prin. investigator 2 Landsat-1 and 2 Skylab earth resources investigation projects NASA, 1972-75. Fellow Geol. Soc. Am.; mem. AAAS, Internat. Assn. Quaternary Research (past mem. Holocene and pedology commns.), Am. Soc. Photogrammetry, Am. Soc. Agronomy, Soil Sci. Soc. Am., Internat. Soil Sci. Soc., Am. Quaternary Assn., Am. Water Resources Assn., Colo. Sci. Soc., Sigma Xi, Colorado Mountain Club. Author 2 books, co-author one book, co-editor 2 books; editor: Quaternary Nonglacial Geology, Conterminous U.S., Geol. Soc. Am. Centennial Series, vol. K-2, 1991; mem. editorial bd. Catena, 1973-88; contbr. over 150 articles to profl. jours. Research includes Quaternary geology and geomorphology, hydrogeology, environ. geology, neotectonics, remote sensing of Earth resources. Office: 13150 W 9th Ave Golden CO 80401-4201

MORRISON, SHIRLEY LINDEN, English language educator, writer, poet; b. Berwyn, Ill., May 2, 1935; d. William John and Florence Marie (Schwartz) Linden; m. Delmont Cleveland Morrison, Aug. 16, 1958; children: Rebecca Linden, Bruce Hunter. Diploma in nursing, Northwestern Meml. Hosp., Chgo., 1956; BS, Northwestern U., Chgo., 1958; MA, U. Wash., 1964. RN, Calif. Jr. pub. health nurse Santa Clara County Health Dept., San Jose, Calif., 1958-59; mem. sr. nursing staff Vets. Hosp., Seattle, 1959-63; instr. ARC, Seattle and Beverly Hills, Calif., 1960-65; sr. lectr., prof. English Coll. Notre Dame, Belmont, Calif., 1966—; rsch. asst. U. Wash., Seattle, 1962; lectr. U. San Francisco, 1968. Author: The Pearl & The Princes, 1985, numerous poems; contbr. articles to profl. jours. Co-chairperson Year-Round Sch. Com., Mill Valley, Calif., 1970; moderator parent-tchr. workshops, Mill Valley, 1970-74; tchr. mythology, gifted program Old Mill Sch., Mill Valley, 1970-74; poetry chair San Mateo (Calif.) County Fair, 1986. NHS scholar, 1953; Danforth grantee Stanford U., 1976, rsch. grantee Coll. Notre Dame, 1988, 90, 92. Mem. Soc. Children's Book Writers, Philological Assn. Pacific Coast, MLA, Jack London Found., AAUW, Friends of Mill Valley Libr., Sierra Club. Office: Coll Notre Dame 1500 Ralston Ave Belmont CA 94002-1908

MORRISON, WILLIAM EDWARD, electronics marketing executive, consultant; b. Powell, Wyo., Sept. 30, 1951; s. Joseph Everett and Mildred Estelle (Cox) M.; m. Lynne Sue Swanson, May 25, 1973; children: Adam Joseph, Alexander Gordon. BS in Elec. Engring., Gen. Motors Inst., Flint, Mich., 1975; MBA, Golden Gate U., 1986. Profl. elec. engr. Project engr. GM Corp., Kokomo, Ind., 1970-77, Lawrence Livermore (Calif.) Nat. Labs., 1977-81; project group mgr. Intel Corp., Santa Clara, Calif., 1981-82; strategic planning mgr. Fujitsu Microelectronics, Santa Clara, 1982-84; product line mgr. Rolm Mil Spec Computers, San Jose, Calif., 1984-87; v.p. sales Magnesys, Santa Clara, 1987-89; pres. Morrison Assocs., Livermore, 1989—; adj. faculty Golden Gate U., San Francisco, 1986—, St. Mary's Coll., Moraga, Calif., 1988. Contbr. articles to tech. bus. publs. Pres. Granada Little League, Livermore, 1988, 89; v.p. Livermore Sports Pk. Com., Livermore, 1990. Republican. Home and Office: Morrison & Assocs 1601 Heidelberg Dr Livermore CA 94550-6108

MORRISON, WILLIAM FOSDICK, electrical company executive, consulting company owner; b. Bridgeport, Conn., Mar. 14, 1935; s. Robert Louis and Helen Fosdick (Mulroney) M.; m. E. Drake Miller, Dec. 14, 1957 (div. Sept. 1972); children: Donna Drake, Deanne Fosdick, William Fosdick; m. Carol Ann Stover, Nov. 20, 1972. BA in Econs., Trinity Coll., Hartford, Conn., 1957. Mgr. purchasing dept. Westinghouse Electric Co., Lima, Ohio, 1960-68; mgr. mfg. Westinghouse Electric Co., Upper Sandusky, Ohio, 1969; gen. mgr. Westinghouse Electric Co., Gurabo, P.R., 1970-71; mgr. tng. Westinghouse Electric Co., Pitts., 1972-84; program mgr. Westinghouse Electric Co., Sunnyvale, Calif., 1984-89, procurement project dir., 1990—; negotiation cons. and trainer, 1969—; instr. San Jose State U., 1993—. Author: The Pre-Negotiation Planning Book, 1985, The Human Side of Negotiations, 1993; contbr. articles to profl. jours. Bd. dirs. Valley Inst. of the Theatre Arts, Saratoga, Calif., 1986-90, Manhattan Playhouse, 1989—. Served to capt. USAFR, 1958-64. Named Man of the Yr. Midwest Lacrosse Coaches Assn., 1983, recipient Service award U.S. Lacrosse Assn., 1982. Mem. Nat. Assn. Purchasing Mgmt. (pres. Lima chpt. 1966-67, dir. nat. affairs 1967-68, dist. treas. 1968-70). Club: Sunnyvale Golf Assn. (vice-chmn. 1985, chmn. 1986, scorer 1992—). Lodge: Elks. Home: 3902 Duncan Pl Palo Alto CA 94306-4550 Office: Westinghouse Electric Co 401 E Hendy Ave Sunnyvale CA 94088-3499

MORRISON, WYNONA MARVEL, psychotherapist. BA in Edn., U. Wash., 1969, MSW, 1974. Bd. cert. in clin. social work. Mental health profl. Community Psychiatric Clinic, Seattle, 1974-84; prin. Wynona Morrison, MSW, Edmonds, Wash., 1984—. Mem. NASW, Wash. State Soc. Clin. Social Work (treas. 1987-93), Internat. Fedn. Psychoanalytic Edn. (charter), N.W. Alliance Psychoanalytic Study (pres. 1993—), Separation and Loss Inst. Office: Wynona Morrison MSW BCD 115 3d Ave N Edmonds WA 98020-3108

MORRISSEY, JOHN CARROLL, lawyer; b. N.Y.C., Sept. 2, 1914; s. Edward Joseph and Estelle (Caine) M.; m. Eileen Colligan, Oct. 14, 1950; children: Jonathan Edward, Ellen, Katherine, John, Patricia, Richard, Brian, Peter. B.A. magna cum laude, Yale U., 1937, LL.B., 1940; J.S.D., N.Y. U., 1951; grad., Command and Gen. Staff Sch., 1944. Bar: N.Y. State 1940, D.C. 1953, Calif. 1954, U.S. Supreme Ct. 1944. Asso. firm Dorsey and Adams, 1940-41, Dorsey, Adams and Walker, 1946-50; counsel Office of Sec. of Def., Dept. Def., Washington, 1950-52; acting gen. counsel def. Electric Power Adminstrn., 1952-53; atty. Pacific Gas and Electric Co., San Francisco, 1953-70; asso. gen. counsel Pacific Gas and Electric Co., 1970-74, v.p., gen. counsel, 1975-80; individual practice law San Francisco, 1980—; dir. Gas Lines, Inc. Bd. dirs. Legal Aid Soc. San Francisco; chmn. Golden Gate dist. Boy Scouts Am., 1973-75; commr. Human Rights Commn. of San Francisco, 1976-89, chmn., 1980-82; chmn. Cath. Social Svc. of San Francisco, 1966-68; adv. com. Archdiocesan Legal Affairs, 1991—. Served to col. F.A., U.S. Army, 1941-46. Decorated Bronze star, Army Commendation medal. Mem. NAS, AAAS, ABA, Calif. State Bar Assn., Fed. Power Bar Assn., N.Y. Acad. Scis., Calif. Conf. Pub. Utility Counsel, Pacific Coast Electric Assn., Pacific Coast Gas Assn., Econ. Round Table of San Francisco, World Affairs Council, San Francisco C. of C., Calif. State C. of C., Harold Brunn Soc. Med. Rsch., Electric Club, Serra Club, Commonwealth Club, Yale Club of San Francisco (pres. 1989-90), Pacific-Union Club, Sometimes Tuesday Club, Sovereign Mil. Order Malta, Phi Beta Kappa. Roman Catholic. Home: 2030 Jackson St San Francisco CA 94109-2840 Office: PO Box 77000 1 California St # 3125 San Francisco CA 94177

MORRISSEY, KYMBERLEE ANNE, nuclear medicine technologist, health educator; b. Denver, June 3, 1957; d. Stephen and Marguerite Louise (Mazzei) Pryor; m. Shawn Michael Morrissey, May 27, 1983. BA in Biology, N.W. Nazarene Coll., 1981; postgrad., St. Anthony Sch. Nuclear Medicine, 1985. Cert. nuclear medicine technologist. Clinic asst. Jefferson County Health Dept., Lakewood, Colo., 1980-84; staff technologist Beth Israel Hosp., Denver, 1984-86, St. Joseph Hosp., Denver, 1986, St. Anthony Healthcare Systems, Denver, 1986—; program dir. St. Anthony Hosp. Sch. Nuclear Medicine Technology. Vol. instr. mile high chpt. Jefferson br. ARC, 1983—, health and edn. team leader, 1986-88, vice chmn. br. coun., 1988—, 1988-91, chmn. exec. coun., 1991—. Exceptional Vol. Svc. award Mile High Chpt. ARC, 1989. Republican. Office: Nuclear Medicine Dept Saint Anthony Hosp Ctr 4231 W 16th Ave Denver CO 80204-1335

MORRISSEY, LEROY EDWARD, artist, sculptor; b. Suisun, Calif., May 10, 1925; s. Thomas L. and Ethel (Forsythe) M.; m. Betty Dolores Keehn, June 16, 1969; children: Jeanne Ryan, Sheila Tharp, Teresa Peterson Turpin. Grad. in comml. art, Calif. Coll. Arts & Crafts, 1951. Illustrator Roy Morrissey's Comml. Art Studio, Salt Lake City, 1951-55; art dir. Smith/Morrissey Advt. Agy., Salt Lake City, 1955-59; art instr. Palomar Coll., San Marcos, Calif., 1960-72; gallery owner Roy Morrissey's Art Show, Temecula, Calif., 1972-78; art dir. The High Country mag., Temecula, 1979-81; ind. artist portraits, western landscape oil paintings Hemet, Calif., 1986—. One-man show in Temecula, Calif.; represented in permanent collection First Ch. Religious Sci., Hemet, Calif.; contbr. articles to profl. jours. With USN, 1941-43, PTO. Recipient 1st Prize award in wood sculpture Nat. Wood Carver Assn./Calif. Carvers Guild, 1992. Home: 1837 E Campus Way Hemet CA 92544

MORRISSEY, WILLIAM THOMAS, financial planner; b. Vancouver, B.C., Can., Sept. 23, 1950; came to U.S., 1951; s. Gerard Majella and Lucy Marie (dela Giroday) M.; m. Stephanie Kathleen Herbaugh, June 23, 1979 (dec. Feb. 1991); children: Travis, Stephen. Student, Shoreline Community Coll., 1968-69, No. Seattle Community Coll., 1970-74, City U., Bellevue, Wash., 1990; cert. fin. planner, Coll. Fin. Planning, Denver, 1984, student advanced studies program, 1990. Assoc. residential real estate Page & Assocs., Seattle, 1971-74; assoc. comml. real estate Westlake Assocs., Seattle, 1975-76, Schwarz & Scott, Seattle, 1977-78; pres., developer Gerke Morrissey, Inc., Bainbridge Island, Wash., 1978-80; owner, mgr. Islander Lopez (Wash.) Resort, 1980-82; pres., cert. fin. planner Sound Fin. Planning, Inc., Mt. Vernon and Friday Harbor, Wash., 1982—; instr. fin. planning workshop Western Wash. U., Bellingham, 1987—; instr. Small Bus. Resource Ctr., Mt. Vernon, 1988—, Am. Assn. Ret. Persons, Anacortes, Wash., 1988—. Contbg. author: Financial Planning Can Make You Rich, 1986, About Your Future, Financial Planning Will Make the Difference, 1988; columnist Skagit Valley Herald; past host bus. radio program Sta. KEZX, Seattle. Bd. dirs. San Juan Pub. Schs. Found. Mem. Inst. for Cert. Fin. Planners (pres. Puget Sound Soc. 1988-89, dir. Pacific region 1991-93), Internat. Assn. for Fin. Planning, Registry Fin. Planning Practitioners, N.W. Wash. Estate Planning Coun. (pres. 1990—), Friday Harbor C. of C., Mt. Vernon C. of C., Friday Harbor Kiwanis. Office: Sound Fin Planning Inc 355 Spring St Friday Harbor WA 98250-8056 also: 227 N 4th #206 Mount Vernon WA 98273

MORROW, JACK B., clergyman; b. Champaign, Ill., July 17, 1927; s. Ralph and Ruth (Bumgartner) M.; m. Jessie Mae Bell, June 19, 1949; children: Robert, Judy. Grad. of Theology, Life Bible Coll., L.A., 1951. Ordained minister Ch. of the Foursquare Gospel, 1951. Founding pastor Desert Chapel, Palm Springs, Calif., 1951-85, pastor emeritus, 1989—. Author: Sex and the Single Saint, 1976. With USN, 1945-46. Mem. Foursquare Ch. Home: 67-330 Rango Rd Cathedral City CA 92234 Office: Desert Chapel 630 S Sunrise Way Palm Springs CA 92264

MORROW, JAMES KIRVEN, marketing and management company executive, consultant; b. Washington, Sept. 20, 1941; s. James Holland and Marie (Moore) M.; m. Joanne Emiko Suzumoto, May 12, 1985; children: Benjamin Trent, Michael James, Ryan William. BS in Nuclear Engring. and Physics, N.C. State U., 1963; MS in Nuclear Engring., Air Force Inst. Tech., 1968; grad., Indsl. Coll. Armed Forces, 1976; MBA, N.Mex. Highlands Coll., 1978; DBA, U.S. Internat. U., 1986. Enlisted USAF, 1961, advanced through grades to col., 1984, ret., 1990; materials engr. Pratt & Whitney, Middleton, Conn., 1963; team leader electronics radiation effects USAF Weapons Lab., Albuquerque, 1963-67; chief trace analysis divsn. USAF Nuclear Engring. Ctr., Dayton, Ohio, 1967-70; dir. command post ops. 7336 munitions support squadron RAF Bruggen, Fed. Republic Germany, 1970-73; chief EMP test dir. USAF Weapons Lab., Albuquerque, 1973-78; dir. bus. mgmt. USAF Civil & Environ. Lab., Panama City, Fla., 1978-83; program mgr. satellite comm. system USAF Space Systems divsn., El Segundo, Calif., 1983-90; pres., CEO Morrow & Assocs., Torrance and Manhattan Beach, Calif., 1990—. Author 15 tng. manuals and tech. reports. Decorated Legion of Merit, 14 other awards, decorations. Mem. Air Force Assn., Manhattan Beach C. of C. Republican. Home: 428 10th St Manhattan Beach CA 90266

MORROW, ROSANNE SURINA, civil engineer; b. L.A., Aug. 5, 1956; d. Daniel and Marjorie Isabel (Klarich) Surina; m. Paul David Morrow, May 11, 1991. BSCE, Calif. State Poly. U., 1979. From asst. engr. to sr. structural engr. Lockheed Corp., Burbank, Calif., 1979-91; mgr. engring. scis. Nordskog Industries, Inc., Van Nuys, Calif., 1991—; designated engring. rep. FAA, Long Beach, Calif., 1992. Office: Nordskog Industries Inc 16000 Strathern St Van Nuys CA 91406

MORROW, SUSAN DAGMAR, psychic, educator, writer, consultant; b. Harrisburg, Pa., July 10, 1932; d. William Lime and Margaret Louise (Deckard) Brubaker; m. Henry Taylor Morrow, June 9, 1952 (div. Mar. 1984); children: Quenby Anne, Christopher Brian. Student Carnegie Inst. Tech., 1950-52, U. Ariz., 1952-54, U. Calif., Berkeley Ext., 1960-72, Foothill Coll., 1980-81. Self-employed psychic, psychic tchr., Palo Alto, Calif., 1976-80, Mountain View, Calif., 1980—; psychic, tchr. Seekers Quest Profl. Ctr., San Jose, Calif., 1983-87; tchr. Sunnyvale Community Ctr., 1977-87; tchr. San Andreas Health Coun., Palo Alto, 1981-83; lectr. U. Calif., Berkeley, 1978, Foothill Coll., Los Altos, Calif., 1980; lectr. in field; medium, cons. in cases of mental disorientation to psychologists, Palo Alto and Mountain View, 1978—, to detectives and police in cases of missing persons, animals or property, 1983—, pvt. tutor, cons. past lives, archeological information, 1990—. Contbr. articles on psychic awareness to various publs. Mem. Assn. Psychic Practitioners (co-founder, v.p. 1982-83, editor and writer newsletter 1982-83), Assn. Rsch. and Enlightenment, Inst. Noetic Sci., Friends of the Animals. Democrat. Methodist. Avocations: physical mediumship, painting, swimming, sailing.

MORROW, WINSTON VAUGHAN, lawyer; b. Grand Rapids, Mich., Mar. 22, 1924; s. Winston V. and Selma (von Egloffstein) M.; m. Margaret Ellen Staples, June 25, 1948 (div.); children: Thomas Christopher, Mark Staples; m. Edith Burrows Ulrich, Mar. 2, 1990. AB cum laude, Williams Coll., 1947; JD, Harvard U., 1950. Bar: R.I. 1950. Assoc. atty. Edwards & Angell, Providence, 1950-57; exec. v.p., asst. treas., gen. counsel, bd. dirs. Avis, Inc. and subs., 1957-61; v.p., gen. mgr. Rent A Car div. Avis, Inc., 1962-64, pres., bd. dirs., 1964-75; chmn., chief exec. officer, bd. dirs. Avis, Inc. and Avis Rent A Car System, Inc., 1965-77; chmn., pres., bd. dirs. Teleflorists Inc. and subs., 1978-80; pres. Westwood Equities Corp., L.A., 1981—, chief exec. officer, 1984—, also bd. dirs.; also bd. dirs. New TC Holding Corp.; chmn., pres., chief exec. officer Ticor Title Ins. Co., 1982-91, also bd. dirs.; chmn. TRTS Data Svcs. Inc., 1985-91; bd. dirs. AECOM Tech. Corp., L.A., 1990—; mem. Pres.'s Industry and Govt. Spl. Travel Task Force, 1968, travel adv. bd. U.S. Travel Svcs., 1968-76, L.A. City-wide Airport Adv. Com., 1983-85; co-chmn. L.A. Transp. Coalition, 1985-91. Mem. juvenile delinquency task force Nat. Coun. Crime and Delinquency, 1985-86, L.A. Mayor's Bus. Coun., 1983-86, Housing Roundtable, Washington, 1983-85; chmn., pres. Spring St. Found., 1991—; bd. dirs. Police Found., Washington, 1983-91; trustee Com. for Econ. Devel., Washington, 1987-91. Decorated Stella Della Solidarieta Italy, Gold Tourism medal Austria). Mem. Fed. Bar Assn., R.I. Bar Assn., Car and Truck Rental and Leasing Assn. (nat. pres. 1961-63), Am. Land Title Assn. (bd. govs. 1989-90), L.A. Area C. of C. (bd. dirs. 1983-90), Bald Peak Colony Club, Williams Club, L.A. Tennis Club, Wilshire Country Club, Calif. Club, Phi Beta Kappa, Kappa Alpha. Home: 4056 Farmouth Dr Los Angeles CA 90027-1314 also: Meadowview Farm Andrews Hill Rd Freedom NH 03836 Office: Westwood Equities Corp 6300 Wilshire Blvd Ste 9020 Los Angeles CA 90048-5202

MORSE, KAREN WILLIAMS, university president; b. Monroe, Mich., May 8, 1940; m. Joseph G. Morse; children: Robert G., Geoffrey E. BS, Denison U., 1962; MS, U. Mich., 1964, PhD, 1967; DSc (hon.), Denison U., 1990. Rsch. chemist Ballistic Rsch. Lab., Aberdeen Proving Ground, Md., 1966-68; lectr. chemistry dept. Utah State U., Logan, 1968-69, from asst. to assoc. prof. chemistry, 1969-83, prof. chemistry dept., 1983-93, dept. head Coll. Sci., 1981-88, dean Coll. Sci., 1988-89, univ. provost, 1989-93; pres. Western Wash. U., Bellingham, 1993—; mem., chair Grad. Record Exam in chemistry com., Princeton, N.J., 1980-89, Gov.'s Sci. Coun., Salt Lake City, 1986-93, Gov.'s Coun. on Fusion, 1989-91, ACS Com. on Profl. Tng., 1984-92; cons. 1993. Contbr. articles to profl. jours.; patentee in field. Mem. Cache County Sch. Dist. Found., Cache Valley, Logan, 1988-93; swim coach, soccer coach; trustee First United Presbyn. Ch., Logan, 1979-81, 82-85; adv. bd. Sci. Discovery Ctr., Logan, 1993. Recipient Disting. Alumni in Residence award U. Mich., 1989. Fellow AAAS; mem. Am. Chem. Soc. (Utah award Salt Lake City and Cen. dists. 1988), Bus. and Profl. Women Club (pres. 1984-85), P.E.O., Phi Beta Kappa, Sigma Xi, Phi Beta Kappa Assocs., Phi Kappa Phi. Office: Western Washington Univ Office of Pres Office of the President Bellingham WA 98225-9000

MORSE, LOWELL WESLEY, banking and real estate executive; b. West Palm Beach, Fla., May 1, 1937; s. Alton and Blanche (Yelverton) M.; B.S., U. Santa Clara, 1968; grad. Def. Lang. Inst., Monterey, Calif., 1959; m. Vera Giacalone, June 22, 1958; children: Lowell Wesley, Stephen D., Michael S. Russian linguist U.S. Army Security Agy., 1957-60; asst. city mgr. City of Pacific Grove (Calif.), 1961-66; city mgr. Town of Los Altos Hills (Calif.), 1967-69; chmn. Morse & Assos., Inc., Portland, Oreg., 1972—; founder, dir. Comerica Bank Calif., San Jose, 1979—; chmn. Cypress Ventures Inc., Portland, The Bagel Basket, Inc.; bd. trustees Regent U. Served with U.S. Army, 1957-60. Home: 21042 Wyndham Hill Ct Tualatin OR 97062 Office: 7155 SW Varns St Portland OR 97223

MORSE, MICHAEL DAVID, chemistry educator, researcher; b. New Martinsville, W.Va., Oct. 6, 1952; s. Harold Lane and Opal Geneva (Nichols) M.; m. Cynthia Jo Brandt, Nov. 26, 1983. BS, Haverford Coll., 1974; MS, U. Chgo., 1977, PhD, 1980. Vis. asst. prof. Rice U., Houston, 1981-83, rsch. assoc., 1983-84; asst. prof. U. Utah, Salt Lake City, 1985-90, assoc. prof., 1990—. Contbr. articles to profl. jours. Mem. AAAS, Am. Phys. Soc., Am. Chem. Soc. Office: Univ Utah Dept Chemistry Salt Lake City UT 84112

MORSE, RICHARD JAY, human resources and organizational development consultant, manufacturers' representative company executive; b. Detroit, Aug. 2, 1933; s. Maurice and Belle Rosalyn (Jacobson) M. BA, U. Va., 1955; MA in Clin. Psychology, Calif. State U., L.A., 1967. Area pers. adminstr. Gen. Tel. Co. of Calif., Santa Monica, 1957-67; sr. v.p. human resources The Bekins Co., Glendale, Calif., 1967-83; pvt. cons. human resources and orgn. devel. Glendale, 1983—. Contbr. articles to profl. jours. Fund raiser various orgns., So. Calif., 1970—. Mem. Nat. Soc. Performance and Instrn. (founding mem. 1958—). Republican. Jewish. Home and Office: 6410 Cambria Pines Rd Cambria CA 93428-2009

MORSE, SCOTT DAVID, international trade research executive, consultant, publisher; b. Sacramento, Dec. 6, 1950; s. David Comestock and Jane Berenice (Derr) M. BSFS in Internat. Econs., Georgetown U., 1974, MSFS in Internat. Trade, 1983. Adminstrv. asst. nat. security coun. Exec. Office of The Pres. of U.S., Washington, 1972-73; internat. trade specialist Calif. Farm Bur. Fedn., Berkeley, Calif., 1975-76; mgr. commodity svc. div. Calif. Farm Bur. Fedn., 1977-81; agrl. trade cons. Patton, Boggs & Blow, Washington, 1983; v.p. agribus. BankAm. World Trade Corp., San Francisco, 1984-85; pres. Morse Mcht. Agribus., San Francisco, 1985-90, Morse Agri-Energy Assocs., San Francisco, 1990-92, World Tariff Ltd., San Francisco, 1991—; adj. lectr. Santa Clara U., 1988—; cons. Calif. Energy Commn., 1990—, Calif. Dept. Food and Agr., 1992—. Contbr. over a dozen articles to profl. jours. Mem. Calif. Coun. for Internat. Trade (bd. dirs.), Georgetown Club (bd. dirs.), Georgetown U. Alumni Assn. Office: World Tarrif Ltd 220 Montgomery St Ste 432 San Francisco CA 94104-3410

MORTENSEN, JAMES DEAN, entrepreneur; b. Logan, Utah, Aug. 11, 1967; s. George Dean and Zella (Hansen) M. Cert. massage technician, Mueller Coll., San Diego, 1987; BS in Psychology and Pre-law, Utah State U., 1992. Foreman Dean Mortensen Painting, Logan, 1979-87; pres. Innovations Unltd., Logan, 1986—; ptnr. Mortensen Family Enterprises, Logan, 1983—. Author: Beat the Sportsbook, 1991; contbr. articles to profl. jours. Mem. Mensa, Intertel., Pi Sigma Alpha, Psy Chi. Office: Innovations Unltd PO Box 130 Providence UT 84332

MORTENSEN, RICHARD EDGAR, engineering educator; b. Denver, Sept. 29, 1935; s. Edgar Steele and Frieda Amalie (Boecker) M.; m. Sarah Jean Raulston, Oct. 12, 1974 (div. 1978). BSEE, MIT, 1958, MSEE, 1958; PhD, U. Calif., Berkeley, 1966. Co-op. engr. GE Co., Schenectady, N.Y., 1955-57; mem. tech. staff Space Tech. Labs., L.A., 1958-61; rsch. asst. U. Calif., Berkeley, 1961-65; prof. engring. UCLA, 1965-91, prof. emeritus, 1991—; cons. TRW, Inc., Redondo Beach, Calif., 1966-70, Aerojet-Gen. Corp., Azusa, Calif., 1970-72, Applied Sci. Analytics, Inc., Canoga Park, Calif., 1980-82. Author: Random Signals and Systems, 1987; contbr. to profl. publs. Team mem. Beyond War, Topanga, Calif., 1986-89; alcoholism counselor. Grantee NSF, 1987-90. Mem. IEEE, Soc. Indsl. and Applied Math., Sigma Xi, Tau Beta Pi, Eta Kappa Nu. Office: Dept Elec Engring 405 Hilgard Ave Los Angeles CA 90024-1594

MORTENSEN, SUSAN MARIE, manufacturing company executive; b. Portland, Oreg., Jan. 24, 1950; d. Leslie Dean Mortensen and Kathryn Merdell Huff; m. José Garcia Ruiz, Oct. 25, 1986. BA, U. Portland, 1972. Advt. dir. B.A.C. Inc., Portland, 1972-76, v.p., 1976-81; exec. dir. Econ. Devel. Assn. Skagit County, Inc., Mt. Vernon, Wash., 1982-86; mgr. Sugiyo U.S.A., Inc., Anacortes, Wash., 1986-87, exec. dir., 1987—. Active Skagit County Tourism Task Force, Washington, 1984; rep. Team Wash. Asian Mission, Japan, 1986; ambassador Wash. Ptnrship. for Econ. Devel., 1984—; mem. Project '90's, 1989; bd. dirs. Taste of Skagit, 1990, Island Hosp. Found., 1992—; mem. adv. bd. Skagit Valley Coll., 1990; mem. Anacortes Water Commn., 1992—. Jansen Found. grantee, 1985, Team Wash. Dept. Trade, 1985, Local Devel. Fund Matching Dept. Com. Devel., Washington, 1986. Mem. Japan-Am. Soc., Econ. Devel. Execs. Wash. (Bd. dirs. 1985—, v.p. 1992—), Anacortes C. of C.

MORTENSEN, WILLIAM S., banking executive; b. 1932. Chmn. bd., pres., CEO 1st Fed. Bank Calif., 1955—. Office: 1st Fed Bank Calif 401 Wilshire Blvd Santa Monica CA 90401-1416*

MORTIMER, DOYLE MOSS, business consultant, state legislator, business owner; b. Idaho Falls, Idaho, Dec. 8, 1954; s. Don and Clara Wanda (Moss) M.; m. Kitty Jean Pearson, Aug. 5, 1976; children: Anna Louise, Suzanne, Daniel Doyle, Julie Jean, Caroline. AA, Ricks Coll., 1977; BS in Sociology, Brigham Young U., 1981. Owner, pres. Randall Book Co., Orem, Utah, 1982-87; cons. IBM, Provo, Utah, 1988-93; owner Mortimer & Assoc., Orem, 1988-93; with Alexander's Print Shop, Orem; state legislator Utah State Legislature, 1993-94. Developer (game) Cues and Clues; editor in field. Rep. county treas., Utah County, 1979-81; Rep. 3d Congl. vice chmn., Utah, 1983-85; pres. LDS Booksellers Assn., 1985; bd. dirs. Latter-day Found. Arts, Salt Lake City, 1990—. Recipient Exemplary Svc. award Utah Co. Rep. Party, 1991. Mem. Rotary.

MORTIMER, KENNETH P., academic administrator. Pres. Western Wash. U., Bellingham, 1988—. Office: Western Wash U Office of President 516 High St Bellingham WA 98225-5946

MORTIMER, WENDELL REED, JR., lawyer; b. Alhambra, Calif., Apr. 7, 1937; s. Wendell Reed and Blanche (Wilson) M.; m. Cecilia Vick, Aug. 11, 1962; children: Michelle Dawn, Kimberly Grace. AB, Occidental Coll., 1958; JD, U. So. Calif., L.A., 1965. Bar: Calif. 1966. Trail atty. Legal div. State of Calif., L.A., 1965-73; assoc. Thelen, Marrin, Johnson & Bridges, L.A., 1973-76, ptnr., 1976—; judge pro tem L.A. Superior Ct., settlement officer. Active San Marino Community Ch. With U.S. Army, 1960-62. Mem. ABA (litigation sect.), State Bar of Calif., L.A. County Bar Assn. (judicial appointments com. 1990-92), Pasadena Bar Assn., Legion Lex., U. So. Calif. Alumni Assn., San Marino City Club, City Club on Bunker Hill (L.A.), Am. Arbitration Assn. (arbitrator). Office: Thelen Marrin Johnson & Bridges 333 S Grand Ave Ste 3400 Los Angeles CA 90071

MORTIMER, WILLIAM JAMES, newspaper publisher; b. Provo, Utah, June 26, 1932; s. William Earl and Margaret (Johnson) M.; m. Paula Ann Deline, Sept. 17, 1956; children: Jeffrey, David, Gregory, Bradley, Judy, William James II, Jennifer. BS, Utah State U., 1954; MS, Columbia U., 1957. Reporter Deseret News, Salt Lake City, 1957-59, pres., pub., 1985—; sales mgr. Deseret News Press, Salt Lake City, 1959-63; gen. mgr. Deseret News Press, 1979-80, Deseret Book Co., Salt Lake City, 1966-79; sr. account exec. Wheelwright Lithographing, Salt Lake City, 1963-66; dir. LSD Ch. Printing Svcs., Salt Lake City, 1980-85; v.p., dir. Newspaper Agy. Corp., Salt Lake City, 1985—; chmn. bd. Murdock Travel, Salt Lake City, Pioneer State Theatre; pres. Printing Industries of Utah, 1964-65, Utah Retail Mchts. Assn., Salt Lake City, 1977-79, Utah Arts Endowment. Author: How Beautiful Upon the Mountains, 1963. Campaign chmn. Salt Lake Area United Way, 1987; hon. col. Utah N.G. 1st lt. U.S. Army, 1954-56, Korea. Named Alumnus of Yr. Utah State U., Logan, 1985. Mem. Utah-Idaho-Spokane Associated Press Assn. (pres. 1993—), Utah Press Assn. (pres.-elect), Salt Lake Area C. of C. (chmn. bd. 1988-89), Alta Club. Mem. LDS Ch. Home: 8763 Kings Hill Dr Salt Lake City UT 84121-6135 Office: Deseret News Pub Co 30 E 1st St PO Box 1257 Salt Lake City UT 84110-1257

MORTON, CHARLES BRINKLEY, retired bishop, former state legislator and lawyer; b. Meridian, Miss., Jan. 6, 1926; s. Albert Cole and Jean (Brinkley) M.; m. Virginia Roseborough, Aug. 26, 1948; children: Charles Brinkley Jr., Mary Virginia. JD with distinction, U. Miss., 1949; MDiv optime merens, U. South, 1959, DD, 1982. Bar: Miss. 1949, Tenn.; ordained to ministry Protestant Episcopal Ch. as deacon and priest, 1959. Sole practice Senatobia, Miss., 1949-56; mem. Thomas & Morton, Senatobia, Miss., 1952-56. Miss. Ho. of Reps., 1948-52, Miss. Senate, 1952-56; priest-in-charge Ch. of Incarnation, West Point, Miss., 1959-62; rector Grace-St. Luke's Ch.,

Memphis, 1962-74; dean Cathedral of Advent, Birmingham, Ala., 1974-82; bishop Episcopal Diocese of San Diego, 1982-92, ret., 1992. Contbr. articles to law and hist. jours. Mem. Miss. Commn. Interstate Coop., 1952-56, Miss. State Hist. Commn., 1952-56; past chmn. bd. Bishop's Sch., La Jolla, Calif., Episcopal Community Svcs., San Diego; past trustee Berkeley Div. Sch., Yale U.; active numerous civic and cultural groups. Served with AUS, World War II, Korea; col., chaplain Res. ret. Decorated Silver Star, Bronze Star medal with cluster, Purple Heart, Combat Inf. Badge; recipient Freedoms Found. Honor medal, 1967, 68, 72. Mem. Mil. Order World Wars, Am. Legion (past post comdr.), Phi Delta Phi, Tau Kappa Alpha, Omicron Delta Kappa, Phi Delta Theta. Lodge: Rotary.

MORTON, DON TOWNLEY, food service company technical director; b. Cordova, Tenn., May 11, 1933; s. Raymond Veazey and Floy (Russell) M.; m. Margaret Helen Leatherwood, July 17, 1953; children: Mark, Michael, Donna, Jeffrey. BS, Memphis State U., 1958. Chemist Kraft Foods, Memphis, 1953-64; quality assurance mgr. Kraft Foods, Buena Park, Calif., 1964-75; tech. dir. Premier Edible Oils Corp., Portland, Oreg., 1975—, v.p. rsch. and devel., 1992—. With USN, 1955-57. Mem. Am. Oil Chemists Soc. (chmn. Smalley com. 1987—), Nat. Inst. Oilseed Products (chmn. lab. certification 1980—), Inst. Food Techs. Republican. Baptist. Office: Premier Edible Oils Corp 12005 N Burgard St Portland OR 97203-6494

MORTON, HUGHES GREGORY, real estate development executive; b. St. Joseph, Mo., Aug. 11, 1923; s. William Marmaduke and Jeanette (Hughes) M.; BS, U. Pa., 1947; postgrad. UCLA, 1949-50; children: William Marmaduke II, Hughes Gregory, Mary Gladys. Lic. real estate broker Calif. Divisional personnel dir. Carnation Co., L.A., 1950-52; contractors rep. Calif. Portland Cement Co., Los Angeles, 1959-64; v.p. Western Fed. Savs. & Loan Assn., L.A., 1964-70; owner Morton and Assos., L.A., 1970—. Lt. (j.g.) USNR, 1941-46. Home: 39015 Indian Rd Anza CA 92539-9068 Office: PO Box 69421 West Hollywood CA 90069-0421

MORTON, LINDA, mayor; b. Dec. 7, 1944; married; 2 children. BA with honors, U. Nebr., 1966. Lic. real estate broker. Tchr. Sunnyvale (Calif.) Elem. Sch., 1967-69, Jefferson County (Colo.) Sch. Dist., 1966-67, 69-70; real estate agt. Crown Realty, Lakewood, Colo., 1979-82, Van Schaack & Co., Lakewood, 1982-83, Re-Max Profls., Lakewood, from 1983. Mem. city council City of Lakewood, 1981-91, now Mayor, Lakewood, Colo., 1991—; represented Lakewood on Bd. Denver Regional Council of Govts., from 1981, chairwoman, 1986-87; chmn. Jefferson C. of C.; appointed by Gov. Colo. to Met. Air Quality Council, 1985; bd. dirs. Nat. Assn. Regional Coun. Govts., 1986-90. Office: City of Lakewood 445 S Allison Pky Lakewood CO 80226-3105

MORTON, THOMAS HELLMAN, organic chemist; b. L.A., Feb. 10, 1947; s. Arthur and Emmy Lou (Hellman) M.; m. Kathryn McCauley, Dec. 28, 1975; children: Gregory Duff, Julia Elizabeth. AB magna cum laude, Harvard Coll., 1968; PhD, Calif. Inst. Tech., Pasadena, 1973. Asst. prof. Dept. Chemistry Brown U., Providence, 1972-80; vis. asst. prof. Brandeis U., Waltham, Mass., 1980-81; asst. prof. Dept. Chemistry U. Calif., Riverside, 1981-85, assoc. prof., 1985-91; prof. U. Calif., Riverside, 1991—; vis. scholar Harvard U., Cambridge, Mass., 1979-80, 86; Fulbright fellow, France, 1991. Contbr. articles to profl. jours. Recipient Allan Maccoll award in Organic Mass Spectrometry, 1992. Mem. Am. Chem. Soc., Am. Soc. for Mass Spectrometry, Soc. for Neurosci., N.Y. Acad. Scis. Office: U Calif Dept Chemistry Riverside CA 92521

MORTON, WALTER GRAYDON, data processing consultant; b. Richmond, Calif., Nov. 29, 1946; s. George Woodrow and Naydeen Ona (Stillions) M.; m. Barbara Gayle Folger, Sept. 23, 1967 (div. Aug. 1987); m. Luzviminda Samatra Rivera, Sept. 5, 1989; children: Caryn, Charlene. AA, Bakersfield Coll., 1967; BS, U. Md. USAFI, 1970, MBA, 1972. Dir. EDP EDP Info. Systems, Buena Park, Calif., 1970-72, WTC, Inc., Newport Beach, Calif., 1972-78; v.p., gen. mgr. OMNUS Computer Corp., Irvine, Calif., 1978-79; pres. SUNMO Corp., Irvine, 1979-82, Interactive Svc. Utility, Costa Mesa, Calif., 1982-86; cons. Hawaii Telesis Group, Honolulu, 1986--; dir. W.T.B.S., Fontana, Calif., 1982-88. Mediator Neighborhood Justice Ctr., Honolulu, 1988 --; sec. Neighborhood Bd., Honolulu, 1988-89. With USN, 1966-72. Mem. Kiwanis Internat. (bd. dirs. 1985, 1989, 1990, pres. 1991-92, lt. gov. 1993—). Baptist. Office: Hawaii Telesis Group 711 Kapiolani Blvd Ste 1150 Honolulu HI 96813-5249

MORTON, WILLIAM EDWARDS, environmental epidemiology educator, occupational medicine specialist; b. Boston, June 30, 1929; s. Arthur Snow and Irma Claire (Edwards) M.; m. Jean Carolee Staley, Aug. 11, 1956; children—Carol, Kristen, Thomas. B.S., U. Puget Sound, 1952; M.D., U. Wash., 1955; M.P.H., U. Mich., 1960, D.P.H., 1962. Diplomate Am. Bd. Preventive Medicine. Sr. asst. surgeon USPHS, Denver, 1956-58; resident Community Hosp., San Mateo, Calif., 1958-59; epidemiologist Colo. Heart Assn., Denver, 1962-67; assoc. prof. pub. health Oreg. Health Sci. U., Portland, 1967-70, prof., 1970-72, prof., head environ. medicine div., 1972—; cons. epidemiology Oreg. State U. Environ. Health Sci. Ctr., Corvallis, 1972-79, Oreg. Comprehensive Cancer Program, Portland, 1973-81; mem. grant rev. panel EPA, Washington, 1979-83; cons. Bonneville Power Adminstrn., Vancouver, Wash., 1980-82; lectr. in field. Contbr. articles to profl. jours. Chmn. occupational health com. Oreg. Lung Assn., Portland, 1982-83; chmn. bd. dirs. Oreg. div. Am. Cancer Soc., Portland, 1975-76; mem. Physicians for Social Responsibility, Portland, 1980—. Recipient certs. of Appreciation Oreg. Lung Assn., 1983, Oreg. Occupational Health Conf., 1981; Outstanding Service plaque Am. Cancer Soc., 1977. Fellow Am. Coll. Epidemiology, Am. Coll. Preventive Medicine, Am. Coll. Occupational Medicine; mem. Northwest Assn. Occupational Medicine (pres. 1974-75), AAUP (pres. chpt. 1982-83), Soc. for Epidemiologic Research, Sigma Xi. Unitarian. Club: Corvair (Beaverton, Oreg.) Office: Oreg Health Scis U 3181 SW Sam Jackson Park Rd Portland OR 97201-3011

MOSBAEK, CRAIG HALL, research manager; b. Santa Barbara, Calif., June 13, 1961; s. Ernest James Mosbaek and Margi Anne Hall. BA in Physics, Reed Coll., 1983. Rsch. assoc. Oreg. Criminal Justice Coun., Portland, 1987-92, rsch. mgr., 1992—; founding pres. Portland Farmers' Market, 1992. Bd. dirs. Hosford-Abernathy Neighborhood Devel. Assn., Portland, 1992. Mem. Am. Assn. Pub. Opinion Rschrs., Reed Coll. Alumni Assn. (steering com. Portland chpt. 1992). Home: 2917 SE 17th Portland OR 97202

MOSBY, DOROTHEA SUSAN, municipal official; b. Sacramento, Calif., May 13, 1948; d. William Laurence and Esther Ida (Lux) M. AA in Sociology, Bakersfield (Calif.) Coll., 1966-69; BS in Recreation, San Jose State U., 1969-72; MPA, Calif. State U. Dominguez Hills, Carson, 1980-82. Asst. dept. personnel officer San Jose Parks and Recreation Dept., 1972-73, neighborhood ctr. dir., 1973-74; sr. recreation leader Santa Monica Recreation and Parks Dept., 1974-76, recreation supr., 1976-83, bus. div. head, 1983-88; bus. adminstr. Santa Monica Cultural & Recreation Svcs., 1988-91; dir. Parks and Recreation, City of South Gate (Calif.), 1991—; bd. dirs., officer Santa Monica City Employees Fed. Credit Union, 1980-89, pres. 1986-87; mem. citizens adv. com. L.A. Olympic Organizing Com., 1982-84. Mem. choir, flute soloist Pilgrim Luth. Ch., Santa Monica, 1974—, treas. Luth. ch. coun., 1984-86; vol. driver XXIII Olympiad, Los Angeles, 1984; contbr. local housing assistance U.S. Olympic Com., Los Angeles, 1984; mem. adv. com. Windsor Sq. Hancock Park Hist. Soc., Los Angeles, 1983, dir. Christmas carolling, 1980—, chmn. Olympic com., 1984, bd. trustees, 1984-90, chmn. pub. programs, 1985, co-chmn. pub. programs, 1986, co-vice chair, 1987, chmn., 1988, 89—; mem. Loyola Marymount U. Continuing Edn. Pub. Sector Adv. Bd., 1991—. Mem. NAFE, Calif. Park and Recreation Soc. (bd. dirs. 1979-82, 86, mem. Calif. bd. park and recreation pers. 1990-92, Scholarship Found. Bd. 1992—), Nat. Recreation and Park Assn., Mgmt. Team Assocs., (sec., treas. 1979-83), L.A. World Affairs Coun., South Gate C. of C., Kiwanis Club, Chi Kappa Rho (pres. 1986), Pi Alpha Alpha. Home: 9139 Elm Vista Dr Apt 103 Downey CA 90242-2992 Office: Parks and Recreation Dept 4900 Southern Ave South Gate CA 90280-3492

MOSEBAR, DONALD HOWARD, professional football player; b. Yakima, Wash., Sept. 11, 1961. Student, U. So. Calif. Center L.A. Raiders, 1983—. Office: L.A. Raiders 332 Center St El Segundo CA 90245

MOSELY, JACK MEREDITH, thoracic and cardiovascular surgeon; b. Hodge, La., July 20, 1917; s. Charles Hodge and Lucille (Hays) M.; m. Kathryn L. Stephenson, Apr. 4, 1954 (div. 1970); children: Kathryn Sue, Jack Meredith Jr. BS, La. State U., 1939; MD, la. State Med. Sch., 1943. Diplomate Am. Bd. of Surgery, Bd. of Thoracic Surgery. Intern Univ. Hosp., Mpls., 1943-44; resident in surgery Univ. Hosp., Syracuse, N.Y., 1946-48; fellow in surgery Lahey Clinic, Boston, 1948-49; instr. in surgery Syracuse U. Med. Sch., 1949-50; surgeon pvt. practice Cleve., 1950-52; resident thoracic surgery Herman Kiefer Hosp., Detroit, 1952-53; thoracic surgeon pvt. practice New Orleans, 1953; instr. thoracic surgery Tulane U. Med. Sch., New Orleans, 1953; surgeon pvt. practice Santa Barbara, Calif., 1953—. Contbr. articles to profl. jours. Past pres. Wood Glen Hall, Santa Barbara; past chmn. Health Sect. Welfare Planning Coun., City of Santa Barbara. Capt. U.S. Army Med. Corps, 1944-46. Mem. Am. Coll. Surgeons, Santa Barbara County Med. Soc., Calif. Med. Soc., Am. Coll. Chest Physicians, Am. Thoracic Soc., S.E. Surg. Congress, Pan Pac Surg. Assn., Valley Club of Montecito. Republican. Office: Mosely Surg Med Group 2420 Fletcher Ave Santa Barbara CA 93105-4840

MOSELY, JOHN DE SOLA, consulting engineer; b. London, Mar. 1933; came to U.S., 1955; s. George H. and E. Louisa (de Sola) M.; m. Mirah Susan Herzog, Dec. 20, 1981; children: Gillian Belle Katherine, Jennifer de Sola. Cons. engr., Hollywood, Calif. Developer 1st comml. stereophonic records, improved sound for films and records. Contbr. articles to profl. publs. Patentee in field. Founding mem., dir. Tech. Found. of Motion Picture & TV Industry. Recipient Sci. and Engring. award Acad. Motion Picture Arts and Scis., 1984. Fellow Soc. Motion Picture and TV Engrs., Inst. of Dirs.; mem. IEEE (sr.), Audio Engring. Soc., Cinema Audio Soc., Brit. Kinematograph Sound and TV Soc.

MOSER, DEAN JOSEPH, accountant; b. San Francisco, Apr. 5, 1942; s. Joseph Edward and Velma Ida (Cruz) M.; BS, U. San Francisco, 1964, postgrad. Law Sch., 1964-66; MA in taxation, Golden Gate U., 1988; m. Michele Patrice Cicerone, June 16, 1963; children: Jay, Lynele, Todd. CPA, Calif.; cert. fin. planner; lic. real estate broker, Calif. Owner, acct. DJM Bookkeeping Svc., 1962-65; asst. contr. Dymo Industries, Internat., Berkeley, Calif., 1965-67; mgr. taxes Arthur Andersen & Co., San Francisco, 1967-76; owner, mgr. Contadora Ltd., Novato, Calif., 1981—, Esprit Realty Co., Novato, 1981—; Dean J. Moser Accountancy Corp., Novato, 1981—, Stellar Properties; gen. mgr. Hal C. Aguirre Co.; founding dir., treas., chief fin. officer Novato Nat. Bank, NorthBay Bancorp; dir. TLC Hosps., Inc., 1990—, Am. Labs. Inc. (CFO), Asst. scout master Boy Scouts Am.; past bd. dirs. Novato Human Needs Center. Mem. AICPA, Calif. Soc. CPAs. Republican. Roman Catholic. Club: Rotary (Paul Harris fellow, past pres. Ignacio, Marin pres.'s coun., dust. area rep.). Office: 1450 Grant Ave Novato CA 94945

MOSER, JANE WEBB, information specialist; b. Prestonsburg, Ky., Aug. 14, 1950; d. Virgil Alonzo and Nancy Watts (Powers) Webb; m. Robert Wallace Moser, Mar. 2, 1985; 1 child, Robert Douglas. BA in Edn., U. Ky., 1972; MA in Edn., U. Tex., San Antonio, 1975; MLS, San Jose State U., 1992. Reading cons. Provincetown (Mass.)-Truro Schs., 1978-80; sec. in dept. tech. USAF Space Divsn., L.A., 1980-82; mgr. data base USAF Space Systems Div., L.A., 1982-91; tech. info. specialist USAF Space Systems Divsn., L.A., 1982-84, intelligence rsch. specialist, mgr. info. systems, 1984-90; ind. cons., secondary and online rschr. Cypress, Calif., 1992—. Tutor Laubach Literacy, Colorado Springs, Colo., 1975-78; mem. commn. on ch. and soc. Los Altos United Meth. Ch., Long Beach, Calif., 1990-92; founding mem. bd. dirs. Air Force Family Support Ctr., L.A., 1980-81; vol. John Douglas French Ctr. Alzheimer Disease. Recipient Sustained Superior Performance award USAF, L.A., 1982-90; named Space Div. Woman of Yr., Fed. Women's Program, L.A., 1987, Air Force Civilian of Yr., Air Force Assn., L.A., 1988. Mem. Spl. Librs. Assn. (various offices 1984-92, Spl. Achievement award 1989), Calif. Libr. Assn., So. Calif. Online Users Group, North Truro Air Force Sta. Wives Club (hon. pres. 1978-80). Home: 13600 Brewerton Ct Chantilly VA 22021

MOSER, ROBERT HARLAN, physician, educator; b. Trenton, N.J., June 16, 1923; s. Simon and Helena (Silvers) M.; m. Linda Mae Salsinger, Mar. 18, 1989; children from previous marriage: Steven Michael, Jonathan Evan. BS, Loyola U., Balt., 1944; MD, Georgetown U., 1948. Diplomate Am. Bd. Internal Medicine. Commd. 1st lt. U.S. Army, 1948, advanced through grades to col., 1966, intern D.C. Gen. Hosp., 1948-49, fellow pulmonary disease D.C. Gen. Hosp., 1949-50; bn. surgeon U.S. Army, Korea, 1950-51; asst. resident Georgetown U. Hosp. U.S. Army, 1951-52, chief resident Georgetown U. Hosp., 1952-53; chief med. service U.S. Army Hosp. U.S. Army, Salzburg, Austria, 1953-55, Wurzburg, Fed. Republic Germany, 1955-56; resident in cardiology Brooke Gen. Hosp. U.S. Army, 1956-57, asst. chief dept. medicine Brooke Gen. Hosp., 1957-59, chief Brooke Gen. Hosp., 1967-68, fellow hematology U. Utah Coll. Medicine, 1959-60, asst. chief U.S. Army Tripler Gen. Hosp., 1960-64, chief William Beaumont Gen. Hosp., 1965-67, chief Walter Reed Gen. Hosp., 1968-69, ret., 1969; chief of staff Maui (Hawaii) Meml. Hosp., 1969-73, chief dept. medicine, 1975-77; exec. v.p. Am. Coll. Physicians, Phila., 1977-86; v.p. med. affairs The NutraSweet Co., Deerfield, Ill., 1986-91; assoc. prof. medicine Baylor U., 1958-59; clin. prof. medicine Hawaii U., 1969-77, Washington U., 1970-77, Abraham Lincoln Sch. Medicine, 1974-75; adj. prof. medicine U. Pa., 1977-86, Northwestern U., 1987-91; adj. prof. Uniformed Services U. Health Scis., 1979—; clin. prof. medicine U. N.Mex. Coll. Medicine, 1992—; flight controller Project Mercury, 1959-62; cons. mem. med. evaluation team Project Gemini, 1962-66; cons. Project Apollo, 1967-73, Tripler Gen. Hosp., 1970-77, Walter Reed Army Med. Ctr., 1974-86; mem. cardiovascular and renal adv. com. FDA, 1978-82; bd. dirs. Pub. Service Satellite Commn., 1980-86; chmn. life scis. adv. com. NASA, 1984-87, mem. NASA adv. coun., 1983-88, chmn. gen. med. panel Hosp. Satellite Network, 1984-86; mem. adv. com. NASA Space Sta., 1988—; mem. Dept. Def. Com. on Grad. Med. Edn., 1986-87; mem. Life Scis. Strategic Planning Study Group, 1986-88; mem. space studies bd. NRC, 1988—, space exploration initiation study, 1990, NASA Space Sta. Commn., 1992—. Author: Diseases of Medical Progress, 1955, rev. edit., 1969, House Officer Training, 1970; co-author: Adventures in Medical Writing, 1970, Decade of Decision, 1992; editor, chief div. sci. publs. Jour. AMA, Chgo., 1973-75; contbg. editor Med. Opinion and Rev., 1966-75; chmn. editorial bd. Diagnosis mag., 1986-89; mem. editorial bd. Hawaii Med. Jour., Family Physicians, Archives of Internal Medicine, 1967-73, Western Jour. Medicine, 1975-87, Chest, 1975-80, Med. Times, 1977-84, Quality Rev. Bull., 1979-91, The Phanos, 1991—, Emergency Med., 1993—; contbr. over 200 articles to med. sci. jours and med. books. Master Am. Coll. Physicians (exec. v.p. 1977-86). Fellow Am. Coll. Cardiology, Royal Coll. Physicians and Surgeons Can. (hon.), Am. Clin. and Climatol. Assn.; mem. Am. Med. Writers Assn., Am. Therapeutic Soc., Am. Osler Soc., Inst. Med., AMA (adv. panel registry of adverse drug reactions 1960-67, council on drugs 1967-73), Chgo. Soc. Internal Medicine, Coll. Physicians Phila., Soc. Med. Cons. to Armed Forces, Alpha Sigma Nu, Alpha Omega Alpha. Democrat. Jewish. Home and Office: Canones Rd # 616 Chama NM 87520

MOSER, ROYCE, JR., physician, medical educator; b. Versailles, Mo., Aug. 21, 1935; s. Royce and Russie Frances (Stringer) M.; m. Lois Anne Hunter, June 14, 1958; children: Beth Anne Moser McLean, Donald Royce. BA, Harvard U., 1957, MD, 1961; MPH, Harvard Sch. Pub. Health, Boston, 1965. Diplomate Am. Bd. Preventive Medicine (trustee), Am. Bd. Family Practice. Commd. officer USAF, 1962, advanced through grades to col., 1974; resident in aerospace medicine USAF Sch. Aerospace Medicine, Brooks AFB, Tex., 1965-67; chief aerospace medicine Aerospace Def. Command, Colorado Springs, Colo., 1967-70; comdr. 35th USAF Dispensary Phan Rang, Vietnam, 1970-71; chief aerospace medicine br. USAF Sch. Aerospace Medicine, Brooks AFB, 1971-77; comdr. USAF Hosp., Tyndall AFB, Fla., 1977-79; chief clin. scis. div. USAF Sch. Aerospace Medicine, Brooks AFB, 1979-81, chief edn. div., 1981-83, sch. comdr., 1983-85; ret., 1985; prof., vice chmn. Dept. Family and Preventive Medicine U. Utah Sch. Medicine, Salt Lake City, 1985—, dir. Rocky Mountain Ctr. for Occupational and Environ. Health, 1987—; cons. in occupational, environ. and aerospace medicine, Salt Lake City, 1985—; presenter nat. and internat. med. meetings. Author: Effective Management of Occupational and Environmental Health and Safety Programs, 1992; contbr. book chpts. and articles to profl. jours. Mem., past pres. First Bapt. Ch. Found., Salt Lake City, 1987-89; mem., chmn. numerous univ. coms., Salt Lake City, 1985—; bd. dirs. Hanford Environ. Health Found., 1990-92; mem. preventive medicine residency review commn. Accredation Coun. Grad. Med. Edn., 1991—; mem. ednl. adv. bd. USAF Human Systems Ctr., 1991—. Decorated Legion of Merit (2). Fellow Aerospace Med. Assn. (pres. 1989-90, Harry G. Mosely award 1981, Theodore C. Lyster award 1988), Am. Coll. Preventive Medicine (regent 1981-82), Am. Coll. Occupational and Environ. Medicine, Am. Acad. Family Physicians; mem. Internat. Acad. Aviation and Space Medicine (selector 1989—), Soc. of USAF Flight Surgeons (pres. 1978-79, George E. Schafer award 1982), Phi Beta Kappa. Home: 664 Aloha Rd Salt Lake City UT 84103-3329 Office: Dept Family & Preventive Medicine 50 N Medical Dr Salt Lake City UT 84132-0001

MOSER, SUZAN ANNE, nurse, researcher, analyst; b. St. Louis, June 21, 1959; d. Mark David Sr. and Betty Jane (Ziercher) Kaskus; m. Charles Edward Moser, May 22, 1981; 1 child, Alexander Charles. Diploma in nursing, Barnes Hosp. Sch. of Nursing, 1980; BSN, SUNY, Albany, 1986; MBA, U. Minn., 1991. RN, Calif., Minn., Pa., Mo. Staff nurse pediatric cardiology unit St. Louis Children's Hosp., 1980-81; staff nurse cardiology dept. U. Mo., Columbia, 1981-83; clin. rsch. rep. Intec Systems, Inc., Pitts., 1983-85; clin. rsch. assoc. Cardiac Pacemakers, Inc., St. Paul, 1985-86, clin. programs specialist, 1986-87, mgr. clin. programs, 1988-89, clin. project mgr., 1989-90, market analyst, 1990-92, bus. analyst, 1992; mgr. clin. evaluation Medtronic CardioRhythm, San Jose, Calif., 1992—; mem. coun. on cardiovascular nursing Am. Heart Assn., Dallas, 1988—. Author: Automatic Implantable Cardioverter Defibrillator System Evaluation, 1988; editor: (chpt. in book) Cardiac Crisis, 1984, Implantable Cardioverter-Defibrillators, 1993; contbr. articles to profl. jours. Brazil out-reach nurse Redeemer Luth. Ch., Fridley, Minn., 1990. Mem. NAFE, Am. Acad. Med. Adminstrs., N.Am. Soc. Pacing and Electrophysiology. Home: 1723 Seville Way San Jose CA 95131-2756 Office: Medtronic CardioRhythm 130 Rio Robles San Jose CA 95134

MOSES, EDWIN, track and field athlete; b. Dayton, Ohio, 1955; m. Myrella Moses. Student, Morehouse Coll. Olympian hurdler; Worlds Top Ranked Intermediate Hurdler, 1976—. Chmn. USOC Substance Abuse Com., 1989—. Holder world record 400 meter hurdle; Olympic gold medalist, 1976, 84; 1st U.S. athlete to be voted delegate to Internat. Amateur Athletic Fedn.; named Sportsman of the Yr. U.S. Olympic Com. Office: Hurdler US Olympic Com 1750 E Boulder St Colorado Springs CO 80909-5746

MOSES, ELBERT RAYMOND, JR., speech and dramatic arts educator; b. New Concord, Ohio, Mar. 31, 1908; s. Elbert Raymond Sr. and Helen Martha (Miller) M.; m. Mary Miller Sterrett, Sept. 21, 1933 (dec. Sept. 1984); 1 child, James Elbert (dec.); m. Caroline Mae Entenman, June 19, 1985. AB, U. Pitts., 1932; MS, U. Mich., 1934, PhD, 1936. Instr. U. N.C., Greensboro, 1936-38; asst. prof. Ohio State U., Columbus, 1938-46; assoc. prof. Ea. Ill. State U., Charleston, 1946-56; asst. prof. Mich. State U., E. Lansing, Mich., 1956-59; prof. Clarion (Pa.) State Coll., 1959-71, chmn. dept. speech and dramatic arts, 1959—, emeritus prof., 1971—; Fulbright lectr. State Dept. U.S. Cebu Normal Sch., Cebu City, Philippine Islands, 1955-56; vis. prof. phonetics U. Mo., summer 1968; hon. sec.'s advocate dept. of aging State of Pa., Harrisburg, 1980-81. Author: Guide to Effective Speaking, 1957, Phonetics: A History and Interpretation, 1964, Three Attributed of God, 1983, Adventure in Reasoning, 1988, Beating the Odds, 1992; poems included in Best Poems of the 90s, 1992; contbr. articles to profl. jours. Del. 3d World Congress Phoneticians, Tokyo, 1976; mem. nat. adv. com. fng. students and tchrs. HEW; del. to Internat. Congress Soc. Logopedics and Phoniatre, Vienna, 1965; liaison rep. to Peace Corps; pres. County Libr. Bd.; past exec. dir. Clarion County United Way; commr. Boy Scouts Am., 1976-77; pres. Venango County Adv. Coun. for Aging, 1978-79. Maj. AUS, 1942-46, lt. col. AUS, ret. Recipient Ret. Sr. Vol. Program Vol. of Yr. award No. Ariz. Coun. Govts., 1989, Spl. award Speech Communication Assn., 1989, Endowment Benefactor award, 1991; 6 Diamond Pin of Melvin Jones Found., Internat. Lions. Fellow United Writers Assn.; mem. Hospitalier Order of St. John of Jerusalem, Knights Hospitalier, Knightly and Mil. Order of St. Eugene of Trebizond (chevalier), Soverign and Mil. Order of St. Stephen the Matyr (comdr.), Knightly Assn. of St. George the Matyr, Ordre Chevaliers du Sinai, Hist. File, VFW (comdr.), Am. Legion (comdr.), Rotary (pres. 1966-67, dist. gov. 1973-74), Order of White Shrine of Jerusalem, Niadh Nask (Marshall of Kilbonane), Internat. Chivalric Inst., Confedn. of Chivalry (life, mem. grand coun.), Ordre Souverain et Militaire de la Milice du Saint Sepulcre (chevalier grand cross), Sovereign World Order of White Cross (lord of knights, dist. commdr. Ariz.), Prescott High Twelve Club (pres. 1990), Phi Delta Kappa (Svc. Key 1978). Republican. Methodist. Home: 2001 Rocky Dells Dr Prescott AZ 86303-5685

MOSHER, GERALDINE LOUISE, computer software educator; b. Detroit, July 8, 1939; d. Andrew Charles and Emily Caroline (Kurgin) M. BA, U. Mich., 1962; MA in Edn., Century U., Albuquerque, 1992. Cert. word perfect resource. Communications officer U.S. Dept. State, Fgn. Svc., Washington, 1962-83; tutor Albuquerque Tech. Vocat. Inst., 1987-89, instr., 1988—; owner Your Computer Tutor, Albuquerque, 1987—. Author: WordPerfect Styles Made Easy, 1993; contbr. articles and poetry to nat. mags. Local coord. Am. Assn. Retired Persons Tax-Aide Program, Albuquerque, 1986—; lit. tutor Mayors Commn. on Lit., Albuquerque, 1990-91. Mem. S.W. Writers Workshop. Democrat. Roman Catholic. Home: 1509 Erbbe NE Albuquerque NM 87112

MOSHER, LOREN CAMERON, geologist, experiential educator; b. Phoenix, Ariz., June 20, 1938; s. Hugh Cameron and Anna Elon (Lively) M.; m. Patricia Ann Fritzsche, June 15, 1963; children: Laura Mosher Biggs, Scott, Todd, Erin, Kindra. BS with honors, Calif. Inst. Tech., Pasadena, 1960; postgrad., Brigham Young U., 1962-63; MS, U. Wis., 1964, PhD, 1967. Asst. prof. geology Fla. State U., Tallahassee, 1967-71; assoc. prof. geosci. U. Ariz., Tucson, 1971-75; rsch. geologist Phillips Petroleum Co. Rsch. Ctr., Bartlesville, Okla., 1975-77, sect. supr., 1977-79; pres., owner Cam Mosher & Assocs., Inc., Pleasant Grove, Utah, 1979-86, 92—, High Challenge, Inc., Pleasant Grove, 1984-92; sales mgr. Binary Data Supply, Inc., Orem, Utah, 1985-88. Contbr. articles to profl. jours. Troop com. mem., scoutmaster, dist. tng. chmn. Boy Scouts Am., various cities, 1963-83; singer Salt Lake (Utah) Mormon Tabernacle Choir, 1982-87. NSF grantee, 1968; fellow Geol. Soc. Am., 1970. Mem. Assn. for Experiential Edn., Am. Soc. for Tng. and Devel. Republican. Mormon. Office: Cam Mosher & Assocs Inc PO Box 74 Orem UT 85059-0074

MOSHER, MICHAEL R(AYMOND), artist, graphic designer, educator; b. July 27, 1955; m. Chrysanthe Johnson. BA, Dartmouth Coll., 1977; MA in Painting, San Francisco State U., 1983, MFA in Conceptual Design, 1988. Salesman Centicore Arts Internat., Ann Arbor, Mich., 1977-78; artist San Francisco, 1978-80; muralist San Francisco Art Commn., 1980-82; art editor North Mission News, San Francisco, 1982-84; computer graphics design cons., 1984-87, 91—; sr. graphic designer Apple Computer, Inc., Cupertino, Calif., 1987-90; adj. faculty Cañada Coll., Redwood City, Calif., 1991—, Community Sch. of Music and Art, Mountain View, Calif., 1991—. Author, artist, performer in "Collaborationation" Interactive Art Kiosk, Franklin Inst., Phila., 1992, "Christopher Cumulonimbus", Small Computers in the Arts Conf., Phila., 1991; artist, mural cycle "The City's Music", Laguna Honda Hosp., San Francisco, 1990; illustrator: Orwell for Beginners, 1984; editorial bd. Community Murals Mag., 1982-84; artwork in collections of Lockard, Phila., Tolhuijs, Zurich, Switzerland, Weilbauer, Quito, Ecuador, Gerald Ford Presdl. Mus., Grand Rapids, Mich.; contbr. articles to profl. jours. Bd. dirs. KMVT Mountain View Community TV, 1989—, Mural Resource Ctr., San Francisco, 1982-84. Home: 302 Easy St # 19 Mountain View CA 94043-2715

MOSHER, SALLY EKENBERG, lawyer; b. N.Y.C., July 26, 1934; d. Leslie Joseph and Frances Josephine (McArdle) Ekenberg; m. James Kimberly Mosher, Aug. 13, 1960 (dec. Aug. 1982). MusB, Manhattanville Coll., 1956; postgrad., Hofstra U., 1958-60, U. So. Calif., 1971-73; JD, U. So. Calif., 1981. Bar: Calif., 1982. Musician, pianist, tchr., 1957-74; music critic Pasadena Star-News, 1967-72; mgr. Contrasts Concerts, Pasadena Art Mus., 1971-72; rep. Occidental Life Ins. Co., Pasadena, 1975-78; v.p. James K. Mosher Co., Pasadena, 1961-82, pres., 1982—; pres. Oakhill Enterprises, Pasadena, 1984—; assoc. White-Howell, Inc., Pasadena, 1984—; real estate broker, 1984—. Contbr. articles to various publs. Bd. dirs. Jr. League

Pasadena, 1966-67, Encounters Concerts, Pasadena, 1966-72, U. So. Calif. Friends of Music, L.A., 1973-76; bd. dirs. Pasadena Arts Coun., 1986—, pres., 1989-92, chair adv. bd., 1992-93; v.p., bd. dirs. Pasadena Chamber Orch., 1986-88, pres., 1987-88; mem. Calif. 200 Coun. for Bicentennial of U.S. Constn., 1987-90; commr. Endowment Adv. Commn, Pasadena, 1988-90; bd. dirs. Calif. Music Theatre, 1988-90, Pasadena Hist. Soc., 1989-91, I Cantori, 1989-91; bd. dirs. Foothill Area Community Svcs., 1990—, treas., 1991, vice-chair, 1992—. Manhattanville Coll. hon. scholar, 1952-56. Mem. ABA, Calif. Bar Assn., Assocs. of Calif. Inst. Tech., Athenaeum, Kappa Gamma Pi, Mu Phi Epsilon, Phi Alpha Delta. Republican. Home: 1260 Rancheros Rd Pasadena CA 91103-2759 Office: 711 E Walnut St Ste 407 Pasadena CA 91101-1676

MOSHER, STEVEN WESTLEY, university administrator; b. Scotia, Calif., May 9, 1948; s. Ralph Donald and Mary Kathryn (Williams) M.; m. Vera Lorraine Cruz; children: Julie Justine, Steven Huang, Matthew Westley, Hannah Elizabeth, Andrew Christian, Moriah Angelica. BS in Oceanography, U. Wash., Seattle, 1970-72; MS in Oceanography, U. Wash., 1973; MA in East Asian Studies, Stanford U., 1977, MA in Anthropology, 1978. Dir. Asian studies The Claremont (Calif.) Inst., 1986—; commr. U.S. Commn. on Broadcasting to PRC, Washington, 1991-92. Author: Broken Earth: The Rural Chinese, 1983, Journey to the Forbidden China, 1985, China Misperceived, 1990, A Mother's Ordeal: Esacpe from One-Child China, 1993. Lt. (j.g.) USN, 1968-76. Recipient Human Rights award Am. Assn. Chinese Polit. Refugees, 1992. Republican. Roman Catholic. Office: Claremont Inst 250 W First St #330 Claremont CA 91711

MOSK, STANLEY, state supreme court justice; b. San Antonio, Sept. 4, 1912; s. Paul and Minna (Perl) M.; m. Edna Mitchell, Sept. 27, 1937 (dec.); 1 child, Richard Mitchell.; m. Susan Hines, Aug. 27, 1982. Student, U. Tex., 1931; Ph.B., U. Chgo., 1933; postgrad., U. Chgo. Law Sch., 1934; JD, Southwestern U., 1935; postgrad., Hague Acad. Internat. Law, 1970, U. Pacific, 1970; LLD, U. San Diego, 1971, U. Santa Clara, 1976, Calif. Western U., 1984, Southwestern U., 1987, Whittier Coll. Law, 1993. Bar: Calif. 1935, U.S. Supreme Ct. 1956. Practiced in Los Angeles, until 1939; exec. sec. to gov. Calif., 1939-42; judge Superior Ct. Los Angeles County, 1943-58; pro tem justice Dist. Ct. Appeal, Calif., 1954; atty. gen. Calif., also head state dept., justice, 1959-64; justice Supreme Ct. Calif., 1964—; mem. Jud. Council Calif., 1973-75, Internat. Commn. Jurists. Chmn. San Francisco Internat. Film Festival, 1967; mem. Dem. Nat. Com., Calif., 1960-64; bd. regents U. Calif., 1940; pres. Vista Del Mar Child Care Service, 1954-58; bd. dirs. San Francisco Law Sch., 1971-73, San Francisco Regional Cancer Found., 1980-83. Served with AUS, World War II. Recipient Disting. Alumnus award U. Chgo., 1958, 93. Mem. Nat. Assn. Attys. Gen. (exec. bd. 1964), Western Assn. Attys. Gen. (pres. 1963), ABA, Calif., Los Angeles, Santa Monica, San Francisco bar assns., Am. Legion, Manuscript Soc., Calif. Hist. Soc., Am. Judicature Soc., Inst. Jud. Administrn., U. Chgo. Alumni Assn. No. Calif. (pres. 1957-58, 67), Order of Coif, Phi Alpha Delta. Mem. B'nai B'rith. Clubs: Hillcrest Country (Los Angeles); Commonwealth, Golden Gateway Tennis (San Francisco); Beverly Hills Tennis. Office: Supreme Ct Calif 303 2nd St San Francisco CA 94107 also: Supreme Ct Calif Sacramento CA 95814

MOSKALSKI, ELTON ALFRED, insurance company executive; b. Clarksburg, W.Va., July 21, 1939; s. Francis John and Gertrude Opal (Everhart) M.; m. Patricia Lynne Black, Apr. 2, 1960; children: Michael Scott, Eric Dana. Student, Lees McRae Coll., Banner Elk, N.C., 1958-60; LLB, U. Richmond, 1965. CPCU. Field claims rep. State Farm Ins. Cos., Richmond, Va., 1965-68; claims supt. State Farm Ins. Cos., Annandale, Va., 1968-70; divisional claim supt. State Farm Ins. Cos., Charlottesville, Va., 1970-73, claims mgr., 1973-81; claims mgr. State Farm Ins. Cos., Rohnert Park, Calif., 1981-83; exec. asst. State Farm Ins. Cos., Bloomington, Ill., 1983-85; dep. regional v.p. State Farm Ins. Cos., Austin, Tex., 1985-89; regional v.p. State Farm Ins. Cos., Greeley, Colo., 1989—. Mem. pres.' adv. bd. U. No. Colo., Greeley, 1989—. Mem. Rotary. Republican. Home: 1269 49th Avenue Ct Greeley CO 80634-2204 Office: State Farm Ins Cos 3001 8th Ave Greeley CO 80638-0001

MOSKOWITZ, DAVID ALEXANDER, conservationist; b. Phila., Dec. 17, 1959; s. Allen David Moskowitz and Margaret Ann (Phillips) Orth; m. Leslie Gail Bottomly, Dec. 30, 1989. BS in Edn., Pa. State U., 1983; JD, Lewis & Clark, 1990. Dir. Project Challenge The Forman Sch., Litchfield, Conn., 1983-87; law clk. Wash. Atty. Gen.'s Office, Olympia, 1988-89; exec. dir. Assn. of Northwest Steelheaders, Portland, Oreg., 1991—; bd. dirs. Northwest Environ. Def. Ctr., Portland, Wildfish PAC, Portland. Bd. dirs. Wildfish Polit. Action Com., Portland, 1992—. Recipient Environ. Leadership award Natural Rsch. Law Inst., Portland, 1990. Office: Assn of NW Steelheaders 6641 SE Lake Rd Milwaukie OR 97222

MOSKUS, JERRY RAY, academic administrator, educator; b. Springfield, Ill., Dec. 10, 1942; s. Raymond Charles and Jean (Riley) M.; m. Virginia Dieckmann Moskus, July 2, 1986; children: Elizabeth, Jane, Jennifer, Julianne, Jonathan. BS in English, Ill. State U., 1965, MS in English, 1968, PhD in Edn. Administrn., 1983. Tchr. English Saybrook (Ill.) Arrowsmith High Sch., 1966-69; instr. Lincoln Land Community Coll., Springfield, 1969-71, asst. to pres., 1971-73, dir. rsch., 1973-75, dean, 1975-84, v.p. acad. svcs., 1984-85; exec. v.p. Des Moines Area Community Coll., Ankeny, Iowa, 1985-90; pres. Lane Community Coll., Eugene, Oreg., 1990—; temp. asst. prof. Iowa State U., Ames, 1989. Bd. dirs. Vachel Lindsay Assn., Springfield, 1983-85, Iowa Children's & Family Svcs., Des Moines, 1986-90; bd. dirs. United Way of Lane County, 1990—. Mem. So. Willamette Pvt. Industry Coun. (bd. dirs. 1990—), League for Innovation in The Community Coll., Springfield Rotary, Phi Delta Kappa, Sigma Tau Delta. Home: 4385 Inwood Ln Eugene OR 97405-4916 Office: Lane Community Coll 4000 E 30th Ave Eugene OR 97405-0640

MOSQUEIRA, CHARLOTTE MARIANNE, dietitian; b. L.A., July 26, 1937; d. Leo and Magdalene Tollefson; B.S., St. Olaf Coll., 1959; postgrad. U. Oreg. Med. Sch., 1959-60; M.A., Central Mich. U., 1980; Registered dietitian; children—Mark, Michael. Chief clin. dietitian, asst. dir. food service Queen of Angels Hosp., Los Angeles, 1968-70; asst. dir. food service Presbyn. Hosp. Ctr., Albuquerque, 1970-73; dir. food service Holy Cross Hosp., Salt Lake City, 1973-77; dir. dietetics Riverside Meth. Hosp., Columbus, Ohio, 1977-79; dir. nutrition and food service Fresno (Calif.) Community Hosp. and Med. Ctr., 1980-91; mem. faculty Dept. Enology and Food Sci., Calif. State U., Fresno, 1984—; dir. nutritional svc. Emanuel Med. Ctr., Turlock, Calif., 1991—. Mem. Am. Dietetic Assn., Calif. Dietetic Assn. Lutheran.

MOSS, CHARLES NORMAN, physician; b. L.A., June 13, 1914; s. Charles Francis and Lena (Rye) M.; A.B., Stanford U., 1940; M.D., Harvard U., 1944; cert. U. Vienna, 1947; M.P.H., U. Calif.-Berkeley, 1955; Dr.P.H., UCLA, 1970; m. Margaret Louise Stakias; children—Charles Eric, Gail Linda, and Lori Anne. Surg. intern Peter Bent Brigham Hosp., Boston, 1944-45, asst. in surgery, 1947; commd. 1st lt. USAF, M.C., 1945, advanced through grades to lt. col., USAF, 1956; Long course for flight surgeon USAF Sch. Aviation Medicine, Randolph AFB, Tex., 1948-49, preventive medicine div. Office USAF Surgeon Gen., Washington, 1955-59; air observer, med., 1954, became sr. flight surgeon 1956; later med. dir., Los Angeles div. North Am. Rockwell Corp., Los Angeles; chief med. adv. unit Los Angeles County, now ret. Decorated Army Commendation medal (U.S.); Chinese Breast Order of Yun Hui. Recipient Physicians Recognition award AMA, 1969, 72, 76, 79, 82. Diplomate in aerospace medicine and occupational medicine Am. Bd. Preventive Medicine. Fellow Am. Pub. Health Assn., AAAS, Am. Coll. Preventive Medicine, Royal Soc. Health, Am. Acad. Occupational Medicine, Western Occupational Med. Assn., Am. Assn. Occupational Medicine; mem. AMA, Mil. Surgeons U.S., Soc. Air Force Flight Surgeons, Am. Conf. Govt. Hygienests, Calif. Acad. Preventive Medicine, (dir.), Aerospace Med. Assn., Calif., Los Angeles County med. assns., Assn. Oldetime Barbell and Strongmen. Research and publs. in field. Home: 7714 Cowan Ave Los Angeles CA 90045-1135

MOSS, DEBRA LEE, school counselor; b. L.A., June 15, 1952; d. Boris and Mildred Rose (Volk) Elkin; divorced; children: Ryan Adam, Lauren Nicole, Rebecca Anne. BA in Psychology, UCLA, 1973; MA in Spl. Edn., Calif. State U., L.A., 1977. Cert. elem. tchr. severely handicapped, learning handicapped and jr. coll. tchr., Calif. Tchr. spl. edn. UCLA Neuropsychiat. Inst., 1972-75, demonstration tchr., curriculum coord., 1975-78; edn. specialist Harbor Regional Ctr. for Developmentally Disabled, Torrance, Calif., 1978-82; ednl. cons. North L.A. Regional Ctr. for Developmentally Disabled, Panorama City, Calif., 1982-87; behavior specialist L.A. Unified Sch. Dist., 1987-91, program specialist, 1991-92, support staff spl. edn. middle schs., 1992—; hon. lectr. West Valley Occupational Ctr., 1986—; tutor spl. edn., L.A., 1973—; behavior specialist to families, 1985—. Contbr. articles to profl. jours. Mem. Am. Assn. on Retardation, Nat. Assn. for Autistic Children and Adults, Coun. for Exceptional Children. Democrat. Office: LA Unified Sch Dist Middle Schools Spl Edn Svc Unit 450 N Grand Los Angeles CA 90012

MOSS, DOUGLAS MABBETT, military officer, aerospace executive; b. Washington, Mar. 21, 1954; s. Lon Harold and Mildred (Mabbett) M. BS in Nuclear Engring., Ga. Inst. Tech., 1976, MS in Mech. Engring., 1981. Teaching asst. Ga. Tech. Mech. Engr. Dept., Atlanta, 1976-77; commd. 2d lt. USAF, 1976, advanced through grades to maj., 1988; instr. pilot 71st Flying Tng. Wing USAF, Vance AFB, Okla., 1977-82; F-15 fighter pilot 18th Tactical Fighter Wing USAF, Kadena AFB, Japan, 1982-84; test pilot 6510 Test Wing USAF, Edwards AFB, Calif., 1984-88; tactical weapons officer USAF, Osan AFB, Korea, 1988-89; instr. test pilot USAF Test Pilot Sch., Edwards AFB, Calif., 1989-90; exptl. test pilotMD-80/MD-90 McDonnell Douglas Corp., Long Beach, Calif., 1990—; project test pilot T-46 Test Force, Edwards AFB, 1986-87; project mgr. Advanced Tactical Fighter, Edward AFB, 1985-88. Mem. Soc. of Exptl. Test Pilots, Martin-Baker Tie Club, Smithsonian Air and Space Soc., Air Force Assn., Order of the Daedalians. Home: 3203 Carolwood Ln Torrance CA 90505-7113 Office: McDonnell Douglas Corp 3855 N Lakewood Blvd Long Beach CA 90846-0001

MOSS, LYNDA BOURQUE, museum director; b. Torrington, Wyo., Mar. 15, 1950; d. Leroy Alfred and Mary (Halley) Bourque; m. Thomas Charles Moss, Jan. 31, 1970; children: Heather, Christopher Eric. BFA, U. Nebr., Omaha, 1977; MA, U. No. Iowa, 1979; MFA, Mont. State U., 1984. Guest lectr. U. Nebr., Omaha, 1977-78; program developer Children's Mus., Omaha, 1977-78; gallery asst. U. No. Iowa, Cedar Falls, 1978-79; curator edn. Western Heritage Ctr., Billings, Mont., 1979-83, dir., 1986—; adj. prof. Ea. Mont. Coll., Billings, 1985-87; curator Mont. Art Gallery Dirs., Kalispell, 1986-87. Represented in pub. and pvt. collections, Am. Northwest. Art scholar Washington U., St. Louis, 1968-70. Mem. Internat. Coun. Mus., Am. Assn. Mus., Coll. Art Assn. Democrat. Home: 2540 Hoover Ave Billings MT 59102-1658 Office: Western Heritage Ctr 2822 Montana Ave Billings MT 59101-2305

MOSS, MARVIN, engineering physicist; b. N.Y.C., Dec. 8, 1929; m. Joan Carolyn Reinhold, Oct. 16, 1957; children: Janine, Diana. BS, Queens Coll., N.Y.C., 1951; PhD, Cornell U., 1963. Jr. engr. Sylvania Electric Products, Inc., N.Y.C., 1951-54; sr. mem. tech. staff Sandia Nat. Labs., Albuquerque, 1963—. Contbr. articles to profl. jours.; inventor fire resistant nuclear fuel cask. Pres. Albuquerque Montessori Soc., 1964-71; chmn. Energy Conservation Coun., Albuquerque, 1980-87; bd. dirs. Explora Found., Albuquerque, 1988—, Explora Adv. Bd., Albuquerque, 1992—; bd. trustees N.Mex. Mus. Natural History and Sci., N.Mex., 1990—. Mem. AAAS, N.Mex. Acad. Sci. (pres. 1990). Home: 8712 Harwood Ave NE Albuquerque NM 87111-3211 Office: Sandia Nat Labs Dept 251 Albuquerque NM 87185

MOSS, MYRA E. See ROLLE, MYRA MOSS

MOSSMAN, ALBERT PRUITT, chemist, consultant; b. Ft. Benning, Ga., June 5, 1937; s. Albert Patterson and Allene (Pruit) M.; m. Martha G. Soto (div.); 1 child, Sabrina A. BS, St. Mary's Coll., 1966. Chemist, Western Regional Rsch. Ctr. USDA, Albany, Calif., 1964—. Author: chpt. on Rice in the Tropics in Handbook of Tropical Foods, 1983; contbr. articles to profl. jours. Mem. Am. Assn. Cereal Chemists, Rice Tech. Working Group. Office: Western Regional Rsch Ctr USDA 800 Buchanan St Berkeley CA 94710-1100

MOSSOFF, JEFFREY, medical administrator, academic administrator; b. Pitts., June 18, 1948; s. Benjamin and Helen B. (Miller) M.; m. Miriam S. Schulman, Dec. 28, 1967; children: Sarra, Adam. BA, Pa. State U., 1970; MBA, Wayne State U., 1978. Asst. dir. housing U. Dayton, Ohio, 1970-72; asst. dir. housing U. Wis., Oshkosh, 1972-74, assoc. dir. housing, 1974-75, acting dir. housing, 1975-76; mng. dir. Wayne State Housing Authority, Detroit, 1976-79; dir. housing Wayne State U., Detroit, 1976-79, exec. adminstr. dept. surgery, 1979-89; exec. adminstr. Univ. Surgeons, Detroit, 1979-89; vice chmn. adminstrn. dept. medicine U. So. Calif., L.A., 1989—; ptnr., cons. Profl. Housing Cons., Troy, 1978-82; v.p. Rehab. and Placement Assocs., Troy, 1980-90; cons. Harper Hosp., Detroit, 1988-89. Speaker at presentations. Trustee Temple Emanu-el, Oak Park, Mich., 1981-85, pres., 1985-87; bd. mem. Met. Detroit Fedn. Reform Synagogues, 1985-87. Mem. Med. Group Mgmt. Assn. (chair acad. practice assembly 1991-92, bd. mem. 1990-92, mem.-at-large exec. com. acad. practice assembly 1988-90), Adminstrs. of Internal Medicine (bd. mem.-at-large 1990-92, by laws com. 1990-91, program com. 1990), Am. Coll. Med. Group Adminstrs., Am. Mgmt. Assn., Assn. Acad. Surg. Adminstrs. (pres. 1988-89), Assn. Am. Med. Colls., Calif. Med. Group Mgmt. Assn., Med. Adminstrs. Assn. of L.A., Soc. Rsch. Adminstrs., Mich. State Med. Soc. (medicaid liaison com. 1987-88). Office: U So Calif Dept Medicine 2020 Zonal Ave # 220 IRO Los Angeles CA 90033

MOST, ROBERT BERNARD, publishing executive; b. Palo Alto, Calif., July 22, 1952; s. Nathan Most and May Rose (Lazarus) Burberik; m. Alice Timoxina Brock, Dec. 1, 1979; children: William, James, Alexander. BA, U. Calif., Santa Barbara, 1973; MA, Wayne State U., 1976, PhD, 1978. Lic. psychologist. Rsch. asst. Wayne State U., Detroit, 1974-78; instr. Learning Resources, San Mateo, Calif., 1978-79; v.p. Behaviordyne, Palo Alto, Calif., 1979-83, Cons. Psychologists Press, Palo Alto, 1983—. Author: Psychological Testing: An Inside View, 1991; contbr. articles to profl. jours. and chpts. to books. Mem. APA, APS. Office: Cons Psychologists Press 3803 E Bayshore Rd Palo Alto CA 94303-4314

MOSTELLER, JAMES WILBUR, III, data processing executive; b. Ft. Riley, Kans., June 21, 1940; s. James Wilbur, Jr., and Ruth Renfro (Thompson) M.; B.S. in Econs., Rensselaer Poly. Inst., 1962; M.B.A., Temple U., 1971; m. Sandra Josephine Stevenson, Oct. 13, 1962; children—Margaret, Steven, Michael. Data processing systems analyst, Philco-Ford, Ft. Washington, Pa., 1966-69; data processing analyst and supr., Merck Sharp & Dohme, West Point, Pa., 1969-75, dir. mgmt. info. systems KELCO div. Merck and Co., San Diego, 1975-87; dir. info. mgmt. Advanced Systems div. United Technologies, San Diego, 1987-88; computer scientist Navy Personnel Research and Devel. Ctr., San Diego, 1988—. Bd. dirs. New Horizons Montessori Sch., Ft. Washington, Pa., 1974-75; leader youth programs North County YMCA, 1977-81; mem. San Diego Research Park Com., 1978-86; 1st. v.p., mem. exec. com. San Diego Space and Sci. Found., 1985-92. With USN, 1962-66, capt. Res., 1966—. Cert. in data processing. Mem. Data Processing Mgmt. Assn., Assn. Systems Mgmt., Naval Res. Assn. (life), U.S. Naval Inst. (life), Beta Gamma Sigma, Sigma Alpha Epsilon (chpt. pres. 1961-62). Office: Navy Pers R & D Ctr San Diego CA 92152-6800

MOSZKOWSKI, LENA IGGERS, educator; b. Hamburg, Mar. 8, 1930; d. Alfred G. and Lizzie (Minden); m. Steven Alexander, Aug. 29, 1952 (div. Oct. 1977); children: Benjamin Charles, Richard David, Ronald Bertram. BS, U. Richmond, 1948; MS, U. Chgo., 1953; PhD candidate, UCLA, 1958. Tchr. Lab. asst. U. Chgo. Ben May Cancer Research Lab., Chgo., 1951-53; biology, sci. tchrs. Bishop Conaty High Sch., Los Angeles, 1967-68; chemistry, sci. tchr. St. Paul High Sch., Santa Fe Springs, Calif., 1968-69; chemistry, human ecology tchr. Marlborough Sch., Los Angeles, 1969-71; biology, sci. ecology tchr. Los Angeles Unified Sch. Dist., 1971—. Author: Termite Taxonomy Cryptotermes Haviland and C. Krybi, Madagascar, 1955, Ecology and Man, 1971, Parallels in Human and Biological Ecology, 1977, American Public Education, An Inside Journey, 1991-92. Founder, adminstr., com. mem. UCLA Student (and Practical Assistance Cooperative Furniture), Los Angeles, 1963-67; active participant UCLA Earth Day Program, Los Angeles, 1970. Recipient Va. Sci. Talent Search Winner Va. Acad. of Sci., 1946; Push Vol. Tchr. award John C. Fremont High Sch., Los Angeles, 1978. Mem. NEA, ASCD, Am. Assn. Individual Investors. L.A. World Affairs Coun. Democrat. Jewish. Home: 2567 S Barrington Ave Los Angeles CA 90064-2828

MOTE, CLAYTON DANIEL, JR., mechanical engineer, educator; b. San Francisco, Feb. 5, 1937; s. Clayton Daniel and Eugenia (Isnardi) M.; m. Patricia Jane Lewis, Aug. 18, 1962; children: Melissa Michelle, Adam Jonathan. BSc, U. Calif., Berkeley, 1959, MS, 1960, PhD, 1963. Registered profl. engr., Calif. Asst. specialist U. Calif. Forest Products Labs., 1961-62; asst. mech. engr., 1962-63; lectr. mech. engring. U. Calif., Berkeley, 1962-63, asst. prof., 1967-69, asst. research engr., 1968-69, assoc. prof., assoc. research engr., 1969-73, prof., 1973—, vice chmn. mech. engring. dept., 1976-80, 83-86, chmn. mech. engring. dept., 1987-91, vice chancellor univ. rels., FANUC chair mech. systems, 1991—; research fellow U. Birmingham, Eng., 1963-64; asst. prof. Carnegie Inst. Tech., 1964-67; vis. prof. Norwegian Inst. Wood Tech., 1972-73, vis. sr. scientist, 1976 '78, '80 '84 '85; cons. in engring design and analysis; sr. scientist Alexander Von Humboldt Found., Fed. Republic Germany, 1988, Japan Soc. for Promotion of Sci., 1991. Mem. editorial bd. Soma Jour. Sound and Vibration, Machine Vibration; contbr. articles to profl. jours.; patentee in field. NSF fellow, 1963-64; recipient Disting. Teaching award, U. Calif., 1971, Pi Tau Sigma Excellence in Teaching award, U. Calif., 1975, Humboldt Prize, Fed. Republic Germany, 1988, Frederick W. Taylor Rsch. medal. Soc. Mfg. Engrs., 1991, Hetenyi award Soc. Exptl. Mechanics, 1992. Fellow NAE, AAAS, ASME (Blackall award 1975, v.p. environ. and transp. 1986-90, nat. chmn. noise control and acoustics 1980-84, chmn. San Francisco sect. 1978-79, Disting. Svc. award 1991), Internat. Acad. Wood Sci., Acoustical Soc. Am.; mem. AIAA, ASTM (com. on snow skiing F-27 1984-87, chmn. new projects subcom.), Am. Soc. Biomechanics, Orthopaedic Rsch. Soc., Internat. Soc. Skiing Safety (v.p., sec. 1977-85, bd. dirs. 1977—, chmn. sci. com. 1985—), Sigma Xi, Pi Tau Sigma, Tau Beta Pi. Office: U Calif Dept Mech Engring Berkeley CA 94720

MOTSCHENBACHER, S(TEVEN) PETER, construction executive; b. Roseburg, Oreg., Sept. 14, 1956; s. Elliott Lee and Jo Anne Lee (Moore) M.; m. Carmel Johnson, Nov. 25, 1978. BBA, U. Oreg., 1980. Staff acct. Coopers & Lybrand, Eugene, Oreg., 1980-81; asst. contr. Pipe Inc., Portland, Oreg., 1982-83; contr. Kniesel Travel, Portland, 1983-84, Columbia Hardwood and Moulding, Tigard, Oreg., 1984-86, KL & K Assocs., Portland, 1986-87; chief fin. officer Johnson Excavating and Utilities, Cornelius, Oreg., 1987—. Mem. U. Oreg. Alumni Assn. (bd. dirs. Portland chpt. 1983, 86-89, treas. 1984, pres. 1985). Republican. Home: 3923 SW Marigold St Portland OR 97219-5359 Office: Johnson Excavating Utilities 1150 S 12th PO Box 371 Cornelius OR 97113

MOTT, JUNE MARJORIE, educator, consultant, elected official; b. Faribault, Minn., Mar. 8, 1920; d. David C. and Tillie W. (Nelson) Shifflett; m. Elwood Knight Mott, Oct. 18, 1958. BS, U. Minn., 1943, MA, 1948. Tchr. high schs. in Minn., 1943-46, 48-53, 54-57; script writer, Hollywood, Calif., 1953-54; tchr. English, creative writing and journalism Mt. Miguel High Sch., Spring Valley, Calif., 1957-86, chmn. English dept., 1964-71, chmn. Dist. English council, 1967-68; mem. Press Bur., Grossmont (Calif.) High Sch. Dist., 1958-86; elected to Grossmont Union High Sch. Governing Bd., 1986, clk. sch. bd., 1989, v.p. governing bd., 1989-90, 93, pres. sch. bd., 1991-92, v.p., 1992-93; scriptwriter TV prodn. Lamp Unto My Feet, Jam Dandy Corp.; free-lance writer, cons. travel writer, photographer; editor, publ Listening Heart, 1989. Author, editor in field. Vice chmn. polit. action San Diego County Regional Resource Ctr., 1980-81; mem. S.D. Bd. of Alcohol and Drug Abuse Prevention, 1990—, Curriculum Com. Grossmont Dist., 1990—, Site Facilities Com., Master Planning Com., 1992—, East County Issues and Mgmt. Com., 1990—, East County Women in Edn.; apptd. del. Calif. Sch. Bds. Assn., 1992—, del. assembly, 1992—; v.p., pub. rels. chmn. Lemon Grove Luth. Ch., 1962-78, 89—, v.p., 1993, pres. 1994. Writing project fellow U. Calif., San Diego, 1978; named Outstanding Journalism Tchr., State of Calif., Outstanding Humanities Tchr., San Diego County, Tchr. of Yr. for San Diego County, 1978; U. Cambridge scholar, 1982; Woman of yr. Lemon Grove Soroptimists, 1990. Mem. ASCD, NEA, AAUW, Nat. Council Tchrs. English, Nat. Journalism Assn., Calif. Assn. Tchrs. English, Calif. Tchrs. Assn., So. Calif. Journalism Assn., Calif. Sch. Bds. Assn. (elected del. region 17, del. assembly 1993—), Calif. Elected Women's Assn. for Edn. Rsch. (ednl. cons. 1990), San Diego County Journalism Educators Assn. (pres. 1975-76), Grossmont Edn. Assn. (pres. 1978-80), Greater San Diego Council Tchrs. English, Nat. Writers Club, Am. Guild Theatre Organists, Calif. Retired Tchrs. Assn. (membership chairwoman 1986-89, pres. chpt. #69 1989-93, parlimentarian 1992-93), Nat. Sch. Bds. Assn., Order Ea. Star, Kiwanis (pres. elect Lemon grove chpt. 1992, program chmn., pres. 1993—), Sigma Delta Chi, Delta Kappa Gamma (chpt Theta Gamma Chi 1993). Democrat. Home and Office: 2885 New Jersey Ave Lemon Grove CA 91945

MOTTA, JOHN JOSEPH, controller; b. Oakland, Calif., Apr. 23, 1949; s. Joseph and Rosemary (King) M.; m. Dianne Yvonne Dyer, Mar. 24, 1979; children: Joseph E., Valerie L. BS in Acctg., Calif. State U., Hayward, 1973; MBA, St. Mary's Coll., 1980. CPA, Wash. Acctg. mgr. Clorox Co., Oakland, 1973-86; contr. Todd Shipyards Corp., Seattle, 1987—. Mem. AICPA. Republican. Office: Todd Shipyards Corp PO Box 3806 Seattle WA 98124-3806

MOTTEK, CARL T., hotel company executive; b. 1928. With Hilton Hotels Corp., 1951—, dir. food and beverage ops., from 1964, v.p., 1965-68, sr. v.p. food and beverage ops., 1968-73, sr. v.p. so. region, 1973-85, exec. v.p., also pres. div. Hilton Hotels, 1985—, also bd. dirs. Office: Hilton Hotels Corp 9336 Civic Center Dr Beverly Hills CA 90210-3964

MOTTELER, ZANE CLINTON, computer science educator; b. Wenatchee, Wash., July 4, 1935; s. Roy Huling and Elizabeth Ann (Stanford) M.; m. Marilynn Rae Ginsbach, June 25, 1960; children: Clinton, Cara, Renee, Seth. BS, Stanford U., 1957, MS, 1962, PhD, 1964; MS, Mich. State U., 1981. Mem. staff Los Alamos (N.Mex.) Nat. Lab., 1957-65; from asst. prof. to prof. math. Gonzaga U., Spokane, Wash., 1965-72, chmn. dept., 1966-71; prof. math. Mich. Tech. U., Houghton, 1972-82, head dept., 1972-80; prof. computer sci., engr. Calif. Poly. State U., San Luis Obispo, 1982-93, prof. emeritus, 1993—, coord. computer engring., 1991-93; sr. computer scientist/math. programmer Livermore (Calif.) Nat. Lab., 1993—; vis. lectr. computer sci. Mich. State U., East Lansing, 1980-81; cons. Los Alamos Nat. Lab., 1965-69; cons., sr. analyst IBM Corp., San Jose, Calif. and Austin, Tex., 1983—; sr. computer scientist Livermore (Calif.) Nat. Lab.,1986—, Chevron Corp., San Francisco, 1983. Author: Introduction to Ordinary Differential Equations, 1972, Introduction to Complex Analysis, 1975; co-author: Assembler Language for Univac 1110, 1982; translator: Partial Differential Equations of Elliptic Type, 1970. Fellow NSF, U. Minn., 1957-58, NASA, Am. Soc. Engring. Edn., Langley, Va., 1982. Mem. IEEE, Assn. Computing Machinery, Computer Scis. Accreditation Commn., Sigma Xi, Phi Beta Kappa, Phi Kappa Phi. Democrat. Roman Catholic. Home: 4094 Blacow St Pleasanton CA 94566-4772 Office: Lawrence Livermore Nat Lab L-472 L-472 PO Box 808 Livermore CA 94550

MOTULSKY, ARNO GUNTHER, geneticist, physician, educator; b. Fischhausen, Germany, July 5, 1923; came to U.S., 1941; s. Herman and Rena (Sass) Molton; m. Gretel C. Stern, Mar. 22, 1945; children: Judy, Harvey, Arlene. Student, Cen. YMCA Coll., Chgo., 1941-43, Yale U., 1943-44; BS, U. Ill., 1945, MD, 1947, DSc (hon.), 1982, MD (hon.), 1991. Diplomate Am. Bd. Internal Medicine, Am. Bd. Med. Genetics. Intern, fellow, resident Michael Reese Hosp., Chgo., 1947-51; staff mem. charge clin. investigation dept. hematology Army Med. Service Grad. Sch., Walter Reed Army Med. Ctr., Washington, 1952-53; research assoc. internal medicine George Washington U. Sch. Medicine, 1952-53; from instr. to assoc. prof. dept. medicine U. Wash. Sch. Medicine, Seattle, 1953-61, prof. medicine, prof. genetics, 1961—; head div. med. genetics, dir. genetics clinic Univ. Hosp., Seattle, 1959-89, Children's Med. Ctr., Seattle, 1966-72; dir. Ctr. for Inherited Diseases, Seattle, 1972-90; attending physician Univ. Hosp., Seattle; cons. Pres.'s Commn. for Study of Ethical Problems in Medicine and Biomed. and Behavioral Research, 1979-83; cons. various coms. NRC, NIH, WHO, others. Editor Am. Jour. Human Genetics, 1969-75, Human Genetics, 1969—. Commonwealth Fund fellow in human genetics Univ.

Coll., London, 1957-58; John and Mary Markle scholar in med. sci., 1957-62; fellow Ctr. Advanced Study in Behavioral Scis., Stanford U., 1976-77, Inst. Advanced Study, Berlin, 1984. Fellow ACP, AAAS; mem. NAS, Internat. Soc. Hematology, Am. Fedn. Clin. Research, Genetics Soc. Am., Western Soc. Clin. Research, Am. Soc. Human Genetics, Am. Soc. Clin. Investigation, Am. Assn. Physicians, Inst. of Medicine, Am. Acad. Arts and Scis. Home: 4347 53d Ave NE Seattle WA 98105 Office: U Wash Div Med Genetics Seattle WA 98195

MOU, LAN, artist; b. Shanghai, China, Aug. 24, 1957; came to U.S., 1988; d. Qijia Mou and Xiangting Qu; m. Hengfu Xin, Feb. 4, 1985. BA, Shanghai (China) Edn. Coll., 1987. Technol. archivist Shanghai Radio Components Factory, Shanghai, 1978-88; distbr. svc. rep. AIM Internat., Inc., Nampa, Idaho, 1991—. Exhibited one-man shows First Security Bank, the Idao Statesman, All Boise; group shows at Nantong City Mus., Shanghai Art Mus., Stewart Art Gallery, Western Idaho Fair. Recipient Spl. award Western Idaho Fair, 1989-92. Mem. Idaho Watercolor Soc. Home: 5162 Blaser Ln 8870 W Lancelot Boise ID 83704

MOUNDS, LEONA MAE REED, educator; b. Crosby, Tex., Sept. 9, 1945; d. Elton Phillip and Ora Lee (Jones) Reed; m. Aaron B. Mounds Jr., Aug. 21, 1965 (div.); 1 dau., Lisa Nichelle. BS in Elem. Edn., Bridgewater State Coll., 1973; MA in Mental Retardation, U. Alaska, 1980. Cert. tchr. Alaska, Colo., Tex., Mass., cert. adminstrv. prin. Tchr., Sch. Dist.# 11, Colorado Springs, Colo., 1973-75; tchr. Anchorage Sch. Dist., 1976-78, 80—, mem. maths. curriculum com., reading contact tchr., mem. talent bank. Tchr. Del Valle (Tex.) Sch. Dist., 1979-80; adminstrv. prin. intern Anchorage Sch. Dist., 1989-90; asst. prin. Spring Hill Elem. Sch., Anchorage, 1990-91; elem. prin. intern.; asst. prin. Turnagain Elem. Sch., Anchorage, 1991—. Bd. dirs. Urban League, 1974; 1st v.p. PTA, Crosby, Tex.; del. Tex. Dem. Conv., 1980; chmn. dist. 13 Dem. Party; mem. Alaska Women Polit. Caucus; bd. dirs. C.R.I.S.I.S. Inc.; tchr. religious edn., lay Eucharist minister St. Martin De Pores Roman Cath. Ch., St. Patrick's Ch.; pres. Black Educators of Pike Peak Region, 1974; mem. social concerns commn. Archidiocese of Anchorage, Coun. for Exceptional Children. With USAF, 1964-66. Alaska State Tchr. Incentive grantee, 1981, Ivy Lutz scholar, 1972. Mem. NEA (human rels. coord. Alaska chpt., region 6 bd. dirs., bd. dirs Alaska chpt., vice-chmn. women's caucus), NAACP, LWV, Anchorage Edn. Assn. (minority chmn. 1982—, mem. black caucus polit. action com., v.p. programs 1986-88), Anchorage Edn. Assn. (v.p. programs com. 1986-87, women's caucus), Assn. Supervision and Curriculum Devel., Alaska Women in Adminstrn., Prins. Assn.

MOUNGER, SCOTT EDWIN, insurance agent; b. Mpls., Nov. 17, 1951; s. Guy Edwina and Marilyn Joy (Lunder) M.; 1 child, Brant Edwin. BS, Moorhead State U., 1973. CLU. Agt. Penn Mut. Life Ins. Co., Davenport, Iowa, 1977-80, D.S. Kane & Assocs., Fargo, N.D., 1980-81; owner, agt. Scott Mounger & Assocs., Fargo, 1981-85; agt. Hektner, Lybeck, Erickson Ins., Fargo, 1985-86; owner, agt. The Canyon Group (formerly Desert Fin. Cos.), Gilbert, Ariz., 1986—; pres. Mesa (Ariz.) Tax Study Group, 1990-91. Mem. Am. Soc. CLU's and ChFC's (local bd. dirs. 1984-86, Pace award 1991, 93), Nat. Assn. Life Underwriters (local bd. dirs. 1983-86, 91-93, numerous awards), Nat. Assn. Health Underwriters (leading prodr.'s round table 1985-87), Million Dollar Round Table, Gilbert C. of C. (chmn. bus. com. 1992). Lutheran. Office: The Canyon Group Inc PO Box 1235 33 S Riata Dr Gilbert AZ 85234

MOUNT, CINDY KAY, small business owner; b. Inglewood, Calif., Aug. 30, 1960; d. Barry Allen and Valora Zell (Dorsey) Pirtle; m. Ross Keenan Mount, Apr. 14, 1984; children: Kelly Ann, Christopher Ross. AA, Glendale Community Coll., 1980. Sr. exec. sec. Bank Am., Newport Beach, Calif., 1979-84; office mgr. McGuinness & Assocs., Newport Beach, Calif., 1984-86; adminstrv. mgr. Bank Am., Laguna Niguel, Calif., 1986-90; owner Ribbons, Ruffles & Lace, Costa Mesa, Calif., 1988—. Organizer Mom & Tot Sunshine Playgroup, Costa Mesa, 1990—. Republican. Home and office: 2250 Vanguard Way #E224 Costa Mesa CA 92626

MOUNT, JOHN WALLACE, music educator; b. Sioux City, Iowa, Nov. 20, 1946; s. George Royal and Dorothy Penelope (Wallace) M.; m. Lorna Joan Bodum, Dec. 28, 1968; children: Sterling George, Megan Melelani. MusB, U. Colo., 1969, MusM, 1972. Prof. voice U. Mont., Missoula, 1973-75; prof. voice U. Hawaii, Honolulu, 1975—, chmn. music dept., 1985—. Performed 47 leading roles Hawaii Opera Theater, 1976—. Bd. dirs. Yacht Club Terrace Owners Assn., Kaneohe, Hawaii, 1977-84. Named nat. finalist Met. Opera, N.Y.C., 1975, San Francisco Opera, 1976, Internat. Competition of Verdian Voices, Busetto, Italy, 1975. Mem. Nat. Assn. Tchrs. Singing (chpt. pres. 1982-86, treas. 1986-92, state gov. 1978-82), Honolulu Youth Symphony (bd. dirs. 1989), Music Educators Nat. Conf., Hawaii Assn. Musical Socs. (bd. dirs. 1985), Hawaii Opera Theater, Nat. Opera Assn. (state gov. 1978—, 1st pl. 1981), Nat. Assn. Schs. of Music (regional chair 1990—, regional chair 1990-92, ethics com. 1992—), State Tchr. Edn. Com. Republican. Methodist. Office: U Hawaii Music 2411 Dole St Honolulu HI 96822-2398

MOURI, MICHAEL PATRICK, physician, surgeon; b. Bridgeton, N.J., June 9, 1955; s. Tadashi Frank and Daisy Tsukiko (Kakoda) M.; m. Jane Celia Busch, June 6, 1982 (div. 1986). DDS, Med. Coll. Va., Richmond, 1982; D of Acupuncture, Acad. Traditional Chinese Medicine, Beijing, 1986; MD, Open Internat. U. Complementary Medicine, Colombo, Sri Lanka, 1988, U. Tex. Med. Br., Galveston, 1989; MPH, U. Calif., Berkeley, 1993. Recruitment dir. Adventure Medicine Internat., Point Reyes, Calif., 1989—; acupuncturist, cons. Nat. Acupuncture Detoxification Assn., N.Y.C., 1989—; vol. physician, dentist Haight-Ashbury Free Clinics, San Francisco, 1989—; mem. staff Mountain Medicine Inst., Oakland, Calif.; vol. physician, dentist Artzen Zonder Grenzen Medicos sin Fronteras, Nicaragua, 1990; with Internat. Health Exchange, Africa Centre, Ghana, 1993. Capt. U.S. Army Dental Corps, 1982-85, maj. USAR Med. Corps, 1985—. Occupational and Environ. Medicine fellow U. Calif., 1992—. Mem. AMA (del. 1990), Acad. Gen. Dentistry, Soc. Am. Magicians, Internat. Brotherhood Magicians, Am. Soc. Clin. Hypnosis, Am. Holistic Med. Assn., World Health Assn. Home: 2737 Forest Ave # 201 Berkeley CA 94705-1360 Office: Inst Toxicology & Environ Health UC Davis School Medicine Davis CA 95616

MOUSEL, DONALD KEE, ophthalmologist; b. McCook, Nebr., Feb. 13, 1932; s. Lloyd Harvey and Beatrix Mizer (Florance) M.; m. Carol Rose Lindstrom, Aug. 20, 1956; 1 child, Lise Beatrix. BA, Whitman Coll., Walla Walla, Wash., 1954; MD, McGill U., Montreal, 1958. Intern Washington Hosp. Ctr., 1958-59, resident in ophthalmology, 1959-62; pediatric ophthalmologist F.D. Costenbader, M.D., Washington, 1962-63; pvt. practice specializing in ophthalmology Reno, Nev., 1965—; clin. prof. surgery and pediatrics U. Nev., Reno, 1983-86, assoc. prof. ophthalmology U. Calif.-San Francisco, 1983—. Contbr. articles to profl. jours. Bd. dirs. Reno Philharmonic, 1982-90. Named Disting. Physician State of Nev., Nev. Med. Soc., 1984. Fellow Am. Acad. Ophthalmology; mem. Am. Assn. Pediatric Ophthalmology and Strabismus, Barraquer Inst. Spain, Reno Surg. Soc., Costenbader Soc. (pres. 1987-89). Home: 180 Southridge Dr Reno NV 89509-3253 Office: Sierra Eye Assocs 90 Ryland St Reno NV 89501

MOWBRAY, JOHN CODE, retired state supreme court chief justice; b. Bradford, Ill., Sept. 20, 1918; s. Thomas John and Ellen Driscoll (Code) M.; m. Kathlyn Ann Hammes, Oct. 15, 1949; children: John, Romy, Jerry, Terry. BA, Western Ill. U., 1940, LHD (hon.), 1976, LLD (hon.), 1977; LLD (hon.), Far Eastern Civil Affairs Tng. Sch., Northwestern U., 1945; JD cum laude, U. Notre Dame, 1949; LLD (hon.), U. Nev., 1978. Bar: Nev. 1949, Ill. 1950. Dep. dist. atty. Clark County, Las Vegas, Nev., 1949-53; U.S. referee Fed. Cts. in Nev., 1955-59; dist. judge for Nev., 1959-67; justice Nev. Supreme Ct., Carson City, 1967—, chief justice, 1986—; founder 1st pub. defender program in Nev., 1967; mem. faculty Nat. Coll. State Judiciary, 1967. V.p. Boulder Dam Area council Boy Scouts Am., 1960-70; bd. dirs. Nev. Area council, 1967—; pres. City of Hope, 1963-64, NCCJ, 1965-66; v.p. YMCA, 1964—; chmn. Nev. Commn. on Bicentennial U.S. Constitution, 1986; nat. trustee Freedoms Found. Valley Forge, Pa. Served to maj. AUS, 1942-46. PTO. Recipient Silver Beaver award Boy Scouts Am., 1966, Outstanding Alumni award Western Ill. U., 1971, Equal Justice award Western regional dept. NAACP, 1970, Minuteman award SAR, 1982, Silver Antelope award Boy Scouts Am., 1983, Jurist of Yr. award Nev. Trial Lawyers Assn., 1986, Judicial Officer of Yr. award State Sheriff and Police Assn., 1986, medal of honor DAR, 1990; Mowbray Hall, Western Ill. U. named in his honor, 1974. Mem. ABA (Liberty Bell award 1991), Nev. Trial Lawyers Assn. (Jurist of Yr. award 1986), Am. Judicature Soc., State Sheriff and Police Assn. (Jud. Officer of Yr. award 1986), SAR (pres. Nev. 1969-70, Nat. Gen. MacArthur medal 1971, nat. trustee 1971—), VFW. Clubs: Rotarian (hon.), Elk. Home: 189 Lake Glen Dr Carson City NV 89703-5133 Address: PO Box 55 Las Vegas NV 89125-0055

MOYA, SARA DREIER, municipal government official; b. N.Y.C., June 9, 1945; d. Stuart Samuel and Hortense (Brill) Dreier; m. P. Robert Moya, May 30, 1966; children: J. Brill, Joshua D. BA, Wheaton Coll., Norton, Mass., 1967; postgrad., Mills Coll., Oakland, Calif., 1967-68, Ariz. State U., 1992—. Mem. Paradise Valley (Ariz.) Town Coun., 1986—, vice mayor, 1990-92; chmn. Gov.'s Homeless Trust Fund Oversight Com., 1991—; pres. Ctr. for Acad. Precosity, Ariz. State U., Tempe, 1987—; bd. dirs. Ariz. Assn. Gifted and Talented, 1990—, Valley Leadership, Inc., Phoenix, 1988—, Data Network for Human Svcs., 1990-93; participant 3d session Leadership Am. Mem. Citizens Adv. Bd. Paradise Valley Police Dept., 1984-86, Valley Citizens League Task Force on Edn.; chair Maricopa Assn. Govts. Task Force on Homeless, 1989-92; mem. FEMA bd. Maricopa County, 1989—; bd. dirs. Valley Youth Theater, 1990—, Maricopa County Homeless Accomodation Sch., 1991—. Mem. Ariz. Women in Mcpl. Govt. (sec. 1988-89, bd. dirs. 1986—, pres. 1989-90), Maricopa Assn. Govts. (regional coun. 1988—, vice-chmn. mag. regional devel. policy com. 1989-91, chair 1992—, mem. mag. joint econ. devel./human resources subcom.), Ariz. Acad., Paradise Valley County Club. Republican. Home: 5119 E Desert Park Ln Paradise Vly AZ 85253-3055 Office: Town Paradise Valley 6401 E Lincoln Dr Paradise Valley AZ 85253-4399

MOYE, ANTHONY JOSEPH, college administrator; b. McAdoo, Pa., Oct. 15, 1933; s. Joseph Frank and Rose (Dvorak) M.; m. Betty Marie Howell, June 16, 1957; children: Vickie Arlene, Julie Ann, Christopher Anthony. BS, Upsala Coll., 1955; MS, Iowa State U., 1957, PhD, 1960. Dean, grad. studies and rsch. Calif. State U., L.A., 1968-71; v.p. acad. affairs Quinnipiac Coll., Hamden, Conn., 1971-72; dep. dean Calif. State U., Long Beach, 1972-74, state univ. dean, 1974-79, asst. vice-chancellor, 1979-84, assoc. vice-chancellor, 1984-89, dep. vice chancellor, 1988—; prof. chemistry Calif. State U., L.A., 1962—; postdoctoral assoc. Harvard U., Cambridge, 1960-62; adv. bd. Calif. Coun. on Competitive Tech., Sacramento, 1989-92. Contbr. articles to profl. jours. Bd. dirs. L.A. Sports Coun., 1988—, Calif. Engring. Fedn., Sacramento, 1986-92; mem. sci. adv. com. Tobacco Related Disease Rsch. Program, 1990—. Fellow Eastman Kodak Co., 1958, Mallinckrodt fellow, Harvard U., 1961-62. Mem. AAAS, Am. Chem. Soc., Calif. Biomedical Rsch. Assn. (exec. com. 1992—), Calif. Math. Project (chair adv. com. 1988—), Calif. Coalition for Math. (sec., bd. trustees, 1991—), History of Sci. Soc., Los Verdes Country Club (pres. 1988). Roman Catholic. Home: 3650 Cliffsite Dr Palos Verdes Peninsula CA 90274-6228 Office: Calif State U 400 Golden Shore St Long Beach CA 90802-4209

MOYER, ALAN DEAN, retired newspaper editor; b. Galva, Iowa, Sept. 4, 1928; s. Clifford Lee and Harriet (Jacques) M.; m. Patricia Helen Krecker, July 15, 1950; children: Virginia, Stanley, Glenn. BS in Journalism, U. Iowa, 1950. Reporter, copy editor Wis. State Jour., Madison, 1950-53; reporter, photographer Bartlesville (Okla.) Examiner-Enterprise, 1953; telegraph editor Abilene (Tex.) Reporter-News, 1954-55; makeup editor Cleve. Plain Dealer, 1955-63; mng. editor Wichita (Kans.) Eagle, 1963-70; exec. editor Wichita Eagle and Beacon, 1970-73; mng. editor Phoenix Gazette, 1973-82, Ariz. Republic, 1982-89; ret., 1989; pres., dir. Wichita Profl. Baseball, Inc., 1969-75; mem. jury Pulitzer Prizes, 1973-74, 85, 86, 88. Mem. AP Mng. Editors Assn. (dir. 1973-78), Am. Soc. Newspaper Editors, Wichita Area C. of C. (dir. 1970-72), Sigma Delta Chi. Office: Phoenix Newspaper Inc 120 E Van Buren St Phoenix AZ 85004-2200

MOYER, CRAIG ALAN, lawyer; b. Bethlehem, Pa., Oct. 17, 1955; s. Charles Alvin and Doris Mae (Schantz) M.; m. Candace Darrow Brigham, May 3, 1986; 1 stepchild, Jason; 1 child, Chelsea A. BA, U. So. Calif., 1977; JD, U. Calif., L.A., 1980. Bar: Calif. 1980, U.S. Dist. Ct. (cen. dist.) Calif. 1980. Assoc. Nossaman, Krueger et al, L.A., 1980-83, Finley, Kumble et al, Beverly Hills, Calif., 1983-85; ptnr. Demetriou, Del Guercio & Lovejoy, L.A., 1985—; instr. Air Resources Bd. Symposium, Sacramento, 1985—, U. Calif., Santa Barbara, 1989—; lectr. Hazmat Conf., Long Beach, Calif., 1986—, Pacific Automotive Show, Reno, Nev., 1989—; lectr. hazardous materials, environ. law UCLA; lectr. environ. law U. Calif., Santa Barbara; lectr. hazardous materials regulatory framework U. Calif., Santa Barbara. Co-author: Hazard Communication Handbook: A Right to Know Compliance Guide, 1990, Clean Air Act Handbook, 1991; contbr. articles to profl. jours. Pres. Calif. Pub. Interest Rsch. Group, L.A., 1978-80. Mem. ABA (natural resources sect.), Calif. Bar Assn., L.A. County Bar Assn. (environ. law sect., chmn. legis. rev. com., mem. exec. com.), Tau Kappa Epsilon (pres. L.A. chpt. 1975-76, Outstanding Alumnus 1983). Republican. Office: Demetriou Del Guercio Chase Pla 801 S Grand Ave Fl 10 Los Angeles CA 90017-4613

MOYER, DEAN LAROCHE, physician, anatomical and clinical pathologist; b. Allentown, Pa., Mar. 17, 1925; s. William Alexander and Florence Phoebe (Moyer) M.; m. Ann Margaret Malkie; children: Michael, Margaret, Catherine. BS, Lehigh U., 1946-48; MD with honors, U. Rochester, 1948-52. Diplomate Am. Bd. Pathology. Intern Childrens' Hosp., Los Angeles, 1952-53, asst. resident in pathology, 1953-54; resident in pathology Mass. Gen. Hosp., Boston, 1954-55, cancer trainee, 1955-56; asst. prof., assoc. prof., prof. pathology UCLA Sch. Med., Los Angeles, 1956-69; chmn. dept. pathology Harbor Gen. Hosp., Torrance, Calif., 1960-69; prof. pathology U. So. Calif. Sch. Med., Los Angeles, 1970-92; chief of pathology at women's hosp. U. So. Calif. Med. Ctr., Los Angeles, 1976-92; med. dir. Nova Med Lab., Canoga Park, Calif., 1992—; mem. subcom. on interns and residents UCLA, 1956-57, subcom. on tissues UCLA, 1960-61, com. on edn. media UCLA, 1965-66, records com. Harbor Gen. Hosp., Torrance, 1961-62, research com., vivarium com. Harbor Gen. Hosp., Torrance, 1961-69, library com. Harbor Gen. Hosp., Torrance, 1963-65; asst. dir. clin. labs UCLA Med. Ctr., 1959-60; rapporteur WHO Div. of Human Reproduction, 1967-68, 71-72; mem. com. on reference ctrs. in reproduction WHO, 1971-72. Editorial bd. dirs. Fertility and Sterility, 1967-74, Jour. of Contraception, 1969-76; editorial asst. Am. Jour. of Obstetrics and Gynecology, 1971-74. Served with USN, 1944-46. Mem. Los Angeles County Med. Soc., Calif. Med. Assn., Pacific Coast Fertility Soc. (bd. dirs. 1966-69, program chmn. 1966-67, pres. elect 1970-71, pres. 1971-72, Squibb award 1960, 66, 69), Am. Fertility Soc. (bd. dirs. 1967-71, chmn. sci. exhibits com. 1967-70, chmn. and assoc. chmn. postgrad. courses 1970-72). Office: Nova Med Lab Canoga Park CA 91304

MOYER, JOHN ARTHUR, obstetrician/gynecologist, state senator; b. Glendive, Mont., Feb. 25, 1922; s. Arthur Boeman Moyer and Nora Elizabeth Moore; m. Caroline Louise Atkinson, Dec. 31, 1947 (dec. 1982); children: Nora, John Jr., David, Julia, Mary Janci, Tim, Vini, Elizabeth, Chris, Susan; m. Joanne Holsted, Jan. 5, 1987. BS, N.D. State U., 1941; MD, U. Ill., 1947. Intern Garfield Bank Community Hosp., Chgo., 1947-49; resident Cook County Hosp., Chgo., 1951-53; pvt. practice Spokane, Wash., 1955-85; chief of staff St. Lukes Hosp., Spokane, 1958; clin. prof. ob-gyn. U. Wash. Med. Sch., Seattle, 1984—; cons., clin. rschr. Group Health Inst., Spokane, 1985; state rep. Wash. State Legislature, Olympia, 1986-92, state senator, 1993; adj. prof. East Wash. U., Spokane, 1987; ob-gyn. cons. Community Clinic, Othello, Wash., 1990—. Dir. Eastern Wash. Hist. Soc., Spokane, 1990—. Cpt. M.C., 1953-55. Fellow Am. Coll. Ob-Gyn. Mem. Wash. State Med. Assn. (pres. 1978), Spokane County Med. Soc. (pres. 1958-59), Spokane Ob-Gyn. Soc. (pres. 1976). Republican. Roman Catholic. Home: 1405 W 9th St Spokane WA 99204

MOYERS, LOWELL DUANE, pipeline company executive; b. Globe, Ariz., June 10, 1930; s. Thomas Jefferson and Alta Beulah (Taylor) M.; m. Phyllis Jean Haviland, Oct. 29, 1951; children: Jennifer, Catherine, Nina. AA, Compton (Calif.) Jr. Coll., 1958, Fullerton Jr. Coll., 1958; student, Fullerton State Coll., 1965-66. Laborer Pacific Pipeline Constrn. Co., Montebello, Calif., 1947-48, timekeeper, 1948-51, foreman, 1953-60, supt., estimater, 1960-69, gen. supt., 1969-73; v.p. Victor Valley Pipeline Co., Victorville, Calif., 1973-77; mgr. Macco Constructors, Apple Valley, Calif., 1977-80; founder, pres., chmn. Ariz. Pipeline Co., Apple Valley, 1980—. Inventor constrn. equipment. Cpl. U.S. Army, 1951-53, Germany. Named among Men of Achievement in Pipeline Industry, Universal News, Inc., 1992. Mem. Pacific Coast Gas Assn., We. Pipe Liners Assn., Apple Valley Country Cub, The Lakes Country Club, Silverlakes Country Club. Republican. Office: Ariz Pipeline Co 17372 Lilac Ct Hesperia CA 92345

MOYERS, WILLIAM TAYLOR, artist; b. Atlanta, Dec. 11, 1916; s. William Taylor and Sarah Frances (McKinnon) M.; m. Neva Irene Anderson, Mar. 20, 1943; children: Joanne, William Taylor, Charles, John. BA, Adams State Coll., Alamosa, Colo., 1939; postgrad., Otis Art Inst., L.A., 1939; Dr. (hon.), Adams State Coll., 1992. Artist Walt Disney Prodns., Burbank, Calif., 1939-40; free lance illustrator, 1946-62. One man show Nat. Cowboy Hall of Fame, 1973; group show Phoenix Art Mus., CAA Shows, 1973-90. Bd. dirs. Albuquerque Arts Bd., 1985, Adams State Coll. Found., 1974—, Cowboy Artists of Am. Mus., Kerrville, Tex., 1984-89. Capt. U.S. Army, 1942-46. Recipient Illustraiton award, Ltd. Editions Club, N.Y.C., 1945, Sculpture awards, Cowboy Artists of Am., 1968-84, Silver medal watercolor, 1989, 91; named Artist of the Yr., Tucson Festival Soc., 1991. Mem. Cowboy Artists of Am. (pres. 1971-72, 83-84, 88-89). Presbyterian. Home: 1407 Morningside Dr NE Albuquerque NM 87110-5639

MOYSKI, STEPHEN MAREK, real estate developer; b. Denver, May 3, 1965; s. John George and Betty Ann (Stylski) M. AB in Econs. with distinction, Stanford U., 1987. Analyst Trammell Crow Co., Denver, 1987-88, staff specialist, 1988-90, fin. mgr., 1990—. Mem. Rocky Mountain Stanford Club, Mullen Alumni Assn. Republican. Roman Catholic.

MOZENA, JOHN DANIEL, podiatrist; b. Salem, Oreg., June 9, 1956; s. Joseph Iner and Mary Teresa (Delaney) M.; m. Elizabeth Ann Hintz, June 2, 1979; children: Christine Hintz, Michelle Delaney. Student, U. Oreg., 1974-79; B in Basic Med. Scis., Calif. Coll. Podiatric Medicine, D in Podiatric Medicine, 1983. Diplomate Am. Bd. Podiatric Surgery. Resident in surg. podiatry Hillside Hosp., San Diego, 1983-84; pvt. practice podiatry Portland, Oreg., 1984—; dir. residency Med. Ctr. Hosp., Portland, 1985-91; lectr. Nat. Podiatric Asst. Seminar, 1990, Am. Coll. Gen. Practitioners, 1991. Contbr. articles to profl. jours.; patentee sports shoe cleat design, 1985. Fellow Am Coll. Ambulatory Foot Surgeons, Am. Coll. Foot Surgeons. Republican. Roman Catholic. Office: Town Ctr Foot Clinic 8305 SE Monterey Ave Ste 101 Portland OR 97266-7728

MRACKY, RONALD SYDNEY, marketing management and media consultant; b. Sydney, Australia, Oct. 22, 1932; came to U.S., 1947, naturalized, 1957; s. Joseph and Anna (Janousek) M.; m. Sylvia Frommer, Jan. 1, 1960; children: Enid Hillevi, Jason Adam. Student, English Inst., Prague, Czechoslovakia, 1943-47; grad., Parsons Sch. Design, N.Y.C., 1950-53; postgrad., NYU, 1952-53. Designer D. Deskey Assocs., N.Y.C., 1953-54; art dir., designer ABC-TV, Hollywood, Calif., 1956-57; creative dir. Neal Advt. Assocs., L.A., 1957-59; pres. Richter & Mracky Design Assocs., L.A., 1959-68; pres., chief exec. officer Richter & Mracky-Bates div. Ted Bates & Co., L.A., 1968-73, pres., chief exec. officer Regency Fin., Internat. Fin. Svcs., Beverly Hills, Calif., 1974-76; sr. ptnr. Sylron Internat., L.A., 1973—; mgmt. dir. for N.Am. Standard Advt.-Tokyo, L.A., 1978-91; chief. exec. officer Standard/Worldwide Cons. Group, Los Angeles and Tokyo, 1981-87; offier, bd. dirs. Theme Rsorts, Inc., Denver, 1979—; prin., offier Prodn. Travel & Tours, Universal City, 1981—, Eques Ltd., L.A., 1988—; mng. ptnr. Internat. Mktg. Media, Beverly Hills, 1989—; cons. in field; exec. dir. Inst. for Internat. Studies and Devel., L.A., 1976-77;. Contbr. articles to profl. jours. With U.S. Army, 1954-56. Recipient nat. and internat. awards design and mktg. Mem. Am. Mktg. Assn., African Travel Assn. (amb.-at-large, pres. So. Calif. chpt.), L.A. Publicity Club, Pacific Asia Travel Assn., S.Am. Travel Assn., Am. Soc. Travel Agents. Office: 3855 Lankershim Blvd Studio City CA 91604

MU, ALBERT T., design engineer; b. Taipei, Taiwan, June 26, 1959; came to U.S., 1984; m. Daisy Wang, Sept. 1989. MSEE, U. Tex., 1985; MS in Engring. Mgmt., Stanford U., 1990. Design engr. Microelectronic Tech., Inc., Hsinchu, Taiwan, 1983-84; sr. design engr. Tex. Instruments Taiwan Ltd., Taipei, 1986-87; sr. packaging engr. Advanced Micro Devices, Inc., Sunnyvale, Calif., 1987-89; sr. design engr. Integrated Devices Tech., San Jose, Calif., 1989-90, Intel Corp., Santa Clara, Calif., 1990-91, Silicon Grahics, Inc, Mountain View, Calif., 1991—; cons. Gould Electronics, Eastlake, Ohio, 1988-89. Contbr. articles to profl. jours.; patentee in field. 2d lt. Taiwan armed forces, 1983-84. Recipient 2d Prize Mini Circuits, 1984. Mem. IEEE, Internat. Electronic Packaging Soc. Home: 1051 Sandalwood Ln Milpitas CA 95035-3233

MUCCILLI, JAY EDWARD, psychologist; b. Duluth, Minn., July 22, 1941; s. Eddie Ormando and Edythe Marie (Stortz) M.; m. Jessie M. Lomoro, Aug. 6, 1965 (div. 1974); children: Lisa, Nicholas, Marcus; m. Alta Jean Merriam, June 21, 1980. BA, U. Minn., 1963; postgrad., George Washington U., 1963-65; MA with honors, U. Colo., 1967, PhD with honors, 1979. Lic. psychologist, marriage, family and child counselor, Calif. Sch. psychologist Boulder (Colo.) Valley Sch. Dist., 1966-67; assoc. dir. counseling svcs. U. Santa Clara (Calif.), 1968-70, acting asst. prof. ednl. psychology, 1969-70, guest prof. Grad. Sch., 1973-79; dir., co-founder Therapeutic Homes, Inc. (now called Community Devel. Svcs.), San Jose, Calif., 1971-73; psychologist, coord. acute psychiat. inpatient units Santa Clara Valley Med. Ctr. and County Hosp., San Jose, 1970-74; pres., co-founder Inst. for Human Svcs., San Jose, 1972-76; clin. psychologist psychiat. dept. Kaiser Permanente Med. Ctr., Santa Clara, 1974-77; pvt. practice San Jose, 1976-1986, Los Gatos, Calif., 1983—; clin. psychologist El Camino Health Ctr., Sunnyvale, Calif., 1969-70; asst. clin. prof. dept. psychiatry Stanford (Calif.) U. Sch. Medicine, 1973-79; chief psychologist psychiat. dept. Kaiser Permanente Med. Ctr. and Hosp., San Jose, 1977-83; mem. instnl. rev. bd. Inst. for Psychosocial Interaction, Palo Alto, Calif., 1981-85; oral exam. commr. psychology exam. com. Calif. Bd. Med. Quality Assurance, 1988—, cons. Atty. Gen.'s Office Justice Dept., 1991—, also cons. to numerous agys., 1970—. Pres., co-founder Found. To Aid Minorities in Human Svc. Careers, San Jose, 1972-76, Advanced Human Studies Inst., Sunnyvale and Palo Alto, Calif.; bd. dirs. Bill Wilson Ctr., Santa Clara, 1977-80. George Washington U. fellow and scholar, 1964-65; USPHS-NIMH fellow, 1965-66; U. Colo. scholar and fellow, 1966-67. Mem. Am. Psychol. Assn., Calif. State Psychol. Assn. (Santa Clara County rep., bd. dirs., Outstanding Grad. Educator award 1986), Santa Clara County Psychol. Assn. (pres. 1986, Outstanding Psychologist award 1987), Am. Psychology and Law Soc., Psi Chi. Office: 405 Alberto Way Ste 4 Los Gatos CA 95032-5406

MUCHA, SUSAN ELIZABETH, marketing executive; b. Fort Bragg, N.C., June 21, 1958; d. Royce Milton and Betty Lou (Love) Powell; m. Phillip Edward Mucha, June 17, 1978. BS in Journalism, U. Fla., 1980; MAS, U. Ala., Huntsville, 1983. Editor SCI Systems, Inc., Huntsville, 1981-86; sr. writer, editor Avco Electronics Textron (now Avex Electronics, Inc.), Huntsville, 1986-88; mgr. mktg. svcs. Flextronics, Inc., Fremont, Calif., 1988-89, dir. mktg. svcs., 1989-90; dir. mktg. svcs. Flextronics Internat., Fremont, 1990—. Bus. cons. Jr. Achievement, Huntsville, 1985-86; mem. allocations com. Huntsville/Madison County United Way, 1987-88, mem. communications com., 1985-86. Mem. Inst. Cert. Profl. Mgrs., Nat. Mgmt. Assn., Internat. Assn. Bus. Communicators (v.p. involvement San Francisco chpt. 1992, accredited bus. communicator 1993), Sigma Kappa. Republican. Home: 1504 Poppybank Ct Pleasanton CA 94566-8401 Office: Flextronics Internat 48001 Fremont Blvd Fremont CA 94538

MUCHNIJ, GREGORY P., chiropractor; b. Detroit, Nov. 22, 1962; s. Boris Peter and Arlene Clair; m. Patricia Shashaty, Nov. 19, 1988;stepdaughter Janessa; 1 child, Michael Anthony. D of Chiropractic, Sherman Coll., 1986. Assoc. Sparacino Chiropractic Ctr., Tucson, 1987-89; dir. My Chiropractor Family Ctr., Phoenix, 1989—. Bd. regents Sherman Coll. Straigh Chiropractic, Spartanburg, S.C., 1990—. Mem. Fedn. Straight Chiropractic Orgn., Chiropractic Assn. Ariz., World Chiropractic Alliance, Nat. Fedn. Ind. Bus., Sherman Coll. Alumni Assn. (sec. 1988-92), Internat. Soc. for Study of Subtle Energies and Energy Medicine, Sherman Ariz. Coll. Roman Catholic. Office: My Chiropractor Family Ctr 350 E Bell Rd Ste 206 Phoenix AZ 85022

MUCKLER, JOHN, professional hockey coach; b. Midland, Ont.; m.; 5 children. Profl. hockey player, Ea. Hockey League, Baltimore, also Long Island Ducks; coach, gen. mgr. Long Island Ducks; 1st pres. N.Y. Jr. Met. League; coach, gen. dir. player pers., mgr. New York Rangers affiliate team, Am. Hockey League, Providence, R.I.; formerly head coach Minnesota North Stars; with Edmonton Oilers, 1981—, formerly co-coach; head coach Edmonton Oilers, 1989-1991, Buffalo Sabres, 1991—. Office: Edmonton Oilers, Northlands Coliseum, Edmonton, AB Canada T5B 4M9

MUECKE, CHARLES ANDREW (CARL MUECKE), federal judge; b. N.Y.C., Feb. 20, 1918; s. Charles and Wally (Roeder) M.; m. Claire E. Vasse; children by previous marriage: Carl Marshall, Alfred Jackson, Catherine Calvert. B.A., Coll. William and Mary, 1941; LL.B., U. Ariz., 1953. Bar: Ariz. 1953. Rep. AFL, 1947-50; reporter Ariz. Times, Phoenix, 1947-48; since practiced in Phoenix; with firm Parker & Muecke, 1953-59, Muecke, Dushoff & Sacks, 1960-61; U.S. atty. Dist. Ariz., 1961-64, U.S. dist. judge, 1964—, now sr. judge.; mem. 9th cir. Jud. Coun. com. review local dist. Ct. Rules. Mem. Phoenix Planning Commn., 1955-61, chmn., 1960; chmn. Maricopa County Dem. Party, 1961-62; trustee U. San Diego Coll. Law; bd. dirs. Phoenix Chamber Music Soc. Served to lst lt. USMCR. 1942-45, to maj. Res. 1945-60. Mem. Fed. Bar Assn., Ariz. Bar Assn., Maricopa Bar Assn., Am. Trial Lawyers Assn., Dist. Judges Assn. Ninth Circuit, Phi Beta Kappa, Phi Alpha Delta, Omicron Delta Kappa. Office: US Dist Ct US Courthouse & Fed Bldg 230 N 1st Ave Ste 7015 Phoenix AZ 85025-0007

MUEH, HANS JUERGEN, chemistry educator; b. Celle, Germany, Jan. 8, 1944; came to U.S. 1951; s. Alfred Eugen and Ilse Elizabeth (Niebuhr) M.; m. Sally Ellis Flax, June 11, 1966; children: Kristine Elizabeth, Kurt David, Deborah Anne. BS, USAF Acad., 1966; MS, U. Wis., 1970, PhD, 1976. Commd. USAF, 1966—, advanced through grades to col.; intelligence analyst HQ Tactical Air Command, Langley AFB, Va., 1966-69; instr. chemistry USAF Acad., Colo., 1970-72; intelligence analyst HQ Mil. Assistance Command, Vietnam, 1972-73; asst. prof. to prof. chemistry USAF Acad., 1976-87, prof. and head dept. chemistry, 1987—; spl. asst. for tech. matters Def. Intelligence Agy., Washington, 1985-86. Contbr. articles to profl. jours. Goethe Inst. fellow, 1979; decorated Meritorious Svc. medal (3). Mem. Am. Chem. Soc., Soc. Com. on Edn., Colo. Assn. Sci. Tchrs., Sigma Xi. Home: 5315 Park Vista Blvd Colorado Springs CO 80918-2450 Office: Dept of Chemistry USAF Academy Colorado Springs CO 80840

MUELLER, BONNIE MAE, social welfare administrator; b. Lewistown, Mont., Oct. 14, 1944; d. Vernon Edmond and Dorothy Mae (Bentel) Kent; m. Freddie Lee Mueller, Apr. 27, 1968; 1 child, Vicki Mae. BS, U. Mont., 1967. Cert. trainer investment in excellence Pacific Inst., 1990. Social worker Lake County Dept. Pub. Welfare, Polson, Mont., 1967-71, county dir., 1971-85; area supr. Region V SRS, Missoula, Mont., 1985—. Active Gov.'s Youth Conf., Helena, Mont., 1990. Mem. Mont. Sheriffs and Peace Officers, Mothers Against Drunk Driving, Mont. Pub. Welfare Assn. (chmn. conf. 1990), Nat. Eligibility Workers, NAFE, Am. Pub. Welfare Assn. Home: 2335 Emory Rd Ronan MT 59864-9747 Office: Dept SRS 2335 Emory Rd Ronan MT 59864-9747

MUELLER, DONALD DEAN, food company executive; b. Columbus, Nebr., Sept. 12, 1937; s. Emil J. and Hulda M. (Cattau) M.; m. JoAnn Ferris, Aug. 17, 1963; children: Bradford Paul, Bartley Brandon. Student U. Nebr., 1956-58, 62-63; BBA, U. Denver, 1965. CPA, Colo. Acct., Ernst & Ernst, Denver, 1965-69; treas. Monfort of Colo., Greeley, 1969-72; v.p. fin. Spencer Foods, Iowa, 1972-79; group v.p. fin. svcs. Monfort, Inc., 1979-83, group v.p. fin. svcs. and lamb ops., 1983-89; exec. v.p. fin. and adminstrn. ConAgra Red Meats, 1989-92, pres. Mapelli Food Distbn. Co., 1990—; bd. dirs. 1st Nat. Bank Greeley. Bd. dirs. Econ. Devel. Action Partnership, Greeley, Weld County, 1984-92, pvt. industry coun., Greeley, 1985-90, chmn. EDAP, 1990, bd. trustees N.C. Med. Ctr., 1992—, pres., 1993, bd. dirs., 1993—. Mem. AICPA, Nat. Assn. Accts., Colo. Soc. CPAs, Greeley Country Club. Republican. Lutheran. Avocations: church activities, singing, sports. Office: Monfort Inc PO Box G Greeley CO 80632-0350

MUELLER, GAIL DELORIES, forensic chemist, toxicologist; b. Chgo., Sept. 30, 1957; d. Roger George and Delories B. (Reppert) Johnson; m. Joseph E. Mueller, Jan. 26, 1991. BS in Chemistry, No. Ill. U., 1980. Quality control chemist Standard Pharmacal Corp., Elgin, Ill., 1980; forensic chemist Ill. Racing Bd. Lab., Elgin, 1980-82, Analytical Techs., Inc., Tempe, Ariz., 1982-84; analytical chemist Nichols Inst., San Juan Capistrano, Calif., 1985-87; forensic chemist, toxicologist, GC/MS group leader Damon Reference Labs., Rancho Cucamonga, Calif., 1987—. Fellow Am. Inst. Chemists; mem. Am. Chem. Soc., Calif. Assn. Toxicologists. Office: Damon Reference Labs PO Box 2279 Rancho Cucamonga CA 91729-2279

MUELLER, GARY ALFRED, software engineer; b. Denver, Oct. 6, 1950; s. Alfred Henry and Verna Mae (Ashmore) M. BS in Mineral Engring. Physics, Colo. Sch. Mines, 1972, BS in Mineral Engring. Math., 1973; BSEE and Computer Sci. with honors, U. Colo., Denver, 1975. Registered profl. engr., Colo. Computer programmer, mathematician U.S. Geol. Survey, Denver, 1977-81; mem. tech. staff AT&T Bell Labs., Denver, 1982-84; sr. software engr. Storage Tech. Corp., Louisville, Colo., 1985—. Mem. IEEE, Tau Beta Pi, Eta Kappa Nu, Kappa Mu Epsilon.

MUELLER, HENRIETTA WATERS, psychologist, artist, painter, printmaker; b. Pitts., Apr. 13, 1915; d. William Sidney and Helen Losey (Kirkwood) Waters; m. Werner A. Mueller, June 15, 1940; children: Christopher Bradford, Richard Kirkwood. BFA with honors, Art Inst. of Chgo., 1938; MA, U. Wyo., 1948, MEd, 1960, studied with Ad Reinhardt, Ilya Bolotowsky, George McNeil, 1990; studied with Helen Frankenthaler, Santa Fe Inst., 1990. Tchr. art U. Nebr., Lincoln, 1956-57; summer art tchr. U. Wyo., Laramie, 1956-62; tchr. art Boulder (Colo.) Valley Sch., 1969-75; sch. clin. psychologist Jefferson County Sch. Dist., Lakewood, Colo., 1973-75; dir. speech and lang. clinic U. Wyo., Laramie, 1976; ednl. cons. Natrona County Sch. Dist., Casper, Wyo., 1976-85; prof. printmaking, art edn. U. of the Pacific, Stockton, Calif., summers 1970-71. Mem. One West Gallery, Ft. Collins, Colo. Marshall grantee Cummington (Mass.) Found., 1953; recipient purchase awards U. N.C., 1958, U. Wyo. Mus. Art, 1975. Mem. Rule Contemporary Gallery (Denver); mem. Internat. Zonta, Alpha Chi Omega. Democrat. Presbyterian. Home: 520 Mapleton Ave Boulder CO 80304-3986 Studio: 1309 Steele St Laramie WY 82070

MUELLER, PETER KLAUS, environmental scientist, researcher. BS in Chemistry, George Washington U., 1950, MS in Environ. Scis., 1953; PhD, Rutgers U., 1955. Rsch. scientist Komline Sanderson Engring. Corp., Peapack, N.J., 1955-57; rsch. chemist air & indusl. hygiene lab Calif. Dept. Health, Berkeley, Calif., 1957-63; chief air & indsl. hygiene lab. State Calif. Dept. Health, Berkeley, 1963-73; chief lab. svcs. region IX U.S. EPA, San Francisco, 1973-74; from tech. mgr. to gen. mgr. environ. chemistry ctr. Environ. Rsch. and Tech., Inc., Thousand Oaks, Calif. and Concord, Mass., 1973-80; sr. project mgr. environ physics. and chemistry program Electric Power Rsch. Inst., Palo Alto, Calif., 1980-85; subprogram mgr. environmental physics and chemistry Electric Power Rsch. Inst., Palo Alto, 1985-87, program mgr. atmospheric sciences, 1987—; mem. rsch. grant adv. coms. for various govt. agys.; chmn. adv. com. Nat. Bur Standards Environ. Measurements, Calif Air Resources Bd. Ozone Measurement Adv. Com.; lectr. U. Calif. Berkeley, Irvine; sci. adv. bd. UCLA; sci. peer review panel for regional air quality devel. Ontario Ministry for Environment; adv. Gov.'s Office State of Colo., Brown Cloud Issues; mem. tech. com. Nat. Acid Deposition program, Peer Review Panel NAPAP; rsch. project reviewer U.S. EPA Office Rsch. and Devel., others. Contbr. numerous articles to profl. jours. Mem. AAAS, Air Pollution Control Assn., Am. Geophys. Union, Am. Chem. Soc. Home: 3801 Magnolia Dr Palo Alto CA 94306 Office: Elec Power Rsch Inst 3412 Hillview Ave Palo Alto CA 94304

MUELLER, RAYMOND JAY, software development executive; b. Denver, Nov. 16, 1959; s. Frank Joseph and JoAnn A. (Seib) M.; m. Hiro K. Abeyta; 1 child, Michael Raymond. A in Acctg. and Computer Sci., Metro State Coll., 1981; cert. in computer sci., Denver U., 1983. cert. data processor, 1985—. Data processing mgr. Bailey Co., Denver, 1980-86; pres. MIS, Inc., Lakewood, Colo., 1986—; cons. to local high schs., 1985-88; speaker in field. Contbr. articles to computer mags.; inventor Touch 2000; patentee in field. Mem. Assn. for Inst. Cert. of Computer Profls., Data Processing Mgmt. Assn., Greater Denver C. of C., Colo. Inst. Artificial Intelligence. Republican. Roman Catholic. Office: MIS Inc 355 Union Blvd # 300 Lakewood CO 80228-1500

MUESSIG, SIEGFRIED, mining company executive, minerals consultant; b. Freiburg, Baden, Fed. Rep. Germany, Jan. 19, 1922; came to U.S., 1927; s. Philipp and Irma (Schönig) M.; m. Mary Catherine Sharp, Mar. 21, 1949; children: Hans, Philipp. BS, Ohio State U., 1947, PhD, 1951. Geologist U.S. Geol. Survey, Mo., Ark., Calif., 1951-55; project chief U.S. Geol. Survey, Spokane, 1956-59; chief geologist U.S. Borax and Chem. Corp., L.A., 1959-66; exploration mgr. Getty Oil Co., L.A., 1966-82; v.p. Getty Mining Co., L.A., 1982-84; pvt. practice cons. Pasadena, Calif., 1984—; pres. Crystal Exploration Inc., Pasadena, 1987—; cons. Borax Consol. Ltd., Chile, Argentina, 1955; bd. dirs. Callahan Mining Corp., Phoenix. Author: Geology of Republic District, Washington, 1969. 2d lt. USAF, 1942-45. Fellow U.S. Atomic Energy, 1950. Fellow Geol. Soc. Am., Soc. Econ. Geologists (v.p. 1974-75, pres. 1978-79, Marsden award 1990); mem. Am. Assn. Petroleum Geologists, Soc. Econ. Geol. Found. (trustee, pres. 1984-85), Soc. Mining Engrs. (disting.), AIME (disting.). Home: 1097 Charles St Pasadena CA 91103-2708 Office: Crystal Exploration Inc 1000 E Walnut St # 117 Pasadena CA 91106-1452

MUFTI, SIRAJ ISLAM, biologist, researcher; b. Bedadi, Hazara, Pakistan, May 10, 1938; came to U.S., 1967; s. Sultan M. and Saeeda M. (Khan) M.; m. Bebe Z. Khan, Jan. 10, 1965; children: Sheereen, Shaheen. BSc, U. Peshawar, Pakistan, 1955; MSc, Am. U., Beirut, 1963; PhD, U. Ariz., 1973. Rsch. asst. Argl. Rsch. Inst., Peshawar, 1955-59, asst. botanist, 1959-61; agr. officer, dir. Ministry of Agr./North Nigeria Devel. Corp., Kaduna, Nigeria, 1963-67; rsch. assoc. in molecular biology Vanderbilt U., Nashville, 1973-75; asst. prof. Pahlavi U., Shiraz, Iran, 1975-77; rsch. asst. prof. Mt. Sinai Med. Ctr., N.Y.C., 1979-81; adj. asst. prof. U. Ariz., Tucson, 1977-79, 198189, assoc. rsch. prof., 1989—. Contbr. numerous articles to profl. jours. Student mentor U. Ariz., Tucson, 1985—; councilor Ariz. State Prison Complex, Tucson, 198—; bd. dirs., sec. Asian-Am. Assn., Tucson, 1988-90. Am. U. scholar, 1961; NIH grantee, 1979, 81, 89, 90, 92. Mem. AAAS, Am. Assn. for Cancer Rsch., AAUP. Democrat. Islam. Home: 7458 E Princeton Dr Tucson AZ 85710-4932 Office: U Ariz Health Sci Ctr Tucson AZ 85721

MUGGENBURG, BRUCE AL, veterinary physiologist; b. St. Paul, May 2, 1937; s. Elmer Carl and Gladys O. (Bakke) M.; m. Marianne Nordgren, June 18, 1960 (dec. 1976); m. Carolyn Seale, July 16, 1977; children: Katherine Ann, Carl Thor, Virginia Hope. B.S., U. Minn.-St. Paul, 1959, D.V.M., 1961; M.S., U. Wis.-Madison, 1964, Ph.D., 1966. Asst. prof. U. Wis., Madison, 1966-69; vis. prof. Universidade do Rio Grande dul Sol, Porto Alegre, Brasil, 1966-68; sr. scientist Lovelace Inhalation Toxicology Research Inst., Albuquerque, 1969—. Contbr. articles to profl. jours. Mem. AVMA, Am. Thoracic Soc., Am. Physiol. Soc., Health Physics Soc., Radiation Rsch. Soc. Lutheran. Club: Scandinavian Club of Albuquerque (pres. 1983, 87, 88). Home: 6812 Kentucky Ct NE Albuquerque NM 87110-3411 Office: Lovelace Inhalation Toxicology Research Inst PO Box 5890 Albuquerque NM 87185

MUGLER, LARRY GEORGE, regional planner; b. Chgo., June 22, 1946; s. Warren Franklin and Elaine Mae (Mittag) M.; m. Judy Ann Allison, Aug. 3, 1968; children: Jonathan, Allison. BSCE, Northwestern U., 1968; postgrad., Evang. Theol. Sem., 1968-70; MS in Urban and Regional Planning, U. Wis., 1972. Planning analyst State of Wis., Madison, 1970-72; dir. community devel. Cen. Okla. Econ. Devel. Dist., Shawnee, 1972-74; planner Denver Regional Council of Govts., 1974-80, dir. environ. services, 1980-83, dir. devel. services, 1983—. Contbre. chpt. on pub. works mgmt. to book. Pres. bd. dirs. Leawood Met. Recreation and Park Dist., Littleton, Colo., 1978—; chair planning and rsch. com. Rocky Mountain Conf. The United Meth. Ch. Named one of Outstanding Young Men in Am., Jaycees, 1974; Lasker Found. fellow, 1971; recipient Disting. Svc. award Spl. Dist. Assn. of Colo., 1989. Mem. Am. Planning Assn. (sec. Colo. chpt.), ASCE (subcom. chmn. 1985-86, 88-91, div. exec. com. 1991—), Urban Land Inst. Republican. Methodist. Office: Denver Regional Coun Govts 2480 W 26th Ave Ste 200B Denver CO 80211-5580

MUHAMMAD, RAQUEL ANNISSA, educator; b. Beggs, Okla., Sept. 3, 1932; d. Gerald John Lovings and Elnora Delores (DuBose) Crenshaw; m. Amos Bradford Muhammad, Nov. 25, 1951; children: Duane Bradford, Sharon Hammond, Valerie Muhammad, Shana Muhammad, Sita Muhammad, Amos Jr. BA, San Diego State U., 1953, BS, 1961; 4eme degree, Alliance Française, 1967; MA, U.S. Internat. U., 1975, PhD, 1980. Instr. San Diego High Sch., 1961-66, 80—; cons., researcher Muhammad Consulting Svcs., San Diego, 1984—; adj. faculty San Diego City Coll., 1988; edn. cons. Operation Ind., Las Vegas, Nev., 1978; coord. ABE Clark County Community Coll., Las Vegas, 1977; dir. edn. Muhammad Univ Islam, San Diego, 1967-75. Editor tchr. guides. Chair Nat. Bd. Edn. Univ. Islam, 1982-85. Fellow UCSD San Diego Writing Program, 1982. Mem. NEA, NAFE, AAUW, Nat. Coun. Tchrs. English, Tchrs. English and Other Langs., Internat. Reading Assn., San Diego Tchrs. Assn. (multicultural com. adv. bd. 1988—), Calif. Tchrs. Assn., Nat. Assn. Black Educators, Nat. Assn. Sch. Adminstrs., Nat. Assn. Sch. Bds., Univ. Women. Democrat. Muslim. Office: San Diego Unified Sch Dist 4100 Normal St San Diego CA 92103-2653

MUIR, WILLIAM KER, JR., political science educator; b. Detroit, Oct. 30, 1931; s. William Ker and Florence Taylor (Bodman) M.; m. Paulette Irene Wauters, Jan. 16, 1960; children: Kerry Macaire, Harriet Bodman. Student, Clifton Coll., Bristol, Eng., 1949-50; B.A., Yale U., 1954, Ph.D., 1965; J.D., U. Mich., 1958. Bar: N.Y. 1960, Conn. 1965. Instr. U. Mich. Law Sch., 1958-59; assoc. firm Davis Polk & Wardwell, N.Y.C., 1959-60; lectr. in polit. sci. Yale U., 1960-64, 65-67; from assoc. to ptnr. Tyler Cooper Grant Bowerman & Keefe, New Haven, 1964-68; prof. polit. sci. U. Calif.-Berkeley, 1968—, dept. chmn., 1980-83; speechwriter v.p. U.S., 1983-85; columnist, 1992-93; sr. cons. Calif. State Assembly, Sacramento, 1975-76; cons. Oakland (Calif.) Police Dept., 1970-72; vis. prof. polit. sci. Harvard U., summers 1976, 79. Author: Prayer in the Public Schools, 1967, later republished as Law and Attitude Change, 1974, Police: Streetcorner Politicians, 1977, Legislature: California's School for Politics, 1982, The Bully Pulpit: The Presidential Leadership of Ronald Reagon, 1993. Active Berkeley Police Rev. Commn., 1981-83, Calif.; chmn. New Haven Civil Liberties Coun., 1965-68. Recipient Hadley B. Cantril Meml. award, 1979, Disting. Teaching award U. Calif., Berkeley, 1974. Mem. Am. Polit. Sci. Assn. (Edward S. Corwin award 1966). Republican. Presbyterian. Home: 59 Parkside Dr Berkeley CA 94705-2409 Office: Dept Polit Sci U Calif Berkeley CA 94720

MULANIX, MITCHELL SCOTT, legislative staff member; b. Vallejo, Calif., Feb. 24, 1965; s. Gary Devon and Carolyn Gayle (Jensen) M. Asset mgr. Security Capital Real Estate, N.Y.C., 1985-87; real estate cons. Frank Howard Allen Co., Santa Rosa, Calif., 1987-89; campaign mgr. Frank Riggs for Congress, Santa Rosa, 1989-91; legis. dir. Office Congressman Frank Riggs, U.S. Ho. of Reps., Santa Rosa, 1991—. Bd. dirs. Big Bros. and Big Sisters, Santa Rosa, 1980—; mem. Santa Rosa Rep. Cen. Com., 1991—; del. Rep. Presdl. Primary. Mem. Odd Fellows. Home: 2258 Guerneville Rd Santa Rosa CA 95401 Office: Office Congressman Frank Riggs 777 Sonoma Ave Ste 329 Santa Rosa CA 95404

MULASE, MOTOHICO, mathematics educator; b. Kanazawa, Japan, Oct. 11, 1954; came to U.S., 1982; s. Ken-Ichi and Mieko (Yamamoto) M.; m. Sayuri Kamiya, Sept. 10, 1982; children: Kimihico Chris, Paul Norihico, Yurika. BS, U. Tokyo, 1978; MS, Kyoto U., 1980, DSc, 1985. Rsch. assoc. Nagoya (Japan) U., 1980-85; JMS fellow Harvard U., Cambridge, Mass., 1982-83; vis. asst. prof. SUNY, Stony Brook, 1984-85; Hedrick asst. prof. UCLA, 1985-88; asst. prof. Temple U., Phila., 1988-89; assoc. prof. U. Calif., Davis, 1989-91, prof., 1991—; mem. Math. Scis. Rsch. Inst., Berkeley, Calif., 1982-84, Inst. for Advanced Study, Princeton, N.J., 1988-89; vis. prof. Max-Planck Inst. for Math., Bonn, Germany, 1991-92. Contbr. articles to profl. jours. Treas. Port of Sacramento Japanese Sch., 1990-91. Mem. Math. Soc. Japan, Am. Math. Soc. Office: U Calif Dept Math Davis CA 95616

MULCAHY, DANIEL MICHAEL, non-profit organization executive; b. Rutland, Vt., Nov. 1, 1953; s. Raymond Michael and Lillian Louise (Noyes) M.; m. Rachel Farias, June 25, 1983; 1 child, Andrew. BA, U. Vt. Patient advocate Dept. of Mental Health and Corrections, Augusta, Maine, 1973, Vt. Assn. for Mental Health, Montpelier, 1974; cottage parent Dept. of Corrections, Vergennes, Vt., 1975-77; citizen advocacy coord. Md. Assn. of Retarded Citizens, Owings Mills, Md., 1978; exec. dir. Vt. Devel. Disabilities, Citizen Advocacy Project, Inc., Montpelier, 1979-81; dir. pub. rels. Cath. Big Bros., Inc., L.A., 1981-86; v.p. community rels. Goodwill Industries of So. Calif., L.A., 1986-93; div. dir. Goodwill Industries of Ventura and Santa Barbara Counties, Oxnard, Calif., 1993—; bd. dirs. Publicity Club of L.A., Rolling Readers USA, Inc., San Diego. Editor (newsletter) Tidings (1st pl. 1992); producer (video) Goodwill and You, 1992, Goodwill Training Program (1st Pl. 1990). Mem. Am. Mgmt. Assn., Internat. Networking Assn. Home: 9507 Stanwin Ave Arleta CA 91331-5535 Office: Goodwill Industries 3130 Paseo Mercado Oxnard CA 93030

MULDARY, PATRICK FARRELL, manufacturing company executive; b. Ft. Wayne, Ind., Sept. 26, 1951; s. George A. and Mary L. (Suelzer) M.; m. Melanie S. Volkert, May 19, 1979; children: Heather N., Megan T. BS in Aero. Engring., Purdue U., 1973; MS in Engring. Mechanics, U. Minn., 1975, MBA in Fin., 1981. Design engr. Chevron U.S.A., San Francisco, 1975-77; project mgr. Gould Inc.-ABD, St. Paul, 1977-79; mgr. engring. Gould Inc.-PBD, St. Paul, 1979-80, plant mgr., 1980-82; mgr. engring. and quality assurance Nichols-Homeshield, Rice Lake, Wis., 1982-90; dir. mfg. Milgard Mfg., Tacoma, Wash., 1990-91; pres. PFM Enterprises, Inc., Sumner, Wash., 1991—. Inventor steam quality measurement device, 1975. Pres. United Way of Rice Lake, Wis., 1983-90. Mem. ASME, Assn. Mfg. Excellence, Am. Archtl. Mfrs. Assn. (dir. 1991-92). Home: 19806 Island Pkwy E Sumner WA 98390 Office: PFM Enterprises Inc PO Box 8174 Bonney Lake WA 98390

MULDOON, NANCY KNIGHT, human resources specialist; b. San Antonio, Mar. 24, 1938; d. Walter John and Estellyn (Allday) Achning; m. William Henry Muldoon III, Aug. 23, 1958; children: William Henry IV, Shevaun Elaine. Student, Vassar Coll., 1956-58, Mary Washington Coll., Fredericksburg, Va., 1958-59; BA, East Texas State U., 1980; MBA, Regis U., 1992. Printing mgr. V.I. Printing Corp., St. Thomas, 1962-71; sales mgr. Press, Inc., St. Thomas, 1971-75; account exec. Commerce (Tex.) Jour., 1979-81; dir. devel. Cystic Fibrosis Found., SanAntonio, 1986; asst. to dir. Mind Sci. Found., SanAntonio, 1986-87; customer svc. rep., account svc. rep. Tex. Health Plan, San Antonio, Austin, 1987; account exec. Agusta (Kans.) Daily Gazette, 1987-89; dir. human resources Park Inn Internat., Sterling, Colo., 1990-91; exec. dir. Logan County United Way, 1991-92; dir. Logan County Family Resource Ctr., 1992—; coord. Parent Profl. Partnerships in N.E. Colo., 1992—; instr. ESL Northeastern Jr. Coll., 1992, internat. edn. adv. bd., 1992—. Docent Dallas Mus. Art, 1984; chmn. bd. Community Health Svc. Agy., Greenville, Tex., 1985; pres., co-founder Louise Drake Garden Club, Commerce, Tex., 1983; treas. Augusta Arts Coun., 1989; bd. dirs. Sterling Arts Coun., 1990-92; mem. Logan County Tourism Com., 1990; mem. strategic planning com. RE-1 Valley Sch. Dist., 1990—. Recipient Dist. Svc. award Commerce C. of C., 1984, Speech award Bus. & Profl. Women. Mem. Logan County Pers. Network (founder, pres. 1990-91), Logan County C. of C. (amb. 1990—), PEO (Colo. chpt.). Republican. Episcopalian. Home: 519 Holly Dr Sterling CO 80751-4645 Office: PO Box 1025 Sterling CO 80751

MULDOON, WILLIAM HENRY, III, newspaper publisher; b. San Antonio, June 14, 1935; s. Wilfrid Edward and Laurie Elizabeth (Battersby) M.; m. Nancy Achning, Aug. 23, 1958; children: William Henry IV, Shevaun Elaine. BA, Dartmouth Coll., 1957; postgrad., U. Tex., 1957-58, Oceanside Carlsbad Coll., 1959-60. Pres. V.I. Printing Corp., St. Thomas, 1961-72, Mountain Top Estates, St. Thomas, 1965-76; pub. St. Thomas Jour., 1972-76, Commerce (Tex.) Jour., Harte-Hanks Co., 1976-85, Copperas Cove (Tex.) Leader Press, 1986-87; mktg. dir. Tex. Weekly mag., Harte-Hanks Co., San Antonio, 1985-86; pub. Augusta (Kans.) Daily Gazette, 1987-90, Jour.-Advocate, Sterling, Colo., 1990—; regional dir. Graphic Arts Tech. Found., St. Thomas, 1966-73. Mem. bd. presdl. advisors East Tex. State U., Commerce, 1978-85; chmn. United Way, Commerce, 1978; dist. chmn. Boy Scouts Am., Commerce, 1980; bus. chmn. San Antonio Symphony Soc., 1986; pres. Commerce C. of C., 1985. Capt. USMC, 1958-62. Recipient Silver Beaver award Boy Scouts Am., 1982; named Ky. col. State of Ky., 1974-91. Mem. Nat. Newspaper Assn., Newspaper Assn. Am., Inter-Am. Press Assn., Colo. Press Assn., NRA (life, master shooter), Marine Corps League, 1st Marine Divsn. Assn., U.S. Marine Corps Combat Corr. Assn., VFW, Am. Legion, San Antonio Country Club, Elks, Rotary, Dartmouth Club (Colo.). Republican. Episcopalian. Home: 519 Holly Dr Sterling CO 80751-4645 Office: Jour-Adv 504 N 3d St PO Box 1272 Sterling CO 80751

MULFORD, RAND PERRY, medical products executive, consultant; b. Denver, Sept. 30, 1943; s. Roger Wayne and Ann Louise (Perry) M.; m. Constance Adel Powell, Mar. 22, 1981 (div. 1987); 1 child, Conrad Perry; m. Paula Marie Skelley, 1987. BS in Basic Engring., Princeton (N.J.) U., 1965; MBA, Harvard U., 1972. Mgmt. cons. McKinsey & Co. Inc., Chgo., 1972-80; v.p. planning and control splty. chem. group Occidental Chem. Co., Houston, 1980-82; pres. Technivest Inc., Houston, 1982-85; exec. dir. corp. planning Merck & Co., Inc., Rahway, N.J., 1985-88; v.p. fin. Advanced Tissue Scis., Inc., La Jolla, Calif., 1989-90; COO Houghten Pharms., Inc., La Jolla, Calif., 1990—; mem. adv. bd. L. Karp & Sons, Inc., Elk Grove Village, Ill., 1980—; bd. dirs. Quest Med., Inc., Dallas. Lt. USN, 1965-70. Home: 2178 Caminito Del Barco Del Mar CA 92014-3619

MULGAONKAR, RANJIT P., marketing manager; b. Kolhapur, Maharashtra, India, Oct. 24, 1957; s. Pandurag and Kamal (Joshi) M.; m. Dana R. Mulgaonkar, Mar. 28, 1987. Diploma in Electronics and Telecommunication Engring., Govt. Poly., Poona, India, 1978; MS, Va. Poly. Inst., 1983. Software engr. Vicom Systems Inc., San Jose, Calif., 1983-84; from software engr. to project leader TAU Corp., Los Latos, Calif., 1984-87; product mgr. Recognition Concepts Inc., Incline Village, Nev., 1987-88; product mktg. mgr. DuPont Design Technologies Inc., Santa Clara, Calif., 1988-90; market devel. mgr. Aldus Corp., Seattle, 1990—. Contbr. articles to profl. jours. Cunningham Found. fellow ,1983. Home: Pioneer Square Sta PO 4164 Seattle WA 98104 Office: Aldus Corp 411 1st Ave S Seattle WA 98104-2860

MULKEY, SHARON RENEE, gerontology nurse; b. Miles City, Mont., Apr. 14, 1954; d. Otto and Elvera Marie (Haglof) Neuhardt; m. Monty W. Mulkey, Oct. 9, 1976; children: Levi, Candice, Shane. BS in Nursing, Mont. State U., 1976. Staff nurse, charge nurse VA Hosp., Miles City, Mont., 1976-77; staff nurse obstetrics labor and delivery Munster (Ind.) Community Hosp., 1982-83; nurse mgr. Thousand Oaks Health Care, 1986-88; unit mgr. rehab. Semi Valley (Calif.) Adventist Hosp., 1988-89, DON TCU, 1989-91; DON Pleasant Valley Hosp. Extended Care Vacility and Neuro Ctr., 1991—. Mem. Am. Nurses Assn., Nat. Gerontol. Nursing Assn., Alpha Tau Delta (pres. 1973-75), Phi Kappa Phi. Home: 3461 Pembridge St Thousand Oaks CA 91360

MULLARKEY, MARY J., state supreme court justice; b. New London, Wis., Sept. 28, 1943; d. John Clifford and Isabelle A. (Steffes) M.; m. Thomas E. Korson, July 24, 1971; 1 child, Andrew Steffes Korson. BA, St. Norbert Coll., 1965; LLB, Harvard U., 1968; LLD (hon.), St. Norbert Coll., 1989. Bar: Wis. 1968, Colo. 1974. Atty.-advisor U.S. Dept. Interior, Washington, 1968-73; asst. regional atty. EEOC, Denver, 1973-75; 1st atty. gen. Colo. Dept. Law, Denver, 1975-79, solicitor gen., 1979-82; legal advisor to Gov. Lamm State of Colo., Denver, 1982-85; ptnr. Mullarkey & Seymour, Denver, 1985-87; justice Colo. Supreme Ct., Denver, 1987—. Recipient Alumni award St. Norbert Coll., De Pere, Wis., 1980. Fellow Colo. Bar Found., ABA Found.; mem. ABA, Colo. Bar Assn., Colo. Women's Bar Assn. (recognition award 1986), Denver Bar Assn. Office: Supreme Ct Colo 2 E 14th Ave Denver CO 80203

MULLEN, CLAUDE ROBERT, JR., meteorologist; b. Quakertown, Pa., Feb. 2, 1931; s. Claude Robert and Estella Jane (Strawn) M.; m. Nadine June Klindt, Sept. 27, 1953; children: Pamela Kay Long, Jeffrey Alan Mullen. Grad. high sch., Coopersburg, Pa. Enlisted USN, 1948, advanced through grades to; master chief aerographer's mate, 1974; ret. USN, 1978; meteorologist Continental Airlines, L.A., 1978-82; meteorology technician U.S. Navy Dept., Pacific Missile Test Ctr., Point Mugu, Calif., 1982—. Decorated Air medal. Mem. Am. Meteorol. Soc., Fleet Rev. Assn., Naval

Weather Svc. Assn. (pres. 1990-91, sec.-treas. 1979-86). Republican. Home: 1506 Kirk Ave Thousand Oaks CA 91360-3516 Office: Naval Aviation Warfare Ctr Code P 3541 Point Mugu Nas CA 93042

MULLER, DAVID WEBSTER, architectural engineer; b. Norwich, Conn., Aug. 25, 1956; s. Richard Johnson and Barbara Alice (Reading) M.; m. Susan Akers, Dec. 31, 1989; 1 stepchild, Shannon. BA in Polit. Sci., George Washington U., 1978. Rsch. assoc. Rep. Nat. Com., Washington, 1978-80, dep. dir. spl. projects, 1981-83; western field dir. Nat. Rep. Congl. Com., Washington, 1983-85; v.p. Russo Watts & Rollins, Sacramento, Calif., 1985-86; campaign mgr. Chavez for U.S. Senate, Silver Spring, Md., 1986; v.p. Russo Watts & Rollins, Sacramento, 1987-89; cons. Sacramento, 1989; pvt. investor Muller/West, Sacramento, 1990—; investor Architectural Design, Muller/West, 1990. Mem. Sacramento C. of C., 1987-89. Mem. Sacramento Club, Capital Club. Home and Office: Muller/West 4835 Hale Ranch Lane Fair Oaks CA 95628

MULLER, JEROME KENNETH, painter, editor, psychologist; b. Amityville, N.Y., July 18, 1934; s. Alphons and Helen (Haberl) M.; m. Nora Marie Nestor, Dec. 21, 1974. BS, Marquette U., 1961; postgrad., Calif. State U., Fullerton, 1985-86; MA, Nat. U., San Diego, 1988; postgrad., Newport Psychoanalytic Inst., 1988-90. Comml. and editorial photographer N.Y.C., 1952-55; mng. editor Country Beautiful mag., Milw., 1961-62, Reprodns. Rev. mag., N.Y.C., 1967-68; editor, art dir. Orange County (Calif.) Illustrated, Newport Beach, 1962-67, art editor, 1970-79, exec. editor, art dir., 1968-69; owner, chief exec. officer Creative Services Advt. Agy., Newport Beach, 1969-79; founder, chief exec. officer Mus. Graphics, Costa Mesa, Calif., 1978—; tchr. photography Lindenhurst (N.Y.) High Sch., 1952-54; tchr. comic art U. Calif., Irvine, 1979; guest curator 50th Anniversary Exhbn. Mickey Mouse, 1928-78, The Bowers Mus., Santa Ana, Calif., 1978; organized Moving Image Exhbn. Mus. Sci. and Industry, Chgo., Cooper-Hewitt Mus., N.Y.C., William Rockhill Nelson Gallery, Kansas City, 1981; collector original works of outstanding Am. cartoonists which are exhibited at major mus. One-man shows include Souk Gallery, Newport Beach, 1970, Gallery 2, Santa Ana, Calif., 1972, Cannery Gallery, Newport Beach, 1974; Author: Rex Brandt, 1972; contbr. photographs and articles to mags. Served with USAF, 1956-57. Recipient two silver medals 20th Ann. Exhbn. Advt. and Editorial Art in West, 1965. Mem. APA, Am. Assn. Profl. Hypnotherapists, Internat. Psychohist. Assn., Newport Harbor Art Mus., Mus. Modern Art (N.Y.C.), Met. Mus. Art, Art Mus. Assn. Am., Laguna Beach Mus. Art, L.A. Press Club, Newport Beach Tennis Club, Alpha Sigma Nu. Home: 2438 Bowdoin Pl Costa Mesa CA 92626-6304 Office: PO Box 10743 Costa Mesa CA 92627-0234

MULLER, RICHARD STEPHEN, electrical engineer, educator; b. Weehawken, N.J., May 5, 1933; s. Irving Ernest and Marie Victoria Muller; m. Joyce E. Regal, June 29, 1957; children: Paul Stephen, Thomas Richard. ME, Stevens Inst. Tech., Hoboken, N.J., 1955; MSEE, Calif. Inst. Tech., 1957, PhD in Elect. Engring. and Physics, 1962. Engr.-in-tng., 1955. Test engr. Wright Aero/Curtiss Wright, Woodridge, N.J., 1953-54; mem. tech. staff Hughes Aircraft Co., Culver City, Calif., 1955-61; instr. U. So. Calif., L.A., 1960-61; asst. prof., then assoc. prof. U. Calif., Berkeley, 1962-72, prof., 1973—; guest prof. Swiss Fed. Inst. Tech., 1993; dir. Berkeley Sensor and Actuator Ctr., 1985—; cons. in field. Co-author: Device Electronics for Integrated Circuits, 1977, 2d rev. edit., 1986, Microsensors, 1990; contbr. more than 200 articles to profl. jours. Vice chmn. Kensington (Calif.) Mcpl. Adv. Coun. Fellow Hughes Aircraft Co. 1955-57, NSF 1959-62, NATO postdoctoral 1958-69, Fulbright 1982-83, Alexander von Humboldt 1993. Fellow IEEE; mem. NAE, Electron Devices Soc. (adv. com. 1984—), Internat. Sensor and Actuator Meeting (chmn. steering com.). Office: U Calif Dept EECS 497 Cory Hall Berkeley CA 94720

MULLER, ROBERT JAMES, software engineer; b. Petaluma, Calif., Apr. 18, 1954; s. Florence Ruth (Junkin) M.; m. Mary L. Swanson, July 21, 1987. AB, U. Calif., Berkeley, 1976; MS, MIT, 1978, PhD, 1982. Cons. MIT, Cambridge, 1979-82; product mgr. Oracle Corp., Menlo Park, Calif., 1983-85; mgr. tech. svcs. Koch Systems Corp., San Francisco, 1985-87; mgr. software project Interactive Devel. Environs., San Francisco, 1987-89; sr. mem. tech. staff Objectivity, Menlo Park, Calif., 1990-92; engring. mgr. Symantec, Novato, Calif., 1992—. Author: ORACLE 7: The Complete Reference; contbr. articles to profl. jours. Mem. IEEE, Assn. for Computing Machinery, Computer Soc., Software Entrepreneurs Forum, Project Mgmt. Inst. Office: Symantec Corp 7200 Redwood Blvd Novato CA 94945

MULLIGAN, WILLIAM ANTHONY, journalist, educator; b. Owensboro, Ky., Sept. 6, 1947; s. James Estell and Marie Claribel (Curran) M.; m. Jian Wang, Apr. 3, 1982; 1 stepchild, CiCi Wang. BS, Brescia Coll., 1970; MS, Murray State U., 1974; PhD, U. Mo., 1986. Editor Tribune Democrat, Marshall Courier, Benton, Ky., 1970-71; mng. and Sunday editor Gleaner Jour., Henderson, Ky., 1971-74; copy editor The Columbus (Ohio) Dispatch, 1974-75; publ. coord. Murray (Ky.) State U., 1975-78; asst. news editor Columbia (Mo.) Missourian, 1978-81, 83-84; instr. journalism U. Mo., Columbia, 1978-81, 83-84; fgn. splist. Xinhua News Agy., Beijing, China, 1981-83; asst. prof. Stephen F. Austin State U., Nacogdoches, Tex., 1984-86; assoc. prof., prof. Calif. State U., Long Beach, 1986—, newspaper option head journalism dept., 1986—, chmn. dept. journalism, 1992—, mag. option head, 1993—; fgn. expert China Daily, Beijing, summer 1988; cons. Quality Times, McDonnell Douglas, Long Beach, 1989-90. Contbr. articles to profl. jours. Mem. Assn. for Educators in Journalism and Mass Comm., Investigative Reporters and Editors, Soc. of Profl. Journalists, Assn. Asian Studies, Internat. Comm. Assn. Office: Journalism Dept 1250 Bellflower Blvd Long Beach CA 90840

MULLIN, CHRIS(TOPHER) PAUL, professional basketball player; b. N.Y.C., July 30, 1963. Student, St. John's U., 1981-85. Basketball player Golden State Warriors, 1985—; mem. U.S. Olympic Team (received Gold medal), 1984, 92. Mem. NBA All-Star team, 1989-93. Office: Golden State Warriors Oakland Coliseum Arena Oakland CA 94621

MULLIN, J. SHAN, lawyer; b. Bellingham, Wash., Mar. 9, 1934; s. Jack D. and Naomi (Smith) M.; m. Lora Jane Fraser, Aug. 9, 1957; children: Barbara, Stephen, John, Anne. BS in Bus., U. Wash., 1956, JD, 1958. Bar: Wash. 1958, U.S. Supreme Ct. 1963. Assoc. Perkins Coie, Seattle, 1958-66, ptnr., 1967—; speaker various nat. and internat. sems. Co-author Legal Compliance Manual chpts. on internat. transactions, rev. edit., 1992. Mem. adv. bd. Pvt. Initiatives in Publ. Edn., Seattle, 1986-93, co-founder, 1980-81; co-founder Leadership Tomorrow, Seattle, 1982-83, bd. chmn., 1991; pres. Mcpl. League Seattle-King County, Seattle, 1976-78; trustee Law Sch. Found. U. Wash., Seattle, 1983-86, 90—, The Seattle Found., 1983-92; bd. dirs., exec. com. United Way King County, 1978-90, chmn. bd. dirs. 1987-88; bd. dirs., counsel Chamber Ctr. for Community Service, Seattle, 1986-90; co-founder, vice chmn. Seattle Alliance for Edn., 1990—; bd. dirs. United for Wash., Seattle, 1985—, Blue Cross Wash. and Alaska, Seattle, 1981-84, Wash. State China Relations Council, Seattle, 1983-85; pres., bd. mgrs. The Archibald Found., 1991—. Served to capt. USAR, 1958-65. Mem. ABA (internat. law and corp. banking and bus. law sects.), Wash. State Bar Assn. (chmn. young lawyers sect. 1963-64, internat. law, corp. banking and bus. law, tax, and intellectual and indsl. property sects.), Seattle-King County Bar Assn. (internat. law sect.), Internat. Bar Assn. (bus. law sect.), Seattle Internat. Tax Roundtable, Greater Seattle C. of C. (gen. counsel 1980-82), Beta Gamma Sigma, Phi Gamma Delta, Phi Delta Phi. Republican. Episcopalian. Clubs: Rainier, Seattle Tennis. Lodge: Rotary. Office: Perkins Coie 1201 3rd Ave 40th Fl Seattle WA 98101-3099

MULLINS, ANDREW J. W., clergyman; b. Charleston, W.Va., July 26, 1939; s. Andrew Jackson and Sallye Elizabeth (Williams) M.; m. Kathy Ellen Conner, June 22, 1962 (div. Mar. 1988); children: Jamie Christine, Megan Abigal, Paige Elizabeth, Melissa Kate. BA, Bethany (W.Va.) Coll., 1962; STM, Gen. Theol. Sem., N.Y.C., 1967; postgrad., NYU, 1972-75; cert. in non-profit mgmt., Columbia U., 1978. Ordained to ministry Episcopal Ch., 1967. Vicar Grace Episcopal Ch., Ravenwood, W.Va., 1967-68; asst. to rector St. Bartholomew's Episcopal Ch., N.Y.C., 1968-80, exec. asst. to rector, 1980-83, assoc. rector, 1983-90; vice dean St. Mark's Cathedral, Seattle, 1990—; vicar St. Simon by Sea, Mantoloking, N.J., summes 1971-88; program host Encounter, Sta. WMVO, W.Va.; cons. to exec. coun. on young adult ministry Episcopal Ch.; exec. dir. Wayne Leeann Found., Seattle, 1993—; founder, past dir. St. Bartholomew's Community Presch. Past mem. bd. dirs. N.Y.C. Parents in Action, Vanderbilt YMCA N.Y., Forum for Corp. Responsibility N.Y., Camp Good News, Bath, Maine, Ind. Citizens N.Y., Appalachian Sch. Religion for Ch. Leaders; founder, past chmn. Performing Arts Cultural Exch.; founding mem., past treas. Counseling and Human Devel. Ctr.; former chmn. Winant/Clayton Vols.; past mem. adv. coun. Sheltering Arms Children's Svc.; past pres. Mental Health Assn. Jackson County, W.Va. Office: St Mark's Cathedral 1245 10th Ave E Seattle WA 98102-4398

MULLINS, BILLY WAYNE, career officer; b. Lubbock, Tex., Mar. 17, 1955; s. Bernie Cleburn and Juanita May (Foster) M.; m. Jill Elizabeth Youngdoff, May 16, 1977; children: Erica Suzanne, Corrinn Rachel. BS in Physics, Angelo State U., 1978; MS in Engring Physics, Air Force Inst. Tech., 1979; PhD in Physics, U. N.Mex., 1989. Commd. 2d. lt. USAF, 1978, advanced through grades to maj., 1989—; tutor physics, Albuquerque, 1991—. Contbr. articles to profl. jours.; inventor in field. Vice chmn. adminstrv. coun. East United Meth. Ch., Colorado Springs, Colo., 1985; various coun. memberships Asbury United Meth. Ch., Albuquerque, 1989—; chancel choir soloist United Meth. Ch., numerous cities, 1978—. Mem. IEEE, Am. Physical Soc., Soc. Physics Students (pres. 1976-77). Office: Phillips Lab PL/WSP Kirtland A F B NM 87117

MULLINS, RUTH GLADYS, nurse; b. Westville, N.S., Can., Aug. 25, 1943; d. William G. and Gladys H.; came to U.S., 1949, naturalized, 1955; student Tex. Womans U., 1961-64; BS in Nursing, Calif. State U.-Long Beach, 1966; MNursing, UCLA, 1973; m. Leonard E. Mullins, Aug. 27, 1963; children: Deborah R., Catherine M., Leonard III. Pub. health nurse, L.A. County Health Dept., 1967-68; nurse Meml. Hosp. Med. Center, Long Beach, 1968-72; dir. pediatric nurse practitioner program Calif. State U., Long Beach, 1973-75, asst. prof., 1975-80, assoc. prof., 1980-85, prof., 1985—; health svc. credential coord. Sch. Nursing, chmn., 1979-81, coord. grad. programs, 1985-92; mem. Calif. Maternal, Child and Adolescent Health Bd., 1977-84; vice chair Long Beach/Orange County Health Consortium, 1984-85, chair 1985-86. Tng. grantee HHS, Calif. Dept. Health; cert. pediatric nurse practitioner. Fellow Nat. Assn. Pediatric Nurse Assocs. and Practitioners (exec. bd., past pres.), Nat. Fedn. Nursing Specialty Orgns. (sec.); mem. Am. Pub. Health Assn., Nat. Alliance Nurse Practitioners (governing body 1990-92), Assn. Faculties Pediatric Nurse Practitioner Programs, L.A. and Orange County Assn. Pediatric Nurse Practitioners and Assocs., Am. Assn. U. Faculty, Ambulatory Pediatric Assn. Democrat. Methodist. Author: (with B. Nelms) Growth and Development: A Primary Health Care Approach; contbg. author: Quick Reference to Pediatric Nursing, 1984; asst. editor Jour. Pediatric Health Care. Home: 6382 Heil Ave Huntington Beach CA 92647-4232 Office: Calif State U Dept Nursing 1250 N Bellflower Blvd Long Beach CA 90840-0001

MULLINS, TRACI LERAE, editor; b. Salem, Oreg., July 1, 1960; d. Lawrence Clinton and Sharon Louise (Searcy) M. BA in Journalism, U. Oreg., 1982. News reporter The Western News, Libby, Mont., 1980; news announcer Sta. KBDF-Radio, Eugene, Oreg., 1982-83; publicist Multnomah Press, Portland, Oreg., 1983-84; head counseling corr. Joyce Landorf Ministries, Del Mar, Calif., 1984-85; publicist NavPress, Colo. Springs, 1985-87, acquisitions editor, 1987—; acquisitions editor NavPress and Piñon Press, 1992—; tchr. various writing confs., 1985—. Contbr. articles to profl. jours. Named one of Outstanding Young Women Am. Mem. Kappa Tau Alpha. Home: 901 N El Paso Colorado Springs CO 80903-9999

MULLIS, KARY BANKS, biochemist; b. Lenoir, N.C., Dec. 28, 1944; s. Cecil Banks Mullis and Bernice Alberta (Barker) Fredericks; children: Christopher, Jeremy, Louise. BS in Chemistry, Ga. Inst. Tech, 1966; PhD in Biochemistry, U. Calif., Berkeley, 1973. Lectr. biochemistry U. Calif., Berkeley, 1972; postdoctoral fellow U. Calif., San Francisco, 1977-79, U. Kans. Med. Sch., Kansas City, 1973-76; scientist Cetus Corp., Emeryville, Calif., 1979-86; dir. molecular biology Xytronyx, Inc., San Diego, 1986-88; cons. Specialty Labs, Inc., Amersham, Inc., Chiron Inc. and various others, Calif., 1988—; chmn. StarGene, Inc., San Rafael, Calif. Contbr. articles to profl. jours.; patentee in field. Recipient Preis Biochemische Analytik award German Soc. Clin. Chem., 1990, Allan award Am. Soc. of Human Genetics, 1990, award Gairdner Found., 1991, Nat. Biotech. award, 1991, Robert Koch award, 1992, Japan prize, 1993, Calif. Scientist of Yr., 1992, Scientist of Yr. R&D Mag., 1991. Mem. Am. Chem. Soc., Inst. for Further Study (dir. 1983—). Office: 6767 Neptune Pl Apt # 5 La Jolla CA 92037

MULVANEY, JAMES FRANCIS, lawyer; b. Chgo., Nov. 2, 1922; m. Mary Ruth Rinderer, 1945; 7 children. BS, Loyola U., Chgo., 1942, JD, 1948. Atty. Chgo., 1948-55, San Diego, Calif., 1956-62; exec. v.p. U.S. Nat. Bank, 1963-72, pres., CEO, 1972-73; pres. San Diego Baseball Co., 1955-68; v.p., gen. counsel San Diego Padres Nat. League, 1968-73; ptnr. Mulvaney, Kahan & Barry, San Diego, 1974—; bd. dirs., chmn. Calif. Higher Edn. Loan Authority, 1983—; bd. dirs. Butler's Mill, Inc. Bd. vis. U. San Diego Sch. Law; chmn. United Way Internat., 1991—, mem. exec. com., United Way Am., 1987—, various officers; co-chmn. San Diego Organizing Project, 1983—; bd. dirs. World SHARE, Inc., 1986—, Old Globe Theatre London, Del mar Charities, 1985—; numerous other civic activities. Officer USN, WWII; lt. comdr. USNR, Korea. Recipient Mr. San Diego award, 1991, First Annual Spirit of Charity award Cath. Community Svcs., 1984, Brotherhood award Nat. Conf. Christians and Jews, Inc., 1983, Citizen of Yr. award Jr. C. of C. and The City Club, 1983, numerous others. Mem. San Diego County Bar Found. (treas., Outstanding Svc. award 1988), ABA, Calif. State Bar Assn., Ill. State Bar Assn., San Diego C. of C., San Diego Coun. on World Affairs, The City Club of San Diego, Navy League. Office: Mulvaney Kahan & Barry 401 West A St 17th Flr San Diego CA 92101-7994

MULVANY, NANCY CLAIRE, small business owner; b. Corpus Christi, Tex., Oct. 23, 1952; d. Herbert Hyland and Audrey Ann (Vevera) M. AB, U. Calif., Berkeley, 1975. Owner, operator Bayside Indexing Svc., Kensington, Calif., 1984—; tchr. U. Calif. Ext., Berkeley, 1988—, Santa Cruz, 1989-90, Grad. Sch. USDA, Washington, 1987—; workshop instr. Assn. for Computing Machinery, Pitts., 1989, Calif. Libr. Assn., San Diego, 1990. Author: Indexing Books, 1993. Mem. Am. Soc. Indexers, Inc. (immediate past pres. 1990-91, pres. 1989-90, v.p. 1988-89, pres. Golden Gate chpt. 1986-87), Assn. for Computing Machinery, Computer Profls. for Social Responsibility.

MULVEY, DENNIS MICHAEL, chemist; b. Lockport, N.Y., Nov. 17, 1938; s. James William and Ruth Elizabeth (Hamilton) M.; m. Diane Holdermiller, Aug. 23, 1963 (div. Nov. 1982); children: Kim, Colleen; m. Beverly June Butler, May 21, 1983; stepchildren: Kenneth Hicks, Karen Hicks, Ronald Hicks. AB in Chemistry, U. Pa., 1960; PhD in Organic Chemistry, SUNY, Buffalo, 1964. NIH postdoctoral rsch. assoc. Columbia U., N.Y.C., 1964-65; sr. rsch. chemist Merck, Sharp and Dohme Rsch. Labs., Rahway, N.J., 1965-70, rsch. fellow, 1970-77; group leader Ortho Pharm. Corp., Raritan, N.J., 1977-80, rsch. mgr., 1980-85; tech. support mgr. Molecular Design Ltd., San Leandro, Calif., 1985-86; polymer design mgr. Pennwalt Corp., King of Prussia, Pa., 1986-88; gen. mgr. fine chems. Vega Biotechs., Inc., Tucson, 1988-89; mgr. peptide mfg. ProCyte Corp., Kirkland, Wash., 1989-92; dir. process scis. ISIS Pharms., Carlsbad, Calif., 1992—; cons. in field. Contbr. articles to profl. publs.; patentee in field. Bd. dirs. Hunt. County Office of Alcoholism, Flemington, 1979-81; vol. fire and rescue squad Oldwick (N.J.) and Milford (N.J.) Squads, 1967-79; v.p. Oak-Tree/Menlo Lions Club, Edison, N.J., 1965-75. Home: 1739 Countryside Dr Vista CA 92083 Office: ISIS Pharms 2280 Faraday Ave Carlsbad CA 92008

MULVIHILL, PETER JAMES, fire protection engineer; b. Honolulu, Jan. 24, 1956; s. James H. and Jane A. (Norton) M. BSCE, Worcester (Mass.) Poly. Inst., 1978. Sr. engr. Indsl. Risk Insurers, San Francisco, 1978-84; fire protection engr. Aerojet Gen. Corp., Sacramento, 1984-87, Reno (Nev.) Fire Dept., 1987-93; fire protection engr., battalion chief Boise (Idaho) Fire Dept., 1993—; instr. part-time Truckee Meadows Community Coll., Reno, 1988-93. Commr. Gov.'s Blue Ribbon Commn. to Study Adequacy of State Regulations Concerning Highly Combustible Materials, Carson City, Nev., 1988. Mem. Soc. Fire Protection Engrs., No. Nev. Fire Marshal's Assn. (pres. 1992-93), Nat. Fire Protection Assn. (tech. com. on fire dept. apparatus), Internat. Assn. Fire Chiefs, Calif. Fire Chiefs' Assn. (fire prevention officers sect. No. divsn.), Fire Marshals' Assn. N. Am. Office: Boise Fire Dept 625 W Idaho St Boise ID 83702

MUMFORD, PATRICIA RAE, religious organization administrator; b. Oklahoma City, Feb. 25, 1932; d. Raymond William and Mildred Louise (Wisdom) Gallagher; m. Donald Earl Mumford, April 6, 1951; children: Raymond Scott, Kenneth Earl, Robert Paul. Columnist The Sapulpan, Sapulpa, Okla., 1949-51; continuity writer Sta. KRMG, Tulsa, 1951-52; with continuity and production TV stas., Phoenix, Las Vegas, Denver, 1953-57; continuity and traffic radio stas. KPOI and KKUA, Honolulu, 1965-71; part-time program asst. Hawaii Council of Chs., Honolulu, 1972-80, assoc. dir., acting dir., 1980-85, exec. coordinator, 1986-87; exec. dir. Hawaii Council of Chs., Kailua, Hawaii, 1987—. Contrib. articles to newspapers, newsletters and mags. Bd. dirs. UNA-Hawaii, Meml. Soc. of Hawaii, Vol. Leadership Devel. program, Hawaii Pub. Broadcasting Authority Adv. Bd., Honolulu, 1978-82; mem. Hawaii State Commn. on Martin Luther King Jr. Holiday, 1988—. Named Outstanding Woman of Yr., City and County of Honolulu, 1982. Mem. Nat. Assn. Ecumenical Staff (svc. award 1987, 92), Ch. Women United (local and state pres., mem. nat. coun. 1965-72). Democrat. Mem. Christian Ch., United Presbyn. Ch.

MUMM, DAVE, labor union administrator; b. Lewiston, Idaho, May 10, 1950; s. Hans August and Phoebe Ruth Mumm; m. Joan Lyn Cooper, Nov. 24, 1984; 1 child, Michael Steven. BA in Polit. Sci., U. Idaho, 1974. Bus. agt. HERE Local Union #8, Seattle, 1981-83, 88-89, sec.-treas., 1989—; adminstrv. aide to gen. pres. Hotel Employees & Restaurant Employees Internat. Union, Washington, 1983—; sec.-treas. Local Union 8 Hotel Employees & Restaurant Employees Internat. Union, Seattle, 1989—; trustee Hotel Emplyees Restaurant Employees Health & Pension Fund, Seattle; pres. food and beverage trades sect. Wash. State Labor Coun. Dir. food and beverage handling panel Wash. State Gov's. Indsl. Health and Safety Adv. Bd., Olympia. Mem. Internat. Found. of Employee Benefits. Democrat. Home: 2023 E Roy St Seattle WA 98112-4038 Office: HERE Local #8 2800 1st Ave Ste 3 Seattle WA 98121-1114

MUN, SANDRA JEAN, marketing coordinator; b. Honolulu, Apr. 23, 1965; d. George K.C. and Jane N.K. (Lau) M. BA, U. Hawaii, 1988. Human resources asst. II GTE Hawaiian Telephone Co., Honolulu, 1988, materials clk., 1988-89, clerical asst., 1989-90; communications asst. Hawaii Dental Svcs., Honolulu, 1991; mktg. coord. Bellamann Svcs., Inc., Honolulu, 1991—. Regional winner Nat. Student Advt. Competition Am. Advt. Fedn., 1988; recipient award Acad. Excellence U. Hawaii, 1987-88, Scholar award Associated Chinese Univ. Women, 1983-84. Mem. Jaycees (individual devel. v.p. 1990-91, personnel dir. 1990, Outstanding Individual Devel. V.P. award 1990-91, Officer-of-the-Quarter award 1990-91, Officer-of-the-Yr. award 1990-91).

MUND, GERALDINE, bankruptcy judge; b. L.A., July 7, 1943; d. Charles J. and Pearl (London) M. BA, Brandeis U., 1965; MS, Smith Coll., 1967; JD, Loyola U., 1977. Bar: Calif. 1977. Bankruptcy judge U.S. Cen. Dist. Calif., 1984—. Past pres. Temple Israel, Hollywood, Calif. Mem. ABA, L.A. County Bar Assn. Office: Roybal Bldg 255 E Temple St Los Angeles CA 90012

MUNDELL, JILL ANN, artist; b. New Prague, Minn., Sept. 3, 1949; d. Richard L. and Margaret (Buster) Mikiska; m. William Russel Mundell, Jan. 9, 1970; children: Russell Allen, Jessica Ann. Student, U. Ariz., 1967-69. Dental technician Kino Starr Dental Lab., Tucson, 1969-71, 75-76, Dental Prosthetics, Tucson, 1990-91; workshop instr. Catalina (Ariz.) Art Coun., 1991-92; freelance artist Tucson, 1990—. Exhibited in groups shows at 3d Ann. Pinal County Invitational Art Exhibit, Casa Grande, Ariz., 1992, 93, Critter and Varmints Show, Prescott's (Ariz.) Phippen Mus. Western Art., 1992, Ariz. Holidays Show, Prescott's Phippen Mus. Western Art, 1992; represented in permanent collections Valley Nat. Bank, Casa Grande, Ariz. (purchase award 1978), Casa Grande Mus. Art, 1993. Mem. Prescott's Phippen Mus. Western Art. U. Ariz. scholar, 1967; recipient Celebrity award Florentine Art Exhibit, 1992, Viewer's Choice award Oracle (Ariz.) Hist.Soc., 1992, One Yr. Exhibit award Casa Grande Ruins Nat. Monument, 1992-93. Mem. Catalina/Golder Ranch Arts Coun. (treas. 1990-91, sec. 1991—), Tucson/Pima Arts Coun. (rural com. 1991—), Colored Pencil Soc. Am. Democrat. Home: HCR 3 Box 1059 Tucson AZ 85737

MUNGER, EDWIN STANTON, political geography educator; b. LaGrange, Ill., Nov. 19, 1921; s. Royal Freeman and Mia (Stanton) M.; m. Ann Boyer, May 2, 1970; 1 child, Elizabeth Stanton Gibson. B.Sc., U. Chgo., 1948, M.Sc., 1949, Ph.D., 1951. Fulbright fellow Makerere U., 1949-50; research fellow U. Chgo.; field assoc. Am. Univs. Field Staff, 1950-60; faculty Calif. Inst. Tech., Pasadena, 1961—; prof. polit. geography Calif. Inst. Tech., 1960—; research fellow Stellenbosch U., 1955-56; vis. prof. U. Warsaw, 1973. Author books including Afrikaner and African Nationalism, 1968, The Afrikaners, 1979, Touched by Africa: An Autobiography, 1983, Ethnic Chess Sets, 1992; editor books including Munger Africana Library Notes, 1969-82; contbr. numerous articles to profl. jours., chpts. to books. Evaluator Peace Corps, Uganda, 1966, Botswana, 1967; chmn. State Dept. Evaluation Team S. Africa, 1971; trustee African-Am. Inst., 1956-62; acting pres. Pasadena Playhouse, 1966; chmn. bd. trustees Crane Rogers Found., 1979-82, fellow, 1950-54; mem. exec. com. NAACP, Pasadena, 1979—, nat. del, 1984, 85; trustee Leakey Found., 1968—, pres., 1971-84; pres. Cape of Good Hope Found., 1985—; pres. Internat. Vis. Coun., L.A., 1991-93, bd. mem., 1979—. RecipientAlumni Citation award for pub. svc. U. Chgo., 1993. Fellow Royal Soc. Arts, African Studies Assn. (founding, bd. dirs. 1963-66); mem. PEN USA West (v.p.), Coun. Fgn. Rels., Cosmos Club, Athenaeum Club, Twilight Club. Office: Calif Inst Tech Div Humanities and Social Scis 1201 E California Blvd Pasadena CA 91125-0001

MUNIR, MOHAMMAD IDREES, genetic engineer, research scientist, consultant; b. Gujranwala, Punjab, Pakistan, Oct. 22, 1954; came to U.S., 1983; s. M. Ismail and Mubarka (Nasreen) M.; m. Samar Z.M. Junjua, Nov. 24, 1984; 1 child, Mnsoora Khullat. BSc, T.I. Coll., Punjab, 1976; MSc, Q.A. U., Islamabad, Pakistan, 1979; PhD, Glasgow (Scotland) U., 1983. Postdoctoral fellow Baylor Coll. Medicine, Houston, 1983-86, sr. rsch. assoc., 1990-92; rsch. assoc. Howard Hughes Med. Inst., Houston, 1986-90; sr. rsch. scientist Biogenex Labs., San Ramon, Calif., 1992—. Developer, creator 1st transgenic mice carrying antisense RNA. Coord., chmn. action com. Ahmadiyya Movement, Washington, 1986-91. Democrat. Islam. Home: 2705 Fountainhead San Ramon CA 94583 Office: Biognex Labs 4600 Norris Canyon San Ramon CA 94583

MUNITZ, BARRY, chief university administrator, English literature educator, business consultant; b. Bklyn., July 26, 1941; s. Raymond J. and Vivian L. (LeVoff) M.; m. Anne Tomfohrde, Dec. 15, 1987. BA, Bklyn. Coll., 1963; MA, Princeton U., 1965, PhD, 1968; cert., U. Leiden, Netherlands, 1962. Asst. prof. lit. and drama U. Calif., Berkeley, 1966-68; staff assoc. Carnegie Commn. Higher Edn., 1968-70; mem. presdl. staff, then assoc. provost U. Ill. System, 1970-72, acad. v.p., 1972-76; v.p., dean faculties Central campus U. Houston, 1976-77, chancellor, 1977-82, chmn. coordinating bd. faculty workload, 1976-80; chmn. Tex. Long Range Planning, 1980-82; pres., chief oper. officer Federated Devel. Co., 1982-91; vice chmn. Maxxam Inc., L.A., 1982-91; chancellor Calif. State U. System, Long Beach, Calif., 1991—; prof. English lit. Calif. State U., L.A., 1991—; bd. dirs. Sta. KCET-TV, Am. Coun. on Edn., ICN Pharmaceuticals, Calif. Econ. Devel. Corp., FHP, Inc.; cons. in presdl. evaluation and univ. governance. Author: The Assessment of Institutional Leadership, 1977, also articles, monographs. Mem. task force NSF. Recipient Disting. Alumnus award Bklyn. Coll., 1979, U. Houston Alumni Pres.'s medal, 1981; Woodrow Wilson fellow, 1963. Mem. Young Pres. Orgn., Heritage Club, Phi Beta Kappa. Office: Calif State U System Office of Chancellor 400 Golden Shore St Long Beach CA 90802-4275

MUNK, WALTER HEINRICH, geophysics educator; b. Vienna, Austria, Oct. 19, 1917; came to U.S., 1933; m. Edith Kendall Horton, June 20, 1953; children: Edith, Kendall. BS, Calif. Inst. Tech., 1939, MS, 1940; PhD, U. Calif., 1947; PhD (hon.), U. Bergen, Norway, 1975, Cambridge (Eng.) U., 1986. From asst. prof. to prof. geophysics Scripps Inst. Oceanography U. Calif. San Diego, La Jolla, 1947—. Contbr. over 200 articles to profl. jours. Recipient Gold medal Royal Astron. Soc., 1968, Capt. Robert Dexter

Conrad award Dept. Navy, 1978, Nat. Medal Sci., 1985, Vetlesen prize, 1993; named Calif. Scientist of Yr. Calif. Mus. Sci. and Industry, 1969; fellow Guggenheim Found., 1948, 55, 62, Overseas Found., 1962, 81-82, Fulbright Found., 1981-82; Sr. Queen's fellow, 1978. Fellow Am. Geophys. Union (Maurice Ewing medal 1976, William Bowie medal 1989), AAAS, Am. Meteorol. Soc. (Sverdrup Gold medal 1966), Accoustical Soc. Am., Marine Tech. Soc. (Compass award 1991); mem. Nat. Acad. Scis. (Agassiz medal 1976, chmn. ocean studies bd. 1985-88), Am. Philos. Soc., Royal Soc. London (fgn. mem.), Deutsche Akademie der Naturforscher Leopoldina, Am. Acad. Arts and Scis. (Arthur L. Day medal 1965), Am. Geol. Soc. Office: U Calif San Diego Scripps Inst Oceanography 0225 La Jolla CA 92093

MUNN, WILLIAM CHARLES, II, psychiatrist; b. Flint, Mich., Aug. 9, 1938; s. Elton Albert and Rita May (Coykendall) M.; student Flint Jr. Coll., 1958-59, U. Detroit, 1959-61; M.D., Wayne State U., 1965; m. Deborah Lee Munn, 1983; children by previous marriage—Jude Michael, Rachel Marie, Alexander Winston. Intern David Grant USAF Med. Center, Travis AFB, Calif., 1965-66; resident in psychiatry Letterman Army Hosp., San Francisco, 1967-70; practice medicine, specializing in psychiatry, Fairfield, Calif., 1972—; chief in-patient psychiatry David Grant Med. Center, 1970-71, chmn. dept. mental health, 1971-72; psychiat. cons. Fairfield-Suisun Unified Sch. Dist., 1971—, Fairfield Hosp. and Clinic, 1971, N. Bay Med. Ctr.(formerly Intercommunity Hosp.), Fairfield, 1971—, Casey Family Program, 1980—, Solano County Coroner's Office, 1981; asst. clin. prof. psychiatry U. Calif., San Francisco, 1976—; cons. Vaca Valley Hosp., Vacaville, Calif., 1988—, VA Hosp., San Francisco, 1976, David Grant USAF Hosp., 1976. Served to maj., M.C., USAF, 1964-72, flight surgeon, chief public health, chief phys. exam. center McGuire AFB, N.J., 1966-67. Diplomate Am. Bd. Psychiatry and Neurology (examiner). Mem. Am. Psychiat. Assn., No. Calif. Psychiat. Soc., E. Bay Psychiat. Assn. Home: 450 Ridgewood Dr Martinez CA 94553-4131 Office: 1245 Travis Blvd # E Fairfield CA 94533-4801

MUNNINGER, MICHAEL JOSEPH, architect; b. Albany, N.Y., Aug. 24, 1948; s. Karl Otto and Margaret Josephine (Craugh) M.; children: John Karl, Michael, Suzanne, Paul, Mark. BArch, U. Tex., 1971; postgrad., Ariz. State U., Phoenix, 1976-77. Registered architect, Ariz., Calif. Founder, ptnr. Archtl. Alliance, Phoenix, 1974—. Contbr. articles to mags., newspapers. Active Hunter Safety Instr. Program, Nat. Trust Hist. Preservation; past chmn. City of Phoenix Visual Improvement Com.; past bd. dirs. Boys Club Met. Phoenix, Ariz. Recipient 2nd prize Art by Architects, 1982, Most Beautiful Home award, Phoenix mag., 1982, Visual Improvement award, City of Phoenix, 1984, Am. Concrete Inst. award, 1989, AIA award of merit Homes of Yr., 1989, City of Tempe Beatification award, 1990. Home: 10001 N 132d St Scottsdale AZ 85259

MUÑOZ, CARLOS, JR., political scientist, educator; b. El Paso, Tex., Aug. 25, 1939; s. Carlos Garcia and Clementina (Contreras) M.; m. Graciela Eulalia Rios, Dec. 18, 1977; children: Carlos Edward, Marina, Genaro, Daniel, Marcelo. AA in Polit. Sci., L.A. City Coll., 1964; BA in Polit. Sci., Calif. State U., 1967; PhD in Govt., Claremont Grad. Sch., 1973. Founding chair and instr. Chicano Studies dept. Calif. State U., L.A., 1968-69; lectr. Pfizer Coll., Claremont, Calif., 1969-70; asst. prof. comparative cultures U. Calif., Irvine, 1970-76; prof. Chicano and ethnic studies U. Calif., Berkeley, 1976—; sr. cons. Documentary Film Project, Nat. Latino Comms. Ctr. entitled "Chicano! History of the Mexican American Civil Rights Movement"; cons. Ford Found., N.Y.C., 1975, U.S. Office Edn., Washington, 1969. Author: Youth, Identity, Power: The Chicano Movement, 1990; contbr. articles to profl. jours., chpts. to books. Advisor Jesse Jackson Presdl. Campaign, Calif., 1988; co-founder LaRaza Unida Party, So. Calif., 1971; founding mem. Nat. Rainbow Coalition, No. Calif., 1984. With U.S. Army, 1959-62. U. Calif. Humanities Rsch. fellow, 1990, Faculty fellow, 1990; Greentree Found. grantee, 1987; Calif. State U. Disting. Scholar Lecture, 1990. Mem. Am. Polit. Sci. Assn., Nat. Assn. for Chicano Studies (co-founder, chair 1972-73), Orgn. Am. Historians, Pi Sigma Alpha. Roman Catholic. Office: Univ of Calif-Berkeley Ethnic Studies Dept Berkeley CA 94720

MUNOZ, JOHN JOSEPH, transportation company executive; b. Salinas, Calif., Jan. 18, 1932; s. John Fernando and Naomal (Smith) M.; m. Phyllis Taylor, Feb. 6, 1961 (div. 1978); children: Sam, Kathy, Toni; m. Rachel Canales, Nov. 24, 1979; children: Michelle, Monique. AA, Allan Hancock Coll., 1956; student, San Jose State U., 1981, Western Sierra Law Sch. Ops. mgr. So. Pacific Milling Co., Santa Maria, Calif., 1971-77; cons. Govt., Venezuela, 1977-78; fleet supt. Granite Rock Co., San Jose, Calif., 1978-80; plant mgr. Granite Constrn. Co., Greenfield, Calif., 1980-85; mgr. transpn. Ball, Ball. & Brosmer Inc., Danville, Calif., 1985-86; ops. mgr., bd. dirs. Sorrento Ready Mix Co., Del Mar, Calif., 1986-89; trans. cons. Greenfield, Calif., 1991—; cons. Dept. Agrl. Devel., Maricaibo, Venezuela, 1976—. Commr. Planning Commn., Greenfield, Calif., 1982-85; mem. fund raising com. Broccoli Festival, Greenfield, 1983-85; dir. Soledad Prison Vocat. Tng., 1982-85. Lt. U.S. Army, 1950-52, Korea. Mem. Am. Concrete Inst., Calif. Trucking Assn., Los Californianos, Rotary, Lions, Elks. Republican. Home: PO Box 3654 Greenfield CA 93927-3654 Office: PO Box 3554 Greenfield CA 93927

MUÑOZ, RICARDO FELIPE, psychology educator; b. Lima, Peru, Apr. 30, 1950; came to U.S., 1961; s. Luis Alberto and Clara Luz (Valdivia) M.; m. Pat Marine, Mar. 31, 1979; children: Rodrigo Alberto, Aubrey Elizabeth Luz. AB, Stanford U., 1972; MA, U. Oreg., 1975, PhD, 1977. Asst. prof. psychology U. Calif., San Francisco, 1977-83, assoc. prof., 1983-89, prof., 1989—; dir. depression clinic San Francisco Gen. Hosp., 1985-90, chief psychologist, 1987—, deputy chief acad. affairs, 1991—; dir. UCSF Clin. Psychology Tng. Program, 1992—; bd. dirs. div. health promotion and disease prevention, Inst. Medicine, NAS, Washington. Co-author: Control Your Depression, 1986, How to Control Your Drinking, 1982, Prevention of Depression: Research and Practice, 1993; editor: Depression Prevention: Research Directions, 1987; co-editor; Social and Psychological Research in Community Settings, 1979. Recipient Health Promotion award Nat. Coalition Hispanic Mental Health and Human Svcs. Orgn., 1984, Dr. Martin Luther King Jr. award, U. Calif., San Francisco, 1991. Fellow Am. Psychol. Assn.; mem. AAAS, Nat. Hispanic Psychol. Assn., Am. Assn. for Artificial Intelligence, Phi Beta Kappa. Office: U Calif 1001 Potrero Ave Ste 7M San Francisco CA 94110-3594

MUNRO, RALPH DAVIES, state government official; b. Bainbridge Island, Wash., June 25, 1943; s. George Alexander and Elizabeth (Troll) M.; m. Karen Hansen, Feb. 17, 1973; 1 son, George Alexander. BA in History and Edn. (scholar), Western Wash. U. Successively indsl. engr. Boeing Co.; sales mgr. Continental Host, Inc.; asst. dep. dir. ACTION Agy.; spl. asst. to gov. of Wash.; gen. mgr. Tillicum Enterprises & Food Services Co.; dir. Found. for Handicapped; pres. Northwest Highlands Tree Farm; now sec. of state State of Wash. Chmn. community service com. Seattle Rotary Club 4; founder 1st pres. Rotary Youth Job Employment Center, Seattle. Named Man of Yr. Assn. Retarded Citizens, Seattle, 1970. Mem. Nat. Assn. Secs. State (pres.), Nat. Assn. Retarded Children, Wash. Historic Mus. (dir.), Wash. Trust Historic Preservation (founder), Nature Conservancy. Republican. Lutheran. Office: Sec of State Legislative Bldg PO Box 40220 Olympia WA 98504-0220*

MUNROE, DONNA SCOTT, insurance executive, management consultant; b. Cleve., Nov. 28, 1945; d. Glenn Everett and Louise Lenox (Parkhill) Scott; m. Melvin James Ricketts, Dec. 23, 1968 (div. Aug. 1979); 1 child, Suzanne Michelle; m. Peter Carlton Munroe, Feb. 14, 1981. BS in Sociology, Portland (Oreg.) State U., 1976, BS in Philosophy, 1978, MS in Sociology, 1983. Lectr. Portland State U., 1977-79; writing, editorial cons. Worth Pubs., N.Y.C., 1978-79; statis. cons. health scis. U. Oreg., Portland, 1979-82; statis. cons. Morrison Ctr. for Youth and Family Svcs., Portland, 1979-82; writer Equitable Savs. & Loan, Portland, 1981-82; mgr. acct. and projects. Electronic Data Systems, Portland, 1982-87; mng. dir. healthcare and ins. fin. group, sr. mgmt. cons. CMSI Inc., Portland, 1987—, mng. dir. ins. and healthcare fin. group. Mem. Am. Mgmt. Assn., Am. Mktg. Assn., Am. Soc. for Quality Control, City Club of Portland, Sigma Xi. Democrat. Episcopalian. Home: 536 SW Cheltenham St Portland OR 97201-2602 Office: Computer Mgmt Systems Inc 0234 SW Bancroft Ct Portland OR 97201-4050

MUNROE, LYDIA DARLENE, jeweler, travel industry executive; b. San Diego, July 9, 1933; d. Daniel O. and Bertha E. (Smith) Thayer; m. H. Flack Jr., July 29, 1949 (div. 1953); children: Debrha Flack Miller, Mona Lynn Flack Pietz; m. Don Evan Heath, Oct. 13, 1953 (dec. 1968); 1 child, Daniel Evan; m. Duskin M. Shears, July 24, 1969 (dec. 1982); m. Albert G. Munroe, Nov. 26, 1982. Student, Sweetwater Adult Edn. Coll. With accounts receivable, payroll Burtrum Yacht Co., Miami, Fla., 1954-55; gen. bookkeeper Stafford and Gardner, 1955-56; bookkepper, switch bd. operator William Creek Copper Mines, 1956-57; with Brisbane (Australia) and Wonderlick, 1957; small bus. owner, miner Coober Pedy South Australia Opal Fields, 1957-72; small bus. owner Down Under Opal, Seattle, 1972—; tour guide, itinerary planner to Australia, 1982—; lectr. on Opals. Author: (VCR and book) Pricing Opal. Active Widowed Info. and Cons. Services. Mem. Maplewood Gem Club (rep. to regional gem show com., dealer chairwoman 1988), West Seattle Gem Club (treas., show chairwoman), N.W. Opal Assn. (v.p., pres., show dealer chairwoman, chairwoman edn. com.), Puyallup Valley Gem Club, OES Juanita Chpt., Am. Mineral Gem Suppliers Assn., Greater Seattle C. of C. Home: 716 SW 179th Ct Seattle WA 98166-3664

MUNSEY, MARGARET RUTH, real estate development company executive; b. Portland, Oreg., Dec. 22, 1924; d. Lyle Emory and Ruth (Holbrook) M.; m. Donald William Thompson, Apr. 16, 1943 (div. 1968); children: Kathie Thompson, Brian Thompson. BA, Fresno State Coll., 1971; MCRP, Calif. State U., Fresno, 1974. Asst. planner City of Fresno, 1973-74; sr. planner Fresno County Assn. Govts., 1974-77; exec. dir. Kern County Coun. Govts., Bakersfield, Calif., 1977-81; ptnr., regional br. mgr. Quad Engrs. and Cons., Bakersfield, Calif., 1981-87; ptnr., planning cons. McGregor/Munsey & Assocs., Davis, Calif., 1987-89; mktg. dir. Fugro McClelland, Sacramento, 1989-91; v.p., CEO Marlon Enterprises, Bakersfield, Calif., 1986—. Pres.-elect AAUW, Fresno, 1976; mem. C. of C., Bakersfield, 1981-86; bd. dirs. Calif. Planning Found., 1982-88. Mem. Am. Planning Assn. (pres. Calif. chpt. cen. sect. 1976-78, Contbn. to Women in Planning 1990), Am. Inst. Cert. Planners (cert.). Democrat. Christian Scientist. Home: 11406 Gold Hill Ct Gold River CA 95670 Office: Marlon Enterprises 5924 Margaret Ct Bakersfield CA 93306

MUNSON, LUCILLE MARGUERITE (MRS. ARTHUR E. MUNSON), real estate broker; b. Norwood, Ohio, Mar. 26, 1914; d. Frank and Fairy (Wicks) Wirick; R.N., Lafayette (Ind.) Home Hosp., 1937; A.B., San Diego State U., 1963, student Purdue U., Kans. Wesleyan U.; m. Arthur E. Munson, Dec. 24, 1937; children—Barbara Munson Papke, Judith Munson Andrews, Edmund Arthur. Staff and pvt. nurse Lafayette Home Hosp., 1937-41; indsl. nurse Lakey Foundry & Machine Co., Muskegon, Mich., 1950-51, Continental Motors Corp., Muskegon, 1951-52; nurse Girl Scout Camp, Grand Haven, Mich., 1948-49; owner Munson Realty, San Diego, 1964—. Mem. San Diego County Grand Jury, 1975-76, 80-81, Calif. Grand Jurors Assn. (charter). Office: 2999 Mission Blvd Ste 102 San Diego CA 92109-8028

MUNSON, RALPH ANDREW, hospital administrator, respiratory therapist; b. Berkeley, Calif., Oct. 14, 1950; s. Andrew Chris and Ruth Ellen (Slager-Post) M.; m. Marilyn Schmieding, Mar. 14, 1974 (div. Sept. 1975); m. Catherine Louise Stout, Apr. 24, 1983; children: Cara Ashley, Trevor Ralph. Cert. in German, Austro Am. Inst., Vienna, Austria, 1971; BA in Biology, Lewis and Clark Coll., 1972; cert. in respiratory therapy, Mt. Hood Community Coll., Gresham, Oreg., 1973; MBA in Health Svcs. Mgmt., Golden Gate U., 1982. Orderly Eugene (Oreg.) Hosp. and Clinic, 1968-72; supr. cardio respiratory Holladay Park Hosp., Portland, Oreg., 1972-74; asst. dir. respiratory care Domincan Santa Cruz (Calif.) Hosp., 1974-76; dir. cardio-respiratory svcs. St. Joseph's Hosp., San Francisco, 1976-79; dir. diagnostic svcs. French Hosp. Med. Ctr., San Francisco, 1979-81; dir. respiratory care Oreg. Health Svcs. Univ., Portland, 1981-86, asst. hosp. adminstr., 1986-87; respiratory therapist Stafflink Legacy Health Svcs., Portland, 1988-91; dir. cardiorespiratory & heart and lung ctr. St. Joseph Hosp., Tacoma, Wash., 1991-93. Contbr. articles to profl. jours., 1985. Recipient Excellence in State Mgmt. award Gov. of Oreg., 1984. Mem. Am. Assn. Respiratory Care (del. 1983-86), Oreg. Soc. Respiratory Care (pres. 1984-86, advocate licensing 1985), Respiratory Care Soc. Oreg. (liaison 1984-85), Respiratory Care Soc. Wash. Republican. Baptist. Home: 25413 163d Pl SW Kent WA 98042-4129

MUNSON, RAY EUGENE, judge; b. Leavenworth, Wash., Sept. 10, 1927; s. Will Keller and Jessie May (Tyler) M.; m. Christine A. Parr, Nov. 13, 1954; children: Mark P., Bradley W., Scott E., Cristofer R. BBA, U. Wash., 1952, JD, 1954. Bar: Wash. 1954, U.S. Dist. Ct. (ea. dist.) Wash. 1957. Spl. agt. FBI, 1954-55; dep. pros. atty. Yakima (Wash.) County Pros. Atty. Office, 1956-57, pros. atty., 1957-61; assoc. Halverson, Applegate, McDonald, Yakima, 1962-65; judge Superior Ct. Wash., Yakima, 1965-69; judge Wash. Ct. Appeals Div. III, Yakima, 1969—, presiding chief judge, 1978, chief judge, 1971-73, 77-79, 83-85, 89. With USN, 1945-48. Home: 821 N 48th Ave Yakima WA 98908-2405 Office: Wash Ct Appeals 500 N Cedar St Spokane WA 99201-1987

MUNSTERTEIGER, KAY DIANE, speech-language pathologist; b. Newcastle, Wyo., June 2, 1956; d. Donald Francis and Janice Mathilda (Emerson) M. BS, U. Wyo., 1978; MS, U. Nev., Reno, 1980. Speech lang. pathologist No. Nev. Speech lang. Clinic, Reno, 1980-82, Washakie County Sch. Dist. 1, Worland, Wyo., 1982—; pvt. practice speech pathologist Worland, 1982—; speech lang. pathologist, cons. Washakie County Sch. Dist. 2, Tensleep, Wyo., 1984-85; speech lang. pathologist Spl. Touch Presch., Worland, 1985-86, 89—; bd. dirs. Spl. Touch Presch./Children Resource Ctr., 1987-89; pres. bd. examiners Speech Pathology and Audiology, 1988—. Mem. Pub. Sch. Caucus. Mem. NEA, State Edn. Assn., Am. Speech Lang. Hearing Assn., Wyo. Speech Lang. Hearing Assn., Nat. Stuttering Project, Pub. Sch. Caucus, Assn. Childhood Edn. Internat., Phi Kappa Phi. Democrat. Roman Catholic. Office: Washakie County Sch Dist # 1 1200 Culbertson Ave Worland WY 82401-3520

MUNTZ, PALMER HAYDEN, college director; b. Pontiac, Mich., Jan. 14, 1960; s. J. Richard and Marietta (Hayden) M.; m. Jeannette Renee Vinje, Feb. 4, 1984; children: Jordan Palmer, Phillip Richard. BS, Western Bapt. Coll., 1982, BTh, 1983; MEd, Oreg. State U., 1990. Admissions counselor Western Bapt. Coll., Salem, Oreg., 1984-87, asst. dir. admissions, 1987-88, dir. admissions and fin. aid, 1991—; fin. aid asst. Oreg. State U., Corvallis, 1988-90; asst. chaplain/resident dir. Whitworth Coll., Spokane, 1990-91. Co-author, editor: How to Survive and Thrive as a Whitworth R.A., 1991; author articles, documents in field. Precinct committeeman Rep. Party of Oreg., Salem, 1992. Mem. Assn. for Christians in Student Devel., Oreg. Assn. Student Fin. Aid Adminstrs. (mem. tng. com. 1992—), Nat. Assn Christian Coll. Admissions Pers., Am. Coll. Pers. Assn., Nat. Assn. Coll. Admissions Counselors. Baptist. Office: Western Bapt Coll 5000 Deer Park Dr SE Salem OR 97301

MUOTO, OLIVER CHUKWUDI, marketing executive, researcher; b. Poznan, Poland, June 29, 1965; came to U.S., 1985; s. Clinton C. and Sylvia S. (Switalska) M. BS in Indsl. Sales Engring., U. So. Calif., L.A., 1988. Analyst Royal Clinic Group, Kano, Nigeria, 1984-85; chief engr. KSCR, L.A., 1986-88; with sales dept. dining scvs. U. So. Calif., L.A., 1988-89, with mgmt. housing scvs., 1989-90; regional dir. Calif. Fin., L.A., 1989—; dir. MIS Davis, Ball & Colombatto Advt., 1990-92; founder, pres. Vetti Comm., 1992; tech. support specialist Coactive Computing, Belmont, Calif., 1993—; cons. U. So. Calif., 1989—. U. So. Claif. scholar, 1988. Mem. IEEE, SAMPE, MENSA, Phi Kappa Phi, Alpha Lambda Delta Honor Soc. (exec. com. 1988-89). Baptist. Home: 2225 Sharon Rd # 121 Menlo Park CA 94025

MURABAYASHI, HARRIS NOZOMU, management analyst; b. Kaneohe, Hawaii, May 10, 1928; s. Junichi and Kaneko (Kodama) M.; widowed' children: Dona Sachie Murabayashi Kang, Fern Miyoko. BA, U. Hawaii, 1950. Jr. acct. Hideo Kajikawa, CPA, Honolulu, 1950; bookkeeping machine operator Dillingham Bros. Ltd., Honolulu, 1950-51; budget analyst Budget and Fin. Dept., State of Hawaii, 1955-59, Planning Dept., City of Honolulu, 1959-64; capital improvement programming analyst Planning and Econ. Devel. Dept., State of Hawaii, 1964-71; chief fiscal analyst Office of Coun. Svcs., City Coun., Honolulu, 1971-91, mgmt. analyst, 1991—; owner, operator McCully Apts., Honolulu, 1976—. Home: 1925 Nehoa Pl Honolulu HI 96822-3069 Office: Office of City Clk 530 S King St Rm 100 Honolulu HI 96813

MURAKAMI, TOSHIO, bishop. Bishop Buddhists Chs. Can., Vancouver, B.C. Office: Buddhist Chs Can, 220 Jackson Ave, Vancouver, BC Canada V6A 3B3

MURANAKA, ALLEN TOKUO, electrical engineer; b. Honolulu, Apr. 8, 1956; s. Roy and Alice (Tanabe) M. BS, U. Hawaii, 1983. Registered profl. engr., Calif., Hawaii. Engr. in tng. Toft Mass Farrow Assocs., Honolulu, 1984-85; engr. Douglas V. MacMahon Ltd., Honolulu, 1986-88, Albert S.C. Chong and Assocs., Honolulu, 1988-89, Engring. Svcs., Honolulu, 1989, Ronald N.S. Ho & Assocs., Honolulu, 1989—.

MURAOKA, DENNIS DEAN, economics educator; b. Santa Barbara, Calif., Nov. 9, 1952; s. Masa and Leora Violet (Macomber) M.; m. Mildred Meredith McKittrick, Dec. 18, 1976. BA, U. Calif., Santa Barbara, 1974, MA, 1976, PhD, 1981. Adminstrv. analyst City of Oxnard, Calif., 1975-79; lectr. Ventura (Calif.) Coll., 1977-80, Oxnard Coll., 1977-80, U. Calif., Santa Barbara, 1979-90, Santa Barbara City Coll., 1979-83; rsch. assoc. Community Orgn. and Rsch. Inst., Santa Barbara, 1980; prof. Calif. State U., Long Beach, 1981—. Co-author: Offshore Lands, 1985; author: (software) Microeconomics Study Wizard Version 1, 1990, Version 2, 1992; Macroeconomics Study Wizard Version 1, 1990, Version2, 1992; contbr. articles to profl. jours. Mem. Sigma Xi. Home: 129 Loureyro Rd Santa Barbara CA 93108 Office: Calif State U Dept Econs Long Beach CA 90840

MURDOCH, WILLIAM RICHARD, television and radio executive; b. Salt Lake City, Oct. 19, 1931; s. David L. and Ora M. (Clark) M.; B.S., U. Utah, 1957; m. Arthel Wilkins, June 11, 1953; children—Deborah, Alison, Rosemary, Matthew. With KSL-TV, Salt Lake City, 1950—, v.p. sales and mktg., 1978-82, v.p., sta. mgr., gen. sales mgr., 1982-86, v.p., gen. mgr., 1986; exec. v.p., gen. mgr. KSL-TV & Radio, 1992—; adv. bd. CBS Affiliates, 1986—, exec. v.p., gen. mgr., 1989-92; chmn. satelite com., mem. govt. relations com.; faculty U. Utah, Salt Lake City, 1963-64. Pres., Forest Meadow Landowners Assn., 1974-78; v.p. Pine and Forest Meadow Landowners Assn., 1980-84; bd. dirs. Salt Lake City chpt. ARC, 1980—; bishop Mormon Ch., 1968-73, mem. High Council, 1966-68, 74-79. Served with U.S. Army, 1953-55; Korea. Mem. Sales and Mktg. Execs. Of Utah (pres. 1978-79), Salt Lake City C. of C. Republican. Clubs: Univ., Salt Lake Ad. Office: Sta KSL-TV Broadcast House Salt Lake City UT 84111

MURDOCK, DAVID H., diversified company executive; b. Kansas City, Apr. 10, 1923; m. Maria Ferrer, Apr., 1992. LLD (hon.), Pepperdine U., 1978; LHD (hon.), U. Nebr., 1984, Hawaii Loa Coll., 1989. Sole proprietor, chmn., chief exec. officer Pacific Holding Co., L.A.; chmn., chief exec. officer Dole Food Co. (formerly Castle & Cooke, Inc.), L.A., 1985—, also bd. dirs. Trustee Asia Soc., N.Y.C., L.A.; founder, bd. dirs. Found. for Advanced Brain Studies, L.A.; bd. visitors UCLA Grad. Sch. Mgmt.;bd. govs. Performing Arts Coun. of Music Ctr., L.A.; bd. govs. East-West Ctr., L.A.; patron of opera Met. Opera, N.Y.C. With USAAC, 1943-45. Mem. Regency Club (founder, pres.) Bel-Air Bay Country Club, Sherwood Country Club (founder, pres.), Met. Club (N.Y.C.). Office: Dole Food Co Inc 31355 Oak Crest Westlake Village CA 91361 also: Pacific Holding Co 10900 Wilshire Blvd Ste 1600 Los Angeles CA 90024*

MURDOCK, DENIS RAY, management consultant; b. Oakland, Calif., Feb. 14, 1948; s. Nymphas Carl and Lillian Wanda (Roberts) M.; m. Jennie Sue Mangum, May 24, 1972; children: Joseph, Esther, Rebekah, Christopher, April, Jessica. BA in Humanities, Brigham Young U., 1974. Owner Murdock's Autobody, Pleasant Grove, Utah, 1973-77; founder, pres. Mountainwest Security Systems, Salt Lake City, 1977-80; gen. staff officer U.S. Army Logistics Ctr., Fort Lee, Va., 1981-82; br. mgr. Robert Jameson & Assocs., Virginia Beach, Va., 1983; chmn., chief exec. officer, pres. The Murdock Group, Inc., Virginia Beach and Salt, Lake City, 1983—; CEO Sports Mgmt., Inc., 1992—; assoc. Econ. Devel. Corp. of Utah, 1992—. Author: What Shape Is Your Parachute In? The Fastest Way to Land a Better Job, 1988, Logex Executive Summary, 1982, numerous instrnl. materials. State del. Rep. party, Salt Lake City, 1976, county del., Orem, Utah, 1990. Maj. USAR, 1966-87. Recipient full tuition scholarship Brigham Young U., Provo, 1966. Mem. Salt Lake City Area C. of C. Republicn. LDS Ch. Home: 9595 S Tarbert Salt Lake City UT 84065 Office: The Murdock Group 5295 S 300 W Ste 475 Salt Lake City UT 84107-4764

MURDOCK, PAMELA ERVILLA, wholesale travel company executive, retail travel company executive; b. Los Angeles, Dec. 3, 1940; d. John James and Chloe Conger (Keefe) M.; children—Cheryl, Kim. BS, U. Colo., 1962. Pres., Dolphin Travel, Denver, 1972-87; owner, pres. Mile Hi Tours, Denver, 1974—, MH Internat., 1987—, Mile-Hi Advt. Agy., 1986— . Named Wholesaler of Yr., Las Vegas Conv. and Visitors Authority, 1984. Mem. NAFE, Am. Soc. Travel Agts., Colo. Assn. Commerce and Industry, Nat. Fedn. Independent Businessmen. Republican. Home: 5565 E Vassar Ave Denver CO 80222-6239 Office: Mile Hi Tours Inc 2120 S Birch St Denver CO 80222-5043

MURDOCK, STEVEN KENT, business consulting executive, consultant; b. Ogden, Utah, May 5, 1946; s. Dell C. and Thea (Johns) M.; divorced; children: Margaret, Kristina, Chanon; stepchildren: Mike, Paul, Lena. AA, Shasta Coll., 1970; BS in Gen. Bus., U. Ariz., 1973; postgrad., U. Calif., Irvine, 1973-74, UCLA, 1975-76, Calif. State U., 1979-80; teaching cert., U. Calif., Berkeley, 1989. Retail fin. mgr. Montgomery Ward's, Sak's Fifth Ave., Amfac Retail Group, 1969-77; mng. ptnr. M & M Bus. Svcs., 1977-81; pres., CEO, sr. cons. Bus. Inc., 1981—. Author: Entrepreneurs How to Manual, 1981, Entrepreneurial Start Ups, How to Have Longevity, 1982, How to Start and Manage Your Own Small Business, 1989, rev. edit. 1991, Business Directory of Illness and Injury Prevention (manual), 1991. Cofounder We the People, 1981; mem. Rowell Ranch Rodeo Assn., 1982, sec., 1987-89; treas. Eden Hosp. Found., 1986; bd. dirs. Boys Club of Castro Valley, 1981. With USMC, 1965-68. Named Boss of the Yr., 1977, Businessman of the Yr., Castro Valley, 1986; nominated for Small Bus. Assn. Advocate of the Yr., 1989, Entrepreneur of Yr., 1991, Smart award for Edn., 1992. Mem. Castro Valley C. of C. (pres. 1982), Dublin C. of C., Pleasanton C. of C., Livermore C. of C., Rotary (pres. Castro Valley chpt. 1986, dist. officer 1989—, Paul Harris fellow, benefactor). Home: 6421 Sunnyslope Ave Castro Valley CA 94552-9704 Office: 7567 Amador Valley Blvd Ste 105 Dublin CA 94568-2442

MURDOCK, VERONICA, television executive; b. San Gabriel, Calif., Apr. 22, 1963; d. Joseph Bernard and Tina (Scinocca) Nocero; m. William James Murdock, July 22, 1989. BA in Broadcast Journalism, U. So. Calif., L.A., 1985, BA in History, 1985. Mgr. of scheduling Schulman Video, Hollywood, Calif., 1985-86; dir. of scheduling The Post Group, Hollywood, 1986-91; ind. TV producer, freelance post-prodn. supr. The Post Group, Redondo Beach, Calif., 1991—; v.p. prodn. Digital Magic, Santa Monica, Calif., 1992—; pres., CEO Magic Image Films subs. Digital Magic, Santa Monica, Calif., 1993—. Mem. Olympic Marching Band, Summer Olympics, L.A., 1984, Rep. Nat. Com.; pres. Trojan Jr. Aux. U. So. Calif., L.A., 1990. Mem. Women in Communications, Am. Film Inst., Women in Show Bus. (exec. v.p. ways and means 1988—, bd.-mem.-at-large 1991—, Woman of the Yr. 1991), Women in Film, Acad. TV Arts Scis., Sigma Delta Chi. Republican. Roman Catholic. Home and Office: 2721 N Myers St Burbank CA 91504 also: Digital Magic 3000 W Olympic Blvd Santa Monica CA 90404

MURGUIA, JOAQUIN FLORENTINO, agricultural company executive, controller; b. Firebaugh, Calif., Oct. 12, 1958; s. Jose Guadalupe Murguia and Sally Delfina (Ayala) Juarez; m. Susan Marie Schroeder, May 16, 1981; children: Teresa Maria, David Joaquin. Student, Bakersfield Coll., 1976-77. Enrolled agt. IRS. Bookkeeper United Farm Workers Am., Keene, Calif., 1977-79; bookkeeper, tax preparer Roger Duran & Co., Yucca Valley, Calif., 1980-82; acctg. asst. Desert Hot Springs (Calif.) County Water Dist., 1982-84; sr. acct., tax preparer Tenen, Cooper & Co., CPAs, Palm Springs, Calif.,

1984-89; contr. Sun and Sands Enterprises, Coachella, Calif., 1989—. Mem. Agrl. Pers. Mgmt. Assn. Jehovah's Witness. Home: 8152 Joshua Ct Yucca Valley CA 92284-6189 Office: Sun and Sands Enterprises 86-695 Ave 54 Ste L Coachella CA 92236

MURIAN, RICHARD MILLER, book company executive; b. East St. Louis, Ill., Sept. 17, 1937; s. Richard Miller Jr. and Margaret Keyes (Gregory) M.; m. Judith Lee, Aug. 11, 1961 (dec. Apr. 1992); 1 child, Jennifer Ann. BA, U. Calif., Davis, 1969; MLS, U. Calif., Berkeley, 1972; MA, Calif. State U., Sacramento, 1975; MDiv, Trinity Evang., 1977. Cert. history instr., libr. sci. instr., Calif. History reader Calif. State U., Sacramento, 1965-66; history reader U. Calif., Davis, 1966-68, philosophy researcher, 1968-69; bibliographer Argus Books, Sacramento, 1970-71; rsch. dir. Nat. Judical Coll., Reno, 1971-72; libr. Calif. State U., Sacramento, 1972-76; tv talk show host Richard Murian Show, L.A., 1979-80; pres. Alcuin Books, Ltd., Phoenix, 1981—; bd. mem. Guild of Ariz. Antiquarian Books; pres. East Valley Assn. Evangs., Mesa, Ariz., 1984-86. Contbr. articles to profl. jours. Active U. Calif. Riverside Libr., 1981-83, KAET (PBS), 1988—, Ariz. State U., 1989—. Recipient Sidney B. Mitchell fellowship U. Calif., Berkeley, 1971. Mem. Phi Kappa Phi. Democrat. Presbyterian. Office: Alcuin Books Ltd 115 W Camelback Rd Phoenix AZ 85013

MURILLO, VELDA JEAN, social worker, counselor; b. Miller, S.D., Dec. 8, 1943; d. Royal Gerald and Marion Elizabeth (Porter) Matson; m. Daniel John Murillo, June 25, 1967 (div. Dec. 1987); 1 child, Damon Michael. BS, S.D. State U., 1965; MA, Calif. State U., Bakersfield, 1980. Cert. marriage, family and child counselor. Social worker adult svcs. Kern County Dept. Welfare, Bakersfield, 1965-78, social worker child protective svcs., 1978-84; asst. coord. sexual abuse program Kern County Dist. Atty., Bakersfield, 1985-91, coord. sexual abuse program, 1991—; Mem. Calif. Sexual Assault Investigators, 1982-84, Kern Child Abuse Protection Coun., Bakersfield, 1982-84; co-developer, presenter Children's Self Help Project, Bakersfield, 1982-87; cons. mem. Sexual Assault Adv. Com., Bakersfield, 1991—. Mem. Soroptimist Internat. Democrat. Home: 114 Spruce St Bakersfield CA 93304 Office: Kern County Dist Atty 1415 Truxtun Ave Bakersfield CA 93301

MURKOWSKI, FRANK HUGHES, senator; b. Seattle, Mar. 28, 1933; s. Frank Michael and Helen (Hughes) M.; m. Nancy R. Gore, Aug. 28, 1954; children: Carol Victoria Murkowski Sturgulewski, Lisa Ann Murkowski Martell, Frank Michael, Eileen Marie Murkowski Van Wyhe, Mary Catherine Murkowski Judson, Brian Patrick. Student, Santa Clara U., 1952-53; BA in Econs, Seattle U., 1955. With Pacific Nat. Bank of Seattle, 1957-58, Nat. Bank of Alaska, Anchorage, 1959-67; asst. v.p., mgr. Nat. Bank of Alaska (Wrangell br.), 1963-66; v.p. charge bus. devel. Nat. Bank of Alaska, Anchorage, 1966-67; commr. dept. econ. devel. State of Alaska, Juneau, 1967-70; pres. Alaska Nat. Bank, Fairbanks, 1971-80; mem. U.S. Senate from Alaska, Washington, Alaska, 1981—, Com. on Energy and Natural Resources, Com. on Fgn. Rels.; ranking Rep. mem. Com. on Vets. Affairs; mem. Select Com. on Indian Affairs; Former v.p. B.C. and Alaska Bd. Trade; Rep. nominee for U.S. Congress from Alaska, 1970. Former v.p. B.C. and Alaska Bd. Trade. Served with USCGR, 1955-57. Mem. Am. Legion, Polish Legion Am. Vets., AMVETS, Ducks Unltd., NRA, Res. Officer's Assn., Army-Navy Club, Pioneers of Alaska, Tower Club, Shilla Club, Internat. Alaska Nippon Kai, Capital Hill Club, Alaska Geographic Soc., Army Athletic Club, Alaska World Affairs Coun., Congl. Staff Club, AAA, Fairbanks Hist. Preservation Found., Coalition Am. Vets., Alaska Native Brotherhood, Diamond Athletic Club, Nat. Wildlife Fedn., Nat. Mining Hall of Fame, Naval Athletic Assn., Am. Bankers Assn, Alaska Bankers Assn. (pres. 1973), Young Pres.'s Orgn., Alaska C. of C. (pres. 1977), Anchorage C. of C. (dir. 1966), B.C. C. of C., Fairbanks C. of C. (dir. 1973-78). Clubs: Elks, Lions, Washington Athletic. Office: US Senate 706 Hart Senate Bldg Washington DC 20510

MUROTAKE, THOMAS HISASHI, emergency medicine technologist; b. Denison, Iowa, July 30, 1955; s. Thomas Hisashi and Nancy May (Morrow) M. EMT. Store mgr. Radio Shack, Van Nuys, Calif., 1980-81; EMT Snyder Ambulance, Van Nuys, Calif., 1981; sales mgr. Radio Shack, Canoga Park, Calif., 1981-82; teletype operator Credit Reports Inc., West L.A., 1982-83; EMT Event Med. Svcs., Los Alamitos, Calif., 1989—; platoon sgt. emergency treatment NCO CoC, 240th Support Bn., Calif. Army Nat. Guard, Long Beach, Calif., 1989—; corp. support svcs. mgr. Informative Rsch., Garden Grove, Calif., 1983—; notary public State of Calif., 1990—. Author: Recollections, 1991, Collected Works, 1991. Vol. EMT Maryland City (Md.) Vol. Fire Dept., 1978-80, asst. publicity chmn. 1979-80. With U.S. Army, 1973-80. Recipient Calif. Commendation medal State of Calif. Mil. Dept., 1991; named Non-Commd. Officer of the Yr., 240th Support Bn., 1991. Mem. Nat. Notary Assn., Am. Legion. Republican. Episcopalian. Home: PO Box 2463 Garden Grove CA 92642 Office: Informative Rsch Ste #220 13030 Euclid St Garden Grove CA 92643

MURPHEY, ROBERT WILLIAM, publishing company executive, educator; b. Oakland, Calif., Oct. 30, 1933; s. John Patrick and Alice Julia (Knudsen) M.; m. Kay Louise Wandmaker, Apr. 13, 1957; children: Diane Murphey Henderson, Karen Murphey George, Maureen Murphey Kuck, John. AA, Coll. San Mateo, 1954; BA, San Jose State U., 1956, MS in Bus. Adminstrn., 1957; postgrad., Iowa State U., 1964. Mgmt. position Pacific Bell Co., Oakland and San Francisco, Calif., 1957-65; dist. mgr. Pacific Bell Co., San Diego, 1965-85; owner, pub. Fireside Pubs., San Diego, 1984—; mem. faculty Chapman Coll., San Diego, 1986-88, assoc. prof., 1988—; mem. faculty Grossmont/Cuyamaca Coll., El Cajon, Calif., 1986-90, Southwestern Coll., Chula Vista, Calif., 1986-87. Author: Methods and Procedures of Handling Employee Grieviences, 1957. Pres. Home of Guiding Hands, Lakeside, Calif., 1972-74, Home of Guilding Hands Found., 1975; 1st v.p. Cystic Fibrosis, San Diego, 1985; officer Grossmont Coll. Acad. Senate, 1988-90; bd. dirs. Friends of San Diego Pub. Libr. Mem. Friends of San Diego Pub. Libr. (life), Navy League (life), Am.'s Finest City Dixieland Jazz Soc., Pi Kappa ALpha (pres. alumni 1957). Republican. Lutheran. Home and Office: 6490 Lake Shore Dr San Diego CA 92119-2528

MURPHY, ARNOLD LEO, printing company executive; b. North Little Rock, Ark., Oct. 24, 1925; s. Arnold Carl and Molly Wilson (Smith) M.; m. Frances Irene Bankhead, Sept. 2, 1944; children: Danny Leo, Michael Wayne, Teresa Lynn. Grad. high sch., North Little Rock. Enlisted USN, 1943, advanced through grades to t/sgt., 1952, sonar operator, 1943-46; B-26 gunner USAF, Korea, 1950-51; B-36 gunner USAF, Ft. Worth, 1951-52; weapons maintenance supt. USAF, Laon, France, 1952-56, Oxnard, Calif., 1956-61; founder, pres. M & N Printing, Inc., Oxnard, 1961—; chief bookkeeper Bank of Am., Compton, Calif., 1947-50; pres., chmn. Acme Addressing, Inc., 1980—. Author: Pictorial History of Ventura County, 1977, Comprehensive Story of Ventura County, 1978. Holder various offices Pleasant Valley Baptist Ch., 1958-80. Recipient 5 Air medals USAF, Korea, 1950-51, Presdl. citation Pres. Truman, 1951, Korean Presdl. citation Pres. Rhee, 1951, 4 Battle Stars USAF, Korea, 1950-51. Mem. El Rio Lions Club (pres. 1962), Am. Legion. Home: 4828 Burson Way Oxnard CA 93030 Office: M & N Printing Inc 174 Lambert St Oxnard CA 93030

MURPHY, FRANCIS SEWARD, journalist; b. Portland, Oreg., Sept. 9, 1914; s. Francis H. and Blanche (Livesay) M.; BA, Reed Coll., 1936; m. Clare Eastham Cooke, Sept. 20, 1974. With The Oregonian, Portland, 1936-79, TV editor, Behind the Mike columnist, 1952-79. Archeol. explorer Mayan ruins, Yucatan, Mex., 1950—, mem. Am. Quintana Roo Expdn., 1965, 66, 68. With AUS, 1942-46. Author: Dragon Mask Temples in Central Yucatan, 1988. Mem. Royal Asiatic Soc., City Club (bd. govs. 1950, 64-66), Explorers Club, Am. Club of Hong Kong. Democrat. Congregationalist. Home: 4213 NE 32nd Ave Portland OR 97211 also: 4-B Block 8, Borrett Mansions 8B Bowen Rd, Hong Kong Hong Kong

MURPHY, FRANKLIN DAVID, physician, educator, publisher; b. Kansas City, Mo., Jan. 29, 1916; s. Franklin E. and Cordelia (Brown) M.; m. Judith Joyce Harris, Dec. 28, 1940; children: Joyce Murphy Dickey, Martha (Mrs. Craig Crockwell), Carolyn (Mrs. Ross Speer), Franklin. A.B., U. Kans., 1936; M.D., U. Pa., 1941. Diplomate: Am. Bd. Internal Medicine. Intern Hosp. U. Pa., 1941-42, instr., 1942-44; instr. medicine U. Kans., 1946-48, dean Sch. Medicine, assoc. prof. medicine, 1948-51, chancellor, 1951-60; chancellor UCLA, 1960-68; chmn. bd., CEO Times Mirror Co., 1968-81, chmn. exec. com., 1981-86; trustee emeritus J. Paul Getty Trust; dir. emeritus Times-Mirror Co. Chmn. Kress Found., Nat. Gallery of Art.; trustee Los Angeles County Mus. Art. Served to capt. AUS, 1944-46. Named One of Ten Outstanding Young Men U.S. Jr. C. of C., 1949; recipient Outstanding Civilian Service award U.S. Army, 1967. Fellow A.C.P.; mem. Phi Beta Kappa, Sigma Xi, Alpha Omega Alpha, Beta Theta Pi, Nu Sigma Nu. Episcopalian. Home: 419 Robert Ln Beverly Hills CA 90210-2631 Office: Times Mirror Co Times Mirror Sq Los Angeles CA 90053

MURPHY, JACQUELINE ADELL, environmentalist, chemist; b. Boykins, Va., Oct. 2, 1948; d. Rufus Roy and Lois (Ricks) M.; m. Scott Haven Bergeson, Jan. 10, 1987. BS in Chemistry, Hampton (Va.) Inst., 1976; BS in Biology, Coll. of William and Mary, 1978. Analyst Dow-Badische Co., Williamsburg, Va., 1975-77; sr. analyst nuclear div. Union Carbide, Paducah, Ky., 1979-83; chemist Placers Temps., Wilmington, Del., 1985-86; toxicological technician DuPont's Stine-Haskell Lab., Wilmington, 1986-87; cons. chemist Talbot Labs., Inc., Upland, Pa., 1987-88; environ. protection specialist U.S. Army Dugway (Utah) Proving Ground, 1989-92, U.S. Bur. Reclamation, 1992—. Pres. Dugway Women's Club, 1989. Mem. Am. Chem. Soc. LDS. Home: 1990 S 2100 E Salt Lake City UT 84108-3179 Office: US Bur Reclamation Upper Colo Regional Office 125 South St Salt Lake City UT 84147

MURPHY, JAMES JEROME, language educator; b. San Jose, Calif., Sept. 9, 1923; s. James Joseph and Marie Therese (Utzerath) M.; m. Kathleen Margaret Woods, Feb. 7, 1948; children: Sheila Maureen, Brian Robert. BA, St. Mary's Coll., Moraga, Calif., 1947; MA, Stanford U., 1950, PhD, 1957. Journalist UPI, San Francisco, 1947-48; tchr. St. Peter's High Sch., San Francisco, 1948-50; instr. St. Mary's Coll., Moraga, 1950-53; asst. prof. Stanford (Calif.) U., 1954-59, Princeton (N.J.) U., 1959-65; assoc. prof., prof. U. Calif., Davis, 1965-91, prof. emeritus; vice chancellor, U. Calif., Davis, 1968-69, assoc. dean, 1972-75, dept. chair, 1966-71, 75-87; pub. Hermagoras Press, Davis, 1983—. Author: Rhetoric in the Middle Ages, 1974 (recipient Yes award 1975); editor: (founding) Rhetorica: A Journal of the History of Rhetoric, 1982-87, (book) Renaissance Eloquence, 1983, numerous others. Served to Major USAF, 1943-45, ETO. Recipient Benemerenti medal Pope John Paul II, 1979, Palmes Academiques Govt. of France, 1987; Am. Coun. Learned Socs. fellow, 1971-72; grantee NEH. Mem. MLA, Internat. Soc. History of Rhetoric (treas. 1989-93), Medieval Acad. Am. (chair nominating com. 1989-90, Speech Communication Assn., Medieval Assn. Pacific (founding chmn. 1966-70). Office: Univ of Calif Dept Rhetoric and Communication Davis CA 95616

MURPHY, JAMES LAWSON, music educator; b. Greenville, S.C., Jan. 30, 1951; s. Marion Wales and Clyde (Morgan) M.; m. Karen Joyce Antolick, May 29, 1973; 1 child, Bethany. MusB, Stetson U., 1973; MusM, Southwestern Sem., 1976; PhD, Tex. Tech U., 1980. Entertainer Walt Disney World, Orlando, Fla., 1973; choral dir. DeLand High Sch., Fla., 1973; asst. prof. music Wayland Bapt. U., Plainview, Tex., 1976-81; chmn. dept. music Temple Jr. Coll., Tex., 1981-87; Esther Becker Simplot prof., chmn. dept. music, chmn. Div. Performing and Fine Arts Coll. Idaho (name changed to Albertson Coll. Idaho), Caldwell, 1987-93; chair dept. music Fort Hays (Kans.) State U., 1993—; choral clinician, various sch. choirs, Tex., 1981-87, Idaho, 1987—. Author: The Choral Music of Halsey Stevens, 1980; contbr. music rev. articles and commentaries to profl. jours. including Idaho Statesman, 1988—; composer various works for miscellaneous media, 1971—. Choir dir., various chs., S.E. U.S., 1970—; bd. dirs. Plainview Civic Theater, 1980, Central Tex. Orchestral Soc., Temple, 1981-83, Community Concert Assn., Temple, 1983-85, Caldwell Fine Arts Series, 1987-91; artistic dir., condr. Boise Master Chorale, 1990—, Boise River Festival Grand Chorale, 1991—; chair Idaho Alliance for Arts Edn., 1990-92,. Named one of Outstanding Young Men Am., U.S. Jaycees, 1980; named Best Actor 1980-81, Plainview Civic Theater, 1981; Tex. Gen. Bapt. Conv. fellow Tex. Tech U., 1977. Mem. Coll. Music Soc. (life), Nat. Assn. Tchrs. Singing, Nat. Assn. Schs. Music, Am. Choral Dirs. Assn. (state chmn. com. for music in jr. colls., gen. chair N.W. honors choir 1990), Tex. Music Educators Assn., Tex. Choral Dirs. Assn., Tex. Assn. Music Schs. (acad. standards commn. 1982-85, dir. 2-yr. schs. 1985-88), Idaho Alliance for Arts Edn. (bd. dirs., chair elect 1988-90, chmn. 1990—, Idaho Music Educators Assn. (govt. rels. chair 1988-89, tech. chair 1989—, bd. dirs.), N.W . Am. Guild Organists (conv. choir dir, clinician 1990), Music Educators Nat. Conf., Idaho Humanities Coun. Speakers Bur., Phi Mu Alpha Sinfornia, Omicron Delta Kappa. Presbyterian. Avocations: travel, photography, tennis, golf. Home: 304 W 40th St Hays KS 67601 Office: Ft Hays State U Dept Music Hays KS 67601

MURPHY, LAWRENCE MARTIN, mechanical engineer; b. Indpls., Dec. 2, 1941; s. Lawrence Stephen and Boniface Marie M.; m. Elonka Kozare, Feb. 19, 1966; children: Timothy Martin, Laura Colleen. BS, U. Notre Dame, 1964, MS, 1966, PhD, 1968. Registered profl. engr., Calif. Mem. tech. staff Sandia Nat. Labs., Livermore, Calif., 1968-77; office mgr. Calif. Energy Commn., Sacramento, Calif., 1977-79; group mgr. Nat. Renewable Energy Lab., Golden, Colo., 1979-85; br. mgr. Nat. Renewable Energy Lab., 1985-89, div. dir., 1989-92, assoc. dep. dir., 1992—; adj. prof. U. Colo., 1983-84. Inventor tensioning device, solar collector, tensioned module, energy conversion system, center post design; contbr. numerous articles to profl. jours. Coach Youth Soccer, Livermore/Sacramento, 1973-76, 78; pres., mem. H.S. Soccer Club, Wheatridge H.S., Colo., 1983-84; co-pres. (K-12) Applewood Swim Club, Lakewood, Colo., 1984. Recipient Outstanding Achievement award Solar Energy Rsch. Inst., 1984, Exceptional Performances awards. Fellow ASME (numerous svc. award, SED exec. com. 1985-89, chmn. 1988, energy com. 1990—); mem. Sigma Xi, Tau Beta Pi. Office: Nat Renewable Energy Lab 1617 Cole Blvd Golden CO 80401-3305

MURPHY, MARY ANN, human services administrator; b. Salt Lake City, Feb. 13, 1943; d. Wallace L. and Irene (Hummer) Matlock; m. Robert A. Glatzer, Dec. 31, 1977; children: Gabriela, Jessica, Nicholas. BA, U. Wash., 1964; MS, Ea. Wash. U., 1975. House counselor Ryther Child Ctr., Seattle, 1966-67; tchr. presch. Head Start, L.A. and Seattle, 1967-70; tchr. presch. Children's Orthopedic Hosp., Seattle, 1970-71, Washington, 1971-72; mem. faculty Ea. Wash. U., Cheney, 1973-82; exec. dir. Youth Help Assn., Spokane, Wash., 1983-88; mgr. regional ctr. for child abuse and neglect Deaconess Med. Ctr., Spokane, 1988—; pres. Wash. State Alliance for Children, Youth & Families, Seattle, 1985-87; chair Gov.'s Juvenile Justice Adv. Commn., Olympia, Wash., 1987—, Spokane Prevention of Child Abuse and Neglect Coun., Spokane, 1988—. Bd. dirs. Vols. of Am., Spokane, 1985—. Named Outstanding Women Leader in Health Care YWCA, 1992. Home: 1950 W Clarke Ave Spokane WA 99201-1306 Office: Deaconess Med Ctr 800 W 5th Ave Spokane WA 99204-2796

MURPHY, MICHAEL ANSELL, optician; b. Salt Lake City, May 12, 1943; s. M. Warner and Coralee (Ansell) M.; m. Vickie P. Murphy, May 27, 1966; children: Stacy, Warner, Rhett, Megan, Lindsay. BS, Brigham Young U., 1968. Pvt. practice Provo, Utah, 1990—. Fellow Nat. Acad. of Optician's; mem. Kiwanis (pres. Timpanegos chpt. 1975-76). LDS Ch. Office: 930 N 500 W Provo UT 84604

MURPHY, PHILIP EDWARD, broadcast executive; b. Chgo., May 11, 1945; s. Edward Curtis and Mary Francis (D'Incecco) M.; m. Carol Jean Sefton, Mar. 11, 1967 (div. 1985); children: Mandy Jean, Patrick Jeffrey. BS, Ind. U., 1967. Prodn. mgr. Sta. WFIU-FM, Bloomington, Ind., 1968; news reporter, photographer, editor Sta. WTHR TV, Indpls., 1969, sr. account exec., 1970-80; account exec. Blair TV, L.A., 1980-81; pres. Am. Spot Cable Corp., Hollywood, Calif., 1981-82; v.p. tech. ops. Paramount Pictures TV, Hollywood, 1982—; spkr. film preservation, in field; advisor Libr. of Congress, Washington, Nat. Archives, Washington. Lighting designer Civic Theatre, Indpls., 1979; tech. dir. Footlite Mus., Indpls., 1970-78; bd. dirs. Cathedral Arts, Indpls., 1978-80. Mem. Internat. Platform Assn., Assn. Moving Image Archivists, Gay and Lesbian Alliance Against Defamation L.A., Hollywood Supports Assn., Soc. Motion Picture and TV Engrs., St. James' Club. Office: Paramount Pictures TV 5555 Melrose Ave Stage # 3/212 Los Angeles CA 90038-3197

MURPHY, ROBERT CARL, pharmacology educator, researcher; b. Seymour, Ind., Dec. 15, 1944; s. Carl E. and Lana L. (Fisher) M.; m. Carol A. Worthington, June 25, 1965; children—Geoffrey R., Elisabeth M. B.S., Mt. Union Coll., 1966; Ph.D., MIT, 1970. Postdoctoral fellow Med. Sch., Harvard U., Boston, 1970-71; asst. prof. pharmacology Med. Sch., U. Colo., Denver, 1971-77, assoc. prof., 1977-80, prof., 1980—; vis. prof. Karolinska Institutet, Stockholm, 1978-79; cons. in field. Assoc. editor Organic Mass Spectrometry, 1972-76; editorial bd. Biomed. Mass Spectrometry, 1982-87, Brit. Jour. Pharmacology, 1987— . Contbr. numerous articles to profl. jours., 1967—. Recipient Research Career Devel. award NIH, 1976-80; NIH grantee, 1973—. Mem. Am. Chem. Soc., Am. Soc. Mass Spectrometry (com. chmn. 1983-85), Am. Soc. Pharmacology and Exptl. Therapeutics, Sigma Xi. Mem. United Ch. of Christ. Office: Nat Jewish Ctr for Immunology and Respiratory Medicine 1400 Jackson St Denver CO 80206-2761

MURPHY, STEVEN PATRICK, systems engineer; b. Williamsport, Pa., Mar. 31, 1960; s. Robert H. and Shirley A. (Haas) M.; m. Jennepher A. Tate, Dec. 24, 1985; children: Daniel O., Chandra A. BSME with honors, Pa. State U., 1986, postgrad., 1986; student, San Diego State U., 1989—. Lic. scuba diver. Engr. Air & Environ. Studies, State College, Pa., 1985-86; systems engr. Naval Rsch., Devel., Test and Evaluation Div., San Diego, 1987—, scuba diver, 1990—; Sci. advisor Bell Jr. High Sch., San Diego, 1991, 92. Author: Over The Side Noise Localization System Update, 1987. Sgt. U.S. Army, 1978-81. Mem. IEEE, ASME. Office: Naval Office R & D Code 785 271 Catalina Blvd San Diego CA 92152-5000

MURPHY, TERESA ANN, information services executive; b. Waverly, N.Y., June 1, 1957; d. Jack Manuel Newbury and Lorraine Catherine (White) Jacobs; m. John Joseph Murphy, May 17, 1986. BSBA, Calif. State U., Hayward, 1989. Cert. mgmt. acct.; cert. data processor. Computer operator fed. systems div. IBM, Owego, N.Y., 1977; data processing controller Data Analysis Corp., Binghamton, N.Y., 1977-78; data processing coord. Am. Cancer Soc., Austin, Tex., 1979; programmer ARTESCO, Phoenix, 1980-81; computer cons. TAP Cons., San Francisco, 1981-83; MIS dir. United Coffee Corp., San Francisco, 1983-85, Marcel Schurman Co., Inc., Fairfield, Calif., 1985-89; pres. Promier, San Mateo, Calif., 1990—. Contbr. articles to profl. jours. Mem. Soroptomists, Burlingame, Calif., 1984. Mem. Nat. Assn. Accts., Am. Mgmt. Assn., Assn. Small Systems Users (co-chair standards com. 1985, dir. edn. com. 1985, pres. 1986, chmn. tech. edn. com., bd. dirs. program com. 1990—), Common Cause, LWV (unit chairperson Burlingame chpt. 1984). Democrat. Roman Catholic. Office: Promier 1670 S Amphlett Blvd Ste 308 San Mateo CA 94402-2513

MURPHY, THOMAS JOSEPH, archbishop; b. Chgo., Oct. 3, 1932; s. Barthomew Thomas and Nellie M. AB, St. Mary of the Lake Sem., 1954, STB, 1956, MA, 1957, STL, 1958, STD, 1960. Ordained priest Roman Cath. Ch., 1958. Various positions with Archdiocese of Chgo.; bishop of Great Falls-Billings Mont., 1978-87; coadjutor archbishop of Seattle, 1987-91, archbishop of Seattle, 1991—. Office: Archdiocese of Seattle 910 Marion St Seattle WA 98104-1274

MURPHY, WARREN CHARLES, rector; b. Phila., May 6, 1944; s. Warren N. and Frances (Stanley) M.; m. Katharine Linde, June 24, 1977; children: Aaron, Malcolm. BA, Bridgewater Coll., 1967, MDiv, Episc. Grad. Sch., 1972; cert., St. George's Coll., Jerusalem, 1987. Community organizer VISTA, Buffalo and Lackawanna, N.Y., 1967-68; legis. asst. U.S. Sen. Birch Bayh, Washington, 1970-71; exec. dir., founder Compass House, Buffalo, 1972-75; dir. community rels. Cambridge (Mass.) Econ. and Opportunity Commn., 1975-76; rector Little Snake River Episc. Ch., Dixon, Wyo., 1977-82, Trinity Episc. Ch., Lander, Wyo., 1982-89, Christ Episc. Ch., Cody, Wyo., 1989—; rector, priest-in-charge Shoshone Episc. Ch., Ft. Washakie, Wyo., 1985-89; chair Wyo. Ch. Coalition, Laramie, 1988—; dep. Gen. Convention of Episc. Ch., Detroit, 1988, 91. Contbr. articles to newspapers, mags.; author nature booklet Under the Firmament, 1989. Bd. dirs. Ring Lake Ranch, Dubois, Wyo., 1984-90; mem. nat. adv. bd., 1990—; organizer Orgn. of Orgns., Lackawanna, 1967-68; vol. Bayh for Pres., Boston, 1976; mem. Dixon Town Coun., 1979-82; mem. psychiat. adv. bd. Pine Ridge Hosp., Lander, 1984-88; bd. dirs. Crisis Intervention Ctr. of Cody, 1991—, Wyo. Coun. for the Humanities, 1993—. Diocese of Wyo. grantee, 1987. Mem. Cody Ministerial Assn. Office: Christ Episc Ch 825 Simpson Ave # 1718 Cody WY 82414-4140

MURRAY, FRANCIS WILLIAM, meteorologist; b. San Antonio, July 29, 1921; s. John Patrick Murray and Mary Myrtle (Clark) Murray Foulke; m. Grace Elizabeth McConnaughey, Aug. 28, 1954 (dec. Sept. 1983); 1 child, John. B.A., U. Tex., 1941; M.A., UCLA, 1948; Ph.D., MIT, 1960. Enlisted U.S. Army Air Force, 1942, advanced through grades to lt. col. U.S. Air Force, 1961; served as weather officer, ret., 1963; sr. scientist Douglas Aircraft Co., Santa Monica, Calif., 1963-66; sr. phys. scientist Rand Corp., Santa Monica, 1966-86, resident cons., 1987—; rsch. assoc. UCLA, 1981-84; lectr. UCLA, 1974. Contbr. articles to profl. jours. Recipient Merewether award Air Weather Service, 1961. Fellow Royal Meteorol. Soc.; mem. Am. Meteorol. Soc. (Los Angeles chpt. Achievement award 1979), Am. Geophys. Union. Presbyterian. Home: 857 Toyopa Dr Pacific Palisades CA 90272-3728 Office: Rand Corp 1700 Main St Santa Monica CA 90406

MURRAY, J(AMES) EDWARD, retired newspaper editor, publisher; b. Buffalo, S.D., Apr. 16, 1915; s. George Edward and Eleanor Lillian (Burshek) M.; m. Miriam Irene Virtanen, Dec. 6, 1940; children: Judith Michaela, James Virtanen. BA in Philosophy, Journalism, U. Nebr., 1938, LLD (hon.), 1974. Reporter UPI, Chgo., 1938-42; war corr., fgn. corr. UPI, London, Rome, Paris, 1943-48; mng. editor L.A. Mirror, 1948-60, Ariz. Republic, Phoenix, 1960-71; assoc. editor, editor Knight News Svc. Detroit Free Press, 1971-75; pres., pub. Daily Camera, Boulder, Colo., 1976-82; ret., 1982. pres. AP Mng. Editors Assn., 1961, Am. Soc. Newspaper Editors, 1972-73; lectr., cons., trainer Nepal, India, Bangladesh, Indonesia, Sri Lanka, Malaysia, New Guinea, Philippines, Fiji, Turkey, Nigeria, Sierra Leone, Kenya, 1982—; lectr. for World Press Freedom Com., Internat. Exec. Svc. Corps., U.S. Info. Svc., Ctr. Fgn. Journalists, Asia Found., East-West Ctr. Recipient John Peter Zenger award for freedom of press U. Ariz., Tucson, 1969. Democrat. Unitarian.

MURRAY, JAMES PATRICK, newspaper columnist; b. Hartford, Conn., Dec. 29, 1919; s. James and Molly (O'Connell) M.; m. Geraldine Norma Brown, Oct. 30, 1945 (dec. Apr. 1984); children: Theodore, Anthony, Pamela, Eric (dec.). AB, Trinity Coll., Hartford, 1943, LittD honoris causa, 1981; LLD honoris causa, Pepperdine U., 1987. Mem. staff New Haven Register, 1943, Los Angeles Examiner, 1944-48, Time, Inc., 1948-61; sports columnist Los Angeles Times, 1961—. Author: The Best of Jim Murray, 1965, The Sporting World of Jim Murray, 1968, The Jim Murray Collection, 1988, Jim Murray: An Autobiography, 1993. Recipient Sportswriter of Yr. award Nat. Assn. Sportscasters and Sportswriters, 1964, 66-77, 79, Headliners Club award, 1965, 76, Alumni medal Trinity Coll., 1972, J.G. Taylor Spink award Baseball Hall of Fame, Cooperstown, N.Y., 1988, Pulitzer prize for disting. commentary, 1990. Mem. Time-Life Alumni Assn., L.A. Press Club (v.p. 1953), PGA West Club, Riviera Country Club. Office: Los Angeles Times Times Mirror Sq Los Angeles CA 90012-3816

MURRAY, JOAN NINA, real estate agent; b. Pueblo, Colo., Dec. 10, 1938; d. Theodore and Sarah (Martino) Iacabone; m. Jesse M. Murray, Apr. 29, 1961; children: Jessica Murray Lancaster, Theodore. BA, Colo. State Coll., 1959, MA, 1962, EdS, 1967. Psychologist Sch. Dist. 60, Pueblo, Colo., 1969—; in-svc. coord. Pueblo, 1975-77; real estate broker Century 21 Summit Realty, Buena Vista, Colo., 1977-82; agt. N.Y. Life Ins. Co., Buena Vista, 1982-93, Believers Realty, Pueblo, Colo., 1993—. Recipient scholarship Colo. State Coll., 1956, Colo. State Merit award, Pi Omega Pi, 1959, Phi Lamda Theta, 1971. Mem. Colo. Assn. for Children with Learning Disabilities, AAUW, Cath. Woman's Orgn., Daughters of Isabella, Delta Gamma, Phi Delta Kappa. Democrat. Home: 27636 County Rd 340 Buena Vista CO 81211-9740 Office: Believers Realty 601 Court Pueblo CO 81003

MURRAY, JOHN B., prevention technology company executive; b. Palo Pinto, Tex., Nov. 8, 1943; s. John Thomas and Myrtle Francis (Darnell) M.; m. Patricia Jean McCormick, Jan. 22, 1966; children: Josh, Jason. Student, Moorpark Coll., 1976. Cert. profl. cons.; cert. protection profl. State traffic officer Calif. Hwy. Patrol, L.A., 1971-78; detective Lane County Sheriff's Office, Eugene, Oreg., 1978-81; asst. dir. loss prevention Jay Jacobs Inc., Seattle, 1981-86; dir. loss prevention Sprouse-Reitz Stores Inc., Portland, Oreg., 1986-92; pres. Prevention Technology Assocs., Beaverton, Oreg.,

1992—. Scoutmaster Boy Scouts Am., Beaverton, 1986-89. With USAF, 1962-70, Vietnam, Greece. Mem. N.W. Retail Loss Prevention Assn. (v.p. 1992-93). Home and Office: 12605 SW Trigger Dr Beaverton OR 97005

MURRAY, JOHN FREDERIC, physician, educator; b. Mineola, N.Y., June 8, 1927; s. Frederic S. and Dorothy Murray; m. Diane Lain, Nov. 30, 1968; children—James R., Douglas S., Elizabeth. A.B., Stanford, 1949, M.D., 1953; D.Sc. (hon.), U. Paris, 1983. From instr. to asso. prof. medicine U. Calif. at Los Angeles, 1957-66; mem. sr. staff Cardiovascular Research Inst., U. Calif., San Francisco, 1966—; asso. prof. medicine Cardiovascular Research Inst., U. Calif. (Sch. Medicine), 1966-69, prof., 1969—; chief chest service San Francisco Gen. Hosp., 1966-89; Vis. prof. Brompton Inst. for Diseases of the Chest, London, 1972-73; Macy faculty scholar Inst. Nat. de la Santé et de la Recherche Medicale, Paris, 1979-80; mem. adv. council and pulmonary disease adv. com. Nat. Heart, Lung and Blood Inst.; mem. clin. studies panel NRC.; bd. govs. Am. Bd. Internal Medicine, Am. Bd. Emergency Medicine. Author: The Normal Lung, 1976, 2d edit., 1986; co-author: Diseases of the Chest, 4th edit., 1980; co-editor: Textbook of Respiratory Medicine, 1988; editor: Am. Rev. Respiratory Disease, 1973-79; contbr. articles to profl. jours. Served with USNR, 1945-46. Sr. Internat. fellow Fogarty Inst. Fellow Royal Coll. Physicians; mem. Assn. Am. Physicians, Am. Soc. Clin. Investigation, Am. Physiol. Soc., Western Soc. Clin. Research, Western Assn. Physicians, Am. Thoracic Soc. (pres. 1981-82), Académie Nationale de Médecine Francaise. Home: 24 Edith Pl San Francisco CA 94133 Office: U Calif PO Box 0841 San Francisco CA 94143-0841

MURRAY, PATTY, U.S. senator; b. Seattle, Wash., Oct. 11, 1950; d. David L. and Beverly A. (McLaughlin) Johns; m. Robert R. Murray, June 2, 1972; children: Randy P., Sara A. BA, Wash. State U., 1972. Sec. various cos., Seattle, 1972-76; citizen lobbyist various ednl. groups, Seattle, 1983-88; legis. lobbyist Orgn. for Parent Edn., Seattle, 1977-84; instr. Shoreline Community Coll., Seattle, 1984—; mem. Wash. State Senate, Seattle, 1989-92; U.S. senator from Washington, 1993—. Mem. bd. Shoreline Sch., Seattle, 1985-89; mem. steering com. Demonstration for Edn., Seattle, 1987; founder, chmn. Orgn. for Parent Edn., Wash., 1981-85; 1st Congl. rep. Wash. Women United, 1983-85. Recipient Recognition of Svc. to Children award Shoreline PTA Coun., 1986, Golden Acorn Svc. award, 1989; Outstanding Svc. award Wash. Women United, 1986, Outstanding Svc. to Pub. Edn. award Citizens Ednl. Ctr. NW, Seattle, 1987. Democrat. Home: 528 NW 203rd Pl Seattle WA 98177-2046 Office: US Senate Office of Senate Mems Washington DC 20510

MURRAY, WILLIAM ALOYSIUS, JR., media services administrator; b. Woodhaven, N.Y., June 29, 1927; s. William Aloysius and Fanny Alina (Hingula) M.; m. June Rose McHardy, Sept. 17, 1950; children: Coqui, Cheri, Christi, William Arthur. Student, Hofstra Coll., 1944-45; AB, MA, Colo. Coll., 1950, 64; postgrad., Denver U., 1968-77, Boston U., 1969. Cert. sch. adminstr. Tchr. Harrison Sch., Colorado Springs, 1950-51; social studies tchr. Antilles Dependent's Sch., San Juan, P.R., 1951-52; English tchr. William Smith Jr. High Sch., Aurora, Colo., 1952-54; mgr. sand mine Bay City (Wis.) Sand Co., 1954-57; secondary tchr., dir. publs. Aurora (Colo.) Pub. Schs., 1957-59, dir. community rels., 1959-70, asst. dir. audio visual publs., 1970-74, edn. specialist media, 1974-80, dir. media svc., 1980-93; cons. B&B Assocs., Aurora, 1980—; ESEA state adv. com. Colo. Dept. Edn., Denver, 1979-81; bd. dirs., pres. Ednl. Film Libr. Assn., N.Y.C., 1975-81; com. mem. chmn. Intellectual Freedom Com., Chgo., 1986-91. Editor: (book) Media Curriculum for Aurora Public Schools, 1980, 86; author: (book) Trustees Handbook, 1979, (manual) Media Manual, 1988. Mem. exec. bd., founder Interfaith Consortium for Pluralism, Denver, 1986—; bd. dirs., dist. chmn. Campfire Girls, Denver, 1968-79; bd. dirs., pres. Arapahoe Pub. Libr. Dist., Littleton, Colo., 1964-82. With USN, 1945-47. Recipient Intellectual Freedom award Assn. for Ednl. Comm. and Tech., 1987, Am. Assn. Sch. Librs., 1989, N.H. Life Mem. award PTA, 1993. Mem. Colo. Libr. Assn. (pres. 1987-88), Colo. Ednl. Media Assn. (chair IFC 1986-91, 93-94), Cen. Colo. Libr. System (pres. 1977), Phi Delta Kappa (pres. Denver U. chpt. 1978, pres. High Plains chpt. 1987, Svc. award 1978, Leadership award 1987, 93). Mem. United Ch. of Christ. Home and Office: 18011 E 14th Dr Aurora CO 80011

MURRAY, WILLIAM DANIEL, federal judge; b. Butte, Mont., Nov. 20, 1908; s. James E. and Viola E (Horgan) M.; m. Lulu Ann MacDonald, Aug. 24, 1938; children—William Daniel, Gael Ann, Timothy. B.S., Georgetown U., 1932; LL.B., U. Mont., 1936, LL.D. (hon.), 1961. Bar: Admitted Mont. bar 1936. Since practiced in Butte; partner firm of Emigh & Murray, 1936—; asst. U.S. atty., Butte, 1938-42; U.S. Dist judge Dist. Mont., 1949—, now sr. U.S. dist. judge. Former chmn. bd. visitors sch. law U. Mont.; mem. bd. regents Gonzaga U.; bd. devel. Georgetown U. Served as lt. UNR, 1942-45. Recipient Barromeo award Carroll Coll., 1960; DeSmet medal Gonzaga U., 1967. Mem. Am., Mont., Silver Bow County bar assns., Bar Assn. D.C. Democrat. Roman Catholic. Office: US Dist Ct Federal Bldg Butte MT 59701

MURREN, DOUGLAS EDWARD, pastor; b. Wenatchee, Wash., July 16, 1951; s. Virgil Edward and Gloria Mae (Humphres) M.; m. Debra Jean Landin, Mar. 27, 1971; children: Matthew Douglas, Raissa Anne. BA in Religion, Seattle Pacific U., 1973; DD (hon.), Internat. Ch. of the Foursquare Gospel, 1991. Lic. pastor Internat. Ch. Foursquare Gospel. Asst. pastor Bethesda Christian Ctr., Wenatchee, 1974-79; founding pastor Eastside Christian Communion, Bellevue, Wash., 1979-80, Eastside Foursquare Ch., Kirkland, Wash., 1981—; conf. speaker, cons. various orgns., Poland, USSR, Norway, Fed. Republic Germany, Haiti, and U.S.; adj. guest faculty Fuller Theol. and Regent Coll., Vancouver; supt. div Foursquare Gospel Ch., N. King County, Wash., 1985-91. Author: Iceman, 1986, Is It Real When It Doesn't Work?, Keeping Your Dreams Alive When They Steal Your Coat, 1993; editor Pastoral Resource, 1985-89, Baby Boomerang, 1990, Is It Real When It Doesn't Work?, 1990; host (radio show) Growing Together; columnist Ministries Today; contbr. articles to profl. jours. Office: Eastside Foursquare Ch PO Box 536 Kirkland WA 98083-0536

MURREY, THOMAS WHITELAW, JR., lawyer; b. Memphis, Oct. 29, 1959; s. Thomas Whitelaw and Betty Joyce (Evans) M.; m. Amy Margueritte Boone, Nov. 7, 1987; 1 child, Joseph Whitelaw. BA in History, Millsaps Coll., 1982; JD, Memphis State U., 1985. Bar: Tenn. 1985, U.S. Ct. Mil. Appeals 1993. Commd. 1st lt. USAF, 1986, advanced through grades to capt., 1990—, promoted to major, 1992. Mem. Heritage Found., Washington, 1989-92; sustaining sponsor Ronald Reagan Presdl. Found., Simi Valley, Calif., 1991. Mem. Am. Numismatic Assn., Tenn. Bar Assn., Federalist Soc., Kappa Alpha. Baptist. Office: QD4A USAF Trial Judiciary Lowry AFB CO 80230-5000

MURTHY, VEERARAGHAVAN KRISHNA, medical educator; b. Pudukottah, India, Feb. 27, 1934; came to U.S., 1964; naturalized citizen; s. Veeraraghavan and Lakshmi Krishnaswamy; m. Anjana Murthy, May 17, 1964 (div. 1977); children: Gayathri, Sakthi, Hari; m. Eileen Ann Hogan, May 26, 1990. BS, U. Madras, India, 1953; MS, U. Bombay, 1960, PhD, 1964. Rsch. assoc., rsch. fellow U. Fla., Gainesville, 1964-68; instr. Banting Inst., U. Toronto, Ont., Can., 1968-74; asst. prof. medicine, then assoc. prof. medicine U. Nebr. Med. Ctr., Omaha, 1974-86; assoc. adj. prof. medicine U. Calif.-San Francisco, Fresno, 1986—; rsch. investigator VA Med. Ctr./U. Calif.-San Francisco, Fresno, 1987—; prof. biology Calif. State U., Fresno, 1991—; cons. to diabetes svc. Valley Med. Ctr. Fresno, 1986—; speaker at nat. and internat. sci. confs. Author numerous rsch. publs. Fellow Royal Soc. Chemistry London; mem. Am. Diabetes Assn., Am. Physiol. Soc. Office: Diabetes Svc Valley Med Ctr 445 S Cedar Ave Fresno CA 93702-2907

MUSCARDINI, MICHAEL CARL, general contractor; b. Modesto, Calif., Sept. 15, 1950; s. John Joseph Muscardini and Theresa (Alchera) Cook; m. Robyn Richards, Sept. 4, 1971; children: Gian Carlo, Marie Kristine. BFA, Calif. Coll. Arts and Crafts, 1972. Lic. contractor. Instr. design dept. Calif. Coll. Arts and Crafts, Oakland, 1976-77; pres., owner Creative Spaces, Inc., Oakland, 1978—; co-founder Bay area bldg. community Splinter Group, 1984—. Trustee, mem. Calif. Coll. Arts and Crafts, 1992. Recipient Design Excellence award AIA, 1986, 87, Outstanding Restoration award Berkeley Archtl. Heritage Assn., 1988, 92, 93; named to Big 50 Hall of Fame Remodeling Mag., 1991. Mem. Calif. Coll. Arts and Crafts Alumni Assn. (pres. 1991—), Berkeley Archtl. Heritage Assn. (bd. dirs. 1993-). Office: Creative Spaces Inc 2500 Magnolia St Oakland CA 94607-2410

MUSCARELLA, VINCENT ALFRED, dermatologist; b. Buffalo, June 21, 1937; s. Gandolph Joseph and Rose Marie (Jelso) M.; children: Vincent Gandolph, Gregory Gustave. Student, U. Buffalo, 1955-58; MD, Loyola U., Chgo., 1962. Diplomate Am. Bd. Dermatology, Nat. Bd. Med. Examiners; cert. of spl. competency in dermatopathology Am. Bds. Dermatology and Pathology. Intern Bernalillo County Indian Hosp., Albuquerque, 1962-63; resident dermatology UCLA, 1965-68; med. dir. Albuquerque Ctr. for Dermatology, 1968—; chmn. N.Mex. Nursing Home Adminstrs. Bd., 1992—; clin. prof. U. N.Mex. Med. Sch., Hosp. Pediatric Dermatology Clinic, 1968-71; attending physician U. N.Mex. Hosp. Dermatologic Surgery Clinic, 1989—; lectr. dermatology, 1976-79; clin. adv. coun. Medicis Pharm. Corp., 1991; mem. staff Presbyn. Hosp., St. Joseph Hosp.; cons. staff Vets. Hosp. Capt. U.S. Army, 1963-65. Fellow Am. Acad. Dermatology, Pacific Dermatol. Assn., Am. Soc. Dermapathology, Am. Acad. Cosmetic Surgery, Am. Soc. Lipo-Suction Surgery, Occuloplastic Fellowship Soc.; mem. AMA, Am. Soc. Dermatologic Surgery, Soc. Investigative Dermatology, Internat. Soc. Dermatol. Surgery, Internat. Soc. Dermatopathology, Southwestern Dermatol. Soc., N.Mex. Dermatol. Soc., N.Mex. Med. Soc., Greater Albuquerque Med. Assn., Am. Acad. Facial Plastic and Reconstructive Surgery. Office: Albuquerque Ctr Dermatology 8100 Constitution Pl NE # 3100 Albuquerque NM 87110

MUSCATELLO, ANTHONY CURTIS, research chemist; b. Princeton, W.Va., Sept. 25, 1950; s. Phillip and Gloria Jean (Peyatt) M.; m. Toni Sue Larsen, Mar. 23, 1985; children: Alyse, Scott, Brian. BS in Chemistry, Concord Coll., Athens, W.Va., 1972; PhD in Inorganic Chemistry, Fla. State U., Tallahassee, 1979. Postdoctoral rsch. assoc. Argonne (Ill.) Nat. Lab., 1979-81; sr. rsch. chemist Rockwell Internat.-Rocky Flats Plant, Golden, Colo., 1981-84, rsch. specialist, 1984-88; tech. staff mem. Los Alamos (N.Mex.) Lab., 1988—; working group leader Tech. Exch. Steering Com., 1987-90. Contbr. articles to profl. jours.; inventor in field. Mem. Am. Chem. Soc., Planetary Soc. New Thought Christian. Home: 2515 W 110th Ave Westminster CO 80234 Office: Los Alamos Tech Office PO Box 4013 Bldg T130A Golden CO 80401

MUSEN, MARK ALAN, computer science educator, physician; b. Providence, Feb. 22, 1956; s. Frederick Norton and Dolores (Shechtman) M.; m. Elyse Ann Barnett, June 5, 1983; 1 child, Jay Derek. BSc in Biology, Brown U., 1977, MD, 1980; PhD in Med. Info. Scis., Stanford (Calif.) U., 1988. Intern in medicine Stanford U. Hosp., 1980-81, resident in medicine, 1981-83, Henry J. Kaiser Family Found. fellow in gen. internal medicine, 1983-87; vis. scientist dept. med. informatics Erasmus U., Rotterdam, Netherlands, 1987-88; asst. prof. medicine and computer sci. Stanford U., 1988—; head sect. on med. informatics Stanford U. Sch. Medicine, 1993—; mem. biomed. libr. rev. com. Nat. Libr. of Medicine, 1992—. Author: Automated Generation of Model-Based Knowledge Acquisition Tools, 1989; mem. editorial bd.: Knowledge Acquisition, 1989—, IEEE Expert, 1990—, Artificial Intelligence in Medicine, 1990—, Internat. Jour. of Expert Systems, 1990—, Methods of Information in Medicine, 1991, Medical Decision Making, 1992-94. Recipient NSF Young Investigator award, 1992. Fellow ACP, Am. Coll. Med. Informatics; mem. Am. Med. Informatics Assn., Am. Assn. for Artificial Intelligence, Assn. for Computing Machinery, Am. Fedn. for Clin. Rsch., Soc. for Med. Decision Making, Soc. for Clin. Trials. Home: 638 Salvatierra St Palo Alto CA 94305-8538 Office: Stanford U Sch of Medicine Sect on Med Informatics Stanford CA 94305-5479

MUSGRAVE, DAVID LESLIE, oceanographer; b. Columbus, Ohio, Jan. 17, 1952; s. Thomas William and Donna La Verne (Robbins) M.; m. Pamela Chaney, Feb. 1970 (div. Nov. 1972); m. Nancy Murphy, Dec. 31, 1990 (div. Dec. 1992). BS in Chemistry, Calif. Inst. Tech., 1974; MS in Oceanography, U. Alaska, 1978, PhD in Oceanography, 1983. Grad. asst. U. Alaska, Fairbanks, 1974-83; post doctoral scholar Woods Hole (Mass.) Oceanographic Instn., 1983-85, asst. scientist, 1985-88; asst. prof. U. Alaska, Fairbanks, 1988—. Contbr. articles to profl. jours. Treas. Common-Ground Alaska, Fairbanks, 1989-92; v.p. Nordic Ski Club Fairbanks, 1990-91, pres., 1991-92. Named Man of Distinction, Fullerton (Calif.) Jr. Coll., 1972. Mem. Am. Geophysical Union, Am. Metorological Assn., U.S. Ski Assn., Nordic Ski Club, Fairbanks Cycle Club, Sigma Xi. Office: Univ Alaska Fairbanks Inst Marine Sci Fairbanks AK 99775-1080

MUSGRAVE, RICHARD ABEL, economics educator; b. Königstein, Germany, Dec. 14, 1910; came to U.S., 1933, naturalized, 1940; s. Curt Abel and Charlotte (Pruefer) M.; m. Peggy Brewer Richman, May 7, 1964. Diploma, U. Heidelberg, 1933; MA, Harvard U., 1936, PhD, 1937; LLD (hon.), Allegheny Coll., 1980; Doktor der Wirtschaftswissenschaften honoris causa, U. Heidelberg, Fed. Republic Germany; Doctoris Oeconomiae honoris causa, Cath. U., Milan, 1989; LLD honoris causa, U. Mich., 1991. Tutor, instr. econs. Harvard, 1936-41; research economist Bd. Govs. Fed. Res. System, Washington, 1941-47; lectr. econs. Swarthmore Coll., 1947-48; prof. econs. U. Mich., 1950-59; prof. polit. economy Johns Hopkins, 1959-62; prof. econs. and pub. affairs Princeton, 1962-65; H.H. Burbank prof. polit. econ. Harvard U., faculty arts and scis. and Law Sch., 1965-81, prof. emeritus, 1981—; adj. prof. U. Calif., Santa Cruz, 1980—; chief economist Internat. Bank Mission to Columbia, 1949; chief ECA Fiscal Mission to Germany, 1951; pres. Colombian Tax Reform Commn., 1968-69; dir. Bolivian Fiscal Reform Mission, 1976-77; at various times cons. bd. govs. Fed. Res. System, Treasury Dept., Council Econ. Advisers, Commn. on Money and Credit. Author: Theory of Public Finance, 1959, Fiscal Systems, 1969, Public Finance in Theory and Practice, 1973; editor Quar. Jour. Econs., 1970-75, Public Finance in a Democratic Soc., 1986; contbr. profl. jours. Recipient Frank E. Seidman award in polit. economy, 1981. Fellow Am. Acad. Arts and Scis.; disting. fellow Am. Econ. Assn. (exec. com. 1956-59, v.p. 1962); mem. NAS, Internat. Seminar in Pub. Econs., Internat. Inst. Pub. Fin. (hon. pres. 1978). Home: 760 Western Dr Santa Cruz CA 95060-3033 Office: Crown College U Calif Santa Cruz Santa Cruz CA 95064

MUSHKIN, LEONARD BARTON, podiatrist; b. Ft. Dodge, Iowa, Apr. 2, 1944; s. Jack and Bernice (Levin) M.; m. Susan Marie Hechtlinger, Aug. 14, 1966 (div. June 1982); children: Jeffrey Phillip, Lawrence Brandon; m. Karen Mildred Meyer, Sept. 27, 1984. BA, U. Calif., Berkeley, 1966; BS, Calif. Podiatry Coll., San Francisco, 1967; D.P.M., Calif Coll. Podiatric Medicine, San Francisco, 1970. Diplomate Am. Coun. Cert. Podiatric Physicians and Surgeons; bd. cert. podiatric surgery and medicine. Preceptor Redwood Empire Podiatric Clinic, Santa Rosa, Calif., 1970-72; podiatrist Monterey (Calif.) Podiatry Group, Inc., 1973—; instr. Calif. Coll. Podiatric Medicine, San Francisco, 1984-86; cons. Productive Podiatry Practices, South San Francisco, 1992—. Recipient 1st place Am. Coll. Foot Roentgenologists, 1970. Fellow Acad. Ambulatory Foot Surgeons, Am. Acad. Podiatric Practice Mgmt. ; mem. Am. Coll. Foot Surgeons (assoc.), Am. Coun. Cert. Podiatric Physicians and Surgeons, Am. Acad. Podiatric Sports Medicine (assoc.), Internat. Coll. Podiatric Laser Surgery (assoc.), Calif. Podiatric Med. Assn., Am. Podiatric Med. Assn. Office: 880 Cass St Monterey CA 93940

MUSIHIN, KONSTANTIN K., electrical engineer; b. Harbin, China, June 17, 1927; s. Konstantin N. and Alexandra A. (Lapitsky) M.; m. Natalia Krilova, Oct. 18, 1964; 1 child, Nicholas; came to U.S., 1967, naturalized, 1973; student YMCA Inst., 1942, North Manchurian U., 1945, Harbin Poly. Inst., 1948. Registered profl. engr., Calif., Colo., N.Y., N.J., Pa., Ill., Wash. Asst. prof. Harbin Poly. Inst., 1950-53; elec. engr. Moinho Santista, Sao Paulo, Brazil, 1955-60; constrn. project mgr. Caterpillar-Brazil, Santo Amaro, 1960-61; mech. engr. Matarazzo Industries, Sao Paulo, 1961-62; chief of works Vidrobras, St. Gobain, Brazil, 1962-64; project engr. Brown Boveri, Sao Paulo, 1965-67; sr. engr. Kaiser Engrs., Oakland, Calif., 1967-73; sr. engr. Bechtel Power Corp., San Francisco, 1973-75; supr. power and control San Francisco Bay Area Rapid Transit, Oakland, 1976-78; chief elec. engr. L.K. Comstock Engring. Co., San Francisco, 1978-79; prin. engr. Morrison Knudsen Co., San Francisco, 1979-84; prin. engr. Brown and Caldwell, Cons. Engrs., Pleasant Hill, Calif., 1984-85; cons. engr. Pacific Gas and Electric Co., San Francisco, 1986-89; sr. engr. Bechtel Corp., San Francisco, 1989—. Mem. IEEE (sr.), Instrument Soc. Am. (sr.), Am. Mgmt. Assn., Nat., Calif. socs. profl. engrs., Nat. Assn. Corrosion Engrs., Instituto de Engenharia de Sao Paulo. Mem. Christian Orthodox Ch. Clubs: Am.-Brazilian, Brit.-Am. Home: 320 Park View Ter Apt 207 Oakland CA 94610-4653

MUSKE-DUKES, CAROL ANNE, writer, educator; b. L.A., Dec. 17, 1945; d. William Howard and Elsie (Kuchera) Muske; m. Edward Healton, June 5, 1972 (div.); m. David C. Dukes, Jan. 31, 1983; 1 child, Anne Cameron; 1 stepchild, Shawn. MA in English, U. Calif., San Francisco, 1970. Adj. prof. Grad. Writing Prog., Columbia U., N.Y.C., 1979-81; vis. poet U. Iowa, Iowa City, 1982; asst. prof. U. N.H., Durham, 1982; vis. prof. U. Calif., Irvine, 1983; prof. English U. So. Calif., L.A., 1984—; dir. Art Without Walls, N.Y.C., 1972-79; vis. disting. poet U. Calif., Irvine. Author: Dear Digby, 1989, Saving St. Germ, 1993, (poetry) Camouflage, 1975, Skylight, 1981, Wyndmere, 1985, Applause, 1989, Red Trousseau, 1993. Bd. advisors L.A. Libr. Assocs., 1987—, P.E.N. West, L.A., 1989—. Grantee NEA, 1984, Creative Artists Svc., 1989; fellow Guggenheim Found., 1981, Ingram Merrill, 1989; recipient Alice F. Castagnola award Poetry Soc. Am., 1979, Pushcart prize, 1992. Mem. PEN, Authors Guild, Poets and Writers Assn., L.A. Library Assn., NOW. Office: Univ of Southern Calif Dept of English Los Angeles CA 90089

MUSKET, RONALD GEORGE, physicist; b. St. Louis, Feb. 4, 1940; s. George Henry and Geraldine (Morris) M.; m. Yvona Marie Hoehne, Aug. 19, 1961; children: Kevin, Brian, Daren. BS in Engring. Physics., U. Colo., 1962; PhD in Engring. Sci., U. Calif., Berkeley, 1967. Physicist Lewis Rsch. Ctr. NASA, Cleve., 1967-69, Sandia Nat. Lab., Livermore, Calif., 1969-77; mgr. surface instruments Kevex Corp., Foster City, Calif., 1977-80; physicist Lawrence Livermore (Calif.) Nat. Lab., 1980—. Contbr. articles to profl. jours. Capt. U.S. Army, 1967-69. Nuclear Sci. and Engring. fellow AEC, 1962-65, Pre-doctoral fellow NASA, 1965-67. Mem. Am. Phys. Soc., Am. Vacuum Soc., Materials Rsch. Soc. Home: 9452 Thunderbird Pl San Ramon CA 94583-3624 Office: Lawrence Livermore Nat Lab East Ave Livermore CA 94550-4726

MUSMANN, KLAUS, librarian; b. Magdeburg, Germany, June 27, 1935; came to U.S., 1957; s. Ernst Hans and Eva (Grunow) M.; m. Gladys H. Arakawa, June 15, 1963 (div. 1973); children: Carlton, Michelle; m. Lois Geneva Steele, Dec. 27, 1986. BA, Wayne State U., 1962; MALS, U. Mich., 1963; MA, Mich. State U., 1967; PhD, U. So. Calif., 1981. Libr. Detroit Pub. Libr., 1962-65; asst. serials libr. Mich. State U., East Lansing, 1965-67; head of acquisitions Los Angeles County Law Libr., L.A., 1968-84; coll. devel. libr. U. of Redlands, Calif., 1984—. Author: Helen and Vernon Farquhar Collection: A Bibliography, 1987, Diffusion of Innovations, 1989, Technological Innovations in Libraries, 1850-1950, 1993; contbr. articles to profl. jours. Grantee Coun. on Libr. Resources, 1990. Mem.ALA, Assn. Coll. and Rsch. Librs., Soc. for History of Tech. Home: 1017 La Hermosa Dr Redlands CA 92373 Office: Univ of Redlands Redlands CA 92374

MUSOLF, DEANNE MARGARET, writer, correspondent for news magazine; b. Duluth, Minn., Nov. 24, 1960; d. Bertram Arthur Musolf and Janice Ann (Wallow) Nephew. BA, Calif. State U., Hayward, 1984; postgrad., U. Bristol, Eng., 1989. Columnist Concord (Calif.) Transcript, 1976-78; fact-checker, writer San Francisco Mag., 1982-83; writer Berkeley (Calif.) Monthly, 1983-84; editor-in-chief Western Ind. Bankers Monthly, 1988; assoc. editor Diablo Mag., 1989; sr. editor Diablo Bus. Mag., Walnut Creek, Calif., 1989-90; contbg. editor Special Events and HomeCare Mags., 1989-90; freelancer The Economist, 1990—; West Coast corr. Life Mag., 1990—; freelancer N.Y. Daily News, 1991—, Am. Airlines Inflight Mags., Southwest Airlines Inflight Mags., 1991—. Home: 874 San Simeon Dr Concord CA 94518-2157

MUSSELMAN, DARWIN B, artist, educator; b. Selma, Calif., Feb. 16, 1916; s. Laban C. and Lola Belle (Banks) M.; m. Ethel Laura Walker, Aug. 30, 1940; children: Ronald Lee, Carol Sue Musselman Woods, Steven Earl. BA, Fresno State Coll., 1938; MFA, Calif. Coll. Arts & Crafts, 1950; MA, U. Calif., Berkeley, 1952; PhD, Calif. State U., 1966. Artist, tchr., art dir. Thomas Advt. Agy., Fresno, Calif., 1945-46, freelance artist, illustrator, 1953-63; tchr. Fresno City Sch., 1946-48; dir. Sch. of Edn. Calif. Coll. Arts & Crafts, Oakland, 1948-53; tchr. Fresno State Coll., 1945-46; prof. Calif. State U., 1953-78; ret. Calif. State U., Fresno, 1978. Exhibitor numerous oil and watercolors regional and statewide shows, 1935—, also one-man and invitational shows U.S., Europe and Mex. Mem. Am. Watercolor Soc., Nat. Watercolor Soc., Am. Soc. Portrait Artists (bd. dirs. 1988—). Republican. Home: 2550 Pecho Rd Los Osos CA 93402-4104

MUSSELMAN, ELIZABETH ANN, lawyer; b. Watertown, N.Y., Feb. 5, 1954; d. John Joseph and Mary Clair (Donahue) M.; m. James Paul Laycock, July 14, 1984; children: Steven Thomas, Matthew Paul, John Carl. BA, Lafayette Coll., Easton, Pa., 1975; JD, U. Denver, 1980. Bar: Colo. 1980, N.Mex. 1985; cert. family law specialist N.Mex. Bd. Legal Specialization. Legal intern Women in Crisis Ctr., Lakewood, Colo., 1978; paralegal specialist Denver Svc. Ctr., Nat. Park Svc., Lakewood, 1979-80; pvt. practice Denver, 1980-84; assoc. Robert D. Morrison, P.C., Taos, N.Mex., 1984-85; pvt. practice Denver, 1985-86; v.p. Leverick & Musselman, Taos, 1986—; dir. jud. affairs asst. dean students U. Denver, 1981-83. V.p., bd. dirs. Battered Women's Project, Taos, 1985-90. Office: Leverick & Musselman PC PO Box 1894 Taos NM 87571-1894

MUSSELMAN, ROBERT CARL, plant physiologist; b. Sioux City, Iowa, June 12, 1942; s. Clarence A. and Verdna S. (Scott) M.; m. Andrea M. Foelske, June 15, 1969; children: Rebecca, Elizabeth, Sarah. BS, Iowa State U., 1964, MS, 1967; PhD, U. Wis., 1972. Rsch. specialist N.Y. State Agrl. Experiment Sta., Geneva, 1973-76; rsch. assoc. N.Y. State Agrl. Experiment Sta., 1976-80; rsch. plant physiologist Air Pollution Rsch. Ctr., U. Calif., Riverside, 1980-88; plant physiologist USDA Forest Svc., Rocky Montain Sta., Fort Collins, Colo., 1988—. With U.S. Army, 1967-69. Recipient George M. Darrow award Am. Soc. Horticulture Sci., 1983. Mem. AAAS, Air and Waste Mgmt. Assn. Lutheran. Home: 717 Scenic Dr Fort Collins CO 80526-5103 Office: USDA Forest Svc Rocky Mountain Forest & Range Expt Sta 240 W Prospect Fort Collins CO 80526

MUSSER, C. WALTON, physical scientist, consultant; b. Mt. Joy, Pa., Apr. 5, 1909; s. Ezra Nissley and Cora Grace (Weidman) M.; m. Edna Mae Hoak, June 23, 1937; children: Lila Darle (Mrs. Richard Hackman), Yvonne Duane (Mrs. Harold Graham), Stanley Walton (dec.). Student, Chgo. Tech. Coll., 1926-28, Leavitt Sch. Psychology, 1928-29, Wharton Sch. Fin. and Commerce, 1929-30, U. Pa., 1930-32, MIT, 1957. Chief engr. product devel. Indsl. Improvement Corp., Phila., 1936-41; rsch. adviser Dept. Def., 1941-56; pres., dir. rsch. Sci. Rsch., Inc., Glenside, Pa., 1945-52; pvt. practice cons., adviser in rsch. and devel., 1936—. Holder of over 162 U.S. Patents in 32 different classes and more than 60 patents in over 28 countries. Recipient Exceptional Civilian Service award for First Working Recoilless Weapon, Sec. of War, 1945; John C. Jones medal for Disting. Svc., Am. Ordnance Assn., 1951; Machine Design award ASME, 1968; named to Ordnance Hall of Fame, 1976. Mem. Acad. Applied Scis., Am. Def. Preparedness Assn. (hon. life), Nat. Soc. Profl. Engrs., Sigma Xi. Address: 1206 Lela Ln Santa Maria CA 93454

MUSSMAN, MICHAEL STEVEN, lawyer; b. Chgo., Dec. 31, 1954; s. Bernard A. and Judith (Yampol) M.; m. Suzanne Ruth Kaiser, Sept. 2, 1979 (div. July 1990); children: Aric Kaiser Mussman, Joshua Kaiser Mussman; m. Sara Gantz, July 17, 1990; stepchildren: Guy A. Tal, Ilanit R. Tal. AB with distinction in Speech Comm., U. Ill., 1976; JD, Washington U., St. Louis, 1979. Bar: Ariz. 1980, U.S. Dist. Ct. Ariz. 1981, U.S. Ct. Appeals (9th cir.) 1981, U.S. Supreme Ct. 1988. Law clk. Pub. Defender's Office, Tucson, 1980-81; trial atty. Pima County Pub. Defender's Office, Tucson, 1981-86, chief trial counsel, 1986-87; dir. Pima County Legal Defender's Office, Tucson, 1987-92; ptnr. Poore, Riddle & Mussman, Tucson, 1992—. Pres. Congregation Bet Shalom, Tucson, 1991—. Mem. Ariz. Bar Assn., Pima County Bar Assn., Nat. Legal Aid and Defenders Assn., Ariz. Attys. for Criminal Justice (chmn. for indigent def. 1988-90), Cardozo Soc. Democrat. Office: Poore Riddle & Mussman 100 N Stone Ste 805 Tucson AZ 85701

MUSSO, ELIZABETH ANN, graphic designer, illustrator; b. Rochester, N.Y., Sept. 15; d. Edward Roy and Dorothy (Evans) Birkicht; m. Frank P.

Musso, Apr. 11, 1978 (div. Aug. 1990); children: C. Scott, Robyn J. AAS in Fine Arts, Rochester Inst. Tech., 1973; BA cum laude, Colo. State U., 1992. Tech. illustrator Eastman Kodak Co., Rochester, N.Y., 1974-77, Environ. Rsch. and Tech., Ft. Collins, Colo., 1979; freelance graphic designer Ft. Collins, 1980-92; graphic designer Concept Systems, Inc., Ft. Collins, 1992—; intern Bob Coonts Design Group, Ft. Collins, 1991. Artist (poster) Wimbledon, 1991 (bronze medal). Vol. Colo. Invitational Internat. Poster Exhbn., Ft. Collins, 1991. Mem. Art Dirs. Club Denver, Golden Key, Phi Kappa Phi. Presbyterian. Home: 2624 Bradbury Ct Fort Collins CO 80521 Office: Concept Systems Inc 2619 Canton Ct Fort Collins CO 80521

MUSTACCHI, PIERO, physician, educator; b. Cairo, Egypt, May 29, 1920; came to U.S., 1947; naturalized, 1952; s. Gino and Gilda (Rieti) M.; m. Dora Lisa Ancona, Sept. 26, 1948; children: Roberto, Michael. BS in Humanities, U. Florence, Italy, 1938; postgrad. in anatomy, Eleve Interne, U. Lausanne, Switzerland, 1938-39; MB, ChB, Fouad I U., Cairo, Egypt, 1944, grad. in Arabic lang. and lit., 1946; D Medicine and Surgery, U. Pisa, 1986; D Honoris Causa, U. Aix-Marseilles, France, 1988; hon. degree, U. Alexandria, Egypt, 1985. Lic. physician, Egypt, Italy; diplomate Am. Bd. Internal Medicine; qualified med. examiner, Calif. House officer English Hosp., Ch. Missionary Soc., Cairo, Egypt, 1945-47; clin. affiliate U. Calif., San Francisco, 1947-48; intern Franklin Hosp., San Francisco, 1948-49; resident in pathology U. Calif., San Francisco, 1949-51; resident in medicine Meml. Ctr. Cancer and Allied Diseases, N.Y.C., 1951-53; rsch. epidemiologist Dept. HEW, Nat. Cancer Inst., Bethesda, Md., 1955-57; cons. allergy clinic U. Calif., San Francisco, 1957-70, clin. prof. medicine and preventive medicine, 1970-90, clin. prof. medicine and epidemiology, 1990—, head occupational epidemiology, 1975-90, head div. internat. health edn. dept. epidemiology and internat. health, 1985-90; med. cons., vis. prof. numerous ednl. and profl. instns., including U. Marseilles 1981, 82, U. Pisa, Italy, 1983, U. Gabon, 1984, U. Siena, Italy, 1985, work clinic U. Calif., 1975-84, Ctr. for Rehab. and Occupational Health, U. Calif. San Francisco, 1984—; qualified med. evaluator Div. Indsl. Accidents, State of Calif., 1990; cons. numerous worldwide govtl. agys. Contbr. chpts. to books, articles to profl. jours. Editorial bd. Medecine d'Afrique Noire, Ospedali d'Italia. Served with USN, USPHS, 1953-55. Decorated Order of Merit (Commander) (Italy), Ordre de la Legion d'Honneur (France), Medal of St. John of Jerusalem, Sovereign Order of Malta, Order of the Republic (Egypt); Scroll, Leonardo da Vinci Soc., San Francisco, 1965; award Internat. Inst. Oakland, 1964; Hon. Vice Consul. Italy, 1971-90. Fellow ACP, Am. Soc. Occupational Medicine, Am. Soc. Environ. and Occupational Health; mem. AAAS, Am. Assn. Cancer Rsch., Calif. Soc. Allergy and Immunology, Calif. Med. Assn., San Francisco Med. Soc., West Coast Allergy Soc. (founding), Mex. Congress on Hypertension (corr.), Internat. Assn. Med. Rsch. and Continuing Edn. (U.S. rep.), Indsl. Accident Commn., Villa Taverna Club, Acad. Italiana della Cucina. Democrat. Home: 3344 Laguna St San Francisco CA 94123-2208 Office: U Calif Parnassus Ave San Francisco CA 94143-0560

MUSTAFA, MOHAMMAD GHULAM, biochemistry educator; b. Dhaka, Bangladesh, Mar. 1, 1940; came to U.S., 1963, naturalized, 1978; s. Mohammad and Quamerunnesa Yaseen; m. Sultana Begum Mustafa, Nov. 6, 1969; 1 child, George E. BS, Dhaka U., 1960, MS summa cum laude, 1962; MA, U. Calif., Berkeley, 1966; PhD, SUNY, Albany, 1969. Asst. research biochemist U. Calif., Davis, 1969-73, asst. adj. prof., 1973-75; adj. asst. prof. UCLA, 1975-78, assoc. prof. in residence, 1978-79, assoc. prof., 1979-84, prof. environ. and occupational health sci., 1984—. Co-editor: Biomedical Effects of Ozone, 1983; mem. editorial bd. Toxicology and Indsl. Health, Princeton, N.J., 1984—; contbr. articles to profl. jours. Recipient Research Career Devel. award NIH, 1976-81; grantee NIH, 1970—. Mem. Am. Chem. Soc., Am. Coll. Toxicology, Air Pollution Control Assn., AAAS, N.Y. Acad. Sci., Sigma Xi. Democrat. Muslim. Home: 10534 Louisiana Ave Los Angeles CA 90025-5918 Office: UCLA Sch Pub Health 405 Hilgard Ave Los Angeles CA 90024-1301

MUTCH, JAMES DONALD, pharmaceutical executive; b. Portland, Oreg., Mar. 6, 1943; s. Keith William and Dorothy (Wones) M.; m. Judith Ann Thompson, June 12, 1965; children: William James, Alicia Kathleen. BS in Pharmacy, Oreg. State U., 1966. Registered pharmacist, Calif., Oreg.; cert. regulatory affairs profl. Mgr. regulatory affairs Syntex Labs., Palo Alto, Calif., 1970-72, assoc. dir. regulatory affairs, 1972-76, dir. regulatory affairs, 1976-80; dir. regulatory affairs and clin. devel. Cooper Vision, Inc., Mt. View, Calif., 1980-86; dir. regulatory affairs and pre-clin. devel. Salutar, Inc., Sunnyvale, Calif., 1987-89, v.p. product devel., 1990-91; pres. Altos Biopharm. Inc., Los Altos, 1991-92; v.p. regulatory affairs and product devel. Pharmacyclics, Inc., Mountain View, Calif., 1992—. Pres. bd. Woodland Vista Swim & Racquet Club, Los Altos, Calif., 1982-83. With USPHS, 1966-68. Mem. AAAS, Am. Pharm. Assn., Regulatory Affairs Profl. Soc. Democrat. Office: Pharmacyclics Inc 265 N Whisman Rd Mountain View CA 94043

MUTOMBO, DIKEMBE, professional basketball player; b. Kinshasa, Zaire, June 25, 1966. Student, Georgetown U. Center Denver Nuggets, 1991—. Office: Denver Nuggets McNichols Sports Arena 1635 Clay St Denver CO 80204

MUTSCHLER, HERBERT FREDERICK, retired librarian; b. Eureka, S.D., Nov. 28, 1919; s. Frederick and Helena (Oster) M.; m. Lucille I. Gross, Aug. 18, 1945; 1 dau., Linda M. B.A., Jamestown Coll., 1947; M.A., Western Res. U., 1949, M.S., 1952. Tchr. history high sch. Lemmon, S.D., 1947-48; asst. librarian Royal Oak (Mich.) Libr., 1952-55; head librarian Hamtramck (Mich.) Libr., 1955-56; head public svcs. Wayne County Libr. System, Wayne, Mich., 1956-59; asst. county librarian Wayne County Libr. System, 1960-62; dir. King County Libr. System, Seattle, 1963-89; library bldg. cons. Wayne County Libr., 1956-62, Wash. State Libr., 1966—; cons. Salt Lake County Libr., Pierce County Libr., North Olympic Libr.; lectr. U. Wash. Sch. Librarianship, 1970-71; bldg. cons. Hoquiam (Wash.) Libr., Olympic (Wash.) Regional Libr., Camas (Wash.) Pub. Libr., N. Cen. (Wash.) Regional Libr., Spokane (Wash.) County Libr., Enumclaw (Wash.) Libr., Puyallup (wash.) Pub. Libr. Contbr. articles profl. jours. Served with AUS, 1941-45; to capt. 1950-52. Decorated Silver Star, Bronze Star with cluster, Purple Heart, Preidential Unit Citation. Mem. ALA (councilor at large 1965-69, chpt. councilor 1971-75, pres. library adminstrv. div. 1974-75), Pacific N.W. Library Assn., Wash. Library Assn. (exec. bd. 1964-65, 69-71, pres. 1967-69). Republican. Lutheran. Club: City, Municipal League. Lodge: Kiwanis. Home: 5300 128th Ave SE Bellevue WA 98006-2952

MYBECK, RICHARD RAYMOND, lawyer; b. Chgo., Dec. 5, 1928; s. Walter Raymond and Genevieve Lucille (Carlsten) M.; m. Betty Jane Engle, Aug. 23, 1952; children: Walter R. II, Wendy Sue, Lucinda Jeanne, Amanda Jane, (dec.), Candace Christine, Sara Melinda. BChE, Purdue U., 1950, BS in Engring. Law, 1953; JD, Ind. U., 1953. Bar: Ind. 1953, Wis. 1954, Ill. 1962, Ariz. 1973; registered U.S. patent atty., patent agt., Can. Patent trainee, atty. Allis Chalmers Mfg. Co., West Allis, Wis., 1953-57, patent atty., 1957-62; atty. Koehring Corp., Milw., 1957; patent atty. Armour and Co., Chgo., 1962-71; sr. patent atty. Greyhound Corp., Chgo., Phoenix, 1971-77; sr. counsel Armour Pharmaceutical Co., Phoenix, Scottsdale, Ariz., 1977-81; pvt. practice Scottsdale, 1981—; pres., bd. dirs. Farmakeia, Inc., Scottsdale, Hoosier Investment Co., Scottsdale. Councilman Town of Paradise Valley, Ariz., 1988-92, commr., chmn. planning and zoning commn., 1981-88, mem. chmn. bd. adjustment, 1974-81; lay speaker United Meth. Ch., 1954—. Named to Hall of Fame Oak Park (Ill.) Youth Baseball, 1987; recipient Degentesh award Forest Park (Ill.) VFW, 1969. Mem. ABA, Ariz. Bar Assn. (chmn. various sects.), Ill. Bar Assn., Wis. Bar Assn., Intellectual Property Assn. Chgo., Purdue Alumni Assn. (dir. region 15 1993—), Elks, Masons, Tau Kappa Epsilon, Sigma Delta Kappa. Methodist. Home: 4901 E Tomahawk Trl Paradise Vly AZ 85253-2030 Office: Mybeck Law Office 8010 E Morgan Trl Ste 10 Scottsdale AZ 85258-1234

MYCUE, EDWARD, writer, publisher, editor, book seller; b. Niagara Falls, N.Y., Mar. 21, 1937; s. John Powers and Ruth Agnes (Taylor) M. AS in Pre-Law, Arlington State Jr. Coll., 1957; BA, North Tex. State U., 1959, postgrad., 1959-60; postgrad., Boston U., 1960-61. Rsch. asst. dept. polit. sci. North Tex. State U., 1958, teaching fellow in govt., 1959-60; endl. TV programming intern Sta. WGBH-TV, Boston, 1960-61; cons. intergovernmental personnel rels. U.S. Dept. Health, Edn., and Welfare, Washington, 1962-68; freelance writer, traveling lectr. Europe, 1968-70; assoc. mgr., pub. Panjandrum Books and Press, 1972-76; asst. mgr. bookshops and publs. dept. Fine Arts Mus. San Francisco, 1976-81; book buyer Grace Cathedral Gift Shop, San Francisco, 1981—; pub. Norton-Coker Press, Took mag., Took Modern Poetry, 1988—; tchr. high sch., asst. headmaster Acherensua Secondary Sch., U.S. Peace Corps., Ghana, 1961.; instr. Am. lit. Internat. People's Coll., Denmark, 1969; instr. writing program Folsom Prison, 1972-73; McDoweel Colony fellow writer-in-residence Peterborough (N.H.) High Sch., 1974. Author: (poetry) Her Children Come Home Too, 1972, Damage Within The Community, 1973, Chronicle, 1974, Root, Route & Range, 1977, Root, Route & Range: The Song Returns, 1979, The Singing Man My Father Gave Me, 1980, Edward, 1987, Unity, 1987, Grate Country, 1988, No One For Free, 1988, The Torn Star (A Vision), 1988, Next Year's Words, 1989, Pink Garden, Brown Trees, 1990, No One 6, 1991, Idolino, 1991, Life Is Built From The Inside Out, 1993; works pub. in (anthologies) The Male Muse, 1973, 14 Voices, 1975, For David Gascoyne, 1981, Poly, 1989, Round Glow of Family Nest, 1989, How The Net Is Gripped, 1992, Rhysling Anthology, 1992, Terminal Velocities, 1993; contbr poetry to Akros, Berleley Poetry Review, COntact II, Detail, European Judaism, Five Leaves Left, Green's Mag., Hippycore, Industrial Sabatoge/Curvd H&2, James White Review, Krax, LINQ, Matilda, Meanjin, Mensuel, New York Quarterly, La Carta de Qliver, Nicolau, Poetry South, Poetry Ireland Review, Barddoni, Exquisite Corpse, Midwest Quarterly, EOTU, Echo Room, Antigonish Review, Fuel, Le Miracle Tatoue, Frank, Euthanesia Roses, Riverside Quarterly, Outrigger, Pearl, My Favorite Sentence, Panjandrum, Beyond Baroque, Xaview Review, Xizquil, Villiage Idiot, Wyoming, Hub of the Wheel, Capilano Review, Washington Review, Stand. MacDowell Colony fellow Peterborough, N.H., 1974, Lowell Inst. fellow Boston, 1960-61. Mem. PEN. Home and Office: P O Box 640543 San Francisco CA 94164-0543

MYER, JON HAROLD, engineering physicist; b. Heilbronn, Germany, Sept. 29, 1922; came to U.S., 1947; naturalized, 1953; s. Oscar Nathan and Greta Cecilie (Wolf) M.; m. Gerda R. Simson, Apr. 20, 1948; children: Gary D., Eric J., Karen B., Kenneth B. BEE, Hebrew Tech. Coll., Haifa, Israel, 1941. Instrument maker Anglo Iranian Oil Co., Abadan, Iran, 1942-44; instrument designer Hebrew Tech. Coll., 1944-46; engring. cons. Haifa, 1946-47; instrumentologist dept. chemistry U. So. Calif., L.A., 1947-53; with Hughes Aircraft Co., L.A., 1953-91; sr. scientist radar systems div. Hughes Aircraft Co., L.A., 1991-92; invention cons. Hughes Rsch. Labs., Malibu, Calif., 1991—; lectr. sci. and tech. in adminstrn. of justice Calif. Luth. Coll., Moorpark, 1979-81. Patentee in engring., physics, magnetics, optics. Pioneering team splty. Explorer program Orange Empire coun. Boy Scouts Am., 1961-66. Recipient Silver Beaver award Boy Scouts Am., 1965. Mem. IEEE, Am. Phys. Soc., Optical Soc. Am., Rsch. Soc. Am., Tau Beta Pi. Home: 22931 Gershwin Dr Woodland Hills CA 91364-3827

MYERS, AL, realtor, property manager, mayor; b. Oakland, Calif., Aug. 6, 1922; s. Alvi A. and Emma (Thoren) M.; student Oreg. Inst. Tech., 1940-41; m. Viola Doreen Wennermark, Sept. 11, 1954; children: Susan Faye, Pamela Ann, Jason Allen. Supt.'s asst. Aluminum Co. Am., Troutdale, Oreg., 1942-44; asst. mgr. Western Auto Supply Co., Portland, 1944-46; owner, operator Al Myers Auto & Electric, Gresham, Oreg., 1946-53; realtor, broker Al Myers Property Mgmt., 1954—; v.p., sec. Oreg. Country, Inc.; faculty Mt. Hood Community Coll. Chmn., Indsl. and Econ. Devel. Com. for Multonomah County, Oreg. Real Estate Ednl. Program, 1961. Mayor Gresham, Oreg., 1972—. Pres. East Multonomah County Dem. Forum, 1965—, mem. exec. com., 1958—. With AUS, 1943. Mem. Portland Realty Bd., Nat. Assn. Real Estate Bds., Christian Bus. Men's Com. Internat., Internat. Platform Assn., Rho Epsilon Kappa (pres. Oreg.). Mem. Evang. Ch. (trustee, treas.). Home: 935 NW Norman Ave Gresham OR 97030-6966 Office: 995 NE Cleveland Ave Gresham OR 97030

MYERS, BARTON, architect; b. Norfolk, Va., Nov. 6, 1934; s. Barton and Meeta Hamilton (Burrage) M.; m. Victoria George, Mar. 7, 1959; 1 child, Suzanne Lewis. BS, U.S. Naval Acad., 1956; MArch with honors, U. Pa., 1964. Commd. 2d lt. USAF, 1956, resigned, 1961; architect Louis I. Kahn, Phila., 1964-65, Bower, Fradley, Phila., 1967-68; architect, prin. A.J. Diamond & Barton Myers, Toronto, Ont., Can., 1968-75; architect, prin. Barton Myers Assocs., Toronto, 1975—, Los Angeles, 1981—; disting. vis. prof. Ariz. State U., Tempe, 1986; sr. prof. UCLA, 1981—; Thomas Jefferson Prof. U. Va., Charlottesville, 1982; vis. prof., lectr., Harvard U., U. Pa., other univs. U.S. and Can., 1968—. Prin. works include Myers Residence, Toronto (Ont. Assn. Architects Toronto Chpt. Annual Design award, 1971, Can. Housing Design Coun. award, 1971), Wolf Residence, Toronto (Architectural Record: Record Houses of 1977, Twenty-Five Yrs. of Record Houses, 1981), Housing Union Bldg., Edmonton (Can. Housing Design Coun. award, 1974, Design in Steel award, 1975), Citadel Theatre, Edmonton (City of Edmonton Design award, 1978, Stelco Design award, 1978), Seagram Mus., Waterloo, Ont., (Gov. Gen.'s Medal for Architecture, 1986), Howard Hughes Ctr. Master Plan and Wang Tower, L.A., 1986, Phoenix Mcpl. Govt. Ctr. (Winning Competition Entry 1985), Portland Ctr. for the Performing Arts, Portland (Progressive Architecture Design award, 1984), Art Gallery Ont. expansion (Winning Competition Entry, 1987), Film and Drama Facility York U., Toronto, 1987, theater and concert hall Cerritos Calif. Arts Ctr., 1987, Cerritos Ctr. Performing Arts, Edmonton (Alta.)úConcert Hall, U.S. Pavilion for Expo '92, Seville, Spain, 1989, N.J. Performing Arts Ctr., Newark, 1990, others. Recipient Gov. Gen.'s award for Architecture Woodsworth Coll., 1992. Fellow Royal Archtl. Inst. Can.; mem. AIA, Soc. Archtl. Historians, Royal Can. Acad. Art, Tau Sigma Delta. Office: Barton Myers Assocs Inc 6834 Hollywood Blvd Fl 2D Los Angeles CA 90028-6175 also: 322 King St, West Toronto, ON Canada M5V 1J2

MYERS, BRADLEY LAWRENCE, project controls engineer; b. Lynwood, Calif., Jan. 27, 1961; s. Larry Dean and Jill Elaine (Ostler) M. BS in Elec. and Electronics Engring., Calif. State U., Chico, 1984; MBA, U. Nev., 1990. Control systems engr. Rexnord/Mathews Conveyor, Chico, 1984-85; custom products engr. Bently Nev. Corp., Minden, 1985-87, mfg. engr., 1987, prodn. supr., 1987-88, mfg. engr., 1989, mktg. engr., 1990-91; cost engr. Bechtel Corp., San Francisco, 1991-93; cost, schedule engr. Bechtel/Chevron Waste Discharge Order Project, Richmond, 1993—. V.p. Carson City (Nev.) Jaycees, 1986-87, state dir., 1987-88, dir., 1988—; v.p., MBA assoc. U. Nev., Reno, 1988-89; dir. Walnut Creek Jaycees, Calif., 1992-93. Mem. IEEE, Am. Assn. Cost Engrs. Office: Bechtel Corp 50 Beale St San Francisco CA 94105-1813

MYERS, CONNIE JEAN, real estate professional; b. Portland, Oreg., Mar. 16, 1946; d. Thomas Arthur and Jennie Maifair (Saunders) M. BS, Oreg. State U., 1968. Asst. contr. Builders Resources Corp., San Mateo, Calif., 1971-73; contr. Little & Blackwell, Menlo Park, Calif., 1973-76; v.p. Landsing Property Corp., Menlo Park, 1976-82; v.p. reg. ptnr. Landsing Property Corp., Denver, 1982-85; cons. Denver, 1985; sr. v.p. De Anza Assets, Inc., Beverly Hills, Calif., 1985-87; v.p., dir. of asset mgmt. Holden Real Estate, Inc., L.A., 1987-88; pres. First Capital Ptnrs. (North) Inc., Bellevue, Wash., 1988—. Author: (procedure manuals) Apartment and Mobilehome Communities, 1986, General Management, Leasing & Marketing, Maintenance & Disaster. Mem. Inst. Real Estate Mgmt. (CPM 1980), Wash. State Bd. Real Estate (broker 1989), Seattle/King County Assn. Realtors (affiliate), Comml. Real Estate Women, Comml. Investment Coun., Women Bus. Owners, Women Bus. Exch. Republican. Office: First Capital Ptnrs (North) 1400 112th Ave SE Ste 100 Bellevue WA 98004

MYERS, DENNIS GILLFORD, marketing professional; b. Canton, Ohio, Apr. 15, 1953; s. Kenneth and Margaret (Wallace) M.; m. Teresa Rose DiCarlo, Nov. 25, 1972; children: Michelle Lynn, April Marie. AA, Orange Coast Coll., 1971-73; AS in Respiratory Therapy, Blair Coll., 1974. Respiratory therapist McKenzie-Willamette Hosp., Springfield, Oreg., 1978-79; asst. mgr. Singer Machine Co., Eugene, Oreg., 1979-80; respiratory therapist Sacred Heart Gen. Hosp., Eugene, 1980-88; sales mgr. Lincare, Eugene, 1988—; computer online specialist CompuServe; owner, pres. Infotrac Cons. Svcs., Springfield, 1984—; dir. mktg. Vital Choice, Eugene, 1991-92. Adv. bd. Home BusinessLine newsletter. Active Metro Area Planning Adv. Com., 1982-83, 85-87, Willamalane Budget Com., 1983-84, Springfield Citizen Involvement Com., 1980-83, Lane County Citizen Involvement Program, 1979-81; mem. adv. bd. Sr. and Disabled Svcs., 1989—; bd. dirs. Am. Heart Assn.; mem. Arbor Day Founds. Mem. World Future Soc. (coordinator Oreg. chpt.), Northwest Info. Profls. (bd. dirs.), Am. Home Bus. Assn. (bd. dirs., editor newsletter). Democrat. Home: 5780 E St Springfield OR 97478-6952

MYERS, DONALD EARL, mathematics educator; b. Chanute, Kans., Dec. 29, 1931; s. Frank Jasper and Electa Bell (Blackburn) M.; m. Ruth Louise Pettit, June 6, 1954; children: Jill Elizabeth, Douglas Lee. BS, Kans. State U., 1953, MS, 1955; PhD, U. Ill., 1960. Assoc. prof. math. Millikin U., Decatur, Ill., 1958-60; asst. prof. math. U. Ariz., Tucson, 1960-64; assoc. prof. math. U. Ariz., 1964-68; prof. math. U. Paris, 1986; mathematician USGS, Denver, 1982-85; maitre de recherche Ecole des Mines, Paris, 1987; prof. math. U. Ariz., 1968—; cons. UN Project, Peoples Republic of China, 1991; referee NSF on math., geology and water resources rsch. Contbr. articles to profl. jours. Squadron comdr. U.S. Power Squadron, 1972, dist. comdr., 1989-90. EPA grantee, 1984-91; named Disting. Alumnus Dept. Math. Kans. State U., 1991. Mem. Math. Assn. Am., Am. Math. Soc., AAAS, Inst. Math. Statistics, Am. Statis. Assn., AAUP (chpt. pres. 1972-74, 92), Internat. Assn. Math. Geology. Office: Univ of Ariz Dept Mathematics Tucson AZ 85721

MYERS, DOUGLAS GEORGE, zoological society administrator; b. Los Angeles, Aug. 30, 1949; s. George Walter and Daydeen (Schroeder) M.; m. Barbara Firestone Myers, Nov. 30, 1980; children: Amy, Andrew. BA, Christopher Newport Coll., 1981. Tour and show supr. Annheuser-Busch (Bird Sanctuary), Van Nuys, Calif., 1970-74, mgr. zool. ops., 1974-75, asst. mgr. ops., 1975-77, mgr. ops., 1977-78; gen. services mgr. Annheuser-Busch (Old Country), Williamsburg, Va., 1978-80, park ops. dir., 1980-81; gen. mgr. wild animal park Zool. Soc. San Diego, 1981-83, dep. dir. ops., 1983-85, exec. dir., 1985—; cons. in field. Exec. com. mem. Ctrl. Balboa Park Assn., San Diego, 1986-87; bd. dirs. San Diego Conv. and Visitors Bur., 1993. Profl. fellow Am. Assn. Zool. Parks & Aquariums, Internat. Union Dirs. Zool. Gardens; mem. Internat. Assn. Amusement Parks and Attractions, Calif. Assn. Zoos and Aquariums (chmn. 1986—). Lodge: Rotary. Office: San Diego Zoo PO Box 551 Zoo Pl & Park Blvd San Diego CA 92112

MYERS, ELIZABETH ROUSE, management consultant; b. Grand Island, Nebr., July 14, 1923; d. William Wayne Rouse and Lulu Zella Trout; m. Richard Roland Myers, June 25, 1943; children: Diane Marie Berndt, Richard Wayne. Student, Kearny State Tchrs. Coll., Nebr., 1942-43. Draftsman Borg-Warner Corp., Kalamazooo, 1944; acct. CFI Steel Corp., Pueblo, Colo., 1950-52; sec., treas. Standard Paint, Yakima, Wash., 1954-86; pres. Pied Piper Childrens Books, Yakima, Wash., 1985—; federal oil leases, 1980—; docent Yakima Valley Mus. & Gilbert House, Wash. 1984—. Editor: High Sch. Paper. Tchr., supt. First Presbyn. Ch., Yakima, Wash., 1958-70; mem. bd. Parent Tchrs.; bd. dirs., teen chmn. YWCA; pres. Gilbert House. Mem. Yakima Valley Mus. (awarded Doll 1985, Show 1986). Republican. Presbyterian. Home: 106 N 25th Ave Yakima WA 98902-2807

MYERS, ELMER, psychiatric social worker; b. Blackwell, Ark., Nov. 12, 1926; s. Chester Elmer Myers and Irene (Davenport) Lewis; widowed; children: Elmer Jr., Keith, Kevin. BA, U. Kans., 1951, MA, 1962; student, U. Calif., Santa Barbara, 1977-78. Psychiat. social worker Hastings (Nebr.) State Hosp., 1960-62; psychiat. social worker State of Calif., Sacramento, 1962-75, supr. psychiat. social worker, 1975-80; supr. psychiat. social worker Alta Calif. Regional Ctr., Sacramento, 1980-85; exec. dir. Tri-County Family Services, Yuba City, Calif., 1966-69; cons. to 3 convalescent Hosps., Marysville, Calif., 1969-71; lectr. Yuba Coll., Marysville, 1971-76; assoc. prof. Calif. State U., Chico, 1972-73; cons. in field, Marysville, 1985—. Juror Yuba County Grand Jury, Marysville, 1965, 87-88; sec. Y's Men's Club, Yuba City, 1964-65; chmn. Tri-County Home Health Agy., Yuba City, 1974-76; vice-chmn. Gateway Projects, Inc., Yuba City, 1974-75; bd. dirs. Yuba County Truancy Bd., Marysville, 1964-67, Golden Empire Health Systems Agy., Sacramento, 1972-76, Youth Services Bur., Yuba City, 1967, Bi County Mental Retardation Planning Bd., Yuba City, 1972, Yuba County Juvenile Justice Commn., Marysville, 1982-90, Am. Cancer Soc., Marysville, 1985-92, Yuba County Rep. Cen. Com., 1983-90, Salvation Army, 1990, facilitator care project, 1992; asst. dir. Marysville Adult Activity Ctr., 1990; active Yuba-Sutter United Way, 1971-73, 1991—, TriCounty Ethnic Forum, sec. 1991—, steering com. Marysville Sr. Ctr. Assn., 1992, bd. dirs. Christian Assistance Network, 1993, Habitat for Humanity, 1993. Recipient Cert. Spl. Recognition Calif. Rehab. Planning Project, 1969, Cert. Spl. Recognition State of Calif., 1967; Cert. Spl. Recognition Alta Calif. Regional Ctrs., 1985. Mem. Nat. Assn. Social Workers (cert.), Kern County Mental Health Assn. (chmn. 1978-79). Lodge: Rotary (bd. dirs. Marysville club 1975-76). Home and Office: 3920 Hwy 20 Marysville CA 95901

MYERS, GREGORY EDWIN, aerospace engineer; b. Harrisburg, Pa., Jan. 1, 1960; s. Bernard Eugene and Joyce (Calhoun) M.; m. Susan Ann Hayslett, Dec. 30, 1983; children: Kimberly, Benjamin. BS in Aerospace Engring., U. Mich., 1981; MS in Aerospace Engring., Air Force Inst. Tech., 1982. Aerospace engr. Sperry Comml. Flight Systems group Honeywell, Inc., Phoenix, 1987-90; sr. project engr. satellite systems ops. Honeywell, Inc., Glendale, Ariz., 1990-92; sr. project engr. air transport systems Honeywell, Inc., Phoenix, 1992-93, prin. engr., 1993—; presenter in field. Contbr. articles to profl. jours. Mem. Aviation Week Rsch. Adv. Panel, 1990-91. Recipient Certs. of Recognition and Appreciation Lompoc Valley Festival Assn., Inc., 1983, Arnold Air Soc. (comdr. 1979), Cert. of Appreciation Instrument Soc. Am., 1991. Mem. AIAA (sr.), Instrument Soc. Am. (cert. Appreciation 1991, aerospace industries div. and test measurement div. 1991—). Lutheran. Office: Honeywell Air Transport Systems Divsn 21111 N 19th Ave Phoenix AZ 85036

MYERS, HELEN DEE, small business owner; b. Denver. Student in med. tech., U. Colo., 1953-55. Cert. meeting profl. Owner Preferred Sales, Inc., Las Vegas, Nev., 1962-81, Creative Convs., Las Vegas, Nev., 1978—; dir. Office of Small Bus. State of Nev., 1989—. Author, publisher: (book) The Business of Seminars, 1982. Coordinator Mary Gojack for Congress, Nev., 1982, Elect Bob Miller, Las Vegas, 1986; chmn. Women Bus. Owners Polit. Action Com., 1987-88; chmn. Gov.'s Small Bus. Coun., 1989—. Mem. Nat. Assn. Women Bus. Owners (sec. 1985-86, bd. dirs. 1983-89), Nat. Speakers Assn., Meeting Planners Internat. Democrat. Home and Office: 2304 Windjammer Way Las Vegas NV 89107-2361

MYERS, HOMER SAMUEL, technology company executive; b. Salina, Kans., Feb. 20, 1916; s. Clarence Benton and Mary Maude (Booth) M.; m. Marie Alma Beauchamp, Dec. 23, 1939 (div. Dec. 1965); children: Booth Richard, Mary Elizabeth, Gertrude Jane, Homer Samuel Jr. Student, Kans. Wesleyan U., 1934-35; BS, Kans. State U., 1942, MS, 1942. Staff mem. radiation lab. MIT, Cambridge, Mass., 1943-46; group leader Engring. Rsch. Inst. U. Mich., Ann Arbor, 1946-48; pres. Radioactive Products, Inc., Detroit, 1948-54, Solvex Corp., Louisville, 1964-78, Fibrex Corp., Humacao, P.R., 1967-78, Easco, Inc., Mt. Juliet, Tenn., 1983-86, Advanced Cooling Tech., Inc., Lexington, Ky., 1988—; exec. v.p. Tracerlab, Inc., Boston, 1954-62; v.p. Spindletop Rsch. Inst., Lexington, 1962-64; cons. U.S. AEC, Washington, 1959-63, mem. isotope and radiation devel. adv. com., 1959-63, mem. labor-mgmt. adv. com., 1961-63. Patentee in field. Home: 2100 Skycrest Dr # 9 Walnut Creek CA 94595

MYERS, JEFFREY DONALD, entrepreneurial inventor; b. Phoenix, Mar. 11, 1955; s. Donald Dean and Joan (Lillevig) M. Student, Scottsdale Community Coll., 1974-76, Ariz. State U., 1977-79. Pres. Commerce Fin. Group Ltd., 1981-86, JDM Interests Ltd., Scottsdale, Ariz., 1985-90, Miidea Co., Scottsdale, 1986—, What a Character Co., Scottsdale, 1988—; owner Little Folks Pub., Scottsdale, Ariz., 1986—; pres. Wax Bean Prodn., Scottsdale, 1986—; pres., chief exec. officer Vasco, Charlotte, N.C., 1987-91; owner JDM Pub., Scottsdale, 1987—; pres. Nat. Crazemaker Studio, Scottsdale, 1988—; pres. Innovation Group, Scottsdale. Author: Don't Leave That Leaf, 1987, Boy Who Lost Sight of His Kite, 1987, Two Kings, 1987; co-inventor internat. lic. characters, Wexler, Little Buddy and The Gang from Grinnington Friends, Desert Dog, Prickly Bear, Wild Hares and Surf Newts from Mars; songwriter: Just Pick One and Dance, Hold Me One Last Time, Next Time You Come Around; creator FotoGun, No Logo. Mem. exec. coun. Phoenix Boys and Girls Clubs. Mem. Phoenix C. of C., Scottsdale C. of C., Licensing Industry Merchants Assn., Nashville Songwriters Assn., Ariz. Songwriters Assn., Sigma Alpha Epsilon. Republican. Home and Office: 12629 N Tatum # 206 Phoenix AZ 85032

MYERS, JOHN RICHARD, strategic planner; b. Balt., Apr. 16, 1945; s. John Richard and Margaret Lee (Plummer) M.; m. Joan Kathryn Plastiras, Apr. 20, 1986; children: Athena Laurie, Philip Richard. BS, Mich. State U., 1967; PhD, Calif. Inst. Tech., 1972. Sr. scientist Systems Applications Inc., San Rafael, Calif., 1972-77; system specialist Stanford U., Palo Alto, Calif., 1977-79; mgr. modeling and planning systems GTE Sprint, Burlingame, Calif., 1979-84; dir. computer ctr. Failure Analysis Assocs., Palo Alto, 1984-85; pres. John R. Myers, Inc., Menlo Park, Calif., 1986—; cons. domestic and internat. telecommunications svc. providers. Contbr. articles on telephone network planning, ops. rsch. to tech. publs. Mem. IEEE, Am. math. Soc. Office: John R Myers Inc PO Box 4011 Menlo Park CA 94026

MYERS, JOHN ROBERT, publishing company executive; b. Kansas City, Mo., Feb. 7, 1947; s. George Henry and Georgiana (Benfey) M.; m. Kerry Brown, Apr. 29, 1978 (div. 1989); children: Katharine Bridget, Kristin Brianne. BA, St. Louis U., 1969, MA, 1970; MBA, So. Ill. U., 1975. Account rep. Xerox Edn. Scis., St. Louis, 1971-72; account mgr. Xerox Pub., St. Louis, 1972-73; mgr. Xerox Learning Systems, St. Louis, 1973-75; dir. human resources Edison Brothers Stores, San Diego, 1975-79; pres. Leadership Studies Prodns., San Diego, 1979-84; sr. v.p. Tracom Corp., Denver, 1984—. V.p. St. Louis Ambs., 1972-75. Roman Catholic. Office: Tracom Corp 3773 Cherry Creek N Dr Denver CO 80209

MYERS, MINDY MORAWETZ, admissions director; b. N.Y.C., Aug. 15, 1955; d. John and Alice (Tauscher) Morawetz; m. Richard Allen Myers, Feb. 25, 1990; 1 child, Jacob Allen. BA, SUNY, Binghamton, 1981. Pub. rels. dir. Parents Mag., N.Y.C., 1978-81, Oakland (Calif.) Parks and Recreation Dept., 1983-86, Jewish Fedn., Oakland, 1986-89; writer Solem & Loeb, San Francisco, 1981-82; TV host, producer KDOL Channel 13, Oakland, 1982-84; admissions dir., coord. student svcs. Wright Inst., Berkeley, Calif., 1989—; founder Mindox Ink, Oakland, 1989—. Author: (children's book) Goldie, 1985, (play) Miller's High, 1973; screenwriter: With Wings I Can Fly, 1990; composer children's music, 1973. Bd. dirs. Jewish Community Rels. Coun., Oakland, 1984-86; bd. dirs. resettlement program Jewish Family Svcs., Oakland, 1988. Mem. Bay Area Screenwriters Assn. (founder, pres. 1987-91). Office: Wright Inst 2728 Durant Berkeley CA 94704

MYERS, RICHARD ALAN, biochemist, researcher; b. Ukiah, Calif., Nov. 29, 1953; s. Donald James and Renée (Call) M.; m. Peggy Riepe, Nov. 25, 1978; children: Isaac James, Emily Mary. BS in Biology, Brigham Young U., 1979, MS in Biology, 1981; PhD in Biochemistry, U. Utah, 1989. Postdoctoral fellow dept. biology U. Utah, Salt Lake City, 1989-91, rsch. asst. prof. Biology Dept., 1991—. Home: 2160 Carolyn Way Bountiful UT 84010 Office: Univ Utah Biology Dept Salt Lake City UT 84112

MYERS, ROBERT EUGENE, educator, writer; b. Los Angeles, Jan. 15, 1924; s. Harold Eugene and Margaret (Anawalt) M.; AB, U. Calif., Berkeley, 1955; MA (Crown-Zellerbach fellow), Reed Coll., 1960; EdD, U. Ga., 1968; m. Patricia A. Tazer, Aug. 17, 1956; children: Edward E., Margaret A., Hal R., Karen I. Employed in phonograph record business, 1946-54; tchr. elem. sch., Calif., Oreg., Minn., 1954-61; rsch. asst. U. Minn., 1961-62; asst. prof. Augsburg Coll., 1962-63, U. Oreg., 1963-66; elem. tchr., Eugene, Oreg., 1966-67; assoc. prof. U. Victoria, 1968-70; assoc. rsch. prof. Oreg. System of Higher Edn., 1970-73; film maker, producer ednl. filmstrips, books and recs., 1973-77; with Oreg. Dept. Edn., Salem, 1977-81, learning resources specialist, 1977-81, with Linn-Benton Edn. Svc. Dist., Albany, Oreg., 1982-87—. Mem. exec. bd. Nat. Assn. Gifted Children, 1974-77. With U.S. Mcht. Marine, 1944-45. Recipient CINE Golden Eagle award Coun. Internat. Nontheatrical Events, 1973. Mem. Internat. Reading Assn. Democrat. Author: (with E. Paul Torrance) Creative Learning and Teaching (Pi Lambda Theta award 1971), 1970, Can You Imagine?, 1965, Invitations to Thinking and Doing, 1964, Invitations to Speaking and Writing Creatively, 1965, Plots, Puzzles, and Ploys, 1966, For Those Who Wonder, 1966; Timberwood Tales, Vol. II, 1977; Wondering, 1984, Imagining, 1985, Myers-Torrace Creative Developments, 1993, What Next?, 1993. Home: 2650 Olive St Eugene OR 97405-3123

MYERS, ROBERT LOUIS, II, electrical engineer; b. Warsaw, Ind., Nov. 26, 1956; s. Robert Louis and Julia Caroline (Gresso) M.; m. M. Jane Brandt, Dec. 30, 1981; 1 child, Meredith Elizabeth. BSEE, Purdue U., 1979. Elec. engr. Hewlett-Packard Co., Ft. Collins, Colo., 1979—; instr. Front Range C.C., Ft. Collins, 1985-91. Mem. Soc. for Info. Display, Soc. of Motion Picture and Television Engrs., Eta Kappa Nu. Office: Hewlett-Packard Co 3404 E Harmony Rd Fort Collins CO 80525

MYERS, THOMAS ANDREW, naval officer; b. China Lake, Calif., Feb. 17, 1966; s. Russell and Margaret Hill (Hubbard) M. BS, U. Wash., 1988. Commd. ensign USN, 1988, advanced through grades to lt.; various duties, 1988-91; traine USS Calif., Bremerton, Wash., 1990-91, RL-div. officer, 1991-92, E-div. officer, 1992—. Republican. Home: 121 Vine St Ste 2405 Seattle WA 98121-1457 Office: USS Calif GN-36 FPO AP WA 96662-1163

MYERSON, RAYMOND KING, investment counseling company executive; b. Chgo., Oct. 21, 1917; s. Harry J. and Minnie (King) M.; m. Natalie Salter, Feb. 20, 1943; children: Bette Kay, Toby Salter. BA, U. Chgo., 1940. Gen. sales mgr. Helene Curtis Industries Inc., Chgo., 1946-60; v.p., dir. mktg. Solo Cup Co., Chgo., 1961-62; v.p. internat. div. Max Factor & Co., Hollywood, Calif., 1963-69; pres., chief exec. officer Myerson Van Den Berg & Co., Santa Barbara, Calif., 1969—. Trustee, treas. Santa Barbara Mus. Natural History, 1975—; bd. dirs., treas. Rec. for Blind, Santa Barbara, 1975-90, U. Calif.-Santa Barbara affiliates, 1990—. treas., active various local polit. campaigns. Lt. USNR, 1942-45. Republican. Office: 3336 Campanil Dr Santa Barbara CA 93109-1017

MYHRE-HOLLERMAN, JANET MARLENE, mathematician; b. Tacoma, Sept. 24, 1932; d. Leif Christian Klippen and Thelma (Fenney) Dickenson; m. Leon Hollerman, May, 1988; 1 child, Karin Myhre. BA, Pacific Luth. U., 1954; MA, U. Wash., 1956; PhD, Fil Lic Inst. Math. Stats., U. Stockholm, Sweden, 1968. Rsch. engr. Boeing Math. Svcs. Unit and Sci. Rsch. Labs., 1956-58; stats. cons. U. Stockholm, 1958-60; instr. math. Harvey Mudd Coll., Claremont, Calif., 1961-62; prof. math. Claremont McKenna Coll., 1962—; pres. Math. Analysis Rsch. Corp., Claremont, 1973—; mem. math. grad. faculty Claremont Grad. Sch., 1968; vis. prof. U. Stockholm, Eidgenossiche Technische, Zurich, Switzerland, 1971-72; dir. Inst. Decision Sci. Claremont McKenna Coll., 1975. Assoc. editor Technometrics, Claremont, 1969-75; editorial bd. Quality Mag., 1981-88; contbr. numerous articles to profl. jours. Recipient Austin Bonis award Am. Soc. for Quality Control, 1984. Mem. Inst. Math. Stats., Statis. Assn. of Am., Am. Assn. Quality Control, Phi Beta Kappa, Sigma Xi. Office: Claremont McKenna Coll Claremont CA 91711

MYHREN, TRYGVE EDWARD, communications company executive; b. Palmerton, Pa., Jan. 3, 1937; s. Arne Johannes and Anita (Blatz) M.; m. Carol Jane Enman, Aug. 8, 1964; children: Erik, Kirsten, Tor; m. 2d Victoria Hamilton, Nov. 14, 1981; 1 stepchild, Paige. BA in Philosophy and Polit. Sci., Dartmouth Coll., 1958, MBA, 1959. Sales mgr., unit mgr. Procter and Gamble, Cin., 1963-65; sr. cons. Glendinning Cos., Westport, Conn., 1965-69; pres. Auberge Vintners, 1970-73; exec. v.p. Mktg. Continental, Westport, 1969-73; v.p., gen. mgr. CRM, Inc., Del Mar, Calif., 1973-75; v.p. mktg. Am. TV and Communications Corp., Englewood, Colo., 1975-78, sr. v.p. mktg. and programming, 1978-79, exec. v.p., 1980, pres., 1981, chmn. bd., chief exec. officer, 1981-88; v.p. then exec. v.p. Time Inc., N.Y.C., 1981-88; treas., vice chmn. then chmn. bd. dirs., mem. exec. com. Nat. Cable TV Assn., Washington, 1982-91; mem. adv. com. on HDTV, FCC, 1987-89; bd. dirs. Advanced Mktg. System, Inc., LaJolla, Citizens Bank Corp., Providence; pres. Myhren Media, 1989—, Greenwood Cable Mgmt., 1989-91, Providence Jour. Co., 1990—; pres. CEO King Broadcast Co., 1991—. Vice chmn. Pub. Edn. Coalition; mem. Colo. Forum, 1984-91, chmn. higher edn. com., 1986; bd. dirs., founder Colo. Bus. Com. for the Arts, 1985-91; mem. exec. coun. Found. for Commemoration U.S. Constn., 1987-90; mem. Nat. GED Task Force, 1987-90; mem. Colo. Baseball Commn., 1989-91; mem. Colo. Film Commn., 1989-91; trustee Nat. Jewish Hosp., 1989—, Rhodes Island Hosp., 1991—. Lt. (j.g.) USNR, 1959-63. Recipient Disting. Leader award Nat. Cable TV Assn., 1988. Mem. Cable TV Adminstrn. and Mktg. Soc. (pres. 1978-79, Grand Tam award 1985), Cable Adv. Bur. (founder 1978), Chrons and Colitis Found. Am. (trustee Rocky Mountain chpt.). Episcopalian.

MYKKANEN, DONALD LEE, engineering company executive; b. Bovey, Minn., Jan. 7, 1932; s. John and Elnor Lillian (Feldt) M.; m. Juanita Mae Follmer, Feb. 4, 1956; children: Ellen M., JoAnn M., Marian J., John W., Susan L. BS, UCLA, 1954; MS, U. Ill., 1956, PhD, 1961. Instr. mech. engrng. U. Ill., Urbana, 1956-61; mgr. materials R & D, McDonnell Douglas Astronautics, Huntington Beach, Calif., 1961-76; pres. ETA Corp., Fallbrook, Calif., 1976—; lectr. Systems Mgmt. Inst. U. Soc. Calif., L.A., 1976-87; cons. on nuclear effects on electronics to Litton Systems, BDM Corp., U.S. Army. Co-author: Metals Selection and Treatment, 1957, Metal and Polymer Matrix Composites, 1987. Speaker on sci. and tech. to civic meetings and schs., 1975—. Mem. IEEE, AIAA (chmn. Orange County sect. 1976, dept. dir. pub. policy region 6, 1976-78), Am. Soc. for Metals, Sigma Xi, Tau Beta Pi, Pi Tau Sigma, Sigma Mu. Office: ETA Corp PO Box 1075 Bonsall CA 92003-1075

MYSELS, KAROL JOSEPH, research chemist, consultant; b. Krakow, Poland, Apr. 14, 1914; came to U.S., 1938; s. Adolf Abraham and Janina Henryka (Rosenberg) Meisels; m. Helen B. Meisels, 1938 (div. 1951); m. Estella Ruth Katzenellenbogen, Mar. 28, 1953. Licencie Sci., U. Lyon (France), 1937, Ingenieur Chemiste, 1937; PhD, Harvard U., 1941. Registered patent agt. Mem. staff patent and engrng. dept. Shell Devel. Co., San Francisco, 1940-42; rsch. asst., assoc. Stanford (Calif.) U., 1941-45; instr. NYU, N.Y.C., 1945-47; from asst. prof. to prof. U. So. Calif., L.A., 1947-66; assoc. dir. rsch. R.J. Reynolds Co., Winston Salem, N.C., 1966-70; sr. rsch. advisor Gen. Atomic Co., San Diego, 1970-79; prin. Rsch. Cons., La Jolla, Calif., 1979—; rsch. chemist U. Calif., San Diego, 1979—; cons. various industries, 1950-66, 79—; vis. prof. Sci. U. Tokyo, 1987; invited lectr. Coll. de France, Paris, 1987, 91, 92; external examiner U. Paris, 1991, 92; assoc. mem. Commn. on Colloid and Surface Chemistry, 1961-69, titular mem., 1969-79, chmn., 1973-79; mem. com. on phys. chemistry Internat. Union of Pure and Applied Chemistry. Mem. editorial bd. Jour. Chem. Edn., 1958-65, Jour. Colloid Sci., 1959-67, Jour. Membrane Biology, 1960-73, Jour. Phys. Chemistry, 1961-62, 75-81, Colloids and Surfaces, 1979—, Langmuir, 1984-90, 92—; author: (with others) Intriduction to the Science of Chemistry, 1952, Introduction to Colloid Chemistry, 1978, Soap Films, Studies of Their Thinning and a Bibliography, 1959, Critical Micelle Contractions of Agueous Surfactant Systems, 1971. With Chem. Corps, U.S. Army, 1042-43. Fellow NSF, 1957-58, 62-63, J.S. Guggenheim Found., 1965-66. Fellow Am. Inst. Chemists (nat. coun. 1969-76, chmn. 1973-79, com. mem. 1975-79); mem. Am. Chem. Soc. (nat. coun. 1961-62, 73-83, Kendall award 1964, co-editor 20 Years of Colloid and Surface Chemistry--The Kendall Award Addresses 1973, 18 Years of Colloid and Surface Chemistry--The Kendall Award Addresses, 1991). Home and Office: 8327 N La Jolla Scenic Dr La Jolla CA 92037-2220

MYSLEWSKI, RIK, magazine editor, writer; b. San Francisco, July 13, 1950; s. Edward Casimir and Julia (Zukowska) M.; m. Marilyn Bancel, Nov. 20, 1983; children: Carolyn, Roxanne. BA in Dramatic Art, U. Calif., Davis, 1976, MFA in Playwriting, 1979. Musician, actor San Francisco, 1973-81; assoc. dir. devel. Exploratorium, San Francisco, 1981-89; exec. editor MacUser, Foster City, Calif., 1989—; pres. Playwrights Found., Mill Valley, Calif., 1987-89. Author: (play) Carmaker, 1982; author and editor numerous magazine articles, 1989—. Mem. World Affairs Coun., San Francisco, 1989—, Gorbachev Found., San Francisco, 1992—. Democrat. Home: 328 Duncan San Francisco CA 94131 Office: MacUser 950 Tower Lane 18th Floor Foster City CA 94404

NACHBAR, JAMES MILTON, plastic surgeon, computer programmer; b. Chgo., Mar. 22, 1956; s. Milton Max Nachbar and Elizabeth Joan Nelson; m. Joyce Ann Irwin, Apr. 16, 1986. BA in Biology, U. Chgo., 1976; MD, Washington U., St. Louis, 1980. Diplomat Am. Bd. Surgery, Am. Bd. Plastic Surgery. Surg. resident U. Ariz., Tucson, 1980-85; plastic surg. resident U. Va., Charlottesville, 1985-88; asst. prof. plastic surgery U. N.Mex., Albuquerque, 1988-91, chief plastic surgery, 1991—. Author: (chpts.) Congenital Craniofacial Malformations, 1991; author (computer programs) Impair, 1989, PSEF 1991-93 Computerized In-Service Review, 1991-93; contbr. articles to profl. jours. Recipient grant Plastic Surgery Ednl. Found., 1990. Mem. AMA, Am. Soc. Plastic & Reconstructive Surgeons, Plastic Surgery Rsch. Coun., Assn. for Computing Machinery, Assn. Acad. Chmn. of Plastic Surgery, Greater Albuquerque Med. Assn., Am. Cleft Palate-Craniofacial Assn. Office: Univ NMex Dept Surgery 2211 Lomas Blvd NE Albuquerque NM 87131

NACHT, SERGIO, biochemist; b. Buenos Aires, Apr. 13, 1934; came to U.S., 1965; s. Oscar and Carmen (Scheiner) N.; m. Beatriz Kahan, Dec. 21, 1958; children: Marcelo H., Gabriel A., Mariana S., Sandra M. BA in Chemistry, U. Buenos Aires, 1958, MS in Biochemistry, 1960, PhD in Biochemistry, 1964. Asst. prof. biochemistry U. Buenos Aires, 1960-64; asst. prof. medicine U. Utah, Salt Lake City, 1965-70; rsch. scientist Alza Corp., Palo Alto, Calif., 1970-73; sr. investigator Richardson-Vicks Inc., Mt. Vernon, N.Y., 1973-76; asst. dir., dir. rsch. Richardson-Vicks Inc., Mt. Vernon, 1976-83; dir. biomed. rsch. Richardson-Vicks Inc., Shelton, Conn., 1983-87; sr. v.p. rsch. and devel. Advanced Polymer Systems, Redwood City, Calif., 1987—; lectr. dermatology dept. SUNY Downstate Med. Ctr., Blkyn., 1977-87. Contbr. articles to profl. jours.; patentee in field. Mem. Soc. Investigative Dermatology, Soc. Cosmetic Chemists (award 1981), Dermatology Found., Am. Physiological Soc., Am. Acad. Dermatology. Democrat. Jewish. Home: 409 Wembley Ct Redwood City CA 94061-4308

NACHT, STEVE JERRY, geologist; b. Cleve., July 8, 1948; s. Max and Elfrida (Kamm) N.; m. Patricia Katherine Osicka, Aug. 3, 1976; 1 child, David Martin. BS in Geology, Kent State U., 1971, MS in Geology, 1973; MS in Urban Studies, Cleve. State U., 1979. Registered geologist, S.C., Va., Wyo.; environ. assessor, Calif.; cert. geologist, Ind.; lic. drinking water treatment class III, Ohio; cert. environ. mgr., Nev. Geologist Cleve. Utilities Dept., 1974-78; geologist, hydrologist Dalton, Dalton & Newport, Cleve., 1979-82; prin. scientist Lockheed-Emsco, Las Vegas, Nev., 1983-86; sr. geologist, project mgr. Earth Tech. Inc., Long Beach, Calif., 1986-87, The MARK Group, Las Vegas, 1987-89; dir. waste tech., sr. geologist Reynolds Elec. & Engring. Co., Las Vegas, 1990-92, acting chief environ. remediation sect., 1992—; mem. tech. adv. com. for cert. of underground storage tank handlers and testers, Nev. Contbr. articles to profl. jours. Mem. AAAS, ASTM (groundwater com., past chmn. sect., well maintenance, rehab. and decommissioning sect.), Am. Inst. Profl. Geologists (cert.), Assn. Ground Water Scientists and Engrs., Assn. Engring. Geologists. Home: 4184 Del Rosa Ct Las Vegas NV 89121-5011 Office: Reynolds Elec & Engring Co PO Box 98521 Las Vegas NV 89193-8521

NADELL, ANDREW THOMAS, psychiatrist; b. N.Y.C., Nov. 3, 1946; s. Samuel Tyler and Bertha Elaine (Trupine) N. MA, Columbia U., 1968; MSc, U. London, 1973; MD, Duke U., 1974. Diplomate Am. Bd. Psychiatry and Neurology. Resident in psychiatry U. Calif., Davis, 1974-77; clin. instr. psychiatry Stanford (Calif.) U. Sch. Medicine, 1979-84, clin. asst. prof. psychiatry, 1984—. Trustee Calif. Hist. Soc., 1989—. Fellow Royal Soc. Medicine; mem. Am. Psychiat. Assn., Am. Assn. History Medicine, Am. Osler Soc., Bay Area History Medicine Soc. (sec. 1984-88, v.p. 1988-90, pres. 1990-92, bd. govs. 1992—), Soc. Social History Medicine, Assn. Internat. de Bibliphilie, Soc. Internat. d'Histoire de la Medicine, Stanford U. Librs. Assocs. (adv. coun. 1988—), Univ. Club, Olympic Club (San Francisco), Grolier Club (N.Y.C.), Roxburghe Club, Colophon Club, Book Club of Calif. (San Francisco). Office: 1828 El Camino Real Burlingame CA 94010-3103

NADY, JOHN, electronics company executive; b. Agfalva, Hungary, Feb. 13, 1945; came to U.S., 1951; s. John and Hermine Nady. BSEE, Calif. Inst. Tech., 1965; MSEE, U. Calif., Berkeley, 1968. Elec. engr. Lawrence Radiation Lab., Livermore, 1966-71, Westinghouse Corp., Oakland, Calif., 1971-72; owner, chief exec. officer Nady Systems, Inc., Oakland, Calif., 1976—, Calif. Concerts, Inc., Oakland, Calif., 1985—. Patentee in field. Mem. Nat. Assn. Broadcasters, Audio Engring. Soc., Nat. Assn. Music Merchants. Office: Nady Systems Inc 6701 Bay St Emeryville CA 94608-1023

NAEGELE, CHARLES JOSEPH, lawyer; b. San Francisco; s. Charles F. and Rosemary Naegele. AB, U. Calif., Berkeley, 1974; JD, U. Calif., San Francisco, 1978. Bar: Calif. 1979. Pvt. practice San Jose, Calif., 1979—. Office: 111 N Market St San Jose CA 95113

NAESER, CHARLES WILBUR, geologist; b. Washington, July 2, 1940; s. Charles Rudolph and Elma (Meyer) N.; m. Barbara Sillcocks, July 13, 1963 (div. Dec. 1979); children: Christiana, Robert; m. Nancy Dearean Cozad, Feb. 6, 1982. BA, Dartmouth Coll., 1962, MA, 1964; PhD, So. Meth. U., 1967. Geologist, U.S. Geol. Survey, Menlo Park, Calif., 1967-71; geologist, U.S. Geol. Survey, Denver, 1971—; adj. prof. Dartmouth Coll., Hanover, N.H., 1979—, U. Wyo., Laramie, 1984—. Contbr. articles to profl. jours. Leader, Cub Scouts, 1981, asst. scoutmaster, 1982, 83, 84. Fellow Geol. Soc. Am.; mem. Am. Geophys. Union, Colo. Sci. Soc. (coun. 1982-84, Best Paper award 1981), Denver Garden Railway Soc. (treas. 1990-93). Republican. Office: US Geol Survey MS-974 Federal Center Denver CO 80225

NAGAO, NORRIS SADATO, political science educator, consultant; b. Sacramento, June 9, 1954; s. Sadao and Misao (Iwahashi) N. AA, Sacramento City Coll., 1973; AB, U. Calif., Berkeley, 1975; MA, Columbia U., 1979, EdM, 1980. Legis. aide Calif. State Assembly, Sacramento, 1976-77; exec. dir. N.Y.-Tokyo-Beijing Nanshiki Baseball Friendship Series, N.Y.C., 1981-84; exec. sec. N.Am.-Japan Promotions, Inc., N.Y.C., 1986-89; pres. Mediagenesis Inc., L.A., 1988-91; asst. prof. polit. sci. Southwestern Coll., Chula Vista, Calif., 1991—. Mem. selection com. The Harvey Milk/Tom Homann Scholarship Fund, Gay and Lesbian Alliance Against Defamation San Diego, Media Action Network Asian Ams., San Diego-Yokohama Sister City Soc. Mem. Japan Am. Soc. of So. Calif., Popular Culture Assn., Pub. Broadcasting KPBS TV/FM San Diego, Calif. Alumni Assn., Alumni of Columbia U., Alumni Fedn. Columbia U., Sacramento City Coll. Alumni Assn., Log Cabin Club, Kappa Delta Pi. Office: Southwestern Coll 900 Otay Lakes Rd Chula Vista CA 91910-7299

NAGEL, DARYL DAVID, retail executive; b. Arlington, Minn., Apr. 13, 1939; s. Paul Charles and Frieda L. (Oldenburg) N.; m. Joan Clare Dacey, Dec. 23, 1961; children: Kelly, Adnrew, Maureen. BME, U. Minn., 1962; diploma in Advanced Mgmt. Program, Harvard U., 1978. Asst. mdse. mgr. Reserus Supply Co., Mpls., 1962-65, mdse. mgr., 1965-66, v.p., gen. mgr., 1966-69; v.p. area gen. mgr. United Bldg. Ctrs., Winona, Minn., 1969-78, exec. v.p., chief ops. officer, 1978-84, pres., chief exec. officer, 1984-87; pres. cheif exec. officer Lanoga Corp., Seattle, 1987—; bd. dirs. Lanoga Corp., Seattle, 1987—, Badger Foundry, Winona, 1984-87. Bd. dirs. United Way, Winona, 1978-84. Mem. Home Ctr. Leadership Coun., C. of C. (bd. dirs. 1964-69, 73, 78), Winona Country Club. Republican. Lutheran. Office: Lanoga Corp 17946 NE 65th St Redmond WA 98052-4963

NAGEL, JEROME KAUB, architect; b. Denver, Dec. 26, 1923; s. Fritz Andrew and Josephine (Gaylord) N.; m. Cynthia Fels, Sept. 1, 1951; children—Peter Barry, James Gaylord. B.Arch., Yale U., 1949. Registered architect, Colo. Prin. J.K. Nagel Architect, Denver, 1953-61, Rogers & Nagel, Denver, 1961-66, Rogers, Nagel, Langhart, Architects, 1966-77, Interplan Inc., 1969-77; pres. Nagel Investment Co.; dir. Bank Western, Denver, Field Devel. Corp., Denver. Mem. Colo. Hwy. Commn., chmn., 1982-83; bd. dirs. Planned Parenthood Fed. Am. Inc., N.Y.C., 1974-78, Rocky Mountain Planned Parenthood, Denver, 1972-76, Colo. chpt. ARC, 1957-60, 80-81, Denver Santa Claus Shop, 1987-91; mem. panel arbitrators Am. Arbitration Assn., 1962—; chmn. Colo. Bicycling Adv., Denver Bicycling Adv. Bd. Bd. Served to 1st lt. AC U.S. Army, 1943-45. Decorated D.F.C., Air medal with 11 oak leaf clusters. Mem. AIA (nat. life; sec. chpt. 1960-61, pres. 1962-63), Denver Country (bd. dirs. 1983-86), University (bd. dirs. 1962-66) Mile High, Denver Rotary Club Found. (pres. 1992-93), Denver Athletic Club. Episcopalian. Home: 67 Eudora St Denver CO 80220-6311

NAGEL, PATRICIA JO, non-profit public policy administrator, lawyer; b. Billings, Mont., Sept. 24, 1942; d. Robert Mark and Evelyn Margaret (Lipsack) McKeown; m. Robert Wells Nagel, Aug. 18, 1963; children: Stacia, Susanna. BA in Polit. Sci., N.Mex. State U., 1965; JD, U. Wyo., 1983. Bar: Wyo. 1984. Interior designer Nassif's Interiors, Cedar Rapids, Iowa, 1965-67, Cedar Rapids Paint, 1973-74; law clk. to presiding justice 7th jud. dist., Casper, Wyo., 1983-84; sole practice Casper, 1984—; dir. Wyo. Futures Project, Casper, 1986—. Sr. editor Land and Water Law Rev., 1982-83. Mem. planning commn. City of Casper, 1980; pres., bd. dirs. Friends of Library, Casper, 1980; pres. Meadowlark Montessori Sch., Casper, 1979; sec. Casper Bicentennial Com., 1976; v.p. Nicolaysen Art Mus., Casper, 1985-86; sec., bd. dirs. Hospice Cancer Treatment Ctr., Casper, 1985-86. Mem. ABA, Natrona County Bar Assn., Wyo. State Bar Assn., Assn. Trial Lawyers Am. Republican. Lutheran. Home: 1105 S Durbin St Casper WY 82601-4327 Office: 300 S Wolcott St Casper WY 82601-2839

NAGEL, RONALD CURTIS, electrical engineer; b. Park Ridge, Ill., June 29, 1961; s. Robert Ira and Edda (Hoerer) N. BSEE, U. Ariz., 1986. Intern engr. GTE R & D Labs., Phoenix, 1980, Motorola Microsystems, Scottsdale, Ariz., 1981-82, IBM, Tucson, 1983, Computer Automation, Tucson, 1983; cons. Nagel Electronics, Chgo., 1984—; engr. Zenith Corp., Chgo., 1985; engr., project leader NATO program Motorola GEG, Scottsdale, Ariz., 1986—. Mem. Nat. Rep. Com., Washington, 1987—. Mem. Mensa, Phi Eta Sigma, Tau Beta Pi. Home: 2853 S El Marino St Mesa AZ 85202-7907 Office: Motorola GEG 8201 E Mcdowell Rd Scottsdale AZ 85257-3893

NAGEL, STANLEY BLAIR, construction executive, investment executive; b. Bklyn., Mar. 19, 1928; s. Robert Arthur and Renee Ann Nagel; children: Scott Alan, Robert Arthur. BBA, U. Oreg., 1950. With constrn. dept. Nagel Investment, Portland, Oreg., 1955-58, pres., 1956—; pres. R.A. Constrn., Portland, 1956—; buyer May Co., Portland, 1958-72; gen. mgr. Portland Outdoor Store, 1972-75; sales rep. maj. accounts Williamson-Dickie Mfg. Co., Ft. Worth, 1975—; pres. E & S Distbrs., Portland, 1982—. Co-inventor pizza machine (patent pending). 2d lt. U.S. Army, 1952-55. Republican. Jewish. Home and Office: 5353 SW Martha St Portland OR 97221-1840

NAGER, NORMAN, communications educator; b. Schuylerville, N.Y., June 2, 1936. BA in Journalism, U. So. Calif., 1957, MA in Journalism, 1970, PhD in Speech Comm., 1978. Publicity writer City of L.A., 1955-57; reporter South Coast News, 1957; info. specialist U.S. Army So. Area Command, Germany, 1957-60; reporter Daily Rev., 1960; pub. rels. writer Prudential Ins. Co. Am., 1961-62; assoc. editor TRW's Space Tech. Labs., 1962-63; adminstrv. asst.to assembly speaker Calif. State Legis., 1963-65, cons. to majority caucus, 1965-67; pub. rels. dir. Meml. Med. Ctr. Long Beach, Calif., 1967-74; lectr. U. So. Calif., 1974-76; pub. rels. counselor Norman R. Nager & Assocs., 1974-76; asst. prof. Calif. State U., Fullerton, 1976-79, assoc. prof., 1979-84, prof., 1984—; chairperson faculty senate, exec. coun. Comm. Sch., Calif. State U., 1992—. Author: Public Relations Management By Objectives, 1984, Strategic Public Relations Counseling, 1987. Recipient Pathfinder award Found. Pub. Relation Rsch. and Edn., 1987,. Fellow Pub. Rels. Soc. Am. (chmn. edn. sect. 1983, co-chmn. ednl. affairs com. 1983, mem. nat. honors and awards com. 1987—, mem. silver anvil com. 1985—, judge 1987—, Outstanding Educator in U.S. 1985); mme. Assn. Edn. in Journalism and Mass Comm. (chair pub. rels. div. 1982-83). Office: Calif State Univ Dept Communications H-230 800 N State College Blvd Fullerton CA 92634-3599

NAGLER, MICHAEL NICHOLAS, classics, comparative literature educator; b. N.Y.C., Jan. 20, 1937; s. Harold and Dorothy Judith (Nocks) N.; m. Roberta Ann Robbins (div. May 1983); children: Jessica, Joshua. BA, NYU, 1960; MA, U. Calif., Berkeley, 1962, PhD, 1966. Instr. San Francisco State U., 1963-65; prof. classics, comparative lit. dept. U. Calif., Berkeley, 1966-91, prof. emeritus, 1991—. Author: Spontaneity and Tradition, 1974, America Without Violence, 1982; co-author: The Upanishads, 1987; contbr. articles to profl. pubs. Fellow Am. Coun. Learned Socs., NIH; MacArthur Found. grantee, 1988. Mem. Am. Philolog. Soc. (editor Oral Tradition). Office: U Calif Classics Dept Berkeley CA 94720

NAGLER, STEWART GORDON, insurance company executive; b. Bklyn., Jan. 30, 1943; s. Henry and Mary N.; m. Bonnie Lawrence, Aug. 9, 1964;

children: David, Ellen. B.S. summa cum laude, Poly. U., 1963. With Met. Life Ins. Co., N.Y.C., 1963—, exec. v.p., 1978-85, sr. exec. v.p., 1985—; chmn. bd. Century 21 Real Estate Corp., Irvine, Calif. Fellow Soc. Actuaries, Acad. Actuaries. Office: Met Life Ins Co 1 Madison Ave New York NY 10010-3603 also: Century 21 Real Estate Corp 2601 SE Main St Irvine CA 92707

NAGLESTAD, FREDERIC ALLEN, legislative advocate; b. Sioux City, Iowa, Jan. 13, 1929; s. Ole T. and Evelyn Elizabeth (Erschen) N.; student (scholar) U. Chgo., 1947-49; m. Beverly Minnette Shellberg, Feb. 14, 1958; children—Patricia Minnette, Catherine Janette. Pub. affairs, pub. relations, newscaster, announcer KSCJ-radio, Sioux City, Iowa, 1949-51; producer, dir., newscaster, announcer WOW-TV, Omaha, 1953-57; program mgr. WCPO-TV, Cin., 1957-58; mgr. KNTV-TV, San Jose, Calif., 1958-61; owner Results Employment Agy., San Jose, 1961-75; legis. advocate Naglestad Assocs., Calif. Automotive Wholesalers Assn., Air Quality Products, Calif. Assn. Wholesalers-Distbrs., State Alliance Bd. Equalization Reform, Quakemaster, many others, 1969—. Pres. Calif. Employment Assn., 1970-72. Asst. concertmaster Sioux City Symphony Orch., 1945-47. Sgt. AUS, 1951-53. Recognized for outstanding contbn. to better employment law, Resolution State Calif. Legislature, 1971. Office: 3991 Fair Oaks Blvd Sacramento CA 95864-7254

NAGOSHI, CRAIG TETSUO, psychology researcher; b. Honolulu, Mar. 9, 1956; s. Kunio and Tokiko (Nonaga) N.; m. Deborah Sparrow, Oct. 26, 1991. BA in Psychology, U. Hawaii, 1978, MA in Psychology, 1980, PhD in Psychology, 1984. Researcher Inst. Behavioral Genetics U. Colo., Boulder, 1984-87; staff fellow Nat. Inst. on Drug Abuse Addiction Rsch. Ctr., Balt., 1987-89; asst. prof. dept. psychology Ariz. State U., Tempe, 1989—; statis. cons., Honolulu, 1980-84. Contbr. articles to profl. jours. Mem. Howard County SANE/FREEZE, 1987-89. Drug Abuse Tng. grantee Nat. Inst. Drug Abuse, 1984-86. Mem. Behavior Genetics Assn., Internat. Soc. Biomed. Research on Alcoholism, Internat. Soc. Study of Individual Differences, Research Soc. on Alcoholism, Sigma Xi. Democrat. Home: 1715 S La Rosa Dr Tempe AZ 85281-6820 Office: Ariz State U Dept Psychology Tempe AZ 85287

NAGY, KENNETH A(LEX), biology educator; b. Santa Monica, Calif., July 1, 1943; s. Alex J. and Phyllis F. Nagy; m. Patricia Vaughan, June 11, 1967; children: Mark S., Erik M. AB in Biology, U. Calif., Riverside, 1967, PhD in Biology, 1971. Asst. prof. biology UCLA, 1971-77, assoc. prof., 1977-83, prof., 1983—. Contbr. articles to profl. jours. Active Boy Scouts Am., Los Angeles, 1982—. Served with U.S. Navy, 1962-64. Grantee NSF, U.S. Dept. Energy. Mem. AAAS, Ecol. Soc. Am., Am. Soc. Ichthyologists and Herpetologists. Home: 11833 Allaseba Dr Los Angeles CA 90066-1112 Office: UCLA Lab Biomed and Environ Scis 900 Veteran Ave Los Angeles CA 90024-1787

NAHAS, WALTER N., metallurgy manager; b. Cairo, Egypt, June 14, 1938; came to U.S., 1964; s. Nadim G. and Nada (Khawam) N.; m. Micheline Ibrahim, Oct. 7, 1972; children: Kareem, Andrew. BS in Chem. Engring., Cairo U., 1961; MS in Chem. Engring., NYU, 1968. Plant engr. Egyptian Iron & Steel Co., Helwan, 1961-63; sr. process engr. The Lummus Co., Bloomfield, N.J., 1965-70, Holmes & Narver Inc., Orange, Calif., 1970-72; from sr. to supervising engr. Fluor Daniel Inc., San Mateo, Calif., 1972-77; mgr. pyro & electrometallurgy Fluor Daniel Inc., Redwood City, Calif., 1977-80; mgr. process tech. Flour Daniel Inc., Redwood City, Calif., 1980-83, mgr. advanced tech. planning, 1983-85, prin. tech. mgr., 1985-89, mgr. metallurgy, 1989—; cons. Fluor Daniel Inc., 1983—. Contbr. articles to profl. jours. Mem. Am. Inst. Mining & Metallurgical Engrs., Am. Inst. Chem. Engrs. Republican. Greek Catholic. Home: 709 Crane Ave Foster City CA 94404

NAHMAN, NORRIS STANLEY, electrical engineer; b. San Francisco, Nov. 9, 1925; s. Hyman Cohen and Rae (Levin) N.; m. Shirley D. Maxwell, July 20, 1968; children: Norris Stanley, Vicki L., Vance W., Scott T. B.S. in Electronics Engring, Calif. Poly. State U., 1951; M.S.E.E., Stanford U., 1952; Ph.D. in Elec. Engring, U. Kans., 1961. Registered profl. engr., Colo. Electronic scientist Nat. Security Agy., Washington, 1952-55; prof. elec. engring., dir. electronics rsch. lab. U. Kans., Lawrence, 1955-66; sci. cons., chief pulse and time domain sect. Nat. Bur. Standards, Boulder, Colo., 1966-73; chief time domain metrology, sr. scientist Nat. Bur. Standards, 1975-83, group leader field characterization group, 1984-85; v.p. Picosecond Pulse Labs, Inc., Boulder, 1986-90; cons. elec. engr., 1990—; prof., chmn. dept. elec. engring. U. Toledo, 1973-75;; prof. elec. engring. U. Colo., Boulder, 1966—; disting. lectr., prin. prof. Centre Nat. d'Etude des Telecommunications Summer Sch., Lannion, France, 1978; disting. lectr. Harbin Inst. Tech., Peoples Republic China, summer 1982; mem. faculty NATO Advanced Study Inst., Castelvecchio, Italy, 1983, Internat. Radio Sci. Union/NRC; chmn. internat. intercommn. group Waveform measurements 1981-90, chmn. Commn. A, 1985-86. Contbr. rsch. articles profl. jours.; patentee in field. Asst. scoutmaster Longs Peak coun. Boy Scouts Am., 1970-73, 75-89. With U.S. Mcht. Marine, 1943-46, U.S. Army, 1952-55. Ford Found. faculty fellow MIT, 1962; Nat. Bur. Standards sr. staff fellow, 1978-79; recipient Disting. Alumnus award Calif. Poly. State U., 1972, Order of Arrow Boy Scouts Am., 1976. Fellow IEEE (life), Internat. Sci. Radio Union; mem. Instrumentation and Measurement Soc. of IEEE (admstrv. com. 1982-84, editorial bd. Trans., 1982-86, Andrew H. chi Best Tech. Paper award 1984, Tech. Leadership and Achievement award 1987), Am. Assn. Engring. Edn., U.S. Mcht. Marine Veterans World War II, Am. Legion, Calif. Poly. State U. Alumni Assn. (life), Stanford U. (life), U. Kans. (life), Am. Radio Relay League Club (life), Sigma Pi Sigma, Tau Beta Pi, Eta Kappa Nu, Sigma Tau, Sigma Xi. Office: 375 Erie Dr Boulder CO 80303-3524

NAHMIAS, VICTOR JAY, architect; b. Woodside, N.Y., May 2, 1951; s. Leon and Judith (Haupt) N.; m. Michal Caspi, June 24, 1975; children: Ariel, Tamar. BA, U. Pa., 1973; BArch, U. B.C., Vancouver, 1977. Registered profl. architect. Carpenter's asst. Weir Constrn., Vancouver, 1973; designer, draftsman Kenn Butts, Northridge, Calif., 1977-78; project mgr. B. Robert Axton, Sherman Oaks, Calif., 1978-79, Howard R. Lane, Woodland Hills, Calif., 1979-81; project architect Rochlin & Baran Assocs., Los Angeles, 1981-84; area architect Kaiser Permanente, Pasadena, 1984-90; ptnr. Wendland-Nahmias AIA & Assocs., Westlake Village, Calif., 1990—; bd. dirs. Kosmic Kids. Bd. dirs., past pres. Cameo Woods Home Owners Assn.; past chmn. Purim Carnival, libr. com. Temple Israel; mem. Nature Conservancy, World Wildlife Fund, Statue of Liberty/Ellis Island Found., L.A. County Mus. Art, Natural History Mus. of L.A. Mem. AIA (co-chmn. L.A. com. on govt. rels., mem. com. on health), AIA Calif. Coun. (steering com., legis. rev. com.), Community Assns. Inst., Am. Philatelic Soc., Nat. Trust for Hist. Preservation, Nat. Audubon Soc., Sierra Club, Conejo Valley C. of C., Westlake Village C. of C. Democrat. Jewish. Home: 3647 Kalsman Dr Apt L Los Angeles CA 90016-4447 Office: 5706 Corsa Ave Thousand Oaks CA 91362-4001

NAHM-MIJO, TRINA, social science educator, dancer, choreographer; b. Honolulu, Sept. 4, 1949; d. Matthew Mai Tai and Elizabeth (Whang) Nahm; m. Jerry Lee Nahm-Mijo, Nov. 18, 1976; children: Rengé, Shayne. BA in Psychology, U. Hawaii, 1969, MEd in Ednl. Psychology, 1971; MPH in Community Mental Health, U. Calif., Berkeley, 1974, PhD in Counseling Psychology, 1979. Dir. dance U. Hawaii, Hilo, 1976-80; lectr. psychology Hawaii Community Coll., Hilo, 1978-79, prof. psychology and sociology, 1979—, chairperson Gen. Edn. and Pub. Svc. div., 1988-91; exchange instr. psychology Santa Monica (Calif.) City Coll., 1985-86; mem. adj. faculty Vt. Coll. of Norwich U., Montpelier, 1987—; coun. chairperson U. Hawaii, Hilo, 1984-85, equal employment opportunity/affirmation action officer, 1991-93. Choreographer (dance/film) Wheels, 1979 (finalist U.S.A. Film Festival 1981, short documentary finalist Acad. Awards 1981). Pres. Family Crisis Shelter, Inc., Hilo, 1987—; mem. adv. bd. Kalani Honua Culture and Conf. Ctr., Kalapana, Hawaii, 1980—; bd. dirs. Kamanawa Sch. Personel Devel., Hilo, 1990-93.. Recipient Leadership in the Arts award YWCA, Hilo, 1984; travel grantee Pres.'s Adv. Com., U. Hawaii, 1990, Humanities grantee NEH, Washington, 1990. Mem. Hawaii State Dance Coun. (grantee 1977, 91), U. Hawaii Commn. on Status of Women (1987-91), Dance 'O Hawaii (founding), 'Ohana O Wahine (founding). Office: U Hawaii Hawaii Community Coll Gen Edn and Pub Svc Div Hilo HI 96720-4091

NAKABAYASHI, NICHOLAS TAKATERU, retired retail executive; b. Honolulu, Feb. 25, 1920; s. Denji and Ume (Teraoka) N. BS, Utah State U., 1949; MS, U. Ill., 1953, PhD, 1959. Rsch. asst. U. Ill., Urbana, 1953-59; jr. rsch. physiologist UCLA, 1959-61, asst. rsch. physiologist, 1961-64; rsch. fellow Calif. Inst. Tech., Pasadena, 1961-64; sec.-treas. Underwater Rsch. Corp., L.A., 1962-64; rsch. asst. dept. ob/gyn U. Mich. Med. Ctr., Ann Arbor, 1964-70; biologist VA Hosp., Wadsworth, 1971-72; instr. San Gabriel Adult Sch., Calif., 1971-78; supr. serology VA Hosp., Long Beach, Calif., 1972-74; owner Regent Liquor Store, L.A., 1974-79; pres., treas. Regent Liquor, Inc., L.A., 1979-85; ret. NIH grantee, 1967, 69. Mem. N.Y. Acad. Sci., 100th Inf. Battalion Vets. Club. Home: 516 Kamoku St Apt 302 Honolulu HI 96826-5102

NAKAGAWA, ALLEN DONALD, radiologic technologist; b. N.Y.C., Mar. 14, 1955; s. Walter Tsunehiko and Alyce Tsuneko (Kinoshita) N. BS in Environ. Studies, St. John's U., Jamaica, N.Y., 1977; MS in Marine Biology, C.W. Post Coll., 1980. Cert. radiologic technologist, in fluoroscopy, Calif.; cert. Am. Registry Radiol. Technologists. Research asst. environ. studies St. John's U., 1976-78; lab. asst. Bur. Water Surveillance, Nassau Co. of Health Dept., Wantaugh, N.Y., 1978; clin. endocrinology asst. U. Calif. VA Hosp., San Francisco, 1981-83; student technologist St. Mary's Hosp., San Francisco, 1985-86; radiologic technologist Mt. Zion Hosp., San Francisco, 1986-88; sr. radiologic technologist U. Calif., San Francisco, 1989—, urosurg. radiologic technologists, 1988-89. Contbr. articles to profl. jours., chpts. to books. Recruiting chmn. hunger project C.W. Post Coll., 1979; participant 33d Annual Radiology Conf., San Francisco, 1990. Mem. AAAS, Calif. Soc. Radiologic Technologists, Marine Mammal Ctr., Calif. Acad. Scis., Planetree Health Resource Ctr., Japanese-Am. Nat. Mus., ACLU, Sigma Xi. Democrat. Methodist.

NAKAGAWA, EILEEN CHIYO, biology educator; b. L.A., Nov. 4, 1959; d. George and Lorraine (Matsuuchi) Kawamura; m. Kevin Saburo, Aug. 18, 1984; 1 child, Chad Isamu. BS in Zoology, Calif. Poly., 1982, MS in Biology, 1985. Substitute tchr. Fullerton (Calif.) Union High Sch. Dist., 1985-86, educator, 1986—. Mem. Sigma Xi. Office: Buena Park High Sch 8833 Academy Dr Buena Park CA 90621

NAKAHATA, TADAKA, retired consulting engineer, land surveyor; b. Kauai, Hawaii, Nov. 24, 1924; s. Tadao and Yae (Ohta) N.; BS in Civil Engring., U. Hawaii, 1951; m. Clara S. Sakanashi, June 23, 1956; children—Leanne A. Nikaido, Holly E. Chung, Merry Y. Ifuku. Engr./surveyor B.H. McKeague & Assos., Honolulu, 1951-55, Harland Bartholomew & Assos., Honolulu, 1955-56, Paul Low Engring. Co., Honolulu, 1956-59, Nakahata, Kaneshige, Imata & Assos., 1959-63; owner T. Nakahata, Honolulu, 1964-83, ret., 1983; mem. Hawaii Bd. Registration of Architects, Engrs. and Land Surveyors, 1980-83. With AUS, 1946-47. Mem. ASCE, Am. Congress Surveying and Mapping, Nat. Soc. Profl. Engrs. Mem. Makiki Christian Ch.

NAKAMOTO, JON MASAO, endocrinologist; b. Dec. 14, 1958. AB, Harvard U., 1981; MD, Yale U., 1985. Diplomate Am. Acad. pediatrics. Intern/resident U. Calif., San Francisco, 1985-88; fellow pediatric endocrinology UCLA, 1988—. Harvard U. scholar, 1977-78; recipient U. Calif.-San Francisco Housestaff Teaching award, 1987, 88, NIH Physician-Scientist award, 1990. Office: UCLA Med Ctr 10833 Le Conte Ave Los Angeles CA 90024

NAKAMURA, MICHAEL S., protective services official. Police chief Honolulu Police Dept. Office: Honolulu Police Dept 1455 S Beretania St Honolulu HI 96814*

NAKANISHI, ALAN, ophthalmologist; b. Sacramento, Mar. 21, 1940. BA, Pacific Union Coll., 1962; MD, Loma Linda U. Intern, L.A. Coutny Med. Ctr. Univ. So. Calif., 1965-66; resident, L.A. County Med. Ctr. Delta Eye Med. Group, 1966-69; ophthalmologist Delta Eye Med. Group, Stockton, Calif. Maj. M.C., U.S. Army, 1969-71. Office: Delta Eye Med Group 1617 St Mark s Plz Stockton CA 95207

NAKANO-MATSUMOTO, NAOMI NAMIKO, social worker; b. Salt Lake City, May 3, 1960; d. Rokuro George and Miyuki (Tashima) N.; m. Robert Hideo Matsumoto. BS in Sociolog and Social Work, Weber State Coll., Ogden, Utah, 1982; MSW, U. Denver, 1986. Lic. social worker, Calif.; lic. clin. social worker, Calif.; cert. social svc. worker, Utah. Student counselor Parkview Community Corrections Ctr., Ogden, 1981-82; caseworker Children's Aid Soc. of Utah, Ogden, 1982-85; intern in social work Asian-Pacific Devel. Ctr., Denver, 1985-86, social worker, 1987; social worker Denver Pub. Schs., 1988-91, Asian-Ams. for Community Involvement, San Jose, Calif., 1991—. Mem. Task Force Monitoring Violence Against Asians, Denver, 1986; mem. com. Japanese-Am. Community Graduation Program, Denver, 1989, 92, Nat. JACL Conf. Workshop, Denver, 1990-91; mem. adv. bd. after sch. program Oasis, Ogden, 1985; bd. dirs. Asian Edn. Adv. Coun., Denver Pub. Schs., 1989-91; vol. friend Denver Girls, Inc., 1989-91; peer counselor tng. workshop Asian/Pacific Ctr. Human Devel., fundraising com., 1986-91. Named One of Outstanding Young Women in Am., 1988, Outstanding Vol.-Denver Girls, Inc., 1990. Mem. NASW, Nat. Assn. Asian-Pacific-Am. Edn., Asian-Am. Psychol. Assn., Asian Women Advocating for Rights & Empowerment, Asian Pacific Islanders for Choice, Coalition for Multicultural Mental Health Svcs., Asian Human Svcs. Assn., Coalition of Asian Pacific Islander Youth. Democrat. Buddhist.

NAKAOKA, JAMES TATSUMI, architect; b. L.A., Nov. 21, 1952; s. Paul and Taeko (Kato) N.; m. Christine Hye-Young Choi, Feb. 17, 1979. BS in Architecture, Calif. Poly. State U., 1978. Lic. architect, U.K. and 19 U.S. states; cert. by Nat. Coun. Archtl. Registration Bd.; lic. interior designer, Tex. Jr. architect Jose Almanza & Assocs., L.A., 1976; urban designer Ruth, Going & Curtis, Inc., San Jose, Calif., 1978-79; sr. designer PAE Internat., L.A., 1979-81, Skidmore, Owings & Merrill, L.A., 1981-82; dir. design Corbin/Yamafuji & Ptnrs., Irvine, Calif., 1982-83; pres. J.T. Nakaoka Assoc. Architects, L.A., 1982—; speaker at numerous confs. in field, U.S., Japan, Singapore. Contbr. articles to mags. and newspapers. Founder, corp. regent Los Angeles County Mus. Art, 1983-93; contbg. founder Mus. Contemporary Art, 1986; mem. Bus. Assocs. Natural History Mus. of L.A. County, 1990-91. Recipient Svc. award Pla. Community Ctr., 1986, New Store of Yr. award Chain Store Age Exec. mag., 1989, Hon. mention Inst. Store Planners/Nat. Retail Merchants Assn, 1989, Outstanding Merit award Nat. Assn. Store Fixture Mfrs., 1989, Store of Yr. award, 1990, 1st award/Specialty Dept. Store, Apparel, inst. Store Planners and Visual Merchandising and Store Design mag., 1990, Store Excellence award Monitor mag., 1990, Superior Achievement in Design and Imaging award Shopping Ctr. World and Retail Store Image mag., 1991, Grand awards Nat. Assn. Store Fixture Mfrs., 1991; named Interior Design Giant, Interior Design mag., 1988-93; award of excellence Archtl. Woodwork Inst., 1991, Gold Nugget Merit award Pacific Coast Builders Conf., 1991, The Best Show award Neocon 23/Showcase of Interior Design, 1991, Calif. Coun. & Nat. Coun. awards, 1991, Store of Yr.-Special Judges award Chain Store Age Executive mag., 1991, Cert. Recognition, Best in Am. Living-Merit award Nat. Assn. Home Builders, 1991, Calif. Coun. and Nat. Coun. awards for Design Excellence Soc. Am. Registered Architects, 1991, L.A. Cultural Heritage Commn. award, 1993, Honor award for Adaptive Re-Use, Calif. Preservation Found., 1993. Mem. AIA, Royal Inst. Brit. Architects, Internat. Coun. Shopping Ctrs., Soc. Am. Registered Architects (cert., Award of Excellence in Interior Design 1991, Hon. Mention 1992, Award of Honor in Design, Interior Design, Industrial Bldg. Design 1992, award for Design Excellence). Republican. Office: J T Nakaoka Assocs 1900 S Sepulveda Blvd Fl 2D Los Angeles CA 90025-5620

NAKASHIMA, JOANNE PUMPHREY, education administrator; b. Broseley, Mo., Feb. 3, 1937; d. Walter and Ola A. (Keener) Pumphrey; m. Christian A. Tirre, Aug. 15, 1959 (div. 1983); 1 foster child, Gary L. Wycuff; m. Masao Nakashima, Dec. 31, 1983; stepchildren: Cathy Reando, Lisa Nakashima. BS in Edn., S. E. Mo. U., Cape Girardeau, 1959; MEd, Miami U., Oxford, Ohio, 1963. Elem Tchr., Sch. Counselor, Sch. Adminstr. Tchr. Green Valley Sch., Ind., 1959-60, Shawnee Sch. System, Camden, Ohio, 1960-62; tchr./counselor Columbus Pub. Sch., Columbus, Ohio, 1982-70; tchr. Eleele Elem. Sch., Eleele, Hawaii, 1970-71, Kaumakani Elem. Sch., Kaumakani, Hawaii, 1971-76; coun. vice prin. Kauai High and Waimea High, Lihue, Waimea, Hawaii, 1976-79; dist. ednl. specialist Kauai Dist., Lihue, Hawaii, 1979-83; prin. Eleele Elem. Sch., Eleele, HI, 1983-86; dist. ednl. specialist Kauai Dist., Lihue, HI, 1986—; part time instr. U. Hawaii, Kauai Site, 1972-75; trainer of facilitative leadership, Dept. of Edn., Kauai, 1990—. Author: Baptist Materials, International Christian Endea. Dem. Party Chair County of Kauai, Hawaii, 1982-84; v.p. Kauai Chorale; co-chair person, Com. to Elect Senator Akaka, Kauai, 1990—. Recipient Adminstr. of Year, High Sch. Counselors Assn., Top Ten Freshman, S.E. Mo. U. Mem. Hawaii Govt. Employee Assn., Hawaii Sch. Counselors Assn., Child and Family Svc., Delta Kappa Gamma (pres. Eta chpt., 2d v.p. Beta Beta state). Democrat. Mem. United Church of Christ. Home: PO Box 965 Kalaheo HI 96741-0965 Office: Kauai Dist Office, DOE 3060 Eiwa St Lihue HI 96766-1310

NAKASHIMA, PATRICIA HATSUYE, educational association administrator; b. Tulelake, Calif., Jan. 24, 1943; d. Harry and Kayo (Shimada) N. BA, San Jose State U., 1964; MA, Stanford U., 1965. Cert. secondary tchr. Dept. head Bret Harte Jr. High Sch., San Jose, Calif., 1967-73, John Steinbeck Jr. High Sch., San Jose, Calif., 1980-83; dept. head Henry T. Gunderson High Sch., San Jose, Calif., 1983-85, faculty rep., 1985-86; affiliate rep. Calif. Fgn. Lang. Tchrs. Assn., San Jose, 1986-87, 2d v.p., 1987-90, pres., 1990-92; curriculum cons. State Dept. Edn. Calif., 1986-87; mem. adv. panel Title II, Pub. Law 98-377 Calif. Post-Secondary Edn. Commn., 1985-88, reader grant proposals, 1985-88; mem. adv. com. for Eisenhower Act. Co-chmn. W. Buddist Sangha, San Jose, 1968-69; advisor San Jose Young Buddhist Assn., 1970-80. Mem. NEA, Am. Assn. Tchrs. French, Calif. Tchrs. Assn., San Jose Tchrs. Assn. (faculty rep. 1977-79), Fgn. Lang. Assn. Santa Clara County (pres. 1985-86), Delta Kappa Gamma (pres. 1992-94). Office: San Jose High Acad 275 N 24th St San Jose CA 95116-1109

NAKKIM, LYNN BOERNER KALAMA, novelist; b. Middletown, N.Y., Aug. 9, 1937; d. Charles Henry and Gertrude (Blochinger) Boerner; m. Per S. Nakkim, July 4, 1960 (div. 1968); 1 child, Eric C. BA, Smith Coll., 1959; MEd, U. Hawaii, 1972. Advt. dir. Gasoline Marketers, San Francisco, 1960-61; real estate broker Calif., 1962-68; tchr. Punahou, Honolulu Jr. Acad., 1966-71, Chaminade U., Honolulu, 1973-74; adminstr. Greenfield (Mass.) C.C., 1977-81; horse breeder 42 horse ranch. Author: The Road to Hana Maui, 1984, Personals, 1986, The Hana Rift Zone, 1991; writer, dir. TV documentaries: Lanai & Kahoolawe, 1986-92, The Koa Question, 1971. Pres. Friends of The Earth, 1972-74; chmn. League Conservation Voters, 1970-74. Mem. Soc. for Hawaiian Archeology, Sierra Club.

NALCIOGLU, ORHAN, radiological science educator; b. Istanbul, Feb. 2, 1944; U.S., 1966, naturalized, 1974; s. Mustafa and Meliha N. BS, Robert Coll., Istanbul, 1966; MS, Case Western Res. U., 1968; PhD, U. Ore., 1970. Postdoctoral fellow dept. physics U. Calif.-Davis, 1970-71; Rsch. assoc. dept. physics U. Rochester, N.Y., 1971-74, U. Wis., Madison, 1974-76; sr. physicist EMI Med. Inc., Northbrook, Ill., 1976-77; prof. depts. radiol. scis., elec. engring. and medicine U. Calif.-Irvine, 1977—, head div. physics and engring., 1985—; dir. Biomedical Magnetic Resonance Rsch., 1987—, dir. Rsch. Imaging Ctr., 1992—; cons. UN, 1980-86. Editor several books; contbr. articles to profl. jours. Mobil scholar, 1961-66. Fellow IEEE, Am. Assn. Physicists in Medicine; pres. IEEE NPSS, 1993—; mem. Soc. Magnetic Resonance Imaging, Soc. Magnetic Resonance in Medicine. Republican. Subspecialty: medical physics. Office: U Calif Irvine Coll Medicine Dept Radiol Sci Irvine CA 92717

NALDER, ERIC CHRISTOPHER, investigative reporter; b. Coulee Dam, Wash., Mar. 2, 1946; s. Philip Richard and Mibs Dorothy (Aurdal) N.; m. Jan Christiansen, Dec. 20, 1968; 1 child, Britt Hillary. BA in Communications, U. Wash., 1968. News editor Whidbey News-Times, Oak Harbor, Wash., 1971; reporter Lynnwood (Wash.) Enterprise, 1972, Everett Herald, Lynnwood, 1972-75; gen. assignment reporter Seattle Post-Intelligencer, 1975-78, edn. writer, 1977-78, investigative reporter, 1978-83; chief investigative reporter Seattle Times, 1983—. Recipient Edn. Writers Assn. award Charles Stewart Mott Found., 1978, Hearst Community Svc. award, 1978, C.B. Blethen awards (12), Outstanding Govt. Reporting award Seattle Mcpl. League, Pub. Svc. in Journalism award Sigma Delta Chi, 1987, Edward J. Meeman award Scripps Howard Found., 1987, Thomas Stokes award, Washington Journalism Ctr., 1990, Pulitzer prize Columbia U., 1990, Nat. Headline award, 1991, Pub. Svc. award, AP Mags. Editors Assn., 1992. Mem. Investigative Reporters and Editors, Pacific N.W. Newspaper Guild. Office: Seattle Times Fairview Avenue St N Seattle WA 98109-5311

NALEWAY, JOHN JOSEPH, biochemist, administrator; b. Chgo., Sept. 8, 1954; s. Anthony Joseph and Margaret Monica (Kowalczyk) N.; m. Alisa Angela Buerger, July 4, 1981; children: Patrick James, Steven Eric, Michael Andrew. Student, Loyola U., 1972-76, Marquette U., 1976-81, U. Alberta, 1981-83. Rsch. assoc. U. Wis., Madison, 1983-86; sr. rsch. chemist Searle Pharm., Monsanto, Chesterfield, Mo., 1986-88; dir. carbohydrate rsch. Molecular Probes, Inc., Eugene, Oreg., 1988—; cons. Carbohydrate Rsch., Eugene, 1991—. Author: (with others) GUS Protocols, 1992. Mem. ACS (carbohydrate div.). Office: Molecular Probes Inc 4849 Pitchford Eugene OR 97402

NANCE, ROBERT LEWIS, oil company executive; b. Dallas, July 10, 1936; s. Melvin Renfro Nance and Ruth Natlie (Seibert) Nowlin; m. Penni Jane Warfel; children: Robert Scott, Amy Louise, Catherine Leslie. BS, So. Meth. U., 1959; LLD (hon.), Rocky Mountain Coll., 1989. V.p. geology Oliver & West Cons., Dallas, 1960-66; ptnr. Nance & Larue Cons., Dallas, 1966-69; pres., CEO Nance Petroleum Corp., Billings, Mont., 1969—; bd. dirs. First Interstate Bank Commerce, Nat. Petroleum Coun., MDU Resources, Mont. Dakota Utilities, Rocky Mountain Coll., Billings, chmn. 1986-91; mem. Nat. Petroleum Coun. Coun. pres. Am. Luth. Ch., Billings, 1980; trustee, chmn. Deaconess Med. Ctr., Billings; chmn. Deaconess Care Corp., Billings. Recipient Hall of Fame award Rocky Mountain Coll. Alumni, 1987, Disting. Svc. Trusteeship, Assn. Governing Bds. Univs. Colls., 1988. Mem. Am. Assn. Petroleum Geologists, Ind. Petroleum Assn. Am. (exec. com., v.p. Mont. chpt. 1975), Ind. Petroleum Assn. Mountain States (v.p. Mont. 1977-79), Mont. Petroleum Assn., Hilands Golf Club, Billings Petroleum Club. Office: Nance Petroleum Corp 550 N 31st St PO Box 7168 Billings MT 59103

NANCE, SANDRA MICHEL, public relations manager; b. Denver, Apr. 26, 1946; d. Wilbert Henry and Bette Caroline (Fick) Michel; m. James O. Branson, June 17, 1972 (div. June 1978); m. John B. Nance, Feb. 20, 1983; 1 child, Tracy. BS in Journalism, U. Colo., 1968. Reporter UPI, Cheyenne, Wyo., 1968, Casper (Wyo.) Star Tribune, Cheyenne, 1969-72; mgr. pub. rels. US WEST Communications (formerly Mountain Bell), Denver, 1973—. Named Women of Achievement YWCA, 1982. Mem. Soc. of Profl. Journalists (pres. 1983-84), Pub. Rels. Soc. of Am. (Colo. chpt. Gold Pick, 1985, 90), US WEST Women (formerly Women in Mgmt., pres. 1979-80), Colo. Press Women.

NANDAGOPAL, MALLUR R., engineer; b. Kolar, Karnataka, India, May 14, 1938; came to U.S., 1976; s. M. Ramanuja Iyengar and Garudammal; m. Sreedharani K. Ramamurthy; children: Radha, Meena, Sudha. BS, Cen. Coll., Bangalore, India, 1958; B of Tech., Indian Inst. Tech., Bombay, 1962; ME, Indian Inst. Sci., Bangalore, 1963, PhD, 1974. Registered profl. engr., Wash. Mem. faculty Indian Inst. Sci., 1963-77; engr. City of Spokane, Wash., 1977—; coord. summer sch. Indian Inst. Sci., 1974-75. Contbr. articles to profl. jours. Mem. IEEE (sr.), Inst. Sci. (sec. Staff Club 1972-74), Fed. Emergency Mgmt. Agy. (mitigation com.). Hindu. Home: 410 E Shiloh Hills Dr Spokane WA 99208-5819

NANDOR, WILLIAM FRANCIS, retail executive; b. Charleroi, Pa., Mar. 5, 1942; s. George Francis and Anna Dorothy (Shemasek) N.; m. Jo-Anne McClellan, Oct. 12, 1962; children: Scott Michael, Mark Joseph, Jennifer Lynn Mi, Christopher George. BA, U. Pitts., 1964; postgrad., Santa Clara (Calif.) U., 1971-72. Mdse. mgr. Sears Roebuck, Pitts., 1963-69; v.p. merchandising Foxmoor Casuals, Brockton, Mass., 1969-75; pres. Apparel Stores Corp., Natick, Mass., 1975-80; v.p. adminstrn. Docktor Pet Ctrs., Wilmington, Mass., 1980-82; v.p. sales and mktg. Fanny Farmer Candy Shops, Bedford, Mass., 1982-86; v.p. ops. Wellpet, Ltd., Scotts Valley, Calif., 1986-87; pres. Gymboree Corp., Burlingame, Calif., 1987-90, Am. Fashion Jewels, South San Francisco, Calif., 1990—; cons. retail firms. Mem.

Common Cause, Washington; tchr. First Bapt. Ch., Pleasanton, Calif. Mem. Internat. Coun. of Shopping Ctrs., Nat. Retail Fedn. (bd. dirs. 1992—). Office: Am Fashion Jewels Inc 651 Gateway Blvd South San Francisco CA 94080

NANDWANA, ASHOK LAKHAJI, communications executive, photographer; b. Ahmedabad, Gujarat, India, Dec. 9, 1951; came to U.S., 1978; s. Lakhaji Kalabhai and Kapur Lakhaji (Dangodara) N.; m. Suvira Satyakam Arya, July 16, 1984; children: Parijat, Shefalee. Grad., Shardamandir, Ahmedabad, 1968. Draftsman Maxwell-Starkman, Beverly Hills, Calif., 1978-79; testing technician Pacific-Bell, L.A., 1979—; photographer L.A., 1979—. Home: 2130 Sheffield Dr La Habra CA 90631

NANSEN, RICHARD RAY, gallery owner; b. Casper, Wyo., July 28, 1956; s. Richard Dean and Karen Lois (Culver) N. Owner Nansen Drywall/Insulation, Jackson, Wyo., 1980-91, Log Cabin Traditions, West Yellowstone, Mont., 1991—; art marketer West Yellowstone Log Cabin, Inc. Ambulance driver, attendant West Yellowstone Ambulance Corps, 1992. Office: Log Cabin Traditions 30 Madison Ave West Yellowstone MT 59758

NANTO, ROXANNA LYNN, career planning administrator, consultant; b. Hanford, Calif., Dec. 17, 1952; d. Lawson Gene Brooks and Bernice (Page) Jackson; m. Harvey Ken Nanto, Mar. 23, 1970; 1 child, Shea Kiyoshi. A, Chemeketa Community Coll., 1976; B, Idaho State U., 1978. PBX operator Telephone Answer Bus. Svc., Moses Lake, Wash., 1965-75; edn. coord. MimiCassia Community Edn., Rupert, Idaho, 1976-77; office mgr. Lockwood Corp., Rupert, Idaho, 1977-78; cost acct. Keyes Fibre Co., Wenatchee, Wash., 1978-80; acctg. office mgr. Armstrong & Armstrong, Wenatchee, Wash., 1980-81; office mgr. Cascade Cable Constrn. Inc., East Wenatchee, Wash., 1981-83; interviewer, counselor Wash. Employment Security, Wenatchee, 1983-84; pres. chief exec. officer Regional Health Care Plus, East Wenatchee, 1986-88; dist. career coord. Eastmont Sch. Dist., East Wenatchee, 1984-90; prin. Career Cons., 1988-90; exec. dir. Wenatchee Valley Coll. Found., 1990-91; ednl. cons. Sunbelt Consortium, East Wenatchee, 1991—; speaker North Cen. Washington Profl. Women, Wenatche, 1987, Wen Career Women's Network, Wenatchee, 1990, Wenatchee Valley Rotary, 1990, Meeting the Challenge of Workforce 2000, Seattle, 1993; cons., speaker Wash. State Sch. Dirs., Seattle, 1987; speaker Wenatchee C. of C., 1989; sec. Constrn. Coun. of North Cen. Washington, Wenatchee, 1981-83; bd. dirs. Gen. Vocat. Adv. Bd., Wenatchee, 1986-88, Washington Family Ind. Program, Olympia, 1989—; mem. econ. devel. coun. Grant County, 1992—. Mem. at large career Women's Network, 1984—, mem. Econ. Devel. Coun. of No. Cen. Washington; mem. Steering Com. to Retain Judge Small. Grantee Nat. Career Devel. Guidelines Wash. State, 1989; named Wenatchee Valley Coll. Vocat. Contbr. of Yr., 1991. Fellow Dem. Women's Club; mem. Nat. Assn. Career Counselors, Nat. Assn. Pvt. Career Counselors, Nat. Coun. Resource Devel., NCW Estate Planning Coun., Family Planning Coun. (treas.). Home: 704 Larch Ct Wenatchee WA 98802-5052 Office: Sunbelt Consortium 704 NE Larch Ct Wenatchee WA 98802

NAPIER, RICHARD STEPHEN, electrical engineering manager; b. Clarksburg, W.Va., May 13, 1949; s. Richard Arthur and Lois Jane (Silcott) N.; m. Barbara Elaine Deems, June 13, 1970; 1 child, Stephen Michael. BSEE, W.Va. U., 1971; MSEE, Stanford U., 1973. Tech. staff mem. Bell Telephone Labs., Holmdel, NY, 1972-73; tech. staff mem. Watkins Johnson Co., San Jose, Calif., 1973-77, head synthesizer equipment sect., 1977-85, mgr. radio frequency automatic test equipment, 1985-88, mgr. antenna dept., 1988—. Author: various newspaper and profl. jour. articles, TV editorials. Mem. Sunnyvale (Calif.) City Coun., 1987—, vice mayor, 1990, mayor, 1990-91; voting mem. Pub. Safety Com. League Calif. Cities, Sacramento, 1987-92; active United Way, Santa Clara County, 1986-87, South Bay Discharges Authority, Santa Clara County, 1987—, Intergovtl. Coun. Solid. Waste Com., Santa Clara County, 1988—; mem. Transp. Commn., Santa Clara County, 1989-91; mem. congestion mgmt. planning agy., Santa Clara County, 1990—. Western Electric Fund scholar, 1973. Mem. Assn. Old Crows, W.Va. U. Alumni Assn., Stanford U. Alumni Assn., Albemerle Hist. Soc., Sunnyvale Hist. Soc., Calif. Theatre Ctr., Tau Beta Pi. Republican. Methodist. Home: 754 Carlisle Way Sunnyvale CA 94087-3429 Office: Watkins Johnson Co 2525 First St San Jose CA 95117-1118

NAPLES, CAESAR JOSEPH, academic administrator, educator; b. Buffalo, Sept. 4, 1938; s. Caesar M. and Fannie A. (Occhipinti) N.; m. Lynda Sequerth, Feb. 1964 (div. Sept. 1971); children: Jennifer, Caesar; m. Sandra L. Harrison, July 16, 1983. AB, Yale U., 1960; JD, SUNY, 1963. Bar: N.Y. 1963, Fla. 1977, Calif. 1988, U.S. Supreme Ct. 1965. Assoc. Moot & Sprague, Buffalo, 1965-69; asst. dir., employee rels. N.Y. Gov. Office, Albany, 1969-71; asst. v. chancellor SUNY, Albany, 1971-75; gen. counsel Fla. State U. System, Tallahassee, 1975-83; v. chancellor Calif. State U., Long Beach, 1983—; prof. pub. policy Grad. Ctr. for Pub. Policy and Adminstrn. Calif. State U., 1983—; cons. Govt. of Australia, U. Nev. System, Reno, Minn. State U. System, Mpls., Assn. Can. Colls. and Univs., Que., various other univs. and colls. Contbr. articles to profl. jours.; co-author: Romanov Succession, 1989 with J.Victor Baldridge. Mem. Metlife Resources Adv. Bd., 19886, chmn, 1992—. Capt. U.S. Army, 1963-65, Germany. Mem. Acad Pers. Adminstrn. (founder), Nat. Ctr. for Study Collective Bargaining Higher Edn. (bd. dirs.). Office: Calif State U 816 N Juanita Ave # B Redondo Beach CA 90277

NAPOLI, WILLIAM JOSEPH, portfolio manager; b. Sao Paulo, Brazil, Apr. 7, 1960; (parents Am. citizens); s. William Leonard Napoli and Isabel Labriola; 1 child, Joseph Alexander. BA, Loyola U., New Orleans, 1981. Propr. William J. Napoli, mem. Pacific Stock Exch., San Francisco, 1983-91; pres. Beyond Limits Trading, San Francisco, 1987-91; founder, pres. Napoli & Assocs. Inc., San Francisco, 1990—; founder, gen. ptnr. Cygnus Investment Ptnrs. L.P., San Francisco, 1991—, Napoli Investment Ptnrs. L.P., San Francisco, 1992—; mem. coms. Pacific Stock Exch., San Francisco. Mem. Com. on Options Proposals (hon.). Office: 220 Montgomery St Ste 500 San Francisco CA 94104

NAPPER, BRIAN WILLIAM, financial consultant; b. Long Beach, Calif., May 31, 1960; s. Karyl Arthur and Barbara Ann (Decker) N.; m. Chantele Louise, Aug. 26, 1986 (div. Oct. 1992); children: Matthew Robert, William Kyle (twins). AA, Long Beach (Calif.) City Coll., 1980; BS, U. Calif., 1982. Ptnr. Peterson Cons., San Francisco, 1982-90, Barrington Cons. Group, San Francisco, 1991—; bd. dirs. World Intellectual Property and Trade Forum, San Francisco. Mem. The Olympic Club, Licensing Execs. Soc., Bay Area Bankruptcy Forum, Assn. of Insolvency Accts., Sigma Nu (ho. bd. 1989-91). Office: Barrington Cons Group Ste 3350 Four Embarcadero Ctr San Francisco CA 94111

NARAMORE, JAMES JOSEPH, family practice physician, educator; b. Gillette, Wyo., Nov. 29, 1949; s. Kenneth Chester and Joan (Biggerstaff) N.; m. Karen Rae Buttermore, July 9, 1972; children: Lindsay, Marissa, Jessica, Marcus. BA with highest achievement in Biology, John Brown U., Siloam Springs, Ark., 1972; MD with family practice honors, U. Utah, 1977. Diplomate Am. Bd. Family Practice. Resident in family practice U. Nebr., Omaha, 1977-80, chief resident; pvt. practice, Gillette, 1981—; mem. staff Campbell County Meml. Hosp., Gillette, 1980—, chief staff, 1986, chief dept. family practice, 1990-91; instr. dept. human medicine U. Wyo., 1983-86, clin. assoc. prof. family practice, 1986—; ptnr., co-founder Med. Arts Lab., Gillette, 1981—; med. dir. Campbell County Detention Ctr., 1988—; med. dir. Pioneer Manor Nursing Home, Gillette, 1989—; aviation med. examiner FAA, Oklahoma City, 1986—; cons. on occupational medicine to numerous industries, Campbell County, 1986—. Charter mem. Gillette Area Leadership Inst., 1986-87; chmn. missions com. Grace Bible Ch., Gillette, 1983—, chmn. bd. elders, 1989—. Mem. Am. Acad. Family Physicians, Wyo. Med. Soc., Campbell County Med. Soc. (pres. 1983-84), Gillette C. of C. (bd. dirs. 1987-90), Toastmasters (pres. Gillette 1992, Competent Toastmaster award 1986—). Republican. Home: 1214 Hilltop Ct Gillette WY 82716 Office: Family Health 407 S Medical Arts Ct Ste D Gillette WY 82716

NARANJO, MICHAEL A., sculptor; b. Santa Fe, N.Mex., Aug. 28, 1944; s. Michael Edward and Rose (Sisneros) N.; m. Laurie Engel, Apr. 29, 1978; children: Jenna Skai, Bryn Mariah. Student, Wayland Bapt. Coll., Las Vegas, N.Mex., 1963, Higlands U., Las Vegas, N.Mex., 1964. One-man shows include Eiteljorg Mus. Southwestern and Indian Art, Indpls., Roswell Mus. and Art Ctr., 1990, Four Winds Gallery, 1991, Mary Duke Biddle Mus., N.C., Colorado Springs Fine Arts Ctr., Colo., Gallery Wall, Phoenix; exhibited in group shows Gov.'s Gallery, Santa Fe, 1979, The Turtle Mus., Niagra, N.Y., Kennedy Ctr. for Performing Arts, World's Fair, Tenn., Smithsonian Inst. Nat. Mus. and Natural History, Washington, 1983, Heard Mus., Phoenix, 1985, 16th World Congress of Rehab. Internat., Tokyo, 1988, Mus. of Man, San Diego, 1989, Mus. Fine Arts, Santa Fe, 1991, Santa Barbara (Calif.) Mus. Art, 1991; represented in permanent collections Heard Mus., Phoenix, Mus. Fine Arts, Santa Fe, Albuquerque Mus., Petro Lewis Oil Co., Denver, Office of the V.P. U.S. Steel, Pitts., former U.S. treas. Francine Neff, Indian Pueblo Cultural Ctr., Albuquerque, The Vatican, The White House. With U.S. Army, 1967-68. Named N.Mex. Vet. of the Yr., DAR, 1986, Outstanding Vietnam Vet, Pres. Jimmy Carter, 1979, Gov.'s award for sculpture, Gov. Jerry Apodaca, N.Mex., 1976. Office: Naranjo Gallery PO Box 747 Espanola NM 87532-0747

NARATH, ALBERT, national laboratory director; b. Berlin, Mar. 5, 1933; came to U.S., 1947; s. Albert Narath and Johanna Agnes Anne (Bruggemann) Bruckmann; m. Worth Haines Scattergood, (div. 1976); children: Tanya, Lise, Yvette; m. Barbara Dean Camp, Aug. 8, 1976; 1 child, Albert. BS in Chemistry, U. Cin., 1955; PhD in Phys. Chemistry, U. Calif., Berkeley, 1959. Mem. tech. staff, mgr. phys. sci. Sandia Nat. Labs., Albuquerque, 1959-68, dir. solid state sci., 1968-71, mng. dir. phys. sci., 1971-73, v.p. rsch., 1973-82, exec. v.p. rsch. and adv. weapons systems, 1982-84, pres., 1989—; v.p. govt. systems AT&T-Bell Labs, Whippany, N.J., 1984-89; vice chmn. basic energy scis. adv. com. Dept. Energy, 1987—; cons. in field. Contbr. sci. articles to profl. jours. Fellow Am. Phys. Soc. (George E. Pake prize 1991); mem. NAE, AAAS. Office: Sandia Nat Labs PO Box 5800 Albuquerque NM 87185-5800

NARAYANAMURTI, VENKATESH, research administrator; b. Bangalore, Karnataka, India, Sept. 9, 1939; came to U.S., 1961; s. Duraiswami and Janaki (Subramaniam) N.; m. Jayalakshmi Krishnayya, Aug. 23, 1961; children: Arjun, Ranjini, Krishna. BSc, MSc, St. Stephen's Coll., Delhi, India, 1958; PhD, Cornell U., 1965. Instr., rsch. assoc. Cornell U., Ithaca, N.Y., 1965-68; mem. tech. staff AT&T Bell Labs., Murray Hill, N.J., 1968-76, dept.head, 1976-81, dir., 1981-87; v.p. rsch. Sandia Nat. Labs., Albuquerque, 1987-92; dean engring. U. Calif., Santa Barbara, 1992—; chmn. adv. bd. Coll. of Elec. Engring., Cornell U., 1989-90, sci. bd. and regional coun. Santa Fe Inst., 1987-90, microelectric bd., Jet Propulsion Lab., Pasadena, Calif., 1988-90, sci. bd. Stanford Synchroton Lab., Stanford, Calif., 1989-92; mem. IUPAP Commn. on Physics for Devel.; engring. directrorate adv. bd. NSF, 1992—; Fermi award com. Dept. of Energy, 1992—; chair Dept. of Energy Inertial Confinement Fusion Adv. Com., 1992—. Author more than 100 publs.; patentee in field. Fellow IEEE, AAAS, Am. Phys. Soc., Indian Acad. Scis.; mem. NAE, Royal Swedish Acad. Engring. Scis. (fgn.). Office: U Calif Office of Dean of Engring Santa Barbara CA 93106

NARDI, PETER MICHAEL, sociology educator; b. Bronx, Nov. 7, 1947; s. Peter John and Jeanne Marie (Mahoney) N. BA, U. Notre Dame (Ind.), 1969; MA, Colgate U., Hamilton, N.Y., 1970; PhD, U. Pa., 1975. Instr. Rutgers U., Camden, N.J., 1974-75, U. Pa., Phila., 1972-75; asst. prof. sociology Pitzer Coll., Claremont, Calif., 1975-81; assoc. prof. sociology Pitzer Coll., 1981-87, prof. sociology, 1987—. Guest editor Calif. Sociologist, 1988; editor: Men's Friendships, 1992; contbr. articles to profl. jours. Co-pres. Gay & Lesbian Alliance Against Defamation, L.A., 1990-91. Durfee Found. grantee, 1989; Haynes Found. grantee, 1988. Mem. Am. Sociol. Assn. (officer Sociologists Lesbian & Gay Caucus 1981-91), ACLU (bd. dirs. Lesbian and Gay Rights chpt.), Acad. Magical Arts. Democrat. Office: Pitzer Coll 1050 N Mills Ave Claremont CA 91711-6101

NARULA, MOHAN LAL, realtor; b. Ferozepur, India, Feb. 2, 1939; came to U.S., 1962; s. Ram Dyal and Pemeshwari Narula; m. Sylvia Conway, Aug. 31, 1968; children: Rabinder, Rajinder. BS, Panjab U., India, 1960; BSME, Calif. Poly. State U., San Luis Obispo, 1965; MS in Engring., Calif. State U., Northridge, 1970. Engr. Abex Corp., Oxnard, Calif., 1965-69; salesman, realtor Walker & Lee, Oxnard, Calif., 1970-73; owner, realtor Narula Co. Realtors, Oxnard, Calif., 1973—. Mem. Cert. Comml. Investment Mem. (designate 1979), Oxnard Harbor Bd. Realtors (mem. profl. standard com. 1980-89), Los Angeles Cert. Comml. Investment Mem. (bd. dirs., treas. 1985). Home: 2830 W Hill St Oxnard CA 93035-2522 Office: Narula Co Realtor 3201 Samuel Ave Ste 7 Oxnard CA 93033-5317

NARY, WILLIAM LLOYD MOSSMAN, lawyer; b. Honolulu, Sept. 15, 1960; s. William L. and Harvalee (Holt) N.; m. Barbra Christensen, Apr. 15, 1989; children: Holli Lyn, Jessica Crysteen. BA, Coll. of Idaho, Caldwell, 1982; JD, U. Idaho, 1985. Assoc. firm Ambrose, Fitzgerald & Crookston, Meridian, Idaho, 1985-87, ptnr., 1987-89; city prosecutor City of Meridian, 1985-89; asst. city atty. Prosecutor, City of Boise, Idaho, 1989-91; dep. city atty. Chief Criminal Deputy, Boise, 1991-93; chief criminal dep. Boise, 1993—. Christian. Office: City of Boise 150 N Capitol Blvd Boise ID 83702

NASBY, BRUCE ALLEN, consultant; b. Fort Dodge, Iowa, Sept. 18, 1948; s. Keith Allan Nasby and Henrietta Ruth (Hanson) Taborowski; m. Carol Elizabeth Briney, Apr. 5, 1975; children: Lisa, Scott. BS in Secondary Edn., U. Ariz., 1974. Sales mgmt. staff Montgomery Ward, Tucson, 1965-74; exec. dir. Jr. Achievement of Tucson, 1974-80; nat. dir. programs Jr. Achievement, Inc., Stamford, Conn., 1980-82; pres. Jr. Achievement of Santa Clar County, San Jose, Calif., 1982-85, Jr. Achievement of So. Calif., L.A., 1985-88; pres., CEO Greater L.A. Zoo Assn., 1988-92, Non-Profit Mgmt. Resources, Woodland Hills, Calif., 1992—, Am. Lung Assn. L.A. County, L.A., 1993—; cons. in field. With USN, 1969-73. Mem. Am. Soc. Assn. Execs., Am. Assn. Zool. Parks and Aquariums, Nat. Soc. Fund Raising Execs., Am. Assn. of Mus., Rotary Club of L.A., Calabasas Country Club. Republican. Episcopalian. Office: Non-Profit Mgmt Resources 21550 Oxnard St Ste 300 Woodland Hills CA 91367

NASH, K(IM) ALAN, broadcast executive; b. Midland, Mich., Nov. 15, 1956; s. Oliver F. and Betty June (Case) N.; m. Mary Sue Gangel, Sept. 4, 1982 (div. June 1991). AS, Ferris State Coll., 1977, BS in TV, 1980; MS in Journalism, Iowa State U., 1985. Announcer WFRS/WRKX campus radio, Big Rapids, Mich., 1976-79, WMPX radio, Midland, Mich., 1978; news and farm dir. KSCB/KEZS radio, Liberal, Kans., 1980; reporter/anchor WOI-TV, Des Moines, 1980-82; prodr. KSNW/Kans. State Network, Wichita, Kans., 1982-83; asst. news dir. KTIV-TV, Sioux City, Iowa, 1983-86; adj. prof. Morningside Coll., Sioux City, Iowa, 1986; news dir. KTVQ-TV/Mont. TV Network, Billings, Mont., 1986-93; dir. news and opinions Sta. KMID-TV, Midland, Tex., 1993—. Mem. Soc. Profl. Journalists, Radio-TV News Dirs. Assn., Mont. AP Broadcasters (pres. 1990-91).

NASH, LEE MARTEN, academic administrator, history educator; b. North Bend, Oreg., Sept. 10, 1927; s. Ray and Grace Gertrude (Miller) N.; m. Grayce Eileen Frey, July 27, 1951; children: Murray Craig, LeAnn Marie, Torrey Scott. AB, Cascade Coll., 1950; MA, U. Wash., 1951; PhD, U. Oreg., 1961. Asst. prof. English and history Cascade Coll., Portland, Oreg., 1951-56, assoc. prof. history, 1959-62, dean of the coll., 1962-67; prof. history No. Ariz. U., Flagstaff, Ariz., 1967-75; prof. history, chair social sci. div. George Fox Coll., Newberg, Oreg., 1975-84, v.p. for acad. affairs, dean of the coll., 1984-92; Herbert Hoover prof. history Geore Fox Coll., Newberg, Oreg., 1992—. Editor: Understanding Herbert Hoover, 1987, River of the West (F. Victor), 1985; contbr. articles and revs. to profl. jours. Elected del. Ariz. State Dem. Conv., Flagstaff, Phoenix, 1972; hist. cons. Gov.'s Ratification Celebration Prodn. Com., Salem, Oreg., 1988. With U.S. Army, 1946-47. Jacobs Found. scholar, 1958; postdoctoral rsch. grantee U. Oreg. Devel. Fund, 1961; history rsch. fellow U. Oreg., 1961-62. Mem. Am. Hist. Assn., Orgn. Am. Historians, Western Hist. Assn., Conf. on Faith and History (exec. bd. 1982-86, editorial bd. 1972—), Oreg. Hist. Soc. (editorial bd. 1990—), Western Lit. Assn., Friends Assn. for Higher Edn. Mem. Friends Ch. Home: 191 Dogwood Dr Dundee OR 97115-9528 Office: George Fox Coll Newberg OR 97132

NASH, M. ELIZABETH, chiropractor; b. Troy, N.Y., July 4, 1960; d. George and Susan (Bourk) N. BA in Phys. Scis., Colgate U., 1983; BS in Bus. Econs., D in Chiropractic, Palmer Coll. of Chiropractic, Davenport, Iowa, 1989. Assoc. chiropractor Hughes Chiropractic, Aneheim, Calif., 1990; intern Forrizzo Chiropractic, Clear Water, Fla., 1990; assoc. chiropractor Holistic Network, Albany, N.Y., 1990-91, Tewson Chiropractic, North Pole, Alaska, 1991, Orlander Chiropractic, Westchester, N.Y., 1991, Koslow Chiropractic, N.Y.C., 1991; head chiropractor, owner North Pole (Alaska) Chiropractic, 1991—. Mem. Alaska Chiropractic Assn., New York State Chiropractic Assn., Alaskan Chiropractic Assn., Calif. Chiropractic Assn. Home and Office: 3375 Badger Rd # 5 North Pole AK 99705

NASH, RICHARD EUGENE, aerospace engineer; b. San Diego, Feb. 18, 1954; s. Clifford Arthur Jr. and Dorothy Fay (Johnson) N.; m. Lynn Elora Martin, Aug. 5, 1978. BSCE, U. Ky., 1981; MCE, U. So. Calif., 1988. Registered profl. civil engr., Calif.; cert. profl. mgr. Mem. tech. staff Rockwell Internat., Downey, Calif., 1982—, lead engr. space shuttle propulsion systems, 1986-88; engr. Nat. Aero-Space Plane, Long Beach, Calif., 1988-89, orbiter project engr., 1989—; pvt. practice civil engring., Buena Park, Calif., 1985—. Scoutmaster Boy Scouts Am., Covington, Ky., 1972-74, Williamstown, Ky., 1976-82, asst. scoutmaster, Ft. Hood, Tex., 1975-76. Sgt. U.S. Army, 1976. Recipient Eagle Scout award Boy Scouts Am., 1972; named to Hon. Order of Ky. Cols. 1985. Mem. NSPE, Nat. Mgmt. Assn., Nat. Eagle Scout Asst. (advisor 1983), Masons (32 degree, sr. deacon), Chi Epsilon. Republican. Office: Rockwell Internat Space Transp and Systems Div 12214 Lakewood Blvd Downey CA 90242-2693

NASH, STELLA B., government nutrition administrator; b. Gould, Ark., Nov. 3, 1942; d. Virgil and Lessie B. (Bonner) Riley; m. Solomon Nash, Mar. 31, 1973; children: Chad, Jereme. BS, Ark. AM & N Coll., 1964; MA, NYU, 1970; postgrad., Pa. State U., 1973-74, U. Mo., 1974-75. Nutritionist/spl. asst. to the dir. Ark. Office on Aging, Little Rock, 1975-76; supr. child nutrition Ark. State Dept. Edn., Little Rock, 1976-79; supr. Coop. Extension Svc. USDA, Denver, 1979-85; regional nutrition dir. Mountain Plains region USDA Food and Nutrition Svc., Denver, 1985—; home mgmt. specialist U. Ark. Coop. Extension, Pine Bluff, 1972-73; nutritionist N.J. Coll. Medicine and Dentistry, Newark, 1970-72; dietitian King County Hosp., Bklyn., 1964-66. Co-author: (coloring book) Nutrition Education, 1972; contbr. newpaper articles to Rocky ' ›untain News, 1992; author (jour.) Ill. Tchr., 1974. State v.p., dist. pres .ew Home Makers Am., Ark., 1958-59; mem. Montbello Optimist Cl..o, Denver, 1987-89, Far NE Neighbors Assn., Denver, 1985—; chairperson worship United Ch. of Montbello, Denver, 1989—. Recipient Nutrition Edn. award Western Dairy Coun., 1986; named Outstanding Educator of Am., Outstanding Educators of Am., 1973, Outstanding Young Woman of Am., Outstanding Young Women of Am., 1976. Mem. Am. Dietetic Assn. (registered dietitian), Colo. Dietetic Assn. (scholarship chairperson 1990-91, pub. rels. 1983-84) Soc. Nutrition Edn., Ark. Gerontol. Soc. (charter), Delta Sigma Theta (undergrad. chpt. sponsor 1972-73). Home: 4743 Chandler Ct Denver CO 80239

NASI, JOHN RODERICK, manufacturing executive; b. Ironwood, Mich., May 8, 1940; s. John Frijolf and Katherine Helen (Uremovick) N.; m. Patricia Ann Hosking, May 28, 1960; children: Jeffrey John, John Patrick, James Marshal. B in Mech. Engring., Gen. Motors Inst. Various mgmt. positions GMC Truck and Coach div. Gen. Motors Corp., Pontiac, Mich., 1964-79, gen. supt. prodn., 1979-81, plant mgr., 1981-82; exec. v.p. Transp. Mfg. Corp., Roswell, N. Mex., 1982—, now pres., chief exec. officer; pres., chief exec. officer MCI, Winnipeg, Man., Can.; bd. dirs. Dallas Smith Transp. Co., Phoenix, Sunwest Bank of Roswell. Bd. dirs. Boy Scouts of Am., Roswell, 1982—, United Way, Roswell, 1982—, St. Mary's Hosp., Roswell, 1984—. Mem. Soc. Automotive Engrs. Republican. Episcopalian. Lodge: Rotary. Home: RR 1 Box 246 Roswell NM 88201-9801 Office: Transp Mfg Corp PO Box 5670 Roswell NM 88202-5670

NASKE, CLAUS-M(ICHAEL), history educator; b. Stettin, Germany, Dec. 18, 1935; came to U.S., 1954; s. Alfred Naske; m. Dinah Ariss, May 20, 1960; children: Natalia-Michelle Nau-geak Naske Carboy, Nathaniel-Michael Noah. BA, U. Alaska, 1961; MA, U. Mich., 1964; PhD, Wash. State U., 1971. Asst. prof. history U. Alaska, Fairbanks, 1969-72, assoc. prof. history, 1972-81, prof. history, 1981—, chair dept. history, 1986-92; exec. dir. U. Alaska Press, Fairbanks, 1987—. Author: E.L. Bartlett of Alaska, 1979, AK: A History of the 49th State, 1979, Fairbanks and Anchorage Pictorial Histories, 1981, Paving Alaska's Trails, 1986. Mem. Alaska Humanities Forum, Anchorage, 1974-80, 88-91, Alaska Growth Policy Coun., Juneau, 1979-82; pres. Alaska Ind. TV, Inc., Anchorage, 1982-85. Named Alaska Historian of Yr., Alaska Hist. Soc., 1980. Mem. Can. Hist. Assn., Western History Assn., Nat. Press Club. Democrat. Home: PO Box 80721 Fairbanks AK 99708

NASKY, H(AROLD) GREGORY, lawyer; b. Titusville, Pa., June 9, 1942; s. Harold G. and Majella Marie (Beck) N.; m. Rosanne Guson, July 22, 1967. AB, St. Bonaventure U., 1964; JD, U. Notre Dame, 1967. Bar: Pa. 1967, Nev. 1972. Assoc. Eaton & Hill, Warren, Pa., 1967-68, Vargas, Bartlett & Dixon, Reno, 1972-73; ptnr. Vargas & Bartlett, Las Vegas, Nev., 1974—, mng. ptnr., 1981-91; corp. sec. Showboat, Inc. (NYSE-SBO), Las Vegas, 1978—, bd. dirs.; bd. dirs. U. Notre Dame Law Assn.; mem. adv. bd. U. Nev. Sch. Medicine.; chmn. 1993—, bd. dirs. Author: Inter Alia Jour. of State Bar of Nevada, A Glimpse of China, 1986; Nev. contbg. author: Real Property, Probate & Trust Law Jour., Disposition of Rents, 1981. Legal advisor Nev. Dance Theatre, Las Vegas, 1977—, bd. dirs. 1988—; legal com. Nev. Resort Assn., Las Vegas, gaming regulations com. 1990—; bd. dirs. Boulder Dam Council Boy Scouts Am., Las Vegas, 1986—; del. People to People Citizen Ambassador Program, People's Republic China, 1985, New Zealand/Australia, 1987, Hungary, Czechoslovakia and Poland, 1990, Russia and Estonia, 1992. Served to capt. JAGC, U.S. Army, 1968-72, Vietnam. Decorated Bronze Star, 1970. Mem. ABA (bus. sect. task force conflicts interest com. 1993), Pa. Bar Assn., State Bar Nev. (mem. chmn. fee dispute com. 1983-89, exec. com. mem. Gaming Law Sect. 1985-93), Am. Soc. Corps. Secs., Internat. Assn. Gaming Attys., Notre Dame Club Las Vegas, 1976— (past pres. 1978-79), U. Nev. Las Vegas Found. (pres. assocs. 1988—, vice chmn. 1992-93). Office: Vargas & Bartlett 3800 Howard Hughes Pkwy 7th Fl Las Vegas NV 89109

NASO, VALERIE JOAN, automobile dealership executive, travel company operator, artist, photographer, writer; b. Stockton, Calif., Aug. 19, 1941; d. Alan Robert and Natalie Grace (Gardner) McKittrick Naso; m. Peter Joralemon, May 31, 1971 (div.). Student pub. schs., Piedmont, Calif. Cert. graphoanalyst. Pres., Naso Motor Co. (formerly Broadway Cadillacs, Oakland, Calif.) Bishop, Calif., 1964—; freelance artist, 1965—; owner, operator Wooden Horse Antiques, Bishop, 1970-82; editor, writer, photographer Sierra Life Mag., Bishop, 1980-83; freelance writer, photographer, 1972—; owner, operator Boredom Tours, Bishop, 1981—; owner, sole photographer, Renaissance Photography, N.Y.C. and Bishop, Calif., 1982—, Keyboard Colors, 1986; cons. graphoanalyst, 1976—. Fiction, non-fiction work pub. in Horse and Horseman, Am. Horseman, Horse & Rider Mag., Cameo Mag., Desert Mag., Sierra Life Mag. Mem. Nat. Assn. Female Execs., Authors Guild, Inc., Authors League Am., Am. Film Inst., Archives of Am. Art, Lalique Soc. Am., Musical Box Soc. Internat., Alliance Francaise (N.Y. chpt.), Bishop C. of C., Victorian Soc. Am., Nat. Trust for Hist. Preservation, Am. Craft Coun., Nat. Rifle Assn. Clubs: Cadillac LaSalle; Wagner Soc. (N.Y.C.). Office: 783 N Main St Bishop CA 93514-2427

NASON, DOLORES IRENE, computer company executive, counselor, eucharistic minister; b. Seattle, Jan. 24, 1934; d. William Joseph Lockinger and Ruby Irene (Church) Gilstrap; m. George Malcolm Nason Jr., Oct. 7, 1951; children: George Malcolm III, Scott James, Lance William, Natalie Joan. Student, Long Beach (Calif.) City Coll., 1956-59; cert. in Religious Edn. for elem tchrs., Immaculate Heart Coll., 1961, cert. teaching, 1962, cert. secondary teaching, 1967; attended, Salesian Sem., 1983-85. Buyer J. C. Penney Co., Barstow, Calif., 1957; prin. St. Cyprian Confraternity of Christian Doctrine Elem. Sch., Long Beach, 1964-67; prin. summer sch. St. Cyprian Confraternity of Christian Doctrine Elem. Sch., Long Beach, 1965-67; pres. St. Cyprian Confraternity Orgn., Long Beach, 1967-69; dist. co-chmn. L.A. Diocese, 1968-70; v.p. Nason & Assocs., Inc., Long Beach, 1978—; pres. L.A. County Commn. on Obscenity & Pornography, 1984—; eucharistic minister St. Cyprian Ch., Long Beach, 1985—; bd. dirs. L.A. County Children's Svcs., 1988—; part-time social svcs. counselor Disabled Resources Ctr., Inc., Long Beach, 1992—; vol. Meml. Children's Hosp., Long Beach, 1977—; mem. scholarship com. Long Beach City Coll., 1984-90, Calif. State U., Long Beach, 1984-90. Mem. Sunland-Tujuna (Calif.)

Citizens-Police Coun., 1987—; mem. adv. bd. Pro-Wilson 90 Gov., Calif., 1990; mem. devel. bd. St. Joseph High Sch., 1987—; pres. St. Cyprian's Parish Coun., 1962—; mem. Long Beach Civic Light Opera, 1973—, Assistance League of Long Beach, 1976—. Mem. L.A. Fitness Club, U. of the Pacific Club, K.C. (Family of the Month 1988). Republican. Roman Catholic.

NASON, PATRICIA ANNE WOODWARD, museum educator, consultant; b. Atlanta, Nov. 1, 1932; d. William Rogers Woodward and Elizabeth (Eugenia) Riley; m. George Frank Nason, III, Feb. 12, 1955; children: Nancy Patricia Nason Guss, Susan Elizabeth Nason Swilley, George Frank IV, Peter Neil. Student, Vanderbilt U., 1950, Brevard C.C., Melbourne, Fla., 1973, UCLA, 1992; BA, Mercer U., 1954. Psychometrist Ga. Inst. Tech., Atlanta, 1954-55; real estate assoc. Fogg/Bancroft Realty, Indialantic, Fla., 1973-78; tchr. econs., psychology, sociology Ctrl. Cath. High Sch., Melbourne, 1977-78; exec. sec. Golden Enterprises, Inc., Melbourne, 1978-81; sr. adminstrv. personnel asst. Info. Systems Am., Atlanta, 1982-87; gift shop staff mem., weekend asst. Maturango Mus., Ridgecrest, Calif., 1987-88, edn. coord., 1988-90, edn. and pub. events coord., 1990-92, program coord., 1992—; bd. dirs., sec., treas. Technical Enterprises, Inc., 1975-82; fundraising cons., Ridgecrest, 1993—. Contbr. articles to newspapers. Active Jr. League South Brevard, Melbourne, 1965—; founder, mgr. Episcopal Book & Gift Shop, Melbourne, 1965-67; v.p. St. Elizabeth Guild, Melbourne, 1966; mem. Tourism Com. Ridgecrest, 1990-92, women's bd. Brevard Symphony, 1978-81. Mem. Am. Assn. Mus. (standing profl. com. edn. 1993—), Phi Mu Alumni Assn. (pres. 1960-62). Home: 627 N Rio Bravo Dr Ridgecrest CA 93555 Office: Maturango Mus 100 E Las Flores Ave Ridgecrest CA 93555

NASR, WALID MERWAN, engineering and investment company executive; b. Monsef, Lebanon, Dec. 31, 1948; came to U.S., 1987; s. Merwan Michel and Bader Adlah (Nassar) N.; m. Victoria Fattouh, July 12, 1975; children: Marwan, Mira, Majed. BSME, Am. U. Beirut, 1971. Pres., owner Sketch Engrng. Co., Beirut, 1978—; WG Farming Co. Sketch Engrng. Co., 1989—, Fana Investment & Trading Inc., Corona, Calif., 1989—; v.p. Sogex Internat., Paris, 1984-88; adviser, owner Needs Devel. Co., Beirut, 1988—; v.p., owner GRF Inc., Corona, 1990—; expert, cons. ILO, Geneva, 1987—; cons. on internat. mgmt. Editor, cons.: International Safety Standards in Industry, 1991. Mem. Soc. Lebanese-Am. Profls. (pres. L.A., 1992—), Lebanese Order Engrs., Am. U. Beirut Alumni N.Am., Internat. Coll. Alumni Am. (co-founder L.A.). Home: 1125 W Citron Corona CA 91720 Office: Fana Investment & Trading 102 E Grand Blvd Corona CA 91719

NATHAN, LAWRENCE CHARLES, chemistry educator; b. Corning, Calif., Nov. 26, 1944; s. Jules Morris and Mildred (Wood) N.; m. Frieda Ruth Bjornson, Aug. 29, 1966 (div. Dec. 1987); children: Kristine M., Cheryl L.; m. Linda Lou Hartman Crabb, June 17, 1988; stepchildren: Anthony W. Crabb, Tammy J. Crabb. BA, Linfield Coll., 1966; PhD, U. Utah, 1971. From asst. prof. to assoc. prof. Santa Clara (Calif.) U., 1970-88, prof., 1988—, chmn. chemistry dept., 1992—; vis. assoc. prof. U. Utah, Salt Lake City, 1976, 77. Contbr. articles to profl. jours. Recipient Disting. Faculty awd. Santa Clara U., 1979. Mem. Am. Chem. Soc., Sigma Xi. Office: Santa Clara U Chemistry Dept Santa Clara CA 95053

NATHAN, LEONARD EDWARD, author, educator; b. Los Angeles, Nov. 8, 1924; s. Israel and Florence (Rosenberg) N.; m. Carol Gretchen Nash, June 27, 1949; children: Andrew Peter, Julia Irene, Miriam Abigail. Student, Ga. Tech., 1943-44, UCLA, 1946-47; BA summa cum laude, U. Calif.-Berkeley, 1950, MA, 1952, PhD, 1961. Instr. Modesto (Calif.) Jr. Coll., 1954-60; prof. dept. rhetoric U. Calif., Berkeley, 1960-91, ret., 1991, chmn. dept., 1968-72. Author: Western Reaches, 1958, The Glad and Sorry Seasons, 1963, The Matchmaker's Lament, 1967, The Day The Perfect Speakers Left, 1969, The Tragic Drama of William Butler Yeats, 1963, Flight Plan, 1971, Without Wishing, 1973, The Likeness, 1975, Coup, 1975, Returning Your Call, 1975, The Transport of Love: The Meghaduta by Kalidasa, 1976, Teachings of Grandfather Fox, 1977, Lost Distance, 1978, Dear Blood, 1980, Holding Patterns, 1982, Carrying On: New and Selected Poems, 1985; also record Confessions of a Matchmaker, 1973, De Meester van Het Winterlandschap, Selected Poems in Dutch transl. by Cees Nooteboom, Uitgeverij de Arbiedspers, Amsterdam, 1990; translator: Songs of Something Else, 1982, Grace and Mercy in Her Wild Hair, 1982, (with Czeslaw Milosz) Happy As a Dog's Tail: Poems by Anna Swir, 1985, (with Czeslaw Milosz) With the Skin: Poems of Aleksander Wat, 1989, (with Arthur Quinn) The Poet's Work: Study of Czeslaw Milosz, 1991. With U.S. Army, 1943-45, ETO. Recipient Phelan award, 1955; Longview prize, 1961; award in lit. Nat. Inst. Arts and Letters, 1971; Poetry medal Commonwealth Club, 1976, 81; U. Calif. Creative Arts fellow, 1961-62, 73-74; U. Calif. Humanities research fellow, 1983-84; Am. Inst. Indian Studies fellow, 1966-67; Guggenheim fellow, 1976-77. Mem. Nat. Coun. Tchrs. English. Office: U Calif Dept Rhetoric Berkeley CA 94720

NATHANSON, THEODORE HERZL, aeronautical engineer; architect; b. Montreal, Que., Can., Apr. 20, 1923; came to U.S., 1949; naturalized, 1983; s. Henry and Minnie (Goldberg) N.; student McGill U., 1940-42; SB in Aero. Engring., MIT, 1944; MArch, Harvard U., 1955. Research engr. Noorduyn Aviation Ltd., Montreal, 1944-45; stress engr. Canadair Ltd., Montreal, 1945-46; structural engr. A.V. Roe (Can.) Ltd., Malton, Ont., 1946-47; with Mies van der Rohe, Chgo., summer 1949, R. Buckminster Fuller, Forest Hills, N.Y., summer 1951; cons. engr. and architect, Montreal, Boston, Los Angeles, 1955—; mem. tech. staff Rockwell Internat., 1979-92, structural analysis and advanced design Space Transp. Systems div., Downey, Calif., 1979-86, mission ops. and advanced concepts Space Sta. Systems div., 1986-87, space sta. elec. power system Rocketdyne div., Canoga Park, Calif., 1987-92; cons. Aerospace Engr., L.A., 1992—; lectr. architecture, McGill U., 1967-68. Fellow Brit. Interplanetary Soc.; mem. Order Engrs. Que., Order Architects Que., Soc. Am. Registered Architects, Nat. Soc. Profl. Engrs., AIAA, Royal Archtl. Inst. Can., Nat. Mgmt. Assn., Copley Soc. of Boston, MIT Club of So. Calif. (bd. govs.), Can. Soc. (Los Angeles). Projects and models included in group shows: Mus. Fine Arts, Springfield, Mass., 1961, N.Y. World's Fair, 1965, Winterfest, Boston, 1966, Boston Artists' Project '70. Jewish. Home and Office: 225 S Olive St Ste 1004 Los Angeles CA 90012

NATHE, DENNIS GERHARDT, ranch executive; b. Scobey, Mont., Dec. 12, 1938; s. Michael Henry and Saralda Sophia (Korf) N.; B.S., St. Benedicts Coll., Atchison, Kans., 1962; M.S., Creighton U., 1966; m. Della Mae Snyder, Dec. 28, 1970; children—Alycia, Michael. Pharm. detail man Lederle Labs., Am. Cyanamid Co., Omaha, 1962-64; clin. research coordinator Med. Products div. 3M Co., St. Paul, 1967; farming, ranching, Redstone, Mont., 1967—; pres. Nathe Ranch Inc., 1973-80 ; pres. Wanmdi Kinyan, Inc., 1981—. Vice-chmn. Mont. Environ. Quality Council, 1977-79, chmn., 1979-81 , public mem., 1981-83 ; Mont. State Rep., 1977-81, 85-88; Mont. state senator, 1989—; Mt. Wiche commr., 1990—; commr. Interstate Commn. Higher Edn., 1990—; chmn. Sheridan County Planning and Improvement Council, 1973-76; del. Economic Devel. Assn. Eastern Mont., 1973-76; chmn. Three Corners Boundary Assn., 1976-77; Democratic Precinct committeeman, 1968-76; vice chmn. Coal Tax Oversight Com., 1985—; mem. Mont. Rural Area Devel. Com., 1976—, Mont. Western Interstate Commn. Higher Edn.; alternate Mo. River Barge Transp. Com., 1980—; mem. Gov.'s Groundwater Task Force, 1983-85; bd. suprs. Sheridan County Conservation Dist., 1969-78; chmn. Eastern Mont. Range Improvement Com., 1973-78; chmn. Sheridan County Republican Central Com., 1980—; mem. Mont. Extension Adv. Council, 1980-82 , participant numerous other civic activities. Served with AUS, 1957-58. Mem. Soc. Range Mgmt., (chmn. Mont. Old West regional range program 1975-79), Durum Growers Assn., K.C. Republican. Roman Catholic. Home: PO Box 4 Redstone MT 59257-0004

NATHWANI, BHARAT NAROTTAM, pathologist, consultant; b. Bombay, Jan. 20, 1945; came to U.S., 1972; s. Narottam Pragji and Bharati N. (Lakhani) N. MBBS, Grant Med. Coll., Bombay, 1969, MD in Pathology, 1972. Intern Grant Med. Coll., Bombay U., 1968-69; asst. prof. pathology Grant Med. Coll., 1972; fellow in hematology Cook County Hosp., Chgo., 1972-73; resident in pathology Rush U., Chgo., 1973-74; fellow in hematopathology City of Hope Med. Ctr., Duarte, Calif., 1975-76, pathologist, 1977-84; prof. pathology, chief hematopathology U. So. Calif., L.A., 1984—; cons. Norris Cancer Hosp., L.A., 1986—. Contbr. numerous articles to profl. jours. Recipient Grant awards Nat. Libr. Medicine, Bethesda, Md., Nat. Cancer Inst., 1991. Mem. AAAS, Internat. Acad. Pathology, Am. Soc. Clin. Pathology, Am. Soc. Hematology, Am. Soc. Oncology. Office: U So Calif Sch Medicine HMR 204 2025 Zonal Ave Los Angeles CA 90033-4526

NATTER, JEFF, health education professional; b. Bklyn., Feb. 3, 1956; s. Abraham George and Nettie (Kaplansky) N. BA, Amherst Coll., 1978; MFA, Yale U., 1981; MPH, Columbia U., 1989. Asst. coord. crisis intervention Gay Men's Health Crisis, N.Y.C., 1985-87; AIDS educator Nat. Hemophilia Found., N.Y.C., 1988-89; edn. mgr. NW AIDS Found., Seattle, 1990—. Mem. APHA, Soc. Pub. Health Educators. Office: NW AIDS Found 127 Broadway E Seattle WA 98102-5711

NAUGHTEN, ROBERT NORMAN, pediatrician; b. Stockton, Calif., Oct. 13, 1928; s. Norman Stafford and Junetta (Doherty) N.; m. Ann Louise Charkins, June 26, 1954; children: Robert James, Annette Marie Naughten-Dessel, Patricia Louise. AA, San Jose City Coll., San Jose, Calif., 1948; BA, U. Calif., Berkeley, 1950; MA, Stanford U., 1955; MD, Hahnemann U., 1959. Lic. physician and surgeon, Calif. Intern Highland-Alameda County Hosp., Oakland, Calif., 1959-60; rsch. fellow Nat. Cancer Inst., Stanford, Calif., 1960-61; resident pediatrics Stanford Med. Ctr., 1961-63; pvt. practice pediatrics Los Gatos, Calif., 1963—; instr. Santa Clara Valley Med. Ctr., San Jose, 1963—, Dept. of Pediatrics, Stanford, 1963-73; cons. drug abuse San Jose Police Dept., 1963-68; cons. child abuse Dist. Atty., San Jose, 1984—; cons. dept. social svcs. State of Calif., 1989—. Contbr. articles to profl. jours. Bd. dirs., v.p. Outreach and Escort, Inc., San Jose, 1985-88. Named Alumnus of Yr. San Jose City Coll., 1967, Chef of the West Sunset Mag., 1989; fellow Coll. of Physicians, Phila., 1986. Mem. AMA, Calif. Assn., Santa Clara Med. Assn. (v.p. 1986-88), Am. Acad. Pediatrics, Am. Acad. Allergy and Clin. Immunology, Calif. Alumni Assn. (Berkeley), Stanford Alumni Assn., Commonwealth Club (San Francisco), Soc. of the Sigma Xi. Democrat. Roman Catholic. Home: 13601 Riverdale Dr Saratoga CA 95070-5229 Office: 777 Knowles Dr Ste 14 Los Gatos CA 95030-1417

NAUMES, PATRICK EDWARD, educator; b. Medford, Oreg., July 12, 1947; s. Robert Arthur and M. Jarvie (Thompson) N. BA, So. Oreg. Coll., 1969; MA, U. Calif., Santa Barbara, 1971. Tchr. St. Mary's Sch., Medford, 1971—, alumni dir., 1989—; bd. dirs. Naumes Equipment and Fuel Co., Medford, Farmers Fin. Corp., Medford. Bd. dirs. Rogue Valley Family YMCA, Medford, 1989—. NEH fellow, 1991. Mem. Am. Classical League. Roman Catholic. Home: 198 Littrell Dr Medford OR 97504 Office: St Mary's Sch 816 Black Oak Dr Medford OR 97504

NAURATH, DAVID ALLISON, engineering psychologist, researcher; b. Houston, Mar. 11, 1927; s. Walter Arthur and Joy Frances (Bradbury) N.; m. Barbara Ellen Coverdell; children: Kathleen Ann, David Allen, Cynthia Ellyn, Randall Austin. BA, Simpson Coll., Indianola, Iowa, 1948; MA, Southern Meth. U., 1949; postgrad., U. Denver, 1955-57. Job analyst U.S. Air Force, San Antonio and Denver, 1951-55; rsch. psychologist U.S. Air Force, Lowry AFB, Colo., 1955-60, Navy, Life Scis. & Systems div., Point Mugu, Calif., 1960-76; engrng. psychologist Navy Systems Engrng., Point Mugu, 1976-83; ret.; presenter at profl. socs. and orgns. in field. Contbr. articles to Jour. Engrng. Psychology, jour. Soc. for Info. Display, jour. Soc. Photo-optical Instrument Engrs. With USAAF, 1944-46. Mem. AAAS (life), IEEE (sr.), Am. Psychol. Assn., Human Factors Soc. (panel mem. Certification of Human Factors Engrs. 1976), Soc. Engrng. Psychologists, Soc. for Info. Display (life). Methodist. Home: 5633 Pembroke St Ventura CA 93003-2200

NAVAJAS, GONZALO, foreign language educator; b. Barcelona, Spain, May 14, 1946; came to U.S., 1970; s. Jose and Carmen (Navarro) N.; 1 child, Paul. PhD, UCLA, 1975. Prof. SUNY, Stony Brook, 1980-83, Tulane U., New Orleans, 1983-85; prof. dept. Spanish and Portuguese U. Calif., Irvine, 1985—; lectr., mem. editorial bd. various jours. in field. Author 7 books; contbr. articles to profl. publs. Mem. Modern Assn. Am., Internat. Assn. Hispanists. Office: U Calif Dept Spanish Irvine CA 92711

NAVARRE, JAMES EARL, business executive; b. Detroit, Feb. 8, 1931; s. Earl Joseph and Florence (Beatty) N.; m. Sarah Rogers, Apr. 30, 1960; children: Sally E., Margot C., Philip J. BA, Albion (Mich.) Coll., 1952; MBA, Columbia U., 1953. Fin. analyst Ford Motor Co., Dearborn, Mich., 1953-58; prin. Cresap, McCormick & Paget, N.Y.C., 1958-62; pres. Sundstrand Data Control, Inc., Redmond, Wash., 1962-69, Mannesmann Tally Corp., Kent, Wash., 1969-73; exec. v.p. New Eng. Fish Co., Seattle, 1973-78; pres. N.W. Med. Resources, Inc., Yakima, Wash., 1980-84, Olympac Foundry Co., Seattle, 1984-86, Spectra Lux Corp., Kirkland, Wash., 1988-90, Ford, Navarre & Assocs., Inc., Bellevue, Wash., 1988-92; chmn. Percon Inc., Eugene, Oreg., 1990—, Lynx Automation, Inc., Lynnwood, Wash., 1991—; chmn., CEO Innovis Techs., Inc., Bellevue, 1991—. Trustee Seattle Opera Assembly, 1968-75, King County United Way, Seattle, 1969-72; bd. dirs. Am. Electronics Assn., Santa Clara, Calif., 1967-70. Cpl. U.S. Army, 1954-56. Mem. Ranier Club, Seattle Tennis Club, Bellevue Athletic Club. Home: 9428 NE 1st St Bellevue WA 98004-5428 Office: Innovis Techs 3245-146th Pl SE Ste 340 Bellevue WA 98007

NAVARRO, ARTEMIO EDWARD, elementary educator; b. Commerce, Calif., Nov. 12, 1950; s. Artemio Gomez and Bertha (Bustamante) N.; m. Sally Jean Ramirez, Aug. 7, 1983; children: Natalie, Julie, Laura, Artemio Jr. AA, East L.A. Coll., 1971; MA, Calif. State U., L.A., 1974, Calif. State U., L.A., 1982. Cert. adminstr. Tchr. Montebello (Calif.) Unified Sch. Dist., 1975—. Coun. mem. City of Commerce, Calif., 1988-91, mayor, 1991—; mem. anti-gang task force, TELACU scholarship com., Regional Occupational Ctr. Com. Mem. Jaycees (pres. East L.A. chpt. 1986-87), Lions Club, St. Marcellinis Holy Name Soc. (past pres.). Office: City of Commerce 2535 Commerce Way Los Angeles CA 90040-1410

NAVARRO, SANTIAGO RAUL, human resources executive; b. San Salvador, El Salvador, Aug. 30, 1954; came to U.S., 1975; s. Santiago and Pilar (Gracia) N.; m. Isabel Victoria Diaz, Oct. 12, 1977; children: Ricardo, Isabel. Student Exec. Mgmt., UCLA, 1989. Machine operator Easton Aluminum Inc., Van Nuys, Calif., 1977-78; lead person Easton Aluminum Inc., Van Nuys, 1979-80, human resources asst., 1980-81, prodn. mgr., 1981-82, human resources mgr., 1982-87, human resources dir., 1987—. Office: Easton Aluminum Inc 7800 Haskell Ave Van Nuys CA 91406

NAY, SAMUEL WESLEY, retired mechanical engineer; b. Steamboat Springs, Colo., May 29, 1914; s. Samuel W. and Josephine L. (Bartz) N.; m. Edythe L. Winberg, May 31, 1942; 1 child: Samuel III (dec.). BS in Engring., Calif. State U., L.A., 1967. Registered profl. engr., Calif. Tooling engr. Lockheed Aircraft, Burbank, Calif., 1940-47; mech. engr. assoc. design and constrn. Dept. Water and Power, L.A., 1947-78; instr. Calif. U. Extension, L.A., 1978-82; cons. engr. S.W. Nay Assocs., Glendale, Calif., 1979-91; ret., 1991. Editor tech. publ. The Flame, 1978-81. Mem. Town Hall, L.A., 1992—. Sgt. USAF, 1942-45. Fellow Inst. for the Advacement Engring. (bd. dirs., treas. 1978-92); mem. ASME, L.A. Coun. Engrng. (v.p., bd. dirs. 1978—, pres. 1990-91), L.A. Coun. Engrs. and Scientists (past pres.), Soc. Fire Pretection Engrs. (life, past pres.). Home: 813 Palm Dr Glendale CA 91202

NAYLOR, GEORGE LEROY, lawyer, rail transportation executive; b. Bountiful, Utah, May 11, 1915; s. Joseph Francis and Josephine Chase (Wood) N.; student U. Utah, 1934-36; student George Washington U., 1937; J.D. (Bancroft Whitney scholar), U. San Francisco, 1953; m. Maxine Elizabeth Lewis, Jan. 18, 1941; children: Georgia Naylor Price, RoseMaree Naylor Hammer, George LeRoy II. Bar: Calif. 1954, Ill. 1968. V.p., sec., legis. rep. Internat. Union of Mine, Mill & Smelter Workers, CIO, Dist. Union 2, Utah-Nevada, 1942-44; examiner So. Pacific Co., San Francisco, 1949-54, chief examiner, 1955, asst. mgr., 1956-61; carrier mem. Nat. R.R. Adjustment Bd., Chgo., 1961-77, chmn., 1970-77; atty. Village of Fox River Valley Gardens, Ill., 1974-77; practice law, legal cons., Ill. and Calif., 1977—, ret. from pvt. practice, 1991; gen. counsel for Can-Veyor, Inc., Mountain View, Calif., 1959-64; adj. instr. dept. mgmt. U. West Fla., 1981. Active Rep. Nat. Com., 1992-93. Served with AUS, World War II. Mem. ABA, Ill. Bar Assn., Calif. Bar Assn., Chgo. Bar Assn., San Francisco Bar Assn. Mormon. Author: Defending Carriers Before the NRAB and Public Law Boards, 1969, Choice Morsels in Tax and Property Law, 1966, Underground at Bingham Canyon, 1944; National Railroad Adjustment Board Practice Manual, 1978. Home and Office: Virginia Lee Rd RR 1 Box 570 Cotter AR 72626-9704

NAYLOR, SCOTT JORDAN, construction executive; b. L.A., Sept. 21, 1952; m. Helen M. Naylor, July 8, 1977; children: Jacob, Anna, Megan, Elizabeth, Michael, Julie. BS, Brigham Young U., 1976. Line dir. Cen. Cartage U.S.A., Salt Lake City, 1972-75; sgt. Utah State Prison, Draper, 1976-81; police officer Draper Police Dept., 1978-82; owner, operator Tactical Security Cons., Salt Lake City, 1979-84, Advanced Security Concepts, Salt Lake City, 1983-85, Naylor Constrn. & Devel., San Diego, 1985—. Author: No Particular Place, 1977. Scoutmaster Boy Scouts Am., Salt Lake City, 1976-85, San Diego, 1987-90. Sgt. U.S. Army, 1970-72, Viet Nam. Mem. Police Officers Assn., Utah Peace Officers Assn. Republican. Office: Naylor Devel PO Box 2148 Alpine CA 91903-2148

NAYLOR, WILLIAM EDWARD, computer scientist; b. Long Beach, Calif., Apr. 18, 1943; s. William Hollis Naylor and Margaret W. Ketteringham; m. Doreen Ellen Berg, June 17, 1967 (div. June 1990); children: W. Jason, Bret Justin. AB in Math., UCLA, 1966, MS in Computer Sci., 1970, PhD in Computer Sci., 1977. Assoc. engr. The Boeing Co., Seattle, 1966; programmer Wolf Rsch. and Devel. Corp., Encino, Calif., 1966-67, System Specialists, Inc., Woodland Hills, Calif., 1967-68; programmer, sr. programmer Inst. Geophysics and Planetary Physics, UCLA, 1968-69; sr. programmer, computer systems designer Sch. Engring. and Applied Sci., UCLA, 1969-78; data communications specialist Xerox Corp., Woodland Hills, Calif., 1978-80; group mgr., dept. mgr. Citicorp TTI, Santa Monica, Calif., 1980-82, computer scientist, sr. computer scientist, 1983—; computer scientist The Aerospace Corp., El Segundo, Calif., 1982-83. Mem. Heal the Bay, Santa Monica, Calif., Greenpeace; fundraiser Walk America, March of Dimes. Mem. IEEE (communications and computer socs.), Assn. Computing Machinery, World Wildlife Fund, LACMA, UCLA Alumni Assn., Bruin Beach, Sierra Club. Office: Citicorp TTI 3100 Ocean Park Blvd Santa Monica CA 90405-3032

NAYLOR-JACKSON, JERRY, entertainer, public relations consultant, producer; b. Chalk Mountain, Tex., Mar. 6, 1939; s. William Guy and Mary Bernice (Lummus) Jackson; m. Pamela Ann Robinson, Jan. 30, 1966; children: Geoffrey K. Naylor, Kelli A. Naylor, Gregory K. Naylor. Grad., Elkins Electronics Inst., Dallas, 1957; student, U. Md., Fed. Republic of Germany, 1957-58. Life first class radio/TV engrng. lic. FCC. Broadcaster various local TV and AM radio stas., San Angelo, Texas, 1955-57; mem. Buddy Holly and the Crickets, 1957-65, lead singer, 1960-65; solo entertainer, performer, recording artist and producer, 1965-83; sr. v.p. corp. devel. Newslink Internat. Satellite Broadcast Comms. Co., Inc., Washington, 1986-88; pres. Internat. Syndications, Inc. subs. Newslink, Inc., Washington, 1986-88; pres., chief exec. officer, owner The Jerry Naylor Co., Inc., Agoura, Calif., 1984—; pres., CEO Media Unlimited/Naylor Prodns., Inc., 1983—; v.p. capital programs, sr. cons. Calif. Luth. Univ., Thousand Oaks, 1990-92; sr. cons., dir. ann. fund Calif. Luth. Univ., 1989-90; polit./media cons. various Rep. candidates and orgns., 1968—; spl. cons. to Violeta Barrios de Chamarro, Pres. of Republic of Nicaragua, 1990-92; disc jockey Sta. KHEY-AM, Sta KINT-AM, El Paso, Tex., 1959; on-air personality Sta. KRLA-AM, Sta. KDAY-AM, L.A., 1960, on-air disc jocky/air personality/celebrity host, KLAC-AM, L.A., Calif., 1974-83; on-camera and voice-over spokesman for Safeway Stores, Inc., Avis Rent-a-Car, Mutual of Omaha, Wrigley Co., 1968-83; U.S. presdl. appointee, chmn. Job Tng. Partnership Act work group/youth at risk subcom. Nat. Commn. for Employemtn Policy, 1985-92. Recording artist maj. labels including CBS Records, Motown Records, Warner Bros. Records, EMI Records, 1965-84; host weekly nat. and internat. radio program Continental Country (Number 1 syndicated country music radio show in Am., Billboard Mag., Country Music Assn., 1974, 77). Active presdl. task force Rep. Nat. Com.; nat. dir. spl. events Reagan for Pres., 1975-76, 79-80; sr. cons. to White House, 1981-88, 89-92. With U.S. Army, 1957-58, Fed. Republic of Germany. Named to Top 40 Male Vocalists of Yr., Billboard Mag., 1970, named #1 Rock Group (Crickets), Billboard Mag./New Musical Express Mag., 1958, 62. Mem. NARAS, Am. Film Inst., Country Music Assn., Acad. Country Music (Telly award for TV Documentary 1991, 92), Phi Kappa Phi (alumni). Home and Office: Jerry Naylor Co Inc 5308 Ambridge Dr Agoura CA 91301

NAZARIAN, IRADJ HASKELL, anatomic and clinical pathologist; b. Teheran, Iran, Apr. 20, 1937; came to U.S., 1985; s. Shalom and Alieh (Rastegar) N.; m. Edna Rastegar, Feb. 14, 1971; children: Shahrzad, Sheila. MD with honors, Shiraz (Iran) U. Med. Sch., 1964. Diplomate Am. Bd. Pathology. Intern Med. Sch. Pahlavi U., Shiraz, Iran, 1963-64, assoc. prof. anatomic and clin. pathology Med. Sch., 1969-73; resident in anatomic and clin. pathology U. Pa. Hosp., 1964-68; splty. tng. in parasitology Columbia U., 1968; ednl. fellow in pathology Mt. Sinai Hosp. Svcs., N.Y., 1968-69; head dept. pathology Tajrish Med. Ctr., Teheran, 1973; head dept. pathology labs. Cardiovascular Med. Ctr., Teheran, 1973-86; physician in charge South Atlantic Med. Group, El Monte, Calif., 1987-92; med. dir. Universal Med. Ctr., South Gate, Calif., 1992—; dir. Metro Med. Lab., L.A., 1988. Contbr. articles to profl. jours. Sec. bd. of anatomic and clin. pathology Ministry of Higher Edn., Iran, 1982-86; bd. dirs. Sapir Jewish Charity Hosp., Teheran, 1981-86. Fellow Coll. Am. Pathologists. Home: 641 N Doheny Dr Beverly Hills CA 90210 Office: Universal Med Ctr 9836 S Atlantic Ave South Gate CA 90280

NAZZARO, DAVID ALFRED, sales executive; b. Malden, Mass., Sept. 15, 1940; s. Alfred Anthony and Louise (Cunningham) N.; m. Jane Valentine, June 26, 1971; one child, David Thomas. BME, U.S. Mcht. Marine Acad., 1962; MS, Columbia U., 1965; MBA, Pepperdine U., 1975. Regional mgr. Turbo Power and Marine Systems div. United Tehcnologies, Hardford, Conn., 1965-74; mgr. bus. devel S & Q Corp., San Francisco, 1974-78; v.p. and gen. mgr. Con-Val, Oakland, Calif., 1978-85; pres. and chief exec. officer Dasa Controls, Belmont, Calif., 1985-87; mgr. bus. devel Johnson Yokogawa Corp., San Francisco, 1987—. Contbr. papers to profl. publs. Bd. dirs. Clearview Homeowners Assn., San Mateo, 1976; pres. St. Bartholomew's Parish Council, San Mateo, 1986. Lt. USNR, 1963-69. Sr. Mem. Instrument Soc. Am. (pres. No. Calif. Sec. 1987-88); mem. ASME, Am. Water Works Assn., Elks, Jaycees, St. Bartholomew's Mens Club (pres. 1977). Home: 30 Tollridge Ct San Mateo CA 94402-3730 Office: Johnson Controls Inc 50 Park Ln Brisbane CA 94005-1375

NEAL, FRED ROY, III, lawyer; b. Wendell, Idaho, Jan. 3, 1950; s. Fred Roy and Fay Margaret (Stacy) N. BA, Pomona Coll., 1972; JD, Lewis and Clark Law Sch., 1976. Bar: Oreg. 1976. Dep. legis. counsel Oreg. Legis. Assembly, Salem, 1976-80; exec. dir. State Ct. Fin. Action Com., Portland, Oreg., 1980-82; legal counsel League of Oreg. Cities, Salem, 1982-87; intergovtl. rels. officer Multnomah County, Portland, 1987—. Founding pres. Washington County Young Dems., Beaverton, Oreg., 1964; pres. The Campaigners, Portland, 1986; bd. dirs. Agri-Bus. Coun. Oreg., Portland, 1986—, Right to Privacy PAC, Portland, 1987—, co-chair, 1993. Mem. ACLU (v.p. Oreg. 1991-93), Oreg. State Bar Assn., Oreg. City Attys. Assn., Nat. Assn. County Intergovtl. Rels. Officers (pres. 1991-93), Nat. Assn. Counties (bd. dirs. 1991-93), City Club Portland (com. mem. 1980—). Home: 3045 NE 9th Portland OR 97212 Office: Multnomah County 1120 SW 5th Ave Rm 1410 Portland OR 97204

NEAL, JAMES MADISON, JR., editor; b. Oklahoma City, Aug. 6, 1925; s. James Madison and Tillie Belle (Milliken) N.; m. Caroline Dorothy Becker (dec. Dec. 1974); children: Charles, James W., Jody, Carolyn. BA, U. Colo., 1949; MA, S.D. State U., 1970. Editor various newspapers, Colo., Nebr. and Okla., 1949-59; wire editor Rapid City Journal, Rapid City, S.D., 1959-67; instr. S.D. State U., Brookings, S.D., 1967-71; asst. prof. U. Nebr., Lincoln, 1971-73, assoc. prof., 1973-90; S.D. chmn. AP Mng. Editors Assn., 1962-64. Mem. Soc. Profl. Journalists, Investigative Reporters and Editors, ACLU (bd. dirs. Nebr. chpt. 1979-82), VFW. Unitarian. Home: 4700 N Kolb #7207 Tucson AZ 85715

NEAL, PHILIP MARK, diversified manufacturing executive; b. San Diego, Aug. 28, 1940; s. Philip Mark and Florence Elizabeth (Anderson) N.; children: Brian, Kevin. B.A., Pomona Coll., 1962; M.B.A., Stanford U., 1964. Mgr. financial planning and analysis CBS, Hollywood, 1964-66; cons.

McKinsey & Co., Los Angeles, 1966-73; v.p., controller Avery Internat. Corp., Los Angeles, 1974-78; sr. v.p. fin. Avery Internat. Corp., Pasadena, 1979-88, group v.p. materials group, 1988-90; exec. pres. Avery Internat. Corp., 1990, pres., chief operating officer, 1990—. Trustee Pomona Coll. Mem. Fin. Execs. Inst. Republican. Episcopalian. Office: Avery Internat Corp PO Box 7090 Pasadena CA 91109

NEAMAN, BRYCENE ALLEN, museum curator; b. Toppenish, Wash., Apr. 7, 1955; s. Lee Allen and Lucille (Albert) N.; m. Beverly W. Dogsleep (div. Apr. 1986); children: Coral Rose Neaman. Gen. studies, Brigham Young U., Provo, UT, 1973-75; music-art, UT State U., Logan, UT, 1978-83. Pub. sch. liaison Adult Edn. Program, Toppenish, Wash., 1978-79; museum curator trainee Yakima Nation Cultural Ctr., Toppenish, Wash., 1980, 84; intake office worker Alcoholism Outreach Program, Toppenish, Wash., 1984-88; museum tech. Yakima Nation Cultural Ctr., Toppenish, Wash., 1988; curator Yakima Indian Nation Cultural Heritage Ctr., Toppenish, Wash., 1988—; coord. Wash. Centennial Com., Olympia, Wash., 1988-89; art commr. State Wash.-Wash. State Arts Commn. Coord. Brochure Art of the Yakima Ind. Art Exhibit, 1989. Exec. officer Wash. State Arts Com. Recipient Art of Y.I.N. An Exhibit of Contemporary Vision, Wash. Centennial Com., 1988-89; Wash. Humanities Art of the Yakima, 1988-89. Mem. Wash. Museum Assn., Western Museum Assn., Nat. Trust for Hist. Pres., Yakima Indian Nation. Mem. LDS. Home and Office: Yakima Nation Mus PO Box 151 Toppenish WA 98948-0151

NEAVES, ROBERT LOUIS, artist, gallery owner; b. Hamilton, Mont., Dec. 15, 1935; s. Walter Edwin and Theresa Joan (Brutto) N.; m. Sheila Rose, Nov. 30, 1956 (div. Apr. 1980); chldren: Anthony B., Marlin L., Melora C., Garry F.; m. Marianne R. Neaves, July 7, 1982; 1 child, Jennifer A. Student, Art Inst. Chgo., 1983-84, U. Mont., 1984-86. Artist, illustrator ITT Fed. Electric Corp., Paramus, N.J., 1962-67; freelance comml. artist Hamilton, 1967-70; art dir. U.S. Forest Svc. Regional Office, Missoula, Mont., 1970-84; owner Neaves Gallery, Hamilton, 1984—. Illustrator (mag. identification guides) Mont. Outdoors, 1984, 92; exhibited at Mus. of the Rockies, 1989-90. Bd. dirs. Daly Mansion Preservation Trust, 1988-90; bd. dirs., pres. Trapper Creek Job Corps Community Coun., 1991-92. Featured Western artist Iowa Wildlife Western Exhbn., Des Moines, 1986; named Artist of Quarter Rocky Mountain Elk Found., Mont., 1987, Artist of Yr. Nat. Bison Soc., S.D., 1988; recipient Top 200 Art Pks. award, 1992. Home and Office: 109 S 4th St Hamilton MT 59840

NEBELKOPF, ETHAN, psychologist; b. N.Y.C., June 13, 1946; s. Jacob and Fannie (Carver) N.; m. Karen Horrocks, July 27, 1976; children: Demian David, Sarah Dawn. BA, CCNY, 1966; MA, U. Mich., 1969; PhD, Summit U., 1989. Social worker Project Headstart, N.Y.C., 1965; coord. Project Outreach, Ann Arbor, 1968-69; program dir. White Bird Clinic, Eugene, Oreg., 1971-75; counseling supr. Teledyne Econ. Devel. Corp., San Diego, 1976-79; dir. planning and edn. Walden House, San Francisco, 1979-89, dir. tng., 1990—; adj. prof. Dept. Social Work, San Francisco State U., 1982-87; cons. Berkeley Holistic Health Ctr., Berkeley, 1979-84, Medicine Wheel Healing Co-op, San Diego, 1976-79; alternate del. Nat. Free Clinic Coun., Eugene, Oreg., 1972-74. Author: White Bird Flies to Phoenix, 1973, The New Herbalism, 1980, The Herbal Connection, 1981, Hope Not Dope, 1990. Mem. Mayor's Task Force on Drugs, San Francisco, 1988; mem. treatment com. Gov.'s Policy Coun. on Drugs, Sacramento, 1989; task force Human Svcs. Tng., Salem, Oreg., 1972; organizer West Eugene Bozo Assn., 1973; founder Green Psychology, 1993. Named Outstanding Young Man of Am., U.S. Jaycees, 1980; recipient Silver Key, House Plan Assn., 1966. Fellow Am. Orthopsychiat. Assn.; mem. Calif. Assn. Family Therapists, World Fedn. of Therapeutic Communities, Nat. Writer's Club, N.Y. Acad. Scis., Internat. Assn. for Human Rels. Lab. Tng., Calif. Assn. of Drug Programs and Profls. (pres. 1988-90), Phi Beta Kappa. Office: 6641 Simson St Oakland CA 94605-2220

NEBGEN, MARY KATHRYN, school superintendent; b. Charlevoix, Mich., Aug. 13, 1946; d. Edward G. and Mary C. (LaBlance) Fochtman; m. Arthur Nebgen, Aug. 8, 1970. BS, U. Ill., 1969; MA, San Jose State U., 1974; EdD, U. Pacific, 1980; MBA, U. Santa Clara, 1983. Tchr. San Jose (Calif.) Unified Sch. Dist., 1969-76, supr. bilingual programs, 1976-79, prin., 1979-82, dir. elem., mid. schs., 1982-84, asst. supt. elem., mid. schs., 1984-85; deputy supt. instructional svc. Albuquerque, 1985-88; deputy supt. Tacoma Pub. Schs., 1988-90; supt. Washoe County Sch. Dist., Reno, 1990—; adj. prof. U. N.Mex., Albuquerque, 1986-88. Contbr. articles to mags. Mem. Boy Scouts Am., Reno. Mem. ASCD, Nat. Sch. Bds. Assn., Nat. Staff Devel. Coun., Am. Assn. Sch. Adminstrs., Western Indsl. Nev., Reno C. of C., Rotary, Phi Delta Kappa. Office: Washoe County Sch Dist 425 E 9th St Reno NV 89520-0106

NEDWIN, GLENN E., biotechnology executive; b. Bklyn., Dec. 9, 1955; s. Richard D. and Joyce I. Nedwin; m. Julie Jarrett, Oct. 20, 1984; children: Alexandra, Elise, Lindsay. BS, SUNY, Buffalo, 1977; PhD, U. Calif., Riverside, 1981; MBA, MIT, 1987. Postdoctoral fellow Genentech, Inc., South San Francisco, Calif., 1982-85; sr. scientist Molecular Therapeutics, Inc., West Haven, Conn., 1985-87; v.p. Ideon Corp., Redwood City, Calif., 1987-89, Xoma Corp., Berkeley, Calif., 1989-91; pres. Novo Nordisk Biotech, Inc., Davis, Calif., 1992—. Contbr. more than 25 sci. articles to profl. jours.; patentee in field. Mem. AAAS, Am. Chem. Soc., Lic. Execs. Soc., Am. Assn. Immunologists, Clin. Immunology Soc., Soc. Indsl. Microbiology. Office: Novo Nordisk Biotech Inc 1445 Drew Ave Davis CA 95616

NEEB, MARTIN JOHN, media executive; b. Austin, Texas, Aug. 16, 1933; s. Martin Jacob and Vera (Basilius) N.; m. Barbara Ann Brauer, Aug. 25, 1956; children: Douglas Martin, John Martin, Kristina Joy. BA, Concordia Theol. Sem, St. Louis, 1955, MDiv in Theology, 1958; MA, St. Louis U., 1959; PhD, Northwestern U., 1967; grad. exec. mgmt. program, U. Pa., 1983. Gen. mgr. sta. WNUR-FM, Northwestern U., Evanston, Ill., 1965-67; dir. pub. rels., assoc. prof. speech Concordia Coll., Chgo., 1959-67; exec. sec. and gen. mgr. Luth. TV, St. Louis, 1967-78; dir. broadcast div. Franciscan Communications Ctr., L.A., 1978-81; exec. dir. univ. communications and gen. mgr. sta. KPLU-FM, Pacific Luth. U., Tacoma, 1981—; bd. dirs. City Club of Tacoma (founding bd.1984), West Coast Pub. Radio; former bd. dirs. Luth. Film Assocs., Templeton Found. Adv. Com.; former bd. dirs., Arthritis Found., U.S. Cath. Conf. Commmications Com. Finalist White House fellowship, 1966, fellow Northwestern U., 1965-66, recipient Nat. TV Emmy Awards, 1974, 77, Gabriel awards, various other media awards from N.Y. Film and TV Festival, Columbus Film Festival, TV Bur. Advt., Freedoms Found., San Francisco Internat. Film Festival, Am. Film Festival, Advt. Club of L.A., Faith and Freedom award Religious Heritage Am., 1985; named One of Outstanding Young Men Am., Jr. C. of C., 1967. Mem. Religious Pub. Rels. Assn., Internat. TV Assn., Pub. Rels. Soc. Am., Nat. Protestant Broadcasters (pres. 1982), South County Coun. C. of C. (past pres., past bd. dirs.), City Club Ta;coma (program chmn. 1984). Lutheran. Home: 18109 28th Ave E Tacoma WA 98445-4354 Office: Pacific Luth U Tacoma WA 98447

NEEDLER, MARTIN CYRIL, university dean, political science educator; b. Manchester, Eng., Mar. 23, 1933; came to U.S., 1948; s. Thomas Anthony and Beatrice Rebecca (Rosenberg) N.; m. Eva Lore Heyman, Mar. 16, 1955 (div. Mar. 1976); children: Stephen, Daniel; m. Jan Knippers Black, July 23, 1976. AB magna cum laude, Harvard U., 1954, PhD, 1960. Instr. Dartmouth Coll., Hanover, N.H., 1959-60; instr. U. Mich., Ann Arbor, 1960-63, asst. prof., 1963-65; rsch. assoc. Harvard Ctr. for Internat. Affairs, Cambridge, Mass., 1965-66; with U. N.Mex., Albuquerque, 1966-90, dir. div. Inter-Am. affairs, 1966-80, prof. polit. sci. and sociology, 1976-90; dean Sch. Internat. Studies U. Pacific, Stockton, Calif., 1990—; vis. sr. rsch. fellow U. Southampton, Eng., 1974; vis. prof. U. Pitts., 1988; sr. assoc. mem. St. Antony's Coll., Oxford, Eng., 1971—; postdoctoral fellow UCLA, 1962. Author: Political Development in Latin America, 1968, Politics & Society in Mexico, 1971, The Problem of Democracy in Latin America, 1987, The Concepts of Comparative Politics, 1991; assoc. editor jour. Armed Forces & Soc., 1983—; contbr. articles to profl. jours. Lectr. Fgn. Svc. Inst., 1967, 80, 81; co-founder N.Mex. Ptnrs. of the Americas, 1969, Border State Univs. Consortium, 1971; founder Internat. Com. for Advanced Latin-Am. Studies, 1974. With U.S. Army, 1954-56. Mem. Latin-Am. Studies Assn. (chmn. program com. 1972-73, exec. coun. 1973-75), Consortium Latin-Am. Studies Program (chmn. steering com. 1970), Am. Polit. Sci. Assn. (comparative politics award com. 1977), Western Polit. Sci. Assn. (exec. coun. 1981-84), Phi Beta Kappa. Democrat. Jewish. Office: U Pacific Sch Internat Studies Stockton CA 95211

NEEFE, DOUGLAS CHARLES, hobby manufacturing executive; b. Coudersport, Pa., Nov. 24, 1944; s. Charles F. and Darlene L. (Anderson) N.; m. Linda K. Green, Mar. 16, 1974; children: Phillip, Gregory, Katherine, Anna, Edwin. BS in Acctg., U. Calif., Long Beach, 1972. Chief acct., Singapore/Nigeria/Egypt Santa Fe Internat. Corp., 1969-77; dir. corp. cash mgmt. systems Santa Fe Internat. Corp., Orange, Calif., 1978-82; treas. Holly Sugar Corp., Colorado Springs, Colo., 1983-87, v.p., chief fin. officer, treas., 1988-90, v.p. adminstrn., 1990-92; v.p., CFO, treas. Centuri Corp., Penrose, Colo., 1992—. With U.S. Army, 1967-69, Korea. Office: Centuri Corp PO Box 227 Penrose CO 81240

NEELAND, ROGER PHILIP, technology application consultant; b. Milw., June 18, 1942; s. Wendell A. and Leta Marie (Baker) N.; m. Linda Lane Ostlin, Feb. 12, 1965; children: Melissa, Kathleen, Michael. BS, USAF Acad., 1964; SM, MIT, 1970; PhD, UCLA, 1974. Registered profl. engr., Colo. Commd. 2nd lt. USAF, 1964, advanced through ranks to lt. col., 1980, ret., 1984; assoc. prof. astronautics USAF Acad., Colo., 1976-80; chief airborne systems br. system R & D FAA, Washington, 1980-82; chief overview div. systems command hdqrs. USAF, Andrews AFB, Md., 1982-83, dir. mission analysis systems command hdqrs., 1983-84; mgr. advanced tech. assessment GE Aerospace, King of Prussia, Pa., 1984-86, mgr. advanced tech. programs, 1986-88; mgr. Colorado Springs (Colo.) ops. GE Aerospace, 1988-90; mgr. devel. and tech. planning GE Aerospace, Colorado Springs, 1990-93; ind. cons., owner Creative Tech. Solutions, Colorado Springs, 1992—. Decorated DFC, 1965, Air medal, 1965, DSM, 1982. Mem. IEEE, AIAA (sr., space systems tech. com. 1985-88, command, control, comm. and intelligence tech. com. 1990—), Sigma Xi. Office: Creative Tech Solutions 1854 Oak Hills Dr Colorado Springs CO 80919

NEELIN, J. DAVID, atmospheric sciences educator; b. Ottawa, Ont., Can., Oct. 31, 1959; came to U.S., 1983; s. James M. and S. Elisabeth (McFaul) N. BSc., U. Toronto (Can.), 1981, MSc., 1983; PhD, Princeton U., 1987. Postdoctoral assoc dept earth, atmospheric & planetary scis. MIT, Cambridge, Mass., 1987-88; prof. dept. atmospheric scis. UCLA, 1988—; UCLA rep. Univ. Corp. for Atmospheric Rsch., Boulder, Colo., 1988—. Contbr. articles to profl. jours. Princeton Honorific fellow, 1986-87; IBM Merit scholar, 1983-84, NSERC Postgrad. scholar, 1981-86; recipient Can. Meteorol. and Oceanographic Soc. award, 1983, Presdl. Young Investigator award, 1991-96. Mem. Geophys. Union, Am. Meteorol. Soc. Office: UCLA Dept Atmospheric Scis 405 Hilgard Ave Los Angeles CA 90024-1301

NEEPER, FREDERIC ALLEN, advertising copywriter; b. Cleve., Apr. 23, 1946; s. Darle Emerson and Mary Lucile (LaMar) N.; m. Mary Lilian Bayliss, Aug. 11, 1970 (div. 1977). BA, Hiram (Ohio) Coll., 1968. Copywriter Pacific Stereo, Emeryville, Calif., 1973-77; sr. tech. writer JBL, Northridge, Calif., 1978-81, communications mgr., 1981-85; copywriter Foote, Cone & Belding, Santa Ana, Calif., 1985-88, sr. copywriter, 1988—. With U.S. Army, 1968-72. Mem. Sierra. Home: 2221 E 1st St Apt I Long Beach CA 90803-2413 Office: Foote Cone & Belding 4 Hutton Center Dr Santa Ana CA 92707-5770

NEESE, RONALD DWAIN, commercial electrician; b. Monroe, Mich., Nov. 13, 1948; s. Dwain Joy and Betty Jean (Bain) N.; m. Zandra Gwen Brown, Feb. 27, 1970 (div. Sept. 1987); children: Erik Ronald, Stephanie Gwen; m. Virginia Lee Martinez, July 7, 1990. AA, Fullerton Coll., 1975. Plant engr. Tungsten Carbide Mftg., Tustin, Calif., 1981-83; plant mgr. Scottdel Industries, Woodland, Calif., 1983-87; comml. electrician Mark III Engring., Sacramento, 1987—; cons. Those Amazing Animals TV program, Hollywood, Calif., 1980; cons.-handler Pat Boone yogurt comml., Hollywood, 1980. Cons. (book) Beekeeping-An Illustrated Handbook, 1983. Leader troop 464 Boy Scouts Am., Woodland, 1985—; bd. dirs. Orange County Farm Bur., Irvine, Calif., 1980-83; pres. Orange County Beekeepers Assn., Santa Ana, 1978, 79. Mem. Western Apicultural Soc. (charter mem., corp. clk.-treas. 1981—, bd. dirs. 1976-78, Roy Thurber award for inventiveness 1987, Spl. Presdl. Recognition award 1981, 87, 89, 90). Republican. Home: 36910 County Road 24 Woodland CA 95695-9355 Office: Western Apicultural Soc PO Box 681 Woodland CA 95776-0681

NEFF, DONALD LEROY, computer software executive; b. Portland, Oreg., Dec. 5, 1950; s. Lester LeRoy and Avon Maxine Neff; m. Josefina S. Carpio, Apr. 23, 1988; 1 child, Justin Leroy. Student, Ambassador Coll., 1972. Cert. data processor. Computer programmer Ambassador Coll., Pasadena, Calif., 1969-78; cons. San Jose, Calif., 1979-92; CEO Tellan Software, Inc., San Jose, 1992—. One man art shows include Carnegie Mus., 1981, Ambassador Coll., 1979. Recipient numerous awards in art shows. Office: Tellan Software Inc 3286 Knightswood Way San Jose CA 95148

NEFF, JOHN, recording engineer, producer; b. Birmingham, Mich., Mar. 13, 1951; s. Robert Leslie Joseph and Mary Therese (McElvarr) N.; m. Nancy Louise Boocks, Aug. 29, 1987; children: Jennifer Lyn Neff, Bryan C. Groves, Kenneth John Neff. Student, Oakland Community Coll., Auburn Hills, Mich., 1970-72. Freelance recording artist, session musician Detroit, 1965-73; freelance record producer Toronto, Phoenix, L.A., 1974-79; radio announcer, engr. Stas. KVIB, KHEI, KMVI, KLHI, KAOI, 1981-88; record producer Maui Recorders, Kula, Hawaii, 1986-92; cons. studio design Roadrunner Audio Svcs., Glendale, Ariz., 1993—; touring musician Detroit, Toronto, Phoenix, L.A., 1969-79. Mem. ASCAP, Audio Engring Soc. (cert.), Am. Fedn. Musicians. Home and Office: Roadrunner Audio Svcs 23846 N 38th Dr Glendale AZ 85310

NEFF, JOHN MICHAEL, health facility administrator, educator, dean; b. Gudalajara, Mex., Dec. 26, 1932; s. Clarence Alvin Neff and Priscilla (Holton) Fenn; m. Lee Cuninggim, Aug. 20, 1961; children: Michael Merriman, Heidi Holton, Joseph Daniel. BA, Pomona Coll., 1955; postgrad., UCLA, 1955-57; MD, Harvard U., 1960. Intern, then resident in pediatrics Sch. Medicine Johns Hopkins U., Balt., 1960-63; epidemic intelligence svc. officer Ctr. for Disease Control USPHS, Atlanta, 1963-65; chief resident in pediatrics Sch. Medicine Johns Hopkins U., Balt., 1965-66, from asst. to assoc. prof. dept. pediatrics, 1968-81, from asst. dean to assoc. dean, 1968-75; fellow in infectious diseases Med. Sch. Harvard U. Children's Hosp., Boston, 1966-68; chief pediatrics Balt. City Hosp., 1975-81; v.p., med. dir. Children's Hosp. Med. Ctr., Seattle, 1981—; prof. pediatrics, assoc. dean Sch. Medicine U. Wash., Seattle, 1981—; founding mem., bd. trustees Broadmead Life Time Care Ctr., Balt., 1975-81; mem. tech. adv. com. Robert Wood Johnson Med. Health Program, 1979-81. Editor: Jour. Infectious Diseases-Evaluation of Smallpox Vaccine, 1977; contbr. articles to profl. jours. Lt. comdr. USPHS, 1963-65. Fellow Infectious Disease Soc. Am.; mem. Soc. Pediatric Rsch., Am. Acad. Pediatrics, Soc. for Epidemiologic Rsch. Office: Childrens Hosp Med Ctr 4800 Sandpoint Way NE PO Box C5371 Seattle WA 98105

NEFF, LESTER LEROY, administrator, minister; b. Medford, Oreg., Nov. 20, 1923; s. James Asher and Ruth (Turnbow) N.; m. Avon Maxine Bostwick, Aug. 15, 1942; children: Lawrence Dale, Carol Lee, Donald Leroy. BA, Ambassador Coll., 1959, MA in Theology, 1962. Inspector Retail Credit Co., Atlanta, 1946-55; dept. mgr. Worldwide Ch. of God, Pasadena, Calif., 1955-64, 1971-73; bus. mgr. Ambassador Coll., Big Sandy, Tex., 1964-71, 73-76; pastor Worldwide Ch. of God, Pasadena, Calif., 1976-79, ministerial adminstr., 1979-81; sec., treas. Ambassador Coll., Pasadena, Calif., 1981-90, Big Sandy, Tex., 1990—. Sec. Worldwide Ch. God, 1981—. Sgt. USAAF, 1943-46. Office: Worldwide Ch of God 300 W Green St Pasadena CA 91105-1852

NEFZGER, TRISTAN ROBERT, computer scientist; b. Denver, Nov. 1, 1950; s. Merle Dean and Maria Cadiz (Livingston) N. BA, Clark U., 1972; MS, Johns Hopkins U., 1985. Chem. analyst Davison Chem., W.R. Grace & Co., Curtis Bay, Md., 1973-85; assoc. staff Johns Hopkins U. Applied Physics Lab., Laurel, Md., 1985-87; rsch. engr. Lockheed Missiles & Space Co., Inc., Sunnyvale, Calif., 1987-91, sr. data systems engr., 1992—. Mem. Inst. for the Study of Human Knowledge (assoc.), Inst. of Noetic Scis., Mensa, Phi Beta Kappa. Home: 1298 W Washington Ave Sunnyvale CA 94086 Office: Lockheed Missiles/Space Co B150 062-37 1111 Lockheed Way Sunnyvale CA 94089-3504

NEGUS-DE WYS, JANE B., science and training management administrator; b. Portland, Oreg., Apr. 24, 1924; d. Howard Curtis and Cleo (Brockhausen) Negus; m. Egbert Christiaan de Wys, Apr. 7, 1949 (div. 1970); children: Wendy, Tanya, Mark, Matthew. BA in Geology with honors, Miami U., Oxford, Ohio, 1946; postgrad. in geology, U. Wis., 1946-48, U. Wyo., 1947, Case Western Res. U., 1949, U. Kans., 1951; postgrad. in geology and thermodynamics, Ohio State U., 1951-53; postgrad. in geology, UCLA, 1964-67; postgrad., Space Physics Inst. NASA, 1965; postgrad. in geology and law, Tex. Tech U., 1969-71; PhD in Geology, W.Va. U., 1980. Geology lab. asst. Miami U., 1945-46; curator geology mus. U. Wis., Madison, 1946-48; geologist, stratigrapher Shell Oil Co., Midland, Tex., 1948-49; geology instr. Case Western Res. U., Cleve., 1949; geol. rsch. asst. U. Kans., Lawrence, 1950-51; geologist Mene Grande Petroleum Corp., Caracas, Venezuela, 1951-53; rsch. assoc., geologist Ohio State U. Rsch. Found., Columbus, 1953-58; geology instr. adult edn. Van Nuys (Calif.) High Sch., 1958-60; engring. geologist, cons. Sierra Engring., Sierra Madre, Calif., 1960-63; sr. scientist, experimenter NASA surveyor program Calif. Inst. Tech. Jet Propulsion Lab, Pasadena, 1962-67; mgr. First Grand Teton Ltd., Mt. Moran Ltd., Jackson, Wyo., 1971-73; mng. dir. Jackson Hole Telecommunications, Jackson, Wyo., 1973-76; asst. dir. environ. studies lab. U. Utah Rsch. Inst., Salt Lake City, 1976-77; rsch. assoc. dept. engring. Devonian shale program W.Va. U., Morgantown, 1977-81; rsch. specialist Exxon Prodn. Rsch. Co., Houston, 1981-86; owner, operator Geosci., Inc., Conroe, Tex., 1986-88; mgr. D.O.E. geopressured-geothermal program Idaho Nat. Engring. Lab., Idaho Falls, 1988-92, dir. indsl. consortium, 1989-92, mgr. nonnuclear space initiative, 1990-92, scientific specialist nuclear ops. and tng. tech., 1992-93; internationally invited spkr. in field, 1991-94. Contbr. numerous articles to profl. jours. Active YWCA, Denver, 1969, organizer Am. Ch., Estado Monagas, Venezuela, 1951-53, various minority rights orgns.; mem. League Women Voters. With U.S. Cadet Nurse Corps, 1943-44. Bio-med. rsch. grantee U. Utah, 1977; recipient NSF award, 1968. Mem. Am. Assn. Petroleum Geologists (continuing edn. com.), Am. Nuclear Soc., Geothermal Resources Coun., DAR, Phi Kappa Phi, Sigma Gamma Epsilon, Phi Sigma, Sigma Xi, Delta Zeta. Home: PO Box 51978 Idaho Falls ID 83405

NEHER, FRED WENDELL, cartoonist; b. Nappanee, Ind., Sept. 29, 1903; s. Jesse Leonard and Anna (Jamison) N.; m. Frances Rutledge, Sept. 7, 1929; children: Fred Jr., James. Student, Acad. Fine Arts, Chgo. Cartoonist Universal Features Syndicate, Chgo., 1922-24, Associated Editors, Chgo., 1925-26, Cen. Press Assocs., Cleve., 1925-30; freelance cartoonist, 1930-34; cartoonist United Feature Syndicate, N.Y.C., 1934-77, ret., 1977. Represented in permanent collections at U. Colo. Libr., Ohio State U., Syracuse U., Albright Coll., Pa., Mus. Cartoon-Art, Rye Brook, N.Y. Mem. Soc. of Illustrators, Cartoonist Soc., Denver Press Club, Boulder Country Club. Home: One Neher Ln Boulder CO 80304

NEIDIG, DONALD FOSTER, JR., astrophysicist; b. Harrisburg, Pa., Aug. 6, 1944; s. Donald Foster and Victoria Elizabeth (Miller) N.; m. Patricia Ann Ferguson, Sept. 8, 1979. BS in Chemistry, Dickinson Coll., 1966; MS in Astronomy, Pa. State U., 1968, PhD in Astronomy, 1976. Instr. Alliance Coll., Cambridge Springs, Pa., 1971-73; astrophysicist Geophysics Directorate Phillips Lab./Nat. Solar Obs., Sunspot, N.Mex., 1976—; mem. sci. working group NASA Orbiting Solar Lab., 1989—; mem. NASA mgmt. ops. working group for solar physics, 1989-90; adj. prof. N.Mex. State U., Las Cruces, 1990—, Park Coll., Holloman AFB Ext., 1992—; co-investigator USAF Space Weather and Terrestrial Hazards Mission, 1993—. Contbr. articles to sci. jours.; editor conf. procs. Recipient Superior Performance awards USAF, 1983-87, 89-920, Bernard A. Schriever Scientist of the Yr. award Air Force Assn., 1992, Loeser Meml. award Phillips Lab. Geophysics Directorate, 1992. Mem. AAAS, Am. Astron. Soc. (solar physics div.), Internat. Astron. Union, Sigma Xi. Home: 1518 Scenic Dr Alamogordo NM 88310-3927 Office: Nat Solar Obs Sunspot NM 88349

NEIL, IAIN ALEXANDER, motion picture equipment supplier; b. Glasgow, Scotland, U.K., July 3, 1956; came to U.S., 1986; s. Claud Alexander and Margaret Kean (Balmer) N.; m. Stella Ana Sanchez, Dec. 9, 1989. BS in Applied Physics with honors, U. Strathclyde, Glasgow, 1976. Head of optical design Barr & Stroud, Ltd., Glasgow, 1977-85; mgr. system engring. Ernst Leitz Can., Ltd., Midland, Ont., Can., 1985-86; v.p. optical div. Panavision, Inc., Tarzana, Calif., 1986-89, sr. v.p., optical div., 1989—. Contbr. articles to profl. jours.; patentee in field. Recipient numerous Acad. Motion Picture Arts awards for cine lenses. Mem. Internat. Soc. Optical Engring., Optical Soc. Am. Office: Panavision Inc 18618 Oxnard St Tarzana CA 91356-1492

NEIL, JOHN MALCOLM, software developer; b. Portland, Oreg., Jan. 8, 1965; s. Carl Reynold and Christina (Smith) N. BS, Yale U., 1987; MS, Stanford U., 1988. CPU hardware engr. Apple Computer Inc., Cupertino, Calif., 1988-91; co-founder, pres. Human Wave Tech., San Francisco, 1991-92; co-founder, chief tech. officer Digital Eclipse Software, Emeryville, Calif., 1992—; ptnr. John Neil & Assocs., San Francisco, 1991—. Author (software) Monopoly for the Macintosh, 1991, Software FPU, 1991, On the Air, 1992. Mem. Assn. for Computing Machinery, Sierra Club. Home: 1397 Church St San Francisco CA 94114 Office: Digital Eclipse Software 5515 Doyle St Emeryville CA 94608

NEILL, ROBERT HAROLD, waste management director; b. Passaic, N.J., Feb. 9, 1930; s. William Jeremiah and Rosemary (Agnes) N.; m. Townley Biddle, July 6, 1963; 1 child, Helen Rosemary. BSME, Stevens Inst. Tech., Hoboken, N.J., 1951; MS, Havard U., 1962. Engr. Foster Wheeler Corp., N.Y.C., 1951-56; assoc. dir. Bur. Radiological Health U.S. Pub. Health Svc., Washington, 1956-78; dir. N.Mex. Environ. Evaluation Group, Albuquerque, 1978—; mem. uranium mill tailings Nat. Acad. Scis. Panel, Washington, 1988-89; mem. adv. com. State Tenn. Radioactive Disposal, 1988; mem. adv. com. office tech. Assessment U.S. Congress, Washington, 1990, 92.; mem. adv. com. on C-14 high level waste U.S. EPA. Trustee Santa Fe Preparatory Sch., 1983-89; capt. U.S. Pub. Health Svc., 1956-78. Fellow Am. Pub. Health Assn., Health Physics Soc. Home: 9409 Thornton NE Albuquerque NM 87109 Office: EEG 7007 Wyoming Blvd Ste F-2 Albuquerque NM 87109

NEIMANN, ALBERT ALEXANDER, statistician, consultant; b. Torrington, Wyo., Nov. 29, 1939; s. Alexander and Lydia (Temple) N.; m. Barbara Jean Maw, May 6, 1962; children: Debbie, Todd, Amy, Kelly,. BA, Willamette U., 1967. Mathematician Keyport (Wash.) Naval Torpedo Sta., 1968-70; math. statistician Concord (Calif.) Naval Weapons Sta., 1970-85, engring. statistician, 1985—. Mgr. Little League Baseball, Antioch, Calif., 1977-84, Little League Softball, Antioch, 1984-87; Sunday sch. tchr. Grace Bapt. Ch., 1979-90; statistician Antioch High Sch., 1985-89. Recipient performance award Concord Naval Weapons Sta., 1979, 88-92. Mem. Am. Statis. Assn., Math. Assn. Am., Am. Soc. for Quality Control, Nat. Coun. Tchrs. Math.

NEISER, BRENT ALLEN, professional association director; b. Cin., Sept. 16, 1954; s. Rodger John and Hazel Jean (Layfield) N.; m. Marion Alice Hutton, Apr. 1, 1978; children: Christy Jean, Steven José. BA in Pub. Affairs, George Washington U., 1976; MA in Urban Studies, Occidental Coll., 1978; MBA, U. Louisville, 1979; postgrad. in internat. affairs, U. Denver, 1987—. Cert. fin. planner, 1985. Project mgr., analyst Legis. Research Com., Frankfort, Ky., 1978-84; pres. Moneyminder, Denver and Frankfort, 1983-91; dir. edn., govt. affairs and ethics Inst. Cert. Fin. Planners, Denver, 1985-91, exec. dir., 1991—; mng. dir. Fin. Products Standards Bd., Denver, 1985-91. Author: EPCOT/World Showcase External Directions, Walt Disney Imagineering, 1977; co-inventor: Trivia Express (game) Denver, 1986. Vol., v.p. Big Bros./Big Sisters, Frankfort, 1982; del. Colo. Model Constnl. Conv., 1987; mem. citizens budget rev. com. Greenwood Village; parent trainer Rocky Moutain Adoption Exch., Denver, 1988, mem. long range planning com., 1992-93, bd. dirs. 1993—; polit. action dir. Frankfort NAACP, 1983, legis. chmn. state conf., 1984; asst. scoutmaster Boy Scouts Am., Littleton, Colo., 1986-89; bd. dirs. Young Ams. Bank Edn. Found., 1993—. Lt. (j.g.) USNR, 1985—. Recipient Outstanding Service award Frankfort NAACP, 1981; named Man of Yr., Frankfort NAACP,

1983; Pub. Affairs fellow Coro Found., 1976-77. Mem. Investors Edn. Assn. Colo. (bd. dirs.), Inst. Cert. Fin. Planners, Internat. Assn. Fin. Planners (bd. dirs. Rocky Mountain chpt. 1990-92), N.Am. Securities Adminstrs. Assn. (investment adviser and fin. planner adv. com.), Nat. Soc. Compliance Profls. (bd. dirs. 1987-89), Am. Film Inst. (writers workshop). Home: 5860 S Big Canyon Dr Englewood CO 80111-3516 Office: Inst Cert Fin Planners 7600 E Eastman Ave Ste 301 Denver CO 80231-4397

NEIWORTH, TRISH LATRISSA LEE, television producer/writer; b. Aberdeen, Wash., Aug. 21, 1959; d. James William and Lorna Darlene (Johnson) Neiworth; m. Joseph Michael Petshow, July 17, 1982; 1 child, Emma Michelle Neiworth-Petshow. AA in Journalism, Mt. Hood Community Coll., Gresham, Oreg., 1979; BA in Journalism, Oreg. State U., 1982. News corres. The Oregonian, Portland, 1982-83; sr. reporter/producer Oreg. Pub. Broadcasting, Portland, 1983-84; TV news reporter KIFI-TV, Idaho Falls, Idaho, 1984-85; polit. reporter KPTV "Ten O'Clock News, Portland, 1985-90; comm. mgr. Employment div. State of Oreg., Salem, 1990-91; TV producer/writer/cons. Neiworth Media, Salem, 1991—. Com. mem. Adult Edn. and Literacy Adv. Com., State of Oreg., Salem, 1990-91, Alumni Adv. Com. Journalism, Oreg. State U., Corvallis, 1987. Recipient AP Broadcast award, 1987; fellow Sears Found.-U.S. Ho. of Reps., 1981. Mem. Internat. Assn. Pers. in Employment Security, Soc. Profl. Journalists, Am. Fedn. Radio and TV Artists, Phi Theta Kappa, Kappa Tau Alpha. Office: Neiworth Media PO Box 4448 Salem OR 97302

NELIPOVICH, SANDRA GRASSI, artist; b. Oak Park, Ill., Nov. 22, 1939; d. Alessandro and Lena Mary (Ascareggi) Grassi; m. John Nelipovich Jr., Aug. 19, 1973. BFA in Art Edn., U. Ill., 1961; postgrad., Northwestern U., 1963, Gonzaga U., Florence, Italy, 1966, Art Inst. Chgo., 1968; diploma, Accademia Universale Alessandro Magno, Prato, Italy, 1983. Tchr. art Edgewood Jr. High Sch., Highland Park, Ill., 1961-62, Emerson Sch. Jr. High Sch., Oak Park, 1962-77; batik artist Calif., 1977—; illustrator Jolly Robin Publ. Co., Anaheim, Calif., 1988—; supr. student tchrs., Oak Park, 1970-75; adult edn. tchr. ESL, ceramics, Medinah, Ill., 1974; mem. curriculum action group on human dignity, EEO workshop demonstration, Oak Park, 1975-76; guest lectr. Muckenthaler Ctr., Fullerton, Calif., 1980, 92, Niguel Art Group, Dana Point, Calif., 1989, Carlsbad A.A., 1990, ARt League, Oceanside Art Group, 1992; 2d v.p. Anaheim Hills Women's Club, 1990-91, rec. sec. 1991-92; fabric designer for fashion designer Barbara Jax, 1987. One-woman shows include Lawry's Calif. Ctr., L.A., 1981-83, Whittier (Calif.) Mus., 1985-86, Anaheim Cultural Ctr., 1986-88, Ill. Inst. Tech., Chgo., 1989, Muckenthaler Cultural Ctr., Fullerton, 1990; also gallery exhibits in Oak Brook, 1982, La Habra, Calif., 1983; represented in permanent collections collections McDonald's Corp., Oak Brook, Glenkirk Sch., Deerfield, Ill., Emerson Sch., Oak Park, galleries in Laguna Beach, Calif., Maui, Hawaii, Mich., N.J.; poster designer Saratoga Fine Arts. Active Assistance League, Anaheim, Calif., 1992—. Recipient numerous awards, purchase prizes, 1979—; featured in Calif. Art Rev., Artists of So. Calif., Vol. II, Nat. Artists' Network, 1992. Mem. AAUW (hospitality chmn. 1984-85), Assistance League Anaheim, Oak Park Art League, Orange Art Assn. (jury chairperson 1980), Anaheim Art Assn., Muckenthaler Ctr. Circle, Anaheim Hills Women's Club. Roman Catholic. Home and Office: 5922 E Calle Cedro Anaheim CA 92807-3207

NELLAMS, JANE HARRIS, director communications, journalist; b. Chgo., May 13, 1955; d. Edward Calvin Harris and Bettejane (Morrow) Kirkpatrick; m. Robert Lee Nellams, Oct. 10, 1987; 1 child, André. BA in Journalism, U. Oreg., 1978. Reporter Seattle Post-Intelligencer, Seattle, 1978-80, Bremerton (Wash.) Sun, 1980-81, Jour.-Am., Bellevue, Wash., 1981-84; pub. info. officer Bellevue Community Coll., 1984-90, dir. coll. rels., 1990-91; dir. pub. rels. North Seattle Community Coll., 1991—. Mem. Jr. League of Seattle, 1988—; precinct chair Dem. Party of Wash., Bellevue, 1988. Mem. Greater Univ. Dist. C. of C. (KUOW adv. com.), Met. Coun. Heart Assn. (communications com.), Nat. Coun. Mktg. and Public Rels. (dir. dist. 7), U. Oreg. Alumni Assn., Sigma Kappa. Office: North Seattle Community Coll 9600 College Way N Seattle WA 98103-3599

NELLINGTON, BLAINE See **MAGNUSON, DONALD RICHARD**

NELSON, ADAM PHILLIP, psychiatrist; b. Queens, N.Y., Mar. 10, 1960; s. Herbert and Harriet (Block) N. BA in Psychology, U. Pa., 1982; MD, U. Pitts., 1986. Diplomate Nat. Bd. Med. Examiners. Resident Hillside Hosp., L.I. Hosp., Glen Oaks, N.Y., 1986-90, supr., 1989-90; physician Holliswood (N.Y.) Hosp., 1988-90, Booth Meml. Hosp., Flushing, 1988-90; staff psychiatrist David Grant USAF Med. Ctr., Travis AFB, Calif., 1990—, Sutter Ctr. Psychiatry, Sacramento, 1993—. Maj. USAF, 1990-93. Mem. AAAS, AMA, Am. Psychiat. Assn., N.Y. Acad. Scis., Psi Chi.

NELSON, ARTHUR ALEXANDER, JR., university dean, pharmacist; b. New Roads, La., June 12, 1946; s. Arthur Alexander Sr. and Ann (Goss) N.; m. Sherida Gail LaCroix, Sept. 4, 1971; children: Bradford Alexander, Jennifer Leigh. BS, N.E. La. U., 1969, MS, 1971; PhD, U. Iowa, 1973. Lic. pharmacist, Idaho, La. Grad. teaching asst. U. Iowa, Iowa City, 1971-73; asst. prof. U. Ill. Med. Ctr., Chgo., 1973-76, assoc. prof., 1976; assoc. prof., program coord. U. S.C., Columbia, 1976-79, assoc. prof., 1980-81, prof., 1981-84, chmn. dept., 1980-84; dean Coll. Pharmacy U. Nebr. Med. Ctr., Omaha, 1984-86, prof. pharmacy, 1986; dean, Coll. Pharmacy Idaho State U., Pocatello, 1987—; cons. Eli Lilly and Co., Indpls., 1984—, Stuart Pharm., Wilmington, Del., 1986-87, Smith Kline and French Lab., Phila., 1979-85, Strategic Mktg. Corp., Bala Cynwick, Pa., 1985. Editor: Research Methods, 1983, Curriculum Guide for Pharmacy, 1988. Recipient Spl. Recognition award Nebr. Hosp. Pharmacists, 1986, Outstanding Svc. award Nebr. Alumni Assn., 1986. Mem. Am. Assn. Colls. Pharmacy, Am. Soc. Hosp. Pharmacists, Idaho State Pharm. Assn., Idaho Soc. Hosp. Pharmacists, Southeastern Idaho Pharm. Assn., Rotary (chmn. exch. students). Baptist. Office: Idaho State U Coll Pharmacy Campus Box 8288 Pocatello ID 83209

NELSON, BARRY VERNON, engineering executive; b. Glendale, Calif., Apr. 8, 1939; s. Vernon Herbert and Jean Leona (Ruliffison) N.; m. Nancy Joyce Cooper, Sept. 14, 1963 (div. Nov. 1984); children: Rodney Norman, Florean Marie, Robert Arthur; m. Nancy Ann Murphy, Dec. 1, 1984. BA, Occidental Coll., 1961; MS, Calif. State U., Northridge, 1973. Project engr. Kurz and Root Co., Anaheim, Calif., 1959-64, Teledyne Corp., Gardena, Calif., 1964-65; project staff engr. Rockwell Corp., Downey, Calif., 1965-67; engr., scientist specialist McDonnell Douglas Corp., Huntington Beach, Calif., 1967-68; adminstrv. asst. Santa Barbara Rsch. Corp., Goleta, Calif., 1968-74; info. systems data mgr. Comprehensive Health Planning Agy., San Diego, 1974-75; data processing mgr. Lucky Stores, Inc., San Diego, 1975-77; CFO Hosp. Mgmt. Svcs., Fullerton, Calif., 1977-80; systems analysis supr. Martin Marietta Corp., Santa Maria, Calif., 1980-82; tech. dir. Sci. Applications Internat. Corp., San Bernardino, Calif., 1982-85; ops. mgr. Frontier Engring. Inc., Concord, Calif., 1985-92; ops. dir. Mgmt. Assistance Corp. of Am., Concord, Calif., 1992—. Office: Mgmt Assistance Corp Am 2280 Diamond Blvd Ste 200 Concord CA 94520

NELSON, BERNARD WILLIAM, foundation executive, educator, physician; b. San Diego, Sept. 15, 1935; s. Arnold B. and Helene Christina (Falck) N.; m. Frances Davison, Aug. 9, 1958; children—Harry, Kate, Anne, Daniel. A.B., Stanford U., 1957, M.D., 1961. Asst. prof., asst. dean medicine Stanford U., Palo Alto, Calif., 1965-67, assoc. dean medicine, 1968-71, cons. assoc. prof., 1980-86; assoc. dean U. Wis., Madison, 1974-77, acting vice chancellor, 1978-79; exec. v.p. Kaiser Family Found., Menlo Park, Calif., 1979-81, 1981-86; chancellor U. Colo. Health Sci. Ctr., Denver, 1986—; mem., v.p., pres. Nat. Med. Fellowships, 1969-77. Trustee Morehouse Med. Sch., 1981-83. Fellow Inst. Medicine; mem. Calif. Acad. Sci., Alpha Omega Alpha (bd. dirs. 1978—). Office: U Colo Health Sci Ctr Office of Chancellor 4200 E 9th Ave Denver CO 80262-0001

NELSON, BRENT CHRISTOPHER, video production executive; b. San Diego, Nov. 16, 1957; s. Elbert Roy and Cecile Dorothy (McMenomy) N.; m. Catherine Michele Hays, Nov. 19, 1988; 1 child, Samantha Michelle. BS in Telecommunications, San Diego State U., 1980. With ride ops. Sea World Calif., San Diego, 1975-78, lead tch. svc., 1978-83, supr. tech. svc., 1983-88, mgr. video prodn., 1988-90; systems engr. Televideo San Diego, 1990-91; dir. tech. ops. La Porta and Co., San Diego, 1991-92; pres. Image Internat., San Diego, 1988—; v.p. prodn. Video Home Sales and Svc., Inc., San Diego, 1992—. Video photographer: International Attractions, China, Taiwan, Manila, Tokyo, Hong Kong, 1985, 87, 88, Sea World corp. video Birth of '85 Killer Whale, 1985 (Cindy award 1986), Birth of '88 Killer Whale, 1988 (Cleo award 1989). Mem. Internat. TV Assn. (award of excellence 1985, 87, 89), Soc. Motion Picture and TV Engrs., San Diego Producers Assn. Republican. Roman Catholic. Office: Video Home Sales and Svc Inc 4420 Hotel Cir Ct Ste 365 San Diego CA 92108

NELSON, BRYAN H(ERBERT), educational association administrator; b. Yakima, Wash., July 3, 1956; s. Herbert B. and Marilyn A. (Cupper) N.; m. Sandra Exley, June 11, 1993; children by previous marriage: Christofer A., Bryanne E. BEd, Ea. Wash. U., 1977, MS in Speech Pathology, 1978. Speech pathologist Ednl. Svc. Dist. 101, Spokane, Wash., 1978-83, coord. speech pathology, 1983-84, coord. inservice tng., 1985; processor fruit broker Herb Nelson Inc., Yakima, 1985-88; coord. early childhood and spl. edn. programs Selah (Wash.) Sch. Dist., 1989-92, coord. spl. edn., 1989-92; dir. New Directions, EPIC, 1992—; gen. ptnr. Nelson Perkins Assocs., Yakima, 1990—; dir. New Directions-Epic, Yakima, Wash., 1992—; guest lectr. Ea. Wash. U., Cheney, 1984-85; chmn. very spl. arts festival Ednl. Svc. Dist 101, 1985, on-site coord. IDEAS conv., 1983. Bd. dirs., chairperson citizens adv. bd. Yakima Vocat. Skill Ctr., 1988-89; mem. gen. adv. com. Yakima Vocat. Coop.; mem. allocation panel United Way, Yakima, 1974, loaned exec., 1990; mem. exec. com. Yakima County Birth to Six, 1989—. Home: 100 N 56th St # 7 Yakima WA 98908 Office: New Directions-Epic 2902 Castlevale Rd Yakima WA 98902

NELSON, CLIFFORD L(EE), JR., company official; b. South Bend, Ind., Feb. 12, 1936; s. Clifford Lee and Margaret (Toops) N.; m. Doris Ann Huber, Aug. 23, 1958; children: Catherine Lynn and Christina Lee (twins), Clifford Lee III. BA, Washington and Jefferson Coll., 1958. Life ltd. svc. teaching credential, Calif. Sales coord. Jessop Steel Co., Washington, Pa., 1958-60; sales engr. Wah Chang Corp., Albany, Oreg., 1960-63; sales engr. metals div. Stauffer Chem. Co., Richmond, Calif., 1963; sr. govt. accounts rep. traffic control materials div. 3M Co., Sacramento, 1964--, field sales trainer, 1967-76. Bd. dirs. Retreat Ministries, Inc., Orange, Calif., 1980--; ruling elder, clk. of session lst Presbyn. Ch., Orange, 1982-85; gift chmn. class of 1958, Washington and Jefferson Coll., 1983--; bd. dirs. Sr. Citizens Community Ctr., Orange, 1985-87; pres. Sister City Assn., Orange, 1989--. Named Jaycee of Yr., Orange Jaycees, 1967. Mem. Am. Pub. Works Assn. (assoc. equipment com. 1982-85), Orange County Traffic Engrs. Coun. (bd. dirs. 1984-85) Maintenance Supts. Assn. Calif. (life, bd. dirs. 1984-85), Riverside-San Bernardino Traffic Engrs., Rotary (pres. Orange chpt. 1989-90, Raotarian of Yr. award 1985). Republican. Home: 1448 N Pine St Orange CA 92667 Office: 3M Co 1010 Hurley Way Sacramento CA 95825

NELSON, CRAIG ALAN, banker; b. San Rafael, Calif., July 11, 1961; s. Kenneth Alfred and Anne Catherine (Laurie) N. BS in Fin., San Diego State U., 1984. Loan assoc. Union Bank, San Diego, 1984-85, comml. loan officer, 1985-86, corp. banking officer, 1986-87, asst. v.p., 1987-89, v.p. corp. banking, 1989—. Corp. recruiter United Way, San Diego, 1988; community group chair San Diego chpt. Am. Cancer Soc., 1989; mem. com. Juvenile Diabetes Assn.; bd. dirs. San Diego State Found., 1989—. Mem. San Diego State U. Young Alumni Assn. (pres. 1988-89, bd. dirs. emeritus 1989). Home: 1233 San Dieguito Dr Encinitas CA 92024-5116 Office: Union Bank 4660 La Jolla Village Dr San Diego CA 92122-4601

NELSON, DANIEL R., bank executive; b. Spokane, Wash., 1938. Wash. State U., 1962; Postgrad., U. Wash. With Ranier Bank, Seattle, 1962-84; pres. West One Bank Corp., Boise, Idaho, 1986-93, CEO, 1986—, chmn. bd. dirs., 1993—. Office: West 1 Bancorp PO Box 8247 Boise ID 83702*

NELSON, DARRYL JAMES, small business owner; b. Detroit, Nov. 9, 1950; s. Herschell James Burns and Madeline Veronica Zidick. Student, Whittier Coll. Warehouseman E.D. Bullard & Co., City of Industry, Calif., 1969-72, C Hagar & Sons Hinge Mfg. Co., City of Industry, 1972-73; mgr. shipping, receiving Rutland Tool & Supply Co., Pico Rivera, Calif., 1974-76, mgr. wholesale traffic, 1983—; owner, mgr. Reno (Nev.) Prospector's Supply Co., 1984—. Mem. Nev. Prospectors, Comstock Prospectors, Motherlode Miners, E Clampus Vitus, Reno C. of C., Winners Circle Breakfast Club (bd. dirs., chmn. Welcome Com.). Office: 315 Claremont St Reno NV 89502-2529

NELSON, DONALD ARVID (NELLIE NELSON), professional basketball coach; b. Muskegon, Mich., May 15, 1940. Student, U. Iowa. Player NBA teams, Chgo. Zephyrs, 1962-63, Los Angeles Lakers, 1963-65, Boston Celtics, 1965-76; from asst. to head coach Milw. Bucks NBA, 1976-87, also dir. player personnel; exec. v.p., part owner Golden State Warriors, NBA, Oakland, Calif., from 1987; mem. Nat. Basketball championship teams, 1966, 68, 69, 74, 76; head coach Golden State Warriors, 1988—, now also gen. mgr. Named Coach of Yr. NBA, 1983, 85. Office: care Golden State Warriors Oakland Coliseum Arena Oakland CA 94621*

NELSON, DOROTHY WRIGHT (MRS. JAMES F. NELSON), federal judge; b. San Pedro, Calif., Sept. 30, 1928; d. Harry Earl and Lorna Amy Wright; m. James Frank Nelson, Dec. 27, 1950; children: Franklin Wright, Lorna Jean. B.A., UCLA, 1950, J.D., 1953; LL.M., U. So. Calif., 1956; JD honoris causa, Georgetown U., 1993, U. So. Calif., 1993, U. Santa Clara, 1993, Western State U., 1993. Bar: Calif. 1954. Research assoc. fellow U. So. Calif., 1953-56; instr., 1957, asst. prof., 1958-61, assoc. prof., 1961-67, prof., 1967, assoc. dean., 1965-67, dean., 1967-80; judge U.S. Ct. Appeals (9th cir.), 1980—; cons. Project STAR, Law Enforcement Assistance Adminstrn.; mem. select com. on internal procedures of Calif. Supreme Ct., 1987—. Author: Judicial Adminstration and The Administration of Justice, 1973; Contbr. articles to profl. jours. Co-chmn. Confronting Myths in Edn. for Pres. Nixon's White House Conf. on Children, Pres. Carter's Commn. for Pension Policy, 1974-80; bd. visitors U.S. Air Force Acad., 1978; bd. dirs. Council on Legal Edn. for Profl. Responsibility, 1971-80, Constnl. Right Found., Am. Nat. Inst. for Social Advancement; adv. bd. Nat. Center for State Cts., 1971-73; chmn. bd. Western Justice Ctr., 1986—. Named Law Alumnus of Yr. UCLA, 1967; recipient Profl. Achievement award, 1969; named Times Woman of Yr., 1968; recipient U. Judaism Humanitarian award, 1973; AWARE Internat. award, 1970; Ernestine Stalhut Outstanding Woman Lawyer award, 1972; Coro award for edn., 1978, Pax Orbis ex Jure medallion World Peace thru Law Ctr., 1975, Hollzer Human Rights award, 1988, medal U. Calif. L.A. , 1993; Lustman fellow Yale U. 1977. Fellow Am. Bar Found., Davenport Coll., Yale U.; mem. Bar Calif. (bd. dirs. continuing edn. bar commn. 1967-74), Am. Judicature Soc. (dir., award 1985), Assn. Am. Law Schs. (chmn. com. edn. in jud. adminstrn.), Am. Bar Assn. (sect. on jud. adminstrn., chmn. com. on edn. in jud. adminstrn. 1973—), Phi Beta Kappa, Order of Coif (nat. v.p. 1974-76), Jud. Conf. U.S. (com. to consider standards for admission to practice in fed. cts. 1976-79). Office: US Ct Appeals Cir PO Box 91510 125 S. Grand Ave Pasadena CA 91109-1510

NELSON, DREW VERNON, mechanical engineering educator; b. Elizabeth, N.J., Oct. 11, 1947; s. Andrew K. and Myra G. (Kempson) N. BSME, Stanford U., 1968, MSME, 1970, PhDME, 1978. Research asst. Stanford U., Calif., 1971-74, asst. prof., 1978-83, assoc. prof., 1983—; engr. Gen. Electric Co., Sunnyvale, Calif., 1975-76, sr. engr., 1977-78; cons. in field. Co-editor: Fatigue Design Handbook, 1989; contbr. articles to profl. jours. Recipient Spergel Meml. award for Most Outstanding Paper, 32nd Internat. Wire and Cable Symposium, 1984. Mem. ASTM, Soc. Automotive Engrs., Soc. for Exptl. Mechanics, Sigma Xi, Tau Beta Pi. Home: 840 Cabot Ct San Carlos CA 94070-3464 Office: Stanford U Dept Mech Engring Stanford CA 94305-4021

NELSON, FRANK EUGENE, microbiology educator; b. Harlan, Iowa, Dec. 5, 1909; s. Frank Daniel and Della Catherine (Meier) N.; m. Carolyn Jane Overholt, Aug. 3, 1940; children: William L., Craig E., Bruce L. BS with honors, U. Minn., 1932, MS, 1934; PhD, Iowa State U., 1936. Instr. U. Minn., St. Paul., 1936-37; asst. prof. Kans. State U., Manhattan, 1937-41, assoc. prof., 1941-43; prof. Iowa State U., Ames, 1943-60; prof. U. Ariz., Tucson, 1960-77, prof. emeritus, 1977—; cons. AID, Fortaleza, Brazil, 1964; vis. prof. U. Reading, Eng., 1972, U. Bath, Eng., 1972. Co-author: Dairy Microbiology, 1990; editor: Jour. Dairy Sci., 1947-52; contbr. chpts. to books. Mem. Am. Soc. Microbiology (nat. coun., pres. north ctrl. br., 1960), Am. Dairy Sci. Assn. (pres. 1966, bd. dirs.). Republican. Home: 3960 E Ina Rd Tucson AZ 85718-1526

NELSON, GARRETT R., retail food company executive. Sr. v.p., CFO, The Vons Cos. Inc., Arcadia, Calif., until 1987, exec. v.p. retail support group, 1987-91, exec. v.p., chief devel. officer. Office: Vons Cos Inc 618 Michillinda Ave Arcadia CA 91007-6300

NELSON, GARY, engineer, state senator; b. Spokane, Wash., Apr. 11, 1936; s. Nels Alfred and Laura Marie (Winberg) Nelson; m. JoAnne Laura Knudson, Nov. 27, 1959; children: Grant, Geoffrey, Gregory. BSEE, Wash. State U., 1958; MSEE, U. Wis., 1963. Engr. RCA, Camden, N.J., 1958-59; officer USAF, Madison, Wis., 1959-62; mgr. U.S. West, Seattle, 1963-90; pvt. practice Edmonds, Wash., 1990—; bd. dirs. Stevens Hosp. Found., Edmonds, Olympic Ballet, United Way of Snohomish County, Everett, 1986-92. planning commn. City of Edmonds, 1964-67, city coun., 1968-74. Capt. USAF, 1959-62. Mem. Sons of Norway, Rotary. Republican. Lutheran. Home: 9710 Wharf St Edmonds WA 98020-2363 Office: State Senate 106A Institutions Olympia WA 98504

NELSON, GENE EDWARD, author, publisher; b. Chgo., Oct. 22, 1944; s. George Arnette and Amelia (Amanda) Malmstrom) N.; m. Sherry Carolyn Nickell, Nov. 6, 1964 (div. Sept. 1980); children: Neil Marshall, Berit Katherine Amanda. BA in Anthropology, So. Ill. U., 1966; postgrad., U. Okla., 1971-77. Asst. dist. mgr. Social Security Adminstrn., Odessa, Tex., 1966-86; v.p. The Magic Brush, Inc., Odessa, 1978-80; gen. ptnr. S & G Automotive Warehouse, Odessa, 1982-85; monk Order of the Holy Cross, Santa Barbara, Calif., 1987-88; author, pub. White Plume Press, Seattle, 1988—; cons. Fircrest Community Found., Seattle, 1991-92; instr. Odessa (Tex.) Coll., 1981-85; columnist Social Security-Fed. Way News, 1990-91; rsch. dir. O'Connor Comm., Seattle, 1992—. Author: Social Security for Business Owners, 1988, Little Flower and Other Love Poems, 1992, Where Do You Go When Love Dies?, 1992; pub.: Finding Oakland, 1992; rsch. dir.: A Field Guide to Health Care Reform, 1993. V.p., meet dir. Odessa (Tex.) Aquatic Club, 1978-80; v.p. Dallas (Tex.) Region Mgmt. Assn., 1977-84; coun. mem. Nat. Coun. Social Security Mgmt. Assn., Balt., 1982-84; pres. Permian Basin Fed. Exec. Assn., Odessa, 1977-86, Ector County Svc. Orgn., Odessa, 1984-86; team leader, fundraiser Santa Barbara (Calif.) YMCA, 1989-90; mem. Bishop's Commn. on Alcoholism & Substance Abuse, 1990-92; vestry mem. St. John Episcopal Ch., Seattle, 1992—; div. chmn., fundraiser Fauntelroy YMCA, Seattle, 1992—. Episcopalian. Home: 2701 California Ave SW Apt 221 Seattle WA 98116 Office: O'Connor Comm 911 Western Ave Ste 330 Seattle WA 98104

NELSON, GEORGE N., petroleum company executive; b. Kansas City, Mo., Oct. 11, 1932; s. Claude and Hazel M. (Smith) N.; m. Cynthia M. Buck; children: Christopher, Georgianne, Stephanie, Amy. BS in Indsl. Mgmt. Engring., U. Okla., 1955; postgrad. in mgmt., MIT, 1983; JD (hon.), U. Alaska, 1990. Petroleum engr. Magnolia Petroleum Co., Okla., Tex. and La., 1955; from drilling engr. to prodn. engr. to prodn. foreman Mobil Oil Co. Venezuela, 1955-61; from prodn. supr. to project engr. to supt. marine terminal and tank farm Superior Oil Co. Venezuela, Lake Maracaibo, 1961-65; project engr. J.F. Pritchard and Co., Kansas City, Mo., 1965; sr. prodn. engr. Arabian Am. Oil Co., Saudi Arabia, 1966; from sr. engr. to sr. supervising engr. to supt. tech. services to mgr. ops. Oasis Oil Co. of Libya, Inc., Tripoli, 1968-75; mgr. prodn. planning British Petroleum of Alaska, Inc., San Francisco, 1975; field mgr. Prudhoe Bay Sohio Alaska Petroleum Co., Anchorage, 1977, asst. gen. mgr. ops., 1978, v.p. ops., 1981; pres. Standard Alaska Prodn. Co./BP Exploration, Anchorage, 1982-90, Pennzoil Caspian Corp., Houston, 1992—. Mem. adv. bd. Alaska Ctr. for Internat. Bus. Devel., U. Alaska, 1986-90; chmn. bd. trustees Govt. Council on Local Hire, Anchorage, 1986; trustee Alaska Pacific U., 1988; bd. dirs. Boys and Girls Club Alaska, Anchorage, 1981—, Alaska Ctr. for Performing Arts, 1988. 2d lt. C.E. U.S. Army, 1957-58. Recipient Alaska Native Community award Alaska Fedn. Natives, 1983, Cert. Appreciation, Gov. of Alaska, 1984, Outstanding Service award NANA Region, 1984, 85, Pub. Service award Municipality of Anchorage, 1986, Cert. Appreciation, Anchorage Star of North C. of C., 1986, Outstanding Service award Alaska chpt. Associated Gen. Contractors Am., 1986, Outstanding Achievement in Environ. Protection award Nat. Environ. Devel. Assn., 1987, Disting. Services award Alaska State C. of C., 1987, Outstanding Service award Alaska Assn. Secondary Prins., 1987, Man and Youth award Boys and Girls Club Alaska, 1988. Mem. Alaska Oil and Gas Assn. (exec. com. 1981-88, bd. dirs. 1981-88, pres. bd. dirs. 1985, 88), Petroleum Club, Tau Beta Pi, Sigma Tau. Democrat.

NELSON, GREGORY JAMES, foundation administrator; b. Tallahassee, Fla., Oct. 22, 1965; s. Richard Harold and Gayle Louise (Taplin) N.; m. Laurie Lynn Anderson, May 28, 1988. BA in English magna cum laude, Seattle Pacific U., 1987; Diploma in African Studies, U. Cape Town, South Africa. Polit. aide James S. Munn, Atty. At Law, Seattle, 1984-85; intern office presdl. pers. The White House, Washington, 1985; exec. dir. U.S. Olympic Acad. Project, community rels. mgr. Seattle C. of C., 1987—; assoc. dir. Ptnrs. in Pub. Edn.; dir. Wash. World Affairs Fellows; tchr. English Ednl. Svc. Exchange, Nanjing, People's Republic of China, summer 1986. Author poetry. Fundraising Reagan-Bush Rep. Campaigns, Seattle, 1983-84; del. Konrad Adenauer Stiftung, Berlin, 1988, Intrnat. Olympic Acad., Olympia, Greece, 1990; elder Presbyn. Ch. Am. Pres.'s Leadership scholar, 1987. Mem. Centurions.

NELSON, HAROLD BERNHARD, museum director; b. Providence, R.I., May 14, 1947; s. Harold B. and Eleanor (Lavina) N. BA, Bowdoin Coll., 1969; MA, U. Del., 1972. Rsch. fellow NMAA Smithsonian Inst., Washington, 1976-77; curator Am. art Mus. Art & Archeol., U. Mo., Columbia, 1977-79; registrar Solomon R. Guggenheim Mus., N.Y.C., 1979-83; exhibition program dir. Am. Fedn. Arts, N.Y.C., 1983-89; dir. Long Beach (Calif.) Mus. of Art, 1989—; juror Annual Art Exhibition Mus. Art, Sci. & Industry, Bridgeport, Conn., 1988, Annual Art Exhibition, Clark County Dist. Libr., Las Vegas, Nev., 1984; speaker Am. Assn. Mus. Annual Conf., Detroit, 1985, annual meeting Western Mus. Conf., Portland, Oreg., 1987, Grantmakers in Art Symposium, N.Y.C., 1986, annual meeting Western Mus. Conf., Salt Lake City, 1985; mem. adv. com. APA, Assn. Sci. and Tech. Ctrs.; panelist Aid to Spl. Exhibitions, NEA, Washington, 1986; participant Am. Legal Assn., ABA Conf., San Francisco, 1986; observer, respondent Mus. Symposium, NEA, Dallas, 1985. Author: Sounding the Depths: 150 Years of American Seascape, 1989. Office: Long Beach Mus Art 2300 E Ocean Blvd Long Beach CA 90803-2442

NELSON, IVORY VANCE, university president; b. Curtis, La., June 11, 1934; s. Elijah H. and Mattie (White) N.; m. Patricia Robbins, Dec. 27, 1985; children: Cherlyn, Karyn, Eric Beatty, Kim Beatty. BS, Grambling (La.) State U., 1959; PhD, U. Kans., 1963. Assoc. prof. chemistry So. U., Baton Rouge, 1963-67, head div. sci., 1966-68; prof. chemistry Prairie View (Tex.) A&M U., 1968-83, asst. acad. dean, 1968-72, v.p. rsch., 1972-82, acting pres., 1982-83; exec. asst. Tex. A&M U. System, College Station, 1983-86; chancellor Alamo C.C. Dist., San Antonio, 1986-92; pres. Cen. Wash. U., Ellensburg, 1992—; DuPont teaching fellow U. Kans., 1959; rsch. chemist Am. Oil Co., 1962; sr. rsch. chemist Union Carbide Co., 1969; vis. prof. U. Autonomous Guadalajara, Mex., 1966, Loyola U., 1967; Fulbright lectr., 1966; cons. evaluation coms. Oak Ridge (Tenn.) Assoc. Univs., NSF, Nat. Coun. for Accreditation Tchr. Edn., So. Assn. Colls. and Schs.; mem. regiona. policy coms. on imoirities Western Interstate Com. on Higher Edn., 1986-88; mem. exec. com. Nat. Assn. State Univs. and Land Grant Colls., 1980-82. Contbr. articles to profl. jours. Bd. dirs. Target 90, Goals San Antonio, 1987-89, United Way San Antonio, 1987-89, Alamo Area coun. Boy Scouts Am., 1987-89, San Antonio Symphony Soc., 1987-91, Key Bank of Wash.; trustee S.W. Rsch. Inst., 1988-91; mem. com. for jud. reform State of Tex., 1991; mem. edn. adv. bd. Tex. Rsch. Park, 1987-89; bd. govs. Am. Inst. for Character Edn., Inc., 1988-91; mem. adv. com. Tex. Ho. of Reps., 1978; chmn. United Way campaign Tex. A&M U. System, 1984; also others. Staff sgt. USAF, 1951-55, Korea. T.H. Harris scholar Grambling State U., 1959; fellow Nat. Urban League, 1969. Mem. AAAS, Am. Chem. Soc., Tex. Acad. Sci., NAACP, Phi Beta Kappa, Sigma Xi, Phi Lambda Upsilon, Beta Kappa Chi, Alpha Mu Gamma, Kappa Delta Pi, Sigma Pi Sigma, Omega Psi Phi. Home: 211 E 10th Ave Ellensburg WA 98926 Office: Office of Pres Cen Wash U Ellensburg WA 98926*

NELSON, JACK RAYMOND, educator, researcher; b. Fargo, N.D., July 25, 1934; s. Frederick Charles and Margaret Ella (Carpenter) Cook; m. Juanita June Cowan, Feb. 6, 1955; children: Dawn R., Jack Raymond, Sandra N., Sheri L., Tammy R. BS, N.D. State U., Fargo, 1960, MS, 1961; PhD, U. Idaho, 1969. Rsch. assoc. Wash. State Agrl. Exptl. Sta./Bur. Land Mgmt., Pullman, Wash., 1964-69; asst. prof. dept. forestry and range Wash. State U., Pullman, 1969-75, assoc. prof. dept. forestry and range, 1975-80, prof. dept. nat. resource sci., 1981—; cons. U.S. Forest Svc., La Grande, Oreg., 1978; assoc. environ. sci. NOVA, Calgary, Alta., 1986. With USN, 1952-59. Mem. Soc. for Range Mgmt., Wildlife Soc., Xi Sigma Pi, Sigma Xi. Home: 946 N Grant St Moscow ID 83843-9411 Office: Wash State U Dept Natural Resource Scis Pullman WA 99164-6410

NELSON, JAMES ALAN, oil company official; b. Toledo, Apr. 29, 1950; s. James O. Nelson and Carolyn A. (Weirich) Swope; m. Diana Lynn Culver (div. Aug. 1987); children: James Brandon, Joel Ryan; m. Mary Ann Hanson, Nov. 11, 1989; 1 child, Courtney Marie. BS, Bowling Green State U., 1971; M Engring. Sci., U. Toledo, 1978. Engring. insp. Standard Oil Co. Ohio, Toledo, 1976-77, lab. chemist, 1977-78, lab. supr., 1978-80, rsch. chemist, 1980-82, project leader, 1982-85; lab. mgr. Alyeska Pipeline Co., Valdez, Alaska, 1985-88; mgr. analytical svcs. Alyeska Pipeline Co., Anchorage, 1988—. Contbr. articles to profl. jours. Recipient cert. of achievement applied tech. div. E.I. Du Pont de Nemours & Co., 1978. Mem. ASTM, Am. Chem. Soc. (cert. of recognition Colo. sect. 1983), Assn. Ofcl. Analytical Chemists, Am. Petroleum Inst. Home: 6109 Camrose Dr Anchorage AK 99504-3226 Office: Alyeska Pipeline Svc Co 1835 S Bragaw St Anchorage AK 99512-0099

NELSON, JAMES WILBUR, contract sales representative retired; b. Silverton, Oreg., Nov. 4, 1925; s. Alfred O. and Mathilda Elizabeth (Thorson) N.; m. Genevieve Ann Mabbott, Oct. 17, 1947 (div. Feb. 1970); children: Brett Alfred, Sue Ann Nelson Franco; m. Frances Marie Boese, Feb. 6, 1970; stepchildren: Sharon Lee Hoevet, Carol Anne Textrum, James Robert Williams. Student, U. Oregon, 1945-47, Oregon State Coll., 1947, Willamette U., 1948; diploma in Acctg., Merritt Davis Sch. of Commerce, 1949. Bookkeeper, office mgr. Gideon Stolz Co., Salem, Oreg., 1949-57; acct. trainee C. Brewer & Co. Ltd., Honolulu, 1957-58; salesperson Sears, Roebuck & Co., Salem, 1958-69; sales rep. Sears, Roebuck & Co., Seattle, 1969-87. Fellow The Oxford Club (life); mem. The Elks Club (life), Illahe Hills Country Club. Lutheran. Home: 4132 Penny Dr S Salem OR 97302

NELSON, KATHLEEN VEENSTRA, marketing, public relations executive; b. Flint, Mich., Sept. 1, 1932; d. Louis Benedict and Cynthia Clare (Aalders) Veenstra; m. Wallace E. Nelson, Sept. 11, 1954. Student, Wheaton Coll., 1950-51. Sec.-treas. Gleed & Co., Seattle, 1963-74; dir. devel. Pacific Sci. Ctr., Seattle, 1976-78; asst. v.p., dir. pub. rels. Rainier Bank, Seattle, 1974-76; pres., chief exec. officer Kathleen Nelson Cons., Kingston, Wash., 1978—; lectr. and cons. in field. Contbr. articles to profl. jours. Chmn. Operation Traingle Parks Project, 1964-71; mem. Downtown Devel.Com., Seattle, 1965-69, chairperson pub. rels. com., 1965-69; mem. Mayor's Seattle St. Tree Com., 1968-71, Mayor's Seattle Waterfront Park Com., 1969-71; trustee Northwest Outward Bound Sch., Portland, Oreg., 1972-79; mem. mktg. com. 13 YMCA's, Seattle-King County, 1976-80; vol. Multi Faith AIDS Project, Seattle, 1989—; elder Presbyn. Ch. Mem. Women's Network (bd. dirs. Seattle chpt. 1984-85, v.p.), Women in Communications (bd. dirs. Seattle chpt. 1978-79), City Club (charter, mktg. com. 1983-84). Home and Office: 10581 NE West Kingston Rd Kingston WA 98346

NELSON, KAY LEROI, chemist, educator; b. Richmond, Utah, Apr. 4, 1926; s. Parley LeRoi and Margaret (Peterson) N.; m. Ina Shepherd, Sept. 4, 1947; children—Marlene, Alan LeRoi, Ronald Leslie, Harold Lynn, Karalee, David LeRoi. B.S., Utah State U., 1948; Ph.D., Purdue U., 1952. AEC thesis research fellow Purdue U., 1950-52, instr., 1953-54; postdoctoral research Office Naval Research fellow UCLA, 1952-53; asst. prof. Wayne State U., 1954-56; asso. prof. Brigham Young U., Provo, Utah, 1956-61; prof. Brigham Young U., 1961-90, prof. emeritus, 1990—, dept. chmn., 1968-71; vis. prof. Oreg. State U., 1971-72; vis. scientist Tex. A&M U., 1985. Author: Laboratory Projects in Organic Chemistry, 1966, Laboratory Excursions in Organic Chemistry, 1969, Correlated Organic Laboratory Experiences, 1972, rev. edit., 1975, Guided Organic Laboratory Experiences, 1983, 3d edit., 1986, ABC Nomograph, 1983; poem My Prayer, 1972. V.p. Desert Villages Assn., Spanish Fork, Utah, 1980-89, exec. dir., 1990—. Served with AUS, 1944-45. Mem. AAAS, Am. Chem. Soc., Deseret Villages Assn. (trustee), Kiwanis, Sigma Xi, Phi Kappa Phi, Phi Lambda Upsilon, Pi Kappa Alpha. Home: Box 15-B RR 3 Sundance UT 84604-9618

NELSON, KENNETH ARTHUR, electrical engineer; b. Coeur d'Alene, Idaho, Apr. 18, 1942; s. Elton Arthur and Maxine Edna (Barnes) N.; m. Sharon Fay Paynter, Sept. 2, 1962; children: Neva Kenine, Krena Krista, Kelina Kara, Kimberly Kay. BSEE, U. Idaho, 1965; cert., Alaxander Hamilton Inst., 1970. Registered profl. engr., Calif. With GE, various locations, 1965-75; sr. mfg. engr. Jenn-Air Corp., Indpls., 1975-79; plant engr. A.O. Smith Corp., Newark, Calif., 1979-82; dir. facilities Memorex Corp., Santa Clara, Calif., 1982-88; with Scenic Mgmt. Corp., Tracy, Calif., 1988—; instr. Profl. Engring. Inst., San Carlos, Calif., 1985-88; founder Scenic Mgmt., Livermore, Calif., 1986—. Inventor in field. Mem. IEEE, Am. Soc. Metals Internat. Republican. Lutheran. Home: 1585 Hoot Owl Ct Tracy CA 95376-4396

NELSON, KIRK RICHARD, telecommunications executive; b. Portland, Oreg., Mar. 30, 1956; s. Richard John and Gloria Mae (Kraxberger) N.; m. Patricia Lee Zech, Aug. 6, 1983; children: Brandon Kirk, Kyle Patrick. BA magna cum laude, Pacific Luth. U., 1978; MBA, Seattle U., 1985; postgrad., U. So. Calif., 1991. Various managerial positions Pacific N.W. Bell, Seattle, 1979-85, dir. regulatory and fin. mgmt., 1985-87; dir. investor rels. US West, Inc., Denver, 1987-88; asst. v.p., exec. dir. external affairs US West Communications, Salt Lake City, 1988-92, exec. dir. rural strategy, 1992—. Chmn. United Way, Salt Lake City, 1987-90, People of Vision, 1990; bd. dirs. Pioneer Meml. Theatre, Salt Lake City, 1987—, Nat. Soc. to Prevent Blindness, Salt Lake City, 1990—; appointed Salt Lake City-County Bd. Health, 1992—. Mem. Utah Mfrg. Assn. (bd. dirs. 1988—, chmn. 1991), U.S. West Pres. Club, Beta Gamma Sigma. Lutheran. Home: 3 Snowstar Ln Sandy UT 84092-4800 Office: US West 250 Bell Plz Rm 1614 Salt Lake City UT 84111-2013

NELSON, KIRK WILLIAM, radio station sales manager; b. San Fernando, Calif., Nov. 16, 1953; s. Culver Hoag and Dolores Ann (Barron) N.; m. Bridget Dufy Finnegan, 1980 (div. 1984); 1 child, Timothy Kirk. Musician, mgr. Nitebank Diner, Phoenix, 1974-79; salesman R.B. Furniture, Tucson, 1979-83; assoc., ptnr. Christianson, Nelson & Assocs., Phoenix, 1983-84; gen. sales mgr. Pulitzer Broadcasting, Inc. KTAR, Phoenix, 1984—; sec., treas. Radio Advt. Met. Phoenix, 1987-88, v.p., 1992—. Mem. Official Bd. Ch. of the Beatitudes, 1989—; bd. dirs. Beatitudes Campus of Care, 1989—. Democrat. Mem. United Church of Christ. Office: Pulitzer Broadcasting Inc 301 W Osborn Phoenix AZ 85013

NELSON, LAWRENCE OLAF, administrative educator; b. Hartford, Conn., Feb. 1, 1926; s. Lawrence Olaf and Gerda Amelia Elizabeth (Hanson) N.; m. Kathleen Alice Brito, Aug. 26, 1950; children: Scott Laurence, Adam Foster. B.S., Central Conn. State U., 1949; M.A., U. Conn., 1953; Ph.D., Mich. State U., 1960. Tchr. pub. schs. Stamford, Conn., 1949-52; asst. dir. U. Conn., 1952-55; asst. to pres. State Coll., Moorhead, Minn., 1956-57; dean of adminstrn. State Coll., 1957-58; cons. Office of Edn., HEW, Washington, 1960; mem. faculty Purdue U., Lafayette, Ind., 1960-74; adminstrv. dean Purdue U., 1967-74; dean Purdue U. (Ft. Wayne Campus), 1969-70, asst. to provost, 1974; prof. higher edn., dean continuing edn. U. Ariz., Tucson, 1974-81; prof. ednl. founds., adminstrn. and higher edn. U. Ariz., 1974—; cons. in field. Mem. planning com. Ind. Gov.'s Regional Correction Center, 1969-71; mem. adv. panel Ind. Higher Edn. Telecommunications System, 1971-74; adv. bd. Midwestern Center, Nat. Humanities Series, 1972-74; mem. Ind. Com. for Humanities, 1972-74, Tucson Com. on Fgn. Relations, 1975-85; bd. dirs. Continuing Edn. for Deaf, 1975-81, Ariz. Consortium for Edn. in Social Services, 1977-81. Author: Cooperative Projects Among Colleges and Universities, 1961. Mem. Am. Assn. Higher Edn., Assn. Continuing Higher Edn., Nat. Assn. Student Personnel Administrators, NEA, Nat. Univ. Continuing Edn. Assn., Nat. Coun. Profs. of Ednl. Adminstrn., Nat. Univ. Extension Assn. (award 1971, dir. 1978-80), Phi Delta Kappa, Epsilon Pi Tau, Delta Chi. Clubs: Kiwanis of Greater Lafayette (pres. 1967), Kiwanis of Moorhead (dir. 1957-58), Rotary of Tucson (dir. 1979-80, pres. 1980-81). Home: 1330 E Indian Wells Rd Tucson AZ 85718-1180 Office: U Ariz 629 Edn Bldg Tucson AZ 85721

NELSON, LINDA ANN, bank commission official; b. Sioux City, Iowa, May 22, 1959; d. C. Howard and Mary Joyce (Forney) N. BA in Bus., U. Wash., 1981; MBA, Boston Coll., 1987. Loan officer Wash. Mut. Savs. Bank, Seattle, 1981-83; ins. rep./agt. Wash. Mut. Service Corp., Seattle, 1983-85; teaching asst. Boston Coll., Chestnut Hill, Mass., 1985-87; bank examiner Fed. Res. Bank Boston, 1987-89, Fed. Res. Bank, San Francisco, 1989—; cons. Manassa Systems Inc., Boston, 1986, Welling & Woodard, 1990. Mem. Nat Assn. Bus. Econs. (v.p. San Francisco chpt. 1993). Office: Fed Res Bank 101 Market St San Francisco CA 94105-1530

NELSON, LINDA RUTH, educator, counselor; b. Kerens, Tex., Apr. 2, 1944; d. Finis Greaves and Sally Oleta (Miller) Hodges; m. Ralph Edward Nelson, June 25, 1967; 1 child, Gretchen. BA, Hastings (Nebr.) Coll., 1965; MA, U. S.D., 1970, Lesley Coll., Cambridge, Mass., 1990. Cert. secondary tchr. and counselor, Wyo. Tchr. speech and English, debate coach Great Bend (Kans.) High Sch., 1965-67; tchr. speech and English Lincoln High Sch., Sioux Falls, S.D., 1967-69; tchr. English, debate coach LeMars (Iowa) Community High Sch., 1974-78; instr. speech and humanities Westmar Coll., LeMars, 1978-81; tchr. English Kittatinny High Sch., Newton, N.J., 1982-83; communication cons. Interact, Newton, 1983-86; tchr. English Mountain Lakes (N.J.) High Sch., 1984-86; ednl. coord. Crest View Hosp., Casper, Wyo., 1987-90; tchr. speech, forensics coach Natrona County High Sch., Casper, 1990-91, counselor, 1993—; vocat. counselor Roosevelt Ctr., Casper, 1991-93; counselor Natrona County High Sch., Casper, 1993—. Columnist LeMars Daily Sentinel, 1973-79; author poems. Vice pres. AAUW, LeMars, 1973; deacon Presbyn. United Ch. of Christ, LeMars, 1979-81; founder Dizzy Disciples, Newton, 1984-86; bd. dirs. Human Sexuality Resource Team, Casper, 1987-89. Ethical Leadership Devel. Conf. scholar, 1983, Wyo. Assn. for Counseling and Devel. scholar, 1990. Mem. NEA, ACA, Am. Soc. Group Psychotherapy and Psychodrama, Wyo. Counseling Assn., Wyo. Writers, Wyo. Poets. Democrat. Office: Natrona County High Sch 930 S Elm Casper WY 82601

NELSON, MAGNUS CHARLES, accountant, former bank executive; b. Richfield, Utah, Dec. 23, 1938; s. Duane Miller and Naomi (Horne) N.; m. Marilyn Kaye Haynie, Mar. 17, 1962; children: Michael D., Thea T., Kristin Nelson Strobelt, Camilla T. Nelson Entote, John D. BS in Acctg., U. Utah, 1962. CPA, Utah; chartered bank auditor. Ptnr. Ernst & Whinney, N.Y.C., 1963-84, 86-89; sr. v.p., dir. control svcs. BankAm. Corp., San Francisco, 1984-86; sr. v.p., contr. DFS Group Ltd., San Francisco, 1989—. Co-author: Implementing Mergers and Acquisitions in the Financial Services Industry, 1985. Treas., bd. dirs. Southeastern Ctr. for Contemporary Art, 1986-89. Served with USAR, 1960-61. Mem. Am. Inst. CPAs (banking com. 1980-83), Utah Assn. CPAs, Bank Adminstrn. Inst. (CPA advisor audit commn. 1976-79, bd. regents 1982-85). Mem. LDS Ch. Office: 655 Montgomery St San Francisco CA 94111-2635

NELSON, MARY CARROLL, artist, author; b. Bryan, Tex., Apr. 24, 1929; d. James Vincent and Mary Elizabeth (Langton) Carroll; m. Edwin Blakely Nelson, June 27, 1950; children: Patricia Ann, Edwin Blakely. BA in Fine Arts, Barnard Coll., 1950; MA, U. N.Mex., 1963. Juror Am. Artist Golden Anniversary Nat. Art Competition, 1987, Don Ruffin Meml. Art Exhbn., Ariz., 1989, N.Mex. Arts and Crafts Fair, 1989; guest instr. continuing edn. U. N.Mex., 1991; curator Shrines, 1988; cons., organizer Affirming Wholeness, The Art and Healing Experience, San Antonio, 1992. Group shows include N.Mex. Mus. Fine Arts Biennial, 1987, N.Mex. Lightworks, 1990, Level to Level, Ohio Layering, 1987, Artist as Shaman, Ohio, 1990, The Healing Experience, Mass., 1991, A Gathering of Voices, Calif., 1991, Art is for Healing, The Universal Link, San Antonio, Tex., 1992, Biennial, Fuller Lodge Art Ctr. Los Alamos, N.Mex., 1993, Layering, Albuquerque, 1993; represented in pvt. collections in: U.S., Fed. Republic of Germany, Eng. and Australia; author: American Indian Biography Series, 1971-76, (with Robert E. Wood) Watercolor Workshop, 1974, (with Ramon Kelley) Ramon Kelley Paints Portraits and Figures, 1977, The Legendary Artists of Taos, 1980, (catalog) American Art in Peking, 1981, Masters of Western Art, 1982, Connecting, The Art of Beth Ames Swartz, 1984, (catalog) Layering, An Art of Time and Space, 1985, (catalog) Layering/Connecting, 1987; contbg. editor Am. Artist, 1976-91, Southwest Art, 1987-91; editor (video) Layering, 1990; arts correspondent Albuquerque Jour., 1991-93. Mem. Albuquerque Arts Bd., 1984-88. Mem. Soc. Layerists in Multi-Media (founder 1982). Home: 1408 Georgia St NE Albuquerque NM 87110-6861

NELSON, MAXINE EVELYN, clinical social worker; b. Cin., June 9, 1947; d. Albert and Marcia (Leenson) Daniels; m. John Albin Nelson, June 30, 1970 (div. 1975); m. Robert Frank Fahrer, Oct. 2, 1993. BA in Biochemistry, Carnegie Mellon U., 1969; MSW, U. Wash., 1986. Clin. social worker. Artist Seattle, 1974—; med. social worker U. Hosp., Seattle, 1986-87; clin. social worker Virginia Mason Med. Ctr., Seattle, 1987—; cons. Northwest Family Tng. Inst., Seattle, 1982-84. Producer: (TV spl.) Labor of Love, 1982, (videos) Corner/Corner'd, 1980, 87 (Seattle Arts Commn. 1980), Profile Self-Confrontation, 1990, 92. Bd. dirs. Northwest Mediation Svc., Seattle, 1983-89. Mem. Am. Soc. Group Psychotherapy and Psychodrama, Acad. Clin. Social Workers. Office: Virginia Mason Clinic 1100 9th Ave Seattle WA 98111

NELSON, NANCY ELEANOR, pediatrician, educator; b. El Paso, Apr. 4, 1933; d. Harry Hamilton and Helen Maude (Murphy) N. B.A. magna cum laude, U. Colo., 1955, M.D., 1959. Intern, Case Western Res. U. Hosp., 1959-60, resident, 1960-63; practice medicine specializing in pediatrics, Denver, 1963—; assoc. clin. prof. U. Colo. Sch. Medicine, Denver, 1977-88, clin. prof., 1988—, asst. dean Sch. Medicine, 1982-88, assoc. dean, 1988—. Mem. Am. Acad. Pediatrics, AMA, Denver Med. Soc. (pres. 1983-84), Colo. Med. Soc. (bd. dirs. 1985-88, judicial coun. 1992—). Home: 1265 Elizabeth St Denver CO 80206-3241 Office: 4200 E 9th Ave Denver CO 80262

NELSON, NEVIN MARY, interior designer; b. Cleve., Nov. 5, 1941; d. Arthur George Reinker and Barbara Phyllis (Gunn) Parks; m. Wayne Nelson (div. 1969); children: Doug, Brian. BA in Interior Design, U. Colo., 1964. Prin. Nevin Nelson Design, Boulder, Colo., 1966-70, Vail, Colo., 1970—; program chmn. Questers Antique Study Group, Boulder, 1969. Coord. Bob Kirscht for Gov. campaign, Eagle County, Colo., 1986; state del. Rep. Nat. Conv., 1986-88; county coord. George Bush for U.S. Pres. campaign, 1988, 92; chmn. Eagle County Reps., 1989-93. Mem. Am. Soc. Interior Designers. Episcopalian. Home: PO Box 1212 Vail CO 81658-1212 Office: 2498 Arosa Dr Vail CO 81657

NELSON, O. EDWARD, marketing executive; b. Portland, Oreg., Mar. 29, 1935; s. Oscar Edward and Hettie Halena (Parker) N.; m. Florence Marlene Arneson, Oct. 23, 1954; children: Stephen, Lynette, Jeffrey, Laurie, Leanne. Student, Calif. State U., Northridge, 1964-67; BS in Mgmt., Marylhurst Coll., Portland, 1977; MBA in Mktg., Portland State U., 1980; PhD in Tech. Mgmt., Columbia Pacific U., San Rafael, Calif., 1990. Buyer Boeing Airplane Co., Renton, Wash., 1957-60; sr. prodn. planner Gen. Dynamics, San Diego, 1960-62; engring. analyst N.Am. Aviation, Downey, Calif., 1962-66; project adminstr. RCA, Van Nuys, Calif., 1966-69; dir. adminstrn. Daystar Communications Inc., Eugene, Oreg., 1969-73; engring. supr. Wagner Mining Equipment Co., Portland, 1973-82; mktg. mgr. Oreg. Metall. Corp., Albany, 1982-92, pres. mktg., 1992—; mem. adj. faculty Oreg. State U., Corvallis, 1984-88; mem. Industry Sector Adv. Com., Washington, 1989—; chmn. Fed. Metals Credit Union, Albany, 1988—. Author: The Product Life Cycle of Engineered Metals, 1989, (proc.) Global Trends in Titanium Trade, 1989; contbr. articles to profl. jours. Mem. com. Mid-Willamette Valley YMCA, 1985—. Mem. Am. Soc. for Metals (chmn. internat. Willamette chpt.), Soc. for Advancement Materials and Process Engring. (internat. speaker 1991), Soc. Automotive Engrs. (speaker 1985), Titanium Devel. Assn. (founding bd. dirs. 1984-86), Am. Def. Preparedness Assn., Smithsonian Assocs., Rotary (bd. dirs. Corvallis 1989—, past pres., 1991-92). Republican. Baptist. Home: 6960 NW Concord Dr Corvallis OR 97330-9564

NELSON, PAULA MORRISON BRONSON, educator; b. Memphis, Mar. 26, 1944; d. Fred Ford and Julia (Morrison) Bronson: m. Jack Marvin Nelson, July 13, 1968; children: Eric Allen, Kelly Susan. BS, U. N.Mex., 1967; MA, U. Colo., Denver, 1985. Physical edn. tchr. Grant Union Sch. Dist., Sacramento, 1967-68; physical edn. tchr. Denver Pub. Schs., 1968-74, with program for pupil assistance, 1974-80, chpt. 1 reading specialist, 1983—; tchr. ESL Douglas County Pub. Schs., Parker, Colo., 1982-83; demonstration tchr. Colo. Edn. Assn., 1970-72; mem. curriculum com. Denver Pub. Schs., 1970-72; mem. Douglas County Accountability Com., Castle Rock, Colo., 1986-92; mem. educators rev. panel Edn. for Freedom; computer trainer Denver Pub. Schs. Tech. Team, 1992—. Co-author: Gymnastics Teacher's Guide Elementary Physical Education, 1973, Applauding Our Constitution, 1989; producer slide shows Brotherhood, 1986, We the People...Our Dream Lives On, 1987, Celebration of Cultures, 1988. Named Pub. Edn. Coalition grantee, Denver, 1987, 88, 89, 90, grantee Rocky Mountain Global Edn. Project, 1987, Wake Forest Law Sch., Winston-Salem, N.C., 1988, 89, 90; recipient chpt. II grant, 1991, Three R's of Freedom award State Dept. Edn., 1987. Mem. Windstar Found., Colo. Coun. Internat. Reading, Internat. Reading Assn., Nat. Soc. for Study of Edn., Colo. Coun. for the Social Studies, Tech. in Edn., Am. Fedn. Tchrs., Denver Fedn. Tchrs. Republican. Methodist. Home: 10488 E Meadow Run Parker CO 80134-6220

NELSON, RANDALL ERLAND, surgeon; b. Hastings, Nebr., Dec. 28, 1948; s. Marvin Erland and Faith Constance (Morrison) N.; m. Carolyn Joy Kaufman, Feb. 28, 1976. BS in Chemistry cum laude, So. Nazarene U., 1971; MD, U. Nebr., 1975; MS in Surgery, U. Ill., Chgo., 1979. Diplomate Nat. Bd. Med. Examiners, Am. Bd. Surgery. Intern in gen. surgery Strong Meml. Hosp., Rochester, N.Y., 1975-76; resident in gen. surgery U. Rochester Affiliated Hosps., 1976-78, Rush-Presbyn.-St. Luke's Med. Ctr., Chgo., 1978-81; gen. surgeon Surg. Group San Jose, Calif., 1981—; instr. gen. surgery U. Rochester Sch. Medicine and Dentistry, 1975-78, Rush Med. Coll., Chgo., 1978-80; adj. attending surgeon Rush-Presbyn.-St. Luke's Med. Ctr., 1980-81. Mem. Rep. Nat. Com., Washington, 1984—. Fellow ACS, Southwestern Surg. Congress; mem. Calif. Med. Assn., Santa Clara County Med. Soc., San Jose Surg. Soc., U.S. C. of C., Circle-K Club, Commonwealth Club Calif., Churchill Club, Phi Delta Lambda. Republican. Office: Surg Group of San Jose 2101 Forest Ave Ste 124 San Jose CA 95128-1489

NELSON, RAYMOND MILFORD, surgeon; b. Loma Linda, Calif., Oct. 10, 1928; s. Hiram Milford Nelson and Eunice Frances Manning Smithwick; m. Carole L. Sundean, Mar. 19, 1932 (dec. 1986); children: Cherie, Cynthia, Kathi, Michael; m. Joni LaVern Denman, May 29, 1988. BS, Pacific Union Coll., 1949; MD, Loma Linda U., 1953. Intern Balboa Naval Hosp., San Diego, 1953-54; resident gen. surg. White Meml. Hosp., L.A., 1957-62; gen. surgeon Belle Vista Mission Hosp., Mayaguez, P.R., 1962-70; pvt. practice surgery Santa Cruz, Calif., 1970—. Lt. USN, 1952-57. Fellow aCS; mem. AMA, Calif. Med. Assn. Home: 520 High St Santa Cruz CA 95060 Office: 602 Frederick St Santa Cruz CA 95062

NELSON, RICHARD LELAND, accountant; b. Ellisville, Miss., July 23, 1945; s. James Leland and Vicia Ree (Cross) N.; m. Laurie Ellen Gaskell, May 18, 1974; children: David C., Leslie C. AA, Columbia Basin Coll., 1971; BA, Eastern Wash. State U., 1973. CPA, Wash. Salesman Nelson's Jewelry & Trophies, Prosser, Wash., 1965-68; mgr. Prosser Bowl, 1968-69; acct. Franklin, Mayhan & Co., Kennewick, Wash., 1973-79, Mayhan & Pfaff, Kennewick, 1973-79; stockholder, officer Mayhan, Pfaff, Borrows & Nelson, Kennewick, 1981-86; pvt. practice Kennewick, 1986—. With USNG, 1965-70. Mem. AICPA, Wash. Soc. CPA. Office: 2630 W Bruneau Pl Kennewick WA 99336

NELSON, ROBERT WILLIAM, real estate executive; b. Eugene, Oreg., May 29, 1942; s. Roy Robert and Alta (Peterson) N.; divorced; 1 child, Erin Michele; m. René O'Bryant. BS in Mgmt., Oreg. State U., 1965; MBA in Real Estate, U. Oreg., 1972. Lic. real estate investment broker; Cert. Comml. Investment Mem. Real estate investor Nelson, Taylor & McCulley, Inc., Eugene, 1968-72; instr. real estate Lane Community Coll., Eugene, 1972—; pres., broker Robert W. Nelson, Real Estate Cons., Inc., Eugene, 1974—; expert witness to value Oreg. Tax Ct. and Lane County Circuit Ct., 1979—; ptnr., broker, exchange cons. PACWEST Real Estate Investments, 1984—; dir. Oreg. Assn. Realtors, 1992; pres. Eugene Assn. Realtors, 1993. Author: Real Estate Law, 1974, Real Estate Finance, 1974, Real Estate Practices, 1974, Tax Deferred Exchanges, 1977, 87, 91. Active Bus. Adv. Counsel, Lane Community Coll., 1975—. Lt. USN, 1965-68. Named Realtor of Yr. Eugene Bd. Realtors, 1983. Mem. Soc. Real Estate Appraisers (nat. grad. fellow 1973), Brokers Million Dollar Club (pres. 1986, 89), Comml. Investment Div. (pres. 1972). Methodist. Office: PACWEST Real Estate Investments 59 E 11th Ave Ste 100 Eugene OR 97401-3510

NELSON, ROGER ELLIS, environment, health and safety manager; b. St. Cloud, Minn., Dec. 10, 1938; s. Walter O. and Alice (Nelson) N.; m. Rosalie Jean Davis, June 25, 1960. BA in Geography, U. Minn., 1960; B Landscape Architecture, U. Calif., Berkeley, 1968. Lancscape architect Bur. Land Mgmt., Dept. Interior, Washington, 1968-73; mgr. environ. qquality BHP-Utah Internat. Inc., San Francisco, 1973—, chmn. polit. action com., 1987—; presenter on environ., environ. mgmt. and environ. policy devel. Contbr. numerous articles to profl. publs. Bd. dirs. Westhaven Christian Adult Retirement, 1975—, Evang. Free Ch. Am., Mpls., 1986—. Comdr. USNR, 1960-63. Mem. ASCE (assoc.), Am. Soc. Landscape Architects, Am. Mining Congress (environ. com. and health and safety com. 1976—, chmn. reclamation tech. com. 1984-85), U.S. C. of C. (natural resources com. 1976—), Commonwealth Club Calif. Republican. Office: BHB Minerals 550 California St San Francisco CA 94104

NELSON, ROSS PETER, software engineer, writer; b. Fargo, N.D., June 12, 1957; s. Robert D. and Ardell (Grefsrud) N.; m. Pamela A. Weiss, July 28, 1979 (div. Apr. 1992). BS in Computer Sci., Mont. State U., 1979. Engr. Intel Corp., Santa Clara, Calif., 1979-83, Gavilan Computer, Campbell, Calif., 1983-84; mgr. Answer Software, Cupertino, Calif., 1984—; sec. Pub. Domain Software Exch., Santa Clara, 1991—. Author: Microsoft's 386/486 Guide, 1989, Running Visual Basic for Microsoft Windows, 1992; co-author: Extending DOS, 1990; contbr. articles to profl. jours. Mem. Computer Profls. for Social Responsibility, Palo Alto, Calif., 1988—, Amnesty Internat. Recipient Silver Pen award San Jose Mecury News, 1991. Mem. ACLU, Assn. for Computing Machinery. Home: 2675 Miller Ave 1 Mountain View CA 94040

NELSON, ROY GUNNAR, pediatrician; b. Hinsdale, Ill., Nov. 9, 1951; s. Gunnar H. and Ingrid (Anderson) N.; m. Nancy G. Brackett, Dec. 23, 1973; children: Lisa, Julie, Kevin. BA in Chemistry, Union Coll., Lincoln, Nebr., 1974; MD, Loma Linda U., 1977. Diplomate Am. Bd. Pediatrics. Intern Loma Linda (Calif.) U. Med. Ctr., 1978, resident, 1979-81; pvt. practice pediatrics and adolescent medicine Flatirons Med. Ctr., Boulder, Colo., 1981—; chmn. dept. pediatrics Boulder United Med. Staff, 1983-84; cons. Boulder and Weld County Health depts., 1982-85, Martin Luther Home, 1982-84; bd. dirs. CompreCare. Mem. sch. bd. Boulder Jr. Acad., 1982-89; mem. Boulder County Child Abuse Team, 1982-85. Home: 633 Sunnyside St Louisville CO 80027-1320 Office: Avista One Med Pla Ste 200 Louisville CO 80027

NELSON, RUSSELL MARION, surgeon, educator; b. Salt Lake City, Sept. 9, 1924; s. Marion C. and Edna (Anderson) N.; m. Dantzel White, Aug. 31, 1945; children: Marsha Nelson McKellar, Wendy Nelson Maxfield, Gloria Nelson Irion, Brenda Nelson Miles, Sylvia Nelson Webster, Emily Nelson Wittwer, Laurie Nelson Marsh, Rosalie Nelson Ringwood, Marjorie Nelson Helsten, Russell Marion, Jr. BA, U. Utah, 1945, MD, 1947; PhD in Surgery, U. Minn., 1954; ScD (hon.), Brigham Young U., 1970; DMS (hon.), Utah State U., 1989. Diplomate: Am. Bd. Surgery, Am. Bd. Thoracic Surgery (dir. 1972-78). Intern U. Minn. Hosps., Mpls., 1947; asst. resident surgery U. Minn. Hosps., 1948-51; first asst. resident surgery Mass. Gen. Hosp., Boston, 1953-54; sr. resident surgery U. Minn. Hosps., Mpls., 1954-55; practice medicine (specializing in cardiovascular and thoracic surgery), Salt Lake City, 1959-84; staff surgeon Latter-day Saints Hosp., Salt Lake City, 1959-84; dir. surg. research lab. Latter-day Saints Hosp., 1959-72, chief cardiovascular-thoracic surg. div., 1967-72, also bd. govs., 1970-90, vice chmn., 1979-89; staff surgeon Primary Children's Hosp., Salt Lake City,

1960; attending in surgery VA Hosp., Salt Lake City, 1955-84, Univ. Hosp., Salt Lake City, 1955-84; asst. prof. surgery Med. Sch. U. Utah, Salt Lake City, 1955-59, asst. clin. prof. surgery, 1959-66, asso. clin. prof. surgery, clin. prof., 1966-69, research prof. surgery, 1970-84, clin. prof. emeritus, 1984—; staff services Utah Biomed. Test Lab., 1970-84; dir. tng. program cardiovascular and thoracic surgery at Univ. Utah affiliated hosps., 1967-84; mem. policyholders adv. com. New Eng. Mut. Life Ins. Co., Boston, 1976-80. Contbr. articles to profl. jours. Mem. White House Conf. on Youth and Children, 1960; bd. dirs. Internat. Cardiol. Found.; bd. govs. LDS Hosp., 1970-90, Deseret Gymnasium, 1971-75, Promised Valley Playhouse, 1970-79. 1st lt. to capt. M.C., AUS, 1951-53. Markle scholar in med. scis., 1957-59; Fellowship of Medici Publici U. Utah Coll. Medicine, 1966; Distinguished Alumni award, 1967; Gold Medal of Merit, Argentina, 1974; named Honorary Prof. Shandong Med. U., Jinan, People's Republic of China, 1985, Old People's U., Jinan, 1986, Xi'an (People's Republic of China) Med. Coll., 1986. Fellow A.C.S. (chmn. adv. council on thoracic surgery 1973-75), Am. Coll. Cardiology, Am. Coll. Chest Physicians; mem. Am. Assn. Thoracic Surgery, Am. Soc. Artificial Internal Organs, AMA, Dirs. Thoracic Residencies (pres. 1971-72), Utah Med. Assn. (pres. 1970-71), Salt Lake County Med. Soc., Am. Heart Assn. (exec. com. cardiovascular surgery 1972, dir. 1976-78, chmn. council cardiovascular surgery 1976-78), Utah Heart Assn. (pres. 1964-65), Soc. Thoracic Surgeons, Soc. Vascular Surgery (sec. 1968-72, pres. 1974), Utah Thoracic Soc., Salt Lake Surg. Soc., Samson Thoracic Surg. Soc., Western Soc. for Clin. Research, Soc. U. Surgeons, Am., Western, Pan-Pacific surg. assns., Inter. Am. Soc. Cardiology (bd. mgrs.), Phi Beta Kappa, Sigma Xi, Alpha Omega Alpha, Phi Kappa Phi, Sigma Chi. Mem. Ch. of Jesus Christ of Latter-day Saints (pres. Bonneville Stake 1964-71, gen. pres. Sunday sch. 1971-79, regional rep. 1979-84, Quorum of the Twelve Apostles 1984—). Home: 1347 Normandie Cir Salt Lake City UT 84105-1919 Office: 47 E South Temple Salt Lake City UT 84150-0001

NELSON, SARAH MILLEDGE, archaeology educator; b. Miami, Fla., Nov. 29, 1931; d. Stanley and Sarah Woodman (Franklin) M.; m. Harold Stanley Nelson, July 25, 1953; children: Erik Harold, Mark Milledge, Stanley Franklin. BA, Wellesley Coll., 1953; MA, U. Mich., 1969, PhD, 1973. Instr. archaeology U. Md. extension, Seoul, Republic Korea, 1970-71; asst. prof. U. Denver, 1974-79, assoc. prof., 1979-85, prof. archaeology, 1985—, chair dept. anthropology, dir. women's studies program, 1985-87; vis. asst. prof. U. Colo., Boulder, 1974. Co-editor: Powers of Observation, 1990; author: Archaeology of Korea, 1993. Active Earthwatch, 1989—. Southwestern Inst. Rsch. on Women grantee, 1981, Acad. Korean Studies grantee, Seoul, 1983, Internat. Cultural Soc. Korea grantee, 1986, Scholarly Communication award People's Republic of China, NAS, 1988; recipient Outstanding Scholar award U. Denver, 1989. Fellow Am. Anthrop. Assn.; mem. Soc. Am. Archaeology, Assn. Asian Studies, Royal Asiatic Soc., Sigma Xi (sec.-treas. 1978-79), Phi Beta Kappa. Democrat. Home: 5878 S Dry Creek Ct Littleton CO 80121-1709 Office: U Denver Dept Anthropology Denver CO 80208

NELSON, THOMAS G., judge; b. 1936. Student, Univ. Idaho, 1955-59, LLB, 1962. Ptnr. Parry, Robertson, Daly and Larson, Twin Falls, Idaho, 1965-79, Nelson, Rosholt, Robertson, Tolman and Tucker, Twin Falls, from 1979; judge U.S. Cir. Ct. (ninth cir.), San Francisco, Calif., 1990—. With Idaho Air N.G., 1962-65, USAR, 1965-68. Mem. ABA (ho. of dels. 1974, 86-88), Am. Bar Found., Am. Coll. Trial Lawyers, Idaho State Bar (pres., bd. commrs.), Idaho Assn. Def. Counsel, Am. Bd. Trial Advocates (pres. Idaho chpt.), Phi Alpha Delta, Idaho Law Found., Internat. Assn. Def. Counsel. Office: US Ct Appeals 9th Circuit PO Box 1339 Boise ID 83701

NELSON, WALTER WILLIAM, computer programmer, consultant; b. Seattle, May 7, 1954; s. Arne A. and Helen R. (Truitt) N.; m. Paula E. Truax, Dec. 21, 1985. BA in Zoology, U. Wash., 1976, BS in Psychology, 1977; PhC in Psychology, U. Minn., 1982. Systems analyst Dept. of Social and Health Svcs., State of Wash., Seattle, 1986-89; computer info. cons. Dept. of Health, State of Wash., Seattle, 1989-90; pres. Data Dimensions, Inc., Seattle, 1990—; cons. The Heritage Inst., Seattle, 1989—; pres. Tech Alliance, Renton, Wash., 1990-91. Contbr. articles to profl. jours. Mem. Tech Alliance, Berkeley Macintosh Users Group, Seattle Downtown Macintosh Bus. Users Group, 4th Dimension Spl. Interest Group (founder, pres. 1990—). Office: Data Dimensions Inc 1100 NW Elford Dr Seattle WA 98177-4129

NELSON, WILLARD GREGORY, veterinarian, mayor; b. Lewiston, Idaho, Nov. 21, 1937; s. Donald William and Eve Mae (Boyer) N.; m. Mary Ann Eklund, Apr. 3, 1965 (div.); children: Elizabeth Ann, John Gregory. BS in Premedicine, Mont. State U., 1959; DVM, Wash. State U., 1961. Lic. veterinarian, Wash., Oreg., Idaho, Mont. Pvt. practice vet. medicine, Kuna, Idaho, 1963-66; asst. to dir. Idaho Dept. Agr., Boise, 1966-78; asst. chief Idaho Bur. Animal Health, 1978-80, chief, 1980-81; adminstr., state veterinarian Idaho Div. Animal Industries, 1981-90; dir. Idaho Dept. Agr., 1990—; mayor City of Kuna (Idaho), 1984—; chmn. Idaho Gov.'s Human and Animal Health Consortium, 1983-90. Kuna city councilman, 1964-68, pres. Planning and Zoning Commn., 1968-72; mem. bd. trustees Joint Sch. Dist. 3, 1970-71, pres., 1972-76; mem. adv. bd. Mercy Med. Hosp., Nampa, Idaho, 1986—; mem. adv. com. Wash., Oreg., Idaho Coll. Vet. Medicine, 1983—; mem. ADA Planning Assn., 1986—, vice chmn., 1991-92, chmn. 1993; mem. Western U.S. Trade Assn., 1990—, treas., 1992; mem. Idaho Emergency Response Commn., 1992—, Idaho Export Coun., 1992—, Idaho Rural Devel. Coun., 1992—, vice-chair, 1993. Served as capt. U.S. Army Vet Corps, 1961-63; lt. col. Idaho Army N.G., 1979-88, col., 1988—. Mem. Idaho Vet. Med. Assn. (v.p. 1987, pres.-elect 1988, pres. 1989, Idaho Veterinarian of Yr. 1989), S.W. Idaho Vet. Med. Assn., U.S. Animal Health Assn. (chmn. anaplasmosis com. 1987-90), AVMA (mem. coun. on pub. health and regulatory medicine 1988—, chmn. 1993, pres. nat. assembly 1988), Western States Livestock Assn., USDA (nat. damage control adv. com. 1992—, nat. dir. animal welfare coalition 1992—), Am. Legion. Lutheran. Club: Lions (Kuna). Home: 793 W 4th St Kuna ID 83634-1941 Office: 2270 Old Penitentiary Rd Boise ID 83712-8298

NELSON, WILLIAM O., pharmaceutical company executive; b. Upland, Calif., Mar. 30, 1941; s. William Orestas and Glenice Irene (Pearson) N.; m. Sue Farmer, Jan. 27, 1962 (div. Jan. 1971); 1 child, Terri Lynn; m. Deborah Marie Goodwin, Oct. 5, 1985. AA, Pima Coll., Tucson, 1976; BS, U. Phoenix, 1980. Sales rep. Sandoz Pharms., Riverside, Calif., 1966-71, Tucson, 1971-79; regional sales mgr. Sandoz Pharms., Phoenix, 1979-87; western area mgr., med. scis. liaison Sandoz Pharms., Rancho Cucamonga, Calif., 1987—. With USN, 1959-63. Republican. Home: 8768 Banyan St Rancho Cucamonga CA 91701

NELSON, WILLIAM RANKIN, surgeon; b. Charlottesville, Va., Dec. 12, 1921; s. Hugh Thomas and Edith (Rankin) N.; m. Nancy Laidley, Mar. 17, 1956 (div. 1979); children: Robin Page Nelson Russel, Susan Kimberly Nelson Wright, Anne Rankin Nelson Cron; m. Pamela Morgan Phelps, July 5, 1984. BA, U. Va., 1943, MD, 1945. Diplomate Am. Bd. Surgery. Intern Vanderbilt U. Hosp., Nashille, 1945-46; resident in surgery U. Va. Hosp., Charlottesville, 1949-51; fellow surg. oncology Meml. Sloan Kettering Cancer Ctr., N.Y.C., 1951-55; instr. U. Colo. Sch. Medicine, Denver, 1955-57; asst. clin. prof. U. Colo. Sch. Medicine, 1962-87, clin. prof. surgery, 1987—; asst. prof. Med. Coll. Va., Richmond, 1957-62; mem. exec. com. U. Colo. Cancer Ctr.; mem. nat. bd., nat. exec. com. Am. Cancer Soc. Contbr. articles to profl. jours. Capt. USAAF, 1946-48. Recipient Nat. Div. award Am. Cancer Soc., 1979. Fellow Am. Coll. Surgeons (bd. govs. 1984-89); mem. AMA, Internat. Soc. Surgery, Brit. Assn. Surg. Oncology, Royal Soc. Medicine (U.K.), Soc. Surg. Oncology (pres. 1975-76), Soc. Head and Neck Surgeons (pres. 1986-87), Am. Cancer Soc. (pres. Colo. div. 1975-77, exec. com., nat. bd. dirs., del. dir. to nat. pres. Colo. div. 1975-77), Am. Soc. Clin. Oncology, Western Surg. Assn. Colo. Med. Soc., Denver Med. Soc., Denver Acad. Surgery, Rocky Mt. Oncology Soc., Univ. Club, Rotary. Republican. Presbyterian. Office: 1801 Williams St Ste 201 Denver CO 80218-1215

NEMETZ, HAROLD, dentist; b. Vancouver, B.C., Can., May 26, 1935; s. Leo and Bessie (Perlman) N.; m. in 1957 (div. 1969); children: Larry, Steven; m. Donna Jean Baker, Aug. 22, 1970. BS, Loyola U., L.A., 1958; DDS, McGill U., Montreal, Can., 1962; Advanced M in Profl. Edn., U. So. Calif., 1977. Dentist pvt. practice Orange County, Calif., 1963—; assoc. prof. U. So. Calif., L.A., 1971-83; prof. Loma Linda (Calif.) U., 1983—; cons. in field. Contbr. articles to profl. jours. Fellow Am. Coll. Dentists, 1970, Internat. Coll. Dentists, 1972, Acad. Gen. Dentistry, 1973. Mem. So. Calif. Acad. Gen. Dentistry (pres.), Am. Acad. Crown and Bridge Prosthodontics, Internat. Assn. Dental Rsch., Am. Dental Soc., Calif. Dental Soc., Orange County Dental Soc. Jewish. Office: Harold Nemetz DDS AMEd 777 S Main St Ste 138 Orange CA 92668

NEMETZ, PETER NEWMAN, policy analysis educator, economics researcher; b. Vancouver, B.C., Can., Feb. 19, 1944; s. Nathan Theodore and Bel Nemetz. BA in Econs. and Polit. Sci., U. B.C., 1966; AM in Econs., Harvard U., 1969, PhD in Econs., 1973. Teaching fellow, tutor Harvard U., Cambridge, Mass., 1971-73; lectr. Sch. Planning, U. B.C., Vancouver, 1973-75, asst. prof., assoc. prof. policy analysis, 1975—, chmn., 1984-90; postdoctoral fellow Westwater Research Centre, Vancouver, 1973-75; vis. scientist, dept. med. stats. and epidemiol. Mayo Clinic, 1986-88, sr. visiting scientist Dept. of Health Scis. Research Mayo Clinic, 1988—; cons. consumer and corp. affairs, Can., 1977-80; program chmn. The Vancouver Inst., 1990—; mem. rsch. mgmt. com. Ctr. Health Svcs and Policy Rsch., U. B.C., 1990—, mgmt. com. S.E. Asia Ctr., 1992—. Mem. bd. mgmt. BC-Yukon divsn. Can. Nat. Inst. for Blind. Editor Jour. Bus. Adminstrn., 1978—. Contbr. articles to sci. jours. Grantee Natural Scis. and Engring. Research Council Can., 1976-92, Consumer and Corp. Affairs Can., 1978-80, Econ. Council of Can., 1979-80, Max Bell Found., 1982-84. Mem. Am. Econ. Assn., AAAS, Assn. Environ. and Resource Economists, Internat. Epidemiol. Assn. Liberal. Jewish. Clubs: Harvard of B.C. (pres. 1986—), University (Vancouver). Avocations: swimming; photography. Office: Univ British Columbia, Faculty of Commerce, Vancouver, BC Canada V6T 1Z2

NEMIR, DONALD PHILIP, lawyer; b. Oakland, Calif., Oct. 31, 1931; s. Philip F. and Mary (Shavor) N.; AB, U. Calif., Berkeley, 1957, JD, 1960. Bar: Calif. 1961. Pvt. practice, San Francisco, 1961—; pres. Law Offices Donald Nemir. Mem. ABA (litigation com.), Calif. State Bar Assn. (litigation com.), Phi Delta Phi. Office: One Bush St Ste 200 San Francisco CA 94104

NEMIRE, KENNETH EUGENE, research psychologist, consultant. BS in Psychobiology, U. Calif., Riverside, 1980; PhD in Exptl. Psychology, U. Calif., Santa Cruz, 1989. Postdoctoral rsch. assoc. NRC/NASA-Ames Rsch. Ctr., Moffett Field, Calif., 1989-91; pres. Interface Techs., Capitola, Calif., 1991—; cons. Calif. State U., Hayward, 1991-92, Monterey (Calif.) Techs., Inc., 1991-93; rsch. psychologist San Jose (Calif.) State U. Found., 1992—; cons. to numerous computer companies; human factors expert witness. Contbr. articles to profl. jours. Founder, chief instr. Shotokan Karate Fedn. of Santa Cruz, Capitola, 1983-92. Postdoctoral rsch. assoc. NRC, 1989-91; recipient Sigma Xi Grant-In-Aid of Rsch., 1988, rsch. grantee NASA, 1992, U.S. Army 1993. Mem. Aerospace Med. Assn., Am. Psychol. Soc., Assn. for Computing Machinery, Human Factors Soc. (mem., v.p. Bay Area chpt. 1992, pres. 1993). Office: 1840 41st Ave Ste # 102 Capitola CA 95010

NEMIROFF, MAXINE CELIA, art educator, gallery owner, consultant; b. Chgo., Feb. 11, 1935; d. Oscar Bernard and Martha (Mann) Kessler; m. Paul Rubenstein, June 26, 1955 (div. 1974); children: Daniel, Peter, Anthony; m. Allan Nemiroff, Dec. 24, 1979. BA, U. So. Calif., 1955; MA, UCLA, 1974. Sr. instr. UCLA, 1974-92; dir., curator art gallery Doolittle Theater, Los Angeles, 1985-86; owner Nemiroff Deutsch Fine Art, Santa Monica, Calif.; leader of worldwide art tours; cons. L'Ermitage Hotel Group, Beverly Hills, Calif., 1982—, Broadway Dept. Stores, So. Calif., 1979—, Security Pacific Bank, Calif., 1978—, Am. Airlines, Calif. Pizza Kitchen Restaurants; art chmn. UCLA Thieves Market, Century City, 1960—, L.A. Music Ctr. Mercado, 1982—; lectr. in field. Apptd. bd. dirs. Dublin (Calif.) Fine Arts Found., 1989; mem. Calif. Govs. Adv. Coun. for Women, 1992. Named Woman of Yr. UCLA Panhellenic Council, 1982, Instr. of Yr. UCLA Dept. Arts, 1984. Mem. L.A. County Mus. Art Coun., UCLA Art Coun., UCLA Art Coun. Docents, Alpha Epsilon Phi (alumnus of yr. 1983). Democrat. Jewish.

NEMIRO-MEAD, BEVERLY MIRIUM ANDERSON, writer, educator; b. St. Paul, May 29, 1925; d. Martin and Anna Mae (Oshanyk) Anderson; m. Jerome Morton Nemiro, Feb. 10, 1951 (div. May 1975); children: Guy Samuel, Lee Anna, Dee Martin; m. William Isaac Mead, Aug. 8, 1992. Student Reed Coll., 1943-44; BA, U. Colo., 1947; postgrad., U. Denver. Tchr., Seattle Pub. Schs., 1945-46; fashion coordinator, dir. Denver Dry Goods Co., 1948-51; fashion model, Denver, 1951-58, 78—; fashion dir. Denver Market Week Assn., 1952-53; free-lance writer, Denver, 1958—; moderator TV program Your Preschool Child, Denver, 1955-56; instr. writing and communications U. Colo. Denver Ctr., 1970—, U. Calif., San Diego, 1976-78, Met. State Coll., 1985—; dir. pub. relations Fairmont Hotel, Denver, 1979-80; free lance fashion and TV model; author: The Complete Book of High Altitude Baking, 1961, Colorado a la Carte, 1963, Colorado a la Carte, Series II, 1966, (with Donna Hamilton) The High Altitude Cookbook, 1969, The Busy People's Cookbook, 1971 (Better Homes and Gardens Book Club selection 1971), Where to Eat in Colorado, 1967, Lunch Box Cookbook, 1965, Complete Book of High Altitude Baking, 1961, (under name Beverly Anderson) Single After 50, 1978, The New High Altitude Cookbook, 1980. Co-founder, pres. Jr. Symphony Guild, Denver, 1959-60; active Friends of Denver Libr., Opera Colo., Achievement Rewards for Coll. Scientists, Sante Fe Opera, Top Hand award Colo. Authors' League, 1969, 72, 79-82, 100 Best Best Books of Yr. award N.Y. Times, 1969, 71; named one of Colo.'s Women of Yr., Denver Post, 1964. Am. Soc. Journalists and Authors, Colo. Authors League (dir. 1969-79), Authors Guild, Authors League Am., Friends Denver Library, Rotary, Sigma Delta Chi, Kappa Alpha Theta. Address: 23 Polo Club Dr Denver CO 80209

NEMMERS, MARY JANE, information specialist; b. Cedar Rapids, Iowa, May 14, 1956; d. Bernard O. and Mary M. (Lockwood) N. BA, Bemidji State U., 1978; MLS, U. Ariz., 1983. Libr. technician Willmar (Minn.) State Hosp., 1978-81; libr. asst., info. specialist Sci. Applications Internat. Corp., Tucson, 1982—. Mem. Spl. Librs. Assn. (nominating com. Ariz. chpt. 1991-92, archivist Ariz. chpt. 1992-93). Democrat. Office: Sci Applications Internat Corp 5151 E Broadway Ste 900 Tucson AZ 85711

NEPPE, VERNON MICHAEL, neuropsychiatrist, author, educator; b. Johannesburg, Transvaal, Rep. South Africa, Apr. 16, 1951; came to U.S., 1986; s. Solly Louis and Molly (Hesselsohn) N.; m. Elisabeth Selima Schachter, May 29, 1977; children: Jonathan, Shari. BA, U. South Africa, 1976; MB, BCh, U. Witwatersrand, Johannesburg, 1973, D in Psychol. Medicine, 1976, M in Medicine, 1979, PhD in Medicine, 1981; MD, U.S., 1982. Diplomate Am. Bd. Psychiatry and Neurology, Am. Bd. Geriatric Psychiatry; registered psychiatry specialist U.S., Rep. South Africa, Can. Specialist in tng. dept. psychiatry U. Witwatersrand, Johannesburg, 1974-80; sr. cons. U. Witwatersrand Med. Sch., Johannesburg, 1980-82, 83-85; neuropsychiatry fellow Cornell U., N.Y.C., 1982-83; div. dir. U. Wash. Med. Sch., Seattle, 1986-92; dir. Pacific Neuropsychiat. Inst., Seattle, 1992—; mem. clin. faculty dept. psychiatry and behavioral scis. U. Wash. Med. Sch.; attending physician Northwest Hosp.; neuropsychiatry cons. South African Brain Rsch. Inst., Johannesburg, 1985—; chief rsch. cons. Epilepsy Inst., N.Y.C., 1989; mem. faculty lectr. Epilepsy: Refining Medical Treatment, 1993. Author: The Psychology of Deja Vu, 1983, Innovative Psychopharmacotherapy, 1990, (text) BROCAS SCAN, 1992; author (with others) 31 book chpts.; editor 14 jours. issues; contbr. articles to profl. jours. Recipient Rupert Sheldrake Prize for Rsch. Design (2d prize) award New Scientist, 1983, Marius Valkhoff medal South African Soc. for Psychical Rsch., 1982, George Elkin Bequest for Med. Rsch. U. Witwatersrand, 1980, Overseas Travelling fellow, 1982-83. Fellow Psychiatry Coll. South Africa (faculty), Royal Coll. Physicians of Can., North Pacific Soc. for Neurology, Neurosurgery and Psychiatry, Coll. Internat. Neuropharmacology, Parapsychologic Assn.; mem. Am. Psychiatric Assn. (U.S. transcultural collaborator diagnostic and statis. manual 1985-86, cons. organic brain disorders 1988—), Am. Epilepsy Soc., Soc. Biol. Psychiatry, Can. Psychiat. Assn., Soc. Sci. Exploration. Jewish. Office: Pacific Neuropsychiat Inst 10330 Meridian Ave N Ste 380 Seattle WA 98133

NERIO, MARK ANTHONY, human resources executive; b. San Antonio, Nov. 26, 1955; s. Reynaldo Lozano and Mary (Munoz) N.; m. Lou Ann Saucedo, July 7, 1979; children: Nicolas, Micah, Mark Adam. BA, So. Meth. U., 1978; EdM, Harvard U., 1979. Asst. to dir. Office of Econ. Devel., City of Dallas, 1979-81; employee rels. assoc. Frito Lay Inc., Dallas, 1981-82, compensation analyst, 1982-84, sr. compensation analyst, 1984-85; mgr. human resources Standard Meat Co. div. Sara Lee Corp., Ft. Worth, 1985-87; dir. compensation Meat group Sara Lee Corp., Memphis, 1988-91; v.p. Gallo Salame div. Sara Lee Corp., San Lorenzo, Calif., 1991—. Bd. dirs. United Meth. Gen. Bd. of Higher Edn. and Ministry, Nashville, 1984-92; trustee Southwestern U., Georgetown, Tex., 1987. Mem. Am. Compensation Assn., Soc. Human Resources Mgmt., No. Calif. Human Resources Coun., Bay Area Compensation Assn. Home: 13 Meadowlark Ct Danville CA 94526 Office: Gallo Salame Inc 2411 Baumann Ave San Lorenzo CA 94580

NEROD, SCHEREPAN ALEXANDER (STEVE NEROD), entrepreneur; b. Anchorage, June 15, 1952; s. Schezepan (Steve) and Eleanor (Maytak) Nierodzik. Student, U. Wash., 1970-72, U. Alaska, 1978-82, U. Calif., Berkeley, 1983-85. Owner Eldorado Placers, Eldorado Creek, Alaska, 1970-83, Nerod & Assocs. Apparel, San Francisco, Seattle, N.Y., 1971-82, Nerod Orthopedics, San Francisco and Seattle, 1982—, DoNots ATV, 1991—, RadGear Bicycles, 1992—; cons. OrthoTech, San Leandro, Calif., Orthopedic Systems, Hayward, Calif., Med. Device Engring., Hayward, Israel Med. Products Devel., Tel Aviv, 1991—. Patentee in field. Mem. Am. Acad. Cosmetic Surgery, Am. Soc. Plastic and Reconstructive Surgery, Am. Orthopedic and Prosthetic Assn., Am. Assn. Orthopaedic Medicine, Am. Acad. Orthopaedic Surgeons, Alaska Miners Assn.

NESBITT, PAUL EDWARD, historian, author, educator; b. Balt., Dec. 25, 1943; s. William Ervin and Margaret Caroline (Shaw) N.; m. Donna Jean Coppock, Aug. 15, 1966 (dec. 1972); children: Erik-Paul A., Janelle M., m. Pamela Jean Lichty, May 25, 1974 (div. 1983); m. Anita Louise Wood, Dec. 8, 1984 (div. 1989). AB, U. Wash., 1965; MA, Wash. State U., 1968, PhD (hon.), 1970; PhD, U. Calgary, 1972. Reader in Anthropology, U. Wash., 1965, grad. research-tchr. Wash. State U., 1966-68, instr., Tacoma Community Coll., Wash., 1968-69; grad. research-tchr. U. Calgary, Alta., Can., 1969-71; exec. Hudson's Bay Co., Calgary, 1971; prof. Western Oreg. U., Monmouth, 1971-74; state historian State of Calif., Sacramento, 1974—; dir. Am. Sch. of Interior Design, San Francisco, 1974, HBC Bow Fort Rsch., Morley, Atla., 1970-71; instr. Am. River Coll., Sacramento, 1980-86; exec. mgr. Calif. State Govt. United Way Campaign, 1986, 87, also bd. dirs., mem. fiscal and communication coms., El Dorado County and Sacramento chpts., 1988—; designer, cultural rsch. cons. pvt. contracts western states, 1960—; exec. dir. Heritage Areas Assn., 1993—. Contbr. articles to prof. jours. Fellow Am. Anthrop. Assn.; mem. Calif. Hist. Soc., Am. Inst. of Interior Designers (profl. 1974-77, bd. dirs. energy planning and devel. cos.), AIA (Cen. Valley chpt. 1975-77). Office: PO Box 942896 Sacramento CA 94296-0001

NESHEIM, ROBERT OLAF, food products executive; b. Monroe Center, Ill., Sept. 13, 1921; s. Olaf M. and Sena M. (Willms) N.; m. Emogene P. Sullivan, July 13, 1946 (div.); children: Barbara Mowry, Susan Yost, Sandra Rankin; m. 2d, Doris Howes Calloway, July 4, 1981. BS, U. Ill., 1943, MS, 1950, PhD, 1951; postgrad. in advanced mgmt. program, Harvard U., 1971. Farm mgr. Halderman Farm Mgmt. Svc., Wabash, Ind., 1946-48; instr. U. Ill., 1951; mgr. feed rsch. The Quaker Oats Co., Barrington, Ill., 1952-64; prof., head of dept. animal sci. U. Ill., 1964-67; dir. nutrition rsch. The Quaker Oats Co., Barrington, Ill., 1967-69, v.p. R & D, 1969-78; v.p. sci. & tech. The Quaker Oats Co., Chgo., 1978-83; sr. v.p. sci. & tech. Avadyne, Inc., Monterey, Calif., 1983-85; pres. Advanced Healthcare, Monterey, 1985-91; ret., 1991. Capt. U.S. Army, 1943-46, South Pacific. Fellow Am. Inst. Nutrition (treas. 1983-86), AAAS; mem. Inst. Food Technologists, Fed. Socs. Exptl. Biologists (treas. 1973-79), APHA, Corral de Tierra Club (Salinas, Calif.).

NESS, RANDALL HANS, data processing consultant; b. Seattle, May 10, 1957; s. Harold Lawrence and Alice Bertina (Tangen) N. BA, U. Wash., 1980, BBA, 1980, MBA, 1985. Cert. data processor, computer programmer, systems profl. Computer system devel. asst. Great Republic Life Ins., Seattle, 1980-82; prin. Randall H. Ness, Bus. Systems Cons., Seattle, 1982-85; cons. Price Waterhouse, Seattle, 1985-87, sr. cons., 1987-90, mgr., 1990—. Mem. Data Processing Mgmt. Assn. (sec. Puget Sound chpt. 1986). Presbyterian. Home: 2510 W Bertona St # 432 Seattle WA 98199 Office: Price Waterhouse 1001 4th Ave # 4200 Seattle WA 98154

NESSELHAUF, LOIS LUCILLE, arena director; b. Dexter, Iowa, Jan. 10, 1938; d. Earl Lavern and Grace Lucille (Percy) Hill; m. Walter Eugene Oliver Nesselhauf, Oct. 26, 1958; children: Cynthia Nesselhauf Somerville, Edward Eugene. Grad. high sch., Colorado Springs, Colo. Stenographer Hdqrs. N.Am. Air Defense Command, Colorado Springs, 1956-60; corp. v.p., sec. E-Z Living Homes, Inc., Colorado Springs, 1971-82; dir. Broadmoor World Arena, Colorado Springs, 1982—; producer Broadmoor Ice Revue, 1982—, Christmas Pops on Ice, 1982—, ice shows for various convs., 1982—; coord. major concerts & spl. events Broadmoor World Arena, 1982—. Mem. NAFE, U.S. Figure Skating Assn. (trophy and medal chmn. 1976-79), Colo. Amateur Sports Corp., Ice Skating Inst. Am., Rocky Mountain Rink Mgrs. Assn., Broadmoor Skating Club, Zonta (Zontian of the Yr. Colorado Springs chpt. 1986, 90, bd. dirs. 1988-90), Colo. C. of C. Office: Broadmoor World Arena 125 El Pomar Rd Colorado Springs CO 80906-4252

NESTY, GLENN ALBERT, manufacturing executive; b. Muncie, Ind., Dec. 23, 1911; s. William Harry and Esther (Peakman) N.; m. Iona Martha Brooks, July 3, 1936; children: Philip, Gregory. BA, DePauw U., 1934; PhD, U. Ill., 1937. Rsch. chemist Allied Chem. Corp., N.Y.C., 1937-42, group leader, 1942-44; asst. dir. cen. rsch. Allied Chem. Corp., Morristown, N.J., 1944-46, assoc. dir. cen. rsch., 1946-55; v.p. R & D Allied Chem. Corp., N.Y.C., 1955-68, bd. dirs., 1957-68; v.p. R & D Internat. Paper Co., N.Y.C., 1968-76, ret., 1976; cons. Internat. Paper Co., N.Y.C., 1976—; bd. dirs. Toth Aluminum Corp., Vacherie, La. Patentee in field. Mem. NSF Study of Industry, Govt. and Univs., Republic of China, 1968; chmn. Dirs. of Indsl. Rsch., 1968, Textile Rsch. Inst., 1964; chmn. rsch. and adv. com. Inst. Paper Chemistry, 1972. DePauw U. scholar, 1930-34; Chem. Found. fellow U. Ill., 1937. Fellow N.Y. Acad. Scis.; mem. AAAS, TAPPI, Am. Chem. Soc. Republican. Methodist. Home: 880 Morningside Dr Apt M226 Fullerton CA 92635

NETTING, ROBERT M., anthropology educator; b. Racine, Wis., Oct. 14, 1934. BA in English summa cum laude, Yale U., 1957; MA in Anthropology, U. Chgo., 1959, PhD in Anthropology, 1963. Lectr. U. Chgo., 1963; from asst. prof. to assoc. prof. U. Pa., 1963-72; prof. anthropology U. Ariz., Tucson, 1972—, Regents' prof. anthropology, 1991—; field researcher Ft. Berthold Reservation, N.D., 1958, Jos Plateau, Northern Nigeria, 1960-62, 66-67, 84, Törbel, Valais, Switzerland, 1970-71, 77, Senegal, Ivory Coast, 1977, Portugal, 1982; cons. AID project Stanford U., USDA, USAID Agrl. Devel. Program.; mem. adv. coun. Wenner-Gren Found. Anthropological Rsch., 1982-86, search com. new dir. rsch., 1985-86; mem. com. human dimensions global change commn. behavioral and social scis. and edn. Nat. Rsch. Coun., 1989-91; pres. Internat. Assn. Study Common Property, 1991-92. Author: Documentary History of the Fox Project, 1948-59, 1960, Hill Farmers of Nigeria; Cultural Ecology of the Kofyar of the Jos Plateau, 1968, Cultural Ecology, 1977, 2d edit., 1986, Balancing on an Alp: Ecological Change and Continuity in a Swiss Mountain Community, 1981, Smallholders, Householders: Farm Families and the Ecology of Intensive Sustainable Agriculture, 1993; editorial com. Annual Rev. Anthropology, 1976-81; bd. editors Ethnohistory, 1983-88; editor Ariz. Studies in Human Ecology, 1984—; contbr. numerous articles to profl. jours. Recipient Robert F. Heizer prize best jour. article ethnohistory Am. Soc. Ethnohistory, 1987; Ctr. Advanced Study Behavioral Scis. fellow, 1986-87, Guggenheim fellow, 1970-71, NSF grantee, 1984-87, 77-78, 71, 58-60, Nat. Inst. Child Health and Human Devel. Ctr. Population Rsch. grantee, 1974-76, Social Sci. Rsch. Coun. grantee, 1966-67, Ford Found. Fgn. Area Studies fellow, 1960-62, Woodrow Wilson fellow, 1957-58. Mem. NAS, Am. Ethnological Soc. (councillor 1976-79), Phi Beta Kappa. Office: Regents Professor Anthropology Haury Bldg Univ of Arizona Tucson AZ 85721

NETTLES, NORA LEE, human resources administrator; b. Kansas City, Kans., Aug. 16, 1955; d. Ernest Sr. and Frances (McQuaid) Voiles. BS in Bus. Adminstrn., Nat. Coll., Denver, 1983; MSS in Applied Communications, U. Denver, 1992. Office mgr. U.S. Army, Anchorage, 1976-79; lease adminstrn. K-N Energy Co., Lakewood, Colo., 1980-83; paralegal Welborn, Dufford, Brown Law Firm, Denver, 1982-84; sec. Colo. N.G., Englewood, 1984-85, staffing specialist, 1985-86, EEO mgr., 1986-88, human resources mgr., 1988—; instr. Nat. Coll., 1992. Mem. U.S. N.G. Assn. Home: 611 Cantril St Castle Rock CO 80104

NETZEL, PAUL ARTHUR, fundraising management executive, consultant; b. Tacoma, Sept. 11, 1941; s. Marden Arthur and Audrey Rose (Jones) N.; BS in Group Work Edn., George Williams Coll., 1963; m. Diane Viscount, Mar. 21, 1963; children: Paul M., Shari Ann. Program dir. S. Pasadena-San Marino (Calif.) YMCA, 1963-66; exec. dir. camp and youth programs Wenatchee (Wash.) YMCA, 1966-67; exec. dir. Culver-Palms Family YMCA, Culver City, Calif., 1967-73; v.p. met. fin. devel. YMCA Met. Los Angeles, 1973-78, exec. v.p. devel., 1979-85; pres. bd. dirs. YMCA Employees Credit Union, 1977-80; chmn. N.Am. Fellowship of YMCA Devel. Officers, 1980-83; adj. faculty U. So. Calif. Coll. Continuing Edn., 1983-86, Loyola Marymount U., L.A., 1986-90, Calif. State U., L.A., 1991—, UCLA Extension, 1991—; chmn., chief exec. officer Netzel Assocs., Inc., 1985—; pvt. practice cons., fund raiser. Chmn. Culver-Palms YMCA, Culver City, 1991-93, vice chmn. 1989-91, bd. mgrs. 1985—; pres. bd. Culver City Guidance Clinic, 1971-74; mem. Culver City Bd. Edn., 1975-79, pres., 1977-78; mem. Culver City Edn. Found., 1982—; bd. dirs. Los Angeles Psychiat. Svc., 1971-74, Goodwill Industries of So. Calif., 1993—; mem. Culver City Council, 1980-88, vice-mayor, 1980-82, 84-85, mayor, 1982-83, 86-87; mem. Culver City Redevel. Agy., 1980-88, chmn., 1983-84, 87-88, vice chmn, 1985-86; bd. dirs. Los Angeles County Sanitation Dists., 1982-83, 85-87, Western Region United Way, 1986-93, vice chmn, 1991-92; chmn. bd. dirs. Calif. Youth Model Legislature, 1987-92; mem. World Affairs Coun., 1989—, Town Hall of L.A., 1991—. Recipient Man of Yr. award Culver City C. of C., 1972. Mem. Nat. Soc. Fund Raising Execs. (nat. bd. dirs. 1989-91, v.p. bd. dirs. Greater L.A. chpt. 1986-88, pres. bd. dirs. 1989-90, Profl. of Yr. 1983), L.A. Athletic, Rotary (L.A. # 5, pres. 1992-93), Mountain Gate Country. Address: Netzel Assocs Inc 9696 Culver Blvd Ste 204 Culver City CA 90232

NETZKY-JOLLY, WENDY HEATHER, director, small business owner; b. Chgo., Feb. 14, 1955; d. Lester and Shirley Ruth (Gorcey) N.; married. BA in Psychology, U. Ariz., 1977, MA in Counseling and Guidance, 1979; cert. in family counseling procedures, ICASSI Inst., 1979. Instr., counselor Devry Inst. Tech., Phoenix, 1984-86; dir., owner Tom Thumb Player's Acting Sch., Tucson, 1986-88; program dir. Arthritis Found., Phoenix, 1988-89; dir., owner Creative Expression Acting Sch., Scottsdale, Ariz., 1989—; pvt. practice counseling, Ariz., 1986-89. Writer, prodr., dir. play "A Child's Dream"; prodr., co-dir., co-writer (video documentary) Creative Expression Acting School; contbr. articles to profl. jours. Mem. Windstar Found., Scottsdale, Ariz., 1989—; co-founder, chmn. Counseling and Guidance Rsch. Fund for Humanitarian Purposes, U. Ariz., Tucson, 1979. Mem. Friends of Jung, Phi Beta Kappa, Phi Kappa Phi, Psi Chi.

NEU, CARL HERBERT, JR., management consultant; b. Miami Beach, Fla., Sept. 4, 1937; s. Carl Herbert and Catherine Mary (Miller) N.; BS, MIT, 1959; MBA, Harvard U., 1961; m. Carmen Mercedes Smith, Feb. 8, 1964; children—Carl Bartley, David Conrad. Cert. profl. mgmt. cons. Indsl. liaison officer MIT, Cambridge, 1967-69; coord. forward planning Gates Rubber Co., Denver, 1969-71; pres., co-founder Dyna-Com Resources, Lakewood, Colo., 1971-77; pres., founder Neu & Co., Lakewood, 1977—; mng. dir. Pro-Med Mgmt. Systems, Lakewood, 1981—; lectr. Grad. Sch. Pub. Affairs, U. Colo. Denver, 1982-84. Mem. exec. coun. Episcopal Diocese Colo., 1974; mem. Lakewood City Coun., 1975-80, pres., 1976; chmn. Lakewood City Charter Commn., 1982, Lakewood Civic Found., Inc., 1986—; pres. Lakewood on Parade, 1978, bd. dirs., 1978-80; pres. Classic Chorale, Denver, 1979, bd. dirs., 1978-83; pres. Lakewood Pub. Bldg. Authority, 1983-93, v.p., 1993—; mem. Metro State Coll. of Denver Found., 1990—, Kaiser Permanente Health Adv. Com., 1990—. With U.S. Army, 1961-67. Decorated Bronze Star medal, Army Commendation medal; recipient Arthur Page award AT&T, 1979; Kettering Found. grantee, 1979-80. Mem. World Future Soc., Internat. City Mgrs. Assn., Lakewood-So. Jefferson County C. of C. (bd. dirs. 1983-89, chmn. 1988, chmn. 1987-88), Jefferson County C. of C. (chmn. 1988). Republican. Episcopalian. Contbr. articles to profl. jours. Home: 8169 W Baker Ave Denver CO 80227-3129

NEUBAUER, MARK ALAN, lawyer; b. Milw., Oct. 28, 1950; s. Edward Daniel and Helene (Levy) N.; m. Diane Rittenberg, Sept. 9, 1979; children: Elisabeth, Jennifer, Alison, Rebecca, Kathryn. B in Journalism, Northwestern U., 1972, M in Journalism, 1973; JD, UCLA, 1976. Bar: Calif. 1977, D.C. 1981. Reporter Knight Ridder Newspapers, Washington, 1975; teaching asst. U. Calif., L.A., 1975-76; reporter Miami (Fla.) Herald, 1976-77; lawyer Buchalter, Nemer, Fields, Chrystie & Younger, L.A., 1977-80; shareholder Stern, Neubauer, Greenwald & Pauly, Santa Monica, Calif., 1980—; adj. lectr. media law Calif. State U., Dominquez Hills, 1979-83; lectr. media law U. Calif. Sch. Mgmt. Extension, L.A., 1983. Contbr. articles to profl. jours. Mem. ABA (assoc. editor Litigation Jour. 1982—), L.A. County Bar Assn., State Bar of Calif. (chmn. litigation sect. 1989-90, vice-chmn. 1988-89, treas. 1987-88, exec. com. mem. 1986-90, adv. 1990—), D.C. Bar, Assn. Bus. Trial Lawyers (pres. 1991-92, v.p. 1990-91, sec. 1989-90, treas. 1988-89, bd. govs. 1985-88, editor Assn. Bus. Trial Lawyers Report 1983-89). Democrat. Jewish. Home: 789 Westholme Ave Los Angeles CA 90024 Office: Stern Neubauer Greenwald & Pauly 1299 Ocean Ave 10th Fl Santa Monica CA 90401

NEUBAUER, MICHAEL GERALD, molecular biologist; b. Santa Monica, Calif., Apr. 25, 1954; s. Hubert Gerald and Barbara Jane (Gazin) N.; m. Donna Gayle Myers, June 22, 1974 (div. Jan. 1988); children: Michelle, Beverly. BA, U. Calif., San Diego, 1977; PhC, U. Wash., 1982. Rsch. assoc. U. Wash., Seattle, 1977-78, 80-84; real estate agent Century 21, Seattle, 1978-80; real estate broker Windemere Real Estate, Seattle, 1985-88; rsch. scientist Bristol-Myers Squibb Phar. Rsch. Inst., Seattle, 1988—. Inventor Beta TGF induced genes; contbr. articles to profl. jours. NIH grantee, 1981-84. Office: Oncogen 3005 First Ave Seattle WA 98121

NEUGEBAUER, GERRY, astrophysicist; b. Gottingen, Germany, Sept. 3, 1932; came to U.S., 1939; s. Otto E. and Grete (Brück) N.; m. Marcia MacDonald, Aug. 26, 1956; children: Carol, Lee. B.S., Cornell U., 1954; Ph.D., Calif. Inst. Tech., 1960. Mem. faculty Calif. Inst. Tech., Pasadena, 1962—, prof. physics, 1970—, Howard Hughes Prof. Physics, 1985—, chmn. divsn. physics, math and astronomy, 1988-93; mem. staff Hale Obs., 1970-80; acting dir. Palomar Obs., 1980-81, dir., 1981—. Served with AUS, 1961-63. Fellow Am. Acad. Arts and Scis.; mem. NAS, Am. Philos. Soc. Office: 320-47 Pasadena CA 91125

NEUHARTH, DANIEL J., II, psychotherapist; b. Sioux Falls, S.D., Nov. 10, 1953; s. Allen Harold and Loretta Faye (Helgeland) N. BA, Duke U., 1975; MS in Journalism, Northwestern U., 1978; MA, John F. Kennedy U., 1988; PhD in Clin. Psychology, Calif. Sch. Profl. Psychology, 1992. Lic. marriage, family and child counselor. Reporter USA Today, Washington, 1982-83; lectr. San Diego State U., 1983-84; talk show host KSDO-TV, San Diego, 1983-84; pres. Dialogues, San Francisco, 1987—; psychotherapist pvt. practice, San Francisco, 1992—; vis. prof. U. Fla., Gainesville, 1980-81, U. Hawaii, Honolulu, 1981-82; adj. faculty U. San Francisco, 1989—. Host, producer radio talk show Saturday Night People, 1984; contbg. author: Confessions of an S.O.B., 1989. Office: Dialogues PO box 1022 Fairfax CA 94978

NEUHAUS, CABLE, journalist, magazine editor; b. Munich, Oct. 5, 1947; came to U.S., 1949; s. Norman Sol and Ruth (Schreiber) N.; m. Carol A. Rosner, Oct. 11, 1983; 1 stepchild, Steven. BS in Journalism, Ohio U., 1969; MA in Journalism, Pa. State U., 1970; postgrad., Carnegie Mellon U., 1977-79. Contbg. editor various regional and nat. publs., 1969-83, reporter, editor, 1969-71; instr. journalism Pa. State U., Wilkes-Barre, Pa., 1971-77; corr. People mag. Time Warner Inc., 1977-80; bur. chief People mag. Time Inc., Pitts., 1980-83, Boston, 1983-88; founding editor TV Entertainment mag. The Crosby Vandenburgh Group, Boston, 1988-90; editorial dir. The Crosby Vandenburgh Group, Boston, 1989-90; bur. chief Entertainment Weekly mag. Time Warner Inc., L.A., 1990—. Editor: A Lively Connection: Intimate Encounters with the Ethical Movement in America, 1978; contbr. numerous nonfiction articles to popular publs. including The Washington Post, Harper's Weekly, The Pittsburgher; contbr. articles to acad. jours.; writer nonfiction basis for TV movie Scorned and Swindled, Phoenix Entertainment, CBS, 1984. Recipient Golden Quill award Pitts. Press Club, 1980.

NEUMAN, B. CLIFFORD, computer scientist; b. N.Y.C., Sept. 27, 1963; s. Peter H-X. Neuman and Barbara Diane (Allen) Gordon. BS, MIT, 1985; MS, U. Wash., 1988, PhD, 1992. With MIT Project Athena, Cambridge, Mass., 1985-86; rsch. assoc. U. Wash., Seattle, 1987-91; scientist U. So. Calif. Info. Scis. Inst., Marina Del Rey, 1991—; rsch. asst. prof. U. So. Calif., L.A., 1992—; participant Internet Rsch. Task Force, 1991—, Internet Engring. Task Force, 1991—. Co-designer Kerberos computer security system; designer Prospero distributed computer system; contbr. articles to profl. jours. Mem. King County (Wash.) Search and Rescue, 1987-91. Mem. IEEE, Assn. for Computing Machinery, Internet Soc., Usenix Assn., Am. Radio Relay League, Aircraft Owners and Pilots Assn. Office: U So Calif Info Scis Inst 4676 Admiralty Way Marina Del Rey CA 90292

NEUMANN, CHARLES AUGUST, regional drainage engineer; b. Walla Walla, Wash., Apr. 10, 1935; s. Elmer Henry Neumann and Thelma Viola (Ostrom) Burgess; m. Mary Martha Havens, June 4, 1960; children: Mary, Bob, Alan, Kelly, Chris, Thomas, Martha. BS in Agrl. Engring., Wash. State U., Pullman, 1957. Tool engr. Boeing Airplane Co., Seattle, 1957-58; hydraulic engr. Bur. of Reclamation, Ephrata, Wash., 1958-59, 60-70, Warden, Wash., 1959-60; chief drainage design br. Bur. of Reclamation, Othello, Wash., 1970-77, 85-87; chief drainage design br. Bur. of Reclamation, Ephrata, 1977-85, regional drainage engr., 1987—. Contbr. articles to profl. jours. Lt. U.S. Army, 1958. Mem. Am. Soc. Agrl. Engrs. (chmn. drainage of irrigated lands com. 1985-88), Res. Officers Assn. (chpt. sec. 1976—). Free Methodist. Home: 952 S Juniper Dr Moses Lake WA 98837 Office: Bur of Reclamation 32 C St NW Ephrata WA 98823

NEUMANN, H. DENIS, machinery and equipment appraiser; b. Kansas City, Mo., Aug. 5, 1938; s. Harold E. and Inez Marie (Johnson) N.; m. Patricia Ann Mueting, Aug. 28, 1975. BA, Baker U., 1961. Copywriter Stowe Hardware & Supply, Kansas City, Mo., 1961-63; acct. U.S. Epperson Underwriting, Kansas City, Mo., 1963-67; sr. appraiser Gen. Appraiser Co., San Francisco, 1967-72, American Appraisal Co., Oakland, Calif., 1974-79; appraiser mgr. Lumberman's Underwriting, Portland, Oreg., 1972-74; pres. Valuation Assocs., San Mateo, Calif., 1979—; pres. Planned Community Cons., San Mateo, 1984-89; ptnr. Auction Data Bank, San Mateo, 1988-91; affiliate Asset Mgmt. Assocs., Martinez, Calif., 1987—, ACI, Inc., Denver, 1984—. Author poetry; editor: The M&E Appraiser, 1983-86; contbr. articles to profl. jours. Mem. Am. Soc. Appraisers (sr. mem., chpt. pres. 1983-84), Am. Arbitration Assn., Internat. Right of Way Assn. (assoc.), Oakland Yacht Club, Rotary Internat. Democrat. Office: Valuation Assocs 2020 Pioneer Ct Ste 6 San Mateo CA 94403

NEUMANN, HERMAN ERNEST, elementary and special education educator; b. Winona, Minn., Nov. 11, 1931; s. Herman Ferdinand and Dena Matilda (Peterson) N.; m. Juanita Evelyn, Sept. 11, 1954; children: Mary Evelyn, Herman Ernest Jr., Martin Andrew, Amy Louise. BS, Winona State U., 1961; MA, Calif. State U., Bakersfield, 1976; postgrad., San Jose U., 1977, Calif. State U., San Barbara, 1978. Cert. early childhood, spl. edn., elem. edn., ESL instr. Classroom tchr. grades K-6, resource specialist Bakersfield (Calif.) City Schs.; classroom tchr. Kern County, Bakersfield; resource specialist Bakersfield (Calif.) City Schs. Contbr. articles to profl. jours. 1st class airman USAF, 1952-56. NSF fellow, 1966, Internat. Biog. Assn. fellow, Cambridge, Eng., 1993; named to Hall of Fame Teaching Excellence Kern County, 1990, Tchr. of Yr., 1990. Mem. NEA (grantee 1969), Bakersfield Elem. Tchrs. Assn., ASCD, Calif. Tchrs. Assn. Home: 5219 Cedarbrook Ln Bakersfield CA 93313-2719

NEUMANN, HERSCHEL, physics educator; b. San Bernardino, Calif., Feb. 3, 1930; s. Arthur and Dorothy (Greenhood) N.; m. Julia Black, June 15, 1951; 1 child, Keith. BA, U. Calif., Berkeley, 1951; MS, U. Oreg., 1959; PhD, U. Nebr., 1965. Theoretical physicist Gen. Electric Co., Richland, Wash., 1951-57; instr. physics U. Nebr., Lincoln, 1964-65; asst. prof. physics U. Denver, 1965-71, assoc. prof. physics, 1971-85, prof., chmn. physics, 1985—; dir. numerous pub. outreach programs in physics. Contbr. over 20 articles to profl. jours. Dir. numerous pub. outreach programs in physics. Mem. Am. Phys. Soc., Am. Assn. Physics Tchrs. Home: 2425 S St Paul St Denver CO 80210-5516 Office: U Denver Dept Physics Denver CO 80208-0202

NEUMANN, NANCY RUTH, studio educator; b. L.A., Feb. 1, 1948; d. Robert Thomas and Frances Andersen; m. Bernd Fritz Dietmar Neumann, June 26, 1971; children: Peter, Christina, Linda, Christoph, Karin. BA, U. Calif., Riverside, 1969; MA, Sorbonne U., Paris, 1971; credentials, Calif. State U., San Bernardino, 1985. Cert. community coll. tchr., various subjects, Calif., studio tchr., Calif. Missionary, reading instr. Maroua, Cameroon, Africa, 1971-73; instr. Pasadena (Calif.) City Coll., 1974-75; secondary tchr. Riverside (Calif.) Christian Sch., 1985-86; studio tchr. Vista Films, Culver City, 1986, Hollywood (Calif.) Studios, 1986-88, Paramount Studios, Hollywood, Calif., 1986-93, MGM - Lorimar Prodns., Culver City, Calif., 1986-90, Universal Studios, Universal City, Calif., 1986-90, R.J. Louis Prodns., Burbank, Calif., 1987, Michael Landon Prodns., Culver City, 1987-88, Carsey-Werner Prodns., L.A., 1988; instr. Riverside Community Coll., 1988; studio tchr. Bob Booker Prodns., Hollywood, 1988-90, Walt Disney Prodns., Burbank, 1992—; exec. producer Am. Pictures, Riverside, 1989—; studio tchr. NBC Prodns., Burbank, 1990; pvt. tutor, Riverside, L.A., 1987—; drama coach Grace Ch., Riverside, 1981-82, Magnolia Ave. Bapt. Ch., Riverside, 1986-89; studio tchr. with NBC, 1991, for Paramount, 1991-92. Author: several plays, 1981-89; writer 70 songs, 1968—. Coach mock trial Riverside Christian High Sch., 1985-86; choir dir. Riverside Christian Sch., 1985-86; Sunday sch. tchr. Grace Bapt. Ch., Harvest Christian Fellowship, Riverside, Vineyard Christian Fellowship, Riverside, 1992, Magnolia Ave. Bapt. Ch., 1968-92, Wheat, Oil and Wine Christian Fellowship, Riverside, Sunday sch. supt.; children's choir dir. Grace Bapt. Ch., 1981-892. Mem. Nat. Assn. Christian Educators, Internat. Alliance of Theatre and Stage Employees, Internat. Platform Assn., Greater L.A. World Trade Ctr. Assn., Sons of Norway (study scholar 1967), Delta Phi Alpha. Republican. Home: 1787 Prince Albert Dr Riverside CA 92507-5852 Office: Walt Disney Studios 500 S Buena Vista Burbank CA 91521

NEUMANN, PETER GABRIEL, computer scientist; b. N.Y.C., Sept. 21, 1932; s. J.B. and Elsa (Schmid) N.; 1 child, Helen K. AB, Harvard U., 1954, SM, 1955; Dr rerum naturarum, Technisch Hochschule, Darmstadt, Fed. Republic Germany, 1960; PhD, Harvard U., 1961. Mem. tech. staff Bell Labs, Murray Hill, N.J., 1960-70; Mackay lectr. Stanford U., 1964, U. Calif., Berkeley, 1970-71; computer scientist SRI Internat., Menlo Park, Calif., 1971—. Contbr. articles to profl. jours. and chpts. to books. Fulbright fellow, 1958-60. Fellow IEEE; mem. AAAS (mem.-at-large sect. com. on info., computing and communications 1991—), Assn. for Computing Machinery (editor jour. 1976—, chmn. com. on computers and pub. policy 1985—). Office: SRI Internat EL-243 333 Ravenswood Ave Menlo Park CA 94025-3493

NEUMANN, RENÉE ANNE, marketing professional; b. Bklyn., Aug. 12, 1951; d. Charles René and Margaret M. (Hoehn) Schmidt. Student, Wagner Coll., 1969-72, Richmond Coll., 1973. Asst. to dir. pub. rels. Nat. Assn. Ins. Agts., N.Y.C., 1972-73; asst. editor S.I. (N.Y.) Register, 1973-74; advt. sales rep. The Staten Islander, 1974-76; outside sales rep. Aamco Transmissions, N.Y., Calif., 1976-81; account exec. UARCO, San Diego, 1982-83; computer sales and mktg. profl. Micro Age of La Jolla (formerly P.C. Specialists), La Mesa, Calif., 1984; self employed, mktg. specialist, automotive aftermarket svcs. San Diego, 1985—; active Women Synergy, 1981-83, Nat. Assn. Profl. Saleswomen, 1983-85, NAFE, 1984-86, San Diego Career Women, 1989-90. Contbr. poetry to lit. mag., columns and articles to gen. interest publs. Winner ann. nationwide pub. rels. contest Gibraltar Transmissions, 1987. Mem. NOW, Am. Humanist Assn., Sierra Club, Mensa (bd. dirs., chair pub. rels. San Diego chpt. 1982-83). Democrat. Buddhist/Wiccan. Office: Apt 1331 15949 Avenida Venusto San Diego CA 92128

NEUMEYER, PETER FLORIAN, English language educator; b. Munich, Aug. 4, 1929; s. Alfred and Eva Maria (Kirchheim) N.; m. Helen Snell, Dec. 28, 1952; children: Zachary, Christopher, Daniel. BA, U. Calif., Berkeley, 1951, MA, 1955, PhD, 1963. Asst. prof. English and edn. Harvard U., Cambridge, Mass., 1963-69; assoc. prof. English SUNY, Stony Brook, 1969-75; prof., chmn. dept. English West Va. U., Morgantown, 1975-78; prof. English San Diego State U., 1978—; disting. vis. prof. English, Chico State U., Calif., 1982; vis. Nat. Endowment for Humanities fellow, Princeton U., 1984. Author: (children's books) Why We Have Day and Night, 1970, The Faithful Fish, 1971, Phantom of the Opera, 1988; (poetry) Homage to John Clare, 1980. Recipient Internat. Youth Libr. stipend, 1985; SUNY Rsch. Found. grantee, 1970, 74, Swedish Bicentennial grantee, 1992; NEH Vis. fellow, 1984. Home: 7968 Windsor Dr La Mesa CA 91941-7808 Office: San Diego State U Dept English San Diego CA 92182

NEURATH, HANS, biochemist, educator; b. Vienna, Austria, Oct. 29, 1909; came to U.S., 1935; s. Rudolf and Hedda (Samek) N.; m. Hilde Bial, June, 1935 (div. 1960); 1 child, Peter Francis; m. Susi Ruth Spitzer, Oct. 11, 1960. PhD, U. Vienna, Austria, 1933; DSc (hon.), U. Geneva, Switzerland, 1970, U. Tokushima, Japan, 1977, Med. Coll. Ohio, 1989, U. Montpellier, France, 1989, Kyoto U., Japan, 1990. George Fisher Baker fellow Cornell U., Ithaca, N.Y., 1936-38; prof. biochemistry Duke U., Durham, N.C., 1938-50; prof. biochemistry U. Wash., Seattle, 1950—, chmn. dept. biochemistry, 1950-75, prof. emeritus biochemistry, 1980—; sci. dir. Fred Hutchinson Cancer Rsch. Inst., Seattle, 1976-80; dir. German Cancer Research Ctr., Heidelberg, Fed. Republic Germany, 1980-81; hon. prof. U. Heidelberg, 1980—; fgn. sci. mem. Max Planck Inst. for Exptl. Medicine, Goettingen, Fed. Republic Germany, 1982—; cons. Battelle Meml. Inst., Columbus, 1970-75. Editor: (compendium) The Proteins (3 edits.), 1953-79; editor Biochemistry Jour., 1962-91, Protein Sci., 1991—; contbr. numerous articles to sci. publs. Advisor NIH, Bethesda, Md., 1954-70; mem. med. adv. bd. Howard Hughes Med. Inst., Miami, Fla., 1969-79, Virginia Mason Rsch. Ctr., Seattle, 1982—. Guggenheim fellow, 1955; named hon. mem. Japanese Biochem. Soc., 1977; recipient Disting. Alumnus award Duke U. Med. Sch., 1970, Stein and Moore award Protein Soc., 1989. Fellow AAAS; mem. NAS (nat. bd. grad. edn. 1971-75). Home: 5752-60th NE Seattle WA 98105 Office: U Wash Dept Biochemistry Seattle WA 98195

NEUTS, MARCEL FERNAND, statistician, educator; b. Ostend, Belgium, Feb. 21, 1935; came to U.S., 1958; s. Achille Jan and Marceline (Neuts) N.; m. Olga Alida Topff, June 27, 1959; children: Chris, Myriam, Catherine, Debbie. Lic. in math., U. Louvain, Belgium, 1956; MS in Stats., Stanford U., 1959, PhD in Stats., 1961. Instr. Lovanium U., Leopoldville, Zaire, 1956-57; researcher U. Louvain, 1960-62; asst. prof. Purdue U., 1962-64, assoc. prof., 1964-68, prof., 1968-76; vis. prof. Cornell U., 1968-69; Unidel prof. U. Del., 1976-85; prof. systems and indsl. engring. U. Ariz., Tucson, 1985—; lectr. math. scis. Johns Hopkins U., Balt., 1979. Author: Probability, 1973, Matrix-Geometric Solutions in Stochastic Models - An Algorithmic Approach, 1981, Structured Stochastic Matrices of M/G/1 Type and Their Applications, 1989; editor: Algorithmic Methods in Probability, 1977; contbr. articles to profl. jours.; coord. editor Jour. Applied Probability and Advances Applied Probability, 1982—; editor in chief, founding editor: Stochastic Models, 1983—. Fellow Commn. Relief Belgium, 1958-60. Recipient Sr. U.S. Scientist award Alexander von Humboldt Found., Fed. Republic of Germany, 1983; Rsch. fellow Ctr. Advanced Study U. Del., 1980-81. Fellow Inst. Math. Stats; mem. Math. Assn. Am. (Lester R. Ford award 1969), Ops. Rsch. Soc. Am. (Rsch. Excellence prize computer sci. tech. sect. 1989), Ops. Rsch. Soc. Israel, Am. Statis. Assn., Internat. Statis. Inst., Bernoulli Soc., Alumnus Assn. Fondation Universitaire Belgium, Alumnus Assn. Founds Nat. Recherche Scientifique Belgium, Sigma XI. Home: 925 N Smoketree Cir Tucson AZ 85745-9666 Office: U Ariz Dept Systems & Indsl Engring Tucson AZ 85721

NEVIN, CROCKER, investment banker; b. Tulsa, Mar. 14, 1923; s. Ethelbert Paul and Jennie Crocker (Fassett) N.; m. Mary Elizabeth Sherwin, Apr. 24, 1952 (div. 1984); children: Anne, Paul, Elizabeth, Crocker; m. Marilyn Elizabeth English, Nov. 3, 1984; 1 child, Jennie Fassett. Grad. with high honors, St. Paul's Sch., 1942; A.B. with high honors, Princeton U., 1946. With Vick Chem. Co., 1949-50, John Roberts Powers Cosmetic Co., 1950-52; with Marine Midland Grace Trust Co. of N.Y., 1952—, exec. v.p., 1964-66, pres., 1966-70, chmn. bd., chief exec. officer, 1968-73; also dir.; vice chmn. bd. Evans Products Co., N.Y.C., 1974-76, Drexel Burnam Lambert Co., investment bankers, N.Y.C., 1976-88; chmn. bd., chief exec. officer CF & I Steel Corp., Pueblo, Colo., 1985—; dir. Medco Containment Services Inc., Magnatck, Inc., BOC Group PLC; bd. govs. U.S. Postal Svc. Chmn. exec. com. ACCION Internat. Lt. (j.g.) AC USN, 1942-46. Clubs: Links (N.Y.C.), N.Y. Yacht (N.Y.C.); Blind Brook. Home: 218 Anderson Hill Rd Purchase NY 10577-9999

NEVIN, DAVID WRIGHT, real estate broker, mortgage broker; b. Culver City, Calif., July 27, 1947; s. Wilbur D. and Anita J. (Hulderman) N.; m. Shirley Grimes, Nov. 12, 1977; children: Jenny, David Wright Jr. BA, Calif. State Poly. U., 1974. Rural manpower asst. employment devel. State Calif., Riverside, 1970-74; pers. mgr. Lindsay Olive Growers, Calif., 1974-79; employee rels. mgr. Morton Salt Co., Newark, Calif., 1979-80; real estate salesman Valley Realty, Fremont, Calif., 1980, The Property Profls., Fremont, Calif., 1980-85; owner Nevin & Nevin, Inc., 1984-88, CitiDesign, 1989—; co-owner Brokers Exch., Inc., 1985-86; dir., officer CitiBrokers Real Estate, Inc., 1986-92; owner Nevin Fin., 1992—. Sustaining mem. Rep. Nat. Com., Washington, 1984; mem. Presdl. Task Force, Washington, 1984. Served with U.S. Army, 1967-69. Mem. Realtors Nat. Mktg. Inst. (real estate brokerage coun.), Internat. Real Estate Fedn., So. Alameda County Bd. Realtors (local govt. rels. com. 1983-86). Mem. Assemblies of God Ch. Address: PO Box 3191 Fremont CA 94539

NEVIN, LEONARD VERNE, state legislator, retired police officer; b. Reno, June 4, 1943; s. Clarence A. and Olive (Lewis) N.; m. Cindy Creighton, Aug. 19, 1983; children: Bridgette, Stephanie. Student, Truckee Meadows C.C., U. Nev. Police officer Reno Police Dept., 1963-86; mem. Nev. State Assembly, 1983-89, assembly asst. majority floor leader, 1987-89; mem. Nev. State Senate from 2d dist., 1991—, minority whip, 1993—; law enforcement coord. Nev. Boys State, Carson City, 1980—; legis. mem. Nev. Hwy. Users Fedn., Las Vegas, 1980—. Mem. adv. bd. Sparks (Nev.) High Sch.; active Heritage Found., U. Nev. Reno Boosters Club. Recipient Law Enforcement Commendation medal City of Reno, 1971, SAR, 1985, Edn. award Washoe County Sch. Dist., 1985, Disting. Svc. award Nev. Gasoline Retailers, 1987; named Police Officer of Yr., Reno/Sparks C. of C., 1979, Hon. Lt. Col., Nev. CAP, 1989, Legislator of Yr., Nev. Conf. Police and Sheriffs, 1989. Mem. Ct. Apptd. Spl. Advs. (chmn. 1985), Sons Italy (Guiseppe Verdi lodge, orator 1988—), Sertoma, 10-42 Club, Elks (Reno). Democrat. Episcopalian. Home: 3372 Lagomarsino Ct Sparks NV 89431-1158 Office: Nev State Senate 401 S Carson St Carson City NV 89710

NEVIN, PAUL EDWARD, small business owner; b. L.A., Oct. 12, 1955; s. W.D. and A.J. Nevin. BS, U. State N.Y., Albany, 1985. Computer specialist Gen. Dynamics Corp., Pomona, Calif., 1980-81; pres. Picture Soft, Riverside, Calif., 1985—. Mem. Oxford Club. Republican. Office: Picture Soft PO Box 7313 Riverside CA 92513

NEWACHECK, DAVID JOHN, lawyer; b. San Francisco, Dec. 8, 1953; s. John Elmer and Estere Ruth Sybil (Nelson) N.; m. Dorothea Quandt, June 2, 1990. AB in English, U. Calif., Berkeley, 1976; JD, Pepperdine U., 1979; MBA, Calif. State U., Hayward, 1982; LLM in Tax, Golden Gate U., 1987. Bar: Calif. 1979, U.S. Dist. Ct. (no. dist.) Calif. 1979, U.S. Ct. Appeals (9th cir.) 1979, U.S. Supreme Ct. 1984, Washington D.C. 1985. Tax cons. Pannell, Kerr and Forster, San Francisco, 1982-83; lawyer, writer, editor Matthew Bender and Co., Oakland, 1983—; tax cons., Walnut Creek, Calif., 1983—; bd. dirs. Aztec Custom Co., Orinda, Calif., 1983—; cons. software Collier Bankruptcy Filing System, 1984. Author/editor: (treatises) Ill. Tax Service, 1985, Ohio State Taxation, 1985, N.J. Tax Service, 1986, Pa. Tax Service, 1986, Calif. Closely Held Corps., 1987, Texas Tax Service, 1988; author: (software) Tax Source 1040 Tax Preparation, 1987, Texas Tax Service 1988, California Taxation, 1989, 2d edit., 1990, Bender's Federal Tax Service, 1989, Texas Litigation Guide, 1993, Family Law: Texas Practice & Procedure, 1993. Mem. youth com. Shepherd of the Valley Luth. Ch., Orinda, 1980-85, ch. coun., 1980-82. Mem. ABA, State Bar Assn. Calif.,

Alameda County Bar Assn., U. Calif. Alumni Assn., U. Calif. Band Alumni Assn., Mensa. Republican. Club: Commonwealth (San Francisco). Home: 21 Tappan Ln Orinda CA 94563-1310 Office: Matthew Bender & Co 2101 Webster St Oakland CA 94612-3027

NEWBERG, DOROTHY BECK (MRS. WILLIAM C. NEWBERG), portrait artist; b. Detroit, May 30, 1919; d. Charles William and Mary (Labedz) Beck; student Detroit Conservatory Music, 1938; m. William C. Newberg, Nov. 3, 1939; children: Judith Bracken, Robert Charles, James William, William Charles. Trustee Detroit Adventure, 1967-71, originator A Drop in Bucket Program for artistically talented inner-city children. Bd. dirs. Bloomfield Art Assn., 1960-62, trustee 1965-67; bd. dirs. Your Heritage House, 1972-75, Franklin Wright Settlement, 1972-75, Meadowbrook Art Gallery, Oakland U., 1973-75; bd. dirs. Sierra Nevada Mus. Art, 1978-80; mem. Nev. Mus. Art; bd. dirs. Nat. Conf. Christians and Jews, northern Nev. region, Gangs Alternatives Partnership; vol. Reno Police Dept. Recipient Heart of Gold award, 1969; Mich. vol. leadership award, 1969, Outstanding Vol. award City of Reno, 1989-90. Mem. No. Nev. Black Cultural Awareness Soc., Sierra Art Found, Serra Club of Reno. Roman Catholic. Home: 2000 Dant Blvd Reno NV 89509-5129

NEWBERG, ELLEN JOYCE, library administrator; b. Wellman, Iowa, Sept. 29, 1941; d. Carl Clarence and Elda Grace (White) Herr; m. Alan Keith Newberg, June 11, 1965. BA, Sioux Falls Coll., 1962; M.L.S., U. Ill., 1963. Asst. dir. libr. Sioux Falls Coll., S.D., 1963-66; libr. cataloger U. Wyo., Laramie, 1966-67, U. Oreg., Eugene, 1967-69; asst. libr. dir. Rocky Mountain Coll., Billings, Mont., 1969-73; head tech. svcs. Parmly Billings Libr., 1973-82, dir., 1982-88; dir. Kitsap Regional Libr., 1989—; Western Libr. Network retrospective conversion trainer, Mont., 1981-82; OCLC installation trainer Dowling Coll. Libr., Oakdale, N.Y., 1978-79; mem. steering com. Gov's. Conf. on Librs. and Info. Svcs., 1990-91; pres. Ctrl. Kitsap Community Schs. Adv. Bd., 1993, 94. Contbr. articles to profl. jours. Mem. ALA (Mont. councilor 1986-88), Wash. Libr. Assn., Pacific Northwest Libr.Assn. (Mont. rep. 1980-82, joint planning team 1981-82). Avocations: gourmet cooking, gardening, hiking. Office: Kitsap Regional Libr 1301 Sylvan Way Bremerton WA 98310-3498

NEWBERG, WILLIAM CHARLES, stock broker, real estate broker, automotive engineer; b. Seattle, Dec. 17, 1910; s. Charles John and Anna Elizabeth (Anderson) N.; B.S. in Mech. Engring., U. Wash., 1933; M. in Mech. Engring., Chrysler Inst. Engring., 1935; LL.B. (hon.), Parsons Coll., 1958; m. Dorothy Beck, Nov. 3, 1939; children—Judith N. Newberg Bookwalter, Robert Charles, James William, William Charles. Salesman, Am. Auto Co., Seattle, 1932-33; student engr. Chrysler Corp., Detroit, 1933-35, exptl. engr., 1935-42, chief engr. Chgo. plant, 1942-45, mem. subs. ops. staff, Detroit, 1945-47, pres. airtemp. div., Dayton, Ohio, 1947-50, v.p., dir. Dodge div., Detroit, 1950-51, pres. Dodge div., 1951-56, group v.p., Detroit, 1956-58, exec. v.p., 1958-60, pres., 1960; corp. dir. Detroit Bank & Trust, Detroit, 1955-60; corp. cons., Detroit, 1960-76; realtor Myers Realty, Inc., Reno, 1976-79; owner Bill Newberg Realty, 1979—; account exec. Allied Capital Corp., Reno, 1980—; chmn. Newberg Corp., 1982; treas. Perfect "10" Industries. Elder, St. John's Presbyterian Ch., Reno, 1976—; exec. bd. Detroit Area council Boy Scouts Am., 1955-74, Nev. Area council Boy Scouts Am., 1976—; Mich. state chmn. March of Dimes, 1967-68. Mem. Soc. Automotive Engrs., Am. Def. Preparedness Assn. (life), Automotive Orgn. Team (life), U. Wash. Alumni Assn. (life), Newcomen Soc., Franklin Inst., Alpha Tau Omega. Clubs: Prospectors, Harley Owners Group, Rider Motorcycle Touring. Home: 2000 Dant Blvd Reno NV 89509-5129

NEWBERRY, ALAN JOHN HESSON, school board association administrator; b. Victoria, B.C., Can., Sept. 4, 1937; s. John Harold Newberry and Hazel Margaret Hesson; m. Janet Christina (McIntosh); children: Christina, Andrea, Alison, Graham. BA, U. Victoria, 1969; MEd, U. Portland, Oreg., 1971; EdD, Ind. U., 1975. Cert. tchr., B.C., Alta., Can. Tchr. Victoria, 1959-60; prin. Sooke Schs., 1961-68, supr., 1968-75; supt. schs. Ministry Edn., Victoria, 1975-79, exec. dir., 1979-85; chief supt. schs. Calgary (Alta.) Bd. Edn., 1985-90; exec. dir. B.C. (Can.) Sch. Trustees Assn., Vancouver, 1990—. Home: 13846 18th Ave, Surrey, BC Canada V4A 1W4 Office: BC Sch Trustees Assn, 1155 W 8th Ave, Vancouver, BC Canada V6H 1C5

NEWBERRY, CONRAD FLOYDE, aerospace engineering educator; b. Neodesha, Kans., Nov. 10, 1931; s. Ragan McGregor and Audra Anitia (Newmaster) N.; m. Sarah Louise Thonn, Jan. 26, 1958; children: Conrad Floyde Jr., Thomas Edwin, Susan Louise. AA, Independence Jr. Coll., 1951; BEME in Aero. Sequence, U. So. Calif., 1957; MSME, Calif. State U., Los Angeles, 1971, MA in Edn., 1974; D.Environ. Sci. and Engring., UCLA, 1985. Registered profl. engr., Calif., Kans., N.C., Tex. Mathematician L.A. div. N.Am. Aviation Inc., 1951-53, jr. engr., 1953-54, engr., 1954-57, sr. engr., 1957-64; asst. prof. aerospace engring. Calif. State Poly. U., Pomona, 1964-70, assoc. prof. aerospace engring., 1970-75, prof. aerospace engring., 1975-90, prof. emeritus, 1990—; staff engr. EPA, 1980-82; engring. specialist space transp. systems div. Rockwell Internat. Corp., 1984-90; prof. aeronautics, astronautics Naval Postgrad. Sch., Monterey, Calif., 1990—, acad. assoc. space systems engring., 1992—. Recipient John Leland Atwood award as outstanding aerospace engring. educator AIAA/Am. Soc. Engring. Edn., 1986. Fellow AIAA (dep. dir. edn. region VI 1976-79, dep. dir. career enhancement 1982-91, chmn. L.A. sect. 1989-90, chmn. Point Lobos sect. 1990-91, dir. tech.-aircraft systems 1990-93), Inst. Advancement Engring, Brit. Interplanetary Soc.; mem.IEEE, AAAS, ASME, NSPE, Royal Aeronautical Soc., Calif. Soc. Profl. Engrs., Am. Acad. Environ. Engrs. (cert. air pollution control engr.), Am. Soc. Engring. Edn. (chmn. aerospace div. 1979-80, div. exec. com. 1976-80, 89-93, exec. com. ocean and marine engring. div. 1982-85, 90—, program chmn. 1991-93, chmn. 1993—), Am. Soc. Pub. Adminstrn., Am. Meteorol. Soc., U.S. Naval Inst., Am. Helicopter Soc., Soc. Naval Architects and Marine Engrs., Air and Waste Mgmt. Assn., Inst. Environ. Scis., Exptl. Aircraft Assn., Water Pollution Control Fedn., Soc. Automotive Engrs., Soc. Allied Weight Engrs., Assn. Unmanned Vehicle Systems, Calif. Water Pollution Control Assn., Nat. Assn. Environ. Profls., Am. Soc. Naval Engrs., Planetary Soc., Tau Beta Pi, Sigma Gamma Tau, Kappa Delta Pi. Democrat. Mem. Christian Ch. (Disciples of Christ). Home: 9463 Willow Oak Rd Salinas CA 93907-1037 Office: Naval Postgrad Sch Dept Aeronautics and Astronautics AA/Ne Monterey CA 93943-5000

NEWBRUN, ERNEST, oral biology and periodontology educator; b. Vienna, Austria, Dec. 1, 1932; came to U.S., 1955; s. Victor and Elizabeth (Reichl) N; m. Eva Miriam, June 17, 1956; children: Deborah Anne, Daniel Eric, Karen Ruth. BDS, U. Sydney (New South Wales), 1954; MS, U. Rochester, 1957; DMD, U. Ala., 1959; PhD, U. Calif., San Francisco, 1965; Odont. Dr. (hon.), U. Lund, Sweden, 1988. Cert. periodontology. Rsch. assoc. Eastern Dental Ctr., Rochester, N.Y., 1955-57, U. Ala. Med. Ctr., Birmingham, 1957-59; rsch. fellow Inst. Dental Rsch., Sydney, Australia, 1960-61; rsch. tchr. trainee U. Calif., San Francisco, 1961-63, postdoctoral fellow, 1963-65, assoc. prof., prof., 1965-70, prof. oral biology, 1970-83, prof. oral biology and periodontology, 1983—; cons. FDA, 1983—. Author: Cariology, 1989, Pharmacology and Therapeutic Dentistry, 1989, (with others) Pediatrics, 1991; editor: Fluorides and Dental Caries, 1986; mem. editorial bd. Jour. Periodontal Rsch., 1985-90, Jour. Peridontology, 1990—. Bd. dirs. Raoul Wallenberg Dem. Club, San Francisco, 1987-92. Mem. AAAS (chmn. dental section, 1988-89), Internat. Assn. Dental Rsch. (pres. 1989-90), Dental Health Foun. (chmn. bd. dirs., 1985-92). Jewish. Office: U Calif San Francisco Divsn Oral Biology San Francisco CA 94143-0512

NEWCOMER, OWEN EUGENE, political science educator; b. Dixon, Ill., Feb. 13, 1948; s. M. Burns and Etholine C. (Clingenpeel) N.; m. Kristina Jean Weis, Apr. 3, 1971. AA, L.A. Valley C.C., 1970; BA, Calif. State U., Northridge, 1971, MA, 1972; PhD, U. So. Calif., 1980. Lectr. polit. sci. Coll. of Canyons, Santa Clarita, Calif., 1973-75; prof. polit. sci. Rio Hondo Coll., Whittier, Calif., 1975—; lectr. polit. sci. L.A. Pierce Coll., Woodland Hills, 1973-75, Moorpark (Calif.) Coll., 1974-75, L.A. City Coll., Hollywood, 1974-75. Author: Governing Los Angeles, 1992. Commr. Whittier City Parks & Recreation Commn., 1987-89; pres. Rio Hondo Coll. Faculty Assn., Whittier, 1989-90; bd. dirs. Whittier City Sch. Dist., 1989—, pres., 1991-92. Mem. Am. Polit. Sci. Assn., Soc. Calif. Hist. Soc., We. Polit. Sci. Assn., Whittier Hist. Soc., Pico Rivera Heritage and Hist. Soc., El Monte Hist. Soc., Model UN of Far West. Democrat. Office: Rio Hondo Coll 3600 Workman Mill Rd Whittier CA 90608

NEWELL, ALMA (LISA NEWELL), company executive, consultant; b. Beaver Falls, Pa., Oct. 21, 1936; d. Charles Edward and Mary Alma (Novak) Kralic; m. Everett William Newell, June 9, 1956 (div. Mar. 1971); children: Lawrence Dean, Debora Lynn, Everett William II. Grad. high sch., Beaver Falls. Lic. real estate agt., Calif. Adminstr. asst. to dir. sales U.S. Stoneware, Tallmade, Ohio, 1969-71; exec. sec. B.F. Goodrich Co., Akron, Ohio, 1971-76; real estate agt. Licensee, L.A., 1977-78, Four Seasons Real Estate, 1978, Am. Calif. Devel., 1978; v.p. E.A.C. Constrn. Corp., L.A., 1978-80; corp. sec., v.p. Bedford Group, Culver City, Calif., 1980—; cons. Pacific Architronics, Pacific Palisades, Calif. Hosp. vol., Ohio, 1972-76; vol. fund raiser for afflicted children, L.A. County, 1977—. Mem. Nat. Notary Assn. Democrat. Roman Catholic. Office: The Bedford Group 600 Corporate Point Ste 1100 Culver City CA 90230-7606

NEWELL, CASTLE SKIP, III, marketing executive, foundation administrator; b. Detroit, Aug. 10, 1940; s. Castle and Leona (Herrick) N.; m. Nancy Elizabeth Taylor, Aug. 7, 1964; children: Andrew Scott, Samantha Suzanne. AA, Orange Coast Coll., Costa Mesa, Calif., 1962. Sports announcer Sta. ABC-TV Wide World of Sports, N.Y.C., 1965-70; dir. pub. rels. Kawasaki Inc., Santa Ana, Calif., 1970-73; shovelman Mendocino County Dept. Pub. Works, Laytonville, Calif., 1973-74; dir. pub. rels. Harwood Products, Branscomb, Calif., 1974-80; v.p. mktg. pub. rels. Bailey's, Inc., Laytonville, Calif., 1980—; pres. Castle Newell & Assocs.; mem. ANSI B 175 com. Comsumer Products Safety Commn., Washington, 1985—. Fireman Laytonville Vol. Fire Dept., 1974—; reserve dep. Mendocino County Sheriff's Dept., 1983—; pres., founder Rural Visions Found., Laytonville, 1986—; mem. bd. govs. Mendocino-Lake Community Coll. Found. Recipient recognition as 237th "Daily Point of Light", U.S. Pres. George Bush, 1990, Community Svc. tribute U.S. Senate, 1990, Commendation award Calif. State Assembly, 1987, Congl. salute U.S. Congress, 1987; nominee Pres.'s Vol. Action award, 1987. Home: PO Box 717 Laytonville CA 95454-0717 Office: Rural Visions Found PO Box 1371 Laytonville CA 95454-1371

NEWELL, MICHAEL STEPHEN, finance company executive, international finance, security-protection consultant; b. Denver, Dec. 22, 1949; s. Henry Michael and Marlene (McRae) N.; m. Linda Margaret Wolfe, Sept. 19, 1987; children: Katherine Margaret, Brittany Nicole; children from previous marriage: Troy, Angela, Michael, Jennifer. Grad., Denver Police Acad., 1972; CO Real Estate Lic., Real Estate Prep., 1977. Cert. peace officer, Colo. Police officer Denver Police Dept., 1972-79; prin. Michael Newell & Assocs., Denver, 1979-82; sr. account exec. Am. Protection Industries, Los Angeles, 1982-84; chief exec. officer Newco Fin., Huntington Beach, Calif., 1984—; chmn. The Newco Internat. Group/Newco Fin., Huntington Beach; founder, bd. dirs. EDEN Philanthropic Found., Fountain Valley, Calif., VALUES Self Improvement Program, Fountain Valley; cofounder, bd. dirs. Self-Love, Sexuality & Spirituality seminars, Fountain Valley; bd. dirs. Lifesong Self-Esteem workshops, Huntington Beach.; chmn. bd., bd. dirs. Steel Head Investment Group; proprietor Steel Head Inn, Michael's Supper Club. Founder, bd. dirs. Law Enforcement Support Assn., Denver, 1981. Served with U.S. Army, 1968-71, Viet Nam. Decorated Bronze Star, Viet Svc. medal with clusters; recipient numerous civilian/police awards Denver Police Dept. Republican. Mem. Religious Sci. Ch. Office: Internat Risk Cons PO Box 621091 Littleton CO 80162-1091

NEWELL, ROGER AUSTIN, mining company executive; b. Portland, Oreg., Mar. 1, 1943; s. Lester Judson and Myrtle Elizabeth (Reisner) N.; m. Mary Anne Norman, June 18, 1965; children: Andrea, Heidi. BSc, U. Oreg., 1965; MSc, Colo. Sch. Mines, 1971; PhD, Stanford U., 1975. Registered profl. geologist, S.C. Geologist, rschr. Kennecott Exploration Ltd., Salt Lake City, 1974-77; exploration geologist Newmont Exploration Ltd., Tucson, 1977-83; exploration mgr. Newmont Exploration Ltd., Danbury, Conn., 1984-89, Gold Fields Mining Co., Reno, Nev., 1989-92; regional mgr. Gold Fields Mining Co., Denver, 1992—. Bd. dirs. Mackey Sch. Mines, Reno, 1989—. Henry DeWitt Smith scholar Stanford U., 1972. Fellow Soc. Econ. Geologists (com. chmn. 1989-92); mem. AIME, Geol. Soc. Am., Sigma Xi. Home: 24344 Paragon Pl Golden CO 80401 Office: Gold Fields Mining Co 1687 Cole Blvd Golden CO 80401

NEWHART, BOB, entertainer; b. Oak Park, Ill., Sept. 29, 1929; m. Virginia Quinn, Jan. 12, 1963; 4 children. BS, Loyola U., Chgo., 1952. Law clk. U.S. Gypsum Co.; copywriter Fred Niles Film Co.; performer Dan Serkin TV show, 1957; appeared on Jack Paar Show, 1960; TV performer numerous guest appearances, 1961—; star TV series Newhart, 1982-90. Rec. artist (album) Button Down Mind on TV; royal command performance, London, 1964, appeared in films Hot Millions, 1968, Catch 22, 1970, Cold Turkey, 1971, First Family, 1980, Little Miss Marker, 1982; TV films include Thursday's Game, 1978, Marathon, 1980. Grand marshall Tournament Roses Parade, 1991. Served with U.S. Army, 1952-54. Recipient Emmy award, 1961, Peabody award, 1961, Sword of Loyola award, 1976; named to Acad. Hall of Fame, 1993. Office: care David Capell 2121 Avenue Of The Stars # 1240 Los Angeles CA 90067-5009

NEWHOUSE, IRVINE RALPH, state legislator; b. Mabton, Wash., Oct. 16, 1920; s. John and Tina (Bos) N.; m. Ruth Martha Gardner, July 14, 1945; children: Joyce, James, Linda, Laura, Daniel, Dorothy. BS, Wash. State U., 1943. County agt. Egrl. Extension Svc., Ellensburg, Wash., 1946; farmer Mabton, 1947—; mem. Wash. Ho. of Reps., Olympia, 1964-80; mem. Wash. State Senate, Olympia, 1980—, Rep. floor leader. Lt. (j.g.) USNR, 1943-45, PTO. Republican. Mem. Christian Reformed Ch. Home: 1160 Murray Rd Box 130 Mabton WA 98935 Office: Wash State Sen 403 Legislative Bldg Olympia WA 98504

NEWHOUSE, WAYNE M., energy company executive. Sr. v.p. Norcen Energy Resources Ltd., Calgary, AB, Can. Office: Norcen Energy Resources Ltd, 715 5th Ave SW, Calgary, AB Canada T2P 2X7

NEWKIRK, RAYMOND LESLIE, management consultant; b. Shreveport, La., July 13, 1944; s. Raymond Clay and Dorothy Emily (Parker) N.; m. Felicisima Guese Calma, Jan. 19, 1985. AA, Dayton Community Coll., 1973; BS in Behavioral Sci., N.Y. Inst. Tech., 1976; MS in Philosophy, Columbia Pacific U., 1980, PhD in Behavioral Sci., 1982; PhD in Human Sci., Saybrook Inst., 1992. Chief exec. officer, cons. Newkirk & Assocs., Ft. Lauderdale, Fla., 1980-84; head dept. ADP Royal Saudi Naval Forces, Jeddah, 1984-86; pres., cons. Internat. Assn. Info. Mgmt., Santa Clara, Calif., 1984; cert. quality analyst Quality Assurance Inst., Orlando, Fla., 1986—; prin. cons. Info. Impact Internat., Nashville, 1988—; exec. dir. Systems Mgmt. Inst., Pleasant Hill, Calif., 1987; pres., COO P.Q. Info. Group, The Netherlands, 1992—. Author: Chronicles of the Making of A Philosopher, 1983; contbr. articles to profl. jours. Speaker, mem. Union for Concerned Scientists, San Francisco, 1988. Fellow Brit. Inst. Mgmt., Internat. Biog. Assn.; mem. Assn. Sytems Mgmt., Assn. Profl. Cons., Planetary Soc., Columbia Pacific Alumni Assn. (pres. Mid-east chpt. 1985), Assn. Computing Machinery, IEEE Computer Soc., Phi Theta Kappa (outstanding scholar award 1973). Roman Catholic. Home: 4395 Snowcloud Ct Concord CA 94518-1938

NEWLAND, RUTH LAURA, small business owner; b. Ellensburg, Wash., June 4, 1949; d. George J. and Ruth Marjorie (Porter) N. BA, Cen. Wash. State Coll., 1970, MEd, 1972; EdS, Vanderbilt U., 1973; PhD, Columbia Pacific U., 1981. Tchr. Union Gap (Wash.) Sch., 1970-71; ptnr. Newland Ranch Gravel Co., Yakima, Wash., 1970—, Arnold Artificial Limb, Yakima, 1981-86; owner, pres. Arnold Artificial Limb, Yakima and Richland, Wash., 1986—; ptnr. Newland Ranch, Yakima, 1969—. Mem. Yakima Greenway Found., Ctr. Marine Conservation, Public Citizen, We The People, Nat. Humane Edn. Soc., Ams. Responsible TV; contbg. mem. Dem. Nat. Com.; charter mem. Nat. Mus. Am. Indian. George Washington scholar Masons, Yakima, 1967. Mem. NAFE, Am. Orthotic and Prosthetic Assn., Internat. Platform Assn., Nat. Antivivisection Soc. (life), Vanderbilt U. Alumni Assn., George Peabody Coll. Alumni Assn., Columbia Pacific U. Alumni Assn., World Wildlife Fund, Nat. Audubon Soc., Greenpeace, Mus. Fine Arts, Humane Soc. U.S., Wilderness Soc., Nature Conservancy, People for Ethical Treatment of Animals, Amnesty Internat., Pub. Citizen, Wilderness Soc., The Windstar Found., Rodale Inst., Sierra Club (life), Emily's List. Democrat. Home: 2004 Riverside Rd Yakima WA 98901-9526 Office: Arnold Artificial Limb 9 S 12th Ave Yakima WA 98902-3106

NEWLIN, DOUGLAS RANDAL, learning products engineer; b. Denver, Mar. 26, 1940; s. Loren Randall and Nola Berneice (Paris) N.; m. Sandra Temple, June 22, 1968; children: Jason Britt, Jeremy Owen. BS in Journalism, U. Colo., 1968. Advt. prodn. mgr. Am. Sheep Producers Council, Denver, 1968-70; promotion dir. Sta. KLZ-AM-FM, Denver, 1970-71; account mgr. Curran-Morton Advt., Denver, 1971-72; advt. and sales promotion specialist Gates Rubber Co., Denver, 1972-78; mktg. communications mgr. Hewlett Packard Co., Ft. Collins, Colo., 1978-90; learning products engr., 1990—; vis. lectr. U. Colo., Boulder, 1972-73, statis. quality control course George Washington U., Washington, 1984. Author hardware and software catalogs, 1984-90, UNIX Tech. Documentation, 1990—; contbr. articles to profl. jours. Pres. Lake Sherwood Homeowners Assn., Ft. Collins, 1982; treas. Lake Sherwood Lake Com., Ft. Collins, 1983-85. Served with U.S. Army, 1959-61. Recipient Gold Key award Bus. and Profl. Advt. Assn., 1976. Democrat. Home: 4112 Mt Vernon Ct Fort Collins CO 80525-3335 Office: Hewlett Packard Co 3404 E Harmony Rd Fort Collins CO 80525-9599

NEWLIN, SHARON DIANNE, aerospace company trainee; b. Ogden, Utah, Oct. 22, 1962; d. Loren Randall and Alice Elizabeth (Haun) N. AS in Secretarial Sci., Weber State U., 1982, BS in Adminstrv. Systems, 1990, postgrad., 1991. Receptionist Boy Scouts Am., Redlands, Calif., 1980; magcard operator MountainWest Savs. & Loan, Ogden, 1982-84; clk. Thiokol Corp., Brigham City, Utah, 1984-86, sec., 1986-90, engring. scheduler, 1990-92, leadership candidate, 1992—; owner, operator SN Enterprises, Willard, Utah, 1991—; computer cons. K & G Splty. Shop, Perry, Utah, 1987—. Sch. coord. for 2 schs. Young Astronaut, 1992; mem. Box Elder Heritage Coun., 1988—. Mem. Am. Bus. Womens Assn., Nat. Arbor Day Found., Good Time Players, Thiokol Ski Club, Thiokol Dance Club. Republican. Mem. LDS Ch. Home: Gen Delivery 55 S Main St Willard UT 84340

NEWMAN, EDGAR LEON, historian, educator; b. New Orleans, Jan. 21, 1939; s. Isidore and Anna (Pfeifer) N.; children: Jonathan, Suzanne; m. Linda Loeb Clark, Apr. 21, 1989. BA, Yale U., 1962; PhD, U. Chgo., 1969. Asst. prof. N.Mex. State U., Las Cruces, 1969-75, assoc. prof. history, 1975—; lectr. U. Peking, 1985; bd. dirs. Am. Congress on Bicentennial of French Revolution of 1989. Fulbright fellow, 1965-66; Am. Philos. Soc. fellow, 1971; Nat. Endowment for Humanities fellow, 1975-76. Mem. Western Soc. for French History (pres. 1977-78, governing coun. 1990-92), Societe d'histoire de la Revolution de 1848 (comite directeur), Soc. Scis. History Assn., French Hist. Studies Assn., Am. Hist. Assn. (annotator for France bibliographical survey 1815-52). Editor: Historical Dictionary of France from the 1815 Restoration to the Second Empire. Office: NMex State U PO Box 3H Las Cruces NM 88003-0001

NEWMAN, FRANK NEIL, federal official; b. Quincy, Mass., Apr. 20, 1942; s. Robert David and Ethel F. N.; 1 child from previous marriage, Daniel. B.A. in Econs. magna cum laude, Harvard U., 1963. Exec. v.p., chief fin. officer Wells Fargo & Co. and Wells Fargo Bank, San Francisco, 1980-86; chief fin. officer Bank Am. Corp, Bank of Am., San Francisco, 1986-1993; under sec of deomestic policy Treasury Dept., Washington, DC, 1993—; vice chmn. bd. dirs. Bank Am. Corp., Bank of Am. Bd. dirs. Japan Soc. of Calif. Club: Harvard (San Francisco). Office: Under Sec of Domestic Finance Treasury Department 15th & Pennsylvania Ave NW Washington DC 20220

NEWMAN, GERARD KEVIN, software engineer; b. New Haven, Sept. 5, 1959; s. Eugene and Joan Barbara (Crosby) N.; m. Victoria Elisabeth Goehner, Jan. 11, 1992. BA in Computer Sci., U. Tenn., 1984. Software engr. Unique Software Devel., Knoxville, Tenn., 1980-83; software engr. II Digital Equipment Corp., Mallborough, Mass., 1983; sr. software engr. SAIC, Oak Ridge, Tenn., 1983-86; prin. scientist San Diego Super Computer Ctr., 1986-92; software engr. TGV, Inc., Santa Cruz, Calif., 1992—. Donor mem. Smithsonian Inst., Washington. Mem. (IEEE), Assn. for Computing Machinery, Internet Soc. Office: TGV Inc 603 Mission St Santa Cruz CA 95060

NEWMAN, GREGORY ALAN, civil engineer; b. Aurora, Ill., Jan. 5, 1953; s. Donald William N. and Marilyn Jean (Lamb) Miller; m. Amy Carolyn Withers (dec. 1989); 1 child, Renee; m. Victoria Anne Barney; 1 child, Christian. BS, U. Denver, 1975; BCE, U. Ariz., 1991. Test chemist I Phelps Dodge Corp., Tucson, Ariz., 1976-79; mem. tech. staff Hughes Aircraft Co., Tucson, 1979-86; civil engr. asst. County of Orange, Santa Ana, Calif., 1986—. Mem. ASCE (assoc.), Aircraft Owners and Pilots Assn., Mensa, Phi Beta Kappa. Democrat. Roman Catholic. Home: 25426 Via Estudio Laguna Niguel CA 92677 Office: County of Orange 400 Civic Center Dr W Santa Ana CA 92702-4048

NEWMAN, J. ROBERT, psychologist, educator; b. Providence, Nov. 24, 1928; s. Edward Francis and Elinor Helene (Cronin) N.; 1 child, Daniel-le. BA in Psychology, U. Mass., 1950, MS in Psychology, 1952; PhD in Psychology, U. Ill., 1955. Lic. psychologist, Calif. Head, human factors Hughes Aircraft, Fullerton, Calif., 1955-62; sr. human factors scientist System Devel. Corp., Santa Monica, Calif., 1962-67; sr. rsch. assoc. Social Sci. Rsch. Inst. U. So. Calif., L.A., 1972-84; prof. psychology Calif. State U., Long Beach, Calif., 1967—; cons. psychologist, Redondo Beach, Calif., 1975—. Author: Evaluation Technology Multiattribute Evaluation, 1983; contbr. articles to profl. jours. Mem. Am. Psychol. Assn., Am. Psychol. Soc., Human Factors Soc., Psychometric Soc. Home: 173 Via Monte Doro Redondo Beach CA 90277-6522 Office: Dept Psychology Calif State U Long Beach CA 90840

NEWMAN, JEFFREY RICHARD, electronics engineer; b. N.Y.C., Nov. 6, 1955; s. Leo and Ellen Ruth (Groer) N.; m. Marushka Wohl, May 29, 1988; 1 child Ariel Jay Wohl. BA in Physics, Calif. State U., Fullerton, 1978; MS in Physics, Calif. State U., Fresno, 1982; postgrad., U. Colo., 1982-85, Fielding Inst., 1990—. Teaching asst. physics dept. Calif. State U., Fresno, 1978-82; rsch. asst. U. Colo., Boulder, 1983-85; mem. tech. staff TRW, Redondo Beach, Calif., 1985-92; ptnr. Donaldson Newman Assocs., Manhattan Beach, Calif., 1993—; cons. L.A. Ednl. Partnership, 1987-88; presenter in field. Coord. speakers South Bay chpt. Beyond War, Redondo Beach, 1987-91; v.p. Beach Cities Dem. Club, Redondo Beach, 1989-91; mem. L.A. County Dem. Cen. Com., 1990. Mem. L.A. Orgnl. Devel. Network, Am. Soc. Tng. and Devel., Sigma Pi Sigma. Democrat. Jewish. Home: 2000 Mathews Ave Apt 5 Redondo Beach CA 90278

NEWMAN, KATHARINE DEALY, author, consultant; b. Phila., Aug. 17, 1911; d. Creswell Victor and Harriet Elizabeth (Hetherington) Dealy; m. Morton Newman, May 11, 1946 (div. 1968); children: Deborah Silverstein, Blaze. BS in Edn. summa cum laude, Temple U., 1933; MA in English, U. Pa., 1937, PhD in English, 1961. Cert. secondary and coll. English educator, Commonwealth of Pa. Tchr. Phila. High Schs., 1933-46, 49-50; asst. prof. U. Minn., Mpls., 1946-47, Temple U. Community Coll., Phila., 1959; assoc. prof. Moore Coll. Art, Phila., 1961-63; tchr. Abington (PA.) High Sch., 1963-67; prof. West Chester (Pa.) State U., 1967-77; cons. Inst. for Ethnic Studies West Chester U., 1975-77; exch. prof. Cheyney State (Pa.) U., 1971; cons. in field. Author: The Gentleman's Novelist: Robert Plumer Ward, 1765-1946, 1961, The American Equation: Literature in a Multi-Ethnic Culture, 1971, Ethnic American Short Stories, 1975, The Girl of the Golden West, 1978, Never Without a Song, 1993; contbr. articles to profl. jours. Named Outstanding Bd. Mem. Jr. League, 1987; Coordinating Coun. Literary Mags. Editor fellow, 1980. Mem. Modern Lit. Assn. (emeritus mem.), Philogical Assn. Pacific Coast, Soc. for the Study of Multi-Ethnic Lit. of U.S. (founder, officer 1973, editor newsletter 1973-77, editor MELUS jour. 1977-81, editor emeritus 1983—, Contbn. award 1982), Inst. for Ethnic Studies (founder, chmn. 1975-77), Episc. Svc. Alliance (co-founder 1978, bd. dirs. 1978-87, v.p. 1982, 86, pres. 1983, 84, cert. appreciation 1987). Democrat. Episcopalian. Home: 910 Bonita Dr Encinitas CA 92024

NEWMAN, LOIS MAE, marketing executive; b. Phoenix, Aug. 16, 1942; d. Harold Orville and Agnes Louise (Rindos) Little; children: Annette Horning, Tyler Katonak. BA, Hamilton Coll., Utica, N.Y., 1964; MA, Hamilton Coll., 1968; postgrad., U. Ariz., 1969, Ariz. State U., 1970. Office mgr. Dunes Hotel and Country Club, Phoenix, 1962-83; prin., treas. Sincere Press, Inc., Phoenix, 1982—; pres., chief exec. officer Euneek, Phoenix, 1983—; staff Ridd Assocs., Inc., Phoenix, 1986—; reg. mktg. exec. Golden Nugget,

Phoenix, 1988—; bd. dirs. Sincere Press, Inc., Internat. Wines & Spirits Ltd., Encino, Calif., Euneek, Inc. Bd. dirs. Sml. Bus. Coun., Phoenix, Congl. Action Com., Phoenix, Israel Bonds, Phoenix; active Better Bus. Bur., Arizonians for Jobs & Energy, Valley Leadership, others; chmn. Phoenix Childrens Hosp. Paragranations; original founder, endorser Maimonides Day Sch.; chmn. Anti-Defamation League; adv. com. vice chmn. Nat. Coun. Christians and Jews; arrangements chmn. City of Hope. Mem. Phoenix Met. C. of C., Ariz. World Trade Assn. Home: 6808 N 26th St Phoenix AZ 85016-1208 Office: Euneek 3104 E Camelback Rd Phoenix AZ 85016-4595

NEWMAN, MARC ALAN, electrical engineer; b. Jasper, Ind., Nov. 21, 1955; s. Leonard Jay and P. Louise (Shainberg) N.; m. Shelley Jane Martin, Aug. 13, 1977; 1 child, Kelsey Renée. BSEE, Purdue U., 1977, MSEE, 1979. Sr. elec. engr. Sperry Corp. Flight Systems, Phoenix, 1979-85; staff engr. Motorola Inc., Tempe, Ariz., 1985-88, Quincy St. Corp., Phoenix, 1988-89; prin. staff scientist Motorola Inc., Chandler, Ariz., 1989-91, Scottsdale, Ariz., 1991—; Prolog and artificial intelligence expert Motorola Inc., Tempe, Chandler and Scottsdale, 1985—. Mem. IEEE, The Assn. for Logic Programming (London), Am. Assn. Artificial Intelligence, Ariz. Artificial Intelligence Assn. (founder), Internat. Platform Assn., Phi Sigma Kappa, Eta Kappa Nu. Home: 1539 N Hobson St Mesa AZ 85203-3653 Office: Motorola Inc 8201 E Mcdowell Rd Scottsdale AZ 85257-3893

NEWMAN, MICHAEL RODNEY, lawyer; b. N.Y.C., Oct. 2, 1945; s. Morris and Helen Gloria (Hendler) N.; m. Cheryl Jeanne Anker, June 11, 1967; children: Hillary Abra, Nicole Brooke. BA, U. Denver, 1967; JD, U. Chgo., 1970. Bar: Calif. 1971, U.S. Dist. Ct. (cen. dist.) Calif. 1972, U.S. Ct. Appeals (9th cir.) 1974, U.S. Dist. Ct. (no. dist.) Calif. 1975, U.S. Dist. Ct. (so. dist.) Calif. 1979, U.S. Dist. Ct. (ea. dist.) Calif. 1983, U.S. Tax Ct. 1979, U.S. Supreme Ct. 1978. Assoc. David Daar, 1971-76; ptnr. Daar & Newman, 1976-78, Miller & Daar, 1978-88, Miller, Daar & Newman, 1988-89, Daar & Newman, 1989—; judge pro tem L.A. Mcpl. Ct., 1982—, L.A. Superior Ct., 1988—. Lectr. Eastern Claims Conf., Eastern Life Claims Conf., Nat. Health Care Anti-Fraud Assn., AIA Conf. on Ins. Fraud; mem. L.A. Citizens Organizing Com. for Olympic Summer Games, 1984, mem. govtl. liaison adv. commn. 1984; mem. So. Calif. Com. for Olympic Summer Games, 1984; cert. ofcl. Athletics Congress of U.S., co-chmn. legal com. S.P.A-T.A.C, chief finish judge; trustee Massada lodge B'Nai Brith. Recipient NYU Bronze medal in Physics, 1962, TAC Disting. Svc. award, 1988, Maths. award USN Sci., 1963. Mem. ABA (multi-dist. litigation subcom., com. on class actions), L.A. County Bar Assn. (chmn. attys. errors and omissions prevention com.), Conf. of Ins. Counsel, So. Pacific Assn., TAC (bd. dirs.), L.A. Athletic Club. Office: 865 S Figueroa St Ste 2500 Los Angeles CA 90017-2567

NEWMAN, MURRAY ARTHUR, aquarium administrator; b. Chgo., Mar. 6, 1924; emigrated to Can., 1953, naturalized, 1970; s. Paul Jones and Virginia (Murray) N.; m. Katherine Greene Rose, Aug. 8, 1952; 1 child, Susan. B.Sc., U. Chgo., 1949; postgrad., U. Hawaii, 1950; M.A., U. Calif., Berkeley, 1951; Ph.D., U. B.C. (Can.), Vancouver, 1960. Curator fisheries UCLA, 1951-53, Ichthyology Museum, U. B.C., 1953-56; curator Vancouver Public Aquarium, 1956-66, dir., 1966-93; pres. Mana Aquarium Cons.; fgn. adv. Nat. Mus./Aquarium Project, Taiwan, Republic of China; past chmn. adv. com. Western Can. Univs. Marine Biol. Soc. Served with USN, 1943-46. Decorated Order of Can.; recipient Man of Yr. award City of Vancouver, 1964; Centennial award Govt. Can., 1967, cert. of merit, 1988; Harold J. Merilees award Vancouver Visitors Bur., 1976, 75 Achievers award, 1987, Silver Bravery medal Royal Soc. Canada, 1992, Canada 125 medal, 1992. Mem. Am. Assn. Zool. Parks and Aquariums, Internat. Union Dirs. Zool. Gardens, Can. Assn. Zool. Pks. and Aquariums (pres. 1978-79), Vancouver Club, Round Table Club. Office: Vancouver Pub Aquarium, PO Box 3232, Vancouver, BC Canada V6B 3X8

NEWMAN, NANCY MARILYN, ophthalmologist, educator, consultant, inventor, entrepreneur; b. San Francisco, Mar. 16, 1941. BA in Psychology magna cum laude, Stanford U., 1962, MD, 1967. Diplomate Am. Bd. Ophthalmology. NIH trainee neurophysiology Inst. Visual Scis., San Francisco, 1964-65; clin. clk. Nat. Hosp. for Nervous and Mental Disease, London, 1966-67; intern Mount Auburn Hosp., Cambridge, Mass., 1967-68; NIH trainee neuro-ophthalmology, from jr. asst. resident to sr. asst. resident to assoc. resident dept. ophthalmology sch. medicine Washington U., St. Louis, 1968-71; NIH spl. fellow in neuro-ophthalmology depts. ophthalmology and neurol. surgery sch. medicine U. Calif., San Francisco, 1971-72, clin. asst. prof. ophthalmology sch. medicine, 1972; asst. prof., chief divsn. neuro-ophthalmology Pacific Med. Ctr., San Francisco, 1972-73, assoc. prof., chief, 1973-88; physician, cons. dept. neurology sch. medicine U. Calif., VA Med. Ctr., Martinez, Calif., 1978—; prof. dept. spl. edn. Calif. State U., San Francisco, 1974-79; vis. prof. Centre Nat. D'Ophtalmologie des Quinze-Vingts, Paris, 1980; clin. assoc. prof. sch. optometry U. Calif., Berkeley, 1990—; bd. dirs., adv. bd. Frank B. Walsh Soc., 1974-91, Rose Resnick Ctr. for the Blind and Handicapped, 1988-92, Fifer St. Fitness, Larkspur, 1990-92; Internat. Soc. for Orbital Disorders, 1983—, North Calif. Soc. Prevention of Blindness, 1978-88, North African Ctr. for Sight, Tunis, Tunisia, 1988—; pres., CEO Minerva Medica; cons. in field. Author: Eye Movement Disorders; Neuro-ophthalmology: A Practical Text, 1992; mem. editoral bd. Jour. of Clin. Neuro-ophthalmology, Am. Jour. Opthalmology, 1980-92, Rapport, Ophthalmology Practice, 1993—; contbr. numerous articles to profl. jours. Recipient NSPI award Self Instrnl. Materials Ophthalmology, Merit award Internat. Eye Found; fellow Internat. Eye Found., San Salvadore, El Salvador, 1971, Smith-Kettlewell Inst. Vis. Scis., 1971-72. Mem. AMA (leader Calif. del. continuing med. edn. 1982, 83), San Francisco Med. Soc., Calif. Med. Assn. (sub com. med. policy coms. 1984—, chair com. on accreditation continuing med. edn. 1981-88, chair quality care rev. commn. 1984), Assn. for Rsch. in Vision and Ophthalmology, Pan Am. Assn. of Ophthalmology, Soc. of Heed Fellows, Pacific Coast Oto-Ophthalmology Soc., Lane Medical Soc. (v.p. 1975-76), Internat. Soc. of Neuro-Ophthalmology (founder), Cordes Soc., Am. Soc. Ophthalmic Ultrasound (charter), Orbital Soc. (founder), West Bay Health Systems Agy., Oxford Opthalmology Soc., Pacific Physician Assocs., Soc. Francaise D'Ophtalmologie (mem. editorial bd. jour.). Home: 819 Spring Dr Mill Valley CA 94941-3924

NEWMAN, OTTO, social science educator; b. Vienna, Austria, July 2, 1922; came to U.S., 1987; s. Jonas and Rosa (Schwarzstein) Neumann; m. June Rose Pattenden, July 6, 1946; children: Paul Anthony, Victoria Rose. Inter BSc, Oxford (Eng.) U., 1940; Dip. Soc., London U., 1964; BSc with honours, London Sch. Econs., 1966, PhD, 1970. Mng. dir. Fanderfield Investments Ltd., London, 1950-64; lectr. U. Stirling, Scotland, 1968-71; chmn. dept. social sci. South Bank U., London, 1972-87; prof. social sci. San Diego State U., 1987-91, disting. vis. scholar, 1990, adj. prof., 1991—; vis. prof. Sangamon State U., Springfield, Ill., 1981-82; vis. prof. U. Calif., San Diego, 1983-84, vis. scholar, 1987-90; dir. Lifestyle Rsch. Inst., London, 1984-87; cons. Coun. for Nat. Acad. Awards, London, 1973-81, Greater London Coun., 1983-86. Author: Gambling: Hazard and Reward, 1972, The Challenge of Corporatism, 1981, (rsch. compendium) Lifestyle Enhancement, 1986; editor 3 books; contbr. articles and revs. to profl. jours. Membership officer Labour Party, London, 1962-66. Mem. Brit. Sociol. Assn. (nat. exec. 1976-84, chmn. publ. com. 1975-80), Phi Beta Delta. Home and Office: 25999 Glen Eden Rd Corona CA 91719

NEWMAN, ROBERT MELVILLE, engineering executive; b. Perth, Australia, Sept. 15, 1963; came to U.S., 1991; s. John Melville and Mary (Lavelle) N.; m. Christine Maree Clarkson, Jan. 5, 1985. BEE with Honors, U. West Australia, Perth, 1985, PhDEE, 1989. Dir. network systems QPSX Comms. Ltd., Perth, 1987-91; group product mgr. Synoptics Comms. Inc., Santa Clara, Calif., 1991—. Inventor, patentee queuing protocol, reassembly protocol. Named Young Achiever of Yr., West Australia, 1985; recipient Pursuit of Excellence (Youth) award BHP Bicentennial Com., Australia, 1987. Mem. IEEE. Office: Synoptics Comms Inc 4401 Great America Pkwy Santa Clara CA 95054

NEWMAN, STANLEY RAY, oil refining company executive; b. Milo, Idaho, Mar. 5, 1923; s. Franklin Hughes and Ethel Amelda (Crowley) N.; student Tex. A&M U, 1944-45; B.S., U. Utah, 1947, Ph.D., 1952. m. Rosa Klein, May 27, 1961 (div. Mar. 1980); children: Trudy Lynn, Susan Louise, Karen Elizabeth, Paul Daniel, Phillip John; m. Madelyn Wycherly, Jan. 10, 1991; children: Heidi, Heather, Amy. With Texaco Res. Ctr., Beacon, N.Y., 1951-82, technologist, 1973-77, sr. technologist research mfg.-fuels, 1977-82, profl. cons. on fuels and chems., 1983—. Chmn., Planning Bd., Village of Fishkill, N.Y., 1973- 77; village trustee, 1990-92; mem. Dutchess County Solid Waste Mgmt. Bd., 1974-76. With inf. Signal Corps U.S. Army, 1944-46. Mem. AAAS, N.Y. Acad. Sci., Dutchess County Geneal. Soc. (pres. 1981-87, exec. v.p. 1987-88), N.Y. Fruit Testing Assn., Sigma Xi (pres. Texaco Res. Ctr. br. 1980-81). Republican. Mormon. Patentee in field. Home: 285 Plantation Cir Idaho Falls ID 83404

NEWMAN, WILLIAM DANIEL, aerospace engineer, consultant; b. Redondo Beach, Calif., Nov. 15, 1963; s. Theodore William and Martha (Seiberling) N.; m. Michele Ann Causley, Sept. 19, 1992. BS in Aerospace Engring., UCLA, 1986; MBA in Mgmt., Loyola Marymount U., L.A., 1991. Cons., engr. Northrop Corp., Pico Rivera, Calif., 1986-91; dir. of cons. Tech. Tng. Corp., Torrance, Calif., 1991-92; cons. DMR Group, Inc., Glendale, Calif., 1992—. Vol. South Bay Young Reps., Torrance, 1990—. Mem. Am. Mgmt. Assn., Data Processing Mgmt. Assn., Project Mgmt. Inst. Home: 5410 W 190th St # 71 Torrance CA 90503

NEWMARK, HERBERT LAWRENCE, real estate investor; b. N.Y.C., Nov. 9, 1924; s. Julius Barney and Augusta (Edelstein) N.; m. Jeanne Lorraine Mittleman, Nov. 9, 1952; children: Richard Dale, Phyllis Marie, Jerome Martin, Miles Roger, Janice Beth. Student, San Diego State U., 1949; JD, Balboa U., San Diego, 1950. V.p. Hoyt Corp., Portland, Oreg., 1953-59; CEO Newtronics, Portland, Oreg., 1959-64, Newmark & Assocs., Portland, Oreg., 1964—. Gov. Am. Jewish Com. Nat. Bd., N.Y.C., 1989—; bd. dirs. Jewish Family & Child Svc., Portland, 1988—, Am. Jewish Com., Portland, 1985—, Cons. of Reed Coll., Portland, 1980—. Lt. USN, 1944-52. Decorated DFC, Air medal. Mem. Griffen Soc., Multnomah Club. Democrat. Jewish. Home: 4646 SW Downsview Ct Portland OR 97221 Office: Newmark & Assocs 610 SW Alder Portland OR 97205

NEWNAM, BRIAN EMERSON, physicist; b. L.A., Aug. 11, 1941; s. George Emerson and Margaret Jeanne (Bumpas) N.; m. Kay Ellen Johnson, June 13, 1975; 1 child, Michael Alexander. BA, Occidental Coll., 1962; MA, U. So. Calif., 1966, PhD, 1972. Engr. thermophysics Douglas Aircraft Co., Santa Monica, Calif., 1962-65; staff mem. thermophysics TRW Systems Group, Redondo Beach, Calif., 1965-68; from staff mem. laserphysics to project leader XUV Fels, XUV Lithographic Techs. and LIDAR systems Los Alamos (N.M.) Nat. Lab., 1972—; vis. scientist Max Planck Inst., Garching, Fed. Republic Germany, 1982; editor, co-chmn. Boulder Damage Symposia, Colo., 1979—. Inventor Extreme-Ultraviolet Reflector, 1990, Tunable XUV coherent source, 1993. Fellow Optical Soc. Am.; mem. Soc. Photo-Optical Instrumentation Engrs. (Kingslake Medal and Prize 1991), Violin Soc. Am., Southern Calif. Assn. Violin Makers. Republican. Office: Los Alamos National Lab MSJ564 PO Box 1663 Los Alamos NM 87545

NEWQUIST, DONALD STEWART, designer, technical director, consultant; b. Frankfort, Ky., May 25, 1953; s. Edward Wallace N. and Jeanne Gayle (Utterback) Caddy; m. Linda Susan Carter, Oct. 10, 1987. BA, Centre Coll. of Ky., Danville, 1975; MA, U. Nev., Las Vegas, 1979; postgrad., U. Nev., 1987—. Grad. fellow Ctr. Coll. of Ky., 1975-76; grad. teaching asst. U. Nev., Las Vegas, 1976-78; instr. tech. theater Clark County Community Coll., N. Las Vegas, Nev., 1978-80; tech. supr. City of Las Vegas, 1979-91; adminstr. Las Vegas Civic Ballet, 1988-90; engring. analyst City of Las Vegas Project Unit, 1991; elec. designer T.J. Krob Cons. Engrs., Las Vegas, 1991—; tech. dir. USAF Base Talent Show, Davis-Monthan AFB, Ariz., 1986, 87; tech. cons. USAF Recreation Ctr., Nellis AFB, Nev., 1982-85; resident designer Ecdysis Dance Theater, Las Vegas, 1980-84; mem. Lorenzi Park Amphitheater Task Force, Las Vegas, 1988. Designer: stage renovation, Reed Whipple Cultural Ctr., 1981; stage addition, Charleston Heights Arts Ctr., 1980. Lic. lay reader, Christ Episcopal Ch., Las Vegas, 1981—. Mem. U.S. Inst. for Theater Tech., Illuminating Engring. Soc. of N.Am. (sect. treas. 1989-90, sect. pres. 1990-92, bi-regional conf. chmn.). Republican. Office: TJ Krob Cons Engrs 1919 S Jones Blvd Ste B Las Vegas NV 89102

NEWSOME, RANDALL JACKSON, judge; b. Dayton, Ohio, July 13, 1950; s. Harold I. and Sultana S. (Stony) N.; B.A. summa cum laude, Boston U., 1972; J.D., U. Cin., 1975. Bar: Ohio 1975, U.S. Dist. Ct. (so. dist.) Ohio 1977, U.S. Ct. Appeals (6th cir.) 1979, U.S. Supreme Ct. 1981. Law clk. to chief judge U.S. Dist. Ct., So. Dist. Ohio, 1975-77; assoc. Dinsmore & Shohl, Cin., 1978-82; judge U.S. Bankruptcy Ct., So. Dist. Ohio, Cin., 1982-88, No. Dist. Calif., Oakland, 1988—. Faculty mem. Fed. Jud. Ctr. ALI-ABA, 1987—; mem. Nat. Conf. of Bankruptcy Judges, 1983—, mem. bd. govs., 1987-88. Fellow Am. Coll. Bankruptcy; mem. Am. Bankruptcy Inst., Phi Beta Kappa. Democrat. Mem. United Ch. of Christ. Office: US Bankruptcy Ct PO Box 2070 Oakland CA 94604-2070

NEWSTEAD, ROBERT RICHARD, urologist; b. Detroit, Sept. 16, 1935; s. Oran Henry and Agnes Audery (Lewandowski) N.; m. Marie Carmela LiPuma, Aug. 5, 1961; children: Elizabeth Marie, Peter Joseph, Angela Agnes, Paul Michael. Student, Coll. Idaho, 1955-57, Quincy Coll., 1957-58; MD, Loyola U., Chgo., 1963. Intern Walter Reed Gen. Hosp., Washington, 1963-64; resident U. Iowa, Iowa City, 1967-71; urologist Urology Clinic Yakima, Wash., 1971-84, pres., 1984—; chief of surgery St. Elizabeth Med. Ctr., Yakima, 1980-81, Yakima Valley Hosp., 1978-79. Bd. dirs. St. Elizabeth Found., Yakima, 1983-93, The Capital Theater, 1987-93, Boy Scouts Am., Yakima, 1982-86. Capt. U.S. Army, 1962-67. Fellow Am. Cancer Soc., Iowa City, 1969-70, Am. Cancer Soc., 1961; named one of Outstanding Young Men Am., 1968. Fellow Am. Bd. Urology, ACS, Am. Urol. Assn., Wash. State Urol. Bd.; mem. AMA, Rubin Flocks Soc. (pres. 1985-86), Yakima Surgical Soc. (pres. 1982-83), Yakima County Med. Soc. (pres. 1989-90), Rotary. Roman Catholic. Home: 814 Conestoga Blvd Yakima WA 98908-2419 Office: Urology Clinic Yakima 206 S 11th Ave Yakima WA 98902-3205

NEWTON, RAY CLYDE, university official; b. Denver, Colo., Sept. 26, 1935; s. Louis Weiss and Thelma (Sipe) N.; m. Patricia Rae (Boekhaus), Dec. 27, 1956; children: Sheri D., Lynn D., William L. (dec.). Grad., Kans. State U., Ft. Hays, 1957; postgrad., S.D. State U., 1959-61, U. Tex., 1970-72. Tchr., chmn. English dept. LaCrosse (Kans.) High Sch., 1957-59; mem. faculty N.Mex. Highlands U., Las Vegas, 1961-63, instr., asst. dean students, 1963-73, dir. pub. info. and pubs., adminstrv. asst. to pres., 1965-73, asst. prof., then assoc. prof. journalism, 1965-73; mem. faculty No. Ariz. U., Flagstaff, 1973—, prof. journalism, asst. dean creative and communication arts, 1984-87, dean, 1987-88, assoc. to pres., 1988—; dir. bilingual mass media program N.Mex. Highlands U., 1972-73; corr. Sta. KGGM-TV, Albuquerque, 1966-71; cons. in field to newspapers and mcpl. govts. Author: (with Newsom and Wellert) Media Writing, 1984, (with Vannette and Cervany) Rethinking Global Education, 1993; contbr. articles and revs. to profl. jours. and popular mags. Mem. adminstrv. bd. Trinity Heights Meth. Ch.; mem. exec. council Grand Canyon council Boy Scouts Am.; bd. dirs. Flagstaff Festival of the Arts; ex-officio bd. dirs. Ariz. Alliance for Arts Edn.; environ. cons. Nat. Park Svc., U.S. Forest Svc., 1990—. Grantee Rotary Found. 1968, Danforth Found., 1969-70; Walter fellow U. Tex., 1971-72; named Journalism Prof. of Yr., Ariz. Newspaper Assn., 1984, Disting. Faculty mem. No. Ariz. U., 1984; recipient Nat. Teaching award Poynter Inst. Media Studies, St. Petersburg, Fla., 1985. Mem. Assn. Edn. Journalism/Mass Communication, Am. Soc. Journalism Sch. Adminstrs., Am. Soc. Newspaper Editors (mem. minorities edn. com.), Aris. Press Assn. (mem. bd. dirs., chmn. edn. com.), Western Social Scis. Assn. (v.p. 1979-80, mem. exec. coun., editorial bd.), Am. Assn. Higher Edn., Inter-Am. Press Assn., 1st Amendment Coalition (past bd. dirs.), Soc. Profl. Journalists, Coll. Sports Info. Dirs. Assn., Flagstaff C. of C., Kiwanis, Phi Eta Sigma, Lambda Iota Tau, Phi Delta Kappa (area coord. Ariz.), Pi Rho Sigma, Phi Kappa Phi (nat. bd. dirs., Disting. Svc. award 1992), Kappa Tau Alpha. Home: 1520 E Appalachian Rd Flagstaff AZ 86004-1714 Office: No Ariz U Office of Pres Box 4092 Flagstaff AZ 86011

NEWTON, RICHARD HOWARD, mechanical engineer; b. Milw., Oct. 12, 1932; s. Howard Leslie and Evelyn Jennie (Shove) N.; m. Martha Jane Dinsmore, Sept. 11, 1954 (dec. Sept. 1964); m. Dorothea Elaine Gregloit, Feb. 19, 1966; children: Scott, Gayle Jensen, Jeffrey, Mark. BSME, Purdue U., 1954; attended AEA Exec. Inst., Stanford U., 1979; MBA, Claremont (Calif.) Grad. Sch., 1984. Engr. Robbins & Myers, Inc., Springfield, Ohio, 1954; project engr. Avionics div. Aerojet, Azusa, Calif., 1956-63; mgr. measurements dept. Astronics div. Aerojet, Azusa, 1963-67, asst. to mgr. Microelectronics div., 1967-68, spl. projects mgr. Astronics div., 1968-79, mgr. Electro Systems, 1979-82, mgr. cen. programs Electro Systems, 1982-88, mgr. spl. ops. Electronics div., 1988—; bd. dirs. Citrus Coll. Found., Glendora, Calif., Rec. for Blind, Inc., Pomona, Calif. Chmn., bd. dirs. Parks and Recreation Commn., Claremont, 1970-72, Planning Commn., 1972-75; mayor City of Clarement, 1978-80; city councilman, 1989-90. Recipient Awards of Honor L.A. County Bd. Suprs., 1980, 1st Dist. L.A. County, 1990. Mem. ASME, AIAA, Am. Def. Preparedness Assn., Air Force Assn., Nat. Space Club, Masonic Lodge. Republican. Presbyterian. Home: 2270 N Tulsa Ave Claremont CA 91711-1604 Office: Aerojet Electronics Div 1100 W Hollyvale St Azusa CA 91702-3333

NEWTON, ROBERT JAMES, naturopath, landscape designer and contractor; b. Pomona, Calif., Oct. 31, 1946; s. Charles Marvin Newton and Nadine Martha (Pickering) Feldheim; m. Charlotte Ann Smith (div. 1986); m. Elizabeth McKinney (div.); 1 child, Charles Robert. BA, Calif. State U., Fullerton, 1968; JD, Am. Coll. Law, Anaheim, Calif., 1975; D Naturopathic Medicine, Clayton Sch. Natural Healing, Birmingham, Ala., 1991. Owner, operator Beautiful Bob's Landscaping, Santa Ana, Calif., 1970-88, Harmonic Environments, 1988—; owner, practitioner Magnetic Healing Ctr., Rixeyville, Va., 1989-91, Huntington Beach, Calif., 1991—. Author: Pathways to God, 1993, (juvenile) Crusing with Charles, 1993. With Calif. Army N.G., 1969-75. Fellow Newport-Irvine Profl. Assn., Assn. Wholistic Healers; mem. Calif. Landscape Contractos Assn. (cert. landscape technician, bd. dirs. Orange County 1979-80, awards 1979, 80, 81), Tibetan Found. (cert. channel and energy practitioner, bd. dirs., v.p. 1984-85), Ch. Universal Knowledge (cert. magnetic healer, assoc.). Home and Office: Harmonic Environs 2301 Florida St Apt 2 Huntington Beach CA 92648

NEWTON, WAYNE, entertainer, actor, recording artist; b. Norfolk, Va., Apr. 3, 1942; s. Patrick and Evelyn (Smith) N.; m. Elaine Okamura, 1968 (div.); 1 child, Erin. L.H.D. (hon.), U. Nev.-Las Vegas, 1981. Owner Tamiment Internat. Resort. Appearances include Sands, Caesar's Palace, Desert Inn, Flamingo and Frontier hotels, Las Vegas, Harrah's Club, Reno and Lake Tahoe, I Love N.Y. Concert, Americana Hotel, N.Y.C., Talk of the Town, London, London Paladium, Grand Ole Oprey House, Nashville, 4th of July, Washington, Astrodome, Houston, Hollywood (Calif.) Bowl, Melodyland, Anaheim, Calif., Circle Star, San Francisco, Sea World, Orlando, Fla., Sherman House, Chgo., Wis. State, Iowa State fairs, Valley Forge Music, Westbury Music fairs, Deauville and Eden Roc hotels, Miami Beach, Carlton Club, Bloomington, Minn., hotels Atlantic City, N.J., before U.S. troops, Beirut; TV appearances on shows of Red, White & Wow, A Christmas Card, miniseries North and South: Book II, 1986; film appearance in 80 Steps to Jonah, 1969; numerous recs; author (with Dick Maurice): Once Before I Go, 1989. A supporter St. John's Indian Mission, Levene, Ariz. Recipient citation as distinguished recording artist and humanitarian, 1971; Freedom Lantern award Commonwealth of Mass., 1979; Entertainer of Yr. award Variety Clubs So. Nev., 1973; Gov.'s award Commonwealth of Mass., 1976; cert. of appreciation Gov. of Nev., 1978; Outstanding Indian Entertainer of Yr. Navajo Nation, 1980; Founders award St. Judes Childrens Hosp.; Humanitarian award AMC Cancer Research Ctr.; Recipient award for Daddy Don't Walk So Fast ASCAP; platinum record for Danke Schoen, also gold album and gold records; also others.; named One of 10 Outstanding Young Men of Am. Nat. Jaycees, 1976, Most Disting. Citizen of Yr. NCCJ. Office: Flying Eagle Inc care Alan Margulies 6000 S Eastern Ave Ste 7B Las Vegas NV 89119-3100

NG, GERALD JOE LUP, marketing professional; b. Honolulu, Apr. 11, 1946; s. Buck Sam and Laura Jun (Lau) N.; m. Cheryl Pidgursky, Aug. 10, 1968; children: Michael Andrew, Amy Allison. Student, U. Calif., Davis, 1964-66; BBA, San Francisco State U., 1978. Sales rep. Beech Nut Foods, Oakland, Calif., 1967-69, Cook and Harms, Mill Valley, Calif., 1969-70, Ideal Toys, N.Y.C., 1970-72; br. mgr. Heads and Threads, Chgo., 1972-77; purchasing mgr. Danforth Screw and Bolt Co., San Carlos, Calif., 1977-81; asst. gen. mgr. Danforth Screw and Bolt Co., San Carlos, 1981-83, gen. mgr., 1983-85, v.p. sales, 1985—. Vice chmn. San Ramon (Calif.) Facilities Group, 1990; pub. rels. chairperson Calif. High Sch. Boosters, 1990—. Mem. U.S. Swimming Northern Calif. (treas. Pacific Swimming). Home: 8 San Pedro Pl San Ramon CA 94583-3017

NG, LAWRENCE CHEN-YIM, electronics engineer; b. Canton, Kowntung, China, Dec. 21, 1946; s. Johnny Fook and Betty Big (Chan) N.; m. Karen Shu, July 21, 1974; children: Edison, Jefferson, Kristina. BS, MIT, 1970, MS, 1973; PhD, U. Conn., 1983. Sr. engr. EB div. Gen. Dynamics, Groton, Conn., 1974-78; project leader Naval Underwater Systems Ctr., New London, Conn., 1978-84; group leader Lawrence Livermore (Calif.) Nat. Lab., 1985—. Mem. IEEE (sr.). Republican. Home: 80 Country Hill Ct Danville CA 94506-6149 Office: Lawrence Livermore Nat Lab PO Box 808 Livermore CA 94551-0808

NG, LAWRENCE MING-LOY, pediatric cardiologist; b. Hong Kong, Mar. 21, 1940; came to U.S., 1967, naturalized, 1977; s. John Iu-cheung and Mary Wing (Wong) N.; B.Med., U. Hong Kong, 1965, B.Surg., 1965; m. Bella May Ha Kan, June 25, 1971; children: Jennifer Wing-mui, Jessica Wing-yee. House physician Queen Elizabeth Hosp., Hong Kong, 1965-66, med. officer, 1966-67; resident physician Children's Hosp. of Los Angeles, 1967-68; resident physician Children's Hosp. Med. Center, Oakland, Calif., 1968-70, fellow in pediatric cardiology, 1970-72, now mem. teaching staff; practice medicine, specializing in pediatrics and pediatric cardiology, San Leandro, Calif., 1972—, Oakland, Calif., 1982—; mng. ptnr. Pediatric Assocs. of East Bay, 1990—; chief of pediatrics Oakland Hosp., 1974-77; chief of pediatrics Vesper Meml. Hosp., 1977-79, sec. staff, 1984, v.p. staff, 1985; chief pediatrics Meml. Hosp., San Leandro, 1986-88; founder Pediatric Assocs. of East Bay, 1990. Active Republican Party. Diplomate Am. Bd. Pediatrics. Fellow Am. Acad. Pediatrics; mem. AMA, Calif. Med. Assn., Am. Heart Assn., Los Angeles Pediatric Soc., East Bay Pediatric Soc., Smithsonian Assos., Nat. Geog. Soc., Orgn. Chinese Ams. (chpt. pres. 1984), Chinese-Am. Physicians Soc. (co-founder, sec. 1980, pres. 1983), Oakland Mus. Assns., Oakland Chinatown C. of C. (bd. dirs. 1986-91), Hong Kong U. Alumni Assn. (sec. No. Calif. chpt. 1992—), Commonwealth Club. Buddhist. Office: 345 9th St Ste 4205 Oakland CA 94607-4206 also: 1234 E 14th St Ste 401 San Leandro CA 94577

NG, WING CHIU, accountant, computer software consultant, educator, activist; b. Hong Kong, Hong Kong, Oct. 14, 1947; came to U.S., 1966; s. Bing Nuen and Oi Ying (Lee) Ng. BS, Yale U., 1969, MS, 1969; PhD, NYU, 1972. CPA, Hawaii. Rsch. assoc. SUNY, Stony Brook, 1972-74; asst. prof. U. Md., College Park, 1974-76; rsch. physicist U. Bonn, Fed. Republic of Germany, 1976-78; chartered acct. Richter, Usher & Vineberg, Montreal, Can., 1978-80; pvt. practice Honolulu, Hawaii, 1980—; pres. Bowen, Ng & Co., Honolulu, 1983-84, Asia-Am. Investment, Inc., Honolulu, 1983—, Mathematica Pacific, Inc., Honolulu, 1984—; part-time prof. U. Hawaii, Honolulu, 1982—; ptnr. Advance Realty Investment, Honolulu, 1980—; dir. S & L Internat., Inc., Honolulu, 1987—. Creator: (computer software) Time Billing, 1984, Dbase General Ledger, 1987, Dbase Payroll, 1987, Dbase Accounts Receivable, 1989. Dir. Orgn. of Chinese Ams., Honolulu, 1984-86, Fedn. for a Dem. China, Honolulu, 1990—, Hong Kong, 1991—. Included in Prominent People of Hawaii, Delta Pub. Co., 1988. Mem. AICPA, Hong Kong Soc. Accts., Hawaiian Trail & Mountain Club (auditor 1987—). Democrat. Buddhist. Office: 1149 Bethel St Ste 411 Honolulu HI 96813

NGUYEN, ANN CAC KHUE, pharmaceutical and medicinal chemist; b. Sontay, Vietnam; came to U.S., 1975; naturalized citizen; d. Nguyen Van Soan and Luu Thi Hieu. BS, U. Saigon, 1973; MS, San Francisco State U., 1978; PhD, U. Calif., San Francisco, 1983. Teaching and research asst. U. Calif., San Francisco, 1978-83, postdoctoral fellow, 1983-86; research scientist U. Calif., 1987—. Contbr. articles to profl. jours. Recipient Nat. Research Service award, NIH, 1981-83; Regents fellow U. Calif., San Francisco, 1978-81. Mem. AAAS, Am. Chem. Soc., N.Y.Acad. Scis., Bay Area Enzyme Mechanism Group, Am. Assn. Pharm. Scientists. Roman Catholic. Home: 1488 Portola Dr San Francisco CA 94127-1409 Office: U Calif Lab Connective Tissue Biochemistry Box 0424 San Francisco CA 94143

NGUYEN, HUE LE, computer company executive, real estate and mortgage consultant; b. Bien Hoa, Vietnam, Sept. 19, 1968; came to U.S., 1985; s. Huan Le Nguyen and That Thi Tran. BS in Elec. Engring., Calif. State U., Fullerton, 1990, postgrad., 1991—. Lic. real estate broker. Sales mgr. VNI Computer, Westminster, Calif., 1990-91; mng. ptnr. KT Mktg. Group, Garden Grove, Calif., 1991-92; pres. Opportunity Land Realty, Garden Grove, 1991—, Merlion Computer, Garden Grove, 1991—; dir. Pho Hoa An, Inc., Garden Grove, 1990—. Mng. editor Non Song Mag., 1988-90; editor: From a Dream, 1990. Dir. Union of Vietnamese Student Assn. So. Calif., Costa Mesa, 1988-90. Mem. Tau Beta Chi. Republican. Roman Catholic. Home: 11772 Seacrest Dr Garden Grove CA 92640

NGUYEN, KING XUAN, educator; b. Hue, Vietnam, Dec. 20, 1930; came to U.S., 1975; s. Duong Xuan Nguyen and Thi Thi Ton-Nu. BA, U. Saigon, 1960, LLB, 1963; MEd, Boise State U., 1980. Tchr. Boise Sch. Dist., 1975—; lectr. S.E. Asian Studies Summer Inst./U. Wash., 1992—; spl. lectr. Boise State U., 1975-77; lectr. Seassi/U. Washington, 1992—. Col. Vietnamese Air Force to 1975. Recipient Red Apple Award for Outstanding Svc. to Edn., Boise, 1990. Mem. NEA, Idaho Edn. Assn., Boise Edn. Assn. Home: 9674 W Pattie Ct Boise ID 83704-2824 Office: Boise Sr High Sch 1010 E Washington St Boise ID 83702-5493

NGUYEN, TAN DINH, pharmacist; b. Saigon, Vietnam, June 3, 1956; came to U.S. 1974; s. Soan Van and Hieu Thi (Luu) N. BA in Chemistry with honors, San Francisco State U., 1980, BS in Biochemistry with honors, 1980; PharmD, U. Calif., San Francisco, 1985. Lic. in pharmacy, Calif. Rsch. asst. San Francisco State U., 1979-80; pharmacy intern U. Calif., San Francisco, 1984-85; staff pharmacist Walgreens Drug Co., Oakland, Calif., 1986-90; pharmacy mgr. Walgreens Drug Co., San Francisco, 1990—; adj. prof. pharmacy practice U. of Pacific, Stockton, Calif., 1991—. Roman Catholic. Home: 1488 Portola Dr San Francisco CA 94127

NGUYEN, THINH VAN, physician; b. Vietnam, Apr. 16, 1948; came to U.S., 1971; s. Thao Van and Phuong Thi (Tran) N.; m. Phi Thi Ho, Jan. 2, 1973; children: Anh-Quan, Andrew. BS, U. Saigon, 1970; MS, U. Mo., 1973; MD, U. Tex., 1982. Diplomate Am. Bd. Internal Medicine, Am. Acad. Pain Mgmt., Fed. Lic. Examination. Rsch. asst. U. Tex. Med. Sch., Dallas, 1974-78; intern U. Tex. Med. Br., Galveston, 1982-83, resident, 1983-85; internist Family Health Plan, Inc., Long Beach, Calif., 1985-88, internist, area chief, 1988-89; pvt. practice San Jose, Calif., 1990—; chmn. interdisciplinary com. Charter Community Hosp., Hawaiian Gardens, Calif., 1988-89. Mem. ACP, Am. Acad. Pain Mgmt., Calif. Assn. of Med. Dirs. (bd. dirs. 1988—), So. Med. Assn. Office: 2470 Alvin Ave Ste 5 San Jose CA 95121

NGUYEN, TIEN MANH, communications systems engineer; b. Saigon, Vietnam, Apr. 5, 1957; came to the U.S., 1975; s. Hung The and Bi Thi (Luu) N.; m. Thu Hang Thi, Dec. 28 1986. BS in Engring., Calif. State U., Fullerton, 1979, MS in Engring., 1980; postgrad., Calif. State U., Long Beach, 1991—, MA in Engring. Math., 1993; MEE, U. Calif., San Diego, 1982; PhD in Engring., Columbia Pacific U., 1986. Cert. EMC engr., Mfg. tech. Teaching asst. U. Calif., San Diego, 1982-83; chief automated mfg. dept. ITT Ednl. Svcs., West Covina, Calif., 1983-85; mem. tech. staff Jet Propulsion Lab., Pasadena, Calif., 1985—; prin. tech. advisor Internat. Consultative Com. for Space Data Systems, Pasadena, 1985-90. Editor: Proceedings of CCSDS RF & Modulation, 1989; contbr. more than 18 articles to profl. jours. Grad. rep. EECS dept. U. Calif., San Diego, 1982-83; NASA del. to internat. CCSDS, 1986—. San Diego fellow, 1980-82, Long Beach Found. scholar Calif. State U.; recipient Bendix Mgmt. Club award, 1987, NASA Honor award, 1988, over 12 NASA monetary awards, 1989—. Mem. IEEE (vice chmn. 1987—, session chmn. internat. symposium on EMC 1986, award 1986), AIAA (sr.), Soc. Mfg. Engrs., Am. Math. Soc., Armed Forces Communications and Electronics Assn., N.Y. Acad. Scis., U.S. Naval Inst., Internat. Platform Assn. Republican. Buddhist. Home: 1501 W Maxzim Ave Fullerton CA 92633 Office: Jet Propulsion Lab 4800 Oak Grove Dr Pasadena CA 91109-8099

NGUYEN, TRUNG DUC, research scientist; b. Saigon, Vietnam, May 14, 1951; came to U.S., 1969; s. Ambrose Q. and Teresa T. Nguyen; m. Susan Bui, Apr. 5, 1975; children: Jason T., Jessica K. BSEE, U. Minn., 1973; MSEE, U. Santa Clara, 1974; PhD in Elec. Engring., Calif. Western U., 1980. Project engr. Systron Donner Corp., Van Nuys, Calif., 1975-79; engring. specialist Litton Data Systems, Van Nuys, 1979-83; sr. engr. Singer Co., Glendale, Calif., 1983-86; sr. tech. staff TRW, Redondo Beach, Calif., 1986-87; sr. rsch. scientist Teledyne Systems Co., Northridge, Calif., 1987—. Contbr. articles on electronics to profl. jours. Mem. IEEE (sr.), Northridge Mgmt. Club. Home: 9430 Gierson Ave Chatsworth CA 91311-4705 Office: Teledyne Systems Co 19601 Nordhoff St Northridge CA 91324-2414

NGUYEN, TUAN ANH, data processing executive; b. Viet Nam, Sept. 2, 1956; came to U.S. 1974; s. Xuan Thanh and Tuyet N. BSEE, BS in Math., BS in Computer Sci., Portland State U., 1979; MS in Computer Engring., Oreg. State U., 1982. Design engr. Tektronix Inc., Beaverton, Oreg., 1979-82; sr. software engr. Intel Corp., Hillsboro, Oreg., 1982-84, Silicon Sys., Inc., Tustin, Calif., 1984-87; cons. TN & Assocs., Orange, Calif., 1987-89; pres. Quicksoft Inc., Orange, 1989—. Mem. Orange 2000 Project, Calif., 1987, Dannemeyer for Congress, Orange, 1990. Mem. IEEE, ACM, Profl., Tech. Cons. Assn., Ind. Computer Cons. Assn. (dir. 1989—).

NGUYEN, VU LINH, mechanical draftsman; b. Saigon, Vietnam, Nov. 4, 1966; came to U.S., 1989; s. Quynh Van and Tam Thi Nguyen. Student, Santa Barbara City Coll., U. Calif., Santa Barbara. Archtl. draftsman Internal Decoration Inc., Saigon, 1986-89; mech. draftsman constrn. co., Saigon, 1986-89, Amber Engring. Corp., Goleta, Calif., 1990—. Winslow Maxwell scholar Santa Barbara City Coll., scholar U. Calif., Santa Barbara. Home: 119 D S Kellogg Ave Goleta CA 93117 Office: Amber Engring Inc 5756 Thornwood Dr Goleta CA 93117-3802

NI, WAYNE WEIJEN, telecommunications executive; b. Taipei, Taiwan, China, May 4, 1961; came to U.S., 1976; s. Fu Yuan and Suh Ling (Hwang) N. BA in Bus. Econs., U. Calif., Santa Barbara, 1983; Exec. MBA, Pepperdine U., 1989. Acct. Valley Provisions, Inc., Goleta, Calif., 1983-84; cost acct. Info. Magnetics, Inc., Goleta, 1984-85; chief acct. Goleta Valley Hosp., 1985-86; chief exec. officer NI Telecommunications, Inc., Santa Barbara, 1985—; corp. controller Signal Tech., Inc., Goleta, 1987-90; v.p., CFO Clamshell Bldgs., Inc., Ventura, 1990—; cons., tax planning Wayne Ni Enterprises, Santa Barbara, 1982—. Mem. Am. Electronics Assn. Republican. Home: 892 Vallecito Dr Ventura CA 93001 Office: Clamshell Bldgs Inc 1990 Knoll Dr Ventura CA 93003

NIBLEY, ROBERT RICKS, retired lawyer; b. Salt Lake City, Sept. 24, 1913; s. Joel and Teresa (Taylor) N.; m. Lee Allen, Jan. 31, 1945 (dec.); children—Jane, Annette. A.B., U. Utah, 1934; J.D., Loyola U., Los Angeles, 1942. Bar: Calif. bar 1943. Accountant Nat. Parks Airways, Salt Lake City, 1934-37, Western Air Lines, Los Angeles, 1937-40; asst. mgr. market research dept. Lockheed Aircraft Corp., Burbank, Calif., 1940-43; asso. firm Hill, Farrer and Burrill, Los Angeles, 1946-53; partner Hill, Farrer and Burrill, 1953-70, of counsel, 1971-78. Served from ensign to lt. comdr. USNR, 1943-46. Mem. Am., Los Angeles bar assns., Phi Delta Phi, Phi Kappa Phi, Phi Delta Theta. Club: California (Los Angeles). Home: 4860 Ambrose Ave Los Angeles CA 90027-1866

NICE, CARTER, conductor, music director; b. Jacksonville, Fla., Apr. 5, 1940; s. Clarence Carter and Elizabeth Jane (Hintermister) N.; m. Jennifer Charlotte Smith, Apr. 4, 1983; children: Danielle, Christian. MusB, Eastman Sch. Music, 1962; MusM, Manhattan Sch. Music., 1964. Asst. condr., concert master New Orleans Philharm., 1967-79; condr., music dir. Sacramento Symphony, 1979-92; music dir., conductor Bear Valley Music Fest., 1985—. Office: 200 P St Ste B36 Sacramento CA 95814

NICE, JAMES WILLIAM, electronics educator; b. La Grande, Oreg., Apr. 10, 1948; s. Glenn Orvin and Jeana Mae (Sullivan) N.; m. Claudia Jo Salzer, Oct. 21, 1967; children: Laura Lee, Chandra Rae. AS in Bus. Mgmt., Mt. Hood Community Coll., Gresham, Oreg., 1979; student, Thomas A. Edison State Coll., 1988—; AS in Electronics Engring. Tech., ITT Tech. Inst., Portland, 1989. Enlisted USN, 1966, electronics technician, 1988-92; student Concordia Coll., Portland, 1993; resigned USN, 1976; field service technician AM Corp., Portland, Oreg., 1976-78; sci. inst. technician State of Oreg., Portland, 1978-81; quality control mgr. Landa Inc., Portland, 1981-83; master electronics instr. ITT Tech. Inst., Portland, 1983—. Mem. Land Use Planning Bd., Gresham, 1977-78; chmn. budget com. Rockwood Water Dist., Gresham, 1982-86; mem. Multnomah County Mounted Sheriff Posse, Portland, 1988—. Mem. IEEE (assoc.), Internat. Soc. Cert. Electronic Technicians, Nat. Assn. Radio and Telecommunications Engrs. Democrat. Mormon. Home: 940 NE Littlepage Rd Corbett OR 97019-9736 Office: ITT Tech Inst 6035 NE 78th Ct Portland OR 97218-2854

NICELY, TIMOTHY, producer, writer; b. Glendale, Calif., Mar. 26, 1944; s. Mario Datious and Dorothy (Machtolf) Paola; married; 1 child, Jesse Dakota. Student, L.A. Community Coll., 1967, 68, 69; grad., Don Martin Sch. Broadcasting & TV Arts, Hollywood, Cali., 1975; student, Calif. State U., Northridge, 1981, SAG Conservatory, Hollywood, 1989-91; cert., Hypnosis Motivation Inst., 1993. Cert. master hypnotist. Talent agt. Webb Agy., Hollywood, 1976; chief oper. officer R.A. Chicken & Assocs., Sherman Oaks, Calif., 1979-87; writer, coord. Toyko TV Spls., 1983, 85, TV Spl./Landsburg Prodn., Hollywood, 1984; producer, host Radio Interview Show, Westlake, Calif., 1986-91; pres. Nicely Co., Woodland Hills, Calif., 1987-91; exec. dir. Solutions Internat., 1992-93; creator, instr. L.T. Univ., Thousand Oaks, Calif., 1988; host, producer Oakwood Industries Incentive Programs, La., Md., Tex., 1988. Author: (children's book) Blast Off, 1982, A New Vaudeville, 1987; creator, writer (cartoon strip) The Good Rumor Man, 1991—; columnist The Good News, 1992—. Mem. counsel YMCA, Reseda, Calif., 1984-87; curator, founder Fowlmania Mus., Reseda, 1984-87; entertainment chmn. March of Dimes/Latina Fiesta, L.A., 1985; host March of Dimes/Reading Champion Progam, L.A., 1985-86; chief brave turkey YMCA Ind. Guide Program, Reseda, 1986-87. With USMC, 1963-66. Recipient Outstanding Achievement award L.A. March of Dimes, 1986. Mem. AFTRA, Screen Actors Guild, Actors Equity Assn., The Hypnosis Union, Am. Hypnosis Assn. Office: Solutions Internat 19528 Ventura Blvd Ste 278 Tarzana CA 91356

NICHOLAS, FREDERICK M., lawyer; b. N.Y.C., May 30, 1920; s. Benjamin L. and Rose F. (Nechols) N.; m. Eleanore Berman, Sept. 2, 1951 (div. 1963); children: Deborah, Jan, Tony; m. Joan Fields, Jan. 2, 1983. AB, U. So. Calif., 1947; postgrad., U. Chgo., 1949-50; JD, U. So. Calif., 1952. Bar: Calif. 1952, U.S. Dist. Ct. Calif. 1952, U.S. Ct. Appeals (9th cir.) 1952. Assoc. Loeb & Loeb, L.A., 1952-56; ptnr. Swerdlow, Glikbarg & Nicholas, Beverly Hills, Calif., 1956-62; pvt. practice Beverly Hills, 1962-80; pres., atty. Hapsmith Co., Beverly Hills, 1980—; bd. dirs. Malibu Grand Prix, L.A., 1982-90; gen. counsel Beverly Hills Realty Bd., 1971-79; founder, pres. Pub. Counsel, L.A., 1970-73. Author: Commercial Real Property Lease Practice, 1976. Chmn. Mus. Contemporary Art, L.A., 1987-93, chmn. com. Walt Disney Concert Hall, L.a., 1987—; trustee Music Ctr. L.A. County, 1993—; trustee L.A. Philharm. Assn., 1987—; chmn. Calif. Pub. Broadcasting Commn., Sacramento, 1972-78; pres. Maple Ctr., 1977-79. Recipient Man of Yr. award Maple Ctr., 1980, Citizen of Yr. award Beverly Hills Bd. Realtors, 1978. Mem. Beverly Hills Bar Assn. (bd. govs. 1970-76, Disting. Svc. award 1974, 81, Exceptional Svc. award 1986), Beverly Hills C. of C. (Man of Yr. 1983). Home: 1011 Cove Way Beverly Hills CA 90210-2818 Office: Hapsmith Co 9300 Wilshire Blvd Beverly Hills CA 90212-3213

NICHOLAS, LAURIE STEVENS, marketing consultant; b. Urbana, Ill., Oct. 2, 1959; d. Richard Charles and Rosemary (Vose) Stevens; m. Robert Arthur Nicholas, Aug. 6, 1983; children: Kali, Connor, Quentin. BS with honors, U. Wyo., 1981, postgrad., 1981-82, MBA, 1983. Asst. product mgr. Unicover Corp., Cheyenne, Wyo., 1983-85, 87-89; mktg. cons. Noble Internat. Travel Agy., Lander, Wyo., 1986, Wyo. State Jour., Lander, 1986; cons. joint legis. and exec. study State of Wyo., Cheyenne, 1987; market researcher Unicover Corp., Cheyenne, 1989-91; instr. Ctrl. Wyo. Coll., Riverton, 1991. Active Econ. Devel. Commn., Lander, 1986, Friends of the Symphony, Cheyenne, 1987. Mem. Fremont County Rep. Women's Club, Local Book Club, Riverton Country Club. Republican. Roman Catholic.

NICHOLAS, THOMAS PETER, library director, community television consultant, producer; b. Laramie, Wyo., Dec. 6, 1948; s. Thomas Lloyd Nicholas and Frances (Collins) Chambers; m. Tanya Michelle Villont; 1 child, Ja'el Michelle. AA in Fine Arts, Cabrillo Coll., 1970; BA in English, U. Colo., 1972; MS in Librarianship and Info. Sci., U. Denver, 1982. Real estate salesperson Sun Country, Lakewood, Colo., 1972-74; v.p. Nicholas Properties, Denver, 1971-77; libr. City of Aurora, Colo., 1975-80, system support mgr., 1981-83, dir. libr. and TV svcs., 1984—; pres. bd. Irving Libr. Network Inc., Denver, 1985—; advisor CL System Inc., Boston, 1985—; acting pers. dir. City of Aurora. Exec. producer TV programs: Election Night 85 (Franny award 1986), Miss Plumjoy's Place, 1988 (Starwards 1988), Aurora's Can't Afford Not To, 1988 (Starwards 1988). Mem. exec. bd., chmn. Arapahoe Pub. Access to Librs., 1984-85; site coordinator Am. Cancer Soc., Aurora, 1988; adv. Youth at Risk, Aurora, 1989; bd. dirs. Cen. Colo. Libr. System, Lakewood, 1985-87; mem. exec. bd. Colo. Libr. Legis. Com., Denver, 1988—; pres. Greater Metro Cable Consortium, 1992—. Mem. ALA, Colo. Libr. Assn. (advisor 1982-83, Programming award 1982, 1st Colo. Childrens Program award 1983, 88), Nat. Assn. Telecommunications Officers and Advisors (regional pres. 1983-84, T.V. Program award 1986), Rotary (program chmn. 1987-88), Eastgate Lions Club (pres. 1989-90). Democrat. Greek Orthodox. Office: Aurora Pub Libr 14949 E Alameda Dr Aurora CO 80012-1500*

NICHOLAW, GEORGE, communications executive; b. Salinas, Calif., Nov. 17, 1927; s. Costas and Anna G. (Melissa) N.; m. Betty Baron. B in Fgn. Trade, Am. Grad. Sch. Internat. Mgmt.; BS, U. Calif., Berkeley. Program dir. Sta. KDON, Salinas, 1953-55; asst. dir. promotion, publicity Sta. KNXT-TV, Los Angeles, 1955-63; dir. info. services and community relations Sta. WBBM-TV, Chgo., 1963-66; dir. community services Sta. WCBS-TV, N.Y.C., 1966-67; v.p. CBS radio div., gen. mgr. Sta. KNX, Los Angeles, 1967—. Commr. Los Angeles Energy Commn.; active Communications Task Force Greater Los Angeles Urban Coalition., Calif. Air Pollution Emergency Traffic Control Com. Served with U.S. Army. Recipient Abe Lincoln award, Peabody award, Ohio State award, Alfred I DuPont award, Columbia U. Mem. Nat. Assn. Broadcasters, Calif. Broadcasters Assn. (dir. Los Angeles chpt.), Hollywood Radio and TV Soc. (dir. Los Angeles chpt.), Arbitron Radio Adv. Council (past chmn.), Calif. Inst. Cancer Research (bd. dirs.), Permanent Charities Com. Entertainment Industries (bd. dirs.). Office: Sta KNX(AM) 6121 W Sunset Blvd Los Angeles CA 90028-6455

NICHOLIA, IRENE KAY, organization administrator; b. Tanana, Ala., Oct. 6, 1956; d. Peter P. and Susie (John) N. Attended, Sheldon Jackson Coll., Ala., 1975-77. Bilingual aid Yukon Sch. Dist., Nenana, 1978-84; programs adminstr. Tanana Ira Native Coun., 1984—. sch. bd. mem. Tanana Sch. Bd., 1988-90; adv. Yukon Salmon Treaty Negotiation, Can./Ala., 1990-92; bd. dirs. Ala. Fedn. of Natives, Anchorage, 1990-92; task force mem. Tanana Chiefs Subsistence Task Force, Fairbanks, 1990-92. Democrat. Episcopalian. Office: State of Alaska State Capitol Juneau AK 99801

NICHOLS, ALAN HAMMOND, lawyer; b. Palo Alto, Calif., Feb. 14, 1940; s. John Ralph and Shirley Weston (Charles) N.; children: Alan Hammond, Sharon Elizabeth, Shan Darwin; m. Nancy A. Mattingly, Mar. 28, 1988; stepchildren: Christopher, McCabe. BA, Stanford U., 1951, JD, 1955; DS (hon.), Calif. Coll. Podiatric Medicine, 1980. Bar: Calif. 1955, U.S. Dist. Ct. (no. dist.) Calif. 1955, U.S. Dist. Ct. (cen. dist.) Calif. 1969, U.S. Dist. Ct. (ea. dist.) Calif. 1978, U.S. Dist. Ct. Ariz. 1978, U.S. Supreme Ct. 1978, U.S. Dist. Ct. Minn. 1979, U.S. Dist. Ct. (so. dist.) Calif. 1980, U.S. Tax Ct. 1981. Assoc. Lillick, Geary, Wheat, Adams & Charles, San Francisco, 1955-61; pres. Nichols & Rogers, San Francisco, 1961-74; pres. Nichols Law Corp., San Francisco, 1974-83, 1992—; pres. Nichols, Doi, Rapaport & Chan, San Francisco, 1987-92; prof. forensic medicine Calif. Coll. Podiatric Medicine, 1975-77. Mem. San Francisco Library Commn., 1962-65; v.p. San Francisco Council Chs., 1965-68; pres. sch. bd. San Francisco Unified Sch. Dist., 1967-71; exec. com. Council Great City Schs. of U.S.; del. Calif. Sch. Bd. Assn. Assembly; mem. Civil Grand Jury, San Francisco, 1975-76; pres. Young Republicans San Francisco, 1957, Calif., 1959; mem. Rep. Central Com., San Francisco, 1961-93, pres., 1976; trustee City Coll. San Francisco, 1966-71, pres. bd. trustees, 1970-71; trustee Calif. Coll. Podiatric Medicine, 1973-85, Cathedral Sch., 1973-74, vice-chmn., 1983-90; bd. govs. Webb Sch., 1992—, Claremont, Calif., 1993—; past trustee Prescott Center Coll.; Rep. candidate Calif. 5th congl. dist. U.S. Congress. Served to lt. AUS, 1951-54. Decorated Commendation medal with 4 clusters; named Young Man of Yr. San Francisco newspapers, 1961. Mem. ABA (local govt. sect., real property probate and trust law sect., urban, state and local govt. sect., corp., banking and bus. law sect., forum com. on health law), San Francisco Bar Assn., State Bar Assn. Calif. (estate planning, trust and probate law sect.), Am. Arbitration Assn. (arbitrator), Phi Beta Kappa, Phi Delta Phi, Sigma Nu, Bohemian Club. Author: (with Harold E. Rogers, Jr.) Water for California, 2 vols., 1967; (poetry) To Climb a Sacred Mountain, 1979, San Francisco Commuter, 1970; (play) Siddartha, 1977, A Gift from the Master, 1978, San Quentin-Inside the Walls, 1991, Journey-A Bicycle Odyssey Through Central Asia, 1992; contbr. articles to profl. jours. including Stanford Law Rev., UCLA Law Rev., Am. Bar Rev. Office: Nichols Law Corp 100 Green St San Francisco CA 94111-1333

NICHOLS, ANDREW WILKINSON, public health physician, educator; b. Bardstown, Ky., Jan. 29, 1937; s. Andrew Wilkinson and Catherine May (Garrison) N.; m. Ann Marie Weaver, June 1965; children: Catherine Ann, Michael Garrison, Miles Andrew. AB, Swarthmore Coll., 1959; MD, Stanford U., 1964; MPH, Harvard U., 1970. Diplomate Am. Bd. Preventive Medicine, Am. Bd. Family Practice. Asst. resident in medicine, then resident in medicine St. Luke's Hosp., N.Y.C., 1964-66, 68-69; med. officer U.S. Peace Corps, Lima, Peru, 1966-68; prof. family & community medicine U. Ariz., Tucson, 1970—, dir. Rural Health Office, 1980—; mem. Ariz. State Ho. Reps., 1992—; pres. Ariz.-Mex. Border Health Found., Tucson, 1985—, U.S.-Mex. Border Health Assn., El Paso, Tex., 1989-90, Nat. Orgn. AHEC Program Dirs., Washington, 1991-93; chmn. bd. dirs. Jour. Rural Health, Kansas City, Mo., 1988, 89, 90; bd. dirs. Ariz. Area Health Edn. Ctr., 1984—, Southwest Border Rural Health Rsch. Ctr., 1988—, WHO Collaborating Ctr. Rural and Border Health, 1992—. Co-author: Public Health and Community Medicine, 1980; contbr. articles to health publs. Bd. dirs. Habitat for Humanity, Tucson, 1979-93, div. higher edn. Christian Ch., St. Louis, 1988-92; exec. com. World Federalist Assn., Washington, 1988—. Robert Wood Johnson Found. Health Policy fellow, 1977-78; sr. fellow Fogaty Internat. Ctr.-NIH, 1985-87; named Outstanding Health Worker of Yr. U.S.-Mex. Border Health Assn., 1986. Fellow Am. Coll. Preventive Medicine, Am. Acad. Family Physicians. Mem. Disciples of Christ Ch. Home: 4556 N Flecha Dr Tucson AZ 85718-6726 Office: Rural Health Office Univ Ariz 3131 E 2d St Tucson AZ 85716

NICHOLS, DAVID NORTON, principal, educator; b. Lancaster, Calif., Mar. 26, 1954; s. Norton Jr. and Sarah Jane (Jones) N. AS, Antelope Valley Coll., 1974; BA, UCLA, 1977; MA, San Diego State U., 1986; postgrad., Long Beach (Calif.) State U., 1977-79. Cert. life sci. tchr., Calif. Adminstrv. intern Carlsbad (Calif.) Unified Sch. Dist., 1985-87, tchr., 1979-90, summer sch. prin., 1987, 88; prin. Lakeside (Calif.) Union Sch. Dist., 1990—; sci. staff developer Calif. Sci. Implementation Network, 1991—; cons. in drug edn., 1986-88; chair dist. curriculum and instrn. com.; coord./advisor phys. edn.; sch. safety patrol, supt. budget task force rep. Quest instr. St. Michael's Episcopal Ch., Carlsbad, 1987, 88, vestry mem., 1988-90. Mem. NEA, ASCD, Assn. Calif. Adminstrs., Heartland Sch. Mgr. Assn. Democrat. Mem. Christian Ch. Home: 6860 Caminito Montanoso Apt 8 San Diego CA 92119-2302 Office: Lindo Park Sch 12824 Lakeshore Dr PO Box 578 Lakeside CA 92040

NICHOLS, DONALD GEORGE, foundation executive; b. Irvington, N.J., Aug. 8, 1943; s. Alfred Boyd and Elizabeth Jane (Titus) N.; m. Marsha Beth Pelley, Nov. 21, 1973; children: Craig, Brian, Tina, Jeffrey, Teri, Hollie. BA in Journalism, U. Ga., 1965; postgrad., U. So. Fla., 1966. Publicist GE Co., Cleve., 1965-69; mgr. corp. communications Gen. Learning Corp. div. GE Co., Morristown, N.J., 1969-71; mgr. advt. and pub. rels. Saga Devel. Corp., Coral Gables, Fla., 1971-72; assoc. dir. devel. Med. Coll. of Ga., Augusta, 1972-78; dir. univ. rels. Univ. Wis., Superior, 1978-81; dir. communications Minn. Med. Found., Mpls., 1981-83; v.p. Medic Alert Found., Turlock, Calif., 1983—; exec. v.p. Medic Alert Implant Registry, Turlock, 1986—; bd. mem. Coun. for Advancement and Support of Edn., Region V, Washington, 1979-81, Nat. Voluntary Health Agy., Washington, 1983—, Emanuel Hosp. Community Cabinet, Turlock, 1991—. Contbr. articles to profl. jours. Mem. of vestry St. Francis Episcopal Ch. Named Outstanding PR Program, Coun. for Advancement and Support of Edn., 1980; recipient Touch Tone award Chgo. (Ill.) Publicity Club, 1992, Silver Anvil, Internat. Bus. Communicators, 1992. Mem. Kiwanis Club Turlock. Office: Medic Alert Found 2323 Colorado Ave Turlock CA 95380

NICHOLS, HUGH, college dean; b. Boise, Idaho, Dec. 5, 1936; s. Jack and Devere (Oliver) N.; m. Lauren Gayle Harrison, Dec. 16, 1983. BA, So. Oreg. Coll., 1961; ArtsD, U. Oreg., 1979. Asst. prof. English Lewis and Clark Coll., Lewiston, Idaho, 1971-77, assoc. prof. English, 1978-82, chair humanities div., 1976-83, prof., dean Sch. Arts and Scis., 1983—. Chmn. Idaho Humanities Coun., 1989-90. Office: Lewis-Clark State Coll Coll Arts & Scis Lewiston ID 83501

NICHOLS, MICHAEL LOWERY, counselor; b. Kansas City, Mo., Aug. 11, 1945; s. Alexander and Ada Dale (Stapleton) N.; m. Doris Jean Griffin, June 2, 1968; children: Michael A., Matthew L. BA, Okla. Bapt. U., 1967; MDiv, Cen. Bapt. Theol. Sem., 1972; DMin, San Francisco Theol. Sem., 1979. Cert. & registered hypnotherapist Am. Bd. Hypnotherapy; endorsed chaplain So. Bapt. Conv.; cert. master practioner (N.L.P.). Tchr. Kansas City Bd. Edn., 1967-73; chaplain Appalachia Regional Hosp., Middlesburg, Ky., 1973-74; chaplain, lt. comdr. USN-West Coast, Calif., 1974-84; pres., sr. pastor Beth-El Bapt. Ch., Fillmore, Calif., 1984-90; chaplain USN Naval Hosp., Portsmouth, Va., 1990; Protestant chaplain Cen. Calif. Women's Facility, Chowchilla, 1990—; pres. Personality Quest Corp., West Lake Village, Calif., 1991—. Author: An Examination of Military Chaplaincy Start-Up Styles: A Guide Book for Chaplains Going Afloat, 1979. Bd. dirs. Boys and Girls Club, Fillmore, 1990-91. Mem. Madera Ministerial Assn. Republican. Home: 1321 Waterford Ln Fillmore CA 93015 Office: Personality Quest Corp 3075 E Thousand Oaks Blvd Ste 100 Thousand Oaks CA 91362

NICHOLS, PHYLLIS D'AMBROSIO, television executive; b. Bronx, N.Y., Dec. 8, 1956; d. James Justin and Rose Mary (Colavito) D'A.; m. Terry Burnett, Nov. 28, 1983 (div. Nov. 1984); m. Timothy Allen Nichols, Mar. 18, 1989; 1 child, Evelyn Nicole. Student, Pace U., Pleasantville, N.Y., 1975-77, Goldenwest Coll, Huntington Beach, Calif., 1990. Cost acct. Burns Security Svcs., Briarcliff Manor, N.Y., 1974-78; adminstrv. asst. Six Star Cablevision, Fort Lee, N.J. and Covina, Calif., 1978-81; office mgr. Seevid, Inc., Huntington Beach, 1982-90, v.p., 1990—. Mem. Com. to Elect Don MacAllister, Huntington Beach, 1988, 92; advocate Calif. Abortion Rights League, Sacramento, 1990—. Mem. Nat. Parks and Conservation League, Huntington Beach C. of C., Friends of Libr. Huntington Beach, Electronic Rep. Assn. Republican. Roman Catholic. Home: 6200 Edinger Huntington Beach CA 92649 Office: Seevid Inc 15178 Transistor Ln Huntington Beach CA 92649

NICHOLS, ROBERT EDMUND, editor, writer, journalist; b. Daytona Beach, Fla., Feb. 14, 1925; s. Joe D. and Edna A. (Casper) N.; m. Diana R. Grosso; children by previous marriage: Craig S., Kim S., Robin K. Student, San Diego State Coll., 1942-43, St. John's Coll., 1944-45, George Washington U., 1948-49. Reporter San Diego Union, 1942-44; corr. Washington bur. N.Y. Herald Tribune, 1945-48, CBS, 1948-51, Time, Inc., 1951-61; contbg. editor Time, asst. edn. dir. Life mag., N.Y.C., 1951-52; corr. representing Time, Life, Fortune, Sports Illus. mags., San Diego area, 1952-61; Sunday editor San Diego Union, 1952-61; fin. editor Los Angeles Times, 1961-68, mem. editorial bd., 1965-68; spl. asst. to bd. govs. Fed. Res. System, 1968-70; v.p., dir. various editorial svcs. Bank of Am., 1970-85; prin. Robert E. Nichols Communications, San Francisco, 1985—. Writer, dir. film and radio documentaries. Mem. U.S. Antarctic Expedition, 1946-47. Recipient Loeb Newspaper Spl. Achievement award, 1963, Loeb award disting. fin. reporting, 1964. Fellow Royal Geog. Soc., Explorers Club; mem. Calif. Scholarship Fedn. (hon., life), Soc. Am. Bus. Editors and Writers (hon., life, pres. 1967-68), South Polar Press Club. Home and Office: 38 Ord Ct San Francisco CA 94114-1417

NICHOLS, ROGER LOUIS, history educator; b. Racine, Wis., June 13, 1933; s. George Calvin and Antoinette Marie (Zegerius) N.; m. Marilyn Jane Ward, July 11, 1959; children: Cynthia Margaret Hawk, Sarah Elizabeth, Martha Catherine Bernth, Jeffrey Roger. BS, Wis. State Coll., LaCrosse, 1956; MS in History, U. Wis., 1959, PhD in History, 1964. Asst. prof. Wis. State U., Oshkosh, 1963-65; assoc. prof. U. Ga., Athens, 1965-69; assoc. prof. U. Ariz., Tucson, 1969-70, prof. history, 1970—; vis. lectr. U. Md., College Park, 1975-76; pres. Coordinating Com. for History in Ariz., Phoenix, 1987-89. Author: General Henry Atkinson, 1965, Black Hawk and the Warrior's Path, 1992; co-author: Stephen Long; (with others) Natives and Strangers, 1979, 90; editor: The Missouri Expedition, 1969, The American Indian, 1971, 81, 86, 92, American Frontier and Western Issues, 1986. Dir. seminar for coll. tchrs. NEH, Tucson, 1981, 88, 93. Rsch. grantee Am. Philos. Soc., 1967, 82, 89. Democrat. Presbyterian. Home: 6661 N Camino Abbey Tucson AZ 85718-2007 Office: U Ariz Dept History 215 Social Science Tucson AZ 85721

NICHOLSON, GLEN IRA, psychology educator; b. Blairsburg, Iowa, Apr. 21, 1925; s. Willis I. and Berneice (McDaniel) N.; m. Phyllis J. Runge, Aug. 9, 1963; children—Marc, Jonathan, Elisabeth. B.A., U. Iowa, 1948, M.A., 1952, Ph.D., 1963. Prin. high sch. Rowan, Columbus Junction and Marion, Iowa, 1948-61; research asst. U. Iowa, 1961-63; asst., then asso. prof. Wichita State U., 1963-67; asso. prof., head dept. ednl. psychology N.Mex. State U., 1967-69; prof. ednl. psychology U. Ariz., Tucson, 1969-92, prof. emeritus, 1992—, head dept., 1969-75, acting div. coord., teaching and tchr. edn. div., 1990-91, acting assoc. dean Coll. Edn., 1991-92; div. head Ednl. Founds., 1986-87. Mem. NEA, Phi Delta Kappa. Home: 9045 E Calle Playa Tucson AZ 85715-5612

NICHOLSON, ISADORE, chemistry educator; b. Phila., Apr. 28, 1925; s. Morris and Sadie (Palmen) N. BA, Temple U., 1949; MSc, Rutgers U., 1952, PhD, 1954. Researcher Uniroyal (U.S. Rubber Co.), Wayne, N.J., 1954-59; prof. L.I. U., Bklyn. and Greenvale, N.Y., 1959-84, ret., 1984. Contbr. articles to profl. jours. With U.S. Army, 1943-46. DuPont fellow Rutgers U., 1953.

NICHOLSON, PAUL EWING, theater executive. MBA, Victoria U., Wellington, New Zealand. Planning mgr., mgmt. acct, systems analyst New Zealand, 1965-74; adminstrv. dir. Downstage Theatre, New Zealand, 1975-80; gen. mgr. Oregon Shakespeare Festival, Ashland, 1980—; guest lectr. Stanford U., Victoria U., New Zealand Ins. Inst., New Zealand Dept. Trade and Industry, Oreg. Ednl. Media Assn., B.C. Touring Coun. Performing Arts; mgmt. cons. various art orgns. including Roanoke Island Hist. Assn., Rogue Valley Symphony, Britt Festivals and Rogue Opera; founding faculty mem. Western Arts Mgmt. Inst.; adj. prof., mem. sch. bus. adv. coun. So. Oreg. State Coll. Active numerous community affairs; participant many local coms. and bds. Office: Oreg Shakespeare Festival office of Gen Mgr Box 158 Ashland OR 97520

NICHOLSON, WILL FAUST, JR., bank holding company executive; b. Colorado Springs, Colo., Feb. 8, 1929; s. Will Faust and Gladys Olivia (Burns) N.; m. Shirley Ann Baker, Nov. 26, 1955; children: Ann Louise Nicholson Naughton, Will Faust III. S.B., M.I.T., 1950; M.B.A., U. Denver, 1956. V.p. Van Schaack & Co., Denver, 1954-66; pntr. N. G. Petry Constrn. Co., Denver, 1966-70; sr. v.p. Colo. Nat. Bankshares, Inc., Denver, 1970-75; pres. Colo. Nat. Bankshares, Inc., 1975—, chmn. bd., chief exec. officer, 1985—; dir. Pub. Svc. Co., Colo.; dir., chmn. VISA USA, Inc., VIAS Internat. Bd. dirs. Boys and Girls Clubs of Metro Denver; active Downtown Denver, Inc., Colo. Assn. of Commerce and Industry, chmn. 1990-91, Denver Urban Renewal Authority, 1958-59, Denver Bd. Water Commrs., 1959-65, pres. 1964, 65; Nat. Western Stock Show; bd. mgrs. Presbyn.-St. Luke's Hosps. With USAF, 1950-53. Mem. Assn. Bank Holding Cos. (bd. dirs. 1979-87, 89-91, exec. com. 1980-85, vice chmn. 1981-82, chmn. 1983-84), U.S. C. of C. (bd. dirs. 1990—), U.S. Golf Assn. (exec. com. 1974-82, v.p. 1978, 79, pres. 1980, 81), Denver Country Club, Denver Club, Univ. Club Colo., Univ. Club N.Y., Castle Pine Golf Club, Royal and Ancient Golf Club (St. Andrews, Scotland), Augusta (Ga.) Nat. Golf Club. Republican. Episcopalian. Home: 30 Cherry St Denver CO 80220-5636 Office: Colo Nat Bankshares PO Box 5168 Denver CO 80217-5168

NICHOLSON, WILLIAM JOSEPH, forest products company executive; b. Tacoma, Aug. 24, 1938; s. Ferris Frank and Athyleen Myrtle (Fesenmaier) N.; m. Carland Elaine Crook, Oct. 10, 1964; children: Courtney, Brian, Kay, Benjamin. SB in ChemE, MIT, 1960, SM in ChemE Practice, 1961; PhD in ChemE, Cornell U., 1965; MBA, Pacific Luth. U., 1969. Registered profl. chem. engr., Wash. Sr. devel. engr. Hooker Chem. Co., Tacoma, 1964-69, Battelle N.W., Richland, Wash., 1969-70; planning assoc. Potlatch Corp., San Francisco, 1970-75, mgr. corp. energy service, 1976—; chmn. electricity com. Am. Paper Inst., 1977—, mem. solid waste task force, 1988-91, mem. air quality com., 1989—; mem. adv. bd. Univ. Calif. Forest Products Lab., 1992—, chmn., 1993—. Mem. Am. Chem. Soc., Am. Inst. Chem. Engrs. (assoc.), Tech. Assn. Pulp and Paper Industry, AAAS, Sigma Xi. Democrat. Clubs: Commonwealth (San Francisco), Cornell (N.Y.). Home: PO Box 1114 Ross CA 94957-1114 Office: Potlatch Corp 244 California St Ste 610 San Francisco CA 94111

NICHTER, LARRY STEVEN, plastic and reconstructive surgeon, educator; b. Cooperstown, N.Y., Nov. 12, 1951; s. Seymour and Beatrice (Sklar) N.; m. Carol Anne Bryant, June 26, 1982; children: Austin Bryant, Bryce Dylan, Travis Drew. AB magna cum laude, Boston U., 1973, MD, 1978; MS in Surgery, U. Va., 1985. Diplomate Am. Bd. Surgery (spl. cert. for competence in hand surgery), Am. Bd. Plastic Surgery. Intern, resident in gen. surgery UCLA Med. Ctr., 1978-82; hand, micro surg. fellow U. Va. Med. Ctr., Charlottesville, 1982-83, resident plastic, maxillofacial, reconstructive surgery, 1983-85, instr. plastic, reconstructive surgery, 1984-85; asst. prof. surgery div. plastic surgery U. So. Calif. Med. Ctr., L.A., 1985-90, dir. plastic surg. rsch. div. plastic surgery, 1985—, assoc. prof. surgery div. plastic surgery, 1990—, faculty mem. craniofacial biology program Sch. Denistry, 1987—. Assoc. editor Annals of Plastic Surgery, 1990-93; mem. editorial adv. bd. Resident and Staff Physician, 1992—; author book chpts., essays (recipient several awards), abstracts, presentations; contbr. numerous articles to profl. jours. Recipient Glaney award Southeastern Soc. Plastic and Reconstructive Surgeons, 1983, Resident's award, 1985, Pfizer award for med. innovation, 1987, Peter B. Samuels award Soc. for Clin. Vascular Surgery, 1985, Spl. Recognition award Women in Show Bus. and Brighter Life for Children's Philanthropic Orgns., 1991, and others. Fellow Am. Coll. Surgeons; mem. AMA, Am. Assn. Plastic Surgeons, Am. Soc. for Surgery of the Hand, Am. Acad. Pediatrics, Am. Soc. for Reconstructive Microsurgery, Am. Cleft Palate Assn., Am. Burn Assn., Calif. Soc. Plastic Surgeons, L.A. County Med. Assn., L.A. Acad. Medicine, L.A. Hand Soc., L.A. Pediatric Soc., L.A. Surg. Soc., Soc. for Head and Neck Surgery, Med. Surfing Assn., Assn. of Acad. Chmn. of Plastic Surgery, Plastic Surgery Rsch. Coun., Sigma Xi, Alpha Omega Alpha, and others. Office: St Josephs Med Plz 1140 W La Veta Ave Ste 810 Orange CA 92668-4202

NICKEL, JAMES WESLEY, philosophy educator; b. Shafter, Calif., Mar. 12, 1943; s. W.H. and Elsie (Sawatsky) N.; m. Phyllis Dick, May 23, 1964 (div. 1982); children: Jonathan Aaron, Philip James; m. Regina Celi, Aug. 24, 1984. BA, Tabor Coll., 1964; PhD, U. Kans., 1968. Prof. Wichita (Kans.) State U., 1968-80; vis. prof. Sch. Law U. Calif., Berkeley, 1980-82; dir. Ctr. for Values and Social Policy U. Colo., Boulder, 1982-88; prof. philosophy U. Colo., 1982—, chair dept. philosophy, 1992—; vis. prof. U. Utah, Salt Lake City, 1988. Author: Making Sense of Human Rights, 1987; contbr. numerous articles to scholarly publs. Recipient fellowship, Nat. Endowment Humanities, 1973, Am. Coun. Learned Socs., 1976, Nat. Humanities Ctr., 1978, Rockefeller Found., 1981. Home: 3055 6th St Boulder CO 80304-2505 Office: U Colo Boulder Campus Box 232 Boulder CO 80309

NICKERSON, WILLIAM ERNEST, author; b. Wilderville, Oreg., Apr. 10, 1908; s. Alonzo Ernest and Estelle Gertrude (Robinson) N.; m. Lucille Willis, Jan. 10, 1910; 1 child, Robert Ernest. D. of Bus. Adminstrn., Peidmont Coll., 1981. Author: How I Turned $1,000 into a Million in Real Estate - In My Spare Time, How to Make A Fortune Today, Starting From Scratch, Nickerson's No Risk Way to Real Estate Fortunes, My Odyssey Around Three Worlds, Did Jesus Survive the Cross?. Republican. Congregationalist.

NICODEMUS, MATTHEW DAVID, activist, educator; b. Evanston, Ill., June 9, 1960; s. Charles Edgar Jr. and Virginia Ann (Gutteridge) N. BA in Philosophy, Stanford U., 1986. With dept. high-energy physics Stanford (Calif.) Linear Accelerator Ctr., 1978-79, lab. technician, 1981-83; lab. technician Harvard U., MIT, Cambridge, Mass., 1979-80; staff organizer Patriots Against Registration and the Draft, Chgo., 1980; organizer, newspaper editor Nat. Resistance Com., Stanford, 1981-82, 84-85; program mgr. Loosening the Ties That Bind, Arcata, Calif., 1986-88; environ. chemistry lab. technician North Coast Labs., Arcata, 1989-90; co-author, project coord. Good Work! Project, Arcata, 1990—; instrnl. aide for learning disabled students Coll. of the Redwoods, Eureka, Calif., 1991—; mediator Humboldt Mediation Svcs., Arcata, 1986—; cons. War Rsch. Info. Svc., Cambridge, 1990—. Author: (booklet) How to Organize an Anti-Draft Group in Your High School, 1979; co-author: A Climber's Guide to Kankakee River State Park, 1979, (booklet) A Graduation Pledge of Responsibility-Organizing Manual, 1988; contbr. articles to profl. jours. Mem. policy bd. Stanford Workshops on Polit. and Social Issues, 1983-84; mem. Stanford Against Conscription, 1979-86, Nat. Resistance Com., 1980—; co-founder Evanston Against Registration and the Draft, 1980-82, Graduation Pledge Alliance, Humboldt State U., Arcata, 1987—. Agape Found. grantee, 1987.

NICOL, MALCOLM F., physical chemistry educator; b. N.Y.C., Sept. 13, 1939; s. John and Hilda E. (Foertner) N.; m. Ann Carolyn Tryon, Aug. 25, 1963 (div. May 1990); children: Barbara, Katherine, Virginia. BA, Amherst Coll., 1960; PhD, U. Calif., Berkeley, 1963. Postdoctoral chemist UCLA, 1963-64, asst. prof. phys. chemistry, 1965-70, assoc. prof., 1970-75, prof., 1975—; cons. Lawrence Livermore (Calif.) Nat. Lab., 1985—, Los Alamos Nat. Lab., 1990—. Assoc. editor Jour. Phys. Chemistry, 1981-90, sr. editor, 1991—; contbr. over 100 articles on chemistry, physics and geophysics to sci. jours. Fellow Alfred P. Sloan Found., 1973-77. Fellow AAAS; mem. Am. Phys. Soc., Am. Chem. Soc. (councilor 1986-88, 91—), Internat. Assn. for the Advancement of High Pressure Rsch. and Tech., Am. Geophys. Union. Home: 412 N Palm Dr Apt 601 Beverly Hills CA 90210-4028 Office: UCLA Dept Chemistry and Biochemistry Los Angeles CA 90024-1569

NICOLAI, EUGENE RALPH, public relations consultant, editor, writer; b. Renton, Wash., June 26, 1911; s. Eugene George and Josephine (Heidinger) N.; student U. Wash., 1929, Whitman Coll., 1929-30; B.A., U. Wash., 1934; postgrad. Am. U., 1942; M.A., George Washington U., 1965; m. Helen Margaret Manogue, June 5, 1935; 1 son, Paul Eugene. Editor, U. Wash. Daily, Seattle, 1934; asst. city editor, writer, nat. def. editor Seattle Times, 1934-41; writer Sta. KJR, Seattle, 1937-39; writer, editor, safety edn. officer Bur. Mines, Washington, 1941-45; news dir. Grand Coulee Dam and Columbia Basin Project, Washington, 1945-50; regional info. dir. Bur. Mines, Denver and Pitts., 1950-55, asst. chief mineral reports, Washington, 1955-61, news dir. office of oil and gas, 1956-57; sr. info. officer, later sr. public info. officer Office Sec. Interior, Washington, 1961-71, staff White House Nat. Conf. on Natural Beauty, spl. detail to White House, 1971, ret.; now public relations cons., tech. editor, writer. Formerly safety policy adviser Interior Dept.; com. mem. Internat. Cooperation Year, State Dept., 1971. With George Washington U. Alumni Found.; founder, mng. dir. Josephine Nature Preserve; pres. Media Assocs. Bd. dirs. Wash. State Council on Alcoholism; adviser Pierce Transit Authority, Pierce County Growth Mgmt., Pierce County Ethics Commn. Named Disting. Alumnus, recipient Penrose award, both Whitman Coll., 1979. Mem. Nature Conservancy, Wash. Environ. Council, Nat. Audubon Soc. (Am. Belgian Tervuren dist. rep.), Crook County (Oreg.) Hist. Soc., Washington State Hist. Soc., Emerald Shores Assn, Sigma Delta Chi, Pi Kappa Alpha. Presbyn. Clubs: George Washington U., Purdy (pres.). Lodge: Masons. Author: The Middle East Emergency Committee; editor: Fed. Conservation Yearbooks. Home: 9809 N Seminole Dr Spokane WA 99208-8608

NICOLAOU, KYRIACOS COSTA, chemistry educator; b. Karavas, Kyrenia, Cyprus, June 5, 1946; came to U.S., 1972; s. Costa and Helen (Yettimi) N.; m. Georgette Karayianni, July 15, 1973; children; Colette, Alexis, Christopher, Paul. BSc, Bedford Coll., London, 1969; PhD, U. Coll., London, 1972. Rsch. assoc. Columbia U., N.Y.C., 1972-73, Harvard U., Cambridge, Mass., 1973-76; from asst. prof. to Rhodes-Thompson prof. chemistry U. Pa., Phila., 1976-89; Darlene Shiley prof. chemistry, chmn. dept. Rsch. Inst. Scripps Clinic, La Jolla, Calif., 1989—; prof. chemistry U. Calif., La Jolla, 1989—; vis. prof. U. Paris, 1986; mem. exec. com. Biann. Cyprus Conf. on Drug Design; mem. med. study sect. B, NIH, 1988-90. Author: (with N. A. Petasis) Selenium in Natural Products Synthesis, 1984; co-editor: Synthesis, Germany, 1984-90; editorial bd. Prostaglandins, Leukotrienes and Medicine, 1978-88, Synthesis, 1990—, Accounts of Chem. Rsch., 1992—, Carbohydrate Letters, 1993—; mem. bd. consulting editors Tetrahedron Publs., 1992—; mem. adv. bd. Contemporoary Organic Synthesis, 1993—; mem. regional adv. bd. J. C. S. Chem. Comm., 1989—, J. C. S. Perkin I, 1991— ; contbr. numerous articles to profl. jours.; patentee in field. Recipient Japan Soc. for Promotion Sci. award, 1987-88, U.S. Sr. Scientist award Alexander von Humboldt Found., 1987-88, Alan R. Day award Phila. Organic Chemisyts Club, 1993; fellow A. P. Sloan Found., 1979-83, J. S. Guggenhiem Found., 1984; Camille and Henry Dreyfus scholar, 1980-84, Arthur C. Cope scholar, 1987. Fellow N.Y. Acad. Scis.; mem. AAAS, Am. Chem. Soc. (Creative Work in Synthetic Organic Chemistry award 1993), Chem. Soc. London, German Chem. Soc., Japanese Chem. Soc. Office: Rsch Inst Scripps Clinic 10666 N Torrey Pines Rd La Jolla CA 92037-1027

NIEDERBRACH, JON, credit company executive; b. Minot, N.D., Jan. 27, 1966; s. Willard Ernest and Florence Mae (Fuhrhop) N.; m. Francisca Cecilia Leon Guerrero, Nov. 18, 1989; children: Peter Trinidad, Joclyn Renee. BA, U. Calif., Irvine, 1988. Staff bulk mail processing, maintenance Western Funding, Inc., Garden Grove, Calif., 1984-86, new accounts processing, 1986-88; asst. v.p. ops. Western Funding, Inc., Garden Grove, 1988-93; data processing supr. Western Funding, Inc., Garden Grove, Calif., 1989—, v.p., 1993—. Editor (newsletter) The Credit Report, 1989—. Bd. dirs., sec., Holy Cross Luth. Ch., Cypress, Calif., 1990-92, dir. fin., 1992—. Mem. Digital Equipment Users Soc., U. Calif. Irvine Alumni Assn. Office: Western Funding Inc PO Box 936 Garden Grove CA 92643-0936

NIEDZIELSKI, HENRI ZYGMUNT, French and English language educator; b. Troyes, France, Mar. 30, 1931; came to U.S., 1956, naturalized, 1963; s. Zygmunt and Anna (Pelik) N.; children: Henri Zygmunt, Daniel Domenic, Robert Nicholas, Anna-Pia Irene. B.A., U. Conn., 1959, M.A., 1963, Ph.D., 1964. Instr. U. Mass., 1962-64, asst. prof., 1965-66; free-lance interpreter, 1960—; asst. prof. U. Laval, Quebec, Can., 1964-65; asso. prof. U. Hawaii, 1966-72, prof., 1972-90, chmn. div. French, 1967-70; linguistic specialist NDEA, Edn. Profl. Devel. Act, 1963-69; Fulbright lectr. linguistics and TESL Krakow, Poland, 1972-74, Bujumbura, Burundi, 1980-81, Poznan, Poland, 1990-92; guest prof. Avignon, France, 1983-84, Bonn, Fed. Republic Germany, 1986-87; Disting. fellow Auckland U., New Zealand, 1989. Author: Le Roman de Helcanus, 1966, Basic French: A Programmed Course, 1968, Handbook of French Structure; A Systematic Review, 1968, Intermediate French: An Individualized Course, 1972, The Silent Language of France, 1975, French Sound Visuals, 1976; Films on Polish Body Language, 1989; editor: Language and Literature in Hawaii, 1968-72, Jean Misrahi Memorial Volume: Studies in Medieval Languages and Literature, 1977, Studies on the Seven Sages of Rome, 1978. Pres. Family Counseling Center Hawaii, 1968-70; chmn. bd. Family Edn. Centers Hawaii, 1969-72. Served with French Armored Cav., 1951-53. Mem. Hawaii Assn. Lang. Tchrs. (pres. 1968-69), Modern Lang. Assn., Polish Inst. Arts and Scis., Chopin Soc. Hawaii (dir. 1990—), Am. Translators Assn., Internat. Sociol. Assn., Alliance Française Hawaii (pres. 1978-80), Hawaii Assn. Translators (founding pres. 1982—), Am. Assn. Tchrs. French (pres. Hawaii 1981-83), Am. Council Teaching Fgn. Langs. (dir. 1970-72), Hawaii Second Lang. Articulation Com. (chmn. 1986-89), Chopin Soc. Hawaii, Phi Beta Kappa, Pi Delta Phi, Phi Kappa Phi, Sigma Delta Pi. Lodge: Rotary.

NIELSEN, DONALD RODNEY, soil and water science educator; b. Phoenix, Oct. 10, 1931; s. Irven Roy and Irma Evelyn (Chase) N.; m. Joanne Joyce Locke, Sept. 26, 1953; children: Cynthia, Pamela, Barbara, Wayne, David. BS, U. Ariz., 1953, MS, 1954; PhD, Iowa State U., 1958; DSc (hon.), Ghent (Belgium) State U., 1986. Asst. prof. soil and water sci. U. Calif., Davis, 1958-63, assoc. prof., 1963-68, prof., 1968—, dir. Kearney Found. of Soil Sci., 1970-75, assoc. dean, 1970-80, dir. Food Protection and Toxicology Ctr., 1974-75, chmn. dept. land, air and water resources, 1975-77, exec. assoc. dean Coll. Agrl. Environ. Scis., 1986-89, chmn. dept. agronomy and range sci., 1989-91; cons. corps. and govtl. agys. Editor Nitrogen in the Environment; co-editor Water Resources Research, 1985-88; mem. editorial bd. Irrigation Sci., Jour. Soil Sci., Soil Sci., Outlook In Agrl., Soil and Tillage Research, contbr. articles to profl. jours. NSF fellow, 1965-66. Fellow Am. Geophys. Union (pres. hydrology sect. 1990-92), Soil Sci. Soc. Am. (pres. 1983-84), Am. Soc. Agronomy (pres. 1990-91); mem. Sigma Xi, Phi Kappa Phi, Gamma Sigma Delta, Phi Lambda Upsilon, Alpha Zeta. Democrat. Home: 1004 Pine Ln Davis CA 95616-1728 Office: U Calif Dept Land Air & Water Resources Veihmeyer Hall Davis CA 95616

NIELSEN, GLADE BENJAMIN, former state senator; b. Hyrum, Utah, Mar. 8, 1926; s. George Benjamin and Katie Ione (Jensen) N.; m. Alpha Fern Strempke, Oct. 15, 1955; children: Karen Lynn, Sharon Kay, Roger Glade, Laura Mae, Lance Eric. BS, Utah State U., 1949. Supt. various constrn. cos., Wyo., Nev., and Calif., 1949-55; pres. Glade Nielsen Builder, Roy, Utah, 1955-86; mem. Utah State Senate, Salt Lake City, 1987-92. Pres. Weber Basin Homebuilders Assn., 1967-68, Home Builders Assn. Utah, 1972-73; v.p. Nat. Assn. Home Builders, Washington, 1974-75, mem. exec. com., 1976-79; pres. Roy C. of C., 1980; bd. dirs. Utah Housing Fin. Agy., Salt Lake, 1975-83. With USN, 1944-46, PTO. Recipient Builder of Yr. award Home Builders Assn. Utah, 1988, Svc. award Utah State Com. Consumer Svcs., 1989, Recognition award Utah State Dept. Commerce, 1989, Hon. Commendation award Ogden Air Logistics Command, 1989, Roy City Outstanding Citizen award, 1993. Mem. Am. Legion, Thunderbird Motor Club Utah (pres.), Elks. Republican.

NIELSEN, LAWRENCE EMORY, small business owner; b. St. Anthony, Idaho, Dec. 21, 1946; s. Orlan Sidney and Bettie Lucille (Miller) N.; m. Catherine Ann Hayden, July 11, 1970; children: Erik Robert, Russell Sidney, Robert Sidney, Laura Ann. Student, Ricks Coll., Rexburg, Idaho, 1969-71; BS, U. Idaho, 1973; MS, Okla. State U., 1974. Health planner Health Planning Coun., Wichita, Kans., 1974-76; sr. planner Idaho Health Systems Agy., Boise, 1976-77; acting exec. dir. Western Oreg. Health Systems Agy., Eugene, 1977-81; exec. dir. Western Ariz. Health Systems Agy., Yuma, 1981-83, No. san Joaquin Valley Health Systems Agy., Modesto, Calif., 1983-86; pres. Millwork of Idaho Inc., Sugar City, 1986—. Patentee in field. mem. coun. City of Sugar City, 1991—; bd. dirs. Fremont County Hosp. Taxing Dist., St. Anthony, Idaho, 1987. With USAR, 1969-75. Mem. Sons of Norway, Phi Theta Kappa. Democrat. LDS. Home: PO Box 211 Sugar City ID 83448-0211 Office: Millwork of Idaho Inc PO Box 60 Sugar City ID 83448-0060

NIELSEN, LELAND C., federal judge; b. Vesper, Kans., June 14, 1919; s. Carl Christian and Christena (Larson) N.; m. Virginia Garland, Nov. 27, 1958; 1 child, Christena. A.B., Washburn U., 1946; J.D., U. So. Calif., 1946. Bar: Calif. 1947. Practice law Los Angeles, from 1947; dep. city atty. City of Los Angeles, 1947-51; judge Superior Ct. Calif. San Diego County, 1968-71, U.S. Dist. Ct. (so. dist.) Calif., San Diego, 1971—. Served to maj. A.C., U.S. Army 1941-46. Decorated Purple Heart, Disting. Svc. Cross, Air medal with oak leaf clusters. Mem. Am. Coll. Trial Lawyers. Republican. Presbyterian. Office: US Dist Ct 940 Front St San Diego CA 92189-0010

NIELSEN, MARK JOSEPH, corporate executive; b. Chgo., Apr. 5, 1959; s. Torben Harold and Nancy Ann (Ingraffia) N. BS, Northwestern U., 1980. Legal asst. Louis G. Davidson & Assocs., Chgo., 1980-83; telecommunications cons. Nielsen & Assocs., Chgo., 1978-84; cable TV contract negotiator City of Chgo., 1983-84; sales, mktg. dir. Cellular Bus. Systems, Inc. div. Cin. Bell Info. Systems, Inc., Chgo., 1984-88; pres. Subscriber Computing Inc., Irvine, Calif., 1988—; faculty mem. dept. engring. profl. devel. U. Wis., Madison, 1985, Nat. Communications Forum, 1987—, Nat. Engring. Consortium, 1988—; pres. Subscriber Computing, Inc., Irvine, 1988—; adv. bd. Nat. Telemarketing Found., 1985-88; exec. producer (cons.) ABA, 1981-82; legis. cons. ACLU, Chgo., 1982-84; incorporator, bd. dirs. Chgo. Access Corp., 1983-89; bd. dirs. Jazz Inst. Chgo. 1987—, Ednl. Overseers Council, Nat. Engring. Consortium, 1987—. Mem. Chgo. Forum, 1982-84; co-convenor, moderator Midwest Conf. on Communications Issues, Chgo., 1979; presbytor, com. chmn. Presbytery of Chgo., 1980-83; bd. dirs., com. chmn. Ch. Fedn. Greater Chgo., 1977-84. Recipient Churchmanship-Can-Be-Creative award Chgo. Sun-Times, 1982; Arthur Baer fellow Chgo. Lit. Club, 1979; named one of Outstanding Young Men in Am., 1987. Mem. Am. Marketing Assn., Am. Mgmt. Assn., Internat. Platform Assn., Chgo. Cable Club, Chgo. Forum, Telecator Network of Am., Cellular Telecommunications Industry Assn. Democrat. Presbyterian. Club: Chgo. Literary. Office: Subscriber Computing Inc 23161 Mill Creek Dr Ste 200 Laguna Hills CA 92653

NIELSEN, NORMAN RUSSELL, computer scientist; b. Pitts., Sept. 8, 1941; s. Russell A. and Lenore (Martin) N.; m. Jeannette Elsener, June 11, 1963; 1 child, Joanne. BA summa cum laude, Pomona Coll., 1963; MBA, Stanford U., 1965, PhD, 1967. Asst. to assoc. prof. Stanford (Calif.) U., 1966-73; rsch. engr., lab dir. Stanford Rsch. Inst./SRI Internat., Menlo Park, Calif., 1973-88; assoc. dir. Info. Tech. Ctr. SRI Internat., Menlo Park, 1988—; bd. dirs., chmn. audit com. Bergstrom Capital Corp. (formerly Claremont Capital Corp.), Seattle, 1976—. Author: Crafting Knowledge-Based Systems, 1988; editor: Artificial Intelligence Simulation and Modeling, 1989; editorial bd. Info. and Mgmt. jour., 1985—; contbr. articles to profl. jours. Mem. AAAS, Am. Assn. Artificial Intelligence (fin. com. 1988—, treas. 1993—), Assn. for Computing Machinery, IEEE Computer Soc., Inst. Mgmt. Scis. Office: SRI Internat BS-276 333 Ravenswood Ave Menlo Park CA 94025-3493

NIELSEN, STEPHEN JAMES, telecommunications industry executive, director; b. Seattle, May 11, 1951; s. James Nielsen, Jr. and Myrtle Irene (Dexter) Smith; m. Elizabeth Ann Allsopp, Aug. 18, 1972; children: Heidi Ann, Daniel Stephen. BS, Western Wash. U., 1973. Media tech. Walla Walla (Wash.) C.C., 1974-76; mem. faculty Bellevue (Wash.) C.C., 1976-78; media specialist US West Comm., Inc., Seattle, 1978-81, comm. cons., 1981-85, mgr. ednl. rels., 1985-87, dir. corp. TV, 1987—, dir., regulatory IDC support, 1987—, dir. ednl. rels., 1988-89, dir. external devel., 1990—; loaned exec., exec. dir. Gov.'s Coun. on Edn. Reform and Funding, State of Wash., 1991—. Co-author Training and Retraining Educators, 1989. Spl. asst. gov. Blue Ribbon Coun. on Edn. Reform, 1991—; bd. dirs. Wash. Inst. Applied Tech., Seattle, 1989—; chmn. Wash. Roundtable Edn. Com., Seattle, 1987—, dep., 1985—; chmn. Ptnrs. in Pub. Edn., Seattle, 1989—; exec. chmn. Gov.'s Task Force on Sch. Drop Outs, State of Wash., Olympia, 1988-89; co-chmn. Mayor's Edn. Summit, City of Seattle, 1990—; mem. supt. search com. Mercer Island Sch., Mercer, Wash., 1990; active King County Econ. Devel. Edn. Com., Early Childhood Edn. Adv. Com. Recipient Emerlald City award Internat. TV Assn., 1984, award of Svc. Supt. Pub. Instrn., Olympia, Wash., 1986, recognition for bd. mem. efforts N.W. Regional Lab., Portland, Oreg., 1987. Fellow World Affairs Coun.; mem. Seattle Alliance for Edn., Seattle C. of C. Office: US West Communications Inc 1600 7th Ave Rm 3203 Seattle WA 98191-0002

NIELSEN, STUART DEE, chemist; b. Green River, Wyo., Oct. 26, 1932; s. Julian Woodruff and Reva May (Stewart) N.; m. Lila Ellen Larett, June 10, 1954; children: Laura May, Martha Ellen, Karl Allen, Jennifer Marie, Isabelle Anne. BS, U. Wyo., 1954; PhD, U. Wash., 1962. Research chemist Rohm & Haas Co., Phila., 1962-66; research scientist Gen. Tire & Rubber Co., Akron, Ohio, 1966-78; chemist Los Alamos (N.Mex.) Nat. Lab., 1978—. Patentee in field. Scoutmaster Boy Scouts Am., Akron, 1970-78. Served with U.S. Army, 1954-56. Allied Chem. Co. fellow, 1960. Mem. Am. Chem. Soc., Soc. Applied Spectroscopy, Am. Soc. Mass Spectrometry, Sigma Xi. Mormon. Home: 114 Sherwood Blvd Los Alamos NM 87544-3425 Office: Los Alamos Nat Lab Group EM-9 MS K484 Los Alamos NM 87545

NIELSEN, WILLIAM FREMMING, district judge; b. 1934. BA, U. Wash., 1956, LLB, 1963. Law clk. to Hon. Charles L. Powell U.S. Dist. Ct. (ea. dist.) Wash., 1963-91; mem. firm Paine, Hamblen, Coffin, Brooke &

Miller, 1964-91; judge U.S. Dist. Ct. (ea. dist.) Wash., Spokane, 1991—. lt. col. USAFR, 1959-82. Fellow Am. Coll. Trial Lawyers; mem. ABA, Wash. State Bar Assn., Spokane County Bar Assn. (pres. 1981-82), Fed. bar Assn. (pres. 1988), Spokane County Legal Svcs. Corp. (past pres.), Lawyer Pilot Bar Assn., Assn. Trial Lawyers Am., Wash. State Trial Lawyers Assn., Assn. Def. Trial Attys., Am. Inns of Ct., Charles L. Powell Inn (pres. 1987), The Spokane Club, Rotary, Alpha Delta Phi, Phi Delta Phi. Office: US Dist Ct PO Box 2208 W920 Riverside Ave Spokane WA 99210-2208

NIELSON, HOWARD CURTIS, former congressman, educator, retired; b. Richfield, Utah, Sept. 12, 1924; s. Herman Taylor and Zula May (Curtis) N.; m. Julia Adams, June 18, 1948; children: Noreen (Mrs. Stephen Astin), Elaine (Mrs. Stanley Taylor), John, Mary Lee (Mrs. Paul Jackson), James, Jean (Mrs. Clay Cundick), Howard Curtis Jr. B.S. in Math, U. Utah, 1947; M.S. in Math, U. Oreg., 1949; M.B.A., Stanford U., 1956, Ph.D. in Bus. Adminstrn. and Statistics, 1958. Statistician C & H Sugar Refining Corp., 1949-51; rsch. economist and statistician Stanford Rsch. Inst., 1951-57; mem. faculty Brigham Young U., Provo, Utah, 1957-82; prof. statistics Brigham Young U., 1961-82, chmn. dept., 1960-63; sr. devel. engr. Hercules, Inc., 1960-66; dir. Ctr. for Bus. and Econ. Rsch., 1971-72; sr. statistician, acting field mgr. C.E.I.R, Inc., 1963-64, mgr., cons., 1964-65; prin. scientist GCA Corp., 1965-67; dir. econ. rsch. Eyring Rsch. Inst., 1974-75; assoc. commr. higher edn. State of Utah, 1976-79; mem. 98th-101st Congresses from 3d dist. Utah; missionary Ch. of Jesus Christ of Latter Day Saints, Australia, 1991-92, Hungary, 1993—; econ. adviser Kingdom of Jordan, Ford Found., 1970-71; prof. Am. U., Beirut, 1970; adj. prof. U. Utah, 1972-76. Author: The Efficiency of Certain Truncated Order Statistics in Estimating the Mean of Various Distributions, 1949, Population Trends in the United States Through 1975, 1955, The Hows and Whys of Statistics, 1963, Experimental Designs Used in industry, 1965, Membership Growth of the Church of Jesus Christ of Latter-Day Saints, 1957, 67, 71, 75, 78, Evaluation of the Seven Year Plan for Economic Development in Jordan, 1971, Economic Analysis of Fiji, Tonga, Western and Am. Samoa, 1972; co-author: The Newsprint Situation in the Western Region of North America, 1952, America's Demand for Wood, 1954, also reports. Mem. Utah Gov.'s Econ. Rsch. Adv. Coun., 1967-72; dir. bur. ch. studies Ch. of Jesus Christ of Latter-day Saints, 1958-63; rsch. dir. Utah Republican Party, 1967-68; mem. Utah Ho. of Reps, 1967-75, majority leader, 1969-71, speaker, 1973-75, mem. legis. budget-audit com., 1967-73, chmn., 1971-73, chmn. legis. coun., 1973-75; mem. Utah 3d Dist., U.S. Ho. of Reps., 1983-91; chmn. Utah County Rep. Com., 1979-81. Mem. Am. Statis. Assn. (pres. Utah 1964-65, nat. council 1967-70), Sci. Research Soc. Am., Order of Artus, Phi Beta Kappa, Sigma Xi, Pi Mu Epsilon, Sigma Pi Sigma, Phi Kappa Phi.

NIEMAN, RICHARD HOVEY, retired plant physiologist; b. Pasadena, Calif., Nov. 7, 1922; s. Charles Percival and Nancy Leigh (Hovey) N.; m. Mary Owens Hall, Apr. 27, 1946; children: Arthur Hall, Edward Hovey. BA, U. So. Calif., 1949, MS, 1951; PhD, U. Chgo., 1955. Postdoctoral fellow in biochemistry U. Chgo., 1955-56; plant physiologist U.S. Salinity Lab., USDA, Riverside, Calif., 1956-88; ret., 1988; adj. prof. biochemistry U. Calif., Riverside, 1987-88. Contbr. articles to profl. jours., chpts. to books. Active environmentalist, Riverside, 1980—; vol. feeding the hungry 1st United Meth. Ch., Riverside, 1986—. Staff sgt. USAAF, 1943-46, PTO. Recipient Outstanding Performance award USDA, 1962, award for contbn. to curriculum study Am. Inst. Biol. Scis., 1963; rsch. grantee Agrl. Rsch. Svc., USDA, 1982, 83. Home: 5755 North View Pl Riverside CA 92506

NIEMI, JANICE, state legislator, lawyer; b. Flint, Mich., Sept. 18, 1928; d. Richard Jesse and Norma (Bell) Bailey; m. Preston Niemi, Feb. 4, 1953 (divorced 1987); children—Ries, Patricia. BA, U. Wash., 1950, LL.B., 1967; postgrad. U. Mich., 1950-52; cert. Hague Acad. Internat. Law, Netherlands, 1954. Bar: Wash. 1968. Assoc. firm Powell, Livengood, Dunlap & Silverdale, Kirkland, Wash., 1968; staff atty. Legal Service Ctr., Seattle, 1968-70; judge Seattle Dist. Ct., 1971-72, King County Superior Ct., Seattle, 1973-78; acting gen. counsel, dep. gen. counsel SBA, Washington, 1979-81; mem. Wash. State Ho. of Reps., Olympia, 1983-87, chmn. com. on state govt., 1984; mem. Wash. State Senate, 1987—; sole practice, Seattle, 1981—; mem. White House Fellows Regional Selection Panel, Seattle, 1974-77, chmn., 1976, 77; incorporator Sound Savs. & Loan, Seattle, 1975. Bd. dirs. Allied Arts, Seattle, 1971—, Ctr. Contemporary Art, Seattle, 1981-83, Women's Network, Seattle, 1981-84, Pub. Defender Assn., Seattle, 1982-84; bd. visitors dept. psychology U. Wash., Seattle, 1983-87, bd. visitors dept sociology, 1988— . Named Woman of Yr. in Law, Past Pres.'s Assn., Seattle, 1971; Woman of Yr., Matrix Table, Seattle, 1973, Capitol Hill Bus. and Profl. Women, 1975. Mem. Wash. State Bar Assn., Wash. Women Lawyers. Democrat. Home: PO Box 20516 Seattle WA 98102-1516

NIEMI, ROBERT JOHN, bank operations manager; b. Lakeheath, Suffolk, Eng., Feb. 27, 1961; came to U.S., 1964; s. Robert Edward and Mary Louise (Lippert) N.; m. Paula MaryAnn Wright, Sept. 19, 1981 (div.). Student, Lorretto Heights Coll., 1979. Ops. mgr. First Colo. Bank & Trust, Denver, 1980-86, Littleton (Colo.) Nat. Bank, 1986-92; CIF coord. Union Bank & Trust, Denver, 1992—. Mem. Littleton Jaycees (treas. 1988, v.p. 1989, bd. dirs. 1990, Presdl. award of Honor 1988, Jaycee of Yr. 1988, award for Outstanding Achievement 1989). Office: Union Bank & Trust 100 Broadway Denver CO 80203

NIENSTEDT, JOHN F, author; b. Emporia, Kans., July 21, 1938; s. John F. and Hazel Pauline (Miller) N.; children: John Brook, Barrie Sue. BA, Kasn. U., 1961. Account exec. WDAF, Kansas City, Mo., 1965-71; dist. rep. J. Walter Thompson Advt., Kansas City, Mo., 1976-82; account exec. Kenyon & Eckhardt Advt., Phoenix, 1984-85; lectr., trainer Performance Enhancement Programs, Phoenix, 1989—. Author: The Outstanding Man, 1992. With U.S. Army, 1972-75, to capt. Res., 1975-91. Mem. Nat. Speakers Assn. (bd. dirs. Ariz. chpt.), Naval Res. Assn., Kans. U. Alumni Assn.

NIERENBERG, NORMAN, urban land economist, retired state official; b. Chgo., May 8, 1919; s. Isadore Isaac and Sadie Sarah (Dorfman) N.; m. Nanette Joyce Fortgang, Feb. 9, 1950; children: Andrew Paul, Claudia Robin. AA, U. Chgo., 1939; AB, Calif. State Coll., L.A., 1952; MA, U. So. Calif., 1956. Lic. real estate broker, Calif.; cert. supr. and coll. instr., Calif. Right-of-way agt. Calif. Dept. Transp., L.A., 1951-61, 85-88; sr. agt. Calif. Dept. Transp., San Francisco, 1988-89; instr. UCLA, 1960-61, 67-75, 81-85; coord. continuing edn. in real estate U. Calif., Berkeley, 1961-64; coord. econ. benefits study Salton Sea, Calif. Dept. Water Resources, L.A., 1968-69; regional economist L.A. dist. CE, 1970-75, chief economist, 1981-85; regional economist Bd. Engrs. for Rivers and Harbors, Ft. Belvoir, Va., 1975-81; faculty resource person Oakland Project, Ford Found., U. Calif., Berkeley, 1962-64; project reviewer EPA, Washington, 1972-73. Editor: History of 82d Fighter Control Squadron, 1945; assoc. editor Right of Way Nat. Mag., 1952-55. Capt. USAAF, 1942-46, ETO, lt. col. USAFR ret. Mem. NEA, Am. Econ. Assn., Calif. Tchrs. Assn., Calif. Assn. Real Estate Tchrs. (bd. dirs. 1962), L.A. Coll. Tchrs. Assn., Res. Officers Assn., Ret. Officers Assn., Omicron Delta Epsilon. Democrat. Jewish. Home: 21931 Burbank Blvd Apt 4 Woodland Hills CA 91367-6456

NIERENBERG, WILLIAM AARON, oceanography educator; b. N.Y.C., Feb. 13, 1919; s. Joseph and Minnie (Drucker) N.; m. Edith Meyerson, Nov. 21, 1941; children—Victoria Jean (Mrs. Tschinkel), Nicolas Clarke Eugene. Aaron Naumberg scholar, U. Paris, 1937-38; B.S., CCNY, 1939; M.A., Columbia U., 1942, Ph.D. (NRC predoctoral fellow), 1947. Tutor CCNY, 1939-42; sect. leader Manhattan Project, 1942-45; instr. physics Columbia U., 1946-48; asst. prof. physics U. Mich., 1948-50; assoc. prof. physics U. Calif. at Berkeley, 1950-53, prof., 1954-65; dir. Scripps Instn. Oceanography, 1965-86, dir. emeritus, 1986—; vice chancellor for marine scis. U. Calif. at San Diego, 1969-86; dir. Hudson Labs., Columbia, 1953-54; assoc. prof. U. Paris, 1960-62; asst. sec. gen. NATO for sci. affairs, 1960-62; spl. cons. Exec. Office Pres., 1958-60; sr. cons. White House Office Sci. and Tech. Policy, 1976-78. Contbr. papers to profl. jours. E.O. Lawrence lectr. Nat. Acad. Sci., 1958, Miller Found. fellow, 1957-59, Sloan Found. fellow, 1958, Fulbright fellow, 1960-61; mem. U.S. Nat. Commn. UNESCO, 1964-68, Calif. Adv. Com. on Marine and Coastal Resources, 1967-71; adviser-at-large U.S. Dept. State, 1968—; mem. Nat. Sci. Bd., 1972-78, 82-88, cons., 1988-89; chmn. USNC/PSA, NRC, 1988—; mem. Nat. Adv. Com. on Oceans and Atmosphere, 1971-77, chmn., 1971-75; mem. sci. and tech. adv. Council Calif. Assembly; mem. adv. council NASA, 1978-83, chmn. adv. council, 1978-82. NATO Sr. Sci. fellow, 1969; Decorated officer Nat. Order of Merit France; recipient Golden Dolphin award Assn. Artistico Letteraria Internazionale, Disting. Pub. Service medal NASA, 1982, Delmer S. Fahrney medal The Franklin Inst., 1987, Compass award Marine Tech. Soc., 1975. Fellow Am. Phys. Soc. (coun., sec. Pacific Coast sect. 1955-64); mem. Am. Acad. Arts and Scis., NAE, NAS (coun. 1973—), Am. Philos. Soc., Am. Assn. Naval Architects, Navy League, Fgn. Policy Assn. (mem. nat. council), Sigma Xi (pres. 1981-82, Procter prize, 1977). Club: Cosmos. Home: PO Box 927269 San Diego CA 92192-7269 Office: U Calif Scripps Instn Oceanography 0221 La Jolla CA 92093

NIESLUCHOWSKI, WITOLD S., cardiovascular and thoracic surgeon; b. Warsaw, Poland, Mar. 2, 1944; came to U.S., 1975; s. Stanislaw Leon and Izabela Anna (Swierczynska) N.; m. Bonnie Jean Thomas, Apr. 15, 1978; children: Jason Brian, Christopher Thomas, Megan Jean, Jennifer Anne. MD, Warsaw Med. Sch., 1967. With Akademicki Zwiazek Sportowy, Warsaw, 1961-75; cardiovascular surgeon Oxnard (Calif.) Hosp., 1975—. Mem. Oxnard Humanitarians, 1987—; bd. dirs. Am. Heart Assn., Camarillo, Calif., 1988—. Fellow ACS, Am. Coll. Cardiologists; mem. Soc. for Thoracic Surgeons. Club: Cabrillo Tennis (Camarillo). Office: 435 S D St # 200 Oxnard CA 93030-5926

NIGAM, BISHAN PERKASH, physics educator; b. Delhi, India, July 14, 1928; came to U.S., 1952; s. Rajeshwar Nath and Durga (Vati) N.; m. Indira Bahadur, Nov. 14, 1956; children—Sanjay, Shobhna, Ajay. B.S., U. Delhi, 1946, M.S., 1948; Ph.D., U. Rochester, N.Y., 1955. Research fellow U. Delhi, 1948-50; lectr. in physics, 1950-52, 55-56; postdoctoral fellow Case Inst. Tech., Cleve., 1954-55; postdoctoral research fellow NRC, Ottawa, Can., 1956-59; research assoc. U. Rochester, 1959-60, asst. prof. physics, part-time 1960-61; prin. scientist Gen. Dynamics/Electronics, Rochester, N.Y., 1960-61; assoc. prof. physics SUNY, Buffalo, 1961-64; prof. physics Ariz. State U., Tempe, 1964—, U. Wis., Milw., 1966-67. Author: (with R.R. Roy) Nuclear Physics, 1967; also articles. Govt. of India scholar U. Rochester, 1952-54. Fellow Am. Phys. Soc. Office: Dept Physics Ariz State U Tempe AZ 85287

NIGRA, ROBERT O., accountant; b. Passaic, N.J., Nov. 2, 1942; s. Louis D. and Catherine B. (Pollara) N.; m. (div. 1975); children: Jeffrey S., Jennifer L. BSBA, Calif. Poly. U., 1965; postgrad., San Jose State U., 1973-75. Cert. tax preparer, Calif. Tchr. physics dept. Calif. Poly. U., San Luis Obispo, 1963-64; asst. comptroler Taylor Steel, Inc., Burlingame, Calif., 1965-67; from acct. to CFO Nine-Six West, Inc., San Jose, Calif., 1967-78; CEO Nine-Six West, Inc., Campbell, Calif., 1978—. Scoutmaster Boy Scouts of Am., San Jose, 1973-83; com. mem. Cub Scouts of Am., San Jose, 1970-73. Mem. Aspen Grove C/P Assn. (bd. dirs. 1983—), Optimist Internat., Campbell Optimist Club (bd. dirs. 1978—), Calif. Poly. U. Alumni Assn. (bd. dirs., CFO 1966—), Survivors Club, Delta Upsilon. Office: Nine-Six West Inc 96 W Campbell Ave Campbell CA 95008-1029

NIIHARA, YUTAKA, physician, educator; b. Tokyo, Oct. 7, 1959; came to U.S., 1973; s. Harushi and Chiyoko (Kang) N.; m. Soomi Song; children: Albert, Hope. BA, Loma Linda U., 1982, MD, 1986. Intern, resident Kettering (Ohio) Med. Ctr., 1986-89; fellow in hematology and oncology Harbor UCLA Med. Ctr., Torrance, Calif., 1989-92; asst. clin. prof. UCLA Sch. Medicine, Torrance and L.A., 1992—. Mem. ACP, N.Y. Acad. Scis. Mem. Seventh Day Adventist Ch. Office: Harbor UCLA Med Ctr 1000 W Carson St Torrance CA 90509

NIIRANEN, VICTOR JOHANNES, professional society administrator; b. Keewatin, Minn., Apr. 24, 1916. DDS, U. Minn., 1940; postgrad., Honolulu Acad. Art, The Foss Sch. Fine Arts; studies with Lau Chun, Hawaii, Hongkong, China. Commd. lt. jr. grade USN, advanced through grades to capt., ret.; nat. pres. Nat. Soc. Arts and Letters, Honolulu; lectr. in field worldwide. Editor Yearbook, editor The Record; contbr. articles to profl. jours. Mem. NSAL. Office: Nat Soc Arts and Letters 469 Ena Rd # 2405 Honolulu HI 96815

NILES, ALBAN ISAAC, judge; b. St. Vincent, W.I., June 10, 1933; s. Isaac N. and Elsie (Lovell) N. BS, UCLA, 1959, JD, 1963. Bar: Calif. 1964, U.S. Dist. Ct. (ctrl. dist.) 1964. Acct. Ernst & Ernst, L.A., 1963-64; pvt. practice law L.A., 1964-82; judge Mcpl. Ct. County of L.A., 1982-92; asst. presiding judge L.A. Mcpl. Ct., 1992—; pres., gen. counsel Kedren Community Health Ctr., L.A., 1971-79; chair L.A. Mcpl. Ct. Judges, 1993—; asst. presiding judge L.A. Mcpl. Ct., 1992, 93. With USAF, 1951-55. Recipient certs. Legislature State of Calif., 1978, Bd. Suprs. L.A. County, 1978, City of L.A., 1979, other numerous community awards from various orgns. Mem. ABA, Nat. Bar Assn. (parliamentarian 1990-91, treas. 1991-93), Am. Legion (commdr. 1987-91), Masons. Office: LA Mcpl Ct Div 110 N Grand Ave Div 8 Los Angeles CA 90012-3014

NILES, GEDDES LEROY, private investigator; b. Haines, Alaska, Oct. 31, 1926; s. Geddes William and Gladys Bell (McCormack) N.; m. Aline Terii Tehei, June 17, 1960; children: Diana Mareva Niles-Hansen, Stephen Lloyd Teva. BA, U. Calif., Berkeley, 1949. Investigator and hearing officer U.S. Civil Service Commn., San Francisco, 1955-62, Honolulu, 1962-78; pres. Niles Realty Ltd., Honolulu, 1979—; dir. The Niles Agy., Honolulu, 1983—. Mem. Neighborhood Bd., Kailua, Hawaii, 1979-80. Club: Iaorana Tahiti (Honolulu) (treas. 1985-89). Office: 350 Ward Ave Ste 106 Honolulu HI 96814-4091

NILLES, JOHN MATHIAS (JACK NILLES), entrepreneur; b. Evanston, Ill., Aug. 25, 1932; s. Elmer Edward and Hazel Evelyn (Wickum) N.; m. Laila Padorr, July 8, 1957. BA magna cum laude, Lawrence Coll., 1954; MS in Engring., U. Calif., Los Angeles, 1964. Sr. engr. Raytheon Mfg. Co., Santa Barbara, Calif., 1956-58; section head. Ramo-Woodridge Corp., L.A., 1958-59; project engr. Space Technology Lab., L.A., 1960; dir. The Aerospace Corp., L.A., 1961-67; sr. systems engr. TRW Systems, L.A., 1967-69; assoc. group dir. The Aerospace Corp., L.A., 1965-72; dir. interdisciplinary programs U. So. Calif., L.A., 1972-81, dir. info. technology program, 1981-89; pres. JALA Internat. Inc., L.A., 1980—; coord. EC Teleforum, Brussels, 1992—; dir. Telecommunicating Adv. Coun., L.A., 1991—, pres. 1993—; chmn. Telecommuting Rsch. Inst., Inc., L.A., 1990—. Author: The Telecommunications Transportation Tradeoff, 1976, Japanese edit., 1977, Exploring the World of the Personal Computer, 1982, French edit., 1985, Micros and Modems, 1983, French edit., 1986. Capt. USAF, 1954-56. Recipient Rod Rose award Soc. Research Adminstrators, 1976, Environ. Pride award L.A. Mag., 1993. Mem. Assn. For Computing Machinery, IEEE Computer Soc., Inst. Mgmt. Sciences, AAAS, World Future Soc., Calif. Yacht. Office: JALA Internat Inc 971 Stonehill Ln Los Angeles CA 90049-1412

NILSEN, ALLEEN PACE, English language educator; b. Phoenix, Oct. 10, 1936; d. Glenn Smith and Maud (Isaacson) Pace; m. Don L. F. Nilsen, Mar. 21, 1958; children: Kelvin, Sean, Nicolette. BA, Brigham Young U., 1958; MEd, Am. U., 1961; PhD, U. Iowa, 1973. Tchr. Fairfax County Schs., Clifton, Va., 1960-61; Eng. instr. Highland Park Jr. Coll., Detroit, 1961-62, Ea. Mich. U., Ypsilanti, Mich., 1963-67, 69-71; tchr. Am. Internat. Sch., Kabul, Afghanistan, 1967-69; teaching instr. U. No. Iowa, Cedar Falls, 1971-72; supr. Tempe (Ariz.) Elem. Sch. Dist.; faculty mem. Ariz. State U., Coll. of Edn., Tempe, 1975-85; asst. dean Ariz. State U., Grad. Coll., 1985-88; prof. Ariz. State U., Dept. of Eng., 1988—; asst. v.p. acad. affairs Ariz. State U., 1988—; speakers bur. Ariz. Humanities Coun., Phoenix, 1987-89; conf. co-chmn. WHIM Humor Confs., Tempe, 1981-88. Author: Presenting M.E. Kerr, 1988; co-author: Literature for Today's Young Adults, 1980, 85, 89, 93, Language Play, 1978. Named Outstanding Woman in English Edn. by Nat. Coun. Tchrs. of English, 1991. Mem. Nat. Coun. Tchrs. English (editor English jour. 1981-88, pres. adolescent lit. assembly 1982-83, ALAN award 1988, One of Outstanding Women in English Edn. award 1991). Democrat. Mem. LDS Ch. Home: 1884 E Alameda Dr Tempe AZ 85282

NILSEN, DON LEE FRED, linguistics educator; b. Palmyra, Utah, Oct. 19, 1934; s. Delles Fredric and Jessie (Parmalee) N.; m. Alleen Pace, Mar. 21, 1958; children: Kelvin, Sean, Nicolette. BA, Brigham Young U., 1958; MA, Am. U., 1961; PhD, U. Mich., 1971. Asst. prof. Eng. SUNY, Oswego, 1964-66; coord. tchr. edn. program U. Mich., Ann Arbor, 1966-67; instr. ESL U. Mich, Ann Arbor, 1969-71; linguistics specialist Kabul (Afghanistan) U., 1967-69; dir. linguistics U. No. Iowa, Cedar Falls, 1971-73; assoc. prof. linguistics Ariz. State U., Tempe, 1973-78, prof. linguistics, 1978—; asst. prof. linguistics U. Redlands, Calif., 1966; instr. French E. Mich. U., Ypsilanti, 1967; interpreter Ariz. Heritage Festival, Phoenix, 1990; plenary speaker Tchrs. Eng. to speakers of other langs., Flagstaff, Ariz., 1988; mem. exec. bd. Workshop Libr. World Humor, Washington, 1985—. Author: English Adverbials, 1972 ; co-author: Pronunciation Contrasts, 1973, Semantic Theory, 1975, Language Play, 1978, Humor in American Literature, 1992, Humor Scholarship: A Research Bibliography, 1993; editor: (newsletter) Humor; mem. editorial bd. Metaphor and Symbolic Activity, Knoxville, Tenn., 1985—; adv. editor Wayne State U. Humor Series, 1987—. With U.S. Army, 1954-56. Recipient grants, World Humor and Irony Membership, Ariz. Humanities Coun., Tempe, 1982-87; named Humanities scholar, Ariz. Humanities Coun., Phoenix, 1985-90. Mem. Internat. Soc. Humor Studies (exec. sec. 1988-91). Democrat. Home: 1884 E Alameda Dr Tempe AZ 85282-2873

NILVA, LEONID, scientist, researcher; b. Leningrad, USSR, Dec. 15, 1956; came to U.S., 1987; s. Alexander and Tamara (Ginzburg) N.; (div. May 1987); 1 child, Maria. BS in Applied Maths., Inst. Elec. Engring., Leningrad, 1977, MS in Computer Sci., 1979; postgrad., Inst. for Control Technique, Leningrad, 1979-81. Cert. handwriting analyst Inst. Integral Handwriting Studies. Programmer Inst. Elec. Equipment, Leningrad, 1981-83; sr. programmer Geol. Inst., Leningrad, 1983-86, Inst. of Hydrotechnology, Leningrad, 1986-87; sr. design engr. Answer Computer, Sunnyvale, Calif., 1987-88; staff scientist Ricoh Calif. Rsch. Ctr., Menlo Park, Calif., 1988-91; mgr. imaging group Harvest Software, Inc., Sunnyvale, Calif., 1991—; rsch. asst. All-Union Astronomic Soc., Leningrad, 1981-87; cons. Informax Inc., Washington, 1990-91; staff scientist Inst. Integral Handwriting Studies, Palo Alto, Calif., 1993—. Patentor variable spectral analysis for OCR, binary tree recognition for OCR. Mem. SPIE, Math. Assn. Am., Assn. for Computing Machinery, Amnesty Internat. Office: Harvest Software Inc 320 Soquel Way Sunnyvale CA 94086-4101

NIMMAGADDA, RAO RAJAGOPALA, materials scientist, researcher; b. Donepudi, Andhra Pradesh, India, July 1, 1944; came to U.S., 1967; s. Suryaprakasa Rao and Bullemma (Venigalla) N.; m. Usha Rani Chava, Nov. 7, 1965 (div. Nov. 1980); children: Sandhya Rani, Pramada Shree; m. Jhansi Rani Talluri, Dec. 18, 1980; children: Sai Chandra and Sri Spandana. B Tech. with honors, Indian Inst. Tech., Bombay, 1965; MS, Mich. Tech. U., 1970; PhD, UCLA, 1975. Jr. sci. officer Def. Metall. Rsch. Labs., Hyderabad, India, 1965-67; postdoctoral scholar UCLA, 1975-78, rsch. engr., 1978-81; rsch. scientist Smith Tool, Irvine, Calif., 1981-83, Burroughs, Westlake Village, Calif., 1983-84; rsch. engr. Memorex Corp., Santa Clara, Calif., 1984-86; staff scientist Lockheed Missiles & Space Co., Palo Alto, Calif., 1986-93; staff engr. Akashic Memories Corp., San Jose, Calif., 1993—. Contbr. articles to profl. jours. Pres. Telugu Assn. So. Calif., 1977, dir. Hindu Temple Soc. So. Calif., 1977-80, pres., 1980. Recipient of Outstanding Tech. Achievement award Strategic Def. Initiative Orgn., Washington, 1989. Mem Am. Vacuum Soc., Materials Rsch. Soc. Republican. Hindu. Home: 120 Gilbert Ave Santa Clara CA 95051-6705 Office: Akashic Memories Corp 305 W Tasman San Jose CA 95134

NINKE, ARTHUR ALBERT, accountant, management consultant; b. Coloma, Mich., Aug. 20, 1909; s. Paul F. and Theresa Grace (Warskow) N.; m. Claudia Wagner, Sept. 13, 1930; children: Doris Ninke Hart, Donald, Marion, George, Arthur Albert, Thomas, Mark, Albert. Student acctg. Internat. Bus. Coll., 1928; diploma commerce Northwestern U., 1932. Auditor, Arthur Andersen & Co., CPA's, Chgo., 1929-36, St. Louis, 1950-55, Midwest Stock Exchange, 1936-41, SEC, 1942-45; expense controller Butler Bros., Chgo., 1946-49; office mgr. Hargis Electronics, 1956-59; auditor HUD, Detroit, 1960-64; owner Urban Tech. Staff Assoc., cons. urban renewal projects and housing devel., Detroit, 1965-81; pres. Simplified Systems & Computer Sales, 1978—, More Benefits Acctg. Svcs., Phoenix, 1991—; exec. dir. Urban Mgmt. Services 1984—, Urban Computerized Services, Inc., 1984-88, Computer Mgmt. Svs., 1985—, Complete Bus. Svc., Dallas, 1979-82, Loving Shepherd Nursing Home, Warren, Mich., 1975-83; sec. Gideons Detroit North Woodward, 1981-83, treas., 1986-87. Author: Family Bible Studies; Computer Networking; dir. Family Bible Hour Club, 1986—; developer simulated machine bookkeeping system; trade mark holder Record-Checks-Systems, 1981—. Controller, Lake Superior R&D Inst., Munising, Mich., 1973-76; lay minister Redford Luth. Ch., 1988-91; pres. Luth. Friendship Homes, Inc., 1975-85; lay evangelist Faith Luth. Ch., 1986-88, treas., 1985-86; mng. dir. Family Evangelism Found., 1977—; controller S.E. Mich. Billy Graham Crusade, 1976-77; pres. Project Compassion Met. Detroit, Inc., 1982-91; bd. dirs. Lutheran Credit Union Greater Detroit, 1982-88; mem. Nat. Council on Aging. Recipient tribute Mich. State Legislature, 1982, 91, tribute City of Warren, 1982, City of Detroit, 1991, Project Compassion of Mich., 1991, Detroit City Coun., 1991, Mich. State Legis., 1991. Mem. Am. Mgmt. Assn., Nat. Soc. Pub. Accts., Nat. Assn. Housing and Redevel. Ofcls. (treas. Mich. 1973-75), Luth. Center Assn. (treas. 1975-81, dir. 1975-81), Internat. Luth. Laymen's League (treas. S.E. Mich. 1971-75, dir. 1976-81), Fairlane Club of Dearborn, Gideon Internat.

NINNEMAN, THOMAS GEORGE, broadcast executive; b. Chgo., Apr. 13, 1950; s. Milton Charles and Bernice Helen (Sharp) N.; m. Nancy Gail Rogers, Aug. 12, 1972; children: Stephanie Christine, Peter Christopher. BA, U. No. Colo., 1972. Dir. news. Sta. KGLN, Glenwood Springs, Colo., 1972-73; program mgr. Sta. KKEP, Estes Park, Colo., 1973-74; ops. mgr. Sta. WMST-AM-FM, Mt. Sterling, Ky., 1974-75; dir. news Sta. KPIK-AM-FM, Colorado Springs, Colo., 1975-77; news stringer AP, UPI, various stas., Colorado Springs, Colo., 1977-78; mgr. driver edn., safety dept. Am. Automobile Assn., Denver, 1978-81; pres. mkt. rschr. Rampart Range Broadcasting Inc., Castle Rock, Colo., 1981-83; news editor Sta. KDEN, Denver, 1983-84; dir. news Stas. KSGT and KMTN-FM, Jackson, Wyo., 1984—; instr. TV Jackson Hole High Sch., Jackson, Wyo., 1989—; panelist Yellowstone Fire Review, Yellowstone Nat. Park, 1989; contract spokesman fire safety, Bridger-Teton Nat. Forest, Jackson, Wyo., 1990—; adv. commn. Wyo. Pub. Radio, 1991—. Asst. scoutmaster, scoutmaster Boy Scouts Am., Castle Rock, Colo., 1979-84, mem. dist. com. 1984—; vice chair Teton County Centennial Com., Jackson, 1989; co-founder, mgr. Jackson Hole Community Band, 1989—; charter mem., coun. mem. Shepherd of the Mountains Lutheran Ch.; active Jackson Hole Brass Quintet, 1985—, Christian Ministry in Nat. Parks local com., 1988—. Recipient Tony Bevinette Friend of Wyo. Tourism award Wyo. Travel Commn., 1993; co-recipient Wyo. News Station of Yr. award AP, 1990; named Broadcast Newsman of Yr. AP, 1976. Home: PO Box 105 Jackson WY 83001 Office: Stas KSGT/KMTN Radio PO Box 100 Jackson WY 83001

NINOS, NICHOLAS PETER, retired military officer, medical consultant; b. Chgo., May 11, 1936; s. Peter Spiros and Ann (Lesczynsky) N. BA in Art, Bradley U., 1958, BS in Chemistry, 1959; MD, U. Ill., Chgo., 1963. Diplomate Am. Bd. Internal Med., Am. Bd. Cardiology, Am. Bd. Critical Care Medicine. Intern Cook County Hosp., Chgo., 1963-64, resident in internal medicine, 1964-67, fellow in cardiology, 1967-68; commd. capt. U.S. Army, 1968, advanced through grades to col., 1979; chief dept. medicine U.S. Army Community Hosp. U.S. Army, Bremerhaven, Fed. Republic Germany, 1968-69, Wurzberg, Fed. Republic Germany, 1969-72; chief critical care Letterman Army Med. Ctr., San Francisco, 1976-91; dep. comdr. San Francisco med. command Letterman Army Med. Ctr./Naval Hosp. of Oakland, San Francisco and Oakland, Calif., 1988-90; ret., 1991; assoc. prof. medicine and surgery Uniformed Svcs., U. Health Scis., Bethesda, Md., 1981—; critical care medicine cons. to U.S. Army Surgeon Gen., 1981-91; lectr. in field. Author (jour.): Ethics, 1988; co-editor: Nutrition, 1988, Problems in Critical Care, Nutrition Support; mem. editorial bd. Jour. Critical Care Medicine, 1988-91; illustrator: Medical Decision Making, 1988. 2d v.p. Twin Springs Condominium Homeowners Assn., Palm Springs, Calif., 1993—; ch. bd. councilman St. George Orthodox Ch. of the Desert, Palm Desert, Calif., 1993—. Decorated Legion of Merit, Meritorious Svc. medal with oak leaf cluster. Fellow Am. Coll. of Critical Care medicine; mem. AMA, Soc. Critical Care Medicine (pres. uniformed svcs. sect. 1987-90, Shubin/Weil award 1988), Am. Coll. Critical Care Medicine (bd. regents 1989—, chmn., 1989-91), Soc. Med. Cons. to Armed Forces (assoc.), Inst. Critical Care Medicine (exec. v.p. 1991-92).

NISH, ALBERT RAYMOND, JR., retired newspaper editor; b. San Bernardino, Calif., Mar. 16, 1922; s. Albert Raymond and Mabel Claire (Shay) N.; m. Lois Maxine Ringgenberg, June 21, 1942; children: Steven Raymond, Richard Henry, Kathleen Lorie Jenner. Student San Bernardino Valley Jr. Coll., 1939-41, U. Calif., Berkeley, 1941-42, Wash. State Coll., 1943; Am. Press Inst., 1977. Pony wire editor AP, San Francisco, 1941-42; reporter Chico Record, Calif., 1945-46, Berkeley Daily Gazette, Calif., 1946-48; valley editor Modesto Bee, Calif., 1948-60, asst. mng. editor, 1960-62, mng. editor, 1962-85. Served as fighter pilot USAAC, 1942-45, PTO. Decorated DFC.

NISHIDA, JANELL ESTHER, artist; b. Seaside, Oreg., Nov. 15, 1948; d. Raymond Jay and Grace Irene (Brown) Stose; . Rodney Shigeo, June 28, 1980; 1 child, Jennica Grace. Student, Foss Sch. of Fine Arts, 1986-88, Honolulu Acad. of Arts, 1987-91. Artist Honolulu, 1986—. Exhibited in shows at Koko Marina, 1987, Windward Artists Guild, 1987, Hawaii Watercolor Soc., 1989, 91, 92, Assn. Hawaii Artists, 1990, 91, 92, Gateway Gallery/Assn. Hawaii Artists, 1991,. Mem. Hawaii Watercolor Soc. (rec. sec. 1993—, Best of Show 1992), Assn. of Hawaii Artists (membership chair 1987-91), Windward Artists, Nat. Watercolor Soc. (assoc.). Home and Studio: 6633 Kauna St Honolulu HI 96825

NISHIOKA, TERUO (TED NISHIOKA), electrical engineer; b. Crystal City, Tex., Sept. 6, 1945; s. Kazuto Benjamin and Kofumi (Shinkawa) N.; m. Suzanne Nayeko Hayashi, June 24, 1978; 1 child, Stephanie. BSEE, Calif. State Poly. U., 1970. Engr. Salt River Project, Phoenix, 1970-72, Pacific Gas and Electric, San Francisco, 1972-74; power plant engr. Wismer and Becker, Sacramento, 1975-78; sr. elec. engr. Ariz. Pub. Svc., Phoenix, 1978—. Author: Underground Cable Thermal Backfill, 1981. Active Japanese-Am. Citizens League, Phoenix, 1978—, bd. dirs. 1991—; v.p. Ariz. Buddhist Ch., Phoenix, 1987-88, pres., 1989-91; mem. Matsuri steering com., 1992—. With U.S. Army, 1966-68. Mem. IEEE, Power Engring. Soc., Elec. Insulation Soc. Office: Ariz Pub Svc PO Box 53999 Phoenix AZ 85072-3999

NISHITANI, MARTHA, dancer; b. Seattle, Feb. 27, 1920; d. Denjiro and Jin (Aoto) N. B.A. in Comparative Arts, U. Wash., 1958; studied with, Eleanor King, Mary Ann Wells, Perry Mansfield, Cornish Sch., Conn. Coll. Sch. Dance, Long Beach State U. Founder, dir. Martha Nishitani Modern Dance Sch. and Co., Seattle, 1950—; dance dir. Helen Bush Sch. and Central YWCA, 1951-54; choreographer U. Wash. Opera Theater, 1955-65, Intiman Theater, 1972—; dance instr. Elementary and Secondary Edn. Act Program, 1966; dance specialist spl. edn. program Shoreline Pub. Schs., 1970-72; condr. workshops and concerts King County Youth Correctional Instns., 1972-73; Dance adv. counsel Wash. Cultural Enrichment Program; dance adv. bd. Seattle Parks and Recreation. Dancer Eleanor King Co., Seattle, 1946-50, dance films, 1946-51, Channel 9, Ednl. TV, 1967-68; lectr. demonstrator numerous colls., festivals, convs., childrens theater.; author articles on dance; one of the subjects: A Celebration of 100 Years of Dance in Washington, 1989. Trustee Allied Arts Seattle, 1967. Recipient Theta Sigma Phi Matrix Table award, 1968, Asian Am. Living Treasure award Northwest Asian Am. Theater, 1984; listed in Dance Archives, N.Y.C. Libr., 1991, N.Y.C. Lincoln Ctr. Dance Archives, 1991. Mem. Am. Dance Guild (exec. com. 1961-63), Com. Research in Dance, Seattle Art Mus., Internat. Dance Alliance (adv. council 1984), Smithsonian Assos., Progressive Animal Welfare Soc. Address: 4205 University Way NE PO Box 45264 Seattle WA 98145-0264

NISKANEN, PAUL MCCORD, travel company executive; b. Bend, Oreg., July 6, 1943; s. William Arthur and Nina Elizabeth (McCord) N.; m. Christine Campbell; 1 son, Tapio. Student U. Freiburg, W. Ger., 1963-64; B.A., Stanford U., 1965; M.B.A., U. Chgo., 1966. Fin. analyst Kimberly-Clark Corp., Neenah, Wis., 1966-68; bus. mgr. Avent Inc. subs. Kimberly-Clark Corp., Tucson, 1968-70; v.p., gen. mgr. Pacific Trailways Bus. Line, Portland, Oreg., 1970-81; chmn. bd., owner Niskanen & Jones, Inc., Moab, Utah, 1982—, Perspectives, Inc., Portland; co-owner Cruise Holidays, Beaverton, Oreg., 1989—. Appointed consul for Finland, 1980—; Mem. Gov.'s Travel Adv. Com., Salem, Oreg., 1976-81; 1st pres. Oreg. Hospitality and Visitors Assn., Portland, 1977-78; bd. dirs. Suomi Coll., Hancock, Mich., 1981—; nat. co-chmn. Dole for Pres. Com., 1987; co-chmn. Vistory 88. Mem. Travel Industry Assn. Am., Am. Assn. Travel Agts., Pacific Northwest Travel Assn. (chmn. 1978-79), Scandinavian Heritage Found. (bd. dirs. 1984). Republican. Home: 4366 SW Hewett Blvd Portland OR 97221-3107 Office: Cruise Holidays 2648 SW Cedar Hills Blvd Beaverton OR 97005

NISSEL, MARTIN, radiologist, consultant; b. N.Y.C., July 29, 1921; s. Samuel David and Etta Rebecca (Ostrie) N.; m. Beatrice Goldberg, Dec. 26, 1943; children: Philippa Lyn, Jeremy Michael. BA, NYU, 1941; MD, N.Y. Med. Coll., 1944. Diplomate Am. Bd. Radiology. Intern Met. Hosp., N.Y.C., 1944-45, Lincoln Hosp., N.Y.C., 1947-48; resident in radiology Bronx Hosp., 1948-50, attending radiologist, 1952-54; resident in radiotherapy Montefiore Hosp., Bronx, 1950-51, attending radiotherapist, 1954-65; attending radiologist Buffalo (N.Y.) VA Hosp., 1951-52; attending radiotherapist Univ. Hosp. Boston City Hosp., 1965-69; asst. prof. radiology Boston U. Sch. of Medicine, 1965-69; chief radiotherapist,dir. radiation ctr. Brookside Hosp., San Pablo, Calif., 1969-77; group leader, radiopharm. drugs FDA, Rockville, Md., 1977-86; pvt. cons. radiopharm. drug devel., 1986—. Contbr. articles to profl. jours. Lectr. Am. Cancer Soc., Contra Costa County, Calif., 1973-76. Capt. MC AUS, 1945-47, Korea. Recipient Contra Costa County Speakers Bur. award Am. Cancer Soc., 1973, 76, Responsible Person for Radiol. Health Program for Radiopharm. Drugs award FDA, 1980-86. Mem. Am. Coll. Radiology, Radiol. Soc. N.Am. Office: PO Box 5537 Eugene OR 97405

NITTA, EUGENE TADASHI, endangered species biologist; b. Lodi, Calif., Aug. 19, 1946; s. Kenji and Emiko (Taguchi) N.; m. Teresa Thelma Tanibe, Dec. 26, 1987; stepchildren: Sheri Y. Yamamoto, Tani-Lyn T. Yamamoto, Staci S. Yamamoto. BA, U. Calif., Santa Barbara, 1969. Observer Internat. Whaling Commn., Cambridge, England, 1972-75; marine mammal and endangered species program coord. NOAA Nat. Marine Fisheries Svcs. Southwest Region, Terminal Island, Calif., 1976-79; protected species program coord. NOAA Nat. Marine Fisheries Svcs. Southwest Region, Honolulu, 1980—; instr. coll. continuing edn. U. Hawaii, Honolulu, 1988-93. Mem. Soc. for Marine Mammalogy (charter mem.), Am. Soc. Mammalogists. Democrat. Episcopalian.

NITZ, FREDERIC WILLIAM, electronics company executive; b. St. Louis, June 22, 1943; s. Arthur Carl Paul and Dorothy Louise (Kahm) N.; m. Kathleen Sue Rapp, June 8, 1968; children: Frederic Theodore, Anna Louise. AS, Coll. Marin, 1970; BS in Electronics, Calif. Poly. State U., San Luis Obispo, 1972. Electronic engr. Sierra Electronics, Menlo Park, Calif., 1973-77, RCA, Somerville, N.J., 1977-79; engring. mgr. EGG-Geometrics, Sunnyvale, Calif., 1979-83; v.p. engring. Basic Measuring Insts., Foster City, Calif., 1983-91; exec. v.p. Reliable Power Meters, Los Gatos, Calif., 1991—; cons. in field, Boulder Creek, Calif., 1978—. Patentee in field. Bd. dirs. San Lorenzo Valley Water Dist., Boulder Creek, 1983—, Water Policy Task Force, Santa Cruz County, Calif., 1983-84. With U.S. Army, 1965-67. Democrat. Lutheran. Home: 12711 East St Boulder Creek CA 95006-9148 Office: Reliable Power Meters 400 Blossom Hill Rd Los Gatos CA 95032-4511

NIX, GARY WILLIAM, special education educator; b. Springfield, Ill., July 6, 1941; s. William H. and Roberta G. (Cass) N.; A.B. in Sociology, Ill. Coll., 1963; M.E.D. in Edn. of Deaf, Smith Coll., 1964; Ph.D. in Spl. Edn., U. Oreg., 1971; m. Rae A. Sapp, Mar. 22, 1964; children: Brian W., Rebecca A., Bradley S. Asst. prof. U. Wis., Stevens Point, 1971-74; assoc. prof. Tex. Tech U., Lubbock, 1975-77; supt. Mystic (Conn.) Oral Sch., 1977-79; assoc. prof. Faculty of Edn., U. B.C., Vancouver, 1979-86; pres., chmn. bd. dirs. Gary W. Nix & Assoc. Ltd., Alexander Graham Bell Assn. for Deaf, 1980-82; dir. Richmond Edn. Clinic, Fraser Valley Edn. Clinic; invited lectr. on mainstreaming Oxford, Eng., Taipei, Taiwan. Exec. bd. Council on Edn. of Deaf, 1980-82. Mem. Internat. Orgn. for Edn. of Hearing Impaired, Britannia Heritage Shipyard Soc. (bd. dirs.), Council for Exceptional Children, Learning Disabilities Assn. Can. (bd. dirs.), Learning Disabilities Assn. of B.C. (past pres.), Can. Psychol. Assn. Unitarian. Author: Mainstream Education of Hearing Impaired Children and Youth (also Spanish and Japanese edits.); contbr. articles to profl. jours. Office: 7451 Elmbridge Way Ste 100, Richmond, BC Canada V6X 1B8

NIX, JAMES RAYFORD, nuclear physicist, consultant; b. Natchitoches, La., Feb. 18, 1938; s. Joe Ebbin and Edna (Guin) N.; m. Sally Ann Wood, Aug. 19, 1961; children—Patricia Lynne, David Allen. B.S. in Physics, Carnegie Inst. Tech., 1960; Ph.D. in Physics, U. Calif.-Berkeley, 1964. Summer physicist Lawrence Livermore Nat. Lab., Livermore, Calif., 1961; research asst. Lawrence Berkeley Lab., Berkeley, Calif., 1961-64, postdoctoral physicist, 1966-68; NATO postdoctoral fellow Niels Bohr Inst., Copenhagen, Denmark, 1964-65; staff mem. Los Alamos Nat. Lab., 1968-77, 89—, group leader, 1977-89 ; vis. prof. Centro Brasileiro de Pesquisas Fisicas, Rio de Janeiro, Brazil, 1974; cons. Calif. Inst. Tech., Pasadena, 1976, 79; chmn. Gordon Research Conf. Nuclear Chemistry, New London, N.H., 1976; chmn. physics div. adv. com. Oak Ridge Nat. Lab., 1976, chmn. nuclear sci. div. vis. com. Lawrence Berkeley Lab., 1979-80. Contbr. articles to numerous publs. Alfred P. Sloan Found. Scholar, Pitts., 1956-60; Phi Kappa Phi fellow, Berkeley, Calif., 1960-61. Fellow Am. Phys. Soc. (exec. com. 1973-75); mem. AAAS, Sigma Xi, Phi Kappa Phi. Democrat. Home: 12 Los Pueblos Los Alamos NM 87544-2659 Office: Los Alamos Nat Lab Nuclear Theory T-2 MS B243 Los Alamos NM 87545

NIX, NANCY JEAN, librarian, designer; b. Denver; d. James Frederik and Josephine (Britt) N. AB in History, U. So. Calif., L.A., 1959, MLS, 1960. Exhibited in group shows at the Iemoto Historical Flower Arrangement Exhibit, 1992. Mem. guiding com. Art Assn. Egg and the Eye Gallery and Restaurant, 1973—; participant Arts & Humanities Symposium, Palm Desert, Calif., 1974; patron cultural symposium L.A. Garden Club, 1975. Recipient Kakan Monpyo award Ikenobo Ikebana Soc. Floral Art, 1988. Mem. Ikebana Internat. (bd. dirs. L.A. chpt. 1978-82, mem. chmn. 1980-82), Japanese Am. Citizens League (historian, exec. bd. L.A. Downtown chpt. 1991—). Republican. Jewish.

NIXON, JAMES JOSEPH, III, telecommunications executive; b. Ogden, Utah, Mar. 26, 1947; s. James Joseph Jr. and Pearl Elizabeth (Day) N.; m. Natalie Stoker, Nov. 18, 1966; children: James Joseph IV, Aaron Duane, Brittney Lee. BS, Weber State Coll., 1980; AS, Mesa Community Coll., 1982. Cert. quality engr. Sr. quality assurance specialist Dept. of Def., Ogden, 1971-80; sr. quality engr. Gen. Dynamics/Convair, San Diego, 1980-82; mgr. quality assurance Teledyne Ryan Aero., San Diego, 1982-85; mgr. supplier quality assurance Magnavox Advanced Systems Co., Torrance, Calif., 1985-87; dir. quality assurance NavCom Def. Electronics, El Monte, Calif., 1987-89; v.p. quality assurance Vitarel Microelectronics, Inc., San Diego, 1989-90; dir. ops. Comstream Corp., San Diego, Calif., 1990-92; pres. Nixon & Assocs., 1992—; pres., CEO Nixon and Assocs., San Diego and Chino, Calif., 1988—. Contbr. articles to profl. jours. Bd. dirs. Calif. Bus. Inst., El Monte, 1988; bd. advisors San Diego Community Colls., 1990. Mem. Am. Soc. for Quality Control (chpt. pres. 1986-87), Soc. Mfg. Engrs., Internat. Soc. Hybrid Mfg., Nat. Mgmt. Assn. (chpt. pres. 1987-89), Soc. Logistical Engrs. Republican. Mem. LDS Ch. Home: 11395 Osoyoos Pl San Diego CA 92126-1443 Office: Comstream Corp 10180 Barnes Canyon Rd San Diego CA 92121

NIXON, JOHN HARMON, economist; b. Mpls., Apr. 7, 1915; s. Justin Wroe and Ida Elisabeth (Wickenden) N. AB, Swarthmore Coll., 1935; AM, Harvard U., 1949, PhD, 1953. Analyst U.S. R.R. Retirement Bd., Washington, 1938-41; economist U.S. Office of Price Adminstrn., Washington, 1941-46; teaching fellow, sr. tutor Harvard Coll., Cambridge, Mass., 1947-50; asst. prof. econs. CCNY, 1953-56; dir. econ. devel. N.Y. State Dept. Commerce, Albany, 1956-59; dir. area devel. Com. for Econ. Devel., N.Y.C., 1959-65; dir. tech. assistance U.S. Econ. Devel. Adminstrn., Washington, 1966-67; urban economist U.S. AID, Saigon, Vietnam, 1967; economist Ralph M. Parsons Co., Washington, 1968-70; chief economist/systems Ralph M. Parsons Co., Pasadena, Calif., 1971-82; mem. adv. bd. U.S. Area Devel. Adminstrn., Washington, 1963-65. Co-author, editor: Community Economic Development Efforts, 1964, Living Without Water (Cairo), 1980. Vice chmn. Mayor's Com. on Econ. Devel., L.A., 1974-75; pres. Pasadena Devel. Corp., 1982-84. Mem. Nat. Economists Club, Nat. Assn. Bus. Economists, Harvard Club N.Y.C., Town Hall of Calif., Phi Beta Kappa. Democrat. Presbyterian. Office: PO Box 76267 Los Angeles CA 90076

NIXON, ROBERT OBEY, SR., business educator; b. Pitts., Feb. 14, 1922; s. Frank Obey and Margurite (Van Buren) N.; m. Marilyn Cavanagh, Oct. 25, 1944 (dec. 1990); children: Nan Nixon Friend, Robert Obey, Jr., Dwight Cavanagh. BS in bus. adminstrn., U. Pitts., 1948; MS, Ohio State U., 1964; MBA, U. Phoenix, 1984. Commd. USAF, 1942, advanced through grades to col., master navigator WWII, Korea, Vietnam; sales, adminstrn. U.S. Rubber Corp., Pitts., 1940-41; asst. engr. Am. Bridge Corp., Pitts., 1941-42; underwriter, sales Penn Mutual Life Ins. Corp., Pitts., 1945-50; capt., nav. instr. USAF Reserves, 1945-50; ret. USAF Col., divsn. chief Joint Chiefs of Staff, 1973; educator, cons. U. Ariz., 1973-79; bus. dept. chmn., coord., founder weekend coll. Pima Community Coll., Tucson, 1979-90, prof. mgmt., coord. Weekend Coll. program, 1991—; founder, pres. Multiple Adv. Group ednl. cons., Tucson, 1978—. Contbr. articles to profl. jours. Mem. Soc. Logistics Engrs. (sr., charter mem.), Phi Delta Theta. Presbyterian. Home: 1824 S Regina Cleri Dr Tucson AZ 85710-8663

NIZZE, JUDITH ANNE, physician assistant; b. L.A., Nov. 1, 1942; d. Robert George and Charlotte Ann (Wise) Swan; m. Norbert Adolph Otto Paul Nizze, Dec. 31, 1966. BA, UCLA, 1966, postgrad., 1966-76; grad. physician asst. tng. program, Charles R. Drew Sch. Postgrad., L.A., 1979; BS, Calif. State U., Dominguez, 1980. Cert. physician asst., Calif. Staff rsch. assoc. I-II Wadsworth Vet. Hosp., L.A., 1965-71; staff rsch. assoc. III-IV John Wayne Clinic Jonsson Comprehensive Cancer Ctr., UCLA, 1971-78; clin. asst. Robert S. Ozeran, Gardena, Calif., 1978; physician asst. family practice Fred Chasan, Torrance, Calif., 1980-82; sr. physician asst. Donald L. Morton prof., chief surg. oncology Jonsson Comprehensive Cancer Ctr., UCLA, 1983-91; administrv. dir. clin. rsch. John Wayne Cancer Inst., Santa Monica, Calif., 1991—. Contbr. articles to profl. jours. Fellow Am. Acad. Physician Assts., Am. Assn. Surgeons Assts., Calif. Acad. Physician Assts.; mem. South Bay Physician Asst. Assn., Am. Sailing Assn. Republican. Presbyterian. Home: 13243 J Fiji Way Marina Dl Rey CA 90292-7079 Office: John Wayne Cancer Inst St John's Hosp & Health Ctr 1328 22d St Santa Monica CA 90404

NOBLE, RICHARD LLOYD, lawyer; b. Oklahoma City, Oct. 11, 1939; s. Samuel Lloyd and Eloise Joyce (Millard) N. AB with distinction, Stanford, 1961, LLB, 1964. Bar: Calif. 1964. Assoc. firm Cooper, White & Cooper, San Francisco, 1965-67; assoc., ptnr. firm Voegelin, Barton, Harris & Callister, Los Angeles, 1967-70; ptnr. Noble & Campbell, Los Angeles, San Francisco, 1970—; dir. Langdale Corp., L.A., Gt. Pacific Fin. Co., Sacramento; lectr. Tax Inst. U. So. Calif., 1970; mem. bd. law and bus. program Stanford Law Sch. Contbr. articles to legal jours. Bd. govs. St. Thomas Aquinas Coll. Recipient Hilmer Dehlman Jr. award Stanford Law Sch., 1962; Benjamin Harrison fellow Stanford U., 1967. Mem. ABA, State Bar Calif., L.A. Bar Assn., San Francisco Bar Assn., Commercial Club (San Francisco), Commonwealth Club (San Francisco), Petroleum Club (L.A.), Capitol Hill Club (Washington), Pi Sigma Alpha. Republican. Home: 2222 Avenue Of The Stars Los Angeles CA 90067-5655 Office: Noble & Campbell 888 W 6th St Los Angeles CA 90017-2703

NOBLE, STUART HARRIS, newspaper executive; b. Vancouver, B.C., Can., Jan. 11, 1941; s. Stewart Ian and Mina Rebecca (Harris) N.; m. Ann Rosalind Thorne, June 20, 1964 (dec. Dec. 1983); children: Kirsten Ann, Kenneth Stuart, William Frank, Catherine Marquerite; m. Susan Carmen Melnechuk, May 12, 1984; 1 child, Justin Arthur. BS in Forestry, U. B.C., Vancouver. From trainee to mgr. employee relations MacMillan Bloedel Ltd., Vancouver, 1965-77; dir. human resources Fording Coal Ltd., Calgary, Alta., Can., 1977-85; v.p. human resources Pacific Pres Ltd., Vancouver, 1985, v.p. human resources and ops., 1988—. Recipient Outstanding Service award Big Bros. of B.C., 1973. Mem. Indsl. Relations Mgmt. Assn., Can. and Am. Newspaper Assns., Vancouver Bd. Trade. Lodge: Rotary (sec., treas. local chpt. 1974-76). Home: 6700 Whiteoak Dr, Richmond, BC Canada V7E 4Z9 Office: Pacific Press Ltd, 2250 Granville St, Vancouver, BC Canada V6H 3G2

NOBLIT, BETTY JEAN, publishing technician; b. St. Elmo, Ill., June 12, 1948; d. Clyde W. and Goldie M. (Haggard) N. Grad. in restaurant and club food mgmt., LaSalle U., 1973; grad., Am. Sch. Travel, 1975. Teletype puncher Sarasota (Fla.) Herald-Tribune, 1968-70, Pueblo Chieftain, 1970—; unified composer; pagination operator Star Jour. Pub. Co., Pueblo, Colo.; personal corr. Prime Min. Indira Gandhi. Mem. NAFE, Internat. Platform Assn., Nat. Geog. Soc., Colo. Hist. Soc., Pueblo Hist. Soc. Home: 1 Cambridge Apt 4B Pueblo CO 81005

NOCE, ROBERT HENRY, neuropsychiatrist, educator; b. Phila., Feb. 19, 1914; s. Rev. Sisto Julius and Madeleine (Saulino) N.; m. Carole Lee Landis, 1987. A.B., Kenyon Coll., 1935; M.D., U. Louisville, 1939; postgrad., U. Pa. Sch. Medicine, 1947, Langley-Porter Neuropsychiat. Inst., 1949, 52. Rotating intern Hamot Hosp., Erie, Pa., 1939-40; resident psychiatrist Warren (Pa.) State Hosp., 1940-41, staff psysician, 1946-48; staff physician Met. State Hosp., Norwalk, Calif., 1948-50; dir. clin. services Pacific State Hosp., Spadra, Calif., 1950-52; dir. clin. services Modesto (Calif.) State Hosp., 1952-58, asst. supt. psychiat. services, 1958-64; pvt. practice medicine specializing in neuropsychiatry, 1965-73; Mem. faculty postgrad. symposiums in psychiatry for physicians U. Calif., 1958, 66. Author: film Reserpine Treatment of Psychotic Patients; Contbr. articles to profl. jours. Served from lt. (j.g.) to lt. comdr. M.C. USNR, 1941-46. Recipient Albert and Mary Lasker award for integration reserpine treatment mentally ill and mentally retarded, 1957; Wisdom award of honor, 1970. Life fellow Am. Psychiat. Assn. (sec. 1954, 55); fellow Royal Soc. Health; mem. Phi Beta Kappa, Delta Psi. Episcopalian. Home: 407 E Colgate Dr Tempe AZ 85283-1809

NODELMAN, JARED ROBERT, real estate investment executive; b. N.Y.C., May 24, 1937; s. George and Ray (Mayerson) N.; children: Seth, Ilisa. BA, Ohio State U., 1958. Pres. Commonwealth Assocs. Inc., San Juan, P.R., 1964-74, Inversiones Metropolitanas, Inc., Santa Rosa, Calif., 1974—. Mem. cabinet Marin Gen. Hosp., Pres.' Coun. Meml. Sloan Kettering Cancer Ctr. Recipient Leadership award Meml. Sloan-Kettering Cancer Ctr., N.Y.C., 1989. Mem. World Trade Club, St. Francis Yacht Club, San Francisco Yacht Club, San Francisco Rotary, Villa Taverna, Olympic Club. Office: 2312 Bethards Dr Ste 5 Santa Rosa CA 95405

NOE, DAVID CLIFFORD, emergency services manager, consultant; b. Cin., Apr. 29, 1964; s. Samuel Van Arsdale and Margerate Lynn (Clifford) N.; m. Stephanie Louise Cooper, June 23, 1990. AAS, U. Cin., 1985; BS, U. Md., 1987. Advanced emergency med. technician Community Medic Rescue, Cin., 1983-85; spl. events mgr. Al-Lin Ambulance, Balt., 1985-87; pub. affairs coord. D.C. Fire Dept.-Emergency Med. Svcs., Washington, 1986-87; asst. ops. mgr. Hall Ambulance Svc., Bakersfield, Calif., 1987-88; dir. pub. rels. Golden Empire Ambulance, Bakersfield, 1988-89; supr. ops. Schaefer Ambulance Svc., Santa Ana, Calif., 1989-90; gen. mgr. Valley Med. Transport, Victorville, Calif., 1990—; cons. Emergency Mgmt. Systems Specialists, Huntington Beach, Calif., 1988—; asst. to the pres. Urban Search and Rescue, Inc., Canyon Country, Calif., 1989—. Bd. dirs. March of Dimes Cen. Valley chpt., 1988-90, mem. adv. coun., High Desert, Calif., 1991—; vis. lectr. emergency med. svcs. Ptnrs. of the Americas, Brazil, 1987. Recipient Presdl. medallion Calif. Jaycees, 1989. Mem. Nat. Assn. Emergency Med. Technicians, Nat. Soc. Emergency Med. Svcs. Adminstrs. Office: Emergency Mgmt Specialists 17231 Kristopher Ln Huntington Beach CA 92392

NOELL, SHARON KAU, electric utility official, researcher; b. L.A., Jan. 18, 1954; d. Clinton and Eleanor (Chin) Kau; m. Gary Richard Noell, June 6, 1985; 1 child, Melinda. BS in Mgmt. Sci., Calif. State U., L.A., 1978, postgrad., 1978-81. Tech. asst. State of Calif., L.A., 1977-79; econs. analyst So. Calif. Edison Co., Rosemead, 1979, human resources analyst, 1980, load rsch. analyst, 1981-83, energy mgmt. analyst, 1983-85, project mgr., 1985—. Contbr. articles to profl. jours. Recipient mayor's commendation City of L.A., 1988, leadership award YWCA, L.A., 1989, commendation Los Angeles County Bd. Suprs., 1989. Mem. Assn. Demand Side Mgmt. Profls., Western States Load Rsch. Group, L.A. Jr. C. of C. (chmn. 1988, bd. dirs. 1989, v.p. 1990). Office: So Calif Edison Co 2244 Walnut Grove Ave Rosemead CA 91770

NOEM, NEAL DAVID, marine corps officer; b. DeSmet, S.D., Dec. 28, 1961; s. Norwood Wayne and Delores Nadine (Stankey) N.; m. Stacey Lee Headley, Jan. 14, 1989. Grad., high sch., 1980. Enlisted U.S. Marine Corps, 1980, advanced through grades to chief warrant officer, 1992; sch. support chief Comm. Officer Sch., Quantico, Va., 1988; radio officer B Co. 7th Comm. Bn., Kaneohe Bay, Hawaii, 1989-90; bn. comm. officer 1st Bn. 12th Marines, Kaneohe Bay, 1990-91; wire officer B Co 7th Comm. Bn., Kaneohe Bay, 1991-92, ops. officer, 1992-93; plans officer Marine Wing Comm. Squadron, Cherry Point, N.C., 1993—. Served in Operation Desert Shield and Desert Storm, Persian Gulf. Decorated Navy Commendation medal, 2 Navy Achievement medals. Mem. Nat. Parks and Conservation Assn., Charles J. Givens Orgn., U.S. Pub. Interest Rsch. Group. Republican. Lutheran. Home: PO Box 543 220 W Main St East Helena MT 59635

NOETH, LOUISE ANN, journalist; b. Evergreen Park, Ill., Nov. 17, 1954; d. Cy John and Alice Rose (Bobrovich) N.; m. Michael T. Lanigan, Aug. 29, 1992. Editor Petersen Pub. Co., Inc., Calif., 1980; assoc. pub., editor Autoscene Mag., Westlake Village, Calif., 1981; investigative editor Four Wheeler Mag., Canoga Park, Calif., 1982—; owner, founder Landspeed Productions, 1985—; automotive writer, columnist Press-Courier Newspaper, Oxnard, Calif., 1992; with EAG&G Inc., 1992, Microlon Corp., 1993; cons. Spirit Am. World Speed Record Team, Pontiac Motor Div., others; mem. Green Mamba Racing Team, Reseda, Calif., 1978—, Spirit of Am. World Speed Racing Record; graphic art commns. for Ferro Corp., Nikon Profl. Svcs., Kodak Profl. Network, Forbes Mag., SEA Sailing. Author: Ventura County Destination Guide: Channel Islands Harbor Retrospect; editor Hot Rod Performance and Custom, 1979; producer: Renewing Pride, Schoolroom in Paradise, Heritage Square; contbr. articles to numerous automotive mags.; photography exhibited at Ventury County Mus. History and Art, 1991, Ventura County Nat. Bank, 1990, 92, Ventura County Fair, 1990 (Spl. Non-Competition award Profl. Category). Mem. project R.A.F.T. Russians and Ams. for Teamwork, Buffalo Bill's West Show. Recipient Moto award in investigative news category, Automotive Journalism Conference, 1983-84, 86. Mem. Tallship Californian Quarter deck Comm., Oxnard C. of C., Edn. Comm. Youth Edn. Motivation Program,Internat. Motor Press Assn. (sec. 1986—), Specialty Equipment Market Assn. (pub. relations com. 1983, suspension and tire com. 1984-85), Am. Auto Racing Writers and Broadcasters Assn.

NOGUCHI, THOMAS TSUNETOMI, author, forensic pathologist; b. Fukuoka, Japan, Jan. 4, 1927; came to U.S., 1952; s. Wataru and Tomika Narahashi N. D of Medicine, Nippon Med. Sch., Tokyo, 1951; LLD (hon.), U. Braz Cubas Fedn. Faculties Mogi Das Cruzes, Sao Paolo, Brazil, 1980; DSc (hon.), Worcester State Coll., 1985. Dep. med. examiner Los Angeles County Dept. Chief Med. Examiner, L.A., 1961-67, coroner, 1967-82; prof. forensic pathology U. So. Calif., L.A., 1982—. Author: Coroner, 1983 (N.Y. Times Bestseller 1984), Coroner At Large, 1985; (fiction) Unnatural Causes, 1988, Physical Evidence, 1990. Fellow Am. Acad. Forensic Sci. (chmn. sect. 1966); mem. Nat. Assn. Med. Examiners (pres. 1983), Calif. State Coroners Assn. (pres. 1974), World Assn. Med. Law (v.p.). Republican. Home: 1110 Avoca Ave Pasadena CA 91105-3405 Office: U So Calif Med Ctr 1200 N State St Rm 2520 Los Angeles CA 90033

NOKES, JOHN RICHARD, retired newspaper editor, author; b. Portland, Oreg., Feb. 23, 1915; s. James Abraham and Bernice Alfaretta (Bailey) N.; m. Evelyn Junkin, Sept. 13, 1936; children: Richard Gregory, William G., Gail (Mrs. William M. Hulden), Douglas J., Kathy E. B.S., Linfield Coll., 1936, LHD (hon.), 1988. With The Oregonian, Portland, 1936-82, city editor, 1950-65, asst. mng. editor, 1965-71, mng. editor, 1971-75, editor, 1975-82; disting. vis. prof. journalism Linfield Coll., 1982-85. Author: American Form of Government, 1939, Columbia's River: The Voyages of Robert Gray 1787-1793, 1991; editor Oreg. Edn. Jour., 1944. Bd. dirs. Portland U.S.O., 1968-72, U.S. Coast Guard Acad. Found., 1972-74, Portland Opera Assn., 1976-78; trustee Linfield Coll., 1977—; v.p. Oreg. UN Assn., 1983-85, chmn. Oreg. UN Day, 1983. Served to lt. (j.g.) USNR, 1944-46; comdr. Res. (ret.). Mem. Navy League U.S. (pres. Portland coun. 1969-

71), Linfield Coll. Alumni Assn. (pres. 1940), World Affairs Coun. Oreg. (pres. 1973-74), AP Mng. Editors Assn. (dir. 1973-80), Am. Soc. Newspaper Editors, N.W. China Coun., Sigma Delta Chi (pres. Willamette Valley chpt. 1975-76). Republican. Methodist. Club: Multnomah Athletic (Portland). Home: 14650 SW 103d Ave Tigard OR 97224

NOLAN, ANITA TORNELLO, nursing administrator; b. San Jose, Calif., Jan. 1, 1947; d. Charles and Frances (Sokolinsky) Tornello; m. Alfred Nolan, Nov. 10, 1979; 1 child, Carly. AS, Evergreen Valley Coll., San Jose, Calif., 1982; BA, St. Mary's Coll., Moraga, Calif., 1989. RN, Calif. Nurse Kaiser Health Found., San Jose, 1980-82, RN, 1982-85; RN Permanente Med. Group, San Jose, 1985-90, nursing supr., 1990-92, mgr. pediatric dept. nursing, 1993—. Author, editor, publisher: (pamphlet) Career Transitions for Nurses Getting Started, 1989. Office: Permanente Med Group 260 International Cir San Jose CA 95119

NOLAN, MARK GREGORY, advertising executive; b. San Francisco, July 3, 1958; m. Robyn Lynn Nolan, June 7, 1980. Mktg. mgr. Shelton-Turnbull, Eugene, Oreg., 1977-80; v.p. mktg. Shelton-Turnbull, Eugene, 1980-81; founder, chief exec. officer Mark Nolan & Assocs., Inc., Citrus Heights, Calif., 1981-87; v.p., ptnr. Nolan Mktg. Group Inc., Citrus Heights, 1987—; mktg. dir., ptnr. Fin. Mktg. Corp., Citrus Heights, 1989—; keynote speaker Marin Self-Pubs. Assn., Ross, Calif., 1986; featured speaker Community Entrepreneurs Assn., Sacramento, 1986, home-based bus. conf., 1991; treas. COSMEP, San Francisco, 1986-88; lectr. UCLA, 1987. Editor: Info. Mktg., 1985-87. Mem. Better Bus. Bur., Eagle Scouts. Mem. S.C. Publicists Assn., Community Entrepreneurs Assn., Internat. Assn. Self-Pubs. (treas. 1986-88), Com. of Small Mag. Editors and Pubs., C. of C., Turtles, Oregon Advt. Club, Entrepreneurs Am., Active 20-30 Club. Office: Mark Nolan & Assocs Inc PO Box 2570 7956 California Ave Fair Oaks CA 95628-2570

NOLAND, PATRICIA ANN, state legislator; b. Seattle, Dec. 30, 1945; d. Gordon F. Watson and Ruth A. (Young) Kalbach; m. C. Glenn Noland, Feb. 3, 1973 (div. 1978); m. John S. Bogers, Jan. 23, 1988. Studeht, Ft. Steilacom Community Coll., 1968-70. Clk., sec. State Wash., Olympia, 1964-67; sec., computer programmer Weyerhaeuser Corp., Tacoma, 1967-70; computer programer City Tucson, 1970-72; adminstrv. asst. ITT Canon Electric, Santa Ana, Calif., 1972-73; city clk. City Casa Grande, Ariz., 1973-76; town mgr. Town Oro (Ariz.) Valley, 1979-83; v.p. HDC, Inc., Tucson, 1983-86; owner Patricia Noland Cons., Tucson, 1983—; state legislator Ariz. Ho. of Reps., Phoenix, 1989—. Pres. Tucson Classics, Inc., 1981-84, Pima County Rep. Club, 1977-78; pres., bd. dirs. Tucson Resident Found., 1978-86; chmn., mem. gov.'s coun. Devel. Disabilities, Phoenix, 1982-85; mem. Pima County Bond Adv. Coun., Tucson, 1978-85. Mem. So. Ariz. Homebuilders (bd. dirs. 1987-89, Assoc. of Yr. 1987), Ariz. Planning Assn., Ariz. Order Women Legislators, Nat. Order Women Legislators. Home: PO Box 30042 Tucson AZ 85751-0042 Office: Arizona State Senate 5356 E 2nd St Tucson AZ 85711

NOLL, WILLIAM NIVEN, retired insurance executive; b. Pasadena, Calif., June 1, 1942; s. William Albrecht and Barbara Jean (Niven) N.; m. Jane Ann Hall, Jan. 17, 1969; children: Jeremy Edward, Kristy Ann, Katy Ann. BA, Pepperdine U., 1969; MDiv, San Francisco Theol. Sem., 1971; MBA, Golden Gate U., San Francisco, 1973; MA, N.Mex. State U. Republican. Baptist. Home: Trout Rd Hot Springs Landin Elephant Butte Lake NM 87935

NOLLMAN, JAMES M., author, communications company executive; b. Boston, Jan. 31, 1947; s. Harris B. and Ruth (Bedrick) N.; m. Kathryn Richey, Aug. 30, 1983; children: Claire, Sasha. BA, Tufts U., 1969. Founder, pres. Interspecies Communication, Friday Harbor, Wash., 1978—; rschr. in field. Composer: (record albums) Playing Music With Animals, 1979, Orcas Greatest Hits, 1986; author: (books) Dolphin Dreamtime, 1987, Spiritual Ecology, 1990, A Sense of Place, 1993. Office: Interspecies Communication 273 Hidden Meadows Ln Friday Harbor WA 98250-9410

NOLTE, JOHN MICHAEL, lawyer, consultant; b. England, Mar. 20, 1941; s. Ernest H. Nolte and Katheryn A. (Reinhart) Robertson; m. S.K. Marren (div. 1979); children: Stephanie Ann, Jennifer Lee, Sarah Sookwang; m. Diane L. Staufenbeil, Apr. 1982. BS, Ariz. State U., Tempe, 1963; MBA in Fin., U. Calif., Berkeley, JD, 1966. Bar: Oreg. 1966, Calif. 1973. Assoc. Keane, Haessler, Bauman & Harper, Portland, Oreg., 1966-71; assoc. gen. counsel Boise Cascade Corp., Palo Alto, Calif., 1972-73, Larwin Group, L.A., 1973-74; mng. ptnr. Leahy, O'Dea & Givens, San Francisco, 1974-81; pvt. practice law and cons. Canterbury and Tunbridge Wells, Eng., 1981-88, Montecito, Calif., 1988—; assoc. mng. dir. Staufenbeil Co., A.G., Boppard, Germany; officer Larwin Co., Encino, Calif.; mem. adv. bd. dirs. IDI, Inc., Savo Electronics Divsn., Corvallis, Oreg. Hon. mem. East Sussex Conservative Party, Buxted, Eng., 1986—; pres. Glen Oaks Community Assn., Montecito, 1990-92. With USMC, 1960-66; lt. comdr. USNR, 1966-70. Mem. ABA, Calif. Bar Assn., Oreg. Bar Assn., L.A. Bar Assn., Am. Judicature Soc., Order of Coif, Phi Kappa Phi. Republican. Home: 1715 Glen Oaks Dr Montecito CA 93108-2111 Office: Larwin Co 16255 Ventura Blvd Ste 900 Encino CA 91436-2371

NOLTE, LAWRENCE WILLIAM, public relations consultant; b. Earlham, Iowa, Sept. 21, 1905; s. Howard Milton and Martha (Sheely) N.; m. Dorothy May Smith, Oct. 6, 1934; 1 child, Patricia Nolte Burdette. BS, Oreg. State U., 1927. Mgr. pub. rels. Am. Dry Milk Inst., Chgo., 1930-41; account exec. Needham, Louis & Brorby, Chgo., 1945-48; advt. mgr. evaporated milk Carnation Co., L.A., 1948-53; mgr. advt. & pub. rels. White King Soap Co., L.A., 1953-57; acct. supr. & dir. pub. rels. Batten Barton Darstine & Osborne, San Francisco, 1957-70; supr. pub. rels. group Cunningham & Walsh, San Francisco, 1970-72; cons. Hillsborough, Calif., 1972—; instr. Coll. San Mateo, 1963-72. Author: Fundamentals of Public Relations, 1974, 1979; coauthor: Effective Publicity, 1984, Public Relations Writing, etc., 1990. Lt. col. U.S. Army, 1941-45. Fellow Pub. Rels. Soc. Am. Republican. Home: 1444 Carlton Rd Burlingame CA 94010-7130

NONG, painter, sculptor; b. Seoul, Korea, Oct. 10, 1930; came to U.S., 1952, naturalized, 1958; Commr. Asian Art Commn. Asian Art Mus. San Francisco, The Avery Brundage Collection, City and County of San Francisco, 1981-84. One-man exhbns. paintings and/or sculpture include Ft. Lauderdale (Fla.) Mus. Arts, Santa Barbara (Calif.) Mus. Art, Crocker Art Mus., Sacramento, Calif., 1965, Ga. Mus. Art, Athens, 1967, El Paso (Tex.) Mus. Art, 1967, Galerie Vallombreuse, Biarritz, France, 1970, Nat. Mus. History, Taiwan, 1971, Nihonbashi Gallery, Tokyo, Japan, 1971, Shinsegye Gallery, Seoul, Korea, 1975, Nat. Mus. Modern Art, Seoul, 1975, San Francisco Zool. Garden, 1975, Tongin Art Gallery, Seoul, 1978, Consulate Gen. Republic of Korea, Los Angeles, 1982, Choon Chu Gallery, Seoul, 1982, Mee Gallery, Seoul, 1984, 86, Leema Art Mus., Seoul, 1985, Tong-A Dept. Store, Taegu, Korea, 1986, Tongso Gallery, Masan, Korea, 1986, Han Kwang Art Mus., Pusan, Korea, 1986, Union de Arte, Bercelona, Spain, 1987, Acad. de Belles Arts, Sabadell, Spain, 1987; numerous group exhibits Mus. and Art Ctr., Douglaston, N.Y., 1961, Nat. Collection Fine Arts, Smithsonian Instn., Washington, 1961, Mus. Fine Arts, Springfield, Mass., 1961, Conn. Acad. Fine Arts, Hartford, Conn., 1962, Charles and Emma Frye Art Mus., Seattle, 1962, The Denver Art Mus., 1965, Jersey City Mus., 1967, U. Santa Clara (Calif.) Mus., 1967, U. Calif., Berkeley, 1968, Maison de la Culture du Havre, Le Havre, France, 1970, Oakland (Calif.) Art Mus., 1971, Gallerie des Champs Elysees, Paris, 1971, Nat. Sculpture Soc., Lever House, N.Y.C., 1971, Taipei Provincial Mus., Republic of China, 1971, San Francisco Mus. Modern Art, 1972, Galerie Hexagramme, Paris, 1975, Galeria de Arte Misrachi, Mexico City, 1979, The Mun Ye Art Ctr., Seoul, 1986, Salon de Artistes Francais, Paris, France, 1971, Salon d'Automne, Paris, 1969-71, Salon Grands et Jeunes d'Aujourd'hui, Paris, 1971-77; represented in numerous permanent collections including, Santa Barbara Mus. Art, Anchorage (Alaska) Hist. and Fine Art Mus., Museo de Arte, Lima, Peru, Govt. Peru, Nat. Mus. History, Govt. of Republic of China, Oakland (Calif.) Art Mus., Ga. Mus. Art, Athens, Korean Embassy, Lima, Peru, Nat. Mus. of Modern Art, Nat. Mus. Korea, Govt. of Republic of Korea, Seoul, Nat. Gallery of Modern Art, New Delhi, India, Asian Art Mus. San Francisco, Govt. of People's Republic China, Beijing and Shanghai, Palacio de la Zarzuela, Madrid, Palacio de la Moncloa, Madrid, The Korean Embassy, Madrid, Mus. Art de Sabadell, Spain, Mus. Nat. des Beaux-Arts, Monte Carlo, Monaco, others; author: Nong Questions, 1982. Chmn. San Francisco-Seoul Sister City Com., City and County San Francisco, 1981-84. Served with U.S. Army, 1956-59; Served with USAF, 1959-60. Recipient numerous awards including citations from Republic of Korea, Cert. Disting. Achievement State of Calif., 1982, Proclamation City and County of San Francisco, 1982. Home: 6816 Clowser Ct Springfield VA 22150

NOOK, GREGORY ERNEST, architect; b. Corning, Iowa, Jan. 24, 1954; s. Clifford Albert N. and Elizabeth Ann (Beach) Brown; m. Rebecca Ann Lundberg, June 6, 1976; children: Jared Gregory, Carissa Ann. BArch, Iowa State U., 1976; MArch, U. Minn., 1981. Registered architect. Intern architect Thorson-Brom-Broshar-Snyder, Waterloo, Iowa, 1976-79; designer, project mgr. Ellerbe, Mpls., 1981-84; project dir., sr. v.p. Ellerbe Becket, Mpls., 1988-90; office dir., sr. v.p. Ellerbe Becket, Santa Monica, Calif., 1990—; assoc. mgr. design Opus, Mpls., 1984-88; speaker in field; instr. seminars, 1989. Trustee Glendale Meth. Ch., Savage, Minn., 1988-90; vol. United Way, Mpls., 1983, 87; youth leader Hudson (Iowa) Meth. Ch., 1978; coach Little League, Savage, Malibu, Calif., 1988-91. Mem. Calif. Coun. AIA, Crest Club, L.A. Bus. Coun. Democrat. Office: Ellerbe Becket 2501 Colorado Ave Santa Monica CA 90404

NOON, JOHN PATRICK, editor, publisher; b. Jersey City, N.J., Oct. 25, 1954; s. John and Margaret Noon; m. Ellen Mary Uphaus, Sept. 5, 1981; children: Patrick, Lisa, Jeffrey. With editorial and mktg. depts. Addison-Wesley Pub. Co., 1979-83; v.p. sales and mktg. Intellisance Corp., 1983-87; pres. PUBLIX Info. Products, Inc., Sunnyvale, Calif., 1987—; founder Syllabus Mag., Query Mag., Higher Edn. Products Mag., Computer Sci. Products, Syllabus-European Edition, Syllabus Japan. Office: PUBLIX Info Products Inc 1307 S Mary Ave Ste 107 Sunnyvale CA 94087

NOONAN, JILL ELIZABETH, lawyer, nurse; b. Valparaiso, Ind., Oct. 8, 1949; d. James Edward and Lorraine Luciele (Pester) Short; m. Charles Andrew Noonan, Dec. 2, 1967; children: Jennifer, Benjamin, Jessica. Diploma, Marion County Gen. Hosp., Indpls., 1975; JD, John F. Kennedy Sch. Law, 1989. Bar: Calif. 1990. RN Woodland (Calif.) Meml. Hosp., 1975-78, Vis. Nurses, LaPorte, Ind., 1979-80; RN, head nurse, CPR instr. Porter Meml. Hosp., Valparaiso, 1980-82; CCRN Mt. Diablo Hosp., Concord, Calif., 1982-85; assoc. Dunn Rogaski & Preovolos, Vallejo, Calif., 1991—. Mem. Am. Nurse Atty. Assn. Office: Dunn Rogaski & Preovolos 241 Georgia St Vallejo CA 94590

NOONAN, JOHN T., JR., federal judge, legal educator; b. Boston, Oct. 24, 1926; s. John T. and Marie (Shea) N.; m. Mary Lee Bennett, Dec. 27, 1967; children: John Kenneth, Rebecca Lee, Susanna Bain. B.A., Harvard U., 1946, LL.B., 1954; student, Cambridge U., 1946-47; M.A., Cath. U. Am., 1949, Ph.D., 1951, LHD, 1980; LL.D., U. Santa Clara, 1974, U. Notre Dame, 1976, Loyola U. South, 1978; LHD, Holy Cross Coll., 1980; LL.D., St. Louis U., 1981, U. San Francisco, 1985; student, Holy Cross Coll., 1980, Cath. U. Am., 1980, Gonzaga U., 1986, U. San Francisco, 1986. Bar: Mass. 1954, U.S. Supreme Ct. 1971. Mem. spl. staff Nat. Security Council, 1954-55; pvt. practice law Boston, 1955-60; prof. law U. Notre Dame, 1961-66; prof. law U. Calif., Berkeley, 1967-86, chmn. religious studies, 1970-73, chmn. medieval studies, 1978-79; judge U.S. Ct. Appeals (9th cir.), San Francisco, 1986—; Oliver Wendell Holmes, Jr. lectr. Harvard U. Law Sch., 1972, Pope John XXIII lectr. Cath. U. Law Sch., 1973, Cardinal Bellarmine lectr. St. Louis U. Div. Sch., 1973, Baum lectr. U. Ill., 1988, Strassberger lectr. U. Tex., 1989; chmn. bd. Games Rsch., Inc., 1961-76. Author: The Scholastic Analyst of Usury, 1957; Contraception: A History of Its Treatment by the Catholic Theologians and Canonists, 1965; Power to Dissolve, 1972; Persons and Masks of the Law, 1976; The Antelope, 1977; A Private Choice, 1979; Bribes, 1984; editor: Natural Law Forum, 1961-70, Am. Jour. Jurisprudence, 1970, The Morality of Abortion, 1970. Chmn. Brookline Redevel. Authority, Mass., 1958-62; cons. Papal Commn. on Family, 1965-66, Ford Found., Indonesian Legal Program, 1968; NIH, 1973, NIH, 1974; expert Presdl. Commn. on Population and Am. Future, 1971; cons. U.S. Cath. Conf., 1979-86; sec., treas. Inst. for Research in Medieval Canon Law, 1970-88; pres. Thomas More-Jacques Maritain Inst., 1977—; trustee Population Council, 1969-76, Phi Kappa Found., 1970-76, Grad. Theol. Union, 1970-73, U. San Francisco, 1971-75; mem. com. theol. edn. Yale U., 1972-77; exec. com. Cath. Commn. Intellectual and Cultural Affairs, 1972-75; bd. dirs. Ctr. for Human Values in the Health Scis., 1969-71, S.W. Intergroup Relations Council, 1970-72, Inst. for Study Ethical Issues, 1971-73. Recipient St. Thomas More award U. San Francisco, 1974, Christian Culture medal, 1975, Laetare medal U. Notre Dame, 1984, Campion medal Cath. Book Club, 1987; Guggenheim fellow, 1965-66, 79-80, Laetare medal U. Notre Dame, 1984, Campion medal, 1987, Alemany medal Western Dominican Province, 1988; Ctr. for advanced Studies in Behavioral Scis. fellow, 1973-74; Wilson Ctr. fellow, 1979-80. Fellow Am. Acad. Arts and Scis., Am. Soc. Legal Historians (hon.); mem. Am. Soc. Polit. and Legal Philosophy (v.p. 1964), Canon Law Soc. Am. (gov. 1970-72), Am. Law Inst., Phi Beta Kappa (senator United chpts. 1970-72, pres. Alpha of Calif. chpt. 1972-73). Office: US Ct Appeals9th Circuit PO Box 547 San Francisco CA 94101-0547

NOONE, TIM BRENNAN, banker; b. Indpls., Dec. 2, 1958; s. Vincent James and Lois Cleo (Shoemaker) N.; m. Maria Patricia Velasquez, Aug.12, 1989; children: Alexandra, Jonathan. BS in Fin., Ind. U., 1981. Mgr. ITT Comml. Fin., Dallas, 1982-84; v.p. Security Pacific Nat. Bank, L.A., 1984-86, Olympic Nat. Bank, L.A., 1986-87; sr. v.p., credit adminstr. Bank of Granada Hills, L.A., 1987—. Sec. Planning & Zoning Com., Granada Hills, 1992. Mem. Kiwanis (treas. 1992—). Republican. Roman Catholic. Office: Bank of Granada Hills 10820 Zelzah Ave Granada Hills CA 91344

NOPAR, ALAN SCOTT, lawyer; b. Chgo., Nov. 14, 1951; s. Myron E. and Evelyn R. (Millman) N. BS, U. Ill., 1976; JD, Stanford U., 1979. Bar: Ariz. 1979, U.S. Dist. Ct. Ariz. 1980, U.S. Ct. Appeals (9th cir.) 1980, U.S. Supreme Ct. 1982, Calif. 1989; CPA, Ill. Assoc. O'Connor, Cavanagh, Anderson, Westover, Killingsworth & Beshears P.A., Phoenix, 1979-85, ptnr., 1985-87; of counsel Tower, Byrne & Beaugureau, Phoenix, 1987-88; ptnr. Minutillo & Gorman, San Jose, Calif., 1989-91, Bosco, Blau, Ward, Nopar & Miller, San Jose, 1991—. Mem. Ariz. Rep. Caucus, Phoenix, 1984-88. Mem. AICPA, ABA (bus. law and law practice mgmt. sects., mem. forum com. on franchising), Ariz. Bar Assn. (bus. law sect.), Calif. State Bar Assn. (bus. law sect.). Office: Bosco Blau Ward Nopar & Miller 2166 The Alameda San Jose CA 95126-1187

NORA, JAMES JACKSON, physician, author, educator; b. Chgo., June 26, 1928; s. Joseph James and May Henrietta (Jackson) N.; m. Barbara June Fluhrer, Sept. 7, 1949 (div. 1963); children: Wendy Alison, Penelope Welbon, Marianne Leslie; m. Audrey Faye Hart, Apr. 9, 1966; children: James Jackson Jr., Elizabeth Hart Nora. AB, Harvard U., 1950; MD, Yale U., 1954; MPH, U. Calif., Berkeley, 1978. Intern Detroit Receiving Hosp., 1954-55; resident in pediatrics U. Wis. Hosps., Madison, 1959-61, fellow in cardiology, 1962-64; fellow in genetics McGill U. Children's Hosp., Montreal, Can., 1964-65; assoc. prof. pediatrics Baylor Coll. Medicine, Houston, 1965-71; prof. genetics, preventive medicine and pediatrics U. Colo. Med. Sch., Denver, 1971—; dir. genetics Rose Med. Ctr., Denver, 1980—; dir. pediatric cardiology and cardiovascular tng. U. Colo. Sch. Medicine, 1971-78; mem. task force Nat. Heart and Lung Program, Bethesda, Md., 1973; cons. WHO, Geneva, 1983—; mem. U.S.-U.S.S.R. Exchange Program on Heart Disease, Moscow and Leningrad, 1975. Author: The Whole Heart Book, 1980, 2d rev. edit., 1989), (with F.C. Fraser) Medical Genetics, 4th rev. edit., 1993, Genetics of Man, 2d rev. edit., 1986, Cardiovascular Diseases: Genetics Epidemiology and Prevention, 1991; (novels) The Upstart Spring, 1989, The Psi Delegation, 1989. Com. mem. March of Dimes, Am. Heart Assn., Boy Scouts Am. Served to lt. USAAC, 1945-47. Grantee Nat. Heart, Lung and Blood Inst., Nat. Inst. Child Health and Human Devel., Am. Heart Assn., NIH; recipient Virginia Apgar Meml. award. Fellow Am. Coll. Cardiology, Am. Acad. Pediatrics, Am. Coll. Med. Genetics; mem. Am. Pediatric Soc., Soc. Pediatric Rsch., Am. Heart Assn., Teratology Soc., Transplantation Soc., Am. Soc. Human Genetics, Authors Guild, Authors League, Acad. Am. Poets, Mystery Writers Am., Rocky Mountain Harvard Club. Democrat. Presbyterian. Home: 6135 E 6th Ave Denver CO 80220-5307 Office: U Colo Sch Medicine A-007 4200 E 9th Ave Denver CO 80262-0001

NORDGREN, WILLIAM BENNETT, engineering executive; b. Salt Lake City, Mar. 5, 1960; s. Kent Widstoe and Eliza (Schmuhl) N.; m. Carolyn B. Erickson, June 26, 1981; 1 child, William Tyson. BS, Brigham Young U., 1986, MS, 1989. Engr. Boeing Airplanes Co., Seattle, 1986-88; pres. CIM Engring. Assocs., Orem, Utah, 1988-89; v.p. engring. Prodn. Modeling Corp., Orem, 1989-93; pres. F & H Simulations, Inc., Orem, 1993—. Developer, polar coordinant mill. Mem. Soc. Mfg. Engrs., Inst. Indsl. Engrs. Republican. Mormon. Office: PO Box 658 Orem UT 84059-0658

NORDHOFF, CHARLES GILBERT, former senatorial staff director; b. Seattle, Feb. 5, 1959; s. Arthur Edward and Nancy Caroline (Skinner) N.; m. Sarah Wessel Birkeland, Dec. 17, 1988 (separated Aug. 1992); children: Emily Grace, Fredric Arthur. AB in Econs., Dartmouth Coll., 1981; MBA, Harvard U., 1985. Asst. legis. asst. Office of U.S. Senator Slade Gorton, Washington, 1981-82, legis. asst., 1982-83; state dir. Office of U.S. Senator Slade Gorton, Seattle, 1989-92; fin. analyst Dole Packaged Foods Co., San Francisco, 1986-87; mgr. fin. analysis Dole Packaged Foods Co., Honolulu, 1987-88; mgr. diversified products Dole Packaged Foods Co., Hua Hin, Thailand, 1988-89. Republican. Roman Catholic. Home: 3439 37th Ave W Seattle WA 98199-1905 Office: 711 Skinner Bldg Seattle WA 98101-2684

NORDLEY, GERALD DAVID, writer, investor; b. Mpls., May 22, 1947; s. V. Gerald and Evelyn May (Whitesel) N.; (div. 1973); 1 child, Sharon; m. Gayle Ann Wiesner, May 9, 1976; children: Jeffrey Goldberg, Andrew Nordley. BA in Physics, Macalester Coll., 1969; MS in System Mgmt., U. So. Calif., L.A., 1980. Enlisted USAF, 1969, commd. 2nd lt., 1970, advanced through grades to maj., 1982; inter-range ops. officer Network Ops. Div., Sunnyvale AFB, Calif., 1973-76; chief orbital ops. br. Def. Satellite Communications Directorate, L.A. AFB, 1976-81; chief spacecraft engr. br. DSCS III Program Office, L.A. AFB, 1981-82; battle dir. Mangilsan Liason Annex, Mang Il San, South Korea, 1983; chief advanced propulsion br. A.F. Rocket Propulsion Lab., Edwards AFB, Calif., 1984-86; rsch. staff mgr. ARIES office Astronautics Lab., Edwards AFB, 1986-89; ret. USAF, 1989; writer, pvt. investor Sunnyvale, 1990—. Membership dir. Macalester Coll. Rep. Club, St. Paul, 1967-68; pres. Park Knowles Estates Property Owners Assn., Boron, Calif., 1988; co-chair Silicon Valley Writers Workshop, Cupertino, Calif., 1992. Decorated Air Force Commendation medal four oak leaf clusters USAF, 1972-82, Meritorious Svc. medal one oak leaf cluster USAF, 1984, 89; recipient Anlab award Analog Mag., 1992. Fellow British Interplanetary Soc.; mem. AIAA (elec. propulsion com. 1984-86), Air Force Assn., Sci. Fiction Writers Am., Whensday People Writers Group, Ft. Mason's Officers Club. Unitarian. Home and Office: 1238 Prescott Ave Sunnyvale CA 94089-2334

NORDLUND, DONALD CRAIG, corporate lawyer; b. Chgo., May 23, 1949; s. Donald E. and Jane (Houston) N.; m. Sally Baum, Sept. 7, 1975; children: Courtney Elizabeth, Michael Andrew, Laurie Katherine. AB, Stanford U., 1971; JD, Vanderbilt U., 1974. Assoc. Ware & Freidenrich, Palo Alto, Calif., 1974-77; atty. Hewlett-Packard Co., Palo Alto, 1977-80, sr. atty., asst. sec., 1980-81, asst. sec., corp. counsel, 1981-85, sec., corp. counsel, 1985-86, sec., asst. gen. counsel, 1986-87, assoc. gen. counsel, sec., 1987—; bd. dirs. Hewlett-Packard Hellas, Palo Alto, Hewlett-Packard European Distbn., Ops., Inc., The Netherlands, Hewlett-Packard Labs. Japan, Inc., Hewlett-Packard Del. Holding Inc., Eon System, Palo Alto, Hewlett-Packard Employees Fed. Credit Union, 1985—; sec. Hewlett-Packard Co. Found., Palo Alto, 1979—, Hewlett-Packard Fin. Co., Palo Alto, 1983—, Apollo Computer, Inc., 1989—; panelist disclosure documents seminar Practicing Law Inst., 1982-93, also contbg. author to course handbook; cons. pub. guide series, CEB, 1991. Mem. exec. com., bd. dirs. Santa Clara County chpt. Jr. Achievement, 1989—. Mem. Am. Soc. Corp. Secs. Inc. (pres. San Francisco region 1986-88, bd. dirs. 1987-90, chmn. sec.'s issues seminar 1986, mem. exec. com. 1988-89), Am. Corp. Counsel Assn. (bd. dirs. San Francisco chpt. 1984—, treas. Bay area chpt. 1986-87, sec. 1987-88, v.p. 1988-89, pres. 1989-90), Foothills Tennis and Swimming Club (Palo Alto). Office: Hewlett-Packard Co 3000 Hanover St Palo Alto CA 94304-1112

NORDMEYER, MARY BETSY, educator; b. New Haven, May 19, 1939; d. George and Barbara Stedman (Thompson) N. ABPhil, Wheaton Coll., Norton, Mass., 1960; MA, San Jose State U., 1968; AS in Computer Sci., West Valley Coll., 1985. Cert. tchr. spl. edn., Calif.; cert. secondary tchr., Calif. Instr. English Santa Clara (Calif.) Unified Sch. Dist., 1965-77, vocat. specialist, 1977—, dir. project work ability, 1984—, also mem. community adv. com.; facilitator Project Work-Ability, Region 5, 1985-86, sec., 1988-90. Author poetry, 1960, Career and Vocat. Edn. for Students With Spl. Needs, 1986; author/designer Career English, 1974, Career Information, 1975. Recipient Outstanding Secondary Educator award, 1975, Award of Excellence, Nat. Assn. Vocat. Edn., 1984; named Tchr. of Yr. in Spl. Edn., Santa Clara Unified Sch. Dist., 1984-85. Mem. Calif. Assn. Work Experience Educators, Sierra Club, Epsilon Eta Sigma. Democrat. Home: 14920 Sobey Rd Saratoga CA 95070-6236 Office: Santa Clara Unified Sch Dist 1889 Lawrence Rd Santa Clara CA 95051-2166

NORDSTROM, BRUCE A., department store executive; b. 1933; married. BA, U. Wash., 1956. With Nordstrom, Inc., Seattle, 1956—, v.p., 1964-70, pres., 1970-75, chmn., 1975-77, co-chmn., 1977—, dir. Office: Nordstrom Inc 1501 5th Ave Seattle WA 98101-1603*

NORDSTROM, JAMES F., apparel company executive; b. 1940; married. BBA, U. Wash., 1962. Various positions Nordstrom, Inc., Seattle, 1960—, exec. v.p., 1975-78, pres., 1975-78, from 1978, co-chmn., also bd. dirs. Office: Nordstrom Inc 1501 5th Ave Seattle WA 98101-1603*

NORDSTROM, JOHN N., department store executive; b. 1937; married. BA, U. Wash., 1958. With Nordstrom, Inc., Seattle, 1958—, v.p., 1965-70, exec. v.p., 1970-75, pres., 1975-77, co-chmn., 1977—, dir.; bd. dirs. Fed. Res. Bank San Francisco. Office: Nordstrom Inc 1501 5th Ave Seattle WA 98101-1603

NORDSTROM, RICHARD DEAN, educator, marketing professional; b. Topeka, Feb. 7, 1933; s. Albert E. and Wanda L. (Officer) N.; m. Margaret Anne Throm Oct. 25, 1958; children: Neal C., Pamela G. BS in Bus., U. Kans., 1954; MBA, Wichita State U., Kansas, 1969; PhD in Bus. Adminstrn., Ark. U., Fayetteville, 1974. Owner, mgr. Nordstrom Ford, Newton, Kans., 1958-70; assoc. prof. Western Ill. U., Macomb, 1974-80; prof. Calif. State U., Fresno, 1980—, chmn. mktg. dept., 1990—; cons. forcasting mktg. and mktg. rsch., 1972—; lectr. Wichita State U., Kans., 1970. Author: Introduction in Selling, 1981; contbr. articles to profl. jours. Mem. Am. Mktg. Assn., Nat. Assn. Forensic Economists. Office: Calif State U Cedar & Shaw Fresno CA 93740

NORGAARD, RICHARD BRUCE, economist, educator, consultant; b. Washington, Aug. 18, 1943; s. John Trout and Marva Dawn (Andersen) N.; m. Marida Jane Fowle, June 19, 1965 (div.); children—Kari Marie, Marc Anders. B.A. in Econs., U. Calif.-Berkeley, 1965; M.S. in Agrl. Econs. Oreg. State U., 1967; Ph.D. in Econs., U. Chgo., 1971. Instr. Oreg. Coll. Edn., 1967-68; asst. prof. agrl. and resource econs. U. Calif.-Berkeley, 1970-76, assoc. prof., 1976-77, 80-87, assoc. prof. energy and resources, 1987-92, prof. energy and resources, 1992—; project specialist Ford Found., Brazil, 1978-79; cons. Ford Found., Calif. Dept. Water Resources, Pub. Interest Econs., Ind. Petroleum Producers of Calif., Plan Sierra Dominican Republic, UN Food & Agrl. Orgn., UN Environment Program, USAID-Thailand, The World Bank; mem. sci. com. on problems of the environment U.S. Nat. Rsch. Coun. Author: Development Betrayed: The End of Progress and a Coevolutionary Revisioning of the Future, 1993; contbr. numerous articles to acad. jours. Active civil rights, environ, and peace orgns. Mem. AAAS, Assn. Pub. Policy and Mgmt., Latin Am. Studies Assn., Am. Econs. Assn., v.p. Internat. Soc. Ecol. Econs., Fedn. Am. Scientists, Assn. Environ. and Resource Econs. Home: 1198 Keith Ave Berkeley CA 94708-1607 Office: U Calif Energy & Resources Program Rm 100 Bldg T-4 Berkeley CA 94720

NORGREN, C. NEIL, manufacturing executive; b. Silt, Colo., Aug. 23, 1923; s. Carl August and Juliet (Lien) N.; m. Carolyn Sutherland, Apr. 12, 1980; children by previous marriage: Jeraldine Leigh, Carol Ann, John Carl, David Laurence. Student, U. Colo., 1941-43. With C.A. Norgren Co. (mfrs. pneumatic products), Englewood, Colo., 1938-84; purchasing agt., office mgr. C.A. Norgren Co. (mfrs. pneumatic products), 1947-49, asst. gen. mgr., 1949-53, v.p., 1953-55, exec. v.p., 1955-62, pres., 1962-84, also dir.; chmn., chief exec. officer Butler Fixture Co., 1984-91; dir. United Bank of Denver (mem. exec. com. 1957-90). Dir. Bus.-Industry Polit. Action Com., 1967-89; pres. Met. Denver chpt. Jr. Achievement, pres. 1954-56; bd. dirs. Denver Mus. Natural History, 1st v.p. 1983-88, pres., 1988-91; bd. dirs. Carl A. Norgren Found., 1955-90; pres. Norsut Found., 1990—; bd. dirs. U. Colo. Found., 1983—, vice chmn., 1985-87, chmn. 1987-90, chmn. exec. com., 1990-92. Staff sgt. USAAF, 1942-46. Mem. NAM (bd. dirs., regional v.p. 1966-70, exec. com. 1968-86, divisional v.p. 1973-78), Nat. Fluid Power Assn., Nat. Coun. Profit Sharing Industries (past chmn. exec. com.), Nat. Western Stock Show Assn. (bd. dirs. until 1991), Inst. Dirs., Met. Denver Execs. Club (co-founder, past pres.), Athletic Club, Pinehurst Country Club, Air Force Acad. Golf Club (Colorado Springs), Met. Club, Greencroft Club, Charlottesville, Va., Beta Theta Pi. Home: 350 Barracks Hill Charlottesville VA 22901

NORKIN, MARK MITCHELL, sales executive; b. Whittier, Calif., Nov. 19, 1955; s. Cleo Donald and Carol Ann (Stewart) Mathis. Grad., Gemmological Inst. Am., 1976. Gemmologist Slavicks Jewelers, Newport Beach, Calif., 1976-77; apprentice Troy Sheet Metal Works, Montebello, Calif., 1977-79, journeyman, 1979-80, foreman, 1980-82, project engr., 1982-85, v.p. sales and engring., 1985—. Republican. Office: Troy Sheet Metal Works 1026 S Vail Ave Montebello CA 90640-6080

NORMAN, DONALD ARTHUR, cognitive scientist; b. N.Y.C., Dec. 25, 1935; s. Noah N. and Miriam F. N.; m. Martha Karpati (div.); children—Cynthia, Michael; m. Julie Jacobsen; 1 child, Eric. B.S.E.E., MIT, 1957; M.S.E.E., U. Pa., 1959, Ph.D. in Psychology, 1962. Lectr. Harvard U., 1962-66; Prof. dept. psychology U. Calif.-San Diego, La Jolla, 1966-92, prof. emeritus, 1992—, prof., chair dept. cognitive sci., 1988-92, chair dept.psychology, 1974-78, dir. cognitive sci. program, 1977-88, dir. Inst. for Cognitive Sci., 1981-89; Apple fellow Apple Computer Inc., Cupertino, Calif., 1993—; mem. sci. adv. bd. Naval Pers. Rsch. Ctr., San Diego, 1982-86; cons. to industry on human computer interaction and user-centered design. Author: Learning and Memory, 1982, Human Information Processing, 2d edit., 1977, User Centered System Design, 1986, The Psychology of Everyday Things, 1988, The Design of Everyday Things, 1989, Turn Signals Are the Facial Expressions of Automobiles, 1992, Things That Make Us Smart, 1993; editor: Perspectives on Cognitive Science, 1981, Exploration in Cognition, 1975, Cognitive Sci. Jour., 1981-85; series editor Cognitive Sci. Series Lawrence Earlbaum Assoc., 1979—. Recipient Excellence in Rsch. award U. Calif., 1984. Fellow Am. Psychol. Soc., Am. Acad. Arts and Scis.; mem. Am. Assn. Arts and Scis., Am. Assn. for Artificial Intelligence, Assn. for Computational Machinery, Cognitive Sci. Soc. (chmn. founding mem.). Office: Apple Computer Inc 1 Infinite Loop Cupertino CA 95014

NORMAN, E. GLADYS, business computer educator, consultant; b. Oklahoma City, June 13, 1933; d. Joseph Eldon and Mildred Lou (Truitt) Biggs; m. Joseph R.R. Radeck, Mar. 1, 1953 (div. Aug. 1962); children: Jody Matti, Ray Norman, Warren Norman, Dana Norman; m. Leslie P. Norman, Aug. 26, 1963; 1 child, Elayne Pearce. Student, Fresno (Calif.) State Coll., 1951-52, UCLA, 1956-59, Linfield Coll., 1986—. Math. aid U.S. Naval Weapons Ctr., China Lake, Calif., 1952-56, computing systems specialist, 1957-68; systems programmer Oreg. Motor Vehicles Dept., Salem, 1968-69; instr. in data processing, dir. Computer Programming Ctr., Salem, 1969-72; instr. in data processing Merritt-Davis Bus. Coll., Salem, 1972-73; sr. programmer, analyst Teledyne Wah Chang, Albany, Oreg., 1973-79; sr. systems analyst Oreg. Dept. Vets. Affairs, Albany, 1979-80; instr. in bus. computers Linn-Benton Community Coll., Albany, 1980—; presenter computer software seminars, State of Oreg., 1991-92, Oreg. Credit Assoc. Conf., 1991, Oreg. Regional Users Group Conf., 1992; computer cons. in field. Mem. Data Processing Mgmt. Assn. (bd. dirs. 1977-84, 89—, region 2 pres. 1985-87, assoc. v.p. 1988, Diamond Individual Performance award 1985). Democrat. Office: Linn Benton CCC Bus Mgmt Dept 6500 Pacific Blvd SW Albany OR 97321-3755

NORMAN, JOHN BARSTOW, JR., designer, educator; b. Paloa, Kans., Feb. 5, 1940; s. John B. and Ruby Maxine (Johnson) N.; m. Roberta Jeanne Martin, June 6, 1967; children: John Barstow III, Elizabeth Jeanne. BFA, U. Kans., 1962, MFA, 1966. Designer and illustrator Advt. Design, Kansas City, Mo., 1962-64; asst. instr. U. Kans., Lawrence, 1964-66; art dir. Hallmark Cards, Inc., Kansas City, Mo., 1966-69; instr. dept. art U. Denver, 1969-73, asst. prof., 1973-78, assoc. prof., 1978—, Disting. prof., 1980; sr. designer Mo. Coun. Arts and Humanities, 1966-67; cons. designer Rocky Mountain Bank Note Corp., Denver, 1971—, Signage Identity System, U. Dever; bd. dirs. communications U. Denver; tech. cons. Denver Art Mus., 1974—, designed exhbns., 1974-75; adv., cons. Jefferson County (Colo.) Sch., System, 1976—; chmn. Design and Sculpture Exhbn., Colo. Celebration of the Arts, 1975-76. One man shows include: Gallery Cortina, Aspen, Colo., 1983; commd. works include: Jedda, Saudi Arabia, Synegistics Corp., Denver; represented in permanent collections Pasadena Ctr. for the Arts, N.Y. Art Dirs. Club, Calif. State U./Fiber Collection, Pasadena (Calif.) Ctr. for the Arts, 1984, N.Y. Art Dirs. Club, 1985 Midland Art Coun./Fiber Collection, 1985, Geologic Soc. Am.; represented in traveling exhbns. L.A. Art Dirs. Show and N.Y. Art Dirs. Show, U.S., Europe, Japan, 1985; fearured in Denver Post, 1984, Post Electric City Mag., 1984, Rocky Mt. News, 1984, Douglas County Press, 1984, Mile High Cable Vision, 1985, Sta. KWGN-TV, 1985, Les Krantz's Am. Artists, 1988, Illustrated Survey of Leading Contemporaries, 1988, U.S. Surface Design Jour., 1988; co-work represented in film collection Mus. Modern Art, N.Y.C.; selected fashion show designs displayed to Sister City dels., Denver, 1987. Co-recipient Silver Medal award N.Y. Internat. Film and Video Competition, 1976, Design awards Coun. Advancement and Support of Edn., 1969, 71, 73, 76, Honor Mention award L.A. Art Dirs. Club, 1984, Honor Mention award N.Y. Art Dirs. Club, 1984, Native Am. Wearable Art Competition, 1985, 5th pl. Nat. Wind Sail Am. Banners Competition, Midland, Mich., 1985, also awards for surface designs in Colo. Ctr. for the Arts Wearable Art Competition, 1984-85, Foothills Art Gallery Nat. Wearable Art Competition, 1984-85, Fashion Group of Denver Competition, 1984-85. Mem. Art Dirs. Club Denver (Gold medals 1974-82, Best of Show Gold medal 1983, Honor Mention award, 1984, 3 Gold medals 1989), Univ. Art Dirs. Assn. Home: PO Box 302 751 Willow Lake Dr Franktown CO 80116 Office: U Denver Sch Art 2121 E Asbury Ave Denver CO 80208-0001

NORMAN, JOHN EDWARD, petroleum landman; b. Denver, May 22, 1922; s. John Edward and Ella (Warren) N.; m. Hope Sabin, Sept. 5, 1946; children—J. Thomas, Gerould W., Nancy E., Susan G., Douglas E. BSBA, U. Denver, 1949, MBA, 1972. Clk., bookkeeper Capitol Life Ins. Co., Denver, 1945-46; salesman Security Life and Accident Co., Denver, 1947; bookkeeper Central Bank and Trust Co., Denver, 1947-50; automobile salesman H.A. Hennies, Denver, 1950; petroleum landman Continental Oil Co. (name changed to Conoco Inc. 1979), Denver, 1950-85; ind. petroleum landman, 1985—. Lectr. pub. lands Colo. Sch. Mines, 1968-85; lectr. mineral titles and landmen's role in oil industry Casper Coll., 1969-71. Mem. Casper Mcpl. Band Commn., 1965-71, mem. band, 1961-71, mgr., 1968-71; former musician, bd. dirs. Casper Civic Symphony; former bd. dirs. Jefferson Symphony, performing mem., 1972-75. Served with AUS, World War II. Mem. Am. Assn. Petroleum Landmen (dir. at large, chmn. publs. for regional dir.), Wyo. Assn. Petroleum Landmen (pres.), Denver Assn. Petroleum Landmen, Rocky Mountain Oil and Gas Assn. (pub. lands com. 1981—), Rocky Mountain Petroleum Pioneers. Episcopalian (mem. choir, vestryman, past dir. acolytes). Club: Elks. Home and Office: 2710 S Jay St Denver CO 80227-3856

NORMAN, LINDSAY DEAN, JR., academic administrator; b. Drexel Hill, Pa., Oct. 14, 1937; s. Lindsay Dean and Julia (Lowe) N.; m. Julie Bossard, May 12, 1990; children: Todd, Julia, Lindsay. BS, U. Md., 1960, MS, 1964, PhD, 1970. Supr. rsch. U.S. Bur. of Mines, College Park, Md., 1961-70; dir. planning U.S. Bur. of Mines, Washington, 1970-74, asst. dir., 1974-79, dir., 1979-81; v.p. J&L Steel Corp., Pitts., 1981-84; v.p., tech. dir. Chase Manhattan Bank, N.Y.C., 1984-86; pres. Mont. Tech., Butte, 1986—; bd. dirs. Pegasus Gold Corp., Spokane, Wash., Butte Mining PC, London, Eng., Mont. Tech. Cos., Butte. Contbr. articles to profl. jours. Chmn. Bedford (Pa.) Symphony, 1982-84. Recipient Meritorious Svc. award U.S. Dept. Interior, 1980, Eminent Engrs. award Tau Beta Pi, 1988. Mem. AIME (Nat. Minerals Econs. award 1988), Butte C. of C. (bd. dirs. 1986—), U. Md. Alumni Assn. Home: 1315 W Park St Butte MT 59701-8997 Office: Mont Tech W Park St Butte MT 59701-1714

NORRIS, ALFRED LLOYD, theological seminary president, clergyman; b. Bogalusa, La., Feb. 6, 1938; s. Leslie Henry Peter and Adele Theresa (Washington) N.; m. Mackie Lyvonne Harper, Sept. 9, 1961; children: Alfred Lloyd II, Angela Renee. BA, Dillard U., 1960; MDiv, Gammon Theol. Sem., Atlanta, 1964, DD (hon.), 1976; DD (hon.), Centenary Coll., 1989; LLD, Dillard U., 1989. Ordained ministry United Meth. Ch., 1963. Pastor Haven United Meth. Ch., New Orleans, 1963-66, Peck United Meth. Ch., New Orleans, 1966-68, First Street United Meth. Ch., New Orleans, 1972-74, Mt. Zion United Meth. Ch., New Orleans, 1980-85; dist. supt. New Orleans dist. United Meth. Ch., New Orleans, 1974-80; dir. recruitment Gammon Theol. Sem., 1968-72, pres., 1985—; now bishop of New Mexico United Methodist Church, Albuquerque, N.Mex.; mem. Am. Preaching Mission, 1967; mem. bd. publs. United Meth. Pub. House, Nashville, 1980—; bd. dirs. Gulfside Assembly, Waveland, Miss., 1975—; mem. La. Conf. Bd. Higher Edn. and Campus Ministry; chmn. bd. ordained ministry La. Ann. Conf., 1980-88; guest preacher Liberia, West Africa, 1988. Trustee Centenary Coll., Shreveport, La., 1979—; mem. exec. com. NAACP, New Orleans, 1980-85; bd. dirs. New Orleans Urban League, 1981-84, Wesley Homes, Inc., Atlanta, 1986—; mem. exec. com. Met. Area Com., New Orleans, 1983-85; chmn. bd. dirs. Lafon Home for Elderly, New Orleans, 1983-85. Crusade scholar, 1961-63. Mem. Assn. United Meth. Theol. Schs. (sec. 1986-88), Adminstrv. Deans' Coun. (v.p. 1986—), Masons, Sigma Pi Phi, Theta Phi. Democrat. *

NORRIS, D. WAYNE, insurance and financial services company executive; b. Portland, Ind., Feb. 9, 1939; s. Leo D. and Mable L. (Miller) N.; m. Bonnie K. Smith, Mar. 6, 1965; children: Julia A., Elizabeth. Student, Ball State U., 1961-64. CLU. Gen. mgr. Am. Gen. Ins., Muncie, Inc., 1964-69; owner D. Wayne Norris CLU and Assocs., Muncie, 1969-73, Tucson, 1973—. Contbr. articles to profl. jours. Bd. dirs. Jr. Achievement Ariz., 1985—; life mem. Nat. Cowboy Hall of Fame, 1981—. Recipient nat. award Jr. Achievement, 1990. Mem. Nat. Assn. Life Underwriters (pres. Ind. chpt. 1971-72, Nat. Quality award 1965, Underwriter of Yr. award 1972), Am. Soc. CLU's (bd. dirs. Tucson 1975-79), Nat. Assn. Security Dealers, Tucson Metro C. of C. (chmn. Los Compadres 1986-88, Bus. Leader of Yr. award 1990), Pime Early Rising Execs. (founder, past pres. 1975—). Office: 5620 N Kolb Rd Ste 166 Tucson AZ 85715-1384

NORRIS, ERIC ALEXANDER, urban planner; b. Frankfurt, Federal Republic of Germany, July 5, 1959; came to U.S., 1960; s. Arthur Francis and Jutta Maria (Kropf) N.; m. Cynthia Pauleen Abell, Aug. 2, 1986; 1 child, Gregory Alexander. BS in Communication Arts, Calif. Poly. U., 1982, MURP, 1992. Assoc. planner Planning Network, Ontario, Calif., 1985-88; planner EDAW, San Bernardino, Calif., 1988; sr. planner, assoc. RHA Inc., Riverside, Calif., 1988-92; planner City of Chino Hills, 1992—. Editor: (profl. newsletter) The Memo, 1987-89; contbr. articles to profl. jours. Chmn. Recreational Trails Com., Highland, Calif., 1990—. Mem. Am. Planning Assn. (Disting. Svc. 1988, 89, Meritorious Planning award 1990, State Outstanding Planning award 1992), Am. Inst. Cert. Planners, Assn. Environ. Profls., Urban Land Inst. Office: City of Chino Hills 2001 Grand Ave Chino Hills CA 92709

NORRIS, MARY BETH, flutist, educator; b. Great Bend, Kans., June 6, 1950; d. Clyde D. and Elizabeth M. (Penner) N.; m. Mark J. Fischer, Nov. 23, 1990. B Music Edn., Ft. Hays State U., 1972. Cert. Suzuki method flute tchr. Tchr. music Hays (Kans.)Pub. Schs., 1975-77; coord. music program Horizons for the Handicapped, Steamboat Springs, Colo., 1978-80; music instr. Colorado Mountain Coll., Steamboat Springs, 1982—; freelance flutist Steamboat Springs, 1981—, ind. flute instr., 1981—; founder, dir. Steamboat Internat. Flute Festival, Steamboat Springs, 1987—, Steamboat String Orch., Steamboat Springs, 1991—. Flute soloist United Meth. Ch., Steamboat Springs. Mem. Suzuki Assn. of the Americas, Music Tchrs. Nat. Assn., Sigma Alpha Iota. Home: 1190 Merritt St Steamboat Springs CO 80477

NORRIS, RICHARD EARL, botanist; b. Seattle, Apr. 13, 1926; s. Ernest and Freda Bertha (Hyden) N.; m. Louisa A. Taylor, June 24, 1951 (div. 1976); children: Richard Earl, Jack Taylor, Laura Ruth; m. Fiona Mary Getliffe, Mar. 25, 1977. BS, U. Wash., 1947; PhD, U. Calif., Berkeley, 1954. Chemist research U. Calif. Radiation Lab., Berkeley, 1953-55; asst. prof., assoc. prof. U. Minn., Mpls., 1955-61; curator algae Smithsonian Inst., Washington, 1961-62; assoc. prof., prof. U. Wash., Seattle, 1962-80; rsch. assoc. U. Witwatersrand, Johannesburg, South Africa, 1980-82, U. Natal, Pietermaritzburg, South Africa, 1982-87; sr. researcher Nat. Botanical Inst., Cape Town, South Africa, 1987-90; rsch. botanist U. Hawaii, Honolulu, 1991-93; ret., 1993. Contbr. articles to profl. jours. Bd. trustees Marine Sci. Soc. Pacific Northwest, Seattle, 1966. Fulbright fellow, 1958, Guggenheim Fellow, 1969; vis. fellow, South Africa, 1976-77. Mem. Phycological Soc. Am. (pres. 1971, editor jour. 1980, Disting. Lectr. 1993), Internat. Phycological Soc. (pres. 1976-77), Phycological Soc. South Africa (pres. 1985-86). Home: 593 Uluhala St Kailua HI 96734

NORRIS, WILLIAM ALBERT, federal judge; b. Turtle Creek, Pa., Aug. 30, 1927; s. George and Florence (Clive) N.; m. Merry Wright, Nov. 23, 1974; children: Barbara, Donald, Kim, Alison. Student, U. Wis., 1945; B.A., Princeton U., 1951; J.D., Stanford U., 1954. Bar: Calif. and D.C. 1955. Assoc. firm Northcutt Ely, Washington, 1954-55; law clk. to Justice William O. Douglas U.S. Supreme Ct., Washington, 1955-56; sr. mem. firm Tuttle & Taylor, Inc., L.A., 1956-80; judge U.S. Ct. Appeals (9th cir.), L.A., 1980—; spl. counsel Pres.' Kennedy's Com. on Airlines Controversy, 1961; mem., v.p. Calif. State Bd. Edn., 1961-67. Trustee Calif. State Colls., 1967-72; pres. L.A. Bd. Police Commrs., 1973-74; Democratic nominee for atty. gen. State of Calif., 1974; founding pres. bd. trustees Mus. Contemporary Art, L.A., 1979—; trustee Craft and Folk Art Mus., 1979—. With USN, 1945-47. Home: 1473 Oriole Dr West Hollywood CA 90069-1155 Office: US Ct Appeals9th Circuit 312 N Spring St Los Angeles CA 90012-4701

NORTH, ANNE VIA, public relations director; b. Clifton Forge, Va., Mar. 15, 1939; d. Charles Ashland Via Jr. and Mary Constance (Scales) Tregenza; m. Richard Conrad Waldburger, Nov. 7, 1964 (div. Nov. 1980); children: Jennifer Radell, Erica Wells; m. Brian Royce North, Oct. 6, 1990. Student, Goucher Coll., 1957-59; cert., Katharine Gibbs Sch., N.Y.C., 1960. Asst. WNEW Radio, N.Y.C., 1960-64, Columbia Rec., N.Y.C., 1964-65; personal asst. Anne Morrow Lindbergh, Darien, Conn., 1978-81, Gerry Mulligan, Darien, 1980-81; asst. to news dir. & exec. producer Satellite News Channel, Stamford, Conn., 1981-83; mgr. bus. devel. & pub. rels. Chapman/Warwick Advt., San Diego, 1983-86; dir. nat. pub. rels. San Diego Conv. & Vis. Bur., 1986—. Mem. Pub. Rels. Soc. Am., Soc. Am. Travel Writers. Office: San Diego Conv & Visitors Bur 401 B St Ste 1400 San Diego CA 92101

NORTH, MARK HUNTINGTON, physicist; b. Evanston, Ill., Nov. 16, 1946; s. Milford Tennyson and Florence Claire (Flinn) N.; m. Alice Marie Black, July 12, 1969 (div. Dec. 1988); children: Matthew Huntington, Sarah Ann. BS in Engring. Physics, U. Ill., 1973, MS in Physics, 1974, PhD in Physics, 1977. Physicist Naval Ocean Systems Ctr., San Diego, 1977-87, 88—; asst. prof. physics Mich. Technol. U., Houghton, 1987-88. With U.S. Army, 1964-68. Mem. Am. Phys. Soc., N.Y. Acad. Scis. Home: 1826 Galveston St San Diego CA 92110-3505 Office: Naval Ocean Systems Ctr Code 524 San Diego CA 92152

NORTH, WHEELER JAMES, marine ecologist, educator; b. San Francisco, Jan. 2, 1922; s. Wheeler Orrin and Florence Julia (Ross) N.; m. Barbara Alice Best, Apr. 25, 1964; children: Hannah Catherine, Wheeler Orrin. BS in Engring, Calif. Inst. Tech., 1944, BS in Biology, 1949; MS in Oceanography, U. Calif. at San Diego, 1953; Ph.D., 1953. NSF postdoctoral fellow Cambridge (Eng.) U.; Electronics engr. U.S. Navy Electronics Lab., Point Loma, Calif., 1947-48; asst. research biologist Scripps Inst. Oceanography, U. Calif. at San Diego, 1953, Rockefeller postdoctoral fellow, 1955-56; asst. research biologist Inst. Marine Resources Scripps Inst. Oceanography, 1956-63; assoc. prof. Calif. Inst. Tech., Pasadena, 1963-70; prof. Calif. Inst. Tech., 1970-92, prof. emeritus, 1992—; Cons. marine biology U.S. Govt., State of Calif., San Francisco, Los Angeles, San Diego, numerous industries, 1957—; Phi Beta Kappa vis. scholar, 1973-74; mem. Calif. Adv. Commn., 1972-73, Nav. and Ocean Devel. Commn., 1973-76; dir. Marine Biol. Cons. Contbr. articles to profl. jours. Recipient NOGI award Underwater Soc. Am., 1975. Mem. Am. Littoral Soc. (James Duggan award), AAAS, Am. Soc. Limnology and Oceanography, Am. Soc. Zoology, Soc. Gen. Physiology, Calif. Acad. Sci., Fish Protective Assn. (dir.), N.Y. Acad. Sci., Am. Geophys. Union, Smithsonian Instn., Am. San Diego museums, Marine Tech. Soc., Western Soc. Naturalists, Calif. Soc. Profl. Engrs., Am. Zoomalac Soc., Internat. Oceanographic Found., Sigma Xi. Home: 205 Carnation Ave Apt 5 Corona Del Mar CA 92625-2807 Office: Calif Inst Tech Div Engring and Applied Sci Pasadena CA 91125

NORTHCUTT, HELENE LOUISE BERKING (MRS. CHARLES PHILLIP NORTHCUTT), artist, educator; b. Hannibal, Mo., July 6, 1916; d. Robert Stanley and Alice Lee (Adkisson) Berking; student Christian Coll., Columbia, Mo., 1932-33; B.S., U. Mo., 1939, A.M., 1940, Ed.D., 1959; m. Charles Phillip Northcutt, June 4, 1938 (dec.); children: John Berking, Francois Lee Northcutt Hedeen. Art tchr., supr. Oakwood High Sch. and Elem. Sch., 1937-39; tchr. jr. high sch. U. Mo. Lab. Sch., 1939-40; tchr. elem. art, Memphis, Mo., 1941; county fine arts supr., Ralls County, Mo., 1941-42; tchr. art high sch., Columbia, 1943-44; tchr. art jr. high sch., Hannibal, Mo., 1951-54; supr. art Ralls County Reorganized Sch. Dist. VI, New London, 1954-56; vis prof. U. Upper Iowa, 1956; instr. U. Mo., 1956-57; prof. art Eastern Mont. Coll. unit U. Mont., Billings, from 1957, now prof. emeritus, mem. grad. faculty; vis. prof. art U. B.C., Vancouver, 1965; cons. in curriculum in art edn.; cons. environ. edn., cons. on Indian edn., early childhood; exhibits fibers and paintings; state dir. Am. Art Week, Am. Artists Profl. League, 1963-65; exhibit chmn. E.M.C. Gallery Fine Arts; program chmn. Becky Thatcher council Girl Scouts U.S.A., 1946-48; bd. dirs., treas. United Christian Campus Ministry; bd. dirs. Growth Through Art. Recipient scholarship Delta Kappa Gamma, 1956-57; Nat. Press award Gen. Fedn. Women's Clubs, 1951; named Outstanding Honor Grad. U. Mo., 1968; citations for distinctive service Eastern Mont. Coll., Helene B. Northcutt Gallery named in her honor. Mem. Nat. Soc. Coll. Profs., AAUP, Mont. Edn. Assn. (past pres. Eastern Faculty unit; v.p. dept. higher edn. 1966-68, dept. pres. 1968-70) Nat., Mont. (sec. 1967-69) art edn. assns., AAUW (past chpt. pres.), Mont. Early Childhood Edn. Assn., Gen. Fedn. Women's Clubs (local past pres.), Delta Kappa Gamma (past chpt. pres., chmn. com., chmn. state world fellowship), Delta Phi Delta, Kappa Delta Epsilon. Methodist (mem. commn. higher edn. ministries, Yellowstone Conf.). Club: Eastern Montana College Faculty (Billings, Mont.). Author: Creative Expression, 1964; Competency base Module-Methods and Materials, 1974; contbr. to publs. in field; reviewer, editor manuscripts on art and art edn. Home: 1140 E 37th Bldg 6 #208 Davenport IA 52807

NORTHROP, GLENN ALLEN, marketing executive; b. Detroit, Aug. 24, 1953; s. Glenn Albert and Sophie R. (Burry) N.; m. Linda Sue Nowlin, July 6, 1977 (div. 1984); m. Sherry Lynn Gravilla, June 8, 1984. BS, Western Mich. U., 1975. Acct. exec. Ross Roy, Inc., Detroit, 1975-77, Yaffe, Stone & August, Southfield, Mich., 1977-79; acct. supr. Young & Rubicam, Detroit, 1979-82; mgr. advt., mktg. Chrysler Corp., Detroit, 1982-85; dir. corp. mktg. Steelcase Inc., Grand Rapids, Mich., 1985-88; v.p. dealer distbn. mktg. Herman Miller, Inc., Zeeland, Mich., 1988-89; COO, dir. bus. ops. Trionix Corp., Kirkland, Wash., 1989—. Mem. Am. Mktg. Assn., Wash. Software Assn., World Future Soc., MIT Forum. Office: 5604 Lakeview Dr NE Ste F Kirkland WA 98033

NORTHRUP, SANDRA JOAN, nurse; b. Indpls., Apr. 22, 1938; d. Clifford LaVern and Christine (Cummingham) Cox; m. Carl Ellis, Feb. 14, 1958 (div. 1968); children: April Lyn, Ronald Murray, Judith Ann Ellis Berezyk; m. John Judson Northrup, Mar. 2, 1979. RN, Clark County (Nev.) Community Coll., 1973; student, U. Nev., 1973-76. Cert. home nurse, 1973. Staff nurse Univ. Med. Ctr., Las Vegas, Nev., 1976-77, Desert Springs Hosp., Las Vegas, 1977-79; supr., coordinator ins. Women's Hosp., Las Vegas, 1977-82; home health nurse Clark County Health Dist., Las Vegas, 1979-83; dir. nursing Tenn. State Prison, Nashville, 1983-85; cons. nursing State of Tenn., Nashville, 1985-86; crisis counselor, sr. psych. nurse State of Nev., Las Vegas, 1987-89; dir. nursing svcs. So. Nev. Adult Mental Health Svcs., Las Vegas, 1989-91, ret., 1991. Recipient Appreciation award ARC. Mem. Am. Nurses Assn., Nev. Nurses Assn., Phi Kappa Phi, Phi Lambda Alpha. Democrat. Baptist. Lodge: Order Ea. Star.

NORTON, DAVID WILLIAM, science educator; b. Wellesley, Mass., Mar. 4, 1944; s. William Bunnell and Mildred Elsie (Smith) N.; m. Carol Ann Chalmers. June 7, 1967; children: Kerry Lynn, Roger Fred, Gail Elaine. AB in Biology, Harvard U., 1967; MS in Zoology, U. Alaska, 1970, PhD in Zoophysiology, 1973. Vis. asst. prof. ecology Boston U., 1973; staff ecologist Dames & Moore, Fairbanks, Alaska, 1973-74; habitat biologist IV Alaska Dept. Fish and Game, Fairbanks, 1974-75; rsch. mgmt. officer Gov. Alaska, Fairbanks, 1975-82, instr., acad. coord. Rural Alaska Honors Inst., 1984-90; exec. sec. Arctic Inst. N.Am., Fairbanks, 1987-91; assoc. prof. natural scis. Arctic Sivunmun Ilisagvik Coll., Barrow, Alaska, 1990—; bd. dirs. Amiq Inst., St. Paul, Alaska, 1991—, Trustees for Alaska, Anchorage, 1987-89. Contbg. editor to various profl. publ.; mem. editorial bd. Arctic, jour. of Artic Inst. N.Am., 1988-91. Co-founder, bd. dirs. Friends of the U. Alaska Mus., Fairbanks, 1981-90. Mem. Sigma Xi. Office: Arctic Sivunmum Ilisagvik Coll 1237 Agvik St Barrow AK 99723-7337

NORTON, DONALD LINN, reporter, journalist, photographer; b. Milw.; s. Francis Wilbur and Eunice Ariel (Hoffman) N. Student, U. Wis., 1958; AA, Wis. Sch. Tech., 1960; cert. Edn. Course, Defense Inst., Ft. Ben Harrison, Ind., 1962. Info. specialist U.S. Army, San Francisco, 1978-80; reporter, photographer NPPA Regional Newspaper # 10, Calif., 1980-82; reporter, photographer, freelance Douglas (Ariz.) Dispatch, 1981-83, Sierra Vista (Ariz.) Dispatch, 1981-83; reporter, photographer Mirror-Sentinel Newspapers, Milw., 1983-85, MM-SR Star News, San Diego, 1986-87; contbr. photographer Entrepreneur Mag., Irvine, Calif., 1988; reporter, photographer Sentinel/MM-Scripps Ranch, San Diego, 1989-91, Scribe & Lens, San Diego, 1991—; feature writer Sorrento-Mira Mesa Times, San Diego, 1993—; gen. mem. NPPA, Durham, N.C., 1972-81, Internat. Photography Orgn., Lewisville, N.c., 1986—. Sgt. U.S. Army, 1960-80. Home and Office: PO Box 711623 San Diego CA 92171-1623

NORTON, DOUGLAS RAY, auditor general; b. Portales, N.Mex., Mar. 23, 1933; s. Clayton G. and Lillian W. (Powers) N.; m. Wanda Jones, May 23, 1951 (div. July 1979); children: Debbie Norton Goodman, Vicki Norton Hulet, Denise Norton Jolley; m. Patricia M. Zins, July 21, 1982. BS, U. Ariz., 1963. CPA, Ariz. Staff acct., audit supr. Ernst & Ernst, Tucson, Ariz., 1963-67; ptnr. Baker, Price & Norton, Prescott, Ariz., 1968-75, Lester Witte & Co., Prescott, Ariz., 1975-76; auditor gen. State of Ariz., Phoenix, 1976—; mem. auditing standards adv. coun. Office of U.S. Comptr. Gen.; mem. Profl. Adv. Bd. Sch. Acctg. Ariz. State U., Tempe; mem. acctg. bd. advisors U. Ariz. Pres. Prescott Bd. Edn., 1976. Served with U.S. Army, 1953-55. Mem. Am. Inst. CPA's, Ariz. Soc. CPA's, Nat. Assn. State Auditors, Comptrollers and Treasurers, Nat. State Auditors Assn. (pres. 1982-83), Nat. Intergovtl. Audit Forum. Lodge: Lions (pres. Prescott chpt. 1973-74). Home: PO Box 1251 Phoenix AZ 85001-1251 Office: Office Ariz Auditor Gen 2700 N Central Ave Ste 700 Phoenix AZ 85004-1140

NORTON, GALE, state attorney general; b. Wichita, Mar. 11, 1954; d. Dale Bentsen and Anna Jacqueline (Lansdowne) N.; m. John Goethe Hughes, Mar. 26, 1990. BA, U. Denver, 1975, JD, 1978. Bar: Colo. 1978, U.S. Supreme Ct. 1981. Jud. clk. Colo. Ct. of Appeals, Denver, 1978-79; sr. atty. Mountain States Legal Found., Denver, 1979-83; nat. fellow Hoover Instn. Stanford (Calif.) U., 1983-84; asst. to dep. sec. U.S. Dept. of Agr., Washington, 1984-85; assoc. solicitor U.S. Dept. of Interior, Washington, 1985-87; pvt. practice law Denver, 1987-90; atty. gen. State of Colo., Denver, 1991—; Murdock fellow Polit. Economy Rsch. Ctr., Bozeman, Mont., 1984; sr. fellow Ind. Inst., Golden, Colo., 1988-90; policy analyst Pres. Coun. on Environ. Quality, Washington, 1985-88; lectr. U. Denver Law Sch., 1989; transp. law program dir. U. Denver, 1978-79. Contbr. chpts. to books, articles to profl. jours. Participant Rep. Leadership Program, Colo., 1988, Colo. Leadership Forum, 1989; chair Nat. Assn. Attys. Gen. Environ. Com. Named Young Career Woman Bus. and Profl. Wome, 1981, Young Lawyer of Yr., 1991. Mem. Federalist Soc., Nat. Environ. Enforcement Coun., Western Water Policy Adv. Commn., Colo. Women's Forum, Order of St. Ives. Republican. Methodist. Office: Colo Dept of Law 1525 Sherman St 5th Fl Denver CO 80203

NORTON, HOWARD CHERRINGTON, leasing company executive; b. Payson, Utah, Apr. 29, 1955; s. Merlin J. Norton and Jane (Cherrington) Hinckley; m. Christine Lynne Stones, July 23, 1982; children: Alexandra, Dax, Mikelle. Grad., Westside High Sch., 1973. Gen. mgr. Transport Leasing, Ltd., Salt Lake City, 1973-75; regional v.p. F-B Truck Line Co., Salt Lake City, 1975-76; pres., chief exec. officer Lester Smith Trucking, Inc., Denver, 1976-78; v.p., then pres. Great Western Leasing, Salt Lake City, 1978-82, chief exec. officer, 1988—; gen. mgr., sec. Oliver Internat., Inc., Salt Lake City, 1983-85; v.p. ops. PST Vans, Inc., Salt Lake City, 1985-88; v.p., bd. dirs. Norton Enterprises, Salt Lake City, 1987-89; mem. lessors conf. com. Ariz. Motor Transport Assn., Phoenix, 1989-90; mem. Nat. Truck Leasing System, Oakbrook, Ill., 1990—. Mem. Young Pres.' Orgn. Mormon. Office: Great Western Leasing Co 1305 W 2100 S Salt Lake City UT 84119-1403

NORTON, JANICE ELIZABETH, air force officer; b. Orlando, Fla., May 3, 1967; d. William Richard and Mary Theresa (Mertsock) N. BS in Aero. Engring., USAF Acad., 1989; MBA, Chapman U., 1992. Commd. 2d lt. USAF, 1989, advanced through grades to 1st lt., 1991; launch systems engr. USAF, L.A., 1989-90, satellite engr., 1991—. Mem. AIAA, Air Force Assn., L.A. Air Force Base Officers' Club. Home: 625 Esplanade Apt 29 Redondo Beach CA 90277 Office: SSD/MHE Los Angeles AFB Los Angeles CA 90091-2960

NORTON, KAREN ANN, accountant; b. Paynesville, Minn., Nov. 1, 1950; d. Dale Francis and Ruby Grace (Gehlhar) N. BA, U. Minn., 1972; postgrad. U. Md., 1978; cert. acctg. U.S. Dept. Agr. Grad. Sch., 1978; MBA, Calif. State Poly. U.-Pomona, 1989. CPA, Md. Securities transactions analyst Bur. of Pub. Debt., Washington, 1972-79, internal auditor, 1979-81; internal auditor IRS, Washington, 1981; sr. acct. World Vision Internat., Monrovia, Calif., 1981-83, acctg. supr., 1983-87; sr. systems liaison coord., Home Savs. Am., 1987—; cons. (vol.) info. systems John M. Perkins Found., Pasadena, Calif., 1985-86. Author (poetry): Ode to Joyce, 1985 (Golden Poet award 1985). Second v.p. chpt. Nat. Treasury Employees Union, Washington, 1978, editor chpt. newsletter; mem. M-2 Prisoners Sponsorship Program, Chino, Calif., 1984-86. Recipient Spl. Achievement award Dept. Treasury, 1976, Superior Performance award, 1977-78; Charles and Ellora Alliss scholar, 1968. Mem. Covenant Ch. Avocations: chess, racquetball, whitewater rafting.

NORWOOD, FREDERICK REYES, applied mechanics engineer; b. Mexico City, Mexico, May 13, 1939; came to U.S. 1954; s. Joseph and Elvira (Reyes) N.; m. Irene Gomez, July 2, 1966 (div. 1982); m. Concepcion Guzman, June 1986; children: Irene, Fred, Angelica. BS, UCLA, 1962; MS, Calif. Inst. Tech., 1963, PhD, 1967. Adj. prof. U. N.Mex., Albuquerque, 1969-85; sr. mem. tech. staff Sandia Nat. Labs., Albuquerque, 1966—. Contbr. articles to profl. jours.; editor proceedings: Techniques and Theory of Stress Measurements for Shock Wave Applications, 1987. Fellow ASME; mem. Am. Geophys. Union, Soc. for Indsl. and Applied Math. Office: Sandia Nat Labs Division 1432 Albuquerque NM 87185

NORWOOD, RONALD EUGENE, auditor, accountant; b. Cresent, Okla., Dec. 24, 1952; s. Jimmie L. and Charlene L. (House) N.; m. Cathy Lynn Reed, Nov. 20, 1971 (div. 1976); children: Katrina, LaFrances, Portia; m. Sandra Norwood; 1 child, Ronald II. AS, Enid (Okla.) Bus. Coll., 1974; BS, Phillips U., 1979. Cert. real estate investigator, fraud examiner. Jr. acct. Phillips Petroleum Co., Bartlesville, Okla., 1974-75; fin. dir. Operation Uplift, Inc., Enid, 1976-79; cons. Nash and Assocs., Tulsa, 1979-80; acct. EDA Corp., Stillwater, Okla., 1980-81, Mitchell Cos., Tulsa, 1981-83; cons. Hill Constrn., Enid, 1983, De'Zanella by J. Scott, Oklahoma City, 1983; examiner, sr. auditor Colo. Real Estate Commn., Denver, 1984—; rsch. analyst U.S. Dept. Labor, Washington, 1978. Sgt. U.S. Army, 1970-73. Named Young Bus. Man of Yr., State of Okla., 1978. Mem. Nat. Assn. Black Accts. Democrat. Home: 4314 Liverpool Ct Denver CO 80249-6966 Office: Colo Real Estate Commn 1776 Logan 4th Fl Denver CO 80203

NOSLER, ROBERT AMOS, sports company executive; b. Ashland, Oreg., Apr. 21, 1946; s. John Amos and Louise (Booz) N.; m. Joan Kathleen Hilliard, July 15, 1967; children: Christie Lynn, Jill Ann, John Robert. Student, U. Oreg., 1965. V.p., gen. mgr. Nosler Bullets, Inc., Bend, Oreg., 1974-88; pres., chief exec. officer Nosler Bullets, Inc., 1988-90; pres., CEO Nosler, Inc., Bend, 1990—. Editor: Nosler Reloading Manual #1, 1976. Bd. dirs. Bend C. of C., 1984-88, treas., 1988; chmn. Central Oreg. Welcome Ctr. Steering Com., 1988. With USN, 1966-70; trustee Ctrl. Oreg. Community Coll. Found., 1992—. Recipient Pres.' award Bend C. of C., 1984, 87, 88. Mem. Nat. Reloading Mfrs. Assn. (bd. dirs. 1982-86, 90-92, pres. 1984-86), Greater Bend Rotary (dir. 1989-91). Republican. Lutheran. Office: Nosler Inc 107 SW Columbia St Bend OR 97702-1014

NOSRATIAN, FARSHAD JOSEPH, internist, cardiologist; b. Tehran, Iran, Sept. 1, 1956; came to U.S., 1979; s. Yahoude Nosrat and Violet (Pousadeh) N.; m. Faranak Daravi, June 24, 1990; 1 child, Michelle. Student, U. Tehran, 1974-78; MD, Albert Einstein Coll. Medicine, Bronx, N.Y., 1983. Diplomate Am. Bd. Internal Medicine, Am. Bd. Cardiovascular Diseases. Resident in internal medicine Harbor-UCLA Med. Ctr., Torrance, 1983-86; fellow in cardiology U. Calif., Irvine, 1986-89, asst. clin. prof., 1989—; clin. staff cardiologist UCLA, 1990—, Centinela Hosp. Med. Ctr., Inglewood, Calif., 1989—, Daniel Freeman Meml. Hosp., Inglewood, 1989—, Little Company of Mary Hosp., Torrance, 1990—, Santa Monica (Calif.) Med. Ctr., 1990—; clin. staff cardiologist Kennedy Med. Ctr., Hawthorne, Calif., 1989—, chmn. critical care com., 1992—. Contbr. chpt. to book, articles to profl. jours. Fellow Am. Coll. Cardiology; mem. Los Angeles County Med. Assn., Alpha Omega Alpha. Office: 4477 118th St # 301 Hawthorne CA 90250

NOTARIANNI, PHILIP FRANK, historian, program coordinator; b. Salt Lake City, July 24, 1948; s. Filippo and Carmela (Angotti) N.; m. Maria Teresa Maletta, Apr. 9, 1983. BS, U. Utah, 1970, MA, 1972; MA, U. Minn., 1976, PhD, 1980. Teaching asst. U. Utah, Salt Lake City, 1972-73; archivist U. Minn., Mpls., 1973-76; history cons. Utah State Hist. Soc., Salt Lake City, 1976-77, preservation historian, 1977-83, coord. mus. svcs., 1983-90, coord. pub. programs, 1990—; adj. prof. U. Utah, 1980—; mem. contract faculty U. Calabria, Italy, 1990. Author: ... The Tintic Minig District, 1982, (with others) The Avenues of Salt Lake City, 1980 (Merit award 1981); editor: Carbon County..., 1981; contbr. articles to profl. jours. Mem. Italian-Am. Civic League, Salt Lake City, 1990—. Unico/Rockefeller Found. grantee, 1973-76, Fulbright Rsch. grantee Italy, 1987-88; recipient Merit award Utah Heritage Found., 1981, Utah Endowment for the Humanities, 1986. Mem. Am.-Italian Hist. Assn. (com. 1990—), Utah State Hist. Soc., Utah Mus. Assn. (pres., bd. dirs. 1983-87). Roman Catholic. Office: Utah State Hist Soc 300 Rio Grande St Salt Lake City UT 84101-1182

NOTHMANN, RUDOLF S., legal researcher; b. Hamburg, Fed. Republic of Germany, Feb. 4, 1907; came to U.S., 1941, naturalized, 1943; s. Nathan and Henrietta G. (Heymann) N. Referendar, U. Hamburg, 1929, PhD in Law, 1932; postgrad. U. Liverpool Law Sch. (Eng.), 1931-32. Law clk. Hamburg Cts., 1929-31, 32-33; export, legal adviser, adviser ocean marine ins. various firms, Ger., Eng., Sweden, Calif., 1933-43, 46-47; instr. fgn. exchange, fgn. trade Extension div. UCLA, 1947-48, vis. assoc. prof. UCLA, 1951; asst. prof. econs. Whittier Coll., 1948-50, assoc. prof., 1950-51; contract work U.S. Air Force, U.S. Navy, 1953-59; contract negotiator space projects, space and missile systems orgn. USAF, L.A., 1959-77; pvt. researcher in internat. comml. law, Pacific Palisades, Calif., 1977—; pres. Hanseatic Devel. Corp., Pacific Palisades, Calif., 1989—. With U.S. Army, 1943-45; ETO. Recipient Gold Tape award Air Force Systems Command, 1970. Mem. Internat. Bar Assn. (vice chmn. internat. sales and related comml. trans. com. 1977-82), Am. Econ. Assn., Calif. Bar Assn. (internat. law sect.), Am. Soc. Internat. Law, Uebersee Club (Hamburg, Germany). Author: The Insurance Certificate in International Ocean Marine Insurance Law and Foreign Trade, 1932; The Oldest Corporation in the World: Six Hundred Years of Economic Evolution, 1949. Home: PO Box 32 Pacific Palisades CA 90272

NOTKIN, DAVID, computer science educator; b. Syracuse, N.Y., Jan. 1, 1955; s. Herbert and Isabell (Schulman) N.; m. Catherine Vaughn Tuttle, July 3, 1988; 1 child, Emma Michael. ScB in computer sci., Brown U., 1977; PhD in computer sci., Carnegie-Mellon U., 1984. Assoc. prof. computer sci. and engring. U. Wash., Seattle, 1984—; vis. assoc. prof. Tokyo Inst. Tech., 1990, Osaka U., 1990-91; chair program com. assoc. computing machinery spl. interest group software engring., Symposium on Founds. of Software Engring., 1993; co-chair program com. 17th Internat. Conf. Software Engring. Assoc. editor: Assn. for Computing Machinery Transactions on Software Engring. and Methodology, 1990—; contbr. articles to profl. jours. Named NSF Presdl. Young Investigator, 1988, others. Mem. IEEE, Assn. Computing Machinery, Sigma Xi. Democrat. Jewish. Home: 4412 Corliss Ave N Seattle WA 98103-7657 Office: U Washington Dept Computer Sci & Engring Seattle WA 98195

NOTKIN, RICHARD T., ceramic sculptor, educator; b. Chgo., Oct. 26, 1948; s. Nathan T. and Thelma N. (Tutilman) N.; children: Jessica, Ethan. BFA, Kansas City (Mo.) Art Inst., 1970; MFA, U. Calif., Davis, 1973. Freelance ceramic sculptor Myrtle Point, Oreg., 1974—; vis. asst. prof. U. Utah, Salt Lake City, 1975; vis. instr. Md. Inst. Coll. of Art, Balt., 1977; vis. artist, lectr. Ohio State U., Columbus, 1982; adj. asst. prof. Mont. State U., Bozeman, 1981; vis. artist Kansas City Art Inst., 1984, Bezalel Acad. of Art & Design, Jerusalem, 1990; artist-in-industry Kohler (Wis.) Co., 1976, 78; artist-in-residence Archie Bray Found., Helena, Mont., 1981. Sculptor nmerous pub. and pvt. collections. Western States Arts Found. fellow, 1976, NEA fellow, 1979, 81, 88, Oreg. Arts Commn. fellow, 1985, John Simon Guggenheim Meml. Found. fellow, 1990, Louis Comfort Tiffany Found. fellow, 1991. Mem. Nat. Coun. on Edn. for the Ceramic Arts, Am. Crafts Coun.

NOTTINGHAM, EDWARD WILLIS, JR., lawyer; b. Denver, Jan. 9, 1948; s. Edward Willis and Willie Newton (Gullett) N.; m. Cheryl Ann Card, June 6, 1970 (div. Feb. 1981); children: Amelia Charlene, Edward Willis III; m. Janis Ellen Chapman, Aug. 18, 1984; 1 child, Spencer Chapman. AB, Cornell U., 1969; JD, U. Colo., 1972. Bar: Colo. 1972, U.S. Dist. Ct. Colo. 1972, U.S. Ct. Appeals (10th cir.) 1973. Law clk. to presiding judge U.S. Dist. Ct. Colo., Denver, 1972-73; assoc. Sherman & Howard, Denver, 1973-76, 78-80, ptnr., 1980-87; ptnr. Beckner & Nottingham, Grand Junction, Colo., 1987-89; asst. U.S. atty. U.S. Dept. Justice, Denver, 1976-78; U.S. dist. judge Dist. of Colo., Denver, 1989—. Bd. dirs. Beaver Creek Met. Dist., Avon, Colo., 1980-88, Justice Info. Ctr., Denver, 1985-87, 21st Jud. Dist. Victim Compensation Fund, Grand Junction, Colo., 1987-89. Mem. ABA, Colo. Bar Assn. (chmn. criminal law sect. 1983-85, chmn. ethics com. 1988-89), Order of Coif, Denver Athletic Club, Delta Sigma Rho, Tau Kappa Alpha. Episcopalian. Office: US Dist Ct 1929 Stout St Denver CO 80294-2900

NOUR, SAMIR, banker, economic consultant; b. Cairo, Egypt, July 9, 1935; m. Layla Enan, June 1, 1963; children: Malak, Karim. BA in Econs., Am. U., Cairo, 1958; MA in Econs., Williams Coll., 1963. Economist Nat. Bank, Cairo, 1960-66; lectr. Am. U., Cairo, 1964-66; economist Bank of Montreal, 1966-69; asst. gen. mgr. UBAF Bank Group, Paris, 1970-79; gen. mgr. UBAF Bank, Seoul, 1979-81, Singapore, 1981-83; pres. Peninsula Investments, Calif., 1983-86.

NOVAK, TERRY LEE, university administrator, professor, former city manager; b. Chamberlain, S.D., Sept. 1, 1940; s. Warren F. and Elaine M. N.; m. Barbara Hosea, Aug. 29, 1981; children: Stephen, David. B.Sc., S.D. State U., 1962; postgrad. (Rotary fellow), U. Paris, 1962-63; M.P.A., Colo. U., 1965, Ph.D., 1970. Asst. city mgr. City of Anchorage, 1966-68; city mgr. City of Hopkins, Minn., 1968-74, City of Columbia, Mo., 1974-78, City of Spokane, Wash., 1978-91; v.p. bus. and fin. Ea. Wash. U., Cheney, 1991-92, prof. public adminstrn., 1992—, dean of extension, 1992—; asst. adj. prof. U. Mo., Columbia, 1975, 77; adj. instr. Gonzaga U., Spokane, 1986-88; mem. nat. adv. coun. on environ. policy and tech. EPA. Author: Special Assessment Financing in American Cities, 1970; contbr. articles to profl. jours. Mem. Internat. City Mgrs. Assn. (Acad. Profl. Devel.), Am. Soc. Public Adminstrn. Episcopalian. Office: Ea Wash U Spokane Ctr MS 1 W MS # 1 W 705 First Ave Spokane WA 99204

NOVICH, CAROLYNN MARY, program analyst; b. Seattle, May 7, 1957; d. Joseph Jaddy and Maria Johanna (Bluhm) N. Student, Western Wash. U., 1975-78; BA in Gen. Studies with honors, Wash. State U., 1980. Tech. editor, writer Battelle, Pacific N.W. Labs., Richland, Wash., 1980-84, adminstrv. specialist, 1984-90, rsch. and devel. program analyst, 1990—, mem. adv. coun. women's com. staff diversity enhancement, 1991-92, mem. women's com. staff diversity enhancement, 1992—. Chairperson fundraising Contact Tri-Cities, Richland, 1992, pres., bd. dirs., 1988. Mem. Soc. for Tech. Communication (sr., co-founder, co-mgr. internat. student tech. writing competition 1986-91 Newsletters Distinction award 1985, 88, Tech. Report Distinction award 1984), Soc. of Women Engrs. (affiliate), Women in Tech. (charter). Office: Battelle Pacific NW Labs Richland WA 99352

NOVICK, STUART ALLAN, advertising agency and marketing executive; b. Savannah, Ga., Aug. 21, 1944; s. Jehiel and Dorothy Ruth (Selicovitz) N.; m. Francesca Julita Lim, June 22, 1986 (div. Mar. 1993); 1 child, Casey Adam. Grad., Stanford U., 1967. Mgr. Chico-San, Inc., Seattle, 1969-72; bus. mgr. Seventh Inn, Boston, 1972-74; owner, mgr. Simulsense, Seattle, 1974-77, More Time! Good Time!, Honolulu, 1977-80; pres. Foodpower, Honolulu, 1980-83, Profitability Cons., Honolulu, 1983-88, Novick and Einstein Advt., Honolulu, 1988—; cons. WorkHawaii, Honolulu, 1990, Am. Lung Assn., Honolulu, 1991. Coord. Gov.'s Energy Awards Program, 1991; chmn. Hunger Project Found., Honolulu, 1977-80; coord. Pau Hunger Found., Honolulu, 1980-81; co-founder, coord. Partnership for the Environment, 1992—. Mem. Exch. Club (coord. Hilo 1990-91). Office: PO Box 26255 Honolulu HI 96825-6255

NOVOGRADAC, MICHAEL JOSEPH, tax accountant; b. Burbank, Calif., Aug. 29, 1961; s. Thomas Matthew and Doris Mae (Hoff) N.; 1 child, Michael J. Student, Calif. State U., Northridge, 1979-80; BA in Econs., UCLA, 1983; MBA, U. Calif., Berkeley, 1984. CPA, MBA. Sr. tax mgr. Arthur Andersen & Co., San Francisco, 1984-89; co-mng. ptnr. Novogradac Fortenbach & Co., San Francisco, 1989—; chmn. bd. Healy Ptnrs. Inc., San Francisco, 1990-91. Co-author: Low Income Housing Tax Credit Handbook and Passive Activity Rules, 1990; pub. newsletter Low Income housing Credit Mosly. Report, 1990. Mem. AICPAs, Calif. Soc. CPAs. Home: 1101 Glenwillow Ln Concord CA 94521 Office: Novogradac Fortenbach & Co 110 Sutter St Ste 100 San Francisco CA 94104

NOWEL, DAVID JOHN, marketing professional; b. New Britain, Conn., Mar. 29, 1935; s. John Joseph and Sophie C. (Nowel) Bonkowski; m. July 20, 1961 (div. 1979); children: Lynn Marie, Bruce Edward. BA in Chemistry and Psychology, Hobart Coll., 1959; MA in Bus., Bklyn. Coll. of Pharmacy, 1964. Neurophysiology rsch. technician Inst. of Living Rsch. Lab., Hartford, 1955-57; sales rep. Sandoz Pharms., Bklyn., 1961-65, Becton Dickenson, Huntington Beach, Calif., 1965-71; sales mgr. Scott Labs., N. Hollywood, Calif., 1971-79; area mgr. Beckman Instruments, Fullerton, Calif., 1979-86; sales rep. Indsl. Tng. Corp.; sales mgr. Pacific Toxicology Lab., L.A., 1987-89, The Mark Group, Santa Ana, Calif., 1989-91; dir. of mktg. Remedial Mgmt. Corp., Newport Beach, Calif., 1991-92; regional acct. mgr. ATEC Environ. Cons., Irvine, Calif., 1992—. Author: Space Station "ARK", 1987. Chairperson energy Orange County C. of C., 1989, mem. air subcom., 1991; co-chairperson environment Irvine C. of C., 1989. With USN, 1959-61. Mem. Assn. of Hazardous Materials Profls. Republican. Unitarian. Home: 19585 Seagull Ln Huntington Beach CA 92648 Office: ATEC Environ Consultants 8 Pasteur Ste 150 Irvine CA 92718

NOWELL, WILLIAM ROBERT, III, journalism educator; b. Raleigh, N.C., Feb. 22, 1949; s. William Robert Jr. and Ruth (Brantley) Nowell; m. Yvonne Lavallee, Aug. 17, 1985; 1 child, Daniella Yvonne. BA, U. N.C., 1971; MS, Northwestern U., 1972; PhD, Ind. U., 1987. Tchr. Garner (N.C.) High Sch., 1972-74; instr. Sandhills Community Coll., Southern Pines, N.C., 1974-77; asst. prof. comm. Elon Coll., N.C., 1981-87; assoc. prof. comm. Calif. State U., Chico, 1987—; tchr. minority editorial tng. program Times-Mirror Corp., L.A., 1992. Contbr. articles to profl. jours. Named Outstanding Journalism Tchr. of the Yr. Calif. Newspaper Pubrs. Assn., 1991. Mem. Soc. Profl. Journalists, Assn. Edn. Jour. Mass Comm. Home: 22 Phlox Way Chico CA 95926 Office: Calif State U 333 Tehama Hall Chico CA 95929

NOWICKI, WILLIAM IAN, software engineer; b. Milw., Apr. 19, 1957; s. Philip Paul and Mary Catherine (McGuire) N.; m. Elizabeth Rosaline Hurd, June 30, 1984. BS, Northwestern U., Evanston, Ill., 1979; MS, Stanford U., 1980, PhD, 1985. Cons. Livermore (Calif.) Nat. Lab., 1978-81, Xerox PARC, Palo Alto, Calif., 1982-84; software engr. Sun Micro Systems, Mountain View, Calif., 1985-89, Legato Systems, Palo Alto, Calif., 1989—. Mem. Assn. Computing Machinery. Libertarian. Office: Legato Systems 260 Sheridan Ave Palo Alto CA 94306

NOYES, RICHARD MACY, physical chemist, educator; b. Champaign, Ill., Apr. 6, 1919; s. William Albert and Katharine Haworth (Macy) N.; m. Winninette Arnold, July 12, 1946 (dec. Mar. 1972); m. Patricia Jean Harris, Jan. 26, 1973. A.B. summa cum laude, Harvard U., 1939; Ph.D., Calif. Inst. Tech., 1942. Research assoc. rocket propellants Calif. Inst. Tech., 1942-46; mem. faculty Columbia U., 1946-58, assoc. prof., 1954-58; Guggenheim fellow, vis. prof. U. Leeds, Eng., 1955-56; prof. chemistry U. Oreg., 1958—, head dept., 1963-68, 75-78, ret., 1984—. Editorial adv. com.: Chem. Revs, 1967-69; editorial adv. com.: Jour. Phys. Chemistry, 1973-80; assoc. editor: Internat. Jour. Chem. Kinetics, 1972-82, Jour. Phys. Chemistry, 1980-82; Contbr. to profl. jours. Fulbright fellow; Victoria U. Wellington, New Zealand, 1964; NSF sr. postdoctoral fellow Max Planck Inst. für Physikalische Chemie, Göttingen, Fed. Republic Germany, 1965; sr. Am. scientist awardee Alexander von Humboldt Found., 1978-79. Fellow Am. Phys. Soc.; mem. Nat. Acad. Scis., Am. Acad. Arts and Scis., Am. Chem. Soc. (chmn. div. phys. chemistry 1961-62, exec. com. div. 1960-75, mem. coun. 1960-75, chmn. Oreg. sect. 1967-68, com. on nominations and elections 1962-68, com. on publs. 1969-72), Chem. Soc. (London), Wilderness Soc., ACLU, Sierra Club (past chmn. Atlantic and Pacific N.W. chpts., N.W. regional v.p. 1973-74), Phi Beta Kappa, Sigma Xi. Home: 2014 Elk Dr Eugene OR 97403-1734 Office: U of Oregon Dept Chemistry Eugene OR 97403

NOZIK, ARTHUR JACK, research physical chemist; b. Springfield, Mass., Jan. 10, 1936; s. Morris and Lillian (Golden) N.; m. Rhoda Ann Fisher, Sept. 6, 1958; children: Eva Sue, Jane Marla. B Chem. Engring., Cornell U., 1958; MS, Yale U., 1962, PhD, 1967. Rsch. engr. McDonnell-Douglas Aircraft Co., Santa Monica, Calif., 1958-60; staff engr. Am. Cyanamid Co., Stamford, Conn., 1961-64, staff scientist, 1967-74; group leader Allied-Signal Corp., Morristown, N.J., 1974-78; sr. scientist Solar Energy Rsch. Inst., Golden, Colo., 1978-80, br. chief, 1980-85, sr. rsch. fellow, 1985—; lectr. over 125 univs. and sci. confs.; mem. sci. rev. coms. U.S. Dept. Energy and NSF; disting. lectr. Dept. Energy and Am. Western Univs., Salt Lake City, 1990. Co-author: Electron Transfer at Surfaces, 1993; editor: Photoeffects at Semiconductor-Electrolyte Interfaces, 1981; sr. editor: Jour. Phys. Chemistry, 1993—; co-editor: Photoelectrochemistry, 1982, 87; mem. editorial bd. Jour. Solar Energy Materials, 1982—; also over 90 articles; patentee in field. Recipient Outstanding Achievement award Solar Energy Rsch. Inst., 1984, H.M. Hubbard award, 1991, Van Morris award Midwest Rsch. Inst., 1985. Mem. Am. Phys. Soc., Am. Chem. Soc., Electrochem. Soc. (chmn. energy tech. group 1984-85), Materials Rsch. Soc., Sigma Xi. Jewish. Office: Nat Renewable Energy Lab 1617 Cole Blvd Golden CO 80401

NOZIK, ROBERT ALAN, ophthalmologist, educator; b. Cleve., Oct. 12, 1934; divorced; 2 children. AB, Western Res. U., 1956, MD, 1960. Diplomate Am. Bd. Ophthalmology (assoc. examiner 1984). Intern Mt. Sinai Hosp., Cleve., 1960-61; resident in ophthalmology Univ. Hosp.-Western Res. U., Cleve., 1961-64; NIH spl. fellow Francis I. Proctor Found., U. Calif., San Francisco, 1966-67, asst., then assoc. rsch. ophthalmologist, 1967-79, rsch. ophthalmologist, 1979—, chief Uveitis Clinic, 1984—, asst. clin. prof., then assoc. clin. prof., 1967-79, clin. prof., 1979—; pvt. practice, San Bruno, Calif., 1967—; chief Uveitis Clinic, Pacific Med. Ctr., San Francisco, 1974—; ophthalmic monitor ALZA Corp., Palo Alto, Calif., 1974-80; numerous presentations in field; vis. prof. U. Autonoma Guadalajara, Mex., 1976, Cleve. Clinic, 1984, U. B.C., Can., 1988. Contbr. over 50 articles to med. jours. Grantee Fight for Sight, Inc., 1970-71, Nat. Soc. for Rsch. To Prevent Blindness, 1972-73, Office of Pres., U. Calif., Berkeley, 1974-75. Mem. ACS, AMA, Am. Acad. Ophthalmology, Frederick C. Cordes Soc., Assn. for Rsch. in Vision and Ophthalmology, Am. Soc. Tropical Medicine and Hygiene, Calif. Med. Assn., San Mateo County Med. Soc., Assn. Proctor Fellows (pres. 1983-85, editor bull. 1983-85),. Office: 1001 Sneath Ln San Bruno CA 94066

NOZISKA, CHARLES BRANT, lawyer; b. Oakland, Calif., Aug. 28, 1953; s. Charles Richard and Shirley Ann (Orme) N. BA, Colo. Coll., 1975; JD magna cum laude, U. San Diego, 1982. Bar: Calif. 1982, U.S. Dist. Ct. (so. dist.) Calif. 1982. Ptnr. Thorsnes, Bartolotta, McGuire & Padilla, San Diego, 1982—. Co-author: Landslide and Subsidence Liability, 1988. Mem. Assn. Trial Lawyers Am., Calif. Trial Lawyers Assn., San Diego Trial Lawyers Assn., San Diego County Bar Assn. Democrat. Office: Thorsnes Bartolotta Mcguire & Padilla 2550 5th Ave Apt 11 San Diego CA 92103-6620

NUCCI, JOSEPH E., JR., electrical engineer; b. Elmhurst, Ill., Mar. 1, 1962; s. Joseph E. and Sharon M. (Knicker) N. AS and AAS, Elgin (Ill.) Community Coll., 1984; BSEE, Ariz. State U., 1986, MSEE, 1989, postgrad., 1990—. Jr. engr./chief draftsman Numeridex Inc., Wheeling, Ill., 1980-84; computer operator Motorola Inc., Schaumburg, Ill., 1983-84; test engr. Codex VLSI Design Ctr., Tempe, Ariz., 1985; asst. engr. Impell Corp., Phoenix, 1986; researcher Ariz. State U., Tempe, 1987-91, tech. asst., 1990—; product devel. engr. mil. divsn. Intel Corp., Chandler, Ariz., 1991-93, quality and reliability engr. mil. and spl. projects divsn., 1993—. Inventor in field. Mem. IEEE, Am. Radio Relay League (N7NOC), Golden Key, Tau Beta Pi, Eta Kappa Nu. Home: 15903 E Redfield Rd Gilbert AZ 85234 Office: Intel CH10-57 5000 W Chandler Blvd Chandler AZ 85226-3699

NUCE, MADONNA MARIE, military officer; b. Denver, Jan. 15, 1952; d. Donald William and Marie Dorothy (Ruscio) N.; m. Edward Ray Geron, Oct. 9, 1982; 1 child, Maria Louise. BA, U. No. Colo., 1974. Enlisted U.S. ANG, 1973; commd. 2d lt. U.S. Army, 1981, advanced through grades to maj., 1989; adminstrv. supply tech. Colo. Army Nat. Guard, Denver, 1974-79; supply technician Colo. Army Nat. Guard, Golden, Colo., 1979-81; tng. officer Colo. Army Nat. Guard, Aurora, Colo., 1981-84, adminstrv. officer, 1984-85; maintenance officer Colo. Army Nat. Guard, Golden, Colo., 1985-86, asst. supply officer, 1986-91, data processing chief, 1991-92, supply mgmt. officer, 1992—. Group leader 5th grade Archdiocese of Denver Jr. Great Books Program, St. Anne Sch., 1987-89, group leader 7th grade Holy Family, 1991-92; bd. dirs. 9 Health Fair, Denver, 1985-90. Mem. Colo. Nat. Guard Assn. (sec. 1981-83, bd. dirs. 1983-85), Assn. of the U.S. Army (treas. 1986-88), Mountainside Art Guild. Roman Catholic. Office: Colo Army Nat Guard Camp George West Golden CO 80401-3997

NUGENT, DEBBIE LEE, sales executive; b. Salt Lake City, Aug. 21, 1963; d. Lerry August and Janice Ray (Alexander) Heath; m. Tad Russell Shaw, Dec. 11, 1982 (div. 1984); 1 child, Lerry Russell; m. Michael Thomas Nugent, May 25, 1985; children: Ian Thomas, Alana Blair. Student, Idaho State U., 1981-83. Assembler Heath Electronic Mfg. Corp., Glenns Ferry, Idaho, 1980-84; pres. Sandyco and Assocs., Idaho Falls, 1984-85; quality assurance inspector Idaho Circuit Tech., Glenns Ferry, 1985-86, sales mgr., 1986—. Tchr. United Meth. Ch., Glenns Ferry, 1977—. Mem. Glenns Ferry C. of C., Jaycees (charter 3 Island chpt. 1992, sec. 1993), Beta Sigma Phi (corr. sec. Alpha Delta chpt. 1992-93, rec. sec. 1993—). Office: Idaho Circuit Tech 401 E 1st St Glenns Ferry ID 83623

NULL, JACK ELTON, superintendent of schools; b. New Haven, Ind., May 22, 1938; s. Clifford Lewis and Violet Alice (Shuler) N.; m. Carolyn Wastjer, June 9, 1962 (div.); 1 child, Richard Lance. BS in Bus. Mgmt., Ind. U., 1960; MA in Elem. Edn., Ball State U., 1963; EdD in Ednl. Adminstrn., Ariz. State U., 1974. Cert. elem. edn. tchr., prin., bus. mgr., supt., Ariz. Adminstrv. asst. to dir. of purchasing Cummins Engine Co., Columbus, Ind., 1960-61; tchr. Randolph Cen. Schs., Winchester, Ind., 1963; tchr., coach East Allen County Schs., New Haven, 1963-66; from prin. to adminstrv. asst. to prin. Wilson Sch. Dist. 6, Phoenix, 1966-73; acting supt., exec. asst. Washington Sch. Dist. 7, Phoenix, 1973-79; supt. Fowler Sch. Dist. 45, Phoenix, 1979—; supt.'s chmn. Westside IMPACT, Phoenix, Tolleson, Avondale, Goodyear and Litchfield, Ariz., 1988-92; All Ariz. Supt., 1992-93. Football ofcl. PAC-10, Big Sky, Ariz. Community Coll. Athletic Conf., 1966—, basketball ofcl., 1963-85; sports statist. Ariz. State U., Tempe,

1968—; clock operator Nat. Football League, Phoenix, 1987—; vice chmn. West Phoenix Cactus League Baseball Coalition, 1991—, edn. reform com., 1993—. Staff sgt. USAFR, 1961-66. Named Football Ofcl. Yr. ACCAC, 1990. Mem. Am. Assn. Sch. Adminstrs., Ariz. Sch. Adminstrs., Inc. (charter mem., active various coms., chmn. legis. com. 1992—), Maricopa County Supt. Assn. (treas. 1970-71, pres. 1971-72), Greater Phoenix Supts. Assn. Democrat. Congregationalist.

NUNN, LESLIE EDGAR, lawyer; b. Evansville, Ind., Oct. 10, 1941. BA, U. Evansville, 1964; JD, U. Denver, 1967. Bar: Colo. 1967, N.Mex. 1977. Lawyer, adminstr. Navajo Tribe of Indians, 1973-76; sole practice, Silverton and Cortez, Colo., 1977-78; ptnr. Nunn & Dunlap, Farmington, N.Mex., 1978-84; sole practice, Denver, 1984-87, Burlington, Colo. 1987—; part-time dep. dist. atty., 1987-92. Served with JAGC, USAF, 1967-73, 89—. Mem. ABA, Colo., N.Mex., S.W. Colo., San Juan County, Navajo Nation bar assns., World Peace Through Law Assn., World Assn. Lawyers (world chmn. law and agr. com.). Decorated Bronze Star. Contbr. articles to legal jours. Home: 4109 Lincoln Ave Evansville IN 47715 Office: PO Box 5678 Evansville IN 47715

NUNNALLY, DON LYNN, agribusiness consultant, cattle and ranching specialist; b. Lamesa, Tex., Apr. 7, 1949; s. Charles Calvin and Florence May (Cowherd) N.; m. Sue King McElvaney (div.); children: Charles Calvin II, Sarah Elizabeth; m. Jennifer Lynn Wolfe, Oct. 21, 1984; stepchildren: Heather Michelle Jobe, Jeffrey Daniel Jobe. BS, Tex. Tech. U., 1973. Asst. mgr. ladder ranch Diamond A Cattle Co., Roswell, N.Mex., 1973-75, div. mgr., 1975-82; owner Nunnally Mgmt., Roswell, N.Mex., 1982-85; gen. mgr. Wichita Land and Cattle Co., Brenham, Tex., 1985-86; EVP, ptnr. S.W. Resource Mgmt., Roswell, 1988—. With U.S. Army. Recipient Tex. Gold Star award Tex. Hdqs. Ext. Svc., 1963, Block and Bridle award Nat. Block and Bridle Tex. tch. chpt., 1969; named Lone Star Farmer, Tex. Assn. Future Farmers, 1965-66, Am. Farmer, Nat. Future Farmers, 1968. Mem. Houston Livestock Show and Rodeo (life), Nat. Guard Assn. Tex., Elks, Rotary. Republican. Episcopalian. Home: 3406 Bandolina Roswell NM 88201 Office: SW Resource Mgmt Inc 700 N Main Ste 414 Roswell NM 88201

NUPEN, BARRY DEAN, data processing executive; b. Spokane, Wash., Sept. 7, 1953; s. Orville Clifford and Georgetta Marie (Kenoyer) N.; m. Judith Anita Reinhardt, Aug. 5, 1978; children: Kari Anita, Bethany Marie, Ryan Eric. BS in Physics, Pacific Luth. U., 1976. Sci. and math. instr. Pierce Coll., Tacoma, 1976-77; tchr. math. Wayneville (Mo.) Sch. Dist., 1977-79; sci. and math. tchr. Washougal (Wash.) Sch. Dist., 1979-80; project mgr. David Taylor Rsch. Ctr. Naval Surface Warfare Ctr., Bremerton, Wash., 1980-85, br. mgr. David Taylor Rsch. Ctr., 1985-93; force silencing advisor for comdr. submarine force U.S. Pacific Fleet Comsubpac, Pearl Harbor, Hawaii, 1993—. Mem. Acoustical Soc. Am., Naval Civilian Mgmt. Assn., Nat. Assn. Naval Tech. Suprs. Presbyterian. Home: 94-531 Alapoai St Mililani HI 96789-1644 Office: Comsubpac Code 42N Bldg 665 Subase Honolulu HI 96860-6550

NUTTALL, MICHAEL LEE, engineer, educator; b. Salem, Mass.; s. Leonard John IV and Ethel (Pecukonis) N.; m. Susan Patricia Wade, July 12, 1988; children: Leonard John VI, Andrew Norman. BSChemE, Brigham Young U., 1987; postgrad., U. Utah, 1992—. Japanese linguist Utah Army N.G., Provo, 1984-87; math tutor Utah Valley C.C., Provo, 1987; engr. Micron Tech., Boise, Idaho, 1988-89, lead engr., 1989-91; instr. Salt Lake C.C., Salt Lake City, 1991-92. Home: 1402 Hollywood Ave Salt Lake City UT 84105

NUTZLE, FUTZIE (BRUCE JOHN KLEINSMITH), artist, author, cartoonist; b. Lakewood, Ohio, Feb. 21, 1942; s. Adrian Ralph and Naomi Irene (Rupert) Kleinsmith; children: Adrian David, Arielle Justine and Tess Alexandra (twins). Author: Modern Loafer, Thames and Hudson, 1981, (authobiography) Futzie Nutzle, 1983, Earthquake, 1989, Run the World: 50 Cents Chronicle Books, 1991; illustrator: The Armies Encamped Beyond Unfinished Avenues (Morton Marcus), 1977, Box of Nothing, 1982, The Duke of Chemical Birds (Howard McCord), 1989, Book of Solutions, 1990; feature cartoonist Rolling Stone, N.Y.C., 1975-80, The Japan Times, Tokyo and L.A., 1986—, The Prague Post, Czechoslovakia, 1991—; contbr. exhbns. include Inaugural, 1966, Cupola, 1967, Rolling Renaissance, San Francisco, 1968, 100 Acres, O.K. Harris 1971, N.Y.C., San Francisco Mus. Art, 1972, Indpls. and Cin. Mus. Art, 1975, Leica, L.A., 1978, Santa Barbara Mus. Annex, Calif., 1978, Swope, Santa Monica, West Beach Cafe, Venice, Calif., 1985, Les Oranges, Santa Monica, Correspondence Sch., 1970-78, 1st Ann. Art-A-Thon, N.Y.C., 1985, Am. Epiphany with Phillip Hefferton, 1986, Polit. Cartoon Show, Braunstein, San Francisco, Komsomolskaya Pravda, 1988, retrospective Eloise Packard Smith, 1990, exemplary contemporary, Cowell, U. Calif. Santa Cruz, 1991, Silicon Graphics Inc., Computor Graphics for NAB, Las Vegas, 1993, Prague Eco-Fair, 1991; represented in pvt. and pub. collections (complete archives) Spl. Collections, McHenry Libr., U. Calif., Santa Cruz, Mus. Modern Art, N.Y.C., San Francisco Mus. Modern Art, Oakland Mus., San Francisco Mus. Cartoon Art, Whitney Mus. Am. Art, N.Y.C. regular contbr. The Japan Times. Ltd., Tokyo, San Francisco Chronicle Sundays "This World", TimesThe Prague Post Prague Czechoslovakia; work pub. in various mags. and newspapers. Address: PO Box 325 Aromas CA 95004

NYBERG, DONALD ARVID, oil company executive; b. Ridgewood, N.J., Aug. 23, 1951; s. Arvid H. and Rita T. (Tenwick) N.; m. Susan Radis, Feb. 14, 1985; children: Matthew D., Ryan T. BA, St. Lawrence U., 1973; MBA, Harvard U., 1975. Mgr. marine ops. Standard Oil, L.A., 1982-83; mgr. ops. planning Standard Oil, Cleve., 1984-85, dir. strategic studies, 1986; divsn. mgr. Brit. Petroleum, Ltd., London, 1987-88; v.p., gen. mgr. U.S. gas bus. BP Exploration, Houston, 1989, v.p., gen. mgr. tech., 1990; v.p. BP Exploration, Anchorage, 1991—; pres., CEO BP Pipelines, Anchorage, 1991—; also bd. dirs. BP Pipelines; v.p. BP Exploration Inc. Office: B P Pipelines Inc 900 E Benson Blvd Anchorage AK 99519

NYBERG, WALTER LAWRENCE, psychology and religion educator emeritus; b. Mpls., Nov. 20, 1922; s. Knute Harold and Helga (Bergman) N.; m. Ruth Brewster Whitney, Dec. 15, 1944; children: Jane, James, Peter, Paul. BA, Macalester Coll., St. Paul, 1946; STB, Boston U., 1949, STM, 1953; PhD, NYU, 1964. Ordained to ministry Meth. Ch., 1949. Pastor Meth. chs. in Mass., Oreg., Kans., 1949-59; assoc. min. Community Ch., Great Neck, N.Y., 1959-61; prof. religious studies U. of the Pacific, Stockton, Calif., 1962-90, emeritus, 1990; therapist Human Achievement Counseling Ctr., Stockton, 1969-86. Dir. Wesley Found, 1951-59. Democrat. Home: 420 Bristol Ave Stockton CA 95204-4330 also: 655 Browns Valley Rd Watsonville CA 95076

NYBORG, JENNIFER KAY, biochemistry educator; b. Loma Linda, Calif., Sept. 2, 1958; d. Alan Orson and Shelby Jean (Fletcher) N. BS, U. Calif., 1981, PhD, 1986. Postdoctoral fellow U. Colo., Boulder, 1986-90; asst. prof. Colo. State U., Ft. Collins, 1990—; cons., mem. sci. adv. bd. Somatogen, Boulder, 1992. Contbr. articles to profl. jours. Bd. dirs. Am. Cancer Soc., Larimer County, 1992. Rsch. grant NIH, 1991, Am. Cancer Soc., 1992. Mem. AAAS, Am. Soc. for Microbiology, Sigma Xi. Democrat. Office: Dept Biochemistry Colo State U Colorado State University CO 80523

NYBORG, LESTER PHIL, physician; b. Twin Groves, Idaho, May 4, 1925; s. Lester Thorsted and LaVernie Mildred (Hathaway) H.; m. LaWana Blanchard, Nov. 23, 1949; children: Jeffrey, Valeah, Vicki. BS, Utah State U., 1951; MD, Northwestern U., 1956; MPH, U. Calif., Berkeley, 1967. Diplomate Am. Bd. Preventive Medicine. Commd. med. officer, lt. USN, 1957, advanced through grades to lt. comdr., 1964; commd. major USAF, 1964, advanced through grades to col., 1970; intern LDS Hosp., Salt Lake City, 1957; resident USAF Sch. Aviation Medicine, 1968-69; chief profl. svcs. 9th Air Force, 1969-70; med. advisor Vietnamese USAF, Vietnam, 1970-71; ret. USAF, 1975; med. dir. Boise (Idaho) State U., 1976—. Decorated Bronze Star, Vietnamese Congressional medal Vietnamese Nat. Air Force, 1971. Mem. Ada County Med. Soc. Home: 660 N Ballantine Eagle ID 83616 Office: Boise State U SHS Boise ID 83725

NYDAM, MARK ALLEN, corporate planner; b. Platte, S.D., June 9, 1958; m. Emily Saxe, May 15, 1982. BS, Yale U., 1980, MS, 1983; MA, U. Chgo., 1990, MBA, 1990. Pres. Geologic Assocs., New Haven, 1981-85; fgn. affairs officer U.S. Dept. State, Washington, 1985-88; corp. planner ARCO, L.A., 1990—; sr. advisor Cen. Europe Inst., Washington, 1990—; sr. cons. R.J. Internat., Washington, 1991—. Mem. L.A. World Affairs Coun. Home: 1406 Bradbury Rd San Marino CA 91108 Office: ARCO 555 S Flower St Los Angeles CA 90071

NYE, W. MARCUS W., lawyer; b. N.Y.C., Aug. 3, 1945; s. Walter R. and Nora (McLaren) N.; m. Eva Johnson; children: Robbie, Stephanie, Philip, Jennifer. BA, Harvard U., 1967; JD, U. Idaho, 1974. Bar: Idaho 1974, U.S. Dist. Ct. Idaho 1974, U.S. Ct. Appeals (9th cir.) 1980. Ptnr. Racine, Olson, Nye, Cooper & Budge, Pocatello, Idaho, 1974—; vis. prof. law U. Idaho, Moscow, 1984. Recipient Alumni Svc. award U. Idaho, 1988. Fellow ABA (mem. ho. dels. 1988—, state chmn. ho. of dels. 1991—), Am. Bar Found. (stat. chmn. 1992—); mem. Am. Bd. Trial Advs., Am. Coll. Trial Lawyers, Idaho Bar Assn. (commr. 1985—, pres. bd. commrs. 1987-88), Idaho Def. Counsel Assn. (pres. 1982), Idaho State Centennial Found. (commr. 1985—), 6th Dist. Bar Assn. (pres. 1982). Home: 173 S 15th Ave Pocatello ID 83201-4056 Office: Racine Olson Nye Cooper & Budge PO Box 1391 Pocatello ID 83204-1391

NYIKOS, MICHAEL STEPHEN, college official; b. South Bend, Ind., Sept. 8, 1933; s. Michael Paul and Elizabeth (Bukovits) N.; m. Doris Louise Hollister, Aug. 16, 1952; children: Michele, Christopher, Stephen, Maureen. BA cum laude, N.Mex. Highlands U., 1957; MA, U. Mich., 1959, PhD, 1970. Tchr., coach Sound Bend Sch. Corp., 1959-61, adminstr., 1962-64; mem. faculty, adminstr. Ft. Lewis Coll., Durango, Colo., 1964-79, dean students, 1970-79; dean student affairs, v.p. external rels. Colo. Sch. Mines, Golden, 1979-89; v.p. instnl. advancement, exec. asst. to pres. Mesa State Coll., Grand Junction, Colo., 1989—; chmn., bd. dirs. Ctr. for Applied Rsch. in Prevention Abuse, Boulder, Colo., 1987—. Bd. dirs. United Way, Grand Junction, 1989-92; mem. Grand Junction Park Adv. Bd., 1990—, Rep. Presdl. Task Force, Nat. Rep. Senatorial Com. Named hon. col. 115th Engr. Rgts., 1986. Mem. NRA, Club 20 (officer, bd. dirs. 1991—), Rotary (past officer Grand Junction, bd. dirs. 1990-91), Phi Delta Kappa. Republican. Roman Catholic. Office: Mesa State Coll Grand Junction CO 81502

NYIRI, JOSEPH ANTON, sculptor, art educator; b. Racine, Wis., May 24, 1937; s. Joseph Anton Nyiri and Dorothy Marion (Larson) Zink; m. Laura Lee Primeau, Aug. 29, 1959 (dec. Mar. 1982); children: Krista, Nicole, Page; m. Melissa Trent, July 28, 1985. BA, U. Wis., 1959, MS, 1961. Tchr. art Madison (Wis.) Sch. Dist., 1959-62; art cons. San Diego Unified Schs., 1962-65, dist. resource tchr., 1965-73, regional tchr. occupational art, 1973-76, mentor tchr., 1985—; sculptor San Diego, 1962—, fine arts cons., 1966—; head dept. art edn. Serra High Sch., San Diego, 1976—; instr. art U. Calif. at San Diego, La Jolla, 1967-80, San Diego State U. Extension, 1969—; fine art restorer, 1963—, lectr. art and art edn., 1963—; pvt. art tchr. San Diego City Zoo. Exhibited sculpture in numerous one-man, two-person, juried and invitational shows, 1960—, U. Mex.-Baja Calif., 1983; rev. Calif. Art Rev., 1989. Active Art Guild San Diego Mus. Art; bd. dirs. San Diego Art Inst. Sgt. Wis. N.G., 1955-61. Named One of 3 Tchrs. of Yr., San Diego County, 1983, One of Outstanding Art Tchrs. in U.S., RISD, 1984, Secondary Tchr. of Yr., San Diego City Schs., 1982; recipient creativity award Pacific Inst., 1969. Mem. Arts/Worth: Nat. Coun. Art (charter), Allied Craftsmen San Diego, Internat. Platform Assn., San Diego Art Inst. (bd. dirs.), San Diego Mus. Art (mem. Art Guild). Democrat. Mem. Christian Ch. Home: 3525 Albatross St San Diego CA 92103-4807 Office: Serra High Sch 5156 Santo Rd San Diego CA 92124-2098

NYMAN, DAVID HAROLD, nuclear engineer; b. Aberdeen, Wash., May 21, 1938; s. Carl Victor and Elsie Ingagord (Laaksonen) N.; m. Lawana Flora Rice, July 19, 1939. Assoc., Grays Harbor Coll., 1958; BSMetE, U. Wash., 1961, MSMetE, 1963. Engr. Gen. Electric Co., Richland, Wash., 1963-68; engring. specialist United Nuclear Corp., New Haven, 1968-73; mgr. Westinghouse Hanford subs. Westinghouse Corp., Richland, 1973—. Contbr. articles to profl jours. Mem. Robotics Internat. of Soc. Mfg. Engrs. (div. chmn. 1985-86, tech. v.p. 1986-88), Robots West Conf. (adv. com. 1984, vice-chmn. 1986, Pres.'s award 1989), Am. Nuclear Soc. (chmn. meetings, proceedings, and transactions com. 1992—), Am. Soc. Metals., Inst. Nuclear Materials Mgmt., Columbia Basin Dog Tng. Club (pres. 1982-84), Richland Kennel Club, West Highland White Terrier Club of Puget Sound, West Highland White Terrier Club Am. (obedience com. 1982-88), Am. Kennel Club (judge tracking dog excellent tests). Republican. Lutheran.

NYPAN, LESTER JENS, retired mechanical engineer; b. Mpls., Oct. 30, 1929; s. Jens and Lillian Louisa (Martinson) N.; m. Yoko Aoki, Dec. 15, 1954 (dec. 1982); m. Dorothy L.M. Koe, Nov. 3, 1982; 1 child, Jade. BS, U. Minn., 1951, MSME, 1952, PhD, 1960. Registered profl. engr., Calif. Instr. U. Minn., Mpls., 1954-60; sr. engr. Lockheed Calif., Burbank, Calif., 1960-62; prof. mech. engring. Calif. State U., Northridge, 1962-91. Contbr. articles to profl. jours. Maj. USAF, 1952-72; PTO. Mem. Am. Soc. Engring. Edn., ASME, Nat. Soc. Profl. Engrs., Tau Beta Pi, Pi Tau Sigma. Home: 9515 Gladbeck Ave Northridge CA 91324-2221 Office: California State Univ 18111 Nordhoff St Northridge CA 91330-0001

NYQUIST, MAURICE OTTO, federal parks agency manager and scientist; b. Fairmont, Minn., May 30, 1944; s. Carl Arther and Wilda Yvette (Freitag) N.; m. Mary Maud Magee, Aug. 8, 1977; children: Gretchen, Beth. BS in Biology, Hamline U., 1966; MA in Biology, Mankato State U., 1968; PhD in Zoology, Wash. State U., 1973. Asst. prof. zoology Wash. State U., Pullman, 1973-74; scientist Nat. Park Svc., Lakewood, Colo., 1974-76, mgr., 1979—; cons. Ch2M-Hill, Seattle, 1972-73. Dir. prodn. interactive computer exhibit on remote sensing for Denver Mus. Nat. History; contbr. sci. articles to profl. jours. Bd. dirs. Nat. Park Service Equal Employment Opportunity Com., Denver, 1981, chmn., 1982. Recipient Mgrs. award Nat. Park Service, Lakewood, 1981, Performance Commendation award, 1988; research grantee Nat. Rifle Assn., 1972. Mem. Am. Soc. Potogrammetry and Remote Sensing (exec. com., bd. dirs., 1988-90, v.p. 1992, pres. elect 1993, asst. dir. remote sensing applications div., 1985-87, dir. 1988-90), Am. Congress on Surveying and Mapping (joint satellite mappingand remote sensing com.), The Wildlife Soc., GRASS Users Group (steering com. 1986—, treas., 1987—), ELAS Users Group (co-chmn. 1985-86, chmn. 1986-87), Sigma Xi. Office: Nat Park Svc GIS Div-WASO PO Box 25287 Denver CO 80225-0287

NYSTROM, CLAIR KARL, electronics engineer; b. Havre, Mont., June 19, 1947; s. Karl A. and Ruth (Cooper) N.; m. Linda L. Haines, Aug. 18, 1968. BS in Indsl. Edn., Walla Walla Coll., 1971; postgrad., No. Mont. Coll., 1988. Owner, prin. avionics shop, Dillingham, Alaska, 1971-74; tchr. electronics Dillingham High Sch., 1973-74; electronics technician Radio Shack, Havre, 1977-78; avionics mechanic Farrell Aircraft Svc., Havre, 1978-79; biomed. electronics technician No. Mont. Hosp., Havre, 1979-83; electronics field svc. engr. Picker Internat., Havre, 1983-92; instr. electronics No. Mont. Coll., Havre, 1983-91; owner Micro Designs, 1989—. Lectr., asst. community health programs Havre Seventh-Day Adventist Ch., 1984—, elder, deacon, tchr., 1984—. Mem. ASME. Republican. Home: 403 19th St PO Box 1 Havre MT 59501 Office: 403 19th St Havre MT 59501

NYSTROM, ROBERT ERIC, computer company executive, consultant; b. San Francisco, July 31, 1954; s. Doyle Duane and Mary Louise (MacDougall) N. BA, U. Calif., Berkeley, 1977. Sr. software engr. Momentum Computer Systems, San Jose, Calif., 1982-84, Counterpoint Computers Inc., San Jose, 1984-88; product mgr. Acer Counterpoint, San Jose, 1988-89; dir. product mgmt. Acer Am. Corp., San Jose, 1989-92, dir. product mktg., 1992—; instr. U. Calif. Santa Cruz Extension, 1991, Northeastern U., San Jose, 1986-87; tng. cons. Gawain Group, San Francisco, 1983—; software cons. Mountain View, Calif., 1983—. Lt. U.S. Navy, 1977-81. Mem. Usenix Assn., Uni Forum. Office: Acer Am Corp 2641 Orchard Pky San Jose CA 95134

OAK, CLAIRE MORISSET, artist, educator; b. St. Georges, Quebec, Can., May 31, 1921; came to U.S., 1945; d. Louis and Bernadette (Coulombe) Morisset; m. Alan Ben Oak, July 2, 1947. Student, Ecole des Beaux Arts, 1938-42, Parsons Sch. Design, N.Y.C., 1945, Art Students League, N.Y.C., 1945-46. Staff artist Henry Morgan & R. Simpson, Montreal, 1942-45; artist illustrator W.B. Golovin Advt. Agy., N.Y.C., 1947-49; freelance illustrator Arnold Constable & Advt. Agy., N.Y.C., 1948-50, Le Jardin des Modes, Paris, 1950-51, May & Co., L.A., 1956, Katten & Marengo Advt. Agy., Stockton, Calif., 1962-84; pvt. practice illustrator, designer San Joaquin Valley, Calif., 1984-92; art instr. San Joaquin Delta Coll., Stockton, 1973—; owner Fashion Illustrator's Workshop, N.Y.C., 1953-54; instr. Bauder Coll., Sacramento, 1975-76; painting workshop leader Lodi Art Ctr., 1991—; watercolor workshop leader D'Pharr Painting Adventures, Virginia City, Nev., 1992. Named S.B. Anthony Woman of Achievement in the Arts, U. Pacific, 1982. Mem. Stockton Art League, Lodi Art Ctr., Ctrl. Calif. Art League, The League of Carmichael Artists, Delta Watercolor Soc. (bd. mem. 1988—). Home: 2140 Waudman Ave Stockton CA 95209

OAKES, TERRY LOUIS, retail clothing store executive; b. Denver, June 12, 1953; s. Robert Walter and Stella Marie (Ray) O.; m. Cynthia Alison Bailey, Jan. 10, 1981; children: Madeleine Bailey, Robert Alan. BBA, So. Meth. U., 1975. Dept. mgr. Woolf Bros., Dallas, 1975-76; buyer I.K.O. Dry Goods, Denver, 1976-79, gen. sales mgr., 1979-81, exec. v.p., mdse. mgr., 1981-86; nat. sales mgr. Fresh Squeeze div. Bayly Corp., Denver, 1986-88; owner, pres. Bolderdash, Denver, 1988—; mem. adv. bd. fashion mdse. divsn. Colo. Inst. Art., Denver, 1991—. Democrat. Presbyterian. Home: 5332 S Geneva Way Englewood CO 80111-6219 Office: Bolderdash 2817 E 3d Ave Denver CO 80206

OAKESHOTT, GORDON B(LAISDELL), geologist; b. Oakland, Calif., Dec. 24, 1904; s. Philip S. and Edith May (Blaisdell) O.; m. Beatrice Clare Darrow, Sept. 1, 1929 (dec. 1982); children: Paul Darrow, Phyllis Joy Oakeshott Martin, Glenn Raymond; m. Lucile Spangler Burks, 1986. BS, U. Calif., 1928, MS, 1929; PhD, U. So. Calif., 1936. Asst. field geologist Shell Oil Co., 1929-30; instr. earth sci. Compton Coll., 1930-48; supervising mining geologist Calif. Div. Mines, 1948-56, dep. chief, 1956-57, chief, 1958; dep. chief Calif. Div. Mines and Geology, 1959-72; cons. geologist, 1973-85, ret.; lectr. geology Calif. State U., Sacramento, 1972-73, Calif. State U., San Francisco, 1975. Author: California's Changing Landscapes—A Guide to the Geology of the State, 1971, 2d edit., 1978, Volcanoes and Earthquakes-Geologic Violence, 1975, Japanese edit., 1981, My California: Autobiography of a Geologist with a Tribute to Don Tocher, 1989; contbr. articles to profl. jours. Fellow AAAS, Geol. Soc. Am., Calif. Acad. Sci.; mem. Seismol. Soc. Am., Nat. Assn. Geology Tchrs. (pres. 1970-71, Webb award 1981), Assn. Petroleum Geologists (hon., Michel T. Halbouty Human Needs award 1993), AIME, Mining and Metall. Soc. Am., Peninsula Geol. Soc. (past pres.), Engrs. Club San Francisco, Geol. Soc. Sacramento (past pres.), Peninsula Gem and Geol. Soc. (hon.), Assn. Engring. Geologists (hon.), Earthquake Engring. Research Inst. (past dir.), Am. Inst. Profl. Geologists (emeritus). Home and Office: Byron Park # 443 1700 Tice Valley Blvd Walnut Creek CA 94595

OAKLEY, CAROLYN LE, state legislator, small business owner; b. Portland, Oreg., June 28, 1942; d. George Thomas and Ruth Alveta Victoria (Engberg) Penketh; m. Donald Keith Oakley, June 27, 1965; children: Christine, Michelle. BS in Edn., Oreg. State U., 1965. Educator Linn County (Oreg.) Schs., 1965-76; owner Linn County Tractor, 1965-90; mem. Oreg. Legis. Assembly, Salem, 1989—, asst. majority leader, 1993—; mem. exec. bd. Oreg. Retail Coun., 1987-90. Chmn. Linn County Rep. Ctrl. Com., 1982-84; chmn. bd. dirs. North Albany Svc. Dist., 1988-90; chair Salvation Army, Linn and Benton Counties, 1987—; vice-chmn. bd. trustees Linn-Benton Community Coll. Found., 1987—; pres. Women for Agr., Linn and Benton Counties, 1984-86; mem. STRIDE Leadership Round Table, 1991—; state chair Am. Legis. Exch. Coun., 1991—, nat. bd. dirs., 1992—; active Edn. Comsn. of the States, 1991—. Named Woman of Yr. Albany chpt. Beta Sigma Phi, 1970. Mem. Nat. Conf. State Legislators (chmn. edn. com. 1992—), Albany C. of C. (bd. dirs. 1986—), Linn County Rep. Women (legis. chmn. 1982-91). Republican. Methodist. Home: 3197 NW Crest Loop Albany OR 97321-9627 Office: Oreg Legis Assembly State Capitol Salem OR 97310

OAKS, DALLIN HARRIS, lawyer, church official; b. Provo, Utah, Aug. 12, 1932; s. Lloyd E. and Stella (Harris) O.; m. June Dixon, June 24, 1952; children: Sharmon, Cheri Lyn, Lloyd D., Dallin D., TruAnn, Jenny June. B.A. with high honors, Brigham Young U., 1954, LL.D. (hon.), 1980; J.D. cum laude, U. Chgo., 1957; LL.D. (hon.), Pepperdine U., 1982, So. Utah U., 1991. Bar: Ill. 1957, Utah 1971. Law clk. to Supreme Ct. chief justice Earl Warren, 1957-58; with firm Kirkland, Ellis, Hodson, Chaffetz & Masters, Chgo., 1958-61; mem. faculty U. Chgo. Law Sch., 1961-71, assoc. dean and acting dean, 1962, prof., 1964-71, mem. vis. com., 1971-74; pres. Brigham Young U., Provo, Utah, 1971-80; also prof. law J. Reuben Clark Law Sch., 1974-80; justice Utah Supreme Ct., 1981-84; mem. Coun. of Twelve Apostles Ch. Jesus Christ of Latter Day Sts., 1984—; legal counsel Bill of Rights com. Ill. Constl. Conv., 1970. Author: (with G.G. Bogert) Cases on Trusts, 1967, 78, (with W. Lehman) A Criminal Justice System and The Indigent, 1968, The Criminal Justice Act in the Federal District Courts, 1969, (with M. Hill) Carthage Conspiracy, 1975, Trust Doctrines in Church Controversies, 1984, Pure in Heart, 1988, The Lord's Way, 1991; editor: The Wall Between Church and State, 1963. Mem. Wilson coun. Woodrow Wilson Internat. Center for Scholars, 1973-80; trustee Intermountain Health Care Inc., 1975-80; mem. adv. com. Nat. Inst. Law Enforcement and Criminal Justice, 1974-76; bd. dirs. Rockford Inst., 1976—, Notre Dame Center for Constl. Studies, 1977-80; bd. dirs. Pub. Broadcasting Service, 1977-85, chmn., 1980-85; bd. dirs. Polynesian Cultural Ctr., 1987—, chmn. 1988—. Fellow Am. Bar Found. (exec. dir. 1970-71); mem. Am. Assn. Pres. Ind. Colls. and Univs. (pres. 1975-78, dir. 1971-78), Order of Coif. Mem. Ch. of Jesus Christ of Latter-day Saints (regional rep. 1974-80; past 1st counselor Chgo. South Stake). Address: 47 E S Temple St Salt Lake City UT 84150

OAKS, M(ARGARET) MARLENE, minister; b. Grove City, Pa., Mar. 30, 1940; d. Allen Roy and Alberta Bell (Pinner) Eakin; m. Lowell B. Chaney, July 30, 1963 (dec. Jan. 1977); children: Christopher Allen, Linda Michelle; m. Harold G. Younger, Aug. 1978 (div. 1986); m. Gilbert E. Oaks, Aug. 3, 1987. BA, Calif. State U., L.A., 1972; religious sci. studies with several instrs. Ordained to ministry Ch. Religious Sci., 1986. Tchr. Whittier (Calif.) Sch. Dists., 1972-74, Garden Grove (Calif.) Sch. Dist., 1974-78; instr. Fullerton Coll., 1974-75; founding min. Community Ch. of the Islands (now Ch. of Religious Sci.), Honolulu, 1978-80; min. Ch. of Divine Sci., Pueblo, Colo., 1980-83; founding min. Ch. Religious Sci., Palo Alto, Calif., 1983-86; min. Ch. Religious Sci., Fullerton, Calif., 1986—; workshop leader Religious Sci. Dist. Conv., San Jose, Calif., 1985, Internat. New Thought Alliance Conf., Las Vegas, 1984, Calgary, Alta., Can., 1985, Washington, 1988, Denver, 1989, Anaheim, Calif., 1990, Las Vegas, Nev., 1992, Golden Valley Unity Women's Advance, Mpls., 1986, 87, Qume Corp., San Jose, 1985. Author: The Christmas in You, 1983, Ki Aikido the Inner Martial Art, 1984, Old Time Religion is a Cult, 1985, Beyond Forgiveness, 1985, 2nd rev. edit. 1992, Service the Sure Path to Enlightenment, 1985, Stretch Marks on My Aura, 1987, Beyond Addiction, 1990, 10 Core Concepts of Science of Mind, 1991, Forgiveness and Beyond, 1992 rev. edit.; contbr. articles to profl. publs. Del. Soviet and Am. Citizens Summit Conf., 1988, 89; pres. Soviet-Am. New Thought Initiatives, 1991chair conf. St. Petersburg, Moscow, 1992, Moscow, 1992, weekly radio program Radio Moscow, Phillipines, 1992—; founder Op. K.I.D.S.; founder, bd. dirs. Awakening Oaks Found., 1990; pres. Santi, 1991—. Named Outstanding Businesswoman, Am. Businesswomen's Assn., 1989. Mem. Fullerton Inerfaith Ministerial Assn. (sec. treas. 1987-89, pres. 1991-92), United Clergy of Religious Sci. (treas. 1991-92, sec. 1992—), Internat. New Thought Alliance (O.C. chpt. pres. 1990), S.Am. New Thought Initiative (pres. 1991—, chair New Thought Conf. 1991), Soroptimists (chair com. internat. coop. and goodwill 1987-88), Kappa Delta Pi. Republican. Office: Ch of Today 117 N Pomona Ave Fullerton CA 92632-1912

OBER, STEPHEN HENRY, entrepreneur, medical company executive; b. Mankato, Minn., Apr. 19, 1949; s. Edgar B. and Ann (Morgan) O.; children: Nathanial, Ann. BA, U. Minn., 1972; MBA, Coll. St. Thomas, St. Paul, Minn., 1984. Mktg. assoc. Am. Med. Systems, Mpls., 1976-80; dir. mktg. Empi, Inc., Mpls., 1980-85; pres. Iomed, Inc., Salt Lake City, 1985-92, also bd. dirs.; mem. indsl. adv. bd. Coll. Engring., Salt Lake City, 1989-92. Patentee in field. V.p. Our Savior's Luth. Ch., 1989-90. Mem. Young Pres.'s Orgn. Democrat. Office: Iomed Inc 1290 W 23d S Salt Lake City UT 84119

OBERG, OWEN HENRY, retired navy officer; b. Athol, Mass., Feb. 3, 1925; s. Elizabeth Ermine (Perry) Oberg. Student, Holy Cross Coll., 1944; BS, Stanford U., 1957; grad., Nat. War Coll., 1969; MS in Internat. Affairs, George Washington U., 1976. Commd. ens. USN, 1946, advanced through grades to rear admiral, 1972, commanding officer USS Caliente, 1969-71, commanding officer USS Kitty Hawk, 1972; chief fleet coord. group USN, Saigon, Vietnam, 1972-73; comdr. carrier group 7 USN, 1973-75, dep. chief of staff for ops. and plans Pacific Fleet Hdqrs., 1975, ret., 1977; program mgr. Hughes Aircraft Co., L.A., 1977-81; product line mgr. Cubic Corp., San Diego, 1981-87. Home: PO Box 1143 Pauma Valley CA 92061-1143

OBERMAN, NORMAN CHARLES, psychoanalyst; b. L.A., May 12, 1929; s. Leon and Anna Greenberg; m. Edna Segal (div. 1966); m. Janet Goodel Winer, Nov. 6, 1966; children: Nina, Matthew. AB, U. Calif., Berkeley, 1952; PhD, Brandeis U., 1964. Pvt. practice clin. psychologist L.A., 1966—; co-founder L.A. Inst. & Soc. for Psychoanalytic Studies, 1966, pres., 1974-75, dean, 1988-91. Mem. APA (psychoanalysis div.), Internat. Psychoanalytical Assn. (tng. analyst). Home and Office: 136 N Formosa Ave Los Angeles CA 90036-2818

OBERSTEIN, MARYDALE, geriatric specialist; b. Red Wing, Minn., Dec. 30, 1942; d. Dale robert and Jean Ebba-Marie (Holmquist) Johnson; children from previous marriage: Kirk Robert, Mark Paul; children: MaryJean. Student, U. Oreg., 1961-62, Portland State U., 1962-64, Long Beach State U., 1974-76. Cert. geriatric specialist, Calif. Florist, owner Sunshine Flowers, Santa Ana, Calif., 1982—; pvt. duty nursing aide Aides in Action, Costa Mesa, Calif., 1985-87; owner, adminstr. Lovelight Christian Home for the Elderly, Santa Ana, 1987—; activity dir. Bristol Care Nursing Home, Santa Ana, 1985-88; evangelist, speaker radio show Sta. KPRZ-FM, Anaheim, Calif., 1985-88; nursing home activist in reforming laws to eliminate bad homes, 1984-86; founder, tchr. hugging classes/healing therapy, 1987—. Bd. dirs. Orange County Coun. on Aging, 1984—; chairperson Helping Hands, 1985—, Pat Robertson Com., 1988, George Bush Presdl. Campaign, Orange County, 1988; bd. dirs., v.p. Women Aglow Orange County, 1985—; evanglist, pub. speaker, v.p. Women Aglow Huntington Beach. Recipient Carnation Silver Bowl Carnation Svc. Co., 1984-85; named Woman of Yr., Kiwanis, 1985, ABI, 1990, Am. Bio. Soc.; honored AM Los Angeles TV Show, Lt. Gov. McCarthy, 1984. Mem. Calif. Assn. Residential Care Homes, Orange County Epilepsy Soc. (bd. dirs. 1986—), Calif. Assn. Long Term Facilities. Home: 2722 S Diamond St Santa Ana CA 92704-6013

OBERTI, SYLVIA MARIE ANTOINETTE, rehabilitation counselor and administrator, career advisor, textile consultant; b. Fresno, Calif., Dec. 29, 1952; d. Silvio Lawrence and Sarah Carmen (Policarpo) O. BA in Communicative Disorders, Calif. State U.-Fresno, 1976, MA in Rehab. Counseling, 1977. Lic. vocat. cons., Calif.; cert. rehab. counselor Commn. Rehab. Counselors; cert. life tchr. community coll., nat. cert. counselor. Sr. rehab. cons. Crawford Rehab. Services, Inc., Emeryville, Calif., 1978-80; vocat. rehab. counselor Rehab. Assocs., Inc., San Leandro, Calif., 1980-81; owner, textile cons. Rugs and Carpets of the Orient, Oakland, Calif., 1979—; exec. dir. TheOberti Co., Oakland and San Jose, Calif., 1981—; cons. to industry, ins. cos., disabled, ADA; tchr. job seeking skills to the disabled. Bd. dirs., treas. Pacific Basin Sch. Textile Arts, 1982-86; active Calif. Assn. Physically Handicapped, Inc., 1976—, Women Entrepreneurs, 1981—. HEW grantee, 1976-77; first woman to solo and finish Mille Miglia, 1992; recipient Pacific Region Community Svc. Trophy Ferrari Club Am., 1992, Silver award Musical Watch Veteran Car Club Mille Miglia Organizers, 1992, 93. Mem. Am. Personnel and Guidance Assn., Am. Rehab. Counseling Assn., Calif. Assn. Rehab. Profls., Indsl. Claims Assn., Internat. Round Table Advancement of Counseling, Nat. Rehab. Assn., Nat. Rehab. Counseling Assn., Nat. Vocat. Guidance Assn., LWV. Office: 3629 Grand Ave Ste 101 Oakland CA 94610-2009

OBNINSKY, VICTOR PETER, lawyer; b. San Rafael, Calif., Oct. 12, 1944; s. Peter Victor and Anne Bartholdi (Donston) O.; m. Clara Alice Bechtel, June 8, 1969; children: Mari, Warren. BA, Columbia U., 1966; JD, U. Calif., Hastings, 1969. Bar: Calif. 1970. Sole practice, Novato, Calif., 1970—; arbitrator Marin County Superior Ct., San Rafael, 1979—; superior ct. judge pro tem, 1988-90. lectr. real estate and ptnrship. law. Author: The Russians in Early California, 1966. Bd. dirs. Calif. Young Reps., 1968-69, Richardson Bay San. Dist., 1974-75, Marin County Legal Aid Soc., 1976-78; baseball coach Little League, Babe Ruth League, 1970-84; mem. nat. panel consumer arbitrators Better Bus. Bur., 1974-88; leader Boy Scouts Am., 1970-84; permanent sec. Phillips Acad. Class of 1962; mem. Phillips Acad. Alumni Council, 1991; bd. community advisors Buck Ctr. for Rsch. on Aging. Mem. State Bar Calif., ABA, Marin County Bar Assn. (bd. dirs. 1985-91, treas. 1987-88, pres.-elect 1989, pres. 1990), Phi Delta Phi, Phi Gamma Delta. Republican. Russian Orthodox. Office: 2 Commercial Blvd Apt 103 Novato CA 94949-6121

O'BRIANT, JENNIFER LYNNE, cosmetics professional; b. Spartanburg, S.C., Sept. 5, 1963; d. Walter Herbert and Mary (Prevette) O'B. BA in Philosophy, U. Pa., 1985. Sales assoc. Macy's, Athens, Ga., 1983-85; buyer Mansour's, La Grange, Ga., 1985-87, div. mdse. mgr., 1988-90; territory mgr. Calvin Klein Cosmetics, Denver, 1990—. Democrat. Home and Office: 7777 E Yale Ave # L308 Denver CO 80231

O'BRIEN, GEORGE DONOGHUE, JR., engineering consultant company executive; b. Detroit, Feb. 4, 1938; s. George Donoghue and Margaret (Foley) O'B.; m. Elise Maria Montilla, May 28, 1961; children: George III, Caroline, Kevin, Roseleen. BS, US Naval Acad., 1960; PhD, Naval Postgrad. Sch., 1970. Commd. ensign USN, 1960, advanced through grades to capt., 1982, naval aviator, test pilot, 1961-75, comdg. officer Attack Squadron 35, 1977-78, comdr. officer nuclear powered aircraft carrier, 1986-89, ret., 1989; pres., ceo Cygna Group, Oakland, Calif., 1990-92; chmn. infrastructure group ICF Kaiser Engrs., Oakland, 1991—. Chmn. Alameda County Bus. Devel. Com., Oakland, 1991-92. Decorated Legion of Merit, others. Mem. Bohemian Club San Francisco, St. Francis Yacht Club. Roman Catholic. Home: 1216 Paru St Alameda CA 94501 Office: ICF Kaiser Engrs 1800 Harrison St Oakland CA 94612-3430

O'BRIEN, HAROLD ALOYSIUS, JR., nuclear chemist, physics researcher, consultant; b. Dallas, May 17, 1936; s. Harold Aloysius and Adelaide (Esser) O'B.; m. Ann Akard, Aug. 22, 1958; children: Walter, Sheri, Matthew. BA, U. Tex., 1959; MS, N.Mex. State U., 1961; PhD, U. Tenn., 1968. Hon. diplomate Am. Bd. Sci. in Nuclear Medicine. Rsch. scientist Oak Ridge (Tenn.) Nat. Lab., 1962-68; mem. rsch. staff Los Alamos Nat. Lab., 1968-74, 86—, asssoc. group leader, 1974-80, group leader, 1980-85; vis. scientist Lawrence Berkeley (Calif.) Lab., 1985-86, Lawrence Livermore (Calif.) Lab., 1985-86, U. Calif., Davis, 1985-86; bd. dirs. Am. Bd. Sci. in Nuclear Medicine, 1976-85, pres., 1983-85; bd. dirs. Rho Med, Inc., Albuquerque; mem. subcom. on nuclear and radio chemistry NAS-NRC, 1974-78; mem. spl. study sect. NIH, 1976. Contbr. numerous articles to profl. jours., chpts. to books; patentee in field. Chmn. N.Mex. Radiation Tech. Adv. Coun., Santa Fe, 1974-85, 90—. Mem. Am. Chem. Soc. (exec. com. 1981-84), AAAS, Soc. Nuclear Medicine (trustee 1975-76, bd. dirs. Edn. and Rsch. Found. 1985—). Home: 107 La Senda Rd Los Alamos NM 87544-3819 Office: Los Alamos Nat Lab Physics Div MS D434 PO Box 1663 Los Alamos NM 87545

O'BRIEN, HOLLY, accountant; b. Chgo., June 22, 1946; d. Albert and Virginia Marjorie (Pyne) Schelling; m. Robert T. O'Brien (div. 1982); children: Becky Jacques, Donald Baber. Student, U. Wash., 1968. Acct. Am. Express, Phoenix, 1970-75, D.C. Speer Constrn., Phoenix, 1975-82, Swiss Am. Corp., Phoenix, 1982-84; sr. account cons. TRW Info. Systems, Phoenix and Pleasanton, Calif., 1984-88; acct. Carson Messinger Elliott Laughling & Ragan, Phoenix, 1988—. Pres. Neighborhood Coalition Greater Phoenix, 1990—; chair Encanto Village Planning Com., Phoenix, 1991—; mem. Indian Sch. Task Force, Phoenix, 1991; bd. dirs. Valley Partnership, Phoenix, 1992. Mem. Ariz. Rose Soc., Ariz. Common Cause, Paradise Rep. Women. Avocations: gardening, reading, watercolors. Office: Neighborhood Coalition Greater Phoenix PO Box 13057 Phoenix AZ 85002

O'BRIEN, JAMES PATRICK, geologist; b. Mt. Kisco, N.Y., Dec. 26, 1961; s. Paul William and Anne P. (Porter) O'B. BS, Ft. Lewis Coll., 1986; MS, Idaho State U., 1991. Geologist E. G. & G. Idao Nat. Engrng. Lab., Idaho Falls, 1988-89; teaching asst. Idaho State U., Pocatello, 1989; geologist Oreg. Dept. Mineral & Geology Industries, Baker, 1990-91; project geologist Ogden Environ. and Energy Svcs., Denver, 1991—. Am. Fedn. Mineral. Socs. scholar, 1989. Mem. Am. Assn. Petroleum Geologists, Geol. Soc. Am., Nat. Groundwater Assn., Sigma Xi. Home: 30 Debra Ann Rd Golden CO 80403 Office: Ogden Environ & Energy Svcs 4582 S Ulster St Pkwy Ste 415 Denver CO 80237

O'BRIEN, JOHN STEVEN, writer; b. Oxford, Ohio, May 21, 1960; s. William Frederick and Judith Rose (Soos) O'B.; m. Lisa Marie Kirkwood, Aug. 11, 1979 (div. May 1993). Grad. high sch., Lakewood, Ohio. Author: (novel) Leaving Las Vegas, 1991, (screenplay) The Rest of Jackie, 1992. Mem. Writer's Guild Am. Democrat. Office: PO Box 10575 Beverly Hills CA 90213

O'BRIEN, KEITH MICHAEL, hydrogeologist, consultant; b. Melrose, Mass., Aug. 11, 1954; s. Edward Joseph O'Brien and Marie Ellen (Moulaison) Drew; m. Amy Virginia Morse, Aug. 10, 1985; children: Reilly Gray Morse, MacKenzie Drew Morse. BA, Hamilton Coll., 1977; MS, U. Mass., 1982; postgrad., N.Mex. Inst. Mining and Tech., 1981-84. Registered geologist, Calif., Ariz., Oreg., Fla. Rsch. assoc. Mass. Water Resources Rsch. Ctr., Amherst, 1978-80; faculty assoc. Hampshire Coll., Amherst, 1980; hydrologist N.Mex. Bur. Mines and Mineral Resources, Socorro, 1981-84; assoc. geologist Stone & Webster Engrng. Corp., Boston, 1984; prin. hydrogeologist Harding Lawson Assocs., Novato, Calif., 1985-89; v.p. PES Environ., Inc., Novato, 1989—. Contbr. articles to profl. jours. Mem. Nicasio (Calif.) Design Rev. Com., 1990-92. Mem. Am. Geophys. Union, Assn. Groundwater Scientists and Engrs., Am. Water Works Assn. Home: 2099 Nicasio Valley Rd Nicasio CA 94946-0807

O'BRIEN, KEVIN CHARLES, product designer; b. Pitts., Dec. 30, 1957; s. Charles James and Minerva A. (Mars) O'B.; m. Ann Marie Poydock, Oct. 9, 1982; children: Michael James, Jessica Lynn, Kaitlyn Theresa. BS in Polymer Engrng., Case Western Res. U., 1979, MS in Macromolecular Engrng., 1981, PhD in Macromolecular Engrng., 1984. Grad. fellow Case Western Res. U., Cleve., 1979-82, staff technician I, 1982-84; postdoctoral research assoc. dept. chem. engrng. U. Tex., Austin, 1984-85; project leader Dow Chem. USA, Walnut Creek, Calif., 1985-89; product devel. engr. Raychem Corp, Menlo Park, Calif., 1989-91, sr. scientist automotive product devel., 1991-92; product devel. mgr. Landec Corp. for Med. Products, 1992—. Contbr. articles to profl. jours.; patentee in field. Instr. religious edn. Newman Cath. Ctr. U. Tex., Austin, 1985; indsl. mentor Industry Initiatives for Sci. and Math. Edn., 1987-88; project leader for Total Award Project of 1990. B.F. Goodrich fellow, 1981. Mem. Am. Phys. Soc., Am. Chem. Soc., Materials Rsch. Soc., N.Am. Membrane Soc., Soc. Automotive Engrs., Nat. Athletic Trainers Assn., Sigma Alpha Epsilon. Office: Landec Corp 3603 Haven Ave Menlo Park CA 94025

O'BRIEN, PAUL JERRY, publishing executive; b. Mpls., Apr. 30, 1925; s. John E. and Lauretta (Carroll) O'B.; divorced; children: John P., James G., Thomas R., Joan T. BA, Gonzaga U., 1951. Reporter Spokane (Wash.) Daily Chronicle, 1947-49; night editor AP, Spokane, 1949-51, bur. mgr., 1951-60; chief of bur. AP, Salt Lake City, 1960-63; asst. to pres. Kearns-Tribune Corp., Salt Lake City, 1963-84, sec., dir., 1969—; pub. The Salt Lake Tribune, Salt Lake City, 1984—; sec., dir. Tele-Communications, Inc., Denver, 1970—, Republic Pictures Corp., L.A., 1984—. Bd. regents Gonzaga U., Spokane, 1975-84; bd. dirs. Holy Cross Hosp., Salt Lake City, 1978-87, Utah Symphony Orch., Salt Lake City, 1982—; trustee Holy Cross Hosp. Found., 1987. Staff sgt. U.S. Army, 1943-45, ETO. Decorated D.F.C. Roman Catholic. Home: 2594 Walker Ln Salt Lake City UT 84117-7729 Office: Salt Lake Tribune 400 Tribune Bldg Salt Lake City UT 84110

O'BRIEN, PHILIP MICHAEL, library administrator; b. Albion, Nebr., Jan. 5, 1940; s. Lawrence Joseph and Mary Helen (Ruplinger) O'B.; m. Christina Bärtling, Jan. 22, 1968; children: Tara, Kirsten; m. Ann Topjon, Mar. 10, 1990. BA, Whittier Coll., 1961; MS in LS, U. So. Calif., 1962, PhD, 1974. Asst. libr. Whittier (Calif.) Coll., 1962-66; social scis. libr. Chico State Coll., 1966-67; spl. collections libr. Whittier Coll., 1970-74, libr. dir., 1974—; libr. U.S. Army, Fed. Republic of Germany, 1967-70. Author: T.E. Lawrence and Fine Printing, 1980, T.E. Lawrence A Bibliography, 1988 (Besterman medal 1989). Recipient Title II fellowship HEW, 1973-74; inducted into Whittier Coll. Athletic Hall of Fame, 1988. Mem. ALA, Assn. Coll. and Rsch. Librs., Calif. Pvt. Acad. Librs. (bd. dirs. 1984-87), Univ. Club Whittier (pres. 1984). Office: Whittier Coll Wardman Libr Whittier CA 90608

O'BRIEN, RAYMOND FRANCIS, transportation executive; b. Atchison, Kans., May 31, 1922; s. James C. and Anna M. (Wagner) O'B.; m. Mary Ann Baugher, Sept. 3, 1947; children: James B., William T., Kathleen A., Christopher R. B.S. in Bus. Adminstrn., U. Mo., 1948; grad., Advanced Mgmt. Program, Harvard, 1966. Accountant-auditor Peat, Marwick, Mitchell & Co., Kansas City, Mo., 1948-52; contr., treas. Riss & Co., Kansas City, Mo., 1952-58; regional contr. Consol. Freightways Corp. of Del., Indpls., also, Akron, Ohio, 1958-61; contr. Consol. Freightways, Inc., San Francisco, 1961—; v.p., treas. Consol. Freightways, Inc., 1962-63, bd. dirs., 1966, v.p. fin., 1967-69, exec. v.p., 1969-75, pres., 1975—, chief exec. officer, 1977-88, 90-91, chmn., 1988—; pres. CF Motor Freight subs. Consol. Freightways, Inc., 1973; dir. Transam. Corp., Watkins-Johnson, Inc.; past chmn. WesternHwy. Inst., Champion Road Machinery, Ltd. Former mem. bus. adv. bd. Northwestern U., U. Calif., Berkeley; bd. dirs., regent, former chmn. bd. trustees St. Mary's Coll.; bd. dirs., regent Charles Armstrong Sch., 1991—; mem. Pres.'s Adv. Herbert Hoover Boys and Girls Club; dir. Boy Scouts Am. Bay Area Coun.; adv. coun. Nat. Commn. Against Drunk Driving. Served to 1st lt. USAAF, 1942-45. Recipient Disting. Svc. Citation Automotive Hall Fame, 1991; named Outstanding Chief Exec. five times Financial World Mag. Mem. Am. Trucking Assn. (bd. dirs. Found., exec. com.), Pacific Union Club, World Trade Club, Commonwealth Club (San Francisco), Burning Tree Country Club, Menlo Country Club. Home: 26347 Esperanza Dr Los Altos CA 94022-2601 Office: Consol Freightways Inc 3000 Sand Hill Rd Menlo Park CA 94025

O'BRIEN, ROBERT S., state official; b. Seattle, Sept. 14, 1918; s. Edward R. and Maude (Ransom) O'B.; m. Kathryn E. Arvan, Oct. 18, 1941 (dec. June 1984). Student public schs. With Kaiser Co., 1938-46; restaurant owner, 1946-50; treas. Grant County, Wash., 1950-65, State of Wash., 1965-89; chmn. Wash. State Fin. Com., 1965-89, Wash. Public Deposit Protection Commn., 1969-89, Wash. Public Employees Retirement Bd., 1969-77, Law Enforcement Officers and Firefighters Retirement System, 1971-77, Wash. State Investment Bd., 1981-89; retired, 1989; mem. Wash. Data Processing Adv. Bd., 1967-73; Gov.'s Exec. Mgmt. and Fiscal Affairs Com., 1978-80, Gov.'s Cabinet Com. on Tax Alternatives, 1978-80; trustee Wash. Tchr.'s Retirement System, 1965-89; bd. dirs. Centennial Bank, Olympia, Wash. Recipient Leadership award Joint Council County and City Employees-Fedn. State Employees, 1970, Eagles Leadership award, 1967. Mem. Nat. Assn. State Auditors, Comptrollers and Treasurers (pres. 1977), Nat. Assn. Mcpl. Fin. Officers, Nat. Assn. State Treasurers, Western State Treasurers Assn. (pres. 1970), Wash. County Treas. Assn. (pres. 1955-56), Wash. Assn. Elected County Ofcls. (pres. 1955-58), Olympia Area C. of C., Soap Lake C. of C. (pres. 1948). Democrat. Clubs: Elks (hon. life); Moose, Eagles, Lions, Olympia Yacht, Olympia Country and Golf; Empire (Spokane); Wash. Athletic (Seattle). Address: 3613 Plummer SE Olympia WA 98503

O'BRIEN, THOMAS JOSEPH, bishop; b. Indpls., Nov. 29, 1935. Grad., St. Meinrad Coll. Sem. Ordained priest Roman Catholic Ch., 1961. Bishop of Phoenix, 1982—. Office: 400 E Monroe St Phoenix AZ 85004-2376*

O'BYRNE, PAUL J., bishop; b. Calgary, Alta., Can., Dec. 21, 1922. Ordained priest Roman Catholic Ch., 1948; bishop of Calgary, 1968—. Office: Cath Pastoral Care Ctr, 1916 2d Ave SW Room 205, Calgary, AB Canada T2S 1S3*

OCCHIATO, MICHAEL ANTHONY, city official; b. Pueblo, Colo.; s. Joseph Michael and Joan Occhiato; m. Peggy Ann Stefonowicz, June 27, 1964 (div. Sept. 1983); children: Michael, James, Jennifer; m. Patsy Gay Payne, June 2, 1984; children: Kim Carr, Jerry Don Webb. BBA, U. Denver, 1961; MBA, U. Colo., 1984; postgrad., U. So. Colo. Sales mgr. Tivoli Brewing co., Denver, 1965-67, acting brewmaster, prodn. control mgr., 1967-68, plant mgr., 1968-69; adminstrv. mgr. King Resources Co., Denver, 1969-70; ops. mgr. Canners Inc., Pepsi-Cola Bottling Co., Pueblo, 1970-76; pres. Pepsi-Cola Bottling Co., Pueblo, 1978-82; gen. mgr. Pepsi-Cola Bottling Group div. PepsiCo., Pueblo, 1982, area v.p., 1982-83; ind. cons. Pueblo, 1983—; pres. Ethnic Foods Internat. dba Taco Rancho, Pueblo, Colo.; chmn. Weifang (China) Sister City del., 1991—; bd. dirs. HMO So. Colo. Health Plan, 1988—. Mem. coun. City of Pueblo, 1978—, pres., 1986, 87, 90, 91; mem. bd. health, 1978-80, regional planning commn., 1980-81, Pueblo Action Inc., 1978-80, Pueblo Planning and Zoning Commn., 1985; chmn. Pueblo Area Coun. Govts., 1980-82; mem. Pueblo Econ. Devel. Corp., 1983-91; chmn. fundraising Pueblo chpt. Am. Heart Assn., 1983—; bd. dirs. El Pueblo Boys Ranch, 1971-73; del. 1st World Conf. Local Elected Officials to 1st UN Internat. Coun. for Local Environ. Initiative. Lt. USN, 1961-65. Mem. So. Colo. Emergency Med. Technicians Assn. (pres. 1975), Pueblo C. of C., Pi Kappa Alpha (v.p. 1960). Lodge: Rotary. Home: 11 Harrogate Ter Pueblo CO 81001-1723 Office: City of Pueblo Office of Mayor 1 City Hall Pl Pueblo CO 81003-4239

OCCHIPINTI, CARL JOSEPH, broadcasting executive; b. New Orleans, Feb. 11, 1931; s. Victor and Anne (Maenza) O.; m. Ila M. Fanning, Nov. 22, 1939; children—Vickie, Michael, Diane. B.S., U. Wyo., 1956. Bus. and advt. mgr. Laramie (Wyo.) Newspapers, Inc., 1957-63; gen. mgr. Sta. KTVS-TV, Sterling, Colo., 1963-75; gen. mgr., v.p. Wyneco Communications, Inc., including Stas. KYCU-TV, Cheyenne, Wyo., KSTF-TV, Scottsbluff, Nebr., KTVS-TV, Sterling, Colo., 1975-86; gen. mgr. Sta. KGWN TV Cheyenne, 1986—, Sta. KSTF TV, Scottsbluff, Nebr., 1986—, Sta. KTVS TV, Sterling, Colo., Sta. KGWC TV, Casper Wyo., 1986—, STa. KGWL TV., Lander-Riverton, Wyo., Sta. KGWR TV, Rock Springs, Wyo., 1986—. With USAF, 1950-53. Mem. Advt. Assn. Denver, Colo. Broadcasters Assn. (past v.p.), Am. Legion, Cheyenne C. of C. (past 1st v.p.). Roman Catholic. Clubs: Cheyenne Country, Sterling Country, Elks. Office: Sta KGWN-TV 2923 E Lincolnway Cheyenne WY 82001-6199

OCHOA, ARMANDO, bishop; b. Oxnard, Calif., Apr. 3, 1943. Grad., Ventura (Calif.) Coll., St. John's Coll., Camarillo, Calif. Ordained priest Roman Cath. Ch., 1970. Titular bishop of Sitifi Calif.; aux. bishop, vicar gen. L.A., 1987—. Office: San Fernando Rectory 15101 San Fernando Mission Blvd Mission Hills CA 91345*

OCHOMOGO, MARÍA GARCÍA, manufacturing company executive; b. Holguin, Oriente, Cuba, Feb. 19, 1950; came to U.S., 1965; d. Ariel A. and Maria del C. (Fernandez) Garcia; m. Oscar Rene Ochomogo, May 29, 1971; children: Mary, Michelle, Oscar Jr. BS, La. State U., 1972, MS, 1974, PhD, 1978. Lab. mgr. Ralston Purina, Campinas, Brazil, 1974-76; rschr. La. State U., Baton Rouge, 1976-78; lab. mgr. Eggo Foods div. Kellogg's, Milpitas, Calif., 1978-85; R&D mgr. Bunge Foods div. Bunge Corp., Atlanta, 1985-87; sr. rsch. chemist Chevron Corp., Richmond, Calif., 1987-92; project mgr. The Clorox Co., Pleasanton, Calif., 1992—. Inventor a low voc pest conc., process stability of Orthene, A new pest tech. Vol. Young Rep. Party, 1968-72; vol. community sci. sch. program Chevron, Richmond, 1991, Clorox, 1992; coord. United Way Chevron Chem., Richmond, 1991. Named First Woman Sanitarian for La. State of La., 1973; T.H. Harris scholarship, La. State U., 1968-72. Mem. Am. Soc. Testing Materials, Chem. Specialty Mfg. Assn., Woeman Engrng. in Bus., Am. Chem. Soc., Inst. Food Technologist, Gamma Sigma Delta, Phi Tau Sigma. Home: 717 Westbrook Ct Danville CA 94506

OCKEY, RONALD J., lawyer; b. Green River, Wyo., June 12, 1934; s. Theron G. and Ruby O. (Sackett) O.; m. Arline M. Hawkins, Nov. 27, 1957; children: Carolyn S. Ockey Baggett, Deborah K. Ockey Christiansen, David, Kathleen M. Ockey Hellewell, Valerie Ockey Sachs, Robert. B.A., U. Utah, 1959, postgrad. 1959-60; J.D. with honors, George Washington U., 1966. Bar: Colo. 1967, Utah 1968, U.S. Dist. Ct. Colo. 1967, U.S. Dist. Ct. Utah 1968, U.S. Ct. Appeals (10th cir.) 1969, U.S. Ct. Claims 1987. Missionary to France for Mormon Ch., 1954-57; law clk. to judge U.S. Dist. Ct. Colo., 1966-67; assoc. ptnr., shareholder, v.p., treas., dir. Jones, Waldo, Holbrook & McDonough, Salt Lake City, 1967-91, pres., IntelliTrans Internat. Corp., 1992—; mem. Utah Ho. Reps., 1988-90, Utah State Senate, 1991—; lectr. in securities, pub. fin. and bankruptcy law. State govtl. affairs chmn. Utah Jaycees, 1969; del. state Rep. Convs., 1972-74, 1976-78, 1980-82, 84-86, del. Salt Lake County Rep. Conv., 1978-80, 88; sec. Wright for Gov. campaign, 1980; legis. dist. chmn. Utah Rep. Party, 1983-87; trustee Food for Poland, 1981—, pres., trustee, Unity to Assist Humanity Alliance, 1992—; bd. dirs. Utah Opera Co., 1991—; trustee, mem. exec. com. Utah Info. Tech. Assn., 1991—. Lt. U.S. Army, 1960-66; to capt. Judge Adv. Gen. USAR, 1966-81. Mem. Utah State Bar Assn. (various coms.), , Nat. Assn. Bond Lawyers (chmn. com. on state legislation 1982-85), George Washington U. Law Alumni Assn. (bd. dirs. 1981-85), Order of Coif, Salt Lake Rotary, Phi Delta Phi. Contbr. articles on law to profl. jours.; mem. editorial bd. Utah Bar Jour., 1973-75; mem. staff and bd. editors George Washington Law Rev., 1964-66. Home: 4502 Crest Oak Cir Salt Lake City UT 84124-3825 Office: 844 S 200 East Ste 150 Salt Lake City UT 84111

O'CONNELL, JOSEPH D., lawyer, magistrate; b. Boston, June 4, 1954; s. James S. and Mary A. (Kelly) O'C.; m. Karla F. Huntington, Aug. 13, 1983; children: Connor J., Jordan E. AB cum laude, Boston Coll., 1975; JD cum laude, Suffolk U., 1979. Bar: Mass. 1979, Ariz. 1980, Alaska 1981, U.S. Dist. Ct. Alaska 1981. Atty., VISTA vol. So. Ariz. Legal Aid, Tucson, 1979-81; atty. Alaska Legal Svcs. Corp., Anchorage, 1981-85; magistrate Alaska Ct. System, Palmer, 1985-90, Anchorage, 1991—. Mem. Amnesty Internat., Anchorage; bd. dirs. Abused Women's Aid in Crisis, Anchorage, 1982-85. Mem. Alaska Bar Assn. (family law com.), Mass. Bar Assn., Ariz. Bar Assn. Democrat. Home: 17720 Juanita Loop N Eagle River AK 99577

O'CONNELL, KATHY L., biochemist, research assistant; b. Saginaw, Mich., July 16, 1964; d. George A. and Jacqueline J. (Reeder) O'C. Student, Delta Coll., 1985; BA in Chemistry, Kalamazoo Coll., 1990. Technologist Dow Chem., Midland, Mich., 1984-86; lab. technician II Upjohn Co., Kalamazoo, Mich., 1986-91, biochemistry asst., 1991; rsch. asst. II Genentech, Inc., South San Francisco, 1991—. Contbr. articles to profl. jours. Kurt D. Kaufman Rsch. fellow Kalamazoo Coll., 1990. Mem. Am. Chem. Soc., Protein Soc., Am. Soc. for Mass Spectrometry. Office: Genentech Inc 460 Point San Bruno Blvd South San Francisco CA 94080-4918

O'CONNELL, KEVIN, lawyer; b. Boston, Sept. 4, 1933; s. Michael Frederick and Kathryn Agnes (Kelley) O'C.; m. Mary Adams, July 14, 1990; children: Tiffany W., Elizabeth H., Dana A., Liesel E. A.B., Harvard, 1955, J.D., 1960. Bar: Calif. 1961. Assoc. firm O'Melveny & Myers, L.A., 1960-63; asst. U.S. atty. criminal div. Cen. Dist. Calif., L.A., 1963-65; staff counsel Gov. Calif. Commn. to Investigate Watts Riot, L.A., 1965-66; ptnr. Tuttle & Taylor, L.A., 1966-70, Coleman & O'Connell, L.A., 1971-75; pvt. practice law L.A., 1975-78; of counsel firm Simon & Sheridan, L.A., 1978-89; ptnr. Manatt, Phelps, Phillips & Kantor, L.A., 1989—. Bd. editors: Harvard Law Rev, 1958-60. Mem. Los Angeles County (Calif.) Democratic Central Com., 1973-74. Served to lt. USMCR, 1955-57. Mem. Am. Law Inst. Home: 426 N Mccadden Pl Los Angeles CA 90004-1026 Office: Manatt Phelps Phillips & Kantor Trident Ctr E Tower 11355 W Olympic Blvd Los Angeles CA 90064-1614

O'CONNER, LORETTA RAE, former court reporter; b. Denver, Dec. 23, 1958; d. Ronald Lee and Norma Jareene (Warner) Barkdoll; m. George Ellis Bentley, Dec. 31, 1976 (div. 1979); m. Donald Hugh O'Conner, Feb. 3, 1987; children: Justin Lee, Brandon Craig. AS, Denver Acad. Ct. Reporting, 1983; BA summa cum laude, Regis U., 1992. Cert. registered profl. reporter. Ct. reporter Denver, 1983-87; dist. ct. reporter Judicial Dept., State of Colo., Pueblo, 1987-91; ct. reporter Pueblo, 1991-93. Chief justice Student Govt. Ct., U. So. Colo., Pueblo, 1992; trained facilitator Kettering Found., Pub. Policy, Dayton, Ohio, 1992; sec. So. Colo. Registered Interpretors for Deaf, Pueblo, 1991. U. So. Colo. Pres.'s scholar, 1991-92, Alumni Assn. scholar, 1991-92; Kettering Found. grantee, 1992; Colo. Legis. grant and scholarship, Regis U., 1992. Mem. Nat. Ct. Reporters Assn., Colo. Ct. Reporters Assn. Home: 1300 30th St D5-16 Boulder CO 80303

O'CONNOR, BRENDA ANNE, museum director, educator; b. Chehalis, Wash., June 27, 1959; d. Charles Rex and Joyce Jean (Hazelrigg) O'C. AA, Centralia (Wash.) Coll., 1979; BA in History, Western Wash. U., 1981, MA in Historic Preservation, 1984. Dir. Lewis County Mus., Chehalis, 1987—; mem. restoration com. Jackson Courthouse, Chehalis, 1989—; mem. Chehalis Hist. Preservation Commn., 1988—. Mem. Twin County Dems., 1990; trustee Sticklin-Greenwood Cemetery, Centralia, Wash. Recipient Citation for Vol. Work City of Chehalis, 1991. Mem. AAUW, Assn. for State and Local History, Wash. Trust for Hist. Preservation (bd. dirs.), St. Helens Club, St. Helens Running Club, Phi Alpha Theta. Office: Lewis County Hist Mus 599 NW Front Way Chehalis WA 98532-2048

O'CONNOR, CAROL ANN, history educator; b. Evanston, Ill., Feb. 14, 1946; d. Joseph L. and Veronica (Keller) O'C.; m. Clyde A. Milner II, Aug. 14, 1977; children: Catherine Carol Milner, Charles Clyde Milner. BA, Manhattanville Coll., 1967; M. Philosophy, Yale U., 1970, PhD, 1976. Instr. Phillips Exeter Acad., Exeter, N.H., 1972-73; asst. prof. Knox Coll., Galesburg, Ill., 1974-77; asst. prof. Utah State U., Logan, 1977-80, assoc. prof., 1980-86, prof., 1986—; dir. grad. studies history dept. Utah State U., Logan, 1988—. Author: A Sort of Utopia, 1983; bd. editors Utah Hist. Quar., 1989-92; contbr. articles to profl. jours. Recipient summer stipend Nat. Endowment for the Humanities, 1986. Mem. Urban History Assn. (exec. bd. 1989-90), Western History Assn., Orgn. Am. Historians, Am. Hist. Assn. Home: 1675 E 1400 N Logan UT 84321-2975 Office: Utah State U Dept History Logan UT 84322-0710

O'CONNOR, ELLEN SWANBERG, management educator, consultant; b. Chgo., May 21, 1954; d. William Harold and Mary (Herschel) S.; m. Richard Francis O'Connor, May 30, 1987; 1 child, Alex William. BA, U. Calif., Berkeley, 1976, MBA, 1983; MA, U. Chgo., 1977, PhD, 1990. Fin. analyst Hexcel Corp., San Francisco, 1980-83; adminstr. Fed. Res. Bank, San Francisco, 1983-85; mgmt. cons. Los Altos, Calif., 1985—; lectr. Calif. State U., San Francisco, 1989-92, Stanford (Calif.) U., 1992—. Contbr. articles to profl. jours. Vol. Project Victory, Palo Alto, Calif., 1985-88, The Trust for Hidden Villa, Los Altos Hills, 1988-89. Weinberg fellow U. Chgo., 1977-79. Mem. Acad. Mgmt., Western Acad. Mgmt., Calif. Alumni Assn. Office: Grad Sch Bus Stanford U Stanford CA 94305

O'CONNOR, JOHN JOSEPH, operations executive; b. Smyrna, Tenn., June 1, 1959; s. John O'Connor and Dolores Jane (Bell) Brem; m. Lea Ann Bradford, Sept. 6, 1986. BS, Tex. A&M U., 1981. Cert. marine engr. 3rd asst. engr. Marine Engrs. Beneficial Assn., Houston, 1981-84; asst. engr. Biehl Ship Mgmt., Houston, 1984; balance technician Hickham Industries, Inc., LaPorte, Tex., 1984-86, prodn. scheduler/Sulzer, 1986-87, project engr./Sulzer, 1987-88, engring. mgr./Sulzer, 1988-89; ops. mgr./Sulzer Hickham Industries, Inc., Huntington Beach, Calif., 1989-93; sr. engr., corp. mergers and acquisitions Hickham Industries, Inc., La Porte, Tex., 1993—; guest speaker Tex. A&M U., Galveston, Tex., College Station, Tex., 1981-89, U. Houston, 1986-89; moderator Power Machinery and Compressor Conf., Houston, 1989. Prin. engr. inventions in field (Achievement awards 1989). Recipient Outstanding Records in Engring., Gulf Oil Corp., Galveston, 1981. Mem. ASME (guest speaker convs.), Pacific Energy Assn. (guest speaker convs. 1990-92), Assn. of Former Students/Tex. A&M.

O'CONNOR, KARL WILLIAM, lawyer; b. Washington, Aug. 1, 1931; s. Hector and Lucile (Johnson) O'C.; m. Sylvia Gasbarri, Mar. 23, 1951 (dec.); m. Judith Ann Byers, July 22, 1972 (div. 1983); m. Eleanor Celler, Aug. 3, 1984 (div. 1986); m. Alma Hepner, Jan. 1, 1987; children: Blair, Frances, Brian, Brendan. BA, U. Va., 1952, JD, 1958. Bar: Va. 1958, D.C. 1959, Am. Samoa 1976, Calif. 1977, Oreg. 1993. Law clk. U.S. Dist. Ct. Va., Abingdon, 1958-59; practice law Washington, 1959-61; trial atty. U.S. Dept. Justice, Washington, 1961-65; dep. dir. Men's Job Corps OEO, Washington, 1965-67; mem. civil rights div. Dept. of Justice, chief criminal sect., prin. dep. asst. atty. gen., 1967-75, spl. counsel for intelligence coordination, 1975; v.p., counsel Assn. of Motion Picture and Television Producers, Hollywood, Calif., 1975-76; assoc. justice Am. Samoa, 1976, chief justice, 1977-78; sr. trial atty. GSA Task Force, Dept. Justice, 1978-81; insp. gen. CSA, 1981-82; spl. counsel Merit Systems Protection Bd., Washington, 1983-86; U.S. atty. for Guam and the No. Marianas, 1986-89, ret.; pvt. practice Medford, Oreg., 1989—; Am. counsel O'Reilly Vernier Ltd., Hong Kong, 1992-93; ptnr. O'Connor & Vernier, Medford, Oreg., 1993—. Served with USMC, 1952-55. Mem. ABA, Oreg. Bar Assn., D.C. Bar Assn., Va. Bar Assn., Calif. Bar Assn., Am. Samoa Bar Assn., Phi Alpha Delta, Sigma Nu. Home: 4828 Dark Hollow Rd Medford OR 97501-9626 Office: 916 W 10th St Medford OR 97501

O'CONNOR, KATHLEEN LUCILLE, health care executive; b. Long Beach, Calif., Nov. 30, 1944; d. Remi Charles and Lucille (Stockwell) O'Connor; m. Ernst O. Kaemke, July 5, 1969 (div. 1983); 1 child, Remi Miles Kaemke. BA, U. Wash., 1966, MA, 1970, postgrad., 1972-78. Spl. asst. to v.p. for acad. affairs U. Wash., Seattle, 1979-81; adminstr. Pacific N.W. Long-term Care Ctr., Inst. of Aging, Seattle, 1981-85; prin. O'Connor Communications, Seattle, 1985—; dir. medicare mktg. Network Health Plan, Mercer Island, Wash., 1988-89; dir. medicare mktg. Network Health Plan, Mercer Island, Wash., 1988-89. Editor: Alzheimer Caregiver, 1987. Pres. Voice for Choice Polit. Action Com., Seattle, 1989—; founding bd. mem. Mil. Retiree Healthcare, 1989—; mem. Seattle Women's Commn., 1972-73. Mem. Pub. Rels. Soc. Am., Leadership Tomorrow Alumni Assn. (governing com. 1987-90, newsletter editor 1987-90), Rotary Internat. Office: O'Connor Communications 911 Western Ave Ste 330 Seattle WA 98104

O'CONNOR, KEVIN THOMAS, archdiocese development official; b. Dubuque, Iowa, Oct. 9, 1950; s. Francis John and Marion Helen (Rhomberg) O'C. BS, Regis Coll., Denver, 1973. Spl. agt. Northwestern Mut. Life, Denver, 1973-78; account exec. Blue Cross/Blue Shield of Colo., Denver, 1978-82; pres., owner O'Connor Ins. Cons., Denver, 1982-92; dir. devel. Archdiocese of Denver, 1992—. Chmn. Regis Coll. Telefund, Denver, 1987-88, 90-91; trustee Serra Trust Fund for Vocations, 1st vice chmn., treas., 1985-92, vice chmn., 1992-93, chmn., 1993—; chmn. St. James Autumn Bazaar, 1985, 87; mem. fin. coun. St. James Parish, Denver, 1988; sec. Mother Teresa Com., 1989. Recipient Share Serra Communications award, Serra Internat., 1989, Spl. Project award, Dist. 6, 1986, 88, Spl. Recognition award, 1989; Alumni Svc. award, Regis Coll., 1990. Mem. Serra Club of Denver (sec. 1986-89, v.p. membership 1989-90, pres.-elect 1990-91, pres. 1991-92, trustee 1992—), Serra Internat. (area rep. to U.S./Can. coun. 1990—). Roman Catholic. Home: 7025 E Costilla Dr Englewood CO 80112-9999 Office: Archdiocese of Denver 200 Josephine St Denver CO 80206

O'CONNOR, MAUREEN, former mayor; b. San Diego, July 14, 1946; d. Jerome and Frances O'Connor; m. Robert O. Peterson, 1977. B in Psychology and Sociology, San Diego State U., 1970. Tchr., counselor Rosary High Sch., 1970-71; council mem. City of San Diego, 1971-79, dep. mayor, 1976, mayor, 1986-92; with Calif. Housing Fin. Agy., 1977-79; mem. Met. Transit Devel. Bd., 1976-81; port commr. San Diego, 1980-85; mem. Rules, Legis., and Intergovtl. Relations com.; chmn. pub. services and safety com. 1974-75; mem. League Calif. Cities' Com. on Human Resources Devel., Natl League Cities' Manpower and Income Support com.; chmn. mayor's crime commn. Roman Catholic. Office: City of San Diego Office of Mayor 202 C St San Diego CA 92101-4806*

O'CONNOR, WILLIAM CHARLES, finance director; b. Poplar Bluff, Mo., July 19, 1943; s. Thomas Francis and Luella Darlene (Davis) O'C.; m. Leigh Volkening, Dec. 21, 1975 (div. May 1992); children: Kelli, Megan, Katie. BA in English, Memphis State U., 1966. High rigger Boiler Makers Union, St. Louis, 1968-70; br. mgr. Pub. Fin. Corp., St. Louis, 1970-74; fin. specialist Pat Ryan & Assocs., Chgo., 1974-77; fin. mgr. Drew Ford, La Mesa, Calif., 1978-80; fin. dir. Honda of Pasadena, Calif., 1980-89, Goudy Honda, Alhambra, Calif., 1989—; cons. Am. Honda Fin. Corp., Torrance, Calif., 1987—. Contbr. articles to profl. jours. Mem. Fin. and Ins. Profls., KC, Jr. C. of C., Young Dems. Orgn. (pres. 1968-69). Home: 613 Camellia Dr Covina CA 91723 Office: Goudy Honda 1400 W Main St Alhambra CA 91801

ODA, YOSHIO, physician, internist; b. Papaaloa, Hawaii, Jan. 14, 1933; s. Hakui and Usako (Yamamoto) O.; AB, Cornell U., 1955; MD, U. Chgo., 1959. Intern U. Chgo. Clinics, 1959-60; resident in pathology U. Chgo., 1960-62, Queen's Hosp., Hawaii, 1962-63, Long Beach (Calif.) VA Hosp., 1963-65; resident in allergy, immunology U. Colo. Med. Center, 1966-67; pvt. practice, L.A., 1965-66; pvt. practice internal medicine, allergy and immunology, Honolulu, 1970—; asst. clin. prof. medicine U. Hawaii, Honolulu, 1970—. Maj., AUS, 1968-70. Diplomate Am. Bd. Internal Medicine. Mem. ACP, Am. Acad. Allergy. Office: Piikoi Med Bldg 1024 Piikoi St Honolulu HI 96814-1925

O'DALY, WILLIAM ANTHONY, instructional designer, poet, translator; b. L.A., Nov. 13, 1951; s. William Louis and Madeline May (Morabito) O'D. Student, U. Calif., Santa Barbara, 1969-72; BA, Calif. State U., Fresno, 1977; MFA, Ea. Wash. U., 1981. Prodn. mgr. market rsch. Gallo Wines, Modesto, Calif., 1977-78; spl. edn. aide Beyer High Sch., Modesto, 1978; poet-in-the-schs. Mont. Arts Coun., Missoula, 1978-79; instr. Ea. Wash. U., Cheney, 1981-83, asst. prof., 1983-86, editor-in-chief Willow Springs mag., 1979-86; internat. prodn. editor Microsoft Corp., Redmond, Wash., 1987-88, tech. editor, 1988-91, sr. instrnl. designer, 1991—; mem. adj. faculty Antioch U., Seattle, 1988—. Author: (book of poems) The Whale in the Web, 1979; translator (poetry vols. by Pablo Neruda) Still Another Day, 1984, The Separate Rose, 1985, Winter Garden, 1986, The Sea and the Bells, 1988, The Yellow Heart, 1990, The Book of Questions, 1991. Recipient citation of achievement Coord. Coun. Lit. Mags., N.Y.C., 1986. Mem. Assn. Computing Machinery, Acad. Am. Poets, Ptnrs. of Americas, World Affairs Coun. Office: Microsoft Corp Rm 1065 Bldg 1 1 Microsoft Way Redmond WA 98052-6399

ODASSO, JAMES VICTOR, chemical engineer; b. Bellflower, Calif., Jan. 18, 1966; s. Leo Blaise and Elizabeth Ann (Nugent) O. Degree, Calif. State U., Long Beach, 1993; postgrad., Mont. State U., 1993—. Plant process control technician Speedy Circuits Inc., Huntington Beach, Calif., 1988-90, plant process control-lab. technician, 1990-93. Insvc. trainer for edn. Santa Ana (Calif.) Sch. Dist., 1992. Recipient Eagle Scout Boy Scouts Am., 1983. Mem. Soc. of Hispanic Profl. Engrs. (youth outreach coord. 1990-92), Am. Inst. Chem. Engrs., Associated Engrs. Student Body Govt. (com. chmn.), Sigma Xi. Republican. Roman Catholic. Home: 5612 Rochelle Ave Westminster CA 92683

ODEGARD, MARK ERIE, geophysicist, consultant; b. Plentywood, Mont., Nov. 1, 1940; s. Harold Theodore and Edna Marcella (Jacobsen) O.; m. Elisabeth Snow, June 17, 1967; 1 child, Liv. AA, Dawson Coll., Glendive, Mont., 1960; BA, U. Mont., 1962; MS, Oreg. State U., 1965; PhD, U. Hawaii, 1975. Asst. prof. Hawaii Inst. Geophysics, Honolulu, 1974-78; dir. geology and geophysics program Office Naval Rsch., Arlington, Va., 1978-81; assoc. prof. N.Mex. State U., Las Cruces, 1981-83; staff rsch. geophysicist Sohio Petroleum Co., Dallas, 1983-86; prin. scientist Basalt Waste Isolation Program, Richland, Wash., 1986-88; rsch. assoc. Unocol Sci. & Tech., Brea, Calif., 1988—. Contbr. over 50 articles to sci. jours. Chmn. San Bernardino County (Calif.) Svc. Area 48 Adv. Com., 1989-91; vice chmn. Chino Hills Planning Commn., 1992—; mem. Chino Hills (Calif.) Mcpl. Adv. Coun., 1990-91. Recipient Antarctica Svc. medal U.S. Congress, 1966. Mem. Soc. Exploration Geophysicists, Am. Geophys. Union, Sigma Xi, Am. Planning Assn. Home: 16121 Valley Springs Rd Chino Hills CA 91709 Office: Unocal Sci & Tech PO Box 76 Brea CA 92621

ODEKIRK, BRUCE, physicist; b. Washington, Apr. 17, 1951; s. Max Dean Odekirk and Kathryn May (Cooper) Negri; m. Rose Marie Murray, Dec. 26, 1979; children: Brandy Danielle. BS in Physics, Sonoma State U., 1978; PhD in Applied Physics, Oreg. Grad. Inst. Sci. & Tech., 1982. Sr. scientist Tektronix, Beaverton, Oreg., 1983-86; prin. device engr. TriQuint Semiconductor, Beaverton, 1986—. Contbr. articles to profl. jours.; patentee in field. Staff sgt. USAF, 1969-73. Mem. IEEE. Democrat. Presbyterian. Home: 430 NE 18th Ave Hillsboro OR 97124-3506 Office: TriQuint Semiconductor PO Box 4935 Beaverton OR 97076-4935

ODELL, ALEXANDRA ROBINSON, artist, body builder; b. Charlotte, N.C., Nov. 10, 1947; d. Arthur Gould Odell and Louise Preston (Robinson) Wilcox; children: Jasmine Grace Dalbeck, Virginia Hayes Dalbeck. Student, Mint Mus., Charlotte, 1955-61; studies with, Marjorie Webster, Washington, 1966-67; student, U. N.C., 1968, Traphagen Sch. Fashion Design, N.Y.C., 1969; jewelry and fashion studies, Ecuador, 1970-73; glaze and lustre studies with, English Potter Tobias Harrison, 1984. Shows and exhibits include: The Mint Mus. Children's Show, 1953, The White House Children's Show, 1954, The Freedon Train Exhibit, 1954-58, Internat. RC European Tour, 1958-60, Spring's Traveling Show, 1984, Zenith Gallery, Washington, 1987, Govinda Gallery, Washington, 1988, (one woman shows) McKenna Gallery, Charlotte, 1985, Deborah Peverall Gallery, Charlotte, 1986, Incorporated Gallery, 1989, Christopher John Gallery, 1990, (permanent collections) Huntington Hartford, The Lejune, Ron Wood of the Rolling Stones, Their Royal Highnesses The Prince and Princess of Wales, President and Mrs. Ronald Reagan, among others. Mem. exec. bd. Children's Mus. of the Desert, Rancho Mirage, Calif., 1991. Mem. DAR, Colonial Dames. Home: 73565 Silver Moon Trl Palm Desert CA 92260-6111

ODELL, JOHN H., construction company executive; b. Toledo, Oct. 31, 1955; s. John H. and Doris Irene (Haskell) O.; m. Kathryn Lau, Oct. 1, 1988; 1 child, Ceara. BS in Environ. Design, U. Miami, Oxford, Ohio, 1977. Staff architect Richard Halford and Assocs., Santa Fe, 1978-79; ptnr. B.O.A. Constrn., Santa Fe, 1980-84; assoc. Stanley Design Works, Santa Fe, 1984-85; owner John H. Odell Constrn., Santa Fe, 1985—; v.p. Los Pintores Inc., Santa Fe, 1990—, Uncle Joey's Food Svcs. Inc., 1991—. Musician Santa Fe Community Orch., 1982, Huntington Community Orch., Huntington, W.Va., 1972-73. Mem. AIA (assoc. mem., treas., bd. dirs. Santa Fe chpt. 1988, 89, 90, 91, 92, 93, mem. liaison Com. on Design, 1987—), Vine and Wine Soc. (pres.), Home Builders Assn. Home: PO Box 2967 Santa Fe NM 87504-2967 Office: John H Odell Constrn 915 Hickox St Santa Fe NM 87501-3689

ODELL, WILLIAM DOUGLAS, physician, scientist, educator; b. Oakland, Calif., June 11, 1929; s. Ernest A. and Emma L. (Mayer) O.; m. Margaret F. Reilly, Aug. 19, 1950; children: Michael, Timothy, John D., Debbie, Charles. AB, U. Calif., Berkeley, 1952; MD, MS in Physiology, U. Chgo., 1956; PhD in Biochemistry and Physiology, George Washington U., 1965. Intern, resident, chief resident in medicine U. Wash., 1956-60, postdoctoral fellow in endocrinology and metabolism, 1957-58; sr. investigator Nat. Cancer Inst., Bethesda, Md., 1960-65; chief endocrine service NICHD, 1965-66; chief endocrinology Harbor-UCLA Med. Center, Torrance, Calif., 1966-72; chmn. dept. medicine Harbor-UCLA Med. Center, 1972-79; vis. prof. medicine Auckland Sch. Medicine, New Zealand, 1979-80; prof. medicine and physiology, chmn. dept. medicine U. Utah Sch. Medicine, Salt Lake City, 1980—. Mem. editorial bds. med. jours.; author 6 books in field; contbr. over 300 artilces to med. jours. Served with USPHS, 1960-66. Recipient Disting. Svc. award U. Chgo., 1973, Pharmacia award for outstanding contbns. to clin. chemistry, 1977, Gov.'s award State of Utah Sci. and Tech., 1988, also rsch. awards, Mastership award ACP, 1987. Mem. Am. Soc. Clin. Investigation, Am. Physiol. Soc., Assn. Am. Physicians, Am. Soc. Andrology (pres.), Endocrine Soc. (v.p., Robert Williams award 1991), Soc. Study of Reprodn. (bd. dirs.), Pacific Coast Fertility Soc. (pres.), Western Assn. Physicians (pres.), Western Soc. Clin. Rsch., Soc. Pediatric Rsch., Alpha Omega Alpha. Office: U of Utah Med Center 50 Medical Dr Salt Lake City UT 84132-0002

ODEN, WILLIAM ARTHUR, minister, artist; b. Dallas, Mar. 27, 1920; s. William Arthur and Mattie Lee (Griffin) O.; m. Dorothy Lee Robinson, Nov. 21, 1941; children: Anna Lee, William Arthur III, Virginia Christina Oden Martin, Nicholas Robinson, Samuel Garner. BA, U. Tex., El Paso, 1953, MA, 1959; BFA, U. N.Mex., 1987. Ordained to ministry, Anglican Cath. Ch., 1991. Clerical N.Am. Aviation Co., Grand Prairie, Tex., 1941-42; examiner, auditor U.S. VA, Dallas, 1948-51; air traffic control specialist CAA and FAA, El Paso, Tex. and Albuquerque, 1951-77; artist Placitas, N.Mex., 1977—; min. Anglican Cath. Ch., Albuquerque, 1991—; chmn. Air Traffic Control Assn., El Paso, 1959-61; catechist Anglican Cath. Ch., Albuquerque, 1987—. Pioneered air traffic control procedures USAF, 1942-46; editor publs. Anglican Cath. Ch., 1990—; author, speaker Air Trafic Control Goes To Coll., 1959; author, editor Fisherman publ., 1990—. Bd. dirs. Ranchos De Placitas Water and Sanitation Dist., 1980—. Sgt. USAF, 1942-46. Mem. Art in the Mountain, Sons of Am. Revolution, Md. Geneol. Soc., Sandoval County Hist. Soc., Vintage Thunderbird Club Internat. Democrat. Home: Star Rt Box 312 Placitas NM 87043 Office: Saint Peters Ch 8100 Hamilton NE Albuquerque NM 87122

ODERMATT, ROBERT ALLEN, architect; b. Oakland, Calif., Jan. 3, 1938; s. Clifford Allen and Margaret Louise (Budge) O.; m. Diana Birtwistle, June 9, 1960; children: Kristin Ann, Kyle David. BArch, U. Calif., Berkeley, 1960. Registered architect, Calif., Oreg., Nev., Colo., Hawaii; cert. Nat. Coun. Archtl. Registration Bds. Draftsman Anderson Simonds Dusel Campini, Oakland, 1960-61; architect James R. Lucas, Orinda, Calif., 1961-62, ROMA Architects, San Francisco, 1962-76; architect, pres. ROMA Architects, 1976-84; prin. ROMA Design Group, San Francisco, 1962-92; pres. The Odermatt Group, Orinda, Calif., 1992—; prin. speaker Internat. Conf. on Rebuilding Cities, Pitts., 1988; mem. U.S. Design in Am. Program, Sofia, Bulgaria, Armenian Disaster Assn. Team, 1989; prin. State of Calif. Bay Area Facilities Plan, 1992; princ. Greece Resort Privatization Program, 1993. Prin. designer Grand Canyon Nat. Park, 1977, Yosemite Nat. Park, 1987; prin. planner hotel complex Westin Hotel, Vail, Colo., 1982, Kaanapali Resort, 1987, Las Montanas Resort, San Diego; master plan U. Calif., Berkeley, 1988, Kohanaiki and Mauna Lani resorts, 1989. Mem. Oakland Mayor's Com. on High Density Housing, 1982; prin. charge Am. Embassy, Bahrain. Fellow AIA (dir. East Bay chpt. 1969-71, pres. 1980-81, dir. Calif. coun. 1979-81, Disting. Svc. award 1991, nat. dir. 1983-86, nat. v.p. 1986-87, chair AIA internat. steering com. 1992-93, graphic stds. adv. com. 1991-92). Office: The Odermatt Group 148 Amber Valley Dr Orinda CA 94563-9999

ODGERS, CHRISTOPHER REYNOLD, computer animation manager; b. Missoula, Mont., June 14, 1955; s. Stephen Lafayette and Glora Cecilia (Morin) O.; m. Anne Michele Tumonis, Aug. 26, 1984. B in Architecture, Cornell U., 1978, postgrad., 1978-80; MBA, Pepperdine U., 1989. Systems designer Hanna-Barbera Prodns., Hollywood, Calif., 1980-82; dir. computer animation systems Hanna-Barbera Prodns., Hollywood, 1982—; cons. George Eastman House, Rochester, N.Y. Contbr. papers and videos on technology. Mem. Soc. Motion Picture and TV Engrs., Assn. Computing Machinery. Home: 976 W Foothill Blvd Apt 294 Claremont CA 91711-3399 Office: Hanna-Barbera Prodns Inc 3400 Cahuenga Blvd W Los Angeles CA 90068-4301

O'DONNELL, CLIFFORD ROBERT, psychology educator; b. Newark, Aug. 28, 1939. BA, Fairleigh Dickinson U., 1964; MS, Okla. State U., 1966; PhD, U. Ky., 1970. Asst. prof. U. Hawaii, Honolulu, 1970-74, assoc. prof., 1974-82, prof., 1982—; asst. rsearcher Ctr. for Youth Rsch. U. Hawaii, 1970-74, assoc. researcher, 1974-82, researcher, 1982—, dir., 1987—. Co-editor: Childhood Aggression and Violence, 1987; contbr. chpts. to books. Mem. Juvenile Justice Interagy. Bd., Honolulu, 1989-91. Rsch. grantee Kamehameha Schs., 1988, Hawaii Dept. Pub. Safety, 1990. Mem. coun. COmmunity Psychology Program Dirs., Consortium Children, Families and Law (exec. com. 1988—), Community Rsch. and Action (exec. coun. 1993—), Soc. Rsch. on Adolescence, Child, Youth and Family Svcs. Office: U Hawaii Dept Psychology 2430 Campus Rd Honolulu HI 96822-2294

O'DONNELL, JOSEPH TIMOTHY, transit consulting company official; b. Whittier, Calif., May 5, 1961; s. James Paul and Cynthia Marie (Narko) O'D. BA, Calif. State U., L.A., 1991; postgrad., U. So. Calif., 1992. Legal asst., expansion coord. Jamko Svc. Corp., L.A., 1982-85; legal asst. Wilzig & Nord, Beverly Hills, Calif., 1985-86; project contracts adminstr. Engring. Mgmt. Cons., L.A., 1986—. Vol. phone bank coord. Californians Against Proposition 102, L.A., 1988, AIDS Cycle Challenge, L.A., 1989-90; canvasser AIDS Tax Credit Initiative, L.A., 1988; bd. dirs. Stonewall Dem. Club, L.A., 1989; pres., newsletter editor Different Spokes/L.A., 1989-91; peer counselor No. Lights Alternatives, L.A., 1990-92. Mem. Different Spokes So. Calif., Gold Key, Phi Kappa Phi.

O'DONNELL, WILLIAM RUSSELL, state senator; b. Quincy, Mass., Jan. 16, 1951; s. Alfred Joseph and Ruth Irene (McCausland) O.; m. Mary Hogan, June 13, 1976; children: Meagan, Patrick, Kevin, Colleen, Kyle. BS in Bus. and Econs., U. Nev., Las Vegas, 1979. Patrolman Las Vegas Met. Police, 1973-74; realtor Coldwell-Banker, Las Vegas, 1988—; pres. Computer System Concepts, Las Vegas, 1980—; Nev. state senator, 1987—. Nev. state assemblyman, Las Vegas, 1985-86; alt. legis. commn. Nev., 1987-89; majority Whip Rep. Party Nev., 1989; mem. Nev. Child Watch Adv. Bd., Assn. for the Handicapped, Pro-Life Nev., Citizens for Responsible Govt.; pres. Sect. 10 Homeowners Assn., Las Vegas, 1986—, Spring Valley Town Bd., 1984—; bd. dirs. Home of the Good Shepherd, St. Rose de Lima Hosp., 1985—. Mem. Las Vegas Bd. Realtors, Rotary. Republican. Roman Catholic. Office: 2995 S Jones Blvd Las Vegas NV 89102

O'DONNELL, WILLIAM THOMAS, radar systems marketing executive, management speaker; b. Latrobe, Pa., Feb. 22, 1939; s. William Regis and Kathryn Ann (Coneff) O'D.; m. Judith Koetke, Oct. 1, 1965; children: William Thomas, William Patrick, Allison Rose, Kevin Raymond. Student Ea. N.Mex. U., 1958-61; student in mktg. John Carroll U., 1961-65, Ill. Inst. Tech., 1965-66; BSBA, U. Phoenix, 1982, MBA with distinction, 1984. Various sales positions Hickok Elec. Instrument Co., Cleve., 1961-65, Fairchild Semicondr., Mpls., 1965-67; Transitron Semicondr., Mpls., 1967-69; regional sales mgr. Burroughs Corp., Plainfield, N.J., 1967-71; mktg. mgr. Owens-Ill. Co., 1972-73, v.p. mktg. Pantek Co., subs. Owens-Ill. Co., Lewistown, Pa., 1973-75, v.p. mktg., nat. sales mgr., Toledo, 1975-76; mktg. mgr. Govt. Electronics div. group Motorola Co., Scottsdale, Ariz., 1976-80, U.S. mktg. mgr. radar positioning systems Motorola Govt. Electronics Group, 1981—; gen. mgr. J.K. Internat., Scottsdale, 1980-81; mgmt. cons. Pres. Cambridge Group, 1987—; v.p. mktg. Pinnacle Surg. Products, 1989, v.p. marketing, Kroy, Inc., 1992—; v.p. mktg. and bus. devel. Kroy Inc., 1992; adj. prof. Union Grad. Sch.; guest lectr. U. Mich. Grad. Sch. Bus. Adminstrn.; instr., chair strategic mgmt. U. Phoenix, 1988, pres. faculty, 1989—; Scottsdale Community Coll., Paradise Valley Community Coll.; talk show host Sta. KFNN, 1992-93. Area chair-gen. mgmt. Union Grad. Sch. Maricopa Community Coll., U. Phoenix. Chmn., Rep. Precinct, Burnsville, Minn., 1968-70; city fin. chmn., Burnsville; dir. community devel. U.S. Jaycees, Mpls., 1968-69; mem. Scottsdale 2000 Com. With USAF, 1957-61. Recipient Outstanding Performance award Maricopa Community Coll. System, 1987, Faciliation award, Maricopa Community Coll., Citation for Faciliation Ability U. Phoenix, 1986, 90, 93; named Hon. Citizen, Donaldsville, La., 1978; others. Mem. Am. Mktg. Assn., Afro-Am. Small Bus. Assn. (bd. dirs.), Amateur Athletic Union (swimming ofcl. 1980-82), Phoenix Ex-ecs. Club, U. Phoenix Faculty Club (bd. dirs., pres. 1988-91, recipient Presdl. Designation award, officer), North Cape Yacht Club, Scottsdale Racquet Club, Toftnees Country Club. Roman Catholic. Home: 8432 E Belgian Trl Scottsdale AZ 85258-1466

O'DOWD, DONALD DAVY, retired university administrator; b. Manchester, N.H., Jan. 23, 1927; s. Hugh Davy and Laura (Morin) O'D.; m. Janet Louise Fithian, Aug. 23, 1953; children: Daniel D., Diane K., James E., John M. BA summa cum laude, Dartmouth Coll., 1951; postgrad. (Fulbright fellow), U. Edinburgh, Scotland, 1951-52; MA, Harvard U., 1955, PhD, 1957. Instr., asst. prof. psychology, dean freshmen Wesleyan U., Middletown, Conn., 1955-60; assoc. prof., prof. of psychology, dean Univ. Oakland Univ., Rochester, Mich., 1960-65, provost, 1965-70; pres. Oakland U., Rochester, Mich., 1970-80; exec. vice chancellor SUNY, Albany, 1980-84; pres. U. of Alaska Statewide System, 1984-90. Chmn. U.S. Arctic Rsch. Commn.; sr. cons. Assn. Governing Bds. of Univs. and Colls.; mem. N.Y. State Regents Commn. Higher Edn. With AUS, 1945-47. Carnegie Corp. fellow, 1965-66. Mem. Am. Psychol. Assn., AAAS, Phi Beta Kappa, Sigma Xi. Home and Office: 1550 La Vista Del Oceano Santa Barbara CA 93109-1739

O'DWYER, TERESA LYNN, business owner; b. Denver, Mar. 18, 1956; d. Lee Merlin and Phyllis Cleo (Menge) Thompson; m. Gordon Dennis Goodell, May 10, 1975 (div. 1981); 1 child, Erin Lee; m. Barton Thomas O'Dwyer, Aug. 20, 1983; 1 child, Kylee Lynn. Student, Aims C.C., 1977-78; cert. mcpl. clk., U. Colo., 1988. Sec., receptionist Majestic Mktg., Denver, 1975-77; sec., receptionist Geriatrics, Inc., Greeley, Colo., 1977-79, asst. to dir. of mktg., 1979-81; program coord. Colo. Assn. of Homes for the Aging, Denver, 1981-83; town clk. Town of Limon, Colo., 1983-91; co-owner Windy Ridge Arts, Inc., Limon, 1991—; treas. REDO, Inc., Limon, 1987—; sec.

Hub City Devel. Corp., Limon, 1985-87. Co-chair precinct 13 Lincoln County Reps., 1986—; mem. fin. com. United Meth. Ch., Limon, 1986—, mem. pastor-parish rels. com., 1991—, chmn. worship com., 1991—; mem. Limon High Sch. Bldg. Com., 1993; chairperson Limon Elem. Accountability Com., 1993, Limon Schs. Dist. Accountability Com., 1993. Recipient Spl. Award of Commendation Nat. Geneal. Soc., 1991, Outstanding Svc. Limon Recovery Agy., 1991. Mem. Limon Promotions Coun., Limon Communty Devel. Assn. (sec., treas. 1987-90), Limon C. of C. (bd. dirs. 1984-86). Office: Windy Ridge Arts Inc 357 D Ave Limon CO 80828

OELKLAUS, WILLIAM FREDERICK, III, wildlife biologist; b. Riverside, Calif., July 15, 1943; s. William Frederick Jr. and LaVonne Mary (Shoemaker) O.; m. Myrna Marie Spracklen, Aug. 30, 1964; children: William Frederick IV, Regan Helen-LaVonne. BS in Wildlife Fishries Rsch., U. Idaho, 1973, MS in Wildlife Mgmt., 1976. Cert. wildlife biologist. Rsch. asst. Idaho Game and Fish Dept., Lewiston, 1973, U. Wyo., Moscow, Idaho, 1974-76; wildlife field dir. VTN-Wyo., Sheridan, 1976-78; wildlife scientist A No. Energy Resource Co., Inc., Portland, Oreg., 1978-81; dir. environ svcs. Nerco, Inc., Portland, 1981-82; environ. dir., corp. wildlife scientist Nerco Mining Co., Sheridan, Wyo., 1982-85; environ./regulatory scientist Nerco-Antelope Coal Co., Douglas, Wyo., 1985—; guest lectr. U. Wyo., Laramie, 1991; negotiating rep. Wyo. Mining Assn., Cheyenne, 1985—; ann. breeding bird survey U.S. Fish and Wildlife Svc., Washington, 1989—. With USAF, 1962-70. Mem. Am. Ornithologist's Union, Audubon Soc., Cooper Ornithol. Soc., Nature Conservancy, Raptor Rsch. Found., Inc., Wildlife Soc., Phi Kappa Phi, Xi Sigma Pi, Phi Sigma. Home: 1239 Frontier Dr Douglas WY 82633 Office: Antelope Coal Co PO Drawer 1450 Douglas WY 82633

OESTMANN, IRMA EMMA, minister, artist, educator; b. Auburn, Nebr., May 6, 1930; d. Martin Edward and Magdalene Augusta (Volkman) O.; m. Allister Roland Behrends, July 29, 1948 (div. 1968); children: John, Allan, Patricia, William, Michael, Russell, Kurt. BS in Edn., U. Nebr., 1972. Ordained min. Unity Ch., Unity Village, Mo., 1982. Dairy farm pvt. farmer Johnson, Nebr., 1948-68; art tchr. Burke High Sch., Omaha, 1972-73, L.A. (Calif.) Pub. Schs., 1974-77; mgr. U-Rent Furniture, Canoga Park, Calif., 1978-80; min. There Is A Way TV Ministry, Palm Springs, Calif., 1982-83, Unity Ch. of Truth, Pomona, Calif., 1983-85, Unity of Del Ray Beach, Fla., 1986-87, Unity of Jupiter, Fla., 1988-90, Unity Ch. of San Gabriel, Calif., 1991—; cert. hypnotist, self-instr., therapist Encino, Calif., 1978-80; pvt. children's art tchr., Upland, Calif., 1986-87. Artist oil and watercolor paintings, 1968—; author, artist: (audio tapes) Self Help and Meditation, 1980—; producer, host: (tv panel series) The Truth Is, 1989; contbr. poems and articles to mags. Mem. San Gabriel (Calif.) Community Coun., 1991—. Office: Unity Church San Gabriel 325 S Pine St San Gabriel CA 91776

OESTREICH, PAUL CHRISTOPHER, electronics engineer; b. Salt Lake City, Dec. 14, 1963; s. Alfred H. and Carol Deane (Salmon) O.; m. Sheryl L. Dirksen, Aug. 20, 1989. BSEE, U. Utah, 1987; MS in Engring. Mgmt., U. Dayton, 1989. Elec. engr. AFMC Ogden Air Logistics Ctr., Hill AFB, Utah, 1987, HQ Air Force Logistics Command, Wright Patterson AFB, Ohio, 1987-88; elec. engr. Indsl. Process Br. HQ Air Force Logistics Command, Wright Patterson AFB, 1989; elec. engr. Software Engring. div. Ogden Air Logistics Ctr., Hill AFB, Utah, 1989—. Mem. IEEE, U.S. Cycling Fedn. Home: 3548 Country Manor Rd Salt Lake City UT 84121-5566 Office: Ogden Air Logistics Ctr Bldg 100 Bay G Hill AFB UT 84056

OFFE, MARTIN ROBERT, software engineer; b. Lincoln, Nebr., Aug. 22, 1964; s. Robert Eldon and Selma Lucile (Barkman) O.; m. Gina Marie Brumbaugh. BA in Computer Sci., Point Loma Nazarene Coll., 1987; MS in Software Engring. with distinction, Nat. U., 1991. Programmer Evolving Tech. Co., San Diego, 1984-86, San Diego State U. Found., 1986-87; software engr. Systems Exploration Inc., San Diego, 1987-92, VisiCom Labs., Inc., San Diego, 1992—. Bd. dirs. Linda Vista Ch. of the Nazarene, San Diego, 1990-92, treas. 1990-92, Sunday sch. tchr., 1992. Mem. Assn. of Computing Machinery. Republican. Home: 14431 NE Alton St Portland OR 97230

O'FLAHERTY, TERRENCE, journalist; b. What Cheer, Iowa, July 15, 1917; s. Leo J. and Lelia (Thomas) O'F. B.A., U. Calif. at Berkeley, 1939. Hist. researcher Metro-Goldwyn-Mayer Studios, 1940-42; columnist San Francisco Chronicle, 1949-86; writer nationally syndicated TV column, 1960-86; mem. bd. Peabody Awards for Radio and TV, 1952-84. Host: TV program PM West, San Francisco, 1961-62; created The Terrence O'Flaherty TV Collection for UCLA TV Archives and Theater Arts Library, 1987; contbr. articles to McCalls, Reader's Digest, TV Guide. Served as lt. USNR, 1942-46. Recipient Gov.'s award (Emmy) NATAS, 1988. Mem. Beta Theta Pi. Home and Office: 4 Whiting St San Francisco CA 94133-2419

OFORI-KYEI, MARK KWAME, systems engineer; b. Tema, Ghana, July 9, 1966; came to U.S., 1981; s. John and Grace (Anti) O. BSBA, U. Ariz., 1990. Intern software engr. GTE Communication Systems, Phoenix, 1987-88; engr., analyst Motorola Inc., Tempe, Ariz., 1990—; tech. advisor African Assn. Ariz., Phoenix, 1991—; com. chair Black Data Processing Assocs., Phoenix, 1991—. Mem. Lifeforce, Phoenix, 1991—. Named All Am. Powerlifter Am. Drug Free Powerlifting Assn., 1987, 89. Mem. IEEE, Black Data Processing Assocs. (com. chair 1991—), Am. Prodn. Inventory Control Soc. Home: 3643 W Grovers Ave Glendale AZ 85308

OFTE, DONALD, management consultant, educator; b. N.Y.C., Aug. 23, 1929; s. Sverre and Ingeborg Ofte; m. Margaret Mae McHenney, July 23, 1955; children: Marc Christian, Nancy Carolyn Ofte Appleby, Kirk Donald Jr. BA in Chemistry, Dana Coll., 1952; postgrad. study metall. engring., Ohio State U., 1958-60. Jr. chemist Inst. Atomic Research, Ames, Iowa, 1952-53; sr. research chemist Monsanto Research Corp., Miamisburg, Ohio, 1958-66; ops. engr. AEC, Miamisburg, 1966-69; br. chief, div. dir. ops. office AEC, Albuquerque, 1969-73; mgr. Pinellas area office AEC, Largo, Fla., 1973-79; mgr. Rocky Flats area office Dept. Energy, Golden, Colo., 1979-82; asst. mgr. devel. and prodn. Dept. Energy, Albuquerque, 1982-83, dep. mgr. ops. office, 1983-84; prin. dep. asst. sec. Dept. Energy Defense Programs, Washington, 1984-87; mgr. ops. office Dept. Energy, Idaho Falls, Idaho, 1987-89; mgmt. cons. Idaho Falls, 1989-92; v.p. govt. ops. United Engrs. and Constructors, Idaho Falls, 1992-93; v.p. Adv. Scis., Inc., 1993—; affiliate prof. Idaho State U., 1990-92; bd. dirs. Denver Fed. Exec. Bd., 1979-82. Author: (with others) Plutonium 1960, 1965, Physiciochemical; contbr. articles to profl. jours. on metallurgy and ceramics. Campaign chmn. United Way Pinellas, St. Petersburg, Fla., 1978; bd. dirs. Bonneville County United Way, Idaho Rsch. Found.; mem. adv. bd. Teton Peaks Council Boy Scouts of Am., 1987-92, Eastern Idaho Tech. Coll.; chmn. Excellence in Edn. Fund Com., 1990-92; vice chmn., bd. dirs. Rio Grande Ch. ARC, Albuquerque, 1982-84. Served to lt. (j.g.) USN, 1953-57. Recipient citation AEC for Apollo 12 SNAP 27 Radioisotope Generator, 1969, High Quality Performance award AEC, 1968, Group Achievement award NASA, 1972; Meritorious Svc. award Dept. Energy, 1985, Disting. Career Svc. award, 1989. Mem. Am. Chem. Soc., Am. Nuclear Soc., Am. Soc. Metals, Nat. Contract Mgmt. Assn., Am. Soc. Pub. Adminstrs., Suncoast Archeol. Soc., Idaho Falls C. of C. (bd. dirs., community svc. award 1990). Home: 2 Amaranth Dr Littleton CO 80127

OGDEN, JAMES DOUGLAS, controller; b. San Diego, June 19, 1950; s. John Blauvelt and Barbara (Wright) O.; m. Michelle Carolyn Avriette, Dec. 1, 1975; children: Douglas Blauvelt, Joy Michelle. BS in Math. and Computer Sci., San Diego State Coll., 1971. Asst. mgr. collections H.F.C., National City, Calif., 1975-77; contr. Elon of Calif., San Diego, 1977-86, Zybex, San Diego, 1986-90, Alturdyne, San Diego, 1990—. Contbr. articles to profl. jours. Mem. La Jolla Regional Group, Phi Eta Sigma. Office: Alturdyne 8050 Armour St San Diego CA 92111

OGDEN, JEAN LUCILLE, sales executive; b. Chgo., Jan. 20, 1950; d. George William and Mary Elizabeth (MacKenzie) Anderson; m. Michael Jude Ogden, Aug. 27, 1977 (div. Dec. 1983). BA with honors, U. Calif., Santa Barbara, 1971. Sales rep. Am. Hosp. Supply Co., Irvine, Calif., 1975-77, Abbott Labs., HPD, L.A., 1977-78, Gillette Co., Albqquerque, 1978-79, Unitek Corp., Monrovia, Calif., 1979-86, Nat. Patent Dental Products, San Diego, 1986-87; area mgr. Branson Ultrasonics Corp., L.A., 1987—. Mem., co-chair Nat. Multiple Sclerosis Soc., San Diego, 1983—; mem. Am. Cancer Soc., San Diego, 1985—, Zool. Soc., San Diego, 1984-85. Named one of Outstanding Young Women in Am., 1984. Mem. Med. Mktg. Assn., Salesmasters Albuquerque, Soroptimist Internat. (officer Carlsbad and Oceanside, Calif. chpt. 1983-85), Alpha Phi (house corp. bd. Long Beach chpt. 1974-75, chpt. advisor 1975-76). Republican. Office: Branson Ultrasonics Corp 12955 E Perez Pl La Puente CA 91746-1414

OGDEN, VALERIA JUAN, management consultant, state representative; b. Okanogan, Wash., Feb. 11, 1924; d. Ivan Bodwell and Pearle (Wilson) Munson; m. Daniel Miller Ogden Jr., Dec. 28, 1946; children: Janeth Lee Ogden Martin, Patricia Jo Ogden Hunter, Daniel Munson Ogden. BA magna cum laude, Wash. State U., 1946. Exec. dir. Potomac Coun. Camp Fire, Washington, 1964-68, Ft. Collins (Colo.) United Way, 1969-73, Designing Tomorrow Today, Ft. Collins, 1973-74, Poudre Valley Community Edn. Assn., Ft. Collins, 1977-78; pres. Valeria M. Odgen, Inc., Kensington, Md., 1978-81; nat. field cons. Camp Fire, Inc., Kansas City, Mo., 1980-81; exec. dir. Nat. Capital Area YWCA, Washington, 1981-84, Clark County YWCA, Vancouver, Wash., 1985-89; pvt. practice mgmt. cons. Vancouver, 1989—; lectr. in field.; adj. faculty pub. adminstrn. program Lewis and Clark Coll. Portland (Oreg.) State U., 1979—; v.p. Pvt. Industry Coun., Vancouver, 1986. Author: Camp Fire Membership, 1980. County V chair Larimer County Dems., Ft. Collins, 1974-75; mem. precinct com. Clark County Dems., Vancouver, 1986—; mem. Wash. State Coun. Vol. Action, Olympia, 1986-90; treas. Mortar Bd. Nat. Found., Vancouver, 1987—; mem. Clark County Coun. Homeless, Vancouver, 1989—. Named Citizen of Yr. Ft. Collins Bd. of Realtors, 1975; recipient Gulick award Camp Fire Inc., 1956, Alumna Achievement award Wash. State U. Alumni Assn., 1988. Mem. Internat. Assn. Vol. Adminstrs. (pres. Boulder 1989-90), Nat. Assn. YWCA Exec. Dirs. Assn. (nat. bd. nominating com. 1988-90), Women in Action, Philanthropic and Ednl. Orgn., Phi Beta Kappa. Unitarian. Home: 3118 NE Royal Oaks Dr Vancouver WA 98662-7435 Office: John L O'Brien Bldg State Capitol Rm 342 Olympia WA 98504

OGG, WILSON REID, poet, curator, publisher, lawyer, educator; b. Alhambra, Calif., Feb. 26, 1928; s. James Brooks and Mary (Wilson) O. Student Pasadena Jr. Coll., 1946; A.B., U. Calif. at Berkeley, 1949, J.D., 1952; Cultural D in Philosophy of Law, World Univ. Roundtable, 1983. Assoc. trust Dept. Wells Fargo Bank, San Francisco, 1954-55; admitted to Calif. bar; pvt. practice law, Berkeley, 1955-78; adminstrv. law judge, 1976-93; real estate broker, cons., 1974-78; curator-in-residence Pinebrook, 1964—; owner Pinebrook Press, Berkeley, Calif., 1988—; research atty., legal editor dept. of continuing edn. of bar U. Calif. Extension, 1958-63; psychology instr. 25th Sta. Hosp., Taegu, Korea, 1954; English instr. Taegu English Lang. Inst., Taegu, 1954. Trustee World U., 1976-80; dir. admissions Internat. Soc. for Phil. Enquiry, 1981-84; dep. dir. gen. Internat. Biographical Centre, Eng., 1986—; dep. gov. Am. Biographical Inst. Research Assn., 1986—. Served with AUS, 1952-54. Cert. community coll. instr. Mem. VFW, AAAS, ABA, State Bar Calif., San Francisco Bar Assn., Am. Arbitration Assn. (nat. panel arbitrators), World Univ. Round Table, World Future Soc. (profl. mem.), Calif. Soc. Psychical Study (pres., chmn. bd. 1963-65), Parapsychol. Assn. (assoc.), Internat. Soc. Unified Sci., Am. Acad. Polit. and Social Sci., Artists Embassy Internat., Internat. Platform Assn., Intertel, Ina Coolbrith Circle, Am. Legion, Mensa, Lawyers in Mensa, Triple Nine Soc., Wisdom Soc., Inst. Noetic Scis., Psychic Sci. Spl. Interest Group, Am. Legion,. Faculty Club (U. Calif.), City Commons Club (Berkeley), Commonwealth Club of Calif., Town Hall Club of Calif., Marines Meml. Club, Masons, Shriners, Elks. Unitarian. Contbr. numerous articles profl. jours; contbr. poetry to various mags. including American Poetry Anthology Vol. VI Number 5, Hearts on Fire: A Treasury of Poems on Love, Vol. IV, 1987, New Voices in American Poetry, 1987, The Best Poems of the 90's, Distinguished Poets of America, The Poetry of Life A Treasury of Moments An. Poetry Anthology, Vol. VII, 1988, The Best Poems Of The 90's, Nat. Libr. Poets, 1992, Disting. Poets Of Am., 1993. Home: 1104 Keith Ave Berkeley CA 94708-1607 Office: 8 Bret Harte Way Berkeley CA 94708-1611

OGIER, WALTER THOMAS, retired physics educator; b. Pasadena, Calif., June 18, 1925; s. Walter Williams and Aileen Vera (Polhamus) O.; m. Mayrene Miriam Gorton, June 27, 1954; children: Walter Charles, Margaret Miriam, Thomas Earl, Kathryn Aileen. B.S., Calif. Inst. Tech., 1947, Ph.D. in Physics, 1953. Research fellow Calif. Inst. Tech., 1953; instr. U. Calif. at Riverside, 1954-55, asst. prof. physics, 1955-60; asst. prof. physics Pomona Coll., Claremont, Calif., 1960-62, assoc. prof., 1962-67, prof. physics, 1967-89, chmn. dept., 1972-89; lectr. Calif. Poly. State U., San Luis Obispo, 1990-92. Contbr. articles on metals, liquid helium, X-rays and proton produced X-rays to profl. jours. Served with USNR, 1944-46. NSF Sci. Faculty fellow, 1966-67. Mem. Am. Phys. Soc., Am. Assn. Physics Tchrs. (pres. So. Calif. sect. 1967-69), Tau Beta Pi. Home: 8555 San Gabriel Rd Atascadero CA 93422-4928

OGIMACHI, NAOMI NEIL, retired chemist; b. L.A., Oct. 20, 1925; s. Tamuro and Yasuko (Togashi) O.; m. Frances Imogene Bennett, July 27, 1956; children: David J., Catharine A., Shawn N., April J. BS, UCLA, 1950; PhD, U. Calif., Berkeley, 1956. Rsch. chemist E.I. DuPont de Nemours, Wilmington, Del., 1955-57, U.S. Naval Ordnance Test Sta., China Lake, Calif., 1957-59; sr. scientist Rocketdyne div. Rockwell Internat., Canoga Park, Calif., 1959-70; rsch. chemist Halocarbon Products Corp., Hackensack, N.J., 1970-75; mgr. chem. process devel. Teledyne McCormick, Hollister, Calif., 1975-89. Contbr. articles to profl. jours.; patentee in field. Sgt. U.S. Army, 1944-46, ETO. Fellow AAAS; mem. Royal Soc. Chemistry (assoc.), Am. Chem. Soc., Sigma Xi, Phi Kappa Phi. Democrat. Methodist. Home: 1218 Santa Clara St Eureka CA 95501

OGLE, JOSEPH WOMACK, composer, retired piano teacher; b. Guthrie, Okla., Oct. 25, 1902; s. James Taylor and Ella (Womack) O.; m. Inez Helen Klein, Aug. 9, 1929; 1 child, Dottie Ella. BA, MusB, Phillips U., 1925; postgrad., Columbia U., 1924-28. Chmn. piano dept. Lon Morris Coll., Jacksonville, Tex., 1928-29, 30, Milligan (Tenn.) Coll., 1929-32; pvt. studio tchr. Santa Ana, Calif., 1932-91; ret., 1991—. Musical compositions published with Boston Music, Schroeder & Gunther, Pro Art Publications, Summy-Birchard and Mills Music, and others. Contbr. profl. jours. Cpl. Nat. Guard, 1921-24. Rhodes scholar Oxford U., 1926. Mem. Music Tchrs. Assn. of Calif., Musical Arts Club of Orange County. Democrat. Office: Joseph Ogle Piano Studio 1710 Greenleaf St Santa Ana CA 92706

OGLE, ROBERT LLOYD, JR., accountant; b. Lakeview, Oreg., Aug. 16, 1955; s. Robert L. and Nancy A. (Hall) O.; m. Pamela C. Ziolkowski, May 6, 1978; children: Caroline E., Robert L. III. BS, U. Oreg., 1977; MBA, Portland State U., 1983, postgrad., 1988. CPA, Oreg. Asst. buyer Macy's, San Francisco, 1977; loan officer First Interstate Bank, Portland, Oreg., 1977-80, employment officer, 1980-84; accounts receivable auditor Key Bank of Oreg., Portland, 1984-89; sr. acct. KPMG Peat Marwick, Portland, 1989-93, Intel Corp., Hillboro, Oreg., 1993—. Loaned exec. United Way, Portland; vol. March of Dimes, Portland, Am. Heart Assn., Portland. Home: 11740 SW Burnett Ln Beaverton OR 97005

OGREAN, DAVID WILLIAM, sports executive; b. New Haven, Feb. 7, 1953; s. Richard Berton and Dorothy (Nystrom) O.; m. Maryellen Harvey, Aug. 10 1974; children: Matthew David, Tracy Erin, Dana Marie. BA in English cum laude, U Conn., 1974; MS in Film, Boston U., 1978. Asa S. Bushnell intern Ea. Coll. Athletic Conf., Centervill, Mass., 1977-78; pub. rels. dir. Amateur Hockey Assn. U.S., Colorado Springs, Colo., 1978-80; mng. editor Am. Hockey and Arena mag., 1979-80; communications rep. ESPN, Inc., Bristol, Conn., 1980-83, program mgr., 1983-88; asst. exec. dir. for TV Coll. Football Assn., Boulder, Colo., 1988-90; dir. of broadcasting U.S. Olympic Com., Colorado Springs, 1990-93; exec. dir. USA Hockey, Colorado Springs, 1993—. Mem. Country Club Colo. Democrat. Mem. Am. Bapt. Ch. Office: US Olympic Com 1750 E Boulder St Colorado Springs CO 80909-5746

OGUNSEITAN, OLADELE ABIOLA, microbiologist, educator; b. Ilesa, Nigeria, Apr. 4, 1961; came to U.S., 1984; s. Olabode Titus and Olanre (Kuteyi) O. PhD, U. Tenn., 1988. Asst. prof. U. Calif., Irvine, 1988—. Mem. AAAS, Am. Soc. Microbiology. Office: U Calif Sch Social Ecology Irvine CA 92717

O'HAGAN, WILLIAM GORDON, automotive repair shop owner; b. Allentown, N.J., Oct. 12, 1943; s. Forrest Allen and Voncile Arline (Linton) O'H.; m. Marcia Helen Beck, Aug. 12, 1947 (div. Oct. 1985). Grad. high sch., Azusa, Calif., 1962. Owner Richfield Oil Co., Baldwin Park, Calif., 1970-72; mgr. Am. Teaching Aids, Covina, Calif., 1972-88; owner Bill's Auto Repair Co., Covina, 1988—. Block commander Neighborhood Watch, Covina. Republican. Baptist. Home: 163 N Marcile Ave Glendora CA 91740-2453 Office: Bills Automotive 678 E San Bernardino Rd Covina CA 91723-1735

OHALETE, CAROL LYNN SCHUSTER, gerontology nurse practitioner; b. Springfield, Ill., Jan. 5, 1947; d. Erich Carl and Eleanor Maxine (Bomke) Schuster; m. Emit Earl Simpson Sr., May 16, 1966 (dec. Dec. 1976); children: E. Earl Jr., Eric E., Carl L.; m. Ifeanyi J. Ohalete May 27, 1978; children: Ifeanyi E., Chioma A. BA, Sangamon State U., Springfield, Ill., 1978; BS in Nursing, Creighton U., Omaha, 1981; postgrad, U. Tex., Galveston, 1988-89; MS in Nursing, U. Tex., Houston, 1991. Cert. sch. nurse, Tex., gerontology nurse practitioner, Tex. Sec. Sch. Practical Nursing, Springfield, 1975-78; clk. State Jour. Register, Springfield, 1978-79; staff nurse, patient edn. coord. U. Nebr. Med. Ctr., Omaha, 1981-82; clin. coord., staff nurse, home health nurse U. Tex. Med. Br., Galveston, 1983-85; mem. faculty LVN program Houston C.C., 1989-90; supplemental staff nurse The Meth. Hosp., Houston, 1978-90; ICU nurse USNR-USNS Mercy, Operation Desert Shield/Storm, 1991; staff nurse Shriners Burns Inst., Galveston, 1988-89; div. officer, adminstrv. head urology clinic USN, Long Beach (Calif.) Naval Hosp., 1991—; mem. radiation com. Naval Hosp., Long Beach, 192—, lectr. edn. dept., 1991—, liaison legal dept., 1992—. Co-author: Career Ladder Advancement Program-Nurses, 1988, Thesis: Influence of Health Promotion on African-American Elders, 1991. Sunday sch. tchr. Covenant Presbyn. Ch., Long Beach, 1992—, choir mem., 1992—, nurse on-call staff, 1992—, vol. homeless meal svc., 1992—. Mem. AACN, Naval Res. Assn., Assn. Mil. Surgeons U.S., U.S. Naval Inst., Nat. Geographic Soc., Smithsonian Inst., Creighton Alumni Assn. Democrat. Home: 98 Coral Sea Ct Los Alamitos CA 90720-5121 Office: Naval Hosp Long Beach Urology Clinic Code 314 7500 E Carson St Long Beach CA 90822

O'HALLORAN, THOMAS ALPHONSUS, JR., physicist, educator; b. Bklyn., Apr. 13, 1931; s. Thomas Alphonsus Sr. and Nora (Sheehan) O'H.; m. Barbara Joyce Hug, June 4, 1954; children: Theresa Joyce, Maureen Ann, Kevin Thomas, Patrick Joseph. Student, San Jose State U., 1948-50; BS in Physics & Math., Oreg. State U., 1953, MS in Physics, 1954; PhD, U. Calif., Berkeley, 1963. Rsch. asst. Lawrence Berkeley Lab., U. Calif., 1963-64; rsch. fellow Harvard U., Cambridge, Mass., 1964-66; asst. prof. physics U. Ill., Urbana, 1966-68, assoc. prof., 1968-70, prof., 1970-93, prof. emeritus, 1993—; vis. scholar U. Utah, Salt Lake City, 1990—; mem. program adv. com. Argonne Nat. Lab., Lemont, Ill., Fermi Lab., Batavia, Ill., Brookhaven Nat. Lab., Upton, L.I.; vis. scientist Lawrence Berkeley Lab., U. Calif., 1979-80; vis. scholar U. Utah, 1990—. Contbr. numerous articles on elem. particle physics to profl. jours. Lt. USN, 1954-58. Guggenheim fellow, 1979-80. Fellow Am. Phys. Soc. Home: 4614 S Ledgemont Salt Lake City UT 84124 Office: U Utah Physics Dept 201 JFB Salt Lake City UT 84112

OHANIAN, BERNARD JAY, writer; b. Tokyo, Apr. 22, 1956; came to U.S., 1956; s. Abraham Sam and Bernadine Jeanette (Preis) O.; m. Catharine Greta Vollmer, July 2, 1983 (div. 1990). Student, U. Degli Studi, Pisa, Italy, 1977-78; BA, U. Calif., Berkeley, 1980. Editor Newsfront Internat., Oakland, Calif., 1978-81; editor-in-chief Mediafile, San Francisco, 1981-83; correspondent RKO Radio, Rome, Italy, 1983-84; English lang. editor Inter Press Svc., Rome, 1983-84; sr. editor Rip N Read News Svc., San Francisco, 1984-85, Mother Jones mag., San Francisco, 1985-88; sr. editor, features MacWeek mag., San Francisco, 1988-89; editorial dir. RX Media Publs., Sausalito, Calif., 1989-90; editorial staff Nat. Geographic mag., Washington, 1992—; freelance editorial cons., Berkeley, Calif., 1990—; vis. faculty mem. Sch. of Journalism U. Calif., Berkeley, 1990—. Author (books) Baseball in America, 1991, A Day in the Life of Italy, 1990; editor (books) The Power to Heal, 1990, A Day in the Life of Ireland, 1991; caption writer (book) In Pursuit of Ideas, 1992. Bd. dirs. Media Alliance, San Francisco, 1986—, pres., 1988-92. Recipient Best Feature Article award Western Publs. Assn., 1990. Mem. Nat. Writers Union, Assn. of Mag. Editors of the Bay Area, U.C. Berkeley Alumni Assn. (life).

OHANIAN, JOHN B., state official; b. Alexandrettse, Turkey, Aug. 29, 1937; came to U.S., 1958; s. Boghos and Khatoun (Djekalian) O.; m. Eileen Ohanian, 1966; children: Nicole, Shant. BS, Northrop U., Inglewood, Calif., 1965. Engr. Teledyne Corp., Calif., 1965-66, Calif. Resources Dept., 1966-69; dep. dir. Office of Gov., State of Calif., Sacramento, 1969-83; engr. Calif. Pub. Utilities Commn., San Francisco, 1969-83, mem., 1987—. Mem. NARUC. Republican. Mem. Armenian Orthodox Ch.

OHARA, JUN-ICHI, physician, immunologist, educator; b. Kyoto, Japan, Feb. 19, 1950; came to U.S., 1983; MD, Okayama U., Japan, 1975; PhD, Osaka U., 1979. Physician Osaka Prefectual Hosp., Habikino, Japan, 1979-80; prof. immunology Saga Med. Sch., Japan, 1980-83; vis. assoc. NIH, Bethesda, Md., 1983-85; vis. scientist NIH, Bethesda, 1985-88; asst. mem. Med. Biology Inst., La Jolla, Calif., 1989-90; physician in rsch. Denver VA Med. Ctr., 1990—; assoc. prof. medicine U. Colo. Sch. Medicine, Denver, 1990—; mem. faculty U. Colo. Health Scis. Cancer Ctr., Denver, 1990—; mem. U. Colo. Cancer Ctr., Denver, 1990—; mem. adv. com. Exptl. Medicine Mag., 1986—. Contbr. articles to profl. jours. Contbr. articles to profl. jours. Mem. Am. Assn. Immunologists (ad hoc referee 1986—), N.Y. Acad. Scis. Home: 5924 S Akron Cir Greenwood Village CO 80111 Office: U Colo Sch Medicine 4200 E 9th Ave Campus Box B-158 Denver CO 80262

O'HARA, MICHAEL J(AMES), physicist; b. Winthrop, Mass., Aug. 7, 1956; s. George J. and Gilda A. (Capone) O. BS in Physics, U. Lowell (Mass.), 1978; MS in Physics, U. Ill., 1980, MS in Computer Sci., 1984. Mem. tech. staff I Hughes Aircraft Co., El Segundo, Calif., 1984-86, mem. tech. staff II, 1986-87; tech. supr. Hughes Aircraft Co., 1987-89, sect. head, 1989-91, asst. dept. mgr., 1991—; software cons. Duosoft Corp., Urbana, 1982-83; bd. dirs. Ednl. Scis. Corp. Am., L.A., 1986—. Mem. N.Y. Acad. Sci., Planetary Soc., Soc. Photo-Optical Instrumentation Engrs., U. Ill. Alumni Club, Soc. Physics Students, Sigma Pi Sigma. Republican. Roman Catholic. Office: Hughes Aircraft Co PO Box 92919 Los Angeles CA 90009-2919

O'HARE, THOMAS EDWARD, chemical engineer, consultant; b. N.Y.C., Sept. 3, 1928; s. Thomas and Ellen (O'Hare) O'H.; m. Claire Hunt, Apr. 25, 1953; children: Nancy E., Terence G., Andrew T., Constance M., Mary Kate. BChE, CCNY, 1951; MBA, NYU, 1956. Process engr. The Lummus Co., N.Y.C., 1951-54; process engr., staff economist, asst. mgr. process engring. The M.W. Kellogg Co., N.Y.C. and London, 1954-66; exec. v.p., dir. Universal Chems. Ltd., Nassau, Bahamas, also Indonesia, 1967-69; mng. ptnr. T.E. O'Hare & Assocs., Huntington Station, N.Y., 1966-78; mng. ptnr. The Intertech Group, Huntington Station, 1971-79, Englewood, Colo., 1989—; assoc. chmn. dept. applied sci. Brookhaven Nat. Lab., Upton, N.Y., 1979-88; U.S. del., participant UN Tech. Confs. in Geneva, Bombany, Teheran, Kiev, 1963-66. Contbr. articles to profl. jours.; patentee in field. Co-chair Citizens Adv. Com. on Urban Renewal, Huntington, N.Y., 1964-66. Cpl. AUS, 1951-53. Mem. ASME, Am. Inst. Chem. Engrs., Am. Econ. Assn., World Future Soc., KC (3d deg.), Sigma Xi. Democrat. Roman Catholic. Home: 7875 E Kettle Ave Englewood CO 80112 Office: The Intertech Group PO Box 3221 Englewood CO 80125

OHARENKO, MARIA T., public relations official; b. Louvain, Belgium, Dec. 25, 1950; came to U.S., 1951; d. Vladimir and Lubomyra (Kotz) O. BS, Northwestern U., 1972, MS, 1973. Pub. info. officer U.S. AEC, ERDA, Dept. Energy, Argonne and Chgo., Ill., 1973-79; pub. info. and news media advance officer U.S. Dept. Energy, Washington, 1980-81; corp. pub. info. mgr. Northrop Corp., Los Angeles, 1981—. Mem. Aviation/Space Writers Assn., Women in Communications, Soc. Profl. Journalists. Ukrainian Catholic. Office: Northrop Corp 1840 Century Park E Los Angeles CA 90067-2101

O'HEARN, MICHAEL JOHN, lawyer; b. Akron, Ohio, Jan. 29, 1952; s. Leo Ambrose and Margaret Elizabeth (Clark) O'H. BA in Econs., UCLA, 1975; postgrad., U. San Diego, 1977; JD, San Fernando Valley Coll. Law,

1979. Bar: Calif. 1979, U.S. Dist. Ct. (cen. dist.) Calif. 1979. Document analyst Mellonics Info. Ctr., Litton Industries, Canoga Park, Calif., 1977-79; pvt. practice Encino, Calif., 1979-80; atty. VISTA/Grey Law Inc., L.A., 1980-81; assoc. Donald E. Chadwick & Assocs., Woodland Hills, Calif., 1981-84, Law Offices of Laurence Ring, Beverly Hills, Calif., 1984-85; atty., in-house counsel Coastal Ins. Co., Van Nuys, Calif., 1985-89; atty. Citrus Glen Apts., Ventura, Calif., 1989-92. Cert. of Appreciation, Agy. for Vol. Svc., 1981, San Fernando Valley Walk for Life, 1988. Mem. Internat. Platform Assn., K.C., Ventura County Bar Assn., Secular Franciscan Order. Republican. Roman Catholic. Home: 3730 Ketch Ave Apt 207 Oxnard CA 93035 Office: 3650 Ketch Ave Oxnard CA 93035

OHL, DONALD CHARLES, news service executive; b. Grand Junction, Iowa, Dec. 19, 1924; s. August and Agnes (Thornburg) O.; m. Evelyn Marie Broadway, Jan. 21, 1955; 1 son, Gary Martin. B.A., U. Iowa, 1950. Formerly mng. editor Guthrie Center (Iowa) Times-Guthrian; Sunday editor Galveston (Tex.) News-Tribune; asst. bur. mgr. UPI, N.Y.C., 1960-64; fgn. editor Copley News Service, San Diego, 1964-69, exec. news editor, from 1969, now gen. mgr. Office: Copley News Svc PO Box 190 San Diego CA 92112-0190

OHLSON, MORTON KAYE, economics educator; b. Denver, June 15, 1931; s. Peter Andrew and Esther Marie (Hesse) O.; m. Elouise Carolyn Spears, Apr. 5, 1952; children: Brent K., Brenda L. BA, U. Colo., 1954, PhD, 1961; MA, U. N.Mex., 1959. Mem. econs. faculty Kans. State Coll., Emporia, 1961-62, U. Wichita, Kans., 1962-65, Met. State Coll., Denver, 1965—; cons. N.Mex. Comprehensive Health Planning Agy., Santa Fe, 1970-72, Denver Urban Observatory, 1970-75; expert witness Med. Malpractice Case, Denver, 1980-81. Author: Economics of Price and Income, 1985, 2d edit., 1991. 1st lt. USAF, 1954-56. Home: 8179 W Louisiana Ave Lakewood CO 80232

OHMAN, DIANA J., school system administrator; b. Sheridan, Wyo., Oct. 3, 1950; d. Arden and Doris Marie (Carstens) Mahin. AA, Casper Coll., 1970; BA, U. Wyo., 1972, MEd, 1977, postgrad., 1979—. Tchr. kindergarten Natrona County Sch. Dist., Casper, Wyo., 1971-72; tchr. rural sch. K-8 Campbell County Sch. Dist., Gillette, Wyo., 1972-80, rural prin. K-8, 1980-82, prin. K-6, 1982-84, assoc. dir. instrn., 1984-87; dir. K-12 Goshen County Migrant Program, Torrington, Wyo., 1988-89; prin. K-2 Goshen County Sch. Dist., Torrington, Wyo., 1987-90; state supt. pub. instrn. State of Wyo., Cheyenne, 1991—; chmn. Campbell County Mental Health Task Force, 1986-87; mem. Legis. Task Force on Edn. of Handicapped 3-5 Yr. Olds, 1988-89. State Committeewoman Wyo. Rep. Party, 1985-88. Recipient Wyo. Elem. Prin. of Yr. award, 1990; named Campbell County Tchr. of Yr. 1980, Campbell County Profl. Bus. Woman of Yr. 1984, Outstanding Young Woman in Am., 1983. Mem. Coun. of Chief of State Sch. Officers (Washington chpt.), Internat. Reading Assn., Wyo. Assn. of Sch. Adminstrs., Kappa Delta Pi, Phi Kappa Phi, Phi Delta Kappa. Republican. Lutheran. Office: Wyo Dept Edn Hathaway Bldg 2d Fl 2300 Capitol Ave Cheyenne WY 82002-0050

OHMERT, RICHARD ALLAN, architect; b. Davenport, Iowa, Apr. 13, 1925; s. Richard George and Jeanette Marie (Ackerman) O.; m. Bonnie Lou Bruyere, June 26, 1948 (div. June 1964); children: Richard, Jennifer, Jan, Kenneth; m. Violet Maria Alto Holmes, Dec. 31, 1971; stepchildren: Candyce, Cynthia. Student, Gallery Fine Arts Sch. Design, 1940-41, UCLA, 1954-56. Registered architect Calif., Nev., accredited Nat. Coun. Archtl. Registration Bds. Assoc. Kistner Wright & Wright, L.A., 1950-71; asst. mgr. architecture Voorhis, Trindle, Nelson Corp., Irvine, Calif., 1971-74; assoc. Davis-Duhaime Assocs., Anaheim, Calif., 1974-89; firm assoc. Neptune-Thomas-Davis, Corona, Calif., 1989—; cons. architect E&O Corp., Irvine, 1985—. Pres. Groves Homeowners Assn., Irvine, 1981-82; bd. mgrs. YMCA, Irvine, 1988-89; pres. bd. dirs. Orange County Child Abuse Prevention Ctr., 1991. Mem. Soc. Am. Registered Architects (sec.-treas. 1990-92, pres. Orange County chpt. 1993—), Irvine Chpt. of Nat. Exch. Club (pres. 1983-84, dist. dir. 1986-87, Calif.-Nev. dist. pres. 1988-89, Exchangite of Yr. award 1990). Democrat. Episcopalian. Home: 5200 Irvine Blvd # 18 Irvine CA 92720 Office: Neptune-Thomas-Davis Architects 357 Sheridan St Ste 101 Corona CA 91720

OHNSTAD, DONALD ALAN, manufacturing executive; b. Estelline, S.D., Oct. 7, 1938; s. Clarence Benjamin and Mary Anna (Aamold) O.; m. Sandra Lee Barnes, Mar. 30, 1962; children: Tiffany Ann, Scott Lee. BA in History, Augustana Coll., 1961; MBA in Fin., Calif. State U., Fullerton, 1971. Program fin. mgr. Ground Systems Group, Hughes Aircraft, Fullerton, Calif., 1968-72; controller Automotive Environ. Systems, Inc., Westminster, Calif., 1972-74; fin. mgr. Acme Ludlow Div. of Ludlow Corp., Temple City, La., 1974-76; cost mgr. Smith Tool Div., Smith Internat., Irvine, Calif., 1976-79; group controller Levi Strauss & Co., San Francisco, 1979-83; gen. mgr. Levi Strauss Fin. Svcs., Basel, Switzerland, 1983-86; group controller Levi Strauss & Co., San Francisco, 1986-87; controller, CFO Fritzi of Calif., Inc., San Francisco, 1987-89; pres., CEO Quality Computer Supplies, Inc., Tempe, Ariz., 1989—; cons. William Goodman Oil & Gas Leases, Villa Park, Calif., 1976-79. Pres. Villa Park (Calif.) Bobby Sox, 1975-76, v.p., 1974-75; commr. Brussels Belgium Sr. League, 1984-85; treas. City of Villa Park, 1977-78. Lt. USN, 1961-64; comdr. USNR, 1964-89. Mem. Naval Res. Assn. Republican. Lutheran. Office: Quality Computer Supplies 2640 S Industrial Park Ave Tempe AZ 85282

OHTAKE, TAKESHI, meteorologist, educator; b. Abiko City, Japan, Jan. 22, 1926; came to U.S. 1964; s. Sakae and Sumiko (Ogawa) O.; m. Kumiko, Jan. 20, 1953; children: Tomoko, Atsuko J., Tadahiro. Diploma, Japan Meteorol. Coll., 1947; BS, Tohoku U., 1952, DSc, 1961. Rsch. asst. Meteorol. Rsch. Inst., Tokyo, 1947-49; rsch. assoc. Geophys. Inst., Tohoku U., Sendai, Japan, 1952-67; lectr. meteorology Coll. Art & Sci., Tohoku U., Sendai, 1961-64; assoc. prof. U. Alaska, Fairbanks, 1964-75, prof. geophysics, 1975-88, prof. emeritus, 1988—; vis. assoc. prof. Colo. State U., Ft. Collins, 1969-71; vis. prof. Nat. Inst. of Polar Rsch., Tokyo, 1979-80, Air Force Geophysics Lab., Bedford, Mass., 1985-87; disting. vis. prof. Nagoya U., 1990-91. Contbr. articles to profl. jours. Fellow Am. Meteorol. Soc., Royal Meteorol. Soc.; mem. Am. Geophys. Union, Meteorol. Soc. Japan, Sigma Xi. Home: 14250 W Warren Dr Lakewood CO 80228-5937

OHTAKI, PETER IWANE, JR., investment banker; b. Seattle, May 2, 1961; s. Peter Iwane and Rose Toshiko (Oda) O. BA, Harvard U., 1983; MBA, Stanford U., 1987. Analyst Merill Lynch Capital Markets, N.Y.C., 1983-85; assoc. Boston Cons. Group, L.A., 1986, Morgan Stanley & Co., N.Y.C., 1987-91; v.p. Unterberg Harris, San Francisco, 1991—. Mem. Am. Electronics Assn.

OHYAMA, HEIICHIRO, music educator, violist, conductor; b. Kyoto, Japan, July 31, 1947; came to U.S., 1970; s. Heishiro and Sumi (Ohara) O.; 1 child, Shinichiro Allen Ohyama. Assocs. degree, Guildhall Sch. Music and Drama, London, 1970. Instr. N.C. Sch. Arts, Winston-Salem, 1972-73; prof. music U. Calif., Santa Barbara, 1973—; prin. violist L.A. Philharm., 1979-91, asst. condr., 1987-90; music dir. Santa Barbara Chamber Orch., 1983—, Crossroads Chamber Orch., Santa Monica, Calif., 1981-93; music dir., condr. Japan Am. Symphony Orch., 1991—; artistic dir. La Jolla (Calif.) Chamber Music Festival, 1986—; condr. Round Top Music Festival, 1983—, N.W. Chamber Orch., 1985-87; vis. lectr. Ind. U., Bloomington, 1972-73; artistic dir. Sante Fe Chamber Music Fair, 1992—. Appearances at Marlboro Music Festival, Vt., 1972-76, Santa Fe Chamber Music Festival, 1977-85, Round Top Music Festival, Tex., 1983—, La Jolla (Calif.) Chamber Music Summer Fest., 1986—; various recordings. Recipient award Young Concert Artist N.Y., 1974, Calif. Artists Mgmt., 1991. Home: 1643 Oramas Rd Santa Barbara CA 93103

OKADA, TSUYOSHI, internist; b. Salinas, Calif., Aug. 3, 1930; s. Kanichi and Haruko (Yokohata) O.; m. Violet Sumiye Shimabukuro, Sept. 10, 1955; children: Cheryl Y., Douglas I., Joan M., Michael H. BA in Chemistry magna cum laude, U. Colo., 1952; MD, Northwestern U., Chgo., 1956. Diplomate Am. Bd. Internal Medicine, Am. Bd. Geriatrics Medicine, Nat. Bd. Med. Examiners. Intern Chgo. Wesley Meml. Hosp., 1956-57; resident, internal medicine UCLA Harbor Gen. Hosp., Torrance, Calif., 1961-64; internist Gardena, Calif., 1964—. Contbr. articles to profl. jours. Capt. U.S. Army Med. Corps, 1957-61, Japan. Fellow ACP; mem. APHA, Calif. Med. Assn., Los Angeles County Med. Assn., Am. Geriatrics Soc., Am. Diabetes Assn., Phi Beta Kappa, Alpha Epsilon Delta. Democrat. Baptist. Office: 16020 S Western Ave Ste 204 Gardena CA 90247

OKASHIMA, MARK ALLEN, healthcare executive, market researcher; b. San Jose, Calif., Oct. 25, 1951; s. John S. and Sumi (Inouye) O. BS, U. Calif., Berkeley, 1973; MBA, U. Santa Clara, 1975. Distbn. analyst Del Monte Corp., San Franisco, 1975-76; vol. V.I.S.T.A., Carson City, Nev., 1976-78; health adminstr. Fallon (Nev.) Tribes, 1978-80; sr. project planner Gov.'s Future Commn., Carson City, 1980-81; data analyst Greater Nev. Health Agy., Reno, 1981-82; dir. rsch. market St. Mary's Regional Med. Ctr., Reno, 1982-92; mgr. fin. planning Seton Med. Ctr., Daly City, Calif., 1992—; cons. Reno Philharm., 1988, 90, Reno Little Theater, 1988. Bd. dir. Internat. Visitor Coun., Reno, 1988, 91, v.p., 1989, pres., 1990. Named Outstanding Young Man of Am., 1987, Internat. Man of Achievement Internat. Biographers, 1989. Mem. Am. Hosp. Assn., Am. Mktg. Assn., Calif. Berkeley Alumni Assn., U. Santa Clara Alumni Assn. Home: 330 Bramble Ct Foster City CA 94404 Office: Seton Med Ctr 1900 Sullivan Ave Daly City CA 94015

OKAZAKI, DONNA SUE, systems analyst; b. Honolulu, Dec. 13, 1959; d. Susumu and Fusako (Itaki) O. BBA, U. Hawaii, 1981, MBA, 1983, postgrad., 1989—. Support analyst Wang Computers, Tokyo, 1984-86; software engr. N.C. State U., CCSP, Raleigh, N.C., 1986-87; cons. Honolulu, 1988-89; systems analyst Seafloor Surveys Internat., Inc., Honolulu, 1989-92; Univ. Hawaii, Honolulu, 1992—. Mem. IEEE Computer Soc., Assn. for Computing Machinery.

O'KEEFE, MARK DAVID, state official; b. Pittston, Pa., July 10, 1952; s. Gervase Frances and Anne Regina (Faltyn) O'K.; m. Lucy Bliss Dayton, Sept. 24, 1983; children: Margaret, Angus, Greer. BA in Environ. Studies, Calif. State U., Sacramento, 1977; MS in Environ. Studies, U. Mont., 1984. Mgr. adjudication program Mont. Dept. Nat. Resources, Helena, 1979-81, dir. water devel., 1981-83; owner, operator Glacier Wilderness Guides, West Glacier, Mont., 1983-89; mem. Mont. Ho. Reps., Helena, 1989-92; state auditor State of Mont., Helena, 1993—. Bd. dirs. Boyd Andrew Chem. Dependency Treatment Ctr., Helena, 1991—. With U.S. Army, 1971-73. Democrat. Home: 531 Power St Helena MT 59601 Office: State Auditors Office Mitchell Bldg Rm 270 PO Box 4009 Helena MT 59604

O'KEEFE, MICHAEL ADRIAN, physicist; b. Melbourne, Australia, Sept. 8, 1942; came to U.S., 1976; s. Peter Francis and Nadezhda O'Keefe; m. Dianne Patricia Fletcher, June 23, 1976; children: Eleanor May, Carlene Frances. Diploma in physics, Royal Melbourne Inst. Tech., 1965; BS, U. Melbourne, 1970, PhD, 1976. Experimental officer Commonwealth Sci. and Indsl. Rsch. Orgn., Melbourne, 1965-69, sci. officer, 1970-76; rsch. assoc. Ariz. State U., Tempe, 1976-79; sr. rsch. assoc. U. Cambridge, Eng., 1979-83; staff scientist U. Calif./LBL, Berkeley, 1983—; cons. Xerox, Palo Alto, Calif., 1989-93, Shell Oil, Houston, 1987-89. Editor: Computer Simulation of Electron Microscope Diffraction and Images, 1989. ;contbr. articles profl. jours. Fellow Royal Microscopical Soc.; mem. Australian Inst. Physics, Electron Microscopy Soc. of Am., Materials Rsch. Soc. Office: U Calif LBL Bldg 72 1 Cyclotron Rd Berkeley CA 94720

OKO, ANDREW JAN, art gallery director, curator; b. London, Sept. 7, 1946; arrived in Can., 1948; s. Jan Kazimierz and Julia Helena (Suska) O.; m. Helen Marie Blanc, Dec. 21, 1972; children: Sonya Celeste, Michelle Kathleen. BA, U. Calgary, 1968; MA, U. Toronto, 1972. Preparator Glenbow Mus., Calgary, Alta., 1972-73, curatorial asst., 1973-74, asst. curator, 1974-77; curator Art Gallery of Hamilton, Ont., 1977-86; dir. MacKenzie Art Gallery, Regina, Sask., 1986—. Author: Country Pleasures: The Angling Art of Jack Cowin, 1984, (with others) Art Gallery Handbook 1982; author/curator: (exhbn. catalogue) The Frontier Art of R.B. Nevitt, 1974, T.R. MacDonald 1908-1978, 1980, The Society of Canadian Painter-Etchers and Engravers in Retrospect, 1981, The Prints of Carl Schaefer, 1983, Canada in the Nineteenth Century: The Bert and Barbara Stitt Family Collection, 1984, Jan Gerrit Wyers 1888-1973, 1989. Mem. Can. Mus. Assn., Can. Art Mus. Dirs.' Orgn., Sask. Arts Alliance (pres. 1991—), Rotary. Office: MacKenzie Art Gallery, 3475 Albert St, Regina, SK Canada S4S 6X6

OKRASINSKI, RICHARD JOSEPH, meteorologist; b. Kingston, Pa., Dec. 24, 1951; s. Joseph and Catherine (Conway) O. BS in Meteorology, U. Utah, 1974, MS in Meteorology, 1977. Phys. scientist Phys. Sci. Lab., Las Cruces, N.Mex., 1977—. Mem. Am. Meteorol. Soc. Office: Phys Sci Lab PO Box 30002 Las Cruces NM 88003-8002

OKRENT, DAVID, engineering educator; b. Passaic, N.J., Apr. 19, 1922; s. Abram and Gussie (Pearlman) O.; m. Rita Gilda Holtzman, Feb. 1, 1948; children—Neil, Nina, Jocelyne. M.E., Stevens Inst. Tech., 1943; M.A., Harvard, 1948, Ph.D. in Physics, 1951. Mech. engr. NACA, Cleve., 1943-46; sr. physicist Argonne (Ill.) Nat. Lab., 1951-71; regents lectr. UCLA, 1968, prof. engring., 1971-91, prof. emeritus, rsch. prof., 1991—; vis. prof. U. Wash., Seattle, 1963, U. Ariz., Tucson, 1970-71; Isaac Taylor chair Technion, 1977-78. Author: Fast Reactor Cross Sections, 1960, Computing Methods in Reactor Physics, 1968, Reactivity Coefficients in Large Fast Power Reactors, 1970, Nuclear Reactor Safety, 1981; contbr. articles to profl. jours. Mem. adv. com. on reactor safeguards AEC, 1963-87, also chmn., 1966; sci. sec. to sec. gen. of Geneva Conf., 1958; mem. U.S. del. to all Geneva Atoms for Peace Confs. Guggenheim fellow, 1961-62, 77-78; recipient Disting. Appointment award Argonne Univs. Assn., 1970, Disting. Service award U.S. Nuclear Regulatory Commn., 1985. Fellow Am. Phys. Soc., Am. Nuclear Soc. (Tommy Thompson award 1980, Glenn Seaborg medal 1987), Nat. Acad. Engring. Home: 439 Veteran Ave Los Angeles CA 90024-1956

OKUMA, ALBERT AKIRA, JR., architect; b. Cleve., Feb. 10, 1946; s. Albert Akira Sr. and Reiko (Suwa) O.; m. Janice Shirley Bono, July 17, 1971; children: Reiko Dawn, Benjamin Scott. BS in Archtl. Engring, Calif. Poly. State U., San Luis Obispo, 1970, BArch, 1975; ednl. facility planning cert., U. Calif., Riverside, 1990. Lic. architect, Calif., Mont., Ariz., Ill., Nev., N.Mex., Oreg., Maine; cert. Nat. Coun. Archtl. Bds. Architect USN, Point Mugu, Calif., 1975-76; designer Wilson Stroh Wilson Architects, Santa Paula, Calif., 1976-79; architect, project mgr. W.J. Kulwiec AIA & Assocs., Camarillo, Calif., 1979-83, Wilson & Conrad Architects, Ojai, Calif., 1983-84, Dziak, Immel & Lauterbach Services Inc., Oxnard, Calif., 1984-85; ptnr. Conrad & Okuma Architects, Oxnard, 1985—; commr. Calif. Bd. Archtl. Examiners, 1985—, City of San Buenaventua Hist. Preservation Commn., 1990—, chmn., 1991-93; peer reviewer Am. Cons. Engrs. Coun., 1987—; lectr. U. Calif. Ext., Riverside, 1991—. Prin. works include Hobson Brothers Bldg. (reconstruction and preservation), Ventura, Calif., (Design for Excellence award 1991, Historic Bldg of Yr. award 1992). Mem. Spiritual Assembly Bahai's of Ventura, Calif., 1978—, treas. 1978-79, 84, 86-88, chmn. 1992-93; treas.'s rep. Nat. Spriritual Assembly Bahai's U.S., Wilmette, Ill., 1981—, mem. dist. teaching com., 1992-93; treas. Parents and Advocates for Gifted Edn., 1988-89; chmn. Ventura Unified Sch. Dist. Citizens Budget Adv. Com., 1990, 92, 92; mem. City of San Buenaventura specific plan citizens com., 1990, 91, 92, 93, multicultural/community heritage task force of the cultural arts plan com. 1991-92. 1st lt. U.S. Army, 1971-73. Mem. AIA (chpt. bd. dirs. 1976-79, 81—, chpt. sec. 1981, v.p. 1982, pres. 1983, Intern Devel. Program Outstanding Firm award 1993), Am. Planning Assn., Internat. Conf. Bldg. Ofcls., Nat. Trust for Hist. Preservation, Calif. Preservation Found., Constrn. Specifications Inst., Design Methods Group, Coalition for Adequate Sch. Housing, Coun. Ednl. Facility Planners Internat., Structural Engrs. Assn. So. Calif. (affiliate), Ventura County Econ. Devel. Assn., Calif. Polytech. State U. Alumni Assn. (life), Toastmasters Internat. Office: Conrad & Okuma Architects 167 Lambert St Oxnard CA 93030-1044

OLAH, GEORGE ANDREW, chemist, educator; b. Budapest, Hungary, May 22, 1927; came to U.S., 1964, naturalized, 1970; s. Julius and Magda (Rasznai) O.; m. Judith Agnes Lengyel, July 9, 1949; children: George John, Ronald Peter. PhD, Tech. U. Budapest, 1949, hon. degree, 1989; DSc honoris causa, U. Durham, 1988, U. Munich, 1990. Mem. faculty Tech. U. Budapest, 1949-54; asso. dir. Cen. Chem. Rsch. Inst., Hungarian Acad. Scis., 1954-56; rsch. scientist Dow Chem. Can. Ltd., 1957-64, Dow Chem. Co., Framingham, Mass., 1964-65; prof. chemistry Case-Western Res. U., Cleve., 1965-69, C.F. Mabery prof. rsch., 1969-77; Donald P. and Katherine B. Loker disting. prof. chemistry, dir. Hydrocarbon Rsch. Inst., U. So. Calif., L.A., 1977—; vis. prof. chemistry Ohio State U., 1963, U. Heidelberg, Germany, 1965, U. Colo., 1969, Swiss Fed. Inst. Tech., 1972, U. Munich, 1973, U. London, 1973-79, L. Pasteur U., Strasbourg, 1974, U. Paris, 1981; hon. vis. lectr. U. London, 1981; cons. to industry. Author: Friedel-Crafts Reactions, Vols. I-IV, 1963-64, (with P. Schleyer) Carbonium Ions, Vols. I-V, 1969-76, Friedel-Crafts Chemistry, 1973, Carbocations and Electrophilic Reactions, 1973, Halonium Ions, 1975, (with G.K.S. Prakash and J. Somer) Superacids, 1984; (with Prakash, R.E. Williams, L.D. Field and K. Wade) Hypercarbon Chemistry, 1987, (with R. Malthotra and S.C. Narang) Nitration, 1989, Cage Hydrocarbons, 1990, (with Wade and Williams) Electron Deficient Boron and Carbon Clusters, 1991, (with Chambers and Prarash) Synthetic Fluorine Chemistry, 1992, also chpts. in books, numerous papers in field; patentee in field. Recipient Leo Hendrik Baekeland award N.J. sect. Am. Chem. Soc., 1966, Morley medal Cleve. sect., 1970; Alexander von Humboldt Sr. U.S. Scientist award, 1979, Pioneer of Chemistry award Am. Inst. Chemists, 1993. Fellow AAAS, Chem. Inst. Can.; mem. NAS, Italian NAS, European Acad. Arts, Scis. and Humanities, Italy Chem. Soc. (hon.), Hungarian Acad. Sci. (hon.), Am. Chem. Soc. (award petroleum chemistry 1964, award Synthetic organic chemistry 1979, Roger Adams award in organic chemistry 1989), German Chem. Soc., Brit. Chem. Soc. (Centenary lectr. 1978), Swiss Chem. Soc., Sigma Xi. Home: 2252 Gloaming Way Beverly Hills CA 90210-1717 Office: U So Calif Dept Chemistry Los Angeles CA 90007

OLAZABAL, GARY STEVEN COYOTE, producer, composer; b. L.A., Sept. 22, 1953; s. Rudolph and Irene Louise (Adante) O.; m. Dena Elizabeth Goodmanson, June 14, 1990. High sch. grad., L.A. Engr. Record Plant, L.A., 1972-74; chief engr. Stevie Wonder, L.A., 1974-91; producer, composer Noisy Neighbors, L.A., 1990—. Co-producer: Woman in Red, 1988 (Academy Oscar award); engr.: (albums) Songs In the Key of Life, 1975 (Grammy award), Characters (Grammy award), Secret Life of Plants (Grammy award). Office: Noisy Neighbors 3435 Primera Ave Los Angeles CA 90068

OLBRECHTS, GUY ROBERT, electrical engineer, consultant; b. Mechelen, Belgium, May 22, 1935; came to U.S., 1967, naturalized, 1978; s. Alphonse and Blanche (Van Coolput) O.; m. Andree Julia Van Nes, Oct. 19, 1961; children: Philippe, Ingrid, Dominique. Ingenieur civil electricien Catholic U. Leuven, Belgium, 1960; MBA, Seattle U., 1976. Lead engr. Ctr. D'Etudes Nucleaires, Mol, Belgium, 1962-65; quality control mgr., chief engr. for magnetics Sprague Electromag., Ronse, Belgium, 1965-67; sr. engr. Boeing Co., Seattle, 1967-79; sect. mgr. data systems engring. and product support Sundstrand Data Control Corp., Redmond, Wash., 1979-88; project engr. memory systems Sundstrand Data Control, 1979-90, rsch. specialist, 1990—; propr., cons., designer Gentronics, Bellevue, Wash., 1970—. Patentee gyro wheel speed modulator, 1981, integrated strapdown/airdata sensor system, 1981, slow-acting phase-locked loop, 1983. Served as cpl. Belgian Army, 1961-62. Recipient inventor award Boeing Co., 1978. Republican. Roman Catholic. Home: 4809 116th Ave SE Bellevue WA 98006-2723 Office: Sundstrand Data Control Corp 15001 NE 36th St Redmond WA 98052-5317

OLCOTT, JOANNE ELIZABETH, naval officer; b. Portland, Oreg., May 12, 1958; d. Richard Hutton and Eleanor (Looker) O. BS, Oreg. State U., 1980; MS, Naval Postgrad. Sch., 1989. Commd. ensign USN, 1980, advanced through grades to lt. comdr., 1991; oceanographic watch officer USN Naval Facility, Guam, 1981-82, USN, Antigua, W.I., 1982-84; adminstrv. officer USN, Antigua, 1983-84, ops. officer, 1984-85; chief testing mgmt. sect. USN Mil. Entrance Processing Sta., Salt Lake City, 1985-87; officer-in-charge Japan detachment Comdr. Naval Forces, Okinawa, 1989-91; ops. officer Naval Facility, Whidbey Island, Wash., 1991—. Mem. NAFE, Kappa Delta. Republican. Episcopalian. Office: 2278 N Fairlane Oak Harbor WA 98277

OLDAKER, WILLIAM HENRY, lawyer; b. Albuquerque, Nov. 9, 1931; s. Merritt W. and Eunice (Rowe) O.; m. Beuna Rasmussen, Aug. 27, 1953; children: Sarah Margaret Oldaker Hammond, William Arthur. LLB, U. Colo., 1955, JD, 1963; student, U. N.Mex., 1988-90. Bar: N.Mex. 1955, U.S. Dist. Ct. N.Mex. 1955, U.S. Ct. Appeals (10th cir.) 1955, U.S. Supreme Ct. 1986. With Albuquerque Nat. Bank, 1948-53, Nat. State Bank, Boulder, Colo., 1953-55; pvt. practice Albuquerque, 1956-68; ptnr. Oldaker & Oldaker, Albuquerque, 1968—; dir. First Interstate Bank. Oil painter of wildlife. Pres., dir., life mem. Salvation Army Bd., Albuquerque, 1962—, mem. adult rehab. bd., San Diego, 1991—; life mem. Albuquerque Econ. Devel., 1965—; chmn. LaJolla Shores Assn., 1992; mem. charter revision com. City of Albuquerque, 1970. Capt. USAF, 1956-59. Recipient various awards for leadership in city and state bds., commns. Mem. ABA, N.Mex. Bar Assn., Albuquerque Bar Assn., Albuquerque C. of C. (dir., pres. elect 1973), Ducks Unltd. (state chmn. 1965-73), Lions Internat. (pres., zone chmn. 1959-70), Rotary (dir.). Republican. Presbyterian.

OLDENBURG, RONALD TROY, lawyer; b. Eldora, Iowa, June 2, 1935; s. Lorenz Frank and Bess Louise (Lewis) O.; m. Vickie Yu; children: John, Keith, Mark. BA, U. N.C., 1957; postgrad., Brunnsvik Folkhogskola, Sorvik, Sweden, 1957-58; JD, U. Miss., 1961. Bar: Miss. 1961, Hawaii 1975. Mgr. Continental Travel Svc., Chapel Hill, N.C., 1956-57, Meridian Travel Svc., Raleigh, N.C., 1961, Linmark Internat. Devel., Seoul, 1972-74; fgn. atty. Li Chun Law Office, Taipei, Taiwan, 1965-67; pvt. practice, Taipei, 1967-72, Honolulu, 1975—. Compiler: International Directory of Birth, Death, Marriage and Divorce Records, 1985; contbr. articles on immigration law to legal jours. Capt. JAGC, USAF, 1962-65. Mem. Am. Immigration Lawyers Assn. Office: 677 Ala Moana Blvd Ste 602 Honolulu HI 96813

OLDFIELD, A(RTHUR) BARNEY, writer, radio commentator; b. Tecumseh, Nebr., Dec. 18, 1909; s. Adam William and Anna Ota (Fink) O.; m. Vada Margaret Kinman, May 6, 1935. AB, U. Nebr., 1933, LittD (hon.), 1992. Commd. 2d lt. U.S. Army, 1932, advanced through grades to lt. col., 1945; advanced through grades to col. USAF, 1947, ret., 1962; columnist, feature writer Jour., Lincoln, Nebr., 1932-40; publicist Warner Bros. Studio, Burbank, Calif., 1946-47; corp. dir. internat. rels. Litton Industries, Beverly Hills, Calif., 1963-89; founder, treas. Radio & TV News Dirs. Found. Author: Never a Shot in Anger, Operation Narcissus, 1991, Those Wonderful Men in the Cactus Starfighter Squadron; contbr. to collections: Yanks Meet Reds, Sale I Made Which Did Most for Me, Road to Berlin. Founder, sec.-treas. Found. of Ams. for Handicapped, Washington; bd. mem., trustee Triple L Youth Ranch Ctr., Colo., 1978-88; trustee USAF Mus.; mem. bd. nominations Aviation Hall of Fame, Dayton, Ohio. Recipient Humanitarian award Am. Rsch. and Med. Svcs. Anaheim, 1978; named Disting. Nebraskalander of Yr., 1983, VFW Disting. Citizen, 1992; inducted Hall of Champions Invent Am., 1989. Mem. Aviation/Space Writers Assn. (founder 1977, Disting. Svc. award), Radio & TV News Dirs. Assn. (Disting. Svc. award 1973), Overseas Press Club Am., Greater L.A. Press Club, Radio & TV News Assn. So. Calif., Writers Guild Am. West, Armed Forces Broadcasters Assn., Air Force Assn. (life), Navy League (life). Republican. Office: PO Box 1855 Beverly Hills CA 90213

OLDHAM, CHRISTOPHER RUSSELL, wine company executive; b. Basingstoke, U.K., Sept. 18, 1946; came to U.S., 1986; s. Henry Russell Oldham and Esme Grace (Craufurd) Anderson; m. Elizabeth Jacoba Graham, Jan. 9, 1971 (div. 1978); 1 child, Justin Mark; m. Janet Patricia Gough, Dec. 9, 1978; children: Carro, Nicholas. Student, Rugby Sch., U.K., 1965, Madrid U., 1967, London Bus. Sch., 1972. Mgmt. exec. Guthrie & Co. (U.K.) Ltd., London and Singapore, 1973-74; mktg. dir. Guthrie & Co. (U.K.) Ltd., London, 1974-75; mng. dir. William Armes & Son, Sudbury, U.K., 1975-76, Transmarine Air Holdings Ltd., Luton, U.K., 1976-80; pres., owner S.C.E.A. Du Chateau De Lacaze, Gabarret, France, 1980-87; corp. devel. dir. Chateaux Shippers Ltd., London, 1984—; pres. Wine Link Inc., San Diego, 1987—, 1990—; cons. Transmarine Holdings Ltd., London, 1980—; bd. dirs. Computerland City of London. Author: Armagnac and Eaux-De-Vie, 1986; author/eidtor (bi-monthly pub.) Wine Line, 1990—; contbr. articles to profl. jours. Hist. rsch. Societe Borda, Pau, France, 1981-87; mem. Worshipful Co. of Glaziers, City of London, liveryman. Capt. U.K. Calvary, 1967-71. Recipient Freedom of City of London by Lord Mayor of London, 1975. Mem. British Inst. of Mgmt., Confrerie Cadets de Gascogne, Cavalry Club

London, Fairbanks Ranch Country Club, S.W. Yacht Club. Office: Chateaux Shippers Group 12526 High Bluff Dr # 300 San Diego CA 92130

OLDHAM, MAXINE JERNIGAN, real estate broker; b. Whittier, Calif., Oct. 13, 1923; d. John K. and Lela Hessie (Mears) Jernigan; m. Laurance Montgomery Oldham, Oct. 28, 1941; 1 child, John Laurence. AA, San Diego City Coll., 1973; student Western State U. Law, San Diego, 1976-77, LaSalle U., 1977-78; grad. Realtors Inst., Sacramento, 1978. Mgr. Edin Harig Realty, LaMesa, Calif., 1966-70; tchr. Bd. Edn., San Diego, 1959-66; mgr. Julia Cave Real Estate, San Diego, 1970-73; salesman Computer Realty, San Diego, 1973-74; owner Shelter Island Realty, San Diego, 1974—. Author: Jernigan History, 1982, Mears Geneology, 1985, Fustons of Colonial America, 1988, Sissoms. Mem. Civil Svc. Commn., San Diego, 1957-58. Recipient Outstanding Speaker award Dale Carnegie. Mem. Nat. Assn. Realtors, Calif. Assn. Realtors, San Diego Bd. Realtors, San Diego Apt. Assn., Internationale des Professions Immobilieres (internat. platform speaker), DAR (vice regent Linares chpt.), Colonial Dames 17th Century, Internat. Fedn. Univ. Women. Republican. Roman Catholic. Avocations: music, theater, painting, geneology, continuing edn. Home: 3348 Lowell St San Diego CA 92106-1713 Office: Shelter Island Realty 2810 Lytton St San Diego CA 92110

OLDS, ROGER ALAN, systems analyst; b. Albuquerque, Nov. 16, 1951; s. Leonard Elmo and Grace Earlene (Hoagland) O.; m. Debra Carmella Romero, Mar. 7, 1981; children: Rachel Ruth, Lisa Kristine. Student, Ricks Coll., 1969-70; BA in Math., Brigham Young U., 1976. Sustitute tchr. Denver Pub. Schs., 1977-82; ins. agt. Am. Nat. Ins. Co., 1982; computer programmer Colo. Compensation Ins. Authority, Denver, 1982-84, systems analyst, 1984—. Mem. Rep. precinct com., Denver, 1980—; sec. Rep. Orgn. Ho. Legis. Dist. 2, 1986-92. Mem. LDS Ch. Home: 1333 S Eliot St Denver CO 80219 Office: Colo Compensation Ins Authority Ste 100N 720 S Colorado Blvd Denver CO 80222

OLDSHUE, PAUL FREDERICK, financial executive; b. Chgo., Nov. 4, 1949; s. James Young and Betty Ann (Wiersema) O.; m. Mary Elizabeth Holl, July 12, 1975; children: Emily Jane, Andrew Armstrong. Abigail Anne. BA, Williams Coll., Williamstown, Mass., 1971; MBA, NYU, 1978. With Chem. Bank, N.Y.C., 1973-78, asst. sec., 1976-78; with Orbanco Fin. Svc. Corp., 1978-83, v.p., treas., 1980-83; exec. v.p. Oreg. Bank, Portland, 1984-88; v.p. syndications PacifiCorp Fin. Svcs., Inc., 1988-90; sr. v.p. U.S. Bancorp, Portland, 1991—. Mem. Fin. Execs. Inst., Multnomah Athletic Club (Portland). Republican.

O'LEARY, DANIEL EDMUND, finance educator; b. White Plains, N.Y., May 19, 1950; s. Daniel Edmund and Dorthea Elizabeth (Reichardt) O'L. BS, Bowling Green U.; MBA, U. Mich.; PhD, Case Western Res. U., 1986; cert. in data processing. CPA, Ohio; cert. info. systems auditor; cert. mgmt. acct. Cons. Peat, Marwick, Mitchell & Co., Cleve., 1977-81; instr. Case Western Res. U., Cleve., 1981-84, Cleve. State U., 1984-85; asst. prof. U. So. Calif., L.A., 1985-90, assoc. prof., 1990—; lectr. Fin. Execs. Inst., L.A., 1990; lectr., cons. Am. Express, N.Y.C., 1988; cons. Computax, 1987. Editor: Artificial Intelligence to Business, 1991, (jour.) Expert Systems Rev., 1986—; author: Artificial Intelligence in Internal Auditing, 1991; mem. editorial bd. Expert Systems Applications, L.A., 1990; contbr. articles to profl. jours. Grantee Expert Systems and Internal Controls Nat. Assn. Accts., 1989, Peat Marwick Found., 1988, 89, Nat. Ctr. for Automated Info. Retrieval, 1986; named Author of Yr. Inst. of Internal Auditors, L.A., 1988. Mem. AICPA (info. tech. subcom. 1990—), Am. Assn. for Artificial Intelligence (pres. artificial intelligence in bus. sect. 1990—), Inst. Mgmt. Scis. (pres. measures in mgmt. sect. 1990—), Am. Acctg. Assn. (pres. artificial intelligence and expert systems sect.). Office: Univ So Calif Grad Sch of Business Los Angeles CA 90089

O'LEARY, PEGGY RENÉ, accountant; b. Billings, Mont., Dec. 6, 1951; d. Paul Eugene and Norma Dean (Metcalf) O'L.; m. Kim Patric Johnson, Mar. 19, 1983. BS, Mont. State U., 1976. CPA, Mont. Staff acct. Peat Marwick Main, Billings, 1976-80; dir. fin. Billings Clinic, 1980—. Div. leader youth support campaign, YMCA, Billings, 1987-88, 92-93, bd. dirs., 1988—, sec. bd., 1989—. Mem. Billings C. of C. (sch. tax com. 1982-88), Pink Chips Investment Club (treas. 1987-88). Republican. Roman Catholic. Home: 4565 Pine Cove Rd Billings MT 59106-1332 Office: Billings Clinic 2825 8th Ave N Billings MT 59101-0998

O'LEARY, THOMAS HOWARD, resources executive; b. N.Y.C., Mar. 19, 1934; s. Arthur J. and Eleanor (Howard) O'L.; m. Cheryl L. Westrum; children: Mark, Timothy, Thomas, Denis, Daniel, Mary, Frances. A.B., Holy Cross Coll., 1954; postgrad., U. Pa., 1959-61. Asst. cashier First Nat. City Bank, N.Y.C., 1961-65; asst. to chmn. finance com. Mo. Pacific R.R. Co., 1966-70, v.p. finance, 1971-76, dir., 1972-82, chmn. finance com., 1976-82; treas. Mo. Pacific Corp., St. Louis, 1968-71; v.p. finance Mo. Pacific Corp., 1971-72, exec. v.p., 1972-74, dir., 1972-82, pres., 1974-82; chmn. bd., chief exec. officer Mississippi River Transmission Corp., 1974-82; vice chmn. Burlington No. , Inc., Seattle, 1982-89; bd. dirs. BF Goodrich, Kroger Co. Served to capt. USMC, 1954-58. Mem. Blind Brook Club (N.Y.C.), Chgo. Club. Office: Burlington Resources Inc 999 3rd Ave Ste 4500 Seattle WA 98104

OLENDER, BEATRIJS TOBI, psychologist, marriage and family therapist; b. Wonosobo, Java, Dutch East Indies, July 30, 1941; came to U.S., 1966; d. Walther Frank Tobi and Ida (Leeuwe) Boehm; m. Irving William Olender, May 15, 1968; children: Derek Steven, Brian David. BA cum laude, Rijks U., Leiden, The Netherlands, 1961, MA cum laude, 1966; MA in Clin. Psychology, U. Mich., 1968, PhD Candidate, 1973. Lic. marriage, family and child counselor, Calif. Rsch. asst. Rijks U., Leiden, 1962-66, lectr., 1966; clin. intern U. Mich., Ann Arbor, 1966-68, 69-71, clin. teaching asst., 1971-73; staff psychologist Merced (Calif.) County Health Clinic, 1968-69; psychotherapy intern Midstream Counseling Ctr., Los Gatos, Calif., 1979-81; pvt. practice psychotherapy Los Gatos, 1981—. Bd. dirs. Santa Clara County Med. Soc. Aux., San Jose, 1976-78, ACLU Santa Clara County, San Jose, 1977-79; vol. dir., pres. bd. Parental Stress Hotline of Greater San Jose, 1976-79; bd. mem. San Jose Symphonic Choir, 1990—. Fulbright exch. grantee Inst. Internat. Edn., 1966; named Outstanding Vol. of Santa Clara County Vol. Action Ctr., San Jose, 1977; recipient Disting. Svc. award Santa Clara County Med. Soc. Aux., San Jose, 1978. Mem. Am. Assn. Marriage and Family Therapists (clin. mem.), Assn. Transpersonal Psychology, Assn. for Past-Life Rsch. and Therapies, Calif. Assn. Marriage and Family Therapists (clin. mem.). Office: 15810 Los Gatos Los Gatos CA 95032

OLES, STUART GREGORY, lawyer; b. Seattle, Dec. 15, 1924; s. Floyd and Helen Louise (La Violette) O.; B.S. magna cum laude, U. Wash., 1947, J.D., 1948; m. Ilse Hanewald, Feb. 12, 1954; children—Douglas, Karl, Stephen. Admitted to Wash. bar, 1949, U.S. Supreme Ct. bar, 1960; dep. pros. atty. King County (Wash.), 1949, chief civil dept., 1949-50; gen. practice law, Seattle, 1950—; sr. partner firm Oles, Morrison & Rinker and predecessor, 1955-90, of counsel, 1991—. Chmn. Seattle Community Concert Assn., 1955; pres. Friends Seattle Pub. Library, 1956; mem. Wash. Pub. Disclosure Commn., 1973-75; trustee Ch. Div. Sch. of Pacific, Berkeley, Calif., 1974-75; mem. bd. curators Wash. State Hist. Soc., 1983; former mem. Seattle Symphony Bd.; pres. King County Ct. House Rep. Club, 1950, U. Wash. Young Rep. Club, 1947; Wash. conv. floor leader Taft, 1952, Goldwater, 1964; Wash. chmn. Citizens for Goldwater, 1964; chmn. King County Rep. convs., 1966, 68, 76, 84, 86, 88, 90, 92, Wash. State Rep. Conv., 1980. Served with USMCR, 1943-45. Mem. ABA (past regional vice chmn. pub. contract law sect.), Wash. Bar Assn., Order of Coif, Scabbard and Blade, Am. Legion, Kapoho Beach Club (pres.), Am. Highland Cattle Assn. (dir.), Phi Beta Kappa, Phi Alpha Delta. Episcopalian (vestryman, lay-reader), Rainier Club, Seattle Yacht Club. Home: 5051 50th Ave NE Apt 40 Seattle WA 98105-2869 Office: Oles Morrison & Rinker 701 5th Ave Ste 3300 Seattle WA 98104-7082

OLEXA, GEORGE RONALD, cellular telecommunication executive; b. West Chester, Pa., Sept. 14, 1955; s. George Paul and Marie Grace (Hanthorn) O.; 1 child, Danielle René. BSEE, Pa. State U., 1977. Cert. 1st class radiotelephone FCC. Cen. office engr. Conestoga Telephone and Telegraph Co., Birdsboro, Pa., 1977-82; chief engr. LIN Broadcasting, N.Y.C., 1982-86; v.p. engring. L.A. Cellular Telephone Co., 1986-88; exec. dir. engring. Pac Tel Cellular, Irvine, Calif., 1988—. Home: 8167 Prestwich Cir Huntington Beach CA 92646 Office: Pac Tel Cellular 3 Park Plz Irvine CA 92714

OLGUIN, JOHN PATRICK, business educator; b. Artesia, N.Mex., Apr. 29, 1959; s. Robert C. and Ruby (Rickner) O. BA, N.Mex. Highlands U., 1986, MBA, 1988, secondary lic., 1990. Foreman Eddy County Community Action Weatherization, Artesia, 1974-75, asst. dir., 1975-78; program coord. Foster Grandparents and Ret. Sr. Vol. Program, Artesia, 1978-80; carpenter Sunshine Constrn., Artesia, 1980-82; truckdriver Alvarado Trucking, Artesia, 1982-84; peer counselor N.Mex. Highlands Univ., Las Vegas, 1984-86, adminstrv. asst., 1986-88, instr., 1988—. Named Outstanding Young Men of Am., 1988-89. Mem. Nat. Acctg. Assn., Nat. Smithsonian Inst. Democrat. Roman Catholic. Home: 104 Alamo Apt 4 Las Vegas NM 87701 Office: N Mex Highlands Univ National Ave Las Vegas NM 87701

OLHOFT, JOHN ERNEST, construction engineer; b. Fallon, Nev., Oct. 28, 1943; s. Karl and Isabelle Kennedy (Oakden) O.; A.S., U. Heidelberg, 1964; student U. Alaska, 1976—; B.S.C.E., Columbia Pacific U., 1982; m. Leona Faye Montgomery, 1981; children—Jonathon Scott, Trask Montgomery. Vice-pres. Consol. Investment Corp., Kodiak, Alaska, 1967—; purchasing agt. Crowley Maritime Corp., Anchorage, 1976-77; constrn. engr. Northwestern Constrn. Inc., Anchorage, 1977-80; project engr. Doyon/Reading & Bates, Fairbanks, Alaska, 1981; insp. Miner & Miner, Cons. Engrs., Inc., Greeley, Colo., 1981; safety engr. Frank Moolin & Assocs., 1982-83; constrn. engr. Matanuska Electric Assn., Palmer, Alaska, 1982-93, dist. engr. Eagle River, 1993—; mem. bd. dirs. Consol. Investment Corp., Kodiak, Alaska. Served with AUS, 1961-64. Decorated Purple Heart. Mem. Nat. Safety Mgmt. Soc., Am. Mgmt. Assn., Smithsonian Instn., Am. Legion, Mensa, Internat. Platform Assn., Am. Film Inst. Mem. Ch. Jesus Christ of Latter-day Saints. Home: 17423 Coronado PO Box 770237 Eagle River AK 99577-0237 Office: Matanuska Elec Assn Inc 11623 Aurora St Eagle River AK 99577

OLIPHANT, CHARLES ROMIG, physician; b. Waukegan, Ill., Sept. 10, 1917; s. Charles L. and Mary (Goss) R.; student St. Louis U., 1936-40; m. Claire E. Canavan, Nov. 7, 1942; children: James R., Cathy Rose, Mary G., William D. Student, St. Louis U., 1936-40, MD, 1943; postgrad. Naval Med. Sch., 1946. Intern, Nat. Naval Med. Ctr., Bethesda, Md., 1943; pvt. practice medicine and surgery, San Diego, 1947—; pres., chief exec. officer Midway Med. Enterprises; former chief staff Balboa Hosp., Doctors Hosp., Cabrillo Med. Ctr.; chief staff emeritus Sharp Cabrillo Hosp.; mem. staff Mercy Hosp., Children's Hosp., Paradise Valley Hosp., Sharp Meml. Hosp.; sec. Sharp Sr. Health Care, S.D.; mem. exec. bd., past. comdr. San Diego Power Squadron. Charter mem. Am. Bd. Family Practice. Served with M.C., USN, 1943-47. Recipient Golden Staff award Sharp Cabrillo Hosp. Med. Staff, 1990. Fellow Am. Geriatrics Soc. (emeritus), Am. Acad. Family Practice, Am. Assn. Abdominal Surgeons; mem. AMA, Calif. Med. Assn., Am. Acad. Family Physicians (past pres. San Diego chpt., del. Calif. chpt.), San Diego Med. Soc., Public Health League, Navy League, San Diego Power Squadron (past comdr.), SAR. Clubs: San Diego Yacht, Cameron Highlanders. Home: 4310 Trias St San Diego CA 92103-1127

OLIPHANT, ERNIE L., safety educator, public relations executive, consultant; b. Richmond, Ind., Oct. 25, 1934; d. Ernest E. and Beulah A. (Jones) Reid; m. George B. Oliphant, Sept. 25, 1955; children—David, Wendell, Rebecca. Student, Earlham Coll., 1953-55, Ariz. State U., 1974, Phoenix Coll., 1974-78. Planner, organizer, moderator confs., programs for various women's clubs, safety assns., 1971-86; nat. field coordinator Operation Lifesaver, Inc., 1986—; assoc. dir. Operation Lifesaver Nat. Safety Council, Phoenix, 1978-86; cons. Fed. R.R. Adminstrn.; lectr. in field.; adviser Am. Ry. Engring. Assn., Calif. Assn. Women Hwy. Safety Leaders, numerous others. Mem. R.R./Hwy. grade crossing com. Ariz. Corp. Commn.; mem. transp. and system com. Ariz. Gov.'s Commn. on Environment; mem. Ariz. Gov.'s Council Women for Hwy. Safety; mem. motor vehicle traffic safety at hwy.-r.r. grade crossings com., roadway environment com., women's div. com. Nat. Safety Council; mem. Phoenix Traffic Accident Reduction Program; task force mem. U.S. Dept. Transp. on Grade Crossing Safety. Recipient Safety award SW Safety Congress, 1973; citation of Merit Adv. Commn. on Ariz. Environment, 1974; Gov.'s award for hwy. safety, 1978; Gov.'s Merit of Recognition Outstanding Service in Hwy. Safety, 1980. Mem. Assn. R.R. Editors, NAFE, Inc., Pub. Relations Soc. Am., R.R. Pub. Relations Assn., committees Nat. Acad. Scis. (dir. transp. research, planning, adminstrn. of transp. safety com., r.r.-hwy. grade crossing safety com.), Women's Transp. Seminar, Ariz. Fedn. Women's Clubs (named pres. of yr. 1968), Ariz. Safety Assn. (safety recognition award 1975), Gen. Fedn. Women's Clubs (internat. bd. dirs.), Nat. Assn. Women Hwy. Safety Leaders, Soc. Govt. Planners, Inc., Phi Theta Kappa. Republican. Quaker. Author of tech. publs.

OLIPHANT, ROBERT THOMPSON, English language educator; b. Tulsa, Oct. 24, 1924; s. Stephen Duncan and Dorothy Ann (Thompson) O.; m. Lois Ann Millett, Apr. 10, 1956 (div. July 1965); children: Matthew Duncan, Jason Stewart; m. Jane H. Johnson, July 26, 1965. AB, Washington and Jefferson Coll., 1949; MA, Stanford U., 1958, PhD, 1962. Asst. prof. Calif. State U., Northridge, 1959-63, assoc. prof., 1964-68, prof. English, 1969—. Author: The Harley Latin-Old English Glossary, 1966, A Piano for Mrs. Cimino, 1980, A Trumpet for Jackie, 1983; author, composer: The Importance of Being Earnest, 1971, Eduardian England: A Pramatic Cantata for Mixed Chorus, 1993. Recipient Lit. Rsch. award U.S. Dept. Edn., 1986-87, 88-89. Office: Calif State U Dept English 18111 Nordhoff St Northridge CA 91330-0001

OLIVA, STEPHEN EDWARD, resource conservationist, lawyer; b. San Rafael, Calif., Jan. 31, 1946; s. George Verdelli Jr. and Dorothy Margaret (Austin) O.; m. Susan Rebecca Ellis, May 5, 1984; children: Stephanie, Mary. BA, U. Calif., Santa Barbara, 1972; JD, U. of the Pacific, 1992. Bar: Calif., U.S. Dist. Ct. (ea. dist.) Calif. Naturalist Calif. Dept. Transp., Sacramento, 1973-76; planner Calif. Energy Commn., Sacramento, 1976, Calif. Air Resources Bd., Sacramento, 1976-79; spl. asst. to sec. The Resources Agy., Sacramento, 1979-80; spl. asst. Calif. Dept. Conservation, Sacramento, 1980, mgr. land conservation unit, 1981-87; spl. asst. Calif. Dept. Forestry, Sacramento, 1980-81; chief Office Land Conservation Calif. Dept. Conservation, Sacramento, 1987-89, dep. chief Calif. div. of recycling, 1989-91, environ. coord., 1991-92, staff counsel, legal office, 1992—; mem. governing bd. Calif. Tahoe Regional Planning Agy., South Lake Tahoe, 1979-81; mem. policy adv. com. Sacramento County Local Agy. Formation Commn., 1988-89. Served with U.S. Army, 1966-68, Vietnam. Mem. ABA, Assn. Environ. Profls., Assn. Am. Geographers, Urban and Regional Info. Systems Assn., Calif. State Bar. Democrat. Office: Calif Dept Conservation 801 K St MS 24-03 Sacramento CA 95814

OLIVAS, DANIEL A., lawyer, deputy state attorney general; b. L.A., Apr. 8, 1959; s. Michael A. and Elizabeth M. (Velasco) O.; m. Susan L. Formaker, Oct. 19, 1986; 1 child, Benjamin Formaker-Olivas. BA, Stanford U., 1981; JD, UCLA, 1984. Bar: Calif., U.S. Dist. Ct. (cen. dist.) Calif., U.S. Ct. Appeals (9th cir.). Law clk., atty. Hunt & Cochran-Bond, L.A., 1984-88; atty. Heller, Ehrman, White & McAuliffe, L.A., 1988-90; dep. atty. gen. dept. of justice antitrust div. State of Calif., L.A., 1990-91, dep. atty. gen. dept. of justice land law sect., 1991—; state apptd. bd. dirs. Western Ctr. Law and Poverty, L.A., 1988—. Mem. Mex.-Am. Bar Assn.Mex.-Am. Bar Found. (bd. dirs. 1993—), L.A. County Bar Assn., Stanford Chicano/Latino Alumni club (pres.-elect 1992-93, pres. 1993-94). Office: State of Calif Ste 5212 300 S Spring St Los Angeles CA 90013-1230

OLIVAS, DAVID ANTONIO, lawyer; b. Santa Fe, Dec. 9, 1952; s. Federico Jake and Rose (Montoya) O.; m. Pauline Marie Collins, June 8, 1985; children: Nicole Rose, Lucas David. BS, U. Colo., 1979, JD, 1982. Bar: Colo. 1983, U.S. Dist. Ct. Colo. 1983. Pres. Solar Heating Systems, Boulder, Colo., 1976-78; mgr. Alternative Heating Systems, Boulder, Colo., 1978-80; dep. dist. atty. City of Denver, 1983-89; sr. assoc. Tilly & Graves, Denver, 1989—; speaker, presenter Denver Dist. Atty. Office, U.S. Atty. Office, 1989, Colo. Hispanic Bar Assn., 1988. With U.S. Army, 1972-74. Mem. ABA, Colo. Bar Assn., Colo. Def. Lawyers Assn., Colo. Hispanic Bar Assn. (v.p. 1986-87, bd. dirs. 1993), Am. Arbitration Assn. (panel mem.). Home: 1025 Waite Dr Boulder CO 80303 Office: Tilly & Graves 3773 N Cherry Creek Dr Denver CO 80209

OLIVER, ANTHONY THOMAS, JR., lawyer; b. San Jose, Calif., July 19, 1929; s. Anthony Thomas and Josephine Gertrude (Bem) O.; m. Beverly J. Wirz, Jan. 27, 1952; children—Jeanne M. Hall, Marilyn M., Cynthia M. Eschardies, Michelle M. Rogan; m. Margaret E. Gurke, Mar. 31, 1984; 1 child, Christopher A. B.S., U. Santa Clara, 1951, J.D., 1953. Bar: Calif. 1954, U.S. Supreme Ct. 1979. Asst. counsel Bank Am. Legal Dept., Los Angeles, 1953-57; assoc. Taylor & Barker, Los Angeles, 1957-58, John F. O'Hara, Los Angeles, 1958-63; sr. pntr., chmn. labor dept. Parker, Milliken, Clark, O'Hara & Samuelian; Los Angeles, 1963—. Mem. Town Hall Calif., 1981—; bd. visitors U. Santa Clara Coll. Law, 1982—. Served to lt. col. USAR. Recipient Edwin J. Owens Lawyer of Year award U. Santa Clara Coll. Law, 1976. Mem. ABA (co-chmn. com. labor arbitration 1985-88), Los Angeles County Bar Assn. (chmn. labor law sect. 1985-86), Indsl. Relations Research Assn., Am. Arbitration Assn. (mem. adv. bd. Los Angeles), N.G. Assn. U.S., N.G. Assn. Calif., State Bar Calif. , Ariz. Indsl. Relations Assn. , Orange County Indsl. Relations Research Assn., Roman Catholic. Club: University, Chancery (Los Angeles). Office: 333 S Hope St 27th Floor Los Angeles CA 90071

OLIVER, DAN DAVID, banker; b. Walla Walla, Wash., Mar. 11, 1952; s. Harold Allen and Nydia Jane (Munns) O.; children: Ana Mary, Whitney Leigh. BA in Pre-Law, Wash. State U., 1974; MBA in Taxation, Golden Gate U., 1979; JD, Western State U., 1978; grad. with trust specialization, U. Wash., Seattle, 1987. Tax acct. John F. Forbes & Co., San Francisco, 1979-81; cat skinner James Francis Munns Farms, Inc., Prescott, Wash., 1981-82; law clk. Sherwood, Tugman, Gose & Reser, Walla Walla, 1975-79; adminstrv. asst. Baker-Boyer Nat. Bank, Walla Walla, 1982-83, asst. trust officer, 1984, trust officer, 1985, asst. v.p., legal counsel, 1986, asst. v.p., legal/complaince officer, 1987, v.p. and legal/compliance officer, 1988—; vice chmn. bd. dirs. Elite Turf Farm, Inc., West Richland, Wash., sr. v.p., sec., legal counsel, 1988—; commr. Walla Walla Housing Authority. Bd. dirs. Prescott (Wash.) Sch. Dist., 1983-87, vice chmn., 1985, chmn. 1986; vol. spirits religious edn. program St. Patrick's Cath. Ch., 1990—; mem. Walla Walla Park and Recreation Adv. Bd., 1991-92, vice chmn., 1992; chmn. Park Improvement Com. for Irrigation, 1992; chair Walla Walla Area Com. for Housing, 1991—. Mem. Am. Bankers Assn., Wash. Bankers Assn. (compliance com. 1990—), Walla Walla Valley Estate Planning Coun. (bd. dirs. 1986-87, treas. 1987-88, sec. 1988-89, v.p. 1989-90, pres. 1990-91), Nat. Arbor Day Found., Columbia Rural Elec. Assn., Walla Walla Men's Group, Walla Walla Exch. Club, Sigma Alpha Epsilon (recorder 1971-72), Nat. Assn. of Underwaters Instrs. (open water I cert. 1992), Bergevin Family Reunion and Edn. Assn. (treas. 1993—). Office: Baker-Boyer Nat Bank Main and 2d Sts Walla Walla WA 99362

OLIVER, JOHN EDWARD, bank training consultant; b. Bedford, Eng., Apr. 14, 1951; came to U.S., 1978; s. Fred K. and Marjorie F. (Brown) O.; m. Jacqueline L. Alcock, Oct. 7, 1972; 1 child, Sophie Rose. Student, Mander Coll., Bedford, 1968-71. Mgr.'s asst. Nat. Westminster Bank, Bedford, 1971-73; credit analyst Kleinwort Benson Ltd., London, 1973-76; mktg. coord. Amex Bank Ltd., London, 1976-78; v.p. Continental Ill. Energy Devel. Corp., Houston, 1978-85; pres. Laurel Mgmt. Systems Inc., San Francisco, 1986—; cons. various U.S. and Internat. banks including Kansallis-Osake-Pankki, London, 1985—; bank edn. cons. Bank Am., San Francisco, 1986—. Author bank tng. programs, utilizing computer simulations. Mem. ASTD, Assn. Bank Trainers and Cons. Office: Laurel Mgmt Systems Inc 235 Pine St Ste 1300 San Francisco CA 94104

OLIVER, JOYCE ANNE, journalist, editorial consultant, columnist; b. Coral Gables, Fla., Sept. 19, 1958; d. John Joseph and Rosalie Cecile (Mack) O. BA in Communications, Calif. State U., Fullerton, 1980, MBA, 1990. Corp. editor Norris Industries Inc., Huntington Beach, Calif., 1979-82; pres. J.A. Oliver Assocs., La Habra Heights, Calif., 1982—; corp. editorial cons. Norris Industries, 1982, Better Methods Cons., Huntington Harbour, Calif., 1982-83, Summit Group, Orange, Calif., 1982-83, UDS, Encinitas, Calif., 1983-84, MacroMarketing, Costa Mesa, Calif., 1985-86, PM Software, Huntington Beach, Calif., 1985-86, CompuQuote, Canoga Park, Calif., 1985-86, Nat. Semicondr. Can. Ltd., Mississauga, Ont., Can., 1986, Maclean Hunter Ltd., Toronto, Ont., 1986-90; Frame Inc., Fullerton, Calif., 1987-88, The Johnson-Layton Co., L.A., 1988-89, Corp. Rsch. Inc., Chgo., 1988, Axon Group, Horsham, Pa., 1990-91, Am. Mktg. Assn., Chgo., 1990-92, Schnell Pub. Co., Inc., N.Y.C., 1992—; mem. Rsch. Coun. of Scripps Clinic and Rsch. Found., 1987-92. Contbg. editor Computer Merchandising/Resell, 1982-85, Computer Reselling, 1985, Reseller Mgmt., 1987-89; contbg. editor Can. Electronics Enging., 1986-90, west coast editor, 1990, Chem. Bus. mag., 1992-93; spl. feature editor Cleve. Inst. Electronics publ. The Electron, 1986-89; bus. columnist Mktg. News, 1990-92; contbr. articles to profl. jours. and mags. Mem. IEEE, Internat. Platform Assn., Soc. Photo-optical Instrumentation Engrs., Inst. Mgmt. Scis., Nat. Writers Club (profl.), Internat. Mktg. Assn., Soc. Profl. Journalists, L.A. World Affairs Coun. Republican. Roman Catholic. Office: 2045 Fullerton Rd La Habra CA 90631-8213

OLIVER, NATHAN JON, systems analyst; b. San Jose, Calif., Oct. 28, 1965; s. Frank M. and Coy A. (Adams) O. BS, Weber State U., Ogden, Utah, 1987; MBA, Westminster Coll., Salt Lake City, 1990. Resident asst. Weber State Coll., 1985-87; sr. systems analyst N.W. Pipeline Corp., Salt Lake City, 1987-92, field support supr., 1992—. Coach Little League Baseball, Ogden, 1986, 87; vol. Salt Lake City Arts Festival, 1990. Mem. Salt Lake City Quality Assurance Assn., N.W. Pipeline Trap and Skeet Club (v.p. 1989).

OLIVER, RICE DONALD, publishing executive; b. L.A., Jan. 23, 1933; s. Claude Frederick and Johnie Mae (Quinn) O.; m. Betty Sue Ewick, Aug. 23, 1952; children: Susan, Steven, Heather, Dana. Student, Calif. Bapt. Sem., 1951-52, Multnomah Coll., 1956-57, Fullerton Coll., 1960-63. Youth leader various chs., Calif., 1950-63; tchr. San Gabriel (Calif.) Christian Sch., 1963-65; prin., founder Maranatha High Sch., Sierra Madre, Calif., 1965-68; pastor various Bapt. chs., Calif., 1968-70; pub. Calif. Weekly Explorer, Tustin, 1979—. Author: Atlas of Calif., 1979, Lone Woman, 1985; produced several live history prodns. including Walk Thru Calif., 1982, Walk Thru West, 1985; contbr. numerous articles to profl. jours. Recipient award Am. Assn. State and Local History. Mem. Nat. Coun. Social Studies, Pacific Ednl. Mktg. Assn. Republican. Office: Calif Weekly Explorer 285 E Main St # 3 Tustin CA 92680

OLIVER, ROBERT WARNER, economics educator; b. L.A., Oct. 26, 1922; s. Ernest Warner and Elnore May (McConnell) O.; m. Darlene Hubbard, July 1, 1946 (dec. Mar. 1987); children: Lesley Joanne Oliver McClelland, Stewart Warner; m. Jean Tupman Smock, July 15, 1989. A.B., U. So. Calif., 1943, A.M., 1948; A.M., Princeton U., 1950, Ph.D., 1958. Teaching asst. U. So. Calif., 1946-47; instr. Princeton U., 1947-50, Pomona Coll., Claremont, Calif., 1950-52; asst. prof. U. So. Calif., Los Angeles, 1952-56; economist Stanford Research Inst., South Pasadena, Calif., 1956-59; mem. faculty dept. econs. Calif. Inst. Tech., 1959-88, prof. econs., 1973-88, prof. emeritus, 1988—; urban economist World Bank, Washington, 1970-71; cons. Brookings Instn., 1961, OECD, Paris, 1979; vis. prof. U. So. Calif., 1985; vis. scholar Pembrook Coll., Cambridge U., Eng., 1989-90. Author: An Economic Survey of Pasadena, 1959, International Economic Cooperation and the World Bank, 1975, Bretton Woods: A Retrospective Essay, 1985, Oral History Project: The World Bank, 1986; contbg. author: Ency. of Econs., 1981. Mem. Human Rels. Com. City of Pasadena, 1964-65, Planning Commn., 1972-75, 91—; bd. dirs. Pasadena City Coun., 1965-69; mem. Utilities Adv. Commn., 1984-88, Strategic Planning Com., 1985; pres. Pasadena Beautiful Found., 1972-74; bd. dirs. Pasadena Minority History Found., 1984—; trustee Pasadena Hist. Soc., 1992—. Lt. (j.g.) USN, 1942-46. Social Sci. rsch. fellow London Sch. Econs., 1954-55; Rockefeller Found. fellow, 1974, 91; Danforth assoc., 1981; recipient Outstanding Teaching award, 1982, Master of the Student Houses, 1987; Hon. Alumnus, 1987—. Mem. Am. Econs. Assn., Royal Econs. Assn., Com. on Fgn. Rels., Western Econs. Assn., Phi Beta Kappa, Phi Kappa Phi, Delta Tau Delta. Democrat. Methodist. Club: Athenaeum. Home: 3197 San Pasqual St Pasadena CA 91107-5330 Office: 1201 E California Blvd Pasadena CA 91125-0001

OLIVER, STEPHEN RONALD, computer science educator; b. Mountain Lake, Minn., Aug. 11, 1947; s. Stephen Thomas and Ella Hulda (Merry) O.; m. Joy Ella Parkinson, Oct. 16, 1976; children: Heather Joy, Shannon Thomas. BA in Math and Philosophy, Morningside Coll., 1970; MS in Computer Sci., U. Kans., 1975; PhD in Computer Sci., Colo. State U., 1988. Application programmer Dana F. Cole & Co., CPA's, Lincoln, Nebr., 1972-73; systems programmer U. Kans. Computation Ctr., Lawrence, 1973-76; custom products engr. Perkin Elmer Computer Systems, Arlington Heights, Ill., 1976-80; tech. staff MITRE, Colorado Springs, Colo., 1980-81; instr. U. Colo. Dept. Computer Sci., Colorado Springs, 1980-85; staff scientist Sci. Applications Internat. Corp., Colorado Springs, 1982-88; assoc. prof. Calif. Poly State U., San Luis Obispo, 1988—; dir., Calif. Polytech. Computer Systems Lab., 1989—. Bd. dirs. Santa Lucia Sch. Bd., Templeton, Calif.; outings chmn. Colo. Mountain Club, Colorado Springs, 1987-88; canvas dir. All Souls Unitarian Ch., Colorado Springs, 1988. NDEA fellow, 1970-72, Sci. Applications Internat. Corp. fellow, 1985-88. Mem. Assn. Computing Machinery (SIG Small/PC treas. 1979-83, chmn. 1983-85, SIG bd. fin. adv. 1984-88, chmn., 1988-90, v.p. 1990—, Small/PC Outstanding Svc. award 1988, lectr. 1986-90). Office: Calif Poly State U Dept Computer Sci San Luis Obispo CA 93407

OLIVER, TERRY VINCENT, utility energy conservation official; b. Pullman, Wash., Jan. 26, 1951; s. Richard Clyde and Virginia (Vincent) O.; m. Marcia Ann Kraft, Sept. 23, 1982; 1 child, Spencer. Student, U.S. Naval Acad., 1969-71, Clark C.C., Vancouver, Wash., 1972; BA, Evergreen State Coll., Olympia, Wash., 1973; postgrad., Oreg. State U., 1981-85. Energy planner Regional Planning Coun. Clark County, Vancouver, 1978-81; mgr. Hood River conservation project Bonneville Power Adminstrn., Portland, Oreg., 1981-85, mgr. local govt. fin. assistance program Office Conservation, 1981-83, project mgr. mktg. environ. for energy conservation in the Pacific Northwest, 1983-85, mgr. residential weatherization program, 1985-87, mgr. energy smart design program, 1987-89, chief conservation sect. comml. design program, 1989—; sr. assoc. H. Gil Peace and Assocs., Beaverton, Oreg., 1988—. Contbr. articles on energy conservation rsch., program design and evaluation to profl. publs. Chmn. Citizens for Solar Wash., Seattle, 1981. With USN, 1969-71. Recipient Spl. Act for Hood River Conservation Project Achievement award U.S. Dept. Energy, 1986. Office: Bonneville Power Adminstrn 905 NE 11th Ave Portland OR 97208

OLIVERE, MARILYN HESS, counselor, actress; b. Wilmington, Del., Oct. 8, 1949; d. William Wilson and Florence Van Dyke (Smith) Hess; m. Robert F. Olivere, Sept. 8, 1973; children: Robin Blythe, Matthew Robert. BA, Duke U., 1972; MS, MEd, U. Del., 1975; postgrad., Glendale Coll. Cert. hypnotherapist. With accounts payable Dupont Co., Wilmington, Del., 1968-71; teller First Nat. Bank Coral Gables, Fla., 1971-72; counselor dept. continuing edn. U. Del., Newark, 1975-77; parole officer State of Del., Wilmington, 1975-77; asst. dir. Mark/Communications Gen. Instrument Co., Chandler, Ariz., 1987-88; office mgr. Robert F. Olivere, M.D., Phoenix, 1981—; counselor Phoenix, 1986—; substitute tchr. Wash Sch. Dist., Phoenix, 1990—; edn. cons., performer Comedy Profls., Phoenix, 1989-91; edn. cons. Moose & Squirrel Prodns., Phoenix, 1989-92; performer Northwest Studios, Phoenix, 1990; cons., bd. dirs. Ctr. for Neurodevel. Studies, Phoenix, 1988—. Performer Playwrites Theatre Workshop, 1990-93, Theatreworks, 1991-93, Phoenix Little Theatre Cookie Co., 1991, Pioneer Mus. Melodrama, 1991-92; asst. dir. Pioneer Mus. Melodrama, 1991-92, Phoenix Children's Hosp. Project Prevention, 1991-93, Theatreworks, 1992-93; instr. children's acting and improvisational comedy 7th St. Theatre & Theatreworks, 1989-93. Health and welfare officer Orangewood Sch. PTA, Phoenix, 1987; chmn. Santa Shop, 1988-90; mem. Washington Sch. Dist., Phoenix, 1983-84; sec. PTA, 1990-92. Nat. Merit scholar, 1968, AAUW scholar, 1972. Mem. APTP, Ariz. Counselor's Assn., Soc. for the Arts, Duke U. Alumni Assn., La Mancha Racquet Club (swim team coord. 1986-89), Mensa.

OLLEY, ROBERT EDWARD, economist, educator; b. Vendun, Que., Can., Apr. 16, 1933; s. Edwin Henry and Elizabeth (Reed) O.; m. Shirley Ann Dahl, Jan. 19, 1957; children—Elizabeth Anne, George Steven, Susan Catherine, Maureen Carolyn. B.A., Carleton U., Can., 1960; M.A., Queen's U., Can., 1961, Ph.D. in Econs., 1969. Vis. asst. prof. Queen's U., Kingston, Ont., Can., 1967-68; asst. prof. econs. U. Sask., Saskatoon, Can., 1963-67, 68-69, assoc. prof., 1969-71, 73-75, prof., 1975—; econ. advisor Bell Can., Montreal, Que., 1971-73, 78-79, Can. Telecommunications Carriers Assn., 1978-85, Sask. Power Corp., 1980-83; econ. advisor AT&T, 1980-90, Waste Mgmt. Inc., 1990—, SaskTel, 1989—; dir. rsch. Royal Commn. on Consumer Problems and Inflation, 1967-68; chmn. adv. com. on consumer standards Standards Coun. Can., 1992-93, Can. rep. to ISO/COPOLCO, Geneva, 1992-93. Author, editor: Consumer Product Testing, 1979; Consumer Product Testing II, 1981; Consumer Credit in Canada, 1966; Economics of the Public Firm: Regulation, Rates, Costs, Productivity Analysis, 1983, Total Factor Productivity of Canadian Telecommunications, 1984; Consumer Reps. Conf. Procs., 1st-4th, 1982-91. Bd. dirs. Can. Found. for Econ. Edn., 1974-82, Can. Gen. Standards Bd., 1977-81. Recipient Her Magesty The Queen Silver Jubilee medal, 1977. Mem. Royal Econ. History Soc., Royal Econs. Assn., Econ. History Assn., Am. Econ. Assn., Can. Econ. Assn., Consumers Assn. Can. (v.p. 1967-75, chmn. 1975-77), Can. Standards Assn. (dir., mem. exec. com. 1971-93, vice chmn. 1985-87, chmn. 1987-89), Consumer's Assn. Found. Can. (v.p. 1989—), Can. Comms. Rsch. Ctr. (dir. 1992—). Home: 824 Saskatchewan Crescent E, Saskatoon, SK Canada S7N 0L3

OLMSTEAD, MARJORIE ANN, physics educator; b. Glen Ridge, N.J., Aug. 18, 1958; d. Blair E. and Elizabeth (Dempwolf) O. BA in Physics, Swarthmore Coll., 1979; MA in Physics, U. Calif., Berkeley, 1982, PhD, 1985. With research staff Palo Alto (Calif.) Research Ctr. Xerox Corp., 1985-86; asst. prof. physics U. Calif., Berkeley, 1986-90; asst. prof. physics U. Wash., Seattle, 1991-93, assoc. prof., 1993—; prin. investigator materials sci. div. Lawrence Berkeley Lab., 1988—; mem. exec. com. Stanford (Calif.) Synchroton Radiation Lab., 1986-90, chmn., 1988-89. Contbr. articles to profl. jours. Named Presdl. Young Investigator, Nat. Sci. Found., 1987; recipient Devel. awards IBM, 1986, 87. Mem. Am. Assn. Physics Tchrs., Am. Phys. Soc., Am. Vacuum Soc., Materials Research Soc., Assn. Women in Sci., Phi Beta Kappa, Sigma Xi. Office: U Wash Dept Physics FM-15 Seattle WA 98195

OLMSTED, RONALD DAVID, foundation executive; b. Portland, Oreg., June 27, 1937; s. Clifford Wolford and Ruth Emily (Driesner) O.; m. Susan Mary Spare, Dec. 27, 1961 (div. June 1972); 1 child, Craig William. Student, Lewis & Clark Coll., 1955-57, U. So. Calif., L.A., 1959-62. V.p., exec. dir. L.A. Ctr. for Internat. Visitors, 1961-67; assoc. dir. devel. U. Chgo., 1967-71; v.p. devel. and pub. affairs Northwestern Meml. Hosp., Chgo., 1971-79; pres. The Ronald Olmsted Co., Mich., Oreg., 1979-89; dir. devel. Marimed Found., Honolulu, 1989—; cons. on health, edn. and human svc. orgns., Mich., Oreg., Hawaii, 1979—. Contbr. articles on African travels and African affair to profl. publs. Co-founder, treas. Civil Found. of Chelsea, Mich., 1982-83; tras. Chelsea Area C. of C., 1981-83; trustee The Harris Sch., Chgo., 1972-73, Ogden Dunes (Ind.) Town Bd., 1970-71; mem. L.A. Com. on Fgn. Rels., 1965-69. Recipient Koa Anvil award Pub. Rels. Soc. Am.-Honolulu, 1992, multiple awards Assn. Am. Colls., 1975-79, multiple MacEachern awards Am. Acad. Hosp. Pub. Rels., 1974-79, multiple awards Nat. Assn. for Hosp. Devel., 1975-79. Mem. Nat. Soc. Fund Raising Execs. Presbyterian. Home: Apt 1506 469 Ena Rd Honolulu HI 96815 Office: Marimed Found Bldg D 1050 Ala Moana Blvd Honolulu HI 96814

OLPIN, ROBERT SPENCER, art history educator; b. Palo Alto, Calif., Aug. 30, 1940; s. Ralph Smith and Ethel Lucille (Harman) O.; m. Mary Florence Catharine Reynolds, Aug. 24, 1963; children: Mary Courtney, Cristin Lee, Catharine Elizabeth, Carrie Jean. BS, U. Utah, 1963; AM, Boston U., 1965, PhD, 1971. Lectr. art history Boston U., 1965-67; asst. prof. U. Utah, Salt Lake City, 1967-72, assoc. prof., 1972-76, prof., 1976—, chmn. dept., 1975-82, dir. art history program, 1968-76, 83-84, dean Coll. Fine Arts, 1987—; cons. curator Am. and English art Utah Mus. Fine Arts, 1973—. Grantee U. Utah, 1972, 85, Utah Mus. Fine Arts, 1975, Utah Bicentennial Commn., 1975, Ford Found., 1975; trustee Pioneer State Theatre Found., 1988—. Mem. Archives Am. Art Smithsonian Instn., Coll. Art Assn. Am., Utah Acad. Scis. Arts Letters, Assn. Historians Am. Art, Phi Kappa Phi, Sigma Nu. Republican. Mormon. Author: Alexander Helwig Wyant, 1836-92, 1968, Mainstreams/Reflections-American/Utah Architecture, 1973, American Painting Around 1850, 1976, Art-Life of Utah, 1977, Dictionary of Utah Art, 1980, A Retrospective of Utah Art, 1981, Waldo Midgley: Birds, Animals, People, Things, 1984, A Basket of Chips, 1985, The Works of Alexander Helwig Wyant, 1986, Salt Lake County Fine Arts Collection, 1987, Signs and Symbols...Utah Art, 1988, J.A.F. Everett, 1989, George Dibble, 1989, Utah Art, 1991. Home: 887 Woodshire Ave Salt Lake City UT 84107-7639 Office: U Utah Coll Fine Arts 250 Art & Architecture Ctr Salt Lake City UT 84112

OLSBY, GREGORY SCOTT, financial executive; b. Seattle; s. Robert G. and M. JoAnn Olsby; m. Carol A. Murphy; children: Joshua, Julia, Jacob. BA, U. Wash., 1979; MBA, George Washington U., 1983. Budget analyst Tracor, Inc., Rockville, Md.; fin. mgr. Concurrent Computer, Rockville; mgr. govt. acctg. US West, Inc., Rockville and Bellevue, Wash., 1985-90; chief fin. officer, contr. MetriCor, Inc., Woodinville, Wash., 1990-92; prin. Wash. Bus. Consulting, Woodinville, 1992—. Mem. Am. Electronics Assn., Wash. Software Assn. Office: 18615 NE 194th St Woodinville WA 98072

OLSCHWANG, ALAN PAUL, lawyer; b. Chgo., Jan. 30, 1942; s. Morton James and Ida (Ginsberg) O.; m. Barbara Claire Miller, Aug. 22, 1965; children: Elliot, Deborah, Jeffrey. B.S., U. Ill., 1963, J.D., 1966. Bar: Ill. 1966, N.Y. 1984, Calif. 1992. Law clk. Ill. Supreme Ct., Bloomington, 1966-67; assoc. Sidley & Austin, and predecessor, Chgo., 1967-73; with Montgomery Ward & Co., Inc., Chgo., 1973-81, assoc. gen. counsel, asst. sec., 1979-81; ptnr. Seki, Jarvis & Lynch, Chgo., 1981-84; v.p., gen. counsel, sec. Mitsubishi Electric Am., Inc., N.Y.C., 1983-91, Cypress, Calif., 1991—. Mem. ABA, Am. Corp. Counsel Assn., Calif. Bar Assn., Ill. Bar Assn., Chgo. Bar Assn., N.Y. State Bar Assn., Bar Assn. of City of N.Y., Am. Arbitration Assn. (panel arbitrators). Office: Mitsubishi Electric Am 5665 Plaza Dr Cypress CA 90630-5023

OLSEN, CHRISTOPHER TED, lawyer; b. L.A., Apr. 1, 1964; s. Donald Theodore Olsen and Janice Marie (Swanson) Present. BA cum laude in Polit. Sci., Elon Coll., N.C., 1986; JD cum laude, Pepperdine U., 1989. Assoc. Shield & Smith, L.A., 1989-91, Hornberger & Criswell, L.A., 1991—. Named Best Oral Adv., Nat. Appellate Advocacy Competition ABA, 1988. Republican. Episcopalian. Office: Hornberger & Criswell 601 S Figueroa Ste 1701 Los Angeles CA 90017

OLSEN, CLIFFORD WAYNE, physical chemist; b. Placerville, Calif., Jan. 15, 1936; s. Christian William and Elsie May (Bishop) O.; m. Margaret Clara Gobel, June 16, 1962 (div. 1986); children: Anne Katherine Olsen Cordes, Charlotte Marie; m. Nancy Mayhew Kruger, July 21, 1990. AA, Grant Tech. Coll., Sacramento, 1955; BA, U. Calif.-Davis, 1957, PhD, 1962. Physicist, project leader, program leader, task leader Lawrence Livermore Nat. Lab., Calif., 1962—; mem. Containment Evaluation Panel, U.S. Dept. Energy, 1984—, mem. Cadre for Joint Nuclear Verification Tests, 1988; organizer, editor procs. for 2nd through 7th Symposiums on Containment of Underground Nuclear Detonations, 1983-93. Contbr. articles to profl. jours. Recipient Chevalier Degree, Order of DeMolay, 1953. Mem. AAAS, Am. Radio Relay League, Seismol. Soc. Am., Sigma Xi, Alpha Gamma Sigma, Gamma Alpha. Democrat. Lutheran. Office: Lawrence Livermore Nat Lab PO Box 808 M/S L-221 Livermore CA 94551

OLSEN, DANIEL PAUL, computer systems professional; b. Butte, Mont., May 31, 1952; s. Paul B. and Rose Patrica (Roe) O.; m. Barbara Diane Nelson, May 28, 1983; children: Lisa Lynn, Christina Danielle, Ashley Dyan. Student, Mont. State U., 1970-72; BS in Computer Sci., U. Mont., 1975; postgrad., Mont. Coll. Mineral Sci. and Tech., 1977-89; cert. in data processing, 1984. Programmer Mont. Power Co., Butte, 1976-77, systems programmer, 1977-78, sr. systems programmer, 1978-83, sr. system support analyst, 1983, supr. prime services, 1983-88, supr. network support, 1988—; adj. instr. Mont. Coll. of Mineral Sci. and Tech., butte, 1977-79. Pres. Echo Lake (Mont.) Homeowners Assn., 1981—; chairman Deerlodge Permittee Assn., 1989—. Mem. Assn. Cert. Computer Profls., Nat. Prime Users Group (sec., treas. 1989-90, pres.-elect 1990-91, pres. 1991-92, exec. cons. 1992-93). Home: PO Box 524 Butte MT 59703-0524 Office: Mont Power Co 40 E Broadway St Butte MT 59701-9394

OLSEN, DAVID MAGNOR, science educator; b. Deadwood, S.D., July 23, 1941; s. Russell Alvin and Dorothy M. Olson; m. Muriel Jean Bigler, Aug. 24, 1963; children: Merritt, Chad. BS, Luther Coll., 1963; MS in Nat. Sci., U. S.D., 1967. Instr. sci., math. Augustana Acad., Canton, S.D., 1963-66; instr. chemistry Iowa Lakes Community Coll., Estherville, Iowa, 1967-69; instr. chemistry Merced (Calif.) Coll., 1969—, instr. astronomy, 1975—, div. chmn., 1978-88, coord. environ. hazardous materials tech., 1989—. Trustee Merced Union High Sch. Dist., 1983—, pres., 1986-87. Mem. NEA, Am. Chem. Soc., Astron. Soc. of the Pacific, Calif. Tchrs. Assn., Planetary Soc., Calif. State Mining & Mineral Mus. Assn. (bd. dirs. 1988—, sec. 1990—), Nat. Space Soc., Merced Coll. Faculty Assn. (pres. 1975, 93, treas. 1980-90, bd. dirs. 1986—, sec. 1990-91), Merced Track Club (mem. exec. bd. 1981), M Star Lodge, Sons of Norway (v.p. 1983). Democrat. Lutheran. Home: 973 Idaho Dr Merced CA 95340-2513 Office: Merced Coll 3600 M St Merced CA 95348-2806

OLSEN, DON LEE, manufacturing executive, author; b. Seattle, June 19, 1928; s. Leonard and Gertrude (Really) O.; m. Joan Lorraine Nickerson, Nov. 15, 1952; children: Nancy Martin, Sandra Olsen. BA, U. Washington, Seattle, 1951. V.p. Pourette Mfg., Seattle, 1965-85, pres., 1986—. Author: Modern Art of Candle Making, 1972, Nature's Candles, 1975, Candles That Earn, 1990. Pres. Roosevelt C. of C., Seattle, 1969, U. Kiwanis, 1972; bd. mem. U. Food Bank, Seattle, 1983-87. Mem. Kiwanis. Republican. Lutheran. Office: Pourette Mfg Inc 6910 Roosevelt Way NE Seattle WA 98115-6635

OLSEN, GLENN WARREN, historian, educator; b. Mpls., Nov. 27, 1938; s. Warren Spandet and Alice Elvira (Lionstone) O.; m. Suzanne Miltner, Aug. 27, 1966; children: Teresa, Catherine, Gregory, John. BA, North Park Coll., Chgo., 1960; MA, U. Wis., 1962, PhD, 1965. Asst. prof. Seattle U., 1965-66, assoc. prof., 1969-72; asst. prof. Fordham U., Bronx, N.Y., 1966-69; prof. U. Utah, Salt Lake City, 1972—; vis. prof. U. Notre Dame, Ind., 1990; v.p. Kairos Found., Erie, Pa., 1970—. Adv. editor: Cath. Hist. Rev., 1971—; cons. editor: Communio: Internat. Cath. Rev., 1988—; contbr. articles to profl. jours. Lectr. internat. sci. bd., confs. on European culture, U. Navarre, Pamplona, 1992—; regent St. Mary's Coll., Notre Dame, 1973-79. Fulbright grantee, 1963-65, travel grantee Am. Coun. Learned Socs., 1979, NEH grantee, 1990; David Piermont Gardner fellow U. Utah, 1977, fellow Inst. for Ecumenical and Cultural Rsch., 1978-79. Mem. Medieval Acad. Am., Am. Hist. Assn., Am. Cath. Hist. Assn., Soc. for Italian Hist. Studies, Medieval Assn. Pacific (councillor 1976-79, 92-95), Rocky Mountain Medieval & Renaissance Assn. (pres., councillor 1984-85), Am. Soc. Ch. History (councillor 1981-84). Roman Catholic. Home: 2233 Bryan Cir Salt Lake City UT 84108-2711 Office: U Utah Dept History 208 Carlson Salt Lake City UT 84112

OLSEN, HARRIS LELAND, real estate and international business executive, educator; b. Rochester, N.H., Dec. 8, 1947; s. Harries Edwin and Eva Alma (Turmelle) O.; m. Mimi Kwi Sun Yi, Mar. 15, 1953; children: Garin Lee, Gavin Yi. AS, SUNY, Albany, 1983, BS, 1988; MA in Polit. Sci., U. Hawaii, 1990. Enlisted USN, 1967, advanced through grades to; served in various nuclear power capacities USN, Conn., 1971-76, Hawaii, 1976-87; ret. USN, 1987; v.p. Waiono Land Corp., Honolulu, 1981-92, dir., 1993—; v.p. Asian Pacific Electricity, Honolulu, 1988-89, Kapano Land Assocs., Honolulu, 1988-92, MLY Networks, Inc., Honolulu, 1989—, THO Consultants Cor., 1991—; staff cons. Mariner-Icemakers, Honolulu, 1982-84, Transpacific Energy Corp., Honolulu, 1982-84; sr. cons. Western Rsch., Honolulu, 1984-87; quality assurance cons. Asian Pacific, Inc., Honolulu, 1987-88; instr., lectr. Asian history and culture U. Chaminade in Honolulu, 1991; instr. nuclear reactor theory Pearl Harbor, Hawaii, 1992—; v.p. Schwartz Inc., 1992—; bd. dirs. Green Gold Corp., 1992—. Inventor, alternate power supply system; contbr. articles to profl. publs. Active Nat. Democratic Com.; head coach USN Men's Softball, Honolulu, 1978-79; pres. Pearl Harbor (Hawaii) Welfare and Recreation Com., 1983-84; mem. Bishop Mus. Mem. USCG Aux., ASCD, Am. Legion, Fleet Res. Assn., Am. Polit. Sci. Assn., Internat. Platform Assn., Navy League, Semiotic Soc. Am., Toronto Semiotics Circle, U.S. Naval Inst., UN Assn., U.S Submarine Vets., Honolulu Acad. Arts, Delta Epsioln Sigma. Democrat. Buddhist. Home: 94-1025 Anania Circle Wahiawa HI 96789 Office: Schwartz Inc 1149 Bethel St Ste 314 Honolulu HI 96813

OLSEN, M. KENT, lawyer, educator; b. Denver, Mar. 10, 1948; s. Marvin and F. Winona (Wilker) O.; m. Nancy Lee Grout, May 1, 1971; children: Kristofor Anders, Alexander Lee, Nikolaus Alrik, Amanda Elizabeth. BS, Colo. State U., 1970; JD, U. Denver, 1975. Bar: Colo., U.S. Dist. Ct. Colo. 1982, U.S. Tax Ct. Law clk. Denver Probate Ct., 1973-75; assoc. ptnr. Johnson & McLachlan, Lamar, Colo., 1975-80; assoc. Buchanan, Thomas and Johnson, Lakewood, Colo., 1981-82, William E. Myrick, P.C., Denver, 1982-83; referee Denver Probate Ct., Denver, 1983-89; ptnr. Haines & Olsen, P.C., Denver, 1989—. Mem. Gov.'s Commn. on Life and the Law, Denver, 1991—; bd. dirs. Adult Care Mgmt., Inc., Denver, 1985—; v.p., bd. dirs. Arc of Denver, Inc., 1990—; bd. dirs. Colo. Guardianship Alliance, Denver, 1990-91. Recipient Outstanding Vol. Svc. award Adult Care Mgmt., 1990, Outstanding Svc. award The Arc of Denver, 1991. Mem. ABA, Colo. Bar Assn. (chair probate sect.), Am. Assn. Home for Aging, Nat. Acad. Elder Law Attys., Denver Bar Assn. Episcopalian. Home: 8112 W Woodard Dr Lakewood CO 80227-2442 Office: Haines & Olsen PC 650 S Cherry St Ste 600 Denver CO 80222-1807

OLSEN, MICHAEL ERIK, fluid dynamics research scientist; b. Butte, Mont., June 20, 1959; s. Paul B. and Rose (Roe) O.; 1990); m. Janet Ellen Bodene, Jan. 1, 1991; 1 child, Pauline Olsen, 1 stepchild, Andrea Terry. BS in Aero. & Astron. Engring., Purdue U., 1982, MS in Aero. & Astron. Engring., 1984. Rsch. asst. NASA-Ames Rsch. Ctr., Moffett Field, Calif., 1979-81; teaching asst. Purdue U., West Lafayette, Ind., 1980, 83-84; rsch. scientist NASA-Ames Rsch. Ctr., Moffett Field, 1984—. Mem. AIAA (sr. mem.), Assn. for Computing Machinery. Roman Catholic. Office: NASA Ames Rsch Ctr N229-1 Moffett Field CA 94035-1000

OLSEN, PHILLIP BUCK, corporate pilot, retired educator; b. Duluth, Minn., Feb. 28, 1931; s. Henry Jomar Olsen and Hjordis (Buck) Henley; m. Frances Ann MacKay, May 22, 1961 (div. Dec. 1984); m. Minnie Eiko Komagome, Aug. 19, 1988. AB, Wesleyan U., Middletown, Conn., 1953; MS in Journalism, UCLA, 1959. Cert. flight instr. FAA. Commd. 2d lt. USAF, 1953, advanced through grades to capt., 1961; pilot various locations, U.S. and Europe, 1953-73; vol. U.S. Peace Corps, Philippines, 1962-64; regional dir. Mindanao/Sulu, Philippines, 1964-66; desk officer Washington, 1966-67; dir., assoc. dean Coll. Arts and Scis. U. Hawaii/Manoa, Honolulu, 1967-86; capt., asst. chief pilot Alexander & Baldwin, Inc., Honolulu, 1986—; pres., ptnr. Aviation Holding, Ltd., Honolulu, 1983—; v.p., bd. dirs. Honolulu Marathon Assn., 1976-80. adj. instr. Embry Riddle Aeronautical U., Hickam AFB, Hawaii, 1992. Editor jour. Western Airlines, 1959-60. Comdr. Aloha State Search and Rescue Squadron, Honolulu, 1972-79. Recipient Estella della Solidarieta, Republic of Italy, 1956. Mem. Asian Studies Assn., Aircraft Owners and Pilots Assn., Elks. Office: Alexander & Baldwin Inc Aviation Dept PO Box 3440 Honolulu HI 96801

OLSEN, ROBERT ARTHUR, finance educator; b. Pittsfield, Mass., June 30, 1943; s. Arthur Anton and Virginia O.; BBA, U. Mass., 1966, MBA, 1967; PhD, U. Oreg., 1974; m. Maureen . Joan Carmell, Aug. 21, 1965. Security analyst Am. Inst. Counselors, 1967-68; rsch. assoc. Center for Capital Market Rsch., U. Oreg., 1972-74; asst. prof. fin. U. Mass., 1974-75; prof. fin., chmn. dept. fin. & mktg. Calif. State U., Chico, 1975—; cons. bus. feasibility studies for Stinson, Isom Assocs. & Career Assocs., Calif. State U., Chico, Endowment Fund, U.S. Forest Svc. Stonier Banking fellow, 1971-72; Nat. Assn. Mut. Savs. Banks fellow, 1975-76; scholar Stanford U., Decision Research, Inc., 1986. Recipient Research award Calif. State U.-Chico, 1983, 86, Profl. Achievement award, 1985. Mem. Am. Fin. Assn., Fin. Execs. Inst., Western Fin. Assn. (Treffizs award 1974), Southwestern Fin. Assn., Fin. Mgmt. Assn., Eastern Fin. Assn., Sierra Club. Contbr. articles to profl. jours. Office: Calif State U Sch Bus Chico CA 95929

OLSEN, ROBERT STEPHEN, home health company executive; b. L.A., Nov. 11, 1946; s. Robert Major and Lillian (Ethel) O.; m. Rosemary Lucas, Oct. 5, 1985; children: Tammy, Gilbert, Christine, Art, Robert, Sonya, Stephanie. PharmD, U. So. Calif., 1975. Resident U. So. Calif.-Los Angeles County Hosp., 1976; dir. pharmacy Greater El Monte Med. Ctr. Pharmacy, El Monte, Calif., 1976-78, Queen Of The Valley Hosp., West Covina, Calif., 1978-80; founding pres. Therafusion, Inc., Santa Fe Springs, Calif., 1981—; pres. S & R Pharmacy Cons. Svcs., Glendora, Calif., 1978—, P.C. Pharmacies, Inc., Alhambra, Calif., 1988-91; cons. surveyor faculty Joint Commn. on Accreditation of Health Care Orgns., Chgo., Ill., 1988—, Quality Healthcare Res., 1992—; chmn. bd. Preferred Care Health Svcs., Santa Fe Springs, 1986—. Contbr. articles to profl. jours. Bd. dirs. Calif. Acad. Home Health Care, Sacramento, 1990; mem. Med. Adv. Task Force Com., Sacramento, 1992. Mem. Am. Soc. Parenteral and Enteral Nutrition, Am. Soc. Hosp. Pharmacies, Am. Pharm. Assn., Calif. Assn. Health Svcs. at Home, Calif. Pharmacy Assn., Calif. I.V. Providers Group (founding pres. 1981-85). Office: Therafusion Inc 11759 E Telegraph Rd Santa Fe Springs CA 90670

OLSEN, ROGER E., language professional/educator english; b. San Francisco, Aug. 23, 1946; s. Perry A. and Elizabeth E. O.; m. Judy E. Winn-Bell, July 29, 1972. BA, U. Pacific, 1967. News reporter KJOY-AM, Stockton, Calif., 1969, KSJO-FM, San Jose, Calif., 1969-71; mktg. cons. pvt. practice, San Francisco, 1969-71; mktg. dir. Country Leathers, San Francisco, 1971-72; mcht. Oakwood Leather Co., San Francisco, 1972-74; comptr. SH Frank & Co., San Francisco, 1974-81; pub. Alemany Press, San Francisco, 1977-83; mktg. mgr. Alemany Press, Hayward, Calif., 1983-90; mktg. dir., west coast Regents/Prentice Hall, Menlo Park, Calif., 1990-91; ind. cons. pvt. practice, San Francisco, 1991—; bd. dirs. Tchrs. of Eng. to Speakers of Other Langs. Bilingual Edn. Interest Sect., Alexandria, Va., 1992-94, pubs. com., 1992-95; bd. dirs. Calif. Assn. for Bilingual Edn., Sacramento, 1991-93. Author: How Many Are There? Enrollment Statistics of LEP Students in the U.S., 1991; (with others) Cooperative Learning & Social Studies, 1992, About Cooperative Learning, 1992. Mem. Am. Assn. for Adult & Continuing Edn. (life, nom. com., 1989-91), Nat. Assn. for Bilingual Edn. (life), Calif. Assn. for Bilingual Edn. (bd. dirs. 1991-93), Commn. on Adult Edn. Office: Independant Consultancies 1282 29th Ave San Francisco CA 94122

OLSEN, STANLEY JOHN, anthropology educator, zooarchaeologist, vertebrate paleontologist; b. Akron, Ohio, June 24, 1919; s. John Mons and Martha Louise (Marquardt) O.; m. Eleanor Louise Vinez, June 20, 1942; 1 child, John Wilfred. Staff dept. vertebrate paleontology Mus. Comparative Zoology, Harvard U., Cambridge, Mass., 1945-56; vertebrate paleontologist Fla. Geol. Survey, Tallahassee, 1956-68; mem. participating faculty dept. geology Fla. State U., Tallahassee, 1957-68, assoc. prof. dept. anthropology, 1968-72, prof., 1972-73; zooarchaeologist Ariz. State Mus., U. Ariz., Tucson, 1973—, prof. dept. anthropology, U. Ariz., 1973—; participant field research Colombia, Belize, Can., U.S., People's Republic of China; condr. seminars in fields. Contbr. numerous articles to profl. jours. Served with USNR, 1942-45. Grants and awards include NSF, 1959, 61-63, 64-66, 67-69, 69-70, Bache Fund Nat. Acad. Scis., 1959, Johnson Fund Am. Philos. Soc., 1966, Am. Philos. Soc., 1970, Guide Found. Peabody Mus. Archaeology and Ethnology Harvard U., 1966, Fla. State U. Faculty for Improvement Social Scis., 1969. Mem. Soc. Mammalogists, Soc. Ichthyologists and Herpetologists, Soc. Vertebrate Paleontology (pres. 1965-66), Soc. Am. Archaeology, Company Mil. Historians, Explorers Club, Sigma Xi (award 1971). Home: 4950 N Camino Arenoso Tucson AZ 85718-6221 Office: U Ariz Dept Anthropology Ariz State Mus Bldg 30 Tucson AZ 85721

OLSHEN, ABRAHAM CHARLES, actuarial consultant; b. Portland, Oreg., Apr. 20, 1913; m. Dorothy Olds, June 21, 1934; children: Richard Allen, Beverly Ann Jacobs. AB, Reed Coll., 1933; MS, U. Iowa, 1935, PhD, 1937. Chief statistician City Plnng. Commn., Portland, Oreg., 1933-34; rsch. asst. math. dept. U. Iowa, 1934-37; biometrics asst. Med. Ctr., 1936-37; actuary, chief examiner Oreg. Ins. Dept., 1937-42, 45-46; actuary West Coast Life Ins. Co., San Francisco, 1946—, chief actuary, 1953-63, v.p., 1947—, 1st v.p., 1963-67, senior v.p., 1967-68, bd. dirs., 1955-68; cons. actuarial and ins. mgmt., pres. Olshen & Assocs., San Francisco, 1979—; bd. dirs. Home Federal Savs. & Loan Assn., San Francisco, 1972-85, vice-chmn. bd. 1979-

85, bd. chmn. 1985-86; guest lectr. various univs. Contbg. writer Ency. Britannica, Underwriters' Report, The Nat. Underwriter, Life Underwriters Mag., Annals of Math. Stats., other publs. Mem. Calif. com. Health Ins. Coun., U. Calif. Med. Care Adminstrn. com., San Mateo County Retirement Bd. (1975-77). Rsch. assoc. Div. of War Rsch., 1942-44, Ops. Rsch. Gp., H/Q Comdr.-in-Chief, U.S. Fleet, 1944-45. Recipient U.S. Navy Ordnance Devel. award, 1945, Disting. Service award U.S. Office of Sci. Rsch. & Devel., 1945, Presdl. Cert. Merit, 1947. Fellow AAAS, Sigma Xi; mem. Health Ins. Assn. Am. (mem., past chmn. Blanks Com., actuarial & stat. com.), Actuarial Club of Pacific States (past pres.), Actuarial Club of San Francisco (past pres.), Am. Acad. of Actuaries (charter), Am. Math. Soc., Am. Risk and Ins. Assn., Calif. Math. Coun., Commonwealth Club (life), Fellow Conf. of Actuaries in Public Practice, Inst. Mgmt. Scis., Inst. Math. Stats., Internat. Actuarial Assn., Internat. Assn. Consulting Actuaries, Internat. Cong. Actuaries, Ops. Rsch. Soc. (charter), San Francisco Press Club (life). Office: Olshen & Assocs 760 Market St Ste 739 San Francisco CA 94102-2302

OLSON, CAL OLIVER, golf architect; b. Grindstone, S.D., Oct. 18, 1939; s. Harold John and Maxine Lorraine (Knutson) O.; m. Paula Lavon Hancock, Dec. 27, 1971. BSCE, Calif. Poly., Pomona, 1974. Prin. Peridian Group, Irving, Calif., 1966-78; v.p. L.D. King Engring., Ontario, Calif., 1978-79; prin. Cal Olson Golf Architect, Costa Mesa, Calif., 1979—. Author: Turftgrass Science, 1983. Mem. ASCE, Am. Soc. Landscape Architects. Republican. Lutheran. Office: Cal Olson Golf Architect 3070 Bristol St #460 Costa Mesa CA 92626

OLSON, CARL ALEXIUS, business executive; b. Newcastle, Calif., Oct. 24, 1919; s. Carl Alexius and Anna Antonia O.; m. Monna Starr Latta, June 14, 1942; children: Chris Anna, Carol Alexius. BS, U. Calif., Berkeley, 1941. Registered profl. engr., Calif. Jr. to chief engr. Kaiser Shipyards, Richmond, Calif., 1941-46; chief tool engr. Kaiser Frazer Corp., Willow Run, Mich., 1946-47; dir. engring. Kaiser Frazer Corp., Detroit, 1947-54; works mgr. Kaiser Frazer Corp., Richmond, Calif., 1954-55; chief engr. to exec. v.p. Industrias Kaiser Argentina, Buenos Aires, 1955-68; mgr. Kaiser Engrs., Oakland, Calif., 1968-69, v.p., 1969-83; pres. Mgmt. Tech. Resources, Alamo, Calif., 1983—; pres., dir.Codem Engring, Berkeley, Calif., 1946—. Mem. AIME, Soc. Automotive Engrs., Am. Baptist Homes West, Oakland, Calif. (dir., treas. 1969—), U. Calif. Berkeley Engring. Alumni Soc., Diablo Country Club. Republican. Baptist. Home: 11 Margaret Ln Danville CA 94526 Office: MTR Internat 3158 Danville Blvd Alamo CA 94507

OLSON, DAVID JOHN, political science educator; b. Brantford, N.D., May 18, 1941; s. Lloyd and Alice Ingrid (Black) O.; m. Sandra Jean Crabb, June 11, 1966; 1 dau., Maia Kari. B.A., Concordia Coll., Moorhead, Minn., 1963; Rockefeller fellow Union Theol. Sem, N.Y.C., 1963-64; M.A. (Brooklings Instn. predoctoral research fellow 1968-69), U. Wis., Madison, 1966, Ph.D. (univ. fellow 1967), 1971. Community planner Madison Redvel. Authority, 1965-66; lectr. U. Wis., 1966-67; from lectr. to asso. prof. polit. sci. Ind. U., Bloomington, 1969-76; prof. polit. sci. U. Wash., Seattle, 1976—; chmn. dept. U. Wash., 1983-88, Harry Bridges endowed chairlabor studies, 1992—, dir.Ctr. Labor Studies, 1992—; vis. prof. U. Bergen, 1987, Harvard U., 1988-89, U. Hawaii, 1989. Co-author: Governing the United States, 1978, Commission Politics, 1977, To Keep the Republic, 1975, Black Politics, 1971; co-editor: Theft of the City, 1974. Recipient Disting. Teaching award Ind. U., 1973, faculty fellow, 1973. Mem. Am. Polit. Sci. Assn., Western Polit. Sci. Assn. (v.p. 1984, pres. 1985), Midwest Polit. Sci. Assn., So. Polit. Sci. Assn. Democrat. Lutheran. Home: 6512 E Green Lake Way N Seattle WA 98103-5418 Office: Univ Wash Dept Polit Sci Seattle WA 98195

OLSON, DAVID MARK, college dean, physical education educator; b. St. Paul, Dec. 13, 1934; s. Vendel W. and Helme D. (Engman) O.; m. Arvis Joyce Garberg, Aug. 7, 1957; children: Jana, Mark, Julie, Michael. BA, Concordia Coll., Moorhead, Minn., 1956; MA, U. Minn., 1957; PhD, U. Iowa, 1966. Tchr. Nicolet High Sch., Milw., 1958-60, Wartburg Coll., Waverly, Iowa, 1960-66; tchr. Pacific Luth. U., Tacoma, 1968—, dean sch. phys. edn., dir. athletics; adj. faculty mem. U.S. Sports Acad., Mobile, Ala., 1985—, Mgmt. Inst. Am. Assn. for Health, Phys. Edn., Recreation and Dance, 1986—; dir. N.W. regional clinic Pres.' Coun. on Phys. Fitness and Sports, 1979, 84; speaker in field. Lay pastor Emmanuel Luth. Ch., Yelm, Wash., 1988—; v.p. Trinity Luth. Ch., Parkland, Wash., 1972, pres., 1973; mem. adminstrv. team World Univ. Games, Sofia, Bulgaria, 1988; mem. steering com. U.S. Olympic Acad. XIII, Olympia, Wash., 1988-89; del. U.S. Olympic Com., L.A., 1986, 88. Mem. Am. Assn. Health, Phys. Edn., Recreation and Dance (pres. N.W. dist. 1981-82), Nat. Assn. Intercollegiate Athletics (dist. chmn. 1970-75, nat. exec. com. 1975-87, nat. pres. 1985-86, award of merit 1979, mem. Hall of Fame), Wash. Assn. Health, Phys. Edn., Recration and Dance (pres. 1975), Wash. Secondary Sch. Athletic Dirs. Assn., Nat. Assn. Coll. Athletic Dirs., Rotary (local v.p. 1970-71, pres. 1971-72), Phi Delta Kappa, Phi Epsilon Kappa. Home: 15810 Lawrence Pl Yelm WA 98597-9103 Office: Pacific Luth U Sch of Phys Edn Tacoma WA 98597

OLSON, DONALD HAROLD, JR., marine engineer; b. San Mateo, Calif., Dec. 8, 1949; s. Donald H. Sr. and Betty Jean (Hemenway) O.; m. Susan Eugenia Youngblood, May 23, 1991. Degree in Geol. Engring., U. Nev., 1977; degree in Marine Engring., Calhoon MEBA Engring. Acad., 1984. Lic. marine engr. Various 2d and 3d asst. engring. positions Marine Engrs. Beneficial Assn., San Francisco, 1984—; cons. S.S. Potomic Restoration, San Francisco, 1985. Cons. State of Nev. Engring. Study Guide, 1984. With U.S. Army, 1970-72, Vietnam. Mem. ASME, Nat. Assn. Underwater Instrs. (advanced diver), Profl. Assn. Diving Instrs. (divemaster), Marine Engrs. Benefical Assn. Republican.

OLSON, DOUGLAS BERNARD, explosives researcher, physical chemist; b. Beeville, Tex., May 14, 1945; s. Paul B. and Winnie R. (Scott) O.; m. Lucie M. Capps, Dec. 28, 1969; children: Eric A., Laura E. BS, S.W. Tex. State U., 1967; MA, U. Tex., 1969, PhD, 1977. Rsch. scientist AeroChem. Rsch. Labs., Princeton, N.J., 1977-88; group leader Ctr. for Explosives Tech. Rsch., N.Mex. Tech., Socorro, 1988-92; group leader chemistry, Energetic Materials Rsch. & Testing Ctr. New Mexico Tech., Socorro, 1992—. Contbr. articles to profl. jours. Office: EMRTC N Mex Tech Campus Sta Socorro NM 87801

OLSON, FERRON ALLRED, metallurgist, educator; b. Tooele, Utah, July 2, 1921; s. John Ernest and Harriet Cynthia (Allred) O.; m. Donna Lee Jefferies, Feb. 1, 1944; children: Kandace, Randall, Paul, Jeffery, Richard. BS, U. Utah, 1953, PhD, 1956. Consecrated Bishop Ch. LDS, 1962. Research chemist Shell Devel. Co., Emeryville, Calif., 1956-61; assoc. research prof. U. Utah, Salt Lake City, 1961-63, assoc. prof., 1963-68, chmn. dept mining, metall. and fuels engring., 1966-74, prof. dept. metallurgy and metall. engring., 1968—; cons. U.S. Bur. Mines, Salt Lake City, 1973-77, Ctr. for Investigation Mining and Metallurgy, Santiago, Chile, 1978; dir. U. Utah Minerals Inst., 1980-91. Author: Collection of Short Stories, 1985; contbr. articles to profl. jours. Del. State Rep. Conv., Salt Lake City, 1964; bishop, 1962-68, 76-82, missionary, 1988. With U.S. Army, 1943-46, PTO. Named Fulbright-Hayes lectr., Yugoslavia, 1974-75, Disting. prof. Fulbright-Hayes, Yugoslavia, 1980, Outstanding Metallurgy Instr., U. Utah, 1979-80, 88-89, Disting. Speaker U. Belgrade-Bor, Yugoslavia, 1974. Mem. Am. Inst. Mining, Metall. and Petroleum Engrs. (chmn. Utah chpt. 1978-79), Am. Soc. Engring. Edn. (chmn. Minerals div. 1972-73), Fulbright Alumni Assn., Am. Bd. Engring. and Tech. (bd. dirs. 1975-82). Republican. Home: 1862 Herbert Ave Salt Lake City UT 84108-1832 Office: U Utah Dept Metallurgy 412 Browning Bldg Salt Lake City UT 84112

OLSON, GERALD THEODORE, educational consultant; b. Rockford, Ill., Mar. 10, 1928; s. Ernest Hjalmer and Irma Lena (Widgren) O.; B.S., U. San Francisco, 1953; M.A., San Francisco State U., 1960; M.Ed., U. So. Calif., 1964; Ph.D., U. Calif., Berkeley, 1974; m. Jean Vujovich, Aug. 28, 1949; children—Gerald Theodore, Kathleen Elaina Olson Groves, John Ernest, Carol Frances Olson Love. Counselor, tchr., dir. student activities Canyon High Sch., Castro Valley, Calif., 1964-70, also lectr. Calif. State U., Hayward, 1971-72 and instr. Chabot Coll., Hayward, 1964-73; cons. counseling and guidance Colo. Dept. Edn., Denver, 1973; cons. career, devel., ednl. services group Los Angeles County Los Angeles County Office of Edn., 1973-92; pvt. cons. and marriage, family, child counselor. Served with USMC, 1946-49, with Army Res. and Calif. Army N.G., 1950-81. Cert. secondary sch. teaching, secondary sch. adminstrn., gen. pupil personnel services, community coll., marriage, family and child counseling, Calif. Contbr. articles to profl. jours. NDEA scholar, 1963-64; NIMH trainee, 1971-72; decorated Meritorious Service medal USAR, 1981. Mem. Am. Psychol. Assn., Calif. Career Edn. Assn. (pres. 1986-87), Calif. Assn. for Counseling and Devel. (editor Compass newsletter 1982-83, 86-87, pres. 1984-85), Calif. Assn. Measurement and Evaluation in Guidance (pres. 1981-82). Democrat. Home and Office: 3366 Tempe Dr Huntington Beach CA 92649-1921

OLSON, JAMES EDWARD, life insurance agent; b. Detroit, Mar. 1, 1933; s. Charles E. and Mildred Dorothy (Schlimme) O.; m. Roberta Woodworth Piatt, Apr. 7, 1956; children: Stephen J., Laura P., Peter J. BBA, U. Mich., 1954, MBA, 1955. CLU, ChFC. Life ins. agt. Fidelity Mut. Life of Pa., San Diego, 1959-64, Northwestern Mut. Life of Wis., San Diego, 1964—. V.p. San Diego Jaycees, 1963-64. Lt. comdr. USNR, 1956-59. Mem. San Diego Assn. Life Underwriters (pres. 1983-84), San Diego Chpt. CLU and ChFC (pres. 1976-77), Estate Planning Coun. San Diego (officer 1992—), U. Mich. Alumni Club (sec. 1966—). Republican. Office: Northwestern Mut Life Ins 3990 Old Town Ave # B 104 San Diego CA 92110

OLSON, JANICE LYNN, real estate executive; b. Washington, Feb. 13, 1946; d. Charles Arthur and Jean Elizabeth (Mudd) O.; divorced; 1 child, Robert. Dir. mktg. Homart Devel. Co., San Bernardino, Calif., 1974-76; property mgr. Homart Devel. Co., Brea, Calif., 1976-82; dir. pub. affairs. Homart Devel. Co., Chgo., 1982-85; gen mgr. Homart Devel. Co., Mesa, Ariz., 1985—. Contbr. articles to profl. jours. Active Mesa Growth Com., 1988—; chmn. of the bd. Mesa unit, bd. dirs. Am. Cancer Soc., 1987—. Recipient Jake award Am. Cancer Soc., 1987, Vol. of Yr. award Am. Cancer Soc., 1989. Mem. Internat. Coun. Shopping Ctrs., Mesa Southwest Mus. Guild, Southwest Archeol. Team, Confederate Air Force (life), 43d Bomb Group Assn. Office: Homart Devel Co 2104 Fiesta Mall Mesa AZ 85202-4888

OLSON, KENNETH HARVEY, computer company executive; b. Souris, N.D., May 7, 1927; s. Oscar L. and Clara (Haugen) O.; m. Darlene R. Gronseth, Aug. 19, 1950 (div. 1987); children: Kenneth David, Martha C., Marie K. BA, Concordia Coll., Moorhead, Minn., 1950; MS, U. N.D., 1953; postgrad., U. Minn., 1955. Instr. math. U. N.D., Grand Forks, 1952-54; programming supr. Convair, San Diego, 1955-59; mgr. software Control Data Corp., Mpls., 1959-61, product mgr., 1961-62; sales mgr. Control Data Corp., San Diego, 1962-70; v.p. Automated Med. Analysts, San Diego, 1970-90; pres., dir. Focus 010 Group, San Diego, 1975—; pres., dir. Health Care Svcs. Corp., San Diego, 1971-74, H.C.S. Corp., San Diego, 1972-75; v.p., trustee Calif. Prepaid Health Plan Coun., 1971-74; trustee HMO Assn. Am., 1974-75; bd. dirs. Touch Techs., Inc., San Diego. Editor: Approximations for the 1604 Computer, 1960. Pres. Lemon Grove (Calif.) Luth. Ch., 1957-59; treas. St. Luke's Luth Ch., La Mesa, Calif., 1992—; founder San Diego Nat. Bank, 1980, mem. bus. adv. com., 1981-85. Named Subcontractor of Yr., Small Bus. Assn. and SAI Corp., 1985; day proclaimed in his honor Mayor of San Diego, 1986; recipient Pres.'s award for disting. svc. Concordia Coll., 1991. Mem. Assn. for Computing Machinery, Sons of Norway. Republican.

OLSON, KENNETH PAUL, rehabilitation counselor; b. Providence, June 26, 1935; s. Gustave Frederick and Beatrice Evelyn (Backstrom) O.; m. Judith Luellan Hazard, Nov. 12, 1965; children: Glenn Edward Johnson. BA in Sociology, U. Denver, 1960; MA in Sociology, U. Colo., 1973. Cert. rehab. counselor, vocat. specialist; lic. profl. counselor, Colo. Exec. dir. Goodwill Industries, Colorado Springs, Colo., 1960-65, San Francisco, 1965, Ft. Worth, 1966-70; counselor II Colo. Div. Rehab., Colorado Springs, 1972-83; pres. Olson Vocat. Svcs., Colorado Springs, 1983—; vocational expert Social Security Adminstn., Denver, 1984—; rehab counselor U.S. Dept. Labor, Denver, 1984-89. V.p. Bus. Arts Ctr., Manitou Springs, 1988-89; councilman Manitou Springs, 1975-78; mem. Econ. Devel. Com., Manitou Springs, 1984-86; chmn. Health Adv. Coun., Pikes Peak Region, 1979-80; commr. Commn. for Rehab. Counselor Cert., 1979-85, Bd. for Rehab. Cert., 1984-86. Fellow Nat. Rehab. Counseling Assn.; mem. Colo. Rehab. Counseling Assn. (pres. 1979, named counselor of yr. 1976), Great Plains Rehab. Assn. (pres. 1982-83), Colo. Rehab. Assn., Colo. Vocational Evaluation Work Adjustment Assn., Colorado Springs C. of C. (Small Bus. Person of Yr. award 1991), Manitou Springs C. of C. (pres. 1986). Home: PO Box 215 Manitou Springs CO 80829-0215 Office: Olson Vocat Svcs 701 S Cascade Ave Colorado Springs CO 80903-4063

OLSON, LUTE, university athletic coach; b. Mayville, N.D., Sept. 22, 1934; s. Albert E. and Alinda E. (Halvorson) O.; m. Roberta R. Russell, Nov. 27, 1953; children: Vicki, Jodi, Gregory, Christi, Steven. B.A., Augsburg Coll., Mpls., 1956; M.A., Chapman Coll., Orange, Calif., 1964. Cert. counselor. Head basketball coach Mahonomen High Sch., Minn., 1956-57, Two Harbors High Sch., Minn., 1957-61; dean of boys Baseline Jr. High Sch., Boulder, Colo., 1961-62; head basketball coach Loara High Sch., Anaheim, Calif., 1962-64, Marine High Sch., Huntington Beach, Calif., 1964-69, Long Beach City Coll., Calif., 1969-73, Long Beach State U., 1973-74, U. Iowa, Iowa City, 1974-83; head basketball coach U. Ariz. Wildcats, 1983—, head coach NCAA Divsn. 1A basketball, ranked #10, 1992. Author: Passing Game Offense, 1980, Multiple Zone Attack, 1981, Pressure Defense, 1981, Match-up Zone, 1983. Crusade chmn. Am. Cancer Soc., Iowa, 1982. Named Coach of Yr. Orange League, 1964; named Coach of Yr. Sunset League, 1968, Coach of Yr. Met. Conf. Calif., 1970-71, Coach of Yr. PCAA, 1974, Coach of Yr. Big Ten Conf., 1979, 80. Mem. Nat. Assn. Basketball Coaches (Coach of Yr. 1980). Lutheran. Office: U Ariz McKale Ctr Tucson AZ 85721

OLSON, MARIAN KATHERINE, emergency management executive, publisher, information broker; b. Tulsa, Oct. 15, 1933; d. Sherwood Joseph and Katherine M. (Miller) Lahman; m. Ronald Keith Olson, Oct 27, 1956, (dec. May 1991). BA in Polit. Sci., U. Colo., 1954, MA in Elem. Edn., 1962; EdD in Ednl. Adminstrn., U. Tulsa, 1969. Tchr. public schs., Wyo., Colo., Mont., 1958-67; teaching fellow, adj. instr. edn. U. Tulsa, 1968-69; asst. prof. edn. Eastern Mont. State Coll., 1970; program assoc. research adminstrn. Mont. State U., 1970-75; on leave with Energy Policy Office of White House, then with Fed. Energy Adminstrn., 1973-74; with Dept. Energy, and predecessor, 1975—, program analyst, 1975-79, chief planning and environ. compliance br., 1979-83; regional dir. Region VIII Fed. Emergency Mgmt. Agy., 1987-93; acting exec. dir., Search and Rescue Dogs of the U.S., 1993—; pres. Marian Olson Assocs., Bannack Pub. Co.; mem. Colo. Nat. Hazards Mitigation Coun. Contbr. articles in field. Grantee Okla. Consortium Higher Edn., 1969, NIMH, 1974. Mem. Am. Soc. for Info. Sci., Am. Assn. Budget and Program Analysis, Internat. Assn. Ind. Pubs., Mont. Assn. Disaster and Emergency Coords., Nat. Inst. Urban Search and Rescue (bd. dirs.), Nat. Assn. for Search and Rescue, Colo. Search and Rescue, Search and Rescue Dogs of U.S., Colo. Emergency Mgmt. Assn., Wyo. Emergency Mgrs. Assn., N.D. Emergency Mgmt. Assn., S.D. Emergency Mgmt. Assn., Colo. State Fire Chiefs Assn., Kappa Delta Pi, Phi Alpha Theta, Kappa Alpha Theta. Republican. Home: 203 Iowa Dr Golden CO 80403-1337 Office: FEMA Denver Fed Ctr Bldg 710 PO Box 25267 Denver CO 80225-0267

OLSON, NANCY SUZANNE, venture capitalist; b. Fort Bragg, Calif., May 9, 1955; d. Noel Ivan and Joan Olson. BA in Bacteriology, U. Calif., Berkeley, 1978; MBA, Wharton Coll., 1985. Biologist Syntex, Palo Alto, Calif., 1979-81; product mgr. Internat. Diagnostic Tech., Santa Clara, Calif., 1981-83; assoc. Sequoia Capital, Menlo Park, Calif., 1985-88, gen. ptnr., 1988-90; gen. ptnr. RX Capital, San Carlos, Calif., 1991-93; exec. v.p. St. Paul Venture Capital, Bloomington, Minn., 1993—; bd. dirs. Vical Inc., San Diego. Mem. Western Assn. Venture Capital, Nat. Assn. Venture Capital, Bay Area Biosci. Assn., Churchill Club.

OLSON, PHILLIP DAVID LEROY, agriculturist, chemist; b. Anchorage, Feb. 3, 1940; s. Marvin Willard and Bernadette (McName) O.; m. Deborah Andreé Butler, Apr. 10, 1982; children from a previous marriage: Jamie Kay, Samuel Phillip, Jill Andre. BS, U. Idaho, 1963; MS, Oreg. State U., 1972. Technician U. Calif., Riverside, 1963-65; rsch. staff Oreg. State U., Corvallis, 1965-75; rsch. and devel. mgr. Hoechst-Roussel Agri-Vet Co., Somerville, N.J., 1975-91; pres. Profl. Agrl. Cons., Hayden Lake, Idaho, 1991—; study investigator Atochem NA, Bryan, Tex., 1991—, Dupont, Wilmington, Del., 1991—, Ciba-Geigy, Greensboro, N.C., 1991—, BASF, Research Triangle Park, N.C., 1991, ISK-Biotech., Fresno, Calif., 1992—, Rhône-Poulenc, Durham, N.C., 1992—; cons. in field rsch. and devel. Mem. Elks. Office: Profl Agricultural Cons Rt 3 Box 125 Hayden Lake ID 83835

OLSON, RICHARD EARL, lawyer, state legislator; b. Elmhurst, Ill., Apr. 24, 1953; s. Earl Leroy and Helen Ellen (Wanamaker) O.; m. Patricia Michelle McKinney, May 16, 1976; children: Shelley, Rachel, Eric. BA, U. Miss., Oxford, 1975; Jd, So. Meth. U., 1978. Bar: N.Mex. 1978. Ptnr. Hinkle, Cox, Eaton, Coffield & Hensley, Roswell, N.Mex., 1978—; mem. N.Mex. Ho. of Reps., 1989—, mem. various coms. Mem. Roswell City Coun., 1986-88, chmn. sts. and alleys com., mem. various other coms.; past chmn. pastor-parish rels. com. 1st United Meth. Ch., Roswell; bd. dirs. Roswell Econ. Forum, Roswell Mus. and Art Ctr. Found., city coun. liaison; bd. dirs. Assurance Home, 1980—, former v.p.; mem. N.Mex. 1st, former bd. dirs. Mem. ABA, Am. Legis. Exec. Coun. (civil justice task force), Def. Rsch. Inst., Noon Optimist Club, Order of Coif, Phi Kappa Phi. Republican. Home: 5003 Thunderbird Lane Roswell NM 88201 Office: Hinkle Cox Eaton Coffield & Hensley PO Box 10 Roswell NM 88202

OLSON, ROBERT HOWARD, lawyer; b. Indpls., July 6, 1944; s. Robert Howard and Jacquline (Wells) O.; m. Diane Carol Thorsen, Aug. 13, 1966; children: Jeffrey, Christopher. BA in Govt. summa cum laude, Ind. U., 1966; JD cum laude, Harvard U., 1969. Bar: Ohio 1969, Fla. 1980, U.S. Dist. Ct. (no. dist.) Ohio 1970, U.S. Dist. Ct. (no. dist.) Ind. 1970, U.S. Dist. Ct. (so. Dist.) Ohio 1971, U.S. Supreme Ct. 1973, Ariz. 1985. Assoc. Squire, Sanders & Dempsey, Cleve., 1969, 70-71, 76-81, ptnr., 1981—, ptnr., Phoenix, 1985—; sr. law clk. U.S. Dist. Ct., No. Dist. Ind. 1969-70; chief civil rights div. Ohio Atty. Gen.'s Office, Columbus, 1971-73, chief consumer protection, 1973-75, chief counsel, 1975, 1st asst. (chief of staff), 1975-76; instr. Law Sch., Ohio State U., Columbus, 1974; mem. Cen. Phoenix com. to advise city council and mayor, 1987-89; bd. dirs., sec. Orpheum Theater Found., 1989-90, pres., 1990—; bd. dirs. The Ariz. Ctr. for Law in the Pub. Interest, 1988—, mem. exec. com., 1990—, treas. 1992-93, v.p., 1993—; mem. Valley Leadership Class XIV. Author monograph on financing infrastructure, 1983; also law rev. articles on civil rights, consumer protection. Bd. dirs. 1st Unitarian Ch. Phoenix, v.p., 1987-89; bd. dirs. 1st Unitarian Ch. Found., 1987-93, pres., 1990-93. Mem. Greater Cleve. Bar Assn. (sec. health law sect. 1984), Am. Acad. Hosp. Attys., Ariz. State Bar Assn., Fla. State Bar Assn., Ohio State Bar Assn., Nat. Assn. of Healthcare Lawyers, Phi Beta Kappa. Democrat. Home: 5201 E Paradise Dr Scottsdale AZ 85254-4746 Office: Squire Sanders & Dempsey 40 N Central Ave Ste 2700 Phoenix AZ 85004-4441

OLSON, ROGER NORMAN, health service administrator; b. Spokane, July 3, 1936; s. Harry Leonard and Evelyn Helen (Pearson) O.; m. Joyce Marlene Markert, June 28, 1959; children: Leonard Mark, Brent Norman. BA, Pacific Luth. U., 1958; MDiv, Augustana Theol. Sem., 1962; MSW, U. Wash., 1970. Pastor Christ Luth. Ch., Des Moines, 1962-64; asst. pastor First Immanuel Luth. Ch., Portland, Oreg., 1964-68; planner Tri-County Community Coun., Portland, 1970-71; project coord. City-County Commn. on Aging, Portland, 1971-73; evaluation coord. Portland Bur. of Human Resources, 1973-74; asst. dir. Multnomah County Project Health Div., 1974-83; interim pastor Augustana Luth. Ch., 1984-85; dir. family support svcs. Met. Family Svc., 1985-91, dir. planning and rsch., 1992—. Rockefeller Bros. fellowship Rockefeller Fund for Theol. Edn., 1958-59, fellowship NIMH, 1968-69, Adminstn. on Aging, 1969-70. Democrat. Lutheran. Home: 3939 NE 21st Ave Portland OR 97212 Office: Met Family Svc 2281 NW Everett Portland OR 97210

OLSON, RONALD CHARLES, aerospace executive; b. Sioux Falls, S.D., Jan. 23, 1937; s. Arthur Helmer and Myrtle Esther (Gustafson) O.; m. Barbara Jean Newcomb, Apr. 7, 1957; children: Bradley Charles, Jodi Lynn. AA, North Idaho Coll., 1956; BS in EE, U. Idaho, 1958; grad. sr. exec. mgmt. program, MIT, 1988. Design engr. Boeing Aerospace, Seattle, 1958-72, engring. mgr., 1973-83; postgrad. in mgmt. MIT, Seattle, 1988; program mgr. Boeing Defense and Space Group, Seattle, 1985—; mem. engring. adv. bd. U. Idaho Coll. Engring., Moscow, 1988—, chmn. bd., 1991—. Recipient Gen. Ira C. Eaker, Air Force Assn., Vandenburg AFB, 1985. Mem. Boeing Mgmt. Assn. (sec. 1981-85), Big Band Dance Club (instr. 1980-85), Twin Lakes Golf & Country Club. Republican. Lutheran. Home: 1123 E Laurel St Kent WA 98031-6227 Office: Boeing Defense Space Group PO Box 3999 Seattle WA 98124-2499

OLSON, RONALD DEAN, Bible translation organization executive; b. Fergus Falls, Minn., Mar. 9, 1934; s. Isack and Laura (Kuchenbecker) O.; m. Frances D. Bundy, Jan. 30, 1960; children: Deborah, Carla, Barbara, Amy. BA, Bethel Coll., St. Paul, 1955; BD, Fuller Theol. Sem., Pasadena, Calif., 1958; ThM, Princeton Theol. Sem., 1959. Translator Wycliffe Bible Translators, Bolivia, S.Am., 1961-85, cons., 1966-85, internat. translation cons., 1969—; dir. Summer Inst. Linguistics, Bolivia, S.Am., 1975-78; internat. translation coord. Wycliffe Bible Translators, Dallas, 1986-89; assoc. dir. Wycliffe Bible Translators, Huntington Beach, Calif., 1990—. Translator: New Testament, 1978; contbr. articles on translation to trade jours. Recipient Ambassador's Svc. award U.S. Consulate, Bolivia, 1985; named Alumnus of Yr. Bethel Coll., St. Paul, 1986. Office: Wycliffe Bible Translators PO Box 2727 Huntington Beach CA 92647

OLSON, STEVEN STANLEY, social service executive; b. Longview, Wash., Aug. 5, 1950; s. Robert Martin and Martha Virginia (Duffin) O.; 1 child, Derek Thomas Dailey. BA, Wash. State U., 1972; MEd, Auburn U., 1977; postgrad., Seattle U., 1981-83. Cert. rehabilitation mgmt. Agrl. extensionist Action/Peace Corps, Popayan, Colombia, 1972-73; supr. Stonebelt Ctr. for the Mentally Retarded, Bloomington, Ind., 1974; adjustment counselor Exceptional Industries, Bowling Green, Ky., 1974-75; vocat. evaluator Exceptional Industries, 1975-76; alcohol counselor E. Ala. Mental Health, Opelika, 1976; intern Auburn Univ./Ptnrs. of the Americas, Guatemala City, Guatemala, 1976; planner, researcher Marion County Mental Health, Salem, Oreg., 1977-79; assoc. dir. Reliable Enterprises, Centralia, Wash., 1979-80; exec. dir. Reliable Enterprises, 1980—; v.p. govt. affairs Rehab. Enterprises Wash., Olympia, 1984-86, chmn. regional rep., 1986-89, pres. 1990-91; treas. Assn. for Retarded Citizens Wash., Olympia, 1983-85, govt. affairs chmn., 1983-89, v.p. 1989-90. Contbr. articles to Vocat. Evaluation and Work Adjustment Bull., 1976, Rehab. World, 1977. Treas. Communities United for Reponsible Energy, Lewis County, Wash., 1979—; vice chairperson Wash. Solar Coun., Olympia, Wash., 1980-83; co-chair Early Childhood Help Orgn., Olympia, 1988. Mem. Am. Assn. Mental Retardation, Assn. for Severely Handicapped, Wash. Assembly for Citizens with Disabilities, Alliance for Children, Youth, and Family. Home: 4333 Maytown Rd SW Olympia WA 98502-9239 Office: Reliable Enterprises 1500 Lum Rd Centralia WA 98531-1822

OLSON, SYLVESTER IRWIN, government official; b. Herman, Minn., Apr. 2, 1907; s. Jacob John and Theresia Mary (Kremer) O.; m. Virginia Varney Colbert, Aug. 19, 1948; children—Karen Therese, Eric Sylvester. Student, Marquette U., 1925-26; B.A., U. Minn., 1929, J.D., 1931. Bar: Minn. bar 1931, Wash. bar 1949, Republic of Korea bar 1954, D.C. bar 1962. Asso. Ewing & Lehmann, St. Paul, 1931-33, Harold E. Stassen, Elmer J. Ryan, Farmington, Minn., 1933-34; mem. firm Stassen, Olson, Kelly & LeVander, South St. Paul, Minn., 1935-39; asst. county atty. Dakota County, Minn., 1933-39; dep. chief counsel Dept. Rural Credit Minn., 1939-42; chief counsel div. adminstrv. mgmt. Minn., 1942-43, atty. and pub. relations counsel, 1944-48; mem. firm Brown, Olson & Clarke, Yakima, Wash.; asso. counsel Graves, Kizer & Graves, Spokane, 1949-54; legal cons. UN Econ. Coordinator, Korea, 1954; minister embassy, dir. U.S. Operations Mission to, Portugal, U.S. Operations Mission to (FOA), 1954-55; dep. dir. U.S. Operations Mission, ICA, also attache Am. Embassy, Tokyo, Japan, 1956-58; asst. dir. office Territories, Dept. Interior, 1959-61; practiced in Washington, 1962-66; program adviser Fed. Water Pollution Control Adminstrn., 1967-68; dir. enforcement div. EPA, 1969-76, spl. asst. dir. water enforcement, 1976-77; Pres. Wells Olson Co., Herman, 1946-78; dir. Pacific N.W., Trans-N.W. Gas, Inc., 1951-55. Chmn. Citation Crusade for Freedom, Central Wash., 1951. Mem. Yakima C. of C. (dir. 1951-53), Fed., Wash.,

Minn., D.C. bar assns., Tau Kappa Epsilon, Phi Alpha Delta. Home: Heatheridge 356 Pikes Peak Dr Grand Junction CO 81503-1740

OLSON, WILLIAM THOMAS, educator, consultant; b. Coeur d'Alene, Idaho, May 1, 1940; s. William Anthony and Julia Glenn (Hunter) O.; BA, U. N.Mex., 1968; postgrad. U. Va., 1968-72; m. Diana Jean Dodds, Aug. 22, 1962; children: Kristin Ann (dec.), Kira Lynn. Intelligence agt. U.S. Army, 1962-65; asso. editor Newspaper Printing Corp., Albuquerque, 1965-66; news and pub. affairs dir. Sta. KUNM-FM, U. N.M., 1966-68; news person KOAT-TV, Albuquerque, 1968; news dir. WCHV Radio, Charlottesville, Va., 1968-69; moderator, producer Radio-TV Center, U. Va., 1969-73; columnist The Jefferson Jour., Charlottesville, Va., 1972; instr. history U. Va., 1971-73; information specialist Wash. State U. Cooperative Ext. Service, Pullman, 1973-77, instr. Sch. Communications, 1976-77, asst. dir., Wash. Energy Ext. Service, 1977-79; dir. Spokane County Head Start, 1979-84; adminstr. Community Colls. of Spokane, 1984-89, dir. critical Thinking Project, 1988-89; pres. Effective Mgmt. Systems Corp., 1987-92, CEO, chmn., bd. dirs., 1992—. Dir. Connoisseur Concerts Assn., 1983-86, pres. 1985-86; dir. West Cen. Community Devel. Assn., pres., 1985-86; dir. Spokane Community Ctrs. Found., 1986—; mem. Mayor's budget com. City of Spokane, 1988-89. Served with AUS, 1962-65. Mem. Am. Soc. Quality Ctrl., advisory bd. Goal/QPC, Wash. Family Independence Program 1990-92. Author TV documentary (with Ken Fielding): The Golden Years?, 1973; film (with B. Dale Harrison and Lorraine Kingdon) New Directions Out of the Culture of Poverty, 1974. Home: 2018 E 14th Ave Spokane WA 99202-3562 Office: Stewart Bldg W-427 First Ave Spokane WA 99204

OLSSON, RONALD ARTHUR, computer science educator; b. Huntington, N.Y., Nov. 16, 1955; s. Ronald Alfred and Dorothy Gertrude (Hofmann) O. BA and MA, SUNY, 1977; MS, Cornell U., 1979; PhD, U. Ariz., 1986. Teaching asst. Cornell U., Ithaca, N.Y., 1977-79, rsch. asst., 1979; lectr. SUNY, Brockport, 1979-81; rsch. assoc. U. Ariz., Tucson, 1981-86; prof. Computer Sci. U. Calif., Davis, 1986—. Author (book) The SR Programming Language: Concurrency in Practice, 1993; contbr. articles to profl. jours. MICRO grantee U. Calif., 1987, 92, NSF grantee, 1988, Dept. Energy grantee, 1988-92. Mem. Assn. for Computing Machinery. Home: 1333 Arlington Blvd Apt 31 Davis CA 95616-2664 Office: U Calif Div Computer Sci Davis CA 95616

O'MALLEY, PETER, professional baseball club executive; b. N.Y.C., Dec. 12, 1937; s. Walter F. and Kay (Hanson) O'M.; m. Annette Zacho, July 10, 1971; children: Katherine, Kevin, Brian. B.S. in Econs, U. Pa., 1960. Dir. Dodgertown, Vero Beach, Fla., 1962-64; pres., gen. mgr. Spokane Baseball Club, 1965-66; v.p. Los Angeles Dodgers Baseball Club, 1967-68, exec. v.p., from 1968; pres. Los Angeles Dodgers, Inc., 1970—, also bd. dirs.; bd. dirs. Tidings newspaper, D.A.R.E. Calif.; sports com. mem. USIA. Bd. dirs. L.A. Police Meml. Found., L. A. World Affairs Coun., Jackie Robinson Found., L.A.-Guangzhou (Republic of China) Sister City Assn., Amateur Athletic Found.; pres. Little League Found.; mem. Music Ctr., L.A. County bd. govs. Office: LA Dodgers 1000 Elysian Park Ave Los Angeles CA 90012-1112 also: Dodger Stadium Los Angeles CA 90012

O'MALLEY, THOMAS PATRICK, university president; b. Milton, Mass., Mar. 1, 1930; s. Austin and Ann Marie (Feeney) O'M. BA, Boston Coll., 1951; MA, Fordham U., 1953; STL, Coll. St.-Albert de Louvain, 1962; LittD, U. Nijmegen, 1967; LLD (hon.), John Carroll U., 1988. Instr. classics Coll. of Holy Cross, Worcester, Mass., 1956-58; asst. prof., chmn. dept. classics Boston Coll., 1967-69, asso. prof., chmn. dept. theology, 1969-73; dean Boston Coll. (Coll. Arts and Scis.), 1973-80; pres. John Carroll U., Cleve., 1980-88; vis. prof. Cath. Inst. W. Africa, 1988-89; assoc. editor AMERICA, N.Y.C., 1989-90; rector Jesuit Com. Fairfield U., 1990-91; pres. Loyola Marymount U., L.A., 1991—. Author: Tertullian and the Bible, 1967. Trustee Boston Theol. Inst., 1969-73, Fairfield U., 1971-82, 89-91, John Carroll U., 1976-88, Xavier U., 1980-86, U. Detroit, 1982-88, Boston Coll. High Sch., 1986-88, Boys Hope, 1986-88. Mem. AAUP, Soc. Bibl. Lit., N.Am. Patristic Soc.

OMAR, SAMIRA AHMAD, range manager, researcher; b. Kuwait, Kuwait, Dec. 19, 1950; came to U.S., 1991; s. Ahmad Sayed Omar and Narjis Munib; m. Aziz Akil Zaman, July 22, 1970; children: Yasmin and Nada. BSc, U. Kuwait, 1972; MSc, U. Calif., Berkeley, 1979, PhD, 1991. Profl. Kiwait Inst. for Sci. Rsch., 1972-79, task leader, 1979-80, project leader, 1980-84, asst. dept. mgr., 1984-86, mgr. agroproduction dept., 1986-88, rsch. scientist, 1991-93; PhD candidate U. Calif., Berkeley, 1988-91, rsch. fellow, 1991—; cons. Environ. Protection Coun., Kuwait, 1984-88, Kuwait Municipality, 1981-84. Author: Spring Plants of Kuwait, 1984. Named Best Researcher in Range Mgmt., 2d Internat. Conf. on Range Mgmt. in the Arabian Gulf, Kuwait, 1990. Mem. Soc. for Range Mgmt., U. Calif. Alumni, Friends of the Earth, Grad. Soc. of Kuwait, Environ. Protection Soc. Office: Univ Calif Berkeley 145 Mulford Hall Berkeley CA 94720

OMENN, GILBERT STANLEY, university dean, physician; b. Chester, Pa., Aug. 30, 1941; s. Leonard and Leah (Miller) O.; m. Martha Darling; children: Rachel Andrea, Jason Montgomery, David Matthew. A.B., Princeton U., 1961; M.D., Harvard U., 1965; Ph.D. in Genetics, U. Wash., 1972. Intern Mass. Gen. Hosp., Boston, 1965-66; asst. resident in medicine Mass. Gen. Hosp., 1966-67; research assoc. NIH, Bethesda, Md., 1967-69; fellow U. Wash., 1969-71, asst. prof. medicine, 1971-74, assoc. prof., 1974-79, Howard Hughes med. inst., 1976-77, prof., 1979—, prof. environ. health, 1981—, chmn. dept., 1981-83, dean Sch. Pub. Health and Community Medicine, 1982—; bd. dirs. Rohm & Haas Co., Amgen, BioTechniques Labs. Inc., Immune Response Corp., Clean Sites, Inc., Population Svcs. Internat., Pacific N.W. Pollution Prevention Rsch. Ctr.; White House fellow/spl. asst. to chmn. AEC, 1973-74; assoc. dir. Office Sci. and Tech. Policy, The White House, 1977-80; assoc. dir. human resources Office Mgmt. and Budget, 1980-81; vis. sr. fellow Wilson Sch. Pub. and Internat. Affairs, Princeton U., 1981; sci. and pub. policy fellow Brookings Instn., Washington, 1981-82; cons. govt. agys., Lifetime Cable Network; mem. Nat. Com. on the Environment, environ. adv. com. Rohm & Haas, Rene Dubos Ctr. for Human Environments, AFL-CIO Workplace Health Fund., Electric Power Rsch. Inst., Carnegie Commn. Task Force on Sci. and Tech. in Jud. and Regulatory Decision Making, adv. com. to dir., Ctrs. Disease Control, 1992—, adv. com. Critical Technologies Inst., RAND; mem. Pres.'s Coun., U. Calif., 1992—. Co-author: Clearing the Air, Reforming the Clean Air Act, 1981. Editor: (with others) Genetics, Environment and Behavior: Implications for Educational Policy, 1972; Genetic Control of Environmental Pollutants, 1984; Genetic Variability in Responses to Chemical Exposure, 1984, Environmental Biotechnology: Reducing Risks from Environmental Chemicals through Biotechnology, 1988, Biotechnology in Biodegradation, 1990, Biotechnology and Human Genetic Predisposition to Disease, 1990, Annual Review of Public Health, 1991, 92, 93, Clinics in Geriatric Medicine, 1992; assoc. editor Cancer Rsch., Cancer Epidemiology, Biomarkers and Prevention, Environ. Rsch., Am. Jour. Med. Genetics, Am. Jour. Preventive Medicine; contbr. articles on cancer prevention, human biochem. genetics, prenatal diagnosis of inherited disorders, susceptibility to environ. agts., clin. medicine and health policy to profl. publs. Mem. President's Council on Spinal Cord Injury; mem. Nat. Cancer Adv. Bd., Nat. Heart, Lung and Blood Adv. Council, Wash. State Gov.'s Commn. on Social and Health Services, Ctr. for Excellence in Govt.; chmn. awards panel Gen. Motors Cancer Research Found., 1985-86; chmn. bd. Environ. Studies and Toxicology, Nat. Rsch. Coun., 1988-91; mem. Bd. Health Promotion and Disease Prevention, Inst. Medicine; mem. adv. com. Woodrow Wilson Sch., Princeton U., 1978-84; bd. dirs. Inst. for Sci. in Society; trustee Pacific Sci. Ctr., Fred Hutchinson Cancer Research Ctr., Seattle Symphony Orch., Seattle Youth Symphony Orch., Seattle Chamber Music Festival, Santa Fe Chamber Music Festival; mem. Citizens for a Hunger-Free Washington; chmn. rules com. Democratic Conv., King County, Wash., 1972. Served with USPHS, 1967-69. Recipient Research Career Devel. award USPHS, 1972; White House fellow, 1973-74. Fellow ACP, AAAS, Nat. Acad. Social Ins., Western Assn. Physicians, Hastings Ctr., Collegium Ramazzini; mem. Inst. Medicine of NAS, White House Fellows Assn., Am. Soc. Human Genetics, Western Soc. Clin. Rsch. Jewish. Home: 5100 NE 55th St Seattle WA 98105-2821 Office: U Wash Dean Sch Pub Health SC-30 Seattle WA 98195

OMER, GEORGE ELBERT, JR., physician, educator; b. Kansas City, Kans., Dec. 23, 1922; s. George Elbert and Edith May (Hines) O.; m. Wendie Vilven, Nov. 6, 1949; children: George Eric, Michael Lee. B.A., Ft. Hays State U., 1944; M.D., Kans. U., 1950; M.Sc. in Orthopaedic Surgery, Baylor U., 1955. Diplomate Am. Bd. Orthopaedic Surgery, 1959, re-cert. orthopaedics and hand surgery, 1983 (bd. dirs. 1983-92, pres. 1987-88), cert. surgery of the hand, 1989. Rotating intern Bethany Hosp., Kansas City, 1950-51; resident in orthopaedic surgery Brooke Gen. Hosp., San Antonio, 1952-55, William Beaumont Gen. Hosp., El Paso, Tex., 1955-56; chief surgery Irwin Army Hosp., Ft. Riley, Kans., 1957-59; cons. in orthopaedic surgery 8th Army Korea, 1959-60; asst. chief orthopaedic surgery, chief hand surgeon Fitzsimons Army Med. Center, Denver, 1960-63; dir. orthopaedic residency tng. Armed Forces Inst. Pathology, Washington, 1963-65; chief orthopaedic surgery and chief Army Hand Surg. Center, Brooke Army Med. Center, 1965-70; cons. in orthopaedic surgery to Surgeon Gen. Army, 1967-70, ret., 1970; prof. orthopaedics, surgery and anatomy, chmn. dept. orthopaedic surgery, chief div. hand surgery U. N.Mex., 1970-90, med. dir. phys. therapy, 1972-90, acting asst. dean grad. edn. Sch. Medicine, 1980-81; mem. active staff U. N.Mex. Hosp., chief of med. staff, 1984-86, Albuquerque; cons. staff other Albuquerque hosps.; cons. orthopaedic surgery USPHS, 1966-85, U.S. Army, 1970—, U.S. Air Force, 1970-78, VA, 1970—, Carrie Tingley Hosp. for Crippled Children, 1970—, interim med. dir., 1970-72, 86-87. Bd. editors: Clin. Orthopaedics, 1973-90, Jour. AMA, 1973-74, Jour. Hand Surgery, 1976-81; contbr. over 200 articles to profl. jours., also 2 books, over 50 chpts. to books. Commd. 1st lt. M.C. U.S. Army, 1949; advanced through grades to col. 1967. Decorated Legion of Merit, Army Commendation medal with 2 oak leaf clusters; recipient Alumni Achievement award Ft. Hays State U., 1973, Recognition plaque Am. Soc. Surgery Hand, 1989, Recognition plaque N.Mex. Orthopaedic Assn., 1991. Fellow ACS, Am. Orthopaedic Assn. (pres. 1988-89, exec. dir. 1989-93), Am. Acad. Orthopaedic Surgeons, Assn. Orthopaedic Chmn., N.Mex. Orthopaedic Assn. (pres. 1979-81), La. Orthopaedic Assn. (hon.), Korean Orthopaedic Assn. (hon.), Peru Orthopaedic Soc. (hon.), Caribbean Hand Soc., Am. Soc. Surgery Hand (pres. 1978-79), Am. Assn. Surgery of Trauma, Assn. Bone and Joint Surgeons, Assn. Mil. Surgeons U.S., Riordan Hand Soc. (pres. 1967-68), Sunderland Soc. (pres. 1981-83), Soc. Mil. Orthopaedic Surgeons, Brazilian Hand Soc., S.Am. Hand Soc. (hon.), Groupe D'Etude de la Main, Brit. Hand Soc., Venezuela Hand Soc. (hon.), South African Hand Soc. (hon.), Western Orthopaedic Assn. (pres. 1981-82), AAAS, Russell A. Hibbs Soc. (pres. 1977-78), 38th Parallel Med. Soc. (Korea) (sec. 1959-60); mem. AMA, Phi Kappa Phi, Phi Sigma, Alpha Omega Alpha, Phi Beta Pi. Home: 316 Big Horn Ridge Rd NE Sandia Heights Albuquerque NM 87122

OMRON, SAM, software publishing executive; b. Buffalo, N.Y., Aug. 17, 1956; s. Issa Salemah and Evelyn S. (Ajlouni) O.; m. Nancy Noel Shunnarah, July 19, 1981; children: Nicole, Christopher, Lauren. BS in Computer Sci., SUNY, Buffalo, 1978. Internat. mktg. Dynabyte, Menlo Park, Calif., 1979-80; dir. Systems Plus, Mountain View, Calif., 1981-92. Republican. Roman Catholic. Office: Systems Plus 500 Clyde Ave Mountain View CA 94043

OMURA, JIMMY KAZUHIRO, electrical engineer; b. San Jose, Calif., Sept. 8, 1940; s. Shomatsu and Shizuko Dorothy (Takesaka) O.; divorced; children: Daniel, Dawn. B.S., MIT, 1963, M.S., 1963; Ph.D. (NSF fellow 1963-66), Stanford U., 1966. Research engr. Stanford Research Inst., 1966-69; mem. faculty UCLA, 1969-85; founder, chmn. bd. Cylink Corp., Sunnyvale, Calif., 1983—; cons. to industry and govt. Co-author: Principles of Digital Communication and Coding, 1979, Spread Spectrum Communications, Vols. I, II, III, 1985; contbr. articles profl. jours. NSF grantee, 1970-78. Fellow IEEE (info. theory group). Office: Cylink Corp 310 N Mary Ave Sunnyvale CA 94086

ONAK, THOMAS PHILIP, chemistry educator; b. Omaha, July 30, 1932; s. Louis Albert and Louise Marie (Penner) O.; m. Sharon Colleen Neal, June 18, 1954. B.A., Calif. State U., San Diego, 1954; Ph.D., U. Cal. at Berkeley, 1957. Research chemist Olin Mathieson Chem. Corp., Pasadena, Calif., 1957-59; asst. prof. Calif. State U., Los Angeles, 1959-63, assoc. prof., 1963-66, prof. chemistry, 1966—. Author: Organoborane Chemistry, 1975; Contbr. articles to profl. jours., chpts. to books. Recipient Research Career award NIH, 1973-78, Nat. award Am. Chem. Soc., 1990; Fulbright research fellow U. Cambridge, Eng., 1965-66. Home: PO Box 1477 South Pasadena CA 91031-1477 Office: Calif State U Dept Chemistry 5151 State U Dr Los Angeles CA 90032

ONASCH, DONALD CARL, business executive; b. New Castle, Pa., July 5, 1927; m. Ruth Ellen Widman; children: Gregory W., Jay W., David R. BA, Washington and Jefferson Coll., 1950; MS in Retailing, U. Pitts., 1952. Div. mgr. mdse. Higbee Co., Cleve., 1953-65, Sibley, Lindsay & Curr, Rochester, N.Y., 1965-70; v.p., gen. mgr. mdse. Liberty House of Hawaii, Honolulu, 1970-72, pres., 1973-77; v.p. Amfac, Inc., Honolulu, 1977-78, exec. v.p., 1978—; bd. dirs. Associated Merchandising Corp. Served with USCG, 1945-46. Club: Oahu Country. Office: Amfac Inc 900 N Michigan Ave # 2860 Chicago IL 60611-1542 Also: Liberty House Inc 1450 Ala Moana Blvd Honolulu HI 96814

O'NEIL, BONNIE IRENE, database architect, engineer; b. Portchester, N.Y., Aug. 7, 1955; d. Tyler G. and Virginia (Ball) Kaus; m. Perry Jay O'Neil, Nov. 22, 1986; 1 child, Tyler William. BA in Psychology, U. So. Calif., L.A., 1976; BS in Computer Sci., Colo. State U., 1985. Sales SCM Corp., Long Beach, Calif., 1976-77; sr. sales rep. Saxon Bus. Products, Carson, Calif., 1977-79; sales rep. AM Internat., L.A., 1979-80; pub. rels. Enterprise Leasing, Torrance, Calif. & Denver, 1981-83; tng. and cons. IBM Corp., Boulder, Colo., 1984-85; tng. coord. Computer Horizons Corp., Golden, Colo., 1985-87; systems engr. Informix Software, Denver, 1988; systems cons. Sybase, Inc., Denver, 1989-91; mem. tech. staff U.S. West Advanced Tech., Boulder, 1991-92; dir. curriculum devel. Miaco Corp., Denver, 1992—; cons. Bell Labs., Denver, 1986-87. Author: Handbook of Data Management, 1993; contbr. articles to profl. jours. Founder, pres. emeritus Opera Buff of Boulder, Colo., 1985—; layreader, choir mem. Calvary Episcopal Ch., Golden, 1992. Mem. DAR, Info. Systems Trainers (bd. dirs. 1986-87), Toastmasters Internat. (CTM 1992), US West Trailtalk Toastmasters (pres. 1992). Republican. Episcopalian. Home: 24771 Westridge Rd Golden CO 80403 Office: Miaco Corp Ste 415 6300 S Syracuse Way Englewood CO 80111

O'NEILL, GARY MARSHALL, securities trader, dealer; b. San Mateo, Calif., July 10, 1952; s. Marshall Davison and Jeanne Louise (Mummert) O'N.; m. Patricia Joan Dunn, Apr. 2, 1986; children: Patrick Marshall, Caroline Elizabeth. BA in History, Pomona Coll., Claremont, Calif., 1974; JD, U. Santa Clara (Calif.), 1978. CLU, Chartered fin. cons. Advanced underwriting cons. N.Y. Life, N.Y.C., 1979-83, dir. field tng., 1983-86; dir. mut. fund sales N.Y. Life Securities, N.Y.C., 1986—. Contbr. articles to La Peninsula mag. Pres. Moraga Manor Homeowners Assn., 1981-83. Mem. Am. Soc. CLUs, Calif. State Bar Assn., San Francisco Planning Coun. (mem. at large), Moraga Tennis and Swim Club. Republican.

O'NEILL, JOHN PATRICK, priest, religious educator, counselor; b. Phila., Dec. 13, 1929; s. John Patrick and Marie Basil (Gill) O'N. AB in History, Niagara U., 1954, MS, 1967; MS, Villanova U., 1965. Ordained priest Roman Cath. Ch., 1959; joined Oblates of St. Francis de Sales. Priest, counselor, 1959—; tchr. secondary Cath. high schs., Pa., Del., N.Y., Mich., 1960-78; adminstr. De Sales Cath. High Sch., Lockport, N.Y., 1961-69. Pres., chair Diocesan Religious Edn. Adv. Bd., Stockton, Calif., 1981-92. Republican. Home and Office: St Jude's Cath Community 3824 Mitchell Rd Ceres CA 95307

O'NEILL, MAURA LOUISE, environmentalist; b. Saratoga, Calif., Sept. 6, 1956; d. Robert John O'Neill and Sunie Cabanne (Birdsall) Creegan; m. Vaho Rebassoo, Nov. 29, 1980; children: Finn, Liisa-Devlin. Student, UCLA, 1973-75; BA, U. Washington, 1977, postgrad., 1977; postgrad., NYU, 1980, Advanced Study Inst. NATO. Legis. intern to Assemblyman Tom Bane, 1974; rsch. asst. King County Pros. Atty.'s Office, 1975-76, Office of Environ. Mediation, 1976-77; environ. analyst Seattle City Light, 1977-78; asst. dir. Consumer Action Now, 1977-80; program dir. mayor's energy office N.Y.C., 1980-82; pres., energy and environ. cons. O'Neill & Co., Inc., Seattle, 1982—. Chair City of Seattle Pub. Safety Civil Svc. Commn., 1987-91; endorsement chair Washington State Women's Polit. Caucus, 1991, chair, 1992-93; treas. Washington Environ. Found.; active strategic planning com. ARC King County, Seattle. Named Bus. Person of Yr. Seattle C. of C./King Broadcasting, 1989. Mem. Seattle Rotary # 4. Office: O'Neill & Co Inc 1201 Third Ave # 2700 Seattle WA 98101

O'NEILL, MAUREEN KELLY, computer research engineer; b. Milw., Feb. 28, 1968; d. Emmet Patrick O'Neill and Katherine Mae (Beauchamp) Campion. BA in Math. and Computer Sci., Cornell U., 1990. Rsch. engr. Electronic Data Systems, Plano, Tex., 1990—. Alumni advisor Cornell Alumni Admissions Amb., Ithaca, 1991—; vol. tutor Boulder United Way, 1991—. Roman Catholic. Office: EDS/Neodata PO Box 4586 Boulder CO 80306-4586

O'NEILL, MICHAEL FOY, business educator; b. Milw., Apr. 16, 1943; s. Edward James and Marcellian (Wesley) O'N.; m. Karen Lynn Shoots, June 13, 1968; children: Kristine, Brenna. BBA, Ohio State U., 1966; PhD in Bus. Adminstrn., U. Oreg., 1978. Cons. Robert E. Miller and Assocs., San Francisco, 1969-73; mem. faculty Calif. State U., Chico, 1971-73, 1980—, U. Oreg., Eugene, 1974-77, U. Ariz., Tucson, 1977-79; pres. Decision Sci. Inst., Atlanta, 1986-87, v.p., 1985-86. Contbr. articles to profl. jours. Served with U.S. Army, 1962-68. Recipient Dean's Research award Calif. State U., Chico, 1981. Home: 2819 North Ave Chico CA 95926-0916 Office: Calif State U Dept Fin and Mktg Chico CA 95926

O'NEILL, NORAH ELLEN, airline pilot; b. Seattle, Aug. 23, 1949; d. John Wilson and Bertha Ellen (Moore) O'N.; m. Scott Reynolds, Jan. 31, 1970 (div. Apr. 1973); m. Scott Edward Byerley, Jan. 29, 1983; children: Cameron, Bren Maxey. Student, U. Calif., Santa Barbara, 1967-68, San Diego State U., 1868-70; BS in Profl. Aeros., Embry-Riddle Aero. U. Lic. airline transport pilot (comml., instrument instr.). Flight instr. Reynolds Aviation, Anchorage, 1973; flight instr. Alaska Cen. Air, Fairbanks, 1973-74, mail, commuter, medivac pilot, 1974-76; DC-8 pilot Flying Tigers, L.A., Seattle, N.Y.C., 1976-80; 747 pilot Flying Tigers, Los Angeles, 1980—. Mem. Airline Pilots Assn., 747 Pilot Fed. Express, Women Airline Pilots Soc. (co-founder 1978, v.p. 1979-80), The 99's (hon.). Home: PO Box 1504 Walla Walla WA 99362-0027 Office: Fed Express PO Box 727 Memphis TN 38194-9999

O'NEILL, SALLIE BOYD, sculptor, educator, business owner; b. Ft. Lauderdale, Fla., Feb. 17, 1926; d. Howard Prindle and Sarah Frances (Clark) Boyd; AA, Stephens Coll., 1945; m. Roger H. Noden, July 8, 1945; children: Stephanie Ann Ballard, Ross Hopkins Noden; m. Russell R. O'Neill, June 30, 1967. Course coord. UCLA Extension, 1960-72, specialist continuing edn. dept. human devel., acad. appointment, 1972-83; pres. Learning Adventures, Inc., 1985-86; v.p., chief fin. officer The Learning Network, Inc., 1985-86; ednl. cons., 1986—; sculptor, 1987—. Bd. dirs. Everywoman's Village, Vn Nuys, 1988—; mem. friends of the UCLA Ctr. for the Study of Women. Mem. Women in Bus. (v.p., bd. dirs. 1976-77, 86-87), Golden State Sculpture Assn. Democrat. Home and Studio: 15430 Longbow Dr Sherman Oaks CA 91403-4910

ONGENA, STEVEN R. G., economist; b. Oostende, Flanders, Belgium, Sept. 2, 1963; came to U.S., 1990; s. Guido and Mady (Wouters) O. Handelsingenieur, K. U., Leuven, Belgium, 1985, MBA, 1986; MA in Econs., U. Alberta, Edmonton, Can., 1988; postgrad., U. Oreg. Faculty dept. econs. U. Oreg., Eugene. With Belgium Spl. Forces, 1989-90. Premier Scholarship Govt. Alberta, 1986-88. Office: Dept Econs U Oreg Eugene OR 97603

ONISHI, YASUO, environmental researcher; b. Osaka, Japan, Jan. 25, 1943; came to U.S., 1969; s. Osamu and Tokiko (Domukai) O.; m. Esther Anna Stronczek, Jan 22, 1972; children: Anna Tokiko and Lisa Michiyo. BS, U. Osaka Prefecture, 1967, MS, 1969; PhD, U. Iowa, 1972. Rsch. engr. U. Iowa, Iowa City, 1972-74; sr. rsch. engr. Battelle Meml. Inst., Richland, Wash., 1974-77, staff engr., 1977-92, mgr. rsch. program office, 1984-92, sr. program mgr., 1992—. Co-author: Principles of Health Risk Assessment, 1985, several other environ. books; contbr. articles to profl. jours.; featured in TV program NOVA. Recipient Best Platform Presentation award ASTM, 1979. Mem. ASCE (chmn. task com. 1986—), IAEA (advisor on environ. issues, U.S. coord. water and soil assessment bilateral joint work on Chernobyl nuclear accident), Nat. Coun. Radiation Protection and Measurements (adj., mem. task com. 1983—), Sigma Xi. Lutheran. Home: 144 Spengler Rd Richland WA 99352-1971 Office: Battelle Pacific NW Labs Batelle Blvd Richland WA 99352

ONO, YONEO, landscape architect; b. Bakersfield, Calif., Apr. 25, 1925; s. George Yoneshiro and Tome (Suenaga) O.; children: Steve M. Ono, M. Miyoko Ono-Moore, Victoria J. Spotts. BS, U. Conn., 1959; postgrad., UCLA, 1954, Calif. State U., 1960-61, 64-68, 70-75. Registered landscape architect, Calif. Nurseryman Evergreen Nursery, Bakersfield, Calif., 1948-50, landscape architect, contractor, 1951-56; landscape architect Yoneo Ono Landscape Architect, Bakersfield, 1956-60; urban/regional planner County of Kern, Bakersfield, 1960-63; city planner City of Bakersfield, 1963, City of Fresno, Calif., 1963-81; landscape architect ONO Design Group, Clovis, Calif., 1984-90; invited speaker on urban renewal and central area planning, Japan, 1975; invited ambassador environ. horticulture del. Peoples Republic of China, 1985. Bd. dirs. County Mental Health Adv. Bd., Fresno, 1980-88; pres. Self Help Enterprises, 1969-71; founder, incorporator Rural Community Assistance Corp., 1978. Recipient Yoneo Ono award Rural Community Assistance Corp., 1984. Fellow Am. Soc. Landscape Architects; mem. Am. Inst. Cert. Planners, Soc. Am. Foresters, Internat. Erosion Control Assn. Home: 10231 Rocking Horse Ln Redding CA 96003 Office: GRR Bear Devel 2950 Beachelli Ln Redding CA 96003

ONSLOW FORD, GORDON MAX, painter; b. Wendover, Buckinghamshire, Eng., Dec. 26, 1912; came to U.S., 1947, naturalized, 1952; s. Max and Maud Elizabeth (Woollerton) Onslow Ford; m. Jacqueline Marie Johnson, May 5, 1941. Grad., Royal Naval Coll., Dartmouth, Eng., 1929; grad., Royal Naval Coll., Greenwich, Eng., 1930. Mem. Surrealist Group, Paris, London, N.Y.C., 1938-43. One-man shows include New Sch. for Social Research, N.Y.C., 1940, Nierendorf Gallery, N.Y.C., 1946, San Francisco Mus. Art, 1948, M.H. DeYoung Mus., San. Francisco, 1962, San Francisco Mus., 1951, 59, 70, Oakland Mus., Calif., 1977, Art Gallery Greater Victoria, B.C., 1971, Samy Kinge Gallery, Paris, 1985; group shows: Paris, 1983, London, 1940, N.Y.C., 1943, Los Angeles County Mus., 1950, 61, 70, 87, Newport Harbor Mus., 1986, Mus. Rath, Geneva, 1987, Centro Atlantico De Arte Moderno, Gran Canaica, Spain, 1989, Laguna Art Mus., 1990, U. Calif. Berkeley Art. Mus., 1990, Malibu Harcourt Gallery, San Francisco, 1992, Pavillion Gallery, Munich, 1993; permanent collections: San Francisco Mus. Modern Art, Tate Gallery, London, M.H. deYoung Mus., Oakland Mus., Guggenheim Mus., N.Y.C., Whitney Mus. Modern Art, N.Y.C., Denver Mus., Fogg Mus., U. Mass., U. Calif.-Davis; author: Toward A New Subject in Painting, 1947, Painting in the Instant, 1964, Creation, 1978, Yves Tanguy and Automatism, 1983, Insights, 1991.

ONSTAD, DAVID O., electrical engineer, power company administrator; b. Spring Grove, Minn., Mar. 17, 1939; s. Oswald S. and Lucille Onstad; m. July 21, 1963; children: Timothy, Daniel. BS in EE, Mont. State U., 1961. Registered profl. engr. Elec. engr. U.S. Bur. Reclamation, Huron, S.D., 1963-68, Boulder City, Nev., 1968-71; supervisory elec. engr. U.S. Bur. Reclamation, Lakewood, Colo., 1972-73, Boulder City, 1974-78; dist. mgr. U.S. Dept. of Energy-Western Area Power Adminstrn., Phoenix, 1978-87; dep. area mgr. U.S. Dept. of Energy-Western Area Power Adminstrn., Boulder City, 1987-89; adminstr. Ariz. Power Authority, Phoenix, 1989—. Cubmaster Boy Scouts Am., Litchfield Park, Ariz., 1981-86. Mem. IEEE (pres. 1985-86), Toastmasters Internat. (div. lt. gov., Disting. Toastmaster 1986), Power Engring. Soc. (pres. Phoenix chpt. 1985-86), Kiwanis Internat. Lutheran. Home: Box 1187 Litchfield Park AZ 85340

ONSTINE WOOD, MARY LOUISE, recreational facility executive; b. Powell, Wyo., Sept. 24, 1963; d. Louis Preston and Mary Susanna (Simpers) O.; m. Dale Raymond Wood, Dec. 29, 1984; 1 child, Mary Elizabeth. Student, Northwest Coll., 1982-83; BS in Microbiology, U. Wyo., 1985. Wyo. 4-H amb. coord. U. Wyo. Coop. Extension Svc., Laramie, Wyo., 1982—; lodge mgr. Two Dot Ranch, Cody, Wyo., 1986—; trip coord. Western Laramie 4-H Roundup, 1992—, U. Wyo. Cooperative Ext. Svc., Laramie. Active Wyo. N.G. Aux., 1987—; state historian Wyo. 4-H Alumni Assn., 1988-91, state sec., 1991-93, dist. coord., 1993—; advisor Natrona County 4-H Jr. Leaders, 1991—; bd. dirs. Natrona County 4-H Found., 1992—, sec. 1992—; amb. Nat. 4-H, 1983. Recipient Molly Pitcher award U.S. Field Artillery Assn., Alumni award Natrona County 4-H, 1992; J.C. Penny scholar Laramie County 4-H Coun., 1990, Key Bank Corp. scholar Natrona County 4-H Coun. Mem. Am. Legion Aux., Alpha Zeta. Republican. Methodist. Home: 4252 Cabin Creek Rd Alcova Rte Casper WY 82604-9245

ONSTOTT, EDWARD IRVIN, research chemist; b. Moreland, Ky., Nov. 12, 1922; s. Carl Ervin and Jennie Lee (Foley) O.; m. Mary Margaret Smith, Feb. 6, 1945; children: Jenifer, Peggy Sue, Nicholas, Joseph. BSChemE, U. Ill., 1944, MS in Chemistry, 1948, PhD in Inorganic Chemistry, 1950. Chem. engr. Firestone Tire & Rubber Co., Paterson, N.J., 1944, 46; research chemist Los Alamos Nat. Lab., 1950—, now guest scientist. Patentee in field. Served with C.E., AUS, 1944-46. Fellow AAAS, Am. Inst. Chemists; mem. Am. Chem. Soc., Electrochem. Soc., N.Y. Acad. Scis., Internat. Assn. Hydrogen Energy, Rare Earth Research Confs., Izaak Walton League, N.Mex. Acad. Scis., Los Alamos Hist. Soc. Republican. Methodist. Home: 225 Rio Bravo Dr Los Alamos NM 87544-3848

ONSTOTT, MARK DOUGLAS, communications educator; b. Denver, Feb. 11, 1954; s. Robert Ernest and Helen Margaret (Spanwell) O.; m. Kim Marie Eby, Dec. 18, 1976; children: Adam Erik, Brittney Kala. BA in Theatre and English, Regis U., 1976; MA in Comm., U. Denver, 1981. Comm. educator Cherry Creek Schs., Englewood, Colo., 1976—. Dist. dir. Colo. High Sch. Activities, Aurora, 1979-85. Mem. ASCD, NEA, Colo. Edn. Assn., Cherry Creek Edn. Assn., Nat. Forensic League (mem. Colo. com. 1982-91, Diamond Key Coach award 1986), Nat. Fedn. Debate Coaches, Nat. Coun. Tchrs. English. Democrat. Roman Catholic. Home: 4043 S Kirk Way Aurora CO 80013 Office: Eaglecrest Sch 5100 S Picadilly St Aurora CO 80015

OPENSHAW, DALE KIM, educator, therapist; b. Salt Lake City, Mar. 10, 1950; s. Richard D. and Naoma Lillian (Tischner) O.; m. Anita B. Evans, Jan. 12, 1973; children: Damian, Cammarie, Derek, Jeffrey, Cody, Shandee, Joshua, Micah. BA, U. Utah, 1973, MSW, 1976; PhD, Brigham Young U., 1978. Prof. human devel. U. Wis.-Stout, 1978-79; child devel. and family life specialist U. Wis.-Madison, 1979-81; prof., dir. marriage and family therapy Utah State U., Logan, 1981—; pvt. practice psychotherapist, Wis. and Utah, 1978—; adj. prof. adolescent devel. psychology. Active Optimist Internat. NIMH grantee U. Utah, 1974-76. Named Tchr. of Yr. Coll. Family Life, 1991-92, 92-93. Mem. Nat. Coun. on Family Rels. (chair family therapy sect.), Soc. Rsch. Child Devel., Am. Assn. Marriage and Family Therapy, Nat. Marriage Consortium, Am. Soc. Clin. Hypnosis, Utah Soc. Clin. Hypnosis (pres. 1991-93), Omicron Nu. Mem. Ch. of Jesus Christ of Latter-Day Saints. Presenter numerous workshops; contbr. articles to profl. jours. Home: 567 E 3700 S PO Box 424 Millville UT 84326-0424 Office: Utah State U Dept Family and Human Devel Logan UT 84322-2905

OPFELL, JOHN BURTON, chemical engineer, educator; b. Cushing, Okla., July 24, 1924; s. Edward Uriah and Carrie Evelyn (Walker) O.; m. Olga Anna Strandvold, Sept. 10, 1954; children: Christopher Kaj, Thane Fredrick, Jon Guido. BS, U. Wis., 1945; MS, Calif. Inst. Tech., 1947, PhD, 1954; MBA, Stanford U., 1951. Registered profl. engr., Calif. Engr. Stanolind Oil and Gas Co., Tulsa, 1947-49, Cutter Labs., Berkeley, Calif., 1955-61, Dynamic Sci. Corp., South Pasadena, Calif., 1961-64, Philco-Ford Corp., Newport Beach, Calif., 1964-69; asst. mgr. corp. planning Sunkist Growers, Sherman Oaks, Calif., 1970-73; asst. to exec. v.p. Henningson, Durham and Richardson, Santa Barbara, Calif., 1980-83; engr. AiResearch Mfg. Co., Torrance, Calif., 1973-80, Allied-Signal Aerospace Co., Torrance, Calif., 1983—; lectr. Calif. Inst. Tech., Pasadena, 1954, U. Calif., Santa Barbara, 1973, 82, Calif. State U., Northridge, 1986. Author: (with others) Momentum Transfer in Fluids, 1956, Equations of State for Hydrocarbons, 1959; contbr. articles to profl. jours. Served as lt. (j.g.) USN, 1944-54. Fellow AAAS, Royal Soc. for Health (London); mem. Am. Inst. Chem. Engrs., Ops. Research Soc. Am., Sigma Xi. Democrat. Lodge: Masons. Home: 1007 Park Circle Dr Torrance CA 90502-2817 Office: Allied Signal Aerospace Co 2525 W 190th St Torrance CA 90509-2960

OPFER, NEIL DAVID, educator, consultant; b. Spokane, Wash., June 3, 1954; s. Gus Chris and Alice Ann (Blom) O. BS in Bldg. Theory cum laude, Wash. State U., 1976, BA in Econs. cum laude, 1977, BA in Bus. cum laude, 1977; MS in Mgmt., Purdue U., 1982. Cert. cost engr. Estimator Standard Oil (Chevron), Richmond, Calif., 1975; gen. carpenter forman Opfer Constrn. Corp., Spokane, 1976; assoc. engr. Inland Steel Corp., East Chgo., Ind., 1977-78; millwright supr. Inland Steel Corp., 1978-79, field engr., 1979-82, project engr., 1982-84, sr. engr., 1984-87; asst. prof. Western Mich. U., Kalamazoo, 1987-89, U. Nev., Las Vegas, 1989—. Contbr. articles to publs. Bd. dirs. Mizpah Boys Home, Las Vegas, 1989—, Habitat for Humanity, 1991—. Mem. Am. Welding Soc. (dir. 1982-87), Am. Inst. Constructors, Am. Assn. Cost Engrs. (Order of Engr. award 1989), Constrn. Mgmt. Assn. Am., Tau Beta Pi (life), Phi Kappa Phi (life). Methodist. Home: 1515 E Reno Ave Las Vegas NV 89119-2116 Office: Univ Nev 4505 S Maryland Pky Las Vegas NV 89154-4018

OPITZ, JOHN MARIUS, clinical geneticist, pediatrician; b. Hamburg, Germany, Aug. 15, 1935; came to U.S., 1950, naturalized, 1957; s. Friedrich and Erica Maria (Quadt) O.; m. Susan O. Lewin; children: Leigh, Teresa, John, Chrisanthi, Felix, Emma. BA, State U. Iowa, 1956, MD, 1959; DSc (hon.), Mont. State U., 1983; MD (hon.), U. Kiel, Fed. Republic of Germany, 1986. Diplomate Am. Bd. Pediatrics, Am. Bd. Med. Genetics. Intern, State U. Iowa Hosp., 1959-60, resident in pediatrics, 1960-61; resident and chief resident in pediatrics U. Wis. Hosp., Madison, 1961-62; fellow in pediatrics and med. genetics U. Wis., 1962-64, asst. prof. med. genetics and pediatrics, 1964-69, assoc. prof., 1969-72, prof., 1972-79; dir. Wis. Clin. Genetics Ctr., 1974-79; clin. prof. med. genetics and pediatrics U. Wash., Seattle, 1979—; adj. prof. medicine, biology, history and philosophy, vet. rsch. and vet. sci. Mont. State U., Bozeman, 1979—; adj. prof. pediatrics, med. genetics U. Wis., Madison, 1979—, Class of 1947 Disting. prof., 1992; coordinator Shodair Mont. Regional Genetic Svcs. Program, Helena, 1979-82; chmn. dept. med. genetics Shodair Children's Hosp., Helena, 1983—; Farber lectr. Soc. Pediatric Pathology, 1987; Joseph Garfunkel lectr. So. Ill. U., Springfield, 1987, McKay lectr. Mont. State U., 1992; Warren Wheeler vis. prof. Columbus (Ohio) Children's Hospital, 1987. Editor, author 12 books; founder, editor in chief Am. Jour. Med. Genetics, 1977—; mng. editor European Jour. Pediatrics, 1977-85; contbr. numerous articles on clin. genetics. Chair Mont. Com. for Humanities, 1991. Recipient Pool of Bethesda award for excellence in mental retardation rsch. Bethesda Luth. Home, 1988, Med. Alumni Citation U. Wis., 1989. Mem. Am. Coll. Med. Genetics (founder), German Acad. Scientists Leopoldina, Am. Soc. Human Genetics, Am. Pediatric Soc., Soc. Pediatric Rsch., Am. Bd. Med. Genetics, Birth Defects Clin. Genetic Soc., Am. Inst. Biol. Scis., Am. Soc. Zoologists, AAAS, Teratology Soc., Genetic Soc. Am., European Soc. Human Genetics, Soc. Study Social Biology, Am. Acad. Pediatrics, German Soc. Pediatrics (hon.), Western Soc. Pediatrics Rsch., Italian Soc. Med. Genetics, Am. Coll. Med. Genetics (founding mem.), Sigma Xi. Democrat. Roman Catholic. Home: 2180 Lime Kiln St Helena MT 59601-5871 Office: Shodair Children's Hosp PO Box 5539 Helena MT 59604-5539

OPOTOWSKY, MAURICE LEON, newspaper editor; b. New Orleans, Dec. 13, 1931; s. Sol and Fannie (Latter) O.; m. Madeleine Duhamel, Feb. 28, 1959 (dec.); children: Didier Sol Duhamel, Joelle Duhamel, Arielle Duhamel (dec.); m. Bonnie Feibleman, May 4, 1991. Student, Tulane U., 1949-51; B.A. cum laude, Williams Coll., 1953. Reporter Berkshire Eagle, Pittsfield, Mass., 1951-53; pub. Sea Coast Echo, Bay St. Louis, Miss., 1953-54; reporter U.P.I., 1956-62; feature editor Newsday, Ronkonkoma, N.Y., 1962-64; Suffolk day editor Newsday, 1964-65, Nassau night editor, 1965-67, nat. editor, 1967-70, Suffolk editor, 1970-72; dir. L.I. Mag., 1972; day editor Press-Enterprise, Riverside, Calif., 1973-84, mng. editor features/adminstrn., 1984-87, sr. mng. editor, 1987-92, mng. editor, 1992—; chief N.Y. State Syndicate Service, 1961-74; mem. Calif. Freedom of Info. Exec. Com., sec., 1979-80, treas., 1980-81, v.p., 1981-82, pres., 1982-83. Trustee Harbor Country Day Sch., 1970-72; bd. dirs. Calif. Newspaper Editor Conf. Bd., 1978-83; mem. Smithtown (N.Y.) Hunt, 1970-73, West Hills Hunt, 1976-80, Santa Fe Hunt, Whip, 1985—; co-chmn. Calif. Bench-Bar Media Com. Served with AUS, 1954-56. Mem. AP News Execs. Calif. (chmn. 1986-87), Calif. 1st Amendment Coalition (pres., treas.), Calif. Soc. Newspaper Editors (bd. dirs., vice chmn. steering com. 1983), AP Mng. Editors Assn., Am. Soc. Newspaper Editors. Office: Press Enterprise Co 3512 14th St Riverside CA 92501-3878

OPPEDAHL, GILLIAN COYRO, occupational therapist; b. Detroit, Feb. 28, 1955; d. Richard Paul Coyro and Joan Audrey (Smith) Sieger; m. John Frederick Oppedahl, Feb. 14, 1987. BS, Wayne State U., 1978. Lic. occupational therapy. Staff occupational therapist Hurley Med. Ctr., Flint, Mich., 1978-80; occupational therapist Wyandotte (Mich.) Gen. Hosp., 1980-84; sr. occupational therapist Baylor U. Med. Ctr., Dallas, 1984-85; occupational therapist Richardson (Tex.) Med. Ctr., 1985-87; adjunctive therapy supr. Glendale (Calif.) Adventist Med. Ctr., 1988-89; occupational therapist Wendy Paine O'Brien Treatment Ctr., Scottsdale, Ariz., 1989—. Bd. dirs. Ariz. Opera League, Phoenix, 1990—, Arizonans for Cultural Devel., Phoenix, 1992. Mem. Am. Occupational Therapy Assn., Ariz. Occupational Therapy Assn., Phoenix Art Mus. Home: 4565 E Lafayette Blvd Phoenix AZ 85018

OPPEDAHL, JOHN FREDRICK, newspaper editor; b. Duluth, Minn., Nov. 9, 1944; s. Walter H. and Lucille (Hole) O.; m. Alison Owen, 1975 (div. 1983); m. Gillian Coyro, Feb. 14, 1987. B.A., U. Calif., Berkeley, 1967; M.S., Columbia U., 1968. Reporter San Francisco Examiner, 1967; reporter, asst. city editor Detroit Free Press, 1968-75, city editor, 1975-80, exec. city editor, 1981, exec. news editor, 1981-82, asst. mng. editor, 1983; nat. editor Dallas Times Herald, 1983-85, asst. mng. editor, 1985-87; mng. editor/news L.A. Herald Examiner, 1987-89; mng. editor Ariz. Republic, Phoenix, 1989-93; exec. editor Phoenix Newspapers, 1993—. Mem. Am. Soc. Newspaper Editors, AP Mng. Editors. Office: Phoenix Newspapers Inc 120 E Van Buren St Phoenix AZ 85004-2200

OPPEDAHL, PHILLIP EDWARD, computer company executive; b. Renwick, Iowa, Sept. 17, 1935; s. Edward and Isadore Hannah (Gangstead) O.; B.S. in Naval Sci., Navy Postgrad. Sch., 1963, M.S. in Nuclear Physics, 1971; M.S. in Systems Mgmt., U. S.C., 1978; m. Sharon Elaine Ree, Aug. 3, 1957 (dec. Aug. 1989); children: Gary Lynn, Tamra Sue, Sue Ann, Lisa Kay. Commd. ensign U.S. Navy, 1956, advanced through grades to capt., 1977; with Airborne Early Warning Squadron, 1957-59, Anti-Submarine Squadron, 1959-65; asst. navigator USS Coral Sea, 1965-67; basic jet flight instr., 1967-69; student Armed Forces Staff Coll., 1971; test group dir. Def. Nuclear Agy., 1972-74; weapons officer USS Oriskany, 1974-76; program mgr. for armament Naval Air Systems Command, Washington, 1977-79; test dir. Def. Nuclear Agy., Kirtland AFB, N.Mex., 1979-82, dep. comdr. Def. Nuclear Agy., 1982-83; pres., chief exec. officer Am. Systems, Albuquerque, 1983—. Pres., bd. dirs. Casa Esperanza, 1990-92. Decorated Disting. Service medal. Mem. Naval Inst., Am. Nuclear Soc., Aircraft Owners and Pilots Assn., Assn. Naval Aviation Navy League. Lutheran. Author: Energy Loss of High Energy Electrons in Beryllium, 1971; Understanding Contractor Motivation and Incentive Contracts, 1977. Home: 1108 Camino Real # 310 Redondo Beach CA 90277

OPPEL, ANDREW JOHN, apparel company executive; b. Kerrville, Tex., Dec. 22, 1952; s. Wallace Churchill and Anne Kathryn (Smith) O.; m. Laura Lee Partridge, Aug. 26, 1972; children: Keith Andrew, Luke Andrew. BA in Computer Sci., Transylvania U., 1974. Computer programmer Johns Hopkins U., Balt., 1974-77; data base programmer Equitable Trust Co., Balt., 1977-78; sr. programmer, analyst Md. Casualty Co., Balt., 1978-79; sr. programmer, analyst Levi Strauss & Co., San Francisco, 1979-82, sr. requirements mgr., 1982-84, tech. cons., 1984-91, tech. advisor, 1991—; instr. U. Calif. Extension, Berkeley, 1983—. Ops. officer Alameda County Radio Amateur Civil Emergency Svc., San Leandro, Calif., 1980—; cub master Boy Scouts Am., Alameda, Calif., 1991-92; referee U.S. Soccer Fedn., Alameda, 1988—. Democrat. Episcopalian. Home: 1308 Burbank St Alameda CA 94501 Office: Levi Strauss & Co 1155 Battery St San Francisco CA 94120

OPPENHEIM, DAVID JOHN, lawyer; b. N.Y.C., Apr. 18, 1923; s. Benjamin and Elizabeth (Smith) O.; m. Mary Martinez, Jan. 16, 1960. BS, U.S. Merchant Marine Acad., 1944; BA, Iona Coll., 1949; JD, Fordham U., 1957. Bar: N.Y. 1958, U.S. Dist. Ct. (so. dist.) N.Y. 1973, U.S. Supreme Ct. 1974. Tchr. Rice High Sch., N.Y.C., 1948-50, Eastchester (N.Y.) High Sch., 1950-60; atty. pvt. practice Bronxville, N.Y., 1958—; pres. Max & Victoria Dreyfuss Found., N.Y.C., 1976—; v.p., gen. mgr. Chappell Music Pub. Co., N.Y.C., 1967-68; pres. Eastchester Tchrs. Assn., 1958-60. Contbr. articles to profl. jours. law and edn. Dist leader, mem. Dem. County Com. Westchester County, Eastchester, 1948-52; counsel Eastchester Fire Dept., 1963-75; trustee Eastchester Pub Libr., 1964-66; mem. supt. coun. U.S. Merchant Marine Acad., King's Point, N.Y., 1983-88; judge Moot Ct. Fordham U. Recipient N.Y. Vets. scholarship, 1953. Mem. N.Y. State Bar Assn., Westchester County Bar Assn., Mission Lake Country Club (various coms.).

OPPENHEIM, SAMUEL AARON, history educator; b. N.Y.C., Nov. 11, 1940; s. Harold A. J. and Dorothy (Sobel) O.; m. Alyne Faye Bernstein, Aug. 15, 1965; children: Michael, Andrew, Dorothy, Sarah. BA in History, U. Ariz., 1962; AM in Soviet Studies, Harvard U., 1964; PhD in History, Ind. U., 1972. Instr. in Russian lang. and history Bishop Coll., Dallas, 1964-67; part-time instr. in Russian lang. and history Austin Coll., Sherman, Tex., 1965-67; from asst. to prof. history Calif. State U.-Stanislaus, Turlock, 1971—, chmn. dept. history, 1985-91. Author: The Practical Bolshevik: A.I. Rykov and Russian Communism, 1881-1938, 1979, Soviet Russia: A History (Lectures & Vignettes), 1991; contbr. articles to profl. jours. Vol. tchr. Russian lang. Beyer High Sch., Modesto, Calif., 1982-86; bd. dirs. Congregation Beth Shalom, Modesto, 1972-79, pres., 1973-75. Recipient Community Svc. award U. Judaism, 1976. Mem. Am. Assn. for the Advancement Slavic Studies, Am. Hist. Assn., Calif. Faculty Assn., B'nai B'rith, Phi Beta Kappa, Phi Alpha Theta, Phi Eta Sigma, Phi Kappa Phi. Democrat. Office: Calif State U History Dept 801 W Monte Vista Ave Turlock CA 95380-0299

OPPENHEIMER, PRESTON CARL, psychologist, counseling agency administrator, psychodiagnostician; b. Jacksonville, Fla., Sept. 17, 1958; s. Dawson N. and Audrey Muriel (Pressman) O.; m. Pilar Apodaca, Oct. 28, 1989; 1 child, Leo Morris. BA in Psychology, U. Calif., San Diego, 1980; MS in Edn., U. So. Calif., 1982, Phd in Counseling, 1988. Registered psychol. asst. Contract counselor Glendale (Calif.) Family Svc. Assn, 1987-88, intake coord., 1988-89, adminstrv. dir., 1989—; psychol. asst. Curtis Psychol. Assocs., L.A., 1988—; assoc. clin. prof. UCLA, 1988—. Narrator, co-editor (documentary) Time Out for Judy--It Beats a Belt, 1984. Active community rels. com. Ea. Region Jewish Fedn. Coun., Covina, Calif., 1987-88, Temple Sinai Glendale, 1989—, bd. dirs., 1991—. Named One of Outstanding Young Men Am., 1986, 87. Mem. Am. Psychol. Assn., Pasadena Jaycees (recipient William D. Sloss award for creative inspiration 1988, project chmn. yr. 1987)/. Republican. Jewish. Office: Glendale Family Svc Assn 3436 N Verdugo Rd Glendale CA 91208-1595

OPPENHEIMER, REX MAURICE, sales and marketing executive, poet, screenwriter; b. Santa Barbara, Calif., Feb. 13, 1949; s. Hans Bernard and Ruth (Lesensky) O.; m. Penelope Lovelock Emmerson, June 5, 1980; children: Elisabeth Lindley, Eliot Yitzhak. Dir. English dept. Yukari Culture Ctr., Toyohashi, Japan, 1983-85; regional sales mgr. ColorView Svcs., Inc., Albuquerque, Mesa, Ariz., 1987-90; mfr.'s rep. Magnavox Comml. Sales, Scottsdale, Ariz., 1990—; chmn., bd. dirs. Slinky Dinky Music Pub., Seres, Inc.; regional sales mgr. So. Calif., N.Am. Philips Consumer Electronics Co.; writer Winmill Entertainment, 1991. Lyricist (records) She's a Goddess, 1972, Come to Me, 1977, 79, Best of Jenifer Warnes, 1983. Mem. ASCAP.

OPSAL, PHILIP MASON, consulting wood scientist; b. Mpls., Oct. 1, 1931; s. Elmer Clement and Mae Hazel (Anderson) O.; children: Pamela Ellen, P. Wade, Claudia Ann. BS, U. Minn., 1956, MS, 1957. Lic. pesticide applicator. Prof. Colo. State U., Ft. Collins, 1957-61; founder, pres., owner Jason Assocs., Inc., Ft. Collins, 1960-86, OHM Chem. Corp., Ft. Collins, 1972-79; v.p. Loadmaster Systems, Inc., Tucson, Ariz., 1986-88; pres., owner Philip Mason Opsal, P.C., Tucson, 1988—; cons. large electric utilities and small utilities, 27 states, 1960—, over 400 attys. at law throughout U.S., 1961—. Author: Lineman's Manual of Wood-Emphasis on Safety, 1990. Pres. 10 Team Little League, Ft. Collins, 1968. With USAF, 1951-53, hon. discharge. Mem. Am. Inst. Timber Constrn., Am. Wood Preservers Assn., Forest Products Soc. (chmn. Rocky Mountain sect. 1980-82), Soc. Forensic Engrs. and Scientists, Soc. Wood Sci. and Tech., Ft. Collins C. of C. (bus. devel. com. 1965). Republican. Lutheran. Office: PO Box 64591 Tucson AZ 85728-4591

ORANS, REN, energy economist, consultant; b. Seattle, Feb. 27, 1959; s. Martin Orans and (Yeh) Tung; m. Meta Uota, Aug. 4, 1990. BA in Econs., U. Calif., Berkeley, 1981; MS in Engring., Stanford U., 1987, PhD in Civil Engring., 1989. Economist Pacific Gas & Electric Co., San Francisco, 1981-86; prin., cons. Energy and Environ. Econs., San Francisco, 1986—. Dean's fellow in engring. Stanford U., 1986. Home: 2 Lupine Apt 4 San Francisco CA 94118

ORBACH, RAYMOND LEE, physicist, educator; b. Los Angeles, July 12, 1934; s. Morris Albert and Mary Ruth (Miller) O.; m. Eva Hannah Spiegler, Aug. 26, 1956; children: David Miller, Deborah Hedwig, Thomas Randolph. B.S., Calif. Inst. Tech., 1956; Ph.D., U. Calif.-Berkeley, 1960. NSF postdoctoral fellow Oxford U., 1960-61; asst. prof. applied physics Harvard U., 1961-63; prof. physics UCLA, 1963-92, asst. vice chancellor acad. change and curriculum devel., 1970-72; chmn. UCLA (Los Angeles div. acad. senate), 1976-77; provost Coll. Letters and Sci. UCLA, 1982-92; chancellor U. Calif., Riverside, 1992—; Cons. Aerospace Corp., 1965-70; mem. physics adv. panel NSF, 1970-73; mem. vis. com. Brookhaven Nat. Lab., 1970-74; mem. materials research lab. adv. panel NSF, 1974-77; mem. Nat. Commn. on Research, 1978-80; chmn. 16th Internat. Conf. on Low Temperature Physics, 1981; Joliot Curie prof, E.S.P.C.I., Paris, 1982, chmn. Gordon Rsch. Conf. on Fractals, 1986; Lorentz prof. U. Leiden, Netherlands, 1987; Raymond and Beverly Sackler lectr. Tel Aviv U., 1989; faculty rsch. lectr. UCLA, 1990; Andrew Lawson lectr. U. Calif., Riverside, 1992. Author: (with A.A. Manenkov) SpinLattice Relaxation in Ionic Solids, 1966; Div. assoc. editor Phys. Rev. Letters, 1980-83, Jour. Low Temperature Physics, 1980-90, Phys. Rev., 1983—; contbr. articles to profl. jours. Alfred P. Sloan Found. fellow, 1963-67; NSF sr. postdoctoral fellow Imperial Coll., 1967-68; Guggenheim fellow Tel Aviv U., 1973-74. Fellow Am. Phys. Soc. (chmn. nominations com. 1981-82, counsellor-at-large 1987-91, chmn. div. condensed matter 1990-91); mem. AAAS (chair-elect steering group, physics sect.), NSF (rsch. adv. com., div. materials 1992-93), Phys. Soc. (London), Univ. Rsch. Assn. (chair coun. pres. 1993), Sigma Xi, Tau Beta Pi, Phi Beta Kappa. Home: 4171 Watkins Dr Riverside CA 92507 Office: U Calif Riverside Chancellor's Office Riverside CA 92521-0101

ORDUNO, ROBERT DANIEL, artist, painter, sculptor; b. Ventura, Calif., Sept. 5, 1933; s. Octavio and Mary G.; children: Patrice Schulman, Nicole Franco. Pvt. practice Artist, Painter, Sculptor; pvt. teaching, Santa Fe, 1990. Exhibited in Great Falls Tribune, J.M. Swanson, 1985, Gazette, Cody Bur, Wyo, Tom Howard, 1987, Aurora, Great Falls Mt., Shirley Edam Diaz, 1988, Southwest Art Mag., J.M. Swanson, 1990; featured artist Shaman's Drum, 1992, featured artist and cover image Internat. Fine Art Collector, 1992. Recipient Best Oil, Denver Indian Mkt., Pine Ridge S.D., 1985, 86, 87, 1st and 2d graphics Red Cloud Indian Sch., Best Painting artists choice Great Falls Native Am. Exhibit, James Bama award Best of Show, Best Contemporary Painting Buffalo Bill Hist. Ctr., Cody, Wyo., 1987, Best Painting Artists Choice award Great Falls Native Am. Exhibit, 1989, Best Show award, 1993. Home: 153 Calle Don Jose Santa Fe NM 87501-2391

O'REILLY, JOHN F., lawyer; b. St. Louis, July 23, 1945; s. John Francis and Marie Agnes (Cooney) O'R.; m. René E. Lee, June 24, 1967; children: Molly, Bryan, Erin, Timothy. BS in Acctg., St. Louis U., 1967, JD cum laude, 1969; MBA cum laude, U. Nev., Las Vegas, 1974. Bar: Mo. 1969, Nev. 1972, U.S. Dist. Ct. Nev. 1972; lic. real estate broker, Nev. Auditor, tax acct. Ernst, Young, Arthur Andersen & Co., St. Louis, 1966-69; pres. Keefer, O'Reilly, Ferrario & Eskin, Las Vegas, Nev., 1972—; atty. Nev. Gaming Policy Commn., Las Vegas, 1983-91; chmn. Nev. Gaming Commn., Las Vegas, 1986-91; pres., bd. dirs. Nev. Fed. Credit Union, Las Vegas, 1974-86. Editor-in-chief Communique mag., 1985. Alt. mcpl. judge City of Las Vegas, 1975-86; mem. adv. bd. Boulder Dam council Boy Scouts Am., Las Vegas, 1977—; pres. adv. bd. Bishop Gorman High Sch., Las Vegas, 1986—; resource speaker Clark County Pub. Sch. System. Served to capt., mil. judge USAF, 1969-73. Mem. ABA, Mo. Bar Assn., Nev. Bar Assn., Clark County Bar Assn. (pres. 1984), So. Nev. Home Builders Assn. (Homer award 1986), Las Vegas C. of C., Knights of Malta, Breakfast Exch. Club, Boys and Girls Club. Democrat. Roman Catholic. Office: Keefer O'Reilly Ferrario Eskin 325 S Maryland Pky Las Vegas NV 89101-5300

OREM, JOSEPH CLIFTON, sales professional; b. Kimberly, Nev., Jan. 3, 1944; s. Clifton Monroe and Lola Mae (Russell) O.; m. Margaret Elizabeth Tarte, June 25, 1966; children: Margaret Katheryn, Andrew Joseph, Teresa Marie Werner. BBA, U. Wash., 1968. Lab. technician U. Wash., Seattle, 1962-68; salesman Bellingham (Wash.) Sash & Door Co., 1968-74, v.p., 1974-80, pres., 1980—. Mem. Western Bldg. Materials Assn. (pres. 1988, Disting. Dealer award 1989), Nat. Lumber and Bldg. Materials Assn. (1st v.p. 1993), Bellingham Yacht Club (commodore 1977), Corinthian Yacht Club, Rotary (Paul Harris fellow, pres. 1991-92). Republican. Episcopalian. Home: 1524 Maple Ln Bellingham WA 98226 Office: Bellingham Sash & Door Co 3801 Hannegan Rd Bellingham WA 98226

OREN, FREDERIC LYNN, educator, financial consultant; b. Gas City, Ind., Aug. 22, 1934; s. William Thompson and Mary Catherine (Nation) O.; m. Aminda Jane Clark, Sept. 2, 1956; children: William Clark, Frederic Wayne. BS, Ind. State U., 1957; postgrad., Calif. State U., Sacramento, 1962, U. Calif., Davis, 1964-65, Calif. State U., Sonoma, 1969-72, U. Ill., 1972, Calif. Luth. U., 1981-82, San Francisco State U., 1982-83, U. Ottawa, 1983. Cert. master tchr., Calif. Tchr. Suisun (Calif.) Valley Elem. Sch. Dist., 1958-60, prin., 1960-64; tchr. Fairfield (Calif.) Elem. Sch. Dist., 1964-68; tchr. Fairfield-Suisun Unified Dist., Fairfield, 1968—, dist. coord., 1968-74, head tchr., 1968—, dir. math network, 1987-92, mentor, 1988-92; chmn. CMT Fed. Credit Union, 1984-89, dir., 1969—; chmn. Assist-A-Grad Scholarship Com., Fairfield, 1968-72; commr. fin. United Meth. Ch., Fairfield, 1987—. Co-author: (textbook) Math 1, 1973; co-author supplemental series B.O.P. 1 thru 16, 1970 (NSF award 1973); author teaching method Nero Math A 1980, Nero Math B, 1992. Chmn. bd. dirs. Meth. Ch., Fairfield, 1964-72, chmn. fin. com., 1986—; chmn. troop com. Boy Scouts Am., Fairfield, 1972-73. Sgt. U.S. Army, 1956-58. Recipient Tchr. of Note award Daily Republic Newspaper, 1977, Bronze award Nat. Acad. Math. Achievement, 1985. Mem. NEA, Calif. Tchr.'s Assn., Calif. Math. Coun., Solano Math. Coun., Fairfield-Suisun Tchrs. Assn. (chmn. polit. action com. 1964-68), Mason, Alpha Phi Omega, Sigma Alpha Omega. Home: 243 E Kentucky St Fairfield CA 94533-5601

ORENSTEIN, (IAN) MICHAEL, philatelic dealer, columnist; b. Bklyn., Jan. 6, 1939; s. Harry and Myra (Klein) O.; m. Linda Turer, June 28, 1964; 1 child, Paul David. BS, Clemson U., 1960; postgrad., U. Calif., Berkeley, 1960-61. Career regional mgr. Minkus Stamp & Pub. Co., Calif., 1964-70; mgr. stamp div. Superior Stamp & Coin Co., Inc., Beverly Hills, Calif., 1970-90; dir. stamp divsn. Superior Stamp and Coin. Co., Inc., Beverly Hills, Calif., 1991-92, dir. space memorabelia, 1992—; stamp columnist L.A. Times, 1965—; bd. Adelphi U. N.Y. Inst. Philatelic & Numismatic Studies, 1978-81. Author: Stamp Collecting Is Fun, 1990; philatelic advisor/creator The Video Guide To Stamp Collecting, 1988. With AUS, 1962-64. Mem. Am. Stamp Dealers Assn., C.Z. Study Group, German Philatelic Soc., Confederate Stamp Alliance, Am. Philatelic Soc. (writers unit 1975-80, 89—), Internat. Fedn. Stamp Dealers, Internat. Soc. Appraisers Space Memorabilia. Republican. Office: Superior Stamp & Coin Co Inc 9478 W Olympic Blvd Beverly Hills CA 90212

ORENSTEIN, MORTON HENRY, lawyer; b. St. Louis, Apr. 22, 1936; s. Jacob Bernard and Evelyn (Essman) O.; m. Grace Emily Manning, Dec. 21, 1962; children: Jeffrey, Manuel, Catherine Clare. BA, Northwestern U., 1958; JD, U. Mich., 1961. Bar: U.S. Dist. Ct. (ea. dist.) Mo. 1961, U.S. Dist. Ct. (no. dist.) Calif. 1973, U.S. Dist. Ct. (ea. dist.) Calif. 1976, U.S. Dist. Ct. (cen. dist.) Calif. 1987, U.S. Ct. Appeals (8th cir.) 1961, U.S. Ct. Appeals (9th cir.) 1973. Field atty. NLRB, San Francisco, 1965-71, supervising atty., 1971-76; ptnr. Voltz, Cook & Orenstein, San Francisco, 1976-82, Schachter,

Kristoff, Ross, Sprague & Curiale, San Francisco, 1982-90, Schachter, Kristoff, Orenstein & Berkowitz, 1991—; asst. prof. San Francisco State U., 1976. Vol. U.S. Peace Corps, Malawi, Africa, 1963-65. With USAR, 1961-62. Mem. ABA (labor and employment sect., exec. com. Calif. labor and employment sect. 1982-87, chmn. 1985-87), San Francisco Bar Assn. (labor and empoyment law sect., exec. com. 1982—, chmn. 1985-87). Democrat. Jewish. Home: 1530 Euclid Ave Berkeley CA 94708-1907 Office: Schachter Kristoff et al 505 Montgomery St Fl 14 San Francisco CA 94111-2552

ORFIELD, ADRIENNE ADAMS, lawyer; b. Memphis, June 14, 1953; d. Vincent Orville and Darlene Jo (Johannes) Adams; m. Michael Bennett Orfield, Sept. 25, 1982; 1 child, Sarah Catherine. BA, Cal. State Coll., San Bernardino, 1975; JD, U. San Diego, 1979. Bar: Calif. 1979, U.S. Dist. Ct. 1979. Assoc. Shifflet & Sharp, San Diego, 1980-82, Ault, Deuprey, Jones, and Gorman, San Diego, 1982-87; ptnr. Ault, Deuprey, Jones & Gorman, San Diego, 1987—. Dir. Crime Victims Fund, San Diego, 1985-90. Mem. San Diego County Bar Assn. (treas. 1992, v.p. 1993, pres. 1994), San Diego Def. Lawyers (v.p. 1985), So. Calif. Def. Lawyers, Calif. Women Lawyers, Lawyers Club San Diego. Republican. Roman Catholic. Office: Ault Deuprey Jones & Gorman 402 W Broadway Ste 1600 San Diego CA 92101

ORGEL, LESLIE ELEAZER, chemist; b. London, Jan. 12, 1927; came to U.S., 1964; s. Simon and Deborah (Gnivish) O.; m. Hassia Alice Levinson, July 30, 1950; children—Vivienne, Richard, Robert. B.A., Oxford (Eng.) U., 1948, D.Phil., 1951. Reader univ. chemistry lab. Cambridge (Eng.) U., 1963-64; fellow Peterhouse Coll., 1957-64; sr. fellow Salk Inst. Biol. Studies, La Jolla, Calif., 1964—; adj. prof. U. Calif., San Diego, 1964—. Author: An Introduction to Transition-Metal Chemistry, Ligand-Field Theory, 1960, The Origins of Life: Molecules and Natural Selection, 1973; co-author: The Origins of Life on the Earth, 1974. Recipient Harrison prize Chem. Soc. London, 1957. Fellow Royal Soc., Am Acad. Arts and Scis., Nat. Acad. Scis. Home: 6102 Terryhill Dr La Jolla CA 92037-6836 Office: Salk Inst PO Box 85800 San Diego CA 92186-5800

ORGEL, STEPHEN KITAY, English language educator; b. N.Y.C., Apr. 11, 1933; s. Samuel Zachary and Esther (Kitay) O. A.B., Columbia, 1954; Ph.D. (Woodrow Wilson fellow), Harvard, 1959. Instr. in English Harvard, Cambridge, Mass., 1959-60; asst. prof. U. Calif., Berkeley, 1960-66, asso. prof., 1966-72, prof., 1972-76; prof. Johns Hopkins U., Balt., 1976-82, Sir William Osler prof., 1982-85; Jackson Eli Reynolds prof. humanities Stanford (Calif.) U., 1987—; bd. suprs. English Inst., 1974-77, chmn., 1976-77. Author: The Jonsonian Masque, 1965, (with Roy Strong) Inigo Jones, 1973, The Illusion of Power, 1975; editor: Ben Jonson's Masques, 1969, Marlowe's Poems and Translations, 1971, The Renaissance Imagination, 1975, (with Guy Lytle) Patronage in the Renaissance, 1981, The Tempest, 1987, (with Jonathan Goldberg) John Milton, 1991; editor-in-chief: English Literary History, 1981-85. Am. Council Learned Socs. fellow, 1968, 73; NEH sr. fellow, 1982-83; Getty scholar, 1986-87. Mem. Modern Lang. Assn., Renaissance Soc. Am., Shakespeare Assn. Am. Office: Stanford U English Dept Stanford CA 94305

ORIENT, JANE MICHEL, physician; b. Tucson, Nov. 2, 1946; d. William Louis and Phyllis Ann Rittman) O. BA, BS, U. Ariz., 1967; MD, Columbia U., 1974. Intern, resident Parkland Meml. Hosp., Dallas, 1974-76; resident U. Ariz., Tucson, 1976-77; asst. prof., instr. Dept. Internal Medcine, U. Ariz. Coll. of Medicine, Tucson, 1977-80; staff physician Tucson VA Hosp.; pvt. practice Tucson, 1981—. Author: Doctor Is Not In, 1992; editor: Art and Science of Bedside Diagnosis, 1991. Mem. Assn. of Am. Physicians and Surgeons (pres. 1986-87, exec. dir. 1989—), Ariz. Med. Assn. (bd. dirs. 1990). Office: 1601 N Tucson Blvd #9 Tucson AZ 85716

ORLAND, TED NORCROSS, artist; b. Berkeley, Calif., Apr. 21, 1941; s. William Hugh and Alice (Sweeny) Organ; m. Linda Ellen Dunne, June 23, 1963 (div. 1976); 1 child, Jon Dunne Orland; m. Frances Dolloff, Dec. 9, 1989. BS in Indsl. Design, U. So. Calif., 1963; MA in Interdiciplinary Creative Arts, San Francisco State U., 1972. Designer Charles Eames Design Office, Venice, Calif., 1965-71; photographic asst. Ansel Adams, Photographer, Carmel, Calif., 1971-75; owner Image Continuum Press, Santa Cruz, Calif., 1973—; instr. U. Calif. Extension, Santa Cruz, 1975—, Maine Photographic Workshops, Rockport, 1985—. Author: Man and Yosemite, 1985, Scenes of Wonder and Curiosity, 1988; editor Image Continuum Jour., 1973-81; co-editor: In A Quiet Voice, 1990. Recipient Cert. of Spl. Congrl. Recognition U.S. Congress, 1988, Roy Acuff Chair of Excellence Austin Peay State U., 1989; Polaroid Print Collection grant, Polaroid Corp., 1978-79, grantee Nat. Endowment for the Arts 1979.

ORLEBEKE, WILLIAM RONALD, lawyer; b. El Paso, Tex., Jan. 5, 1933; s. William Ronald and Frances Claire (Cook) O.; m. Barbara Raye Pike, Aug. 29, 1954 (div. 1988); children: Michelle, Julene, David; m. Kathie Waterson, 1989. BA, Willamette U., 1956; MA, Kans. U., 1957; JD, Willamette U., 1966. Bar: Calif. 1966, U.S. Dist. Ct. (no. dist.) Ill. 1989 (cen. dist.) Calif. 1989, U.S. Ct. Appeals (9th cir.) 1967. Assoc. Eliassen & Postel, San Francisco, 1966-69; ptnr. Coll, Levy & Orlebeke, Concord, Calif., 1969-77, Orlebeke & Hutchings, Concord, 1977-86, Orlebeke, Hutchings & Pinkerton, 1986-88, Orlebeke & Hutchings, 1988-89; prin. Law Offices W. Ronald Orlebeke, 1989—; hearing officer Contra Costa County, Calif., 1981—; arbitrator Contra Costa County Superior Ct., 1977—, U.S. Dist. Ct. No. Calif., 1978—; judge pro tem Mt. Diablo Mcpl. Ct., 1973-77. Alumni bd. dirs. Willamette U., 1978-81, trustee, 1980-81; scholarship chmn. Concord Elks, 1977-79; del. Joint U.S/China Internat. Trade Law Conf., Beijing, Peoples Republic of China, 1987. Served with USMCR, 1952-59. Sr. scholar, Willamette U., 1955-56; Woodrow Wilson fellow, Kans. U., 1956-57; U.S. Bur. Nat. Affairs fellow, 1966, others. Mem. SAR, Am. Legion, Sons of Confederate Vets. (Award of Merit 1989), Sons of Union Veterans Civil War, U.S. Navy League, First Marine Divsn. Assn. Republican. Lodges: Order Ea. Star (worthy patron 1980), Masons, Shriners, Elks, Rotary (charter pres. Clayton Valley/Concord Sunrise club 1987-88, chmn. dist. 5160 Calif. membership devel. 1989-90, dist. govs. liaison dist. 5160 1990-92, dist. 5160 Rotarian of Yr. 1989-90, Paul Harris fellow 1988, 1992 dist. conf. chmn. benefactor 1990, award of merit 1990). Office: 3330 Clayton Rd Ste B Concord CA 94519-2894

ORLOFF, CHET, cultural organization administrator; b. Bellingham, Wash., Feb. 22, 1949; s. Monford A. and Janice (Diamond) O.; m. Wendy Lynn Lee, Sept. 20, 1970; children: Callman Labe, Hannah Katya. BA, Boston U., 1971; MA, U. Oreg., 1978; postgrad., Portland State U. Tchr. Peace Corps, Afghanistan, 1972-75; asst. dir. Oreg. Hist. Soc., Portland, 1975-86, dir., 1991—; dir. Ninth Cir. Hist. Soc., Pasadena, Calif., 1987-91. Editor: Western Legal History, 1987-91, Law for the Elephant, 1992; sr. editor: Oreg. Hist. Quar.; contbr. articles to profl. jours. Commr. Met. Arts Commn., Portland, 1981-84, Portland Planning Commn., 1989-92. Mem. Phi Alpha Theta. Office: Oregon Historical Society 1200 SW Park Ave Portland OR 97205

ORLOFF, NEIL, lawyer; b. Chgo., May 9, 1943; s. Benjamin R. and Annette (Grabow) O.; m. Jan Krigbaum, Oct. 9, 1971 (div. 1979); m. Gudrun Mirin, Oct. 2, 1992. BS, MIT, 1964; MBA, Harvard U., 1966; JD, Columbia U., 1969. Bar: D.C. 1969, N.Y. 1975, Calif. 1989, Utah 1993. Ops. officer World Bank, Washington, 1969-71; dir. regional liaison staff EPA, Washington, 1971-73; legal counsel Pres.'s Council on Environ. Quality, Washington, 1973-75; prof. dept. environ. engring. Cornell U., Ithaca, N.Y., 1975-88, UCLA, 1992; dir. Ctr. for Environ. Research, 1984-87, Am. Ecology Corp., 1986-88; of counsel Morgan, Lewis & Bockius, N.Y.C., 1986-87; ptnr. Irell & Manella, Los Angeles, 1986-892, Parsons, Behle & Latimer, Salt Lake City, 1992—; vice chmn. bd. dirs. S.W. Research and Info. Ctr., Albuquerque, 1975-84; vice chmn. ABA Air Quality Commn., Chgo., 1983—. Author: The Environmental Impact Statement Process, 1978, The National Environmental Policy Act, 1980, Air Pollution-Cases and Materials, 1980, Community Right-to-Know Handbook, 1988; mem. editorial bd. Natural Resources and Environment, 1984-87. Adviser Internat. Joint Com. Can., 1979-81; governing bd. N.Y. Sea Grant Inst., 1984-87; vice chmn. City of Ithaca Environ. Commn., 1976-77; adviser N.Y. Dept. Environ. Conservation, 1984-87.

ORMAN, DAVID ALLEN, oil company corporate communications executive; b. Phila., Jan. 5, 1943; s. Jack Morton and Rose Orman; m. Marsha Leslie Sheldon, July 27, 1990; children: Terry, Susan. BA in English, Franklin and Marshall Coll., 1964. Sportswriter St. Petersburg (Fla.) Times, 1964-65; mgr. employee comm. ARCO, Phila., 1968-72, L.A., 1972—; cons. 2d Thoughts, L.A., 1986—. Chmn. gt. Am. smokeout steering com. Calif. div. Am. Cancer Soc., 1986. Sgt. U.S. Army, 1965-68. Fellow Internat. Assn. Bus. Communicators (pres. L.A. 1976, Communicator of Yr. award 1976, Chmn.'s award 1988); mem. Coun. Comm. Mgmt. (pres. 1989). Office: ARCO 515 S Flower St Los Angeles CA 90071

ORMAN, JOHN LEO, software engineer, writer; b. San Antonio, Mar. 19, 1949; s. Alton Woodlee and Isabel Joan (Paproski) O. BS in Physics, N.Mex. Inst. Mining & Tech., 1971, BS Math., MS Physics, 1974. Rsch. asst. N.Mex. Inst. Mining & Tech., Socorro, 1967-74; computer programmer State of N.Mex., Santa Fe, 1974-76; computer analyst Dikewood Corp., Albuquerque, 1976-83; nuclear engr. Sandia Nat. Labs., Albuquerque, 1983-88, software engr., 1988—. Author numerous poems. NSF fellow, 1971-74; recipient 2d place award N.Mex. State Postry Soc., 1987. Mem. IEEE Computer Soc., Am. Assn. Physics Tchrs., Assn. for Computing Machinery, Nat. Writer's Club (poetry award 1987), Southwest Writers Workshop (3d place award non-fiction 1987), N.Mex. Mountain Club. Home: 900 Solar Rd NW Albuquerque NM 87107-5750 Office: Sandia Nat Labs Orgn 9226 PO box 5800 Albuquerque NM 87185

ORMASA, JOHN, retired utility executive, lawyer; b. Richmond, Calif., May 30, 1925; s. Juan Hormaza and Maria Inocencia Olondo; m. Dorothy Helen Trumble, Feb. 17, 1952; children: Newton Lee, John Trumble, Nancy Jean Davies. BA, U. Calif.-Berkeley, 1948; JD, Harvard U., 1951. Bar: Calif. 1952, U.S. Supreme Ct. 1959. Assoc. Clifford C. Anglim, 1951-52; assoc. Richmond, Carlson, Collins, Gordon & Bold, 1952-56, ptnr., 1956-59; with So. Calif. Gas Co., L.A., 1959-66, gen. atty., 1963-65, v.p., gen. counsel, 1965-66; v.p., system gen. counsel Pacific Lighting Service Co., Los Angeles, 1966-72; v.p., gen. counsel Pacific Lighting Corp., Los Angeles, 1973-75, v.p., sec., gen. counsel, 1975. Acting city atty., El Cerrito, Calif., 1952. Served with U.S. Navy, 1943-46. Mem. ABA, Calif. State Bar Assn., Kiwanis (v.p. 1959). Republican. Roman Catholic.

ORME, MAYNARD EVAN, broadcasting executive; b. Fresno, Calif., Dec. 7, 1936; s. Otis Lowe and Lila (Morton) O.; m. Joan Frances King, Apr. 2, 1966; children: Jennifer Ariana, Juliana Alaire. MusB, U. Calif., Berkeley, 1961; MA in Theatre Arts, UCLA, 1967, PhD in Edn., 1978. Cert. community coll. tchr., Calif. Research asst. Instructional Media Ctr. Dept. Edn. UCLA, 1965-66; producer-dir., instructional TV coordinator, news dir. Sta. KVCR-TV San Bernardino (Calif.) Valley Coll., 1966-68; learning resources coordinator, dir. Sta. KCET-TV, Los Angeles, 1968-73; gen. mgr., dir. media services, exec. dir. Sta. KTEH-TV, San Jose, Calif., 1973-86; exec. dir., pres., chief exec. officer Oreg. Pub. Broadcasting, Portland, 1986—, pres., chief exec. officer, 1990—; mem. TV adv. com. Calif. State Instructional TV, 1977-82, chmn. 1979-80. Vice chmn. San Jose Police Activities League, 1982-83, chmn., bd. dirs., 1983-85; bd. dirs. Music Theater, Oreg., 1990-91. Vice chmn. San Jose Police Activities League, 1982-83, chmn., bd. dirs. 1983-85. Served to capt. U.S. Army, 1961-66. Mem. Assn. Calif. Pub. TV Stas. (pres. 1982-86), Calif. Media and Library Educators Assn., Nat. Acad. TV Arts and Scis., Pacific Mountain Network (bd. dirs. 1981-88, v.p. 1984-86, chmn. 1986-88), Calif. Pub. Broadcasting Commn. (chmn. TV adv. com. 1978-79), Pub. Broadcasting Service (bd. dirs. 1984-90, chmn. membership com. 1985-86, vice chmn. bd. 1987-89, chmn. satellite interconnection com. 1987-90, mem. exec. com.), Assn. Pub. TV Stas (bd. dirs. 1992—), Orgn. State Broadcast Execs. (vice chair 1991-93, chair 1993—), UCLA Doctoral Alumni Assn., Big C Soc., Rotary (bd. dirs. 1990—, treas. 1992-93, v.p.-elect 1993-94), Los Gatos Athletic Assn. (v.p. 1975, pres. 1976, bd. dirs.), West Valley Joggers and Striders, Order of Golden Bear, Phi Delta Kappa, Alpha Epsilon Rho. Home: 2726 Rivendell Rd Lake Oswego OR 97034-7390 Office: Oreg Pub Broadcasting 7140 SW Macadam Ave Portland OR 97219-3013

ORNELLAS, DONALD LOUIS, chemist researcher; b. San Leandro, Calif., July 7, 1932; s. Louis Donald and Anna (Gerro) O.; children: Timothy Donald, Kathryn Ann, Melinda Dawn. BS in chemistry, Santa Clara U., 1954. Chemist Kaiser Gypsum Co, Redwood City, Calif., 1954-55, Kaiser Aluminum & Chem. Co., Permanente, Calif., 1957-58, Lawrence Livermore (Calif.) Nat. Lab., 1958—. Patentee in field; contbr. articles to profl. jours., presentations to tech. meetings. Capt. U.S. Army, 1955-57. Recipient Annual medal award, Am. Inst. Chemist, 1954. Mem. Parents Without Ptnrs. (chpt. 53 pres. 1971-73, chpt. 458 bd. dirs. 1982-91). Democrat. Roman Catholic. Home: 559 S N St Livermore CA 94550-4365 Office: Lawrence Livermore National Lab PO Box 808 L-282 Livermore CA 94550

ORNSTEIN, DONALD SAMUEL, mathematician; b. N.Y.C., July 30, 1934; s. Harry and Rose (Wisner) O.; m. Shari Richman, Dec. 20, 1964; children—David, Kara, Ethan. Student, Swarthmore Coll., 1950-52; Ph.D., U. Chgo., 1957. Fellow Inst. for Advanced Study, Princeton, N.J., 1955-57; faculty U. Wis., Madison, 1958-60; faculty Stanford (Calif.) U., 1959—, prof. math., 1966—; faculty Hebrew U., Jerusalem, 1975-76. Author: Ergodic Theory Randomness and Dynamical Systems, 1974. Recipient Bocher prize Am. Math. Soc., 1974. Mem. NAS, Am. Acad. Arts and Sci. Jewish. Office: Dept Math Stanford U Stanford CA 94305

O'ROURKE, BRIAN JAY, lawyer; b. Colorado Springs, Colo., Feb. 9, 1946; s. Dennis and Ruth (Rouss) O'R.; m. Bayita Teresa Garoffolo, Jan. 6, 1969; children: Simon, Anthony, Virginia. BA, Yale U., 1967; MA, U. N.Mex., 1970; JD, U. Colo., 1973. Law clk. to chief judge U.S. Dist. Ct. Denver, 1973-74; atty. Foley, Hoag & Eliot, Boston, 1974-78; shareholder Keleher & McLeod, P.A., Albuquerque, 1978—, also bd. dirs. mem., past pres. Balletwest of N.Mex./D.A.N.C.E., Inc., Albuquerque, 1985—, Chamber Orch. of Albuquerque, 1987—. Mem. ABA (Mexican law com.), Internat. Bar Assn. Office: Keleher & McLeod PA PO Drawer AA Albuquerque NM 87103

O'ROURKE, J. TRACY, manufacturing company executive; b. Columbia, S.C., Mar. 14, 1935; s. James Tracy and Georgia Adella (Bridges) O'R.; m. Lou Ann Turner, Mar. 19. 1954; 1 son, James Tracy. BSME, Auburn U., 1956. Teflon specialist duPont Co., Wilmington, Del., 1957-62; pres., chief exec. officer LNP Corp., Malvern, Pa., 1962-72; v.p. Carborundum, Niagara Falls, N.Y., 1972-76; exec. v.p. Chemetron, Chgo., 1976-78; sr. v.p. Allen Bradley Co. subs. Rockwell Internat. Corp., Milw., 1978-81, pres., chief oper. officer, 1981-86, also chief exec. officer, dir., 1986-90; chmn., chief exec. officer Varian Assocs., Palo Alto, Calif., 1990—. Served as 1st lt. USAF, 1957-59. Office: Varian Assocs PO Box 10800 3050 Hansen Way Palo Alto CA 94304

O'ROURKE, RONALD EUGENE, computer and electronics industry executive; b. Loma Linda, Calif., Jan. 31, 1957; s. Eugene Lawrence and Marilyn Jean (Rickert) O'R.; m. Victoria Lippincott, Apr.16, 1988; 1 child: Ryan Lawrence. BS in Computer Systems Engring., Stanford U., 1980; MS in Computer Sci., San Diego State U., 1993. Registered engr.-in-tng., Calif.; lic. pvt. pilot. Asst. computer programmer Fluor Corp., Irvine, Calif., 1977; systems engr. intern IBM Corp., San Francisco, 1978; computer programmer Ford Aerospace & Communications Corp., Newport Beach, Calif., 1979; mktg. rep. IBM Corp., San Francisco, 1980-82; program mgr. Gen. Atomics, Sorrento Electronics, San Diego, 1989—. Chmn. reconstrn. com. LaJolla (Calif.) Village Homeowners' Assn., Inc., Southpointe, 1991, dir., 1991—. Lt.. USN, 1983-89, USNR, 1989—. Mem. IEEE, Am. Nuclear Soc., Naval Res. Assn., Naval Submarine League, U.S. Naval Inst., Stanford Alumni Assn. (life), Mensa, Theta Delta Chi (v.p. 1977-78). Republican. Presbyterian. Home: 3388 Caminito Vasto La Jolla CA 92037-2919 Office: Sorrento Electronics 10240 Flanders Ct San Diego CA 92121-3990

OROYAN, SUSANNA ELIZABETH, artist, author; b. Portland, Oreg., May 24, 1942; d. Louis B. and Marjorie E. (Hibbert) Scruggs; m. Thomas Oroyan; 1 child, Martin Thomas. BA in English, Calif. State U., Sacramento, 1967; MA in English, U. Oreg., 1971. Tchr. English Eugene (Oreg.) High Sch., 1968-72; artist, owner Fabricat Design, Eugene, 1979—; cons., contbg. editor Doll Artistry Mag., 1990—; lectr. Original Doll Artist Invitation Seminar, 1977, 78, 80; instr. Search prog. U. Oreg., 1975-76; artist, instr. Jr. League Art in Schs. Progs., 1976, 77, 78, guest instr. sculpture, 1990—; editor: Original Doll Artist Coun. Am. News, 1980—; columnist Dollmaker's Notebook, Doll Rev., 1975-78; author: Dollmaker's Notebook, 1981, Fabric Figures, 1989, Paperclay, 1992, Business and Marketing, Competitions and Critique, Polymer Clay Contracts, 1993, Ideas and Techniques for Dollmaking, 1993; co-author: (with Carol-Lynn Waugh) Contemporary Artist Dolls, 1986; contbr. to various publs. One man shows at Keller Gallery, Salem, Oreg., Contemporary Crafts Gallery, Portland, Springfield (Oreg.) Mus.; exhibited in group shows at Internat. Dollmaker's Assn., 1974-75, United Fedn. Doll Clubs, 1976, 77, 79, 80, Original Doll Artist Coun. Am., 1979-80, Oreg. Art Exhbn., 1975-76, Lane Co., 1975, Wenham Mus., Mass., 1988, Dollmaker's Magic, Houston, N.Y.C., 1988-90, Dolls of 21st Century, Springfield, Oreg., 1990, Artique, Anchorage, 1993, Contemporary Artists Mulvane, Topeka, Kans., 1993. eka; represented in pvt collections. Chmn. Emerald Empire Doll and Toy Festival, 1975, 77, 80. Recipient 1st award Internat. Dollmarker's Assn., 1974, 75, All Oreg. Art Exhibit, 1975, United Fedn. Doll Clubs, 1976. Mem. Original Doll Artist Coun. of Am., Nat. Inst. Am. Doll Artists (pres. 1987—), United Fedn. of Doll Clubs (chmn. region I conf. 1985), Acad. Dollmakers Internat. Home and Office: Fabricat Design 3270 Whitbeck Blvd Eugene OR 97405

ORR, JACK DEMILT, accountant; b. Pueblo, Colo., Oct. 17, 1952; s. Yale C. and Winifred R. (Dall) O. BS, Biola Coll., 1975; MS in Taxation, Colo. State U., 1976. CPA, Colo. Inventory acct. Farmland Foods, Cheraw, Colo., 1975; staff acct. Dunham & Swanson, PC, Denver, 1977-80; mgr. Nelson & Co., Denver, 1980-84; pres. Jack D. Orr, PC, CPA, Lakewood, Colo., 1985—. Mem. Nat. Fedn. Ind. Bus., Colo. CPAs, Nat. Assn. Tax Practictioners, West Chamber, Kiwanis. Office: 3615 South Kipling Lakewood CO 80235

ORR, MICHAEL P., finance company executive; b. 1947. BA, Cen. U. of Iowa, 1969; MBA, Ind. U., 1971. With John Deere Credit Co., Moline, Ill., 1974—; v.p. John Deere Capital Corp., 1982—; pres. John Deere Capital Corp., Reno. Office: John Deere Capital Corp 1 E 1st St Ste 600 Reno NV 89501-1691

ORROK, FRANCENE FELDMAN, retired clinical psychologist; b. Chgo., June 10, 1937; d. Harold and Sylvia (Moteff) Feldman; m. Herman Silbiger, June 17, 1956 (div. 1975); children: Russell William, Julie Ann Silbiger Kenoff; m. G. Timothy Orrok, Nov. 23, 1984. BA, U. Mich., 1957; PhD, Wayne State U., 1964. Lic. psychologist, N.J. Asst. prof. Drew U., Madison, N.J., 1964-67, Fairleigh Dickinson U., Madison, 1967-71; assoc. prof. Brookdale Community Coll., Lincroft, N.J., 1971-74; clin. psychologist Riverview Hosp., Red Bank, N.J., 1973-76; pvt. practice Red Bank, 1972-88; ret., 1988; pres. Big Rock Investments, Inc. Pres. bd. dirs. 1st Unitarian Ch., Lincroft, 1986-88; vice-chmn. bd. dirs. Rogue Valley Unitarian Universalist Fellowship, Ashland, Oreg., 1989-90; pres. Big Rock Investments Inc., 1991—. Mem. APA, Toastmasters Internat. (chpt. pres. 1990).

ORSATTI, ALFRED KENDALL, organization executive; b. Los Angeles, Jan. 31, 1932; s. Alfredo and Margaret (Hayes) O.; m. Patricia Decker, Sept. 11, 1960; children: Scott, Christopher, Sean. B.S., U. So. Calif., 1956. Assoc. producer, v.p. Sabre Prodns., Los Angeles, 1957-58; assoc. producer Ror Vic Prodns., Los Angeles, 1958-59; bus. rep. AFTRA, Los Angeles, 1960-61; Hollywood exec., sec. Screen Actors Guild, Los Angeles, 1961-81, nat. exec. sec., 1981—; trustee Pension Welfare Plan Screen Actors Guild; del. Los Angeles County Fedn. Labor, Los Angeles, Hollywood Film Council, Los Angeles; v.p., mem. exec. Calif. Fedn. Labor; v.p. Calif. Theatrical Fedn.; chmn. arts, entertainment and media com. dept. profl. employees AFL-CIO. Mem. Mayor's Film Devel. Com., Los Angeles. Mem. Hollywood C. of C. (bd. dirs.), Actors and Artists Am. Assn. (1st v.p.). Office: Screen Actors Guild 7065 Hollywood Blvd Los Angeles CA 90028-6064

ORT, ROSALYN MARIA, business owner; b. L.A., Nov. 8, 1942; d. David Wayne Carpenter and Catherine (Carastathis) Simmons; m. Donald Wayne Ort, July 28, 1959; children: Lani Susan, Brian David. Student, Scottdale Community Coll., 1974-78. Interior designer Kiva Fls. & Interiors, Phoenix, 1976-79; with archtl. sales Facings of Am., Phoenix, 1979-84; founding ptnr. First Team, Inc., Phoenix, 1984—, pres., 1989-92; founding ptnr. The Duckmint Partnership (subs. First Team, Inc.), 1992—; agt. coun. rep. Dow Chem. Co., Midland, Mich., 1989-90, Balco, Inc., Wichita, 1990; vol. mentor Women's Network Entrepreneurial Tng. program SBA, 1993. Vol. Dallas Cares-Vietnam POW's, 1970-72, UNICEF, 1992, St. Mary's Food Bank, 1992. Mem. Constrn. Products Mfrs. (pres. 1986-87, Elliot Spratt award 1985, Mem. of Yr. 1985, 1st v.p. 1985-86, Best Nat. Program Activity 1984), Constrn. Specifications Inst. (S.W. region conf. chmn. 1984-85, program chmn. 1982-83, Mem. of Yr. 1983), Nat. Assn. Women Bus. Owners (bd. dirs. Phoenix chpt.), Nat. Speakers Assn., Toastmasters Internat. Republican. Greek Orthodox. Office: The First Team Inc P.O. Box 17017 Phoenix AZ 85011-0017

ORTEGA, ANTHONY DAVID (TONY ORTEGA), visual artist; b. Sante Fe, Feb. 24, 1958; s. Victor Rodriguez and Mary (Ortega) Ortega; m. Sylvia Francis Mortero; 1 child, Cipriano. BA, U. Colo., 1980; AA, Rocky Mountain Sch. Art, 1982. Visual artist Denver, 1982—. Active Big Brothers of Denver, 1984-92. Grantee Co-Vision Colo. Coun. Arts, 1991, New Forms Regional Initiative, 1990, 92; recipient Afkey award Denver Art Mus., 1991-92, Big Brother of Yr. award, 1988-89, Minora Yasui Community Vol. award, 1989, Colo. 100 Certificate of Recognition award Historic Denver, Inc. and Denver Past, 1993. Mem. Chicano Humanities & Arts Coun. Democrat. Roman Catholic. Office: PO Box 11559 Denver CO 80211

ORTEGA, RUBEN BAPTISTA, police chief; b. Glendale, Ariz., July 17, 1939; s. Epifanio Dominguez and Clara (Baptista) O.; B.S. in Criminal Justice and Police Adminstrn., No. Ariz. U., 1980; m. Nellie Ann Alvarado, Nov. 23, 1958; children—Karen Ann, Jeffrey Randal. With Phoenix Police Dept., 1960—, police chief, 1980—; instr. Phoenix Police Regional Tng. Acad., 1969-73; cons. Juvenile Crime Prevention Task Force, Phoenix, 1975-79. Bd. dirs. NCCJ, 1979-81. Recipient Outstanding Community Service awards Am. Legion, 1979, also others. Mem. Ariz. Organized Crime Prevention Council, Ariz. Law Enforcement Office Adv. Council, Internat. Assn. Chiefs of Police. Roman Catholic. Office: Police Dept 315 E 200 South Salt Lake City UT 84111

ORTEGA, RUBEN FRANCISCO, state representative; b. Douglas, Ariz., Feb. 14, 1956; s. Ruben and Natalia (Escobar) O. BA in Polit. Sci., Ariz. State U., 1978. Congressional staff asst. Jim McNulty, 1983-84; mgr. Ortega's Boot Shop, 1984—; vol. Am. Cancer Soc.; rep. Dist. 8 Legislature, 1989; com. Judiciary, Transp., COunties & Municipalities and Human Resources & Aging. Mem. Nat. Conf. State Legislatures, Nat. Assn. Latino Elected Officials, World COun. Young Polit. Leaders, Mexican Am. State Legislators Policy Inst. (bd. mem.). Democrat. Roman Catholic. Office: Ariz State Legislature Babocomari Estates Huachuca City AZ 85616

ORTEGO, GILDA BAEZA, librarian, information professional; b. El Paso, Tex., Mar. 29, 1952; d. Efren and Bertha (Singh) Baeza; m. Felipe de Ortego y Gasca, Dec. 21, 1986. BA, Tex. Woman's U., 1974, graduate, 1974-75; MLS, U. Tex., 1976, postgrad., 1990-93; cert., Hispanic Leadership Inst., 1988. Stack maintenance supr. El Paso Libr. U. Tex., 1974-75; pub. svcs. libr. El Paso Community Coll., 1976-77; ethnic studies libr. U. N.Mex., Albuquerque, 1977-81; br. head El Paso Pub. Libr., 1981-82; dep. head Mex.-Am. Svcs., El Paso Pub. Libr., 1982-84; libr. Mex.-Am. Studies U. Tex. Libr., Austin, 1984-87; libr. Phoenix Pub. Libr., 1987-89; assoc. libr., west campus Ariz. State U., Phoenix, 1989-90; Proyecto Leer libr. Tex. Woman's U., Denton, 1991-92; dir. learning resources Sul Ross State U., Alpine, Tex., 1992—; speaker and cons. in field. Founding editor jour. La Lista, 1983-84; founding indexer Chicano Periodical Index, 1981-86; reviewer jour. Voices of Youth Advocates, 1988-90; contbr. poetry and articles to books and jours. Mem. ALA, Assn. for Libr. and Info. Sci. Edn., Tex. Libr. Assn., Ariz. State Libr. Assn. (pres. svcs. Spanish speaking Roundtable 1980-90), Reforma (pres. El Paso chpt. 1983, pres. Ariz. chpt. 1989-90), Unltd. Potential, Inc. (treas. 1988-89), Hispanic Leadership Inst. Alumni Assn., Modern Lang. Assn.

ORTIZ, ANTONIO IGNACIO, public relations executive; b. Mexico City, Feb. 22, 1961; came to U.S., 1988; s. Antonio and Sylvia (Vega) O.; m. Socorro Chinolla, June 12, 1982. B in Bus., Universidad Autonoma de Baja

Calif., Tijuana, 1984. With acctg. dept. Bank of the Atlantic, Tijuana, 1979-83; mgr. Aldaco, Tijuana, 1983-84; dir. pub. rels. Oh! Laser Club, Tijuana, 1984-88, Iguanas, Tijuana, 1988-90, Euebe, S.A., Tijuana, 1990—; cons. DDBSA Corp., Chula Vista, Calif., Calif. Alson Ltd., San Diego, Exim Trading Co., San Diego, R.P. Noble Enterprises, La Jolla, Ca.; dir. pub. rels. R. Noble Enterprises. Home: PO Box 431859 San Deigo CA 92143-1859 Office: Exim Trading Corp PO Box 435108 San Diego CA 92143-5108

ORTIZ, CHARLES FRANCIS, federal government official; b. N.Y.C., Mar. 29, 1951; s. William and Guillermina (Alvarado) O.; m. Irma Delia Bosch, June 6, 1986. BA, InterAmerican U., 1973; postgrad., Syracuse U., 1974-76. Assoc. editor P.R. Indsl. Dir., San Juan, 1976-77; claims rep. Social Security Adminstrn., Bayamon, P.R., 1977-88; svc. rep. Social Security Adminstrn., Phoenix, 1988—. Author: Self-Concept and the Problem of Alienation, 1972; author (short stories) Leviathan, 1982, The Prisoner's Escape, 1984. Mem. Paz de Cristo, Mesa, Ariz., 1990, Amnesty Internat., 1990. Roman Catholic. Home: 814 W Sun Coast Dr Gilbert AZ 85234-8968 Office: Social Security Adminstrn PO Box 4217 Phoenix AZ 85030-4217

ORTIZ, JAMES GEORGE, data information services company executive; b. Boston, June 6, 1961. BA suma cum laude, Monterey Inst. Internat. Studies, 1989, MA, 1990. Instr. lang. Blue Mountain C.C., Pendleton, Oreg., 1990—; pres., CEO, Data Info. Svc., Inc., Toppenish, Wash., 1991—; founder JGO Internat., Hermiston, Oreg., 1992—. Regional dir. CASA of Oreg., Hermiston, 1990. Scholar Chevron Co., 1988-89. Mem. Wall Street Edge, Consumer Buyline (affiliate), Charles J. Givens Orgn. Republican. Adventist. Office: Data Info Svcs Inc 881 Blue Heron Rd Toppenish WA 98948

ORTLOFF, TODD WAYNE, radio program director; b. Port Angeles, Wash., Apr. 30, 1968; s. Cecil Wayne and Joan Kay (Hoff) O.; m. Kimberly Kristine Zook, June 29, 1991. AA, Peninsula Coll., Port Angeles, 1988; BA, Wash. State U., 1991. Radio announcer KAPY Radio, Port Angeles, 1983-87; sales rep. Angeles Music, Port Angeles, 1987-88; radio announcer KONP Radio, Port Angeles, 1987-91, program dir., 1991—; intern news reporter KAPP-TV, Yakima, Wash., 1991. Recipient Edward r. Murrow award Wash. State U., 1991, Excellence in Broadcast News award, 1991. Mem. Radio-TV News Dirs. Assn. Lutheran. Home: 2115 W 16th St Port Angeles WA 98362 Office: KONP Radio 313 W 1st St Port Angeles WA 98362

ORTON, WILLIAM H (BILL), congressman, lawyer; b. North Ogden, Utah, Sept. 22, 1948. BS, Brigham Young U., 1973, JD, 1979. Adj. prof. Portland (Oreg.) State U./Portland C.C., 1974-76; tax auditor IRS, 1976-77; atty., 1980-90; adj. prof. Brigham Young. U., Provo, Utah, 1984-85; mem. 103rd Congress from 3rd Utah dist., Washington, D.C., 1990—; mem. budget com., banking, fin. & urban affairs com.; Mem. Banking, Fin. and Urban Affairs Com., Budget Com. Democrat. Mormon. Office: 1122 Longworth House Office Bldg Washington DC 20515-4312

ORULLIAN, B. LARAE, bank executive; b. Salt Lake City, May 15, 1933; d. Alma and Bessie (Bacon) O.; cert. Am. Inst. Banking, 1961, 63, 67; grad. Nat. Real Estate Banking Sch., Ohio State U., 1969-71. With Tracy Collins Trust Co., Salt Lake City, 1951-54; sec. to exec. sec. Union Nat. Bank, Denver, 1954-57; exec. sec. Guaranty Bank, Denver, 1957-64, asst. cashier, 1964-67, asst. v.p., 1967-70, v.p., 1970-75, exec. v.p., 1975-77, also bd. dirs.; pres., chief exec. officer, dir. The Women's Bank N.A., Denver, 1977-88, chair, chief exec. officer, dir., 1989—, Equitable Bankshares of Colo., 1980—; vice chmn. Equitable Bank Littleton; chmn. bd., dir. Colo. Blue Cross/Blue Shield, lectr.; bd. dirs. Pro Card, Inc.Treas. Girl Scouts U.S.A., 1981-87, 1st. nat. v.p., chair exec. com., 1987-90, nat. pres., 1990—; bd. dirs., chair fin. Rocky Mountain Health Care Corp.; bd. dirs. Ams. Clean Water Found., Denver Improvement Assn.; bd. dirs., advisor Care Internat. Named to Colo. Women Hall of Fame, 1988, Colo. Entrepreneur of Yr., Inc. Mag. and Arthur Young and Co., 1989, Woman of the Yr., YWCA, 1989. Mem. Bus. and Profl. Women Colo. (3d Century award 1977), Colo. State Ethics Bd., Denver C. of C. (bd. dirs., chair state and local affairs), Am. Inst. Banking, Am. Bankers Assn. (mem. adv. bd. Community Bankers Coun.), Nat. Assn. Bank Women, Internat. Women's Forum, Com. of 200, Denver Partnership. Republican. Mormon. Home: 10 S Ammons St Lakewood CO 80226-1331

OSBORN, RALPH STEPHEN, military officer; b. Santa Monica, Calif., Oct. 5, 1952; s. Francis Carlyle and Shirley (Oviatt) O.; m. Ellen Marie Zook, Apr. 20, 1974; children: Katherine Claire, Stephen Colin. BS, No. Ariz. U., 1974, MS, 1982. Dep. sheriff Coconino County Sheriffs Office, Flaggstaff, Ariz., 1976-78; commd. 2d lt. USMC, 1979, advanced through grades to capt., 1984, communications officer MWCS-38, 1980-83; dist. comdr. Camp S.D. Butler Mil. Police, Okinawa, Japan, 1984-85; co. comdr. First Force Svc. Support Group, Camp Pendelton, Calif., 1987-89; provost marshal Mil. Police Dept. Marine Corps Logistics Base, Barstow, Calif., 1989-91; leadership program mgr. Oreg. Bd. Pub. Safety Standards and Tng., 1991—. Contbr. articles to profl. jours. Decorated Overseas Svc. Ribbon with 2 Bronze stars, Navy Achievement medal with 1 Gold star, Meritorious Svc. medal. Mem. Internat. Assn. of Chiefs of Police, FBI Nat. Acad. Assocs. Republican. Home: 922 Olive Way Monmouth OR 97361 Office: BPST 550 N Monmouth Ave Monmouth OR 97361

OSBORN, SIMEON JAMES, lawyer; b. Seattle, June 21, 1958; s. Arthur Vern and Allie Marcelia (Paxman) O. BA, Whitman Coll., Walla Walla, Wash., 1980; JD, U. Puget Sound, 1984. Bar: Wash. 1984, U.S. Dist. Ct. (we. dist.) Wash. 1984. Ptnr. Anderson & Osborn, Seattle, 1984-86, Osborn & Gosanko, Seattle, 1986-87; assoc. Kargianis, Austin & Erickson, Seattle, 1987—; bd. dirs. Coastall Softball, Inc., Seattle, DOA, Inc., ACE Mgmt., Inc. Author: (student handbook) Your Civil Rights and Responsibilities, 1987. Mem. Assn. Trial Lawyers Am., Wash. State Trial Lawyers, Harbor Club. Office: Kargianis Austin & Erickson 4700 Columbia Ctr 701 5th Ave Seattle WA 98104-7016

OSBORNE, GAYLE ANN, corporate executive; b. Bossier City, La., Feb. 1, 1951; d. Walker Henry and Marjorie Evelyn (Cook) Pyle; m. Paul A. Huelsman, June 28, 1969 (div. Jan. 1976); children: Ginger, Paula; m. Luther L. Osborne, Sept. 10, 1976 (div. Aug. 1989). Sales assoc. Model City Real Estate, Midwest City, Okla., 1972-73; mgr. adminstrn. Equipment Renewal Co., Oklahoma City, 1973-76, Gulfco Industries, Inc., Casper, Wyo., 1976-77; v.p. B&B Tool and Supply Co., Inc., Casper, 1977, 79, 81; br. v.p. B&B Tool and Supply Co., Inc., Williston, N.D., 1983-90, pres., 1990—; pres. BOP Repair & Machine, Inc., Casper, 1981—; owner Osborne Leasing Co. Mem. Casper Petroleum Club, Nat. Skeet Shoot Assn. (All Am. Skeet Team), Amateur Trapshooting Assn. Democrat.

OSBORNE, PHILLIP LEE, air force officer; b. Chattanooga, Tenn., Mar. 31, 1959; s. Floyd Wilburn and Emma Gene (Delaney) O.; m. Sarah Elizabeth Drayton, Apr. 14, 1984; children: Christopher Phillip, Sarah Emily, Matthew Joseph. BS in Edn., Jacksonville State U., 1981; MEd, MA, Valdosta State Coll., 1983. Commd. 2d lt. USAF, 1983, advanced through grades to capt., 1987; dep. comdr. ICBM crew USAF, Little Rock AFB, 1984-87, comdr. ICBM crew, 1987; instr. history USAF Acad. USAF, Colorado Springs, Colo., 1987-89, asst. prof. history, 1989-91; intelligence officer USAF Kelly AFB, San Antonio; speaker in field. Editor: American Studies at USAFA, 1988; contbr. revs. to various publs. Choir mem. St. Michael's Episc. Ch., Colorado Springs, 1987—, St. Francis Episcopal Ch., San Antonio; judge Colo. Coll. History Day, Colorado Springs, 1987-91; vol. Colorado Springs Food Pantry, 1988-91, Joint Intel Staff, Somalia, Africa, 1992-93. Named Outstanding Young Man in Am., Outstanding Young Men of Am., Montgomery, Ala., 1988, USAF Intel Cmd. Co. Grade Officer of the Quarter. Mem. Nat. Trust Historic Preservation, So. Hist. Assn., USAF Acad. History Club (officer in charge 1990-91), Nat. Military Intelligence Assn., Phi Alpha Theta, Phi Delta Kappa, Phi Mu Alpha, Pi Gamma Mu.

OSBORNE, THOMAS JOE, history educator; b. Long Beach, Calif., May 17, 1942; s. Thomas Jefferson and Dorothy Marie (Jacksie) O.; m. Ginger Tredway, June 28, 1975; children: Brooks Tredway Osborne, Todd Tredway Osborne. BA, Calif. State U., L.A., 1965; MA, Claremont Grad. Sch., 1968, PhD, 1979; negotiation cert., Harvard U., 1991. Instr. history Rancho Santiago Coll., Santa Ana, Calif., 1969—, dir. Oxford program, 1989-90, chmn. history dept., 1990-91, 92-93; asst. prof. Chapman U., Orange, Calif., 1970, U. Hawaii, Honolulu, 1981; cons. Libr. Congress, Washington, 1981-82. Co-author: Paths to the Present, 1973; author: Empire Can Wait, 1981; contbg. author: American National Biography; also articles. Mem. adv. bd. Orange County Educators for Social Responsibility, 1987—; bd. dirs. Beyond War Found., Palo Alto, Calif., 1989-91. Recipient Disting. Faculty Lectr. award Rancho Santiago Coll., 1987, Nat. Teaching Excellence award U. Tex., 1988; fellow Ford Found., 1975, NEH, 1981. Mem. Soc. for Historians Am. Fgn. Rels., Found. for Global Community, Am. Mensa, Sierra Club, Phi Alpha Theta. Democrat.

OSBORNE, THOMAS WALKER, software engineer; b. Oak Park, Ill., Mar. 12, 1961; s. Robert Patton and Marian Juanita (Vinyard) O. BS in Computer Sci., History, Trinity U., San Antonio, 1983; MS in Computer Sci., DePaul U., 1990. Programmer mdbs, Inc., Schaumburg, Ill., 1985-86; sr. tech. analyst United Airlines/Covia, Denver, 1986—. Co-author numerous papers. Mem. IEEE, Assn. for Computing Machinery. Home: 6398 S Louthan St Littleton CO 80120 Office: Covia 5350 S Valentia Way Englewood CO 80111

O'SCANNLAIN, DIARMUID FIONNTAIN, federal judge; b. N.Y.C., Mar. 28, 1937; s. Sean Leo and Moira (Hegarty) O'S.; m. Maura Nolan, Sept. 7, 1963; children: Sean, Jane, Brendan, Kevin, Megan, Christopher, Anne, Kate. AB, St. John's U., 1957; JD, Harvard U., 1963; LLM, U. Va., 1992. Bar: Oreg. 1965, N.Y. 1964. Tax atty. Standard Oil Co. (N.J.), N.Y.C., 1963-65; assoc. Davies, Biggs, Strayer, Stoel & Boley, Portland, Oreg., 1965-69; dep. atty. gen. Oreg., 1969-71; public utility commr. of Oreg., 1971-73; dir. Oreg. Dept. Environ. Quality, 1973-74; sr. ptnr. Ragen, Roberts, O'Scannlain, Robertson & Neill, Portland, 1978-86; judge, U.S. Ct. Appeals (9th cir.), San Francisco, 1986—, mem. exec. com., 1988-89, mem. Jud. Coun. 9th Cir., 1991—; mem. U.S. Judicial Conf. Com. on Automation and Tech., 1990—; cons. Office of Pres.-Elect and mem. Dept. Energy Transition Team (Reagan transition), Washington, 1980-81; chmn. com. adminstrv. law Oreg. State Bar, 1980-81. Mem. council of legal advisers Rep. Nat. Com., 1981-83; mem. Rep. Nat. Com., 1983-86, chmn. Oreg. Rep. Party, 1983-86; del. Rep. Nat. Convs., 1976, 80, chmn. Oreg. del., 1984; Rep. nominee U.S. Ho. of Reps., First Congl. Dist., 1974; team leader Energy Task Force, Pres.'s Pvt. Sector Survey on Cost Control, 1982-83, trustee Jesuit High Sch.; mem. bd. visitors U. Oreg. Law Sch., 1988—; mem. citizens adv. bd. Providence Hosp., 1986-92. Maj. USAR, 1955-78. Mem. Fed. Bar Assn., ABA (sec. Apellate Judges Conf. 1989-90, exec. com. 1990—), Arlington Club, Multnomah Club. Roman Catholic. Office: US Ct Appeals 313 Pioneer Courthouse 555 SW Yamhill St Portland OR 97204-1396

OSEDACZ, RICHARD PHILIP, air force officer, astronautical engineer; b. Central Falls, RI, Feb. 24, 1962; s. Stanley Philip and Phyllis Ann (Kwasniewski) O.; m. Carol Ann Marcellino, Mar. 18, 1989. BS, USAF Acad., 1984; MS, Air Force Inst. Tech., Dayton, Ohio, 1989. Commd. 2d lt. USAF, 1984, advanced through grades to capt., 1988; missile performance engr. fgn. tech. div. USAF, Dayton, 1984-87, dept. br. chief, 1987-88; staff astronautical engr. Hdqrs. Air Force Space Command, Peterson AFB, Colo., 1989-90, dept. div. chief, 1990—, instr., 1989—; programmer 1st Command & Control Squadron, Cheyenne Mountain AFB, Colorado Springs, Colo., 1990—; software cons. Loral Aerospace, Colorado Springs, 1991—. Contbr. articles to profl. jours. Coach Dayton Christian Mid. Sch., 1984-89; guitarist St. Adalbert's Ch., Dayton, 1984-89. Recipient cert. Dayton Christian Schs., 1989. Mem. Acad. Model Aeros., Am. Numismatics Assn. Office: HQ AFSPACECOM/DOJY Mail Stop 7 Peterson AFB CO 80914

OSGOOD, FRANK WILLIAM, urban and economic planner; b. Williamston, Mich., Sept. 3, 1931; s. Earle Victor and Blanche Mae (Eberly) O.; children: Ann Marie, Frank William Jr. BS, Mich. State U., 1953; M in City Planning, Ga. Inst. Tech., 1960. Prin. planner Tulsa Met. Area Plnning Commn., 1958-60; sr. assoc. Hammer & Co. Assocs., Washington, 1960-64; econ. cons. Marvin Springer & Assocs., Dallas, 1964-65; sr. assoc. Gladstone Assocs., Washington, 1965-67; prof. urban planning Iowa State U., Ames, 1967-73; pres. Frank Osgood Assoc./Osgood Urban Rsch., Dallas, 1973-84; dir. mktg. studies MPSI Americas Inc., Tulsa, 1984-85, Comarc Systems/Roulac & Co., San Francisco, 1985-86; pres. Osgood Urban Rsch., Millbrae, Calif., 1986—; adj. prof. U. Tulsa, 1974-76; lectr. U. Tex., Dallas, 1979, U. Tex., Arlington, 1983. Author: Control Land Uses Near Airports, 1960, Planning Small Business, 1967, Continuous Renewal Cities, 1970; contbr. articles to profl. jours. Chmn. awards Cub Scouts Am., Ames, 1971-73; deacon Calvary Presbyn. Ch., San Francisco, 1987-90. 1st lt. USAF, 1954-56. Recipient Community Leaders and Noteworthy Americans award 1976. Mem. Am. Planning Assn. (peninsula liaison 1987-89, dir. pro-tem 1990 No. Calif. sect., edn. coord. 1991-92, Calif., dir. N. Cen. Tex. sect., Tex. chpt. 1983), Am. Inst. Planners (v.p. Okla. chpt. 1975-77), Okla. Soc. Planning Cons. (sec., treas. 1976-79), Urban Land Inst., Le Club. Republican. Presbyterian. Home and Office: 12 Elder Ave Millbrae CA 94030-2425

O'SHAUGHNESSY, BILL, designer; b. San Francisco, Jan. 9, 1954; s. James William and Frances Rose (Schula) O'S.; m. Evelyn Johanna Schweinfurter, July 17, 1982. AS, Coll. San Mateo, 1983; student, San Jose State U., 1991—. Designer Insul-8 Corp., San Carlos, Calif., 1983-89, Toshiba Am. MRI, South San Francisco, Calif., 1989-90, Magna Design, San Jose, Calif., 1989—. Home: 947 Holly St San Carlos CA 94070 Office: Magna Design 1740 Technology Dr # 100 San Jose CA 95110

OSINSKI, MAREK ANDRZEJ, physicist, researcher; b. Wroclaw, Poland, May 28, 1948; came to U.S., 1985; naturalized, 1993; s. Seweryn and Jadwiga (Osinska) O.; m. Elizabeth Balieiro, Dec. 19, 1984 (dec. Aug. 1985); m. Joanna Grazyna Morska, Mar. 20, 1987; children: Boleslaw Leszek, Jacek Ksawery. MSc in Physics, U. Warsaw (Poland), 1971; PhD in Phys. Scis., Polish Acad. Scis., Warsaw, 1979. Asst. prof. Inst. Physics, Polish Acad. Scis., Warsaw, 1974-80; rsch. fellow dept. electronics U. Southampton (Eng.), 1980-84; sr. rsch. assoc. dept. engring. U. Cambridge (Eng.), 1984-85; vis. rsch. prof. Ctr. for High Tech. Materials, U. N.Mex., Albuquerque, 1985-87; NTT vis. prof. RCAST, U. Tokyo, 1988-89; assoc. prof. EECE and physics depts. U. N.Mex., Albuquerque, 1988—; guest scientist dept. electronic engring. U. Tokyo, 1989; cons. Raynet Corp., Menlo Park, Calif., 1988-89, Fuji-Xerox Co., Ltd., Ebina, Japan, 1989. Contbr. over 160 sci. rsch. papers in refereed jours. and conf. procs.; N.Am. editor Progress in Quantum Electronics, 1991—. Mem. bd. advisors Am. Freedom Coalition of N.Mex., Albuquerque, 1987—; chmn. bd. dirs. Polish-Am. Sch. Albuquerque, 1987—. Mem. IEEE (sr.), Optical Soc. Am., Soc. Photo-Optical Instrumentation Engrs., Materials Rsch. Soc., Sigma Xi. Office: U NMex Ctr for High Tech Materials Albuquerque NM 87131-6081

OSSEWAARDE, ANNE WINKLER, real estate developer; b. Dallas, June 2, 1957; d. Lowell Graves and Ruth Lenore (Lind) Winkler; m. Kirk L Ossewaarde, Apr. 27, 1991. BBA in Fin. with honors, Emory U., 1979; MBA in Acctg. and Fin., U. Tex., 1983; MS in Real Estate Devel., MIT, 1988. Mgmt. trainee Citizens & So. Nat. Bank, Atlanta, 1979-81; banking assoc. Continental Ill. Nat. Bank, Chgo. and Dallas, 1983-85; asst. v.p., devel. assoc. Trammell Crow Residential, Dallas, 1985-87, Seattle, 1988-91; devel. mgr. Blackhawk Port Blakely Communities, Issaquah, Wash., 1991—. Charles Harritt Jr. Presdl. scholar U. Tex., 1982, Alexander Grant scholar, 1982. Mem. NAFE, Jr. League of Seattle, Comml. Real Estate Women, MIT Ctr. for Real Estate Devel. Alumni Assn., Alpha Epsilon Upsilon. Methodist.

OST, MICHAEL BRIAN, small business owner; b. Elmhurst, Ill., Apr. 26, 1959; s. Borje Wilhelm Alexander and Raili Tuulikki (Nissinen) O. Student, Northrop U., 1984-85, Calif. State U., Northridge, 1987. Crew mem. McDonalds, Lake Zurich, Ill., 1975-77; fork lift operator Jewel Tea Co., Barrington, Ill., 1977-79; mgr. Young's Aquarium, Glendale, Calif., 1984-90; owner Tropical Fish Safari, Lakewood, Calif., 1990—; active global leadership and global family consulting. Designer, inventor marine technology wet day filter. With USAF, 1979-84. Office: Tropical Fish Safari 20949 Norwalk Blvd Lakewood CA 90715

OSTASHEK, JOHN, government leader. Leader Govt. of Yukon Territory, Whitehorse, YT. Office: Office of the Leader, PO Box 2703, Whitehorse, YK Canada Y1A 2C6*

OSTER, ERIC THOMAS, manufacturing executive; b. Phila., May 14, 1945; s. Richard James and Eva May (Gesnaker) O.; m. Gloria Carmela Alduenda, May 5, 1966; 1 child, Michele Yvette. Student, San Diego State U., 1962-63; AS in Bus., Grossmont Coll., El Cajon, Calif., 1977; BSBA, Calif. Coast U., 1982. Reliability analyst Pacific S.W. Airlines, San Diego, 1967-72, supr. reliability engring., 1972-77, mgr. systems engring. and tng., 1977-81, mgr. prodn. planning and control, 1981-84; materials mgr. Cyclomatic/Pow Con Inc., San Diego, 1984-85, mfg. mgr., 1985-86; mgr. ops. planning PPG Industries, Torrance, Calif., 1986-88; plant mgr. Herman Miller Inc., Irvine, Calif., 1988-90; v.p. mfg. Harpers Office Furniture Mfg., Torrance, 1990-92; plant mgr. Lightolier/Forecast Lighting Mfg., Compton, Calif., 1992—; cons. Transamerica Airlines, Oakland, Calif., 1985, Pres.'s Pvt. Sector Survey on Cost Control. Cons. book: War on Waste, 1984. With USMC, 1963-67. Recipient Presdl. Letter of Appreciation, Pres. Ronald Reagan, 1982; named to U.S. Sen. Commn. Inner Circle, 1991. Mem. Am. Mgmt. Assn., Am. Prodn. and Inventory Control Soc., Soc. Mfg. Engrs. Republican. Methodist. Home: 27775 Hidden Trail Rd Laguna Hills CA 92653 Office: Lightolier/Forecast 501 W Walnut St Compton CA 90220

OSTERBROCK, DONALD E(DWARD), astronomy educator; s. William Carl and Elsie (Wettlin) O.; m. Irene L. Hansen, Sept. 19. 1952; children: Carol Ann, William Carl, Laura Jane. Ph.B., U. Chgo., 1948, B.S., 1948, M.S., 1949, Ph.D., 1952; DSc (hon.), Ohio State U., 1986, U. Chgo., 1992. Mem. faculty Princeton, 1952-53, Calif. Inst. Tech., 1953-58; faculty U. Wis.-Madison, 1958-73, prof. astronomy, 1961-73, chmn. dept. astronomy, 1966-67, 69-72; prof. astronomy U. Calif., Santa Cruz, 1972-92, prof. emeritus, 1993—; dir. Lick Obs., 1972-81; mem. staff Mt. Wilson Obs., Palomar Obs., 1953-58; vis. prof. U. Chgo., 1963-64, Ohio State U., 1980, 86; Hill Family vis. prof. U. Minn., 1977-78. Author: Astrophysics of Gaseous Nebulae, 1974, James E. Keeler, Pioneer American Astrophysicist and the Early Development of American Astrophysics, 1984, (with John R. Gustafson and W.J. Shiloh Unruh) Eye on the Sky: Lick Observatory's First Century, 1988, Astrophysics of Gaseous Nebulae and Active Galactic Nuclei, 1989, Pauper and Prince: Ritchey, Hale, and Big American Telescopes, 1993; editor: (with C.R. O'Dell) Planetary Nebulae, 1968, (with Peter H. Raven) Origins and Extinctions, 1988, (with J.S. Miller) Active Galactic Nuclei, 1989; Stars and Galaxies: Citizens of the Universe, 1990; letters editor Astrophys. Jour., 1971-73. Served with USAAF, 1943-46. Recipient Profl. Achievement award U. Chgo. Alumni Assn., 1982; Guggenheim fellow Inst. Advanced Studies, Princeton, N.J., 1960-61, 82-83, Ambrose Monnell Found. fellow, 1989-90; NSF Sr. Postdoctoral Rsch. fellow U. Coll., London, 1968-69. Mem. NAS (chmn. astronomy sect. 1971-74, sec. class math. and phys. sci. 1980-83, chmn. class math and phys. sci. 1983-85, councilor 1985-88), Am. Acad. Arts and Scis., Internat. Astron. Union (pres. commn. 34 1967-70), Royal Astron. Soc. (assoc.), Am. Astron. Soc. (councilor 1970-73, v.p. 1975-77, pres. 1988-90, vice chmn. hist. astronomy div. 1985-87, chmn. 1987-89, Henry Norris Russell lectr. 1991), Astron. Soc. Pacific (chmn. history com. 1982-86, Catherine Wolfe Bruce medal 1991), Wis. Acad. Scis. Arts and Letters, Am. Philos. Soc. Congregationalist. Home: 120 Woodside Ave Santa Cruz CA 95060-3422

OSTERMILLER, JOHN VICTOR, real estate company executive; b. Lincoln, Nebr., Nov. 4, 1910; s. John and Louise (Bernhardt) O.; m. Margaret Ellen Kerr, June 17, 1934; children: Karen Rea, John Kerr. Student, U. Nebr., 1927-28; BS, Colo. State U., 1932. Tchr. vocat. agr., pub. sch. Colo., 1934-42; agrl. fieldman Gt. Western Sugar Co., Brush, Colo., 1942-49; asst. mgr. Gt. Western Sugar Co., Brush and Ft. Morgan, 1949-57; mgr. Gt. Western Sugar Co., Longmont, Colo., 1957-63; agrl. mgr. Gt. Western Sugar Co., Ft. Morgan, 1963-70, N.E. Colo. asst. dist. agrl. mgr., 1970-73; v.p. Gt. Western Sugar Export Co., 1973-75; mgr. farm and ranch dept. Crown Realty Co., Denver, 1975-78, Carriage House Realtors, Ft. Morgan, 1978-83, Realty Assocs., Ft. Morgan, 1984-87, Accent Real Estate, Ft. Morgan, 1987—; bd. dirs. Lower South Platte Water Conservancy Dist. Contbr. articles to profl. jours. Instr. Adult Edn., Yuma, Colo., 1935-38, Brush, 1938-42. Rep. precinct committeeman, Morgan County, 1950-57, 64-74, Boulder County, 958-63; mem. St. Vrain Valley Sch. Bd., Longmont, 1961-63; bd. dirs. Brush Civic Club, 1944-50, Ft. Morgan Heritage Found., pres. 1969-75; bd. dirs., pres. Colo. State U. Found., 1973-86. Mem. Ft. Morgan C. of C. (dir. 1965-69, pres. 1968), Colo. State U. Alumni (dir. 1971-82, pres. 1975-76), Am. Sugar Beet Soc. Technologists, Masons, Lions, Alpha Tau Alpha, Lamda Gamma Delta, Sigma Phi Epsilon. Presbyterian. Home: 4 Yates Ter Fort Morgan CO 80701-9217

OSTROGORSKY, MICHAEL, historian, archaeologist; b. Hamilton, Ont., Can., Sept. 11, 1951; came to U.S., 1952; s. William and Hedy Ostrogorsky. BA, Boise State Coll., 1973; MA, San Francisco State U., 1976; PhD, U. Idaho, 1993. Cons., ptnr. Idaho Archaeol. Cons., Boise, 1976-80; instr. history U. Alaska, Dillingham, 1985; historian Nat. Park Svc., Anchorage, 1986, Alaska Office History and Archaeology, Anchorage, 1987-91; sr. historian INFOTEC Rsch., Inc., Fresno, Calif., 1991—; media cons., ptnr. Planet Earth Prodns.; freelance cons., 1981-85. Contbr. articles to archaeol. and hist. jours. Cons. N.W. Office, Sierra Club, Seattle, 1984, mem. exec. com. Alaska chpt., 1987-91, chmn., 1988-90, sec., 1991; bd. dirs. Alaska Ctr. for Environ., Anchorage, 1989, Prince Williams Sound Fund, 1989-92. Whittenberger Found. fellow, 1982-83, John Calhoun Smith fellow, 1983-84; Charles Redd Ctr. grantee Brigham Young U., 1987. Mem. Mining History Assn. (coun. 1990-93), Am. Hist. Assn. (Beveridge grantee 1982), Soc. for Hist. Archaeology, Western History Assn., Nat. Trust for Hist. Preservation, Phi Alpha Theta. Democrat. Office: INFOTEC 5088 N Fruit Ave Ste 101 Fresno CA 93711

OSTROM, PHILIP GARDNER, computer company executive; b. New Haven, Aug. 8, 1942; s. David McKellar and Barbara (Kingsbury) O.; m. Toni Hammons, Dec. 21, 1965; n. Nancy Jean Kahl, Apr. 2, 1983; children: Eric Craig, Paige Lynne. BS, U. Ariz., 1965. Sales mgr. Procter & Gamble Co., Louisville, 1968-70, Dun & Bradstreet, L.A., 1970-71; internat. sales mgr. Memorex Corp., Santa Clara, Calif., 1971-82; dir. ops. Memtek Products, Campbell, Calif., 1982-86, Victor Techs., Scotts Valley, Calif., 1986-88; ops. mgr. Apple Computer, Cupertino, Calif., 1988—. Capt. USMC, 1965-68, Vietnam. Home: 1099 Maraschino Dr San Jose CA 95129 Office: Apple Computer 750 Laurelwood Dr Santa Clara CA 95054

OSTWALD, VENICE ELOISE VARNER, librarian, educator, minister, writer; b. Denver, July 19, 1928; d. Earl Robert and Madeline (Shoemaker) Varner; m. Leonard F. Ostwald (div.). BA, U. Colo.-Boulder, 1946; MS, U. So. Calif., 1954. Librarian, tchr. Long Beach Pub. Schs., Calif., 1954-61; asst. prof. U. Oreg., Eugene, 1961-63; dir. libr. and audio-visual Hillsborough Pub. Schs., Calif., 1963-65; adminstrv. asst. to libr. dir. San Jose State U., 1965-67; instrn. specialist/librarian DeAnza Coll., Cupertino, Calif., 1967-87, emeritus, 1987—. Founder, bd. dirs. Singles in Service, Santa Clara, Calif., 1972; co-founder Casa Serena Hospice, San Jose, 1981; co-founder, pres. Spiritual Edn. Endeavors Publ. Co., 1984; chmn. bd. SHARE Found., 1985. Lyricist songs include Part of Me, Oasis, Peru, Caliente, Hyano Cucarumba, Esclava. Mem. Beta Phi Mu, Kappa Delta. Office: SHARE Found 1556 Halford Ave # 288 Santa Clara CA 95051-2694

OSWALD, DELMONT RICHARD, humanities council executive, writer; b. Idaho Falls, Idaho, Oct. 7, 1940; s. Philip Fredrick and Lucille (Andrus) O.; m. Jean Stringam, June 17, 1967 (div. Jan. 1979); children: Sarah Mary, Benjamin Philip. BA, Idaho State U., 1962; MA, Brigham Young U., 1967. Instr. history Brigham Young U., Provo, Utah, 1967-71, asst. to dean social sci., 1971-74; exec. dir. Utah Humanities Coun., Salt Lake City, 1974—; pres. elect Utah Acad. Sci., Arts, Letters, Salt Lake City, 1989-90, pres. 1991-93; nat. bd. dirs. Nat. Fedn. State Humanities Couns., Washington 1988-93, chmn. Nat. meeting, Portland, Oreg., 1990. Author: Autobiography of James Beckwourth, 1972 (U.S. Amb. Book 1972); mem. editorial bd. Dialogue Mag., 1992—. U.S. Senate Reauthorization N.E.H. testifier Fedn. State Humanities Coun., Washington 1990, mem. gov.'s commn. Martin Luther King Jr. Day; mem. edn. com. Project 2000, 1989-90; pres. elect Bd. of Utah Alliance for Arts and Humanities. Recipient N.E.H. Merit awards 1984, 86, 88, Exemplary award, 1990, 91; Dedicatory Address Jewitt Ctr. Humanities, Salt Lake City, 1989. Mem. Nat. Fedn. State Humanities coun. (bd. dirs.), Utah Hist. Assn., Mormon Hist. Assn., Salt Lake City C. of C. (Honors in Arts 1990), Wasatch Westerners. Home: 209 4th Ave Salt

Lake City UT 84103-2484 Office: Utah Humanities Coun 350 S 400E # 110 Salt Lake City UT 84111

OTA, ROY TSUNEO, traffic technician; b. Hilo, Hawaii, June 18, 1942; s. Hideo and Miyako (Hamazu) O.; married, 1970. BBA in Bus. Rsch., U. Hawaii, 1965; BA in Humanities, West Oahu Coll., 1983. From traffic technician III to traffic technician V Dept. Transp. Svcs., Honolulu, 1972-76, traffic technician VI, 1976—. Donor Blood Bank Hawaii, Honolulu, 1990. Lt. USN, 1965-72, capt. Res. Mem. U.S. Naval Inst. (life), Res. Officers Assn. (life, pres. Hawaii dept. 1982-83), Naval Res. Assn. (life, v.p. 1985), Ret. Officers' Assn. (life), Grand Lodge Calif. (inspector 1982-89), Grand Lodge Hawaii (sr. deacon 1992). Christian Scientist. Home: 3215 Ala Ilima St A-801 Honolulu HI 96818-2905 Office: City and County Honolulu Dept Transp Svcs 650 S King St Honolulu HI 96813-3017

OTOMO, STACY AKIO, civil engineer, consultant; b. Lanaina, Hawaii, Oct. 17, 1955; s. Futoshi and Ruth Shizue (Higashi) O.; m. Carole Fumie Saito, Dec. 3, 1983; children: Jordan, Ashley. BS, U. Hawaii, 1977, MS, 1979. Registered profl. engr., Hawaii. Grad. teaching asst. Univ. Hawaii, Honolulu, 1977-79; jr. engr. R.M. Towill Corp., Honolulu, 1979; sr. design engr. Warren S. Unemori Engring. Inc., Wailuku, Hawaii, 1979-85; chief engr. Richard M. Sato and Assocs., Inc., Wailuku, 1985-88; projects mgr. Warren S. Unemori Engring., Inc., Wailuku, 1988-91; pres. Otomo Engring., Inc., Wailuku, 1992—. Mem. Maui County Urban Design Rev. Bd., Wailuku, 1988—, West Maui Casting Club, Lahaina, Hawaii, 1983—, Maui Bus. Coun., Kahului, 1988; coach tee ball league Wailuku, 1992; bd. dirs. Waikulu Elem. Sch. PTA, 1992, Maui United Way , Kalului, 1993—. Mem. Hawaii Soc. Profl. Engrs. (Maui chpt. treas. 1985-86, sec. 1986-87, v.p. 1987-88, pres. 1988-89, state dir. 1989-90, Young Engr. of Yr. 1986, 88, Hawaii State Young Engr. of Yr. 1989, Engr of Yr. 1989, 92). Home: 895 Noela Pl Wailuku HI 96793-9677

O'TOOLE, JOSEPH WILLIAM, aircraft sales executive; b. Leominster, Mass., May 15, 1931; s. Charles Stuart and Josephine Margaret (McLaughlin) O'T.; m. Sara Elizabeth Copeland, Dec. 29, 1956; children: Mary, Patricia, Katherine, Joseph Jr. BS in Econs., History, U. Md., 1966; postgrad., U. Utah, 1970-71; diploma, Indsl. Coll. Armed Forces, Va., 1971, Air Force War Coll., Ala., 1974. Commd. 2d lt. USAF, 1952, advanced through grades to col., 1971, various positions, 1952-78, dir. procurement, 1978, ret., 1978; dir. bus. devel. Gould Electronics, El Marte, Calif., 1978-83; v.p. Astro Vista Inc., Irvine, Calif., 1983-86; pres. Inland Mktg., Claremont, Calif., 1986—; mng. dir. FXC Aircraft Sales, Santa Ana, Calif., 1986—; cons. mktg. Loral, Inc., N.Y., 1983-86, cons. contracts Northrop Aircraft Inc., Hawthorn, Calif., 1983-86, Gould Inc., Chgo., 1984-88, Perkin Elmer, Pomona, Calif., 1988-90. Bd. dirs. C. of C., Pasadena, Calif., 1974-76, Claremont, 1983-89; dir. City Devel. Programs, Claremont, 1987-89. Decorated Air medals (16), DFC (4). Mem. Gould Club (pres. 1978-80, Svc. award), Navy League, Air Force Assn., MIA-POW Assn., Claremont Rotary (bd. dirs., Svc. award), Nat. Contract Mgmt. Assn. (v.p. Langley AFB, Svc. award). Roman Catholic. Home: 647 W Sage St Claremont CA 91711 Office: FXC Internat Aircraft Sales 3410 S Susan St Santa Ana CA 92704

O'TOOLE, ROBERT JOHN, II, telemarketing consultant; b. Binghamton, N.Y., Mar. 24, 1951; s. Robert John and Joan Ceclia (Martin) O'T.; m. Donna Sue Stevenson, Jan. 28, 1978 (div. 1984); children: Irene Grace, Erin Colleen, Robert John III. Student, Corning (N.Y.) C.C., 1969-71, SUNY, Brockport, 1970-71; BA, Wake Forest U., 1973; MBA, Southwestern Coll., 1986. Asst. dir. devel. Duvall Home for Children, DeLand, Fla., 1978-81; gen. mgr. Royale Art Advt., Odessa, Tex., 1981-82; v.p. Barnes Assocs. Advt., Odessa, 1982-84, Tex. Assn. for Blind Athletes, Austin, 1985-86; sales mgr. Los Amables Pub., Albuquerque, 1987-88; dir. devel. Albuquerque (N.Mex.) Help for the Homeless, 1988-91; chmn., CEO Advantage Mktg., Inc., Albuquerque, 1991—; cons. Nat. Child Safety Coun., Austin, 1985, Assoc. Profl. Fire Fighters, Austin, 1985, Reynolds Aluminum, Austin, 1986, Found. for AIDS Rsch., Vista, Calif., 1991-92. Author: Telemarketing Tickets, 1988; founder, editor: (newspaper) Albuquerque Street News, 1990; publisher: (newspaper) The New Mexican, 1991; contbr. articles to jours. Founder Permian Basin Rehab. Ctr., Odessa, 1983, Albuquerque (N.Mex.) Help for the Homeless, Inc., 1988. Recipient Cert. of Merit, Small Bus. Adminstrn., Odessa, 1984. Mem. Direct Mktg. Assn., Amnesty Internat. Home: Historic Coke House 1023 2nd St SW Albuquerque NM 87102 Office: Advantage Mktg Inc 201 Pacific SW Albuquerque NM 87102

OTOSHI, TOM YASUO, electrical engineer; b. Seattle, Sept. 4, 1931; s. Jitsuo and Shina Otoshi; m. Haruko Shirley Yumiba, Oct. 13, 1963; children: John, Kathryn. BSEE, U. Wash., 1954, MSEE, 1957. With Hughes Aircraft Co., Culver City, Calif., 1956-61; mem. tech. staff Jet Propulsion Lab., Calif. Inst. Tech., Pasadena, 1961—; cons. Recipient NASA New Tech. awards. Mem. Wagner Ensemble of Roger Wagner Choral Inst., L.A. Bach Festival Chorale. Mem. IEEE (sr., editorial bd. Transactions on Microwave Theory and Techniques), Sigma Xi. Contbr. articles to profl. jours; patentee in field. Home: 3551 Henrietta Ave La Crescenta CA 91214-1136 Office: Jet Propulsion Lab 4800 Oak Grove Dr Pasadena CA 91109-8099

OTT, DAVID MICHAEL, engineering company executive; b. Glendale, Calif., Feb. 24, 1952; s. Frank Michael and Roberta (Michie) O.; m. Cynthia Dianne Bunce. BSEE, U. Calif., Berkeley, 1974. Electronic engr. Teknekron Inc., Berkeley, 1974-79; chief engr. TCI, Berkeley, 1979-83; div. mgr. Integrated Automation Inc., Alameda, Calif., 1983-87, Litton Indsl. Automation, Alameda, 1987-92; founder, chmn. Picture Elements Inc., Berkeley, 1992—. Inventor method for verifying denomination of currency, method for processing digited images, automatic document image revision. Mem. IEEE, AAAS, Assn. Computing Machinery, Union of Concerned Scientists. Office: Picture Elements Inc 777 Panoramic Way Berkeley CA 94704

OTT, WAYNE ROBERT, environmental engineer; b. San Mateo, Calif., Feb. 2, 1940; s. Florian Funstan and Evelyn Virginia (Smith) O.; m. Patricia Faustina Bertuzzi, June 28, 1967 (div. 1983). BA in Econs., Claremont McKenna Coll., 1962; BSEE, Stanford U., 1963, MS in Engring, 1965, MA in Communications, 1966, PhD in Environ. Engring., 1971. Commd. lt. USPHS, 1966, advanced to comdr., 1982; chief lab. ops. br. U.S. EPA, Washington, 1971-73, sr. systems analyst, 1973-79, sr. rsch. engr., 1981-84, chief air toxics and radiation monitoring rsch. staff, 1984-90; vis. scientist dept. stats. Stanford (Calif.) U., 1979-81; vis. scholar Ctr. for Risk Analysis and dept. stats., civil engring., 1990-93; sr. environ. engr., EPA Atmospheric Rsch. and Exposure Assessment Lab, 1993—; dir. field studies Calif. Environ. Tobacco Smoke Study, 1993—. Author: Environmental Indices: Theory and Practice, 1976, Environmental Statistics: Probability Theory Applied to Environmental Problems; contbr. articles on indoor air pollution, total human exposure to chems., stochastic models of indoor exposure, motor vehicle exposures, personal monitoring instruments, and environ. tobacco smoke to profl. jours. Decorated Commendation medal. Mem. Internat. Soc. of Exposure Analysis (v.p. 1989-90), Am. Statis. Assn., Am. Soc. for Quality Control, Air and Waste Mgmt. Assn., Phi Beta Kappa, Sigma Xi, Tau Beta Pi, Kappa Mu Epsilon. Democrat. Clubs: Theater, Jazz, Sierra. Avocations: hiking, photography, model trains, jazz recording. Developer nationally uniform air pollution index, first total human exposure activity pattern models. Home: 1008 Cardiff Ln Redwood City CA 94061-3678 Office: Stanford U Dept Stats Sequoia Hall Stanford CA 94305

OTTEN, ARTHUR EDWARD, JR., lawyer, corporate executive; b. Buffalo, Oct. 11, 1930; s. Arthur Edward Sr. and Margaret (Ambrusko) O.; m. Mary Theresa Torri, Oct. 1, 1960; children: Margaret, Michael, Maureen Staley, Suzanne, Jennifer. BA, Hamilton Coll., 1952; JD, Yale U., 1955. Bar: N.Y. 1955, Colo. 1959. Assoc. Hodges, Silverstein, Hodges & Harrington, Denver, 1959-64; ptnr. Hodges, Kerwin, Otten & Weeks (predecessor firms), Denver, 1964-73, Davis, Graham & Stubbs, Denver, 1973-86; pres., mem. Otten, Johnson, Robinson, Neff & Ragonetti, P.C., Denver, 1986—; rec. sec. Colo. Nat. Bankshares, Inc., Denver, 1983-93. Lt. USN, 1955-59. Mem. ABA, Colo. Bar Assn., Denver Bar Assn., Am. Arbitration Assn. (panel arbitrators, large complex case panel), Law Club, Univ. Club, Denver Mile High Rotary (pres. 1992-93), Phi Delta Phi. Republican. Roman Catholic. Home: 3774 S Niagara Way Denver CO 80237-1248 Office: Otten Johnson Robinson Neff & Ragonetti PC 1600 Colorado Blvd Denver CO 80220-1056

OTTENBERG, SIMON, anthropology educator; b. N.Y.C., June 6, 1923; s. Reuben Isaac Ottenberg and Clarisse Chène; m. Carol Perry Barnard, June 14, 1986. BA in Anthropology, U. Wis., 1948; PhD in Anthropology, Northwestern U., 1957; DLitt (hon.), U. Nigeria, Africa, 1992. Instr. anthropology U. Chgo., 1954; instr. Wash. State Coll., Pullman, 1954-55; from instr. to prof. U. Wash., Seattle, 1955-90, prof. emeritus, 1990—; hon. vis. prof. U. Ghana, Lagos, 1970-71. Author: Double Descent in an African Society, 1968, System of Authority in an African Society, 1972, The Masked Rituals of Afikpo, 1975, Boyhood Rituals in an African Society, 1989. Pres. African Studies Assn., 1988-89, pres. Arts Coun. of the African Studies Assn., 1992—. Sgt. U.S. Army, 1943-46. NSF grantee, 1959-60; Guggenheim Found. fellow, 1970-71, Social Sci. Rsch. Found. African fellow, 1963-64, NEH fellow, 1978-79, Regents fellow Smithsonian Inst., Wash., 1993-94. Home: 2317 22nd Ave E Seattle WA 98112-2604 Office: U Wash Dept Anthropology Seattle WA 98195

OTTER, CLEMENT LEROY, lieutenant governor; b. Caldwell, Idaho, May 3, 1942; s. Joseph Bernard and Regina Mary (Buser) O.; m. Gay Corinne Simplot, Dec. 28, 1964; children: John Simplot, Carolyn Lee, Kimberly Dawn, Corinne Marie. BA in Polit. Sci., Coll. Idaho, 1967; PhD, Mindanao State U., 1980. Mgr. J.R. Simplot Co., Caldwell, Idaho, 1971-76, asst. to v.p. adminstrn., 1976-78, v.p. adminstrn., 1978-82, internat. pres., from 1982, now v.p.; lt. gov. State of Idaho, Boise, 1987—. Mem. Presdl. Task Force-AID, Washington, 1982-84; com. mem. invest tech. devel. State Adv. Council, Washington, 1983-84; mem. exec. council Bretton Woods Com., 1984—; mem. U.S. C. of C., Washington, 1983-84. Mem. Young Pres.' Orgn., Sales and Mktg. Execs., Idaho Assn. Commerce and Industry, Idaho Agrl. Leadership Council, Idaho Ctr. for Arts, Idaho Internat. Trade Council, Pacific N.W. Waterways Assn., N.W. Food Producers, Ducks Unltd. Republican. Roman Catholic. Clubs: Arid, Hillcrest Country. Lodge: Moose, Elks. Office: Office of the Lt Gov State House Rm 225 Boise ID 83702*

OTTLEY, JEROLD DON, choral conductor, educator; b. Salt Lake City, Apr. 7, 1934; s. Sidney James and Alice (Warren) O.; m. JoAnn South, June 22, 1956; children: Brent Kay, Allison. B.A., Brigham Young U., Provo, Utah, 1961; M.Mus., U. Utah, 1967; Fulbright study grantee, Fed. Republic Germany, 1968-69; D.M.A. (grad. teaching fellow), U. Oreg., 1972. Tchr. public schs. Salt Lake City area, 1961-65; mem. faculty U. Utah, Salt Lake City, 1967—, asst. prof. music, 1971-78, adj. assoc. prof. music, 1978-81, adj. prof. music, 1981—; assoc. conductor Salt Lake Mormon Tabernacle Choir, 1974-75, conductor, 1975—; also guest conductor throughout U.S. Conducted Mormon Tabernacle Choir in 12 concert tours U.S., 24 fgn. countries; rec. artist CBS Masterworks, London/Decca Records, Bonneville Records and Laserlight; prepared choirs for Eugene Ormandy, Maurice Abravanel, Stanislaw Skrowaczewski, Michael Tilson Thomas, Robert Shaw, Julius Rudel, Sir David Willcocks, Ling Tung. Past mem. gen. music coms. Mormon Ch., cultural arts com. Salt Lake City C. of C. (Honors in the Arts award), past bd. advs. Barlow Endowment Music Composition; v.p., bd. dirs., com. chair Chorus Am. Served with U.S. Army, 1957-59. Faculty Study grantee U. Utah, 1971-72; recipient Brigham Young U. Alumni Achievement award, 1990. Mem. Am. Choral Dirs. Assn., Am. Choral Found., Master Tchr. Inst. Arts. (past trustee). Office: Mormon Tabernacle Choir 50 E North Temple Fl 20 Salt Lake City UT 84150-0001

OTTO, HARRY CLAUDE, manufacturing executive; b. Chgo., Feb. 7, 1957; s. Edward and Carol (Greengard) Urbanski; m. Linda Jean Schneller, Sept. 13, 1980. Diagnostic ctr. mgr. Panafax Corp., Chgo., 1979-83; spl. project mgr. Panafax Corp., Melville, N.Y., 1983-86; product mgr. Brother Internat. Corp., Piscataway, N.J., 1986—. Contbr. articles to profl. jours. Mem. Facsimile Systems Equipment Engring., Electronic Industries Assn., Telecommunications Industry Assn., Am. Mgmt. Assn. Republican. Methodist. Office: Telautograph Corp 8700 Bellanca Ave Los Angeles CA 90045

OU, JING-HSIUNG JAMES, virology educator; b. Taipei, Taiwan, June 10, 1954; came to U.S., 1977; s. Shang-ling and Jin-yeh (Lin) O.; m. Ker-hwa Susan Tung, June 20, 1979; children: Elaine, Yee-ping. BS, Nat. Taiwan U., Taipei, 1976; PhD, Calif. Inst. Tech., 1982. Asst. biochemist U. Calif., San Francisco, 1982-86; asst. prof. U. So. Calif., L.A., 1986-92; assoc. prof., 1992—. Contbr. articles to profl. jours. Am. Cancer Soc. Rsch. grantee, 1987, NIH Rsch. grantee, 1988—, Coun. for Tobacco Rsch. grantee, 1989—. Mem. AAAS, Am. Soc. for Microbiology, Am. Soc. for Virology, Am. Soc. for Chinese Biochemists (life.). Office: U So Calif Dept of Microbiology 2011 Zonal Ave Los Angeles CA 90033-1054

OUTLAND, ORLAND T, civic leader, retired army officer; b. Dennison, Ohio, Apr. 27, 1923; s. Orland and Mary Alice (Chambers) O.; m. Anna Mae Greer, May 29, 1961; 1 child, Orland V. Joined U.S. Army, 1940, advanced through grades to maj.; intelligence officer U.S. Army, various cities and, countries, 1962; ret., 1962; ins. cons. Met. Life Ins. Co., Fresno, Calif., 1962-63; ins. broker, Fresno, 1963-64; sr. adminstrn. analyst Pacific Fidelity Life Ins. Co., L.A., 1964-66; agy. mgr. Pacific Fidelity Life Ins. Co., Downey, Calif., 1966-67; office mgr. H & R Block, San Bernardino, Calif., 1969; owner, mgr., cons. Outland's Tax and Bus. Svc., Reno, 1969-75. Pres. Consumer Action No. Nev., Reno, 1975; chmn. Common Cause Nev., 1976, 81-83, Washoe County Bd. Equalization, Reno, 1981-82; lobbyist on campaign financing, ethics in govt., health care, and taxation, 1974—; chmn. platform com. Washoe County Rep. Com., 1977-78; chmn. John Anderson Nev. Presdl. Campaign, Nev., 1980; trustee Washoe County Sr. Citizens Svc. Ctr., 1991—; vice chmn. citizens adv. com. Regional Transp. Commn., Reno, 1991—; mem. cen. com. Washoe County Dem. Com., 1992, quality of life task force Truckee Meadows Regional Planning Agy, 1992—; others. Decorated Bronze Star Medal. Mem. Nat. Coun. Sr. Citizens (v.p. Nev. coun. chpt. 4539, 1991—), Am. Assn. Ret. Persons (chmn. Nev. legis. com. 1989-90, trustee chpt. 416, 1991—, activist Nev. health care and long term care campaign 1988—), Ret. Officers Assn., 37th Div. Assn. Home: 2675 Valmar Pl Reno NV 89503-2130

OUWEHAND, WILLIAM, airline executive; b. Amsterdam, The Netherlands, May 27, 1932; came to U.S., 1954; s. Huig and Martha (Teeuwsen) O.; m. Elizabeth Nina Gallo, Mar. 21, 1959 (div. Mar. 1969); m. Patricia Ann Fuhr, June 21, 1969; children: Terre Sue, Michael Todd. Student, U. Groningen (Holland), 1956, McMaster U., Toronto, 1959. Currency expert Amsterdam/Rotterdam Bank, 1955-56; owner, mgr. Universal Travel Svc., Dundas, Ont., 1956-59; sales mgr. Cont Am. Trs, San Francisco, 1959; group devel. mgr. Phillip Martin & Assocs., Oakland, Calif., 1959-61; passenger sales mgr. Pacific S.W. KLM Royal Dutch Airlines, L.A., 1961-84; v.p., gen. mgr. GO Am. Inc., Anaheim, Calif., 1984-87; passenger sales mgr. U.S.A. and Mexico Austrian Airlines, Newport Beach, Calif., 1987—. Author: Successful Marketing, 1972. Chmn. Traffic Commn., Garden Grove, 1974-76; mem. Transp. Action Com., So. Calif., 1985. 1st lt. Dutch Army, 1951-54. Recipient Svc. to State award E. Evans Sec. State N.Mex., Albuquerque, 1968. Mem. Assn. Internat. Skal Clubs (past pres.), L.A. Transp. Club (bd. dirs. 1974—), Sertoma (hon. life, Centurian award 1972), Orange County Interline Club (hon. life), Masons. Republican. Home: 3 Carriage Hill Ln Laguna Beach CA 92653-6041 Office: Austrian Airlines 4000 Macarthur Blvd Ste 740 Newport Beach CA 92660-2532

OVERALL, RICHARD PALMER, quality assurance professional; b. Dyersburg, Tenn., May 13, 1946; s. Jesse Ulin III and Helen Lucile (Bunch) O.; 1 child, Sean Richard. Student, Kans. State U., 1964-66; BS in Journalism, U. Tenn., 1968; MPA, U. No. Colo., 1977; postgrad., Laramie County Community Coll., 1990—. Adminstrv. officer II Wyo. Disaster and Civil Def. Agy., Cheyenne, 1974-75; asst. mgr. Zale Corp., Cheyenne, Wyo., 1975-76; quality rev. examiner dept. employment unemployment ins. div State of Wyo., Cheyenne, 1981—; owner, operator Overall Enterprises Wyo., Cheyenne, 1984—; ptnr. Overall Farms, Dyersburg, 1989—, Overall Properties, Dyersburg, 1989—. Contbr. articles and photographs to newspapers. Pres. Successful Cheyenne Christian Singles, 1980-86. Capt. USAF, 1968-74, USAFR, 1974-83. Office: Wyo Dept Employment PO Box 447 Cheyenne WY 82003

OVERGAARD, WILLARD MICHELE, political scientist, jurisprudent; b. Montpelier, Idaho, Oct. 16, 1925; s. Elias Nielsen and Myrtle LaVerne (Humphrey) O.; m. Lucia Clare Cochrane, June 14, 1946; children: Eric Willard, Mark Fredrik, Alisa Claire. B.A., U. Oreg., 1949; Fulbright scholar, U. Oslo, 1949-50; M.A. (non-resident scholar 1954-55), U. Wis., Madison, 1955; Ph.D. in Polit. Sci. (adminstrv. fellow 1955-56, research fellow 1962-64), U. Minn., 1969. Instr., Soviet and internat. affairs Intelligence Sch., U.S. Army, Europe, 1956-62; dir. intelligence rsch. tng. program Intelligence Sch., U.S. Army, 1958-61; asst. prof. internat. affairs George Washington U., 1964-67; sr. staff polit. scientist Ops. Research Inst., U.S. Army Inst. Advanced Studies, Carlisle, Pa., 1967-70; assoc. prof. polit. sci., chmn. dept., dir. Internat. Studies Inst., Westminster Coll., New Wilmington, Pa., 1970-72; prof. polit. sci. and pub. law Boise (Idaho) State U., 1972—, chmn. dept., 1972-87, acad. dir. M.P.A. degree program, personnel adminstr., mem. humanities council interdisciplinary studies in humanities, 1976-87, dir. Taft Inst. Seminars for Pub. Sch. Tchrs., 1985-87, coord. Legal Asst. Program, 1990—; mem. comml. panel Am. Arbitration Assn., 1974—; cons. in field. Mem. Consortium for Idaho's Future, 1974—; adv. com. Idaho Statewide Tng. Program Local Govt. Ofcls., 1974-78; adv. group Gov. Idaho Task Force Local Govt., 1977; co-dir. Idaho State Exec. Inst., Office of Gov., 1979-83; grievance hearing officer City of Boise, 1981-85; arbitrator U.S. Postal Svc., 1988-90. Author: The Schematic System of Soviet Totalitarianism, 3 vols, 1961, Legal Norms and Normative Bases for the Progressive Development of International Law as Defined in Soviet Treaty Relations, 1945-64, 1969; co-author: The Communist Bloc in Soviet Europe, 1959; editor: Continuity and Change in International Politics, 1972; chief editor: Idaho Jour. Politics, 1974-76. Served with USAAF, 1943-45; with AUS, 1951-54; ret. maj. USAR. Named Disting. Citizen of Idaho Idaho Statesman, 1979; named Outstanding Prof. of Sch. Social Scis. and Pub. Affairs, Boise State U., 1988. Mem. ABA (assoc.). Home: 2023 S Five Mile Rd Boise ID 83709-2316 Office: Boise State U Dept Polit Sci 1910 University Dr Boise ID 83725-0001

OVERHOLT, MILES HARVARD, cable television consultant; b. Glendale, Calif., Sept. 30, 1921; s. Miles Harvard and Alma Overholt; A.B., Harvard Coll., 1943; m. Jessie Foster, Sept. 18, 1947; children: Miles Harvard, Keith Foster. Mktg. analyst Dun & Bradstreet, Phila., 1947-48; collection mgr. Standard Oil of Calif., L.A., 1948-53; br. mgr. RCA Svc. Co., Phila., 1953-63, ops. mgr. Classified Aerospace project RCA, Riverton, N.J., 1963; pres. CPS, Inc., Paoli, Pa., 1964-67; v.p. Gen. Time Corp.; mem. pres.'s exec. com. Gen. Time Corp., Mesa, Ariz., 1970-78; gen. mgr., dir. svc. Talley Industries, Mesa, 1967-78; v.p., gen. mgr. Northwest Entertainment Network, Inc., Seattle, 1979-81; v.p., dir. Cable Communication Cons., 1982—; mcpl. cable cons., 1981—; pub. The Mcpl. Cable Regulator. Served with USMCR, 1943-46. Decorated Bronze Star, Purple Heart (two). Mem. Nat. Assn. TV Officers and Advisors. Home: 8320 Frederick Pl Edmonds WA 98026-5033 Office: Cable Communication Cons 4517 California Ave SW Ste B Seattle WA 98116-4110

OVERHOLTZER, PHYLLIS JO, health planner, consultant; b. Walsenburg, Colo., Sept. 16, 1954; d. Gilbert G. and Evelyn M. (Roybal) Wilkins; m. Gary A. Overholtzer, July 17, 1975 (div. 1984); children: Shaun M., Ryan P. AA, U. Alaska, 1990; BA, Alaska Pacific U., 1991. EMT. Safety dir. ARC, Anchorage, 1975-76; divsn. dir. Cook Inlet Native Assn., Anchorage, 1978-84; health planner Cook Inlet Tribal Coun., Anchorage, 1984; health dir. South Ctrl. Found., Anchorage, 1985-89; programs dir. Armed Svcs. YMCA, Elemendorf AFB, Alaska, 1990-91; spl. projects coord. North Pacific Rim, Anchorage, 1991-92; assoc. exec. dir. Health-Link TV broadcast, Anchorage, 1992—; cons. ASE Cons., Anchorage, 1980—, instr., cons. Standard Oil Co., Prudoue Bay, Alaska, 1982-84, Atlantic Richfield Oil Co., Prudoue Bay, 1980-84. Nat. task force mem. Indian Health Svcs., Washington, 1987, congrl. task force mem., 1983-84 (Emergency Med Svcs. Adminstr of Yr. 1989); panel mem. United Way, Anchorage, 1981. Mem. Nat. Ski Patrol System, Alaska Profl. Health Assn., Alaska Ctr. Blind/Deaf Adults (bd. dirs. 1992). Home: 6804 Cape Lisburne Cir Anchorage AK 99504 Office: TNPR 3300 C St Anchorage AK 99503

OVERTON, EDWIN DEAN, campus minister, educator; b. Beaver, Okla., Dec. 2, 1939; s. William Edward and Georgia Beryl (Fronk) O. B.Th., Midwest Christian Coll., 1963; M.A. in Religion, Eastern N.Mex. U., 1969, Ed.S., 1978; postgrad. Fuller Theol. Sem., 1980. Ordained to ministry Christian Ch., 1978. Minister, Christian Ch., Englewood, Kans., 1962-63; youth minister First Christian Ch., Beaver, Okla., 1963-67; campus minister Central Christian Ch., Portales, N.Mex., 1967-68, Christian Campus House, Portales, N.Mex., 1968-70; tchr. religion, philosophy, counseling Eastern N.Mex. Univ., Portales, 1970—, campus minister, Christian Campus House, 1968—, dir., 1980—; farm and ranch partner, Beaver, Okla., 1963—. State dir. Beaver Jr. C. of C., 1964-65; pres. Beaver High Sch. Alumni Assn., 1964-65; elder Cen. Christian Ch., Portales, 1985-88, 1990—; chmn. Beaver County March of Dimes, 1966; pres. Portales Tennis Assn., 1977-78. Mem. U.S. Tennis Assn. Republican. Club: Lions. Home: 1129 Libra Dr Portales NM 88130-6123 Office: 223 S Avenue K Portales NM 88130-6643

OVERTON, LEWIS MARVIN, JR., crisis management consultant; b. Des Moines, July 2, 1937; s. Lewis Marvin and Helen Jane (Thomas) O.; m. Helen Virginia Hawthorne, Sept. 9, 1961 (div. Feb. 1984); children: Thomas William, Anne Hawthorne; m. Priscilla Craig Franklin, Dec. 28, 1985. BS in Chemistry, Stanford U., 1961; MBA with honors, Pace U., 1967. Assoc. A.T. Kearney Cons., N.Y.C., 1967-72, Alan Patricof Assocs., N.Y.C., 1972-75; v.p. fin. Jon-T Chem., Inc., Houston, 1975-79, CEO, receiver, 1981-85; pres. Lewis Overton, Jr., Cons., Houston, 1979-93; prin. Lewis Overton Jr. Cons. Inc., Pasadena, Calif., 1993—; pres., CEO D-Cemco, Inc., Burbank, Calif., 1984-87, Microwave Products Am., Memphis, 1989-91; ptnr. Belet Ptnrs., Newport Beach, 1989-91; mng. dir. Menumaster, Inc., Sioux Falls, S.D., 1991-93; receiver Dist. Ct., State of Tex., 1981-93. Acting exec. dir. Am. Lung Assn. of Los Angeles County, 1993. Mem. Nat. Assn. Bankruptcy Trustees, Am. Bankruptcy Assn., Turnaround Mgmt. Assn., Calif. Yacht Club. Episcopalian. Home: 180 State St Pasadena CA 91105-3445 Office: Lewis Overton Jr Cons Inc 130 W State St Pasadena CA 91105

OVESON, W(ILFORD) VAL, state official, accountant; b. Provo, Utah, Feb. 11, 1952; s. Wilford W. and LaVon Oveson; m. Emilee Nebeker, Sept. 1, 1973; children: Polly, Libby, Peter, Benjamin. Student, U. Utah, 1973-74; BS in Acctg., Brigham Young U., 1976. CPA, Utah. Acct. Squire and Co., Orem, Utah, 1975-79; pvt. practice acctg. Squire and Co., Orem, 1979-80; state auditor State of Utah, Salt Lake City, 1981-84, lt. gov., 1985-93; sr. mgr. KPMG Peat Marwick, 1993; chmn. Utah Tax Commn., Salt Lake City, 1993—; mem. dist. export coun. U.S. Dept. Commerce, 1985—, mem. bd. examiners, State of Utah, 1981-84; chmn. State Records Com., 1981-84. Bd. dirs., unit campaign dir. United Way of Greater Salt Lake, 1985-86; trustee Travis Found., 1985-88; treas. Utah County Rep. Party; mem. State Platform Com., 1982, 84; mem. exec. com. Utah State Rep. Party, 1981—. Mem. AICPA (mem. governing coun. 1986), Utah Assn. CPAs (Pub. Svc. award 1984). Republican. Mem. LDS Ch. Home: 2125 S 900 E Bountiful UT 84010-3105

OVIATT, LARRY ANDREW, educator; b. Boone, Iowa, Mar. 13, 1939; s. Eli Charles and T. Mae (Lathrop) O.; children: Julia, Vanessa, Dana. BA, Drake U., Des Moines, 1962; MS, San Diego State U., 1975. Tchr. art San Diego City Schs., 1969—, mentor tchr., 1992—; owner Perfect Travel of Lajolla, 1989—. San Diego dir. Anderson for Pres., 1976; dist. coord. Hedgecock for Mayor, San Diego, 1984; dir. Elder Help Corp., San Diego, 1988; v.p. African Am. Mus., 1989—; pres. Sushi Gallery, Inc., 1980—; bd. dirs. Mingei Internat. Mus., 1983-87; pres. Community Svc. Assn., 1984—; pres. Diversionary Theatre, Africian Am. Mus.; dir. AIDS Walk for Life, 1988, 89; bd. dirs. AIDS Art Alive. Named 1986 Tchr. of Yr. Urban League, 1986, Sec. Art Tchr. of Yr. Calif. Art Tchrs. Assn., 1988, Art Tchr. of Yr. Calif. Art Tchrs. Assn., 1992, Vol. of Yr. San Diego City Schs., 1993. Mem. So. Calif. Art Tchrs. Assn. (pres. 1984-89), Calif. Art Edn. Assn. (dir. 1984-89, conf. adminstr., Art Edn. Tchr. of Yr. award 1992), Nat. Art Edn. Assn. (dir. 1987—). Home: 1611 29th St San Diego CA 92102-1419 Office: San Diego City Schools 4100 Normal St San Diego CA 92103-2653

OWEN, CAROL THOMPSON, artist, educator; b. Pasadena, Calif., May 10, 1944; d. Sumner Comer and Cordelia (Whittemore) Thompson; m. James Eugene Owen, July 19, 1975; children: Kevin Christopher, Christine Celese. Student, Pasadena City Coll., 1963; BA with distinction, U. Redlands, 1966; MA, Calif. State U., L.A., 1967; MFA, Claremont Grad. Sch., 1969. Cert. community coll. instr., Calif. Head resident Pitzer Coll.,

Claremont, Calif., 1967-70; instr. art Mt. San Antonio Coll., Walnut, Calif., 1968—; dir. coll. art gallery Mt. San Antonio Coll., 1972-73. Group shows include Covina Pub. Libr., 1971, U. Redlands, 1964, 65, 66, 70, 78, 88, 92, Am. Ceramic Soc., 1969, Mt. San Antonio Coll., 1991, The Aesthetic Process, 1993, others; ceramic mural commd. and installed U. Redlands, 1991. Mem. Calif. Scholarship Fedn., Faculty Assn. Mt. San Antonio Coll., Coll. Art Assn. Am., Calif. Tchrs. Assn., Friends of Huntington Library, L.A. County Mus. Art, Heard Mus. Assn., Sigma Tau Delta. Republican. Presbyterian. Home: 534 S Hepner Ave Covina CA 91723-2921 Office: Mt San Antonio Coll Grand Ave Walnut CA 91789

OWEN, DAVID, computer engineer; b. Torrance, Calif., July 27, 1968; s. Philsun and Won Sook (Yoon) O. BS in Computer Sci., U. Calif., Irvine, 1990. Engr. I Northrop, Pico Rivera, Calif., 1990; assoc. engr. Versyss, Inc., Torrance, 1990-91, engr. I, 1991-93; engr. NCR Corp., El Segundo, Calif., 1993—. Mem. So. Calif. Quality Assurance Assn.

OWEN, GILBERT EUGENE, health facility administrator; b. Hawthorne, Calif., June 21, 1949; s. Lester Neal and Evelyn May (Lemen) O.; m. Kathryn Lorraine Williams, Nov. 1, 1969 (dec. Oct. 1979); m. Deborah Ann Barnes, July 18, 1981; children: Damon Shawn, Epiphany, Bryan Daniel, Austin Lee. BA in English, Calif. State U., Long Beach, 1976. Surfboard sander Infinity Surfboards, Santa Ana, Calif., 1970-79; claims adjuster State Compensation Ins. Fund, Santa Ana, 1979-82, account rep., 1982; v.p. ops. Redhill Med. Mgmt. Corp., Santa Ana, 1982—. Author (short story): On the Borderline, 1971. Mem. Orange County Workers' Compensation Def. Assn., Yosemite Assn. Democrat. Home: 105 S Milton St Anaheim CA 92806-3110 Office: Redhill Med Mgmt Corp 2953 Pullman St Santa Ana CA 92705-5818

OWEN, JOHN, journalist; b. Helena, Mont., June 10, 1929; s. John Earl and Ella Jean (McMillian) O.; m. Alice Winnifred Kesler, June 9, 1951; children—David Scott, Kathy Lynn. B.A. in Journalism, U. Mont., 1951. Sports editor Bismarck (N.D.) Tribune, 1953-55; wire editor Yakima (Wash.) Herald, 1956; with Seattle Post-Intelligencer, 1956—, sports editor, 1968—, asso. editor, 1980—. Author: Intermediate Eater Cookbook, 1974, Gourmand Gutbusters Cookbook, 1980, Seattle Cookbook, 1983, Great Grub Hunt Cookbook, 1989; also short stories. Served with AUS, 1951-52. Named Top Sports Writer in Wash. Nat. Sportswriters Orgn., 1966, 68, 69, 71, 74, 85, 88. Home: 611 Bell # 4 Edmonds WA 98020 Office: 101 Elliott Ave W Seattle WA 98119-4220

OWEN, ROBERT BARRY, research scientist; b. Chgo., Oct. 16, 1943; s. Jack Saunders and Dorothy Colen (Riley) O.; m. Lyn Irwin Owen, Oct. 31, 1970; children: Catherine Anne, Ruth Riley. BS, Va. Polytechnic Inst. State U., Blacksburg, 1966, PhD, 1972; MA, U. Colo., Boulder, 1989. Rsch. sci. NASA/Marshall Space Flight Ctr., Hunstville, Ala., 1962-87; chief sci. Optical Rsch. Inst., Inc., Boulder, Colo., 1982-92; sci./pres. Owen Rsch., Boulder, Colo., 1990—; visiting sci. Nat. Ctr. for Atmos. res., Boulder, 1982; sci. visitor, nat. Bur. of Standards, 1985. Contbr. articles to profl. jours. Recipient Sci. Merit, NASA, (2) Small Bus. Innovative Rsch. awards. Mem. Optical Soc. of Am., Soc. for Am. Archeol., Am. Assn. for Artifical Intelligence. Office: Owen Rsch Ste E4-262 2525 Arapahoe Ave Boulder CO 80302-6700

OWEN, SCOTT ARNOLD, mechanical engineer; b. Oakland, Calif., May 24, 1961; s. John Arnold and Renata Christa (Henneberg) O. BSME, U. Calif., Berkeley, 1983. Registered profl. engr., Calif. Supervising air quality engr. Bay Area Air Quality Dist, San Francisco, 1984—. Mem. ASME, Soc. Automotive Engrs., South of Market Boys. Home: 370 Turk St Apt 283 San Francisco CA 94102 Office: Bay Area Air Quality Dist 939 Ellis St San Francisco CA 94109

OWEN, WILLIAM FREDERICK, engineering and management consultant; b. Pontiac, Mich., July 27, 1947; s. Webster Jennings and Elizabeth (Hayes) W.; m. Delores T. Owen, Mar. 30, 1974 (div. Dec. 1978); m. Janice L. Pierce, July 29, 1983. BS, Mich. Tech. U., 1972; MS, U. Mich., 1973; PhD, Stanford U., 1978. Research engr. Neptune Microfloc, Corvallis, Oreg., 1973-75, process applications engr., 1975-76; process applications engr. Dr. Perry McCarty, Stanford, Calif., 1976-78; sr. engr. Culp/Wesner/Culp, Cameron Park, Calif., 1978-82; pres. Owen Engring. and Mgmt. Cos., Denver, 1982—. Author: Energy in Wastewater Treatment, 1982, Turbo Mainenance Manager. Del. People-to-People, People's Republic China, 1986. Served with USN, 1965-68. Recipient Local Govt. Innovations award Denver Regional Council Govt., 1983, Boettcher Innovations award Denver Regional Council Govt., 1984, Energy Innovations award Colo. Council Energy Ofcls., 1983. Club: Pinehurst Country (Denver). Home: 3829 S Chase St Denver CO 80235-2953 Office: Owen Engring and Mgmt Cons Inc 5353 W Dartmouth Ave Denver CO 80227-5515

OWEN-RIESCH, ANNA LOU, economics and history educator; b. West Bend, Wis., Apr. 16, 1919; d. Louis J. and Emily (Dexheimer) Reisch; children: Deann, Todd, John. BE, U. Wis., Whitewater, 1940; PhM, U. Wis., 1942, PhD, 1952. Mem. faculty U. Wis., Milw., 1948-52; asst. dean L. and S. U. Wis., Madison, 1954-57, mem. faculty, 1954-56; vis. lectr. U. Colo., Boulder, 1958-69, asst. prof., 1969-83, assoc. prof., 1983-89, prof., 1989—; social dir. Meml. Union, U. Wis., Madison, 1948-49; faculty advisor to student groups, U. Colo., Boulder, 1965-81; chmn. social studies Intedisciplinary Studies U. Colo., Boulder, 1983-85, honors dir., 1984-85. Author: Perlman's Lectures on Capitalism and Socialism, 1970, Conservation Under F.D. Roosvelt, 1983; contbr. articles to profl. jours. Lectr., workshop leader Benevolent Corps., West Bend, Wis., 1976-81; lectr. Intensive English Ctr., Boulder, 1978-82; vol. YMCA, Heart Assn., Cancer Found., Boulder, 1982-89. Named Hyde Park scholar, 1950; recipient Disting. Alumni Svc. award, U. Wis., Whitewater, 1983. Mem. AAUP, Miss. Valley Hist. Assn., Orgn. Am. Historians, Am. Hist. Assn., Am. Econ. Assn., Acad. Ind. Scholars, Delta Kappa Pi. Home: 200 Devon Pl Boulder CO 80302 Office: U Colo Econs Dept University Of Colorado CO 80309 also: U Colo Honors-Norlin Libr University Of Colorado CO 80309

OWENS, DORIS A., controller; b. Waukegan, Ill., June 8, 1950; d. Benjemin H. and Annie (Haisma) Bloede; m. Brian E. Owens, Aug. 28, 1971; children: Teresa, Kelly. BS in Acctg., So. Ill. U., 1972; MBA in Mgmt., Roosevelt U., 1979. Voucher audit VA Hosp., N. Chgo., 1972-74; cost acct. Kleinschmidt Div., Deerfield, Ill., 1974-79; sr. acct. Andes Candies, Delavan, Wis., 1980; acct. mgr. Andes Candies, Delavan; contr. Tobler Suchard, USA, Delavan; fin. mgr. Jacobs Suchard, USA, Delavan, contr.; contr. Egg Products, Inc., Muskego, Wis., 1987-88; chief fin. officer Monogram Chocolates, Palm Beach, Fla., 1988-89; contr. Michael Angelo's Gourmet Foods, Inc., Vista, Calif., 1989—.

OWENS, ERNEST SIBLEY, III, research program manager; b. Pensacola, Fla., Oct. 11, 1945; s. Ernest S. Jr. and Edna L. (Kell) O.; m. Anita Kay Wagoner, Nov. 29, 1968; children: Heather Renee, Jonathan Michael. BS in Biology, Memphis State U., 1967; MS in Mgmt., Troy State U., 1977; MA in Psychology, Ball State U., 1979. Comd. base inspector gen. USAF, 1975; advanced through grades to chief air base operability div. USAF, Offutt AFB, Nebr., 1985-87; sr. rsch. scientist Battelle, Edgewood, Md., 1987-89; prog. and environ. permitting mgr. Battelle Tooele Ops., Tooele, Utah, 1990—. Author: NBC vols., 1985; editor: AUS Aviation and NBC Integration Compendium, 1988. Deacon, Calvary Bapt. Ch., Bel Air, Md., 1987-89, S.E. Bapt. Ch., Salt Lake City, 1990—; chmn. campaign United Way, Edgewood, 1988-89. Decorated Air Force Commendation medal, Air Force Meritorious Svc. medal with two oak leaf clusters. Republican. Baptist.

OWENS, GWENDOLYN RENNETTA, speech and language therapist; b. Martinsville, Va., Sept. 28, 1940; d. Clarence and Virginia Caroline (Staples) Self; m. Theodore R. Owens, July 1, 1961; children: Sharon Owens Harrison, Christopher. BS, Hampton U., 1961; MA, Oakland U., Rochester, Mich., 1980. Cert. spl. edn. tchr., Calif. Speech therapist El Paso (Tex.) Treatment Ctr., 1961-62, Cerebral Palsy Assn., Niagara Falls, N.y., 1966-68, Med. Coll. of Va., Richmond, 1968-69, San Francisco Schs., 1968-77, Southfield (Mich.) Pub. Schs., 1979-80, San Mateo (Calif.) Sch. Dist., 1980—. Contbg. author: Speech and Language Handbook, 1987. Mem. Calif. Speech and Hearing Assn., San Mateo County Speech Assn. (v.p. 1987—), The Links, Inc. (corr. sec. 1987—), Delta Sigma Theta. Home: 1109 Blythe St Foster City CA 94404-3603

OWENS, K. BUCK, art educator; b. San Antonio, Dec. 7, 1949; s. Kenneth Norwood Owens and Blanche (Buck) Price; m. Kathie Mae Anderson, June 11, 1978; children: Jamie Tera Owens-May, Shawna Christine Owens. BA in Art Edn., Western State Coll., 1971; MA in Visual Art, U. No. Colo., 1992. Cert. art tchr., K-12. Art tchr. Gunnison (Colo.) High Sch., 1971-72; elem. art tchr. Boulder Valley Pub. Schs., 1972-78; middle sch. art tchr. Aurora (Colo.) Pub. Schs., 1978—; middle dist. resource tchr. Aurora Pub. Schs., 1992; K-12 dist. resource tchr. Boulder Pub. Schs., 1977-78. Mem. NEA (Aurora chpt.), Am. Crafts Coun., Colo. Art Edn. Assn. (rep. 1990-94). Democrat. Home: 2178 S Clarkson Denver CO 80210-4502 Office: East Middle Sch 1275 Fraser Aurora CO 80011

OWENS, ROBERT PATRICK, lawyer; b. Spokane, Wash., Feb. 17, 1954; s. Walter Patrick and Cecile (Phillippay) O.; m. Robin Miller, Aug. 12, 1978; children: Ryan Barry, Meghan Jane. BA, Wash. State U., 1976; JD, Gonzaga U., 1981; LLM in Admiralty Law, Tulane U., 1983. Bar: Wash. 1982, Alaska 1984, U.S. Dist. Ct. (ea. dist.) Wash. 1982, U.S. Dist. Ct. Alaska 1984, U.S. Ct. Appeals (5th cir.) 1983. Assoc. Groh, Eggers & Price, Anchorage, 1983-88; mng. atty. Taylor & Hintze, Anchorage, 1988-90; assoc. Copeland, Landye, Bennett and Wolf, Anchorage, 1990—. Coord. supplies Insight Seminars, Anchorage, 1985-86. Mem. ABA (dist. 27 rep. young lawyers div. 1988-90), Alaska Bar Assn., Wash. State Bar Assn., Anchorage Bar Assn. (pres. 1991-92, v.p. 1990-91, pres. young lawyers sect. 1986-88), Alaska Fly Fishers, Phi Alpha Delta. Roman Catholic. Office: Copeland Landye Bennett & Wolf Ste 1350 550 W 7th Ave Anchorage AK 99501-6613

OWENS, STEVEN RALPH, dentist; b. Safford, Ariz., Feb. 2, 1950; s. J. Marvin and Irene (Damron) O.; m. Jammie Stromberg, Aug. 9, 1972; children: Christopher M., Ryan A., Amanda, Ashley. BS, U. Ariz., 1976; DDS, U. Pacific, 1980. Pvt. practice dentistry Alamogordo, N.Mex., 1982-92, Ahwatukee, Ariz., 1993—. Mem. ADA, White Sands Soaring Assn. (pres. 1991-92). Mormon. Home: 1300 N Sycamore Ct Chandler AZ 85224 Office: Ste 114 12020 S Warner-Elliot Loop Phoenix AZ 85044

OWENS, WARNER BARRY, physical therapist; b. Detroit, Apr. 29, 1939; s. Wendell Lee and Flora Lucille (Maddox) O.; m. Frances Hutton, June 11, 1960 (div. May 1973); children—Jeffrey, Karen; m. Sandra Irene Olstyn, Nov. 16, 1974. B.S., UCLA, 1962. Staff phys. therapist Valley Phys. Therapy Ctr., Van Nuys, Calif., 1962-63; chief phys. therapist St. Joseph Med. Ctr., Burbank, Calif., 1963-70, dir. rehab., 1970—, bd. dirs. Credit Union, 1974-76, 83-91, pres., 1986-91; pres. Therapeutic Assocs. Inc., Sherman Oaks, 1992—; dir. Tetrad and Assocs., Sherman Oaks, 1972—; chmn. bd. dirs. Am. Rehab. Network, Inc.; mem. admissions com. phys. therapy option Calif. State U.-Northridge, 1976—. Childrens Hosp. Sch. Phys. Therapy Kate Crutcher scholar, 1961; recipient Outstanding Contbn. to Profession award Calif. State U.-Northridge, 1983. Mem. Am. Phys. Therapy Assn. (chmn. jud. com. 1981-82), Am. Coll. Sports Medicine, Phys. Therapy Dirs. Forum, Internat. Wine and Food Soc. (bd. dirs. San Fernando Valley 1979—, pres. 1980). Republican. Home: 3680 Alomar Dr Sherman Oaks CA 91423-4947 Office: Therapeutic Assocs Inc 4827 N Sepulveda Blvd Sherman Oaks CA 91403

OWINGS, DONALD HENRY, psychology educator; b. Atlanta, Dec. 7, 1943; s. Markley James and Loyce Erin (White) O.; m. Sharon Elizabeth Calhoun, Jan. 29, 1966; children: Ragon Matthew, Anna Rebekah. BA in Psychology, U. Tex., 1965; PhD, U. Wash., 1972. Asst. prof. psychology U. Calif., Davis, 1971-78, assoc. prof., 1978-83, prof., 1983—, chair dept., 1989-93. Contbr. articles to profl. jours., book chpts. NSF rsch. grantee, 1978-80, 82-84. Mem. Animal Behavior Soc., Internat. Soc. for Ecol. Psychology, Internat. Soc. for Behavioral Ecology, Internat. Soc. for Comparative Psychology. Democrat. Home: 815 Oeste Dr Davis CA 95616 Office: U Calif Dept Psychology Davis CA 95616-8686

OWINGS, MARGARET WENTWORTH, conservationist, artist; b. Berkeley, Calif., Apr. 29, 1913; d. Frank W. and Jean (Pond) Wentworth; m. Malcolm Millard, 1937; 1 child, Wendy Millard Benjamin; m. Nathaniel Alexander Owings, Dec. 30, 1953. A.B., Mills Coll., 1934; postgrad., Radcliffe Coll., 1935; LHD, Mills Coll., 1993. One-woman shows include Santa Barbara (Calif.) Mus. Art, 1940, Stanford Art Gallery, 1951, stitchery exhbns. at M.H. De Young Mus., San Francisco, 1963, Internat. Folk Art Mus., Santa Fe, 1965. Commr. Calif. Parks, 1963-69, mem., Nat. Parks Found. Bd, 1968-69; bd. dirs. African Wildlife Leadership Found., 1968-80, Defenders of Wildlife, 1969-74; founder, pres. Friends of the Sea Otter, 1969-90; chair Calif. Mountain Lion Preservation Found., 1987; trustee Environmental Def. Fund, 1972-83; Regional trustee Mills Coll., 1962-68. Recipient Gold medal, Conservation Svc. award U.S. Dept. Interior, 1975, Converva-tion award Calif. Acad. Scis., 1979, Am. Motors Conservation award, 1980, Joseph Wood Krutch medal Humane Soc. U.S., Nat. Audubon Soc. medal, 1983, A. Starker Leopole award Calif. Nature Conservancy, 1986, Gold medal UN Environment Program, 1988, Conservation award DAR, 1990, Disting. Svc. award Sierra Club, 1991. Home: Grimes Point Big Sur CA 93920

OWREN, MICHAEL J., psychologist; b. Oslo, July 19, 1955; s. Leif and Ingrid (Rømming) O. BA, Reed Coll., Portland, 1977; PhD, Ind. U., 1986. Researcher U. Calif., Davis, 1986-90, U. Pa., Phila., 1986-90; asst. prof. psychology U. Colo., Denver, 1990—. Contbr. articles to profl. jours. Nat. Insts. Health fellow, 1986-88. Mem. Am. Psychol. Soc., Am. Soc. Primatologists, Animal Behavior Soc., Acoustical Soc. Am., Sigma Xi. Office: U Colo Dept Psychology Campus Box 173 PO Box 173364 Denver CO 80217-3364

OXENHANDLER, DAVID, college administrator; b. New Britain, Conn., May 31, 1958; s. Issac Benyamin and Tehila (Berenstien) O.; m. Nancy Sue Fineberg, June 10, 1984; children: Daniel, Jenna-Beth. BS in Bus., U. Conn., 1980; MBA, U. Mass., 1985. CFO Am. br. Internat. Artists, Northampton, Mass., 1981-83; planning and control mgr. Tex. Instruments, Dallas, Colorado Springs, Colo., 1985-90; v.p. fin., CFO Colo. Tech., Colorado Springs, 1990—. Office: Colo Tech 4435 N Cedar St Colorado Springs CO 80907

OZANICH, CHARLES GEORGE, real estate broker; b. Fayette County, Pa. Aug. 11, 1933; s. Paul Anthony and Alma Bertha (Sablotne) O.; student Am. River Coll., Sierra Coll.; m. Betty Sue Carman, Feb. 20, 1955; children: Viki Lynn, Terri Sue, Charles Anthony, Nicole Lee. Owner, broker Terrace Realty, Basic Realty, Grass Valley, Calif., 1971—; compliance inspector Dept. Vets. Affairs. Mem. Grass Valley Vol. Fire Dept., 1965-93. Served with USAF, 1951-55; Korea. Decorated Bronze Star with three oak leaf clusters, Korean Presdl. citation, UN citation. Mem. Neveda County Bd. Realtors (dir. 1973-74). Lodges: Masons, Shriners. Nat. Champion award Truck Drivers Roadeo class 5 semi-trailer 18 wheeler div., 1954. Home: 15053 Chinook Ln Grass Valley CA 95945-8846 Office: 10113 Alta Sierra Dr Ste 100 Grass Valley CA 95949-9408

OZANNE MARSH, RICHARD, artist; b. St. Louis, May 20, 1959; s. Ozan J. and Patricia (Benkman) M. Student, Gustave Nebel European Atalier, Cannes, France, 1981; BFA, U. Ariz., 1982; MFA, Ariz. State U., 1992; postgrad, Columbia U. Intern instr. Fairbanks (Alaska) Summer Festival of Arts, 1981; asst. instr. Art Student League, N.Y.C., 1982-86; instructors asst. Chautaugua (N.Y.) Inst., 1982-86; pvt. tchr. Divsn. Related Arts PFA, N.Y.C., 1984-86; pub. demonstrations, lectures various locations, 1986, 88, 90. One-man shows include Hall of Fame Gallery, Ariz., 1982, Mona Bishop Gallery, Sierra Vista, Arizona., 1988, Cantebury Sch. Fine Arts Gallery, 1988, Christchurch New Zealand, 1988, Arizona State U., 1992, Munger Hall, Chautauqua; exhibited in group shows at Indep. Art Exhibitions, 1983-86, Nancy Stein Gallery, N.Y.C., 1985-86, Ariel Galley, N.Y.C., 1990, National Atrs Club, N.Y.C., AAO Gallery, Buffalo, Am. Soc. Fine Arts., N.Y.C., CAA Gallery, Abney Gallery, N.Y.C., 1992-93, Chautaugua, Salmagundi Club, N.Y.C.; represented in permanent collections USSR Ministy Culture, Moscow, Cantebury Soc. Arts, First Christian Ch., Lifequest Corp.; contbr. covers to books, mags., records. Recipient First Prize award Chautaugua Soc. for Peace, Bestor Plaza Festival, 1985; Helen Tempe Logan scholar, 1984, Divsn. Related Arts Traveling scholar, 1990.. Mem. Art Students League N.Y., N.Y. Art Equity Assn. Home: 122 S Hardy Tempe AZ 85281

OZERNOY, LEONID MOISSEY, astrophysicist; b. Moscow, May 19, 1939; came to U.S., 1986, naturalized citizen; m. Marianne Rosen; 2 children. BS in Physics, Moscow State U., 1961, MS in Astronomy, 1963; PhD in Astrophysics, Shternberg Astron. Inst., Moscow, 1966; DSc in Astrophysics, Lebedev Phys. Inst., USSR Acad. Scis., Moscow, 1971. Rsch. scientist, dept. theoretical physics Lebedev Phys. Inst., 1966-71, sr. rsch. scientist, 1971-86; asst. then assoc. prof. Moscow Physics and Tech. Inst., 1968-79, fired after applying for emigration from USSR; prof. astrophysics, disting. vis. scientist Ctr. for Astrophysics, Harvard Coll. Obs. and Smithsonian Astrophys. Obs., Cambridge, Mass., 1986-89; prof. astrophysics, disting. vis. scholar Inst. Geophysics and Planetary Physics, Los Alamos (N.Mex.) Nat. Lab., 1989-91; sr. assoc. Nat. Rsch. Coun.-NAS Goddard Space Flight Ctr., NASA, Greenbelt, Md., 1991-92, sr. rsch. scientist Univ. Space Rsch. Assn., 1993—; prof. computational sci. and space sci. Inst. Computational Sci. and Informatics, George Mason U., Fairfax, Va., 1993—; vis. prof. Boston U., 1986-87, Harvard U., 1987; mem. sci. coun. on plasma astrophysics, Presidium of USSR Acad. Scis., 1971-75. Co-editor Astrophysics and Space Scis. mag., 1976-86; author several books and over 200 sci. papers in theoretical astrophysics and related fields. Recipient Silver medal USSR Exhbn. of Achievements in Nat. Economy, 1968; NRC/NASA rsch. assoc., 1991. Fellow Am. Phys. Soc. (com. on internat. freedom of scientists 1988-90); mem. AAAS, Internat. Astron. Union, N.Y. Acad. Scis., Am. Astron. Soc. (exec. com. high energy astrophysics div. 1989-90), Astron. Soc. Pacific, COSPAR (Com. Space Rsch., Internat. Coun. Sci. Unions), The Planetary Soc., Internat. Platform Assn. Office: NASA Goddard Space Flight Ctr Lab Astronomy and Solar Physics Code 685 Greenbelt MD 20771 also: George Mason U Inst Computat Sci & Inform Sci and Tech Bldg I Fairfax VA 22030-4444

PABST, RALPH MALCOM, import-export, publishing and mining executive; b. Macon, Ga., Nov. 2, 1920; s. Eugene Price and Beatrice I. (Kenney) Jernigan; adopted s. George A. Pabst; children: Genevieve A. Martinez, Yvonne M. Pierce, George P. BFA, Bradley U.; postgrad., Brigham Young U., Jones Bus. Coll., Fla.; DO, Anglo-Am. Inst. Drugless Therapy, Eng. Owner, mgr. Bam's Overseas Treasures; pres. The Augury Press; pres., chmn. bd. Greater Denver-Phoenix Mining Co., Inc.; chmn. bd. Am. Entertainment Corp., Commodity Exch. U.S.A.; mem. Consular Corps, Washington. Author: Plodding toward Terror, Away and Beyond, Executive Handbook, The Spoofiness Lexicon, Match Wits, I Rementer Cuisine's Finest Moments, Zodiac of Life, Renew Your Life through God, The Handiwork of God in the Holy Land, Mental Telepathy, Astral Peer, God's Handwriting, Hitler the Occultist, Top Hat, Bugsy Siegel/Betty Woods Memories, Jacob von Walzer, Facts: Then and Now, J F K, "The Whole Trust...So Help Me...," Kenney and Allied Families, The Cowart/Jernigan Allied Families. Dep. sheriff, Ariz., Nev., Mass. Officer USN, World War II. Decorated knight grand officer Ancient and Imperial Order of Crescent (Eng.), knight Order St. Dennis of Zante, (Greece), King Peter of Yugoslavia; recipient award Freedoms Found. at Valley Forge, Acad. Palms class A, Internat. Am. Inst.; named Ky. col., lt. col. Ala., marshall Phoenix Rep. Com. Mem. Nat. Sheriffs Assn. (life), Navy League (life), SAR (past treas. gen., gold citizenship medal, Patriot's medal, Minute Man award), Mayflower Soc., Sons and Daus. Pilgrims (life), Soc. Colonial Wars, Soc. Founders and Patriots, Desc. Colonial Clergy (life), Huguenot Soc., St. Andrew's Soc., St. George's Soc., Nat. Sojurners (life), Masons (32d degree), Son of a Witch (pres. gen.). Address: PO Box 40355 Phoenix AZ 85067

PACAL, JOSEPH FRANK, human ecology educator, lifestyle consultant; b. Glendale, Calif., Oct. 5, 1952; s. Albert John and Irma (Frey) P.; m. Marlies Schade, July 26, 1983 (div. Sept. 1990); children: Maluhia, Naniola. Field support Arctic Rsch. Lab., U. Ala., Barrow, 1975-76; actor Twentieth Century Fox, Telluride, Colo., 1978; instr. Telluride Ski Sch., 1978-79; project mgr. Winterstash Food Coop., Telluride, 1979-80; dir. Ctr. for Ecol. Living, Haiku, Hawaii, 1983-92; presenter Lifestyle Ecology, Telluride, 1992—. Author: The Art of Living, 1991; actor, writer (play) Hatching Out, 1988; writer, editor Lifestyle Ecology newsletter, 1988—. Democrat. Home and Office: Lifestyle Ecology PO Box 1955 Telluride CO 81435

PACE, BROOKS, real estate executive; b. St. George, Utah, Dec. 1, 1942; s. Andrew B. and Verda (Follett) P.; m. Sephanie Fish, Sept. 6, 1966 (div. Apr. 1974); 1 child, Nicola; m. June Bob Owens, Oct. 8, 1983; children: Andy, Matt, Cris. BS, U. Utah, 1966. Pres. The Dammeron Corp., Dammeron Valley, Utah, 1976—. Chairman adv. panel Redevelopment Agy. City of St. George, 1990-91. Capt. U.S. Army, 1960-71, ETO. Office: The Dammeron Corp 1 Dammeron Valley Dr Dammeron Valley UT 84783-5149

PACE, DENNY F., business consultant, educator; b. Clemenceau, Ariz., Aug. 27, 1926; s. LeRoy and Mauretta (Eager) P.; m. Eleanor Ruth Brown, May 19, 1946 (div. 1988); children: Cynthia Ann Nicholson, Susan C. Groscup, Taina Pace Bucci. BA, U. So. Calif., 1955, MPA, 1964; EdD, Tex. A&M U., 1975. Police officer City of L.A., 1947-64; dep. regional adminstr. U.S. Dept. Justice, Dallas, 1971-73; prof. Long Beach City Coll., Calif. State U., 1975-89; owner, cons. Pace & Assocs., Huntington Beach, Calif., 1985—; cons. Westinghouse Electric Co., Washington, 1974-75, Pub. Adminstrn. Svc. Chgo., 1973-75. Author: (with Denny) Concepts of Organized Crime, 1975, rev., 1991, (award 1991), Concepts of Community Relations, 1985, rev. 1991, (award 1991), (with others) Vice Control, 1974, rev., 1991, Narcotics Control, 1973, rev., 1991. With USMC, 1942-45; staff sgt. U.S. Army, 1951. Decorated Purple Heart L.A. Police Dept. Mem. Am. Social. Assn., Calif. Assn. Criminal Justice Edn., Masons. Home and Office: 3842 Montego Dr Huntington Beach CA 92649-2006

PACE, LORIN NELSON, lawyer, state official; b. Miami, Ariz., Aug. 15, 1925; s. Levi Wilson and Sentella (Nelson) P.; m. Marylynn Haymore, July 26, 1950; children: Grant F., Lee W., Stanley L., Mark L. Lorraine Brown, Maurine Worsham, Lynn H., Deanna Lambson, Bradley W., Teresa Segura. Student, Kans. State Tchr. Coll., 1944; BA, Brigham Young U., 1951; LLB, JD, U. Utah, 1952. Bar: Utah 1953. Ins. adjuster Gen. of Am., Salt Lake City, 1953-54; pvt. practice law Richfield, Utah, 1954-55, Salt Lake City, 1960—; vice consul, 3rd. sec. U.S. State Dept., Washington, 1955-56; mission pres. Ch. Jesus Christ of Latter-day Saints, Buenos Aires, Argentina, 1956-60; cons. on mcpl. tax code and nat. assembly reform COMURES, ISDEM, El Salvador, 1992. Author: There Ought to Be a Law--and Why There Isn't, 1972. State legislator Utah House Reps., Salt Lake City, 1968-86; state senator Utah State Senate, Salt Lake City, 1986—. 2nd lt. USAAF, 1943-45. Republican. Mem. LDS Church. Home: 2386 Olympus Dr Salt Lake City UT 84124-2812 Office: 36 S State 12th St Salt Lake City UT 84111-1401

PACE, ROBERT KELLEY, JR., finance educator; b. Wichita Falls, Tex., Mar. 19, 1957; s. Robert Kelley Sr. and Armour Katrine (Grey) P.; m. Shuifen Shen, Dec. 28, 1986. BA, Coll. Idaho, 1979; PhD, U. Ga., 1985. Asst. prof. U. Houston, 1982-85; asst. prof. U. Alaska, Fairbanks, 1986-89, assoc. prof., 1990—; mem. pension planning com. U. Alaska, Fairbanks, 1988—, mem. optional retirement com., 1990—. Contbr. articles to profl. jours. Herbert U. Nelson scholarship Nat. Assn. of Realtors, 1979, Mellon Found. grant, 1987, Internat. Assn. of Assessing Officers grant. Mem. Am. Stats. Assn., Inst. of Math. Stats., Am. Real Estate and Urban Econs. Assn., Am. Real Estate Soc., Fin. Mgmt. Assn. Home: PO Box 84574 Fairbanks AK 99708 Office: U Alaska Fairbanks AK 99775

PACELA, ALLAN FRED, publisher, editor; b. Chgo., Oct. 5, 1938; s. John Paul and Eleanor M. (Sorge) P.; children from previous marriage: Elizabeth Jean, David Allan, John Allan; m. Ramona Bachich, Feb. 14, 1987. BSEE, MIT, 1960; MS in Math., U. Miami, Coral Gables, Fla., 1962; DS Med. Engring., Ind. No. U., 1971. Sr. scientist Lear Siegler Med. Lab., Santa Monica, Calif., 1963-64; rsch. scientist Beckman Instruments, Fullerton, Calif., 1964-72; pres., gen. mgr. Interscience Tech. Corp., Brea, Calif., 1972-88; editor, pub. Quest Pub. Co., Brea, 1970—; tech. and editorial cons. Inventor Bilateral Impedance Plethysmograph, Apnea Alarm for monitoring premature sudden infant death syndrome. Mem. IEEE, Assn. for the Advancement of Med. Instrumentation. Office: Quest Pub Co 1351 Titan Way Brea CA 92621-3708

PACHECO, MANUEL TRINIDAD, university president; b. Rocky Ford, Colo., May 30, 1941; s. Manuel J. and Elizabeth (Lopez) P.; m. Karen M. King, Aug. 27, 1966; children: Daniel Mark, Andrew Charles, Sylvia Lois Elizabeth. BA, N.Mex. Highlands U., 1962; MA, Ohio State U., 1966, PhD, 1969. Prof. edn., univ. dean Tex. A&I U., Laredo, 1972-77, exec. dir. Bilingual Edn. Ctr., Kingsville, 1980-82; prof. multicultural edn., chmn. dept. San Diego State U., 1977-78; prof. Spanish and edn. Laredo State U., 1978-80, pres., 1984-88; assoc. dean Coll. Edn. U. Tex., El Paso, 1982-84, exec. dir. for planning, 1984; chief policy aide for edn. to gov. N.Mex., 1984; pres. U. Houston-Downtown, 1988-91, U. Ariz., Tucson, 1991—; bd. trustees Ednl. Testing Svc., Princeton, N.J., 1987—; cons. lang. div. Ency. Britannica, 1965-72; bd. dirs. Valley Nat. Bank Corp. Co-editor: Handbook for Planning and Managing Instruction in Basic Skills for Limited English Proficient Students, 1983; producer: (videotapes) Teacher Training, 1976. Treas. adv. com. U.S. Commn. on Civil Rights, L.A., 1987-91; trustee United Way of Houston, 1988-91; chmn. pub. rels. Buffalo Bayou Partnership, Houston, 1988-91; bd. dirs. Ctr. for Addiction and Substance Abuse, Greater Tucson Econ. Coun., Ariz. Econ. Coun., Ariz. Town Hall. Recipient Disting. Alumnus award Ohio State U., Columbus, 1984; named Most Prominent Am.-Hispancis Spanish Today mag., 1984, one of 100 Outstanding Hispanics Hispanic bus., 1988, Man of Yr. Hispanic Profl. Action Com., 1991; Fulbright fellow U. de Montepellier, France, 1962. Mem. Am. Assn. State Colls. and Univs., Nat. Acad. of Pub. Adminstrn., Hispanic Assn. Colls. and Univs., Tex. Assn. of Chicanos in Higher Edn., Rotary, Phi Delta Kappa. Office: U Ariz Office of Pres Tucson AZ 85721

PACHECO, ROBERT CHARLES, estate planner; b. Providence, R.I., Oct. 18, 1944; s. Charles C. and Rita E. (Rezendes) P.; m. Anita L. Grow, Oct. 30, 1976; children: Michael W., Stephen C., Christopher R. B of Bus., U. Nev., 1965. From agt. to mgr. to regional v.p. various ins. cos., San Jose, Calif., 1965-78; pres. The Pacheco Agy., Sparks, Nev., 1978—; cons. Kaskie and Rand, Reno, 1990—; advisor Interstate Assurance, Des Moines, 1987—; speaker in field. Contbr. articles to profl. jours. Mem. Jr. C. of C., Reno, 1972. Staff sgt. U.S. Army res., 1965-72. Republican. Roman Catholic. Office: The Pacheco Agy 731 Greenbrae Dr Sparks NV 89431

PACIFIC, JOSEPH NICHOLAS, JR., educator; b. Honolulu, Oct. 27, 1950; s. Joseph Nicholas Sr. and Christine Mary (Mondelli) P.; m. Paulette Kay Miller, July 7, 1975. BA in Math., BS in Biology, BSEE, Gonzaga U., 1974; MMSc in Clin. Microbiology, Emory U., 1978. Cert. tchr., Hawaii, Wash. Rsch. specialist Ctr. Disease Control, Atlanta, 1978-82; supr. Joe Pacific Shoe Repair, Honolulu, 1983; lab. technician Mont. State U., Bozeman, 1984; sci. tchr. Hawaii Preparatory Acad., Kamuela, 1985-87; unit mgr. Hawaii Med. Service Assn., Honolulu, 1987-88; tchr. biology St. Andrew's Priory Sch., Honolulu, 1988—. Mem. Nat. Registry Microbiologists, Sigma Xi, Pi Mu Epsilon, Phi Sigma, Kappa Delta Pi, Alpha sigma Nu. Home: 2313 Kaola Way Honolulu HI 96813 Office: St Andrew's Priory Sch 224 Queen Emma Sq Honolulu HI 96813-2388

PACK, PHOEBE KATHERINE FINLEY, civic worker; b. Portland, Oreg., Feb. 2, 1907; d. William Lovell and Irene (Barnhart) Finley; student U. Calif., Berkeley, 1926-27; B.A., U. Oreg., 1930; m. Arthur Newton Pack, June 11, 1936; children: Charles Lathrop, Phoebe Irene. Layman referee Pima County Juvenile Ct., Tucson, 1958-71; mem. pres.'s council Menninger Found., Topeka; mem. Alcoholism Council So. Ariz., 1960—; bd. dirs. Kress Nursing Sch., Tucson, 1957-67, Pima County Assn. for Mental Health, 1958—, Ariz. Assn. for Mental Health, Phoenix, 1963-—, U. Ariz. Found., Casa de los Niños Crisis Nursery; co-founder Ariz.-Sonora Desert Mus., Tucson, 1975—, Ghost Ranch Found., N.Mex.; bd. dirs. Tucson Urban League, Tucson YMCA Youth Found. Mem. Mt. Vernon Ladies Assn. Union (state vice regent, 1962-84),Mt. Vernon One Hundred (founder), Nature Conservancy (life), Alpha Phi. Home: Villa Compana 6653 E Carondelet Dr Apt 415 Tucson AZ 85710-2153

PACK, RUSSELL T, theoretical chemist; b. Grace, Idaho, Nov. 20, 1937; s. John Terrell and Mardean (Izatt) P.; m. Marion Myrth Hassell, Aug. 21, 1962; children: John R., Nathan H., Allen H., Miriam, Elizabeth, Quinn R., Howard H. BS, Brigham Young U., 1962; PhD, U. Wis., 1967. Postdoctoral fellow U. Minn., Mpls., 1966-67; asst. prof. Brigham Young U., Provo, 1967-71; assoc. prof. Brigham Young U., 1971-75, adj. prof., 1975—; staff scientist Los Alamos (N.Mex.) Nat. Lab., 1975-83, fellow, 1983—, assoc. grp. leader, 1979-81; vis. prof. Max Planck Institut, Gottingen, 1981; chmn. Gordon Rsch. Conf., 1982; lectr. in field. Contbr. articles to profl. jours. Named Sr. U.S. Scientist, Alexander Vol Humboldt Found., 1981. Fellow Am. Phys. Soc. (sec.-treas. div. Chem. Physics 1990-93); mem. Am. Chem. Soc., Sigma Xi. Mem. Ch. of Jesus Christ of Latter Day Saints. Home: 240 Kimberly Ln Los Alamos NM 87544-3526 Office: Los Alamos National Lab T-12 MS B268 Los Alamos NM 87545

PACKARD, DAVID, manufacturing company executive, electrical engineer; b. Pueblo, Colo., Sept. 7, 1912; s. Sperry Sidney and Ella Lorna (Graber) P.; m. Lucile Salter, Apr. 8, 1938 (dec., 1987); children: David Woodley, Nancy Ann Packard Burnett, Susan Packard Orr, Julie Elizabeth Stephens. B.A., Stanford U., 1934, EE, 1939; LLD (hon.), U. Calif., Santa Cruz, 1966, Catholic U., 1970, Pepperdine U., 1972; DSc (hon.), Colo. Coll., 1964; LittD (hon.), So. Colo. State Coll., 1973; D.Eng. (hon.), U. Notre Dame, 1974. With vacuum tube engrng. dept. Gen. Electric Co., Schenectady, 1936-38; co-founder, ptnr. Hewlett-Packard Co., Palo Alto, Calif., 1939-47, pres., 1947-64, chief exec. officer, 1964-68, chmn. bd., 1964-68, 72—; U.S. dep. sec. defense Washington, 1969-71; dir. Genetech, Inc., 1981-92; bd. dirs. Beckman Laser Inst. and Med. Clinic; chmn. Presdl. Commn. on Def. Mgmt., 1985-86; mem. White House Sci. Coun., 1982-88. Mem. President's Commn. Pers. Interchange, 1972-74, President's Coun. Advisors on Sci. and Tech., 1990-92, Trilateral Commn., 1973-81, Dirs. Coun. Exploratorium, 1987-90; pres. bd. regents Uniformed Svcs. U. of Health Scis., 1975-82; mem. U.S.-USSR Trade and Econ. Coun., 1975-82; mem. bd. overseers Hoover Instn., 1972—; bd. dirs. Nat. Merit Scholarship Corp., 1963-69, Found. for Study of Presdl. and Congl. Terms, 1978-86, Alliance to Save Energy, 1977-87, Atlantic Coun., 1972-83, vice chmn., 1972-80, Am. Enterprise Inst. for Public Policy Rsch., 1978—, Nat. Fish and Wildlife Found., 1985-87, Hitachi Found. Adv. Coun., 1986—; vice chmn. The Calif. Nature Conservancy, 1983-90; trustee Stanford U., 1954-69, pres., 1958-60, David and Lucile Packard Found., pres., chmn. 1964—, Herbert Hoover Found., 1974—, Monterey Bay Aquarium Found., chmn., 1978—, The Ronald Reagan Presdl. Found., 1986-91, Monterey Bay Aquarium Rsch. Inst., chmn., pres. 1987—. Decorated Grand Cross of Merit Fed. Republic of Germany, 1972, Medal Honor Electronic Industries, 1974; numerous other awards including Silver Helmet Def. award AMVETS, 1973, Washington award Western Soc. Engrs., 1975, Hoover medal ASME, 1975, Gold Medal award Nat. Football Found. and Hall of Fame, 1975, Good Scout award Boy Scouts Am., 1975, Vermilye medal Franklin Inst., 1976, Internat. Achievement award World Trade Club of San Francisco, 1976, Merit award Am. Cons. Engrs. Council Fellows, 1977, Achievement in Life award Ency. Britannica, 1977, Engrng. Award of Distinction San Jose State U., 1980, Thomas D. White Nat. Def. award USAF Acad., 1981, Disting. Info. Scis. award Data Processing Mgmt. Assn., 1981, Sylvanus Thayer award U.S. Mil. Acad., 1982, Environ. Leadership award Natural Resources Def. Council, 1983, Dollar award Nat. Fgn. Trade Council, 1985, Gandhi Humanitarium Award, 1988, Roback Award Nat. Contract Mgmt. Assn., 1988, Pub. Welfare Medal NAS, 1989, Chevron Conservation Award, 1989, Doolittle Award Hudson Inst., 1989, Disting. Citizens Award Commonwealth Club San Francisco, 1989, William Wildback award, Nat. Conf. Standards Labs., Washington, 1990; named to Silicon Valley Engrng. Hall of Fame, Silicon Valley Engrng. Coun., 1991, Pueblo (Colo.) Hall of Fame, 1991. Fellow IEEE (Founders medal 1973); mem. Nat. Acad. Engrng. (Founders award 1979), Instrument Soc. Am. (hon. lifetime mem.), Wilson Council, The Bus. Roundtable, Bus. Council, Am. Ordnance Assn. (Crozier Gold medal 1970,) Henry M. Jackson award 1988, Nat. Medal Tech. 1988, Presdl. Medal of Freedom 1988, Sigma Xi, Phi Beta Kappa, Tau Beta Pi, Alpha Delta Phi (Disting. Alumnus of Yr. 1970). Office: Hewlett-Packard Co PO Box 10301 Palo Alto CA 94304-1112

PACKARD, JULIE, aquarium administrator; d. David and Lucile P. Exec. dir. Monterey Bay Aquarium, Monterey, Calif., 1984—. Office: Monterey Bay Aquarium 886 Cannery Row Monterey CA 93940-1085

PACKARD, ROBERT GOODALE, III, planner; b. Denver, Apr. 12, 1951; s. Robert and Mary Ann (Woodward) P.; m. Jane Ann Collins, Aug. 25, 1973; children: Jessica Nelson, Robert Gregg. BA, Willamette U., 1973; M in Urban and Regional Planning/Community Devel., U. Colo., 1976. Project mgr. Environ. Disiciplines, Inc., Portland, Oreg., 1973-75; asst. dir. planning Portland Pub. Schs., 1976-78; dir. planning Bur. of Parks, Portland, 1978-79; dir. planning and urban design Zimmer Gunsul Frasca, Portland, 1979-81, dir. project devel., 1981-84, mng. ptnr., 1984—; pres. Art Celebration, Inc. 1986-88. Co-author: The Baker Neighborhood/Denver, 1976. Contbr. articles to profl. jours. Mem. City of Portland Waterfront Commn., 1982-83; mem. Mayor's Task Force for Joint Use of Schs., Portland, 1979-80; mem. Washington Park Master Plan Steering com., Portland, 1980-81; bd. dirs. Washington Park Zoo, 1983-86, pres. Arts Celebration Inc./Artquake, 1986—. New Rose Theatre, 1981-83; dir., pres. Grant Park Neighborhood Assn., Portland, 1981-83; mem. Pioneer Sq. Bd., 1992, Archtl. Found. Oreg., 1992. Recipient Spl. Citation, Nat. Sch. Bds. Assn., 1978; Meritorious Planning Project award Am. Planning Assn., 1980, Nat. Am. Planning Assn., 1981; Meritorious Design award Am. Soc. Landscape Architects, 1981; Honor award Progressive Arch., 1983. Mem. AIA (assoc.), Am. Planning Assn., Soc. Mktg. Profls. Clubs: City. Home: 3313 SW Fairmount Blvd Portland OR 97201-1478 Office: Zimmer Gunsul Frasca Ptnrship 320 SW Oak St Ste 500 Portland OR 97204-2737

PACKARD, RONALD, congressman; b. Meridian, Idaho, Jan. 19, 1931; m. Jean Sorenson, 1952; children: Chris, Debbie, Jeff, Vicki, Scott, Lisa, Theresa. Student, Brigham Young U., 1948-50, Portland State U., 1952-53; D.M.D., U. Oreg., Portland, 1953-57. Gen. practice dentistry Carlsbad, Calif., 1959-82; mem. 98th-103rd Congresses from 43rd (now 48th) Dist. Calif., 1983—; mem. appropriations com. 103rd Congress from 43rd Dist. Calif., mem. pub. works and transp. com., sci., space and tech. com. Mem. Carlsbad Sch. Dist. Bd., 1960-72; bd. dirs. Carlsbad C. of C., 1972-76; mem. Carlsbad Planning Commn., 1974-76, Carlsbad City Coun., 1976-78; Carlsbad chmn. Boy Scouts Am., 1977-79; mayor City of Carlsbad, 1978-82; mem. North County Armed Svcs. YMCA, North County Transit Dist., San Diego Assn. Govts., Coastal Policy Com., Transp. Policy Com.; pres. San Diego div. Calif. League of Cities. Served with Dental Corps USN, 1957-59. Republican. Mem. Ch. LDS. Office: House Office Bldg 2162 Rayburn Washington DC 20515

PACKER, BOYD K., church official. Mem. Quorum of the Twelve, Ch. of Jesus Christ of Latter-Day Saints. Office: LDS Church 50 E North Temple Salt Lake Cty UT 84150-0001

PACKER, MARK BARRY, lawyer, financial consultant, foundation official; b. Phila., Sept. 18, 1944; s. Samuel and Eve (Devine) P.; AB magna cum laude, Harvard U., 1965, LLB, 1968; m. Donna Elizabeth Ferguson; children—Daniel Joshua, Benjamin Dov, David Johannes. Bar: Wash. 1969, Mass. 1971. Assoc. Ziontz, Pirtle & Fulle, Seattle, 1968-70; pvt. practice, Bellingham, 1972—; bd. dirs., corp. sec. BMJ Holdings (formerly No. Sales Co., Inc.), 1977—; trustee No. Sales Profit Sharing Plan, 1977—; bd. dirs., corp. sec., gen. counsel Dr. Cookie, Inc., 1981-92. Mem. Bellingham Planning and Devel. Commn., 1975-84, chmn., 1977-81, mem. shoreline subcom., 1976-82; pres. Congregation Beth Israel, Bellingham, 1980-82; mem. Bellingham Mcpl. Arts Commn., 1986-91, landmark rev. bd., 1987-91; chmn. Bellingham campaign United Jewish Appeal, 1979-90; bd. dirs. Whatcom Community Coll. Found., 1989-92; lit. tutor Whatcom Lit. Coun., 1988-90; trustee, chmn. program com. Bellingham Pub. Sch. Found., 1991—; discussion leader, short story/novella reading group, 1988-92; active Heavy Culture classic lit. group, 1991—, Jewish studies group, 1993—; mng. trustee Bernard M. & Audrey Jaffe Found. Recipient Blood Donor award ARC, 1979, 8-Gallon Pin, 1988, Mayor's Arts award City of Bellingham, 1993. Mem. ABA (sec. real property probate and trust), Wash. State Bar Assn. (sec. environ. and land use law, com. law-related edn. 1990-92, sec. bus. law, sec. real property, probate and trust, com. law examiners 1992—).

PACKNETT, DON STEVENSON, meteorologist; b. DeQueen, Ark., Mar. 9, 1931; s. William S. and Edith L. (Maddry) P.; m. June Stires, June 19, 1954; children: Mark, Sandra. BS, Ariz. State U., 1953; postgrad., UCLA, 1953-54, U. Mich., 1962-64; MS, Tex. A & M U., 1959. Commd. 2d lt. USAF, 1953, advanced through grades to lt. col., 1971, advanced weather officer, 1953-73, ret., 1973; staff meteorologist Stearns-Roger Engrng., Denver, 1973-83; meteorol. cons. Colorado Springs, Colo., 1983-85; sr. environ. scientist Gen. Rsch. Corp., Colorado Springs, 1985-90; forensic meteorol. cons. Colorado Springs, 1990—; cons. PPG Industries, Pitts., 1973-85, United Engrs., Denver, 1983-85, Dept. Energy, Columbus, Ohio, 1980-85. Author over 250 tech. reports. Mem. Am. Meteorol. Soc. (cert. cons. meteorologist 1974, chmn. tech. sessions 1978-83), Nat. Coun. Indsl. Meteorologists (pres. 1982-83). Home and Office: 1607 Babcock Ln Colorado Springs CO 80915-1427

PACKWOOD, BOB, senator; b. Portland, Oreg., Sept. 11, 1932; s. Frederick William and Gladys (Taft) P.; children: William Henderson, Shyla. BA, Willamette U., 1954; LLB, NYU, 1957; LLB (hon.), Yeshiva U., 1982, Gallaudet Coll., 1983. Bar: Oreg. Law clerk to Justice Harold J. Warner Oreg. Supreme Ct., 1957-58; pvt. atty., 1958-68; Chmn. Multnomah County Rep. Cen. Com., 1960-62; mem. Oreg. Legislature, 1963-69; U.S. senator from Oreg., 1969—, chmn. small bus. com., 1981-84, chmn. commerce com., 1981-85, chmn. fin. com., 1985-86, ranking min. mem. fin. com., 1987—. Mem. Internat. Working Group of Parliamentarians on Population and Devel., 1977; mem. Pres.'s Commn. on Population Growth and the Am. Future, 1972; chmn. Nat. Rep. Senatorial Com., 1977-78, 81-82; bd. dirs. NYU, 1970; bd. overseers Lewis and Clark Coll., Portland, 1966. Named One of Three Outstanding Young Men of Oreg., 1967; Portland's Jr. 1st Citizen, 1966; Oreg. Speaker of Yr., 1968; recipient Arthur T. Vanderbilt award NYU Sch. Law, 1970; Anti-Defamation League Brotherhood award, 1971; Torch of Liberty award B'nai B'rith, 1971; Richard L. Neuberger award Oreg. Environ. Coun., 1972; Conservation award Omaha Woodmen Life Ins. Soc., 1974; Monongahela Forestry Leadership award, 1976; Solar Man of Yr., Solar Energy Industries Assn., 1980; Guardian of Small Bus. award Nat. Fedn. Ind. Bus., 1980; Forester of Yr., Western Forest Industries Assn., 1980; Am. Israel Friendship award B'nai Zion, 1982; Grover C. Cobb award Nat. Assn. Broadcasters, 1982; Religious Freedom award, Religious Coalition for Abortion Rights, 1983; 22d Ann. Conv. award, Oreg. State Bldg. and Constrn. Trade Council, 1983; United Cerebral Palsy Humanitarian award, 1984; Am. Heart Assn. Pub. Affairs award, 1985; Margaret Sanger award Planned Parenthood Assn., 1985; Worth his Wheat in Gold award for leadership on tax reform Gen. Mills., 1986; Am. Assn. Homes for the Aging for Outstanding Svc. in cause of elderly, 1987; NARAL award for congrl. leadership, 1987; James Madison award Nat. Broadcast Editorial Assn., 1987; Pub. Excellence award First Ann. Jacob K. Javits, 1987; Golden Bulldog award Watchdogs of Treasury, Inc., 1988, 90; Sound Dollar award, 1989; Golden Eagle award Nurse Anesthetists, 1990; John. F. Hogan Disting. Svc. award Radio-TV News Dirs. for def. of First Amendment, 1991; Nat. Conf. Soviet Jewry recognition, 1992, numerous others. Mem. Oreg. Bar Assn., D.C. Bar Assn., Beta Theta Pi. Office: US Senate 259 Russell Senate Bldg Washington DC 20510-3702

PADDEN, ROBIN REINHARD, electrical engineer; b. Boulder City, Nev., Aug. 17, 1951; s. Thomas J. and Janet Merritt (Harris) P.; m. Pamela Annette Hilbert, June 27, 1981; children: Edward, Michael, Elizabeth. AA, U. Nev., 1971; BS, Calif. Poly. Inst., 1976; MS, Stanford U., 1978. Engr. USN Postgrad. Sch., Monterey, Calif., 1978; rsch. engr. SRI Internat., Palo Alto, Calif., 1978-84; engr. Algotek, Redwood City, Calif., 1984-85, Iomega Corp., Roy, Utah, 1985—; cons. Eyring Rsch. Inst., Provo, Utah, 1990-91. Patentee in field. Cons. Deaf Info. Citizens Orgn., Fremont, Calif., 1984; deaf interpreter State of Utah, Bountiful, 1992. Mem. IEEE. Democrat. LDS Ch. Home: 5141 S 2975 W Roy UT 84067 Office: Iomega Corp 1821 W 4000 S Roy UT 84067

PADGET, JOHN E., insurance executive; b. L.A., Aug. 26, 1948; s. LeRoy and Gladys (Black) P. BA, U. Kans., 1969, postgrad., 1970. Instr. bridge Am. Contract Bridge League, 1971-77; owner Hectors, Kirkland, Wash., 1978-84; producer TV show Sta. 2, Oakland, 1985-88; regional mgr. Keithwood Agy.-Am. Health Care Adv., Pleasanter, Calif., 1988—; also bd. dirs. Author: Winning Style, 1977, The Brothers, 1990. Mem. AAAS, Mensa, Internat. Platfrom Soc. Jewish. Office: KWA 4683 Chabot Dr Ste 201 Pleasanton CA 94588-2755

PADGETT, ALAN GREGORY, theology and philosophy educator, clergyman; b. Washington, Sept. 25, 1955; s. C.W. and Mary Louise (Cavalier) P.; m. Sally Victoria Bruyneel, Apr. 30, 1977; 1 child, Luke Edward. BA, So. Calif. Coll., 1977; MDiv, Drew U., 1981; DPhil, Oxford (Eng.) U., 1989. Ordained to ministry United Meth. Ch., 1979. Youth pastor Bloomfield (N.J.) Presbyn. Ch., 1978-79; assoc. pastor San Dieguito United Meth. Ch., Encinitas, Calif., 1981-82; pastor San Jacinto (Calif.) United Meth. Ch., 1982-86; adj. prof. So. Calif. Coll., Costa Mesa, 1984-90, Orange Coast Coll., Costa Mesa, 1989-90; asst. prof. philosophy Bethel Coll., St. Paul, 1990-92; assoc. prof. theology and philosophy of sci. Azusa (Calif.) Pacific U., 1992—; vis. lectr. U. Durham, Eng., 1989; theology cons. Pew Charitable Trust, 1992-93; coord. Minn. Student Philosophy Conf., 1992. Author: God, Eternity and the Nature of Time, 1992, The Mission of the Church in Methodist Perspective, 1992; contbr. articles to religious jours. John Wesley fellow, 1986-89; rsch. grantee Ralph L. Smith Found., 1986-89; Dillistone scholar Oriel Coll., Oxford U., 1988. Mem. Christian Theol. Rsch. Fellowship (founder, pres. 1992—), Am. Acad. Religion, Soc. Christian Philosophers, Philosophy of Sci. Assn., Ctr. for Theology and Natural Sci., Tyndale Fellowship. Democrat. Office: Azusa Pacific U 901 E Alosta St Azusa CA 91702

PADGETT, FRANK DAVID, former associate state supreme court justice; b. Vincennes, Ind., Mar. 9, 1923. LLB, Harvard U., 1948. Bar: Hawaii 1949, U.S. Supreme Ct. 1967. Assoc., then ptnr. Robertson, Castle & Anthony, Honolulu, 1949-66; ptnr. Padgett & Greeley, Honolulu, 1966-67, Padgett, Greeley & Marumoto (and predecessor firms), Honolulu, 1968-74; assoc. judge Intermediate Ct. Appeals State Hawaii, Wailuku and Maui, 1980-82; assoc. justice Hawaii Supreme Ct., Honolulu, 1982-92. Mem. ABA, Hawaii Bar Assn., Assn. Trial Lawyers Am. Office: Supreme Ct Hawaii PO Box 2560 Honolulu HI 96804-2560

PADGETT, JOHN DWAIN, II, small business owner; b. Anchorage, Sept. 25, 1968; s. John Dwain Padgett and Toni Marie (Elmore) Smith. AA, Green River C.C., Auburn, Wash., 1990. Owner, mgr. El Tiburón, Kent, Wash., 1990—. Vol. Ferrets N.W., Mercer Island, Wash., 1989—. With USN, 1988-89. Office: El Tiburón PO Box 3276 Kent WA 98032

PADIAN, KEVIN, paleontologist, educator; b. 1951. BA, Colgate U., 1972, MAT, 1973; M.Phil., Yale U., 1978, PhD, 1980. Assoc. prof. U. Calif., Berkeley, 1980—; cons. mus. and ednl. inst. Author, editor: The Beginning of the Age of Dinosaurs, 1986; contbr. articles to profl. jours. Grantee NSF, 1978-80, 85-89, Nat. Geographic Soc., 1981-82, Am. Chem. Soc., 1981-82, DAAD, 1986. Fellow Calif. Acad. Scis.; mem. Soc. Vertebrate Paleontology, Soc. for the Study of Evolution, Soc. for Systematic Zoology, Nat. Ctr. Sci. Edn. (bd. dirs.), Sigma Xi. Office: U Calif Dept Integr Biol Mus Paleontology Berkeley CA 94720

PADVE, MARTHA BERTONNEAU, urban planning and arts consultant, fundraiser; b. Scobey, Mont., Feb. 22; d. Henry Francis and Marie (Vaccaro) Bertonneau; m. Jacob Padve, May 9, 1954 (div. 1980). Student, Pasadena Jr. Coll., 1938-40; cert., S.W. U. Bus. Coll., L.A., 1940-41, Pasadena Inst. for Radio, 1946-47; student, Claremont Colls., 1972-74, U. So. Calif., 1983-84, Community Coll., Pasadena, 1987-88. Juvenile roles Pasadena (Calif.) Community Playhouse, 1935-37; ptnr., bus. mgr. restaurant devel. ventures, Pasadena, 1940-50; club dir. Red Cross, Nfld., Can., 1944-45; leading roles Penthouse Theatre, Altadena, Calif., 1946-48; club dir. armed forces spl. svcs. Red Cross, Austria, 1949-52; head dept. publs. Henry E. Huntington Libr., San Marino, Calif., 1953-57; cons. art planning Model Cities program, Omaha, 1975; founding instr. contemporary art collecting class, 1979-80; dir. devel. Bella Lewitzky Dance Found., L.A., 1980-81; instr. Art. Ctr. Coll. Design, Pasadena, 1981-82, assoc. dir. devel., 1981-83; instr. Coll. Continuing Edn. U. So. Calif., L.A., 1983-84; urban planning and arts cons. The Arroyo Group, Pasadena, 1979—; cons. in field, 1984—; developer edn. program Mus. Contemporary Art, L.A., 1984-86. Contbr. articles to newspapers; author (the arts segment) Pasadena Gen. Plan, 1980-83. Trustee, v.p. Pasadena Art Mus., 1967-74; co-chmn. bldg. fund Norton Simon Mus. Art, Pasadena 1968-70; chmn. Pasadena Planning commn., 1973-81, Pasadena Street Tree Plan, 1975-76, Pasadena High Rise Task Force, 1979, San Gabriel Valley Planning Coun., 1977-78; mem. Pasadena Downtown Urban Design Plan, 1980-83; founding mem. Arts, Pks. & Recreation Task Force, 1978-80; vice-chmn. Pasadena Design Review commn., 1974-78; founding chmn. So. Calif. Fellows of Contemporary Art, 1976-78; mem. adv. com. U. So. Calif. art galleries, 1976-82, UCLA oral history program contemporary art, 1983—; chmn. audit com. L.A. County Grand Jury, 1986-87; founder Pasadena Robinson Meml. Fund, Inc., 1990-92, bd. dirs. 1992—; curator Vroman's Art on the Stairwell, 1992—. Named Woman of the Yr., Pasadena Women's Civic League, 1980; recipient Gold Crown award Tenth Muse, Pasadena Arts Coun., 1983, Commendation awards Pasadena City Dirs., 1975, 80, 82, 83, Commendation award L.A. County Bd. Suprs., 1987, Graphic Arts award Southern Calif. Fellows Contemporary Art, 1978. Mem. Calif. Inst. Tech. Assocs. Republican. Roman Catholic. Home and Office: 80 N Euclid Ave Pasadena CA 91101-1711

PADWE, CAROL, investments executive; b. Bklyn., July 14, 1944; d. Sol and Esther (Goldberg) Vogelman; m. Stephen Alan Padwe, Aug. 26, 1967; children: Marc Philip, Melissa Dawn. BA, CUNY, 1967; MS, Bklyn. Coll., 1973. Tchr. N.Y.C. Bd. of edn., Bklyn., 1967-70; program dir. Cystic Fibrosis Found., Phoenix, Ariz., 1980-82; assoc. v.p. Dean Witter Reynolds, Inc., Scottsdale, Ariz., 1983—. Fin. columnist: Today's Ariz. Women, 1988-89. Volunteer child life dept. Phoenix Children's Hosp., 1990—; mem. Scottsdale Town Enrichment Program, 1985; del. Ariz. Women's Town Hall, 1990, 91; treas. planned giving com. Am. Cancer Soc., Phoenix met. area. Mem. Stock and Bond Club. Office: Dean Witter Reynolds Inc 5225 N Scottsdale Rd Scottsdale AZ 85250-7092

PAGANI, ALBERT LOUIS, aerospace system engineer; b. Jersey City, Feb. 19, 1936; s. Alexander C. and Anne (Salvati) P.; m. Beverly Cameron, Feb. 23, 1971; children: Penelope, Deborah, Michael. BSEE, U.S. Naval Acad., 1957; MBA, So. Ill. U., 1971. Commd. 2d lt. USAF, 1957, advanced through grades to col., 1978; navigator USAF, Lake Charles, La., 1957-63; pilot USAF, McGuire AFB, N.J., 1963-65; command pilot USAF, Anchorage, Alaska, 1965-68; mgr. airlift USAF, Saigon, Socialist Republic of Vietnam, 1968-69; chief spl. missions USAF, Scott AFB, Ill., 1969-74; commd. tactical airlift group USAF Europe, Mildenhall, Eng., 1974-76; dep. comdr. Rhein Main Air Base USAF Europe, Frankfurt, Fed. Republic Germany, 1976-78; chief airlift mgmt. USAF Military Airlift Command, Scott AFB, Ill., 1978-81, dir. tech. plans and concepts, 1981, dir. command and control, 1982-85; ret., 1985; program mgr. Lockheed Missile and Space Co., Sunnyvale, Calif., 1985—. V.p. Cath. Ch. Council, Mildenhall, 1974, pres., 1975. Decorated Legion of Merit, Bronze Star, Air medal, Vietnam Cross of Gallantry. Mem. Nat. Def. Transp. Assn., Soc. Logistics Engrs., Air Force Assn., Armed Forces Communication and Electronics Assn., Air Lift Assn., Daedalions, Mensa. Home: 41090 Driscoll Ter Fremont CA 94539-3872 Office: Lockheed Missile & Space Co Advanced Programs 69-90 1111 Lockheed Way Sunnyvale CA 94089-1212

PAGANI, BEVERLY DARLENE, government administrator; b. Compton, Calif., Aug. 29, 1937; d. Donald Marshell Cameron and Irene Von (Kirkendoll) Good; m. Albert Louis Pagani, Feb. 21, 1971; children: Penelope Collins, Deborah Anne, Michael Stuart. BS, So. Oreg. Coll., 1967; MBA, So. Ill. U., Edwardsville, 1972. Cert. cost estimator and analyst. Enlisted USAF, 1959, advanced through grades to capt., 1962, resigned, 1971; chief mgmt. analysis USAF, Mildenhall, Eng., 1974-76; personnel classifier USAF, Scott AFB, Ill., 1979-80; housing mgmt. analyst USAF, Scott AFB, 1980-81, cost analyst, 1981-85; chief manpower analyst USN, Moffett Field, Calif., 1985—; chief mgmt. support office Army Aviation Research and Tech. Activity, Moffett Field, Calif., 1986-88; project control mgr. NASA-AMES Rsch. Ctr., Moffett Field, Calif., 1988—. Mem. Soc. Logistic Engrs., Inst. Cost Analysts, Am. Soc. Mil. Comptrollers, Soc. Cost Estimating and Analysis. Republican. Roman Catholic. Office: Numerical Aerodynamic Simulation Systems NASA-AMES Rsch Ctr Moffett Field CA 94503-1099

PAGE, CURTIS MATTHEWSON, minister; b. Columbus, Ohio, Oct. 24, 1946; s. Charles N. and Alice Matthewson P.; m. Martha Poitevin, Feb. 12, 1977; children: Allison, Charles, Abigail. BS, Ariz. State U., 1968; MDiv, San Francisco Theol. Sem., 1971, D Ministry, 1985. Ordained to ministry Presbyn. Ch., 1971. Pastor Ketchum (Idaho) Presbyn. Ch., 1972-80, Kirk O'The Valley Presbyn. Ch., Reseda, Calif., 1980-90; campaign dir. Kids 1st Edn. Reform Partnership, L.A., 1990-91; sr. pastor Orangewood Presbyn. Ch., Phoenix, 1991—; bd. dirs. Express Pub., Ketchum. Bd. dirs. Mary Magdalene Home, Reseda; moderator Kendall Presbytery, 1978; chmn. com. on preparation for the ministry, San Fernando, Calif., 1988-90; chmn. Ketchum City Zoning Commn., 1979-80; mem. Ketchum Master Planning Commn., 1974, Mayor's Citizen's Adv. Task Force on Ethics, 1990; co-chmn. Voice Community Orgn. in San Fernando Valley, 1988-90.

PAGE, DON NELSON, theoretical gravitational physics educator; b. Bethel, Alaska, Dec. 31, 1948; s. Nelson Monroe and Zena Elizabeth (Payne) P.; m. Catherine Anne Hotke, June 28, 1986; children: Andrew Nicolaas Nelson, John Paul Weslie. AB in Physics and Math., William Jewell Coll., 1971; MS in Physics, Calif. Inst. Tech., 1972, PhD in Physics and Astronomy, 1976; MA, U. Cambridge, Eng., 1978. Rsch. asst., assoc. Calif. Inst. Tech., Pasadena, 1972-76, 87; rsch. asst., NATO fellow U. Cambridge, 1976-79; rsch. fellow Darwin Coll., Cambridge, 1977-79; asst. prof. physics Pa. State U., University Park, 1979-83, assoc. prof., 1983-86, prof., 1986-90; prof. U. Alta., Edmonton, Can., 1990—; vis. rsch. faculty, assoc. U. Tex., Austin, 1982, 83, 86; vis. rsch. assoc. Inst. Theoretical Physics U. Calif., Santa Barbara, 1988; vis. prof. U. Alta., Edmonton, Can., 1989-90; mem. Inst. Advanced Study, Princeton, N.J., 1985; assoc. Can. Inst. Advanced Rsch., Toronto, 1987-91, fellow, 1991—; cons. Time-Life, Alexandria, Va., 1990—; assoc. editor Can. Jour. Physics, 1992—. Editorial bd. jour. Classical and Quantum Gravity, 1988-91; assoc. editor Can. Jour Physics, 1992—; contbr. articles to The Phys. Rev., Physics Letters, Phys. Rev. Letters, Nuclear Physics. U.S. Presdl. scholar, 1967; Danforth Found. grad. fellow, 1971-76; Alfred P. Sloan Found. rsch. fellow, 1982-86; John Simon Guggenheim Found. fellow, 1986-87. Fellow Am. Sci. Affiliation, Can. Inst. Advanced Rsch.; mem. Am. Phys. Soc. Baptist. Home: 5103-126 St, Edmonton, AB Canada T6H 3W1 Office: U Alta, 412 Physics Lab, Edmonton, AB Canada T6G 2J1

PAGE, JAKE (JAMES K. PAGE, JR.), writer, editor; b. Boston, Jan. 24, 1936; s. James Keena Page and Ellen Van Dyke (Gibson) Kunath; m. Aida de Alva Bound, Nov. 28, 1969 (div. 1974); children: Dana de Alva Page-Brooks, Lea Gibson Page Kuntz, Brooke Bound Page; m. Susanne Calista Stone, Mar. 10, 1974; stepchildren: Lindsey Truitt, Sally Truitt, Kendall Barrett. BA, Princeton U., 1958; MA, NYU, 1959. Asst. sales promotion mgr. Doubleday & Co., 1959-60; editor Doubleday Anchor Books, 1960-62, Natural History Press, Doubleday, N.Y.C., 1962-69; editorial dir. Natural History Mag., N.Y.C., 1966-69; editor-in-chief Walker & Co., N.Y.C., 1969-70; sci. editor Smithsonian Mag., Washington, 1970-76; founder, dir. Smithsonian Books, Washington, 1976-80; start-up editor Smithsonian Air & Space Mag., Washington, 1985; pvt. practice as writer Waterford, Va., Corrales, N.Mex., 1980—; mag. cons. Denver Mus. Nat. History, 1989-90; contract text editor Doubleday, 1992. Author: (with Richard Saltonstall Jr.) Brown Out & Slow Down, 1972, (with Larry R. Collins) Ling-Ling & Hsing Hsing: Year of the Panda, 1973, Shoot the Moon, 1979, (with Wilson Clark) Energy, Vulnerability and War: Alternatives for America, 1981, Blood: River of Life, 1981, (with Susanne Page) Hopi, 1982, Forest, 1983, Arid Lands, 1984, Pastorale: A Natural History of Sorts, 1985, Demon State, 1985, (with Eugene S. Morton) Lords of the Air: The Smithsonian Book of Birds, 1989, Smithsonian's New Zoo, 1990, Zoo: The Modern Ark, 1990, (with Eugene S. Morton) Animal Talk: Science and the Voices of Nature, 1992, The Stolen Gods, 1993, Songs to Birds, 1993, (with Charles B. Officer) Tales of the Earth, 1993; editor: (with Malcolm Baldwin) Law and the Environment, 1970; contbg. editorships Science Mag., 1980-86, Oceans Mag., 1987, Mother Earth News, 1990, National Geographic Traveler, 1990—, TDC (now Destination Discovery), 1991—; contbg. author to numerous books and mags. Mem. nat. bd. advisors Futures For Children, Albuquerque, 1980—; bd. dirs. Wildlife Rescue N.Mex., Albuquerque, 1993—. Democrat. Home and Office: PO Box 78 345 Chimaja Rd Corrales NM 87048

PAGE, JOHN BOYD, physics educator; b. Columbus, Ohio, Sept. 4, 1938; s. John Boyd and Helen (Young) P.; m. Norma Kay Christensen, July 28, 1966; children: Rebecca, Elizabeth. BS, U. Utah, 1960, PhD, 1966. Rsch. assoc. Inst. for Theoretical Physics U. Frankfurt/Main, Fed. Republic of Germany, 1966-67; rsch. assoc. Cornell U., Ithaca, N.Y., 1968-69; asst. prof. physics Ariz. State U., 1969-75, assoc. prof., 1975-80, prof., 1980—; vis. prof. dept. physics Cornell U., 1989. Contbr. articles to profl. jours. Recipient Humboldt Rsch. award, 1991; NSF grantee, 1972-77, 77-80, 80-82, 82-86, 90-92, 91—. Fellow Am. Phys. Soc.; mem. Am. Assn. Physics Tchrs., Phi Beta Kappa, Sigma Xi, Phi Kappa Phi, Phi Eta Sigma. Office: Ariz State U Physics Dept Tempe AZ 85287-1504

PAGE, LESLIE ANDREW, disinfectant manufacturing company executive; b. Mpls., June 5, 1924; s. Henry R. and Amelia Kathryn (Steinmetz) P.; m. DeEtte Abernethy Griswold, July 6, 1952 (div. Sept. 1975); children: Randolph, Michael, Kathryn, Caroline; m. Mary Ellen Decker, Nov. 26, 1976. BA, U. Minn., 1949; MA, U. Calif., Berkeley, 1953; PhD, U. Calif., 1956. Asst. microbiologist, lectr. U. Calif., Davis, 1956-61; microbiologist, research leader Nat. Animal Disease Ctr., USDA, Ames, Iowa, 1961-79; ret., 1979; med. text cons. Bay St. Louis, Miss., 1979-85; founder, pres. Steri-Derm Corp., Escondido, Calif., 1987—; specialist in Chlamydial nomenclature and disease. Editor: Wildlife Diseases, 1976, Jour. Wildlife Diseases, 1965-68; contbr. chpts. to med. texts, numerous articles to profl. jours.; patentee Liquid Antiseptic Composition. Pres. Garden Island Community Assn., Bay St. Louis, 1980-81; chief commr. East Hancock Fire Protection Dist., Bay St. Louis, 1982-83; sec., treas. Woodridge Escondido Property Owners Assn., 1986-88. With AUS, 1943-46, ETO. Fellow Am. Acad. Microbiology; mem. Wildlife Disease Assn. (pres. 1972-73, Disting. Service award 1980), Am. Soc. for Microbiology, Zool. Soc. San Diego, Sigma Xi, Phi Zeta (hon.). Home and Office: 1723 Cypress Point Gln Escondido CA 92026-1063

PAGE, MARTHA POITEVIN, management and publishing consultant; b. Idaho Falls, Idaho, May 24, 1948; d. John Joseph and Doris Claire (Gregory) Poitevin; m. Curtis Matthewson Page, Feb. 12, 1977; children: Allison Rose, Charles Joseph, Abigail Anne. BA, U. Calif., Berkeley, 1970; MBA, Calif. State U., Northridge, 1987. News dir. KSKI Radio, Hailey, Idaho, 1972-74; reporter, sales rep. Idaho Mountain Express, Ketchum, 1974-77; pub., editor Express Pub., Ketchum, 1977-80; pubs. coord. L.A. Children's Mus., 1981-83; ptnr. Gates.Phoenix, Ltd., 1992—; chmn. bd. dirs., pres. Express Pub., 1977—. Chair Winnetka Elem. Sch. Site Coun., Canoga Park, Calif., 1976-80; publicist, lobbyist, mem. Valley Organized in Community Efforts, San Fernando Valley, Calif., 1979-80; pres. Ketchum City Coun., 1974-77; mem. Blaine County Planning and Zoning Bd., Ketchum, 1975-77. Democrat. Presbyterian. Office: Gates.Phoenix Ltd 341 W Montecello Phoenix AZ 85013

PAGE, THOMAS ALEXANDER, utility executive; b. Niagara Falls, N.Y., Mar. 24, 1933; m. Evelyn Rainnie, July 16, 1960; children: Christopher, Catherine. B.S. in Civil Engring, Purdue U., 1955, M.S. in Indsl. Adminstrn, 1963. Registered profl. engr., N.Y. C.P.A., Wis., Tex. Comptroller, treas. Wis. Power & Light Co., Madison, 1970-73; treas. Gulf States Utilities Co., Beaumont, Tex., 1973-75, sr. v.p. fin., 1975, exec. v.p., 1975-78, also bd. dirs.; exec. v.p., chief operating officer San Diego Gas & Electric Co., 1978-81, pres., chief exec. officer, 1981-92, chmn., 1983-92, chmn., chief exec. officer, 1992—, also bd. dirs. Mem. Dane County Bd. Suprs., Wis., 1968-72. Served to capt. USAF, 1955-57. Home: 1904 Hidden Crest Dr El Cajon CA 92019-3653 Office: San Diego Gas & Electric Co 101 Ash St San Diego CA 92101-3096

PAGET, JOHN ARTHUR, mechanical engineer; b. Ft. Frances, Ont., Can., Sept. 15, 1922; s. John and Ethel (Bishop) P.; B. in Applied Sci., Toronto, 1946; m. Vicenta Herrera Nunez, Dec. 16, 1963; children: Cynthia Ellen, Kevin Arthur, Keith William. Chief draftsman Gutta Percha & Rubber, Ltd., Toronto, Ont., 1946-49; chief draftsman Viceroy Mfg. Co., Toronto, 1949-52; supr., design engr. C.D. Howe Co. Ltd., Montreal, Que., Can., 1952-58, sr. design engr. Combustion Engring., Montreal, 1958-59; sr. staff engr. Gen. Atomic, Inc., La Jolla, 1959-81. Mem. ASME, Soc. Mfg. Engrs., Profl. Engrs. Ont., Soc. for History Tech., Inst. Mech. Engrs., Newcomen Soc., Brit. Nuclear Energy Soc. Patentee in field. Home: 3183 Magellan St San Diego CA 92154-1515

PAGLIARINI, JAMES, broadcast executive. AB, Princeton U., 1975; MEd, Temple U., 1976. Asst. to gen. mgr. Sta. KTEH-TV, San Jose, Calif., 1976-80; co-founder Sta. KNPB-TV, Reno, Nev., 1980—, sta. mgr., 1982-83, gen. mgr., CEO, 1983—; bd. dirs. Agy. Instrnl. T.V., Pub. Broadcasting, Western Indsl. Nev.; chmn. bd. govs. Pacific Mountain Network, 1987—; mem. Cable Access Bd., Reno, PBS assessment policy com., 1988-89, funding task force, 1991, task force on nat. prodns., 1992-93. Chmn. community adv. com. U. Nev. Sch. Engring., Reno; past bd. dirs. Planned Parenthood No. Nev., Boy Scouts Am., We. Nev. Clean Cities Com. Mem. Nev. Pub. Broadcasting Assn. (pres.), Small Sta. Assn. (pres. 1991-92). Office: Station KNPB Box 14730 Reno NV 89507

PAIGE, ALFRED LEE, small business owner; b. Bklyn., Nov. 4, 1950; s. David B. and Myrtle (Chappel) P.; 1 child, Munyaradzi Tungamirai. Student, Seattle Ctrl. Community Coll., 1984-86; BA in Govt., Columbia Coll., 1992. Lic. refrigeration engr. Nursing asst. Portsmith (N.Mex.) Hosp., 1972-76; radar operator Pearl Harbor, Pearl City, Hawaii, 1978-84; boiler engr. City of Seattle, 1985-86; maintenance repair Mil. Sealift Command Pacific, Oakland, Calif., 1987-88; mgr., owner Small Engine Repair, Oakland, Calif., 1988—. Support mem. ARC, Seattle, 1984-92, CARE, N.Y.C., 1992, Planned Parenthood, 1992, Am. Legion, San Francisco, 1992. With USN, 1972-92. Recipient Sea Svc. Deployment ribbon, 1973-90, Navy Expeditionary medal, 1987-90, Humanitarian Svc. medal, 1982. Mem. U.S. Naval Inst., Navy League. Republican. Home: 1942 47th Ave Oakland CA 94601 Office: Small Engine Repair PO Box 2534 Oakland CA 94614

PAIGE, GLENN DURLAND, political scientist, educator; b. Brockton, Mass., June 28, 1929; s. Lester Norman and Rita Irene (Marshall) P.; m. Betty Gail Grenier, Jan. 2, 1949 (div.); children: Gail, Jan, Donn, Sean, Sharon, Van; m. Glenda Hatsuko Naito, Sept. 1, 1973. Grad., Phillips Exeter Acad., 1947; A.B., Princeton U., 1955; M.A., Harvard U., 1957; Ph. D., Northwestern U., 1959. Asst. prof. pub. adminstrn. Seoul Nat. U., 1959-61; asst. to assoc. prof. politics Princeton U., 1961-67; prof. polit. sci. U. Hawaii, Honolulu, 1967-92, prof. emeritus, 1992—. Author: The Korean Decision, 1968, The Scientific Study of Political Leadership, 1977; editor: Political Leadership, 1972, To Nonviolent Political Science, 1993; co-editor: (with George Chaplin) Hawaii 2000, 1973, (with Sarah Gilliatt) Nonviolence in Hawaii's Spiritual Traditions, 1991, Buddhism and Nonviolent Global Problem-Solving, 1991, Nonviolence Speaks to Power (Petra K. Kelly), 1992; social sci. editor: Biography, 1977—; mem. internat. editorial coun.: Magisterium (Moscow), 1991—. Program chmn. Hawaii Gov.'s Conf. on Yr. 2000, 1970; leader U.S. Group 103, Amnesty Internat., 1977-78; cons. UN Univ., 1980-86; coord. planning project Ctr. for Global Nonviolence, U. Hawaii Spark M. Matsunaga Inst. for Peace, 1988—; mem. nat. adv. group Martin Luther King Jr. Inst. for Nonviolence, State of N.Y., 1989-90. With U.S. Army, 1948-52. Decorated Commendation medal; recipient Seikyo Culture prize, 1982, Dr. G. Ramachandran award for internat. understanding, 1986, Anuvrat award for internat. peace, 1987; named Woodrow Wilson Nat. fellow, 1955-56, Princeton U. Class fo 1955 award, 1987, 3d Gandhi Meml. lectr., New Dehli, 1990, Disting. life fellow Delhi Sch. Nonviolence, 1992. Mem. Interant. Peace Rsch. Assn. (co-covenor nonviolence study group 1989-91), Interant. Polit Sci. Assn., World Future Studies Fedn., Phi Beta Kappa. Home: 3653 Tantalus Dr Honolulu HI 95822

PAIGE, LOWELL J., mathematics educator; b. Wheatland, Wyo., Dec. 10, 1919; s. Constant Antone and Electa Dot (Hastings) P.; m. Margaret Connor, Oct. 19, 1942 (dec. 1965); children: Richard Michael, Steven Hastings; m. Betty McIntosh, Feb. 10, 1967; stepchild, Michael Edwards. BS, U. Wyo., 1939; PhM, U. Wis., 1940, PhD, 1947; LLD (hon.), U. Wyo., 1974. Instr. dept. math. UCLA, 1947-49, asst. prof., 1949-55; vis. mem. Inst. Adv. Study, Princeton, N.J., 1953-54; assoc. prof. math. UCLA, 1955-62, prof. dept. math., 1962—, chmn. dept. math., 1964-68, dean div. phys. sci., Coll. Letters and Sci., 1968-73, chmn. acad. senate, 1968-70; vis. lectr. Yale U., New Haven, 1956-57; asst. dir. edn. NSF, 1973-75, acting dep. dir., 1974; spl. asst. to pres. for govtl. rels. U. Calif., 1975-82; mem. Gov.'s Staff/Asst. Advisor Edn., 1983-87; mem. Calif. Postsec. Edn. Commn., 1987—, chmn., 1991-92. Contbr. articles to profl. jours.; mng. editor Pacific Jour. Math., 1959-64; author: Elements of Linear Algebra, 1960. Lt. USN, 1942-46. Mem. Am. Math. Soc., Math. Assn. Am., AAAS (fellow), Sigma Xi, Phi Kappa Phi, Sigma Tau. Home: 44710 Garden Ct El Macero CA 95618-1002

PAIGE, PAUL, music educator; b. Boston, July 4, 1934; s. Herman A. and Sara (Richards) P.; m. Alice McDowell, July 9, 1960; children: Alan, David, Rebecca. North Park Coll., Chgo., 1954; BMus, Boston U., 1956, PhD, 1967; MMus, Northwestern U., 1959. Chmn. music dept. Ricker Coll., Houlton, Maine, 1963-66, Cazenovia (N.Y.) Coll., 1966-69, Marymount Coll., Salina, Kans., 1969-71; prof. music Grand Canyon U., Phoenix, 1971—; adjudicator Music Tchr. Nat. Assn., Am. Guild Organists, Am. Choral Dirs. Assn.; organ recitalist. Reviewer, The Choral Jour. Mem. Music Tchrs. Nat. assn., Music Educators Nat. Conf., Coll. Music Soc., Am. Choral Dirs. Assn., Am. Guild Organists, Ariz. State Music Tchrs. Assn. (pres., 1992-94). Mem. Evang. Covenant Ch. Office: Grand Canyon Univ 3300 W Camelback Rd Phoenix AZ 85017-1097

PAIGE, VICTORIA HAHNE, public relations consultant; b. Palo Alto, Calif., Oct. 29, 1965; d. Henry Victor and Iris Helen (Suppik) Hahne; m. Kirk Brundage Paige, Nov. 9, 1991. BA in Pub. Rels., San Jose State U., 1988. Jr. assoc. Neale-May and Ptnrs., Los Altos, Calif., 1987-89; pub. rels. mgr. Software Pub. Corp., Santa Clara, Calif., 1989-92; pub. rels. cons. Los Altos, 1992—. Recipient Best award for high tech/high touch comms. Internat. Assn. Bus. Communicators, Bay Area, Calif., 1992.

PAINE, ROBERT TREAT, chemistry educator; b. Colorado Springs, Colo., Dec. 15, 1944; Robert T. and Marietta H. Paine; m. Bonnie Pauly Paine, Aug. 20, 1967; children: Andrew S., Matthew H., Joanna M. BS, U. Calif., Berkeley, 1966; PhD, U. Mich., 1970. Postdoctoral work Northwestern U., Evanston, Ill., 1970-72; postdoctoral work Los Alamos (N.Mex.) Nat. Lab., 1972-74, cons., 1974—; asst. prof. U. New Mex., Albuquerque, 1974-78, assoc. prof., 1978-82, prof., 1982—. Contbr. articles to profl. jours. Trainee NASA, 1966-69. Mem. AAAS, Am. Chem. Soc., Materials Research Soc. Office: U NMex Dept Chemistry Albuquerque NM 87131

PAINE, TIMOTHY FRANCIS, clinical researcher; b. Torrance, Calif., May 28, 1965; s. Russell Gene and Cornelia Dominica (Duran) P. BS in Microbiology, Calif. Poly. Pomona, 1988. Midwest coord. Phenomenex, Inc., Torrance, 1988-89; quality assurance supr. Spectrum Med. Industries, Long Beach, Calif., 1989-90; clin. rsch. assoc. Alpha Therapeutic Corp., L.A., 1990-92, Amgen, Inc., Thousand Oaks, Calif., 1992—. Mem. Sigma Chi. Democrat. Roman Catholic. Office: Amgen Inc 17-2-C-391 Amgen Ctr Thousand Oaks CA 91320-1789

PAINTER, AMELIA ANN, marketing professional; b. Hot Springs, Ark., Oct. 26, 1946; d. Jack H. and Emily C. (Hosmer) Chapman; m. Douglas M. Painter, June 12, 1988; children: Katrina, Bruce, Emily Grace. Sales mgr. Comml. Mktg. Systems, Houston, 1984-85; mktg. dir. Southmark Mgmt., Dallas, 1985-86; dir. of sales Noble Design and Set Constrn., San Diego, Calif., 1986-89; mktg. dir. Scenic Drive Set Design and Constrn., L.A., 1990-93; writer, columnist Jump Mag., Del Mar, Calif., 1993—. Asst. editor Houston Motion Picture Coun. mag., 1985. Office: PO Box 154 San Luis Rey CA 92068

PAISLEY, DAVID DUANE, sales executive; b. Dayton, Ohio, July 21, 1961; s. Dalton Duane and Carol Elaine (Lockard) P.; m. Patience Lea Wickersham, Sept. 20, 1986. BS in Natural Resources, Ohio State U., 1984; postgrad., Nat. Exec. Inst., 1986. Distbn. supr. Youthland, Inc., Columbus, Ohio, 1981-86; mktg. exec. Pikes Peak Coun., Boy Scouts Am., Colorado Springs, Colo., 1986-87; dist. exec. Pikes Peak Coun., Boy Scouts Am., Colorado Springs, 1987-89, sr. dist. exec., 1990-91; sales mgr. Grand West Outfitters, Colorado Springs, 1991—; outdoor pursuits program instr. Ohio State U., Columbus, 1980-85; program dir. Philmont Scout Ranch, Cimarron, N.Mex., 1982-84. Author: (climbing guide book) Miners Park: A Climbers Guide, 1984; editor: (newsletters) Summit, 1986-91, High Trails, 1991—, (tng. manual) Philmont Rock Staff Handbook, 1987. Fundraiser U.S. Olympic Tng. Ctr., Colorado Springs, 1991. Named Outstanding Young Man of Am., 1987. Mem. Nat. Pks. and Conservation Assn., East Colorado Springs Rotary (srs. chmn. 1988-91), High Adventure Explorers Post (adult advisor 1986-92), Sierra Club, Wilderness Soc., Colo. Mountain Club. Episcopalian. Home: 916 Bonfoy Ave Colorado Springs CO 80909 Office: Grand West Outfitters 3250 N Academy Blvd Colorado Springs CO 80917

PAKISER, LOUIS CHARLES, JR., geophysicist; b. Denver, Feb. 8, 1919; s. Louis C. and Lila E. (Hanson) P.; m. Helen L. Meineke, Oct. 9, 1939. Geol. Engr., Colo. Sch. Mines, 1937-42; postgrad., U. Nancy, France, 1945, Stanford, U. Colo., 1958-60. Geophysicist Carter Oil Co., 1942-49; first nat. exec. dir. Am. Vets. Com., 1949-52; also mng. editor AVC Bull.; mem. nat. planning com.; geophysicist U.S. Geol. Survey, 1952-92; rep. geophysics br. U.S. Geol. Survey, Denver, 1958-60; chief maj. crustal studies U.S. Geol. Survey, 1960-61, chief br. crustal studies, 1961-65; acting chief Nat. Center Earthquake Research, 1965-67, chmn. exec. com. of center, 1967-68; chief Office Earthquake Research and Crustal Studies, 1967-70, research geophysicist, 1970-79, annuitant research geophysicist, 1979-92, chief br. seismicity and earth structure and nat. earthquake info. service, 1975-77; ad hoc panel on earthquake prediction OST, 1964-68; disting. lectr. Soc. Exploration Geophysicists, 1964; spl. lectr. U. New Orleans, 1982-83; chmn. interagy. staff group on minority participation in sci. and engring. U.S. Dept. Interior, 1972-74; adv. com. Am. Indian Ednl. Opportunity Program U. Colo., 1981-84; vis. com. geophysics dept. Colo. Sch. Mines, 1986—. Chmn. land use adv. com. Douglas County, Colo., 1975-76, chmn. mineral extraction planning task force, 1989-90; bd. dirs. Nat. Consortium for Black Profl. Devel., 1976-79; mem. adv. coun. Am. Vets. Com., 1960-61; mem. steering com. Nat. Civil Liberties Clearing House, 1950-52. Pvt. AUS, 1943-45. Recipient Distinguished Service award U.S. Dept. Interior, 1970. Mem. NAACP (exec. com. Tulsa br. 1949, co-chmn. membership com. 1949), Am. Indian Sci. and Engring. Soc., Am. Geophys. Union, Soc. Advancement Chicanos and Native Ams. in Sci., Am. Geol. Inst. (chmn. adv. com. to minority participation program 1973-75), Geol. Soc. Am. (chmn. com. on minority participation in geol. scis. 1975-80), AAAS. Mem. United Ch. Christ (state social action bd. 1964-66). Home: 2710 S Sandy Ridge Rd Sedalia CO 80135-8470

PAKVASA, SANDIP, physicist; b. Bombay, India, Dec. 24, 1935; came to U.S. 1961; s. Sirish V. and Sumitra (Surti) P.; m. Heide Miller, Nov. 19, 1978. BSc, M.S. U. Baroda, India, 1954; MSc, M.S. U. Baroda, 1957; PhD, Purdue U., 1966. Rsch. assoc. Syracuse (N.Y.) U., 1965-67; asst. prof. U. Hawaii, Honolulu, 1968-70, assoc. prof., 1970-73, prof. physics, 1974—; vis. prof. U. Wis., Madison, 1978, 81, Nat. High Energy Physics Lab., Japan, 1983, 89, U. Melbourne, Australia, 1986, TAta Inst. Fund Rsch., Bombay, 1983, 88; vis. assoc. CERN, Geneva, 1982. Contbr. articles to profl. jours., chpts. to books. Japan Soc. for Promotion of Sci. fellow, 1981, 85. Fellow Am. Phys. Soc. Office: Univ Hawaii 2505 Correa Rd Honolulu HI 96822-2286

PALACIOS, PEDRO PABLO, lawyer; b. Santo Tomas, N.Mex., June 29, 1953; s. Luis Flores and Refugio (Hernandez) P.; m. Kelle Haston, July 2, 1983; children: Pedro Pablo II, Charles Rey, Jose Luis. BA, Yale U., 1975; JD, U. N.Mex., 1979. Bar: N.Mex. 1979. Pvt. practice Las Cruces, N.Mex., 1983—. Mem. N.Mex. State Bar Assn. Democrat. Roman Catholic. Home: PO Box 16335 Las Cruces NM 88004-6335 Office: 1980 E Lohman Ste D-3 Las Cruces NM 88001-1236

PALADE, GEORGE EMIL, cell biologist, educator; b. Jassy, Romania, Nov. 19, 1912; came to U.S., 1946, naturalized, 1952; s. Emil and Constanta (Cantemir) P.; m. Irina Malaxa, June 12, 1941 (dec. 1969); children—Georgia Teodora, Philip Theodore; m. Marilyn G. Farquhar, 1970. Bachelor, Hasdeu Lyceum, Buzau, Romania; M.D., U. Bucharest, Romania. Instr., asst. prof., then assoc. prof. anatomy Sch. Medicine, U. Bucharest, 1935-45; vis. investigator, asst. assoc., prof. cell biology Rockefeller U., 1946-73; prof. cell biology Yale U., New Haven, 1973-83; sr. research scientist Yale U., 1983-89; prof.-in-residence, dean sci. affairs Med. Sch., U. Calif., San Diego, 1990—. Author sci. papers. Recipient Albert Lasker Basic Research award, 1966, Gairdner Spl. award, 1967, Horwitz prize, 1970, Nobel prize in Physiology or Medicine, 1974, Nat. Medal Sci., 1986. Fellow Am. Acad. Arts and Scis.; mem. Nat. Acad. Sci., Pontifical Acad. Sci., Royal Soc. (London), Leopoldina Acad. (Halle), Romanian Acad., Royal Belgian Acad. Medicine.

PALECEK, GEORGE THOMAS, retail store executive; b. Tokyo, Japan, Sept. 5, 1952; s. George John and Miho (Kishi) P. BS, Met. State Coll., Denver, 1980; M of Computer Info. Systems, U. Denver, 1992. Indsl. engr. Safeway Stores Inc., Denver, 1984-87, programmer analyst, 1987-89; systems suppor mgr. Safeway, Inc., Denver, 1989-90, network operation mgr., 1990—; lectr. Arapahoe C.C., Littleton, Colo., 1989—; instr. U. Denver, 1993—. With U.S. Army, 1972-75. Mem. Assn. for Computing Machinery, Uniforum. Home: 5554 S Datura St Littleton CO 80120 Office: Safeway Inc 6900 S Yosemite St Englewood CO 80112

PALEN, THEODORE EDWARD, science education professional, medical informatics consultant; b. St. Paul, July 26, 1954; s. Elmer and Herwanna (Gross) P.; m. Karen Dianne Berg, Aug. 19, 1980; children: Eric, Nicolle. BA in Chemistry, Bethel Coll., 1976; PhD in Biochemistry, U. Colo., 1983, MD, 1993. Postdoctoral fellow Nat. Jewish Ctr. for Immunology, Denver, 1983-84; vis. asst. prof. Bethel Coll., St. Paul, 1984-85; rsch. assoc. U. Colo., Boulder, 1985-89; sci. advisor office of pub. rels. U. Colo. Health Scis. Ctr., Denver, 1989—. Contbr. articles to profl. jours. Deacon, chmn. Immanuel Bapt. Ch., Denver, 1986-89. Recipient Meritorious Rsch. award Western Regional Soc. for Clin. Rsch., 1990; U. Colo. scholar 1976, 89, Am. Soc. for Quality Control scholar, 1989, Whitehead scholar, 1991-93, ARCS scholar, 1991-93, Adler scholar, 1992-93. Mem. AAAS, Am. Soc. Molecular Biologists and Biochemistry, Phi Lambda Upsilon. Baptist. Office: U Colo Health Scis Ctr 4200 E 9th Ave # 092A Denver CO 80262-0001

PALIWODA, STANLEY JOSEPH, marketing educator; b. Renfrew, Strathclyde, Scotland, June 2, 1948; came to Can., 1990; s. Stanislaw and Helen Buchanan (Rome) P.; m. Helen McIsaac, Mar. 1989. BA with honors, Ulster U., Londonderry, Northern Ireland, 1974; MSc, Bradford (Eng.) U., 1975; PhD, Cranfield Inst. Tech., Bedford, Eng., 1980. Sales/relief br. mgr. Glasgow, Scotland, 1966-70; mktg. researcher London, England, 1975-76; lectr. mktg. U. Westminster, London, England, 1979-80; lectr. mktg. and internat. bus. U. Manchester (Eng.) Inst. Sci. and Tech., England, 1980-90; prof. mktg., chair U. Calgary, Alta., Can., 1990—; occasional lectr. various funding bodies, 1980-90. Author: Essence of International Marketing, 1993, Directions in International Marketing, 1993, Investment Opportunities in Eastern Europe, 1993, International Marketing, 2d edit. 1992, AMBA Guide to Business Schools, 8th edit., 1990, New Perspectives in International Marketing, 1992; co-author: Research in International Marketing, 1986. Constituency chmn. Liberal Democrats, Manchester, Wythenshawe, 1988-90. Recipient Doctoral Scholarship, Econ. and Social Rsch. Coun., London, 1976-77, 78-79, Polish State scholar, 1977-78, Export Rsch. prize Cranfield (Bedford, Eng.) Inst. Tech., 1980, Case Study of Yr. prize Unilever/Case Clearing House, Bedford, 1981, Commemorative plaque Indsl. Mktg. Rsch. Assn., Lichfield, Staffs., Eng., 1984. Mem. Acad. Internat. Bus. (U.K. treas. 1980-90), Assn. MBAs London (dir. 1979-90), Inst. Export London (examiner mktg. 1987-88), Am. Mktg. Assn., Brit. Inst. Mgmt., Brit. Assn. Slavic and Eastern European Studies, Chartered Inst. Mktg., European Mktg. Acad., European Internat. Bus. Assn., Adminstr. Scis. Assn. Canada, Internat. Mgmt. Devel. Assn. Presbyterian. Office: U Calgary Faculty of Mgmt, 2500 University Dr NW, Calgary, AB Canada T2N1N4

PALLASCH, THOMAS JOHN, periodontist, pharmacologist, educator; b. Milw., June 15, 1936; s. Joseph John and Stella (Zavis) P. D.D.S., Marquette U., 1960; M.S. in Pharmacology, certificate in periodontics, U. Wash., 1967; m. Christine Peterson, May 14, 1977; children: Brian, Jennifer, Robert. Rotating dental intern U.S. Navy, 1960-61; assoc. prof. pharmacology and periodontics, chmn. dept. pharmacology Sch. Dentistry, U. So. Calif., L.A.,

1967—, dir. oral biology grad. program, 1968-77, dir. pain and anxiety control program, 1972-76, chmn. dept. periodontics, 1981-83, prof. pharmacology and periodontics, 1989—, sec. faculty senate, 1990—; pvt. practice periodontics Burbank, Calif., 1968—; expert witness on dental malpractice, 1970—; With USN, 1960-64. Named Disting. Practitioner Nat. Acads. of Practice, 1991. Fellow Am. Coll. Dentists, Pierre Fauchard Acad.; mem. Am. Dental Assn., Am. Coll. Dentists, AAAS, Delta Sigma Delta (dep. supreme grand master 1968-71), Omicron Kappa Epsilon. Author: Clinical Drug Therapy in Dental Practice, 1973, Synopsis of Pharmacology for Students in Dentistry, 1974, Pharmacology for Dental Students and Practitioners, 1980; editor, pub. Dental Drug Service Newsletter; contbg. editor Dentist's Med. Digest, 1986—. Home and Office: 1411 W Olive Ave Burbank CA 91506-2405

PALMATIER, MALCOLM ARTHUR, editor, consultant; b. Kalamazoo, Nov. 11, 1922; s. Karl Ernest and Cecile Caroline (Chase) P.; m. Mary Elizabeth Summerfield, June 16, 1948 (dec. Oct. 1982); children: Barnabus, Timothy K., Duncan M.; m. Marie-Anne Suzanne van Werveke, Jan. 12, 1985. BS in Math., Western Mich. U., 1945; MA in English, UCLA, 1947; MA in Econs., U. So. Calif., 1971. Instr. English Pomona Coll., Claremont, Calif., 1949-51; editor Naval Ordnance Test Sta., Pasadena, Calif., 1951-54; head editorial unit Rocketdyne, L.A., 1954-55; editor The RAND Corp., Santa Monica, Calif., 1955-87; cons. editor The RAND Corp., Santa Monica, 1987—; instr. English UCLA, L.A., summer 1950. Mng. editor, cons. editor Jour.: Studies in Comparative Communism, L.A., 1968-80; co-editor Perspectives in Economics, 1971; contbr. chpts. to book, book revs. and articles to profl. jours. Chmn. bd. New Start, West L.A., 1980-82. With USNR, 1943-45. Mem. Jonathan Club. Home: 516 Avondale Ave Los Angeles CA 90049-4804 Office: The RAND Corp 1700 Main St Santa Monica CA 90407-2138

PALMER, ALAN, epidemiologist; b. South Shields, Durham, Eng., May 2, 1936; came to U.S., 1959; s. Joseph and Hilda (Cullin) P.; m. Adora Jean Rees, July, 1963; children: Cameron, Kevin, Kendra. BA, San Francisco State U., 1964; MPH, UCLA, 1967; PhD, U. Utah, 1974. Physiologist chronic respiratory disease control program USPHS, Washington, 1964-69; chief field studies Nat. Inst. for Occupational Safety and Health, CDC, USPHS, 1970-76; sr. scientist, mgr. Ctr. for Occupational Safety/Health SRI Internat., Menlo Park, Calif., 1976-80; pvt. practice Respiratory Health Surveillance Screening, Quality Control and Epidemiology, La Honda, Calif., 1980—; expert witness; bd. dirs. Broadleaf Industries, San Diego. Contbr. articles to profl. jours. Mem. edn. com. Rotary, Half Moon Bay, Calif., 1987, 88. Comdr. USPHS, 1964-76. Mem. Am. Indsl. Hygiene Assn., N.Y. Acad. Scis. Home: 7 Heritage Rd La Honda CA 94020 Office: Box 118 S R-2 La Honda CA 94020

PALMER, BEVERLY BLAZEY, psychologist, educator; b. Cleve., Nov. 22, 1945; d. Lawrence E. and Mildred M. Blazey; m. Richard C. Palmer, June 24, 1967; 1 child, Ryan Richard. PhD in Counseling Psychology, Ohio State U., 1972. Lic. clinical psychologist, Calif. Adminstrv. assoc. Ohio State U., Columbus, 1969-70; research psychologist Health Services Research Ctr. UCLA, 1971-77; commr. pub. health Los Angeles County, 1978-81; pvt. practice clin. psychology Torrance, Calif., 1985—; prof. psychology Calif. State U., Dominguez Hills, 1973—. Reviewer manuscripts for numerous textbook pubs; contbr. numerous articles to profl. jours. Recipient Proclamation County of Los Angeles, 1972, Proclamation County of Los Angeles, 1981. Mem. Am. Psychol. Assn. Office: Calif State U Dominguez Hills Dept Psychology Carson CA 90747

PALMER, CHARLES RAY, graphics arts administrator; b. New Orleans, Oct. 17, 1940; s. Zack and Amy Cecilia Palmer; m. Jeanette Francis Smith, Oct. 24, 1964; 1 child, Bridgette Latrice. AA in Art, Southwest City Coll., 1975; BA in Art with honors, Calif. State U., Dominguez Hills, 1979. Binderyman System Devel. Corp., Santa Monica, Calif., 1964-66; duplicator operator System Devel. Corp., Santa Monica, 1966-73, Northrop Corp., Hawthorne, Calif., 1973-75; printing press operator Northrop Corp., Hawthorne, 1975-79, visual aid artist, 1979-83, graphics prodn. control specialist, 1983-87, graphic art service mgr., 1987—; ltd. partnership, Crenshaw Graphics, L.A., 1979-82. With USAF, 1960-64. Mem. Am. Legion. Democrat. Roman Catholic. Home: 7630 Cimarron St Los Angeles CA 90047-2319 Office: Northrop Corp One Northorne Ave Orgn/Zone 1553/87 Hawthorne CA 90250

PALMER, DANIEL LEE, data communication manufacturing company executive; b. Norman, Okla., July 6, 1958; s. James Daniel and Margret (Kupka) P.; m. Kathleen Marie Connolly, Aug. 31, 1985; children: Jonathan Daniel, Elizabeth Marie. BSEE, U. Colo., 1980; MSEE, U. Santa Clara, 1985. Engr. GTE Lenkurt, San Carlos, Calif., 1980-82; div. mgr. Granger Assocs., Santa Clara, Calif., 1982-84; v.p. DSC Comm., Santa Clara, 1984-89; v.p. engring., corp. officer Digital Link, Sunnyvale, Calif., 1989—. Contbr. articles to profl. jours. Mem. IEEE, Eta Kappa Nu. Home: 36532 Montecito Dr Fremont CA 94536 Office: Digital Link Corp 252 Humboldt Ct Sunnyvale CA 94089

PALMER, DENNIS ALAN, advertising executive; b. Mt. Vernon, Wash., Aug. 26, 1953; s. David Harrison and Marylou (Sasser) P.; m. Nola Tam Henderson, Aug. 30, 1981; children: Skyler Dennison, Sara Jeanette. BA, Evergreen State Coll., 1975. Mktg. dir. Simpak Corp., Seattle, 1976-78; nat. sales and mktg. dir. Sekai Bicycle Co., Seattle, 1978-80; acct. supr. Ehrig & Assocs., Seattle, 1980-82; v.p. Evans/Kraft Advt., Seattle, 1982-88; pres., prin. Pacific Rim Advt., Seattle, 1988-92; advt. mgr. Time Oil Co., Seattle, 1992—. Mem. ad industry com. United Way, Seattle, 1986-89; mem. promotion com. Seattle Pike Place Market, 1985-87. Recipient S.D.A. award, Seattle Design Assn., 1987. Mem. Seattle Advt. Fedn. (bd. dirs. 1987-89, Addy award 1987), World Trade Club (bd. dirs. 1989-90), Japan Am. Soc. (com. mem.), Lions. Methodist. Office: Time Oil Co 2737 W Commodore Way Seattle WA 98199

PALMER, JAMES DANIEL, inspector; b. Oklahoma City, Okla., Aug. 11, 1936; s. Athol Ford and Marjorie Lorraine (Ward) P.; m. Gail Dorothy Myers, June 1954 (div. Sept. 1956); 1 child, James Douglas; m. Gloria Jean West, Dec. 14, 1963; children: Diana Lorraine, Elana Louise, Sheri Francis. AB in Police Sci. with honors, San Jose (Calif.) State U., 1963, AB in Psychology, 1964; MPA, Golden Gate U., 1972. Cert. Calif. police officers standards and tng. Asst. foreman Hunts Foods, Inc., Hayward, Calif., 1959-64; spl. investigator Dept. A.B.C. State of Calif., Oakland, 1964-67; criminal inspector Contra Costa County Dist. Atty., Martinez, Calif., 1967-72, lt. of inspectors, 1972-92; ret., 1992; pres. Contra Costa County Peace Officers, Richmond, 1974-75; past v.p. Contra Costa County Dist. Atty's Inv. Assn., Martinez, 1971, tng. officer, 1990-92. Contbr. articles to profl. jours. Past pres. South Hayward (Calif.) Dem. Club, 1976, 77, San Leandro (Calif.) Dems., 1975; mem. Gov's Law Enforcement Adv. Commn., Sacramento, Calif., 1972-76, Calif. Dem. Coun., 1972-73; rev. Am. Fellowship Protestant Ch., 1990—, min., 1990—. With USAF, 1955-58. Home: 2788 Sydney Way Castro Valley CA 94546

PALMER, PATRICIA ANN TEXTER, English language educator; b. Detroit, June 10, 1932; d. Elmer Clinton and Helen (Rotchford) Texter; m. David Jean Palmer, June 4, 1955. BA, U. Mich., 1953; MEd, Nat.-Louis U., 1958; MA, Calif. State U.-San Francisco, 1966; postgrad. Stanford U., 1968, Calif. State U.-Hayward, 1968-69. Chmn. speech dept. Grosse Pointe (Mich.) Univ. Sch., 1953-55; tchr. South Margerita Sch., Panama, 1955-56, Kipling Sch., Deerfield, Ill., 1955-56; grade level chmn. Rio San Gabriel Sch., Downey, Calif., 1957-59; tchr. newswriting and devel. reading Roosevelt High Sch., Honolulu, 1959-62; tchr. English, speech and newswriting El Camino High Sch., South San Francisco, 1962-68; chmn. ESL dept. South San Francisco Unified Sch. Dist., 1968-81; dir. ESL Inst., Millbrae, Calif., 1978—; adj. faculty New Coll. Calif., 1981—, Skyline Coll., 1990—; Calif. master tchr. ESL Calif. Coun. Adult Edn., 1979-82; cons. in field. Recipient Concours de Francais Prix, 1947; Jeanette M. Liggett Meml. award for excellence in history, 1949. Mem. AAUW, NAFE, TESOL, ASCD, Am. Assn. of Intensive English Programs, Internat. Platform Assn., Calif. Assn. Tchrs. English to Speakers Other Langs., Nat. Assn. for Fgn. Student Affairs, Computer Using Educators, Speech Commn. Assn., Faculty Assn. of Calif. C.C., U. Mich. Alumnae Assn., Nat.-Louis U. Alumnae Assn., Ninety Nines (chmn. Golden West chpt.), Cum Laude Soc., Soroptimist Internat., Peninsula Lioness Club (pres.), Chi Omega, Zeta Phi Eta. Home: 2917 Franciscan Ct San Carlos CA 94070-4304 Office: 450 Chadbourne Ave Millbrae CA 94030-2499

PALMER, PAULA LARAINE, librarian; b. Pawnee, Okla., Oct. 3, 1954; d. Paul Wallace and Rachel Alphia (Christopher) P.; m. Robert Gene Goad, Mar. 23, 1980 (div. 1984); m. David Robert Jones, Mar. 28, 1992. BA in Anthropology, U. Wash., 1991, postgrad., 1991—. Sales rep. Olga Co., Van Nuys, Calif., 1974-79; program asst. U. Wash., Seattle, 1983-86; owner Domestic Svcs., Seattle, 1987-92; ethnology mus. collections asst. Thomas Burke Meml. Mus., Seattle, 1992—; cons. Domestic Svcs., Seattle, 1992, editor, 1992—. Vol. KUOW Nat. Pub. Radio, U. Wash., Seattle, 1980—, A Contemporary Theater, Seattle, 1985-92, Folklife Festival, Seattle, 1989—, Burke Mus., 1991-92, U.S. Postal Svc., 1991—. Mem. Am. Libr. Assn., Wash. Mus. Assn., Spl. Librs. Assn., Phi Beta Kappa.

PALMER, ROBERT ARTHUR, private investigator; b. St. Augustine, Fla., May 20, 1948; s. Kenneth and Elizabeth Jane (Taylor) Anderson; m. Christine Lynn Creger, May 14, 1974. AA, Glendale C.C., 1975; BS, U. Phoenix, 1981; MA, Prescott Coll., 1993. Lic. pvt. investigator, Ariz. Dep. sheriff Maricopa County Sheriff's Office, Phoenix, 1971-79; owner Palmer Investigative Svcs., Prescott, Ariz., 1980-90; pres. The Magnum Corp., Prescott, 1990—. V.p. Mountain Club Homeowners, Prescott, 1986—. Mem. Internat. Assn. Chem. Testing, World Assn. Detectives, Nat. Assn. Legal Investigators, Nat. Assn. Profl. Process Servers, Ariz. Assn. Lic. Pvt. Investigators (pres. 1984), Ariz. Process Servers Assn. (pres. 1985-86), Prescott C. of C. (v.p. 1987-90). Office: Palmer Investigative Svcs PO Box 10760 Prescott AZ 86304

PALMER, VINCENT ALLAN, construction consultant; b. Wausa, Nebr., Feb. 18, 1913; s. Victor E. and Amy (Lindquist) P.; AA, Modesto Jr. Coll., 1933; BSCE, U. Calif., Berkeley, 1936; m. Louise V. Cramer, Mar. 12, 1938 (dec. June 1979); children: Margaret, Georgia, Vincent Allan; m. 2d, Hope Parker, Jan. 23, 1982. Constrn. engr. Kaiser Engrs., 1938-63, constrn. mgr., 1963-69, mgr. constrn., 1970-75, project mgr., 1975-76; project mgr. reef runway Universal Dredging Corp., Honolulu, 1975-76; pvt. practice constrn. cons., Walnut Creek, Calif., 1976—. Mem. ASCE (life), Project Mgmt. Inst., Monterey Bay Aquarium, Sierra Club. Home and Office: 1356 Corte Loma Walnut Creek CA 94598-2904

PALMER, WILLIAM JOSEPH, accountant; b. Lansing, Mich., Sept. 3, 1934; s. Joseph Flammin Lacchia and Henrietta (Yagerman) P.; m. Judith Pollock, Aug. 20, 1960 (div. Nov. 1980); children: William W., Kathryn E., Leslie A., Emily J.; m. Kathleen Francis Booth, June 30, 1990. BS, U. Calif., Berkeley, 1963. CPA. With Coopers and Lybrand, 1963-80, mng. ptnr., Sacramento, 1976-80; ptnr. Arthur Young & Co., San Francisco, 1980-89; ptnr. Ernst & Young, San Francisco, 1989—; guest lectr. U. Calif., Berkeley, 1971, Stanford U. Engring. Sch., 1976; lectr. Golden Gate Coll., 1975. Author: (books) Businessman's Guide to Construction, 1981, Construction Management Book, 1984, Construction Accounting & Financial Management 4th Edition, 1988, Construction Litigation-Representing The Contractor, 1992. Bd. dirs. Sacramento Met. YMCA, 1976-82, v.p., 1979-82; bd. dirs. Sacramento Symphony Found., 1977—; asst. state fin. chmn. Calif. Reagan for Pres., 1980. Served to lt. USN, 1953-59. Mem. AICPA (vice chmn. com. constrn. industry, 1975-81), Nat. Assn. Accts. (pres. Oakland/East Bay chpt. 1972, Man of Yr. 1968), Calif. Soc. CPAs., Assn. Gen. Contractors Calif. (bd. dirs. 1971-74), World Trade Club, Commonwealth Club (San Francisco), Del Paso Country Club, Sutter Club, Comstock Club (Sacramento), Lambda Chi Alpha. Presbyterian. Avocations: antique boats, sailing, tennis, book collecting, pipe collecting. Home: 6 Heather Ln Orinda CA 94563-3508 Office: Ernst & Young 1 Sansome St San Francisco CA 94104-4405

PALMIERI, DEBORAH ANNE, business and political consultant, writer, educator; b. Milford, Mass., July 15, 1953; d. Anthony Joseph and Eleanor M. (Fuller) P. BA with distinction, U. Colo., 1976; MA, U. Denver, 1980; MPhil, Columbia U., 1984, PhD, 1986. Cert., Kiev State Pedagogical Inst. for Fgn. Langs., Kiev, Ukraine, 1981. Vis. asst. prof. govt. dept. Pomona (Calif.) Coll., 1987; asst. dean Grad. Sch. U. So. Calif., L.A., 1987-90; v.p. Demographic Rsch. Co., El Segundo, Calif., 1990-92; cons., writer, 1992—; adj. prof. U. Denver, 1992—; vis. rsch. scholar London Sch. Econs., 1980-81; cons. Rockefeller Found., N.Y.C., 1984-85; MacArthur scholar Ctr. on East-West Trade, Duke U., 1989-90; lectr. in field. Co-author: The Dynamics of Soviet Foreign Policy, 1989; author, editor: The USSR in the World Economy, 1992; contbr. articles to profl. jours. Jr. fellow Harriman Inst., Columbia U., 1984-85; Presdl. fellow Columbia U., 1983-84; Elizabeth Fackt fellow U. Denver, 1978-79, Anderson fellow, 1979, Russian Lang. study grantee, 1979, Joseph Korbel fellow, 1979-80, Internat. Studies fellow, 1980-81; named to Outstanding Young Women of Am., 1986. Mem. Am. Polit. Sci. Assn., Am. Assn. for Advancement of Slavic Studies, Calif.-Russia Trade Assn., Internat. Studies Assn., Colo. Hist. Soc.

PALMIERI, RODNEY AUGUST, state agency administrator, pharmacist; b. Santa Rosa, Calif., July 12, 1944; s. August John and Olga (Giusti) P.; m. Phyllis Scott, Aug. 14, 1965; children: Christopher August, Joshua Scott. AA, Santa Rosa Jr. Coll., 1964; B of Pharmacy, U. Colo., 1968. Pvt. practice pharmacy, Santa Rosa, 1968-71; pharm. cons. State of Calif., San Jose, 1971-75; chief pharm. cons. State of Calif., Sacramento, 1975-80, sr. mgr., 1980-91; project dir. Vital Record Improvement Project, 1991—; gen. ptnr. Cold Springs Office Devel., Placerville, Calif., 1984—. Mem. El Dorado County Grand Jury, 1990; Weblos leader Boy Scouts Am., 1976-77, scoutmaster, 1977-82; referee, coach El Dorado (Calif.) Youth Soccer League, 1977-83; dir. El Dorado County Fair. Mem. Rho Chi (pres. 1967-68), Phi Delta Chi. Office: Cold Springs Cons 2900 Cold Springs Rd Placerville CA 95667-4220

PALOMBI, BARBARA JEAN, psychologist; b. Rockford, Ill., May 28, 1949; d. Frank and Vira Lavina (Gornet) P. BA, Luther Coll., Decorah, Iowa, 1971; MA, Pacific Lutheran U., Tacoma, Wash., 1974; PhD, Mich. State U., 1987. Career counselor Wright State U., Dayton, Ohio, 1974-77; asst. dean, dir. U. Calif., Irvine, 1977-80; grad. asst. Mich. State U., E. Lansing, 1980-83, clin. intern, 1983-84; clin. intern Colo. State U., Fort Collins, 1984-85; psychologist Ariz. State U., Tempe, 1985—, sr. psychologist, 1991—; cons. in field. Contbr. articles and papers to profl. jours. Mem. U.S. Wheelchair Olympic Team, 1976, U.S. Wheelchair Team to the Interna.t Stoke-Mandelville Games, 1979; alternative mem. U.S. Wheelchair Olympic Team, 1980; U.S. rep. Internat. Symposium on Sports, Physical Edn. and Recreation for the Handicapped, UNESCO, 1982. Grantee Nat. Sci. Found., U. Calif., 1977, 79; named Outstanding Handicapped Citizen Rock County 1982, Handicapped Profl. Woman of the Yr. Western Region, 1987. Mem. Am. Assn. Counseling and Devel. (Glen E. Hubele Nat. Grad. Student Research award 1988), Am. Coll. Personnel Assn. (bd. dirs. Div. VII-Counseling, mem. Div. VIII-Wellness, Burns B. Crookston Research award 1988, Commn. VII Grad. Student Research award 1988), Am. Psychology Assn. (rep. div. 17 handicapped task force). Democrat. Home: 1140 E Marny Rd Tempe AZ 85281-1809 Office: Ariz State U Counseling & Consultation Tempe AZ 85287

PALSMA, MARY J(ACOBSON), educator; b. Webster, S.D., Jan. 16, 1942; d. M. Sherman and Shirley Mae (Amsden) Jacobson; m. Wayne H. Palsma, Dec. 23, 1967; 1 child, Robert Wayne. BS, Northern State Coll., Aberdeen, S.D., MS, 1967. Cert. tchr., Community Coll., Ariz., Secondary High Schs., Ariz. & S.D. Eng. tchr. & libr. Northwestern High Sch., Northville, S.D., 1962; Math. tchr. Milbank (S.D.) High Sch., 1962-64; Math. & Eng. tchr. Riggs High Sch., Pierre, S.D., 1964-68, Mitchell (S.D.) Jr. High Sch., 1969-70, Bourgade Catholic High Sch., Phoenix, 1975—; with Madeline Hunter's Essential Elements of Instrn., Phoenix, 1987-88. Pres. Inter-Club Coun. of Ariz., 1987-88. Mem. Am. Assn. of U. Women (several offices, 1965—, pres. 1977-79; fellowship grant, 1980), Nat. Catholic Edn. Assn. Republican. Lutheran.

PALUMBO, MICHAEL ARNOLD, music educator; b. Denver, Nov. 12, 1945; s. Anthony Palumbo and Mary Jean (Molzer) Brackeen; m. Cynthia Ann Orsborn, June 9, 1968; children: Eric Michael, Allison Paige. B Music Edn., U. Denver, 1967, MA, 1971; ArtsD, Ball State U., 1981. Orch. dir. Cedar Falls (Iowa) High Sch., 1971-73; dir. orchs. Wayne (Nebr.) State Coll., 1973-81, Weber State U., Ogden, Utah, 1981—; conductor New Am. Symphony Orch., Ogden, 1989—; profl. violist orchs., Nebr., Iowa, Ind., Utah, Colo., 1971—; clinician, adjudicator music festivals, 1973. With U.S. Army, 1968-70. Ball State U. fellow, 1978-81. Mem. Utah Music Educators Assn. (v.p. 1984-86, pres. 1989-91), Am. Fedn. Musicians, Am. Viola Soc. (pres. Utah chpt. 1992—), Am. String Tchrs. Assn. (pres. Utah chpt. 1986-88), Phi Mu Alpha, Pi Kappa Lambda. Home: 5171 Fillmore Ave Ogden UT 84403-4612 Office: Weber State U Ogden UT 84408-1905

PAMPLIN, ROBERT BOISSEAU, SR., holding company executive; b. Sutherland, Va., Nov. 25, 1911; s. John R. and Pauline (Beville) P.; m. Mary K. Reese, June 15, 1940; 1 child, Robert Boisseau Jr. BBA, Va. Poly. Inst. & State U., 1933; postgrad., Northwestern U., 1933-34; LLD (hon.), U. Portland (Oreg.), 1972; LHD (hon.), Warner Pacific Coll., 1976. With Ga.-Pacific Corp., Portland, 1934-76, sec., from 1936, adminstrv. v.p., 1952-55, exec. v.p., 1955-57, pres., 1957-67, chmn. bd., chief exec. officer, from 1967; ret., 1976; with R.B. Pamplin Corp., 1957—, chmn. bd., chief exec. officer; also chmn. bd., chief exec. officer Mt. Vernon Mills Inc. (subs. R.B. Pamplin Corp.), Greenville, S.C. Office: R B Pamplin Corp 900 SW 5th Ave Ste 1800 Portland OR 97204-1259 also: Mt Vernon Mills Inc PO Box 3478 1 Insignia Fin Plz Greenville SC 29602

PAN, WILLIAM JIAWEI, import/export company executive, consultant; b. Shanghai, People's Republic of China, July 24, 1935; came to U.S., 1985; s. You-Yuan Pan and Ruth Li Tien; m. Fengqiu Liu, Dec. 26, 1965; 1 child, Song. BS, Peking U., People's Republic of China, 1958. Cert. sr. engr., People's Republic of China. Engr. Beijing Radio Factory, 1958-78, Dong Feng TV Factory, Beijing, 1978-80; asst. gen. mgr. Beijing br. China Nat. Electronics Import/Export Corp., 1980-91; mgr. electronics dept. China Resource Products, N.Y.C., 1985-91; pres., chief exec. officer King Trading, Inc., San Francisco, 1987-91; pres., CEO Kings Internat., Inc., San Jose, Calif., 1991—. Office: Kings Internat Inc Ste 150 467 Saratoga Ave San Jose CA 95129

PANASCI, NANCY ERVIN, speech pathologist, cookbook writer, communications consultant; b. Fairborn, Ohio, Mar. 24, 1954; d. Lindsay James and Frances E. (Erickson) Ervin; m. Ernest James Panasci, Aug. 7, 1976; children: Caitlin Alba, Adele Frances, Carissa Anne. BS, Colo. State U., 1976; MA, Cath. U., Washington, 1979. Tchr. Montessori Sch., Rome, N.Y., 1971-72, Fairfax (Va.) Sch. Dist., 1976-77; speech pathologist Littleton (Colo.) Pub. Schs., 1979-92, pvt. practice, 1992—; communication cons. speech pathology Trial Attys., Denver, 1986—. Com. chairperson. Jr. League in Denver, 1982-91; com. chmn. Make-A-Wish Found. of Colo., 1991; com. chairperson. Denver Victims Svc. Ctr., Share Our Strength. Named Best Cook in West, Rocky Mountain Newspaper, Denver, 1982. Mem. Am. Speech Hearing Lang. Assn. (cert. clin. competence 1980), Colo. Speech Hearing Assn. (com. chairperson 1982-86), Racquet World Club (Englewood, Colo.), Cherry Hills Country Club. Roman Catholic. Home: 5191 S Hanover St Englewood CO 80111-6244 Office: Littleton Pub Schs Littleton CO 80120

PANDO, ALAN OSCAR, advertising company executive; b. Iowa City, Nov. 13, 1931; s. Oscar Benjamin and Eva Marie (Schillig) P.; m. Elizabeth Harlow, June 22, 1956; children: Karen, Scott, Robert; m. Stacie Hunt, Oct. 17, 1981. B.S., U. Notre Dame, 1953. Product mgmt. cons. Chesebrough Ponds, N.Y.C., 1956-60; v.p. Benton & Bowles, N.Y.C., 1960-66; sr. v.p. Kenyon & Eckhardt, N.Y.C., 1966-68; group sr. v.p. Doyle Dane Bernbach, N.Y.C., 1968-82; pres. Della Femina Travisano & Ptnrs., Los Angeles, 1982-85, DDB Needham West, Los Angeles, 1986—. Served to lt. (j.g.) USN, 1953-56. Office: DDB Needham Worldwide Inc 11601 Wilshire Blvd Los Angeles CA 90025

PANELLI, EDWARD ALEXANDER, associate justice; b. Santa Clara, Calif., Nov. 23, 1931; s. Pilade and Natalina (Della Maggiora) P.; m. Lorna Christine Mondora, Oct. 27, 1956; children: Thomas E., Jeffrey J., Michael P. BA cum laude, Santa Clara U., 1953, JD cum laude, 1955, LLD (hon.), 1986; LLD (hon.), Southwestern U., L.A., 1988. Bar: Calif. 1955. Ptnr. Pasquinelli and Panelli, San Jose, Calif., 1955-72; judge Santa Clara County Superior Ct., 1972-83; assoc. justice 1st Dist. Ct. of Appeals, San Francisco, 1983-84; presiding justice 6th Dist. Ct. of Appeals, San Jose, 1984-85; assoc. justice Calif. Supreme Ct., San Francisco, 1985—; instr. Continuing Legal Edn., Santa Clara, 1976-78. Trustee West Valley Community Coll., 1963-72; trustee Santa Clara U., 1963—, chmn. bd. trustees, 1984—. Recipient Citation, Am. Com. Italian Migration, 1969, Community Legal Svcs. award, 1979, 84, Edwin J. Owens Lawyers of Yr. award Santa Clara Law Sch. Alumni, 1982, Merit award Republic of Italy, 1984, Gold medal in recognition of Italians who have honored Italy, Lucca, Italy, 1990, St Thomas More award, San Francisco, 1991, Filippo Mazzei Internat. award, Florence, Italy, 1992; Justice Edward A. Panelli Moot Courtroom named in his honor Santa Clara U., 1989. Mem. ABA, Nat. Italian Bar Assn. (inspiration award 1986), Calif. Trial Lawyers Assn. (Trial Judge of Yr. award Santa Clara County chpt. 1981), Calif. Judges Assn. (bd. dirs. 1982), Jud. Coun. Calif. (vice-chair 1989-93), Alpha Sigma Nu, Phi Alpha Delta Law Found. (hon. mem. Douglas Edmonds chpt.). Republican. Roman Catholic. Office: Supreme Ct Calif 303 2nd St San Francisco CA 94107-1366

PANETTA, JOSEPH DANIEL, biotechnology executive; b. Syracuse, N.Y., Mar. 1, 1954; s. Salvatore and Josephine Mary (Sbardella) P.; m. Karin Ann Hoffman, Oct. 21, 1978; children: Lauren Marie, Christopher Daniel. BS, LeMoyne Coll., 1976; MPH, U. Pitts., 1979. Environ. protection specialist U.S. EPA, Washington, 1979-82, sr. policy analyst, 1982-84; project leader Schering Corp./NorAm Chem Co., Wilmington, Del., 1984-85; mgr. regulatory affairs agrchems. divsn. Pennwalt Corp., Phila., 1985-88; mgr. corp. regulatory affairs Mycogen Corp., San Diego, 1988-90; dir. corp. regulatory affairs and quality assurance Mycogen Corp., 1990-92; dir. corp. regulatory, environ. affairs Mycogen Corp., San Diego, 1992—; chmn. agr. and environment subcom. Internat. Bioindustry Forum; chmn. maneb data task force Inter-industry, Washington, 1985-88; guest lectr. biotech. U. Calif., San Diego, and Calif. Western Law Sch. Contbr. articles to profl. jours. Mem. Rep. State Com. Del., 1987. Mem. Nat. Agrl. Chems. Assn. (mem. registrations com. 1986-89), Indsl. Biotech. Assn. (mem. govt. rels. com., internat. affairs com.), Calif. Indsl. Biotech. Assn. (mem. agrl. affairs com.), Am. Chem. Soc. (mem. agrl. div.). Roman Catholic. Home: 4324 Corte Al Fresco San Diego CA 92130-2160 Office: Mycogen Corp 4980 Carroll Canyon San Diego CA 92121-1764

PANETTA, LEON EDWARD, federal official, former congressman; b. Monterey, Calif., June 28, 1938; s. Carmelo Frank and Carmelina Maria (Prochilo) P.; m. Sylvia Marie Varni, July 14, 1962; children: Christopher, Carmelo, James. B.A. magna cum laude, U. Santa Clara, Calif., 1960, LL.B., J.D., 1963. Bar: Calif. bar 1965, U.S. Supreme Ct. 1965, U.S. Dist. Ct. (no. dist.) Calif. 1965, U.S. Ct. Appeals 1965. Legis. asst. to U.S. Sen. Thomas Kuchel, Washington, 1966-69; dir. U.S. Office Civil Rights, HEW, Washington, 1969-70; exec. asst. to Mayor of N.Y.C., 1970-71; ptnr. Panetta, Thompson & Panetta, Monterey, 1971-76; mem. 95th-103d Congresses from 17th Calif. dist., 1977-93, chmn. budget com., mem. agr. com., adminstrn. com., also com. dep. majority whip for budget issues, mem. select com. on hunger; dir. U.S. Office Mgmt. and Budget, Washington, 1993—. Author: Bring Us Together, 1971. Counsel Monterey Regional Park Dists.; counsel NAACP, 1971-76; bd. trustees U. Santa Clara Law Sch.; founder Monterey Coll. Law; mem. Monterey County Dem. Cen. Com., 1972-74; v.p. Carmel Valley Little League, 1974-75. Served with AUS, 1964-66. Recipient Lincoln award NEA, 1970, Disting. Svc. award NAACP, 1972, Bread for World award, 1978, Nat. Hospice Orgn. award, 1984, Golden Plow award Am. Farm Bur. Fedn., Pres.'s award Am. Coun. on Tchr. of Fgn. Langs., 1991, Coastal and Ocean Mgmt. award Coastal Zone Found., 1991, Food Rsch. and Action Ctr. award, 1991; named Lawyer of Yr., Law Sch. U. Santa Clara, 1970. Mem. Calif. Bar Assn. Roman Catholic. Office: 252 Old Executive Office Bldg Washington DC 20503

PANETTI, RAMON STANLEY, investment company executive, consultant, lawyer; b. Akron, Ohio, Sept. 18, 1931; s. Augustine and Margaret Ruth (Sirdefield) P.; m. Bernadette S. Browne, Oct. 21, 1967; 1 child, Robert Lincoln. BBA, John Carroll U., 1954; MBA, U. Pa., 1958; JD, Cleve. State U., 1964. Bar: Ohio 1964. Fin. exec. Standard Oil Co. (Ohio), Cleve., 1957-65; mgmt. cons. Alspaugh & Co., Cleve., 1965-66; CEO, bd. dirs. Intersvc.

Corp., Cleve., 1966-73; fin. cons., Cleve., 1973-77; CEO, investment cons. Capital Res. Advisors Inc., Newport Beach, Calif., 1978—; lectr. econs., fin. and bus. policy John Carroll U., Cleve., 1965-67. 1st lt. U.S. Army, 1954-56. Mem. Chancellor's Club (U. Calif., Irvine). Office: Capital Res Advisors Inc 1500 Quail St Ste 470 Newport Beach CA 92660

PANG, HERBERT GEORGE, ophthalmologist; b. Honolulu, Dec. 23, 1922; s. See Hung and Hong Jim (Chuu) P.; student St. Louis Coll., 1941; BS, Northwestern U., 1944, MD, 1947; m. Dorothea Lopez, Dec. 27, 1953. Intern Queen's Hosp., Honolulu, 1947-48; postgraduate course ophthalmology N.Y.U., Med. Sch., 1948-49; resident ophthalmology Jersey City Med. Ctr., 1949-50, Manhattan Eye, Ear, & Throat Hosp., N.Y.C., 1950-52; practice medicine specializing in ophthalmology, Honolulu, 1952-54, 56—; mem. staffs Kuakini Hosp., Children's Hosp., Castle Meml. Hosp., Queen's Hosp., St. Francis Hosp.; asst. clin. prof. ophthalmology U. Hawaii Sch. Medicine, 1966-73, now asso. clin. prof. Cons. Bur. Crippled Children, 1952-73, Kapiolani Maternity Hosp., 1952-73, Leahi Tb. Hosp., 1952-62. Capt. M.C., AUS, 1954-56, Diplomate Am. Bd. Ophthalmology. Mem. AMA, Am. Acad. Ophthalmology and Otolaryngology, Assn. for Rsch. Ophthalmology, ACS, Hawaii Med. Soc. (gov. med. practice com. 1958-62, chmn. med. speakers com. 1957-58), Hawaii Eye, Ear, Nose and Throat Soc. (pres. 1960), Pacific Coast Oto-Ophthalmological Soc., Pan Am. Assn. Ophthalmology, Mason, Shriner, Eye Study Club (pres. 1972—). Home: 346 Lewers St Honolulu HI 96815-2345

PANG, KEVIN D., astronomer; m. Sue T.S., July 23, 1981; children: Denise Leilani. BA, U. Hawaii, 1962; MS, U. Calif., L.A., 1963, PhD, 1970. Rsch. geophysicist U. Calif., L.A., 1964-70; rsch. assoc. U. Colo., Boulder, 1970-73; staff scientist Computer Scis. Corp., N.Y.C., 1973-74; rsch. assoc. The Jet Propulsion Lab., Pasadena, Calif., 1974-76, astronomer, 1980—; staff scientist Sci. Applications Internat. Corp., Pasadena, 1976-80; cons. The Rand Corp., Santa Monica, Calif., 1964-65; lectr. Gordon Rsch. Confs. Author numerous works. With U.S. Army, 1957-65. Recipient Group Achievement award NASA Viking Project to Mars, 1976, Herbert C. Pollock award The Dudley Observatory, 1988; Woodrow Wilson fellow, 1962; numerous grants. Mem. Internat. Astronomical Union (commr. 1982—), Am. Astronomical Soc., Am. Geophysical Union, Am. Meteorological Soc., Am. Assn. Advancement for Sci., Sigma Xi, Phi Beta Kappa. Democrat. Office: Jet Propulsion Lab 4800 Oak Grove Dr T1182 Pasadena CA 91109-8099

PANG, KIN MAN (ANDY), physician; b. Hong Kong, China, Jan. 10, 1948; came to U.S., 1969; s. Kwong Yuen and Chiu Wah (Li) P.; m. Pamela Yinping Chan, Feb. 11, 1976; children: Wyming Lee, Wyson Jonathon, Wyki Gina. BS, Ill. Inst. Tech., 1973; MS, U. Chgo., 1977; MD, Rush Med. Coll., 1983. Intern, resident Southern Ill. U., Springfield, 1983-85; intern St. Joseph Hosp., Chgo., 1985-86, Cook County Hosp., Chgo., 1986-87; resident St. Joseph Hosp., 1987-89; physician group practice, Manteca, Calif., 1989-91, pvt. practice, Manteca, Calif., 1991—. Fellow Am. Coll. Ob-gyn.; mem. AMA, Am. Inst. Ultrasound in Medicine, Am. Assn. Gynelogic Lapardoscopists, Calif. Med. Assn., San Joaquin County Med. Soc., Sigma Xi. Office: 505 E Center Manteca CA 95336

PANKOVE, JACQUES ISAAC, physicist; b. Chernigov, Russia, Nov. 23, 1922; came to U.S., 1942, naturalized, 1944; s. Evsey Leib and Miriam (Simkine) Pantchechnikoff; m. Ethel Wasserman, Nov. 24, 1950; children: Martin, Simon. B.S.E.E., U. Calif., Berkeley, 1944, M.S.E.E., 1948; Ph.D. in Physics, U. Paris, 1960. Mem. tech. staff RCA Labs., Princeton, N.J., 1948-70; physicist, fellow RCA Labs., 1970-85; prof. U. Colo., Boulder, 1985—, Hudson Moore Jr. Univ. prof., 1989—, program mgr. materials and devices Ctr. for Optoelectronic Computing Systems, 1986-89; Disting. rsch. fellow Nat. Renewable Energy Lab. (formerly Solar Energy Rsch. Inst.), 1985—; vis. McKay lectr. U. Calif., Berkeley, 1968-69; vis. prof. U. Campinas, Brazil, 1975; Disting. vis. prof. U. Mo. at Rolla, 1984; participant NAS sci. exch. program with: Romania, 1970, Hungary, 1972, Yugoslavia, 1976. Mem. hon. editorial bd. Solid State Electronics, 1970—, Solar Energy Materials, 1984—, Optoelectronics, 1986—; regional editor Crystal Lattice Defects and Amorphous Materials, 1984-90; author: Optical Processes in Semiconductors, 1971, 75; editor: Electroluminescence, 1977, Display Devices, 1980, Hydrogenated Amorphous Silicon, 1984; co-editor: Hydrogen in Semiconductors, 1991, Wide Bandgap Semiconductors, 1992; author: (ednl. film) Energy Gap and Recombination Radiation, 1962; laser sculpture, Bklyn. Mus., 1968; contbr. articles to profl. jours.; organizer sci. confs.; patentee in field. Trustee Princeton Art Assn., 1970-82; mem. Experiment-in-Arts-and-Tech., Berkeley, 1968-69. Served with U.S. Army, 1944-46. Recipient RCA achievement awards, 1952, 53, 63; David Sarnoff scholar, 1956. Fellow IEEE (J. J. Ebers award 1975, assoc. editor Jour. Quantum Electronics 1968-77, mem.-at-large IEEE awards bd. 1992—), Am. Phys. Soc.; mem. AAAS, NAE (hon.), Materials Rsch. Soc., Internat. Soc. for Optical Engring., Sigma Xi. Home: 2386 Vassar Dr Boulder CO 80303-5763 Office: U Colo Dept Elec Engring Boulder CO 80309-0425 also: Nat Renewable Energy Lab 1617 Cole Blvd Golden CO 80401

PANNER, OWEN M., federal judge; b. 1924. Student, U. Okla., 1941-43, LL.B., 1949. Atty. Panner, Johnson, Marceau, Karnopp, Kennedy & Nash, 1950-80; judge U.S. Dist. Ct. Oreg., Portland, 1980—. Office: US Dist Ct 602 US Courthouse 620 SW Main St Portland OR 97205-3023*

PANOPOULOS, LINDA LOUISE, mathematics educator; b. Omaha, Nov. 6, 1949; d. Roy Thomas and Eleanor Ernestine (Hobbs) Gage; m. Nick A. Panopoulos, May 26, 1979; children: Jeannine, Elizabeth. Student, U. Nebr., Omaha, 1967-69, Coll. St. Mary, 1970-72; BS, U. Wyo., 1981. Acctg. clk. Omaha Pub. Power Dist., 1971-79; adj. instr. Laramie County C.C., Cheyenne, 1979—; tchr. Laramie County Sch. Dist., Cheyenne, Wyo., 1981-82; v.p. Panopoulos Enterprises, Cheyenne, 1989—. Vol. Cheyenne Frontier Days Com., 1992. Mem. Daus. of Penelope (treas. 1989—), Ch. Women United, Philoptochos (corr. sec. 1991—). Greek Orthodox. Office: Panopoulos Enterprises 6811 Valley View Pl Cheyenne WY 82009

PANSKY, EMIL JOHN, entrepreneur; b. Manhattan, N.Y., June 1, 1921; s. Stanislaus and Anna (Jankovic) P.; m. Bill B. Byrne, May 27, 1955; 1 adopted child, Jimmy. BME, Cooper Union Coll., 1941; MBA, Harvard U., 1949; MADE, NYU, 1950. Registered profl. engr., Mich. Chief insp. flight line Republic Aviation, Farmingdale, L.I., 1941-45, salvage engr., 1946-47; product control supr. to product control mgr. Ford Motor, Detroit, 1949-51; asst. plant mgr. Anderson Brass, Birmingham, Ala., 1951-53; asst. v.p. to v.p. mfg. Cummins Engine, Columbus, Ind., 1953-54; pvt. practice Emil J. Pansky Assoc., San Leandro, Calif., 1954—; pres. Calif. Mfrs. Tech. Assn., San Francisco, 1978-80. Patentee die cast auto wheels, 1965. Pres. Menlo Circus Club, Menlo Park, Calif., 1974-81, Home Owners Assn., Kanuela, Hawaii, 1989-92; bd. dirs. No. Calif. Tennis Assn., San Francisco, 1984-87. Mem. ASME (life), Harvard Club San Francisco (bd. dirs. 1986-92), Harvard Bus. Sch. Club San Francisco (bd. dirs. 1970-73). Democrat. Home: 901 Jackling Dr Hillsborough CA 94010 Office: Emil J Pansky Assoc 1666 Timothy Dr San Leandro CA 94577

PANTOS, WILLIAM PANTAZES, mechanical engineer, consultant; b. Ann Arbor, Mich., May 15, 1957; s. William Van and Lillian William (Skinner) P. BS in Mech. Engring., Northwestern U., Evanston, Ill., 1979; MS in Mech. Engring., San Diego State U., 1991. Registered profl. engr., Calif. Owner Signs & Symbols, Niles, Ill., 1975-80; engr. Hughes Aircraft, El Segundo, Calif., 1980-83, Gen. Dynamics, San Diego, 1983-85; staff engr. TRW, San Diego, 1985-90; pres. Tekton Industries, Carlsbad, Calif., 1990—. NROTC scholar USN, 1975. Mem. Am. Soc. Mech. Engrs., Nat. Soc. Profl. Engrs., Alpha Delta Phi. (pres. 1978). Greek Orthodox. Home: 6857 Seaspray Ln Carlsbad CA 92009-3738

PANY, KURT JOSEPH, accounting educator, consultant; b. St. Louis, Mar. 31, 1946; s. Joseph Francis and Ruth Elizabeth (Westerman) P.; m. Darlene Dee Zabish, June 3, 1971; children: Jeffrey, Michael. BSBA, U. Ariz., 1968; MBA in Mgmt., U. Minn., 1971; PhD in Accountancy, U. Ill., 1977. CPA, Ariz., cert. fraud examiner. Staff auditor Arthur Andersen & Co., Mpls., 1968-69, Touche Ross & Co., Phoenix, 1971-73; teaching asst. U. Minn., Mpls., 1969-71; teaching asst. auditing and acctg. U. Ill., Urbana, 1972-76; asst. prof. acctg. Ariz. State U., Tempe, 1977-81, assoc. prof., 1981-85, Arthur Andersen/Don Dupont prof. acctg., 1985-93; mem. acctg. and auditing standards com. State of Ariz., Phoenix, 1989—. Contributor: CPA Examination Review, 1983--, Principles of Auditing, 1988; editor (with Andrew D. Bailey, Jr.) Auditing: A Journal of Practice & Theory, 1984-88; mem. editorial bd. Advances in Acctg., 1982--, Jour. Acctg. Edn., 1983--; reviewer Jour. Acctg. and Pub. Policy, 1983--; reviewer Acctg. Rev., 1984--, ad hoc editor, 1989--; contbr. numerous articles to profl. jours. Active various child-related orgns. Peat, Marwick, Mitchell & Co. Found. grantee, 1985. Fellow AICPA (auditing standards div. 1989-90, acctg. lit. selection com. 1989-90, acctg. lit. awards com. 1979-83); mem. Am. Acctg. Assn. (tech. program com. 1980-81, chairperson Western region auditing sect. 1981-83, acctg. lit. nominating com. 1982-84, 88-89, acctg. lit. selection com. 1989-90, dir. auditing standards, chmn. auditing standards com. 1989-90), Ariz. Soc. CPA's (auditing standards com. 1978-81, ethics com. 1981-84). Office: Ariz State U Sch of Accountancy Tempe AZ 85287

PANZER, JOEL RUSSELL, geographer; b. Hanover, N.H., June 23, 1958; s. Milford Donald and Joan Gail (Bartholomew) P.; m. Maureen Louise Wruck, Apr. 25, 1992. BA in Geography, Trenton State Coll., 1982; MA in Geography, Calif. State U., Chico, Calif., 1989. Planning intern City of Chico (Calif.) Planning Dept., 1983, Butte County Planning Dept., Oroville, Calif., 1984; planner III Monterey County Planning Dept., Salinas, Calif., 1985-90; pres. Carmel Valley (Calif.) Seed Co., 1988—; environ. planner Rancho San Carlos, Carmel, Calif., 1990—; pres., dir. Cachagua Community Ctr., Carmel Valley, Calif., 1986—; cons. M.L. Wruck & Assocs., Carmel Valley, 1992—. Author: Cachagua Area Plan, 1983. Sec. Cachagua Community Ctr., Carmel Valley, 1986-91; class of 1992 Leadership Monterey Peninsula, 1991-92. Mem. Leadership Monterey Peninsula Alumni Assn., Assn. Pacific Coast Geographers, Assn. of Am. Geographers, Am. Planning Assn. Democrat. Jewish. Home: 33750 E Carmel Valley Rd Carmel Valley CA 93924 Office: Pacific Union Co Rancho San Carlos PO Box 222707 Carmel CA 93922

PAPARIAN, MICHAEL, environmental advocate; b. L.A., Aug. 30, 1955; s. William Joseph and Serpouhi Mary (Dickranian) P.; m. Catherine Eleanor Sproul, Mar. 23, 1991; 1 child, Matthew Sproul. BA in Psychology, BA in Biology, U. Calif., Santa Cruz, 1977; MA in Environ. Planning, Calif. State U., Sacramento, 1987. Legis. rep. Sierra Club Calif., Sacramento, 1978-84, state dir., 1984—; mem. toxic substances rsch. and tng. program pub. adv. com. U. Calif., 1990—. Editor: California Energy Directory, 1980; also articles. Mem. Calif. Gov.'s Solarcal Coun., 1979-82; mem. Sacramento support com. Am. Youth Hostels, 1988—; pres. Coun. for Justice in Cyprus and Near East, Sacramento, 1983—. Recipient Flak Catchers award Calif. Common Cause, 1988. Mem. Internat. Union for Conservation Nature and Natural Resources (commn. on strategy and planning 1984—), Natural Resources Def. Coun., Calif. League Conservation Voters (bd. dirs. 1983—), Calif. Inst. Pub. Affairs (trustee 1985—), Calif. Hazardous Waste Mgmt. Coun. (coun. 1983-84). Mem. Armenian Apostolic Ch. Office: Sierra Club Calif 923 12th St Ste 200 Sacramento CA 95814

PAPCUN, GEORGE, linguistics research scientist, consultant; b. N.Y.C., Nov. 2, 1939; s. George John and Alice (Falik) P.; m. Judith Celia Kaye, July 10, 1977. BA in Math., U. Ariz., 1961; MA in Formal Linguistics, UCLA, 1969, PhD in Acoustic Phonetics, 1980. Mem. tech. staff Aerospace Corp., El Segundo, Calif., 1973-76; sr. instr., course author Integrated Computer Systems, Santa Monica, Calif., 1980-83; sr. instr., course author Los Alamos (N.Mex.) Nat. Lab., 1982—, mem. exec. com. Ctr. for Nonlinear Studies, 1986—, assoc. and dep. dir. Ctr. for Nonlinear Studies, 1987-88, speech project leader computing and comm. div., 1992—; cons. L.A. Sheriff Dept., 1984-85, Orange County Pub. Defender's Office, Santa Ana, Calif., 1992; presenter and expert witness in field; cons. on practical applications of speech tech. to pvt. cos. Author: Voice Input/Output for Computers, 1980, Forensic Lineups, 1992; also articles; inventor animated display of mouth. Bd. dirs. La Tierra Nueva, Santa Fe, 1992-94. Recipient award for one of 100 most significant technol. innovations R & D Mag., 1992; fellow Ford Found., 1968, NDEA, 1970-71. Mem. Acoustical Soc. Am. Home: 1081 Buckman Rd Santa Fe NM 87501

PAPE, ARNIS WESTON, minister; b. Portales, N.Mex., Dec. 24, 1950; s. Arnis Wilson and Lella Mae (Berry) P.; m. Lucena Ann Molzen, May 31, 1975; children: John Dayton, Jennifer Marie. BA in Psychology, U.N.Mex., 1974. Ordained to ministry Church of Christ, 1972. Assoc. minister Ch. of Christ, Plainview, Tex., 1974-76; pulpit minister Ch. of Christ, Artesia, N.Mex., 1976-85, Ft. Collins, Colo., 1985—; tchr. Pepperdine U., Malibu, 1991, 93. Editor bull. Meadowlark Messenger, 1985—; contbr. articles to profl. jours.; author booklet: Happy Though Married, 1988, rev. edit., 1992. Co-founder Am. Children's Transplant Fund, Ft. Collins, 1987; mem. Parent Adv. Bd., Artesia, 1983-84; mem. pres.'s coun. Lubbock Christian U., 1985—. Recipient award for outstanding svc. Ch. of Christ, 1985. Home: 2212 Shawnee Ct Fort Collins CO 80525-1849 Office: Church of Christ 2810 Meadowlark Ave Fort Collins CO 80526-2838

PAPE, THOMAS EMIL, marketing professional, consultant; b. Redbud, Ill., Apr. 28, 1959; s. Gilbert Raymond and Delphine (Mehrtens) P. BA, So. Ill. U., 1981. Cert. energy auditor, Ill., residential conservation svc. trainer, Calif., master water auditor. Energy cons. VISTA, Carbondale, Ill., 1979-80; design cons. Applied Alternatives, Desoto, Ill., 1980-83; energy auditor DMC Energy Inc., Springfield, Ill., 1981-83, field cons., 1983-84; project supr. DMC Energy Inc., Santa Monica, Calif., 1984-85; mktg. rsch. cons. DMC Energy Inc., L.A., 1985-88; conservation specialist City of Pasadena, Calif., 1988-90; dir. Volt Delta Resources, Orange, Calif., 1990—; mem. solar speaker bur. Ill. Dept. Energy and Natural Resources, 1979-82. Mem. Assn. Profl. Energy Mgrs., Am. Water Works Assn. (chmn. water conservation com. on interior plumbing), Pacific Coast Electric Assn. (exec. dir.), Pacific Coast Gas Assn. (exec. dir.). Roman Catholic. Home: 1704 Elm St El Cerrito CA 94530-1909

PAPERNO, HERBERT, quality assurance engineer; b. N.Y.C., Mar. 10, 1933; s. Joseph Paperno and Celia (Holtsman) Brodsky; m. Judith Price Paperno, Nov. 24, 1975; children: Roger Ian, Adam Michael, Timothy Blake. B Chem. Engring., CCNY, 1955. Registered profl. engr., Calif., Tex. Test engr. Aberdeen (Md.) Proving Grounds, 1955-56; design engr. Douglas Aircraft Co., Santa Monica, Calif., 1956-59; quality engr. Aerojet Gen., Sacramento, 1959-70; quality assurance engr. Bechtel Corp., San Francisco, 1970-77; quality assurance mgr. Brown & Root, Houston, 1977-80; v.p. Dynatech Nuclear, San Francisco, 1980-84; mgr. nuclear program Pacific Gas & Electric, San Francisco, 1984—. Mem. Am. Soc. for Quality Control (chmn. standards control energy div. 1988—, Regional Counsilor of Yr. award 1989), B'nai B'rith (pres. San Francisco 1983). Home: 508 Stone Dr Novoto CA 94947 Office: Pacific Gas & Electric One California F-1800 San Francisco CA 94106

PAPERNY, VLADIMIR, designer, writer; b. Moscow, May 19, 1944; came to U.S., 1981; s. Zinovy Paperny and Kaleria Ozerova; m. Gulnora Khoshmukhamedova (div. May 1973); 1 child, Dmitry; m. Katya Kompaneyets, Feb. 10, 1979; 1 child, Tanya; stepchildren: Yelena, Marc. MA in Indsl. Design, Stroganov Art Sch., Moscow, 1969; PhD in Archtl. History, Inst. Theory and History Architecture, Moscow, 1979. Designer, rsch. assoc. Rsch. Inst. Indsl. Design, Moscow, 1969-73; free-lance art dir. Moscow Drama Theatre, 1973-75, Moscow State Lit. Mus., 1979-81; sr. rsch. fellow Cen. Inst. Theory and History Architecture, Moscow, 1975-79; assoc. art dir. Orange Coast Mag., Irvine, Calif., 1981-83; dir. advt. and graphic arts Integrated Ceilings, Inc., L.A., 1983-86; dir. advt. Lavi Industries, Valencia, Calif., 1986-88; pres. Vladimir Paperny & Assocs., L.A., 1988—; guest scholar Woodrow Wilson Internat. Ctr. Scholars, Washington, 1984. Author: The Future of Dwelling, 1973, Culture Two, 1985; designer electronic equipment. Recipient Cert. of Merit, Illustration West-29, L.A., 1990, Soc. Dimensional Illustration, 1990, Top 10 award Archtl. Record Mag., 1985, AD-Q award Progressive Archtl. Mag., 1983, Pewter award, Gold Ink awards, 1990. Office: Vladimir Paperny & Assoc 5818 W Third St Los Angeles CA 90036

PAPIER, BRUCE LEE, educator, consultant, artist; b. Columbus, Ohio, May 31, 1940; s. Abe Papier and Fannie Lehrer. BFA, Ohio State U., 1966, MA, 1967, MFA, 1969. Designer Israel Aircraft Industries, Tel Aviv, 1969-71; asst. prof. U. Denver, Colo., 1971-78, Purdue U., West Lafayette, Ind., 1978-83, Ariz. State U., Tempe, 1983-87; assoc. prof. N.Mex. Highlands U., Las Vegas, 1987—; coord. design program N.Mex. Highlands U., Las Vegas, 1987—, cons. computer graphics, 1987—. Vol. designer for devel. Mus. for Children, Denver, 1974. With USAF, 1959-63. Mem. AAUP, Rio Grand SIGGRAPH (edn. coord.). Office: N Mex Highlands Univ Visual Communications Bldg Las Vegas NM 87701

PAPIKE, JAMES JOSEPH, geology educator, science institute director; b. Virginia, Minn., Feb. 11, 1937; s. Joseph John and Sistine Marie (Tassi) P.; m. Pauline Grace Maras, Sept. 6, 1958; children: Coleen, Coreen, Jimmy, Heather. BS in Geol. Engring. with high honors, S.D. Sch. Mines and Tech., 1959; PhD, U. Minn., 1964. Rsch. geologist U.S. Geol. Survey, Washington, 1964-69; assoc. prof. dept. earth and space scis. SUNY, Stony Brook, 1969-71, prof., 1971-82, chmn. dept., 1971-74; prof. dept. geology and geol. engring. S.D. Sch. Mines and Tech., Rapid City, 1982-87, Disting. prof., 1987-90, dir. Inst. for Study Mineral Deposits, 1982-90, dir. Engring. and Mining Expt. Sta., 1984-90; Regents' prof. dept. geology, dir. Inst. Meteoritics, U. N.Mex., Albuquerque, 1990—; mem. adv. com. for earth scis. NSF, 1985-89, Continental Sci. Drilling Rev. Group, Dept. Energy, 1986-87, Lunar and Planetary Sample Team, 1990—, Lunar Outpost Site Selection Com., 1990-91, organizing com. for FORUM for Continental Sci. Drilling, 1990—, adv. com. Inst. Geophysics and Planetary Physics, Los Alamos Nat. Lab., 1991—. Assoc. editor procs. 4th Lunar Sci. Conf., 1973, Jour. Geophys. Rsch., 1975-77, 82-84; editor procs. Internat. Conf.: The Nature of Oceanic Crust, 1976, Luna 24 Conf., 1977, Conf. on Lunar Highlands Crust, 1980; guest editor spl. issue Geophys. Rsch. Letters, 1991; mem. editorial bd. Procs. Lunar and Planetary Sci. Confs., 1987; contbr. numerous articles to profl. jours. Recipient NASA medal, 1973, Centennial Alumni award S.D. Sch. Mines and Tech., 1985; grantee NSF, NASA, Dept. Energy, 1969—. Fellow Geol. Soc. Am., Mineral. Soc. Am. (life, MSA medal 1974, past mem. coun.), Soc. Econ. Geologists (mem. coun.); mem. Am. Geophys. Union (past sec.), Geochem. Soc. (v.p. 1988-89, pres. 1989-91), Meteoritical Soc., Mineral. Assn. Can. Roman Catholic. Home: 103 La Mesa Placitas NM 87043 Office: U NMex Inst Meteoritics Northrop Hall Rm 313 Albuquerque NM 87131-1126

PAPPAS, COSTAS ERNEST, aeronautical engineer, consultant; b. Providence, Oct. 14, 1910; s. Ernest and Sofie (Rose) P.; m. Thetis Hero, June 9, 1940; children: Alceste, Conrad. B.S., NYU, 1933, M.S., 1934. Registered profl. engr., N.Y., Calif. Stress analyst, aerodynamicist Republic Aviation Corp. (formerly Seversky Aircraft Corp.), 1935-39, chief aerodynamics, 1939-54, chief aerodynamics and thermodynamics, 1954-57, asst. dir. sci. research, 1957-59, asst. to v.p. research and devel., 1959-64; cons. to aerospace industry, 1964—; cons. sci. adv. bd. USAF-Aero Space Vehicles Panel. Author: Design Concepts and Technical Feasibility Studies of an Aerospace Plane, 1961, (with Thetis H. Pappas, memoirs) To the Rainbow and Beyond, 1992; contbr. articles to profl. jours.; patentee in field. Mem. NYU Alumni Vis. Com.; mem. San Mateo County Devel. Assn.; mem. grievance com. San Mateo-Burlingame Bd. Realtors, 1982-83, mem. legis. com., 1985-86; planning commr. City of Redwood City (Calif.), 1984-87, vice chmn. planning commn., 1986; mem. adv. council Growth Policy Counc., 1985-90. Recipient Wright Bros. award Soc. Automotive Engr., 1943; award Rep. Aviation Corp., 1944; Certificate of Distinction NYU Coll. Engring., 1955. Mem. NASA (subcom. high speed aerodynamics 1947-53, spl. subcom. research problems transonic aircraft design 1948), Inst. Aero Scis. (asso. fellow, mem. adv. bd. and membership com.), Inst. Aerospace Scis. (chmn. vehicle design panel 1960), Am. Inst. Aeros. and Astronautics (mem. ram jet panel, chmn. workshop profl. unemployed), Calif. Soc. Profl. Engrs., Air Force Assn., Tau Beta Pi (founder, 1st pres. San Francisco Peninsula alumnus chpt. 1971, asst. dir. Dist. 15 1979—), Redwood City-San Mateo County C. of C. (econ. devel. and govtl. rels. com. 1987—), Iota Alpha. Club: Commonwealth of Calif. Address: PO Box 5633 San Mateo CA 94402

PAPPAS, JOHN STEPHEN, educator, Greek folk musician/dance ethnologist; b. San Francisco, July 13, 1943; s. Státhis and Florence Edith (Arrington) P.; m. Paula Louise Surber, Aug. 17, 1968; children: Kaliópi, Státhis. AA, City Coll. San Francisco, 1963; BA, U. Calif., Berkeley, 1965; MA, San Francisco State, 1969. English tchr. Frondistirion Klitsáki, Athens, 1970-71; instr. English, ethnic dance and soccer San Joaquin Delta Coll., Stockton, Calif., 1972—; soccer coach, instr. folk dance for disabled San Joaquin Delta Coll., 1972—; com. U. of the Pacific Folk Dance Camp, Stocton, 1969—; choreographer Duquesne U. Tamburitzans, Pitts., 1980; tchr., performer Smithsonian Inst., Washington, 1976, San Francisco's Western Regional Am. Folk Life Festivals, N.W. Folk Music Festival, Seattle; tchr., lectr., performer in U.S., Can., Mex., 1965—. Author: Ethnic Dances of Greece, 1978; contbr. folklore articles to various pubs.; writer, prodr., performer ethnic music recordings including Greek Dances, 1990, Greek Dances # 2, 1991. Leader cub scouts Boy Scouts Am., Stockton, 1986-89, asst. scoutmaster, Boy Scouts, 1989—, brotherhood mem., assoc. advisor, chpt. advisor, 1993, Nat. Jamboree, adv. Order of Arrow, assoc. mgr. Buckskin games; asst. coach Little League Baseball, Stockton, 1990; sec. ch. coun. St. Basil's Greek Orthodox Ch., Stockton, 1992-93; St. Basil's Greek Orthodox Ch. parish coun. sec. 1992-93. Mem. NRA, United Arcadian Soc., Hellenic Profl. Soc., Golden Gate Live Steamers, Sacramento Valley Live Steamers, Lodi Hellenic Soc., U. Calif. Berkeley Alumni Assn. (life). Office: San Joaquin Delta Coll 5151 Pacific Ave Stockton CA 95207-6370

PAPPAS, NICHOLAS, psychiatrist; b. Bklyn., June 30, 1937; s. Michael George and Chrisanthy Anna (Nikolakakis) P.; m. Margaret Carol, Nov. 24, 1963; children: Katina Michelle, Christine Reneé. BA in Physiology and Anatomy, Ind. U., 1959; MD, Ind. U., Indpls., 1962. Diplomate Am. Bd. Psychiatry. Intern Detroit Receiving Hosp., 1962-63; resident Ind. U. Med. Ctr., 1963-65, Napa St. Hosp., Imola, Calif., 1968-70; staff psychiatrist Ctrl. State Hosp., Indpls., 1965-66, Napa State Hosp., Imola, 1970-73; pvt. practice Novato, Calif., 1971—; supr. Sonoma St. U. Nursing students, 1973—, Calif. Sch. Profl. Psychology interns, Berkeley, Calif., 1976—; staff sec. Novato Community Hosp., 1974; med. dir. Canyon Manor Hosp., Novato, Calif., 1974-75; med. cons. Erickson Inst., Santa Rosa, Calif., 1982—. Contbr. articles to profl. jours. With US Army, 1966-68. Mem. Calif. Biofeedback Soc. Republican. Greek Orthodox. Office: 1025 5th St Novato CA 94945

PARADY, JOHN EDWARD, information systems executive, consultant; b. Inglewood, Calif., Sept. 26, 1939; s. Raymond Oliver and Ella Louise (Timm) P.; m. Barbara Lyn Pettit, Aug. 13, 1966; children: John, Renee, Stacy. BS, Calif. State U., Los Angeles, 1966; MS, U. So. Calif., 1969. Cert. data processing. Dir. info. systems Weyerhauser Co., Tacoma, Wash., 1975-82; exec. dir. McKenna, Conner & Cuneo, Los Angeles, 1982-83; sr. v.p. Bank of Am., San Francisco, 1983-85; pvt. practice cons. L.A., 1986-88; exec. v.p. Pacific Stock Exchange, Los Angeles, 1988—; mem. The Rsch. Bd., N.Y.C., 1983-86; bd. dirs. The Ctr. for Info. Systems Rsch., Cambridge, Mass., 1977-85; bd. dirs. The Molding Corp. Am. Served to 2d lt., U.S. Army, 1959-64. Republican. Mormon. Home: 1004 Vista Del Valley Rd La Canada Flintridge CA 91011-1805 Office: 233 S Beaudry Ave Los Angeles CA 90012-2000

PARAMORE, JAMES MARTIN, church executive; b. Salt Lake City, May 6, 1928; s. James Frank and Ruth Colorado (Martin) P.; m. Helen Heslington, Dec. 7, 1951; children: James Richard, Jolene, David, Christine, Lisa, Paul. Student, Monterey Peninsula Coll., 1947-48; BA in Sociology and Econs., Brigham Young U., 1961; postgrad., U. Utah, 1963. Missionary Ch. of Jesus Christ of Latter Day Saints, France and Belgium, 1946-51; ch. seminary tchr. Ch. of Jesus Christ of Latter Day Saints, Pleasant Grove, Utah, 1962-63; mission pres. Ch. of Jesus Christ of Latter Day Saints, Brussels, 1966-69; exec. sec. coun. of 12 apostles Ch. of Jesus Christ of Latter Day Saints, Salt Lake City, 1970-77, gen. authority, 1977—, mem. Presidency of the Seventy, 1987—; elec. distbn. engr. Geneva works U.S. Steel, Provo, Utah, 1955-57, process engr., 1957-62; cons. U. Utah, Salt Lake City, 1963-66; mem. adv. bd. Bonneville Telecomm., Salt Lake City, 1983-87; regional rep. LDS Ch. in Western USA and France, 1971-77. Vice chmn. Utah Com. on Children and Youth, Salt Lake City, 1970-75; bd. dirs. Nat. Com. on Children and Youth, Washington, 1965-66; pres., bd. dirs. Sharon Community Edn. and Recreation Assn., Orem, Utah, 1960-66; mem. devel. com. Orem Golf Course, 1960-63; mem. Orem City Coun., 1963-66. Sgt. U.S. Army, 1946-48, USNG; 1st lt. USNG, 1946, 57-61. Republican. Home: PO Box 24 Draper UT 84020-0024 Office: Ch of Jesus Christ LDS 47 E South Temple St Salt Lake City UT 84150

PARDO, SCOTT ALBERT, statistician; b. Phila., Dec. 13, 1957; s. Murray S. and Betty R. (Rothenberg) P.; m. Gail Covitt, June 3, 1990; children: Michael Avraham, Yehudah Aryeh. BA in Anthropology, Calif. State U., Northridge, 1979; MS in Stats., Rochester Inst. Tech., 1983; MS in Ops. Rsch., U. So. Calif., 1987, PhD in Indsl. Engring., 1992. Ops. rsch. analyst U.S. Army Communications, Ft. Huachuca, Ariz., 1980-83; systems modeling analyst Aerospace Corp., El Segundo, Calif., 1983-88; ops. researcher Rand Corp., Santa Monica, Calif., 1988-91, cons., 1991—; sr. statistician Siemens Pacesetter, Inc., Sylmar, Calif., 1991—. Mem. Inst. Indsl. Engrs., Am. Statis. Assn.,Ops. Rsch. Soc. Am., Am. Soc. Quality Control, Armed Forces Comms. and Electronics Assn., Sigma Xi, Omega Rho, Alpha Pi Mu. Home: 1603 Corning St Los Angeles CA 90035 Office: Siemens Pacesetter Inc 15900 Valley View Ct Sylmar CA 91392-9221

PARDUE, A. MICHAEL, plastic and reconstructive surgeon; b. Nashville, June 23, 1931; s. Andrew Peyton and Ruby (Fly) P.; m. Jeanette Mabry, June, 1961 (div. Mar. 1964). BS, U. of the South, 1953; MD, U. Tenn., 1957. Resident in gen. surgery Pittsfield (Mass.) Affiliated Hosps., 1966; resident in plastic surgery N.Y. Hosp./Cornell Med. Ctr., 1968; plastic surgeon A. Michael Pardue, M.D., Thousand Oaks, Calif., 1968—. Lt. comdr. USN, 1956-62. Fellow ACS; mem. Am. Soc. Plastic and Reconstructive Surgeons, Am. Soc. Aesthetic Plastic Surgery, Calif. Soc. Plastic Surgeons. Episcopalian. Office: 327 S Moorpark Rd Thousand Oaks CA 91361-1086

PAREDES, BERT (NORBERT PAREDES), computer systems engineer; b. Frankfurt, Fed. Republic Germany, Dec. 27, 1947; s. George and Elfriede (Kleebach) P.; m. Linda L. Stubblefield, July 5, 1968 (div. 1986); m. Katherine Blacklock, Feb. 4, 1989. BS in Computer Sci., SUNY, Albany, 1970; postgrad., U. Colo., 1977-78. Enlisted U.S. Army, 1970, programmer/analyst, 1970-79, resigned, 1979; staff engr. Martin Marietta, Denver, 1979-81, sr. staff engr., 1984-92; regional analyst, mgr. Gould Computer Systems, Denver, 1981-84; mgr. tech. analysis and support Denelcor, Inc., Aurora, Colo., 1984; v.p. C-Quad Systems, Inc., Littleton, Colo., 1992—; Pres., chief exec. officer A.C.T., Inc., Denver, 1982-84. Contbr. articles to profl. jours. Vol. cons. Opera Colo., Denver, 1982—. Nat. Merit scholar, 1966. Mem. Assn. Computing Machinery, Armed Forces Communications and Electronics Assn., Am. Rose Soc., Mensa, Denver Bot. Gardens. Libertarian. Lutheran. Home: 6859 N Beaver Run Littleton CO 80125-9202 Office: C-Quad Systems Inc Ste 600 26 W Dry Creek Cir Littleton CO 80120

PARENT, ELIZABETH ANNE, educator; b. Bethel, Alaska, Jan. 12, 1941; d. Joe and Evelyn (Halverson) P.; divorced; children: Brian Wescott, Liam Wescott, Siobhan Wescott. MEd, Harvard U., 1973, CAS, 1974; MA, Stanford U., 1978, PhD, 1984. Dir. Fairbanks (Alaska) Headstart Assn., 1970-72; lectr. Harvard U., Cambridge, Mass., 1973-74, U. Calif., Berkeley, 1976-79; lectr. San Francisco State U., 1979-80, asst. prof., 1980-85, assoc. prof., 1985—; mem. information and tech. com. Smithsonian Inst., 1990—. Columnist Tundra Times, Anchorage, Alaska. Mem. Univ. Com. on Minorities, Stanford, 1988-90, Commn. on Racism, San Francisco State U., 1989—. Am. Indian Program fellow, 1972-74; Ford fellow, 1975; Danforth fellow, 1975. Mem. Am. Higher Edn. Assn. Home: PO Box 280954 San Francisco CA 94128-0954 Office: San Francisco State U Am Indian Studies 1600 Holloway Ave San Francisco CA 94132-1722

PARENTI, KATHY ANN, interior designer; b. Gary, Ind., Sept. 24, 1957; d. Lee Everett Huddleston and Barbara Elizabetrh (Daves) Tilley; m. Michael A. Parenti, Mar. 31, 1979 (div. Sept. 1990). Student, Ind. U., Gary, 1977; cert., U. Nev., Las Vegas, 1978; diploma, Interior Design Inst., Las Vegas, 1984. Supr. Circus Circus Hotel, Las Vegas, 1980-87; owner Interior Views, Las Vegas, 1984-87; sales rep. Win-Glo Window Coverings, 1987-88; owner Dimension Design, 1988-90; sales rep. Sidney Goldberg & Assoc., Las Vegas, 1990—. Mem. Internat. Brotherhood of Teamsters, Chauffeurs, Warehousemen, Network of Exec. Women in Hospitality, Internat. Soc. Interior Designers, Internat. Design Inst. Soc., The Rep Network.

PARER, JULIAN THOMAS, obstetrics and gynecology educator; b. Melbourne, Australia, Sept. 2, 1934; m. Robin M.W. Fletcher, Apr. 23, 1962; 1 child, William John. B Agr. Sci., U. Melbourne, 1959; M Rural Sci. in Bioclimatology, U. New Eng., Australia, 1962; PhD, Oreg. State U., 1965; MD, U. Wash., 1971. Diplomate Am. Bd. Ob-Gyn, Am. Bd. Maternal and Fetal Medicine. Grad. fellow and asst., summer and rsch. fellow U. Oreg. Med. Ch., Portland, 1961-63; vis. scientist Oreg. Regional Primate Rsch. Ctr., Portland, 1964-66; instr. dept. ob-gyn U. Wash., Seattle, 1966-68, sr. fellow, mem. med. rsch. unit, mem. Anesthesia Rsch. Ctr., 1969-71; resident Los Angeles County-U. So. Calif. Sch. Medicine, L.A., 1971-74; asst. prof., assoc. prof. U. Calif., San Francisco, 1974-82, prof., 1982—, dir. obstetrics, 1980-87, dir. maternal-fetal medicine fellowship tng. program, 1983—, assoc. vice chmn dept., 1987—; rsch. affiliate Regional Primate Ctr., Seattle, 1969-71; assoc. staff Cardiovascular Rsch. Inst., U. Calif., 1976—; vis. scientist Nuffield Inst. for Med. Rsch., Oxford (Eng.) U., 1981-82; vis. scientist U. Chile, Santiago, 1985-89, Devel. Physiology Lab., U. Auckland, New Zealand, 1988-89. Author: Handbook of Fetal Heart Rate Monitoring, 1983; editor: (with P.W. Nathanielsz) Research in Perinatal Medicine, 1984; Antepartum and Intrapartum Management, 1989; contbr. numerous articles and abstracts to med. jours. Fellow Am. Coll. Obstetricians and Gynecologists; mem. Am. Physiol. Soc., Australian Perinatal Soc., Soc. for Gynecol. Investigation, Soc. Perinatal Obstetricians (bd. dirs. 1988-91), Soc. for Study Fetal Physiology, Chilean Soc. Ob-Gyn (fgn. corr.), Phi Kappa Phi, Phi Sigma. Office: U Calif 505 Parnassus Ave San Francisco CA 94143-0001

PARFREY, ADAM, publishing executive; b. N.Y.C., Apr. 12, 1957; s. Sydney Woodrow and Rosa Shirley (Ellovich) P.; m. Robin Boyarsky, Aug. 15, 1983 (div. 1986). Student, UCLA, 1975-77, U. Calif., Santa Cruz, 1978-79. Pub., editor Idea Mag., San Francisco, 1979-81; mng. editor PAJ Publs., N.Y.C., 1984-87; editor Exit Mag., N.Y.C., 1984-86; pub. Amok Press, N.Y.C., 1986—, Feral House, L.A., Portland, Oreg., 1987—. Author: Apocalypse Culture, 1987, Cult Rapture, 1993; co-editor: Rants & Incendiary Tracts, 1988; contbr. articles to profl. jours. Office: Feral House PO Box 3466 Portland OR 97208

PARIS, DAVID ANDREW, dentist; b. Milw., Jan. 16, 1962; s. John Baptistia and Geraldine Louella (Grosso) P. BA, UCLA, 1985, DDS, 1989. Oral surgery extern VA, Phoenix, 1989; primary practitioner Aids Project L.A. Dental Clinic, 1990—; assoc. M. Marchese D.D.S., Sun Valley, Calif., 1990-92, D. Pickrell DMD, West Hollywood, Calif., 1992—. Mem. ADA, Calif. Dental Assn., San Fernando Valley Dental Assn., Acad. Gen. Dentistry, Delta Sigma Delta.

PARIS, EDWARD MARVIN, education researcher, information systems consultant; b. Denver, Oct. 7, 1951; s. Marvin E. and Winifred A. (West) P.; m. Carol L. Powell, Aug. 2, 1975; 1 child, Julia. BA, U. Colo., Boulder, 1973, MPA, 1979; postgrad., U. Colo., Denver. Adminstrv. officer Colo. Dept. Revenue, Denver, 1979-80, Colo. Dept. Social Svc., Denver, 1980; budget analyst U. Colo., Boulder, 1980-84; instl. analyst U. Colo., Colorado Springs, 1984-89, dir. instl. rsch., 1989—, interim dir. fin. svcs., 1991—; cons. in info. systems, Colorado Springs; instl. rep. Am. Coll. Testing prog. Mem. Assn. Instnl. Rsch. (mem. workshop selection com. for nat. conv. 1989), Pi Alpha Alpha. Home: 2614 Farragut Cir Colorado Springs CO 80907-6406 Office: U Colo PO Box 7150 Colorado Springs CO 80933-7150

PARIS, KENNETH JOEL, software company executive; b. N.Y.C., Mar. 10, 1947; s. Paul L. and Fanny L. (Cohen) P. BS in Math., Clarkson U., 1973; BBA, West Conn. State Coll., 1974; MS in Computer Sci., Poly. Inst. of N.Y., 1980. Cert. data processor. Systems cons. Bundy Corp., Norwalk, Conn., 1974-78; dir. database adminstr. KPMG Peat Marwick, N.Y.C., 1978-85, Montvale, N.J., 1986-89; dir. product devel. Pansophic Systems Inc., Naperville, Ill., 1985-86, Forecross Corp., San Francisco, 1989—. Contbr. articles to profl. jours. Mem. Assn. for Computing Machinery, Internat. DB2 User Group (pres. 1991-92). Home: 564 Mission St #338 San Francisco CA 94105 Office: Forecross Corp 90 New Montgomery St San Francisco CA 94105

PARIS, RICHARD WAYNE, forester; b. Corning, N.Y., July 22, 1956; s. Robert Lee and Ann (Seeley) P.; m. Alberta E. Blanchard, Mar. 21, 1992. BS in Forest Resource, Iowa State U., 1978; postgrad., Everett C.C., 1984. Forester Colville Tribal Forestry, Nespelem, Wash., 1979-81, U.S. Bur. Indian Affairs, Nespelem, 1986—; fire warden, forester State of Utah, Kamas, 1982; law enforcement park technician U.S. Nat. Park Svc., Coulee Dam N.R.A., Wash., 1983-85; park technician U.S. Corps Engrs., Somerset, Ky., 1985-86; instr. Inland Empire EMS Tng. Coun. EMT, ambulance dir. Grand Coulee (Wash.) Vol. Fire Dept., 1981—; first aid instr. ARC, Ephrata, Wash., 1980—; instr.-trainer CPR, Am. Heart Assn., Grant County, Wash., 1980—; mem. Wash. State EMS Edn. Com. Recipient Outstanding Svc. award ARC, 1982. Mem. Soc. Am. Foresters, Am. Forestry Assn., Coulee Med. Found. (sec. 1987-88), Grant County EMS Coun. (pres. 1984-86, sec. 1987-93), N.Cen. Wash. Regional EMS Coun. (pres. 1990-93, EMS Adminstr. of Yr. 1989, 91). Baptist. Home: 417 Grand Coulee Ave W Grand Coulee WA 99133-0471 Office: US Bur Indian Affairs Colville Indian Agy Nespelem WA 99155

PARK, CHUI SUH, pharmacist; b. Sinuiju, Dem. People's Rep. Korea, Aug. 26, 1941; came to U.S., 1969; s. Seung Ryong and Jong Nam (Kim) P.; m. Youn Jin Kim, May 4, 1968; children: Clara, Sharon. BS, Seoul Nat. U., 1964, MS, 1967; MS, Purdue U., 1972; BS, U. Utah, 1976. Pharmacist Hanil Pharm. Industrial Co. Ltd., Seoul, Rep. of Korea, 1966-69, De Jay Drugs, L.A., 1976-79, Disco Drugs, Riverside, Calif., 1979-80, Clark Drugs, L.A., 1980—. Mem. Korean Pharmacist Assn. Calif., Am. Pharm. Assn. Democrat. Roman Catholic. Home: 1236 Cranbrook Pl Fullerton CA 92633 Office: Clark Drugs #7 650 E El Segundo Blvd Los Angeles CA 90059

PARK, DAVID DUCK-YOUNG, small business owner; b. Seoul, Korea, Feb. 3, 1942; came to U.S., 1971; s. Chang Hyun and Yong In (Shin) P.; m. Sue Hyae-Sun Kim, Dec. 23, 1968; children: Lisa, Tina, Brian. BA, Yon Sei U., Seoul, 1964. Mgr. Cathay Pacific Airways, Seoul, 1966-71; supr Am. Express Co., Washington, 1971-81; owner, operator All Seasons Gift Shop, L.A., 1981-84, Hairpros/Hair Cuttery, Agoura Hills, Calif., 1984—; instr. Cathay Pacific Airways, 1967-70. 2d lt. Korean Army, 1964-66. Home and Office: 1340 Tottenham Ct Oak Park CA 91301-4732

PARK, EDWARD CAHILL, JR., physicist; b. Wollaston, Mass., Nov. 26, 1923; s. Edward Cahill and Fentress (Kerlin) P.; m. Helen Therese O'Boyle, July 28, 1951. AB, Harvard U., 1947; postgrad., Amherst Coll., 1947-49; PhD, U. Birmingham, Eng., 1956. Instr. Amherst (Mass.) Coll., 1954-55; mem. staff Lincoln Lab., Lexington, Mass., 1955-57, Arthur D. Little, Inc., Cambridge, Mass., 1957-60; group leader electronic systems Arthur D. Little, Inc., Santa Monica, Calif., 1960-64; sr. staff engr., head laser system sect. Hughes Aircraft Co., Culver City, Calif., 1964-68; sr. scientist Hughes Aircraft Co., El Segundo, Calif., 1986-88; mgr. electro optical systems sect. Litton Guidance and Control Systems, Woodland Hills, Calif., 1968-70; sr. phys. scientist The Rand Corp., Santa Monica, 1970-72; sr. scientist R&D Assocs., Marina Del Rey, Calif., 1972-1986, cons., 1986-89; sr. tech. specialist Rockwell Internat., N.Am. Aircraft, El Segundo, Calif., 1988—. Contbr. articles to profl. jours.; patentee in field. Served to 1st lt. USAAF, 1943-46. Grantee Dept. Indsl. and Sci. Research, 1953. Fellow Explorers Club (sec. So. Calif. chpt. 1978-79); mem. IEEE, Optical Soc. Am., N.Y. Acad. Scis., Armed Forces Communications and Electronics Assn., Assn. Old Crows, Sigma Xi. Democrat. Clubs: 20-Ghost (Eng.), Harvard (So. Calif.). Home: 932 Ocean Front Santa Monica CA 90403-2406 Office: Rockwell Internat North Am Aircraft 201 N Douglas St El Segundo CA 90245-4637

PARK, JOSEPH CHUL HUI, computer scientist; b. Seoul, Korea, Aug. 6, 1937; s. Don Gil and Eui Kyung (Shin) P.; m. Young Ja Yoon, Aug. 17, 1968; children: Esther Y.J., Maria Y.S., David Y.W., Jonathan Y.S. BA, Coll of Wooster, Ohio, 1959; BS, MIT, 1959; MS, U. Ill., 1961, PhD, 1967. Mem. rsch. staff Stanford Linear Accelerator Ctr Stanford U., 1969-72, 73-75; assoc. prof., then prof. computer sci. Korea Advanced Inst. of Sci., Seoul, 1975-82; mem. tech. staff Braegen Corp., Milpitas, Calif., 1982-86, Hewlett-Packard Labs., Palo Alto, Calif., 1986-92; mgr. compiler R&D Advanced Processor div. Intergraph Corp., Palo Alto, 1992—; lectr. in computer engring. Santa Clara (Calif.) U., 1987—; head Computer Sci. Rsch. Ctr., Korea Advanced Inst. Sci., Seoul, 1980-82. Mem. IEEE, Assn. Computing Machinery. Baptist. Home: 14800 Masson Ct Saratoga CA 95070

PARK, RODERIC BRUCE, university official; b. Cannes, France, Jan. 7, 1932; came to U.S., 1932; s. Malcolm Sewell and Dorothea (Turner) P.; m. Marijke DeJong, Aug. 29, 1953; children: Barbara, Marina, Malcolm. AB, Harvard U., 1953; PhD, Calif. Inst. Tech., 1958. Postdoctoral fellow Calif. Inst. Tech., 1958, Lawrence Radiation Lab., Berkeley, Calif., 1958-60; prof. botany U. Calif., Berkeley, 1960-89, prof. plant biology, 1989-93, prof. emeritus, 1993—; chmn. dept. instrn. in biology U. Calif., 1965-68; provost, dean U. Calif. (Coll. Letters and Sci.), 1972-80, vice chancellor, 1980-90; pres. Brickyard Cove Harbors, Inc., 1975-77; dir. William Kaufmann, Inc., 1976-86; mem. corp. Woods Hole Oceanographic Instn., 1974-80; mem. Harvard vis. com. Biochem. and Molecular Biology, 1990—; acting dir. U. Herbarium and Jepson Herbarium, 1991—. Co-author: Cell Ultrastructure, 51967, Papers on Biological Membrane Structure, 1968; Biology editor, W.H. Freeman & Co., 1966-74; Contbr. articles to profl. jours. Pres. bd. trustees Athenian Sch., 1980—; trustee U. Calif.-Berkeley Found., 1986-90, Jepson Endowment, 1992—; dir. Associated Harvard Alumni, 1976-79; bd. overseers Harvard U., 1981-87; mem. exec. com. Coun. Acad. Affairs, 1986-90, chmn. 1988-89, Nat. Assn. State Univs. and Land Grant Colls., 1988-90; mem. vis. com. Arnold Arboretum, 1981-88, chmn., 1986-88; acting dir. Univ. and Jepson Herbaria, 1991-93. Recipient New York Bot. Gardens award, 1962. Fellow AAAS; mem. Am. Soc. Plant Physiologists, Am. Bot. Soc., Am. Soc. Photobiology, Danforth Assn. (pres. San Francisco chpt. 1972), Richmond Yacht Club (commodore 1972, dir. Found. 1992—), Transpacific Yacht Club, Explorers Club. Home: 531 Cliffside Ct Richmond CA 94801-3766 Office: U Calif Koshland Hall Berkeley CA 94720

PARK, ROY HAMPTON, communications company executive; b. Dobson, N.C., Sept. 15, 1910; s. I.A. and Laura Frances (Stone) P.; m. Dorothy Goodwin Dent, Oct. 3, 1936; children—Roy Hampton, Adelaide Hampton Park Gomer. BBA, N.C. State U., Raleigh, 1931; LHD (hon.), Keuka Coll., 1967; HHD (hon.), N.C. State U., 1978; LLD (hon.), Ithaca Coll., 1985, Wake Forest U., 1985. Dir. pub. relations Farmers Coop. Exchange, N.C. Cotton Growers Coop. Assn., Raleigh, 1931-42; founder, editor, pub. Coop. Digest, Farm Power, 1939-66; sr. editor Rural Electrification Adminstrn., 1936-37; pres., also bd. dirs. RHP Ind. Inc., Ithaca, 1945—; pres. Hines-Park Foods, Inc., Ithaca, N.Y., Hines-Park Foods, Ltd., Can. and Duncan Hines Inst., Inc., 1949-56, v.p., 1956-63; pres., also bd. dirs. Avalon Citrus Assocs., Inc., Orlando, Fla., 1962—, Roy H. Park Broadcasting Inc., Greenville, N.C., 1962—, Sta. WDEF-TV-AM-FM, Chattanooga, Tenn., 1963—, Sta. WJHL-TV, Johnson City, Tenn., 1964—, Sta. WTVR-TV-AM-FM, Richmond, Va., 1965—, Sta. WNAX-AM, Yankton, S.D., 1968—, Sta. WUTR-TV, Utica-Rome, 1969—, Sta. WSLS-TV, Roanoke, 1969—, Cob-bHouse of Rock Hill (S.C.) Inc., 1968, Sta. WBMG-TV, Birmingham, 1973—, Sta. KWJJ-AM/FM, 1973—, Sta. KJJO-AM/FM, Mpls., 1974, Sta. KEZX-AM/FM, KWLO/KFMW, Waterloo, Iowa, 1987, Sta. WHEN-AM, Syracuse, N.Y., 1976—, Sta. WRHP-FM, Syracuse, 1977—; chmn., dir. Park Outdoor Advt. and Park Displays, Ithaca, 1964-88, also bd. dirs.; pres. Park Outdoor Advt., Inc., Scranton, Pa., 1969-84; pres., also bd. dirs. Warner Robins Ga. Inc., 1972, Park Newspapers, Inc., Ithaca, 1972—; and Ga., 1972—, Manassas, Va., 1972—, Nebraska City, Nebr., 1975—, Brooksville, Fla., 1975—, Ogdensburg, N.Y., 1975—, Plymouth, Ind., 1977—, Norwich, N.Y., 1977—, McAlester, Okla., 1978, Macomb, Ill., 1979, Newton, Morganton and Statesville, N.C., 1979, Perry, Ga., 1980, Mich., 1980, Ark., 1981, Moore County, Lumberton, Marion and Devils Lake, N.C., 1982, Waynesboro, Va., 1983, Medina, N.Y., 1984, Clark County, Ind., 1984, Hudson, N.Y., 1985, Ky., 1985, Pa., 1986, Iowa, 1986, Blackduck, Minn., 1991; pres., also bd. dirs. RHP Newspapers Inc., Ithaca, 1973—, Lockport (N.Y.) Pubs. Inc., 1973—, Kannapolis (N.C.) Pub. Co., 1978—; pres., also bd. dirs. State and Aurora Inc., Broken Arrow, Okla., 1979, Sapulpa, Okla., 1979; chmn., chief exec. officer Park Comm., Ithaca, N.Y.; bd. dirs. Molinos de P.R., Tompkins County Area Devel. Corp., Ithaca, First Research Devel. Corp., Ithaca; pres. Upstate Small Bus. Investment Co., Ithaca, 1960-66; assoc. chmn. laymen's nat. Bible com. Nat. Bible Week, 1972; chmn. pub. relations com. N.C. State U. Devel. Council, 1963-72, vice chmn. council, 1964-72, chmn., 1972—; trustee Endowment Funds N.C. State U. Found., Ithaca Coll., 1973—, mgr. exec. com., 1977—, chmn. exec. com., 1981—. Asso. chmn. laymen's nat. Bible com. Nat. Bible Week, 1972; chmn. pub. relations com. N.C. State U. Devel. Council, 1963-72, vice chmn. council, 1964-72, chmn., 1972—; trustee N.C. State U., 1977-85; bd. dirs. N.C. State U. Found., 1962-66, trustee endowment funds; trustee, chmn. exec. com. Ithaca Coll., 1973—. Recipient spl. citation Am. Inst. Coops., 1947; Disting. Service award Tompkins County United Fund, 1961; Meritorious Service award N.C. State U. Alumni Assn., 1970; Abe Lincoln award So. Bapt. Radio-TV Commn., 1971, Gold Plate award Am. Acad. Achievement, 1984; named Country Squire by Gov. N.C., 1953, hon. citizen New Orleans, 1958, hon. citizen Tenn., 1961, Ky. col., 1963, adm. in Gt. Navy Neb., 1961, Soc. Prodigal Son by Gov. N.C., 1964. Mem. N.C. State U. Alumni Assn. (pres. 1960-61, gen. fund chmn. 1962), Pub. Relations Soc. Am., Am. Agrl. Editors Assn., Am. Assn. Agrl. Coll. Editors, Agrl. Relations Council, Sales Execs. Club N.Y.C., Friends Ithaca Coll., Lucullus Circle, Les Amis D'Escoffier Soc., Confrerie de la Chaines des Rotissuers, Antique Automobile Club Am., Va., N.C., Nat. assns. broadcasters, Am., So. newspaper pubs. assns., es. 1981), Ga. Press Assn., N.Y. State Pubs. Assn. (dir.), Phi Kappa Phi, Pi Sigma Epsilon, Alpha Phi Gamma, Pi Phi Pi. Presbyn. (ruling elder 1969—). Clubs: Nat. Press, Capitol (Washington); Sales Execs. (dir. 1980, v.p. 1981-82), N.Y. Athletic, Cornell, Marco Polo (N.Y.C.); Union League (N.Y.C.); City, Capital City, Sphinx (Raleigh); Ithaca Country; Statler (Cornell U.); Commonwealth (Richmond); Shenandoah (Roanoke). Home: 205 Devon Rd Ithaca NY 14850-1409 Office: Park Comm Inc Terrace Hill PO Box 550 Ithaca NY 14851-0550

PARK, SEUNG KOOK, flavor chemist; b. Seoul, Korea, Dec. 4, 1957; s. Won Byung Park and Hyungsook Cha Park; m. Hyeran Park, July 1, 1986. BS in Food Tech., Kyung Hee U., 1981; MS in Food Sci., U. Calif., 1989, PhD in Agrl., Environ. Chemistry, 1993. Analytical flavor chemist Dong Suh Foods Corp., Seoul, 1981-86; rsch. assoc. U. Calif., Davis, 1991—. Mem. Inst. of Food Technologists, Am. Soc. for Viticulture and Enology, Am. Chem. Soc., the Korean Scientists and Engrs. Assn. in U.S.A. Office: U Calif Dept Viticulture/Enology Davis CA 95616

PARKER, ALBERTA WEST, physician, educator; b. Bakersfield, Calif., Nov. 1, 1917; d. James Henry and Laura Rebecca (West) P.; m. Walter W. Horn, Apr. 14, 1950; children: Michael, Rebecca. BA, U. Calif., Berkeley, 1938, MD, 1942, MPH, 1963; postgrad., U. Calif., Berkely. Pediatric clinician Berkeley, Calif., 1945-50; dir. maternal and child health Berkeley City Health Dept., 1950-55; lectr. Sch. Pub. Health U. Calif. Berkeley, 1955-66, clin. prof. community health, 1966-76, clin. prof. emerita, 1976—; cons. Office of Health, Office of Econ. Opportunity, Washington, 1969-73, Health programs WHO, Geneva, 1972-78, mem. adv. com. on health care, 1970-78; cons. in field. Mem. WHO. Home: 337 Western Dr Richmond CA 94801

PARKER, ALICE ANNE, writer; b. Eugene, Oreg., Aug. 29, 1939; d. Alvan Perry and Holly (Seavey) P.; m. Don Severson, Sept. 28, 1957 (div. 1960); m. Henry Holthaus, Dec. 26, 1982; 1 child, April Anne Holthaus Severson. BA, CUNY, 1974; MA, Columbia U., 1965; postgrad., U. Calif., Berkeley, 1966. Tchr. English Sch. Visual Arts, N.Y.C., 1964-65, Rutgers (N.J.) U., 1964-65; prof. San Francisco Art Inst., 1970-75. Author: Understand Your Dreams, 1991; (jour.) Metapsychology: The Jour. of Discarnate Intelligence, 1985-87; producer audio tapes Beyond Your Wildest Dreams, 1984; (films) I Change I Am the Same, 1970, Introduction to Humanities, 1972, Near the Big Chakra, 1973, The Struggle of the Meat, 1974, Animals Running, 1974, Riverbody, 1970. Mem. Phi Beta Kappa. Home: 53-086 Halai Rd Hau'ula HI 96717 Office: Real Dreams PO Box 1214 Haleiwa HI 96712

PARKER, BRIAN PRESCOTT, forensic scientist; b. Norfolk, Va., Aug. 31, 1929; s. Milton Ellsworth and Louise Randall (Smith) P.; BS in Quantitative Biology, M.I.T., 1953; JD, Northwestern U., 1957; M.Criminology, U. Calif., Berkeley, 1961, D.Criminology, 1967; m. Sonia Garcia Rosario, Dec. 23, 1960; children: Robin Marie, Augustin Keith. Research asst. U. P.R. Med. Sch., 1961; cons. P.R. Justice Dept., 1961-63; spl. asst. FDA, Washington, 1964; lectr., then asst. prof. criminology U. Calif., Berkeley, 1964-70; sr. criminalist, then sr. forensic scientist Stanford Research Inst., Menlo Park, Calif., 1971-73; prof. forensic sci. and criminal justice Calif. State U., Sacramento, 1973-92; prof. emeritus, 1988—; project dir. phys. evidence Dept. Justice, 1969-70; vis. fellow Nat. Police Research Unit, Australia, 1985; vis. prof. Elton Mayo Sch. Mgmt., South Australia Inst. Tech., 1985. Fellow Am. Acad. Forensic Scis.; mem. Am. Chem. Soc., Acad. Criminal Justice Scis., Calif. Assn. Criminalists, Forensic Sci. Soc. London. Co-author: Physical Evidence in the Administration of Criminal Justice, 1970, The Role of Criminalistics in the World of the Future, 1972; asso. editor Law, Medicine, Science—and Justice, 1964; contbr. to Ency. Crime and Justice, 1983. Home: 5117 Ridgegate Way Fair Oaks CA 95628-3603

PARKER, CATHERINE SUSANNE, psychotherapist; b. Norwood, Mass., Nov. 4, 1934; d. George Leonard and Hazel Olga (Remmer) P. BA, Bates Coll., 1956; MSW, U. Denver, 1961. Diplomate Acad. Cert. Social Workers; cert. social worker, Colo. Social worker Taunton (Mass.) State Hosp., 1956-59; social worker Ft. Logan Mental Health Ctr., Denver, 1961-66, clin. team leader, 1966-72; dir. adult services Western Inst. Human Resources, Denver, 1973-74; pvt. practice psychotherapy Denver, 1974—; instr. U. Denver, 1977-79; workshop facilitator Arapahoe Community Coll., 1986—. Mem. Nat. Assn. Social Workers, Internat. Transactional Analysis Assn. Home: 6453 S Downing St Littleton CO 80121-2517 Office: Denver Mental Health 165 Cook St Ste 100 Denver CO 80206-5308

PARKER, CHARLES EDWARD, lawyer; b. Santa Ana, Calif., Sept. 9, 1927; s. George Ainsworth and Dorothy P.; m. Marilyn Esther Perrin, June 23, 1956; children—Mary, Catherine, Helen, George. Student, Santa Ana Coll., U. So. Calif.; J.D., S.W. U.-La. Bar: Calif. 1958, U.S. Dist. Ct. (cen. dist.) Calif. 1958, U.S. Supreme Ct. 1969, D.C. 1971, U.S. Dist. Ct. (no. and so. dists.) Calif. 1981. Prof. law Western State U., Fullerton, Calif., 1973-83; spl. counsel Tidelands, First Am. Title Co., 1980-82; dir. First Am. Fin. Corp., 1981-82. Served to sgt. U.S. Army, 1951-53. Author: (book) Tidelands and The Public Trust, 1991. Mem. ABA (com. improvement land records, sect. real property), Orange County Bar Assn., Calif. Bar Assn., D.C. Bar Assn. Club: Santa Ana Kiwanis, Lodge: Elks (Santa Ana). Contbr. articles in field to profl. jours. Office: 18101 Charter Rd Orange CA 92667-2638

PARKER, CHARLYN DEETTE, educator; b. Stillwater, Okla., June 4, 1947; d. Emmett J. and Jaclyn Louise (Sanford) Hyde; m. Robert Sheldon Parker, Oct. 28, 1970; children: Robin Lynn, Cheryl Lee. BS in Home Econs., Biochemistry, Calif. Poly. State U., 1969. Cert. tchr., Calif. Tchr. sci. Copperas Cove (Tex.) Unified Sch. Dist., 1973-75; tchr. sci. Elk Grove (Calif.) Unified Sch. Dist., 1984—, mentor tchr., 1987—; leader dept. sci. James Rutter Middle Sch., Sacramento, 1987-91; leader sci. div. Samuel Jackman Middle Sch., Sacramento, 1991—; mem. sci. steering com., family life edn. com., Elk Grove. Mem. NEA, Calif. Tchrs. Assn., Elk Grove Edn. Assn., Calif. Sci. Tchrs. Assn., Alpha Phi. Office: Samuel Jackman Middle Sch 7925 Kentwal Dr Sacramento CA 95823

PARKER, C(RAIG) STEPHEN, computer and programming consultant; b. Evanston, Ill., May 6, 1949; s. R. Sam and Clois (James) Papa; m. Jane Ann Saare, Aug. 28, 1971; children: Brandon E., Todd S. BA, Calif. State U., Northridge, 1971, MA, 1975. Cert. data processor, cert. profl. cons. to mgmt. Tchr. Alemany High Sch., San Fernando, Calif., 1971-72, Simi Valley (Calif.) Unified Sch. Dist., 1972-75, Sweetwater Union High Sch. Dist., Chula Vista, Calif., 1975-77, San Diego Community Coll., 1977-80; owner Coin Laundry, Encinitas, Calif., 1978-81; bookkeeper First Presbyn. Ch., San Diego, 1980-85; computer cons. Parker Computer Svcs., San Diego, 1984-91, Covill, Gerzytn, Lotherinton & Parker, San Diego, 1991—. Mem. Ind. Computer Cons. Assn. (chpt. treas. 1985-86, chpt. pres. 1986-88, nat. v.p. 1989-90, nat. pres. 1990-91, nat. chmn. 1991-92, rep. Inst. for Cert. of Computer Profls. 1988—), Data Processing Mgrs. Assn., Cons. Roundtable San Diego, Nat. Bur. Profl. Mgmt. Cons. Office: Covill Gersztyn Lotherington and Parker 2145 Garnet Ave San Diego CA 92109

PARKER, DENISE RENEE, computer programmer analyst; b. Long Beach, Calif., Dec. 5, 1964; d. Grant Richard and Judith Ann (Johnson) P. BA, U. Calif., Irvine, 1988; MBA, U. Calif., 1990—. Model Kathy Clark Agy., Santa Ana, Calif., 1987-90; programmer analyst Bergen Brunswig Corp., Orange, Calif., 1988—; mgr., waitress Fio Rita's Restaurant, Los Alamitos, Calif., 1980-89; computer specialist Office Dean Humanities, U. Calif., 1987-88. Howard Hughes Meml. scholar Hughes Helicopter Co., 1983. Mem. NAFE, Am. Mgmt. Assn., Delta Delta Delta. Republican. Home and Office: 114 Echo Run Irvine CA 92714

PARKER, DONN BLANCHARD, information security consultant; b. San Jose, Calif., Oct. 9, 1929; s. Donald William and Miriam Estelle (Blanchard) P.; m. Lorna Ruth Schroeder, Aug. 16, 1952; children: Diane Parker Wisdom, David. B.A., U. Calif, Berkeley, 1952, M.A., 1954. Sr. engr. Gen. Dynamics Co., San Diego, 1954-62; staff cons. Control Data Corp., Palo Alto, Calif., 1962-69; sr. mgmt. systems cons. SRI Internat., Menlo Park, Calif., 1969—; speaker San Francisco Commonwealth Club, 1991. Author: Crime by Computer, 1976, Ethical Conflicts in Computer Technology, 1977, 89, Computer Security Management, 1982, Fighting Computer Crime, 1983. Rsch. grantee NSF, 1971-79, U.S. Dept. Justice, 1979—; recipient Individual Achievement award Info. Systems Security Assn., 1991-92. Mem. Assn. Computing Machinery (sec. 1969-75), Am. Fedn. Info. Processing Socs. (bd. dirs. 1974-76), Am. Soc. Indsl. Security. Republican. Lutheran. Office: SRI Internat Menlo Park CA 94025

PARKER, G. JOHN, fire chief. AS in Polit. Sci., Ill. Ctrl. Coll., 1975, AS in Fire Sci. Tech., 1979. Cert. fire officer II, prevention officer I, Ill. From firefighter to capt., 1965-81, fire investigator II, 1981-83, battalion chief, 1983-86, asst. fire chief, 1986-88; fire chief City of Peoria, Ill., 1988-91, City of Pomona, Calif., 1991—. Bd. dirs. Pomona Valley ARC, Christman in April; mem. adv. com. Pomona Adult Sch. Dep. fire chief Ill Air Nat. Guard. Recipient Arson Investigator Outstanding Svc. award, 1982, Outstanding Alumni award Am. Coun. on Edn., 1989, Dr. Martin Luther King Commemorative Svc. award, 1990. Mem. Internat. Assn. Fire Chiefs and Black Profl. Fire Fighters, Am. Heart Assn., Nat. Assn. Black Pub. Adminstrs., Calif. Fire Chiefs Assn., L.A. County Fire Chiefs Assn., Foothill Fire Chiefs Assn., Greater Pomona Kiwanis. Address: 13375 Cardinal Ridge Rd Chino CA 91709 Office: Fire Dept 505 S Garey Ave Pomona CA 91766*

PARKER, HARRY S., III, art museum administrator; b. St. Petersburg, Fla., Dec. 23, 1939; s. Harry S. Parker and Catherine (Baillie) Knapp; m. Ellen McCance, May 23, 1964; children: Elizabeth Day, Thomas Baillie, Samuel Ferguson, Catherine Allan. A.B. magna cum laude, Harvard U., 1961; M.A., NYU, 1966. Exec. asst., adminstrv. asst. to dir. Met. Mus. Art, N.Y.C., 1963-66, exec. asst. to pres., 1966-67, exec. asst. to dir., 1967, chmn. dept. edn., 1967-71, vice dir. edn., 1971-73; dir. Dallas Mus. Art, 1974-87, Fine Arts Mus. San Francisco, 1987—. Mem. Am. Assn. Mus. (v.p.) Assn. Art Mus. Dirs., Century Assn., Bohemian Club. Home: 171 San Marcos San Francisco CA 94116 Office: Fine Arts Mus/San Francisco Calif Palace Legion of Honor Lincoln Pk San Francisco CA 94121

PARKER, JAMES AUBREY, judge; b. Houston, Jan. 8, 1937; s. Lewis Almeron and Emily Helen (Stuessy) P.; m. Florence Fisher, Aug. 26, 1960; children: Roger Alan, Pamela Elizabeth. BA, Rice U., 1959; LLB, U. Tex., 1962. Bar: Tex. 1962, N.Mex. 1963. With Modrall, Sperling, Roehl, Harris & Sisk, Albuquerque, 1962-87; judge U.S. Dist. Ct. N.Mex., Albuquerque, 1987—; mem. N.Mex. Bd. Bar Commrs., 1982-83, Commn. on Professionalism, 1986—. Articles editor Tex. Law Rev., 1961-62. Mem. ABA, Am. Judicature Soc., Am. Bd. Trial Advs., Tex. Bar Assn., N.Mex. Bar Assn., Albuquerque Bar Assn., Tennis Club, Order of Coif, Chancellors, Phi Delta Phi. Office: US Dist Ct PO Box 566 Albuquerque NM 87103-0566

PARKER, JAMES WILLIAM, science educator; b. Elk City, Okla., Dec. 8, 1951; s. James William and Barbara Jean (Heavener) P.; m. Susan Gail Meckel, June 23, 1979; children: Ryan David, Kristen Gail. BA in Sociology, San Diego State U., 1987, MA in Edn., 1991. Cert. lang. devel. specialist. From box boy to grocery buyer Am. Stores/Skaggs-Alpha Beta, San Diego and La Habra, Calif., 1968-88; ESL tchr. Grossmont Adult Sch., 1990; sci., history, math tchr. La Presa Middle Sch., Calif., 1988-90; sci. tchr. Spring Valley Middle Sch., Calif., 1990—, Gateways Sch., San Diego, 1991; master tchr. San Diego State U. Sch. Tchr. Edn., 1990—; mem. Student Assistance Team, Spring Valley, 1989—; advisor Sci. Olympiad, San Diego, 1988-90. Mem. Anza-Borrego Found., Co-founder pack 319 Boy Scouts of Am., den leader, cubmaster, 1988, asst. scoutmaster, 1991. San Diego State U. scholar, 1989. Mem. San Diego Zool. Soc., San Diego Sci. Educators Assn., Nat. Sci. Tchrs. Assn., Defenders of Wildlife, Sierra Club. Democrat. Unitarian/Roman Catholic. Home: 4767 Boulder Pl La Mesa CA 91941 Office: Spring Valley Middle Sch 3900 Conrad Dr Spring Valley CA 91977

PARKER, JOHN BRIAN, broadcast executive; b. L.A., July 3, 1959; s. John Egar and Iris (Landry) P.; m. Dorothy Lynn McCorkle, Aug. 18, 1981; 1 child, Jennifer Lynn. BA in Econs., San Diego State U., 1982. V.p., gen. mgr. Parker Industries, San Diego, 1982—, v.p., 1986—, MIS dir., 1988—; asst. dir. Ctr. for Total Health, Solana Beach, Calif., 1982-83; v.p. Parker Broadcasting, San Diego, 1986—. Foster parent San Diego Social Svcs., 1989—. Recipient Fredrick Lynn Ryan award San Diego State U., 1982. Mem. Nat. Assn. Broadcasting. Republican. Mem. Christian Ch. Home: 1330 Caminito Laura Encinitas CA 92024-9624 Office: Parker Industries 2408 First Ave San Diego CA 92101

PARKER, JOHN MARCHBANK, consulting geologist; b. Manhattan, Kans., Sept. 13, 1920; s. John Huntington and Marjorie Elizabeth (Marchbank) P.; m. Agnes Elizabeth Potts, Mar. 17, 1978; m. Jan Goble, July 18, 1941 (div. 1968); children—Susan Kelly, Elizabeth Douglass, Deirdre Parker, John Eric; m. Nancy Booth, Jan. 24, 1970 (div. 1974). Student U. Minn., 1937, U. Wyo., 1938; B.S., Kans. State U., 1941. Cert. petroleum geologist Am. Inst. Profl. Geologists. Geologist, U.S. Pub. Roads Adminstrn., Alaska Hwy., Can., 1942-43; Field geologist Imperial Oil Ltd., Northwest Ter., Can., 1943-44; dist. geologist Stanolind Oil & Gas Co., Casper, Wyo., 1944-52; v.p. exploration Kirby Petroleum Co., Houston, 1952-74; v.p. exploration Northwest Exploration Co., Denver, 1974-75; cons. geologist Denver, 1975—. Contbr. articles to profl. jours. Recipient Disting. Service in Geology award Kans. State U., 1983. Fellow AAAS, Geol. Soc. Am.; mem. Am. Assn. Petroleum Geologists (pres. 1982-83, adv. council Tulsa 1983-84, Hon. Mem. award), Rocky Mountain Assn. Geologists (explorer of yr. 1979; pres. 1980-81). Home: 2615 Oak Dr No 32 Lakewood CO 80215 Office: PO Box 150187 Lakewood CO 80215

PARKER, JOHN WILLIAM, pathology educator, investigator; b. Clifton, Ariz., Jan. 5, 1931; s. Vilas William and Helen E. Parker; m. Barbara A. Atkinson, June 8, 1957; children: Ann Elizabeth, Joy Noelle, John David, Heidi Susan. BS, U. Ariz., 1953; MD, Harvard U., 1957. Diplomate Am. Bd. Pathology. Clin. instr. pathology U. Calif. Sch. Medicine, San Francisco, 1962-64; asst. prof. U. So. Calif. Sch. Medicine, L.A., 1964-68, assoc. prof., 1968-75, prof., 1975—, dir. clin. labs., 1974—, vice chmn. dept. pathology, 1985—, dir. pathology reference labs., 1991—; assoc. dean sci. affairs U. So. Calif., 1987-89, v.p. univ. faculty senate, 1991-92; co-chmn. 15th Internat. Leucocyte Culture Conf., Asilomar, Calif., 1982; chmn. 2d Internat. Lymphoma Conf., Athens, Greece, 1981; v.p. faculty senate U. So. Calif., 1991-92; bd. dirs. ann. meeting Clin. Applications of Cytometry, Charleston, S.C., 1988—. Founding editor (jour.) Hematological Oncology, 1982-93; assoc. editor Jour. Clin. Lab. Analysis, 1985—; co-editor: Intercellular Communication in Leucocyte Function, 1983; founding co-editor (jour.) Communications in Clin. Cytometry, 1994—; contbr. over 150 articles to profl. jours., chpts. to books. Named sr. oncology fellow Am. Cancer Soc., U. So. Calif. Sch. Medicine, 1964-69, Nat. Cancer Inst. vis. fellow Walter and Eliza Hall Inst. for Med. Research, Melbourne, Australia, 1972-73. Fellow Coll. Am. Pathologists, Am. Soc. Clin. Pathologists; mem. Am. Assn. Pathologists, Am. Soc. Hematology, Internat. Acad. Pathology, Phi Beta Kappa, Phi Kappa Phi. Office: U So Calif Sch Medicine CSC 107 2250 Alcazar St Los Angeles CA 90032

PARKER, JOYCE STEINFELD, social worker; b. Neptune, N.J., Dec. 11, 1946; d. Milton Donald and Lillian (Sonia) Steinfeld; m. Lawrence Neil Parker, Sept. 18, 1970 (div. Sept. 1990); children: Jill Monica, Gregory Robert. MEd, Boston U., 1969; MSW, UCLA, 1976; PhD, U.S.C., 1992. Lic. social worker. Tchr. spl. edn. Dearborn Sch., Boston, 1969-70, Christ Ch. Child Ctr., Bethesda, Md., 1970-71; tchr. 1st grade Hiroshima (Japan) Internat. Sch., 1971-72; clin. social worker Orange County Mental Health, Westminster, Calif., 1976-80; employee asst. affiliate Human Affairs Internat., L.A., 1987—; instr. U. So. Calif. Sch. Social Work, L.A., 1988-90; pvt. practice clin. social work Redondo Beach, Calif., 1981—; community speaker parenting, marriage, psychol. topics, So. Bay of La., 1983—. Fellow NASW, Soc. Clin. Social Work.

PARKER, JULIA LYNNE, military reserve officer; b. Ventura, Calif., Apr. 23, 1966; d. James Anthony Parker and Patricia Joan (Burnett) Petersen. BS, U.S. Merchant Marine Acad., 1990. 3d officer Mil. Sealift Command USN, 1990—. Editor Yearbook, 1990. With USN, 1985-86. Mem. Internat. Orgn. Masters, Mates and Pilots. Home: 19916 Old Owen Rd Apt 111 Monroe WA 98272

PARKER, KENNETH DEAN, toxicologist, criminalist; b. Menan, Idaho, Feb. 27, 1935; s. Kenneth Lewis and Bernedene (Nichols) P.; m. Gay Hemmerling, June 16, 1961; 1 child, Dean Walter. BS, U. Calif., Berkeley, 1958, M Criminology, 1960. Diplomate Am. Bd. Forensic Toxicology. Rsch. asst. U. Calif., 1957-62; rsch. assoc. toxicologist Med. Ctr. U. Calif., San Francisco, 1969-70; toxicologist, criminalist, dir. Probe div. Hine Inc., San Francisco, 1973-81; owner, dir. Probe Sci., El Cerrito, Calif., 1981—; relief toxicologist to coroner City and County San Francisco, 1957-70; lab. inspector Coll. Am. Pathologists, Northfield, Ill., Am. Assn. Clin. Chemists; cons. in field. Fellow Am. Acad. Forensic Sci.; mem. AAAS, Am. Chem. Soc., Internat. Assn. Forensic Toxicologists, Western Pharmacology Soc., Calif. Assn. Toxicologists (chartered). Democrat. Home: 2109 Pinehurst Ct El Cerrito CA 94530-1879 Office: Probe Sci 2109 Pinehurst Ct El Cerrito CA 94530-1879

PARKER, KIMBERLY JANE, non-profit association executive, paralegal; b. Ann Arbor, Mich., Sept. 24, 1958; d. John Richard and Jane Eleanor (Twichell) P. BA in Polit. Sci., U. Redlands, 1980; Cert. in Legal Assistantship, U. Calif. Irvine, 1983, Cert. in Non-Profit Exec. Mgmt., 1990; Cert. in Adminstrn. Non-Profit Programs, Calif. State U. Long Beach, 1991. Hostess Disneyland, Anaheim, Calif., 1976-80; legal sec., asst. John R. Parker Law Corp., Orange, Calif., 1976-81; legal asst. C.D. Daly Law Corp., Newport Beach, Calif., 1981-83; exec. dir. Christian Conciliation Svc., Anaheim, 1983—. Editor: Peacemaker's Handbook; contbr. articles to profl. jours. Bd. dirs. YWCA Ctrl. Orange, 1991—; mem. So. Calif. Head Injury Found., Downey, 1990—; chair women's forum Trinity United Presbyn. Ch., 1992—. Recipient Cert. of Appreciation, County of Orange, 1992; grantee Christian Conciliation, 1985. Mem. Christian Legal Soc., Christian Ministry Mgmt., So. Calif. Mediation Assn., County Assn. Dispute Resolution, Christian Conciliation Svc. (bd. dirs. 1983—), Vol. Ctr. of Orange County. Republican. Presbyterian. Office: Christian Conciliation Svc 3855 E La Palma Ste 125 Anaheim CA 92807-1700

PARKER, KRISTIN LUAN MARTIN, critical care nurse; b. Des Moines, Aug. 27, 1967; d. Stevan Jon and Linda Ann (Butelli) M.; m. Gary S. Parker, May 1, 1992. Diploma, Iowa Meth. Sch. Nursing, Des Moines, 1988; student, Calif. State U., Carson. RN, Iowa, Calif. Staff nurse CCU Mercy Med. Ctr., Des Moines, 1988-89, staff nurse CCU, acute myocardial intervention transport team, 1989-90; transport nurse Heart Inst., Heart Inst., Hosp. Good Samaritan, L.A.; clin. coord. L.A. Cardiology, 1990—. Mem. ANA, AACN. Office: LA Cardiology 1245 Wilshire Blvd Ste 703 Los Angeles CA 90017

PARKER, LARRY LEE, electronics company executive, consultant; b. St. Paul, Oct. 21, 1938; s. Clifford Leroy and Evelyn Elaine (McArtor) P.; m. Esperanza Victoria Delgado, Aug. 7, 1965; children: Sean Lawrance, Nicole Kathleen. AA in Engring., Antelope Valley Coll., Lancaster, Calif., 1964; BS in Indsl. Engring., U. Calif., Berkeley, 1966, MS in Ops. Rsch., 1968. Prin., cons. Ted Barry & Assocs., L.A., 1968-73; v.p. mfg. Pacific div. Mark Controls, Long Beach, Calif., 1973-79; v.p. world ops. ARL div. Bausch & Lombe, Sunland, Calif., 1979-84; pres. control products div. Leach Corp., Buena Park, Calif., 1984-88, exec. v.p., chief operating officer parent co., 1988-90, pres., chief exec. officer, bd. dirs., 1990—; advisor engring. coun. U. Calif., Long Beach, 1990—; bd. dirs. So. Calif. Tech. Exec. Network. With USN, 1956-59. Recipient Outstanding Achievement award Los Angeles County Bd. Suprs., 1964. Mem. APICS (mem. exec. com. mfg.), Am. Electronics Assn. (pres.'s round table), Orange County Performing Arts Frat. Home: 2711 Canary Dr Costa Mesa CA 92626-4747 Office: Leach Corp PO Box 5032 Buena Park CA 90622-5032

PARKER, MICHAEL DAVID, computer scientist, consultant; b. Ft. Wayne, Ind., Feb. 27, 1954; s. Milton Duane and Katherine Elizabeth (Sours) P. BS in Systems Engring., U. Ariz., 1976, MS in Computer Science, 1977. Systems programmer Grumman Data Systems, Oxnard, Calif., 1978-80; project mgr. Omnidata, Thousand Oaks, Calif., 1980-82; test specialist Raytheon Data Systems, Thousand Oaks, 1982-83; lead designer Logicon, San Diego, 1983-85; computer security mgr. Gen. Dynamics, San Diego, 1985-86; pres. MDPC, San Diego, 1986—. Office: MDPC PO Box 2558 Vista CA 92085-2558

PARKER, PATRICK JOHNSTON, entrepreneur, educator; b. London, Apr. 4, 1931; came to U.S., 1942; s. Russell Johnston and Mildred Grace (Best) P.; m. Evelyn Heims, Nov. 12, 1952 (div. Aug. 1985); children: Karen, Russell; m. Patricia Marie Sobchak, Sept. 3, 1985 (div. May 1992); children: Katherine, Michael; m. Sally Fulton, Aug. 1992. BA, U. Chgo., 1955, MBA, 1957. Asst. prof. U. Calif., Berkeley, 1957-61; assoc. dean, prof. U. Rochester (N.Y.) Grad. Sch. Mgmt., N.Y., 1966-69; prof. U.S. Naval Postgrad. Sch., Monterey, Calif., 1961, 74—; mem. rsch. staff Ctr. for Naval Analysis, Arlington, Va., 1962-64; dir. tactical air program Dept. Def., Washington, 1964-66, dep. asst. sec. def., 1972-74; pres., chief exec. officer Hickok Mfg. Co., Rochester, 1969-72; chmn. bd. dirs., chief exec. officer Cameron Scott Cosmetics, Menlo Park, Calif., 1988—; pres., chmn. bd. trustees Aequus Inst., Montclaire, Calif., 1985—; mem. chief of naval ops. exec. panel USN, 1971-87, chmn., 1971-73. Author: (with Brian Dailey) Soviet Strategic Deception, 1988; contbr. articles to profl. jours. Trustee Shimer Coll., Mt. Carroll, Ill., 1968-72, St. John's Coll., Annapolis, Md., 1992—; dep. dir. Def. Transition Team, Pentagon, 1980; bd. overseers Ctr. Naval Analysis, 1966-72. Republican. Episcopalian. Home: 1993 Orchard Rd Hollister CA 95023-9420 Office: 163 Constitution Dr Menlo Park CA 94025

PARKER, PAUL HENRY, environmental consultant, mediator; b. Logan, Utah, Mar. 8, 1949; s. Reese Redford and Melna (Stuaffer) P.; m. Colleen Baker, June 8, 1973; children: Lorielle, Joshua, Patrick, Leslie. B Landscape Architecture, Utah State U., 1974; M Landscape Architecture, Harvard U., 1976. Community planner Terracor, Salt Lake City, 1973-74; rsch. asst. Harvard U. Grad. Sch. Design, Cambridge, Mass., 1975; dep. state plan coord. State of Utah, Salt Lake City, 1976-81; land planner Tosco Corp., Boulder, Colo., 1981-83; v.p. Inst. for Rsch. Mgmt., Salt Lake City, 1983-91, Ctr. for Resource Mgmt., Salt Lake City, 1991—; cons. to Russian Forest Ministry, Moscow, 1990-92. Office: Ctr for Resource Mgmt 1104 E Ashton Ave Salt Lake City UT 84106

PARKER, ROBERT AARON, sales executive; b. Wolfeboro, N.H., Nov. 20, 1948; s. Howard and Betty (McCauley) Blodgett; divorced; children: William, Aaron, Seth, Christopher. Student, New Eng. Inst., Boston, 1969. Pres. Physicians & Surgeons Funeral & Ambulance Systems, Tavares/Altamonte, Fla., 1970-78; founder, pres. Pacific Rim Investments, Hollywood, Calif., 1981-90; nat. dir. Le Tip Internat., Inc., San Diego, 1990—; mem. disaster relief team Cruz Roja (earthquake), Mexico City, 1985. Disaster coord. Benton-Franklin ARC, Kennewick, Wash., 1972-73; disaster care chmn. Seminole County ARC, Sanford, Fla., 1973-74. Recipient Charter award Am. Assn. Trauma Specialists, 1976. Mem. Assn. for Rsch. and Enlightenment. Reincarnationist. Home: 8721 Santa Monica Blvd #308 Hollywood CA 90069 Office: Le Tip Internat Inc 4926 Savannah St Ste 175 San Diego CA 92110

PARKER, ROBERT DANIEL, engineering executive; b. Carmel, Calif., May 23, 1945; s. Robert Jesse and Edna Mae (Monch) P.; m. Adrianne Catherine Doyle, Oct. 1980 (div. Mar. 1985). BS in Engring., Calif. Inst. Tech., 1967; MSEE, U. So. Calif., 1969, PhD in Elec. Engring., 1972. Rsch. engr. laser and advanced systems engring. Electronics div. Northrop Corp., Hawthorne, Calif., 1986-87; sr. staff engr. Electro Optical and Data Systems group Hughes Aircraft Co., El Segundo, Calif., 1972-82; head power subsystem engring. sect. Space and Communications group Hughes Aircraft Co., El Segundo, Calif., 1982-85, sr. project engr. systems engring. labs., 1985-86, mgr. spacecraft systems engring. dept. comml. systems div., 1987—. Patentee in field; contbr. articles to profl. publs. Recipient IR-100 award Indsl. Rsch. Mag., 1977. Mem. IEEE (sr., chairperson various programs), AIAA (sr.), Sigma Xi. Republican. Presbyterian. Home: 29501 Oceanport Rd Palos Verdes Peninsula CA 90274-5702 Office: Hughes Aircraft Co 200 N Sepulveda Hawthorne CA 90250 also: PO Box 92919 Los Angeles CA 90009

PARKER, ROY ALFRED, transportation engineer, planner; b. Conway, Ark., Apr. 6, 1930; s. Walter Lane and Harriett Mae (Diffee) P.; m. Dixie Anna Dean, June 9, 1953; children: Walter Lane II, David Dean, Shauna Amyr. BS, U. Idaho, 1953; cert. in hwy. traffic, Yale U., 1958. Registered profl. traffic engr., Calif. Asst. planning programming engr. Bur. Pub. Roads (now Fed. Hwy. Adminstrn.), Sacramento, 1958-59; asst. city traffic engr. City of Phoenix, 1959-62; city traffic engr. Palo Alto, Calif., 1962-66; sr. transp. engr. Wilbur Smith & Assocs., London, 1966-68; project mgr. Wilbur Smith & Assocs., Sacramento, 1980; sr. transp. engr. F.R. Harris Engring. Corp., São Paulo, Brazil, 1968-69; prin. assoc. R.W. Crommelin & Assocs., Los Angeles, 1969-70; dep. transp. dir. City and County of Honolulu, 1970-75, dir. dept. transp. services, 1981-83; exec. dir. Oahu Met. Planning Orgn., Honolulu, 1975-79; sr. traffic engr. Lyon Assocs., Inc., Damascus, Syrian Arab Republic, 1979; pres. Roy A. Parker and Assocs., La Jolla, Calif., 1980; transp. engr. City of Concord, Calif., 1983-84, dep. pub. works dir., 1984-88; transp. adminstr. City San Leandro (Calif.), Calif., 1988-90, 91—; acting dir. dept. engring. and transp. City San Leandro (Calif.), 1990-91; lectr. dept. civil engring., Coll. Engring. U. Hawaii, 1971-75; lectr. Inst. Transp. Studies, U. Calif., Berkeley, 1983—. Served with USAF, 1953-57. Fellow Inst. Transp. Engrs. (pres. western dist. 1975-76, pres. San Francisco Bay Area sect. 1991-92); mem. Phi Eta Sigma, Sigma Tau. Democrat. Home: 1160 Sunrise Hl Concord CA 94518-1731 Office: San Leandro Engring & Transp Dept 835 E 14th St San Leandro CA 94577-3767

PARKER, THEODORE CLIFFORD, electronics engineer; b. Dallas, Oreg., Sept. 25, 1929; s. Theodore Clifford and Virginia Bernice (Rumsey) P.; B.S.E.E. magna cum laude, U. So. Calif., 1960; m. Jannet Ruby Barnes, Nov. 28, 1970; children: Sally Odette, Peggy Claudette. V.p. engring. Telemetrics, Inc., Gardena, Calif., 1963-65; chief info. systems Northrop-Nortronics, Anaheim, Calif., 1966-70; pres. AVTEL Corp., Covina, Calif., 1970-74, Aragon, Inc., Sunnyvale, Calif., 1975-78; v.p. Teledyne McCormick Selph, Hollister, Calif., 1978-82; sr. staff engr. FMC Corp., San Jose, Calif., 1982-85; pres. Power One Switching Products, Camarillo, Calif., 1985-86; pres. Condor D.C. Power Supplies, Inc., 1987-88, pres. Intelligence Power Tech. Inc., Camarillo, 1988—. Mem. IEEE (chmn. autotestcon '87), NRA (life), Am. Prodn. and Inventory Control Soc., Am. Def. Preparedness Assn., Armed Forces Communications and Electronics Assn., Tau Beta Pi, Eta Kappa Nu. Home: 1290 Saturn St Camarillo CA 93010-3520 Office: Intelligence Power Tech Inc 829 Flynn Rd Camarillo CA 93012-8702

PARKER, THOMAS GOOCH, retired surgeon; b. Dallas, Aug. 27, 1925; s. Buford M. Parker and Opal-Love Burckhalter; m. Martha Lea Reams, July 18, 1953; children: Melissa Parker Draper, Thomas R., Diana. Student, U. Tex., 1943-46; MD, Harvard U., 1949. Diplomate Am. Bd. Surgery, Am. Bd. Thoracic Surgery. From surg. intern to chief resident Mass. Meml. Hosp., Boston, 1949-56; mem. staff San Mateo (Calif.) Med. Clinic, 1958-71; pvt. practice gen. and thoracic surgery San Mateo, 1971-91; ret., 1991; mem. joint adv. commn. Korea, 1952; clin. nstr. Boston U. Sch. Medicine, 1956; asst. in surgery Stanford Med. Sch., Calif., 1960—. 1st lt. USAF, USNR, 1943-53. Fellow Am. Coll. Surgeons, San Francisco Surg. Soc.; mem. Bohemian Club, Burlingame Country Club. Republican. Home: 531 Ravenscourt Rd Hillsborough CA 94010

PARKER, WALLACE CRAWFORD, computer consultant; b. Pitts., Apr. 16, 1937; s. Wallace McCullough and Virginia (Crawford) P.; m. Marilyn J. Styrwold Kelly, May 11, 1985; stepchildren: Susan M. Kelly, Ryan W. Kelly. BS in Math., U. Pitts., 1968; BS in Computer Sci., U. Oreg., 1986. Computer instr. Lane C.C., Eugene, Oreg., 1987-90; cons. Eugene, 1989—; advisor Boston Computer Soc./Macintosh Users Group, 1989—. Author: Putting MS Works to Work, 2d edit., 1989; manuscript and tech. editors for chpts. to books; contbr. numerous articles to profl. jours. With U.S. Army, 1957-59. Mem. IEEE, Eugene Macintosh Users Group (bd. dirs. 1988—, editor monthly jour. 1992—). Home and Office: 30825 Blanton Rd Eugene OR 97405-9402

PARKER, WAYNE CHARLES, city manager; b. Sacramento, Nov. 14, 1956; s. Allen B. and Marilyn Kay (Alt) P.; m. Julie Ann Fife, June 29, 1979; children: Spencer, Alycia, Kara, Taylor. BA, Brigham Young U., 1979, MPA, 1981. Adminstrv. intern City of Santa Ana, Calif., 1981; pub. mgmt. intern City of Kansas City, Mo., 1981-82; city adminstr. City of Smithville, Mo., 1982-85, City of Merriam, Kans., 1985-88; city mgr. City of Roy, Utah, 1988—; adj. prof. Mo. Internat. U., Kansas City, 1987-88. Bd. dirs. Merrian C. of C., 1987-88; chmn. Fire Dept. Consolidation Task Force, Ogden, Utah, 1989—; exec. com. Weber Econ. Devel. Corp., Ogden, 1990; LDS Bishop 1992—. David M. Kennedy scholar, 1980. Mem. Inter-at. City Mgmt. Assn., Utah City Mgmt. Assn. (sec. 1990—), Kiwanis, Beta Gamma Sigma (life). Mem. LDS Ch. Office: Roy City Corp 5051 S 1900 W Roy UT 84067-2936

PARKER, WILLIAM ELBRIDGE, consulting civil engineer; b. Seattle, Mar. 18, 1913; s. Charles Elbridge and Florence E. (Plumb) P.; m. Dorris Laurie Freeman, June 15, 1935; children—Dorris Laurie, Jane Elizabeth. B.S., U.S. Naval Acad., 1935. Party chief King County Engrs., 1935-39; exec. sec., cons. engr. State Wash., 1946-49; city engr., chmn. Bd. Pub. Works, City of Seattle, 1953-57; cons. City of San Diego, 1957; ptnr. Parker-Fisher & Assocs., 1958-66; cons. engr. Minish & Webb Engrs., Seattle, 1966-70; city engr. City of Bremerton (Wash.), 1970-76; owner Parker & Assocs., Seattle, 1976—. Served to capt. C.E.C., USNR, 1939-45, 51-53. Named to Broadway Hall of Fame. Registered profl. engr., Wash. Mem. Am. Pub. Works Assn., U.S. Naval Inst., Pioneers of State Wash. (pres.), U.S. Naval Acad. Alumni Assn. (chpt. pres.), College Club (Seattle). Lodges: Masons, Shriners.

PARKER, WINIFRED ELLIS, nuclear physicist; b. New Haven, Conn., Apr. 19, 1960; d. Johnson and Dorothy Joan (Sergeant) P.; m. Peter Edward Palmieri, Aug. 9, 1986 (div. Oct. 1991). BS, Dickinson Coll., 1982; MS, Carnegie Mellon U., 1985, PhD, 1989. Postdoctoral assoc. Los Alamos (N.Mex.) Nat. Lab., 1989-92, Lawrence Livermore (Calif.) Nat. Lab., 1992—. Contbr. articles to profl. jours. Mem. AAAS, Am. Phys. Soc., Sigma Xi. Office: Lawrence Livermore Nat Lab PO Box 808 L-41 Livermore CA 94550

PARKHURST, CHARLES LLOYD, electronics company executive; b. Nashville, Aug. 13, 1943; s. Charles Albert Parkhurst and Dorothy Elizabeth (Ballou) Parkhurst Crutchfield; m. Dolores Ann Oakley, June 6, 1970; children: Charles Thomas, Deborah Lynn, Jere Loy. Student, Hume-Fogg Tech. Coll., 1959-61; AA, Mesa Community Coll., 1973; student, Ariz. State U., 1973-76. Mem. design staff Tex. Instruments, Dallas, 1967-68; mgr. design Motorola, Inc., Phoenix, 1968-76; pres. LSI Cons., Inc., Tempe, Ariz., 1976-85, LSI Photomasks, Inc., Tempe, 1985—. Mem. Rep. Congl. Leadership Coun., Washington, 1988; life mem. Rep. Presdl. Task Force, 1990. Served as cpl. USMC, 1961-64. Mem. Bay Area Chrome Users Soc., Nat. Trust Hist. Preservation, Ariz. State U. Alumni Assn. (life). Baptist. Office: LSI Photomasks Inc 406 S Price Rd Ste 5 Tempe AZ 85281-3195

PARKINSON, DEL R., music educator, pianist; b. Blackfoot, Idaho, Aug. 6, 1948; s. Douglas R. and Jane (Peck) P.; m. Glenna M. Christensen, Aug. 6, 1986. MusB, Ind. U., 1971, MusM, 1972, MusD, 1975; diploma, Juilliard Sch., N.Y.C., 1977. Asst. prof. Furman U., Greenville, S.C., 1975-76; assoc. prof. Ricks Coll., Rexburg, Idaho, 1977-85; prof. Boise (Idaho) State U.,

1985—; tchr., performer Dixie Festival of the Performing Arts, St. George, Utah, 1986—; performer Hsu & Parkinson duo pianists, 1986—, Am. Piano Quartet, 1989—; pianist Boise Philharmonic, 1988—. Recording pianist Am. Piano Quartet, 1992. Fulbright-Hays grantee, London, 1974-75; recipient Gov. of Idaho Excellence award, 1988. Mem. Music Tchrs. Nat. Assn. (master, state chmn.), Nat. Guild Piano Tchrs. (adjudicator), Am. Liszt Soc. (jour. contbr.). Office: Boise State U Dept of Music Boise ID 83725

PARKINSON, THOMAS BRIAN, marketing executive; b. Lytham-St. Annes, Lancashire, Eng., Oct. 14, 1935; came to U.S., 1966; s. Alfred and Marjorie (Wright) P.; m. Margaret Moore, Oct. 12, 1957; children: Karen, Lynn, Stephen David. Cert. Mech. Engring., Harris Coll. Further Edn., Preston, Lancashire, Eng., 1962. Apprentice tool maker English Electric Co. Ltd., Preston, Lancashire, Eng., 1951-57; designer aircraft structure British Aircraft Corp., Warton, Lancashire, Eng., 1957-63, stress engr. aircraft, 1963-66; stress engr. aircraft Douglas Aircraft Co., Long Beach, Calif., 1966-76, sales engr. commercial mktg., 1976-78, project mgr. commercial mktg., 1978-85, sales mgr. comml. mktg. Pacific and Asia, 1985-89, exec. asst. comml. mktg. Pacific and Asia, 1989—. Commr. Planning Commn., City of Huntington Beach (Calif.), 1975-77, Underground Utilities Commn., Huntington Beach, 1975-77; chmn. City Charter Revision Com., Huntington Beach, 1977; campaign mgr. Com. to Re-Elect Jerry Matney, Huntington Beach, 1973. With Royal Navy, 1953-55. Mem. Instn. Engring. Designers (assoc.), Pacific Area Travel Assn. (chmn. rsch. authority, bd. dirs. 1983-85, award of merit 1985). Episcopalian. Home: 9042 Annik Dr Huntington Beach CA 92646-2760 Office: Douglas Aircraft Co 3855 N Lakewood Blvd Long Beach CA 90846-0001

PARKISON, ROGER CLYDE, computer scientist; b. Oakland, Calif., May 19, 1949; s. Duane W. and Mary M. (Trotter) P.; m. Carole J. Suzuki, Aug. 7, 1971; children: Brian C., Diana L. BA, U. Calif., 1971; PhD, Stanford U., 1980. Rsch. asst. Stanford U., 1972-75; prin. programmer UCLA, 1975-84; sr. software engr. Isitec Corp., Sunnyvale, Calif., 1984-87; prin. software engr. Digital Equipment Corp., Cupertino, Calif., 1987-92; software designer Tandem Computers, Cupertino, Calif., 1992—. Contbr. articles to profl. jours. Mem. Assn. for Computing Machinery (spl. interest group on artificial intelligence), Am. Assn. for Artificial Intelligence (spl. interest group in mfg.), Assn. for Computational Linguistics. Home: PO Box 1179 Felton CA 95018

PARKS, DOROTHY PATRICIA, tax preparation firm owner; b. Sebastopol, Calif., Jan. 28, 1956; d. William Clifford Feht and Evelyn (Bohling) Harris; m. Glenn Allen Parks, Mar. 28, 1981; children: Denise Marie, William Randle. Grad. high sch., El Sobrante, Calif. Various positions Bank of Am., Calif., 1974-83; owner Shoreline Fin. Svcs., Tomales, Calif., 1984—. Treas. Tomales Presbyn. Ch., 1987—, Shoreline Acres Presch., Tomales, 1988—, bd. dirs. 1988—, Hope Counseling Svcs., Petaluma, Calif., 1989—. Office: Shoreline Fin Svcs 27005 Maine St Upstairs Tomales CA 94971

PARKS, GERALD THOMAS, JR., lawyer, business executive; b. Tacoma, Wash., Feb. 25, 1944; s. Gerald Thomas and Elizabeth (Bell) P.; m. Susan Simenstad, July 22, 1967; children: Julie, Christopher; m. Bonny Kay O'Connor, Jan. 15, 1979, children: Garrett, Ardrienne. BA in Polit. Sci., U. Wash., 1966; JD, U. Oreg., 1969. Bar: Wash. 1969. Assoc. Graham & Dunn, 1972-77, ptnr., 1977-82; sole practice, 1982—; sec., treas. Holaday-Parks Fabricators, Inc., 1972-78, v.p., gen. mgr. (named changed to Holaday-Parks, Inc.), 1978-84; pres., chief exec. officer, 1984—. Served to lt. with USN, 1969-72. Mem. Wash. State Bar Assn., Sheet Metal and Air Conditioning Contractors of Western Wash., Inc. (pres. 1989-91), Sheet Metal and Air Conditioning Contractors Nat. Assn. (dir. 1989-92, v.p. 1992-93), Seattle Yacht Club, Broadmoor Golf Club, Seattle Tennis Club. Office: PO Box 69208 4600 S 134th Pl Seattle WA 98168

PARKS, HAROLD RAYMOND, mathematician, educator; b. Wilmington, Del., May 22, 1949; s. Lytle Raymond Jr. and Marjorie Ruth (Chambers) P.; m. Paula Sue Beaulieu, Aug. 21, 1971 (div. 1984); children: Paul Raymond, David Austin; m. Susan Irene Taylor, June 6, 1985; 1 stepchild, Kathryn McLaughlin. AB, Dartmouth Coll., 1971; PhD, Princeton U., 1974. Tamarkin instr. Brown U., Providence, 1974-77; asst. prof. Oreg. State U., Corvallis, 1977-82, assoc. prof., 1982-89, prof. math., 1989—; vis. assoc. prof. Ind. U., Bloomington, 1982-83. Author: Explicit Determination of Area Minimizing Hypersurfaces, vol. II, 1986, (with Steven G. Krantz) A Primer of Real Analytic Functions, 1992; contbr. articles to profl. publs. Cubmaster Oregon Trail Coun. Boy Scouts Am., 1990-92. NSF fellow, 1971-74. Mem. Am. Math. Soc., Math. Assn. Am., Soc. Indsl. and Applied Math., Phi Beta Kappa. Republican. Mem. Soc. of Friends. Home: 33194 Dorset Ln Philomath OR 97370-9555 Office: Dept Math Oreg State Univ Corvallis OR 97331-4605

PARKS, MICHAEL CHRISTOPHER, journalist; b. Detroit, Nov. 17, 1943; s. Robert James and Rosalind (Smith) P.; m. Linda Katherine Durocher, Dec. 26, 1964; children: Danielle Anne, Christopher, Matthew. AB, U. Windsor, Ont., Can., 1965. Reporter Detroit News, 1962-65; corr. Time-Life News Service, N.Y.C., 1965-66; asst. city editor Suffolk Sun, Long Island, N.Y., 1966-68; polit. reporter, foreign corr. The Balt. Sun, Saigon, Singapore, Moscow, Cairo, Hong Kong, Peking, 1968-80; fgn. corr. L.A. Times, L.A., Peking, Johannesburg, Moscow, Jerusalem, 1980—. Recipient Pulitzer Prize, 1987. Mem. Royal Commonwealth Soc. London. Club: Foreign Corr. (Hong Kong). Home: Box 17, BEIT Agron (Govt Press Office), Jerusalem Israel 94581 Office: L A Times Times Mirror Sq Los Angeles CA 90012-3816

PARKS, RICHARD KEITH, clinical social worker; b. Rock Springs, Wyo., Oct. 13, 1947; s. Keith Andrew and Mildred Ann (Matkovich) P.; m. Debra D. Thomas, Sept. 21, 1968 (div. Nov. 1971); m. Alberta Dea Henderson, Feb. 26, 1974; children: Heather, Richell. AA, Western Wyo. Coll., 1969; BSW, U. Wyo., 1985; MSW, Denver U., 1988. Lic. social worker. Owner, mgr. Rich's Britches, Rock Springs, 1974-77; asst. mgr. Wyo. Bearing, Rock Springs, 1976-82; residential counselor Southwest Wyo. Rehab. Ctr., Rock Springs, 1983-85; community care worker, therapist Southwest Counseling Svc., Rock Springs, 1985-89; sch. social worker Sch. Dist. #1, Rock Springs, 1989-90; mental health counselor State of Nev. Rural Clinics, Fernley, 1990—; inpatient clin. social worker Nev. Mental Health Inst., Reno, 1992—; social work cons. Pershing Gen. Hosp., Lovelock, Nev., 1991—; program mgr. Transitional Living Ctr., 1985-87; workshop presenter in field, 1986. Vol. counselor Sweetwater Crisis Intervention Ctr., Rock Springs, 1973-83, bd. dirs., 1979-83; v.p. Downtown Mchts. Assn., 1975. Mem. NASW, Alumni Assn. U. Wyo. Congregationalist.

PARKS, ROBERT HOWARD, JR., sculptor; b. Hollywood, Calif., Feb. 10, 1943; s. Robert Howard and Edna Mable (Omischer) P.; m. Linda Lee, Nov. 18, 1966; children: Stephanie J., Harland M. Grad. high sch., Burbank, Calif. Pres. Bob Parks Gallery, Scottsdale, Ariz., 1978—. Prin. works include bronze sculptures Power & Performance, 1989, Perpetual memorial Trophy, 1981, Royal Trust Trophy, 1985, Gene Autry Bronze, 1978, Trophy For West Va. Breeders Classic, Ltd., 1992-96; represented in permanent collections of Favell Art Mus., Birmingham Art Mus., Chgo. Art Inst., City of Scottsdale. Recipient Purchase award Amoco Corp., 1992, Award of Excellence, Deerpath Art League, 1991, Best of Show award Long Grove Art Fest, 1992, Gallery award Long Grove Art Fest, 1992, Pard'ners award Mira Arabians, 1992. Office: Bob Parks Gallery 7072 5th Ave Scottsdale AZ 85251

PARKS, THOMAS NORVILLE, neurobiologist; b. Berkeley, Calif., May 27, 1950; s. Herbert Otho and Wilma Jean (Strong) P.; m. Patricia Legant, July 6, 1980; 1 child, Anna Legant. B.S., U. Calif., Irvine, 1972; Ph.D., Yale U., 1978. Lectr. psychology Yale U., New Haven, 1977; postdoctoral fellow U. Va., Charlottesville, 1977-78; asst. prof. anatomy U. Utah, Salt Lake City, 1978-83, assoc. prof., 1983-87, prof., 1987—, George and Lorna Winder prof. Neuroscience and chair, dept. Neurobiology and Anatomy, 1992—; bd. dirs. NPS Pharmaceuticals Inc., v.p., 1987-88. Mem. NIH (hearing rsch. study sect. 1986-90, Claude pepper award 1993—). Office: U Utah Sch Medicine Dept Neurobiology and Anatomy Salt Lake City UT 84132

PARKS, TOM HARRIS, association executive; b. L.A., Aug. 18, 1932; s. Samuel Harris and Virginia Marion (Cummings) P.; m. Cornelia Sue Legg, Mar. 26, 1964; children: Tom H., Therese Ann Pond, Patrick, Ryan. Student, El Camino Coll., Torrance, Calif., 1951. With Horseshoe & Gardena Clubs, Gardena, Calif., 1958-83; gen. ptrn. Rainbow Club, Gardena, 1983-85; exec. v.p. Gardena C. of C., 1985—. Columnist, Gardena Ramblings. Chmn. Meml. Hosp. Trustees, Gardena, 1988—. With USN, 1951-55; co-chmn. United Way UGA Project, 1990, Cultural Arts Corp., 1990. Mem. S.C. Assn. Chamber Execs. (bd. dirs. 1990—), Calif. Assn. Chamber Execs. (bd. dirs. 1991—), South Bay Assn. Chambers (pres. 1989-90), Am. Legion, Toastmasters. Republican. Office: Gardena C of C 1204 W Gardena Blvd Gardena CA 90247-4871

PARKS, WILLIAM HAMILTON, supply company executive; b. South Bend, Ind., July 15, 1934; s. Hamilton and Elizabeth Ann (Osborne) P.; m. Sue Ann Fenske, Apr. 1, 1965 (div. 1971). B.A., Mich. State U., 1957, M.A., 1960, Ph.D., 1967. Mem. staff Cadillac div. Gen. Motors, 1958-60; asst. prof. U. Oreg., Eugene, 1965-72; assoc. prof. U. Idaho, Moscow, 1972-78, prof., 1977—; owner, pres. Northwest River Supplies, Moscow, 1972—. Served with U.S. Army, 1954-56. Mem. Fin. Mgmt. Assn., Acad. of Mgmt. Home: 1205 Orchard Ave Moscow ID 83843-9420 Office: 2009 S Main St Moscow ID 83843

PARLETTE, CAROL HOLLAND, management firm executive; b. Springfield, Mo., Feb. 21, 1944; d. Marvin Benjamin and Georgia Genevieve (Hager) Holland; m. G. Nicholas Parlette, May 23, 1975. BS in Edn., Southwest Mo. State U., 1966; MPH, U. Calif., Berkeley, 1976. Exec. dir. Calif. Soc. Internal Medicine, San Francisco, 1972-85; owner and pres. Holland-Parlette Assocs., San Francisco, 1985—. Named Assn. Exec. of Yr., No. Calif. Soc. Assn. Execx., 1989. Western Occupational Med. Assn. (exec. dir. 1990—), Kite Trade Assn. (exec. dir. 1988—, Western Office Am. Soc. Assn. Execs. (dir. 1985—), exec. dir., Structural Engrs. Assn. No. Calif., Am. Assn. Med. Soc. Execs., Commonwealth Club. Office: Holland Parlette Assocs 50 1st St Ste 300 San Francisco CA 94105-2411

PARMA, FLORENCE VIRGINIA, magazine editor; b. Kenilworth, N.J., Aug. 30, 1940; d. Howard Frank and Mildred Faye (Lister) von Finkel; m. Wilson Henry Parma, June 15, 1973 (div. Aug. 1986). Studies with pvt. tutor, Chaumont, France, 1961-62; student, NYU, 1962-63. Copywriter Schless & Co., N.Y.C., 1963-65; editor, researcher Barchas Lab., Stanford, Calif., 1969-73; adminstrv. exec. Crater Inc., Honolulu, 1974-79; mgr., editor Off Duty mag., Honolulu, 1979—; v.p. Mapasa, Inc. (dba The Prides of New Zealand), 1992—. Editor: Welcome to Hawaii Guide, 1985—; co-editor: Serotonin and Behavior, 1972; freelance columnist. Republican. Episcopalian. Home and Office: Off Duty Hawaii 3771 Anuhea St Honolulu HI 96816-3849

PARMENTER, ROBERT HALEY, physics educator; b. Portland, Maine, Sept. 19, 1925; s. LeClare Fall and Esther (Haley) P.; m. Elizabeth Kinnecom, Oct. 27, 1951; children: David Alan, Douglas Ian. B.S., U. Maine, 1947; Ph.D., Mass. Inst. Tech., 1952. Mem. staff solid state and molecular theory group Mass. Inst. Tech., 1951-54; guest scientist Brookhaven Nat. Lab., 1951-52; mem. staff Lincoln Lab., 1952-54, RCA Labs., 1954-66; vis. scientists RCA Labs., Zurich, Switzerland, 1958; acting head solid state research group RCA Labs., 1962-65; prof. physics U. Ariz., 1966—, chmn. dept., 1977-83; mem. NASA rsch. adv. com. electrophysics, 1964-68, chmn., 1966-68, mem. rsch. and tech. adv. com. basic rsch., 1966-68; vis. lectr. Princeton (N.J.) U., 1960-61. Served with USNR, 1944-46. Fellow AAAS, Am. Phys. Soc. (chmn. div. condensed matter physics 1967-68); mem. Sigma Xi, Tau Beta Pi. Home: 1440 E Ina Rd Tucson AZ 85718-1175 Office: U Ariz Physics Dept Tucson AZ 85721

PARMETER, DIANA LYNN, musician; b. Modesto, Calif., Mar. 26, 1963; d. Robert Clyde Parmeter and Isla Ruth (Anna) Sanchez. MusB, Calif. State U., Northridge, 1988; MusM, Rice U., 1990. Cellist Fresno (Calif.) Philharm., 1980-81, Naples String Trio, Long Beach, Calif., 1982-92, Harrah's Hotel, Lake Tahoe, Nev., 1987-88, Rapides Symphony, Lake Charles, La., 1989-90, Galveston (Tex.) Symphony, 1989-90, Mantovani Orch., 1990-92, South Coast Symphony, Irvine, Calif., 1991-92, Santa Barbara (Calif.) Symphony, 1991-93, Nidom String Quartet, Tomakomai, Japan, 1992-93; cello tchr. Sterling High Sch., Baytown, Tex., 1989-90, Gentry Jr. High Sch., Baytown, 1989-90. Active So. Poverty Law Ctr., Montgomery, Ala., 1991-92, Long Beach Coalition Choice, 1992, Sierra Club, 1992-93; demonstrator L.A. Coalition Against Intervention Mid. East, 1991. Scholar Bell T. Ritchie Found., 1987, Calif. State U.-Northridge, 1987, San Fernando Valley Teaching Orgn., 1987, Shepherd Sch., 1990. Mem. Am. String Tchrs. Assn., Long Beach Musicians Assn. Home: 5923 Lemon Ave Long Beach CA 90805

PARNALL, EDWARD, retired orthopedic surgeon; b. Ann Arbor, Mich., Oct. 18, 1904; m. Erma Hills: children: Theodore, Carolyn, William. BA cum laude, U. Mich., 1924; AM, Harvard U., 1925, MD, 1929. Pvt. practice Rochester, N.Y., 1932-39; with N.W. Clinic, Minot, N.D., 1939-42; pvt. practice Albuquerque, 1946-76. Lt. col. U.S. Army, 1942-46. Democrat. Home: 1216 Mesilla SE Albuquerque NM 87110

PARNELL, GREGORY ELLIOTT, physicist, technical policy analyst; b. Ranger, Tex., Dec. 22, 1953; s. Shelby Delbert and Carleta Joy (Elliott) P. BS, Tex. A&M U., 1976, MS, 1978, PhD, 1987. Exploration geophysicist Shell Oil Corp., Houston, 1980-83; assoc. phys. scientist RAND Corp., Santa Monica, Calif., 1987—. Author monograph; contbr. articles to profl. jours. Mem. IEEE, IEEE Communs. Soc., IEEE Electromagnetic Compatibility Soc., IEEE Soc. on Social Implications of Tech., Am. Phys. Soc. (forum on physics and society, div. nuclear physics). Office: RAND Corp 1700 Main St Santa Monica CA 90407-2138

PARNICKY, WILLIAM, estate and financial planning executive; b. N.Y.C., Dec. 31, 1921; s. Peter and Eudokia (Hutzolo) P.; m. Winnifred Lois Heleve (dec. June 1970); children: Michael W., Peter C.; m. Juanita Eloise Thomas, Mar. 13, 1972. BS, U. Calif., Davis, 1947. CLU, CFP. Instr. Curtiss Wright Tech. Inst., Glendale, Calif., 1940-41; commd. 2d lt. USAAF, 1941, advanced through grades to capt., 1943, resigned, 1949; stress analyst Lockheed Aircraft (Vega), Burbank, Calif., 1941-43; owner operator Parnicky Farms, Imperial, Calif., 1948-72; mgr. ins. sales Farm Bur., El Centro, Calif., 1953-61; pres. William Parnicky Inc. dba Fiscal Fitness, Grants Pass, Oreg., 1961—. Pres. Kiwanis, Grants Pass, 1968, Rogue Valley Life Underwriters, Medford, Oreg., 1977, Grants Pass Life Underwriters, 1982, Calif. Farm Bur. Fedn. Young People, 1950. Named Boss of Yr., Am. Bus. Women's Assn., 1977, Agt. of yr., Rogue Valley Life Underwriters, 1980, Grants Pass Life Underwriters, 1983. Mem. So. Oreg. Estate Planners, Nat. Assn. Life Underwriters, Internat. Assn. Fin. Planners, Million Dollar Round Table. Office: Fiscal Fitness 950 SW 6th St Grants Pass OR 97526

PARONI, GENEVIEVE MARIE SWICK, retired science educator; b. Eureka, Nev., July 27, 1926; d. William Jackson and Myrtle Rose (Smith) S.; m. Walter Andrew Paroni, Dec. 26, 1954; 1 child, Andrea Marie. BA, U. Nev., Reno, 1948; MEd, U. Idaho, 1978; postgrad., MIT, Oreg. State U., U. Oreg., U. Wash., Ft. Wright Coll., U. Portland. Cert. elem. and secondary sect., Nev. Tchr., vice prin. Eureka County High Sch., 1948-66; coast geodetic U.S. Govt., Eureka, 1950's; tchr. biol. and phys. scis., facilitator Pub. Schs. Dist. #393, Wallace, Idaho, 1968-91; ret., 1991; regional dir. NSTA, Idaho, Panhandle, 1982-90; chmn. in svc. adv. State Dept. Edn., Boise, Idaho, 1980-83, mem. state sci. commn., 1981-82; mem. Idaho Sci. Curriculum Guide Com., 1987, Univ. Idaho Commn. on Math/Sci. Edn., 1988-89, Inland Empire Physics Alliance, 1989-90, Idaho Sci. Alliance Com., 1990. Contbr. history articles to profl. jours. Active Wallace City Council, 1970-80; bd. mem. Wallace Pub. Library, 1983—, Silver Valley Arts and Crafts Assn., 1991; precinct chmn. Republicans, Wallace, 1970-80; bd. dirs. Greater Wallace, 1980—, Wallace Dist. Arts Coun., 1993; bishop's warden, Episcopal Ch., 1990—. Grantee Idaho Power, 1985; named Outstanding Tchr., Dist. #393. 1975; finalist Presdl. awards in High Sch. Sci. Teaching. Mem. NEA, Idaho Edn. Assn., Wallace Edn. Assn. (sec. 1970's), AAUW (pres. 1970's), Bus. and Profl. Women Assn. (v.p. Nev. chpt. 1953-55), Delta Kappa Gamma (pres. 1980-82), Phi Delta Kappa. Lodge: Pythian Sisters (Grand Guard, 1950), Order of Eastern Star (matron Nev. chpt.). Home: PO Box 229 Wallace ID 83873-0229

PARPIA, ZAKIR HUSAIN, home builder; b. Bombay, India, Jan. 16, 1948; came to U.S., 1975; s. Sultan Rahim and Zarin Sultan (Patel) P.; m. Chitra Z. Parpia; children: Zarina, Aliza, Raheem. BCE with 1st class honors, U. Bombay, 1972; MCE magna cum laude, Wash. State U., Pullman, 1976. Gen. mgr. R C Constrn. Co., Spokane, 1976-79; pres. Himalaya Homes, Inc., Spokane, 1979-89, Everett, Wash., 1989—; pres. Home Owners Warranty Corp., Spokane, 1981, also bd. dirs. Mem. oversight com. U. Wash. Component Testing Program, 1985-87; del. to energy and planning coms. Wash. State Bldg. Code Adv. Coun. Mem. Bldg. Industry Assn. Wash. (pres. 1988), Home Builders Assn. Wash. (pres. 1988), Home Builders Assn. Wash. (bd. dirs. 1982—, Wash. State Builder of Yr. 1986, Spokane Builder of Yr. 1983, 85, 88), Home Builders Assn. Spokane (chmn. energy task force 1983—, pres. 1983), Nat. Assn. Home Builders (nat. bd. dirs. 1982—), Rotary Club of Lynnwood. Home: 22530 76th Ave SE Woodinville WA 98072 Office: Himalaya Homes Inc 10217 19th Ave SE Everett WA 98208

PARQUETTE, JACK ROBERT, lawyer; b. Des Moines, July 2, 1934; s. Robert West and Helen (Cox) P.; m. Eva Miersch, Sept. 11, 1965; children: Jonathan R., Brian K. Student, U. Colo., 1959; LLB, Lincoln U., 1977. Bar: Calif. 1978, U.S. Ct. Appeals (9th cir.) 1978, U.S. Dist. Ct. (ea. dist.) Calif., 1978. Claims mgr. Unigard Ins. Calif., Sacramento, 1966-77; ptnr. Barker, Mikel & Parquette, Sacramento, 1979-81; pvt. practice, 1981—. Mem. Calif. State Bar Assn., No. Calif. Def. Assn. Home: 7748 Guenivere Way Citrus Hills CA 95610-6761

PARRENAS, CECILIA SALAZAR, educator; b. San Jose de Buenavista, Antique, Philippines, July 17, 1945; came to U.S., 1983; d. Angel Xavier Salazar and Lourdes Quibing (Jabile); m. Florante Y. Parrenas, Dec. 24, 1964; children: Rolf, Celine, Rhacel, Rhanee, Cerissa, Rheana, Margarita, Cecille. BS in Elem. Edn., Philippine Normal Coll., Manila, 1966; MA in Adminstrn., Nat. Tchrs. Coll., Manila, 1971, EdD in Edn. Mgmt., 1977; postgrad., Boston U., 1979. Faculty mem. Internat. Sch., Inc., Metro Manila, 1967-81; dept. head English and art Woodrose, Pvt. Sch. for Girls, Metro Manila, 1981-83; assoc. prof. De LaSalle U., Manila, 1983-84; program asst. sr. edn. programs MIT Sloan Sch., Cambridge, 1984-85; resource tchr. San Bernardino (Calif.) City Unified Sch. Dist., 1986-91; bilingual tchr., unit leader Pomona (Calif.) Unified Sch. Dist., 1991—; cons. Boston Pub. Schs. and Boston U. Bilingual Resource Tng. Ctr., 1978-79; presenter 20th Internat. Conf. on Bilingual/Bicultural Edn., 1991. One-woman painting and brushworks shows Brush, Ink and Color, Manila, 1981, Touchen and Calligrafen, Innsbruck, Austria, 1981, Seasons, Manila, 1982. Philippine Normal Coll. Alumni Assn. grantee, Manila, 1962-66, grantee Curso para profesores Agencia de Cooperacion Internacional, Madrid, 1991; postdoctoral fellow Boston U., 1978-79. Mem. Nat. Assn. Bilingual Edn. (presenter 22nd internat. conf. 1993). Home: 2283 La Salle Ave San Bernardino CA 92407-2497 Office: Pomona Unified Sch Dist Allison Elem Sch 1011 Russell Pl Pomona CA 91767

PARRO, DOUGLAS ARTHUR, non-profit child care center administrator; b. Denver, Dec. 29, 1954; s. Russell James and Theresa Viola (Zapp) P.; m. Jamie Lou Sherberg, May 21, 1976. BA in Psychology and Sociology, U. Colo., 1978, MA in Clin. Psychology, 1987. Lic. profl. counselor. Delivery driver various cos., Denver, 1970-74; postal clk. U.S. Postal Svc., Denver, 1974-75; oil well roughneck Wildcat Driller, Nebr., 1975; liquor clk. Mayfair Liquors, Denver, 1980-82; counselor/asst. dir., 1977-80; exec. dir. Jefferson Hall, Arvada, Colo., 1983—; cons., trainer Community Learning Ctrs., Gemini Shelter, Shalom House, Adolescent Treatment Program, All My Children Homes, Denver, 1987—; grant writer, adminstr., Jefferson Hall, Arvada, 1983—; field instr. Colo. State U., 1987—, U. Denver, 1988—. Treas. Shadow Wood Homeowners Assn., Denver, 1986-93; assoc. mem. Denver Zool. Found., 1991—; commr. Placement Alternatives Commn., Jefferson County, Colo., 1983-89; mem. Colo. Juvenile Coun., Denver Youth Agy. Network. Mem. Child Welfare League of Am., Phi Beta Kappa. Office: Jefferson Hall 7695 W 59th Ave Arvada CO 80004-5501

PARROTT, DENNIS BEECHER, sales executive; b. St. Louis, June 13, 1929; s. Maurice Ray and Mai Ledgerwood (Beecher) P.; m. Vivian Cleveland Miller, Mar. 24, 1952; children: Constance Beecher, Dennis Beecher, Anne Cleveland. BS in Econs., Fla. State U., Tallahassee, 1954; postgrad. Princeton U., 1964; MBA, Pepperdine U., 1982. With Prudential Ins. Co. Am., 1954-74, v.p. group mktg., L.A., 1971-74; sr. v.p. Frank B. Hall Cons. Co., L.A., 1974-83; v.p. Johnson & Higgins, L. A., 1983—; speaker in field. Chmn. Weekend with the Stars Telethon, 1976-80; chmn. bd. dirs. United Cerebral Palsy/Spastic Children's Found. Los Angeles County, 1979-82, chmn. bd. govs., 1982-83; bd. dirs. Nat. United Cerebral Palsy Assn., 1977-82, pres., 1977-79; bd. dirs. L.A. Emergency Task Force, 1992; mem. community adv. council Birmingham High Sch., Van Nuys, Calif., 1982-85 ; sect. chmn. United Way, Los Angeles, 1983-84; bd. dirs. The Betty Clooney Found. for Brain Injured, 1986-88; mem. com. to fund an endowed chair in cardiology at Cedars-Sinai Med. Ctr., 1986-88; adv. council Family Health Program Inc., 1986-88; bd. Deacons Bel Air Presbyn. Ch., 1990-92, chmn. 1991-92; elder Bel Air Presbyn. Ch. 1993—. Served to 1st lt. AUS, 1951-53. C.L.U. Mem. Am. Soc. C.L.U.s, Internat. Found. Employee Benefits, Merchants and Mfrs. Assns. 44th Annual Mgmt. Conf. (chmn. 1986), Employee Benefits Planning Assn. So. Calif. Republican. Presbyterian. Clubs: Los Angeles, Woodland Hills Country, Jonathan (Los Angeles). Office: One Century Pl 2029 Century Park E Los Angeles CA 90067

PARRY, ATWELL J., JR., state senator, retailer; b. Ogden, Utah, June 14, 1925; s. John Atwell and Nina Virginia (McEntire) P.; m. Elaine Hughes, Feb. 6, 1946; children—Bonnie, Michael, Jay, Donald, David, Delbert, Kent. Student pub. schs., Nampa, Idaho. Salesman, King's Packing Co., Nampa, 1947-54, credit mgr., 1954-55; plant mgr. Stone Poultry Co., Nampa, 1955-56; salesman Nestle Chocolate Co., 1956-64; owner, mgr. Melba Foods, Idaho, 1964-82; mem. Idaho Senate, 1981—; bd. dirs. Western Idaho Tng. Ctr., 1987-90; chmn. Senate Finance Com. and co-chmn. Joint Fin. and Appropriations Com., 1987—; chmn. Idaho State Bd. for Nat. Ctr. for Constl. Studies, 1988-90. Bd dirs. Alcohol Treatment Ctr., Nampa, 1978-82; mem. adv. bd. Mercy Med. Ctr., Nampa, 1976-81; mem. Melba City Council, 1971-74. Recipient Silver Beaver award Boy Scouts Am., 1959, Service award Mercy Med. Ctr. Republican. Mormon.

PARRY, PAMELA JEFFCOTT, association executive, art librarian; b. Forest Hills, N.Y., Mar. 6, 1948; d. Richard Francis and Florence Ida (Michels) J.; m. Ellwood Comly Parry III, Nov. 20, 1971; children: Janna, Evan, Taylor. B.A., U. Ariz., 1969; M.A. in Art History, Columbia U., 1971, M.L.S., 1973. Asst. curator slide collection dept. art history Columbia U., N.Y.C., 1970-72, asst. fine arts librarian, 1972-76; editorial asst. Archives of Neurology, Iowa City, 1976-78; bibliographer Internat. Dada Archive, U. Iowa, Iowa City, 1979-81; exec. dir. Art Librs. Soc. N.Am., Tucson, 1980-93; editor newsletter Art Libraries Soc. N. Am., Tucson, 1978-81. Editor Art Documentation, 1982, 85-86, The Art Reference Collection Series, 1976-82; author: Contemporary Art and Artists: An Index to Reproductions, 1978, Photography Index: A Guide to Reproductions, 1979 (ALA award 1979), (with others): Print Index: A Guide to Reproductions, 1983. Mem. Tucson Unified Sch. Dist. Community Partnership Coun., 1987, sec., 1989, Spl. Edn. Parents Orgn., 1991-92, chair, 1991-92, parents adv. coun., 1992—. N.Y. State Regents fellow, 1969-71. Mem. Am. Soc. Assn. Execs., Visual Resources Assn., Assn. Archtl. Librs., Soc. Am. Archivists, Mus. Assn. Ariz., Ariz. State Libr. Assn., U. Ariz. Assoc. Art History (community bd. 1991—, v.p. 1993-94), Phi Kappa Phi. Democrat. Home: 3775 N Bear Creek Cir Tucson AZ 85749-9454 Office: 3900 E Timrod St Tucson AZ 85711-4169

PARRY, ROBERT TROUTT, bank executive, economist; b. Harrisburg, Pa., May 16, 1939; s. Anthony C. and Margaret R. (Troutt) P.; m. Brenda Louise Grumbine, Dec. 27, 1956; children: Robert Richard, Lisa Louise. BA magna cum laude, Gettysburg (Pa.) Coll., 1960; MA in Econs., U. Pa., 1961, PhD, 1967. Asst. prof. econs. Phila. Coll. Textiles and Sci., 1963-65; economist Fed. Res. Bd., Washington, 1965-70; v.p., chief economist Security Pacific Nat. Bank, Los Angeles, 1970-76, sr. v.p., chief economist, 1976-81, exec. v.p., chief economist, 1981-86; pres., chief exec. officer Fed. Res. Bank San Francisco, 1986—; bd. dirs. Nat. Bur. Econ. Rsch.; mem. adv. bd. Pacific Rim Bankers Program, Ctr. for Fin. System Rsch. Ariz. State U.; mem. policy adv. bd. Ctr. for Real Estate and Urban Econs., U. Calif., Berkeley, mem. exec. com. Inst. Bus. and Econs. Rsch.; bd.

dirs. San Francisco Bay Area Coun.; mem. Bay Area Econ. Forum; lectr. Pacific Coast Banking Sch., 1976-78; adv. panel Pacific Econ. Outlook Project of Asia Found.; mem. adv. coun. SRI Internat. Mem. econ. vis. com. U. Pa.; mem. exec. bd. Boy Scouts Am., 1993—. NDEA fellow, 1960-63. Mem. Nat. Assn. Bus. Economists (pres. 1979-80), Am. Bankers Assn. (chmn. econ. adv. com.), Calif. Bankers Assn. (bd. dirs. 1982-83), Am. Econs. Assn., Western Econs. Assn. Home: 90 Overhill Rd Orinda CA 94563-3123 Office: Fed Res Bank San Francisco PO Box 7702 San Francisco CA 94120-7702

PARRY, ROBERT WALTER, chemistry educator; b. Ogden, Utah, Oct. 1, 1917; s. Walter and Jeanette (Petterson) P.; m. Marjorie J. Nelson, July 6, 1945; children: Robert Bryce, Mark Nelson. BS, Utah State Agr. Coll., 1940; MS, Cornell U., 1942; PhD, U. Ill., 1946; DSc (hon.), Utah State U., 1985. Research asst. NDRC Munitions Devel. Lab., U. Ill. at Urbana, 1943-45, teaching fellow 1945-46; mem. faculty U. Mich., 1946-69, prof. chemistry, 1958-69; Distinguished prof. chemistry U. Utah, 1969—; indsl. cons., 1952—. Chmn. com. teaching chemistry Internat. Union Pure and Applied Chemistry 1968-74. Recipient Mfg. Chemists award for coll. teaching, 1972, Sr. U.S. Scientist award Alexander Von Humboldt-Stiftung (W. Ger.), 1980, First Govs. Medal of Sci. State Utah, 1987. Mem. Am. Chem. Soc. (Utah award Utah Sect. 1978, past chmn. inorganic div. and div. chem. edn. award for distinguished service to inorganic chemistry 1965, for chem. edn., 1977, dir. 1973-83, bd. editors jour. 1969-80, pres.-elect 1981-82, pres. 1982-83, Priestly medal 1993), Internat. Union Pure and Applied Chemistry (chmn. U.S. nat. com.), AAAS, Sigma Xi. Founding editor Inorganic Chemistry, 1960-63. Research, publs. on some structural problems of inorganic chemistry, and incorporation results into theoretical models; chemistry of phosphorus, boron and fluorine. Home: 5002 Fairbrook Ln Salt Lake City UT 84117 Office: U Utah Dept Chemistry Henry Eyring Bldg Salt Lake City UT 84112

PARSHLEY, PHILIP FORD, JR., surgeon; b. Hartford, Conn., Oct. 13, 1931; s. Philip F. and Dorothy Jane (Parker) P.; m. Barbara Jane Vaughan, Aug. 2, 1932; children: Marianne, Jeffrey V., Philip P., Dorothy E. AB, Dartmouth Coll., 1953 ; MD, Harvard U., 1956. Diplomate Am. Bd. Surgery. Intern, then resident in surgery Boston City Hosp., 1956-62; surgeon Bodine Cantrel Clinic, Portland, Oreg., 1964-67, The Surg. Ctr., Portland, 1967—; med. dir. Oreg. Burn Ctr., Portland, 1973—, Oreg. Tissue Bank, Portland, 1989-91; clin. prof. surgery Oreg. Health Scis. U., 1992—. Capt. USAF, 1962-64. Fellow ACS (pres. Oreg. chpt. 1988-89); mem. Am. Burn Assn., Portland Surg. Soc. (pres. 1982-83), North Pacific Surg. Assn., Pacific Coast Surg. Assn. Office: The Surg Ctr 2800 N Vancouver Ave Portland OR 97227-1630

PARSONS, BRUCE JAMES, optometrist; b. Salt Lake City, Dec. 24, 1922; s. Percy James and Beatrice (Rordame) P.; m. Thelma Bagnell, May 26, 1950; children: Cheryl Ann, Wendy Jean, Craig Bruce, Vaughn James. BS, U. Calif., Berkeley, 1949, OD, 1949. Optometrist Murray, Utah, 1949—. Mem. Rotary (dist. gov. 1984-85). Office: Murray Vision Ctr 120 E 4800 S Murray UT 84107

PARSONS, GIBBE HULL, medical educator; b. Turlock, Calif., Dec. 1, 1942; s. Beck and Charlene (Hull) P.; m. Ann MaGuire, Apr. 6, 1969; children: Christopher, Craig, Kerry. BA, Calif. State U., San Jose, 1964; MD, George Washington U., 1968; prof. medicine. Intern St. Vincents Hosp., N.Y.C., 1968-69; resident in internal medicine U. Calif. Davis Med. Ctr., Sacramento, 1971-73, fellow, 1973-75, asst. prof., 1975-90, prof. of medicine, 1990—; med. dir. respiratory care U. Calif. Davis Med. Ctr., Sacramento, 1975-83. Bd. dirs. Am. Lung Assn., Sacramento, 1975—, Arden Park Recreation and Park Dist., Sacramento, 1984-90. Lt. USN, 1969-71. Mem. Am. Thoracic Soc., Calif. Thoracic Soc., DaVinci Soc. for Study Bronchial Circulation, Am. Physiol. Soc. Methodist. Office: U Calif Davis Med Ctr Pulmonary Critical Care Div 4301 X St Sacramento CA 95817-2214

PARSONS, MICHAEL LOEWEN, research and development executive; b. Oklahoma City, Apr. 20, 1940; s. O.L. and Eva (O'Neill) P.; m. Karen O. Bridwell, Aug. 1958 (div. 1970); children: Stephen M., David R.; m. Virginia E. Thomas, Mar. 23, 1971; children: LaGuinn E., Lynn Erin. Student, Austin Coll., 1958-61; BA, Kans. State Coll. (Pitts. State U.), 1962, MS, 1963; PhD, U. Fla., 1966. Rsch. chemist Phillips Petroleum, Bartlesville, Okla., 1966-67; asst. prof. Ariz. State U., Tempe, 1967-71, assoc. prof., 1971-77, prof., 1977-84; dep. group leader Los Alamos (N.Mex.) Nat. Lab., 1984-88; dir. R & D Pacific Scientific Co. HTL/Kin-Tech Div., Duarte, Calif., 1988-91; v.p. tech. and new product devel. Pacific Scientific Co. HTL/Kin-Tech. Div., Duarte, Calif., 1990—. Contbr. articles to profl. jours. Mem. Soc. Applied Spectroscopy (pres. 1979, William F. Meggos award 1967, 75), Am. Chem. Soc. (chmn. local sec. 1972, Outstanding Chemist award 1981), Optical Soc. Am., Soc. Photo Optical Instrumentation Engring., Sigma Xi. Office: Pacific Sci Co 1800 Highland Ave Duarte CA 91010-2895

PARSONS, STUART OVERTON, JR., human factors scientist, consultant, educator; b. Denver, Aug. 11, 1926; s. Stuart Overton Sr. and Gladys (East) P.; m. Harriet Jaggard, July 11, 1955; children: Carol, Cynthia, Pamela. BA, U. Colo., 1948; MA, U. So. Calif., 1950, PhD, 1958. Profl. engr., Calif.; lic. psychologist, Calif. Aviation electronics technician USN, 1944-46; psychometrician Colo. Merit System, Denver, 1947-48; pers. technician City of Denver, 1950-51; rsch. assoc. Psychol. Svcs. Inc., L.A., 1951-53; indsl. rels. specialist Lockheed Corp. Offices, Burbank, Calif., 1954-57; engring. mgr. Lockheed Missile & Space Co., Sunnyvale, Calif., 1958-87; pres. Parsons and Assocs., Saratoga, Calif., 1987—; adj. prof. U. Denver, 1987—; adj. assoc. prof. U. So. Calif., L.A., 1969-92; researcher Waseda U., Tokyo, 1988-89; lectr. San Jose State U., 1964-92, Coll. Notre Dame, 1970, 93. Author over 40 books and jour. articles, 1960-91. Col. USAFR, 1950-83. Fellow Human Factors Soc. (sec.-treas. 1964-66, bd. dirs. Bay Area chpt. 1969, 75, 78); assoc. fellow Am. Inst. Aero. & Astronautics; mem. Internat. Ergonomics Assn. (U.S. del. 1991—). Episcopalian. Home and Office: 19740 Via Escuela Dr Saratoga CA 95070-4445

PARTLOW, FRANK ALMOND, JR., army officer; b. San Francisco, Sept. 1, 1938; s. Frank A. and Nina Esther (Bateman) P.; m. Kay Eleanor Sunderman, Nov. 10, 1960; children: Tamara Lynne Zoscak, Michele Anne Caruso. BS in Engring., U.S. Mil. Acad., 1960; MA in European Studies, Stanford U., 1967. Commd. 2d. lt. U.S. Army, 1960, advanced through grades to brigadier gen., 1986; asst. prof. social scis. U.S. Mil. Acad., 1967-70; exec. asst. to sr. internat. ofcl. U.S. Army, 1971-73, bn. comdr., 1975-77, sr. analyst, 1977-78; staff asst. internat. security affairs Dept. Def., 1979-80; brigade comdr. U.S. Army, 1980-82; dep. dir. planning Dept. Army, 1983-84; chief staff Multinat. Force, 1985-86; sr. mem. U.S. Arms Control Delegation, Geneva, 1986-88; dir. estimates Def. Intelligence Agy., 1988-90, ret., 1990; bus. analyst, cons., 1991-92. Contbr. articles to profl. jours. Harvard U. sr. fellow, 1982-83. Mem. Internat. Inst. Strategic Studies (assoc.), Phi Kappa Phi. Republican. Home and Office: No Nev Network 15 Scattergun Reno NV 89509

PARTOW-NAVID, PARVIZ, information systems educator; b. Iran, July 24, 1950; came to U.S., 1974; s. Mohammad and Parvin (Maleki) P.-N.; m. Mahroo Changizi, July 6, 1976; children: Puya, Rod. BBA, Tehran Bus. Coll., 1973; MBA, U. Tex., 1976, PhD, 1981. Asst. prof. Mich. Tech. U., Houghton, 1981-83; assoc. prof. Calif. State U., L.A., 1983-87, prof., 1987—; cons. Nichols Inst., San Juan Capistrano, Calif., 1987-89, Security Pacific Bank, L.A., 1990—; assoc. dir. Ctr. for Info. Resource Mgmt., L.A., 1987—; presenter in field. Author: Microcomputer Software Tools, 1987; contbr. articles, revs. to profl. publs. Mem. Inst. Mgmt. Sci., Soc. Info. Mgmt., Beta Gamma Sigma. Office: Calif State U LA Dept Info Svcs 5151 State University Dr Los Angeles CA 90032-4221

PARVANKIN, JOSEPH DANIEL, education administrator; b. Portland, Oreg., Feb. 23, 1963; s. Ivan Angel and Connie (King) P. BA in Econs. and Polit. Sci., Linfield Coll., 1985. Mem. sr. staff Multnomah Edn. Svc. Dist., Portland, 1985-86, asst. site supr., 1987-88, 89-91; program dir. youth coord. Wash. County Edn. Svc. Dist., Portland, 1991-93; v.p. Highlights Restaurants, Inc., Portland, 1993—; cons. Urban Japanese Soc., Tokyo, 1988-89; bd. dirs. Pacific Wonderland, Portland. Mem. Environ. Edn. Assn. Portland. Office: Highlights Restaurants Inc 539 NE 106th Pl Portland OR 97220

PASCAL, C(ECIL) BENNETT, classics educator; b. Chgo., May 4, 1926; s. Jack and Goldie (Zeff) P.; m. Ilene Joy Shulman, Feb. 1, 1959; 1 child, Keith Irwin. BA, UCLA, 1949, MA, 1950; MA, Harvard U., 1953, PhD, 1956. Instr. U. Ill., Champaign, 1955-56, Cornell U., Ithaca, N.Y., 1957-60; asst. prof. U. Oreg., Eugene, 1960-75, prof. classics, 1975—, head dept., various years - 1965-85. Author: Cults of Cisalpine Gaul, 1964; contbr. articles to profl. jours. Mem. Eugene Bicycle Com., 1971-83. Served with USN, 1944-46. Traveling fellow, Italy, Harvard U., 1956-57, Fulbright-Hays fellow, Rome, 1967-68. Mem. Am. Philol. Assn., Classical Assn. Pacific N.W. (pres. 1965-66), AAUP, Archeol. Inst. of Am. (past pres., sec. Eugene Soc.). Democrat. Jewish. Home: 330 Fulvue Dr Eugene OR 97405-2788 Office: U of Oreg Dept Classics Eugene OR 97403

PASCARELLI, FRED JOSEPH, marketing and advertising executive; b. Bklyn., Sept. 14, 1950; s. Joseph and Alma Louise (Unger) P.; m. Judith Anne Lundgren, June 17, 1973 (div. Aug. 1984); 1 child, Matthew Ryan; m. Jayne Ellen Polk, May 18, 1990. AAS, No. Nev. C.C., Elko, Nev., 1973; BBA, Boise State U., 1975. Sales mgr. Safeway Stores, Inc., Elko, 1967-75; sales rep. Gen. Foods Corp., Boise, Idaho, 1975-78; territory sales mgr. Homelite Textron, Boise, 1978-84; dist. sales mgr. Homelite Textron, Detroit, 1984-88; mktg. mgr. Homelite Textron, Charlotte, N.C., 1988-90; dir. mktg., mgmt. cons. Inertia Dynamics Corp., Chandler, Ariz., 1990-92; dir. bus. devel. Ryobi Outdoor Products, Chandler, 1992; dir. product planning and advt. Adobeair, Phoenix, 1992-93; sr. account exec. product devel. Ariz. Pub. Svc., Phoenix, 1993—; dir., ptnr. P & H Properties, Boise, 1978—. Author, editor, pub.: (newsletter) Dealer Update, 1986-88. Sec., treas. Sports Boosters, Elko, 1972-73; fundraiser Cath. Ch. Bldg. Fund, Boise, 1979; pres. Homeowners Assn., Boise, 1983-84. Home: 2516 E Cathedral Rock Dr Phoenix AZ 85044 Office: Ariz Pub Svc PO Box 53999 Mail Sta 8638 Phoenix AZ 85072-3999

PASCH, ANNE DUDLEY, geology educator; b. Wisconsin Rapids, Wis., Sept. 20, 1936; d. Gordon Delos and Agnes Carson (Vanneman) Shipman; m. Kurt R.M. Pasch, June 11, 1960; children: Barbara Vanneman Pasch Racine, Karl Dittrich. BS, U. Wis., 1958; MAT, Alaska Meth. U., 1972; postgrad., U. Calif., Berkeley, 1988-89. Tchr. sci. Milw. Pub. Schs., 1958-60, Anchorage Sch. Dist., 1960-67; geologist U.S. Geol. Survey, Anchorage, 1977-83; tchr. geology Anchorage Community Coll., 1973-87; assoc. prof. U. Alaska, Anchorage, 1987-88, prof. geology, 1988—, chmn. dept. geology, 1989-91; cons. Anchorage Sch. Dist., 1989-91. Author: Investigations in Environmental Geology, 1987; co-author: National History of Alaska, 1988. Bd. dirs. Anchorage Symphony Orch., 1971-74, double bass player, 1973-88; pres. Anchorage Symphony Women's League, 1970-71; double bass player Anchorage Chamber Orch., 1989-91; mem. commn. Profl. Tchrs. Practicum Commn., State of Alaska, 1967. Recipient Pres.'s Spl. Project award U. Alaska, Fairbanks, 1990, Faculty Devel. award, Anchorage, 1990, grantee, 1984. Mem. Alaska Geol. Soc. (bd. dirs. 1987-89), Alaska Ctr. for the Environment, Alaska Miner's Assn., Geol. Soc. Am. (campaign rep. 1987-91), Soc. for Sedimentary Geology, Nat. Assn. Geology Tchrs., Southcentral Alaska Mus. Natural History. Lutheran. Home: 7661 Wandering Dr Anchorage AK 99502-1932 Office: Univ of Alaska 3211 Providence Dr Anchorage AK 99508

PASCOE, PATRICIA HILL, writer, state senator; b. Sparta, Wis., June 1, 1935; d. Fred Kirk and Edith (Kilpatrick) H.; m. D. Monte Pascoe, Aug. 3, 1957; children: Sarah, Ted, Will. BA, U. Colo., 1957; MA, U. Denver, 1968, PhD, 1982. Tchr. Sequoia Union High Sch. Dist., Redwood City, Calif. and Hayward (Calif.) Union High Sch. Dist., 1957-60; instr. Met. State Coll., Denver, 1969-75; instr. Denver U., 1975-77, 81, research asst. bur. ednl. research, 1981-82; tchr. Kent Denver Country Day, Englewood, Colo., 1982-84; freelance writer Denver, 1985—; mem. Colo. Senate, Denver, 1989-93; commr. Edn. Commn. of the States, Denver, 1975-82. Contbr. articles to numerous publs. and jours. Bd. dirs. Samaritan House, Cystic Fibrosis Found.; pres. East High Sch. Parent, Tchr. and Student Assn., Denver, 1984-85; mem. Moore Budget Adv. Com., Denver, 1966-72; legis. chmn. alumni bd. U. Colo., Boulder, 1987-89; del. Dem. Nat. Conv., San Francisco, 1984, N.Y.C., 1992. Mem. Soc. Profl. Journalists, Common Cause (bd. dirs. Denver chpt. 1986-88), Phi Beta Kappa. Presbyterian. Home: 744 Lafayette St Denver CO 80218-3503

PASCOTTO, ALVARO, lawyer; b. Rome, Mar. 8, 1949; came to U.S., 1984; s. Antonio and Anna Ludovica (Habig) P.; m. Linda Haldan, July 20, 1985. JD, U. Rome, 1973. Bar: Italy 1976, Calif. 1987, U.S. Dist. Ct. (cen. dist.) Calif. 1987, U.S. Ct. Appeals (9th cir.) 1987. Ptnr. Studio Legale Pascotto, Rome, 1976-86, Pascotto, Gallavotti & Gardner, L.A. and Rome, 1986-90, Pascotto & Gallavotti, L.A., 1990—; counsel, cons. Quantum Inc., Reno, Nev., 1980-87, Execucorp Mgmt. Cons., Miami, Fla., 1980-85; official counsel Consulate Gen. Italy, L.A., 1987—. Mem. ABA, Calif. Bar Assn., Italian-Am. Bar Assn., Am. Mgmt. Assn., Consiglio dell'Ordine Degli Avvocati e Procuratori di Roma. Clubs: Circolo del Golf (Rome); Malibu (Calif.) Racquet Club, Regency Club (L.A.). Home: 6116 Merritt Dr Malibu CA 90265-3847 Office: Pascotto & Gallavotti 11111 Santa Monica Blvd Los Angeles CA 90025-7296

PASCULLI, MARK ANDRE, accountant; b. Jersey City, Nov. 16, 1962; s. Morris Charles and Dolores (Abeal) P.; m. Lori Elizabeth Cole, Jan. 7, 1989; 1 child, Mark Daniel. Student, Fresno State U., 1988; student, top 5 in class, San Joaquin Coll. Law, 1991—. CPA, Calif. Staff acct. Borchardt, Wiley and Co., Fresno, Calif., 1988-89; acct. DeMera DeMera Cameron, Fresno, 1989—. Mem. AICPA, Calif. Soc. CPAs, Beta Alpha Psi Alumni, Sigma Chi Alumni. Republican. Office: DeMera DeMara Cameron 5080 N Fruit Ste 101 Fresno CA 93711

PASICH, KIRK ALAN, lawyer; b. La Jolla, Calif., May 26, 1955; s. Chris Nick and Iva Mae (Tormey) P.; m. Pamela Mary Woods, July 30, 1983; children: Christopher Thomas, Kelly Elizabeth. BA in Polit. Sci., UCLA, 1977; JD, Loyola Law Sch., L.A., 1980. Bar: Calif. 1980, U.S. Dist. Ct. (no., so., ea. and cen. dists.) Calif. 1981, U.S. Ct. Appeals (9th cir.) 1982, U.S. Ct. Appeals (1st cir.) 1992. Assoc. Paul, Hastings, Janofsky & Walker, L.A., 1980-88, ptnr., 1988-89; ptnr. Hill Wynne Troop & Meisinger, L.A., 1989—. Author: Casualty and Liability Insurance, 1990, 92; entertainment law columnist, ins. law columnist L.A. and San Francisco Daily Jour., 1989—; contbr. articles to profl. jours. Active bd. dirs. Nat. Acad. Jazz, L.A., 1988-89, chmn. bd. dirs. Woody Herman Found., L.A., 1989-92, active L.A. City Atty's. Task Force for Econ. Recovery, 1992—. Named to Calif's. Legal Dream Team as 1 of state's top 25 litigators, Calif. Law Bus., 1992. Mem. ABA (mem. Task Force on Complex Insurance Coverage Litigation, co-chair Insurer Insolvency subcom.), L.A. County Bar Assn. Office: Hill Wynne Troop & Meisinger 10940 Wilshire Blvd Los Angeles CA 90024-3902

PASIN, SELENA ANN, sales and marketing executive; b. Ellensburg, Wash., Mar. 28, 1963; d. J.A. and Carlene Rose (Scammon) P. BS in Internat. Bus. Mgmt., U. San Francisco, 1987. Mktg. dir. Money Mailer Pacific N.W., Gig Harbor, Wash., 1988-90, dir. franchise sales, 1990—. Mem. Tacoma Execs., Gig Harbor C. of C. (v.p. bus. and econ. devel. 1991—, tourism chair 1989-92, sec. 1991—). Office: Money Mailer Pacific NW 3206 50th St Ct NW # 210 Gig Harbor WA 98335

PASLOV, EUGENE, state education official. Supt. edn. Nevada. Office: Nev Dept Edn 400 W King St Carson City NV 89710-0001

PASQUA, THOMAS MARIO, JR., journalism educator; b. L.A., Aug. 13, 1938; s. Thomas Mario and Ann Ione (Anderson) P.; m. Sandra Mae Liddell; children: Bruce Burks, Julie Burks, Geoffrey, Alexis. BA, Whittier (Calif.) Coll., 1960; MA, UCLA, 1961; PhD, U. Tex., 1973. Cert. secondary tchr. Reporter, photographer Whittier Daily News, 1954-65; tchr. LaSerna High Sch., Whittier, 1961-63, 64-65; lectr. Calif. State U., Fullerton, 1973-75, Mesa Coll., San Diego, 1978-83, U. San Diego, 1979-80, San Diego State U., 1985; prof. Southwestern Coll., Chula Vista, Calif., 1965—. Co-author: Excellence in College Journalism, 1983, Mass Media in the Information Age, 1990, Historical Perspectives in Popular Music, 1993; editor C.C. Journalist, 1983—; bibliographer Journalism Quar., 1974-92; contbr. articles to profl. jours. Mem. ch. coun. St. Andrew Luth. Ch., Whittier, 1965; mem. Chula Vista Bd. of Ethics, 1978-86; mem. Chula Vista Charter Rev. Com., 1969; mem. adv. bd. Bay Gen. Hosp., Chula Vista, 1985-87; mem. ch. coun. Victory Luth. Ch., Chula Vista, 1989-90. Wall St. Jour. Newspaper Fund fellow U. Wash., 1962; recipient Nat. Teaching award Poynter Inst. Media Studies, 1987. Mem. C.C. Journalism Assn. (archivist 1989—), Journalism Assn. C.C.'s (exec. sec. 1975-81), Assn. for Edn. in Journalism and Mass Comm. (Markham prize 1974), Internat. Comm. Assn., Coll. Media Advisers, Am. Fedn. Tchrs. (pres. Southwestern Coll. 1977-78, 81-87), Phi Kappa Phi, Kappa Tau Alpha, Pi Sigma Alpha. Democrat. Home: 760 Monterey Ave Chula Vista CA 91910-6318 Office: Southwestern Coll 900 Otay Lakes Rd Chula Vista CA 91910-7223

PASSENHEIM, BURR CHARLES, physicist; b. St. Louis, Dec. 15, 1941; s. Carlton Donald and Georgia (Elenor) P.; m. Kathryn E. Kirkland, 1964 (div. 1976); children: John Burr, Susan Jean; m. Jeannine Vivian Berger, Sept. 25, 1982. BA, U. Calif., Berkeley, 1963; MA, U. Calif., Riverside, 1965, PhD, 1969. Physicist Gen. Atomic, San Diego, 1969-72, IRT Corp., San Diego, 1972-78, Mission Rsch., San Diego, 1978-83, Jaycor, San Diego, 1983—. Editor: Jour. of Radiation Effects, 1985-86; author: How to Do Radiation Tests, 1988. Mem. IEEE (session chmn. conf. 1991). Home: 5838 Camber Dr San Diego CA 92117 Office: Jaycor 9775 Towne Centre Dr San Diego CA 92121

PASSMAN, STEPHEN LEE, theoretical mechanics scientist; b. Suffolk, Va., Sept. 3, 1942; s. Milton Lawrence and Jean (Lehrman) P.; m. Anita Joy Greenwald, June 12, 1965; children: Michael, Rebecca, Sara, Rachel. BSEM, Ga. Inst. Tech., 1964, MSEM, 1966, PhD, 1968. Instr. U.S Naval Acad., Annapolis, Md., 1968-70; postdoctoral fellow Johns Hopkins U., Balt., 1970-71; from asst. to assoc. prof. Ga. Inst. Tech., Atlanta, 1971-78; sr. mem. tech. staff Sandia Nat. Labs., Albuquerque, 1978—; lectr. George Washington U., Washington, 1969-70; vis. mem. Math. Research Ctr. U. Wis., Madison, 1972, Inst. Math. and Its Applications, U. Minn., Mpls., 1984, 89, Math Sci. Inst., Cornell U., 1987-90; cons. Bell Labs., Norcross, Ga., 1975-78; vis. scientist Pitts. Energy Tech. Cen., 1988-90, cons., 1990—; vis. scholar Carnegie Mellon U., 1988-90; adj. prof. engring. U. Pitts., 1990—; U.S. Rep. multiphase flow com., Internat. Energy Agy., 1992. Contbr. articles to profl. jours. Served to capt. U.S. Army, 1968-70. Scholar Johns Hopkins U., 1990. Mem. ASME (elasticity com. 1987—, multiphase flow com. 1990—), Soc. Natural Philosophy (treas. 1977-78, dir. 1978—, chmn. bd. dirs. 1985-86), Soc. Engring. Sci. (bd. dirs. 1986—, treas. 1987—), Am. Acad. Mechanics, Am. Phys. Soc., Soc. Rheology, Sigma Xi. Home: 6005 Concordia Rd NE Albuquerque NM 87111-1328 Office: Sandia Nat Labs Dept 6212 Box 5800 Albuquerque NM 87185

PASSOVOY, SUSAN JANE, lawyer; b. Stockton, Calif., Apr. 10, 1946; d. Aaron and Ann (Hackman) P.; m. Timothy Charles Blackburn, Oct. 3, 1992. BA, Stanford U., 1967; JD, U. Calif., Berkeley, 1971. Bar: Calif. 1972, U.S. Dist. Ct. (no. dist.) 1972, U.S. Ct. Appeals (9th cir.) 1972, U.S. Supreme Ct. Asst. counsel Trimont Land Co., San Francisco, 1971-72; staff Raymond D. Nasher Co., Dallas, 1973; assoc. Brobeck, Phleger & Harrison, San Francisco, 1974-76; ptnr. Ellman, Passovoy, Burke & Cassidy, San Francisco, 1976-82, Howard, Rice, Canady, Robertson & Falk, San Francisco, 1982-84, Coblentz, Cahen, McCabe & Breyer, San Francisco, 1984—; gen. counsel Episcopal Community Svcs. of San Francisco, 1983-93; gov. Am. Coll. Real Estate Lawyers, 1991—; adv. commn. Practising Law Inst., 1991—. Trustee San Francisco Art Inst., 1982-84; pres. San Francisco Moving Co., 1978-82, Women's Forum West, 1993, dir., 1976-78, 84-86, 92-93, pres., 1993—. Fellow Am. Bar Found.; mem. ABA, Calif. Bar Assn. Office: Coblentz Cahen McCabe et al 222 Kearny St San Francisco CA 94108

PASTEGA, RICHARD LOUIS, retail specialist; b. Klamath Falls, Oreg., Mar. 25, 1936; s. Louie and Jennie (Borgialli) P. BS, So. Oreg. State Coll., 1960; MS, Mont. State U., Bozeman, 1961. Tchr. social studies Henley High Sch., Klamath Falls, Oreg., 1962-63, Juneau (Alaska) Douglas High Sch., 1964-67, Thessaloniki (Greece) Internat. High Sch., 1967-69; editor, pub. Breakdown Newspaper, Klamath Falls, Oreg., 1971-73; mgr. Pastega's Market, Klamath Falls, 1975—. Del. Dem. Nat. Conv., N.Y.C., 1976, Oreg. Dem. Platform conv., Eugene, Beaverton and Ashland, 1978-80, 82; councilor City of Klamath Falls, 1986-88; bd. dirs. Basin Transit Svc., Klamath Falls, 1981-87; chair Klamath County Dem. Cen. Com., 1983-86, sec. 1992—. Mem. Sons of Italy. Democrat. Home: 428 S 9th St Klamath Falls OR 97601-6126

PASTER, JANICE D., state legislator; b. St. Louis, Aug. 4, 1942. BA, Northwestern U., 1964; MA, Tufts U., 1967; JD, U. N.Mex., 1984. Pvt. practice, 1984—; mem. N.Mex. State Senate from 10th dist. Democrat. Home: 5553 Eakes Rd NW Albuquerque NM 87107-5529 address: Box 1966 Albuquerque NM 87103

PASTERNACK, ROBERT HARRY, school psychologist; b. Bklyn., Nov. 30, 1949; s. William and Lillian Ruth (Levine) P.; m. Jeanelle Livingston, Apr. 10, 1980; children: Shayla, Rachel. BA, U. South Fla., 1970; MA, N.Mex. Highlands U., 1972; PhD, U. N.Mex., 1980. Dir. Eddy County Drug Abuse Program, Carlsbad, N.Mex., 1972-73; adminstrv. intern U.S. Office Edn., Washington, 1975-76; exec. dir. Villa Santa maria, Cedar Crest, N.Mex., 1976-78; clin. dir. Ranchos Treatment Ctr., Taos, N.Mex., 1978-79; sch. psychologist N.Mex. Boys Sch., Springer, 1980—, supt., 1991; pres. Ensenar, Inc., Taos, 1980—; instr. N.Mex. Highlands U., Las Vegas, 1980—, U. N.Mex., Albuquerque, 1980—; cons. N.Mex. Youth Authority, Santa Fe, 1988—, N.Mex. Devel. Disabilities Bur., Santa Fe, 1986—, various sch. dists. Author: Growing Up: The First Five Years, 1986; contbr. articles to profl. publs. Pres., bd. dirs. Children's Lobby, N.Mex., 1978, N.Mex. Spl. Olympics, 1986-88, Child-Rite, Inc., Taos, 1990; mem. Gov.'s Mental Health Task Force, Albuquerque, 1988—. Mem. Nat. Assn. Sch. Psychologists, Correctional Edn. Assn., Nat. Alliance Mentally Ill, N.Mex. Coun. on Crime and Delinquency. Home and Office: Enseñar Inc PO Box 3126 Taos NM 87571-3126 Office: New Mexico Boys Sch PO Box 38 Springer NM 87747-0038

PASTERNAK, DERICK PETER, physician, medical center executive; b. Budapest, Hungary, Apr. 21, 1941; s. Leslie Laszlo and Hedvig Eva (Hecht) P.; came to U.S., 1956, naturalized, 1962; BA, Harvard U., 1963, MD cum laude, 1967; MBA, U. N.Mex., 1985; m. Nancy Jean Clark, June 6, 1969; children: Kenneth Zoltan, Katherine Renee, Sarah Marie. Intern, jr. resident Bronx Municipal Hosp., N.Y.C., 1967-69; resident in internal medicine U. Calif. Hosps., San Francisco, 1971-73; mem. staff Lovelace Med. Center, Albuquerque, 1973—, med. dir. quality assurance program, 1976-80; med. dir. Lovelace Med. Found., 1980-86, pres., chief exec. officer, 1986—; pres. N.Mex. PSRO, Inc., 1980-82; clin. assoc. prof. medicine U. N.Mex. Referee U.S. Soccer Fedn.; v.p. N.Mex. Symphony Orch. Capt. M.C., AUS, 1969-71; lt. col. USAR. Decorated Bronze Star, Army Commendation Medal. Diplomate Am. Bd. Internal Medicine. Fellow AMA, Am. Coll. Physicians, Am. Coll. Physician Execs. (bd. dirs.); mem. AMA, N.Mex. Med. Soc., Greater Albuquerque Med. Assn., Am. Group Practice Assn. (trustee). Office: Lovelace Inc 5400 Gibson Blvd SE Albuquerque NM 87108-4763

PASTIN, MARK JOSEPH, university educator, executive consultant; b. Ellwood City, Pa., July 6, 1949; s. Joseph and Patricia Jean (Camenite) P.; m. Joanne Marie Reagle, May 30, 1970 (div. Mar. 1982); m. Carrie Patricia Class, Dec. 22, 1984 (div. June 1990); m. Christina M. Brecto, June 15, 1991. BA summa cum laude, U. Pitts., 1970; MA, Harvard U., 1972, PhD, 1973. Asst. prof. Ind. U., Bloomington, 1973-78, assoc. prof., 1978-80; prof. mgmt., dir. Ariz. State U., Tempe, 1980—; founder, bd. CTG, Inc., Tempe, 1983—; mem. adv. bd. Aberdeen Holdings, San Diego, 1988-90; dir. Sandpiper Group, Inc., N.Y.C., 1987—, S.W. Projects, Inc., San Diego, 1988-90, Learned, Nicholson, Ltd., 1990-91; chmn. bd. Coun. Ethical Orgns., Phoenix, 1986—, Japan Am. Soc. Phoenix; chmn. bd. Found. for Ethical Orgns.; cons. GTE, Southwestern Bell, St. Louis, 1987-89, Tex. Instruments, MicroAge Computers, Med-Tronic, Blood Systems, Inc., Opus Corp., GTE, NyNex, Am. Express Bank, Kaiko Bussan Co., Japan, Century Audit Co., Japan, Scottsdale Meml. Hosp., Cosanti Found.; vis. faculty U. Mich., Ann Arbor, 1978, Harvard U, 1980; invited presenter Australian Inst. Mgmt., Nippon Tel. & Tel., Hong Kong Commn. Against Corruption, 1984, Young Pres.'s Orgn. Internat. U., 1990, Nat. Assn. Indsl. & Office Parks,

1990, ABA, 1991, Govt. of Brazil, 1991. Author: Hard Problems of Management, 1986 (Book of Yr. award Armed Forces Mil. Comptrs. 1986), Power By Association, 1991, The State of Ethics in Arizona, 1991, Planning Forum, 1992; editor: Public-Private Sector Ethics, 1979; columnist Bus. Jour.; contbr. articles to jours. Founding bd. mem. Tempe Leadership, 1985-89; bd. mem. Ctr. for Behavioral Health, Phoenix, 1986—, Tempe YMCA, 1986—, Valley Leadership Alumni Assn., 1989—; mem. Clean Air Com., Phoenix, 1987—. Nat. Sci. Found. fellow, Cambridge, Mass., 1971-73; Nat. Endowment for the Humanities fellow, 1975; Exxon Edn. Found. grant, 1982-83. Mem. Strategic Mgmt. Soc. (invited presenter 1985), Am. Soc. Assn. Execs. (invited presenter 1987-91), Bus. Ethics Soc. (founding bd. mem. 1983), Found. Ethical Orgns. (chmn. 1988), Pres.'s Assn., Am. Mgmt. Assn., Ariz. Club, Golden Key Nat. Hon. Club, Harvard Club, Ariz. Club, Phi Beta Kappa. Home: 14436 S 34th Way Phoenix AZ 85044-7046 Office: PO Box 24838 Tempe AZ 85285-4838

PASTOR, ED, congressman; b. June 28, 1943. Mem. Maricopa County Bd. Suprs., Phoenix, Ariz., 1976-91; mem. 102nd-103rd Congresses from Ariz. 2nd dist., 1991—. Office: House of Representatives Washington DC 20515*

PASTORE, MICHAEL ANTHONY, college administrator; b. Fresno, Calif., Aug. 31, 1932; s. Michele Costantino and Rosa Maria (Damiani) P.; A.A., Coll. of Sequoias, Visalia, Calif., 1952; B.S., U. San Francisco, 1954; M.A., Fresno State Coll., 1969; Ph.D., U. Wash., 1976; m. Elizabeth Anne York, Dec. 23, 1955; children—Michael Anthony, Christi Anna, Maria Delisa. Agt., M.A. Pastore Ins. Co., Fresno, 1963-69; instr., coordinator, div. chmn. Edmonds Community Coll., Lynwood, Wash., 1969-73; founder, pres. City Univ. Seattle, 1973—. Served with U.S. Army, 1956-57. Roman Catholic. Clubs: Wash. Athletic, Rainier (Seattle); Glendale Country (Bellevue, Wash.). Home: 618 175th Pl NE Bellevue WA 98008-4242 Office: 16661 Northup Way Bellevue WA 98008-3045

PASTORE, THOMAS MICHAEL, telecommunications sales executive; b. Bronx, N.Y., Jan. 25, 1959; s. Philip J. and Olga E. (DeGenito) P.; m. Kimberly A. Coppersmith, Dec. 13, 1986; 1 child, Gabriela Maria. BA in Bus., Western State Coll., 1981. Sales rep. Victor Technologies Inc., Denver, 1981-84; account mgr. No. Telecom Inc., Denver, 1984-87, v.p. sales coun., 1985—, sales engr., 1987-92, dist. sales mgr., 1992—. Mem. Better Air Campaign, 1990—; sec. Warren Sq. Homeowners Assn., Denver, 1987-92; player, contbr. Dale Tooley Tennis Tournament, 1991-92; fundraiser Am. Cancer Soc., Denver, 1991—; mem. Denver Art Mus., 1991-92. Republican. Roman Catholic. Home: 3520 S Quintero St Aurora CO 80013-3026 Office: No Telecom Inc 5575 Dtc Pky Ste 150 Englewood CO 80111-3012

PASTREICH, PETER, orchestra executive director; b. Bklyn., Sept. 13, 1938; s. Ben and Hortense (Davis) P.; m. Jamie Garrard Whittington; children by previous marriages: Anna, Milena, Emanuel, Michael. A.B. magna cum laude, Yale Coll., 1959; postgrad., N.Y. U. Sch. Medicine, 1959-60; studied trumpet, with Robert Nagle at Yale U., with Raymond Sabarich, Paris. Asst. mgr. Denver Symphony, Balt. Symphony; Mgr. Greenwich Village Symphony, N.Y.C., 1960-63; gen. mgr. Nashville Symphony, 1963-65, Kansas City Philharmonic, 1965-66; asst. mgr., mgr. St. Louis Symphony, 1966-78, exec. dir., 1966-78; exec. dir. San Francisco Symphony, 1979—; instr. orch. mgmt. Am. Symphony Orch. League; bd. dirs. Nat. Com. for Symphony Orch. Support; founder San Francisco Youth Orch.; rep. planning and constrn. Davies Symphony Hall, San Francisco Symphony, 1980. Author: TV comml., 1969 (CLIO award); contbr. articles to various newspapers. Mem. recommendation bd. of the Avery Fisher Artist Program, Yale U. Council com. on music; past mem. adv. panel Nat. Endowment for the Arts, co-chmn. music panel, 1985; founding mem. bd. dirs. St. Louis Conservatory, mem. policy com. Maj. Orch. Mgrs. Conf., chmn., 1980; bd. dirs. Laumeier Sculpture Park, St. Louis, Stern Grove Festival, San Francisco Conv. and Visitors Bur.; chmn. fund campaign French-Am. Internat. Sch., San Francisco. Served with U.S. Army, 1960. Recipient First Disting. Alumnus award Yale U. Band, 1977, cert. Merit Yale Sch. Music, 1984. Mem. Am. Symphony Orch. League (dir., chmn., former chmn. task force on mgmt. tng.; mem. exec. and long-range planning com., chmn. standing com. on adminstrv. policy), Assn. Calif. Symphony Orchs. (dir.), Bankers Club of San Francisco. Club: Yale (N.Y.C.). Office: San Francisco Symphony Davies Symphony Hall San Francisco CA 94102*

PATE, LINDA KAY, sales executive; b. Morehead City, N.C., Feb. 4, 1949; d. Leon Jr. and Mildred E. (Lawrence) P. Student, East Carolina U., 1967, 68; diploma, Hardbarger Bus. Coll., Raleigh, N.C., 1970; AA, Coll. of Marin, Kentfield, Calif., 1978; BSBA summa cum laude, San Francisco State U., 1984. Adminstr. shareholder rels. Cameron Brown Co., Raleigh, 1970-74; legal asst. Itel Corp., San Francisco, 1974-75; ops. mgr. Trans Meridian, San Francisco, 1977-81; sales rep. Candle Corp., Larkspur, Calif., 1981, sales mgr. nat. accounts, 1992—. Recipient award Soc. Super Software Sellers, 1985-91. Mem. Beta Gamma Sigma. Republican. Office: Candle Corp 200 Tamal Pla Corte Madera CA 94925

PATEL, JYOTI SHIVABHAI, biophysicist; b. Patna, Bihar, India, Aug. 15, 1943; came to the U.S., 1968; s. Shivabhai Pushottamdas and Kamla Patel; 1 child, Sarita. BA in Physics and Math., Youngstown State U., 1974; MS in Health Physics, Tex. A&M U., 1988, postgrad., 1988. With Med. Rsch. Inst., 1978-83, Tex. A&M U., 1984-88, Westinghouse Hanford Co., 1989-91; coord. EG&G Rocky Flats, 1991—. Recipient Cert. of Appreciation Kingdom of Saudi Arabia, 1991. Mem. Health Physics Soc. Home: 10424 W 44th Ave # 3A Wheat Ridge CO 80033 Office: EG&G Rocky Flats MS T690A PO Box 464 Golden CO 80402-0464

PATEL, MARILYN HALL, federal judge; b. Amsterdam, N.Y., Sept. 2, 1938; d. Lloyd Manning and Nina J. (Thorpe) Hall; m. Magan C. Patel, Sept. 2, 1966; children: Brian, Gian. B.A., Wheaton Coll., 1959; J.D., Fordham U., 1963. Mng. atty. Benson & Morris, N.Y.C., 1963-65; sole practice N.Y.C., 1965-67, San Francisco, 1971-76; atty. Dept. Justice, San Francisco, 1967-71; judge Alameda County Mcpl. Ct., Oakland, Calif., 1976-80, U.S. Dist. Ct. (no. dist.) Calif., San Francisco, 1980—; adj. prof. law Hastings Coll. of Law, San Francisco, 1974-76. Author: Immigration and Nationality Law, 1974; also numerous articles. Mem. bd. of visitors Fordham U. Sch. of Law. Mem. ABA (litigation sect., jud. adminstrn. sect.), ACLU (former bd. dirs.), NOW (former bd. dirs.), Am. Law Inst., Am. Judicature Soc. (bd. dirs.), Calif. Conf. Judges, Nat. Assn. Women Judges (founding mem.), Internat. Inst. (bd. dirs.), Advs. for Women (co-founder). Democrat. Office: US Dist Ct PO Box 36060 450 Golden Gate Ave San Francisco CA 94102

PATEL, NARESH MAGANLAL, computer engineer, writer; b. Manchester, Eng., Feb. 24, 1965; s. Maganlal R. and Kusumben M. Patel; m. Hina Nanu, Sept. 14, 1986. Assoc. City and Guilds Inst., U. London, Eng., 1986; BS in Engring., U. London, 1986, Diploma Imperial Coll., 1989, PhD, 1989. Programmer UNISYS, London, 1985; rsch. assoc. U. London, 1986-90; performance engr. Tandem Computers Inc., Cupertino, Calif., 1990—. Author: Performance Modelling of Communication Networks and Computer Architectures, 1992; contbr. articles to profl. jours. Mem. Assn. Computer Machinery. Office: Tandem Computers Inc 19333 Valloo Pky Loc 3-22 Cupertino CA 95014-2599

PATEL, NAVIN J., electronics engineer, consultant; b. Chitravad, Gujarat, India, Sept. 4, 1949; came to U.S., 1970; s. Jamnadas R. and Diwali (Ghetiya) P.; m. Lalita Dadhania, Nov. 13, 1980; children: Nimish, Mitul. BSc in Physics, Math., Gujarat (India) U., 1969; BSEE, Pacific States U., L.A., 1973. Engr. Data Products Corp., Woodland Hills, Calif., 1973-81; cons. Internat. Svcs., Newburry Park, Calif., 1981-84; sr. engr. Librascope Corp., Glendale, Calif., 1984—; Cons. engr. Amtech Internat., Agoura Hills, Calif., 1987—. Democrat. Hindu. Home: 21333 Lassen St Chatsworth CA 91311-4203 Office: Librascope Corp 833 Sonora Ave Glendale CA 91201-2433

PATHAK, VIBHAV GAUTAM, electrical engineer; b. Bhavnagar, India, July 7, 1964; s. Gautam Yeshwantrai and Jyoti (Gautam) P. BSEE, Calif. State U., Long Beach, 1985, MSEE, 1987. Registered profl. engr., Calif. Mem. tech. staff Logicon, Inc., San Pedro, Calif., 1987-89; elec. systems engr. Rockwell Internat. Corp., Canoga Park, Calif., 1990—; founder Softouch, Inc., Norwalk, Calif., 1988—. Calif. State U. scholar, 1983. Mem. Cerrito's Music Circle (co-bd. dirs. 1989—), Workstation Users Group, Toastmasters Internat., Eta Kappa Nu.

PATINO, ISIDRO FRANK, law enforcement educator; b. San Antonio, Mar. 10, 1943; s. Isidro F. and Maria (Narro) P.; children: Michael, Rebecca, Karleen; m. Carol Macotte, 1989. BS, Calif. State U., L.A., 1973. Records comdr. Placentia (Calif.) Police Dept., 1980-85; asst. dean Criminal Justice Tng. Ctr. Golden West Coll., Huntington Beach, Calif., 1986-89, assoc. dean instrn., 1989-90; divsn. dean dept. pub. svc. Rio Hondo Coll., Whittier, Calif., 1990—; pres., mem. State Chancellors Adv. Com. Pub. Safety Edn., 1991—. Mem. Calif. Law Enforcement Assn. of Records Suprs. (pres. so. chpt. 1985-87, state pres. 1986-87), Calif. Acad. Dirs. Assn. (vice-chmn. 1987-88, chmn. 1988-89), Acad. Criminal Justice Scis., Western and Pacific Assn. Criminal Justice Educators, Calif. Assn. Adminstrn. of Justice Educators, Calif. Peace Officers Standards and Tng. Basic Course Consortium (chmn. instrn. com. 1987-88), World Future Soc., Nat. Assn. Field Tng. Officers (nat. pres. 1992-93). Roman Catholic.

PATINO, MANUEL LUIS, utility company executive; b. Havana, Cuba, Jan. 19, 1933; came to U.S., 1962, naturalized, 1967; s. José and María (Mosquera) P.; m. Aurora Amparo Feliu, Oct. 21, 1961; children: Manuel Antonio, Juan Carlos, Susan Marie. E.E., U. Havana, Cuba, 1959; postgrad. in applied math., U. Colo., 1963-68, M.B.A., 1972. Engr.-in-tng. Pub. Service Co. of Colo., Denver, 1962-63, planning engr., 1963-68, sr. planning engr., 1968-72, supr. system planning, 1972-74, budget coordinator, 1974-76, planning coordinator, 1976-80, econs. and forecasting coordinator, 1980-83, strategic planning dir., 1983-85, staff asst., fin. and corp. devel., 1985-86, project mgr. bus. devel., 1986-88, bus. devel. dir., 1988—; mem. Gov.'s Revenue Estimating Adv. Com., 1980-86; mem. econs. com. Edison Elec. Inst., Washington, 1982-86; econ. rev. advisor Denver Regional Coun. Govts., 1982-86; advisor energy analysis and environ. divisional com. Electric Power Rsch. Inst., Palo Alto, Calif., 1980-86; assoc. exec. dir. Boulder (Colo.) Tech. Incubator, 1991—. Mem. Denver Dem. Cen. Com., 1982-88; adv. bd. Machebeuf Cath. High Sch., 1990-92, small bus. coun. Colo. Assn. Commerce and Industry, 1991—, Denver adv. coun. Small Bus. Adminstrn., 1992-94; summer fellowship mentor Colo. Alliance for Sci., 1991—. Mem. Nat. Assn. Bus. Economists, IEEE, Lions, Denver Club (dir. 1992-94). Roman Catholic. Home: 1268 Locust St Denver CO 80220-2829 Office: Pub Service Co of Colo PO Box 840 1225 17th St Denver CO 80202

PATMORE, GERALDINE MARY (BOBBE PATMORE), real estate developer; b. Vancouver, B.C., Can.; came to U.S., 1968; d. Oscar Andrew and Geraldine Mary (Whalen) Jorgenson; m. Alan Max Patmore; children: Alan Barry, Paul Richard (dec.), Rosemary Anne Marta. Student, U B.C., Vancouver, Marylhurst Coll. Realtor George Beebe Co., Palm Springs, Calif., 1971-75; v.p. realtor Frank Bogert Co., Palm Springs, Calif., 1975-77; realtor West World Properties, Palm Springs, Calif., 1978-87; dir. sales Golden Mile Investment Co., Palm Springs, Calif., 1987—; pres. Patmore Assocs. Real Estate Investments, Palm Springs, 1989—. Charter mem. Child Help-USA (bd. dirs., desert chpt. 1976-80), Palm Springs; v.p. Humane Soc. Desert, Palm Springs, 1984-86; bd. dirs. SPCA-Animal Samaritans, Palm Springs, 1986—. Named Liaison Officer for work on sister city program between U.S. and Can. City of Palm Springs, 1973—. Mem. Palm Springs C. of C. (charter mem. sister city program 1972—), Nat. Bd. of Realtors (mem. Palm Springs Bd. Realtors 1972—), Internat. Council Shopping Ctrs. Roman Catholic. Clubs: Racquet (Palm Springs,Calif.), Vancouver Lawn Tennis and Badminton (B.C.). Home: 1466 Plato Cir Palm Springs CA 92264-9225 Office: Golden Mile Investment Co 559 S Canyon Dr Palm Springs CA 92264-9504

PATNER, RICHARD, translator; b. Chgo., Nov. 7, 1946; s. Alfred Harold and Evelyn (Goldstein) P.; m. Toshiko Tsunekuni, Feb. 28, 1972; children: Naomi, Ken. BS, U. Wis., 1969, MA, 1978. Translator Madison, Wis., 1974-84, Edmonds, Wash., 1984—. Mem. Am. Translators Assn. Home and Office: 14613 60th Pl W Edmonds WA 98026-3612

PATRICK, LESLIE DAYLE, hydrologist; b. Grand Island, Nebr., Nov. 20, 1951; d. Robert Norman and Charlotte Ruth (Thomas) Mayfield; m. Jeffrey Rogan Patrick, July 1, 1972. BA in Geology, U. Alaska, Anchorage, 1975, MS in Mgmt., 1991. Data base mgr. U.S. Geol. Survey, Anchorage, 1975-78, with digital modeling, 1980-85, with water use studies, 1978-91, chief computer sect., systems analyst, 1985-91, asst. dist. chief mgmt. ops., 1991—. Mem. Alaska Groundwater Assn. (sec./treas. 1980). Office: US Geol Survey Water Resources Div 4230 University Dr Ste 201 Anchorage AK 99508-4664

PATRICK, LYNDA LEE, financial executive; b. Hollywood, Calif., Mar. 6, 1938; d. Leland Walton and Ruth Katherine (Pooree) Davis; children: Leslie Escalera, Leisa Young, Theresa Gomez, Frederick Escalera. Grad. mgmt. effectiveness program, U. So. Calif., 1988-89. Bus driver Garden Grove (Calif.) Unified Sch. Dist., 1969-73, Orange County Transit Dist., Garden Grove, 1973-77; sch. bus. instr. Modoc Unified Sch. Dist., Alturas, Calif., 1977-81; transit mgr. Daves Sys., Santa Ana, Calif., 1981-83; instr./charger mgr. ATE/Ryder, Long Beach, Calif., 1983-89; fin. exec. v.p. Tuit Internat., Inc., Paso Robles, Calif., 1989—; owner, v.p. Tite-Line Valve Products Inc., 1992—; cons. ATE/RYDER, Cin., 1989—. Mem. U. So. Calif. Alumni Assn. Office: Tuit Internat Inc PO Box 1823 Paso Robles CA 93447-1823

PATRIE, PETER HUGO, banker; b. Dayton, Ohio, Dec. 19, 1946; s. C. Hugo and Margaret (Penny) P.; m. Janis Lee Yates, Feb. 5, 1968; children: Peter Todd, Brent, Ryan. BSBA, Miami U., Oxford, Ohio, 1968; postgrad., U. Fla., 1968-69. Mgr. credit dept. Atlantic Nat. Bank, Jacksonville, Fla., 1970-72; regional credit mgr. Kaiser Cement & Gypsum, Long Beach, Calif., 1972-73; dist. mgr. ITT Consumer Fin., Denver, 1973-80; sr. v.p. Nev. First Bank, Reno, 1981-89, Bank of Am. Nev., Reno, 1989-90; gen. mgr. Silver State Thrift & Loan, Reno, 1990—; grad. asst. U. Fla. Grad. Sch., Gainesville, 1968; prof. Reno Bus. Coll., 1991. Mem. Western Indsl. Nev., Reno, 1989-91; tchr. Jr. Achievement-Bus. Alliance, Reno, 1990. Recipient Grad. Fellowship U. Fla. Grad. Sch., Gainesville, 1969. Mem. Sparks C. of C., Greenbrae Lions. Republican. Office: 545 Nichols Blvd Sparks NV 89431

PATRIQUIN, EDWARD LEROY, JR., software developer, computer architect; b. Upland, Calif., Sept. 30, 1958; s. Edward Leroy Sr. and Margaret Winifred (Robertson) P.; m. Linda Susan King, Mar. 30, 1985; 1 child, Thomas Edward. Grad. high sch., Bishop, Calif. Computer operator U. So. Calif., L.A., 1978-79; software engr. Moss Motors, Santa Barbara, Calif., 1979-80, RKA, Sacramento, 1980; pvt. practice cons. Sacramento, 1980-82; sr. engr. Convergent Techs., San Jose, Calif., 1982-85; mgr. operating systems Valid Logic, San Jose, 1985-86; prin. engr. Cydrome, Milpitas, Calif., 1986-88; mgr. sofware devel. Plus Devel., Milpitas, 1988-91; mgr. software devel. Quantum Comml. Products, Milpitas, 1990-92, mgr. devel. engring., 1992—. With USN, 1976-78. Republican. Home: 1492 Kiner Ave San Jose CA 95125-4844 Office: Quantum Comml Products 500 Mccarthy Blvd Milpitas CA 95035-7908

PATSAKOS, GEORGE, physicist; b. N.Y.C., Mar. 24, 1942; s. James and Stella (Krias) P. AB in Physics summa cum laude, Columbia Coll., 1962; PHD in Physics, Stanford U., 1969. Teaching asst. Stanford U., 1962-68; rsch. asst. Los Alamos (N.Mex.) Sci. Lab., 1963; rsch. assoc. Ind. U., Bloomington, 1968-70; asst. prof. physics U. Idaho, Moscow, 1970-76; vis. faculty New Sch. Social Rsch., N.Y.C., 1979-80; assoc. prof. astronomy Wash. State U., Pullman, 1981; staff engr. Hughes Aircraft Co., El Segundo, Calif., 1985-86; assoc. prof. physics U. Idaho, Moscow, 1976—; cons. local attys. Contbr. articles to profl. jours. Bd. dirs. Moscow Recycling Ctr., 1975-76, Friends Mus. of Art, Wash. State U., Pullman, 1986-89; wilderness vol. U.S. Forest Svc., Enterprise, Oreg., 1979, wilderness guard, 1981. NSF predoctoral fellow, 1962-67, Am. Soc. Engring. Edn. summer faculty fellow, 1984-85. Mem. AAAS, Am. Assn. Physics Tchrs., Am. Phys. Soc., Astronomical Soc. Pacific, N.Y. Acad. Scis., Sigma Xi, Phi Beta Kappa. Office: Dept Physics U Idaho Renfrew Hall Rm 2 Moscow ID 83843

PATTEN, BEBE HARRISON, minister; b. Waverly, Tenn., Sept. 3, 1913; d. Newton Felix and Mattie Priscilla (Whitson) Harrison; m. Carl Thomas Patten, Oct. 23, 1935; children: Priscilla Carla and Bebe Rebecca (twins), Carl Thomas. D.D., McKinley-Roosevelt Coll., 1941; D.Litt., Temple Hall Coll. and Sem., 1943. Ordained to ministry Ministerial Assn. of Evangelism, 1935; evangelist in various cities of U.S., 1933-50; founder, pres. Christian Evang. Chs. Am., Inc., Oakland, Calif., 1944—, Patten Acad. Christian Edn., Oakland, 1944—, Patten Bible Coll., Oakland, 1944-83; chancellor Patten Coll., Oakland, 1983—; founder, pastor Christian Cathedral of Oakland, 1950—; held pvt. interviews with David Ben-Gurion, 1972, Menachim Begin, 1977, Yitzhak Shamir, 1991; condr. Sta. KUSW world-wide radio ministry, 70 countries around the world, 1989-90, Stas. WHRI and WWCR world coverage short wave, 1990—. Founder, condr.: radio program The Shepherd Hour, 1934—; daily TV, 1976—, nationwide telecast, 1979—; Author: Give Me Back My Soul, 1973; Editor: Trumpet Call, 1953—; composer 20 gospel and religious songs, 1945—. Mem. exec. bd. Bar-Ilan U. Assn., Israel, 1983; mem. global bd. trustees Bar-Ilan U., 1991. Recipient numerous awards including medallion Ministry of Religious Affairs, Israel, 1969; medal Govt. Press Office, Jerusalem, 1971; Christian honoree of yr. Jewish Nat. Fund of No. Calif., 1975; Hidden Heroine award San Francisco Bay council Girl Scouts U.S.A., 1976, Golden State award Who's Who Hist. Soc., 1988; Ben-Gurion medallion Ben-Gurion Research Inst., 1977; Resolution of Commendation, Calif. Senate Rules Com., 1978; hon. fellow Bar-Ilan U., Israel, 1981; Dr. Bebe Patten Social Action chair established Bar-Ilan U., 1982. Mem. Am. Assn. for Higher Edn., Religious Edn. Assn., Am. Acad. Religion and Soc. Bibl. Lit., Zionist Orgn. Am., Am. Assn. Pres. of Ind. Colls. and Univs., Am. Jewish Hist. Soc., Am.-Isreal Pub. Affairs Com. Address: 2433 Coolidge Ave Oakland CA 94601

PATTEN, BEBE REBECCA, college dean, clergywoman; b. Berkeley, Calif., Jan. 30, 1950; d. Carl Thomas and Bebe (Harrison) P. BS in Bible, Patten Coll., 1969; BA in Philosophy, Holy Names Coll., 1970; MA in Bibl. Studies New Testament, Wheaton Coll., 1972; PhD in Bibl. Studies New Testament, Drew U., 1976; MA in Philosophy, Dominican Sch. Philosophy & Theology, 1990. Ordained to ministry Christian Evang. Ch., 1963. Co-pastor Christian Cathedral, Christian Evang. Chs. Am., Inc., 1964—; assoc. prof. Patten Coll., Oakland, Calif., 1975-82, dean, 1977—, prof. N.T., 1982—; presenter in field. Author: Before the Times, 1980, The World of the Early Church, 1990; contbg. author: Internat. Standard Bibl. Ency., rev. edit., 1983. Active Wheaton Coll. Symphony, 1971-72, Drew U. Ensemble, 1971-75, Young Artists Symphony, N.J., 1972-75, Somerset Hill Symphony, N.J., 1973-74, Peninsula Symphony, 1977, 80-81, Madison Chamber Trio, N.J., 1973-75. Named one of Outstanding Young Women of Am., 1976, 77, 80-81, 82; St. Olaf's Coll. fellow, 1990. Mem. AAUP, Am. Acad. Religion, Soc. Bibl. Lit., Internat. Biographical Assn., Christian Evang. Chs. of Am., Inc. (co-pastor Christian Cathedral, bd. dirs. 1964—), Christian Assn. for Student Affairs, Assn. for Christians in Student Devel., Inst. for Bibl. Rsch., Phi Delta Kappa.

PATTEN, RICHARD E., personnel recruiting company executive; b. Seattle, May 17, 1953; s. Donald Wesley and Lorraine Louise (Kienholz) P.; m. Monica Rose Bourg, Mar. 20, 1976; children: Richard Douglas, Wesley Bourg, Melinda Rose. BA, U. Wash., 1976. Exec. v.p. Microfilm Svc. Co., Seattle, 1976-84, gen. mgr., 1985-87, chmn. bd., 1988-90; pres. Express Svcs. Temporary and Permanent Pers., Seattle, 1990—. Candidate for U.S. Ho. of Reps., 1982; deacon Bethany Bapt. Ch., Seattle, 1983-86; co-chmn. fin. com. Wash. State Billy Graham Crusade, 1990-91. Mem. Nat. Micrographics Assn. (pres. N.W. chpt. 1979-80, bd. dirs. 1978-79), Assn. Image and Info. Mgmt. (chmn. svc. co. 1987), Assn. Records Mgrs. and Adminstrs., Wash. Athletic Club, Rotary. Republican. Baptist. Home: 7012 NE 161st St Bothell WA 98011-4265 Office: Express Svcs Co Westlake Ctr Ste 715 1201 4th Ave S Ste 101 Seattle WA 98134

PATTERSON, DANIEL WILLIAM, dentist; b. Minot, N.D., Aug. 12, 1948; s. Girdell William and Fern Lemay (Sullivan) P. DDS, Northwestern U., 1972; Alumnus degree (hon.), U. Colo., 1977; BS in Biology, U.N.Y., 1993; postgrad, U. Denver, 1993. Cert. health industry orgn., ops. U. Denver, 1993. Dentist Dan L. Hansen, DDS, P.C., Lakewood, Colo., 1974-75; pvt. practice dentistry Littleton, Colo., 1975-88; clin. instr. dept. applied dentistry U. Colo., Denver, 1981-86, lectr., 1983, clin. asst. prof. depts. restorative and applied dentistry, 1989-91, dir. advanced dentistry program, 1989-90, asst. prof. clin. track dept. restorative dentistry, 1991—. Mem. editorial adv. panel Dental Econs. Jour., 1981; also articles. Active Chatfield Jaycees, Littleton, 1976-81; vocal soloist, mem. Denver Concert Chorale, 1978-82. Lt. USN, 1968-74. Fellow Acad. Gen. Dentistry (bd. eligible certifying bd. gen. dentistry); mem. ADA, Met. Denver Dental Soc., Colo. Dental Assn. (Pres.'s Honor Roll 1982-84), Mensa, Sedalia Wild Game Club. Lutheran. Home: 6984 N Fargo Trl Littleton CO 80125-9270 Office: U Colo Health Scis Ctr Sch Dentistry 4200 E 9th Ave Denver CO 80262-0001

PATTERSON, DAVID, geneticist, biologist, educator; b. Medford, Mass., Aug. 24, 1944; s. David and Mildred (Hughes) P.; m. Norma Jean Riggs, June 3, 1967; children: Matthew, Jennifer. B.S., MIT, 1966; Ph.D., Brandeis U., 1971. Assoc. dir. Eleanor Roosevelt Inst. Cancer Rsch., Denver, 1978—, v.p. sci. affairs, 1980-84, pres., 1984—; prof. dept. biochemistry U. Colo. Health Scis. Ctr., Denver, 1983—, prof. dept. medicine, 1984—; mem. adv. com. M.D. Anderson Hosp., Houston ; mem. editorial Somatic Cell and Molecular Genetics, 1983—; contbr. numerous articles and abstracts to profl. jours. Bd. dirs. Community Outreach Therapeutic Day Care, Denver, 1981-83; mem. biotech. subcom. Colo. Commn. Higher Edn., Denver, 1982. Grantee study chromosome 21, NIH, 1979-93, aging process NIH, 1981-93, cell biology NIH, 1983-88; Damon Runyon-Walter Winchell fellow, 1971-74; recipient Theodore T. Jossem Rsch. award Nat. Down Syndrome Congress, 1989, Sci. award for sci. Bonfils-Stanton Found., 1992. Mem. Am. Soc. Cell Biology, Am. Soc. Human Genetics, AAAS, Gerontol. Soc., Nat. Down Syndrome Soc. (scientific adv. bd.), Sigma Xi. Office: E Roosevelt Inst for Cancer Rsch 1899 Gaylord St Denver CO 80206-1299

PATTERSON, DAVID ANDREW, computer scientist, educator, consultant; b. Evergreen Park, Ill., Nov. 16, 1947; s. David Dwight and Lucie Jeanette (Ekstrom) P.; m. Linda Ann Crandall, Sept. 4, 1967; children: David Adam, Michael Andrew. BS in Math., UCLA, 1969, MS in Computer Sci., 1970, PhD, 1976. Mem. tech. staff Hughes Aircraft Co., L.A., 1972-76, Thinking Machines Corp., Cambridge, Mass., 1979; prof. computer sci. div. U. Calif., Berkeley, 1977—, chmn., 1990-93, Pardee chair, 1992—; cons. Sun Microsystems Inc., Mountain View, Calif., 1984—, Thinking Machines Corp., Cambridge, 1988—; mem. sci. adv. bd. Data Gen. Corp., Westborough, 1984—; com. to study scope and role of computer sci. NAS, Washington, 1990-92; chmn. program com. 4th Symposium on Archtl. Support for Oper. Systems and Computer Architecture, Santa Clara, Calif., 1991; mem. Mgmt. Ops. Working Group NASA, 1992—; co-chair program com. Hot Chips Symposium IV, Stanford, Calif., 1992. Author: A Taste of Smalltalk, 1986, Computing Unbound, 1989, Computer Architecture: A Quantative Approach, 1990, Computer Organization & Design: The Hardware/Software Interface, 1993. Recipient Disting. Teaching award U. Calif., Berkeley, 1982, corp. fellow Thinking Machines Corp., Cambridge, 1989, ACM Karl V. Karlstrom Outstanding Educator award, 1991. Fellow IEEE; mem. NAE, Computing Rsch. Assn. (bd. dirs. Washington 1991—), Spl. Interest Group on Computer Architecture of Assn. Computing Machinery (bd. dirs. 1987-90). Office: U Calif Computer Sci Div 571 Evans Hall Berkeley CA 94720

PATTERSON, DAWN MARIE, dean, consultant, writer; b. Gloversville, N.Y., July 30; d. Robert Morris and Dora Margaret (Perham) P.; m. Robert Henry Hollenbeck, Aug. 3, 1958 (div. 1976); children: Adrienne Lyn, Nathaniel Conrad. BS in Edn., SUNY, Geneseo, 1962; MA, Mich. State U., 1973, PhD, 1977; postgrad., U. So. Calif. and Inst. Ednl. Leadership. Librarian Brighton (N.Y.) Cen. Schs., 1962-67; asst. to regional dir. Mich. State U. Ctr., Bloomfield Hills, 1973-74; grad. asst. Mich. State U., East Lansing, 1975-77; cons. Mich. Efficiency Task Force, 1977; asst. dean Coll. Continuing Edn., U. So. Calif., Los Angeles, 1978-84; dean, assoc. prof. continuing edn. Calif. State U., Los Angeles, 1985—; pres. Co-Pro Assocs. Mem. Air Univ. Bd. Visitors, 1986-90, Commn. on Extended Edn. Calif. State U. Calif., 1988-91; Hist. Soc., Los Angeles Town Hall, Los Angeles World Affairs Council. Dora Louden scholar, 1958-61; Langworthy fellow, 1961-62; Edn. Professions Devel. fellow, 1974-75; Ednl. Leadership Policy fellow, 1982-83; Leadership Calif., 1992-93. Mem. AAUW (pres. Pasadena br. 1985-86), Am. Assn. Adult and Continuing Edn. (charter), Nat. Univ. Continuing Edn. Assn., Internat. Assn. Continuing Edn. and Tng. (bd. dirs. 1990—), Calif. Coll. and Mil. Educators Assn. (pres.), Los Angeles Airport

Area Edn. Industry Assn. (pres. 1984), Rotary Club of Alhambra (bd. dirs.), Fine Arts (Pasadena), Zonta (v.p. 1992—), Kappa Delta Pi, Phi Delta Kappa, Phi Beta Delta, Phi Kappa Phi. Republican. Unitarian. Office: 5151 State University Dr Los Angeles CA 90032-4221

PATTERSON, DENNIS GLEN, Canadian government official, lawyer; b. Vancouver, B.C., Can., Dec. 30, 1948; common law wife: Marie Uviluq; children: Bruce, George, Jessica, Alexander. BA with distinction, U. Alta., Edmonton, 1969; LLB, Dalhousie U., Halifax, N.S., 1972. Bar: N.S., 1972, B.C., 1974. Exec. dir. Maliiganik Tukisinniavik, Iqaluit, N.W.T., Can., 1975-81; mem. legis. assembly, Iqaluit Govt. of N.W.T., Yellowknife, 1979-93, minister edn., 1981-88, minister aboriginal rights and constl. devel., 1981-87, minister responsible for women, 1985; govt. leader, 1987-91, mem. cabinet, 1991-92, now mem. legis. assembly. Office: Legis Assembly of NWT, PO Box 1320, Yellowknife, NT Canada X1A 2L9

PATTERSON, DENNIS JOSEPH, management consultant; b. Honolulu, Apr. 13, 1948; s. Joseph John and Dorothy Elizabeth (Snajkowski) P.; m. Susan Tyra Pedlow, Dec. 31, 1981; children: Valerie Jean, Christina Elizabeth. BA, Elmhurst (Ill.) Coll., 1970; MA, George Washington U., 1973. Asst. dir. Vancouver (B.C.) Gen. Hosp., 1973-76, dir., 1975-76; v.p. Shaugnessy Hosp., Vancouver, 1976-79; pres. Westcare, Vancouver, 1979-84; mgr. Ernst & Whinney, Chgo., 1984-86, sr. mgr., 1986-88, ptnr., 1988-93; pres. FHP Internat. Consulting, Fountain Valley, Calif., 1993—. Contbr. articles to profl. jours. fin. mgr. Electoral Action Movement, Vancouver, 1978; trustee George Washington U., Calif. Sch. Profl. Psychology. Fellow Am. Coll. Healthcare Execs.; mem. Am. Assn. Healthcare Cons., Phi Gamma Mu. Republican. Anglican. Clubs: Royal Vancouver Yacht, Va. Country. Office: FHP Internat Consulting 9900 Talbert Ave Fountain Valley CA 92708

PATTERSON, FRANCINE G. P., foundation administrator; b. Chgo., Feb. 13, 1947; d. Cecil H. and Frances L. (Spano) P. AB in Psychology, U. Ill., 1970; PhD in Devel. Psychology, Stanford U., 1979. Rsch. asst. U. Ill. Children's Rsch. Ctr., Urbana, 1969-70; pres., rsch. dir. The Gorilla Found., Woodside, Calif., 1976—; adj. rsch. assoc. dept. anthropology and ctr. anthrop. rsch. San Jose (Calif.) State U., 1982—; adj. assoc. prof. dept. psychology U. Santa Clara (Calif.), 1984—; bd. consultants Ctr. for Cross-Cultural Communications, Washington. Author: Koko's Kitten, 1985 (Tex. Bluebonnet award 1987), Koko's Story, 1987 (N.J. Libr. Assn. award 1990); co-author: The Education of Koko, 1981. Grantee for gorilla lang. rsch. Nat. Geog. Soc., 1976-83, 85; recipient Rolex award for enterprise Rolex, Geneva, 1978, Award for Outstanding Profl. Svc., Preservation of the Animal World Soc., 1986. Mem. Am. Soc. Primatologists, Am. Ednl. Rsch. Assn. Am. Assn. Zool. Parks and Aquariums, Am. Assn. Zookeepers, Animal Behavior Soc., Phi Beta Kappa. Office: The Gorilla Found PO Box 620530 Redwood City CA 94062-0530

PATTERSON, JOHN REUBEN, journey man; b. Glendale, Calif., Apr. 20, 1928; s. John Wilson and Margeret Francis (McCall) P.; m. Colleen E. Mohr, Aug. 25, 1956; children: John M., Robin Lynn, Patrick Jay, Molley Ann. Student, L.A. City Coll., 1947-50, L.A. State Coll., 1953-54. Foreman Oreg. State Forestry, Tillamook, 1954-55; line man Pacific Power and Light, various locations, Oreg., 1956-69; foreman Pacific Power and Light, Cottage Grove, Oreg., 1969-90. Elected Cottage Grove City Councilor, 1985—; leader Boy Scouts Am., Oreg., 1957—; mem. Cottage Grove Planning Com., 1973-81. With USN, 1946-53. Mem. Order of Arrow (sect. advisor 1985), Jaycees, Kiwanis, Moose, Masons. Republican.

PATTERSON, MARK JEROME, computer systems designer; b. Inglewood, Calif., July 23, 1960; s. Jerry Lee Patterson and Robin Helen McCracken Steely. Programmer Green & Assocs., L.A., 1985-87; systems analyst The Software Works, Glendale, Calif., 1987-90; programmer Snow Software, Clearwater, Fla., 1990; systems designer Pelican Corp., Altadena, Calif., 1990—; design cons. Prestige Station, Inc., 1990-92, Petro-Can., Inc., Calgary, Alta., 1988-90. Author computer programs: Set of Dataflex Macros, 1990, Ultimate File Viewer, 1992. Libertarian. Scientologist. Home: 3278 Tonia Ave Altadena CA 91001-4435

PATTON, AUDLEY EVERETT, retired business executive; b. Eve, Mo., Nov. 9, 1898; s. Charles Audley and Letitia Virginia (Earhart) P.; BS in Indsl. Adminstrn., U. Ill., 1921, MS in Bus. Orgn. and Operation, 1922, PhD in Econs., 1924; m. Mabel Dickie Gunnison, Aug. 5, 1930 (dec. Feb. 1976); 1 child, Julie Ann Patton Watson; m. Mary Ritchie Key, June 24, 1977. Auditor, Mfg. Dealers Corp., Cambridge, Mass., 1921; instr. econs. public utilities U. Ill., Champaign-Urbana, 1924-25, asst. prof. econs. Coll. Commerce and Bus. Adminstrn., 1925-26; asst. to pres. Chgo. Rapid Transit Co., Chgo. South Shore & South Bend R.R. Co., Chgo. North Shore & Milw. R.R. Co., Chgo. Aurora & Elgin R.R. Co., 1926; asst. to pres. Public Service Co. No. Ill., Chgo., 1926-43, sec., 1928-52, asst. treas., 1928-44, v.p., 1943-53; v.p., dir. No. Ill. Gas Co., Aurora, 1953-54; v.p. Commonwealth Edison Co., Chgo., 1952-63, ret., 1963; asst. to pres. Presbyn-St. Luke's Hosp., Chgo., 1963-65; former v.p., dir. Big Muddy Coal Co.; past dir. Gt. Lakes Broadcasting Co., Chgo., Chgo. & Ill. Midland Ry. Co., Allied Mills, Inc., Chgo., Am. Gage & Machine Co., Elgin, Ill., HMW Industries, Inc., Stamford, Conn. Treas., Katherine Kreigh Budd Meml. Home for Children, Libertyville, Ill., 1929-36; mem. adv. com. on pub. utilities U. Ill., 1937-40, mem. gen. adv. com., 1943-46. Bd. dirs. Am. Cancer Soc. Ill. div., 1948-76, pres., 1957-59, chmn. bd., 1959-62, mem. fin. com., 1970-76; bd. dirs. Civic Fedn. Chgo., 1945-63, v.p., 1954-63; bd. dirs. South Side Planning Bd. Chgo., 1950-58; bd. dirs., mem. exec. com. Ill. C. of C., 1957-61; trustee Kemper Hall Sch. for Girls, Kenosha, Wis., 1929-37, Highland Park (Ill.) Hosp., 1946-51, Christine and Alfred Sonntag Found. for Cancer Research, 1965-81. Recipient Am. Cancer Soc. medal, 1951. Mem. U. Ill. Found., U.S. Men's (dir. 1958-62, v.p. 1960-65), Midwest (dir. 1956-60) curling assns., OX5 Aviation Pioneers (life mem.), Beta Gamma Sigma, Phi Eta, Delta Sigma Pi, Phi Kappa Phi, Delta Chi. Episcopalian. Clubs: Univ. Chgo. (bd. dirs. 1944-46, treas. 1945-46); Chgo. Curling (pres. 1956-57) (Northbrook, Ill.). Contbr. articles to profl. jours. Home and Office: 14782 Canterbury Ave Tustin CA 92680-6753

PATTON, CARL E., physics educator; b. San Antonio, Sept. 14, 1941; s. Carl Elliott and Geraldine Barnett (Perry) P. BS, MIT, 1963; MS, Calif. Inst. Tech., 1964, PhD, 1967. Sr. scientist Raytheon Co., Waltham, Mass., 1967-71; assoc. prof. physics Colo. State U., Ft. Collins, 1971-75, prof., 1975—; IEEE Magnetics Soc. Disting. lectr., 1993. editor-in-chief IEEE Transactions on Magnetics, 1987-91. Fellow IEEE (Magnetics Soc. Disting. lectr. 1993), Am. Phys. Soc. Office: Colo State Univ Dept Physics Fort Collins CO 80523

PATTON, KENNETH WARD, college dean; b. L.A., Aug. 12, 1946; s. William Edward and Mildred Evelyn (Peterson) P.; m. Barbara Patton, June 10, 1969 (div. 1980); 1 child, Nicole Ann; m. Shirley Ellen, June 17, 1982. BA, Fresno State U., 1969; MS, Calif. Poly. San Luis Obispo, 1971. Tchr. Santa Ana (Calif.) Unified Sch. Dist., 1969-71; asst. prof. Calif. State U., Northridge, 1970-71; dir. vocat. instrn. and econ. devel. L.A. Community Coll., 1976-90; dean career edn., econ. devel. Glendale (Calif.) Community Coll., 1990—; contract edn. com. Ed/NET, Sacramento, 1986-92; mem. Calif. Sch. Leadership Coun., Sacramento, 1992. Mem. Verdugo Pvt. Industry Coun., Glendale, 1990-92; chair careers in trnasition com. C. of C., Glendale, 1990-92, mem. bus. edn. com., 1990-92. Office: Glendale Community Coll 1500 N Verdugo Rd Glendale CA 91208

PATTON, STUART, biochemist, educator; b. Ebenezer, N.Y., Nov. 2, 1920; s. George and Ina (Neher) P.; m. Colleen Cecelia Lavelle, May 17, 1945; children—John, Richard, Gail, Thomas, Mary Catherine, Patricia, Joseph. B.S., Pa. State U., 1943; M.S., Ohio State U., 1947, Ph.D., 1948. Chemist Borden Co., 1943-44; research fellow Ohio State U., Columbus, 1946-48; mem. faculty Pa. State U., University Park, 1949-80, prof., 1959-80; Evan Pugh rsch. prof. agr. Pa. State U., 1966-80; adj. prof. neurosci. Sch. Medicine U. Calif., San Diego, 1981—; vis. scientist Scripps Instn. Oceanography; cons. in field, 1950—. Author: (with Robert Jenness) Principles of Dairy Chemistry, 1959, (with Robert G. Jensen) Biomedical Aspects of Lactation, 1975. Served to lt. (j.g.) USNR, 1944-46. Recipient Borden award chemistry milk Am. Chem. Soc., 1957, Agrl. and Food Chemistry award, 1975; Alexander von Humboldt sr. scientist award, 1981. Mem. Am. Chem. Soc., Am. Dairy Sci. Assn. (bd. dirs. 1963-66), Am. Oil Chemists Assn., Am. Soc. Biochemistry and Molecular Biology, Am. Soc. Cell Biology. Home: 6208 Avenida Cresta La Jolla CA 92037-6510 Office: U Calif San Diego Ctr Molecular Genetics 0634-J La Jolla CA 92093

PATTON, WILLIAM WALLACE, JR., research geologist; b. Vancouver, B.C., Can., May 25, 1923; came to U.S. 1924; s. William Wallace Sr. and Mary Lombard (Magoun) P.; m. Margaret Ellen Braidwood, Jan. 13, 1951; children: James K., Amelia Patton Haworth, Elizabeth Reid. BA, Cornell U., 1945, MS, 1948; PhD, Stanford (Calif.) U., 1959. Geologist U.S. Geol. Survey, Washington, 1948-51; geologist U.S. Geol. Survey, Menlo Park, Calif., 1951-90, asst. chief Alaska br., 1990-91, scientist emeritus, 1992—. Contbr. numerous articles to profl. jours. With USMC, 1943-45. Fellow AAAS, Geol. Soc. of Am.; mem. Am. Assn. Petroleum Geologists, Am. Geophys. Union. Office: US Geol Survey MS/904 345 Middlefield Rd Menlo Park CA 94025-3591

PATZER, ERIC JOHN, biological chemist; b. N.Y.C., Apr. 12, 1949; s. Henry and Ruth Louise (Littman) P.; children: Eric Brett, Drew Michael, Scott Jeffrey. BS, Pa. State U., 1971; PhD, U. Va., 1978. Postdoctoral fellow Stanford (Calif.) U., 1978-81; scientist Genentech, Inc., South San Francisco, Calif., 1981-85, sr. scientist, 1985-88, sci. dir., 1988-90, sr. dir., 1990-93, v.p. product devel., 1993—. Mem. editorial bd. Viral Immunology, 1987—; contbr. articles to profl. jours., chpts. to books. Pres. Bishop Estates Swim Team, Concord, Calif., 1986, 87; judge Symposium on Sci. and Societal Issues, Lawrence Berkeley (Calif.) Hall of Sci., 1987, 89. Fellow NIH, 1974-78, Helen Hay Whitney Found., 1978-81. Mem. Am. Soc. Microbiology, Am. Soc. Virology, N.Y. Acad. Scis. Home: 6575 Ascot Dr Oakland CA 94611 Office: Genentech Inc 460 Point San Bruno Blvd South San Francisco CA 94080-4918

PAUKER, GUY JEAN, political analyst; b. Bucharest, Romania, Sept. 15, 1916; s. Jean Jacques and Coralie P.; m. Mirona Cochinescu, 1944 (div. Aug. 1960); 1 child, Randolph Guy; m. Ewa Teresa Toczylowska, Sept. 11, 1960; 1 child, Anthony John Henry. MA, U. Bucharest, Romania, 1937, LLB, 1938, Doctorate, 1946; MA, PhD, Harvard U., 1950, 52. Editorial writer Adeverul & Dimineata Newspapers, Bucharest, Romania, 1934-37, Jurnalul Newspaper, Bucharest, Romania, 1944-47; correspondent United Press of Am., Bucharest, Romania, 1946-47; instr. lectr. Harvard U., Cambridge, Mass., 1952-56; rsch. assoc. MIT/C.I.S., Cambridge, Mass., 1953-56; asst. prof. U. Calif. Berkeley, 1956-59, assoc. prof., 1959-63; sr. staff mem., cons. The Rand Corp., Santa Monica, Calif., 1960-82, 82—; faculty rsch. assoc. Calif. Inst. Tech., Pasadena, Calif., 1970-74; rsch. assoc. East-West Ctr. Resource Systems Inst., Honolulu, 1979-82; sec. gen. Romanian Inst. Internat. Affairs, Bucharest, 1945-47; co-founder Friends of the U.S., Bucharest, 1945. Author of about 112 books, monographs, essays; contbr. articles to profl. jours. Recipient Ford Faculty fellowship Ford Found., 1954-55. Mem. Coun. on Fgn. Rels., Internat. Inst. for Strategic Studies, The Asia Soc., Bel Air Bay Club. Home: 21423 Colina Dr Topanga CA 90290-9401

PAUL, AUGUSTUS JOHN, III, marine biologist, educator; b. Oneida, N.Y., July 19, 1946; s. Augustus J. and Marjorie Lucille (Malm) P.; m. Elaine Ann Rogers, Aug. 10, 1968 (div. 1972); 1 child, Oran Andrew; m. Judy McDonald, Jan. 19, 1975. BS, U. Mass., Amherst, 1969; MS, U. Alaska, 1973; PhD, Hokkaido U., Hakodate, Japan, 1987. Rsch. assoc. U. Alaska Inst. Marine Sci., Fairbanks, 1971-89, assoc. prof., 1989—. Contbr. articles to profl. jours. Sci. advisor Prince William Sound Regional Citizen's Adv. Coun., Anchorage, Alaska, 1990—. Scholar Hakodate-Alaska Friendship Soc., 1988. Mem. Am. Assn. Limnology and Oceanographers, Crustacean Soc. (assoc. editor 1991—), Nat. Shellfish Assn. (editorial bd. 1990—), Pacific Sci. Assn. Office: U Alaska PO Box 730 Seward AK 99664

PAUL, DAVID JACOB, nuclear energy industry executive; b. Wilmington, Del., Sept. 19, 1932; s. Benjamin Paul and Betty (Weinburg) Katz; m. Rachel Mercia Ibbetson, Oct. 8, 1967; children: Benjamin, Sara. B in Chem. Engring., U. Del., 1956; MS in Nuclear Engring., U. Va., 1960. Lic. profl. mech. and profl. nuclear engr., Calif. Rsch. engr. United Aircraft Rsch. Labs., East Hartford, Conn., 1961-64; sr. scientist NUMEC, Apollo, Pa., 1964-65; sr. engr. Westinghouse Electric, Pitts., 1965-69; safety project mgr., breeder reactor Atomics Internat., Canoga Park, Calif., 1969-70; group supr. General Atomics, LaJolla, Calif., 1970-75; systems integration project mgr. GE, San Jose, Calif., 1975-77; fusion project mgr. Electric Power Rsch. Inst., Palo Alto, Calif., 1977-80; v.p. ENTOR Corp., Campbell, Calif., 1980—; also bd. dirs. ENTOR Corp., Campbell; bd. dirs. Utility Computernet Corp., Campbell, 1986—. Author: (paper for European Nuclear conf.) HTGR Safety Characteristics, 1975; editor, project mgr. several rsch. reports. Mem. Am. Israeli Pub. Affairs Com., San Francisco, 1989—, Jewish Fedn. Greater San Jose, 1989—. Engring. fellow U. Va., 1959. Mem. AAAS, Am. Nuclear Soc. (chpt. v.p. 1959-60), Bibl. Archeol. Soc. Jewish. Office: ENTOR Corp 1901 S Bascom Ave Ste 1240 Campbell CA 95008

PAUL, DAVID PATRICK, insurance company executive; b. Minot, N.D., July 12, 1959; s. Herbert Lawrence and Dolores (Sawatzke) P.; m. Joanne Frances Kochis, May 4, 1985; 1 child, Alexander David. BS in Agrl. Econs., N.D. State U., 1981. Field underwriter Fed. Crop Ins. Corp., Billings, Mont., 1981-86; field statistics coordinator Fed. Crop Ins. Corp., 1986-88, dir., 1988; dir. St. Paul Compliance Office, Eagan, Minn., 1988—; asst. v.p. Home Farmers Mut. Ins. Assn., Bloomington, Minn., 1990-92; br. chief Fed. Crop Ins. Corp., Billings, Mont., 1992—. Mem. liturgy com. St. Patrick's Ch., Billings, 1988-89, lector and Eucharistic minister, 1988—. Recipient Superior Svc. award, USDA, 1985, Overholt Outstandinc Achievement award, 1991. Office: FCIC Billings Field Underwriting Office 2110 Overland Ave Ste 106 Billings MT 59102

PAUL, JUSTIN, JR., test engineer; b. Keams Canyon, Ariz., Oct. 23, 1966; s. Justin and Alice (Jackson) P. BS, No. Ariz. U., 1990. Underground transmission designer Ariz. Pub. Svcs., Phoenix, 1988; mentor Am. Indian sci. & engring. NSF and No. Ariz. U., Flagstaff, 1989; test engr. Toch Dineh Inds. Inc., Leupp, Ariz., 1990—. Mem. Am. Indian Engring. Soc. (v.p. 1985-90). Home: Box # 275 2542 N 4th St Flagstaff AZ 86004 Office: TOch Dineh Inds Inc HC-61 Box 58 Winslow AZ 86047

PAUL, RICHARD WILLIAM, philosophy educator; b. Chgo., Jan. 2, 1937; s. Arthur Palczynski and Helen Winslow Paul; children: Richard, Jeremy. BA in English, No. Ill. U., 1960; MA in English, U. Calif., Santa Barbara, 1961, MA in Philosophy, 1964, PhD in Philosophy, 1968. Assoc. in English U. Calif., Santa Barbara, 1961; asst. in English St. Louis U., 1961-62; assoc. in English U. Calif., Santa Barbara, 1963, asst. in philosophy, 1963-64; asst prof. philosophy Fresno (Calif.) State Coll., 1966-69; assoc. prof. philosophy Sonoma State U., Rohnert Park, Calif., 1969-74, dir. Ctr. for Critical Thinking and Moral Critique, 1981—, chmn. dept. philosophy, 1980-84, prof. philosophy, 1974—; lectr. in field of ednl. reform; test developer in critical thinking. Author: Critical Thinking: What Every Person Needs to Survive in a Rapidly Changing World, 2d rev. edit., 1992; Contbr. numerous articles to profl. jours. and books; editorial bd. Jour. of Informal Logic. Mem. Calif. State Senate Task Force on Moral Edn. Named Distinguished Philosopher, Coun. for Philos. Studies, 1987; Lansdowne Vis. scholar, U. Victoria, 1987, Alfred Korzybski Meml. Lectr., Inst. Gen. Semantics, 1987, others. Mem. Nat. Coun. for Excellence in Critical Thinking (chmn.), Found. for Critical Thinking (pres.). Office: The Ctr for Critical Think 1801 E Cotati Ave Rohnert Park CA 94928-3609

PAUL, ROBIN ELIZABETH, environmental protection specialist; b. Pitts., Nov. 16, 1955; d. Banks Issac and Bernice Elizabeth (Sampica) P.; 1 child, Marshall Austin. BA in Anthropology, U. Tex., Arlington, 1984; MA in Anthropology, N.Mex. State U., 1988. Pers. asst. IRS, Anchorage, 1978-80; adminstrv. asst. U. Tex., Dallas, 1980-83; anthropologist U.S. Army C.E., Albuquerque, 1985-86; environ. protection specialist Def. Logistics Agy., Holloman AFB, N.Mex., 1988-90, U.S. Army, White Sands Missile Range, N.Mex., 1990—. With U.S. Army, 1975-78. Recipient Sustained Superior Performance award Def. Logistics Agy., 1990. Mem. Alpha Chi, Psi Chi. Republican. Roman Catholic. Office: STEWS-EL-N (Environ Office) White Sands Missle Range NM 88002

PAUL, SHALE, author, management consultant; b. Wilson, Pa., July 15, 1931; s. Ralph Wilmer and Blanche (Shale) P.; m. Carolyn Dain Canham, Aug. 29, 1951 (div. 1984); children: Lisa, Kenneth, Julie Grace, Jennifer; m. Candace Paul, Nov. 10, 1984. BA in Econs., Cornell U., 1953, MBA, 1954. Estimator/expeditor R.W. Paul Constrn. Co., Pitts., 1958-60; mgmt. cons. McKinsey & Co., Washington, 1960-64; sr. staff analyst Com. for Econ. Devel., Washington, 1964-66; dir. planning Rsch. Analysis Corp., McLean, Va., 1966-72; pres. Salisbury South, Inc., Salisbury, Md., 1972-76, Continental Restaurants, Inc., Denver, 1977-80, Ctr. for Individual Effectiveness, Golden, Colo., 1980-83; pres. The Delta Group, McLean, 1984-86, Evergreen, Colo., 1986—. Co-author: Men Near the Top, 1966; author: The Warrior Within. 1983, Maybe It's Not Your Fault, But You Can Do Something About It, 1993; co-author (with Candace Paul) Tough/Nice, 1988, Discovering Your Inner Power: A Workbook for the Warrior Within, 1992. 1st lt. USMC, 1954-57. Mem. Nat. Speakers Assn., Colo. Authors League. Home: 28106 Meadowlark Dr Golden CO 80401 Office: The Delta Group PO Box 40 Evergreen CO 80439-0040

PAULE, LAWRENCE DAVID, chiropractor; b. Chgo., Sept. 29, 1960; s. Herbert Isidore and Joyce (Friedman) P. BA, U. Ariz., 1983; BS, L.A. Coll. Chiropractic, Whittier, Calif., 1987, D of Chiropractic, 1987. Diplomate Nat. Bd. Chiropractic Examiners. Chaplain Boy Scouts Am., Payson, Ariz., 1982-84; assoc. dr. Neurological Orthopaedic Assocs., Panorama City, Calif., 1989—. Recipient Jewish Community Svc. award Hillel, 1983. Mem. Young Demo., City of Hope, Kiwanis, Toastmasters.

PAULING, LINUS CARL, chemistry educator; b. Portland, Oreg., Feb. 28, 1901; s. Herman Henry William and Lucy Isabelle (Darling) P.; m. Ava Helen Miller, June 17, 1923 (dec. Dec. 7, 1981); children: Linus Carl, Peter Jeffress, Linda Helen, Edward Crellin. BS, Oreg. State U., Corvallis, 1922; ScD (hon.), Oreg. State Coll., Corvallis, 1933; PhD, Calif. Inst. Tech., 1925; ScD (hon.), U. Chgo., 1941, Princeton, 1946, U. Cambridge, U. London, Yale U., 1947, Oxford U., 1948, Bklyn. Poly. Inst., 1955, Humboldt U., 1959, U. Melbourne, 1964, U. Delhi, Adelphi U., 1967, Marquette U. Sch. Medicine, 1969; LHD, Tampa U., 1950; UJD, U. N.B., 1950; LLD, Reed Coll., 1959; Dr. h.c., Jagiellonian U., Montpellier (France), 1964; DFA, Chouinard Art Inst., 1958; also others. Teaching fellow Calif. Inst. Tech., 1922-25, research fellow, 1925-27, asst. prof., 1927-29, assoc. prof., 1929-31, prof. chemistry, 1931-64; chmn. div. chem. and chem. engring., dir. Calif. Inst. Tech. (Gates and Crellin Labs. of Chemistry), 1936-58, mem. exec. com., bd. trustees, 1945-48; research prof. (Center for Study Dem. Instns.), 1963-67; prof. chemistry U. Calif. at San Diego, 1967-69, Stanford, 1969-74; pres. Linus Pauling Inst. Sci. and Medicine, 1973-75, 78—, research prof., 1973—; George Eastman prof. Oxford U., 1948; lectr. chemistry several univs. Author several books, 1930—, including How to Live Longer and Feel Better, 1986; contbr. articles to profl. jours. Fellow Balliol Coll., 1948; Fellow NRC, 1925-26; Fellow John S. Guggenheim Meml. Found., 1926-27; Recipient numerous awards in field of chemistry, including; U.S. Presdl. Medal for Merit, 1948, Nobel prize in chemistry, 1954, Nobel Peace prize, 1962, Internat. Lenin Peace prize, 1972, U.S. Nat. Medal of Sci., 1974, Fermat medal, Paul Sabatier medal, Pasteur medal, medal with laurel wreath of Internat. Grotius Found., 1957, Lomonosov medal, 1978, U.S. Nat. Acad. Sci. medal in Chem. Scis., 1979, Priestley medal Am. Chem. Soc., 1984, Chem. Edn. award, 1987,Tolman medal, 1991, award for chemistry Arthur M. Sackler Found., 1984, Vannevar Bush award Nat. Sci. Bd., 1989. Hon., corr., fgn. mem. numerous assns. and orgns. Home: Salmon Creek 15 Big Sur CA 93920 Office: Linus Pauling Inst Sci and Medicine 440 Page Mill Rd Palo Alto CA 94306-2025

PAULLIN, JOANN MARIE, accountant, educator; b. Spokane, Wash., July 25, 1946; d. Carl Victor and Gladyls Marie (Soderstrom) Koford; m. William Charles Paullin, Oct. 14, 1967 (div. Jan. 1986); children: Kimberly Rae, Angela Rae. BS in Bus., Mont. State U., 1968. Tchr. bus. various locations, 1968-83; office mgr. Century 21/Jim Bennetts Realty, Kalispell, 1981, Flathead Land Cons., Kalispell, 1981-83; acctg. mgr. Semltool, Inc., Kalispell, 1983-84; office mgr. Ureco Inc., Columbia Falls, Mont., 1984-86; controller Glacier View Hosp., Kalispell, 1986; acct. Kalispell Regional Hosp., 1987-91, Serac Inc., Spokane, 1991-92, Pentzer Devel. Corp., Spokane, 1992—. Mem. fin. com. Epworth United Meth. Ch., Kalispell, 1986-91, mem. loan and grant com., 1986-88; chairperson CORE team Region XII Assn. of Div., Separated and Widowed Caths., Kalispell, 1988-90. Mem. AAUW (chmn. edn. com. 1990-91), Hosp. Fin. Mgrs. Assn., Kalispell C. of C. (ambassador, community edn. com.), Exec. Women Internat. Democrat.

PAULOS, PETER ERNEST, orthodontist; b. Salt Lake City, May 7, 1943; s. Ernest Gus and Katherine Joann (Dizikes) P.; m. Arthea Marie Buckman, Sept. 11, 1966; children: Andrew Peter, Peter Ernest Jr., Stephanie Katherine. BS, U. Utah, 1965; DDS, Northwestern U., 1969; MS, U. Mich., 1973. Diplomate Am. Bd. Orthodontics. Pvt. practice Salt Lake City, 1973—. Lt. U.S. Armed Forces, 1969-71. Recipient Award of Merit, Am. Coll. Dentists, 1969. Mem. ADA, Am. Assn. Orthodontists, Utah Dental Assn., Utah Orthodontic Soc., Salt Lake Dist. Dental Soc., Rocky Mountain Soc. Orthodontists, Hon. Cols. (pres. 1990-92), Valley West C. of C. Greek Orthodox. Office: 2940 West 3650 South Salt Lake City UT 84119

PAULSEN, VIVIAN, magazine editor; b. Salt Lake City, May 10, 1942; d. Paul Herman and Martha Oline (Blattman) P. B.A., Brigham Young U., 1964, postgrad., 1965; postgrad., U. Grenoble, France, 1966. Cert. tchr., Utah. Tchr. French Granite Sch. Dist., Salt Lake City, 1966-67; assoc. editor New Era mag., Salt Lake City, 1970-82; mng. editor Friend mag., Salt Lake City, 1982—. Contbr. numerous articles to mags. Am. Field Service scholar, 1959; grad. fellow Brigham Young U., 1964-66. Mem. Soc. Children's Book Writers. Republican. Mem. Ch. of Jesus Christ of Latter-day Saints. Office: The Friend 50 E North Temple Salt Lake City UT 84150-0001

PAULSON, DONALD ROBERT, chemistry educator; b. Oak Park, Ill., Sept. 6, 1943; s. Robert Smith and Florence Teresa (Beese) P.; m. Elizabeth Anne Goodwin, Aug. 20, 1966; children: Matthew, Andrew. BA, Monmouth Coll., 1965; PhD, Ind. U., 1968. Asst. prof. chemistry Calif. State U., Los Angeles, 1970-74, assoc. prof., 1974-78, prof., 1979—, chmn. dept., 1982-90; vis. prof. U. B.C., Vancouver, Can., 1977-78, U. Sussex, Brighton, Eng., 1984-85. Author: Alicyclic Chemistry, 1976; contbr. articles to profl. jours. Named Outstanding Prof., Calif. State U., Los Angeles, 1978. Mem. Am. Chem. Soc., Chem. Soc. (London), InterAm. Photochem. Soc., Nat. Assn. Sci. Tchrs., Sigma Xi. Democrat. Episcopalian. Home: 1627 Laurel St South Pasadena CA 91030-4710 Office: Calif State U Dept Chemistry 5151 State University Dr Los Angeles CA 90032-4221

PAULSON, GREGORY STEPHEN, entomologist; b. Amittyville, N.Y., Jan. 5, 1955; s. Neil Albert and Louise (LaValle) P. BA in Zoology, Miami U., Oxford, Ohio, 1977; MS in Entomology, U. Hawaii, 1983; PhD in Entomology, Washington State U., 1990. With U.S. Peace Corps World Health Orgn., Apia, Western Somoa, 1977-80; grad. rsch. asst. dept. of Entomology U. Hawaii, Honolulu, 1981-83; rsch. assoc. dept. of plant pathology U. Hawaii, Kula, 1984-85; grad. rsch. asst. dept. Entomology Wash. State U., Pullman, 1985-90, instr. Biology, 1985-90; faculty advisor, coach hockey club Wash. State U., Pullman, 1992. Author (book) Insects Did It First, 1992; contbg. photographer 10 books or articles, 1989—; contbr. articles to profl. jours. Recruiter Coll. Knowledge for the Mind, Spokane, Wash., 1992; mem. com. Alliance of States Supporting Indians in Sci. & Tech., 1992. Recipient Grand Prize and 1st Prize Polaroid Internat. Photomicrography Competition, 1992. Mem. Entomol. Soc. Am. (Best Presentation award 1990), Wash. State Entomol. Soc., Nat. Coun. of Returned Peace Corps. Vols., Hawaii Entomol. Soc., Sigma Xi. Office: dept Biology Wash State U Pullman WA 99164-4235

PAULSON, TERRY LEE, clinical psychologist; b. Panama City, Fla., Oct. 23, 1945; s. Homer Frederick and Ann Marie (Carlson) P.; m. Kathleen Wyna Hiebert, Mar. 19, 1968 (div. 1976); 1 child, Sean Douglas; m. Valorie Ann Leland, June 19, 1976. BA in Psychology, UCLA, 1968; MA in Lay Theology, Fuller Theol. Sem., 1975; PhD in Clinical Psychology, Fuller Grad. Sch. Psychology, 1974. Lic. clinical psychologist; cert. speaking profl. Prin. Paulson & Assocs., Inc., North Hollywood, Calif., 1975-80, Agoura Hills, Calif., 1980—; adv. bd. Wellness Community, Conejo Valley, Calif.,

1989—. Author: ABC's for Teachers, 1976, Making Humor Work, 1989, Secrets of Life Every Teen Needs to Know, 1990, They Shoot Managers Don't They, 1991. Coun. mem. Westlake Luth. Ch., Westlake Village, Calif., 1986-89. Mem. Am. Soc. Tng. & Devel., Nat. Speakers Assn. (nat. bd. dirs. 1991—, Coun. Peers award Excellence 1991). Republican. Office: PO Box 365 Agoura Hills CA 91376-0365

PAULSON-EHRHARDT, PATRICIA HELEN, laboratory administrator; b. Moses Lake, Wash., June 10, 1956; d. Luther Roanoke and Helen Jane (Baird) Paulson; m. Terry Lee Ehrhardt, Mar. 12, 1983. Student, Pacific Luth. U., 1974-76; BS in Med. Tech., U. Wash., 1976; BS in Biology, MS in Biology, Eastern Wash. U., 1982. Med. technologist Samaritan Hosp., Moses Lake, 1979-81; lab. supr. Moses Lake Clinic br. Wenatchee Valley Clinic, 1983-87; with Kalispell (Mont.) Regional Hosp., 1987—; account exec. Pathology Assocs. Med. Lab., Spokane, Wash., 1988—; mem. med. lab. tech. adv. com. Wenatchee (Wash.) Valley Coll., 1984-85, chmn., 1985-86. Mem. Flathead Valley Community Band, 1987-90. Mem. Am. Soc. Med. Technologists (hematology judge 1986 Wash. State Student Bowl), Wash. State Soc. Med. Techologists (coordinator sci. assembly small lab. 1986), Wash. Assn. Diabetic Educators, Am. Soc. Clin. Pathologists (cert.), Pan Players Flute Soc., AAUW, Flathead Tennis Assn., Sigma Xi, Kappa Delta (pledge class pres. 1976). Republican. Lutheran. Club: Moses Lake Volleyball Assn. (pres. 1985-86). Lodge: Rotary (active wive's br. Moses Lake, 1985). Home: RR 3 Box 157E Milton Freewater OR 97862-9803

PAULUS, NORMA JEAN PETERSEN, lawyer; b. Belgrade, Nebr., Mar. 13, 1933; d. Paul Emil and Ella Marie (Hellbusch) Petersen; LL.B., Willamette Law Sch., 1962; LL.D., Linfield Coll., 1985; m. William G. Paulus, Aug. 16, 1958; children—Elizabeth, William Frederick. Sec. to Harney County Dist. Atty., 1950-53; legal sec., Salem, Oreg., 1953-55; sec. to chief justice Oreg. Supreme Ct., 1955-61; admitted to Oreg. bar, 1962; of counsel Paulus and Callaghan, Salem, mem. Oreg. Ho. of Reps., 1971-77; sec. state State of Oreg., Salem, 1977-85; of counsel firm Paulus, Rhoten & Lien, 1985-86; supt. pub. instrn. State of Oreg., 1990—; Oreg. exec. bd. US West, 1985—; adj. prof. Willamette U. Grad. Sch, 1985. Fellow Eagleton Inst. Politics, 1971; mem. Pacific NW Power Planning Council, 1987-89; adv. com. Defense Adv. Com. for Women in the Service, 1986, Nat. Trust for Hist. Preservation, 1988—; trustee Willamette U., 1978—; bd. dirs. Benedictine Found. of Oreg., 1980—, Oreg. Grade. Instn. Sci. and Tech., 1985—, Mid Willamette Valley council Camp Fire Girls, 1985-87; overseer Whitman Coll., 1985—; bd. cons. Goodwill Industries of Oreg.; mem. Salem Human Relations Commn., 1967-70, Marion-Polk Boundary Commn., 1970-71; mem. Presdl. Commn. to Monitor Philippines Election, 1986. Recipient Distinguished Service award City of Salem, 1971; Path Breaker award Oreg. Women's Polit. Caucus, 1976; named One of 10 Women of Future, Ladies Home Jour., 1979. Woman of Yr., Oreg. Inst Managerial and Profl. Women, 1982, Oreg. Women Lawyers, 1982, Woman who Made a Difference award Nat. Women's Forum, 1985. Mem. Oreg. State Bar, Nat. Order Women Legislators, Women Execs. in State Govt., Women's Polit. Caucus Bus. and Profl. Women's Club (Golden Torch award 1971), Zonta Internat., Delta Kappa Gamma.

PAULY, JAMES ROSS, retail executive; b. Bakersfield, Calif., Apr. 8, 1927; s. Leo Antone and Alice Louise (Medlock) P.; m. Katherine Francis Iriart, June 29, 1947; children: Rhond Rae Prout, Kathy Sue Carlton. Student, Chaffey Coll., Ontario, Calif., 1946-47. Salesman Emersons Mens Store, Corona, Calif., 1942-44, buyer, salesman, 1947-67, buyer, salesman, owner, 1967-69; ptnr., pres. Emerson-Pauly Mens Wear, Corona, 1969—; chmn. Solicitation Com., Corona, 1952-59. Dir., v.p. Corona Redevel Agy., 1963-78; trustee Corona-Norco Sch. Dist., 1966-76; chmn. Parking Authority, Corona, 1966-80. With USN, 1945-46. Mem. Corona C. of C. (dir. 1951-54, Citizen of Yr. 1972), Downtown Bus. Assn. (chmn. 1948-52, 67-77), Twenty-Thirty Svc. Club (pres. 1951-52), Corona Elks (exalted ruler 1959), Corona Rotary (pres. 1965-66). Home: 1819 S Main St Corona CA 91720-4963

PAUP, MARTIN ARNOLD, real estate and securities investor; b. Seattle, Aug. 30, 1930; s. Clarence Jacob and Emaline Ethel (Lodestein) P.; m. Mary Jean Iske, Apr. 4, 1959; children: Barbara Ann Paup Soriano, Jennifer Marie, Elizabeth Paup Gail. BS, U. Wash., 1952. Indsl. engr. Boeing Airplane Co., Seattle, 1954-60; owner Coopers Unfinished Furniture, Seattle, 1960-63; claims rep. Unigard Ins., Seattle, 1963-66; asst. benefits mgr. Equitable Life Assurance, Seattle, 1966-85; owner Paup Ventures, Seattle, 1974--, Paup Investment Co., Seattle, 1963--, Ella Paup Properties, Seattle, 1963--. Bd. dirs. Denny Regrade Property Owners' Assn., Seattle, Denny Regrade Bus. Assn., Seattle, First Ave. Assn., Seattle. Seattle Dept. Community Devel. grantee, 1980. Mem. Greenwood C. of C., Stanwood Camano Yacht Club, Seattle, Enological. Democrat. Roman Catholic. Home: 2021 1st Ave Ste 4G Seattle WA 98121-2135 Office: Paup Co 2021 1st Ave # 4G Seattle WA 98121-2135

PAVEY, JANET SUE, gift shop manager, buyer; b. Phoenix, July 1, 1954; d. Earl Leroy and Helen Mae (Davio) Waters; m. Trevan Leroy Woolbright Jr., Oct. 16, 1976 (div. 1984); m. Geoffrey Alan Pavey, June 17, 1989. BS, No. Ariz. U., 1976; Dipl., Dale Carnegie Mgmt. Seminar, Flagstaff, Ariz., 1989. With Northgate Fabrics, Flagstaff, 1976-79; asst. store mgr. Malcolm's Dept. Store, Flagstaff, 1979-83; store mgr. Hartfields, Flagstaff, 1983-84; gift shop mgr., buyer Little America Hotel, Flagstaff, 1984—. Mem. Cardinal Key (alumni advisor 1976—), Beta Sigma Phi (rep. city coun., pres. 1989-90, chpt. pres. 1988-89). Republican. Methodist. Office: Little America Hotel 2515 E Butler Ave # 3900 Flagstaff AZ 86004-6099

PAVIN, RANDALL BROOKE, electrical engineer; b. Whittier, Calif., Feb. 17, 1953; s. Joesph Meyer and Elaine Ethelene (Hirsch) P.; m. Patricia Martinez Reyes, Oct. 11, 1986. BSEE, Calif. State U., Long Beach, 1975, MSEE, 1981; cert. in intelligent systems, U. Calif., Irvine, 1989, cert. in advanced software tech., 1992. Mem. tech. staff Rockwell Internat., Anaheim, Calif., 1976-91, engrng. specialist, 1991—. Inventor frequency control device. Bd. dirs., treas. Fullerton Plz. Homeowners Assn., Fullerton, Calif., 1980—. Mem. IEEE, Engrng. Alumni Assn. Calif. State U.-Long Beach. Home: 914 Cobb Ave Placentia CA 92670 Office: Rockwell Internat FB15 3370 Miraloma Ave Anaheim CA 92803

PAVLAK, FRANK JAMES, federal government accountant; b. Paterson, N.J., Mar. 23, 1947; s. Alexander John Sr. Margaret Eleanor (Gillespie) P.; m. Linda Lee Breen, July 24, 1976; children: Brian Christopher, Heather Christine. BS in Acctg., U. No. Colo., 1975. Auditor U.S. Gen. Acctg. Office, Washington, 1975-80, U.S. Gen. Svcs. Adminstr., Denver, 1980-81; examiner, br. chief U.S. Securities & Exch. Commn., Denver, 1981—; founder Assn. for Recognizing the Life of Stillborns. Roman Catholic. Office: Assn for Recognizing the Life of Stillborns 11128 W Frost Ave Littleton CO 80127

PAVLATH, ATTILA ENDRE, research chemist; b. Budapest, Hungary, Mar. 11, 1930; came to U.S., 1958; s. Eugene Rudolph and Yolanda Elizabeth (Hortobagyi) P.; m. Katalin Wappel, July 27, 1951; children: George, Grace. Diploma in chem. engring., Tech. U., Budapest, 1952; D in Chemistry, Hungarian Acad. of Sci., Budapest, 1955. Asst. prof. Tech. U., Budapest, 1952-56; group leader Cen. Chem. Rsch. Inst., Budapest, 1954-56; rsch. fellow McGill U., Montreal, Can., 1957-58; sr. group leader Stauffer Chem. Co., Richmond, Calif., 1958-67; project leader Western regional rsch. ctr. USDA, Albany, Calif., 1967-78, rsch. leader Western regional rsch. ctr., 1979—. Author three books; contbr. articles to profl. jours; patentee in field. Fellow Am. Inst. Chemists (councilor 1985—, dir. 1993—); mem. Am. Chem. Soc. (councilor 1973-90, dir. 1991—), Royal Chem. Soc. Great Britain, N.Am. Thermonalysis Soc., Internat. Union of Pure and Applied Chemistry. Office: USDA Western Regional Rsch Ctr 800 Buchanan St Berkeley CA 94710-1100

PAVLICK, HARVEY NAYLOR, financial executive; b. San Francisco, May 29, 1942; s. Leopold Ferdinand and Anna Cathrine (Naylor) P. BA, San Francisco State U., 1965; MA, U. Chgo., 1968; D in Philosophy, Claremont Grad. Sch., 1974. Dir. ann. fund Union Coll., Schenectady, N.Y., 1968-70; dir. corp. and found. funding U. Calif., Berkeley, 1975-78; prin. Hyde Park Properties, Ltd., San Francisco, 1979-83; pres. Am. Equity Coun., Inc., Irvine, Calif., 1984—; chmn. bd. dirs. Investment Grade Real Estate Coun., Inc., Irvine; chmn. exec. com. Ahwahnee-Pacific Corp., Napa, Calif., 1990—. Sponsor Friends Huntington Libr., San Marino, Calif., 1986—, Children, Inc., Alexandria, Va., 1984—; mem. World Affairs Coun. of Orange County, Santa Ana, Calif., 1986, L.A. County Mus. Art, 1988—; donor Friends of San Francisco Symphony, 1990—. Mem. World Affairs Coun. L.A., Pi Sigma Alpha.

PAVLIK, NANCY, convention services executive; b. Hamtramck, Mich., July 18, 1935; d. Frank and Helen (Vorobojoff) Phillips; m. G. Edward Pavlik, June 30, 1956; children: Kathleen, Christine, Laureen, Michael, Bonnie Jean. Student, U. Ariz., 1956-80. Exec. sec. Mich. Bell, Detroit, 1951-56, RCA, Camden, N.J., 1956-58; owner, pres. Southwest Events Etc., Scottsdale, Ariz., 1969—. Chmn. hospitality industry com. Scottsdale City Coun., 1989—; bd. dirs. Scottsdale Curatorial Bd., 1987-89. Mem. Soc. Incentive Travel Execs., Meeting Planners Internat., Am. Soc. Assn. Execs., Indian Arts and Crafts Assn., Scottsdale C. of C. (bd. dirs., tourism steering com. 1984-88), Contemporary Watercolorists Club. Democrat. Roman Catholic. Home: 7500 E Mccormick Pky # 33 Scottsdale AZ 85258-3454 Office: SW Events Etc 8233 E Paseo Del Norte A-600 Scottsdale AZ 85258

PAWULA, KENNETH JOHN, artist, educator; b. Chgo., Feb. 4, 1935; s. John and Clara (Brzezinski) P.; student Northwestern U., 1956, Art Inst. Chgo., 1956; B.F.A., U. Ill., 1959; M.A. in Painting, U. Calif., Berkeley, 1962. Graphic designer Motorola, Inc., Chgo., 1959-60; grad. asst. printmaking U. Calif., Berkeley, 1961-62, asso. in art, 1962-63; archaeol. delineator for Islamic excavation Am. Research Center, Egypt, 1964-65; instr. Sch. of Art, U. Wash., Seattle, 1965-67, asst. prof., 1967-73, asso. prof., 1974—; participant artist-in-residence program of Ecole Superieure Des Beaux-Arts D'Athenes at Rhodos Art Center, Greece, 1978; cons. to Wydawnictwo Interpress, Warsaw, Poland, 1978; mem. art jury ann. painting, drawing and sculpture show Art Mus. of Greater Victoria, Can., 1971, Unitarian Art Gallery, Seattle, 1968, Cellar Gallery, Kirkland, Wash., 1968, Lakewood Artist's Outdoor Exhibit, Tacoma, Wash., 1968; participant Painting Symposium, Janow Podlaski, Poland, 1977. One-man shows of paintings include: Univ. Unitarian Fine Arts Gallery, Seattle, 1970, Polly Friedlander Gallery, Seattle, 1970, Lynn Kottler Galleries, N.Y.C., 1971, U. Minn. Art Gallery, Mpls., 1971, Art Mus. of Greater Victoria, Can., 1972, Second Story Gallery, Seattle, 1972, Yuuhigaoka Gallery Osaka, Japan, Universidade Federal Fluminense Niteroi, Rio de Janiero, Brazil, 1990, Pyramid Gallery, N.Y.C., 1991; group shows include: Worth Ryder Gallery, U. Calif., Berkeley, 1962, Seattle Art Mus., 1964, 70, 65, 66, Frye Art Mus., Seattle, 1966, San Francisco Art Ins., 1966, Henry Gallery, U. Wash., Seattle, 1966, 67, 70, State Capitol Mus., Olympia, Wash., 1967, Attica Gallery, Seattle, 1967, 69, Sec. of State's Office, Olympia, 1968, Eastern Mich. U., Ypsilanti, 1968, Rogue Gallery, Medford, Oreg., 1968, Marylhurst Coll., Oreg., 1968, Spokane Art Mus., 1968, Cheney Cowles Mus., Spokane, 1969, Jade Gallery, Richland, Wash., 1969, Alaska U., 1970, Polly Friedlander Gallery, Mpls., 1971, Anchorage Art Mus., 1972, U. Nev. Art Gallery, 1972, Juneau (Alaska) Art Mus., 1972, Springfield (Mo.) Art Mus., 1973, U. N.D., Grand Forks, 1974, Washington and Jefferson Coll., Washington, Pa., 1975, MacMurray Coll., Jacksonville, Ill., 1976, Gallery of Fine Arts, Eastern Mont. Coll., 1976, Inst. of Culture, Janow Podlaski, Poland, 1977, Seattle Arts Commn., 1978, Polish Cultural Center, Buffalo, 1979, Cabo Frio Internat. Print Biennial, Brazil, 1983, Sunderland (Eng.) Poly. U. Faculty Exchange Exhbn., 1984, Internat Art Biennial Mus. Hosio Capranica-Viterbo, Italy, 1985; represented in permanent collections: San Francisco Art Mus., Seattle Art Mus., Henry Gallery, U. Wash., Seattle, Highline Coll., Midway, Wash., Marylhurst Coll., Art Mus., Janow Podlaski, Poland, Tacoma Nat. Bank, Fine Arts Gallery of San Diego. Mem. Coll. Art Assn., AAUP. Home: 2242 NE 177th St Seattle WA 98195-0001 Office: U Wash Coll Arts & Scis Sch Art DM-10 Seattle WA 98195

PAY, HOWARD RICHARD, operations executive; b. Sioux Falls, S.D., June 1, 1951; s. Richard H. Pay. BS, Colo. State U., 1973; MBA, U. Mont., 1982. Mgr. Computer Mgmt. Svcs., Portland, Oreg., 1977-81; cons. Price Waterhouse, Portland, 1981-88; prin. The Pringle Co., Portland, 1988-92; v.p. ops. Supra Products, Inc., Salem, Oreg., 1992—. V.p. Oreg. Trout, Portland, 1984-89, pres., 1989, The Old Ch. Soc., Portland, 1991-92; bd. trustees Leukemia Soc. Am., Portland, 1990. Recipient George Washington Meml. award Freedom Found., 1973. Mem. Univ. Club. Office: Supra Products Inc PO Box 3167 Salem OR 97302-0167

PAYANT, V. ROBERT, legal association administrator, educator, judge; b. Iron Mountain, Mich., June 25, 1932; s. Vital Alexander and Anna Jane (Freele) P.; m. Virginia Henneberry, June 23, 1956; children: Margaret, Thomas More, Mary Adele, Ned, Robert. BS in English, Marquette U., 1954, JD, 1956. Bar: Wis. 1956, Mich. 1957, Nev. 1985. Atty. City of Iron Mountain (Mich.), 1959-63; probate judge County of Dickinson, Iron Mountain, 1963-68; 95th dist. judge State of Mich., Iron Mountain, 1968-77, 41st cir. judge., 1977-82; ct. adminstr. State of Mich., Lansing, Mich., 1985-88; assoc. dean Nat. Jud. Coll., Reno, Nev., 1982-85; dean Nat. Jud. Coll., Reno, 1990—; mem. faculty Nat. Jud. Coll., Reno, 1973—, dean 1990—, Inst. for Ct. Mgmt., Denver, 1982—. Mem. ABA, Nev. Bar Assn., Mich. Bar Assn., Am. Judicature Soc., K.C. Republican. Roman Catholic. Office: U Nevada Nat Judicial Coll Nat Jud Coll Reno NV 89557

PAYEA, NORMAN PHILIP, II, plastic surgeon; b. Detroit, May 11, 1949; s. Norman Philip and Helen (Kucera) P.; 1 child, Heather Marie. BS in Biology, Mich. State U., 1970, MD, 1974; JD, U. Denver, 1991, MBA, 1992. Diplomate Am. Bd. Plastic Surgery. Intern, gen. surgery Loyola U. Med. Ctr., Chgo., 1974-75, resident, gen. surgery, 1975-77; resident, plastic/reconstructive and hand surgery McGill U. Teaching Hosps., Montreal, Que., Can., 1977-79; plastic surgeon East Tawas, Mich., 1979-81, Wheat Ridge, Colo., 1981-82, Lakewood, Colo., 1983—; aviation med. examiner Fed. Aviation Agy.; lectr. in field. Contbr. articles to profl. jours. Active numerous civic orgns. and founds. including Denver Art Mus., Denver Botanical Gardens, Denver Art Mus., Denver Mus. of Natural History, Denver Zool. Found., Internat. Soc. for Athletic Plastic Surgery, others. Fellow Royal Coll. Physicians and Surgeons of Can.; mem. ABA, AMA, Flying Physicians Assn., Am. Coll. Legal Medicine, Assn. Trial Lawyers Am., Colo. Bar Assn., Colo. Trial Lawyers Assn., Colo. State Soc. Plastic and Reconstructive Surgeons (various offices), Clear Creek Valley Med. Soc. (various offices), Colo. Med. Soc., Am. Soc. Plastic and Reconstructive Surgeons, Am. Burn Assn., Rocky Mountain Hand Surgery Soc., Am. Assn. for Hand Surgery. Home: 3470 Ward Rd Wheat Ridge CO 80033-5225 Office: Lakewood Med Ctr 8805 West 14th Ave Denver CO 80215

PAYNE, ANCIL HORACE, retired broadcasting executive; b. Mitchell, Oreg., Sept. 5, 1921; s. Leslie L. and Pearl A. (Brown) P.; m. Valerie Dorrance Davies, Apr. 6, 1959; children—Anne Sparrow, Alison Louise, Lucinda Catherine. Student, Willamette U., 1939-41, U. Oreg., 1941, U. Notre Dame, Ohio State U., 1943; B.A., U. Wash., 1947; postgrad., Am. U., 1950-51; hon. PhD, Willamette Univ., 1991. Adminstrv. asst. to congressman, Washington, 1949-52; gen. mgr. Martin Van Lines, Anchorage, 1952-56; mgr. Frontiers-Oreg. Ltd., Portland, Oreg., 1956-59; asst. v.p. bus. div. King Broadcasting Co., Seattle, 1959-63, v.p., 1963-70, exec. v.p., 1970-71, pres., 1971-87; chmn. bd. affiliates NBC, 1975-79; bd. dirs. Airborne Freight Co., AdExpress Co. Mem. Oreg. Bd. Higher Edn., 1966-70; pres. Centrum Found.; bd. dirs. Sr. Svcs. Seattle King County, Oreg. Shakespeare Festival; trustee Whitman Coll., 1984-92. Served to lt. (j.g.) USNR, 1942-45, PTO. Mem. Phi Beta Kappa, Alpha Delta Sigma. Episcopalian. Clubs: Monday, Rainier, Columbia Tower (Seattle). Home: 1107 First Ave # 2001 Seattle WA 98101 Office: 1107 1st Ave Apt 606 Seattle WA 98101

PAYNE, BILLY (WILLIAM A. PAYNE), real estate lawyer, sports association executive; m. Martha Payne. JD, U Ga Law School. Head Atlanta Com. for the Olympic Games 1996, 1992—. Office: US Olympic Com 1750 E Boulder St Colorado Springs CO 80909

PAYNE, CLAIRE MARGARET, molecular and cellular biologist; b. N.Y.C., Mar. 2, 1943; d. Frederick John Luscher and Florence Muriel (Seiler) Nothdurft; m. Thomas Bennett Payne, Apr. 19, 1969. BS, SUNY, Stony Brook, 1963; MS, Adelphi U., 1965; PhD, SUNY, Stony Brook, 1971. Biology tchr. North Babylon (N.Y.) High Sch., 1970-72; rsch. asst. Dept. Pathology U. Ariz., Tucson, 1972-73, lectr. Dept. Pathology, 1973-86, rsch. assoc. prof. Pathology, 1986-89, rsch. prof. Pathology, 1989-93; rsch. prof. Ariz. Rsch. Labs. and Dept. Microbiology & Immunology, Tucson, 1993—; supr. Clin. Electron Microscopy Lab., U. Ariz., Tucson, 1973-86, adminstrv. chief, 1986-93. Vol. Am. Cancer Soc., 1988—. Ariz. Disease Control Rsch Commn. grantee, 1990-93, grantee Mathers Found., 1992—. Mem. AAAS, Soc. for Diagnostic Ultrastructural Pathology (sec.-treas. 1991—), Ariz. Soc. for Electron Microscopy and Microbeam Analysis (pres. 1983-84), Ariz. Soc. Pathologists, Tucson Soc. of Pathologists, Am. Soc. Cell Biology, European Soc. for Cutaneous Ultrastructure Rsch., Biomedical Diagnostics & Rsch. (pres.). Office: Dept Microbiology & Immunology 1501 N Campbell Ave Tucson AZ 85724-0001

PAYNE, DARRELL LEE, small business owner; b. Houston, Oct. 21, 1948; s. Alvis Lee and Freddie Jean (Harmeier) P.; m. Carol Jo Quesenbury, Dec. 15, 1967 (div. 1973); children: Patricia Ann, Alan Chandler; m. Karen Nadine Brown, Feb. 29, 1980; children: Kari Ann, Sara Jean. Grad., James Madison High Sch., Houston, 1976. Customer engr. Control Data Corp., Houston, 1969-73; asst. mgr. City Wide TV, Houston, 1972-74; prodn. mgr. JRW Electronics, Sunnyvale, Calif., 1975-77; test engr. Compression Labs., Inc., San Jose, 1977, Apple Computer Inc., Cupertino, Calif., 1977-82; test engring. cons. San Martin, Calif., 1982-85; test mfg. engring. mgr. Headland Tech., Fremont, Calif., 1985-88; gen. ptnr. Digital Image Duplication, San Martin, 1988—. Mem. So. County Alano Club (v.p. 1988-89). Home and Office: Digital Image Duplication 240 Hindiyeh Ln San Martin CA 95046

PAYNE, JOHN HARMAN, portfolio manager; b. Welch, W.Va., Apr. 2, 1955; s. Hobart Elkins and Phyllis (Rau) P. BA, Ind. U., 1979; MS, U. Wyo., 1986. CFA. Portfolio specialist Rainier Investment Advisors, Seattle, 1987-88; portfolio mgr. Security Pacific Bank, Seattle, 1988-89; portfolio mgr., asst. v.p. Sterling Pvt. Investment Mgmt., Seattle, 1989-91; exec. portfolio mgr., v.p. Bank of Am.-Ariz., Tucson, 1991—; rsch. asst. U. Wyo., Laramie, 1984-86; heavy equipment operator Thunder Basin Coal Co., Gillette, Wyo., 1979-84; cons. Small Bus. Inst., Laramie, 1987. mem. fin. com. Ariz.-Sonora Dessert Mus., Tucson, 1992—, investment com. Tucson Community Found., 1992—. Mem. Assn. Investment Mgmt. and Rsch., Phoenix Soc. Fin. Analysts. Office: Bank of Am Ariz 6401 B N Campbell Tucson AZ 85718

PAYNE, JOHN HOWARD, television producer, director; b. Fukuoka, Japan, Aug. 13, 1951; came to U.S., 1951; s. John and Libby Lee (Small) P.; m. Elizabeth gigi Duis, Aug. 26, 1972; children: Nathan, Jessica. BS in Comm., U. No. Colo., 1974, MA in Ednl. Media, 1983. Audio/visual asst. U. No. Colo., Greeley, 1974-79, audio/visual dir., 1979—; faculty AIMS C.C., Greeley, 1981-82. Writer, producer, dir. (video) Olgame, Olgame, 1991, Art and Community, 1989, The Turn of Our Century, 1989. Bd. dirs. Greeley Boys Club, 1974; loaned exec. Wild County United Way, Greeley, 1988; mktg. comm. Wild County United Way, Greeley, 1990; bd. dirs. United Way of Weed County, 1991, 92. Mem. Assn. of Ednl. Comm. Technologists, No. Colo. Media Profls., Internat. TV Assn. (pres.-elect No. Colo. 1991-92, pres. No. Colo. 1992-93), Colo. Film Video Assn. Democrat. Home: 4023 W 14th St Greeley CO 80634 Office: U No Colo 130 Candelaria Greeley CO 80639

PAYNE, MICHAEL, state legislator; b. Ontario, Oreg., Apr. 5, 1969; s. Arthur and Shirley Payne. Student, Ea. Oregon State Coll., Oxford (Eng.) U.; BA in Polit. Sci. and Philosophy, Duke U., 1991. Legis. asst. State Rep. Mike Nelson, 1989, 91; mem. Oreg. Ho. Reps., 1993—. Democrat. Office: Oreg Ho Reps Ho Office 369 Salem OR 97310

PAYNE, WARREN GILBERT, advertising director; b. Portland, Oreg., Mar. 26, 1954; s. William G. and Charlene (Gilbert) P.; m. Reen Weiler, Oct. 14, 1973; children: Cara Charlene, Sean Weiler. AA, Highline Coll., 1975; BFA in Music, Seattle U., 1977. Profl. musician Seattle, 1971-78; sales asst. Klopman Mills div. Burlington Industries, L.A., 1978-79; advt./mktg. dir. The Weekly, Seattle, 1979-86; advt. dir. Inside The Seahawks Mag., Kirkland, Wash., 1986; assoc. pub. The Rocket Mag., Seattle, 1987-88; prin., creative dir. PD&G Direct Mktg., Seattle, 1988-89; advt. dir. Aldus Mag., Aldus Corp., Seattle, 1989-91; advt. mgr. Aldus Corp., Seattle, 1991-92; advt. mgr. Hard Copy Group Hewlett-Packard, San Diego, Calif., 1992; adj. faculty Seattle U., 1989-92. Contbr. articles to mags. Mem. Am. Mktg. Assn. (bd. dirs. Puget Sound chpt. 1989-90), Assn. Alternative News Weeklies (bd. dirs. 1981-84), Seattle Advt. Fedn. (bd. dirs. 1984-89, pres. 1987-88), Am. Advt. Fedn. (dist. XI gov. 1991—, Silver medal), Seattle Ad 2 Club (life). Office: Hewlett-Packard MS: GOU12 16399 W Bernardo Dr San Diego CA 92127

PAYTON, JAMES EDWARD, JR., engineer; b. Huntington Park, Calif., Oct. 11, 1957; s. James Edward and Norma Jean (Boydston) P.; m. Peri Melissa Simpson, Oct. 20, 1984; children: Shaun, Shane, Serena. BS in Environ. Sci., U. Calif., Riverside, 1979; BSME, Calif. State U., Fullerton, 1984, MSEE, 1992. Mgr. Straw Hat Pizza, Corona, Calif., 1974-80; applications engr. L.A. Water Treatment, City of Industry, Calif., 1980-81; mem. tech. staff Rockwell Internat. Autonetics Strategic Systems Div., Anaheim, Calif., 1981—. Mem. Norco (Calif.) Elem. PTA, 1987—; coach Norco Little League, 1989, 90. Lt. (j.g.) USNR, 1988—. Named Outstanding Young Man of Am., 1989. Mem. Naval Res. Officers Assn. Home: 950 3d St Norco CA 91760

PEACH, PHILIP RAY, association executive; b. Chgo., June 14, 1956; s. Stanley Willard and Elna (Brown) P. BS in Polit. Sci., Oreg. State U., 1979. Mem. ops. mgmt. staff Merrill Lynch, Portland, 1982; campaign mgr. Howe for Senate, Portland, 1982; chief asst. Eugene D. Timms, State Senator, Salem, Oreg., 1983; fin. dir. Moshofsky for Congress, Portland, 1984; dir. govt. affairs Oreg. Lodging Assn., Portland, 1984-87, exec. dir., 1987—; exec. dir. Travel Industry Coun. Oreg., Portland, 1987—. Editor: Oregon Innkeeper's Manual, 1990; contbr. articles to profl. publs. Bd. dirs. Portland-Oreg. Visitors Assn., 1990—; mem. hospitality com. Mt. Hood C.C., Gresham, Oreg., 1987—, Portland C.C., 1987-92, So. Oreg. State U., 1992—; mem. precinct com. Oreg. Rep. Com., 1979—. Recipient Outstanding Membership award Am. Hotel and Motel Assn., 1990, 92. Mem. Am. Soc. Assn. Execs. (Excellence in Membership award 1990, Excellence in Edn. award 1991), Oreg. Soc. Assn. Execs. (Mgmt. Excellence award 1991), Internat. Soc. Hotel Assn. Execs. (exec. com. 1987—, sec. 1992—). Baptist. Office: Oreg Lodging Assn 12724 SE Stark St Portland OR 97233

PEACOCK, RICHARD BECK, film educator, writer; b. Detroit, Apr. 18, 1933; s. E. J. and Mildred (Beck) P.; children: Jerome, Martin, Zeke, Avia; m. Carol Pharo, Dec. 3, 1987. BA, U. Windsor, Ont., Can., 1961; MA, Wayne State U., 1964; postgrad., Praestegaard Film Sch., Denmark, 1972-73. Instr. English U. San Diego, 1964-66; assoc. prof. film Palomar Coll., San Marcos, Calif., 1966—, chmn. communications dept., 1990—; program dir. N. San Diego Film Series, San Marcos, 1970-90. Author: Learning to Leave, 1983, rev. edit., 1993, Art of Moviemaking, 1993; contbr. articles to mags. Cand. state assembly Calif. 42d dist. Peace and Freedom Party, 1970. Sgt. USMC, 1953-56, Korea. Mem. Univ. Film Assn., Soc. Cinema Studies. Home: 3152 Levante Carlsbad CA 92009 Office: Palomar Coll Dept Communications 1140 W Mission Rd San Marcos CA 92069-1415

PEARCE, DRUE, state legislator; b. Fairfield, Ill., Apr. 2, 1951; d. H. Phil and Julia Detroy (Bannister) P. AB, Ind. U., 1973; MPA, Howard U., 1984. Sch. tchr. Clark County, Ind., 1973-74; curator Louisville Zoo, 1974-77; dir. Summerscene, Louisville, 1974-77; asst. v.p. Alaska Nat. Bank of the North, 1977-82; legis. aide to Alaska State Rep. John Ringstad, 1983; mem. Alaska Ho. of Reps., 1984-88; state senator Alaska Senate, 1988—. Mem. Alaska Resource Devel. Coun., Alaska Women's Polit. Caucus. Mem. DAR, Alaska C. of C. Republican. Home: 6035 Tanaina Dr Anchorage AK 99502-1832 Office: Office of the State Senate 3111 C St # 535 Anchorage AK 99503

PEARCE, JANICE, health sciences educator; b. Salt Lake City, Aug. 8, 1931; d. Kelly Bradford and Thyra (Morgan) P. BS in Physical Edn., U. Utah, 1952; MS in Physical Edn., Wash. State U., 1959; postgrad., Stanford U., 1966-67; PhD in Health Scis., U. Utah, 1974. Tchr. Arrowview Jr. High., San Bernardino, 1952-53, Olympus High Sch., Salt Lake City, 1953-56; teaching asst. Wash. State U., Pullman, 1956-57; prof. health edn. Utah State U., Logan, 1957-92, instr., 1992—; health internship in Israel program

Brigham Young U., 1985, 86; Utah coord. S.W. Regional Ctr. for Drug-Free Schs. and Communities, 1989; cons. Mill Hollow Workshop for Health Edn., Utah State Office of Edn., 1981, Sci. and Health Conf., Colo. Sch. Health Coun., Estes Park, 1983; presenter numerous state, regional and nat. conf. papers on health edn. Mem. Logan Mcpl. Coun., 1990—, chmn. 1992; bd. trustees U. Utah Sch. on Alcoholism and Other Drug Dependencies, 1987-90, vice chmn. 1988, 89, 90, state policy bd. on substance abuse, 1976-91; mem. adv. com. to Senator Orrin Hatch, 1987-91; trustee Cache Valley Health Care Found., 1977-81; vice chmn. Bear River Assn. of Govt.'s Human Resources Adv. Bd., 1982-88; pub. edn. chmn. Utah Cancer Soc., Cache County chpt., 1977-79; bd. dirs. Hospice of Cache Valley, 1979-81; mem. Logan Transit Bd., 1991—; active Task Force Cache County 2010, 1992-93. Fellow Am. Sch. Health Assn. (v.p. 1980-81, pres. elect 1981-82, pres. 1982-83, Disting. Svc. award 1980); mem. ASCD, Assn. for Advancement of Health Edn., Am. Alliance for Health, Physical Edn., Recreation and Dance, Nat. Assn. Parliamentarians, Utah Assn. for Health, Physical Edn., Recreation and Dance, Utah Acad. of Arts, Scis. and Letters, Alpha Lambda Delta, Nat. Fedn. Bus. and Profl. Women (nat. found. chmn. 1983-84, 84-85, pres. Utah br. 1981-82). Mem. LDS Ch. Home: 727 N 150 W Logan UT 84321-3269

PEARCE, ROBERT WAYNE, university adminstrator, education educator; b. Enid, Okla., May 9, 1944; s. Howard K. and Pearl V. (Metz) P.; m. Marie F. Knopp, May 29, 1965; children: Kimberly, Robert Wayne II, Eric, John, Gretchen. BS in Bus., Phillips U., Enid, 1965, EdM, 1967; EdD, Okla. State U., 1972. Acct. Pan Am. Petroleum Co., Tulsa, 1965-66; mgmt. trainee Sears, Roebuck and Co., Enid, 1966-67; registrar, admissions dir., asst. prof. Phillips U., 1967-69; asst. to the pres. Kans. Newman Coll., Wichita, 1969-77; v.p. adminstrn. and fin. So. Ark. U., Magnolia, 1977-87, v.p. acad. affairs, 1987-88; v.p. fin. svcs., prof. edn. Idaho State U., Pocatello, 1988—; cons. in field. Chmn. Ark. Commn. on Health Care Cost Effectiveness, Little Rock, 1980-84, Cert. Need Appeals Commn., Little Rock, 1986-88; mem., chmn. various ch. couns., Enid, Wichita, Magnolia, Ark., 1966-88; mem. Ark. Fire Tng. Adv. Bd., Camden, 1986-88. Named Outstanding Young Educator, Jr. C. of C., Ark., 1980. Mem. Nat. Assn. Coll. and Univ. Bus. Officers, Phi Kappa Phi. Roman Catholic. Home: 1205 College Rd Pocatello ID 83204-5021 Office: Idaho State U Pocatello ID 83209

PEARCE, RUTH ANNE, retired elementary educator; b. Fayetteville, N.C., Oct. 26, 1942; d. Cecil Merle and Annie Margaret (Blackwelder) Lamb; m. William Gordon Pearce, July 8, 1969. BS in Edn., Ill. State U., 1964; M in Creative Arts, Lesley Coll., 1987. Cert. elem. educator, Colo. Tchr. Sch. Dist. 61, Decatur, Ill., 1964-65; tchr. Sch. Dist. 60, Pueblo, Colo., 1965-91, ret., 1992; owner Pueblo Mdse. Spltys., 1980-92. Sec. Pueblo Civic Ballet Bd., 1977-80; sec., vice chair Colo. Edn. Polit. Action Com., Denver, 1976-80; del. Rep. Cen. Com., Pueblo, 1972-90; deacon Cen. Christian Ch. Mem. Pueblo Edn. Assn. (v.p. 198--82, 83-84, contract negotiator 1980-90, curriculum coun. 1974-86), Colo. Edn. Assn. (del. 1976-87), NEA (del. 1981, 82), Shriners Ladies (2d v.p.), Daus. of Nile. Home: 9 Knightsbridge Pl Pueblo CO 81001

PEARL, ELLIOT DAVID, lawyer; b. L.A., Aug. 17, 1932; s. John and Anna Marion (Lehrfeld) P.; m. Arlene Joan Adelberg, Sept. 30, 1956; children: Sharon Pearl Jacobvitz, Robin Pearl Fine, Jeffrey. BA, U. Calif., Berkeley, 1953, JD, 1956. Bar: Calif., U.S. Dist. Ct. (so. dist.) Calif. Atty. criminal div. U.S. Dept. Justice, Washington, 1956; ptnr. Malone, Dennis, Schotty & Pearl, Sacramento, 1960-75; pres. Elliot D. Pearl, P.C., Sacramento, 1975—; judge pro tempore Sacramento Superior Ct., 1982—; presenter at legal symposia. Contbr. to Calif. Law Rev.; contbr. articles to profl. publs. Trustee Sacramento Jewish Fedn., 1960-78, Mosaic Law Synagogue, Sacramento, 1960—; co-chair Young Citizens for Johnson, Sacramento County, 1964. Capt. JAGC USAF, 1957-60. Mem. Calif. Lawyers Assn. (cert. trial lawyer), Calif. State Bar, Sacramento County Bar Assn., Calif. Assn. Trial Lawyers. Democrat. Jewish. Office: Elliot D Pearl PC 3500 American River Dr Sacramento CA 95864

PEARSALL, THOMAS PERINE, educator; b. Richmond, Va., Nov. 2, 1945. BEng, Dartmouth Coll., 1968; MSc in Solid-State Physics, U. London, 1970; PhD in Applied Physics, Cornell U., 1973. With Bell Labs., Holmdel, N.J., 1973-76, Laboratoire Central de Recherches, Thomson/CSF, Orsay, France, 1976-80; program mgr. optical electronics systems Bell Labs., Murray Hill, N.J., 1980—, mgr. European mktg. for optical communications, 1986-88, mgr. internat. bus. devel. Far East, 1988-89; Boeing chair semiconductor electronics U. Washington, Seattle, 1989—; dir. Ctr. for Compound Semicondr. Tech. Wash. Tech. Ctr., Seattle. Patentee GaInAsP long wave LED, 1976; long-wavelength GaInAs photodiode, 1978; noise-free, high temperature photodetector, 1980; developer long distance optical fiber telecommunications. Recipient Design News award; NSF Fellow to India, 1983-87; James B. Reynolds fellow. Office: U Wash Dept Elec Engring Seattle WA 98195

PEARSON, BELINDA KEMP, economist, consultant; b. Kansas City, Mo., Apr. 14, 1931; d. William Ewing and Margaret Norton (Johnson) Kemp; m. Carl Erik Pearson, Sept. 15, 1953; children: Erik, Frederick, Margaret. BA, Wellesley Coll., 1952; MA, Tufts U., 1954, PhD, 1958. Rsch. asst. Harvard U., Cambridge, Mass., 1954-55; instr. econs. Suffolk U., Boston, 1956-59; lectr. econs., Wellesley Coll., Mass., 1964-65; econ. analyst, asst. econs. Seafirst Bank, Seattle, 1966-79, v.p., 1974-85; chief economist, 1979-85; dir. Lektor, Inc., Bellevue, Wash., 1984—, pres., 1987—; mem. Wash. Gov's Coun. Econ. Advisors, Olympia, 1979—; dir. Pacific N.W. Regional Econ. Conf., 1979—, chair, Seattle Conf., 1987; mem. Western Blue Chip Econ. Forecast Panel, 1988—; mem. bd. regents Wash. State U., Pullman, 1985-90, v.p., 1988-90, Regents Found. Investment Com. of Wash. State U., 1987-91; mem. Wash. State Libr. Commn., Olympia, 1976-84. Fulbright scholar London Sch. Econs., 1952-53. Mem. Am. Econ. Assn., Nat. Assn. Bus. Economists (chmn. arrangements 1982 ann. meeting), Seattle Economists Club (pres. 1973-74), Mcpl. League, City Club (Seattle) (chmn. reports com. 1986-88), pres. LWV, Lake Wash. East, 1993—. Office: Lektor Inc PO Box 312 Medina WA 98039-0312

PEARSON, CLAUDE MEREDITH, legal consultant; b. Hudson, Wyo., Dec. 20, 1921; s. Claude Meredith and Golda May (King) P.; m. Helen Lucille Adams, Feb. 1, 1947; children: Susan Mae Pearson-Davis, Marcia Kay Pearson Vaughan. BA, Jamestown Coll., 1943; JD, U. Mich., 1948. Bar: Wash. 1949, U.S. Dist. Ct. (we. dist.) Wash., 1950. Ptnr. Pearson & Anderson, Tacoma, 1946-52, Pearson Anderson & Pearson, Tacoma, 1953-60, Davies Pearson & Anderson, Tacoma, 1960-72; shareholder Davies Pearson P.C., Tacoma, 1972-91, legal cons., 1991—; chair bus. sect. Wash. State Bar, Seattle, 1972, chair specialization bd., 1985-87, chair alternate dispute resolution sect., 1990. Pres. United Good Neighbor Fund, Tacoma, 1964. With USNR, 1942-73, capt. 1966. Mem. Mich. Alumni Assn. (past dir.-at-large, 1st v.p., citation 1984), Vashon Golf and Country Club. Home: 3419 N 24th St Tacoma WA 98406 Office: Davies Pearson PC 920 Fawcett Tacoma WA 98402

PEARSON, ERWIN GALE, educator, consultant; b. McMinnville, Oreg., July 19, 1932; s. Emil Walburg and Clarice Francis (Hurner) P.; m. Evelyn May Kohler, Sept. 4, 1954 (div. 1966); children: Julie, Deborah, Timothy, Cheri; m. Marianne R. Mackay, Jan. 8, 1982; children: Jennifer, Kyle. BS, Oreg. State U., Corvallis, 1954, MS, 1979; DVM, Cornell U., 1958. Assoc. vet. H.M. Adams, Astoria, Oreg., 1960-61, G.E. Schwenke, Woodburn, Oreg., 1961-65; vet. Santiam Vet. Clinic, 1965-78; asst. prof. vet. Cornell U., Ithaca, N.Y., 1979-82; assoc. prof. vet. Oreg. State U., 1982-88, prof. vet., 1988—. Mem. editorial bd. Compendium on CE for Vets., 1982—, Cornell Vet., 1988-92; contbr. articles to profl. jours. Pres. Woodburn Jaycees, 1964, Morgan House Assn. Oreg., Eugene, 1968. 1st lt. U.S. Army, 1958-60. Named Key Man, Woodburn Jaycees, 1966. Mem. Am. Coll. Vet. Internal Medicine (diplomate), Am. Vets. Med. Assn., Williamtic Vet. Med. Assn. (pres. 1963). Republican. Baptist. Home: 34364 Iris Circle Philomath OR 97370-9005 Office: Oreg State U Coll Veterinary Medicine Corvallis OR 97331

PEARSON, FRAIN GARFIELD, communications educator; b. Richfield, Utah, Aug. 29, 1936; s. A.J. and Leola (James) P.; m. Laree B. Pearson, Sept. 15, 1959; children: Timothy, Russell, Michael, Mary Lee, Betsey, Jamie, Julie. BS, Brigham Young U., 1960; MS, U. Utah, 1967; PhD, U. Oreg., 1976. Tchr. Sevier Sch. Dist., Richfield, Utah, 1960-61; with Hercules Powder Co., Magna, Utah, 1961-64; prof. communications, dept. chmn. So. Utah U., Cedar City, Utah, 1966—; cons. in field. Author: Interactive Communication, 1982, Indian Head, 1993. Coach Boys Little League Football, Cedar City, Utah, 1972-80. With USNG, 1958-62. Mem. Western States Communication Assn., Speech Communications Assn. Office: So Utah U 350 W Center St Cedar City UT 84720-2473

PEARSON, GARY DEAN, dentist; b. Rockford, Ill., Dec. 25, 1952; s. Miles Addison and Pauline (Hammond) P.; m. Marcea Lou Schlensker, Dec. 4, 1981 (div. 1989); 1 child, Grant Addison. BS cum laude, Rockford Coll., 1974; DDS, U. Ill., Chgo., 1978. Lic. dentist, Ill., Mich., N.H., Wis., Ariz. Pvt. practice dentistry Rockton, Ill., 1978-93; group practice dentistry Tucson, 1993—. Recipient Gen. Assembly Scholarship, State of Ill., 1977. Mem. Am. Dental Assn., Ill. State Dental Soc., Winnebago County Dental Soc., U. Ill. Alumni Assn., Rockton C. of C., Phi Theta Kappa. Lutheran. Club: Rockford Coll. Alumni. Home: 5144 N Whitehurst Pl Tucson AZ 85715 Office: Dental-Net Inc 7202 E Rosewood Ste 150 Tucson AZ 85710

PEARSON, JOHN, mechanical engineer; b. Leyburn, Yorkshire, U.K., Apr. 24, 1923; came to U.S., 1930, naturalized, 1944; s. William and Nellie Pearson; m. Ruth Ann Billhardt, July 10, 1944; children—John, Armin, Roger. B.S.M.E., Northwestern U., 1949, M.S., 1951. Registered profl. engr., Calif. Rsch. engr. Naval Ordnance Test Sta., China Lake, Calif., 1951-55, head warhead rsch. br., 1955-58, head solid dynamics br., 1958-59, head detonation physics group, 1959-67; head detonation physics div. Naval Weapons Ctr., China Lake, Calif., 1967-83, sr. rsch. scientist, 1983—; cons., lectr. in field; founding mem. adv. bd. Ctr. for High Energy Forming, U. Denver; mem. bd. examiners Sambalpur U., India, 1982-83. Author: Explosive Working of Metals, 1963; Behavior of Metals Under Impulsive Loads, 1954; contbr. articles to profl. publs; patentee impulsive loading, explosives applications. Charter mem. Sr. Exec. Svc. U.S., 1979. With C.E., U.S. Army, 1943-46, ETO. Recipient L.T.E. Thompson medal, 1965, William B. McLean medal, 1979, Superior Civilian Svc. medal USN, 1984, Haskell G. Wilson award, 1985, cert. of recognition Sec. Navy, 1975, merit award Dept. Navy, 1979, cert. of commendation Sec. Navy, 1981, Career Svcs. award Sec. Navy, 1988, John A. Ulrich award Am. Def. Preparedness Assn., 1991; 1st disting. fellow award Naval Weapons Ctr., 1989. Fellow ASME; mem. Am. Soc. Metals, Am. Phys. Soc., N.Y. Acad. Scis., AIME, NSPE, Fed. Exec. League, Sigma Xi, Tau Beta Pi, Pi Tau Sigma, Triangle. Home and Office: PO Box 1390 858 N Primavera Rd Ridgecrest CA 93556

PEARSON, KEITH LAURENCE, environmental scientist; b. Chgo., Apr. 1, 1929; s. Victor R. and Ingeborg E. (Olson) P.; m. Ellen M. O'Dell, May 28, 1955; 1 child, Brian V. BA, Augustana Coll., 1951; MA, U. Ariz., 1965, PhD, 1969. Asst. prof. U. Wis., Superior, 1967-68; assoc. prof. No. Ariz. U., Flagstaff, 1968-76; environ. analyst Bur. Land Mgmt., Washington, 1976-78; environ. planner Bur. Land Mgmt., Phoenix, 1979—. Author: The Indian in American History, 1973; contbg. author: A Slice of Life, 1975; contbr. articles to profl. jours. Fellow Am. Anthropol. Assn.; mem. Soc. for Applied Anthropology. Democrat. Episcopalian. Home: 12634 N Rosewood Ave Phoenix AZ 85029-2125

PEARSON, LARRY LESTER, journalism educator, communication consultant; b. Sioux Falls, S.D., Sept. 27, 1942; s. Lester Loren and Lois Ursula (Cochran) P.; m. Alice Marie Simons, Sept. 15, 1979; children: Gregory Eric, Hillary Yvette, Andrew Todd. BA cum laude, U. Minn., 1964, PhD, 1990; MA, U. Wis., 1969. Newsman UPI, Mpls., 1962-63; newsman Daily American, Rome, Italy, 1964-65; instr. Journalism Sch., U. Wis., 1965-67; with Mpls. Tribune, 1967-85, wire editor, 1970-72, news editor, 1972-82; news editor Mpls. Star & Tribune, 1982; asst. prof. U. Alaska, Anchorage, 1985-92, assoc. prof., 1992—, dir. Ctr. for Info. Tech., 1990-92; spl. cons. to Alaska Ho. Com. on Telecomm., 1985-90. Mem. Internat. Communication Assn., Am. Soc. Newspaper Design, Assn. Edn. in Journalism and Mass Communication. Lutheran. Home: 2410 E 16th Ave Anchorage AK 99508-2906 Office: U Alaska Anchorage AK 99508

PEARSON, ROBERT ALLEN, optometrist; b. Scottsbluff, Nebr., Dec. 8, 1946; s. William Franklin and Hope Jacqueline (Williams) P.; m. Sue Ione Parmelee, Sept. 6, 1969. BS, BA, U. Wyo., 1970; OD, So. Calif. Coll. Optometry, 1986. Microbiologist State of Nev., Las Vegas, 1970-82; optometrist S.W. Vision, Las Vegas, 1982—. Mem. LIGA Internat. Inc., Santa Ana, Calif. 1992, Vision U.S.A., St. Louis, 1992. Mem. APHA, Am. Optometric Assn., Nev. Optometric Assn. (Optometrist of Yr. 1988)., Nev. State Bd. Optometry. Home: 3404 El Cortez Ave Las Vegas NV 89102 Office: SW Vision PO Box 15645 Las Vegas NV 89114

PEARSON, WALTER HOWARD, marine biologist, researcher; b. Troy, N.Y., Mar. 25, 1946; s. Howard Stevenson and Mazel Mott (Brownhill) P.; m.. Cynthia-Ruth Egan, June 16, 1972 (div. Oct. 1989); children: Kristin Turnbull, Jeffrey Mott; m. Terri L. Sumner, Nov. 28, 1992. BS in Biology, Bates Coll., 1967; MS in Biology, U. Alaska, 1970; PhD in Oceanography, Oreg. State U., 1977. Fishery biologist, rschr. Nat. Marine Fisheries Svc., Sandy Hook Lab., Highlands, N.J., 1975-78; sr. rsch. scientist Battelle Marine Rsch. Lab., Sequim, Wash., 1978-88, tech. group leader marine scis. lab., 1988-91, mgr. tech. devel. program, 1991—; tech. leader large multidisciplinary studies of oil spill effect. Contbr. articles on behavior of marine organisms and effects of pollution and human activity to jours. Sgt. U.S. Army, 1969-71. NSF grantee, 1967-69. Mem. Assn. Chemoreception Scis. (charter), AAAS, N.Y. Acad. Sci., Animal Behavior Soc., Crustacean Soc., Western Soc. Naturalists. Episcopalian. Home: PO Box 1858 Sequim WA 98382-1858 Office: Battelle Marine Scis Lab 439 W Sequim Bay Rd Sequim WA 98382-9099

PEARSON, WARREN THOMAS, surgeon; b. Burlington, Iowa, Dec. 8, 1929; s. George John and Elma Ann (Pollock) P.; m. Margaret Louise Kofoed, Sept. 5, 1965; children: George Maxwell, Ralph Warren. MD, U. Iowa, 1955. Diplomate Am. Bd. Surgery, Am. Bd. Thoracic Surgery. Intern Grasslands Hosp., Valhalla, N.Y., 1955-56; resident in gen. surgery Bronx (N.Y.) VA Hosp., 1956-60; resident in thoracic and cardiovascular surgery Walter Reed Army Hosp., Washington, 1963-65; fellow dept. cardiovascular surgery Upstate Med. Ctr., Syracuse, N.Y., 1960-61; instr. surgery NYU, N.Y.C., 1968-79; pvt. practice N.Y.C., 1968-79; asst. clin. prof. Mt. Sinai Coll. Medicine, CUNY, 1974-79; pvt. practice Encino, Calif., 1979-86; pvt. practice, Santa Monica, Calif., 1986—; clin. instr. cardiothoracic surgery UCLA, 1989—. Contbr. articles to med. jours. Maj. M.C., U.S. Army, 1961-67. Fellow ACS, Am. Coll. Chest Physicians, Am. Coll. Cardiology; mem. AMA, Soc. Thoracic Surgeons, N.Am. Soc. for Pacing and Electrophysiology, Internat. Soc. for Study Lung Cancer, Am. Thoracic Soc., Am. Heart Assn. (coun. on cardiovascular surgery), Pan-Am. Med. Assn., Calif. Med. Assn., N.Y. Acad. Medicine, N.Y. Acad. Scis., Los Angeles County Med. Assn., L.A. Trudeau Soc. Republican. Episcopalian. Home: 1701 Midvale Ave Los Angeles CA 90024 Office: 2021 Santa Monica Blvd Santa Monica CA 90404

PEASE, NICKOLAS ALLEN, science educator, basketball coach; b. Ione, Wash., Aug. 10, 1954; s. Edwin Drake and Viola Mae (Manley) P.; m. Jean Susan Rasmussen, June 10, 1979; 1 child, Trevor Allen. AA, Spokane Falls C.C., Spokane, Wash., 1974; BA in Edn., Ea. Wash. U., 1977. Cert. tchr., Wash. Tchr., coach Cusick (Wash.) Sch. Dist., 1977—. Mem. Wash. Edn. Assn., Wash. State Coaches Assn. (nominee state coach of yr. 1991), Cusick Edn. Assn. (chmn. negotiations 1989-90, Tchr. of Yr. 1984). Democrat. Home: 1201 Pease Rd Usk WA 99180

PEASLAND, BRUCE RANDALL, financial executive; b. Buffalo, N.Y., Mar. 24, 1945; s. Kenneth Arthur and Edith Grace (Bristow) P.; m. Debra Myers Peasland, June 13, 1981; children: Michael John, Timothy Scott, Amanda Jean. BS, U. So. Calif., 1971, MBA in Fin., 1978; JD, Western St. U., 1983. Price and cost analyst McDonnell Douglas Corp., Long Beach, Calif., 1966-70; cost mgr. The Gillette Co., Santa Monica, Calif., 1971-78; controller Lear Siegler Inc., Santa Ana, Calif., 1978-85, British Petroleum, Hitco, Newport Beach, Calif., 1986-87; v.p. fin., dir. Control Components Inc., Rancho Santa Margarita, Calif., 1987-90; chief fin. officer MacGillivray Freeman Films, Laguna Beach, Calif., 1990-91; exec. v.p., chief fin. officer Prevue Systems Corp., Irvine, Calif., 1992—. Youth advisor YMCA, Dana Point, Calif., 1985—. With USMC, 1963-69. Recipient of Mgr. of Yr. award Nat. Mgmt. Assn., 1984. Fellow U. So. Calif. MBA Assn.; mem. Nat. Assn. of Accts., Nat. Mgmt. Assn. (dir. 1978-85), U. So. Calif. Trojan Club, U. So. Calif. Alumni Club. Republican. Episcopalian. Home: 25211 Yacht Dr Dana Point CA 92629-1439 Office: Prevue Systems Corp 2102 Business Center Dr Irvine CA 92715-9999

PECCEI, ROBERTO DANIELE, physicist, educator; b. Torino, Italy, Jan. 6, 1942; came to U.S., 1958; s. Aurelio Guido and Annetta (Migliorero) P.; m. Jocelyn Scott, June 10, 1962; children: Alessandra, Aurelio. BS, MIT, 1962, PhD, 1969; MS, NYU, 1964. Asst. prof. physics Stanford (Calif.) U., 1971-78; mem. staff Max Planck Inst., Munich, Fed. Republic Germany, 1978-84; head theory group Deutsche Electron Synchrotron, Hamburg, Fed. Republic Germany, 1984-88; prof. dept. physics UCLA, 1988—, chmn. dept., 1989; Schroedinger prof. U. Vienna, Austria, 1984; mem. sci. policy com. Stanford Linear Accelerator Ctr., 1990—, physics adv. com. Fermi Lab., Batavia, Ill., 1990—; E. Segré prof. Tel Aviv U., Israel, 1992. Fellow Am. Phys. Soc.; mem. Club of Rome. Office: UCLA Dept Physics 405 Hilgard Ave Los Angeles CA 90024-1301

PECHMANN, CORNELIA ANN RACHEL, marketing professional; b. Binghamton, N.Y., May 22, 1959; d. Karl and Helen (Guley) P. BA, Bucknell U., 1981; MS, Vanderbilt U., 1985, MBA, 1985, PhD in Mgmt., 1988. Asst. prof. mktg. Calif. State U., Fullerton, 1986-88, U. Calif., Irvine, 1988—; rsch. asst. Vanderbilt Diabetes Rsch. & Tng. Ctr., Nashville, 1982-83, Neighborhood Housing Svcs., Nashville, 1982-83, Nashville Cons. Group, 1984-86. Contbr. articles to profl. jours. Recipient Alden G. Clayton Doctoral Dissentation award Mktg. Science Inst., 1987. Mem. Assn. for Consumer Rsch., Am. Mktg. Assn., Am. Acad. of Advt., Soc. for Consumer Psychol., Phi Beta Kappa, Beta Gamma Sigma. Democrat. Office: U Calif Grad Sch Mgmt Irvine CA 92717

PECHTEL, CURTIS THEODORE, psychology educator; b. Milw., June 30, 1920; s. William Christian and Myrtle (Ruby) P.; m. Jeanne DeBarr, June 29, 1948; 1 child, Loren Eric. BA, Lewis & Clark Coll., 1941; MA, U. Wis., 1947; PhD, Northwestern U., 1951. Rsch. assoc. Med. Sch. Northwestern U., Chgo., 1947-60; assoc. prof. Chgo. Med. Sch., 1964-68; cons. Mt. Sinai Hosp., Milw., 1964-68; assoc. prof. Loop Community Coll., Chgo., 1968; prof. Glendale (Ariz.) Community Coll., 1968-90, ret., 1990. Contbr. articles to profl. jours. Candidate state legis. and congress, Milw., 1964-66; county rep. Rep. Party, Milw., 1964-68; pres. Milw. Local Community Coun., 1963-67. Home and Office: 4224 W Lawrence Ln Phoenix AZ 85051-3666

PECK, CHARLES S., realty company executive; b. Glen Cove, N.Y., Dec. 10, 1947; s. William H. and Polly Peck; m. Shawn Hayward; children: Christopher S., William Taylor, Stephen C. BA, Yale U., 1969; MBA in Fin., Harvard U., 1974. Treas. WED Enterprises; exec. v.p., chief fin. officer Cushman Realty Corp., L.A., 1978—; also chmn. Cushman Investment and Devel. Corp., pres., 1984—. Dir. Am. Found. for Internat. Mountaineering & Rsch.; active L.A. Music Ctr., U.S. Olympic Com. Lt. USN, 1969-72. Mem. Urban Land Inst., Harvard Bus. Ch. Alumni Assn., Valley Hunt Club, Jonathan Club. Republican. Home: 776 S Orange Grove Blvd Apt 4 Pasadena CA 91105-1775 Office: Cushman Realty Corp 601 S Figueroa St 47th Fl Los Angeles CA 90017-5752

PECK, DONALD HARVEY, chiropractor; b. Oak Park, Ill., July 18, 1945; s. Donald Ray and Dorothy Sylvia (LaFlamme) P.; m. Mary Evelyn Lamb, June 15, 1964 (div. 1971); children: Donald Lee, Nancy Ellen; m. Cheryl Jean Cox, July 7, 1973; children: Richard Krom Watkins Jr., Bradley Alan, Steven Edward. AA, Mt. San Antonio Coll., 1966; DC, Palmer Coll. of Chiropractic, 1970. Diplomate Nat. Bd. Chiropractic Examiners. Engring. technician Besteel Corp., Industry, Calif., 1965-66, City of Ontario, Calif., 1966-67; supr. Mercy Hosp., Davenport, Iowa, 1967-70; pvt. practice chiropractor San Bernardino and Redlands, Calif., 1971-81; pvt. practice Cottonwood, Ariz., 1981—; instr. Yavapai Coll. Clarkdale, Ariz., 1982-88. Scoutmaster Calif. Inland Empire coun. Boy Scouts Am., 1974-81, Grand Canyon coun. Boy Scouts Am., 1981—; active Am. Youth Soccer Orgn., Cottonwood, 1977-92, regional commr., 1984-88; instr. trainer, chief instr. Ariz. Game and Fish Dept., Cottonwood, 1983—. Recipient Award of Merit Boy Scouts Am., 1980, Silver Beaver award, 1988; named Vol. of Yr. Verde Valley C. of C., 1987. Mem. Kiwanis (bd. dirs. 1985-87), Order of Arrow (chpt. adviser, vigil honor mem., Cert. Merit Boy Scout Am. Nat. Ct. of Honor 1990). Republican. Office: 703 S Main St Cottonwood AZ 86326-4615

PECK, ELLIE ENRIQUEZ, consultant, retired state administrator; b. Sacramento, Oct. 21, 1934; d. Rafael Enriquez and Eloisa Garcia Rivera; m. Raymond Charles Peck, Sept. 5, 1957; children: Reginaldo, Enrico, Francisca Guerrero, Teresa, Linda, Margaret, Raymond Charles, Christina. Student polit. sci. Sacramento State U., 1974. Tng. services coord. Calif. Div. Hwys., Sacramento, 1963-67; tech. and mgmt. cons., Sacramento, 1968-78; expert examiner Calif. Pers. Bd., 1976-78; tng. cons. Calif. Pers. Devel. Ctr., Sacramento, 1978; spl. cons. Calif. Commn. on Fair Employment and Housing, 1978; community svcs. rep. U.S. Bur. of Census, No. Calif. counties, 1978-80; spl. cons. Calif. Dept. Consumer Affairs, Sacramento, 1980-83, project dir. Golden State Sr. Discount Program, 1980-83; dir. spl. programs for Calif. Lt. Gov., 1983-90, ret., 1990; pvt. cons., 1990—. Author Calif. Dept. Consumer Affairs publ., 1981, U.S. Office Consumer Affairs publ., 1982. Bd. dirs Sacramento/Sierra Am. Diabetes Assn., 1989-90. Author: Diabetes and Ethnic Minorities: A Community at Risk. Trustee, Stanford Settlement, Inc., Sacramento, 1975-79; bd. dirs. Sacramento Emergency Housing Ctr., 1974-77, Sacramento Community Svcs. Planning Coun., 1987-90, Calif. Advs. for Nursing Home Reform, 1990—, Calif. Legis. Coun. for Older Ams., 1990-91; v.p. Comision Femenil Nacional, Inc., 1987-90; del. Dem. Nat. Conv., 1976; mem. exec. bd. Calif. Dem. Cen. Com., 1977-89; chairperson ethnic minority task force Am. Diabetes Assn., 1988-90; steering com. Calif. Self-Esteem Task Force Minority Coalition, 1990-93. Recipient numerous awards including Outstanding Community Svc. award Comuicaciones Unidos de Norte Atzlan, 1975, 77, Outstanding Svc. award, Chicano/Hispanic Dem. Caucus, 1979, Vol. Svc. award Calif. Human Devel. Corp., 1981, Dem. of Yr. award Sacramento County Dem. Com., 1987, Outstanding Advocate award Calif. Sr. Legis., 1988, 89, Calif. Assn. of Home for Aging, Advocacy award, 1989, Resolution of Advocacy award, League Latin-Ams. Citizens, 1989, Meritorious Svc. to Hispanic Community award Comite Patriotico, 1989, Meritorious Svc. Resolution award Lt. Gov. of Calif., 1989, Cert. Recognition award Sacramento County Human Rights Commn., 1991. Mem. Hispanic C. of C., CongressCalif. Srs., Sacramento Gray Panthers, Hispanic Dem. Club Sacramento County (v.p. 1982-83). Home and Office: 2667 Coleman Way Sacramento CA 95818-4459

PECK, ERNEST JAMES, JR., college dean; b. Port Arthur, Tex., July 26, 1941; s. Ernest James and Karlton Maudean (Luttrell) P.; divorced; children: David Karl, John Walter. BA in Biology with honors, Rice U., 1963, PhD in Biochemistry, 1966. Rsch. assoc. Purdue U., West Lafayette, Ind., 1966-68, asst. prof., 1968-73; asst. prof. Baylor Coll. Medicine, Houston, 1973-74, assoc. prof., 1974-80, prof., 1980-82; prof., chmn. biochemistry Sch. Med. Sci., U. Ark., Little Rock, 1982-89; dean sci. and math. U. Nev., Las Vegas, 1989—; adj. prof. U. Ark., Pine Bluff, 1988-89; program dir. NSF, Washington, 1988-89, advisor, 1979—; mem. editorial bd. Jour. Neurosci. Rsch., N.Y.C., 1982—. Co-author: Female Sex Steroids, 1979, Brain Peptides, 1979. Fellow NSF, 1962, NIH, 1964-66; recipient Rsch. Career Devel. award NIH, NICHD, 1975-80. Fellow AAAS; mem. Am. Chem. Soc., Am. Soc. Biochemistry and Molecular Biology, Am. Soc. Neurochemistry, Endocrine Soc., Am. Soc. Zoologists, Sigma Xi. Office: Univ Nev Las Vegas Box 454001 4505 S Maryland Pkwy Las Vegas NV 89154-4001

PECK, GAILLARD RAY, JR., aerospace business and healthcare consultant; b. San Antonio, Oct. 31, 1940; s. Gaillard Ray and Lois (Manning) P.; m. Jean Adair Hilger, Dec. 23, 1962 (div. Oct. 1969); children: Gaillard III, Katherine Adair; m. Peggy Ann Lundt, July 3, 1975; children: Jennifer Caroline, Elizabeth Ann. BS, Air Force Acad., 1962; MA, Cen. Mich. U., 1976; MBA, U. Nev. Las Vegas, 1990. Lic. comml. pilot, flight instr. Commd. 2d lt. USAF, 1962, advanced through grades to col., 1983, ret., 1988, air force instr. pilot, fighter pilot, 1963-72; instr. Fighter Weapons Sch. USAF, Nellis AFB, 1972-75; fighter tactics officer Pentagon, Washington, 1975-78; aggressor pilot, comdr. 4477th Test & Evaluation Squadron, Nellis AFB, Nev., 1978-80; mil. advisor Royal Saudi Air Force, Saudi Arabia,

1980-82; student Nat. War Coll., Washington, 1982-83; dir. ops., vice comdr. Kadena Air Base, Japan, 1983-85; wing comdr. Zweibrucken Air Base, Germany, 1985-87; dep. dir. Aerospace Safety directorate USAF, Norton AFB, Calif., 1987-88; rsch. asst. U. Nev., Las Vegas, 1988-90; mktg. cons. Ctr. for Bus. & Econ. Rsch. U. Nev., Las Vegas, 1990; adminstr. Lung Ctr. of Nev., Las Vegas, 1991-93; cons. Las Vegas, 1993—. Author: The Enemy, 1973. Recipient Silver Star, Legion of Merit, DFC (3), Air medal. Mem. Phi Kappa Phi Nat. Honor Soc., Order of Daedalians, Red River Fighter Pilots Assn., Air Force Assn., Ky. Col., U. Nev. Las Vegas and Air Force Acad. Alumni Assn., The Ret. Officers Assn. Home: 1775 Sheree Cir Las Vegas NV 89119-2716

PECK, JOHN THOMAS, newspaper editor; b. Tucson, June 6, 1950; s. George Thomas and Treva Lorraine (Myers) P. Student in philosophy, Colo. Coll., 1968-71; student, U. Ariz., 1973—. Theater/dance writer, critic Ariz. Daily Star, Tucson, 1974-80, news desk utility editor, 1980-83, arts editor, 1984-85, features editor, 1985-86, mng. editor, 1987—; program coord. Nat. Critics Inst./Nat. Playwrights Conf., Waterford, Conn., 1975, 76, 77; adj. prof. in journalism U. Ariz., Tucson, 1981, 89; cons. in field. Contbr. articles, columns to profl. publs. Mem. grante com. Tucson Community Found., 1986—; bd. dirs. Friends of Tucson Libr., 1988—, Sportsman's Fund, Tucson, 1985-88; mem. Primavera Found., Tucson, 1989—. Critic fellow Nat. Cortex Inst., 1974, Am. Dance Festival, 1975; fellow NEH, 1978, Western States Arts Found. Mem. Parke County Hist. Co., Monzú Soc., Anzona Press Club, Old Pueblo Club. Democrat. Home: 239 W Franklin St Tucson AZ 85701-1021 Office: Ariz Daily Star 4850 S Park Ave PO Box 26807 Tucson AZ 85714

PECK, PAUL LACHLAN, minister; b. Glens Falls, N.Y., Sept. 11, 1928; s. Paul Lee and Caroline Jeannette (Stanton) P.; children: Paul Barrett, Kathryn Elizabeth Peck Kadick. BS, U. Conn., 1952; ThD, Bernadean U., 1976; MEd, Westfield State Coll., 1983. Ordained to ministry Truth Ctr., 1972. With Proctor and Gamble Co., Watertown, N.Y., 1956-60; dir. deferred giving programs Syracuse (N.Y.) U., 1960-68, v.p., 1968-70; v.p. Fairleigh-Dickinson U., N.J., 1970-71, Manhattan Coll., Bronx, N.Y., 1971-75; founder, pastor Arete' Truth Ctr., San Diego, 1975—. Author: Footsteps Along the Path, 1978, Inherit the Kingdom, 1978, Milestones of the Way, 1978, Freeway to Health, 1980, Freeway to Work and Wealth, 1981, Freeway to Human Love, 1982, Freeway to Personal Growth, 1982, Your Dreams Count, 1990, Heroic Love Poems, 1990. Bd. dirs. Girl Scouts U.S.A., Syracuse, 1967-70; trustee, bd. dirs. Erickson Ednl. Found., 1970-75; vol. chaplain Auburn (N.Y.) State Prison, 1967-68; mem. chaplains' coun. Syracuse U., 1960-70; co-founder suicide and drug abuse prevention program Syracuse U., 1968-71, Fairleigh-Dickinson U., 1970-71, Manhattan Coll., 1971-75. Staff sgt. USNG, 1947-50. Mem. Internat. New Thought Alliance, SAR, Rotary, Knights of Malta (svc. award 1973), Masons, Shriners, Spiritual Frontiers Fellowship. Home and Office: 6996 Camino Revueltos San Diego CA 92111-7642

PECK, RAYMOND CHARLES, SR., driver and traffic safety research specialist; b. Sacramento, Nov. 18, 1937; s. Emory Earl and Margaret Helen (Fiebiger) P.; m. Ellie Ruth Enriquez, Sept. 5, 1957; children: Teresa M. Peck Montijo, Linda M. Peck Heisler, Margaret H. Peck Henley, Raymond C., Christina M. BA in Exptl. Psychology, Calif. State U., Sacramento, 1961, MA in Exptl. Psychology, 1968. Jr. rsch. tech. Calif. Dept. Motor Vehicles, Sacramento, 1962-63, asst. social rsch. analyst, 1963-64, staff rsch. analyst, 1967-71, sr. rsch. analyst, program mgr., 1971-80, rsch. program specialist II, 1980, acting, chief rsch., 1980-81, rsch. program specialist II, 1981-84, chief of rsch., 1984—; cons. to Computing and Software, Inc., Mentoris Co., Sims & Assocs., Pub. Systems, Inc., Planning Rsch. Corp., Nat. Pub. Svcs. Rsch. Inst., Dunlap & Assocs., Sacramento Safety Council, Nat. Safety Council, Boston U., Sch. Pub. Health, Vt. Alcohol Rsch. Ctr., Ctr. for Disease Control, Nat. Inst. Health, Miss. State U. Chmn. com. on operator regulation Transportation Rsch. Bd., Nat. Acad. Scis., 1976-82; past mem. editorial adv. bd. Accident Analysis and Prevention, Traffic Safety Evaluation Rsch. Review; mem. editorial bd. Jour Safety Research, Alcohol, Drugs and Driving; contbr. articles to profl. jours. Recipient Met. Life award of Hon., Nat. Safety Council, 1970, Met. Life Cert. of Commendation, 1972, A.R. Lauer award Human Factor Soc., 1981, award of Hon., award of Merit Traffic Safety Evaluation Rsch. Rev., 1983. Mem. Am. Statis. Assn., Am. Assn., Assn. Automotive Medicine, Am. Pub. Health Assn. Democrat. Home: 2667 Coleman Way Sacramento CA 95818-4459 Office: Calif Dept Motor Vehicles 2415 First Ave Sacramento CA 95818

PECK, RICHARD EARL, academic administrator, playwright, novelist; b. Milw., Aug. 3, 1936; s. Earl Mason and Mary Amanda (Fry) P.; m. Donna Joy Krippner, Aug. 13, 1960; children: Mason, Laura. AB magna cum laude, Carroll Coll., Waukesha, Wis., 1961; MS, U. Wis., 1962, PhD, 1964. Asst. prof. U. Va., Charlottesville, 1964-67; assoc. dean, prof. Temple U., Phila., 1967-84; dean arts and scis. U. Ala., 1984-88; provost, v.p. academic affairs Ariz. State U., Tempe, 1988-89, interim pres., 1989-90; pres. U. N.Mex., Albuquerque, 1990—. Editor: Poems/Nathaniel Hawthorne, 1967, Poems/Floyd Stovall, 1967; author: (books) Final Solution, 1973 (nominated for John W. Campbell award as Best Sci. Fiction Novel of 1973 by Sci. Fiction Rsch. Assn.), Something for Joey, 1978, Passing Through, 1982, (plays) Sarah Bernhardt and the Bank, 1972, Don't Trip over the Money Pail, 1976, The Cubs Are in fourth Place and Fading, 1977, Phonecall, 1978, Bathnight, 1978, Prodigal Father, 1978, Lovers, Wives and Tennis Players, 1979, Curtains, 1980, A Party for Wally Pruett, 1982, Allergy Tests, 1982, Your Place or Mine, 1987, (films) Starting over Again, 1982, What Tangled Webs, 1974, Tutte le Strade Portanno a Roma, 1974, Il Diritto, 1974; contr. numerous scholarly articles to lit. jours., book revs., travel articles and humor columns to newspapers and mags., papers to univ. orgns. and witers' confs. Bd. dirs. East Valley Partnership (Econ. Devel. Orgn.), Sci. and Tech., Samaritan Health Svcs.; gubernatorial appointee, bd. dirs. Ala. Humanities Found.; mem. Nat. Found. for Post-Secondary Edn.; bd. dirs. Phila. Alliance for Teaching Humanities in the Schs., Dela. Valley Faculty Exch.; adv. bd. Ea. Pa. Theater Coun.; chmn. Temple U. Bicentennial Festival of Am. Arts, 1976; mem. Univ. Negotiating Team in re: Temple-AAUP faculty contract. Capt. USMC, 1954-59. Recipient Whitman Pub. scholarship, 1959-63, Woodrow Wilson fellowship, 1961-62, Knapp Found. fellowship, 1962-63, C. Brooks Fry award Theater Americana, Altadena, Calif., 1979. Mem. MLA, Northeast MLA. Conf. Univs. and Colls. Arts, Letters and Scis., Coun. Colls. Arts and Scis., Nat. Assn. State Univs. and Land-Grant Colls. Home: 1901 Roma Ave NE Albuquerque NM 87106-3824 Office: U NMex Office of Pres Albuquerque NM 87131

PECK, SHAUNA ARLENE, sculptor, educator; b. Cin., Aug. 28, 1955; parents: Maurice and Mary (Tingue) P. BA in Studio ARt, U. Calif., Santa Barbara, 1978, BA in Psychology, 1979; MFA, Claremont Grad. Sch., 1986. vis. lectr. Coll. Creative Studies, Santa Barbara, 1988-89, U. Calif. Irvine, 1990-91; adj. prof. Otis Art Inst., L.A., 1993—, New Sch. Architecture, San Diego, 1993—. Solo shows include Coll. Creative Studies, 1978, So. Exposure Gallery, San Francisco, 1980, Installations Gallery, San Diego, 1982, Claremont Grad. Sch., 1984, 86, Pence Gallery, L.A., 1987, Santa Monica, Calif., 1989, Mincher/Wilcox Gallery, San Francisco, 1989, 90, 93, Daniel Saxon Gallery, L.A., 1990; exhibited in group shows at Foster Goldstrom Fine Arts, San Francisco, 1979, Source Gallery, San Francisco, 1980, San Diego Art Inst., 1981, Maple Creek Gallery, San Diego, 1982, Claremont Grad. Sch., 1984, U. Calif., Irvine, 1986, 88, Calif. State U., Fullerton, 1986, Jeffrey Linden Gallery, L.A., 1987, Pence Gallery, 1987, 89, L.I. U., N.Y., 1988, Beaver Coll. Art Gallery, Phila., 1988, Oakland (Calif.) Mus., 1989, Shosana Wayne Gallery, Santa Monica, 1989, Mincher/Wilcox, 1990. Westaf fellow, 1990. Mem. NOW. Democrat. Home: 2219 32d St San Diego CA 92104

PECORA, ROBERT, chemistry educator; b. Bklyn., Aug. 6, 1938; s. Alfonso Edward and Helen (Buscavage) P. A.B., Columbia U., 1959, A.M., 1960, Ph.D., 1962. Asst. prof. chemistry Stanford U., 1964-71, assoc. prof., 1971-78, prof., 1978—; chmn. chemistry, 1992—; vis. prof. U. Manchester, (Eng.), 1970-71, U. Nice, (France), 1978; cons. chemistry to maj. corps. Co-author: Dynamic Light Scattering, 1976; contbr. articles to profl. jours. Recipient Sr. Scientist award Alexander von Humboldt Found., 1985; NSF fellow, 1960-62, Am. Acad. Scis. postdoctoral fellow U. libre de Bruxelles, Belgium, 1963. Fellow AAAS, Am. Phys. Soc.; mem. Am. Chem. Soc. Home: 707 Continental Circle Mountain View CA 94040-3366 Office: Stanford U Dept Chemistry Stanford CA 94305

PECSOK, ROBERT LOUIS, chemist, educator; b. Cleve., Dec. 18, 1918; s. Michael C. and Katherine (Richter) P.; m. Mary Bodell, Oct. 12, 1940; children: Helen Pecsok Wong, Katherine, Jean Pecsok Nagle, Michael, Ruth Pecsok Hughes, Alice, Sara Pecsok Lima. S.B. summa cum laude, Harvard, 1940, Ph.D., 1948. Prodn. foreman Procter & Gamble Co., Balt., 1940-43; instr. chemistry Harvard, 1948; asst. prof. chemistry U. Calif. at Los Angeles, 1948-55, asso. prof., 1955-61, prof., 1961-71, vice chmn. dept., 1965-70; prof., chmn. dept. U. Hawaii, Honolulu, 1971-80; dean natural scis. U. Hawaii, 1981-89; sci. adviser FDA, 1966-69. Author: Principles and Practice of Gas Chromatography, 1959, Analytical Methods of Organic and Biochemistry, 1966, Modern Methods of Chemical Analysis, 1968, 2d edit., 1976, Modern Chemical Technology, 1970, rev. edit. 1989, Physicochemical Applications of Gas Chromatography, 1978. Served as lt. USNR, 1943-46. Recipient Tolman medal, 1971; Guggenheim fellow, 1956-57; Petroleum Research Fund Internat. fellow, 1963-64. Mem. Am. Chem. Soc., Am. Inst. Chemists, Phi Beta Kappa, Alpha Chi Sigma, Phi Lambda Upsilon. Home: 6009 Haleola St Honolulu HI 96821-2113

PEDEN, MARK RENICK, computer company executive; b. Redding, Calif., Sept. 5, 1966; s. Samuel Stephen and Judith Ann (Reedy) P.; m. Nataly El-Haj, Jan. 6, 1990. Student, Pacific Christian Coll., 1984-86; BSBA, BS in Speech Communications, Portland State U., 1991. Trainer, cons. Oz Computer Tng. Ctr., Bellevue, Wash., 1981-83; retail support rep. Apple Computer, Inc., Bellevue, 1983-85; pres. Computer Profls., Aloha, Oreg., 1985—; comml. real estate investor. Mem. Assn. for Systems Mgmt., Distributive Edn. Clubs Am. (pres. 1984), Japan Ryobu-Kai Karate Fedn. (2d degree black belt). Office: Computer Profls PO Box 7354 Beaverton OR 97007-7354

PEDERSEN, DONALD LEE, radiologist; b. Omaha, June 17, 1932; s. Henry William and Frances (Isom) P.; m. Kathleen Helen Smail, Dec. 28, 1958 (div. 1978); children: Brian David, Jeffrey Lee; m. Teresa Ann Sampson, July 7, 1983. BS in Pharmacy, Creighton U., 1954; MS in Chemistry, U. Nebr., 1956; MD, Northwestern U., 1960. Diplomate Am. Coll. Radiology. Asst. prof. radiology Med. Sch. U. Ky., Lexington, 1966-69; radiologist Helena (Mont.) Radiol. Assoc., 1969-90; chief, dept. radiology Ft. Harrison VA Med. Ctr., Ft. Harrison, 1990—. Capt. USAF, 1964-66. Home: 635 S Harris Helena MT 59601 Office: Ft Harrison VA Med Ctr Fort Harrison MT 59636

PEDERSEN, GAYLEN, executive; b. Salt Lake City, Mar. 4, 1934; s. Oliver Cowdery and Phoebe Gold (Gedge) P.; m. Mary Ann Hunter, Sept. 13, 1957; children: Mark Alan, Gordon Hunter, Gay Lynn, Eric David, Scott Douglas, Julie Ann, Dale Ryan. BS in Physics, Brigham Young U., 1959. Missionary Ch. of Jesus Christ of Latter-day Saints, New England states, 1954-56; instr. math. Cen. Utah Vocat. Sch., Provo, Utah, 1958-59; assoc., design engr. Boeing Co., Seattle, Washington, 1959-62; gen. mgr. Ogden Air Logistics Ctr., Hill Air Force Base (Utah), 1962-87; sr. instr. Shipley Assocs., Bountiful, Utah, 1987-89; pres., chief exec. officer Pedersen Pub., Bountiful, 1987-89; pres., chmn. bd. Gaylen Pedersen Family Orgn., Bountiful, 1976—; dir. mktg. Redcon-Resource Data Consultants, Bountiful, 1989-90; USAF sr. mgmt. staff Ogden Air Logistics Ctr., Hill Air Force Base, 1983-87, USAF mid. mgr., 1976-83; pvt. cons., 1990—. Author: System Level, Post Production Support: Tendencies, Conditions and Principles, 1988; editor: Nutritional Herbology, Vol. I, 1987, Vol. II, 1988. Instl. rep. Boy Scouts Am., Bountiful, 1965-67, basketball coach Explorer Scouts, 1980-87; bishop Ch. Jesus Christ Latter-day Saints, 1969-73. With U.S. Army, 1956-58. Republican. Office: Gaylen Pedersen Family Orgn 1311 Indian Trail Cir Bountiful UT 84010

PEDERSEN, MARTIN ALBERT, consulting engineer, surveyor; b. Rawlins, Wyo., Dec. 2, 1946; s. Rasmus and Ella (Rasmussen) P.; m. Karen Louise Bond, Aug. 26, 1967 (div. 1978); children: David Frank, Jennifer Louise; m. Patricia Ann Smith, Mar. 1, 1980; 1 child, Hans Rasmus. Student, U. Wyo., 1965. Registered land surveyor, Wyo., Mont., Idaho, Nev., Ariz., N.Mex., N.D., S.D., Colo., Calif., U.S. mineral surveyor. Surveyor Robert Jack Smith & Assocs., Rawlins, 1966-75, prin., 1975—. Scoutmaster Boys Scouts Am., Rawlins, 1969-75, dist. chmn., 1975-81; head Rawlins Search and Rescue Dive Team, 1984; mem. Christ Luth. Ch. Mem. Wyo. Assn. Cons. Engrs. and Surveyors (pres. 1978), Profl. Land Surveyors Wyo. (pres. 1980-81), Am. Congress Surveying and Mapping, Wyo. Engring. Soc. (sec.-treas. 1988—), Ducks Unltd., Elks. Home: 207 E Heath St Rawlins WY 82301-4307 Office: Robert Jack Smith Assocs Inc PO Box 1104 1015 Harshman St Rawlins WY 82301-1104

PEDERSEN, THOMAS JOHN, healthcare services executive; b. Evergreen Park, Ill., Sept. 11, 1949; s. Ernest Thomas and Mildred Rose (Ondrak) P.; m. Karen Ann Krzystofiak, Sept. 12, 1970 (div. Oct. 1982); 1 child, Bryan Thomas; m. Traci Lea Herman, Sept. 7, 1986; 1 child, Amy Lea. BA, U. Ill., 1970. Sr. sales exec. Dun & Bradstreet, Inc., Chgo., 1970-72; dist. mgr. Xeroradiography Ops., Oak Brook, Ill., 1972-76; regional mgr. EMI Med., Inc., Northbrook, Ill., 1976-79; divsn. mgr. Siemens Med. Systems, Inc., Iselin, N.J., 1979-80; exec. v.p., COO Ami Diagnistic Svcs., Inc., L.A., 1980-82; founder, v.p., corp. sec. Am. Health Svcs. Corp., Newport Beach, Calif., 1982-88; pres., CEO, bd. dirs. Ameritech Devel., Ltd., Newport Beach, 1988—, CSI Holding Corp., Cerritos, Calif., 1989-92; bd. dirs. Imagenet, Inc., Princeton, N.J.; adv. bd. Teal Electronics, Inc., San Diego, 1991—. Mem. Corona del Mar (Calif.) Homeowners Assn., 1987—; sr. referee Am. Youth Soccer Assn., Newport Beach, 1990—. Mem. Orange County Venture Network (bd. dirs. 1991—), So. Calif. Tech. Network. Office: 304 Narcissus Ave Corona Del Mar CA 92625-3005

PEDERSON, ROBERT DAVID, lawyer; b. Gallup, N.Mex., Oct. 23, 1953; s. Robert Leo and Alice (Montoya) P.; m. Jamie Gene Jonas, July 8, 1975; children: Jessica, Erik. B of Univ. Studies, U. N.Mex., 1975, JD, 1978; postgrad., Northwestern U., 1983. Bar: N.Mex., 1978, U.S. Dist. Ct. N.Mex. 1978. Assoc. Schuelke, Wolf & Rich, Gallup, 1978-81; v.p. 1st Interstate Bank, Gallup, 1981-84; sole practice Gallup, 1984-85; chief dep. dist. atty. 11th Judicial Dist., McKinley County, N.Mex., 1985—; cons. 1st Interstate Bancorp., Gallup, 1984—; chief children's ct. atty. 11th Judicial Dist., McKinley County, 1985—. State cen. com. N.Mex. Dems., 1984—. Mem. ABA, State Bar Assn. N.Mex.(mock trial judge 1986), McKinley County Bar Assn. (pres. 1982), Northwest Interagency Narcotics Task Force. Democrat. Lutheran. Office: 11th Jud Dist Dist Atty McKinley County Courthouse Gallup NM 87301

PEDERSON, SANFORD LLOYD, psychologist; b. Lynwood, Calif., July 13, 1952; s. Alan Fay and Maryalice (Faulkner) P.; m. Lisa Ellen Collins, Sept. 7, 1975; children: Clifford Collins, Craig Alan. BA in Psychology, U. CAlif., Riverside, 1974; postgrad., Calif. State U., San Bernardino, 1975-78; PhD in Psychology, U. Maine, 1984. Lic. psychologist, Ill., Wis. Instr. Unity (Maine) Coll., 1982-83; psychologist VA Med Ctr., Togus, Maine, 1983-85, VA Med. Ctr., North Chicago, Ill., 1985-91; coop. asst. prof. dept. psychology U. Maine, Orono, 1985; clin. asst. prof. dept. psychology Chgo. Med. Sch., North Chicago, Ill., 1986-91; pvt. practice clin. psychology Arlington Heights, Ill., 1987-91; chief psychologist VA Med. Ctr., Livermore, Calif., 1991—; presenter in field. Contbr. articles to profl. publs. NIMH fellow, 1978-81. Mem. Am. Psychol. Assn., Nat. Orgn. VA Psychologists (trustee 1988-91, chair tng. and edn. com. 1988—, cert. of recognition 1989), Internat. Neuropsychol. Soc., Midwestern Psychol. Assn., Assn. Psychology Internship Ctrs. (assoc. editor newsletter 1988-92, editor 1992—, bd. dirs. 1991—), Assn. VA Chief Psychologists, Psi Chi. Office: VA Med Ctr Psychology Svc 4951 Arroyo Rd Livermore CA 94550

PEEBLES, CAROL LYNN, immunology researcher; b. Wellington, Kans., Jan. 20, 1941; d. Harry Alexander and Phyllis Dorothy (Pyle) P. BA, Kans. State Coll. of Pittsburg, 1962, MS, 1964; cert. med. technology, St. Francis Hosp., Wichita, Kans., 1965. Med. technologist St. Francis Hosp., Wichita, 1965-74; lab. supr. allergy and immunology Scripps Clinic and Rsch. Found., La Jolla, Calif., 1974-77; sr. rsch. asst. autoimmune disease ctr. Scripps Clinic and Rsch. Found., La Jolla, 1982—; lab. supr. rheumatology lab. U. Colo. Health Scis. Ctr., Denver, 1977-82. Author workshop manual; contbr. articles to sci. publs. Mem. Am. Coll. Rheumatology, AAAS, Am. Soc. Microbiology, Am. Soc. Med. Tech., Am. Soc. Clin. Pathology. Office: Scripps Rsch Inst 10666 N Torrey Pines Rd SBR-6 La Jolla CA 92037

PEEBLES, LUCRETIA NEAL DRANE, principal; b. Atlanta, Mar. 16, 1950; d. Dudley Drane and Annie Pearl (Neal) Lewis; divorced; 1 child, Julian Timothy. BA, Pitzer Coll., 1971; MA, Claremont Grad. Sch., 1973, PhD, 1985. Special edn. tchr. Marshall Jr. High Sch., Pomona, Calif., 1971-74; high sch. tchr. Pomona High Sch., 1974-84; adminstr. Lorbeer Jr. High Sch., Diamond Bar, Calif., 1984-91; prin. Chapparal Mid. Sch., Moorpark, Calif., 1991-92, South Valley Jr. High Sch., Gilroy, Calif., 1992—; co-dir. pre-freshman program, Claremont (Calif.) Coll., 1974; dir. pre-freshman program, Claremont Coll., 1975; cons., Claremont, 1983—. Author: Negative Attendance Behavior: The Role of the School, 1985. Active Funds Distbn. Bd.-Food for All, 1987—, Funds Distbn. Task Force-Food for All, 1986; mem. Adolescent Pregnancy Childwatch Task Force. Named Outstanding Young Career Woman Upland Bus. and Profl. Women's Club, 1978-79; Stanford U. Sch. Edn. MESA fellow, 1983, NSF fellow Stanford U., 1981, Calif. Tchrs. Assn. fellow, 1979, Claremont Grad. Sch. fellow, 1977-79, fellow Calif. Edn. Policy Fellowship Program, 1989-90; recipient Woman of Achievement award YWCA of West Edn., 1991. Mem. Assn. Calif. Sch. Adminstrs. (Minigrant award 1988), Assn. for Supervision and Curriculum Devel., Nat. Assn. Secondary Sch. Principals, Phi Lambda Theta. Democrat. Am. Baptist. Home: 790 Upton Ct San Jose CA 95136 Office: South Valley Jr High Sch Gilroy United Sch Dist 7810 Arroyo Cir Gilroy CA 95020

PEELER, STUART THORNE, petroleum industry executive and independent oil operator; b. Los Angeles, Oct. 28, 1929; s. Joseph David and Elizabeth Fiske (Boggess) P.; m. Sylvia Frances Townley, Nov. 5, 1985. B.A., Stanford U., 1950, J.D., 1953. Bar: Calif. 1953. Ptnr. Musick, Peeler & Garrett, Los Angeles, 1958-73; with Santa Fe Internat. Corp., Orange, Calif., 1973-81; v.p., sec., assoc. gen. counsel Santa Fe Internat. Corp., 1973-74, sr. v.p., gen. counsel, dir., 1975-81; vice-chmn. bd., chmn. exec. com. Supron Energy Corp., 1978-82; chmn. bd., chief exec. officer Statex Petroleum, Inc., 1982-89; chmn., pres. and chief exec. officer Putumayo Prodn. Co., 1989—; bd. dirs. Cal Mat Co., Homestake Mining Co., Homestake Gold of Australia Ltd., Chieftain Internat. Inc. Trustee J. Paul Getty Trust; mem. U.S. Tuna Team, 1957-67, capt., 1966. Served with U.S. Army, 1953-55. Decorated Army Commendation medal. Mem. State Bar Calif., Am. Judicature Soc., AIME, Theta Chi, Phi Delta Phi, Tucson Country Club. Republican. Congregationalist. Office: PO Box 35852 Tucson AZ 85740-5852

PEEPS, CLAIRE VICTORIA CALDER, arts administrator, writer; b. Vancouver, B.C., Oct. 24, 1956; d. John Calder and Gertrude (Davies) P.; m. Nathan Birnbaum, June 24, 1989. BA, Stanford U., 1978; MFA, U. N.Mex., 1982. Exec. asst., mng. editor The Friends of Photography, Carmel, Calif., 1982-84, edn. dir., 1984-86; exec. dir. High Performance Mag., L.A., 1986—; assoc. artistic dir. L.A. Festival, 1989—; bd. dirs. High Performance Mag., Arts, Inc., Fringe Festival, L.A.; cons. Andy Warhol Found. for Visual Arts. Author: Judith Golden - Cycles, 1988; co-author: Mario Giacomelli, 1986; work displayed in various exhibitions, 1982—. Panelist Nat. Endowment for Arts, Washington, 1989, 90, site visitor, N.Y., Mpls., Tex., 1988, 89, 90, cons., Washington, 1987, 89; panelist Nat./State/County Partnership, L.A., 1989, 90. Mem. Art Table. Office: 1055 Wilshire Blvd Ste 810 Los Angeles CA 90017

PEETE, RUSSELL FITCH, JR., aircraft appraiser; b. Memphis, Tenn., June 15, 1920; s. Russell Fitch and Louise Gift (Edmondson) P.; m. Esther Eletha Mosley, Feb. 7, 1942 (dec. Jan. 1987); children: Miriam, Russell III, William; m. Margery May George, Sept. 2, 1988. BS in Aerospace Engring., Miss. State U., 1942. Dredge hand U.S. Corp. Engrs., West Memphis, Ark., 1937; rodman U.S. Corp. Engrs., Mobile, Ala., 1939; rsch. engr. Chicago & Southern Airlines, Memphis, 1941-51; tech. sales rep. Lockheed Corp., Burbank, Calif., 1951-82; ops. analyst Flying Tiger Line, L.A., 1982; dir. sales engring. Cammacorp, El Segundo, Calif., 1982-85, Anacorp, Marina Del Rey, Calif., 1977-89; aviation cons. Avcons, Sedona, Ariz., 1985—; aircraft appraiser Nat. Aircraft Appraiser Assn., Sedona, 1992—; cons. Avcons, Camarillo, Calif., 1985-86. Sec. Conejo Y's Mens Clubs, Thousand Oaks, Calif., 1960-63. With U.S. Army, 1944-46. Mem. Soc. Automotive Engrs., Exptl. Aircraft Assn., Aircraft Owners and Pilots Assn., Confederate Air Force, Internat. Aerobatic Club, Nat. Aircraft Appraisers Assn. Republican. Lutheran. Office: Avcons 110 Mission Rd Sedona AZ 86336

PEETS, BARBARA AILEEN, wildlife and western artist; b. Gowanda, N.Y., Oct. 1, 1943; d. Albert Evertt Grover and Katherine Aileen (Weber) Christensen; m. Thomas Michael Peets, June 19, 1965 (div. May 1989); children: Thomas R., Carmen L., Morgan K., Aaron L., Tamarack I. BFA, Kent State U., 1965. Controls dept. API Instrument Co., Stevensville, Ohio, 1965-66; adult art instr. Salmon, Idaho, 1971-78, western and wildlife artist, 1970—. Cover artist Am. Buffalo Jour., 1983, 87, 92, Nat. Bison Mag., 1987, Steamboat Mag., 1992 (Ozzie award 1992); numerous exhbns. throughout U.S. and Europe, 1970—; Hamilton Collection/series of ltd. edit. plates, 1993—. Speaker Rotary, Salmon, 1992. Mem. Ultima Art and Media Programs, Rocky Mountain Elk Found. Home: Rt 1 Box 67D Salmon ID 83467 Office: Country Gallery 909 Main St Salmon ID 83467

PEETZ, JONATHAN EMIL, counselor; b. Longview, Wash., Jan. 31, 1952; s. Ferdinand Emil and Pricilla Isabell (Bate) P.; m. Carol LeAnne Cherrington, June 9, 1978; children: Mark Root, Lisa Root, Jamie Abercrombie. AA, Lower Columbia Coll., Longview, 1987. Lic. counselor, Wash.; cert. clin. hypnotherapist; cert. chem. dependency specialist. Heavy equipment operator Weyerhaeuser, Longview, 1970-86; alcohol and drug counselor Community Alcohol and Drug Ctr., Longview, 1986-88; lead counselor Recovery N.W., Vancouver, Wash., 1988-92; clin. dir. Starting Point Inc., Longview, 1992—. Home: 133 Cherrington Rd Castle Rock WA 98611 Office: Starting Point Inc 1315 Hemlock Longview WA 98632

PEEVEY, MICHAEL ROBERT, electric company executive; b. N.Y.C., Feb. 8, 1938; s. Willard Michael Bliss and Miriam Gardiner (Cooke) Bliss Peevey; m. Lauretta Ann Peevey, Mar. 17, 1961 (div. 1976); children: Darcie Ann, Maria Beth; m. Carole Jean Liu, May 27, 1978; 1 child, Jared Liu. BA in Econs., U. Calif.-Berkeley, 1959, MA in Econs., 1961. Economist U.S. Dept. Labor, Washington, 1961-65; coord. community programs Inst. Indsl. Rels., U. Calif.-Berkeley, 1969-70; dir. rsch. Calif. Labor Fedn., AFL-CIO, 1971-73, 65-69; pres. Calif. Coun. for Environl./Econ. Balance, San Francisco, 1973-84; v.p. So. Calif. Edison Co., Rosemead, 1984-85, sr. v.p., 1985-86, exec. v.p., 1986-90, pres., 1990—; chmn. Electric Transp. Coalition, 1991—; chmn. electric transp. steering com. Edison Electric Inst., 1991—. Bd. dirs. Calif. Housing Fin. Agy., Sacramento, 1984-86; mem. Commn. to Rev. the Master Plan for Higher Edn., Calif., 1985-88; trustee Calif. State U. and Colls., 1977-85; mem. Gov.'s Infrastructure Rev. Task Force, Sacramento, 1983-84; bd. govs. Econ. Literacy Coun. of Calif., 1982—; bd. visitors Calif. Maritime Acad., 1980-83; mem. steering com. State Solid Waste Mgmt. Bd., 1980-83; commr. Nat. Commn. on State Workmen's Compensation Laws, Washington, 1971-72; bd. dirs. Consumer Fedn. Calif., 1972-78; co-chmn. Citizens for Adequate Energy, 1979-82; chair Commn. on Innovation, Calif. Community Colls. Mem. Calif. C. of C. (bd. dirs.), L.A. C. of C. (bd. dirs.), World Trade Club, Sutter Club, Calif. Club. Democrat. Episcopalian. Office: So Calif Edison Co PO Box 800 2244 Walnut Grove Ave Rosemead CA 91770-3714

PEHL, RICHARD HENRY, physicist, researcher; b. Raymond, Wash., Nov. 27, 1936; s. Henry Leopold and Annabelle (Moyer) P.; m. Paula Bhatia, July 1, 1980. B.S. in Chem. Engring., Wash. State U., 1958, M.S. in Nuclear Engring., 1959; Ph.D. in Nuclear Chemistry, U. Calif.-Berkeley, 1963. Grad. asst. Lawrence Berkeley Lab., Calif., 1960-63, research assoc., 1963-65, staff mem., 1965-78, staff sr. scientist, 1978—; mem. instrument devel. sci. team, NASA, 1984—; adj. staff physicist Ind. U. Cyclotron Facility, Bloomington, 1987—. Co-contbr. chpt. to Nuclear Spectroscopy and Reactions, 1974; contbr. articles to sci. jours. AEC fellow, 1958-59. Mem. Am. Phys. Soc., Sigma Xi, Phi Lambda Upsilon, Sigma Tau, Tau Beta Pi, Phi Kappa Phi. Home: 2550 Dana St Apt 6D Berkeley CA 94704-2867 Office: Lawrence Berkeley Lab Bldg 29 Berkeley CA 94720

PEIRANO, LAWRENCE EDWARD, civil engineer; b. Stockton, Calif., May 13, 1929; s. Frank Lloyd and Esther Marie (Carigiet) P.; m. Mary Ellen

Alabaster, July 26, 1952; children: Thomas Lawrence, Ellen Marie. BSCE, U. Calif., Berkeley, 1951, MSCE, 1952. Registered profl. engr., Calif., Nev.; diplomate Am. Acad. Environ. Engrs. Assoc. civil engr. Calif. Div. Water Resources, 1952-53; with Kennedy Engrs., Inc., San Francisco, 1955—, project mgr., 1960—, v.p., chief environ. engr., 1974—; dir. ops. Kennedy/Jenks Engrs., Inc., San Francisco, 1979—; sr. v.p., regional mgr. Kennedy/Jenks/Chilton, Inc. (formerly Kennedy Engrs., Inc.), San Francisco, 1986—; exec. v.p., chief tech. officer Kennedy/Jenks Cons., Inc., San Francisco, 1990—, also chmn. bd. dirs.; spl. lectr. san. engring. U. Calif., Berkeley, 1976. Served with U.S. Army, 1953-55, Korea. James Monroe McDonald scholar, 1950-51. Fellow ASCE; mem. Water Environment Fedn., Am. Water Works Assn., Cons. Engrs. and Land Surveyors Calif., Internat. Assn. on Water Quality, Sierra Club, U.S. Ski Assn., U. Calif. Alumni Assn., Tau Beta Pi, Chi Epsilon. Republican. Roman Catholic. Home: 3435 Black Hawk Rd Lafayette CA 94549-2326 Office: Kennedy Jenks Cons Inc 303 2nd St San Francisco CA 94107-1366

PEIRCE, FREDERICK FAIRBANKS, lawyer; b. Torrington, Conn., Jan. 28, 1953; s. Everett L. and Frederica (Fairbanks) P.; m. Sandra Marie MacMillan, Dec. 16, 1989. BS, Colo. State U., 1975; JD, U. Colo., 1979. Bar: Colo. 1979, U.S. Dist. Ct. Colo. 1979. Assoc. Bratton & Zimmerman, Gunnison, Colo., 1979-80; staff atty. Holland & Hart, Aspen, Colo., 1980-82; assoc. Austin, McGrath & Jordan, Aspen, 1982-84, Austin & Jordan, Aspen, 1984-87; ptnr. Austin, Jordan, Young & Peirce, Aspen, 1987-89, Austin & Peirce, Aspen, 1989-92, Austin, Peirce & Smith, Aspen, 1992—. Bd. dirs. Aspen Nordic Coun. Inc., 1985-88, Aspen Velo Club Inc., 1986-88, Aspen Cycling Club Inc., 1988-93, Aspen Ctr. for Environ. Studies, 1991—, v.p., 1992—; bd. dirs. Pitkin County Parks Assn., 1990—, v.p., 1991, pres., 1992—. NSF grantee, 1975. Colo. Bar Assn., Pitkin County Bar Assn. (v.p. 1985-86, pres. 1986-88, bd. govs. rep. 1989-91, exec. coun. 1993—), Phi Kappa Phi. Office: Austin Peirce & Smith 600 E Hopkins Ave Ste 205 Aspen CO 81611-2933

PEISER, RICHARD BONDY, real estate developer, educator; b. Houston, Aug. 12, 1948; s. Maurice Bondy and Patricia (Levy) P.; m. Beverly Siegal, May 26, 1981; children: Allison, Michael. BA, Yale U., 1970; MBA, Harvard U., 1973; PhD, Cambridge U., 1980. Planner N.Y.C. Planning Commn., 1970-71, Gerald D. Hines Interests, Houston, 1974-75; ptnr. Peiser Bldg. Co./Doyle Stuckey Homes, Houston, 1975-77; asst. prof. So. Meth. U., Dallas, 1978-85; assoc. prof., dir. Lusk Ctr. for Real Estate Devel. U. So. Calif., L.A., 1986—; owner Peiser Corp., Dallas, 1984—. Bd. dirs. South Coast Botanical Garden, L.A., 1988—, Bus. Policy Coun., L.A., 1988—, YMCA Camp Grady Spruce, Dallas, 1982—. Fellow Urban Land Inst.; mem. Yale Club L.A. (bd. dirs. 1988—). Office: U So Calif Sch Urban and Regional 351 Von Kleinsmid Ctr Los Angeles CA 90089-0042

PEJZA, JOHN PHILIP, priest, academic administrator; b. Neshkoro, Wis., Aug. 5, 1934; s. Philip Peter and Regina Rosalie (Dombrowski) P. BA, Villanova U., 1957, MA, 1961, MSSS, 1964; MA, U. San Francisco, 1981; postgrad., U. San Diego, 1982, EdD, 1987. Joined Order of St. Augustine, Roman Cath. Ch., 1952; ordained priest, 1961; cert. tchr. and adminstr., Calif. Tchr. Malvern (Pa.) Prep Sch., 1961-63; tchr. St. Augustine High Sch., San Diego, 1963-64, 70-75, prin., 1983-88; tchr., asst. prin. Villanova Prep. Sch., Ojai, Calif., 1964-70, pres., 1988—; prin. Cen. Cath. High Sch., Modesto, Calif., 1975-80, Marian High Sch., San Diego, 1981-83; secondary cons. Diocese of Stockton, Calif., 1977-80; exec. sec. province planning commn. Province of St. Augustine, Los Angeles, 1974-75; counselor Province of St. Augustine, Order of St. Augustine, Los Angeles, 1975-79; mem. priests' senate Diocese of San Diego, 1983-85. Contbr. articles to profl. jours. Mem. Nat. Cath. Ednl. Assn. (regional assoc. secondary div. 1987—), Augustinian Secondary Edn. Assn. (exec. sec. 1989—), Coun. Advancement and Support of Edn., Internat. Radio Club Am. (pres. 1977-79), Rotary, Phi Delta Kappa. Home: 185 St Thomas Dr Ojai CA 93023-2399 Office: Villanova Prep Sch 12096 N Ventura Ave Ojai CA 93023-3999

PELLA, JEROME JACOB, statistician; b. Pierz, Minn., Mar. 13, 1939; s. Joseph Pella and Louisa Petronella (Schommer) Thrasher; m. Judith Suzanne Annable, Dec. 8, 1979; children: John Knull, Kathleen Knull, Daniel Knull. BS, U. Minn., 1961; MS, U. Wash., 1964, PhD, 1967. Statistician Inter-American Tropical Tuna Commn., La Jolla, Calif., 1965-69, Nat. Marine Fisheries Svc., Auke Bay, Alaska, 1969—; cons. Pacific Salmon Commn., Vancouver, B.C., Can., 1982—. Author: (with others) Stock Mixtures, 1987. Mem. Am. Inst. Fishery Biologists, Sigma Xi. Office: Nat Marine Fisheries Svc 11305 Glacier Hwy Juneau AK 99801-8626

PELLEGRINI, CLAUDIO, physics educator, researcher; b. Rome, May 9, 1935; came to U.S., 1978; s. Edmondo and Margherita (Sabatini) P.; m. Maria Grazia Tomassetti, Dec. 27, 1961; children: Luca, Matteo, Flavia. Laurea, U. Rome, 1958, libera docenza, 1965. Physicist Frascati (Italy) Nat. Lab., 1959-63, physicist, group leader, 1963-76, div. head, 1976-78; sr. scientist Brookhaven Nat. Lab., Upton, N.Y., 1978-89; assoc. chmn. Nat. Synchrotron Light Source, 1985-89; prof. UCLA, 1989—, dir. ctr. advanced accelerators, 1989—; assoc. chmn. Nat. Synchrotron Light Source, 1985-89; mem. DOE High Energy physics adv. panel, 1992—. Editor: High Power Laser and Applications, 1978, Laser Handbook: Free Electron Laser, 1991. Fellow Am. Phys. Soc. (exec. com. particle beam div. 1988—). Office: U Calif Los Angeles CA 90024-1547

PELLEGRINI, ROBERT J., psychology educator; b. Worcester, Mass., Oct. 21, 1941; s. Felix and Teresa (Di Muro) P.; 1 child, Robert Jerome. BA in Psychology, Clark U., 1963; MA in Psychology, U. Denver, 1966, PhD in Social Psychology, 1968. Prof. San Jose (Calif.) State U., 1967—; rsch. assoc. U. Calif., Santa Cruz, 1989-90; pres. Western Inst. for Human Devel., San Jose, 1985—. Author: Psychology for Correctional Education; contbr. articles to profl. jours. Mem. Phi Beta Kappa. Office: San Jose State U Dept Psychology San Jose CA 95192

PELLONE, DAVID THOMAS, financial executive; b. Ashtabula, Ohio, Mar. 15, 1944; s. Frank Joseph and Shirley Edna (Foster) P.; m. Sunny Jewel Unfug, May 28, 1977; children: Todd Gary, Michelle Christine. BBA in Indsl. Mgmt., Kent State U., 1967; MBA in Acctg. and Fin., U. Santa Clara, 1973. Product supr., indsl. engr. Owens Corning Fiberglass, Santa Clara, Calif., 1970-72; line contr. Fairchild Semiconductor, Mountain View, Calif., 1973-74; corp. contr. Cermetek, Inc., Mountain View, 1974-76; various mgmt. positions 3M Co., Ventura, Calif., 1976-83; cons. J&P Assocs., Menlo Park, Calif., 1983-84; area fin. mgr. GenRad, Inc., Milpitas, Calif., 1984-86; v.p., contr. Genus, Inc., Mountain View, 1986-90; v.p. fin. and adminstrn. AG Processing Techs., Inc., Sunnyvale, Calif., 1990—; instr. U. San Francisco, 1990—, DeAnza Coll., 1991—. With U.S. Army, 1967-69. Mem. Am. Mgmt. Assn., Am. Acctg. Assn., Inst. Internal Auditors, Inst. Indsl. Engrs. (sr.), U. Santa Clara MBA Alumni (bd. dirs.), Churchill Club, Commonwealth Club (Calif.), World Forum of Silicon Valley. Republican. Episcopalian. Office: AG Processing Techs Inc 1325 Borregas Ave Sunnyvale CA 94089-1072

PELOSI, NANCY, congresswoman; b. Balt., Mar. 26, 1941; d. Thomas J. D'Alesandro Jr.; m. Paul Pelosi; children: Nancy Corinne, Christine, Jacqueline, Paul, Alexandra. Grad., Trinity Coll. Former chmn. Calif. State Dem. Com., 1981; committeewoman Dem. Nat. Com., 1976, 80, 84; fin. chmn. Dem. Senatorial Campaign Com., 1987; mem. 99th-102d Congresses from 5th Calif. dist., 1987-1992, 103rd Congress from 8th Calif. dist., 1993—; mem. appropriations com., subcoms. labor, HHD & edn., fgn. ops., D.C.; intelligence (select) com., standard official conduct com. Office: US Ho of Rep 240 Cannon Bldg Washington DC 20515-0508*

PELOTTE, DONALD EDMOND, bishop; b. Waterville, Maine, Apr. 13, 1945; s. Norris Albert and Margaret Yvonne (LaBrie) P. AA, Eymard Sem. and Jr. Coll., Hyde Park, N.Y., 1965; BA, John Carroll U., 1969; MA, Fordham U., 1971, PhD, 1975. Ordained priest Roman Cath. Ch., 1972. Provincial superior Blessed Sacrament, Cleve., from 1978; ordained coadjutor bishop Diocese of Gallup, N.Mex., 1986-90, bishop, 1990—; nat. bd. dirs. Maj. Superiors of Men, Silver Spring, Md., 1981-86, Tekakwitha Conf., Great Falls, Mont., 1981—. Author: John Courtney Murray: Theologian in Conflict, 1976. 1st native Am. bishop. Mem. Cath. Theol. Soc. Am., Am. Cath. Hist. Soc. Address: Bishop of Gallup PO Box 1317 Gallup NM 87305-1317

PELTASON, JACK WALTER, university administrator; b. St. Louis, Aug. 29, 1923; s. Walter B. and Emma (Hartman) P.; m. Suzanne Toll, Dec. 21, 1946; children: Nancy Hartman, Timothy Walter H., Jill K. BA, U. Mo., 1943, MA, 1944, LLD (hon.), 1978; AM, Princeton U., 1946, PhD, 1947; LLD (hon.), U. Md., 1979, Ill. Coll., 1979, Gannon U., 1980, U. Maine, 1980, Union Coll., 1981, Moorehead (N.D.) State U., 1980; LHD (hon.), 1980, Ohio State U., 1980, Mont. Coll. Mineral Scis. and Tech., 1982, Buena Vista Coll., 1982, Assumption Coll., 1983, Chapman Coll., 1986, U. Ill., 1989. Asst. prof. Smith Coll., Mass., 1947-51; asst. prof. polit. sci. U. Ill., Urbana, 1951-52, assoc. prof., 1953-59, dean Coll. Liberal Arts and Scis., 1960-64, chancellor, 1967-77; vice chancellor acad. affairs U. Calif., Irvine, 1964-67, chancellor, 1984-92; pres. U. Calif. System, Oakland, 1992—, Am. Coun. Edn., Washington, 1977-84; Cons. Mass. Little Hoover Commn., 1950. Author: The Missouri Plan for the Selection of Judges, 1947, Federal Courts in the Political Process, 1957, Fifty-eight Lonely Men, 1961, Understanding the Consitution, 12th edit. 1990, (with James M. Burns) Government By The People, 14th edit. 1990; contbr. articles, rev. to profl. jours. Recipient James Madison medal Princeton U., 1982. Fellow Am. Acad. Arts and Scis.; mem. Am. Polit. Sci. Assn. (council 1952-54), Phi Beta Kappa, Phi Kappa Phi, Omicron Delta Kappa, Alpha Phi Omega, Beta Gamma Sigma. Home: 6 Gibbs Ct Irvine CA 92715-4030 also: 70 Rincon Rd Kensington CA 94707 Office: U Calif Office of Pres 300 Lakeside Dr Oakland CA 94612-3550

PELTON, HAROLD MARCEL, mortgage broker; b. Montreal, Que., Can., Jan. 24, 1922; s. Grover Cleveland and Denise (Pigeon) P.; m. Frances Farley, June 1947 (div. 1968); children: Mary Virginia Joyner, Diane Jean Slagowski; m. Virginia L. King, July 11, 1970. Student, L.A. City Coll., 1948-49, Anthony Schs., Van Nuys, Calif., 1966. Lic. real estate real broker, Calif. Stockbroker, agt. Mitchum, Jones, Templeton Assurance Co., L.A., 1957-60; owner Assurance Investment Co., Van Nuys, Calif., 1960-65; sales syndicator TSI Investment Co., L.A., 1965-69; pres., owner Univest Co., Beverly Hills, Calif., 1970-72, Am. Oil Recovery, L.A., 1973-79; v.p. Newport Pacific Funding Co., Newport Beach, Calif., 1979-81; chmn. bd. dirs. TD Publs., El Toro, Calif., 1981-83; pres., broker HP Fin., Inc., Laguna Hills, Calif., 1983--. Contbg. editor Am. Oil Recovery newspaper, 1973-79; editor Trust Deed Jour., 1981-83. Served with U.S. Army, 1942-46, PTO. Mem. L. A. Mus. Art, Laguna Hills C. of C., Kiwanis, Toastmasters. Republican. Office: HP Fin Inc 24942 Georgia Sue Laguna Hills CA 92653-4323

PELTON, JOSEPH NEAL, communications executive; b. Tulsa, Oct. 29, 1943; s. Irmal Walker and Flora Elizabeth (Buser) P.; m. Eloise Christine Janssen, Sept. 10, 1965; children: Emily Daniele, Elaine Gabrielle, Alexander Joseph. BS in Physics, U. Tulsa, 1965; MA in Polit. Sci., NYU, 1967; PhD in Internat. Relations, Georgetown U., 1972. Quality assurance engr. N.Am. Rockwell, Tulsa, 1965; intern in internat. affairs NASA Hdqrs., Washington, 1967; research assoc. in sci. policy George Washington U., Washington, 1967-68; staff asst. COMSAT Corp., Washington, 1968-70, mgr. Internat. Telecommunications Satellite Orgn. affairs, 1971-73; exec. asst. to dir. gen. Internat. Telecommunications Satellite Orgn., Washington, 1974-83, dir. strategic policy, 1984-89; dir. grad. telecommunications program and telecommunications rsch. ctr. U. Colo., Boulder, 1989—; adj. prof. communication Am. U., 1983-84; dir. grad. telecommunications program, dir. Ctr. for Advanced Rsch. in Telecommunications, U. Colo.-Boulder; invited speaker U.S. Sen. Judiciary Com., 1987; bd. dirs. Internat. Space U. at MIT, chmn., 1993—, WETA Channel 26, Washington; chmn. pub. com. Pacific Telecommunications Coun., 1986-89. Author: Global Communications Satellite Policy, 1977, Global Talk, 1981 (Pulitzer nomination 1982, lit. award Am. Astronaut Soc. 1982), The INTELSAT Global Satellite Network, 1984, Satellites International, 1987, Space 30, 1989, Future Talk, 1990, How To Book of Satellite Communications, 1991, Future View, 1992; exec. editor: Journal of Space Communication, 1987—, Future Vision, 1992. Chmn. Parks and Recreation Bond Drive, Arlington County, 1977; 1st vice-chmn. Democratic Party, Arlington, 1975-76; bd. dirs. Arlington Retirement Housing Corp., 1975-78, 83; founder Project SHARE (Satellites for Health and Rural Edn., INTELSAT and IIT), 1985; bd. dirs., chmn. strategic planning com. Nat. Univ. Teleconf. Network, 1990—. Recipient Disting. Alumnus award U. Tulsa, 1986, Sr. Exec. Top Productivity award INTELSAT, 1985, Global Devel. award Miami Children's Hosp.; named Arlington Citizen of the Yr. Washington Star/Jour. newspapers, 1977. Mem. AIAA, Soc. Satellite Profls. (founding pres. 1983-84, co-chmn. Internat. Adv. Bd. 1985—), World Future Soc., Internat. Inst. Communications (trustee 1987-90), Internat. Acad. Astronautics, Internat. Platform Assn. Democrat. Unitarian. Home: 520 Aurora Ave Boulder CO 80302-7128

PELTON, VALERIE JEAN, air force officer; b. Charleston, S.C., Aug. 5, 1964; d. Lawrence Elmer and Bernardine Joyce (Walker) P.; m. Daniel Joseph Hicken, Dec. 14, 1987. BA in French and Modern European Studies, Vanderbilt U., 1986; MA in Polit. Sci., U. Nev., 1992; postgrad., Whittier Coll. Sch. Law, 1993—. Commd. 2nd lt. USAF, 1986, advanced through grades to capt., 1990; flight comdr. 6922 Electronic Security Squadron USAF, Angeles City, The Philippines, 1987-89; chief electronic combat ops. det 3 693IW USAF, Las Vegas, Nev., 1989-91, chief plans, programs and tests det 3 693 IW, 1991—; resigned USAF. Voting officer det 3 693 IW, Las Vegas, 1990-92, 6922nd ESS, Clark AFB, The Philippines, 1987-89. Capt. USAFR. Recipient Exxon Found. scholarship Exxon Corp. Vanderbilt U., 1985, AFROTC scholarship. Mem. NAFE, Federally Employed Women, Vanderbilt Alumni Assn., U. Nev. Las Vegas Alumni Assn., Alpha Sigma Pi. Republican. Roman Catholic. Home: 21340 Alder Dr # 204 Santa Clarita CA 91321

PELTZER, DOUGLAS LEA, semiconductor device manufacturing company executive; b. Clinton, Ia., July 2, 1938; s. Albert and Mary Ardelle (Messer) P.; m. Nancy Jane Strickler, Dec. 22, 1959; children: Katharine, Eric, Kimberly. BA, Knox Coll., 1960; MS, N.Mex. State U., 1964; MBA, U. Phoenix, 1990. Rsch. engr. Gen. Electric Co., Advanced Computer Lab., Sunnyvale, Calif., 1964-67; large scale integrated circuit engr. Fairchild Camera & Instrument, Rsch. & Devel. Lab., Palo Alto, Calif., 1967-70, supervisory engr. bipolar memory devel., Mountain View, Calif., 1970-73, process engring. mgr., bipolar memories div., 1973-83, tech. dir., 1977-83; v.p. tech. ops. Trilogy Systems Corp., Cupertino, Calif., 1983-85 ; pres. Tactical Fabs, Inc., 1985-89; v.p. process devel. Chips and Techs. Inc., 1989-92; pres, CEO CAMLAN, Inc., San Jose, Calif., 1992—. NSF fellow, 1962-63; recipient Sherman Fairchild award for tech. excellence, 1980, Semiconductor Equipment and Materials Inst. award, 1988; Inventor of Yr. award Peninsula Patent Law Assn., 1982. Mem. AAAS, IEEE, Sigma Pi Sigma. Inventor in field; patentee in field. Home: 10358 Bonny Dr Cupertino CA 95014-2908 Office: CAMLAN Inc 2381 Zanker Rd Ste 100 San Jose CA 95131-1122

PEMBERTON, MATTHEW ANTHONY, insurance agent; b. Vallejo, Calif., Apr. 2, 1947; s. Matthew I. and Mildred (Commottor) Cotabish; m. Mary Lafollette, Nov. 24, 1972 (div. 1978); 1 child, Sally Elizabeth; m. Suzan Leigh Kutchins, June 5, 1982; children: Alexandra, Vanessa. BA in Econs. with honors, U. Calif., Berkeley, 1969; MA in Econs., Northwestern U., Ill., 1971. CLU; Chartered Fin. Cons. Instr. econs. U. Ky. & U. Louisville, Ft. Knox, 1971-73; spl. agt. NML Ins. Co., San Francsico, 1974—; investment officer Robert W. Baird & Co., Inc., San Francisco, 1984—. 1st lt. U.S. Army, 1971-73. Office: Northwestern/Baird 1 Sansome St Ste 1700 San Francisco CA 94104-4432

PEÑA, FEDERICO FABIAN, U.S. secretary of transportation, lawyer; b. Laredo, Tex., Mar. 15, 1947; s. Gustavo J. and Lucille P.; m. Ellen Hart, May 1988. BA, U. Tex., Austin, 1969, JD, 1972. Bar: Colo. 1973. Ptnr. Pena & Pena, Denver, 1973-83; mayor City and County of Denver, 1983-91; pres. Peña Investment Advisors, Inc., Denver, 1991-93; sec. U.S. Dept. of Transp., Washington, 1993—; assoc. Harvard U. Ctr. for Law and Edn., Cambridge, Mass.; mem. Colo. Bd. Law Examiners. Mem. Colo. Ho. of Reps., 1979-83, Dem. leader, 1981. Named Outstanding House Dem. Legislator, Colo. Gen. Assembly, 1981. Roman Catholic. Office: Dept of Transportation Office Sec 400 7th St SW Washington DC 20590*

PENA, JUAN JOSE, interpreter; b. Hagerman, N.Mex., Dec. 13, 1945; s. Rosa Pena; m. Petra Cervantes, Dec. 22, 1974 (div. 1982); children: Federico Ezequiel, Margarita Blea. BA, N.Mex. Highlands U., 1968, MA, 1972, postgrad. With Albert Garcia Gen. Contr., Las Vegas, N.Mex., 1955-67; teaching asst. N.Mex. Highlands U., Las Vegas, 1971-72, prof. Spanish, Chicano studies, 1972--78; teaching asst. U. N.Mex., Albuquerque, 1978-79; attendant N.Mex. State Mental Hosp., Las Vegas, 1982-83; staff and supervisory interpreter U.S. Dist. Ct. N.Mex., Albquerque, 1983—; head Raza Unida delegation to PLO in Lebanon, 1971, head negotiator with Iranians for release of 2 Chicanos and 1 Indian. Author collection of poetry: Angustias y Remembranzas; contbr. articles to profl. jours.; author play: Canto a La Raza, 1978. Pres. Dads Against Discrimination, Albuquerque, 1987-89; chmn. bd. trustees No. N.Mex. Legal Svcs., Las Vegas, 1972-81; mem. exec. com. Ind. Socialist Parties of Latin Am. With U.S. Army, 1969-70. Decorated Bronze Star medal. Mem. N.Mex. Translator and Interpreters Assn. (pres. 1984-86), Nat. Assn. Judiciary Interpreters (sec. 1986-88), Nat. Partido Raza Unida (pres. 1976-81), N.Mex. Partido Raza Unida (pres. 1972-75, 77-78), Vietnam Vets. Am. (vice chmn. chpt. 318 1993—), Vietnam Vets. N.Mex., Albuquerque No. 1/Am. GI Forum (vice chmn. 1990-91, 92-93, chmn. civil rights com. and vietnam vets. com. 1991-92), Nat. Assn. Chicano Studies (founding mem.), N.Mex. Chicano Studies Assn. (pres. 1972-78), Phi Sigma Iota. Democrat. Roman Catholic. Home: 1115 9th St SW Albuquerque NM 87102-4027 Office: US Dist Ct Dist of NM Rm 13022 500 Gold Ave SW Albuquerque NM 87103

PENCE, MARTIN, federal judge; b. Sterling, Kans., Nov. 18, 1904; m. Eleanor Fisher, Apr. 12, 1975. Bar: Calif. 1928, Hawaii 1933. Practice law Hilo, Hawaii, 1936-45, 50-61; judge 3d Circuit Ct., Hawaii, 1945-50; chief judge U.S. Dist. Ct., Hawaii, 1961-74; sr. judge U.S. Dist. Ct., 1974—. Office: US Dist Ct 1036 Maunawili Loop Kailua HI 96734-4621

PENDERGHAST, THOMAS FREDERICK, business educator; b. Cin., Apr. 23, 1936; s. Elmer T. and Dolores C. (Huber) P.; BS, Marquette U., 1958; MBA, Calif. State U., Long Beach, 1967; D in Bus. Adminstrn. Nova U., 1987; m. Marjorie Craig, Aug. 12, 1983; children: Brian, Shawna, Steven, Dean, Maria. Sci. programmer Autonetics, Inc., Anaheim, Calif., 1960-64; bus. programmer Douglas Missile & Space Ctr., Huntington Beach, Calif., 1964-66; computer specialist N.Am. Rockwell Co., 1966-69; asst. prof. Calif. State U., Long Beach, 1969-72; prof. Sch. Bus. and Mgmt., Pepperdine U., Los Angeles, 1972—; spl. adviser Commn. on Engring. Edn., 1968; v.p. Visual Computing Co., 1969-71; founder, pres. Scoreboard Animation Systems, 1971-77; exec. v.p. Microfilm Identification Systems, 1977-79; pres. Data Processing Auditors, Inc., 1981—; data processing cons. designing computer system for fin. health and mfg. orgns., 1972—. Mem. Orange County Blue Ribbon Com. on Data Processing, 1973; mem. Orange County TEC Policy Bd., 1982-87. Served to lt. USNR, 1958-60. Cert. in data processing. Mem. Users of Automatic Info. Display Equipment (pres. 1966). Author: Entrepreneurial Simulation Program, 1988. Home: 17867 Bay St Fountain Valley CA 92708-4443

PENDLETON, OTHNIEL ALSOP, fundraiser, clergyman; b. Washington, Aug. 22, 1911; s. Othniel Alsop and Ingeborg (Berg) P.; m. Flordora Mellquist, May 15, 1935; children: John, James (dec.), Thomas, Ann, Susan. AB, Union Coll., Schenectady, N.Y., 1933; BD, Eastern Bapt. Theol. Sem., 1936; MA, U. Pa., 1936, PhD, 1945; postgrad., Columbia U., 1937-38. Ordained to ministry Bapt. Ch., 1936. Pastor chs. Jersey City, 1935-39, Phila., 1939-43; dean Sioux Falls Coll., S.D., 1943-45; fund raiser Am. Bapt. Ch., N.Y.C., 1945-47; fund-raiser Mass. Bapt. Ch., Boston, 1947-54; fund-raiser Seattle, Chgo., Boston, Washington, N.Y.C. and Paris, France, 1955-64, Westwood, Mass., 1971-84; staff mem. Marts & Lundy, Inc., N.Y.C., 1964-71; lectr. Andover-Newton (Mass.) Sem., 1958, Boston U. Sch. Theology, 1958, Harvard U., Cambridge, Mass., 1977-84; cons. Grant MacEwan Coll., Edmonton, Alta., Can. Author: New Techniques for Church Fund Raising, 1955, Fund Raising: A Guide to Non-Profit Organizations, 1981; contbr. articles in field to profl. jours. Address: 529 Berkeley Ave Claremont CA 91711

PENDLETON, RONALD KENNETH, education educator; b. L.A., Dec. 17, 1940; s. Kenneth Harry and Pauline B. (Delaney) P.; m. Peggy Jean Williams, Dec. 24, 1988. AA, El Camino Coll., Torrance, Calif., 1961; BA, Calif. State U., Arcata, 1963; MA, Calif. State U., Long Beach, 1978; PhD, Ariz. State U., 1981. Social worker Humboldt County Welfare Dept., Eureka, Calif., 1964-66; comml. pilot Continental Air Svcs., Vientiane, Laos, 1971-73; mgr., chief pilot Santa Fe Charter Air Svc., Hooper Bay, Alaska, 1975; indsl. arts tchr. Stavanger (Norway) Am. Sch., 1976-78; rsch. assoc. Ariz. State U., Tempe, 1978-81; prof., coord. of vocat. tchr. edn. Calif. State U., San Bernardino, 1981—; cons. Vocat. Mentor Svcs., San Bernardino, 1990—, pub. Faultline Publs. San Bernardino, 1991—; res. dept. sheriff San Bernardino County Sheriffs Dept., 1986—, tng. cons., 1991—. Author: Readings for Vocational Instructors, 1990; contbr. articles to profl. jours. Pres. Inland Empire Symphony League, 1984-86, sec., bd. dirs., 1986-88. Capt. USAF, 1966-71. Mem. Rotary (pres. 1990-91, bd. dirs.), C. of C. (vocat. edn. adv. coun.). Home: 6659 Ridgeline Ave San Bernardino CA 92407-2083 Office: Calif State U Dept Edn 5500 University Pky San Bernardino CA 92407-2318

PENDLETON, VERNE H., JR., geologist; b. Medford, Oreg., Sept. 17, 1945; s. Verne H. and Ilene Clara Koepsell) P.; m. Paula Jean Obenshain, June 22, 1968. BS in Geology, Oreg. State U., 1973. Geologist/engring. inspector/tech. Soils Testing Lab., Inc., Medford, 1976-81; rsch. tech. Dept. Civil Engring., U. Idaho, Moscow, 1982-84; constrn. geologist, lab. mgr. Soils Testing Lab., Inc., Medford, 1984-88; quality control insp. LTM Inc., Medford, 1988-91; sr. materials specialist/coord. Hwy. div. Oreg. Dept. Transp., 1991-92; ATE region materials inspector hwy. div. Oreg. Dept. Transp., Bend, 1992—. With U.S. Army, 1966-69. Republican. Ch. of the Nazarene. Home: 1834 NE Todd St Roseburg OR 97470

PENG, ZHONG, electrical engineer; b. Tianjin, China, May 20, 1946; came to U.S, 1981; s. Shichang and Rungeng (Bu) P. BSEE, Tianjin U., 1968; MSEE, Purdue U., 1982; MS in Computer Engring., U. So. Calif., 1984. Registered profl. engr., Calif. Elec. engr. Henan Power Adminstrn., Anyang, China, 1968-78; rsch. assoc. Electric Power Rsch. Inst., Beijing, 1980-81; lectr. Calif. State U., L.A., 1985; power system analyst CAE Electronics, Montreal, Que., Can., 1987-89; power system engr. Pacific Gas & Electric, San Francisco, 1085-87, elec. engr., 1989—. Contbr. articles to profl. jours. Coord. alumni svcs. Grad. Sch. Chinese Acad. Scis., 1991—. Mem. IEEE (sr., prize paper award 1987, 88). Office: Pacific Gas & Electric 150 Spear # 661 San Francisco CA 94105

PENHUNE, JOHN PAUL, science company executive, electrical engineer; b. Flushing, N.Y., Feb. 13, 1936; s. Paul and Helene Marguerite (Beux) P.; m. Nancy Leigh Peabody, Sept. 6, 1958 (div. Apr. 1982); children: Virginia Burdet, James Peabody, Sarah Slipp; m. Marcellite Helen Porath, Feb. 15, 1986; 1 child, Marcellite Helen Broadhurst. BSEE, MIT, 1957, PHDEE, 1961; postgrad., U. Grenoble, France, 1959, Harvard U., 1973. Asst. prof. elec. engring. MIT, Cambridge, Mass., 1962-64; mem. tech. staff Lincoln Lab. MIT, Lexington, Mass., 1964-66; supr. radar group Bell Telephone Labs., Whippany, N.J., 1966-68; asst. dir. Advanced Ballistic Missile Def. Agy., Washington, 1968-69; pres. Concord Rsch. Corp., Burlington, Mass., 1969-73; pvt. practice sci. cons. Carlisle, Mass., 1973-79; bd. dirs. Phys. Dynamics, Inc., La Jolla, Calif., 1979-81; sr. v.p. for rsch. Sci. Applications Internat. Corp., San Diego, 1981—; indsl. adv. bd. Inst. for biomed. Engring., U. Calif., San Diego, 1992—, connect. steering com., 1993—. Author: Case Studies in Electromagnetism, 1960; patentee in field. Bd. dirs. La Jolla Chamber Music Soc., 1985-87. 1st lt. U.S. Army, 1961-62. Recipient Meritorious Civilian Svc. award Dept. Army, 1968. Mem. Cosmos Club (Washington), San Diego Yacht Club., Eta Kappa Nu, Tau Beta Pi, sigma Xi, Phi Kappa Sigma. Home: 6730 Muirlands Dr La Jolla CA 92037-6315 Office: Sci Applications Internat Corp 1241 Cave St La Jolla CA 92037

PENKOFF, DIANE WITMER, educator; b. Pasadena, Jan. 20, 1945; d. Stanley Lamar and Mary Evelyn Witmer; m. Robert D. Joyce (div. 1987); 1 child, David William Penkoff. AA, Golden West Coll., Huntington Beach, Calif., 1977; BS in BA, U. LaVerne (Calif.), 1980; MS in Sys. Mgmt., U. So. Calif., L.A., 1989; MA in Communication Arts, U. So. Calif., 1993. Dir. pub. rels. Weight Watchers, Santa Ana, Calif., 1980-84; dir. communications March of Dimes, Costa Mesa, Calif., 1986-90; prin. Penkoff Communication Resources, Laguna Hills, Calif., 1990—; instr. Calif. State U., Fullerton,

1990—; asst. lectr.communication arts and scis. U. So. Calif., University Park, 1991—. Editor, The Paper Weight, 1981-84. Chmn. awd. com. March of Dimes, Costa Mesa, nat. vol., 1980—. Mem. Pacific Chorale, Pub. Rels. Soc. Am. (acredited mem., legis. action com.), U. So. Calif. Alumni Assn.

PENN, ZACHARY OWEN, screenwriter; b. N.Y.C., Mar. 23, 1968; s. Arthur Steven and Marilyn (Spicehandler) P. BA, Wesleyan U., 1990. Co-author: (screenplay) Central Park, 1990, The Last Action Hero, 1991, P.C.U., 1992. Mem. Writers Guild of Am.

PENNAK, ROBERT WILLIAM, biologist, educator; b. Milw., June 13, 1912; s. William Henry and Ella Sophia (Clemeson) P.; m. Alberta Vivian Pope, Sept. 7, 1935; children: Richard Dean, Cathy Ann. BS, U. Wis., 1934, MS, 1935, PhD, 1938. Instr. biology U. Colo., Boulder, 1938-40, prof. biology, 1941-74, prof. emeritus, 1974—; cons. numerous nat. and internat. corps. Author: Fresh-water Invertebrates of the U.S., 1953, Collegiate Dictionary of Zoology, 1964; contbr. over 120 articles to profl. jours. Rsch. grantee various orgns. Mem. Am. Microscopical Soc., Am. Benthological Soc. (Excellence in Benthic Sci. award 1991), Am. Soc. Limnology and Oceanography, Am. Soc. Zoologists, Internat. Assn. Meiobenthologists. Home: 14215 E Marina Dr Aurora CO 80014

PENNER, STANFORD SOLOMON, engineer; b. Unna, Germany, July 5, 1921; came to U.S., 1936, naturalized, 1943; s. Heinrich and Regina (Saal) P.; m. Beverly Preston, Dec. 28, 1942; children: Merilynn Jean, Robert Clark. BS, Union Coll., 1942; MS, U. Wis., 1943, PhD, 1946; Dr. rer. nat. (hon.), Technische Hochschule Aachen, Fed. Republic Germany, 1981. Research asso. Allegany Ballistics Lab., Cumberland, Md., 1944-45; research scientist Standard Oil Devel. Co., Esso Labs., Linden, N.J., 1946; sr. research engr. Jet Propulsion Lab., Pasadena, Calif., 1947-50; mem. faculty Calif. Inst. Tech., 1950-63, prof. div. engring., jet propulsion, 1957-63; dir. research engring. div. Inst. Def. Analyses, Washington, 1962-64; prof. engring. physics, chmn. dept. aerospace and mech. engring. U. Calif. at San Diego, 1964-68, vice chancellor for acad. affairs, 1968-69, dir. Inst. for Pure and Applied Phys. Scis., 1968-71, dir. Energy Ctr., 1973-91; bd. dirs. Ogden Corp., Optodyne Corp.; U.S. mem. adv. group aero. rsch. and devel. NATO, 1952-68, chmn. combustion and propulsion panel, 1958-60; mem. adv. com. engring. scis. USAF-Office Sci. Rsch., 1961-65; mem. subcom. combustion NACA, 1954-58; rsch. adv. com. air-breathing engines NASA, 1962-64; mem. coms. on gas dynamics and edn. Internat. Acad. Astronautics, 1969-80; mem. coms. NRC; cons. to govt., univs. and industry, 1953—; nat. lectr. Sigma Xi, 1977-79; spl. guest Internat. Coal Sci. Confs., 1983, 85, 87, 89; mentor Defense Sci. Studies Group, 1985—; chmn. Studies Municipal Waste Incineration NSF, 1988-89, Calif. Coun. Sci. Tech., 1992. Author: Chemical Reactions in Flow Systems, 1955, Chemistry Problems in Jet Propulsion, 1957, Quantitative Molecular Spectroscopy and Gas Emissivities, 1959, Chemical Rocket Propulsion and Combustion Research, 1962, Thermodynamics, 1968, Radiation and Reentry, 1968; sr. author: Energy, Vol. I (Demands, Resources, Impact, Technology and Policy), 1974, 81, Energy, Vol. II (Non-nuclear Energy Technologies), 1975, 77, 84, Energy, Vol. III (Nuclear Energy and Energy Policies), 1976; Editor: Chemistry of Propellants, 1960, Advanced Propulsion Techniques, 1961; Detonations and Two-Phase Flow, 1962, Combustion and Propulsion, 1963, Advances in Tactical Rocket Propulsion, 1968, In Situ Shale Oil Recovery, 1975, New Sources of Oil and Gas, 1982, Coal Combustion and Applications, 1984, Advanced Fuel Cells, 1986, Coal Gasification: Direct Applications and Syntheses of Chemicals and Fuels, 1987, CO2 Emissions and Climate Change, 1991; assoc. editor Jour. Chem. Physics, 1953-56; editor Jour. Quantitative Spectroscopy and Radiative Transfer, 1960-92, Jour. Def. Research, 1963-67, Energy, The Internat. Jour, 1975—. Recipient spl. awards People-to-People Program, sp. awards NATO, pub. service award U. Calif. San Diego, N. Manson medal Internat. Colloquia on Gasdynamics of Explosions and Reactive Systems, 1979, Internat. Columbus award Internat. Inst. Communications, Genoa, Italy, 1981, Disting. Assoc. award U.S. Dept. Energy, 1990; Guggenheim fellow, 1971-72. Fellow Am. Phys. Soc., Optical Soc. Am., AAAS, N.Y. Acad. Scis., AIAA (dir. 1964-66, past chmn. com., G. Edward Pendray award 1975, Thermophysics award 1983, Energy Systems award 1983), Am. Acad. Arts and Scis.; mem. Nat. Acad. Engring., Internat. Acad. Astronautics, Am. Chem. Soc., Combustion Inst., Sigma Xi. Home: 5912 Ave Chamnez La Jolla CA 92037 Office: U Calif San Diego 9500 Gilman Dr La Jolla CA 92093-0310

PENNEY, BRYAN LE ROY HUMPHREY, lay pastor, nursing assistant; b. Port Hueneme, Calif., Mar. 8, 1954; s. Chester Ulysses Jr. and Carlene (Fisher) Humphrey; m. Judith Deanna Klann, Apr. 14, 1990. Lay preacher, pulpit supply First So. Bapt. Ch., Red Bluff, Calif., 1986-88; lay pastor Fairvale Bapt. Ch., Fair Oaks, Calif., 1988-89; security officer Carrow's Restaurant, Citrus Heights, Calif., 1990-91; nursing asst. Stat Nurses Svc., Sacramento, Calif., 1991—, Sutter Oaks Nursing Ctr., Carmichael, Calif., 1992—; ind. distbr. Herbalife. Author: (poems) Heartfelt Reflections, 1988, God...My Father, My Inspiration, 1990. Dir. Santa Clarita Valley Jaycees, Canyon Country, Calif., 1980-81. Sgt. USAF, 1973-76. Named Patriot of Christian Liberty, 1989, Poet of Merit, Am. Poetry Assn., 1989, Golden Poet, World of Poetry Press, 1985, 90, Silver Poet, 1986; recipient Presdl. Medal of Merit, Presdl. Task Force, 1989. Home and Office: 34 Goodwin Cir Sacramento CA 95823-5141

PENNINGTON, DOROTHY CAROLYN, financial planner; b. Imogene, S.D., Dec. 24, 1921; d. Ruben Allan and Ida Millie (Obst) Haggart; m. Charles J. Pennington, May 31, 1947 (dec. Oct. 1955); m. James E. Shreffler. Student, Black Hills Tchrs. Coll., 1939-41; BBA, Golden Gate U., 1965, MBA, 1968. Cert. fin. planner. Adminstrv. asst. Crowley Enterprises, San Francisco, 1955-70; registered rep. Putnam Fin. Svcs., San Rafael, Calif., 1968-73, Waddell & Reed, Kansas City, Mo., 1973-74, Pace Securities Inc., San Francisco, 1974-76, Ind. Fin. Planners, Parsippany, N.J., 1976-80, Judy & Robinson Securities, Menlo Park, Calif., 1980-87; br. mgr. Planned Investments, Inc., Murphys, Calif., 1987—. V.p. Faith Luth. Ch., Murphys, 1988-90, pres., 1990-92; auditor Republican Women, Calaveras County, Calif., 1989-92; mem. AAUW, Calaveras County, 1987-92. Mem. Internat. Assn. for Fin. Planning. Home: PO Box 2637 Murphys CA 95247-2637 Office: Planned Investments Inc 202 Sunnyhills Ln Murphys CA 95247

PENNISTON, GREGORY KENT, chiropractor; b. Omaha, June 23, 1957; s. Lloyd Martin and Beverly Jennette Penniston; m. Shelley Lynn Yogman, July 5, 1981 (div. Aug. 1987); 1 child, Benajmin West; m. May Joan Smith, Apr. 2, 1988; children: Ruth Cameron, Zachery Lloyd, Helen Grace. Student, U. Mo., 1975-77; Dr of Chiropractic, Sherman Coll., Spartanburg, S.C., 1980. Intern Kansas City, Mo., 1980-81; assoc. Dr. John DeMent, Tucson, 1982-83; owner, dir. Lifeline Chiropractic, Tucson, 1983—; bd. dirs. Ariz. Chiropractic Alliance, Tucson, 1988-91. Mem. Ariz. Assn. Chiropractic (com. mem.), So. Ariz. Chiropractic. Libertarian. Home: 4955 N Calle Bendita Tucson AZ 86718 Office: Lifeline Chiropractic 702 S Craycroft Ste A Tucson AZ 86711

PENNOCK, CECIL ALAN, electronic engineer; b. Siloam Springs, Ark., Mar. 20, 1946; s. Cecil Floyd and Wanda (Perkins) P.; m. Melody Pennock (div. Feb. 1983); 1 child, Joseph Alan. AS in Engring. Tech., Grantham Coll., 1978, BS in Electronics Engring., 1981; AA in Math., Butte Coll., 1981. Broadcast engr. Sta. KHSL-TV, Chico, Calif., 1969—. Sgt. USAF, 1966-69. Mem. Soc. Broadcast Engrs. (cert. chmn.). Home: 701 E Lassen Sp 174 Chico CA 95926

PENTONY, DEVERE EDWIN, social sciences educator; b. Manchester, Iowa, Sept. 10, 1924; s. Joseph Clive and Amber Leora (Davis) P.; m. Isabel Susan Hoag, Sept. 28, 1933 (div.); children: Bryan DeVere, Elisabeth Ann; m. JoAnn Meriwether Craig, Jan. 17, 1991. PhD, U. Iowa, 1955. Chair, prof. dept. internat. rels. San Francisco (Calif.) State U., Sch. Behavioral Social Sci., 1958—, dean, 1966-82; bd. dirs. Overseas Tng. and Orientation Program, San Francisco. Editor: Underdevelope Lands, 1963; author: Unfinished Rebellions, 1970; contbr. articles to profl. jours. Sgt. U.S. Army, 1943-46. Mem. Internat. Studies Assn. Democrat. Home: 460 Arlington St San Francisco CA 94131 Office: San Francisco State U Internat Rels Dept 1600 Holloway San Francisco CA 94132

PENWELL, JONES CLARK, real estate appraiser, consultant; b. Crisp, Tex., Dec. 19, 1921; s. Clark Moses and Sarah Lucille (Jones) P.; B.S., Colo. State U., 1949; m. A. Jerry Jones, July 1, 1967; children—Dale Maria, Alan Lee, John Steven, Laurel Anne, Tracy Lynn. Farm mgmt. supr. Farmers Home Adminstrn., Dept. Agr., 1949-58; rancher 1958-61; real estate appraiser/realty officer Dept. Interior, Tex., Calif., Ariz., Colo., Washington, 1961-78, chief appraiser Bur. Reclamation, Lakewood, Colo., 1978-80; ind. fee appraiser, cons., 1980—. Served with USN, 1940-46. Accredited rural appraiser; cert. review appraiser, gen. appraiser; recipient Outstanding Performance awards U.S. Bur. Reclamation, 1964, 75, 80. Mem. Am. Soc. Farm Mgns. and Rural Appraisers, Internat. Right-of-Way Assn., Nat. Assn. Rev. Appraisers (regional v.p. 1978-79), Jefferson County Bd. Realtors. Democrat. Presbyterian. Clubs: Elks, Rotary, Mt. Vernon Country. Author: Reviewing Condemnation Appraisal Reports, 1980; The Valuation of Easements, 1980. Home and office: 10100 W 21st Pl Lakewood CO 80215-1406

PEPE, BARBARA EILENE, writer, television producer; b. Pitts., Sept. 30, 1951; d. Michael Thomas and Patricia Ann (Crump) P. BA in Journalism, Duquesne U., 1973. Dir. publicity London Records, 1975-77; head East Coast music div. Solters/Roskin/Friedman, N.Y.C., 1977-79; dir. contemporary publicity RCA Records, N.Y.C., 1979-84; freelance writer, TV producer, cons. N.Y.C., 1984-88; sr. producer Movietime, E! Entertainment TV, L.A., 1988—; radio interviewer. Contbr. articles, chpt. to profl. publs. Mem. Women in Communications, Sigma Delta Chi. Democrat. Office: 5670 Wilshire Blvd Los Angeles CA 90036

PEPPER, DARRELL WELDON, mechanical engineer; b. Kirksville, Mo., May 14, 1946; s. Weldon Edward and Marjorie Louise (Dove) P.; m. Jeanne Evelyn Limbacher, Aug. 16, 1969; 1 child, Erik Weldon. BS, U. Mo.-Rolla, 1968, MS, 1970, PhD, 1973. Postdoctoral U. Mo., Rolla, 1973-74; research engr. E.I. duPont, Aiken, S.C., 1974-78, research supr., 1978-84, research staff engr., 1984-87, chief scientist Marquardt, Van Nuys, Calif., 1987-90; pres. Softcrunch Inc., Aiken, 1984-88; co-founder, chief exec. officer Advanced Projects Rsch., Inc., Moorpark, Calif., 1988—; assoc. prof. U. Nev., Las Vegas, 1992—. Author: (with others) Finite Elements 1-2-3, 1991, The Finite Element Method, Basic Concepts and Applications, 1992. Contbr. articles to profl. jours. Bd. dirs. Aiken United Way, 1983-87 , Aiken Community Playhouse, 1977-78. Served to capt. USAR, 1968-76. NSF fellow 1969-73; U. Mo. scholar 1964. Named one of Outstanding Young Men Am., 1975. Fellow ASME; mem. AIAA (sr. mem.), Sigma Xi, Pi Tau Sigma. Republican. Congregationalist. Avocations: golf; white water rafting; woodworking; personal computing.

PEPPER, DAVID M., physicist, educator, author, inventor; b. L.A., Mar. 9, 1949; s. Harold and Edith (Kleinplatz) P.; m. Denise Danyelle Koster, Mar. 19, 1992. BS in Physics summa cum laude, UCLA, 1971; MS in Applied Physics, Calif. Inst. Tech., 1974, PhD in Applied Physics, 1980. Mem. tech. staff Hughes Rsch. Labs., Malibu, Calif., 1973-87, sr. staff physicist, 1987-91, head nonlinear and electro-optic devices sect., 1989-91, sr. scientist, 1991—; adj. prof. math. and physics Pepperdine U., Malibu, 1981—. Co-author: Optical Phase Conjugation, 1983, Laser Handbook, Vol. 4, 1985, Physics and Applications of Spatial Light Modulators, 1993, Contemporary Topics in Optical Phase Conjugation, 1993, CRC Handbook of Lasers, 1993; tech. referee profl. jours.; contbr. articles to tech. jours. including Sci. Am.; holder 13 patents. Mem. Sons and Daughters of 1939 Club, 2d Generation of Martyrs Meml., Mus. Holocaust. Recipient Rudolf Kingslake award Soc. Photo-Optical Instrumentation Engrs., 1982, Publ. of Yr. award Hughes Rsch. Lab., 1986; NSF trainee Calif. Inst. Tech., 1971; Howard Hughes fellow Hughes Aircraft Co., 1973-80. Fellow Optical Soc. Am.; mem. AAAS, IEEE (guest editor, assoc. editor), SPIE (guest editor), N.Y. Acad. Scis., Am. Phys. Soc., Internat. Coun. Sci. Unions (com. on sci. and tech. in developing countries), Sigma Xi (v.p. 1986-87, chpt. pres. 1987-88, 90-91, 91-92), Sigma Pi Sigma. Jewish. Office: Hughes Rsch Labs RL 65 3011 Malibu Canyon Rd Malibu CA 90265-4797

PEPPER, JOHN ROY, oil and gas executive; b. Denver, Feb. 24, 1937; s. Wesley Wayne and Lucille (Stith) P.; m. Sallie K. Force, Dec. 13, 1958 (div. July 1970); m. Judithea Lawrence, Sept. 24, 1977; stepchildren: Sarah Douglas-Broten, Kenneth R. Douglas. BBA, U. Denver, 1961; postgrad., UCLA, 1962, U. Denver, 1965. Analyst Texaco, Inc., L.A., 1962-63; landman Texaco, Inc., Bakersfield, Calif., 1963-65; prin. John Pepper, Landman, Denver, 1965-75; owner, operator John R. Pepper Oil & Gas Co., Denver, 1975—; bd. dirs. Trans-Telecom, Miami, Fla.; cons. Organizer Friends of Bob Crider campaign, Denver, 1985. Mem. Ind. Petroleum Assn. Mountain States, Ind. Petroleum Assn. of Ams. (pub. lands com. 1968-74). Republican. Lutheran. Home: 2499 S Colorado Blvd # 608 Denver CO 80222 Office: John R Pepper Oil & Gas Co 1800 Glenarm Pl Ste 200 Denver CO 80202-3829

PEPPERCORN, JOHN EDWARD, chemical company executive; b. Hutchinson, Kans., Sept. 3, 1937; s. John Edward and Lorena Fay (Hirt) P.; m. Mary Claire Purcell, July 25, 1961; children: Michael Edward, Mark Purcell. BSBA, U. Kans., 1960; grad. Tuck Exec. Program, Dartmouth Coll., 1978. Mgr. plastic sales Gulf Oil Chems., Houston, 1966-69, mktg. mgr., 1973-77, v.p. U.S. plastics, 1977-81, v.p. aromatics and derivatives, 1981-83; gen. mgr. Gulf Plastic Products Co., Morristown, N.J., 1969-72; v.p. domestic mktg. Gulf Oil Products, Houston, 1983-85; v.p., gen. mgr. aromatics Chevron Chem. Co., Houston, 1985; sr. v.p. indsl. chems. Chevron Chem. Co., San Francisco, 1985-86, sr. v.p., 1986-89, pres., chief exec. officer, 1989—. Served to capt. U.S. Army, 1960-61. Mem. Soc. Plastic Industry (bd. dirs. 1978-81), Flexible Packaging Assn. (bd. dirs. 1980-82). Office: Chevron Chem Co 575 Market St San Francisco CA 94105-2823

PERALTA, EVERETT FIGUEROA, social sciences educator; b. Hermosillo, Sonora, Mex., May 20, 1954; came to U.S., 1958; s. Everado Grijalva and Dora (Figueroa) P. BS, SUNY, Albany, 1985. Resident dir. Ariz. State U., Tempe, 1979-82; coord. leadership devel. program U. Bridgeport, Conn., 1982-85; dir. Grad. Student Assn. Ariz. State U., Tempe, 1985-87; vice-chmn. Ariz. State Bd. Econ. Planning and Devel., Phoenix, 1987-88; sr. mgmt. cons. Crystal Resources, Tempe, 1984-88; v.p. adminstrn. N.Am. Group-Investment Ins. Sch., Phoenix, 1988-89; sub. tchr. Willcox (Ariz.) Pub. Schs., 1990—; coll. instr. Cochise Coll., Douglas, Ariz., 1991—; chmn., cons. Scholar Devel. Systems, Willcox, 1992—; presenter leadership skills workshops, 1985, 92, professionalism, 1986 Immigration Act, university responsibility to community; cons., developer workshops on developing capable people Willcox Middle Schs. Author: College Study Skills, 1992, Organizational Development and Leadership Skills, 1985. Bd. dirs. Rural Schs. Project, Willcox, 1972-73, Cochise County Learning Adv. Coun., Bisbee, Ariz., 1991—; election bd. clk. City of Willcox, 1992; mem. commn. Tempe City Transp. Commn., 1989; precinct committeeman, dep. registrar Rep. Cen. Com., Maricopa County, Ariz., 1983; lector, altar server Sacred Heart Cath. Parish, 1992—; mem. St. Jude Parish Coun., 1990-91; exec. dir. Coun. Family Concerns and Resources, 1993—. Recipient Leadership award Omicron Delta Kappa; named one of Outstanding Young Men Am. Fellow Am. S.W. Found. (vice chmn. 1987-89), UN Assn. (state treas., bd. dirs. Conn. chpt. 1984-85), Ctr. for Study of Presidency, Wilson Ctr. for Scholars, K.C. (3d degree knight), Theta Kappa Epsilon. Roman Catholic. Home: HCR 3 Box 5963 Willcox AZ 85643 Office: Scholar Devel System 222B N Bowie Willcox AZ 85643

PERALTA, RICHARD CARL, agricultural engineer; b. Enid, Okla., Nov. 8, 1949; s. John Francis and Christina Margareta (Reinl) P.; m. Ann Wilson Blanchard, Mar. 27, 1972; children: Dia, Samantha, Nancy, Hugh. BS, U. S.C., 1971; MS, Utah State U., 1977; PhD, Okla. State U., 1979. Registered profl. engr., Ark. Grad. research assoc. Oklahoma State U., Stillwater, 1977-79; from asst. prof. to assoc. prof. agrl. engring. U. Ark., Fayetteville, 1980-88; assoc. prof. dept. biol. & irrigation engring. Utah State U., Logan, 1988-91, prof., 1991—; cons. hydrologist, U.S. Geological Survey, Fayetteville, 1985-87; cons. engr. Mid-Am. Internat. Corp., Lima, Peru, 1986-87; cons. engr. ARD, FAO, 1989. Contbr. articles to sci. jours. Co-dir. Citizens for Responsible Legis., Stillwater, 1979; elders quorum, counsellor, pres., exec. sec., fin. asst. clk., activities com. chmn., Ch. of Jesus Christ of Latter-Day Saints, 1979—; scoutmaster, 1988-89; cubmaster, 1989-91. Served as 1st lt. with USAF, 1971-75; served to lt. col. USAFR. Mem. ASCE, Am. Soc. of Agrl. Engrs., Am. Water Resources Assn., Gamma Sigma Delta, Sigma Xi. Home: PO Box 412 Millville UT 84326-0412 Office: Utah State U Dept Biol & Irrigation Engring Logan UT 84322

PERATT, ANTHONY LEE, electrical engineer, physicist; b. Belleville, Kans., Feb. 26, 1940; s. Galvin Ralph and Arlene Frances (Friesen) P.; m Glenda Delores White, Dec. 19, 1966; children: Sarah, Galvin, Mathias. BSEE, Calif. State Poly. U., 1963; MSEE, U. So. Calif., L.A., 1967, PhD, 1971. Staff The Aerospace Corp., El Segundo, Calif., 1971-72, Lawrence Livermore (Calif.) Nat. Lab., 1972-79; guest scientist Max Planck Inst. fur Plasmaphysik, Garching, Germany, 1975-77; sr. scientist Maxwell Labs., San Diego, 1979-81; staff Los Alamos (N.Mex.) Nat. Lab., 1981—; vis. scientist Royal Inst. Tech., Stockholm, 1985, 88; adv. bd. Mus. Sci. and Industry, Chgo., 1990—; mem. Excom, IEEE Nuclear and Plasma Sci. Soc., 1987, 88, 89, 90; gen. chmn. IEEE Internat. Conf. on Plasma Sci., 1994. Author: Physics of the Plasma Universe, 1992; editor IEEE Transactions on Plasma Sci. Jour., 1986, 89, 90, 92, Laser and Particle Beams, 1988. Recipient Award of Excellence, Dept. Energy, 1987. Mem. IEEE, Am. Phys. Soc., Am. Astron. Soc., Eta Kappa Nu. Office: Los Alamos Nat Lab MS-D406 Los Alamos NM 87545

PERATT, KAREN LEE, publishing company executive; b. York, Nebr., Mar. 17, 1954; d. Terrence Dean and Naomi Rey (Railsback) P.; m. James Edward Svatko, Sept. 6, 1975. BA in Polit. Sci., U. Calif., Irvine, 1976; MA in Applied Linguistics, UCLA, 1978. Editor Time-Life Books, Tokyo, 1978-82; gen. mgr. Collier Macmillan Internat., N.Y.C., 1982-85; dir. ESL, Macmillan Pub. Co., N.Y.C., 1986-88, asst. v.p., 1988-89, v.p., 1989-91; dir. lang. products Maxwell Multi Media, Boulder, Colo., 1991-92; asst. v.p., dir. multimedia projects Simon & Schuster, Englewood Cliffs, N.J., 1992-93; pres. Internat. Media Access, Boulder, Colo., 1993—; internat. rsch. fellow Am. U. Cairo, 1978. Project dir. TV-radio series Family Album, U.S.A., 1989. Edn. Abroad fellow Chinese U. Hong Kong, 1974-75. Mem. Tchrs. English to Speakers Other Langs., Assn. Am. Pubs. (chmn. English to speakers other langs. com. 1987-89). Methodist. Office: Regents Prentice Hall 113 Sylvan Ave Englewood NJ 07632

PERAZZO, GLEN THOMAS, educator; b. Fallon, Nev., May 19, 1963; s. John T. and Nancy A. Perazzo; m. Elizabeth Ann Jervis, Jan. 21, 1989; children: Andrew Glen, Eric Charles. BA, Brigham Young U., 1987; postgrad., Western Nev. C.C., 1990, U. Nev., 1990. Cert. secondary tchr., Nev. With Perazzo Bros. Dairy, Fallon, 1970—; substitute tchr. Clark County Sch. Dist., Las Vegas, Nev., 1988-89; tchr. Churchill County Sch. Dist., Fallon, 1989—; instr. Western Nev. C.C., Fallon, 1990. Named Outstanding Tchr., Churchill County High Sch., 1990. Mem. Nev. Edn. Assn., Internat. Theatre Assn., Intercollegiate Knights (life). Republican. Mem. LDS Ch. Office: Churchill County High Sch 1222 S Taylor Fallon NV 89406

PERCY, LEE EDWARD, motion picture film editor; b. Kalamazoo, Feb. 10, 1953; s. Richard Noyes and Helen Louise (Sheffield) P. Student, Goodman Sch., Chgo., 1971, Juilliard Sch., 1972; AB, U. Calif., Santa Cruz, 1977. Radio news reporter McGovern Campaign, Chgo., 1972; cons. Kjos Pub. Co., Chgo., 1973-74; dir. VisArt, Ltd., San Francisco, 1977; ind. film editor L.A., 1978—. Editor motion pictures: Re-Animator, 1984, Kiss of the Spiderwoman, 1985, Slam Dance, 1987, Checking Out, 1988, Blue Steel, 1989, Reversal of Fortune, 1990, Year of the Gun, 1991, Single White Female, 1992. Mem. Am. Cinema Editors, Editors Guild Hollywood, Motion Picture Editors N.Y.

PEREGRIN, MAGDA ELIZABETH, artist; b. Budapest, Hungary, Jan. 2, 1923; came to U.S. 1937; d. Stephen and Anna (Csukas) Wiesner; m. William Thomas Peregrin, Sept. 4, 1950. Student, Pasadena City Coll., 1955-57, Pasadena Art Mus., 1960-62. Staff artist Am. Greetings, Inc., Cleve., 1945-50; free lance artist Am. Greetings, Inc., 1950-55, Greetings, Inc., Joliet, Ill., 1950-60; tchr. Creative Arts Grp., Sierra Madre, Calif., 1980—, Yosemite Art Activity Ctr., Yosemite, Calif., 1980—. One-man shows include Hillcrest Invitational, Whittier, Calif., 1975-91, Fresno (Calif.) Met. Mus., 1987, Brea Cultural Ctr., 1985, 90, Creative Arts Group, Sierra Madre, Calif., 1980-91, L.A. City Hall, 1980, San Bernardino (Calif.) County Mus., 1988, 89, Downey Art Mus., Calif., 1990, Fairplex Fine Arts Exhibit, 1990, Pasadena Arts Coun., 1991, Watercolor West XXIII-Brand Libr., Glendale, Calif., 1991; represented in permanent collections Smithsonian Inst., Washington, Arcadia Meth. Hosp., Arcadia, Calif., Home Savs. and Loan, L.A. (Purchase award 1975), Unocal, L.A. (Purchase award 1978), City of Hope (Purchase award 1975), Duarte, Calif., Hillcrest Congl. Ch., Whittier. Recipient Purchase award Hillcrest Presbyn. Ch., 1988, 3d Pl. award Hillcrest Invitational, 1990, 91, 2d Pl. award, 1992, 2d and 3d Pl. awards, 1993. Mem. Mid-Valley Arts League (bd. dirs. 1970-73), Watercolor West (bd. dirs. 1970-73), Pasadena Soc. Artists, Yosemite Renaissance Exhibit. Republican. Roman Catholic. Home: 8517 E Ravendale Rd San Gabriel CA 91775-1121

PERELL, WILLIAM SIMON, information services executive; b. N.Y.C., Oct. 27, 1952; s. Arthur and Betty Sylvia (Simon) P.; m. Cheryl Elizabeth Harrison, Aug. 24, 1986. BA, Dartmouth Coll., 1974, MBA, 1975. Pres. Agraport, Inc., San Francisco, 1981-84; sr. v.p. Marketel Internat., Inc., San Francisco, 1985-91; v.p. mktg. E-FAX Comms. Inc., Oakland, Calif., 1992—. Mem. Internat. Assn. Bus. Communicators, Nat. Investor Rels. Inst. Jewish. Office: E-FAX Comms Inc 1611 Telegraph Ave # 555 Oakland CA 94612

PERELSON, GLENN HOWARD, health facility administrator; b. Bklyn., Oct. 10, 1954; s. Bruce Irwin and Shirley May (Bergman) P. AB, Hamilton Coll., 1975; MD, Boston U., 1979; MBA, U. Phoenix, 1991. Diplomate Am. Bd. Internal Medicine, sub-bd. Cardiovascular Disease; bd. cert. in med. mgmt. Fellow in medicine Tufts U., Boston, 1983-85; chmn., founder Zero-G Industries, Boston, 1985-88; med. dir. FHP, Inc., Fountain Valley, Calif., 1988—; cons. Manor Assocs., Buckingham, Pa., 1985—. Editor, author: (test) Appleton's Rev. for Nat. Bds., 1985; author: Appleton's Rev. for FLEX, 1985. Mem. Am. Coll. Physician Execs., Am. Heart Assn., Cardiac Space Rsch. Soc. Home: 2333 Camino del Rio S # 250 San Diego CA 92108

PEREYRA-SUAREZ, CHARLES ALBERT, lawyer; b. Paysandu, Uruguay, Sept. 7, 1947; came to U.S., 1954, naturalized, 1962; s. Hector and Esther (Enriquez-Sarano) P.-S.; m. Susan H. Cross, Dec. 30, 1983. BA in History magna cum laude, Pacific Union Coll., 1970; postgrad., UCLA, 1970-71; JD, U. Calif., Berkeley, 1975. Bar: Calif. 1975, D.C. 1980. Staff atty. Western Ctr. Law and Poverty, Inc., Los Angeles, 1976; trial atty. civil rights div. U.S. Dept. Justice, Washington, 1976-79; asst. U.S. atty., criminal div. U.S. Dept. Justice, Los Angeles, 1979-82; sr. litigation assoc. Gibson, Dunn & Crutcher, Los Angeles, 1982-84; sole practice Los Angeles, 1984-86; ptnr. McKenna & Cuneo, Los Angeles, 1986—. Democrat. Office: McKenna & Cuneo 444 S Flower St Los Angeles CA 90071-2901

PEREZ, ANTHONY MARTIN, JR., lawyer; b. San Francisco, Sept. 7, 1953; s. Anthony Martin and Alice Mercedes (Roque) P.; m. Alice Mary Phillips, Nov. 30, 1985; children: Caitlin, Elizabeth. BA, Calif. State U., Sacramento, 1976; JD, U. Pacific, 1983. Bar: Calif. 1984. Adminstrv. law judge, cons. State of Calif., Sacramento, 1980-84; pvt. practice Sacramento, 1984—; assoc., co-founder Adminstrv. Law Group, Sacramento, 1987—. Co-author: Child Care and Development, 1990. Bd. dirs. Legal Ctr. for Handicapped and Disabled, Sacramento, 1989l; gen. counsel Sacramento Local Conservation Group, 1989. Mem. ABA, Calif. State Bar Assn. Democrat. Office: Wells Fargo Ctr 400 Capitol Mall Ste 2390 Sacramento CA 95814

PEREZ, REINALDO JOSEPH, electrical engineer; b. Palm River, Cuba, July 25, 1957; came to U.S., 1975; s. Reinaldo I. and Palminia Ulloa (Rodriguez) P.; m. Madeline Kelly Reilly, Mar. 11, 1989; children: Alexander, Laura-Marie. BSc in Physics, U. Fla., 1979, MSc in Physics, 1981; MScEE, Fla. Atlantic U., 1983, PhD, 1989. Communications engr. Kennedy Space Ctr., NASA, Cape Canaveral, Fla., 1983-84; rsch. engr. jet propulsion lab. JPL, Calif. Inst. Tech., Pasadena, 1988—; instr. engring. UCLA, 1990—. Contbr. articles to profl. publs. Mem. AAAS, IEEE (book rev. editor 1990—), NSPE, Electromagnetic Compatibility Soc. (assoc. editor jour.), Am. Soc. Physics Tchrs., N.Y. Acad. Scis., Applied Computational Electromagnetic Soc. (assoc. editor jour.), Phi Kappa Phi. Republican. Baptist. Office: JPL Calif Inst Tech 4800 Oak Grove Dr MS: 301-460 Pasadena CA 91109

PEREZ, RICHARD LEE, lawyer; b. Los Angeles, Nov. 17, 1946; s. Salvador Navarro and Shirley Mae (Selbrede) P.; children: Kristina, Kevin, Ryan. BA, UCLA, 1968; JD, U. Calif., Berkeley, 1971. Bar: U.S. Dist. Ct. (no. dist.) Calif. 1974, U.S. Ct. Appeals (9th cir.) 1974, U.S. Dist. Ct. (ea. dist.) Calif. 1982, U.S. Dist. Ct. (no. dist.) Tex. 1984, U.S. Dist. Ct. (so. dist.) Calif. 1991. Assoc. McCutchen, Doyle, Brown & Enersen, San Francisco, 1972-74, John R. Hetland, Orinda, Calif., 1974-75; ptnr. Lempres & Wulsfberg, Oakland, Calif., 1975-82, Perez & McNabb, Orinda, 1982—; speaker real estate brokerage and computer groups and seminars; mem. adv. bd. Computer Litigation Reporter, Washington, 1982-85, Boalt Hall High Tech. Law Jour., 1984-90. Assoc. editor U. Calif. Law Rev., 1970-71. Served to capt. U.S. Army, 1968-79. Mem. ABA, Alameda County Bar Assn., Contra Costa County Bar Assn. Office: Perez & McNabb 140 Brookwood Rd Orinda CA 94563-3000

PEREZ, STEVEN RANDALL, journalist; b. Indio, Calif., June 20, 1960; s. Jose O. and Elizabeth Marie (Brake) P. BA in Journalism, San Diego State U., 1985. Reporter radio and TV stations, Calif., 1980-89; instr. U. Calif., Santa Cruz, Calif., 1989-91; writer Santa Cruz Sentinel, 1990—; owner APEX Prodns., Santa Cruz, Calif., 1991—. Bd. dirs. Santa Cruz Community Counseling Ctr., 1991-92. Mem. Calif. Chicano News Assn., Nat. Assn. Hispanic Journalists. Home: 625 Bonnie St Santa Cruz CA 95062 Office: Santa Cruz Sentinel 207 Church St Santa Cruz CA 95062

PEREZ, TIMOTHY ALLEN, software company administrator; b. Carmel, Calif., Apr. 30, 1961; s. Robert L. and Karen G. (Stanfield) P.; m. Cynthia Lorraine Whipple, June 1, 1984; children: Dansell, Robert, Steven. BS, Brigham Young U., 1987. Instructional trainer Missionary Tng. Ctr., Provo, Utah, 1983-86, MIS tng. supr., 1986-87; mktg. rep. IBM Corp., Denver, 1987-92; account mgr. Interactaive Software Systems, Inc., Denver, 1992—; fin. industry specialist IBM Corp., Denver, 1988-89, law enforcement cons., 1990-92. Missionary, Ch. of Jesus Christ of Latter-Day Saints, Fla., 1980-82; dir. youth job hunt Colo. Alliance of Bus., 1988. Recipient Duty to God award Ch. of Jesus Christ of Latter-Day Saints, 1978. Republican. Home: 4862 S Salida Ct Aurora CO 80015-1981 Office: Interactive Software Systems Inc 7175 W Jefferson Ave # 2500 Denver CO 80235

PEREZ-MENDEZ, VICTOR, physics educator; b. Guatemala, Aug. 8, 1923; came to U.S., 1946; m. 1949; 2 children. MS, Hebrew U., Israel, 1947; PhD, Columbia U., 1951. Rsch. assoc. Columbia U., N.Y.C., 1951-53, staff physicist, 1953-61; sr. scientist Lawrence Berkeley Lab., U. Calif., Berkeley, 1960—; vis. lectr. Hebrew U., 1959—; prof. physics dept. radiology U. Calif., San Francisco, 1968—. Fellow IEEE, AAAS, Am. Phys. Soc., N.Y. Acad. Sci.; mem. Soc. Photo Instrumentation Engrs. Office: U Calif Lawrence Berkeley Lab Berkeley CA 94720

PERIC-KNOWLTON, WLATKA, nurse practitioner; b. Nürmberg, Germany, Oct. 29, 1955; came to U.S., 1957; d. Vladimir and Zlata (Mihaljevic) Peric; m. Gregory Dean Knowlton, May 1, 1983. BSN, Ariz. State U., 1977, MSN, 1986. RN, Ariz.; cert. adult nurse practitioner CCRN, CDE; CEN. Gen. surgery staff nurse St. Joseph's Hosp., Phoenix, 1977-78, staff nurse cardiovascular oper. room, charge nurse, 1978-80; staff nurse surg. ICU, charge nurse Carl Hayden VA Med. Ctr., Phoenix, 1980-83, dir. anticoagulation clinic, 1984—; nurse practitioner ambulatory care dept. Phoenix VA Hosp., 1983—; mem. adj. clin. faculty Ariz. State U., Tempe, 1986—. Editor-in-chief newsletter VA Nurse Practitioner News, 1989-91; guest editor Nurse Practitioner Forum; contbr. articles to nursing jours. Named Nat. Nurse Practitioner of Yr., Syntex, 1989, Fed. Employee of Yr., Phoenix Fed. Exec. Assn., 1989; recipient award for excellence in nursing western region VA, 1991. Mem. ANA (Search for Excellence award 1991), Am. Acad. Nurse Practitioners (Ariz. rep. 1991-93), Ariz. Nurse Practitioner Coun. (treas. 1985-87, v.p. 1989-90, pres. 1990-91, legis. chmn. 1992—), Ariz. Nurses Assn. (vice chmn. legis. com. 1985-87, bd. dirs. 1982-83), Am. Heart Assn. (coun. on thrombosis 1989—, community speaker Phoenix 1989—), Sigma Theta Tau. Democrat. Roman Catholic. Office: Carl Hayden VA Med Ctr 650 E Indian School Rd Phoenix AZ 85012

PERILLOUX, BRUCE EDGAR, product line manager, optical engineer; b. New Orleans, Mar. 24, 1961; s. Louis Francis and Edna Eloise (Zirkle) P.; m. Anne Mary Jeansonne, Jan. 19, 1985. BSEE, U. New Orleans, 1983, MS in Engring., 1984. Registered engr.-in-tng., La. Thin film R & D engr. Coherent, Inc., Auburn, Calif., 1985-87, project engr., 1987-88, product line mgr., 1988—. Inventor polar preserving reflector, multilayer optical filter, chromatic invariant coating, diffractive laser resonator, optical engineering related. La. Land Exploration and Devel. scholar, 1984. Mem. Optical Soc. Am., Phi Kappa Phi, Sigma Xi. Home: 17328 Vintage Dr Grass Valley CA 95949-8512 Office: Coherent Inc 2301 Lindbergh St Auburn CA 95602-9595

PERKINS, CHERYL GREEN, certified public accountant; b. Spokane, Wash., Dec. 16, 1945; d. Philip Benjamen and Vera Kay (Broyles) Green; m. T. Don Perkins, Sept. 27, 1976; 1 child, Alan Kent. BBA, Wash. State U., 1968; MBA, U. Oreg., 1969. CPA, Oreg. CPA KPMG Peat Marwick, San Francisco, Portland, Oreg., 1969-75; CPA, ptnr. Isler & Co., Portland, Oreg., 1976-81; CPA, shareholder Perkins Jeddeloh & Acheson, Portland, Oreg., 1981-86, Perkins & Co., P.C., Portland, Oreg., 1986—. Co-author: Real Estate Taxation, 1982. Community bd. mem. Meridian Park Hosp.; mem. deferred giving com. St. Vincent Hosp., Portland, 1987—, Am. Lung Assn., Portland, 1991—; trustee Marylhurst (Oreg.) Coll., 1984-86. Named One of Best Tax Practioners in Oreg., Money Mag., 1987. Mem. AICPA, Oreg. Soc. CPAs (chmn. various coms. 1974—), Portland Tax Forum (bd. dirs. 1989—), Portland Estate Planning Coun. (bd. dirs. 1989—), Multnomah Athletic Club. Republican. Office: Perkins & Co PC 111 SW 5th Ave Ste 2000 Portland OR 97204

PERKINS, DOROTHY A., marketing professional; b. Weiser, Idaho, Aug. 13, 1926; d. Ross William and Josephine Stanford (Gwilliam) Anderson; m. Leonard Taylor Perkins, Nov. 16, 1948; children: Larry Taylor, Michael A., Drew A., Nancy. Grad. high sch., Boise, Idaho. Sec. Meadow Gold Dairies, Boise, 1944-46; sec. to supt. Idaho State Police, Boise, 1946-48, Idaho State Dept. Edn., Boise, 1952-56; sec. to maintenance engr. Idaho State Dept. Hwys., Boise, 1956-58; adminstrv. sec., asst. mgr. Casper (Wyo.) C. of C., 1962-72, exec. v.p., 1972-91; mktg. rep. World Wide Travel, Casper, 1991—. Mem. Wyo. Ho. of Reps., 1982—, chmn. house labor, health and social svcs. com., 1990—. Mem. Wyo. C. of C. Execs. (sec.-treas. 1978-91, past pres.), Mountain States Assn. (bd. dirs. 1979-91, past pres.), Wyo. Hwy. Users Fedn. (bd. dirs. 1978—, pres. 1993—). Republican. Home: 1014 Surrey Ct Casper WY 82609-3270 Office: World Wide Travel PO Box 9370 Casper WY 82609

PERKINS, FLOYD JERRY, theology educator; b. Bertha, Minn., May 9, 1924; s. Ray Lester and Nancy Emily (Kelley) P.; m. Mary Elizabeth Owen, Sept. 21, 1947 (dec. June 1982); children: Douglas Jerry, David Floyd, Sheryl Pauline; m. Phyllis Genevra Hartley, July 14, 1984. AB, BTh, N.W. Nazarene Coll., 1949; MA, U. Mo., 1952; MDiv, Nazarene Theol. Sem., 1952; PhD, U. Witwatersrand, Johannesburg, South Africa, 1974. Ordained to Christian ministry, 1951. Pres. South African Nazarene Theol. Sem., Florida Transvaal, Africa, 1955-67; pres. Nazarene Bible Sem., Lourenzo Marques, Mozambique, 1967-73, Campinas, Brazil, 1974-76; prof. missions N.W. Nazarene Coll., Nampa, Idaho, 1976; prof. theology Nazarene Bible Coll., Colorado Springs, Colo., 1976—; chmn., founder com. higher theol. edn. Ch. of Nazarene in Africa, 1967-74; sec. All African Nazarene Mission Exec., 1967-74; ofcl. Christian Council Mozambique, 1952-74. Author: A History of the Christian Church in Swaziland, 1974. Served with USN, 1944-46. Mem. Soc. Christian Philosophers, Evang. Theol. Soc., Am. Schs. Orientan Rsch., Am. Soc. Missiology, Assn. Evang. Missions Profs. Republican. Home: 1529 Lyle Dr Colorado Springs CO 80915-2009 Office: Nazarene Bible Coll 1111 Chapman Dr Colorado Springs CO 80916-1902

PERKINS, GLADYS PATRICIA, retired aerospace engineer; b. Crenshaw, Miss., Oct. 30, 1921; d. Douglas and Zula Francis (Crenshaw) Franklin; m. Benjamin Franklin Walker, Sept. 26, 1952 (dec.); m. William Silas Perkins, Sept. 16, 1956 (dec.). BS in Math., Le Moyne Coll., 1943; postgrad., U. Mich., 1949, U. Calif., L.A., 1955-62. Mathematician Nat. Adv. Com. for Aeronautics (now NASA), Hampton, Va., 1944-49, Nat. Bur. of Standards, L.A., 1950-53, Aberdeen Bombing Mission, L.A., 1953-55; assoc. engr. Lockheed Missiles Systems Div., Van Nuys, Calif., 1955-57; staff engr. Hughes Aircraft Co., El Segundo, Calif., 1957-80; engring. specialist Rockwell Internat., Downey, Calif., 1980-87, ret., 1987. Contbr. articles to profl. publs. Named Alumnus of Yr. Le Moyne-Owen Coll., 1952. Mem. Soc. of Women Engrs., Assn. of Computing Machinery, Le Moyne-Owen Alumni Assn. (pres. 1984), U. Mich. Alumni Club, Alpha Kappa Alpha. Democrat. Congregationalist. Home: 4001 W 22nd Pl Los Angeles CA 90018-1029

PERKINS, PHYLLIS HARTLEY, college official; b. Bluffton, Ind., Feb. 24, 1934; d. Enoch B. and Velda C. (Williams) Hartley; m. Melza H. Brown, Jan. 6, 1973 (dec. Mar. 1977); m. Floyd J. Perkins, July 14, 1984. BA, NW Nazarene Coll., Nampa, Idaho, 1956; MEd, Oreg. State U., 1961; EdD, Ariz. State U., 1983. Sec. to Senator Henry Dworshak, U.S. Senate, Washington, 1957-58; prof. NW Nazarene Coll., 1959-62, 67-68, 1974-79; prof. Japan Christian Jr. Coll., Chiba, Japan, 1962-67; field dir. Sahuara coun. Girl Scouts U.S., Tucson, 1969-72; tchr. Canyon-Oywhee Sch.-Sch. Agy., Caldwell, Idaho, 1972-74; dir. Nazarene World Mission Soc., Kansas City, Mo., 1980-86; dir. admissions Nazarene Bible Coll., Colorado Springs, Colo., 1985-93, dir. admissions, v.p. acads., 1993—; mem. Nazarene Denomination Book Com., Kansas City, 1985—. Author: The Bible Speaks to Me About My Service and Mission, 1990, Together in Ministry, 1992. Recipient citation of merit NW Nazarene Coll., 1985. Mem. Nat. Assn. Evangelicals (bd. adminstrn. 1985—, vice-chmn. women's commn. 1992—), Delta Pi Epsilon. Republican. Office: Nazarene Bible Coll PO Box 15749 Colorado Springs CO 80935-5749

PERKINS, ROY FRANK, internist, former university official; b. Rock Island, Ill., Aug. 31, 1918; s. Frank and Jennie (Baker) P.; m. Marion Karen Mazursky, Mar. 13, 1942; children: Marc, Nancy, Franklin, John, James. BS, U. Ill., Urbana, 1939; MD, U. Ill., Chgo., 1941; MS, U. Minn., 1949. Diplomate Am. Bd. Internal Medicine. Intern LA County Hosp, 1941-42; fellow Mayo Clinic, Rochester, Minn., 1942-48, staff physician, 1948-49; pvt. practice, Alhambra, Calif., 1949-79; staff physician Scripps Clinic and Rsch. Found., La Jolla, Calif., 1979-87; v.p. for med. affairs Baylor U. Med. Ctr., Dallas, 1988-92; ret., 1992; dir. health care svcs. AMA, Chgo., 1966-67; sr. mgmt. counsel Booz, Allen & Hamilton, Chgo., 1967-90; clin. prof. medicine U. So. Calif., L.A., 1968-92. Contbg. author: The New Health Care Market, 1985; also articles. Capt. M.C., U.S. Army, 1944-46. Mem. Am. Coll. Physician Execs., Am. Diabetes Assn. (bd. govs. So. Calif. 1955-57), L.A. Diabetes Assn. (pres. 1955, San Gabriel br. 1960-61). Home: 6427 Caminito Aronimink La Jolla CA 92037

PERKINS, THOMAS JAMES, venture capital company executive; b. Oak Park, Ill., Jan. 7, 1932; s. Harry H. and Elizabeth P.; m. Gerd Thune-Ellefsen, Dec. 9, 1961; children: Tor Kristian, Elizabeth Siri. B.S.E.E., M.I.T., 1953; M.B.A., Harvard U., 1957. Gen. mgr. computer div. Hewlett Packard Co., Cupertino, Calif., 1965-70, dir. corp. devel., 1970-72; gen. partner Kleiner & Perkins, San Francisco, 1972-80; sr. ptnr. Kleiner Perkins Caufield & Byers, San Francisco, from 1980; chmn. bd. Tandem Computers, Inc., Cupertino, Calif.; chmn. bd. Tandem Computers, Genentech; dir. Spectra Physics., Corning Glass Works, Collagen Corp., LSI Logic Corp., Hybritech Inc., Econics Corp., Vitalink Communications Corp. Author: Classic Supercharged Sports Cars, 1984. Trustee San Francisco Ballet, 1980—. Mem. Nat. Venture Capital Assn. (chmn. 1981-82, pres. 1980-81). Clubs: N.Y. Yacht, Links, Am. Bugatti (pres. 1983—). Office: Tandem Computers Inc 10435 Tantau Ave Cupertino CA 95014-3548 also: Genentech Inc 460 Point San Bruno San Francisco CA 94080*

PERKINS, TIM, engineering executive; b. Torrance, Calif., May 5, 1958; s. Robert and Thelma (Cole) P.; m. Patricia Ann Chong, Aug. 9, 1986; 1 child, Danielle Yim Chong. BS in Physics, Calif. State U., San Luis Obispo, 1980; MS in Electrical Engring., U. Calif., Santa Barbara, 1983, MA in Psychology, 1985, PhD in Psychology, 1987. Calif. Instructor's credential. Physicist Burroughs Corp., Westlake, Calif., 1980-82; staff scientist Applied Magnetics Corp., Goleta, Calif., 1982-88, sr. scientist, 1988-90, mgr., 1990-92; dir. Internat. Test Instruments, Irvine, Calif., 1992; instr. Santa Barbara (calif.) City Coll., 1982-84. Contbr. articles to profl. jours.; inventor paraphase signal analyser, 1989. Democrat. Home: 2909 Paseo del Refugio Santa Barbara CA 93105 Office: Applied Magnetics Corp 75 Robin Hill Rd Santa Barbara CA 93117

PERKINS, WILLIAM CLINTON, company executive; b. Decatur, Ill., Mar. 7, 1920; s. Glen Rupert and Frances Lola (Clinton) P.; m. Lillian Wuollet, Sept. 7, 1955 (div. 1965); m. Shirley Thomas, Oct. 24, 1969; children: William Rea, Howard Christy, Clinton Colcord. BS Mil. Sci. and Meteorology, U. Md., 1954; MS in Bus. and Pub. Adminstrn., Sussex Coll., Eng., 1975. Commd. USAF, 1943-73, advanced through grades to col.; with Ship Systems div. Litton Ind., Culver City, Calif., 1973-75; dir. material Hughes Aircraft Co., Tehran, Iran, 1974-78; mgr. internat. s/c Northrop Corp., Dahran, Saudi Arabia, 1978-81; dir. materiel CRS, Riyadh, Saudi Arabia, 1981-83; head major subcontracts Lear Ziegler Corp., Santa Monica, Calif., 1984-88; pres., CEO Ice Village Ctrs., Inc., L.A., 1988—; bd. dirs. Ice Village Ctrs., Inc., L.A., Forefront Industries, Maywood, Calif. Bd. dirs. World Children's Transplant Fund, L.A., 1987—; mem. Mayor's Space Adv. Com., L.A., 1970-74; mem. aerospace hist. com. Mus. Sci. and Industry, L.A., 1988—. Mem. AIAA (sect. chmn. 1970), Ret. Officers Assn. (pres. 1992—), Soc. for Non-destructive Testing (program chmn. 1973), Am. Soc. Quality Control, Am. Meteorol. Soc., Sigma Alpha Epsilon (alumni chpt. pres. 1974-76). Home: 8027 Hollywood Blvd Hollywood CA 90046

PERKO, WALTER KIM, computer consultant, systems analyst; b. Mpls., Dec. 8, 1950; s. Eero Nestor and Lorene (Hanson) P. AA in Computer Sci., U. Minn., 1975. Test technician hard disc drives Control Data Corp., Magnetic Peripherals Inc., Mpls., 1979-83; computer contractor NASA/Ames-Singer/Link Corp., Moffett Field, Calif., 1983-84; field engr. Multi Metrics Inc., Redwood City, Calif., 1984-85; computer cons., contractor Bay Alarm Co., Oakland, Calif., 1985-87; computer cons. Interocean Steamship Corp., San Francisco, 1986—; cabinet maker, designer Per Madsen Design, San Francisco, 1987-89; computer telephone support Computer Hand Holding, San Francisco, 1990-91; contrator Mil. Sealift Command, Oakland, Calif., 1991-92, Navy Pub. Works Ctr., Oakland, 1992—; cons. SysOp of the Midi and Multi Media Exch. BBS, San Francisco, 1987—. Author product info. and evaluators; editor product descriptions. With USN, 1968-72, Korea and Vietnam. Mem. Soc. Automotive Engring. Lutheran. Office: Midi & Multi Media Exch BBS PO Box 640608 San Francisco CA 94164-0608

PERKOWSKI, MAREK ANDRZEJ, electrical engineering educator; b. Warszawa, Poland, Oct. 6, 1946; came to U.S., 1981; s. Adam Perkowski and Hanna (Zielinska) Mystkowska; m. Ewa Kaja Wilkowska, Oct. 26, 1974; 1 child, Mateusz Jan. MS in Electronics with distinction, T.U. of Warsaw, 1970, PhD in Automatics with distinction, 1980. Sr. asst. Inst. of Automatics, T.U. of Warsaw, 1973-80, asst. prof., 1980-81; vis. asst. prof. Dept. Elec. Engring., U. Minn., Mpls., 1981-83; assoc. prof. Dept. Elec. Engring., Portland State U., 1983—. Co-author: Theory of Automation, 3rd edit., 1976, Problems in Theory of Logic Circuits, 4th edit., 1986, Theory of Logic Circuits-Selected Problems, 3rd edit., 1984; contbr. 9 book chpts. and 120 articles to profl. jours. Mem. Solidarity, Warsaw, 1980-81. Recipient Design Automation award SIGDA/ACM/DATC IEEE, 1986-91; rsch. grantee NSF, 1991, Commn. for Familites Roman Cath. Ch., Vatican, 1981. Mem. IEEE (Computer Soc.), Polish Nat. Alliance, Assn. for Computing Machinery, Am. Soc. for Engring. Edn. Roman Catholic. Home: 15720 NW Perimeter Dr Beaverton OR 97006 Office: Dept Elec Engring Portland State U 1800 SW 6th Ave PO Box 751 Portland OR 97207-0751

PERLBERGER, MARTIN, lawyer, international motion picture industry specialist; b. Amsterdam, The Netherlands, Mar. 17, 1928; came to U.S., 1946, naturalized, 1952; s. Oscar and Claire (Untermans) P.; m. Lily Ann Barancik, Apr. 15, 1954 (div. 1980); children, Carol, Mark; m. Karina Nilsen, May 15, 1982 (div. 1992). AB in Econs., Stanford (Calif.) U., 1951; postgrad., Columbia U., 1951-52; JD, Stanford U., Stanford, Calif., 1954. Bar: Calif. 1954, D.C. 1954, N.Y., 1980, U.S. Supreme Ct. 1976. Assoc. David Lloyd Kreeger, Washington; from assoc. to ptnr. Kaplan, Livingston, Goodwin, Berkowitz & Selvin, Beverly Hills, Calif.; pvt. practice L.A.; exec. producer maj. motion picture ventures in People's Republic of China, Australia, Japan; rep. West Coast Toni Mendez, Inc. N.Y. Literary Agy.; founder, bd. dirs. Ctr. for Internat. Comml. Arbitration; cons. mergers, acquisitions, joint ventures, venture capital and corp. fin. various nat. and internat. orgns. Bd. dirs. Internat. Vis. Coun., L.A., 1989—. Mem. ABA (internat. law sect., past mem. coun., past chmn. European law com.), Calif. Bar Assn. (internat. law sect. exec. com. 1992), L.A. Bar Assn. (exec. com. internat. law sect., 1968—, chmn. 1976-77, exec. com. intellectual property and entertainment law sect. 1992—), L.A. Copyright Soc. (past trustee 1978-80), Am. Arbitration Assn. (nat. panel), D.C. Bar Assn., Am. Film Mktg. Assn. (internat. arbitration panel 1984—), Netherlands Am. Bus. Assn. L.A. (bd. dirs. 1992—), Netherlands Am. Soc. So. Calif. (v.p. 1982-84, exec. sec. 1992—), Belgian Bus. Club, Order of Coif. Office: 3251 Bennett Dr Los Angeles CA 90068-1704

PERLIS, MICHAEL FREDRICK, lawyer; b. N.Y.C., June 3, 1947; s. Leo and Betty F. (Gantz) P.; children: Amy Hannah, David Matthew; m. Angela M. Rinaldi, Dec. 23, 1988. BS in Fgn. Svc. , Georgetown U., 1968, JD, 1971. Bar: D.C. 1971, U.S. Dist. Ct. D.C. 1971, U.S. Ct. Appeals 1971, D.C. Ct. Appeals 1971, Calif. 1980, U.S. Dist. Ct. (no. dist.) Calif. 1980, U.S Dist. Ct. (cen. dist.) Calif. 1985, U.S. Ct. Appeals (9th cir.) 1980, U.S. Supreme Ct., 1980. Law clerk D.C. Ct. Appeals, Washington, 1971-72; asst. corp. counsel D.C., Washington, 1972-74; counsel U.S. SEC, div. enforcement, Washington, 1974-75, br. chief, 1975-77, asst. dir., 1977-80; ptnr. Pettit & Martin, San Francisco, 1980-89, Stroock & Stroock & Lavan, L.A., 1989—; adj. prof. Cath. U. Am., 1979-80. Mem. ABA (co-chmn. subcom. securities and commodities litigation 1982-83), D.C. Bar Assn., Calif. State Bar Assn. Office: Stroock & Stroock & Lavan 2029 Century Park E Los Angeles CA 90067-2901

PERLMAN, DAVID, science editor, journalist; b. Balt., Dec. 30, 1918; s. Jess and Sara P.; m. Anne Salz, Oct. 15, 1941; children: Katherine, Eric, Thomas. A.B., Columbia U., 1939, M.S., 1940. Reporter Bismarck (N.D.) Capital, 1940; reporter San Francisco Chronicle, 1940-41, reporter, sci. editor, 1952-77, city editor, 1977-79, assoc. editor, sci. editor, 1979—; reporter New York Herald Tribune, Paris, N.Y.C., 1945-49; European corr. Colliers mag. and New York Post, 1949-51; Regents prof. human biology U. Calif., San Francisco 1974; vis. lectr. China Assn. Sci. and Tech., Beijing, Chengdu and Shanghai, 1983; sci. writer-in-residence U. Wis., 1989. Contbr. articles to major mags. Founding dir. Squaw Valley (Calif.) Community of Writers; dir. Alan Guttmacher Inst., 1985—; trustee Scientists Inst. for Pub. Info., 1986—. Served with inf. USAAF, 1941-45. Recipient Atomic Indsl. Forum award, 1975, Westinghouse Sci. Writing award, 1976, Ralph Coates Roe medal ASME, 1978, Margaret Sanger Community Svc. award, 1981, Fellows' medal Calif. Acad. Scis., 1984, Career Achievement award Soc. Profl. Journalists, 1989; Poynter fellow Yale U., 1984, Carnegie fellow Stanford U., 1987. Fellow Calif. Acad. Scis.; mem. AAAS (adv. bd. Science-81-86 mag., com. Pub. Understanding of Sci. 1985-90), Coun. for Advancement Sci. Writing (pres. 1976-80), Nat. Assn. Sci. Writers (pres. 1970-71), Astron. Soc. of Pacific (dir. 1976-78), Sigma Xi. Office: Chronicle Pub Co 901 Mission St San Francisco CA 94103-2988

PERLMAN, MITCHEL DEAN, clinical psychologist; b. Miami, Fla., Mar. 31, 1955; s. Ivan Perlman and Helene (Greenfield) Alberts; m. Phyllis Breitbart, Apr. 6, 1973 (div. Apr. 1986); children: Christopher, Jordanna, Bethany. Student, Miami Dade Jr. Coll., 1971-73, Dallas Bible Coll., 1978-79; BA in Psychology summa cum laude, U. Tex., Dallas, 1980; PhD in Clin. Psychology, Calif. Sch. Profl. Psychology, 1986. Counselor Santa Fe Christian Community Sch., 1984-85, Christian Unified Sch. Dist., Temple Beth Israel Day Sch., Santa Fe Montessori Sch., 1985-87; rsch. cons. Am. Guidance Svc., San Diego, L.A., 1984-89; pvt. practice San Diego, 1984—; adj. faculty U.S. Internat. U., 1986—; leader K-SOS workshops, 1984-87; leader workshops in field, 1986—. Contbg. author: (textbook) Handbook of Psychological Assessment, 1989, Innovations in Child Behavior Therapy, 1989; syndicated columnist: Perlman on Chaos; contbr. articles to profl. jours. Mem. APA. Home: 3958 La Jolla Village Dr La Jolla CA 92037 Office: Clin Resource Cons 411 Brookes Ave San Diego CA 92103

PERLMUTTER, LEONARD MICHAEL, concrete construction company executive; b. Denver, Oct. 16, 1925; s. Philip Permutter and Belle (Perlmutter); m. Alice Love Bristow, Nov. 17, 1951; children: Edwin George, Joseph Kent, Cassandra Love. B.A., U. Colo., 1948, postgrad., 1948-50. Ptnr. Perlmutter & Sons, Denver, 1947-58; v.p. Prestressed Concrete of Colo., Denver, 1952-60; pres. Stanley Structures, Inc., Denver, 1960-83; chmn. bd. Stanley Structures, Inc., 1983-87; dir. Colo. Nat. Bankshares, Inc.; adj. prof. Grad. Sch. Pub. Affairs U. Colo., Denver, 1987—; chief exec. officer Econ. Devel. Gov.'s Office State of Colo., 1987-88; chmn. bd. Colo. Open Lands, 1989. Chmn. bd. U. Colo. Found., Boulder, 1979-81; dir. Santa Fe Opera Assn., N.Mex., 1976-85; v.p. Santa Fe Fedn., 1979-87; chmn. bd. Nat. Jewish Hops.-Nat. Asthma Ctr., Denver, 1983-86; pres. Denver Symphony Assn., 1983-84, chmn. bd., 1985; trustee Midwest Rsch. Inst., 1989—; pres. Nat. Jewish Ctr. for Immunology and Respiratory Medicine, 1991-93. Recipient Humanitarian Am. Jewish Com., 1981. Mem. Prestressed Concrete Inst. (pres. 1977, dir. 1973-74). Club: Rolling Hills Country (Golden) (pres. 1966-68). Home: 15125 Foothill Rd Golden CO 80401 Office: LAP Inc Three Park Ctrl Ste 440 1515 Arapahoe Denver CO 80202

PERLMUTTER, LYNN SUSAN, neuroscientist; b. N.Y.C., Oct. 12, 1954; d. David Louis and Audrey Marilyn (Cherkoss) P.; m. Howard Jay Deiner, May 30, 1976; 1 child, Jocelyn Rae Perldeiner. BA with highest honors, SUNY, Stony Brook, 1976; MA, Mich. State U., 1980, PhD, 1984. Postdoctoral fellow U. Calif., Irvine, 1984-87; asst. prof. neurology & pathology U. So. Calif., L.A., 1987—, sec. med. faculty assembly, 1990-92; science coord. USC Bravo Med. Magnet High Sch. Partnership, 1993—; ad hoc reviewer John Douglas French Found., L.A., 1988, 91, Calif. Dept. Alzheimer's Disease Program, Sacramento, 1990, 92, NIH Neurology Rev. Panel; chmn. blood-brain barrier session Internat. Conf. Alzheimer's Disease, Italy, 1992. Contbr. articles to sci. jours. Travel fellow Internat. Conf. on Alzheimer's Disease, 1990, 92. Mem. AAAS, Soc. for Neurosci., Electron Microscopy Soc. Am., N.Y. Acad. Scis., Med. Faculty Women's Assn. (chmn. membership 1989-91), Phi Kappa Phi. Democrat. Jewish. Office: U So Calif Sch Medicine 1333 San Pablo St MCA-243 Los Angeles CA 90033

PERLMUTTER, MILTON MANUEL, chemist, accountant, financial consultant, property manager, real estate appraiser; b. Montreal, Que., Can., July 21, 1956; s. Max and Edith (Liszauer) P. Student, Dawson Coll., Montreal, 1975; BSC, McGill U., Montreal, 1978; PhD, Queen's U., Kingston, Ont., 1984. Cert. profl. chemist. Lectr./tutor Queen's U., Kingston, 1984-85; postdoctoral scholar UCLA Sch. Medicine, 1986-89; sr. chemist P.G. & E. Co., L.A., 1989-92; pres., chief exec. officer MMP Chem. and Environ. Cons. Svcs. Co., L.A., 1992—; sr. rsch. scientist U. So. Calif. Sch. Dentistry, L.A., 1993—; cons. in field. Contbr. articles to profl. jours. Vol. UCLA Sch. Medicine, 1989—, Chabad House, L.A., 1986—. R. Samuel McLaughlin scholar, 1978-79, Natural Scis. and Engring. Rsch. Coun. scholar, 1979-82, 92—. Fellow Am. Inst. Chemists; mem. AAAS, Am. Chem. Soc., Internat. Union Pure and Applied Chemists, N.Y. Acad. Sci., Soc. Nuclear Medicine. Jewish. Home: 741 Gayley Ave Apt 416 Los Angeles CA 90024-2410 Office: MMP Chem Environ Cons Svcs Co 1015 Gayley Ave Ste 1260 Los Angeles CA 90024-3424

PERLOFF, JEFFREY MARK, agricultural and resource economics educator; b. Chgo., Jan. 28, 1950; s. Harvey S. and Miriam (Seligman) P.; m. Jaqueline B. Persons, Aug. 15, 1976; 1 child, Lisa. BA, U. Chgo., 1972; PhD, MIT, 1976. Asst. prof. U. Pa., Phila., 1976-80; asst. prof. U. Calif., Berkeley, 1980-82, assoc. prof., 1982-89, prof., 1989—. Author: (with Dennis Carlton) Modern Industrial Organization, 1990; contbr. numerous articles to profl. jours. Office: U Calif Dept Agrl Econs 207 Giannini Hall Berkeley CA 94720

PERNA, FRANK, JR., manufacturing company executive; b. Detroit, Jan. 15, 1938; s. Frank and Mary (Cataldo) P.; m. Monika Doering, May 10, 1960; children: Laura, Reneé, Christopher. BSME, Gen. Motors Inst., 1960; MSEE, Wayne State U., 1966; MBA in Mgmt. (Sloan fellow), MIT, 1970. Asst. to dir. reliability Gen. Motors Corp., Detroit, 1955-70; v.p., dir. engring. Sun Electric Corp., Crystal Lake, Ill., 1971-77, exec. v.p. ops., 1977-78, pres., chief exec. officer, 1978-81; v.p., group exec. Whittaker Corp., Los Angeles, 1983-85; pres. MagneTek, Inc., Los Angeles, 1985—; bd. dirs. 1st State Bank and Trust, Hanover Park, Ill., 1st Nat. Bank of Hoffman Estates,

Ill. Named one of Outstanding Young Man of Am., 1968. Mem. Bd. Profl. Engrs. Office: MagneTek Inc 11150 Santa Monica Blvd Los Angeles CA 90025-3333*

PEROFF, RONALD PETER, otolaryngologist, head and neck surgeon; b. Toronto, Ont., Can., Aug. 8, 1942; came to U.S., 1973; s. William and Diane (Karstoff) P.; m. Karen Virginia Hastings, Jan. 5, 1980; 1 child, Roderick John William. Sr. matriculation, Lawrence Park Collegiate, Toronto, 1961; MD, U. Toronto, 1967. Intern Montreal Gen. Hosp., 1967-68; gen. practice intern Charlotte (N.C.) Meml. Hosp., King Edward VII Meml. Hosp., Bermuda, 1968-69; resident in otolaryngology, head and neck surgery McGill U., Montreal, 1969-70, 70-71, 71-73; resident in gen. surgery Queens Med. Ctr., Honolulu, 1970-71; otolaryngologist, head and neck surgeon Honolulu Med. Group, 1973-79. Mem. AMA, Am. Acad. Otolaryngology, Head and Neck Surgery, Hawaii Med. Assn., Hawaii Soc. Otolaryngology, Head and Neck Surgery, Honolulu County Med. Soc. Office: Queens Physicians Office Bldg II 1329 Lusitana # 307 Honolulu HI 96813

PERRELLA, ANTHONY JOSEPH, electronics engineer; b. Boulder, Colo., Sept. 16, 1942; s. Anthony Vincent and Mary Domenica (Forte) P.; B.S., U. Wyo., 1964, postgrad., 1965; postgrad. U. Calif. at San Diego, 1966-67, U. Calif. at Irvine, 1968-70; m. Pamela Smith, July 19, 1980; 1 child, Kathleen. Flight engr. U.S. Naval Tng. Devices Center, San Diego, 1965-67; rsch. engr. Collins div. Rockwell Internat. (formerly Collins Radio Co.), Newport Beach, Calif., 1967-69, electromagnetic interference and TEMPEST group head, 1969-74, supr., 1974-75, mgr., 1975-77, mgr. systems integration, 1977, mgr. space communication systems, 1977-78; sr. mem. tech. staff ARGOSystems Inc., Sunnyvale, Calif., 1978—, program mgr., 1978-81, dep. dept. mgr. EW Systems, 1980-83, div. EW staff engr., 1983-84, dept. mgr., 1984-87, Sun Microsystems Inc., Mountain View, 1987-89; prin. A.J. Perrella-Cons., Cupertino, Calif., 1989—; v.p. rsch. and devel. Things Unlimited, Inc., Laramie, Wyo., 1965-72, pres., 1972-75; bd. dirs. Columbian Credit Union. Mem. IEEE, AAAS, Am. Mgmt. Assn., N.Y. Acad. Scis., Assn. Old Crows, KC, Tau Kappa Epsilon. Roman Catholic. Home: 931 Brookgrove Ln Cupertino CA 95014-4667 Office: 2550 Garcia Ave Mountain View CA 94043-1100

PERRET, JOSEPH ALOYSIUS, banker, consultant; b. Phila., Feb. 26, 1929; s. Joseph Henry and Mary Rose (Martin) P.; m. Nancy S. Bott, June 24, 1950; children—Kathlyne, Robert, Susan, Michael. Student, U. Pa., 1953-57, Temple U., 1957-58, Stonier Grad. Sch. Banking, 1966. Head analyst Phila. Nat. Bank, 1953-57; spl. banking rep. Burroughs Corp., Phila., 1957-59; v.p. First Pa. Banking & Trust Co., Phila., 1959-66, Md. Nat. Bank, Balt., 1966-70; sr. v.p. Md. Nat. Bank, 1970-75, Comml. Credit Co., Balt., 1975-78, Sanwa Bank Calif., Los Angeles, 1978-91; cons., 1991—; chmn. bd. Star System, Inc., San Diego. Mem. Am. Bankers Assn., Data Processing Mgmt. Assn., Balt.-Washington Regional Clearing House (chmn. 1970), Calif. Bankers Cleanring House Assn. (chmn. 1990). Clubs: Country of Md; Merchants (Balt.); Friendly Hills Country (Whittier, Calif.). Home and Office: 3023 S Rio Claro Dr La Puente CA 91745-5954

PERRIER, BARBARA SUE, artist; b. Akron, Ohio, Oct. 7, 1937; d. Willis Austin and Mary Gladys (Campbell) Bibler; m. David John Perrier, July 14, 1956 (div. Nov. 1972); children: David John Jr., Kenneth James, Mark Richard; m. Gary Dean Warren, June 26, 1981 (div. May 1993). AA in Comml. Art, AA in Liberal Arts, Ventura Coll., 1991. Artist Anointed Brush Studio, Oxnard, Calif., 1987—; tchr. pvt. art classes. One-woman show at Columbia Arts Ctr., Vancouver, Wash., 1988, Gallery Los Olivos, 1993; exhibited in group shows at Franky's Place, Ventura, 1992, Santa Paula Soc. of Arts 3d Annual Fall Show, 1992, Gloria Dei Art Show, Camarillo, Calif., 1992, 13th Annual Nat. Bald Eagle Conf. Art Show, 1992, Gloria Dei Art Festival, Camarillo, 1991, Ventura Coll. Student Art Show, 1990, 53d Annual City of Santa Paula Art Show, 1989, 5th Annual Buenaventura Art Assn. Art Show, Ventura, 1988, Westlake Village 15th Annual Art Show, 1988. Mem. Buenaventura Art Assn., Oxnard Art Assn., Santa Paula Soc. of Arts, Calif. Gold Coast Watercolor Soc. (charter, pres. 1992), So. Calif. Wildlife Artist Assn. Baptist. Home and Office: Anointed Brush Studio 1231 Masthead Dr Oxnard CA 93035

PERRILL, FREDERICK EUGENE, information systems executive; b. Charlotte, N.C., Sept. 11, 1939; s. Frederick Eugene and Dorothy (Miller) P.; m. Kathryne Sims, June 1, 1963. BS in Engring., U.S. Naval Acad., 1962; MS in Bus., Naval Postgrad. Sch., 1969. Commd. ensign USN, 1962, advanced through grades to capt., 1982; supply officer USS Biddle DDG-5, 1962-63, USS Hermitage LSD-34, 1963-64; comptr. Amphibious Staff, 1964-68; dir. systems, acctg., transp. Naval Supply Depot, Yokouka, Japan, 1969-72; project mgr. fin. systems design Asst. Sec. of Navy, 1973-76; dir. logistics USS Concord, 1976-78; project mgr. Fin. Systems, Washington, 1978-81; commanding officer Fin. and Acctg. Ctr., San Diego, 1981-83; dir. ops. Naval Supply Depot, Oakland, 1984-85; asst. chief of staff MIS, COMMS. Naval Airforce Pacific, Coronado, Calif., 1985-86; ret. Naval Airforce Pacific, Coronado, 1986; sr. group mgr. Planning Rsch. Corp., San Diego, 1986-87; v.p. R.D. Ram Corp., San Diego, 1987-88; dir. Fourth Generation Tech., LaJolla, Calif., 1988-90; pres. Perrill Info. Systems, San Diego, 1990—; cons. Titan Corp., LaJolla, 1991—, Monger Industries, San Diego, 1988—, Delfin Corp., San Jose, 1990-91, Dobbs Ho., Memphis, 1986. Contbr. articles to profl. jours. Asst. scout master Boy Scouts Am., Yokosuka, Japan, 1969-72; Protestant lay leader USS Concord AFS-5, Norfolk, Va., 1976-78. Mem. VFW, Naval Sailing Assn., Am. Legion, Humane Soc. of U.S., Disabled Am. Vets. Presbyterian. Home: 4785 Seda Dr San Diego CA 92124

PERRIN, EDWARD BURTON, health services researcher, biostatistician, public health educator; b. Greensboro, Vt., Sept. 19, 1931; s. J. Newton and Dorothy E. (Willey) P.; m. Carol Anne Hendricks, Aug. 18, 1956; children: Jenifer, Scott. B.A., Middlebury Coll., 1953; postgrad. (Fulbright scholar) in stats, Edinburgh (Scotland) U., 1953-54; M.A. in Math. Stats, Columbia U., 1956; Ph.D., Stanford U., 1960. Asst. prof. dept. biostats. U. Pitts., 1959-62; asst. prof. dept. preventive medicine U. Wash., Seattle, 1962-65; asso. prof. U. Wash., 1965-69, prof., 1969-70, prof., chmn. dept. biostats., 1970-72, prof. dept. health services, 1975—, chmn. dept., 1983—; prof. (hon.) West China U. of Med. Scis., Szechwan, Peoples Republic of China, 1988—; overseas fellow Churchill Coll., Cambridge U., 1991-92; clin. prof. dept. community medicine and internat. health Sch. Medicine, Georgetown U., Washington, 1972-75; dep. dir. Nat. Center for Health Stats., HEW, 1972-73, dir., 1973-75; research scientist Health Care Study Center, Battelle Human Affairs Research Centers, Seattle, 1975-76, dir., 1976-78; dir. Health and Population Study Center Battelle Human Affairs Research Centers, Seattle, 1978-83; sr. cons. biostats. Wash./Alaska regional med. programs, 1967 -72; biometrician VA Co-op Study on Treatment of Esophageal Varices, 1961-73; mem. Epidemiology and Disease Control Study Sect., NIH, 1969-73; chmn. health services research study sect., HEW, 1976-79; chmn. health services research and devel. field program rev. panel, VA, 1988-91. Contbr. articles on biostats., health services and population studies to profl. publs.; mem. editorial bd.: Jour. Family Practice, 1978-90, Public Health Nursing, 1992—. Mem. tech. bd. Milbank Meml. Fund, 1974-76. Recipient Outstanding Service citation HEW, 1975. Fellow AAAS, Am. Public Health Assn. (Spiegelman Health Stats. award 1970, program devel. bd. 1971, chmn. stats. sect. 1978-80, governing council 1983-85, stats. sect. recognition award 1989), Am. Statis. Assn. (mem. adv. com. to div. statis. policy 1975-77); mem. Inst. Medicine of Nat. Acad. Sci. (chmn. membership com. 1984-86, mem. bd. on health care svcs. 1987—, chmn. com. on clin. evaluation 1990—), Biometrics Soc. (pres. Western N.Am. Region 1971), Inst. Math. Stats., Internat. Epidemiologic Assn., Sigma Xi, Phi Beta Kappa. Home: 4900 NE 39th St Seattle WA 98105 Office: U Wash Dept Health Svcs SC-37 Seattle WA 98195

PERRIS, ELIZABETH L., federal judge; b. 1951. AB, U. Calif., 1972; JD, U. Calif., Davis, 1975. Admitted to bar, 1976. Bankruptcy judge U.S. Dist. Ct. Oreg., 1984—. Office: US Dist Ct 900 Security Pacific Plz 1001 SW 5th Ave Portland OR 97204-1118

PERRO, MARY ELIZABETH, systems programmer; b. North Kingstown, R.I., Oct. 25, 1964; d. Michael Alexander and Dorothy Edna (Mayer) Perro. BA in Computer Sci., Rutgers U., Camden, N.J., 1986. Assoc. programmer Phila. Life Ins., 1986-87; programmer, analyst CIGNA, Voorhees, N.J., 1987; assoc. programmer IBM Corp., Manassas, Va., 1987-90; sr. assoc. programmer IBM Corp., San Jose, Calif., 1990—. Coach Spl. Olympics, Santa Clara County, 1991—; tutor English lang. and reading, 1991—.

PERROT, PAUL NORMAN, museum director; b. Paris, France, July 28, 1926; came to U.S., 1946, naturalized, 1954; s. Paul and K. Norman (Derr) P.; m. Joanne Stovall, Oct. 23, 1954; children—Paul Latham, Chantal Marie Claire, Jeanine, Robert. Student, Ecole du Louvre, 1945-46, N.Y. U. Inst. Fine Arts, 1946-52. Asst. The Cloisters, Met. Mus. Art, 1948-52; asst. to dir. Corning (N.Y.) Mus. Glass, 1952-54, asst. dir. mus., 1954-60, dir., 1960-72; editor Jour. Glass Studies, 1959-72; asst. sec. for mus. programs Smithsonian Instn., Washington, 1972-84; dir. Va. Mus. Fine Arts, 1984-91; lectr. glass history, aesthetics, museology; past v.p. Internat. Coun. Mus. Found.; past pres. N.E. Conf. Mus.; past pres. Internat. Centre for Study of Preservation and Restoration of Cultural Property, Rome, mem. coun., 1974-88. Author: Three Great Centuries of Venetian Glass, 1958, also numerous articles on various hist. and archael. subjects. Former trustee Winterthur Mus.; former trustee, treas. Mus. Computer Network; mem. Internat. Cons. Com. for the Preservation of Moenjodaro; chmn. adv. com. World Monuments Fund. Mem. Am. Assn. Mus. (past v.p., coun. 1967-78), N.Y. State Assn. Mus. (past pres.), Internat. Assn. History Glass (past v.p.) Corning Friends of Library (past pres.), So. Tier Library System (past pres.). Office: Santa Barbara Museum of Art 1130 State St Santa Barbara CA 93101-2746

PERROTT, PAMELA RUNDLE, systems analyst, data processing trainer; b. Miles City, Mont., Sept. 5, 1941; d. Neil Donald and Ethel (Rundle) Sharp; divorced; children: Gordon, Michael. BA in Biology, Bryn Mawr Coll., 1962; MA in Biochemistry, Cambridge U., Eng., 1964; cert. in data processing, North Seattle C.C., 1982; M in Software Engring., Seattle U., 1992. Rsch. tech. U. Wash., Seattle, 1964-72, assoc. in biology, 1972-82; programmer analyst Grange Ins. Group, Seattle, 1982-85; programmer analyst Family Life Ins., Seattle, 1985-86, software programmer, 1986-89, sr. systems analyst, 1989-91; systems analyst Boeing Computer Svcs., 1991—; facilitator Seattle Area Tech. Edn. Coords., 1990. Mem. Assn. Computing Machinery, Computer Soc. of IEEE, Assn. for Women in Computing (v.p. membership 1983-84).

PERRY, ANTOINETTE KRUEGER, pianist, instructor; b. Manhattan, N.Y., Sept. 21, 1954; d. Paul Krueger and Lillian (Haslach) Teddlie; m. John Perry, Dec. 29, 1984; 1 child, Sean Paul. Student, Kans. U., 1972-74; MusB, U. Tex., 1976, MusM, 1978; postgrad., Munchen Hochschule Für Musk, 1979-80. Instr. Community Sch. Performing Arts (name changed R.D. Colburn Sch. of the Performing Arts), L.A., 1981—; lectr. UCLA, 1984—; summer faculty artist Aspen (Colo.) Music Sch., 1985—; mem. summer workshop faculty Idyllwild (Calif.) Sch. Music and the Arts, 1987—; concert artist in field. U. Tex. fellow, 1976-79; German-Am. Club Exch. scholar, 1979-80. Mem. Phi Kappa Phi. Office: UCAL Music Dept 405 Hilgard Ave Los Angeles CA 90024-1301

PERRY, BONNE LU, county public welfare administrator; b. Miles City, Mont., Mar. 26, 1929; d. Daniel Glenn and Mabel Jane (Scriven) Harris; adopted d. Albert Hartford and Bertha Gertrude (Erickson) P. Student, No. Mont. Coll., 1947-49; BA in English, U. Mont., 1951; postgrad., Queens Coll., 1966. Tchr. English Whitefish (Mont.) High Sch., 1951-53; tchr. English and drama Great Falls (Mont.) High Sch., 1953-58; tchr. English Northport (N.Y.) High Sch., 1958-67; social worker Roosevelt County Dept. Pub. Welfare, Wolf Point, Mont., 1969-74; social worker supr. I Roosevelt, Sheridan, and Daniels Counties Dept. Pub. Welfare, Wolf Point, Mont., 1974-78; county dir. II Richland County Dept. Pub. Welfare, Sidney, Mont., 1978—. Author: (poetry) Winter, 1978. Mem. Mont. Pub. Welfare Assn., Am. Pub. Welfare Assn., Mont. County Dirs., Eastern Mont. Mental Health Assn., Community Health Mtg., U. Mont. Alumni Assn., Whitefish Edn. Assn. (pres. 1952-53), Alpha Phi. Democrat. Congregationalist. Lodges: Order of Eastern Star, PEO (recording sec. 1984-85. Home: 120 7th St SW Trlr 25 Sidney MT 59270-4943 Office: Richland County Dept Pub Welfare 221 5th St SW Sidney MT 59270-4900

PERRY, DAVID NILES, public relations executive; b. Utica, N.Y., Mar. 7, 1940; s. Francis N. and Marion H. P.; B.S., Utica Coll. Syracuse U., 1962; m. Jacqueline J. Adams, Dec. 21, 1962. Pub. affairs rep. Allstate Ins. Co., Pasadena, Calif., 1966-67; dir. press rrels. L.A. C. of C., 1968; rep. pub. rels. Lockheed Propulsion Co., Redlands, Calif., 1968-70; mgr. pub. rels. Bozell & Jacobs Inc., L.A., 1970-73, Phoenix, 1974; pres. David Perry Pub. Rels. Inc., Scottsdale, Ariz.; exec. dir. Ariz. Water Quality Assn., Cert. Collision Repair Assn. Mem. Ariz. Commn. Ariz. Environment, 1972—. Served with USNR, 1962-65. Mem. Pub. Rels. Soc. Am. (accredited, dir. Phoenix chpt. 1975-82, pres. 1978). Office: 6819 E Diamond St Scottsdale AZ 85257-3233

PERRY, DONALD LESTER, II, venture capitalist; b. Culver City, Calif., Jan. 21, 1958; s. Donald Lester Sr. and Joyce Estella (Kirklin) P.; m. Michael Albert Behn, July 24, 1982. BA in Econs. and Polit. Sci., Williams Coll., 1979; MBA in Strategic Mgmt., Claremont (Calif.) Grad. Sch., 1990. Fgn. exch. trader Morgan Guaranty Trust Co., N.Y.C., 1979-80; exec. recruiter Benson-McBride & Assoc., Beverly Hills, Calif., 1980-82; asst. v.p. money markets div. Nat. Australia Bank, L.A., 1982-86; v.p., eurodollar trader Sanwa Bank of Calif., L.A., 1986-88; v.p. comml. loans Union Bank, L.A., 1989-90; mng. ptnr. Pine Cobble Ptnrs., L.A., 1990—; speaker Pacific Coast Regional SBDC, L.A., 1989—, Nat. Assn. Black MBAs, L.A., 1990—, So. Calif. Edison/Joint Coun., L.A., 1990—. Mem. Town Hall of Calif., L.A., 1990. Named Positive Black Role Model, Assn. of Black Women Entrepreneurs, 1993. Mem. L.A. Venture Assn., L.A. Urban Bankers, Pacific Coast Regional Small Bus. Devel. Corp. (loan com. 1990—), L.A. World Affairs Coun. Republican. Office: Pine Cobble Ptnrs 1533 E Edgecomb St Covina CA 91724-2807

PERRY, GAIL WALBORN, human resources executive; b. Wiesbaden, Germany, Mar. 9, 1952; d. William Edward and Eloise (Walborn) P. BA, Tulane U., 1974. Restaurant and personnel mgr. Village Inn Pancake Houses of Tucson, Inc., 1974-78; sr. personnel counselor Temporaries Inc., L.A., San Francisco, 1978-80; human resources mgr. Group Health Med. Assocs., Tucson, 1980-85; personnel dir. The Tucson Nat. Resort and Spa, 1985-86, Northwest Hosp., Tucson, 1986-88; human resources dir. Charter Hosp. of Tucson, 1988-89, Thomas-Davis Med. Ctrs., P.C., Tucson, 1989—. Bd. dirs. Big Bros./Big Sisters of Tucson, 1992—, v.p. planning and program devel., 1993—. Recipient Excellence in Community Svc. award Hosp. Corp. of Am., 1986. Mem. Soc. for Human Resource Mgmt. (Ariz. state coun. dir. 1989, state coun. 1986-91), Soc. for Human Resource Mgmt. of Greater Tucson (pres. 1984-85, bd. dirs. 1982-86), Jr. League of Tucson (v.p. of tng. 1986-87, bd. dirs. 1985-87, exec. coun. 1986-87). Democrat. Episcopalian. Office: Thomas-Davis Med Ctrs PC PO Box 12650 655 N Alvernon Way Tucson AZ 85732

PERRY, HUBERT CARVER, bank executive, community volunteer, retired; b. Whittier, Calif., June 11, 1911; s. Herman Lee Perry and Lola Carver; m. Louise Curtis Bacon, 1945; children: Lee, Brian, Ellen, Mark. AB, Whittier Coll., 1935; MBA, Stanford U., 1937. Loan officer Bank of Am., L.A., 1938, v.p., 1955-70, regional v.p., 1970-72; cons. Intex Corp., Long Beach, Calif., Exec. Svc. Corp.; bd. dirs. Hosp. Billing and Collection Svc., Wilmington, Del.; trustee Not-For-Profit Hosps., Washington, Richard M. Nixon Library and Birthplace, Inc.; trustee and past chmn. Presbyn. Intercommunity Hosp. Audit Com.; mem. Com. on Governance of Hosp. Coun. of South Calif., 1981—. Contbr. articles to mags. Lt. comdr. USNR, 1942-46. Mem. Lions Club (past pres.). Republican. Quaker. Home: 14221 Mar Vista Whittier CA 90602

PERRY, JAMES GREGORY, sales and marketing executive; b. Missoula, Mont., Oct. 4, 1952; s. Joseph Tarsisus and Mary Cathrine (Schneider) P.; m. Diana Sue Coen, May 24, 1974; 1 child, Natalie Shureé. Student, Yuba Coll., Marysville, Calif., 1970-72. Credit supr. CBS Mus. Instruments, Fullerton, Calif., 1975-76, mktg. rep., 1976-80, sales rep., 1980-82; mktg. rep. Paiste Am., Inc., Brea, Calif., 1982-85, nat. sales mgr., 1985-91; field sales mgr. Am. Med. Sales, 1991—; caption chief percussion So. Calif. Judges Assn., 1983—; percussion judge So. Calif. Sch. Band Orch. Assn., 1985—. With USN, 1972-75. Mem. NRA, Greenpeace, Costeau Soc., Mu Sigma Kappa (pres. 1972), Jaycess (pres. Castleton, Ind. chpt. 1981). Office: Am Med Sales Inc 4928 W Rosecrans Ave Hawthorne CA 90250

PERRY, JEAN LOUISE, dean; b. Richland, Wash., May 13, 1950; d. Russell S. and Sue W. Perry. BS, Miami U., Oxford, Ohio, 1972; MS, U. Ill., Urbana, 1973, PhD, 1976. Cons. ednl. placement office U. Ill., 1973-75; adminstrv. intern Coll. Applied Life Studies, 1975-76, asst. dean, 1976-77, assoc. dean, 1978-81, asst. prof. dept. phys. edn., 1976-81; assoc. prof. phys. edn. San Francisco State U., 1981-84, prof., 1984-90, chair, 1981-90; dean Coll. of Human and Community Scis. U. Nev., Reno, 1990—. Named to excellent tchr. list U. Ill., 1973-79. Mem. AAHPERD (fellow research consortium, pres. 1988-89), Am. Assn. Higher Edn., Am. Ednl. Research Assn., Nat. Assn. Phys. Edn. in Higher Edn., Nat. Assn. Girls and Women in Sports (guide coordinator, pres.), Delta Psi Kappa, Phi Delta Kappa. Home: 3713 Ranchview Ct Reno NV 89509 Office: U Nev Coll Human and Community Scis Mail Stop 136 Reno NV 89557

PERRY, JOHN, senator, lawyer; b. Buffalo, Nov. 12, 1954; s. Robert John and Katherine (Marros) P.; m. Peggy Truesdale, Aug. 23, 1980; children: Alexandra, Joanna. BA, U. Utah, 1977; JD, U. Wyo., 1980. Legal intern City of Buffalo, 1979; dep. cty., prosecuting atty. Johnson County, Wyo., 1980—; partner Goddard, Perry & Vogel, Buffalo, Wyo., 1980—; state senator State of Wyo., 1985-92. Chmn. Senate Jud. Com., 1988-92, v. chmn. Wyo. Govt. Reorganization Coun., 1988-92, bd. dirs. Buffalo Day Care, Buffalo Helping Hands, Johnson County YMCA, Johnson County Community Concert Assn., legis. coord. Am. Legis. Exchange Coun., mem. Johnson County Child Protection Team, 1981—. Mem. Wyo. Bar Assn., Wyo. Peace Officers Standards and Tng. Com., Johnson County Bar Assn., U. Utah Beehive Honor Soc. Home: 112 Cummings Ave Buffalo WY 82834 Office: Goddard Perry & Vogel 412 N Main St Buffalo WY 82834

PERRY, JOHN SPENCER, newspaper editor; b. Evanston, Ill., July 28, 1951; s. John S. and Patricia L. (Hogan) P.; m. Tena M. Kessler, June 17, 1973 (div. Oct. 1981); 1 child, Sean K.; m. Diane M. Wasner, Sept. 21, 1985; stepchildren: Tiffany, Tony. AA, Canada Jr. Coll., Redwood City, Calif., 1971; BJ, U. Oreg., 1973. Reporter, news editor West Lane News, Veneta, Oreg., 1973-76; copy dest chief East Oregonian, Pendleton, 1976-78; copy editor Jour. Am., Bellevue, Wash., 1978-80, news editor, 1980-83, Sunday editor, 1983-84, city editor, 1984-86, mng. editor, 1986-88, editor, 1988-92, exec. editor, asst. to pub., 1992—, also chmn. editorial bd., 1992—. Sr. editor: Volcano: The Eruption of Mount St. Helens, 1980. Mem. steering com. Bellevue Econ. Summit, 1982; bd. dirs. Forum Eastside, Bellevue, 1990; mem. Leadership Redmond, Wash., 1990. World Affairs fellow, Seattle, 1989. Mem. Investigative Reporters and Editors, Am. Soc. Newspaper Editors, AP Mng. Editors Asns., Redmond C. of C. (bd. dirs. 1992—), The Lake Club. Office: Jour Am 1705 132d Ave NE Bellevue WA 98009

PERRY, JOHN VAN BUREN, historian, educator; b. Aberdeen, S.D., Feb. 7, 1928; s. Van Buren and Elise (Andersen) P. B.Sc., No. State U., S.D., 1954; postgrad. Law Sch., N.Y. U., 1954-55; M.A., U. Calif., Berkeley, 1959; postgrad. U. So. Calif., 1965-66. Instr. history Calif. State U. Fresno and Sonoma, 1963-65; asst. prof. Kern Community Coll. Dist., Bakersfield and Porterville, Calif., 1969-71; prof. social scis. and humanities Central Wyo. Coll., Riverton, 1971-75; prof. history, humanities and social scis. Lake Tahoe Community Coll., South Lake Tahoe, Calif., 1975—, pres. faculty senate, 1979-80, senate sec., 1983-84, advisor Truman Scholarship, 1979-89, founder/advisor Lambda Tau chpt. Alpha Gamma Sigma Soc. Pres., Lake Tahoe Community Concert Assn., 1977-79, 81-89, bd. dirs., 1975-89, campaign mgr., 1979-81; pres. Arts in Action, 1973-75; del. Wyo. Council on Arts, 1972-75, Wyo. Council for Humanities, 1973-75; bd. dirs. Riverton Community Concert Assn., 1972-75, Assn. to Restore Tallac Sites, 1981-83; bd. dirs. Lake Tahoe Cultural Arts Alliance, 1981-89, treas., 1982-84, 86-88, co-pres., 1984-86; founder, exec. dir. Perry Found. for Humanities Lake Tahoe Community Coll., 1988—. Served with USN, 1946-50. Root-Tilden fellow, 1954-55. Mem. Am. Hist. Assn., Community Coll. Humanities Assn., Mus. Soc. San Francisco, Los Angeles County Mus. Art, Met. Mus. N.Y.C., Am. Philatelic Soc., Am. Assn. Mus., Sons of Norway, Smithsonian Instn. Home: PO Box 14266 South Lake Tahoe CA 96151-4266 Office: PO Box 14445 South Lake Tahoe CA 95151

PERRY, L. TOM, church official, merchant. Mem. Quorum of the Twelve, Ch. of Jesus Christ of Latter-Day Saints, Salt Lake City; co-chmn. ZCMI, Salt Lake City. Office: LDS Church 47 E South Temple St Salt Lake City UT 84150-0001

PERRY, LEE ROWAN, lawyer; b. Chgo., Sept. 23, 1933; s. Watson Bishop and Helen (Rowan) P.; m. Barbara Ashcraft Mitchell, July 2, 1955; children: Christopher, Constance, Geoffrey. B.A., U. Ariz., 1955, LL.B., 1961. Bar: Ariz. 1961. Since practiced in Phoenix; clk. Udall & Udall, Tucson, 1960-61; mem. firm Carson, Messinger, Elliott, Laughlin & Ragan, 1961—. Mem. law rev. staff, U. Ariz., 1959-61. Mem. bd. edn. Paradise Valley Elementary and High Sch. Dists., Phoenix, 1964-68, pres., 1968; treas. troop Boy Scouts Am., 1970-72; mem. Ariz. adv. bd. Girl Scouts U.S.A., 1972-74, mem. nominating bd., 1978-79; bd. dirs. Florence Crittenton Services Ariz., 1967-72, pres., 1970-72; bd. dirs. U. Ariz. Alumni, Phoenix, 1968-72, pres., 1969-70; bd. dirs. Family Service Phoenix, 1974-75; bd. dirs. Travelers Aid Assn. Am., 1985-89; bd. dirs. Vol. Bur. Maricopa County, 1975-81, 83-86, pres., 1984-85; bd. dirs. Ariz. div. Am. Cancer Soc., 1978-80, Florence Crittenton div. Child Welfare League Am., 1976-81; bd. dirs. Crisis Nursery for Prevention of Child Abuse, 1978-81, pres., 1978-80. Served to 1st lt. USAF, 1955-58. Mem. ABA, State Bar Ariz. (conv. chmn. 1972), Rotary (dir. 1971-77, pres. 1975-76, West Leadership award 1989), Ariz. Club, Phoenix Country Club, Phi Delta Phi, Phi Delta Theta (pres. 1954). Republican. Episcopalian. Office: Citibank Tower PO Box 33907 Phoenix AZ 85067-3907

PERRY, MICHAEL DENNIS, software educator; b. Providence, June 23, 1953; s. John K. and Sonya C. (Susi) P. BA in Bus. Adminstrn., Maharishi Internat. U., 1982. Account exec. Coastal Securities, L.A., 1983-84; programmer, clk. Exec. Life Ins. Co., L.A., 1984-88; programmer Gt. Am. Life Ins. Co., L.A., 1989-90; tech. support rep. Sterling Software-Dylakor Div., Chatsworth, Calif., 1990-92; software educator Sterling Software-Dylakor Divsn., Chatsworth, Calif., 1992—. Tchr. Westside Spl. Religious Edn., Pacific Palisades, 1986—. Roman Catholic. Office: Sterling Software Dylakor Divsn 9340 Owensmouth Ave Chatsworth CA 91311

PERRY, MICHAEL THOMAS, state official; b. Kalispell, Mont., Mar. 2, 1950; s. Joseph T. and Mary Catherine (Schneider) P.; m. Arna Claire Kaufmann, Sept. 5, 1971 (div. 1992); children: Gregory Evan, Colby Alan-Joseph. AA, Yuba Coll., Marysville, Calif., 1970; BA, Calif. State U., Sacramento, 1974; MPA, Nat. U., Sacramento, 1984. With Calif. State Bd. Equalization, Sacramento, 1976—, program tech. III, 1989-90, tax rep., 1990-92, sr. tax rep., 1992—. Sr. league v.p. Rancho Cordova (Calif.) Little League, 1990, sr. league players agt., 1988, publicity dir., 1986. With USAFR, 1972—. Home: 4001 S Watt Ave # 104 Sacramento CA 95826

PERRY, RICHARD LEE, academic administrator, physics educator; b. Portland, Oreg., Jan. 22, 1930; s. William McGuire and Emily Ruth (Usher) P.; m. Ruth Corrine Ferrell, June 13, 1952; children: Dawn, Glenn, Craig, Stella. BA, Linfield Coll., 1952; MS, Oreg. State Coll., 1955; PhD, Oreg. State U., 1961. Assoc. physicist Linfield Rsch. Inst., McMinnville, Oreg., 1956-61; asst. prof. U. of the Pacific, Stockton, Calif., 1961-65, assoc. prof., 1965-71, prof., 1971—; chair physics dept. U. of the Pacific, Stockton, 1987—; cons. Thompson Ramo-Wooldridge, Inc., Canoga Park, Calif., 1962-63; cons. physicist Tektronix, Inc., Beaverton, Oreg., summers 1963, 64, U.S. Army Nuclear Def. Lab., Edgewood Arsenal, Md., 1968-69; rsch. scientist, cons. NASA/Ames Rsch. Ctr., Moffett Field, Calif., summers 1978, 79, 80, 81, 83, 84. Contbr. articles to profl. jours. AEC fellow, 1967, NASA/ASEE fellow, 1975, 76. Mem. Am. Assn. Physics Tchrs., Soc. Photo-Optical Instrumentation Engrs., Sigma Xi. Republican. Home: PO Box 48 Valley Springs CA 95252-0048 Office: U of the Pacific Physics Dept 3601 Pacific Ave Stockton CA 95211-0197

PERRY, ROBERT L., nurse; b. Cedar Rapids, Iowa, Mar. 25, 1957; s. Robert Lee and Odleen Gladys (Wallace) P.; m. Leslie Diane Bingham, Feb.

18, 1983; children: Robert Lace, Gary Bingham, Spencer Wallace. AS, Lee's McRae Coll., 1978; BSN, A&T State U., 1981; postgrad., U. Phoenix. RN, Utah, N.C. Staff nurse New River Mental Health, Boone, N.C., 1981-88; charge nurse Logan (Utah) Regional Hosp., 1988—, chmn. behavioral health unit, 1992—; CPR instr. trainer Am. Heart Assn., N.C., 1980-88; found. employee dr. chairman Cache Valley Health Care Found., Logan, 1982—. Zoning officer Town of Banner Elk, N.C., 1984. Republican. Mormon. Home: 2715 S 600 W Nibley Logan UT 84321 Office: Logan Regional Hosp 1400N 500E Logan UT 84321

PERRY, ROBERT MICHAEL, consulting engineering company executive; b. N.Y.C., Dec. 5, 1931; s. Jerome and Rose P.; m. Frances Diane Gross, Feb. 2, 1957; children—Karen, David, Janice. B.S.E., U. Mich., 1953; postgrad., Columbia U., 1955-57. Engr. Dames & Moore (Cons. Engrs.), Los Angeles, 1955-60; asso. Dames & Moore (Cons. Engrs.), 1960-65, partner, 1965-75, mng. partner, 1975—, chief fin. officer, 1980—, dir., 1981—; pres., dir. RMP Inc., 1972—. Served with C.E. U.S. Army, 1953-55. Mem. ASCE (dir., treas. N.Y. sect. 1964-68), Profl. Services Mgmt. Assn. Club: University (Los Angeles). Home: 2736 Via Victoria Palos Verdes Peninsula CA 90274-4478 Office: 911 Wilshire Blvd Los Angeles CA 90017-3409

PERRY, SUZANNE CHRISTL, writer; b. Sacramento, Calif., Sept. 5, 1952; d. William Edward and Mary Virginia (Fahey) P.; m. William Brown Huston, Jr., Feb. 1, 1991. BA in Computer Sci., Film Studies, U. Calif., Santa Cruz, 1975; postgrad. in Seismology, Pasadena City Coll., 1990—. Acctg. sec. Am. Internat. Pictures, Beverly Hills, Calif., 1975; motion picture story analyst Disney, Universal, Lorimar, Am. Internat., L.A., 1976-83; producer Divorce Court syndicated TV program, Hollywood, Calif., 1984-86, Triumph ABC-TV Secrets & Mysteries, Hollywood, 1987; free lance writer Pasadena, Calif., 1988; motion picture story analyst Touchstone, Disney Pictures, Burbank, Calif., 1989-90; seismic data analyst U.S. Geol. Survey, Pasadena, 1991—. Author: (novel) Was It a Rat I Saw?, 1992; story editor 500 TV episodes Divorce Court, 1984-86. Mem. People for the Ethical Treatment of Animals, Washington, 1986—, Greenpeace, Washington, 1988—. Recipient Miller scholarship Pasadena City Coll., 1991, Van Amringe scholarship, 1992. Office: US Geol Survey 525 S Wilson Ave Pasadena CA 91106

PERRY, TIMOTHY J., manufacturing company executive, consultant; b. Rumford, Maine, Oct. 14, 1929; s. Ernest Joseph and Louise Ann (Walsh) P.; m. Dawn Lorraine Loewen, June 6, 1966; children: Louise Anne, Timothy J. Jr., Lorraine A., Ronald L., Vincent M. BS, Maine Maritime Acad., 1951; postgrad., U.S. Naval Postgrad. Sch., Monterey, Calif., 1961. Engr. States Marine Lines, N.Y.C., 1951-53; instr. Maine Maritime Acad., Castine, 1953-55; commd. officer USN, 1955, advanced through grades to capt.; ret., 1978; gen. mgr. Century Computer Corp., Concord, Calif., 1978-80; pres. Mello Mfg. Inc., Richmond, Calif., 1981—; bd. dirs. Mercury Tech., Inc., Hayward, Calif.; cons. on pneumatic conveying. Inventor vacuum tech. filtration, mercury separation tube crushing, pneumatic separator interceptor. Republican. Roman Catholic. Home: 1875 Piedras Cir Danville CA 94526 Office: Mello Mfg Inc 623 S 32d St Richmond CA 94804

PERRY, WILLIAM JOSEPH, food processing company executive; b. Sacramento, Calif., Nov. 4, 1930; s. Joseph Nasciemeto and Jennie (Nunez) P.; m. Beverly Ann Styes, Dec. 9, 1956 (div. May 1981); children: Katherine, Bill Jr., Kathleen, Barbara; m. Leslie Z. Blumberg, June 30, 1986. BS, U. Calif., Berkeley, 1953. Quality control supr. Stokely Van Camp, Oakland, Calif., 1953-54; plant mgr. Safeway Stores, Brookside div., Grandview, Wash., 1954-61, Gallo Winery, Modesto, Calif., 1961-62; gen. mgr. Bocca Bella Olive Assoc., Wallace, Calif., 1962-65; v.p. Early Calif. Ind., L.A., 1965-74, Fairmont Foods, Santa Ana, Calif., 1974-75; pres. Cal Agra Ind., Stockton, Calif., 1975-76; exec. v.p. Food Brokers Internat., L.A., 1976—; pres., co-owner G.F.F., Inc., L.A., 1981—; dir. G.F.F., Inc., L.A., 1981—, Food Brokers, Inc., L.A., 1976—, Cozad & Assoc. Ad Agy., Encino, Calif., 1985-87. Wrestling com., dir. protocol, L.A. Olympic Com., 1981-84. Mem. Nat. Food Brokers Assn., Assn. of Dressings and Sauces, Nat. Juice Processing Assn., Nat. Single Service Assn., Am. Chem. Soc., Westlake Tennis & Swim Club. Republican. Roman Catholic. Home: 9370 Flicker Way West Hollywood CA 90069-1728 Office: GFF Inc 5443 E Washington Blvd Los Angeles CA 90040-2105

PERRYMAN, BRUCE CLARK, college dean; b. Laramie, Wyo., Jan. 28, 1939; s. Homer F. and Phyllis C. (White) P.; m. Sharon Lynn Lungren, June 28, 1958; children: Kimberly Jo, Bruce Homer. BBA, BA in Mktg. Edn., U. Wyo., 1965, MS in Bus. and Edn., 1966; PhD in Coll. Adminstrn., Colo. State U., 1993. Cert. tchr. and adminstr., Wyo., Minn., Colo. Dir. research unit Wyo. State Dept. Edn., Cheyenne, 1966-67, state dir. of vocat. edn., 1968-71; asst. prof. bus. Adams State Coll., Alamosa, Colo., 1967-68; pres., exec. dir. Mountain Plains Edn. Ctr., Glasgow, Mont., 1971-77; field underwriter N.Y. Life Ins. Co., Worland, Wyo., 1977-79; v.p., mgr. United Savs. Bank, Worland, 1979-84; curriculum facilitator Washakie County Sch. Dist. #1, Worland, 1984-86; pres., dir. Hibbing (Minn.) Tech. Coll., 1986-89; dean bus. and govt. studies C.C. Denver, 1989—. Trustee local sch. bd., 1980-84, pres. 1982-84; council mem. Zion Luth. Ch., 1977-84, pres. 1980-82; mem. City Recreation Bd., treas., 1979, Pub. Utilities Bd., 1980-84; mem. Farm Bur. Fedn. Sgt. USAF, 1958-62. Wyo. Tchrs. scholar (2); Kellog doctoral fellow Tex. Tech U., 1979; I/O/E/A fellow, 1988. Mem. NEA (life), ACD, Am. Assn. Community and Jr. Colls., Am. Assn. Sch. Adminstrs., Am. Vocat. Assn., Am. Vocat. Edn. Rsch. Assn. (charter), Nat. Coun. Occupational Edn., Nat. Coun. Instrnl. Adminstrs., Elks, Masons, Rotary Internat. (past pres.), Phi Delta Kappa. Home: 3623 E Fremont Pl Littleton CO 80122-1921 Office: CC Denver So Classroom 313 E 1111 W Colfax Ave Denver CO 80204-9999

PERRYMAN, KENT MICHAEL, neurophysiologist; b. St. Louis, Dec. 13, 1940; s. Kenith Dale Perryman and Juanita I. (McArthy) Mellor; m. Mary Nancy Montano, July 29, 1990. BA in Psychology, Hayward State U., 1969; MA in Psychology, UCLA, 1970, PhD in Physiol. Psychology, 1974. Asst. rsch. psychologist UCLA, 1976-78, asst. rsch. neurophysiologist, 1978-92, assoc. rsch. neurophysiologist, 1992—; co-prin. investigator dept. neurosurgery Harbor/UCLA Med. Ctr., Torrence, 1979-82; chief psychiatry depts. Cognitive Neurophysiology Lab. Sepulveda (Calif.) VA Med. Ctr., 1982—; lectr. in field. Author: (with D.F. Lindsley, D.B. Lindsley) Neural Mechanisms of Goal-Directed Behavior and Learning, 1980, (with L.J. Fitten, P. Gross) Advances in Alzheimer's Therapy: Cholinestyerase Inhibitors, 1988; contbr. articles to profl. jours. With USN, 1958-61. VA Merit Rev. grantee, 1983, 87. Mem. N.Y. Acad. Scis. Office: Sepulveda VA Med Ctr 16111 Plummex St Sepulveda CA 91343

PERSON, EVERT BERTIL, newspaper and radio executive; b. Berkeley, Calif., Apr. 6, 1914; s. Emil P. and Elida (Swanson) P.; m. Ruth Finley, Jan. 26, 1944 (dec. May 1985); m. 2d, Norma Joan Betz, Mar. 12, 1986. Student, U. Calif., Berkeley, 1937; LHD, Calif. State Univs., 1983. Co-publisher, sec.-treas. Press Democrat Pub. Co., Santa Rosa, Calif., 1945-72, editor, 1972-73, pres., pub., editor-in-chief, 1973-85; sec.-treas. Finley Broadcasting Co., Santa Rosa, 1945-72; pres. Finley Broadcasting Co., 1972-89, Kawana Pubs., 1975-85; pub. Healdsburg Tribune, 1975-85; prin. Evert B. Person Investments, Santa Rosa, 1985—; pres. Person Properties Co., Santa Rosa, 1945-70; v.p. Finley Ranch & Land Co., Santa Rosa, 1947-72, pres., 1972-79; pres. Baker Pub. Co., Oreg., 1957-67, Sebastopol (Calif.) Times, 1978-81, Russian River News, Guerneville, Calif., 1978-81; pres. publ. Kawana Pubs., 1978-85; mem. nominating com. AP, 1982-84, mem. auditing com., 1984-85. Bd. dirs. Empire Coll., Santa Rosa, 1972—, Sonoma County Taxpayers Assn., 1966-69, San Francisco Spring Opera Assn., 1974-79; bd. dirs. San Francisco Opera, 1986—, v.p., 1988—; pres. Calif. Newspaperboy Found., 1957-58; chmn. Santa Rosa Civic Arts Commn., 1961-62; pres. Santa Rosa Sonoma County Symphony Assn., 1966-68, Luther Burbank Meml. Found., 1979, Santa Rosa Symphony Found., 1967-77; adv. bd. Santa Rose Salvation Army, 1959-67; commodore 12th Coast Guard Dist. Aux., 1969-70; trustee Desert Mus., Palm Springs, 1987-92, v.p., 1988-92; mem. adv. bd. Sonoma State U., 1988—, v.p. pres.'s adv. bd., 1991—; v.p. Nat. Bd. Canine Companions, Inc., 1989-92. Mem. Calif. Newspaper Pubs. Assn. (pres. 1981-82), Internat. Newspaper Fin. Execs. (pres. 1961-62), Navy League U.S., Bohemian Club, Sonoma County Press Club, Santa Rosa Golf and Country Club, The Springs Club, Santa Rosa Rotary, Masons (32 degrees KCCH), Shriners. Roman Catholic. Home: 1020 McDonald Ave Santa Rosa CA 95404 Office: The Oaks 1400 N Dutton Ave Ste 12 Santa Rosa CA 95401-4644

PERTHOU, ALISON CHANDLER, interior designer; b. Bremerton, Wash., July 22, 1945; d. Benson and Elizabeth (Holdsworth) Chandler; m. A.V. Perthou III, Sept. 9, 1967 (div. Dec. 1977); children: Peter T.R., Stewart A.C. BFA, Cornish Coll. Arts, 1972. Pres. Alison Perthou Interior Design, Seattle, 1972—, Optima Design, Inc., Seattle, 1986-89; treas. Framejoist Corp., Bellevue, Wash., 1973-90; pres. Classics: Interiors & Antiques, Inc., 1988—; cons. bldg. and interiors com. Children's Hosp., Seattle, 1976—; guest lectr. U. Wash., Seattle, 1980-81. Mem. bd. trustees Cornish Coll. Arts, Seattle, 1973-80, sec. exec. com., 1975-77; mem. procurement com. Patrons of N.W. Cultural and Charitable Orgn., 1985—, mem. antiques com., 1991—. Mem. Am. Soc. Interior Design, Seattle Tennis Club (mem. house and grounds com. 1974-75), City Club. Office: 4216 E Madison St Seattle WA 98112-3237

PERTICA, ALEXANDER JOSÉ, physicist; b. Buenos Aires, Dec. 7, 1961; came to U.S., 1967; s. Horacio N. and Nilda (Altuna) Pertica; m. Elona H. Hamarich, May 25, 1990. BA in Physics, Cornell U., 1984; MS in Physics, U. So. Calif., 1986. Assoc., Tech. Staff The Aerospace Corp., L.A., 1985-86; engr. Lawrence Livermore (Calif.) Nat. Lab., 1986-91, project leader, 1991—. Contbr. articles profl. jours. Mem. Optical Soc. of Am. Office: Lawrence Livermore Nat Lab PO Box 808 Livermore CA 94551-0808

PESAPANE, JOHN, air force officer; b. Long Branch, N.J., Dec. 3, 1946; s. Louis and Mary (Richichi) P.; m. Sandra L. Brown, June 15, 1968; children: John S., Gina M. BSEE, N.J. Inst. Tech., 1968; MS in Aero. Engring., U. Mich., 1972. Commd. 2d lt. USAF, 1968, advanced through grades to col.; ICBM evaluator/ISTRAD USAF, Vandenberg AFB, Calif., 1978-81; ops. rsch. analyst The Pentagon USAF, Washington, 1981-85; program mgr. for testing BSD/Small ICBM USAF, Norton AFB, Calif., 1985-90; dir. devel. ASD/SRAM II USAF, WP AFB, Ohio, 1990-92, dir. integration ASD/B-2 program, 1992-93; dep. program dir. Follow-on Early Warning System, Los Angeles AFB, CA, 1993—. Asst. scoutmaster Boy Scouts Am., Woodbridge, Va., 1981-85. Home: 3A Officers Rd San Pedro CA 90731

PESKIN, GARY LEE, computer consulting company executive; b. Chgo., Oct. 20, 1952; s. Albert Abraham and Ruth (Raff) P.; m. Janet Lynn Kramer, Dec. 4, 1983; children: Brynn Michelle, Jenna Gail, Elan Aaron. SB, MIT, 1974; JD, U. So. Calif., 1977. Bar: Calif. 1977. Pres. The Firstech Corp., Beverly Hills, Calif., 1978—; sr. v.p. Prin. Portfolio Svcs., L.A., 1984-92. Bd. dirs. Temple Valley Beth Shalom, Encino, Calif., 1989-91; pres. Concern Found. for Cancer Rsch., L.A., 1991-92. Democrat. Jewish. Office: The Firstech Corp 9595 Wilshire Blvd Ste 212 Beverly Hills CA 90212

PESQUEIRA, RALPH RAYMOND, retail executive; b. Calexico, Calif., Feb. 5, 1935; s. Rafael Ramon and Alfa (Parmer) P.; m. Rosilee Indermill, Oct. 28, 1958 (div. 1981); children: Melinda, Becky, Jennifer. Student, Abilene Christian U., 1957-58; BS, San Diego State U., 1957. Owner, pres. El Indio Shops, Inc., San Diego, 1971—. Trustee Calif. State U.; bd. dirs. America's Cup Organizing Com., Leap Into the Future Scholarships, St. Vincent DePaul; mem. econ. devel. task force City of San Diego; mem. citizen adv. group San Diego Police Dept.; bd. advisers San Diego Sports Arena; mem. Centre City Planning Com. San Diego, Corp. Fin. Coun. San Diego; pilot San Diego Police Dept. Air Res.; chmn. appeals com. United Way; del. Rep. Nat. Conv., 1992; mem CAP Search and Rescue. Mem. AirLifeLine, Alba 80 Soc., Mex.-Am. Bus. and Profl. Assn., Navy League of U.S., San Diego Zool. Soc. (pres.'s assoc.), San Diego Mus Art, San Diego Starlight Opera. Mem. Ch. of Christ. Office: El Indio Shops Inc 3695 India St San Diego CA 92103

PETER, ARNOLD PHILIMON, lawyer; b. Karachi, Pakistan, Apr. 3, 1957; came to U.S., 1968; s. Kundan Lal and Irene Primrose (Mall) P. BS, Calif. State U., Long Beach, 1981; JD, Loyola U., L.A., 1984; MS, Calif. State U., Fresno, 1991. Bar: Calif. 1985, U.S. Dist. Ct. (ea., so., no. and cen. dists.) Calif. 1986, U.S. Ct. Appeals (9th cir.) 1989, U.S. Ct. Appeals (11th cir.) 1990. Law clk. appellate dept. Superior Ct., L.A., 1984-85, U.S. Dist. Ct. (ea. dist.) Calif., Fresno, 1986-88; assoc. Pepper, Hamilton & Scheetz, L.A., 1988-89, McDermott, Will & Emery, P.A., L.A., 1989-90, Cadwalader, Wickersham & Taft, L.A., 1990-91; labor and employment counsel City of Fresno, Calif., 1991—. Contbr. articles to profl. jours. Mem. ABA, L.A. County Bar Assn. (mem. conf. of dels., com. on fed. cts.), Calif. State Bar Assn. (chmn. com. on fed. cts.), L.A. Athletic Club. Office: Office of City Atty City Hall Fresno CA 93721

PETERS, BARBARA HUMBIRD, writer, editor; b. Santa Monica, Calif., Sept. 26, 1948; d. Philip Rising and Caroline Jean (Dickason) Peters. AA, Santa Monica Coll., 1971; BS, San Diego State U., 1976; postgrad. UCLA, 1981-82, 84. Ptnr. Signet Properties, L.A., 1971-85; tech. editor C. Brewer & Co., Hilo, Hawaii, 1975; editor The Aztec Engineer mag., San Diego, 1976-77; regional publicist YWCA, San Diego, 1977-78; campaign cons. Rep. Congl. and Assembly Candidates San Diego; Pollster, Los Angeles Times, 1983; pres., dir. Humbird Hopkins Inc., San Clemente, Calif., 1978-91; pub. rels. cons. ASCE, San Diego, 1975-76, Am. Soc. Mag. Photographers, San Diego, 1980. Author: The Layman's Guide to Raising Cane: A Guide to the Hawaiian Sugar Industry, 1975, The Students' Survival Guide, 1976, 2d edit. 1977. Mem. Mayor's Coun. on Librs., L.A., 1969; mem. Wilshire Blvd. Property Owners Assn., Santa Monica, 1972-78; docent Mus. Sci. and Industry, L.A., 1970; founding mem. Comml. and Indsl. Properties Assn., Santa Monica, 1982-89. Recipient Acting award Santa Monica Coll., 1970. Mem. NAFE, Internat. Assn. Bus. Communicators, Sales and Mktg. Execs. Assn. Avocations: travel, opera, puns.

PETERS, BARBARA M. STRATTON, career counselor, administrator; b. Pocatello, Idaho, Apr. 18, 1949; d. Richard Wendell and Margaret Mae (Harris) Stratton; m. Thomas Henry Peters, Aug. 7, 1984. BA in Polit. Sci., Idaho State U., 1967, MEdn in Student Personnel Work, 1976. Asst. dir. career planning and placement Idaho State U., Pocatello, 1972-77; assoc. dir. Career Devel. Ctr., Humboldt State U., Arcata, Calif., 1977-90, career counselor, 1990—, mem. academic senate, 1984-87, 1992—, cooperative edn. adv. bd., 1980—, student retention com., 1984—, adv. com. on services to disabled students, 1980—. Campaign worker Bosco for Congress Campaign, Arcata, 1982; mem. Redwoods Occupational Edn. Council, Eureka, 1977—, pres., 1985-86. Mem. Am. Assn. Counseling and Devel., Am. Coll. Personnel Assn., Western Assn. Student Employment Adminstrs., Idaho Personnel and Guidance Assn., AAUW (Mitchell-Loux scholarship 1967-68), Phi Kappa Phi. Democrat. Roman Catholic. Avocations: singing, camping, baseball. Home: 221 Dollison St Eureka CA 95501-4307 Office: Humboldt State U Career Devel Ctr Arcata CA 95521

PETERS, DEANNA JEAN, paralegal company executive; b. Fremont, Nebr., Mar. 9, 1964; d. Leslie Lee and Bernice (Knorr) Focht; m. Mark Alan Peters, Nov. 5, 1988; 1 child, Brooke Lauren. Cert., North Am. Coll., 1983. Legal asst. various law firms Phoenix, 1982-89; pres., co-founder Consumer Legal, Inc., Phoenix, 1989—. Author: Divorce and Child Custody, 1992. Vol. arbitrator State Bar of Ariz., Phoenix, 1990—. Mem. Maricopa County Bar (vol. paralegal 1990—), Entrepreneurial Mothers Assn., Christian Bus. Women, Nat. Assn. Bus; Women, Ariz. Assn. Ind. Paralegals (founder). Republican. Roman Catholic. Office: Consumer Legal Inc 3520 E Indian School # 3 Phoenix AZ 85018

PETERS, DOUGLAS CAMERON, mining engineer, geologist; b. Pitts., June 19, 1955; s. Donald Cameron and Twila (Bingel) P. BS in Earth and Planetary Sci., U. Pitts., 1977; MS in Geology, Colo. Sch. Mines, 1981, MS in Mining Engring., 1983. Technician, inspector Engring. Mechanics Inc., Pitts., 1973-77. Research asst. Potential Gas Agy., Golden, Colo., 1977-78; geologist U.S. Geol. Survey, Denver, 1978-80; cons. Climax Molybdenum Co., Golden, 1981-82; cons., Golden, 1982-84; mining engr., prin. investigator U.S. Bur. Mines, Denver, 1984—; bur. rep. to Geosat Com., 1984—; program chmn. GeoTech Conf., Denver, 1984-88, mem. long. range planning subcom., 1989-92, gen. chmn., 1991; engr. in tng. #11800, Colo., Wyo., profl. geologist #367. Author: Physical Modeling of Draw of Broken Rock in Caving, 1984, Bur. Mines Articles and Reports; editor COGS Computer Contbns., 1986—, Geology in Coal Resource Utilization, 1988-91; assoc. editor Computers & Geosciences, 1989—; contbr. articles to profl. jours. Recipient AAPG Energy Minerals Divsn. pres. award, 1993, Cert. of Appreciation Am. Inst. Profl. Geologists, 1984, 85, 86, Appreciation award, 87, Spl. award Denver Geotech Com., 1988, Appreciation award, 1989. Mem. Computer Oriented Geol. Soc. (charter, com. chmn. 1983—, pres. 1985, dir. 1986, contbg. editor newsletter 1985—), Geol. Soc. Am., Rocky Mountain Assn. Geologists, Am. Inst. Profl. Geologists (cert. profl. geologist #8274), Soc. Mining Metallurgy and Exploration, Am. Assn. Petroleum Geologists (com. mem. 1984—, astrogeology com., remote sensing com. Energy Mineral div. v.p. 1990-91, pres. 1991-92, Cert. of Merit award 1992, 93, Pres.'s award 1993), Am. Soc. Photogrammetry and Remote Sensing, Nat. Space Soc., Colo. Mining Assn., Pitts. Geol. Soc. Republican. Office: US Bur Mines Denver Fed Ctr PO Box 25086 Denver CO 80225-0086

PETERS, GERALDINE JOAN, astrophysicist; b. San Diego; d. Gerald John and Olga (Peloff) Duffner; m. Philip James Peters, Aug. 11, 1968. BS, Calif. State U., Long Beach, 1965; MA, UCLA, 1966, PhD, 1974. Rsch. and teaching asst. UCLA, 1969-72, rsch. assoc., lectr., 1974-76; physicist Ctr. for Astrophysics, Cambridge, Mass., 1976-78; adj. asst. prof. U. So. Calif., 1978-83, assoc. rsch. scientist, 1983—; vis. asst. and assoc. prof. UCLA, 1983-86; vis. prof. Pomona Coll., 1992-93. Editor Be Star Newsletter, 1987—; referee for jours., books, granting agys., 1976—; contbr. articles to profl. jours. NASA grantee, 17 times, 1976—. Mem. Internat. Astron. Union (sci. organizing com. 1985—), Am. Astron. Soc., Astron. Soc. of the Pacific (bd. dirs. 1984-87), Sigma Xi. Office: U So Calif Space Scis Ctr University Park Los Angeles CA 90089-1341

PETERS, HENRY H., state legislator; b. Honolulu, Feb. 5, 1941; married; 1 child. Grad., Brigham Young U. Dir., adv. Waianae Model Cities; mem. Hawaii Ho. of Reps., 1975—, speaker, from 1981. Served with U.S. Army, 1967-69. Home: 87-641 Farrington Hwy Waianae HI 96792

PETERS, JOHN ERIC, management consultant; b. Greenvile, Pa., July 2, 1962; s. Joseph Harold and Patricia Louise (Flannery) P.; m. Stephanie Marie Singer, July 1, 1989. BS in Indsl. Engring., Pa. State U., 1984. Indsl. engr. Carolina Power & Light, Huntsville, S.C., 1984-85; engring. mgr. Tompkins Associates, Inc., Raleigh, N.C., 1985-89; gen. mgr. Tompkins Associates, Inc., Soquel, Calif., 1989—. Contbg. author: Warehouse Management Handbook, 1986. Mem. Inst. Indsl. Engrs. (sr.). Republican. Methodist. Home: 330 Doris Ave Aptos CA 95003 Office: Tompkins Assocs Inc 3065 Porter St Ste 200 Soquel CA 95073

PETERS, JON FLEMING, marketing professional; b. Newton, Kans., Feb. 16, 1945; s. Albert Andrew and Uelma Marie (Fleming) Unger; m. Carol Lyn Karle, Jan. 29, 1966. BS, U. Iowa, 1968; MA, U. Houston, 1970; PhD, Simon Fraser U., 1976. Asst. prof. U. Nebr. Med. Sch., Omaha, 1976-80; internat. mktg. mgr. Nicolet Biomed., Madison, Wis., 1980-88, Neurocom Internat. Inc., Clackamas, Oreg., 1988—. Contbr. over 100 articles on brain elec. activity to profl. jours. Office: Neurocom Internat Inc 9570 SE Lawnfield Rd Clackamas OR 97015

PETERS, JOYCE EILEEN, automotive electronics executive; b. L.A., May 22, 1953; d. Arthur and Paula Lois (Levine) Gordon; m. David Jack Peters, Jan. 7, 1972 (div. June 1981); 1 child, Megan Alisa Holdaway. Student, West Valley Coll., 1971-82, Orange Coast Coll, 1991-92. Sales rep. Ohbach's, L.A., 1971-74; mgr. Alan Austin, Beverly Hills, Calif., 1974; ptnr. Communication Unltd., Inglewood, Calif., 1973-74, Radioland, Inglewood, 1976-79, Inglewood Electronics, Inglewood, 1979-81, Auto Systems, Gardena, Calif., 1981-84; owner Houst Plant Parties, L.A., 1975; chief exec. officer, owner Auto Systems, Mobile Excelleration Corp., Hermosa Beach, Calif., 1985-91; comm. cons. Raycom, Paramount, Calif., 1992—; judge Alpine Electronics, Torrance, Calif., 1988. Author short stories. Mem. NAFE.

PETERS, KENNETH DARRYL, SR., contracts administrator; b. Englewood, N.J., Jan. 27, 1949; s. John Conna Jr. and Lena Ponease (Jones) P.; m. Katie M. Coleman, Nov. 27, 1976; children: Kenneth Jr., Kevin. BA, Fisk U., 1971; MSW, U. Kans., 1973; postgrad., U. Calif., Berkeley, 1974, U. Calif., Davis, 1979. Sch. cons. Cath. Social Svcs., Stockton, Calif., 1973-78; placement coord. Dept. Devel. Disabilities, Stockton, Calif., 1978-80; program cons. Dept. Devel. Disabilities, Sacramento, Calif., 1980-84, program analyst, 1984-87; contracts adminstr. Dept. Transp., Stockton, 1987—; mem. Mental Health Adv. Bd., Stockton, 1978-90, Child Health & Disability Prevention, Stockton, 1979-90, Nat. Conf. Social Welfare, San Francisco, 1983. Lt. col. U.S. Army res., 1980—. Recipient Comendation Calif. State Senate, 1983, Calif. State Assembly, 1983. Mem. NAACP, Nat. Assn. Black Social Workers (bd. dirs.), Orgn. Black Calif. Voters (bd. dirs.), Calif. Bd. Respiratory Care (subcom. chmn. 1990—), Alpha Phi Alpha (sec. 1992—). Democrat. Baptist. Home: 2663 Fallenleaf Dr Stockton CA 95209 Office: Dept Transp 1976 E Charter Way Stockton CA 95205

PETERS, RAYMOND EUGENE, computer systems company executive; b. New Haven, Aug. 24, 1933; s. Raymond and Doris Winthrop (Smith) P.; m. Mildred K. Mather, July 14, 1978 (div. Nov. 1983). Student, San Diego City Coll., 1956-6l; cert., Lumbleau Real Estate Sch., 1973, Southwestern Coll., Chula Vista, Calif., 1980. Cert. quality assurance engr. Founder, pub. Silhouette Pub. Co., San Diego, 1960-75; news dir. Sta. XEGM, San Diego, 1965-67, Sta. XERB, Tijuana, Mex., 1973-74; founder, chief exec. officer New World Airways, Inc., San Diego, 1974-75; co-founder, exec. vice chmn. bd. San Cal Rail, Inc.-San Diego Trolley, San Diego, 1974-77; founder, pres. Ansonia Sta., micro systems, San Diego, 1986—; co-founder, dir. S.E. Community Theatre, San Diego, 1960-68; commr. New World Aviation Acad., Otay Mesa, Calif., 1971-77; co-founder New World Internat. Trade & Commerce Commn., Inc., 1991—. Author: Black Americans in Aviation, 1971, Profiles in Black American History, 1974, Eagles Don't Cry, 1988; founder, pub., editor Oceanside Lighthouse, 1958-60, San Diego Herald Dispatch, 1959-60. Co-founder, bd. dirs. San Diego County Econ. Opportunity Commn., 1964-67; co-founder Edn. Cultural Complex, San Diego, 1966-75; co-founder, exec. dir. S.E. Anti-Poverty Planning Coun., Inc., 1964-67; mem. U.S. Rep. Senatorial Inner Circle Com., Washington, 1990; mem. United Ch. Crist. With U.S. Army, 1950-53, Korea. Mem. Am. Soc. Quality Control, Nat. City C. of C., Internat. Biog. Soc., Afro-Am. Micro Systems Soc. (exec. dir. 1987—), Negro Airmen Internat. (Calif. pres. 1970-75, nat. v.p. 1975-77), Internat. Masonic Supreme Coun. (Belgium), Internat. Platform Assn., U.S. C. of C., Greater San Diego Minority C. of C. (bd. dirs. 1974—, past chmn. bd.), Masons (Most Worshipful Grand Master), Shriners (Disting. Community Svc. award 1975), Imperial Grand Potentate, Nubian Order. Republican. Home: 6538 Bell Bluff Ave San Diego CA 92119-1015

PETERS, ROBERT WAYNE, direct mail and catalog sales specialist; b. LaPorte, Ind., Jan. 2, 1950; s. Harry Carl and Dorothy May (Fischer) P.; m. Frances Kay Cooley, Aug. 21, 1971; children: Carolyn Marie, Angela Lynn. BA, Purdue U., 1972. CLU. Mgr. pension adminstrn. Gen. Life Ins. Corp., Milw., 1973-75; dir. qualified plan devel. Cen. Life Assurance Co., Des Moines, 1976-84; v.p. individual ops. First Farwest Ins. Co., Portland, Oreg., 1984-90; pres. CAF Enterprises, Inc., Portland, 1990—; lectr. various govt. agys. Contbr. articles to profl. jours. Mem. N.W. Vintage Thunderbird (v.p. 1988, pres. 1989-90, exec. bd. 1991, sec. 1992-93), Optimists (treas. West Des Moines chpt. Iowa Club 1983-84. Office: CAF Enterprises Inc 9997 SW Avery Tualatin OR 97062

PETERS, WILLIAM FRANK, art educator; b. Oakland, Calif., Nov. 8, 1934; s. Clifford Leslie and Gladys Fay (Parrish) P.; m. Patricia Ann Redgwick, June 3, 1956 (div. 1973); 1 child, David William. B. Art Edn. with honors, Calif. Coll. Arts & Crafts, 1961; postgrad., various schools, various locations. Cert. spl. secondary art edn. life, gen. jr. high life. Summer campus art dir., instr. Richmond (Calif.) Unified Sch. Dist., 1961-66, Sch. of Fine Arts, Mt. Diablo Unified Sch. Dist., Concord, Calif., 1967-74; instr. Liberty Union High Sch. Dist., Brentwood, Calif., 1961—, chmn. arts & crafts dept., 1976-91; dist. rep. Pacific Art Assn., East Contra Costa County, Calif., 1967-70, Calif. Art Assn., East Contra Costa County, 1970-74; accreditation team mem. Western Assn. Schs. and Colls., Albany, Calif., 1981; film evaluator Contra Costa County Schs., 1965-84. Artist (oil painting) Contra Costa County Fair (Best of Show, 1968), (watercolor Best of

Show 1990), (jewelry) Delta Art Show, Antioch, Calif. (1st. pl. 1979), (ceramic) Festival of Color, Concord, Calif. (1st pl. 1963); photographer Contra Costa County Fair (1st pl. 1987, 88, 89, 90, 91, 92). Fundraiser United Crusade, Brentwood, Calif., 1980-83; publicity vol. East Contra Costa County Soroptimist Club, East County Rape/Crisis Ctr., Kappa Beta, John Marsh Meml. Assn., Knightsen 4-H, Delta Rotary Club, Delta Recreation Dept., Oakley Women's Club, Town of Byron, others. Named Contra Costa County Tchr. of Yr. AAUW, 1981; postgrad scholar Calif. Coll. of Arts and Crafts, 1962-63. Mem. NEA, Calif. Tchrs. Assn., Liberty Edn. Assn. (chmn. salary com., past v.p., chmn. evaluation com., chmn. pers. policies com., chmn. scholarship com.), Delta Art Assn. (past bd. dirs.), Brentwood C. of C. (dir. Brentwood Christmas decorations 1968-92). Democrat. Office: Liberty Union High Sch 850 2D St Brentwood CA 94513

PETERSEN, ARTHUR MEREDITH, language educator, consultant; b. Bakersfield, Calif., Jan. 8, 1942; s. Peter Arthur and Valerie Agnus (Swink) P.; m. Marcia Denise Petersen, July 4, 1969 (div. 1977); m. Tina S. Pasteris, Aug. 24, 1990. AA in English, Sierra Coll., 1965; BA in English with honors, Calif. State U., Sacramento, 1971, MA in English, 1972; PhD in English, Union Inst., 1983. Part-time tchr. English, supr. English lab. Sierra Coill., Rocklin, Calif., 1968-73; with U. Alaska S.E., Juneau, 1975—, asst. dean Sch. Edn., 1984-85, asst. vice chancellor acad. affairs, 1985-87, pres. faculty senate, 1990-91, chmn. B Liberal Arts Degree com., 1990-92, prof. English, 1990—. Author poetry, textbooks on writing. Humanities cons. Perseverance Theatre, Juneau, 1977—, Alaska Humanities Forum, 1990-93. With U.S. Army, 1960-63. Mem. Modern Lang. Assn., N.W. Conf. on Brit. Studies, Keats/Shelley Assn. Am., AAUP, Emily Dickenson Soc. Home: PO Box 210174 Auke Bay AK 99821 Office: U Alaska SE 11120 Glacier Hwy Juneau AK 99801-8671

PETERSEN, DONALD FELIX, consultant; b. Centralia, Wash., Nov. 16, 1928; s. Otto Anders and Martha Hilda (Peck) P.; m. Norma Ingeborg Wise, Jan. 17, 1954; children: Marilyn, Ronald, Kenneth. BBA, U. Wash., 1950. Transp. rate analyst Pub. Utility Commr., Salem, Oreg., 1953-57; mgmt. effectiveness analyst Dept. of Fin. and Adminstrn., Salem, 1958, mgmt. analyst, 1958-61, supr., fiscal analyst, 1962-67; prin. fiscal analyst Legis. Budget Com., Olympia, Wash., 1967-79, legis. auditor, 1980-86; program analysis mgr. Dept. of Social and Health Svcs., Olympia, 1986-91; mem. state career exec. program dept. pers. State of Wash., Olympia, 1986-89; team mem. Price-Waterhouse, Olympia, 1987. Freeholder Thurston County Bd. of Freeholders, 1978-79; chair Tanglewilde Park and Recreation Dist., Lacey, 1987, 89-90, vice chair, 1988; active Dem. Party, Thurston County, 1987—; vol. RSVP, 1988-92; 3rd congl. dist. coord. Am. Assn. Ret. Persons Vote Program, 1990—. With U.S. Army, 1951-52. Cert. of Appreciation, North Thurston Kiwanis, 1988, State of Wash., 1988, Dept. Social and Health Svcs., 1989, ACTION, 1990. Mem. Tangewilde Recreation Ctr., Inc., Masons, Kiwanis (pres. 1973-74, sec. 1970-71). Democrat. Home and Office: 423 Ranger Dr SE Olympia WA 98503-6728

PETERSEN, EDWIN L., aerospace safety management; b. Logan, Utah, Dec. 13, 1944; s. Edwin LeGrande and Hazel (Cassity) P.; Carla Knighton, June 2, 1979; children: Ronald, Richard, Brady, Chad, Shellece, Steven. AA in Automotive Engring. Tech., Weber State Coll., 1980; BS in English, Computers, Weber State U., 1986. Cert. safety program auditor. Engr. Thiokol Corp., Brigham City, Utah, 1970-84, supr. safety Space Ops., 1984—. Author: novelette Memorautmobilia, 1981 (pub. award 1981). Recipient NASA Flight Safety award, 1992, George M. Low trophy, 1991, NASA Silver Snoopy award, 1992. Mem. Am. Soc. Safety Engrs., Am. Soc. Quality Engrs., Internat. Loss control Inst., Nat. Safety Coun., Lambda Iota Tau. Mem. LDS Ch. Home: 4072 N 900 W Ogden UT 84414-1008 Office: Thiokol Corp Space Ops PO Box 707 Brigham City UT 84302-0707

PETERSEN, FINN BO, oncologist, educator; b. Copenhagen, Mar. 26, 1951; came to U.S., 1983; s. Jorgen and Ebba Gjeding (Jorgensen) P.; m. Merete Secher Lund, Mar. 7, 1979; children: Lars Secher, Thomas Secher, Andreas Secher. BA, Niels Steensen, Copenhagen, 1971; MD, U. Copenhagen, 1978. Intern in internal medicine Copenhagen, 1978-79, resident in hematology, 1980-83; fellow oncology Fred Hutchinson Cancer Rsch. Ctr. U. Wash., Seattle, 1983-85, assoc. researcher oncology, 1985-87, asst. mem. in clin. rsch., 1987-91, asst. prof., 1988-91, prof. medicine, 1992—; clin. dir. bone marrow transplant program U. Utah Sch. Medicine, 1992—. Author: Hematology, 1977; contbr. articles to profl. jours. Mem. AMA, AAAS, Am. Soc. Hematology, Danish Med. Assn., Assn. Gnotobiology, Exptl. Soc. Hematology. Office: U Uath Bone Marrow Transplant Program Div of Hematology and Oncology Salt Lake City UT 84132

PETERSEN, GREGG EMIL, army officer; b. Ft. Atkinson, Wis., Sept. 15, 1956; s. Albert Verner and Donna Lucile (Draeger) P.; m. Shirley Elizabeth Reddoch, Jan. 25, 1986; children: Rebecca Michele, John Albert. BA in Biology, Ripon Coll., 1978; MS in Info. Systems Mgmt., George Washington U., Washington, 1988. Commd 2nd lt. US Army, 1978, advanced through grades to major; from signal platoon leader to bn. signal officer 3rd bn. 60th Air Defense Artillery, Grafenwoehr, Germany, 1979-80; from asst ops. officer to company commdr. company C 11th Air Defense Signal Bn., Darmstadt, Germany, 1981-83; brigade signal officer 2nd brigade 5th Infantry Div., Ft. Polk, La., 1984-85; bn. ops./intel officer 5th Signal Bn., Ft. Polk, 1985-86; electronic engr. Pentagon, Washington, 1988-89; asst. div. signal officer 25th Infantry Div., Schofield Barracks, Hawaii, 1990-91; exec. officer 125th Signal Bn., Schofield Barracks, 1991-93; tactical comm. staff officer Pacific Command, Camp Smith, Hawaii, 1993—. Mem. Assn. of the U.S. Army, Armed Forces Communications Electronics Assn. Home: 94-343 Hakamoa St Mililani HI 96789 Office: J62, PACOM Camp Smith HI 96861

PETERSEN, MICHAEL KEVIN, osteopath; b. Petaluma, Calif., Aug. 11, 1959; s. Richard Frederick and Marilyn Floy (Hough) P.; m. Marianne Cook, Apr. 24, 1981; children: Alayna, Natalie, Jessica. Student, Brigham Young U., 1977-78, Santa Rosa Jr. Coll., 1981-83; BA, Sonoma State U., 1986; DO, U. Osteo. Medicine and Health, 1991. Missionary Canada Toronto Mission, 1979-81; data quality control analyst Union Pacific R.R., San Francisco, 1981-83; rsch. assoc. U. Calif., San Francisco, 1984-86; scientist Henkel Rsch. Corp., Santa Rosa, Calif., 1987; intern U. Nev., Reno, 1991, resident, 1992—, chief resident of internal medicine, 1993—. Author: (computer software) Heart sounds and phonocardiogram simulator, 1989. Capty. U.S. ANG, 1989—. Mem. AMA, Am. Osteo. Assn., Assn. Mil. Surgeons U.S., Coll. Gen. Practitioners, ACP (assoc.), Sigma Xi. LDS Ch. Office: U Nev Sch Medicine Dept Internal Medicine 1000 Locust Ave Reno NV 89520

PETERSEN, ROLAND, painter, printmaker; b. Endelave, Horsens, Denmark, 1926; came to U.S., 1928; m. Sharane Havlina, Aug. 12, 1950; children—Dana Mark, Maura Brooke, Julien Conrad, Karena Caia. B.A., U. Calif.-Berkeley, 1949, M.A., 1950; postgrad., Han Hofmann's Sch. Fine Arts, summers 1950-51, S.W. Hayter's Atelier 17, Paris, 1950, 63, 70, Islington Studio, London, 1976, The Print Workshop, London, 1980. Tchr. State Coll. Wash., Pullman, 1952-56; mem. faculty U. Calif., Davis, 1956-91, prof. art, 1991; ret., 1991. Exhibited one-man shows: Gump's Gallery, San Francisco, 1962, Staempfli Gallery, N.Y.C., 1963, 65, 67, Adele Bednarz Gallery, Los Angeles, 1966, 69, 70, 72, 73, 75, 76, Crocker Art Gallery, Sacramento, 1965, de Young Mus., San Francisco, 1968, La Jolla Mus., 1971, Phoenix Mus., 1972, Santa Barbara Mus., 1973, USIS sponsored touring one-man exhbn., Turkey, U. Reading, Eng., 1977, 80, U. Calif., Davis, 1978, Brubaker Gallery, Sarasota, Fla., 1979, Rorick Gallery, San Francisco, 1981, 82, 83, 84, 85, Himovitz-Salomon Gallery, Sacramento, 1987-88, 91, Vanderwoude Tananbaum Gallery, N.Y.C., 1987-89, Harcourts Gallery, San Francisco, 1989, 91, 93, U. Calif., Davis, 1992; group shows include Calif. Palace Legion of Honor, San Francisco Art Inst., 1962, Mus. Art, Carnegie Inst., Pitts., 1964, Obelisk Gallery, Washington, John Herron Art Inst., Indpls., 1964, Pa. Acad. Fine Arts, Phila., Crocker Art Gallery, Sacramento, 1965, 81, Art Inst. Chgo., 1965, Va. Mus. Fine Arts, Richmond, 1966, U. Ariz. Art Gallery, Tucson, 1967, Am. Cultural Center, Paris, 1971, Nat. Gallery, Washington, 1972, Otis Art Inst. Gallery, Los Angeles, 1974, Auerbach Fine Art Gallery, London, 1977, U. Wis., Madison, 1977, Bklyn. Mus., 1978, U. Ill., 1978, U. Nev., Las Vegas, 1980, Brubaker Gallery, Sarasota, Fla., 1983, U.S.A. World Print Council, San Francisco, Nat. Mus., Singapore, Nat. Gallery, Bangkok, Thailand, Amerika Haus, Berlin, Malmo Konsthall, Sweden, Museo Carrillo Gil, Mexico City, all 1984-86, Crocker Art Mus., 1991, Fresno Met. Mus., 1992, Hall of Pictures, Uman, Russia, 1992, Calif. State U., L.A., 1992, San Bernardino, 1993 Pence Gallery, Davis, Calif., 1993; represented in permanent collections: de Young Mus., San Francisco, San Francisco Mus. Modern Art, Va. Mus. Fine Arts, Richmond, Mus. Modern Art, N.Y.C., Phila. Mus. Art, Whitney Mus. Am. Art, Phoenix Mus., Santa Barbara Mus., Musée Municipal, Brest, France, Smithsonian Instn. Nat. Collection Fine Arts & Archives of Am. Art, others. Served with USN, 1944-46, PTO. Recipient numerous prizes and awards, 1950—; Guggenheim fellow, 1963; U. Calif. creative arts fellow, 1967, 70, 77; Fulbright grantee, 1970. Mem. AAUP, San Francisco Art Assn., Calif. Soc. Printmakers. Home: 6 Lanai Way PO Box 1 Dillon Beach CA 94929

PETERSEN, VERNON LEROY, communications and engineering corporation executive; b. Mason, Nev., Nov. 3, 1926; s. Vernon and Lenora Eloise (Dickson) P.; children: Anne C., Ruth F. Cert. naval architecture, U. Calif., 1944, cert. in plant engring., adminstrn. and supervision UCLA, 1977; cert. in real estate exchanging Orange Coast Coll., 1978. Philippines Real Estate Office, U.S. C.E., 1950-55; pres., gen. mgr. Mason Merc. Co., 1956-62; pres., gen. mgr. Mason Water Co., 1956-62; pres. Petersen Enterprises, Cons. Engrs., Nev. and Calif., Downey, 1962-79, Vernon L. Peterson, Inc., 1980—; pres., chief exec. officer Castle Communications Co. Inc., 1985—; Sta. KCCD-TV, 1985-89; installation mgr. Pacific Architects & Engrs., L.A. and South Vietnam, 1969-72, facilities engr., ops. supr., acting contract mgr. L.A. and Saudi Arabia, 1979-82; bldg. engr. Purex Co., Inc., Lakewood, Calif., 1975-79; lectr. plant engring., various colls. in Calif., 1975—. Candidate for U.S. Congress, 1956, del. Rep. State Conv., 1960-64; candidate for U.S. Presidency, 1980. With AUS, 1944-47. Inducted into the Order of the Engrs. Fellow Soc. Am. Mil. Engrs. (life mem., named Orange County Post's Engr. of Year 1977, founder Da Nang Post 1969, Orange County Post 1977, pres. 1978-79, Red Sea Post, Jeddah, Saudi Arabia 1980), Internat. Platform Assn., Orange County Engr. Coun. (pres. 1978-79), Am. Inst. Plant Engrs. (chpt. 38 Engring. Merit award 1977-78), Soc. Women Engrs. (assoc.), AIAA. Mormon. Office: Castle Communications PO Box 787 Temecula CA 92593-0787

PETERSON, ANITA ANN, educational evaluator; b. Shell Lake, Wis.; m. Emery J. Cardenas II, July 26, 1982. BA, Marquette U., 1983; MEd, Harvard U., 1987; postgrad., U. So. Calif. Cert. family and marriage therapist. Pvt. practice counseling and cons., Boston, 1987-88; cons., evaluator State of Hawaii, Honolulu, 1988-89; ednl. evaluator Kamehameha Schs.-Bishop Estate, Honolulu, 1990—; cons., Honolulu, 1988—. Author: Development of a Criterion-Referenced, Performance-Based Assessment of Reading Comprehension in a Whole Literacy Program, 1991, Performance Based Assessment in the KEEP whole literacy curriculum, 1992. Rep. Com. on Human Svcs., Honolulu, 1989; active neighborhood bd., 1992. Mem. Am. Ednl. Rsch. Assn., Assn. for Moral Edn., Assn. for Supervision and Curriculum Devel., Nat. Soc. Study Edn., Polit. Edn. Assn., Harvard Club (v.p. Hawaii chpt.) Phi Beta Kappa. Office: Kamehameha Schs EED Eval Kapalama Heights Honolulu HI 96817

PETERSON, BARBARA ANN BENNETT, history educator; b. Portland, Oreg., Sept. 6, 1942; d. George Wright and Hope (Chatfield) Bennett; m. Frank Lynn Peterson, July 1, 1967. BA, BS, Oreg. State U., 1964; MA, Stanford U., 1965; PhD, U. Hawaii, 1978; PhD (hon.), London Inst. Applied Rsch., 1991. Prof. history U. Hawaii, Honolulu, 1967—, chmn. social scis. dept., 1971-73, 75-76, asst. dean, 1973-74; prof. Asian and European colonial history and world problems Chapman Coll. World Campus Afloat, 1974; prof. European overseas exploration, expansion and colonialism U. Colo., Boulder, 1978; assoc. prof. U. Hawaii-Manoa Coll. Continuing Edn., 1981; Fulbright prof. history Wuham (China) U., 1988-89; Fulbright rsch. prof. Sophia U., Japan, 1967; lectr. Capital Speakers, Washington, 1987—. Coauthor: Women's Place Is in the History Books, Her Story, 1620-1980: A Curriculum Guide for American History Teachers, 1980; author: Notable Women of Hawaii, 1984, America in British Eyes, 1988; editor: (with W. Solheim) The Pacific Region, 1990, 91; assoc. editor Am. Nat. Biography.; also numerous articles. Participant People-to-People Program, Eng., 1964, Expt. in Internat. Living Program, Nigeria, 1966; chmn. 1st Nat. Women's History Week, Hawaii, 1982; mem. Hawaii Commn. on Status of Women; mem. coun. Bishop Mus. Recipient state proclamations Gov. of Hawaii, Mayor City of Honolulu, Outstanding Tchr. of Yr. award Wuhan (People's Republic China) U., 1988; Fulbright scholar, Japan, 1967, People's Republic China, 1988-89; NEH-Woodrow Wilson fellow Princeton U., 1980, Medallion of Excellence award Am. Biog. Assn., 1989, named Woman of Yr., 1991. Fellow Internat. Biog. Assn., (Cambridge, Eng. chpt.); mem. AAUW, Am. Studies Assn., Fulbright Alumni Assn. (founding pres. Hawaii chpt. 1984-88, mem. nat. steering com. chairwomen Fulbright Assn. ann. conf. 1990), Am. Hist. Assn. (mem. numerous coms.), Maison Internat. des Intellectuals, Hawaii Found. History and Humanities (mem. editorial bd. 1972-73), Hawaii Found. Women's History, Hawaii Hist.Assn., Nat. League Am. Pen Women (contest chairperson 1986), Pi Beta Phi, Phi Kappa Phi. Home: 1341 Laukahi St Honolulu HI 96821-1407 also: East-West Ctr 1777 East-West Rd Honolulu HI 96848

PETERSON, BERGEN VOROS, group product manager; b. Salt Lake City, Sept. 12, 1959; d. Gerald John and Carla Marie (Olson) Voros; m. James Robert Peterson, Mar. 13, 1983; children: Kathryn Marie, Robert Gerald. BS in Bus. Adminstrn., Marquette U., 1981; MBA, Portland State U., 1989. Mktg. coord. Elaine Powers Figure Salons, Milw., 1981-83; sales coord. WJDQ/Q101 Radio, Meridian, Miss., 1983-85; account supr. Campus Dimensions, Phila., 1986-88; instr. Portland (Oreg.) State U., 1989-91, 92; sr. product mgr. First Interstate Bank, Portland, 1991—; cons. Oreg. Credit Union League, Beaverton, 1990. Adv. coun. mem. Human Svc. Coun., Vancouver, Wash., 1990, 91; bd. mem. Crime Stoppers, Portland, 1992. Mem. Am. Mktg. Assn. (bd. mem., membership 1992-93). Democrat. Roman Catholic. Home: 3100 NE 108th Circle Vancouver WA 98686

PETERSON, BILL, editor; b. Saskatoon, Sask., Can., May 25, 1954; s. Robert Oscar and Dorothy H.M.(Stevenson) P. BBA, U. Sask., 1986. Reporter The Star Phoenix, Saskatoon, 1972-80, editorial writer, 1981-83, city editor, 1984-86, spl. projects coord., 1986-87, editor, 1988-93; dir. comm. Sask. Mining Devel. Corp., Saskatoon, 1980-81; pres. Perk Holdings Can., Saskatoon, 1987-88; mem. adv. com. U. Regina Sch. Journalism, 1988—; pres. Nat. Newspaper Awards, 1989-92. Journalism fellow U. Toronto, 1983-84; Commonwealth Journalism fellow City Univ., London, 1986. Mem. Can. Assn. Journalism. Office: Star Phoenix, 204 5th Ave N, Saskatoon, SK Canada S7K 2P1

PETERSON, BROOKE ALAN, lawyer; b. Omaha, Dec. 6, 1949; s. Lloyd Earl and Priscilla Anne (Bailey) P.; m. Diane Louise Tegmeyer, Aug. 19, 1990. BA, Brown U., 1972; JD, U. Denver, 1975. Bar: Colo. 1975, U.S. Dist. Ct. Colo. 1975. Assoc. Garfield & Hecht, Aspen, Colo., 1975-77, Robert P. Grueter, Aspen, 1977-78; ptnr. Wendt, Grueter & Peterson, Aspen, 1978-79; prin. Brooke A. Peterson, P.C., Aspen, 1979—; mcpl. judge, Aspen, 1980—. Chmn. election commn., Pitkin County, 1979—. Mem. ABA, Colo. Bar Assn. (bd. govs. 1984-86, exec. council 1986-87), Pitkin County Bar Assn. (pres. 1981-83), Am. Trial Laywers Assn., Colo. Trial Lawyers Assn. Avocations: skiing, surfing, softball, squash, music. Home: 222 Roaring Fork Dr Aspen CO 81611-2239 Office: 315 E Hyman Ave Aspen CO 81611-1946

PETERSON, CARL HERBERT, banker, air force officer; b. Moline, Ill., Nov. 7, 1922; s. Carl John and Evelyn Marie (Nordmark) P.; m. Helen May Walker, Aug. 30, 1942; children: Susan Marie, Patricia Ann, Judith Lee, Cynthia Kathleen. BS, U. Md., 1959. Commd. 2d lt. USAAF, 1944; advanced through grades to col. USAF, 1967; fighter pilot, flight comdr. USAF, Munich and Pitts., 1949-54; dir. flying safety Air Force Acad., 1955-58; plans officer Alascan Air Command, Elmendorf AFB, Alaska, 1959-62; prof. aerospace sci. U. Puget Sound, Tacoma, 1962-66; direct air support ctr. dir. USAF, Danang and Bien Hoa, Vietnam, 1966-67; chief Air Force Doctrine Div., Pentagon, Washington, 1968-72; ret., 1972; v.p., trust officer Puget Sound Nat. Bank, Tacoma, 1972-90; ret., 1990. Decorataed Air medal, DFC, Legion of Merit with oak leaf cluster. Mem. Kiwanis (pres. Tacoma 1983). Republican. Lutheran. Home: 7221 Zircon Dr SW Tacoma WA 98498

PETERSON, CARL STUART, computer software engineer; b. Portland, Oreg., Jan. 4, 1966; s. Norman Dale and Evelyn Joyce (Kelly) P. BS in Computer and Info. Sci., U. Oreg., 1990. Software test engr. programming langs. Microsoft Corp. Internat., Redmond, Wash., 1991-92, software test engr. applications programmability unit, 1992—. Mem. Assn. for Computing Machinery. Office: Microsoft Corp Bldg 18/2 One Microsoft Way Redmond WA 98052-6399

PETERSON, CHARLES ERIC, senator, automotive executive; b. Ogden, Utah, June 4, 1914; s. Charles Eric and Dora Ann (Brown) P.; m. Harriet Robinson, Oct. 4, 1935; children: Charles E., Joan Peterson Fisher, Kent D., Steven V. Student, Weber Coll., 1931-33; BA, U. Chgo., 1935; AA, Utah Tech. Coll., 1985. Personnel supr. Kimberly-Clark, Neenah, Wis., 1935-42, U.S. Steel Co., Provo, Utah, 1942-46; mgr. Barbizon Co., Provo, 1946-49; ptnr. Utah Office Supply, Provo, 1949-59; owner, mgr. Chuck Peterson Motors, Provo, 1959-84; senator State of Utah, Provo, 1984-92; pres. Utah Auto Dealers, Salt Lake City, 1965. Speaker Utah Ho. of Reps., 1951-55; vice chmn. Utah Bd. Regents, 1969-79; mgr. Provo C. of C., 1959; pres. Provo Jaycees, 1957, Chgo. Mission Mormon Ch., 1980-83. Recipient Pub. Service award Brigham Young U., 1978, Presdl. citation Weber Coll., 1980, 93, Quality Dealer award Time Mag., 1973; named Hon. Alumnus Brigham Young U., 1975, Citizen of Yr., Utah County, 1978. Republican. Clubs: Riverside Country, Brigham Young U. Cougar. Lodge: Kiwanis. Home: 2737 Edgewood Provo UT 84604-5930

PETERSON, CHASE N., university president; b. Logan, Utah, Dec. 27, 1929; s. E.G. and Phebe (Nebeker) P.; m. Grethe Ballif, 1956; children: Erika Elizabeth, Stuart Ballif, Edward Chase. A.B., Harvard U., 1952, M.D., 1956. Diplomate: Am. Bd. Internal Medicine. Asst. prof. medicine U. Utah Med. Sch., 1965-67; assoc. Salt Lake Clinic; dean admissions and fin. aids to students Harvard U., 1967-72, v.p. univ., 1972-78; v.p. health scis. U. Utah, Salt Lake City, 1978-83, prof. medicine, 1983—, pres., 1983-91, clin. prof. medicine, 1991—; pres. emeritus U. Utah, Salt Lake City, 1992—; bd. dirs. First Security Corp., Utah Power & Light Co., O.C. Tanner Co.; chair Office Tech. Assessment. Mem. Nat. Assn. State Univs. and Land-Grant Colls. (chmn. 1988-89). Home: 66 Thaynes Canyon Dr Park City UT 84060-6711 Office: U Utah Salt Lake City UT 84112

PETERSON, CURTIS GERALD, broadcast executive; b. Council Bluffs, Iowa, Nov. 24, 1952; s. Scott William and Margaret Helen (Hansen) P.; m. Vicky Lynn McGee, Aug. 18, 1973; 1 child, Cory Scott. BA, U. Nebr., Omaha, 1976. Acct. exec. KMGC/KNUS, Dallas, 1977-80; gen. sales mgr. KESY Radio, Omaha, 1981-82; v.p., gen. mgr. KFRX Radio, Lincoln, Nebr., 1982-86, KAYI Radio, Tulsa, 1987-88. Republican. Roman Catholic. Office: Sta KIDO AM 1109 Main St Ste 570 Boise ID 83702-5641

PETERSON, DEAN MCCORMACK, mechanical engineer; b. Wessington, S.D., Dec. 12, 1931; s. Walter Henry and Era Faye (McCormack) P.; m. Mary Joan Drake, Oct. 20, 1954; children: Michael Dean, Marshall Drake. BS in Gen. Engring., S.D. Sch. Mines, Rapid City, 1954; MS in Mech. Engring., U. Rochester, 1963. Sr. project engr. Eastman Kodak Co., Rochester, 1954-68; mgr. engr. Honeywell, Inc., Denver, 1968-78, Fisher Price Toys, San Diego, 1978-81; dir. engring. Nimslo Corp., Atlanta, 1981-83, Spin Physics, San Diego, 1983-87, Am. Optical, San Diego, 1987-89, Signet Armorlite, San Marcos, Calif., 1989-90; pvt. engring. cons. Pacific Innovations Co., Escondido, Calif., 1990-91; v.p. engring. Galen Med., Escondido, 1991—; instr. Rochester Inst. Tech., 1963-68, Arapaho Community Coll., Littleton, Colo., 1972-76. Patentee in field. Election asst. Rep. Party, Escondido, 1985. With U.S. Army, 1954-56. Fellow Soc. Photo Scientists & Engrs.; mem. ASME, Soc. Plastics Engrs., Soc. Photo-Optical Engrs., Triangle, Sigma Tau. Republican. Presbyterian. Home: 2730 Peet Ln Escondido CA 92025-7431 Office: Galen Med 3220 Avenida Roposo Escondido CA 92029

PETERSON, DONALD WILLIAM, geologist; b. San Francisco, Mar. 3, 1925; s. Herman William and Alice M. (Korslund) P.; m. Betty Ann Leitch, Mar. 21, 1948; children: Karen, Kristine, Susan. BS, Calif. Inst. Tech., 1949; MS, Wash. State U., 1951; PhD, Stanford U., 1961. Geologist U.S. Geol. Survey, Globe, Ariz., 1952-57, Menlo Park, Calif., 1957-68, 1975-80, 85—; dep. chief office of mineral resources U.S. Geol. Survey, Washington, 1968-70; scientist-in-charge, Hawaiian Volcano Obs. U.S. Geol. Survey, Hawaii Nat. Park, 1970-75; scientist-in-charge, Cascades Volcano Obs. U.S. Geol. Survey, Vancouver, Wash., 1980-85; cons. in volcanology Volcanological Survey Indonesia, Yogyakarta, 1983, Bandung, 1985, 86. Contbr. numerous articles to profl. jours. With USN, 1944-46, 51-52. Recipient Meritorious Svc. award U.S. Dept. Interior, 1983. Fellow Geol. Soc. Am., Calif. Acad. Scis.; mem. AAAS, Am. Geophys. Union, Internat. Assn. Volcanology (sec. commn. on mitigation of volcanic disasters 1988—). Lutheran. Office: US Geol Survey MS-910 345 Middlefield Rd Menlo Park CA 94025-3591

PETERSON, DOROTHY HAWKINS, artist, educator; b. Albuquerque, Mar. 14, 1932; d. Ernest Lee and Ethel Dawn (Allen) Hawkins; m. John W. Peterson, July 9, 1954; children: John Richard, Dorothy Anne. BS in Edn., U. N.Mex., Albuquerque, 1953; MA, U. Tex., 1979. Freelance artist, 1960—; educator, instr. Carlsbad (N.Mex.) Ind. Elem. Sch. Dist., 1953-54; instr. Charleston (S.C.) County Schs., 1955-56; instr. in painting Midland (Tex.) Coll., 1971-76, Roswell (N.Mex.) Mus. Sch., 1981-83, 91—; instr. in art history Ea. N.Mex. U., Roswell, 1989—; instr. painting N.Mex. Mil. Inst., Roswell, 1992—; bd. dirs. N.Mex. Arts Commn., Santa Fe; cons. Casa de Amigos Craft Guild, Midland, Tex., 1971-73. Tutor Roswell Literacy Coun., 1988-89; bd. dirs. N.Mex. Arts & Crafts Fair, Albuquerque, 1983-85. Named Best of Show, Mus. of the S.W., 1967, 69; recipient Top award, 1973, 75, Juror award N.Mex. Arts & Crafts Fair, 1986, 1st pl. award Profl. Watercolor N.Mex. State Fair, 1988. Mem. N.Mex. Watercolor Soc. (2d Pl. award 1981, San Diego Watercolor Soc. award 1988, 1st Pl. award state fair, 1988). Office: PO Box 915 Roswell NM 88202-0915

PETERSON, EDWIN J., state supreme court justice; b. Gilmanton, Wis., Mar. 30, 1930; s. Edwin A. and Leora Grace (Kitelinger) P.; m. Anna Chadwick, Feb. 7, 1971; children: Patricia, Andrew, Sherry. B.S., U. Oreg., 1951, LL.B., 1957. Bar: Oreg. 1957. Assoc. firm Tooze, Kerr, Peterson, Marshall & Shenker, Portland, 1957-61; mem. firm Tooze, Kerr, Peterson, Marshall & Shenker, 1961-79; assoc. justice Supreme Ct. Oreg., Salem, 1979-83, chief justice, 1983-91; mem. standing com. on fed. rules of practice and procedure, 1987-93; bd. dirs. Conf. Chief Justices, 1985-87, 88-91. Chmn. Portland Citizens Sch. Com., 1968-70; vice chmn. Young Republican Fedn. Orgn., 1951; bd. visitors U. Oreg. Law Sch., 1978-83, 87—, chmn. bd. visitors, 1981-83. Served to 1st lt. USAF, 1952-54. Mem. ABA, Am. Judicature Soc., Oreg. State Bar (bd. examiners 1963-66, gov. 1973-76, vice chmn. profl. liability fund 1977-78), Multnomah County Bar Assn. (pres. 1972-73), Phi Alpha Delta, Lambda Chi Alpha. Episcopalian. Home: 3365 Sunridge Dr S Salem OR 97302-5950 Office: Oreg Supreme Ct Supreme Ct Bldg Salem OR 97310

PETERSON, ERLE VIDAILLET, retired metallurgical engineer; b. Idaho Falls, Idaho, Apr. 29, 1915; s. Vier P. and Marie (Vidaillet) P.; m. Rosemary Sherwood, June 3, 1935; children: Kent Sherwood, Pamela Jo. BS in Mining Engring., U. Idaho, 1940; MS in Mining Engring., U. Utah, 1941. Tech. advisor Remington Arms Co., Salt Lake City, 1941-43; constrn. engr. plutonium plant duPont, Hanford, Wash., 1943-44; R & D engr. exptl. sta. duPont, Wilmington, Del., 1944-51; plant metallurgist heavy water plant duPont, Newport, Ind., 1951-57; rsch. metallurgist metals program duPont, Balt., 1957-62, prin. project engr. USAF contracts, 1962-68; devel. engr. duPont, Wilmington, 1969-80; ret., 1980. Patentee in field; contbr. articles to profl. jours. Candidate for State Senate-Am. Party, Wilmington, 1974; com. chmn. Boy Scouts Am., Wilmington, 1975-78; treas. Local Civic Assn., Wilmington, 1977-79. Rsch. fellow U. Utah, 1940. Mem. Am. Soc. Metallurgists Internat., Del. Assn. Profl. Engrs. Republican. Home: PO Box 74 Rigby ID 83442

PETERSON, FRANK ROBERT, game warden; b. Great Falls, Mont., Sept. 13, 1951; s. Adrian Fredrick and Thelma R. (Isakson) P.; m. Linda Carol Jordan, Feb. 7, 1976; children: Ashley Paige, Brekke Lane. BS in Wildlife Mgmt., U. Wyo., 1973. Cert. profl. peace officer. Game warden trainee Wyo. Game & Fish Dept., Elk Mountain, 1974-75; game warden Wyo. Game & Fish Dept., Jeffrey City, Wyo., 1976-78, Dayton, Wyo., 1978—. Mem. N.Am. Wildlife Enforcement Officers Assn. (bd. dirs. 1980-81, exec. com. 1980—), Wyo. Game Wardens Assn., Big Horn Mountain Peace Officers. Home and Office: Wyo Game & Fish Dept PO Box 27 Dayton WY 82836

PETERSON, GLENN VIGGO, industrial arts educator; b. Gothenburg, Nebr., Oct. 16, 1928; s. Peter and Nellie D. (Young) P.; m. Dorothy Bernice Pollat, June 4, 1948; children: Connie Anne, Kent Leon, Sandra Kay. BA, Kearney State Coll., 1952; MA, U. No. Colo., 1956-61. Cert. secondary tchr. Tchr. indsl. arts Kearney, Nebr., 1956-62, Colorado Springs, Colo., 1962-89. Mem. Colorado Springs Coin Club (pres. 1990-92), Colorado Springs Numismatic Soc., Rob Morris #46 (3d degree 1962-92), Phi Delta Kappa. Republican. Presbyterian. Home: 7504 Gillen Rd Colorado Springs CO 80919

PETERSON, HARRY LEROY, academic administrator; b. Duluth, Minn., Feb. 22, 1940; s. Harry Leonard and Pearl Vivian (Rhode) P.; m. Sylvia K. Brinkley, Sept. 1, 1963; 1 child, Aaron B. BA in Sociology, San Diego State U., 1963; MSW, U. Calif., Berkeley, 1966; PhD in Ednl. Policy Studies, U. Wis., 1977. Psychiat. social worker Brown County Guidance Clinic, Green Bay, Wis., 1966-68; dir. student life programs U. Wis., Green Bay, 1969-75; exec. asst. to sec. Wis. Dept. of Transp., Madison, 1975-77, Wis. Dept. of Industry Labor & Human Rels., Madison, 1977-78; sr. spl. asst. U. Wis., Madison, 1978-87, exec. asst. to chancellor, 1988-90; v.p. Univ. Rels. and Devel. U. Idaho, Moscow, 1990—. Contbr. articles to profl. jours. Home: 776 Indian Hills Dr Moscow ID 83843-9308 Office: U Rels & Devel U Idaho Moscow ID 83843

PETERSON, HOWARD COOPER, lawyer, accountant; b. Decatur, Ill., Oct. 12, 1939; s. Howard and Lorraine (Cooper) P.; BEE, U. Ill., 1963; MEE, San Diego State Coll., 1967; MBA, Columbia U., 1969; JD, Calif. Western Sch. Law, 1983; LLM in Taxation NYU, 1985. Bar: Calif., cert. fin. planner.; CPA, Tex.; registered profl. Engr., Calif.; cert. neuro-linguistic profl. Elec. engr. Convair div. Gen. Dynamics Corp., San Diego, 1963-67, sr. electronics engr., 1967-68; gen. ptnr. Costumes Characters & Classics Co., San Diego, 1979-86; v.p., dir. Equity Programs Corp., San Diego, 1973-83; pres., dir. Coastal Properties Trust, San Diego, 1979-89, Juno Securities, Inc., 1983—, Juno Real Estate INc., 1974—, Scripps Mortgage Corp., 1987-90, Juno Transport Inc., 1988—; chief fin. officer and dir. Imperial Screens of San Diego, 1977—, Heritage Transp. Mgmt. Inc., 1989-91, A.S.A.P. Ins. Svcs. Inc., 1983-85. Mem. ABA, Interamerican Bar Assn., Nat. Soc. Public Accts., Internat. Assn. Fin. Planning, Assn. Enrolled Agts.

PETERSON, HOWARD GEORGE FINNEMORE, sports executive; b. Presque Isle, Maine, Mar. 23, 1951; s. George Conrad and Valeda (Finnemore) P. Student New Eng. Conservatory of Music, 1967-68, Andrews U., 1968-71, Orson Welles Film Sch., 1971-72, Loma Linda U., 1972-75. Pres., Nat. Ski Touring Operators Assn., 1977-79; exec. v.p. mktg. U.S. Ski Assn., 1979-81, exec. dir., 1981-85, sec. gen., 1985—; chief exec. officer U.S. Ski Team, 1988—, U.S. Ski Ednl. Found., 1988—; dir. Mountain Rescue Svc., Inc. Mem. U.S. Ski Coaches Assn. (dir.), Nat. Ski Touring Operators Assn. (dir.), Internat. Ski Fedn. (eligibility com., TV and sponsorship freestyle com., chmn. expert's group for pool questions 1988—), U.S. Olympic Properties Com., Winter Olympic Sports Coun. (sec. 1988—, olympic tng. ctrs. com. 1988—), U.S. Skiing Found. (exec. dir., trustee), Pan Am. Sports Orgn. (winter games adv. com. 1988—). Author: Cross Country Citizen Racing, 1980; I Hope I Get a Purple Ribbon, 1980; Cross Country Ski Trails, 1979; Cannon: A Climber's Guide, 1972. Office: US Ski Assn PO Box 100 Park City UT 84060-0100

PETERSON, IRENE RENIE, record and publishing company executive; b. Lynden, Wash., Jan. 6, 1927; d. John Earl and Mary Magdalene (Weeda) Sluys; m. Glenn Harold Blakely, Jan. 12, 1944 (div. 1962); children: Sharon Elaine Edkins, Sandra Lynne Wiggins, Steven Lane Blakely; m. Harold Alfred Peterson, July 3, 1965. Grad., Success Bus. Coll., 1962. Waitress various restaurants, Wash., 1944-52, Bellingham Hotel, 1952-62; legal sec. Law Office, Lynden, Wash., 1963-64; editorial sec. Georgia-Pacific Corp., Bellingham, 1964-76; record co. exec., owner L.P.S. Records, Inc., Bellingham, 1976—; pub., writer, designer, owner, songwriter Heartstone & Fourth Corner Music, 1976—. Author: Life in the Ruff, 1960 (Collector's Item 1962); composer various albums and singles; author children's books, designer of postcards Heartstone Prints, Bellingham, 1970—. Blue Bird leader Campfire Girls, Bellingham, 1952, campfire leader, 1954; queen chaperone Blossomtime Festival, Bellingham, 1960-62, campaign worker Sheriff of Whatcom County, Bellingham, 1976-80; pres. Jimmy Murphy Fan Club, Bellingham, 1985—. Office: Heartstone Music/BMI 2140 St Clair St Bellingham WA 98226-4016

PETERSON, JAMES ALGERT, geologist, educator; b. Baroda, Mich., Apr. 17, 1915; s. Djalma Hardaman and Mary Avis (McAnally) P.; m. Gladys Marie Pearson, Aug. 18, 1944; children—James D., Wendy A., Brian H. Student, Northwestern U., 1941-43, U. Wis., 1943; B.S. magna cum laude, St. Louis U., 1948; M.S. (Shell fellow), U. Minn., 1950, Ph.D., 1951. Mem. staff U.S. Geol. Survey, Spokane, Wash., 1949-51; instr. geology Wash. State U., Pullman, 1951; geologist Shell Oil Co., 1952-65; geologist div. stratigrapher, 1958-63, sr. geologist, 1963-65; instr. geology N. Mex. State U., San Juan, (P.R.), br., 1959-65; prof. geology U. Mont., Missoula, 1965—; cons. U.S. Geol. Survey, 1976-82, rsch. geologist, 1982—. Editor: Geology of East Central Utah, 1956, Geometry of Sandstone Bodies, 1960, Rocky Mountain Sedimentary Basins, 1965, (with others) Pacific Geology, Paleotectonics and Sedimentation, 1986; Contbr. (with others) articles to profl. jours. Served to 1st lt. USAAF, 1943-46. Recipient Alumni Merit award St. Louis U., 1960. Fellow AAAS, Geol. Soc. Am.; mem. Am. Assn. Petroleum Geologists (pres. Rocky Mountain sect. 1964, Pres.'s award 1988, Disting. Svc. award 1992), Rocky Mountain Assn. Geologists (Outstanding Scientist award 1987), Four Corners Geol. Soc. (hon., pres. 1962), Am. Inst. Profl. Geologists (pres. Mont. sect. 1971), Soc. Econ. Paleontologists and Mineralogists (hon. 1985, sec.-treas. 1969-71, editor 1976-78, Disting. Pioneer Geologist award 1988), Mont. Geol. Soc. (hon. 1987), Utah Geol. Soc. Club: Explorers. Home: 301 Pattee Canyon Dr Missoula MT 59803-1624

PETERSON, JAMES ALMA, business analyst; b. Safford, Ariz., Jan. 18, 1950; s. Chester John and Virginia (Christenson) P.; m. Barbara Lynette Cornelius, Aug. 24, 1973; children: Shannon, William, Steven, Ashley. BS in Computer Info. Systems, S.W. Mo. State U., 1985. Sr. programmer analyst Tanner Southwest, Inc., Phoenix, 1985-87; systems analyst Western Savs., Phoenix, 1987-88; chief fin. officer Nat. Citizenship Inst., Phoenix, 1988-92; corp. mgr. Lockheed IMS, Phoenix, 1992—; pvt. practice computer cons., Phoenix, 1985-92. Republican. Church of Jesus Christ of Latter Day Saints. Home: 1038 E Le Marche Phoenix AZ 85022 Office: Lockheed Info Mgmt Systems 40 N Central #2250 Phoenix AZ 85004

PETERSON, JAN KENT, architect; b. Kewanee, Ill., June 18, 1945; s. Alton Gerald and Rubye Charlotte (Johnson) P.; m. Suzanne Lynn Clark, Dec. 29, 1968 (div. 1982); children: Kristen, Jeremy. BS in Archtl. Sci., Washington U., St. Louis, 1967; MArch, Washington U., 1969. Registered architect, Colo., Mo., Ill., Ariz. Draftsman Schwarz & Henmi, St. Louis, 1969-72; comprehensive planning dir. Community Devel. Agy., East St. Louis, Ill., 1975-77; architect Hastings & Chivetta, Clayton, Mo., 1977-82, Peckham Guyton Albers & Viets, St. Louis, 1982-83, Henmi-Jen-Enderling, St. Louis, 1983-89; prin. Peterson Design, St. Louis, 1987-91; instr. night sch. Washington U., 1987-92. Prin. works include St. Charles (Mo.) Police Hdqrs. Bldg., 1979 (AIA nat. exhibit), Westgate Shopping Ctr., 1981 (design award Nat. Mall Monitor mag.), St. Louis U. recreation complex, 1984 (Constrn. Products & Mfrs'. Coun. Honor award), Wentzville (Mo.) Community Hosp. 1987. (Masonry Inst. St. Louis design excellence award). Chmn. tech. planning adv. task force East-West Gateway Coordinating Coun., St. Louis, 1976-77. rem. AIA, Sigma Phi Epsilon (pres. alumni bd. Mo. Beta chpt. 1987-91, mem. alumni bd. Co. Gamma chpt., 1992—). Office: 4921 Sandstone Dr Fort Collins CO 80526

PETERSON, JOHN ERIC, physician, educator; b. Norwalk, Ohio, Oct. 26, 1914; s. Charles Augustus and Fannie Helen (Stanford) P.; m. Lodene C. Pruett, Aug. 18, 1938; children—Carol Peterson Haviland, John Eric. Student, Columbia Jr. Coll., 1932-34; M.D., Coll. Med. Evangelists, 1938. Diplomate: Nat. Bd. Med. Examiners, Am. Bd. Internal Medicine. Intern Henry Ford Hosp., Detroit, 1938-39; resident Henry Ford Hosp., 1939-42; practice medicine specializing in internal medicine Los Angeles, 1942-56, Loma Linda, Calif., 1956—; mem. staff Los Angeles County Hosp., Riverside (Calif.) County Gen. Hosp.; mem. faculty Sch. Medicine, Loma Linda U., 1942—, prof. medicine, 1967-88, prof. medicine emeritus, 1988—, chmn. dept., 1969-80; assoc. dean Sch. Medicine, Loma Linda U. (Sch. Medicine), 1965-75; mem. staff Loma Linda U. Hosp., 1967—, chief medicine service, 1969-80; rsch. assoc. Harvard Med. Sch., 1960-61; cons. to univs. and fgn. govts. Contbr. articles to various publs. Fellow A.C.P.; mem. AMA, Calif., San Bernardino County med. assns., Am. Heart Assn., Calif., Inland socs. internal medicine, Am. Diabetes Assn., Western Soc. Clin. Research, Assn. Profs. of Medicine, Los Angeles Acad. Medicine, Diabetes Assn. So. Calif., Sigma Xi, Alpha Omega Alpha. Office: Loma Linda U Med Ctr Dept Medicine Rm 1576 Loma Linda CA 92350

PETERSON, JOHN LEONARD, lawyer, judge; b. Butte, Mont., Sept. 11, 1933; s. Roy Victor and Lena Pauline (Umhang) P.; m. Jean Marie Hollingsworth, June 10, 1957; children: Michael R., John Robert, Carol Jean. BA in Bus., U. Mont., 1957, JD, 1957. Bar: Mont. 1957, U.S. Supreme Ct. 1964, U.S. Ct. Appeals (9th cir.) 1974, U.S. Tax Ct. 1978. Assoc., McCaffery, Roe, Kiely & Joyce, 1957-63; ptnr. McCaffery & Peterson, 1963-79; sole practice, Butte, Mont., 1979-85; part-time U.S. bankruptcy judge, 1963-85; U.S. bankruptcy judge, Mont., 1985—. Bd. govs. Nat. Conf. Bankruptcy Judges, 1989-92; mem. Mont. Bd. Regents Higher Edn., 1975-82; del. Democratic Nat. Conv., 1968. Mem. Nat. Conf. Bankruptcy Judges, Assn. Trial Lawyers Am., Mont. Bar Assn., Silver Bow County Bar Assn., Butte Country Club, Butte Town Club, Butte Exch. Club, VASA Order Am., Scandinavia Fraternity of Am. Democrat. Lutheran. Office: US Dist Ct 215 Fed Bldg Butte MT 59701

PETERSON, KENNER CHARLES, environmental contractor, consultant; b. Trona, Calif., May 4, 1945; s. Oliver C. Peterson and Kim Stratton Pace; m. RanDee Dorine Cochell, Aug. 9, 1965 (div. Dec. 1990); children: Maerae Alania, Rebecca Diane, Romona Sue. Student, Ga. Inst. Tech., 1985-90, U. Calif., Davis, 1991. Registered environ. assessor. Park ranger Land County Parks, Cottage Grove, Oreg., 1979-83; mgr. Grove Christian Svc. Camp, Dorina, Oreg., 1980-84; ops. mgr. Roberts Environ., Eugene, Oreg., 1984-86; pres., CEO Kenner Inc., Cottage Grove, 1986—. Sgt. USAF, 1965-68. Mem. Nat. Asbestos Coun. (bd. dirs. 1988-90, pres. 1989-90), Asbestos Abatement Assn. (bd. dirs. 1987-90). Office: Kenner Inc 80110 Sears Rd Cottage Grove OR 97424

PETERSON, KEVIN BRUCE, newspaper editor, publishing executive; b. Kitchener, Ont., Can., Feb. 11, 1948; s. Bruce Russell and Marguerite Elizabeth (Hammond) P.; m. Constance Maureen Bailey, Feb. 11, 1975 (dec. May 1975); m. Sheila Helen O'Brien, Jan. 9, 1981. B.A., U. Calgary, Alta., Can., 1968. Chief bur. Calgary Herald, 1972-75, city editor, 1976-77, news editor, 1977-78, bus. editor, 1978, mng. editor, 1978-86, editor, asst. pub., 1986-87, gen. mgr., 1987-88, pub., 1989—; pres. Canadian U. Press, Ottawa, Ont., Can., 1968-69. Harry Brittain Meml. fellow Commonwealth Press Union, London, 1979. Mem. Can. Mng. Editors (bd. dirs. 1983-87), Am. Soc. Newspaper Editors, Horsemen's Benevolent and Protective Assn., Alta. Legis. Press Gallery Assn. (v.p. 1971-76), Can. Daily Newspaper Assn. (bd. dirs. 1990—, vice chmn., treas. 1992, chmn.-elect 1993). Clubs: Calgary Petroleum, Ranchmen's, 100-to-1 (Arcadia, Calif.). Office: Calgary Herald, 215 16th St Se, Calgary, AB Canada T2P 0W8

PETERSON, KEVIN MERLE, investment banker; b. Salt Lake City, Sept. 1, 1950; s. Merle J. and Louise (Johnston) P.; m. Deborah Ann Peterson, June 23, 1973. BA, N.W. Nazarene Coll., 1973; MA, U. Idaho, 1975. Mcpl. bond analyst First Nat. Bank Oreg., Portland, 1976-78; dir. mcpl. bond div. Oreg. State Treasury, Salem, 1978-80; dir. rev. bonds The Port of Portland, 1980-83; v.p., mgr. western region pub. fin. dept. A.G. Edwards and Sons, Portland, 1983-87; v.p., dir. pub. fin. Paulson Investment Co., Inc., Portland, 1988-91; v.p., pres. pub. fin. First Security Bank, Salt Lake City, 1991—. Office: First Security Bank 61 S Main 6th Fl Salt Lake City UT 84130

PETERSON, LARRY CHARLES, fishery biologist; b. Wakefield, Nebr., July 8, 1940; s. Lawrence Earl and Erma (Gabelman) P.; m. Cheryl Sue Armstrong, June 7, 1959; children: Layne T., Lynae S. Student, U. Minn., 1959; BA in Biology & Fisheries Mgmt., U. S.D., 1961; postgrad., Colo. State U., 1967. Fish mgmt. biologist U.S. Fish & Wildlife Svcs., Jackson, Wyo., 1962-63, Tishomingo, Okla., 1963-65, Springville, Utah, 1965-66, Vernal, Utah, 1966-68, Kalispell, Mont., 1968-84, Anchorage, Alaska, 1984—. Co-author surveys, rsch. in field. Mem. Am. Fish Soc., Wildlife Soc. Home: 5404 W Dimond Blvd # 3 Anchorage AK 99515 Office: US Fish & Wildlife Svc 1011 E Tudor Rd Anchorage AK 99503

PETERSON, LEROY, educator; b. Fairfield, Ala., Feb. 15, 1930; s. Leroy and Ludie Pearl (Henderson) P.; m. Theresa Petite, Apr. 6, 1968 (div. Oct. 1984); children: Leroy III, Monica Teresa; m. Ruby Willodine Hopkins, July 21, 1985. Cert. in piano, Bavarian State Acad., Wuerzburg, Fed. Republic Germany, 1954; BS in Music Edn., Miami U., Oxford, Ohio, 1957. Life credential music tchr., Calif. Tchr. music Cleve. Pub. Schs., 1957-62, L.A. Unified Schs., 1963—. Song composer. With U.S. Army, 1952-54. Mem. Phi Mu Alpha Sinfonia. Democrat. Mem. Ch. of Christ. Home: 12600 Cobalt Rd Victorville CA 92392-6277 Office: Chester W Nimitz Jr High 6021 Carmelita Ave Huntington Park CA 90255-3399

PETERSON, LEVI SAVAGE, English language educator; b. Snowflake, Ariz., Dec. 13, 1933; s. Joseph and Lydia Jane (Savage) P.; m. Althea Grace Sand, Aug. 31, 1958; 1 child, Karrin. BA, Brigham Young U., 1958, MA, 1960; PhD, U. Utah, 1965. Asst. prof. Weber State U., Ogden, Utah, 1965-68, assoc. prof., 1968-72, prof., 1972—; dir. honors program Weber State U., 1973-82. Author: Canyons of Grace, 1982, The Backslider, 1986, Juanita Brooks, 1988 (Evans award 1988), Night Soil, 1990; editor: Greening Wheat, 1983. Trustee Weber County Libr., Ogden, 1988—. Mem. Assn. for Mormon Letters (bd. dirs., pres. 1981-90), Rocky Mountain Modern Lang. Assn., Utah Acad. of Scis., Arts and Letters (editor Encyclia 1976-81, Disting. Coll. Svc. award 1984), Western Lit. Assn. Democrat. Home: 1561 25th St Ogden UT 84401-2923 Office: Weber State U Dept English Ogden UT 84408

PETERSON, LOWELL, cinematographer; b. L.A., Feb. 1, 1950; s. Lowell Stanley and Catherine Linda (Hess) P.; m. Deanna Rae Terry, Aug. 2, 1981. Student, Yale U., 1968; BA in Theater Arts, UCLA, 1973. Asst. cinematographer, Hollywood, Calif., 1973-83; camera operator Hollywood, 1983-92, dir. photography, 1992—. Asst. cinematographer various prodns. including Blind Ambition, 1979, Hawaii Five-O, 1979-80, White Shadow, 1980-81, Lou Grant, 1981-82, Two of a Kind, 1982, Remington Steele, 1982-83, Something About Amelia, 1983; camera operator various prodns. including Tourist Trap, 1979, Newhart, 1983, Scarecrow and Mrs. King, 1983-85, Children in the Crossfire, 1984, Stranded, 1986, Knots Landing, 1986-87, 89-92, Like Father Like Son, 1987, Star Trek: The Next Generation, 1987-89, Coupe de Ville, 1990, Show of Force, 1990, Postcards from the Edge, 1990, Guilty by Suspicion, 1991, The Mambo Kings, 1992, Dracula, 1992; dir. photography Knots Landing, 1992-93; contbr. articles to Film Comment, 1974, Internat. Photographer, 1984—. Mem. Soc. Motion Picture and TV Engrs., Internat. Photographers Guild, L.A. Music Ctr. Opera League, Friends of UCLA Film Archive, Am. Cinematheque, U.S. Chess Fedn. Home and Office: 3815 Ventura Canyon Ave Sherman Oaks CA 91423-4710

PETERSON, MICHAEL CHARLES, pilot; b. Manitowoc, Wis., July 17, 1960; s. Charles Desmond and Marilyn Jane (Byrum) P.; m. Jessica Lillian Manwaring, May 18, 1985. Student, U. Minn., 1978-79; BS magna cum laude, Met. State U., 1982. Cert. airline transport pilot, flight instr., flight engr. turbojet (FAA). Flight instr. P.C. Flyers Inc., Englewood, Colo., 1981-84; asst. chief pilot Air Center One, Englewood, Colo., 1981-84; pilot Intensive Air Care, Denver, 1982-84, Burlington No. Aviation, Englewood, 1983-84, Corp. Jets, Scottsdale, Ariz., 1984; flight officer Key Airlines Inc., Las Vegas, 1984-85; capt. U.S. West Aviation, Englewood, 1985—; v.p. Aviation Resources Inc., Castle Rock, Colo., 1990-92, Colo. Alpine Designs, Inc., Littleton, 1992—. AOPA scholar, 1981. Republican. Home: 62 Peachtree Cir Castle Rock CO 80104-2727 Office: US West Aviation 7425 S Peoria St Englewood CO 80112 also: Colo Alpine Designs Inc 9748 S Ashleigh Ln Littleton CO 80126

PETERSON, MILLIE M., state legislator; b. Merced, Calif., June 11, 1944. BS, U. Utah, 1979, MSW, 1984. Mem. Utah State Senate from 12th dist., 1991—. Mem. NASW, Assn. Am. Med. Colls. Democrat. Address: 7131 W 3800 S West Valley City UT 84120

PETERSON, RICHARD EDWARD, nursing administrator; b. Chgo., Feb. 11, 1946; s. Otto Edward and Dorothy (Ziegler) P.; m. Catherine Libert Peterson, May 28, 1972; children: Christine, Janis. RN, Alexian Bros. Hosp. Sch., Chgo., 1968; BS in Nursing, DePaul U., Chgo., 1970; MEd, U. San Diego, 1976, MS in Nursing, 1982. Cert. advanced nursing adminstrn., staff devel. Faculty San Diego City Coll., 1980—; administrv. dir. nursing, dir. edn. and quality programs Green Hosp. of Scripps Clinic, LaJolla, Calif., 1987—; faculty mem. U. Phoenix, 1991—. With N.C., USN, 1969-77. Mem. Phi Delta Kappa, Sigma Theta Tau, Alpha Tau Delta, Chi Sigma Iota. Home: 2526 Pheasant Dr San Diego CA 92123-3324

PETERSON, RICHARD HERMANN, history educator; b. Berkeley, Calif., Jan. 16, 1942; s. William Martin and Dorothy Jean (Heyne) P.; m. Nora Ann Lorenzo, June 21, 1970; 1 child, Nina Elizabeth. AB, U. Calif., Berkeley, 1963; MA, San Francisco State U., 1966; PhD, U. Calif., Davis, 1971. Calif. community coll. teaching credential. Asst. prof. history Ind. U., Kokomo, 1971-76; instr. social studies Coll. of the Redwoods, Ft. Bragg, Calif., 1976-78; assoc. prof. history San Diego State U., 1978-82, prof. history, 1982—. Author: Manifest Destiny in the Mines, 1975, The Bonanza Kings, 1977, 91, Bonanza Rich, 1991; book rev. editor Jour. of San Diego History, 1978-82, editorial cons., 1980-82; contbr. articles to profl. jours. Judge for papers Internat. History Fair, San Diego, Tijuana, Mex., 1983-88. Faculty Summer fellow Ind. U., 1975, 76, San Diego State U., 1980; rsch. grantee Sourisseau Acad., 1977, Am. Assn. State/Local History, 1988; named Golden Poet of Yr., World of Poetry, 1987-89. Mem. Calif. Hist. Soc., Hist. Soc. of So. Calif., Western History Assn., Calif. Studies Assn. Home: 7956 Lake Adlon Dr San Diego CA 92119-3117 Office: San Diego State U History Dept 5300 Campanile Dr San Diego CA 92182-0380

PETERSON, ROBERT WILLIAMS, physicist; b. July 14, 1925; s. Thomas A. and Elsie H. (Pfeil) P.; m. Clara Schwartz, May 23, 1981. BS summa cum laude, Rutgers U., 1950; PhD, Calif. Tech. Inst., 1954. Mem. staff Los Alamos (N.Mex.) Nat. Lab., 1954—. With U.S. Army, 1943-45, ETO. Mem. Sigma Xi, Phi Beta Kappa. Office: PO Box 83 Los Alamos NM 87544-0083

PETERSON, ROLAND OSCAR, retired electronics company executive; b. Bklyn., Jan. 18, 1932; s. Oscar Gustaf and Klara Ingegerd (Lindau) P.; m. Agnes Frances Walsh, Sept. 12, 1953; children: Joan, Lauren, Paul, Michael. BEE, Poly. Inst. N.Y., 1953, MEE, 1954. Registered profl. engr., N.Y. Research fellow Microwave Research Inst., Bklyn., 1953-54; sr. engr. Sperry Gyroscope Co., Great Neck, N.Y., 1956-60; with Litton Industries, Inc., Woodland Hills, Calif., 1961—; v.p. advanced systems engring. Guidance and Control Systems div., Litton Industries, Inc., Woodland Hills, Calif., 1973-76; v.p. bus. devel. Guidance and Control Systems div., Litton Industries Inc., Woodland Hills, Calif., 1976-77, pres., 1977-83; v.p. Litton Industries, Inc., 1979-83; sr. v.p., group exec. Litton Industries, Inc., Beverly Hills, Calif., 1983-88, pres., chief operating officer, 1988-90, sr. v.p., group exec., chief scientist, 1990-92; retired, 1992. Regional chmn. Los Angeles United Way campaign , 1985-86. Served to 1st lt. U.S. Army, 1954-56. Recipient Disting. Alumni award Poly. Inst. N.Y., 1986. Mem. Am. Electronics Assn., Inst. Navigation (western regional v.p. 1975-76, Hays award 1982). Roman Catholic.

PETERSON, RONALD ARTHUR, emeritus business law educator; b. Valley, Nebr., June 21, 1920; s. Arthur Lawrence and Hazel McClellan (Foster) P.; m. Patricia Marguerite North, Aug. 29, 1942; children: Ronald, Kathleen, Patrick, James, John, Thomas, Mary, Joseph. B.A. in Poly. Sci., U. Omaha, 1943; J.D. in Law, Creighton U., 1948; postgrad. U. Wash., 1963-64. Bar: Nebr. 1948, Wash. 1949. Asst. prof. Seattle U., 1963-76, dir. legal studies, 1973-83, assoc. prof., 1976-84, prof. emeritus dept. bus. law, 1984—. Author: The Old English Year Books. Dir. high sch.-coll. and alumni rels. Seattle U., 1950-58, dir. admissions, 1958-73; founding mem. Wash. State Coun. on High Sch.-Coll. Rels., 1953-73, chmn., 1962-63; founding mem. Seattle Archdiocese Sch. Bd., Western Wash., 1969; mem. Spl. Task Force on Legis. for Wash. System of Pub. Librs., 1971-73; assoc. dir. Wash. Criminal Justice Edn. and Tng. Ctr., 1973; mem. editorial bd. Introduction to Law and the Legal Process, 1980, mem. Oreg.-Wash. Commn. on the Pub. of Mapping Your Education; vol. chaplain juvenile ct. King County Dept. Youth Svcs., 1991. Lt. USNR, 1943-46. Recipient Exemplary Tchr. award Alpha Kappa Psi, 1964. Mem. Am. Bus. Law Assn. (del. 1980), Pacific Northwest Bus. Law Assn. (pres. 1984-85), Seattle U. Alumni Assn. (Campus Svc. award 1989), Beta Gamma Sigma. Roman Catholic. Home: 1625 McGilvra Blvd E Seattle WA 98112-3119

PETERSON, RONALD DUANE, computer science educator; b. Ogden, Utah, Mar. 10, 1948; s. Arthur Daniel Peterson and Gwen (Davis) Tesch; m. Debra Quinn, June 10, 1971; children: Emily, Sarah, Eric, Joy. Student, U. Utah, 1970-71; BA, Weber State Coll., Ogden, Utah, 1971; PhD, Cornell U., 1980. Dir. Computer Ctr., Parks Coll., Cahokia, Ill., 1976-80; asst. prof. computer sci. Weber State U. (formerly Coll.), 1980-84, assoc. prof., 1984—; NSF trainee, U. Utah, Salt Lake City, 1971; project engr. TRW, Ogden, 1985—. Recipient Outstanding Faculty Mem. data processing dept. Weber State Coll., 1982. Mem. IEEE Computer Soc., Assn. for Computing Machinery (chpt. sponsor 1981—), Am. Mensa. Mem. LDS Ch. Office: Weber State U Computer Sci Dept 2401 Ogden UT 84408-2401

PETERSON, SHARON ELIZABETH, marketing professional; b. Tuskegee, Ala., Feb. 3, 1958; d. Malcolm Norman and Amy Elizabeth (Danner) B. BS in Archtl. Engring., N.C. A&T State U., Greensboro, N.C., 1981; MS in Indsl. Administrn., Carnegie Mellon U., Pittsburgh, 1988. Structural design engr. Stone and Webster Engring. Corp., Boston, 1981-87; mfg. project mgr. Hughes Aircraft Co., Fullerton, Calif., 1988-90; mktg. rep. Hughes Data Systems., Anaheim, Calif., 1990-93; product mgr. Day Runner, Inc., Fullerton, Calif., 1993—. Mem. NAFE, Am. Mktg. Assn. Methodist.

PETERSON, SPENCER ALAN, ecologist; b. Sioux Falls, S.D., Jan. 6, 1940; s. Earl Harold and Josephine Henrietta (Giebink) P.; m. Shirley Ann White, Sept. 16, 1961; children: Scott Joseph, Sheila Marie. BS, Sioux Falls Coll., 1965; MS, U. N.D., 1967, PhD, 1971. Project leader Mich. Dept. Natural Resources, Lansing, 1971-72; rsch. biologist U.S. EPA, Corvallis, Oreg., 1972-74, team leader, 1974-77, program leader, 1977-81, br. chief, 1981-89; regional scientist U.S. EPA, Seattle, 1989-90; program leader U.S. EPA, Corvallis, Oreg., 1990—. Co-author: Role of Water Urban Ecology, 1979; author: Restoration of Lakes and Reservoirs, 1986, 1993. Chair bd. trustees 1st United Meth. Ch., Corvallis, 1971-72. Staff sgt. U.S. Army, 1961-62. Nat. Def. Grad. fellow U.S. Dept. HEW, 1966-69, Nat. Wildlife Fedn. fellow, 1970. Mem. North Am. Lake Mgmt. Soc. (bd. dirs. 1970, Tech. Excellence award 1990), Sigma Xi. Office: US EPA 200 SW 35th St Corvallis OR 97333

PETERSON, STANLEY LEE, artist; b. Viborg, S.D., Mar. 26, 1949; s. Norman and Neva Jean (Harns) P.; m. Katherine Anne Burnett. BFA, U. S.D., 1971. Artist W.H. Over Museum, Vermillion, S.D., 1971-72; graphic artist S.D. Pub. TV, Brookings, 1972-76; free lance artist San Francisco, 1976-77; engring. technician City of Tracy, Calif., 1977-85; artist Stanley Peterson Graphics, Los Banos, Calif., 1985—; contract engring. technician, system mgr. City of Tracy, 1985-89, system mgr., 1989-90; engring. technician IV County of Sacramento, 1991, prin. engring. technician, 1991—; cons. in field. Artist/designer Nat. History Diorama, W.H. Over Museum, 1972. Democrat. Home: 427 N Santa Monica St Los Banos CA 93635-3223

PETERSON, VANCE TULLIN, academic administrator, educator; b. Santa Monica, Calif., Nov. 4, 1944; s. William Tullin and Chanuth Joy (Griggs) P.; m. Anne Rose Breck, Apr. 7, 1968; children: Sara Rose, Theresa Pauline. BA, Occidental Coll., 1966; MS, George Washington U., 1971; PhD, Stanford (Calif.) U., 1976. Instr. Stanford U., 1972-73; researcher Carnegie Commn. on Higher Edn., Berkeley, Calif., 1973-74; asst. prof. U. Toledo, 1974-77; exec. dir. univ. rels. U. So. Calif., L.A., 1977-83; assoc. provost UCLA, 1983-89; v.p. Occidental Coll., L.A., 1989—. Editor: The Law &

Higher Education, 1976; contbr. articles to profl. jours. Trustee CASE Dist. VII, 1980-83, Arcadia Ednl. Found., 1989—; mem. Pasadena (Calif.) 2000 Commn., 1988. Capt. USNR (ret.). World ranked track 400m IH, 1965-66. Mem. Nat. Soc. Fundraising Execs., Coun. for Advancement and Support of Edn., Jonathan Club, Rotary, Alpha Tau Omega. Republican. Episcopalian. Office: Occidental Coll 1600 Campus Rd Los Angeles CA 90041-3314

PETERSON, VICTOR LOWELL, aerospace engineer, research center administrator; b. Saskatoon, Sask., Can., June 11, 1934; came to U.S., 1937; s. Edwin Galladet and Ruth Mildred (McKeeby) P.; m. Jacqueline Dianne Hubbard, Dec. 21, 1955; children: Linda Kay Peterson Landrith, Janet Gale, Victor Craig. BS in Aero. Engring., Oreg. State U., 1956; MS in Aerospace Engring., Stanford U., 1964; MS in Mgmt., MIT, 1973. Rsch. scientist NASA-Ames Rsch. Ctr., Moffett Field, Calif., 1956-68, asst. chief hypersonic aerodyns., 1968-71, chief aerodyns. br., 1971-74, chief thermo and gas dynamics div., 1974-84, dir. aerophysics, 1984-90, dep. dir., 1990—; mem. nat. adv. bd. U. Tenn. Space Inst., Tullahoma, 1984—. Contbr. numerous articles to profl. jours. Treas. Woodland Acres Homeowners Assn., Los Altos, Calif., 1978—. Capt. USAF, 1957-60. Recipient medal for outstanding leadership NASA, 1982; Alfred P. Sloan fellow MIT, 1972-73. Fellow AIAA. Republican. Methodist. Home: 484 Aspen Way Los Altos CA 94024-7126 Office: NASA-Ames Rsch Ctr Mail Stop 200-2 Moffett Field CA 94035

PETERSON, WILLARD JAMES, lawyer; b. San Jose, Calif., Feb. 4, 1955; s. Marlowe Theodore and Lauretta Marie (Flaig) P. Student, U. Santa Clara, 1973-75; BA in English with hons., U. Wash., 1977; JD, U. Puget Sound, 1980. Bar: Wash., Hawaii; U.S. Cir. Ct. Appeals (9th cir.); U.S. Supreme Ct. Asst. atty. gen. Office of the Atty. Gen./Commonwealth No. Mariana Islands, Saipan, 1981-82; assoc. Dinman & Yokoyama, Honolulu, 1983-84; dep. prosecutor Honolulu Prosecutor, 1984-88; ptnr. Peterson & Esser, Honolulu, 1989—. Contbg. author: Hawaii Criminal Procedure Digest, 1989. Recipient O'Connor scholarship U. Santa Clara, 1974. Mem. Wash. Bar Assn., Hawaii State Bar Assn. Office: Peterson & Esser 500 Ala Moana Blvd Ste 400 Honolulu HI 96813

PETERZELL, PAUL ROBERT, marketing executive; b. Santa Monica, Calif., Apr. 26, 1961; s. Harry Labe and Joyce Naomi (Moore) P. BS in Bus. Adminstrn., U. Calif., Berkeley, 1982. Project mgr. Warren Weiss Co., Canoga Park, Calif., 1982-84; sr. rsch. analyst Carnation/Nestle, L.A., 1984-87; mktg. cons. PRP Cons., L.A., 1988-89; asst. v.p. mktg. First Interstate Bank, L.A., 1989-91, v.p. mktg., 1991—. Mem. Am. Mktg. Assn., Phi Beta Kappa, Beta Gamma Sigma. Home: 205-A 44th St Manhattan Beach CA 90266 Office: First Interstate Bank 633 W 5th St T12-60 Los Angeles CA 90071

PETICOLAS, WARNER LELAND, physical chemistry educator; b. Lubbock, Tex., July 29, 1929; s. Warner Marion and Beulah Francis (Lowe) P.; m. Virginia Marie Wolf, June 30, 1969; children—Laura M., Alicia B.; children by previous marriage—Cynthia M., Nina P., Phillip W. B.S., Tex. Technol. Coll., 1950; Ph.D., Northwestern U., 1954. Research asso. DuPont Co., Wilmington, Del., 1954-60; research div. IBM, San Jose, Calif., 1960-67; cons. IBM, 1967-69, mgr. chem. physics group, 1965-67; prof. phys. chemistry U. Oreg., 1967—; vis. prof. U. Paris-Pierre and Marie Curie, 1980-81; cons. in field. Committeeman Democratic party, Eugene, Oreg., 1967-70. Served with USPHS, 1955-57. Recipient Alexander von Humboldt award, W. Ger., 1984-85. Guggenheim fellow Max von Laue-Paul Langevin Inst., Grenoble, France, 1973-74. Fellow Am. Phys. Soc.; mem. Am. Chem. Soc., Am. Phys. Soc., Sigma Xi, Alpha Chi Sigma, Tau Beta Pi. Episcopalian. Home: 2829 Arline Way Eugene OR 97403-2527 Office: U Oregon Dept Of Chemistry Eugene OR 97403

PETR, CONSTANCE F., mental health counselor; b. Waukegan, Ill., Apr. 29, 1950; d. Douglas Van Anden and Muriel (Newkirk) Frost; m. Georg Petr, Jr., Dec. 29, 1973 (div. Nov. 1978); children: Tavis Van Anden, Katrina Mitzi Barbara. BA, U. Vt., 1971; MEd., U. Wash., 1986. Cert. counselor. Rsch. asst. Psychopharmacology U. Wash., Seattle, 1987-88; case mgr. Counterpoint Mental Health Ctr., Edmonds, Wash., 1988-92; pvt. practice Everett, Wash., 1992—. Mem. Am. Counseling Assn. Home: 11201 3rd Ave SE Everett WA 98208

PETRACCA, MARK PATRICK, political scientist, educator; b. Melrose, Mass., Oct. 6, 1955; s. Pasquale George and Frances (Pavuk) P.; m. Terry B. Schuster, June 24, 1979; children: Gina, Joseph. AB, Cornell U., 1977; AM, U. Chgo., 1979, PhD, 1986. Instr. U. Chgo., 1980-81; asst. prof. Amherst (Mass.) Coll., 1982-84; asst. prof. polit. sci. U. Calif., Irvine, 1984-92, assoc. prof. polit. sci., 1992—; vis. prof. Beijing (China) U., 1987; panelist Lobdell Group, Cosa Mesa, Calif., 1991—. Editor: The Politics of Interests, 1992; co-author: The American Presidency; columnist Orange Coast Daily Pilot, 1991—; contbg. editor Orange County Metropolitan, Newport Beach, Calif., 1989—. Mem. Com. on Election Reform, City of Irvine, 1991-92; mem. exec. com. Irvine Tomorrow, 1990—; mem. Blue Ribbon Com. on Housing, City of Irvine, 1989-90; trustee Calif. State U. Fullerton Coll. Legal Clinic. Recipient Lauds and Laurels award for disting. teaching U. Calif. Irvine Alumni Assn.; ABA Fund for Justice and Edn. grantee, 1988; U.Calif.-Irvine teaching exch. fellow, 1987. Mem. Am. Polit. Sci. Assn., Midwest Polit. Sci. Assn., Western Polit. Sci. Assn. (editorial bd. 1990), So. Polit. Sci. Assn., Presidency Rsch. Group, Acad. Polit. Sci. Office: Univ of Calif - Irvine Sch Social Sci Irvine CA 92717

PETRAITIS, RIMTAUTAS A., civil engineer; b. Kaunas, Lithuania, Dec. 19, 1935; came to U.S., 1949; s. Antanas and Irena (Jackevicia) P.; m. Giedre Maria Fledzinskas, June 11, 1966; children: Toland, Erik. BS, Gonzaga U., 1957; MS, U. So. Calif., 1961. Registered profl. engr., Calif. Hydrographer So. Calif. Edison Co., L.A., 1958; city traffic engr. City of Vernon, Calif., 1958-72; dir. traffic and parking City of Beverly Hills, Calif., 1972-79; owner, mgr. Petraco, L.A., 1979—; ptnr. Trident Devel., Baldwin Park, Calif., 1979-84; chmn. Beverly Hills Environ. Rev. Bd., 1973-74; mem. Beverly Hills Mgmt. Assn., 1972-79, pres., 1975-76. Mem. parking and traffic com. Beverly Hills C. of C., 1972-79, Baldwin Park C. of C., 1982-84. Capt. U.S. Army, 1957-58. Mem. ASCE, Am. Pub. Works Assn., Inst. Traffic Engrs., Soc. Am. Mil. Engrs., Res. Officers Assn. Republican. Roman Catholic. Home and Office: 1479 Westerly Ter Los Angeles CA 90026-1651

PETRAKIS, NICHOLAS LOUIS, physician, medical researcher, educator; b. San Francisco, Feb. 6, 1922; s. Louis Nicholas and Stamatina (Boosalis) P.; m. Patricia Elizabeth Kelly, June 24, 1947; children: Steven John, Susan Lynn, Sandra Kay. BA, Augustana Coll., 1943; BS in Medicine, U. S.D., 1944; MD, Washington U., St. Louis, 1946. Intern Mpls. Gen. Hosp., 1946-47; physician-researcher U.S. Naval Radiol. Def. Lab., San Francisco, 1947-49; resident physician Mpls. Gen. Hosp., 1949-50; sr. asst. surgeon Nat. Cancer Inst., USPHS, San Francisco, 1950-54; asst. research physician Cancer Research Inst., U. Calif., San Francisco, 1954-56; asst. prof. preventive medicine U. Calif. Sch. Medicine, San Francisco, 1956-60, assoc. prof., 1960-66, prof., 1966-91, prof. emeritus, 1991—; prof. epidemiology U. Calif. Sch. Pub. Health, Berkeley, 1981—; assoc. dir. G.W. Hooper Edn., U. Calif., San Francisco, 1970-74, acting dir., 1974-77, chmn. dept. epidemiology and internat. health, 1979-89; co-dir. Breast Screening Ctr. of No. Calif., Oakland, 1976-81; cons. Breast Cancer Task Force, Nat. Cancer Inst., Bethesda, Md., 1972-76; chmn. Biometry & Epidemiology Contract Rev. Com., Bethesda, 1977-81; mem. bd. sci. counselors, div. cancer etiology Nat. Cancer Inst., Bethesda, 1982-86; mem. scientific adv. com. Calif. State Tobacco-Related Disease Rsch. Program, 1991—; cons. U. Crete Sch. Medicine, Heraklion, Greece, 1984; bd. dirs. No. Calif. Cancer Ctr., 1991. Contbr. over 200 research papers on breast cancer, med. oncology and hematology. Eleanor Roosevelt Internat. Cancer fellow Am. Cancer Soc., Comitato Reserche Nucleari, Cassacia, Italy, 1962; U.S. Pub. Health Service Spl. fellow Galton Lab., U. London, 1969-70; recipient Alumni Achievement award Augustana Coll., Sioux Falls, S.D., 1979, Axion award Hellenic-Am. Profl. Soc. of Calif., San Francisco, 1984, Lewis C. Robbins award Soc. for Prospective Medicine, Indpls., 1985. Mem. Am. Soc. Preventive Oncology (founding, pres. 1984-85, Disting. Achievement award 1992), Soc. for Prospective Medicine (founding), Am. Assn. Cancer Rsch., Am. Epidemiol. Soc., Am. Soc. Clin. Investigation, Am. Bd. Preventive Medicine (cert.). Home: 335 Juanita Way San Francisco CA 94127-1657 Office: U Calif Sch Medicine Dept Epidemiology and Biostats 1699 HSW San Francisco CA 94143-0560

PETRARCA, SANDRA MARIA, software instructional designer, nursing educator; b. Cooperstown, N.Y., Jan. 19, 1948; d. William Marion and Helen Margaret (Barnes) Biggis; m. Daryl Shawn Petrarca, Mar. 18, 1972 (div. Dec. 1982). Diploma in nursing, Hosp. of U. Pa., Phila., 1968; BSN, U. Pa., 1971; MSN, U. Ill., 1980; postgrad., U. Wash., 1986—. RN, Wash. Home care nurse Home Health Care Chgo. North, 1975-78, Community Home Health Care, Seattle, 1980-87; mem. faculty Loyola U., Chgo., 1978-80; mem. nursing faculty City U., Bellevue, Wash., 1984—; mem. clin. faculty U. Wash., Seattle, 1982-86, mem. nursing faculty, 1985-86, rsch. and teaching asst., 1987-90, cons., designer, 1989; pub. health nurse Seattle-King County Health Dept., 1986-90; computer based tng. designer and developer Microsoft Corp., Redmond, Wash., 1990—. Co-author: (computer based tng. program) Pediatric Patient Management Problems, 1978. Mem. Am. Ednl. Rsch. Assn., Pi Lambda Theta (sec. 1989-91), Sigma Theta Tau. Home: 323 N 83 St Seattle WA 98103

PETRIE, ALLAN KENDRICK, insurance company executive; b. Buffalo, Mar. 14, 1928; s. William Alexander and Hazel Victoria (Ball) P.; student U. Idaho, 1948-50; MS in Program Mgmt., West Coast U., 1978. Vice pres. Western Internat. Ins. Brokers, Newport Beach, Calif., 1979-91; pres. Kendrick Ins. Offices, Inc., Redondo Beach, Calif., 1983—. Served to capt. U.S. Army, 1945-48. Mem. Am. Soc. Safety Engrs., Wine and Food Soc. So. Calif., Lambda Chi Alpha. Contbr. articles to mags. and newspapers. Home: 27808 Palos Verdes Dr E Palos Verdes Peninsula CA 90274-5151

PETRON, DONALD ROBERT, magazine editor; b. South Bend, Ind., Sept. 21, 1946; s. Robert Henry and Margaret Henrietta (Ostrowski) P.; m. Carmen Gloria Rodriguez, Feb. 15, 1969 (div. Nov. 1982); children: Gloria Louise, Margaret Evelyn. AA, Am. River Coll., 1974; BA, Calif. State U., Sacramento, 1991. Mcht. Kroger Co., South Bend, 1964-66; enlisted USAF, 1966, advanced through grades to master sgt., 1986; electronic technician USAF Air Weather Svc., Southwestern U.S., 1966-71, Western U.S., 1972-74; technician, instr. USAF Royal Thai Air Base, Ubon, Thailand, 1971-72; instr. electronics Chanute Tech. Tng. Ctr., Rantoul, Ill., 1974-78; mgr. installations USAF Comm. Command, Pacific area, 1978-84; dir. pub. rels. 1849th Electronic Installation Squadron USAF, Sacramento, 1984-86; ret. USAF, 1986; writer, photographer Country Music Forum mag., Sacramento, 1986-87, editor, 1987-88; electronic tech. Sacramento Army Depot, 1988—. Contbr. articles to profl. jours. Mem. Air Force Assn., Golden Key. Republican. Roman Catholic. Office: Sacramento Army Depot Fruitridge Rd Sacramento CA 95813

PETRONIO, RONALD ANTHONY, military officer, lawyer; b. Pitts., Nov. 25, 1956; s. Ronald Harry and Patricia (Kerr) P. BA, Muskinghum Coll., 1978; JD, U. Akron, 1981. Bar: Pa. 1981, Calif. 1991. Commd. USN, 1981, advanced through grades to lt. commdr., 1989; trial-defense counsel USN, Guam, 1981-83; command judge advocate USS Fulton (AS-11), New London, Conn., 1983-85; spl. asst. U.S. atty. U.S. Atty's Office, Honolulu, 1985-86; sr. trial counsel USN, Pearl Harbor, Hawaii, 1986-88; Naval Hosp., Camp Pendleton, Calif., 1989-91; ret. USN, 1991; assoc. Belsky & Assocs., San Diego, 1991—. V.p. Young Coll. Reps., New Concord, Ohio, 1976-78, Muskingum Coll. Student Union, 1977; rep. Muskingum Coll. Bd. Trustees, 1976; vol. atty. U.S. Naval Hosp. H.I.V. Ward, San Diego, 1988—, AIDS Found., San Diego, 1991—; atty Vol. Lawyers Program, San Diego County, 1991—. Mem. Allegheny County Bar Assn., San Diego County Bar Assn., Nat. Health Lawyers Assn. Roman Catholic. Home: 3385 Palm St San Diego CA 92104 Office: Belsky & Assocs 610 W Ash St Ste 700 San Diego CA 92101

PETRUNOFF, VANCE T., publisher; b. Sofia, Bulgaria, Feb. 29, 1956; came to U.S., 1985; s. Troyan Nakov and Jordanka Paneva (Zareva) P.; m. Christine Virginia Judge, Feb. 17, 1989; 1 child, Troyan Hudson.. Anika. Student, Inst. Econs./G.V. Plechanov, Moscow, 1978, Inst. Encons./K. Marx Sofia, Bulgaria, 1983. Export/import cons. Western Consolidated Energy, Denver, 1985-86; publisher Internat. Trade Press, San Francisco, 1987—; internat. trade cons. VTP IMPEX, San Francisco, 1987—; sr. ptnr., gen. mgr. Am. Imports & Investments Ltd., Soflia, Bulgaria. Pub./editor: Directory of Foreign Trade Organizations in Eastern Europe, 1988, 3d edit., 1990, The Soviet Economy: 1970-1990: A Statistical Analysis, 1990. Dir. pub. rels. Com. for Dem. Bulgaria, San Francisco, 1989—. Mem. Calif. Coun. for Internat. Trade. Office: Internat Trade Press 2 Townsend St # 2-304 San Francisco CA 94107 also: AII Ltd, 40 Vasil Levski Blvd., 1142 Sofia Bulgaria

PETRUSKA, GREGORY JAMES, oil company executive; b. Chgo., Jan. 4, 1958. BS in Petroleum Engring., U. Tulsa, 1980; MBA, UCLA, 1989. Registered profl. engr., Colo., Calif. Petroleum engr. Chevron U.S.A., Inc., Denver, 1980-84; rsch. engr. Chevron Oil Field Rsch. Co., La Habra, Calif., 1984-87; internat. banking officer First Interstate Bank, Ltd., L.A., 1989-91; engring. mgr. L.A. dist. Groundwater Tech., Inc., Torrance, Calif., 1991-92; dir. environ. affairs World Oil Corp., South Gate, Calif., 1993—. Shell scholar U. Tulsa, 1976-77, Reading and Bates scholar, 1977-80, Univ. scholar, 1977-80. Mem. Calif. Soc. Profl. Engrs., Anderson Alumni Assn., Tau Beta Pi (sec. 1978-79), Phi Gamma Kappa, Pi Epsilon Tau (v.p. 1979-80). Office: World Oil Corp 9302 S Garfield Ave South Gate CA 90280-3896

PETRUZZI, CHRISTOPHER ROBERT, business educator, consultant; b. Peoria, Ill., July 28, 1951; s. Benjamin Robert and Mary Katherine (Urban) P.; m. Therese Michele Vaughan, Aug. 21, 1982 (div.1987); m. Georgina Sailer, June 20, 1992. BA, Wabash Coll., 1972; MBA, U. Chgo., 1974; PhD, U. Southern Calif., 1983. Lectr. bus. U. Wis., Milw., 1975-77; cons. H.C. Wainwright, Boston, 1978-79; lectr. U. So. Calif., 1978-81; prof. bus. U. Pa., Phila., 1981-84; prof. acctg. NYU, 1984-89, Calif. State U., Fullerton, 1989—; dir. Health Hut, Inc., L.A.; Bow-Tie Food Svcs., Inc., L.A.; pres. ECON, N.Y.C., L.A., 1987—. Earhart fellow, 1972-73; U. Chgo. fellow, 1974-76. Libertarian. Home: 800 E Ocean Blvd Apt 1101 Long Beach CA 90802-5455

PETRZILKA, HENRY See FILIP, HENRY

PETTERS, SAMUEL BRIAN, air force officer; b. Lakeland, Fla., Feb. 7, 1967; s. Clement Edward and Joan Agnes (Barthle) P.; m. Vicki Jean LaBauve, Dec. 17, 1988; children: John Clement, Benjamin Howard. BA, La. State U., 1989. Commd. 2d lt. U.S. Air Force, 1990, advanced through grades to 1st lt., 1992; edn. and tng. officer 323 Ops. Support Squadron, Mather AFB, Calif., 1991-93; historical officer Air Force Historical Rsch. Agency, Maxwell AFB, Ala., 1993—. Mem. MacNexus Macintosh Users Group. Republican. Roman Catholic. Home: 1926 Kingsbury Dr Montgomery AL 36106 Office: AFHRA/RSQ 600 Cherrault Circle Maxwell AFB AL 36112-6424

PETTERSEN, THOMAS MORGAN, accountant, finance executive; b. Poughkeepsie, N.Y., Nov. 9, 1950; s. Olsen Thomas and Reva Frances (Palmer) P. BS, U. Albany, 1973. CPA, N.Y. Sr. acct. Arthur Andersen and Co., N.Y.C., 1973-76; sr. ops. auditor Gulf and Western Inc., N.Y.C., 1977, fin. analyst, 1978; adminstr. auditing NBC, N.Y.C., 1979; mgr. auditing NBC, Burbank, Calif., 1980, dir. auditing, 1981-88, dir. acctg. systems and ops. analysis, 1988-90; v.p. fin. and adminstrn. Data Dimensions, Inc., Culver City, Calif., 1991-92; cons. Westwood One, Inc., Culver City, 1992—. Mem. AICPA, Fin. Execs. Inst. Republican. Roman Catholic. Home: 217 1st Pl Manhattan Beach CA 90266-6503 Office: Westwood One Inc 9540 Washington Blvd Culver City CA 90232-2689

PETTIGREW, STEVEN LEE, healthcare management company executive, consultant; b. Colorado Springs, May 8, 1949; s. Wesley N. and Mary Ellen (Howard) P.; m. Elise Woodcock, Dec. 12, 1987. BS in Mech. Engring., Colo. State U., 1972. Regional dir. Mgmt. Engring. Svcs. Assn. Program, Inc., Phoenix, 1972-76; v.p. Ariz. Hosp. Assn., Phoenix, 1976-79; corp. exec. dir. Samaritan Health Svc., Phoenix, 1979—; lectr. Ariz. State U., Tempe, 1976-78, 93. Contbr. articles to tech. publs. Bd. dirs. Hospice of Valley, Phoenix, 1981-88, pres., 1986-88, trustee endowmentfund, 1983—; Valley Leadership Class X11, 1990-91. NSF rsch. grantee, 1971-72. Fellow Healthcare Info. and Mgmt. Systems Soc. (bd. dirs. 1980-81); mem. Healthcare Fin. Mgmt. Assn. (sr.), Inst. Indsl. Engrs. (sr.), Sigma Tau, Kiwanis (bd. dirs. Phoenix chpt. 1985-86, Spl. Svc. award 1986). Methodist. Office: Samaritan Health Svc 1441 N 12th St Phoenix AZ 85006-2887

PETTIGREW, THOMAS FRASER, social psychologist, educator; b. Richmond, Va., Mar. 14, 1931; s. Joseph Crane and Janet (Gibb) P.; m. Ann Hallman, Feb. 25, 1956; 1 son, Mark Fraser. A.B. in Psychology, U. Va., 1952; M.A. in Social Psychology, Harvard U., 1955, Ph.D., 1956; D.H.L. (hon.), Governor's State U., 1979. Rsch. assoc. Inst. Social Rsch., U. Natal, Republic South Africa, 1956; asst. prof. psychology U. N.C., 1956-57; asst. prof. social psychology Harvard U., Cambridge, Mass., 1957-62, lectr., 1962-64, assoc. prof., 1964-68, prof., 1968-74, prof. social psychology and sociology, 1974-80; prof. social psychology U. Calif., Santa Cruz, 1980—, U. Amsterdam, 1986-91; mem. com. status black Ams. NRC, 1985-88. Author: (with E.Q. Campbell) Christians in Racial Crisis: A Study of the Little Rock Ministry, 1959, A Profile of the Negro American, 1964, Racially Separate or Together?, 1971, (with Frederickson, Knobol, Glazer and Veda) Prejudice, 1982, (with Alston) Tom Bradley's Campaigns for Governor: The Dilemma of Race and Political Strategies, 1988; editor: Racial Discrimination in the United States, 1975, The Sociology of Race Relations: Reflection and Reform, 1980 (with C. Stephan & W. Stephan) The Future of Social Psychology: Defining the Relationship Between Sociology and Psychology, 1991; mem. editorial bd. Jour. Social Issues, 1959-64, Social Psychology Quarterly, 1977-80; assoc. editor Am. Sociol. Rev, 1963-65; mem. adv. bd. Integrated Edn, 1963-84, Phylon, 1965—, Edn. and Urban Society, 1968-90, Race, 1972-74, Ethnic and Racial Studies, 1978—, Rev. of Personality and Social Psychology, 1980-85, Community and Applied Social Psychology, 1989—, Individual and Politics, 1989—; contbr. articles to profl. pubs. Chmn. Episcopal presiding Bishop's Adv. Com. on Race Relations, 1961-63; v.p. Episcopal Soc. Cultural and Racial Unity, 1962-63; mem. Mass. Gov.'s Adv. Com. on Civil Rights, 1962-64; social sci. cons. U.S. Commn. Civil Rights, 1966-71; mem. White House Task Force on Edn., 1967; mem. nat. task force on desegregation policies Edn. Commn. of States, 1977-79; trustee Ella Lyman Cabot Trust, Boston, 1977-79; mem. Emerson Book Award com. United Chpts. Phi Beta Kappa, 1971-73. Guggenheim fellow, 1967-68; NATO sr. scientist fellow, 1974; fellow Center Advanced Study in Behavioral Scis., 1975-76; Sydney Spivack fellow in intergroup relations Am. Sociol. Assn., 1978; Netherlands Inst. Advanced Study fellow, 1984-85; recipient Kurt Lewin Meml. award Soc. for Psychological Study of Social Issues, 1987, (with Martin) Gordon Allport Intergroup Rels. Rsch. prize, 1988, Faculty Rsch. award U. Calif., Santa Cruz, 1988; Bellagio (Italy) Study Ctr. resident fellow, Rockefeller Found., 1991. Fellow Am. Psychol. Assn., Am. Sociol. Assn. (council 1979-82); mem. Soc. Psychol. Study Social Issues (council 1962-66, pres. 1967-68), NRC (com. status black Ams. 1985-88), European Assn. Social Psychology. Home: 524 Van Ness Ave Santa Cruz CA 95060-3556 Office: U Calif Kerr Hall Santa Cruz CA 95064

PETTIS, RONALD EUGENE, lawyer; b. Williston, N.D., Sept. 5, 1939; s. Elmer Roy and Hildur Ann (Olson) P.; m. T. Mary Whitehead, June 12, 1961; children: Anna T. Scott, Phillip A. BA, U. Idaho, 1961; JD, U. Calif., Berkeley, 1969. Bar: Calif. 1970, U.S. Dist. Ct. (cen. dist.) Calif. 1974, U.S. Supreme Ct. 1978. Assoc. Hennigan, Butterwick & Clepper, Riverside, Calif., 1971-74, ptnr., shareholder, 1974-79; ptnr., shareholder Butterwick, Bright, Pettis & Cunnison, Inc., Riverside, 1979-82; ptnr. Gray, Cary, Ames & Frye, San Diego, 1982—. Mem. bd. dirs., chmn., environ com. Border Trade Alliance. Served to capt. USMC, 1961-66. Mem. ABA, Internat. Bar Assn., Border Trade Alliance, U.S.-Mex. C. of C. (bd. dirs. Pacific chpt.), Masons. Presbyterian. Office: Gray Cary Ames & Frye 1700 1st Interstate Plz 401 B St San Diego CA 92101-4219

PETTIS-ROBERSON, SHIRLEY MCCUMBER, former congresswoman; b. Mountain View, Calif.; d. Harold Oliver and Dorothy Susan (O'Neil) McCumber; m. John J. McNulty (dec.); m. Jerry L. Pettis (dec. Feb. 1975); m. Ben Roberson, Feb. 6, 1988; children: Peter Dwight Pettis, Deborah Neil Pettis Moyer. Student, Andrews U., U. Calif., Berkeley. Mgr. Audio-Digest Found., L.A., Glendale; sec.-treas. Pettis, Inc., Hollywood, 1958-68; mem. 94th-95th Congresses from 37th Calif. Dist., mem. coms. on interior, internat. rels., edn. and labor; pres. Women's Rsch. and Edn. Inst., 1979-80; bd. dirs. Kemper Group, 1979—. Mem. Pres.'s Commn. on Arms Control and Disarmament, 1980-83, Commn. on Presdl. Scholars, 1990-92; active Children's Hosp. Found.; trustee U. Redlands, Calif., 1980-83, Loma Linda (Calif.) U. and Med. Ctr., 1990—, also chair; bd. dirs. Former Mems. Congress, Capitol Hill Club (Washington), Congressional Club, Morningside Country Club (bd. govs.). Mem. Nat. Women's Econ. Alliance Found., Capitol Hill Club (Washington), Morningside Country Club (bd. govs.).

PETTIT, GEORGE ROBERT, chemistry educator, cancer researcher; b. Long Branch, N.J., June 8, 1929; s. George Robert and Florence Elizabeth (Seymour) P.; m. Margaret Jean Benger, June 20, 1953; children: William Edward, Margaret Sharon, Robin Kathleen, Lynn Benger, George Robert III. B.S., Wash. State U., 1952; M.S. Wayne State U., 1954, Ph.D., 1956. Teaching asst. Wash. State U., 1950-52, lecture demonstrator, 1952; rsch. chemist E.I. duPont de Nemours and Co., 1953; grad. teaching asst. Wayne State U., 1952-53, rsch. fellow, 1954-56; sr. rsch. chemist Norwich Eaton Pharms., Inc., 1956-57; asst. prof. chemistry U. Maine, 1957-61, assoc. prof. chemistry, 1961-65, prof. chemistry, 1965; vis. prof. chemistry Stanford U., 1965; chmn. organic div. Ariz. State U., 1966-68, prof. chemistry, 1965—; vis. prof. So. African, Univs., 1978; dir. Cancer Rsch. Lab., 1974-75, Cancer Rsch. Inst., 1975—; lectr. various colls. and univs.; cons. in field. Contbr. articles to profl. jours. Mem. adv. bd. Wash. State U. Found., 1981-85. Served with USAFR, 1951-55. Recipient Disting. Rsch. Professorship award Ariz. State U., 1978-79, Alumni Achievement award Wash. State U., 1984; named Dalton Prof. Medicinal Chemistry and Cancer Rsch., 1986—, Regents Prof. Chemistry, 1990—. Fellow Am. Inst. Chemists (Pioneer award 1989); mem. Am. Chem. Soc. (awards com. 1968-71, 78-81), Chem. Soc. (London), Pharmacognosy Soc., Am. Assn. Cancer Rsch., Sigma Xi, Phi Lambda Upsilon. Office: Ariz State U Cancer Rsch Inst Tempe AZ 85287-1604

PETTIT, GHERY DEWITT, veterinarian; b. Oakland, Calif., Sept. 6, 1926; s. Hermon DeWitt Pettit and Marion Esther (St. John) Menzies; m. Frances Marie Seitz, July 5, 1948; children: Ghery St. John, Paul Michael. BS in Animal Sci., U. Calif., Davis, 1948, BS in Vet. Sci., 1951, DVM, 1953. Diplomate Am. Coll. Vet. Surgeons (recorder 1970-77, pres., chmn. bd. dirs. 1978-80). Asst. prof. vet. surgery U. Calif., Davis, 1953-61; prof. vet. surgery Wash. State U., Pullman, 1961-91, prof. emeritus, 1991—; mem. Wash. State Vet. Bd. Govs., 1981-88, chmn., 1987; vis. fellow Sydney (Australia) U., 1977. Author/editor: Intervertebral Disc Protrusion in the Dog, 1966; cons. editoral bd. Jour. Small Animal Practice, Eng., 1970-88; mem. editoral bd. Compendium on C.E., Lawrenceville, N.J., 1983-86, editoral rev. bd. Jour. Vet. Surgery, Phila., 1984-86, editor 1987-92; contbr. articles to profl. jours., chpts. to books. Elder Presbyn. Ch., Pullman, 1967—. Served with USN, 1944-46. Recipient Norden Disting. Tchr. award Wash. State U. Class 1971, Faculty of Yr. award Wash. State U. Student Com., 1985. Mem. Am. Vet. Med. Assn., Sigma Xi, Phi Zeta, Phi Kappa Sigma (chpt. advisor 1981—). Republican. Office: Wash State U Coll Vet Medicine Pullman WA 99164-7010

PETTIT, WILLIAM DUTTON, JR., bank executive; b. Princeton, N.J., Apr. 9, 1949; s. William Dutton and Carol Helene P.; BA cum laude, Princeton U., 1971; MBA, U. Oreg., 1973; m. Katherine King Lambert, Aug. 14, 1971; children: William Dutton, Timothy Donaldson, Christopher Thomas. Mktg. officer U.S. Bancorp, Portland, Oreg., 1974; fin. analysis officer Seattle First Nat. Bank, 1974, asst. v.p., 1975; v.p., chief credit officer Seafirst Mortgage Corp., Seattle, 1976-77, sr. v.p., mgr. fin. and adminstrn., 1978-80, exec. v.p., chief oper. officer, 1980-81; sr. v.p., mgr. strategic planning Seafirst Corp., Seattle, 1981-82, exec. v.p., chief fin. officer, mgr. real estate group, 1982-87, sr. v.p., mgr. fin. insts., corp. fins. E.F. Hutton, 1987; pres., dir. Pacific First Fin. Corp., Tacoma, Washington, 1988-92; pres. R.D. Merrill Co., 1992—. Bd. dirs. Jr. Achievement, Boy Scouts Am., King County United Way; bd. advisors sch. bus. adminstrn. U. Oreg.; bd. regents Seattle U.; trustee Corp. Coun. for Arts. Mem. Seattle Golf Club, Rainier Club, Wash. Athletic Club. Office: Pacific First Fin Corp 1420 5th Ave Seattle WA 98101-2333

PETTITE, WILLIAM CLINTON, public affairs consultant; b. Reno, Nev.; s. Sidney Clinton and Wilma (Stibal) P.; m. Charlotte Denise Fryer; children: Patrick Keane, William Ellis, Joseph Clinton. Owner, Market Lake Citizen & Clark County Enterprise Newspapers, Roberts, Idaho, 1959-70, pub., 1959-61; publicity dir. Golden Days World Boxing Champs, Reno, 1970; pub. Virginia City (Nev.) Legend newspaper, 1970; public affairs cons., Fair Oaks, Calif., 1966—, owner PT Cattle Co., Firth, Idaho; dir. of bus. studies made in Wales, France, Can., 1984—. County probate judge, Idaho, 1959-61; acting County coroner, 1960-61; sec., trustee Fair Oaks Cemetery Dist., 1963-72; bd. dir. Fair Oaks Water Dist., 1964-72, v.p., 1967-68, pres., 1968-70; dir., v.p. San Juan Community Svcs. Dist., 1962-66, 68-72; exec. sec. Calif. Bd. Landscape Architects, 1976-77, Calif. Assn. Collectors, 1966-68. Cons. Senate-Assembly Joint Audit Com. Calif. Legislature, 1971-73; exec. officer Occupational Safety and Health Appeals Bd., 1981-83; mem. regulatory rev. commn. Calif. FabricCare Bd., 1981-82; mem. Sacramento County Grand Jury, 1981-82, cons. bd. supvs. Sacramento County, 1985-86; chmn. bus. adv. bd. East Lawn Corp, 1991—. Election campaign coord. for E.S. Wright, majority leader Idaho Senate, 1968, Henry Dworshak, U.S. Senator, 1960, Hamer Budge, U.S. Rep., 1960, Charles C. Gossett, former Gov. Idaho, 1959-74; asst. sgt. at arms Rep. Nat. Conv., 1956; chmn. Rep. County Cen. Com., 1959-61; del. Rep. State Conv., 1960. Chmn. Idaho County Centennial Commn., 1959-61. Recipient Idaho Centennial award, 1968, 69. Mem. Assn. Sacramento County Water Dists. (bd. dir. 1967-72, pres. 1970-72), No. Calif. Peace Officers Assn., Nat. Coun. Juvenile Ct. Judges (com. 1959-61), Sacramento Law Enforcement Adminstrs. Club. Author: Memories of Market Lake, Vol. I, 1965; A History of Southeastern Idaho, Vol. II, 1977, Vol. III, 1983, Vol. IV, 1990; contbr. articles to newspapers, profl. jours. Home: PO Box 2127 Fair Oaks CA 95628-2127 Office: 2631 K St Sacramento CA 95816-5178

PETTY, DONALD GRIFFIN, research administrator; b. Montgomery, Ala., Nov. 4, 1949; s. William Henry and Ellen Marie (Ford) P.; m. Patricia Marie Sanchez, Sept. 1, 1984; children: Zachary Allan, Kimberly Nicole. BS in Chemistry, Colo. State U., 1972; MA in Tech. Journalism, U. Colo., 1976; MBA, Regis Coll., 1988. Geochemist Hazen Research Inc., Golden, Colo., 1973-75; mktg. specialist Tech. Dynamics Corp., Denver, 1976-77; publ. specialist Community Coll. Denver, 1977-78; mktg. coordinator Micro Motion Inc., Boulder, Colo., 1978; project mgr. Solar Energy Research Inst., Golden, 1978-88; adminstr. Sch. Medicine U. Colo., Denver, 1988—; instr. Community Coll. Denver, Met. State Coll., 1977—. Pres., chmn. bd. Front Range Literacy Action, 1985—; Rep. precinct capt., Denver, 1984—. Named one of Outstanding Young Men Am., Jaycees, 1981. Mem. AAAS, Soc. Tech. Communication (sr.), Am. Chem. Soc., Am. Inst. Chemists. Republican.

PETTY, KEITH, lawyer; b. Swan Lake, Idaho, June 13, 1920; s. William Dorris and Emma Louise (Johnson) P.; m. Gail Wells, Jan. 11, 1943; children—Kaye Wells Paugh, Jane Wells Taylor, Richard Keith, Scott Robert. B.S., U. Idaho, 1942; J.D., Stanford U., 1948; postgrad. Harvard U., 1943. Bar: Calif., 1949, Idaho, 1948. Tax acct. Pacific Telephone Co., San Francisco, 1948-50; acct. John F. Forbes & Co., San Francisco, 1950-54; partner Petty, Andrews, Tufts & Jackson and predecessor firms, San Francisco, San Jose and Palo Alto, Calif., 1954-86; sole practice Palo Alto, 1986—; lectr. in field. Served to lt. USNR, 1942-46. Mem. Calif. Soc. C.P.A.s, San Francisco Bar Assn. Mormon. Clubs: Commonwealth, Univ., Bankers. Home: 1420 Pitman Ave Palo Alto CA 94301-3055 Office: 1755 Embacadero Rd Ste 110 Palo Alto CA 94303

PETZEL, FLORENCE ELOISE, educator; b. Crosbyton, Tex., Apr. 1, 1911; d. William D. and A. Eloise (Punchard) P.; Ph.B., U. Chgo., 1931, A.M., 1934; Ph.D., U. Minn., 1954. Instr., Judson Coll., 1936-38; vis. instr. Tex. State Coll. for Women, 1937; asst. prof. textiles Ohio State U., 1938-48; asso. prof. U. Ala., 1950-54; prof. Oreg. State U., 1954-61, 67-75, 77, prof. emeritus, 1975—, dept. head, 1954-61, 67-75; prof., div. head U. Tex., 1961-63; prof. Tex. Tech U., 1963-67; vis. prof. Wash. State U., 1967. Effie I. Raitt fellow, 1949-50. Mem. Seattle Art Mus., Oreg. Art Mus., Textile Mus., Met. Opera Guild, San Francisco Opera Assn., Portland Opera Assn. Sigma Xi, Phi Kappa Phi, Omicron Nu, Iota Sigma Pi, Sigma Delta Epsilon. Author Textiles of Ancient Mesopotamia, Persia and Egypt, 1987; contbr. articles to profl. jours. Home: 625 NW 29th St Corvallis OR 97330-5255

PEVSNER, WILLIAM JACOB, osteopath; b. L.A., Apr. 29, 1958; s. Samuel and Elizabeth (Breplau) P. DO, Coll Osteo Medicine of Pacific, 1986. Intern Rio Hondo Meml. Hosp., Downey, Calif., 1986-87; pvt. family practice osteopathy Hacienda Heights, Calif., 1987—. V.p. Stillpointe Ctr. for Counseling and Growth, Hacienda Heights, 1990. Office: 2219 Hacienda Blvd # 101 Hacienda Heights CA 91745

PÉWÉ, TROY LEWIS, geologist, educator; b. Rock Island, Ill., June 28, 1918; s. Richard E. and Olga (Pomrank) P.; m. Mary Jean Hill, Dec. 21, 1944; children—David Lee, Richard Hill, Elizabeth Anne. AB in Geology, Augustana Coll., 1940; MS, State U. Iowa, 1942; PhD, Stanford U., 1952; DSc (hon.), U. Alaska, 1991. Head dept. geology Augustana Coll., 1942-46; civilian instr. USAAC, 1943-44; instr. geomorphology Stanford, 1946; geologist Alaskan br. U.S. Geol. Survey, 1946-93; chief glacial geologist U.S. Nat. Com. Internat. Geophys. Year, Antarctica, 1958; prof. geology, head dept. U. Alaska, 1958-65; prof. geology Ariz. State U., 1965-88, prof. emeritus, 1988—, chmn. dept., 1965-76; dir. Mus. Geology, 1976—; lectr. in field, 1942—; mem. organizing com. 1st Internat. Permafrost Conf. Nat. Acad. Sci., 1962-63, chmn. U.S. planning com. 2d Internat. Permafrost Conf., 1972-74, chmn. U.S. del. 3d Internat. Permafrost Conf., 1978, chmn. U.S. organizing com. 4th Internat. Permafrost Conf., 1979-83; com. to study Good Friday Alaska Earthquake Nat. Acad. Scis., 1964-70, mem. glaciological com. polar research bd., 1971-73, founding chmn. permafrost com., mem. polar research bd., 1975-81; organizing chmn. Internat. Assn. Quarternary Research Symposium and Internat. Field Trip Alaska, 1965; mem. Internat. Commn. Periglacial Morophology, 1964-71, 80-88 ; mem. polar research bd. NRC, 1975-78, late Cenozoic study group, sci. com. Antarctic research, 1977-80. Contbr. numerous papers to profl. lit. Recipient U.S. Antarctic Service medal, 1966; Outstanding Achievement award Augustana Coll., 1969; recipient Internat. Geophysics medal USSR Nat. Acad. Sci., 1985; named second hon. internat. fellow Chinese Soc. Glaciology and Geocryology, 1985. Fellow AAAS (pres. Alaska div. 1956, com. on arid lands 1972-79), Geol. Soc. Am. (editorial bd. 1975-82, chmn. cordilleran sect. 1979-80, chmn. geomorphology div. 1981-82), Arctic Inst. N.Am. (bd. govs. 1969-74, exec. bd. 1972-73), Iowa Acad. Sci., Ariz. Acad. Sci. (pres. 1982-83); mem. Assn. Geology Tchrs., Glaciological Soc., N.Z. Antarctic Soc., Am. Soc. Engring. Geologists, Internat. Permafrost Assn. (founding v.p. 1983, pres. 1988—), Am. Quaternary Assn. (pres. 1984-86), Internat. Geog. Union. Club: Cosmos. Home: 538 E Fairmont Dr Tempe AZ 85282-3723

PEYTON, CAROLYN SUE (CARRIE PEYTON), journalist; b. Washington, May 20, 1955; d. Wesley Grant and Jewel (Schneider) P. BA in Journalism, San Jose State U., 1977. Reporter Penisula Times Tribune, Palo Alto, Calif., 1977-80; European rsch. editor Off Duty Mag., Frankfurt, Germany, 1981-82; from asst. news editor to news editor V.I. Daily News, St. Thomas, 1982-84; asst. city editor Niagara Falls (N.Y.) Gazette, 1984; from copy editor to asst. city editor Contra Costa Times, Walnut Creek, Calif., 1984-87; copy editor Sacramento (Calif.) Bee, 1987-89, wire editor, 1989-91, copy desk chief, 1991—; tchr. editing class Calif. State U., Sacramento, 1988-89. Vol., fundraiser Sta. KXPR/KXJZ Pub. Radio, Sacramento, 1991-93; active Laguna Creek Community Assn., Elk Grove, Calif., 1991-93. Mem. Sacramento Bee Women's Caucus. Democrat. Jewish. Office: Sacramento Bee 2100 Q St Sacramento CA 95852

PEZESHKI, KAMBIZ ALI, metallurgical engineer; b. Tabriz, Iran, Sept. 30, 1949; came to U.S., 1970; s. Amir Aziz Allah and Azam (Mazi) P.; m. Shiron Cashmir Wisenbaker, Apr. 7, 1976; children: Shahene A., Shahla J. BS in Metall. Engring., U. Utah, 1977; MBA in Mktg. and Human Rels., U. Phoenix, 1982. Cert. tchr., Ariz. Process metallurgist Amax, Inc., Golden, Colo., 1977-79; process, rsch. engr. Cities Svcs. Co./Oxidental, Miami, Ariz., 1979-84; tech. svcs. engr. Am. Cyanamid, Wayne, N.J., 1984-87; mgr. western mining Rhone-Poulenc, Inc., Salt Lake City, 1987-93; nat. sales engr. Hychem, Inc., Salt Lake City, 1993—; polymerization cons. RTZ/Kennecott Copper, Salt Lake City, 1989—. Fund raiser Jake Garn for Senate, Salt Lake City, 1976; fund raiser, motivator Barry Goldwater for Senate re-election, 1980-81; vol. Ted Wilson for Gov., Salt Lake City, 1988. Mem. Am. Mining Engrs. Soc. Republican. Home: 2101 Cresthill Dr Salt Lake City UT 84117

PFAELZER, MARIANA R., federal judge; b. 1926. AB, U. Calif.; LLB, UCLA, 1957. Bar: 1958. Assoc. Wyman, Bautzer, Rothman & Kuchel, 1957-78, ptnr., 1969-78; judge U.S. Dist. Ct. (ctrl. dist.) Calif., 1978—. Mem. ABA. Office: US Dist Ct 312 N Spring St Los Angeles CA 90012-4701

PFEIFER, WILLIAM DANIEL, chiropractor; b. Juneau, Alaska, Oct. 28, 1956; s. Dan William Pfeifer and Pauline R. (Greenewald) Hinchman; m. Mary Lorene Price, Oct. 3, 1981; children: Angela, Chelsea, Billy, Jason, Natalie. Dr of Chiropractic, Palmer Coll. Chiropractic, Davenport, Iowa, 1982. Chiropractor Family Chiropractic Clinic, Ketchikan, Alaska. Mem. campus adv. coun. U. Alaska S.E., Ketchikan, 1986-92. Mem. Am. Chiropractic Assn., Ketchikan C. of C., Ketchikan Rotary 2000 (pres. 1991-92, Rotary dist. 5010 Russian task force 1993-94). Office: Family Chiropractic Clinic 130 Carlama 130 Carlanna Ste 200 Ketchikan AK 99901

PFEIFFER, GERALD G., human resources consultant; b. Bowling Green, Ohio, Oct. 23, 1939; s. Harry A. and Velma C. (Morrow) P.; m. Jill S. Kimber, Apr. 20, 1980. BS, George Washington U., 1962; MBA, Wayne State U., Detroit, 1970. CLU. With FBI, Washington, Detroit, 1960-63, Am. Std. Corp., Detroit, 1963-70; labor rels. supr. to dir. personnel ITT Corp., various cities, 1970-76; labor rels. and safety advisor to sr. e.r. cons. various cities Mobil Oil Corp., 1976-85; exec. v.p., gen. mgr. HAP Ent., Inc., San Diego, 1985-90; human resources cons. Merit Resource Group, San Francisco, 1991—. Contbr. articles to profl. jours. Advisor Jr. Achievement, 1967-84; human resources cons. Joan Kroc Homeless Ctr., San Diego, 1989-92, United Way, San Diego, 1989-92. Capt. USAF, 1962. W.I.N. grantee, 1968. Mem. Rotary. Home: 5067 Cabrillo Pt Byron CA 94514

PFEIFFER, JOHN WILLIAM, publisher, management consultant; b. Wallace, Idaho, July 10, 1937; s. John William and Mary Loretta (Schmidt) P.; m. Judith Ann Cook, Dec. 14, 1973; children: Heidi Erika, Charles Wilson. BA, U. Md., 1962; PhD (fellow), U. Iowa, 1968; JD, Western State U., 1982; DABS (hon.), Calif. Am. U., Escondido, 1980. Instr. U. Md., 1965-67; dir. adult edn. Kirkwood (Iowa) Community Coll., 1967-69; dir. ednl. resources Ind. Higher Edn. Telecommunications Systems, Indpls., 1969-72; pres. Univ. Assocs., San Diego, 1972-90, Pfeiffer & Co., San Diego, 1991—; adj. tchr. Ind. U., 1969-72, Purdue U., 1971-72. Author: Instrumentation in Human Relations Training, 1973, 2d edit. 1976, Reference Guide to Handbooks and Annuals, 1975, 2d edit. 1977, 3d. edit. 1981, (With Goodstein and Nolan) Applied Strategic Planning, 1986, 2d edit. 1988, (with Judith A. Pfeiffer) LBP, 1990; editor: A Handbook of Structured Experiences for Human Relations Training, 10 vols., 1969-85, The Annual Handbook for Facilitators, 10 vols. 1972-81, Group and Orgns. Studies Internat. Jour. for Group Facilitators, 1976-79, The Annual for Facilitators, Trainers and Consultants, 1982-91, Strategic Planning: Selected Readings, 1986, The Instrumentation Kit, 1988, Shaping Strategic Planning, 1988, Training Technology, 7 vols., 1988, Theories and Models, 4 vols., 1992, Plan or Die, 1993, Pfeiffer Library, 28 vols., 1993. Served with U.S. Army, 1958-62. Office: Pfeiffer & Co 8517 Production Ave San Diego CA 92121-2280

PFEIFFER, ROBERT JOHN, business executive; b. Suva, Fiji Islands, Mar. 7, 1920; came to U.S., 1921, naturalized, 1927; s. William Albert and Nina (MacDonald) P.; m. Mary Elizabeth Worts, Nov. 29, 1945; children—Elizabeth Pfeiffer Tumbas, Margaret Pfeiffer Hughes, George, Kathleen. Grad. high sch., Honolulu, 1937; DSc (hon.), Maine Maritime Acad.; HHD (hon.), U. Hawaii; DHL (hon.), Hawaii Loa Coll. With Inter-Island Steam Navigation Co., Ltd., Honolulu, (re-organized to Overseas Terminal Ltd. 1950); with (merged into Oahu Ry. & Land Co. 1954), 1937-55, v.p., gen. mgr., 1950-54, mgr. ship agy. dept., 1954-55; v.p., gen. mgr. Pacific Cut Stone & Granite Co., Inc., Alhambra, Calif., 1955-56, Matcinal Corp., Alameda, Calif., 1956-58; mgr. div. Pacific Far East Line, Inc., San Francisco, 1958-60; with Matson Nav. Co., San Francisco, 1960—, v.p., 1966-70, sr. v.p., 1970-71, exec. v.p., 1971-73, pres., 1973-79, 84-85, 89-90, CEO, 1979-92; chmn. bd., bd.dirs. Matson Nav. Co., 1979—; chmn. bd. Matson Nav. Co., San Francisco, 1979—; v.p. The Matson Co., San Francisco, 1968-70; also bd. dirs., chmn. Matson Nav. Co.; pres. The Matson Co., 1970-82; v.p., gen. mgr. Matson Terminals, Inc., San Francisco, 1960-62; pres. Matson Terminals, Inc., 1962-70, chmn. bd., 1970-79; chmn. bd. Matson Svcs. Co., 1973-79, Matson Agys., Inc., 1973-78; sr. v.p. Alexander & Baldwin, Inc., Honolulu, 1973-77; exec. v.p. Alexander & Baldwin, Inc., 1977-79, chmn. bd., 1980—, CEO, 1980-92, pres., 1979-84, 89-91; chmn. bd., pres., dir. A&B-Hawaii, Inc., 1988-89, chmn. bd., 1989—, also bd. dirs.; bd. dirs. Matson Nav. Co., Alexander & Baldwin, Inc., 1st Hawaiian Inc., 1st Hawaiian Bank; mem. Gov.'s commn. on exec. salaries State of Hawaii, com. on jud. salaries. Past chmn. maritime transp. rsch. bd. Nat. Acad. Sci.; former mem. select com. for Am. Mcht. Marine Seamanship Trophy Award, commn. sociotech. systems NRC.; mem. adv. com. Joint Maritime Congress; trustee Pacific Tropical Bot. Garden, Pacific Aerospace Mus., also bd. dirs.; mem. Japan-Hawaii Econ. Coun., Army Civilian Adv. Group; vice-chmn. Hawaii Maritime Ctr.; former chmn. A Commitee on Excellence (ACE), Hawaii; mem. adv. coun. Girl Scouts U.S.A. coun. of the Pacific; bd. govs. Hugh O'Brian Youth Found.; mem. exec. com. Rsch. Round Table Alameda County chpt. Am. Heart Assn.; bd. govs. Japanese Cultural Ctr. Hawaii; mem. bd. nominators Am. Inst. for Pub. Svc.; life mem. Vets. Fgn. Wars U.S.; hon. co-chmn. McKinley High Sch. Found.; mem. adv. bd. Hawaii Bldg. and Constrn. Trades Coun., AFL-CIO Ednl. and Charitable Found. Lt. USNR, World War II; comdr. Res. ret. Mem. Nat. Assn. Stevedores (past pres.), Internat. Cargo Handling Coordination Assn. (past pres. U.S. com.), Propeller Club U.S. (past pres. Honolulu), Nat. Def. Transp. Assn., Conf. Bd., Containerization & Intermodal Inst. (hon. bd. advisors), 200 Club, Maui C. of C., Aircraft Owners and Pilots Assn., Standard Steamship Owners' Protection and Indemnity Assn. Ltd. (bd. dirs.) (Bermuda), Pacific Club, Outrigger Club, Oahu Country Club, Maui Country Club, Pacific Union Club, Bohemian Club, World Trade Club (San Francisco), Masons, Shriners. Republican. Home: 535 Miner Rd Orinda CA 94563-1429 Office: Alexander & Baldwin Inc 822 Bishop St Honolulu HI 96813-3925

PFEUFFER, JOSEPH JOHN, electrical engineer, director; b. N.Y.C., Nov. 18, 1944; s. Joseph and Florence (Gucwa) P.; m. Geraldine Rodi, Oct. 30, 1971; children: Evan Joseph, Marc Stewart, Carey Paul. B of Engring., Stevens Inst. of Technology, 1967; postgrad., E. Wash. State U., Cheney, 1990—. Engr. Potter Instrument Co., Plainview, N.Y., 1967-72; mgr. Qantex, Plainview, 1973-79, Documation, Melbourne, Fla., 1979-82; dir. Medicomp, Palm Bay, Fla., 1982-84, Centronics, Hudson, N.H., 1984-85, Storage Tech., Melbourne, Fla., 1985-88, Megascan, Gibsonia, Pa., 1988-89, Bruning, Martinez, Calif., 1989-90, Output Tech., Spokane, Wash., 1990—; dir. Indian River Rsch., Melbourne, Fla., 1981—, Gonzaga U. Engring. Ctr. Spokane, Wash., 1992. Inventor magnetic record, 1970, voice recognition, 1982, laser printing, 1990. Fellow IEEE; mem. Am. Radio Relay League. Republican. Roman Catholic. Home: 4838 S Bella Vista Dr Veradale WA 99037 Office: Output Tech Corp 2310 N Fancher Rd Spokane WA 99206

PFITZNER, KURT PATRICK, military officer; b. Sacramento, Calif., Jan. 7, 1958; s. Raymond Richard Pfitzner and Marion Anne (Luning) Jordahl. Diploma, FBI AntiSniper, San Angelo, Tex., 1978; BA, Angelo State U., 1982; diploma, Squadron Officer, Montgomery, Ala., 1986; postgrad., Webster U., 1992—. Enlisted USAF, 1977; policeman USAF, San Angelo, 1977-80; commd. USAF, 1982, advanced through grades to capt., 1987; student pilot USAF, Lubbock, Tex., 1983; officer in charge law enforcement USAF, Wichita Falls, Tex., 1983-85, sect. comdr. tech. tng. group, 1985-86; chief edn. Air Force Space Command USAF, Colorado Springs, Colo., 1986, protocol officer Air Force Space Command, 1986—, patrol officer, 1989; congl. liaison officer The Pentagon, Washington, D.C., 1990—; planning cons. U.S. Space Found., Colorado Springs, 1986; exec. chmn. Security Police Cadet Post, Wichita Falls, 1983; instr. presidential classroom, Washington D.C., 1992, 93, Lt's. Profl. Devel. Program, 1992, Literacy Vol. Am., 1992; mil. asst. Presdl. Inaugural Com., 1993. Instr. Peterson AFB Chapel, 1987; CPR instr. ARC, Wichita Falls, 1986, first-aid instr., 1986, swimming instr., 1986; CPR instr. Am. Heart Assn., 1981; vol. radio personality CARE Christian Radio, San Angelo, 1980; Sunday Sch. instr., Fain Presbyn. Ch., Wichita Falls, 1985. Named Officer of Yr. Hdqrs. Air Force Space Commmand, 1987. Mem. Air Force Assn., North Tex./So. Okla. Criminal Investigators Assn. Republican. Home: 904 Commonwealth Ave Alexandria VA 22301-2312 Office: Office of Legis Liaison Office of Sec of USAF Washington DC 20330

PFLIBSEN, KENT PAUL, optical scientist, research director; b. Ft. Dodge, Iowa, Nov. 28, 1955; s. Donald Richard and Betty Elaine (Schock) P.; m. Dell Patrice Lavin, Aug. 16, 1980; children: David Paul, Peter James. BS, Iowa State U., 1978; MS, U. Ariz., 1980, PhD, 1984. Mem. tech. staff Hughes Aircraft Co., Tucson, Ariz., 1979-84; asst. scientist Eye Rsch. Inst., Boston, 1984-88; optical scientist Kaman Aerospace Corp., Tucson, 1989-92, dir. electro-optics rsch., 1992—. Author: The Retina, 1988. DuNoy fellow U. Ariz., 1978-79, German Acad. fellow, 1982-83. Mem. N.Y. Acad. Scis., Optical Soc. Am., AAAS, Phi Kappa Phi, Sigma Xi. Lutheran. Home: 3532 N Calle Floreada Tucson AZ 85715-2701 Office: Kaman Aerospace Corp 3480 E Brittania Dr Tucson AZ 89706-3644

PFLUG, RAYMOND JOHN, retired educator; b. Cin., Jan. 24, 1919; s. Raymond Wilard and Clara Josephine Pflug; m. Alma Scott (div. June 1966); m. Jane Elizabeth Hanigan; children: John, Scott, Charles. BA, Stanford U., 1947, MA, 1949; postgrad., U. Calif., Berkeley, 1955. Instr. U. Nev., Reno, 1949-51; with U. Oreg., Eugene, 1951-52, Berked, 1954, Stanford (Calif.) U., 1948, Coll. of San Mateo, Calif., 1956, U. Damascas, Syria, 1962, Bir Zeit, 1965. Editor: Basic Course in Model Engineering, 1965, Ways of Language, 1967, Huck Finn, The Making of a Classic, 1969. Capt. USAF, 1942-45, 51-52. Democrat. Home: 3769 Laurel Way Redwood City CA 94062-3113

PFLUGFELDER, HALA O., mathematics educator; b. Dec. 3, 1921; came to U.S., 1954.; d. Peter S. and Maria Orlik; m. Wolfgang F. Pflugfelder; children: Tanya Torres, Gregory M. M, U. Gottinggen, Fed. Republic of Germany, 1947; PhD, U. Freiburg, Fed. Republic of Germany, 1949. Rsch. asst. U. Freiburg, 1947-50; prof. Temple U., Phila., 1956-85. Author: Quasigroups and Loops-Introduction, 1990; editor: Quasigroups and Loops-Theory and Application, 1990; contbr. articles to profl. jours. Mem. Am. Math. Soc. Home: 42 Oak Forest Pl Santa Rosa CA 95409-6314

PFORTMILLER, SANDRA CLAIR, magazine editor; b. Mpls., Sept. 22, 1939; d. Clarence Peterson and Vida May (Boggs) Barnacle; m. Jerome Carlton Hansen, June 18, 1960 (div. Jan. 1979); m. Gene Pfortmiller, May 26, 1979; children: Derik and Keith (dec.), Kimberlie Lyn Prescott. AA, Stephens Coll., 1959; student, Phoenix Coll.; degree in ministry, Morris Pratt Inst., Milw., 1990. Ordained to ministry Nat. Spiritualist Assn. of Churches, 1992. Asst. jewelry buyer Donaldson's Dept. Store, Mpls., 1959-60; asst. buyer Allied Purchasing, N.Y.C., 1960-61; freelance model Stern's, Hanes, Bamberger's, Bridal House, N.Y., N.J., 1966-67; display designer Hansen Studio, Maplewood, N.J., 1967-69; owner, pres. Decorating on a Velvet Shoestring, South Orange, N.J., 1969-76; real estate sales rep. Kalla Realty Comml., Phoenix, 1977-79; mag. editor The Nat. Spiritualist, Phoenix, 1990—; rep. for The Nat. Spiritualist at Parliament for World Religions, 1993. Contbr. articles to profl. jours. Actress, maker costumes for film, The N.J. Found. Retarded Children, 1974; bd. dirs. YES, South Orange, 1976. Mem. LM and CM Soc. (sec., treas.). Office: The Nat Spiritualist PO Box 56039 Phoenix AZ 85079-6039

PFORZHEIMER, HARRY, JR., oil consultant; b. Manila, Nov. 19, 1915; s. Harry and Mary Ann (Horan) P.; BS in Chem. Engring., Purdue U., 1938; postgrad. Case Inst. Tech., Law Sch., George Washington U., Case Western Res. U.; m. Jean Lois Barnard, June 2, 1945; children: Harry, Thomas. with Standard Oil Co. (Ohio), various locations, 1938-80, pres. White River Shale Oil Corp., 1974-76, v.p. Sohio Natural Resources Co., 1971-80, program dir. Paraho oil shale demonstration, Grand Junction, 1974-80; pres., chmn. bd., chief exec. officer Paraho Devel. Corp., 1980-82, sr. mgmt. advisor and dir., 1982-85, cons., 1985—; pres. Harry Pforzheimer Jr. and Assocs., 1983—, Ind. Colo. West Fin., Inc.; dir. IntraWest Bank Grand Junction; adj. prof. chem. engring. Cleve. State U. Contbr. articles to tech. and trade jours. Mem. planning adv. bd. St. Mary's Hosp. and Med. Ctr.; long-range planning com. Immaculate Heart of Mary Ch.; bd. dirs. Colo. Sch. Mines Research Inst.; mem. Petroleum Adminstrn. for War, Washington, 1942-45, Purdue U. Pres.'s Coun.; chmn. Wayne N. Aspinall Found.; mem. long range planning com. Immaculate Heart Mary Ch. Mem. Am. Inst. Chem. Engrs. (chmn. Cleve. 1955, gen. chmn. internat. meeting, Cleve. 1961), Am. Petroleum Inst., Am. Mining Congress, Colo. Mining Assn., Rocky Mountain Oil and Gas Assn., Denver Petroleum Club, Purdue Alumni Assn., Sigma Alpha Epsilon. Clubs: Army and Navy (Washington), Bookcliff Country, Rio Verde Country. Lodge: Kiwanis. Home: 2700 G Rd # 1-C Grand Junction CO 81506 Office: 743 Horizon Ct Grand Junction CO 81506-8714

PFUEHLER, SUSAN GULLBERG, theatre educator; b. Kirkwood, Ill., May 6, 1930; d. Karl Arthur and Susie Cornelia (Brown) Gullberg; m. Edwin E. Pfuehler, Aug. 5, 1961; 1 child, Erich. BA, Monmouth (Ill.) Coll., 1951; MA, U. Iowa, 1956. Instr. Eng., drama Winola High Sch., Viola, Ill., 1951-54; grad. assistantship, theatre U. Iowa, Iowa City, 1955-56; asst. prof. theatre U. Ariz., Tucson, 1956-61; prof. theatre Eastern Wash. U., Cheney, 1963—; costume dir. Wilderness Rd., Berea, Ky., 1957; faculty, costume designer, dir. Nat Music Camp, Interlochen, Mich., 1958-60, 63-65, 68-70, 72, 75-86;costume designer, dir. The Stephen Foster Story, Bardstown, Ky., 1961, 62; cons. Trails West, Walla Walla, Wash., 1974. Mem. AAUP, Assn. Theatre in Higher Edn., N.W. Drama Assn., Interplayers (bd. dirs. Spokane, Wash. 1991—). Home: PO Box 88 Cheney WA 99004-0088

PFUND, EDWARD THEODORE, JR., electronics company executive; b. Methuen, Mass., Dec. 10, 1923; s. Edward Theodore and Mary Elizabeth (Banning) P.; BS magna cum laude, Tufts Coll., 1950; postgrad U. So. Calif., 1950, Columbia U., 1953, U. Calif., L.A., 1956, 58; m. Marga Emmi Andre, Nov. 10, 1954 (div. 1978); children: Angela M., Gloria I., Edward Theodore III; m. Ann Lorenne Dille, Jan. 10, 1988. Radio engr., WLAW, Lawrence-Boston, 1942-50; fgn. svc. staff officer Voice of Am., Tangier, Munich, 1950-54; project. engr. Crusade for Freedom, Munich, Ger., 1955; project mgr., materials specialist United Electrodynamics Inc., Pasadena, Calif., 1956-59; cons. H.I. Thompson Fiber Glass Co., L.A., Andrew Corp., Chgo., 1959, Satellite Broadcast Assocs., Encino, Calif., 1982; teaching staff Pasadena City Coll. (Calif.), 1959; dir. engring., chief engr. Electronics Specialty Co., L.A. and Thomaston, Conn., 1959-61; with Hughes Aircraft Co., various locations, 1955, 61-89, mgr. Middle East programs, also Far East, Latin Am. and African market devel., L.A., 1971-89, dir. internat. programs devel., Hughes Communications Internat., 1985-89; mng. dir. E.T. Satellite Assocs. Internat., Rolling Hills Estates, Calif., 1989—; dir. programs devel. Asia-Pacific TRW Space and Tech. Group, Redondo Beach, Calif., 1990—. With AUS, 1942-46. Mem. AIAA, Phi Beta Kappa, Sigma Pi Sigma. Contbr. articles to profl. jours. Home: 25 Silver Saddle Ln Palos Verdes Peninsula CA 90274-2437

PFUND, RANDY (RANDELL), professional basketball coach; b. Oak Park, IL, Dec. 29, 1951. Student, Wheaton Coll. Former high sch. tchr. and coach Ill.; former asst. coach, dir. booster orgn. Westmont Coll., Santa Barbara, Calif.; asst. coach L.A. Lakers, 1985-92, head coach, 1992—. Office: LA Lakers PO Box 10 Inglewood CA 90301

PFUNTNER, ALLAN ROBERT, entomologist; b. Buffalo, May 19, 1946; s. Robert James and Verna May (Colton) P.; m. Sri Hartini Hartono, Aug. 23, 1970; children: Nicolis Dean, Erin Tristina. BA in Biology, San Jose State U., 1969, MA in Biology, 1977. Cert. entomologist. Sanitarian Monterey County Health Dept., Salinas, Calif., 1972-73; vector control asst. Santa Clara County Health Dept., San Jose, Calif., 1973-75; entomologist Northwest Mosquito Abatement Dist., Riverside, Calif., 1975-84; asst. mgr. West Valley Vector Control Dist., Chino, Calif., 1984-89, mgr., 1989—. Contbr. articles to jours. Served with U.S. Army, 1969-72. Mem. Entomol. Soc. Am., Am. Mosquito Control Assn., Soc. Vector Ecologists. Office: West Valley Vector Control Dist 13355 Elliot Ave Chino CA 91710-5255

PHAM, KINH DINH, electrical engineer, educator, administrator; b. Saigon, Republic of Vietnam, Oct. 6, 1956; came to U.S., 1974; s. Nhuong D. and Phuong T. (Tran) P.; m. Ngan-Lien T. Nguyen, May 27, 1985. BS with honors, Portland State U., 1979; MSEE, U. Portland, 1982; postgrad., Portland State U., 1988—. Registered profl. engr., Oreg., Calif., Ariz., Fla. Elec. engr. Irvington-Moore, Tigard, Oreg., 1979-80; elec. engr. Elcon Assocs., Inc., Beaverton, Oreg., 1980-87, sr. elec. engr., assoc. ptnr., 1987—; adj. prof. Portland (Oreg.) Community Coll., 1982—. Contbr. articles to profl. jours. Recipient Cert. Appreciation Am. Pub. Transit Assn. and Transit Industry, 1987. Mem. IEEE, Eta Kappa Nu. Buddhist. Office: Elcon Assocs Inc 12670 NW Barnes Rd Portland OR 97229-6016

PHAN, CHUONG VAN, biotechnologist; b. Trungthanh, Vinhlong, Vietnam, July 6, 1942; came to U.S. 1988; s. Nhac Van and Lua Thi (Nguyen) P.; m. Bang Tam Tran; 1 child, Trongvan; m. Hitomi Shimono; children: Maichi, Milan, Mica. BSc in Agr., Nat. Ctr. Agr., Saigon, Vietnam, 1969; MSc in Agr., Kyushu U., Japan, 1976, PhD in Agr., 1980. Instr. U. Cantho, Vietnam, 1969-73; rsch. scientist U. Guelph, Can., 1982-87, Hoechst Can., Inc., Regina, 1987-88; sr. rsch. scientist Agrigenetics Co., Madison, Wis., 1988-89, Sungene Tech., San Jose, Calif., 1989-90, Petoseed Co., Inc., Woodland, Calif., 1990—. Contbr. articles to profl. jours. Mem. Internat. Assn. Plant Tissue Culture, In Vitro, Japanese Jour. Breeding. Buddhist. Home: 413 Grande Ave Davis CA 95616-0213 Office: Petoseed Co 37437 State Hwy 16 Woodland CA 95695-9353

PHAN, PHILLIP VU TRAN, computer company executive; b. Bien Hoa, Vietnam, Oct. 25, 1968; came to U.S., 1979; s. Dao Tran Phan and Thien-Huong Tran. AS, Grossmont Coll., El Cajon, Calif., 1989; BS, San Diego State U., 1992. Printing ops. asst. Grossmont Coll, 1986-92; sales mgr. Microdex, Escondido, Calif., 1988—; pres. The VP Cons. Co., Santee, Calif., 1990-91, Innovative Mgmt. Systems, Santee, 1991—; programmer analyst Grossmont Coll., 1993; cons. Nat. Computer Corp., Escondido, 1987-88. Author software The VP Systems, In-Trak version 1.0. Advisor Vietnamese Assoc. Students, 1989—. Mem. Data Processing Mgmt. Assn., Am. Mgmt. Assn., Alpha Iota Epsilon, Alpha Gamma Sigma. Republican. Mem. Christian and Missionary Alliance. Home: 9164 Paseo Cresta Santee CA 92071 Office: Innovative Mgmt Systems PO Box 293 La Mesa CA 91944-0293

PHANSIRI, BETTY JO, medical technologist, consultant, educator; b. Grand Island, Nebr., Aug. 2, 1950; d. Helen Doris (Koertje) P.; m. Thosaporn Phansiri, July 26, 1974; children: Krisanna, Melisa, Kirk. BS, Wayne (Nebr.) State Coll., 1972; MS, Cen. Mich. U., 1990. Instr. Aims Community Coll., Greeley, Colo., 1979-92; diagnostic svc. mgr. Meml. Hosp., Greeley, 1983, mgr. ancillary div., 1983-86; buyer North Colo. Med. Ctr., Greeley, 1986-88; med. technologist Platte Valley Med. Ctr., Brighton, Colo., 1988—; cons. technologist Internal Medicine, Greeley, 1983-84; instr. Planned Parenthood, Denver, 1989-90. Mem. Am. Soc. Med. Technologists, Am. Soc. Clin. Pathologists, Nat. Notary Assn., Colo. Soc. Med. Technologists, Colo. Assn. Continuing Edn. Lutheran. Home: 3927 13th St Greeley CO 80634-2721 Office: Platte Valley Med Ctr 1850 E Egbert St Brighton CO 80601-2404

PHARR, MICHAEL MILTON, retail executive; b. Oklahoma City, Oct. 10, 1940; s. Marion Milton and Helen (Kleeman) P.; m. Jane Louise Erickson, June 21, 1969; 1 son, Matthew Milton. B.S., Yale U., 1962; M.B.A., Stanford U., 1966. Analyst, mgr. The Pillsbury Co., Mpls., 1966-72; analyst, mgr., dir. Dayton Hudson Corp., Mpls., 1972-73; asst. controller Dayton Hudson Corp., 1973-78, sr. v.p. control and strategic planning, 1979-84; sr. v.p. fin. and adminstrn. B. Dalton Bookseller, Mpls., 1978-79; vice chmn., chief adminstrv. officer Mervyn's, Hayward, Calif., 1985-88; exec. v.p., chief adminstrv. officer, CFO, Safeway Inc., Oakland, Calif., 1988-92, vice chmn., chief adminstrv. officer, CFO, 1992—, also bd. dirs. Bd. dirs. Minn. Opera, Mpls., 1972-76, U. Minn. Acctg. Adv. Coun., 1979-82, Minn. Acctg. Aid Soc., 1983-84, Minn. Pub. Radio, St. Paul, 1983-84, YMCA, 1986—; bd. dirs., treas. The Bridge for Runaway Youth, 1980-84; mem. adv. bd. Puente Project, 1986—, United Way Cabinet, 1990-92. Roman Catholic. Clubs: Minneapolis; Minikahda (Mpls.); Peninsula Golf and Country. Office: Safeway Inc 201 4th St Oakland CA 94660-0001

PHELAN, JEFFREY PATRICK, obstetrician-gynecologist; b. Boston, Apr. 7, 1946; m. Marilyn Marcy, May 3, 1969; children: Kelly Elizabeth, Shane Patrick, Shannon Leigh. MD, U. Miami, 1973; JD, Loyola Law Sch., 1988. Diplomate Am. Bd. Ob-Gyn. Intern, resident Naval Regional Med. Ctr., Portsmouth, Va., 1973-77; obstet. cons. Pregnant Cardiac Clinic U. So. Calif.-L.A. County Med. Ctr., 1981-83, dir. Normal Birth Ctr., 1981-88, dir. External Cephalic Version Clinic, 1982-85, obstet. cons. Post Date Clinic, 1984-86, assoc. dir. Women's ICU, 1984-88, dir. antepartum fetal surveillance, 1984-88; dir. maternal-fetal medicine Queen of the Valley Hosp., West Covina, Calif., 1987-91; co-dir. maternal-fetal medicine Pomona (Calif.) Valley Hosp. Med. Ctr., 1987—; dir. maternal-fetal medicine San Antonio Hosp., Upland, Calif., 1991—. Editor: Critical Care Obstetrics, 1987, Cesarean Delivery, 1988, Prevention in Prematurity, 1992; editor jour. Ob-Gyn. and the Law, 1989. Fellow Am. Coll. Ob-Gyn. (1st award for sci. presentation 1989), Am. Coll. Legal Medicine; mem. ABA, Calif. Bar Assn., Soc. Perinatal Obstetricians (Soc. award 1989). Office: 1030 S Arroyo Pky # 110 Pasadena CA 91105

PHELAN, MICHAEL ABEEL, consulting company executive; b. Anchorage, Jan. 2, 1949; s. Donald Abeel and Henriette Cecilia (Darrieulat) P.; m. Susan Bonynge Strange; m. Rebecca Carson, Mar. 30, 1989. BS, Georgetown U., 1975, PhD, 1983. Biologist, technologist Litton Bionetics, Kensington, Md., 1976-77; biologist, technologist Bur. Biologics, FDA, Bethesda, Md., 1977-79, biologist, 1979-85, rsch. biologist, 1985-89; cons. Diagnostic Resources Group, Chevy Chase, Md., 1989—, dir. western office, 1991—, v.p., 1992—; cons. Dept. Health Svcs., State of Calif., 1991—. Contbr. sci. articles to profl. jours and books. With U.S. Army, 1967-70, Vietnam. Recipient Commendable Svc. awards FDA, Washington, 1979, 84. Home and Office: 2010 Nelson Rd Scotts Valley CA 95066

PHELPS, ROBIN MCCANN, clinical social worker; b. Cleveland, Tenn., Dec. 7, 1957; d. William Donald and Joyce Ann (Guffey) McC.; m. Neal Harris Phelps III, Dec. 18, 1981; children: Amber Rae, Miranda Brooke, Neal Harris IV. BS, Brigham Young U., 1979; MS, U. Utah, 1983. Lic. social worker. Psychiat. technician Utah State Hosp., Provo, 1980-81, children and youth coord., 1984-86; psychiat. social worker Hiwassee Mental Health Ctr., Cleveland, 1983-86; social svc. cons. Omni Home Health, Cleveland, 1985-87; psychiat. social worker Kenneth E. Shoemaker, M.D., Cleveland, 1985-89, Davidson Clinic, Farmington, Utah, 1989-91, Mountain Heights Clinic, 1991—; presenter in field. Mem. C.A.P.P., Inc., Cleveland, 1985, Child Abuse Rev. Bd., Cleveland, 1985; mem. treatment com. Child Sexual Abuse Investigative Team, Cleveland, 1985. Mem. NASW. Home: 1594E 2475 Layton UT 84040 Office: Mountain Hts Clinic 535 Medical Dr Bountiful UT 84010-4929

PHELPS, WILLARD, Canadian government official. Min. Justice, Health and Social Svcs. and Energy Yukon Terr., Can., 1993—. Office: Govt Yukon, PO Box 2703, Whitehorse, YK Canada Y1A 2C6

PHIBBS, CIARAN SARGENT, health economist; b. Syracuse, N.Y., Feb. 7, 1957; s. Roderic H. and Jane (Sargent) P.; m. Jill Ann Sullivan, July 7, 1990. BA in Econs., St. Lawrence U., 1979; MA in Econs., U. Calif.-San Diego, La Jolla, 1982, PhD in Econs., 1987. Nat. Ctr. for Health Svcs. Rsch. postdoctoral fellow U. Calif., San Francisco, 1987-89, rsch. assoc., 1990-91; asst. prof. Columbia U., N.Y.C., 1989-90; health economist VA, Menlo Park, Calif., 1991—; presenter in field, 1982—; reviewer Med. Car, 1988—, Rev. Econs. and Stats., 1989, Jour. AMA, 1989—, Family Planning Perspectives, 1989, Social Sci. and Medicine, 1990, Pediatrics, 1991—, Am. Jour. Epidemiology, 1991, Am. Jour. Pub. Health, 1991—; reviewer Agy. for Health Care Policy and Rsch. Contbr. articles to profl. jours. Mem. adv. com. March of Dimes, San Francisco, 1990—, Coleman Advs. for Children, San Francisco, 1990-91. Grantee Agy. for Health Care Policy and Rsch., 1991-92. Mem. APHA, Am. Econ. Assn., Assn. for Health Svcs. Rsch. Office: VA Med Ctr HSR&D (152) 795 Willow Rd Menlo Park CA 94025

PHILIP, WILLIAM WARREN, banker; b. Tacoma, Oct. 26, 1926; s. Warren F. and Lillian (Lehman) P.; m. Dorothy Mary Mitchell, Oct. 14, 1954; children: Cynthia Ann, Susan Kelly. Student, U. Wash., 1946-47; grad., Pacific Coast Banking Sch., 1961; postgrad., Pacific Luth. U., 1987. With Puget Sound Nat. Bank, Tacoma, 1951—; pres. Puget Sound Nat. Bank, 1971—, chmn., 1979—; bd. dirs. Fed. Res. Bd. San Francisco; chmn. Pierce County, Savs. Bond div. Treasury Dept. Bd. dirs. Lakewood Water Dist., Tacoma Pierce County Econ. Devel.; chmn. Multicare Hosp. Tacoma; chmn. bus. adv. bd. Pacific Luth. U.; past chmn. bd. Mary Bridge Children's Hosp. Mem. Wash. Roundtable, Tacoma Golf and Country Club, Rainier Club, Columbia Tower Club, Canterwood Golf and Country Club. Office: Puget Sound Nat Bank 1119 Pacific Ave Tacoma WA 98402-4374

PHILIPP, MARILYN OETJEN, law firm administrator; b. Columbus, Ohio, May 9, 1947; d. Robert Adrian and Dorothy Mae (Myers) Oetjen; m. Edward William Philipp, Jan. 3, 1976. BA, Hope Coll., 1969; M. in Internat. Mgmt., Am. Grad. Sch. Internat. Mgmt., 1975. Adminstrv. asst. internat. programs office Earlham Coll., Richmond, Ind., 1969-74; mktg. writer Sony Corp., Tokyo, 1976-77; litigation support specialist O'Melveny & Myers, L.A., 1978-80; pers. mgr. Hahn & Cazier, L.A., 1981-84; adminstr. Atkinson, Andelson, Loya, Ruud & Romo, Cerritos, Calif., 1984—; mem. symposium com. Computer Law Systems, Inc., Eden Prairie, Minn., 1989, 90; co-owner Neil's Schwinn Cyclery, Anaheim, Calif. Mem. Assn. Legal Adminstrs., Nat. Bicycle Dealer's Assn. Presbyterian. Office: Atkinson Andelson et al 13304 Alondra Blvd Cerritos CA 90701

PHILIPPI, ERVIN WILLIAM, mortician; b. Lodi, Calif., June 4, 1922; s. William and Rebecca (Steinert) P.; m. Emma Grace Mosely, May 8, 1958 (div. Mar. 1979); m. Helen Jo Hunt, June 3, 1979. Grad., Calif. Coll. Motuary Sci., 1948. Embalmer, mortician, mgr. Salas Bros. Chapel, Modesto, Calif., 1946-92; dep. coroner Stanislaus County, Calif., 1955-75. With U.S. Army, 1942-46.

PHILIPS, DANIEL JOSEPH, computer generated imagery company executive; b. Detroit, Oct. 14, 1948; s. Charles Edward and Ellen Marie (Kitchen) P.; m. Theresa Mary Houston, Dec. 26, 1970; children: Eric Mason, Tyler Andrew. Student, Soc. of Arts and Crafts, Detroit, 1966-67, Wayne State U., 1967-68, Carleton U., Ottawa, Ont., Can., 1971. Designer Can. Broadcasting Corp., Ottawa, 1972-74, Vancouver, B.C., Can., 1974-80; creative dir. Omnibus Computer Graphics, Toronto, Ont., Can., 1980-87; designer, owner Prodn. Design, Toronto, 1987-90; mgr. computer generated imagery Walt Disney Pictures, Feature Animation, Glendale, Calif., 1990—. Recipient Nomination Acad. Award Acad. of Motion Picture Scis., 1991. Mem. Assn. Computing Machinery, Toronto Animation Soc. Office: Walt Disney Pictures 1420 Flower St Glendale CA 91221

PHILIPSBORN, JOHN TIMOTHY, lawyer, author; b. Paris, Oct. 19, 1949; s. John David and Helen (Worth) P. AB, Bowdoin Coll., 1971; MEd, Antioch Coll., 1975; JD, U. Calif., Davis, 1978. Bar: Calif. 1978, U.S. Dist. Ct. (no. and ea. dists.) Calif. 1978, U.S. Ct. Appeals (9th cir.) 1985, U.S. Supreme Ct. 1985; cert-specialist in criminal law State of Calif., 1985. VISTA vol. Office of Gov. State of Mont., Helena, 1972-73; cons. U.S. Govt., Denver, 1974; lectr. Antioch New Eng. Grad. Sch., Keene, N.H., 1973-75, U. N.H., Durham, 1973-75; ptnr. Philipsborn & Cohn, San Jose, Calif., 1978-80; atty., supr. Defenders Inc., San Diego, 1980-83; assoc. Garry, Dreyfus & McTernan, San Francisco, 1983-87; pvt. practice, San Diego and San Francisco, 1987—; cons. Nicaraguan ct. evaluation projects, 1987—; coord. Internat. Conf. Adversarial System, Lisbon, Portugal, 1990; mem. adj. faculty New Coll. Law, San Francisco, 1991—; legal asst. project refugee camps S.E. Asia, 1992—. Contbr. articles to profl. jours. Founder trial program San Francisco Schs., 1986; bd. dirs. Calif. Indian Legal Svcs., 1990—. Fulbright scholar, Portugal, 1989. Mem. Nat. Assn. Criminal Def. Lawyers (assoc., co-chmn. death penalty impact litigation group 1989, co-chmn. govtl. misconduct com. 1990-92, vice chmn. task force on emerging democracies 1990-91), Calif. State Bar (evaluation panel criminal law specialists 1986—, com. on continuing edn. of bar 1991—), Calif. Attys. for Criminal Justice (bd. govs. 1989—, assoc. editor jour. 1987—, chmn. Amicus Curiae com. 1992—, co-chmn. govtl. misconduct com. 1989-92,), World Affairs Coun. Office: 1231 Market St San Francisco CA 94103-4805

PHILIPSBORN, RANDALL H., disaster preparedness consultant; b. Chgo., Nov. 14, 1952; s. Herbert F. and Margery (Lederer) P.; m. Mary E. Brooks, July 5, 1986. Student, Boston U., 1971-73; BA, Northwestern U., 1975; MA, U. Colo., 1978. Rsch. asst. U. Colo., Boulder, 1976-78; planner Disaster Preparedness Office, V.I., 1979; hazard mitigation specialist Fed. Emergency Mgmt. Agy., Denver, 1978-87; pres. Mitigation Assistance Corp., Boulder, 1987—; presenter workshops, symposia; lectr. in field. Author articles on emergency mgmt. to various publs., conf. procs. Recipient Gov.'s Cert. Appreciation, Utah, 1986, Wyo., 1989, 90, Legislature Citation of Honor, Alaska, 1990, Citation award Applied Geography Group, 1984. Mem. Assn. State Floodplain Mgrs. (assoc. del. 1986-89, bd. dirs. 1989, chair mitigation com., 1991—), Internat. Disaster and Emergency Specialists, Colo. Assn. Stormwater and Floodplain Mgrs., Colo. Emergency Mgmt. Assn., Colo. Soc. Natural Hazards Rsch., Wyo. Emergency Mgmt. Assn. Home and Office: Mitigation Assistance Corp PO Box 382 Boulder CO 80306-0382

PHILIPSON, JOSEPH, chemist; b. Chgo., Aug. 30, 1918; s. Isador and Minnie (Haas) P.; m. Amy Goldstein, Apr. 11, 1942 (dec. Oct. 1985); children: David, Alice, Robert, Jean; m. Stella Rudnick, Jan. 14, 1990. BS, U. Wis., 1940; MS, U. Minn., 1941; PhD, U. So. Calif., 1944. Registered profl. engr., Calif. Rsch. chemist Sanitary Dist. Chgo., N.Am. Aviation, Inglewood, Calif., 1945-47, Aerojet Gen. Corp., Azusa, Calif., 1947-52; chief chemist Grand Cen. Rocket Co., Pocoima, Calif., 1952-54; div. dir. Atlantic Rsch. Corp., Pasadena, Calif., 1957-64; cons. chemist, Pasadena, 1964—. Contbr. articles to profl. jours.; patentee in field. Mem. AIAA, Am. Chem. Soc., Soc. Plastic Engrs., Soc. Aerospace Material and Process Engrs., Cons. Chemists Assn. Home and Office: 2250 Kinclair Dr Pasadena CA 91107-1022

PHILLIPS, ALAN GUY, ceramics engineer, artist; b. Colorado Springs, Colo., Apr. 18, 1949; s. Hilda H. (Guy) P. BA in Chemistry, U. Colo., 1971. Chemist Diamond Shamrock, Houston, 1972; with new product R & D Kaman Scis., Colorado Springs, 1973-77, Rockwell Internat. EG&G Rocky Flats, Golden, Colo., 1978—; owner Alan Phillips, Inc., Arvada, Colo., 1980-85, The Ambrosial Woods Gallery, Arvada, 1990—. Mem. Nature Conservancy, Wilderness Soc., Sierra.

PHILLIPS, ALMA BERCOVITZ, secondary education educator; b. L.A., Mar. 30, 1923; d. Jack Louis and Pauline (Perlman) Bercovitz; m. G. L. Phillips, Feb. 21, 1957; children: Clayton Arthur, Bradley Edward. BA, UCLA, 1944; postgrad., U. Mex., Domingus Hills, 1947. Cert. secondary edn. tchr., Calif. With Reggio Emilia High Sch., 1958-59; tchr. Barstow (Calif.) Secondary Sch., 1948-49; tchr. L.A. Unified Sch. Dist., 1949-86, ret. Author poems; contbr. recipes to cookbooks. With U.S. Army, 1944-46. Fulbright grantee Italy, 1957-58. Mem. AAUW, Temple Beth El, Bus. and Profl. Women's Group. Democrat. Home: 1927 S Moray Ave San Pedro CA 90732-4317

PHILLIPS, ANNA, publisher, editor-in-chief newspaper; b. Oakalla, Tex., Nov. 19, 1936; d. Edward C. and Barbara W. (Roberts) Spinks; 1 child, Kenny E. Phillips. Asst. sales mgr. Am. Legion Newspaper, San Antonio, 1961-68; sales profl. Sta. KLRN-TV Ednl. Broadcasting, San Antonio, 1969-73; sales mgr. Victor Bloom Advt. Agy., L.A., 1973-77, Non-Commd. Officers Assn., Oceanside, Calif., 1977-80; asst. sales mgr. Marshals Assn., San Diego, 1978-81; editor-in-chief, founder World of Entertainment, 1981-90; founder, pub. Associated News of So. Calif., San Bernardino, 1985-93. Editorial columnist City Police and Sheriffs of San Bernardino, 1987-93. Mgr. pub. rels. dept. Student Coun. Trinity U., San Antonio, Funds for Nat. Celebrity Jazz Concerts. Recipient Nat. Pub. award Nat. Fedn. of Fed. Employees, 1967. Home: 800 W Trenton St San Bernardino CA 92405-4232 Office: Associated News PO Box 3104 San Bernardino CA 92413-3104

PHILLIPS, ARTHUR MORTON, III, botanist, consultant; b. Cortland, N.Y., Jan. 20, 1947; s. Arthur Morton Jr. and Ruth (Mason) P.; m. Diedre Weage, Sept. 3, 1988. BS, Cornell U., 1969; PhD, U. Ariz., 1977. Instr., dept. biol. sci. U. Ariz., Tucson, 1971-73, rsch. asst., dept. geosciences, 1973-76; rsch. botanist Mus. No. Ariz., Flagstaff, 1976-80, curator biology, 1980-89; environ. cons. Flagstaff, 1990—; mem. Ariz. plant recovery team U.S. Fish & Wildlife Svc. Endangered Species, Phoenix, 1981—, Natural Areas Adv. Coun. Ariz. State Pks., Phoenix, 1980-89, chmn. 1985-86; adj. prof. No. Ariz. U., Flagstaff, 1984—. Author: Grand Canyon Wildflowers, 2d edit., 1990; co-author: Checklist, Vascular Plants, Grand Canyon National Park, 1987, High Country Wildflowers, 1987, Expedition to San Francisco Peaks, 1989, 4 endangered plants recovery plans, 1984-87. Fellow Ariz.-Nev. Acad. Sci.; mem. Ecol. Soc. Am., Am. Quaternary Assn., Soc. for Conservation Biology, Flagstaff Rotary Club (sec. 1989-92, achievement 1990, pres. 1993-94). Home and Office: Bot & Environ Cons PO Box 201 Flagstaff AZ 86002-0201

PHILLIPS, BETTY LOU (ELIZABETH LOUISE PHILLIPS), author; b. Cleve.; d. Michael N. and Elizabeth D. (Materna) Suvak; m. John S. Phillips, Jan. 27, 1963 (div. Jan. 1981); children: Bruce, Bryce, Brian; m. John D.C. Roach, Aug. 28, 1982. BS, Syracuse U., 1960; postgrad. in English, Case Western Res. U., 1963-64. Cert. elem. and spl. edn. tchr., N.Y. Tchr. pub. schs. Shaker Heights, Ohio, 1960-66; sportswriter Cleve. Press, 1976-77; spl. features editor Pro Quarterback Mag., N.Y.C., 1976-79; freelance writer specializing in books for young people, 1976—; interior designer residential and comml.; bd. dirs. Cast Specialties Inc., Cleve. Author: Chris Evert: First Lady of Tennis, 1977; Picture Story of Dorothy Hamill (ALA Booklist selection), 1978; American Quarter Horse, 1979; Earl Campbell: Houston Oiler Superstar, 1979; Picture Story of Nancy Lopez, (ALA Notable book), 1980; Go! Fight! Win! The NCA Guide for Cheerleaders (ALA Booklist), 1981; Something for Nothing, 1981; Brush Up on Your Hair (ALA Booklist), 1981; Texas ... The Lone Star State, 1989, Who Needs Friends? We All Do!, 1989; also contbr. articles to young adult and sports mags. Bd. dirs. The Children's Mus., Denver; mem. Friends of Fine Arts Found., Denver Art Mus., Cen. City Opera Guild. Mem. Soc. Children's Book Writers, Am. Soc. Interior Designers (allied), Delta Delta Delta. Republican. Roman Catholic. Home: 125 Guilford Rd Piedmont CA 94611-3804

PHILLIPS, BILLY SAXTON, artist, designer, painter; b. Louisville, Nebr., June 20, 1915; d. Charles William and Georgia Hazel (de le Zene) Tremblay; m. John Henry Phillips, Sept. 3, 1937; 1 child, Terry. Grad., Art Ctr. Coll. of Design, 1950. Free-lance artist L.A., 1951—; package designer Wilson Paper-Disneyland, Anaheim, Calif., 1952-56; inventor Vernon (Calif.) Container Corp., 1952-56; instr. Clatsop Community Coll., Astoria, Oreg., 1990-92; painter Reva-Reva Gallery, Papeete, French Polynesia, 1972-92; artist P.M. Prodns., L.A., 1951-90; instr., motivator Maoridom, New Zealand, 1980—. Designer, patentee Ukili, 1967, packages, 1960 (zipper openings on cardboard containers); designer Disneyland's Tinkerbell. Developer Cultural Exchange Program First Ams.-Maori, S.W. Am. and New Zealand, 1986. Mem. Art Ctr. Alumni (charter, life), Trail's End Art Assn., Lady Elk, Inventors and Scientists Am.

PHILLIPS, CHARLES RICHARD, real estate executive; b. St. Louis, June 24, 1947; s. Leonard Russell Phillips and Doris Lucille (Pipkin) Woodward; m. Sonia Eileen Lujan, Oct. 31, 1990; 1 child, Breonna. BS, U. Mo., St. Louis, 1973; MBA, U. Colo., Denver, 1981. Lic. real estate broker. Real estate specialist VA, St. Louis and Denver, 1972-78; pres. Chaves Bank, Denver, 1979-83; owner Carriage House Properties, Denver, 1983—; mem. U. Colo.-Denver Alumni Bd., 1983-85; bus. advocate SBA, Colo., 1985. Appointee Leadership Denver, 1983; bd. mem. Regional Transp. Dist., Small Bus. Adv. Coun., Denver, 1984; bd. dirs. Queen City Housing, Denver, 1984—; lifetime presdl. appt. Selective Svc. Bd. Mem. Colo. Hispanic C. of C. (comptroller 1983—), Mensa, Intel.

PHILLIPS, DARRELL, retail executive; b. Hamilton, Ohio, Oct. 7, 1956; s. Bill L. and Lois J. (Marcum) P. Student, Western State Coll., Gunnison, Colo., 1974-77; BSBA, U. No. Colo., Greeley, 1979. Sales rep. Econ. Lab., White Plains, N.Y., 1979, Color Tile, Inc., Denver, 1980-81; store mgr. Color Tile, Inc., Lake Charles, La., 1981-82; v.p. Phillips Stationers, Inc., Denver, 1982-87; pres. Pro-Dispatch Office Supply, Denver, 1988—; bd. dirs. U.S. Bus. Inc. Mem. Nat. Office Produts Assn. Republican.

PHILLIPS, DAVID MORGAN, minister; b. Whittier, Calif., Oct. 10, 1951; s. Daniel and Elsie (Morgan) P.; m. Christine Estelle George, June 9, 1972; children: Kimberly, Danny, Wesley. BA in Religion, Point Loma Nazarene Coll., 1973; MA in Religion, Azusa Pacific U., 1986, cert. ministry mgmt., 1987, MDiv, 1989. Ordained to ministry, Nazarene Ch., 1975. Part-time youth and Christian edn. minister Ch. of the Nazarene, Wilmington, Calif., 1971-73; sr. pastor Ch. of the Nazarene, Hawthorne, Nev., 1973-74, Moreno Valley, Calif., 1976-82, Apple Valley, Calif., 1981—; asst. pastor Ch. of the Nazarene, Brea, Calif., 1974-76; Bible quiz dir. S.W. region Nazarene Youth Internat., 1975-77, sec.-treas., 1977-91; chaplain, treas. res. unit San Bernardino County Sheriff's Dept., 1991—, res. sworn dep. sheriff, mem. pers. officer unit 135, 1992—; dist. treas., fin. mgr., chmn. dist. fin. com., mem. ministerial credentials com., So. Calif. dist. Ch. of Nazarene, 1987—, mem. dist. ch. planting com., 1988—, mem. dist. adv. bd., 1989-92, chmn. dist. youth camps bd., dir. Nazarene Bible Coll. extension, 1989—. Trustee Nazarene Bible Coll., 1990—, Idyllwild Pines Christian Conf. Ctr., 1990—; pres. Hawthorne Ministerial Assn., 1972-73; bd. dirs. Rotary, 1975-76. Recipient City Proclamation for Svc., City of Brea, 1976, Community award for Vol. Svc. Town of Apple Valley, Comdr.'s Outstanding Svc. award Sheriff Dept. San Bernardino, 1992, Lifesaving medal San Bernardino County Sherrif Dept.; named Reserve Deputy of Yr. Apple Valley, Reserve Comdr. Apply Valley Police San Bernardino County Sherrif Dept. Mem. Stephen Manley Evangelistic Assn. (sec. bd. dirs. 1982-85, 91—, chmn. bd. dirs. 1985-89, treas. 1990-91; adj. prof. leadership and fin. Nazarene Bible Coll., Colorado Springs, Colo., 1990—;. Home: PO Box 1281 Apple Valley CA 92307 Office: Ch of Nazarene PO Box 2636 Apple Valley CA 92307

PHILLIPS, DAVID PARKER, legal foundation executive, lawyer; b. Buffalo, Apr. 7, 1934; s. David Harvey and Mary Louise (Parker) P.; m. Elizabeth Ann Edwards, Mar. 30, 1964; children: Elizabeth P., David Page, Sara Ann. BS in Engring. with honors, Princeton U., 1956; MA, U. Wyo., 1958; JD, U. Colo., 1966. Bar: Colo. 1966. Geologist Exxon U.S.A., Inc., Mont., Colo., Tex., 1958-63; atty. Indsl. Resources, Inc., Golden, Colo., 1966-70; exec. dir. Rocky Mountain Mineral Law Found., Denver, 1971—. Bd. dirs. Natural Resources Law Ctr., U. Colo., 1981—; bd. dirs. Denver chpt. Amigos de Ams., 1985-92, pres., 1988-90. Mem. Denver Petroleum Club, Sigma Xi. Office: Rocky Mountain Mineral Law Found 7039 E 18th Ave Denver CO 80220

PHILLIPS, DONALD JAMES, artist; b. Oakland, Calif., Nov. 25, 1924; s. Thomas Francis and Mary Elizabeth (Rose) P.; m. Virginia May Schmidt, Sept. 3, 1949; children: Ann Katherine Phillips Barber, Jane Louise Phillips McFann. BA, Calif. Coll. Arts and Crafts, Oakland, 1950. Designer constrn. co., Oakland, 1950; archtl. delineator major chain, Oakland, 1952-62, indsl. designer, 1962-82; watercolor artist Fireside Gallery and Mulberry Gallery, Carmel and Aptos, Calif.; art exhibit judge art socs. and fair competitions; instr. adult watercolor study. With USMC, 1942-45, 50-51. Recipient Honorarium award USCG, Governor's Island, N.Y., 1991, 18 nat. and internat. awards painting, 1982-92, 30 various local awards, 1982-98, Adirondack Rouse Gold Medallion, The Arts Guild of Old Forge (N.Y.) Inc., 1985. Mem. Watercolor West, Am. Watercolor Soc. Democrat. Roman Catholic. Home: 1755 49th Ave Capitola CA 95010

PHILLIPS, DONALD LEWIS, marriage and family therapist; b. Hartshorne, Okla., Oct. 6, 1933; s. Guy and Hazel Leona (Barnes) P.; m. Ruthanne Hammers, Dec. 19, 1954; children: Donna Ruelayne (dec.), Rodney Eugene, Denton Jay. BA, Grand Canyon U., 1964; MDiv, Golden Gate Bapt. Theol. Sem., 1967; PhD in Ednl. Psychology, U. Beverly Hills, 1982; MA in Marriage and Family Therapy, Azusa Pacific U., 1988. Dir. chaplainery Juvenile Probation Dept. Santa Clara County, San Jose, Calif., 1968-79; dir. Christian Community Counseling Ctr., San Jose, 1971—, Barhabas House, San Jose, 1989—. Author: Family and Personal Growth, 1978, Christian Counselors Training Manual, 1979. Mem. Ministers Fellowship Internat., Calif. Assn. Marriage and Family Therapy. Republican. Home and Office: Barnabas House Ministries 4198 Rosenbaum Ave San Jose CA 95136-2137

PHILLIPS, DONNA ROSE, production artist, writer; b. Cheyenne, Wyo., June 16, 1961; d. Leyson Kirk and Leona Anna (Rasmussen) P.; m. Steven Gary Steinsapir, May 17, 1992; 1 child, Andrew Trevor Steinsapir. Student,

Mt. San Antonio Coll., Walnut, Calif., 1982-83, Citrus Coll., Azusa, Calif., 1988. Prodn. artist Treasure Chest Advt., Pomona, Calif., 1986-89, Rutland Tool & Supply Co. Inc., Industry, Calif., 1989-92; pvt. practice Baldwin Park, Calif., 1992—. Author, editor: Book of Days, 1989; contbr. articles to mags. Recipient award for art Bank of Am., Covina, Calif., 1979. Mem. Sons of the Desert. Republican. Lutheran. Home: 3700 Baldwin Park Blvd Unit D Baldwin Park CA 91706-4101

PHILLIPS, DOROTHY REID, library technician; b. Hingham, Mass., Apr. 21, 1924; d. James Henry and Emma Louise (Davis) Reid; m. Earl Wendell Phillips, Apr. 22, 1944; children—Earl W., Jr., Betty Herrera, Carol Coe. Cert., Durham Vocat. Sch., 1952; B.S. in Comml. Edn., N.C. Central U., 1959; postgrad. U. Colo., 1969; M.Human Relations, Webster Coll., 1979; postgrad. Grad. Sch. Library Sci., U. Denver, 1983. Vocat. nurse Meml. Hosp., U. N.C., Chapel Hill, 1955-59; vol. work, Cairo, Egypt, 1965-67; library technician Base Library, Lowry AFB, Colo., 1960-65, Fitzsimons Med. Library, Aurora, Colo., 1976—; mem. Denver Mus. Natural History, Denver Art Mus., Mariners. Mem. AAUW (chpt. community rep. 1982-83, state chmn. edn. found. 1982-84, pres. Denver br. 1984-86), Altrusa Internat. (corr. sec. Denver 1982-83, bd. dirs. 1984-85, pres. Denver chpt. 1988), Friends of Library, Colo. Library Assn., Council Library Technicians, Federally Employed Women, Delta Sigma Theta (corr. sec. Denver 1964-66). Democrat. Presbyterian. Home: 3085 Fairfax St Denver CO 80207-2714 Office: Fitzsimmons Army Med Ctr Med Tech Library Aurora CO 80045

PHILLIPS, EDWIN ARTHUR, meteorologist; b. Alton, Ill., July 30, 1952; s. Edwin Charles and Ada Mae (Russell) P.; m. Anne Mildred Hasse, May 23, 1981; children: Alexander, Jacob. BA in Aeronautics, Parks Coll., 1973. bd. dirs. World Affairs Coun., Scottsdale, Ariz., 1992—, Clark Candy Co., Phoenix. Author: Koy/Ed Phillips Almanac, 1980-92, Ktar/Ed Phillips Almanac, 1983-93, Crisis in the Atmosphere, 1990. Mem. Am. Meteorological Soc., Nat. Assn. for the Advancement of Sci., Ariz. Pilots Assn. Republican. Jewish. Office: Arizona State Senate 1700 W Washington Phoenix AZ 85007

PHILLIPS, ELDON FRANKLIN, newspaper editor; b. Louisville, Dec. 19, 1941; s. George Walter and Vada Belle (Dixon) P.; m. Nancy Rose Chambers, Nov. 27, 1968 (div. Nov. 1984). BA, U. Ky., 1966. Mag. editor Cin. Post, 1970-77; night news editor Miami (Fla.) News, 1977-80, asst. news editor, 1983-88; asst. news editor Hollywood (Fla.) Sun-tattler, 1981-83; asst. mng. editor Tribune Newspapers, Mesa, Ariz., 1989—; adj. prof. Ariz. State U., Tempe, 1990. Sgt. USAF, 1966-70. Mem. Soc. Newspaper Design, Aircraft Owners and Pilots Assn. Democrat. Baptist. Office: Tribune Newspapers 120 W 1st Ave Mesa AZ 85210-1372

PHILLIPS, FRANK SIGMUND, business executive; b. Anchorage, June 17, 1952; s. Charles W. and Kirsten H. (Alsos) P. BA, U. Calif., San Diego, 1973; JD, NYU, 1976; postgrad., U. Mo., 1977. Bar: Calif. 1977. Atty. Nat. Labor Rels. Bd., Washington, 1976-77; ptnr. Phillips and Phillips, San Diego, 1978-83; sr. atty. Namco of Am., Inc., Sunnyvale, Calif., 1983-85; v.p., gen. counsel Hang Ten Internat., San Diego, 1985-89; ptnr. Scenic Visuals Publs., San Diego, 1988—; exec. v.p. Licensing Enterprises, Inc., San Clemente, Calif., 1990—; instr. U. San Diego, 1979-83; gen. counsel San Diego Booksellers Assn., 1986—; bd. dirs. Green Found. for Earth Scis., La Jolla, Calif., 1986—. Bd. regents U. Calif., 1981-83; mem. chancellors assocs. U. Calif. San Diego, La Jolla, 1982—. Root-Tilden scholar NYU, 1973-76. Mem. Calif. State Bar, San Diego County Bar Assn., World Trade Assn. of San Diego, U. Calif. San Diego Faculty Club, U. Calif. San Diego Alumni Assn. (pres. 1981-83). Democrat. Home: PO Box 633090 San Diego CA 92163

PHILLIPS, GENEVA FICKER, editor; b. Staunton, Ill., Aug. 1, 1920; d. Arthur Edwin and Lillian Agnes (Woods) Ficker; m. James Emerson Phillips, Jr., June 6, 1955 (dec. 1979). B.S. in Journalism, U. Ill., 1942; M.A. in English Lit., UCLA, 1953. Copy desk Chgo. Jour. Commerce, 1942-43; editorial asst. patents Radio Research Lab., Harvard U., Cambridge, Mass., 1943-45; asst. editor adminstrv. publs. U. Ill., Urbana, 1946-47; editorial asst. Quar. of Film, Radio and TV, UCLA, 1952-53; mng. editor The Works of John Dryden, Dept. English, UCLA, 1964—. Bd. dirs. Univ. Religious Conf., Los Angeles, 1979—. UCLA teaching fellow, 1950-53, grad. fellow 1954-55. Mem. Assn. Acad. Women UCLA, Friends of Huntington Library, Friends of UCLA Library, Renaissance Soc. So. Calif., Samuel Johnson Soc. of So. Calif., Assocs. of U. Calif. Press., Conf. Christianity and Lit., Soc. Mayflower Descs. Lutheran. Home: 213 First Anita Dr Los Angeles CA 90049 Office: UCLA Dept English 2225 Rolfe Hall Los Angeles CA 90024

PHILLIPS, GEOFFREY KENT, research biologist; b. Poughkeepsie, N.Y., June 11, 1956; s. Charles Edward and Shirley May (Paquet) P.; m. Elizabeth Ann Jasmine, June 7, 1980. BA in Environ. Sci., Marist Coll., 1978; MPH in Environ. Health, U. Hawaii, 1992. Food researcher, health and safety coordinators com. U.S. Army Natick (Mass.) Rsch. Devel. and Engring. Ctr., 1980-90; rsch. biologist, chem. hygiene officer Tripler Army Med. Ctr., Honolulu, 1990—; mem. hazardous material response team Natick Rsch., Devel. and Engring. Ctr., 1989-90; hazardous comm. instr. Tripler Army Med. Ctr., Honolulu, 1990—. Firefighter Roosevelt Engine Co. # 3, Hyde Park, N.Y., 1976-80; rescue worker Roosevelt Rescue Squad, Hyde Park, 1976-80. Recipient Meritorious Svc. medal Dept. of the Army, Natick, 1990, U.S. Army Safety award Tripler Army Med. Ctr. Comdr., Honolulu, 1992, Nat. Inst. Occupational Safety and Health Study Grant U. Hawaii, Honolulu, 1991. Mem. Sigma Xi. Office: Tripler Army Med Ctr Dept Clin Investigation HSHK-CI Tripler HI 96859

PHILLIPS, GERTRUDE MARILYNN, fine artist, educator, transformational psychologist; b. Niagara Falls, N.Y., Feb. 22, 1931; d. James Dickens and Gertrude Myrtle (Anderson) Phillips; m. Thomas Conant Davis, June 3, 1953 (div. Nov. 1961); children: Christian Conant Davis, Cary Phillips Davis; m. Gordon Archer Wood (div. 1975); 1 child, Gordon Anderson Wood. AB, BSc, Hood Coll., Frederick, Md., 1953; postgrad., Syracuse U., 1966-68, U. Pitts., 1962; MA, U. Wash., 1974. Cert. tchr., Wash. Fine artist, cons. Orcas Island, Wash., 1984—; edn. cons. in pvt. practice Orcas Island, 1989—; rschr. in child growth and devel., 1968-84, in expansion of IQ and creativity, 1962—. Artist, including ltd. edit. of prints, 1990. Mem. Establishment of Presbyn. Mission, Orcas Island, 1989-90; chair Bellevue (Wash.) Art Commn., 1974-81; founder art fairs B.C. Arts League, Ottawa, Ont., 1964, West Coast Jazz Festivals, 1974-81. Recipient award Nat. Gallery of Art, Ottawa, 1983. Mem. AAUW (v.p. Orcas Island br. 1990-92, program chair 1990-92), N.Y. Acad. Sci., Jung Soc. Office: PO Box 772 Eastsound WA 98245

PHILLIPS, JILL META, author, critic; b. Detroit, Oct. 22, 1952; d. Leyson Kirk and Leona Anna (Rasmussen) P. Student pub. schs., Calif. Lit. counselor Book Builders, Charter Oak, Calif., 1966-77. Author: (with Leona Phillips) A Directory of American Film Scholars, 1975, The Good Morning Cookbook, 1976, G.B. Shaw: A Review of the Literature, 1976, T.E. Lawrence: Portrait of the Artist as Hero, 1977, The Archaeology of the Collective East, 1977, The Occult, 1977, D.H. Lawrence: A Review of the Literature and Biographies, 1978, Film Appreciation: A College Guide Book, 1979, Annus Mirabilis: Europe in the Dark and Middle Centuries, 1979, (with Leona Rasmussen Phillips) The Dark Frame: Occult Cinema, 1979, Misfit: The Films of Montgomery Clift, 1979, Butterflies in the Mind: A Précis of Dreams and Dreamers, 1980; The Rain Maiden: A Novel of History, 1987, Walford's Oak: A Novel, 1990, The Fate Weaver: A Novel in Two Centuries, 1991, Saturn Falls: A Novel of the Apocalypse, 1993; contbr. book revs. to New Guard mag., 1974-76. Mem. Young Ams. for Freedom, Am. Conservative Union, Elmer Bernstein's Film Music Collection, Ghost Club London, Count Dracula Soc., Dracula Soc. London, Richard III Soc. Republican. Home: 851 N Garsden Ave Covina CA 91724-2636 Office: PO Box 260 Glendora CA 91740-0260

PHILLIPS, JOHN RICHARD, engineering educator; b. Albany, Calif., Jan. 30, 1934; s. Eric Lester and Adele Catherine (Rengel) P.; m. Joan Elizabeth Soyster, Mar. 23, 1957; children: Elizabeth Huntley, Sarah Rengel, Catherine Hale. BS, U. Calif., Berkeley, 1956; M in Engring., Yale U., 1958, PhD in Engring., 1960. Registered profl. engr., Calif. Chem. engr. Stanford Rsch. Inst., Menlo Park, Calif., 1960; rsch. engr. Chevron Rsch. Co., Richmond, Calif., 1962-66; mem. faculty Harvey Mudd Coll., Claremont, Calif., 1966—, prof. engrng., 1974—, James Howard Kindleberger prof. engrng., 1991—, dir. engring. clinic, 1977-93, chmn. engring. dept., 1993—; vis. prof. U. Edinburgh, Scotland, 1975, Cambridge (Eng.) U., 1981, ESIEE, France, 1981, Naval Postgrad. Sch., 1984-85, Calif. Poly. U., San Luis Obispo, 1992; vis. scientist So. Calif. Edison Co., 1980; founder Claremont Engring., 1973; cons. in field. Contbr. articles to profl. jours. 1st lt. AUS, 1960-62. Mem. Am. Inst. Chem. Engrs., Sigma Xi, Alpha Delta Phi, Tau Beta Pi. Home: 911 W Maryhurst Dr Claremont CA 91711-3320

PHILLIPS, OWEN RICHARD, economics educator, antitrust consultant; b. Gt. Falls, Mont., Aug. 23, 1953; s. Owen Albert Phillips and Dorothy June (Austin) West; m. Lori Jo Yerger, Aug. 24, 1974; children: Jillian Kate, Jonathan Lloyd. BA in Econs., Stanford U., 1974, PhD, 1980. Asst. prof. econs. Tex. A&M U., College Station, 1979-85; asst. prof. econs. U. Wyo., Laramie, 1985-88, assoc. prof., 1988—; econ. cons. antitrust div. U.S. Dept. Justice, Washington, 1988-91. Author: Economic Analysis, 1992; also articles. Rsch. grantee NSF, 1984, 89. Office: U Wyo Dept Econs Laramie WY 82071-3985

PHILLIPS, PATRICK EDWARD, fire protection engineer; b. Birmingham, Ala., May 5, 1931; s. John Bunyon and Frances (Fede) P.; m. Fern L. Schalund, Nov. 24, 1954 (div. May 1979); children: Matthew, Craig, Tracey, Karla; m. Paula Lynn Jacobson, Nov., 1990. B.S. in Fire Protection and Safety Engrng., Ill. Inst. Tech. Registered profl. engr., Calif., Mass. with Mich. Inspection Bur., Detroit, 1950-65, AEC, Richland, Wash., 1965-68, U.S. Dept. Energy, Las Vegas, 1968-91, ret., 1991; cons., Las Vegas, 1975—; cons. consulting svc. in fire protection. Co-author: Fire Protection for the Design Professional, 1975. Served with U.S. Army, 1953-55. Named Man of Yr. Automatic Fire Alarm Assn., 1975. Fellow Soc. Fire Protection Engrs.; mem. Am. Soc. Safety Engrs., System Safety Soc., Cert. Safety Profls., Nat. Fire Protection Assn. (life, chmn. signalling systems correlating com., com. on detection devices, halon com., former mem. com. systems concepts for bldg. fire safety, NFPA Standards medal 1993), Underwriter's Labs. Fire Council. Lodges: Elks , Masons (master 1979), (pres. 1980, capt. 1977, 90, Scottish Rite, York Rite), Order of the Eastern Star, 1991—. Home and Office: 1963 Sycamore Trl Las Vegas NV 89108-1947

PHILLIPS, ROBIN, director, actor; b. Haslemere, Surrey, Eng., Feb. 28, 1942; arrived in Can., 1973; s. James William and Ellen Ann (Barfoot) P. Studied with Duncan Ross, Bristol Old Vic. Theatre Sch. Dir. gen. Citadel Theatre, Edmonton, Alberta, Can.; chmn. and exec. prodr. Theatre Unmasked Ltd. First profl. acting role in The Critic, 1959; TV appearences include: The Forsyte Saga, BBC, The Seagull, BBC; assoc. dir. Bristol Old Vic, 1960; asst. dir. Royal Shakespeare Co., Stratford-upon-Aron, 1965; dir. Two Gentlement of Verona; assoc. dir. Northcott Theatre, 1967-68; dir. The Seagull, Leatherhead, 1969, Tiny Alice, Royal Shakespeare Co., Aldwych, 1970, Two gentleman of Verona, Abelard and Heloise, London and Broadway, 1970, Caesar and Cleopatra, also Dear Antoine, Chichester, 1971, The Lady's Not for Burning, 1972; artistic dir. Greenwich Theatre, 1973, Stratford Festival Theatre, Can., 1974-80; dir. Virginia Haymarket Theatre, London, 1980-81; world premiere Farther West, Calgary, Alta., 1982, The Jeweller's Shop, Westminster Theatre, London, 1982; artistic dir. Grand Theatre Co., London, Ont., from 1982; dir. Tonight at 8:30, New World, for CentreStage Co., Toronto; dir. A Midsummer Night's Dream, The Crucible, The Philadelphia Story, Citadel Theatre, Edmonton, Alta., 1989-90 season; dir. Richard III, N.Y.C., 1990; dir. gen. Citadel Theatre, 1991; actor, dir. numerous others. Active task force on profl. tng. in cultural sector Marcel Masse comm. dept., exec. com. Can. Artists Com. Can. Coun., Ottawa, adv. com. Office: Citadel Theatre, 9828 101A Ave, Edmonton, AB Canada T5J 3C6

PHILLIPS, RONALD EDWARD (RON), sales executive; b. Clovis, N.Mex., Apr. 10, 1937; s. Rodney Vernon and Ethel Edna (Huff) P.; m. May Frances Willingham, Aug. 27, 1957; children: Rhonda Louise, Russell Kent, Teresa Gail; m. Janet Irene Johnsonbaugh Smith, July 4, 1938; stepchildren: Steven, Gregg, Laura. Student, Ea. N.Mex. U., 1955-56, U. N.Mex., 1957, Famous Artist Schs., 1963-64, North Light Art Sch., 1989-90. Group merchandiser women's fashions J.C. Penney Inc., Albuquerque, 1957-64; chem. salesman Take Over Products, Clovis, N.Mex., 1964-65; with International Auto Leasing, Albuquerque, 1965; salesman Pennsalt Chems., N.Mex. div., Albuquerque, 1965-67; N.Mex. sales rep. W.W. Grainger Inc., Chgo., 1967-72; founder Pueblo Arts, Inc., Albuquerque, 1972—; mgr. Dairy Queen, Santa Rosa and Lovington, N.Mex., 1982-85; owner, mgr. Western Pit n Grill & Food Gallery, Lovington, 1985-88; owner Pueblo Arts Inc./Trailwest Gallery, Albuquerque, 1988—; tchr. quick draw, continuous line drawing, 1990; artist, guide Pueblo Arts Inc. Trailwest Paintouts, Guide for Artists, 1990-92. Artist, author: (sketchbook) Traveling Mans Old Town Sketchbook, 1990; movie extra Whitesands, 1991, Next Fire on Earth, 1992. Pres. Albuquerque Wildlife and Conservation, 1963-64; mem. Albuquerque Conv. & Vis. Bur., 1988—. With N.Mex. Air Nat. Guard, 1955-61. Mem. N.Mex. Art League (hon. life, pres. 1964-65), Indian Arts and Crafts Assn. (mem. ethics com. 1973-74), Albuquerque Press Club. Republican. Office: Pueblo Arts Inc 5555 Zoni SE # 154 Albuquerque NM 87108

PHILLIPS, RONALD FRANK, legal educator, law school dean; b. Houston, Nov. 25, 1934; s. Franklin Jackson and Maudie Ethel (Merrill) P.; m. Jamie Jo Bottoms, Apr. 5, 1957; children: Barbara Celeste Phillips Oliveira, Joel Jackson, Phil Edward. B.S., Abilene Christian U., 1955; J.D., U. Tex., 1965. Bar: Tex. 1965, Calif. 1972. Bldg. contractor Phillips Homes, Abilene, Tex., 1955-56; br. mgr. Phillips Weatherstripping Co., Midland and Austin, Tex., 1957-65; corp. staff atty. McWood Corp., Abilene, 1965-67; sole practice law Abilene, 1967-70; mem. adj. faculty Abilene Christian U., 1967-70; prof. law Pepperdine U. Sch. Law, Malibu, Calif., 1970—; dean Pepperdine U. Sch. Law, 1970—; bd. dirs. PNB Fin. Group. Deacon North A and Tenn. Ch. of Christ, Midland, 1959-62; deacon Highland Ch. of Christ, Abilene, 1965-70; elder Malibu Ch. of Christ, 1978—; mgr., coach Little League Baseball, Abilene, Huntington Beach and Malibu, 1968-78, 90—; coach Youth Soccer, Huntington Beach, Westlake Village and Malibu, 1972-80, 85-86, 91. Recipient Alumni citation Abilene Christian U., 1974. Fellow Am. Bar Found.; mem. ABA, State Bar Tex., State Bar Calif. (com. on law sch. edn. 1970—), Christian Legal Soc., L.A. Bar Assn., Assn. Am. Law Schs. (chmn. sect. on adminstrn. law schs. 1982, com. on cts. 1985-87), Am. Law Inst., Nat. Conf. Commrs. on Uniform State Laws. Republican. Office: Pepperdine U Sch Law 24255 Pacific Coast Hwy Malibu CA 90263

PHILLIPS, RONDALL VAN, town manager; b. Beech Grove, Ind., June 24, 1945; s. Gene Edwin and Inez Pearl (Perry) P.; m. Karen Louise Nichols, Aug. 18, 1966; children: Kristen, Jarrod, Allison, Scott, Monica. BS, So. Nazarene U., 1967; M of Regional and City Planning, U. Okla., 1970. Fed. aid coord. City of Aurora, Colo., 1970-71; planning dir., exec. dir. San Luis Valley Coun. of Govts., Alamosa, Colo., 1971-79; v.p., gen. mgr. Wespro, Inc., Oklahoma City, 1979-82; mgr., govt. rels. Wilson Foods Corp., Oklahoma City, 1982-84, dir., foodservice mktg., bus. devel., 1982-84; town mgr. Town of Vail, Colo., 1984—; bd. dirs. Colo. Mcpl. League, Denver, Colo. Nuclear Materials Transp. Com., Denver. Mem. Colo. Assn. Ski Towns, 1984— (former sec., treas.), 1989 World Alpine Ski Championships Orgn. Com., Vail, 1985—, Colo. Tourism Bd. Adv. Coun., Denver, 1989—, Vail Br. Latter-day Sts. Ch. (pres. 1985—). Recipient Outstanding Young Man of Am. award, 1976. Mem. Internat. City Mgrs. Assn., Okla. City Internat. Trade Assn. (pres. 1980-83). Republican.

PHILLIPS, SANDRA SAMMATARO, curator, educator. AB in Art and History, Bard Coll., 1967; MA, Bryn Mawr (Pa.) Coll., 1969; PhD in Art History with honors, CUNY, 1985. Curator, assoc. in art dept. Bard Coll., 1968-77; photographic historian Catskill Ctr. for Photography, 1980-85; curator Vassar Coll. Art Gallery, Poughkeepsie, N.Y., 1986-87; curator of photography San Francisco Mus. of Modern Art, 1987—; lectr. in art history ind. study program Bard Coll., 1971-77, Met. Mus. Art, 1986, Internat. Ctr. Photography, 1986, cons., 1989, Goethe Inst., San Francisco, 1988; guest lectr. in art history Mills Coll., Oakland, Calif., spring 1980; part-time lectr. art history SUNY, New Paltz, 1977-86; tchr. history and photography courses Parsons Sch. of Design/New Sch. for Social Rsch., 1981-86; part-time lectr. in contemporary art San Francisco State U., fall 1989, in contemporary photography San Francisco Art Inst., 1993; bd. dirs. San Francisco Camerawork. Author: An Uncertain Grace: Photographs by Sabastiao Salgado, 1990, The MacMillan Dictionary of Art, 1991, Helen Levitt, 1991, Wright Morris: Origin of a Species, 1992; author: (with others) The Eyes of Time: Photojournalism in America, 1988, Perpetual Motif, 1988; contbr. articles to profl. jours. Am.-Hungarian Found. grantee Budapest, 1982, NEA grantee, 1989. Mem. The Coll. Art Assn., Hudson River Heritage. Office: San Francisco Mus Modern Art San Francisco CA 94102

PHILLIPS, STEPHEN CHASE, systems engineer, consultant; b. Misawa AFB, Japan, Jan. 6, 1960; s. Charles Wayne and Margaret Talmadge (Maxwell) P.; m. Shanna Ruth Nuffer, Mar. 20, 1993. BSEE, Rice U., 1987, BA in Math. Sci., 1987. Systems engr. Celerity Computing, Houston, 1987-88; software developer, cons. Chase Cons., Houston and Seattle, 1988—; cons. Compu-Mentor, Seattle, 1992—. Activist Sierra Club, Seattle, 1988-90; tutor City of Seattle, 1991. With USN. Mem. IEEE, Assn. Computing Machinery, The Mountaineers.

PHILLIPS, TED RAY, advertising agency executive; b. American Falls, Idaho, Oct. 27, 1948; s. Virn E. and Jessie N. (Aldous) P.; m. Dianne Jacqulynne Walker, May 28, 1971; children: Scott, Russell, Stephen, Michael. BA, Brigham Young U., 1972, MA, 1975. Account exec. David W. Evans, Inc., Salt Lake City, 1972-75; dir. advt. Div. Continuing Edn., U. Utah, Salt Lake City, 1975-78; sr. v.p. Evans/Lowe & Stevens, Inc., Atlanta, 1978, exec. v.p., 1979; pres., chief exec. officer David W. Evans/Atlanta, Inc., 1979-80; dir. advt. O.C. Tanner Co., Salt Lake City, 1980-82; pres. Thomas/Phillips/Clawson Advt., Inc., Salt Lake City, 1982-86; pres. Hurst & Phillips, Salt Lake City, 1986—; advt. instr. div. continuing edn. Brigham Young U., 1983-85. Dir. publicity, promotion Western States Republican Con., 1976. Mem. Am. Advt. Fedn. (8 Best-in-West awards, 2 nat. Addy awards, Clio finalist 1984, Telly award 1991, 92), Utah Advt. Fedn. (bd. dirs. 1976-78, 80-87, pres. 1984-85), Rotary. Mormon. Home: 1792 Cornwall Ct Sandy UT 84092 Office: Hurst & Phillips Advt & Pub Comm Inc 1440 Foothill Dr Salt Lake City UT 84108

PHILLIPS, WADE, professional football team coach; b. Orange, Tex., June 21, 1947; s. Bum Phillips; m. Laurie Phillips; children: Tracey, Wesley. Student, U. Houston. Asst. football coach U. Houston, 1969; football coach Orange (Tex.) High Sch., 1970-72, Okla. State U., 1973-74, U. Kans., 1975; linebacker coach Houston Oilers, 1976, defensive line coach, 1977-80; defensive coord. New Orleans Saints, 1981-85, Phila. Eagles, 1986-88; defensive coord. Denver Broncos, 1989-93, head coach, 1993—. Office: Denver Broncos 13655 E Dove Valley Pkwy Englewood CO 80112

PHILLIPS, WILLIAM MICHAEL, computer operator, consultant; b. Ely, Nev., Jan. 28, 1966; s. Lloyd Eugene and Dorothy Bess (McCoy) P.; m. Beverely Dianne Mayhall, Aug. 17, 1986; children: Tiffany Nicole, Kirk David. Student, So. Utah State Coll., 1984-85. Computer technician So Utah Office Supply, Cedar City, 1984-85; computer operator Newmont Gold Co., Carlin, Nev., 1992—; personal computer cons., Elko, Nev., 1992—. Mem. LDS Emergency Svcs. Network, Elko, 1992—. With USN, 1987-92, Desert Storm. Mem. Ea. Nev. Amateur Radio Soc., Navy Mil. Afiliate Radio Svc., Elko Amateur Radio Club. Democrat. Home: 376 S Valley Bend Dr Elko NV 89801

PHILLIPS, WILLIAM REVELL, retired geology educator; b. Salt Lake City, Jan. 9, 1929; s. William L. and Della (Weight) P.; m. LaRue Vail, July 21, 1950; children: Lee Revell, Lyle Vail, Lane William, Kathryn Ann. BS, U. Utah, 1950, MS, 1951, PhD, 1954. Petrographer Kennecott Copper Corp., Salt Lake City, 1954-56; asst. prof. La. Poly. Inst., Ruston, 1956-57; prof. geology Brigham Young U., Provo, 1957, prof. emeritus, chmn. dept., 1972-75; asst. dir. archaeol. expdn. Brigham Young U., Fayum, Egypt, 1981-92; pres. faculty acad. Brigham Young U., 1988-89, prof. emeritus, 1991—; sr. seasonal ranger U.S. Park Svc., Mammoth, Wyo., 1956-66; cons. geologist U.S. Forest Svc., Provo, 1969-71; Fulbright prof. U. Sind, Hyderabad, Pakistan, 1963-64, Mid. East Tech. U., Ankara, Turkey, 1966-67; vis. prof. Waterloo U., Ont. Can., 1971-72; vis. rsch. prof. Haceteppe U., Ankara, Turkey, 1975-76. Author: Mineral Optics, 1971, Optical Mineralogy, 1981; also articles. Dir. hosting Ramses II Exhbn., Provo, 1985-86. Recipient Karl G. Maeser teaching award Brigham Young U., 1986. Fellow Geol. Soc. Am.; mem. Am. Mineral. Soc., Utah Geol. Soc. (asst. editor), Sigma Xi (pres. Brigham Young U. 1978-79). Mem. LDS Ch. Home: 1839 North 1500 East Provo UT 84604 Office: Brigham Young U Dept Geology Provo UT 84602

PHILLIPS, ZAIGA ALKSNIS, pediatrician; b. Riga, Latvia, Sept. 13, 1934; came to U.S., 1949; d. Adolfs and Alma (Ozols) Alksnis; (div. 1972); children: Albert L., Lisa K., Sintija. BS, U. Wash., 1956, MD, 1959. Fellow Colo. Med. Ctr., Denver, 1961-62; sch. physician Bellevue and Issaquah (Wash.) Sch. Dists., 1970-77; pvt. practice Bellevue, 1977—; staff pediatrician Swedish Overlake Ctr., 1977—, Childrens Hosp. and Med. Ctr., Seattle, 1977—, Evergreen Med. Ctr., 1977—; cons. physician, Allergy Clinic, Childrens Hosp., Seattle, 1988—; cons. and contact to pediatricians in Latvia, 1988—. Mem. Am. Latvian Assn., 1972—, Wash. Latvian Assn., Seattle, 1972—; pres. Latvian Sorority Gundega, Seattle, 1990-93; bd. dirs. Sister Cities Assn.,Bellevue, 1992—. Fellow Am. Acad. Pediatricians; mem. Am. Latvian Physicians Assn., Wash. State and Puget Sound Pediatric Assn. Office: Pediatric Assn 2700 Northup Way Bellevue WA 98004

PHILLIPS-JONES, LINDA, consulting psychologist; b. South Bend, Ind.; d. Robert Milton and Priscilla Alicia (Tancy) Phillips; m. G. Brian Jones, Feb. 16, 1980; stepchildren: Laurie Darian Jones, Tracy Leigh Jones. BS, U. Nev., Reno, 1964; AM, Stanford U., 1965; PhD, UCLA, 1977. Lic. psychologist. Tchrs.' trainer Edn. Consultants Ltd. Internat. Tng. Consultants, Saigon, Vietnam, 1966-71; rsch. scientist Am. Insts. for Rsch., Palo Alto, Calif., 1979-83; sr. trainer, orgn. devel. cons. SRI Internat., Menlo Park, Calif., 1984-88; psychologist, cons. Coalition of Counseling Ctrs., Grass Valley, Calif., 1980—; cons. Clairol Nat. Mentor Program, N.Y.C., 1989—. Author: Mentors and Proteges, 1982, The New Mentors and Proteges, 1993; co-author: Men Have Feelings, Too!, 1988, A Fight to the Better End, 1989; contbr. articles to profl. jours.; editorial bd. Mentoring Internat., Vancouver, B.C., Can., 1989—. Recipient Civilian Svc. award Govt. of South Vietam, 1971; grad. fellow UCLA, 1964-65, 72-77. Mem. Am. Soc. for Tng. & Devel. Home and Office: Coalition of Counseling Ctrs 13560 Mesa Dr Grass Valley CA 95949-8132

PHILLIPSON, PAUL GUSTAVE, warehouse executive, avalanche control specialist; b. Hackensack, N.J., Jan. 18, 1947; s. Doris (Druding) P.; m. Maggie Louise Cummings, Nov. 30, 1980; 1 child, Amber Rae. BS in Fin., U. Colo., 1974. Engr. Boulder Fire Control Products, Denver, 1970-76; v.p., treas. MTL, Inc., Reno, 1979-90, pres., 1990—. With USN, 1966-69. Mem. Am. Assn. Avalanche Profls., Far West Prof. Ski Patrol Assn. Office: MTL Inc PO Box 11950 Reno NV 89510

PHILPOT, JOHN WILLIAM (BILL), JR., sales executive; b. Salem, Oreg., June 9, 1942; s. John William and Ruth Etta (Purvis) P.; m. Diane Antoinette Piombo, Nov. 6, 1965; children: William Nicholas, Christopher Richard. Student, Calif. State U., Sacramento, Hayward, 1970. Owner Valley Fluid Handling, Inc., Sacramento, 1975-87; mgr. sales Berthoud Sprayers, Elk Grove, Calif., 1988-91, Ger Van Co., Internat., Modesto, Calif., 1992-93; sales profl. Kuker-Parker Industris, Inc., Modesto, Calif., 1993—. Republican. Baptist.

PHILPOTT, DELBERT EUGENE, research scientist; b. Loyal, Wis., Sept. 24, 1923; s. Lacey D. and Nettie A. (Goehring) P.; m. Donna A. Clark, Jan. 1985. BA, Ind. U., 1948, MS, 1949; PhD, Boston U., 1963; PhT (hon.), Coll. Optometry, 1976. Rsch. assoc. U. Ill. Med. Sch., Chgo., 1949-52; head electron microscope lab. Inst. Muscle Rsch., Woods Hole, Mass., 1952-63; asst. prof. U. Colo. Med. Sch., Denver, 1963-66; co-dir. Inst. Biomed. Rsch., Denver, 1966; head ultrastructure rsch. NASA, Ames Rsch. Ctr., Moffett Field, Calif., 1966-90; rsch. assoc. Ames Rsch. Ctr., 1990—; sci. coord. Student Space and Biology, NASA, Moffett Field, 1974—; chmn. radiation chmn. Ames Rsch. Ctr., NASA, 1987—; sci. coord. black colls., 1989-90; faculty advisor Delta Coll., Stockton, Calif., 1982—; flown 7 expts. on Russian space craft, 5 on Am. space crafts. Author over 230 scientific papers. Ham radio operator City of Sunnyvale, Ames Rsch. Ctr., 1976—. With U.S. Army, 1942-45. Mem. No. Calif. Soc. Electron Microscopy (v.p., pres.), Electron Microscope Soc. Am. (biol. dir.), N.Y. Acad. Scis., Sigma Xi.

Home: PO Box 2014 Sunnyvale CA 94087-0014 Office: NASA Ames Rsch Ctr Moffett Field CA 94035

PHILPOTT, LARRY LA FAYETTE, horn player; b. Alma, Ark., Apr. 5, 1937; s. Lester and Rena (Owens) P.; m. Elise Robichaud, Nov. 24, 1962 (div. June 1975); children: Daniel, Stacy; m. Anne Sokol, Feb. 14, 1984. B.S., Ga. So. Coll., 1962; Mus.M., Butler U., 1972. Instr. in horn Butler U., De Pauw U.; dir. music Cedarcrest Sch., Marysville, Wash., 1991—. Mem., N.C. Symphony, 1960, Savannah (Ga.) Symphony, L'Orchestre Symphonique de Quebec, Que., Can., 1962-64, prin. horn player, Indpls. Symphony Orch., 1964-89, Flagstaff Summer Festival, 1968—; artist in-residence Ind.-Purdue Indpls.; appeared with, Am. Shakespeare Theatre, summer 1965, Charlottetown Festival, summers 1967-68, Flagstaff Summer Festival, 1968-85, Marrowstone Music Festival, 1985—. Served with USN, 1956-60. Mem. Music Educators Nat. Conf., Am. Fedn. Musicians, Internat. Conf. Symphony and Opera Musicians, Internat. Horn Soc., Coll. Music Soc., Phi Mu Alpha Sinfonia. Home: 18115 Vineway Pl Arlington WA 98223-7407 Office: Cedarcrest Sch 6400 88th St NE Marysville WA 98270-2800

PHILPOTT, LINDSEY, civil engineer, researcher; b. Bridestowe, Devonshire, Eng., Aug. 2, 1948; came to U.S., 1983; s. George Anthony and Joyce Thirza (Teeling) P.; m. Christine May Pembury, Aug. 20, 1974 (div.); children: David, Elizabeth; m. Kathleen Linda Matson, Feb. 17, 1982 (div.); children: Nicholas, Benjamin; m. Kim Elaine Moore, Nov. 24, 1991. Higher Nat. Cert. in Civil Engring., Bristol (Eng.) Poly., 1973; BSCE, U. Ariz., 1986, MSCE, 1987. Registered profl. engr., Calif. Area structural engr. Dept. Environment (Property Svcs. Agy.), Bristol, 1971-73; civil engr. Webco Civil Engring., Exeter, Eng., 1973-75; tech. mgr. Devon & Cornwall Housing Assn., Plymouth, Eng., 1975-79; prin., architect S.W. Design, Plymouth, 1979-81; archtl. engr. United Bldg. Factories, Bahrain, 1981-83; jr. engr. Cheyne Owen, Tucson, 1983-87; civil engr. Engring. Sci. Inc., Pasadena, Calif., 1987-89; project engr. Black & Veatch, Santa Ana, Calif., 1989-90; sr. engr. Brown & Caldwell, Irvine, Calif., 1990-91; environ. engr. Met. Water Dist. So. Calif., 1991—. Foster parent Foster Parents Plan, Tucson, 1985-87; vol. reader tech. books Recording for the Blind, Hollywood, Calif., 1988-89, South Bay, Calif., 1990-91, Pomona, Calif., 1991—. Mem. ASCE, Am. Water Works Assn., Am. Water Resources Assn. (water quality com. 1990—), Internat. Ozone Assn., Water Pollution Control Fedn., Mensa, Engrs. Soc. (pres. 1985-86). Office: Met Water Dist Environ Compliance Divsn PO Box 699 San Dimas CA 91773

PHIPPS, CLAUDE RAYMOND, research scientist; b. Ponca City, Okla., Mar. 15, 1940; s. Claude Raymond Louis and Deva Pauline (DeWitt) P.; m. Lynn Malarney, Dec. 1, 1962 (div. Feb. 1989); 1 child, David Andrew. BS, MIT, 1961, MS, 1963; PhD, Stanford U., 1972. Rsch. staff Lawrence Livermore (Calif.) Nat. Lab., 1972-74, Los Alamos (N.Mex.) Nat. Lab., 1974—; assoc. dir. Alliance for Photonic Tech., Albuquerque, 1992; co-instr. "Pairs" Relationship Tng., Santa Fe, N.Mex., 1990—; dir. Santa Fe Investment Conf., 1987; mem. program com. MIT Workshop on High Temperature Superconductors, Cambridge, 1988; mem. Instl. R & D Com., Los Alamos Nat. Lab., 1990-92, project leader laser effects, 1982-87, mem. internat. rsch. tour, Australia, Japan, Scotland, 1988-89; invited discussion leader Gordon Conf. on Laser Particle Interactions, N.H., 1992. Co-author: Laser Ionization Mass Analysis, 1993; author internat. lecture series on laser surface interactions, Berlin, Antwerp, Marseilles, Xiamen, Cape Town, Durban, 1987—; contbr. articles to profl. jours. Lt. USN, 1963-65. Grad. fellow W. Alton Jones Found., N.Y.C., 1962-63. Home: 1621 Calle Torreon Santa Fe NM 87501 Office: Los Alamos Nat Lab Mail Stop E543 Los Alamos NM 87545

PI, WEN-YI SHIH, aircraft company engineer, researcher; b. Peiping, People's Republic of China, Feb. 28, 1935; came to U.S., 1959; d. Chih-Chuan and Hsiu-Yun (Yang) Shih; m. William Shu-Jong Pi, July 2, 1961; 1 child, Wilfred. BS, Nat. Taiwan U., Taipei, Republic of China, 1956; MS, Stanford U., 1961, PhD, 1963. Research assoc. Stanford (Calif.) U., 1963-64; engring. specialist Northrop Corp., Hawthorne, Calif., 1965-83, sr. tech. specialist, 1983—. Contbr. articles to profl. jours. Recipient Silver Achievement award Los Angeles YWCA, 1983; Amelia Earhart Scholar Zonta Internat., 1961-62. Fellow: AIAA (assoc.); mem. Sigma Xi. Office: Northrop Corp Aircraft Divsn One Northrop Ave Dept 3852/MF Hawthorne CA 90250-3277

PIAZZA, DUANE EUGENE, biomedical researcher; b. San Jose, Calif., June 5, 1954; s. Salvador Richard and Mary Bernice (Mirassou) P.; m. Sandra Patrignani, Sept. 19, 1992. BS in Biology, U. San Francisco, 1976; MA in Biology, San Francisco State U., 1986. Staff rsch. assoc. I U. Calif., San Francisco, 1975-81; sr. rsch. technician XOMA Corp., San Francisco, 1981-82; biologist II Syntex USA Inc., Palo Alto, Calif., 1982-85; pres., cons. Ryte For You, Oakland, Calif., 1985—; rsch. assoc. I Cetus Corp., Emeryville, Calif., 1986-90; rsch. assoc. II John Muir Cancer and Aging Rsch. Inst., Walnut Creek, Calif., 1991-92; rsch. assoc. Pharmagenesis, Palo Alto, Calif., 1993—. CPR instr. ARC, San Francisco, 1980-86, vol. 1st aid sta. instr., Santa Cruz, 1985-86, vol. 1st aid sta. disaster action team, Oakland, 1986—, br. chmn. disaster action team, 1987-88; treas. Reganti Homeowner Assn., 1990-92. Mem. AAAS, Am. Soc. Microbiology, N.Y. Acad. Scis., Astron. Soc. Pacific, Planetary Soc., Mt. Diablo Astronomy Soc. Republican. Roman Catholic. Home: 613 Malarin Ave Santa Clara CA 95050

PIAZZA, MICHAEL JOSEPH, professional baseball player; b. Norristown, Pa., Sept. 4, 1968. Student, Miami (Fla.)-Dade C.C. Player L.A. Dodgers, 1992—; mem. Nat. League All-Star Team, 1993. Office: LA Dodgers Dodger Stadium Los Angeles CA 90012

PICARD, ROBERT GEORGE, educator, writer; b. Pasadena, Calif., July 15, 1951; s. Robert William and Roberta Marlene (Robertson) P.; m. Terry Jean Haverstock, Dec. 28, 1971 (div. May 1979); m. Elizabeth Louise Carpelan, Sept. 15, 1979; children: Anna Elisabeth, Helena Caroline, Alexander William. BA, Loma Linda U., 1974; MA, Calif. State U., Fullerton, 1980; PhD, U. Mo., 1983. Editor Riverside (Calif.) Community News, 1977-79; copy editor, wire editor Ontario (Calif.) Daily Report, 1979-80; publs. editor Freedom of Info. Ctr., Columbia, Mo., 1980-83; from asst. to assoc. prof. La. State U., Baton Rouge, 1983-87; assoc. prof., dir. communication industries mgmt. Emerson Coll., Boston, 1987-90; prof. Calif. State U., Fullerton, 1990—; chair Com. for Media Diversity, Boston, 1987—; vis. prof. Turku (Finland) Sch. Econs., 1993—. Author: The Press and the Decline of Democracy, 1985, The Ravens of Odin: The Press in the Nordic Nations, 1988, Media Economics: Concepts and Issues, 1989, In the Camera's Eye: News Coverage of Terrorist Events, 1991, Media Portrayals of Terrorism, 1993; editor: Press Concentration and Monopoly, 1988, The Cable Network's Handbook, 1993; editor Jour. Media Econs., 1988—; assoc. editor Polit. Communication and Persuasion, 1988-91. Chpt. pres. ACLU, Baton Rouge, 1985-87; bd. dirs. New England Inst. for Peace, Boston, 1988-90; coord. publicity Habitat for Humanity, Riverside, 1991-92. Recipient Internat. Rsch. award Assn. for the Advancement of Policy, Rsch. and Devel., 1984, Outstanding Rsch. award Phi Kappa Phi, 1986. Mem. Assn. for Edn. in Journalism and Mass Communication (chair profl. freedom and responsibility com. 1992-93). Home: 2806 Gertrude St Riverside CA 92506 Office: Calif State U Dept Communications Fullerton CA 92634

PICCININI, ROBERT M., grocery store chain executive. Chief exec. officer Save Mart Supermarkets, Modesto, Calif. Office: Save Mart Supermarkets PO Box 4278 Modesto CA 95352-4278

PICCONE, JOSEPH ANTHONY, industrial engineer; b. Louisville, Colo., Dec. 19, 1935; s. Joseph Piccone and Lucille Elizabeth (Johnson) Shepherd; m. Linda M. Ingemarson, July 28, 1955; children: Sharon Louise, Aaron Arthur. Student, U. Colo., 1963-65, Ariz. State U., 1965-66, Phoenix Coll., 1966-67, Glendale Community Coll., 1967-69. Methods engr. Martin Marietta Corp., Denver, 1957-64, Goodyear Aerospace Corp., Litchfield Park, Ariz., 1964-65; cost engr. Sperry Flight Systems, Phoenix, 1965-70; cons. engr. M.E.S.A. Program Inc., Phoenix, 1970-73; indsl. engr. Goodyear Aerospace Corp., Litchfield Park, 1973-76; mgmt. engr. St. Mary's Hosp., Tucson, 1976-77; mgr. design devel. Bapt. Hosps. and Health Systems, Phoenix, 1977-88; prin. Costcomp, Glendale, Ariz., 1988-91; mgr. indsl. engring. Tooh Dineh Industries, Leupp (Navajo Nation), Ariz., 1991—. Contbr. articles to profl. jours. Pres. St. Jerome's PTO, 1970; v.p. Washington Schs. PTA, Phoenix, 1969; mem. exec. com. Boy Scouts Am. Manzanita Sch., Phoenix, 1968; precinct capt. Dem. Com., Phoenix, 1969-72. Mem. Inst. Indsl. Engrs. (pres. 1980-81, v.p. 1979-80, dir. 1967-78, Excellence award 1978, 81), Soc. Health Systems, Healthcare Info. Mgmt. Systems Soc. Roman Catholic. Home: Apt 4G 3850 N Fanning Dr Apt G4 Flagstaff AZ 86004-2289 Office: Tooh Dineh Industries Inc HC-61 Box 58 Winslow AZ 86047

PICK, ARTHUR JOSEPH, JR., chamber of commerce executive; b. Louisville, Mar. 22, 1931. BS, U. Calif., Riverside, 1959; grad., Coro Found., L.A., 1960; MA in Urban Studies, Occidental Coll., 1969. Pres. Greater Riverside C. of C., 1972—. Mem. pres. Riverside Monday Morning Group, 1991—; pres. Young Life Riverside, 1966-68; pres. Riverside Symphony Orch. Soc. 1966-69; founding pres. Riverside Cultural Arts Coun., 1969-71; elected Riverside City Coun., 1967, re-elected, 1971; founder Friends of Calif. Bapt. Coll., 1978, Friends of La Sierra U., Riverside, 1978, Friends of Sherman Indian High Sch., 1988, Friends of Calif. Sch. for the Deaf, Riverside, 1988 . With U.S. Army, 1953-55; trustee La Sierra U., 1992—; mem. Calif./Nev. Super Speed Train Commn., 1992—. Recipient Disting. Svc. award Riverside Jaycees, 1966, Patron of Arts award Cultural Arts Coun., 1977, Vernon Jordan Humanitarian award Riverside Area Urban League, 1989, Citizen of Yr. award Riverside Police Officers Assn., 1990, Atlas award Riverside YWCA, 1990, Community Svc. award, 1990; named Young Man of Yr. Riverside Jaycees, 1966, Citizen of Yr. Internat. Rels. Coun., 1992. Mem. Mayors and Councilmen Assn. Riverside County (pres. 1968-69), Inland Area Urban League (founder, bd. dirs., Pacesetter award 1982), U. Calif. Alumni Assn. Riverside (bd. dirs. 1981-87), Riverside Jaycees (life), Riverside Raincross Club. Office: Greater Riverside C of C 4261 N Main St Riverside CA 92501-3886

PICK, DANIEL LLOYD, mathematician; b. San Diego, Apr. 21, 1959; s. Richard Allen and Gracia (Molina) P. AB, Brown U., 1982; postgrad., San Diego State U., 1983-84, 89, U. Calif., Irvine, 1992. Documentation writer Software Products Internat., San Diego, 1984-85; tech. writer Ashton-Tate, Torrance, Calif., 1985-86; product info. analyst Unisys, Camarillo, Calif., 1986-87; freelance tech. writer San Diego, 1987-92; judge Soc. for Tech. Comm. San Diego Tech. Publs. Competition, 1991. Author: (manual) Using dBASE Mac, 1986. Cubmaster Pack 261, Boy Scouts Am., La Jolla, Calif., 1990-92. Named Eagle Scout, Boy Scouts Am., 1975; grad. fellowship U. Calif., Irvine, 1992—. Mem. SIAM, Associated Alumni Brown U. Office: 408 Verano Pl Irvine CA 92715

PICK, JAMES BLOCK, management and sociology educator; b. Chgo., July 29, 1943; s. Grant Julius and Helen (Block) P. BA, Northwestern U., 1966; MS in Edn., No. Ill. U., 1969; PhD, U. Calif., Irvine, 1974, C.D.P., 1980. C.S.P., 1985, C.C.P., 1986. Asst. rsch. statistician, lectr. Grad. Sch. Mgmt. U. Calif., Riverside, 1975-91, dir. computing, 1984-91; co-dir. U.S.-Mex. Database Project, 1988-91; assoc. prof. mgmt. and bus., dir. info. mgmt. program U. Redlands, 1991—; cons. U.S. Census Bur. Internat. Div., 1978: mem. Univ. Commons Bd., 1982-86; mem. bd. govs. PCCLAS, Assn. Borderlands Studies, 1989-92. Trustee Newport Harbor Art Mus., 1981-87, 88—, chmn. permanent collection com., 1987-91, v.p., 1991—. Recipient Thunderbird award Bus. Assn. Latin Am. Studies, 1993. Mem. AAAS, Assn. Computing Machinery, Assn. Systems Mgmt. (pres. Orange County chpt. 1978-79), Am. Statis. Assn., Population Assn. Am., Internat. Union for Sci. Study of Population, Soc. Info. Mgmt. Club, Standard (Chgo.). Author: Geothermal Energy Development, 1982, Computer Systems in Business, 1986, Atlas of Mexico, 1989; condr. research in info. systems, population, environ. studies; contbr. sci. articles to publs. in fields.

PICKEL, FREDERICK HUGH, energy company executive; b. Seattle, June 12, 1952; s. Hugh E. Jr. and Dorothy J. (Miller) P.; m. Carol Chilk, Jan. 15, 1983. BS in Engring. and Econs., Harvey Mudd Coll., Claremont, Calif., 1974; MS in Ops. Rsch., MIT, 1978, MCE, 1978, PhD in Engring. Econs., 1982. Gen. engr. FPC, Washington, 1974-75; mgmt. cons. SRI Internat. Decision Analysis Group, Menlo Park, Calif., 1976-77; adminstr. spl. energy projects New Eng. Electric, Westboro, Mass., 1981-84; dir. bus. devel. and energy sales Pacific Enterprises/Pacific Energy, L.A., 1984-86; mgr. strategy and devel. Pacific Enterprises, L.A., 1986-89; mgr. gas acquisition policy Pacific Enterprises/So. Calif. Gas Co., L.A., 1989—; cons. New Eng. Electric, others, Cambridge, Mass., 1978-81. Contbr. articles to profl. jours. Trustee Harvey Mudd Coll., 1989-92, campaign cabinet, 1991—; mem. La Brea Hancock Homeowners Assn., L.A., 1990—; mem. Gov.'s Commn. on Cogeneration, Boston, 1977-78. NSF scholar, 1975-76. Mem. L.A. Athletic Club, Internat. Assn. Energy Econs. (pres. L.A. chpt. 1989, Boston chpt. 1984), Am. Econs. Assn., Harvey Mudd Coll. Alumni Assn. (gov. 1986—, treas. 1988-89). Home: 618 S Mansfield Ave Los Angeles CA 90036-3514 Office: So Calif Gas Co 555 W 5th St ML 28E0 Los Angeles CA 90013-1011

PICKENS, ALEXANDER LEGRAND, education educator; b. Waco, Tex., Aug. 31, 1921; s. Alex LeGrand and Elma L. (Johnson) P.; m. Frances M. Jenkins, Aug. 20, 1955. B.A., So. Methodist U., 1950; M.A., North Tex. State U., Denton, 1952; Ed.D., Columbia U., 1959. Tchr. art public schs. Dallas, 1950-53, Elizabeth, N.J., 1953-54; mem. faculty Coll. Architecture and Design U. Mich., 1954-59; mem. faculty dept. art U. Ga., Athens, 1959-62; mem. faculty Coll. Edn. U. Hawaii, Honolulu, 1962—, prof. edn., 1968—, chmn. doctoral studies curriculum instrn. Coll. Edn., 1984-89, asst. to dean for coll. devel., 1989—; dir. children's classes Ft. Worth Children's Museum, 1951-53; head art Nat. Music Camp, Interlochen, Mich., summers 1957-58, U. Oreg., Portland, summers 1959-60, 62; cons. youth art activities Foremost Dairies, 1964-74; cons. art films United World Films, 1970-75; art edn. cons. Honolulu Paper Co., 1970-76, Kamehameha Sch., Bishop Estate, 1978—. Exhibited ceramics, Wichita Internat. Exhbn., Syracuse (N.Y.) Nat. Exhbn., St. Louis Mus., Dallas Mus., San Antonio Mus., Detroit Art Inst., Hawaii Craftsmen, also others; editorial bd.: Arts and Activities mag, 1955-82; editor: U. Hawaii Ednl. Perspectives, 1964—; contbr. articles to profl. jours. Memm. adult com. Dallas County chpt. Jr. ARC, 1951-53; exec. com. Dallas Crafts Guild, 1950-53; v.p., publicity chmn. U. Ga. Community Concert Assn., 1960-62, mem., program chmn. Gov.'s Commn. Observing 150 Yrs. Pub. Edn. in Hawaii, 1990-91. Served with USAAF. Recipient award merit, Tex. State Fair, 1957, All-Am. award, Ednl. Press Assn. Am., 1968, 70, 72, 75, 79, Regents' medal for excellence in teaching, U. Hawaii, 1989, Gov.'s Commn. Observance of 150 Yrs. Pub. Edn., 1990-91. Mem. Internat. Soc. Edn., NEA, Nat. Art Edn. Assn., AAUP, Phi Delta Kappa, Kappa Delta Pi. Address: 1471 Kalaepohaku St Honolulu HI 96816

PICKENS, WILLIAM H., university administrator; b. Albuquerque, June 24, 1946; s. William H. Pickens and Sammie Bratton Johnson; m. Monica Neville; children: Rena Michelle, Bryan Thomas. BA in History magna cum laude, U. N.Mex., 1968, MA in Econ. History, 1971; PhD in U.S. Econ. History, U. Calif., Davis, 1976. Acting dir. plant facilities Los Rios Community Coll. Dist., Sacramento, 1983-84; dep. dir. fiscal analysis Calif. Postsecondary Edn. Commn., 1978-86, exec. dir., 1986-88; vis. scholar Ctr. for Studies in Higher Edn., U. Calif., Berkeley, 1989; assoc. v.p. adminstrn. Calif. State U., Sacramento, 1989—; vis. lectr. U. Calif., Berkeley, 1981-82, 89-90; cons. temporary com. on edn. policies State of Wash., 1983; mem. adv. bd. Nat. Forum Coll. Financing Alternatives, Nat. Ctr. for Postsecondary Governance and Fin., Columbia Tchrs. Coll., 1986-91; nat. coord. State Higher Edn. Fin. Officers, 1982-84, exec. com., 1981-85; mem. Western Interstate Commn. on Higher Edn. Task Force on Minorities in Higher Edn., 1986-87; cons. L.A. Community Coll. Dist., 1984, San Francisco Community Coll. Dist., 1991. Cons. editor Jour. Higher Edn., 1989—; contbr. articles to profl. jours. Bd. dirs., CFO Davis Community Housing Corp., 1989—; mem. sch. site coun. Emerson Jr. High, Davis, 1991—. U. Calif. regents fellow, 1972, 74-75; recipient Community Achievement Recognition, Sacramento Med. Found. Blood Ctr., 1989. Mem. Nat. Assn. Coll. and Univ. Bus. Officers (fin. mgmt. com. 1991—), Phi Beta Kappa, Phi Kappa Phi. Presbyterian. Office: 1525 3d St Sacramento CA 95814

PICKERING, AVAJANE, specialized education facility executive; b. New Castle, Ind., Nov. 5, 1951; d. George Willard and Elsie Jean (Wicker) P. BA, Purdue U., 1974; MS in Spl. Edn., U. Utah, 1983, PhD, 1991. Cert. spl. edn. Co-dir. presch. for gifted students, 1970-74; tchr. Granite Community Edn., Salt Lake City, 1974-79; tchr. coordinator Salt Lake City Schs., 1975-85; adminstrv. dir., owner Specialized Ednl. Programming Svc., Inc., Salt Lake City, 1976—; mem. Utah Profl. Adv. Bd.; adj. instr. U. Utah, Salt Lake City, 1985—. Rep. del. Utah State Conv., also county conv.; vol. tour guide, hostess Temple Square, Ch. Jesus Christ of Latter-Day Saints, 1983-88. Mem. Coun. for Exceptional Children, Coun. for Learning Disabilities, Learning Disability Assn., Ednl. Therapy Assn. Profl., Learning Disabilities Assn. Utah (profl. adv. bd.), Attention Deficit Coalition Utah (treas.), Hadassah, Delta Kappa Gamma, Phi Kappa Phi. Home: 1595 S 2100 E Salt Lake City UT 84108-2750 Office: Specialized Ednl Programming Svcs 1760 S 1100 E Salt Lake City UT 84105-3430

PICKETT, DAVID FRANKLIN, JR., aerospace company executive; b. Littlefield, Tex., May 3, 1936; s. David Franklin and Dottie Ardell (Britton) P.; m. B. Christine Klop, Aug. 21, 1971. AA, Del Mar Coll., Corpus Christi, 1960; BS in Chem., U. Tex., 1962, MA, 1965, PhD, 1970. Rsch. chemist Am. Magnesium Co., Snyder, Tex., 1969-70; chemist, chem. engr. Air Force Aero Propulsion Lab., Dayton, Ohio, 1970-78; sect. head Hughes Aircraft Co., El Segundo, Calif., 1978-84; asst. dept. mgr. Hughes Aircraft Co., El Segundo, 1984-86, dept. mgr., 1986-89, prodn. line mgr., 1990-91, program mgr., 1991—; ECS coordinator ann. battery conf. Calif. State U., Long Beach, 1987-89. Inventor preparation of nickel electrodes, 1974, prodn. of cadmium electrodes, 1975; author: Nickel Electrode & NiCd Cell Technology, 1984-88. With USN, 1955-57. Mem. Southern Calif./Nev. Electrochem. Soc. (sec. 1980-81, vice chmn. 1981-82, chmn. 1982-83), Am. Chem. Soc., Am. Inst. Aeronautics and Astronautics, Phi Lambda Upsilon. Baptist. Home: 4 Hilltop Cir Palos Verdes Peninsula CA 90274-3432 Office: Hughes Indsl Electronics Co Electron Dynamics Divsn 3100 Lomita Blvd Torrance CA 90505-5104

PICKETT, MICHAEL D., computer hardware and software distributor; b. 1947. BSBA, U. So. Calif. With Deloitte Haskins & Sells, 1969-83; v.p. fin., chief fin. officer Merisel Internat. (formerly Softsel Computer Products), 1983-86, pres., chief oper. officer, 1986-88, pres., chief exec. officer, bd. dirs., 1988—. Office: Merisel Internat 200 Continental Blvd El Segundo CA 90245-4510

PICKETT, THEODORE R., JR., professional consultant, arbitrator, director; b. Columbus, Nebr., May 8, 1923; s. Theodore Roy and Maude Ether (Lieber) P.; m; Mary Eleanor Brown Pickett, July 18, 1947; children: Theodore III, Mary C., Christine S., Forrest B. AB, San Diego State, 1949; MBA, Harvard, Cambridge, Mass., 1957. CPA,Ariz. and Calif.; Community Coll. Teaching Cert. U.S. Army, 1950-61; asst. dean and prof. acct. Ariz. State U., Tempe, Ariz., 1961-62; logistical mgr. Litton Systems, L.A., 1962-63; partner Regional CPA Firm, Phoenix, 1964-78; pres. CEO Limited Consulting, Tempe, Ariz., 1979—; adv. bd. mem. Am. Arbitration Assn., 1991—; pres. Ariz. Bd. Acctg., Phoenix, 1977-78. Contbr. articles to profl. & mil. jours. With U.S. Navy, 1942-44, U.S. Marine Corps, 1944-46; col. U.S. Army, 1950-61. Decorated Legion of Merit, Purple Heart, Air medal with oak leaf cluster, Meritorious Svc. medal. Mem. Nat. Assn. State Bds. Acctg. (bd. dirs. 1976-77), Nat. Assn. Corp. Dirs. (charter), Ariz. Soc. CPAs (pres. 1972-73), Assn. U.S. Army, Ret. Officers Assn., Mil. Order Purple Heart, Mil. Order World Wars, Tempe C. of C. (mil. affairs com.), Masons. Home: PO Box 24775 Tempe AZ 85285-4775

PICKLE, JOSEPH WESLEY, JR., religion educator; b. Denver, Apr. 8, 1935; s. Joseph Wesley and Wilhelmina (Blacketor) P.; m. Judith Ann Siebert, June 28, 1958; children: David E., Kathryn E., Steven J. BA, Carleton Coll., 1957; B.D., Chgo. Theol. Sem., 1961; MA, U. Chgo., 1962, PhD, 1969. Ordained to ministry Am. Bapt. Conv., 1962. Asst. pastor Judson Meml. Ch., N.Y.C., 1959-60; acting dean summer session Colo. Coll., Colorado Springs, 1969-70, from asst. prof. to prof. religion, 1964—; vis. prof. theology Iliff Sch. Theology, Denver, 1984; vis. prof. religious studies U. Zimbabwe, Harare, 1989; cons. Colo. Humanities Program, Denver, 1975-89; coord. Sheffer Meml. Fund, Colo. Coll., Colorado Springs, 1983—. Co-editor Papers of the 19th Century Theology Group, 1978, 88, 93. Pres. bd. dirs. Pikes Peak Mental Health Ctr., Colorado Springs, 1975; chmn. Colo. Health Facilities Rev. Coun., Denver, 1979-84; mem. Colo. Health Facilities Rev. Coun., Denver, 1976-84, Colo. Bd. Health, Denver, 1986-91. Am. Bapt. Conv. scholar, 1953-59; Fulbright Hays Grad. fellow Fulbright Commn., U. Tübingen, Fed. Republic Germany, 1963-64, Danforth fellow, 1957-63, Joseph Malone fellow, 1987. Fellow Soc. for Values in Higher Edn.; mem. Am. Theol. Soc., Am. Acad. Religion (regional pres. 1983-84, 92-93), Cath. Theol. Soc. Am. Democrat. Home: 20 W Caramillo St Colorado Springs CO 80907-7314 Office: Colo Coll 14 E Cache La Poudre St Colorado Springs CO 80903-3243

PICKLE, JUDITH ANN, college official; b. Chgo., Apr. 28, 1935; d. Frederick William and Evelyn J. (Deinhart) Siebert; m. Joseph Wesley Pickle Jr., June 28, 1958; children: David Edward, Kathryn Evelyn, Steven Joseph. BA, Carleton Coll., 1957; MEd, Goucher Coll., 1958. Cert. tchr., Colo. Elem. tchr. Woodmere (N.Y.) Acad., 1959-60, Harvey (Ill.) Pub. Schs., 1958-59, 60-61; supr. student tchrs. The Colo. Coll., Colorado Springs, 1966-80, coord. vol. aide program, 1974-80; dir. vols. and community edn. The Pikes Peak Hospice, Colorado Springs, 1981-87; program coord. Colo. Coll., Colorado Springs, 1988—, coord. elderhostel, 1989-90, 92—; bd. dirs. Pikes Peak Hospice, Colorado Springs. Co-editor: Helen Hunt Jacksons' Colorado, 1989; editor: (newsletter) La Tertulia, 1989—. Mem. Open Space Adv. Coun., Colorado Springs (Colo.) Pk. Dept., 1980-83, chmn., 1982. Recipient Faculty Rsch. and Devel. grants The Colo. Coll., Colorado Springs, 1973, 79, Excellence in Ednl. Programming award Nat. Hospice Orgn., Washington, 1986. Mem. Woman's Ednl. Soc., Woman's Literary Club (pres. 1991-92), Springs Area Beautiful Assn. (sec. 1979-81), Phi Delta Kappa. Democrat. Congregationalist. Home: 20 W Caramillo Colorado Springs CO 80907 Office: Colo Coll 14 E Cache la Poudre Colorado Springs CO 80903

PICKMAN, PHILLIP, data processing executive; b. Mpls., May 6, 1938; s. Sam and Rose G. (Chiat) P.; m. 1962; children: Michael, Kara, Todd. BS, U. Minn., 1960, MSME, 1962. Supr. oper. systems Bell Telephone Labs., Whippany, N.J., 1962-68; mgr. systems planning Dayton Hudson Corp., Mpls., 1968-73; dir. info. svcs. Red Owl Stores, Inc., Mpls., 1973-74; dir. systems and mgmt. info cook United, Cleve., 1974-77; regional v.p. May Dept. Stores, L.A., 1977-79; sr. assoc., exec. recruiter Westlake Group, Westlake Village, Calif., 1980-81; pres. and founder Info. Resources Group, Westlake Village, Calif., 1981-87; dir. product mgmt. Cap Gemini Am., Canoga Park, Calif., 1987—. Treas. Foxmoor Hills Homeowners Assn., Westlake Village, 1989—90, pres. 1991-92, Morris County (N.J.) Dem. County Com., 1965-68; vice chmn. Parsippany-Troy Hills (N.J.) Planning Bd., 1967-68; mem. adv. bd. B'nai Brith Hillel Found., U. Minn., 1972-73. Mem. Tau Beta Pi, Pi Tau Sigma. Jewish. Home: 1815 Stonegate St Westlake Village CA 91361 Office: Cap Gemini Am 21107 Vanowen St Canoga Park CA 91303-2852

PICKRELL, THOMAS RICHARD, retired oil company executive; b. Jermyn, Tex., Dec. 30, 1926; s. Mont Bolt and Martha Alice (Dodson) P.; m. M. Earline Bowen, Sept. 9, 1950; children—Thomas Wayne, Michael Bowen, Kent Richard, Paul Keith. B.S., North Tex. State U., 1951, M.B.A., 1952; postgrad., Ohio State U., 1954-55; advanced mgmt. program, Harvard U., 1979. CPA, Tex. Auditor, acct. Conoco, Inc., Ponca City, Okla., 1955-62; mgr. acctg. Conoco, Inc., Houston, 1965-67; asst. controller Conoco, Inc., Ponca City, 1967-81; v.p., controller Conoco, Inc., Stamford, Conn., 1982-83, Wilmington, Del., 1983-85; asst. prof. Okla. State U., Stillwater, Okla., 1962-63; controller Douglas Oil Co., Los Angeles, 1963-65; mem. adv. bd. dept. acctg. North Tex. State U., Denton, 1978-85; mem. adv. bd. Coll. Bus., Kansas State U., Manhattan, 1979-81. Bd. dirs. YMCA, Ponca City, 1976-78, Kay Guidance Clinic, Ponca City, 1971-74, United Way, Ponca City, 1979-81; chmn. Charter Rev. Com., Ponca City, 1971-72. Served to sgt. U.S. Army, 1944-46; ETO. Mem. AICPA, Fin. Execs. Inst. (pres. Okla. chpt. 1972), Am. Petroleum Inst. (acctg. com., gen. com.), Ponca City Country Club (pres. 1980-81), Rotary (pres. Ponca City club 1973-74), Beta Gamma Sigma, Beta Alpha Psi. Republican. Presbyterian. Home: RR 4 Box 209B Santa Fe NM 87501-9804

PIDGEON, CHRISTOPHER WILLIAM, computer scientist, consultant; b. Balt., Jan. 24, 1950; s. John Leeds and Sally Louise (Trow) P.; m. Virginia Estrada, Nov. 16, 1991; 1 child, Jennifer Virginié. BSBA, Calif. State Poly. U., 1976, MBA, 1980; MS in Info. and Computer Sci., U. Calif., Irvine,

1983, PhD in Info. and Computer Sci., 1990. Programmer, analyst Press-Enterprise Newspaper, Riverside, Calif., 1971-77; systems analyst County of Riverside, 1977-78; mgr. Sun-Telegram Newspaper, San Bernardino, Calif., 1978-79; prof. computer info. systems Calif. State Poly. U. Coll. Bus., Pomona, Calif., 1979—; chief technologist Hughes Aircraft Co. Space and Communications Group, L.A., 1987—; software engring. cons. Christopher W. Pidgeon, Inc., Riverside, 1985-87. Author: Structured Analysis Methods for Computer Information Systems, 1985. With USN, 1973-75, Vietnam. Mem. IEEE, Assn. for Computing Machinery. Home: 13242 Mindanao Way Marina Del Rey CA 90292

PIEPER, DAROLD D., lawyer; b. Vallejo, Calif., Dec. 30, 1944; s. Walter A. H. and Vera Mae (Ellis) P.; m. Barbara Gillis, Dec. 20, 1969; 1 child, Christopher Radcliffe. AB, UCLA, 1967; JD, USC, 1970. Bar: Calif. 1971. Ops. rsch. analyst Naval Weapons Ctr., China Lake, Calif., 1966-69; assoc. Richards, Watson & Gershon, L.A., 1970-76, ptnr., 1976—; spl. counsel L.A. County Transp. Commn., 1984—; commr. L.A. County Delinquency and Crime Commmn., 1983—, pres., 1987—; chmn. L.A. County Delinquency Prevention Planning Coun., 1987-90. Contbr. articles to profl. jours. Peace officer Pasadena (Calif.) Police Res. Unit, 1972-87, dep. comdr., 1979-81, comdr., 1982-84; chmn. pub. safety commn. City of La Canada Flintridge, Calif., 1977-82, commr. 1977-88; bd. dirs. La Canada Flintridge Coordinating Council, 1975-82, pres. 1977-78; exec. dir. Cityhood Action Com., 1975-76; active Calif. Rep. Party, Appellate Circle of Legion Lex U. So. Calif.; sponsoring mem. L.A. County Mus. Art; active La Canada Flintridge Tournament of Roses assn., Verdugo Hills Hosp. Assocs., Verdugo Hills Hosp. Found.; chmn. Youth Opportunities United, Inc., 1990—, vice-chmn. 1988-89, bd. dirs. 1988—; mem. L.A. County Justice Systems Adv. Group, 1987-92; trustee Lanterman Hist. Mus. Found., 1989—. Recipient commendation for Community Service, L.A. County Bd. Suprs., 1978. Mem. La Canada Flintridge C. of C. and Community Assn. (pres. 1981, bd. dirs. 1976-83), Navy League U.S., Pacific Legal Found., Peace Officers Assn. L.A. County, UCLA Alumni Assn. (life), U. So. Calif. Alumni Assn. (life), L.A. County Bar Assn., Calif. Bar Assn., ABA, U. So. Calif. Law Alumni Assn., Calif. Club. Office: Richards Watson & Gershon 333 S Hope St 38th Fl Los Angeles CA 90071

PIERCE, DEBORAH MARY, educator; b. Charleston, W. Va.; d. Edward Ernest and Elizabeth Anne (Trent) P.; m. Henry M. Armetta, Sept. 1, 1967 (div. 1981); children: Rosse Matthew Armetta, Stacey Elizabeth Pierce. Student, U. Tenn., 1956-59, Broward Jr. Coll., 1968-69; BA, San Francisco State U., 1977. Cert. elem. tchr., Calif. Pub. relations assoc. San Francisco Internat. Film Festival, 1965-66; account exec. Stover & Assocs., San Francisco, 1966-67; tchr. San Francisco Archdiocese Office of Cath. Schs., 1980-87; with The Calif. Study, Inc. (formerly Tchr's. Registry), Tiburon, Calif., 1988—; pvt. practice as paralegal San Francisco, 1989—; tchr. Jefferson Sch. Dist., Daly City, Calif., 1989-91. Author: (with Frances Spatz Leighton) I Prayed Myself Slim, 1960. Pres. Mothers Alone Working, San Francisco, 1966, PTA, San Francisco, 1979, Parent Teacher Student Assn., San Francisco, 1984; apptd. Calif. State Bd. Welfare Community Rels., Com., 1964-66; active feminist movement. Named Model of the Yr. Modeling Assn. Am., 1962. Mem. People Med. Soc., Assn. for Rsch. and Enlightenment, A Course in Miracles, Commonwealth Club Calif, Angel Club San Francisco. Democrat. Home: 1479 48th Ave Apt # 2 San Francisco CA 94122

PIERCE, GEORGE ADAMS, university administrator, educator; b. Carlsbad, N.Mex., May 21, 1943; s. Jack Colwell and Shirley (Adams) P.; m. Margaret Mary Brakel, Feb. 10, 1980; children: Christopher, Catherine Rose. BA in Polit. Sci., Fairleigh Dickinson U., 1969; MA in Polit. Sci., New Sch. Social Rsch., 1971; PhD in Higher Edn., Claremont Grad. Sch., 1976. Asst. dir. promotion Afco, N.Y.C., 1969-71; dir. spl. programs U. Calif., Riverside, 1971-73; asst. to pres. Claremont (Calif.) Grad. Sch., 1973-75; asst. to pres. Seattle U., 1975-78, dir. planning, 1978-83, v.p. adminstrn., 1983-87, v.p. planning, 1987-89; v.p. bus. and fin. affairs Western Wash. U., Bellingham, 1989—; chmn. regional rev. panel Truman Scholarship Found., 1977-90. Chmn. Seattle Ctr. Adv. Commn., 1977-83; bd. dirs. N.W. Kidney Found., Seattle, 1986—, YMCA, Bellingham, 1990—; chmn. pack 41 Boy Scouts Am., Bellingham, 1992—. With USAF, 1963-65. Recipient Cert. Merit Riverside County Comprehensive Health Planning, 1972, Cert. Appreciation Office Mayor City of Seattle, 1983, Nat. Truman Scholarship Found., 1986. Mem. Am. Assn. Higher Edn., Assn. Instnl. Rsch. (regional pres. 1977), Nat. Assn. Coll. and Univ. Bus. Officers (chmn. pers. and benefits com. 1992—), Rotary. Democrat. Roman Catholic. Home: 421 Morey Ave Bellingham WA 98225-6606 Office: Western Wash U Old Main 300 Bellingham WA 98225

PIERCE, HILDA (HILDA HERTA HARMEL), painter; b. Vienna, Austria; came to U.S., 1940; 1 child, Diana Rubin Daly. Student, Art Inst. of Chgo.; studied with Oskar Kokoschka, Salzburg, Austria. Art tchr. Highland Park (Ill.) Art Ctr., Sandburg Village Art Workshop, Chgo., Old Town Art Center, Chgo.; owner, operator Hilda Pierce Art Gallery, Laguna Beach, Calif., 1981-85; guest lectr. major art museums and Art Tours in France, Switzerland, Austria, Italy. One-woman shows include Fairweather Hardin Gallery, Chgo., Sherman Art Gallery, Chgo., Marshall Field Gallery, Chgo.; exhibited in group shows at Old Orchard Art Festival, Skokie, Ill., Union League Club (awards), North Shore Art League (awards), ARS Gallery of Art Inst. of Chgo.; represented in numerous private and corporate collections; commissioned for all art work including monoprints, oils and murals for superliner Carnival Cruise Lines 70,000 ton megaliner M.S. Fantasy, 1990; commd. 17 large murals for M.S. Imagination by Carnival Cruise Lines; contbr. articles to Chgo. Tribune Mag., American Artist Mag., Southwest Art Mag., SRA publs., others. Recipient Outstanding Achievement in Field of Art for Citizen Foreign Birth award Chgo. Immigrant's Svc. League. Mem. Arts Club of Chgo. Office: Hilda Pierce Studio PO Box 7390 Laguna Niguel CA 92607-7390

PIERCE, JEFFREY LEO, power systems engineer, consultant; b. Pitts., Nov. 27, 1951; s. Francis Leo and Hilda Elizabeth (Swartzer) P.; m. Vicki Lynn Freeman, Sept. 20, 1976 (div. Mar. 1985); 1 child, Rebecca Lynn; m. Samantha Elizabeth Cannon, Mar. 16, 1986; 1 child, Jonathan Leo. BSCE, U. Pitts., 1973, MSCE, 1977. Registered profl. engr. Asst. mgr. planning/studies Chester Engrs., Pitts., 1973-77; mgr. environ./indsl. engring. SE Techs., Inc., 1977-84; mgr. ind. power engr. SE Techs., Inc., L.A., 1984—. Contbr. articles to profl. jours. Mem. ASCE, ASME (chmn. western chpt. solid waste divsn. 1991-93), Assn. Energy Engrs. (charter), Water Pollution Control Fedn. Home: 4500 Spencer St Torrance CA 90503 Office: SE Techs Inc 98 Vanadium Rd Bridgeville PA 15017

PIERCE, LESTER LAURIN, retired pilot, aviation consultant; b. Merlin, Oreg., Sept. 26, 1907; s. Frank Arthur and Charlotte (Allen) P.; m. Helen Ramona Thomas, Mar. 22, 1937; children: Adrienne C. Freeman, Nancy E. Johnson. Grad. high sch., 1925. Theatre mgr. Redwood Theatres, Inc., Fortuna and Eureka, Calif., 1927-28; salesman, bookkeeper Thomas Furniture House, Eureka, 1930-39; pilot, mgr. Pierce Bros. Flying Svc., Eureka, 1934-41; aerial photographer Pierce Flying Svc., Eureka, 1934-75; chief flight instr. Govt. Approved Flight Sch., Eureka, 1947-60; aerial seeder, mgr., pres., salesman Pierce Flying Svc., Inc., Eureka, 1946-68; flight examiner FAA, Eureka, 1948-68, aircraft maintenance insp., 1950-68; mapping pilot Stand Aerial Surveys, Newark, 1948. Lt., flight tng., safety officer, USN, 1942, comdr. 1950. Mem. Soc. Aircraft Safety Investigators and Aviation Cons., OX-5 Club, Eureka Rotary Club, Elks. Home and Office: 3428 Jacoby Creek Rd Bayside CA 95524-9304

PIERCE, MARY LEE, financial planner; b. Mpls., Dec. 5, 1955; d. Patrick Bernard and Dona Jean (Henderscheid) P. BA in Geography and Sociology cum laude, U. Utah, 1978, M Human Resource Econs., 1985, cert. in urban planning, 1978; CFP, Coll. for Fin. Planning, Denver, 1991. CFP; lic. ins. saleswoman, Minn., Calif., Utah, Wash., Tex.; lic. Nat. Assn. Securities Dealers. Mem. design team IDS Fin. Svcs., Mpls., 1992-93.; fin. planner IDS Fin. Svcs., Murray, Utah, 1984—, bus. fin. planner, dist. mgr., 1986—; cons. West Side Community Coun., Salt Lake City, 1984. Vol. fundraiser Primary Children's Hosp., Salt Lake City, 1989, Sta. KUED-TV, Salt Lake City, 1989; mem. Profls. for Reperatory Dance Theatre, Salt Lake City, 1988—. Mem. LWV (off bd. chmn. Salt Lake City 1982-84), Salt Lake Area C. of C. (Leadership Utah). Democrat. Office: IDS Fin Svcs 6985 Union Park Ctr Ste 600 Midvale UT 84047

PIERCE, RICHARD AUSTIN, history educator; b. Manteca, Calif., July 26, 1918; s. J. Austin and Catherine (Treat) P.; m. Vera Hilda Morris, Jan. 5, 1955; 1 child, Catherine Hilda. BA, U. Calif., Berkeley, 1940, MA, 1952, PhD, 1956. Prof. Queen's U., Kingston, Ont., Can., 1959-83, prof. emeritus, 1983—; prof. history U. Alaska, Fairbanks, 1988—. Author: Russian Central Asia 1867-1917, 1960, Russia's Hawaiian Adventure 1815-1817, 1965, Eastward to Empire, Explorations and Conquest on the Russian Open Frontier to 1750, 1973 (with G.V. Lantzeff), Russian America: A Biographical Dictionary, 1990; editor/pubr.: Alaska History Series, vols. 1-40, 1972—. With U.S. Army, 1941-45. Fulbright fellow, 1953-54, Guggenheim fellow, 1965, U. Moscow Exch. Fellow, 1992. Home: 237 Yonge St, Kingston, ON Canada K7M 1G2 Office: Univ of Alaska Dept History Fairbanks AK 99775

PIERCE, ROBERT LORNE, petrochemical, oil and gas company executive. Chmn. and chief exec. officer Foothills Pipe Lines Ltd., Calgary, Alta., Can.; chmn. Pan-Alta. Gas.; bd. dirs., sr. v.p., NOVA Corp. of Alta.; bd. dirs. Bank of N.S. Mem. Can. C. of C. (bd. dirs.), Internstate Natural Gas Assn. Am. (bd. dirs.). Office: Nova Corp Alta, 801 7th Ave SW PO Box 2535, Calgary, AB Canada T2P 2N6

PIERCE, ROBERT WILLIAM, geology educator; b. Des Moines, Feb. 26, 1940; s. Robert William and Iona Ruth (Harris) P.; m. M. Jeanne Traastad, June 27, 1964; children—Robert Daniel, Joanna Ruth. A.B. Monmouth (Ill.) Coll., 1962; M.S., U. Ill., 1967, Ph.D., 1969. Instr. U. Ill., Urbana, 1967-69; asst. prof. then assoc. prof. U. Fla., Gainesville, 1969-82; assoc. prof. geology Eastern N.Mex. U., Portales, 1982—, chmn. dept. phys. scis., 1987—; vis. scientist N.Mex. Acad. Sci., 1984-87; dir. Electron Microscope Facility Eastern N.Mex. U., 1986—. Author articles on paleontology and stratigraphy. Leader Llano Estacado council Boy Scouts Am., 1982; coach Am. Youth Soccer Orgn., Portales, 1984—, referee, 1984—, instr., 1986—; referee U.S. Soccer Fedn., 1990—, N.Mex. High Schs., 1989—. Mem. Am. Assn. Petroleum Geologists, Geol. Soc. Am., Internat. Paleontol, Union, Soc. Econ. Paleontotogists and Mineralogists, Internat. Assn. Math. Geologists. Lodge: Kiwanis. Office: Ea NMex U Dept Phys Sci-Geology Portales NM 88130

PIERCE, RONALD LEE, accounting educator; b. El Paso, Tex., Jan. 8, 1939; m. Lorraine Schwendiman, June 15, 1964; children—Ronald Merlin, Julene, Kristin, Lee Alvin, Larry Thomas. B.A., Brigham Young U., 1963, M. Accountancy, 1965; postgrad. U. So. Calif., 1972-75. C.P.A., Utah, Calif. Staff acct. Peat, Marwick, Mitchell & Co., Salt Lake City, 1964-66; asst. to Corp. div. controller Boise Cascade Corp., 1966-67; pvt. practice tax, auditing, gen. acctg., Logan, Utah, 1967-72, Claremont, Calif., 1972—; asst. prof. acctg. Utah State U., Logan, 1967-72; mem. faculty Calif. State U.-Los Angeles, 1972—, assoc. prof. acctg., 1977—. Mem. Am. Inst. C.P.A.s, Am. Acctg. Assn., Inst. Internal Auditors. Mem. LDS Ch. Office: Calif State U Dept Acctg 5151 State University Dr Los Angeles CA 90032

PIERCE, SUSAN RESNECK, academic administrator, English educator; b. Janesville, Wis., Feb. 6, 1943; d. Elliott Jack and Dory (Block) Resneck; m. Kenneth H. Pierce; 1 child, Alexandra. AB, Wellesley Coll., 1965; MA, U. Chgo., 1966; PhD, U. Wis., 1972. Counselor 5 yr. program U. Wis., Madison, 1969-70, teaching asst., 1970-71, specialist program educationally disadvantaged children, part-time 1970-71; lectr. U. Wis., Rock County, 1970-71; from asst. prof. to prof. English Ithaca (N.Y.) Coll., 1973-83, chmn. dept., 1976-79, 81-82; dean Henry Kendall Coll. Arts and Scis., prof. English U. Tulsa, 1984-90; v.p. acad. affairs, prof. English Lewis and Clark Coll., Portland, Oreg., 1990-92; pres. U. of Puget Sound, Tacoma, 1992—; vis. assoc. prof. Princeton (N.J.) U., 1979; program officer div. ednl. programs NEH, 1982-83, asst. dir., 1983-84; bd. dirs. Janet Elson Scholarship Fund, 1984-1990, Tulsa Edn. Fund, Phillips Petroleum Scholarship Fund, 1985-90, Okla. Math. & Sci. High Sch., 1984-90, Hillcrest Med. Ctr., 1988-90; cons. U. Oreg., 1985, Drury Coll., Springfield, Mo., 1986; mem. Middle States and N. Cen. Accreditation Bds., 1986; mem. adv. com. Fed. Women's Program, NEH, 1982-83; participant Summit Meeting on Higher Edn., Dept. Edn., Washington, 1985; speaker, participant numerous ednl. meetings, sems., commencements; chair Frederick Ness Book Award Com. Assn. Am. Colls., 1986; mem. award selection com. Dana Found., 1986, 87; mem. Acad. Affairs Council, Univ. Senate, dir. tchr. edn., chmn. adv. group for tchr. preparation, ex-officio mem. all Coll. Arts and Scis. coms. and Faculty Council on Internat. Studies, all U. Tulsa; bd. dirs. Am. Conf. Acad. Deans; bd. trustees Hillcrest Med. Ctr. Author: The Moral of the Story, 1982, also numerous essays, jour. articles, book sects., book revs.; co-editor: Approaches to Teaching "Invisible Man"; reader profl. jours. Bd. dirs. Arts and Humanities Council, Tulsa, 1984-90; trustee Hillcrest Hosp., Tulsa, 1986-90 mem. cultural series com., community relations com. Jewish Fedn., Tulsa, 1986-90. Recipient Best Essay award Arix. Quar., 1979, Excellence in Teaching award N.Y. State Edn. Council, 1982, Superior Group Service award NEH, 1984, other teaching awards; Dana scholar, Ithaca Coll., 1980-81; Dana Research fellow, Ithaca Coll., 82-83; grantee Inst. for Ednl. Affairs, 1980, Ford Found., 1987, NEH, 1989. Mem. MLA (adv. com. on job market 1973-74), South Ctrl. MLA, Soc. for Values in Higher Edn., NCCJ (bd. dirs. Tulsa 1986-90), Assn. Am. Colls. (bd. dirs.), Am. Conf. Acad. Deans (bd. dirs. 1988-91), Phi Beta Kappa, Phi Kappa Phi, Phi Gamma Kappa. Office: U of Puget Sound 1500 N Warren Tacoma WA 98416

PIERCE, WILLIAM GAMEWELL, geologist; b. Gettysburg, S.D., Sept. 24, 1904; s. Lee I. and Mary Clyde (Gamewell) P.; m. May Bell Henry, Oct. 6, 1930; children: William Henry, Kenneth Lee, Diane May. AB, U. S.D., 1927; MA, Princeton U., 1929, PhD, 1931. Jr. to assoc. geologist U.S. Geol. Survey, Washington, 1929-39; geologist U.S. Geol. Survey, 1939-54, Menlo Park, Calif., 1954-74; scientist emeritus U.S. Geol. Survey, 1974—. Contbr. articles to profl. jours. Active Pub. Works Com., Los Altos Hills, Calif., 1976-84, Roads and Drainage Com., 1984-90. Recipient Disting. Svc. award Dept. Interior, 1965; named Centenial Geologist Wyo. Geol. Assn., 1990; grantee Nat. Sci. Found., 1962-63. Fellow Geol. Soc. Am.; mem. Am. Assn. Petroleum Geologists, Geol. Soc. Washington (sec. 1951). Democrat. Congregationalist. Home: 23200 Via Esplendor Villa 35 Cupertino CA 95014 Office: US Geol Survey 345 Middlefield Rd Menlo Park CA 94025-3591

PIERCE, WILLIAM RODGERS, retired educator; b. Topeka, Aug. 13, 1915; s. Robert Stevens and Esther (Rodgers) P.; m. Joann Geddes Randall, Sept. 19, 1942; children: Patricia Martha, John Randall. BSF, U. Wash., 1940, PhD, 1958; MF, Yale U., 1947. Inspector Dept. of Justice-Border Patrol, El Paso, Tex., 1940-42, Vaughn, N.Mex., 1940-42, Missoula, Mont., 1940-42; dist. ranger Dept. Agrl. Forest Svc. Region One, Mont. and Idaho, 1946-55; prof. forestry U. Mont., Missoula, 1955-81, ret., 1981; expert witness Quinault Indians, Tahola, Wash., 1971-87; computer programmer State of Mont., Missoula, 1981-85. chmn. Gig Harbor Penninsula Adv. Commn., Gig Harbor, 1986—. Lt. USNR, 1943-45. Mem. AAAS, Soc. of Am. Foresters (club and chpt. chmn., Golden Mem. 1991), Gig Harbor Lions (bd. dirs.), Nature Conservency, Sigma Xi. Home: 5801 28th Ave NW Gig Harbor WA 98335

PIERCY, GORDON CLAYTON, bank executive; b. Takoma Park, Md., Nov. 23, 1944; s. Gordon Clayton and Dorothy Florence (Brummer) P.; m. Roberta Margaret Walton, 1985; children: Elizabeth Anne, Kenneth Charles, Virginia Walton, Zachary Taylor Walton. BS, Syracuse U., 1966; MBA, Pace U., 1973. Mgmt. trainee Suburban Bank, Bethesda, Md., 1962-66; mktg. planning assoc. Chem. Bank, N.Y.C., 1966-70; sr. market devel. officer Seattle-First Nat. Bank, 1970-74; product expansion adminstr., mktg. planning mgr. VISA, Inc., San Francisco, 1974-76; v.p., dir. mktg. Wash. Mut. Savs. Bank, Seattle, 1976-82; v.p., mktg. dir. First Interstate Bank of Wash. N.A., 1983-86; sr. v.p. mktg., dir. Puget Sound Nat. Bank, Tacoma, 1986-92; sr. v.p., dir. mktg. and sales Key Bank, 1993—. Bd. dirs. Tacoma Pierce County Visitor & Conv. Bur., Seattle Better Bus. Bur. Mem. Am. Mktg. Assn. (bd. dirs.), Bank Mktg. Assn., Mktg. Communications Execs. Internat., Seattle Advt. Fedn. (chmn.), Am. Bankers Assn. (communications coun.), Sigma Nu, Alpha Kappa Psi, Delta Mu Delta. Episcopalian. Home: 17302 SE 45th St Issaquah WA 98027-7809 Office: PO Box 11500 Tacoma WA 98411-0500

PIERIK, MARILYN ANNE, librarian; b. Bellingham, Wash., Nov. 12, 1939; d. Estell Leslie and Anna Margarethe (Onigkeit) Bowers; m. Robert Vincent Pierik, July 25, 1964; children: David Vincent, Donald Lesley. AA, Chaffey Jr. Coll., Ontario, Calif., 1959; BA, Upland (Calif.) Coll., 1962; cert. in teaching, Claremont (Calif.) Coll., 1963; MSLS, U. So. Calif., L.A., 1973. Tchr. elem. Christ Episcopal Day Sch., Ontario, 1959-60; tchr. Bonita High Sch., La Verne, Calif., 1962-63; tchr., libr. Kettle Valley Sch. Dist. 14, Greenwood, Can., 1963-64; libr. asst. Monrovia (Calif.) Pub. Libr., 1964-67; with Mt. Hood Community Coll., Gresham, Oreg., 1972—, reference libr., 1983—, chair faculty scholarship com., 1987—; mem. site selection com. Multnomah County (Oreg.) Libr., New Gresham br., 1987, adv. com. Multnomah County Libr., Portland, Oreg., 1988-89; bd. dirs. Oreg. Episcopal Conf. of Deaf, 1985-92. Bd. dirs. East County Arts Alliance, Gresham 1987-91; vestry person, jr. warden St. Luke's Episc. Ch., 1989-92; founding pres., bd. dirs. Mt. Hood Pops, 1983-91, bd. dirs., 1983-91, bd. dirs., 1991—. Recipient Jeanette Parkhill Meml. award Chaffey Jr. Coll., 1959, Svc. award St. Luke's Episcopal Ch., 1983, 87, Edn. Svc. award Soroptimists, 1989. Mem. AAUW, NEA, Oreg. Edn. Assn., Oreg. Libr. Assn., ALA, Gresham Hist. Soc. Office: Mt Hood Community Coll Libr 26000 SE Stark St Gresham OR 97030-3300

PIERRE, DONALD ARTHUR, electrical engineering educator; b. Bloomington, Wis., July 2, 1936; s. Joseph J. and Odile M. (LeGrave) P.; m. Mary Louise Albin, Nov. 21, 1959; children: Michael, Louise, John. BSEE with honors, U. Ill., 1958; MSEE, U. So. Calif., 1960; PhDEE, U. Wis., 1962. Registered profl. engr., Mont. Mem. tech. staff Hughes Aircraft Co., L.A., 1958-62; asst. prof. elec. engring. Mont. State U., Bozeman, 1962-65, assoc. prof., 1965-69, prof., 1969—, head elec. engring. and computer sci. dept., 1979-84; prin. investigator numerous rsch. projects. Author: Mathematical Programming and Augmented Lagrangians, 1975, Optimization Theory with Applications, 1986; mem. editorial adv. bd. Jour. Computers and Elec. Engring., 1972—; contbr. over 100 articles to profl. jours. Recipient Wiley award Mont. State U., 1982, Teaching and Commitment to Honors award, 1987; award for outstanding achievement Am. Acad. Higher Edn., 1984. Fellow IEEE (chmn. Mont. sect. 1986); mem. IEEE Control System Soc. (chmn. edn. com. 1981-84, bd. govs. 1990-92), Am. Soc. for Engring. Edn., Sigma Xi, Tau Beta Pi, Eta Kappa Nu, Pi Mu Epsilon, Phi Kappa Phi. Home: 6343 Aajker Creek Rd Bozeman MT 59715-9102 Office: Mont State U Elec Engring Dept Bozeman MT 59717

PIERRE, JOSEPH HORACE, JR., commercial artist; b. Salem, Oreg., Oct. 3, 1929; s. Joseph Horace and Miriam Elisabeth (Holder) P.; m. June Anne Rice, Dec. 20, 1952; children: Joseph Horace III, Thomas E., Laurie E., Mark R., Ruth A. Grad., Advt. Art Sch., Portland, Oreg., 1954, Inst. Comml. Art, 1951-52. Lithographic printer Your Town Press, Inc., Salem, Oreg., 1955-58; correctional officer Oreg. State Correctional Instn., 1958-60; owner Illustrators Workshop, Inc., Salem, 1960-61; advt. mgr. North Pacific Lumber Co., Portland, 1961-63; vocat. instr. graphic arts Oreg. Correctional Instn., 1963-70; lithographic printer Lloyd's Printing, Monterey, Calif., 1971-72; illustrator McGraw Hill, 1972-73; owner Publishers Art Svc., Monterey, 1972-81; correctional officer Oreg. State Penitentiary, 1982-90; ret. Editor/publisher: The Pro Cartoonist & Gagwriter; author: The Road to Damascus, 1981, The Descendants of Thomas Pier, 1992, The Origin and History of the Callaway and Holder Families, 1992; author numerous OpEd cols. in Salem, Oreg. Statesman Jour., others; pub. cartoons nat. mags.; mural Mardi Gras Restaurant, Salem; cartoon strip Fabu, Oreg. Agr. mo. Mem. Rep. Nat. Com., Citizens Com. for Right to Keep and Bear Arms. Served with USN, 1946-51. Decorated Victory medal, China Svc. medal, Korea medal. Mem. U.S. Power Squadron, Nat. Rifle Assn., Acad. of Model Aeronautics, Oreg. Correctional Officers Assn. (co-founder, hon. mem.), Four Corners Rod and Gun Club. Republican. Home: 4822 Oak Park Dr NE Salem OR 97305-2931

PIERSON, CAROL ANNE, broadcast executive; b. Santa Monica, Calif., Jan. 10, 1945; d. David Waltz and Florence Edith (Hoeg) P.; life ptnr. Janice Lynne Thyer. BA, Antioch Coll., 1975. Pub. affairs dir. Sta. WYSO, Yellow Springs, Ohio, 1973-75, asst. mgr., 1975-76; asst. radio mgr. Sta. WGBH, Boston, 1976-84; program dir. Sta. KQED, San Francisco, 1985-91, dir. radio prodns., 1991—; pres. Media Works, Somerville, Mass., 1976-91. Musician: (rec.) Solid Ground, 1983. Recipient GLAAD media award, San Francisco, 1991. Mem. Western Pub. Radio, Women's Philharm. (treas.), Nat. Lesbian and Gay Journalists Assn. (treas.). Office: Sta KQED-FM 2601 Mariposa St San Francisco CA 94110

PIES, RONALD E., city official; b. Rochester, N.Y., Mar. 21, 1940; s. Herman S. and Sylvia P.; m. Bernita Orloff, Aug. 27, 1964; children—Cara Jean, David Paul; B.S., Ariz. State U., 1963; Recreation leader City of Phoenix, Ariz., 1962-64; head recreation div. City of Scottsdale (Ariz.) Parks and Recreation Dept., 1964-69; dir. parks and recreation, City of Tempe, Ariz., 1969-84, community services dir., 1984—; guest lectr. Ariz. State U. Mem., pres. Kyrene Sch. Dist. Governing Bd., 1979-82. Chmn., bd. regents Pacific Revenue Sources Mgmt. Sch. NRPA; gen. chmn. Fiesta Bowl Soccer Classic, 1982—; founding mem. Tempe YMCA bd. mgrs.; apptd. mem. Ariz. State Parks Bd., 1987-93, chair, 1991. Named Outstanding Young Man, Jaycees; recipient Superior Svc. Mgmt. award Am. Soc. for Pub. Adminstrn., Ariz. chpt., 1988. Mem. Tempe C. of C., Ariz. Parks and Recreation Assn. (bd. dirs. 1986—, pres. adminstrs., Disting. Fellow award 1983), Nat. Recreation and Parks Assn. (Outstanding Profl. 1991), Sigma Alpha Epsilon. Club: Tempe Diablos. Office: Rural Box 3500 Tempe AZ 85282-5482

PIET, STEVEN JAMES, research engineer, research; b. Greenville, N.C., Mar. 1, 1956; s. James Vincent and Diane (Wallace) P.; m. Robin Lou Ramsthaler, July 7, 1984; children: Monica (dec.), Valerie, Alexander. SB, MIT, 1979, SM, 1979, ScD, 1982. Sr. engr. EC&G Idaho, Idaho Falls, 1982-86; sr. program specialist EG&G Idaho, Idaho Falls, 1986-88; sr. engring. specialist EC&G Idaho, Idaho Falls, 1988-93; prin. engr. EC&G Idaho, 1993—. Mem. Am. Nucleau Soc., Soc. Risk Analysis, Fusion Power Assoc. (Rose award 1987), Nature Conservancy (Ordway Assoc.), Sigma Xi (life mem.). Republican. Roman Catholic. Home: 1129 Santa Madera Ct Solana Beach CA 92075-1620

PIGOTT, CHARLES MCGEE, transportation equipment manufacturing executive; b. Seattle, Apr. 21, 1929; s. Paul and Theiline (McGee) P.; m. Yvonne Flood, Apr. 18, 1953. B.S., Stanford U., 1951. With PACCAR Inc, Seattle, 1959—, exec. v.p., 1962-65, pres., 1965-86, chmn., pres., 1986-87, chmn., chief exec. officer, 1987—, also bd. dirs.; dir. The Seattle Times, Chevron Corp., The Boeing Co. Pres. Nat. Boy Scouts Am., 1986-88, mem. exec. bd. Mem. Bus. Council. Office: Paccar Inc PO Box 1518 777 106th Ave NE Bellevue WA 98004*

PIHL, JAMES MELVIN, electrical engineer; b. Seattle, May 29, 1943; s. Melvin Charles and Carrie Josephine (Cummings) P.; m. Arlene Evette Housden, Jan. 29, 1966 (div. Dec. 1990); 1 child, Christopher James. AASEE, Seattle, 1971; postgrad., City Univ., Bellevue, Wash., 1982—. 1st class operators lic.; lic. in real estate sales. Journeyman machinist Svc. Exch. Corp., Seattle, 1964-67; design engr. P.M. Electronics, Seattle, 1970-73, Physio Control Corp., Redmond, Wash., 1973-79; project engr. SeaMed Corp., Redmond, 1979-83; sr. design engr. Internat. Submarine Tech., Redmond, 1983-85; engring. mgr. First Med. Devices, Bellevue, Wash., 1985-89; rsch. engr. Pentco Products, Bothell, Wash., 1989—. Inventor, patentee protection system for preventing defibrillation with incorrect or improperly connected electrodes, impedance measurement circuit. With U.S. Army,, 1961-64. Mem. N.Y. Acad. Scis. Home: 14303 82d Ave NE Bothell WA 98011

PIHLAJA, MAXINE MURIEL MEAD, orchestra executive; b. Windom, Minn., July 19, 1935; d. Julian Wright and Mildred Eleanor (Ray) Mead; m. Donald Francis Pihlaja, Jan. 4, 1963; children: Geoffrey Blake, Kirsten Louise, Jocelyn Erika. BA, Hamline U., 1957; postgrad., Columbia U., 1957-58. Group worker Fedn. of Chs., L.A., 1956; case worker St. John's Guild Floating Hosp. Ship, N.Y.C., 1957-59; Y-Teen program dir. YWCA, Elizabeth, N.J., 1957-60, Boulder, Colo., 1964-65; spl. svcs. program and club dir. U.S. Army, Ingrandes and Nancy, France, 1960-62; music buyer, salesperson Guinn's Music, Billings, Mont., 1977-78, N.W. Music, Billings, 1978-79; office adminstr. Am. Luth. Ch., Billings, 1979-84; mgr. Billings Symphony Soc., 1984—; substitute tchr. Community Day Care and Enrichment Ctr., Billings, 1971-76. Dir. Handbell choir 1st Presybn. Ch., Billings, 1972—, Am. Luth. Ch., 1981-84, 1st English Luth. Ch., 1982—; mem. Billings Symphony Chorale, 1965-91, Bellissimo!, 1983-93. Mem. Nat. Soc. Fund Raising Execs. (sec. Mont. 1988), Mont. Assn. Female Execs., Am. Guild English Handbell Ringers (state chmn. 1988-89, treas. Area X bd. dirs. 1990—), Mont. Assn. Symphony Orchs. (treas. 1987-92). Lutheran. Office: Billings Symphony Orch 401 N 31st St Box 7055 Billings MT 59101 Office: Billings Symphony Orch Box 59103 401 N 31st St Billings MT 59101

PIIRTO, DOUGLAS DONALD, forester, educator; b. Reno, Nev., Sept. 25, 1948; s. Rueben Arvid and Martha Hilma (Giebel) P.; BS, U. Nev., 1970; MS, Colo. State U., 1971; PhD, U. Calif., Berkeley, 1977; m. Mary Louise Cruz, Oct. 28, 1978. Rsch. asst. Colo. State U., 1970-71, U. Calif., Berkeley, 1972-77; forester, silviculturist U.S. Dept. Agr., Forest Svc., Sierra Nat. Forest, Trimmer and Shaver Lake, Calif., 1977-85; assoc. prof. natural resources mgmt. dept. Calif. Poly. State U., San Luis Obispo, 1985-90, prof. 1990—; researcher in field; instr. part-time Kings River Community Coll., Reedley, Calif.; forestry cons., expert witness. Registered profl. forester, Calif.; cert. silviculturist USDA Forest Svc. Recipient Meritorious Performance and Profl. Promise award CalPoly, 1989. Mem. Soc. Am. Foresters, Am. Forestry Assn., Forest Products Rsch. Soc., Soc. Wood Sci. and Tech., Alpha Zeta, Xi Sigma Pi, Sigma Xi, Beta Beta Beta, Phi Sigma Kappa. Lutheran. Contbr. articles to sci. and forestry jours. Home: 7605 El Retiro Ave Atascadero CA 93422-3721 Office: Calif Poly State U Dept Natural Resources Mgmt San Luis Obispo CA 93710

PIKE, CHRISTOPHER DORAN, secondary education educator; b. Upland, Calif., Apr. 11, 1953; s. Kenneth Lester and Judith Carolyn (Wise) P.; m. Elizabeth Jane King (div.). BS in Edn., No. Ariz. U., 1976; cert. jewelery, Mohave C.C., Kingman, Ariz., 1984; MS, No. Ariz. U., 1990. Tchr. Kingman (Ariz.) High Sch., 1976—, sci. dept. chmn., 1992; tchr. Mohave C.C., Kingman, 1980—. Dorm pres. No. Ariz. U., Flagstaff, 1974-76, judical chmn., 1976; scout craft dir. Boy Scouts Am., Flagstaff, 1974; asst. girl scout leader Girl Scouts Am., Kingman, 1988-89. Recipient Order of the Arrow, Boy Scouts Am., San Bernardino, 1968, Eagle Scout, 1971. Mem. AAAS. Home: 4579 Vickie Ln Kingman AZ 86401 Office: Kingman High Sch 400 Grandview Kingman AZ 86401

PIKE, RICHARD JOSEPH, JR., geologist; b. Nantucket, Mass., June 28, 1937; s. Richard Joseph and Idolize Evelyn (Roderick) P.; m. Jane Ellen Nielson, Sept. 2, 1967 (div. 1982); children: Benjamin R., Owen S.; m. Linda Hutchinson Grossman, May 4, 1986. BS, Tufts Coll., 1959; MA, Clark U., 1963; PhD, U. Mich., 1968. Geographer U.S. Army, Natick, Mass., 1962-63; ops. analyst Cornell Aero Labs., Buffalo, 1964; geologist astrogeology br. U.S. Geol. Survey, Flagstaff, Ariz. and Menlo Park, Calif., 1968-86; geologist br. of regional geology U.S. Geol. Survey, Menlo Park, 1987—; mem. various NASA panels, Ariz., Calif., and Tex., 1968-70, 74-78; vis. prof. Instituto di Ricerce per la Protezione Idrogeologica nell Italia centrale del Consiglio Nazionale delle Ricerche, Perugia, Italy, 1988-89. Author: (with others) Impact Craters on Mercury, 1988, (with G.P. Thelin) Digital Shaded-Relief Map of the U.S., 1991 (represented in map exhibit Cooper-Hewitt Mus., N.Y.C., 1992-93; contbr. articles to profl. jours. Recipient Apollo medallion NASA Hdqrs., 1971. Mem. AAAS, Am. Geophys. Union, Geol. Soc. Am., 356 Registry (essayist, editor 1978-93), Sigma Xi. Office: US Geol Survey M/S 975 345 Middlefield Rd Menlo Park CA 94025-3591

PILKINGTON, SANDRA JAYNE, mortgage company executive; b. Corpus Christi, Tex., Sept. 4, 1943; d. Glenn William and Jayne (Jones) Burger; m. Bobby Eugene Pilkington, Dec. 22, 1963 (div. Feb. 1977); children: Timothy Robert, Jillene Leslie. AA, Mesa Coll., Grand Junction, Colo., 1963; BS in Bus. Adminstrn./Econs., Regis Coll., Denver, 1982. Pub. rels. account exec. PR Svcs., Longmont, Colo., 1974-77; aerospace cost analyst Beech Aircraft, Boulder, Colo., 1977-84; cost acct. Thousand Trails, Bellevue, Wash., 1984-86; loan officer Lynnwood Am. Mortgage, Bellevue, 1986-88, Pacific First Fed. Bank, Bellevue, 1988-89; pres., mortgage broker Mortgage Assocs., Bellevue, 1989—. Bd. mem. Cancer Lifeline, Seattle, 1987-91. Mem. Wash. Assn. Mortgage Brokers (mem. edn. com. 1988—). Mem. Unity Ch. Home: 7495 Old Redmond Rd Redmond WA 98052 Office: Mortgage Assocs 11711 SE 8th St Ste 303 Bellevue WA 98005

PILLA, THOMAS VICTOR, civil rights analyst, consultant, writer; b. Jackson Heights, N.Y., July 23, 1944; s. Nicholas George and Jeanette Mary (Corrado) P.; m. Mary Tarrant White, July 15, 1972; children: Thomas Lynn, Caitlin Julianna. BS, SUNY, New Paltz, 1966; MA, UCLA, 1971. Life credential in C.C. counseling, secondary teaching, C.C. instrn., Calif.; cert. probate paralegal. Secondary tchr. East Islip (N.Y.) Union Free Sch. Dist., 1966-67; cons. U.S. Commn. on Civil Rights, L.A., 1971-72, community rels. specialist, 1972, rsch. specialist, 1972-78, equal opportunity specialist, 1978-79, civil rights analyst, 1979—; bd. dirs. Cts. and Records Fed. Credit Union, L.A., 1986—, chmn. bd., 1989-91. Asst. scoutmaster troop 26, Boy Scouts Am., L.A., 1988—; bd. dirs. Griffith Park Boys Camp Adv. Coun., L.A., 1991—. Grantee Japan Soc. N.Y., 1967, UCLA, 1969. Mem. UCLA Edn. Alumni Assn., U. West L.A. Alumni Assn., Phi Delta Kappa. Democrat. Roman Catholic. Home: 1015 S Carmelina Ave Los Angeles CA 90049 Office: US Commn on Civil Rights WRO 3660 Wilshire Blvd Ste 810 Los Angeles CA 90010

PILLAR, CHARLES LITTLEFIELD, retired mining consultant; b. Denver, May 25, 1911; s. Charles and Alice May (Littlefield) P.; m. Elizabeth Reed Broadhead, Sept. 10, 1932 (div. May 1939); m. Gwendola Elizabeth Lotz, Sept. 16, 1939; children: Ann, Catherine, Pamela. Engr. mines, Colo. Sch. Mines, 1935. Registered profl. engr., B.C., Ariz. Various positions in field, 1935-75; mine cons. Pillar, Lowell & Assocs., Tucson, Ariz., 1976-83; cons. Bechtel Corp., San Francisco, 1976-79, Fluor Corp., Redwood City, Calif., 1979-83; mem. Colo. Sch. Mines Rsch. Inst., Golden, 1975-83, pvt. practice Tucson, 1985-89; bd. dir. Internat. Geosystems Corp., Vancouver, B.C. Contbr. articles to profl. jours. Mem. Nat. Rep. Senatorial com.; rep. Presdl. Task Force. Capt. USAF, 1942-45. Mem. AIME (William Saunders Gold Medal award, Disting. mem. award), Can. Inst. Mining and Metallurgy, Profl. Engrs. B.C., Heritage Found., Smithsonian Assocs., Nat. Exch. Club, U.S. Senatorial Club (presdl. task force), Vancouver Club, Tucson Nat. Country Club. Republican. Episcopalian. Home: 9460 N Camino Del Plata Tucson AZ 85741-9070

PILLAY, SIVASANKARA K.K., research scientist; b. Puliyoor, India, Jan. 28, 1935; came to U.S., 1960; s. Raman T.N. and Janaki Amma Pillay; m. Revathi Krishnamurthy, Mar. 22, 1964; 1 child, Gautam. BS with honors, U. Mysore, Bangalore, India, 1955, MS, 1956; PhD, Pa. State U., 1965. Lectr. U. Mysore, 1956-60; teaching asst. Pa. State U., University Park, 1960-65, assoc. prof. nuclear engring., 1971-81; research assoc. Argonne (Ill.) Nat. Lab., 1965-66; sr. research scientist Western N.Y. Nuclear Research Ctr., Buffalo, 1966-71; program mgr., scientist Los Alamos (N.Mex.) Nat. Lab., 1981-92, program mgr., 1992—; cons. Pa. State Police, Harrisburg, 1971-75, Brookhaven Nat. Lab., Upton, N.Y., 1976-80, U.S. Dept. Energy, Washington, 1977-80, Radiation Mgmt. Corp., Phila., 1978-81. Author: Laboratory Experiments in Applied Nuclear and Radiochemistry, 1979, Nuclear Technology Laboratory Experiments, 1979; editor Pa. State Cosmopolitan, 1962-63; contbr. articles to profl. jours. Sec. Boy Scouts India, Chitradurga, 1957-60; trainer Boy Scouts Am., University Park, 1975-76; warden Silver Jubilee Orphanage, Chitradurga, 1958-60. Fellow Kopper Chem. Co., 1962-63, ERDA, 1976. Fellow Am. Inst. Chemists (cert. chemist), Am. Nuclear Soc. (asst. tech. program 1982, chmn. isotopes and radiation div. 1990-91), chmn. honors and awards 1991—); mem. AAAS, ASTM, Inst. Nuclear Materials Mgmt., Am. Chem. Soc., N.Y. Acad. Scis., Sigma Xi. Home: 369 Cheryl Ave Los Alamos NM 87544-3637 Office: Los Alamos Nat Lab Nuclear Materials Tech Divsn Mail Stop E500 Los Alamos NM 87545

PINCKARD, MARA, library administrator; b. Lawrence, Mass., Apr. 14, 1941; d. James Joseph and Mary Anderson (Long) Forrest; m. R. Neal Pinckard (div.) J. Keith, Kathryn. BS in Microbiology, U. N.H., 1963; MLS, U. Ariz., 1975. Grad. rsch. asst. U. Hawaii, Honolulu, 1963-64; rsch. asst. U. Edinburgh (Scotland) Med. Sch., 1964-67, Scripps Clinic & Rsch. Found., LaJolla, Calif., 1967-68; ref. libr., sci. bibliographer U. Tex., San Antonio, 1977-82; head of sci. ref. Ariz. State U., Tempe, 1982—; asst. head Noble Libr., Ariz. State U., Tempe, 1990—. Vol. Desert Samaritan Hosp., Mesa, Ariz., 1988. Mem. Spl. Libr. Assn. (pres. Ariz. chpt. 1989-90, also Sci. Tech. div., Libr. Mgmt. div., Info. & Tech. div.), Am. Libr. Assn., Assn. Coll. & Rsch. Libr. Office: Ariz State Univ Tempe AZ 85287-1006

PINCUS, HOWARD JONAH, geologist, educator; b. N.Y.C., June 24, 1922; s. Otto Max and Gertrude (Jankowsky) P.; m. Maud Lydia Roback, Sept. 6, 1953; children: Glenn David, Philip E. BS, CCNY, 1942; AM, Columbia U., 1948, PhD, 1949. Mem. faculty Ohio State U., 1949-67, successively instr., asst. prof., assoc. prof., 1949-59, prof., 1959-67, chmn. dept. geology, 1960-65; rsch. geologist U. S. Bur. Mines, summers 1963-67; geologist, rsch. supr. U.S. Bur. Mines, 1967-68; prof. geol. sci. and civil engring. U. Wis., Milw., 1968-87, prof. emeritus, 1987—, dean Coll. Letters and Sci., 1969-72; rsch. assoc. Lamont Geol. Obs., Columbia, 1949, 50, 51; geologist Ohio Dept. Natural Resources, summers 1950-61; cons. geology and rock mechanics, 1954-67, 68—; mem. U.S. nat. com. on tunnelling tech. NAE, 1972-74, mem. U.S. Nat. com. on rock mechanics, 1975-78, 80-89, chmn., 1985-87; mem. U.S. com. Internat. Assn. Engring. Geology-NAS, chmn., 1987-90; sr. postdoctoral fellow NSF, 1962. Editor Geotech. Testing Jour., 1993—; contbr. articles to profl. jours. Served to 1st lt. C.E. AUS, 1942-46. Recipient award for teaching excellence U. Wis.-Milw. Alumni Assn., 1978. Fellow ASTM (tech. editor Geotech. Testing Jour. 1993—, Reinhart award 1987, Award of Merit 1989), AAAS, Geol. Soc. Am.; mem. NSPE, AAUP (pres. Ohio State U. chpt. 1955-56, mem. coun. 1965-67, pres. U. Wis.-Milw. chpt. 1976-77), Am. Geophys. Union, Geol. Soc. Am. (chmn. engring. geology divsn. 1973-74), Soc. Mining Engrs., Internat. Assn. Engring. Geology (mem. U.S. com.), Internat. Soc. Rock Mechanics, Assn. Engring. Geologists, Am. Inst. Profl. Geologists (pres. Ohio sect. 1965-66), Computer Oriented Geol. Soc., Phi Beta Kappa (pres. Ohio State U. chpt. 1959-60, pres. U. Wis.-Milw. chpt. 1976-77), Sigma Xi. Home: 17523 Plaza Marlena San Diego CA 92128-1807 Office: PO Box 27598 San Diego CA 92198-1598

PINE, CHARLES JOSEPH, clinical psychologist; b. Excelsior Springs, Mo., July 13, 1951; s. Charles E. and LaVern (Upton) P.; m. Mary Day, Dec. 30, 1979; children: Charles Andrew, Joseph Scott, Carolyn Marie. BA in Psychology, U. Redlands, 1973; MA, Calif. State U.-L.A., 1975; PhD, U. Wash., 1979; postdoctoral UCLA, 1980-81. Diplomate in Clinical Psych. Am. Bd. Profl. Psych. Lic. psychologist, Calif., Fla. Psychology technician Seattle Indian Health Bd., USPHS Hosp., 1977-78; psychology intern VA Outpatient Clinic, L.A., 1978-79; instr. psychology Okla. State U., 1979-80, asst. prof., 1980; asst. prof. psychology and native Am. studies program Wash. State U., 1981-82; dir. behavioral health services Riverside-San Bernardino County Indian Health Inc., Banning, Calif., 1982-84; clin. psychologist, clin. co-dir. Inland Empire Behavioral Assocs., Colton, Calif., 1982-84; clin. psychologist VA Med. Ctr., Long Beach, Calif., 1984-85; clin. psychologist, psychology coordinator Psychiatry div. VA Med. Ctr., Sepulveda, Calif., 1985-93; clin. dir. Traumatic Stress Treatment Ctr., Thousand Oaks, Calif., 1985-93; assoc. clin. prof. UCLA Sch. Medicine, 1985—, Fuller Grad. Sch. Psychology, Pasadena, Calif., 1985-93, indep. practitioner Orlando, 1993—; adj. assoc. prof. Calif. Sch. Profl. Psychology, L.A., 1989—; rsch. assoc. Nat. Ctr. for Am. Indian and Alaska Native Mental Health Rsch., U. Col. Health Sci. Ctr., Denver, 1989—; psychologist alcohol and drug abuse treatment program, Orlando VA Outpatient divsn. Tampa VA Med. Ctr., 1993—; cons. NIH, 1993—; mem. L.A. County Am. Indian Mental Health task force, 1987-92. Editorial cons. White Cloud Jour., 1982-85; cons. Dept. Health and Human Services, USPHS, NIMH, 1980. Vol. worker Variety Boys Clubs Am., 1973-75; coach Rialto Jr. All-Am. Football League, 1974, Conejo Youth Flag Football Assn., pres., 1990, coach, bd. dirs. Westlake Youth Football, 1991-92; coach. Conejo Valley Little League, Dr. Phillips Little League, 1993—; co-commr., coach Dr. Phillips Pop Warner Football, 1993—. U. Wash. Inst. Indian Studies grantee, 1975-76, UCLA Inst. Am. Cultures grantee, 1981-82. Fellow Am. Psychol. Assn. (chair task force on service delivery to ethnic minority populations bd. ethnic minority affairs 1988—, bd. ethnic minority affairs 1985-87); mem. Soc. Indian Psychologists (pres. 1981-83), Nat. Register Health Svc. Providers in Psychology, Calif. Psychol. Assn. Found. (bd. dirs. 1990-92), N.Y. Acad. Sci., Soc. for Psychol. Study Ethnic Minority Issues (exec. com. 1987-88), Sigma Alpha Epsilon. Republican. Baptist. Contbr. psychol. articles to profl. lit.

PINES, ALEXANDER, chemistry educator, researcher; b. Tel Aviv, June 22, 1945; came to U.S., 1968.; s. Michael and Neima (Ratner) P.; m. Ayala Malach, Aug. 31, 1967 (div. 1983); children: Itai, Shani; m. Ditsa Kafry, May 5, 1983; children: Noami, Jonathan, Talia. BS, Hebrew U., Jerusalem, 1967; PhD, MIT, 1972. Asst. prof. chemistry U. Calif., Berkeley, 1972-75, assoc. prof., 1975-80, prof., 1980—, Pres.'s chair, 1993; faculty sr. scientist materials scis. div. Lawrence Berkeley Lab., 1975—; cons. Mobil Oil Co., Princeton, N.J., 1980-84, Shell Oil Co., Houston, 1981—; chmn. Bytel Corp., Berkeley, Calif., 1981-85; vis. prof. Weizmann Inst. Sci., 1982; adv. prof. East China Normal U., Shanghai, People's Rep. of China, 1985; sci. dir. Naloræ, Martinez, Calif., 1986—; Joliot-Curie prof. Ecole Superieure de Physique et Chemie, Paris, 1987; Walter J. Chute Disting. lectr. Dalhousie U., 1989, Charles A. McDowell lectr. U. B.C., 1989, E. Leon Watkins lectr. Wichita State U., 1990; Hinshelwood lectr., U. Oxford, 1990, A.R. Gordon Disting. lectr. U. Toronto, 1990, Venable lectr. U. N.C., 1990, Max Born lectr. Hebrew U. of Jerusalem, 1990; William Draper Harkins lectr. U. Chgo., 1991, Kolthoff lectr. U. Minn., 1991; Md.-Grace lectr. U. Md., 1992; mem. adv bd. Nat. High Magnetic Field Lab., Inst. Theoretical Physics, U. Calif. Santa Barbara; mem. adv. panel chem. Nat. Sci. Found.; Randolph T. Major Disting. Lectr. U. Conn., 1992; Peter Smith lectr. Duke U., 1993, Arthur William Davidson lect. U. Kansas, 1992, Arthur Birch lect. Australian Nat. U., 1993. Editor Molecular Physics, 1987-91; mem. bd. editors Chem. Physics, Chem. Physics Letters, Nmr: Basic Principles and Progress, Advances in Magnetic Resonance; adv. editor Oxford U. Press; contbr. articles to profl. jours.; patentee in field. Recipient Strait award North Calif. Spectroscopy Soc., Outstanding Achievement award U.S. Dept. of Energy, 1983, 87, 89, R & D 100 awards, 1987, 89, Disting. Teaching award U. Calif., E.O. Lawrence award, 1988, Pitts. Spectroscopy award, 1989; Guggenheim fellow, 1988, Christensen fellow St. Catherine's Coll., Oxford, 1990, Wolf Prize for chemistry, 1991, Donald Noyce Undergrad. Teaching award U. Calif., 1992, Robert Foster Cherry award for Great Tchrs. Baylor U. Fellow Am. Phys. Soc. (chmn. div. chem. physics), Inst. Physics; mem. NAS (adv. panel chem.), Am. Chem. Soc. (mem. exec. com. div. phys. chemistry, Signature award, Baekeland medal, Harrison Howe award 1991), Royal Soc. Chemistry (Bourke lectr.), Internat. Soc. Magnetic Resonance (v.p.). Office: U Calif Chemistry Dept D 64 Hildebrand Hall Berkeley CA 94720

PINGS, ANTHONY CLAUDE, architect; b. Fresno, Calif., Dec. 16, 1951; s. Clarence Hubert and Mary (Murray) P.; m. Carole Clements, June 25, 1983; children, Adam Reed, Rebecca Mary. AA, Fresno City Coll., 1972; BArch, Calif. Poly. State U., San Luis Obispo, 1976. Lic. architect, Calif.; cert. Nat. Council Archtl. Registration Bds. Architect Aubrey Moore Jr., Fresno, 1976-81; architect, prin. Pings & Assocs., Fresno, 1981-83, 86—, Pings-Taylor Assocs., Fresno, 1983-85. Prin. works include Gollaher Profl. Office (Masonry Merit award 1985, Best Office Bldg. award 1986), Fresno Imaging Ctr. (Best Instnl. Project award 1986, Nat. Healthcare award Modern Health Care mag. 1986), Orthopedic Facility (award of honor Masonry Inst. 1987, award of merit San Joaquin chpt. AIA 1987), Modesto Imaging Ctr. (award of merit San Joaquin chpt. AIA 1991). Mem. Calif. Indsl. Tech. Edn. Consortium Calif. State Dept. Edn., 1983, 84. Mem. AIA (bd. dirs. Calif. chpt. 1983-84, v.p. San Joaquin chpt. 1982, pres. 1983, Calif. Coun. evaluation team 1983, team leader Coalinga Emergency Design Assistance team), Fresno Arts (bd. dirs., counsel 1989—, pres. 1990-93). Democrat. Home: 4350 N Safford Ave Fresno CA 93704-3509 Office: Anthony C Pings AIA 1640 W Shaw Ave Ste 107 Fresno CA 93711-3506

PINIELLA, LOUIS VICTOR, professional baseball team manager; b. Tampa, Fla., Aug. 28, 1943; m. Anita Garcia, Apr. 12, 1967; children: Lou, Kristi, Derrick. Student, U. Tampa. Baseball player various minor-league teams, 1962-68, Cleve. Indians, 1968, Kansas City Royals, 1969-73; baseball player N.Y. Yankees, 1974-84, coach, 1984-85, mgr., 1985-87, 1988, gen. mgr., 1987-88, spl. advisor, TV announcer, 1989; mgr. Cin. Reds, 1990-92, Seattle Mariners, 1992—. Named to All-Star team, 1972; recipient Ellis Island Medal of Honor, 1990. Office: Seattle Mariners PO Box 4100 411 First Ave South Seattle WA 98104

PINK, ERNEST EDWIN, insurance agency executive; b. Rochester, N.Y., Apr. 1, 1942; s. Ernest Hugh and Bertha (Frachel) P.; m. Sharon K. German, Dec. 27, 1961 (div. July 1978); children: Ernest R., Stacy L. BSBA, Tri-State U., Angola, Ind., 1964; M Fin. Svcs., Am. Coll., Bryn Mawr, Pa., 1991. CLU; chartered fin. cons., ins. counselor. Claim investigator Lincoln Nat. Life Ins. Co., Ft. Wayne, Ind., 1964-70; ins. salesman Lincoln Nat. Sales Corp., Missoula, Mont., 1970-76, sr. v.p., sales mgr., 1976-80; ptnr. Toole & Easter Agy., Missoula, 1984-86; owner, mgr., life underwriter Pink Ins. Agy., Inc., Missoula, 1980-84, 87—; bd. dirs. Mont. Ins. Edn. Found., Helena, 1981-90, pres., 1989-90. Chmn. Ducks Unltd., Missoula, 1978—; commr. Missoula Housing Authority, 1985—, chmn. 1993. Mem. Nat. Assn. Life Underwriters (nat. quality awards), Mont. Assn. Life Underwrriters (sec.-treas. 1976-77), Western Mont. Assn. Life Underwriters (pres. 1975-76), Am. Soc. CLU's and Chartered Fin. Cons., Western Mont. Estate Planning Coun., Ind. Ins. Agts. (adj. mem. strategic planning com. 1988-90), NRA (life), Nat. Skeet Shooting Assn. (life), Missoula Trap and Skeet Club (bd. dirs. 1990), Rotary. Office: PO Box 9139 127 E Front St Ste 302 Missoula MT 59801

PINKERT, TED CHARLES, pathologist, nuclear medicine physician; b. Ames, IA, Oct. 4, 1947; s. Paul August and Elinor Caroline (Schultz) P.; m. Joan Marie Sliger, Dec. 12, 1972 (div. Apr. 1989); m. Susan Delle Rooney, June 22, 1989; children: Emery, Vincent. BA, U. Minn., Mpls., 1970, MD, 1974. Am. Bd. of Pathology. Resident pathologist St. Mary's Hosp., Duluth, Minn., 1974-75, Providence Med. Ctr., Portland, Oreg., 1975-78; fellow in nuclear medicine Oreg. Health Sci. U., Portland, Oreg., 1978-79; pathologist Tuality Community Hosp., Hillsboro, Oreg., 1979—, nuclear medicine physician, 1979—. Mem. Oreg. Pathologists Assn., Oreg. Med. Assn., Coll. of Am. Pathologists. Home: 11801 SW Langley Dr Gaston OR 97119 Office: Tuality Community Hosp 335 SE 8th Ave Hillsboro OR 97123-4248

PINKERTON, ALAN SCOTT, forest ranger; b. Yosemite, Calif., Apr. 24, 1949; s. Jack Dana and Beverly Eileen (Preston) P.; m. Kim Teresa Klebe, Mar. 27, 1976; children: Jessica Alaine, Preston Scott. BS, Colo. State U., 1981. Firefighter Calif. Div. Forestry, Mariposa, 1967-70; foreman USDA Forest Svc., El Portal, Calif., 1971-74; fire mgmt. officer USDA Forest Svc., Burley, Idaho, 1975-78; forester-planning USDA Forest Svc., Twin Falls, Idaho, 1981-82; forester-oil/gas USDA Forest Svc., Afton, Wyo., 1982-84; forester-recreation USDA Forest Svc., Las Vegas, 1984-88; dist. ranger USDA Forest Svc., Ketchum, Idaho, 1988—; mem. budget team USDA Forest Svc., Ogden, Utah, 1989-91, mem. orgn. team, 1991—; mem. comprehensive plan team Blaine County, Hailey, Idaho, 1989—; mem. steering com. Blaine County Recreation Dist., Hailey, 1990-91. Bd. dirs. Environ Resource Ctr., Ketchum, 1992—. Delano F. Scott scholar Colo. State U., 1979. Mem. Sun Valley-Ketchum C. of C. (bd. dirs. 1990—), Lions Club Internat. Republican. Methodist. Office: USDA Forest Svc 206 Sun Valley Rd Box 2356 Ketchum ID 83340

PINKERTON, CLAYTON DAVID, artist; b. San Francisco, Mar. 6, 1931; s. David B. and Kathryn Irene (Davies) P. B.A. in Edn, Calif. Coll. Arts and Crafts, 1952, M.F.A., 1953; postgrad., U. N.Mex., 1952, U. Paris, 1957. Former curator and former dir. coll. internship program Richmond Art Ctr.; mem. faculty Calif. Coll. Arts and Crafts. One-man exhbns. include Calif. Palace Legion of Honor, San Francisco, 1960, M.H. de Young Meml. Mus., San Francisco, 1962, Everett Ellin Gallery, Los Angeles, 1961, Esther Robles Gallery, Los Angeles, 1968, San Francisco Mus. Art, 1956, 67, Arleigh Gallery, San Francisco, 1970, Richmond (Calif.) Art Ctr., 1976, Himovitz/Salomon Gallery, Sacramento, 1985, 86, 88, Monterey Penisula Mus. Art, 1988, U. of Pacific, Stockton, 1988, Calif. State U., Chico, 1989, Michael Himovitz Gallery, 1991, 93, Spectrum/Himovitz Gallery, San Francisco, 1991-92, (figurative-narrative works) 1991, Am. Cultural Ctr., Brussels, 1991, Spectrum/Himovitz Gallery, San Francisco, 1992; group exhbns. include Mus. Modern Art, N.Y.C., 1962, Whitney Mus. Modern Art, N.Y.C., Mus. Contemporary Art, Chgo., 1971, Mus. Fine Arts, Richmond, Va., 1970, San Francisco Mus. Fine Arts, 1978, Los Angeles County Mus., 1979, Phoenix Art Mus., 1970, Oakland (Calif.) Mus., 1979, Bolles Gallery, 1981, Monterey Peninsula Mus. Art, 1985, 86, Art Bridge, Kobe, Japan, 1986, The Human Form Galeria Mesa, Ariz., 1987, (figurative works) Sierra Coll., Rocklin, Calif., 1989, Calif. Eccentrics U. Ill., 1990, Triton Mus., San Jose, 1992, Am. Cultural Ctr., Brussels, 1992, Am. Embassy, Calcutta, New Delhi, 1993, 3 Painters-4 Decades, Sacramento, 1993, others; represented in permanent collections: Ill. Bell Telephone Co., Chgo., M.H. De Young Meml. Mus., San Francisco, Crocker Art Mus., Sacramento, others. Recipient James D. Phelan award, 1957, 61; Fulbright scholar, 1957-58. Home: PO Box 77 Amador City CA 95601-0077

PINKERTON, GUY CALVIN, savings and loan executive; b. Seattle, Aug. 1, 1934; s. John L. and Dorothy V. (Kock) P.; children: Deborah, Lisa. BA, U. Wash., 1959. CPA, Wash. Supr. Touche Ross & Co., Seattle, 1959-65; pres., CEO Wash. Fed. Savs., Seattle, 1965—. With USN, 1956-58. Mem. Fin. Mgrs. Soc. (dist. gov.), Fin. Execs. Inst. (sec.). Republican. Presbyterian. Office: Wash Fed Savs 425 Pike St Seattle WA 98101-2334

PINKHAM, CLARKSON WILFRED, structural engineer; b. L.A., Nov. 25, 1919; s. Walter Hampden and Dorothy Rebecca (Burdorf) P.; m. EmmaLu Hull, May 8, 1942; children: Nancy Pinkham Ballance, Timothy Hull, Anthony Hull. B in Applied Sci., U. Calif., Berkeley, 1944, BS, 1947. Registered civil and structural engr., Calif., Wash.; registered structural engr., Ill., Ariz.; registered profl. engr., Fla., Ga., Ind., Iowa, Kans., Md., Oreg., Tex., Wis. Designer S.B. Barnes and Assocs., L.A., 1947-54, assoc., 1954-68, pres., 1968—. Contbr. articles to profl. jours. Active L.A. County Earthquake Commn., 1971-74, Town Hall. With USN, 1941-46, lt. comdr. USNR, 1946-54. Fellow ASCE (life), Am. Concrete Inst. (bd. dirs. 1975-78, Henry L. Kennedy award 1986); mem. ASTM, Structural Engrs. Assn. So. Calif. (hon., pres. 1971) Structural Engrs. Assn. Calif. (pres. 1975, chmn. seismology com. 1967-70), Internat. Assn. Bridge and Structural Engring., Earthquake Engring. Rsch. Inst., Bldg. Seismic Safety Commn., Am. Welding Soc., Masonry Soc. (bd. dirs. 1986-87), Structural Stability Rsch. Coun., Am. Arbitration Assn., Seismol. Soc. Am., Internat. Conf. Bldg. Officials, Am. Inst. Steel Constrn. Office: SB Barnes Assocs 2236 Beverly Blvd Los Angeles CA 90057-2292

PINKNEY, D. TIMOTHY, financial planner; b. Long Beach, Calif., June 6, 1948; s. Robert Patten and Mary (Chernus) P.; m. Nancy Dianne Fisher, Aug. 21, 1971; 1 child, Heather Anne. BA, Calif. Luth. U., 1980; MA, Pepperdine U., 1976. Cert. fin. planner. Membership mgr. Seattle C. of C., 1977-79; v.p. mktg. John L. Scott Investment, Bellevue, Wash., 1980-81, SRH Fin., Bellevue, 1981-82, Foster Investment Co., Bellevue, 1982-83; pres., chief exec. officer Footprint Fin. Planning, Bellevue, 1983-88, Sheppard & Assocs. Personal Fin. Advs., Bellevue, 1988-91; mgr. and v.p. asset mgmt. div. U.S. Bank, 1991-92; v.p., Calif. mgr. asset mgmt. div. U.S. Bank of Calif., Sacramento, 1992—; founder, chief exec. officer Wealth Link Enterprises. Author: book, video and cassete series Pathways to Wealth, Yes IRA's Still Make Cent$?, 1988. Co-chmn. Fin. Independence Week, Western Wash., 1987; bd. dirs. Traveler's Aid Soc., A United Way Agy., Seattle, 1988, pacesetter United Way, 1988-91; alumni class steward Calif. Luth. U., 1992, 93. Lt. USN, 1970-77, comdr. USNR, ret., 1992. Selected as Jr. Officer of Yr., USNR, 1984, 85. Mem. Nat. Speakers Assn. (bd. dirs. N.W. chpt. 1992), Internat. Assn. Fin. Planning (chmn. West Region 1987-90, pres. Western Wash. chpt. 1986-87), Seattle Soc. CFPs (bd. dirs. 1985-86), Inst. CFPs, Real Estate Securities and Syndication Inst. (v.p. 1980-83), East King County and Pierce County Estate Planning Coun., Seattle Res. Officer Assn. (pres. and v.p. 1983-85), Puget Sound Naval Res., Assn. (v.p. 1985-90), Rotary (membership devel. com. Sacramento, chmn. edn. com., bd. dirs. Seattle 1992).

PINNELL, ROBERT PEYTON, chemistry educator; b. Fresno, Calif., Dec. 5, 1938; s. Paul Peyton and Iris Ione (Shepherd) P.; m. Sharron Lyne Gregory, Aug. 18, 1962; children: Jason Peyton, Sabrina Lyne. BS, Calif. State U., Fresno, 1960; PhD, U. Kansas, 1964. Postdoctoral fellow U. Tex., Austin, 1964-66; asst. prof. chemistry Claremont (Calif.) McKenna Coll., Scripps Coll. and Pitzer Coll., 1966-72, assoc. prof., 1972-78, prof., 1978—, chmn. joint sci. dept., 1974-77; rsch. affiliate Jet Propulsion Lab., 1986—, vis. assoc. prof. chemistry Calif. Inst. Tech., 1973-74. Postdoctoral fellow U. Calif. at Santa Barbara, 1980-81, NASA-Am. Soc. for Engring. Edn. fellow,

1982, 83, 86, 87. Mem. Nat. Sci. Tchrs. Assn., Am. Assn. for the Advancement Sci., Am. Chem. Soc., Calif. Assn. Chemistry Tchrs., Sigma Xi. Democrat. Office: Claremont McKenna Scripps & Pitzer Colls Joint Sci Dept Claremont CA 91711

PINNEY, EDMUND, educator, mathematician; b. Seattle, Aug. 19, 1917; s. Henry Lewis and Alice (Joy) P.; m. Eleanor Russell, Mar. 10, 1945; children—Henry Russell, Gail Shiela. B.S., Calif. Inst. Tech., 1939, Ph.D., 1942. Research asso. Radiation Lab., Mass. Inst. Tech., 1942-43; research analyst Consol.-Vultee Aircraft Corp., 1943-45; instr. Ore. State Coll., 1945-46; mem. faculty U. Calif., Berkeley, 1946—, prof. math., 1959—; cons. in field. Author: Ordinary Difference-Differential Equations, 1958. Fellow AAAS; mem. Am. Math. Soc., Am. Phys. Soc. Home: 66 Scenic Dr Orinda CA 94563-3412 Office: Univ Calif 839 Evans Hall Berkeley CA 94720

PINNOW, ARNO LEE, quality assurance executive; b. Milw., July 21, 1941; s. Roy Lee and Lila Viola (Uphoff) P.; m. Leta Sheila Williams, Dec. 28, 1963 (dec. Mar., 1992); children: Christopher Gene, Marjorie Lee. BS in Chem. Engring., Ill. Inst. Tech., 1964. Registered profl. engr., Ill. Mgr. systems and tng. Amp-vial project Abbott Labs., North Chicago, Ill., 1971-72, mfg. quality mgr. Hosp. div., sr. v.p. ops., Rocky Mount, N.C., 1972-74, sect. mgr. quality audits, North Chicago, 1974-77, ops. mgr. quality evaluation, 1977-82; dir. quality assurance Hollister, Inc., Libertyville, Ill., 1981-85; mgr. quality engring. Advanced Cardiovascular Systems subs. Eli Lilly & Co., Temecula, Calif., 1985-88; mgr. quality assurance Medtronic Interventional Vascular, San Diego, Calif., 1989-93; mgr. quality and regulatory affairs, Lenexa Plant, Puritan-Bennett, Kans.; dist. mgr. A.L. Williams Assocs., San Diego, 1988-91; distbr., Nat. Safety Assocs., San Diego, 1988—; cons. in field, 1984-85, 88—. Patent applications in field. Judge Sci. Fair Gurnee Schs., 1968-70; leader Boy Scouts Am., 1959-77; mem. ch. council Lutheran Chs., Waukegan, Ill., 1971-72, Rocky Mount, N.C., 1973-74, Fallbrook, Calif., 1989-91; mem. Citizens Adv. Bd. Warren Twp. High Sch., Gurnee, 1979-81. Mem. Nat. Soc. Profl. Engrs., Am. Soc. Quality Control, Am. Prodn. and Inventory Control Soc., Am. Inst. Chem. Engrs., Marquetry Soc. Am., Woodworkers Assn. N.Am., Pi Kappa Phi, Alpha Phi Omega. Lutheran. Avocations: woodworking, stained glass, construction, locksmithing, landscaping. Home: 10441 W 116th St # 261 Overland Park KS 66210

PINO, GIANCARLO, food products executive; b. Brunico, Italy, June 30, 1954; came to the U.S., 1987; s. Letterio and Benedetta (Moschella) P.; m. Daniela Grecchi, Aug. 9, 1989; 1 child, Giorgia. Cert. computer programming, C.H.T., Verona, Italy, 1968; perito tecnico, 1st Tecnico Industriale, Trento, Italy, 1970. V.p. Tele Radio Ara Inc., Trento, 1970-74; pres. Panasound Inc., Trento, 1974-79; v.p. Videoteam Inc., Trento, 1979-84, pres., 1984-87; pres. Pasta Fresca Co., Inc., Arcadia, Calif., 1987—, Italfin, Inc., Irwindale, Calif., 1987—. Lt. Italian Army, 1970-72. Home: 1354 Deborah Ave Azusa CA 91702 Office: Pala Fresca Co Inc 119 W Live Oak Ave Arcadia CA 91007

PINOLI, BURT ARTHUR, airline executive; b. Santa Rosa, Calif., Nov. 23, 1954; s. Norris L. and Grace G. (Williams) P.; m. So Yen, May 9, 1987; 1 child, Lucas. BS in Agri-Bus., Calif. State U., Fresno, 1979; M. Internat. Mgmt., Am. Grad. Sch. Internat. Mgmt., Glendale, Ariz., 1988. Loan officer, mgmt. trainee Lloyds Bank Calif., Sanger, 1979-81; mgr. sales/bus. devel. Transamerica Airlines, Oakland, Calif., 1981-86; credit analyst, comml. loan officer Farm Credit Bank System, Ukiah, Calif., 1986-87; city mgr. Northwest Airlines, Beijing, 1988-90, Shanghai, People's Rep. of China, 1991—. Del. to India, Internat. Youth Exch. Named Nat. 4-H Coun. Nat. winner health project, 1974; recipient Blue Key, 1978. Mem. Alpha Gamma Rho (pres. 1978-79), Alpha Zeta. Home: 1551 Boonville Rd Ukiah CA 95482-9303

PINTA, WANDA BOHAN (MRS. R. JACK PINTA), municipal official; b. Greenfield, Ia., Sept. 11, 1918; d. Edward Philip and Stella (Plymesser) Bohan; B.S., Ia. State U., 1943; postgrad. Los Angeles State Coll., 1956-59; m. R. Jack Pinta, Apr. 17, 1948 (dec. Sept. 1982). Tech. writer, editor Gen. Motors Corp., Milford, Mich., 1943-45; sr. home economist Los Angeles Dept. Water and Power, 1956-61, dir. home econs., 1961—, dir. ednl. services, 1981-86, ret., 1986. Sec. Assn. for UN, Des Moines, 1953-55. Mem. mayor's Community Adv. Com. Recipient Laura McCall Home Service Achievement award, 1960; acceptor Aham's Alma award, 1970-72. Mem. Am. (consumer interests com. 1968-70), Cal. (exec. council, pres. Los Angeles dist. 1966-67) home econs. assns., Los Angeles Home Economists in Bus., Elec. Women's Round Table (dir. 1974, nat. pres. 1978-80), Soc. Consumer Affairs Profls. in Bus. (sec. So. Calif. chpt. 1978-79), Los Angeles City/County Energy Edn. Council (communications chmn. 1981-83, pres. 1983-84), Calif. Energy Edn. Forum, LWV (exec. bd. Des Moines 1953-55), Los Angeles World Affairs Council, Town Hall, Iowa State U. Alumni Assn. Episcopalian. Mem. Order Eastern Star. Club: Pilot (pres. Van Nuys 1962-63). Home: 5744 Vantage Ave North Hollywood CA 91607-1729

PINTER, JOSEPH KALMAN, mathematician; b. Janoshalma, Hungary, Jan. 12, 1953; arrived in Can., 1981; s. József and Teréz (Hoványi) P.; m. Mary Tan, Oct. 12, 1985; children: Kálmán Bonaventure, Elizabeth Anne. MS in Elec. Engring., Tech. U. Budapest, Hungary, 1976, PhD in Elec. Engring., 1979; MS in Math., U. Calgary, Can., 1986. Researcher Sefel Geophys., Calgary, Alta., Can., 1981-82; applied geophysicist Sci. and Exploration Computer Applications, Dome Pete Ltd., Calgary, Alta., Can., 1982-87, sr. applied geophysicist, 1987-88; researcher Amoco Can., Ltd., Calgary, Alta., 1988-92. Author: Propositions on the Geophysical Applications of the Radon Integral, 1990; inventor fully automated interpreter for refraction data, direct and inverse scattering in the Radon domain. Mem. Am. Math. Soc., N.Y. Acad. Scis., Soc. for Indsl. and Applied Math., Assn. of Profl. Engrs. Geologists and Geophysicists of Alta. Roman Catholic. Home: # 864 Lake Lucerne Dr SE, Calgary, AB Canada T2J 3H4

PINTER, NICHOLAS, geologist; b. Palma, Mallorca, Spain, July 27, 1964. BA, Cornell U., 1986; MS, Penn State U., 1988; PhD, U. Calif., Santa Barbara, Calif., 1992. Exploration geologist Mobil Oil, Bakersfield, Calif., 1989, Mobil New Exploration Ventures, Dallas, 1990; rsch. asst. Penn State U., University Park, Pa., 1986-88; rsch., teaching asst. U. Calif., Santa Barbara, 1988-92, researcher, lectr., 1992—. Co-author: Active Tectonics, 1994; contbr. numerous articles to profl. jours. Recipient Dissertation fellowship U. Calif., 1991, Rsch. fellowship White Mtn. Rsch. Sta., 1991, 92, Mathias Rsch. award U. Calif. Natural Res. System, 1990, Pacific Rim fellowship, 1990. Mem. Geol. Soc. of Am., Sigma Xi. Office: U of Calif Dept of Geol Scis Santa Barbara CA 93106

PINTO, FAUSTO JOSE, cardiologist; b. Santarem, Portugal, Nov. 3, 1960; came to U.S. 1989; s. Fausto Alexandre and Emilia (Conceicao) P.; m. Margarida Maria Silva, Oct. 5, 1985; children: Ana Margarida Silva, Maria Rita, Fausto Silva. MD, Lisbon Med. Sch., 1984. Intern/resident Univ. Hosp. Sta. Maria, Lisbon, 1984-86, fellow in cardiology, 1987-89; fellow in cardiology Stanford (Calif.) U. Med. Ctr., 1990-92, invasive fellow cardiology, 1992—, clin. attending echocardiography lab., 1991—. Contbr. articles to profl. jours. Calouste Gulbenkian fellow, 1990-92; Stanford U. Med. Ctr. postdoctoral fellow, 1991. Mem. Am. Coll. Cardiology, Am. Soc. Echocardiography, European Soc. Cardiology, N.Y. Acad. Sci., Am. Assn. for Devel. of Sci., Portuguese Soc. Cardiology, San Francisco Zool. Soc. Office: Stanford U Med Ctr Divsn Cardiology 300 Pasteur Dr Stanford CA 94305

PIPER, ARTHUR RUSSELL, insurance agent; b. Saye, Wyo., Sept. 29, 1942; s. Russell Alvin and Mary Ella (Stotts) P.; m. Carol Louise Price, July 23, 1969; children: John, Andrea, Jean, Aimee, Julie, Adam. BS in Sociology, Brigham Young U., 1969, MBA, 1972; CLU, The Am. Coll., 1977. Ins. agt. Met. Life, Morriston, N.J., 1972-74, Oakland, Calif., 1972-74; unit mgr. Met. Life, San Jose, Calif., 1974-77; agy. mgr. Beneficial Life, San Jose, 1977-79, Portland, Oreg., 1979-85; owner The Piper Planning Group, Beaverton, Oreg., 1985—. Bishop LDS Ch., Beaverton, 1991—, exec. sec. to state pres., Beaverton, 1985-89. Republican. Home: 7990 SW Barnard Dr Beaverton OR 97007 Office: The Piper Planning Group 14475 SW Allen BLW Ste A Beaverton OR 97006

PIPER, LEW EDWARD, JR., accountant; b. Miami, Fla., July 31, 1960; s. Lew Edward and Allura Louise (Flora) P.; m. Kathy Robin Link, June 15, 1985; 1 child, Lew Edward III. AA, St. Petersburg (Fla.) Jr. Coll, 1982; BBA, U. South Fla., 1984. CPA, Calif. Staff acct. Price Waterhouse CPAs, Little Rock, 1984-85; audit and acctg. mgr. Lund & Guttry, CPAs, Palm Springs, Calif., 1986—. Chmn. Coachella Valley Muscular Dystrophy Assn. Telethon, Palm Springs, 1990-92; campaign staff Com. to Elect Will Kleindienst for Mayor, Palm Springs, 1992. Recipient Shiny Apple award Palm Springs Unified Sch. Dist., 1990. Mem. AICPAs, Calif. Soc. CPAs (quality reviewer quality rev. div. 1990—), Palm Springs C. of C. (treas. bd. dirs. 1992—, chmn. edn. com. 1990-92). Republican. Office: Lund & Guttry CPAs 415 S Palm Canyon Dr Palm Springs CA 92262

PIRAHESH, HAMID, computer scientist; b. Tehran, Iran, June 8, 1950; s. Ebrahim and Effat (Nadim) P.; m. Parvin Katebi, Mar. 3, 1976; 1 child, Payom. BEE, U. Tech., Tehran, 1972; MS, UCLA, 1978, PhD, 1983. Electronics researcher U. Tech., 1971-74; system analyst Hepco, Tehran, 1974-76; system architect Transaction Tech. Inc., Santa Monica, Calif., 1979-85; computer scientist IBM Almaden Rsch. Ctr., San Jose, Calif., 1985—. Contbr. articles to profl. jours. Mem. IEEE, ACM. Office: IBM Almaden Rsch Ctr 650 Harry Rd San Jose CA 95120

PIRO, PAMELA JEAN, accounting manager; b. Butte, Mont., Aug. 23, 1960; d. Duane R. and Jean Ann (Hawe) Pacheco; m. Daniel Eugene Piro, July 21, 1989. BBA in Acctg., Internat. Bus., Gonzaga U., 1983. CPA, Colo. Sr. auditor Price Waterhouse, Denver, 1984-89; gen. acctg. mgr. Entenmann's div. of Gen. Foods Baking Cos., Denver, 1989-90; acctg. mgr. Invesco Funds Group, Inc., Denver, 1990—. Mem. AICPA, Colo. Soc. CPAs. Democrat. Roman Catholic. Office: Invesco Funds Group Inc 7800 E Union Ave # 800 Denver CO 80237

PIROLLI, PETER LOUIS THOMAS, education educator, cognitive scientist; b. Oshawa, Ont., Can., Apr. 27, 1959; came to U.S., 1981; s. Remo and Elizabeth (Blakemore) P. BS in Psychology and Anthropology, Trent U., Can., 1980; BS in Cognitive Psychology, Trent U., 1981; MS in Cognitive Psychology, Carnegie Mellon U., 1982, PhD in Cognitive Psychology, 1985. Asst. prof. to assoc. prof. U. Calif., Berkeley, 1985—; rsch. assoc. Xerox Palo Alto (Calif.) Rsch. Ctr., 1985-91, mem. rsch. staff, 1992—; rsch. assoc. Inst. for Rsch. on Learning, Palo Alto, 1985-91; Prin. NSF, Office of Naval Rsch., Nat. Ctr. for Vocat. Edn.. Editor: Instructional Science, 1990—; contbr. articles to profl. jours. NAE fellow Nat. Acad. Edn., 1986. Mem. AAAI, Cognitive Sci. Soc., Am. Ednl./Rsch. Assn., Am. Psychol. Assn., Am. Psychol. Soc., AAAS, Assn. Computing Machinery, others.

PISAROWICZ, JAMES ALEXANDER, human resources specialist, educator, consultant; b. St. Paul, June 28, 1951; s. Antoni Kashmer and Patricia Charlotte (Olson) P.; m. Patricia Marie Ayd, Aug. 19, 1973 (div. 1980); m. Karen Sue Rosga, May 19, 1990. BA in Math. and Psychology, Hamline U., 1973; MA in Psychology, U. Denver, 1976, PhD in Psychology, 1981. Cons. Denver, Austin, Tex., 1973-83; asst. prof. Antioch U., Denver, 1982-84; park ranger Nat. Park Svc., Wind Cave Nat. Park, S.D., 1984-88; geographer U.S. Census Bur., Boston, 1988-89; resource specialist Minn. Dept. Natural Resources, Spring Valley, 1989-90; exec. dir. Death Valley (Calif.) Natural History Assn., 1990-92; employment tng. rep. The Tng. Advantage, Montrose, Colo., 1992—; asst. prof. Mesa State Coll., 1993—. Author: Caving Basics, 1982, 87; editor: Processes of Transition, 1980, Death Valley Prehistory and History, Vol. 1, 1987, Vol. 2, 1988, Vol. 3, 1992, (jours.) NSS Bull., 1989, Death Valley Telescope, 1990-92; contbr. over 130 articles to profl. jours. COSIP Rsch. fellow NSF, 1972-73. Fellow Nat. Speleological Soc. (Lew Bicking award 1990), The Explorers Club; mem. Psi Chi. Office: The Tng Advantage 11 S Park Ave Ste C Montrose CO 81402

PISCIOTTA, SAMUEL JAMES, small business owner; b. Pueblo, Colo., Dec. 10, 1938; s. Sam Jr. and Eva May (Padula) P.; m. Cynthia Diane Garrett, Aug. 8, 1961; children: Samuel, Pamela, Richard, Michael. BA, Western State Coll., 1967. Pres., mgr. Pueblo (Colo.) Bus. Men's Club, Inc., DBA Capt. Sam's Family Athletic Club, Inc., 1961—. Composer symphonic music. Co-founder, v.p. Pueblo Performing Arts Guild, 1986—; founder, co-organizer Pubelo office So. Colo. Better Bus. Bur., 1985—, chmn. bd. 1987-88). Named one of Outstanding Young Men of Am., 1970, Small Bus. Yr., Pueblo C. of C., 1988, Colo. C. of C., 1988; recipient Scoutmaster Order of the Arrow, Boy Scouts Am., 1972. Mem. Nat. Swim and Recreation Assn. (pres. 1976-77), Greater Pueblo Sports Assn., Pueblo Jaycees (state bd. dirs. 1973-75), Pueblo Bus. Exch. (co-founder, pres. 1984), Kiwanis (bd. dirs. 1986), Elks, Masons, KT, Jesters, Shriners (potentate 1992), Dante Alighieri Soc., Royal Order Scotland, Order of Quetzalcoatl (charter camaxtli 1992), Tau Kappa Epsilon. Republican. Home: 27 Pedregal Ln Pueblo CO 81005-2917 Office: Capt Sam's Family Athletic Club Inc 1500 W 4th St Pueblo CO 81004-1271

PISTER, KARL STARK, engineering educator; b. Stockton, Calif., June 27, 1925; s. Edwin LeRoy and Mary Kimball (Smith) P.; m. Rita Olsen, Nov. 18, 1950; children: Francis, Therese, Anita, Jacinta, Claire, Kristofer. B.S. with honors, U. Calif., Berkeley, 1945, M.S., 1948; Ph.D., U. Ill., Urbana, 1952. Instr. theoretical and applied mechanics U. Ill., 1949-52; mem. faculty U. Calif., Berkeley, 1952-91, prof. engring. scis., 1962—, Roy W. Carlson prof. engring., 1985-90, dean Coll. Engring., 1980-90; chancellor U. Calif., Santa Cruz, 1991—, now pres., chancellor; Richard Merton guest prof. U. Stuttgart, W. Ger., 1978; cons. to govt. and industry; bd. dirs. Monterey Bay Aquarium Rsch. Inst.; bd. trustees Monterey Inst. Internat. Studies; chmn. bd. Calif. Coun. Sci. and Tech. Author research papers in field; assoc. editor: Computer Methods in Applied Mechanics and Engring, 1972, Jour. Optimization Theory and Applications, 1982; editorial adv. bd. Encyclopedia Phys. Sci. and Tech. Served with USNR, World War II. Recipient Wason Research medal Am. Concrete Inst., 1960, Vincent Bendix Minorities in Engring. award Am. Soc. for Engring. Edn., 1988; Fulbright scholar Ireland, 1965; Fulbright scholar W. Ger., 1973. Fellow Am. Acad. Mechanics, ASME; mem. Nat. Acad. Engring., ASCE, ASME, Earthquake Engring. Research Inst., Soc. Engring. Sci. Office: U Calif Santa Cruz Office of Chancellor 1156 High St Santa Cruz CA 95064-1026

PISTON, WADE ANTHONY, medical association executive, consultant; b. L.A., Jan. 14, 1953; s. Anthony Walter and Amy (Gilbert) P.; m. Claudia May Rode, Nov. 15, 1986. AB, U. So. Calif., 1975, MPA, 1977. Adminstr. health resources Los Angeles County Med. Assn., 1978-84, pub. affairs officer, 1984-86, dir. pub. affairs and govt. rels., 1986—; founder, prin. Horton Cons., L.A., 1986—, L.A. Vancouver Sister City Assn., 1986—; bd. dirs. L.A. st. Petersburg Sister City Assn. Pres. civil svc. commn. Los Angeles County, 1992; pres. L.A. Jr. C. of C., 1983-84; mem. Calif. commn. on Primary Care Clinics Adv. Coun., Sacramento, 1988-90. Mem. Am. Assn. Med. Soc. Execs., Am. Soc. Assn. Execs., Am. Assn. Polit. Cons., L.A. Pub. Affairs Officers Assn. (chmn. 1992—), Healthcare Execs. So. Calif., Rotary (chmn.). Home: 1745 Carlson Ln Redondo Beach CA 90278 Office: Los Angeles County Med Assn 1925 Wilshire Blvd Los Angeles CA 90057

PITCHER, HELEN IONE, advertising executive; b. Colorado Springs, Colo., Aug. 6, 1931; d. William Forest Medlock and Frankie La Vone (Hamilton) Tweed; m. Richard Edwin Pitcher, Sept. 16, 1949; children: Dushka Myers, Suzanne, Marc. Student, U. Colo., 1962-64, Ariz. State U., 1966, Maricopa Tech. Coll., 1967, Scottsdale Community Coll., 1979-81. Design draftsman Sundstrand Aviation, Denver, 1962-65; tech. illustrator Sperry, Phoenix, 1966-68; art dir. Integrated Circuit Engring., Scottsdale, Ariz., 1968-71, dir. advt., 1981—; advt. artist Motorola Inc., Phoenix, 1971-74; pres. Pitcher Tech. Pubs., Scottsdale, 1974-81. Profl. advisor Paradise Valley Sch. Dist., Phoenix, 1984—; mem. bd. advisors graphic arts dept. Ariz. State U., Tempe. mem. Nat. Audio Visual Assn., Bus. Profl. Advt. Assn. (treas. 1982-86), Direct Mktg. Club. Democrat. Mem. Ch. Christ. Home: 13681 N Pima Rd Scottsdale AZ 85260-4105

PITKIN, ROY MACBETH, physician, educator; b. Anthon, Iowa, May 24, 1934; s. Roy and Pauline Allie (McBeath) P.; m. Marcia Alice Jenkins, Aug. 17, 1957; children: Barbara, Robert Macbeth, Kathryn, William Charles. B.A. with highest distinction, U. Iowa, 1956, M.D., 1959. Diplomate Am. Bd. Obstetrics & Gynecology, 1967. Intern King County Hosp., Seattle, 1959-60; resident in ob-gyn U. Iowa Hosps. and Clinics, Iowa City, 1960-63; asst. prof. ob-gyn U. Ill., 1965-68; assoc. prof. ob-gyn U. Iowa, Iowa City, 1968-72; prof. U. Iowa, 1972-87, head dept. ob-gyn, 1977-87; prof., chmn. dept. ob-gyn. UCLA, 1987—; mem. residency rev. com. ob-gyn, 1981-87, chmn. 1985-87. Editor-in-chief: Year Book of Obstetrics and Gynecology, 1975-86; editor-in-chief: Clinical Obstetrics and Gynecology, 1979; editor: Obstetrics and Gynecology, 1985. Contbr. articles to med. jours. Served to lt. comdr. M.C. USNR, 1963-65. NIH career awardee, 1972-77. Fellow Royal Coll. Obstetricians and Gynecologists (ad eundem); mem. AMA (Goldberger award in clin. nutrition 1982), Am. Coll. Obstetricians and Gynecologists, Am. Gynecol. and Obstet. Soc., German Soc. Gynecology and Obstetrics (hon. 1992), Central Assn. Obstetricians and Gynecologists, Soc. Gynecologic Investigation (pres. 1985-86), Soc. Perinatal Obstetricians (pres. 1978-79), NAS, Inst. of Medicine. Presbyterian. Office: UCLA Sch Medicine Dept Ob-Gyn Los Angeles CA 90024-1740

PITLAK, ROBERT THOMAS, sales and marketing executive; b. Jersey City, May 4, 1938; s. John Francis Pitlak and Estelle Dorothy (Marciniak) Oesch; m. Faith Sarah Phillips, June 30, 1962; children: George, Sarah. BS in Physics, St. Peters Coll., 1960; MS in Physics, Fairleigh Dickenson U., 1968; MBA, Pepperdine U., 1979. Optical engr. Bausch & Lomb, Inc., Rochester, N.Y., 1960-61; product mgr. Isomet Corp., Palisades Park, N.J., 1961-65; program engr. Kollsman Instruments Corp., Syosset, N.Y., 1965-69; product line mgr. Holobeam, Inc., Paramus, N.J., 1969-72; field sales engr. Oretec div. EG&G, Oak Ridge, Tenn., 1972-73; mgr. sales/mktg. Apollo Lasers, Inc., L.A., 1973-79; v.p. mktg. Interactive Radiation, INc., North Vale, N.J., 1979-81; mgr. laser products Allied-Signal Corp., Chatsworth, Calif., 1981-86; pres., CEO Pitlak Corp., Thousand Oaks, Calif., 1986—; also bd. dirs., chmn. bd. Pitlak Corp., Thousand Oaks; bd. dirs. Deltron Laser Corp., Palo Alto. Author: Computer Programs for Use in Electro Optics, 1984, (computer program) Media Evaluation and Analysis Under Restrained Resources, 1988. Mem. Optical Soc. of Am., K.C. (dep. grand knight). Republican. Roman Catholic. Office: Pitlak Corp PO Box 7835 Thousand Oaks CA 91359

PITT, CHARLES HORACE, metallurgy educator, consultant; b. Fremont, Wis., Aug. 9, 1929; s. Horace B. and Nelda Ruby (Sommer) P.; m. Margaret Louise Park, June 8, 1956; children—Roland, William, Jennifer, Rosanne, Barbara. B.S., U. Wis., 1951; Ph.D., U. Utah, 1959. Registered profl. engr., Wash., Utah. Engr. Gen. Electric Co., Richland, Wash., 1951-53; asst. prof. metallurgy dept U. Utah, Salt Lake City, 1959-65, assoc. prof., 1965-71, prof., 1971—. Served with U.S. Army, 1954-56. Mem. Nat. Assn. Corrosion Engrs., Am. Soc. Metals (chmn. Utah chpt. 1967-68), AIME, Phi Kappa Phi (pres. Utah chpt. 1980-81). Mem. Ch. of Jesus Christ of Latter-day Saints. Home: 3082 S 400 W Bountiful UT 84010-7813 Office: U Utah Metallurgy Dept 412 WBB Salt Lake City UT 84112

PITT, STEPHEN HAROLD, software management executive; b. Sydney, NSW, Australia, Aug. 28, 1954. BA in Mgmt., St. Mary's, Moraga, Calif., 1992. Cert. acct. Mgr. customer svc. Ultradata Corp., Pleasanton, Calif., 1981-84, v.p. customer svcs., 1984-86, sr. v.p., 1986-87, COO, 1987—; bd. dirs. Prodata, Inc., Bismarck, N.D. Mem. Nat. Inst. Accts. Home: 63 Rainbow Bridge Way San Ramon CA 94583

PITT, WILLIAM ALEXANDER, cardiologist; b. Vancouver, B.C., Can., July 17, 1942; came to U.S., 1970; s. Reginald William and Una Sylvia (Alexander) P.; m. Judith Mae Wilson, May 21, 1965; children: William Matthew, Joanne Katharine. MD, U. B.C., Vancouver, 1967. Diplomate Royal Coll. Physicians Can. Intern, Mercy Hosp., San Diego, 1967-68, resident, 1970-71; resident Vancouver Gen. Hosp., 1968-70, U. Calif., San Diego, 1971-72; assoc. dir. cardiology Mercy Hosp., San Diego, 1972-92; with So. Calif. Cardiology Med. Group, San Diego, 1984—; bd. trustees San Diego Found. for Med. Care, 1983-89, pres., chmn. bd. trustees, 1986-88, med. dir., 1991—; bd. dirs. Mut. Assn. for Profl. Services, Phila., 1984-92; pres. Alternet Med. Svcs., Inc., 1992—. Fellow Royal Coll. Physicians Can., Am. Coll. Cardiology (assoc.); mem. AMA, Am. Heart Assn., Calif. Med. Assn., San Diego County Med. Soc., San Diego County Heart Assn. (bd. dirs. 1982-88). Episcopalian. Office: So Calif Cardiology Med Group 6386 Alvarado Ct Ste 101 San Diego CA 92120-4906

PITTMAN, EDWARD DALE, geology consultant; b. Dublin, Tex., Feb. 17, 1930; s. Cle Dale and America Faye (Tatum) P.; m. Alva K. Anderton, Sept. 2, 1955; children: Sheri Lynn, Susan Kay. BA, UCLA, 1956, MA, 1958, PhD, 1962. Geologist Amoco Prodn. Co., Okla. City, 1962-65; various rsch. positions to group supr. Rsch. Ctr. Amoco Prodn. Co., Tulsa, 1965-89; prof. geology U. Tulsa, 1989-91; geology cons., Sedona, Ariz., 1991—; adjunct prof. U. Tulsa, 1979, '81, '84. With U.S. Army, 1951-53. Mem. Am. Assn. Petroleum Geologists (hon., A.I. Leverson award 1989, disting. svc. award), Soc. for Sedimentary Geology (v.p. 1988-89, best paper award 1977, excellence of presentation award 1978, outstanding oral presentation award 1987), Tulsa Geol. Soc. (hon., pres. 1981-82). Home and Office: 222 Bowstring Dr Sedona AZ 86336

PITTS, BERNARD RAY, judge; b. Lampe, Mo., June 16, 1944; s. Charles Edward Antonie and Helen Agnes (Schwyhart) P.; m. Tua Emmeline Katter, Dec. 30, 1970; children: Olga Marie, Helen Linnea, Olivia Tatiana, Galadriel Alexandra, Alex Christian. AA, Yuba Coll., Marysville, Calif., 1964; BA, Brigham Young U., Provo, Utah, 1968; JD, U. Wyo., Laramie, 1973; MA, U. No. Colo., 1981. Bar: Wyo. 1974, U.S. Dist. Ct. Wyo. 1974, U.S. Ct. Mil. Appeals 1975, U.S. Ct. Appeals (10th cir.) 1980. Assoc. Patrick E. Hacker & Assocs., Cheyenne, Wyo., 1978-79; asst. city atty. City of Cheyenne, 1979-84; assoc. Robert L. Nelson & Assocs., Cheyenne, 1985-88; adminstrv. asst. Clk. of Laramie County, Cheyenne, 1985-90; asst. county atty. Laramie County, Cheyenne, 1990-92; mcpl. judge Town of Pine Bluffs, Wyo., 1984—, Town of Burns, Wyo., 1983—, City of Cheyenne, 1986—; with LDS Ch. Mission to Finland, 1965-68; Wyo. state senate attorney budget session 49th Legislature, 1988; instr. criminal justice Warren acad. ctr. Chapman U., Cheyenne. Bd. dirs. Meals on Wheels of Cheyenne, 1985-89, treas., 1986-87, pres., 1987-88; precinct com. Rep. Party, 1986—; del. Rep. State Conv., 1990. With U.S. Army, 1968-70, 75-78. Mem. Wyo Bar Assn., Wyo. Conf. Special Ct. Judges, Laramie County Bar Assn. Latter Day Saints. Ch. Office: 2101 O'Neil Ave Rm 304 Cheyenne WY 82001

PITTS, WILLIAM CLARENCE, physicist; b. Seattle, Apr. 19, 1929; s. Clarence H. and Emily B. (Kepp) P.; m. Joanne R. Lawson, May 18, 1952 (dec. Jan. 1978); children: Starr R., Nancy H.; m. Patricia A. Kirkland, May 1, 1981. BS in Physics, U. Wash., 1951; postgrad., Stanford U., 1951-58. Rsch. scientist NACA/NASA, Moffett Field, Calif., 1951-86, Eloret Inst., Moffett Field, 1986—. Contbr. numerous articles to profl. publs.; inventor two-force measuring balance for earth orbit application. Office: NASA Ames Rsch Ctr N 234-1 Moffett Field CA 94035

PIZZORNO, JOSEPH EGIDIO, JR., college president; b. San Gabriel, Calif., Dec. 7, 1947; s. Joseph Egidio Sr. and Mary (Carmela) P.; m. Mavis Bonnar (div. Oct. 1983); 1 child, Raven Muir; m. Lara Elise Udell, Sept. 28, 1985; 1 child, Galen Udell. BS with Distinction, Harvey Mudd Coll., Claremont, Calif., 1969; Naturopathic Doctor with honors, Nat. Coll. Naturopathic Medicine, Portland, Oreg., 1975. Rsch. asst. Lockheed Aircraft, Ontario, Calif., 1968; rsch. technologist U. Wash., Seattle, 1970-75; practice naturopathic medicine Seattle, 1975-80, practice midwifery, 1978-82; pres., researcher Bastyr Coll., Seattle, 1978—; pres. Coun. on Naturopathic Med. Edn., Portland, Oreg., 1985-87; apptd. adv. panel safety and efficacy of dietary supplements U.S. Office of Tech. Assessment, 1993—. Co-author: A Textbook of Natural Medicine, 1985, Encyclopedia of Natural Medicine, 1990; contbg. editor Let's Live mag., Los Angeles, 1987—; contbr. articles to profl. jours. Mem. Am. Assn. Naturopathic Physicians (bd. dirs. 1984—), Wash. Assn. Naturopathic Physicians (edn. dir. 1976), Seattle Midwifery Sch. (edn. com. 1978-91), Northwest Sci. Fiction Soc. Libertarian. Home: 13502 42d St NE Seattle WA 98125 Office: Bastyr Coll 144 NE 54th St Seattle WA 98105-3753

PLANK, GEORGE, performing arts company executive; b. L.A., Jan. 26, 1956; s. John Franklin and Evelyn M. (Freeman) P. Student, U. Calif. Berkeley, 1973-75; BA, Pomona Coll., 1978; MA Theater Arts, UCLA, 1988. Dir. Am. Theaters Overseas, West Germany, 1981-85, Tokyo, 1987-89, Veneto, Italy, 1989-90; dir., prodr., v.p. Myriad Shows Ltd, L.A., 1985-87; dir. George Plank, Beverly Hills, Calif., 1990—; cons. Eliot Concept Design, Venice, Calif., 1990—, N.L. Budinger, San Francisco, 1992—, Andrew J.

Carroll, San Francisco, 1992; actor films and commls., Calif. and overseas, 1978—; with Look Talent Agy., San Francisco, 1992—, Actors' Group, Seattle, 1990—. Author: American Theaters in Europe, 1988; dir., playwright mus. revues and dramas, 1981—. Vol. devel. dept. San Francisco AIDS Found., 1993—. Named Best Dir. U.S. Play Tournaments, West Germany, 1982-85, Michael Harris shows, Seattle, 1991; performed Outstanding performances for U.S. govt., Tokyo, 1989. Mem. AFTRA, Kenneth Wallace-Smith Blue Stocking Found. (scribe, v.p. 1992), Theater Bay Area San Francisco, UCLA Theater Alumni Assn., Actors Equity Assn., Pomona Coll. Theater Dept. Alumni Assn., Jean-Marc Barr Franco-Am. Cinematique (v.p. 1993), Red Lodge (Mont.) Hist. Soc. Home: PO Box 94 Berkeley CA 94701 Office: PO Box 123 Beverly Hills CA 90213

PLANTING, PETER JOHN, manufacturing engineer; b. Kouvola, Finland, Aug. 23, 1937; s. Harvey Alvin and Irma Hagar Linnea (Manninen) P.; m. Lois Rita Tourtelot, May 29, 1969 (div. Aug. 1982); children: John David, Anna Liisa; m. Marilyn Jo Wahl, Jan. 29, 1983; 1 child, Kristina; stepchildren: Theresa Echols, Mark Echols. BS in Chemistry, San Jose (Calif.) State U., 1962. Staff chemist, project engr. SRI Internat., Menlo Park, Calif., 1962-70; R&D and mfg. engr. Hewlett-Packard, Palo Alto, Calif., 1972—; guest lectr. U. Oulu (Finland), 1983; con. various corps., Finland, 1983—; engring. liaison Hewlett-Packard/Microwave Tech., Hsinchu Taiwan, 1988—. Contbr. articles to profl. jours.; patentee in field. Mem. Am. Vacuum Soc., Finnish Am. Home Assn. (bd. dirs. 1985-88), Internat. Soc. Hybrid Mfrs. Office: Hewlett-Packard Co 1400 Fountain Grove Pky Santa Rosa CA 95403-1738

PLATE, THOMAS GORDON, newspaper editor; b. N.Y.C., May 17, 1944; s. John William and Irene (Henry) P.; m. Andrea I. Margolis, Sept. 22, 1979; 1 child, Ashley Alexandra. AB, Amherst Coll., 1966; MPA, Princeton U., 1968. Writer Newsweek, N.Y.C., 1968-70; editor Newsday, L.I., N.Y., 1970-72; sr. editor N.Y. Mag., N.Y.C., 1972-75; editor edit. page L.A. Herald Examiner, 1978-82; sr. editor Time Mag., N.Y.C., 1982-83; editor in chief Family Weekly, N.Y.C., 1984-85; editor edit. pages N.Y. Newsday, N.Y.C., 1986-90, L.A. Times, 1990—. Author: Secret Police, 1981, Crime Days!, 1975, Understanding Doomsday, 1971; co-author: Commissioner, 1978. Recipient Best Deadline Writing award Am. Soc. Newspaper Editors, 1981, Best Edit. awards L.A. Press Club, 1979, 80, 81. Mem. Century Assn. (N.Y.), Phi Beta Kappa. Office: LA Times Times Mirror Sq Los Angeles CA 90053

PLATT, JAMES ROBERT, business executive; b. Batavia, N.Y., Oct. 23, 1948; s. Robert John and Mildred J. (Foote) P.; m. Shelly A. Tunis, May 24, 1980; children: Shane Christopher, Tristan Robert. BS, SUNY, Brockport, 1970; MA, Ariz. State U., 1982. Cert. tchr., N.Y. Inside sales supr. Mallco Distbrs., Phoenix, 1972-77; grad. teaching asst. Ariz. State U., Tempe, 1978-79; sales rep. Wisco Equipment Co., Inc., Phoenix, 1979-82, sales mgr., 1984-88; sales rep. Clyde Hardware Co., Tucson, 1982-84; v.p. Wistech Controls, Phoenix, 1988—. Mem. Ariz. Coun. Excellence. Regents scholar SUNY, 1966-70. Mem. Instrument Soc. Am., Young Execs.-Fluid Power Distbrs. Assn., Am. Soc. Environ. History, Soc. Mfg. Engrs., Phi Alpha Theta. Office: Wistech Controls 4810 S 36th St Phoenix AZ 85040-2905

PLATT, JOHN STODDARD, electrical engineer; b. Portland, Oreg., Aug. 3, 1943; s. John Williams Stoddard and Jane (Kerr) P.; m. Doris Rodriguez, June 28, 1975; children: John, Peter, Victor. BA, Havard Coll., 1966; BS, Oreg. State U., 1981, MS, 1983. Coord. physics Nat. Program for Improvement of Sci. Teaching, Lima, Peru, 1971-78; engr. Hewlett Packard Co., McMinnville, Oreg., 1983—. Vol. U.S. Peace Corps, Peru, 1967-70. Mem. IEEE, Corvallis United Soccer Club (v.p. for selection 1991), Tau Beta Pi. Home: 330 NW 29th Corvallis OR 97330

PLATT, JOSEPH BEAVEN, former college president; b. Portland, Oreg., Aug. 12, 1915; s. William Bradbury and Mary (Beaven) P.; m. Jean Ferguson Rusk, Feb. 9, 1946; children: Ann Ferguson Walker, Elizabeth Beaven Garrow. BA, U. Rochester, 1937; PhD, Cornell U., 1942; LLD, U. So. Calif., 1969, Claremont McKenna Coll., 1982; DSc, Harvey Mudd Coll., 1981. Instr. physics U. Rochester, N.Y., 1941-43, from asst. prof. to prof., 1946-56, assoc. chmn. dept. physics, 1954-56; staff mem. radiation lab. MIT, Cambridge, 1943-46; pres. Harvey Mudd Coll., Claremont, Calif., 1956-76, now part-time sr. prof. physics; pres. Claremont U. Ctr., 1976-81; trustee Aerospace Corp., 1972-85, Consortium for Advancement of Pvt. Higher Edn., 1985-92; chief physics br. AEC, 1949-51; cons. U.S. Office Ordnance Rsch., NSF, 1953-56; mem. com. on sci. in UNESCO, Nat. Acad. Scis.-NRC, 1960-62, mem. com. on internat. orgns. and programs, 1962-64; sci. advisor U.S. Del., UNESCO Gen. Conf., Paris, 1960, alt. del., 1962; mem. panel on internat. sci. Pres.'s Sci. Adv. Com., 1961; chmn. Subcom. on Sino-Am. Sci. Cooperation, 1965-79; trustee Analytic Svcs., Inc., 1958-89, chmn., 1961-89; mem. adv. com. on sci. edn. NSF, 1965-70, 72-76, chmn., 1969-70, 73-74, 74-75; bd. dirs. Lincoln Found., 1979-85, Bell & Howell Corp., 1978-88, Am. Mut. Fund, 1981-88, DeVry, Inc., 1984-87, Sigma Rsch., 1983-87. Trustee China Found. for Promotion of Edn. and Culture, 1975—, Carnegie Found. for Advancement Teaching, 1970-78; chmn. select com. Master Plan for Higher Edn. Calif., 1971-73; mem. Carnegie Coun. for Policy Studies in Higher Edn., 1975-80. Fellow Am. Phys. Soc.; mem. IEEE, Automobile Club So. Calif. (bd. dirs. 1973-90, chmn. bd. dirs. 1986-87), Calif. Club, Sunset Club, Twilight Club, Cosmos Club, Bohemian Club, Phi Beta Kappa, Sigma Xi, Phi Kappa Phi. Home: 452 W 11th St Claremont CA 91711-3833

PLATT, STUART FRANKLIN, defense industry executive; b. N.Y.C., Nov. 9, 1933; s. Samuel Adams and Rose Ann (Cohan) P.; m. Melanee Ann Daniels, Mar. 29, 1980. BS, U. Rochester, 1955; MBA, U. Mich., 1956; MS in Systems Analysis, U. Rochester, 1970. Commd. ensign USN, 1956, advanced through grades to rear admiral, 1979, ret., 1987; asst. dep. chief Naval Material, Procurement and Prodn., 1975-79; subsistence field activities Def. Pers. Support Ctr., 1977-79; dep. comdr. Naval Systems Command HQ, 1979-83; competition adv. gen., 1983-86; sr. v.p. Continental Maritime Industries, 1987-88; pres. Found. Health Fed. Svcs., 1988-90; chmn., CEO LA-LB Shipyards, Inc., L.A., 1990—; mng. dir. FPBSM Investments, San Francisco, 1990—; pres. Precision Echo, Inc., Santa Clara, 1992—; bd. dirs. Axel Electronics, Inc., Sigma Power, Inc., DRS Diagnostic/Retrieval Systems, Inc., Harding Assocs., Inc., SPD Techs., Indian Wells Water Co., Inc. Pres. Neva Russian Dance Ensemble, San Francisco, Nat. Assn. Uniformed Svcs. and Surviving Widows, Calif. chpt.; mem. bd. governing advisors U.S. Merchant Marine Acad., 1991-94. Decorated DSM, Legion of Merit, Bronze Star. Mem. U.S. C. of C. Office: Stuart Platt & Ptnrs 870 Market St Ste 1141 San Francisco CA 94102

PLATZ, HOWARD RICHARD, financial executive; b. Denver, Mar. 10, 1961; s. Howard Richard Sr. and Juanita E. (Sale) P.; m. Jolene Sue Fisher, Aug. 17, 1985; children: David, William. BS in Acctg., Greenville (Ill.) Coll., 1983. CPA, Calif. Acct. Jeffrey L. Cummings, CPA, St. Louis, 1983-86; acct., MIS mgr. Mary L. Dietz, J.D., San Diego, 1986-88; sr. acct. Hardy, Oswald & Co., CPAs, Vista, Calif., 1988-91; dir. fin. Park Pl. Prodns., Carlsbad, Calif., 1992—. Mem. AICPA (tax div.), Calif. Soc. CPAs. Republican. Home: 4726 Ingraham St San Diego CA 92109 Office: Spirit of Discovery Park Place Prodns 5421 Avenida Encinas Ste J Carlsbad CA 92008

PLATZKER, ARNOLD C.G., medical educator; b. N.Y.C., Aug. 26, 1936; m. Marjorie Sanek, June 9, 1963; 2 children. AB, žBrown U., 1958; MD, Tufts U., 1962. Intern Boston City Hosp., 1962-63, resident in pediatrics, 1963-64; resident in pediatrics Stanford U., 1964-66; fellow U. Calif. Sch. Medicine, San Francisco, 1968-71; instr. dept. pediatrics Stanford U. Sch. Medicine, 1965-66; assoc. dir. Pediatrics Pulmonary Function Lab. U. Calif., San Francisco, 1971-73; asst. prof. dept. pediatrics U. Calif. Med. Sch., 1971-73; asst. prof. pediatrics U. So. Calif., 1974-77, assoc. prof. pediatrics, 1977-85, prof. pediatrics, 1985—; head, div. neonatology and pediatric pulmonology U. Soc. Calif., 1973—; pres. Childrens Hosp. Med. Group, 1982-86, bd. dirs., mem. exec. com., 1981-93; vis. fellow Clare Hall, Cambridge U., 1986, life mem., 1986; steering, exec. com. NHLBI study pediatric pulmonary and cardiac complications of vertically transmitted HIV infection, 1989—, chmn. pulmonary subcommittee, 1989—. Contbr. articles to profl. jours. Bd. dirs. Am. Lung Assn. Los Angeles County, 1989-93, exec. com., 1992-93, Am. Lung Assn. Calif., 1990-93. Fellow Am. Coll. Chest Physicians, Am. Acad. Pediatrics, Royal Soc. Medicine (U.K.); mem. Western Soc. Pediatric Rsch., Am. Thoracic Soc. (chmn. pediatric sci. assembly 1979), European Soc. Pneumonology, Calif. Perinatal Assn. (pres. 1978, bd. dirs. 1977-80), European Respiratory Soc., AAAS, N.Y. Acad. Scis., AAUP. Office: Childrens Hosp of LA PO Box 54700 Los Angeles CA 90054-0700

PLAYER, GARY FARNSWORTH, geologist; b. San Francisco, Jan. 30, 1943; s. Lawrence Lynden and Laura (Farnsworth) P.; m. Corrie Lynne Oborn, June 18, 1965; children: Dolly, Sherri, Gary, Roch, Eric, Linda, Micah, Nathan. BS in Geology, Stanford U., 1964; MA, UCLA, 1966. Cert. petroleum geologist; registered geologist, Calif. Geologist Union Oil Co. Calif., Anchorage, Alaska, 1965-68, Stauffer Chem Co., Richmond, Calif., 1968-69, Gulf Oil Co., Bakersfield, Calif., 1969-70, Dames and Moore, Anchorage, 1970-73; cons. mechanics rsch. U. Alaska, Anchorage, 1973-77; geologist Atlantic Richfield Co., Anchorage, 1977-81; exploration mgr. MAPCO Oil and Gas Co., Tulsa, Okla., 1981-83; cons. Tahoma Resources, 1983-92; geologist LDS Ch., Salt Lake City, 1992—. Contbr. articles to profl. jours. Precinct chmn. Rep. Cen. Com., Anchorage, 1979; trumpet soloist numerous bands and orchs., 1967—. Mem. Utah Geol. Assn., Am. Assn. Petroleum Geologists (assoc. editor 1982-85). Mem. LDS Ch. Office: LDS Ch 50 E North Temple Salt Lake City UT 84150

PLEMING-YOCUM, LAURA CHALKER, religion educator; b. Sheridan, Wyo., May 25, 1913; d. Sidney Thomas and Florence Theresa (Woodbury) Chalker; m. Edward Kibbler Pleming, Aug. 25, 1938 (dec. Nov. 1980); children: Edward Kibbler,lam Rowena Pleming Chamberlin, Sidney Thomas; m. William Lewis Yocum, Dec. 19, 1989. BA, Calif. State U., Long Beach, 1953, MA in Speech and Drama, 1954; postgrad., U. So. Calif., L.A., 1960-63; D Religion, Grad. Sch. Theology, Claremont, Calif., 1968. Internat. lectr. Bibl. studies, 1953—, adult seminar resource person, 1953—; Bibl. lectr. Principia Coll., Elsah, Ill., 1968-90; Bible scholar 1st Ch. of Christ, Scientist, Boston, 1970-75; tchr. adult edn. Principia Coll., summers, 1969-71; tour lectr. to Middle East, 1974—; mem. archaeol. team, Negev, Israel. Author: Triumph of Job, 1979; editor (newsletter) Bibleletter, 1968-84. Mem. AAUP, Am. Acad. Religion, Soc. Bibl. Lit. and Exegesis, Am. Schs. Oriental Rsch., Inst. Mediterranean Studies, Religious Edn. Assn., Internat. Platform Assn., Congress Septuagint and Cognate Studies, Religious Edn. Assn., Zeta Tau Alpha (alumni pres. Long Beach chpt. 1960), Gamma Theta Upsilon (pres. Long Beach chpt. 1952).

PLENK, AGNES MERO, psychologist; b. Budapest, Hungary, Jan. 28, 1917; d. Julian and Rose (Szesci) Mero; m. Henry P. Plenk, June 17, 1938; children: Bruce, Penny Plenk Dalrymple, Timothy. BA, Northwestern U., 1945, MA, 1947; PhD, U. Utah, 1967. Lic. psychologist, Utah, Nat. Registered Health Care Providers. Sr. psychologist dept. psychiatry Med. Sch. U. Utah, 1947-50; pvt. practice Salt Lake City, 1950-62; adj. prof. ednl. psychology U. Utah, 1972—; adj. prof. clin. psychology Brigham Young U.; founder, dir. Holladay Community Nursery Sch., Salt Lake City, 1953-62; founder The Children's Ctr., Salt Lake City, 1962, now cons., supr. Contbr. articles to profl. jours. Bd. dirs. Legal Aid Soc. Recipient Jane Adams award, 1968, Susan Gates award, 1985, Minuteman award, 1989, Merit of Honor Alumni Assn., 1990, Ped. Soc. Svc. to Children award, 1992; named to Children's Hall of Fame, 1985, Educator of Yr., 1985. Mem. APA, Utah Psychol. Assn. (pres. 1976), Am. Orthopsychiat. Assn., Am. Assn. Psychiat. Svcs. for Children, Salt Lake City Tennis Club. Unitarian. Home: 865 S Monument Park Cir Salt Lake City UT 84108 Office: 1855 Medical Cir Salt Lake City UT 84112

PLENK, HENRY P., radiation oncologist; b. Vienna, Austria, May 19, 1917; came to U.S., 1938; m. Agnes Mero, June 17, 1938; children: Bruce, Penny Plenk Dalrymple, Tim. Candidate Med., U. Vienna Med. Sch., Austria, 1938; MB, Northwestern U., 1941, MD, 1942, MS in Pathology, 1946. Diplomate Am. Bd. Radiology. Assoc. prof. radiology U. Utah, Salt Lake City, 1947-52, clin. prof. radiology, 1970—; head dept. radiology U. Utah Med. Sch., Salt Lake City, 1948-52; dir. dept. radiology St. Mark's Hosp., Salt Lake City, 1952-69; founder radiation ctr. LDS Hosp., Salt Lake City, 1969-80, pres. radiology ctr. oncologists, 1980-86; prin. investigator Radiation Therapy Oncology Group, Phila., 1972-86. Author: History of Radiology in Utah, 1990; editor: Medicine in the Beehive State 1940-90, 1992. Capt. USAMC, 1944-46. Named Fellow emeritus Am. Coll. Radiology, 1988, Outstanding Contbr., Am. Cancer Soc., 1978, 88, Physician of Yr., LDS Hosp., 1991; recipient Spl. award of Merit Salt Lake County Med. Soc., 1988. Democrat. Unitarian. Home: 865 Monument Park Circle Salt Lake City UT 84108

PLETCHER, PEGGY JO, program director; b. Wheeler, Tex., Apr. 2, 1932; d. Robert Lee and Carrie Leola (McClain) Rodgers; m. Bernard A. Pletcher, Nov. 10, 1955 (div. 1989); children: Robert A., George F., David J. BS, Baylor U., 1953; MEd in Counseling, Coll. Idaho, 1974; PhD, U. Idaho, 1979. Cert. home economist, secondary tchr., counselor. Tchr. Perryton (Tex.) High Sch., 1953-55; home economist S.W. Pub. Svc., Lubbock, Tex., 1955-56; extension home economist U. Idaho, Boise, 1968-80; dir. Dist. I Coll. Agr. U. Idaho, Moscow, 1980-89, head communications Coll. Agr., 1983-84, dir. Sch. Home Econ., 1986-92; dir. Dist. II Coll. Agriculture U. Idaho, Boise, 1992—; cons. Postharvest Inst. Perishables U. Idaho, Moscow, 1983-84. Author: Implementation of Technology in Rural Areas, 1983, Influencing Legislation, 1979, Electronic Mail, 1983. Dir. U. Idaho Credit Union, Moscow, 1984-89; pres. Soroptimists Internat., Boise, Idaho, 1980; mem. Toastmasters Internat., Moscow, Idaho, 1989-92, Boise, 1992—. Nat. Assn. Extension Home Economists fellow, 1974; recipient Superior Svc. award USDA, 1973, provost's fellow Bryn Mawr Summer Inst. for Women in Higher Edn. Adminstrn., 1992. Mem. AAUW, Am. Home Econs. Assn. (leader award 1993), Nat. Assn. Home Econ. Adminstrs., Idaho Home Econs. Assn. (Disting. Svc. award 1987), Epsilon Sigma Phi, Gamma Sigma Delta, Phi Delta Kappa. Office: Univ Idaho Boise Ctr 800 Park Blvd Boise ID 83712

PLISKA, EDWARD WILLIAM, lawyer; b. Rockville, Conn., Apr. 13, 1935; s. Louis Boleslaw and Constance (Dombrowski) P.; m. Luisa Anne Crotti, Nov. 29, 1958; children: Gregory, John, Thomas, Laura. AB, Princeton (N.J.) U., 1956; LLB, U. Conn., 1964; LLD (hon.), San Mateo (Calif.) U., 1975. Bar: Calif. 1965. Dep. dist. atty. Santa Barbara (Calif.) County, 1965; dep. dist. atty. San Mateo County Dist. Atty., Redwood City, Calif., 1965-71, chief trial dep., 1970-71; pvt. practice San Mateo, 1971-72; judge San Mateo County Mcpl. Ct., 1973-86; ptnr. Corey, Luzaich, Gemello, Manos & Pliska, Millbrae, Calif., 1986—; officer Am. Judges Assn., 1983-86; prodr. and host (TV and Radio show) Justice Forum, 1973-78; prof. criminal and contitutional law San Mateo LAw Sch., 1971-76. Editor Ct. Rev., 1981-88. Trustee Belmont (Calif.) Sch. Dist., 1987-91, pres. 1990; chmn. San Mateo County Cultural Arts Commn., 1987-90; mem. Peninsula Community Found. Arts Fund, 1988—; v.p. Hillbarn Theatre, 1989—. With U.S. Army, 1957. Mem. Calif. Judges Assn., Calif. State Bar Assn., Nat. Assn. Criminal Def. Lawyers, Calif. Attys. for Criminal Justice, San Mateo County Bar Assn., San Mateo County Trial Lawyers (bd. dirs. 1990-91). Democrat. Roman Catholic. Home: 1567 Escondido Way Belmont CA 94002 Office: Corey Luzaich Gemello Manos Pliska PO Box 669 700 El Camino Real Millbrae CA 94030

PLOG, STANLEY C., marketing research and consulting executive; b. L.A., Apr. 12, 1930; s. Clifton George and Edith Christine (Swanson) P.; m. Georgia Perrin, Sept. 5, 1953; children: Stephen, Gregory. BA, Occidental Coll., 1957; MA, PhD, Harvard U., 1961. Pres. Behavior Sci. Corp., 1963-73; chmn., CEO Plog Rsch., Inc., Reseda, Calif., 1974—; chmn. Showcase Rental Cars, Reseda, 1981-91, Showcase Limousine Svc., Reseda, 1989-91. Author, editor: Changing Perspectives, 1969, State Mental Hospitals, 1976, Principles and Techniques, 1977, Mental Health and the, 1980, Leisure Travel: Making, 1991. Cons. Rep. State Ctrl. Com., 1965-67; campaign advisor, cons. Ronald Reagan Gubernatorial Campaign, 1965-66. With USAF, 1950-53. Mem. APA, Am. Mktg. Assn., Travel & Tourism Rsch. Assn. Republican. Presbyterian. Office: Plog Rsch Inc 18631 Sherman Way Reseda CA 91335

PLONKEY, KENNETH DALE, theatre educator; b. Detroit, Sept. 23, 1937; s. Alvin F. and Loretta E. (Baumgarten) P.; m. Carol Ann Nelson, Feb. 11, 1962 (div. Mar. 1980); children: Shannon, Erik, Carla; m. Janet C. Vialpando, Dec. 28, 1980 (div. Feb. 1990); m. Norma G. Livingston, Mar. 24, 1990. BA, Colo. State Coll., 1959; MA, So. Ill. U., 1964; PhD, So. Ill. U., Carbondale, 1968. Cert. life tchr. Tchr. Palisade (Colo.) High Sch., 1959-62; grad. asst., fellow So. Ill. U., Carbondale, 1962-64; instr. La. State U., Baton Rouge, 1964-68; dir. theatre U. So. Colo., Pueblo, 1968—; dir. Proscenium One, Inc., Carbondale, 1963-64, U. So. Colo. Summer Theatre, Pueblo, 1968—; pres. Iron Springs Chateau, Manitou Springs, Colo., 1978-79; dir. So. Colo. Drama Quartet, Pueblo, 1970-74. Author plays: Inspector General, 1976, Heavenly Hash, 1978, Bayou Battles, 1978, Sourstone Medicine Mine, 1979, Wizard Who Wanted Happiness, 1984, Empress's New Clothes, 1986; actor stage and film appearing in Outlaw, The Return, The Chisholms, The Frisco Kid, The Sacketts, Centennial, How the West Was Won, The White Buffalo, Taming of the Shrew, The Male Animal, Someone Waiting, Arsenic and Old Lace, Camelot, The Odd Couple, The Moon is Blue, J.B., Heritage, Hillside Dairy Milk Barns, others. John Golden Traveling fellow, N.Y.C, 1964; Colo. humanities grantee, 1971. Mem. SAG, NEA, Colo. Edn. Assn., Rocky Mountain Theatre Conf., Pueblo Performing Arts Guild (pres. 1989-91). Office: U So Colo 2200 Bonforte Blvd Pueblo CO 81001-4990

PLOOG, HOLLI ILENE, information services company executive; b. N.Y.C., Dec. 11, 1947; d. A.R. Goldin and Molly Beth (Greenberg) P.; m. Bertrand Charles Campbell, Nov. 20, 1941. BA, George Washington U., 1969; JD, Golden Gate U., 1980. Writer, prodn. assoc. Marvel Comics Group, N.Y.C., 1970-74; planner Marin County Criminal Justice Agy., San Rafael, Calif., 1975-76; dir., dist. atty. Marin County, San Rafael, Calif., 1976-80; atty. jud. coun. State of Alaska, Anchorage, 1980; legis. coun. State of Alaska, Juneau, 1981; ptnr. Dichter & Ploog Law Offices, 1981-84; dir. Anchorage Dept. Revenue, 1984-88; v.p. Lockheed Datacom Systems Corp., L.A., 1988-90; sr. v.p. Lockheed Info. Mgmt. Svcs. Co. (formerly Lockheed Datacom), L.A., 1990—; bd. dirs. Nat. Coun. State Child Support Adminstrs. 1987-88, Washington; pres. Nat. Child Support Enforcement Assn. 1989-90. Bd. dirs. Blood Bank Alaska, Anchorage, 1983-88; chmn. Alaska Woman's Polit. Caucus, Anchorage, 1982-84; mem. Dem. state cen. com., Anchorage, 1986-88; del. Dem. Conv., San Francisco, 1984. Recipient citation for excellence Dept. Human and Health Svcs./Child Support Enforcement, 1986, Book award Constitutional Law, 1978. Mem. ABA, Alaska Bar Assn., L.A. County Bar Assn. (fee arbitration panel 1988—), Am. Arbitration Assn. (community svcs. mediation panel 1978-80). Democrat. Office: Lockheed Info Mgmt Svcs 5120 W Goldleaf Cir Ste 200 Los Angeles CA 90056-1288

PLOPPER, CHARLES GEORGE, anatomist, cell biologist; b. Oakland, Calif., June 16, 1944; s. George Eli and Josephine Viola (Gates) P.; m. Suzanne May, Aug. 1, 1944. AB, U. Calif., Davis, 1967, PhD, 1972. Chief. electron microscopy br. U.S. Army Med. Research Nutrition Lab., Denver, 1972-73; vis. scientist Calif. Primate Research Ctr., Davis, 1974-75; chief. electron microscopy div. Letterman Army Inst. Research, San Francisco, 1974-75; asst. prof. U. Hawaii Sch. Medicine, Honolulu, 1975-77; assoc. prof. Kuwait U. Sch. Medicine, 1977-78; sr. staff fellow Nat. Inst. Environ. Health Sci. Research, Triangle Park, N.C., 1978-79; from asst. to assoc. prof. U. Calif. Sch. Vet. Medicine, Davis, 1979-86, dept. chmn., 1984-88, prof., 1986—; mem. study sect. NIH div. Research Grants, Bethesda, Md., 1986-90; Paley vis. prof. Boston U. Sch. Medicine, 1985; vis. pulmonary scholar Duke U., U. N.C., N.C. State U., 1991. Served to capt. U.S. Army, 1972-75. Mem. Am. Soc. Cell Biology, Am. Thoracic Soc., Am. Assn. Antomists, Am. Assn. Pathologists, Anat. Soc. Great Britain and Ireland, Davis Aquatic Masters (bd. dirs.). Democrat. Club: Davis Aquatic Masters. Home: 511 Hubble St Davis CA 95616-2720 Office: Univ of Calif Sch of Vet Medicine Dept of Anatomy Davis CA 95616

PLOTHOW, ROGER HENRY, college official, consultant; b. Peru, Ind., Nov. 21, 1934; s. Anthony Fredrick Jr. and Wilma Lavon (Henry) P.; m. Lenora Dean Damron, May 24, 1957; children: Roger D., Phillip A., Kathleen L., Melissa A., Amy L. BS, Purdue U., 1956, MS, 1965; EdD, Brigham Young U., 1974. Tchr. vocat. agr. Gilead (Ind.) High Sch., 1956-58; tchr. vocat. agr. Lewis Cass High Sch., Walton, Ind., 1958-62, dir. counseling, 1962-65, asst. prin., 1965-66; state sxec. dir. Agrl. Stblzn. and Conservation Svc., USDA, Indpls., 1966-68; asst. to pres. Indpls. Campus, Purdue U., 1968-70; adult edn. cons. Utah Office Edn., Salt Lake City, 1970-72; dean continuing edn. Utah Valley C.C., Provo, 1972-84, dir. devel., 1984—; cons., owner Henry Dean Pub., Provo, 1989—. Author: Philanthropic Foundations of Utah, 1989, 2d edit., 1991, (software) Proposal Writing, 1991-92. Bd. dirs. Utah County Fair, Provo, 1974-78; cons. USA Volkschule Evaluation Team, Germany, 1982; scoutmaster Boy Scouts Am., Provo, 1974-80. Capt. USAR, 1957-66. Scholar Purdue U., 1952, Manchester (Ind.) Coll., 1962. Mem. Nat. Coun. for Resource Devel. (nat. bd. dirs. 1988—), Adult Edn. Assn. U.S.A. (nat. bd. dirs. 1978-82), Kiwanis (pres. 1990-91). Democrat. Mem. LDS Ch. Avocations: gardening, reading, travel, family history. Home: 1254 North 1220 West Provo UT 84604 Office: Utah Valley CC 800 West 1200 South Orem UT 84058

PLOTKIN, BRUCE ANDREW, lawyer, real estate broker; b. Athol, Mass., Oct. 7, 1951; s. Charles S. and Natalie P.; m. Debra Schneider, Aug. 24, 1991. BA, U. Denver, 1973, JD, 1988. Bar: Colo. 1988, D.C. 1990; lic. real estate broker. Pvt. practice lawyer Denver. Office: 1675 Broadway # 1000 Denver CO 80202

PLOTT, CHARLES R., economics educator; b. Frederick, Okla., July 8, 1938; s. James Charles and Flossie Ann (Bowman) P.; m. Marianna Brown Cloninger, May 30, 1961; children: Rebecca Ann, Charles Hugh. B.S., Okla. State U., 1961, M.S., 1964; Ph.D., U. Va., 1965. Asst. prof. econs. Purdue U., 1965-68, assoc. prof., 1968-70; vis. prof. econs. Stanford U., 1968-69; Edward S. Harkness prof. econs. and polit. sci. Calif. Inst. Tech., Pasadena, 1970—, dir. Program for Study of Enterprise and Public Policy, 1979—, dir. Lab. for Exptl. Econs. and Polit. Sci., 1987—; vis. prof. law U. So. Calif. Law Center, 1976; vis. prof. U. Chgo., 1980; dir. Lee Pharms. Author works in fields of econs., polit. sci., philosophy, exptl. methods, math. methods; contbr. articles to profl. jours.; bd. editors: Social Sci. Research, 1976-77, Public Choice, 1973—, Jour. Econ. Behavior, 1983—. Named to Coll. Bus. Hall of Fame Okla. State U.; Ford Found. fellow, 1968, Guggenheim fellow, 1981, fellow Ctr. for Advanced Studies in Behavioral Scis., 1981; NSF grantee, 1972, 74, 78, 79, 80, 83, 86, 88, 92. Fellow Am. Acad. Arts and Scis., Econometric Soc., Huntington Library and Art Gallery; mem. Am. Econ. Assn., Econ. Sci. Assn. (pres. 1987), So. Econ. Assn. (exec. com. 1978-79, v.p. 1985-87, pres. 1989-90), Pub. Choice Soc. (pres. 1977-78), Royal Econ. Assn., Am. Polit. Sci. Assn., Econs. Sci. Assn. (pres. 1987-88). Clubs: Cosmos, Mont Pelerin Soc. Home: 881 El Campo Dr Pasadena CA 91107-5565 Office: Calif Inst Tech Divsn Humanities & Social Scis Pasadena CA 91125

PLOUGH, CHARLES TOBIAS, JR., electronic research and development executive; b. Oakland, Calif., Sept. 7, 1926; s. Charles Tobias Sr. and Miriam Lucille (Miller) P.; m. Jean Elizabeth Rose, June 13, 1950 (div. May 1969); children: Charles III, Cathleen, Mark, Barbara; m. Janet Mary Ansell Lumley, July 5, 1969; children: Mark Ansell Lumley, Simon John Lumley. AB with honors, Amherst Coll., 1950; BSEE with honors, U. Calif., Berkeley, 1953. Mgr. tech. devel. Fairchild Semiconductor, Palo Alto, Calif., 1958-71; v.p. Multi-State Devices, Montreal, Can., 1971-78; mgr. research and devel. Dale Electronics, Norfolk, Nebr., 1978-89, ret., 1989. Patentee in field. Mem. IEEE. Lodge: Lions (sec. Norfolk 1982-86). Home: 2030 Quail Run Dr NE Albuquerque NM 87122-1100

PLOVNICK, MARK STEPHEN, business educator; b. N.Y.C., June 8, 1946. s. Jacob and Dorothy Edith (Berger) P.; m. Daisy Shulan Chan, Mar. 13, 1982. BS in Mech. Engring., Union Coll., 1968, BA in Econs., 1968; MS in Mgmt., MIT, 1970, PhD in Mgmt., 1975. Instr., researcher MIT, Cambridge, 1970-76; asst. prof. Clark Univ., Worcester, Mass., 1976-79, assoc. prof., 1979-89, chmn. dept. mgmt., 1979-82, assoc. dean Grad. Sch. Mgmt., 1982-89; prof., dean Sch. Bus. and Pub. Adminstrn. U. Pacific, Stockton, Calif., 1989—; cons. to various orgns., 1970—; dir. Devel. Rsch. Assocs., Reston, Va., 1979-82; adj. assoc. prof. U. Mass. Med. Sch., Worcester, Mass., 1982-89; adj. asst. prof. Boston Univ. Sch. Medicine, 1974-75; clin. instr. Harvard Med. Sch., Boston, 1977-78. Mem. Civil Svc. Commn., San Joaquin County, 1989—. Author 5 books; contbr. numerous articles to profl. jours. Trustee Art Inst. Boston, 1983-90, Worcester Vis. Nurse Assn., 1985-89; bd. dirs. Goodwill Industries, 1991—, Jr. Achievement, 1991—, United Way of San Joaquin, 1992—, Boy Scouts of Am. (San Joaquin chpt.),

1992—. Mem. Acad. Mgmt., Assn. Info. and Decision Scis., Orgn. Devel. Inst., Greater Stockton C. of C. (bd. dirs.). Office: U Pacific Sch Bus & Pub Adminstrn Stockton CA 95211

PLUM, RICHARD EUGENE, retired flight engineer; b. Alliance, Ohio, Feb. 24, 1928; s. Vernon and Mida Lucile (Halverstadt) P.; m. Bea Hernandez; children: Pamela Sue Lachman, Patricia Ann Quaranto, Peggy Lynn, Richard John. Grad., Calif. Flyers Sch. Aeronautics. Cert. master aircraft mechanic, flight engr. Flight engr. Am. Airlines, Inc., Dallas, Ft. Worth, 1951-90, ret., 1990; check airman Am. Airlines, Chgo., 1968-70. Editor Pub Newsletter, 1964-68. Served with USN, 1945-47. Recipient Top Gun award Western Fast Draw Assn., 1969. Mem. NRA, Calif. Rifle and Pistol Assn., World Fast Draw Assn. (chmn. 1984-89, editor-pub. newsletter 1984-89, Top Gun award 1988), Mid-Western Fast Draw Assn. (chmn. 1964-68, Mid-Am. champion 1967, Chgo. conf. champion 1968), Old Frontier Thumbers Conf., Ohio Fast Draw Assn., Ariz. Fast Draw Assn., Kans. Fast Draw Assn., Restless Guns Fast Draw Club, Bordertown Fast Draw Club. Republican. Home: 83 Cargil Dr Sierra Vista AZ 85635

PLUMMER, CHARLES MCDONALD, community college administrator; b. Garibaldi, Oreg., Mar. 21, 1934; s. Earl Carlos and Florence Elta (Lamb) P.; m. Diane Hansen, July 7, 1957; children: Jeffrey Earl, Susan Lynn Plummer Johnson. BS in Edn., So. Oreg. State Coll., 1957; MEd, U. Oreg., 1967. Tchr. Canyonville (Oreg.) High Sch., 1957-59, Glendale (Oreg.) High Sch., 1959-60; tchr. Roseburg (Oreg.) High Sch., 1960-66, dir. student activities, pub. info., 1963-66; registrar Umpqua C.C., Roseburg, 1966-68, dean admissions and records, 1968-74, dean instrn., 1974-86, v.p. instructional svcs., 1986—; exec. bd. N.W. Student Success Conf., Portland, 1989-92; co-founder, staff Pacific NW Great Tchrs. Seminar, Portland, 1979—. Pres. Greater Douglas United Way, 1989, bd. dirs. 1983-92; pres. Roseburg Concert Chorale, 1982-92; bd. dirs. Roseburg Community Concert Assn., 1989—. Mem. Kiwanis Club (pres. 1979, bd. dirs. 1973-79), Oreg. Coun. of Instrnl. Adminstrs. (chair 1990), Roseburg Area C. of C. (bd. dirs. 1982-85, Roseburg First Citizen 1991), Phi Delta Kappa. Presbyterian. Home: 567 NE Winchester St Roseburg OR 97470 Office: Umpqua CC PO Box 967 Roseburg OR 97470

PLYMATE, ROBERT RUSSEL, chemist, health industry consultant; b. Wahoo, Nebr., Aug. 4, 1936; s. Thomas R. and Margret (Johnson) P.; m. Barbara Ann Curtis, Aug. 9, 1957; children: Jorjia, Robert, Julian, Janine, Rachel, Gale. BS, Reish Coll., Mason City, Iowa, 1965; MA, Columbia Coll., Irvine, Calif., 1979; D Naturopathy, Naturopathic Coll., Renfro, S.C., 1985. Rsch. head John F. Kennedy Coll., Wahoo, 1975-77; chemist, owner Alpha-Lac Inc., Albany, Oreg., 1980—; fellow Nutramed. Examiners, Boulder, Colo., 1988—. Patentee in field. Chmn. Ark. Found. for Environ. Issues, Rogers, 1991-92. Mem. Brit. Guild Drugless Practitioners (assoc.). Jehovah's Witness. Home and Office: 3940 Scenic Dr Albany OR 97321

POCKER, YESHAYAU, chemistry, biochemistry educator; b. Kishinev, Romania, Oct. 10, 1928; came to U.S., 1961; naturalized, 1967.; s. Benzion Israel and Esther Sarah (Sudit) P.; m. Anna Goldenberg, Aug. 8, 1950; children: Rona, Elon I. MSc, Hebrew U., Jerusalem, 1949; PhD, Univ. Coll., London, Eng., 1953; DSc, U. London, 1960. Rsch. assoc. Weizmann Inst. Sci., Rehovot, Israel, 1949-50; humanitarian trust fellow Univ. Coll., 1951-52, asst. lectr., 1952-54, lectr., 1954-61; vis. assoc. prof. Ind. U., Bloomington, 1960-61; prof. U. Washington, Seattle, 1961—; bicentennial lectr. Mont. State U., Bozeman, 1976, U. N.C., Chapel Hill, 1977, guest lectr. U. Kyoto, Japan, 1984; Edward A. Doisy vis. prof. biochemistry St. Louis U. Med. Sch., 1990; plenary lectr. N.Y. Acad. Sci., 1983, Fast Reactions in Biol. Systems, Kyoto, Japan, 1984, NATO, 1989, Consiglio nat. delle Richerche, U. Bari, Italy, 1989, Sigma Tau, Spoleto, Italy, 1990; Internat. lectr. Purdue U., 1990; cons. NIH, 1984, 86, 88; Spl. Topic lectr. on photosynthesis, Leibniz House, Hanover, Fed. Republic Germany, 1991; enzymology, molecular biology lectr., Dublin, Ireland, 1992. Mem. editorial adv. bd. Inorganica Chimica Acta-Bioinorganic Chemistry, 1981-89; bd. reviewing editors Sci., 1985—; contbr. numerous articles to profl. jours.; pub. over 220 papers and 12 revs. Numerous awards worldwide, 1983-90. Fellow Royal Soc. Chemistry; mem. Am. Chem. Soc. (nat. speaker 1970, 74, 84, chmn. Pauling award com. 1978; plaque awards, 1970, 74, 84, outstanding svc. award 1979), Soc. Exptl. Biology, Am. Soc. Biol. Chemists, N.Y. Acad. Sci., Sigma Xi (nat. lectr. 1971). Office: U Wash Chemistry Dept BG-10 Seattle WA 98195

POCKLINGTON, PETER H., business executive; b. Regina, Sask., Can., Nov. 18, 1941; s. Basil B. and Eileen (Dempsey) P.; m. Eva d. Jack McAvoy, June 2, 1974; 4 children. Pres. Westown Ford, Tilbury, Ont., Can., 1967-69; pres. Chatham, Ont., 1969-71, Edmonton, Alta., Can., 1971-82; chmn. Pocklington Fin. Corp., Edmonton, 1982—; owner, gov. Edmonton Oiler Hockey Club, 1976—; owner Edmonton Trapper Triple A Baseball Club, 1981—; formed Hartford Properties, Inc., 1985, Edmonton, Club Fit Inc., 1990; purchased Superior Furniture Systems Mfg., Inc., 1987, Canbra Foods Ltd., 1988, Green Acre Farms, Sabastool, Miss., 1988, Green Acre Foods Inc., Nacadoches, Tex., 1988. Mem. Mayfair Golf and Country Club, Edmonton Golf and Country Club, Vintage Golf Club, Indian Wells, Calif. Office: Pocklington Fin Corp Ltd, 2500 Sun Life Pl 10123-99 St, Edmonton, AB Canada T5J 3H1 also: Edmonton Oilers, Edmonton, AB Canada T5B 4M9*

PODBOY, JOHN WATTS, psychologist, educator; b. York, Pa., Sept. 27, 1943; s. August John and Harriett Virginia (Watts) P.; 1 son, Matthew John. B.A., Dickinson Coll., 1966; M.S., San Diego State Coll., 1971; Ph.D., U. Ariz., 1973. Dir., Vets. Counseling Center, U. Ariz., Tucson, 1972-73; project dir. San Mateo County (Calif.) Human Relations Dept., Redwood City, 1974; staff psychologist Sonoma State Hosp., Eldridge, Calif., 1975-81; cons. clin. psychologist Comprehensive Care Corp., Newport Beach, Calif., 1974-75, Sonoma County (Calif.) Probation Dept., 1976-88; pvt. practice, 1982—; cons. to Sonoma County Superior Cts., 1983—; asst. prof. Sonoma State U., 1977-81; dir. Sonoma Diagnostic and Remedial Center, 1979-82. Chmn. San Mateo County Diabetes Assn., 1975. Served to lt. USNR, 1966-69. Fellow Am. Coll. Forensic Psychology, Am. Bd. Med. Psychotherapists (fellow); mem. Am. Psychol. Assn., Western Psychol. Assn., Redwood Psychol. Assn. (pres. 1983), Nat. Council Alcoholism, Nat. Rehab. Assn. Home: PO Box 488 Kenwood CA 95452-0488

POEDTKE, CARL HENRY GEORGE, JR., management consultant; b. Chgo., Jan. 12, 1938; s. Carl H. Sr. and Irene F. (Eskilson) P.; m. Marie-Paule M. Thiriet, Mar. 10, 1962 (dec.); children: Gislaine Canavan, Carl Henry George III; m. Janice M. Barron, Aug. 26, 1991. BS, MIT, 1959. Mgr. value engring. Chgo. Rawhide Mfg. Co., Chgo., 1962-66; ptnr. Price Waterhouse, Chgo., Paris, N.Y.C., 1966-91; ret. Price Waterhouse, Chgo., 1991. Author: Managing and Accounting for Inventories, 1980; contbr. articles to profl. jours. Bd. dir. Guild Bd. Lyric Opera, Chgo., 1984-92; mem. vis. adv. com. sch. acctg. De Paul U., Chgo., 1986-91. 1st lt. U.S. Army, 1959-62. Fellow Am. Prodn. and Inventory Control Soc.; mem. AIIE (sr., cert.), Inst. Mgmt. Cons. (bd. dirs. 1987-90), Coun. Cons. Orgns. (bd. dirs. 1989-90), Union League Club, Masons. Home: PO Box 677 Tesuque NM 87574

POEHLS, AILEEN ORIANNA, applied physicist; b. Chgo., Aug. 21, 1951; d. Ching Chang and Sze Lu (Hsiang) Woo; m. Kenneth A. Poehls, Dec. 13, 1974; 1 child, Diane K. BS, Beloit Coll., 1973. Edn. intern Mus. of Sci., Boston, 1972; elem. tchr. Nathan Hale Elem. Sch., Lansing, Ill., 1973; rsch. asst. Woods Hole (Mass.) Oceanographic Inst., 1973-75; computer programmer Phys. Dynamics, Inc., Santa Monica, Calif., 1975-76; programmer Arete Assocs., Inc., Santa Monica, 1976-80; programmer/analyst Arete Assocs., Inc., Encino, Calif., 1981-87; sr. programmer/analyst Arete Assocs., Inc., Sherman Oaks, Calif., 1988-90, mem. rsch. staff, 1990-92, staff scientist, 1992—. Contbr. poetry to Brilliant Star mag. Troop leader Girl Scout Am., Culver City, Calif., 1989—; support campaigner YMCA, Culver City, 1986—; nation chief YMCA and Y-Indian Program, Culver City, 1987-88; mem., sec. Local Spiritual Assembly of the Baha'i Faith, Beloit, Wis., Falmouth, Mass., Culver City, 1972—; chmn. Farragut Site coun. Culver City Unified Sch. Dist., 1987-89. Named to Outstanding Young Women of Am., 1987; recipient Neighborhood award Girl Scouts Am., 1992, Hon. Svc. award, 1993. Mem. Am. Geophys. Union, Am. Inst. Physics, Woods Hole Oceanographic Inst. Affiliates. Office: Arete Assocs 5000 Van Nuys Blvd Sherman Oaks CA 91403

POEHNER, RAYMOND GLENN, retired bank executive; b. Cleve., Oct. 2, 1923; s. Raymond Frank and Winifred (Kirchbaum) P.; student pub. schs., Chgo. and Cleve.; m. Frances E. Dunaway Gillespie, Jan. 4, 1958; children: R. David, Jacquline Diane, Leslie Marie, Jon Anthony, Rebecca Glen; stepchildren: Bruce Gillespie, Tony Gillespie. Enlisted U.S. Navy, 1941, advanced through grades to chief petty officer, 1957, ret., 1965; with Security Pacific Nat. Bank, San Diego, 1966—, loan officer, 1971-74, credit card officer, 1975-81, asst. br. mgr., 1974-80, asst. mgr., 1981—. Mem. U.S. Naval Inst. (assoc.), Sierra Club, VFW, Nat. Hist. Soc., Fla. Sheriff's Assn., Am. Biog. Soc. (nat. bd. advisors), R.I. Research (cert. assoc.), Fleet Res. Assn., Nat. Geographic Soc., Am. Legion, Animal Protection Inst. Am., Nat. Assn. Civilian Conservation Corps Alumni, Fla. Sheriff's Assn., Optimist Club (dir. 1978), Fraternal Order Police (booster Fla. chpt.). Republican.

POERTNER, LEE ANNE, English language educator; b. Salt Lake City, Nov. 4, 1936; d. Robert Gail Beckstrand and Norma Ruth (Tobias) Beckstrand Bueche; m. Jerry Vance Horner, July 8, 1954 (div. 1968); children: Jeri Lynn Horner, Alan Dale Horner; m. Kenneth Wayne Poertner, Dec. 26, 1979. BA, U. St. Thomas, Houston, 1963; MA, Ind. U., 1965. Tchr. McTigue Sch., Toledo, 1964-65, dean of girls, 1965-67; cellist Long Beach (Calif.) Symphony Orch., 1970-74; English prof. Long Beach City Coll., 1967—. cellist Long Beach Community Orchestra, 1992—. Mem. Aquinas Honor Soc., U. St. Thomas, 1960-63. Mem. NEA, Calif. Tchrs. Assn. Republican. Mormon. Office: Long Beach City Coll 4901 E Carson St Long Beach CA 90808-1706

POESCHL, BRIAN K., sales representative; b. Santa Ana, Calif., Dec. 17, 1964; s. Gary C. and Zeta Rae (Nichols) P. BS in Biology, U. Calif., Irvine, 1988; MBA, U. So. Calif., 1993. Sales rep. Parke Davis, Morris Plains, N.J., 1989—. Mem. Sigma Chi. Republican. Presbyterian. Home: 8 Blue Heron Ln Aliso Viejo CA 92656 Office: Parke Davis 201 Tabor Rd Morris Plains NJ 07950

POFFENBERGER, DAVID JOHN, plant manager; b. Auburn, Ind., Sept. 12, 1959; s. John Phillip and Barbara Lou (Rice) P.; m. Lori Lynn Burger, Nov. 28, 1981; children: Ryan, Kelsie. AS, Ind. U., Ft. Wayne, 1981, 82; BS, Purdue U., 1984. Salesman Edison Bros., Ft. Wayne, Ind., 1978-81; warehouse shipping clk. Dana Corp., Ft. Wayne, 1978-81; product engr. Dana Corp., Churubusco, Ind., 1981-84, catalog mgr., 1984-87; product mgr. Dana Corp., Toledo, Ohio, 1987-89, mktg. mgr., 1990-91; mktg. mgr. Brown Bros. Ltd.-Dana Corp., Swindon, Eng., 1990-91; mgr. Dana Corp., Manteca, Calif., 1991—. Office: Dana Corp 105 Industrial Dr Manteca CA 95336

POGÁNY, GÁBOR LÁSZLÓ, biochemist, cancer researcher; b. Satoraljaujhely, Hungary, June 20, 1957; s. Sándor and Ilona (Görgey) P.; m. Susan Bojtor, June 30, 1979; children: Orsolya, Krisztina, Anna. BSc, Tech. U. Budapest, Hungary, 1979; MSc, Eötvös U. Sci., Budapest, 1981; PhD, Semmelweis Med. U., Budapest, 1990. Rsch. asst. Inst. Enzymology, Biol. Rsch. Ctr. Hungarian Acad. Scis., Budapest, 1981-86; rsch. assoc. Joint Rsch. Assn. Hungarian Acad. Scis./Semmelweis Med. U., Budapest, 1986-91; sr. rsch. assoc. dept. biology U. N.Mex., Albuquerque, 1991—. Contbr. articles to sci. jours. Trainee Fedn. European Biochem. Socs., 1986; fellow European Assn. Cancer Rsch., 1991. Mem. Hungarian Biochem. Soc., Hungarian Oncol. Soc. Office: Univ N Mex Dept Biology Castetter Hall Albuquerque NM 87131

POGGIONE, WILLIAM JOSEPH, public administration consultant, law educator; b. Glendale, Calif., May 7, 1935; s. Joseph Frank and Una Etta Lee (Marshall) P.; m. Joan Ireland, June 7, 1978; children: Pamela, Lorraine, William M. JD, Southwestern U., 1970; BA, U. Redlands, 1977; MPA, U. La Verne, 1980; PhD, Pacific Western U., 1986. Cert. protection profl. Capt. Los Angeles County Dept. Sheriff, L.A., 1957-88; instr. Mt. San Antonio Coll., Walnut, Calif., 1972-80; prof. U. La Verne, Calif., 1977—; instr. Calif. Poly. U., Pomona, 1980—; prof. U. Redlands, Calif., 1981—, Kensington U., Glendale, 1988—; pres. William J. Poggione & Assocs., Placentia, Calif., 1988—. Mem. Inmate Welfare Commn., L.A., 1988-91, Al Maliahak Temple. Served with U.S. Army. Named to Order of the White Elephant (Thailand), 1989, Internat. Hall of Fame, 1987; recipient Disting. Svc. award Govt. Honduras, 1988, Royal Pouch medal Thailand, 1987. Mem. Am. Soc. for Indsl. Security, FBI Nat. Acad. Assn., L.A. World Affairs Coun., People-to-People Internat., Scottish Rite. Republican. Home and Office: 342 Georgia Cir Placentia CA 92670

POGOREL, BARRY ROBERT, management consultant, painter; b. L.A., May 9, 1948; s. Bernard Sydney and Bernice Love (Enenberg) P. BFA, UCLA/U. Calif., Santa Cruz, 1971; MFA, UCLA, 1974. Mgmt. cons. C.N.I., L.A., 1984-89, Pogorel & Assocs., L.A., 1989—. Exhibited paintings at Whitney Mus., N.Y.C., 1974; poetry includes Self Portrait, 1972. Whitney Mus. scholar, 1974. Jewish. Office: 4020 Colonial Ave Los Angeles CA 90066

POHL, JOHN HENNING, chemical engineer, consultant; b. Ft. Riley, Kans., May 29, 1944; s. Herbert Otto and Ellen Irene (Henning) P.; m. Judith Lynn Sykes, Aug. 10, 1968; children: J. Otto, Clint. AA, Sacramento City Coll., 1964; BS, U. Calif., Berkeley, 1966; MS, MIT, 1973, DSci, 1976. Inspector constrn. C.O. Henning Cons. Engrs., Sacramento, 1965; engr. E.I. du Pont Nemours, Wilmington, Del., 1966-70; rsch. asst. MIT, Cambridge, 1971-75, lectr., 1975-76; mem. tech. staff Sandia Nat. Labs., Livermore, Calif., 1976-81; dir. fossil fuels Energy and Environ. Rsch., Irvine, Calif., 1981-86; dir. R & D Energy Systems Assocs., Tustin, Calif., 1986-89; sr. scientist energy W.J. Schafer Assocs., Irvine, 1989-91; pres. Energy Internat., Mission Viejo, Calif., 1988—; sr. cons. ESA Engring., Laguna Hills, Calif., 1989—; pres. Green Burner Co., 1991—. Contbr. articles to profl. jours.; patentee in field. Treas. Headstart, Cambridge, 1975-76. Recipient Sci. and Tech. Achievement award U.S. EPA, 1987, Best Energy Projects award Energy Commn., Taiwan, coal evaluation, 1989, Low NOx Burner, 1992. Mem. ASME (advisor corrosion and deposits com. 1989—), Am. Flame Rsch. Com., Am. Chem. Soc., Am. Inst. Chem. Engrs. (combustion advisor 1988—), Combustion Inst. Western States (exec. com. 1988—), Combustion Inst. (program subcom. 1976—), Engring. Found. (steering com. ash deposits 1989—). Home: 26632 Cortina Dr Mission Viejo CA 92691-5429

POHLMAN, DAVID LAWRENCE, training systems consultant; b. Detroit, May 17, 1944; s. Lawrence Luther and Lois Betty (Huffeut) P.; m. Diane Lee Ewing, Dec. 27, 1967 (div. 1980); children: Scott David, Anne Kiersten; m. Katherine Margaret Wattigney, Dec. 11, 1981; children: Ann Margaret Williams, David Joseph Williams. BS in Edn., Ohio U., 1967; MA in Psychology, U. No. Colo., 1977. Commd. officer USAF, 1967, advanced through grades to lt. col.; instr. pilot USAF, Chandler, Ariz., 1975-78, rsch. pilot., 1978-82; div. chief USAF, San Antonio, 1982-87; ret., 1987; tng. div. mgr. Gallegos Rsch. Group, Wheatridge, Colo., 1987-88; mgr. fed. systems div. Andersen Consulting, Denver, 1988-90; pres. Dave Pohlman Assocs., Aurora, 1990—; com. chmn. Dept. Def., Washington, 1982-87, subcom. chmn. industry panel, 1988-92; subcom. mem. intersvc.-Industry Tng. System, Orlando, Fla., 1987; industry co-chmn. Computer-Aided Acquisition and Logistics Human Systems Components com., 198-92; mem. Aurora Vets. Affairs Commn., 1993; mem. 6th Congrl. Dist. Vets. Adv. Coun., 1993. Contbr. articles to profl. publs. Mem. Am. Ednl. Rsch. Assn., Am. Def. Preparedness Assn., Nat. Security Indsl. Assn., Air Force Assn. Roman Catholic. Home: 2557 S Evanston St Aurora CO 80014-2519 Office: 15200 E Girard Ave Ste 1850 Aurora CO 80014-5039

POIRIER, CAROL SUE, nurse; b. Oakland, Calif., June 3, 1963; d. Ivo James and Betty Jean (Centner) Van Asten; m. Michael John Poirier, June 23, 1984; children: David Michael, Amanda Rose. AS, Contra Costa Coll., 1988. RN, Calif. RN Home Health Agy. Med. Personnel Pool, Fairfield, Calif., 1989; nurse Sutter Meml. Hosp., Sacramento, 1988—. Republican.

POIRIER, RICHARD OVEILA, talent agent, personal manager, motion picture investment company executive; b. Boston, Dec. 10, 1947; s. Oveila A. and Evelyn G. (Sullivan) P. Student, George Washington U., 1968; diploma in Law, City of London Coll., 1969; BS summa cum laude, Boston U., 1976. Exec. producer Kaleidescope Records, Boston, 1979-81; acct., law office mgr. William R. Dickerson & Assocs., L.A., 1981; artist royalty supr. Capitol Records, Hollywood, Calif., 1981-83; dir. royalties Warner/Elektra/Atlantic Internat. Records, Warner Home Video, Burbank, Calif., 1983-86; pres. Richard Poirier Model & Talent Agy., L.A., 1986—; cons. in field; guest speaker various functions; judge various beauty contests. Contbr. articles to Boston U. Pubs., The Daily Free Press, 1975-76; contbr. photographs to First Models Directory of L.A., Acad. Motion Picture Arts and Scis. Acad. Players Directory, 1988—; featured on Sta. ABC TV Inside Edition, 1990; editor, pub. Model Call mag. Mem. Ford Hall Forum, Boston, 1974-79, Boston Mus. Fine Art, 1973-79. With U.S. Army, 1967-69. Recipient Film and TV Actors Symposium award, 1990. Mem. Nat. Acad. Rec. Arts and Scis., Nat. Acad. Video Arts and Scis., Beverly Hills Bar Assn. (entertainment law sect., legis. com.), Music Industry Network, Hollywood C. of C., 5 Percent Club of L.A., Mondrian Models and Photographers Club, The Actors Ctr., Club de L'Ermitage. Office: Richard Poirier Model & Talent Agy 3575 Cahuenga Blvd W Bldg 254 Los Angeles CA 90068-1341

POIRIER, ROBERT JAMES, technical marketing engineer; b. Hemet, Calif., June 27, 1947; s. Robert G. and Katherine A. (Gauthé) P.; m. Cecilia M. Worland, June 20, 1970; children: Glennon, Amanda. AS in Engring., Barstow Jr. Coll., 1969; BS in Indsl. Engring., U. Pomona, 1973; postgrad., Calif. State Poly., 1987—. Engr. in tng.; cert. supervision. Indsl. engr. TiTech Internat., Pomona, Calif., 1973-76; sr. indsl. engr. TEKFORM Products Inc., Anaheim, Calif., 1976-80; sr. indsl. engr., customer svc. product specialist ITT Pomona, 1980—. Patentee Integrated Circuit test clip.

POIROT, JAMES WESLEY, engineering company executive; b. Douglas, Wyo., 1931; m. Raeda Poirot. BCE, Oreg. State U., 1953. With various constrn. firms, Alaska and Oreg.; with CH2M Hill Inc., 1955, v.p., Seattle and Atlanta, from 1967; chmn. bd. CH2M Hill Inc., Englewood, Colo., 1983-93; former chmn. Western Regional Coun., Design Profls. Coalition. Chmn. Accreditation Bd. for Engring. and Tech., Indsl. Adv. Coun., mem. Oreg. joint Grad. Schs. of Engring., Engring. Coun. Named ENR Constrn. Man of Yr., 1988. Fellow ASCE (c.p. 1991-93, chmn. steering com. quality manual from 1985, past bd. dirs., pres.-elect 1992), Am. Cons. Engrs. Coun. (pres. 1989-90), Nat. Acad. Engring. Office: CHZM Hill Inc PO Box 22508 Denver CO 80222-0508

POLADIAN, ARA A., obstetrician and gynecologist; b. Kessab, Syria, Dec. 12, 1953; came to U.S., 1976; s. Apraham and Zarouhie (Baboujian) P. BSc, Haigazian Coll., Beirut, 1975; MD, St. George's U., Grenada, W.I., 1981; postdoctoral student, Rutgers U., 1985. Diplomate Am. Bd. Ob.-Gyn. Intern Rutgers U., 1981, residen in ob-gyn., 1982-85; pvt. practice ob-gyn., 1985—; dir. Am. Fertility Ctr., North Hollywood, Calif., 1987—; asst. clin. prof. dept. ob.-gyn. Woman's Hosp., U. So. Calif. Sch. Medicine, L.A., 1988—; chmn. quality assurance dept. ob.-gyn. Med. Ctr. North Hollywood, 1988-92, dept. chmn., 1989-92; vis. prof. Wyeth-Ayerst Labs., L.A., 1990—. Editor med. sect. Youth Mag., 1973-75; contbr. articles to profl. pubis. Mem. fin. com. Meridian Sch., L.A., 1986-89. Fellow ACOG; mem. Am. Fertility Soc., Am. Assn. Gynecologic Laparoscopists, Calif. Med. Assn., L.A. County Med. Assn. Evangelical. Office: Am Fertility Med Ctr 10876 Riverside Dr North Hollywood CA 91602

POLAKOFF, KEITH IAN, historian, university administrator; b. N.Y.C., Dec. 12, 1941; s. Irwin L. and Edna (Sopkin) P.; m. Carol J. Gershuny, June 21, 1964; children: Amy Ellen, Adam Matthew. BA magna cum laude, Clark U., 1963; MA, Northwestern U., Evanston, Ill., 1966, PhD, 1968. Lectr. Herbert H. Lehman Coll., CUNY, 1967-69; asst. prof. history Calif. State U., Long Beach, 1969-73, assoc. prof. 1973-78, prof., 1978—, assoc. dean instrnl. support Sch. Social and Behavioral Scis., 1980-81, assoc. dean ednl. policy, 1981-84, dean, 1985-86; dean Sch. Fine Arts, 1984-85, asst. v.p. acad. affairs, dean grad. studies, 1986-90, assoc. v.p. acad. affairs, dean grad. studies, 1991—; co-chair Calif. Minority Grad. Edn. Forum, 1990—; mem. coun. Big West Conf. (formerly Pacific Coast Athletic Assn.), 1982-90, Western Collegiate Athletic Assn., 1982-85. Author: The Politics of Inertia, 1973, (with others) Generations of Americans, 1976, Political Parties in American History, 1981; contbg. author: The Presidents: A Reference History, 1984; editor: The History Tchr., 1972-77, prodn. mgr., 1977-80. Mem., clk. bd. trustees Los Alamitos Sch. Dist., 1980-81; mem. Los Alamitos Unified Sch. Dist. Bd. Edn., 1990—, pres. 1992—; chmn. adv. com. on facilities, Los Alamitos Sch. Dist., 1989, chair steering com. for measure K for kids, 1990; bd. dirs. Long Beach Opera Assn., 1981-89, pres. 1982-83, treas., 1987-88; bd. dirs. Los Alamitos Jr. Baseball, 1988-90, Los Alamitos Basball, 1990-92. Avocations: travel, photography. Home: 2971 Druid Ln Los Alamitos CA 90720-4948 Office: Calif State U 1250 N Bellflower Blvd Long Beach CA 90840-0118

POLAN, DAVID JAY, lawyer; b. Chgo., Feb. 16, 1951; s. Julius and Jeanne Warsaw (Fox) P.; m. Terri Susan Lapin, Aug. 3, 1980; children: Adam Michael, Daniel Jacob, Jennifer Leigh. BA, U. Ill., 1972; JD, John Marshall Law Sch., Chgo., 1975. Bar: Ill. 1975, Ariz. 1990, U.S. Dist. Ct. (no. dist.) Ill. 1975, U.S. Dist. Ct. Ariz. 1990, U.S. Ct. Appeals (7th cir.) 1977. Atty., Pritzker & Glass, Ltd., Chgo., 1975-78, Barnett, Ettinger, Glass, Berkson & Braverman, Chgo., 1978-79; gen. mgr. Y.P. Aurora, Ltd., Ill., 1979-83; counsel, corp. sec. JP Communications Co., Tucson, 1981-90; sta. mgr. KPOL-TV, Tucson, 1983-86, gen. mgr., 1986-90; gen. counsel Northtown Bus Svc., Ltd., Lincolnwood, Ill., 1975-88; gen. ptnr. THC Ptnrs., Chgo., 1980—; co-owner LV Pictures, Las Vegas, 1984-86. Active Orchard Village Assn. for Handicapped, Skokie, Ill., 1981-87, co-owner Rockford Lightning Continental Basketball Assn., 1986-91; mem. Soviet Jewry commn., Jewish Fedn. So. Ariz., Tucson, 1984, leadership devel. program, 1984-87, chmn., 1985-87, bd. dirs., 1985-91, active various coms.; mem. bd. Congregation Bet Shalom, 1984; assoc. mem. Hadassah, Tucson, 1984; mem. nat. com. for leadership devel. Coun. Jewish Fedn., 1986-91, chmn. western area 1988-91; bd. dirs. Jewish Family and Children's Svcs., 1986-92, also sec. 1988-89, v.p. 1989-92; bd. dirs. Jewish Community Found., 1987-91, Tucsonans Say No to Drugs, 1986-87; bd. dirs., vice chmn. Ping-Welch's Championship LPGA Tournament, 1992. Recipient Community Svc. Award Jewish Fedn. So. Ariz., 1987, Meritorious Svc. award, 1988, Gary I. Sarver Young Man of Yr. award, 1989. Mem. Ariz. State Bar, Pima County Bar Assn., Tucson Pks. Found. (bd. dirs.), Volk Jewish Community Ctr. Club, Diehard Cubs Fan Club, Ventana Canyon Golf and Racquet Club. Office: 1200 E Ajo Way Ste 105 Tucson AZ 85713-5056

POLAREK, JAMES WALLACE, pharmaceutical company research administrator; b. Evanston, Ill., Jan. 26, 1957; s. Andrew John and Thelma Elizabeth (Wallace) P.; m. Laurel Marie Bunce, Aug. 21, 1988. BS, UCLA, 1979; PhD, U. Chgo., 1986. Product mgr. Biogenex Labs., Dublin, Calif., 1986-87; rsch. scientist Telios Pharms., San Diego, 1987-89, dir., 1989-93; sr. dir., 1993—; gen. mgr. Telios Pharma, GmbH, Hamburg, Germany, 1991-92. Contbr. chpt. to book, articles to profl. jours.; patentee in field. NIH grantee, 1984, 90, 91. Mem. Am. Acad. Dermatol. Surgery, Wound Healing Soc., Soc. for Investigative Dermatol. Democrat. Office: Telios Pharms 4757 Nexus Ctr San Diego CA 92121

POLESE, RICHARD LOUIS, editor, publisher, writer, author; b. Berkeley, Calif., Nov. 16, 1941; s. James Paul and Esther Miriam (Holman) P.; m. Margaret Ann Coates, Jan. 18, 1964 (div. 1976); children: Tamsin, Vanessa, Martin. BA, Hanover (Ind.) Coll., 1964. Weekly newspaper editor Santa Fe (N.Mex.) News, 1966-68; editor of pubs. Museum of N.Mex. Press, Santa Fe, 1968-72, editor El Palacio Mag., 1976-80; sr. editor John Muir Pubs., Santa Fe, 1980-83; pub. Ocean Tree Books, Santa Fe, 1983—; pub. cons. Ocean Tree Svcs., Santa Fe, 1973-75; bd. dirs. Friends Of Peace Pilgrim. Author: Discovering Dixie, 1991, Prayers of the World, 1993; editor numerous books, 1968—. Recipient Charles and Dorothy Lynn Lit. award Hanover Coll., 1964. Mem. Pubs. Assn. of the South, Santa Fe Hist. Soc. (founding), Rocky Mountain Book Pubs. Assn. (catalog and dir. editor 1986—, chair pubs. and mktg. com. 1985-93). Democrat. Unitarian. Home: 1325 Cerro Gordo Road Santa Fe NM 87501 Office: Ocean Tree Books P O Box 1295 Santa Fe NM 87504

POLIS, SAMUEL, chemical company executive; b. Phila., Feb. 15, 1926; s. Abraham and Reba (Shalita) P.; m. Bette Jane Oaks, Dec. 27, 1950; children: Stephen Guy, Diane Gayle. BSChemE, U. Pa., 1950; MBA, U. Conn., 1980.

Plastics engr. Naval Air Exptl. Sta., Phila., 1952-56; tech. svc. rep. flexible urethane foam Mobay Chem. Co., Pitts., 1956-60; mgr. urethane rsch. and devel. Olin Corp., New Haven, 1960-82; tech. dir. western region Crain Industries, Compton, Calif., 1982-87; ret. Crain Industries, Compton, 1987. Contbr. articles to profl. jours.; patentee in field. Served to capt. U.S. Army, 1944-45, ETO, 1950-52, Korea. Decorated Bronze Star medal with oak leaf cluster; recipient Superior Accomplishment award Naval Air Exptl. Sta. 1956. Mem. Soc. Plastics Industry (asst. chmn. flexible foam tech. com. 1968-69, chmn. 1970-71, 78-80), Am. Legion (vice comdr. Wilton, Conn. chpt. 1981-82). Home: 170 Grumman Hill Rd Wilton CT 06897-4621

POLK, BENJAMIN KAUFFMAN, retired architect, educator; b. Des Moines, May 18, 1916; s. Harry Herndon and Alice (Kauffman) P.; m. Emily Despain Isaacs, Aug. 23, 1946. Student, Amherst Coll., 1933-35, U. Chgo., 1935-36, Iowa State Coll., 1936-38. Ptnr. Polk and Malone, San Francisco, 1948-53; propr. Benjamin Polk, Architect & Planner, New Delhi, Calcutta, Karachi, 1952-64; assoc. W.R. Ewald Jr., Regional Planning, Washington, 1965-66; mem. architecture & planning faculty Calif. Poly. State U., San Luis Obispo, 1966-80; ret., 1980. Author: Architecture and the Spirit of the Place, 1961, Building for South Asia, An Architectural Autobiography, 1992, (with Emily Polk) India Notebook, 1986, (with Seneviratna) Buddhist Monastic Architecture, 1992, A Figure in a Landscape, An Architectural Autobiography, Vol. 2, 1993; also booklets, articles. Vice-pres. Service Civile Internat., East India, 1957-63; advisor Small Wilderness Area Preservation, Calif., 1970-80. Tech. sgt. U.S. Army, 1942-46. Recipient Gold medal Prime Min. of Burma, 1961. Republican. Presbyterian. Home: 2361 Claranita Ave Los Osos CA 93402

POLLACK, ALAN MYRON, physician; b. N.Y.C., Feb. 16, 1958; s. Samuel and Jean Anna (Friedman) P. BS in Biochemistry, UCLA, 1979; MD, U. Tex., 1983. Diplomate Am. Bd. Internal Medicine. Intern Cedars Sinai Med. Ctr., L.A., 1983-84, resident, 1984-86; physician internal medicine Kaiser Permanente, Panorama City, Calif., 1986—. Mem. Phi Beta Kappa, Alpha Omega Alpha. Home: 24502 Skyridge Dr Santa Clarita CA 91321-3551 Office: Kaiser Permanente 13652 Cantara St Panorama City CA 91402-5423

POLLACK, MARK JOEL, systems analyst, financial consultant; b. Milw., Nov. 8, 1957; s. Jacob (Jack) and Blema Harriet (Marcus) P. AS in Math. and Sci., Victor Valley Coll., 1979; BSBA, U. La Verne, 1990. Analyst Allied Signal Aerospace Co., Torrance, Calif., 1981—; fin. cons. Primerica Fin. Svcs., Upland, Calif., 1992—. Author: (software) Time and Attendance Utilities, 1990. With USAF, 1976-80.

POLLAK, NORMAN L., accountant; b. Chgo., Aug. 16, 1931; s. Emery and Helen (Solomon) P.; m. Barbara Zeff, Aug. 21, 1955 (div. 1980); m. Jean Lambert, Sept. 21, 1986 (div. 1991); children: Martin Joel, Elise Susan McNeal, Rhonda Louise. BS, Northwestern U., 1955. CPA, Calif.; lic. real estate agt. Calif. Sr. acct., 1951-58, pvt. practice acctg., 1958-86; semi-ret. acct., fin. and mgmt. cons., pres. Norman L. Pollak Accountancy Corp., Westlake Village, 1958-86, prin., 1986—; expert witness on dissolution matters; lectr. profl. orgns. Former pres. Ventura County Estate Planning Coun., 1975-78, 78-79); past treas. com. to elect Sybil Nisenholz for Councilwoman City of Westlake Village; founder Valley Estate Planning Coun., 1962, chpt. pres., 1964-65; founder Ventura Co. Estate Planning Coun.; chmn. Comm. Contest for Hearing Impaired, emegency com. Disaster Preparedness, Oak Forest Mobile Estates Assn.; compiled disaster preparedness plan; dir. AmeriVox; coach Braile Olympics for Blind; bd. dirs. Oak Forest Homeowners Assn. Mem. AICPA, Interant. Planning Coun. Fin. Planners, Calif. Soc. CPA's (former chmn. San Francisco tech. discussion group 1960-61), Nat. Assn. Accts., Westlake Village C. of C., Conejo C. of C., Conejo Future Found., Honokowai Palms Homeowners Assn. (bd. dirs.), Northwestern U. Alumni Club, Optimist, Delta Mu Delta. Home and Office: 143 Sherwood Dr Westlake Village CA 91361-4814

POLLAK, ROBERT ANDREW, economist; b. N.Y.C., Dec. 1, 1938; s. Harold R. and Carol (Prager) P.; m. Vivian Rogosa; children: Steven, Edward. BA, Amherst Coll., 1960; PhD, MIT, 1964. Asst. prof. econs. U. Pa., Phila., 1964-68; economist U.S. Bur. Labor Statistics, Washington, 1968-69; assoc. prof. econs. U. Pa., Phila., 1968-72, prof. econs., 1972-83, prof. econs. and social scis., 1983-90; prof. econs. U. Wash., Seattle, 1990—; vis. prof. econs. U. Wash., Seattle, 1985-89. Author: The Theory of the Cost of Living Index, 1989, (with T.J. Wales) Demand System Specification and Estimation, 1992; also articles in profl. jours.; editor Internat. Econ. Rev., 1976-85, assoc. editor 1985—; mem. bd. editors Jour. Economic Lit., 1985—; assoc. editor Rev. Econs. and Stats., 1987—, Demography, 1990—. Grantee Rockefeller Found., NSF, NIH. Fellow AAAS, Econometric Soc.; mem. Internat. Union for the Sci. Study of Population. Office: U Wash Dept Econs DK-30 Seattle WA 98195

POLLARD, JANN DIANN, artist, interior designer; b. Mt. Pleasant, Iowa, Apr. 11, 1942; d. Donald Robert and Mary (Young) Lawrence; m. Gene A. Pollard, Apr. 25, 1970; children: Brittany, Natalie. BFA in Interior Design, U. Colo., 1963; postgrad., Coll San Mateo. Interior designer Dohrmann Co., Brisbane, Calif., 1964-68, H. Janders Design Cons., San Francisco, 1968-70, Jann Pollard Design, Burlingame, Calif., 1970-90; artist The Gallery, Burlingame, 1985—, Cottage Gallery, Carmel, Calif., 1991—. One-person shows include The Gallery, Burlingame, 1987, 88, 91; SWA Zellerbach Show, San Francisco, 1985 (hon. mention) Soc. Western Artists Ann., 1985, 91, San Diego Internat. Watercolor Show, 1990; artist for bookcovers Karen Brown Travel Books, 1991-92. Active Hillsborough Aux. to Family Svc. Agy., Burlingame, 1983-93. Recipient 2d prize Soc. Western Artists, 1973. Mem. Am. Soc. Interior Designers (profl.), Watercolor Soc. Marin County, Watercolor Soc. Santa Cruz, Watercolor Soc. Santa Clara, Soc. Western Artists. Home and Studio: 105 La Mesa Dr Burlingame CA 94010

POLLARD, KENNETH MICHAEL, molecular immunologist, researcher; b. Dubbo, Australia, June 11, 1952; came to U.S., 1982; s. Jack and Norma M. (Bourke) P. BS with honors, Australian Nat. U., Canberra, 1975; PhD, U. Sydney, Australia, 1983. Scientific officer Sutton Rheumatism Rsch. Lab. Royal North Shore Hosp., St. Leonards, NSW, Australia, 1975-78; rsch. assoc. Scripps Clinic and Rsch. Found., La Jolla, Calif., 1982-85, sr. rsch. assoc., 1987-91; rsch. officer Sutton Rheumatism Rsch. Lab. Royal North Shore Hosp., St. Leonards, NSW, Australia, 1985-87; asst. mem. Scripps Clinic and Rsch. Found., La Jolla, 1992—. Contbr. articles to profl. jours. Named Eleanor Sophia travelling fellow U. Sydney, Australia Scripps Clinic and Rsch. Found., 1982-83, fellow Terri Gotthelf Lupus Rsch. Inst., 1988-91. Mem. Am. Coll. Rheumatology, Am. Soc. Microbiology. Office: Scripps Clinic & Rsch Found 10666 N Torrey Pines Rd La Jolla CA 92037-1027

POLLEY, HARVEY LEE, retired missionary and educator; b. Wapato, Wash., Aug. 14, 1924; s. Edward Prestley and Alda June Polley; m. Corinne Weber; children: Catherine, David, Corinne, Robert. BA, Whitworth Coll., Spokane, Wash., 1951; postgrad., East Wash. Coll., 1953, Berkeley Bapt. Div. Sch., 1958-59; MEd, Cen. Wash. Coll., 1958; postgrad., Ecole d'Adminstrn. des Affaires Africaines, Brussels, 1959-60. Tchr. Quincy (Wash.) Pub. Schs., 1953-57, N.W. Christian Schs., Spokane, 1958; missionary Am. Bapt. Fgn. Missionary Soc., Zaire, 1958-89; tchr. Evang. Pedagogical Inst., Kimpese, Zaire, 1961-69, asst. legal rep., dir., prin., supt., 1969-72; dir. BIM Hostel, Kinshasa, Zaire, 1972-73; mem. staff Ctr. for Agrl. Devel. Lusekele, Zaire, 1975-85, dir., 1976-79, 83-85; dir. Plateau Bateke Devel. Program, Kinshasa, 1985-89; ret., 1989. Author: Rural Development Guide, 1989. Mem. Coun. Elders, Kimpese, 1969-72; pres. bd. adminstrn. Vanga (Zaire) Hosp., 1981-83; mem. exec. com. Nat. Human Nutrition Planning Coun. Govt. Zaire-AID, Kikwit, 1983-85. Home: W2405 Johannsen Rd Spokane WA 99208

POLLEY, TERRY LEE, lawyer; b. Long Beach, Calif., June 2, 1947; s. Frederick F. and Geraldine E. (Davis) P.; m. Patricia Yamanoha, Aug. 4, 1973; children: Todd, Matthew. AB, UCLA, 1970; JD, Coll. William and Mary, 1973. Bar: Calif. 1973, U.S. Tax Ct. 1974, U.S. Supreme Ct. 1987. Assoc. Loeb & Loeb, Los Angeles, 1973-78; ptnr. Ajalat, Polley & Ayoob, Los Angeles, 1978—; lectr. taxation law U. So. Calif., 1978-87. Author (with Charles R. Ajalat) California's Water's Edge Legislation, 1987; contbr. articles to profl. jours, legal jours.; editorial bd. William and Mary Law Rev. Chmn. sch. bd. Greater Long Beach Christian Schs., 1988-92; elder Grace Brethren Ch., Long Beach, 1988—. Mem. ABA (state and local tax com. 1973-92), Calif. Bar Assn. (chmn. taxation sect. 1990-91, exec. com. 1987-92, state and local tax com. 1975—, taxation sect.), L.A. County Bar Assn. (exec. com. 1980-87, chmn. exec. com. 1985-86, taxation sect.), Omicron Delta Epsilon. Republican. Office: Ajalat Polley & Ayoob 643 S Olive St Bldg 200 Los Angeles CA 90014-1685

POLLOCK, JOHN PHLEGER, lawyer; b. Sacramento, Apr. 28, 1920; s. George Gordon and Irma (Phleger) P.; m. Juanita Irene Gossman, Oct. 26, 1945; children: Linda Pollock Harrison, Madeline Pollock Chiotti, John, Gordon. A.B., Stanford U., 1942; J.D., Harvard U., 1948. Bar: Calif. 1949, U.S. Supreme Ct. 1954. Ptnr. Musick, Peeler & Garrett, L.A., 1953-60, Pollock, Williams & Berwanger, L.A., 1960-80; ptnr. Rodi, Pollock, Pettker, Galbraith & Phillips, L.A., 1980-89, of counsel, 1989—. Contbr. articles to profl. publs. Active Boy Scouts Am.; former trustee Pitzer Coll., Claremont, Calif., 1968-76; trustee Fletcher Jones Found., Good Hope Med. Found. Served with AUS, 1942-45. Fellow Am. Coll. Trial Lawyers; mem. ABA, L.A. County Bar Assn. (trustee 1964-66). Home: 30602 Paseo del Valle Laguna Niguel CA 92677-2317 Office: 801 S Grand Ave Los Angeles CA 90017-4613

POLLOCK, RICHARD EDWIN, former county administrator; b. Phila., Aug. 27, 1928; s. Ernest Edwin and Evelyn Marie (Scarlett) P. Student Armstrong Coll., 1947, U. Calif., Berkeley, 1949-51, 55; BA in Recreation, San Jose State U., 1961; postgrad. San Fernando Valley State U., 1969-70, U. Calif., Davis, 1963-77, UCLA, 1964, U. Calif., Santa Barbara, 1970, U. Redlands, 1979; m. Yvonne May Graves, Oct. 11, 1952 (div. Aug. 1989); children: Colleen May, Karen Marie, Richard Irvin, Annette Yvonne, Mary Ann. Swim pool mgr. and instr. Berkley Tennis Club, 1955-56; police officer City of Berkeley, 1956; recreation and aquatic supr. Pleasant Hill (Calif.) Recreation and Park Dist., 1956-62; gen. mgr. Pleasant Valley Recreation and Park Dist., Camarillo, Calif., 1962-68; bldg. insp. Ventura County (Calif.), 1969-71; adminstr. Sacramento County-Carmichael Recreation and Park Dist., 1971-73; dir. parks and recreation Imperial County (Calif.), 1973-81; ret.; mem. faculty Imperial Valley Jr. Coll., 1974—; aquatic cons., 1957—; real estate investor, 1984—; chmn. San Francisco Bay Area Conf. for Cooperation in Aquatics, 1958-59. Adviser/scoutmaster Desert Trails council Boy Scouts Am.; bd. dirs., instr. ARC; work with devel. disabled and handicapped children and adults; res. dep. Sheriff, 1981— Served from pvt. to lt. U.S. Army, 1951-55; Korea. Recipient recognition for 52 years vol. service ARC, 1989; registered recreator and park mgr.; cert. elem., secondary and community coll. tchr., Calif.; reg. hypnotherapist. Mem. Nat. Recreation and Park Assn., AAHPER, Calif. Park and Recreation Soc., Calif. County Dirs. Parks and Recreation Assn., Calif. Boating Safety Officers Assn., Aircraft Owners and Pilots Assn., Nat. Assn. Emergency Med. Technicians. Democrat. Mormon. Author: Bibliography: A Pool of Aquatic Sources, 1960. Home: PO Box 3011 El Centro CA 92244-3011

POLON, LINDA BETH, educator, writer, illustrator; b. Balt., Oct. 7, 1943; d. Harold Bernard and Edith Judith Wolff; m. Marty I. Polon, Dec. 18, 1966 (div. Aug. 1983). BA in History, UCLA, 1966. Elem. tchr. L.A. Bd. Edn., 1967—; writer-illustrator Scott Foresman Pub. Co., Glenview, Ill., 1979—, Frank Schaffer Pub. Co., Torrance, Calif., 1981-82, Learning Works, Santa Barbara, Calif., 1981-82, Harper Row Co.; editorial reviewer Prentice Hall Pub. Co., Santa Monica, Calif., 1982-83. Author: (juvenile books) Creative Teaching Games, 1974, Teaching Games for Fun, 1976, Making Kids Click, 1979, Write up a Storm, 1979, Stir Up a Story, 1981, Paragraph Production, 1981, Using Words Correctly, 3d-4th grades, 1981, 5th-6th grades, 1981, Whole Earth Holiday Book, 1983, Writing Whirlwind, 1986, Magic Story Starters, 1987, (teacher's resource guides) Just Good Books, 1991, Kid's Choice/Libraries, 1991. Mem. Soc. Children's Book Writers. Democrat. Home: 1515 Manning Ave Apt 3 Los Angeles CA 90024-5831 Office: L A Bd of Edn 980 S Hobart Blvd Los Angeles CA 90006-1299

POLSON, DONALD ALLAN, surgeon; b. Gallup, N.Mex., May 12, 1911; s. Thomas Cress and Carrie Fern (Cantrall) P.; student Stanford U.; M.D., Northwestern U., 1936, M.Sc., 1947; m. Cecily, Lady Avebury, Nov. 9, 1946; 1 dau., Carolyn Kathleen. Intern, then resident in surgery St. Luke's Hosp., Chgo., 1936-38; practice medicine specializing in gen. surgery, Phoenix, 1947-83; formerly chmn. Drs. Polson, Berens & Petelin, Ltd.; chief staff Maricopa County Hosp., 1952-53, St. Joseph's Hosp., 1961; bd. dirs. Ariz. Blue Shield, 1950-55, pres., 1956. Served to col. M.C., AUS, World War II. Diplomate Am. Bd. Surgery. Mem. AMA, A.C.S., Ariz. Med. Assn. (dir. 1955-60), Maricopa County Med. Soc. (pres. 1954), Phoenix Surg. Soc. (pres. 1959), Alpha Omega Alpha, Nu Sigma Nu. Republican. Episcopalian. Clubs: Paradise Valley Country, White Mountain Country. Home: 7619 N Tatum Blvd Paradise Vly AZ 85253-3378 Office: 550 W Thomas Rd Phoenix AZ 85013

POLUS, JUDITH ANN, art educator; b. Reedsburg, Wis., Apr. 16, 1943; d. Allan Milton and Leona Christina (Gadow) Jenkins; m. Gerald Edward Polus, Oct. 26, 1973 (div. 1987); 1 child, Jessica Lynette. BA, St. Olaf Coll., Northfield, Minn., 1964; postgrad., U. Iowa, 1965-66. Elementary art tchr., supr. Wauwatosa (Wis.) Pub. Sch. Sys., 1964-65; high sch. art tchr. Oakfield (Wis.) Pub. Sch. System, 1969-74; curator of edn. Leigh Yawkey Woodson Art Mus., Wausau, Wis., 1983-86; dir. Bemis Art Sch., Colo. Springs (Colo.) Fin Arts Ctr., 1987-89, acting exec. dir., 1989-90, dir. Bemis Art Sch., 1991—; art juror 5th Congl. Dist. High Sch. Art Competition, Colorado Springs, 1988, Fred Wells 15-12 State Juried Competition, Lincoln, Nebr., 1990-91; coord. Kennedy Ctr. Imagination Celebration, 1988, Robert Bateman Master Classes, Wausau, Wis., 1986, Colorado Springs, 1991; workshop presenter R.T. Peterson Inst., Jamestown, N.Y., 1992. Mem. steering com. Arts/Bus./Edn. Com., Colorado Springs, 1988—, Kennedy Ctr. Imagination Celebration, 1987—. Mem. Nat. Art Edn. Assn., Colo. Art Edn. Assn., Met. Mus. Art (assoc. mem.), Nat. Mus. of Women in the Arts (charter mem.). Office: Bemis Art Sch of Colo Spgs 30 W Dale St Colorado Springs CO 80903-3249

POLYZOS, GEORGE CONSTANTINE, computer science educator; b. Athens, Greece, Apr. 4, 1959; came to U.S., 1988; s. Constantine G. and Eftyhia Polyzos; m. Anthoula I. Paizanou, Aug. 31, 1984. Diploma in Elec. Engring., Nat. Tech. U., Athens, 1982; MASc, U. Toronto, Can., 1985, PhD, 1989. Asst. prof. computer sci. and engring. U. Calif., San Diego, 1988—; faculty investigator Project Sequoia 2000. Contbr. articles to profl. jours. Mem. IEEE, Assn. Computing Machinery. Office: U Calif CSE La Jolla CA 92093-0114

POLZER, CHARLES WILLIAM, curator; b. San Diego, Dec. 1, 1930; s. Charles W. and Rosalie Marie (Kane) P. BA, Santa Clara U., 1952; MA, St. Louis U., 1960; BA/MA, Alma Coll., 1965; PhD, U. Ariz., 1972. Instr. Brophy Coll. Prep. Sch., Phoenix, 1958-61; priest Soc. of Jesus, 1964—; lectr., instr. U. Ariz., Tucson, 1971-73; curator ethnohistory Ariz. State Mus./U. of Ariz., Tucson, 1973—; project dir., editor Documentary Rels. of S.W., Tucson, 1975—; cons. Times Books Ltd., London, 1989-91, History House, Chgo., 1989—; founder, pres. AmeriSearch Inc., Tucson, 1987—. Author: A Kino Guide: His Missions and Monuments, 1968, A Kino Guide II, 1982; co-author: The Presidio & the Militia on the Northern Frontier of New Spain, 1987, Pedro de Rivera& the Military Regulations for Northern New Spain, 1988. Fed. commr. Christopher Columbus Quin. Jubilee Commn., 1985—. Recipient Isabel La Catolica award, 1987, Tucson-Mexico Rels. award, 1982, Citation of Merit, 1982. Mem. Ariz.-Mexico Commn., AmeriSearch Inc. (founder, pres. 1987—), Explorer's Club. Roman Catholic. Home: 2844 E First St Tucson AZ 85716 Office: Ariz State Mus Univ of Ariz Tucson AZ 85721

POMBO, RICHARD, congressman, farmer, rancher; b. Tracy, Calif., 1961; m. Annette, 1983; children: Richard Jr., Rena. Student, U. Calif., Pomona, 1981-83. Councilman City of Tracy, 1991-92; mayor pro-tem Tracy City Coun., 1992; mem. 103rd Congress from 11th Calif. dist., 1993—. Co-founder, v.p. San Joaquin County Citizen's Land Alliance, Calif., 1986—; active San Joaquin County Econ. Devel. Assn., Tracy Bus. Improvement Dist., City Coun. (vice chmn. Community Devel. Agy., Community Parks Com., and Waste Mgmt. Com.), San Joaquin County Rep. Ctrl. Com. Mem. Rotary Club. Roman Catholic. Office: US Ho of Reps House of Representatives Washington DC 20515

POMERANZ, YESHAJAHU, cereal chemist, technologist; b. Tlumacz, Poland, Nov. 28, 1922; came to U.S., 1959, naturalized, 1967; s. David and Rysia (Bildner) P.; m. Ada Waisberg, Oct. 27, 1948; children: Shlomo, David. B.S., Israeli Inst. Tech., Haifa, 1946; Chem. Engr., Israeli Inst. Tech., 1947; student, U. London, 1954-55; Ph.D., Kans. State U., 1959-62. Dir. Central Food Testing Lab., Haifa, 1948-59; research chemist Agrl. Research Service, U.S. Dept. Agr., Manhattan, Kans., 1962-69; dir. Barley and Malt Lab. Agrl. Research Service, U.S. Dept. Agr., Madison, Wis., 1969-73; dir. U.S. Grain Mktg. Research Ctr. Agrl. Research Service, U.S. Dept. Agr., Manhattan, 1973-86; research prof. dept. food sci. Wash. State U., Pullman, 1986—; vis. prof. U.S. and abroad. Sci. editor, Am. Assn. Cereal Chemists; author, co-author, editor numerous book, symposia procs. in cereal sci., tech., food sci. tech. analysis; patentee high protein bread lipid syntheses and uses. Von Humboldt awardee, 1981; recipient Wiley award, 1980, Osborne award, 1981, W.F. Geddes medal, 1982, Disting. Svc. award U.S. Dept. Agr., 1983, Nat. Assn. Wheat Growers, 1990. Fellow AAAS, Inst. Food Technologists, Assn. Cereal Chemists; mem. Am. Chem. Soc. (Food Agr. award 1984), Assn. Ofcl. Analytical Chemists, Sigma Xi, Gamma Sigma Delta. Home: 1405 SW Wadleigh Dr Pullman WA 99163-2048 Office: Wash State Univ Dept Food Sci & Human Nutrition Pullman WA 99164-6376

POMEROY, HORACE BURTON, III, accountant, corporate executive; b. Bronxville, N.Y., July 11, 1937; s. Horace Burton Jr. and Juhn (McCalla) P.; m. Margarita Maria Benavidez, July 14, 1973; children: Josephine, Emily. BS in Bus Adminstrn., U. Ariz., 1964; MBA, Boise State U., 1982. Comml. bank officer Continental Bank, Chgo., 1964-67; cons. Morgan Olmstead Kennedy Gardner, L.A., 1967-74; mgr. cash and banking Morrison Knudsen Corp., Boise, Idaho, 1974—; rep. Idaho State Legistature Dist. 16, 1988—. With U.S. Army, 1959-60. Mem. Nat. Assn. Accts., Nat. Corp. Cash Mgrs. Assn., Nat. Philatelic Assn., Masons, Elks. Republican. Episcopalian. Home: 6822 Kingsdale Dr Boise ID 83704-7343 Office: Morrison Knudsen Corp 1 MK Pla Boise ID 83729

POMEROY, JOHN SELTZER, retired geologist; b. Bethlehem, Pa., May 7, 1929; s. Harold Buchanan and A. Mildred (Seltzer) P.; m. Sara Kathryn Black, Dec. 28, 1957; children: Jeffrey, Stephen, Richard, Susan. BA, Lehigh U., 1951; postgrad., U. Utah, 1955-56. Geologist U.S. Geol. Survey, Washington, 1953-58; geologist Alaskan geology br. U.S. Geol. Survey, Menlo Park, Calif., 1958-64; geologist Ky. geology br. U.S. Geol. Survey, Lexington, 1964-68; supervisory geologist tech. reports br. U.S. Geol. Survey, Washington, 1968-70; geologist ea. regional geology br. U.S. Geol. Survey, Reston, Va., 1970-89. Contbr. 125 articles and maps to profl. jours. With U.S. Army, 1951-53. Republican. Presbyterian. Home: 1568 Katella Way Escondido CA 92027-3638

POMEROY, KENT LYTLE, physical medicine and rehabilitation physician; b. Phoenix, Apr. 21, 1935; s. Benjamin Kent and LaVerne (Hamblin) P.; m. Karen Jodelle Thomas (dec. Dec. 1962); 1 child, Charlotte Ann; m. Margo Delilah Tuttle, Mar. 27, 1964 (div. Jan. 1990); children: Benjamin Kent II, Janel Elise, Jonathan Barrett, Kimberly Eve; m. Brenda Pauline North, Sept. 1, 1990. BS in Phys. Sci., Ariz. State U., 1960; MD, U. Utah, 1963. Diplomate Am. Bd. Phys. Medicine and Rehab. Rotating intern Good Samaritan Hosp., Phoenix, 1963-64; resident in phys. medicine and rehab. Good Samaritan Hosp., 1966-69, asst. tng. dir. Inst. Rehab. Medicine, 1970-74, dir. residency tng., 1974-76, asst. med. dir., 1973-76; dir. Phoenix Phys. Medicine Ctr., 1980-85, Ariz. Found. on Study Pain, Phoenix, 1980-85; pvt. practice, Scottsdale, Ariz., 1988—; lectr. in field. Contbr. articles to med. jours. Leader Theodore Roosevelt coun. Boy Scouts Am.; mem. exec. posse Maricopa County Sheriff's Office, Phoenix, 1981—, posse comdr., 1992—; mem. med. adv. bd. Grand Canyon-Saguaro chpt. Nat. Found. March of Dimes, 1970-78. Capt. M.C., U.S. Army, 1964-66. Recipient Scouter's Tng. award Theodore Roosevelt coun. Boy Scouts Am., 1984, Scouter's Woodbadge, 1985. Mem. AMA, Am. Acad. Phys. Medicine and Rehab., Internat. Rehab. Medicine Assn., Am. Assn. Orthopaedic Medicine (co-founder, sec.-treas. 1982-88, pres. 1988-90), Pan Am. Med. Assn. (diplomate), Prolotherapy Assn. (pres. 1981-83), Am. Pain Soc., Western Pain Soc., Am. Assn. for Study Headache, Am. Thermographic Soc. (charter), Am. Soc. Addiction Medicine (sec. Ariz. chpt.), Am. Acad. Pain Medicine, Wilderness Medicine Soc., Acad. Clin. Neurophysiology, Ariz. Soc. Phys. Medicine (pres. 1977-78), Ariz. Med. Assn., Maricopa County Med. Soc., Mil. Officers World Wars (1st vice comdr. Phoenix chpt. 1993—), others. Mem. LDS Ch. Office: Royal Orthopedic & Pain Rehab Assocs 9755 N 90th St Ste A-205 Scottsdale AZ 85258 also: 2536 N 3rd St Ste 3 Phoenix AZ 85004

POMPEA, STEPHEN M., astronomer; b. Biloxi, Miss., July 18, 1953; s. Edward Tinari and Irene (Nagurney) P.; m. Nancy L. Regens, Mar. 21, 1986; children: Cynthia, Bradley. BA, Rice U., 1975; MAT, Colo. State U., 1977; PhD, U. Ariz., 1989. Sci. tchr. Air Acad., Colorado Springs, Colo., 1977-80; physicist Martin Marietta Corp., Denver, 1980-89; instrument scientist U. Ariz., Tucson, 1989-92; adj. faculty U. Ariz., 1992—; assoc. scientist Gemini 8 Meter Telescopes Project; cons. in optical physics and telescope design, 1986—; cons. in sci. edn. Ednl. Svc. Unit #11, Holdredge, Nebr., 1978-88; affiliate faculty Colo. State U. Dept. Physics, 1978-88. Patentee in field. Mem. Am. Astron. Soc., Astron. Soc. of the Pacific, Optical Soc. Am., Soc. of Photo-Optical Instrumentation Engs., Sigma Xi. Office: U Ariz Gemini Project 950 N Cherry Ave Tucson AZ 85719

POMPEY, SHERMAN LEE, historian, researcher; b. L.A., June 26, 1930; s. Alfred William George and Mira Nellie (Vornburg) P.; m. Idamae Erickson (div.); 1 child, Timothy Lee; m. Barbara Jean Bergman (div.); children: Pamilea Dawn, Marian Angel; m. Judith Dee Larson (div.); 1 child, Sherri Lory Rose. AA in English, Pasadena (Calif.) City Coll., 1967; BA in Social Sci., Fresno (Calif.) State U., 1969. Storekeeper USN, 1948-57; Navy rep. Guam Coun. 800 Boy Scouts Am., 1949-50; procurement asst. Fed. Civil Svc., 1957-61, 66-70; freelance rsch. historian Albany, Oreg., 1973—. Author, contbr. over 450 books, booklets and rsch. papers to Libr. of Congress, over 250 Family History Libr., Salt Lake City. Bd. dirs. Seek and Find, Albany, Oreg., 1987—; advisor zone 2 Albany Sch. Dist., 1987-93; Dem. precinct committeeman, Albany, 1988-91. Mem. Ofcl. Mail Study Group (pres. 1988-90, editor jour. 1988-90), Linn County Philatelic Soc. (bd. dirs. 1985-90, pres. 1978-80), Tonga/Tin Can Mail Study Cir. Pentecostal. Home: 725 Davidson St SE Apt 30 Albany OR 97321-5034

POMPHREY, MICHAEL KEVIN, software engineer; b. Ramey AFB, Puerto Rico, Aug. 22, 1947; s. Patrick James Sr. and Marie Louise (Eschenbrenner) P.; m. Lori Nicholson, June 12, 1971; children: Michael Kevin Jr., Katie Marie. BS, USAF Acad., 1970; MS in Human Resource Mgmt., U. Utah, Bitburg, Germany, 1978; postgrad., City Coll. Chgo., Madrid and Sembach, Germany, 1981-84. Cert. data processor, systems profl. Commd. 1st lt. USAF, 1971, advance through grades to maj., 1982, ret., 1990; various tactical fighter squadrons Utah, 1977-80; weapon systems officer, 1979; flight comdr. for tactical fighter squadron Torrejon AFB, Spain, 1980-81; computer systems dir. Nellis AFB, Nev., 1984-90; sr. software engr. SofTech, Inc., Layton, Utah, 1990—. Decorated D.F.C., Bronze Star, Air medal. Mem. Mem. Assn. the Inst. for Cert. Computer Profls., Data Processing Mgmt. Assn. (Las Vegas chpt. v.p. 1989-90, bd. dirs. 1991—, Great Salt Lake chpt. v.p. 1991-92, pres. 1993—, Spl. Recognition award 1989, Individual Performance award 1990), Utah Computer Soc., Utah Info. Tech. Assn., Assn. for Systems Mgmt., Armed Forces Comm. and Electronics Assn., Air Force Acad. Grad., Air Force Assn., Red River Valley Fighter Pilots Assn. Roman Catholic. Office: SofTech Inc 50 N Main St Layton UT 84041-2236

POMRANING, GERALD CARLTON, nuclear engineering educator; b. Oshkosh, Wis., Feb. 23, 1936; s. Carlton Chester and Lorraine Helen (Volkman) P.; m. Gayle Ann Burkitt, May 27, 1961 (div. 1983); children: Linda Marie, Sandra Lee. BS, U. Wis., 1957; cert., Technische Hogeschool, Delft, Holland, 1958; Ph.D. (NSF fellow), MIT, 1962. Mgr. GE, Pleasanton, Calif., 1962-64; group leader Gen. Atomic Co., La Jolla, Calif., 1964-69; v.p. Sci. Applications, La Jolla, 1969-76; prof. engring. UCLA, 1976—; cons. to govt. and industry. Author: Radiation Hydrodynamics, 1973, Transport in Stochastic Mixtures, 1991; editor: Reactor Physics, 1966; contbr. articles to profl. jours. Fulbright fellow, 1957-58. Fellow AAAS, Am. Nuclear Soc. (Mark Mills award 1963), Am. Phys. Soc.; mem. Math.

Assn. Am., Soc. Indsl. Applied Math., Am. Math. Soc., Sigma Xi, Alpha Xi Sigma, Phi Eta Sigma, Phi Kappa Phi, Tau Beta Pi, Phi Lambda Upsilon.

POND, DANIEL JAMES, technology planning and analysis program manager, technical leader; b. Bklyn., Oct. 24, 1949; s. Jack Jacob and Helen (Bartholomew) P.; m. Diane Louise Lippman, Sept. 5, 1971 (div. Oct. 1982); children: David Alan, Steven Douglas; m. Linda Rae Smith, June 18, 1983; stepchildren: Timothy Joseph Wood, Melissa Jill Wood. AA, Nassau Community Coll., Garden City, N.Y., 1969; BS in Psychology, Adelphi U., 1971; MS in Counselor Edn., L.I. Univ., 1975; PhD in Ergonomics, N.C. State U., 1981. Operating engr. for several indsl. firms, 1968-77; assoc. prin. engr. Harris Govt. Systems, Melbourne, Fla., 1981-83; sr. human factors engr. Lockheed-Ga. Co., Marietta, Ga., 1983-84; chmn. engring. psychology Fla. Inst. Tech., Melbourne, 1984-90; chief adminstr. Ctr. for Interdisciplinary Rsch. on Aging, Fla. Inst. Tech., Melbourne, 1988-89; cons. Grumman, Melbourne, 1990; sr. program mgr., human factors tech. group leader Pacific N.W. Lab., Richland, Wash., 1990—; cons. Fla. Power & Light Nuclear Tng., Ft. Pierce, 1987-90; mem. Dept. Def. Human Factors Engring. Tech. Adv. Group Tech. Soc./Industry Group rep. of Assn. of Aviation Psychologists. Reviewer Ergonomists, Human Factors Engrs. Mem. Human Factors Soc. (rep. to the edn. com. AAAS, 1985-91, profl. standards com. 1985-91, chmn. 1988-91, chmn. tech. adv. group, 1991-93, coun. tech. groups chmn. 1987-88, educators' profl. group chmn. 1985-87, Paul M. Fitts educators' award com. chmn. 1985-87, edn. com.-internship subcom. chmn. 1984-85, pub. rels. com. 1983-85), Am. Soc. Safety Engrs., Assn. Aviation Psychologists, Sigma Xi. Home: RR 3 Box 3885 Prosser WA 99350-9541 Office: Pacific NW Lab Tech Planning & Analysis Ctr PO Box 999 MS K8-24 Richland WA 99352-0999

PONDER, RANDALL SCOTT, financial planner, money manager, consultant; b. Oklahoma City, Oct. 3, 1959; s. Curtis Phalen Ponder and Carol Ann (Butler) McFall. BS in Mgmt., Oklahoma City U., 1981; MBA in Fin., Golden Gate U., 1985. Registered investment advisor. Mktg. rep. Ford Aerospace Corp., Sunnyvale, Calif., 1981-87; cons. Vector Enterprises, Solvang, Calif., 1987-88; fin. counselor Cigna Corp., San Francisco, 1988-89; pres. Ponder Fin. Group, Redwood City, Calif., 1989—; chief fin. officer CAT AIR Corp., Belmont, Calif., 1989-92; tchr. investments Sequoia Adult Edn. Program, Redwood City, 1990—; fin. con. to various start-up cos., Redwood City, 1985—. Mem. Internat. Assn. Fin. Planners, Kiwanis (pres. Redwood City club 1993—). Republican. Office: Ponder Fin Group 720 University Ave Palo Alto CA 94301

PONTAROLO, MICHAEL JOSEPH, lawyer; b. Walla Walla, Wash., Sept. 1, 1947; s. Albert and Alice Mary (Fazzari) P.; m. Elizabeth Louise Onley, July 18, 1970; children: Christie, Amy, Nick, Angela. BA, Gonzaga U., 1969, JD, 1973. Bar: Wash. 1973, U.S. Dist. Ct. (ea. dist.) Wash. 1974. Assoc. Mullin & Etter, Spokane, Wash., 1973-75, William Iunker, Spokane, 1974-75, Delay, Curran & Boling, Spokane, 1975-77; prin. Delay, Curran, Thompson & Pontarolo, P.S., Spokane, 1977—; mem. Spokane County Med. Legal Com., 1987, 88, 91; chair Superior Ct. Liaison Com., 1987-88; mem. Bench Bar Com., 1987-88; mem. Superior Ct. Arbitration Bd., 1987—; adj. prof. Gonzaga U. Sch. Law, 1987. Bd. dirs. Community Ctrs. Found., Spokane, 1986-89; active Spokane C.C. Legal Secretary Adv. Com.; mem. adv. bd. Spokane C.C., 1992—. Recipient Cert. of Recognition, Superior Ct. Clk., Spokane, 1986. Mem. ABA, Am. Arbitration Assn., Wash. State Bar Assn. (interprofl. com. 1987-90, character and fitness com. 1991—, jud. recommendation com. 1990-92, spl. dist. counsel 1984), Wash. State Trial Lawyers Assn. (v.p. east 1979-80, Cert. Appreciation 1982, 90, 92, Leadership award 1984, CLE program chmn. 1984), Assn. Trial Lawyers Am., Assn. Personal Injury Lawyers, Western Assn. Workers' Compensation Bds., Spokane County Bar Assn. (v.p., sec.-treas. 1986-89, pres. 1989-90, bd. trustees 1984-86., membership com., chair 1992-93). Office: Delay Curran Thompson Pontarolo W 601 Main Ste 1212 Spokane WA 99201

PONTERIO, FRANK JULIAN, healthcare administrator, consultant; b. San Mateo, Calif., Sept. 6, 1961; s. Arthur Edward and Beatrice L. (Dougherty) P. BS in Bus. Adminstrn./Healthcare Mgmt., San Diego State U., 1989. Mgr. San Mateo Med. Clinic, 1982-86; bus. mgr. San Mateo Cardiovascular Cons. Inc., 1986-89; healthcare cons. Practice Mgmt. Systems, Inc., Burlingame, Calif., 1989-91; practice adminstr. San Mateo Orthopedic Med. Group, Inc., 1991—; healthcare cons. Ponterio & Assocs., San Mateo, 1990—. Mem. Med. Group Mgmt. Assn., Am. Coll. Med. Group Adminstrs. Republican. Roman Catholic. Home: 19 Dory Ln Foster City CA 94404 Office: San Mateo Orthopedic Med Group Inc 77 N San Mateo Dr San Mateo CA 94401

POOL, JEANNIE GAYLE, music historian, arts administrator; b. Paris, Ill., Nov. 6, 1951; d. Raymond E. and Betty N. (Elliott) P.; m. Kevin J. Barker, July 16, 1983; children: Amelia Barker, Elliott Barker. BA in Music, Hunter Coll., 1977; postgrad., Columbia U., 1977-80; MA in History, Calif. State U., Northridge, 1987. Dir. Internat. Congress on Women in Music, N.Y.C., L.A., 1979-90; co-dir. Internat. Inst. for the Study of Women in Music Calif. State U., Northridge, 1986—; exec. dir. Soc. for the Preservation of Film Music, L.A., 1990—; broadcaster Sta. KPFK-FM Radio, L.A., 1980—; producer Cambria Records, L.A., 1986—. Named for Disting. Svcs. Local 47 Am. Fedn. Musicians, 1987; recipient Am. Music Broadcasting award Sigma Alpha Iota, 1982-88. Office: PO Box 8192 La Crescenta CA 91224-0192

POOL, JOHN THOMAS, health services coordinator, consultant; b. Spokane, Wash., July 13, 1943; s. Dean Layton and Alice Gwendalyn (Rygg) P.; m. Elaine W. Wirkkunen, Mar. 25, 1972; children: Matthew, Erik. BA in Econs., U. Wash., 1966. Detective Univ. Police Dept., Seattle, 1970-74; spl. agt. Drug Enforcement Adminstrn., Seattle and El Paso, Tex., 1976-83; tng. coord. Drug Enforcement Adminstrn., Dallas, 1983-88; demand reduction coord. Drug Enforcement Adminstrn., Seattle, 1988—; vice chairman bd. Wash. State Drug Free Bus., Seattle, 1989—; bd. dir. Alaskans for Drug Free Youth, Ketchikan, Alaska, 1989—, Gov.'s Substance Abuse Coun., Olympia, Wash., 1991; bd. advisor Wash. State Substance Abuse Co-action, Bellevue, Wash., 1989—. Author: (book) Creating The Drug Free Business, 1990. Intelligence officer USN, 1966-70. Mem. Alpha Sigma Phi. Office: Drug Enforcement Adminstrn 220 W Mercer Ste 104 Seattle WA 98119

POOLE, BARBARA ANN, mathematics educator; b. Harrison, Mich., Aug. 31, 1935; d. Maxwell Eugene and Ethel Marie (Graub) Stanley; m. Donald Ray Poole, July 31, 1954; children: James, Julia. BS, U. Oreg., 1957; MEd, U. Wash., 1973. Tchr. N. Eugene (Oreg.) High Sch., 1957-59; mathematician Naval Weapons Ctr., China Lake, Calif., 1962-63; tchr. N. Seattle Community Coll., 1973—. Author: Introductory Algebra, 1989, Intermediate Algebra, 1989. Mem. Am. Math. Assn. 2-Yr. Colls. (NW v.p. 1987-91), Math. Assn. Am., Nat. Coun. Tchrs. Math., Pi Mu Epsilon, Pi Lambda Theta. Lutheran. Home: PO Box 525 Woodinville WA 98072-0525 Office: N Seattle Community Coll 9600 College Way N Seattle WA 98103-3599

POOLE, CECIL F., federal judge; b. Birmingham, Ala.; children: Gayle, Patricia. LL.B., U. Mich.; LL.M., Harvard U., 1939. Practice of law San Francisco, former asst. dist. atty., 1951-58; clemency sec. to Gov. Brown of Calif., 1958-61; U.S. atty. No. Dist. Calif., 1961-70; Regents prof. Law U. Calif., Berkeley, 1970; counsel firm Jacobs, Sills & Coblentz, San Francisco, 1970-76; judge U.S. Dist. Ct., No. Dist. Calif., 1976-79, U.S. Ct. of Appeals for 9th Circuit, 1979—; adj. prof. Golden Gate U. Sch. Law, 1953-58; mem. adv. com. Nat. Commn. for Reform Fed. Criminal Laws, 1968-70. Served to 2d lt. AUS, World War II. Mem. ABA (chmn. sect. individual rights 1971-72, ho. of dels. 1972-74), San Francisco Bar Assn. (dir. 1975-76). Office: US Ct Appeals 9th Cir PO Box 193939 San Francisco CA 94119-3939

POOLE, HARRY WENDELL, county group probation counselor; b. Paces, Va., Jan. 29, 1953; s. Charlie Washington and Minnie Beatrice (Oliver) P. AA, Riverside Community Coll., 1981; BS, U. Redlands, 1983; MS, Calif. State U., Dominuez Hills, Calif., 1985. With payroll Kaiser Steel Corp., Fontana, Calif., 1975-83; group counselor I Riverside County Probation, Riverside, Calif., 1983-86; group counselor II Riverside County Probation, 1986—; youth counselor Calif. Youth Authority, Chino, 1978. Democrat. Baptist. Office: Riverside County Probation 3933 Harrison St Riverside CA 92503-3597

POOLE, HENRY JOE, JR., business executive; b. Rocky Point, N.C., July 5, 1957; s. Henry Joe Sr. and Marjorie (Morse) P.; m. Loretta Lynn Scott, Sept. 12, 1981; children: Robert Howard, Amanda Lynn. AA, Cypress Coll., 1977; student, San Diego State U., 1978, Calif. State U., Fullerton, 1978-79. Pres. Poole Ventura Inc., Ventura, Calif., 1979-92; gen. mgr. W.I.C. PVI systems divsn., Ventura, Calif., 1992—. Inventor in field. Mem. ASME, Soc. Mfg. Engrs., Am. Vacuum Soc., Am. Welding Soc., Soc. Vacuum Coaters. Office: WIC PVI Systems Divsn 5301 N Ventura Ave Ventura CA 93001

POOLE, ROBERT ANTHONY, journalist; b. St. Austell, Cornwall, Eng., Dec. 17, 1944; arrived in Can., 1977; m. Valerie Avril Taggart, Apr. 14, 1973; children—Claire Lucy, Emma Louise. Irish editor Press Assn., Belfast, Northern Ireland, 1970-77; gen. reporter Calgary Herald, Alta., Can., 1977-79; city editor Calgary Albertan, 1979-80; city editor Calgary Sun, 1980-81, mng. editor, 1981-84, editor-in-chief, 1984—. Office: Calgary Sun, 2615 12th St NE, Calgary, AB Canada T2P 7W9

POONAWALA, ISMAIL KURBANHUSEIN, Near Eastern language professor; b. Godhra, Gujarat, India, Jan. 7, 1937; came to U.S., 1964; s. Kurbanhusein Fidahusein and Sakina Sultanali (Sakina) P.; m. Oumayma Hasan Ali Ahmad, Jan. 6, 1981; 1 child, Qays Hasanayn. MA, Bombay U., 1959, Cairo U., 1964; PhD, UCLA, 1968. Asst. prof. McGill U., Montreal, Can., 1968-71; rsch. assoc. Harvard U., Cambridge, Mass., 1971-74; Author: Biobibliography of Ismaili Literature, 1977; translator History of al-Tabari: Last Years of the Prophet, 1990; editor Al-Urjuza al-Mukhtara, 1970; author/editor Al-Sultan al-Khattab, 1967. Muslim. Office: UCLA Dept Near Eastern Langs Los Angeles CA 90024

POONJA, MOHAMED, business reorganization, financial and management consultant; b. Mombasa, Kenya, Nov. 8, 1948; came to U.S., 1984; s. Abdulrasul and Maleksultan (Dharsee) P.; m. Zaitun Virji, Feb. 24, 1979; children: Jamil Husayn, Karim Ali. Student, Inst. Chartered Accts., Eng., Wales; MS in Mgmt. and Organizational Behavior, U.S. Internat. U. CPA. Audit supr. Ernst & Young (formerly Ernst & Whinney), Dublin, Ireland, 1966-72, Coopers & Lybrand, Dublin, 1973-76; group controller Diamond Trust of Kenya, Nairobi, 1976-78; chief operating officer Kenya Uniforms, Ltd., Nairobi, 1978-81; sr. mgr. Coopers & Lybrand, Calgary, Alta., Can., 1981-84; ptnr. Coopers & Lybrand, San Jose, Calif., 1984-92; chpt. 7 panel bankruptcy trustee No. Dist. Calif., San Jose, Calif., 1991—; with Poonja & Co., 1992—; ptnr. Menzenita Capital Ptnrs. Ltd., 1993—; v.p. Bay Area Bankruptcy Forum; bd. dirs. Calif. Bankruptcy Forum. Mem. ABA, Brit. Inst. Mgmt., Am. Bankruptcy Inst., Assn. Insolvency Accts., Inst. Bus. Appraisers, Cert. Fraud Examiners, Rotary. Home: 630 Milverton Rd Los Altos CA 94022-3930 Office: Poonja & Co 167 S San Antonio Rd Ste 17 Los Altos CA 94022-3930

POOR, CLARENCE ALEXANDER, physician; b. Ashland, Oreg., Oct. 29, 1911; s. Lester Clarence and Matilda Ellen (Doty) P.; AB, Willamette U., 1932; MD, U. Oreg., 1936. Diplomate Am. Bd. Internal Medicine. Intern U. Wis., Madison, 1936-37, resident in internal medicine, 1937-40, instr. dept. pathology Med. Sch., 1940-41, clin. instr., clin. asst. dept. internal medicine, 1942-44; pvt. practice medicine specializing in internal medicine, Oakland, Calif., 1944—; mem. emeritus staff Highland Alameda County Hosp., Oakland, 1949—; mem. staff Providence Hosp., Oakland, 1947—, pres. staff, 1968-69; staff mem. Samuel Meritt Hosp., Oakland, 1958—; staff mem. Summit Med. Ctr. (merger Providence Hosp. and Samuel Merritt Hosp.), 1991—. Mem. Nat. Council on Alcoholism, 1974—, bd. dirs. Bay Area, 1977—. Mem. Am., Calif., Alameda-Contra Costa med. assns., Alameda County Heart Assn. (trustee 1955-62, 72-82, pres. 1960-61), Calif. Heart Assn. (dir. 1962-72), Soc. for Clin. and Exptl. Hypnosis, Am. Soc. Clin. Hypnosis, San Francisco Acad. Hypnosis (dir. 1966—, pres. 1973). Home and Office: 400 29th St Ste 201 Oakland CA 94609-3547

POPE, EDWARD JOHN ANDREW, corporate executive, consultant; b. N.Y.C., July 18, 1962; s. Thomas Andrew and Barbara (McInnes) P. BS, U. Calif., L.A., 1983, MS, 1985, PhD, 1989. Engring. asst. U. Calif., 1979-83, rsch. asst., 1984-89; pres. MATECH, Westlake Village, Calif., 1989—; cons. Orion Labs., Inc., Camarillo, Calif., 1988-89, Refractory Composites, Inc., Whittier, Calif., 1989-90, ENSCI, Inc., Woodland Hills, Calif., 1990—; bd. dirs. Ventura County World Affairs Coun. Contbr. numerous articles to profl. jours. Assoc. mem. State Ctrl. Com. of Rep. Party, Calif., 1981-83; pres. UCLA Bruin Reps., L.A., 1981-82; active UCLA Chem. Adv. Coun., 1993; appointed Ventura County Coun. on Econ. Vitality, 1993. Regent's scholar U. Calif., 1979, Chancellor's scholar, 1979; IBM Corp. fellow Watson Rsch. Ctr., 1988. Mem. Am. Ceramic Soc. (chair edn. com. 1990—), Nat. Inst. Ceramic Engrs., Materials Rsch. Soc. (acad. affairs com. 1987-89), UCLA chpt. Materials Rsch. Soc. (pres. 1982-89). Office: MATECH 31304 Via Colinas Ste 102 Thousand Oaks CA 91362-3901

POPE, JOHN WILLIAM, judge, law educator; b. San Francisco, Mar. 12, 1947; s. William W. and Florence F. (Kline) P.; m. Linda M. Marsh, Oct. 23, 1970; children: Justin, Ana, Lauren. BA, U. N.Mex., 1969, JD, 1973. Bar: N.Mex. 1973, U.S. Dist. Ct. N.Mex. 1973, U.S. Ct. Appeals (10th cir.) 1976. Law clk. N.Mex. Ct. of Appeals, Santa Fe, 1973; assoc. Chavez & Cowper, Belen, N.Mex., 1974; ptnr. Cowper, Bailey & Pope, Belen, 1974-75; pvt. practice law Belen, 1976-80; ptnr. Pope, Apodaca & Conroy, Belen, 1980-85; dir. litigation City of Albuquerque, 1985-87; judge State of N.Mex., Albuquerque, 1987-92, Dist. Ct. (13th jud. dist.), N.Mex., 1992—; instr. U. N.Mex., Albuquerque, 1983—, prof. law , 1990—; lectr. in field. Mem. state cen. com. Dem. Party, N.Mex., 1971-85; state chair Common Cause N.Mex., 1980-83; pres. Valencia County Hist. Soc., Belen, 1981-83. Mem. Valencia County Bar. Home: 400 Godfrey Belen NM 87002 Office: Valencia County Courthouse PO Box 1089 Los Lunas NM 87301

POPE, MAX LYNDELL, public utility official; b. Clinton, N.C., Nov. 5, 1932; s. William Walter and Maggie (Honeycutt) P.; B.A., Idaho State Coll., 1962; grad. U.S. Army Command and Gen. Staff Coll., 1977, Security Manpower Program, Indsl. Coll. Armed Forces, 1980; m. Sarah Jane Norris, Dec. 10, 1954. City mgr. City of Rangely (Colo.), 1963-66, City of Seaside (Oreg.), 1966-69, City of Pasco (Wash.), 1969-70; city adminstr. City of Coeur d'Alene (Idaho), 1971-72; planner State of Idaho, Boise, 1972-75; city adminstr. City of Woodburn (Oreg.), 1975-85; gen. mgr. Woodinville Water Dist., Wash., 1986-90; tech. specialist U.S. EPA, 1991-92; gen. mgr. Vandenberg Village Community Svcs. Dist., 1992—. Ordained elder Presbyn. Ch., 1958, elder, Woodburn, 1976-80. With U.S. Army, 1953-56, 70-71. Recipient Disting. Svc. award Rangely Jaycees, 1964. Mem. Internat. City Mgmt. Assn., Am. Soc. Public Adminstrn., Am. Public Works Assn., Am. Water Works Assn., Civil Affairs Assn., Res. Officers Assn., Woodinville C. of C., Woodburn C. of C. Clubs: Rotary. Home and Office: 1300 North L St Lompoc CA 93436

POPE, PETER T., forest and paper products company executive; b. 1934; married. BA, Stanford U., 1957, MBA, 1959. With Pope & Talbot Inc., Portland, Oreg., 1960—, asst. sec., 1964-68, v.p., 1968-69, v.p., gen. mgr., 1969-71, chmn. bd., chief exec. officer, 1971-90, chmn., pres., chief exec. officer, 1990—. With USAR, 1957-58. Office: Pope & Talbot Inc 1500 SW 1st Ave Portland OR 97201-5815

POPE, WENDELL LAVON, computer science educator; b. Arco, Idaho, Jan. 16, 1928; s. Wendell Stephen and Berniece (Hadden) P.; m. Dorothy Nancy Hill, Sept. 17, 1950 (div. Apr. 1979); children: Keith L., Kathryn N., Mary Ann, Marcus D., Linda C., Anna T., Malcolm W., Kevin W., Tamara L.; m. Shirlene R. Mason, Dec. 13, 1979. BS in Math., Utah State Agrl. Coll., Logan, 1956; MS in Math., Stanford U., 1958; MS in Computer Sci., U. Wis., 1968. Advanced study scientist Lockheed Missile & Space Div., Sunnyvale, Calif., 1956-58, math. analyst, 1958-59; asst. prof. Utah State U., Logan, 1959-69, assoc. prof., 1969-77, dir. Computer Ctr., 1969-77, prof. computer sci., 1977-89, prof. emeritus, 1990—; mgr. systems analysis and design Water Rsch. Ctr., U.S. AID Project, Colo. State U., Cairo, 1990-91. Contbr. articles to profl. jours. Pres. Hyrum (Utah) Lincoln Sch. P.T.A., 1962-64; chmn. dist. 2 Rep. party, Hyrum, 1962-64, sec., 1964-66. 1st lt. U.S. Army, 1946-48, 50-53. NSF sci. faculty fellow U. Wis., Madison, 1966-67. Mem. LDS Ch. Home: 1545 E 2000 N Logan UT 84321 Office: Utah State U Computer Sci Dept Logan UT 84322

POPEJOY, WILLIAM J., savings and loan association executive; b. 1938; married. B.A., Calif. State U., 1961, M.A., 1962. Pres. Fed. Home Loan Mortgage Corp., 1971-74; pres. Am. Savs. & Loan Assn. subs. Fin. Corp. Am., Los Angeles, 1974-80; chmn., pres., chief exec. officer Am. Savs. & Loan Assn. subs. Fin. Corp. Am., Irving, Calif., 1984-89, also bd. dirs.; pres. Far West Savs. & Loan Assn., 1980-81; pres., chief fin. officer Fin. Fedn. Inc., Culver City, Calif., from 1981; chmn., pres., chief exec. officer Fin. Corp. Am., Irvine, 1984-89, also bd. dirs. Office: Fin Corp Am 18401 Von Karman Ave Irvine CA 92715-1542

POPOVAC, GWYNN, artist, writer; b. Wilmington, Del., Dec. 1, 1948; d. William Jackson and Lora (Taylor) Miller;m. Vladimir Popovac, June 20, 1976; 1 child, Lola. Student, UCLA, 1966-71. Presenter program on artists, David Knight Prodns., San Francisco, 1989; speaker on mask art St. Mary's Coll., Moraga, Calif., 1991; co-founder Second Sundays lit. enterprise, 1990—. Author: Wet Paint, 1986; group exhbns. mixed media art include Rod Rumsey Gallery, L.A., 1967-69, Gagosian's The Open Gallery, L.A., 1970-74; Turtle Bay Trading Co., Beverly Hills, Calif., 1971, Benton/Rosamond Gallery, Carmel, Calif., 1988, Mountain Matters Gallery, Sonora, Calif., 1989-92, The Gallery, Sonora, 1992, Wellspring Gallery, Santa Monica, Calif., 1992; Drawings published in Conversations with Bugs, 1993. Home: 17271 Robin Ridge St Sonora CA 95370

POPPA, RYAL ROBERT, manufacturing company executive; b. Wahpeton, N.D., Nov. 7, 1933; s. Ray Edward and Annabelle (Phillips) P.; m. Ruth Ann Curry, June 21, 1952; children: Sheryl Lynn, Kimberly Marie. BBA, Claremont Men's Coll., 1957. Sales trainee IBM, L.A., 1957-59, sales rep., 1959-62, product mktg. rep., 1963, sales mgr., 1964-66; v.p., gen. mgr. Comml. Computers Inc., L.A., 1966-67; v.p. Greyhound Computer Corp., Chgo., 1967-68, pres., chief exec. officer, bd. dirs., 1969-70; pres., chief exec. officer, bd. dirs., mem. exec. com. Data Processing Fin. & Gen., Hartsdale, N.Y., 1970-72; exec. v.p., chief fin. officer, bd. dirs., mem. exec. com. Mohawk Data Sci. Corp., Utica, N.Y., 1972-73; chmn., pres., chief exec. officer Pertec Computer Corp., L.A., 1973-81, BMC Industries, Inc., St. Paul, 1982-85; pres., chmn., chief exec. officer Storage Tech. Corp., Louisville, Colo., 1985—; founder Charles Babbage Inst.; past dir. Spacelabs, Inc. Trustee Claremont Men's Coll.; mem. Chmn.'s Circle Colo. Reps.; past mem. Pres. Com. Nat. Medal of Sci. Recipient Exec. of Yr. award U. Colo. MBA Alum Assn., 1986, Community Svc. award Inst. Human Rels. Am. Jewish Com., 1980, Colo. Bus. Leader of Yr. award CACI, 1991. Mem. Computer and Comm. Industry Assn. (chmn., past bd. dirs., mem. exec. com., vice chmn.), Am. Electronics Assn. (past bd. dirs., mem. exec. com. Colo. chpt.), Electronic Mfrs. Club, Boulder Country Club. Office: Storage Tech Corp 2270 S 88th St Louisville CO 80028-0002

POPPOFF, ILIA GEORGE, science writer, consultant; b. San Diego, Apr. 9, 1924; s. George Ilia and Stamatka P.; m. Betty Ann Sieh, Oct. 19, 1944; children: Mark David, Robin Marie, Christine Lea. Student, San Diego State U., 1942-43; BA, Whittier (Calif.) Coll., 1947; postgrad., U. Calif., Berkeley, 1947-48, Stanford U., 1954-55. Radiol. physicist U.S. Naval Radiol. Def. Lab., San Francisco, 1948-53; chmn. atmospheric scis., sr. physicist Stanford Rsch. Inst., Menlo Park, Calif., 1953-67; chief stratospheric projects NASA/Ames Rsch. Ctr., Mt. View, Calif., 1967-79; freelance sci. writer Carnelian Bay, 1980-90, Pebble Beach, Calif., 1990—; organizer, editor of proceedings, chmn. Mountain Watershed Symposium, Crystal Bay, Nev., 1988. Co-author: (monograph) Physics of the Lower Ionosphere; (textbook) Fundamentals of Aeronomy; editor proceedings Internat. Mountain Watershed Symposium, 1990; contbr. articles to profl. jours. Commr. Tahoe Regional Planning Agy. Adv. Planning Commn., Zephyr Cove, Nev., 1983—; bd. mem. Calif. Regional Water Quality Control Bd., South Lake Tahoe, Calif., 1984—; bd. dirs., pres. Tahoe Resource Conservation Dist., South Lake Tahoe, 1982-88. Mem. AAAS, Am. Geophys. Union, Am. Cetacean Soc.

PORAD, LAURIE JO, jewelry company official; b. Seattle, Dec. 19, 1951; d. Bernard L. and Francine J. (Harvitz) P. BA, U. Wash., 1974; postgrad., Seattle Pacific U., summers 1975-76. Cert. standard tchr., Wash. Substitute tchr. Issaquah (Wash.) Sch. Dist., 1974-77; with data processing dept. Ben Bridge Jeweler, Seattle, 1977-83, auditing mgr., 1983-87, systems mgr., 1987-92, MIS special project mgr., 1992—; mem. adv. bd. computer sci. dept. Highline Community Coll., Midway, Wash., 1985—, mem. tech. prep. leadership com. 1993—. Tchr. religion sch. Temple de Hirsch Sinai, Seattle, 1972-76, 84—, coord. computerized Hebrew learning ctr., 1987-88, coord. of religion sch. city facility, 1988—; tutor Children's Home Soc. Wash., Seattle, 1976-77. Mem. Assn. for Women in Computing (life mem., chmn. chpt. workshop 1985-88, nat. chpts. v.p. 1985-88, nat. pres. 1988-90, nat. chpt. v.p. 1992—), Wash. Women United. Home: 14616 NE 44th St Apt # M-2 Bellevue WA 98007-7102 Office: Ben Bridge Jeweler PO Box 1908 Seattle WA 98111-1908

PORCARO, MICHAEL FRANCIS, advertising agency executive; b. N.Y.C., Apr. 3, 1948; s. Girolamo M. and Marianna (DePasquale) P.; m. Bonnie Kerr, Apr. 7, 1972; children: Sabrina, Jon. BA in English, Rockford (Ill.) Coll., 1969. Broadcaster Sta. KFQD, Anchorage, 1970-71, Sta. KENI, Anchorage, 1972-73; v.p. ops. Cook Inlet Broadcasters, Anchorage, 1973-74; owner Audio Enterprises, Anchorage, 1974-75; asst. Alaska Pub. Broadcasting Commn., Anchorage, 1975-76; exec. dir. Alaska Pub. Broadcasting Commn., 1976-81; chief exec. officer, ptnr. Porcaro Blankenship Advt. Corp., Anchorage, 1981—; cons. Arco Alaska TV sta., Anchorage, 1981; expert witness U.S. Sen. Subcom. on Telecommunications, Washington, 1978; mem. citizens adv. com. U. Alaska Dept. Journalism. Chmn. Municipality of Anchorage Urban Design Commn., 1990-93; mem. mayor's transition team Municipality of Anchorage, 1987-88; bd. dirs. Anchorage Glacier Pilots Baseball Club, 1987-88; mem. citizens adv. com. dept. journalism U. Alaska, Anchorage; bd. dirs. Brother Francis Shelter for the Homeless. Recipient Silver Mike award Billboard mag., 1974, Bronze award N.Y. Film Critics, 1981, Best of North award Ad. Fedn. Alaska, 1982—, Addy award, 1985, 91, Grand Addy award 1990, Cable TV Mktg. award 1986; Paul Harris fellow. Mem. Advt. Fedn. Alaska. Republican. Roman Catholic. Office: Porcaro Blankenship Advt 433 W 9th Ave Anchorage AK 99501-3519

PORDON, WILLIAM PHILIP, music educator; b. Buffalo, Aug. 4, 1925; s. William Peter Pordon and Victoria Regina (Valenches) Dobson; m. Eleanor Grace, Sept. 28, 1951; children: Judith, Dorothy, Gregory. MusB, Chgo. Conservatory of Music, 1950, MusM, 1951. Violinist Atlanta Symphony, 1951-55; music tchr. Augusta (Ga.) Pub. Schs., 1955-59; dir. music Wayland (Mass.) Pub. Schs., 1960-69; asst. prof. music edn. U. Lowell, Mass., 1969-85. Author: String Starter, 1983. With U.S. Army, 1942-44, ETO. Recipient Lowell Mason award Mass. Music Educators Assn., 1981. Mem. Am. String Tchrs. Assn. (pres. San Diego sect. 1985—). Home: 3154 Old Heather Rd San Diego CA 92111-7714

POROSKY, MICHAEL, real estate and investment company executive; b. Detroit, Mar. 28, 1930; s. Walter Michael and Ruth (Hanny) P.; m. Paula Lea Dickinson; children: Michael Winston, Patrick Dickens, Wendy Christine. BA in Journalism, U. Wash., 1953. Agt. Phoenix Mut. Life Ins. Co., Seattle, 1957-66; pres. Profl. Cons. Cos., Seattle, 1967—. V.p. N.W. region Pacific N.W. Lawn Tennis Assn., 1974-78. Lt. commdr. USN, 1952-57; USNR, '57-68. Mem. Seattle Tennis Club. Republican.

PORRERO, HENRY, JR., computer company executive; b. Upland, Calif., Aug. 16, 1945. AA, Chaffey Coll., 1970; BS, Calpoly Pomona U., 1973. Bus. mgr. Guy F. Atkinson Co., South San Francisco, 1973-83; controller Laird Constrn. Co., Inc., R. Cucamonga, Calif., 1983-85; pres., founder PLT Computer Systems, Inc., Upland, Calif., 1986—; fin. cons. Parrott & Wright Constrn., Corona, Calif., 1987—. Treas. Boy Scouts Am., Upland, 1987-89. With USN,1966-69. Mem. Am. Legion, Friends Upland Library, Calif. Sheriffs Assn. Republican. Home: 854 W Carson St Upland CA 91786-3704

PORTER, A. DUANE, mathematics educator; b. Detroit, Dec. 31, 1936; s. Alphonse Walter and Nelda (Hoffman) P.; m. Carol Burt, Aug. 12, 1960; children: Lisa Luane, Joshua Duane. BS, Mich. State U., 1960, MS, 1961; PhD, U. Colo., 1964. Statistician Gen. Motors, Flint, Mich., 1960; asst. prof. U. Wyo., Laramie, 1964-67, assoc. prof., 1967-69, prof., 1969—, acting head math. dept., 1976-79; vis. prof. Clemson (S.C.) U., 1977, Humboldt

State U., Arcata, Calif., 1978; dir. Sci. & Math. Teaching Ctr., Laramie, 1979-83, RMMC Summer Sch., Laramie, 1982—, NSF Faculty Enhancement, Laramie, 1988—. Contbr. articles to profl. jours. Grantee NSF. Mem. Am. Math. Soc., Math. Assn. Am. (gov. 1978-81), Nat. Coun. Tchrs. Math., N.Y. Acad. Scis. Office: U Wyo Math Dept Laramie WY 82071

PORTER, ALBERT WRIGHT, author, artist, educator; b. Bklyn., Nov. 25, 1923; s. Arthur and Gertrude (Wright) P.; m. Shirley Alberta Owens, Feb. 2, 1946; children: Kim Kronfeld, Todd. AA, Compton Jr. Coll., 1942; BA, UCLA, 1950; MA, Calif. State U., L.A., 1957. Tchr. L.A. Pub. Schs., 1950-58, art supr., 1958-71; freelance artist, lectr. L.A., 1958—, author, 1974—; prof. art Calif. State U., Fullerton, 1971-89, prof. emeritus, 1989—. Author: (textbooks) Shape and Form, 1974, Pattern, 1975, Art of Sketching, 1977, Expressive Watercolor Techniques, 1982; co-author: Exploring Visual Design, 1987. Capt. USAF, 1944-45, ETO. Recipient 1st pl. award Palos Verdes Art Festival, 1977. Mem. Nat. Watercolor Soc. (v.p. 1977-78, award 1972), Watercolor West, Calif. Art Educators Assn., Art Educators L.A. (Outstanding Achievement award 1988). Home: 8554 Day St Sunland CA 91040-1812

PORTER, BRIAN STANLEY, police chief; b. Seattle, May 2, 1938; s. Jack D. and Margaret I. (Tuter) P.; grad. U. Alaska, 1970, Northwestern U. Traffic Inst., 1970-71, FBI Nat. Exec. Inst., 1981; m. Bette K. Schakohl, Apr. 26, 1958; children—Kelle, Kerry, Kory. With Anchorage Police Dept., 1960—, chief of police, 1980—; chmn. Alaska Police Standards Council, 1978-80. Served with U.S. Army, 1957-58. Office: The House of Representatives 3430 Fordham Dr Anchorage AK 99508

PORTER, DAVID TAYLOR, physical education educator; b. Des Moines, May 14, 1951; s. Blaine Robert and Elizabeth (Taylor) P.; m. Lorrie Parker, May 25, 1976; children: Tara, Lincoln, Dillon, Taylor. BS, Brigham Young U., 1975, MS, 1977; EdD, U. Hawaii, 1993. Instr. Brigham Young U., Provo, Utah, 1976-82; asst. prof. Brigham Young U., Laie, Hawaii, 1982—; pres., dir. tennis Hawaii Aces, Oahu, 1991—. Mem. U.S. Profl. Tennis Assn. (regional v.p. 1988—, Newcomer award 1987, Coach award 1990, 91, 92), U.S. Racquet Stringers Assn. (cert.), Am. Alliance Phys. Edn., Recreation and Dance, Mensa. Republican. Church of Jesus Christ of Latter-Day Saints. Home and Office: 55-220 Kulanui St # 1722 Laie HI 96762

PORTER, DIXIE LEE, insurance executive, consultant; b. Bountiful, Utah, June 7, 1931; d. John Lloyd and Ida May (Robinson) Mathis. B.S., U. Calif. at Berkeley, 1956, M.B.A., 1957. Personnel aide City of Berkeley (Calif.), 1957-59; employment supr. Kaiser Health Found., Los Angeles, 1959-60; personnel analyst U. Calif. at Los Angeles, 1961-63; personnel mgr. Reuben H. Donnelley, Santa Monica, Calif., 1963-64; personnel officer Good Samaritan Hosp., San Jose, Calif., 1965-67; fgn. service officer AID, Saigon, Vietnam, 1967-71; gen. agt. Charter Life Ins. Co., Los Angeles, 1972-77, Kennesaw Life Ins. Co., Atlanta, from 1978, Phila. Life Ins. Co., San Francisco, from 1978; now pres. Women's Ins. Enterprises, Ltd.; cons. in field. Co-chairperson Comprehensive Health Planning Commn. Santa Clara County, Calif., 1973-76; bd. dirs. Family Care, 1978-80, Aegis Health Corp., 1977-92, U. Calif. Sch. Bus. Adminstrn., Berkeley, 1974-76; mem. task force on equal access to econ. power U.S. Nat. Women's Agenda, 1977—. Served with USMC, 1950-52. C.L.U. Mem. C.L.U. Soc., U. Calif. Alumni Assn., U. Calif. Sch. Bus. Adminstrn. Alumni Assn., AAUW, Bus. and Profl. Women, Prytanean Alumni, The Animal Soc. Los Gatos/Saratoga (pres. 1987-90), Beta Gamma Sigma, Phi Chi Theta. Republican. Episcopalian.

PORTER, GENE LAVON, writer, artist; b. L.A., Aug. 24, 1935; s. Robert Brown and Mamie (Pollon) P.; m. Doris Ann Dunlap, Dec. 21, 1957; children: Ronald, Mark. BA in Psychology, Calif. State U., L.A., 1961; MA in Humanities, Calif. State U., Dominguez Hills, 1977; MA in Creative Arts: Interdisciplinary, Calif. State U., San Francisco, 1980. Registered environ. health specialist, Calif. Programs specialist Los Angeles County, 1966-78, City and County of San Francisco, 1980-90; writer/artist Burbank, Calif., 1991—. Author: The Nature of Form in Process, 1969, Conceptual Art Books, 1976-80; author computer art book; inventor non-parallel sided kaleidoscopes. With U.S. Army, 1954-57, Japan, Korea.

PORTER, JAMES NEIL, marketing executive; b. Sacramento, Oct. 3, 1931; s. Neil Lendell and Alice Elizabeth (Hummell) P.; m. Susan Elizabeth Moore, Apr. 16, 1955 (div. Feb. 1990); children: David James, Mary Katherine, Anne Elizabeth. BA, San Jose State U., 1953. Mgr. product mgmt. Memorex Corp., Santa Clara, Calif., 1968-71; dir. mktg. planning Cartridge TV, Inc., San Jose, Calif., 1971-73; dir. mktg. CMX Systems, joint venture CBS and Memorex, Sunnyvale, Calif., 1973-74; product mgr. Unicom Systems subs. Rockwell Internat., Sunnyvale, 1974-75; mgmt. cons. Mountain View, Calif., 1975-77; pres. Disk/Trend, Inc., Mountain View, 1977—. Prin. contbr. (annual market study) Disk/Trend Report, 1977—. With U.S. Army, 1953-55. Mem. IEEE, Internat. Data Storage Equipment and Materials Assn. (bd. dirs. 1986—, v.p. 1988—). Office: Disk/Trend Inc 1925 Landings Dr Mountain View CA 94043-0810 :

PORTER, JONATHAN, history educator and department chair; b. Boston, Mar. 25, 1938; s. Eliot Furness and Aline (Kilham) P.; m. Zoe Barter, June 20, 1959. AB, Harvard U., 1960; MA, U. Colo., 1963; PhD, U. Calif., Berkeley, 1971. Instr. history U. Colo., Boulder, 1964-65; instr. history U. N.Mex., Albuquerque, 1969-71, asst prof. history, 1971-74, assoc. prof. history, 1974-87, chair history dept., 1986—, prof. history, 1987—. Author: Tseng Kuo-fan's Private Bureaucracy, 1972, All Under Heaven, 1983; contbr. articles on Chinese sci. and history to profl. jours. NDEA Title VI (Chinese) grantee U.S. Dept. Edn., 1965-66, Am. Coun. Learned Socs. grantee, 1976-77; Social Sci. Rsch. Coun. fellow, 1968-69. Mem. Assn. for Asian Studies (exec. sec. western conf. 1974-79, pres. western conf. 1984-85), Sports Car Club Am. Home: 199 Mirasol Corrales NM 87048 Office: U NMex Dept History Albuquerque NM 87131-1181

PORTER, MICHAEL PELL, lawyer; b. Indpls., Mar. 31, 1940; s. Harold Troxel and Mildred Maxine (Pell) P.; m. Alliene Laura Jenkins, Sept. 23, 1967 (div.); 1 child, Genevieve Natalie; m. Janet Kay Smith Hayes, Feb. 13, 1983 (div.). Student, DePauw U., 1957-58; BA, Tulane U., 1961, LLB, 1963. Bar: La. 1963, U.S. Ct. Mil. Appeals 1964, N.Y. 1969, Hawaii 1971. Clk. U.S. Ct. Appeals (5th cir.), New Orleans, 1963; assoc. Sullivan & Cromwell, N.Y.C., 1968-71, Cades Schutte Fleming & Wright, Honolulu, 1971-74, ptnr., 1975—; mem. deans coun. Law Sch. Tulane U., 1981-88; dep. vice chancellor Episcopal Diocese Hawaii, 1980-88, chancellor, 1988—; chancellor Episcopal Ch., Micronesia, 1988—. Author: Hawaii Corporation Law & Practice, 1989, Nat. Corp. Law Series, 1989. Bd. dirs. Jr. Achievement Hawaii, Inc., 1974-84, Inst. Human Svcs., Inc., 1980-88; donor Michael P. Porter Dean's Scholastic award U. Hawaii Law Sch., 1977—. With JAGC, U.S. Army, 1963-66, Vietnam. Tulane U. fellow, 1981. Mem. ABA, Assn. of Bar of City of N.Y., Hawaii State Bar Assn., Pacific Club. Republican. Office: Cades Schutte Fleming & Wright 1000 Bishop St Honolulu HI 96813-4212

PORTER, RICHARD ERNEST, speech educator, author; b. Long Beach, Calif., Dec. 7, 1933; s. Ernest Long and Arlene Mary (Dietz) P.; m. Rosemary Jean Macias, June 18, 1957; children: Tamre Lynn Cardozo, Gregory Richard. BA, Calif. State U., Long Beach, 1956; MA, San Diego State U., 1968; PhD, U. So. Calif., L.A., 1974. Commd. ensign USN, 1956, advanced through grades to lt. comdr., 1965, resigned, 1967; prof. Calif. State U., 1970—. Author: Understanding Intercultural Communication, 1981, Communication Between Cultures, 1990; editor: Intercultural Communication: A Reader, 1972-93 (Best Book award 1986). Mem. Speech Communication Assn., Western Speech Communication Assn., Assn. Communication Administrs., Internat. Community Coun., Long Beach Yacht Club. Office: Calif State U Dept Speech Communication Long Beach CA 90840

PORTER, STEVEN HAROLD, credit manager; b. Vancouver, Wash., Apr. 5, 1958; s. Quentin Zebedee and Margie Ann (Storm) P.; m. Jennifer Sue Buriff, July 28, 1979; children: Jeremiah, Matthew, Joshua, Michael, Benjamin, Isaac. AA in Bus. Adminstrn., Warner Pacific Coll., 1978. Asst. mgr. Fotomart, Inc., Portland, Oreg., 1978-79; owner Marque Printing, Vancouver, 1979-80; acct. mgr. Harvest States Coops., Portland, 1980-84; acctg. systems analyst Harvest States Coops., St. Paul, 1984-85; credit mgr. Americold Corp., Portland, 1985—. Bd. mem. Salmon Creek Little League, Vancouver, 1988—; coord. Crossroads Community Ch., Vancouver, 1990—. Office: Americold Corp Ste 135 7007 SW Cardinal Ln Portland OR 97224

PORTER, THEODORE MARK, history educator; b. Kelso, Wash., Dec. 3, 1953; s. Charles Clinton and Shirley Isobel (Tolle) P.; m. Diane Rita Campbell, Aug. 19, 1979; 1 child, David Campbell. AB, Stanford U., 1976; PhD, Princeton U., 1981. Postdoctoral instr. Calif. Inst. Tech., Pasadena, 1981-84; rsch. mem. Zentrum fur interdisziplinaere Forschung der U. Bielefeld, Germany, 1982-83; asst. prof. history U. Va., Charlottesville, 1984-91; assoc. prof. history UCLA, 1991—. Author: The Rise of Statistical Thinking, 1986; co-author: The Empire of Chance, 1989; contbr. numerous articles to profl. jours. Grantee Guggenheim Found., 1989-90, Nat. Sci. Found., 1991-92. Mem. History of Sci. Soc. (mem. coun. 1991-93), Am. Hist. Assn. Home: 18 Virgil Ct Irvine CA 92715 Office: UCLA Dept of History 405 Hilgard Ave Los Angeles CA 90024

PORTER, VERNA LOUISE, lawyer; b. L.A., May 31, 1941. B.A., Calif. State U., 1963; JD, Southwestern U., 1977. Bar: Calif. 1977, U.S. Dist. Ct. (cen. dist.) Calif. 1978, U.S. Ct. Appeals (9th cir.) 1978. Ptnr. Eisler & Porter, L.A., 1978-79, mng. ptnr., 1979-86, pvt. practice law, 1986—; judge pro-tempore L.A. Mcpl. Ct., 1983—, L.A. Superior Ct., 1989—, Beverly Hills Mcpl. Ct., 1992—; mem. state of Calif. subcom. on landlord tenant law, panelist conv., mem. real property law sect. Calif. State Bar, 1983; speaker on landlord-tenant law to real estate profls., including San Fernando Bd. Realtors; vol. atty. L.A. County Bar Dispute Resolution, mem. client rels. panel, fee arbitrator. Editorial asst., contbr. Apt. Owner Builder; contbr. to Apt. Bus. Outlook, Real Property News, Apt. Age; mem. World Affairs Coun., Mem. ABA, L.A. County Bar Assn. (client-rels. vol. dispute resolution and fee arbitration, 1981—), L.A. Trial Lawyers Assn., Wilshire Bar Assn., Women Lawyer's Assn., Landlord Trial Lawyers Assn. (founding mem., pres.), da Camera Soc. Republican. Office: 2500 Wilshire Blvd Ste 1226 Los Angeles CA 90057-4320

PORTER, WILLIAM EMME, state legislator, small business owner; b. Lucknow, India, Mar. 29, 1925; (parents Am. citizens); s. Ruben Boring and Lenore Carolyn (Emme) P.; m. E. Caryl Wilbur, June 3, 1947; children: Elisabeth, Katherine, Kristin. Student, Doane Coll., 1945-47; AB, Albion Coll., 1949; MS, Kans. State U., 1950. Tchr. Garden City (Kans.) Pub. Schs., 1951-53; prin. pub. schs. Wilson, Kans., 1953-55; tchr., head sci. dept.pub. schs. Las Cruces, N.Mex., 1955-84, farmer-mgr., 1975—; mem. N.Mex. Ho. Reps., Santa Fe, 1990—; Mem. agriculture and water com., N.Mex. State Ho. Reps., 1990—, tax and revenue com., 1990—, tax equalization com., 1990—, border devel. com., 1992—, internat. spaceport com., 1992—, agriculture and forestry com. Nat. Conf. State Legis., 1993—. Contbr. articles to newspapers; patentee Porter Bermuda Grass. Pres. Community Concert Assn., Las Cruces, 1989-91; founder Friends of Fort Selden, N.Mex., 1988. With U.S. Army, 1943-45, ETO. Mem. N.Mex. Acad. Sci. (pres. 1960-61), Beta Beta Beta. Democrat. Home: 5200 N Hwy 85 Las Cruces NM 88005

PORTNEY, JOSEPH NATHANIEL, aerospace executive; b. L.A., Aug. 15, 1927; s. Marcus and Sarah (Pilson) P.; m. Ina Mae Leibson, June 20, 1959; children: Philip, Jeffrey. BS, U.S. Naval Acad., 1952. Commd. 2d lt. USAF, 1952, advanced through grades to capt., 1956, resigned, 1960; with Litton Systems, Inc., Woodland Hills, Calif., 1960—; project engr. Litton Aero Products Litton Systems, Inc., Woodland Hills, 1967-68, program mgr. Litton Aero Products, 1968-72, advanced program mgr. guidance and control systems, 1972-85, mgr. advanced programs guidance and control systems, 1985—. Creator solar compass, pilot and navigator calendar. Mem. Inst. of Navigation (v.p. 1988-89, pres. 1989-90), U.S. Naval Acad. Alumni Assn. (trustee 1980-83). Jewish. Home: 4981 Amigo Ave Tarzana CA 91356-4505 Office: Litton Systems Inc 5500 Canoga Ave Woodland Hills CA 91367-6621

POSIN, DANIEL Q., physics educator, television lecturer; b. Turkestan, Aug. 13, 1909; came to U.S., 1918, naturalized, 1927; s. Abram and Anna (Izritz) P.; m. Frances Schweitzer, 1934; children: Dan, Kathryn. A.B., U. Cal., 1932, A.M., 1934, Ph.D., 1935. Instr. U. Cal., 1932-37; prof. U. Panama, 1937-41; dean natural scis. U. Mont., prof., 1941-44, chmn. dept. physics and math., 1942-44; staff Mass. Inst. Tech., 1944-46; prof. physics, chmn. dept. N.D. State Coll., Fargo, 1946-55; prof. dept. physics DePaul U., 1956-67; prof. phys. sci. dept. Calif. State U., San Francisco, 1967—; chmn. dept. interdisciplinary scis. Calif. State U., 1969—; dir. Schwab Sci. Lecture Series, Atoms for Peace exhibit Mus. Sci. and Industry, Chgo.; Chief cons. Borg Warner Sci. Hall and Allied Chem. Sci. Hall, Times Square; scientific cons. CBS-TV. (Recipient 6 Emmy awards for best educator on TV in Chgo., and best ednl. TV programs). Author: Trigonometria, 1937-41, Fisica Experimental, Fisica, 1937-41, Mendeleyev—The Story of a Great Scientist, 1948, I Have Been to the Village, with Introduction by Einstein, 1948, rev. edit., 1974, Out of This World, 1959, What is a Star, 1961, What is Chemistry, 1961, What is a Dinosaur, 1961, The Marvels of Physics, 1961, Find Out, 1961, Chemistry for the Space Age, 1961, Experiments and Exercises in Chemistry, 1961, What is Matter, 1962, What is Electronic Communication, 1962, What is Energy, Dr. Posin's Giants, 1962, Life Beyond our Planet, 1962, Man and the Sea, 1962, Man and the Earth, 1962, Man and the Jungle, 1962, Man and the Desert, 1962, Science in the Age of Space, 1965, Rockets and Satellites, Our Solar System, The Next Billion Years, 1973; contbr. to: Today's Health; sci. cons.: Compton's Yearbook; contbr. to: feature articles Chgo. Tribune, (book) After Einstein-Remembering Einstein, 1981; co-contbr. to book The Courage to Grow Old, 1989; appearances, CBS Radio-TV, WTTW-WGN-TV, 1956-67, NET; ABC TV series Dr. Posin's Universe. Chmn. edn. com. Chgo. Heart Assn., 1963-67; Trustee Leukemia Soc. James T. Grady award Am. Chem. Soc., 1972. Fellow Am. Phys. Soc.; mem. A.A.A.S., Phi Beta Kappa, Sigma Xi. Office: Calif State Univ San Francisco CA 94132

POSNER, LINDA ROSANNE, charity volunteer, educator; b. Rockford, Ill., Sept. 24, 1940; d. Lawrence George and Genevieve Annette (Reecher) Turnquist; m. Christian John Posner, Oct. 14, 1972; children: Katrina E., Christian L. BA, Rockford Coll., 1962; MEd, U. Md., 1970. Elem. sch. tchr. Elmhurst and Villa Park, Ill., 1962, 68; spl. edn. tchr. Christ Ch. Child Ctr., Bethesda, Md., 1970-72. Chmn. Heart Ball, 1988—, Golden Thimble IX, Hosp. of Good Samaritan, L.A., 1986-87, Heart of Gold recognition dinner; chmn. Am. Heart Assn. Greater L.A., 1983, now bd. dirs.; pres. St. Vincent Med. Ctr. Auxiliary, L.A., 1983-84; trustee St. Alban's Episc. Ch., L.A., 1985-87; bd. dirs. Claremont Young Musicians Orch., Claremont Heritage, home tour 1991-93, Los Angeles County Med. Assn., pres. aux. dist. 14, 1992-93. Mem. U. So. Calif. Med. Faculty Wives (pres. 1986-87). Home: 3455 Spring Hill Dr Janesville WI 53545

POST, AUGUST ALAN, economist, artist; b. Alhambra, Calif., Sept. 17, 1914; s. Edwin R. and Edna (Stickney) P.; m. Helen E. Wills, Nov. 21, 1940; 1 child, David Wills. AB, Occidental Coll., 1938; student Chouinard Inst. Art, 1938; MA, Princeton, 1940; LLD, Golden Gate U., 1972, Occidental Coll., 1974, Claremont Grad. Sch., 1978. In banking bus., 1933-36; instr. econs. Occidental Coll., 1940-42; asst. prof. Am. U., 1943; economist Dept. State, 1944-45; rsch. dir. Utah Found., 1945-46; chief economist, adminstrv. analyst State of Calif., 1946-50, state legis. analyst, 1950-77; cons. to commn. studying higher edn. Wells Commn., N.Y.; cons. Milton Eisenhower Com. Higher Edn. and State, 1964; mem. Nat. Com. Support of Public Schs., 1967; mem. nat. adv. panel Nat. Center Higher Edn. Mgmt. Systems, 1971-72; chmn. Calif. Gov.'s Commn. on Govt. Reform, 1978—; mem. faculty U. So. Calif. Grad. Sch. Pub. Adminstrn., 1978-80; Regents' prof. U. Calif., Davis, 1983, vis. prof., 1984-85; spl. cons. Touche Ross and Co., 1977-87; cons., interim exec. dir. Calif. Commn. for Rev. of Master Plan for Higher Edn., 1985 ; mem. adv. bd. Calif. Tomorrow nat. shows and one-man shows; dir. Crocker Art Gallery Assn., pres., 1966-67. Trustee U. Calif., Berkeley, Art Mus., 1986-91; mem. adv. com. on future ops. Coun. State Govts., 1965; bd. mgrs., pres. YMCA; bd. dirs. Sacramento Civic Ballet Assn.; trustee Calif. Coll. Arts and Crafts, 1982-86; chmn. Calif. State Task Force on Water Future, 1981-82, Sacramento Regional Found., bd. dirs., 1983-91; bd. dirs. Calif. Mus. Assn., pres., 1976-77; bd. dirs. Policy Analysis for Calif. Edn., 1985—, Senate Adv. Commn. on Control of Cost of State Govt., 1986—; chmn. Citizens Commn. on Ballot Initiatives, 1992—; Catalonia Sister State Task Force, 1988—, Calif. Citizens Budget Commn., 1992, co-chmn., Commn. on Innovation, Calif. Community Colls., 1992; chmn. Californians for Pension Protection, 1992—, Judicial Coun. Select com. on Judicial Retirement, 1993—. With USNR, 1943-44. Mem. Nat. Acad. Public Adminstrn., Phi Beta Kappa, Kappa Sigma. Home: 1900 Rockwood Dr Sacramento CA 95864-1527

POST, GAINES, JR., college educator, dean, administrator; b. Madison, Wis., Sept. 22, 1937; s. Gaines and Katherine (Rike) P.; m. Jean Wetherbee Bowers, July 19, 1969; children—Katherine Doris, Daniel Lawrence. B.A., Cornell U., 1959; B.A., Oxford U., 1963; M.A., Stanford U., 1964, Ph.D., 1969. Instr. Stanford U., 1966-69; asst. prof. history U. Tex., Austin, 1969-74, assoc. prof., 1974-83; dean faculty, sr. v.p. Claremont McKenna Coll., Calif., 1983-88, prof., 1988—; exec dir. Rockefeller Found. Commn. on Humanities, 1978-81; fellow Interuniv. Seminar on Armed Forces and Society. Author: The Civil Military Fabric of Weimar Foreign Policy, 1973; (with others) The Humanities in American Life, 1980, Dilemmas of Appeasement: British Deterrence and Defense, 1934-37, 1993; Editor: German Unification: Problems and Prospects, 1992. Mem. exec. com. Forming the Future Project, Austin Ind. Sch. Dist., 1982; mem. Tex. Com. for Humanities, 1981-83; mem. council Calif. Congl. Recognition Program, 1984-88. Rhodes scholar, 1961-63; Am. Council Learned Socs. fellow, 1982-83; Am. Philos. Soc. grantee, 1974. Mem. Community Coll. Humanities Assn. (bd. dirs. 1981-89), Am. Hist. Assn. Home: 2254 N Navarro Dr Claremont CA 91711-1758 Office: Claremont McKenna Coll Dept History 890 Columbia Ave Claremont CA 91711

POST, KEVIN EUGENE, aviation analyst; b. Falls Church, Va., Sept. 23, 1963; s. Philip Holmes and Leola Ann (Olson) P.; m. Lynette Marie Bowen, June 13, 1987; children: Tiffany Lynette, Shelby Anne. BS in Aviation, Le Tourneau U., 1986. Mechanic Boeing Modification, Everett, Wash., 1987-89; factory analyst Boeing Change Mgmt., Everett, 1989-91, inter-div. analyst, 1991-92, contracts change bd. analyst, 1992—; factory rep. career team Boeing Change Mgmt., 1991-92, change mgmt. rep. quality improvement team Boeing Customer Engrng., Everett, 1992—. Office: Boeing Co 3003 W Casino Rd Everett WA 98203

POSTMA, JAMES LEE, computer software engineer, consultant; b. Chgo., Aug. 9, 1934; s. John Jr. and Grace E. (Lee) P.; m. Yukiko Honda, Dec. 21, 1960 (div. Feb. 1980); children: Monica Lee, Cindy Jane, Joy Marie; m. Frances Ann Speers, July 26, 1980. BSME, Purdue U., 1956; postgrad., Alexander Hamilton Inst., 1962. Registered profl. engr., Calif; cert. flight instr., FAA. Sr. engr. North Am. Aviation, Canoga Park, Calif., 1960-67; mgr. CELESCO, Costa Mesa, Calif., 1967-72, Calif. Computer Corp., Anaheim, 1972-73; pvt. practice investment adviser Anaheim, 1973-78, pvt. practice computer software engineering cons., 1978-80; pvt. practice computer software engineering cons. Steilacoom, Wash., 1980—; pres. Brainware Corp., Anaheim, 1967-77; dir. 2003 Corp., Steilacoom, 1992. 1st lt. USAF, 1957-60, Japan. Recipient Sci. award Bausch & Lomb, 1952. Mem. ASME (pres. student chpt. 1955), Theta Xi. Republican. Lutheran.

POSTREL, VIRGINIA INMAN, editor; b. Asheville, N.C., Jan. 14, 1960; d. Samuel Martin and Sue Sanders (Lile) Inman; m. Steven Robert Postrel, June 22, 1986. AB, Princeton U., 1982. Staff reporter The Wall St. Jour., Phila., 1982-84; staff writer Inc mag., Boston, 1984-86; asst. editor Reason Mag., Santa Monica, Calif., 1986-88, assoc. editor, 1988-89; editor Reason Mag., L.A., 1989—. Contbr. articles to profl. jours. Office: Reason Mag 3415 S Sepulveda Blvd # 400 Los Angeles CA 90034

POTASH, STEPHEN JON, international public relations specialist; b. Houston, Feb. 25, 1945; s. Melvin L. and Petrice (Edelstein) P.; m. Jeremy Warner, Oct. 19, 1969; 1 son, Aaron Warner. BA in Internat. Rels., Pomona Coll., 1967. Account exec. Charles von Loewenfeldt, Inc., San Francisco, 1969-74, v.p., 1974-80; founder, pres. Potash & Co., Pub. Rels., Oakland, Calif., 1980-87; cons. Am. Pres. Lines and Am. Pres. Cos., 1979-87; exec. dir. Calif. Coun. Internat. Trade, 1970-87; v.p. corp. communications Am. Pres. Cos., Oakland, 1987-90; chmn. Potash & Co., Oakland, 1990—. Bd. dirs. Calif. Coun. Internat. Trade, 1987—, Calif.-Southeast Asia Bus. Coun., 1992—, Temple Sinai, Oakland, 1979-81. Mem. Pub. Rels. Soc. Am., Commonwealth Club of Calif., World Trade Club San Francisco. Office: Potash & Co 1946 Embarcadero Oakland CA 94606-5213

POTHITT, KATHLEEN MARIE, physical oceanography researcher; b. Santa Monica, Calif., Jan. 11, 1964; d. John Andrew and Eileen Sharon (Melcher) Alexander; m. Richard Pothitt, Jan. 22, 1993; children from a pervious marriage: Richard Alexander Island, Timothy Demetrius Island. Student, UCLA, 1981-83; BS in Applied Math. summa cum laude, Calif. State U., Northridge, 1986. Rsch. analyst Arete Assocs., Sherman Oaks, Calif., 1985-91, mem. rsch. staff, 1991—; property mgr. Ronald Craig, Inc., Northridge, 1987-90; tutor math. Culver City 1986—. Recipient Acad. Achievement award, Calif. State U., 1986. Mem. Am. Geophys. Union, Am. Math. Assn., Soc. for Indsl. and Applied Math., Soc. Women Engrs., Women in Sci. and Engrng., Nat. Parks Conservation Assn. Republican. Home: 3873 Girard Ave # 4 Culver City CA 90232 Office: Arete Assocs PO Box 6024 Sherman Oaks CA 91413-6024

POTOCKI, JOSEPH EDMUND, marketing company executive; b. Jersey City, Jan. 31, 1936; s. Joseph and Estelle (Bielski) P.; m. Margaret Mary Shine, May 21, 1960; children: Joseph, Meg, David. BS, Seton Hall U., 1957. Asst. regional sales mgr. Gen. Mills Inc., Valley Stream, N.Y., 1960-67; group mgr. merchandising Warner Lambert Co., Morris Plains, N.J., 1967-84; dir. merchandising svcs. Beatrice Hunt/Wesson, Fullerton, Calif., 1974-83; pres., chief exec. officer Joseph Potocki & Assocs., Irvine, Calif., 1983-92; pres. Mktg. Fulfillment Svcs., Tustin, Calif., 1985-87; sr. exec. Gage Mktg., 1992—; bd. dirs. Schmidt Cannon, L.A., Clarke Hooper Am., Irvine, Clark Hooper PLC, London; sec. Nat. Premium Sales Exec., Union, N.J., 1982-87. 1st lt. U.S. Army, 1957-59. Recipient Mktg. Motivator award L.A. Mktg. Exhbn., 1981, Mktg. Gold medal Am. Mktg. Assn. 1957. Mem. Promotion Mktg. Assn. (chmn. bd. dirs. 1977-79, v.p. West sect. 1980-87, bd. dirs. 1990, chmn. edn. com., Reggie award 1984, 85, 87), Promotion Mktg. Assn. Am. (bd. dirs. exec. com. 1978-87, Chmn.'s Bowl 1979, Named to Chmn.'s Circle 1986), Nat. Premium Sales Execs. (sec. 1985-86, Pres. award 1985). Republican. Roman Catholic. Home: 22772 Azure Sea Monarch Pky Laguna Niguel CA 92677 Office: Gage Mktg Group 18200 Von Karman Ste 200 Irvine CA 92715

POTTER, DAVID ERIC, computer executive; b. San Jose, Calif., Sept. 12, 1949; s. Charles Devere and Ada (Ranelli) P.; m. Lauren Fins, Sept. 22, 1974; 1 child, Tracy Brianne. BA, U. Calif., 1971, MA, 1974, postgrad., 1978. Tng. instr. Intel Corp., Santa Clara, Calif., 1978-79; sales devel. mgr. Intel Corp., Santa Clara, 1979-80; pres., chief exec. officer Concurrent Sciences, Inc., Moscow, Idaho, 1980—. Contbr. articles to profl. jours. Mem. Assn. Computing Machinery, Internat. RMX User's Group (v.p. 1985-87). Home: 1191 Tolo Trl Moscow ID 83843-8707 Office: Concurrent Scis PO Box 9666 530 S Asbury St Moscow ID 83843-2228

POTTER, DAYNA MAE, anthropologist, human osteologist; b. Albany, Oreg., Sept. 22, 1954; d. Daniel and Evelyn Mae (Troxel) P.; 1 child, Daniel Jacob Gillentine. BA in Anthropology, N.Mex. State U., 1990, postgrad., 1990—. Refinery worker Payne & Keller, Houston, 1973-78; owner, operator Small Tavern, Dickinson, Tex., 1978-79; customer svc. worker Group W Cable, Santa Ana, Calif., 1983-84; with Storer Cable, Houston, 1984-85; grad. asst. N.Mex. State U., Las Cruces, 1991-93; human osteologist Human Systems Rsch., Las Cruces, 1990—; rsch. scientist, archeologist U. Tex., El Paso, 1993—. Illustrator: (lab. manual) Lab Manual for SkelMAP, 1990. Mem. Explorations in Human Endeavors (bd. mem. 1992—), Soc. for Creative Anachronism. Office: 1630 Wyoming # 10 Las Cruces NM 88001

POTTER, J(EFFREY) STEWART, property manager; b. Ft. Worth, July 8, 1943; s. Gerald Robert Potter and Marion June (Mustain) Tombler; m. Dianne Eileen Roberb, Dec. 31, 1970 (div. Aug. 1983); 1 child, Christopher Stewart; m. Deborah Ann Blevins, Oct. 20, 1991. AA, San Diego Mesa Coll., 1967. Cert. apartment mgr., apartment property supr. Sales mgr. Sta. KJLM, La Jolla, Calif., 1964-67; mgr. inflight catering Host Internat., San Diego, 1967-69; lead aircraft refueler Lockheed Co., San Diego, 1969-70; property mgr. Internat. Devel. and Fin Corp., La Jolla, 1970-72; mgr. bus.

property BWY Constn. Co., San Diego, 1972-73; mgr. residents Coldwell Banker, San Diego, 1973-74; mgr. Grove Investments, Carlsbad, Calif., 1974-76, Villa Granada, Villa Seville Properties Ltd., Don Cohn, Chula Vista, Calif., 1976-83; gen. mgr. AFL-CIO Bldg. Trades Corp., National City, Calif., 1983—; instr., Cert. Apt. Mgmt. San Diego Apt. Assn. Fellow Nat. City C. of C., Toastmasters, Founding Families San Diego Hist. Soc., La Jolla Monday Night Club (treas. 1984-89). Roman Catholic. Home: 4616 Granger St San Diego CA 92107-4012 Office: AFL-CIO Bldg Trades Corp 2323 D Ave National City CA 91950-6798

POTTER, JOHN HOWELL, radio entertainer; b. Rochester, N.Y., June 17, 1954; s. John Howell and Joanne (Winne) P.;m. Julea Hancock, Dec. 8, 1979 (div. Dec. 1984); 1 child, James Stephan; m. Anne Cleveland Hadley, Dec. 28, 1990. BA, Valparaiso (Ind.) U., 1977. Morning show host KCBN Radio, Reno, Nev., 1979-81, WOYK Radio, York, Pa., 1980-81, WVIC Radio, Lansing, Mich., 1981-82; afternoon show host KJR Radio, Seattle, 1982-83; morning show host WMJQ Radio, Rochester, N.Y., 1983-86; TV weathercaster WROC-TV, Rochester, 1983-86, KTNV-TV, Las Vegas, Nev., 1986-90; morning show host KWNR Radio, Las Vegas, 1990—, 1990—; stand-up comic Bally's Catch a Rising Star, Las Vegas, 1990. Columnist Fun-Time Mag., Rochester, 1983-84. Telethon host Humane Soc., Las Vegas, 1991—, Easter Seals Soc., Rochester, N.Y., 1983-86; dir. Easter Seals Soc. Monroe County, Rochester, 1985-86; co-chmn. Big Bros./Big Sisters Bowlathon, Rochester, 1985. Recipient Gannett Found. award, Rochester, 1972, Best of Las Vegas award Las Vegas Rev.-Jour., 1990. Repubican. Presbyterian. Home: 9109 Emerald Cove Ct Las Vegas NV 89117-2405 Office: KWNR Radio 1515 E Tropicana Ave Las Vegas NV 89119-6517

POTTRUCK, DAVID S., brokerage house executive; b. 1948. BA, U. Pa., 1970, MBA, 1972. Now pres., CEO U.S. Govt., 1972-74; with Arthur Young & Co., 1974-76, sr. cons.; with Citibank N.Am., 1976-81, v.p.; with Shearson/Am. Express, 1981-84, sr. v.p. consumer mktg. and advt.; with Charles Schwab & Co., San Francisco, 1984—; exec. v.p. mktg., br. adminstr. Charles Schwab and Co., Inc.; now pres. Charles Schwab & Co. Office: Charles Schwab & Co Inc 101 Montgomery St San Francisco CA 94104-4122

POTTS, ERWIN REA, newspaper executive; b. Pineville, N.C., Apr. 20, 1932; s. Jennings Bryan and Edith Maxine (Matthews) P.; m. Silvia Antuna Montalbo, Feb. 18, 1961; children: Matthew Kingsley, Jeffrey Manuel, Bryan Erwin (dec.). Student, Mars Hill (N.C.) Jr. Coll., 1950-52; A.B. in Journalism, U. N.C., 1954. Reporter, editor Knight Newspapers, Miami, Fla., 1958-70; city editor Miami Herald, 1967-70; v.p., gen. mgr. Tallahassee Democrat, 1970-73, Charlotte (N.C.) Observer, News, 1973-75; pres. McClatchy Newspapers (Sacramento Bee, Fresno Bee, Modesto Bee, Anchorage Daily News, Tri-City Herald, Tacoma News Tribune, Rock Hill Herald, Beaufort Gazette, Hilton Head Island Packet, 10 other newspapers), Sacramento, Calif., Wash., S.C., 1975—; chief exec. officer McClatchy Newspapers (Sacramento Bee, Fresno Bee, Modesto Bee, Anchorage Daily News, Tri-City Herald, Tacoma News Tribune, 13 other newspapers), Sacramento, Calif., Wash., S.C., 1989—. Bd. dirs. Nespaper Advt. Bur.; bd. visitors U. N.C. Sch. Journalism, Stanford U. Knight fellowships. With USMC, 1955-58. Mem. Calif. Newspaper Pubs. Assn., Am. Newspaper Assn. (govt. affairs com.), API (regional adv. bd.). Office: McClatchy Newspapers PO Box 15779 2100 Q St # 95816 Sacramento CA 95852 also: The Modesto Bee PO Box 3928 1325 H St Modesto CA 95352

POUGH, FREDERICK HARVEY, mineralogist; b. Bklyn., June 26, 1906; s. Francis H. and Alice H. (Beckler) P.; m. Eleanor C. Hodge, Oct. 14, 1938 (dec. May 1966); children: Frederick Harvey, Barbara Hodge. SB, Harvard, 1928, PhD, 1935; MS, Washington U., 1932; student, Ruperto Carola, Heidelberg, Germany, 1932-33. Asst. curator mineralogy Am. Mus. Natural History, N.Y.C., 1935-40; acting curator Am. Mus. Natural History, 1941, curator, 1942-44, curator phys. geology and mineralogy, 1942-52, cons. mineralogist, 1953-64, 66—; gem cons. Jewelers Circular-Keystone, 1940-85; dir. Santa Barbara Mus. Natural History, 1965-66; pres. Mineralogy, Inc., 1978—. Author: Jewelers Dictionary, 1945, 50, 76, Field Guide to Rocks and Minerals, 1953, 76, All About Volcanoes and Earthquakes, 1953, All about Volcanoes and Earthquakes (Hindi translation), 1958, All About Volcanoes and Earthquakes (Persian translation), 1959, All About Volcanoes and Earthquakes (Bengali translation), 1959, All About Volcanoes and Earthquakes (Italian translation), 1960, All About Volcanoes and Earthquakes (Arabic translation), 1962, All About Volcanoes and Earthquakes (Portuguese translation), 1964, Our Earth, 1961, The Story of Gems and Semi-Precious Stones, 1967, Guide des Roches et Mineraux, 1969, 79, First Guide to Rocks and Minerals, 1991; contbg. editor: Lapidary jour., 1984—. Recipient Bronze medal Royal Geol. Soc., Belgium, 1948, Derby medal Brazilian Geol. Survey, Hanneman award for outstanding contbns. in lit. of mineralogy and gemology, 1988, Mineral. award Carnegie Mus. Nat. History, Pitts., 1989, Lifetime Achievement award Accredited Gemologist Assn., 1993; named Mineralogist of Yr., Am. Fedn. Mineral Soc., 1966. Fellow Mineral Soc. Am., Geol. Soc. Am.; mem. Mineral Soc. Gt. Britain., Gemmological Assn. All Japan (Am. rep. 1985—). Clubs: Harvard (N.Y.C.); Explorers. Address: PO Box 7004 Reno NV 89510

POULOS, DARWIN ROBERT, research scientist; b. L.A., Mar. 22, 1959; s. Robert Annis and Victoria Mary (Baba) P.; m. Donna Elizabeth Long, Mar. 21, 1987. AS in Chemistry, West Valley Coll., 1980; AA in Math., W. Valley Coll., 1981; BS in Chem. Engring., U. Calif., 1982; MS in Chem. Engring., San Jose State U., 1985. Registered profl. engr., Calif.; cert. tchr., Calif. Tchr. asst. West Valley Coll., Saratoga, Calif., 1977-80; asst. rsch. dept. chmn. Dept. Chmn. U. Calif., Berkeley, 1982; formulation chemist IBM Amaden Rsch. Ctr., San Jose, 1983-85; rsch. chemist Lifescan Inc., Milpitas, Calif., 1986—. NSF grantee, 1976. Mem. Am. Chem. Soc., Am. Assn. Clin. Chemistry. Republican. Lutheran. Office: Lifescan Inc 1000 Gibraltar Dr Milpitas CA 95035-6312

POULSEN, DENNIS ROBERT, environmentalist; b. Boston, Jan. 17, 1946; s. Stephen Dudley and Dorothy Hope (Davis) P.; m. Bonnie Lou Reed; children: David, Zachery, Patrick. AS in Forestry, U. Mass., Stockbridge-Amherst, 1965; AS in Indsl. Supervision, Chaffey Coll., Alta Loma, Calif., 1977; BS in Bus. Adminstrn., U. Redlands (Calif.), 1979; postgrad., U. Calif., Riverside, 1986, U. Calif., Davis, 1991-93. Cert. environ. profl., registered environ. profl., registered environ. assessor, Calif., cert. hazardous materials mgr., cert. lab. technolgoist; diplomate Inst. Hazardous Materials Mgmt. Water control technician Weyerhaeuser Co. Chem. Lab., Fitchburg, Mass., 1965-69; environ. rsch. technician Kaiser Steel Corp., Fontana, Calif., 1969-78, environ. rsch. engr., 1978-83, asst. environ. dir., 1983-87; mgr. environ. svcs. Calif. Steel Industries Inc., Fontana, 1987—; mem. adv. group Calif. EPA (CAL EPA), 1993—; originator AISE Nat. Environ. Com., Pitts., papers chmn., 1993; mem. adv. group Calif. Environ. Protection Agy., 1993—. Contbr. articles and papers on environmental issues to profl. publs. Del. U.S. Environ. Delegation, Soviet Union, 1990; mem. U.S. Citizens Network of the UN Conf. on Environment and Devel. Mem. Nat. Assn. Environ. Profls. (cert. review bd., mem. internat. com. 1992—), Air and Water Mgmt. Assn., Nat. Environ. Health Assn., Environ. Info. Assn., Hazardous Materials Control Rsch. Inst., Water Environment Fedn. (groundwater com.), World Safety Orgn. (cert. hazardous materials supr.), Assn. Energy Engrs. (environ. engrs. mgrs. inst., environ. project of yr. award 1992), Chino Basin Water Dist. Watermaster Adv. Coun., Calif. Water Pollution Control Assn., Inst. Hazardous Materials Mgmt. (ethics com., publs. sub-com.), People to People Internat., U. Redlands Alumni Assn. (bd. mem., nominee Gordon Adkins award for profl. achievement). Home: 5005 Hedrick Ave Riverside CA 92505-1425 Office: Calif Steel Industries Inc 14000 San Bernardino Ave Fontana CA 92335-5259

POULSHOCK, NORMAND GARBER, educator; b. Phila., Feb. 7, 1926; s. Morton Meyer and Esther Ruth (Garber) P.; m. Barbara Lee Baker, Oct. 14, 1947; children: David Noel, Deborah Ann, Joseph Warren. BA, U. Calif., Long Beach, 1954, MA, 1955; postgrad., U. Wash., 1970, Cen. Wash. U., 1971-73. Cert. tchr., Calif., Oreg., Wash. Tchr. Garden Grove (Calif.) Schs., 1955-58, Klamath Falls (Oreg.) Pub. Schs., 1959-69, Shoreline Sch. Dist., Seattle, 1969-71, Bellevue (Wash.) Pub. Schs., 1971-77; lectr. music dept. Pacific Luth. U., Tacoma, 1976—; tchr. U. Wash., 1972, U. Portland, 1972; pianist various clubs, Honolulu, Calif., Oreg., Wash., 1946-76; condr. Klamath Community Symphony, Klamath Falls, Oreg., 1962-68; 2nd French Horn, Honolulu Symphony, 1946-47, 4th French Horn, Anaheim, Calif. and Long Beach, Calif. Symphonies, 1953-54; violist Cascade Symphony, Edmonds, Wash., 1969-77, Pacific Luth. U. Orch., Tacoma, 1985-86; clin. adjudicator pub. schs., western Wash.; composer-in-residence Cispus (Wash.) Summer Music Camp, 1973-85. Composer A Short Symphony for Synthesizer and Orch., 1971 (commd. and performed by Seattle Symphony), Viola Concerto, 1975, Sonata for Violin and Piano, 1990, pieces for various instrumental combinations; developed 1st individualized gen. music course in Wash. pub. schs.; contbr. articles to profl. jours. Pres. Unitarian fellowship, Klamath Falls, 1964-65; v.p. Musicians Union, Klamath Falls, 1965-66. With USN, 1944-49. Mem. Soc. of Composers, Music Tchrs. Nat. Assn. (Composer of Yr. 1990), Wash. Music Tchrs. Assn. (adjudicator 1970—). Home: 14009 18th Ave S Tacoma WA 98444 Office: Pacific Luth U Tacoma WA 98447

POULSON, SANDRA LOUISE, convention and visitors bureau administrator; b. Denver, Aug. 20, 1947; d. Joseph Warren Zimmerman and Gwenn Louann (Merz) Kuhn. BFA, U. Ariz., 1970. Asst. mgr. art prodn. The Emporium, San Francisco, 1970-71; graphic artist Papago Printing, Phoenix, 1971-72; publs. dir. Courier Terminal Systems, Phoenix, 1972-73; communications illustrator Sperry Flight Systems, Phoenix, 1973-76; advt. dir. Phoenix Racquets, Phoenix, 1976-77; sales rep. Pointe Resorts, Phoenix, 1977-78; pub. rels. mgr. Phoenix Conv. and Visitors Bur., 1978-81; v.p. Mission Travel, Phoenix, 1981-88; exec. dir. Tempe (Ariz.) Conv. and Visitors Bur., 1988—. Mem. East Valley Partnership, Tempe, 1989—; mem. class VI Valley Leadership, Phoenix, 1984; mem. Rep. John McCains Mariners, Phoenix, 1984, Maricopa County Sports Authority Adv. Bd., Phoenix, 1989—; pres. Juvenile Diabetes Found., 1988-90, bd. dirs. 1988—; mem. internat. lay review com., 1991—; mem. Super Bowl '96 Com., 1989-93, World Cup '94 Com., 1990-94, Fiesta Bowl Com., 1980—; chmn. Juvenile Diabetes Found Golf Classic, 1988-90, Juvenile Diabetes Pro-Football Legends, 1990, chmn. Ad Club Man/Women of Yr., 1983, Fiesta Bowl Speakers Bur., 1982-85, publicity com. 1980-82; mem. CEO search com. Internat. Assn. Conv. & Visitors Bureaus, 1992-93. Mem. Meeting Planners Internat., Phoenix, 1989—, Am. Soc. Assn. Execs., Valley Innkeepers, ATIA (bd. dirs. 1988-90). Office: Tempe Conv & Visitors Bur 51 W 3rd St # 105 Tempe AZ 85281-3633

POUND, JOHN BENNETT, lawyer; b. Champaign, Ill., Nov. 17, 1946; s. William R. and Louise Catherine (Kelly) P.; m. Mary Ann Hanson, June 19, 1971; children: Meghan Elizabeth, Matthew Fitzgerald. BA, U. N.Mex., 1968; JD, Boston Coll., 1971. Bar: N. Mex. 1971, U.S. Dist. Ct. N. Mex. 1971, U.S. Ct. Appeals (10th cir.) 1972. Law clk. to Hon. Oliver Seth, U.S. Ct. Appeals, 10th Cir., Santa Fe, 1971-72; shareholder Montgomery & Andrews, P.A., Santa Fe, 1972—; asst. counsel Supreme Ct. Disciplinary Bd., 1977-83, dist. rev. officer, 1984—; mem. Supreme Ct. Com. on Jud. Performance Evaluation, 1983-85. Contbr. articles to profl. jours. Pres. bd. dirs. N.Mex. Ind. Coll. Fund, Santa Fe; chmn. N.Mex. Dem. Leadership Coun., 1991—; bd. dirs. Santa Fe Boys Club, 1989—; mem. rules com. N.Mex. Dem. Party, 1982—; v.p. Los Alamos Nat. Lab. Comm. Coun., 1985—. Fellow Am. Coll. Trial Lawyers, N.Mex. Bar Found.; mem. ABA, Am. Bd. Trial Advocates, N.Mex. Bar Assn. (health law sect. 1987—), Santa Fe County Bar Assn. Democrat. Roman Catholic. Office: Montgomery & Andrews PA 325 Paseo De Peralta Santa Fe NM 87501-1860

POUND, LELAND EARL, communications company executive; b. Chico, Calif., July 23, 1945; s. Raymond Lyons and Jessie Ruth (Glabe) P.; m. Rita Elaine Morefield, Oct. 2, 1982 (div. Nov. 1989). BA, U. Calif., Riverside, 1967. Reporter Daily News Tribune, Fullerton, Calif., 1969-70; editor News-Times Newspapers, Placentia, Calif., 1970-77, The Newport Ensign, Newport Beach, Calif., 1977-83; contr. Coast Media Inc., Culver City, Calif., 1983-85; CFO Baker Communications Inc., Beverly Hills, Calif., 1985—. Author: History of Glabe Family, 1969. Home: 20 Seton Irvine CA 92715 Office: Baker Communications Inc 4010 Palos Verdes Dr N # 208 Rolling Hills Estates CA 90274

POURNELLE, JERRY EUGENE, author; b. Shreveport, La., Aug. 7, 1933; s. P. Eugene and Ruth (Lewis) P.: m. Roberta Jane Isdell, July 17, 1959; children: Jennifer, Alexander, Francis Russell, Phillip Eugene, Richard Stefan. BS, U. Wash., 1954, MS, 1957, PhD, 1964. Instr. U. Wash., Seattle, 1956-57; research engr., aviation psychologist Boeing Co., Seattle, 1958-64; mgr. spl. studies Aerospace Corp., San Bernardino, Calif., 1964; prof., dir. research inst. Pepperdine U., Los Angeles, 1965-69; exec. asst. to mayor City Los Angeles, 1969; author, lectr., cons. Studio City, Calif., 1970—; cons. Directorate of Plans USAF, 1968; chief cons. Profl. Educators Los Angeles, 1970; cons. to chancellor Calif. State Colls., 1970—. Author: Human Temperature Tolerance in Astronautic Environments, 1959, Stability and National Security, 1968, (with Stefan Possony) The Stategy of Technology, 1970, Congress Debates Viet Nam, 1971, The Right to Read, 1971, Red Heroin, Red Dragon, 1971; (with Larry Niven) The Mote in God's Eye, 1974, (with Larry Niven) Inferno, 1976; West of Honor, 1976, The Mercenary, 1977, High Justice, 1977, (with Larry Niven) Lucifer's Hammer, 1977, Janissaries, 1979, King David's Spaceship, 1980, (with Larry Niven) Oath of Fealty, 1981, Prince of Mercenaries, 1989, (with Roland Green) Janissaries: Clan and Crown, 1982, (with Dean Ing) Mutual Assured Survival, 1984, (with Larry Niven) Footfall, 1985, (with Larry Niven, Stephan Barnes) Legacy of Heorot, 1987, (with Roland Green) Storms of Victory, 1987, Prince of Mercenaries, 1989, Falkenberg's Legion, 1990; (with S.M. Stirling) Go Tell the Spartans, 1991, (with S.M. Stirlings) The Children's Hour, 1991; (with Larry Niven and Michael Flynn) Fallen Angels, 1991, (with S.M. Stirling) Prince of Sparta, 1992, (with Larry Niven) The Gripping Hand, 1992; editor: 2020 Vision; sci. editor, columnist Galaxy Sci. Fiction, 1975-78, Byte mag., 1978—; (anthologies) (with John F. Carr) Black Holes, 1978, Endless Frontier, 1979, Survival of Freedom, 1982, Endless Frontier Vol. II, 1982, There Will Be War, 1983, Men At War, 1984, Blood and Iron, 1984, Day of The Tyrant, 1985, Warrior, 1986, Imperial Stars, 1986, Guns of Darkness, 1987, Imperial Stars: Republic and Empire, Vol. II; InfoWorld columnist, 1986-92, War World, 1988, There Will Be War: Call to Battle, 1988, Imperial Stars: Clash of Empire Vol. III, 1989, Armageddon!, 1989, After Armageddon, 1990, War World: Death's Head Mutiny, Vol. II, 1990, (with John F. Carr) Endless Frontier III: Cities in Space, 1991, War World: Sauron Dominion, Vol. III, 1991; editor: (with John F. Carr) Codomium: Revolt on War World, 1992, (with John F. Carr) Endless Frontier IV: Life in the Asteroid Belt, 1992. Scoutmaster Boy Scouts Am., 1958; chmn. bd. dirs. Seattle Civic Playhouse Assn., 1960-63; asst. chmn. San Bernardino County Rep. Com., 1964; assoc. dir. Sam Yorty for Mayor Campaign, 1969; bd. dirs. Pepperdine Research Inst., 1966-69. Served with AUS, 1950-52; mem. Rep. Bd. Govs., 1962-63. Decorated Bronze medal; recipient Excellence award Am. Security Council, 1969, John W. Campbell award 1973. Fellow AAAS; mem. Inst. Strategic Studies, AIAA, Ops. Research Soc. Am., Univ. Prof. for Acad. Order (bd. dirs. 1971), Sci. Fiction Writers Am. (pres. 1973-74). Episcopalian. Home and Office: 12190 1/2 Ventura Blvd Box 372 Studio City CA 91604

POVHE, THOMAS JEROME, educational consultant; b. Grand Forks, N.D., Oct. 19, 1950; s. Frank Fred and Mollie Anne (Zgonc) P. BS in Edn., Bemidji (Minn.) State U., 1972; MEd in Library Sci., Ariz. State U., 1988. Educator St. Leo's Cath. Sch., Hibbing, Minn., 1973-77; realtor Ryan Real Estate, Glendale, Ariz., 1978-81; investment advisor Investwave, Glendale, Ariz., 1985-88; sch. library media specialist Unified Sch. Dist. 21, Coolidge, Ariz., 1987-93, dist. resources coord., planner, 1989-93; mem. Lit. Essential Skills Ariz. Bd. Edn., 1988-90, Ariz. dept. edn. Libr. Guidelines Steering Com., 1988-90, chmn. sub0com. Devel. Info. Skills, 1989-90; evaluator for organizational effectiveness of gen. adult reference svcs. Velma Teague Br. Libr., 1993. Contbr. articles to profl. jour. Mem. Info. Literacy Outcome Measures Project, 1991-92; mem. NCSS Elem./Early Childhood Com., 1992—, mem. curriculum stds. for social studies, 1993—, mem. nat. stds. for civics and govt. project, 1993—. Recipient Young Teen's Childrens Lit. award. Mem. ALA, Am. Assn. Sch. Librs. (nat. task force on info. skills, 1989-93), Internat. Churchill Soc., Assn. for Libr. Collections and Tech Svcs., Spl. Librs. Assns. Democrat. Roman Catholic. Home: 4443 W Solano Dr N Glendale AZ 85301-6311

POVONDRA, WILLIAM FRANK, JR., advertising and marketing consultant; b. Astoria, N.Y., Oct. 24, 1943; s. William F. and Leona Povondra; m. Maryann Witting, Feb. 14, 1985 (dec. Mar. 1992). Student, Santa Monica Coll., 1961-62, 63-65, Coll. of Marin, Kentfield, Calif., 1968-71. Regional mgr. Ticketron, Inc., San Francisco, 1968-76; v.p. mktg. Spl. Event Entertainment, L.A., 1976-80; v.p. Hillyer & Assocs. Advt., Inc., L.A., 1980-84; dir. mktg. Josephson/Kluwer BRC, Culver City, Calif., 1985-87; v.p. mktg. So. Pacific Exhbn. Group, Inc., L.A., 1987-91; dir. mktg. Whole Life Expo, Venice, Calif., 1992—; cons. Worldwide Events, Inc., L.A., 1990, Russian Ministry of Culture, Moscow, 1990, Calif. Exhbn. Internat., Bejing, 1990. Mem. Beverly Hills Optimists. Home and Office: PO Box 9877 Marina Del Rey CA 90295

POWELL, BETTY JEAN, marketing and advertising consultant; b. Grand Junction, Colo., Sept. 16, 1928; d. A. Gene and Ruth H. (Tobin) Southerland; m. Larry Allan Powell, Feb. 15, 1949 (dec. Mar. 1956); children: Larry Jr., Patricia A., April S. BS in Bus. Adminstrn., Lewiston (Idaho) Bus. Coll., 1949; MA in Mktg., UCLA, 1956; BS in Fashion Merchandising, Patricia Stevens, Phoenix, 1960; D Nutripathy, Am. Coll. Nutripathy, Phoenix, 1980. Pub. rels. dir. Pleasure World, Inc., Little Rock, 1961-65; pres. Lovely Lady of Aquarius Mktg., Kansas City, Mo., 1965-71; mktg. dir. Combined Retail Svcs. Internat., San Rafael, Calif., 1971-74; employment mgr. permanent divsn. Western Employment, Denver, 1974-76; advt. cons. Johnson Pub. Co., Loveland, Colo., 1976-79; bus. adminstr. Natural Health Outreach, Scottsdale, Ariz., 1979-81; nat. field coord. Pop-ins-Maid & Carpet Franchises, West Palm Beach, Fla., 1981-86; regional mgr. 50 State Dirs., Wash., 1987-90; cons., lectr., 1990—; cons. Panda Corp., Phoenix, 1990-91, Windstar, Inc., Scottsdale, 1991-92. Author: The White Raven, 1958; editor fin. investment newsletter Money Wise, 1965, Wildlife Mag., 1962; contbr. articles on travel and mktg. to profl. jours. Regional dir. Bluebirds, Girl Scouts U.S.A., Palm Springs, Calif., 1960; pres. PTA, Peoria, Ariz., 1961. Home and Office: 8730 E Hazelwood Scottsdale AZ 85251-1819

POWELL, EARL ALEXANDER, III, art museum director; b. Spartanburg, S.C., Oct. 24, 1943; s. Earl Alexander and Elizabeth (Duckworth) P.; m. Nancy Landry Powell, July 17, 1971; children—Cortney, Channing, Sumner. AB with honors, William Coll., 1966; AM, Harvard U., 1970, PhD, 1974. Teaching fellow in fine arts Harvard U., 1970-74; curator, Michener Collection U. Tex., Austin, 1974-76, asst. prof. art history, 1974-76; mus. curator, sr. staff asst. to asst. dir. and chief curator Nat. Gallery Art, Washington, 1976-78, exec. curator, 1979-80; dir. Los Angeles County Mus. Art, 1980-92, Nat. Gallery Art, Washington, 1992—; mem. So. Calif. Adv. Coun. Archives of Am. Art, 1980—; career advisor Harvard U. Author: American Art at Harvard, 1973, Selections from the James Michener Collection, 1975, Abstract Expressionists and Imagists: A Retrospective View, 1976, Milton Avery, 1976, The James A. Michener Collection: Twentieth Century American Painting, catalogue raisonne, 1978, Thomas Cole monograph, 1990. Trustee Pitzer Coll. Served with U.S. Navy, 1966-69, comdr. Res., 1976-80. Harvard U. traveling fellow, 1973-74; recipient King Olav medal, 1979; decorated chevalier Arts and Letters. Mem. Fine Arts Adv. Panel, Fed. Reserve Bank, Commn. President of the White House, President's Commn. on Arts and Humanities, Coun. Arts and Humanities, Fed. Coun. on Arts and Humanities, Nat. Portrait Gallery Commn., Pa. Ave. Devel. Corp., Scholarly Adv. Coun., Japan Am. Nat. Mus., USIA Commn. for Arts Bus. Commn. for the Arts, Walpole Soc., Am. Assn. Museums (co-chmn. commn. on mus. for a new century); trustee Am. Assn. Mus. Dirs., Am. Fedn. Arts, White House Hist. Assn., The Newport Art Mus.

POWELL, GARY ALLISON, facilities and development administrator; b. Waialua, Hawaii, June 22, 1954; s. Glen Allan and Ruth Elizabeth (Still) P.; m. Masako Hokazono, Jan. 31, 985; children: Alicia Megumi, Allison Kaoru, Alena Akari. Mgr. Powell's Gardening Svc., Haleiwa, Pupukea Garden Ctr./Nursery, Haleiwa, North Shore Farm and Garden, Haleiwa; groundskeeper Waimea Falls Park, Haleiwa, 1980, sect. head, 1980, horticulturalist, 1981, bot. horticulturalist, 1982, supt. of grounds, 1985, ops. mgr., 1987-89, mgr. facilities and devel., 1989—, mgr. product devel., 1992; cons. Pacific Consultants, Wahiawa, 1991—; former cons. Hawaii Hort. Rsch., Haleiwa. Contbr. articles to publs.; author: (with others, poems) Free-Verse Poetry, 1982. Bd. dirs. Hawaii Christian Camp and Conf. Assn., 1978-81; pres. Sunset Beach Ch. of Christ and Sch., Hawaii, 1982-89. Mem. Profl. Grounds Mgmt. Soc., Am. Zookeepers Assn., Global Instn. Mgmt. Soc. Baptist. Office: Pacific Consultants 949 Hanau St Wahiawa HI 96786

POWELL, JULIA GERTRUDE, volunteer; b. Fenton, Mich., Jan. 25, 1907; d. Thomas James and Leila May (Bishop) Selman; m. Ronald Douglas Powell, June 25, 1924 (div. May 4, 1961); 1 child, Nelda Dorothea (dec.). BA in Edn., Colo. Coll., 1949, MA in Edn., 1949; M in Adminstrn., UCLA, 1950; postgrad., Chapman Coll. Tchr. kindergarten Garden Grove (Calif.) Elem. Sch., Garden Grove Unified Sch. Dist., 1950-71. Pres. Garden Grove Tchrs. Assn., Calif., 1961, Ebell of Laguna Hills, Leisure World, 1983, Beethoven chpt. Guild, Orange County, 1984; Worthy Matron Hermosa chpt. Eastern Star, Santa Ana, Calif., 1972; Worthy High Priestess White Shrine of Jerusalem, 1976; Queen Merret Temple Daus. of Nile, Anaheim, Calif., 1988-89. Mem. Calif. Retired Tchrs. Assn., NEA-Am. Assn. Retired Persons, Am. Assn. Univ. Women. Republican. Presbyterian.

POWELL, LANE ALAN, editor; b. Alamogordo, N.Mex., Mar. 8, 1955; s. Cecil Lane Holmes and Janet Marie (LeRoux) Powell; m. Mari Catherine Priemesberger, July 15, 1989; 1 child, Lane Cody. BS in Journalism, U. Fla., 1984. Info. specialist Engring. Coll. U. Fla., Gainesville, 1983-85; editor Windsor Publs., L.A., 1985-89; coord. publs. East Bay Regional Park Dist., Oakland, Calif., 1989—. Editor: Jacksonville and Florida's First Coast, 1989. Named Outstanding Hard Cover Pub. of Yr. Am. Chambers of Commerce Execs., 1989, Best Spl. Facility Brochure in Calif. Calif. Park and Recreation Soc., 1990. Home: 1882 N 5th St Concord CA 94519 Office: East Bay Regional Park Dist 2950 Peralta Oaks Ct Oakland CA 94605

POWELL, MEL, composer; b. N.Y.C., Feb. 12, 1923. Studied piano from age 4; studied composition with Ernst Toch, L.A., 1946-48; with Paul Hindemith, Yale U., from 1948, MusB, 1952. Mem., chmn. faculty composition Yale U., 1957-69; mem. staff, head faculty composition, formerly dean Calif. Inst. Arts, Valencia, provost, 1972-76, now Inst. fellow, Roy E. Disney chair in mus. composition. Albums include Six Recent Works, 1982-88; composer: Duplicates: A Concerto for Two Pianos and Orchestra (premier L.A. Philharm. 1990, Pulitzer prize 1990), Modules for chamber orch. (recorded L.A. Philharm. 1991), Woodwind Quintet (recorded 1991), Setting for Two Pianos (recorded 1992), Settings for Small Orch., 1992 (commissioned by chamber orchs. of St. Paul, L.A., N.J.), Settings for Guitar (recorded 1993), numerous other compositions; subject of profile in New Yorker mag. Recipient Creative Arts medal Brandeis U., 1989; Guggenheim fellow; Nat. Inst. Arts and Letters grantee. Mem. Arnold Schoenburg Inst. (hon. life). Office: Calif Arts Inst Dept Composition 24700 Mcbean Pky Santa Clarita CA 91355-2397

POWELL, MELCHIOR DANIEL, educational administrator, lawyer; b. N.Y.C., July 7, 1935; children: Anthony, Vanessa. BS, N.J. State U., 1957; MA, George Washington U., 1963; JD, U. Balt., 1966; PhD, U. Md., 1968. Bar: Md. 1966. Atty., City of Greenbelt, Md., 1966-67; dir. contract rsch. Nat. Assn. Counties, 1967-71; assoc. prof. urban affairs U. No. Colo., Greeley, 1971-72; dir. Office of Evaluation and Mgmt. Improvement, Appalachian Region Com., Washington, 1972-73; dean Grad. Ctr. Pub. Policy and Adminstrn., Calif. State U.-Long Beach, 1973-92, prof. emertius, 1992—; with We. Govtl. Rsch. Assn., 1992—; cons. in field. Author: Education for the Future Pub. Svc., 1981; Achieving Closer Ties, 1984. Contbr. articles to profl. jours. Mem. Mayor's Task Force City of Long Beach, 1978, mem. charter comm., 1979, bd. dirs. poverty program, 1980; mem. Calif. workers compensation rate setting commn., 1991. Served to lt. (j.g.), U.S. Navy, 1959-63. Mem. Western Govt. Rsch. Assn. (pres. 1980-82, exec. sec. 1982—), Am. Soc. Pub. Adminstrn. (pres. Md. chpt. 1972-73, program chmn. Nat. Conf. 1980, conf. chmn. 1986, pres. L.A. Metro chpt. 1976-77, Dykstra award 1977, Will Baughman award 1982), Urban Affairs Assn. (pres. 1986-87, nat. conf. program chmn. 1984), Internat. Assn. Schs. and Insts. of Adminstrn. (v.p. N.Am. 1989-92). Democrat. Roman Catholic. Home: 16491 Tropez Ln Huntington Beach CA 92649-1873 Office: We Govtl Rsch Assn 10900 Los Alamos Blvd Los Alamitos CA 90720

POWELL, ROBERTA A., medical social worker; b. Eugene, Oreg., Aug. 9, 1952; d. Robert A. and Ruthann B. (Cartier) Saul; m. Robert B. Powell,

Apr. 12, 1980. BA, U. Oreg., 1974; MSW, Portland State U., 1978. Lic. clin. social worker, Oreg. Psychiat. technician St. John's Hosp., Longview, Wash., 1974-76; vets. counselor Portland (Oreg.) Military and Vets. Counseling Ctr., 1976-79; mental health counselor Adult Rehab. Svcs./Ind. Living Svc., Portland, 1979-84; social worker Rehab. Inst. Oreg. Outpatient Porgram, Portland, 1983-89; lead social worker Rehab. Inst. Oreg., Portland, 1989-91; social worker Legacy Rehab. Svcs., 1991—; Mem. Region I Adv. Bd. Vocat. Rehab. Div., Portland, 1983-89, NW Med. Case Mgmt. Group, Portland, 1992—. Vol. Bklyn. Action Corps., Portland, 1984-86; mem., lector Holy Trinity Parish, Beaverton, Oreg., 1986-92; mem. St. Cecilia Parish, Beaverton, 1993—. Mem. Nat. Assn. Social Workers Med. and Health Coun., Good Samaritan Hosp. Employee Activities Assn., Oregon Road Runners Club, Sierra Club. Office: Rehab Inst Oreg 1040 NW 22d St Ste 550 Portland OR 97210

POWELL, RONALD JAMES, special education administrator; b. L.A., May 12, 1949; s. John George and Lena Faye (Haley) P.; m. Jacyln Marie Oliver, Nov. 16, 1974; children: Haley Marie, Nathan James, Adam John. BS, John Brown U., 1972; MA, U. Calif., Riverside, 1980, PhD, 1992. Tchr. Victor Valley Union High Sch. Dist., Victorville, Calif., 1972-81; program specialist Desert Mountain Spl. Edn. Local Plan Area, Victorville, 1981-83, program mgr., 1983—; cons. Calif. State Dept. of Edn., Sacramento, 1988-93; rsch. coord. State of Calif./U.S. Dept. Edn., Sacramento, 1990-91; instr. Calif. State U., San Bernardino, 1993—; mem. Dept. Mental Health Interagy Task Force, San Bernardino, 1989-90. Author: The California Principal Leadership Scale. 1989. Mem. Victor Valley Child Abuse Task Force, Victorville, 1989-90; mem. exec. bd. Victor Valley Community Svcs. Coun., Victorville, 1983-89, v.p., 1987-89. Recipient Dr. Gordon S. and Anna Watkins Commencement award U. Calif. Riverside, 1992. Mem. Assn. Calif. Sch. Adminstrs., Coun. for Exceptional Children, Am. Assn. on Mental Retardation, San Bernardino County Schs. Office Adminstrv. Pers. (v.p. 1985-87). Democrat. Baptist. Home: 13288 Choco Rd Apple Valley CA 92308-6141 Office: Desert Mountain Spl Edn Local Plan Area 16519 Victor St Ste 301 Victorville CA 92392-3967

POWELL, STEPHANIE, visual effects director; b. Dayton, Ohio, Sept. 27, 1946; d. Harley Franklin and Evelyn Luella (Reed) Pence. Pres., CEO Video Assist Systems, Inc., North Hollywood, Calif., 1979—, Out of the Blue Visual Effects, 1979—. Developer using 3/4-inch videotape for broadcast; co-developer color videotap for motion picture work. Mem. Acad. TV Arts and Scis., Acad. Magical Arts and Scis. Office: Video Assist Systems Inc 11030 Weddington St North Hollywood CA 91601

POWELL, TED FERRELL, micrographics specialist; b. Rexburg, Idaho, Feb. 2, 1935; s. Edward Lewis and Thelma Mae (Arnold) P.; m. Nedra Scoresby, Jan. 15, 1954; children: Janeal, Julia, Greg F., Megan, Kara, N. Elizabeth. BS in Acctg., U. Utah, 1962; MBA, U. Phoenix, 1987. Supr. geneal. libr. LDS Ch., Salt Lake City, 1967-70; supr. granite mountain records vault Ch. Jesus Christ Latter Day Sts., Salt Lake City, 1970-71, dir. microfilming field ops., 1971-85, ops. analyst geneal. dept., 1985—; chmn. East Canyon Resort, Inc., 1988—; chmn., chief exec. officer Bus. Edn. and Cons. Inst., 1991; mem. com. on preservation of hist. records NRC, Washington, 1984—. Co-author: A Guide to Micrographics, 1984; also articles. Mem. Assn. Info. and Image Mgmt. (chpt. pres. 1976-77, bd. dirs. 1977-80, Disting. award 1978), Inst. Internal Auditors (cert.), Internat. Council Archives (com. reprography 1976—). Republican. Home: 3144 S 160 W Bountiful UT 84010-6501 Office: Ch Jesus Christ Latter-Day Saints 50 E North Temple Salt Lake City UT 84150-0001

POWELSON, JOHN PALEN, economist, educator; b. N.Y.C., Sept. 3, 1920; s. John Abrum and Mary Elizabeth Rennie (Stephen) P.; m. Alice Williams Roberts, May 31, 1953; children: Cynthia (dec.), Judith, Kenneth, Carolyn, Lawrence. A.B., Harvard U., 1941, A.M., 1947, Ph.D., 1950; M.B.A., U. Pa., 1942. CPA, N.Y. Acct. Haskins & Sells, N.Y.C., 1942-44; instr. acctg. U. Pa., 1944-45; teaching fellow econs. Harvard U., Cambridge, Mass., 1946-48; sr. acct. Price, Waterhouse & Co., Paris, 1948-49; asst. prof. U. Buffalo, 1949-50; economist IMF, 1950-54, asst. chief tng., 1954-58; prof. econs. Sch. Advanced Internat. Studies, Johns Hopkins U., 1958-64; prof. econ. devel. U. Pitts., 1964-66; prof. econs. U. Colo., Boulder, 1966-91; ret., 1991; chmn. econs. dept. Inter-Am. U. Air, 1966-67; dir. tng. program nat. accounts Centro de Estudios Monetarios Latinamericanos, Mexico City, 1963-64; econ. adviser Govt. Bolivia, 1960; vis. prof. econs. U. San Andres, La Paz, Bolivia, 1960; vis. scholar Harvard U., 1981-82; cons. Inter-Am. Devel. Bank, Washington, 1967-68; econ. adviser Ministry of Finance and Planning, Kenya, 1972-74. Author: Economic Accounting, 1955, National Income and Flow-of-Funds Analysis, 1960, Latin America-Today's Economic and Social Revolution, 1964, Institutions of Economic Growth, 1972, A Select Bibliography on Economic Development, 1979, (with others) Economics of Development and Distribution, 1981, (with others) Threat to Development: Pitfalls of the N.I.E.O., 1983, Facing Social Revolution: The Personal Journey of a Quaker Economist, 1987, (with others) The Peasant Betrayed: Agriculture and Land Reform in the Third World, 1987, The Story of Land: A World History of Land Tenure and Agrarian Reform, 1988, Dialogue with Friends, 1988; co-editor: Economic Development, Poverty, and Income Distribution, 1977. Treas. Internat. Student House, Washington, 1952-59. Home: 45 Bellevue Dr Boulder CO 80302-7813

POWELSON, STEVEN E., data systems company executive; b. Tucson, Aug. 18, 1954; s. Roy A. and Neva (Carut) P.; m. Sandra K. Powelson, Apr. 28, 1985; 1 child, Michael. AAS, Pima C.C., 1976; BS, Ariz. State U., 1992. V.p., CFO Diversified Data Systems, Tucson, 1976-88; prin. Valley Wide Ins. Agy., Phoenix, 1987—; CFO Valley Wide Budget Fin., Inc., Phoenix, 1986—; owner, cons. Revelation Data Systems, Phoenix, 1985—. Lay leader Ch. Jubilee Fellowship, Phoenix, 1992. Scholarship Anaheim Pub. Co., 1992. Mem. NCSL, Am. Prodn. and Inventory Control Soc. (v.p. 1982), Am. Mktg. Assn. Republican. Office: Revelation Data Systems 10820 N Cavecreek Rd Phoenix AZ 85020

POWER, DENNIS MICHAEL, museum director; b. Pasadena, Calif., Feb. 18, 1941; s. John Dennis Power and Ruth Augusta (Mott) Zwicky; m. Kristine Moneva Fisher, Feb. 14, 1965 (div. Aug. 1984); children: Michael Lawrence, Matthew David; m. Leslie Gabrielle Baldwin, July 6, 1985; 1 stepchild, Katherine G. Petrosky. B.A., Occidental Coll., 1962, M.A., 1964; Ph.D. (NSF fellow), U. Kans., 1967. Asst. curator ornithology Royal Ont. Mus.; also asst. prof. zoology U. Toronto, 1967-71; asso. curator Royal Ont. Mus., Toronto, 1971-72; exec. dir. Santa Barbara (Calif.) Mus. Natural History, 1972—; biol. researcher; cons. ecology. Editor: The California Islands: Proceedings of a Multidisciplinary Symposium, 1980, Current Ornithology, vol. 6, 1989, vol. 7, 1990, vol. 8, 1991, vol. 9, 1992, vol. 10, 1993; contbr. articles to sci. jours. Bd. dirs. Univ. Club Santa Barbara, 1989-92, v.p., 1991-92; bd. dirs. Santa Barbara Chamber Orch., 1990—, v.p., 1991—; mem. adv. coun. Santa Cruz Island Found., 1989—; mem. discipline adv. com. for museology Coun. for Internat. Exch. of Scholars, 1991—. Grantee NRC Can., 1968-72, 1974-78. Fellow Am. Ornithologists Union (life, sec. 1981-83, v.p. 1988-89), Am. Assn. Mus. (coun. 1980-83); mem. Cooper Ornithol. Soc. (dir. 1976-79, pres. 1978-81, hon. mem. 1993), Calif. Assn. Mus. (dir. 1990-91, chmn. 1987-89), Western Mus. Conf. (dir. 1977-83, pres. 1981-83), AAAS, Am. Soc. Naturalists, Assn. Sci. Mus. Dirs., Ecol. Soc. Am. Soc. Study Avolution, Soc. Systematic Zoology, Sigma Xi. Office: Santa Barbara Museum of Natural History 2559 Puesta Del Sol Santa Barbara CA 93105-2998

POWER, JOHN BRUCE, lawyer; b. Glendale, Calif., Nov. 11, 1936; m. Ann Power, June 17, 1961 (div. 1980); children: Grant, Mark, Boyd. AB magna cum laude, Occidental Coll., 1958; JD, NYU, 1961; postdoctoral, Columbia U., 1972. Bar: Calif. 1962. Assoc. O'Melveny & Myers, Los Angeles, 1961-69, ptnr., 1969—; resident ptnr. O'Melveny & Myers, Paris, 1973-75; lectr. in field. Contbr. articles to jours. Dir. Met. L.A. YMCA, 1988—; mem. bd. mgrs. Stuart Ketchum Downtown YMCA, 1985-92, pres., 1989-90; mem. Los Angeles County Rep. Ctrl. Com., 1962-63; trustee Occidental Coll., 1992—. Root Tilden scholar. Mem. ABA (vice chmn. internat. fin. subcom. 1984-91, comml. fin. svcs. com., com. 3rd party legal opinions, bus. law sect.), Am. Bar Found. (life), Calif. Bar Assn. (chmn. partnerships and unincorp. assns. com. 1982-83, chmn. uniform commn. code com. 1984-85, exec. com. 1987-91, treas. bus. law sect. 1988-89, vice chmn. 1989-90, chmn. 1990-91, chmn. coun. sect. chairs 1992-93), L.A. County Bar Assn. (exec. com. comml. law and bankruptcy sect. 1970-73, 86-89), Internat. Bar Assn., Fin. Lawyers Conf. (bd. govs., pres. 1984-85), Exec. Svc. Corps. (sec. 1985—), Occidental Coll. Alumni Assn. (pres. 1967-68, pres. circle, exec. com. 1979-82, 91—, vice chair 1991—), Phi Beta Kappa (pres. 1988-90 So. Calif.). Club: California. Office: O'Melveny & Myers 400 S Hope St Los Angeles CA 90071-2801

POWER, MIMI (MARY ANNE POWER), business owner, counselor; b. N.Y.C., June 20, 1935; d. Monte James and Viola Mary (Murray) P.; children: Michael James, Katie Ann, Monica. BA, Rosary Coll., 1958; MSW, St. Louis U., 1960; AAS, Elisabeth Kubler Ross Inst., 1990. Foster care worker Cath. Social Svc., Cin., 1963-65; supr. Women's Christian Alliance, Phila., 1965-69; psychiat. counselor Cumberland County Mental Health Ctr., Vineland, N.J., 1969-71; supr. adoption office Spaulding for Children, Westfield, N.J., 1972-74; rancher MJK Ranch, Belen, N.Mex., 1974-88; owner Cottonwood Counseling Ctr., Albuquerque, 1981—; workshop mothers who sexually abuse N.Mex. Sexual Assault Conf., Albuquerque, 1985-86; mem. workshop on sexual abuse of handicapped children Navajo Nation, Window Rick, Ariz., 1990-92; mem. disability workshop U. N.Mex., 1992. Facilitator workshop on homophobia Women's Ch. Conf., 1993; bd. dirs. Camino Real, Belen, 1985-86. Named Mother of Yr. N.Mex. Sch. of Visually Handicapped, 1982; NSF scholar, 1958-60. Mem. Rosary Coll. Alumnae Assn., Pilot Club (Award of the Yr. 1982). Democrat. Office: Cottonwood Ctr PO Box 4532 Albuquerque NM 87196-4532

POWERS, ALAN DALE, geologist, federal government executive; b. Eugene, Oreg., June 10, 1929; s. Thomas Richard and Gwenn Beryl Stivers P.; m. Lelah Phena Hall, Mar. 23, 1951; children: Sandra L., Thomas R., Janice M. Powers Yankus, Karen A. Powers Jones. BS in Geology, U. Oreg., 1951. Geologist Dept. Interior Bur. Reclamation, Stockton and Sacramento, Calif., 1952-60; water resource project planner Dept. Interior Bur. Reclamation, Sacramento, 1960-63; recreation resource planner Dept. Interior Bur. Outdoor Recreation, Washington, 1963-65; budget analyst Bur. Budget, Office of Mgmt. and Budget, Washington, 1966-75; dir. office of outer continental shelf program coordination Dept. Interior, Washington, 1976-82; deputy assoc. dir. offshore leasing Dept. of Interior Minerals Mgmt. Svc., Washington, 1982; regional dir. Minerals Mgmt. Svc., Anchorage, 1983—. Recipient Disting. Svc. award Sec. of Interior, 1985. Mem. Sr. Exec. Svc. (Meritorious Exec. 1982, Disting. Exec. 1987, Presdl. awards). Home: PO Box 210116 Anchorage AK 99521-0116 Office: Minerals Mgmt Svc 949 E 36th Ave Anchorage AK 99508-4362

POWERS, DAVID LEON, university administrator; b. Portland, Maine, June 22, 1932; s. Leon Herbert and Alice Mary (Batchelder) P.; m. Runie Ann Gibson, Dec. 21, 1958; children: David L. Jr., Brian G. BA, St. Lawrence U., 1956. Assoc. dir. admissions St. Lawrence U., Canton, N.Y., 1958-62, asst. to v.p. devel., 1962-65, adminstrv. asst. to pres., 1965-71; dir. devel. St. Paul's Sch., Concord, N.H., 1971-73; v.p. devel., external affairs Colby-Sawyer Coll., New London, N.H., 1973-84; assoc. v.p., campaign dir. Bucknell U., Lewisburg, Pa., 1984-88; v.p. instl. advancement Colo. Sch. of Mines, Golden, 1988—. Bd. dirs. Gov. Dummer Acad., Byfield, Mass., 1972-88, Nat. Easter Seal Soc., Chgo., 1979-85, N.H. Fund-Raising Coun., Concord, 1979-84, Susquehanna Valley Vis. Br., 1985-88; v.p., dir. Ea. Union County United Fund, Lewisburg, Pa., 1985-88. Recipient Outstanding Svc. award No. N.Y. Heart Assn., Canton, 1969, Appreciation Resolution award Nat. Easter Seal Soc., 1985. Mem. Coun. Advancement Support and Edn., Sigma Chi. Republican.

POWERS, EDWIN MALVIN, consulting engineer; b. Denver, July 20, 1915; s. Emmett and Bertha Malvina (Guido) P.; m. Dorothy Lavane Debler, Jan. 18, 1941; children: Dennis M., Kenneth E., James M., Steven R. BS in Chem. Engring., U. Denver, 1939, MS, 1940. Registered profl. engr., N.J., Colo., Fall Out Analysts Engr., U.S. Fed. Emergency Mgmt. Agency, 1975-87. Prodn. supr. Nat. Aniline Div., Buffalo, 1940-45; engr., project supr. Merck & Co., Rahway, N.J., 1945-67, chief project coordinator, 1967-72, purchasing engr., 1972-82; ret., 1982; cons. engr., Conifer, Colo., 1982—. Capt. Air Raid Wardens, River dist., Buffalo, 1942-45. Mem., del. Conifer Home Owners Assns. Protect Our Single Homes, 1984-86, Regional Environ. Assn. Concerned Home Owners, 1985-86, task force area devel. Hwy. 285/ Conifer Area County Planning Bd. Community, 1986-88. Mem. NSPE, Am. Chem. Soc. (emeritus), Am. Inst. Chem. Engrs. (treas. N.J. 1960, exec. com. 1961-63). Home and Office: 26106 Amy Circle Dr Conifer CO 80433-6102

POWERS, HURSHAL GEORGE, chemical engineer; b. Vona, Colo., Oct. 8, 1933; s. Charles Edward and Carrie A. (Carpenter) P.; m. Rosemary A. Gutschmidt, Dec. 9, 1956; children: Lori A., Keith A., Sheryl L. BSChemE, U. Denver, 1956. Lic. profl. engr. Engr. GE, Richland, Wash., 1956-57, 59-65; sr. engr. Douglas United Nuclear, Richland, 1965-67; sr. engr., mgr. Battelle Pacific N.W. Lab., Richland, 1967-70, staff engr., 1989—; fellow engr., mgr. Westinghouse Hanford Co., Richland, 1970-89; cons. Westinghouse Hanford Co., 1989, Westinghouse Specialty Metals Plant, Blairsville, Pa., 1983-88; mem. stats. coun. nuclear energy div. Westinghouse, Pitts., 1986-88. Contbr. numerous articles to profl. jours.; 2 patents in field. 1st lt. U.S. Army, 1957-59. Mem. Intercollegiate Knights, Pi Delta Theta, Pi Lambda Epsilon. Baptist. Home: RR 4 Box 4001 Kennewick WA 99336-9810 Office: Battelle NW Labs PO Box 999 Richland WA 99352-0999

POWERS, JOANNE PATRICIA, software engineer, systems analyst, information scientist; b. Riverside, Calif., Jan. 9, 1953; d. Otis Kemp and Margaret Louise (Schaffer) P. BA in Math., BS in Computer Sci., U. Calif., Irvine, 1974; MBA in Mgmt., Calif. State U., Fullerton, 1987; postgrad., U. So. Calif., 1989-90. Computer programmer Rockwell Internat., Anaheim, Calif., 1974-76, Los Angeles, 1976-77; lead software engr. Anaheim, 1978-87, Seal Beach, Calif., 1987-91; software analyst Computer Sci. Corp., Santa Ana, Calif., 1977-78; prin. INFOPOWER, Garden Grove, Calif., 1990—, Pet Mart, Tustin, Calif., 1992—. Sponsor Immigration and Refugee Ctr. St. Anselm's, Garden Grove, Calif., 1979-82; soprano in ch. choir. Mem. NAFE, Beta Gamma Sigma. Democrat. Episcopalian. Home: 12292 Lesley St Garden Grove CA 92640-3236

POWERS, MARCUS EUGENE, lawyer; b. Cedarville, Ohio, Apr. 7, 1929; s. Frederick Armajo and Elizabeth Isabel (Rumbaugh) P. B.A., Ohio Wesleyan U., 1951; J.D. (Root-Tilden scholar), NYU, 1954, LL.M., 1958. Bar: Ohio 1954, N.Y. 1959, Calif. 1964. Asst. prof. law NYU Sch. Law, 1956-60; atty. Am. Brake Shoe Co., N.Y.C., 1959-63; asst. gen. counsel Dart Industries Inc., Los Angeles, 1963-81; sr. v.p., gen. counsel Nat. Med. Enterprises, Inc., Los Angeles, 1981-93; exec. v.p., sec. Health Care Property Investors Inc., Santa Monica, Calif., 1985-87; cons. Nat. Med. Enterprises, Inc., Los Angeles, 1993—. Served with U.S. Army, 1954-56. Mem. ABA (mem. com. on corp. law depts. 1985-93), Los Angeles County Bar Assn. (past chmn. corp. law depts. sect., Outstanding Corp. Counsel 1990), Inst. Corp. Counsel (bd. dirs. 1979-92, chmn. 1984-86), Assn. Bar City N.Y., Calif. State Coastal Conservancy, Phi Beta Kappa, Omicron Delta Kappa, Phi Delta Theta, Kappa Sigma, Pi Sigma Alpha, Theta Alpha Phi. Office: Nat Med Enterprises Inc 2700 Colorado Ave PO Box 4070 Santa Monica CA 90404

POWERS, PAULLETE, small business owner; b. Greensburg, Pa., July 10, 1941; m. William Louis Powers. BS in Polit. Sci., Duquesne U., Pitts., 1967; JD, U. Va., 1970. Group facilitator Atlantic U., Virginia Beach, Va., 1970-76; sr. social worker City of Virginia Beach, 1976-81; pres. All Discovery Inc., L.A., 1981-87, Creative Designs, Albuquerque, 1988-90; pres. human resource devel. InPowerment, Albuquerque, 1989—; assoc. in fin. svcs. Nyhbert & Assocs., Albuquerque, 1993—; clin. dir. Inst. for Breakthrough Counseling, 1992; co-dir. Money for Ednl. Growth of Am. (MEGA), 1992; assoc. trainee Highbert & Assocs. Fin. Planning, 1993. Interfaith min., 1985; mem. The Spiritual Coun. Internat. Children's Villages Project, 1991. Mem. Exec. Women Internat. (bd. dirs. 1990), Internat. Platform Assn., Greater Albuquerque C. of C. (diplomat), Internat. Trade Coun., J.B. Moore Internat. Law Soc. (sec. 1969). Office: 3815 Eubank NE Albuquerque NM 87111

POWERS, RAY LLOYD, state senator, dairy farmer, rancher; b. Colorado Springs, Colo., June 27, 1929; s. Guy and Cora (Hill) P.; student public schs.; m. Dorothy Parrish, Dec. 14, 1975; 1 dau., Janet. Dairy farmer, Colorado Springs, 1947—; mem. Colo. Ho. of Reps., 1978-80; mem. Colo. Senate, 1981—. Bd. dirs. Mountain Empire Dairyments Coop., Denver, 1967-81. Mem. Colo. Cattlemen. Clubs: Republican Men's; Lions. Home: 5 N Marksheffel Rd Colorado Springs CO 80929-9302

POWERS, SHARON A., chamber of commerce executive; b. Pitts., May 28, 1955; d. Raymond Gerald and Florence Rosella (Kelly) Coffman. BBA, Nat. U., Las Vegas, Nev., 1991. Br. auditor Union Nat. Bank, Pitts., 1974-78; office mgr. Hawaii-Nev. Investment Co., Las Vegas, 1978-81; full chg. bookkeeper Stewart, Archibald & Barney, Las Vegas, 1981-84; ops. mgr. BRS, Inc./LeMaron Corp., Las Vegas, 1984-87; bus. mgr. Las Vegas C. of C., Las Vegas, 1987—; dir. fin. and bus. Las Vegas C. of C., 1988—, asst. v.p. fin. and adminstrn., 1993. Mem. adv. com. So. Nev. chpt. Muscular Dystrophy Assn., 1988, v.p. exec. bd., 1989-91; bd. dirs. Nev. Animal Soc., Las Vegas, 1985-87; mem. host com. Nat. Bill of Rights Tour, 1991; grad. Leadership Las Vegas, 1991. Mem. NAFE (metro use of force review bd.), Las Vegas Success Network, Toastmasters. Office: Las Vegas C of C 711 E Desert Inn Rd Las Vegas NV 89109

POWERS, STEPHEN, educational researcher, consultant; b. Bakersfield, Calif., June 10, 1936; s. Robert Boyd and Mildred (Irwin) P.; m. Gail Marguerite Allen, Dec. 28, 1968; children: Rick, Joseph, Rebecca. B.S in Edn., No. Ariz. U., 1959; M.A., U. Ariz., Tucson, 1970, M.Ed., 1972, Ph.D., 1978. Cert. tchr., Calif.; cert. tchr., adminstr., jr. coll. tchr., Ariz. Policeman, City of Bakersfield, 1967-69; tchr. Marana (Ariz.) Pub. Schs., 1969-72; dir. Am. Sch. Belo Horizonte, Brazil, 1972-73; tchr. Nogales (Ariz.) Pub. Schs., 1973-75; rsch. specialist Tucson Unified Sch. Dist., 1975—; prof. Walden U., U. Ariz., 1981, U. Phoenix, 1990; founder Creative Rsch. Assocs., 1991—; bd. dirs. Manchester Coll., Oxford U. Contbr. articles to profl. jours. Nat. Inst. Edn. grantee, 1980. Mem. Am. Ednl. Rsch. Assn., Royal Statis. Soc. (U.K. chpt.), Am. Statis. Assn. Bahai. Office: 1010 E 10th St Tucson AZ 85719-5813

POY, GLENN DERRICK, corporate executive; b. Johannesburg, South Africa, Apr. 23, 1957; arrived in Can., 1966; BCommerce/Fin. and Acctg., McMaster U., 1980. Staff acct. Touche Ross & Co., Toronto, Ont., 1979-82; sports cons. Peter Burwash Internat., Houston, 1983-85; dir., fin. Magna Internat., Inc., Toronto, 1985-88; mng. dir. Designworks/USA (A Magna Co.), Newbury Park, Calif., 1988-92, Inside Leadership, Agoura Hills, Calif., 1992—. Editor: Open Forum, 1990—; contbr. articles to profl. jours. Mem. Soc. Mgmt. Accts. of Ont. (bd. dirs. 1986-88), So. Calif. Planning Forum (co-chmn., mark of excellence com. 1990, v.p. communications 1990—), Calif. Luth. U. (Pres.'s Coun. of Advisors 1990—), ASTD (leadership devel. com. 1992). Office: Inside Leadership 4240 Lost Hills Rd Ste 1108 Agoura Hills CA 91301

POYNOR, LANA PAULETTE, import company executive; b. Wichita Falls, Tex., Sept. 15, 1963; d. Garland Max and Janelle (Jackson) P. BA, Tex. A&M U., 1986; postgrad., Western State U., San Diego, Cambridge (Eng.) U., 1990. Pres., chmn. bd. The Westbound Corp., San Diego, 1991—; bd. dirs. Go Oil Corp., Jacksboro, Tex. Co-author: (cookbook) Pure and Simple, 1991. Vol. Coll. Reps., College Station, Tex., 1984-86, Meals-on-Wheels, La Jolla, Calif., 1991-92. Mem. San Diego Mus. Arts, Voices for Children. Presbyterian. Office: The Westbound Corp PO Box 8274 La Jolla CA 92038

POYNTER, JAMES MORRISON, travel educator; b. Kansas City, Mo., July 27, 1939; s. Lewis Alderson and Patricia Connely (Dunn) P.; m. Sorore; children: Lewis, Robert, Michael. BA, George Washington U., 1969, MA, 1975. Cert. travel counselor (honorary). Adminstrv. dir. Inst. Cert. Travel Agents, Arlington, Va., 1967-72; ednl. cons. Saudi Arabian Airlines, Jeddah, 1972-77; specialist employment and trng. Leon County Dept. Human Resources, Tallahassee, 1977-79; pres., CEO Fla. Profl. and Econ. Devel. Corp., Tallahassee, 1979-81; mgr., co-owner The Travel Ctr., Tallahassee, 1979-82, Adventures in Travel, Tallahassee, 1979-82; assoc. prof. travel adminstrn. Met. State Coll. Denver, 1982—; pres. Travel Analysis, Denver, 1988—. Author: Foreign Independent Tours, 1989, Corporate Travel Management, 1990, Travel Agency Accounting Procedures, 1991, Tour Design Marketing and Management, 1992, Travel and Tourism Books in Print, 1992, (with others) Travel Industry Business Management, 1986. With U.S. Army, 1957-60. Mem. Am. Soc. Travel Agts., Assn. Corp. Travel Execs. (edn. cons. 1988-89), Soc. Travel and Tourism Educators (bd. dirs. 1989-91), Profl. Guides Assn. Am., Rocky Mountain Bus. Travel Assn. (bd. dirs. 1986-87), Rocky Mountain Profl. Guides Assn. (bd. dirs. 1989-90, v.p. 1989-90), Colo. Author's League (treas. 1992). Republican. Presbyterian. Office: Met State Coll Denver HMTA Dept Campus Box 60 PO Box 173362 Denver CO 80217-3362

PRACKO, BERNARD FRANCIS, II, artist, business owner; b. Jan. 17, 1945. AA, N.Mex. Mil. Inst., 1965; BA, U. Colo., 1970. Pres. Art Access, Inc., Phoenix, 1974—. Office: Art Access Inc 6991 E Camelback Rd Ste B111 Scottsdale AZ 85251-2432

PRAG, ARTHUR BARRY, physicist, space researcher; b. Portland, Oreg., Apr. 14, 1938; s. Arthur Edwin and Margaret (Twombly) P.; m. Mary Ann Tomaschko, Aug. 10, 1986; 1 child, Patrick William. BS in Physics, U. Portland, 1959, MS in Physics, 1962; PhD in Physics, U. Washington, 1964. Mem. tech. staff The Aerospace Corp., L.A., 1964-70, rsch. scientist, 1970—. Contbr. articles to profl. jours. Mem. AAAS, Am. Phys. Soc., Am. Geophys. Union, Sigma Xi. Office: The Aerospace Corp MS MS/255 PO Box 92957 Los Angeles CA 90009-2957

PRAGER, SUSAN WESTERBERG, law educator; b. Sacramento, Dec. 14, 1942; d. Percy Foster Westerberg and Aileen M. (McKinley) P.; m. James Martin Prager, Dec. 14, 1973; children: McKinley Ann, Case Mahone. AB, Stanford U., 1964, MA, 1967; JD, UCLA, 1971. Bar: N.C. 1971, Calif. 1972. Atty. Powe, Porter & Alphin, Durham, N.C., 1971-72; acting prof. law UCLA, 1972-77; prof. UCLA Sch. Law, 1977—; assoc. dean law sch. UCLA, 1977-92; Arjay and Frances Fearing Miller prof. of law, 1992—; dean UCLA, 1982—; Arjay and Frances Fearing Miller prof. of law, 1993—; bd. dirs. Pacific Mut. Life Ins. Co., Newport Beach, Calif., 1979—. Editor-in-chief, UCLA Law Rev., 1970-71. Trustee Stanford U., 1976-80, 87—. Mem. ABA (council of sect. on legal edn. and admissions to the bar 1983-85), Assn. Am. Law Schs. (pres. 1986), Order of Coif. Office: UCLA Sch Law 405 Hilgard Ave Los Angeles CA 90024-1476

PRASAD, JAYASIMHA SWAMY, electrical engineer; b. Pavagada, India, Oct. 18, 1948; came to U.S. 1978; BE, Indian Inst. Sci., Bangalore, 1971; MTech, Indian Inst. Tech., Madras, 1973; MS, Oreg. State U., 1980, PhD, 1985. Sr. engr. Hindustan Aeronatucis Ltd., Hyderabad, India, 1973-74; asst. prof. Indian Inst. Tech., Madras, 1974-78; sr. engr. Nat. Semiconductor Corp., Santa Clara, Calif., 1980-82; tech. fellow Tektronix Inc., Beaverton, Oreg., 1985—; cons. Internat. Microelectronic Products, San Jose, 1982-83, Textronix, 1983-85; adj. prof. Oreg. State U., 1985—. Contbr. articles to profl. jours.; inventor in field. Chevron scholar, 1983-84. Mem. IEEE (sr.), SPIE. Home: 11265 SW Morgen Ct Portland OR 97223-3967

PRASAD, RAJENDRA, hematologist, oncologist; b. Madras, India, Aug. 31, 1945; married; 2 children. Student, St. Joseph's Coll., Tiruchirapalli, India, 1960-61; MD, Kastruba Med. Coll., Manipal and Magnalore, India, 1966; postgrad., U. Karnataka, 1966, Mysore U., 1966. Diplomate Am. Bd. Internal Medicine, Am. Bd. Hematology, Am. Bd. Oncology. Rotating house surgeon U. Madras, 1967-68; rotating intern St. John's Riverside Hosp., Yonkers, N.Y., 1968-69; resident in internal medicine VA Hosp., Bklyn., 1969-71; fellow in hematology and oncology VA Hosp., Long Beach, Calif., 1971-73; pvt. practice specializingin hematology and oncology Long Beach, 1973—; mem. staff Long Beach Community Hosp., 1973—, chief dept. medicine, 1977; mem. staff Woodruff Community Hosp., Long Beach; cons. hematologist, oncologist Long Beach Meml. Hosp., St. Mary's Med. Ctr., Pacific Hosp., Long Beach Dr.'s Hosp., Dr.'s Hosp. of Lakewood, Bellwood Gen. Hosp.; vice chmn. cancer therapy com. Long Beach Community Hosp., 1978; asst. clin. prof. dept. hematology and oncology U. Calif., Irvine, 1979-88, assoc. clin. prof., 1988—; ind. stock broker, investment advisor, 1992—. Contbr. articles to profl. pubs. Chmn. Calif. chpt. Tamilnadu Found., 1985. Fellow Royal Coll. Physicians; mem. Am. Soc. Clin. Oncology, Am. Soc. of Hematology, Long Beach soc. Internal

Medicine (v.p. 1981, sec.-treas. 1982), Fillmore Condit Founder's Club. Office: 3816 Woodruff Ave # 306 Long Beach CA 90808

PRATER, WALTER LLOYD, mechanical engineer; b. Tulsa, Apr. 11, 1955; s. Samuel Lewis and Patricia (Gaylor) P.; m. Shari Lynn Loeffler, July 28, 1985. BSME, U. Kans., 1978; MSME, San Jose State U., 1985. Registered mechanical engr., registered mfg. engr. Mfg. engr. IBM, San Jose, Calif., 1978-80, test engr., 1980-83; adv. prodn. devel. engr. IBM, San Jose, 1983—. Contbr. articles to profl. jours. Scholar Amoco, 1977-78; recipient First Pl. award in Zoology Long's Peak Sci. Fair, 1973. Mem. ASME, Soc. Mfg. Engrs., Tau Beta Pi, Pi Tau Sigma. Republican. Home: 325 El Portal Way San Jose CA 95119-1416 Office: IBM H28/70B 5600 Cottle Rd San Jose CA 95193-0001

PRATHER, CHARLES EDWARD, radiologist, educator; b. Sterling, Kans., June 18, 1938. BA in Psychology, U. Okla., 1956-60, MD, 1960-64. Diplomate Am. Bd. Medical Examiners, Am. Bd. Therapeutic Radiology; lic. med. examiner Okla., Md. Straight medicine intern Good Samaritan Hosp. and Med. Ctr., Portland, Oreg., 1964-65; radiation therapy and nuclear medicine resident U. Okla. Med. Ctr., Oklahoma City, 1965-67, chief resident radiation therapy and nuclear medicine, 1967-68; staff assoc. radiation therapist Walter Reed Gen. Hosp., 1969-70, asst. chief radiation therapy, 1970-71; radiation therapy cons. Veterans Adminstrn Hosp., Fresno, Calif., 1972—; assoc. staff. dept. nuclear medicine Vallty Med. Ctr., Fresno, 1971, 72, St. Agnes Hosp., Fresno, 1972; active staff Fresno Community Hosp., 1972; co-dir. dept. radiation therapy Fresno Community Hosp., 1972-79; staff observer provisional staff Fresno Community Hosp., 1973; radiation therapy cons. Valley Children's Hosp. Tumor Bd., Fresno, 1974—, Hanford Community Hosp. Tumor Bd. 1976; bd. trustee Cen. Calif. Cancer Coun., 1978; head and neck cancer com. No. Cali. Oncology Group, 1978;. Speaker and author in field. Chmn. profl. edn. com. Am. Cancer Soc., 1972-76, program chmn. Fresno, 1973, 75, v.p. programs, 1973; numerous com. and hosp. appointments 1972-92. Major USMC, 1969-71. Radiation Therapy and Nuclear Medicine fellow Am. Cancer Soc., Mount Zion Hosp. and Med. Ctr., San Francisco, 1968-69; recipient Certificate of Merit award Am. Cancer Soc., 1970, 71, Order of the Golden Sword award, 1972, Disting. Svc. award, 1973, Certificate of Appreciation, 1974-75, Vol. of Yr. award 1977; Certificate of Appreciation Lions Club of Am., 1972, Bronze award St. Agnes Med. Ctr. Founs, 1987, Spl. Recognition for Cancer Program award St. Agnes Med. Ctr., 1992. Mem. AMA, Am. Club Therapeutic Radiologists, Am. Coll. Radiology, Am. Soc. Therapeutic Radiologists, Am. Endocurietheraphy Soc., Am. Soc. Law and Medicine, Okla. County Med. Soc., Okla. State Med. Soc., Soc. Nuclear Medicine (cen. Okla. Sect.), Fresno County Med. Soc., Calif. Med. Assn., No. Calif. Acad. Clin. Oncology, Union Am. Physicians, Cen. Calif. Cancer Coun., Royal Soc. Medicine (affiliate), U. Calif. San Francisco Assn. Clin. Faculty, Assn. Freestanding Radiation Oncology Ctr., U. Calif.

PRATT, CLARA COLLETTE, gerontology educator; b. Boise, Idaho, Mar. 30, 1948; d. Tony A. and Bertha A. (West) Collette; m. David Sheldon Pratt, June 27, 1975; children: Hannah Louise, Jacob Anthony. BS summa cum laude, Gonzaga U., 1970; MS, U. Oreg., 1972, PhD, 1974. Asst. prof. Oreg. State U. Extension Svc., Corvallis, 1974-76, U. Wash., Seattle, 1976-78; asst. prof. Oreg. State U., Corvallis, 1978-82, assoc. prof., 1982-86, prof., 1986—, dir. gerontology program, 1978—; evaluation cons. various ednl., health and svc. orgns. in Oreg. and Wash., 1980—. Contbr. chpts. to books, articles to profl. jours. Bd. dirs., v.p. Benton Hospice, Corvallis, 1986-91; bd. dirs. Oreg. Sr. Svcs. TAsk Force, Salem, 1991—; vice chair, chair Tri-County Area Agy. on Aging, Corvallis, 1980-86. Fellow Gerontol. Soc. Am.; mem. Western Gerontol. Soc., Am. Soc. on Aging, Nat. Coun. on Family Rels., Oreg. Gerontol. Soc., Assn. Gerontology in Higher Edn., Omicron Nu. Office: Oreg State U/Gerontology Milam Hall Corvallis OR 97331

PRATT, GEORGE JANES, JR., psychologist, author; b. Mpls., May 3, 1948; s. George Janes and Sally Elvina (Hanson) P.; BA cum laude, U. Minn., 1970, MA, 1973; PhD with spl. commendation for overall excellence, Calif. Sch. Profl. Psychology, San Diego, 1976; 1 dau., Whitney Beth. Psychology trainee Ctr. for Behavior Modification, Mpls., 1971-72, U. Minn. Student Counseling Bur., 1972-73; predoctoral clin. psychology intern San Bernardino County (Calif.) Mental Health Svcs., 1973-74, San Diego County Mental Health Services, 1974-76; affiliate staff San Luis Rey Hosp., 1977-78; postdoctoral clin. psychology intern Mesa Vista Hosp., San Diego, Calif., 1976; clin. psychologist, dir. Psychology and Cons. Assocs. of San Diego, 1976—; chmn. Psychology and Cons. Assocs. Press, 1977—; bd. dirs. Optimax, Inc., 1985—; pres. George Pratt Ph.D., Psychol. Corp., 1979—; chmn. Pratt, Korn & Assocs., Inc., 1984—; mem. staff Scripps Meml. Hosp., 1986—; founder La Jolla Profl. Workshops, 1977; clin. psychologist El Camino Psychology Ctr., San Clemente, Calif., 1977-78; grad. teaching asst. U. Minn. Psychology and Family Studies div., 1971; teaching assoc. U. Minn. Psychology and Family Studies div., Mpls., 1972-73; instr. U. Minn. Extension div., Mpls., 1971-73; faculty Calif. Sch. Profl. Psychology, 1974-83, San Diego Evening Coll., 1975-77, Nat. U., 1978-79, Chapman Coll., 1978, San Diego State U., 1979-80; vis. prof. Pepperdine U., L.A., 1976-80; cons. U. Calif. at San Diego Med. Sch., 1976—, also instr. univ., 1978—; psychology chmn. Workshops in Clin. Hypnosis, 1980-84; cons. Calif. Health Dept., 1974, Naval Regional Med. Ctr., 1978-82, ABC-TV; also speaker. Mem. South Bay Youth Svcs. Com., San Diego, 1976-80. With USAR, 1970-76. Licensed and cert. psychologist, Calif. Fellow Am. Soc. Clin. Hypnosis; mem. Am. Psychol. Assn., Calif. Psychol. Assn., Internat. Soc. Hypnosis, San Diego Psychology Law Soc. (exec. com.), Am. Assn. Sex Educators, Counselors and Therapists (cert.), San Diego Soc. Sex Therapy and Edn. (past pres.), San Diego Soc. Clin. Hypnosis (past pres.), Acad. San Diego Psychologists, Soc. Clin. and Exptl. Hypnosis., U. Minn. Alumni Assn., Nat. Speakers Assn., Beta Theta Pi. Author: HyperPerformance, 1987; A Clinical Hypnosis Primer, 1984, 88; Release Your Business Potential, 1988; Sensory/Progressive Relaxation, 1979; Effective Stress Management, 1979; Clinical Hypnosis: Techniques and Applications, 1985; contbr. chpts. to various books. Office: Scripps Hosp Med Bldg 9834 Genesee Ave Ste 321 La Jolla CA 92037-1216

PRATT, HENRY LUCIUS, retired industrial engineer; b. L.I., Oct. 31, 1920; s. henry l. and L.H. (Hindley) P. BS, U. So. Calif., 1950. Mfg. engr. Lockheed Aricraft Co., Burbank, Calif., 1951-58, 1958-66, indsl. engr., 1966-76, ret., 1976. Sgt. Inf., 1944-46. Home: 708 H St # 47 Chula Vista CA 91910

PRATT, JOHN CLARK, English language educator, publisher; b. St. Albans, Vt., Aug. 19, 1932; s. John Lowell and Katharine (Jennison) P.; m. Dolores Barghausen, Jan. 27, 1955 (div. Feb. 1968); children: Karen, Sandra, Pamela, John; m. Doreen Joyce Kleerup, June 28, 1968; stepchildren: Lynn, Christine. Student, Dartmouth Coll., Hanover, N.H., 1950-53; BA, U. Calif., Berkeley, 1954; MA with honors, Columbia U., 1960; PhD, Princeton U., 1965. Commd. 2nd lt. USAF, 1955, advanced through grades to lt. col., 1971, ret., 1974; instr. to prof. English USAF Acad., Colorado Springs, Colo., 1960-74; chmn. English dept. Colo. State U., Ft. Collins, 1974-80, prof. English, 1974—; pres. Pratt Pub. Co., Ft. Collins, 1988—; Fulbright lectr. CIES/Washington, Portugal, 1974-75, USSR, 1980; honors prof. Colo. State U., Ft. Collins, 1989. Author: The Meaning of Modern Poetry, 1962, John Steinbeck, 1970, 76, The Laotian Fragments, 1974, 85, Vietnam Voices: Perspectives on the War Years, 1941-82, 84, Writing From Scratch: The Essay, 1987; (with Tim Lomperis) Reading The Wind: The Literature of the Vietnam War, 1986; gen. editor Writing from Scratch Series, 1988—; editor: (with Victor Neufeldt) George Eliot's Middlemarch Notebooks: A Transcription, 1979, One Flew Over the Cuckoo's Nest, 1973; contbr. articles to profl. jours., chpts. to books. Decorated Bronze Star, Air medal; recipient Oliver C. Pennock award, Colo. State U., 1989. Republican. Lutheran. Office: Colo State U Dept English Fort Collins CO 80523

PRATT, RANDALL ADEN, insurance agent; b. Rising City, Nebr., Dec. 27, 1921; s. Thomas Elgrande and Margaret (Aden) P.; married, June 6, 1948; children: John, Victoria, Kathleen. BS, U. Nebr., 1943; CLU, Am. Coll., 1957, M of Fin. Sci., 1985, ChFC, 1987. Agt. br. mgr. Sun Life Assurance Co. of Can., Honolulu, 1947-77; agy. mgr. Standard Ins. Co. of Portland, Oreg., 1977-82; v.p., mgr. Executive Ten Ins. Agy., Honolulu, 1982—; pres. Mktg. One-Hawaii Inc., Honolulu, 1980—. 1st lt. U.S. Army, 1943-46, Korea. Mem. Mgrs. Assn. (pres. 1977-78), Assn. Life Underwriters (pres. 1954-55), CLU's (pres. 1962-63), Rotary Club of Honolulu (pres. 1962-63). Republican. Methodist. Home: 1599 Ulupuni St Kailua HI 96734

PRATT, RONALD FRANKLIN, public relations executive; b. Savannah, Ga., July 15, 1948; s. Frank Tecumseh and Lila Elizabeth (Lee) P. BA, Washington U., St. Louis, 1972. Reporter Savannah News-Press, 1972; news dir. WSOK Radio, Savannah, 1973; editor Hilton Head News, Hilton Head Island, S.C., 1974-77; account exec. Russom & Leeper, San Francisco, 1978-80; sr. account exec. Russom & Leeper, 1981-83, v.p., 1983-85; sr. v.p., prin. The Leeper Grp., San Francisco, 1985-86; pres. Ronald Pratt Pub. Rels., San Francisco, 1987-90; sr. v.p., mgmt. supr. Porter/Novelli, L.A., 1990-92, sr. v.p., group exec., 1993—; cons. Coro Found., San Francisco, 1989-90. Bd. dirs. Hilton Head Jazz Festival, 1976-77; pres. Hilton Head Inst. for the Arts, 1976-77; dir., v.p. San Francisco Coun. on Entertainment, 1985-87. Recipient Enterprise award, AP, Ga., 1973. Mem. Internat. Assn. Bus. Communicators (Gold Quill 1983), Internat Foodsvc. Editorial Coun., Agrl. Relations Coun., Produce Mkgt. Assn. Office: Porter/Novelli 12100 Wilshire Blvd Ste 1800 Los Angeles CA 90025-1168

PRATT, ROSALIE REBOLLO, harpist, educator; b. N.Y.C., Dec. 4, 1933; d. Antonio Ernesto and Eleanor Gertrude (Gibney) Rebollo; Mus.B., Manhattanville Coll., 1954; Mus.M., Pius XII Inst. Fine Arts, Florence, Italy, 1955; Ed.D., Columbia U., 1976; m. George H. Mortimer, Esquire, Apr. 22, 1987; children: Francesca Christina Rebollo-Sborgi, Alessandra Maria Pratt Jones. Prin. harpist N.J. Symphony Orch., 1963-65; soloist Mozart Haydn Festival, Avery Fisher Hall, N.Y.C., 1968; tchr. music public schs., Bloomfield and Montclair, N.J., 1962-73; mem. faculty Montclair State Coll., 1973-79; prof. Brigham Young U., Provo, Utah, 1984—, coord. grad. studies dept. music, 1985-87. Co-author: Elementary Music for All Learners, 1980; editor Internat. Jour. Arts Medicine, 1991—, (proceedings) 2d, 3d, 4th Internat. Symposia Music Edn. for Handicapped; contbr. articles to Am. Harp Jour., Music Educators Jour., others. Fulbright grantee, 1979; Myron Taylor scholar, 1954. Mem. Am. Harp Soc. (Outstanding Service award 1973), AAUP (co-chmn. legis. rels. com. N.J. 1978-79), Internat. Soc. Music Edn. (chair commn. music in spl. edn., music therapy, and medicine 1985—), Internat. Soc. Music in Medicine (v.p. 1993—), Internat. Assn. of Music for the Handicapped (co-founder, exec. dir., jour. editor), Coll. Music Soc., Music Educators Nat. Conf., Brigham Young U. Grad. Coun., Phi Kappa Phi, Sigma Alpha Iota. Office: Brigham Young U Harris Fine Arts Ctr Provo UT 84602

PRATT, WALDEN PENFIELD, research geologist; b. Columbus, Ohio, Mar. 22, 1928; s. Julius William and Louisa Gabriella (Williamson) P.; m. Janice May Eddy, Dec. 21, 1957; children: Julius William II, Susan Elizabeth, David Milton. AB, U. Rochester, 1948; postgrad. Yale U., 1948-49; MS, Stanford U., 1956, PhD, 1964. Geologist, U.S. Geol. Survey, Iron River, Mich., 1949-51, Claremont, Calif., 1953-55, research geologist, Lakewood, Colo., 1956-89, scientist emeritus, 1989—; geologist Pacific Coast Borax Co., Salta, Argentina, 1955. Co-editor: United States Mineral Resources, 1973 (U.S. Geol Survey monetary award), Proceedings, Internat. Conf. on Miss. Valley-type lead-zinc deposits, 1984; editor Soc. Econ. Geologists Newsletter, 1986-91; contbr. articles to U.S. Geol. Survey publs. Served with U.S. Army, 1951-53. Recipient Meritorious Service award Dept. Interior, 1983. Fellow Geol. Soc. Am., Soc. Econ. Geologists (hon.); mem. Am. Assn. Petroleum Geologists, Rocky Mountain Assn. Geologists, Colo. Sci. Soc. Republican. Presbyterian. Office: U S Geol Survey MS 905 PO Box 25046 Denver CO 80225-0046

PRAUSNITZ, JOHN MICHAEL, chemical engineer, educator; b. Berlin, Jan. 7, 1928; came to U.S., 1937, naturalized, 1944; s. Paul Georg and Susi Prausnitz; m. Susan Frieda Prausnitz, June 10, 1956; children: Stephanie, Mark Robert. B. in Chem. Engring., Cornell U., 1950; MS, U. Rochester, 1951; Ph.D., Princeton, 1955; Dr. Ing., U. L'Aquila, 1983, Tech. U. Berlin, 1989. Mem. faculty U. Calif., Berkeley, 1955—, prof. chem. engring., 1963—; faculty rsch. lectr. U. Calif., Berkeley, 1981; Warren K. Lewis lectr. MIT, 1993; cons. to cryogenic, polymer, petroleum and petrochem. industries. Author: (with others) Computer Calculations for Multicomponent Vapor-Liquid Equilibria, 1967, (with P.L. Chueh) Computer Calculations for High-Pressure Vapor-Liquid Equilibria, 1968, Molecular Thermodynamics of Fluid-Phase Equilibria, 1969, 2d edit., 1986, (with others) Regular and Related Solutions, 1970, Properties of Gases and Liquids, 3d edit., 1977, 4th edit., 1987, Computer Calculations for Multicomponent Vapor-Liquid and Liquid-Liquid Equilibria, 1980; contbr. to profl. jours. Recipient Alexander von Humboldt Sr. Scientist award, 1976, Carl von Linde Gold Meml. medal German Inst. for Cryogenics, 1987, Solvay prize Solvay Found. for Chem. Scis., 1990, Corcoran award Am. Soc. for Engring. Edn., 1991, D.L. Katz award Gas Processors Assn., 1992; named W.K. Lewis lectr. MIT, 1993; Guggenheim fellow, 1962, 73, fellow Inst. Advanced Study, Berlin, 1985; Miller rsch. prof., 1966, 78. Mem. Am. Inst. Chem. Engrs. (Colburn award 1962, Walker award 1967), Am. Chem. Soc. (E.V. Murphree award 1979), NAE, NAS, Am. Acad. Arts and Scis. Office: U Calif 308 Gilman Hall Berkeley CA 94720

PRAY, RALPH EMERSON, metallurgical engineer; b. Troy, N.Y., May 12, 1926; s. George Emerson and Jansje Cornelius (Owejan) P.; student N.Mex. Inst. of Mining and Tech., 1953-56, U. N.Mex., 1956; BSMetE, U. Alaska, 1961; DScMetE. (Ideal Cement fellowship, Rsch. grant), Colo. Sch. of Mines, 1966; m. Beverley Margaret Ramsey, May 10, 1959; children: Maxwell, Ross, Leslie, Marlene. Engr.-in-charge Dept. Mines and Minerals, Ketchikan, Alaska, 1957-61; asst. mgr. mfg. rsch. Universal Atlas Cement div. U.S. Steel Corp., Gary, Ind., 1965-66; rsch. metallurgist Inland Steel Co., Hammond, Ind., 1966-67; owner, dir. Mineral Rsch. Lab., Monrovia, Calif., 1968—; pres., Keystone Canyon Mining Co., Inc., Pasadena, Calif., 1972-79, U.S. Western Mines, 1973—, Silveroil Rsch. Inc., 1980-85; v.p. Mineral Drill Inc., 1981-90; pres., CEO Copper de Mex. S.A. de C.V.; prime contractor def. logistics agy. U.S. Dept. Def., 1989-92; owner Precision Plastics, 1973-82; bd. dirs. Bagdad-Chase Inc., 1972-75; ptnr. Mineral R&D Co., 1981-86; lectr., Purdue U., Hammond, Ind., 1966-67, Nat. Mining Seminar, Barstow (Calif.) Coll., 1969-70; guest lectr. Calif. State Poly U., 1977-81, Western Placer Mining Conf., Reno, Nev., 1983, Dredging and Placer Mining Conf., Reno, 1985, others; v.p., dir. Wilbur Foote Plastics, Pasadena, 1968-72; strategic minerals del. People to People, Republic of South Africa, 1983; vol. Monrovia Police Dept.; city coord. Neighborhood Watch, 1990—. With U.S. Army, 1950-52. Fellow Geol. Mining and Metall. Soc. India (life), Am. Inst. Chemists, South African Inst. Mining and Metallurgy; mem. Soc. Mining Engrs., Am. Chem. Soc., Am. Inst. Mining, Metall. and Petroleum Engrs., NSPE, Can. Inst. Mining and Metallurgy, Geol. Soc. South Africa, Sigma Xi, Sigma Mu. Achievements include research on recovery of metals from refractory ores, benefication plant design, construction and operation, underground and surface mine development and operation, mine and process plant management; syndication of natural resource assets with finance sources; contbr. articles to sci. jours.; guest editor Calif. Mining Jour., 1978—; patentee chem. processing and steel manufacture. Office: 805 S Shamrock Ave Monrovia CA 91016-3651

PREACHER, STEPHEN PRESTON, academic administrator; b. Washington, Mar. 14, 1949; s. Brooks Connor and Grace Littleton P.; m. Ronda Ruth Radford, July 17, 1971; children: Ryan Alexander, Reagan Radford. BA in Religion, Bob Jones U., 1971; MBA, Nat. U., San Diego, Calif., 1976, MS in Edn., 1980; D of Bus. Adminstrn., U.S. Internat. U., San Diego, 1986. V.p. Brooks Preacher & Assocs. Real Estate, Greenville, S.C., 1972-74; pres. Chieftan Enterprises, Greenville, 1974-75; ops. mgr. Radford Overhead Doors, San Diego, 1975-78; pvt. practice fin. planner San Diego, 1976-80; prof. bus. Liberty U., Lynchburg, Va., 1980-86, chmn. dept. bus. mgmt., 1985-86; chmn. dept. bus. Christian Heritage Coll., El Cajon, Calif., 1986-89, acad. v.p., 1989—; owner, pub. The Rugged Individualist. Office: Christian Heritage College 2100 Greenfield Dr El Cajon CA 92019-1157

PREBLE, DUANE, artist, art educator; b. National City, Calif., May 20, 1936; s. Bennett and Mary Salome (Williams) P.; m. Sarah Ann Hamilton, Mar. 13, 1961; children: Jeffrey Hamilton, Malia. BA, UCLA, 1959; MFA, U. Hawaii, Honolulu, 1963. Lectr. U. Hawaii, Honolulu, 1963-64, prof., 1964-91, prof. emeritus art, 1991—; vis. prof. U. Colo., 1979, 80; bd. trustees Honolulu Acad. Arts, 1973—; chair dept. art U. Hawaii, Honolulu, 1985-87; bd. dirs. Hawaii Alliance Arts Edn. Author: (college textbook) Artforms, 4th edit., 1989. Mem., chair City Commn. on Culture & the Arts, Honolulu, 1971-73. Mem. ASCD, Internat. Soc. for Edn. Thru Art, Am. Coun. for the Arts, Coll. Art Assn. Home: 3347 Anoai Pl Honolulu HI 96822-1419 Office: U Hawaii Dept Art 2535 The Mall Honolulu HI 96822-2233

PREECE, DEREK ALAN, management consultant, entrepreneur; b. San Diego, Jan. 11, 1953; s. Richard K. and Dorothy (Jurgens) P.; m. Rita Burrell, May 27, 1976; children: Daniel, Kathryn, Jeffrey, Alan, John. BA, Brigham Young U., 1978, MBA, 1981. Mng. ptnr. Sunstar Comm. Group, Laurel, Mont., 1981-85; regional mgr. Medivision, Inc., Boston, 1985-87; pres. Enhancement Dynamics, Inc., El Cajon, Calif., 1987—. Mem. Phi Kappa Phi. Mem. Ch. Latter Day Saints.

PREECE, MCCOY D., travel corporation executive, high school official; b. Moab, Utah, May 5, 1954; s. Charles Merlin and Jacqulyn (Swain) P.; m. Karen Lucille Gividen, Aug. 20, 1976; children: Justin Coy, Joshua Charles, Nicolas Bert, Nikita Karen. Student, Utah State U., 1972-73, 76; completion cert., Branif Airlines, 1975. Cert. Travel Agent, 1988, Weather Observer, 1979, Weight Balance Instr., 1979-81. Ramp agent Frontier Airlines, Rock Springs, Wyo., 1978-79; ticket and ramp agent Frontier Airlines, Vernal, Utah, 1979-80, ops. instr., 1980-81; gen. mgr. Frontier Travel and Tours, Vernal, Utah, 1981-82; ticket and ramp agent Frontier Airlines, Seattle, 1982-84; asst. mgr. system aircraft appearance Frontier Airlines, Denver, 1984-85; mgr. Nomad Travel, Inc., Salt Lake City, 1985-86, pres., gen. mgr., 1986—; group coord. Inst. of Cert. Travel Agts., Salt Lake City, 1985-88; bd. dirs. Nomad Travel Inc. Mem. Ind. Travel Agts. Alliance (com. mem. 1988—, chmn. 1989—). Republican. Ch. of Jesus Christ of Latter Day Saints. Home: 3536 Piera Cir West Jordan UT 84084-2745 Office: Nomad Travel 2100 S 140 W #102 Salt Lake City UT 84115-3137

PREECE, NORMA, executive secretary; b. Kaysville, Utah, May 19, 1922; d. Walter and Wilma (Witt) Buhler; m. Joseph Franklin Preece, July 26, 1946 (dec. 1991); children: Terry Joe, Shannette Preece Keeler. Grad. high sch., Kaysville, 1940. Telephone operator Mountain States Telephone & Telegraph Co., Kaysville, 1940-43; clk. Civil Svc., Ogden, Utah, 1943-50; newspaper corr. Davis County Clipper, North Davis County, Utah, 1954-85; pub. communication dir. Latter-day Saints Ch., Kaysville, 1988-89; exec. sec. Kaysville Area C. of C., Kaysville, 1985-90; stake missionary Latter-Day Saints Ch., Kaysville, 1991—. Publicty chmn. Boy Scouts Am., Kaysville, 1965-69, Am. Cancer Dr., Davis County, 1967, Kaysville Civic Assn., 1960-80; mem. Utah Press Women Assn., Salt Lake City, 1973-75; active publicity Utah Congress PTA, Salt Lake City, 1977p; judge Future Farmers Am., Davis County, 1968; campaign com. mem. Republican Party, Davis County, 1990; ordinance worker LDS Temple, Ogden, Utah, 1992—. Recipient award for outstanding contbn. Davis High Sch., Kaysville, 1979, Total Citizen award Utah C. of C., 1988, Disting. Svc. award Kaysville Arts Coun., 1981; Outstanding Svc. award Kaysville Jaycees, 1972, Disting. Svc. award, 1985; named Citizen of Yr., City of Kaysville, 1985. Mem. Lit. Club (Athens, pres. 1990), Fine Arts Club (pres. 1964). Mem. LDS Ch. Home: 347 E 200 N Kaysville UT 84037-2039 Office: Kaysville Area C of C 44 E 100 N Kaysville UT 84037-1910

PREGERSON, HARRY, federal judge; b. L.A., Oct. 13, 1923; s. Abraham and Bessie (Rubin) P.; m. Bernardine Seyma Chapkis, June 28, 1947; children: Dean Douglas, Kathryn Ann. B.A., UCLA, 1947; LL.B., U. Calif.-Berkeley, 1950. Bar: Calif. 1951. Pvt. practice Los Angeles, 1951-52; Assoc. Morris D. Coppersmith, 1952; ptnr. Pregerson & Costley, Van Nuys, 1953-65; judge Los Angeles Mcpl. Ct., 1965-66, Los Angeles Superior Ct., 1966-67, U.S. Dist. Ct. Central Dist. Calif., 1967-79, U.S. Ct. Appeals for 9th Circuit, Los Angeles, 1979—; faculty mem., seminar for newly appointed distr. Judges Fed. Jud. Center, Washington, 1970-72; mem. faculty Am. Soc. Pub. Adminstrn., Inst. for Ct. Mgmt., Denver, 1973—; panelist Fed. Bar Assn., L.A. chpt., 1989, Calif. Continuing Edn. of Bar, 9th Ann. Fed. Practice Inst., San Francisco, 1986, Internat. Acad. Trial Lawyers, L.A., 1983; lect. seminars for newly-appointed Fed. judges, 1970-71. Author over 450 published legal opinions. Mem. Community Rels. Com., Jewish Fedn. Coun., 1984—, Temple Judea, Encino, 1955—; bd. dirs. Marine Corps Res. Toys for Tots Program, 1965—, Greater Los Angeles Partnership for the Homeless, 1988—; bd. trustees Devil Pups Inc., 1988—; adv. bd. Internat. Orphans Inc., 1966—, Jewish Big Brothers Assn., 1970—, Salvation Army, Los Angeles Met. area, 1988—; worked with U.S. Govt. Gen. Svcs. to establish the Bell Shelter for the homeless, the Child Day Care Ctr., the Food Partnership and Westwood Transitional Village, 1988. 1st lt. USMCR, 1944-46. Decorated Purple Heart, Medal of Valor Apache Tribe, 1989; recipient Promotion of Justice Civic award, City of San Fernando, 1965, award San Fernando Valley Jewish Fedn. Coun., 1966, Profl. Achievement award Los Angeles Athletic Club, 1980, Profl. Achievement award UCLA Alumni Assn., 1985, Louis D. Brandeis award Am. Friends of Hebrew U., 1987, award of merit Inner City Law Ctr., 1987, Appreciation award Navajo Nation and USMC for Toys for Tots program, 1987, Humanitarian award Los Angeles Fed. Exec. Bd., 1987-88, Grateful Acknowledgement award Bet Tzedek Legal Svcs., 1988, Commendation award Bd. Suprs. Los Angeles County, 1988, Others award Salvation Army, 1988, numerous others. Mem. ABA (vice-chmn., com. on fed. rules of criminal procedure and evidence sect. of criminal 1972—, panelist Advocacy Inst., Phoenix, 1988), L.A. County Bar Assn., San Fernando Valley Bar Assn. (program chmn. 1964-65), State Bar Calif., Marines Corps Res. Officers Assn. (pres. San Fernando Valley 1966—), DAV (Birmingham chpt.), Am. Legion (Van Nuys Post),. Office: US Ct Appeals 9th Cir 21800 Oxnard St Ste 1140 Woodland Hills CA 91367-3633

PRELL, JOEL JAMES, medical group administrator; b. L.A., Aug. 16, 1944; s. Samuel and Mary Devorah (Schwartz) P.; children: Vanessa S., Matthew. BA, U. So. Calif., L.A., 1967; cert. fin. mgmt., Ohio State U., 1979; M. Pub. Health, UCLA, 1981. Various positions, 1967-72; chief adminstrv. office sr. adminstrv. analyst L.A. County, 1972-73; dep. regional dir. for planning and community rels. L.A. County Dept. Health Svcs. Region, 1973-75; adminstr. ambulatory care L.A. County Harbro Gen. Hosp., 1975-76; assoc. dir. hosp. and clinics ambulatory care svcs. U. Calif.-Irvine Med. Ctr., 1976-78; asst. to the dir. rsch. and analysis unit U. Calif., Davis, 1978-80; v.p. profl. svcs. San Pedro Peninsula Hosp., 1981-84; sr. v.p. South Coast Med. Ctr., 1984-87; pres., CEO Harbor Health Systems, Inc., 1987-90; CEO Santa Monica (Calif.) Plz. Med. Group, Inc., 1990-93; administrator Pathology Cons. Med. Group, Torrance, Calif., 1993—; spl. asst. to the contr. UCLA Hosp. and Clinics, 1980-81, adminstr. emergency medicine ctr., 1981. Mem. Hosp. Coun .So. Calif. (polit. action steering com., chmn. legis. affairs com.), Calif. Hosp. Polit. Action Com. (bd. dirs.), Health Care Execs. So. Calif., UCLA Health Svcs. Adminstrs. Alumni Assn. (pres.), Med. Group Mgmt. Assn., Am. Coll. Health Care Adminstrs., Friends of Castle Heights. Office: Pathology Cons Med Group 20221 Hamilton Ave Torrance CA 90502

PRENDERGAST, WILLIAM JOHN, ophthalmologist; b. Portland, Oreg., June 12, 1942; s. William John and Marjorie (Scott) P.; m. Carolyn Grace Perkins, Aug. 17, 1963 (div. 1990); children: William John, Scott; m. Sherryl Irene Guenther, Aug. 25, 1991. BS, U. Oreg., Eugene, 1964; MD, U. Oreg., Portland, 1967. Diplomate Am. Bd. Ophthalmology. Resident in ophthalmology U. Oreg., Portland, 1970-73; pvt. practice specializing in ophthalmology Portland, 1973-82; physician, founder, ptnr. Oreg. Med. Eye Clinic, Portland, 1983—; founder, pres. Med. Eye Assocs., Inc. Ophthalmic Clinic Networking Venture, Portland, 1992—; clin. asst. prof. dept. ophthalmology Oreg. health Sci. Ctr., 1985—; pres. Med. Eye Assocs. Vol. surgeon N.W. Med. Teams, Oaxaca, Mexico, 1989, 90. With USPHS, 1968-70. Fellow Am. Acad. Ophthalmology; mem. Met. Bus. Assn., Multnomah Athletic Club, Mazamas Mountaineering Club, Portland Yacht Club, Phi Beta Kappa, Alpha Omega Alpha. Office: Oregon Med Eye Clinic 1955 NW Northrup St Portland OR 97209-1689

PREOVOLOS, PENELOPE ATHENE, lawyer; b. San Francisco, Sept. 16, 1955; d. James Peter and Lorraine Lucille (Tiscornia) P.; m. Richard Gonzalo Katerndahl, Mar. 24, 1984. AB, U. Calif., Berkeley, 1976; JD, Harvard U., 1979. Bar: Calif. 1979, U.S. Dist. Ct. (no. dist.) Calif. 1979, U.S. Ct. Appeals (9th cir.) 1979. Law clk. to Hon. Charles M. Merrill U.S. Ct. Appeals (9th cir.), San Francisco, 1979-80; assoc. Morrison & Foerster, San Francisco, 1980-85; ptnr. Morrison & Foerster, San Franciso, 1985—. Contbr. articles to profl. jours. Bd. dirs. San Francisco Neighborhood Legal

Assistance Found., 1990—; mem. exec. com. antitrust and trade regulation law sect. State Bar Calif. Mem. ABA (antitrust sect.). Democrat. Roman Catholic. Home: 225 Evergreen Dr Kentfield CA 94904-2707 Office: Morrison & Foerster 345 California St San Francisco CA 94104-2606

PRESCOTT, DAVID MARSHALL, biology educator; b. Clearwater, Fla., Aug. 3, 1926; s. Clifford Raymond and Lillian (Moore) P.; m. Gayle Edna Demery; children: Lavonne, Jason, Ryan. BA, Wesleyan U., 1950; PhD, U. Calif., Berkeley, 1954. Asst. prof. UCLA Med. Sch., 1955-59; biologist Oak Ridge (Tenn.) Nat. Lab., 1959-63; prof. U. Colo. Sch. Medicine, Denver, 1963-66; prof. molecular, cell and devel. biology U. Colo., Boulder, 1966—, Disting. prof., 1980—; pres. Am. Soc. Cell Biology, 1966. Author: Cell Reproduction, 1976, Cancer: The Misguided Cell, 1986, Cells, 1988; also numerous rsch. reports; editor: Methods in Cell Biology, 15 vols., 1963-78. Adv. com. March of Dimes, 1979-90. Recipient von Humboldt prize Fed. Republic Germany, 1979; grantee NIH, 1985—, Nat. Found. Cancer Rsch., 1985-89, NSF, 1990-91; John Simon Guggenheim Meml. Found. fellow, 1990-91. Fellow Am. Acad. Arts and Scis.; mem. NAS. Home: 285 Brook Pl Boulder CO 80302-8031 Office: Univ Colo Dept Biology Boulder CO 80309

PRESCOTT, JOEL HENRY, advertising executive, writer; b. Detroit, Apr. 10, 1941; s. Joel Henry Prescott Jr. and Millicent (French) Bennett. BA in Polit. Sci., U. Mich., 1963. Advt. copy supr. Young & Rubicam, Inc., Detroit, 1968-70; co-creative dir. Parker Advt., Inc., Palos Verdes, Calif., 1972-76; creative dir. Marsteller Advt., L.A., 1979-84, Robert Elen & Assocs., Hollywood, Calif., 1984-86; creative supr. Grey Advt., Inc., L.A., 1976-79; sr. writer Grey Advt., Inc., Cypress, Calif., 1986-92; founder, chief exec. officer Prescott & Assocs., 1990—. Writer Hitsory of Cadillac/ Lincoln, Car Collector mag., 1990, Mitsubishi TV comml. series (Telly award 1989), various Honda car ads (Belding award 1980, 82); contbr. articles to Classic Car mag., Old Cars Weekly newspaper, (book) The Classic Car. Mem. Classic car Club Am. (life mem.), CHVA (bd. dirs. So. Calif. 1987-90). Republican. Episcopalian. Home: 29 Calle Cienega Placitas NM 87043

PRESCOTT, LAWRENCE MALCOLM, medical and health writer; b. Boston, July 31, 1934; s. Benjamin and Lillian (Stein) P. BA, Harvard U., 1957; MSc, George Washington U., 1959, PhD, 1966; m. Ellen Gay Kober, Feb. 19, 1961 (dec. Sept. 1981); children: Jennifer Maya, Adam Barrett; m. Sharon Lynn Kirshen, May 16, 1982; children: Gary Leon Kirshen, Marc Paul Kirshen. Nat. Acad. Scis. postdoctoral fellow U.S. Army Rsch., Ft. Detrick, Md., 1965-66; microbiologist/scientist WHO, India, 1967-70, Indonesia, 1970-72, Thailand, 1972-78; with pub. rels. Ted Klein & Co., Van Vechten, Smith, Kline, Beecham, others, 1984—; cons. health to internat. orgns., San Diego, 1978—; author manuals; contbr. articles in diarrheal diseases and lab. scis. to profl. jours., numerous articles, stories, poems to mags., newspapers, including Living in Thailand, Jack and Jill, Strawberry, Bangkok Times, Sprint, 1977-81; mng. editor Caduceus, 1981-82; pub., editor: Teenage Scene, 1982-83; pres. Prescott Pub. Co., 1982-83; med. writer numerous jours. including Modern Medicine, Dermatology Times, Cope, ACP Observer, Medical Tribune, American Family Physician, Ophthalmology Times, Group Practice News, Newspaper of Cardiology, Paacnotes, Genetic Engineering News, Medical Week, Medical World News, Urology Times, Gastroenterology and Endoscopy News; author: Curry Every Sunday, 1984. Home and Office: 18264 Verano Dr San Diego CA 92128-1262

PRESLER, GERALD ALLEN, county government official; b. Seattle, Mar. 22, 1945; s. Charles H. and Dourthy (Zolatz) P.; m. Sharon Olden (div. 1970); 1 child, Stacy Lynn; m. Vickie Ray Beard, Aug. 12, 1972; children: Kevin Jay, Corey Allen. Student, Bellingham (Wash.) Tech., 1963, U. Wash., 1969-70; BA in Bus. Adminstrn., City U., Bellevue, Wash., 1993. Engr. City of Bellingham, 1962-70, Stevens Thompson & Ruyan, Seattle, 1970-73; community devel. dir. City of Anacortes, Wash., 1973-76; city adminstr., pub. works dir. City of Blaine, Wash., 1976-80; v.p. program devel. Olympic Ctr. Bellingham, 1980-85; v.p. Medi-Fitness/Tol-Tec, Portland, Oreg., 1984-88; supr., mgr. Snohomis County, Everett, Wash., 1988—; cons. various bus. and polit. campaigns, 1984—. Author: 2 Land Use Commperhensae Land Use Plans, 2 Shoreline Management Plans, 2 Coastal Zone Management Plans, 3 Community Development Block Grants; co-author 18 City/Co. Traffic Safety Programs. Campaign mgr. for county treas., Whatcom County, 1987; chmn. citizen com. Better Roads, Whatcom County, 1980; organizer Border Town Funding/City of Blaine, 1980. Sgt. U.S. Army N.G., 1962-66. Recipient spl. recognition Wash. Traffic Safety Commn., 1991. Home: 3844 Cindy Ln Bellingham WA 98226 Office: Snohomish County 2930 Wetmore Ave Everett WA 98201

PRESLEY, ROBERT BUEL, state senator; b. Tahlequah, Okla., Dec. 4, 1924; s. Doyle and Annie (Townsend) P.; grad. FBI Nat. Acad., Washington, 1962; student Riverside City Coll., 1960; A.A., UCLA, m. Ahni Ratliff, Aug. 20, 1944; children—Donna Thurber, Marilyn Raphael, Robert Buel. Various positions Riverside County Sheriff's Dept. (Calif.), 1950-62, undersheriff, 1962-74; mem. Calif. Senate, 36th Dist., 1974—; lectr. ethics. Served with U.S. Army, 1943-46. Decorated Bronze Star. Mem. FBI Nat. Acad. Assn. (pres. Calif. chpt. 1974). Baptist. Clubs: Lions, Elks, Am. Legion, V.F.W., Moose, Riverside County Democratic Century (pres. 1972-73). Home: 5508 Grassy Trail Dr Riverside CA 92504-1214 Office: Office of State Senate State Capitol Rm 4048 Sacramento CA 95814

PRESS, BARRY HARRIS JAY, plastic surgeon, educator; b. Marshalltown, Iowa, Apr. 10, 1951; s. Robert Alfred and Phyllis Elaine (Rovner) P.; m. Cynthia Jane Witz, Aug. 11, 1973; children: Sarah Jane, Rachel Ann. BS, U. Iowa, 1973, MD, 1977. Diplomate Am. Bd. Med. Examiners, Am. Bd. Surgery, Am. Bd. Plastic Surgery. Intern U. Minn. Hosps., Mpls., 1977-78, resident in gen. surgery, 1978-85; resident in plastic surgery Inst. for Reconstructive Plastic Surgery, NYU Med. Ctr., N.Y.C., 1985-87; asst. prof. Sch. of Medicine Stanford (Calif.) U., 1987—; dir. burn ctr., assoc. chief plastic surgery Santa Clara Valley Med. Ctr., San Jose, Calif., 1987—. Fellow ACS; mem. AMA, Am. Soc. Plastic and Reconstructive Surgeons, Am. Burn Assn., Calif. Med. Assn., Santa Clara County Med. Assn., Calif. Soc. of Plastic Surgeons, Am. Soc. for Surgery of the Hand, San Jose Surg. Soc. Office: Santa Clara Valley Med Ctr Div Plastic Surgery 751 S Bascom Ave San Jose CA 95128-2604

PRESS, LLOYD DOUGLAS, JR. (SKIP PRESS), screenwriter, producer, author; b. Commerce, Tex., July 26, 1950; s. Lloyd Douglas Press Sr. and Bettie Eleanor (Jacobs) Davidson; m. Debra Ann Hartsog, July 30, 1989; children: Haley Alexander, Holly Olivia. Mng. editor Today's Profls. mag., L.A., 1979-80; editor Entertainment Monthly, L.A., 1984; writer, producer How-to-Videos, 1986—; freelance writer, 1978—; writer, tech. ops. manuals Franchise Cons. Group, L.A.; writer, cons. First Interstate Bank, L.A. Author: Cliffhanger, 1992, Knucklehead, 1992, The Devil's Forest Fire, 1992, The Big Picture, 1993, The Importance of Mark Twain, 1993, Amazing Almanac (California), 1993; co-writer Fair Game feature, Braunstein-Hamady Prodns., 1991, Allure feature Chessler Prodn., 1991; writer TV Zoobilee Zoo, 1986; writer, packager video Jan Stephenson's How to Golf, 1986; writer, co-producer video A Woman's Guide to Firearms, 1987; writer, cons. video Wedding Helper, 1989; writer radio show Alien Worlds, 1978; mng. editor Entertainment Monthly, 1984; contbr. articles to profl. jours.; producer, dir., playwright several plays. Dir. Ind. Writers of So. Calif. Script-a-thon, Century City, Calif., 1990. Mem. Dramatists Guild, PEN, Poets and Writers, Ind. Writers of So. Calif. (bd. dirs. at large 1989-90, v.p. 1990-91). Home and Office: 710 E Palm Ave Burbank CA 91501

PRESSEL, ESTHER JOAN, anthropologist; b. Loysburg, Pa., Jan. 15, 1937; d. J. William and Rachel Pressel. PhD, Ohio State U., 1971. Assoc. prof. anthropology Colo. State U., Fort Collins, 1968—. Fellow Am. Anthropol. Assn.; mem. Soc. for Psychol. Anthropology, Soc. for Med. Anthropology, Sigma Xi. Home: 829 Juniper Ln Fort Collins CO 80526 Office: Colo State U Dept Anthropology Fort Collins CO 80523

PRESSLEY, JAMES RAY, electrical engineer; b. Ft. Worth, July 14, 1946; s. Loy Dale and Dorothy Helen (Foust) P.; m. Barbara Kay McMillin, Oct. 9, 1968 (div. 1981); children: James Foust Pressley, Kreg Milam Pressley; m. Susan Marie Straw, Apr. 27, 1985 (div.); children: Shaye Eugene Straw, Rebecca Alycen Straw, Rachel Leilani Straw. BSEE, U. Tex., Arlington, 1970. Registered profl. engr., Alaska, Hawaii, Oreg., Wash. Designer/ draftsman Romine & Slaughter, Ft. Worth, 1967-71; engr. Crews MacInnes & Hoffman, Anchorage, 1971-73, O'Kelly & Schoenlank, Anchorage, 1973-75, Theodore G. Creedon, Anchorage, 1975-77; v.p. Fryer, Pressley Elliott, Anchorage, 1977-80, Fryer/Pressley Engring., 1980-91, FPE/Roen Engrs., Inc., 1991—, also chmn. bd., 1991—; mem. elec. constrn. and maintenance industry evaluation panel, 1982—. Mem. IEEE, Illuminating Engring. Soc. (sustaining), Internat. Assn. Elec. Inspectors, Nat. Assn. Corrosion Engrs., Alaska Profl. Design Coun. Office: FPE/Roen Engrs Inc 560 E 34th Ave Ste 300 Anchorage AK 99503-4184

PRESSMAN, THANE ANDREW, consumer products executive; b. San Diego, Calif., June 6, 1945; s. Harold Andrew and Audrey Ethelyn (Negus)P.; m. Caroline Hannah Hood Snyder, Nov. 23, 1966; children: Sean, Steven. BS, Springfield (Mass.) Coll., 1967; MS, Syracuse U., 1969. Various to brand mgr. Procter & Gamble Co., Cin., 1968-76, assoc. mgr. advt., 1976-79; v.p. Lamalie Assocs., Inc. Chgo., 1979-81; dir. new products Alberto Culver Co., Melrose Park, Ill., 1981-84; group staff, v.p. Sara Lee Corp., Northbrook, Ill., 1984-85; pres., COO Kitchens of Sara Lee Can., Bramalee, Ont., 1986-88; exec. v.p. Sara Lee Bakery Co., Bramalee and Deerfield, Ill., 1988-90; pres., CEO Crestar Food Products, Inc. (affiliate of H.J. Heinz Co.), Eugene, Oreg., 1991-92, Crestar Food Products Inc. & Crestar Food Products Can. Ltd., Eugene, Oreg./Mississauga, Ont., Can., 1992—; guest lectr. U. Mich. Grad. Sch. Bus., Ann Arbor, 1977-79. Bd. dirs. Am. Field Svc. U.S.A., N.Y.C., 1986-89; trustee Am. Field Svc. Intercultural Programs, N.Y.C., 1988—, Springfield Coll., 1988—; campaign co-chmn. United Way, Cin., Chgo., Bramalea, Deerfield, 1976-90. Mem. Assn. Governing Bds. Univs. Colls., Eugene Country Club, David Allen Reed Soc., Grocery Product Mfrs. of Can., Internat. Dairy Deli Assn., Dixie Curling Club, Brentwood C.C., Richland C.C.

PRESTON, JAY WILSON, telephone company executive; b. Missoula, Mont., Jan. 14, 1956; s. Jay William and Elizabeth H. (Cummings) P.; m. Deborah Korn, Sept. 10, 1983; children: Matthew Alexander, David Jonathon, Ezra Jeremiah. BSEE, Mont. State U., 1978; MBA, Columbia U., 1983. Asst. gen. mgr. Ronan (Mont.) Tel.Co., 1978-81; v.p. Ronan (Mont.) Tel. Co., 1983-88, pres., COO, 1988—; founding treas., b.d dirs. Telephone Exch. Carriers Mont., Gt. Falls, 1986-87; mem., vice chmn., chmn. Mission Valley Power Consumer Coun., Polson, Mont., 1990—. Prin. organizer Ronan community certification effort Mont. Cert. Communities Program, Helena, 1987-88; founder, pres. Cen. Lake County Community Devel. Corp., Ronan, 1988—; founding bd. dirs. Fund for Rural Edn. and Devel., Washington, 1988-93, Flathead Reservation Human Rights Coalition, Flathead Indian Reservation, Mont., 1989—; mem. Mont. Ambs., 1987—. Mem. U.S. Tel. Assn. (small co. com. 1985-88), Orgn. for Protection and Advancement Small Telephone Co. (bd. dirs. 1986-88), Ronan C. of C. (bd. dirs., v.p., pres. 1983-88, Man of Yr. award 1989). Democrat. Home: 717 2d Pl SW Ronan MT 59864 Office: Ronan Tel Co 312 Main St SW Ronan MT 59864

PRESTON, MARTHA SUE, quality assurace director; b. Washington, Oct. 15, 1952; d. George Millard and Martha Preston. BA in Biology cum laude, Lycoming Coll., 1974; postgrad., U. Md., 1981-85. Lab. asst. biology dept. Lycoming Coll., Williamsport, Pa., 1973-74; biologist arthritis and rheumatism br. NIH, Bethesda, Md., 1974-75, biologist nutrition and endocrinology lab., 1975-80; biologist div. blood and blood products FDA, Bethesda, Md., 1980-88; mgr. regulatory affairs Baxter Healthcare Corp., Glendale, Calif., 1988-90; dir. regulatory affairs, quality assurance Trancel Corp., Santa Anna, Calif., 1990—. Presenter in field, 1977-89. Mem. Drug Info. Assn., Am. Heart Assn. (thrombosis coun.), Tissue Culture Assn., Regulatory Affairs Profls. Soc. Office: Trancel Corp 1202 E Wakeham Ave Santa Ana CA 92705

PRESTON, ROBERT ARTHUR, astronomer; b. N.Y.C., June 29, 1944; s. Arthur Lloyd and Dorothy Elizabeth (Smith) P.; m. Ann Lee Archer, July 18, 1970; 1 child, Karen Ann. BS, Cornell U., 1966, MS, 1967; PhD, MIT, 1972. Rsch. scientist Lockheed Rsch. Lab., Palo Alto, Calif., 1972-73; astronomer Jet Propulsion Lab., Calif. Inst. Tech., Pasadena, 1973—, supr. astronomical measurements group, 1975—, mgr. astrophysics rsch. program, 1983-92, project scientist Space VLBI project, 1991—; leader U.S. Sci. teams for Vega Venus Balloon and Phobos Lander Missions, 1982-90. Recipient Exceptional Svc. award NASA, 1986; rsch. grantee NASA, 1975—, Nat. Park Svc., 1980—. Mem. Am. Astron. Soc., Internat. Astron. Union. Home: 24618 Golf View Dr Santa Clarita CA 91355-2301 Office: Calif Inst Tech Jet Propulsion Lab 4800 Oak Grove Dr Pasadena CA 91109-8099

PRESTON, TOBIAS JAMES, commercial fisherman; b. Walden, Colo., May 10, 1962; s. James Everett and Janice Ellen (Plum) P.; m. Cecelia Theresa, Nov. 8, 1986; 1 child: Caleb Jake. Assoc. of N.T., Canyonview Sem., Silverton, Oreg., 1983; EdB, U. AK., Fairbanks, 1991. Elem. Edn. Boat skipper J.E. Preston Fisheries, Homer, Alaska, 1980-85; vessel owner Preston Fisheries Inc., Homer, Alaska, 1986—; cons., J.E. Preston, Homer, AK, 1986—; v.p. Preston Fisheries Inc., 1989—; founded McKinley Mortgage, 1992. Voting mem. Rep. Caucus, Fairbanks, AK, 1990. Named Chancellors List, Dean's List, U. AK., Fiarbanks, AK, 1988, 89;. Mem., treas. Prince William Sound Setnetters Assn., 1987—. Republican. Baptist. Office: Preston Fisheries Inc PO Box 394 Homer AK 99603-0394

PRESTRUD, STUART H., management consultant; b. Seattle, Apr. 18, 1919; s. Einar and Agnes (Holm) P.; m. Victoria Hart, Jan. 28, 1956 (div. 1968); children: Douglas, Jack, Charles; m. Barbara Bye, Oct. 28, 1980; stepchildren: William Brinkley Jr., Elizabeth Brinkley. BA cum laude, U. Wash., 1946. From trust adminstr. to v.p. 1st Interstate Bank Wash. (formerly Pacific Nat. Bank Wash.), Seattle, 1946-81; v.p., cons. Aldarra Mgmt. Co., Seattle, 1987—. Sec., bd. dirs. Norman Archibald Charitable Found., Seattle, 1981—; trustee Mus. of Flight, Seattle, 1985—, Mus. History & Industry Endowment Trust, Seattle, 1990—; com. chair United Way Seattle-King County, 1989; pres. Seattle Opera Endowment Trust, Seattle, 1985-90. Lt. USNR, 1943-44. Recipient Sr. Citizen award Seattle Sr. Citizens, 1990. Mem. Seattle Golf Club, Seattle Tennis Club, Wash. Athletic Club, Phi Beta Kappa (asst. treas. Puget Sound Assn. 1980—). Office: 1st Interstate Bank PO Box 21927 Seattle WA 98111-3927

PREVITE, RICHARD, computer company executive; b. Boston, 1935. BS, San Jose State U., 1956, MA. Contr. Sierra Elec. Corp., Menlo Park, Calif., 1961-69; with Advanced Micro Devices, Inc., Sunnyvale, Calif., 1969—, sr. v.p., treas., chief adminstrv. officer, pres., COO, bd. dirs.; bd. dirs. Robinson Nugent, Inc. Office: Advanced Micro Devices Inc 901 Thompson Pl Sunnyvale CA 94086-4518*

PREVO, MARY ELLEN, toxicologist; b. Belleville, Ill., June 27, 1947; d. Roy Arthur and Ellen (Weber) Knobeloch; m. Ralph W. Prevo, Mar. 21, 1970; children: Brian Geoffrey, Shelly Nicole. BS, Ea. Ill. U., 1969; student, So. Ill. U., 1969-70; MA, San Jose State U., 1985. Biologist ALZA Corp., Palo Alto, Calif., 1974-77, sr. biologist, 1977-79, mgr. toxicology, 1979-87, dir. toxicology, rsch. scientist, 1987-91, dir. toxicology and microbiology, rsch. fellow, 1991—. Coach AYSO, Sunnyvale, Calif., 1982, 84, 86, 90. Mem. Am. Coll. Toxicology, Soc. Toxicology (No. Calif. chpt.), Soc. Comparative Ophthalmology, No. Calif. Pharm. Discussion Group, Genetic and Environ. Toxicology Assn. Office: ALZA Corp PO Box 10950 950 Page Mill Rd Palo Alto CA 94303-0802

PRIBILSKY, KEVIN ANDREW, food products executive; b. Walla Walla, Wash., Apr. 11, 1963; s. Wilber Ehrhardt and Karen Elaine (Elder) P.; m. Kirsten Anne Peterson, Apr. 11, 1987; 1 child, Stefan Martin. BBA, Pacific Luth. U., 1985; MBA, UCLA, 1990. Fin. systems analyst The Boeing Co., Seattle, 1985; mktg. intern higher edn. Ashton-Tate Software, Torrance, Calif., 1989; student sales rep. Apple Computer, LA., 1989-90; account rep. Physio-Control Corp., Rowayton, Conn., 1990-91; v.p. mktg. and adminstrn. The Bur-Bee Co., Inc., Walla Walla, 1992—. Author, editor: (newsletter) PC News, 1985-88, Bur-Bee News, 1992—. Vol. Salvation Army, Bridgeport, Conn. 1991. Fellow UCLA, 1989. Mem. Am. Wholesale Marketers Assn., Instl. Foodsvc. Distbrs. Am., Rotary Internat., Alpha Kappa Psi, Beta Gamma Sigma. Republican. Office: Bur-Bee Co Inc PO Box 797 Walla Walla WA 99362

PRICE, ANN HESSE, writer, editor; b. Portland, Oreg., Aug. 6, 1955; d. Louis Farver and Margaret (Putnam) H.; m. David A. Price, Aug. 8, 1981 (dec. Dec. 1987). Student, U. Minn., 1977; BS, Oreg. State U., 1977. Asst. mgr. The Gap Stores, Portland and Seattle, 1977-79; promotion coord. Unicorn Textiles, Ltd., Seattle, 1979-80; sales rep. United Specialty Advt., Seattle, 1980-82; br. store mgr. Liberty of London, Dallas, 1982-84; ednl. mgr. Bernina of Am., Hinsdale, Ill., 1984-86; seminar leader Palmer/Pletsch Assoc., Portland, 1986-90; freelance writer Seattle, 1987—; cons./conv. planner Tacony Corp., St. Louis, 1989; TV spokesperson Am. Home Sewing Assn., Seattle, 1989; editor Home Economists in Bus., 1989-91; keynote speaker Goodwill Industries, Seattle, 1990; seminar leader Clemson U., Seattle, 1992. Author: The Serger Idea Book, 1989; contbr. over 150 article to profl. publs. Program chair Trinity Luth. Ch., 1990—. Mem. Internat. Assn. Bus. Communicators, Nat. Speakers Assn. (asst. editor 1991-92), Toastmasters Internat. (pres. 1991, treas. 1990, editor 1989), Pacific N.W. Writers. Home and Office: 2224 Sunset Dr W Tacoma WA 98466

PRICE, ARTHUR RICHARD, petroleum company executive; b. Calgary, Alta., Can., Oct. 22, 1951; married; 3 children. BSc, U. Alta., 1973. With NOVA Corp. of Alta., 1973-79; v.p. Husky Oil Ltd., Calgary, 1979-84, pres., 1984-93, CEO, 1992-93; pres. Husky Oil Ops. Ltd., Calgary, 1984-93; spl. advisor internat. investment Hutchinson Whampoa Ltd. Bd. Dirs. Office: Husky Oil Ltd, 707 8th Ave SW, Calgary, AB Canada T2P 1H5

PRICE, CYNTHIA ANN See BATTIN, CYNTHIA ANN

PRICE, EDWARD DEAN, federal judge; b. Sanger, Calif., Feb. 12, 1919; s. Earl Trousdale and Daisy Shaw (Biggs) P.; m. Katherine S. Merritt, July 18, 1943; children: Katherine Price O'Brien, Edward M., Jane E. B.A., U. Calif., Berkeley, 1947, LL.B., 1949. Bar: Calif. 1949. Assoc. Cleary & Zeff, Modesto, Calif., 1949-51; assoc. Zeff & Halley, Modesto, Calif., 1951-54; ptnr. Zeff, Halley & Price, Modesto, Calif., 1954-63, Zeff & Price, Modesto, Calif., 1963-65, Price & Martin, Modesto, Calif., 1965-69, Price, Martin & Crabtree, Modesto, Calif., 1969-79; judge U.S. Dist. Ct., Fresno, Calif., 1980-90, sr. judge, 1990—; mem. adv. bd. governing com. Continuing Edn. of Bar, San Francisco, 1963-71, governing bd. Calif. State Bar, 1973-76; v.p. Jud. Council, Calif., 1978-79. Contbr. articles to profl. jours. Served with U.S. Army, 1943-46. Mem. ABA, Am. Coll. Trial Lawyers, Am. Bd. Trial Advocates. Democrat. Methodist. Home: 1012 Wellesley Ave Modesto CA 95350-5042 Office: US Dist Ct 5554 US Courthouse 1130 O St Fresno CA 93721-2201

PRICE, FRANK, motion picture and television company executive; b. Decatur, Ill., May 17, 1930; s. William F. and Winifred A. (Moran) P.; m. Katherine Huggins, May 15, 1965; children: Stephen, David, Roy, Frank. Student, Mich. State U., 1949-51. Writer, story editor CBS-TV, N.Y.C., 1951-53, Columbia Pictures, Hollywood, Calif., 1953-57, NBC-TV, Hollywood, Calif., 1957-58; producer, writer ZIV-TV, Hollywood, Calif., 1958; producer, writer Universal Television, Universal City, Calif., 1959-64, v.p., 1964-71, sr. v.p., 1971-73, exec. v.p. in charge of production, 1973-74, pres., 1974-78; v.p., dir. MCA, Inc., 1976-78; pres. Columbia Pictures Prodn., 1978-79; chmn., chief exec. officer Columbia Pictures, 1979-84, also bd. dirs.; chmn. MCA Motion Picture Group, 1984-86; chmn., chief exec. officer Price Entertainment Inc., 1987-90; chmn. Columbia Pictures, 1990-91; also bd. dirs. Sony Pictures Entertainment; chmn., chief exec. officer Price Entertainment, 1991—; bd. dirs. Savoy Pictures; bd. dirs. Savory Pictures. Writer, story editor, CBS-TV, N.Y.C., 1951-53, Columbia Pictures, Hollywood, Calif., 1953-57, NBC-TV, 1957-58, Hollywood, producer, writer, ZIV-TV, 1958, Universal Television, Universal City, Calif., 1959-64, v.p., 1964-71, sr. v.p., 1971-73, exec. v.p. in charge of production, 1973-74, pres., 1974-78. With USN, 1948-49. Mem. Writers Guild Am., West. Office: Price Entertainment Inc 10202 Washington Blvd Culver City CA 90232-3119

PRICE, GAYL BAADER, title insurance company executive; b. Gothenburg, Sweden, Mar. 1, 1949; came to U.S., 1951; d. Harold Edgar Anderson and Jeanette Helen (Hallberg) Akeson; m. Daniel J. Baader, Nov. 27, 1971 (div. Sept. 1980); m. Leigh C. Price, Feb. 28, 1983; foster children: Heidi, Heather. BA in Fgn. Lang., U. Ill., 1971. Asst. buyer The Denver, 1971-73, buyer, 1973-75; escrow sec. Transam. Title, Evergreen, Colo., 1975-76, escrow officer, 1976-78, sr. escrow officer, 1978-79, br. mgr., 1979-84; sr. account mgr. Transam. Title, Denver, 1984-87, sales mgr., 1987-91, v.p., 1989—. Vol. Safehouse for Battered Women, Denver, 1986—, Spl. Olympics, 1986—. Mem. Home Builders Assn. Met. Denver (bd. dirs. 1989—, exec. com. 1992, assoc. mem. coun. chair 1991, Arthur Gaeth Assoc. of Yr. 1989), Sales and Mktg. Coun. Met. Denver (chair, Most Profl. award 1989), Douglas County Econ. Devel., Zonta Club (Denver II, pres. 1990, Zontian of Yr. 1988), Colo. Assn. of Homebuilders (Assoc. of Yr. 1992). Home: 1975 Linda Ln Evergreen CO 80439-9528 Office: Transam Title Ins 6 W Dry Creek Cir # 110 Littleton CO 80120-8031

PRICE, HUMPHREY WALLACE, aerospace engineer; b. San Antonio, Sept. 25, 1954; s. Humphrey Rodes and Ruth (Wallace) P. BS in Engring., U. Tex., 1976, MS in Engring., 1978. Rsch. asst. nuclear reactor lab. U. Tex., Austin, 1976; nuclear engr. EDS Nuclear, Inc., San Francisco, 1977-78; engr. Jet Propulsion Lab., Pasadena, Calif., 1978-82, tech. group leader, 1984-89; configuration engr. NASA's Mariner Mark II spacecraft Jet Propulsion Lab., 1989—; rsch. engr. SW Rsch. Inst., San Antonio, 1982-84; cons. Am. Rocket Co., Camarillo, Calif., 1986-87; tech. staff World Space Found., Pasadena, 1980—. Patentee in field; contbr. to tech. papers in field. Mem. AIAA (sr.), Brit. Interplanetary Soc. Office: HW Price Cons PO Box 454 La Canada Flintridge CA 91012-0454

PRICE, JEANNINE ALLEENICA, clinical psychologist; b. Cleve., Oct. 29, 1949; d. Q. Q. and Lisa Denise (Wilson) Ewing; m. T. R. Price, Sept. 2, 1976. BS, Western Res. U., 1969; MS, Vanderbilt U., 1974; MBA, Stanford U., 1985. Cert. alcoholism counselor, Calif. Health Service coordinator Am. Profile, Nashville, 1970-72; exec. dir. Awareness Concept, San Jose, Calif., 1977-80; mgr. employee assistance program Nat. Semiconductor, Santa Clara, Calif., 1980-81; mgmt. cons. employee assistant programs; counselor Awareness Concept, 1989—, exec. dir., 1989-90. Mem. Gov.'s Adv. Council Child Devel. Programs. Mem. Am. Bus. Women's Assn., NAFE, AAUW, Coalition Labor Women, Calif. Assn. Alcohol counselors, Almaca. Author: Smile a Little, Cry a Lot, Gifts of Love, Reflection in the Mirror, The Light at the Top of the Mountain, The Dreamer, The Girl I Never Knew, An Act of Love, Walk Toward the Light.

PRICE, JOE, artist, educator; b. Ferriday, La., Feb. 6, 1935; s. Edward Neill and Margaret (Hester) P. BS, Northwestern U., 1957; postgrad., Art Ctr. Coll., L.A., 1967-68; MA, Stanford U., 970. Free-lance actor, artist N.Y.C., 1957-60; free-lance illustrator, actor, L.A., 1960-68; free-lance comml. artist, San Carlos, Calif., 1968-69; package designer Container Corp. Am., Santa Clara, Calif., 1969; prof. studio art and filmmaking, chmn. dept. art Coll. San Mateo, Calif., 1970—. One man shows include Richard Sumner Gallery, Palo Alto, Calif., 1975, San Mateo County Cultural Ctr., 1976, 82, Tahir Galleries, New Orleans, 1977, 82, Kerwin Galleries, Burlingame, Calif., 1977, Edits. Gallery, Melbourne, Australia, 1977, Ankrum Gallery, Los Angeles, 1978, 84, Edits. Ltd. West Gallery, San Francisco, 1981, Miriam Perlman Gallery, Chgo., 1982, San Mateo County Arts Council Gallery, 1982, Candy Stick Gallery, Ferndale, Calif., 1984, Assoc. Am. Artists, N.Y.C. and Phila., 1984, Gallery 30, Burlingame, 1991, San Mateo, 1984, Triton Mus. Art, Santa Clara, Calif., 1986, Huntsville (Ala.) Mus. Art, 1987, Gallery 30, San Mateo, 1988-91, Concept Art Gallery, Pitts., 1991; exhibited in groups shows at Berkeley Art Ctr., Calif., 1976, Burlingame Civic Art Gallery, 1976, Syntex Gallery, Palo Alto, Calif., 1977, Gump's Gallery, San Francisco, 1976, 77, Nat. Gallery of Australia, 1978, Sonoma County Gallery, 1979, Gov. Dummer Acad. Art, Byfield, Mass., 1979, Miss. Mus. Art, 1982, C.A.A. Galleries, Chautauqua, N.Y., 1982, Huntsville Mus. Art, 1983, Tahir Gallery, New Orleans, 1983, Hunterdon Art Ctr., N.J., 1984, Editions Galleries, Melbourne, Australia, 1988, Van Straaten Gallery, Chgo., 1988, 6th Internat. Exhbn., Carnegie-Mellon U., Pa., 1988, Forum Gallery, Jamestown, N.Y., 1988, 5th Internat. Biennale Petite Format de Papier, Belgium, 1989, 4th Internat. Biennial Print Exhibit, Taipei Fine Arts Mus., People's Republic China, 1990, Interprint, Lviv '90, USSR, 1990, New Orleans Mus. Art, 1990, Internat. Print Triennale, Cracow, Poland, 1991, 15th Ann. Nat. Invitational Drawing Exhbn. Emporia State U., Kans., 1991, Haggar U. Gallery, U. Dallas, 1991, Directions in Bay Area Printmaking: Three Decades Palo Alto Cultural Ctr., 1992, Am. Prints: Last Half 20th Century, Jane Haslem Gallery, Washington, 1992, Wenniger Graphics, Boston, 1993; represented in permanent collections San Francisco Mus. Modern Art, Achenbach Found. Graphic Arts, San Francisco, Phila. Mus. Art, New Orleans Mus. Art, Portland Mus. Art, Maine, The Library of Congress, Washington. Huntsville Mus. Art, Midwest Mus. Am. Art, Ind., Cracow Nat. Mus., Poland, Cabo Frio Mus., Brazil, Nat. Mus. Am. Art, Smithsonian Inst., Washington. Recipient Kempshall Clark award Peoria Art Guild, 1981, Paul Lindsay Sample Meml. award 25th Chautauqua Nat. Exhbn. of Am. Art, 1982, 1st Ann. Creative Achievement award Calif. State Legislature/Arts Coun. San Mateo County, 1989. Mem. Am. Color Print Soc., Audubon Artists (Louis Lozowick Meml. award 1978, Silver medal of honor award 1991), Boston Printmakers (Ture Bengtz Meml. award 1987), Calif. Soc. Printmakers (mem. council 1979-81), Los Angeles Printmaking Soc., Phila. Print Club (Lessing J. Rosenwald prize 1979), Arts Council of San Mateo Count, Theta Chi. Democrat. Home: PO Box 3305 Sonora CA 95370-3305 Office: Coll San Mateo 1700 W Hillside Blvd San Mateo CA 94402

PRICE, JOSEPH EARL, physics educator; b. Denver, Sept. 23, 1930; s. Joseph Elias and Gladys May (Hagar) P.; m. Nola Ann Iverson, Aug. 10, 1963; children: Rodney Jay, Andrea Jo. BA, Colo. Coll., 1952; MA, Rice U., 1954, PhD, 1956. Asst. prof. Lamar U., Beaumont, Tex., 1956-59; from asst. prof. to prof. Idaho State U., Pocatello, 1959-92, prof. emeritus, 1992—; engr. Westinghouse Rsch. Lab., Pitts., 1956, Phillips Petroleum Co., Idaho Falls, Idaho, 1963; Assn. Western Univ. fellow Idaho Nat. Engring. Lab., Idaho Falls, 1970, 76, 78. Contbr. articles to profl. jours. Mem. various coms. United Meth. Ch., Pocatello, Idaho, 1964—; trustee Bannock County Hist. Soc., 1992—. Recipient Atomic Energy Commn. grant, Idaho State U., Pocatello, 1965, NSF grant, Idaho State U., 1965, Faculty rsch. grant, Idaho State U., 1970, 74, 78. Mem. AAUP (treas. 1973-75), Am. Assn. Physics Tchrs. (Idaho-Utah sect. pres., v.p. 1985-87, program chmn.), Idaho Acad. Sci., Idaho Sci. Tchrs. Assn., AEC (edn. com. 1968-71), Phi Beta Kappa, Sigma Xi (v.p., pres. 1981-84). Home: 26 Davis Dr Pocatello ID 83201-3244

PRICE, KATHLEEN MCCORMICK, book editor; b. Topeka, Kans., Dec. 25, 1932; d. Raymond Chesley and Kathleen (Shoffner) McCormick; m. William Faulkner Black, Aug. 25, 1956 (div. 1961); 1 child, Kathleen Serena; m. William Hillard Price, Aug. 13, 1976. BA, U. Colo., Denver, 1971. Book reviewer Denver Post, 1971-78; book editor San Diego Mag., 1978-92; cons. editor St. John's Cathedral, Denver, 1985—. Author: There's a Dactyl Under My Foot, 1986. Historian, Altar Guild, St. John's Cathedral, Denver. Mem. PEN Internat., Denver Women's Press Club, Denver Country Club, La Garita Club, Phi Beta Kappa. Episcopalian. Home: 27 Crestmoor Dr Denver CO 80220-5853

PRICE, KEITH GLENN, accountant; b. Ft. Morgan, Colo., Nov. 24, 1941; s. George Felt and Irene Lois (Gibbs) P.; m. Norma Helen Witt, Feb. 28, 1970; children: Diana, Michael, Troy, Aaron, Christopher. BS, BA, Colo. State U., 1968. CPA. Auditor IRS, Casper, Wyo., 1968-75; ptnr. Hines, Price and Co., Cheyenne, Wyo., 1975-76, Fisher, Hines and Price, Cheyenne, Wyo., 1976-80; sole practice Cheyenne, Wyo., 1980—; co-founder, pres. High Plains Mortgage Co., 1990—; chmn. bd. dirs. Goodwill Industries of Wyo., 1980-87. Treas. North Christian Ch., 1986—, Salesman with a Purpose, 1980; mem. Heels, 1975—; founder Cheyenne Typing Svc. Served to sgt. USMCR, 1963-71. Mem. AICPA, Wyo. Soc. CPAs, Nat. Soc. Pub. Accts., Nat. Fedn. Ind. Bus., U.S. C. of C. Republican. Mem. Ind. Ch. of Christ. Home: 5333 Frederick Dr Cheyenne WY 82009-3335 Office: 721 E 16th St Cheyenne WY 82001-4772

PRICE, LAWRENCE CRAIG, auditor; b. Ontario, Oreg., June 9, 1953; s. Lawrence Doyn and Patty Patricia (Chard) P. BS in Math., Computer Sci., Acctg., Portland State U., 1984. Auditor U.S. Dept. of Def., Mountain View, Calif., 1986-90; auditor office inspector gen. U.S. Dept. of Justice, San Bruno, Calif., 1990—. Home: 655 S Fair Oaks K212 Sunnyvale CA 94086 Office: DOJ-OIG-Audit 1200 Bayhill Dr Ste 222 Sunnyvale CA 94066

PRICE, MARGARET RUTH, financial services company executive; b. Phoenix, Sept. 12, 1956; d. James John and Mavis Marie (Anderson) Knopp; m. Michael Reid Price, Sept. 15, 1979. BS in Instl. Food Svc. and Mgmt., Mont. State U., 1978. CFP. Dir. nutrition programs Human Resource Devel. Coun., Bozeman, Mont., 1979-82; investment cons. Shearson Lehman Bros., Anchorage, 1982-85; v.p., investment cons. Boettcher & Co.-Kemper Fin. Svcs., Anchorage, 1985-88; v.p., investment cons., fin. planner Kemper Securities, Inc.-Kemper Fin. Svcs., Anchorage, 1988—; nutrition cons., Bozeman, 1979-82; presenter radio talk show Sta. KENI, Anchorage, 1987. Bd. dirs. Alaska Bot. Garden, 1987—; mem. Anchorage Employee Retirement Income Security Act, 1987—, Anchorage Estate Planning Coun., 1991—. Mem. Amnesty Internat., Anchorage Nordic Ski Club. Home: 831 Harbor Cir Anchorage AK 99515-3641 Office: Kemper Securities Inc 550 W 7th Ave Ste 1980 Anchorage AK 99501-6606

PRICE, PATRICIA ANNE, artist; b. Tulsa, Feb. 4, 1950; d. Max Edward and Katharine (Jordan) P. BA, Oral Roberts U., 1974. Pvt. practice oil and gas lease broker Burleson County, Tex., 1978-84; rsch. and sale clk. The Kiva Indian Arts, Santa Fe, 1984-90; owner Singing Coyote-Southwestern crafts, 1992—. Exhibited in Romanian Libr., N.Y.C., 1975, Boston (Mass.) Coll., 1975, S.W. Tex. State, San Marcos, 1977, Ohio State U., Columbus, 1977. Recipient East European scholarship S.W. Tex. State U., San Marcos, 1977. Mem. C. of C. Santa Fe, Mex. (women's divsn. 1991—), The Cherokee Nation (tribal mem.). Home and Office: 142 Verano Loop Eldorado Santa Fe NM 87505

PRICE, PAUL BUFORD, physicist, educator; b. Memphis, Nov. 8, 1932; s. Paul Buford and Eva (Dupuy) P.; m. JoAnn Margaret Baum, June 28, 1958; children—Paul Buford III, Heather Alynn, Pamela Margaret, Alison Gaynor. BS summa cum laude, Davidson Coll., 1954, DSc, 1973; MS, U. Va., 1956, PhD, 1958. Fulbright scholar U. (Eng.) Bristol, 1958-59; NSF postdoctoral fellow Cambridge (Eng.) U., 1959-60; physicist R&D Ctr. GE, Schenectady, 1960-69; vis. prof. Tata Inst. Fundamental Rsch., Bombay, India, 1965-66; adj. prof. physics Rensselaer Poly. Inst., 1967-68; prof. physics U. Calif., Berkeley, 1969—, chmn. dept. physics, 1987-91, McAdams prof. physics, 1990-92, dean phys. scis., 1992—, dir. Space Scis. Lab., 1979-85; bd. dirs. Terradex Corp., Walnut Creek, Calif.; cons. to lunar sample analysis planning team NASA; mem. space sci. bd. Nat. Acad. Scis.; vis. prof. U. Rome, 1983; sci. assoc. Centre d'Etude Recherche Nucleaire, 1984; Miller rsch. prof. U. Calif., Berkeley, 1972-73; researcher in space and astrophysics, nuclear physics. Author: (with others) Nuclear Tracks in Solids; Contbr. (with others) articles to profl. jours. Recipient Disting. Svc. award Am. Nuclear Soc., 1964, Indsl. Rsch. awards, 1964, 65, E.O. Lawrence Meml. award AEC, 1971, medal for exceptional sci. achievement NASA, 1973; John Simon Guggenheim fellow, 1976-77. Fellow Am. Phys. Soc., Am. Geophys. Union; mem. Nat. Acad. Scis. (chmn. geophysics sect. 1981-84, sec. class phys.-math. scis. 1985-88, chmn. 1988-91).

PRICE, RICHARD TAFT, JR., manufacturing company executive; b. San Diego, June 7, 1954; s. Richard Taft and Murial Martha (Weinhold) T. Student, Brigham Young U., 1972-76; BS, Ariz. State U., 1978. Sales mgr. Imperial Metals, Los Angeles, 1978-83; pres. Alumatone, Inc., No. Hollywood, Calif., 1983-88; acquisitions mgr. Calif. Custom Shapes Inc., Los Angeles, 1988-90, pres., 1990—; bd. dirs. IMCOA, Inc., Los Angeles, 1988—, Vulcan Metal Products, Inc., Birmingham, Ala., 1990—. Republican. Office: Calif. Custom Shapes Inc 1800 Talbot Way Anaheim CA 92805

PRICE, ROBERT CONRAD, II, museum director; b. Landstuhl, Ger., June 19, 1958; s. Robert Conrad and Billie Lou (Brummell) P.; m. Carolee McHolland, Oct. 6, 1984; children: Cory, Matthew, Emily. BS in Bus., Ariz. State U., 1981. Retail mgr. Assoc. Distbrs., Phoenix, 1979-81; asst. editor Valley Life Rev., Fresno, Calif., 1981-82; head writer Ariz. State Fair, Phoenix, 1983; mus. publicist Mesa (Ariz.) S.W. Mus., 1982-84, mus. shop mgr., 1982-84, curator pub. progs., 1984-92, asst. dir., 1993—; lectr. in field. Author: Mesa: Beneath the Shadow of the Superstitions, 1988; author newspaper col., New Times, 1983. Recording sec. Arts in Mesa, 1985-86; treas. Friends of Mesa Youtheatre, 1989—. Mem. Mus. Assn. Ariz. (mem. conf. planning com. 1989). Democrat. Office: Mesa Southwest Mus 53 N Macdonald St Mesa AZ 85201-7325

PRICE, ROBERT E., manufacturing company executive; b. 1942. BA, Pomona Coll., 1964. V.p. Fed-Mart Corp., 1964-75; pres., chief exec. officer Price Corp., San Diego, 1976-89, pres., chmn. bd., chief exec. officer, 1989-91, chmn. bd., chief exec. officer, 1991—, also bd. dirs. Office: Price Co PO Box 85466 San Diego CA 92186-5466*

PRICE, ROY CANTRELL, minister; b. L.A., May 23, 1935; s. Walter and Wilma Harlan (Nance) P.; m. Sandra Lee Burns, Aug. 27, 1957; children: Steven R., Cynthia Price Long. BA, Westmont Coll., 1957; ThM, Luther Rice Sem., Lithonia, Ga., 1977; D Ministry, Luther Rice Sem., Jacksonville, Fla., 1978; DPhil, Oxford Grad. Sch., Dayton, Tenn., 1988. Ordained to ministry Christian and Missionary Alliance, 1962. Youth pastor Grace Ch., Santa Barbara, 1957-58; pastor Valley Neighborhood Ch., San Jose, 1958-60, Williams Community Ch., Williams, Oreg., 1960-63; assoc. pastor Portland Alliance Ch., 1963-64; pastor Arbor Hts. Alliance Ch., Seattle, 1964-68; asst. pastor Allegheny Ctr. Alliance Ch., Pitts., 1968-71; sr. pastor Christian and Missionary Alliance, Wadsworth, Ohio, 1971-75; pastor Internat. Protestant Ch., Saigon, Vietnam, 1975; sr. pastor First Alliance Ch., Louisville, 1975-81, Paradise (Calif.) Alliance Ch., 1981-91, Monte Vista Chapel, Calif., 1992—; bd. mgrs. Christian and Missionary Alliance, Colorado Springs, 1985-91, mem. dist. exec. com., Oakland, Calif., 1982-86; guest lectr. Pippert Alliance Theol. Sem., 1984; adj. lectr. Pastoral Theology and Ch. Polity, 1988. Contbr. articles to profl. jours. Trustee Feather River Health Found., Paradise, 1986-91; mem. Community Drug Abuse Task Force, Paradise, 1987; bd. dirs., trombonist Paradise Symphony Orch.; bd. regents Oxford Grad. Sch. Mem. Internat. Soc. for Systems Scis., Nat. Assn. Evangelicals, Ministerial Assn. of Paradise (pres. 1987), Paradise C. of C., Lions (1st v.p. 1974-75), Rotary. Republican. Home: 1680 N Quincy Rd Turlock CA 95380 Office: Monte Vista Chapel PO Box 1001 Turlock CA 95381

PRICE, THOMAS FREDERICK, theatre educator; b. Salt Lake City, June 19, 1937; s. Thomas William P. and Caryl Susan (Brown) Wood; children: Devin, Jennifer. BA in Drama, Pomona Coll., 1960; MA in Theatre, San Francisco State U., 1962; PhD in Drama, Stanford U., 1968. Asst. prof. English U. of the Pacific, Stockton, Calif., 1968-70; asst. prof. drama U.S. Internat. U., Sch. Performing Arts, San Diego, 1970-74; archivist, curator The Philibrick Libr., Los Altos Hills, Calif., 1975-85; prof. English Tianjin (China) Normal U., 1985-87; adj. prof. theatre So. Oreg. State Coll., Ashland, 1991—; assoc. prof. English Tanmkang U., Taipei, Taiwan, 1993—; ednl. broadcaster KPFA-FM, L.A., 1960-62, KSRO-FM, Ashland, Oreg. Author: Dramatic Structure and Meaning, 1992; contbr. articles to profl. jours. Mem. Calif. Scholarship Fedn. (hon. life), Assn. for Theatre in Higher Edn., Nat. Trust for Historic Preservation. Home: 345 Ravenwood Pl Ashland OR 97520

PRICE, THOMAS MUNRO, computer consultant; b. Madison, Wis., Oct. 2, 1937; s. John Edward and Georgia Winifred (Day) P.; m. Judith Ann Holm, Aug. 8, 1959; children: Scott Michael, Andrea Lynn. BS, Carroll Coll., Waukesha, Wis., 1959; MS, U. Wis., 1961, PhD, 1964. Prof. math. U. Iowa, 1964-77, U. Wyo., Laramie, 1978-79; computer user cons. U. Wyo., 1979-85, MIS prof., 1985-89; computer cons. Laramie, 1989—. Contbr. articles to profl. jours. Home: 1315 E Park Ave Laramie WY 82070-4145 Office: Computer Support 1315 E Park Ave Laramie WY 82070-4145

PRICE, WARREN, III, state official; b. Washington, June 19, 1943; s. Warren II and Frances (Davis) P.; m. Johna Kanoho, Mar. 21, 1967 (div. Mar. 1987); children: Warren Price IV, Brandon Phillip Price. BA in Econs., U. N.C., 1965; JD, U. Calif., San Francisco, 1972. Ptnr. Goodsill, Anderson, Quinn and Stifel, Honolulu, 1972-87; atty. gen. State of Hawaii, Honolulu, 1987—; mem. Jud. Selection Commn., Honolulu, 1985-87. Served to lt. USNR, 1965-69. Mem. Nat. Inst. of Trial Advocacy (faculty 1984-87), Pacific Law Inst. (bd. dirs., faculty 1985—), Order of the Coif, Am. Inns of Ct. Democrat. Episcopalian. Office: Atty Gen's Office 415 S Beretania St Rm 405 Honolulu HI 96813-2407

PRICE, WESTCOTT WILKIN, III, health care executive; b. Glendale, Calif., May 6, 1939; s. Westcott Wilkin Jr. and Edna Johnson (Lange) P.; m. Hillary Clark Haney, Apr. 12, 1941; children: Christopher, Gretchen, Wendy. BS in Bus., U. Colo., 1961; MBA, U. So. Calif., 1967. V.p., chief operating officer Calif. Med. Ctrs., Los Angeles, 1970-73; pres., chief exec. officer Wm. Flaggs Inc., Commerce, Calif., 1973-80; pres., vice chmn. FHP Inc., Fountain Valley, Calif., 1981—. Bd. dirs. FHP Found., Long Beach, Calif., 1985—; bd. govs. U. So. Calif. Sch. Pub. Adminstrn., Los Angeles, 1987—. Served to lt. (j.g.) USN, 1961-63. Republican. Episcopalian. Club: Calif. (Los Angeles). Office: FHP Internat Corp 9900 Talbert Ave Fountain Valley CA 92708-5153

PRICER, JAMIE LEE, magazine editor; b. Pomona, Calif., Oct. 22, 1948; d. James Mevin Parker and Delcie Erma (Hobson) Vuncannon; m. Leslie Stuart Pricer, June 18, 1988; children: Adam, Blake, Morgan. AA in Social Scis., Col. of Desert, Palm Springs, Calif., 1978; BS in Bus. Adminstrn., Bloomsburg U., 1987. Writer Hi-Desert Pub. Co., 29 Palms, Calif., 1974-77; asst. editor Hi-Desert Pub. Co., Yucca Valley, Calif., 1977-78; copy editor Lubbock (Tex.) Evening Jour., 1981-83; copy editor, writer Press-Enterprise, Bloomsburg, Pa., 1983-87; writer, editor Underwater USA, Bloomsburg, 1984-87; copy editor, writer N.E. Pa. Bus. Jour., Bloomsburg, 1985-87; exec. editor Post Newspapers, Palm Desert, Calif., 1987-89; editor Palm Springs (Calif.) Life Mag., 1989—; pub. speaker numerous civic orgns., Palm Springs, 1989—; workshop leader ednl. insts., So. Calif., 1989—. Editor: History of Indian Wells, 1990. Mem. San Bernardino County Econ. Devel. Commn., San Bernardino, Calif., 1979-80. Named Best Feature section Calif. Newspaper Publishers Assn., Sacramento, 1975; Maggie finalist We. Publishers Assn., Sherman Oaks, Calif., 1990, 91. Office: Palm Springs Life 303 N Indian Canyon Palm Springs CA 92263

PRICKETT, DAVID CLINTON, physician; b. Fairmont, W.Va., Nov. 26, 1918; s. Clinton Evert and Mary Anna (Gottschalk) P.; m. Mary Ellen Holt, June 29, 1940; children: David C., Rebecca Ellen, William Radcliffe, Mary Anne, James Thomas, Sara Elizabeth; m. Pamela S. Blackstone, Nov. 17, 1991. AB, W.Va. U., 1944; MD, U. Louisville, 1946; MPH, U. Pitts., 1955. Lab. asst., instr. in chemistry, W.Va. U., 1943; intern, Louisville Gen. Hosp., 1947; surg. resident St. Joseph's Hosp., Parkersburg, W.Va., 1948-49; gen. practice, 1949-50, 55-61; physician USAF, N.Mex., 1961-62, U.S. Army, Calif., 1963-64, San Luis Obispo County Hosp., 1965-66, So. Calif. Edison Co., 1981-84; assoc. physician indsl. and gen. practice Los Angeles County, Calif., 1967—; med. dir. S. Gate plant GM, 1969-71; physician staff City of L.A., 1971-76; relief med. practice Applachia summer seasons, 1977, 1986, 1988-92. Med. Officer USPHS, Navajo Indian Reservation, Tohatchi (N.Mex.) Health Ctr., 1953-55, surgeon, res. officer, 1957-59; pres. W.Va. Pub. Health Assn., 1951-52, health officer, 1951-53, sec. indsl. and pub. health sect. W.Va. Med. Assn., 1956. Author: The Newer Epidemiology, 1962, rev., 1990, Public Health, A Science Resolvable by Mathematics, 1965. Served to 2d lt. AUS, 1943-46. Dr. Thomas Parran fellow U. Pitts. Sch. Pub. Health, 1955; named to Hon. Order Ky. Cols. Mem. Am. Occupational Med. Assn., Western Occupational Med. Assn., Am. Med. Assn., Calif. Med. Assn., L.A. County Med. Assn., Am. Acad. Family Physicians, Phi Chi. Address: PO Box 4032 Whittier CA 90607

PRIDHAM, THOMAS GRENVILLE, research microbiologist; b. Chgo., Oct. 10, 1920; s. Grenville and Gladys Etheral (Sloss) P.; m. Phyllis Sue Hokamp, July 1, 1943; children: Pamela Sue, Thomas Foster, Grenville Thomas, Rolf Thomas, Montgomery Thomas. BS in Chemistry, U. Ill., 1943, PhD in Bacteriology, 1949. Instr. bacteriology U. Ill., Champaign-Urbana, 1947; rsch. microbiologist No. Regional Rsch. Lab., USDA, Peoria, Ill., 1948-51, 53-65, U.S. Indsl. Chems., Balt., 1951-52; supr. tech. ops. Acme Vitamins, Inc., Joliet, Ill., 1952-53; sr. rsch. biologist U.S. Borax Rsch. Corp., Anaheim, Calif., 1965-67; supervisory rsch. microbiologist No. Regional Rsch. Ctr., No. Regional Rsch. Ctr., USDA, Peoria, 1967-81; head agrl. rsch. culture collection No. Regional Rsch. Lab. USDA, Peoria, 1967-81; ret., 1981; cons. Mycogen Corp., San Diego, 1985-87; U.S. sr. scientist Fed. Republic Germany, Darmstadt, 1977. Contbg. author: Actinomycetales: The Boundary Microorganisms, 1974, Bergey's Manual of Determinative Bacteriology, 1974, Synopsis and Classification of Living Organisms, 1982; mem. editorial bd. Jour. Antibiotics, 1969-81; contbr. articles to Jour. Bacteriology, Applied Microbiology, Phytopathology, Actinomycetes, Mycologia, Devel. Indsl. Microbiology, Jour. Antibiotics, Internat. Bull. Bacteriological Nomenclature Taxonomy, Antibiotics Ann., Antimicrobial Agts., Chemotherapy, also others. With USNR, 1943-45, with Rsch. Res., 1945-54, lt. ret. Fulbright scholar, Italy, 1952; grantee Soc. Am. Bacteriologists, 1957. Fellow Am. Acad. Microbiology (ASM state network 1991—); mem. Am. Soc. Microbiology (com. mem., workshop presenter), Soc. Indsl. Microbiology, Mycol. Soc. Am., U.S. Fedn. Culture Collections (v.p. 1981). Episcopalian. Home: 980 Looking Glass Ln Las Vegas NV 89110-2711

PRIMACK, MARVIN HERBERT, anesthesiologist; b. Detroit, Mar. 20, 1931; s. Abraham and Florence (Zeman) P.; m. Bune Fay Rothbart, Sept. 4, 1955; children: Todd, Teri, Daren, Heidi. BS, Wayne State U., 1953; MD, U. Mich., 1957. Diplomate Am. Bd. Anesthesiology. Intern Sinai Hosp., Detroit, 1957-58; resident Harper Hosp., Detroit, 1958-60; ptnr. Associated Anesthesiologists Detroit, 1960-66; v.p., chief exec. officer Stockton Anesthesia Med. Group Inc., Stockton, Calif., 1966-79; pres. Marvin H. Primack M.D. Inc., Stockton, 1979-88; chief of staff St. Joseph's Med. Ctr., Stockton, 1975-76; v.p., chief exec. officer Stockton Anesthesia Med. Group Inc., 1989—. Bd. trustees Found. for Med. Care San Joaquin, Stockton, 1970-85, chmn. bd. trustees, 1980-83. Fellow Am. Coll. Anesthesiologists; mem. AMA, Am. Soc. Anesthesiologists, Calif. Soc. Anesthesiologists, Calif. Med. Soc., San Joaquin Med. Soc. Office: Stockton Anesthesia Med Group Inc 2626 N California St Ste G Stockton CA 95204-5527

PRINCE, ALEXINE, business owner, educator; b. Chico, Calif., Jan. 9, 1938; d. Peter and Bernice (Abel) Cazassa; m. Ralph H. Prince, Mar. 17, 1963 (div. 1983); children: Renee Kathleen, Timothy Peter. BA, Occidental Coll., 1957; MA, U. Calif., Berkeley, 1959; JD, Western State Coll. of Law, Fullerton, 1987. High sch. tchr. English Grossmont Dist., San Diego, 1959-61, Santa Ana (Calif.) Dist., 1961-63, Big Bear Lake (Calif.) Dist., 1963-65, San Bernardino (Calif.) Dist., 1965-67. Elder First Presbyn. Ch., San Bernardino, 1970-92; mem. Nat. Assistance League, San Bernardino, 1973-92, Nat. Charity League, San Bernardino, 1978-83. Office: Singles Connection PO Box 3737 San Bernardino CA 92413

PRINCE, JAMES W. (BILL), psychiatrist; b. Atlanta, May 3, 1953; s. Harold Bailey Sr. and Sarah Evelyn (Houck) P.; m. G.R. Sharpe, Nov. 18, 1991. BA in Psychology, Yale U., 1977; MD, Emory U., 1981. Diplomate Am. Bd. Psychiatry and Neurology. Resident in psychiatry U. Wash., Seattle, 1981-85; psychiatrist Roanoke-Chowan Human Svcs. Ctr., Ahoskie, N.C., 1985-88, Good Samaritan Mental Health Ctr., Puyallup, Wash., 1988—; psychiatrist Highline-West Seattle Mental Health Ctr., Seattle, 1989—, lead psychiatrist, 1991—. Recipient Svc. award Nat. Health Svc. Corps, 1987. Mem. NAACP, ACLU, So. Poverty Law Ctr., United Negro Coll. Fund, Am. Psychiat. Assn. Office: Highline-West Seattle Mental Health Ctr PO Box 69080 Seattle WA 98168

PRINCE, KATHLEEN CORINNE, cartoonist; b. Ann Arbor, Mich., Apr. 18, 1948; d. Richard Prince and Alice Kathryn Feasal; m. Alex Frank Blendl, June 27, 1973. Student, U. Mich., 1966-67. Circulation asst. Oreg. Mag., Portland, 1979-81, events editor, 1981-88; free lance writer, cartoonist Oreg., 1988—. Author: pub. short stories, humor pieces, non-fiction articles, cartoons, editorial cartoons. Home: 1055 Westward Ho Rd Lake Oswego OR 97034-2837

PRINCE, PATRICIA, lawyer; b. Redwood City, Calif., May 16, 1959; d. Frederick Seaton Jr. and Anne (Armstrong) P. BA, Stanford U., 1981; JD, U. San Francisco, 1991. Bar: Calif. 1991; U.S. Dist. Ct. (no. dist.) Calif., 1991; U.S. Ct. Appeals (9th cir.), 1992. Dir. sales and mktg. Stein Eriksen Lodge, Park City, Utah, 1982-84; v.p. mktg. Tower Mgmt. Co., Park City, 1984-86; cons. Laventhol & Horwath, San Francisco, 1986-87; mktg. mgr. Innkeeper Assocs., San Francisco, 1987; assoc. Feldman, Waldman & Kline, San Francisco, 1991-93, Cohen, Nelson & Makoff, Triburon, San Francisco, 1993—; summer assoc. Bartko, Welsh, Tarrant & Miller, San Francisco, 1990. Mem. U. San Fransisco Students for Choice, 1989-91, Queen's Bench and reproductive rights com., San Francisco, 1992—. Recipient Am. Jurisprudence award Lawyers Coop. Pub. Co. and Bancroft-Whitney Co., 1988. Mem. State Bar of Calif., Bar Assn. San Francisco, Marin County Women Lawyers. Democrat. Home: 1410 Vistazo W # 2 Tiburon CA 94920 Office: Cohen Nelson & Macoff 1660 Tiburon Blvd Ste G Tiburon CA 94920

PRINCIPE, HELEN M., medical case manager; b. Santa Monica, Calif., May 18, 1953; d. William John and Bessie Sylvia (Amsden) McGonagle; 1 child, Francis Edward. AS, Northeastern U., 1978; BSN cum laude, Worcester (Mass.) State Coll., 1981. RN, Mass., Calif. Critical care nurse Mt. Auburn Hosp., Cambridge, Mass.; adminstrv. nurse, critical care nurse, instr. Alta Bates Hosp., Berkeley, Calif.; clin. instr. med.-surg. devel., critical care nurse Valley Hosp., Las Vegas, Nev.; med. case mgr., supr. Intracorp, Oakland, Calif.; spl. case cons. Lincoln Nat., Pleasanton, Calif.; with Conservco, Walnut Creek, Calif., PruCare of No. Calif., San Mateo, Calif. Mem. AAUW, Rehab. Ins. Nurses Group, Case Mgmt. Soc. Am. (founding pres. No. Calif. chpt., nat. bd. dirs.), Individual Case Mgmt. Assn.

PRINDLE, ROBERT WILLIAM, geotechnical engineer; b. L.A., Nov. 19, 1950; s. Robert Edward and Margaret Elizabeth (Johnson) P.; m. Nancy K. Hayden, Apr. 5, 1986; children: William Robert, Amy Elizabeth. Student St. John's Coll., Camarillo, Calif., 1968-70; BSCE summa cum laude, Loyola U., L.A., 1974; MS, Calif. Inst. Tech., 1975; 40-hours hazardous waste ops. and emergency response tng.; 8-hours hazardous waste ops. supr./mgr. tng. Lic. geotechnical engr., Calif.; registered profl. civil engr., Calif., Colo., N. Mex. Engring. aide L.A. County Sanitation Dists., 1973-74; student engr. L.A. Dept. Water and Power, 1974, 75; staff engr. Fugro, Inc., Long Beach, Calif., 1976-78; sr. staff engr. Woodward-Clyde Consultants, Orange, Calif., 1978-79; mem. tech. staff Sandia Nat. Labs., Albuquerque, 1980-89; v.p. engring. Deuel & Assocs, Inc., Albuquerque, 1989-90, pres., 1990—; pres. Prindle-Hinds Environ., Inc., 1990—. Contbr. articles to profl. jours. Mem. N. Mex. Symphony Orch. Chorus, 1981-84. Calif. State Grad. fellow, 1974-75, Calif. Inst. Tech. Inst. fellow, 1974-75. Mem. ASCE, NSPE, Internat. Soc. for Soil Mechanics and Found. Engring., N.Mex. Hazardous Waste Mgmt. Soc., Tau Beta Pi. Republican. Roman Catholic. Office: Prindle-Hinds Environ Inc 7208 Jefferson St NE Albuquerque NM 87109-4309

PRINGLE, BRUCE D., judge; b. Denver, June 17, 1944; s. Edward E. and Pauline (Judd) P.; children: Jeffrey, Jennifer; m. Gail G. Pringle, Jan. 5, 1992. Student, Northwestern U., 1962-63; BA, U. Colo., 1966, JD, 1969. Bar: U.S. Ct. Appeals (10th cir.), Colo. Supreme Ct. Law clk. to Hon. William Doyle U.S. Dist. Ct. (Colo. dist.), Denver, 1969-70; assoc. Winner, Berge, Martin & Clark, Denver, 1970-75; ptnr. Clark, Martin & Pringle, Denver, 1975-81, Baker & Hostetler, Denver, 1981-91; U.S. Magistrate judge U.S. Dist. Ct., Denver, 1991—; instr. law, lectr. U. Denver Law Sch., Fed. Bar Assn., Aurora C.C., Met. State Coll., Aurora C.C. Author of treatise Colo. Law Annotated (7 vols.), 1984-88, (2 vols.), 91. Mem. com. conduct of U.S. Dist. Ct., 1981-84; mem. Colo. Supreme Ct. com. on Colo. Rules of Civil Procedure; former mem. Litigation Subcom. for Freedom of Info. Coun. Mem. Am. Judicature Soc., U.S. Magistrates Assn., Colo. Bar Assn., Aurora Bar Assn., Order of Coif. Office: US Dist Ct C-160 1929 Stout St Denver CO 80294

PRINGLE, ROBERTA FRANCES, social worker; b. Cheyenne, Wyo., Dec. 17, 1944; d. Stanley J. and Clementena J. (Paul) Sheldon; m. John B. Vallejos, Apr. 1, 1987 (div.); children: Juanita M., John B.; m. Robert C. Pringle, Apr. 23, 1991. BSEd, Chadron State Coll., 1966; BA in Social Work, Colo. State U., 1981, MSW, 1986. From caseworker to gen. social svc. supr. III Huerfano County Dept. Social Svc., Walsenburg, Colo., 1966-93; social worker Caring Unltd.-Hospice, Human Svc. Coun., LaVeta, Colo., 1993—; developer, cons. Domestic Violence Elimination Program, Walsenburg, 1985-89; chmn. Human Svc. Coun., Walsenburg, 1984—. Contbr. articles to profl. pubs. Chmn. sr. svcs. adv. coun. AAA, 1989—. Mem. Nat. Assn. Social Workers (area rep. 1987—), Am. Pub. Welfare Assn., NAFE. Home: Box 10 La Veta CO 81055 Office: Caring Unltd La Veta CO 81055

PRINJA, ANIL KANT, nuclear engineering educator; b. Mombasa, Kenya, Apr. 9, 1955; came to U.S., 1980; s. Kapil Dev and Kushal (Dharney) P.; m. Renu Mohan, Sept. 18, 1983; children: Vivek Kapil, Akash Prinja. BSc in Nuclear Engring. with 1st class honors, London U., 1976, PhD in Nuclear Engring., 1980. Asst. rsch. engr. UCLA, 1980-87; asst. prof. nuclear engring. U. N.Mex., Albuquerque, 1987-89, assoc. prof., 1989—; chmn., host Internat. Conf. Transport Theory, 1991, U.S. Edge Plasma Physics: Theory and Applications Workshop, 1993; cons. Sandia Nat. Labs., Albuquerque, 1987—, Sci. Applications Internat., Inc., Albuquerque, 1987—. Contbr. chpts. to books and articles to profl. jours. Recipient Outstanding Acad. Achievement award Brit. Nuclear Energy Soc., 1976; grantee Dept. of Energy, Sandia Nat. Lab., Los Alamos Nat. Lab., Culham Labs., U.K., KFA Julich, Germany, 1989—, others. Mem. Am. Phys. Soc., Am. Nuclear Soc., Materials Rsch. Soc., Brit. Nuclear Energy Soc., N.Y. Acad. Sci. Hindu. Office: U New Mex 209 Farris Engring Ctr Albuquerque NM 87131

PRIOR, DAVID JAMES, college dean; b. Anniston, Ala., Dec. 13, 1943; m. Merry Lucille; children: Andrea Suzanne, Christopher Sutton. AB, Olivet (Mich.) Coll., 1965; MS, Ctrl. Mich. U., 1968; PhD, U. Va., 1972. Postdoctoral fellow-neurobiology Princeton (N.J.) U., 1972-73; asst. prof. biolg. scis. U. Ky., Lexington, 1973-78, prof. biology, 1985-87, assoc. prof. physiology and biophysics, 1984-87, prof. physiology and biophysics Coll. Medicine, 1987; prof., chair biology No. Ariz. U., Flagstaff, 1987-92, dean Coll. Arts and Scis., 1992—. Office: No Ariz U Coll Arts and Scis PO Box 5621 Flagstaff AZ 86011

PRIOR, LINDA GAY, legal assistant, educator; b. L.A., Nov. 24, 1942; d. Edward Langdon Haar and Martha Jayne (Horsley) Cuzner; m. Thomas E. Prior, June 7, 1980 (div. June 1984); children: Lorrie May White, Lisa Lee Fuller, Terri Lynn Preston. Student, Pima Coll., 1979-81. Cert. jr. coll. level tchr., Ariz.; cert. profl. legal sec. Exec. sec., adminstrv. asst. Davis Constructors & Engrs., Albany, Ga., 1968; legal sec. Haas, Holland, Freeman, Levison & Gibert, Atlanta, 1969-71, Steinberg, Levkoff, Spitz & Goldberg, Charleston, S.C., 1971-73; exec. sec., adminstrv. asst. WCBD-TV ABC Affiliate Sta., Charleston, 1973; legal asst., office mgr. Uricchio, Groose & Paul, Charleston, 1974-79; trial asst. Molloy, Jones, Donahue, Tucson, 1979-82; freelance paralegal Geri Land Assocs., Tucson, 1982-83; legal asst. Karp, Stolkin & Weiss, PC, Tucson, 1983—; sole proprietor Sunshine Daisy Ltd., Tucson, 1991—; mem. adv. bd. legal asst. program Pima C.C., 1981—, assoc. faculty, instr., 1981—; rsch. dir. Broadcast Intelligence, Tucson, 1984-86; mem. Pres.'s Club, U. Ariz., 1992; lectr. in field. dir. leadership devel. Christian Chs. of S.C., 1977-79; supr., counselor Hotline Crisis Intervention, Charleston, 1978-79; 1st vice-chmn. Broadway Christian Ch. Bd. Dirs., Tucson, 1981-83. Recipient 2d Pl. trophy Tucson (Ariz.) City Pool League, 1989, Silver and Bronze medals Perimeter Bicycle Assn., 1990, 92, Club Champion award Am. Contract Bridge Assn., 1992. Mem. Nat. Assn. Legal Assts. (cert. litigation specialist, cert. legal asst., certifying bd. 1984-88, regional dir. bd. dirs. 1984-86), Tucson Assn. Legal Assts. (founder, pres. 1980-83), Greater Ariz. Bicycle Assn., Flecha Caida Homeowners' Assn. (sec.), Pima County Bar Assn. (social devel. com.). Republican. Home: 4830 E Calle Chueca Tucson AZ 85718 Office: Karp & Weiss PC 33 N Stone Ave Ste 1800 Tucson AZ 85701

PRISBREY, REX PRINCE, insurance agent, underwriter, financial consultant; b. Washington, Utah, Mar. 18, 1922; s. Hyrum William and Susanne (Prince) P.; m. Pinka Julieta Lucero, Nov. 16, 1943; children: Karol Sue Prisbrey Lewallen, Pamela Blanche Prisbrey Ebert, Michael Rex. BA in Acctg., Denver U., 1949. CLU. Ptnr. Allen Stamm & Assocs., home builders, Farmington, N.Mex., 1949-52; acct. Linder Burke & Stevenson, Santa Fe, N.Mex., 1949-52; agt. State Farm Ins. Cos., Farmington, 1952-56; mgr. State Farm Ins. Cos., Phoenix, 1956-60; contractor, agt. State Farm Ins. Cos., Scottsdale, Ariz., 1960—; v.p., treas. Original Curio Store Inc., Santa Fe. Pres. Farmington Jr. C. of C., 1952; v.p. N.Mex. Jr. C. of C., 1953. 1st lt. USAAF, 1942-46, CBI. Decorated DFC, Air medal with oak leaf cluster; recipient Disting. Life Underwriter award Cen. Ariz. Mgrs. Assn., 1979. Mem. Am. Soc. CLU's, Scottsdale Assn. Life Underwriters (pres. 1980-81), Airplane Owners and Pilots Assn., Hump Pilots Assn. (life, speaker at meml. of Hump Flyers, Kunming, China 1993), Pinewood Country Club (bd. dirs., treas., v.p. 1985—), Civitans (pres. Scottsdale 1962-63). Home: 4011 N 65th St Scottsdale AZ 85251 Office: State Farm Ins Cos 6730 E McDowell Rd Scottsdale AZ 85257

PRITCHARD, ARTHUR OSBORN, retired business administrator; b. Scarsdale, N.Y., Oct. 7, 1910; m. Dorothy E. White (dec.); m. Virginia R. Cunningham (div.). AB, Pomona Coll., 1932; MA in Internat. Rels., Columbia U., 1934. With Dept. Agr. and Gen. Acctg. Office U.S. Govt., Washington, 1934-36, Berkeley, Calif., 1936-41; staff sgt., Army Med. Corp. U.S. Army, 1941-45; pub. acctg. pvt. practice, 1945; acct. and office mgr. Talbot Bird & Co., SF, 1946-60; treas. and bus. mgr. No. Calif. Conf. of United Ch. of Christ, 1960-76; ret., 1976; participant UN Film Study Guide project, 1991-93. Mem. Outlook Club of Calif. 1948—, sec., 1967-93; bd. dirs, Berkeley City Club, 1977-83, pres., 1978-82; instr. of adult edn. Berkeley YMCA; pres. 1989 program, City Commons Club of Berkeley; program dir., 1991-93; active mem. First Congl. Ch. of Berkeley, 1938—; life mem. Commonwealth Club, 1939—. Decorated Bronze Star; Team Facilitator grantee U.S. Inst. of Peace, Washington, 1991-93. Mem. Am. Assn. for the UN, UN Assn. of the U.S. of Am. (pres. Alameda County chpt., 1956-59, No. Calif. Divsn. of UNA-USA, 1959-65, received citation), World Affairs Coun. of No. Calif. (charter mem. 1947). Home: 989 Tulare Ave Berkeley CA 94707

PRITCHARD, JOEL, state lieutenant governor; b. Seattle, May 5, 1925; m. Damaris Pritchard; children: Peggy, Frank, Anne, Jeanie. Student, Marietta Coll.; PhD (Hon.), Seattle U. Pres. Griffin Envelope Co., Seattle; mem. Wash. Ho. of Reps., Olympia, 1958-66, Wash. State Senate, 1966-70, U.S. Ho. of Reps., Washington, 1972-84; dir. govt. rels. Bogle & Gates, 1985-88; lt. gov. State of Wash., Olympia, 1989—; mem. Merchant Marine and Fisheries Com. U.S. Ho. of Reps., subcom. on Asia and the Pacific Fgn. Rels. Com., Panama Canal Consultative Commn., 1987-88; U.S. del. to UN Gen. Assembly, 1983. With U.S. Army, PTO, WWII. Office: Lt Gov's Office PO Box 40400 304 Legislative Bldg Olympia WA 98504-0400

PRITCHETT, B(RUCE) MICHAEL, SR., economics educator, consultant; b. American Fork, Utah, Nov. 3, 1940; s. Melrose Jed and Lois (Watson) P.; m. Patricia Louise Sunderland, June 19, 1964; children: Bruce Michael Jr., Laura, Steven Louis. BS, Brigham Young U., 1965; MS, Purdue U., 1967, PhD, 1970. Bd. dirs. Pritchett Constrn. Co. Inc., Provo, Utah, 1954—; grad. instr. in econs. Purdue U., West Lafayette, Ind., 1967-68; asst. prof. econs. Brigham Young U., Provo, 1969-76, assoc. prof. econs., 1977-90, prof. managerial econs., 1990—; cons. in field. Author: A Study of Capital Mobilization..., 1977, Financing Growth..., 1985, Applications of the GB2 Distribution in Modeling Insurance Loss Processes, 1990. NDEA fellow Purdue U., 1966-68, Krannert fellow Purdue U., 1968-69. Mem. Am. Econ. Assn., Western Econ. Assn., Nat. Assn. Bus. Economists. Office: Brigham Young U 614 Tanner Bldg Provo UT 84602

PRITZ, MICHAEL BURTON, neurological surgeon; b. New Brunswick, N.J., Oct. 8, 1947; s. John Ernest and Helen Violet (Rockoff) P.; m. Edmay Marie Gregorcy, Feb. 18, 1973; children: Edmond Louis, Benjamin David. BS, U. Ill., 1969; PhD, Case Western Res. U., 1973, MD, 1975. Diplomate Am. Bd. Neurol. Surgery. Asst. prof. neurol. surgery U. Calif. Irvine Med. Ctr., Orange, 1981-85, assoc. prof., 1985—. Contbr. articles to profl. jours. Recipient Herbert S. Steuer award Case Western Res. U., Cleve., 1975; NSF fellow, 1968; Edmund J. James scholar U. Ill., Champaign, 1968-69. Mem. Soc. Neurosci., Am. Assn. Anatomists, Am. Assn. Neurol. Surgeons, Congress Neurol. Surgeons, Soc. Neurol. Surgeons of Orange County (pres. 1985-86, sec.-treas. 1984-85). Office: Ind Univ Med Ctr Sect Neurosurgery 545 Barnhill Dr Indianapolis IN 46202-5124

PRO, PHILIP MARTIN, federal judge, lawyer; b. Richmond, Calif., Dec. 12, 1946; s. Leo Martin and Mildred Louise (Beck) P.; m. Dori Sue Hallas, Nov. 13, 1982; 1 child, Brenda Kay. BA, San Francisco State U., 1968; JD Golden Gate U., 1972. Bar: Calif. 1972, Nev. 1973, U.S. Ct. Appeals (9th cir.) 1973, U.S. Dist. Ct. Nev. 1973, U.S. Supreme Ct. 1976. Pub. defender, Las Vegas, 1973-75; asst. U.S. atty., Dist. Nev., Las Vegas, 1975-78; ptnr. Semenza, Murphy & Pro, Reno, 1978-79; dep. atty. gen. State of Nev., Carson City, 1979-80; U.S. magistrate U.S. Dist. Ct. Nev., Las Vegas, 1980-87; U.S. dist. judge, 1987—; instr. Atty. Gen.'s Advocacy Inst., Nat. Inst. Trial Advocacy, 1992; mem. com. administrn. Magistrate Judges System Jud. Conf. U.S., 1992—. Bd. dirs. NCCJ, Las Vegas, 1982—, mem. program com. and issues in justice com.; mem. com. administrn. of magistrate judge system of Jud. Conf. of U.S., 1992—. Mem. ABA, Fed. Judges Assn. (bd. dirs. 1992), Nev. State Bar Assn., Calif. State Bar Assn., Nev. Judges Assn. (instr.), Assn. Trial Lawyers Am., Nev. Am. Inn Ct. (pres. 1989—), Ninth Cir. Jury (instructions com.), Nat. Conf. U.S. Magistrates (sec.), Nev. Am. Inn of Ct. (pres. 1989-91). Republican. Office: US Dist Ct 341 Fed Bldg 300 Las Vegas Bldv S Las Vegas NV 89101

PROBASCO, DALE RICHARD, management consultant; b. Ogden, Utah, July 23, 1946; s. Robert Vere and Dorleen E. (Oppliger) P.; m. Joan Michele Takacs, Dec. 20, 1969; children: Todd Aaron, Brad Dillon. BS, Utah State U., 1975; MS, U. Phoenix, 1988. Inventory asst. Moore Bus. Form, Logan, Utah, 1973-75; systems engr. Electronic Data Systems, Dallas, 1975-76, Bechtel Corp., San Francisco, 1976-78; supr. project scheduling Toledo Edison Co., 1978-80; mgr. project controls Utah Power and Light Co., Salt Lake City, 1980-87, mgr. mktg. strategy, 1987-89; pres. Probasco Cons., Inc., West Jordan, Utah, 1989-90; sr. assoc. Metzler & Assocs., Deerfield, Ill., 1990—. Contbr. articles to profl. publs. Pres. Emery County Little League, Castledale, Utah, 1981-84; coach Little League Baseball, West Jordan, Utah, 1985-86. With USN, 1965-72. Mem. Am. Econ. Devel. Conf., Nuclear Info. and Records Mgmt. Assn., Assn. for Info. and Image Mgmt. Lutheran.

PROBER, ALEXANDRA JAWORSKI, education educator; b. Nadryb, Poland, Dec. 11, 1907; came to U.S., 1912; d. Leon and Wladyslawa (Bojkowska) Jaworski; m. Theodore Prober (dec. 1961); children: Walter, Martha, Thomas. AA, Pasadena (Calif.) City Coll., 1954, BA, 1957; MA, L.A. State U., 1965. Cert. tchr., Calif. Buyer raw materials Princess Pat Cosmetic Co., Chgo., 1934-39; treas., mgr. AR-EX Cosmetics, Chgo., 1937-43; performer Sta. WIND, Chgo., 1940-42; with counter intelligence U.S. Army, Salt Lake City, Calif., 1943; tchr. Sierra Madre (Calif.) Schs., 1960-61, Pasadena Unified Sch. Dist., 1962-73, L.A. City Coll., 1980-81; reader Nat. Edn. Assn., 1988—. Author: (poetry) Awakened Echoes, 1990; contbr. articles to profl. jours. Vol. UCLA Hosp., 1981-84; lectr. for various civic groups, 1980; active Friends of Huntington Libr.; mem. Masquers Theatre Group, Chgo., Pacific Asia Mus. Huntington Libr.; performer plays; mem. World Acad. Arts and Culture, 1987—. With U.S. Army, 1944. Recipient 4th prize Nat. Writers Club Article Contest, 1983, 5th prize poetry, 1988, 1st prize for poetry Vega mag., 1983, Golden Poet award World of Poetry, 1985, 87, 88, 89, 90, 91, 92. Mem. AAUW, Nat. League Am. PEN Women, Calif. State U. Alumni Assn., UCLA Alumni Assn., Calif. Tchrs. Assn. (life, Tchr. Edn. and Profl. Standards com. 1938-43, hiring com, 1942), Variety Club Charities (pub. chmn. 1982), Calif. Ret. Teachers (life), Sherlock Holmes Club, Pi Lambda Theta. Home: 1274 Sonoma Dr Altadena CA 91001-3152

PROBST, KEVIN FORBES, physicist; b. Salt Lake City, Aug. 27, 1950; s. Gerald G. and Betty F. (Nelson) P.; m. Peggy Dietz, June 13, 1972; children: Jennifer, Matthew. BS in Physics, USAF Acad., 1972; MS in Physics, Ohio State U., 1973. Rschr. C.S. Draper Lab., Cambridge, Mass., 1979-81; dir., engr. BDM Corp., Albuquerque, 1981-85; v.p., engr. Titan Corp., Albuquerque, 1985-88; dep. dir. Strategic Def. Initiative Orgn., Washington, 1988-90; pres., engr. The CORE Group, Inc., Albuquerque, 1990—; cons. numerous govt. and def. orgns., 1985-88, 90—. Patentee in field. Maj. USAF, 1972-79. Mem. AIAA (chmn. Ann. Fire Control Symposium 1990), IEEE, Am. Defense Preparedness Assn. Office: The CORE Group Inc 2301 Yale Blvd SE B-3 Albuquerque NM 87119

PROCUNIER, RICHARD WERNER, environmental scientist, administrator; b. Dallas, Tex., Oct. 27, 1936; s. Werner Richard and Dorothy (Koch) P.; m. Janet Mesing, Sept. 5, 1958 (div. Aug. 28, 1984); children: Nancy, Carol, Ellen; m. Carolyn Harris, June 25, 1988. BSEE, MIT, 1958; PhD, Univ. Coll. London, 1966. Prof. U. London, 1966-68; rsch. scientist Lockheed, Palo Alto, Calif., 1968-72; mgr. Hewlett Packard, Santa Clara, Calif., 1972-74; chief of noise control U.S. EPA, San Francisco, 1974-82, sci. advisor, 1982-83, environ. scientist, 1990—; prof. U. Calif., Davis, 1984-85; adminstr. County Health Svcs., Martinez, Calif., 1986-89; mem. Nat. Edn. Com., Nat. Environ. Health Assn., Denver, 1980-87; enforcement coord., U.S. EPA, San Francisco, 1990. Contbr. many articles to profl. jours. Proponent to incorporate Orinda, Calif., 1984. Recipient Presidential citation, Nat. Environmental Health Assn., 1981. Fellow Royal Soc. London; mem. World Affairs Coun., Commonwealth Club, Kappa Sigma (Leadership award 1958).

PROFFER, KATHLEEN ANNE, geologist; b. Santa Monica, Calif., Apr. 10, 1955; d. Perry Lawrence and Marilyn May (Winbigler) Ehlig; m. Terril Ray Proffer, Aug. 24, 1984; children: Jacob, Clayton, Evan. AA in Geology, Pasadena City Coll., 1975; BS in Geology, UCLA, 1977; MS in Geolgy, Calif. State U., L.A., 1986. Registered geologist, Calif.; cert. engring. geologist, Calif. Staff geologist Robert Stone and Assocs., Canoga Park, Calif., 1978-80, R&M Cons., Inc., Irvine, Calif., 1980-82, Earth Tech. Corp., Long Beach, Calif., 1983-84, Hansen Engring., Bakersfield, Calif., 1986-87; geologist WZI, Inc., Bakersfield, 1987-92. Mem. Geol. Soc. Am., Assn. Engring. Geologists (assoc.), Am. Assn. Petroleum Geologists. Home: 3713 Margalo Ave Bakersfield CA 93313

PROFFITT, LAWRENCE ALAN, secondary school educator; b. Encino, Calif., July 1, 1959; s. George Leslie and Cleah (James) Proffitt; m. Melissa Sue. BS, U. Utah, 1982; MA, U. Calif., Riverside, 1988. Cert. tchr., adminstr., Calif. Sterilization technician Deseret Med., Inc., Sandy, Utah, 1977-82; tchr. Jordan Sch. Dist., Sandy, 1982-85, Yucaipa-Calimesa Joint Unified Sch. Dist., Yucaipa, Calif., 1985—; pres. Citrus Belt Uniserv, Rialto, Calif., 1991—. Named to Outstanding Young Men of Am., 1989. Mem. Calif. Tchrs. Assn. (task force on extremist attacks on edn. 1990—), Yucaipa-Calimesa Educators Assn. (fin. dir. 1987, v.p. 1988, pres. 1988—), Yucaipa-Calimesa C. of C. Democrat. Home: 1003 7th Pl Calimesa CA 92320

PRONKO, LEONARD CABELL, theater educator; b. Cebu, Philippines, Oct. 3, 1927; s. Stephen Michael and Alice Lee Ludwell (Beal) P. BA, Drury Coll., 1947; MA, Washington U., St. Louis, 1951; PhD, Tulane U., 1957. Asst. prof. langs. Lake Erie Coll., Painesville, Ohio, 1955-56; from asst. prof. to prof. romance langs. Pomona Coll., Claremont, Calif., 1957-84, prof. to theater, 1985—, chair theater dept., 1991—; dir. kabuki Mixed Blood Theatre, Mpls., 1984. Author: The World of Jean Anouilh, 1961, Avante-Garde, 1962, Eugene Ionesco, 1965, Theatre East and West, 1967, Guide to Japanese Drama, 1973, George Feydeau, 1975, Eugene Labiche and Georges Feydeau, 1982; contbr. articles to profl. publs. Fellow Guggenheim Soc., 1963-64, Japan Found., 1976; recipient award L.A. Drama Critics Circle, 1972, award of excellence Am. Coll. Theatre Festival, 1974, Order of Sacred Treasure, Govt. of Japan, 1986. Democrat. Home: 1543 N Bates Pl Claremont CA 91711-3107 Office: Pomona Coll Theater Dept 300 E Bonita 333 N College Way Claremont CA 91711-6328

PRONOVE-IRREVERRE, PACITA, medical officer; b. Manila, Philippines, Oct. 12, 1919; d. Ricardo Avenido and Dolores (Laico) Pronove; m. Filadelfo Irreverre, Dec. 30, 1950. AA, U. Philippines, 1939, MD, 1944. Diplomate Am. Acad. Pediatrics. Physician Pasay City Health Dept., Philippines, 1946-52; pediatric resident Childrens Hosp., Washington, 1952-54; rsch. assoc. NIH, Bethesda, Md., 1959-61, scientist, adminstr., 1961-73. co-discoverer Bartter's Syndrome. Pres. Pasay City Jr. Women's Club, Manila, 1948, Philippine Jr. Women's Clubs, Manila, 1950. Outstanding Alumnae award U. Philippines Coll. Medicine, 1987. Home: 4470 N Camino de Carrillo Tucson AZ 85715

PRONZINI, BILL JOHN (WILLIAM PRONZINI), author; b. Petaluma, Calif., Apr. 13, 1943; s. Joseph and Helene (Guder) P. Coll. student, 2 years. Author 50 novels (including under pseudonyms), 3 books of non-fiction, 6 collections of short stories, 1971—; first novel The Stalker, 1971; editor 80 anthologies; contbr. numerous short stories to publs. Recipient Scroll award, Best First Novel, Mystery Writers Am., 1972, Life Achievement award Pvt. Eye Writers Am., 1987. Mem. Writers Guild Am.-West. Democrat. Office: PO Box 2536 Petaluma CA 94953

PROPHET, MATTHEW WALLER, JR., school superintendent; b. Okolona, Miss., Apr. 4, 1930; s. Matthew Waller and Elzira Elise (Walker) P.; m. Freddye Maxine Adams, Jan. 17, 1954; children—Michael, Matthew, Tony Michelle. B.Gen. Edn., U. Omaha, 1960; M.A. in Ednl. Supervision and Adminstrn., Roosevelt U., 1970; Ph.D., Northwestern U., 1972. Enlisted U.S. Army, 1951; commd. 2d lt., 1952; advanced through grades to comdr.; various assignments in Germany, Korea, other countries; advisor to Ohio N.G., 1964-65; personnel mgmt. advisor, Vietnam, 1965-66; chief ind. tng. 5th U.S. Army, Fort Sheridan, Ill., 1967-71; dep. supt. Lansing Sch. Dist., Mich., 1972-1978, supt., 1978-82; supt. Portland Pub. Schs., Oreg., 1982—; adj. prof. Coll. Edn. Mich. State U., East Lansing, Mich., 1974-82; coordinator Edn. Policy Fellowship Program, Mich., 1975-82; dir. Inst. Ednl. Leadership, Inc., Washington. Active United Way, Jr. Achievement, Mich. Soc. to Prevent Blindness, others. Decorated Bronze Star, Air medal, Legion of Merit, others. Mem. Mich. Assn. Sch. Adminstrs. (former nat. del.), Am. Assn. Sch. Adminstrs., Nat. Program for Ednl. Leadership, Mich. Middle Cities Edn. Assn., Area Educators Committed to Cooperation (former chmn.), Roundtable (Ingham County), Edn. Policy Fellowship Program, Adv. Council for Equal Ednl. Opportunity, Ret. Officers Assn. (U.S. Army), Alpha Chi, Phi Delta Kappa. Office: Portland Pub Schs PO Box 3107 Portland OR 97208-1804*

PROPP, DALE HARTLEY, railroad director; b. Graceville, Minn., Oct. 23, 1935; s. George Hartley and Esther (Annette Swenson) P.; children: Michael Dale, Heidi Lynn Propp DesMouneaux. BS in Chemistry, Gustavus Adolphus Coll., 1957; post-grad., U. Minn., 1960-62. Chemist oil lab. No. Pacific R.R., Livingston, Mont., 1957-58; chief chemist, engr. tests No. Pacific R.R., St. Paul, 1958-70; with Burlington No. R.R., 1970—; gen. supt. locomotive ops. Burlington No. R.R., Denver, 1990—. State dele. Rep. Com., St. Paul, 1968. Mem. Nat. R.R. Lubrication Coun. (chmn. 1982—), Soc. Tribology Lubrication Engrs., Locomotive Maintenance Officers Assn. (pres. 1985-86). Republican. Presbyterian. Home: 2501 Twelve Oak Dr Colleyville TX 76034 Office: Burlington No R R 777 Main St Fort Worth TX 76102

PROPST, MICHAEL TRUMAN, pathologist; b. Lebanon, Oreg., July 3, 1940; s. Lynn Edward and Vera Ruth (Forbes) P.; m. Susan Jean Joesting, Dec. 26, 1974; children: Christopher M., Andrew J., Matthew A., Michael Jonathan, Edwin Cam. BS, Oreg. State U., 1962; MD, U. Oreg., 1966. Diplomate Am. Bd. Pathology. Pathologist Humana Hosp., Anchorage, 1974-84; med. examiner State of Alaska, Anchorage, 1975—; med. dir. Physicians Med. Lab., Anchorage, 1984—. Served to maj. USAF, 1971-74. Fellow Coll. Am. Pathologists, Am. Soc. Clin. Pathologists, Am. Acad. Forensic Scientists, Royal Soc. Medicine (Gr. Britain), ; mem. Nat. Assn. Med. Examiners, Alaska State Med. Assn. Episcopalian. Office: Physicians Med Lab 4335 Laurel St Anchorage AK 99508-6336

PROTACIO, ROMEO ROMUALDO, personnel executive; b. Pasay, Philippines, Oct. 5, 1941; came to U.S. 1982; s. Pedro Reyes and Josefa (Romualdo) P. BA, U. of East, Manila, 1972, MA, 1981; EdD, Pepperdine U., 1991. Cert. profl. human resources. Assoc. prof. U. of the East, Manila, 1972-82; instr. Sierra Coll. of Bus., L.A., 1983-86, Am. Bus. Inst., L.A., 1986-88; pers.-risk mgr. Queen of Angels-Hollywood Presbyn. Med. Ctr., L.A., 1988—; cons. Ministry of Edn., Republic of Singapore, 1974. Vol. Pira, L.A. Mem. healthcare Human Resource Mgmt. Assn., So. Calif. Assn. Healthcare and Risk Mgmt., Pers. and Indsl. Rels. Assn., Am. Soc. of Law and Medicine. Office: QAHP Med Ctr 1300 N Vermont Ave Los Angeles CA 90027

PROTZMAN, GRANT DALE, unierity administrator, state legislator; b. Ogden, Utah, May 3, 1950; s. Paul L. and Maxine E. (Nelson) P.; m. Linda Sue Gerasta, Mar. 30, 1985; children: Heather Sue, Kristen Marie, Erin Elizabeth. BA, Utah. State U., 1976; MS, Calif. Am. U., 1979; MA, U. No. Colo., 1987, EdD, 1988. Coord. student activities Weber State U., Ogden, 1976-81, coord. student govt., 1981-82, assoc. dir. student life, 1982-84, dir. co-curricular learning, 1984-87, planning and devel. officer, dir. drug and alcohol program, 1987-91, asst. to v.p., 1991—; mem., asst. minority whip Utah State Ho. of Reps., Salt Lake City, 1986—; sr. cons. Inst. for Leadership Devel., Ogden, 1978—. Author: An Examination of Select Motivational Variables of Members in Three Different Types of Volunteer Organizations in a Collegiate Setting, 1988, An Investigation of the State of Motivation Management and Assessment in Volunteer Organizations, 1988; contbr. articles to profl. jours. Mem. adv. bd. Wasatch Care Ctr., Ogden, 1986—, Families in Edn., 1992, Weber Sch. Dist., 1992; mem. Weber Area Emergency Planning Com., Ogden, 1988—, critical workplace skills adv. bd. Applied Tech. Ctr., 1991—. Named Outstanding Young Man of the Year, Jay Cees; Recipient Ptnrs. in Edn. Recognition award Weber Sch. Dist., 1987, Appreciation award Utah Vocat. Leadership Orgns., 1987, Extended Svc. award Ogden Sch. Dist., 1988, Outstanding Legislator award Utah Democratic Party Chmn's. award, 1988, Utah Sch. Employees Assn. Scroll of Honor award as Outstanding legislator, 1990, Weber State U. Student Svcs. Soar award, 1991, Utah Edn. Assn. Honor Roll award as Outstanding legislator, 1991, Utah Ednl. Libr. Media Assn. award for Outstanding Dedication and Svc. to Utah Lib. Media programs, 1992, Utah Assn. of Rehabilitative Facilities award for Svc. to Persons with disabilities, 1992, U.B.A.T.C. award for Support of Vocational Edn., 1992. Mem. Nat. Assn. Campus Activities (regional coord. 1982-85, conf. educator 1980-83, Nat. Outstanding Unit of Yr. 1986, Regional Outstanding Unit of Yr. 1985), Utah Edn. Assn. (honor roll award 1991), Rotary, Kappa Delta Pi, Phi Sigma Alpha, Phi Delta Kappa. Democrat. Mormon. Home: 3073 N 575 E Ogden UT 84414-2077 Office: Weber State U 3750 Harrison Blvd Ogden UT 84408-2109

PROUD, JOHN FREDERICK, manufacturing executive, consultant, educator; b. New Prague, Minn., Apr. 11, 1942; s. John Cranston and Avis Catherine (Kamish) P.; m. Marsha Anne Ross, Feb. 29, 1964 (div. Feb. 1979); children: Karen Lynn Allen, Michael James; m. Darlene Elizabeth Sundal, July 4, 1980. BS, Calif. Polytech. State U., San Luis Obispo, 1964; MS, West Coast U., 1973. Systems analyst Burroughs Corp., City of Industry, Calif., 1968-72; mgr. info. systems Century Data Systems, Anaheim, Calif., 1972-76; regional cons., educator Xerox Corp., L.A., 1976-79, mgr. nat. customer edn., 1981-86, mgr. just-in-time mfg., 1986-87; pres. Proud Enterprises Corp., Palm Desert, Calif., 1987—; prin. Oliver West, Protland, Oreg., 1988—; internat. educator, 1988—, Xerox Corp., L.A., 1982-87. Author: (with others) The Proven Path, 1989; contbr. articles to profl. jours. Lt. (j.g.) USNR, 1965-68, Vietnam. Mem. Am. Prodn. and Inventory Control Soc. (Orange County pres. 1985-86, internat. conf. com. 1986-87, internat. nominating com. 1987, nat. adv. com. 1988—, internat. conf. com. 1991-92, past pres., Orange Badge 1986, Appreciation 1986-87). Republican. Office: The Oliver West Cos 1011 SE Division St Ste 307 Portland OR 97266 Office: Proud Enterprises Corp 260 Dester Holly Dr Palm Desert CA 92260

PROUDFOOT, JAMES MICHAEL, research and development executive; b. Oakland, Md., Feb. 12, 1955; s. James Milton and Mary Rose (Gallagher) P.; m. Cynthia Louise Ross, Nov. 7, 1987. BA in Polit. Sci., Internat. Rels. summa cum laude, Am. U., 1976. Sytems analyst, engr. Sci. Applications, Inc., Norfolk, Va., 1978-81; sr. program mgr. Sci. Applications Internat. Corp., Torrance, Calif., 1981-91, v.p. for bus. devel., 1991—. Mem. AIAA, Am. Astronautical Soc., Am. Assn. Ind. Investors, CATO Inst. Mem. LDS Ch.

PROUGH, STEPHEN W., savings and loan executive; b. 1945. COO Westcorp, Irvine, Calif., 1983—, bd. dirs. Office: Westcorp PO Box 19733 23 Pasteur Irvine CA 92718*

PROULX, MICHAEL JOHN, food service executive; b. Stillwater, Minn., Oct. 12, 1948; s. Vital George and Irene Helen (Maier) P.; m. Germaine Peters, July, 19, 1969; children: Jennifer Germaine, Michael John II. AA, Mesa Community Coll., 1969. With Bashas' Supermarket, 1966—; from stock clk./cashier to grocery mgr. Bashas' Supermarket, Phoenix, 1967-76, store mgr., 1976-81; div. supr. Bashas' Supermarket, Chandler, Ariz., 1981—. V.p., mem. Phoenix Civitan Club, 1973-77; dir. coun. Boy Scouts Am., Grand Canyon, 1978-80. Mem. Rotary (charter pres. Sedona Midday club 1980-81, bd. dirs. 1981-82, Paul Harris fellow 1984). Republican.

Roman Catholic. Home: PO Box 56 Sedona AZ 86339-0056 Office: Bashas' Supermarket PO Box 488 Chandler AZ 85244-0488

PROUT, CARL WESLEY, history educator; b. Bakersfield, Calif., Apr. 19, 1941; s. George Hecla and Ruth (King) P. BA, U. Calif., Santa Barbara, 1964, MA, 1965; postgrad., U. Tenn., Knoxville, 1968-71, Am. U., Cairo, 1974, U. So. Calif., 1981, Ain Shams U., Cairo, 1981. Instr. history Santa Barbara Coll., 1965-66, U. Tenn., Knoxville, 1968-71; instr. Orange Coast Coll., Costa Mesa, 1966-68, asst. prof., 1971-73, assoc. prof., 1973-75, prof., 1975—; treas. Willmore Corp., 1980-81, sec., 1984-85, v.p., 1985-86, pres., chmn., 1988-89, also bd. dirs.; group facilitator Coastview Meml. Hosp., Long Beach, 1986-89. Research and publs. in field. Pres., chmn. bd. Alamitos Heights Improvement Assn., 1979-80, bd. dirs., 1980-82; mem. East Long Beach Joint Council, 1979-80, Local Coastal Planning Adv. Com., 1979-80. Recipient Salgo Outstanding Tchr. award, 1974-76. Mem. Am. Hist. Assn., Meml. West Alumni Club, Sigma Nu. Office: Orange Coast Coll 2701 Fairview Rd Costa Mesa CA 92626-5561

PROUT, RALPH EUGENE, physician; b. Los Angeles, Feb. 27, 1933; s. Ralph Byron and Fern (Taylor) P.; m. Joanne Morris, Sept. 17, 1980; children: Michael, Michelle. BA, La Sierra Coll., 1953; MD, Loma Linda U., 1957; D of Nutri-Medicine (hon.), John F. Kennedy Coll., 1987. Diplomate: Nat. Bd. Med. Examiners. Intern Los Angeles County Hosp., 1957-58; resident internal medicine White Meml. Hosp., Los Angeles, 1958-60; resident psychiatry Harding Hosp., Worthington, Ohio, 1960-61; practice medicine specializing in internal medicine Napa, Calif., 1961-63; staff internist Calif. Med. Facility, Vacaville, 1963-68, chief med. officer, 1968-84; chief med. cons. Calif. Dept. Corrections, 1977-86, chief med. services, 1983; med. cons. Wellness Cons., Placerville, Calif., 1986—; pres. Total Living Inc., 1984—; instr. Sch. Medicine, Loma Linda U., 1965-66; clin. assoc. U. Calif.-Davis Sch. Medicine, 1978-84; med. cons. Substance Abuse Pine Grove Camp, 1985-90. Treas. Vacaville Republican Assembly, 1972-75; del. Republican Central Com. Solano County, 1975-78; Bd. dirs. Napa-Solano County United Crusade, Vallejo, Calif., 1969-71, v.p., 1970-71; bd. dirs. Project Clinic, Vacaville, 1974-77, Home Health Com. Inter-Community Hosp., Fairfield, 1978-80; pres. MotherLode Citizens for Drug-Free Youth, Amador County, 1985—. Named One of Outstanding Young Men of Am., 1968. Mem. AMA, Internat. Acad. Nutrition and Preventive Medicine, Calif. Soc. Internal Medicine, Am. Soc. Internal Medicine, Am. Assn. Sr. Physicians, Mother Lode Citizens for Drug-Free Youth, Native Sons of Golden West, Alpha Omega Alpha. Republican. Home and Office: 24405 Shake Ridge Rd Volcano CA 95689-9728

PROVOW, JEFFREY STEVEN, transportation specialist; b. St. Louis, June 6, 1957; s. Donald Rece and Denelda Arlene (Main) P.; children: Brian Jeffrey, Brenden Scott, Christopher Michael. Student, W.Va. U., 1975-76; BS in Food Sci. and Chemistry, Rutgers U., 1979. Intercoastal supr. U.S. Lines, Staten Island, N.Y., 1980-81; equipment container mgr. U.S. Lines, Chgo., 1981-82, M.W. ops. mgr., 1982-84; port ops. mgr. U.S. Lines, Long Beach, Calif., 1984-86; v.p. drainage svcs. TransPacific Intermodal Inc., Long Beach, 1986-87; mgr. intermodel Containerfreight Inc., Long Beach, 1987-88; terminal mgr. CSX Intermodal, Long Beach, 1988-89; asst. gen. mgr. West region CSL Intermodal, Long Beach, 1989-92, gen. mgr. West/Southwest region, 1992—. Wrestling referee Manalapan (N.J.) Recreation, 1971-81, football coach, 1978-81; mgr., umpire Stanton (Calif.) Little League, 1990—. Mem. Harbor Transp. Club. Office: CSX Intermodal Inc 111 W Ocean Blvd # 1600 Long Beach CA 90802-4632

PROYECT, MARTIN H., investment banker; b. N.Y.C., Oct. 24, 1932; s. Max and Fay (Madison) P.; children—Christopher T., Michele F. B.A., Columbia U., 1954, L.D., 1956. Bar: N.Y. bar 1956. Assoc. Reavis & McGrath, N.Y.C., 1956-59; exec. v.p. Calvin Bullock Ltd., N.Y.C., 1959-79; chmn., pres. Venture Advisers, Inc., Santa Fe, 1968—, N.Y. Venture Fund, Inc., 1968—, Venture Income Plus, Inc., 1980—, Venture Muni Plus, Inc., 1984—, Retirement Planning Funds Am., Inc., 1984—; bd. govs. Investment Co. Inst. Author: Investors Guide to the Economic Recovery Tax Act of 1981; editor: How to Succeed in Spite of Yourself. Home: 4963 Crooked Stick Las Vegas NV 89113 Office: 124 E Marcy St Santa Fe NM 87501-2019

PRUDHOMME, RONALD EDWARD, food processing executive; b. San Jose, Calif., June 3, 1941; s. Edward L. and Julie M. Prudhomme; m. Paula L. Pimentel, Nov. 1, 1987. BS, U. Calif., Davis, 1964, MS, 1966; MBA, Pepperdine U., 1977. Asst. head micro div. Nat. Food Processing Assn., Berkeley, Calif., 1966-72; quality control mgr. Gentry Internat. Inc., Gilroy, Calif., 1972-74; new product devel. staff Tri Valley Growers, Modesto, Calif., 1974-76, asst. prodn. mgr., 1976-83; plant mgr. Ingomar Packing Co., Los Banos, Calif., 1983-89, gen. mgr., 1989—. Mem. Calif. League of Food Processors (bd. dirs. 1989—), Am. Inst. Plant Engrs., Sportsmen of Stanislaus. Office: Ingomar Packing Co PO Box 1448 Los Banos CA 93635

PRUEITT, MELVIN LEWIS, physicist, computer graphicist; b. Wickes, Ark., Oct. 17, 1932; s. Ernest E. and Bessie (Parsons) P.; m. Susi Rosmarie Hufschmid, Dec. 5, 1956; children: Roger, Cynthia, Daniel, Linda, Stanley, Shawn. BS in Physics, Brigham Young U., 1960; MS in Physics, U. Ariz., 1962; PhD in Physics, U. N.Mex., 1971. Rscher. EG & G, Nevada Test Site, Nev., 1960; rsch asst. U. Ariz., Tucson, 1961-62; staff mem. Los Alamos (N.Mex.) Nat. Lab., 1962—; pres. Innovar Corp., Los Alamos, 1980—; speaker in field. Author: Computer Graphics, 1975, Art and the Computer, 1984, Hansen-Roach Cross Sections: A Graphical Representation, 1988; exhibits include N.Y. Mus. Natural History, Expo '86, Vancouver, B.C., Can., ET Nouvelles Technologies, Que., Can., Forum des Arts de l'Univers Scientifique et Technique, France, Everson Mus. Art, Miami Yout Mus.; contbr. articles to profl. jours.; 4 patents in field. Republican. Mem. LDS Ch. Home: 161 Cascabel St Los Alamos NM 87544-2515 Office: Los Alamos Nat Lab MS-B295 Los Alamos NM 87545

PRUSINER, STANLEY BEN, neurology and biochemistry educator, researcher; b. Des Moines, May 28, 1942; s. Lawrence Albert and Miriam (Spigel) P.; m. Sandra Lee Turk, Oct. 18, 1970; children: Helen Chloe, Leah Anne. AB cum laude, U. Pa., 1964, MD, 1968. Diplomate Am. Bd. Neurology. Intern in medicine U. Calif., San Francisco, 1968-69, resident in neurology, 1972-74, asst. prof. neurology, 1974-80, assoc. prof., 1980-84, prof., 1984—, prof. biochemistry, 1988—, acad. senate faculty rsch. lectr., 1989-90; prof. virology U. Calif., Berkeley, 1984—; mem. neurology rev. com. Nat. Inst. Neurol. Disease and Strokes, NIH, Bethesda, Md., 1982-86, 90-92; mem. sci. adv. bd. French Fedn., L.A., 1985—; mem. sci. rev. com. Alzheimer's Disease Diagnostic Ctr. & Rsch. Grant Program, State of Calif., 1985-89; chmn. sci. adv. bd. Am. Health Assistance Fedn., Rockville, Md., 1986—. Editor: The Enzymes of Glutamine Metabolism, 1973, Slow Transmissible Diseases of the Nervous System, 2 Vols., 1979, Prions - Novel Infectious Pathogens Causing Scraple and CJD, 1987, Prion Diseases of Humans and Animals, 1992, Molecular and Genetic Basis of Neurologic Disease, 1992; contbr. over 170 rsch. articles to profl. jours. Mem. adv. bd. Family Survival Project for Adults with Chronic Brain Disorders, San Francisco, 1982—, San Francisco chpt. Alzheimer's Disease and Related Disorder Assn., 1985—. Lt. comdr. USPHS, 1969-72. Alfred P. Sloan Rsch. fellow U. Calif., 1976-78; Med. Investigator grantee Howard Hughes Med. Inst., 1976-81; grantee for excellence in neurosci. Senator Jacob Javits Ctr., NIH, 1985-1990; recipient Leadership and Excellence for Alzheimer's Disease award NIH, 1990—, Potamkin prize for Alzheimer's Disease Rsch., 1991, Med. Rsch. award Met. Life Found., 1992, Christopher Columbus Discovery award NIH and Med. Soc. Genoa, Italy, 1992, Charles A. Dana award for pioneering achievements in health, 1992, Dickson prize for outstanding contbns. to medicine U. Pitts., 1992, Max Planck Rsch. award Alexander von Hamboldt Found. and Max Planck Soc., 1992, Gairdner Found. Internat. award, 1993. Mem. NAS (Inst. Medicine, Richard Lounsberg award for extraordinary achievements in biology and medicine 1993), Am. Acad. Arts and Scis., Am. Acad. Neurology (George Cotzias award for outstanding rsch. 1987, Presdl. award 1992), Assn. Am. Physicians, Am. Soc. Microbiology, Am. Soc. Neurochemistry, Internat. Soc. Neurochemistry, Am. Soc. Virology, Am. Neurol. Assn., Concordia Argonaut Club.

PRYOR, CAROLYN ANN, church musician, educator; b. Auburn, Ind., Aug. 13, 1934; d. Leland Alvin and Ruth Alberta (Norton) P.; children: Maria Vanessa, Anthony Hugh. BA in Music, Occidental Coll., 1957. Organist, dir. Goodsell Meth. Ch., Bklyn., 1959-63; organist Boro Park Prog. Synagogue, Bklyn., 1959-63; kindergarten tchr. L.A. City Schs., 1966-67; tchr., adminstr. St. Michael's Ch., N.Y.C., 1967-69, various schs., N.Y.C., 1969-77; organist, dir. United Meth. Ch., Seacliff, N.Y., 1970-78; sr. sec. to rsch. doctors Columbia U., N.Y.C., 1978-79; dir. music ministries 1st United Meth. Ch., Campbell, Calif., 1979—. Contbr. articles to profl. jours. Mem. Am. Guild Organists, Choral Condrs. Guild, Choristers Guild.

PRYOR, DOUGLAS KEITH, clinical psychologist, consultant; b. Oakland, Calif., Aug. 12, 1944; s. Richard Smith and Clara Margaret (Ford) P.; m. Roxanne Rae, Oct. 14, 1990. BA, Calif. State U., Chico, 1967; MA, U. Pacific, 1971; PhD, U. So. Calif., 1976. Lic. psychologist, marriage, family and child counslor, ednl. psychologist, Calif. Social svc. worker Dept. Pub. Assistance, Stockton, Calif., 1967-70; asst. to program dir. Stockton State Hosp., 1970-72; sch. psychologist, vice prin. Mesrobian Elem. and High Sch., Pico Rivera, Calif., 1972-74; sch. psychologist Pasadena (Calif.) Unified Sch. Dist., 1974-83; pvt. practice clin. psychology, Santa Ana, Calif., 1980-87, Sacramento, 1987—; pres. Behavior Mgmt. Cons., Sacramento, 1982—; mgr. Calif. Behavior Modification Workshop, Stockton, 1972; clin. fellow Human Factors Programs, Santa Ana, 1977-79, Milton Erikson Advanced Inst. Hypnotherapeutic and Psychotherapeutic Studies, Santa Ana, 1979-80; presenter, lectr. in field. Mem. APA, Calif. Assn. Sch. Psychologists (rep. region V, 1982-88, officer 1992), Calif. Psychol. Assn. (officer 1992), Sacramento Valley Psychology Assn. (bd. dirs. 1990—, treas. Div. 1, 1990, pres. Div. 1, 1992). Democrat. Buddhist. Office: Behavior Mgmt Cons 650 Howe Ave Ste 560 Sacramento CA 95825-4732

PRYOR, MARK ALLAN, telecommunications specialist, consultant; b. Alameda, Calif., Aug. 24, 1954; s. Roger Phelps and Dorris Elaine (Freitas) P.; m. Janet Karen Chang, May 23, 1987; 1 child, Karen. Student, U. Calif., Berkeley, 1972-75; BS in Info. Systems Mgmt., U. San Francisco, 1988. Programmer Pacific Bell Customer Records, San Francisco, 1979-81, systems analyst, 1982-83, group mgr., 1984-85; project leader Pacific Bell Customer Svcs., San Ramon, Calif., 1986-88; mgr. applications devel. Pacific Bell Customer Svcs., San Ramon, 1988-90; intern in tech. Bellcore, Livingston, N.J., 1990-91; product mgr. customer network mgmt. products Pacific Bell Data Communications Group, San Ramon, 1991—; cons. Bellcore, Morristown, N.J., 1990-92. Mem. IEEE. Office: Pacific Bell Data Comm Group 2600 Camino Ramon 45051 San Ramon CA 94583

PRYOR, PETER PATRICK, newspaper editor; b. N.Y.C., Mar. 5, 1946; s. Thomas Mathew and Marie (Schmidt) P. Student, Pierce Jr. Coll., Woodland Hills, Calif., 1964-65. With editorial dept. L.A. Times, 1968-71; news editor Daily Variety Ltd., Hollywood, Calif., 1971-73, mng. editor, 1973-88, editor, 1988-91, editor-at-large, 1991—. With USN, 1965-68, including Vietnam. Office: Daily Variety Ltd 5700 Wilshire Blvd # 120 Los Angeles CA 90036

PTASYNSKI, HARRY, geologist, oil producer; b. Milw., May 26, 1926; s. Stanley S. and Frances V. (Stawicki) P.; m. Nola G. Whitestine, Sept. 15, 1951; children: Ross F., Lisa Joy. BS, Stanford U., 1950. Cert. profl. geologist; cert. petroleum geologist. Dist. geologist Pure Oil Co., Amarillo, Tex., 1951-55, Casper, Wyo., 1955-58; ind. geologist, Casper, 1958—. With USN, 1944-46, PTO. Mem. Am. Assn. Petroleum Geologists, Am. Inst. Profl. Geologists, Ind. Petroleum Assn. Am. (v.p., bd. dirs. 1976—), Ind. Petroleum Assn. Mountain States (v.p., bd. dirs. 1976-80, Rocky Mountain Oil and Gas Assn. (bd. dirs., exec. com. 1980—). Republican. Episcopalian. Home: 1515 Brookview Dr Casper WY 82604-4852 Office: 123 W First St Ste 560 Casper WY 82609-1916

PUCK, THEODORE THOMAS, geneticist, biophysicist, educator; b. Chgo., Sept. 24, 1916; s. Joseph and Bessie (Shapiro) Puckowitz; m. Mary Hill, Apr. 17, 1946; children: Stirling, Jennifer, Laurel. B.S., U. Chgo., 1937, Ph.D., 1940. Mem. commn. airborne infections Office Surgeon Gen., Army Epidemiol. Bd., 1944-46; asst. prof. depts. medicine and biochemistry U. Chgo., 1945-47; sr. fellow Am. Cancer Soc., Calif. Inst. Tech., Pasadena, 1947-48; prof. biophysics U. Colo. Med. Sch., 1948—, chmn. dept., 1948-67, disting. prof., 1986—; dir. Eleanor Roosevelt Inst. Cancer Research, 1962—; Disting. research prof. Am. Cancer Soc., 1966—; nat. lectr. Sigma Xi, 1975-76. Author: The Mammalian Cell as a Microorganism: Genetic and Biochemical Studies in Vitro, 1972. Mem. Commn. on Physicians for the Future. Recipient Albert Lasker award, 1958, Borden award med. rsch., 1959, Louisa Gross Horwitz prize, 1973, Gordon Wilson medal Am. Clin. and Climatol. Assn., 1977, award Environ. Mutagen Soc., 1981, E.B. Wilson medal Am. Soc. Cell Biology, 1984, Bonfils-Stanton award in sci., 1984, U. Colo. Disting. Prof. award, 1987, Henry M. Porter medal, 1992; named to The Colo. 100, Historic Denver, 1992; Heritage Found. scholar, 1983; Phi Beta Kappa scholar, 1985. Fellow Am. Acad. Arts and Scis.; mem. Am. Chem. Soc., Soc. Exptl. Biology and Medicine, AAAS (Phi Beta Kappa award and lectr. 1983), Am. Assn. Immunologists, Radiation Research Soc., Biophys. Soc., Genetics Soc. Am., Nat. Acad. Sci., Tissue Culture Assn. (Hon. award 1987), Paideia Group, Santa Fe Inst. Sci. Bd., Phi Beta Kappa, Sigma Xi. Office: Eleanor Roosevelt Inst Cancer Rsch 1899 Gaylord St Denver CO 80206-1299

PUCKETT, RICHARD EDWARD, artist, consultant, retired recreation executive; b. Klamath Falls, Oreg., Sept. 9, 1932; s. Vernon Elijah and Leona Belle (Clevenger) P.; m. Velma Faye Hamrick, Apr. 14, 1957 (dec. 1985); children: Katherine Michelle Briggs, Deborah Alison Bolinger, Susan Lin Rowland, Gregory Richard. Student So. Oreg. Coll. Edn., 1951-56, Lake Forest Coll., 1957-58; Hartnell Jr. Coll., 1960-70; B.A., U. San Francisco, 1978. Asst. arts and crafts dir., Fort Leonard Wood, Mo., 1956-57; arts and crafts dir., asst. spl. services officer, mus. dir., Fort Sheridan, Ill., 1957-59; arts and crafts dir., Fort Irwin, Calif., 1959-60, Fort Ord, Calif., 1960-86; dir. arts and crafts br. Art Gallery, Arts and Crafts Center Materials Sales Store, 1960; opening dir. Presidio of Monterey Army Mus., 1968. Recipient First Place, Dept. Army and U.S. Army Forces Command awards for programming and publicity, 1979-81, 83-85, 1st and 3d place sculpture awards Monterey County Fair Fine Arts Exhibit, 1979, Comdrs. medal for civilian svcs., 1986, numerous other awards, Golden Acad. award, Internat. Man of Yr. award, 1991-92. Mem. Am. Craftsman Assn. (former), Glass Arts Soc., Monterey Peninsula Art Assn., Salinas Fine Arts Assn., Am. Park and Recreation Soc. One-man shows: Seaside City Hall, 1975, Fort Ord Arts and Crafts Center Gallery, 1967, 73, 79, 81, 84, 86, Presidio of Monterey Art Gallery, 1979; Glass on Holiday, 1981, 82; also pvt. collections; designed and opened first Ft. Sheridan Army Mus. Home: 1152 Jean Ave Salinas CA 93905-3321 also: PO Box 7 Keno OR 97627

PUDNEY, GARY LAURENCE, television executive; b. Mpls., July 20, 1934; s. Lawrence D. and Agnes (Hansen) P. BA, UCLA, 1956. V.p. ABC, Inc., N.Y.C., 1968—; v.p., sr. exec. in charge of spls. and talent ABC Entertainment, 1979-89; pres. The Gary L. Pudney Co., Beverly Hills, Calif., 1988—; chief oper. officer Paradigm Entertainment, Beverly Hills, 1989-92; exec. producer World Musics Awards, ABC-TV, 1993—. Exec. producer for United Cerebral Palsy Aspen and Lake Tahoe Pro-Celebrity Tennis Festivals, 4 yrs., AIDS Project L.A. Dinner, 1985, The 25th Anniversary of the L.A. Music Ctr. Bd. dirs. nat. Cerebral Palsy Found., Ctr. Theatre Group Ahmanson Theatre, L.A., Ctr. Theatre Group of L.A. Music Ctr.; mem. bd. La Quinta Arts Found., 1991—. Recipient Helena T. Deveraux Meml. award, 1985, Humanitarian award Nat. Jewish Ctr. for Immunology and Respiratory Medicine, 1986, Gift of Love award Nat. Ctr. Hyperactive Children, 1988, Winner award Excellence The L.A. Film Adv. Bd. Mem. Hollywood Radio and TV Soc. (bd. dirs.), Acad. TV Arts and Scis. (exec. com.), Met. Mus. Art, Mus. Modern Art. Democrat. Lutheran.

PUENTE, JOSE GARZA, safety engineer; b. Cuero, Tex., Mar. 19, 1949; s. Roque Leos and Juanita Vela (Garza) P.; m. Francisca Rodriguez Estrada, Sept. 7, 1969; 1 son, Anthony Burk. B.A., W. Tex. State U., Canyon, 1972; postgrad. U. Ariz.-Tucson, 1980; grad. U.S. Army transp. courses, 1972, 78, postgrad., 1989. Cert. U.S. Council Accreditation in Occupational Hearing; cert. Audiometric Technicians of Am. Indsl. Hygiene Assn. Asst. gen. mgr. Am. Transit Corp., Tucson, 1972-75; pub. transp. supt. City of Tucson, 1975-77; asst. safety coord., Tucson, 1977-81; safety coord. Mesa, Ariz., 1981-88; corp. safety dir. Am. Fence Corp., Phoenix, 1988-89; safety adminstr. Ariz.-ADOT, Phoenix, 1989—; owner La Paz Gospel Supplies & Gift shop, Tucson, 1979-80. Mem. Tucson Child Care Assn., 1973-74; mem. Citizen Task Force, Sunnyside sch. bd., 1977; mem. minority selection for Hispanic seatbelt program vendor Govs. Office of Hwy. Safety, 1989—; mem. Mayors Task Force on seatbelt awareness City of Mesa, 1988-89. Maj. USAR, 1971—. Fellow Advanced Mgmt. Seminar Urban Mass Transp. Adminstrn., Northeastern U., Boston, 1976-77; recipient Excellence award Ariz-Safety Assn., 1984. Mem. Am. Soc. Safety Engrs. (pres. elect Ariz. chpt. 1989-90, pres., 1990-91, Safety Profl. of Yr. 1984), Mexican-Am. Govtl. Employees (charter Tucson chpt.), Res. Officers Assn., Ariz. Safety Engrs., Ariz. Mcpl. Safety Assn. (Profl. of Yr. 1986), Internat. Platform Assn. Democrat. Baptist. Clubs: Internat. Order DeMolay (charter), Lions, Mesa Bowling League, Toastmasters. Home: PO Box 90 Mesa AZ 85211-0090 Office: 206 S 17th Ave Phoenix AZ 85007-3213

PUFFER, RUTH RICE, statistician, epidemiologist; b. Berlin, Mass., Aug. 31, 1907; d. J. Adams and Emily Hope (Rice) P. BA, Smith Coll., 1929, ScD (hon.), 1970; posgrad., Johns Hopkins U., 1937-38; DPH, Harvard U., 1943. Dir. statis. svcs. Tenn. Dept. Pub. Health, Nashville, 1933-53; chief dept. health stats. Pan Am. Health Orgn., regional office WHO, Washington, 1953-70, cons., 1970—; cons. U.S. Dept. State, New Delhi, India, 1981, 85, Jakarta, Indonesia, 1983. Author: Familial Susceptibility to Tuberculosis, 1944, Practical Statistics for Health and Medical Workers, 1950, Patterns of Urban Mortality, 1967, Caracteristicas de Mortalidad Urbana, 1968, Patterns of Mortality in Childhood, 1973, Caracteristicas de la Mortalidada en la Ninez, 1973, Patterns of Birthweights, 1987, Caracteristicas del Peso al Nacer, 1988; author numerous papers. Recipient Centennial award Tenn. Dept. Pub. Health, 1977, Abraham Horwitz award for Internat. Health Pan-Am. Orgn., 1978. Fellow Am. Pub. Health Assn. (v.p. 1950), Am. Statis. Assn.; mem. Delta Omega. Unitarian. Home: 900 N Hill Rd Apt 490 McMinnville OR 97128

PUGAY, JEFFREY IBANEZ, mechanical engineer; b. San Francisco, June 26, 1958; s. Herminio Salazar and Petronila (Ibanez) P. BSME, U. Calif., Berkeley, 1981, MSME, 1982; MBA, Pepperdine U., 1986, MS in Tech. Mgmt., 1991. Registered profl. engr., Calif. Engring. asst. Lawrence Berkeley Nat. Lab., 1978-80; assoc. tech. staff Aerospace Corp., L.A., 1981; mem. tech. staff Hughes Space & Comm. Co., El Segundo, Calif., 1982-85, project engr., 1985-88, tech. head, 1988-89, sr. staff engr., 1989-90, mgr. tech. ops. and strategic systems, 1991-92, ops. leader, 1992—. White House Fellow regional finalist, 1991, 92. Mem. ASME, Soc. Competitor Intelligence Profls., Am. Mgmt. Assn., L.A. World Affairs Coun., Make A Wish Found., Pi Tau Sigma, Delta Mu Delta. Republican. Roman Catholic. Home: 8180 Manitoba St Unit 120 Playa Del Rey CA 90293-8651 Office: Hughes Space & Comm Co PO Box 92919 Los Angeles CA 90009-2919

PUGH, HELEN PEDERSEN, realtor; b. San Francisco, Feb. 17, 1934; d. Christian Edward and Gladys Phoebe Zumwalt Pedersen; m. Howard Brooks Pugh, Sr., Oct. 11, 1974; children: Catherine Collier, Stephen Leach, Matthew Leach, Virginia Schmitt. AA, U. Calif., Berkeley, 1953. Cert. real estate appraiser; cert. real estate instr. Pvt. sec. to exec. dir. Rep. party, Phoenix, 1972, Henderson Realty, Phoenix, 1973; sta. mgr. Mobil Oil Co., Phoenix, 1973-74; realtor, John Hall and Assocs., Scottsdale, Ariz., 1978—, pres. luxury homes div. Vol. coord. William Baker for Congress, Phoenix, 1972; vol. Phoenix Meml. Hosp., Scottsdale Hosp. North Devel. Com.; master tchr. Presbyn. Ch., youth leader; troop leader Cactus-Pine coun. Girl Scouts U.S., 1960-74; asst. den leader Roosevelt coun. Boy Scouts Am.; instr. Jr. Achievement; v.p. Planned Parenthood Aux., Family Svc. Agy. Aux.; bd. dirs. Phoenix Symphony Aux., Phoenix Art Mus.; sec. Scottsdale Bus. Assn. Bd.; deacon Presbyn. Ch. Mem. Scottsdale Bd. Realtors, Scottsdale Comml. Bd., Ariz. Assn. Realtors (bd. dirs.), Phoenix Comml. Bd. (Multiple Listing Service Forms Com. award 1981), Internat. Real Estate Fedn. (Ariz. chpt. pres.), Nat. Assn. Realtors, Fiabci, Farm and Land Inst., Valley of Sun Real Estate Exchangers, LWV, Scottsdale C. of C. (amb.), U. Calif. Alumni Assn. (Ariz. chpt. pres.), Scottsdale Rep. Forum, Cactus Wren Rep. Women, Palo Verde Rep. Women, Toastmasters (past pres., youth leader, gov. area 7, disting. toastmaster), Delta Zeta, Alpha Tau Rho. Home: 7463 E Raintree Ct Scottsdale AZ 85258-2005 Office: 8777 E Via De Ventura Ste 290 Scottsdale AZ 85258-3396

PUGH, JAMIE KATHLEEN, statistician, researcher; b. Redlands, Calif., Oct. 30, 1946; d. James Richard and Martha Grace (Lewis) Caudle; m. William Marshell Pugh, June 24, 1967; children: Kimberly Ann, Alice Louise. BS in Physics, San Diego State U., 1969, MS in Stats., 1982. Mem. tech. staff Computer Scis. Corp., San Diego, 1977-80; scientist Rsch., Devel., Test and Evaluation div. Naval Command Control and Ocean Surveillance Ctr., San Diego, 1980—; lect. San Diego State U., 1985-86. Mem. AAAS, Am. Soc. Quality Control, Soc. Indsl. and Applied Math., Am. Statis. Assn.

PUGH, KYLE MITCHELL, JR., musician, music educator; b. Spokane, Wash., Jan. 6, 1937; s. Kyle Mitchel, Sr. and Lenore Fae (Johnson) P.; m. Susan Deane Waite, July 16, 1961; children: Jeffray, Kari. BA in Edu., East Wash. U., 1975. Cert. tchr., Wash. Tuba player Spokane Symphony Orch., 1958-63; rec. assoc. Century Records, Spokane, 1965-73; tuba player World's Fair Expo '74, Spokane, 1974; bass player Russ Carlyle Orch., Las Vegas, 1976, Many Sounds of Nine Orch., northwest area, 1969-81; band tchr. Garry Jr. High School, Spokane, 1976-79, Elementary Band Program, Spokane, 1979—; bass player Doug Scott Cabaret Band, Spokane, 1982-91; dept. head Elem. Band Dept., Spokane, 1984-89. Editor (newsletter) The Repeater, 1987 (Amateur Radio News Svc. award 1987); extra in movie Always, 1989. Active in communications Lilac Bloomsday Assn., Spokane, 1977. Served to E-5 USNR, 1955-63. Recipient Disting. Service award Wash. State Commn., 1974, Nev. Hollerin' Champ Carl Hayden Scribe, 1979. Mem. Am. Fedn. Musicians (life), Spokane Edn. Assn. (rec. sec. 1987), Music Educator's Nat. Conf., Am. Radio Relay League (asst. dir. 1987), Ea. Wash. Music Educator's Assn. (pres. 1978-79), Dial Twisters Club (pres. 1979-80), VHF Radio Amateurs (dir. 1980-83), Elks, Moose. Home: 5006 W Houston Ave Spokane WA 99208-3728 Office: Elem Mus Office 503 W 4th Ave Spokane WA 99204-2603

PUGH, RICHARD CRAWFORD, lawyer; b. Phila., Apr. 28, 1929; s. William and Myrtle (Crawford) P.; m. Nanette Bannen, Feb. 27, 1954; children: Richard Crawford, Andrew Lembert, Catherine Elizabeth. AB summa cum laude, Dartmouth Coll., 1951; BA in Jurisprudence, Oxford (Eng.) U., 1953; LLB, Columbia U., 1958. Bar: N.Y. 1958. Assoc. firm Cleary, Gottlieb, Steen & Hamilton, N.Y.C., 1958-61; ptnr. Cleary, Gottlieb, Steen & Hamilton, 1969-89, counsel, 1989—; disting. prof. law U. San Diego, 1989—; mem. faculty Law Sch. Columbia U., 1961-89, prof., 1964-69, adj. prof., 1969-89; lectr. Columbia-Amsterdam-Leyden (Netherlands) summer program Am. law, 1963, 79; dep. asst. atty. gen. tax div. U.S. Dept. Justice, 1966-68; Cons. fiscal and fin. br. UN Secretariat, 1962, 64. Editor: Columbia Law Rev., 1957-58; editor: (with W. Friedmann) Legal Aspects of Foreign Investment, 1959, (with others) International Law, 1993, Taxation of International Transactions, 1993, Taxation of Business Enterprises, 1993. Served with USNR, 1954-56. Rhodes scholar, 1953. Mem. ABA, Am. Law Inst., Am. Coll. Tax Counsel, Am. Soc. Internat. Law, Coun. Fgn. Rels., Internat. Fiscal Assn. (pres. U.S. br. 1978-79). Home: 7335 Encelia Dr La Jolla CA 92037-5729 Office: Univ San Diego Sch Law Alcala Park San Diego CA 92110-2429

PUGHE, BRONWYN GINGER, writer educator; b. Natick, Mass., Dec. 27, 1955; de. Earle Wells and Mary Louise (Miller) P.; childern: Conor, Chris; stepchildren: Mary, Elizabeth, David. BA in English, U. Mont., 1985, MFA in Writing, 1988, MA in Lit., 1989. Adminstrv. asst., Architecture Dept. Carnegie Mellon U., Pitts., 1979-80; art dir. Mesa Quick Copy & Printing, El Paso, Tex., 1982-83; editor, art. dir. Cutbank Mag., Missoula, Mont., 1985-88; music tchr. Primrose Montessori, Missoula, Mont., 1983-89; tutor pvt. practice, Missoula, Mont., 1986-87; teaching asst. U. Mont., 1987-89; dir., Creative Writing Charles Wright Acad., Tacoma, 1989-92; instr. Tacoma C.C., 1992—; adj. faculty Pierce Coll., Tacoma, 1992—; instr. Pacific Luth. U., 1993—. Author: Oasis, 1985, Lord John 10, 1988, Young Voices at Risk, 1993; contbr. Three Rivers Poetry Jour., Amphora Review., High Plains Lit. Review, Bloomsbury Review, Vanderbilt Review; editor: Polyhymnia: A Mag. of the Fine Arts, 1989-92. Helper Steilacoom Hist. Soc., Wash., 1992; bd. dir. Women's Place (adv. coun.), 1988-89; mem., provider Mont. Childcare Assn., 1986-89; cit's. review bd. United Way, 1986. Cultural Infusion in Coll. grantee Northwest Indian Coll., Pierce Coll., 1992, Native Am. Lit. grantee, 1992; best of show, 2nd pl. award,

JEA, 1992. Founder Steilacoom Writer's Group; mem. Am. Assn. of Women in Community & Junior Colls., Nat. Coun. of Tchrs of English (Superior Recognition award with State Supt. Pub. Instrn. 1993), Associated Writing Programs, Poets and Writers.

PUGMIRE, GREGG THOMAS, optical engineer; b. Montpelier, Idaho, Sept. 23, 1963; s. Vaughn Rich and Yvonne (Thomas) P.; m. Linda Lee Harris, July 17, 1987; children: Lindsay, Stephanie. BS, MS, Brigham Young U., 1990. Summer rsch. engr. Nat. Security Agy., Ft. Meade, Md., 1988; rsch. asst. Brigham Young U., Provo, Utah, 1988-90; optical engr., scientist ESL Inc., Sunnyvale, Calif., 1990—; 1993 conf. presenter in field. Engring. scholar Brigham Young U., 1989-90. Mem. Optical Soc. Am., Golden Key, Eta Kappa Nu. Mem. LDS Ch. Home: 2184 Royal Dr Santa Clara CA 95050-3610 Office: ESL Inc 495 E Java Dr Sunnyvale CA 94088-3510

PULLEN, KENT EDWARD, state legislator, chemist; b. El Paso, Tex., May 4, 1942; s. Eugene Hoyt and Maris Morie (Glover) P.; m. Fay Lynnette Endres, June 13, 1964; children: Katherine Ann, Walter David. BS, U. N.Mex., 1963; PhD, U. Wash., 1967. Asst. prof. chemistry U. Idaho, Moscow, 1967-68; engr. Boeing Co., Seattle, 1968-90; mem. Wash. Ho. Reps., Olympia, 1973-75, Wash. Senate, 1975-90; chmn. Senate Law and Justice com., 1988-89; mem. King County Coun., 1990—. Bd. dirs. Citizen Taxpayers Assn., Kent, Wash., 1979-85; chmn. Citizens Against Crime, 1975; co-chmn. Com. for Honest Elections, Kent, 1977. Mem. Mountaineers Club. Wash. State Chess Champion, 1985. Office: King County Coun King County Courthouse Seattle WA 98104

PULLIAM, EUGENE SMITH, newspaper publisher; b. Atchison, Kans., Sept. 7, 1914; s. Eugene Collins and Myrta (Smith) P.; m. Jane Bleecker, May 29, 1943; children—Myrta, Russell, Deborah. A.B., DePauw U., 1935, LL.D., 1973. Reporter, UP, Chgo., Detroit, Buffalo, 1935-36; news editor Radio Sta. WIRE, Indpls., 1937-41; city editor Indpls. Star, 1947-48; mng. editor Indpls. News, 1948-62; asst. publisher Indpls. Star and News, 1962-76; pres. Phoenix Newspapers, 1979—; exec. v.p. Central Newspapers, Indpls., 1979—. Mem. Am. Soc. Newspaper Editors, Am. Newspaper Pubs. Assn. Found. (past pres.), Hoosier State Press Assn. (treas.), Soc. Profl. Journalists, Delta Kappa Epsilon. Club: Crooked Stick Golf. Office: Indpls Star Indpls Newspapers Inc 307 N Pennsylvania St Indianapolis IN 46204-1899 also: Phoenix Newspapers Inc 120 E Van Buren St Phoenix AZ 85004

PULLIAM, FRANCINE SARNO, real estate broker and developer; b. San Francisco, Sept. 14, 1937; d. Ralph C. Stevens and Frances I. (Wilson) Sarno; m. John Donald Pulliam, Aug. 14, 1957 (div. Mar. 1965); 1 child, Wendy; m. Terry Kent Graves, Dec. 14, 1974. Student, U. Ariz., 1955-56, U. Nev., Las Vegas, 1957. Airline stewardess Bonanza Airlines, Las Vegas, 1957; real estate agt. The Pulliam Co., Las Vegas, 1958-68, Levy Realty, Las Vegas, 1976-76; real estate broker, owner Prestige Properties, Las Vegas, 1976—; importer, exporter Exports Internat., Las Vegas, 1984—; Citicorp Bank; mem. adv. bd. to Amb. to Bahamas Chic Hect. Bd. dirs. Las Vegas Bd. Realtors, Fedn. Internat. Realtors, Nat. Kidney Found., Assistance League, Cancer Soc., Easter Seals, Econ. Rsch. Bd., Children's Discovery Mus., New Horizons Ctr. for Children with Learning Disabilities, Girl Scouts, Home of the Good Shepard, St. Jude's Ranch for Homeless Children; pres., bd. dirs. Better Bus. Bur.; chmn. Las Vegas Taxi Cab Authority; pres. Citizens for Pvt. Enterprises. Mem. Las Vegas C. of C. (bd. dirs., developer). Republican. Roman Catholic. Office: 3100 Charleston Ste 202 Las Vegas NV 89102

PULLIN, JORGE ALFREDO, physics researcher; b. Buenos Aires, Feb. 26, 1963; came to U.S., 1989; s. Archie Ernest and Evangelina (Rostagno) P.; m. Gabriela Ines Gonzalez, Oct. 7, 1989. MSc in Physics, Inst. Balseiro, Bariloche, Argentina, 1986, PhD in Physics, 1988. Asst. prof. U. Cordoba, Argentina, 1988—, mgr. computer systems physics dept., 1988-89; rsch. assoc. Syracuse (N.Y.) U., 1989-91, U. Utah, 1991-93; asst. prof. Pa. State U., Collegeville, 1993—; grant reviewer ANEP, Govt. of Spain, 1991—. Reviewer Math. Revs., 1988—, Soc. for Indsl. & Applied Math. Rev., 1991—, Cambridge U. Press, 1991—; referee Physics Letters, 1990—, Phys. Rev., 1990—, Am. Jour. Physics, 1991—, Jour. Math. Physics, 1991—; contbr. articles to profl. jours. Mem. Internat. Soc. Gen. Relativity.

PULLUM, GEOFFREY KEITH, linguistics educator; b. Irvine, Scotland, Mar. 8, 1945; came to U.S., 1980; s. Keith Francis and Marjorie Joan (Horsey) P.; m. Joan Elona, Sept. 29, 1967; 1 child, Calvin James. BA with 1st honors, U. York, Eng., 1972; PhD, U. London, 1976. Lectr. Univ. Coll., London, 1974-81; prof. linguistics U. Calif., Santa Cruz, 1981—. Author: The Great Eskimo Vocabulary Hoax, 1991; author, editor 12 books, 150 articles, 1970-93. Fellow Ctr. for Advanced Study in Behavioral Scis., Stanford, Calif., 1990-91. Office: U Calif Cowell Coll 1156 High St Santa Cruz CA 95064

PUNCH, SANDRA LEE, academic administrator; b. Pekin, Ill., Apr. 18, 1952; d. Jack B. Sarff and Marcella Mae (Petrie) Owens; m. William Joseph Punch, Sept. 16, 1979. Multiple subject credential, San Diego State U., 1974, BA in Geography and Art, 1974, MS in Counseling, 1989. Educator Chula Vista (Calif.) City Schs., 1975-77; dept. mgr. Bullocks Dept. Store, San Diego, 1976-79; bus. svcs. rep. Pacific Telephone, San Diego, 1979-80; clerical asst. San Diego State U., San Diego, 1980-82, registration coord., 1982-85, registration and records coord., 1985-87; coord. student svcs. North County br. San Diego State U., San Marcos, Calif., 1987-91; dir. career ctr. Calif. State U., San Marcos, 1991—; bd. dirs. leadership isnt. San Diego State U.; mem. presdl. search com. San Diego State U., San Marcos, 1989. Mem. San Diego Zool. Soc., 1979-93. Mem. Women's Coun. of the State U., Advocates for Women in Academia, Coll. Placement Coun., Western Coll. Placement Assn., Calif. Ednl. Placement Assn. (exec. bd. mem.), North County Pers. Assn. Office: Calif State U San Marcos CA 92096

PUNCHARD, LIONEL, mortgage banking company executive; b. L.A., July 30, 1952; s. T.J. and Ethel (Fields) P. Student, Fullerton Coll., 1973, Whittier Coll., 1976. Sr. loan officer The Mortgage Guild, Garden Grove, Calif., 1983-85; prodn. mgr. Internat. Mortgage, Orange, Calif., 1985; pres. 1st Republic Mortgage, Santa Ana, Calif., 1985—. Mem. Nat. Assn. Home Builders, Bldg. Industry Assn. Orange County, Sales and Mktg. Coun. (bd. dirs. 1989—), Orange Assn. Mortgage Bankers. Office: 1st Republic Mortgage 2020 E 1st St Ste 205 Santa Ana CA 92705

PURCELL, ALEXANDER HOLMES, entomologist, educator; b. Summit, Miss., Oct. 12, 1942; s. Alexander H. and Dorothy (Adams) P.; m. Rita Hall, Oct. 14, 1946. BS, USAF Acad., 1964; PhD, U. Calif., Davis, 1974. Commd. capt. USAF, 1964, officer, pilot, 1964-70, resigned, 1970; grad. research asst. U. Calif., Davis, 1971-74; prof. entomology U. Calif., Berkeley, 1974—, dept. chair, 1993—; cons. FAO (UN), 1981. Contbr. articles to profl. jours. Mem. AAAS, Entomological Soc. Am., Am. Phytopath. Soc. Office: U Calif Dept Entomol Scis 201 Wellman Hall Berkeley CA 94720

PURCELL, CHARLES KIPPS, lawyer; b. Bellefonte, Pa., Mar. 15, 1959; s. Geoffrey and Alice (Kipps) P. BA, U. Va., 1981; JD, Harvard U., 1984. Bar: N.Mex. 1986, U.S. Dist. Ct. N.Mex. 1986, U.S. Ct. Appeals (D.C. and 10th cirs.) 1986, U.S. Supreme Ct. 1991. Law clk. to Hon. Ruth Bader Ginsburg U.S. Ct. Appeals (D.C.) Cir., Washington, 1984-85; lawyer Rodey, Dickason, Sloan, Akin & Robb, Albuquerque, 1986—. Bd. dirs. Quintessence-Choral Artists of the S.W., Albuquerque, 1990. Home: 1406 Atrisco Dr NW Albuquerque NM 87105-1110 Office: Rodey Dickason et al PO Box 1888 Albuquerque NM 87103-1888

PURCELL, STUART MCLEOD, III, financial planner; b. Santa Monica, Calif., Feb. 16, 1944; s. Stuart McLeod Jr. and Carol (Howe) P. AA, Santa Monica City Coll., 1964; BS, Calif. State U., Northridge, 1967; grad., CPA Advanced Personal Fin. Planning Curriculum, San Francisco, 1985. CPA, Calif. Sr. acct. Pannell Kerr Forster, San Francisco, 1970-73; fin. cons. Purcell Fin. Services, San Francisco, 1973-74, San Rafael, Calif., 1980-81; controller Decimus Corp., San Francisco, 1974-76, Grubb & Ellis Co., Oakland, Calif., 1976-78, Marwais Steel Co., Richmond, Calif., 1979-80; owner, fin. counselor Purcell Wealth Mgmt., San Rafael, 1981—; guest lectr. Golden Gate U., San Francisco, 1985—; leader ednl. workshops, Larkspur, Calif., 1984. Contbr. articles to profl. jours. Treas. Salvation Army, San Rafael-San Anselmo-Fairfax, Calif., 1987—; chmn. fin. planners div. United Way Marin County, Calif., 1984; mem. fundraising com. Marin County March of Dimes, 1987—, Marin County Arthritis Found., 1988—; mem. Marin Estate Planning Council. Served to lt. (j.g.) USNR, 1968-76. Named Eagle Scout, 1959, Best Fin. Advisor Marin County Independent-Jour. newspaper, 1987, Top Producer Unimarc, 1986; recipient Outstanding Achievement award United Way, 1984. Mem. Am. Inst. CPAs, Calif. Soc. CPAs, Nat. Speakers Assn., Internat. Assn. for Fin. Planners (exec. dir. North Bay chpt., San Francisco 1984), Internat. Soc. Pre-Retired Planners, Soc. CPA-Fin. Planners (dist. membership chmn. San Francisco 1986), Sigma Alpha Epsilon. Presbyterian. Home: 45 Vineyard Dr San Rafael CA 94901-1228 Office: Purcell Wealth Mgmt 1811 Grand Ave Ste B San Rafael CA 94901-1925

PURDIE, ROBIN STANFORD, retired air force officer; b. Cambridge, Eng., Feb. 14, 1940; came to U.S., 1943; s. Donald and Mary Carol (Brown) P.; m. Marian Zola Abbott, June 24, 1959; children: Scott, Michael, Jeffrey. BA, San Diego State U., 1961; MS, Auburn U., 1973. Commd. 2nd lt. USAF, 1961, advanced through grades to col., retired, 1991; pilot tng. USAF, Williams AFB, 1962; pilot instr., examiner USAF, Travis AFB, Calif., 1962-69, Altus AFB, Okla., 1969-72; pilot EC-47 USAF, Nakhan Phanom, Thailand, 1973-74; from C-5 squadron commdr. to dep. commdr. ops. USAF, Dover AFB, Del., 1979-85; chief pilot military airlift command USAF, Scott AFB, Ill., 1985-89; dep. chief of staff, ops. 22nd Air Force, Travis AFB, Calif., 1989-91. Editor: (textbook) Tongue and Quill, 1976; contbr. articles to profl. jours. Decorated with Legion of Merit with 1 oak leaf cluster, Air medal with 3 oak leaf clusters. Mem. AARP, Air Force Assn., Order of Daedalians (vice flight capt.), Retired Officers' Assn., Airlift Assn.

PURDY, JOSEPH DONALD, small business owner; b. Oklahoma City, May 28, 1942; s. Allen B. and Ruth (Sanders) P.; m. Annelie S. Purdy, Sept. 7, 1969; 1 child, Kimberly. BA, Calif. State U., Long Beach, 1960; MA, Chapman Coll., Orange, Calif., 1965; PhD, U. Okla., 1968. Asst. prof. U. Miss., Oxford, 1969-71; assoc. prof., head dept. Okla. State U., Weatherford, 1971-75; assoc. supt. Santa Barbara County (Calif.) Schs., 1975-81; chief exec. officer, owner Purdy Enterprises, Santa Maria, Calif., 1981—. Author: Selling, 1990; contbr. articles to profl. jours. Pres. bd. dirs. Santa Maria Symphony Orch., 1986-87. With U.S. Army, 1955-57. Mem. Internat. Reading Assn., Santa Maria Valley Developers (chmn. membership com. 1987-89), Lake Maria Valley Club (pres. 1984-86). Office: PO Box 2802 Santa Maria CA 93457-2802

PURSEL, HAROLD MAX, SR., mining engineer, civil engineer, architectural engineer.; b. Fruita, Colo., Sept. 15, 1921; s. Harold Maurice and Viola Pearl (Wagner) P.; m. Virginia Anna Brady, May 6, 1950; children: Harold Max, Leo William, Dawn Allen, Helen Virginia, Viola Ruth. BS in Civil Engring., U. Wyo., 1950. Asst. univ. architect U. Wyo., 1948-50; with Sharrock & Pursel, Contractors, 1951-55; owner Max Pursel, Earthwork Constrn., 1955-59; project engr. Farson (Wyo.) Irrigation Project, 1960-61; owner Wyo. Builders Service, Casper, 1962-66; head dept. home improvement Gamble Stores, Rawlins, Wyo., 1967; resident work instr. Casper (Wyo.) Job Corps Conservation Center, 1968; P.M. coordinator Lucky Mc Uranium Mine, Riverton, Wyo., 1969-80; constrn. insp. U.S. Bur. Reclamation, 1983—; cons. freelance heavy and light constrn., 1984—. Served with U.S. Army, 1942-45. Mem. Nat. Rifle Assn., Internat. Platform Assn., Mensa. Lodges: Eagles, Masons, Shriners. Exptl. research with log, timber and frame constrn. in conjunction with residential applications.; expanded experimental research to develop methods to up-date and modernize early area residences while retaining period styles, materials and general construction methods. Home: PO Box 572 Riverton WY 82501-0572

PURSELL, PAUL DENNIS, rehabilitation director; b. Altadena, Calif., Jan. 26, 1950; s. Robert Ralph and Thelma (Winifred) P. BS, Calif. State U., 1972. Registered phys. therapist. Asst. athletic trainer Orange County Ramblers Football, Inc., Anaheim, Calif., 1968, Calif. State U., Long Beach, 1968-71; athletic trainer U.S. Olympic Track & Field Tng. Camp, San Diego, 1971; phys. therapy aide Fountain Valley (Calif.) Community Hosp., 1971-72; chief phys. therapy Tustin (Calif.) Community Hosp., 1972-78; disaster planning coord. St. Joseph Hosp., Orange, Calif., 1984-90, dir. human devel., 1987-91, dir. phys. rehab. svcs., 1978—; instr. Calif. State U., Long Beach, 1989—; pres. Calif. Phys. Therapy Fund, Inc., Sacramento, 1983-84; chmn. bd. Orange County/Long Beach Health Edn. Ctr., 1984-85, Health Assocs. Fed. Credit Union, 1985-86. Chmn. Calif. Allied Health Coalition, Sacramento, 1983-84; speaker of assembly Orange County (Calif.) Health Planning Coun., 1986-87; trustee Gail Pattison Youth Leadership Trust, Orange, 1990-91; mem. mgmt. audit com., City of Orange, 1991—; chmn. bd. Leadership Orange, 1992-93; mem. Orange Citizen of Yr. Selection Com., 1988-89; pres. adv. coun. phys. therapy Calif. State U., Long Beach, chmn., 1987—. Recipient Commendation for Volunteerism, Carnation Found., 1984. Mem. Am. Coll. Sports Medicine, Am. Phys. Therapy Asn. (pres. Calif. chpt. 1983-84, Outstanding Svc. award 1980, 84), Nat. Fire Protection Assn., Orange County/Long Beach Health Consortium (chmn. bd. 1984-85), Orange C. of C. (pres. 1990-91),. Democrat. Roman Catholic. Office: St Joseph Hosp 1310 W Stewart Dr Ste 203 Orange CA 92667

PURSINGER, MARVIN GAVIN, classified advertising executive; b. Terre Haute, Ind., Dec. 23, 1923; s. Walter E. and Nellie V. (Coleman) Persinger; m. Elizabeth Jane Pursinger, Dec. 24, 1950; children: Gavin, Karen, Kristen, Beth, Bradley, Susannah. AB, Bowling Green State U., 1946, MA, 1947; PhD, U. So. Calif., 1961. Prof., Calif. State U., Northridge, 1957-60; staff Surgeon Gen. of U.S., Washington, 1961-62; prof. U. Minn., Mpls., 1962-63; pres. Gavin Internat. Corp., Morris, Minn., 1963-68, T. L. Lords Internat. Corp., Mpls., 1968-70, Asset Enhancement Corp., 1983—, Brendon Marshall Inc., 1992—; pres., owner Pursinger Co., Portland, 1970-82; strategic planning cons., Portland, 1982-84; pres. Bradward Thomas, Inc., 1984-87; pres. Bradward Vancouver (Wash.), Ltd., 1987-91; pres., dir. Brendon Marshall Inc., 1991—. Author syndicated column Bradward on Classifieds, in 1461 newspapers U.S. and Canada. Mem. White House Conf. on Edn., 1957. Capt. USMC, 1942-51. Ford Found. fellow, 1956-57. Named Eagle Scout with Palms Boy Scouts Am. Democrat. Episcopalian. Office: 600 SE Maritime Ave Stes 170-209 Vancouver WA 98661

PURVIS, JOHN ANDERSON, lawyer; b. Greeley, Colo., Aug. 31, 1942; s. Virgil J. and Emma Lou (Anderson) P.; m. Charlotte Johnson, Apr. 3, 1976; 1 child, Whitney; children by previous marriage: Jennifer, Matt. B.A. cum laude, Harvard U., 1965; J.D., U. Colo., 1968. Bar: Colo. 1968, U.S. Dist. Ct. Colo. 1968, U.S. Ct. Appeals (10th cir.) 1978, U.S. Ct. Claims, 1980. Dep. dist. atty. Boulder, Colo., 1968-69; asst. dir. and dir. legal aid U. Colo. Sch. Law, 1969; assoc. Williams, Taussig & Trine, Boulder, 1969; head Boulder office Colo. Pub. Defender System, 1970-72; assoc. and ptnr. Hutchinson, Black, Hill, Buchanan & Cook, Boulder, 1972-85; ptnr. Buchanan, Gray, Purvis and Schuetze, 1985—; acting Colo. State Pub. Defender, 1978; adj. prof. law U. Colo., 1981, 84-88, others; lectr. in field. Chmn., Colo. Pub. Defender Commn., 1979-89; mem. nominating commn. Colo. Supreme Ct., 1984-90; chmn. Boulder County Criminal Justice Com., 1975-81, Boulder County Manpower Coun., 1977-78. Recipient Ames award Harvard U., 1964; Outstanding Young Lawyer award Colo. Bar Assn., 1978. Mem. Internat. Soc. Barristers, Am. Coll. of Trial Lawyers, Colo. Bar Assn., Boulder County Bar Assn., Colo. Trial Lawyers Assn., Am. Trial Lawyers Assn., Trial Lawyers for Pub. Justice. Democrat. Address: 1050 Walnut St Ste 501 Boulder CO 80302

PUST, DAVID RICHARD, broadcaster; b. Olympia, Wash., July 29, 1940; s. Edgar Herman and Margaret Rae (Dodds) P.; m. Charlotte Jean Armstrong, June 25, 1963; children: Jeffrey, Steven. BA, St. Martins Coll., 1975. Morning announcer Sta. KGY Inc., Olympia, 1967—, gen. mgr., 1991—. Mem. Olympia Planning Commn., 1982-85. Named Hon. Grand Marshall Lakefair, 1991. Mem. West Olympia Rotary, Wash. State Assn. of Broadcasters (bd. dirs. 1989—). Baptist. Home: 2234 Crestline Blvd NW Olympia WA 98502 Office: KGY Inc 1240 N Washington Olympia WA 98501

PUTINAR, MIHAI IOAN, mathematician; b. Risnov, Brasov, Romania, Nov. 7, 1955; came to U.S., 1990; s. Ioan G. and Artensia (Tihan) P.; m. Gabriela G. Teodosiu, Mar. 3, 1989; 1 child, Corina. MA, U. Bucharest, Romania, 1979; PhD, Inst. of Math., Bucharest, 1984. Sci. researcher dept. math. Increst, Bucharest, 1980-90; vis. prof. dept. math. U. Iowa, Iowa City, 1990; vis. assoc. prof. dept. math. U. Kans., Lawrence, 1991; asst. prof. of math. U. Calif., Riverside, 1991-93, assoc. prof., 1993—. Author: Lectures on Hyponormal Operators, 1989; contbr. articles to publs. 2d lt. Romania Arty., 1974-75. Fellow Alex von Humboldt Found., Bonn, 1992; recipient Simion Stoilow prize romanian Acad. Sci., Bucharest, 1987; Internat. Math. Union grantee, Helsinki, 1990. Mem. Am. Math. Soc. Home: 41484 Ave de la Reina Temecula CA 92592 Office: U Calif Dept Math Riverside CA 92521

PUTMAN, CAROL JEAN, photographer; b. San Francisco, Jan. 1, 1943; d. Joe Alfred and Jessie Jane (Harris) P. BA, Calif. State U., Hayward, 1968. Freelance photographer Clayton, Calif., 1975—; exec. sec. Bank of Am., San Francisco, 1980; group sec. physics dept. U. Calif., Berkeley, 1974-75, sec. civil engring. dept., 1981-84, faculty sec. journalism dept., 1984-85, adminstrv. asst. math. dept., 1985-86, 87-88. Mem. Humane Soc. U.S., Thyroid Found. Am., Inc.

PUTNAM, BARRETT GRAHAM, architect; b. Eldora, Iowa, Apr. 22, 1919; s. Bennett William and Genevieve Azalea (Speers) P. Student, L.A. City Coll., 1937-40. Archtl. draftsman Louis H. Yade, Architect, L.A., 1937-39; machine tool designer Douglas Aircraft Co., Santa Monica, Calif., 1939-44; design/engring. staff Jet Propulsion Lab./Calif. Inst. Tech., Pasadena, 1946; archtl. designer Roy Kent Constrn. Co., Glendale, Calif., 1946-52; drafting/design staff Merrill Baird, Architect, Glendale, Calif., 1952-53; archtl. designer Frank W. Green, Architect, Reno, Nev., 1954-62; pres. Putnam Assocs., Architects, Reno, Nev., 1962—. Comdr. No. Nev. Sheriff's Aero Squadron. With USN, 1944-45. Mem. Lions. Republican. Home: 215 Taurus Cir Reno NV 89511 Office: Putnam Assocs Ltd 215 Taurus Cir Reno NV 89511

PUTNAM, CLARA JOYCE, small business owner; b. Vallejo, Calif., May 31, 1943; d. Brownie Butler and Vera Merle (Parker) Barger; m. Paul Richard Putnam, July 29, 1964; children: Rory, Dennis, Richard, Craig, Shannon. Owner Love Is Homemade, Eugene, Oreg. Leader Campfire, 1972-82. Mem. St. Mark's Women's Club (various offices), Carmel of Maria Regina (aux. bd., various offices). Democrat. Roman Catholic. Home and Office: 598 Baxter St Eugene OR 97402

PUTNAM, DAVID FRANK, small business owner, engineer; b. Mt. Kisco, N.Y., Feb. 8, 1932; s. Oliver Osmond and Mae Dorothy (Severance) P.; m. Barbara Louise Goodwin, Aug. 25, 1956; children: Katherine Jean, Laurie Mae, David Oliver, Sean Ernest. BE, Yale U., 1953. Registered profl. engr., Oreg. Engr. Gen. Dynamics/Electric Boat, Groton, Conn., 1955-62, United Technologies/Hamilton Std., Windsor Locks, Conn., 1962-66, McDonnell Douglas Astronautics, Huntington Beach, Calif., 1966-73; pres. Umpqua Rsch. Co., Myrtle Creek, Oreg., 1973—. Lt. (j.g.) USNR, 1953-55. Methodist. Home: 1594 Springbrook Rd Myrtle Creek OR 97457 Office: Umpqua Rsch Co 125 Volunteer Way Myrtle Creek OR 97957

PUTNAM, JACKSON KEITH, historian; b. Emmons County, N.D., Feb. 10, 1929; s. Hugh Gordon and Mary Lucille (Jackson) P.; divorced; children: Roy, Zona, Zreata, Mike. BS, U. N.D., 1952, MA, 1956; PhD, Stanford U., 1964. From instr. to asst. prof. Oreg. State U., Corvallis, 1958-65; from asst. prof. to prof. Calif. State U., Fullerton, 1965-91, prof. emeritus, 1991—. Author: Old-Age Politics in California, 1970, Modern California Politics, 3d edit., 1990. With U.S. Army, 1952-54. Mem. Am. Hist. Assn. (Pacific Coast br.), Calif. Studies Assn., Calif. Hist. Soc., Hist. Soc. So. Calif., Western Hist. Assn. (Oscar Winter award 1977). Democrat. Home: 3112 E Yorba Linda Blvd C-2 Fullerton CA 92631 Office: Calif State U 800 N State College Blvd Fullerton CA 92634

PUTNAM, VIRGINIA ALICE, real estate trade association administrator; b. N.Y.C., Feb. 21, 1952; d. Frank Amador and Kathryn Rose (Graham) Garay; m. Barry Alan Wichmann (div. Oct. 1979); 1 child, Stephanie Mara; m. Gary Richard Putnam, Mar. 7, 1987. BSBA in Acctg., San Francisco State U., 1983. Ward clk. Rockingham Meml. Hosp., Harrisonburg, Va., 1971-72; acct. Garden Sullivan Hosp., San Francisco, 1972-77; office mgr. Pierce & Strain Advt., San Francisco, 1977-78, Luth. Coun. U.S.A., San Francisco, 1978-80; acct. Luth. Social Svcs., San Francisco, 1979-82; co-owner, cons. Carrell, Willits & Stewart, Fremont, Calif., 1981-82; auditor Peat, Marwick & Mitchell CPA's, San Francisco, 1983; asst. exec. v.p. Spokane Bd. of Realtors, 1983-85; exec. v.p. Skagit County Assn. of Realtors, Burlington, Wash., 1986—; pres. N.W. Coun. of Multiple Listing Svc., Seattle, 1983, conf. coord. 1985, 92, profl. stds. trainer Wash. Assn. of Realtors, 1992. Pres. Skagit Women's Alliance and Network, Mt. Vernon, Wash., 1990; co-chmn. Friendship Ho., Mt. Vernon, 1991-92; fundraising chmn. Fire Safety Ho. Program, Mt. Vernon, 1991. Recipient Pres. award Skagit County Assn. of Realtors, 1989, Outstanding Contbn. Skagit County Fire Chiefs' Assn., 1991, Officer's Merit award Kiwanis Club of Skagit Valley, 1987. Mem. Am. Soc. of Assn. Execs., Wash. Soc. of Assn. Execs., Skagit Women in Bus., Kiwanis Club of Mt. Vernon, Skagit Valley Alternative Sch. (mentor program 1992). Office: Skagit County Assn Realtors 108 Century Ln Burlington WA 98233

PYBRUM, STEVEN MARK, tax specialist, accountant; b. Santa Cruz, Calif., Mar. 12, 1951; m. Belinda J. Pybrum, Sept. 18, 1987. BS, Calif. Poly. U., 1973; MBA, Golden Gate U., 1988. CPA, Calif. Cost acct. William Wrigley Co., Santa Cruz, 1973-75; tax acct. Ackerman Stranuhal and Co. CPAs, Santa Cruz, 1975-77; prin., mgmt. cons. Pybrum and Co., Santa Barbara, Calif., 1979—. Nat. speaker Tax Tips radio program, 1980; contbr. articles to mags., newspapers. Mem. Calif. Soc. CPAs, Elks, C. of C. Office: Pybrum and Co PO Box 23209 Santa Barbara CA 93121-3209

PYE, DAVID THOMAS, life sciences company executive; b. Darby, Pa., June 12, 1942; s. David and Grace Marie (Dale) P. B.S., Widener U., 1964. C.P.A., Pa., Calif. Tax cons. Price Waterhouse & Co., Phila., 1964-70; dir. taxes AID, Inc., Phila., 1970-75; dir. tax adminstrn. Syntex Corp., Palo Alto, Calif., 1975—. Mem. Am. Inst. C.P.A.s, Calif. C.P.A. Soc., Pa. Inst. C.P.A.s, Tax Execs. Inst. Home: 2210 Jackson St # 103 San Francisco CA 94115 Office: Syntex Corp 3401 Hillview Ave Palo Alto CA 94304-1397

PYLE, WALTER ROBERT, mechanical engineer, consultant; b. Orange, Calif., Sept. 10, 1944; s. Larry Thomas and Muriel Dorothy (Korb) P. BSME and Elec. Engring., Calif. Polytech. Inst., 1966. Rsch. engr. Chevron Rsch. Co., Richmond, Calif., 1966-86, sr. rsch. engr., 1986-88, engring. assoc., 1988-90, sr. engring. assoc., 1990-92, staff engr., 1992—; cons. Shadowbox Constrn. Co., Richmond, Calif., 1979—, Ebonex Techs. Inc., Emeryville, Calif., 1986-89, Electrochlor Co., San Anselmo, Calif., 1984-86; bd. dirs. H-Ion Solar Co., Richmond. Inventor gasoline nozzles, photoseparatory nozzle, 1983. Mem. Sane Freeze, Washington, 1988—; supporter Calif. Polytech. Alumni Found., San Luis Obispo, 1966—; trustee UHF Engring. Soc., San Pablo, Calif., 1976—. Mem. Am. Ceramic Soc., Am. Solar Energy Soc., Nat. Hydrogen Assn., Am. Hydrogen Assn., Soc. Automotive Engrs., Internat. Hydrogen Energy Assn. Mormon and Buddhist. Office: Chevron Rsch & Tech Co 100 Chevron Way Richmond CA 94802

PYPER, JAMES WILLIAM, chemist; b. Wells, Nev., Sept. 5, 1934; s. William Jones and Wilma (Bjelke) P.; m. Phyllis Diane Henry, Aug. 30, 1957; children: Scott, Mark, Gregory, Heather, Melanie, Tara, Tammy, Wendy, Michael, Tanya, David. BS, Brigham Young U., 1958, MS, 1960; PhD, Cornell U., 1964. Ordained bishop Ch. Jesus Christ of Latter-day Saints, 1973. Research chemist Lawrence Livermore (Calif.) Nat. Lab., 1963-84, mass spectrometry group leader, 1973-75, tritium tech. group leader, 1977-78, applied phys. chemistry group leader, 1979-80, sect. leader for analytical chemistry, 1980-83, dep. sect. leader for analytical chemistry, 1983-87, assoc. div. leader condensed matter and analytical scis. div., 1987-89, quality assurance mgr., 1989-90, ret., 1990. Contbr. articles to sci. jours. Presided over local congregations, 1973-75, 87-91; mem. stake high coun., 1976-87, missionary Ch. of Jesus Christ of Latter Day Saints, Thessaloniki, Greece, 1991-93. Republican.

QUACKENBUSH, JUSTIN LOWE, federal judge; b. Spokane, Wash., Oct. 3, 1929; s. Carl Clifford and Marian Huldah (Lowe) Q.; m. Marie McAtee; children: Karl Justin, Kathleen Marie, Robert Craig. B.A., U. Idaho, 1951;

LL.B., Gonzaga U., Spokane, 1957. Bar: Wash. 1957. Dep. pros. atty. Spokane County, 1957-59; ptnr. Quackenbush, Dean, Bailey & Henderson, Spokane, 1959-80; dist. judge U.S. Dist. Ct. (ea. dist.) Wash., Spokane, from 1980, now chief judge; part-time instr. Gonzaga U. Law Sch., 1960-67. Chmn. Spokane County Planning Commn., 1969-73. Served with USN, 1951-54. Mem. ABA, Wash. Bar Assn., Spokane County Bar Assn. (trustee 1976-78), Internat. Footprint Assn. (nat. pres. 1967), Spokane C. of C. (trustee, exec. com. 1978-79). Episcopalian. Club: Spokane Country. Lodge: Shriners. Office: US Dist Ct PO Box 1432 Spokane WA 99210-1432

QUALE, MARK CHRISTOPHER, marketing executive; b. Boston, Oct. 14, 1948; s. Andrew Christopher and Luella (Meland) Q.; m. Clareen Heim, Mar. 25, 1989. BA, Princeton U., 1970; MBA, Harvard U., 1975. Asst. product mgr. Richardson-Vicks, N.Y.C., 1970-72, product mgr., 1972-73; product mgr. The Dial Corp., Phoenix, 1975-78, sr. product mgr., 1978-81; v.p. mktg. Thompson Industries, Phoenix, 1981-82, v.p. sales, mktg., 1982-88; v.p. gen. mgr. Rockford Corp., Tempe, Ariz., 1988-90, v.p. corp. mktg., 1990—. Home: 6029 E Calle Del Sud Scottsdale AZ 85251 Office: Rockford Corp 546 S Rockford Dr Scottsdale AZ 85251

QUALLEY, CHARLES ALBERT, fine arts educator; b. Creston, Iowa, Mar. 19, 1930; s. Albert Olaf and Cleora (Dietrick) Q.; m. Betty Jean Griffith, Nov. 26, 1954; children: Janet Lynn, John Stuart. B.F.A., Drake U., 1952; M.A., U. Iowa, 1956, M.F.A., 1958; Ed.D., Ill. State U., 1967. Art tchr. Des Moines Pub. Schs., 1952,, 54-55; critic art tchr. U. Iowa, 1955-57; prof. fine arts U. Colo., Boulder, 1958-90, prof. emeritus, 1990—; chmn. dept. fine arts U. Colo., 1968-71, assoc. chmn., 1981-82; vis. prof. Inst. for Shipboard Edn., semester at sea, 1979, Ill. State U., 1985. Author: Safety in the Art Room, 1986; contbg. editor Sch. Arts, 1978-85, mem. editorial adv. bd., 1985-87; author column Safetypoint, 1981-85. Served with AUS, 1952-54, Korea. Mem. Nat. Art Edn. Assn. (v.p. 1980-82, pres. 1987-89, dir. conv. svcs. 1990—), Colo. Art Edn. Assn. (editor 1965-67, 75, pres. 1976-78), Delta Phi Delta, Omicron Delta Kappa, Pi Kappa Delta. Home: 409 Fillmore Ct Louisville CO 80027-2273

QUAN, LISA LING, school administrator; b. Stockton, Calif., June 2, 1967; d. Wing You and Yim Yung Quan. BS in Sociology with honors, Oreg. State U., 1989; MS in Curriculum and Instrn. with honors, U. Oreg., 1990—; TEFL/TESL, Transworld Tchrs. Coll., 1991. Cert. tchr., Oreg. Nursery attendant Zion Luth. Ch., Stockton, 1986-87; tchr. asst. Linn-Benton Community Coll., Corvallis, Oreg., 1988-89, Early Childhood Ctr., Eugene, Oreg., 1989-90; dir. Wah Mei Sch., San Francisco, 1990—; peer reviewer child devel. divsn. Calif. Dept. Edn., 1992—, grant reader, 1992. Recipient Gladys Benard Edn. award Delta Kappa Gamma, 1988, 89, 90. Mem. Nat. Assn. for Edn. of Young Children, Assn. Childhood Edn. Internat., Profl. Assn. for Childhood Edn., Soc. for Asian Art.

QUATE, CALVIN FORREST, engineering educator; b. Baker, Nev., Dec. 7, 1923; s. Graham Shepard and Margie (Lake) Q.; m. Dorothy Marshall, June 28, 1945 (div. 1985); children: Robin, Claudia, Holly, Rhodalee; m. Arnice Streit, Jan., 1987. B.S. in Elec. Engring, U. Utah, 1944; Ph.D., Stanford U., 1950. Mem. tech. staff Bell Telephone Labs., Murray Hill, N.J., 1949-58; dir. research Sandia Corp., Albuquerque, 1959-60, v.p. research, 1960-61; prof. dept. applied physics and elec. engring. Stanford (Calif.) U., 1961—, chmn. applied physics, 1969-72, 78-81, Leland T. Edwards prof. engring., 1986—; assoc. dean Sch. Humanities and Scis., 1972-74, 82-83; sr. research fellow Xerox Research Ctr., Palo Alto, Calif., 1984—. Served as lt. (j.g.) USNR, 1944-46. Recipient Rank prize for Opto-electronics, 1982, Pres.'s 1992 Nat. medal of Sci. Fellow IEEE (medal of honor 1988), Am. Acad. Arts and Scis., Acoustical Soc.; mem. NAE, NAS, Am. Phys. Soc., Royal Microscop. Soc. (hon.), Sigma Xi, Tau Beta Pi. Office: Stanford Univ Dept Electrical Engineering ERL Palo Alto CA 94305

QUE HEE, SHANE STEPHEN, environmental health sciences educator; b. Sydney, N.S.W., Australia, Oct. 11, 1946; came to U.S., 1978; s. Robert Que Hee and Beris Elizabeth Byers. BSc with honors, U. Queensland, Brisbane, Australia, 1968, MSc, 1971; PhD, U. Sask., Saskatoon, 1976. Postdoctoral fellow chemistry dept. McMaster U., Hamilton, Ont., Can., 1976-78; asst. prof. dept. environ. health U. Cin., 1978-84, assoc. prof., 1984-89; assoc. prof. dept. environ. health sci. UCLA, 1989—; mem. editorial bd. Jour. of Biol. Monitoring, CRC Press, Boca Raton, Fla., 1989—, Lab. Methodology in Biochemistry, CRC Press, Boca Raton, 1988—; mem. peer rev. com. hazardous materials data base Nat. Libr. Medicine, Bethesda, Md., 1985-89, FAIC, 1987. Author: The Phenoxyalkanoic Herbicides: Chemistry, Analysis and Environmental Pollution, 1981, Biological Monitoring: An Introduction, 1993; contbr. more than 80 articles to profl. jours. Active Coalition Against Apartheid, Cin., 1984-85, Gay/Lesbian March Activists, Cin., 1987-89; chmn. membership com. Rainbow Coalition, Cin., 1988-89. NIOSH grantee, 1980, 92. Mem. AAAS, Am. Chem. Soc., Am. Coll. Toxicology, Am. Indsl. Hygiene Assn., Am. Conf. Govt. Indsl. Hygienists, Am. Water Works Assn. Home: 923 Levering Ave Unit 102 Los Angeles CA 90024-6608 Office: UCLA Sch Pub Health Dept Environ Hlth Scis Ctr Occup/Environ Health 10833 Le Conte Ave Los Angeles CA 90024-1772

QUENZER, MIQUE, film and television director, consultant, writer; b. L.A., Dec. 4, 1943; s. Arthur Joseph Quenzer and Marcoreta (Hellman) Starr; m. Alberta F. Robertsax; 1 child, M. Kleo. V.p. Sta. KGMB-TV, Honolulu, 1964-75, Hawaii Prodn. Ctr., Honolulu, 1964-75; pres. Quenzer Driscoll Dawson, Inc., Honolulu, 1976—. With U.S. Army, 1966-72. Recipient Sweepstakes award Am. Advt. Fedn., 1981, silver medal, 1982, 2 1st place and 1 2d place awards, 1982; Best of Show award Honolulu Advt. Fedn., 1989. Mem. Film and Video Assn. Hawaii (pres. 1992), Assn. Ind. Comml. Prodrs. (bd. dirs.). Office: 816 Queen St Honolulu HI 96813

QUERCIA, PETER WADE, JR., investor, consultant; b. Norwich, Conn., Feb. 7, 1954; s. Peter Wade and Dorothy (Heath) Q.; m. Lisa LaSalle; 1 stepson, Bradford. AS, Mohegan Coll., 1975; BA, U. So. Calif., 1977; MBA, Nat. U., 1981; postgrad., San Diego State U. Writer, editor Wall St. Jour., N.Y.C., 1970-71; cons., investor PQ Enterprises, Brookdale, Calif., 1971—. Democrat. Roman Catholic. Home: 101 Bobcat Ln Boulder Creek CA 95005-9365

QUIBAN, ESTELITA CABRERA, controller; b. Manila, Sept. 3, 1938; came to U.S., 1969; d. Apolonio and Regina (Lacasmana) Cabrera; m. Teodoro Quiban Jr., June 20, 1964; children: Erwin James, Theodelinde, Joyce Ann, Rina Francis. Assoc. Bus., Phillipine Coll. Commerce, Manila, 1956; BS in Acctg., Far Ea. U., Manila, 1958. Cost acct. Associated Pharms., Manila, 1959-65; chief acct. Allied Travels, Manila, 1965-69; acct. Allied Outlets, San Francisco, 1969-70, Chalet 21, San Francisco, 1970-75; head acct. Anna Millers Inc., San Francisco, 1976-81, contr., 1981—; v.p. Pacific Outlets Inc., San Francisco, 1985—; corp. sec. Anna Millers Inc., San Francisco, 1989—; trustee Anna Millers Pension Plan, San Francisco, 1990—. Treas. St. Augustine Choralle, 1990-92. Democrat. Roman Catholic. Home: 2926 Dublin Dr South San Francisco CA 94080 Office: Anna Millers Inc 86 Dorman Ave San Francisco CA 94124

QUICK, VALERIE ANNE, sonographer; b. Alta., Can., Feb. 14, 1952; came to U.S., 1953; d. Kenneth Conrad and Kathryn (Maller) Bjorge. Grad. high sch., Salinas, Calif. Registered adult and pediatric echocardiographer, abdomen, small parts and ob-gyn sonographer. Chief EKG technician Natividad Med. Ctr., Salinas, 1978-81, chief ultrasound dept., 1981—. Mem. Am. Inst. Ultrasound in Medicine, Am. Soc. Echocardiography, Nat. Soc. for Cardiopulmonary Technicians, Soc. Diagnostic Med. Sonographers, Am. Heart Assn. Office: PO Box 6694 Salinas CA 93912-6694

QUICK, WILLIAM THOMAS, executive, writer; b. Muncie, Ind., May 30, 1946; s. Clifford Willett and Della May (Ellis) Q. Student, Ind. U., 1964-66. Pres. Iceberg Prodns., San Francisco, 1986—. Author: Dreams of Flesh and Sand, 1988, Dreams of Gods and men, 1989, Yesterday's Pawn, 1989, Systems, 1989, Singularities, 1990, (as Quentin Thomas) Chains of Light, 1992, (as Margaret Allan) The Mammoth Stone, 1993. Mem. Sci. Fiction Writers Am. Home and Office: 1558 Leavenworth St San Francisco CA 94109-3220

QUIGLEY, KEVIN WALSH, lawyer, state legislator; b. Everett, Wash., Feb. 23, 1961; s. David W. Quigley and Mary (Cernetig) Thoreson; m. Suzanne Marion Bakke. BA with spl. honors, George Washington U., 1983; JD cum laude, NYU, 1986; LLM, Harvard U., 1992. Jr. fellow ctr. internat. studies NYU Law Sch., N.Y.C., 1986; assoc. Perkins Coie, Seattle, 1987—; mem. Wash. State Senate from 39th dist., 1993—; mem. various coms. Wash. State Senate. Bd. dirs. Teen Parent Housing Coun., Lake Stevens, Wash., 1992—. Grad. fellow Harvard Law Sch., 1987. Mem. Rotary, Phi Beta Kappa. Democrat. Home: 1029 Springbrook Rd Lake Stevens WA 98258

QUIGLEY, PHILIP J., telecommunications industry executive; b. 1943. With Advanced Mobile Phone Svc. Inc., 1982-84, v.p., gen. mgr., Pacific region; with Pac Tel Mobile Access, 1984-86, pres., chief exec. officer; with Pac Tel Personal Communications, 1986-87, pres., chief exec. officer; exec. v.p., chief oper. officer Pac Tel Corp., 1987; with Pacific Bell, San Francisco, 1987—; now pres., chief exec. officer Pacific Bell Group, Pacific Telesis, San Francisco. Office: Pacific Bell 140 New Montgomery St San Francisco CA 94105-3705

QUIJADA, ANGÉLICA MARÍA, elementary educator; b. Tijuana, Mex., Mar. 22, 1963; came to U.S., 1967; d. Juan José and Paula (Magallanes) Q. AA, L.A. Harbor Coll., Wilmington, Calif., 1985; BA, Calif. State U., Carson, 1990, MA, 1993. Tchr. asst., tutor L.A. Harbor Coll., 1982-85; elem. tchr. asst., tutor Ambler Avenue Sch., Carson, 1985-90; bilingual elem. tchr. Hooper Avenue Sch., L.A., 1991—. Counselor Pathfinders, Carson 7th Day Adventist Ch., 1980. Mem. Tchrs. English to Speakers Other Langs., Phi Kappa Phi. Democrat. Home: 320 E 181st St Carson CA 90746

QUILICO, JACK ANDREW, author, composer; b. Helena, Mont.; s. John and Madeline (O'Berto) Q. BS, Eastern Mont. Coll., 1953; MA, Mont. State U., 1971; postgrad., Mont. State Coll. Tchr. Wyo. Edn., S.D. Edn., Mont. Edn. Author: Iran, America and the Middle East Today and Tomorrow; composer: The Music Master, Scarlet and Gold, Shaman, Guardians, Eagles of the Sea. Deputy state treas. Mont., 1963-64; candidate for treas. 1964; chmn. region 9 Young Reps. Nat. Fedn., 1961, chmn. fgn. affairs com., 1962-63; insp. gen. Mont CAP; dep. wing comdr. S.D. CAP. Lt. USN. Mem. ASCAP, World Assn. Band Educators. Home: PO Box 994 Billings MT 59103

QUILLEN, EDWARD KENNETH, III, freelance writer, columnist; b. Greeley, Colo., Nov. 12, 1950; s. Edward Kenneth II and Dorothy May (Wollen) Q.; m. Martha Alice Patterson, June 26, 1969; children: Columbine Kay, Abigail Cynara. Student, U. No. Colo., 1968-74. Reporter Longmont (Colo.) Scene, 1972; editor Middle Park Times, Kremmling, Colo., 1974-77, Summit County Jour., Breckenridge, Colo., 1977-78; mng. editor Mountain Mail, Salida, Colo., 1978-83; freelance writer, Salida, 1983—; columnist Denver Post, 1986—. Author: The White Stuff, 1985; also 11 westerns under pseudonym; contbr. numerous articles to mags. Recipient award for best personal column Colo. Press Assn., 1983, 88. Democrat. Office: PO Box 548 Salida CO 81201

QUILLIGAN, EDWARD JAMES, medical school administrator; b. Cleve., June 18, 1925; s. James Joseph and Maude Elvira (Ryan) Q.; m. Betty Jane Cleaton, Dec. 14, 1946; children—Bruce, Jay, Carol, Christopher, Linda, Ted. B.A., Ohio State U., 1951, M.D., 1951; M.A. (hon.), Yale, 1967. Intern Ohio State U. Hosp., 1951-52, resident, 1952-54; resident Western Res. U. Hosps., 1954-56; asst. prof. obstetrics and gynecology Western Res. U., 1957-63, prof., 1963-65; prof. obstetrics and gynecology UCLA, 1965-66; prof., chmn. dept. Ob-Gyn Yale U., 1966-69; prof., chmn. dept. Ob-Gyn U. So. Calif., 1969-78, asso. v.p. med. affairs, 1978-79; prof. Ob-Gyn. U. Calif., Irvine, 1980-83, vice chancellor health affairs, dean Sch. Medicine, 1987-89, prof., 1987—; prof., chmn. ob.-gyn. dept. U. Wis., 1983-85; prof., chmn. Ob-Gyn Davis Med. Ctr. U. Calif., Sacramento, 1985-87; vice chancellor Health Scis., dean Coll. Med. U. Calif., Irvine, 1987-89, prof. ob-gyn, 1987—. Contbr. articles to med. jours.; co-editor-in-chief: Am. Jour. Obstetrics and Gynecology. Served to 2d lt. AUS, 1944-46. Recipient Centennial award Ohio State U., 1970. Mem. Soc. Gynecologic Investigation, Am. Gynecol. Soc., Am. Coll. Obstetrics and Gynecology, Sigma Xi. Home: 24 Urey Ct Irvine CA 92715-4038 Office: NC Irvine Med Ctr Dept Ob-Gyn 101 City Blvd W Bldg 26 Orange CA 92668-2901

QUINLAN, JAMES JOSEPH, mining geologist, consultant; b. Wallace, Idaho, Oct. 16, 1924; s. James Ernest and Clara (Carson) Q.; m. Patricia Luann Ziegler, Nov. 29, 1952; children: James P., Claudia, Timothy, Daniel, Michael, Bradley, Robert, Sean. BS in Mining, U. Wash., 1945, postgrad., 1946-47. Mine geologist Sunshine Mining Co., Kellogg, Idaho, 1947-51; geologist U.S. Geol. Survey, Spokane, 1951-57; exploration geologist Hecla Mining Co., Spokane, Tucson and Salt Lake City, 1957-69; chief geologist, chief mine engr. Lakeshore Project Hecla Mining Co., Casa Grande, Ariz., 1969-74; project mgr. Red Mountain Project Kerr-McGee Corp., Patagonia, Ariz., 1974-78; sr. staff geologist Kerr-McGee Corp., Oklahoma City, 1978-86; cons. geologist J.J. Quinlan and Sons, Norman, Okla. and Tucson, 1986—; co-chair ad hoc task force for Red Mountain Continental Sci. Drilling Com., Oklahoma City, 1984-85. Contbr. articles to profl. jours. Docent Arizona-Sonora Desert Museum. Lt. (j.g.) USNR, 1943-46. Mem. AIME (sr. mem.; chmn. Columbia sect. 1964, chmn. geology br. Ariz. sect. 1975), Ariz. Geol. Soc. Republican. Roman Catholic. Home and Office: 5626 E Holmes St Tucson AZ 85711

QUINN, CINDY LEE, communications consultant; b. Bloomington, Ill., Mar. 22, 1949; d. Ray R. and Jane Adele (Lartz) Q. BA, U. Colo., 1972. Mgr. communications Capitol Life Ins., Denver, 1978-82, Am. TV & Communications, Englewood, Colo., 1987-88; dir. communications Guaranty Nat. Ins., Englewood, Colo., 1982-86; prin. Quinn Communications, Denver, 1988—. Mem. Internat. Assn. Bus. Communicators (dir. 1989, Bronze Quill award 1988), Pub. Rels. Soc. Am.

QUINN, FRANCIS A., bishop; b. L.A., Sept. 11, 1921. Ed., St. Joseph's Coll., Mountain View, Calif., St. Patrick's Sem., Menlo Park, Calif., Cath. U., Washington, U. Calif., Berkeley. Ordained priest Roman Cath. Ch., 1946; ordained titular bishop of Numana and aux. bishop of San Francisco, 1978; bishop Diocese of Sacramento, 1979—. Office: PO Box 1706 1119 K St Sacramento CA 95812-1706

QUINN, JOHN EDWARD, steel fabrication company executive; b. Worcester, Mass., June 20, 1947; s. John Edward and Anne (Torrey) Q.; m. Celia Word Hogan, June 13, 1967 (div. 1972); children: Kevin Patrick, Kelly Anne; m. Sally Anne Kerr, Aug. 9, 1975. AS, Broward Community Coll., 1967. Cert. project mgmt. profl. Steel detailer Metal Fabricators, Inc., Denver, 1974-76; steel detailer self-employed Denver, 1976-78; chief draftsman Zimkor Industries, Inc., Littleton, Colo., 1978-81, drafting dept. mgr., 1981-84, v.p. ops., 1984-90, exec. v.p., 1990—. Mem. Project Mgmt. Inst., Am. Soc. for Quality Control, Am. Inst. Steel Constrn., Am. Welding Soc. Office: Zimkor Industries Inc PO Box 1006 Littleton CO 80160

QUINN, JOHN R., archbishop; b. Riverside, Calif., Mar. 28, 1929; s. Ralph J. and Elizabeth (Carroll) Q. Student, St. Francis Sem., Immaculate Heart Sem., San Diego, 1947-48; Ph.B., Gregorian U., Rome, 1950, Licentiate in Sacred Theology, 1954, S.T.L., 1954. Ordained priest Roman Cath. Ch., 1953, as bishop, 1967. Assoc. pastor St. George Ch., Ontario, Calif., 1954-55; prof. theology Immaculate Heart Sem., San Diego, 1955-62, vice rector, 1960-62; pres. St. Francis Coll. Sem., El Cajon, Calif., 1962-64; rector Immaculate Heart Sem., 1964-68; aux. bishop, vicar gen. San Diego, 1967-72; bishop Oklahoma City, 1972-73, archbishop, 1973-77; archbishop San Francisco, 1977—; provost U. San Diego, 1968-72; pastor St. Therese Parish, San Diego, 1969; apptd. consultor to Sacred Congregation for the Clergy in Rome, 1971; pres. Nat. Conf. Cath. Bishops, 1977-80, chmn. Com. of Liturgy; chmn. com. on Family Life U.S. Cath. Conf.; chmn. Bishops' Com. on Pastoral Rsch. and Practices, Bishops' Com. on Doctrine; mem. Bishops' Com. on Sems., Pontifical Commn., Seattle, 1987-88, Bishops' Com. for Pro-Life Activies, 1989—; apptd. pontifical del. for religious in U.S., 1983; pres. Calif. Cath. Conf., 1985; elected Nat. Conf. Catholic Bishops, Rome, 1994. Trustee U. San Diego, 1991-93. Mem. Cath. Theol. Soc. Am., Canon Law Soc. Am., Am. Cath. Hist. Soc. Address: 445 Church St San Francisco CA 94114-1799

QUINN, LEBRIS SMITH, cell biologist; b. Norwalk, Conn., Apr. 13, 1954; s. James Edward and Jean Marie (Kuzenski) Smith; m. Thomas Peter Quinn, Aug. 25, 1979 (div. 1983); m. Travis C. Gamble, June 8, 1985. BA in Biology with distinction, Swarthmore Coll., 1976; PhD in Anatomy and Cell Biology, U. Wash., 1982. Rsch. asst. prof. Dept. Biol. Structure, U. Wash., Seattle, 1986—. Contbr. articles to profl. jours. Rsch. grantee USDA, ACS and others. Mem. AAAS, Women in Sci., Women in Cell Biology, Am. Soc. for Cell Biology, Am. Soc. of Animal Sci., Sigma Xi. Office: U Wash SM-20 Seattle WA 98195

QUINN, PAT (JOHN BRIAN PATRICK QUINN), professional sports team manager; b. Hamilton, Ont., Can., Jan. 29, 1943; s. John Ernest and Jean (Ireland) Q.; m. Sandra Georgia Baker, May 1, 1963; children: Valerie, Kathleen. BA in Econs., York U., 1972; JD, Del. Law Sch., 1987. Player Toronto Maple Leafs, Ont., 1968-70, Vancouver Canucks, B.C., Can., 1970-72, Atlanta Flames, 1972-77; coach Phila. Flyers, 1977-82, L.A. Kings, 1984-86; head coach Team Canada, 1986; pres., gen. mgr. Vancouver Canucks, 1987—, head coach, 1990—; player rep. NHL, Atlanta, 1973-77, bd. govs., 1987—. Named Def. Man of Yr., Vancouver Canucks, 1971; named Coach of Yr. NHL, 1979-80; Coach of Yr., Sporting News, 1980, 92, Hockey News, 1980, 92; recipient Jack Adams Trophy NHL Coach of the Year; named Coach of Yr. Acad. Awards of Sports; best Canucks record in history of franchise, 1991-92. Roman Catholic. Office: care Vancouver Canucks, Pacific Coliseum, 100 N Renfrew St, Vancouver, BC Canada V5K 3N7

QUINN, PATRICK JAMES, embryologist; b. Strathalbyn, Australia, Mar. 13, 1946; came to U.S., 1986; s. Allen Edward and Lucy Christina (Morrison) Q.; m. Kay McLaren, May 18, 1968; children: Joanne, Katherine. B of Agr. Sci., U. Adelaide, South Australia, 1968; PhD, U. Sydney, New South Wales, 1973. Internat. postdoctoral fellow The Jackson Lab., Bar Harbor, Maine, 1972-73; sr. lectr. U. Newcastle, New South Wales, 1974-81; hon. rsch. fellow Med. Rsch. Coun., London, 1980; sr. rsch. fellow U. Adelaide, 1982-86; chief PhD Cedars-Sinai Med. Ctr., L.A., 1986-88; dir. Inst. for Reproductive Rsch., L.A., 1988-91, IVF Lab., Tarzana, Calif., 1991—; cons. Irvine Scientific, Santa Ana, Calif., 1987—. Author numerous scientific papers, 1969—; patentee in field. Recipient Internat. Postdoctoral fellowship NIH, 1972-73, award Royal Soc. Commonwealth Bursary, London, 1980. Mem. Australian Soc. Reproductive Biology (coun. mem. 1982-83), Fertility Soc. Australia (coun. mem. 1986), Am. Fertility Soc.

QUINN, TOM, communications executive; b. Los Angeles, Mar. 14, 1944; s. Joseph Martin and Grace (Cooper) Q.; m. Amy Lynn Friedman, Nov. 24, 1982; children—Douglas, Lori. B.S., Northwestern U., 1965. Reporter, newswriter ABC Radio, Chgo. and Los Angeles, 1965; reporter, producer Sta. KXTV, Sacramento, 1966; day editor City News Service, Los Angeles, 1966-68, chmn., 1980-85; pres. Americom, Inc., Los Angeles, 1985—; pres. Radio News West, Los Angeles, 1968-70; campaign mgr. Jerry Brown for Sec. State, Los Angeles, 1970; dep. sec. state Calif., Sacramento, 1971-74; campaign mgr. Brown for Gov., Los Angeles, 1974; sec. Calif. Dept. Environ. Affairs, Sacramento, 1975-79; pres. Sta. KFSO Radio, Fresno, 1985—; pres. K-HITS Radio, Reno, Nev.; dir. Parallel Communications Co. Chmn. Tom Bradley Mayoral Campaign, 1985. Recipient Headliner of Yr. award Greater Los Angeles Press Club, 1978; Environ. Protection award Calif. Trial Lawyers Assn., 1979. Democrat. Office: 6255 W Sunset Blvd Bldg 1901 Los Angeles CA 90028-7420

QUIÑONES, EDGAR A., oil company executive; b. Moniquira, Boyaca, Colombia, Dec. 19, 1935; came to U.S., 1952; s. Eduardo and Graciela (Pinilla) Quiñones-Neira; m. Myriam Cecilia, Oct. 13, 1962; children: Carlos E., Myriam L., Felipe, Ana Maria. Petroleum Engr., Colo. Sch. Mines, Golden, 1957; student exec. program, UCLA, 1989. Exec. trainee Cities Svc. Co., Bartlesville, Okla., 1957-58; engr., chief engr. Cities Svc. Co., Colombia, S.Am., 1958-69; mgr. prodn. Cities Svc. Co., Argentina, S.Am., 1969-73; mgr. ops. Cities Svc. Co., Peru, S.Am., 1973-76; staff drilling mgr. Cities Svc. Co., Tulsa, 1976-80; pres., gen. mgr. Cities Svc. & Occidental, Colombia, 1980-88; dir. govtl. rels. Occidental Exploration & Prodn. Co., Bakersfield, Calif., 1988-90; pres., gen. mgr. Occidental Exploration & Prodn. Co., Quito, Ecuador, 1990—; pres. Colombia Info. Ctr. for Petroleum Industries, Bogota, 1983-85; mem. adv. bd. Coun. of Americas, N.Y.C., 1988-90; dir. Colombia-Am. Assn., N.Y.C., 1988-90; trustee Caribbean Cen. Am. Action, Washington, 1988-90. Mem. Soc. Petroleum Engrs., Colombia-Am. C. of C. (dir. 1985-86). Roman Catholic. Office: Occidental Exploration & Prodn Co PO Box 11174 1200 Discovery Way Bakersfield CA 93389

QUINTANA, JEAN, clinical hypnotherapist; b. Newark, Dec. 31, 1951; d. Anthony and Mary Lee (Hemdrick) Jackson; m. Ronald Vasquez, 1973 (div. 1975); 1 child, Anthony Vasquez; m. Ronald Leo Quintana, Nov. 19, 1979. Student, Bryman Sch., 1975-76, Behavior Sci. Rsch. Edn. Ctr., 1992—. Cert. clin. hypnotherapist. Med. asst. Dr. De Cuir, Long Beach, Calif., 1976-77; artist Artistic Endeavors, Long Beach, 1977—; hypnotherapist Hypnotherapeutics, Ventura, Calif., 1991—. Chaplain Reps. Womans Club, 1990; corr. sec. The Channel Islands Gulls, Oxnard, 1992. Recipient Golden Poet award World of Poetry, 1989, 92; scholarship Behavior Sci. Rsch. and Edn. Ctr., 1992. Mem. Gold Coast Assn. of Hypnotherapists (pres. 1992—), The Pro-Speakers Toastmasters, Ventura County Profl. Women's Network, Am. Bd. Hypnotherapy, Anacapa Yacht Club. Home: 1111 Janetwood Dr Oxnard CA 93030 Office: Hypnotherapeutics PO box 50238 Oxnard CA 93031

QUINTON, PAUL MARQUIS, physiology educator, researcher; b. Houston, Tex., Sept. 17, 1944; s. Curtis Lincoln and Mercedes Genale (Danley) Q.; m. Bonnie Sue Casey, Aug. 5, 1967 (div. 1988); 1 child, Marquis; m. Lisbet Joris, Dec. 31, 1992. B.A., Univ. Tex., 1967; Ph.D., Rice U., 1971. Asst. prof. physiology and medicine UCLA Med. Sch., 1975-79; asst. prof. biomed. scis. U. Calif., Riverside, 1979-81, assoc. prof., 1981-84, prof., 1984—; assoc. prof. physiology UCLA, 1981-91. Recipient Paul di Sant'Agnese Disting. Sci. Achievement award Nat. Cystic Fibrosis Found., 1991. Office: U Calif Biomed Scis Weber Hall W Riverside CA 92521

QUIROGA, FRANCISCO GRACIA, surgeon; b. P de Nacozari, Son, Mexico, Feb. 26, 1930; came to U.S., 1956; s. Jose M. and Teresa (Gracia) Q.; m. Fernanda Mino, Oct. 18, 1958; children: Juan Carlo, Richard, Teresa. MD, Nat. U. Mexico, Mexico City, 1955. Diplomate Am. Bd. Surgery. Intern, resident surgery Sydenham Hosp., N.Y.C., 1960-65; pvt. practice surgery Tucson, 1965—. Fellow ACS, N.Y. Acad. Medicine. Roman Catholic. Home and Office: 1302 Thunderhead Circle Tucson AZ 85718

QUIROS, CARLOS FRANCISCO, plant genetics educator; b. Lima, Peru, Mar. 17, 1946; came to U.S., 1970; s. Carlos A. and Hilda (Raffo) Q.; m. Ana Raquel Velando, Mar. 15, 1970; children: Carlos M., Cesar S. BSc, Agrarian U., Lima, 1967, AE, 1968; MSc, U. N.H., 1972; PhD, U. Calif., Davis, 1975. Researcher Nat. Inst. Agr., Celaya, Mex., 1976-77; postdoctoral researcher U. Sherbrooke, Que., Can., 1976-77; rsch. assoc. U. Alta., Edmonton, Can., 1977-81; assoc. scientist Internat. Plant Rsch. Inst., San Carlos, Calif., 1981-83; asst. prof. vegetable crops U. Calif., 1983-87, assoc. prof., 1987-91, prof., 1991—. Contbr. articles to sci. jours., chpts. to books. Grantee Calif. Celery Rsch. Bd., 1983—, USDA, 1984—, AID, 1987-90, NSF, 1990; Fulbright fellow, France, 1990-91. Mem. AAAS, Am. Assn. Hort. Sci., Am. Potato Assn., Econ. Bot. Soc. Roman Catholic. Office: U Calif Dept Vegetable Crops Davis CA 95616

QUISENBERRY, ROBERT MAX, architect, researcher; b. Eugene, Oreg., Nov. 18, 1956; s. Clifford Hale and Annemaria Gertrude (Frank) Q.; m. Dawnese Elaine Tarr, Sept. 18, 1982. BArch, U. Oreg., 1982. Registered architect, Wash. Intern R. Merriman Assocs., Tacoma, 1978-81; owner Solar Design Assocs., Tacoma, 1981-83; job capt. Robert Jones, AIA, Tacoma, 1983; project architect Merritt & Pardini, Tacoma, 1984-87; project mgr. Lorimer-Case, San Diego, 1987-89; project design architect The Austin Hansen Group, San Diego, 1989-91; prin. Studio Q Architecture, Chula Vista, Calif., 1991—. Recipient Washington State Passive Solar Design and Building award Western Solar Utilization Network, 1981. Mem. AIA, Earthquake Engring. Rsch. Inst. Republican. Home: 644 Hartford St Chula Vista CA 91913-2456

QUISMORIO, FRANCISCO P., JR., physician, medical educator, researcher; b. San Fernando, The Philippines, Jan. 21, 1941; s. Francisco N. Sr. and Cristina (Parpana) Q.; m. Violeta Consolacion; children: James Patrick, Anne Violet. BS, U. Philippines, Quezon City, 1960, MD, 1964. Fellow in rheumatology U. Pa., Phila., 1966-68; fellow in immunology L.A. County and So. Calif. Med. Ctr., L.A., 1969-70; chief clin. rheumatology lab. LAC and U. So. CAlif. Med. Ctr., L.A., 1978—; assoc. prof. sch. med. U. So. Calif., L.A., 1976-83, prof. med., 1983—, prof. pathology, 1986—, vice chief div. rheumatology and immunology, 1986—; counselor Am. Fedn. Clin. Rsch., 1980; mem. Scientific and Med. Com. Arthritis Found., 1979-83; dir. Clin. Immunology Lab., L.A., 1984—; commnr. oral exams. Calif. Med. Bd., 1981—. Contbr. articles to profl. jours. Recipient rsch. award Am. Lupus Soc., 1980, svc. award Arthritis Found., 1980, Borie Fibrositis Rsch. award, 1989, Fleur de Lis award, 1991; named Outstanding Alumnus, U. Philippines, 1990. Fellow Am. Coll. Rheumatology, Am. Coll. Physicians; mem. So. Calif. Rheumatism Soc. (pres. 1969, 70), Am. Assn. Immunologists, N.Y. Acad. Sci., Clin. Immunology Soc., Philippine Med. Soc. So. Calif. (rsch award). Office: Univ So Calif Sch Medicine 2025 Zonal Ave Los Angeles CA 90033-4526

QURAISHI, MARGHOOB A., management consultant; b. Jaipur, India, July 15, 1931; s. Nazir A. Quraishi and Khudija B. Khan; married; 4 children. B of Commerce, U. Karachi, Pakistan, 1955, postgrad., 1956; cert. in bus. fin., indsl. mgmt. & rels., McGill U., Montreal, Que., 1958; MBA, Stanford U., 1959. Rsch. economist Riches Rsch., Inc., 1960-61; acct., auditor Webb & Webb, CPAs, 1961-62; contr., adminstrv. asst. to pres. Capcom, 1963; v.p., sr. cons. CPM Internat., Inc., 1964-65; mgr., contr. Woodside Homes, 1965-66; founder, pres. Associated Mgmt. Systems, Palo Alto, Calif., 1966—; guest speaker, tchr. in field. Author numerous publs. in field. Mem. Inst. Mgmt. Cons., Am. Arbitration Assn., Am. Mgmt. Assn., Am. Mktg. Assn., Am. Soc. Appraisers. Office: Associated Mgmt Systems 974 Commercial St Ste A Palo Alto CA 94303

QURESHEY, SAFI U., electronics manufacturing company executive; b. Karachi, Pakistan, Feb. 15, 1951; s. Razi and Ishrat (Temuri) Q.; m. Anita Sue Savory, Sept. 19, 1976; children: Uns, Zeshan, Anisa. BS in Physics, U. Karachi, 1971; BSEE, U. Tex., 1975. Test specialist Documentor div. A.M. Internat., Santa Ana, Calif., 1975-77; test engr. Computer Automation, Irvine, Calif., 1977-78; design engr. Telefile Computer Products, Irvine, 1978-80; founder, pres. AST Research, Inc., Irvine, 1980—; CEO AST Research Inc., 1988—. Mem. So. Calif. Tech. Execs. Network (bd. dirs.). Islamic. Office: AST Rsch Inc PO Box 19658 Irvine CA 92713-9658

RAABE, WILLIAM WALLACE, foreign language professional, educator; b. Columbus, Ohio, Mar. 23, 1928; s. John Christian Spencer and Chrystal Rae (Limes) R.; m. Karon LeAnne Howard, Sept. 2, 1961; 1 child, William Wallace II. BA, Ohio State U., 1949; MS in Edn., Ea. N. Mex. U., Portales, 1973. Educator Hobbs (N. Mex.) Pub. Schs. System, 1971—. Author: (poetry) Troika (Golden Poet of Year award), 1991, Autumn Fields (Golden Poet of Year award), 1992, Famine, 1989. Rep. Precinct Chmn., Lea County N. Mex., 1975-81; mem. Hobbs Community Players (bd. mem. 1976-78). Lt. U. S. Army, 1951-71. Recipient Purple Heart (2 awards), U. S. Army, Korea, 1971, 72, Air Medal, U. S.Army, Korea, 1972, Letter of Commendation, U. S. Army, Germany, 1970, Army Commendation Medal, Ft. Bliss, Tex., 1971. Mem. NEA-Hobbs (exec. bd. 1974-78), N. Mex. Assn. Class Room Tchrs. (exec. bd. 1974-78). Republican. Russian Orthodox. Home: 1714 Rose Ln Hobbs NM 88240

RABINOVICH, SEMYON, retired meteorologist; b. USSR, Jan. 1, 1922; came to U.S., 1988; s. Girsh and Gita (Chernomordik) R.; m. Yevgenya Treyster, Apr. 15, 1950; 1 child, Michael. MSc, Elec. Engring. Inst., 1949; PhD, Leningrad State Elec. Enring. Inst., 1958, All-Union State Rsch. Inst., 1969. Engr. elec. measuring instruments Design Bur. Vibrator, Leningrad, USSR, 1949-50, sr. engr. elec. measuring instrument design, 1950-51; project leader Elec. Measuring Instrument Design Bur. Vibrator, Leningrad, USSR, 1951-53; head lab. elec. measuring instruments Design Bur. Vibrator, Leningrad, USSR, 1953-60, head rsch. dept. elec. measuring instruments design, 1960-64; head lab. theoretical metrology D.I. Mendeleev All-Union State Rsch. Inst. Metrology, Leningrad, 1964-80, prof., 1972-76; ret., 1982; assoc. prof. Leningrad State Elec. Engring. Inst., 1958-59, 64-65. Author: Photocell Galvanometrical Self-balancing Instruments, 1964, Galvanometrical Self-balancing Instruments, 1972, Measurement Errors, 1978, Measurement Errors: Theory and Practice, 1993, (with L.F. Kulicovsky and others) Galvanometrical Compensators, 1964; also numerous articles to jours. and conf. procs.; patentee in field. Recipient silver medals Nat. Econs. Achievements Exhbn., 1960, 61, bronze medal, 1979. Home: 7705 Romaine St Apt 6 Los Angeles CA 90046

RABINOVITZ, JASON, film and television producer, consultant; b. Boston, Aug. 17, 1921; s. Morris J. and Martha (Leavitt) R.; m. Frieda Pearlson, July 18, 1948; children: Abby, Judith, Daniel, Jonathan. B.A. magna cum laude, Harvard U., 1943, M.B.A. with distinction, 1948. With Chase Nat. Bank, N.Y.C., 1948-49; asst. to sec.-treas. United Paramount Theatres, Inc., N.Y.C., 1949-53; dir. Microwave Assocs., Burlington, Mass., 1952-54; asst. controller ABC, N.Y.C., 1953-56; adminstrv. v.p. ABC-TV Network, N.Y.C., 1956-57; with Metro-Goldwyn-Mayer, Inc., N.Y.C., 1957-69; treas., CFO Metro-Goldwyn-Mayer, Inc., 1963, financial v.p., 1967-69; dir., exec. v.p., gen. mgr. Ency. Brit. Edni. Corp., Chgo., 1971-73; sr. v.p., gen. mgr. Am. Film Theatre, N.Y.C., 1974-75; v.p., asst. to pres. Metro-Goldwyn-Mayer, Inc., Culver City, Calif., 1976-79; v.p. fin. Metro-Goldwyn-Mayer, Inc., 1979-83; sr. v.p. fin. and corp. adminstrn. MGM/UA Entertainment Co., 1983-84; cons. motion picture and TV, 1984—, 1952-54. Served to capt., parachutist AUS, 1942-46. Decorated Bronze Star. Mem. Phi Beta Kappa, Phi Eta Sigma. Home: 1675 Stone Canyon Rd Los Angeles CA 90077-1912

RABINOWITZ, JAY ANDREW, state supreme court justice; b. Phila., Feb. 25, 1927; s. Milton and Rose (Rittenberg) R.; m. Anne Marie Nesbit, June 14, 1957; children: Judith, Mara, Max, Sara. B.A., Syracuse U., 1949; LL.B., Harvard, 1952. Bar: N.Y. 1952, Alaska 1958. Pvt. practice law N.Y.C., 1952-57; law clk. to presiding judge U.S. Dist. Ct., Fairbanks, Alaska, 1957-58; asst. U.S. atty. Fairbanks, 1958-59; dep. atty. gen., chief civil div. State of Alaska, 1959-60; judge Superior Ct. Alaska, 1960-65; justice Alaska Supreme Ct., 1965—; chief justice Alaska Supreme Ct., Juneau, 1972-75, 78-81, 1984-87, 90-92. Served with AUS, 1945-46. Mem. N.Y. Bar Assn., Alaska Bar Assn. (commr. on uniform laws 1971—). Office: Alaska Supreme Ct PO Box 70850 Fairbanks AK*

RABINOWITZ, MARIO, physicist; b. Mexico City, Mex., Oct. 24, 1936; came to U.S., 1939; s. Laib and Rachel (Loschak) R.; m. Laverne Marcotte; children: Daniel L., Benjamin M., Lisa B. BS in Physics, U. Wash., 1959, MS in Physics, 1960; PhD in Physics, Washington State U., 1963. Electronics engr. Collins Radio Co., Burbank, Calif., 1957; rsch. engr. Boeing Co., Seattle, 1958-61; rsch. asst. Physics dept. Wash. State U., Pullman, 1961-63; sr. physicist Westinghouse Rsch. Ctr., Pitts., 1963-66; mgr. gas discharges and vacuum physics Varian Assocs., Palo Alto, Calif., 1966-67; rsch. physicist Stanford (Calif.) Linear Accelerator Ctr., 1967-74; sr. scientist and mgr. Electric Power Rsch. Inst., Palo Alto, 1974—; adj. prof. Ga. Inst. Tech., Atlanta, 1987—, U. Houston, 1990—, Va. Commonwealth U., Richmond, 1990—, Case Western Res. U., Cleve., 1975-77, Boston U., 1975-77. Contbr. numerous articles to profl. jours.; patentee in field. Del., counselor Boys State, Ellensburg, Wash., 1953-55. Scholarship Baker Found., 1955-58; recipient Alumni Achievement award Wash. State U., 1992. Home: 715 Lakemead Way Redwood City CA 94062-3922

RABORG, CHRISTOPHER HENRY, food company executive; b. N.Y.C., Jan. 19, 1950; s. Frederic Birchal and Stephanie (Sydlowski) R.; m. Maria Christina da Silveira Cardoso, May 31, 1980; children: Bianca, Christopher Henry Jr. BS in Econs., U. Pa., 1973. Sr. systems analyst Andersen Cons., Sao Paulo, Brazil, 1973-76; mgr. fin. planning/analysis Schering-Plough, Latin America, 1976-77; mgr. strategic planning R.J. Reynolds, Rio de Janeiro, 1977-79; mgr. econ. planning Coca-Cola, Sao Paulo, 1979-81; exec. v.p. Swensen's, Sao Paulo, 1981-84; v.p., chief fin. officer Warner-Lambert, Sao Paulo, 1984-88; dir. fin. and planning Oral-B Labs., Redwood City, Calif., 1989-90; v.p., chief fin. officer Ruiz Food Products, Inc., Dinuba, Calif., 1990—; chmn., bd. advisors CIM Inst. Calif. State U., Fresno, 1992—. Named Entrepreneurial Success SBA, 1992. Mem. Wharton Club Brazil (founder, v.p. 1986-88), Wharton Clubs No. and So. Calif. Republican. Roman Catholic. Home: 31162 Hacienda Rd Visalia CA 93292 Office: Ruiz Food Products Inc 501 S Alta Ave Dinuba CA 93618

RABOVSKY, JEAN, toxicologist; b. Balt., Aug. 18, 1937. BS in Chemistry, U. Md., 1959; PhD in Biochemistry, Brandeis U., 1964. Asst. rsch. biologist U. Calif., Irvine, 1972-76; postdoctoral assoc. U. Fla., Gainesville, 1976-78; rsch. chemist Nat. Inst. Occupational Safety & Health, Morgantown, W.Va., 1978-89; staff toxicologist Calif. EPA, Sacramento, 1989—. Contbr. sci. lit., prepare risk assessments and other govtl. documents. Mem. AAAS, Am. Chem. Soc., N.Y. Acad. Scis., Soc. Toxicology, Sigma Xi. Office: Calif EPA Office Environ Health Hazzard Assessment 601 N 7th St PO Box 942732 Sacramento CA 94234-7320

RABY, WILLIAM LOUIS, author; b. Chgo., July 16, 1927; s. Gustave E. and Helen (Burgess) R.; m. Norma Claire Schreiner, Sept. 8, 1956; children: Burgess, Marianne, Marlene. BSBA, Northwestern U., 1949; MBA, U. Ariz., 1961, PhD, 1971. Ptnr. VAR CPA Firms, 1950-76, Touche Ross & Co., N.Y.C., 1977-87; pres. Ariz. State Bd. Accountancy. Author: The Income Tax and Business Decisions, 1964, 4th edit., 1978, Building and Maintaining a Successful Tax Practice, 1964, The Reluctant Taxpayer, 1970, Tax Practice Management, 1974, Introduction to Federal Taxation, annually, 1980-91, Tax Practice Managment: Client Servicing, 1986; editor: Raby Report on Tax Practice, 1986—, PPC Guide To Successful Tax Practice, 1991; mem. editorial adv. bd. Taxation for Accountants, The Tax Adviser; contbr. articles to profl. jours. Served with USN, 1942-45. Mem. AICPA (chmn. fed. tax div. 1980-83, v.p. 1983-84, coun. 1983-90), Am. Acctg. Assn., Am. Taxation Assn. (pres. 1980-81), Tax Ct. Bar, Ariz. C. of C. (chmn. 1987), Inst. CFPs, U. Club Phoenix, ASU U. Club, Beta Gamma Sigma (past pres. Ariz. alumni chpt.), Delta Mu Delta, Beta Alpha Psi, Alpha Kappa Psi. Presbyterian (elder, chmn. adv. coun. on ch. and soc. 1979-81). Office: PO Box 26846 Tempe AZ 85285-6846

RACE, LISA ANNE, environmental chemist; b. Casper, Wyo., Nov. 10, 1961; d. George L. and Sherry L. (Scheafermeyer) R. BS in Biochemistry, U. Wyo., 1984. Biol. aide High Plains Grassland Rsch. STa., USDA, Cheyenne, Wyo., 1990-91; chem. analyst technician divsn. labs. Wyo. Dept. Agr., Laramie, 1984-87; chemist Chem. Rsch. Labs., Santa Maria, Calif., 1987-88; chemist, environ. health and safety officer Enseco-Chem. Rsch. Labs., Santa Maria, 1988-90, acting lab. mgr., 1990, quality control and assurance officer, 1990; mobile lab. mgr. Coast to Coast Analytical Svcs., San Luis Obispo, Calif., 1991—. Home: 269 E Waller Ln Santa Maria CA 93455-2061 Office: Coast to Coast Analytical Svcs 141 Suburban Rd San Luis Obispo CA 93401

RACHIELE, ARTHUR HENRY, estate planning professional; b. Pitts., Aug. 24, 1928; s. Harry Henry and Lena Susie (Franklin) R.; m. Lena Marie Zuccher, Jan. 1, 1947 (div.); children: Leonard Lee, Arlene Ann Rachiele Florjancic; m. Janice Arline Jackson, July 27, 1990. BSBA, Duquesne U., 1942. Officer, treas. Sharpsburg Theatre Enterprise, Pitts., 1946-49; pres. Estate Planning for Physicians, Pitts., 1953—. Capt. U.S. Army, 1942-47, 50-52. Mem. NALU, Nat. Assn. Security Dealers, Royal Gardens Assn. (bd. dirs., treas. 1991—), Univ. Club, Variety Club, Elks, Rotary, Ariz. Club, Alpha Phi Delta. Home: 4822 N 72d Way Scottsdale AZ 85251-1302

RACHMELER, MARTIN, university administrator; b. Bklyn., Nov. 21, 1928; s. Jack and Sophie (Rosenbloom) R.; m. Elizabeth Karkalis, June 9, 1956; children: Susan, Ann, Helen. AB, Ind. U., 1950; PhD, Case Western Res. U., 1960. USPHS postdoctoral researcher U. Calif., Berkeley, 1959-61, asst. rsch. geneticist, 1961-62; asst. prof. Northwestern U. Med. Sch., Chgo., 1962-67, assoc. prof., 1967-89; dir. rsch. svcs. adminstrn. Northwestern U., Evanston, Ill., 1977-89; dir. tech. transfer U. Calif., San Diego, 1989—. Author: Lectures in Medical Genetics, 1966; contbr. article to profl. jours. With U.S. Army, 1952-54. Recipient USPHS Rsch. Career Devel. award, 1968-72. Mem. Assn. Univ. Tech. Mgrs. (v.p. 1983-85, trustee 1986-88, pres.-elect 1990, pres. 1991), Licensing Exec. Soc., Am. Soc. for Microbiology, Nat. Coun. Univ. Rsch. Adminstrs. (regional chair 1988), Sigma Xi (sec.-treas. 1982-86, chpt. pres. 1988). Office: U Calif Mail Code 0093 9500 Gilman Dr La Jolla CA 92093

RACICOT, MARC F., governor; b. Thompson Falls, Mont., July 24, 1948; s. William E. and Patricia E. (Bentley) R.; m. Theresa J. Barber, July 25, 1970; children: Ann, Timothy, Mary Catherine, Theresa, Joseph. BA, Carroll Coll., Helena, Mont., 1970; JD, U. Mont., 1973; postgrad., U. Va., 1973, Cornell U., 1977. Bar: Mont. 1973. With U.S. Army, 1973-76; advanced through grades to capt., 1973; legal assistance officer U.S. Army, Ft. Lewis, Wash., 1973; chief trial counsel U.S. Army, Kaiserslautern, Fed. Republic of Germany, 1975-76; resigned, 1976; dep. county atty. Missoula (Mont.) County, 1976-77; bur. chief County Prosecutor Svcs. Bur., Helena, Mont., 1977-89; asst. atty. gen. State of Mont., Helena, 1977-89; spl. prosecutor for the Atty. Gen.'s Office State of Mont., atty. gen., 1989-93, gov., 1993—. Founder Missoula Drug Treatment Program, 1977; bd. dirs. Carroll Coll. Pres.'s Coun., United Way, Helena; bd. visitors U. Mont. Sch. Law. Inducted into Basketball Hall of Fame Carroll Coll., 1982. Mem. Mont. Bar Assn., Nat. Assn. Attys. Gen, Carroll Coll. Century Club (bd. dirs.). Republican. Roman Catholic. Office: State of Mont Office of the Governor 204 State Capitol Helena MT 59620*

RACINA, THOM (THOMAS FRANK RAUCINA), writer, editor; b. Kenosha, Wis., June 4, 1946; s. Frank G. and Esther May (Benko) Raucina. B.F.A., Goodman Sch. Drama, Art Inst. Chgo., 1970, M.F.A. in Theatre Arts and Directing with honors, 1971. TV writer Hanna-Barbera Co., Hollywood, Calif., 1973-74, MTM Enterprises, Inc., Hollywood, 1974-76; head writer General Hospital ABC-TV, Hollywood, 1981-84; head writer Days of Our Lives NBC-TV, 1984-86, head writer Another World, 1986-88, co-head writer Generations daytime series, 1988-91, head writer syndicated Dangerous Women night-time TV series, 1991-92; assoc. head writer daytime TV series Santa Barbara, 1992-93. Author: Lifeguard, 1976, The Great Los Angeles Blizzard, 1977, Quincy, M.E., 2 vols., 1977, Kodak in San Francisco, 1977, F.M., 1978, Sweet Revenge, 1978, The Gannon Girls, 1979, Nine to Five, 1980, Tomcat, 1981, Secret Sex: Male Erotic Fantasies (as Tom Anicar), 1976, Magda (as Lisa Wells), 1981; ghost writer: non-fiction The Happy Hustler (Grant Tracy Saxon), 1976, Marilyn Chambers: My Story (Marilyn Chambers), 1976, Xaviera Meets Marilyn (Xaviera Hollander and Marilyn Chambers), 1977; musical plays A Midsummer Night's Dream, music and lyrics, 1968, Allison Wonderland, music and lyrics, 1970, The Marvelous Misadventure of Sherlock Holmes, book, music and lyrics, 1971; TV scripts Sleeping Over segment of Family, ABC, 1978, Russian Pianist segment, ABC, 1979, 1 Child of the Owl, NBC After-Sch. Spl., 1979; contbr. articles to Playboy, Cosmopolitan, Penhouse, Oui, Los Angeles, Gentleman's Quar., Westways; West Coast editor: Grosset & Dunlap, Inc., N.Y.C., 1978—; theatre dir., pianist, organist, composer. Recipient Emmy award nomination 1982, 83, 84, 85, 87; U.S. Nat. Student Assn. grantee, 1965. Mem. Authors Guild Am., Writers Guild Am. West. Democrat. Roman Catholic. Home: 3449 Waverly Dr Los Angeles CA 90027-2526

RACITI, CHERIE, artist; b. Chgo., June 17, 1942; d. Russell J. and Jacque (Crimmins) R. Student, Memphis Coll. Art, 1963-65; B.A. in Art, San Francisco State U., 1968; M.F.A., Mills Coll., 1979. Assoc. prof. art San Francisco State U., 1984-89, prof., 1989—; lectr. Calif. State U., Hayward, 1974, San Francisco Art Inst., 1978; mem. artist com. San Francisco Art Inst., 1974-85, sec., 1980-81. One woman show U. Calif., Berkeley, 1972, Nicholas Wilder Gallery, Los Angeles, 1975, San Francisco Art Inst., 1977, Marianne Deson Gallery, Chgo., 1980, Site 375, San Francisco, 1989, Reese Bullen Gallery, Humboldt State U., Arcata, Calif., 1990; group shows include Whitney Mus. Art, 1975, San Francisco Sci. Fiction, The Clocktower, N.Y.C., Otis-Parsons Gallery, Los Angeles, 1984-85, San Francisco Art Inst., 1985, Artists Space, N.Y.C., 1988, Angles Gallery, Santa Monica, 1987, Terrain Gallery, San Francisco, 1992, Ctr. for the Arts, San Francisco, 1993. Bd. dirs. New Langton Arts, 1988-92. Recipient Adaline Kent award San Francisco Art Inst., 1976; Eureka fellow Fleishhacker Found., San Francisco, 1988. Home: 1045 17th St San Francisco CA 94107-2508 Office: San Francisco State U Art Dept 1600 Holloway Ave San Francisco CA 94132-1722

RADA, ALEXANDER, university official; b. Kvasy, Czechoslovakia, Mar. 28, 1923; s. Frantisek and Anna (Tonnkova) R.; came to U.S., 1954, naturalized, 1959; M.S., U. Tech. Coll. of Prague, 1948; postgrad. Va. Poly. Inst., 1956-59, St. Clara U., 1966-67; Ed.D., U. Pacific, 1975; m. Ingeborg Solveig Blakstad, Aug. 8, 1953; children: Alexander Sverre, Frank Thore, David Harald. Head prodn. planning dept. Mine & Iron Corp., Kolin, Czechoslovakia, 1941-42; mgr. experimenting and testing dept. Avia Aircraft, Prague, 1943-45; sec.-gen. Central Bldg. Office, Prague, 1948; head metal courses dept. Internat. Tech. Sch. of UN, Grafenaschau, W.Ger., 1949-50; works mgr. Igref A/S, Oslo, 1950-51; cons. engr., chief sect. machines Steel Products Ltd., Oslo, 1951-54; chief engr., plant supr. Nelson J. Pepin & Co., Lowell, Mass., 1954-55; sr. project engr., mfg. supt. Celanese Corp. Am., Narrows, Va., 1955-60; mgr. mfg., facilities and maint. FMC Corp., San Jose, Calif., 1960-62; mgr. adminstrn. Sylvania Electronic Systems, Santa Cruz, Calif., 1962-72; asst. to pres., devel. officer Napa (Calif.) Coll., 1972-88; chief exec. officer NAVCO Pacific Devel. Corp., Napa, 1984-91; pres. NAVCO Calif. Co., 1991—; prof. indsl. mgmt. Cabrillo Coll., Aptos, Calif., 1963-72; mgmt. and engring. cons., 1972—. Pres. ARC, Santa Cruz, 1965-72, bd. dirs., pres., Napa, 1977-88; mem. Nat. Def. Exec. Res., U.S. Dept. Commerce, Washington, 1966—, chmn. No. Calif. region 9, 1981-88; mem. President's Export Council-DEC, San Francisco, 1982—. Recipient Meritorious Service citation ARC, 1972, Etoile Civique l'Ordre de l'Etoile Civique, French Acad., 1985; registered profl. engr., Calif. Mem. NSPE, Calif. Soc. Profl. Engrs., Am. Def. Preparedness Assn., Assn. Calif. Community Coll. Adminstrs., Nat. Assn. Corp. Dirs., World Affairs Council No. Calif., Phi Delta Kappa. Editor-in-chief Our Youth, 1945-48; co-editor (with P. Boulden) Innovative Management Concepts, 1967. Home and Office: 1019 Ross Cir Napa CA 94558-2118

RADA, ALEXANDER SVERRE, video technician; b. Lowell, Mass., Feb. 21, 1955; s. Alexander and Ingeborg S. (Blakstad) R.; m. Wipada Kooaroon, Dec. 31, 1987. AS in Telecommunications Tech., Napa Valley Coll., Napa, Calif., 1979. Gen. class lic. FCC; cert. broadcast TV technologist. Factory technician Internat. Video Corp., Sunnyvale, Calif., 1979-80; test engring. supr. Sony Broadcast Co., San Jose, Calif., 1980-82; sr. technician Precision Echo, Inc., San Jose, 1982-83; engr. One Pass Film and Video, Inc., San Francisco, 1983; broadcast svcs. engr. Audio Visual Co., Honolulu, 1984-85; owner, pres. ITN Tech. Svcs. Co., Honolulu, 1986—. Mem. Soc. Broadcast Engrs. (vice chmn. Hawaii chpt. 1992—), Soc. Motion Picture and TV Engrs., 1986—, Audio Engring. Soc. Home: 444 Nahua St Penthouse 12 Honolulu HI 96815

RADASHAW, SHARON LEE, music educator, entertainer; b. Grosse Pointe, Mich., Mar. 7, 1937; d. Henry Paul and Daisy (Hein) Fleischmann; m. Denny Dmitri Radashaw, July 25, 1959; children: Todd Warren, Joy Noelle, Shana Lee. B Music Edn., Ea. Mich. U., 1959; M Music, Mich. State U., 1962; postgrad., U. Calif., Santa Barbara, 1965-90, U. San Diego, 1992—. Cert. Calif. special secondary music credential, Calif. gen. secondary credential. Music tchr. Mason (Mich.) Pub. Schs., 1959-60; music tchr., cons. Waverly Schs., Lansing, Mich., 1960-62; music tchr. Garden Grove (Calif.) Unified Sch. Dist., 1962-63; music cons. Valley Oak Dist. & Ventura County, Thousand Oaks, Calif., 1965-67; creative arts tchr. Calif. Lutheran U., Thousand Oaks, Calif., 1969, 70, 80; music cons. Conejo Unified Sch. Dist., Thousand Oaks, Calif., 1978-80; music, drama, math tchr. L.A. Unified Sch. Dist., Chatsworth, Calif., 1980—; master tchr. Calif. State U., Northridge, 1990—; music specialist The Calif. Arts Project, Northridge, 1991—; chair music dept. Lawrence Jr. High, Chatsworth, Calif., 1988—; extra actress, singer T.V. stage, movies, L.A., Hollywood, 1965—; music & drama counselor Boy Scouts of Am., Ventura County, 1981—; singer Ventura County Master Chorale, 1965-70. Actress, singer: (ednl. TV) Dido and Aeneas, The Mikado; appeared in plays Kismet, Born Yesterday, The Stingiest Man in Town, The Mikado, A Little Night Music, Evita, La Cage Aux Folles, Desert Song, The Medium, Dido and Aeneas, Oklahoma, Fiddler on the Roof, The Music Man; appeared in films The Quitters, People's Coice of the Oscars; dir.: (musicals) Guys and Dolls, Pipe Dream, Finian's Rainbow, How to Succeed in Business Without Really Trying, Oliver, Fiddler on the Roof, The Music Man, Annie, Grease, Peter Pan, Kiss Me Kate, Brigadoon, Fame, (plays) Our Town, Willie Wonka and the Chocolate Factory, Blithe Spirit, Arsenic and Old Lace, The Pink Panther Strikes Again, Scrooge. arts commissioner Thousand Oaks Art Commission, 1985—; exec. producer Conejo Players Theatre, 1980-92; art show judge Thousand Oaks City Coun., 1985—; mem. team Calif. Towards Arts Assessment Project, Sacramento, 1993. Recipient Bravo award L.A. Music Ctr., 1992. Mem. Nat. Educators Assn., Nat. Music Educators Assn., Calif. Tchr's. Assn., Calif. Music Educators Assn., Calif. Math Educators Assn., Drama Tchr's Assn. of So. Calif., United Tchr's of L.A. Home: 3879 Abbey Ct Thousand Oaks CA 91320 Office: Lawrence Jr High 10100 Variel Chatsworth CA 91311

RADEBAUGH, ALAN PAINE, artist; b. Boston, May 2, 1952; s. John Franklin and Dorothy (Paine) R.; m. Ann Harrison Craig, Feb. 13, 1981 (div. 1987); m. Karen Rae Olson, Dec. 3, 1991. Student, Coll. Wooster, 1970-72, U. N.Mex., 1992. Custom jeweler Black Dog Jewelry, Canton, N.Y., 1972-73; arts and crafts tchr. Brentwood Stables Summer Camp, Angelica, N.Y., 1973; pvt. practice designer, builder Santa Barbara, Calif., 1974-76, Portland, Oreg., 1976-79; pvt. practice furniture designer Pueblo, Colo., 1980; pvt. practice visual artist Albuquerque, 1981—; juror N.Mex. Annual Woodworkers Show, Santa Fe, 1984; cons. Albuquerque (N.Mex.) Conv. and Visitors Bur., 1992. Exhibited in group shows McNeese State U., 1991, Mus. Albuquerque, 1991, Ctrl. Mo. State U., 1991, Cork Gallery, Avery Fisher Hall, Lincoln Ctr., 1992, EMU Gallery, U. Oreg., 1992, others; represented in permanent collections including Albuquerque Mus. Fine Arts; prin. works include model of mus. and exhibition spaces N.Mex. Mus. Natural History, 1983, clay miniatures Archeol. Mus. Andros, Greece, 1983, graphic image Nat. Med. Assn. Dartmouth Med. Sch., 1993. Donated graphic image Manzano State Park, N.Mex. Pks. & Recreation, Mountainaire, N.Mex., 1990; donated crafted birdhouse Habitat for Humanity Internat., Santa Fe, 1992; donated painting Traveling Art Gallery, Albuquerque (N.Mex.) Conv. and Visitors Bur., 1992, 93. Recipient 1st pl. in design N.Mex. Annual Woodworkers Show, Santa Fe, 1982, Merit award Paxton Co., Albuquerque, 1983, Albuquerque (N.Mex.) United Artists, 1983, Purchase award Albuquerque (N.Mex.) Mus. Fine Arts, 1984, hon. mention award Art Ctr., Los Alamos, N.Mex., 1993. Mem. Albuquerque/State N.Mex. Artists Slide Registry, Maine Arts Commn. Slide Registry.

RADEBAUGH, RAY, physicist; b. South Bend, Ind., Nov. 4, 1939; s. Vernon and Velma (Johnson) R.; m. Judy Kalmbach, Aug. 20, 1962 (div. 1975); children: Michael, Keith, Carol, James. BS in Engring. Physics, U. Mich., 1962; MS in Physics, Purdue U., 1964, PhD in Physics, 1966. Rsch. asst. Purdue U., West Lafayette, Ind., 1962-66; postdoctoral fellow Nat. Bur. Stds., Boulder, Colo., 1966-68; physicist/project leader Nat. Bur. Stds., 1968—; group leader Nat. Inst. Standards and Tech., Boulder, 1989-91; lectr. UCLA, 1980—; chmn. Cryogenic Engring. Conf., 1985-87, program com., 1982-91; chmn. Internat. Cryocooler Conf., 1983-84, program com., 1984—. Editorial bd. Cryogenics, 1985—; editor-in-chief Modern Instrumentation and Measurements in Physics and Engineering, Am. Inst. Physics, 1992—; contbr. articles to profl. jours; patentee in field. Adv. bd. Salvation Army, Boulder, 1973-88, chmn. bd., 1983-87. Home: 335 Gorham Ct Louisville CO 80027-1219 Office: Nat Inst Stds and Tech 325 Broadway St Boulder CO 80303-3328

RADER, RALPH WILSON, humanities educator; b. Muskegon, Mich., May 18, 1930; s. Ralph McCoy and Nelle Emily (Fargo) R.; m. June Willadean Warring, Sept. 3, 1950; children—Lois Jean, Eric Conrad, Michael William, Nancy Anne, Emily Rose. B.S., Purdue U., 1952; Ph.D., Ind. U., 1958. Instr. dept. English U. Calif., Berkeley, 1956-58, asst. prof., 1958-63, assoc. prof., 1963-67, prof., 1967—, chmn. dept., 1976-80; F.I. Carpenter vis. prof. English U. Chgo., 1970; dir. seminar NEH, summer 1975, 83, 85, 93; editorial com. U. Calif. Press, 1963-72, co-chmn., 1968-72; mem. exec. com. Assn. Depts. English, 1978-80; mem. budget and interdepartmental rels. com. U. Calif., Berkeley, 1986-80, chmn. 1988-89; mem. pres. English dept. adv. com. Harvard U., 1989-91, chmn. vis. com. 1985-91, chmn., 1991—. Author: Tennyson's Maud: The Biographical Genesis, 1963, reprinted, 1978. Co-author: Essays in Eighteenth Century Biography, 1968; New Approaches to Eighteenth Century Literature, 1974. Editor: (with Sheldon Sacks) Essays: An Analytic Reader, 1964; adv. bd. Yale edit. Private Papers of James Boswell; editorial bd. Critical Inquiry; Prose Studies. Am. Council Learned

Socs. grantee, 1959; Guggenheim fellow, 1972-73; recipient Disting. Teaching award U. Calif.-Berkeley, 1975-76. Mem. MLA, Phi Beta Kappa. Democrat. Home: 465 Vassar Ave Berkeley CA 94708-1215

RADLER, FRANKLIN DAVID, publishing holding company executive; b. Montreal, Que., Can., June 3, 1942; m. Rona Lassner, Mar. 26, 1972; children: Melanie, Melissa. MBA, Queen's U., Can., 1967. Pres., chief oper. officer, dir. Hollinger Inc., Toronto; exec. v.p. Argus Corp. Ltd., Toronto; chmn. Am. Pub. Co., Jerusalem Post Ltd., Palestine Post Ltd. Office: Hollinger Inc, 1827 W 5th Ave, Vancouver, BC Canada V6J 1P5 also: Hollinger Inc, 10 Toronto St, Toronto, ON Canada M5C 2B7

RADY, ERNEST S., thrift and loan association executive; b. 1938. Chmn. bd. Western Thrift & Loan, Orange, Calif., 1973—; chmn. bd., CEO Westcorp, Irvine, Calif., 1975—. Office: Westcorp 23 Pasteur Rd Irvine CA 92718*

RADYS, RAYMOND GEORGE, laser scientist; b. Kaunas, Lithuania, Aug. 30, 1940; came to U.S., 1949; s. Valerian Felix and Ella Lydia (Heinrich) R. BSEE, U. Ill., 1963. Engr. Hughes Aircraft, Culver City, Calif., 1963-76; scientist Hughes Aircraft, El Segundo, Calif., 1985—; sr. engr. Transaction Tech., Santa Monica, Calif., 1976-83; participant GM electric vehicle impact project, 1991-93. Recipient tech. award NASA, 1980, 89. Mem. U.S. Chess Found., Hughes Chess Club (champion 1971). Libertarian. Office: Hughes Aircraft Bldg E1 MS B122 PO Box 902 El Segundo CA 90245-0902

RADZIEMSKI, LEON JOSEPH, physics educator; b. Worcester, Mass., June 18, 1937; s. Leon Joseph and Josephine Elizabeth (Janczukowicz) R.; married; children: Michael Leon, Timothy Joseph. BA, Coll. Holy Cross, 1958; MS, Purdue U., 1961, PhD, 1964. Staff physicist Los Alamos (N.Mex.) Nat. Lab., 1967-83; head dept. physics N.Mex. State U., Las Cruces, 1983-88, assoc. dean, dir. arts and scis. rsch. ctr. Coll. of Arts & Scis., 1988-90; dean of scis. Wash. State U., Pullman, 1990—, prof. physics, 1990—; vis. scientist Laboratoire Aime Cotton, Orsay, France, 1974-75; vis. assoc. prof. dept. nuclear engring. U. Fla., Gainesville, 1978-79; bd. dirs. Astrophysical Rsch. Consortium, Seattle, 1988—, Wash. Tech. Ctr., Seattle, 1990—. Editor Marcel Dekker Series: Laser Advances; contbr. articles and books to profl. jours.; also Applications of Laser Plasmas, 1989; patentee in field. 1st lt. USAF, 1964-67. Hughes Aircraft Co. fellow, 1958-59. Fellow Optical Soc. Am., Soc. Applied Spectroscopy; mem. Am. Phys. Soc., Laser Inst. Am. Home: 440 SW City View St Pullman WA 99163-2760 Office: Wash State U Divsn Scis Pullman WA 99164-3520

RAE, MATTHEW SANDERSON, JR., lawyer; b. Pitts., Sept. 12, 1922; s. Matthew Sanderson and Olive (Waite) R.; m. Janet Hettman, May 2, 1953; children: Mary-Anna, Margaret Rae Mallory, Janet S. Rae Dupree. AB, Duke, 1946, LLB, 1947; postgrad., Stanford U., 1951. Bar: Md. 1948, Calif. 1951. Asst. to dean Duke Sch. Law, Durham, N.C., 1947-48; assoc. Karl F. Steinmann, Balt., 1948-49, Guthrie, Darling & Shattuck, L.A., 1953-54; nat. field rep. Phi Alpha Delta Law Frat., L.A., 1949-51; research atty. Calif. Supreme Ct., San Francisco, 1951-52; ptnr. Darling, Hall & Rae (and predecessor firms), L.A., 1955—; mem. Calif. Commn. Uniform State Laws, 1985—, chmn. drafting com. for revision Uniform Prin. and Income Act of Nat. Conf., 1991—. V.p. L.A. County Rep. Assy., 1959-64; mem. L.A. County Rep. Cen. Com., 1960-64, 77-90, exec. com., 1977-90; vice chmn. 17th Congl. Dist., 1960-62, 28th Congl. Dist., 1962-64; chmn. 46th Assy. Dist., 1962-64, 27th Senatorial Dist., 1977-85, 29th Senatorial Dist., 1985-90; mem. Calif. Rep. State Cen. Com., 1966—, exec. com., 1966-67; pres. Calif. Rep. League, 1966-67; trustee Rep. Assocs., 1979—, pres., 1983-85, chmn. bd. dirs., 1985-87. Served to 2d lt. USAAF, WWII. Fellow Am. Coll. Trust and Estate Counsel; academician Internat. Acad. Estate and Trust Law (exec. coun. 1974-78); mem. ABA, Los Angeles County Bar Assn. (chmn. probate and trust law com. 1964-66, Arthur K. Marshall award probate and trust law sect. 1984, chmn. legislation com. 1980-86, chmn. program com. 1981-82, chmn. membership retention com. 1982-83, trustee 1983-85, Shattuck-Price Meml. award 1990, dir. Bar Found. 1987-93), South Bay Bar Assn., State Bar Calif. (chmn. state bar jour. com. 1970-71, chmn. probate com. 1974-75, exec. com. estate planning trust and probate law sect. 1977-83, chmn. legislation com. 1977-89, co-chmn. 1991-92, probate law cons. group Calif. Bd. Legal Specialization 1977-88, chmn. conf. dels. resolutions com. 1987, exec. com. conf. dels. 1987-90), Lawyers Club of Los Angeles (bd. govs. 1981-87, 1st v.p. 1982-83), Am. Legion (comdr. Allied post 1969-70), Legion Lex (dir. 1964—, pres. 1969-71), Air Force Assn., Aircraft Owners and Pilots Assn., Town Hall (gov. 1970-78, pres. 1975), World Affairs Coun., Internat. Platform Assn., Los Angeles Com. on Fgn. Rels., Breakfast Club (law, pres. 1989-90), Commonwealth Club, Chancery Club, Rotary, Phi Beta Kappa (councilor Alpha Assn. 1983—, v.p. 1984-86), Omicron Delta Kappa, Phi Alpha Delta (supreme justice 1972-74, elected to Disting. Service chpt. 1978), Sigma Nu. Presbyterian. Home: 600 John St Manhattan Beach CA 90266-5837 Office: Darling Hall & Rae 777 S Figueroa St Fl 34 Los Angeles CA 90017-2513

RAEDEKE, LINDA DISMORE, geologist; b. Great Falls, Mont., Aug. 20, 1950; d. Albert Browning and Madge (Hogan) Dismore; m. Kenneth John Raedeke, Dec. 26, 1971 (div. 1982); m. Charles Moore Swift, Jr., Mar. 14, 1992. BA in History, U. Wash., 1971, MS in Geology, 1979, PhD, 1982. Geomorphologist, park planner Corporacion Nacional Forestal and U.S. Peace Corps, Punta Arenas, Chile, 1972-74; glacial geologist Empresa Nacional del Petroleo, Punta Arenas, 1972-75; geologist FAO, UN, Punta Arenas, 1974; geologist Lamont-Doherty Geol. Obs., Columbia U., Tierra del Fuego, Chile, 1974-75; Wetlands evaluation project coord. Wash. Dept. Agr., U. Wash., Seattle, 1975-76; geomorphol. cons. Okanogan County Planning, Oceanographic Inst. Wash., Seattle, 1976; curator Remote Sensing Applications Lab., U. Wash., 1976-77; geol. cons. Amoco, Denver, 1978; petrologist Lamont-Doherty Geol. Obs., 1979; geol. cons. Empresa Minera de Mantos Blancos, Tierra del Fuego, 1980; geol. rsch. asst. U. Wash., Seattle, 1977-81; exploration geologist Chevron Resources Co., Denver, 1981-84; rsch. geologist Chevron Oil Field Rsch. Co., La Habra, Calif., 1984-89; sr. compensation analyst Chevron Corp., San Francisco, 1989-90; staff geologist Chevron Overseas Petroleum, Inc., San Ramon, Calif. 1990-91, project leader, 1991—. Contbr. articles to profl. jours. Recipient Cert. of Achievement YWCA, 1988. Mem. Am. Geophys. Union, Geol. Soc. Am., Am. Assn. Petroleum Geologists (poster chmn. 1987). Office: Chevron Overseas Petroleum Inc PO Box 5046 San Ramon CA 94583-0946

RAE-DUPREE, JANET SANDERSON, journalist; b. Redondo Beach, Calif., Sept. 14, 1962; d. Matthew Sanderson and Jane Hettman Rae; m. David Edward Dupree, Sept. 8, 1984. BA in Polit. Sci., U. Mich., 1984. Intern, news staff Beach Cities Newspapers, Hermosa Beach, Calif., 1981, UPI, L.A., 1982; intern Wash. bur. L.A. Times, 1982, intern suburban staff, 1983; reporter trainee L.A. Times Valley Edition, Chatsworth, Calif., 1984-86; staff writer Daily News of L.A., Woodland Hills, Calif., 1986-87, The Daily Breeze, Torrance, Calif., 1987-89, L.A. Times South Bay Edition, Torrance, 1989—. Recipient In-depth reporting 2d pl. award Nat. Headliners, 1988, 3d pl. news reporting, Copley Ring of Truth award, 1989; 2d pl. in-depth reporting award Valley Press Club, 1986, 2d pl. student div. Robert F. Kennedy award, 1984. Mem. Soc. Profl. Journalists (regional membership chair, past pres. L.A. chpt.), Investigative Reporters & Editors. Office: LA Time South Bay Edit 23133 Hawthorne Blvd Ste 200 Torrance CA 90505

RAE-HALLCOM, JUDY, publisher; b. Hollywood, Calif., Feb. 9, 1945; d. Eli and Sylvia (Goldvarg) Litman; m. Roger Alan Rothberg, Nov. 1965 (div. 1975);m. Dale Hallcom, Mar. 30, 1981; children: Suzanne Bock, Jason Rothberg. Sales mgr. Travel Host Mag., L.A., 1975-76; pub. Big Valley Now Valley Mag., Van Nuys, Calif., 1976-80; ptnr. Boeckmann Rsch. & Devel., Agoura, Calif., 1981-85; sales mgr. Ventura County Cable Ad Sales, Westlake Village, Calif., 1986-90; pub. Earth News, Agoura Hills, Calif., 1990—. Democrat. Jewish. Office: Earth News 5126 Clarston Dr # 200 Agoura Hills CA 91301

RAEL, HENRY SYLVESTER, health administrator; b. Pueblo, Colo., Oct. 2, 1928; s. Daniel and Grace (Abyeta) R.; m. Helen Warner Loring Brace, June 30, 1956 (dec. Aug. 1980); children: Henry Sylvester, Loring Victoria Bush. AB, U. So. Colo., 1955; BA in Bus Adminstrn., U. Denver, 1957, MBA, 1958. Sr. boys counselor Denver Juvenile Hall, 1955-58; adminstrv. asst. to pres. Stanley Aviation Corp., Denver, 1958-61; Titan III budget and fin. control supr. Martin Marietta Corp., Denver, 1961-65; mgmt. adv. services officer U. Colo. Med. Center, Denver, 1965-72; v.p. fin., treas. Loretto Heights Coll., Denver, 1972-73; dir. fin. and adminstrn. Colo. Found. for Med. Care, 1973-86, Tri-County Health Dept., Denver, 1986—; bd. dirs. State Colo. Pub. Employees Retirement Assn., 1993—; instr. fin. mgmt., mem. fin. com. Am. Assn. Profl. Standards Rev. Orgn., 1980-85 ; speaker systems devel., design assns., univs., 1967-71. Mem. budget lay adv. com. Park Hill Elem. Sch., Denver, 1967-68, chmn., 1968-69; vol. worker Boy and Girl Scouts, 1967-73; bd. dirs. Community Arts Symphony, 1981-83, 85-87; controller St. John's Episcopal Cathedral, 1982-83; charter mem. Pueblo (Colo.) Coll. Young Democrats, 1954-55; block worker Republican party, Denver, 1965-68, precinct committeeman, 1978-84 ; trustee Van Nattan Scholarship Fund, 1974—; bd. dirs. Vis. Nurse Assn., 1977-84, treas., 1982-84. Served with USAF, 1947-53; res. 1954-61. Recipient Disting. Service award Denver Astron. Soc., 1968, Citation Chamberlin Obs., 1985; Stanley Aviation masters scholar, 1957; Ballard scholar, 1956. Mem. Assn. Systems Mgmt. (pres. 1971-72), Hosp. Systems Mgmt. Soc., Budget Execs Inst. (v.p. chpt. 1964-65, sec. 1963-64), Colo. Pub. Employees Retirement Assn. (bd. dirs. 1993—), Denver Astron. Soc. (pres. 1965-66, bd. dirs. 1982—), Am. Assn. Founds. for Med. Care (fin. com. 1981-82), Nat. Astronomers Assn. (exec. bd. 1965—). Epsilon Xi, Delta Psi Omega. Episcopalian. Home: 70 S Albion St Denver CO 80222-1002

RAFAEL, RUTH KELSON, archivist, librarian, consultant; b. Wilmington, N.C., Oct. 28, 1929; d. Benjamin and Jeanette (Spicer) Kelson; m. Richard Vernon Rafael, Aug. 26, 1951; children—Barbara Jeanette Rafael Martinez, Brenda Elaine. B.A., San Francisco State U., 1953, M.A., 1954; M.L.S., U. Calif.-Berkeley, 1968. Cert. archivist, 1989; life credential. Libr. Tchr. San Francisco Unified Sch. Dist., 1956-57; libr. Congregation Beth Sholom, San Francisco, 1965-83; archivist Western Jewish History Ctr. of Judah L. Magnes Mus., Berkeley, Calif., 1968, head archivist, librarian, 1969—; cons. NEH, Washington, NHPRC, Congregation Sherith Israel, San Francisco, Mount Zion Hosp., San Francisco, Benjamin Swig archives project, San Francisco, Camp Swig, Saratoga, Calif.; project dir. Ethnicity in Calif. Agriculture, 1989, San Francisco Jews of European Origin, 1880-1940, an oral history project, 1976. Author: Continuum, San Francisco Jews of Eastern European Origin, 1880-1940, 1976, rev. edit., 1977; (with Davies and Woogmaster) poetry book Relatively Speaking, 1981; Western Jewish History Center: Archival and Oral History Collections, Judah L. Magnes Meml. Mus., 1987; contbg. editor Western States Jewish History, 1979—. Mem. exec. bd. Bay Area Library Info. Network, 1986-88. Bur. Jewish Edn. scholar, San Francisco, 1983; NEH grantee, 1985. Mem. ALA, Soc. Am. Archivists, Soc. Calif. Archivists, Calif. Library Assn., No. Calif. Assn. Jewish Librarians (pres. 1975-76), Jewish Arts Council of the Bay (bd. dirs. 1981-83). Office: Western Jewish History Ctr Judah L Magnes Mus 2911 Russell St Berkeley CA 94705-2333

RAFEEDIE, EDWARD, federal judge; b. Orange, N.J., Jan. 6, 1929; s. Fred and Nabeeha (Hishmeh) R.; m. Ruth Alice Horton, Oct. 8, 1961; children: Fredrick Alexander, Jennifer Ann. BS in Law, U. So. Calif., 1957, JD, 1959; LLD (hon.), Pepperdine U., 1978. Bar: Calif. 1960. Pvt. practice law Santa Monica, Calif., 1960-69; mcpl. ct. judge Santa Monica Jud. Dist., Santa Monica, 1969-71; judge Superior Ct. State of Calif., Los Angeles, 1971-82; dist. judge U.S. Dist. Court for (cen. dist.) Calif., Los Angeles, 1982—. Trustee Santa Monica Hosp. Med. Ctr., 1979—; bd. dirs. UniHealth of Am., Los Angeles, 1985; mem. adv. bd. Greater Western council Boy Scouts Am., Los Angeles, 1980—. Served with U.S. Army, 1950-52, Korea. Office: US Dist Ct 312 N Spring St Los Angeles CA 90012-4701

RAFFERTY, KEVIN ALFRED, educator; b. Albany, N.Y., Aug. 21, 1953; s. Edward Michael and Marie Teresa (Walsh) R.; m. Rhonda Olivia Salkin, Aug. 10, 1975; children: Jessica Alison, Melissa Ann, Matthew Kevin. BA in Liberal Arts, Eisenhower Coll., 1975; MA in Anthropology, SUNY, Stony Brook, 1978, PhD in Archaeology, 1982. Field archaeologist Ariz. State U., Tempe, 1977-80; resource area archaeologist Bur. of Land Mgmt., Las Vegas, 1980-83; dir. archaeology Div. of Anthropol. Studies, U. Nev., Las Vegas, 1983-89; prof. ethnology Community Coll. of So. Nev., North Las Vegas, 1989-91, chmn. dept. of behavioral scis., 1991—; owner, prin., investigator Archaeol. Rsch. of So. Nev., 1990—; chmn. Nev. Coun. of Profl. Archaeologists, North Las Vegas, 1988—; vice-chmn. Adv. Coun. for Historic Preservation, Carson City, Nev., 1988—. Contbr. articles to profl. publs. Eucharistic min. Christ the King Cath. Community, Las Vegas, 1982-86, lector, 1989-92, mem. pro-life com., 1989—. Grad. fellowship SUNY, 1975-78. Mem. Soc. for Am. Archaeology, Southwestern Anthropol. Assn., Nev. Coun. of Profl. Archaeologists, Nev. ARchaeol. Assn., Ariz.-Nev. Acad. of Sci., Great Basin Anthropol. Conf. Democrat. Roman Catholic. Home: 1600 Camarillo Dr North Las Vegas NV 89031 Office: Community Coll of So Nev 3200 E Cheyenne Ave North Las Vegas NV 89030

RAFI, MALIK MOHAMMED, agronomist; b. Trichy, India, Jan. 15, 1963; came to the U.S., 1988; s. Sharfudin and Mumtaz (Begum) R.; m. Rehana Sultana Rafi, July 30, 1992. BS in Agriculture, Tamil Nadu Agriculture Univ., India, 1984, MS in Plant Breeding and Genetics, 1987; MS in Plant Sci., U. Calif., Riverside, 1990, postgrad. rsch. asst. U. Calif., Riverside, 1989, teaching asst., 1990. Contbr. articles to profl. jours. Games sec. Agrl. Coll. and Rsch. Inst., Madurai, India, 1984. Fellow Indian Coun. Agrl. Rsch., 1985, 88; recipient Student Travel award Tissue Culture Assn., 1992, Excellent Presentation award World Congress on Cell and Tissue Culture, 1992. Mem. Crop Sci. Soc. Am., Agronomy Soc. Am., Western Soc. Crop Sci., Tissue Culture Assn., Western Wheat Workers Assn., Sigma Xi. Home: # 11 Park Village Moscow ID 83843 Office: U Idaho Dept PSES Moscow ID 83843

RAFN, ELEANOR YOLANDA (ELEONORA D'ANNUNZIO), freelance writer, publications specialist; b. Glen's Falls, N.Y., Sept. 18, 1932; d. Arturo Marius and Anna Mary (Gennamore) D'Annunzio; 1 child, Robert K Rafn II. Engring. writer GE Engring. Rsch., Schenectady, N.Y., 1950-53; artist, publs. designer Cushing-Malloy Lithographers, Ann Arbor, Mich., 1953-55; sr. technical writer Rockwell Internat. Space Div., Downey, Calif., 1955-63; freelance writer Robert Rafn & Assocs., Sherman Oaks, Calif., 1963-85; acting br. chief NASA Ames-Dryden Flight Rsch., Edwards AFB, Calif., 1985-87; head of publs. Photomatrix Corp., Culver City, Calif., 1987—; Author children's plays for ednl. TV. Pub. info. officer CAP, 1950-53; exec. v.p., preview chmn. So. Calif. Motion Picture Coun., 1975-80; mem. exec. bd. Com. on Children's Television, 1976-78; exec. v.p. HAVE Humanitarian Awards, 1976-78, Film Adv. Bd., 1977-80; exec. coord. Childhelp USA, 1978-79. Named Poet of Merit, Am. Poetry Assn., 1989. Home: 5444 Bellingham Ave # 34 Valley Village CA 91607

RAFSNIDER, GILES THOMAS, economics educator; b. Dayton, Ohio, Oct. 18, 1941; s. Lowell Bruce and Cyrilla Stella Katrina (Strothman) R.; m. Donna Jean Fry, Dec. 27, 1964; children: Erica Christine, Gillian Helene. Student, Deep Springs Coll., 1959-62, Oreg. State U., 1962-63; BS, Utah State U., 1965; MS, U. Nev., Reno, 1967; PhD, U. Mass., 1974. Rsch. dir. Ins. div. Nev. Dept. Commerce, Carson City, 1973-74; forest economist USDA Forest Svc., Broomall, Pa., 1974-78; agrl. economist Econ. Rsch. Svc., USDA, Ft. Collins, Colo., 1978-85; adj. assoc. prof. Colo. State U., Ft. Collins, 1978-85; assoc. prof. agrl. econs. U. Nebr., Lincoln, 1985-91; vis. assoc. prof. agrl. econs. U. Wyo., Laramie, 1992—; adj. prof. Ecole Nationale d'Agriculture, Meknes, Morocco, 1987-91; cons. The World Bank, 1993—. Contbr. articles to profl. jours. Harry J. Loman fellow, Media, Pa., 1973-74. Mem. Am. Econ. Assn., Am. Mgmt. Assn., Western Agrl. Econ. Assn., Internat. Assn. Agrl. Econs. Greek Orthodox. Home: 2024 Custer Dr Fort Collins CO 80525 Office: U Wyo Dept Agrl Econs Laramie WY 82071-3354

RAGAB, MOHAMED MAHMOUD, aerospace engineer; b. Cairo, Dec. 7, 1952; came to U.S., 1982; s. Mahmoud Mostafa Ragab and Gazbeya Mohamed El-Alayli; m. Nancy Abdel-Rahim, July 17, 1986; children: Cindy Mohamed, Sami Mohamed. BS in Aero. Engring., Cairo U., 1975; Diplome d'Ingenieur, Ecole Nat. Superieure de l'Aeronaut. et de l'Espace, Toulouse, France, 1980, Docteur Ingenieur, 1982. Rsch. and devel. engr. Arab Orgn. Industrialization, Cairo, 1977-78; grad. rsch. asst. French Space Agy., Toulouse, 1980-82; teaching asst. Ecole Nat. Superieure de l'Aeronaut. et de l'Espace, 1981-82; sr. engr. Beech Aircraft Corp., Wichita, Kans., 1983-88; engring. specialist Gen. Dynamics, San Diego, 1988-93, sr. engring. specialist, 1993—, flight instr., 1986—. Author numerous tech. papers. With Egyptian Army, 1975-76. Diplome des Etudes Approfondies grantee, 1980. Mem. AIAA (sr.). Republican. Home: 14123 Capewood Ln San Diego CA 92128-4208 Office: Gen Dynamics Space Systems MZ 22-8301 PO Box 85990 San Diego CA 92186-5990

RAGGIO, WILLIAM JOHN, state senator; b. Reno, Oct. 30, 1926; s. William John and Clara M. (Cardelli) R.; student La. Poly. Inst., 1944-45, U. Okla., 1945-46; BA, U. Nev., 1948; JD, U. Cal. at Hastings, 1951; m. Dorothy Brigman, August 15, 1948; children: Leslie Ann, Tracy Lynn, Mark William. Admitted to Nev. bar, 1951, U.S. Supreme Ct. bar, 1959; since practiced in Reno and Las Vegas; asst. dist. atty. Washoe County, Nev., 1952-58, dist. atty., 1958-71; ptnr. firm Wiener, Goldwater, Galatz & Raggio, Ltd., 1971-72, Raggio, Walker & Wooster Reno and Las Vegas, 1974-78, Raggio, Wooster & Lindell, 1978-92, sr. ptnr. Vargas & Bartlett, 1992—; mem. Nev. Senate, 1973—, minority floor leader, 1977-81, 82-87, 91, majority flr. leader, 1987—; mem. legis. commn., vice chmn. criminal law and adminstrn. com. Council State Govts., 1972-75. Bd. dirs. Am. Savs. & Loan Assn., 1967-70. Adv. bd. Salvation Army, Reno; mem. Nev. Am. Revolutionary Bicentennial Commn., 1975-81; mem. Republican State Cen. Com. Bd. dirs. YMCA, Reno chpt. NCCJ, Salvation Army; nat. chmn. Am. Legislative Exchange Council, v.p., dir. Sahara Resorts, Casino Properties, Inc., Sahara Las Vegas, Inc.; trustee Nat. Dist. Attys. Found. (vice chmn. 1962-65); trustee Community Action Program Washoe County. Republican candidate for U.S. Senate, 1970. Served with USNR, 1944-46; to 2d lt. USMCR, 1946-47. Named Young Man of Yr., Reno-Sparks Jr. C. of C., 1959; recipient Disting. Nevadan award, 1968, Fellows award The Salvation Army, Torch of Liberty award The Anti-Defamation League. Fellow Am. Bd. Criminal Lawyers (v.p. 1978—); mem. ABA (state chmn. jr. bar conf. 1957-60, ho. dels.) Am. Judicature Soc., Navy League, Air Force Assn., Nat. (nat. pres. 1967-68; named Outstanding Prosecutor 1965), Nev. State (sec. 1959, pres. 1960-63) Dist. Attys. Assn., NCCJ (Brotherhood award 1965), Nev. Peace Officers Assn., Internat. Assn. Chiefs Police, Am. Legion, Elks, Lion Club, Prospectors Club, Alpha Tau Omega, Phi Alpha Delta. Republican. Roman Catholic. Home: PO Box 281 Reno NV 89504-0281

RAGHAVENDRA, CAULIGI SRINIVASA, computer engineering educator; b. Kurnool, India, Mar. 23, 1955; came to U.S., 1979; s. C.R. Srinivasa Murthy and S. Janaki Bai. BSc in Physics, Bangalore (India) U., 1973; BE, Indian Inst. of Sci., Bangalore, 1976, ME, 1978; PhD, UCLA, 1982. Asst. prof. U. So. Calif., L.A., 1982-87, assoc. prof., 1987-91; Boeing Centennial chair, prof. computer engring. Wash. State U., Pullman, 1992—; cons. Hughes Aircraft Co., L.A., 1985-88, TRW, Aerospace Corp., Aerojet, L.A. Contbr. articles to profl. jours. Presdl. Young Investigator award NSF, 1985. Mem. IEEE, Assn. Computing Machinery. Office: Wash State U Sch of EECS Pullman WA 99164

RAGLAND, SAMUEL CONNELLY, industrial engineer; b. Nashville, July 12, 1946; s. Julian Potter and Stella (Thompson) R.; m. Marilyn Margaret Oppelt, July 15, 1967; children: Sherry Anne, David Michael. BSBA, Ariz. State U., 1974; MBA U. Phoenix, 1991. Indsl. engr. First Interstate Bank, Phoenix, 1966-76, Beckman Instruments, Scottsdale, Ariz., 1976-78; mgmt. analyst Ariz. Legislative Budget Com., Phoenix, 1978; indsl. engr. mgmt. systems ITT Courier Terminal Systems, Tempe, Ariz., 1978-81; project control adminstr. Gen. Host Corp., Phoenix, 1981; sr. cons. Arthur Young & Co., Phoenix, 1981-82; ops. analyst City of Phoenix, 1982-84; project leader Garrett Engine div. Allied-Signal Corp. (formerly Garrett Turbine Engine Co.), Phoenix, 1984-92, cons., program mgr., TRW, Mesa, 1992—; dir. Mary Moppets of Highland Inc., 1977-81. Mem. Inst. Indsl. Engrs. (sr. mem. cen. Ariz. chpt., dir. community rels. 1983-85, dir. chpt. devel. 1985-86, v.p., pres.-elect 1986-87, pres. 1987-88), Inst. Indsl. Engrs. (nat. chpt. devel. com. 1988-91, chmn.), Assn. Systems Mgmt. (div. dir. 1989-92, pres. 1992-93), Phoenix Philatelic Assn. Contbr. articles to profl. publs. Address: 11319 E Jenan Dr Scottsdale AZ 85259

RAGSDALE, KATHLEEN MARY, educator; b. St. Paul, Oct. 16, 1964; d. Leslie Richard and Patricia Ann (Oursland) Kupris; m. Larry John Ragsdale, Nov. 18, 1983. BS in Child Devel., Calif. State U., Fullerton, 1988. Presch. asst. Montessori Edn. Ctr., Garden Grove, Calif., 1984-85; teaching asst. Anaheim (Calif.) City Sch. Dist., 1985, Garden Grove Unified Sch. Dist., 1985-87; telephone operator Target Store, Anaheim, 1988; substitute tchr. Lynwood (Calif.) Unified Sch. Dist., 1989; substitute tchr. spl. edn. Orange County (Calif.) Dept. Edn., 1990-91, Garden Grove Unified Sch. Dist., 1990—. With U.S. Army, 1982-84. Mem. Nat. Honor Soc. Roman Catholic.

RAGUINDIN, SHIRLEY SAOIT, meteorologist; b. Wahiawa, Hawaii, Sept. 25, 1964; d. Isabelo Alonzo and Maria (Saoit) R. BS in Meteorology, U. Hawaii, 1986; MPA, U. Okla., 1989. Meteorological trainee Nat. Weather Svc., Honolulu, 1982-86; weather forecaster Dept. Air Force, Fussa, Japan, 1986-88; counselor substance abuse Dept. Air Force, Washington, 1988-89; chief social actions Dept. Air Force, Spokane, Wash., 1989-91; project engr., mgr. Procter & Gamble, Phoenix, 1991—. Editor: Hawaiian Tropical Fishes, 1981. Mem. Asian-Pacific Heritage Club, Tucson, 1989-91; model African Am. Club Scholarship, Tucson, 1989-90; Capt. USAF, 1986-91. Mem. NAFE, Air Force Assn., Air Force Res. Officer Tng. Corp (commdr. 1985-86, Disting. Grad., 1986, Gov.'s award 1986), Phi Eta Sigma. Roman Catholic. Office: Procter & Gamble 2050 S 35th Ave Phoenix AZ 85009

RAHR, TAMMY SUE, artist, educator; b. Rochester, N.Y., Dec. 20, 1958; d. Richard A. and Beverly M. (Fanton) R.; 1 child, David John. Assoc. in Fine Arts and Mus. Studies, Inst. Am. Indian Arts, Santa Fe, 1987. Artist-in-residence N.Mex. Arts Div., Santa Fe, 1987-90; pvt. practice artist-in-residence various locations, 1990-92; ethnobotanical trail coord. Wheelwright Mus. of the Am. Indian, Santa Fe, 1992—; artist-in-residence Opera Am./Very Spl. Arts, N.Mex., 1991, Mus. of N.Mex. Artist Retreat, 1991, 92, Inst. Am. Indian Arts Mus. Collection of Contemporary Indian Art, 1992; lectr. DAR, Cin. Art Mus., 1992; presenter in field. One-woman shows include Nat. Mus. of the Am. Indian, Smithsonian Instn., N.Y.C., 1991, Champaign-Urbana (Ill.) U. YMCA, 1991, Women's City Club, Cin., 1989; group shows include Wheelwright Mus. of the Am. Indian, Santa Fe, 1991; represented in permanent collections Mus. Natural History, Cin., Seneca-Iroquois Nat. Mus., Salamanca, N.Y., Inst. Am. Indian Arts Mus., Santa Fe, Mus. Indian Arts and Culture, Santa Fe, Wheelwright Mus. of the Am. Indian, Santa Fe. Mem. com. Children's Pow-Wow Wheelwright Mus., Santa Fe, 1991-92. Mem. Inst. Am. Indian Arts Alumni Assn. (exec. coun. 1987-92). Home: PO Box 15201 Santa Fe NM 87506-5001

RAIBLE, PETER SPILMAN, minister; b. Peterborough, N.H., Nov. 22, 1929; s. Robert Jules and Mildred (Galt) R.; m. Dee Dee Rainbow, June 18, 1950 (div. 1968); children: Stephen M., Robin S., Robert R., Deborah R.; m. Marcia McClellan Barton, June 5, 1987. PhB, U. Chgo., 1949; BA, U. Calif., Berkeley, 1952; MDiv, Starr King Sch. Ministry, 1953, D in Sacred Theology (hon.), 1974. Ordained to ministry Unitarian Ch. Asst. minister First Unitarian Ch., Providence, 1953-55; minister Unitarian Ch., Lincoln, Nebr., 1955-61, Univ. Unitarian Ch., Seattle, 1961—; bd. pres. Starr King Sch., Berkeley, 1967-68; mem. exec. com. Council Chs., Seattle, 1982-88; adj. prof. Meadville Lombard, 1987-88, Northwest Theol. Union, 1989; bd. dirs. First Ave. Svc. Ctr., 1990—. Author: How to Case a Church, 1982; book editor Jour. Liberal Ministry, 1965-71; editor: UU Polity Manual, 1992. Bd. dirs. Council Planning Affiliates, Seattle, 1969-73, Wash. State chpt. ACLU, Seattle, 1963-67; chmn. ministerial adv. com. Planned Parenthood Ctr., Seattle, 1963-68; pres. United Nations Assn., Lincoln, 1959-61. Served as cpl. USAF, 1948-49. Merrill fellow Harvard U., Cambridge, Mass., 1972. Mem. Unitarian Universalist Ministers Assn. (pres. 1973-75), Pacific N.W. dist. Unitarian Universalist Assn. (exec. 1962-64, pres. 1985-87, mem. commn. on appraisal 1977-81). Office: U Unitarian Ch 6556 35th Ave NE Seattle WA 98115-7393

RAINES, LEONARD HARLEY, marketing and communications executive; b. Beaumont, Tex., Feb. 13, 1947; s. Leonard Harley and Annie Sue (Nix) R.; m. Sherry Yvette Brown, Mar. 12, 1972 (div. 1976); m. Marcia Lynn Riska, Sept. 20, 1986. AA, Dept. of Def. Info. Coll., 1966; student, U. Houston, 1982, 83, UCLA, 1984—. Publs. mgr. Wailua U., Kauai, Hawaii, 1970-72; prodn. mgr. Wattenmaker Advt., Cleve., 1972-73; art dir. Creative

Advt., Houston, 1973-74; pres. Raines Advt., Houston, 1974-78; exec. v.p. Martin, McCray, Raines and Scott Advt., Houston, 1978-84; pres. Team Equinox USA, L.A., 1987-89, Raines Mktg. Group, L.A., 1984—, Mediamark, Lake Arrowhead, Calif., 1991—; cons. Spur Products, Inc., Boise, 1988-92, UCLA Med. Ctr., L.A., 1986—, Lake Arrowhead, 1991—; pres. San Bernardino Nat. Forest Assn. Art dir, editor: Rarities in American Cut Glass, 1975; author (screenplay) The Short Timer, 1987, co-author (screenplay) The Thanatos Program, 1987. Mem. Vietnam Vets of Am., Lake Arrowhead, 1991—, Rep. Presdl. Task Force, 1985, 86; sec. UCLA Mountain Bruins Club/UCLA Alumni Assn., Lake Arrowhead, 1991-92. With USN, 1965-70. Decorated Silver Star, Legion of Merit with V, Bronze Star with V and 1 gold star, Purple Heart with 2 gold stars, Air medal with 1 gold star. Mem. U.S. Naval Inst., U.S. Jaycees (bd. dirs., Keyman 1979-80), Lake Arrowhead Communities C. of C., UCLA Mountain Bruins Club (pres.). Home: PO Box 190 Lake Arrowhead CA 92352 Office: Mediamark PO Box 1110 Twin Peaks CA 92391

RAINEY, ANTHONY HAROLD, financial executive; b. Riverside, Calif., Feb. 28, 1958; s. Harold and Joan Helen (Bryan) R.; m. Janice Kumi Akitomo, Aug. 10, 1985; children: Allison P., Christopher A., Jordan I. BA in Polit. Economy of Indsl. Socs., U. Calif., Berkeley, 1980; MPA, U. Wash., 1982; diploma mgmt. def. acquisition contracts, U.S. Army Logistics Ctr., Ft. Lee, Va., 1983; MS in Info. Systems Mgmt., Seattle Pacific U., 1991. Asst. resident dir. U. Calif., 1977-79, affirmative action advisor ednl. opportunity program, 1979-80; asst. resident dir. U. Wash., Seattle, 1980-82; mgr. regional info. resources SBA, Seattle, 1984-87; dir. planning and budget Seattle Mcpl. Ct., 1987—; mem. adj. faculty City U., Bellevue, Wash., 1982—; bus. cons. Bus. Info. Devel., Seattle, 1988—. Bd. dirs. Cen. Area Pub. Devel. Authority, Seattle, 1990—, Cen. Area Youth Authority/RMU, Cen. Area Motivation Program, Seattle, 1990—; trustee Mcpl. League King County, Seattle, 1991; commr. King County Children's and Family Commn., 1992. Pub. affairs fellow U.S. Dept. Edn., 1980; recipient Seattle Children and Youth Commn. Vol. award, 1992. Mem. Am. Mgmt. Assn., Inst. Mgmt. Accts., Govt. Fin. Officers Assn., Assn. Systems Mgmt., Am. Planning Assn., Am. Payroll Assn., Seattle Mgmt. Assn., Breakfast Group. Democrat. Home: 4531 NE 201st Pl Seattle WA 98155 Office: Seattle Mcpl Ct 600 3d Ave Rm 1510 PSB Seattle WA 98104

RAINEY, BARBARA ANN, sensory evaluation consultant; b. Fond du Lac, Wis., Nov. 11, 1949; d. Warren and Helen Eileen (Ginther) Bradley; m. Phillip Michael Rainey, Sept. 5, 1970; 1 child, Nicolette. BS, Kans. State U., 1975. Group leader Armour & Co. R&D Ctr., Scottsdale, Ariz., 1976-80; owner Barbara A. Rainey Cons., Manteca, Calif., 1980—. Contbr. articles to profl. jours. Kans. State Alumni fellow Kans. State U. Alumni Assn., 1990. Mem. ASTM, Inst. Food Technologists (prof., chmn. sensory div. 1984-85, sec. 1980-82, chmn.-elect, sec. Ctrl. Valley subsect. 1991-92, chmn. 1992-93, treas. 1989-91, speaker short course 1979-81, chmn. 50th anniversary SED 1989), Phi Kappa Phi, Beta Sigma Phi, Delta Zeta Iota (treas. 1984-85, sec. 1989-90, chmn.-elect 1992-93, Best Program award 1989, 90, 92, 93). Office: PO Box 622 Manteca CA 95336-0622

RAINWATER, JANETTE, clinical psychologist; b. Summit, N.J., Sept. 11, 1922; s. Cameron and Lell Anna (Bitzer) Munkittrick; m. Clarence Saunders Rainwater, Oct. 3, 1942 (div. Mar. 1969); 1 child, Michael Vance; m. William Walter Parsons, Sept. 3, 1982 (dec. Sept. 1991). BS, Birmingham So., 1943; postgrad., Johns Hopkins U., 1947-49; PhD in Clin. Psychology, U. Calif., 1964. Psychologist Ctr. for Spl. Problems, San Francisco, 1965-67; pvt. practice Berkeley, Calif., 1965-69; counselor San Francisco State Coll. Counseling Ctr., 1966-69; instr. in psychology UCLA Extension, 1969-83; pvt. practice L.A., 1969—; workshop leader, U.S., Mex., Western Europe, Czechoslovakia, Hungary, USSR, Yugoslavia, Brazil, Iran, Malaysia, 1966—; asst. clin. prof. Neuro Psychiat. Inst., UCLA, 1972-76; trainer in gestalt therapy Gestalt Inst. of L.A., 1970-85; developer tng. program of USSR and Czechoslovakian psychotherapists by U.S. psychotherapists, 1988—. Author: You're in Charge: A Guide to Becoming Your Own Therapist, 1979, A Dragon in a Wagon, 1966, Vision: How, Why, What We See, 1962; author (cassette) The Art of Self Observation, 1983. Mem. APA, Internat. Soc. Polit. Psychology, PEN. Home: PO Box 640 Pacific Palisades CA 90272-0640

RAINWATER, NANCY GREGG, clinical psychologist; b. Pensacola, Fla., Dec. 17, 1951; d. Crawford and Betty (Gregg) R.; m. Andrew A. Sweet, May 19, 1984; 1 child, Adrienne. BA, Wellesley Coll., 1973; MA, Ga. State U., 1975, PhD, 1979. Lic. psychologist, Colo. Allied health profl. Children's Hosp., Denver, 1980-87; asst. clin. profl. U. Colo. Health Sci. Ctr., Denver, 1980-87; clin. affiliate U. Denver, 1987—; pvt. practice Denver, 1989—. Co-editor: (continuing edn. series) The Diabetes Educator, 1988-90; contbr. articles to profl. jours. Bd. dirs. Colo. Nat. Abortion Rights Action League, Denver, 1986-90, pres., 1989. NIH postdoctoral traineeship Nat. Asthma Ctr., Denver, 1979-80. Mem. APA, Assn. for the Advancement of Behavior Therapy, Soc. of Behavioral Medicine, Colo. Psychol. Assn., Colo. Soc. for Behavior Analysis and Therapy. Office: 1720 S Bellaire St Ste 808 Denver CO 80222

RAISBECK, JAMES DAVID, aircraft design executive; b. Milw., Sept. 29, 1936; s. Clifford Clinton and Minnie (Hommersand) R.; BS in Aero. Engring., Purdue U., 1961; m. Sherry Bylund; 1 child, Jennifer Lee Raisbeck Hunter. Aero. rsch. engr. Boeing Co., Seattle, 1961-69, rsch. aerodynamist, 1961-64, commercial aircraft preliminary design, 1965-66; liaison to U.S. Air Force, 1966-68, program mgr. comml. STOL programs, 1968-69; chmn. bd., chief exec. officer Robertson Aircraft Corp., Renton, Wash., 1969-73; v.p. tech. Am. Jet Industries, L.A., 1973-74; chmn. bd., chief exec. officer, founder Raisbeck Group, L.A., 1974-80; founder, chmn. bd., chief exec. officer Raisbeck Engring., Inc., 1981—; cons. Served with SAC, USAF, 1955-58. Recipient Disting. Engring. Alumnus in Aeronautics, Purdue U. Fellow AIAA (assoc.); mem. Soc. Automotive Engrs., Tau Beta Pi, Sigma Gamma Tau, Phi Eta Sigma. Patentee in field of wing design, propellors and aircraft systems; designs, builds aerodynamic cleanup packages for business and corp. turbine-powered airplanes. Address: 7536 Seward Park Ave S Seattle WA 98118

RAISIAN, JOHN, public policy institute executive, economist; b. Conneaut, Ohio, July 30, 1949; s. Ernest James and Ruby Lee (Owens) R.; m. Joyce Ann Klak, Aug. 17, 1984; children: Alison Kathleen, Sarah Elizabeth. BA, Ohio U., 1971; PhD, UCLA, 1978. Rsch. assoc. Human Resources Rsch. Ctr., U. So. Calif., L.A., 1972-73; cons. Rand Corp., Santa Monica, Calif., 1974-75, 76; vis. asst. prof. econs. U. Wash., Seattle, 1975-76; asst. prof. econs. U. Houston, 1976-80; sr. economist Office Rsch. and Evaluation, U.S. Bur. Labor Stats., Washington, 1980-81; spl. asst. for econ. policy Office Asst. Sc. for Policy, U.S. Dept. Labor, Washington, 1981-83, dir. rsch. and tech. support, 1981-84; pres. Unicon Rsch. Corp., L.A., 1984-86; sr. fellow Hoover Instn., Stanford, Calif., 1986—, assoc. dir., dep. dir., 1986-90, dir., 1990—; exec. dir. Presdl. Task Force on Food Assistance, Washington, 1983-84; mem. faculty steering com. Haas Ctr. for Pub. Svc., Stanford U., mem. adv. bd. Students for East European Democracy. Mem. editorial bd. Jour. Labor Rsch., 1983—; contbr. articles to profl. jours. Advisor Nat. Coun. on Handicapped, Washington, 1985-86, Nat. Commn. on Employment Policy, Washington, 1987-88; chmn. minimum wage bd. Calif. Indsl. Welfare Commn., 1987; mem. nat. adv.com. Student Fin. Assistance, Washington, 1987-89. Recipient Best Publ. of Yr. award Econ. Inquiry, Western Econ. Assn., 1979, Disting. Teaching award U. Houston Coll. Social Scis., 1980, Disting. Svc. award U.S. Dept. Labor, 1983; predoctoral fellow Rand Corp., 1976; rsch. grantee U. Houston, 1977. Mem. Am. Econs. Assn., Western Econ. Assn. (chmn. nominating com. 1992), Commonwealth Club of Calif., World Affairs Coun., Coun. Fgn. Rels., Mont Pelerin Soc., Phi Beta Kappa. Republican. Office: Stanford U Hoover Inst War Revolution Peace Stanford CA 94305-6010

RAJABI-ASL, ALI, information systems specialist, consultant; b. Abadan, Iran, June 13, 1963; came to U.S., 1979; s. Saleh and Mary R.-A.; m. Maryam Shahab, July 5, 1991. Student, L.A. Pierce Coll., 1982-83; BS, U. So. Calif., L.A., 1986. Part-time software and system cons. Falcon United Industries, Van Nuys, Calif., 1986-89, DejBan Structural Engring. Firm, Encino, Calif., 1986-88, Accu-Link Corp., Northridge, Calif., 1988-89; software engr. Orion Info. Systems, Sylmar, Calif., 1987-88, Am. Benefit Plan Adminstrs., L.A., 1988-89; sr. info. systems officer Security Pacific Automation Co., L.A., 1989—. Mem. Assn. for Computing Machinery, Digital Equipment Computer Users Soc. Office: Security Pacific Automation Corp 333 S Beaudry Ave # 2950W Los Angeles CA 90017-1466

RAJARATNAM, RICHARD G., surgeon, otolaryngologist; b. Colombo, Sri Lanka; came to U.S., 1980; s. Sidney N. and Esther G. (Tevathasan) R.; m. Chrishantina Rajakone, Jan. 21, 1980; children: Crisanjali, David. Degree, St. Thomas Coll., 1967, MBBS, 1972; FRCS, St. Bartholomews Med. Sch., London, 1978. Diplomate Am. Coll. Surgeons, Am. Bd. Otolaryngology. Registrar St. Bartholomewes Hosp., London, Eng., 1976-82; chief resident otolaryngology Loma Linda (Calif.) U. Med. Ctr., 1982-85; cons. So. Clalif. Med. Group, Kaiser Permante, Fontana, Calif., 1985-89; chief of otolaryngolgy So. Clalif. Med. Group, Kaiser Permante, Riverside, Calif., 1989—; asst. prof. Loma Linda U. Med. Ctr. Commonwealth Med. scholar, Brit. Govt., 1978. Fellow ACS, Royal Coll. Surgeons (Eng.); mem. Am. Acad. Otolaryngology. Methodist.

RAKUTIS, RUTA, chemical economist; b. Marijampole, Lithuania, Aug. 16, 1939; came to U.S., 1949; s. Juozas Rakutis and Natalia Pavilcius. BS cum laude, U. Ill., 1961; PhD, U. Iowa, 1968; MBA, Northeastern U., 1974. Sr. scientist Jet Propulsion Lab, Pasadena, Calif., 1968-70; scientist color lab. Polaroid Corp., Cambridge, Mass., 1970-74; sales mgr. Am. Cyanamid Co., Wayne, N.J., 1974-79; mktg. mgr. Lignin Chems., Am. Can. Co., Greenwich, Conn., 1979-81; cons. SRI Internat., Menlo Park, Calif., 1981-88; mgr. tech. devel. Imperial West Chem. Co., Antioch, Calif., 1988-92; product mgr. polymers Garratt-Callahan Co., Millbrae, Calif., 1992—. Contbr. articles to profl. jours. Dunlop fellow, 1967-68. Mem. Chem. Mktg. Rsch. Assn. of Am. Chem. Soc., Lakeview Assocs., Sigma Xi.

RALEIGH, CECIL BARING, geophysicist; b. Little Rock, Aug. 11, 1934; s. Cecil Baring and Lucile Nell (Stewart) R.; m. Diane Lauster, July 17, 1982; children: Alison, Marianne, Lawrence, David. B.A., Pomona (Calif.) Coll., 1956; M.A., Claremont (Calif.) Grad. Sch., 1958; Ph.D., UCLA, 1963. Fellow Research Sch. Phys. Sci., Australian Nat. U., Canberra, 1963-66; geophysicist U.S. Geol. Survey, Menlo Park, Calif., 1966-80; program mgr. for earthquake prediction research program U.S. Geol. Survey, 1980-81; dir. Lamont-Doherty Geol. Obs. and prof. geol. scis. Columbia U., Palisades, N.Y., 1981-89; dean Sch. Ocean and Earth Sci. and Tech. U. Hawaii, Honolulu, 1989—; chmn. bd. dirs. DOSECC, Inc., 1985-88; mem. NAS/NRC Ocean Studies Bd.; bd. dirs. JOI, Inc.; chmn., bd. dirs. Nat. Energy Lab. Hawaii Authority; chmn. NAS/NRC Yucca Mt. Panel. Author papers control earthquakes, rheology of the mantle, mechanics of faulting, crystal plasticity. Recipient Interdisciplinary award U.S. Nat. Com. Rock Mechanics, 1969, 74; Meritorious Service award Dept. Interior, 1974; Barrows Dist. Alumnus award Pomona Coll. Fellow Am. Geophys. Union, Geol. Soc. Am. Democrat. Office: U Hawaii Sch Ocean Earth Sci & Tech Honolulu HI 96822

RALSTON, GILBERT ALEXANDER, writer, educator; b. L.A., Jan. 5, 1912; s. Alexander Gilbert and Jeanette (Johnston) R.; grad. Pasadena Coll., 1929-32; grad. Am. Acad. Dramatic Arts, 1935; B.C.A., Sierra Nev. Coll., 1972; D in Psycholog, Fielding Inst., 1983, PhD in Health Sci., 1987, Columbia Pacific U., 1986; m. Mary K. Hart, Dec. 20, 1938; children—Michael, David. Actor, stage mgr. theatre prodns. N.Y.C., 1931-35; writer, dir. radio shows NBC, N.Y.C., 1936-38; prodn. supr. Compton Advt., Inc., N.Y.C., West Coast, 1939-42; organizer, mgr. radio dept. Proctor & Gamble, Cin., 1943-47, exec. producer inc. TV div., 1947-50; free lance producer TV films, 1950-55; exec. producer in charge TV drama CBS, 1955, dir. network programs originating in N.Y.C., 1956; producer High Adventure documentaries with Lowell Thomas, 1957; chmn. sch. communication arts Tahoe (Cal.) Paradise Coll., 1968; dean sch. communicative arts Sierra Nevada Coll., Incline Village, Nev., 1960-73, pres., 1973-83, pres. emeritus, 1983—; pres. Ralston Sch. Communicative Arts, Genoa, Nev., 1971—, Ralston Sch. Massage; v.p. Rule of Three Prodns., Los Angeles, 1973—; lectr. Fordham U., City Coll. City U. N.Y., Loyola U. of Los Angeles, St. Mary's Coll. of Calif. Mem. Authors Guild, ASCAP, Western Writers Am., Writers Guild Am., Am. Massage and Therapy Assn. Author: Ben, 1972; (with Richard Newhafer) The Frightful Sin of Cisco Newman, 1972; Dakota Warpath, 1973; Dakota: Red Revenge, 1973; Dakota Cat Trap, 1974; Dakota Murder's Money, 1974; Dakota: Chain Reaction, The Deadly Art, 1975, The Third Circle, 1976, The Tao of Touch, 1983, Gods Fist, 1989, Hamelin House, 1989, Hunter Fentress, 1990, Fattura Della Morte, 1990, others. Author screenplays: No Strings Attached, 1962; A Gallery of Six, 1963; A Feast of Jackals, 1963; Cockatrice, 1965; Kona Coast, 1967; Night of the Locust, 1969; Ben, 1971, Third Circle, 1975, Sure, 1975. Author screen adaptations: Willard (by Stephen Gilbert), 1970; Bluebonnet (by Boris Sobelman and Jack H. Robinson), 1971; Dakota Red, 1987. Author scripts for TV under sometime pseudonym Gil Alexander: High Adventure, Naked City, Route 66, Follow the Sun, Bus Stop, The Untouchables, Alcoa Theatre, Ben Casey, Richard Boone Show, 12 O'Clock High, The Name of the Game, Daktari, Laredo, Combat, Big Valley, Gunsmoke, Amos Burke, Slattery's People, Alfred Hitchcock, Star Trek, It Takes a Thief, O'Hara, Cannon, numerous others. Address: PO Box 490 Sullivans Island SC 29482

RALSTON, LENORE DALE, academic policy and program analyst; b. Oakland, Calif., Feb. 21, 1949; d. Leonard Earnest and Emily Allison (Hudnut) R. BA in Anthropology, U. Calif., Berkeley, 1971, MPH in Behavioral Sci., 1981; MA in Anthropology, Bryn Mawr Coll., 1973, PhD in Anthropology, 1980. Asst. researcher anthropology inst. internat. studies U. Calif., Berkeley, 1979-82, rsch. assoc. Latin Am. Study Ctr., 1982-83, acad. asst. to dean Sch. of Optometry, 1990—; assoc. scientist, rsch. adminstr. Med. Rsch. Inst., San Francisco, 1982-85; cons. health sci. Berkeley, 1986-90; mem. fin. bd. Med. Rsch. Inst., 1983-84; speaker in field. Co-author: Voluntary Effects in Decentralized Management, 1983; contbr. articles to profl. jours. Commr. Community Health Adv. Com., Berkeley, 1988-90; vice chair, commr. Community Health Commn., Berkeley, 1990—; bd. mem. safety com. Miles, Inc., Berkeley, 1992—. Grantee Nat. Rsch. Svc. Award, WHO, NIMH, NSF. Fellow Applied Anthropology Assn.; mem. Am. Pub. Health Assn., Am. Anthropology Assn., Sigma Xi. Home: 1232 Carlotta Ave Berkeley CA 94707-2707

RALSTON, RACHEL WALTERS, developmental psychologist; b. Max, N.D., June 13, 1915; d. Lewis David and Wilhelmina May Bertha (Freitag) Walters; m. William Clifton Hollowell, May 22, 1944 (div. May 1962); m. John Elvin Ralston, June 24, 1964. AA, Foothill Jr. Coll., 1964; BA, San Francisco State U., 1969; postgrad., Can. Coll., 1975-81. Chair North Fair Oaks Adv. Coun., Redwood City, Calif., 1975-77; initiator Community Concern for Sr. Citizens, Menlo Park and San Mateo County, Calif., 1975-80; organizer, pres. Concerned Srs., Inc., San Mateo County, 1980-86; chair exec. bd. Concerned Srs., Inc., Redwood City, 1987—; peer counselor for the elders Mental Health div. Health Dept., San Mateo County, 1986—; Mem. Older Adults Com., Mental Health Adv. Bd., 1985—; mem. adv. bd. Emeritus Inst. Coll. of San Mateo, 1987—. Mem. Com. on Aging San Mateo County, 1978-90; del. State House Conf. on Aging, Sacramento, 1980. Recipient Commendation Pvt. Sector Initiative, Washington, D. C., 1986; named Citizen of The Day Sta. KABL, San Francisco, 1985. Mem. AAUW, Am. Soc. on Aging, Am. Assn. Ret. Persons. Republican. Home: 610 17th Ave Menlo Park CA 94025-2039

RALSTON, ROY B., petroleum consultant; b. Monmouth, Ill., June 7, 1917; s. Roy Crews and Helen Ruth (Boggs) R.; m. Catherine Elizabeth Thompson, Aug. 6, 1940; 1 child, John Richard. BA, Cornell Coll., 1939; student, Iowa U., 1938; postgrad., U. Ill., 1940-41. Pretroleum cons. Scottsdale, Ariz., 1977—; dist. mgr. exploration Skelly Oil Co., Evansville, Ind., 1941-46; div. mgr. exploration and prodn. Ashland Oil & Refinery Co., Henderson, Ky., 1946-50; mgr. exploration and prodn. Ashland Oil & Refinery Co., Ashland, Ky., 1950-54; div. mgr. exploration Phillips Petroleum Co., Evansville, 1955-58, Amarillo, Tex., 1958-65, Oklahoma City, 1965-69; v.p. exploration and prodn. Phillips Petroleum Can. Ltd., Calgary, Alta., Can., 1969-72; exploraton mgr. North Am. Phillips Petroleum Co., Bartlesville, Okla., 1973-75; regional mgr. exploration and prodn. Phillips Petroleum Co., Denver, 1975-77; petroleum cons. 1st Nat. Bank, Amarillo, Tex., 1977—, Valley Nat. Bank, Phoenix, 1977—, 1st Interstate Bank, Phoenix, 1977-86. Youth career dir. Oklahoma City C. of C., 1966-68. Recipient Disting. Svc. award Okla. Petroleum Coun., 1968, Svc. award Land Mgmt. Sch. Okla. U., 1978. Mem. Am. Assn. Petroleum Geologists (publicity dir. nat. conv. Oklahoma City 1968, cert. petroleum geologist), Am. Assn. Petroleum Landmen, Soc. Petroleum Engrs. AIME, Ariz. Geol. Soc., N.Mex. Geol. Soc., Rotary. Republican. Presbyterian.

RAMASAMY, SAVAKKATTU MUNIAPPAN, chemical researcher, educator; b. Savakkattupalayam, India, Apr. 14, 1942; came to U.S., 1984; s. S.P. and Palanithai S. Muniappan; m. Saroja Ramasamy, Mar. 13, 1968; children: Sumathy, Vimala, Venkatesh. BSc, U. Madras, India, 1964, MSc, 1966; PhD, Okla. State U., 1981. Asst. prof. PSG Coll. Arts and Sci., Coimbatore, India, 1966-74; prof. Gobi (India) Arts Coll., 1974-77, 82-84; rsch. assoc. dept. chemistry U. Wyo., Laramie, 1984—. Mem. Am. Chem. Soc. Office: U Wyo Dept Chemistry University Sta Laramie WY 82071-3838

RAMASWAMY, PADMANABHAN, materials scientist; b. Ambattur, India, Mar. 5, 1953; came to U.S., 1977; s. Ramaswamy Iyer and Bhagavathy (Narayanan) Padmanabhan. BSc in Physics, Loyola Coll., Madras, India, 1972; B of Engring. in Metallurgy, Indian Inst. Sci., Bangalore, 1975; PhD in Materials Sci., Oreg. Grad. Ctr., 1982. Research and devel. engr. Bharat Electronics, Ltd., Bangalore, 1975-77; research scientist Oreg. Grad. Ctr., Beaverton, 1982-83; sr. staff engr. Motorola, Inc., Phoenix, 1984-86, prin. staff scientist, 1987-91, mem. tech. staff, mgr. materials and characterization lab., adv. pkg. deve. ctr., 1991—. Contbr. articles to profl. jours. Mem. Electron Microscopy Soc. Am., Electrochem. Soc., Materials Rsch. Soc. Home: 1325 E Grandview St Mesa AZ 85203-4427 Office: Motorola Inc B-136 5005 E McDowell Phoenix AZ 85026

RAMER, BRUCE M., lawyer; b. Teaneck, N.J., Aug. 2, 1933; s. Sidney and Anne S. (Strassman) R.; m. Ann Greenberg Ramer, Feb. 15, 1965; children: Gregg B., Marc K., Neal I. BA, Princeton U., 1955; LLB, Harvard U., 1958. Bar: Calif. 1963, N.J. 1958. Assoc., Morrison, Lloyd & Griggs, Hackensack, N.J., 1959-60; ptnr. Gang, Tyre, Ramer & Brown, Inc., L.A., 1963—. Exec. dir. Entertainment Law Inst., Law Ctr. of U. So. Calif.; bd. of councilors Law Ctr. U. So. Calif.; past pres. L.A. chpt.; bd. govs., chmn. nat. exec. coun. Am. Jewish Com. (nat. v.p. 1982-88, pres. L.A. chpt. 1980-83, chair Western region 1984-86, community svc. award, 1987); chmn. Pacific Rim Inst.; trustee Loyola Marymount U.; vice chair United Way, 1991-93, corp. bd. dirs., 1981-93, chair coun. pres. 1989-90, mem. community issues coun., 1989-90, chair discretionary fund distbn. com., 1987-89; bd. dirs. L.A. Urban League, 1987—, Jewish Fedn. Coun. of greater L.A. (mem. Community Rels. com.), Jewish TV Network, Sta. KCET-TV; mem., bd. dirs. Rebuild L.A.; vice chmn., bd. govs. Calif. Community Found.; recipient Ann. Brotherhood award Nat. Conf. on Christians and Jews, 1990; mem. Fellows of Am. Bar Found. Pvt. U.S. Army, 1958-59, 2d lt., 1961-62. Mem. ABA, L.A. County Bar Assn., Calif. Bar Assn., Beverly Hills Bar Assn. (exec. dirs. award 1988), L.A. Copyright Soc. (pres. 1974-75), Calif. Copyright Conf. (pres. 1973-74), Princeton Club (pres. 1975-78). Office: Gang Tyre Ramer & Brown Inc 6400 Sunset Blvd Los Angeles CA 90028-7392

RAMEY, FELICENNE HOUSTON, dean academic affairs, educator; b. Phila.; m. Melvin R. Ramey, Sept. 5, 1964; 2 children. BS, Pa. State U., University Park, 1961; MS, Duquesne U., 1967; JD, U. Calif., Davis, 1972; MA, Calif. State U., Sacramento, 1978. Bar: Calif. Microbiologist Pa. Dept. of Labs., Phila., Walter Reed Army Med. Ctr., Washington; chemist Calgon Corp., Pitts.; instr. Carnegie-Mellon U., Pitts.; dep. atty. gen. Calif. Dept. of Justice, Sacramento; clk. U.S. Dist. Ct. Calif., Sacramento; asst. prof. Calif. State U., Sacramento, assoc. prof., chair dept. behavior and environment, assoc. dean Sch. Bus.; dir. litigation Human Rights Commn., Sacramento; bd. dirs. Legal Aid Soc., Sacramento mag.; vis. scholar Ga. Inst. Tech., 1981, Boston Coll., 1988. Mem. edn. com. Blacks for Effective Community Action, 1978—. ACE fellow U. Calif., Santa Cruz, 1992—. Mem. Calif. Agrl. Alumni Assn. (bd. dirs.), Western Bus. Law Assn. (pres., pres. elect, v.p., exec. sec. Calif. and Nev. chpts. 1983-89), Nat. Assn. Women Deans and Adminstrs., Sacramento Black C. of C. (edn. com. 1990—, bd. dirs. 1989—). Home: 612 Cleveland St Davis CA 95616-3128 Office: Calif State U Sch Bus Adminstrn Sacramento CA 95819-6088

RAMEY, ROBERT COLIN, artist; b. Kenosha, Wis., Mar. 15, 1958; s. Archibald Lee and Elaine (Smith) Hileman. Exhibited in shows at Wustum Mus., Racine, Wisc., Lewis & Clark Coll., Lewiston, Idaho, Art Inst. Chgo., La Quinta (Calif.) Festival, Human Form Oreg. Coast Mus. Art, Newport; represented in permanent collections The Winthers Family Trust, Napa, Calif., The Nestle Corp., U.S. Bank Corp. Oreg., Standard Brands Inc.

RAMIER, DOUGLAS WILLIAM, computer services professional; b. North Tonawanda, N.Y., Nov. 29, 1958; s. Fergus Frederick and Marilyn (Pierce) R. AS in Liberal Arts, Genesee C.C., 1980; BS in Computer Sci., U. Wyo., 1983, MS in Computer Sci., 1985. Comm. systems specialist Rockwell Internat., Cedar Rapids, Iowa, 1986-87; dir. computer svcs. N.W. Coll., Powell, Wyo., 1987—; math/computer sci. instr. Coe Coll., Cedar Rapids, 1986-87; instr. computer applications N.W. Coll., 1992—. Recipient Ryan-Dewitt Math-Sci. award Exxon, Genesee C.C., 1980. Mem. Assn. for Computing Machinery (spl. interest group on univ. and coll. computing svcs.), Phi Kappa Phi, Phi Beta Kappa. Home: 680 Shoshone St Powell WY 82435 Office: NW Coll 231 W 6th St Powell WY 82435

RAMÍREZ, JOSÉ LUIS, quality management executive, engineer, chemist; b. Chamácuaro, Mex., Sept. 28, 1955; came to U.S., 1970; s. José and Maria Santos (Ugalde) R.; m. Judy Elaine Simmons, Nov. 4, 1984; children: Dawn, Sharon, Delia, José Luis II, Jesus. BS, U. Calif., San Diego, 1979. Chem. technician U. Calif., San Diego, 1978-79; engring. technician Fairchild Semiconductors., Healdsburg, Calif., 1979-80, process engr., 1981-82; quality engr. Optical Coating Labs., Santa Rosa, Calif., 1982-84; sr. devel. engr. Materials Progress Corp., Santa Rosa, 1984-85, quality mgr., 1985-87; process engring. mgr. Sola Optical U.S.A., Petaluma, 1987-89, total quality mgmt. exec., 1989—. Co-inventor removal of impurities from semiconductors. Mem. Am. Soc. for Quality Control, Am. Chem. Soc., Total Quality Mgmt. User's Group (chmn. 1990-91). Home: 2309 Donahue Ave Santa Rosa CA 95401-9045 Office: Sola Optical USA 1500 Cader Ln Petaluma CA 94954-6905

RAMIREZ, RICARDO, bishop; b. Bay City, Tex., Sept. 12, 1936; s. Natividad and Maria (Espinosa) R. B.A., U. St. Thomas, Houston, 1959; M.A., U. Detroit, 1968; Diploma in Pastoral Studies, East Asian Pastoral Inst., Manila, 1973-74. Ordained priest Roman Catholic Ch., 1966; missionary Basilian Fathers, Mex., 1968-76; exec. v.p. Mexican Am. Cultural Ctr., San Antonio, 1976-81; aux. bishop Archdiocese of San Antonio, 1981-82; bishop Diocese of Las Cruces, N.M., 1982—; cons. U.S. Bishop's Com. on Liturgy, from 1981; advisor U.S. Bishop's Com. on Hispanic Affairs, from 1981. Author: Fiesta, Worship and Family, 1981. Mem. N.Am. Acad. on Liturgy, Hispanic Liturgical Inst., Padres Asociada Derechos Religiosos Educativos y Sociales. Lodges: K.C; Holy Order Knights of Holy Sepulcher. Office: Diocese of Las Cruces 1280 Med Park Dr Las Cruces NM 88005-3239

RAMIREZ, STEVEN ADRIAN, city official; b. San Diego, Apr. 19, 1961; s. Ponciano Jr. and Josephine (Campos) R.; m. Dora Ann Perez, Feb. 20, 1993. AA in Psychology, San Diego Mesa Coll., 1984; BA in Indsl. Psychology, San Diego State U., 1985, MA in Indsl. Psychology, 1989. Orgn. devel. specialist City of San Diego, 1987—; cultural diversity trainer, 1992—; soccer coach, counselor Samuel F.B. Morse High Sch., San Diego, 1981-91. Vol. Logan Hts. Family Health Ctr., San Diego, 1985—, Alba 80 Soc., San Diego, 1984—, charter pres., bd. dirs. Named Vol. of the Yr., Logan Hts. Family Health Ctr., 1990. Mem. Orgn. Devel. Network (chmn. 1992—), Latino City Employees Assn. (charter pres. 1991). Office: City of San Diego 4950 Murphy Canyon Rd San Diego CA 92123-4325

RAMO, ROBERTA COOPER, lawyer; b. Denver, Aug. 8, 1942; d. David D. and Martha L. (Rosenblum) Cooper; m. Barry W. Ramo, June 17, 1964. BA magna cum laude, U. Colo., 1964; JD, U. Chgo., 1967. Bar: N.Mex., 1967, Tex. 1971. With N.C. Fund, Durham, N.C., 1967-68; nat. teaching fellow Shaw U., Raleigh, N.C., 1968-70; mem. Sawtelle, Goode, Davidson & Troilo, San Antonio, 1970-72, Rodey, Dickason, Sloan, Akin & Robb, Albuquerque, 1972-74; sole practice law, Albuquerque, 1974-77; mng.

ptnr. Poole, Kelly & Ramo, Albuquerque, 1977-93; bd. dirs. United N.Mex. Bank of Albuquerque, 1983-88. Bd. dirs., past pres. N.Mex. Symphony Orch., 1977-86; bd. dirs. Albuquerque Community Found., N.Mex. First, 1980-90; trustee Manzano Day Sch., 1975-77; bd. regents U. N.Mex., 1988—, pres. 1990-93. Fellow Am. Bar Found.; mem. Albuquerque Bar Assn. (dir., pres. 1980-81), N.Mex. Bar Assn. (chmn. bus., banking sect. 1979-80, Outstanding Contbn. award 1981, 84), ABA (vice chmn. 1981-82, chmn. law practice sect. 1984, ALI/ABA com.), AM. Bar Retirement Assn. (bd. dirs.), Am. Judicature Soc. (bd. dirs. 1988-91), Greater Albuquerque C. of C. (bd. dirs. exec. com. 1987-91). Contbr. articles to profl. jours. Address: Poole Kelly & Ramo PO Box 1769 Albuquerque NM 87103

RAMO, SIMON, engineering executive; b. Salt Lake City, May 7, 1913; s. Benjamin and Clara (Trestman) R.; m. Virginia Smith, July 25, 1937; children: James Brian, Alan Martin. BS, U. Utah, 1933, DSc (hon.), 1961; PhD, Calif. Inst. Tech., 1936; DEng (hon.), Case Western Res. U., 1960, U. Mich., 1966, Poly. Inst. N.Y., 1971; DSc (hon.), Union Coll., 1963, Worcester Polytechnic Inst., 1968, U. Akron, 1969, Cleve. State U., 1976; LLD (hon.), Carnegie-Mellon U., 1970, U. So. Calif., 1972, Gonzaga U., 1983, Occidental Coll., 1984, Claremont U., 1985. With Gen. Electric Co., 1936-46; v.p. ops. Hughes Aircraft Co., 1946-53; with Ramo-Woolridge Corp., 1953-58; dir. U.S. Intercontinental ballistic missile program, 1954-58; dir. TRW Inc., 1954-85, exec. v.p., 1958-61, vice chmn. bd., 1961-78, chmn. exec. com., 1969-78, cons., 1978—; pres. The Bunker-Ramo Corp., 1964-66; chmn. bd. TRW-Fujitsu Co., 1980-83; bd. dirs. Arco Power Techs.; vis. prof. mgmt. sci. Calif. Inst. Tech., 1978—; Regents lectr. UCLA, 1981-82, U. Calif. at Santa Cruz, 1978-79; chmn. Center for Study Am. Experience, U. So. Calif., 1978-80; Faculty fellow John F. Kennedy Sch. Govt., Harvard U., 1980-84; mem. White House Energy Research and Devel. Adv. Council, 1973-75; mem. adv. com. on sci. and fgn. affairs U.S. State Dept., 1973-75; chmn. Pres.'s Com. on Sci. and Tech., 1976-77; mem. adv. council to Sec. Commerce, 1976-77, Gen. Atomics Corp., 1988—, Aurora Capital Ptnrs., 1991—, Chartwell Investments, 1992—; co-chmn. Transition Task Force on Sci. and Tech. for Pres.-elect Reagan; mem. roster consultants to adminstr. ERDA, 1976-77; bd. advisors for sci. and tech. Republic of China, 1981-84; chmn. bd. Aetna, Jacobs & Ramo Venture Capital, 1987-90, Allenwood Ventures Inc., 1987—. Author: The Business of Science, 1988, other sci., engring. and mgmt. books. Bd. dirs. L.A. World Affairs Coun. 1973-85, Mus. Ctr. Found., L.A., L.A. Philharm. Assn., 1981-84; life trustee Calif. Inst. Tech., Nat. Symphony Orch. Assn., 1973-83; trustee emeritus Calif. State Univs.; bd. visitors UCLA Sch. Medicine, 1980—; bd. dirs. W.M. Keck Found., 1983—; bd. govs. Performing Arts Coun. Mus. Ctr. L.A., pres., 1976-77. Recipient award IAS, 1956; award Am. Inst. Elec. Engrs., 1959; award Arnold Air Soc., 1960; Am. Acad. Achievement award, 1964; award Am. Iron and Steel Inst., 1968; Disting. Svc. medal Armed Forces Communication and Electronics Assn., 1970; medal of achievement WEMA, 1970; awards U. So. Calif., 1971, 79; Kayan medal Columbia U., 1972; award Am. Cons. Engrs. Coun., 1974; medal Franklin Inst., 1978; award Harvard Bus. Sch. Assn., 1979; award Nat. Medal Sci., 1979; Disting. Alumnus award U. Utah, 1981; UCLA medal, 1982; Presdl. Medal of Freedom, 1983; named to Bus. Hall of Fame, 1984; recipient Aesculapian award UCLA, 1984, Durand medal AAIA, 1984, John Fritz medal, 1986, Henry Townley Heald award Ill. Inst. Tech., 1988, Nat. Engring. award Am. Assn. Engring. Socs., 1988, Franklin-Jefferson medal, 1988, Howard Hughes Meml. award, 1989. Fellow IEEE (Electronic Achievement award 1953, Golden Omega award 1975, Founders medal 1980, Centennial medal 1984), Am. Acad. Arts and Scis.; mem. N.Y. Acad. of Sci., Nat. Acad. Engring. (founder, coun. mem. Bueche award), Nat. Acad. Scis., Am. Phys. Soc., Am. Philos. Soc., Inst. Advancement Engring., Internat. Acad. Astronautics, Eta Kappa Mu (eminent mem. award 1966). Office: 9200 Sunset Blvd Ste 801 Los Angeles CA 90069-3506

RAMO, VIRGINIA M. SMITH, civic worker; b. Yonkers, N.Y.; d. Abraham Harold and Freda (Kasnetz) Smith; B.S. in Edn., U. So. Calif., D.H.L. (hon.), 1978; m. Simon Ramo; children—James Brian, Alan Martin. Nat. co-chmn. ann. giving U. So. Calif., 1968-70, vice chmn., trustee, 1971—, co-chmn. bd. councilors Sch. Performing Arts, 1975-76, co-chmn. bd. councillors Schs. Med. and Engring.; vice-chmn. bd. overseers Hebrew Union Coll., 1972-75; bd. dirs. The Muses of Calif. Mus. Sci. and industry, UCLA Affiliates, Estelle Doheny Eye Found., U. So. Calif. Sch. Medicine; adv. council Los Angeles County Heart Assn., chmn. com. to endow Chair in cardiology at U. So. Calif.; vice-chmn., bd. dirs. Friends of Library U. So. Calif.; bd. dirs., nat. pres. Achievement Rewards for Coll. Scientists Found., 1975-77; bd. dirs. Les Dames Los Angeles, Community TV So. Calif.; bd. dirs., v.p. Founders Los Angeles Music Center; v.p. Los Angeles Music Center Opera Assn.; v.p. corp. bd. United Way; v.p. Blue Ribbon-400 Performing Arts Council; chmn. com. to endow chair in gerontology U. So. Calif.; vice chmn. campaign Doheny Eye Inst., 1986. Recipient Service award Friends of Libraries, 1974; Nat. Community Service award Alpha Epsilon Phi, 1975; Disting. Service award Am. Heart Assn. 1978; Service award U. So. Calif.; Spl. award U. So. Calif. Music Alumni Assn., 1979; Life Achievement award Mannequins of Los Angeles Assistance League, 1979; Woman of Yr. award PanHellenic Assn., 1981; Disting. Service award U. So. Calif. Sch. Medicine, 1981; U. So. Calif. Town and Gown Recognition award, 1986; Asa V. Call Achievement award U. So. Calif., 1986; Phi Kappa Phi scholarship award U. So. Calif., 1986. Mem. UCLA Med. Aux., U. So. Calif. Pres.'s Circle, Commerce Assos. U. So. Calif., Cedars of Lebanon Hosp. Women's Guild (dir. 1967-68), Blue Key, Skull and Dagger.

RAMOS, ALBERT A., electrical engineer; b. L.A., Feb. 28, 1927; s. Jesus D. and Carmen F. (Fontes) R.; B.S. in Elec. Engring., U. So. Calif., 1950, M.S. in Systems Mgmt., 1972; Ph.D., U.S. Internat. U., 1975; m. Joan C. Pailing, Sept. 23, 1950; children—Albert A., Richard R., James J., Katherine. With guided missile test group Hughes Aircraft Co., 1950-60; with TRW DSG, 1960—, sr. staff engr. Norton AFB, San Bernardino, Calif., 1969-91, ret., 1991. Served with USNR, 1945-46. Registered profl. engr., Calif. Mem. IEEE, NSPE, Air Force Assn., Mexican-Am. Engring. Soc., Mexican-Am. Profl. Mgmt. Assn. (mem. administering commn. dept. community svcs.), Sigma Phi Delta, Eta Kappa Nu, Tau Beta Pi. Home: 1457 W Cypress Ave Redlands CA 92373-5612

RAMOS, J. MARIO, opera director, conductor; b. Volta Redonda, Brazil, June 23, 1956. MusB, Tex. Christian U., 1982; MA, MBA, So. Meth. U., Dallas, 1985. Assoc. producer Motion Graphics, Rio de Janeiro, 1972-74; gen. dir. Teatro Poeira, Volta Redonda, 1975-77; dir. devel. Pub. Opera Dallas, 1985; gen. mgr. Ft. Worth Opera, 1985-86, gen. dir., 1986-91; gen. dir. Hawaii Opera Theatre, Honolulu, 1991—. Southwestern Petroleum Corp. scholar Tex. Christian U., 1977-78, Walsh scholar, 1977-82. Mem. Opera Am. Office: Hawaii Opera Theatre 987 Waimanu St Honolulu HI 96814-3319

RAMOS, LINDA MARIE, endoscopy technician; b. San Jose, Calif., July 8, 1961; d. Albert Sequeira and Catherine Marie (Souza) Vieira; m. John Bettencourt Ramos, June 12, 1982. AA, De Anza Coll., 1986; BA, St. Mary's Coll. Calif., Moraga, 1988. Cert. gastrointestinal clinician, aerobic instr. Endoscopy technician O'Connor Hosp., San Jose, 1979—; aerobic instr. Mountain View Athletic Club, 1984—, Decathalon Club, Santa Clara, 1984—. Contbr. articles to profl. jours. Vol. O'Connor Hosp., 1975-79; active campaign Santa Clara City Council, 1980-81. Fellow Irmandade Da Festa Do Espirito Santo (sec. 1974-82, queen 1975-76), Soc. Gastrointestinal Assts., No. Soc. Gastrointestinal Assts., Soc. Espirito Santo of Santa Clara, Luso Am. Fraternal Fedn. (state youth pres. 1979-80, youth leader local coun. Santa Clara Mountain View 1979-87, scholar, 1979, founder, organizer Mountain View-Santa Clara chpt. 1980, pres. local region 1980-84, state 20-30 pres. 1984-85, state dir. youth programs 1988—); mem. Aerobics and Fitness Assn. Am. Republican. Roman Catholic. Home: 141 Saratoga Ave Apt 1123 Santa Clara CA 95051-7359 Office: O'Connor Hosp 2105 Forest Ave San Jose CA 95128-1471

RAMOS, LUIS ROBERTO, military serviceman; b. Ponce, P.R., Sept. 29, 1964; s. Freddie and Elba (Ramos) R.; m. Aida Luz Gonzalez, Dec. 21, 1985; 1 child, Hedrick Yanick. Student, Cath. U. P.R., Ponce, 1982-83, Chgo. City Coll., 1985-87, Monterey Peninsula Coll., 1991—. Lic. automotive servicing technician. Commd. U.S. Army, advanced through grades; with field arty. fire support U.S. Army, Fort Ord, Calif., 1989—. With USN, 1983-89. Roman Catholic. Home: Jardines Del Caribe 17 St # 123 Ponce PR 00731

RAMOS, NELSON HERBERT, healthcare executive; b. Bklyn., Oct. 14, 1950; s. Herbert and Asia (Perez) R.; m. Penny Helene Williams, Sept. 4, 1982; children: Katalyn, Kelsey. BS in Econs., BS in Engring., Renseelaer Poly. Inst., Troy, N.Y., 1972; M in Engring., Rensealner Poly. Inst., Troy, N.Y., 1973. Engring. supr. Air Force Systems Command, Edwards AFB, Calif., 1973-76; mgmt. engr. Sharp Meml. Hosp., San Diego, 1976-79; supr. mgmt. engring. Kaiser Found. Hosp., San Diego, 1977-80; dir. mgmt. engring. Meml. Hosps. Assn., Modesto, Calif., 1980-83; ptnr. MMC Healthcare, Modesto, 1983-86; dir. mgmt. svcs. Mercy Gen. Hosp., Sacramento, Calif., 1986-89; v.p. mgmt. systems Meml. Hosps. Assn., Modesto, 1989—; pres. Am. Inst. Indsl. Engr., San Diego, 1978-79. Mem. Calif. Hosps. Polit. Action Com., Sacramento, 1992. Lt. USAF, 1973-76. Mem. Am. Hosp. Assn., Hosp. Fin. Mgmt. Assn., Ctrl. Calif. Hosp. Mgmt. Systems Soc. (pres.-elect 1993), Renseelaer Alumni Assn. (class pres. 1972-77), Alpha Phi Omega, Modesto C. of C. Office: Meml Hosps Assn 1700 Coffee Rd Modesto CA 95355

RAMPIL, IRA JAY, physician, educator, medical engineer; b. N.Y.C., Dec. 14, 1953. BS, SUNY, Stony Brook, 1975; MS, U. Wis., 1976; MD, Columbia U., 1983. Diplomate Am. Bd. Anesthesiology, Nat. Bd. Med. Examiners. Asst. prof. U. Calif., San Francisco, 1987—, med. dir. Neurophysiologic Monitoring Svc, 1992—. Office: U Calif Dept of Anesthesia San Francisco CA 94143

RAMSAY, ERIC GUY, surgeon; b. Accrington, England, Sept. 22, 1927; came to U.S., 1954; s. Robert Guy and Gertrude Elizabeth (Osborne) R.; m. Lois Clark, July 25, 1953; children: Michael, Timothy, Jennifer, Peter. M.B.Ch.B., U. Glasgow (Scotland), 1950. Diplomate Am. Bd. Surgery. Intern Falkirk Royal Infirmary, Glasgow Western Infirmary, Scotland, 1950-51; resident surgery Mo. Pacific Hosp., St. Louis, 1954-58; pvt. practice surgeon Tucson, 1959—; chief surgery Kino Community Hosp., Tucson, 1966—; dir. med. edn. St. Mary's Hosp., Tucson, 1963-65, Tuscon Hosps. Med. Edn. Program, 1966—; clin. prof. surgery U. Ariz. Coll. Medicine, 1972—. Flight lt. RCAF, 1951-54. Mem. Am. Coll. Surgeons, AMA, Assn. for Hosp. Med. Edn., Southwestern Surg. Congress, Ariz. Med. Assn., Pima County Med. Soc., Tucson Surg. Soc. Home: 5476 E River Rd Tucson AZ 85718-7246 Office: Tucson Hosps Med Edn Program PO Box 42195 Tucson AZ 85733-2195

RAMSAY, JOHN BARADA, research chemist, educator; b. Phoenix, Dec. 28, 1929; s. John A. and Helen G. Ramsay; m. Barbara Ann Hilsenhoff, Apr. 18, 1953; children: Bryan J., Kathleen L., Carol A., David A. BS in Chemistry, Tex. Western U., 1950; PhD in Analytical Chemistry, U. Wis., 1954. Mem. staff Los Alamos Nat. Lab., 1954-70, 73—; assoc. prof. Coll. Petroleum and Minerals, Dhahran, Saudi Arabia, 1970-73; cons. U.S. Navy, USAF, 1980—; adj. prof. U. N.Mex., Los Alamos, 1980-85. Author sci. articles. Recipient award of excellence U.S. Dept. Energy, 1984, 92. Mem. AAAS, N.Mex. Acad. Sci. (pres. 1988), Am. Archeol. Soc. (chpt. pres. 1979), National Ski Patrol, Westerners Internat. (chpt. pres. 1988-90), Sigma Xi. Democrat. Home: 6 Erie Ln Los Alamos NM 87544-3810 Office: PO Box 1663 Los Alamos NM 87545-0001

RAMSAY, ROBERT HENRY, investment manager; b. Atchison, Kans., June 18, 1925; s. Ronald and Dorcas (Carlisle) R.; m. Margaret Packard, Aug. 16, 1952 (dec. Dec. 1989); children: Margaret R. Gray, William P., David C.; m. Carolyn McKillop, Dec. 8, 1991. BS in Aeronautical Engring., U. Kans., 1945; M in Retailing, U. Pitts., 1948. Br. mgr. Boettcher & Co., Grand Junction, Colo., 1956-65, Colorado Springs, Colo., 1965-71; pres. Robert H. Ramsay Fin. Svcs., Colorado Springs, 1971-74, Ramsay & Ellsworth, Inc., Colorado Springs, 1974-87, Ramsay Investment Counsel Inc., Colorado Springs, 1987—; bd. dirs. Norwest Bank of Colorado Springs. Bd. dirs. Colorado Springs Sch. Mem. Rotary Club of Colorado Springs. Office: Ramsay Investment Counsel Inc 810 Holly Sugar Bldg Colorado Springs CO 80903

RAMSBY, MARK DELIVAN, lighting designer and consultant; b. Portland, Oreg., Nov. 20, 1947; s. Marshall Delivan and Verna Pansy (Culver) R.; divorced; children: Aaron Delivan, Venessa Mercedes. Student, Portland (Oreg.) State U., 1966-67. With C.E.D., Portland, 1970-75; minority ptnr. The Light Source, Portland, 1975-78, pres., 1978-87; prin. Illume Lighting Design, Portland, 1987-90; ptnr. Ramsby, Dupuy & Seats, Inc., Portland, 1990-91; dir. lighting design PAE Cons. Engrs., Inc., Portland, 1991—; pvt. practice cons. Portland, 1979—. Recipient Top Ten Outstanding Achievement award Metalux Lighting, 1981-85, 100% award, 1985, Edwin F. Guth award of merit, 1990, Edison award of excellence, 1990, 93. Mem. Illuminating Engring. Soc. Am. (sec.-treas. Oreg. sect. 1978-79, Oreg. Section and Regional award 1989, Lighting Design awards), Internat. Assn. Lighting Designers. Republican. Lutheran. Office: PAE Cons Engrs 808 SW 3rd Ave Ste 300 Portland OR 97204-2426

RAMSEY, JERRY VIRGIL, educator, financial planner; b. Tacoma, July 24, 1940; s. Virgil Emory and Winifred Victoria (Carothers) R.; m. Elaine Sigrid Perdue, June 24, 1967; 1 child, Jason Perdue. BA in Elem. Edn., U. Puget Sound, 1967; MEd in Tchr. Tng. and Curriculum Devel., U. Wash., 1971; PhD in Econ. Geography, Columbia Pacific U., 1993. Tchr. Tacoma Pub. Schs., 1967—; fin. planner Primerica Corp., Tacoma, 1986-90, Waddell & Reed, Inc., Tacoma, 1990—; real estate investor, CEO Ramsey Properties, Gig Harbor, Wash., 1970—; lectr. Pacific Luth. U., Tacoma, 1972-86. Precinct committeeman Pierce County Rep. Com., Tacoma, 1968-78; mem. steering com. Peninsula Neighborhood Assn., Gig Harbor, Wash., 1991-92. With USAF, 1959-62. Recipient Golden Acorn award PTA, 1975, Meritorious Teaching award Nat. Coun. Geog. Edn., 1978, achievement award Rep. Nat. Com., 1985; grantee U.S. Office Edn., 1971. Mem. NEA (life), Knife and Fork Club (pres. 1983), Kiwanis (pres. Tacoma 1976), Phi Delta Kappa. Methodist. Office: Ramsey Properties PO Box 1311 Gig Harbor WA 98335

RAMSEY, LELAND KEITH, petroleum engineer; b. Topeka, May 31, 1952; s. Keith G. and Darlene (Berndt) R.; m. Kimberly M. Milner, Mar. 31, 1979; children: Jessica Ray, Jeremy Lee. BS, Kans. State U., 1974. Field engr. Dowell div. Dow Chem. Corp., Rock Springs, Wyo., 1975-78, dist. engr., Williston, N.D., 1978-80, sr. dist. engr., 1980-81; dist. sales supr. Dowell/Schlumberger Inc., Williston, 1981-85, field svc. mgr., 1985-88, div. sales engr., Casper, Wyo., 1988-89, sales engr. Roswell, N.Mex., 1989-92; tech. specialist, Midland, Tex., 1992. Mem. Soc. Petroleum Engrs. (chpt. membership chmn. 1982-83, sec.-treas. 1983-84, vice-chmn., 1984-85, chmn. 85-86, scholarship chmn. 1986-88), Am. Assn. Petroleum Geologists, Roswell Geol. Soc. Republican. Baptist. Avocations: golf, racquetball.

RAMSEY, ROSS LAMAR, music educator; b. Logan, Utah, Aug. 29, 1937; s. Ross Brown and Lola (Mortensen) R.; m. Christine Louise Ware, Sept. 26, 1959; children: Rex William, Heather Dee, Holly Lee. BFA, U. N.Mex., 1960; MA, N.Mex. State U., 1968. Cert. tchr., N.Mex. Band dir. Las Cruces (N.Mex.) Pub. Schs., 1964-86; adj. prof. music N.Mex. State U., Las Cruces, 1987—; v.p. for bands, N.Mex. Music Educators Conf., 1973. Arranger Sonata for Two Oboes and Wind Ensemble (Vivaldi), 1983; contbr. articles to profl. publs. Chmn. internat. student exchaqnge, Rotary Internat., Las Cruces, 1987—. Capt. USAF, 1961-63. Cited for exceptional accomplishment, N.Mex. legislature, 1976, for outstanding contbn. to bands, World of Music, 1981, 83, 85; named Outstanding Dir., Six Flags over Tex., 1978, Internat. Music Festivals, 1979; named to N.M. Music Educators Hall of Fame, 1992; Paul Harris fellow Rotary Internat., 1993. Mem. Music Educators Nat. Conf., Band Dirs., Nat. Bandmasters Assn. (citation of excellence 1978), Phi Beta Mu. Democrat. Unitarian. Home: 344 Phillips Dr Las Cruces NM 88005-1661

RANCE, QUENTIN E., interior designer; b. St. Albans, Eng., Mar. 22, 1935; came to U.S., 1981; s. Herbert Leonard and Irene Ann (Haynes) R.; m. India Perlin, May 17, 1974. Grad., Eastbourne (Eng.) Sch. Art, 1960. Soft furnishings buyer Dickeson & French Ltd., Eastbourne, 1960-61, outside sales mgr., 1961-62; design dir. Laszlo Hoenig, Ltd., London, 1962-73; mng. dir. Quentin Rance Interiors Ltd., London, 1973-81; pres. Quentin Rance Enterprises, Inc., Encino, Calif., 1981—. Works featured in Designers West, 1983, Design House Rev., 1983, Profiles mag., 1987, Nat. Assn. Mirror Mfrs. Jour., 1988, Designer Specifier, 1990. Mem. Founders for Diabetic Research/City of Hope. Served with RAF, 1953-55. Fellow Chartered Soc. Designers (Eng.); mem. Am. Soc. Interior Designers (profl., chpt. bd. dirs. 1983-87, 89-91, chmn. Avanti 1983-85, admissions chmn. 1985—, Presdl. citations 1984-87, 91), Knights of Vine. Home and Office: 18005 Rancho St Encino CA 91316-4214

RANCE, THOMAS P., music educator; b. Council Bluffs, Iowa, June 4, 1961; s. Patrick Thomas and Carolyn Ann (Pass) R. BMus, U. Iowa, 1983. Cert. elem. and secondary tchr., Iowa. Instr. Santa Clara (Calif.) U.; sect. percussionist Monterey County Symphony, Carmel, Calif., Santa Cruz County Symphony, Sacramento (Calif.) Symphony; prin. percussionist Modesto (Calif.) Symphony Orch., West Bay Opera, Palo Alto, Calif., Fremont (Calif.)/Newark Philharm. Mem. Percussive Arts Soc. (pres. no. Calif. chpt. 1984-87). Home: 2032 Benita Dr # 2 Rancho Cordova CA 95670

RANCK, JOHN STEVENS, human resources executive, consultant; b. Warren, Ohio, Sept. 14, 1945; s. Charles Thomas and Helen Marie (Weir) R.; m. Bibbie-Ann Rose Robertson, Dec. 25, 1975; children: James L., Edward L. BS, USAF Acad., 1971; MS in Human Resources, Gonzaga U., 1979, MBA, 1984. Cert. adminstrv. mgr.; sr. profl. in human resources mgmt. Salesman Neal's Family Shoes, Warren, 1964-65; prodn. staff Packard Elec. div. GMC, Warren, 1965-66; personnel mgr. United Paint Mfg., Inc., Greenacres, Wash., 1981-82; personnel dir. Sheraton-Spokane Hotel, 1982-83; personnel mgr. Students Book Corp., Pullman, Wash., 1984-87; personnel analyst Spokane Co., 1988-90; pres. Top Ranck Mgmt., Spokane and Loon Lake, Wash., 1990—; v.p., sec.-treas. TONGA Coffee, Co., 1993—. Active Stevens County Rep. Com. Capt. USAF, 1966-80. Mem. ASTD, Adminstrv. Mgmt. Soc. (chpt. dir. 1982-84, sec. 1983), Am. Compensation Assn., Internat. Pers. Mgmt. Assn., N.W. Human Resource Mgmt. Assn. (exec. bd. 1989-93, treas. 1993, legis. liaison 1991-92, v.p. programs 1990, coll. rels. com. 1989), Soc. Human Resource Mgmt., Spokane Valley C. of C., Chewelah C. of C., Masons (Kinght York Grand Cross of Honor, Order of Purple Cross, Knight Comdr. Ct. of Honor), K.T. (grand comdr. 1987-88), Red Cross Constantine, Royal Order Scotland, Shriners, Grotto. Lutheran. Home: 40151 Morgan Rd PO Box 297 Loon Lake WA 99148-0297 Office: Top Ranck Mgmt PO Box 501 Loon Lake WA 99148-0501

RANDALL, JANET ANN, biology educator, researcher; b. Twin Falls, Idaho, July 3, 1943; d. William Franklin and Bertha Silvia (Kalousek) Orr; m. Bruce H. MacEvoy. BS, U. Idaho, 1965; MEd, U. Wash., 1969; PhD, Wash. State U., 1977. Postdoctoral fellow U. Texas, Austin, 1977-79; from asst. to assoc. prof. biology Ctrl. Mo. State U., Warrensburg, 1979-87; assoc. prof. biology San Francisco State U., 1987-92, prof., 1992—; vis. prof. Cornell U., Ithaca, N.Y., 1984-85. Contbr. 25 articles to profl. jours. Rsch. grantee Nat. Geog. Soc., 1982, 86, NSF, 1984, 87, 88-89, 89-91, 91-93, 93—. Fellow Calif. Acad. Sci.; mem. Animal Behavior Soc. (mem. at large 1986-89), Am. Soc. Zoologists (program officer), Am. Soc. Mammalogists, Internat. Soc. Behavioral Ecologists, Sigma Xi. Home: 3137 Monterey St San Mateo CA 94403 Office: San Francisco State U Dept Biology San Francisco CA 94132

RANDALL, JOHN ERNEST, marine biologist; b. L.A., May 22, 1924; s. John Ernest and Mildred Adeline (McKibben) R.; m. Helen Au, Nov. 9, 1951; children: Loreen Ann, Rodney Dean. BA, UCLA, 1950; PhD with honors, U. Hawaii, 1955. Rsch. fellow U. Hawaii, Honolulu, 1953-55, Yale U./Bishop Mus., Tahiti, 1955-57; prof. Inst. Marine Biology U. P.R., Mayaguez, 1961-65; dir. Inst. Marine Biology, Mayaguez, 1962-65; rsch. asst. prof. marine lab. U. Miami (Fla.), 1957-61; dir. The Oceanic Inst., Waimanalo, Hawaii, 1965-66; marine biologist U. Hawaii, Hawaii Inst. Marine Biology, Kaneohe, 1967-69; ichthyologist B.P. Bishop Mus., Honolulu, 1965-75, chmn. zoology dept., 1975-79, sr. ichthyologist zoology dept., Linus Allen Bishop disting. chair in zoology, 1979—; grad. faculty zoology dept. U. Hawaii, 1966-75, 83—; rsch. assoc. vertebrate zoology Smithsonian Inst., ichthyology Natural History Mus. of L.A. County. Bd. editors Revue Francaise d'Aquariologie, Caribbean Jour. Sci.; editor Freshwater and Marine Aquarium, Sea Frontiers, 1961-78, Indo-Pacific Fishes; mem. editorial bd. Micronesica, 1963—; adv. bd. Fauna of Saudi Arabia; contbr. articles to profl. jours. 2nd lt. Med. Adminstrv. Corps, U.S. Army, 1943-46. Recipient Robert H. Gibbs. Jr. Meml. award for excellence in systematic ichthyology, 1990. Mem. Am. Assn. Zool Nomenclature, Am. Elasmnbranch Soc., Am. Soc. Ichthyologists and Herpetologists, Assn. Island Marine Labs. of the Caribbean, Assn. Pacific Systematists, Australian Coral Reef Soc., Biol. Soc. Wash., European Ichthyological Union, Hawaiian Acad. Scis., Ichthyological Soc. Japan, Indian Soc. Ichthyology, Internat. Gamefish Assn., Internat. Oceanographic Found., Phi Beta Kappa, Phi Kappa Sigma, Sigma Xi. Office: Bernice Pauahi Bishop Mus PO Box 19000-A Honolulu HI 96817-0916

RANDALL, ROBERT GORDON, computer consultant; b. Walla Walla, Wash., May 23, 1966; s. Ronald Lloyd and Kathleen Marie (Dill) R. BA in Theatre Mgmt., Ea. Wash. U., 1988, postgrad., 1992—. Dir. publicity Univ. Theatre Ea. Wash. U., Cheney, 1985-87, resident advisor Univ. Housing, 1987-90; mem. sales staff Video Giant, Walla Walla, various summers, mgr., 1990—; computer cons. Computer Resources Corp., Walla Walla, 1991—. Mem. Walla Walla Little Theatre, 1992—; tchr. Trinity Bapt. Ch., Walla Walla, 1990—; co-dir. Insight Players Ednl. Theatre for Child Abuse and Neglect, Walla Walla, 1990—; mem. computer support Walla Walla High Sch. Alumni Assn., 1990—. Republican. Baptist. Home: 1011 Puff Ln # K College Place WA 99324 Office: Computer Resources Corp 2316 Eastgate N Ste 160 Walla Walla WA 99362

RANDALL, ROGER PAUL, religious organization consultant; b. Cottage Grove, Oreg., Nov. 3, 1946; s. Vinal Truman and Janet Louise (Peterson) R.; m. Sara Holt Clemmons, Sept. 26, 1968; 1 child, Allison L. BS, Oreg. State U., 1968; postgrad., Internat. Grad. Sch. Theology, San Bernardino, Calif., 1968, 71, Regis U., 1991—. Campus dir. Auburn U. Campus Crusade for Christ, Auburn, Ala., 1969-72; Tex. area dir. Campus Crusade for Christ, Dallas, 1972-73; so. regional dir. Campus Crusade for Christ, San Bernardino, 1973-75, univ. ministry nat. dir., 1980-85; dir. internat. univ. resources Campus Crusade for Christ, Boulder, Colo., 1988—; nat. dir. Student Venture, San Bernardino, 1975-80; Africa univ. ministry coord. Life Ministry, Nairobi, Kenya, 1985-88; founder, dir. Nat. Network of Youth Ministries, San Diego, 1977-79; co-founder, dir. World-wide Student Network, Orlando, Fla., 1986—; cons. Internat. Leadership Devel. Task Force, Laguna Niguel, Calif., 1991—. Editor: Make Your Mark, 1981, International University Resource Manual, 1986; contbr. articles to profl. jours. Long range planning cons. Platt Jr. High Sch., Boulder, 1989; resource person U.S. Dept. HHS, Washington, 1980-88; commn. mem. UN Internat. Youth Yr. Commn., N.Y.C., 1983. Home: 1302 S Gibson Ct Superior CO 80027

RANDALL, WILLIAM B., manufacturing company executive; b. Phila., Jan. 8, 1921; s. Albert and Ann (Fine) R.; m. Geraldine Kempson, Aug. 10, 1943; children: Robert, Erica Lynn, Lisa. Student, Rider Coll., Trenton, N.J., 1940-41. Gen. Sales mgr. Lowres Optical Mfg. Co., Newark, 1946-49; pres., founder Rand Sales Co., N.Y.C., 1949-58; gen. mgr. Sea & Ski Co. div. Botany Industries, Inc., Millbrae, Calif., 1958-61; pres., dir. Botany Industries, Inc., 1961-66, v.p., 1961-65; pres. Renauld of France, Reno, 1967-68; chmn. bd. Renauld Internat., Reading, Pa., 1963-65; pres., chief operating officer Renauld Internat., Ltd., Burlingame and Reno, 1966-67; pres., chmn. bd. Randall Internat., Ltd., 1967-68; sr. exec. v.p. Forty-two Prods. Ltd., 1969-71; pres. Exec. Products Internat. Ltd., 1969-71, New Product Devel. Ctr., Carlsbad, Calif., 1971—; pres. Internat. Concept Ctr. Exec. Products Internat. Ltd., Irvine, 1971—, pres. Sun Research Ctr., 1974—; pres. La Costa Products Internat., 1975-86; mng. dir. merchandising La Costa Hotel and Spa, 1986-88; pres., chief exec. officer Randall Internat., Carlsbad, 1989—; bd. dirs. Bank of La Costa, Am. Body Care, Inc. Served to 1st lt., navigator USAAF, 1942-45. Mem. Am. Mgmt. Assn., Nat. Wholesale Druggists Assn., Nat. Assn. Chain Drug Stores, Hon. Order Ky. Cols., Baja Beach and Tennis Club (bd. dirs.). Home: 7150 Arenal Ln Carlsbad CA 92009-6701

RANDALL, WILLIAM THEODORE, state official; b. Seattle, July 8, 1931; s. Heaton Henry Randall and Mabel Maud (Johnson) Landstrom; m. Barbara Ann Bouffard; children: Julie Randall Waybright, Linda A. Randall Wiggins, Mary Lee Randall Lane. BA in Far Ea. Studies, U. Wash., 1953,

BA in Polit. Sci., 1959, MEd in Edn. Adminstrn., 1966; EdD in Edn. Adminstrn., Ariz. State U., 1969. Agt. Aetna Ins. Co., Seattle, 1957-59; tchr. Shoreline Pub. Schs., Seattle, 1959-61, prin., 1961-66, dir. rsch., 1969-70; asst. supt. Wash. Sch. Dist., Phoenix, 1970-73; supt. Scottsdale (Ariz.) Pub. Schs., 1973-80; pres. William Randall Assocs., Phoenix, 1980-83; supt. Creighton Sch. Dist., Phoenix, 1983-88; commr. edn. State of Colo., Denver, 1988—; cons. Edge Learning Corp., Tempe, Ariz., 1978-82; edn. advisor Gov. of Ariz., 1985; pres.-elect Ariz. Adminstrs., Inc., 1986-88. Author: Stress Management, 1978; co-author: Role of Teacher, 1979, Management Development, 1980. Chmn. Ariz. Child Care Coalition, Phoenix, 1986; bd. dirs. Colo. Childrens Trust, Denver, 1989—; mem. exec. bd. Communities for Drug Free Colo., Denver, 1988. Sgt. U.S. Army, 1955-57. Named Adminstr. of Yr. Shoreline Edn. Assn., Seattle, 1966, Ariz. Supt. of Yr. Ariz. Sch. Adminstrs., Phoenix, 1988. Office: Colo Dept Edn 201 E Colfax Ave Denver CO 80203-1704

RANDHAWA, BIKKAR SINGH, educational psychologist, educator; b. Jullundur, India, June 14, 1933; came to Can., 1961, naturalized, 1966; s. Pritam S. and Sawaran K. (Basakhi) R.; m. Leona Emily Bujnowski, Oct. 8, 1966; children—Jason, Lisa. B.A. in Math., Panjab U., 1954, B.T. in Edn., 1955, M.A. in History, 1959; B.Ed., U. Alta., Can., 1963; M.Ed. in Measurement and Evaluation, U. Toronto, Ont., Can., 1967, Ph.D., 1969. Tchr. secondary sch. math. Panjab, 1955-61; asst. headmaster, then headmaster, 1955-61; tchr. high sch. math. and sci. Beaver County, Riley, Alta., 1964-65, Camrose County, Alta., 1961-64; tchr. high sch. math. and sci. Edmonton (Alta.) Public Schs., 1965-67; tutor in math. for social sci. Ont. Inst. Studies in Edn., Toronto, 1968-69; mem. faculty U. Sask., Saskatoon, 1969-76, 77—; prof. ednl. psychology U. Sask., 1977—, asst. dean research and field services, 1982-87; prof., coord. Visual Scholars' Program, U. Iowa, 1976-77; cons. in field. Contbr. articles profl. jours. Fellow Am. Psychol. Assn., Am. Psychol. Soc. (charter), Can. Psychol. Assn., mem. Am. Ednl. Research Assn., Can. Soc. Study Edn., Nat. Coun. Measurement in Edn., Sask. Psychol. Assn., Phi Delta Kappa (pres. Saskatoon chpt. 1971, 85). Home: 510 Forsyth Crescent, Saskatoon, SK Canada S7N 4H8 Office: U Sask, 3116 Edn Bldg, Saskatoon, SK Canada S7N 0W0

RANDISI, ELAINE MARIE, law corporation executive; b. Racine, Wis., Dec 19, 1926; d. John Dewey and Alveta Irene (Raffety) Fehd; A.A., Pasadena Jr. Coll., 1946; B.S. cum laude (Giannini scholar), Golden Gate U., 1978; m. John Paul Randisi, Oct. 12, 1946 (div. July 1972); children—Jeanine Randisi Manson, Martha Randisi Chaney, Joseph, Paula, Catherine Randisi Carvalho, George, Anthony (dec.). With Raymond Kaiser Engrs., Inc., Oakland, Calif., 1969-75, 77-86, corp. acct., 1978-79, sr. corp. acct., 1979-82, sr. payroll acct., 1983-86, acctg. mgr., Lilli Ann Corp., San Francisco, 1986-89, Crosby, Heafey, Roach & May, Oakland, Calif., 1990—; corp. buyer Kaiser Industries Corp., Oakland, 1975-77; lectr. on astrology Theosophical Soc., San Francisco, 1979—; mem. faculty Am. Fedn. Astrologers Internat. Conv., Chgo., 1982, 84. Mem. Speakers Bur., Calif. Assn. for Neurologically Handicapped Children, 1964-70, v.p. 1969; bd. dirs. Ravenwood Homeowners Assn., 1979-82, v.p., 1979-80, sec., 1980-81; mem. organizing com. Minority Bus. Fair, San Francisco, 1976; pres., bd. dirs. Lakewood Condominium Assn., 1984-87; mem., trustee Ch. of Religious Sci., 1992—. Mem. Am. Fedn. Astrologers, Nat. Assn. Female Execs., Calif. Scholarship Fedn. (life), Alpha Gamma Sigma (life). Mem. Ch. of Religious Science (lic. practioner pres. 1990-91, sec. 1989-90). Initiated Minority Vendor Purchasing Program for Kaiser Engrs., Inc., 1975-76. Home: 742 Wesley Way Apt 1C Oakland CA 94610-2338 Office: Crosby Heafey Roach & May 1999 Harrison St Oakland CA 94612-3515

RANDLE, ELLEN EUGENIA FOSTER, opera and classical singer, educator; b. New Haven, Conn., Oct. 2, 1948; d. Richard A.G. and Thelma Lousie (Brooks) Foster; m. Ira James William, 1967 (div. 1972); m. John Willis Randle. Student, Calif. State Coll., Sonoma, 1970; studied with Boris Goldovsky, 1970; student, Grad. Sch. Fine Arts, Florence, Italy, 1974; studied with Tito Gobbi, Florence, 1974; student, U. Calif., Berkeley, 1977; BA in World History, Lone Mountain Coll., 1976, MA in Performing Arts, 1978; studied with Madam Eleanor Steber, Graz, Austria, 1979; studied with Patricia Goehl, Munich, Fed. Republic Germany, 1979; MA in Counseling and Psychology, U. San Francisco, 1990, MA in Marriage, Family, Child Counseling, 1991; postgrad., U. San Francisco, 1991—. Clin. case mgr. Oakland, Calif., 1991—; instr. East Bay Performing Art Ctr., Richmond, Calif., 1986, Chapman Coll., 1986; clin. case mgr. Kairos Unlimited Group Home, Oakland. Singer opera prodns. Porgy & Bess, Oakland, Calif., 1980-81, LaTraviata, Oakland, Calif., 1981-82, Aida, Oakland, 1981-82, Madame Butterfly, Oakland, 1982-83, The Magic Flute, Oakland, 1984, numerous others; performances include TV specials, religous concerts, musicals; music dir. Natural Man, Berkeley, 1986; asst. artistic dir. Opera Piccola, Oakland, Calif., 1990—. Art commr. City of Richmond, Calif. Recipient Bk. Am. Achievement award. Mem. Music Tchrs. Assn., Internat. Black Writers and Artists Inc. (local #5), Nat. Coun. Negro Women, Nat. Assn. Negro Musicians, Calif. Arts Fedn., Calif. Assn. for Counseling and Devel. (mem. black caucus), Nat. Black Child Devel. Inst., The Calif.-Nebraskan Orgn., Inc., San Francisco Commonwealth Club, Gamma Phi Delta. Democrat. Mem. A.M.E. Zion Ch. Home: 5314 Boyd Ave Oakland CA 94618-1112

RANDLE, MICHAEL CHARLES, computer scientist; b. Clarksdale, Miss., Apr. 28, 1952; s. Jesse Frank Sr. and Eleanor Marjana (Mothershed) R.; m. Jan Ceile Parry, Jan. 27, 1973. BS in Biology, Rhodes Coll., 1973; MS in Natural Sci., Memphis State U., 1976. Programmer/analyst NORAD, 1977-81; chief of applications 1155th Tech. Ops. Squadron, 1981-82; sr. systems programmer Planning Rsch. Corp., Honolulu, 1982-85, test and evaluation chief, 1985-88, system integrator intelligence work sta., 1988-90; sr. software engr. Systems Exploration Inc., Kailua, Hawaii, 1990-91; computer scientist U.S. Govt., Naval Ocean Systems Ctr., Kailua, Hawaii, 1991—; designer, programmer computer application and multicast communications software. Active Citizens Against Noise, Honolulu, 1986-88. Capt. USAF, 1976-82. Mem. Assn. for Computing Machinery. Republican. Home: 46-362 Nahewai St Kaneohe HI 96744 Office: Naval Command Control & Ocean Surveillance Ctr RDT&E Divsn Detachment Kailua HI 96734-0997

RANDLE, WILLIAM CRAWFORD, software engineer; b. Portland, Oreg., May 2, 1952; s. Jack C. and Georgia L. (Lynes) R.; m. Susan K. Stivers, June 13, 1987; 1 child, Michelle J. BS in Electronic Computer Engring., Oreg. State U., 1974. Design engr. I and II Tektronix, Inc., Beaverton, Oreg., 1974-79, software engr. II, 1979-84; software engr. III Tektronix, Inc., Redmond, Oreg., 1984-88, sr. software engr., 1988-90, prin., software engr., 1990—. Inventor data communications analyzer, method for generating distorted signals. Mem. IEEE, Assn. for Computing Machinery, Fraternal Order of Eagles, Sigma Tau, Eta Kappa Nu. Home: 3562 SW 34th St Redmond OR 97756-9450 Office: Tektronix Inc 625 SE Salmon Ave Redmond OR 97756-9580

RANDOL, GEORGE CEDRIC, human resources administrator, consultant; b. Clinton, Okla., Dec. 3, 1930; s. John Cedric Randol and Helen (Graves) Taaffe; m. Judith M. Knab, May 14, 1955; children: Peter, John, Stephen, JAmes, Mary. BA, U. San Francisco, 1954, postgrad., 1960-61. Tchr. English and history Riordan High Sch., San Francisco, 1954-55; copy editor San Francisco Chronicle, 1955-61; lay theologian Cath.U., Fresno, Calif., 1961-66; textbook cons. Ginn and Co. and Silver Burdette, San Francisco, 1966-68; wire news editor The Fresno Bee, 1968-74, copy editor, 1985-87, dir. human resources, 1987—; internat. rep. The Newspaper Guild-AFL-CIO, Washington, 1974-76; adminstrv. officer Cen. Calif. Newspaper Guild-Local 92 AFL-CIO, Sacramento, 1976-85. Board dirs. Alcoholism & Drug Abuse Coun., Fresno, 1988-91, pres., 1991—. Mem. Valley Employers Assn. (exec. bd. dirs. Fresno chpt. 1991—). Democrat. Roman Catholic. Office: The Fresno Bee 1626 E St Fresno CA 93786

RANDOLPH, KEVIN H., marketing executive; b. Seattle, July 6, 1949; s. Howard Amos and Betty Elaine (Leahy) R.; m. Deborah Lou Newell, Sept. 18, 1976; children: Heather, Lyndsay. BA, Wash. State U., 1972. Mgr. Computers for Mktg., L.A., 1972-74; data processing mgr. Parker Rsch., Pasadena, Calif., 1974-77; prin. Randolph & Assocs., L.A., 1977-79; v.p. Bank Am. Corp., San Francisco, 1979-87, Interactive Network, Mountain View, Calif., 1987-91; sr. v.p. ICTV, Santa Clara, Calif., 1991—; cons. R & T Rentals, Ephrata, Wash., 1979—, Randolph Home Ctr., Ephrata, 1972—. Mem. Am. Mktg. Assn., Am. Mgmt. Assn., Am. Electronics Assn. Home: 371 Arbor Ct Benicia CA 94510

RANDOLPH, STEVEN, insurance and estate planning agent; b. Nebr., Oct. 14, 1946; m. Sherri Hamrick, 1980 (div. 1989); children: David, John, Michelle; m. Kathleen Riley, 1991. BS, U. Nebr., 1971. Registered rep., SEC; variable annuities license; ins. and disabilities license. Rep. Real Estate Consulting Svcs., Inc., Newport Beach, Calif., 1971-86; fin. svcs. advisor Prudential Fin. Group, Laguna Hills, Calif., 1986—. With USMC, 1964-68, Vietnam. Mem. Nat. Assn. Securities Dealers, Nat. Assn. Life Underwriters (Nat. Sales Achievement award, Nat. Quality award), Million Dollar Round Table Club, Pres.'s Club (awards). Home and Office: PO Box 9612 Newport Beach CA 92658-9612

RANDOLPH, VALERIE ROBIN, lawyer; b. Evanston, Ill., July 19, 1962; d. Robert Manice and Valerie (Vandaveer) R. BBA, Okla. U., 1984; JD, U. Va., 1987. Bar: Calif. 1987. Assoc. Gibson, Dunn & Crutcher, L.A., 1987—. Mem. ABA, Calif. Bar Assn., Jr. League of L.A. Office: Gibson Dunn & Crutcher 333 S Grand Ave Bldg 4810 Los Angeles CA 90071-1552

RANER, GUY HAVARD, retired educator; b. Vicksburg, Miss., Nov. 7, 1919; s. Guy Havard and Caroline Lorraine (Campbell) R.; m. Jane Anne Law, Dec. 13, 1941; children: Daniel Law, Janice Anne; m. Dolores Altman Deutsch, June 20, 1985. BJ, U. Mo., 1942; secondary teaching credential, UCLA, 1946; M Polit. Sci., U. So. Calif., 1956; secondary adminsrv. credential, Calif. State U., Northridge, 1958. Tchr. social studies, dept. chmn., curriculum advisor L.A. Unified Sch. Dist., 1946-80; ret., 1980. Contbr. articles to various publs. Former pres., newsletter editor Reseda Dem. Club, Reseda-West Valley Dem. Club, Chatsworth Dem. Club; mem. Los Angeles County Dem. Ctrl. Com., 1968—, also mem. resolutions com.; Dem. candidate for Calif. Assembly, 1968; mem. exec. bd. San Fernando Valley Dem. Com., 1981-92; Clinton del./alt. Dem. Nat. Conv., 1992. Lt. USNR, 1942-45, 51-52. Mem. Zero Population Growth. Home: 22244-2 James Alan Cir Chatsworth CA 91311-7137

RANFTL, ROBERT MATTHEW, management consulting company executive; b. Milw., May 31, 1925; s. Joseph Sebastian and Leona Elaine (Goetz) R.; m. Marion Smith Goodman, Oct. 12, 1946. BSEE, U. Mich., 1946; postgrad. UCLA, 1953-55. Product engr. Russell Electric Co., Chgo., 1946-47; head engring. dept. Radio Inst. Chgo., 1947-50; sr. project engr. Webster Chgo. Corp., 1950-51, product design engr., 1951-53, head equipment design group, 1953-54, head electronic equipment sect., 1954-55, mgr. product engring. dept., 1955-58, mgr. reliability and quality control, 1958-59, mgr. adminstrn. 1959-61, mgr. product effectiveness lab., 1961-74; corp. dir. engring./design mgmt., 1974-84, corp. dir. managerial productivity Hughes Aircraft Co., Los Angeles, 1984-86; pres. Ranftl Enterprises Inc., Mgmt. Cons., Los Angeles, 1981—; guest lectr. Calif. Inst. Tech., Cornell U., U. Calif.; mem. White House Conf. on Productivity, 1983; mem. human resources productivity task force Dept. of Def., 1985-86. Author: R&D Productivity, 1974, 78; (with others) Productivity: Prospects for Growth, 1981; contbr. articles to profl. jours. Mem. AAAS, AIAA, Am. Soc. Engring. Edn., Am. Soc. Tng. and Devel., IEEE, Inst. Mgmt. Scis., Acad. Mgmt., N.Y. Acad. Scis., U. Mich. Alumni Assn., UCLA Alumni Assn. Office: Ranftl Enterprises Inc PO Box 49892 Los Angeles CA 90049-0892

RANGILA, NANCY ARNEVNA, investment consultant; b. Petrozavodsk, Russia, Mar. 23, 1936; came to U.S., 1937; d. Henry Hjalmar and Myrtle Marie (Jacobson) R. B.A. in Am. History, U. S.C., 1958, M.A. in Am. History, 1964; M.B.A. in Fin., U. So. Calif., 1973. Chartered fin. analyst; cert. employee benefit specialist, cert. fin. planner, chartered investment counselor. Fin. analyst Capital Rsch. Co., L.A., 1964-73; v.p., portfolio mgr., fin. analyst Capital Cons., Inc., Portland, Oreg., 1973-82; sr. v.p., Franklin Fin. Svcs. (subs. Bank of Am. Fed. Savs. Bank), Portland, 1982-91; v.p. rsch., exec. asst. to chair Cutler & Co., Medford, Oreg., 1992—; lectr. investments, retirement plans. Chmn. City of Portland Hosp. Facilities Authority. Mem. Portland Soc. Fin. Analysts, Assn. Investment Mgmt. and Rsch., L.A. Soc. Fin. Analysts, Oreg. Women's Forum, City Club, Multnomah Athletic Club (Portland). Republican. Home: 2221 SW 1st Ave Apt 1625 Portland OR 97201-5019 Office: Cutler & Co 503 Airport Rd Medford OR 97504

RANGWALA, ZOAIB ZAINUDDIN, electronics executive; b. Karachi, Pakistan, Aug. 22, 1951; came to U.S., 1973; s. Zainuddin Asgherally and Fizza (Abbasbhoy) R.; m. Jumana Zoaib Ebrahim, Aug. 14, 1977; children: Fatema, Maryam, Zainab. BEE, Ned Engring. U., 1972; MSEE, U. Calif., Berkeley, 1975; MBA, U. Santa Clara, 1979. Design engr. Signetics Corp., Sunnyvale, Calif., 1976-78; design mgr. Data Gen., Sunnyvale, Calif., 1978-81; computer-aided design and applications mgr. Raytheon, Mountain View, Calif., 1981-85; product line mgr. Semi-Custom Logic, San Jose, Calif., 1985-89, pres., CEO, 1989—. Contbr. tech. articles to profl. jours. Named Outstanding Tchg. Assoc. U. Calif., Berkeley, 1976. Mem. Beta Gamma Sigma. Islamic. Office: Semi Custom Logic Inc 555 N Mathilda Ave Ste 110 Sunnyvale CA 94086

RANISH, DONALD ROSEMAN, political science educator, political consultant; b. Newburgh, N.Y., Nov. 19, 1943; s. Harry and Sylvia (Roseman) R.; m. Leslee Ann Guttman, Aug. 29, 1970. BA, Calif. State U., Fullerton, 1970; MA, U. Calif., Santa Barbara, 1972, PhD, 1975. Prof. polit. sci. Alma (Mich.) U., 1975-76, Calif. State U., San Bernardino, 1976-77; prof. polit. sci. and law Antelope Valley Coll., Lancaster, Calif., 1977—, Kyung Hee U., Seoul, 1987—; Fulbright lectr., Republic of Korea, 1987. Author: American Political Process, 1982, 5th edit., 1993, Rhetoric of a Rebel, 1975; contbr. articles and papers to profl. publs. Bd. dirs. United Way Antelope Valley, Lancaster, 1986-88. U.S. Sea grantee, 1974-75; U.Calif. Regents grantee, 1975. Mem. Am. Polit. Sci. Assn., Acad. Criminal Justice Scis., Fulbright Alumni Assn., Phi Kappa Phi, Pi Sigma Alpha. Democrat. Home: 42953 Cherbourg Ln Lancaster CA 93536-4827

RANKEN, J. THOMAS, public affairs manager; b. Coronado, Calif., May 2, 1956; s. John Thomas and Corinne Diana (Lauriente) R.; m. Melissa Flotree, Oct. 24, 1987; children: R. Michelle, John Thomas. BA in Econs., U. Va., 1978; MBA, U. Wash., 1981. Store mgr. Summit Corp., Falls Church, Va., 1978-79; asst. v.p. Wash. Mut., Seattle, 1981-87; spl. credits officer Gibraltar Savs., Bellevue, Wash., 1987-89; mgr. pub. affairs Immunex Corp., Seattle, 1989—. Bd. dirs., 1st v.p. Harborview Med. Ctr.; past mem. bd. dirs., also pres. Seattle Mental Health Crisis Clinic; past mem. Seattle Bd. Ethics; pres. Wash. P & A. Mem. Wash. State Biotech. Assn. (bd. dirs., chmn. external affairs com. 1989—), Indsl. Biotech. Assn. (chmn. state rels. com. 1989—), Rotary (past pres. Univ. Sunrise club). Republican. Methodist. Home: 3228-43d Ave W Seattle WA 98199 Office: Immunex Corp 51 University St Seattle WA 98101-2936

RANKIN, WILLIAM PARKMAN, educator, former publishing company executive; b. Boston, Feb. 6, 1917; s. George William and Bertha W. (Clowe) R.; m. Ruth E. Gerard, Sept. 12, 1942; children: Douglas W., Joan W. BS, Syracuse U., 1941; MBA, NYU, 1949, PhD, 1979. Sales exec. Redbook mag., N.Y.C., 1945-49; sales exec. This Week mag., N.Y.C., 1949-55, adminstrv. exec., 1955-60, v.p., 1957-60, v.p., dir. advt. sales, sales devel. dir., 1960-63, exec. v.p., 1963-69; gen. exec. newspaper div. Time Inc., N.Y.C., 1969-70; gen. mgr. feature svc. Newsweek, Inc., N.Y.C., 1970-74, fin. and ins. advt. mgr., 1974-81; prof., asst. to the dir. Walter Cronkite Sch. Journalism and Telecommunication, Ariz. State U., Tempe, 1981—; lectr. Syracuse U., NYU, Berkeley Sch. Author: Selling Retail Advertising, 1944; The Technique of Selling Magazine Advertising, 1949; Business Management of Consumer Magazines, 1980, 2 ed. 1984, The Practice of Newspaper Management, 1986. Mem. Dutch Treat Club. Home: 1220 E Krista Way Tempe AZ 85284-1545 also: Bridge Rd Bomoseen VT 05732 Office: Ariz State U Walter Cronkite Sch Journalism/Telecom Tempe AZ 85287-1305

RANSMEIER, DENIS SIRERA, university administrator; b. Hanover, N.H., Sept. 23, 1947; s. Joseph Sirera and Margaret (Mitchel) R.; m. Deborah Carter (div. 1988); m. Ethel Atkins, Apr. 2, 1989. BA, Amherst (Mass.) Coll., 1970; MEd, Boston Coll., 1973; MBA, Columbia U., 1975. Staff acct. Price Waterhouse & Co., Washington, 1975-78; asst. dean for adminstrn. Law Ctr. Georgetown U., Washington, 1978-87; v.p. fin. and adminstrn., treas. Seattle U., 1987—. Mem. Fin. Execs. Inst., Assn. Jesuit Colls. and Univs. (exec. com. 1988—), Nat. Assn. of Coll. and Univ. Bus. Officers, N.W. Ind. Colls. Bus. Officers. Office: Seattle Univ Seattle WA 98122

RANSOM, RICHARD E., state supreme court chief justice; b. Hampton, Iowa, Dec. 9, 1932. BA, U. N.Mex., 1954; LLB, Georgetown U., 1959. Bar: N.Mex. 1959, D.C. 1959. Lawyer Albuquerque, 1959-86; justice N.Mex. Supreme Ct., Santa Fe, 1986-92; state chief justice N. Mex. Supreme Ct., 1992—. Editor: N. Mex. Trial Lawyers Assn. Jour., 1967-82. 1st lt. USMC, 1954-56. Fellow Am. Coll. Trial Lawyers, Internat. Soc. Barristers, Internat. Acad. Trial Lawyers. Office: N Mex Supreme Ct PO Box 848 237 Don Gaspar Ave Santa Fe NM 87503-0001*

RAO, MING, chemical engineering and computer science educator; b. Gejiu, Yunnan, Peoples Republic of China, June 24, 1954; came to U.S., 1984; s. Jin Rao and Lie Zhang; m. Xiaomei Zheng, Oct. 28, 1981; children: Mai Rao, Diana Rao. BS, Kunming Inst. of Tech., 1976; MS, U. Ill., 1987; PhD, Rutgers U., 1989. Engr. Kaiyuan Chemicals Inc., Yunnan, 1976-78; lectr. Yunnan Inst. Tech., 1981-84; rsch. engr. FAA Tech. Ctr., Atlantic City, N.J., 1989; supr. Rutgers U., Piscataway, N.J., 1988-89, asst. prof., 1989-91, assoc. prof., 1991—; dir. Intelligence Engring. Lab. U. Alta., Edmonton, Can., 1989—. Author: Integrated System for Intelligent Control, 1991, Process Control Engineering, 1993, Integrated Distributed Intelligent Systems in Manufacturing, 1993; guest editor Intelligent Process Control, 1992; contbr. 200 articles to profl. jours. and conf. procs. Recipient Doctoral Excellence fellowship Rutgers U., Piscataway, 1987-89. Mem. Am. Assn. Artificial Intelligence, IEEE, Can. Soc. Chem. Engrs., Can. Paper and Pulp Assn., Am. Inst. Chem. Engrs., Sigma Xi, Tau Beta Pi. Office: U Alberta, Dept Chem Engring, Edmonton, AB Canada

RAO, RAMACHANDRA MIRYALA, hypertension researcher; b. Chennur, Andhra, India, June 15, 1953; came to U.S., 1982; s. Chenchuramaiah and Suseelamma (Kotta) M.; m. Suchitra Tadikonda, Dec. 21, 1980; children: Sukhesh, Sudheshna. BS, Sri Venkateswara, Tirupati, India, 1973, MS, 1975, PhD, 1980; diploma in yoga and therapeutics, Yoga Inst. Sri Venkateswara, 1980. Postdoctoral fellow Post Grad Inst. Basic Med. Sci., Madras, India, 1981-82; Rockefellor fellow Health Sci. Ctr. U. Tex., San Antonio, 1982-84; sch. fellow Med. Sch. U. Tex., Houston, 1984-87; sch. assoc. Oreg. Health Scis. U., Portland, 1987-89; asst. prof. Drew U. Medicine, L.A., 1990—; cons. Bio-Systems Rsch., Lake Oswego, Oreg., 1987-89. Author rev. Calcium Bringing Proteins, 1989; contbr. articles to rsch. publs. NIH fellow, 1989. Mem. AAAS, N.Y. Acad. Sci., Endocrine Soc. Office: Drew U Medicine & Sci 1621 E 120th St Los Angeles CA 90059

RAPHAEL, MARTIN GEORGE, research wildlife biologist; b. Denver, Oct. 5, 1946; s. Jerome Maurice and Alys (Salmonson) R.; m. Susan Williams, August 4, 1967; 1 child, Samantha Marie. BA, Sacramento State U., 1968; BS, U. Calif., Berkeley, 1972, MS, 1976, PhD, 1980. Staff research assoc. U. Calif., Berkeley, 1974-80, assoc. specialist, 1980-84; project leader USDA Forest Svc., Laramie, 1984-89, Olympia, Wash., 1989—; adj. prof. U. Wyo., Laramie, 1986-89; cons. ecologist Pacific Gas and Electric Co., San Ramon, Calif., 1981-84. Contbr. articles to sci. jours. Mem. AAAS, Am. Soc. Mammalogists (recipient Best Poster award 1984), Am. Ornithologists' Union, Cooper Ornithol. Soc. (chmn. membership com. 1985-90, asst. sec. 1986—, bd. dirs. 1989-92), The Wildlife Soc. (local pres. publs. com. 1983-84, assoc. editor Wildlife Soc. Bull. 1987-90), Phi Beta Kappa, Sigma Xi, Xi Sigma Pi. Home: 3224 Biscay Ct NW Olympia WA 98502 Office: Pacific NW Rsch Sta 3625 93d Ave SW Olympia WA 98512

RAPIER, PASCAL MORAN, chemical engineer, physicist; b. Atlanta, Jan. 11, 1914; s. Paul Edward and Mary Claire (Moran) R.; m. Martha Elizabeth Doyle, May 19, 1945; children: Caroline Elizabeth, Paul Doyle, Mollie Claire, John Lawrence, James Andrew. BSChemE, Ga. Inst. Tech., 1939; MS in Theoretical Physics, U. Nev., 1959; postgrad., U. Calif., Berkeley, 1961. Registered profl. engr., Calif., N.J. Plant engr. Archer-Daniels-Midland, Pensacola, Fla., 1940-42; group supr. Dicalite div. Grefco, Los Angeles, 1943-54; process engr. Celatom div. Eagle Picher, Reno, Nev., 1955-57; project mgr., assoc. research engr. U. Calif. Field Sta., Richmond, 1959-62; project mgr. sea water conversion Bechtel Corp., San Francisco, 1962-66; sr. supervising chem. engr. Burns & Roe, Oradell, N.J., 1966-74; cons. engr. Kenite Corp., Scarsdale, N.Y., Rees Blowpipe, Berkeley, 1960-66; sr. cons. engr. Sanderson & Porter, N.Y.C., 1975-77; staff scientist III Lawrence Berkeley Lab., 1977-84; bd. dirs. Newtonian Sci. Found.; v.p. Calif. Rep. Assembly, 1964-65; discoverer phenomena faster than light, origin of cosmic rays and galactic red shifts. Contbr. articles to profl jours.; patentee agts. to render non-polar solvents electrically conductive, direct-contact geothermal energy recovery devices. Mem. Am. Inst. Chem. Engrs., Gideons Internat., Lions Internat., Corvallis, Sigma Pi Sigma. Presbyterian. Home and Office: 8015 NW Ridgewood Dr Corvallis OR 97330-3026

RAPP, GENE EDWARD, consultant; b. San Francisco, Aug. 6, 1930; s. Gene H. and Helen E. (Stegemann) R.; m. Marilyn J. Soncini, Feb. 5, 1949 (div. 1989); children: Stephen Arthur, Christine Lynn Rapp Losey, Craig Alan; m. April J. Nelson, July 28, 1990. BS, U. Calif., Davis, 1952, MEd, 1959; PhD, Ohio State U., 1971. Agrl. instr. Escalon (Calif.) Union High Sch., 1953-60; agriculturalist, student advisor U. Calif., Davis, 1960-72; exec. dir. Coun. of Calif. Growers, Davis, 1972-74; exec. v.p. Agrl. Edn. Found., Davis, 1974-88; pvt. practice cons. Davis, 1988—; statewide internat. vis. dir. div. agrl. U. Calif., Berkeley, 1968-70; bd. dirs. Agrl. Edn. Found., Templeton, Calif.; mentor Sacramento (Calif.) Personal Computer Group, 1987—. Named Young Man of Yr., C. of C., Escalow, Calif., 1959, Hon. mem. Calif. Agrl. Leadership Assn., Pomona, Calif., 1984. Mem. Nat. Soc. for the Study Edn., Kiwanis Club Davis (past pres.), Alpha Zeta, Alpha Tau Alpha, Phi Delta Kappa.

RAPP, LAWRENCE KEITH, cruise line executive; b. San Francisco, June 28, 1947; s. Lawrence Keith and Gertrude Lydia (Campbell) R.; m. Julie Maxine Dodd, Apr. 24, 1971; 1 child, Heather. BA, U. Calif., Berkeley, 1969. Mgr. spl. projects Royal Viking Line, San Francisco, 1972-81; mng. dir. Pearl Cruises, Hong Kong, 1981-86; v.p. hotel Am. Hawaii Cruises, Honolulu, 1986-87, Seabourn Cruise Line, San Francisco, 1987—. Contbr. svcs. mgmt. and human resources articles to profl. jours. Mem. Am. Mgmt. Assn., Phi Beta Kappa. Office: Seabourn Cruise Line 55 Francisco St San Francisco CA 94133

RAPSON, RICHARD L., history educator; b. N.Y.C., Mar. 8, 1937; s. Louis and Grace Lillian (Levenkind) R.; m. Susan Burns, Feb. 22, 1975 (div. June 1981); m. Elaine Catherine Hatfield, June 15, 1982; 1 child, Kim Elizabeth. BA, Amherst Coll., 1958; PhD, Columbia U., 1966. Asst. prof. Amherst (Mass.) Coll., 1960-61, Stanford (Calif.) U., 1961-65; from assoc. prof. to prof. history U. Hawaii, Honolulu, 1965—, founder, dir. New Coll., 1968-73; bd. dirs. Semester at Sea, U. Pittsburgh, 1979—; psychotherapist, Honolulu, 1982—. Author: Individualism and Conformity in the American Character, 1967, Britons View America, 1971, The Cult of Youth, 1972, Major Interpretations of the American Past, 1978, Denials of Doubt, 1980, Cultural Pluralism in Hawaii, 1981, American Yearnings, 1989; co-author: (with Elaine Hatfield) Love, Sex and Intimacy: Their Psychology, Biology and History, 1993; mem. editorial bd. Univ. Press Am., 1981—. Woodrow Wilson fellow, Wilson Found., Princeton, 1960; Edward Perkins scholar, Columbia U., 1961; Danforth tchr., Danforth Found., St. Louis, 1965; recipient E. Harris Harbison for Gifted Teaching award, Danforth Found., 1973, Outstanding Tchr. award Stanford U. 25th Reunion Class, 1992. Mem. Am. Hist. Assn., Orgn. Am. Hist., Nat. Womens Hist. Project, Phi Beta Kappa, Outrigger Canoe Club, Honolulu Club. Office: U Hawaii Dept History 2530 Dole St Honolulu HI 96822-2310

RAPUANO, MARY ANNE, public school administrator; b. New Haven, June 6, 1934; d. Rosario and Concetta (Tisci) Scalise; m. Philip Joseph Rapuano, July 2, 1960; 1 child, Marc Ross. BS, So. Conn. U., 1955; postgrad., U. So. Calif., L.A., 1969-71; MA, Calif. State U., Northridge, 1974. Cert. tchr., Calif., Conn. Tchr. Wallingford (Conn.) Pub. Schs., 1955-60, Culver City (Calif.) Unified Sch. Dist., 1962-65, Palos Verdes (Calif.) Unified Sch. Dist., 1965-67; spl. edn. tchr. L.A. Unified Sch. Dist., 1971-74, Simi Valley (Calif.) Unified Sch. Dist., 1974-76; resource specialist Manhattan Beach (Calif.) City Sch. Dist., 1974-76, dir. spl. svcs., 1976-87; dir. pupil svcs. Conejo Valley Unified Sch. Dist., Thousand Oaks, Calif., 1987—; cons. Marc Ross Enterprises, Camarillo, Cambria, Calif., 1985—; coll. instr. Calif. State U., Northridge, 1981—; panelist Fourth Ann. Dubnoff Conf., L.A., 1980; participant First Internat. Conf. on Handicapped Children, Stirling, Scotland, 1978. Mem. Assn. of Calif. Sch. Adminstrs., L.A. Calif. Adminstrs. of Spl. Edn., Learning Disabilities Assn. (formerly Calif. Assn. for Neurologically Handicapped Children, Waldie scholar 1971), Phi Delta Kappa (East Ventura County chpt. 1989—). Office: Conejo Valley Unified Sch 1400 E Janss Rd Thousand Oaks CA 91362-2198

RASBAND, RONALD A., chemical manufacturing company executive; b. 1951. Student, U. Utah. V.p. Keyes Fibre Inc., 1979-82; with Huntsman Chem. Corp., Salt Lake City, 1982—, chief oper. officer, from 1988, pres., 1988—. Office: Huntsman Chem Corp 2000 Eagle Gate Tower Salt Lake City UT 84111

RASCHKE, CARL ALLAN, humanities educator, college program director, author, educator; b. N.Y.C., Sept. 11, 1944; s. Charles Frederick and Grace Evelyn (Van Nostrand) R.; m. Lorita Elaine Lagiglia, Mar. 2, 1968 (div.); 1 child, Erik; m. Susan Kay Doughty, Sept. 9, 1981. BA, Pomona Coll., 1966; MA, Grad. Theol. Union, 1969; PhD, Harvard U., 1973. Staff reporter Livermore (Calif.) Herald and News, 1967-68; teaching asst. U. Mass., Boston, 1970-71; asst. prof. religious studies U. Denver, 1972-77, prof. religious studies, 1984—, dir. Inst. for the Humanities, 1987—; mem. adv. group on pub. humanities Nat. Endowment for the Humanities, Washington, 1988. Author: Interruption of Eternity, 1980, Theological Thinking, 1988, Painted Black, 1990; editor: Lacan and Theological Discourse, 1989. Sr. fellow Independence Inst., Golden, Colo., 1986—; columnist Colorado Springs Gazette Telegraph, 1987-90; pres. Omega Found., 1981-84. Fellow German Acad. Exch. Svc., 1974-75, Nat. Endowment for the Humanities, 1978-79. Mem. Am. Acad. Religion (pres. Denver chpt. 1977-78, editor 1982—), Am. Philos. Assn., Am. Assn. for Advancement Core Curriculum (pres.), Inst. for Advanced Philos. Rsch. (advisor), Colo. Innovation Soc. Office: U Denver Dept Religious Studies Denver CO 80208

RASCHKO, BETTYANN BERNADETTE, interior designer, consultant; b. Salem, Oreg., June 13, 1925; d. Otto A. and Paula J. (Skopil) Boetticher; m. Jamaes Michael Raschko, Aug. 22, 1950 (dec. 1985); children: Paula, Michael. BA in Interior Design, Marylhurst Coll., 1947; MA in Interior Design, Calif. State U., San Jose, 1959; post-grad., U. Calif., Davis, 1970-71, Stanford U., 1967. Interior designer Fromlath's Interiores, Long Beach, Calif., 1959-60, Anne Phillips Design Studio, Long Beach, Calif., 1960-63; asst. prof. art dept. Marymount/Loyola U., L.A., 1960-63; asst. prof. interior design Calif. State U., Long Beach, 1960-65; prof. interior design Calif. State U., San Francisco, 1964-77, prof. emeritus, 1977—; prin. Raschko Cons., Tigard, Oreg., 1977—; presenter in field. Author: Housing Interiors for the Disables and Elderly, 1982; contbr. articles to profl. jours.; exhibited at group show San Francsico Internat. Design, 1972. Del., Pres.'s Com. on Employment of the Handicapped, 1987—. Recipient Joel Polsky award Housing Interiors for the Disabledand Elderly, 1985; scholar faculty Marylhurst Coll., 1946, Fulbright scholar, 1975-76, Fulbright Sr. Rsch. scholar, Sweden, 1986; Nat. Inst. Rehab. fellow, 1985-86; named D.D. Eisenhower Found. del. leader, 1991, 92. Mem. AIA (corres.), Am. Soc. Interior Designers (edn. com. No. Calif. 1968-69, nat. govt. affairs com. 1987-89, barrier free com. 1986-87, consumer protection com. 1986-88, health care design com. 1985-88), Environ. Design Rsch. Assn., Am. Soc. of Aging, Interior Design Educators Coun. (western regional chair 1976, guidance com. 1978, barrier free curriculum com. 1986), Human Factors Soc. & Econs., Fulbright Alumni Assn. Home and Office: 16645 SW Queen Mary Ave King City OR 97224-2323

RASHEDI, SAEED, bank officer; b. Tehran, Iran; came to U.S., 1965; s. Mohammad Ali and Azizeh (Rasouli) R.; m. Jean L. Kemp; children: Shandiz Thomas, Karie Anoushan. BA in Philosophy, Tehran U.; MBA, West Coast U.; PhD, USIU. Br. mgr. 1st Fed. Bank Calif., Santa Monica, 1990—; instr. Inst. Fin. Edn., 1988—, area coord., 1990-92, regional dir., 1992—. Mem. Mar Vista Optimists Club (program chair 1990—). Office: 1st Fed Bank 12654 Washington Blvd Mar Vista CA 90066

RASHER, GEORGE JOSEPH, sales executive; b. Northridge, Calif., Apr. 18, 1956; s. Clarence Emerson and Berta (Sturm) R.; m. Kim Eileen Abel, Mar. 27, 1978. BA in Radio, TV & Film with highest honors, Calif. State U., Northridge, 1978; MBA magna cum laude, Pepperdine U., 1981. Account exec. various advt. agys., L.A., 1978-81; product mgr. Mattel Electronics, Hawthorne, Calif., 1981-83; dir. product mktg. Epson Am., Torrance, Calif., 1983-90; v.p. sales and mktg. Parana Supplies Corp., Torrance, 1990—. Mem. Am. Motor Cyclist Assn., Nat. Office Products Assn., Nat. Office Machine Dealers Assn., A Better Computer Dealer Channel, Torrance C. of C., L.A. C. of C. Office: Parana Supplies Corp 3625 Del Amo Blvd Torrance CA 90503

RASK, MICHAEL RAYMOND, orthopaedist; b. Butte, Mont., Oct. 24, 1930; s. Barth John and Marguerite Sadie (Joseph) R.; m. Elizabeth Anne Shannon, May 21, 1948; children: Dagny Marguerite Rask-Regan, Badih John, Patrick Henry, Molly Michelle. BS, Oreg. State U., 1951; MD, Oreg. Health Scis. U., 1955; PhD, 1978, U. Humanistic Studies, 1986. Diplomate Am. Bd. Orthopaedic Surgery, Am. Bd. Neurological Orthopaedic Surgery, Am. Bd. Bloodless Surgery, Am. Bd. Medical-Legal Analysts, Am. Bd. Hand Surgery, Am. Bd. Sportsmedicine Surgery, Am. Bd. Spinal Surgery. Intern Kings County Hosp., Bklyn., 1955-56; orthopaedic resident U. Oreg. Med. Sch., Portland, 1959-63; with neurological orthopaedic surgery preceptorships Oreg. Emmanuel Hosp., Portland, 1962-76; pvt. practice in neurol. orthopedic surgery Las Vegas, 1976—; clin. instr. orthopaedics U. Oreg., 1964-71; prof. Am. Acad. Neurological and Orthopaedic Surgery, 1985—; editorial reviewer Clin. Orthopaedics & Related Rsch., 1978—, Am. Med. Reports, 1985—, Muscle & Nerve, 1987—, Am. Jour. Cranio-Mandibular Practice. Author: Seminoma, 1970, Orthopod, 1972; editor in-chief: Jour. Neurological Orthopedic Medicine & Surgery, 1976—; editorial rev. bd. Jour. Craniomandibular Practice; numerous lectures in field. Lectr. Arthritis Found., Las Vegas, 1976-78, cons. orthopaedist Easter Seal Ctr. for Crippled Children & Adults, Las Vegas, 1978-81, med. advisor so. Nev. chpt. Nat. Multiple Sclerosis Soc.; bd. dirs. Gov.'s Com. on the Employment of the Handicapped, Nev., 1980-82. Capt. USAF, 1956-63. Fellow Cuban Soc. Orthopaedics Traumatology; mem. Am. Acad. Neurological Orthopaedic Surgeons (hon. 1979, course chmn. 1977-79, pres. 1978, chmn. bd. dirs. 1976—), Nev. State Pharmacy Assn., Am. Back Soc. (bd. dirs. 1983-88), Semmelweiss Sci. Soc. (pres. Nev. chpt. 1980—), Am. Fedn. Med. Accreditation (chmn. 1979—), Neurol. Orthopaedic Inst. (chmn. 1979—), Bd. Neurol. Orthopaedic Surgeons (chmn. 1977—), Sundry Primary Certifying Bds. (chmn. bd. dirs. 1976—), Silkworm Club, Caterpillar Club. Democrat. Office: Am Acad Neurol & Orthopaedic Med Surgeons 2320 N Rancho Dr Ste 108 Las Vegas NV 89102-4510

RASKIN, JEF, inventor; b. N.Y.C., Mar. 9, 1943; s. William Benjamin and Frieda (Botfeld) R.; m. Linda Sara Blum, July 27, 1982; children: Aza Benjamin, Aviva Frieda, Aenea Hannah. BS in Math., SUNY, Stony Brook, 1965; MS in Computer Sci., Pa. State U., 1967. Prof. U. Calif. at San Diego, LaJolla, 1969-74; pres. Bannister & Crun, Brisbane, Calif., 1974-78; mgr. advanced systems Apple Computer Inc., Cupertino, Calif., 1978-82; chmn., CEO Info. Appliance Inc., Palo Alto, Calif., 1982-89; cons. Pacifica, Calif., 1989—; cons. Hewlett Packard, IBM, NCR, Fujitsu, Ricoh, others; vis. scholar Stanford Artifical Intelligence Lab., Stanford, 1973; creator Apple's MacIntosh Project, 1979-82. Patentee in field; contbr. articles to profl. jours. Bd. dirs. Pacifica Land Trust, 1991—, Pacifica Arts and Heritage Coun., 1990—, Chanticleer, San Francisco, 1982-85; mem. San Mateo Regional Planning Commn., Redwood City, Calif., 1975-78. Grantee in thermal scis. NSP, 1962; Acad. Senate Rsch. Com. grantee U. Calif. San Diego, 1971; rsch. grant in computer music Pa. State U., 1966; fellow Creative Arts Inst., 1973. Mem. AAAS, Assn. for Computing Machinery, Acad. of Model Aeronautics, Calif. Acad. of Scis. Home: 8 Gypsy Hill Rd Pacifica CA 94044

RASKIN, SARAH ANNE, neuropsychologist; b. Washington, July 15, 1962; d. Allen and Theol Joyce (Shayne) R.; m. Brian Waddell, Sept. 13, 1991. BA, Johns Hopkins, 1984; PhD, CUNY, 1990. Neuropsychology asst. dept. neurology Mt. Sinai Med. Ctr., 1985-86; intern dept. rehab. medicine Mt. Sinai Med. Ctr., N.Y.C., 1986-88, staff psychologist, 1987-91; staff neuro psychologist Good Samaritan Neuropsychol. Svcs., Puyallup, Wash., 1991—. Contbr. articles to profl. jours. Mem. Anonymous Women for Peace, N.Y.C., 1987-91; adv. and facilitator Mt. Sinai Rape Crisis Intervention Program, N.Y.C., 1989-91; facilitator Queens Head Injury Support Group, Good Samaritan Mild Head Injury Support Group, 1992—, Ptnrs. for Health, Seattle, 1991—. Helena Rubenstein Found. Tuition fellow, 1988-90; Sigma Xi rsch. grantee, 1989; recipient Am. Psychol. Assn. Dissertation award, 1990. Mem. Internat. Neuropsychological Soc., Nat. Head Injury Found., Nat. Brain Injury Rsch. Group, N.Y. Head Injury Assn. (N.Y.C. region steering com. 1984-86, 91), Asociación de Neuropsicologia de Nicaragua (hon.), Pacific Northwest Neuropsychological Soc., Wash. State Head Injury Found. Home: 712 Summit Ave E # 7 Seattle WA 98102-5925 Office: Good Samaritan Neuropsychol 1420 Meridian St S Ste A Puyallup WA 98371-6905

RASMUS, DANIEL WAYNE, knowledge engineer, writer; b. L.A., Oct. 28, 1961; s. Arthur Lee and Shirley Ann (Ottosen) R.; m. Janet Aileen Marer, Mar. 1, 1987; children: Rachel Michelle, Alyssa Suzzette. Student, U. Calif., Santa Cruz, 1979-82; cert. in intelligent systems, U. Calif., Irvine, 1989. Supr. EDP Christie Electric Corp., Torrance, Calif., 1980-83; supr. system devel. Dataproducts Corp., Irvine, Calif., 1983-85; systems analyst ITT Cannon, Santa Ana, Calif., 1985; material systems analyst Cipher Data Products, Garden Grove, Calif., 1985-87; mgr. CAM Western Digital, Irvine, 1987-90; leader, info. systems engring. Hughes Aircraft, Fullerton, Calif., 1990—; western regional editor Mfg. Systems Mag., 1990—; cons. Nat. Commn. on Indsl. Innovation, L.A., 1985; planning com. mem. 3d and 4th Internat. Confs. on Expert Systems are the Leading Edge in Prodn. Planning and Ops. Mgmt., Charleston, S.C., 1988-89. Co-author: Understanding Artificial Intelligence, 1988; contbr. editor PC AI, 1987—; contbr. articles to profl. jours. Congl. dist. coord. Gary Hart for Pres., Orange County, Calif., 1984; strategic planning advisor Carol Ann Bradford for Congress, Orange County, 1984; bd. dirs. Jewish Fedn. of Orange County, 1988-93. Undergrad. fellow U. Calif. Pres.'s Office, Santa Cruz, 1982. Mem. Am. Assn. for Artificial Intelligence, Am. Prodn. Inventory Control Soc., Internat. Assn. Knowledge Engrs., Orange County Ask Users Group (bd. dirs. 1988-89), Neuron Data Users Group (bd. dirs. 1989—), Assn. for Computing Machinery, Burroughs PC53 Users. Democrat. Office: Hughes Aircraft Fullerton CA 92634

RASMUSON, BRENT (JACOBSEN), photographer; b. Logan, Utah, Nov. 28, 1950; s. Eleroy West and Fae (Jacobsen) R.; m. Tess Bullen, Sept. 30, 1981; children: John, Mark, Lisa. Grad. high sch. Pre-press supr. Herald Printing Co., Logan, 1969-79; profl. drummer, 1971-75; owner Valley Automotive Specialties, 1971-76; exec. sec. Herald Printing Co., 1979-89; owner Brent Rasmuson Photography, Smithfield, Utah, 1986—. Author photo prints of LDS temples: Logan, 1987, Manti, 1989, Jordan River, 1989, Provo, 1990, Mesa, Ariz., 1990, Boise, Idaho, 1990, Salt Lake LDS Temple, 1990, Idaho Falls, 1991, St. George, 1991, Portland, Oreg., 1991, L.A., 1991, Las Vegas, Nev., 1991, Seattle, Wash., 1992; photographs featured in Best of Photography Ann., 1987, 88, 89. Mem. Assoc. Photographers Internat. Republican. Mem. Ch. of Jesus Christ of Latter Day Saints. Home and Office: 40 N 200 E Smithfield UT 84335-1543

RASMUSON, ELMER EDWIN, banker, former mayor; b. Yakutat, Alaska, Feb. 15, 1909; s. Edward Anton and Jenny (Olson) R.; m. Lile Vivian Bernard, Oct. 27, 1939 (dec. 1960); children: Edward Bernard, Lile Muchmore (Mrs. John Gibbons, Jr.), Judy Ann; m. Col. Mary Louise Milligan, Nov. 4, 1961. B.S. magna cum laude, Harvard U., 1930, A.M., 1935; student, U. Grenoble, 1930; LL.D., Alaska Pacific U., 1993, Alaska Pacific U., 1993. C.P.A., N.Y., Tex., Alaska. Chief accountant Nat. Investors Corp., N.Y.C., 1933-35; prin. Arthur Andersen & Co., N.Y.C., 1935-43; pres. Nat. Bank of Alaska, 1943-65, chmn. bd., 1966-74, chmn. exec. com., 1975-82, now chmn. emeritus; mayor City of Anchorage, 1964-67, dir., emeritus and cons., 1989; civilian aide from Alaska to sec. army, 1959-67; Swedish consul Alaska, 1955-77; Chmn. Rasmuson Found.; Rep. nominee U.S. Senate from Alaska, 1968; U.S. commr. Internat. N. Pacific Fisheries Commn., 1969-84; mem. Nat. Marine Fisheries Adv. Com., 1974-77, North Pacific Fishery Mgmt. Council, 1976-77, U.S. Arctic Research Commn., 1984-92. Mem. City Council Anchorage, 1945, chmn. city planning commn., 1950-53; pres. Alaska council Boy Scouts Am., 1953; sec.-treas. Loussac Found.; regent U. Alaska, 1950-69; trustee King's Lake Camp, Inc., 1944—, Alaska Permanent Fund Corp., 1980-82. Decorated knight first class Order of Vasa, comdr. Sweden; recipient silver Antelope award Boy Scouts Am., Japanese citation Order of the Sacred Treasure, Gold and Silver Star, 1988; outstanding civilian service medal U.S. Army; Alaskan of Year award, 1976. Mem. Pioneers Alaska, Alaska Bankers Assn. (past pres.), Defense Orientation Conf. Assn., NAACP, Alaska Native Brotherhood, Explorers Club, Phi Beta Kappa. Republican. Presbyn. Clubs: Masons, Elks, Anchorage Rotary (past pres.); Harvard (N.Y.C.; Boston); Wash. Athletic (Seattle), Seattle Yacht (Seattle), Rainier (Seattle); Thunderbird Country (Palm Desert, Calif.); Bohemian (San Francisco); Eldorado Country (Indian Wells, Calif.); Boone & Crockett. Home: PO Box 100600 Anchorage AK 99510-0600

RASMUSSEN, ERIC ASHBY, chief financial officer; b. Salt Lake City, May 28, 1956; s. Julian Woodhouse and Nina (Ashby) R.; m. Robynn Diane Page, Dec. 14, 1979; children: Beau Ryan, Gregory Eric, Haley Page. BA in Fin. (cum laude), U. Utah, 1981; MBA, Nova U., 1983. Sr. acct. Am. express, N.Y.C., 1981-83; supr. acctg. Am. express, Salt Lake City, 1983-85, mgr. acctg., 1985-86; dir. devel. ops. Harrington Mgmt. Inc., Salt Lake City, 1986-88; chief fin. officer Courier Control Ctr. Inc., Salt Lake City, 1988—; pres. Unitel, Salt Lake City, 1989—, also bd. dirs.; bd. dirs. Courier Control Ctr., Inc., Salt Lake City, Unishippers Assn., Salt Lake City, San River Corp., Salt Lake City, PCC, Inc. Appeared in Community Play, 1986. Mem. Hinckly Inst. of Politics, U. Utah, Salt Lake City, 1979—. Named to Dean's List, Nova, 1983. Office: Courier Control Ctr Inc 675 E 2100 S # 350 Salt Lake City UT 84106-1887

RASMUSSEN, GAIL MAUREEN, critical care nurse; b. Can., Feb. 22, 1941; d. Thomas Alfred and Bernice Hilda (Sayler) Salisbury; m. Byron Karl Rasmussen, June 28, 1964; children: Stephen, Carla, Wade, Gregory. AS, Riverside City Coll., 1961; BSN, U. Phoenix, 1987; MS in Health Professions Edn., Osteo. Coll. the Pacific, 1991. RN, Calif.; CCRN. Staff nurse Meml. Med. Ctr., Long Beach, Calif., 1961-63, UCLA Med. Ctr., 1963-64; clin. nurse ICU, critical care unit Intercommunity Med. Ctr., Covina, Calif., 1964-71, 78-83; instr. advanced cardiac life support L.A. Counties, 1991—. Mem. AACCN.

RASMUSSEN, MICHELE VINCENT, gifted and talented education and communication educator; b. Murray, Utah, Apr. 18, 1963; d. Kent Bryan and Theone Edith (Paxton) V.; m. Kevin Dee Rasmussen, June 26, 1992. BS, U. Utah, 1984, endorsemesnt in gifted edn., 1988. Tchr. 3d grade South Jordan (Utah) Elem. Sch., 1985-89; gifted tchr. 3d grade Peruvian Park Elem. Sch., Sandy, Utah, 1989—; instr. pub. speaking Brigham Young U., Provo, Utah, 1989-91. Mem. Salt Lake Jr. League, 1990—; mem. exec. com. Nat. Young Reps., nat. committeewoman; mem. exec. com. Utah State Rep. Party. LDS. Home: 294 Roosevelt St Midvale UT 84047-3257

RASMUSSEN, MIKE JOSEPH, college financial aid administrator; b. Avalon, Calif., Aug. 1, 1947; s. Herman Joseph and Nina (Walker) R.; m. Phyllis Ann Freedman; children: Dawn Michelle, Stephen Michael. AA, West Valley Coll., 1967; AA (two), Butte Coll., 1980, 83; BA, San Jose State Coll., 1969; MA, San Jose State Univ., 1976. Cert. community coll. counselor, instr., chief adminstrv. officer, super., Calif. Vets. counselor San Jose (Calif.) State Univ., Office of Vets. Affairs, 1976-77; vets. counselor, program coord. Butte Coll., Office of Vets. Affairs, Oroville, Calif., 1977-80; dir. fin. aid and vets. affairs Butte Coll., Oroville, 1980-92, dir. spl. programs and svcs., 1993—; bd. dirs. Chico (Calif.) Community Hosp. Found. With USN, 1970-74, Vietnam. Recipient Cert. Appreciation Butte-Glenn County Vets. Employment Com., 1979, Boy Scouts Am. Troop 770, Paradise, Calif., 1985, Paradise (Calif.) Lioness Club, 1986, Pub. Svc. award State of Calif. Oroville Employment Devel. Dept., 1980. Mem. Calif. Community Coll. Student Fin. Aid Adminstrs. Assn. (treas. 1984-86, coord. region I, 1985-87, bd. dirs. No. Calif. 1986-87, pres.-elect 1988-89, pres. 1989-90, immediate past pres. 1990-91, Outstanding Svc. award 1985, 87, cert. of appreciation 1985, 86, 89, 90). Home: 2209 Mariposa Ave Chico CA 95926-1539 Office: Butte Coll 3536 Butte Campus Dr Oroville CA 95965-8399

RASMUSSEN, NEIL WOODLAND, insurance agent; b. Portland, Oreg., Sept. 14, 1926; s. Ernest Roy and Lulu Mildred (Woodland) R.; m. Mary Ann Cannon, Aug. 10, 1957; children: Kirk, Sally, P. Cannon, Eric (dec.). BA, Stanford U., 1949. Registered mut. funds rep. Warehouseman Consol. Supply Co., Portland, Oreg., 1949-50, sales rep., 1955-56; sales rep. Consol. Supply Co., Eugene, Oreg., 1950-52; sales rep. Consol. Supply Co., Salem, Oreg., 1956-64, br. mgr., 1964-82; agt. life and health ins. N.Y. Life Ins. Co., Salem, 1982—. Commdg. officer Navel Res. Constrn. Battalion Div., Salem, Oreg., 1958-63, Naval Res. Surface Div., Corvallis, Oreg., 1963-67; officer Selective Svc. Res., Salem, 1969-74. Lt. USN, 1952-55. Recipient Nat. Quality award Nat. Assn. Life Underwriters, 1986-88. Mem. Salem Assn. Life Underwriters, Res. Officers Assn. (dir. 1988-91, v.p. 1988-91), East Salem Rotary Club (dir. 1980-83, sr. active mem. 1990-92). Republican. Episcopalian. Office: NY Life Ins Co 530 Center St NE Salem OR 97301

RASMUSSEN, THOMAS VAL, JR., lawyer, small business owner; b. Salt Lake City, Aug. 11, 1954; s. Thomas Val and Georgia (Smedley) R.; m. Donita Gubler, Aug. 15, 1978; children: James, Katherine, Kristin. BA magna cum laude, U. Utah, 1978, JD, 1981. Bar: Utah 1981, U.S. Dist. Ct. Utah 1981, U.S. Supreme Ct. 1985. Atty. Salt Lake Legal Defender Assn., Salt Lake City, 1981-83, Utah Power and Light Co., Salt Lake City, 1983-89, Hatch, Morton & Skeen, Salt Lake City, 1989-90; ptnr. Morton, Skeen & Rasmussen, Salt Lake City, 1991—; co-owner, developer Handi Self-Storage, Kaysville, Utah, 1984—; instr. bus. law Brigham Young U., Salt Lake City, 1988-90. Adminstrv. editor Jour. Contemporary Law, 1980-81, Jour. Energy Law and Policy, 1980-81. Missionary Ch. of Jesus Christ of Latter-Day Sts., Brazil, 1973-75. Mem. Utah, Salt Lake County Bar Assn., Intermountain Miniature Horse Club (pres. 1989, 2d v.p. 1990), Phi Eta Sigma, Phi Kappa Phi, Beta Gamma Sigma. Home: 7079 Pine Cone Cir Salt Lake City UT 84121-4311 Office: Morton Skeen & Rasmussen 1245 Brickyard Rd Ste 600 Salt Lake City UT 84106-2564

RASMUSSON, ERIC DANA, government relations director; b. Fargo, N.D., Mar. 5, 1961; s. Richard Allen and Mary Ann (Wakely) R.; m. Tricia Lynnette Tucker; children: Kristen Lee, Allison Ann. BA, Calif. State u., Stanislaus, 1984. Field rep. Calif. State Assemblyman Norm Waters, Sacramento, 1982-84; legis. adv. Los Gatos-Saratoga (Calif.) Bd. Realtors, 1984-89; exec. v.p. Sunnyvale (Calif.) Bd. Realtors, 1989; dir. govt. rels. Sacramento Assn. Realtors, 1989—. Contbr. articles to mags. Co-founder, dir. PAC, Los Gatos (Calif.) C. of C., 1987; chair govt. affairs com. Nat. Assn. Realtors, Washington, 1991; active Clean Air Partnership. Mem. Sacramento Mutual Housing Assn. (bd. dirs. 1989—). Democrat. Lutheran. Home: 612 Cardigan Ct Roseville CA 95747 Office: Sacramento Assn Realtors 2003 Howe Ave Sacramento CA 95825

RASOF, HENRY LEPLIN, editor; b. Santa Monica, Calif., Nov. 16, 1946; s. Bernard and Beatrice R. BA in Music, UCLA, 1971; MFA in Creative Writing, Bklyn. Coll., 1977. Prodn. editor Plenum Press, N.Y.C., 1974-75; adj. prof. English Hofstra U., Hempstead, N.Y., 1977-78; asst. editor Arco Pub., N.Y.C., 1982-84; sr. editor Franklin Watts, N.Y.C., 1984-88; sr. project editor Houghton Mifflin, Boston, 1988-89; editor pvt. practice Boulder, Colo., 1989—; cons. editor ABC-CLIO, Denver. Author: The Folk, Country, and Bluegrass Musician's Catalogue, 1982, The Picture Life of Charles and Diana, 1988; contbr. articles to profl. jours. Home: 4800 Osage Dr Boulder CO 80303-3932 Office: ABC CLIO 50 S Steele St Denver CO 80209

RASPORICH, ANTHONY WALTER, university dean; b. Port Arthur, Ont., Can., Jan. 9, 1940; s. Milan and Sophia (Grgurich) R.; m. Beverly Jean Matson. BA, Queen's U., Kingston, Ontario, 1962, MA, 1965; PhD, U. Man., Winnipeg, 1970. Tchr. Kingston Bd. Edn., 1962-63; prof. history U. of Calgary, Alta., 1966—, dean social scis. faculty, 1986—. Author: For A Better Life, 1982, Oil and Gas in Western Canada 1900-80, 1985; editor: The Making of the Modern West, 1984; co-editor Canadian Ethnic Studies, 1980-93, Sports in the West, 1990. C.D. Howe postdoctoral fellow, fellow Assn. Univs. Colls. Can., Thunder Bay, Ontario, 1970, Vis. Can. Studies, Sussex, Eng., 1979, Killam Found., Calgary, 1979, Social Scis. Human Rsch. Coun., Ottawa, Can., 1981. Mem. Canada Ethnic Studies Assn., Can. Hist. Assn., Ont. Hist. Soc. Office: U of Calgary, Faculty Social Scis, Calgary, AB Canada T2N 1N4

RASSEKH, NOSRATOLLAH, history educator; b. Tehran, Iran, Nov. 22, 1924; came to U.S. 1944; s. Ahmad and Fatimeh (Dai) R.; m. Valerie Latham, Feb. 8, 1952 (div. 1973; children: William, Paree, Laleh, Michael; m. Mona Rassekh, Mar. 21, 1979. BA in Polit. Sci., Stanford U., 1942, MA in Internat. Rels., 1950, PhD, 1960. Instr. Stanford U., 1954-58, Verde Valley Sch., Sedona, Ariz., 1958-60; asst. prof. Lewis and Clark Coll., Portland, 1960-64; assoc. prof. history Lewis and Clark Coll., 1964-70, prof. history, 1970—, chmn. dept. history, 1964-79; cons., book reviewer ALA, Washington, 1973—. Contbr. articles to profl. jours. Bd. dirs. Portland Habilitatio Ctr., 1988—. Ray Lyman Wilbur fellow, 1952-54, Hoover Libr. fellow, 1970, NDEA grantee, 1966-68. Mem. Am. hist. Assn., Am. Assn. for Mid-East Studies, Acad. Polit. Sci., Inst. of Mid-East-N. African Affairs (bd. dirs.), Internat. Collegiate Orgn. for Asian Studies in the U.S. Baha'i. Home: 3939 SW Vesta St Portland OR 97219-7464 Office: Lewis and Clark Coll Dept History Portland OR 97219

RATCLIFF, BRUCE EPHLIN, hoist company executive; b. Canton, Ill., Oct. 3, 1941; s. Ralph A. and Margaret H. (Buck) R.; student Coll. San Mateo, 1960-62, U. Ariz., 1962, U. Calif. at Santa Barbara, 1965; B.A. in Econs., San Francisco State U., 1967. Vice pres. sales Ratcliff Hoist Co., Belmont, Calif., 1967-69, exec. v.p., 1969-75, pres., chief operating officer, 1975—, also dir.; pres., chief exec. officer Ratcliff Co., 1977—. Club: San Francisco Bachelors. Home: 1308 Sunnyslope Ave Belmont CA 94002-3728 Office: 1655 Old County Rd San Carlos CA 94070-5205

RATCLIFFE, ALFONSO FRED, academic dean, engineering consultant; b. St. Louis, Oct. 21, 1928; s. William Morgan and Alice Elizabeth (Carter) R.; m. Josephine Jay Johnson, Sept. 1963 (div. 1967); m. Dolores Corita Potter, Jan. 16, 1969. AB in Physics, UCLA, 1951, MS in Engring., 1963, PhD in Engring., 1970. Profl. engr., Calif. Engr., mgr. Rototest Labs., Lynwood, Calif., 1955-63; scientist, cons. Ogden Tech. Labs., Monterey Park, Calif., 1963-69; staff engr. linguistics UCLA, 1964-67; staff engr., mgr. Mattel, Inc., Hawthorne, Calif., 1969-74; assoc. prof., dept. chair dept. elec. engring. Calif. State U., Northridge, 1975-79, assoc. dean sch. engring. & computer sci., 1980-81, dean engring. & computer sci., 1981-92; ind. cons. L.A., 1992—; cons. RCA, Reseda, Calif., 1977, Info. Terminals, San Jose, Calif., 1979, Burroughs Corp., Westlake Village, Calif., 1980, Calif. Dept. Commerce, Pasadena, 1988-90. Contbr. articles to profl. jours.; patentee in field. Mem. state bd. Math., Engring. & Sci. Achievement Program, Berkeley, Calif. 1988—. With U.S. Army, 1946-48. Named to Charles Sumner High Sch. Hall of Fame, St. Louis, 1987. Mem. NSPE, Am. Soc. Engring. Edn. (chair Pacific sect. 1986-87), San Fernando Valley Engrs. Coun. (chair 1988-90), Inst. for Advancement for Engring., Soc. Mfg. Engrs., Tau Beta Pi. Home: 1301 N Kenter Ave Los Angeles CA 90049 Office: Calif State U Sch Engring 18111 Nordhoff St Northridge CA 91330

RATEAVER, BARGYLA, writer, international consultant; b. Ft. Dauphin, Madagascar, Aug. 3, 1916; came to U.S., 1935; d. Eugene Alaric and Margaret (Schaffnit) R.; 1 child, Gylver. AB, U. Calif., Berkeley, 1943, MS in Libr. Sci., 1959; MS, U. Mich., 1950, PhD, 1951. lectr. organic gardening, radio and TV, exhibits and demonstrations, 1968—; liaison with internat. activities in organic gardening and farming, 1972—. Author: Organic Method Primer, 1973, A Condensation of E E Pfeiffer's B D Farming, 1974. Organic Method Primer Update, 1993. Mem., bd. dirs. Price Pottenger Nutrition Found. Mem. Internat. Fedn. of Organic Agriculture Movements. Home and Office: 9049 Covina St San Diego CA 92126-3717

RATHLESBERGER, JAMES HOWARD, public administrator; b. Pitts., May 2, 1948; s. Howard Erwin and Jean Edna (Heiden) R.; m. M. Elizabeth Ware, Jan. 2, 1988. BA, U. Calif., Berkeley, 1971; MPA, NYU, 1986. Staff dir. environ. study conf. U.S. Congress, Washington, 1974-75; v.p. Nat. Limestone Inst., Washington, 1975-76; mem. Carter-Mondale Transition Team, Atlanta and Washington, 1976-77; spl. asst. to the asst. sec. U.S. Dept. of the Interior, Washington, 1977-81; spl. asst. to dean of the faculty of arts and scis. NYU, 1981-85; asst. exec. v.p. Nat. Health Coun., N.Y.C., 1985-89; exec. officer Bd. of Podiatric Medicine, Sacramento, Calif., 1989—. Editor: Nixon and the Environment, 1972; contbr. articles to profl. jours. Vol. VISTA, Charleston, W.Va., 1968-69. Named Hon. Citizen Paola, Kans., 1968. Home: 1014-2 P St Sacramento CA 95814 Office: Bd of Podiatric Medicine 1420 Howe Ave #8 Sacramento CA 95825

RATHMANN, GEORGE BLATZ, genetic engineering company executive; b. Milw., Dec. 25, 1927; s. Louis and Edna Lorle (Blatz) R.; m. Frances Joy Anderson, June 24, 1950; children: James, Margaret, Laura, Sally, Richard. BS with honors, Northwestern U., 1948; MS, Princeton U., 1950, PhD in Phys. Chemistry, 1952. With 3M Co., St. Paul, 1951-72, various positions including rsch. chemist, rsch. dir., group tech. dir., mgr. X-ray products; with Litton Med. Systems, Des Plaines, Ill., 1972-75; v.p. R & D diagnostics div. Abbott Labs., North Chicago, Ill., 1975-80; pres., chief exec. officer Amgen Inc., Thousand Oaks, Calif., 1980-88; chmn. Amgen Inc., Newbury Park, Calif., 1988—; chmn. ICUS Corp., 1990—. Mem. AAAS, Am. Chem. Soc., Indsl. Biotech. Assn. (bd. dirs.), Phi Beta Kappa, Sigma Xi. Home: Greystone 60 Beaver Creek CO 81620 Office: Amgen Ctr Thousand Oaks CA 91320

RATIU, TUDOR STEFAN, mathematician, educator; b. Timisoara, Romania, Mar. 18, 1950; came to U.S., 1975; s. Mircea Dimitrie and Rodica P. (Bucur) R.; m. Lilian Massoud, Mar. 26, 1978; children: Victor I., Marius M., Julia L. BA, U. Timisoara, 1973, MA, 1974; PhD, U. Calif., Berkeley, 1980. Programmer Cen. Inst. Mgmt., Bucharest, Romania, 1974-75; T.H. Hildebrandt rsch. asst. prof. U. Mich., Ann Arbor, 1980-83; assoc. prof. U. Ariz., Tucson, 1983-87; assoc. prof. U. Calif., Santa Cruz, 1987-88, prof., 1988—. Editor: Algebras, Groups and Geometries, 1988-91; co-author: Manifolds, Tensor Analysis and Applications, 1983, 2d edit., 1989. A.P. Sloan Found. fellow, 1984-87, NSF postdoctoral fellow, 1983-86. Mem. Am. Math. Soc., Am. Romanian Acad. Arts and Scis. (exec. com. 1989—), World Union Free Romanians. Roman Catholic. Office: U Calif Santa Cruz CA 95064

RATKOVIC, JOSEPH ANTHONY, product developer; b. Phila., Sept. 8, 1945; s. Joseph Anthony and Mary Constance (Yayac) R.; m. Dolores Tomas, Oct. 9, 1971; children: Anthony, Michael, Lynette. BSEE, Villanova U., 1967; MS, Purdue U., 1968; postgrad. engr., UCLA, 1972; PhD, Rand Grad. Inst., 1980. Group mgr. Hughes Aircraft Co., L.A., 1968-74; project mgr. Rand Corp., Santa Monica, Calif., 1975-80; dir. Aerospace Corp., El Segundo, Calif., 1980-84; prin. Ratkovic Consulting, L.A., 1988-90; gen. mgr. Litton Advanced Systems, Van Nuys, Calif., 1984-88; dir. Litton Guidance & Control, Woodland Hills, Calif., 1990—; bd. dirs. Hyperformanc Armor, Marina Del Ray, Calif. Coach baseball team, L.A., 1980-86. Home: 1316 Armacost Ave Los Angeles CA 90025 Office: Litton Systems 5500 Canoga Ave Woodland Hills CA 91367-6698

RATLIFF, JAMES CONWAY, hotel executive; b. Evanston, Ill., Mar. 28, 1940; s. Harold Sugart and Marjorie (Elmore) R. BA, Mich. State U., 1967. Dir. food & beverage ops. Detroit Hilton, 1970-71; dir. food & beverage purchasing Hilton Hotels Corp., N.Y.C., 1972-77; corp. dir. procurement Hilton Hotels Corp., Beverly Hills, Calif., 1977—; treas. Am. Inst. Food Distbn., Fair Lawn, N.J., 1989-90, bd. dirs., 1984—, vice-chmn. 1991—; instr. Calif. State Poly. U., Pomona, 1987, 88. With U.S. Army, 1963-65. Mem. Food Svc. Purchasing Assn. Canada (hon. mem.), Produce Mktg. Assn. (bd. dirs. 1986-88, v.p. 1989-90, sec./treas. 1991—, chmn. elect, 1992, chmn. 1993), Produce Mktg. Assn. (chmn. foodservice div. 1989-90, bd. dirs. foodservice div. 1985-88), Nat. Restaurant Assn. Foodservice Purchasing Mgrs. (bd. dirs. 1977-81, chmn. 1981-83), Pacific Corinthian Yacht Club. Republican. Methodist. Office: Hilton Hotels Corp 9336 Civic Center Dr Beverly Hills CA 90210-3964

RATLIFF, LEIGH ANN, pharmacist; b. Long Beach, Calif., May 20, 1961; d. Harry Warren and Verna Lee (Zwink) R. D in Pharmacy, U. Pacific, 1984. Registered pharmacist, Calif., Nev. Pharmacist intern Green Bros. Inc., Stockton, Calif., 1982-84, staff pharmacist Thrifty Corp., Long Beach, Calif., 1984-85, head pharmacist, 1986-87, pharm. buyer, 1987-92; pharmacy. mgr. Kmart Pharmacy, Long Beach, Calif., 1992—. Mem. Pacific Alumni Assocs., Nat. Trust for Hist. Preservation, Friends of Rancho Los Cerritos; treas. Bixby Knolls Ter. Homeowners Assn., 1988-92, pres. 1992—; vol. Docent Rancho Los Cerritos Hist. Site, 1988— Mem. Am. Pharm. Assn., Am. Inst. History Pharmacy, Calif. Pharmacist Assn., Lambda Kappa Sigma. Republican. Methodist. Avocations: creative writing, raising aquarium fish, house plants, collecting Lladro pieces. Home: 3913 N Virginia Rd Unit 301 Long Beach CA 90807-2670 Office: Kmart Pharmacy 5450 Cherry Ave # 4472 Long Beach CA 90805

RATLIFF, LOUIS JACKSON, JR., mathematics educator; b. Cedar Rapids, Iowa, Sept. 1, 1931; s. Louis Jackson and Ruth Sara (Sidlinger) R. BA, State U. Iowa, 1953, MA, 1958, PhD, 1961. Lectr. Ind. U., Bloomington, 1961-63, U. Calif., Riverside, 1963-64; asst. prof. U. Calif., 1964-67, assoc. prof., 1967-69, prof. math., 1969—. Author: Chain Conjectures in Ring Theory, 1978; contbr. articles to profl. jours.; assoc. editor Procs. of AMS, 1987-92, Communications in Algebra, 1990—. 1st lt. USAF, 1953-57. NSF fellow, 1960-62, grantee, 1965-69, 71-88; recipient Disting. Teaching award, U. Calif.-Riverside, 1983. Mem. Am. Math. Soc., Phi Beta Kappa. Democrat. Seventh Day Adventist. Home: 3139 Newell Dr Riverside CA 92507-3147 Office: U Calif Dept Math Riverside CA 92521

RATLIFF, WILLIAM ELMORE, curator, researcher; b. Evanston, Ill., Feb. 11, 1937; s. Harold Shugart and Marjorie (Elmore) R.; m. Lynn Louise Robbins, June 1959; children: Sharon, Paul, Susan, David, John. BA, Oberlin Coll., 1959; MA, U. Wash., 1968, PhD, 1974. Rsch. fellow Hoover Instn., Stanford, Calif., 1968-79; cons., dir. rsch. Rsch. Internat., San Francisco, 1976-82; critic, chief editorial writer Times Tribune, Palo Alto, Calif., 1979-86; sr. rsch. fellow Hoover Instn., Stanford, 1986—; music stringer L.A. Times, 1975—, Opera News, 1978—; cons., lectr. U.S. Info. Agy., Washington, 1986, 88, 89, 90; lectr. U.S. Dept. Def. confs./seminars, Washington, 1984—. Author: Castroism in Latin America, 1978; author/ editor Media and Cuban Revolution, 1987; co-author: Capitalist Revolution in Argentina, 1990, The Civil War in Nicaragua, 1992; co-editor Juan Peron Cartas del exilio, 1991; area editor: Yearbook on Internat. Communist Affairs, 1968-91; contbr. articles to profl. jours. Office: Stanford U Hoover Inst Stanford CA 94305

RATLIFF-GARRISON, TONYA ANNETTE, editor; b. Temple, Tex., June 25, 1963; d. Mackie Gene and Felicia Ethel (Camp) Ratliff; m. Ivor Robert Green, Aug. 8, 1981 (div. May 1988); children: Tobe Nichole Green, Britton Ratliff Green; m. Robin Lee Garrison, Sept. 9, 1988; children: James Tyler Garrison, Teysha Noel Garrison. BA in Mass Comm., St. Edwards U., 1987. Editorial asst. Austin (Tex.) Am.-Statesman, 1982-89; editor, reporter Idaho State Jour./Ag Jour., Pocatello, 1990-92. Editor (mags.) Ea. Idaho Farm and Ranch, 1992—, Intermountain Horse & Rider; editor, designer Barbwire Barbs: A Collection of Works from Poets in the Cowboy Poets of Idaho. Recipient Best in Ag Writing award Nat. Press Women, 1992, Hon. Mention Light Features, Utah-Idaho-Spokane AP, 1992, Idaho Conservation Writer Yr., 1992, 1st place award Nat. Press Women, 1993. Mem. NAFE, Soc. Profl. Journalists, Soc. Environ. Journalists, Idaho Press Women (Best in Ag Writing 1992, 93), Idaho Press Club. Democrat. Office: Ea Idaho Farm & Ranch 301 Northgate Mile Idaho Falls ID 83403

RATNER, BUDDY DENNIS, bioengineer; b. Bklyn., Jan. 19, 1947; s. Philip and Ruth Ratner; m. Teri Ruth Stoller, July 7, 1968; 1 child, Daniel Martin. BS in Chemistry, Bklyn. Coll., 1967; PhD in Polymer Chemistry, Polytech. Inst. Bklyn., 1972. Postdoctoral fellow U. Wash., Seattle, 1972-73, from rsch. assoc. to assoc. prof., 1973-86, prof., 1986—; dir. Nat. ESCA and Surface Analysis Ctr., Seattle, 1984—. Editor: Surface Characterization of Biomaterials, 1988; mem. editoral bds. 8 jours. and book series; contbr. more than 200 articles to profl. jours. Recipient faculty achievement/outstanding rsch. award Burlington Resources Found., 1990, Perkin Elmer Phys. Electronics award for excellence in surface sci.; grantee NIH. Fellow Am. Inst. Med. Biological Engring (founding), Am. Vacuum Soc.; mem. AAAS, Adhesion Soc., Am. Chem. Soc., Am. Inst. Chem. Engrs., Internat. Soc. Contact Lens Rsch. (coun. mem.), Materials Rsch. Soc., Soc. Applied Spectroscopy, Soc. for Biomaterials (pres. 1991, 1992, Clemson award 1989). Office: U Wash Dept Chem Engring BF-10 Seattle WA 98195

RATNER, MARC LEONARD, English language educator, retired; b. N.Y.C., Jan. 19, 1926; s. Abraham Bret and Nadine (Blumberg) R.; m. Margaret Patrick, June 10, 1951 (div. Jan. 1983); children: Megan, Nicolas, Shelagh; m. Marjorie Eleanor Locklear, May 27, 1983. BA, Fordham U., 1950; MA, U. Pa., 1951; PhD, NYU, 1958. Instr. U. Colo., Boulder, 1955-60; from asst. to assoc. prof. U. Mass., Amherst, 1960-67; prof. Calif. State U., Hayward, 1967-92; dir. Atlantic studies program U. Mass., Amherst, 1966-67. Author: William Styron, 1972; contbr. articles, essays to profl. publs. Cpl. USAAF, 1943-46, PTO. Fulbright grantee, 1963-65, 71-72, 74-75, 85-86. Mem. MLA, Am. Film Inst., Mark Twain Soc. Democrat. Home: 1652 Countrywood Ct Walnut Creek CA 94598-1010 Office: Calif State U Carlos Bee Blvd Hayward CA 94542-1510

RATZLAFF, VERNON PAUL, educator, consultant; b. Mt. Lake, Minn., May 16, 1925; s. Peter Benjamin and Helen (Dick) R.; m. Bonnie Lou Sommers, Dec. 17, 1955; children: Paul, Gwen, Jay, Peter. BA in Elem. Edn., German, Goshen Coll., 1954; MA, U. N.D., 1971; student, U. Minn., 1956-57, U. Oreg., 1965, U. No. Ariz., 1968. Cert. tchr. Elem. tchr. Richfield (Minn.) Pub. Schs., 1954-74; tchr. Tuba City (Ariz.) Pub. Sch., 1975—; resource person to tchrs., Grand Forks, N.C., 1970-72, resource person to upper elem. tchrs. and children, Richfield, 1967-70; adminstr. of Christian Sch. Hopi Mission, Oraibi, Ariz., 1971-75; math tchr. Nortland Pioneer Coll.; established "Look Folks-No Fail" classrooms. Author: Side by Side " Up from the Pit to Become a Shining Star" (Where Students Take Responsibility for Learning), 1990; contbr. articles to numerous jours. Mem. NEA, Ariz. Edn. Assn., Am. Assn. Retired People. Republican. Home: Grandview # 153 PO Box 947 Tuba City AZ 86045

RAU, HARRY MILTON, III, chef; b. Medford, Mass., Nov. 12, 1950. Student, Brevard Coll., 1972. Dir. Muir Tech. Coll., 1985-88; owner Harry M. Rau Assocs., San Diego, 1988—. Office: 7770 Regents Rd Ste 113-281 San Diego CA 92122

RAUB, WALTER B., systems analyst, consultant; b. Easton, Pa., Dec. 18, 1959; s. George Francis and Anne Louise (Jarema) R.; m. Naomi Lynn Minarcik, Jan. 23, 1988; children: Kelli, Kerri. BS in Computer Sci., Shippensburg U., 1981. Analyst Sperry Univac, Parsippany, N.J., 1981-82; database adminstr. Mountain Bell, Denver, 1982-84; sr. system analyst, ptnr. Mechanized System Consulting Design Svcs., Denver, 1984-92; pres. Gator Enterprises Inc., Lakewood, Colo., 1992—. Patentee in field.

RAUCH, LAWRENCE LEE, aerospace and electrical engineer, educator; b. L.A., May 1, 1919; s. James Lee and Mabel (Thompson) R.; m. Norma Ruth Cable, Dec. 15, 1961; children: Lauren, Maury Rauch. A.B., U. So. Calif., 1941; postgrad., Cornell U., 1941; A.M., Princeton U., 1948, Ph.D., 1949. Instr. math. Princeton U., 1943- 49; faculty U. Mich., 1949—, prof. aerospace engring., 1953-79, emeritus, 1979, chmn. instrumentation engring. program, 1952-63, chmn. computer, info. and control engring. program, 1971-76, asso. chmn. dept. elec. and computer engring., 1972-75; chief technologist telecommunication sci. and engring. div. NASA/Calif. Inst. Tech. Jet Propulsion Lab., 1979-85; vis. prof. Ecole Nationale Supérieure de L'Aéronautique et de l'Espace, Toulouse, France, 1970, Calif. Inst. Tech., Pasadena, 1977-85, U. Tokyo, 1978; cons. govt. and industry, 1946—; chmn. telemetering working group, panel test range instrumentation Research and Devel. Bd. Dept. Def., 1952-53; mem. exec. com. (Nat. Telemetering Conf.), 1959-64; Western Hemisphere program chmn. (1st Internat. Telemetering Conf.), London, 1963, program chmn., U.S.A., 1967; supr. air blast telemetering, Bikini, 1946; mem. project non-linear differential equations Office Naval Research, 1947-49; mem. research adv. com. on communications, instrumentation and data processing NASA, 1963-68. Author: Radio Telemetry, 1956; also numerous sci. articles and papers on radio telemetry. Recipient award for outstanding contbn. to WWII Army and Navy, 1947, annual award Nat. Telemetering Conf., 1960; Donald P. Eckman award for disting. achievement in edn. Instrument Soc. Am., 1966; Pioneer award Internat. Telemetering Conf./USA, 1985. Fellow IEEE (spl. award contbns. radio telemetry 1957, adminstrv. com. profl. group space electronics and telemetry 1958-64), AAAS, Explorers Club; mem. Am. Math. Soc., AIAA, U. Mich. Research Club, Phi Beta Kappa, Sigma Xi, Phi Eta Sigma, Phi Kappa Phi. Address: 759 N Citrus Ave Los Angeles CA 90038-3401

RAUCINA, THOMAS FRANK See RACINA, THOM

RAUE, JORG EMIL, electrical engineer; b. Stettin, Germany, June 13, 1936; came to U.S., 1952; s. Ludwig and Liselotte (Barth) R.; m. Anke Volkmann, June 29, 1957; children: Monika Kay, Jennifer Faye. BSEE, Milw. Sch. Engring., 1961; MSEE, Marquette U., 1965, PhDEE, 1968. Mem. faculty Milw. Sch. Engring., 1961-68, chmn. dept., 1968-69; research engr. TRW Systems, Redondo Beach, Calif., 1969-76; mgr. dept. TRW Systems, Redondo Beach, 1976-79; sr. research scientist TRW Electronic Systems, Rendondo Beach, Calif., advanced systems mgr., 1980—; chmn. dept. elec. engring. Calif. Polytech State U., San Luis Opispo, 1979-80; mem. faculty Marquette U., Milw., 1968-69, Loyola U., Los Angeles, 1970-72, U. So. Calif., Los Angeles, 1983—. Contbr. articles to profl. jours. Served with U.S. Army, 1955-58. Recipient Disting. Tchr. award Milw. Sch. Engring., 1968; named Outstanding Alumnus Milw. Sch. Engring., 1985. Fellow IEEE; mem. Microwave Soc. of IEEE (sec. adminstrn. com. 1985—), Sigma Xi. Home: 28813 Rothrock Dr Palos Verdes Peninsula CA 90274-3060

RAUGHTON, JIMMIE LEONARD, urban planner, educational administrator; b. Knoxville, Tenn., Oct. 9, 1943; s. George L. and Ann (Simotes) R.; B.A. in Urban and Regional Planning, U. No. Colo., 1974, M.A., 1976, postgrad. U. Colo., 1986. Mgr., Flexitran div. Gathers, De Vilbliss Architects and Planners, 1966-68; asst. dir. planning City of Aurora, Colo., 1970-71; planner City of Lakewood, Colo., 1971-73; planner City of Boulder, Colo., 1973-74; instr. urban planning Community Coll. of Denver, 1974-76, div. dir. human resources and svcs., 1976-81, div. dir. sci. and tech., 1981-85; v.p. State of Colo. Community Colls., 1985—; exec. dir. Edn. Found. Colo., 1989—; coord. devel. Rocky Mountain Energy and Environ. Tech. Center, 1980. cons. Denver Regional Council of Govts. for Model Sign Code, 1973, City of Boulder Transp. Dept., 1975—; chmn. profl. advisory com. to Colo. Gov.'s Land Use Adviser, 1973; also public speaker. Mem. exec. bd. Civic Center Assn., Denver, 1973-75; supervisory com. Colo. State Employees Credit Union, 1986—;mem. bd. Support Systems Consol., 1984, Bridge Industry, 1984-85; candidate Denver City Council, 1975; bd. dirs. Plan Metro Denver, 1975-76, Four Corner Art Collection, 1973—. Recipient Citizen Award of Honor, Assn. of Beautiful Colo. Roads, 1972. Mem. Am. Inst. of Planners (mem. exec. bd. Colo. 1970-75, treas. 1972-73), Colo. City Mgrs. Assn., Am. Soc. Planning Ofcls., Am. Vocat. Assn., Am. Soc. for Tng. and Devel., Pi Alpha Alpha. Methodist. Contbr. articles to local newspapers. Home: 2501 High St Denver CO 80205-5565 Office: State of Colo Community Colls 1391 N Speer Blvd Denver CO 80204-2552

RAUH, J. RANDALL, physician; b. Hardtner, Kans., June 30, 1947; s. John Harry and Dorothy Mae (Dimmick) R.; m. Janice Yvonne Weigand, July 1, 1967 (div. Jan. 1989); children: HEather Elaine, Sarah Elaine, Travis Randall, Joshua Blaine. BS in Chemistry and Biology, Northwestern Okla. State U., 1969; MD, U. Okla., 1973. Diplomate Am. Bd. Ob-Gyn. Resident Tulsa Med. Coll. U. Okla., 1973-76; pvt. practice Okmulgee, Okla., 1976-80; pvt. group practice Stillwater Women's Clinic, Okla., 1980; pvt. practice Miles City, Mont., 1981--; clin. instr. Tulsa Med. Coll., 1977—, U. N.D. Sch. Medicine; chief of staff Holy Rosary Hosp., Miles City, 1981-82, 88-89, trustee, 1983-89; mem. Ethics Com. Presentation Health System, Aberdeen, S.D., 1986-90. Contbr. articles to profl. jours. Pres. Little League Com. Miles City Youth Baseball Assn., 1988-90. Recipient Excellence in Clin. Tchg. award Am. Acad. Fam. Practice, 1977. Fellow ACOG, ACS, mem. AMA, Nat. Rural Health Assn., Am. Fertility Soc., Mont. Med. Assn., U. Okla. Coll. Med. Alumni Assn. (life mem.), Miles City Area C. of C. Republican. Lutheran. Office: 219 N Merriam Ave Miles City MT 59301-2794

RAUSCHKOLB, ROY SIMPSON, soil scientist; b. St. Louis, Apr. 18, 1933; s. Roy Simpson and Sibyl Charity (Williams) R.; m. Joan Inez Marshall, May 31, 1953; children: Sibyl Ann, Roy Simpson III, Jean May. B.A. in Chemistry, Ariz. State U., 1961; M.S. in Agrl. Chemistry, U. Ariz., 1963, Ph.D., 1968. Cotton specialist Coop. Extension U. Ariz., Tucson, 1965-66; soil specialist, 1967-69, assoc. dean, dir., 1981-88, resident dir., 1988—; supt. Exptl. Farm, Safford, Ariz., 1966-67; soil specialist Coop. Extension U. Calif., Davis, 1969-77, asst. dir., 1977-81; cons. FAO, Rome, 1972, 74, EPA, Ada, Okla., 1976, AEC, Aleppo, Syria, 1977, Ministry of Agrl., Cairo, Egypt, 1991. Author: Land Degradation (in 3 langs.), 1993; Nitrogen Management in Irrigated Agriculture, 1976. Served with USAF, 1952-56. Grantee Dept. Water Resources (Calif.), 1980, W.K. Kellogg Found., 1982. Fellow Soil Sci. Soc. Am., Am. Soc. Agronomy (Calif. chpt. council mem. 1975-77); mem. Alpha Zeta (v.p. 1960-61), Gamma Sigma Delta. Office: U Ariz Coll Agr Maricopa Agricultural Ctr 37860 W Smith-enke Rd Maricopa AZ 85239-3010

RAUSER, VICKIE SUE, auditor; b. Townsend, Mont., Jan. 19, 1959; d. Walter Frank and Anna Winifred (Etzwiler) R. BS in Bus., Mont. State U., 1981. CPA, Mont. From staff auditor to audit supr. Mont. Office of the Legis. Auditor, Helena, 1981-91, audit mgr., 1991—. Mem. Order Ea. Star (assoc. conductress 1987-88, 91-92, conductress 1988-89, 92-93, assoc. matron 1989-90, worthy matron 1990-91), Toastmasters Internat. (sec.-treas. 1990, v.p. edn. 1992-93). Episcopalian. Office: Office Legis Auditor Capitol Bldg Rm 135 Helena MT 59601

RAUTENBERG, ROBERT FRANK, consulting statistician; b. Milw., Sept. 14, 1943; s. Raymond Clarence and Anna Josephine (Winter) R.; m. Meredith Taylor, June 2, 1965 (div. Feb. 1975); 1 child, Matthew Carl. PhD in Bus. Adminstrn., Pacific Western U., 1983; post doctorate rsch., Sorbonne U., Paris. Pvt. practice acctg. Kansas City, Mo., 1975-76; pres. Seven Diamond Enterprises, San Francisco, 1976-78; chief exec. officer Assurance Systems, San Francisco, 1984—. Author: The Analytical Management Handbook, 1985, Supplement to the Analytical Management Handbook, 1991; contbr. articles to profl. jours. and conf. proceedings. Mem. Internat. Soc. Bayesian Analysis (charter), European Fedn. Mgmt. Consulting Assns., Royal Statistical Soc. Episcopalian. Home: 711 Leavenworth St San Francisco CA 94109 Office: Assurance Systems 220 Montgomery St Ste 3036 San Francisco CA 94104-4715

RAVAGE, JOHN WILLIAM, mass media educator; b. Anderson, Ind., Mar. 15, 1937; s. John and Velma Louise (McClelland) R.; m. Linda Dawn Ravage, Nov. 2, 1958; children: Christopher, Jeffrey. BA in English/Speech, Ball State U., 1959, MA in English, 1962; MA in Theatre, U. Ill., 1965; PhD in Communications, Purdue U., 1974. Tchr. English/speech Madison Heights High Sch., Anderson, Ind., 1959-61; prof. English/speech Elgin (Ill.) Community Coll., 1961-64; prof. speech/communications St. Joseph's Coll., Rensselaer, Ind., 1966-73; prof. mass media U. Wyo., Laramie, 1974—; lectr. on African-Ams. in the western U.S. Author: Television: The Director's Viewpoint, 1980, Singletree, 1990, (play) Murder Springs Up, 1991. Mem. Western Writer's of Am., Am. Film Inst., Broadcast Edn. Assn. Home: 2332 Cottonwood Dr Laramie WY 82070-7311 Office: Dept Comms/Mass Media PO Box 3904 Laramie WY 82071-3904

RAVELING, GEORGE, university athletic coach. Head coach NCAA Divsn. 1A basketball, ranked #8 U. So. Calif. Trojans, 1992. Office: U So Calif Univ Park Los Angeles CA 90089

RAVELY, VICTORIA ALLINE, postal clerk; b. Seattle, Nov. 22, 1946; d. Ganam Emergy and Wilma Edith (Bressie) Dodson; m. William L. Rose, 1963 (div. 1967); m. Norman W. Ravely, 1967; children: Romy Roseann, Caryn Alice, John-William Harold. AA in Liberal Arts, Columbia Basin Coll., 1979, AS in Legal Secretarial, 1979; BA in Law magna cum laude, Cen. Wash. U., 1981. Clk. U.S. Postal Svc., Costa Mesa, Calif., 1965-68, Pasco, Wash., 1968-75; legal sec. Port of Posco, 1979-80; gen. office clk. U.S. Post Office, Richland, Wash., 1980—. Guardian ad litem Benton Franklin Counties Juvenile Ct. System, Kennewick, Wash., 1983—; tutor with literacy coun. ESL; mem. Grace Gospel fellowship, Westside Presbyn. Ch. Named Outstanding Wash. State Vol. as guardian ad litem, 1987. Mem. Am. Postal Workers Union (OWCP counselor 1980—), Concerned Women Am., Eagle Forum, Berean Bible Soc., Human Life. Republican. Office: PO Box 135 Richland WA 99352-0135

RAVEN, BERTRAM H(ERBERT), psychology educator; b. Youngstown, Ohio, Sept. 26, 1926; s. Morris and Lillian (Greenfeld) R.; m. Celia Cutler, Jan. 21, 1961; children: Michelle G., Jonathan H. BA, Ohio State U., 1948, MA, 1949; PhD, U. Mich., 1953. Research assoc. Research Ctr. for Group Dynamics, Ann Arbor, Mich., 1952-54; lectr. psychology U. Mich., Ann Arbor, 1953-54; vis. prof. U. Nijmegen, U. Utrecht, Netherlands, 1954-55; psychologist RAND Corp., Santa Monica, Calif., 1955-56; prof., chmn. dept. psychology UCLA, 1956—; vis. prof. Hebrew U., Jerusalem, 1962-63, U. Wash., Seattle, U. Hawaii, Honolulu, 1968, London Sch. Econs. and Polit. Sci., London, 1969-70; external examiner U. of the West Indies, Trinidad and Jamaica, 1980—; participant Internat. Expert Conf. on Health Psychology, Tilburg, Netherlands, 1986; cons., expert witness in field, 1979—. co-dir. Tng. Program in Health Psychology, UCLA, 1979-88; cons. World Health Orgn., Manila, 1985-86; cons., expert witness various Calif. cts., 1978—. Author: (with others) People in Groups, 1976, Discovering Psychology, 1977, Social Psychology, 1983; editor: (with others) Contemporary Health Services, 1982; Policy Studies Review Annual, 1980; editor Jour. Social Issues, 1969-74; contbr. articles to profl. jours. Guggenheim fellow, Israel, 1962-63; Fulbright scholar The Netherlands, 1954-55, Israel, 1962-63, Britain, 1969-70; Citation from Los Angeles City Council, 1966, Rsch. on Soc. power by Calif. Sch. of profl. psychology, L.A., 1991; NATO sr. fellow, Italy, 1989. Fellow Am. Psychol. Assn. (chair bd. social and ethical responsibility 1978-82), Am. Psychol. Soc., Soc. for Psychol. Study of Social Issues (pres. 1973-74); mem. AAAS, Am. Sociol. Assn., Internat. Assn. Applied Psychology, Soc. Exptl. Social Psychology, Assn. Advancement of Psychology (founding, bd. dirs. 1974-81), Internat. Soc. Polit. Psychology, Interam. Psychol. Soc., Am. Psychology-Law Soc. Home: 2212 Camden Ave Los Angeles CA 90064-1906 Office: UCLA Dept Psychology Los Angeles CA 90024-1563

RAVENSCROFT, VERNON FRANK, consultant; b. Buhl, Idaho, Jan. 26, 1920; s. William Francis and Fern (Gould) R.; m. Harriett Elnora Burkhard, Dec. 28, 1940; children: Marilyn, Carolyn, Lynell (dec.), Allan, Gordon, Bryan. BS in Forestry, U. Idaho, 1943. Extension forester Idaho Agrl. Extension Svc., Moscow, 1942-51; gen. mgr. Penta Post & Treating Co., Tuttle, Idaho, 1951-73; farming & cons. pvt. practice, Tuttle & Boise, 1973-79; pres. Consulting Assocs. Inc., Boise, 1979—. Contbr. articles to profl. jours. Mem. sch. bd. Hagerman (Idaho) Sch. Dist., 1956-64; state rep. Idaho State Legis., Boise, 1962-74; state party chmn. Idaho Reps., Boise, 1975-77; mem. adv. bd. Sawtooth Nat. Forest, Shoshone Dist. B.L.M., State of Idaho B.L.M. Recipient NAt. Outstanding 4-H Leadership award. Mem. Idaho Pvt. Power Coun. (state chmn. 1982-84), Idaho Ind. Energy Coun. (bd. dirs. 1992). Office: Consulting Assocs Inc 1843 Broadway Ave Boise ID 83706

RAVEY, DONALD LEE, educator; b. San Diego, July 22, 1929; s. Robert Lee and Marian Adelaide (Hyams) R. BS, San Diego State U., 1950; MS, MIT, 1961. Mfg. facilities engr. Convair, a Div. Gen. Dynamics, San Diego, 1955-59; unit chief procurement planning/control Boeing, Seattle and New Orleans, 1961-63; tchr. Sacramento Bus. Coll., 1964-65; sr. systems analyst Matson Navigation Co., San Francisco, 1965-67; mgr. systems and data svcs. Ampex Corp., Redwood City, Calif., 1967-72; adminstrv. svcs. mgr. Sunland Mktg., Inc., Menlo Park, Calif., 1972-73; mgmt. analyst Tri-Valley Growers, Inc., San Francisco, 1973-76; mgr. engring. systems Unisys Peripherals Div., Santa Clara, Calif., 1976-89; adj. prof. San Mateo County Community Coll. Dist., 1990—. Patentee on sequence switching circuit with latching alarm, 1978. Lt. USNR, 1951-55. Mem. Commonwealth Club of Calif., MIT Club of No. Calif. Home: 127 Chukker Ct San Mateo CA 94403-1306

RAWAT, BANMALI SINGH, electrical engineering educator; b. Garhwal, India, July 2, 1947; came to U.S., 1981; s. Dilwan Singh and Narda (Negi) R.; m. Shanti Parmar, Feb. 6, 1977; children: Manita, Sahit. BSEE, Banaras Hindu U., Varanasi, India, 1968, MSEE, 1970; PhD in Elec. Engring., Sri Venkateswara U., Tirupati, India, 1976. Lectr. dept. elec. engring. U.

Gorakhpur, India, 1970-71; instrumentation engr. West Coast Paper Mills, Dandeli, Karnataka, India, 1971-72; sr. rsch. fellow BITS, Pilani and S.V. Univ, Tirupati, India, 1972-75; sr. scientist Def. R & D Orgn., Dehra Dun, India, 1975-78; assoc. prof., then prof., chair dept. electronics engring. Univ. Gorakhpur, 1978-81; assoc. prof., then prof. dept. elec. engring. U. N.D., Grand Forks, 1981-88; prof. U. Nev., Reno, 1988—, chmn. dept. elec. engring., 1988-91. Author rsch. papers on microwaves. Coach Am. Youth Soccer Orgn., Sparks, Nev. Fellow Inst. Electronic and Telecommunications Engrs., Chinese Inst. Electronics; mem. IEEE (sr. mem., sec.-treas. Red River Valley sect. 1987, vice-chmn. 1988, chmn. No. Nev. sect. 1990-91), Internat. Microwave Tech. Symposium (chmn. 1989—), Electromagnetics Acad. Hindu. Office: U Nev Dept Elec Engring Reno NV 89557

RAWITCH, ROBERT JOE, newspaper editor; b. L.A., Oct. 11, 1945; s. Sam and Jean (Reifman) R.; m. Cynthia Z. Knee, Oct. 27, 1968; children—Dana Leigh, Jeremy Aaron, Joshua Eric. BA in Journalism, Calif. State U.-Northridge, 1967; MS in Journalism, Northwestern U., 1968. Reporter L.A. Times, 1968-80, asst. met. editor, 1980-82, editor Valley sect., 1982-83, suburban editor, 1983-89, exec. editor Valley and Ventura County edits., 1989-93; dir. editorial ops. Valley & Venture County edits., 1993—; lectr. Calif. State U.-Northridge, 1971-83. Co-author: Adat Ari El, The First Fifty Years, 1988. Chmn. Calif. Freedom of Info. Com., 1978-79; pres. Calif. First Amendment Coalition, 1991-93; bd. dirs. Temple Adat Ari El, 1987-92; sec., treas. Calif. Soc. Newspaper Editors, 1991—. Recipient Eagle Scout award Boy Scouts Am., 1959, Greater L.A. Press Club award, 1973, 75, 79, Jewish Youth of Yr. award United Jewish Fund, 1963, Clarence Darrow Found. award, 1979. Mem. Soc. Profl. Journalists (nat. bd. dirs. 1979-82). Office: L A Times 20000 Prairie St Chatsworth CA 91311-6595

RAWLINGS, ROBERT HOAG, newspaper publisher; b. Pueblo, Colo., Aug. 3, 1924; s. John W. and Dorothy (Hoag) R. Student Colo. U., 1943-44; BA, Colo. Coll., 1947; m. Mary Alexandra Graham, Oct. 18, 1947; children: Jane Louise, John Graham, Carolyn Anne, Robert Hoag II. Reporter Pueblo Chieftain and Pueblo Star-Jour., 1947-51, advt. rep. 1951-62, gen. mgr., 1962-79, pub. and editor, 1980—; sec. Star-Jour. Pub. Corp., 1962-84, pres., 1984—; Bd. dirs. Colo. Nat. Bank-Pueblo, chmn. adv. bd., Colo. Pub. Expenditures Coun., Colo. Leadership Forum, Air Force Acad. Found., U. So. Colo. Found., Colo. Water Edn. Found.; mem. activity reuse com. Pueblo Depot, chem. demilitarization citizens adv. com.; adv. bd. El Pomar Ctr., Colo. Pub. Affairs Coun.; pres. Robert Hoag Rawlings Found. Served with USNR, 1942-46. Named Colo. Newspaper Person of 1989, Disting. Univ. Fellow Pres. Club U. So. Colo., 1993; recipient Outstanding Svc. to Univ. award U. So. Colo. Alumni Assn., 1993. Mem. Colo. Press Assn., (dir. 1963-66, 76-78, pres. 1985, chmn. bd. dirs. 1986), Rocky Mountain Ad Mgrs. (past pres.), Colo. AP (past pres.), Elks, Rotary. Presbyterian. Office: Star-Jour Pub Corp PO Box 4040 Pueblo CO 81003-0040

RAWLINSON, STUART ELBERT, geologist; b. Oakland, Calif., Dec. 2, 1950; s. Bradford Stevon and Margaret Edna (Lisman) R.; m. Carol Ann Baran, Jan. 6, 1979 (div. Jan. 1993); children: Karen Lynn, Kathryn Marie. AA, Los Angeles Harbor Coll., 1972; BS, Calif. State U., Long Beach, 1974; MS, U. Alaska, 1979, PhD, 1990. Field asst. Holmes and Narver, Inc., McMurdo Sta., Antarctica, 1970-71; supply and logistics coord. Holmes and Narver, Inc., South Pole Sta., Antarctica, 1974-75; instr. geology Tanana Valley Community Coll., Fairbanks, Alaska, 1977; diver, technician U. Alaska, Fairbanks, 1978-79, rsch. asst., 1977-80; geologist Dept. Natural Resources, State of Alaska, Fairbanks, 1980-88; sr. project engr. Holmes & Narver, Inc., Las Vegas, Nev., 1988-90; sr. project engr. Raytheon Svcs. Nev., Las Vegas, 1990-91, mgr. environ. ops. dept., 1991-92, mgr. waste mgmt. dept., 1992, mgr. environ. site characterization, 1992—; liaison mem. Permafrost com. NRC, Washington, 1984-88, U.S. Permafrost del. to China, 1984; leader field trip to Prudhoe Bay Oilfield 4th Internat. Conf. on Permafrost, 1983. Contbr. articles to profl. jours. Recipient U.S. Antarctic Svc. medal NSF, 1975. Mem. Am. Assn. Petroleum Geologists, Soc. Econ. Paleontologists and Mineralogists, Am. Inst. Profl. Geologists, Phi Kappa Phi. Republican. Methodist. Office: Raytheon Svcs Nev Environ Site Characterization 222 S Rainbow Blvd Ste 115 Las Vegas NV 89128

RAWLS, JAMES JABUS, history educator; b. Washington, Nov. 10, 1945; s. Jabus W. and Jane Kathleen (Brumfield) R.; m. Linda Joyce Higdon, Dec. 29, 1967; children: Benjamin Jabus, Elizabeth Jane Kathleen. BA with honors in History, Stanford U., 1967; MA, U. Calif., Berkeley, 1969, PhD, 1975. Instr. history San Francisco State U., 1971-75, Diablo Valley Coll., Pleasant Hill, Calif., 1975—; vis. lectr. U. Calif., 1977-81, vis. assoc. prof., 1989; scholar-in-residence Calif. State U., Sacramento, 1987; moderator Chautauqua program NEH, Calif., Oreg., 1992; radio personality Dr. History, Sta. KNBR, NBC, San Francisco, 1990—. Co-author: Land of Liberty: A United States History, 1985, California: An Interpretive History, 1993; author: Indians of California, 1986, Dr. History's Whizz-Bang, 1992, Dame Shirley and the Gold Rush, 1993, Never Turn Back: Father Serra's Mission, 1993; editor: Dan De Quille of the Big Bonanza, 1980, New Directions in California History, 1989; co-editor: California: A Place, A People, A Dream, 1986; contbr. Worldmark Ency. of the States, 1981; World Book Ency., 1993. Recipient faculty lectr. award Diablo Valley Coll., 1988, Nat. Teaching Excellence award U. Tex., 1989. Fellow Calif. Hist. Soc. (book rev. editor Calif. History 1983—); mem. Am. Hist. Assn. Democrat. Office: Diablo Valley Coll Dept History Pleasant Hill CA 94523

RAWSON, RAYMOND D., dentist; b. Sandy, Utah, Nov. 2, 1940; s. James D. and Mable (Beckstead) R.; m. Linda Downey, July 23, 1959: children: Raymond Baline, Mark Daniel, Pamela Ann, David James, Kristi Lynn, Kenneth Glenn, Richard Allen. B.S., U. Nev. at Las Vegas, 1964; D.D.S., Loma Linda U., 1968; M.A., U. Nev., 1978; m. Linda Downey, July 23, 1959; children: Raymond Blaine, Mark Daniel, Pamela Ann, David James, Kristi Lynn, Kenneth Glenn, Richard Allen. Diplomate Am. Bd. Forensic Odontology (pres. 1984), Am. Bd. Oral Medicine. Gen. practice dentistry, Las Vegas, 1968—; instr. dental hygiene, dental dir. Clark County Community Coll., 1977—, dep. coroner, chief dental examiner, 1977—; adj. prof. U. Nev., 1977—, adj. assoc. prof. oral diagnosis and forensic dentistry Northwestern U., Chgo., 1985—. Contbr. articles to profl. jours. Active Boy Scouts Am., 1968—; pres. Red Rock Stake; bishop Ch. Jesus Christ Latter-day Saints, 1978-84; asst. majority leader Nev. State senator. Fellow Am. Acad. Forensic Scis. (pres., chmn.), ADA (editorial rev. bd. jour.), Federation Dentaire International, Omicron Kappa Upsilon (commr. edn. commn. of the states). Republican. Office: 6375 W Charleston Blvd Las Vegas NV 89102-1124

RAY, BRUCE DAVID, lawyer; b. Denver, Dec. 19, 1955; s. John Denver Ray and Jane (Guiney) Mitchell; m. Faith Theofanus, Aug. 20, 1978; children: Ellena, Constance, Christian. BA magna cum laude, U. Colo., 1978; JD, Union U., Albany, N.Y., 1981. Bar: Colo. 1981. Spl. environ. counsel URS-Berger, San Bernardino, Calif., 1982-84; asst. regional counsel EPA, Denver, 1984-90; spl. asst. U.S. atty. U.S. Dept. Justice, Denver, 1987-90; environ. counsel Manville Corp., Denver, 1990—. Asst. editor Natural Resources and Environment, 1989—; contbr. articles to legal jours. Recipient bronze medal EPA, 1986, 91, gold medal, 1989, Environ. Excellence award, 1987, Best Article award, 1988, Roasch prize Albany Law Sch., 1981. Mem. ABA (sect. on natural resources, energy and environ. law), Colo. Bar Assn. (environ. law coun. 1987—), Aurora Bar Assn., Environ. Law Inst., Air and Waste Mgmt. Assn., Phi Beta Kappa. Office: Manville Corp 717 17th St Denver CO 80202-3330

RAY, DAVID CHRISTIAN, aerospace engineer; b. Northridge, Calif., July 31, 1961; s. Don Brandon and Laurel Irene (Epstein) R. BA in Phys. Sci., U. Calif., Berkeley, 1984. Aerospace engr. Space Scis. Lab. U. Calif., Berkeley, 1984—, cons. high voltage, high vacuum systems, contamination control, 1987—. Contbr. articles to profl. jours. and mags.; presenter rsch. studies to profl. soc. Office: U Calif Space Sci Lab Centennial at Grizzly Peak Blvd Berkeley CA 94720

RAY, DAVID LEWIN, lawyer, accountant; b. Los Angeles, June 17, 1929; s. Herbert and Beatrice (Lewin) R.; m. Arlene Opas, July 15, 1951; children: Stephan, Robyn. BS, UCLA, 1954; JD, U. LaVerne, 1970. Bar: U.S. Dist. Ct. (so., no. and cen. dists.) Calif.; CPA, Calif. Ptnr., acct. Ray & Ray, Los Angeles, 1957-71, Zigmond, Ray & Co., Beverly Hills, Calif., 1971-73; ptnr. Ray, Rolston & Ress, Beverly Hills, 1970-80, Ray & Murray, Beverly Hills, 1973-80, Saltzburg, Ray & Bergman, Los Angeles, 1980—. Contbr. articles to profl. jours. Served with U.S. Army, 1951-53. Mem. AICPA, Calif. Soc. CPA's, Am. Assn. Attys.-CPA's, Beverly Hills Bar Assn., L.A. County Bar Assn. (chair exec. com. of provisional and postjudgement ren=medies sect.), L.A. Trial Lawyers Assn., Am. Arbitration Assn., Brentwood Country Club, Masons. Office: Saltzburg Ray & Bergman 10960 Wilshire Blvd Fl 10 Los Angeles CA 90024-3702

RAY, JAMES A., management consulting company executive; b. San Francisco, June 27, 1960; s. Raymond H. and Marge A. (Fusco) R.;. AA, City Coll. San Francisco, 1980; student, San Francisco State U., 1980-83, U. San Francisco, 1983-84. Ops. mgr. Selix Formal Wear, Hayward, Calif., 1981-82, Macy's Calif., Daly City, 1982-86; gen. mgr. Fugitive Prodns., San Francisco, 1987; store mgr. Best Products, South San Francisco, Calif., 1989-90; pres. Integrated Capital Mgmt. Group, San Francisco, 1988—; bd. dirs. ARION Group, San Francisco; ptnr. Computer Mgmt. Group, San Francisco, 1990—; cons. Mike Pritchard Prodns., San Rafael, Calif., 1990—; editor, pub. Real Estate Digest. Author: Foreclosure, 1990; editor Bus. Times newsletter. Mgr. field ops. Arlo Smith for BART Bd., San Francisco, 1986; campaign coord. Proposition V-Save the Horses, San Francisco, 1988; campaign mgr. Arlo Smith for Supr., 1990. Mem. Assn. Former Intelligence Officers, Olympic Club. Republican. Catholic. Office: Integrated Capital Mgmt Group 2555 20th Ave San Francisco CA 94116

RAY, LEO ELDON, fish breeding and marketing company executive; b. Logan County, Okla., Dec. 9, 1937; s. Wilbur Houston and Florence Ivy (Doggett) R.; B.S. in Zoology, U. Okla., 1963; m. Judith Kay Croddy, Aug. 29, 1959; children—Tana Kim, Tod Kent, Kacy Kay. Research asst. U. Okla., 1961-63; tchr. public schs., Dumas, Tex., 1963-64, Grants, N.Mex., 1964-65, Anaheim, Calif., 1965-69; co-owner Fish Breeders, Niland, Calif., 1969-87; owner, pres. Fish Breeders of Idaho, Inc., Buhl, 1971—, Fish Processors, Inc., 1971—. Served with U.S. Army, 1957-60. Mem. Calif. Catfish Farmers Am. (past pres.), Catfish Farmers Am. (past pres., dir.), U.S. Trout Farmers Assn. (past pres., dir.). Address: Rte 3 Box 234 Buhl ID 83316

RAY, MARIANNE YURASKO, social services administrator; b. Mpls., Sept. 25, 1934; d. Andrew George and Ann (Rusinko) Yurasko; m. Raymond Robert Ray, Nov. 22, 1962 (div. July 1980); children: Joel Christopher, Angela Christine. BA, U. Utah, 1956; student, U. Wash., 1975; MA, Pacific Lutheran U., 1978. Case worker, vol. agy. liaison State of Wash. Dept. Social and Health Services, Tacoma, Wash., 1963-65, 1971-79, 1983; child placement project dir. State of Wash. Dept. Social and Health Services, Olympia, Wash., 1979-80; casework supr. Child Protective Service State of Wash. Dept. Social and Health Services, Tacoma, Wash., 1980-81, foster home recruiter and licenser, 1981-83; owner, cons. Myray Focuses, Seattle, 1983—; pres. Delta Dynamics Inc., Seattle, 1984-86; mental health therapist Children's Indsl. Home, Tacoma, 1985-86, Good Samaritan Mental Health, Puyallup, Wash., 1986-87; part-time faculty Cen. Wash. U., Ellensburg, 1985—, Highline Community Coll., Midway, Wash., 1985-87, Renton (Wash.) Vocational Tech. Inst., 1985—, Lake Washington Vocational Tech. Inst., Kirkland, Wash., 1985—; dir. child abuse treatment Cath. Community Services, Seattle, 1987—; cons. Tacoma Sch. Dist., 1985-86; presenter nat. conferences and workshops. Creator workshops: Humor Techniques for Stress Management in the Classroom, 1985, Humor in Stress Management: Applications in Helping Professions, 1987, Kicking the Holiday Blues, 1986, Humor for the Health of It, 1987, Laughing Matters--It Really Does!, 1984—, Relocation: What it means for the Employee and Family, 1984—, Humor in the Workplace for Higher Productivity and Team Building, 1984—, Laughter and Liberation in the Classroom to Promote Learning, 1987—, Creative Imagery in Relaxation Techniques, 1987—. Mem. Am. Psychol. Assn. (assoc.), Pacific Northwest Orgn. Devel. Network, Pacific Northwest Speakers Assn. Office: Myray Focuses Counseling/Consulting PO Box 98570 Seattle WA 98198-0570 also: Cath Community Svcs 100 23d Ave S Seattle WA 98144

RAY, PAUL LEO, venture capital and consulting company executive; b. Grinnell, Iowa, Nov. 3, 1946; s. Robert Russell and Julia Barbara (Conrad) R.; children: Cameron Conrad, Jennifer Kirsten. BS in Mktg., Ball State U., Muncie, Ind., 1969. With Dow Corning Corp., 1969-71, V. Mueller div. Am. Hosp. Supply Corp., 1971; co-founder, pres. Gt. Lakes Surg., Inc., Milw., 1978-80; dir. sales Collagen Corp., Palo Alto, Calif., 1980-82, Allergenetics div. Axonics, Inc. (now 3M Diagnostic Systems), Mountain View, Calif., 1982-84; founder, pres., chief exec. officer AllerTech, Inc., Denver, 1984-88; chief exec. officer Alamar Bioscis. Labs., Inc., Napa, Calif., 1988; mng. ptnr. MedCap Venture Ptnrs., Ltd., Englewood, Colo., 1989—, also bd. dirs.; acting gen. mgr. Hemotec, Englewood, 1989-90; ptnr. Paradigm Ptnrs., Boulder, Colo.; bd. dirs. Primus Corp., Kansas City, Mo., TMJ Implants, Inc., Golden, Colo., Surginetics, Inc., Pixsys, Inc. Bd. dirs. Interplast Inc., nonprofit orgn. providing free plastic surgery to children, 1985-89, mem. adv. coun., 1989—; co-chmn. bd. Colo. Bio/Med. Venture Ctr., Denver, 1990-92. Mem. Rockies Venture Capital Club, Beta Theta Pi. Office: Paradigm Ptnrs 1911 11th St Boulder CO 80302

RAY, RICHARD STANLEY, accountant; b. Miami, Ariz., June 12, 1937; s. Milton Sevier and Anne Elizabeth (Mickelson) R.; m. Laura Ann Young, Apr. 11, 1963; children: Denise, Mark, Melanie, Laura, Jordon. AA, Ea. Ariz. Jr. Coll., 1957; BS in Acctg., Ariz. State U., 1962, MS in Acctg., 1964. CPA, Ariz. Staff acct. Deloitte, Haskins & Sells, Phoenix, 1963-65; controller AMECO, Phoenix, 1965-70, U-Haul Co., Phoenix, 1970-76; dir. audit svcs. Ariz. Pub. Service Co., Phoenix, 1976—; advisor to bd. Credit Data of Ariz., Phoenix, 1981—, chmn. bd., 1980-81; dir. Arcoa Internat., Phoenix, 1973-76. Treas., bd. mem. Big Sisters of Ariz., Phoenix, 1972-78; dist. coun. Boy Scouts Am., Phoenix, 1982-84; stake pres. Mormon Ch., Tempe, Ariz. 1987—. Grad. rsch. fellowship, Ariz. Bankers Assn., Phoenix, 1962. Mem. Am. Inst. CPA's, Ariz. Soc. CPA's (Acctg. Achievement award 1962), Ariz. State Bd. Accountancy (continuing profl. edn. com. 1986—), Edison Electric Inst. (com. mem. 1976—), Rotary. Republican.

RAY, SANKAR, opto-electroic device scientist; b. Calcutta, India, Dec. 30, 1953; came to U.S., 1976; s. Asok Kumar and Sumitra (Dey) R.; m. Diana Konaszewski, June 8, 1985; children: Krishanu, Monisha. BSc in Physics with honors, U. Calcutta, 1974; MSc in Physics, Indian Inst. Tech., Kanpur, 1976; PhD in Physics, Brown U., 1981. Prin. rsch. scientist Honeywell Corp. Tech. ctr., Bloomington, Minn., 1981-87; lead rsch. scientist Boeing High Tech. Ctr., Bellevue, Wash., 1987-90, mgr. advanced components for fiber optic networks, 1990—; evaluator rsch. proposals Jet Propulsion Lab., Pasadena, Calif., 1990, Simon Fraser U., Vancouver, B.C., Can., 1990; chmn. organizing com. Boeing Photonics Symposium, Seattle, 1991; mem. Compound Semiconductor Adv. Com., Wash. Tech. Ctr., U. Wash., 1992. Contbr. articles to Phys. Rev. Letters, Applied Physics Letters, IEEE Electron devices; author, co-author over 25 jour. articles, conf. procs. Mem. IEEE, Am. Phys. Soc., Indian Physics Assn., Sigma Xi. Office: Boeing Def & Space Group PO Box 3999 Seattle WA 98124-2499

RAYBOULD, BARRY JOHN, computer software company executive; b. Stourbridge, Eng., Jan. 14, 1956; came to U.S., 1984; s. Arthur Wesley and Edna (Tromans) R.; m. Jacqueline Seddon, June 19, 1981. Grad. with honors, U. Cambridge, Eng., 1977, BA and MA in Engring., 1978. Supt. prodn. Delta Metal Group, Manchester, U.K., 1980-81, mgr. overseas mfg., 1981-82; sr. engr. Prime Computer Inc., Stevenage, U.K., 1982-85; product mgr. Prime Computer Inc., Natick, Mass., 1985-88; pres. Ariel PSS Corp., Mountain View, Calif., 1989—, pres., CEO, 1991—. Editor: International Directory of Peformance Support Authoring Systems, 1991. Mem. Nat. Soc. for Performance and Instrn. (bd. dirs. 1990-91), Applied Learning Tech., Internat. Interactive Communications Soc., Soc. for Tech. Communication (highest award of distinction 1990, 92). Office: Ariel PSS Corp 100 View St Ste # 114 Mountain View CA 94041-1366

RAYBURN, JAMES CHALMERS, III, jewelry store owner; b. Dallas, Oct. 31, 1945; s James Chalmers Jr. and Helen Maxine (Stanley) R.; m. Lucia Pires de Carvalho, June 28, 1969; children: Shannon Kathleen, Michelle Ciara. BA, Colo. U., 1969. Pres. Youth Rsch. Internat., Colorado Springs, Colo., 1970-72; mem. staff Young Life Campaigns, Colorado Springs, 1972-74; area dir. Young Life Campaigns, West Phoenix, Ariz., 1974-76, Naples, Fla., 1976-77; self-employed Colorado Springs, 1978-86; pres. Spectrum Gems, Colorado Springs, 1986—. Author: Dance Children, Dance, 1984. Pres. Erindale Park Homeowners Assn., Colorado Springs, 1973, 78. Named Coach of Yr., Colorado Springs, 1973, 78. Home: 1947 Forest Ridge Dr Colorado Springs CO 80918-3486 Office: Spectrum Gems 333 N Tejon St Colorado Springs CO 80903

RAYBURN, MARGARET, state legislator; b. North Powder, Oreg., Apr. 5, 1927; d. John Alexander and Pearl Laurel (Wicks) Shaw; m. Glenn Albert Rayburn, July 19, 1946; children: Jeffrey John, Mary Jane Victoria Rayburn Ahlbeck. BA, Eastern Wash. U., 1949. Elem. tchr. Harriett Thompson Elem. Sch., Grandview, Wash., 1949-63; jr. high tchr. Grandview Jr. High, 1963-76, counselor, 1976-83; mem. Wash. Legislature, 1985—; chair Agr. Comm., Olympia, Wash., 1987—, Edn. Commn., Olympia, 1985-89, Local Gov. Comm., Olympia, 1985—, Energy and Utilities Commn., 1991-92, Higher Edn. Commn., 1993—. Bd. dirs. Crisis Ctr., Sunnyside, Wash., 1979-89, Wash. State Policy Inst., 1989—; vice chair agr. and timber com. Nat. Conf. State Legis. Named Outstanding Elected Official Grandview C. of C., 1985. Mem. AAUW, Dem. Club, Fedn. Women's Club, Grandview Grange, Delta Kappa Gamma (pres. 1974-76). Home: Box 3799 1610 S Euclid Rd Grandview WA 98930-9999 Office: John O'Brian Bldg # 310 Olympia WA 98504

RAY-LYNCH, LEOPOLD AUGUSTUS, architect; b. Port Antonio, Jamaica, Oct. 30, 1951; came to U.S., 1959, naturalized, 1961; s. Robert, Jr. and Doris Beatrice (Byrd) R.; B.Arch. (AIA scholar Ariz. chpt. 1971, Sun Angel Found. archtl. scholar 1974, Dubois Found. scholar 1975, Dougherty scholar 1975), Ariz. State U., 1976; M.A. in Urban Planning (grad. fellow 1979), UCLA, 1980. Architect-in-tng. firms in Las Vegas, Nev., 1976-78; asst. economist L.A. Office Econ. Devel., 1980; assoc. A.K. Ngai & Assocs., architects/planners, Los Angeles, 1980-82; urban design cons. Vitalize Van Nuys, Inc., 1980; coord. Sat. scholar program UCLA, 1979-80; architect/rehab. specialist Mark Briggs & Assocs., 1982; ptnr. The AEP Partnership, Architects and Engrs., 1986, Alexander Haagen Co., 1987—. project developer/mall mgr.; prin. works include Baldwin Hills Mall, DeMille Dr. Residence, Spreading Oak Residence, Blue Residence (L.A.) and various others. Mem. AIA, Am. Inst. Cert. Planners, Rotary. Democrat. Roman Catholic. Co-author: Earth-Integrated Architecture, 1975. Office: 3650 W Martin Luther King Jr Blvd Los Angeles CA 90008-1700

RAYMOND, EUGENE THOMAS, technical writer, consultant, retired aircraft engineer; b. Seattle, Apr. 17, 1923; s. Evan James and Katheryn Dorothy (Kranick) R.; m. Bette Mae Bergeson, Mar. 1, 1948; children: Joan Kay Hibbs, Patricia Lynn Adams, Robin Louise Flashman. BSME, U. Wash., 1944; postgrad., 1953-55; registered profl. engr., Tex. Rsch. engr. The Boeing Co., Seattle, 1946-59, sr. group engr., 1959-63, 66-71, sr. specialist engr., 1971-81, prin. engr. flight control tech., 1982-88; project design engr. Gen. Dynamics, Ft. Worth, 1963-66. Lt., USNR, 1943-46, 49-52; PTO. Recipient prize Hydraulics and Pneumatics mag., 1958. Mem. Soc. Automotive Engrs. (cert. of appreciation, chmn. adv. bd. com. A-6 nat. com. for aerospace fluid power and control tech. 1983-88, vice-chmn. com. 1986-88, cons.), Fluid Power Soc. (dir. northwest region 1973-74), Puget Sound Fluid Power Assn., AIAA, Beta Theta Pi, Meridian Valley Country Club, Masons, Shriners. Lutheran. Aircraft editorial adv. bd. Hydraulics and Pneumatics mag., 1960-70; achievements include 5 patents in Fluid Sealing Arrangements, Quasi-Open-Loop Hydraulic Ram Incremental Actuator with Power Conserving Properties, Rotary Digital Electrohydraulic Actuator, Two-Fluid Nonflammable Hydraulic System and Load-Adaptive Hydraulic Actuator System and Method for Actuating Control Surfaces; designed and developed mechanical systems for the XB-47 and B-52 jet bombers, 707 airliner and many other aircraft; contbr. over 20 technical papers and articles to profl. jours. Home and Office: 25301 144th Ave SE Kent WA 98042-3401

RAYMOND, GEORGE THOMAS, programmer, analyst; b. Lakeland, Fla., Dec. 4, 1960; s. George Barr and Marie Agnes (DuPont) R. AA in Mgmt., AS in Data Processing, Polk C.C., 1981; BS in Systems Sci., U. West Fla., 1983; MBA in Telecommunications, U. San Francisco, 1991. Computer specialist Naval Regional Data Automation Ctr., Jacksonville, Fla., 1982-83, computer programmer, 1984; computer programmer Tempo Homes, Inc., Pensacola, Fla., 1983; tech. support supr. Dynamac Internat. Corp., Rockville, Md., 1984-87; sr. programmer, analyst TDS Healthcare Systems Corp., Santa Clara, Calif., 1987-89; McLaren fellow U. San Francisco, 1989-91; sr. programmer, analyst Ross Stores, Inc., Newark, Calif., 1991—; LAN database architecture rev. com. Ross Stores, Inc., 1991, case tool task force, 1992—. Clk. Office of Registrar of Voters, San Jose, Calif., 1989, San Francisco, 1990-92. Mem. Am. Mgr.'s Assn., Sierra Club, U. San Francisco Alumni Assn., Sigma Alpha Epsilon (Dr. James A. Bell scholar 1984). Democrat. Presbyterian. Office: Ross Stores Inc 8333 Central Ave Newark CA 94560

RAYMOND, KENNETH NORMAN, chemistry educator, research chemist; b. Astoria, Oreg., Jan. 7, 1942; s. George Norman and Helen May (Dunn) R.; m. Jane Galbraith Shell, June 19, 1965 (div. 1976); children: Mary Katherine, Alan Norman; m. Barbara Gabriele Sternitzke, June 17, 1977; children: Gabriella Petra, Christopher Norman. B.A., Reed Coll., 1964; Ph.D., Northwestern U., 1968. Asst. prof. chemistry U. Calif.-Berkeley, 1968-74, assoc. prof., 1974-78, prof., 1978—; vice chmn. dept. U. Calif. Berkeley, 1982-84, chmn., 1993—; mem. study sect. NIH, 1983; mem. chemistry adv. com. NSF, 1985-87. Editor: Bioinorganic Chemistry II, 1977; assoc. editor Biology of Metals, 1987-91; mem. bd. editors Topics in Current Chemistry, 1981—; mem. editorial bd. Inorganic Chemistry, 1979-86, Accounts Chem. Rsch., 1982-90, Inorganica Chimica Acta f-Block Elements, 1984-90, Jour. Coordination Chemistry, 1981—, Jour. Inorganic and Nuclear Chemistry, 1974-81, Jour. Am. Chem. Soc., 1983—, Metallobiochemistry, 1992—; U.S. editorial advisor Springer-Verlag in Chemistry, 1972-91; contbr. over 220 articles to profl. jours.; 8 patents in field. Alfred P. Sloan research fellow, 1971-73; Miller research prof., 1977-78; Guggenheim fellow, 1980-81; recipient E.O. Lawrence award, Dept. of Energy. 1984. Mem. Am. Chem. Soc., Am. Crystallographic Soc., Sigma Xi. Democrat. Office: U Calif Berkeley Dept Chemistry Berkeley CA 94720

RAYMOND, ROBERT EDWARD, reliability engineer; b. Huntington, N.Y., Nov. 29, 1936; s. Edward Launtz and Helen (Getman) R.; m. Mary Jane Schwaller, Mar. 30, 1970; children: Kristina Marie, Jennifer Louise. B in Elec. Engring., Ga. Inst. Tech., 1960. Profl. engr., Calif. Jr. engr. Bendix York Div., York, Pa., 1959-63; engr. Bendix Missile Div., Mishawaka, Ind., 1963-69; sr. engr. Bendix Brake Div., South Bend, Ind., 1969-78; staff engr. Bendix Engine Controls Div., South Bend, 1978-90; mem. tech. staff V McDonnell-Douglas Helicopter Co., Mesa, Ariz., 1990—. Mem. IEEE, Am. Soc. for Quality Control (cert. quality engr. and RE), Inst. Environ. Scis. Home: 3448 E Harmony Ave Mesa AZ 85204-6452

RAYMOND, SUSAN GRANT, sculptor; b. Denver, May 23, 1943; d. Edwin Hendrie and Marybelle (McIntyre) G; m. Macpherson Raymond Jr., Aug. 18, 1967 (div. Mar. 1987); children: Lance Ramsay, Mariah McIntyre. BA in English, Cornell U., 1965; MA in Anthropology, U. Colo., 1968. Curator of anthropology Denver Mus. of Nat. History, 1968-71, contract artist, 1976-77, 79, 81, 83; instr. in anthropology U.S. Internat. U., Steamboat Springs, Colo., 1971-73. Sculpted monumental bronze sculpture for Littleton Colo., 1987, Vail, Colo., 1986, inspirational sculpture Childrens Hosp., 1977, diorama figures for Denver Mus. of Nat. History, 1971, 76, 77, 79, 81, 83; other prin. works include sculptures Routt Meml. Hosp, 1977, U. Denver, 1982, Craig Hosp. 1984, Lakewood Westernaires, 1984, Stonegate swimming hole, Scottsdale, 1989, 10th Mtn. div. Monument, Ft. Drum, N.Y.; exhibited at Western Heritage Art Fair, Littleton, 1991. Mem. Nat. Ski Patrol, 1965-75; bd. dirs. Tread of Pioneers Mus., Steamboat Springs, 1971-87. Recipient Maurice Hexter award Nat. Sculpture Soc., 1984, Art Castings award N. Am. Sculpture Exhibition, 1982, Summerart award Steamboat Springs Arts and Humanities, 1984; winner 10th Mountain Div. Monumental Sculpture at Ft. Drum, Watertown, N.Y., 1990: named hon. mem. 10th Mountain Division at work's completion, 1992.

RAYNER, ARNO ALFRED, investment executive, consultant; b. San Francisco, Sept. 23, 1928; s. Kurt Hugo and Angela (Flasch) R.; m. Kenyon Lee Reid, June 14, 1951; children—Eric, Jill, Neal. B.S. in Econs., U. Calif.,

Berkeley, 1949, M.B.A., 1954. Security analyst Bank of Calif., San Francisco, 1950-54; various positions to sr. v.p. Indsl. Indemnity, San Francisco, 1954-74; v.p. Bechtel internat. services Bechtel Group, San Francisco, 1975-76; pres. Rayner Assocs., Inc., Mill Valley, Calif., 1977—; dir. Invest-in-Am., San Francisco; cons. Bechtel Power, San Francisco, 1976—, Citation Ins., 1989—. Fellow Fin. Analysts Fedn.; mem. Inst. Chartered Fin. Analysts, San Francisco Bond Club, Am. Fin. Assn., Tiburon Peninsula Club (pres., dir.), Bohemian Club, World Trade Club, Harbor Point Club, Kiwanis (v.p., dir.). Republican. Lutheran. Home: 450 E Strawberry Dr Mill Valley CA 94941-2506

RAYNOLDS, DAVID ROBERT, buffalo breeder, author; b. N.Y., Feb. 15, 1928; s. Robert Frederick and Marguerite Evelyn (Gerdau) R.; m. May (Kean) Raynolds, May 12, 1951; children: Robert, Linda, Martha, Laura, David A.F. AB, Dartmouth Coll., 1949; MA, Wesleyan U., Middletown, Conn., 1955; predoctoral, Johns Hopkins Sch. Advanced Internat. Studies, Washington, 1956; grad., Nat. War Coll., Washington, 1973. Account exec. R.H. Morris Assoc., Newtown, Conn., 1949-50; fgn. svc. officer Dept. of State, Washington, 1956-76; pres. Ranch Rangers, Inc., Lander, Wyo., 1976—; pres. Nat. Buffalo Assn., Ft. Pierre, S.D., 1987-88. Author: Rapid Development in Small Economies (Praeger); contbr. articles to profl. jours. Mem. mgmt. com. Wyo. Heritage Soc.; bd. dirs. Liberty Hall Found., Wyo. Community Found. With U.S. Army, 1950-53. Recipient Meritorious Svc. Award, Dept. of State, Washington, 1966. Mem. The Explorers Club, Fremont County Farm Bur., Fgn. Svc. Assn., Am. Legion, Rotary, Elks. Republican. Episcopalian. Office: Table Mountain Group PO Box 1310 Lander WY 82520-1310

RAZOUK, RASHAD ELIAS, retired chemistry educator; b. Dumiat, Egypt, Aug. 22, 1911; came to U.S., 1968; s. Elias A. and Martha A. (Israfil) R.; m. Emily S. Habib, Aug. 24, 1946 (dec. Dec. 1988); children: Reda R., Rami R.; m. Henrietta Doche, July 8, 1990. BSc with honors, Cairo U., 1933, MSc, 1936, PhD, 1939. Asst. prof. Cairo U., 1939-46, assoc. prof., 1946-50; prof. chemistry, chmn. dept. Ain Shams U., Cairo, 1950-66; prof. Am. U. Cairo, 1966-68; prof. Calif. State U., L.A., 1968-78, emeritus prof., 1978—; vice dean Faculty Sci. Ain Shams U., Cairo, 1954-60; acting dir. div. surface and coll. chem. Nat. Rsch. Ctr., Cairo, 1954-68; cons. Lockheed Aircraft Co., L.A., 1971-73. Contbr. articles on adsorption, active solids, wetting and wettability, solid reactions, surface tension, and contact angles to profl. jours. Fellow Am. Inst. Chemists (emeritus); mem. Am. Chem. Soc. (emeritus), Royal Soc. Chemistry (life). Democrat. Roman Catholic. Home: 1140 Keats St Manhattan Beach CA 90266-6810 Office: Calif State U 5151 State University Dr Los Angeles CA 90032-4221

REA, ROBERT HALL, environmental, business consultant; b. Sherman, Tex., Sept. 19, 1934; s. Leonard B. and Cleo Mae (Hall) R.; m. Maureen Louise Boshier, May 23, 1987. BS in Civil Engring., Tex. A&M U., 1956; MS in Aero. Engring., Air Force Inst. Tech., 1960; Civil Engr., Columbia U., 1961; MBA, U. Phoenix, Albuquerque, 1987. Registered profl. engr., Ohio, N.Mex., Ariz. V.p., dir. Abt Assocs., Inc., Cambridge, Mass., 1964-73; prin. Resource Planning Assocs., Inc., Cambridge, 1973-76; pres. Resource Communities, Inc., Santa Fe, N.Mex., 1976-80; v.p. Santa Fe div. Energy Transition Corp., 1980-84; asst. dir. N.Mex. Rsch. & Devel. Inst., Santa Fe, 1984-87; v.p. New Bus. Assocs., Inc., Rio Rancho, N.Mex., 1987-89; sr. engr. Sci. Applications Internat. Corp., Albuquerque, 1989—; cons. NEDA Bus. Cons., Inc., Albuquerque, 1989—; prin. N.Mex. Cons. Grp., Albuquerque, 1988—; faculty U. Phoenix, Albuquerque, 1988—, Webster U., Albuquerque, 1988—. Contbr. articles to profl. jours. Mem. N.Mex. Symphony Orch. Chorus, Albuquerque, 1985—. Capt. USAF, 1956-64. Decorated Air Force Commendation medal; Guggenheim Found. scholar, 1960. Mem. Tech. Cons. Inst. (bd. dirs. 1988—), Nat. Soc. Profl. Engrs., N.Mex. Soc. Profl. Engrs. (chmn. audit com., treas. Albuquerque Chpt.), Coll. on Innovation Mgmt. & Entrepreneurship, Inst. Mgmt. Scis., Albuquerque C. of C. (Achievement award 1990), Kiwanis. Unitarian.

REA, WILLIAM J., district judge; b. 1950; BA, Loyola U., 1942, LLB, U. Colo., 1949. With U.S. Census Bur., Denver, 1949-50; adjuster Farmers Ins. Group, L.A., 1950; pvt. practice law, L.A., 1950-64, Santa Ana, Calif., 1964-68; juege Superior Ct., L.A., 1968-84; judge U.S. Dist. Ct. (cen. dist.) Calif., L.A., 1984—. Past pres. L.A. chpt. Nat. Exec. Com.; chmn. Constn. and By-Laws Com. With USN, WWII. Mem. L.A. County Bar Assn. (Outstanding Jurist award 1985), So. Calif. Def. Counsel Assn. Disting. Svc. award 1982), Internat. Acad. Trial Lawyers (Trial Judge of Yr. 1982), L.A. Trial Lawyers Assn., Am. Bd. Trial Advs. (nat. pres.). Office: US Dist Ct 312 N Spring St Los Angeles CA 90012-4701*

READ, CHARLES RAYMOND, SR., business executive; b. Clovis, N.Mex., Apr. 21, 1915; s. Charles Edward and Mary Ellen (Elder) R.; m. Elenore Littlefield, Oct. 10, 1936 (dec. July 1985); children: Charles Raymond Jr., Nancy Ann Read Clendenin; m. Debra Rae Stutzman, Mar. 30, 1989. Baker, candymaker Peter-Paul's Candy, Clovis, 1932-34; baker Holsum Bakery, Boise, Idaho, 1934-35, Elsner's Bakery, Everett, Wash., 1935-37; head baker United Bakery, Ellensburg, Wash., 1937-40; owner, baker Read's Royal Bakery, Ellensburg, 1940-42; mgr., baker Clark's Bakery, Seattle, 1945-57; owner, baker Read's Bakery, Seattle, 1957-62; pres. Read Products, Inc., Seattle, 1962—; ptnr. Peasley-Read, Seattle, 1968—; guest TV programs KING-5, Seattle, 1950-62; distbr. Richlite, 1962—. With USN, 1942-45. Seattle Pacific U. fellow; recipient trophies, plaques for cake decorating Pacific N.W. Clinary Arts Exhibit, 1950-62. Mem. United Comml. Travelers, Smithsonian Inst., Masons (3d degree). Office: Read Products Inc 3615 15th Ave W Seattle WA 98119

READ, FRANK THOMPSON, lawyer, university dean; b. Ogden, Utah, July 16, 1938; s. Frank Archie and Fay Melrose (Thompson) R.; m. Lenet Hadley; 5 children. BS with high honors, Brigham Young U., 1960; JD, Duke U., 1963. Bar: Minn. 1963, Mo. 1966, N.Y. 1968, Okla. 1975. Pvt. practice Mpls., St. Paul, 1963-65; atty. AT&T, Kansas City, Mo., and N.Y.C., 1965-68; asst. prof. law, asst. dean Law Sch., Duke U., 1968-70, assoc. prof., asst. dean, 1970-72, prof., assoc. dean, 1972-73, prof., 1973-74; dean, prof. law U. Tulsa Coll. Law, 1974-79, Ind. U. Sch Law., Indpls., 1979-81, U. Fla. Coll. Law, 1981-88; dean, chief exec. officer Hastings Coll. Law, U. Calif., San Francisco, 1988—; Trustee Law Sch. Admission Coun., 1976—, pres., 1984-85; chmn. Okla. Jud. Coun., 1976-78, pres., 1984-85; vis. prof. U. N.C., So. Meth. U., Brigham Young U. Author: Let Them Be Jugged: The Judicial Integration of the Deep South, 1978, The Oklahoma Evidence Handbook, 1979, Read's Florida Evidence, 2 vols., 1987; contbr. articles to profl. jours. Mem. ABA (sect. legal edn.), Am. Law Inst., Assn. Am. Law Schs., Order of Coif, Phi Kappa Phi. Home: 1215 Greenwich St Apt 4A San Francisco CA 94109-1508 Office: U Calif Hastings Coll Law 200 McAllister St San Francisco CA 94102-4978

READ, ROBERT LOGAN, real estate professional; b. Portland, Oreg., Sept. 27, 1938; s. Logan Acton Read and Florence May (Brosnan) Neuheisel. Cadet, U.S. Mil. Acad., West Point, N.Y., 1960-63; BA, U. Oreg., 1963-64, postgrad., 1968-70. Instr. math. Peace Corps, Indore, India, 1965-67; officer pub. affairs Peace Corps, San Francisco, 1967-68; anchorman, reporter, news dir. various NBC, CBS affiliates, Portland, Medford, Oreg., Reno, Nev., Santa Maria, Calif., 1970-77; realtor various cos., Portland, 1978-83; realtor Profls. 100, Portland, 1983—, assoc. broker. Producer, author, anchorman TV documentaries. Served with AUS, 1959-62. Ford Found. fellow U. Oreg., 1969; recipient John Swett award Calif. Pub. Schs., 1976. Mem. Nat. Assn. Realtors, Oreg. Assn. Realtors, Wash. County Bd. Realtors (cert.), West Point Soc. of Oreg. (pres.). Democrat. Club: Bergfreunde Ski (Beaverton, Oreg.). Office: Profs. 100 Realtors Lincoln Tower 250 10260 SW Greenburg Rd Portland OR 97223

READE, ROBERT MELLOR, advertising consultant, retired convenience store executive; b. Elmhurst, Ill., Jan. 9, 1940; s. M.G. and Virginia A. (Mellor) R.; m. Carol Jean Coon, May 26, 1962; children: Christopher, Gregory. BA in Liberal Arts, U. Ariz., 1962. Charting mgr. Eller Outdoor Advt., Phoenix, 1964-69; sales mgr. Mullins Neon, Denver, 1969-70; pres. Gannett Outdoor Co. Ariz., Phoenix, 1970-84; sr. v.p. Gannett Outdoor Group, N.Y.C., 1984-85; sr. v.p. real estate and devel. Circle K Corp., Phoenix, 1985-86; pres., chief operating officer Circle K Internat., Phoenix, 1986-90; ret., 1990; cons. Outdoor Sys. Co., Phoenix, 1992—; bd. dirs. Western Savs. and Loan. Chmn. Phoenix chpt. Am. Humanics, 1983, Valley Youth Coalition, 1981, Phoenix City Bond Election, 1984; active Thunderbirds, 1978-83, Theodore council Boy Scouts Am., Community Council, Phoenix United Way, Camelback Mental Health Found. With USAR, 1963-69. Recipient U. Ariz. Alumni Appreciation award, 1975, 77, Slouaker award, 1977; Anti Defamation League Torch of Liberty award, 1981. Mem. Ariz. Safety Assn. (pres. 1981), Young Pres. Orgn., Outdoor Assn. Am., Inst. Outdoor Advt., Phoenix Advt. Club (pres. 1974), Rotary (pres. 1982).

REAGAN, GARY DON, lawyer; b. Amarillo, Tex., Aug. 23, 1941; s. Hester and Lois Irene (Marcum) R.; m. Nedra Ann Nash, Sept. 12, 1964; children: Marc, Kristi, Kari, Brent. AB, Stanford U., 1963, JD, 1965. Bar: N.Mex. 1965, U.S. Dist. Ct. N.Mex., 1965, U.S. Supreme Ct. 1986. Assoc. Smith & Ransom, Albuquerque, 1965-67; ptnr. Smith, Ransom, Deaton & Reagan, Albuquerque, 1967-68, Williams, Johnson, Houston, Reagan & Porter, Hobbs, N.Mex., 1968-77, Williams, Johnson, Reagan, Porter & Love, Hobbs, 1977-82; sole practice, Hobbs, 1982—; city atty. City of Hobbs, 1978-80; City of Eunice, N.M., 1980—; instr. N.Mex. Jr. Coll. and Coll. of S.W., Hobbs, 1978-84. Mayor, City of Hobbs, 1972-73, 76-77, city commr., 1970-78; pres., dir. Jr. Achievement of Hobbs, 1974-85; pres., trustee Landsun Homes, Inc., Carlsbad, N.Mex., 1972-84; trustee Lydia Patterson Inst., El Paso, Tex., 1972-84, N.Mex. Conf. United Meth. Ch., 1988—, Coll. of S.W., Hobbs, 1989—; chmn. County Democratic Com., 1983-85. Mem. ABA, State Bar N.Mex. (coms. 1989—, v.p. 1992-93, pres.-elect 1993—), Lea County Bar Assn. (pres. 1976-77), Hobbs C. of C. (v.p. 1986-87, pres. 1989-90), Rotary (pres. Hobbs 1985-86), Hobbs Tennis (pres. 1974-75, state senator, 1993—). Home: 200 E Eagle Dr Hobbs NM 88240-5323 Office: 501 N Linam St Hobbs NM 88240-5715

REAGAN, JANET THOMPSON, psychologist, educator; b. Monticello, Ken., Sept. 15, 1945; d. Virgil Joe and Carrie Mae (Alexander) Thompson; m. Robert Barry Reagan, Jr., Aug. 7, 1977; children: Natalia Alexandria, Robert Barry. B.A. in Psychology, Berea Coll., 1967; Ph.D. in Psychology, Vanderbilt U., 1972. Mgr. research and eval. Nashville Mental Health Center, 1971-72; mgr. eval. Family Health Found., New Orleans, 1973-74; asst. prof. dept. health systems mgmt. Tulane U., New Orleans, 1974-77; dir. eval. Project Heavy West, Los Angeles, 1977-78; asst. prof. health adminstrn. Calif. State U.-Northridge, 1978-83, assoc. prof., director health adminstrn., 1983-87, prof., dir. health adminstrn., 1987—; cons. in field. Mem. Am. Pub. Health Assn., Am. Coll. Health Care Adminstrn., Assn. Health Svcs. Rsch., Am. Coll. Health Care Execs. (com. on higher edn. 1987, chmn. 1991), Assn. Univ. Programs in Health Adminstrn. (task force on undergrad. edn. 1985-90, chn.n. 1988-90), Psi Chi, Phi Kappa Phi. Mem. editorial adv. bd. Jour. of Long Term Care Administrn.; contbr. articles to profl. jours., papers to profl. assns. Home: 9354 Encino Ave Northridge CA 91325-2414 Office: Calif State U Dept Health Sci Northridge CA 91330

REAGAN, NANCY DAVIS (ANNE FRANCIS ROBBINS), volunteer, wife of former President of U.S.; b. N.Y.C., July 6, 1923; d. Kenneth and Edith (Luckett) Robbins; step dau. Loyal Davis; m. Ronald Reagan, Mar. 4, 1952; children: Patricia Ann, Ronald Prescott; stepchildren: Maureen, Michael. BA, Smith Coll.; LLD (hon.), Pepperdine U., 1983; LHD (hon.), Georgetown U., 1987. Contract actress, MGM, 1949-56; films include The Next Voice You Hear, 1950, Donovan's Brain, 1953, Hellcats of the Navy, 1957; Author: Nancy, 1980; formerly author syndicated column on prisoner-of-war and missing-in-action soldiers and their families; author: (with Jane Wilkie) To Love a Child, (with William Novak) My Turn: The Memoirs of Nancy Reagan, 1989. Civic worker, visited wounded Viet Nam vets., sr. citizens, hosps. and schs. for physically and emotionally handicapped children, active in furthering foster grandparents for handicapped children program; hon. nat. chmn. Aid to Adoption of Spl. Kids, 1977; spl. interest in fighting alcohol and drug abuse among youth: hosted first ladies from around the world for 2d Internat. Drug Conf., 1985; hon. chmn. Just Say No Found., Nat. Fedn. of Parents for Drug-Free Youth, Nat. Child Watch Campaign, President's Com. on the Arts and Humanities, Wolf Trap Found. bd. of trustees, Nat. Trust for Historic Preservation, Cystic Fibrosis Found., Nat. Republican Women's Club; hon. pres. Girl Scouts of Am. Named one of Ten Most Admired Am. Women, Good Housekeeping mag., ranking #1 in poll, 1984, 85, 86; Woman of Yr. Los Angeles Times, 1977; permanent mem. Hall of Fame of Ten Best Dressed Women in U.S.; recipient humanitarian awards from Am. Camping Assn., Nat. Council on Alcoholism, United Cerebral Palsy Assn., Internat. Ctr. for Disabled; Boys Town Father Flanagan award; 1986 Kiwanis World Service medal; Variety Clubs Internat. Lifeline award; numerous awards for her role in fight against drug abuse. Address: 11000 Wilshire Blvd Los Angeles CA 90024

REAGAN, RONALD WILSON, former President of United States; b. Tampico, Ill., Feb. 6, 1911; s. John Edward and Nelle (Wilson) R.; m. Jane Wyman, Jan. 25, 1940 (div. 1948); children: Maureen E., Michael E.; m. Nancy Davis, Mar. 4, 1952; children: Patricia, Ronald. AB, Eureka Coll., 1932. Gov. State of Calif., 1967-74; businessman, rancher, commentator on public policy, 1975-80, Pres. of U.S., 1981-89. Sports announcer, motion picture and TV actor, 1932-66. Author: Where's The Rest of Me?, Speaking My Mind: Selected Speeches, 1989, An American Life: The Autobiography, 1990. Served as capt. USAAF, 1942-45. Mem. Screen Actors Guild (pres. 1947-52, 59), Tau Kappa Epsilon. Republican. Address: Fox Plaza 2121 Ave of the Stars 34th fl Los Angeles CA 90067

REAL, MANUEL LAWRENCE, federal judge; b. San Pedro, Calif., Jan. 27, 1924; s. Francisco Jose and Maria (Mansano) R.; m. Stella Emilia Michalik, Oct. 15, 1955; children: Michael, Melanie Marie, Timothy, John Robert. B.S., U. So. Calif., 1944, student fgn. trade, 1946-48; LL.B., Loyola Sch. Law, Los Angeles, 1951. Bar: Calif. 1952. Asst. U.S. Atty.'s Office, Los Angeles, 1952-55; pvt. practice law San Pedro, Calif., 1955-64; U.S. atty. So. Dist. Calif., 1964-66; judge U.S. Dist. Ct. (cen. dist.) Calif., L.A., 1966—, now chief judge. Served to ensign USNR, 1943-46. Mem. Am., Fed., Los Angeles County bar assns., State Bar Calif., Am. Judicature Soc., Chief Spl. Agts. Assn., Phi Delta Phi, Sigma Chi. Roman Catholic. Club: Anchor (Los Angeles). Office: US Dist Ct 312 N Spring St Los Angeles CA 90012-4701*

REARDANZ, LESLIE ELMER, III, lawyer; b. Urbana, Ill., Aug. 22, 1965; s. Leslie Elmer II and Eileen Ann (Gondolfi) R.; m. Diane Elizabeth Crowley, Nov. 17, 1990. BA, U. Calif., Davis, 1987; JD, Southwestern U. Sch. Law, L.A., 1990. Bar: Calif. 1990; U.S. Dist. Ct., 1990; U.S. Ct. Mil. Appeals. Law clk. Sacramento Army Depot, 1985-86, Selvin Weiner & Ruben, L.A., 1988; summer assoc. Lynberg & Watkins, L.A., 1989, assoc., 1990-91; lt. JAGC, USN, 1991—. Mem. Rep. Presdl. Task Force, Washington, 1990—; active Spl. Olympics, Davis, 1985—; mem. Rep. Nat. Com., 1988—. Recipient Am. Jurisprudence Book award, 1989, Exceptional Achievement award Southwestern Law Sch., 1989. Mem. ABA, Calif. Bar Assn., Calif. Young Lawyers Assn., Am. Soc. Internat. Law, Ctr. for Study of Presidency, Acad. Polit. Sci. Republican. Roman Catholic. Office: USN Naval Sta Naval Legal Svc Office San Diego CA 92136-5138

REARDEN, CAROLE ANN, clinical pathologist, educator; b. Belleville, Ont., Can., June 11, 1946; d. Joseph Brady and Honora Patricia (O'Halloran) R. BSc, McGill U., 1969, MSc, MDCM, 1971. Diplomate Am. Bd. Pathology, Am. Bd. Immunohematology and Blood Banking. Resident and fellow Children's Meml. Hosp., Chgo., 1971-73; resident in pediatrics U. Calif., San Diego, 1974, resident then fellow, 1975-79, dir. histocompatability and immunogenetics lab., asst. prof. pathology, 1979-86, assoc. prof., 1986-92, prof., 1992—, head div. lab. medicine, 1989—; prin. investigator devel. monoclonal antibodies to erythroid antigens. Contbr. articles to profl. jours. Mem. Mayor's Task Force on AIDS, San Diego, 1983. Recipient Young Investigator Rsch. award NIH, 1979; grantee U. Calif. Cancer Rsch. Coordinating Com., 1982, NIH, 1983. Mem. Am. Assn. Pathologists, Am. Fed. Clin. Rsch., Am. Soc. Hematology, Am. Assn. Blood Banks (com. organ transplantation and tissue typing 1982-87), Am. Soc. Histocompatibility and Immunogenetics, Am. Soc. Transplant Physicians. Office: U Calif San Diego Dept Pathology 0612 9500 Gilman Dr La Jolla CA 92093-0001

REASER, RICHARD LEE, small business owner, consultant, engineer; b. Detroit, Dec. 28, 1932; s. Alpha Burrell and Elsie Jane (Parrish) R.; m. Kathryn Joan Britten, June 11, 1955; children: Richard Lee Jr., Ruth Jane, Ann Marie Firth, Ellen Rose Reaser Choi. BSEE, Mich. State U., East Lansing, 1955; BS in Engring., UCLA, Westwood, 1958. Program mgr. Hughes Aircraft Co., Culver City, Calif., 1955-88; owner Svc. Unltd., L.A., 1983—. Secretary Aid Assn. for Luths., Inglewood, Calif., 1960—; bd. dirs. L.A. Luth. High Sch., 1964-70; pres. So. Calif./So. Nev. Fedn. Aid Assn. for Luths., 1980-82; adminstr. Ladera Ch. of the Brethren, L.A., 1990—. State of Mich. scholar, 1951-55, Square D Co. scholar, 1954-55; recipient MS fellowship Hughes Aircraft Co. Mem. IEEE, Am. Inst. Profl. Book Keepers, Southern Calif. Genealogy Soc., Greater South Bay Computer User Group, L.A. West Side Genealogy Soc. (publicity com. 1991—), L.A. Computer Soc. (coord. 1989—), Hughes PC Users Group (editor 1988—), Hughes Aircraft Retiree Assn. (bd. dirs. L.A. chpt. 1988—), Phi Kappa Phi, Pi Mu Epsilon, Tau Beta Pi, Eta Kappa Nu. Republican. Home and Office: 5611 S Sherbourne Dr Los Angeles CA 90056-1318

REAVES, GIBSON, astronomer, astronomy educator; b. Chgo., Dec. 26, 1923; m. Mary Craig Kerr, Apr. 2, 1955; 1 child, Benjamin Kerr. BA in Astronomy, U. Calif., L.A., 1947; PhD in Astronomy, U. Calif., Berkeley, 1952. Mem. faculty U. So. Calif., L.A., 1952—; prof. astronomy U. So. Calif., L.A., 1965—. With C.E., U.S. Army, 1942-46, PTO. Fellow AAAS, Royal Astron. Soc.; mem. Am. Astron. Soc., Astron. Soc. Pacific, Internat. Astron. Union; assoc. meritus Lowell Observatory. Office: U So Calif Dept Astronomy Los Angeles CA 90089-1342

REAVEY, WILLIAM ANTHONY, III, lawyer; b. Springfield, Mass., Dec. 27, 1944; s. William A. Jr. and Deborah M. (Clancy) R.; Jacqueline R. Beauvais, Sept. 2, 1967; children: Patrick, Kevin, Brian, Michael. BS, USAF Acad., 1966; MA, Yale U., 1968, JD, 1976. Bar: Calif. 1976. Assoc. Latham & Watkins, Newport Beach, Calif., 1976-81; ptnr. Aylward, Kintz & Stiska, San Diego, 1981-87, Lillick & McHose, San Diego, 1987-90, Pillsbury, Madison & Sutro, San Diego, 1991—. Bd. dirs. Am. Liver Found., San Diego, 1991, Kind Found., San Diego, 1992, San Diego Comml. Indsl. Coun. Bldg. Industry Assn., 1992. Capt. USAF, 1966-73, Vietnam. Decorated Bronze Star. Mem. ABA. Roman Catholic. Home: 10515 Livewood Way San Diego CA 92131 Office: Pillsbury Madison & Sutro 101 W Broadway Ste 1800 San Diego CA 92101

REAVILL, DAVID WILLIAM, financial investment company executive; b. Los Angeles, Sept. 18, 1948; s. William Arthur and Marian Elizabeth (Stocks) R.; m. Karen McDonnell, Mar. 6, 1993. BA, Westmont Coll., 1971; MA, U. Calif., Santa Barbara, 1978, Calif. State U., Los Angeles, 1988. Registered fin. & ops. prin., gen. securities prin., mcpl. securities prin. Assoc. prof. U. Calif., Santa Barbara, 1975-78; pres. First Los Angeles Securities, 1979-86; cons. Wedbush Securities, Los Angeles, 1986-87; regional dir. Fidelity Investments, Los Angeles, 1988—. TV broadcaster KWHY-TV, 1980-85, KSCI-TV, 1981-83; commentator Am. Radio Network, 1985-86; editor-in-chief Univ. Times newspaper, 1987. Mem. County Art Mus., Los Angeles, 1979-88. Mem. Nat. Assn. Securities Dealers, Securities Industry Assn., Fin. Mgrs. Assn., Greater L.A. Zoo Assn., Sunset Hills Country Club (Thousand Oaks, Calif.). Office: Fidelity Investments 811 Wilshire Blvd Ste 1675 Los Angeles CA 90017

REAVIS, ROBERT ARTHUR, software engineer, consultant; b. Fresno, Calif., Mar. 23, 1949; s. Glynn Martin and Meredith Elizabeth (Henry) R.; m. Carol Sue Neider, June 30, 1973; children: Richard Alan, Renee Alyssa. AA, Fresno City Coll., 1969; BS in Electronic Engring., Calif. Poly. State U., 1972; postgrad, Nat. U., 1992—. Mem. tech. staff Hughes Aircraft Co., Culver City, Calif., 1972-77; sr. programmer analyst Link div. Singer Corp., Sunnyvale, Calif., 1977-78; engring. supr. Applied Tech. div. Litton Systems, Inc., San Jose, Calif., 1978-91; v.p. engring. also bd. dirs. Inter Bus. Tech., San Jose, 1983-87, corp. sec., 1985-87; owner Warm Springs Computer Works, Fremont, Calif., 1981—; sr. software engr. Kaiser Electronics, San Jose, 1991-93. Elder Irvington Presbyn. Ch., Fremont, 1982-87, pres. 1985-87. Mem. IEEE, Assn. of Old Crows. Republican.

REAVIS, THEODORE EDWARD, training and organization development consultant; b. Valhalla, N.Y., Nov. 2, 1937; s. Lawrence Edward and Theodosia Cordelia (Madison) R.; m. Geraldine Rita Le Boeuf, July 3, 1964. BA, Va. State U., 1962; MA, San Francisco State U., 1970. Orgn. devel. specialist Kaiser Aluminum & Chem., Oakland, Calif., 1969-72; assoc. dir. orgn. research & devel. Kaiser Permanente, Oakland, 1972-79; mgr. coll. relations Kaiser Aluminum & Chem., Oakland, 1979-81; cons. training and orgn. devel. Berkeley, Calif., 1981-82; mgr. training and orgn. devel. Kaiser Permanente Med. Ctr., Oakland, 1982—; mem. faculty J. F. Kennedy U., Walnut Creek, Calif. 1991-93; cons. in field. Mem. Mayor's Task Force on Employment and Training, Oakland, 1983; bd. mgrs. YMCA, 1992. Recipient Cert. of Appreciation Nat. Urban League, N.Y., 1971-72, Mayor's Council on Youth Opportunity, Oakland, 1970. Democrat.

RECHARD, OTTIS WILLIAM, mathematics and computer science educator; b. Laramie, Wyo., Nov. 13, 1924; s. Ottis H. and Mary (Bird) R.; m. Dorothy Lee Duble, Nov. 19, 1943; children—Katherine L. (Mrs. Larry V. Baxter), Carol G. (Mrs. David P. Reiter), Nancy L. (Mrs. William Moore), Elizabeth A. B.A., U. Wyo., 1943; postgrad., U. Calif., Los Angeles, 1943; M.A., U. Wis., 1946, Ph.D., 1948. Instr. U. Wis., 1948; instr., asst. prof. Ohio State U., 1948-51; staff mem. Los Alamos (N.Mex.) Nat. Lab., 1951-56; prof., dir. computing ctr. Wash. State U., Pullman, 1956-68; prof., chmn. dept. computer sci. Wash. State U., 1963-76, prof., dir. systems and computing, 1968-70; prof. math. and computer scis. U. Denver, 1976—, dir. computing services, 1976-79; vis. prof., chmn. dept. computer sci. U. Wyo., 1986-87; cons. NSF, Idaho Nuclear Corp., Los Alamos Nat. Lab.; program dir. computer sci. program NSF, 1964-65, chmn. adv. panel on instl. computing facilities, 1969-70. Mem. Los Alamos Sch. Bd., 1954-56; mem. Pullman Sch. Bd., 1967-74; Trustee, past pres. Westminster Found., Synod Wash.-Alaska. Served to 1st lt. USAAF, 1943-45. Decorated Order of Leopold II Belgium). Fellow AAAS; mem. Assn. for Computing Machinery, Am. Math. Soc., Math. Assn. Am., IEEE Computer Soc., Soc. Indsl. and Applied Math., AAUP, Phi Beta Kappa, Sigma Xi, Phi Kappa Phi. Presbyn. (elder). Club: Rotarian. Home: Rt 3 Box 369 Calder ID 83808 also: 6980 E Girard Ave # 405 Denver CO 80224

RECHTIN, EBERHARDT, aerospace educator; b. East Orange, N.J., Jan. 16, 1926; s. Eberhardt Carl and Ida H. (Pfarrer) R.; m. Dorothy Diane Denebrink, June 10, 1951; children: Andrea C., Nina, Julie Anne, Erica, Mark. B.S., Calif. Inst. Tech., 1946, Ph.D. cum laude, 1950. Dir. Deep Space Network, 1949-67; asst. dir. Calif. Inst. Tech. Jet Propulsion Lab., 1949-67; dir. Advanced Research Projects Agy., Dept. Def., 1967-70, prin. dep. dir. def. research and engring., 1970-71, asst. sec. def. for telecommunications, 1972-73; chief engr. Hewlett-Packard Co., Palo Alto, Calif., 1973-77; pres., chief exec. officer Aerospace Corp., El Segundo, Calif., 1977-87; prof. U. So. Calif., 1988—. Served to lt. USNR, 1943-56. Recipient major awards NASA, Dept. Def., USN; Disting. Alumni award Calif. Inst. Tech., 1984. Fellow AIAA (Robert H. Goddard Astronautics award 1991), IEEE (Alexander Graham Bell award 1977); mem. NAE, Tau Beta Pi. Home: 1665 Cataluna Pl Palos Verdes Estates CA 90274 Office: U So Calif University Park Los Angeles CA 90089-2565

RECKERS, PHILIP MERLE, accounting and business educator; b. Quincy, Ill., May 1, 1946; s. Merle Joseph and Frances Adelaide (Friye) R.; m. Patricia Ann Polchinski, May 12, 1979; children: Brian, Colleen, Ashley. BS, Quincy Coll., 1968; MBA, Washington U., St. Louis, 1972; PhD, U. Ill., 1978. Asst. prof. U. Md., College Park, 1976-80; assoc. prof. Ariz. State U., Tempe, 1980-83, prof. acctg. and bus., 1983—. Assoc. editor Advances in Acctg., 1985-92; mem. editorial bd. Auditing, 1987-92, Behavioral Rsch. in Acctg., 1992; contbr. articles to profl. jours. Coach, Little League, Tempe, 1989-92. With U.S. Army, 1970-72, Viet Nam. Peat Marwick Found. auditing rsch. grantee, 1976, 85, 89, 90, 91; Ernst and Young Found. tax rsch. grantee, 1991; Am. Acctg Assn. edn. rsch. grantee, 1982. Mem. Am. Acctg. Assn. Roman Catholic. Home: 2067 E Hermosa Dr Tempe AZ 85282 Office: Ariz State U Coll Bus Sch Accountancy BA267C Tempe AZ 85287

REDDEN, JAMES ANTHONY, federal judge; b. Springfield, Mass., Mar. 13, 1929; s. James A. and Alma (Cheek) R.; m. Joan Ida Johnson, July 13, 1950; children: James A., William F. Student, Boston U., 1951; LL.B., Boston Coll., 1954. Bar: Oreg. bar 1955. Since practiced in Medford; mem. firm Collins, Redden, Ferris & Velure, 1957-73; treas. State of Oreg., 1973-

77; atty. gen., 1977-80; U.S. dist. judge U.S. Dist. Ct. Oreg., Portland, 1980—. Chmn. Oreg. Pub. Employee Relations Bd.; mem. Oreg. Ho. of Reps., 1963-69, minority leader, 1967-69. With AUS, 1946-48. Mem. ABA, Mass. Bar Assn., Oreg. State Bar. Lodge: KC. Office: US Dist Ct 612 US Courthouse 620 SW Main St Portland OR 97205-3023*

REDDIEN, CHARLES HENRY, JR., lawyer, corporate professional, consultant; b. San Diego, Aug. 27, 1944; s. Charles Henry and Betty Jane (McCormick) R.; m. Paula Gayle, June 16, 1974; 1 child, Tyler Charles. BSEE, U. Colo., Boulder, 1966; MSEE, U. So. Calif., 1968; JD, Loyola U., L.A., 1972. Bar: Calif. 1972, Colo. 1981, U.S. Dist. Ct. 1981. Mgr., Hughes Aircraft Co., 1966-81; pvt. practice, 1972—; pres., broker R&D Realty Ltd., 1978-91; mem. spl. staff, co-dir. tax advantage group OTC Net Inc., 1981-82; pres., chmn. Heritage Group Inc., investment banking holding co., 1982-84, Plans and Assistance Inc., mgmt. cons., 1982-83, Orchard Group Ltd., investment banking holding co., 1982-84, J.W. Gant & Assocs., Inc., investment bankers, 1983-84; mng. ptnr., chief exec. officer J.W. Gant & Assocs., Ltd., 1984-85; chmn. bd. Kalamath Group Ltd., 1985-87, Heritage group Ltd. Investment Bankers, 1985-87; dir. Virtusonics Corp., 1985-92; v.p., dir. Heritage Fin. Planners Inc., 1982-83; pres., chmn. PDN Inc., 1987-89; pub., exec. v.p., dir. World News Digest Inc., 1987-90, LeisureNet Entertainment, Inc., 1989-90; chief exec. officer, Somerset Group Ltd., 1988-93, Inland Pacific Corp., 1989-91, World Info. Network, Inc., 1990-92, pres., CEO, chmn., Europa Cruises Corp., 1992—; CEO, chmn. Casino World Inc., 1993—. Recipient Teaching Internship award, 1964. Mem. Calif. Bar Assn., Nat. Assn. Securities Dealers, IEEE (chmn. U. Colo. chpt. 1965), Am. Inst. Aero. and Astronautical Engrs., Phi Alpha Delta, Tau Beta Pi, Eta Kappa Nu. Contbr. articles to profl. jours. Office: 2305 E Arapahoe Rd Ste 200 Littleton CO 80122-1538

REDDING, GREGORY J., pediatric respiratory specialist, medical researcher, educator; b. Patuxent River, Md., Dec. 8, 1948; s. Lester Allen and Leta Eileen (James) R. BA, U. Calif., La Jolla, 1970; MD, Stanford U., 1974. Diplomate Am. Bd. Pediatrics. Pediatric resident Harbor Gen. Hosp.-UCLA, Torrance, Calif., 1974-77; pediatric pulmonary fellow U. Colo. Sch. Medicine, Denver, 1977-80; asst. prof. pediatrics U. Wash. Sch. Medicine, Seattle, 1980-86, assoc. prof. pediatrics, 1986—, dir. pediatric pulmonary tng. ctr., 1986—; dept. head pulmonary medicine Children's Hosp. and Med. Ctr., Seattle, 1980—, dir. pulmonary sect., 1980—, med. dir., respiratory care dept., 1980—. Contbg. author: (book) Pediatric Pulmonology, 1992; co-editor: (textbook) With Chronic Lung Disease Practice of Pediatrics, 1980-85; editor: (monograph) The Pediatric Airway, 1984. Mem. Cystic Fibrosis Found., 1988—, chmn. profl. edn. com. 1990-92, Am. Heart Assn., 1988-91; exec. bd. mem Am. Lung Assn. Wash. NIH grantee, 1987-92, Bureau of Maternal and Child Health grantee, 1986—; recipient Nat. Rsch. Svc. award NIH, 1979. Mem. Am. Thoracic Soc. (chmn. pediatrics 1990-93), Soc. Critical Care, Soc. Pediatric Rsch., Am. Soc. Respiratory Care, Wash. Thoracic Soc. (pres. 1989-91)., Office: Children's Hosp and Med Ctr Box C5371 4800 Sand Point Way NE Seattle WA 98105

REDDY, NAGENDRANATH K., biochemist, researcher; b. Bangalore, India, Nov. 18, 1937; came to U.S., 1968; s. K. Rami and K. (Gnanamma) R.; m. Saraswati K., May 11, 1967; children: Kalpana, Sandip. BS, SRI Venkateswara U., Andhra, India, 1957; MS, U. Saugor, Madhya Pradesh, India, 1959; PhD, Indian Inst. Sci., Bangalore, 1971. Jr. research asst. Nat. Dairy Research Inst., Bangalore, 1959-60; sr. research asst. Indian Inst. Sci., Bangalore, 1965-68; research assoc. Roswell Park Meml. Inst., Buffalo, 1968-73; asst. prof. U. Cin., 1975-80; asst. prof. research biochemistry U. So. Calif., L.A., 1980—. Editor: Fibrinolysis, 1980; contbr. articles to profl. jours. Recipient Research Career Devel. award NIH, 1978. Mem. AAAS, Am. Soc. Biol. Chemists. Home: 3402 S Punta Del Este Dr La Puente CA 91745-6634

REDDY, RAM KADIRI, electronics executive; b. Madras, India, Jan. 4, 1949; came to U.S., 1970; s. Venkata Kadiri and Seshamma (Kadiri) R.; m. Pratibha Kadiri, May 20, 1973; children: Aditya K., Meghana K. BSEE, Indian Inst. Tech., Madras, 1970; MEE, U. Wis., 1972. Sect. mgr. Am. Microsystems Inc., Santa Clara, Calif., 1977-82; pres. Proximity Designs Corp., Sunnyvale, Calif., 1982-85, Lotus Designs Corp., Sunnyvale, 1985-88, Silicon Logic, San Jose, Calif., 1988-90, Startech Semiconductor, San Jose, 1990—. Home: 18766 Cabernet Dr Saratoga CA 95070-3561

REDENTE, EDWARD FRANCIS, environmental engineer, educator; b. Derby, Conn., Feb. 18, 1951; s. Lawrence A. and Frances E. (Sorrentino) R.; m. Kyle Elizabeth Stubenvoll, June 9, 1973; children: Elizabeth F., Jessica G., Kate B. BA, Western Mich. U., 1972; MS, Colo. State U., 1974, PhD, 1980. Environ. engr. Utah Internat., Inc., San Francisco, 1974-76; rsch. assoc. Colo. State U., Ft. Collins, 1976-79, instr., 1979-80, asst. prof., 1980-84, assoc. prof., 1984-88, prof. dept. range sci., 1988—; pres. Redente and Assocs, Inc., Ft. Collins, 1986—. Author sci. reports; contbr. articles to profl. jours., chpts. to books. Deacon Ch. of Christ, Ft. Collins, 1985—; mem. Gov.'s Commn. on Mountain Scars, Denver, 1989-90. Grantee U.S. Dept. Energy, 1979-91, NSF, 1986-87, Nat. Park Svc., 1988—. Mem. Am. Soc. Surface Mining and Reclamation, Soc. Range Mgmt. (sec.-treas. 1989-90), Ecol. Soc. Am., Sigma Xi. Office: Colo State Univ Dept Range Sci Fort Collins CO 80523

REDFIELD, JOHN DUNCAN, computer programmer; b. Hackensack, N.J., Sept. 27, 1947; s. Daniel Smith and Shirley Carolyn (Gray) R. AA, San Bernardino Valley Jr. Coll., Colton, Calif., 1971, Westark C.C., Ft. Smith, Ark., 1984. Free-lance programmer Phoenix, 1975-78, San Bernardino, 1978-80, Ft. Smith, Ark., 1980-90, Las Vegas, Nev., 1990—. With USN, 1966-70, Vietnam. Mem. DAV (life), Mobile Riverine Forces Assn. Moravian/Presbyterian.

REDHEFFER, RAYMOND MOOS, mathematician, educator; b. Chgo., Apr. 17, 1921; s. Raymond L. and Elizabeth (Moos) R.; m. Heddy Gross Stiefel, Aug. 25, 1951; 1 son, Peter Bernard. S.B., MIT, 1943, S.M., 1946, Ph.D., 1948; DSc (hon.), U. Karlruhe, 1991. Rsch. assoc. MIT Radiation Lab., 1942-45, Rsch. Lab. of Electronics, 1946-48; instr. Harvard U., Radcliffe Coll., 1948-50; mem. faculty UCLA, 1950—, prof. math., 1960—; guest prof. Tech. U. Berlin, 1962, Inst. for Angewandte Math., Hamburg, 1966, Math. Inst. U. Karlsruhe, 1971-72, 81, 88, 91; U.S. sr. scientist Alexander von Humboldt Found., Karlsruhe, 1976, 85. Author: (with Ivan Sokolnikoff) Mathematics of Physics and Modern Engineering, 1958, (with Charles Eames) Men of Modern Mathematics, 1966, (with Norman Levinson) Complex Variables, 1970, Differential Equations, Theory and Applications, 1991, Introduction to Differential Equations, 1992; film author, animator, 1972-74; contbr. articles to profl. jours. Pierce fellow Harvard U., 1948-50; sr. postdoctoral fellow NSF, Göttingen, Germany, 1956; Fulbright rsch. scholar Vienna, 1957, Hamburg, 1961-62; recipient Disting. Teaching award UCLA Alumni Assn., 1969. Mem. Deutsche Akademie der Naturforscher (Leopoldina), Sigma Xi. Home: 176 N Kenter Ave Los Angeles CA 90049-2730 Office: UCLA Dept Mathematics 6224 Math Sci Bldg Los Angeles CA 90024

REDMOND, KELLY THOMAS, climatologist; b. Wausau, Wis., Jan. 5, 1952; s. Clarence James and Joyce Alice (Sagstetter) R. BS in Physics, MIT, 1974; MS in Meteorology, U. Wis., 1977, PhD in Meteorology, 1982. Asst. state climatologist Oreg. State U., Corvallis, 1982-84; state climatologist Oreg. State U., 1984-89; reg. climatologist Western Reg. Climate Ctr., Desert Rsch. Inst., Reno, Nev., 1989—, reg. climatologist, dep. dir., 1992—. Mem. Am. Assn. State Climatologists (pres. 1989-90). Home: 2570 Polk St Reno NV 89503-1328 Office: Western Reg Climate Ctr PO Box 60220 Reno NV 89506-0220

REDONDO, ANTONIO, physicist; b. Guatemala City, Guatemala, Dec. 10, 1948; came to U.S., 1968; s. Mariano and Paz (Muiño) R.; m. Shelby Lynn Dinteman, June 18, 1971; children: Tomás P., Michael D., Rebecca M. BS magna cum laude, Utah State U., 1971; MS, Calif. Inst. Tech., 1972, PhD, 1977. Asst. prof. physics U. de Los Andes, Mérida, Venezuela, 1977-78, assoc. prof. physics, 1978-80; rsch. assoc. Calif. Inst. Tech., Pasadena, 1980-83; mem. staff Los Alamos (N.Mex.) Nat. Lab., 1983—. Contbr. sci. articles to profl. jours. Woodrow Wilson fellow Calif. Inst. Tech., 1972, IBM Predoctoral fellow IBM Corp., 1975. Democrat. Office: Los Alamos Nat Lab Mail Stop D429 Los Alamos NM 87544

REECE, MONTE MEREDITH, lawyer, judge; b. Jackson, Tenn., May 29, 1945; s. Jerrel Rexford Sr. and Marjorie (Ricks) R.; m. Melanie Fleshman; children: Hugh, Bryan, Andrew, Jerrel, Rebecca. Student, La. State U., 1963-64, 66, La. Coll., 1964-65; LLB, Western State U., 1974. Atty. English & Marotta A.P.C., Downey, Calif., 1974-78; pvt. practice, 1978—; magistrate judge U.S. Dist. Ct. (ea. dist.) Calif., South Lake Tahoe, 1983—; judge pro tem El Dorado County Mcpl. Ct., South Lake Tahoe, 1983—; cons. assembly judiciary com., Sacramento, 1993. Advisor Tahoe Human Svcs., South Lake Tahoe, 1986—; pres. Sudden Infant Death syndrome, South Lake Tahoe, 1988—. With USNR, 1968-70, Vietnam. Mem. Fed. Magistrate Judges Assn., El Dorado County Search and Rescue (pres. 1989), Lions (pres. 1985—, Lion of Yr. 1988-89). Office: US Dist Ct PO Box 20000 3330 Lake Tahoe Blvd Ste 10 South Lake Tahoe CA 96151

REED, DALE DEVON, engineering executive; b. Veedersburg, Ind., July 22, 1931; s. Clyde and Aline (Jones) R.; m Donna Ellen Bartley, Apr. 16, 1955; children, Katherine, Richard, Ann. BS in Engring., Purdue U., 1953. Engr. John Deere, Waterloo, Iowa, 1953-54; lt. U.S. Army Engrs., 1954-56; field engr. LeTourneau Westinghouse, Peoria, Ill., 1956-62; pres. Blakemore Equipment, Oakland, Calif., 1962-66, Buran Equipment Co., San Leandro, Calif., 1966-84; Buran and Reed Inc. Buram and Reed Inc., San Leandro, 1984—; bd. dirs. Civic Bank Corp., Oakland. Planning commr. City of San Leandro, 1984—; dir. Goodwill of East Bay, Oakland, 1988—, Humana Hosp. of San Leandro, 1986—; pres. San Leandro Scholarship Fund, 1990—. Mem. San Leandro C. of C. (officer 1986-87). Republican. Home: 1560 Daily Ct San Leandro CA 94577 Office: Buran and Reed Inc 1801 Adams Ave San Leandro CA 94577

REED, DALLAS JOHN, criminal justice educator; b. Missoula, Mont., May 23, 1929; s. Dallas J. and Bess (Rocek) R.; m. Joyce E. Clark, June 22, 1962; children: Steven P., Pamela J., Allison E. BA, U. Mont., 1951, MA, 1955; PhD, U. Minn., 1968; postgrad., Rutgers, 1973. Instr. sociology U. Mont., Missoula, 1959-61; instr. to assoc. prof. sociology Idaho State U., Pocatello, 1961-70; exec. dir. West Area Alcohol Edn. and Tng. Program Inc., NIAAA, Reno, Nev., 1975-77; assoc. prof. sociology U. Nev., Las Vegas, 1970-75, assoc. prof. criminal justice, 1977-90; vis. prof. Jacksonville (Ala.) State U., 1990-91. Treas. bd. dirs. Community Action Against Rape, Las Vegas, Nev., 1984-90; chmn.bd. dir. Nevada State Advisory on Alcohol and Drug Abuse, 1976-77; capt. U.S. Army, 1951-53. Nevada Div. Alcoholism fellow, 1973. Mem. Am. Sociol. Assn., Acad. Criminal Justice Scis., Am. Correctional Assn., Am. Soc. Criminology, Nev. Arbitration Assn. (charter mem.), Phi Kappa Phi, Phi Lambda Alpha, Alpha Kappa Delta, Pi Gamma Mu.

REED, DAVID GEORGE, entrepreneur; b. Alameda, Calif., July 19, 1945; s. David Francis and Anna Amelia Vangeline (Paulson) R.; m. Marianne Louise Watson, Apr. 7, 1971 (div. June 1975); m. Michele Ann Hock, June 28, 1989; 1 child, Casey Christine Michele. AA in Bus. Adminstrn., Diablo Valley Coll., Pleasant Hill, Calif., 1965; BA in Design and Industry, San Francisco State U., 1967, MBA in Mktg., 1969; cert. res. police officer, Los Medanos Coll., Pittsburg, Calif., 1977. Owner Western Furs, Ltd., Walnut Creek, Calif., 1963-72; mgmt. cons. Controlled Interval Scheduling, Rolling Hills Estates, Calif., 1972-73; owner Dave Reed's Texaco, Concord, Calif., 1973-76; mgmt. cons. Mgmt. Scheduling Systems, Houston, 1974-76, Thomas-Ross Assocs., Mercer Island, Wash., 1972-82; plant mgr. Bonner Packing, Morgan Hill, Calif., 1981; mfg. engr. Systron Donner, Concord, 1982-84, Beckman Instruments, San Ramon, Calif., 1984-90; owner Dave Reed & Co. Water Ski Sch., White Water Rafting, Pittsburg, Calif., 1987—, Dave Reed & Co., design, market, mfg. Contender boats, Pittsburg, 1976—; lectr. wildlife mgmt. Dave Reed & Co., Pittsburg, 1965—, lectr. mgmt. seminars, 1982—; coach Japanese Water Ski Team, Bluff Water Ski Club, Tokyo, 1984; fin. mgr. Japanese investors Dave Reed & Co., Pittsburg, 1986—. Res. dep. sheriff Contra Costa County Sheriff's Dept., Martinez, Calif., 1977-80. With U.S. Army, 1969-71, Vietnam. Recipient Gold medal internat. freestyle wrestling Sr. Olympics, Fullerton, Calif., 1983. Mem. Am. Water Ski Assn. (Calif. state water ski champion 1977, 86, western region water ski champion 1977, silver medal nat. water ski championships 1977), Nat. Wildlife Fedn., Can. Nature Fedn., Calif. Wildlife Fedn., Bay Area Tournament Assn. (chmn. 1968—), Diablo Water Ski Club (bd. dirs. 1968—). Republican. Home: PO Box 336 Chiloquin OR 97624

REED, DWIGHT THOMAS, brokerage executive, lawyer; b. Singapore, Feb. 25, 1955; came to U.S., 1960; s. Marvin C. Reed; 1 child, Josh Simmons. BA/BS, U. Calif., Berkeley, 1977, JD, 1981. Asst. export trade officer U.S. Fgn. Svc., Am. Embassys, Singapore, China, Japan, 1981-90; litigation dir. Horowitz and Reed, Berkeley, 1990-92; CEO Dwight Inc., Richmond, Calif., 1992—. Author: The Growth of Cocaine, 1981, The State Dept. for Blacks, 1992. Recipient Law Firm of Yr. award ACLU, Berkeley, 1991. Mem. Nat. Assn. Criminal Def. Lawyers, Nat. League Black Lawyers (Man of Yr. 1991), Calif. Trial Lawyers Assn. Democrat. Office: Dwight Inc 2224 Ohio Ave Richmond CA 94804-2706

REED, EDWARD CORNELIUS, JR., federal judge; b. Mason, Nev., July 8, 1924; s. Edward Cornelius Sr. and Evelyn (Walker) R.; m. Sally Torrance, July 14, 1952; children: Edward T., William W., John A., Mary E. BA, U. Nev., 1949; JD, Harvard U., 1952. Bar: Nev. 1952, U.S. Dist Ct. Nev. 1957, U.S. Supreme Ct. 1974. Atty. Arthur Andersen & Co., 1952-53; spl. dep. atty. gen. State of Nev., 1967-69; judge U.S. Dist. Ct. Nev., Reno, 1979—, now chief judge. Former vol. atty. Girl Scouts Am., Sierra Nevada Council, U. Nev., Nev. Agrl. Found., Nev. State Sch. Adminstrs. Assn., Nev. Congress of Parents and Teachers; mem. Washoe County Sch. Bd., 1956-72, pres. 1959, 63, 69; chmn. Gov.'s Sch. Survey Com., 1958-61; mem. Washoe County Bd. Tax Equalization, 1957-58, Washoe County Annexation Commn., 1968-72, Washoe County Personnel Com., 1973-77, chmn. 1973; mem. citizens adv. com. Washoe County Sch. Bond Issue, 1977-78, Sun Valley, Nev., Swimming Pool Com., 1978, Washoe County Blue Ribbon Task Force Com. on Growth, Nev. PTA (life); chmn. profl. div. United Way, 1978; bd. dirs. Reno Siver Sox, 1962-65. Served as staff sgt. U.S. Army, 1943-46, ETO, PTO. Mem. ABA (jud. adminstrn. sect.), Nev. State Bar Assn. (adminstrv. com. dist. 5, 1967-79, lien law com. 1965-78, chmn. 1965-72, probate law com. 1963-66, tax law com. 1962-65), Am. Judicature Soc. Democrat. Baptist. Office: US Dist Ct 5147 US Courthouse 300 Booth St Reno NV 89509-1316

REED, FRANK FREMONT, II, retired lawyer; b. Chgo., June 15, 1928; s. Allen Martin and Frances (Faurot) R.; m. Jaquelin Silverthorne Cox, Apr. 27, 1963; children: Elizabeth Matthiessen Mason, Laurie Matthiessen Stern, Mark Matthiessen, Jeffrey, Nancy, Sarah. Student Chgo. Latin Sch.; grad. St. Paul's Sch., 1946; A.B., U. Mich., 1952, J.D., 1957. Bar: Ill., 1958. Assoc. Byron, Hume, Groen & Clement, 1958-61, Marks & Clerk, 1961-63; pvt. practice law, Chgo., 1963-78; dir. Western Acadia (Western Felt Works), 1960-75, chmn. exec. com., 1969-71. Rep. precinct capt. 1972-78; candidate for 43d ward alderman, 1975; bd. dirs., sec. Chgo. Found. Theater Arts, 1959-64; vestryman St. Chrysostom's Ch., 1975-79, mem. ushers guild, 1964-79, chmn., 1976-78; bd. dirs. North State, Astor, Lake Shore Dr. Assn., 1975-78, pres. 1977-78; bd. dirs. Community Arts Music Assn. of Santa Barbara, 1984-93, treas. 1988-93; bd. dirs. Santa Barbara Arts Coun., 1987-89. Cpl. AUS, 1952-54. Mem. ABA, Ill. Bar Assn., Phi Alpha Delta, Racquet Club, Wausaukee Club (sec., dir. 1968-71, 92-) (Chgo.); Birnam Wood Golf Club (Santa Barbara, Calif.). Episcopalian. Author: History of the Silverthorn Family, 4 vols., 1982, Allen Family of Allen's Grove, 1983, Goddard and Ware Ancestors, 1987, Faurot Family, 1988. Contbr. articles to The Am. Genealogist, 1972-73, 76-77. Home: 1944 E Valley Rd Santa Barbara CA 93108-1428

REED, FRANK METCALF, bank executive; b. Seattle, Dec. 22, 1912; s. Frank Ivan and Pauline B. (Hovey) R.; student U. Alaska, 1931-32; B.A., U. Wash., 1937; m. Maxine Vivian McGary, June 11, 1937; children: Pauline Reed Mackay), Frank Metcalf. Vice pres. Anchorage Light & Power Co., 1937-42; pres. Alaska Electric & Equipment Co., Anchorage, 1946-50; sec., mgr. Turnagain, Inc., Anchorage, 1950-56; mgr. Gen. Credit Corp., Anchorage, 1957; br. mgr. Alaska SBA, Anchorage, 1958-60; sr. v.p. First Interstate Bank of Alaska, Anchorage, 1960-87, also dir., corp. sec.; dir. First Interstate Corp. of Alaska, pres., dir. Anchorage Broadcasters, Inc.; past pres., chmn. Microfast Software Corp.; ptnr. R.M.R. Co.; dir. Anchorage Light & Power Co., Turnagain, Inc., Alaska Fish and Farm, Inc., Life Ins. Co. Alaska, Alaska Hotel Properties, Spa Inc. Pres., Anchorage Federated Charities, Inc., 1953-54; mem. advisory bd. Salvation Army, 1948-58; mem. Alaska adv. bd. Hugh O'Brian Youth Found., 1987—; trustee Anchor Age Endowment Fund, 1988—, chmn., 1991; mem. City of Anchorage Planning Commn., 1956; mem. City of Anchorage Coun., 1956-57; police commr. Ter. of Alaska, 1957-58; chmn. City Charter Commn., 1958; mem. exec. com. Greater Anchorage, Inc., 1955-65; pres. Sch. Bd., 1961-64; mem. Gov.'s Investment adv. com., 1970-72; mem. Alaska State Bd. Edn.; mem. citizens adv. com. Alaska Meth. U.; chmn. Anchorage Charter Commn., 1975; apptd. by Mayor as co-chmn. charter rev. commn. Municipality of Anchorage, 1990; chmn. bldg. fund dr. Community YMCA, 1976—; bd. dirs., mem. exec. com. Arts Alaska, 1976-78; sec.-treas. Breakthrough, 1976-78; bd. dirs. Anchorage Civic Opera, 1978, Rural Venture Alaska, Inc.; bd. dirs Alaska Treatment Ctr., 1980-87, pres. 1985-86; trustee Marston Found., Inc., 1978, exec. dir. 1988; pres. Sunset Balloon Flights, Inc., Del Mar, Calif., 1990. Served as lt. USNR, 1942-46. Elected to Hall Fame, Alaska Press Club, 1969; named Outstanding Alaskan of Year Alaska C. of C., 1976, Alaskan of Yr., 1990, Outstanding Vol. in Philanthropy Alaska chpt. Nat. Soc. Fundraising Execs, 1991; recipient Community Svc. award YMCA, 1975-78. Mem. Am. Inst. Banking, Am. (exec. council 1971-72) Alaska (pres. 1970-71) bankers assns., Nat. Assn. State Bds. Edn. (sec.-treas. 1969-70), C. of C. U.S. (Western region legislative com.), Anchorage C. of C. (pres. 1966-67, dir.), Pioneers of Alaska, Navy League (pres. Anchorage council 1961-62). Clubs: Tower (life), San Francisco Tennis. Lodges: Lions (sec. Anchorage, 1953-54, dir. 1988, pres., 1962-63), Elks. Home: 1361 W 12th Ave Anchorage AK 99501-4252

REED, GERARD ALEXANDER, theology educator, history educator; b. Colorado Springs, Colo., Jan. 19, 1941; s. Paul Alexander and Lula (Taylor) R.; m. Roberta Kay Steininger, May 26, 1963. BA, So. Nazarene U., 1963; MA, Okla. U., 1964, PhD, 1967. Ordained to ministry Nazarene Ch., 1977. Asst. prof. So. Nazarene U., Bethany, Okla., 1966-68; prof. MidAm. Nazarene Coll., Olathe, Kans., 1968-82; prof., chaplain Point Loma Nazarene Coll., San Diego, 1982—. Contbr. articles to profl. publs. Parriott Found. fellow, 1964; summer seminar grantee NIH, 1979. Mem. Am. Maritain Assn., Am. Soc. Environ. History, Conf. of Faith and History, Wesleyan Theol. Soc., Western History Assn. Office: Point Loma Nazarene Coll 3900 Lomaland Dr San Diego CA 92106-2810

REED, HELEN BERNICE, artist; b. Watsonville, Calif., Dec. 22, 1917; d. Harry James and Loretta Elizabeth (Morgan) Aguirre; m. Clarence Varnick Reed, Sept. 8, 1944 (dec. Aug. 1988). Grad. high sch., Watsonville. Demonstrator Long Beach (Calif.) Art Assn., 1984; lectr., demonstrator Muckenthaler Cultural Ctr., Fullerton, Calif., 1984; juror Nat. Date Festival, Indio, Calif., 1987, Lakewood (Calif.) Art Guild, 1984; demonstrator San Bernardino (Calif.) Art Assn., 1984, Whittier (Calif.) Art Assn., 1984; art instr. Fullerton, 1967—. Exhibited in group shows with The Nat. Watercolor Soc., Stockholm, 1972, Farmington, N.Mex., Grants Pass, Oreg., Spokane, 1985, Am. Watercolor Soc., N.Y.C., 1979, Springville (Utah) Mus., 1983; art represented in books, 1986, 88. Recipient Strathmore Paper award Okla. Watercolor Soc., 1984, Arches Paper Cash award Watercolor West, 1984, Purchase award Tex. Fine Arts Assn., 1974. Mem. Watercolor West Transparent Watercolor Soc. (bd. dirs. 1979-84), Nat. Watercolor Soc. Republican.

REED, JAMES ANTHONY, hotel industry executive, consultant; b. Marion, Ohio, June 12, 1939; s. James E. and Sue (McCurdy) R. Student, Fla. State U., 1956-59, U. N.H., 1978. Food and beverage mgr. Caneel Bay Plantation, St. John, Virgin Islands, 1960-64; mgr. Mauna Kea Beach Hotel, Kamuela, Hawaii, 1964-72; v.p. C. Brewer & Co., Ltd., Honolulu, 1972-77, Dunfey Hotel Corp., Hampton, N.H., 1977-80, Marriott Hotels & Resorts, Calif., Hawaii and Asia, 1980-89; pres. The Reed Group, Irvine, Calif., 1989; gen. mgr. La Posada de Santa Fe, 1990-91, Hotel Santa Fe, 1991-93; pres. Reed Group, Santa Fe, 1993—; pres. Kilauea Volcano House Inc., Mackensie Hawaii Ltd., Augustine's Decor Spain; vice-chmn., bd. dirs. Picuris Pueblo Enterprises, cons. to Native Am. Tribes. Named Outstanding Young Men of Am., 1969. Mem. Calif. Thoroughbred Breeders Assn., Calif. Hotel Assn., Sch. Am. Rsch., Community Leaders of Am., Appaloosa Horse Club. Home and Office: 8111 Camino Del Oro La Jolla CA 92037

REED, JAMES EARL, fire department captain; b. San Francisco, Mar. 21, 1957; s. Arlen Earl and Louise (Gibbs) R.; m. Jody Lynn Bales, Feb. 14, 1976 (div. Aug. 1978); 1 child, Darci Lynn. Student, Casper Coll., 1989—. State cert. fire fighter I, II, III, state cert. fire svc. instr. I, state cert. fire prevention officer I. Shop worker, shop foreman, salesman Becker Fire Equipment, Casper, Wyo., 1975-78; safety equipment maintance Bell H2S Safety and Oilind Safety Engring., Casper, 1978-80; tchr. outreach program Casper Coll., 1988-90; owner operator J.R.'s Custom Hand Planted Signs, 1980-93; capt. Casper Fire Dept., 1978—; artist Images Studio, Casper, 1991—; instr. CPR courses Am. Heart Soc., ARC, 1980—; instr. SCBA courses, 1983-85. Active fund raisers City/County Fire Fighters Burn Fund, 1982, 84—, fund raisers Muscular Dystrophy Assn., 1981, 82, 85-89, fund raisers March of Dimes, 1984, 85, 87, fund raisers Casper Mountain Racers Youth Olympics, 1985-87, Casper Event Ctr.'s "Spl. Christmas for Spl. Kids," 1984-87. Named Firefighter of Yr. Casper Fire Dept., Casper Ladies Auxiliary, Am. Legion Regional and Post 2, 1984. Mem. Casper Fire Fighters Assn. (entertainment com. 1980—, exec. com. 1988-90), City County Fire Fighters Burn Fund (trustee 1985-86, treas. 1986-89, sec. 1989-91, pres. 1992—). Republican. Seventh-day Adventist. Home: 1847 Jim Bridger Casper WY 82604

REED, MARY LOU, state legislator; m. Scott Reed; children: Tara, Bruce. BA, Mills Coll. Mem. Idaho State Senate, 1985—; Senate Minority Leader; coord. Com. for Fair Rates. Democrat. Office: 10 Giesa Rd Coeur D Alene ID 83814

REED, NICHOLAS (RATHBURN), business executive; b. Virginia, Minn., Feb. 9, 1943; s. Lawrence Lester and Rose Ursula (Campagnale) R.; m. Gena Marie Hazelip, Mar. 5, 1983; 1 child, Dana. BS in Biology, Niagara U., 1966. Clin. rsch. assoc. Norwich (N.Y.)-Eaton Pharms., 1968-70; sr. clin. rsch. assoc. Merrell-Dow Pharms., Cin., 1971-85; cons. Clin. Rsch. Svcs., Grapevine, Tex., 1985-86; dir. field ops. Inst. Biol. Rsch. and Devel., Newport Beach, Calif., 1986-88; v.p., CFO Rsch. Mgmt. Assocs., Irvine, 1988-89; pres. Profl. Rsch. Network, Irvine, 1989—. Office: Profl Rsch Network 6 Venture Ste 206 Irvine CA 92718-3316

REED, PATRICK NORMAN, automobile industry executive; b. Aberdeen, Wash., Oct. 25, 1947; s. Charles William and Majory Francis (Borum) R.; m. Debra Gail Walker, Feb. 11, 1978; 1 child, Christopher. BS in Psychology, Wash. State U., 1972. V.p. sales. Mech. Ins. Assocs., Encino, Calif., 1984-86; pres. Reed Lombardi, Inc., Westlake Village, Calif., 1986-90, Chandler, Ariz., 1986-90; v.p. sales Western Nat. Warranty Corp., Scottsdale, Ariz., 1990—. Home: 3043 E Mallory Mesa AZ 85213 Office: Western Nat Warranty Corp 4141 N Scottsdale Rd Scottsdale AZ 85252

REED, RAY PAUL, engineering mechanics measurement consultant; b. Abilene, Tex., May 26, 1927; s. Raymond Roseman and Gladys Daisy (Reddell) R.; m. Mary Antoinette Wied, Oct. 7, 1950; children: Mary Kathryn, Patricia Lynn. BSME, Tex. A&M U., 1950; MS in Engring. Mechanics, U. Tex., 1958, PhD, 1966. Registered profl. engr., N.Mex., Tex. Rsch. engr. S.W. Rsch. Inst., San Antonio, 1950-54; rsch. scientist U. Tex., Austin, 1954-56; mem. tech. staff Sandia Nat. Labs., Albuquerque, 1956-61, rsch. fellow, 1961-66, disting. mem. tech. staff, 1966—. Author: manual on the use of thermocouples; contbr. numerous reports and articles on shock measurement and thermometry to profl. jours. With USNR, 1945-46, PTO. NIH grantee U. Tex., 1962-66. Mem. ASTM (chmn. com. 1985—), ASME, Sigma Xi. Office: Sandia Nat Labs Field Scis Dept PO Box 5800 Albuquerque NM 87185-5800

REED, REBECCA S., college activities administrator; b. Denver, Feb. 16, 1964. BA, U. Denver, 1987. Dir. program devel. Chicago Creek Rds., Inc., Idaho Springs, Colo., 1987-89; job placement coord., instr. Community Coll. Denver, 1989-91, dir. student activities, 1991—; coord. spl events Denver Art Mus., 1987—. Grantee Comprecare, 1988, Colo. State Programs of Excellence, 1992-93. Mem. Pub. Rels. Soc. Am., Colo. Assn. Job Devel. & Placement Individuals, Nat. Assn. Student Personnel Adminstrs. Office:

Community Coll Denver PO Box 173363 Campus Box 205 Denver CO 80217-3363

REED, ROBERT GEORGE, III, petroleum company executive; b. Cambridge, Mass., Aug. 9, 1927; s. Robert George and Marjorie B. Reed; m. Maggie L. Fisher, Mar. 22, 1974; children: Sandra McNickle, Valerie Sloan, Jonathan J., John-Paul. BA in Econs., Dartmouth Coll., 1949; AMP, Harvard U., 1970. Mktg. mgr. Tidewater Oil subs. Getty Oil Co., L.A., 1957-64; v.p. mktg. Cities Svc. Oil Co., Tulsa, 1964-72; exec. v.p. Tesoro Petroleum Corp., San Antonio, 1972-79; chmn. bd., chief exec. officer Clark Oil & Refining Corp., Milw., 1979-81, pres., chief exec. officer div. Apex Oil Co., St. Louis, 1981-85; chmn., pres., chief exec. officer Pacific Resources, Inc., Honolulu, 1985-92; bd. dirs. Alexander and Baldwin, Inc., Honolulu, BHP Petroleum Pty. Ltd., First Hawaiian Bank. With USN, 1945-46. Mem. Nat. Petroleum Refiners Assn., Nat. Petroleum Council, Hawaii C. of C. Clubs: Pacific, Plaza, Waialae Country. Office: Petroleum Americas Inc 733 Bishop St PO Box 3379 Honolulu HI 96842

REED, WILLIAM ARTHUR, aerospace company executive; b. Santa Monica, Calif., Jan. 2, 1947; s. Galen Wade and Dorothy Reed; m. Lynne Marie Thilberg, May 2, 1987. AA, Antelope Valley Coll., Lancaster, Calif., 1976; BS, Calif. State U., Dominquez Hills, 1978, MS, 1986. Requirements mgr. Lockheed Advanced Devel. Co., Burbank, Calif., 1978-84, procurement mgr., 1984-89, dir. material F117 program, 1989—. Sgt. U.S. Army, 1966-68, Vietnam. Mem. Lockheed Mgmt. Assn. Republican. Home: 4040 West Ave N Quartz Hill CA 93551

REEDER, RANDY MARCELLE, food products executive; b. Modesto, Calif., May 4, 1956; s. Gene and Betty Jo (Pipkin) R.; m. Teresa Reeder, Feb. 27, 1982; children: Tara, Natasha, Cescelly, Ryan. Student, Modesto Jr. Coll., 1976. Car washer Calif. 5 Minute Car Wash, Modesto, 1972-73; tire man Wayne Bayle Trucking, Penrose, Colo., 1974; with Nagel Landscaping, Modesto, 1974; janitor West Mart, Ceres, Calif., 1975; laborer Del Monte, Modesto, 1975, fork lift driver, 1976-79, fork lift mechanic, 1980-91, supr. lift shop, 1991—. Home: 309 Fortuna Ave Modesto CA 95354 Office: Del Monte 4000 Yosemite Blvd Modesto CA 95354-9726

REEDER, SAMUEL KENNETH, analytical laboratory executive; b. Vinita, Okla., July 25, 1938; s. Dwight Cecil and Melba Mae (Mattox) R.; m. Camille Augusta Goepfert, Aug. 17, 1959; children: Jerold, Jeanne, Jodi. BA, La Sierra Coll., Riverside, Calif., 1960; PhD, Mont. State U., 1971. Tchr. Seventh-day Adventist Schs., San Diego and Springfield, Org., 1961-66; chief scientist R&D Sunkist Growers, Inc., Ontario, Calif., 1971-79; lab. mgr. R&D Beatrice/Hunt-Wesson, Inc., Fullerton, Calif., 1979-90; v.p. tech. svcs. C.L. Tech., Inc., Corona, Calif., 1990—. Contbr. sci. papers to profl. jours. Trustee Ontario City Libr., 1976-80, pres. bd. trustees, 1978-80. Recipient Bank of Am. award, 1956. Mem. Nat. Food Processors Assn. (chmn. chemistry div. western lab. com. 1989-90), Am. Chem. Soc., Inst. Food Technologists, Assn. Ofcl. Analytical Chemists (assoc.). Seventh-day Adventist. Home: 3253 Crystal Ridge Cir Corona CA 91720-7943 Office: C L Tech Inc 280 N Smith Ave Corona CA 91720-1740

REED-GRAHAM, LOIS L., administrator, secondary education educator; b. Muscogee, Okla., Jan. 19, 1933; d. Louis G. and Bonnie (Hill) Reed; children: Harold Gibson, Kathryn Ann Graham. RN, San Diego County Hosp., 1953; BA, Calif. State U., Sacramento, 1972, MPA, 1978; postgrad., Calif. State U., Sacremento; EdD, U. Laverne. Tchr., adminstr., job developer CETA, Sacramento; bus. instr. Los Rios Community Coll., Sacramento; tchr. grade 6 Mark Hopkins Sch., Sacramento; acting adminstr. Fern Bacon Sch., Sacramento; adminstr. Sacramento City Schs.; tchr. grades 7,8, mentor tchr. Fern Bacon Sch., Sacramento; cons. Prentice Hall Pub. Co. Contbr. articles to profl. publs. Mem. Calif. State Fair Employment and Housing Commn. Mem. AAUW (bd. dirs., pres. Sacramento chpt. 1990), Nat. Assn. Univ. Women (pres.). Home: 7408 Toulon Ln Sacramento CA 95828-4641

REEDS, ROBERT TERRILL, construction executive; b. Montebello, Calif., Nov. 24, 1932; s. John William and Maxine (Keifer) R.; m. Elizabeth Isaacs, June 26, 1960; children: Judith, Leonard. BS in Mech. Enging., U. Calif., Berkeley, 1960; postgrad., Ind. U., 1960-62, UCLA, 1962-64. Registered profl. engr., Calif. Engr. RCA Corp., Indpls., 1960-63; quality control engr. Endevco Corp., Pasadena, Calif., 1963-67; quality control mgr. Raytheon Corp., Santa Ana, Calif., 1967-73; constrn. cons. Am. Inspection, Mission Viejo, Calif., 1974—; lectr. U. Calif., Irvine, Santa Ana Coll., Saddleback Coll., Irvine Coll., Orange Coast Coll., 1978—; speaker in field, 1978—. Columnist: Around the House, 1979-86; editor: (newsletter) The Inspector, 1977-84, 91—; co-editor: Home Maintenance, 1990, Home Time, 1990. Staff sgt. USAF, 1949-53. Named one of Top 50 Bus. Orange County Register, 1985. Mem. Calif. Real Estate Inspection Assn. (pres. 1979-80, bd. dirs. 1981-90, John Daly award 1989), Am. Soc. Home Inspectors (standards com. 1985-86, bylaws com. 1988-89, P. Monohan award 1990), Calif. Hist. Preservation, Nat. Hist. Preservation. Office: Am Inspection 26916 Pueblonuevo Dr Mission Viejo CA 92691

REENTS, SUE, state legislator. Mem. Idaho State Senate from dist. 19, 1989—. Home: 908 N 18th St Boise ID 83702

REES, LANE CHARLES, industrial relations consultant; b. Longview, Tex., June 23, 1951; s. Holly Elias and Charlene Elizabeth (Quin) R.; m. Brenda Faye Anderson, July 1, 1978; children: Brian Andrew, Lauren Catherine. BBA in Mgmt. magna cum laude, Tex. A&M U., 1973, MEd in Ednl. Adminstrn., 1978. Personnel rep. Tex. A&M U., College Sta., 1973-77; v.p. Brazos Gen. Svcs., Bryan, Tex., 1977-78; successively personnel office supr., wage and salary administrator, employee relations rep., sr. employee relations rep. ARCO, various cities, Tex., 1979-83; from sr. employee relations rep. to employee relations dir. ARCO, Anchorage and Kuparuk, Alaska, 1983-87; dir. employee relations ARCO, Prudhoe Bay, Alaska, 1987-90, dir. human resources dept. engring., 1990—; ptnr. Rees and Assocs., Anchorage and Tex., 1978—. Mem. editorial staff (jour.) Conference Leadership, 1978. Precinct committeeman Rep. Party of Alaska, Anchorage, 1988-90, v. chmn. 1993—; chmn. Dist. 8 Rep. Party, 1990-92, Dist. 10, 1992-93; mem. cen. com. State of Alaska, 1990—; chmn. utility regulatory commn. Municipality of Anchorage, 1989-91; mem., com. sec. United Meth. Communication Commn., Nashville, 1988—; evangelism chmn., mem. adv. coun. St. John United Meth. Ch., Anchorage, 1986-91, chmn. adminstrv. bd. 1991—; trustee Nat. Found. Evangelism, Lake Junaluska, N.C., 1988—; conf. lay leader Alaska Missionary Conf.-Meth. Ch., 1992—. Recipient Denman award Alaska Missionary Conf. of United Meth. Ch., 1989, Legis. citation State of Alaska, 1989. Mem. Acad. Mgmt., Tex. A&M U. Assn. Former Students (nat. councilman 1987-91), Am. Numismatic Assn., Alaska Soc. SAR (pres. 1989-90, trustee Nat. Soc. 1991—, Silver Good Citizenship award 1989), Phi Eta Simga, Phi Kappa Phi, Sigma Iota Epsilon (pres. 1972-73), Beta Gamma Sigma. Home: 2430 Nancy Cir Anchorage AK 99516-2635 Office: ARCO Alaska Inc PO Box 100360 Anchorage AK 99510-0360

REES, RAYMOND F., military officer; b. Pendleton, Oreg., Sept. 29, 1944; s. Raymond Emmett and Lorna Doone (Gemmell) R.; m. Karen Kristine Young, Nov. 1966 (div. Mar. 1974); children: Raymond Gordon, Christian Frederick; m. Mary Len Middleton, Dec. 30, 1977; 1 child, Carrie Evelyn. BS, U.S. Mil. Acad., 1966; JD, U. Oreg., 1976. Commd. 2d lt. U.S. Army, 1966; platoon leader, troop exec. officer, co. comdr. 3d Armored Cavalry Regiment, Bamberg, Fed. Republic Germany; resigned U.S. Army, 1973; with Oreg. Army Nat. Guard, 1973—, advanced through grades to maj. gen., 1990; asst. ops. officer Infantry Brigade; co. comdr. 2d Battalion, 162d Infantry, Corvallis, Oreg.; with 116th Armored Calvary Regiment, 1976-87; adjutant gen. Oreg. Army Nat. Guard, 1987-91; dir. Army N.G., 1991-92; vice chief N.G. Bur., Washington, 1992—. State rep. Hometown Heroes Project for Congl. Medal of Honor Soc.; bd. dirs. Oreg. Hist. Soc. Decorated Bronze Star. Mem. Adjutant Gen. Assn. U.S., Nat. Guart Assn. U.S., Assn. of U.S. Army, Oreg. Nat. Guard Assn., U.S. Armor Assn., Oreg. Bar Assn., Am. Legion, Rotary, Mil. Order World Wars, West Point Soc. Oreg., 101st Airborne Div. Assn., 116th Armored Cavalry Assn., 41st Infantry Div. Assn., Elks. Office: Chief N G Bur Attn NGB-ZB 2500 Army Pentagon Washington DC 20310-2500

REES, WILLIAM JAMES, dermatologist, consultant; b. Kansas City, Mo., July 13, 1922; s. John Archibald and Blanche Evelyn (Watson) R.; m. Marybeth Smith, Jan. 31, 1950; children: Virginia Lee, Diane Elizabeth, Carolyn Marie, Karen Jean, Mary Noel. BA, Rockhurst Coll., 1942; MD, St. Louis U., 1946; M in Pub. Health, U. Minn., 1950. Diplomate Am. Bd. Dermatology. Med. administrator Dept. of Army and Upjohn, Germany, Austria, U.S., 1952-61; clin. investigator Abbott Labs., North Chgo., Ill., 1961-63; resident in dermatology U. Calif. Med. Ctr., San Francisco, 1963-65; chmn. biomed. rsch. Stanford Rsch. Inst., Menlo Park, Calif., 1965-69; dir. life scis. Stanford Rsch. Inst., Zurich, Switzerland, 1969-71; asst. dir. Stanford Rsch. Inst., Washington, 1971-72; dir. internat. clin. rsch. G.D. Searle & Co., Chgo., 1972-83; dir. clin. rsch. Chemex Pharms., Denver, 1983-86; pres., mng. dir. Rhys Internat. Assocs., Edmonds, Wash., 1988—; cons. State of Calif. Div. Occupational Health, Berkeley, 1963-68; clin. instr. dermatology U. Calif. Med. Ctr., San Francisco, 1965-68, asst. prof., 1969-71. Col. U.S. Army, 1942-87. Mem. Am. Acad Dermatology (life, assoc.), Am. Acad. Med. Dirs., Am. Soc. Tropical Medicine and Hygiene, Am. Med. Soc. Vienna, Am. Pub. Health Assn., Assn. Mil. Dermatologists, Assn. of Mil. Surgeons U.S.; (charter) Am. Acad. Clin. Toxicology. Home: 550 Seamont Ln Edmonds WA 98020 Office: Rhys Internat Assocs 9792 Edmonds Way Ste 248 Edmonds WA 98020

REESE, ALBERT MOORE, tourism executive; b. Morgantown, W.Va.; s. Albert M. Reese; m. Susan Holt. BA, W.Va. U., 1954; MS in Communications, Boston U., 1958. Dir. pub. rels. United Way of San Diego County, 1968-74; v.p. pub. affairs San Diego Conv. and Visitors Bur., 1975-92. Chmn. San Diego County Quincentennial Commn.; bd. dirs. San Diego County unit Am. Cancer Soc., 1981—. Capt. USAF, 1954-56. Mem. Pub. Rels. Soc. Am. (pres. San Diego chpt. 1973, accredited), San Diego Press Club. Democrat. Episcopalian. Home: 5317 E Palisades Rd San Diego CA 92116-2047

REESE, GARY FULLER, librarian; b. Logan, Utah, Aug. 2, 1938; s. Perry Leland and Edith Mary (Fuller) R. BS, Brigham Young U., 1959, MS, 1961; MLS, U. Wash., Seattle, 1965. With Tacoma (Wash.) Pub. Libr., 1965—, mgr. spl. collections, 1980—. Author: Documentary History of Fort Steilacoom, 1982, Origins of Pierce County Name Origins, 1989, Who We Are, A History of Tacoma's Black Community, 1992, The George Washington Bush Reader, 1992; editor: Diaries of August V. Kautz., 1978, Journals of Edward Huggins, 1982. Trustee Steilacoom (Wash.) Hist. Mus., 1988-91. Recipient Living Landmark, Pierce County Landmarks Commn., 1988, John Binns award Tacoma Community Coll., 1989; David Douglas fellow, 1982. Mem. ALA, Tacoma Hist. Soc. (bd. dirs. 1990-91), Tacoma-Pierce County Geneal. Soc. (hon.). Mem. LDS Ch. Office: Tacoma Pub Libr 1102 Tacoma Ave S Tacoma WA 98402-2098

REESE, ROBERT JENKINS, senator, lawyer; b. Lovell, Wyo., June 2, 1947; s. William David and Elsa Edith (Bluhm) R.; divorced; 1 child, William Derek; m. Mary Lynn Cockriel, Dec. 24, 1986; children: Tyler Eric, Whitney Elsa, Kelley Cockriel, Meagan Cockriel. BA, Harvard U., 1969; JD, U. Wyo., 1978. Bar: Wyo. 1978, U.S. Dist. Ct. Wyo. 1978, U.S. Ct. Appeals (10th cir.) 1984. Tchr. Stratford Jr. High Sch., Arlington, Va., 1971-75; dep. county atty. Sweetwater County, Green River, Wyo., 1978-82; pvt. practice Green River, 1983-86; senator State of Wyo., Cheyenne, 1985-93; ptnr. Reese & Mathey, Green River, 1986—. Dem. chmn. Sweetwater County, Green River, 1983-85. Mem. Wyo. Trial Lawyers Assn. (bd. dirs. 1985-86), Green River C. of C. (bd. dirs. 1984-86), Sweetwater County Bar Assn. (pres. 1985-86, v.p. 1991-92). Democrat. Office: Reese & Mathey PO Box 1060 Green River WY 82935-1060

REESER, ROBERT DUANE, educator; b. Freeport, Ill., Mar. 4, 1931; s. James M. and Erma B. (Kyler) R. BS, N. Ill. U., 1953; MA, U. Denver, 1959; PhD, Ohio State U., 1974. Art tchr. Rockford (Ill.) Pub. Schs., 1955-59, Kern County Union High Sch. Dist., Bakersfield, Calif., 1959-62, Santa Cruz (Calif.) City Schs., 1962-69; teaching assoc. Ohio State U., 1969-71; prof. art Calif. State U., L.A., 1971-87, assoc. dean sch. arts and letters, 1987—; princ. cons. art edn. Painter and ceramic artist on-going exhibits. Chair L.A. County Art Edn. Coun., 1984-85. With U.S. Army, 1953-55. Recipient outstanding art educator award, Ruth Jansen found., 1986. Mem. Internat. Soc. for Edn. Through Art, U.S. Soc. for Edn. Through Art, Nat. Art Edn. Assn. (Pacific dir. 1989-91), Artists Equity Assn., Calif. Humanities Assn. (bd. govs.1989), Calif. Art Edn. Assn. (Award of Merit 1978, Douc Langur award 1985, pres. 1976-78); Kappa Pi, Cavaliers. Democrat. Office: Calif State U 5151 State University Dr Los Angeles CA 90032-4221

REEVE, ALISON, psychiatrist; b. Paris, Feb. 19, 1956; came to U.S., 1956; d. Franklin d'Olier and Helen (Schmidinger) R.; m. Victor C. Strasburger, Aug. 18, 1984; children: Max Arthur, Katya Bess. BA, Conn. Coll., New London, 1977; MD, U. Conn., Farmington, 1983. Cert. psychiatrist Am. Bd. Psychiatry and Neurology, 1988. Fellow NIMH, Washington, 1987-89; asst. prof. U. N. Mex. Sch. Medicine, Albuquerque, 1989—; dir. Neuropshchiat. Clinics, Albuquerque, 1991—. Mem. Am. Psychiat. Assn., Am. Neuropsychiat. Assn., Physicians for Social Responsibility, Psychiat. Med. Assn., Nat. Alliance for Mentally Ill. Office: U NMexs Mental Health Ctr Neuropsychiat Clinics 1000 Stanford NE Albuquerque NM 87131

REEVES, BRUCE, social worker; b. Centerville, Utah, Jan. 8, 1955; s. Leon W. and Maxine (Hodson) R. BA, U. Utah, 1979, MSW, 1983. Mental health caseworker Traveler's Aid Soc. Salt Lake, Salt Lake City, 1983-86; socialwork cons. Home Health of Utah, Bountiful, 1985-86; victim svcs. counselor Salt Lake County Atty's. Office, Salt Lake City, 1986-87; crisis line supr., mgr., cons. AIDS assistance program Aetna and Human Affairs Internat., Salt Lake City, 1987—; presenter in field. Bd. dirs. Walk-ons, Inc., Salt Lake City, 1989—; mem. appropriations com. United Way Greater Salt Lake, Salt Lake City, 1990—, bd. assocs. Ririe-woodbury Dance Co., Salt Lake City, 1991—, human svcs. com. Utah Stonewall Ctr., Salt Lake City, 1992—. Mem. NASW, APHA. Democrat. Office: Aetna/HAI 488 E 6400 S # 300 Salt Lake City UT 84105

REEVES, CARLA MARIANNE, women's health and midwife nurse; b. San Francisco, June 25, 1949; d. Robert Dwight and Irma Marianne (Nelson) R. BS in Nursing, U. Md., Balt., 1971; MS in Nursing, U. Ky., 1975. RN, Ariz., Calif.; cert. nurse midwife, Ariz., Calif. Commd. officer U.S. Army, 1967-77; commd. officer USAF, 1978, advanced through grades to maj., 1971-83; nurse, midwife USAF Hosp. Luke, Luke AFB, Ariz., 1978-84, sr. nurse, midwife, 1985-88; sr. nurse, midwife Regional Med. Ctr., Clark Air Base, The Philippines, 1984-85; ret., 1988; nurse, midwife S.W. Women's Health Svcs., Phoenix, 1988—; pvt. duty-clinic nurse Homemakers Upjohn, Santa Maria, Calif., 1978; ob-gyn nurse practitioner Planned Parenthood Santa Barbara (Calif.), Inc., 1978. Decorated Meritorious Svc. medal with oak leaf cluster; named Ariz. Outstanding Achievement-PMH Physician Office Nurse of Yr., 1992. Mem. Am. Coll. Nurse Midwifes (cert.), Nurses Assn. of Am. Coll. Obstetricians and Gynecologists, Am. Pub. Health Assn., World Wildlife Fund, Ariz. Humane Soc., Doris Day Animal League, Cousteau Soc. Home: 9609 N 34th Dr Phoenix AZ 85051-1208 Office: SW Women's Health Svcs 2850 N 24th St Ste 500B Phoenix AZ 85008-1043

REEVES, EMERY IRVING, aeronautics and astronautics educator, consultant; b. Kansas City, Mo., Nov. 10, 1929; s. Irving Emery and Edith Catherine (Starrett) R.; m. Emily Louise Townsend, Aug. 14, 1954; children: John F., James T., David C., William E. BEEE, Yale U., 1951; MSEE, MIT, 1954. Mem. tech. staff TRW, Redondo Beach, Calif., 1958-85, project mgr. FLTSATCOM, 1977-81, mgr. engring. ops. Space Systems div., 1977-81, v.p., gen. mgr. Spacecraft Engring. div., 1981-85; cons. prof. Stanford (Calif.) U., 1985-91. Author: Space Mission Analysis and Design Handbook, 1990; contbr. articles to profl. jours. Scoutmaster Boy Scouts Am., 1977-85. Lt. (j.g.) USN, 1955-58. Recipient Disting. Pub. Svc. medal NASA, 1984. Fellow AIAA (assoc.), Sigma Xi, Tau Beta Pi. Republican. Home: 401 Yarmouth Rd Palos Verdes Peninsula CA 90274-2647

REEVES, JOHN ALLEN, financial services company executive, lawyer; b. Des Moines, July 5, 1950; s. M.L. and Doris M. Reeves; m. Susan J. Richtsmeier, Sept. 11, 1971; children: J.C., Andrew, Benjamin. BA, Lewis and Clark Coll., 1972; JD, Drake U., 1975. Bar: Iowa 1975, U.S. Supreme Ct. 1979, Calif. 1984. Staff atty. St. Paul Fire & Marine Ins. Co., Des Moines, 1975-76; assoc. atty. Fairall, Fairall & Kaplan, Marshalltown, Iowa, 1976-78, ptnr., 1978-82; mgr. Farm Credit Banks, Sacramento, 1982-85; asst. corp. counsel The Money Store Investment Corp., Sacramento, 1985-88; COO Educaid subs. The Money Store Investment Corp., Sacramento, 1988-93, pres., 1993—. Adult leader Boy Scouts Am., Roseville, Calif., 1990—. Mem. ABA, Calif. Lenders for Edn. (pres. 1991—), Nat. Coun. Higher Edn. Loan Programs (mem. fed. regulations com. 1989—), Nat. Assn. Govt. Guaranteed Lenders (bd. mem. 1987—), Calif. Bar Assn., Sacramento Bar Assn. Office: Educaid 3301 C St Sacramento CA 95816

REEVES, MARCIA ELLEN, insurance agent; b. Framingham, Mass., Mar. 27, 1949; d. Robert F. and Lois Ann (Walker) R. Grad. high sch., Scotia, N.Y. Cert. gen. agt.; acredited customer svc. rep.; errors and omissions cert. trainer. Account exec. Nat. Mortgage and Fin. Co. Ltd., Honolulu, 1980-82; ind. ins. agt. Ins. Specialist of Hawaii, Inc., Honolulu, 1982-89, Beck, Kuklich & Swartman, Inc., Honolulu, 1989-90; gen. ptnr., mgr. Mutual Gen. Underwriters, Honolulu, 1990—. Pres. Kapiolani Jaycees, Honolulu, 1984-86. Recipient Warrior Club Recruitment award Hawaii Jaycees, Honolulu, 1984, 85; named 1st Female Chpt. Pres., Hawaii Jaycees, Honolulu, 1984, Pres. of Month, 1985, Outstanding Young Woman of Am., 1985. Mem. Hawaii Ind. Ins. Agts. Assn. (conv. chmn. 1987-89, edn. chmn. 1989-91, v.p. 1990, pres.-elect 1991, pres. 1992, Disting. Svc. award 1989). Home: 53C-2 S Kuakini St Honolulu HI 96813 Office: Mutual Gen Underwriters 680 Iwilei Rd Ste 528 Honolulu HI 96817

REEVES, SUSAN ELIZABETH, afterschool program director; b. Burley, Idaho, Apr. 20, 1956; d. Adolph and Patricia Jane (Howard) Korb; m. Roy Chester Reeves, Aug. 14, 1987; stepchildren: Tony, Hana. Student, Boise State U., 1974-77. Mgr. Siderail Restaurant, Boise, 1977-78; warranty adminstr. Cummins Intermountain, Boise, 1978-82; mech. parts specialist Morrison-Knudsen Railroad Divsn., Boise, 1982-85; aftersch. program dir. Tender Loving Care Unltd., Pocatello, Idaho, 1985—; workshop presenter Early Childhood Conf., Pocatello, 1987, 89, 90, 93. Mem. Pocatello Jaycees (sec.-treas. 1986-87, bd. dirs. 1986-93, mgmt. v.p. 1990-91, pres. 1990-92, chmn. bd. dirs. 1992-93, Jaycee of Month 1986-92, Jaycee of Yr. 1990, Outstanding Chpt. Pres. 1991-92), Idaho Jaycees (state program mgr. 1987-90, Outstanding Young Women Am. 1991). Home: 973 Highland Blvd Pocatello ID 83204 Office: Tender Loving Care 200 N 15th Pocatello ID 83201

REFSLAND, GARY ARLAN, sociology educator; b. Big Timber, Mont., May 5, 1944; s. William Anton and Agnes Eline (Freeberg) R.; m. Judith Estelle Hall, Aug. 20, 1969 (div. Aug. 1974); m. Marjorie Gillette Shaw, Dec. 12, 1977. BS in Sociology, Mont. State U., 1970, MS in Sociology, 1971; postgrad., Internat. Grad. Sch., Stockholm, 1970; AA in funeral directing, Calif. Coll. Mortuary Sci., 1973. Cert. funeral dir., mortician. Instr. sociology Mont. State U., Bozeman, 1971-72, lectr., 1976—, coord. aging svcs., 1976-77, acting dir. Ctr. Gerontology, 1977-79, dir. Mont. Ctr. Gerontology, 1979—; mortician Dokken Nelson Funeral Service, Bozeman, 1974-76; cons. State Agy. Aging, 1979—, Legacy Legis., 1987—; program coordinator Mont. Area Health Edn. Ctr./Office Rural Health, 1987—; mem. adv. bd. Sr. Community Services Employment program, Mont., 1983—, Regional Edn. and Tng. program Fed. Region VIII, 1980-82, Mont. State U., 1986—, Mont. Area Health Edn. Ctr., 1987; mem. planning com. Gov's. Adv. Council, Mont. Aging Policy Perspectives: 1990, 1987—; mem. Gov's. Third Priorities for People, 1988; state coordinator White Ho. Conf. on Aging, 1981-82. Writer, producer (TV show) Mont.'s Priorities for Aging, 1981; producer The Mental health Problems of Older Adults, 1988; writer, exec. producer (videotape) Senior Centers.: Opportunities for Older Montanans. Pres. Gallatin County Housing Authority Bd., Bozeman, 1981-82, sec. 1978-81; pres. Sourdough Ridge Property Owners Assn., Bozeman, 1982-84, Gallatin County Council on Aging, 1978-80. With USN, 1962-66. Recipient Armed Forces Community award San Diego C. of C., 1966, Cert. Appreciation U.S. Dept. HHS, 1982, Community Achievement award, 1989; named one of Outstanding Young Men Am. U.S. Jaycees, 1981. Mem. Am. Soc. Aging, Mont. Gerontology Soc. (charter officer 1982-83), Nat. Council on Aging (del. council 1982-83), Am. Legion, Alpha Kappa Delta. Home: 212 Ridge Trl Bozeman MT 59715-9253 Office: Mont State U Ctr Gerontology Bozeman MT 59717

REGAN, ANN ELLEN, computer scientist; b. Mineola, N.Y., Dec. 18, 1962; d. James J. and Mary E. (Deegan) R. BS in Computer Sci., Ariz. State U., 1985; MS in Computer Sci., Northwestern U., 1988. Jr. programmer Comsystems div. SAIC, San Diego, 1981-85; systems analyst, programmer Computer Scis. Corp., San Diego, 1985-86; computer scientist Four Pi Systems, San Diego, 1988-90, sr. applications engr., 1990-93; sr. software engr. HNC, San Diego, 1993—. Mem. Assn. for Computing Machinery, Am. Assn. for Artificial Intelligence, Calif. Scholastic Fedn. (life), Upsilon Pi Epsilon. Office: HNC 5501 Oberlin Dr San Diego CA 92121

REGAN, JOHN BERNARD (JACK), community relations executive, assemblyman; b. Chgo., Feb. 2, 1934; s. Andrew J. and Frances (O'Born) R.; m. Rosemary E. Seger, Aug. 17, 1980. BA, So. Ill. U., 1960. V.p. Collins Bros., Las Vegas, Nev., 1971-76; pres. Terra, Inc., Las Vegas, 1973-80; owner Jack's Place, Las Vegas, 1980-93; govt. and mil. affairs liaison C.C. So. Nev., North Las Vegas, 1984-93; dist. dir. Nat. Coun. for Community Rels., 1984-86; nat. treas. Nat. Coun. Mktg. and Pub. Rels., 1986-88; state dir. Internat. Coun. of Shopping Ctrs., Nev., 1976. State assemblyman Nev. State Legis., Carson City, 1988-90, 92-93; mem. Am. Legis. Exchange Coun., 1990-93; arts, tourism and cultural resources com. mem. Nat. Coun. of State Legis., 1990-93; active Las Vegas Habitat for Humanity. With USN, 1951-55. Recipient Lion of Yr. award Las Vegas Lions Club, 1978, Paragon award Nat. Coun. for Community Rels., 1985. Mem. Thunderbird Chpt. Air Force Assn. (pres. 1989-90, named hon. Thunderbird, Nighthawk, stealth fighter), North Las Vegas C. of C. (v.p. 1986). Democrat. Jewish. Home: 1650 Cookson Ct Las Vegas NV 89115-6948 Office: C C So Nev 3200 E Cheyenne Ave # 2na North Las Vegas NV 89030-4228

REGELE, MICHAEL BRUCE, minister, information and marketing services executive; b. Corvallis, Oreg., Mar. 30, 1952; s. William and Geneva (Chapman) R.; m. Debra S. Brog, June 26,1976; children: Jonathan, Justin, Jordan, Kiersten, Elissa. BA, Seattle Pacific U., 1975; MDiv, Fuller Theol. Sem., 1986. Ordained to ministry Presbyn. Ch. U.S.A., 1987; cert. tchr., Wash. Child care worker Griffin Home for Boys, Renton, Wash., 1973-74; tchr. Grace Acad., Kent, Wash., 1975-76, Columbia Sch., Seattle, 1976-78; assoc. pastor Mariners Ch., Newport Beach, Calif., 1980-84; exec. dir. Congress on Bibl. Exposition, Irvine, Calif., 1984-86; cons. Ministry Consulting, Irvine, 1986-87; pres. Ch. Info. and Devel. Svcs. (name changed to Percept), Costa Mesa, Calif., 1987—; bd. dirs. Com. on Bibl. Exposition, Wheaton, Ill., 1983-88. Author: Your Church and Its Mission, 1988; co-author study guides. Bd. dirs. Irvine Unified Sch. Dist., 1990—. Republican. Office: Ch Info and Devel Svcs 151 Kalmus Dr Ste 104A Costa Mesa CA 92626-5900

REGINATO, ROBERT JOSEPH, soil scientist; b. Palo Alto, Calif., Apr. 13, 1935; s. Guiseppe Primo and Carolina Theresa (Boccignone) R.; m. Donna Marie LeStum, Aug. 26, 1956; children: Richard Lynn, David Lewis, Christopher Michael, Michael Jeffrey. B.S., U. Calif., Davis, 1957; M.S., U. Ill., 1959; Ph.D., U. Calif., Riverside, 1973. Rsch. asst. U. Calif., Davis, 1956-57, U. Ill., Urbana, 1957-59; soil scientist U.S. Water Conservation Lab., USDA-Agrl. Rsch. Svc., Phoenix, 1959-89 , rsch. leader, 1980-89; assoc. dir. Pacific W. Area USDA Agrl. Rsch. Svc., Albany, Calif., 1989-91, dir., 1991—; vis. scientist U. Calif., Davis, 1977-78; USDA collaborator U. Ariz., Tucson, 1959-89. Contbr. over 180 articles to tech. jours. Active Roosevelt coun. Boy Scouts Am., 1960-76. Fellow Am. Soc. Agronomy, Soil Sci. Soc. Am.; mem. Am. Geophys. Union, Internat. Soil Sci. Soc., Western Soil Sci. Soc., Sigma Xi, Alpha Zeta, Kappa Sigma. Roman Catholic. Home: 1494 London Cir Benicia CA 94510-1353 Office: Pacific West Area 800 Buchanan St Berkeley CA 94710

REGUERO, EDWARD ANTHONY, financial services executive; b. Honolulu, Jan. 20, 1960; s. Edward Louis and Lillie Bell (Sanders) Chavez; m. Melodie Lyn Huber, Oct. 3, 1987. Grad. pub. schs. CLU, ChFC. Agt. Provident Mutual Life Ins., Irvine, Calif., 1981-82; fin. svcs. profl. Baker Knox Fin. Svcs., Costa Mesa, Calif., 1981-84; pres. Fin. Engring. Concepts, Inc., Irvine, 1984—; reg. dir. Fin. Network Investment Corp., Torrance, Calif., 1989-93; chief exec. officer Worldwide Investment Network, Irvine, 1989—; lectr. Successful Money Mgmt. seminars, Irvine, 1988—; profl.

speaker, 1981—. Author: The No-Limit Sales Person, 1991. With U.S. Army, 1978-81. Mem. Nat. Speakers Assn., Internat. Platform Assn., Irvine C. of C., Internat. Assn. Fin. Planning, Million Dollar Roundtable, Top of Table, Orange County Life Underwriters, Center Club (Costa Mesa), Racquet Club of Irvine. Republican. Office: Worldwide Investment Network 8001 Irvine Center Dr Ste 1200 Irvine CA 92718-2934

REHART, BURTON SCHYLER, journalism educator, freelance writer; b. Pacific Grove, Calif., July 24, 1934; s. Burton Schyler Sr. and Ruth Evelyn (Whitaker) R.; m. Catherine Loverne Morison, Apr. 14, 1962 (div. Aug. 1983); children: William, Anne Marie, Catherine Evelyn; m. Felicia Rose Cousart, June 30, 1984. BA in Journalism, Fresno (Calif.) State Coll., 1957; MA in History, Calif. State U., Fresno, 1966; cert., Coro found., 1961, Stanford U., summer 1975. Cert. adult edn. tchr., Calif. Reporter Bakersfield Californian, 1955; reporter, photographer Fresno Bee, 1957, Madera (Calif.) Daily Tribune, 1960-61, Ventura (Calif.) Free Press, 1961-62; from instr. to prof. journalism Calif. State U., Fresno, 1963—, prof. journalism, 1979—, chmn. dept. journalism, 1992—. Author: M. Theo. Kearney-Prince of Fresno, 1988, (with others) Fresno in the 20th Century, 1986; editor, chmn. editorial bd. Fresno City, County Hist. Soc. Jour.; contbr. articles to profl. jours. Asst. foreman Fresno County Grand Jury, 1969. With U.S. Army, 1958-60. Coro Found. grantee, 1960-61. Mem. Soc. Profl. Journalists (pres. 1987-89), World Future Soc. (writer), Phi Kappa Phi (pres. 1977-78, Calif. State U. Fresno chpt.). Democrat. Episcopalian. Home: 1557 E Roberts Ave Fresno CA 93710 Office: Calif State U Dept Journalism Shaw and Cedar Avenues Fresno CA 93740-0010

REHBERG, DENNIS R., state official; b. Billings, Mont., Oct. 5, 1955; m. Janice; 1 child. Student, Mont. State U., Wash. State U. Rancher and businessman, legis. aide, 1977, fin. dir. Congl. Campaigns, 1980-82; Mont. state rep. Dist. 88, 1985-89; lt. gov. Mont., from 1991. Home: 4401 Hwy 3 Billings MT 59106

REHG, KENNETH LEE, linguistics educator; b. East St. Louis, Ill., Nov. 21, 1939; s. Theophil Albert and Kathryn Louise (George) R.; 1 child, Laura Leolani. BA, U. Ill., 1962; MA, So. Ill. U., 1965; PhD, U. Hawaii, 1986. Tng. officer Internat. Ctr. for Lang. Studies, Washington, 1966-67; lang. officer U.S. Peace Corp, Saipan, Micronesia, 1967-70; asst. rschr. social sci. rsch. inst. U. Hawaii, Honolulu, 1974-83, asst. prof., 1984—; cons. Samoa Dept. Edn., Pago Pago, 1978, U.S. Geol. Survey, Menlo Park, Calif., 1979-81, Japan Nat. Mus. Ethnology, Osaka, 1986; participant Fulbright-Hays Study Group, Ea. Indonesia, 1991. Author: Ponapean Reference Grammar, 1981; co-author: Kitail Lokaiahn Pohnpei, 1969, Ponapean-English Dictionary, 1979; mng. editor Oceanic Linguistics; contbr. articles to profl. jours. Rsch. fellow U. Hawaii, 1981-82; recipient Excellence in Teaching award Hawaii Tchrs. ESL, 1984, Mortar Bd., 1990. Mem. AAAS, Linguistic Soc. Am., Linguistic Soc. Hawaii, Hawaii Acad. Sci. Office: U Hawaii Dept Linguistics Moore Hall 1890 East-West Rd Honolulu HI 96822

REHORN, LOIS MARIE SMITH, nursing administrator; b. Larned, Kans., Apr. 15, 1919; d. Charles and Ethel L. (Canaday) Williamson; m. C. Howard Smith, Feb. 15, 1946 (dec. Aug. 1980); 1 child, Cynthia A. Huddleston; m. Harlan W. Rehorn, Aug. 25, 1981. RN, Bethany Hosp. Sch. Nursing, Kansas City, Kans., 1943; BS, Ft. Hays Kans. State U., Hays, 1968, MS, 1970. RN, N.Mex. Office nurse, surg. asst. Dr. John H. Luke, Kansas City, Kans., 1943-47; supr. nursing unit Larned (Kans.) State Hosp., 1949-68, dir. nursing edn., 1968-71, dir. nursing, 1972-81, ret., 1981. Named Nurse of Yr. DNA-4, 1986. Mem. Am. Nurses Assn., Kans. Nurses Assn. (dist. treas.), N.Mex. Nurses Assn. (dist. pres. 1982-86, dist. bd. dirs. 1992-94). Home: 1436 Brentwood Dr Clovis NM 88101-4602

REIBER, GREGORY DUANE, forensic pathologist; b. Loma Linda, Calif., May 25, 1955; s. Clifford D. and Anna M. (Field) R.; m. Faustina Mae Davis, Feb. 10, 1980; children: Jenessa Anne, Zachary Duane. BS magna cum laude, Andrews U., Berrien Springs, Mich., 1977; MD, Loma Linda (Calif.) U., 1981. Diplomate Am. Bd. Pathology. Resident in pathology Loma Linda U. Med. Ctr., 1981-85; fellow in forensic pathology Root Pathology Lab., San Bernardino, Calif., 1985-86; assoc. pathologist Root Pathology Lab., 1986-90, No. Calif. Forensic Pathology, Sacramento, 1990—; asst. clin. prof. pathology Loma Linda U. Sch. Medicine, 1987-90, U. Calif., Davis, 1990—; apptd. Calif. SIDS Autopsy Protocol Com. Contbr. articles to profl. jours. Fellow Am. Soc. Clin. Pathologists; mem. AMA, Internat. Wound Ballistics Assn., Nat. Assn. Med. Examiners, Am. Acad. Forensic Scis., N.Y. Acad. Sci., Calif. Med. Assn., Sacramento-El Dorado Med. Soc., Alpha Omega Alpha. Republican. Seventh-day Adventist. Office: No Calif Forensic Pathology 2443 Fair Oaks Blvd Ste 311 Sacramento CA 95825-7630

REICH, SIMEON, mathematics researcher, educator; b. Cracow, Poland, Aug. 12, 1948; came to U.S., 1975; s. Moshe and Amalia (Alter) R.; m. Hayuta Cohen, Mar. 26, 1974; children: Uri, Daphna, Shelley. BSc summa cum laude, Israel Inst. Tech., Haifa, 1970, DSc, 1973. Lectr. Tel Aviv (Israel) U., 1973-75; L. E. Dickson instr. U. Chgo., 1975-77; asst. prof. U. So. Calif., L.A., 1977-79, assoc. prof., 1979-84, prof., 1984-; vis. scientist Argonne (Ill.) Nat. Lab., 1978; vis. assoc. prof. U. Calif., Berkeley, 1981; acting chmn. dept. of math U. So. Calif., L.A., 1983-84; prof. Israel Inst. Tech., Haifa, 1987-88, 90. Co-author: Uniform Convexity, Hyperbolic Geometry and Nonexpansive Mappings, 1984; co-editor: Optimization and Nonlinear Analysis, 1992; author 140 rsch. papers. NSF rsch. grantee, 1976-84, U. So. Calif. faculty rsch. grantee, 1983-84, grantee San Diego SuperComputer Ctr., 1987-91. Mem. Am. Math. Soc., Math. Assn. Am., Soc. for Indsl. and Applied Math. Office: Univ So Calif Dept Math Los Angeles CA 90089

REICHARD, DAVID WARK, electronics consultant; b. San Francisco, Oct. 18, 1948; s. Ken and Gerrie (Griffith) R. AS, Coll. of Marin, 1972. Owner The Photo Shop, San Rafael, Calif., 1976-86, RNA, Oakland, Calif., 1966—; technician Sears Roebuck, San Bruno, Calif., 1989—, Renaissance Faire, Novato, Calif., 1982-89. Pres. San Rafael Bus. Improvement Dist., 1984-85; vol. KALX-FM, Berkeley ARC, Oakland. Mem. East Bay Amatuer Radio Club, Marin Amatuer Radio Club. Home and Office: 2783 E 12th St # C Oakland CA 94601-1505

REICHARTZ, W. DAN, hotel executive; b. 1946. With Hilton Hotels Corp., N.Y.C., 1967-87, Desert Palace Inc. doing bus. as Caesars Palace, Las Vegas, 1987—; now pres., chief oper. officer Caesars Palace, Las Vegas. Office: Caesars Palace 3570 Las Vegas Blvd S Las Vegas NV 89109-8933

REICHBACH, NAOMI ESTELLE, social service administrator; b. N.Y.C., Apr. 19, 1934; d. Nathaniel S. and Sara (Hirsch) R. BS in Edn., SUNY, New Paltz, 1955; MS in Spl. Edn., CCNY, 1969. Tchr. Shield Inst., Bronx, N.Y., 1956-58; tchr., parent educator Shield Inst., 1961-63; head tchr., program developer Oakland (Calif.) Unified Sch. Dist., 1959-60; edn. dir. N.Y.C. Assn. Retarded Children, 1963-67, 1967-69; co-founder, exec. dir. Burt Children Ctr., Psychiatric Residential Treatment Ctr. and Sch., San Francisco, 1969—. Fellow Am. Orthopsychiat. Assn., Royal Soc. Health; mem. Calif. Svcs. for Children. Office: Burt Ctr 940 Grove St San Francisco CA 94117-1798

REICHE, MARVIN GARY, restaurant executive; b. Sacramento, Sept. 2, 1949; s. Robert A. and Kate Kathleen (Groo) R.; m. Kathleen Louise Price, Feb. 10, 1968; children: Bradford, Renee, Darren, Michelle, Ryan, Brandon. With Harman Mgmt. Corp., 1967-79, cook and pie shell operator, Lodi, Calif., 1967, cook, Carmichael, Calif., 1967-68, store mgr., Sacramento, 1968-72, Fair Oaks, Calif., 1972-77, dist. mgr. Central Sacramento, 1977-79; owner, investor Kentucky Fried Chicken, Covina, West Covina, Long Beach, Lakewood, Bellflower, Los Angeles County, Garden Grove and Anaheim, Calif., 1979—; sole owner Kasmar Enterprises; dir. So. Calif. Kentucky Fried Chicken Advt. Assn. Judge Bank Am. Achievement Awards Program, 1983. Mem. Assn. Kentucky Fried Chicken Franchisee (nat. dir. 1989-91, pres. So. Calif. chpt. 1989-90, 91—, bd. dirs. So. Calif., advt. assoc.), Republican. Mormon.

REICHEK, JESSE, artist; b. Bklyn., Aug. 16, 1916; s. Morris and Celia (Bernstein) R.; m. Laure Guyot, May 16, 1950; children—Jonathan, Joshua. Student, Inst. Design, Chgo., 1941-42; diploma, Academie Julian, Paris, 1951. Instr. dept. architecture U. Mich., Ann Arbor, 1946-47; prof. Inst. Design Ill. Inst. Tech., Chgo., 1951-53; prof. dept. architecture U. Calif., Berkeley, 1953-87, prof. emeritus, 1987—; cons. Nat. Design Inst. Ford Found. project, Ahmedabad, India, 1963, San Francisco Redevel. Agy. Embarcadero Center, 1966—; lectr. Nat. Inst. Architects, Rome, 1960, U. Florence, 1960, U. Naples, 1960, Israel Inst. Tech., 1960, Greek Architects Soc., Athens, 1960, U. Belgrade, 1960, MIT, 1965, U. N.Mex., 1964, Am. Cultural Center, Paris, 1960, 64, Gujarat Inst. Engrs. and Architects, 1963, U. Colo., 1961, Harvard, 1962, U. Minn., 1962, U. Coll. London, 1967, Inst. Contemporary Arts, London, 1967, Ecole Nationale des Beaux-Ats, 1967; artist in residence Tamarind Lithography Workshop, 1966, Am. Acad. in Rome, 1971-72; research prof. Creative Arts Inst. U. Calif., 1966-67; artist in residence IBM Los Angeles Sci. Center, 1970-71. Exhibited one man shows at, Galerie Cahiers d'Art Paris, 1951, 59, 68, U. Calif. at Berkeley, 1954, Betty Parsons Gallery, N.Y.C., 1958, 59, 63, 65, 67, 69, 70, Molton Gallery, London, 1962, Am. Culture Center, Florence, Italy, 1962, Bennington Coll., 1963, U. N.Mex., 1966, U. So. Calif., 1967, Axiom Gallery, London, 1968, Yoseido Gallery, Tokyo, 1968, Los Angeles County Mus. Art, 1971; exhibited in group shows, Bklyn. Mus., 1959, Mus. Modern Art, N.Y.C., 1962, 65, 69, Knox-Albright Art Gallery, 1962, Art Inst. Chgo., 1963, Cin. Art Mus., 1966, Balt. Art Mus., 1966, Yale Art Gallery, 1967, Grand Palais, Paris, 1970, Nat. Mus. Art, Santiago, Chile, 1970, art and tech. exhibit, Los Angeles County Mus. Art, 1971, Maeght Found., St. Paul de Vence, France, 1971, Mus. Modern Art, Paris, 1971; represented in permanent collections, Mus. Modern Art, Art Inst. Chgo., Bibliotheque Nationale, Paris, Victoria & Albert Mus., London, Los Angeles County Art Mus., Grunwald Graphic Arts Found., U. Calif. at Los Angeles, San Diego Mus. Art, Amon Carter Mus., Fort Worth; Author: Jesse Reichek-Dessins, 1960, La Monte de la Nuit, 1961, Fontis, 1961, Etcetera, 1965, Le Bulletin Des Baux, 1972; e.g., 1976. Served to capt. C.E. AUS, 1942-46. Home: 5925 Red Hill Rd Petaluma CA 94952-9437

REICHEL, JOHN KENTO, medical care organization official, writer; b. Oakland, Calif., Dec. 28, 1959; s. David and Hisae (Kawashima) R. BA, U. Calif., Berkeley, 1982. Lab. asst. Kaiser Permanente Med. Care Program, Berkeley, 1978-84; editor Kaiser Permanente Med. Care Program, Oakland, Calif., 1984-91; standards analyst, contbr. to corp. mag. Kaiser Permanente Med. Care Program, Walnut Creek, Calif., 1991—; advisor to editor Teen Assn. Model Railroaders, Oakland, 1990—. Contbr. music revs. and articles to various publs. Named Pivot Pin, Teen Assn. Model Railroaders. Democrat. Home: 1800 E 38th St Oakland CA 94602

REICHEL, PHILIP LEE, sociology educator; b. Bakersfield, Calif., Oct. 8, 1946; s. Joseph J. and Virginia (Spry) R.; m. Paula Jean Hauschild, June 1969 (div. 1980); children: Scott Andrew, Matthew Jason; m. Eva Maria Jewell, Dec. 15, 1983. BS, Nebr. Wesleyan U., 1969; MA, Kans. State U., 1972, PhD, 1979. Classification officer Nebr. Penal and Correctional Complex, Lincoln, 1970-71; assoc. prof. Augusta (Ga.) Coll., 1972-83, U. No. Colo., Greeley, 1983-91; full prof. U. No. Colo., 1991—; dir. criminal justice studies U. No. Colo., Greeley, 1983—. Author book on fgn. justice systems; contbr. articles to profl. jours. Advisor United Way Greeley, 1989, 93; bd. dirs. Planned Parenthood, Augusta, 1982, Legal Aid Soc., Greeley, 1993—. Named Favorite Prof., Mortar Bd., U. No. Colo., 1990. Mem. Acad. Criminal Justice Scis. (local host 1989-90), Am. Soc. Criminology, Western Social Sci. Assn. Democrat. Home: 3412 Belmont Ave Evans CO 80620-2442 Office: U No Colo Sociology Dept Greeley CO 80639

REICHENBACH, THOMAS, veterinarian; b. N.Y.C., Jan. 6, 1947; s. Henry J. and Helen M. (Kelly) R.; m. Cleda L. Houmes, Nov. 23, 1984. BS in Chemistry, U. Notre Dame du Lac, 1968; MS in Chemistry, U. Calif., Davis, Calif., 1973; AA, Shasta Coll., 1975; DVM, U. Calif., Davis, Calif., 1981. Doctor of Veterinary Medicine, Diplomate Am. Bd. Veterinary Practitioner. Sentry dog handler U.S. Army, 1970-71; indsl. chemist Syntex, Palo Alto, Calif., 1973-75; gestation herd mgr. Llano Seco Rancho, Chico, Calif., 1975-76; pres. Veterinary Mgmt. Svcs., Salinas, Calif., 1981—; chief exec. officer Santa Barbara Vet. Emergency Group, 1991—; lectr. in field; adv. bd. Veterinary Post Grad. Inst., Santa Cruz, Calif., 1988. Contbr. articles to profl. jours.; author computer software Personal Wedding Planner, 1985, Veterinary Clinical Simulation, 1988. With U.S. Army, 1969-71. Mem. Am. Vet. Med. Assn., Calif. Vet. Med. Assn., Nat. Notre Dame Monogram Club. Republican. Roman Catholic. Office: Vet Mgmt Svcs 1887 Cherokee Dr # 1 Salinas CA 93906-2394

REICHENBERG, CHERRI JANN, advertising executive; b. Bassett, Nebr., Feb. 11, 1951; d. Lloyd James and Laura May (Hutcheson) Alderman; m. Robert Edwin Reichenberg Jr., Oct. 23, 1971. Student, Colo. State U., 1970-71; BA in Psychology and Sociology, Chadron (Nebr.) State Coll., 1974. Head libr. Chadron Pub. Libr., 1972-75; newspaper reporter, advt. rep. Western Editorial Svcs., Inc., Glenwood Springs, Colo., 1976-77; editor, advt. mgr. Chadron Record Newspapers, Inc., 1977-79; pub., owner Crawford (Nebr.) Clipper Newspapers, 1979-86; owner Western Comm. Assocs., Crawford, 1979-86; account exec., asst. spl. sects. editor Orange Coast Daily Pilot, Costa Mesa, Calif., 1988-89, retail advt. mgr., 1989-90; account exec. Hershey Comm., Inc., Irvine, Calif., 1990—. Sec. Dawes County Tourism Bd., Chadron, 1983-84; instr. Roadmasters Motorcycle Safety Tng., Chadron, 1982-85. Recipient Best Spl. Edition Nebr. Press Assn., 1982, 83, Best Editorial Color, 1982, 84, 86, Best Advt. Color, 1982, Best Advt. Idea, 1982. Democrat. Episcopalian.

REICHHOLD, JANET E., poet, artist; b. Lima, Ohio, Jan. 18, 1937; d. John Howard and Erma Marie (Bible) Styer; m. Robert L. Steiner (div.); children: Heidi Lynn Vetter, Bambi, Hans; m. Werner Reichhold, Oct. 21, 1971. Attended, Bluffton (Ohio) Coll., 1955-56, 57, Ohio IU., 1956, Reedley (Calif.) Jr. Coll., 1962-64, Fresno State U., 1964, San Francisco State U., 1968. Founder AHA Books, Gualala, Calif., 1987—; pubr. Mirrors - Internat. Haiku Spirit, Gualala, Calif., 1987—; editor Yuki Teikei Haiku Soc., Gualala, Calif., 1990—. Author: Shadows on an Open Window, 1979, From the Dipper...Drops, 1983, Duet for One Mirror, 1984, Thumbtacks on a Calendar, 1985, Reissnaegal auf einen Kalender, 1985, Cherries/Apples, 1986, Graffiti, 1986, As Stones Cry Out, 1987, Tigers in a Tea Cup, 1988, The Land of Seven Realms, 1988, A Literary Curiosity: The Pyramid Renga "Open" (with Bambi Walker), 1989, Narrow Road to Renga, 1989, A Gift of Tanka, 1990, Round Renga Round, 1990, A Dictionary of Haiku, 1992. Recipient award for best unpublished poem Mus. of Haiku Lit., Tokyo, 1984, 86, Encouragement award Itoen Tea Co., Tokyo, 1992. Mem. Haiku Soc. Am. (Merit Book award 1988, 90), Poetry Soc. of Japan, Haiku Writers of Gualala Arts, German Haiku Soc., Holland Cir. of Haiku, Romanian Haiku Soc., Haiku Internat. Assn.

REICHLIN, LOUISE, choreographer, educator; b. Bordentown, N.J., Aug. 15, 1941; d. Albert and Ida (Bloom) R.; m. Alfred Desio, Sept. 30, 1967. BA, Bennington (Vt.) Coll., 1963; MFA, U. Calif., Irvine, 1977. Broadway shows N.Y., 1967-71; faculty dance dept. Loyola Marymount, L.A., 1972-73; faculty drama dept. U. So. Calif., L.A., 1972-87; faculty dance dept. U. Calif., Irvine, 1973-75; producer/presenter Brand Art Ctr., Glendale, 1986-88, 91—; faculty music dept. U. So. Calif., 1974—; founder, artistic dir. L.A. Choreographers & Dancers, 1979—; choreographer Shakespeare Festival L.A., 1975, 90; vis. faculty Colls. and Sch. workshops, 1971-91; choreographer, writer L.A. Zoo series spl. programs., 1984. Choreographer: The Tennis Dances, 1979, Celtic Suite, 1983-90, Urban and Tribal Dances, 1990-92. Sec. L.A. Area Dance Alliance. Mem. Dance Resource Ctr., Western Alliance of Arts Administrs. Home and Office: LA Choreographers 1807 Rodney Dr Los Angeles CA 90027-4307

REICHMAN, FREDRICK THOMAS, painter; b. Bellingham, Wash., Jan. 28, 1925; s. Frederick and Ilma Lucia (Yearing) R.; m. Michela Madelene Robbins, Sept. 24, 1955; children: Alexandra Ilma, Matthew Nathaniel. BA cum laude, U. Calif., Berkeley, 1950, MA in Art, 1952; postgrad., San Francisco Art Inst., 1946-47. Instr. art San Francisco Art Inst., 1952, U. Calif., Davis, 1963-66, Dominican Coll., San Rafael, Calif., summer 1974, Calif. Coll. Arts and Crafts, Oakland, 1976, U. Calif. extension, San Francisco, 1966—; lectr. U. Calif., Berkeley, 1953; dir. children's art classes Jr. Center Art and Sci., Oakland, 1953-64, 66-77. One-man exhbns. include Rose Rabow Galleries, San Francisco, 1958, 61, 63, 65, 69, 73, 75, San Francisco Mus. Modern Art, 1969, Benson Gallery, Bridgehampton, N.Y., 1966-72, Silvan Simone Gallery, L.A., 1971-73, Santa Barbara (Calif.) Mus. Art, 1974, Rose Rabow Galleries-James Willis Gallery, San Francisco, 1976, Gallery Paule Anglim, San Francisco, 1979-81, Chikyudo Gallery, Tokyo, 1980, Espace Doyoo, Tokyo, 1982, Ki-Do-Ai-Raku, Tokyo, 1982, Maeitetsu-Marukoshi, Kanazawa, Japan, 1982, The New Gallery, Taos, N.Mex., 1982, Charles Campbell Gallery, San Francisco, 1984, 86, David Barnett Gallery, Milw., 1985, 89, Artform Gallery, 1985, The New Gallery, Houston, 1985, Mekler Gallery Inc., L.A., 1988, Galerie B. Haasner, Wiesbaden, 1990, 92, Ruth Siegel Gallery, N.Y., 1991, U. Calif., Santa Cruz, Ann Porter Sesnon Art Gallery, 1991, Galerie B. Haasner, Germany, 1992, Harcourts Contemporary, San Francisco, 1992, Louis Newman Galleries, Beverly Hills, Calif., 1993; 2-man show, Iannetti-Lanzone Gallery, San Francisco, 1989, Miyagi Mus. Art, Sendai, Japan, 1982, 3-man show, Milw. Art Mus., 1982, group exhbns. include, Esther Robles Gallery, L.A., 1961, Whitney Mus. Am. Art traveling exhbn., 1962-63, Expo '70, Osaka, Japan, 1970, Oakland Mus., 1971, Joslyn Art Mus. traveling exhbn., 1973-74, San Francisco Mus. Modern Art, 1974, Martha Jackson Gallery, N.Y.C., 1978, New Gallery, 1981, Forum Gallery, N.Y.C., 1984, Smith Andersen Gallery, Palo Alto, 1986, Ruth Siegel Gallery, N.Y.C., 1986, Kultorvert Galerie, Copenhagen, 1986, Richmond (Calif.) Art Ctr., 1987, Nat. Mus. Am. Art, Washington, 1989, Arte 7, San Francisco, 1990, Harcourts Contemporary, San Francisco, 1991; represented in permanent collections throughout U.S., including Nat. Mus. Am. Art, San Francisco Mus. Modern Art, Oakland Mus., Univ. Art Mus., Berkeley, Santa Barbara Mus. Art, Milw. Art Mus., Ulrich Mus. Art, Wichita, Fine Arts Museums San Francisco, Okla. Art Center, Oklahoma City, Bank Am. World Hdqrs., San Francisco, Achenbach Found., San Francisco, Mills Coll. Art Gallery, Oakland, U. Calif., San Francisco; works rep. art publs.; commns. include stage set for, San Francisco Mime Troupe, The Exception to the Rule, 1965; mural, Boche Pediatrics Outpatient Clinic, Stanford U. Med. Sch., 1961, San Francisco Civic Center, 1968. Served with USNR, 1943-45. Recipient Purchase prize San Francisco Art Festival, 1964, One-Man Show award, 1968; Irving prize Am. Wit and Humor U. Calif., Berkeley, 1951; Taussig traveling fellow U. Calif., Berkeley, 1952; profiled in 50 West Coast Artists by Henry Hopkins, 1981, Art in the San Francisco Bay Area 1945-80 by Thomas Albright, 1985.

REID, ALAN CLIFFORD, marine non-commissioned officer; b. Durango, Colo., Nov. 11, 1961; s. Clifford Edward and Mary Ellen (Poole) R. Enlisted USMC, 1979, advanced to SSGT sgt., 1992; driver/dispatcher 1st Tanks BN/USMC, Camp Pendleton, Calif., Okinawa, Japan, 1980-83, 1st Recon BN/USMC, Camp Pendleton, Calif., 1983-84; avionics technician USMC, Cherry Point, N.C., 1985; material cont., maintenance cont. USMC, Cherry Point, 1988, Iwakuni, Japan, 1986, 87-88; instr. USMC, Oak Harbor, Wash., 1988-92; with computer systems tech. schs. command USMC, Mare Island, Calif., 1992—. Vol. Am. Cancer Soc., Oak Harbor, 1989. Mem. Soc. Am. Mil. Engrs. (Washington Post programs 1988-89, L.A. Post pres. 1990—), Nat. Soc. Profl. Engrs., Masons. Republican. Roman Catholic. Office: Computer Systems Tech Schs Command CSTSC Box 1304 Mare Island CA 94592-5050

REID, BARRY JONATHAN, financial planner; b. Hamilton, Ont., Can., Feb. 12, 1957; s. Herbert John and Donna Jean (Harding) McLeod; m. Becky Jo Pendleton, Sept. 1, 1977. BA in History, Polit. Sci., UCLA, 1979. Cert. employee benefit specialist. Commodities rep. Smith Barney, Seattle, 1981-82; owner, mgr. Intervest Cons., Seattle, 1982-83; fin. planner Waddell & Reed, Inc., Federal Way, Wash., 1983-84; dis. mgr. Waddell & Reed, Inc., Tacoma, 1984-87; div. mgr. Waddell & Reed, Inc., Tacoma and Olympia, Wash., 1987-88; fin. planner Waddell & Reed, Inc., Tacoma, 1988—. Researcher, editor debate handbooks. Bd. dirs. Seattle Tree Preservation, 1988—, Pierce County Alliance, 1992—; speaker ARC Counsel on Elder Abuse, Tacoma, 1988—; mem. Mayor's Task Force for Community Standards, Tukwila, Wash., 1988. Home: 5103 S 164th St Seattle WA 98188-3224 Office: Waddell and Reed Inc 15 S Oregon Ave Tacoma WA 98409-7461

REID, BELMONT MERVYN, brokerage house executive; b. San Jose, Calif., May 17, 1927; s. C. Belmont and Mary Irene (Kilfoyl) R. BS in Engring., San Jose State U., 1950, postgrad.; m. Evangeline Joan Rogers, June 1, 1952. Pres., Lifetime Realty Corp., San Jose, 1969-77, Lifetime Fin. Planning Corp., San Jose, 1967-77; founder, chmn. bd. Belmont Reid & Co., Inc., San Jose, 1960-77; pres., registered investment advisor JOBEL Fin. Inc., Carson City, Nev., 1980—; pres., chmn. bd. Data-West Systems, Inc., 1984-85. County chmn. 1982-85, Carson City Rep. Cen. Com., treas., 1979-81; chmn. Carson City Gen. Obligation Bond Commn., 1986—; rural county chmn. Nev. Rep. Cen. Com., 1984-88; mem. Carson City Charter Rev. Com., 1986-91, chmn., 1988-91. With USN, 1945-46, 51-55. Decorated Air medals. Mem. Nat. Assn. Securities Dealers, Mcpl. Securities Rulemaking Bd., Carson City C. of C. (pres. 1986-87, bd. dir. 1982-88), Capital Club of Carson City, Rotary (chpt. sec. 1983-84, 86-87, pres. 1988-89, Paul Harris fellow). Home: 610 Bonanza Dr Carson City NV 89706-0201 Office: 711 E Washington St Carson City NV 89701-4063

REID, DIXIE LEE, city councilwoman; b. Coeur d'Alene, Idaho, Dec. 27, 1942; d. Richard E. and Elsie M. (Lenz) Johnson; m. Thomas R. Reid, Sept. 9, 1961; children: Toni Capaul, Raini Cherry, Michael. Student, U. Idaho, 1960, North Idaho Coll., 1961. City cashier City of Coeur d'Alene, 1962-63, city councilwoman, 1974-77, 83—, coun. pres., 1983—; advtg. assoc. Coeur d'Alene Press, 1978-80; owner, mgr. Gish's Corner, Post Falls, Idaho, 1980-88; owner Shopping Svcs., Coeur d'Alene, 1988—; assoc. designer Chapman Interior Design, Coeur d'Alene, 1990—; 1st v.p. Assn. of Idaho Cities, Boise, 1990-91, pres., 1991-92. Chmn. Park & Recreation Commn., Coeur d'Alene, 1970-80. Mem. PEO (pres. 1980-82, 90-91), Nat. League Cities (small cities coun. 1987—, environ. com. 1989—). Roman Catholic. Home: 1144 Lambert Ln Coeur D Alene ID 83814-6043

REID, FRANCES MARION PUGH, retired educator; b. LaGrange, Mo., Dec. 18, 1910; d. Bert Allison and Johanna Fredericke (Schroeter) Pugh; m. Garth Oscar Reid, Aug. 27, 1940; children: Garth Oscar Jr., James Allison. AB, Drury Coll., 1931. Tchr. Eng. Diamond (Mo.) High Sch., 1931-32, Castleford (Idaho) High Sch., 1935-36; tchr. Eng., speech Filer (Idaho) Rural High Sch., 1936-39, Clinton Jr. High Sch., Tulsa, 1939-40; tchr. Eng., creative writing Borah High Sch., Boise, Idaho, 1958-76; ret., 1976. Author: None So Small, 1958, Thy Word in My Heart, 1962, Walk a Rainbow Trail, 1974, In the Lee of Mountains, 1976, Given to Time, 1978, No Leave-Taking, 1982. Mem. AAUW (book rev. chmn. 1978-79, 93-94), Idaho Writers League (Writer of Yr. award 1975, Poet of Yr. award 1982), Idaho Ret. Tchrs. Assn. (pres. 1989-91, Hall of Fame 1980), Boise Ret. Tchrs. Assn. (co-pres. 1977-78, Co-Community Svc. award 1986), Delta Kappa Gamma (publicity chmn. 1980-90). Baptist. Home: 6117 Lubkin St Boise ID 83704-7563

REID, GERALD ALAN, financial executive, controller; b. Sweetwater, Tex., Aug. 9, 1961; s. Gerald Norris and Lenora Arlene (Gallas) R.; m. Tina Ann Shaw, May 15, 1988; children: Gerald Wayne, Britton Carrol. BBA in Acctg., Tex. Tech U., 1988. CPA, N.Mex. Staff acct. Ernst & Young, Roswell, N.Mex., 1988-91; asst. v.p., contr. First Fed. Savs. Bank N.Mex., Roswell, 1991—. Mem. N.Mex. Fin. Mgrs. Soc. (v.p. 1992, pres. 1993), N.Mex. Taekwondo Fedn. (liaison 1992—), World Taekwondo Fedn., Golden Key Nat. Honor Soc.

REID, HARRY, senator; b. Searchlight, Nev., Dec. 2, 1939; s. Harry and Inez Reid; m. Landra Joy Gould; children—Lana, Rory, Leif, Josh, Key. AS, Southern Utah State U., 1959; LLD (hon.), U. So. Utah, 1984; BA, Utah State U., 1961; JD, George Washington U., 1964. Bar: Nev. 1963, U.S. Supreme Ct. City atty. Henderson, Nev., 1964-66; trustee So. Nev. Meml. Hosp. Bd., 1967-69, chmn. bd. trustees, 1966-68; mem. Nev. Assembly, 1969-71; lt. gov. Nev., 1971-75; chmn. Nev. Gaming Commn., 1977-81; mem. 98th-99th Congresses, 1983-87; U.S. senator from Nev. U.S. Senate, 1987—, mem. appropriations, environ. and pub. works, aging, select com. on POW/MIA affairs, Indian affairs, Hispanic affairs coms., 1987—, mem. joint com. orgn. congress, 1992-93, chmn. toxic substances subcom. of Senate Environ. and Pub. Works com., chmn. legis. subcom. of Senate Appropriations com.; sec. Indian Affairs com. Calif. Dem. Congl. Del., 1983-86. Active Helsinki Commn.; bd. dirs. So. Nev. Meml. Hosp., 1966-68. Named Nev. Jaycees Outstanding Young Man of Yr., 1970, Man of Yr., City of Hope, 1970; recipient Nat. Jewish Hosp.-Asthma Ctr. Humanitarian award,

1984, Honor award Am. Lung Assn., 1987. Mem. Nev. Bar Assn., Am. Bd. Trial Advocates, Phi Kappa Phi. Office: US Senate 324 Hart Senate Bldg Washington DC 20510

REID, J. STEPHEN, insurance and estate planning executive; b. Detroit, Apr. 9, 1939; s. Horace Jeter and Viola A. (Israelson) R.; m. Alice Virginia Allen, June 3, 1965; children: Kristen Elisa, Sonja Kaiulani. BA, Dartmouth Coll., 1962; MBA, U. Mich., 1964; MS in Fin. Svcs., Am. Coll., Bryn Mawr, Pa., 1983. CLU, ChFC. Br. mgr. Met. Life, Chgo., 1968-69, Honolulu, 1969-75; pres. Reid Ins. Agy. Inc., Honolulu, 1975—, Profl. Estate Planning, Inc., Seattle, 1992—. Mem. Million Dollar Round Table (Top of Table, Ct. of Table), Hawaii Estate Planning Coun. (all incl. pres. 1981), Hawaii Assn. Life Underwriters, CLU and ChFC (pres. Hawaii chpt. 1985, 86), Dartmouth Club Hawaii (pres. 1980-82), Oahu Country Club (Honolulu), Plaza Club Hawaii-Honolulu. Episcopalian.

REID, JOSEPH LEE, physical oceanographer, educator; b. Franklin, Tex., Feb. 7, 1923; s. Joseph Lee and Ruby (Cranford) R.; m. Freda Mary Hunt, Apr. 7, 1953; children: Ian Joseph, Julian Richard. BA in Math., U. Tex., 1942; MS, Scripps Instn. Oceanography, 1950. Rsch. staff Scripps Instn. Oceanography, La Jolla, Calif., 1957-74; prof. oceanography Scripps Instn. Oceanography, La Jolla, 1974-91, ret., 1991; dir. Marine Life Rsch. Group, 1974-87; assoc. dir. Inst. Marine Resources, 1975-82; cons. Sandia Nat. Labs., Albuquerque, 1980-86. Author: On the Total Geostrophic Circulation of the South Pacific Ocean: Flow Patterns, Tracers and Transports, 1986, On the Total Geostrophic Circulation of the South Atlantic Ocean: Flow Patterns, Tracers and Transports, 1989; contbr. articles to profl. jours. Lt. USNR, 1942-46, ETO, PTO. Recipient award Nat. Oceanographic Data Ctr., Washington, 1984, Albatross award Am. Miscellaneous Soc., 1988, Alexander Agassiz medal NAS, 1992. Fellow AAAS, Am. Geophys. Union (pres. Ocean Scis. sect. 1972-74, 84-86); mem. Am. Meteorol. Soc., Oceanography Soc. Home: 1105 Cuchara Dr Del Mar CA 92014-2623

REID, MARION TAYLOR, library director; b. Balt., Oct. 27, 1944; d. Richard Milton and Margaret (Sawyer) Taylor; m. K. Brooks Reid, Sept. 3, 1966; children: Kathryn Margaret, Kristina Brooks. BS in English Edn., U. Ill., 1966, MLS, 1968. Sch. libr. Urbana (Ill.) Community Schs., 1966-68; asst. libr. Ill. Natural History Survey, Urbana, 1968; supr. book processing La. State U. Librs., Baton Rouge, 1968-69, head order dept., 1969-78, asst. dir. tech. svcs., 1978-84, assoc. dir., 1984-89; interim libr. dir. Calif. State U., San Marcos, 1989-90, dir. of libr. svcs., 1990—, acting dir. computing and telecom.; cons. Johns Hopkins U. Libr., Balt., 1982, Emory U. Libr., Atlanta, 1982, Ga. State U. Libr., Atlanta, 1986, U.S. Naval Acad. Nimitz Libr., Annapolis, Md., 1991, Southeastern La. U. Libr., 1992, U. Ill. Libr., Chgo., 1993. Contbr. articles to profl. publs., chpts. to books. Coun. on Libr. Resources fellow, 1974, La. State U. Sch. Bus. Adminstrn. fellow, 1982, UCLA Grad. Sch. Libr. and Info. Sci. sr. fellow, 1989. Mem. ALA, Assn. Libr. Collections and Tech. Svcs. (pres. 1988), Assn. Coll. and Rsch. Librs., Calif. Libr. Assn. (coun. rep. 1992, mem. exec com. 1993-94), Beta Phi Mu (nat. bd. dirs. 1991—). Home: 1092 Cima Dr San Marcos CA 92069 Office: Calif State U Library San Marcos CA 92096

REID, MEGAN BETH, museum administrator; b. Durango, Colo., May 1, 1954; d. Charles Henry Jr. and Jean Phyllis (Siegfried) R. BA in Studio Art, Ft. Lewis Coll., 1975; postgrad., U. Minn., 1977-79. Intern U. Minn. Gallery, Mpls., 1978-79; curator Dacotah Prairie Mus., Aberdeen, S.D., 1980, dir., 1981-82; exhibit technician Fulton (Tex.) Mansion State Hist. Structure, Tex. State Pks., 1983-84, pk. supt./mus. dir., 1985; dir. Rio Colo. div. Ariz. Hist. Soc., Yuma, 1985—; exhibit designer and constuctor, 1980—. Living history researcher and performer, 1985—; contbr. articles to profl. publs., 1985—. Bd. dirs. cultural coun. and hist. designation rev. com. City Yuma, 1985—, bd. dirs. Main St. com., 1988—; cons. S.D. Arts Coun., 1982, Ariz. Arts Coun.-Tribal Mus. Assessment Program, 1990. Art purchase grantee Nat. Endowment for Arts, 1981-82; gen. operating grantee Inst. Mus. Svcs., 1981-82; oral history grantee Ariz. Humanities Coun., 1987; recipient various bldg. preservation grants Ariz. State Hist. Preservation Office, 1985—. Mem. Am. Assn. Mus., Nat. Trust for Hist. Preservation, Assn. State and Local History, Western Assn. Mus., Ariz. Mus. Assn. (cons. 1990), Mt. Plains Mus. Assn. Office: Ariz Hist Soc 240 S Madison Ave Yuma AZ 85364-1421

REID, RICHARD ALAN, management science educator; b. Cleve., May 15, 1938; s. Harry William Palmer and Leenore (Weber) R.; m. Janice Marie Maline; children: Adam R., Kevin D., Bradley H. BSME, Case Inst. Tech., 1962; MBA, Ohio State U., 1967, PhD, 1970. Engr. field svc. AC Electronics, Milw., 1962-65; asst. prof. mgmt. sci. U. N.Mex., Albuquerque, 1969-75, assoc. prof. mgmt. sci., 1975-83, prof. mgmt. sci., 1983—; cons. Los Alamos (N.Mex.) Nat. Lab., 1979—, Sandia Nat. Labs. Albuquerque, 1987-89, VA Hosp., Albuquerque, 1978-79, Presbyn. Hosp. Ctr., Albuquerque, 1971-74. Co-author: Competitive Hospitals, 1986; contbr. articles to profl. jours. Ed Wood lectureship Anderson Sch. Mgmt., U. N. Mex., 1990. Mem. Decision Sci. Inst., Operations Rsch. Soc. Am. Office: Univ N Mex Anderson Sch Mgmt Albuquerque NM 87131

REIDER, HARRY ROBERT, management consultant; b. Phila., Nov. 28, 1940; s. Benjamin and Esther (Weiss) R. BSBA, Drexel U., 1963, MBA, 1966; PhD in Organizational and Mgmt. Psychology, Southwest U., Phoenix, 1982. CPA, Pa. Corp. systems analyst Campbell Soup Co., Camden, N.J., 1963-66; mgr. corp. systems devel. Leeds & Northrup, North Wales, Pa., 1966-69; mgr., mgmt. cons. Peat, Marwick, Mitchell & Co., Phila., 1969-76; pres. Reider Assocs., mgmt. cons., Santa Fe, 1976—; lectr., cons. in field. Author: Operational Auditing, 1983, EDP Auditing, 1983, Developing a Consulting Practice, 1985, General Practice Management, 1985, Microcomputer Fundamentals, 1985, Microcomputer Hardware and Software Selection Process, 1985, Developing an MAS Practice, 1987, How to Conduct the Single Audit, 1990, Advising and Consulting to the Small Business, 1991, Self-study audio cassette courses: Developing A MAS (Consulting) Practice, 1992, Operational Auditing: A Tool For Positive Improvement, 1992, Effective Audit of Net-For-Profit Organizations, 1993, Current Developments in Goverment Auditing, 1993, Managing your Practice for Success, 1993, Managing in Today's Environment, 1993, Improving Organizational Communications, 1993, The Complete Guide to Operational Auditing, 1993; contbr. articles to profl. jours.; guest commentator (video) The CPA Report. Mem. AICPA (Discussion Leader of Yr. 1986-87), Pa. Inst. CPAs (chmn. social responsibility com. 1980-81), N.Mex. Soc. CPAs. Office: Reider Assocs RR 9 Santa Fe NM 87505-9805

REIDLINGER, CHARLES RONALD, academic administrator; b. New Orleans, Jan. 18, 1929; s. Charles August Reidlinger and Jewel (Gardner) Milazzo; m. Natalie Sykes, Aug. 7, 1950; children: Christopher, Ray, Craig Ronald. BS in Zoology, McNeese State U., 1957; MS in Zoology, U. Tenn., 1958; PhD in Adult Edn., Kans. State U., 1978. Asst. prof. zoology The Citadel, Charleston, S.C., 1958-60, Murray (Ky.) State U., 1960-62, Ky. So. Coll., Louisville, 1965-68; assoc. prof. zoology Brunswick (Ga.) Jr. Coll., 1968-71; instr. zoology Johnson County Community Coll., Overland Park, Kans., 1971-73; off campus coord. Kans. State U., Manhattan, 1973-79; profl. devel. coord. St. Mary's U., San Antonio, 1979-82; provost, prof. N.Mex. State U., Alamogordo, 1982—. Pres. United Way Otero County, Alamogordo, 1990, campaign chmn., 1991. NSF summer scholar, 1960, acad. yr. scholar, 1962-64. Mem. Am. Assn. Community and Jr. Colls., N.Mex. Assn. Community and Jr. Colls., Coun. Two Yr. Colls. Four Yr. Instns. (pres. 1991—), Alamogordo C. of C. (bd. dirs. 1986-90), Rotary (pres. Alamogordo chpt. 1989-90). Home: 1409 Plaza Del Prado Alamogordo NM 88310-3972 Office: NMex State U 2400 N Scenic Dr Alamogordo NM 88311

REIDY, RICHARD ROBERT, publishing company executive; b. Patchogue, N.Y., May 9, 1947; s. Joseph Robert and Irene (Jennings) R.; m. Carolyn Alyce Armstrong, Mar. 21, 1970; children: Dawn Patricia, Shawn Patrick, Christopher Keith. Student, Suffolk County Community Coll., 1966-68, L.I. Tech. Sch., 1969-70, Scottsdale Community Coll., 1983-84, 85-86. Lic. real estate agt., Ariz. Restaurant owner Reidy's, Patchogue, 1973-77; design draftsman Sverdrop & Parcel, Tempe, Ariz., 1978-79, Sullivan & Masson, Phoenix, 1979-81; pres. Success Pub. Co., Scottsdale, Ariz., 1983—; with U.S. Postal Dept., 1980—. Editor, owner, pub.: Who's Who in Arizona, 1984-85, 89-90. Chief Scottsdale YMCA, 1983-84; eucharistic minister St. Daniel the Prophet Cath. Ch., Scottsdale, 1985—; mem. World Wide Marriage Encounter, 1986—; pres. Coronado High Sch. Band Boosters, 1988-89. Mem. Scottsdale C. of C., Phoenix Better Bus. Bur. Office: Success Pub Co PO Box 3431 Scottsdale AZ 85271-3431

REIF, (FRANK) DAVID, artist, educator; b. Cin., Dec. 14, 1941; s. Carl A. and Rachel L. (Clifton) R.; m. Ilona Jekabsons, July 30, 1966; 1 child, Megan Elizabeth. BFA, Art Inst. Chgo., 1968; MFA, Yale U., 1970. Asst. prof. art U. Wyo., Laramie, 1970-74, assoc. prof., 1974-81, prof., 1981—; assoc. prof. U. Mich., Ann Arbor, 1980-81; acting head dept. art U. Wyo., Laramie, 1986-87; selection cons. Ucross Found. Residency Program, Wyo., 1983—; exhibit juror Artwest Nat., Jackson, Wyo., 1986; panelist Colo. State U., Ft. Collins, 1981; lectr. U. Mich., 1980. One-man shows include Dorsky Galleries N.Y.C., 1980, Colo. State U., 1978, No. Ariz. U., 1977, 87, U. Mich., 1980, 81, One West Ctr. Contemporary Art, Ft. Collins, 1991; exhibited in group shows at First, Second and Third Wyo. Biennial Tour, 1984-88, U.S. Olympics Art Exhibition, L.A., 1984, Miss. Mus. Art and NEA Tour., 1981-83, La. Invitational Sculpture Tour Exhibition, 1991-92. With USAR, 1963-69. Recipient F.D. Pardee award Yale U., 1970; Best Sculpture award Joslyn Art Mus. Omaha, 1978; Nat. Endowment Arts grantee, 1978-79, Wyo. Basic Rsch. grantee, 1983-84, 86-87. Mem. Coll. Art Assn., Internat. Sculpture Ctr. Democrat. Home: 3340 Aspen Ln Laramie WY 82070-5702 Office: U Wyo Dept Art PO Box 3138 Laramie WY 82071-3138

REIF, JOHN STEVEN, epidemiologist, veterinarian; b. N.Y.C., Sept. 18, 1940; s. Hans V. and Anne (Marie) R. DVM, Cornell U., 1963; MSc in Epidemiology, U. Pa., 1966. NIH postdoctoral fellow U. Pa., Phila., 1966-68, asst. prof., 1969-73, assoc. prof., 1974-78; prof., chief comparative medicine sect. Inst. Rural Environ. Colo. State U., Ft. Collins, 1979—; prof. U. Otago Sch. Medicine, Wellington, N.Z., 1987-88. Contbr. numerous articles to profl. jours. Mem., pres. Larimer County Bd. Health, Ft. Collins, 1980-85; mem. Colo. Bd. Health, Denver, 1982-87. Fogarty fellow NIH, 1987-88; recipient Recognition award Tchrs. Preventive Medicine, 1989. Fellow Am. Coll. Epidemiology; mem. APHA, Internat. Epidemiology Assn., Internat. Soc. Environ. Epidemiology, Soc. for Epidemiologic Rsch. Office: Colo State U Dept Environ Health Fort Collins CO 80523

REIF, LAURIE LOUISE, psychotherapist; b. L.A., May 5, 1929; d. Theron Wenton and Dorothy Virginia (Kimmey) Aslin; m. William Klein, Apr. 24, 1948 (div. 1972); m. Kurt Reif, Oct. 10, 1977; children: Elizabeth, Bella Marie Stephen, Teresa, Thomas, Alana, Maranda, Jennifer, Adrian, Stephanie. BS, Calif. Poly. U., Pomona, 1972; MA in Psychology, Ea. N.Mex. U., 1985; PhD in Psychology, Kensington U., Glendale, Calif., 1991. Cert. med. psychotherapist; cert. mediator. Dir. admissions Ednl. Tutoring Inst. of Calif., 1972-73; recruiter Assoc. Colls. of Calif., 1973-74; placement counselor Employment Rsch., Calif., 1974-78; dir. admissions Legal Adminstrv. Ctr., Calif., 1978-80; paralegal Kurt Reif, Atty.-at-Law, 1980-84; grad. asst., counselor, tchr. Ea. N.Mex. U., Portales, 1984-85; counselor M.L.P. Assocs., Inc., Portales, 1985; counselor, coord. geriatric svcs. Carlsbad (N.Mex.) Mental Health Ctr., 1986; program therapist Life Mgmt. Program Guadalupe Med. Ctr., 1986-91; pvt. practice psychotherapy Carlsbad, 1991—; instr. N.Mex. State U., Carlsbad, 1991—; dir. of treatment Compassionate Friends, Inc., 1991—. Recipient Cert. of Recognition for Excellence in Rsch., Svc. award Psi Chi. Mem. APA, Am. Assn. for Counseling and Devel., Internat. Psychogeriatric Assn., Am. Mental Health Counselors Assn., Forum on Death and Dying, N.Mex. Psychol. Assn., Reality Therapy Assn., Trans Pecos Assn. for Counseling and Devel., Hospice, Downtown Businessmen's Assn., Kiwanis. Democrat. Home: 1712 Trevino Ct Carlsbad NM 88220 Office: 516 N Canal Carlsbad NM 88220

REIFF, SIDNEY, internist; b. N.Y.C., June 10, 1918; s. Israel Joshua and Yetta (Halonbrenner) F.; m. Renee Polansky, Feb. 3, 1946; children: Isabel, Kenneth, Russell. BA, NYU, 1938, MD, 1942. Diplomate Am. Bd. Internal Medicine. Intern Lincoln Hosp., N.Y.C., 1942-43, med. resident, 1946-48; pvt. practice internal medicine Bklyn., 1948-71; staff internist So. Calif. Permanente Med. Group, L.A., 1971—; asst. clin. prof. medicine SUNY Downstate Med. Sch., Bklyn., 1949-70. Contbr. articles to profl. publs. Capt. U.S. Army, 1943-46, PTO. Decorated Bronze Star. Fellow ACP; mem. L.A. Soc. Internal Medicine, Physicians for Social Responsibility. Democrat. Jewish. Home: 768 Glenmont Ave Los Angeles CA 90024 Office: So Calif Permanente 4950 Sunset Blvd Los Angeles CA 90027

REIFF, THEODORE CURTIS, investment banker; b. Cleve., Aug. 6, 1942; s. William Fred and Dorothy Louise (Knauer) R.; m. Janis Lynn Brunk, May 6, 1966 (div. Aug. 1980); m. Theresa Dolores Baranello, Oct. 30, 1982. BS, Ohio State U., 1969. Lic. real estate broker. Dir. adminstrv. svcs. Mgmt. Horizons, Inc., Columbus, Ohio, 1969-73; v.p. Danco Mgmt. Co., Lancaster, Ohio, 1973-74; sr. v.p. Anchor Lighting Corp., Columbus, 1974-75; ptnr. Curtis-Lee & Assocs., Delaware, Ohio, 1974-77; pres. Cartunes Corp., San Diego, Calif., 1977-91; also bd. dirs. Cartunes Corp., San Diego; facilities coord. Raytheon Co., Burlington, Mass., 1979-82; ptnr. Greenstone & Reiff, San Diego, 1982-86; ptnr. Creative Bus. Strategies, Inc., San Diego, 1986-91, pres., bd. dirs.; pres. Bus. Pubs. Inc., San Diego, 1989-91, also bd. dirs.; mng. dir. PM Co., Tijuana, B.C., Mex., 1991—; bd. dirs. Integrated Ceramic Tech., San Marcos, Calif., 1986-88, Pacific Rim Interface Mems. Enterprises Inc., 1988-90, Distributed Communications Corp., San Diego, 1986-91, Paradox Devel. Corp., San Diego, 1990-91, Phoenix Systems & Techs., Chula Vista, Calif., 1990-91; instr. Miramar Coll., San Diego, 1984-90. Mem. Friends of San Diego Zoo, 1980—; chmn. bus. adv. com. San Diego State U. Coll. of Bus., 1979-82; mem. adv. com. Coll. Bus. Calif. State U., 1992—. With Ohio N.G., 1966-72. Named Outstanding Businessman City of Columbus, Ohio, 1974; recipient Recognition award San Diego State U. Coll. of Bus., 1983, Appreciation award Am. Mktg. Assn., 1984, IEEE, 1986. Mem. Am. Electronics Assn. (chmn. small bus. com. 1988-89, chmn. fin. com. 1989-91), San Diego World Trade Assn., High Tech. Found. Home: 4356 Vivaracho Ct San Diego CA 92124-2225

REILLEY, KATHLEEN PATRICIA, lawyer; b. Pitts., Oct. 31, 1948; d. Edward Michael and Mary Elizabeth (Davidson) R. BA, U. Calif., Berkeley, 1976; JD, Golden Gate U., 1979. Bar: Calif. Staff atty. Fresno County Legal Svcs., Calif., 1979-85, Santa Monica (Calif.) Rent Control Bd., 1985-89; asst. city atty. City of Berkeley, 1990-91; atty. Linda DeBene Inc., Danville, Calif., 1991—. Co-founder Calif. Housing Action & Info. Network, 1976. Mem. Calif. State Bar Assn. (real property sect.), Contra Costa County Bar Assn. (real property sect.). Democrat. Episcopalian. Office: Linda DeBene Inc 4135 Blackhawk Plz Circle Danville CA 94506

REILLY, ROBERT JOSEPH, counselor; b. Spokane, Wash., Mar. 7, 1936; s. John Francis and Vivian Helen (White) R.; m. Joan Steiner, June 20, 1960; children: Sean Michael, Patrick Joseph, Bridget Colleen. BA in Psychology, Seattle U., 1985. Pvt. U.S. Army, 1953, advanced through grades to maj., 1981, ret.; counselor Schick Shadel Hosp., Seattle, 1984-89; dir. Canyon Counseling, Puyallup, Wash., 1987-92; counselor Wash. State Employee Adv. Svc., Olympia, 1992—; bd. dirs. Chem. Dependency Counselors Wash. State, 1985-89, cert. bd., 1990-92, 93—; exec. v.p. Coll. Therapeutic Hypnosis, Puyallup, 1989—. Pres. Irish Cultural Club, Tacoma, 1983-85; sec. Retired Officers Assn., 1983-87, pres. 1993—. Mem. Wash. State Chpt. Nat. Bd. for Hypnotherapy & Hypnotic Anaesthesiology (pres. 1991—). Office: Wash State Employee Adv Svc 3400 Capital Blvd Olympia WA 98504-7540

REIM, RUTHANN, career and personal counselor, corporate trainer; b. Fresno, Calif., Oct. 4, 1943; d. F. Wayne and Charlene Marie (Young) Howd; m. Terry D., Nov. 29, 1963; children: Tracey, Brandon. BA in Sociology, San Jose State U., 1966; MA Guidance & Counseling, Pacific Luth. U., 1984. Cert. counselor, nat. Tchr., elem. sch. Dupont Sch. Dist., Tacoma, 1966-67, Prince Georges Sch. Dist., Lanham, Md., 1967-68, Franklin Pierce sch. Dist., Tacoma, 1968-70; owner Rainbow Glassworks, Tacoma, 1973-76, Creative Womanlife, Tacoma, 1976-78; dir., counselor Individual Devel. Ctr., Tacoma, 1984-88; pres. Career Mgmt. Inst., Tacoma, 1989—; adj. faculty mem. dept. edn. Pacific Luth. U., 1980-84. Author: (career booklet) Career Change Made Easy, 1990; artist 5' round stained glass window "Dogwood", 1980. Trainer Jr. League Tacoma, 1977-79. Mem. Rotary (1st woman pres. 1991-92, bd. dirs. 1988—), Phi Kappa Phi. Office: Career Mgmt Inst 8404 27th St W Tacoma WA 98466-2723

REIMANN, BERNHARD ERWIN FERDINAND, biologist; b. Berlin, Germany, May 30, 1922; s. Phlilip Bernhard Ferdinand and Margarete (Kutzleb) R.; m. Beate Eleonore Hedwig, Sept. 1, 1949; 1 child, Joachim Oscar Ferdinand. Grad., Paulsen Oberschule, 1941; Lic., Berlin, 1949; D in Botany, Zoology, Geology, Freie U., Berlin, 1959. Supr. electo microscopy facility Scripps Inst. Oceanography, La Jolla, Calif., 1961-67; chief electron microscopy dept. pathology and area lab. svcs. William Beaumont Army Med. Ctr., El Paso, Tex., 1967-87; ret.; assoc. grad. faculty U. Tex. El Paso, 1968-69, assoc. prof. biology dept. N.Mex. State U., Las Cruces, 1967-87; assoc. clin. prof. dept. patholgy Tex. Tech. U., El Paso, 1980-87. Contbr. articles to profl. jours. Vol. environ. adviser liquid waste disposal problems Village of Capitan N.Mex. and Lincoln County, 1988—. With German Air Force, 1941-47. Named Civil Servant of Yr. Fed. Bus. Assn., 1981; recipient Commanders Civilian Svc. award William Beaumont Army Med. Ctr., 1987. Fellow AAAS; mem. Electron Microscopy Soc. Am. Democrat. Home: 115 E Lobo Rd Capitan NM 88316

REIMER, NEIL JOSEPH, entomologist, consultant; b. Petaluma, Calif., Nov. 14, 1954; s. Gale Reuben and Donna Marie (DeDecker) R.; m. Carol Ann Jackson, Jan. 8, 1983; children: Claire, Timothy. Student, Calif. State U., Northridge, 1972-75; BS, U. Calif., Riverside, 1976, MS, 1980; PhD, U. Hawaii, 1985. Rsch. asst. U. Hawaii, Honolulu, 1981-85, asst. entomologist, 1986—, mem. grad. faculty, 1990; cons. Hawaii Pest Control Assn., Honolulu, 1985—, Hawaii Coffee Growers Assn., Kona, 1989—. Contbr. articles to profl. jours.; contbr. chpts. to numerous books. Erhorn scholar U. Hawaii, 1985; rsch. grantee Hawaii Gov.'s Agrl. Coordinating Com., 1989, 91, 92, Hawaii Dept. Land and Natural Resources, 1990. Mem. Entomol. Soc. Am., Am. Inst. Biol. Sci., Internat. Union for Study Social Insects, Internat. Orgn. for Biol. Control, Hawaiian Entomol. Soc. (treas. 1991-93), Sigma Xi. Office: U Hawaii 3050 Maile Way Rm 310 Honolulu HI 69822

REIMER, STEVEN JAMES, investment company executive; b. Hutchinson, Kans., July 7, 1957; s. Delmer James and Geraldine Louise (Toews) R.; m. Stephanie Ann Heinrichs, June 19, 1982; children: Kyle Daniel, Jeffrey Paul, Laura Christine, John Alexander. BA in Edn. and Bus., Tabor Coll., 1980; postgrad., Wichita State U., 1984. Securities broker SunAmerica Securities, Inc, Wichita, Dallas, 1985-89; dir., shareholder ISM Fin. Group, Inc., Wichita, Kans., 1988-89; pres. CEO Cottonwood Fin. Svcs., Inc., Wichita, 1989-90; securities broker Laney and Co., Vancouver, Seattle, Wash., 1989-92; registered investment advisor Fin. Rsch., Inc., Seattle, 1990—; dir. Churchill Mortgage Co., Vancouver, Wash., 1990—; v.p., dir. Churchill Cos., Inc., Vancouver, 1990—; sec., officer, dir. Churchill Energy Corp., Vancouver, 1992—; securities broker Andover Securities, Inc., Kansas City, Vancouver, Mo., Wash., 1992—; pres. Blue Rhino Trading Co., Inc., 1993—; adv. councilman Churchill Cos., Inc., Vancouver, 1992—. Mem. taskforce substance abuse team Wichita Pub. Schs., 1984-85; chmn. elect Tabor Coll. Alumni Bd., 1986-89; bd. dirs. Clark County Chaplaincy, Vancouver, 1992—. Mem. Nat. Assn. Securities Dealers, Internat. Assn. Fin. Planners. Mem. Mennonite Brethren. Office: Churchill Cos Inc 1104 Main St Ste 500 Vancouver WA 98660

REIMNITZ, ELROI, minister; b. Porto Alegre, Brazil, June 20, 1948; s. Elmer and Kordula Luise (Schelp) R; Ruth Weimer, June 1973; children: Patrick, Kristeen, Nicholas. Diploma, Seminario Concordia, Porto Alegre, 1966; postgrad., Faculdade Porto-Alegrense E.C.L., 1968; MDiv, Concordia Sem., St. Louis, 1971, ThD, 1975; postdoctoral studies, Faculdade de Direito I.R.R., Canoas, Brazil, 1976-77, Faith Luth. Sem., Tacoma, 1990—. Ordained to ministry Luth. Ch.-Mo. Synod, 1975. Vicar Immanuel Luth. Ch., Bristol, Conn., 1969-70; asst. to pastor Our Savior's 1st Luth. Ch., Granada Hills, Calif., 1974-75; pastor Zion Luth. Ch., Alamo, Tex., 1975, St. John's Luth. Ch., Canoas, 1976-78; pastor, dir. ministries Trinity Luth. Ch., Grand Island, Nebr., 1978-86; pastor Redeemer Luth. Ch., Thousand Oaks, Calif., 1986—; instr. U. Luterana do Brasil, Canoas, 1976-78; adminstrv. dir. Cultural Lang. Inst., Canoas, 1976-78; supt. Trinity Luth. Sch., Grand Island, 1978-86; treas. Grand Island cir. Nebr. dist. Luth. Ch.-Mo. Synod, 1984-86; chaplain police, sheriff and fire depts. City of Grand Island, 1985-86; counselor campus ministry Calif. Luth. U., Thousand Oaks, 1986—; adj. faculty mem. Trinity Theol. Sem., Newburgh, Ind., 1993—. Contbr. articles to religious jours. Adv. mem. Grand Island Luth. Family and Social Svcs., 1985-86; mem. programs com. Cen. Platte Natural Resources Dist., 1985-86, site coun. Cypress Elem. Sch., Newbury Park, Calif., 1987-88, Community Devel. Allocation Com., Thousand Oaks, 1991-92; bd. dirs. Casas De La Senda Homeowners Assn., Newbury Park, 1986—, Citizens Quality of Life Action Alliance, Thousand Oaks, 1992—; alt. mem. ad hoc com. Newbury Park Libr., 1987-90, Newbury Park High Sch. Site Coun., 1992—; treas. circ. one pacific s.w. dist. Luth. Ch. Mo., Synod, 1991—. Mem. Am. Assn. Christian Counselors, United Assn. Christian Counselors Internat. Home: 3883 San Marcos Ct Newbury Park CA 91320-3725 Office: Redeemer Luth Ch 667 Camino Dos Rios Thousand Oaks CA 91360-2399

REINCE, MARTHA MARY, human resources manager; b. Milw., Dec. 11, 1962; d. George Richard and Alice Kathleen (Hayes) Seidenstricker; m. Kevin Robert Reince, Nov. 10, 1990. BBA in Accting., St. Norbert Coll., DePere, Wis., 1985. Tax acct. Arthur Anderson & Co., Milw., 1985-87; mgmt. devel. program Arthur Anderson & Co., L.A., 1987-89; human resources mgr. Learning Group Internat., L.A., 1989—. Roman Catholic. Home: 5834 Dunrobin Ave Lakewood CA 90713-1030

REINDERS, JAMES W., petroleum consultant; b. Alliance, Nebr., Sept. 20, 1927; s. Herman I. and Catherine L. (Tickner) R.; m. Violet A. Strong, Nov. 13, 1948; children: James M., Janice K., Jody M. BSEE, U. Nebr., 1950. Registered profl. engr. Mktg. mgr. Schlumberger, New Orleans, 1965-69; div. mgr. Schlumberger, Shreveport, La., 1969-71; tech. mgr. Schlumberger, Houston, 1971-73; mgr. Schlumberger, Tehran, Iran, 1973-75; tech. mgr. Schlumberger, London, 1975-81; pres. Geo Vann, Inc., Houston, 1982-84; petroleum cons. Houston, 1984-91, Albuquerque, 1991—. Sculpture entitled Carhenge, 1987. With USNR, 1944-46. Mem. Soc. of Petroleum Engrs., Nat. Forensic Ctr., Toastmasters, Pi Mu Epsilon. Republican. Home: 13215 Circulo Largo NE Albuquerque NM 87112

REINER, JAMES ANTHONY, marketing executive; b. Orange, Calif., Sept. 12, 1958; s. Earl Arthur and Mary Ann (Cuff) R. BBA in Acctg., U. Mo., 1983, MBA in Mktg., 1984. Mktg. intern The Seven-UP Co., St. Louis, 1984-85; mktg. analyst Rawlings Sporting Goods, St. Louis, 1985-86; mktg. mgr. Rawlings Sporting Goods Co., St. Louis, 1986-88; product mgr. Con Agra Consumer Frozen Food Co., St. Louis, 1988-89, sr. product mgr., 1989-90, group product mgr., 1990-91, dir. mktg., 1991-92; exec. v.p. mktg. Luigiho's Inc., Duluth, Minn., 1992; dir. diversification Samsonite Corp., Denver, 1992—. Mem. Am. Mktg. Assn., Alpha Mu Alpha (hon.). Republican. Home: 9888 E Vassar Dr I204 Denver CO 80231 Office: 11200 E 45th Ave Denver CO 80239

REINFELDS, JURIS, computer science educator; b. Riga, Latvia, Apr. 1, 1936; came to U.S., 1989; s. Nikolais Janis and Irma (Kaulins) R.; m. Lauma Petersons, Sept. 15, 1962; children: Peteris Maris, Ivars Valdis, Martins Nikolais. BSc, U. Adelaide, Australia, 1959; PhD, U. Adelaide, 1963. Postdoctoral fellow U. Edinburgh, Scotland, 1961-64; postdoctoral rsch. fellow U. Adelaide, Australia, 1964-65; NSF postdoctoral rsch. assoc. NASA, Huntsville, Ala., 1965-66; asst. prof. computer sci. U. Ga., Athens, 1966-72; vis. scientist CERN, Geneva, 1972-75; found. prof. computer sci. U. Wollongong NSW, Australia, 1975-89; prof. computer sci. N.Mex. State U., Las Cruces, 1989—; cons. Australian Internat. Devel. Program, Hat Yai, Thailand, 1983-91, Los Banos, Philippines, 1983-90. Mem. IEEE Computer Soc., Assn. for Computer Machinery, Australian Computer Soc., Las Cruces Rotary Club. Office: N Mex State U Computer Sci Dept Box 30001 Dept CS Las Cruces NM 88003

REINHARDT, BRUCE STEVEN, natural resources specialist; b. Pasadena, Calif., Nov. 16, 1951; s. Wesley Earl II and Verna Lou (Furry) R.; m. Katherine Rose Wilson, Feb. 14, 1991; 1 child, Katie Analiese. BA in Biology, Sonoma State U., Rohnert Park, Calif., 1973; MS in Range Mgmt., U. Calif., Davis, 1978. Botanist Forest Svc. USDA, Eureka, Calif., 1974-76; agrl. rschr. Agrl. Rsch. Svc., USDA, Davis, 1976-77; range conservationist Forest Svc., USDA, Tulelake, Calif., 1978-79; range conservationist Soil Conservation Svc., USDA, Santa Maria, Calif., 1981; range conservationist

Bur. Land Mgmt., U.S. Dept. Interior, Susanville, Calif., 1979-80; natural resources planner USAF, Vandenberg AFB, Calif., 1981-82, Beale AFB, Calif., 1982-86, Andersen AFB, Guam, 1986-89; environ. protection specialist USAF, Beale AFB, 1989—; cons. botanist, Eureka, 1976; instr. Lassen Coll., Susanville, 1979-81. Recipient Natural Resources Conservation award SAC, 1985, USAF, 1985, Natural Resources Conservation Program award Sec. Def., 1985. Mem. Soc. for Range Mgmt., Wildlife Soc., Nat. Assn. Mil. Wildlife Mgrs., Profl. Assn. Diving Instrs. Republican. Nazarene. Home: 17671 Candlewood Ct Penn Valley CA 94946 Office: USAF 9 CES/CEV 6451 B St Beale AFB CA 95903-1708

REINHARDT, DOMINGO HAROLDO, agronomist; b. Paraisopolis, Brazil, Apr. 27, 1952; came to U.S., 1989; s. Otto and Margrit (Gassner) R.; m. Solange Brandao, Aug. 4, 1979; children: Renata, Rodolfo, Daniel. BS, Fed. U. of Bahia, Salvador, 1976; MS, Fed. U. of Ceara, Fortaleza, Brazil, 1984. Rsch. exec. Nat. Rsch. Ctr. on Cassava and Fruit Crops, Bahia, Brazil, 1986-89; rschr. Brazilian Corp. for Agrl. Rsch., Bahia, Brazil, 1977-86, 89—; tropical fruit crops cons. Agropecuaria Gaviao Ltd., Bahia. Contbr. articles to profl. jours. Pres. Assn. of Employees at Embrapa/Nat. Rsch. Ctr. for Cassava and Fruit Crops, Bahia, 1980-82. Mem. Sigma Xi. Home: 411 Russell Park 6 Davis CA 95616-5165

REINHARDT, STEPHEN ROY, federal judge; b. N.Y.C., Mar. 27, 1931; s. Gottfried and Silvia (Hanlon) R.; children: Mark, Justin, Dana. B.A. cum laude, Pomona Coll., 1951; LL.B., Yale, 1954. Bar: Calif. 1958. Law clk. to U.S. Dist. Judge Luther W. Youngdahl, Washington, 1956-57; atty. O'Melveny & Myers, L.A., 1957-59; partner Fogel Julber Reinhardt Rothschild & Feldman (L.C.), L.A., 1959-80; judge U.S. Ct. Appeals (9th cir.), L.A., 1980—; Mem. exec. com. Dem. Nat. Com., 1969-72, nat. Dem. committeeman for Calif., 1976-80; pres. L.A. Recreation and Parks Commn., 1974-75; mem. Coliseum Commn., 1974-75, L.A. Police Commn., 1975-78, pres., 1978-80; sec., mem. exec. com. L.A. Olympic Organizing Com., 1980-84; bd. dirs. Amateur Athletic Found. of L.A., 1984-92; adj. prof. Loyola Law Sch., L.A., 1988—. Served to 1st lt. USAF, 1954-56. Mem. ABA (labor law coun. 1975-77).

REINHARDT, WILLIAM PARKER, chemical physicist; b. San Francisco, May 22, 1942; s. William Oscar and Elizabeth Ellen (Parker) R.; m. Katrina Hawley Currens, Mar. 14, 1979; children: James William, Alexander Hawley. BS in Basic Chemistry, U. Calif., Berkeley, 1964; AM in Chemistry, Harvard U., 1966, PhD in Chem. Physics, 1968; MA (hon.), U. Pa., 1985. Instr. chemistry Harvard U., 1967-69, asst. prof. chemistry, 1969-72, assoc. prof., 1972-74; prof. U. Colo., Boulder, 1974-84, chmn. dept. chemistry, 1977-80; prof. chemistry U. Pa., Phila., 1984-91, chmn. dept., 1985-88, D. Michael Crow prof., 1987-91; prof. chemistry U.Wash., Seattle, 1991—, assoc. chmn. undergrad. program, 1993—; vis. fellow Joint Inst. for Lab. Astrophysics of Nat. Bur. of Standards and U. Colo., 1972, 74, fellow, 1974-84; dir. Telluride Summer Rsch. Ctr., 1986-89, treas., 1989—; mem. com. on atomic, molecular and optical scis. NRC, 1988-90. Editorial bd. Phys. Rev. A, 1979-81, Chem. Physics, 1985—, Jour. Chem. Physics, 1987-89, jour. Phys. B (UK), 1992—; researcher theoretical chem. physics, theoretical atomic and molecular physics for numerous publs. Recipient Camille and Henry Dreyfus Tchr. Scholar award, 1972; Alfred P. Sloan fellow, 1972; J.S. Guggenheim Meml. fellow, 1978; Coun. on Rsch. and Creative Work faculty fellow, 1978. Fellow AAAS, Am. Phys. Soc.; mem. Am. Chem. Soc., Phi Beta Kappa, Sigma Xi (nat. lectr. 1980-82), Phi Lambda Upsilon (Fresenius award 1977). Office: U Wash Dept Chemistry BG-10 Seattle WA 98195

REINHOLD, ALLEN KURT, graphic design educator; b. Salt Lake City, Feb. 21, 1936; s. Eric Kurt and Lillian (Hansen) R.; m. Irene Laura Rawlings, May 4, 1962; children: Cindy Anne, David, Alyce, Bryce, Eugene Patrick. BA, Brigham Young U., 1961, MA, 1962. Cert. secondary and post secondary tech. and indsl., Utah, color cons. Freelance artist Allen Reinhold Art & Design Studio, American Fork, Utah, 1962—; tchr. art Emery County High Sch., Castle Dale, Utah, 1962-63; graphic artist Brigham Young U., 1954-56, 63-66; prodn. artist Evans Advt. Agy., Salt Lake City, 1968; dir. ednl. media Olympus High Sch., Salt Lake City, 1966-68; art dir. Telelecture Utah div. Family Svcs., Salt Lake City, 1968-69; art instr. Utah Tech. Coll., Salt Lake City, 1969-85; prof. graphic design Salt Lake Community Coll., 1985—; advisor, coach Vocat. Indsl. Clubs of Am., Salt Lake City, 1978-91. Illustrator: Book of Mormon Stories, 5 vols., 1971-76; exhibited in group shows at Pagent of the Arts, Am. Fork, 1980-89, Salt Lake Art Festival, 1982; executed mural Walter Talbot, 1986. Active Boy Scouts Am., American Fork, 1975-90; bd. dirs. art Am. Fork City, 1976-80; team mem. Utah State Bd. for Vocat. Edn. Accreditation, Salt Lake city, 1990. With USAR, 1953-62. Fellow Delta Phi Kappa (historian 1961-62), Salt Lake Community Coll. Faculty Senate, Utah Watercolor Soc. Republican. Mem. Ch. of Jesus Christ of Latter Day Saints. Home: 590 N 200 E American Fork UT 84003-1711 Office: Salt Lake Community Coll PO Box 31808 Salt Lake City UT 84131-0808

REINING, DONALD JAMES, construction supply company executive, retired; b. Bridgeport, Ill., Nov. 11, 1923; s. Henry James and Cora Augustine (Ramsey) R.; m. Jane Ann Linkogle, Aug. 23, 1948. BS in Edn., Ind. U., 1950. Mgr. Jeffersonville C. of C., Ind., 1950-53; exec. dir. Lafayette C. of C., Ind., 1953-61; mgr. Torrance C. of C., Calif., 1961-62; pres. So. Calif. Rock Products Assn., South Pasadena, 1963-91, So. Calif. Ready Mixed Concrete Assn., South Pasadena, 1963-91, San Bernardino Riverside Rock Products Assn., South Pasadena, 1966-74; govt. appointee Western Miners Adv. Coun., Calif., 1967. Commr. Clark County Planning Commn., Jeffersonville, Ind., 1950-51, West Lafayette Traffic Commn., Ind., 1957-61, Pub. Works Commn. LaCañada Flintridge, Calif., 1987—; dir. Little Co. of Mary Hosp., Torrance, 1962-64; sec. and treas. Calif. Transp. Found., 1992—. Recipient Mgmt. Achievement Merit award Am. Soc. Assn. Execs. 1967; named Man of Yr. So. Calif. Soc. Execs., L.A., 1983-84. Mem. Press Club, University Club, Masons, Elks. Republican. Presbyterian. Home: 5535 Rockcastle Dr LaCanada Flintridge CA 91011 Office: So Calif Rock Products Assn 1811 Fair Oaks Ave South Pasadena CA 91030

REINISCH, NANCY RAE, therapist, consultant; b. Chgo., Mar. 31, 1953; d. Charles Richard and Marianne (Gross) R.; m. Paul A. Salmen, June 14, 1980; children: Chas, Marcus. BA in Sociology cum laude, Colo. Coll., 1975; cert. drug and alcohol counseling, U. Minn., 1980; MSW, U. Denver, 1982. Cert. relationship therapist; lic. clin. social worker. Counselor Rampart Boys' Home, Colorado Springs, Colo., 1975; advocate bilinqual community Migrants in Action, St. Paul, 1976; therapist Chrysalis Ctr. for Women, Mpls., 1979; team leader and prevention specialist Project Charlie, Edina, Minn., 1977-80, also trainer, cons., 1985—; mental health worker Bethesda Mental Health Ctr. and Hosp., Denver, 1980-83; therapist Gateway Alcohol Recovery Ctr., Aurora, Colo., 1983-84; pvt. practice therapy, also dir. Family Practice Counseling Service, Glenwood Springs, Colo., 1984—; co-dir. Valley Sexual Abuse Ctr.; bd. dirs. Adv./Safehouse Project, Glenwood Springs; mem. Valley View Hosp. Ethics com., Glenwood Springs, 1986—. Mem. sch. accountability com. Glenwood Springs, Human Svcs. Commn., Garfield County. Mem. Nat. Assn. Social Workers, NOW, Nat. Abortion Rights Action League, ACLU, Colo. Pub. Interest Research Group. Democrat. Jewish. Office: Family Practice Counseling Svc 1905 Blake Ave Glenwood Springs CO 81601-4250

REINMUTH, JAMES E., college dean. Dean Coll. Bus. Adminstrn. U Oreg., Eugene. Office: Dean Business Administration Iniversity of Oregon Eugene OR 97403

REINSTEIN, HENRY ALLEN, real estate management and franchising consultant, mail order executive; b. Bklyn., July 8, 1922; s. Harry M. and Jennie (Blam) R.; m. Claire Steckman, Nov. 9, 1947; children: Jon Eric (Rick), Lisa. BA, Bklyn. Coll., 1949; MBA, Wichita U., 1954; postgrad., UCLA; grill master cert. (hon.), McDonald's Hamburger U., Los Angeles, 1975. Gen. mgr. Hurley Distbg., Jamaica, N.Y., 1946-50; ptnr. Geneva Electronics, Elmhurst, N.Y., 1950-55; regional sales mgr. Philco-Bendix Laundercenters, Woodside, N.Y., 1955-68; real estate and franchise dir. Internat. House of Pancakes, Los Angeles, 1969-76; real estate dir. West Winchell's Donuts, La Mirada, Calif., 1976-80; pres. Henry Allen Co., Northridge, Calif., 1980—; cons. Papallini Hair Inst., Los Angeles, 1965-67, Permac Dry Cleaner, Los Angeles, 1968-69, Gibraltar Transmission, San Diego, 1980-84, Auto Oil Changers, Long Beach, Calif., 1985—. Served with U.S. Army Air Corps, 1942-46, ETO. Mem. City of Hope (Northridge, Calif. chpt.), Assn. Corp. Real Estate Execs., Am. Entrepreneurs Assn., Kitco Internat. Inc. Import-Export Assn., Am. Cons. League (chartered cons., accredited profl. cons.). Democrat. Jewish. Home and Office: Henry Allen Co PO Box 5475 Sherman Oaks CA 91413-5475

REIS, JEAN STEVENSON, administrative secretary; b. Wilburton, Okla., Nov. 30, 1914; d. Robert Emory and Ada (Ross) Stevenson; m. George William Reis, June 24, 1939 (dec. 1980). BA, U. Tex., El Paso, 1934; MA, So. Meth. U., 1935; postgrad., U. Chgo., summers 1937-38, U. Wash., 1948-49. Tchr. El Paso High Sch., 1935-39; safety engr., trainer Safety and Security Div., Office of Chief Ordnance, Chgo., 1942-45; tchr. Lovenberg Jr. High Sch., Galveston, Tex., 1946; parish sec. Trinity Parish Episcopal Ch., Seattle, 1950-65; adminstrv. sec., asst. Office Resident Bishop, United Meth. Ch., Seattle, 1965—. Mem. AAUW, Beta Beta Beta. Home: 9310 42nd Ave NE Seattle WA 98115-3814 Office: Office of Bishop 2112 3d Ave #301 Seattle WA 98121

REISBERG, LEON ELTON, education educator; b. Dallas, Sept. 1, 1949; s. Morris Abraham and Gertrude (Turner) R.; m. Iris Fudell, July 3, 1973 (div. 1986); children: Joshua Fudell, Leah Fudell; m. Donna Brodigan, July 11, 1993. BS in Edn., U. Tex., Austin, 1971; MEd, U. Ark., Fayetteville, 1972; EdD, U. Kans., Lawrence, 1981. Tchr. Oklahoma City Sch. Dist., 1972-75, Putnam City Sch. Dist., Oklahoma City, 1975-78, U. Kans. Med. Ctr., Kansas City, 1978-79; asst. prof. Pacific Luth. U., Tacoma, 1981-88; tchr. Tacoma (Wash.) Sch. Dist., 1989-90; assoc. prof. edn. Pacific Luth. U., 1988—; chmn. dept. spl. edn. Pacific Luth. U., Tacoma, 1986-93, chmn. profl. edn. adv. bd., 1992—; project dir., Consulting Spl. Edn. Personnel Tng. Project, Tacoma, 1983-86; chmn. Profl. Edn. Adv. Bd. Cons. editor Learning Disability Quar., 1981-89, Acad. Therapy, 1988-90, Intervention, 1990—; contbr. articles to profl. publs. Mem. Coun. Exceptional Children, Coun. Learning Disabilities (Pacific Rim region rep.), Assn. Trainer Spl. Edn. Pers., Pi Kappa Phi. Democrat. Jewish. Office: Pacific Luth U Sch Edn Tacoma WA 98447

REISCH, MICHAEL STEWART, social work educator; b. N.Y.C., Mar. 4, 1948; s. Joseph and Charlotte (Rosenberg) R.; m. Amy Jane Lewis, May 21, 1972; children: Jennifer, Nikki. BA in History with highest honors, NYU, 1968; JD, Cornell U., 1971; PhD in History, SUNY, Binghamton, 1975; MSW, CUNY, 1979. Youth worker Washington-Heights-Inwood YM-YWHA, N.Y.C., 1965-66; editor, columnist Heights Daily News, Bronx, N.Y., 1966-68; rsch./teaching asst. SUNY, Binghamton, 1970-72; unit dir., program cons. Child Study Assn.-Wel Met, Inc., N.Y.C., 1970-72; asst. dir. youth div. Mosholu-Montefiore Community Ctr., Bronx, 1972-73; project dir. Silverman Found./N.Y. Assn. Deans, N.Y.C., 1973-74; asst. dean Sch. Social Welfare, asst. prof. SUNY, Stony Brook, 1974-79; asst. prof., then assoc. prof. Sch. Social Work U. Md., Balt., 1979-86; dir. Sch. Social Work and Pub. Adminstrn., prof. San Francisco State U., 1986—; cons. in field. Author: From Charity to Enterprise, 1989 (Social Sci. Book of Month); editor, author various books in field; contbr. articles to profl. publs., chpts. to books. Cons. to numerous local, state and fed. polit. campaigns, 1971—; mem. Gov.'s Adv. Coun. Human Resources, Md., 1983-86; pres. Welfare Advs., Md., 1983-86; campaign mgr. Rep. Barbara Mikulski, Balt., 1982; bd. dirs. Coleman Advs. for Children and Youth, 1986—; chair Children's Budget Task Force City of San Francisco, 1989-92; mem. Mayor's Adv. Coun. on Drug Abuse, San Francisco, 1988-91. Woodrow Wilson Found. fellow, 1972-73. Mem. NASW (del. 1990-92, peace and justice commn. 1992—), Coun. on Social Work Edn. (com. on status of women 1989-92, bd. dirs. 1993—), Am. Hist. Assn., Nat. Assn. Deans/Dirs. of Schs. of Social Work (sec. 1993—), Calif. Assn. Deans/Dirs. of Schs. of Social Work (pres. 1992—).

REISINGER, GEORGE LAMBERT, management consultant; b. Pitts., Aug. 28, 1930; s. Eugene Merle and Pauline Jane (Lambert) R.; m. Judith Ann Brush, Nov. 24, 1967; children—Douglas Lambert, Christine Elizabeth. B.S. in Bus. Adminstrn., Central Coll., 1953; postgrad., Cleveland-Marshall Law Sch., 1962-67. Asst. personnel mgr. Continental Can Co., Houston, 1958-60; mgr. labor relations The Glidden Co., Cleve., 1960-67; dir. employee relations Mobil Oil Corp., N.Y.C., Caracas, Dallas, Denver, 1967-78; sr. v.p. Minton & Assocs., Denver, 1978-82; v.p., ptnr. Korn-Ferry Internat., Denver, 1982-86; pres. The Sigma Group, Inc., Denver, 1986—. Bd. dirs. Ponderosa Hills Civic Assn., 1977-80, Arapahoe County Youth League, Parker Action Team for Drug Free Colo.; pres. Douglas County Youth League; bd. dirs., steering com. Rocky Mountain Lions Eye Inst. With USAF, 1953-58. Mem. Am. Soc. Personnel Adminstrs., N.Y. Personnel Mgmt. Soc., Colo. Soc. Personnel Adminstrn., Am. Soc. Profl. Cons., Rocky Mountain Inst. Fgn. Trade and Fin., Employment Mgmt. Assn., Denver Den, Lions Internat. (bd. dirs.). Republican. Methodist. Clubs: Denver Petroleum, Pinery Country, Republican 1200. Lodge: Lions (bd. dirs. Denver den). Home: 7924 Deertrail Dr Parker CO 80134-8262 Office: The Sigma Group Inc 717 17th St Ste 1440 Denver CO 80202-3335

REISNER, PHYLLIS, computer researcher; b. N.Y.C., Jan. 14, 1934; d. Max and Ruth (Polikoff) R. BA, Hunter Coll., 1955; MS, Lehigh U., 1970, PhD, 1972. Various positions, 1956-60; mem. rsch. staff IBM, Yorktown Heights, N.Y., 1960-67, San Jose, Calif., 1972-91; sr. human factors engr. IBM, Palo Alto, Calif., 1991—; presenter in field. Mem. editorial staff Interacting with Computers, 1988—; contbr. articles to profl. jours., chpts. to books. Fulbright travel grantee, 1956, Govt. of France travel grantee, 1956. Mem. Assn. for Computing Machinery (vice chmn. spl. interest group on computer human interaction 1987-88, chmn. 1988-89, mem. exec. com. 1989-91. Office: ISSC IBM Subs 1510 Page Mill Rd Palo Alto CA 94304-1195

REITAN, HAROLD THEODORE, management consultant; b. Max, N.D., Nov. 3, 1928; s. Walter Rudolph and Anna Helga (Glesne) R.; m. Margaret Lucille Bonsac, Dec. 29, 1954; children: Eric, Karen, Chris, Jon. B.A., St. Olaf Coll., 1950; M.A. in Social Psychology, U. Fla., 1962, Ph.D., 1967. Commd. officer U.S. Air Force, 1951, advanced through grades to col.; comdr., U.S. Air Force Spl. Treatment Ctr., Lackland, Tex., 1971-74, U.S. Air Force Corrections and Rehab. Group, Lowry, Colo., 1974-76, Tech. Tng. Wing, 1976-78, ret., 1978; mgr. health services Coors Industries, Golden, Colo., 1978-84, mgr. tng. and organizational devel., 1984-89, cons. mgmt. assessment, tng. and devel., 1989—. Decorated Legion of Merit with oak leaf cluster, D.F.C. with oak leaf cluster, Bronze Star, Meritorious Service medal, Air medal with four oak leaf clusters. Mem. Am. Psychol. Assn., Phi Kappa Phi. Republican. Lutheran. Contbr. articles to profl. jours. Office: 116 S Nome St Aurora CO 80012-1242

REITEMEIER, (TIMOTHY) GEORGE, chamber of commerce executive, public relations exective; b. Pueblo, Colo., Jan. 17, 1931; s. Paul John and Ethel Regina (McCarthy) R.; m. JoAnn Lillian Perkins, May 19, 1952 (dec. July 1977); children: Michael Douglas, Ann Ellen Loutzenhiser; m. Joy Arlene Little Duvall, Nov. 16, 1985. A of Arts and Scis., U. So. Colo., 1951. Cert. chamber exec. Mgr. Florence (Colo.) C. of C., 1952-53; asst. mgr. Cheyenne (Wyo.) C. of C., 1953; mgr. Longmont (Colo.) C. of C., 1953-55; dist. mgr. southwest div. Washington C. of C., 1955-57; mgr. Canon City (Colo.) C. of C., 1957-59, Casper (Wyo.) C. of C., 1959-64; exec. v.p. Niagara Falls (N.Y.) C. of C., 1965-70; pres., gen. mgr. Spokane (Wash.) C. of C., 1970-93; pres. Reitemeier Stedman, Inc., Spokane, 1993—; bd. dirs. Spokane Unltd., Spokane Stock Exch. Bd. dirs. Expo '74 Worlds Fair, Spokane, SEACAB; mem. Gov.'s Small Bus. Improvement Coun., 1988-90. With USAF, 1949-50. Mem. Assn. of Wash. Bus. (past bd. dirs.), U.S. C. of C. (local chamber com.), Wash. C. of C. Execs. (past v.p., pres.), Colo. C. of C. Execs. (v.p.), Oreg.-Wash. Idaho Chamber Officers/Mgrs. Assn. (pres. 1973-74). Republican. Roman Catholic. Office: Reitemeier Stedman Inc 6105 Excell Spokane WA 99208-3785

REITEN, RICHARD, electric power industry executive; b. 1939. BA, U. Wash., 1962. With Simpson Timber Co., Seattle, 1962-64, St. Regis Paper Co., Tacoma, 1964-66, Hearin Products, Inc., Portland, Oreg., 1966-71; with Di Giorgio Corp., San Francisco, 1971-79, pres. bldg. material group; with Nicoli Co., Portland, 1979-87; dir. Oreg. Econ. Devel. Dept., Salem, 1987-89; pres. Portland Gen. Corp., 1989-92, Portland Gen. Electric Co., 1992—. Office: Portland Gen Electric 121 SW Salmon St Portland OR 97204-2901

REITZ, RONALD CHARLES, biochemistry educator; b. Dallas, Feb. 27, 1939; s. Percy A. and Hazel (Thomison) R.; B.S., Tex. A&M U., 1961; Ph.D., Tulane U., 1966. NIH postdoctoral fellow U. Mich., Ann Arbor, 1966-69; vis. scientist Unilever Research Labs., Welwyn Herts, U.K., 1968; asst. prof. biochemistry U. N.C., Chapel Hill, 1969-75; assoc. prof. biochemistry U. Nev., Reno, 1975-80, prof., 1980—; vis. scientist DuPont de Nemours, Wilmington, Del., 1985, Nagoya (Japan) City U., 1990; vis. prof. Max Planck Institut für Biophys. Chem., Göttingen, Germany, 1990-91. Contbr. articles to profl. jours. Ski instr. Reno Recreational Dept., 1977-86. Mem. Am. Soc. Biol. Chemists, Research Soc. on Alcoholism, Am. Soc. Pharmacology and Exptl. Therapeutics, Am. Oil Chemists Soc., Sigma Xi. Methodist. Home: 3237 Susileen Dr Reno NV 89509-3859 Office: U Nev Dept Biochemistry Howard Med Sci Bldg Reno NV 89557

RELIGA, JAMES PAUL, software engineer; b. Berwyn, Ill., Sept. 11, 1953; s. John James and Stella Gertrude (Pavlis) R.; m. Peggy Lee Partlow, Mar. 15, 1982. BA in Physics, U. Calif., Irvine, 1975. Sci. programming specialist Lockheed Missiles and Space Co., Sunnyvale, Calif., 1983, sr. rsch. engr., 1983-85, rsch. specialist, 1985—. Office: Lockheed Missiles/Space Co 1111 Lockheed Way Sunnyvale CA 94089

RELYEA, ROBERT GORDON, management consultant; b. Bloomington, N.Y., Nov. 10, 1917; s. Aaron Dewitt and Margaret (Smedes) R.; m. Eleanor Florence Caminiti, June 2, 1938 (dec. Feb. 1984); children: Robert Paul, Peter Douglas, Paula Florence Relyea Holsinger; m. Ann P. Delmonico, June 23, 1985. BGS, Rollins Coll., 1966; MS, Fla. State U., 1969; PhD, Clayton U., 1987. Mgr. UTC div. United Aircraft, Inc., Cape Canaveral, Fla., 1964-69; pres. Better Mgmt. Assocs. Inc., Satellite Beach, Fla., 1969-71, Sun Lakes, Ariz., 1973—; mgr. quality and svc. United Mobile Homes, Inc., Chandler, Ariz., 1971-73; instr. Maricopa Community Colls., PHoenix, 1974—; quality mgr. IMC Magnetics, Inc., Tempe, Ariz., 1979-80; asst. to pres. Ecotronics Labs., Inc., Scottsdale, Ariz., 1980-81; quality mgr. Parker-Hannifin Co., Goodyear, Ariz., 1981-83; sr. quality auditor Govt. Electronics Group/Radar Systems Div. Motorola, Inc., Tempe, 1983-88; bd. dirs. SanTan Adobe, Inc., Sun Lakes. Contbr. articles to profl. publs. Scoutmaster Boy Scouts Am., Ridgewood, N.J., 1946-57; bd. dirs. Sun Lakes Home Owners Assn., 1974-78, Adult Action, Inc., Mesa, 1975-91, Cactus-Pine coun. Girls Scouts U.S.A., Phoenix, 1980-83. Mem. Nat. Contract Mgmt. Assn., Am. Soc. for Quality Control (del. to USSR, Bulgaria and Hungary 1988), Missile, Space and Range Pioneers (life), Order of Arrow, Masons, Shriners, Pi Lambda Theta. Home and Office: Better Mgmt Assocs Inc 9003 N Citrus Ln Sun Lakes AZ 85248

REMACLE, ROSEMARY, marketing professional; b. Yuma, Ariz., Oct. 2, 1942; d. Gale Wendell and Sarah (Myer) Monson; m. David Scott Remacle, Michael Andrew. BA in French/BS in Edn., Ariz. State U., 1964; MA in History, San Jose State U., 1978. Tchr. Phoenix Union Sch. Dist., 1964-66, Santa Clara (Calif.) Unified Sch. Dist., 1967-74; bus. owner Retail Bus., Saratoga, Calif., 1974-78; mgr. computer ops. Memorex Corp., Santa Clara, Calif., 1978-80; with Intel Corp., Santa Clara, 1980-86, with strategic staff, mktg. mgr., dir. tng. and devel. worldwide; dir., distbr. sales and mktg. No. Am. Zilog, Campbell, Calif., 1986-89; ptnr. Regis McKenna, Inc., Palo Alto, Calif., 1989—. Editor: Technology Marketing Insights, 1990—. Democrat.

REMINGTON, DELWIN WOOLLEY, soil conservationist; b. Vernal, Utah, May 10, 1950; s. Lyle H. and Muriel (Woolley) R.; m. Sylvia Bendixsen, July 20, 1973 (div. Nov. 1990); children: Holly, Reed Lyle, Roger Delwin, Kevin Bendixsen, Kollin Scott, Heidi; m. Marcia C. Cebull, June 1991. BS, Utah State U., 1975. Nurseryman Millcreek Gardens, Salt Lake City, 1975-79; yard foreman Brown Floral, Salt Lake City, 1979-82; agrl. salesman Steve Regan Co., Vernal, 1982-85; plant protection and quarantine aid APHIS USDA, Salt Lake City, 1986; soil conservationist USDA Soil Conservation Svc., Vernal, 1986—. Active Take Pride in Am., Vernal, 1989, Op. Desert Shield, Saudi Arabia, 1990. With Air NG, 1971-92. Mem. Utah Cert. Nurseryman, Soil & Water Conservation Soc. (fin. com. Utah chpt. 1989-90). Mem. LDS Ch. Home: 860 N 1500 E Apt A Vernal UT 84078-4623 Office: USDA Soil Conservation Svc 475 W 100 N Vernal UT 84078-2093

REMPLE, TIMOTHY KIRK, software engineering administrator; b. Colorado Springs, Colo., Nov. 5, 1955; s. Thomas King and Brooksie N. (Collins) R.; m. Ruth Ann Meydrech, Sept. 22, 1984. BSEE and Computer Sci., U. Colo., 1978, MS in Computer Sci., 1980, MBA, 1993. Programmer System Devel. Corp., Colorado Springs, 1973-75; student assoc. IBM, Boulder, Colo., 1976-77; rsch. asst. U. Colo., Boulder, 1977-79; engr. Storage Tech. Corp., Louisville, Colo., 1979-80; sr. rsch. scientist Honeywell, Mpls., 1980-84; mgr. Hewlett-Packard Co., Ft. Collins, Colo., 1984—. Contbr. articles to sci. jours. Mem. IEEE, Eta Kappa Nu. Home: 2954 Spinnaker Pl Longmont CO 80503-9263 Office: Hewlett-Packard Co 3404 E Harmony Rd Fort Collins CO 80525-9599

REMY, RAY, chamber of commerce executive; b. San Francisco. B in Polit. Sci., Claremont Men's Coll. (now Claremont McKenna Coll.); M in Pub. Adminstrn., U. Calif., Berkeley. Adminstrv. intern City of Berkeley, 1962-63; with So. Office League of Calif. Cities, 1963, then asst. to exec. dir. and mgr., to 1969; exec. dir. So. Calif. Assn. Govt., 1969-76; appointed dep. mayor City of L.A., 1976-84; pres. L.A. Area C. of C., 1984—; also prin. spokesman Los Angeles Area C. of C. Sec. Mus. Sci. and Industry; past chmn. bd. councilors Sch. Pub. Adminstrn. U. So. Calif., L.A.; vice chmn. bd. dirs. Rose Inst. for State and Local Govt.; commr. Met. Transp. Authority; vice chmn. bd. turstees, Claremont McKenna Coll., Calif. Trust for the Environ., Bay Delta Overnight Coun.; pres. Inst. for Local Self Govt.; bd. dirs. RLA; exec. com. 2000 ptnrship.; mem. bus. adv. coun. U.S. Dept. Transp. Recipient numerous awards including Fletcher Bowron award, Donald Stone award, Mus. of Sci. and Industry Fellowship award, others. Mem. Nat. Acad. Pub. Adminstrn., Jr. Statesmen Found., Am. Soc. Pub. Adminstrn. (past pres.), Metro Transit Authority. Office: Los Angeles Area C of C PO Box 3696 404 S Bixel St Los Angeles CA 90017

RENARD, RONALD LEE, allergist; b. Chgo., July 31, 1949; s. Robert James and Dorothy Mae (Fruik) R.; m. Maureen Ann Gilmore, Aug. 5, 1972 (div. Mar. 1992); children: Jeffrey, Stephen, Justin, Leigh Ellen; m. Catherine L. Walker, Apr. 1, 1992; children: Morgan, Michal, Luke. 1 & 2 Degre de la Langue, U. de Montepellier, France, 1970; BS in French, U. San Francisco, 1971; MD, Creighton U., 1976. Dir. med. ICU, lt. U.S. Army Hosp., Ft. Leonard Wood, Mo., 1980-81; dir. respiratory therapy, asst. chief allergy svc. Walter Reed Med. Ctr., Washington, 1981-84; staff allergist Chico (Calif.) Med. Group, 1984-86; allergist pvt. practice Redding, Calif., 1986—; dir. ACLS program Enloe Hosp., Chico, 1988-91; bd. dirs. Am. Lung Assn. of Calif., 1989-91; asst. prof. medicine USPHS, Bethesda, Md., 1982-84; asst. prof. family medicine U. Calif. Davis Med. Sch., Redding, 1990-93; med. dir. asthma camp Am. Lung Assn., Chico, Redding, 1986-93. Contbr. articles to profl. jours. Fellow Am. Acad. Allergy & Immunology, Am. Coll. Allergists; mem. Alpha Omega Alpha Nat. Honor Med. Soc., Assn. Mil. Allergists, Calif. Thoracic Soc. Republican. Roman Catholic. Office: Ste A 1950 Rosaline Ave Redding CA 96001

RENDU, JEAN-MICHEL MARIE, mining executive; b. Tunis, Tunisia, Feb. 25, 1944; s. Paul C. and Solange M. (Krebs) R.; m. Karla M. Meyer, Aug. 18, 1973; children: Yannick P., Mikaël P. Ingénieur des Mines, Ecole des Mines St. Etienne, France, 1966; MS, Columbia U., 1968, D. Engring. Sci., 1971. Mgr. ops. rsch. Anglovaal, Johannesburg, Republic of South Africa, 1972-76; assoc. prof. U. Wis., Madison, 1976-79; assoc. Golder Assocs., Denver, 1979-84; dir. tech. and sci. systems Newmont Mining Corp., Danbury, Conn., 1984-89; v.p. Newmont Gold Co., Denver, 1989-93, Newmont Mining Corp., Denver, 1993—. Author: An Introduction to Geostatistical Methods of Mineral Evaluation, 1978, 81; contbr. tech. papers to profl. jours. Fellow South African Inst. of Mining and Metallurgy (corr. mem. of coun.); mem. N.Y. Acad. Sci., Internat. Assn. for Math. Geology, Soc. Mining Engrs., Sigma Xi. Roman Catholic. Office: Newmont Gold Co 1700 Lincoln St Denver CO 80203-4501

RENETZKY, ALVIN, publisher; b. Bklyn., Aug. 2, 1940; s. Sam and Anna (Preiser) R.; m. Phyllis Ann (div.); 1 child, Davida; m. Cheryl Linden. PhD, U. Southern Calif., 1966. Publisher Academic Media, Los Angeles, 1967-70, Ready Reference Press, Santa Monica, Calif., 1974—. Editor: Directory of

Career Resources for Women, 1980, Directory of Career Resources for Minorities, 1981, Career Employment Opportunities Directory, 1985, Directory of Internships. Mem. Am. Soc. Tng. and Devel. Office: Ready Reference Press PO Box 5879 Santa Monica CA 90409-5879

RENFRO, DONALD WILLIAM, architect; b. Bakersfield, Calif., Nov. 13, 1931; s. Donald Francis and Lennie Lorraine (Despain) R.; student Bakersfield Coll., 1949-51; cert. energy auditor, Calif.; registered, cert. Nat. Council Archtl. Registration Bds.; m. Nancy M. Henry, Aug. 6, 1982; children—Dayna, Trisha, Donna. Staff designer Whitney Biggar, Architect, 1955-61; asso. Eddy & Paynter Assos., Bakersfield, Calif., 1961-70; prin. Eddy Paynter Renfro & Assos., Bakersfield, 1970-78; pres. Donald Renfro & Assocs., Bakersfield, 1978-84; pres. Renfro-Russell & Assocs., Inc., 1984—; pres., dir. Design Research Assos., Inc. Mem. Bakersfield Coll. Archtl. Adv. Com.; mem. Bakersfield Design Rev. Bd. Served with U.S. Army, 1952-54. Mem. AIA (past pres. Golden Empire chpt.) past dir. So. Calif. chpt.). Republican. Lodge: Kiwanis (past dir.). Office: 4800 Stockdale Hwy Ste 304 Bakersfield CA 93309-2636

RENGARAJAN, SEMBIAM RAJAGOPAL, electrical engineering educator, researcher, consultant; b. Mannargudi, Tamil Nadu, India, Dec. 12, 1948; came to U.S., 1980; s. Srinivasan and Rajalakshmi (Renganathan) Rajagopalan; m. Kalyani Srinivasan, June 24, 1982; children: Michelle, Sophie. BE with honors, U. Madras, India, 1971; MTech, Indian Inst. Tech., Kharagpur, 1974; PhD in Elec. Engring., U. N.B., Fredericton, Can., 1980. Mem. tech. staff Jet Propulsion Lab., Pasadena, Calif., 1983-84; asst. prof. elec. engring. Calif. State U., Northridge, 1980-83, assoc. prof., 1984-87, prof., 1987—; vis. prof. UCLA, 1987-88, vis. researcher, 1984—; cons. Hughes Aircraft Co., Canoga Park, Calif., 1982-87, NASA/Jet Propulsion Lab., Pasadena, 1987-90, 92, Ericsson Radar Electronics, Sweden, 1990-92; guest researcher Chalmers U., Sweden, 1990, UN Devel. Program, 1993. Contbr. sci. papers to profl. publs. Recipient Outstanding Faculty award Calif. State U., Northridge, 1985, Meritorious Performance and Profl. Promise award, 1986, 88, Merit award San Fernando Valley Engrs. Coun., 1989, cert. of recognition NASA, 1991, 92; Nat. Merit scholar Govt. India, 1965-71. Fellow Inst. Advancement Engrs.; mem. IEEE (sr. L.A. chpt. sec., treas. antennas and propagation soc. 1981-82, vice chmn. 1982-83, chmn. 1983-84), Internat. Union Radio Sci. (U.S. nat. com.), N.Y. Acad. Scis., Sigma Xi. Office: Calif State U 18111 Nordhoff St Northridge CA 91330-0001

RENNE, JANICE LYNN, interior designer; b. Los Angeles, July 16, 1952; d. George Joseph and Dolly Minni (Neubaurer) R.; m. William Lee Kile, Dec. 6, 1975 (div. Sept. 1983). BA, Sweet Briar Coll., 1974; AA, Interior Designers Inst., 1985. cert. interior designer 1992; Lic. gen. contractor 1989. Exec. trainee Bullock's, Santa Ana, Calif., 1974, Pub. Fin., Inc., Huntington Beach, Calif., 1975; bookkeeper William L. Kile DDS, Inc., Santa Barbara, Calif., 1979-81, Nelson & Hamilton, Inc., Santa Barbara, 1981-82; interior designer Ultimate Designs, Irvine, Calif., 1984-85, sr. designer, 1985-86; draftsperson JBI Inc., Long Beach, Calif., 1984-85; prin. designer Janice Renne Interior Designs, Newport Beach, Calif., 1986—; space planner Design Pak II, Newport Beach, 1987-88; State of Calif. rep. task force for developing self-cert. process for Calif. interior designers, Internat. Soc. Interior Design, 1991. Created utility room design for Easter Seals Design House, 1985; weekly radio show host on restaurant design, 1986; work published in Orange County mag. and L.A. Times., 1988. Recipient scholarship Calif. Inst. Applied Design, Newport Beach, 1984. Mem. Internat. Soc. Interior Designers (grad. assoc. designer butler's pantry, assoc. designer Design House powder rm. 1988, Orange County chpt. 1988-89, asst. editor Orange County chpt. Quar. Newsletter, Orange County chpt. gen. bd. 1991—, chair licensing com. 1991—, bd. dirs. 1991-92), Color Assn. of U.S., Constrn. Specifier Inst., Nat. Exec. Women in Hospitality, Calif. Legis. Conf. in Interior Design (gen. bd. 1991—, v.p. communications 1992-93), Orange County and Newport Beach, Letip Internat. (sec. 1987, 89, 90, treas. 1991, pres. 1993). Republican. Lutheran. Office: 2915 Redhill Ave Ste B201-G 2234 Newport Blvd Costa Mesa CA 92626

RENNER, DANIEL SEGISMUNDO, research and development electronics manager; b. Santiago, Chile, Sept. 21, 1953; came to U.S. 1985; s. Armando and Ines Ruth (Margolius) R.; m. Catherine Barbara Platovsky, Sept. 10, 1977; children: Ines Ruth, Andrea Sharon, Monica Sarah. BEE, U. Chile, Santiago, 1976; PhD, U. Cambridge, Eng., 1979. Chartered engr., Engring. Council, England. Research engr. Standard Telecommunications Labs., Harlow, Essex, Eng., 1980-85; research group mgr. Rockwell Internat., Dallas, 1985-89; dir. opto-electronic engring. Rockwell Internat., Newbury Park, Calif., 1989-91; dir. engring. Ortel Corp., Alhambra, Calif., 1991—. Contbr. articles to profl. jours. Inventor of optoelectronic devices. Recipient Hamilton prize, U. Cambridge, England, 1979. Mem. IEE, IEEE (assoc. editor Jour. Quantum Electronics 1990—, chmn. LEOS semiconductor laser workshop 1993), Internat. Semiconductor Laser Conf. (tech. prog. com. 1988, 90, 92), Conf. Lasers and Electro-optics (tech. prog. com. 1987-88), Conf. Optical Fiber Communication (tech. program com. 1990, 91, 92), Conf. Semiconductor LAsers and Applications (chmn. 1991, 92, 93). Jewish. Office: Ortel Corp 2015 W Chestnut St Alhambra CA 91803-1542

RENOUF, ALICE, Asian studies specialist, educator; b. Chgo., July 19, 1946; d. William and Esther Otis (Pace) R.; m. Jon Granville Rush, Sept. 17, 1983; children: Cassidy Pace Rush, Whitney Renouf Rush. BA, U. Colo., 1969, MA, 1971, PhD candidate, 1974. Asst. to dean, internat. fellowship advisor U. Colo., Boulder, 1976-82, asst. dir. fgn. student and scholar program, 1982-83, asst. to dir. Asian studies program, 1987—; dir. Colo. China Coun., Boulder, 1977—. Author: Modern Chinese History, 1979. Bigelow Found. grantee U. Colo., Boulder, 1973, 74; fellow to Tunghai U., Taichung, Taiwan, 1970. Mem. Asian Art Coord. Coun. (pres. 1987—), Conf. on World Affairs (mem. exec. com. 1985—), Denver Com. on Fgn. Rels. (bd. dirs. 1985—). Democrat. Home and Office: 932 Marine St Boulder CO 80302

RENSON, JEAN FELIX, psychiatry educator; b. Liège, Belgium, Nov. 9, 1930; came to U.S., 1960; s. Louis and Laurence (Crahai) R.; m. Gisèle Bouillenne, Sept. 8, 1956; children: Marc, Dominique, Jean-Luc. MD, U. Liege, 1959; PhD in Biochemistry, George Washington U., 1971. Diplomate Am. Bd. Psychiatry. Asst. prof. U. Liège, 1957-60; rsch. fellow U. Liege, 1966-72; clin. assoc. prof. dept. psychiatry U. Calif., San Francisco, 1978—; pvt. practice Lakeview Psychotherapy Ctr., Stockton, Calif., 1986—; vis. asst. prof. Stanford U., Palo Alto, Calif., 1972-77. Assoc. editor: Fundamentals of Biochemical Pharmacology, 1971. NIH fellow, 1960-66. Democrat. Office: Lake View Psychotherapy Ctr # 12 2389 W March Ln Stockton CA 95207-5239

RENZAS, JAMES HOWARD, relocation company executive, consultant; b. Elmhurst, Ill., June 6, 1951; s. George Howard and Marion Margaret (Bowers) R.; m. Ellen Nolan Dietzler, Dec. 30, 1978; children: Brooke, Russell, Erin, Jennifer. BS, U. Ill., 1973; MS, No. Ill. U., 1978. Sr. cons. Don Kane and Assoc., Chgo., 1978-80, PHH Fantus Co., Chgo., 1980-83; exec. dir. Commn. Econ. Devel. in Orem, Utah, 1983-86; dir. PHH Fantus Co., San Mateo, Calif., 1986-88; pres. Location Mgmt. Svc., Irvine, Calif., 1988-90; mng. cons. Premier Relocation, Irvine, Calif., 1990-91; exec. v.p. Paragon Decision Resources, Irvine, Calif., 1991—; guest speaker numerous seminars. Contbr. articles to profl. jours. Mem. Indsl. Devel. Reserve Coun., Nat. Assn. Corp. Real Estate Execs. (bd. dirs. 1991-92, comml. coun. 1991-92). Office: Paragon Decision Resources 1 Park Pla # 325 Irvine CA 92691

REPLOGLE, DANA MICHAEL, musical instruments company executive; b. San Francisco, May 26, 1954; s. Ellsworth E. and Gwendolyn Mae Replogle. Student, Santa Clara U., 1972-73. Pvt. practice mgmt./fin. cons. L.A., 1976-82; v.p. bus. devel. R.G. Stewart & Co., L.A., 1982-85, Stewart Mgmt. Corp., L.A., 1985-88; bus. mgr. Valley Arts USA, L.A., 1989-92; exec. mgr. guitar sales Saynick Music Corp., L.A., 1992—; fin. cons. Straightline Mortgage, Sherman Oaks, Calif., 1985—. Editor: Modern Arnis, 1983; contbr. articles to mags. Home: PO Box 41484 Los Angeles CA 90041

REPLOGLE, JOHN ASHER, research hydraulic engineer, irrigation consultant; b. Charleston, Ill., Jan. 13, 1934; s. Clifford Cleo and Cleda Annabel (Kibler) R.; m. Louisa Ruth Roudebush, Feb. 2, 1957; children: Neal Keith, Brent John. BS, U. Ill., 1956, MS, 1958, PhD in Civil Engring., 1964. Registered profl. engr., Ill., Calif. Grad. asst. U. Ill., Urbana, 1956-58, instr., 1958-63; rsch. agrl. engr. U.S. Water Conservation Lab. Agrl. Rsch. Svc.-USDA, Phoenix, 1963-66, rsch. hydraulic engr. U.S. Water Conservation Lab., 1966-75, rsch. leader U.S. Water Conservation Lab., 1975-85, rsch. leader, rsch. hydraulic engr. U.S. Water Conservation Lab., 1985-90, sr. rsch. hydraulic engr. U.S. Water Conservation Lab., 1990—; cons. USAID, New Delhi, 1982, 83, Dacha, Bangladesh, 1986, 88, Kathmandu, Nepal, 1989, Lahore, Pakistan, 1990. Co-Author: Flow Measuring Flumes for Open Channel Systems, 1984; contbr.over 100 articles to profl. jours.; patentee in field. Recipient Nat. Technology Transfer award Agrl. Rsch. Svc.-USDA, 1990; named one of top 10 nat. Fed. Engr. Yr. NSPE, 1991. Fellow AAAS; mem. ASCE (nat. chmn., vice-chmn., sec. irrigation and drainage engring. div. 1984-89, best tech. paper award 1988, James R. Croes Medal 1977), Am. Soc. Agrl. Engrs. (engr. yr. award western region 1987, chmn. Ariz. sect. 1970, The Hancor Soil and Water Engring. award, 1992), Internat. Com. Irrigation and Drainage, Irrigation Assn., Kiwanis Internat. Presbyterian. Office: Agrl Rsch Svc-USDA US Water Conservation Lab 4331 E Broadway Rd Phoenix AZ 85040-8807

REQUICHA, ARISTIDES ADELINO GUALBERTO, computer scientist; b. Monte Estoril, Portugal, Mar. 18, 1939; came to U.S., 1965; s. Adelino P. and Ana (Gualberto) R.; m. Shahin A. Hakim, Sept. 5, 1970. Engring. Diploma, Univ. Lisbon, Portugal, 1962; PhD, U. Rochester, 1970. Lectr. Univ. Lisbon, 1961-63; rsch. scientist NATO Saclantcen, La Spezia, Italy, 1970-73; scientist to sr. scientist Univ. Rochester, N.Y., 1973-83; assoc. prof. Univ. Rochester, 1983-86; prof. U. So. Calif., L.A., 1986—. Editor: CVGIP-Graphic Models & Image Processing, 1989—, Springer Book Series on Computer Graphics, 1982—, Jour. Design & Mfg., 1991—; contbr. sci. articles to profl. jours. Lt. Portuguese Air Force, 1963-65. Fellow IEEE (editor Transactions on Robotics and Automation 1991—); mem. AAAS, Soc. Mfg. Engrs. (sr.), Assn. Computing Machinery (editor Transactions on Graphics 1984-90), Am. Assn. Artificial Intelligence, Sigma Xi. Office: U So Calif Dept Computer Sci Los Angeles CA 90089-0781

RESEN, W. PATRICK, lawyer, law educator; b. Walla Walla, Wash., June 15, 1946; s. John W. and Mary Ellen (Coughlin) R.; m. Karen Jo Thomas, Aug. 26, 1967 (div. 1975). BA, U. Tex.-El Paso, 1973; JD, U. Mo., 1973, BS, SUNY, Albany, 1987. Bar: N.Mex. 1974, U.S. Dist. Ct. N.Mex. 1974, U.S. Ct. Mil. Appeals 1974, U.S. Dist. Ct. (we. dist.) Tex. 1975, U.S. Ct. Appeals (10th cir.) 1975, U.S. Tax Ct. 1978, U.S. Supreme Ct. 1978, U.S. Ct. Claims 1979, Calif. 1981, D.C. 1981, U.S. Dist. Ct. (no. dist.) Calif. 1981, U.S. Ct. Appeals (5th, 9th, 11th cirs.) 1981, U.S. Ct. Internat. Trade 1982, Nebr. 1983, N.Y. 1983, U.S. Dist. Ct. Nebr. 1983, U.S. Ct. Appeals (fed. cir.) 1983, U.S. Ct. Vets. Appeals 1990, U.S. Army Ct. Mil. Rev. 1990. Joined U.S. Army, 1968, served to sgt., 1970, to maj. JAGC, 1974-82, active Res. LTC Mil. Judge, 1982—; pvt. practice, Danville, Calif., 1982-89, San Ramon, Calif., 1989—; instr. law St. Mary's Coll., Moraga, Calif., 1982—; prof John F. Kennedy Sch. Law, Walnut Creek, Calif. Decorated Meritorious Svc. medal with 2 oak leaf cluster, Army Commendation medal, Army Achievement medal. Roman Catholic. Office: 18 Crow Canyon Ct Ste 390 San Ramon CA 94583-1669

RESENDEZ, ARNOLDO HORACIO, federal agency administrator; b. La Ascencion, Nuevo Leon, Mexico, June 11, 1953; came to the U.S., 1964; s. Jesus and Lucinda (Ortega) R.; m. Blanca Bustamante, Apr. 28, 1984; 1 child, Marcos. Student, Calif. State U., 1972-75; BA in Mgmt., Nat. Louis U., 1990. Assoc. dir. Campesinos Unidos, Brawley, Calif., 1975-80; v.p. tech. assistance and constituency support Nat. Coun. La Raza, Washington, 1980-88, v.p. office spl. and internat. projects, 1988-91; regional dir. Peace Corps, L.A., 1991—; sec. Nat. Youth Employment Coalition, Washington, 1984-89; bd. dirs. United Svc. Agys., Washington, 1985-90. Treas. Am. G.I. Forum, Washington, 1985. Roman Catholic. Home: 1529 Ellsmere Los Angeles CA 90019 Office: Peace Corps Ste 8104 11000 Wilshire Blvd Los Angeles CA 90024

RESMER, MARK ANTHONY, university official; b. Stoke on Trent, Eng., Dec. 12, 1954; came to U.S., 1980; s. Brunon and Danuta (Koziell-Poklewski) R.; m. Emily Powell, June 10, 1989. Licenciate, Trinity Coll., London, 1974; BA, Vassar Coll., 1985. Dir. acad. computing Vassar Coll., Poughkeepsie, N.Y., 1984-88; dir. computing, media and telecommunications svcs. Sonoma State U., Rohnert Park, Calif., 1988-92, assoc. v.p. info. tech., 1993—, dir. Guide, Calif. tech. project, 1993—; orgn. rep. Inter-Univ. Consortium for Ednl. Computing, Pitts., 1985-88, EDUCOM, Washington, 1986—. Contbr. articles to profl. jours. Episcopalian. Office: Sonoma State U 1801 E Cotati Ave Rohnert Park CA 94928-3609

RESNICK, CINDY, state legislator; b. Three Rivers, Mich., July 31, 1949; married; 4 children. Former mem. Ariz. Ho. of Reps., dist. 14; mem. Ariz. State Senate. Mem. Am. Assn. Bus. and Profl. Women, Orgn. Women Legis., Tucson Assn. Child Care, B'nai B'rith Women. Democrat. Jewish. Office: State Senate 9649 E Baker Tucson AZ 85748

RESNICK, JEFFREY I., plastic surgeon; b. Jersey City, Mar. 2, 1954; s. Victor and Regina (Bistritz) R.; m. Michele Gail Zinger, July 12, 1981; children: Andrew Gregory, Daniel Zachary. BS, Yale U., 1975; MD, U. Pa., 1980. Diplomate Am. Bd. Surgery, Am. Bd. Plastic Surgery. Resident in surgery Mass. Gen. Hosp., Boston, 1980-85, resident in plastic surgery, 1985-87; fellow in craniofacial surgery UCLA, 1987-88; pvt. practice plastic surgery Santa Monica, Calif., 1989—; asst. clin. prof. plastic surgery UCLA, 1987—. Contbr. articles to profl. jours. Surgeon Indochina Surg. Ednl. Exch., Vietnam, 1992. Mem. Am. Soc. Plastic and Reconstructive Surgeons, Am. Soc. Maxillofacial Surgeons, Am. Cleft Palate-Craniofacial Assn., Plastic Surgery Ednl. Found., Sigma Xi, Alpha Omega Alpha. Office: 1301 20th St Ste 470 Santa Monica CA 90404

RESNICK, SOL DONALD, civil engineering consultant; b. Milw., June 15, 1918; s. Samuel and Esther (Schneiderman) R.; m. Susan Kay Golden, June 21, 1981; children: Harry, Rachel. BS in Agrl. Engring., U. Wis., 1941, BSCE, 1942, MSCE, 1949; DSc (hon.), U. Ariz., 1993. Registered profl. engr., Ariz., Colo. Asst. hydrology engr. TVA, Knoxville, 1942-43; asst. prof. civil engring. Colo. State U., Ft. Collins, 1949-52; irrigation engr. U.S. Agy. for Internat. Devel., Nagpur, India, 1952-57; dir. water ctr. U. Ariz., Tucson, 1957-84; water rsch. engr. AID, Bicol, Philippines, 1969; prof. hydrology Asian Inst. Tech., Bangkok, 1959; prof. agrl. engring. U. Ceara, Fortaleza, Brazil, 1964-66; vis. scientist Ben-Gurion U., Sede Boker, Israel, 1984, 92; dir. emeritus U. Ariz., Tucson, 1984—; vis. sci. Ben-Gurion U., Sede Boker, Isreal, 1990, 92. Co-author: More Water for Arid Land, 1974; co-editor: Advances in Hydrologic Science, 1990. Bd. dirs. Ariz. Nature Conservancy, Tucson, 1965—; chmn. U. Ariz. Negev Com., 1975—; pres. Zionist Orgn. Am., 1986—, Tucson YMCA Y's Men Club, 1976-77. 1st lt. U.S. Army, 1943-47. Mem. ASCE, Am. Soc. Agrl. Engring., The Nature Conservancy, War Vets, U. Ariz. Investment Club (pres. 1968—), Ariz. Hydrologic Soc., So. Ariz. Water Rsch. Assn. (founding mem. 1986). Jewish. Home: PO Box 37258 Tucson AZ 85740-7258 Office: Univ Ariz Tucson AZ 85721

RETALLACK, GREGORY JOHN, geologist, educator; b. Hobart, Australia, Nov. 8, 1951; came to U.S., 1977; s. Kenneth John Retallack and Moira Wynn (Dean) Gollan; m. Diane Alice Johnson, May 21, 1981; children: Nicholas John, Jeremy Douglas. B.A., Macquarie U., Sydney, 1973; B.Sc. with honors, U. New Eng., 1974, Ph.D., 1978. Vis. asst. prof. Northern Ill. U., Dekalb, 1977-78; vis. scholar Ind. U., Bloomington, 1978-81; asst. prof. U. Oreg., Eugene, 1981-86, assoc. prof., 1986-92, prof., 1992—. Author: Geological Excursion Guide to the Sea Cliffs North of Sydney, 1978, Late Eocene and Oligocene Paleosols from Badlands National Park, South Dakota, 1983, Soils of the Past, 1990, Miocene Paleosols and Ape Habitats in Pakistan and Kenya, 1991; contbr. numerous articles in field to profl. jours. Grantee NSF, 1979, Wenner-Gren Found., 1983. Mem. Geol. Soc. Am., Geol. Soc. Australia, Bot. Soc. Am., Paleontol. Soc. (pres. Pacific sect. 1986), Oreg. Acad. Sci. (pres. 1986), Soc. Econ. Paleontologists and Mineralogists, Sigma Xi (pres. U. Oreg. chpt. 1983-84). Home: 2715 Elinor St Eugene OR 97403-2513

RETHORE, BERNARD GABRIEL, diversified company executive; b. Bklyn., May 22, 1941; s. Francis Joseph and Katharine Eunice (MacDwyer) R.; BA, Yale U., 1962; MBA, U. Pa., 1967; m. Marilyn Irene Watt, Dec. 1, 1962; children: Bernard Michael, Tara Jean, Kevin Watt, Alexandra Marie, Rebecca Ann, Christopher Philip, Abigail Lyn. Assoc., McKinsey & Co., Inc., Washington, 1967, then sr. assoc., 1973; v.p./gen. mgr. Greer div. Microdot, Inc., Darien, Conn., 1973-77, v.p. ops. connector group, 1977-78, pres. bus. devel. group, 1978-82, pres. fastening systems and sealing devices groups, 1982-84, pres. Microdot Industries, 1984-87, pres., chief exec. officer, 1988; pres. Microdot Europe Ltd., 1984-88; sr. v.p. Phelps Dodge Corp., Phoenix, 1989—; group exec. Phelps Dodge Industries, 1989-90, pres., 1990—; dir. Blue Cross/Blue Shield of Conn., 1989-90; cons. U.S. Govt., UN; mem. World Bus. Coun., Am. Internat. Grad. Sch. Mgmt., 1990—, chmn., 1991—. Mem. dean's adv. bd. Wharton Sch. Bus., U. Pa., 1972-80; chmn. Emmaus adv. bd. Fairfield Prep. Sch.-Lauralton Hall Acad., 1981-85; elected mem. bd. fin. Town of Westport, Conn., 1986-90; trustee Ballet Arizona, 1989—, vice chmn. 1991—; bd. dirs. Boys Hope of Phoenix, 1989—; trustee Phoenix Country Day Sch., 1992—. Served to capt., inf., AUS, 1962-65. Decorated Bronze Star. Mem. Yale Club (N.Y.C.), Union League (Chgo.), Plaza Club (Phoenix). Home: 6533 E Maverick Rd Paradise Valley AZ 85253 Office: Phelps Dodge Corp 2600 N Central Ave Phoenix AZ 85004-3050

RETHY, VICTOR STEPHEN, software engineer; b. San Francisco, July 3, 1960; s. Emery Imre and Katharina (Koestner) R.; m. Mary Emelia Ludloff, Sept. 21, 1991. AB, U. Calif., 1986. Computer analyst Globe Turbocharger, Inc., San Francisco, 1982-85; software engr. Ask Computer Systems, Mountain View, Calif., 1986-88, project leader, 1988—. Mem. Assn. Computing Machinery, Am. Prodn. Inventory Control Soc. Office: Ask Computer Systems 2440 W El Camino Real Mountain View CA 94039

RETSKY, MICHAEL CHARLES, programmer, analyst; b. Chgo., Jan. 18, 1957; s. Jack and Jayce Bernice (Holtz) P. BS, Ark. Tech. U., 1987. Programmer analyst Data Processing Co., Van Nuys, Calif., 1987—, Summation Data, L.A., 1990-92; sr. programmer analyst Santa Fe Pacific Pipeline Ltd., L.A., 1992—. Mem. Sierra Club. Democrat. Lutheran. Home: PO Box 7205 Van Nuys CA 91409-7205

RETTERSON, KATHLEEN B., biopharmaceutical marketing executive; b. Phila., May 5, 1958; d. Leo C. and Jane E. Bezdziecki. BA, Brown U., 1980; MBA, Stanford U., 1987. Bus. mgr. dept. biochemistry U. Mass. Med. Ctr., Worcester, 1981-85; fin. analyst Brian M. Freeman & Co., Washington, 1987-88; assoc. product mgr. Amgen Inc., Thousand Oaks, Calif., 1988, product mgr., 1988-89, mktg. mgr., 1989-92, assoc. dir., 1992—. Mem. Anglican Ch. Office: Amgen Inc 1840 Dehavilland Dr Thousand Oaks CA 91320-1789

REUBER, JAMES LOUIS, psychotherapist; b. Clinton, Okla., Oct. 23, 1947; s. Louis and Esther Leona (Hinz) R.; 1 child, James Keith Reuber. BA, U. Okla., 1970, MA, 1972. Cert. marriage and family therapist. Staff therapist Community Counseling and Guidance Ctr., Oklahoma City, 1972-74; assoc. vis. prof. human rels. U. Okla., Norman, 1973-74; bldg. supr. Penny Lane Residential Treatment Ctr., L.A., 1978; contracting officer Def. Logistics Agy., L.A., 1979—; psychotherapist L.A., 1978—. Gaylord philanthropy scholarship E.K. Gaylord, 1965; Monsanto scholar, 1965, U. Okla. scholar, 1965. Mem. Am. Assn. of Marriage and Family Therapists (clin. mem.), Mensa. Home: 6400 Primrose N 3 Los Angeles CA 90068 Office: DCMAO El Segundo 222 N Sepulveda El Segundo CA 90245

REUER, BARBARA LOUISE, music therapy company executive, therapist, consultant; b. Hoven, S.D., Apr. 12, 1952; d. Erwin Walter and Elvera (Ziebart) R. BS in Music Edn., No. State U., Aberdeen, S.D., 1970; M Music Edn., U. Kans., 1976; PhD in Music Therapy, U. Iowa, 1987. Instr. credential, Calif. Music therapist Mental Health Inst., Clarinda, Iowa, 1976-77; music therapist, tchr. Dubuque (Iowa) Sch. Dist., 1977-80; grad. asst. U. Iowa, Iowa City, 1980-83, 86, vis. instr., 1984-85; cons. Cons. Svcs./Ultimate Networks, Carlsbad, Calif., 1987; sales trainer Dan McBride & Assocs., Carlsbad, 1987; health facilitator Better Lifeplans Inst. Calif., San Diego, 1988-90; realtor, mktg. cons. Coldwell Banker and Prudential, Encinitas, Calif., 1990-92; cons., owner Music Works Calif., Solana Beach, Calif., 1992—; cons. wellness program San Diego City Schs., 1988—; coord., cons. Rhythm for Life, Mesa, Ariz., 1992—; mktg. cons. Prudential Calif. Realty, Encinitas, 1992—; cons., vol. Kaiser Hospice Program, San Diego, 1992—. Co-auhtor: (handbooks) Ultimate Legal Handbook, 1985, 87, Music Works, 1986.; contbr. articles to profl. publs. Mem. Leads, Carlsbad, 1989; mem. choir Calvary Luth. Ch., Solana Beach, 1990—, edn. min., 1992-94; vol. Am. Cancer Soc., San Diego, 1991—. Grantee Bureau Edn. and Health, 1981, HIV/AIDS project grantee Neil Seymour Meml. Fund. Mem. Nat. Assn. for Music Therapy (v.p. 1992-94, Outstanding Contbn. award 1991, grantee western region), Music for All People (task force 1992—), Rhythm for Life (coun. coord. 1992—), Soc. for Advancement Music Therapy (founder, pres. 1991—), Networks, Toastmasters. Republican. Office: Music Works Calif PO Box 1674 Solana Beach CA 92075

REUTHER, WALTER, horticulture educator; b. Manganoui County, North Is., New Zealand, Sept. 21, 1911; came to U.S., 1919; s. Arthur W.G. and Martha (Kruger) R.; m. Flora Astbury Nelson, Aug. 4, 1935; children: David Walter, Charles Arthur. BS in Chemistry, U. Fla., 1933; PhD in Plant Physiology, Cornell U., 1940. Asst. horticulturist Agrl. Experiment Sta., U. Fla., Gainesville, 1933-37; rsch. asst. in pomology Cornell U., Ithaca, N.Y., 1937-40; asst. prof. pomology Cornell U., Ithaca, 1940; assoc. horticulturist, then prin. horticulturist USDA, Orlando, Fla., 1941-55; head dept. horticulture U. Fla., Gainesville, 1955-56; prof., chmn. dept. horticulture, researcher Citrus Ctr., U. Calif., Riverside, 1956-66, prof., horticulturist, 1966-72, 74-79; coord. regional rsch. Inst. Nat. Investigations in Agriculture, Valencia, Spain, 1972-74; prof. emeritus U. Calif., Riverside, 1979—; cons. Del Monte Corp., 1962-72, Govt. of Greece, 1963, 64, Rockefeller Found., 1965, 66-67, 69, UN, 1970, 75, 77, Govt. of Spain, 1972-74, Govt. of Brazil, 1975, 81, Govt. of Indonesia, 1977-78, 84, Govt. of Republic of China, 1979, Govt. of Honduras, 1980, Govt. of Mex., 1982, Govt. of Colombia, 1982. Editor (5 vol. series) The Citrus Industry, 1966-77; contbr. 130 articles to profl. jours. Fellow Am. Soc. Hort. Sci. (pres. 1962-63, chmn. bd. dirs. 1963-64). Democrat. Home: 4005 Haverford Ave Riverside CA 92507-4817 Office: U Calif Dept Botany and Plant Sci Riverside CA 92521

REVELL, JOHN HAROLD, dentist; b. Lead, S.D., Dec. 12, 1906; s. Aris LeRoy and Margaret (O'Donnell) R.; AB in Engring., Stanford, 1930; postgrad. McGill Med. Sch., 1930; DDS summa cum laude, U. So. Calif., 1941; postgrad. in Maxillo Facial and Plastic Surgery, Mayo Found., U. Minn., 1944; m. Catherine Cecelia Gerrard, Sept. 14, 1936; children: Mary Margaret, Kathleen Dianne Revell, Timothy John, Maureen Frances Brown, Dennis Cormac. Engaged as instr. U. So. Calif. Dental Coll., L.A., 1941-42; practice oral surgery, maxillo facial-plastic surgery, Shafter, Calif., 1946—; mem. staff Mercy Hosp., Bakersfield, Calif., 1948—, chmn. dental sect., 1955-60, 70-71; mem. surg. staff San Joaquin Hosp., Bakersfield; lectr. on applied nutrition; internat. pioneer lectr. surg. orthodontics. Served with AUS, 1932-37, 42-46; now maj. ret. Recipient of Special Clinic award Am. Soc. Dentistry for Children, 1964; Rotary Internat. Presdl. citation, 1982. Diplomate Internat. Bd. Applied Nutrition. Fellow Internat. Coll. Applied Nutrition; mem. ADA (life), Calif. Dental Assn. (life), Ventura Dental Soc. (life), So. Calif., Kern County (dir.), Los Angeles County (award 1941), Santa Barbara-Ventura County dental assns., Am. Acad. Dental Medicine, Am. Acad. Applied Nutrition, Am. Soc. Dentistry for Children (life), Pierre Fauchard Acad., Shafter C. of C. (dir. 1948-50), Alpha Tau Epsilon, Omicron Kappa Upsilon, Phi Kappa Phi, Theta Xi. Republican. Roman Catholic. Rotarian (pres. Shafter 1950-51, dir. 1951-52). Patentee precisioner. Rsch. on maxillary dental papilloma, rotation unerupted impacted teeth, channeling for extensive movement of teeth; also clin. rsch. in cleft palate surgery; inventor rapid fabrication device for infant feeding; pioneer in prefab. bldgs. and homes while constrn. officer U.S. Army, 1932-37; developer prototype WW-2 Jeep machine gun mount. Author publs. in field; all rsch. data presented to and housed at La. State U. Dental Coll., New Orleans. Home: 81 620 Ave 49 Indio CA 92201

REVERAND, CEDRIC DWIGHT, II, English language educator; b. Bklyn., Dec. 3, 1941; s. Cedric Dwight and Muriel (Cestare) R.; m. Jane Myers, July 24, 1965. BA, Yale U., 1963; MA, Columbia U., 1964; PhD, Cornell U., 1972. Prof. English, dir. cultural programs U. Wyo., Laramie,

1983—. Author: Dryden's Final Poetic Mode, 1988; editor: 18th-Century English Literature: A Current Bibliography; contbr. articles to profl. jours. Recipient Ellbogen Outstanding Teaching award U. Wyo., 1987; hon. Cambridge fellow, Clare Hall, 1993—; named Ford Found. fellow Cornell U., 1967-72, Mellon fellow UCLA and Yale U., 1978, 85. Mem. MLA, Am. Soc. for 18th-Century Studies, Western Alliance Arts Adminstrs., Phi Beta Kappa. Home: 412 Garfield St Laramie WY 82070-3739 Office: U Wyo Dept English PO Box 3353 Laramie WY 82071-3353

REY, JUAN CARLOS, engineer; b. Oberá, Misiones, Argentina, Feb. 25, 1957; s. Juan Carlos and Dolly Beatriz (Prytz Nilsson) R.; m. Ema Beatriz Rocchi, Feb. 28, 1980; children; Diego Ariel, Javier Alejandro. Nuclear Engr. Degree, Inst. Balseiro, Bariloche, Rio Negro, 1981. Registered profl. engr. Sr. researcher INVAP S.E., Bariloche, 1981-89; vis. Scholar Stanford (Calif.) U., 1989-90, sci. and engring. assoc., 1990—. Office: Stanford U AEL # 224 Stanford CA 94305

REYES, BIENVENIDO CASTRO, internist; b. Aparri, Cagayan, The Philippines, Oct. 15, 1944; came to U.S., 1971; s. Felicisimo P. and Maria (Castro) R.; children: Bienvenido Jr., Joan, Matthew, Mark. BS, Far Eastern U., Manila, 1965, MD, 1970. Diplomate Am. Bd. Internal Medicine. Intern St. Clare's Hosp., Schenectady, 1971-72; resident in internal medicine VA Ctr., Dayton, Ohio, 1972-74, Ohio State U., Columbus, 1975; pvt. practice, Long Beach, Calif. AMA. Office: 2820 E 4th St Long Beach CA 90814

REYNA, VALERIE FRANCES, psychologist, educator, researcher; b. Miami Beach, Fla., Apr. 20, 1955; d. Benjamin Villa and Patricia Ruth (Wilson) R.; m. Charles J. Brainerd, Oct. 5, 1985; 1 child, Bertrand Reyna-Brainerd. BA, Clark U., 1976; PhD, Rockefeller U., 1981. Asst. prof. U. Tex., Dallas, 1981-87; adj. prof. U. Ariz., Tucson, 1987-88, asst. prof. dept. ednl. psychology, 1988-92, assoc. prof., 1992—; vis. scientist Stanford (Calif.) U., 1982-83. Editor: Developmental Psychology, 1985, Development of Long-Term Retention, 1991; contbr. articles to profl. jours.; author books. Mem. AAAS, APA, Am. Psychol. Soc., Ariz. Ednl. Rsch. Org., Soc. Advancement Chicanos and Native Ams. in Sci., Hispanic Profls. Action Com. Edn., Faculty Network Higher Edn., Psychonomic Soc., Soc. for Rsch. in Child Devel., Sigma Xi. Democrat. Home: 6060 E Calle Ojos Verde Tucson AZ 85715-1947 Office: U Ariz Dept Ednl Psychology Tucson AZ 85721

REYNOLDS, CHARLES PATRICK, pediatric oncologist, researcher; b. El Paso, Tex., Aug. 8, 1952; s. Charles Albert and Lallah Elizabeth (Munro) R.; m. Debra Dawn Adams, Feb. 3, 1979; children: Amy Elizabeth, Jennifer Ann. BA in Biology, U. Tex., 1974; MD, U. Tex. Southwestern Med. Sch., Dallas, 1979; PhD, U. Tex., 1979. Lic. Tex., Calif. Postdoctoral fellow U. Tex. Southwestern Med. Sch., Dallas, 1979-80; pediatric intern Nat. Naval Med. Ctr., Bethesda, Md., 1980-81; battalion surg. Third Marine Div., Okinawa, Japan, 1981-82; rsch. med. officer Naval Med. Rsch. Inst., Bethesda, 1982-87; asst. prof. UCLA, 1987-89; assoc. prof. U. So. Calif., L.A., 1989—; dir. Neuroblastoma Marrow Purging Lab. Childrens Cancer Group, L.A., 1988—; team physician U.S. Shooting Team, 1991—. Patentee in field; contbr. articles to profl. jours. Mem. 1992 USA Olympic Shooting Team, Barcelona, Spain. Grantee Nat. Cancer Inst., Am. Inst. Cancer Rsch. Mem. NRA, Am. Soc. Clin. Oncology, Am. Assn. Cancer Rsch., Soc. Analytical Cytology. Roman Catholic. Office: Childrens Hosp LA Div Hematology Oncology PO Box 54700 Los Angeles CA 90054-0700

REYNOLDS, DONALD DEAN, retired civil engineering technician; b. Bristol, Colo., Sept. 1, 1921; s. Charles Lloyd and Clara Lillian (Whitehead) R.; m. Jo Ann Vernon, Oct. 14, 1951; children: Paul Lloyd, Deana Jean Reynolds Mounts. BA, Northwestern State Coll., Okla., 1947. Jr. high tchr., coach Bonner Springs (Kans.) Bd. Edn., 1948-49; surveyor Kans. Dept. Hwys., Topeka, 1948; civil engr. technician U.S. Bur. Reclamation, Ephrata, Wash., 1950-54, Ephrata & Othello, Wash., 1964-84; civil engr. technician, conservationist U.S. Dept. Agr., Othello, 1954-57; lab. inspector Harza Engring., Ephrata, 1957-61; developer, owner Columbia Basin Farm, Wash., 1954-84; civil engr. tech. Cortez Co., 1984-86; retired Colo., 1986. With USAF, 1943-45. Home: 349 5th Ave SE Ephrata WA 98823-2247

REYNOLDS, JERRY OWEN, professional basketball executive; b. French Lick, Ind., Jan. 29, 1944. Student, Vincennes U., Oakland City Coll., Ind. U., Ind. State U. Coach Rockhurst Coll., Kansas City, Mo., 1975-84, Pittsburg (Kans.) State U., 1984-85; asst. coach Sacramento Kings, 1985-86, 86-87, 87-88, head coach, 1988-89, dir. player personnel, 1989-92, gen. mgr., 1992—. Office: Sacramento Kings 1 Sports Pky Sacramento CA 95834-2301•

REYNOLDS, JO-ANNE ELAINE, banker; b. Kingston, Jamaica, July 1, 1956; d. Arthur Eugene Brooks and Barbara Fay Arscott Williams; m. Randolph Paul Reynolds, Aug. 11, 1977 (div. 1990); 1 child, Jason Dominic. BSC in Quantitative Decision Analysis, U. Redlands, 1977. Lic. real estate salesperson, Calif. Fgn. exch. trader Mercury Internat., Toronto, Ont., Can., 1977-82; fgn. exch. trader Bank of Am. Can., Toronto, Ont., 1982-83, ops. mgr., 1983-85; ops. mgr. Fgn. Currency Svcs., Bank of Am., L.A., 1985-89, v.p., mgr., 1989—; cons. Vincent Bugliosi, Author, L.A., 1989-91. Pres. Home Owners Assn. of Winnetka, Calif., 1987-88, treas., 1986-87; fundraiser United Way, L.A., 1990-91. Mem. Nat. Assn. Realtors. Office: Bank of America 525 S Flower St B-Level Los Angeles CA 90071

REYNOLDS, JOHN CURBY, sales representative; b. San Jose, Calif., Aug. 15, 1948; s. Ivan Randolph and Lillie Murrel (McBrown) R.; m. Sharon Taylor, June 12, 1982; children: Brian James, Chris John. AA, Cabrillo Jr. Coll., Aptos, Calif., 1969; student, Calif. Polytechnic U., 1969-71. Sales rep. Equitable of Iowa Ins. Co., Sacramento, 1973-79, Grand Auto Inc., Sacramento, 1979-82, Princess House, Sacramento, 1982-84; sales telemktg. Montgomery Ward, Sacramento, 1984-85; sales rep. Sanitary Supply Co., Tucson, 1986—; mem. SVEA Bus. Group, Sierra Vista, Ariz., 1986—. Mem. First So. Bapt. Ch., Sierra Vista, 1989—; deacon bd. dirs., moderator ch. bd. dirs., sec. Evang. Free Ch. Mem. Sierra Vista C. of C. (mil. affairs com.). Democrat. Office: Sanitary Supply Co Inc 360 S 7th St Sierra Vista AZ 85635-2506

REYNOLDS, KATHLEEN DIANE FOY (KDF REYNOLDS), transportation executive; b. Chgo., Dec. 9, 1946; d. David Chancy Foy and Vivian Anne (Schwartz) R. Student, San Francisco State U., 1964-68. Studio coord. KTVU-TV, Oakland, Calif., 1968-70; assoc. prodr. KPIX-TV, San Francisco, 1970-72; music publicist Oakland, 1966-78; writer PLEXUS, West Coast Women's Press, Oakland, 1974-82, gen. mgr., 1984-86; screen writer Oakland, 1970—; v.p. Designated Driver Transport Group, Inc., Oakland, 1991—; coun. mem. West Coast Women's Press, Oakland, 1975-86; founding assoc. Women's Inst. for Freedom of the Press, Washington, 1976—. Author of periodical news, reviews, features, 1974-82; author of six documentaries for comml. and PBS-TV, 1968-73. Mem. Soc. Mayflower Descendants, Casper, Wyo., 1967—. Mem. Profl. Businesswomen's Conf., Ind. Feature Project. Home: PO Box 2742 Oakland CA 94602

REYNOLDS, PATRICK, foundation administrator, fundraiser, lecturer, author; b. Miami Beach, Fla., Dec. 2, 1948; s. Richard Joshua Jr. and Marianne (O'Brien) R. Student, U. Calif., Berkeley, 1967-70, UCLA, 1970-71, U. So. Calif., 1973-74. Founder Citizens for a Smokefree Am., Beverly Hills, Calif., 1989—; spokesperson Neuropsychology of Smoking Cessation, SyberVision Systems; speaker on smoking ordinances and cigarette tax increases to univs., health groups and state and mcpl. legislatures; appeared in numerous TV radio and print interviews on dangers of smoking. Co-author: The Gilded Leaf: Three Generations of the R.J. Reynolds Family and Fortune; appeared in film Eliminators, 1986. Recipient Humanitarian of Yr. award Chgo. Mt. Sinai Hosp., 1988, Spl. Svc. award WHO, 1989. Office: 505 S Beverly Dr Ste 1000 Beverly Hills CA 90212-3898

REYNOLDS, RICHARD HENRY, art educator; b. N.Y.C., May 16, 1913; s. Raymond R. and Sarah Alice (Weeks) R.; m. Marjorie Merrihew Sharrer, Aug. 10, 1939; 1 dau., Barbara Gwynne Nagata. A.B., U. Calif., 1936; student U. Calif., Los Angeles, 1939, Mills Coll., 1940; M.A., Coll. Pacific, 1942; postgrad. Oreg. State U., 1962; D.F.A., Morningside Coll., Sioux City, Iowa, 1976. Window display artist Emporium, San Francisco, 1936-37, Foreman-Clark, 1937, Hastings Clothing Co., 1937-38; asst. chmn. div. arts and letters Stockton Jr. Coll., 1939-43; prof. art, chmn. dept. U. of the Pacific, 1948-73, sr. prof., 1973-80, prof. emeritus, 1980, faculty research lectr., 1960, chairman academic council (senate), 1967-68, chmn. president's task force on acad. programs, 1980; mem. Stockton Arts Commn., 1980-81; guest lectr. Alaska Meth. U., Liberal Arts Inst., Anchorage, 1962; lectr. in field; judge numerous competitive art exhbns.; judge art sect. Ariz. State Fair, 1971; one-man show (sculpture) John Muir Gallery, Modesto, Calif., 1956, (painting) Lanai Gallery, Sacramento, 1956, (polychromed wood-reliefs) Stockton Fine Arts Gallery, 1972, 74, U. Pacific Alumni House Gallery, 1972; mem. show, Five Artists, invited E. B. Crocker Gallery, Sacramento, 1956; sculpture accepted for national exhbn. 10th Ann. New Eng. Exhbn., New Canaan, Conn., 1958; invited exhibit sculpture Eric Locke Gallery, San Francisco, 3d Ann. West Coast Sculptors, 1960; exhibited painting Purdue U., 1966; 2-man show (with wife) Stockton Savs. Loan Bank Invitational, 1968; exhibited paintings at No. Calif. Arts Exhbn., Sacramento, 1970; exhibited selected paintings Mother Lode Art Assn. Annual Show, Sonora, Calif., 1968; commd. sculptures buildings and campus U. of the Pacific, 1958, 60, 62, 63, bronze relief Swenson Golf Course, Stockton, 1968, metal falcon sculpture Atwater (Calif.) High Sch., 4 foot bronze relief for Stockton Record Bldg., bronze plaque Quemado (N.Mex.) Library, 1973; TV and radio lectr., 1955—; pvt. architectural sculpture commns., 1956—; exhibited Da Vinci Internat. Exhbn., N.Y.C., 1970, U. Pacific, 1973, Modesto Jr. Coll., 1973, Unitarian Arts Festival, Stockton, 1976-92, Ann. Delta Art Assn. show, Pittsburgh, Calif., 1976, Stockton Art League Show, annually, 1976-91; judge Merced Art Assn., 1976. Bd. dirs. Stockton Art League, 1978-79 hon. bd. dirs. Stockton Symphony Ballet Assn., 1978-84, San Joaquin Concert Ballet Assn. Served as lt. (j.g.), U.S. Naval Res., active duty, 1943-46. Awarded prize in oils Spring Art Festival, Stockton Art League, 1951; Bronze medal sculpture, Oakland Art Gallery's Oil Painting-Sculpture Ann. Exhbn., 1952; Kingsley award for sculpture Crocker Art Gallery, Sacramento, 1952, 53, 79; San Joaquin Pioneer Museum, 1953; 2d prize, Nat. Mag. Cover Contest, 1957; sculpture prizes Unitarian Arts Festival, Stockton, 1959, 61, 91; jurors mention Nat. Exhbn. Small Paintings, Tour Gallery Assos., N.Mex., 1962; hon. mention Stockton Art League, 1964, 68; Best of Show award, 2d prize (painting), honorable mentions in Calif. exhibitions, 1966; Transparent Painting award No. Calif. Spring Art Festival Haggin Mus., Stockton, Calif., 1968; columnist Senior Spectrum, 1989, 90—. Acrylic Painting award Unitarian Arts Festival, Stockton, 1968; purchase prize, painting Lodi Art Ann., Acampo, 1971, 79, 91, 92; 2d prize, painting San Joaquin County Fair and Expn., 1972, drawing and painting awards, 1974, 3d award, mixed media, 1981; 3 painting awards Stockton Art League Ann., 1974, purchase award, 1975; 1st prize sculpture San Joaquin County Fair and Expn. Art Show, 1976, 82; spl. award sculpture Crocker Kingsley Exhbn., 1982. 2d prize and hon. mention Bank of Stockton, 1976; 2d prize, other media San Joaquin County Fair, 1978; 2d award Lodi Spring Wine Show, 1982, 3d award, 1983; hon. mention Lodi Grape Festival and Nat. Wine Show, 1982; 2d award Unitarian Arts Festival, Stockton, 1982; hon. mention No. Calif. Arts, Inc. Exhbn., Sacramento, 1982; 2d award painting San Juin County Fair, also hon. mention graphics, 1983, 3rd prize sculpture Joaquin County Fair, 1988; 1st prize junk sculpture Alan Short Gallery, Stockton, Calif., 1983; 3d award Lodi Spring Wine Show Art Exhbn., 1983, 2 Exhibitor awards No.Calif. Arts Exhbn., Sacramento, 1983, 3d award San Joaquin County Fair Art Exhbn., 1984, Bronze Relief plaque for San Joaquin County Hosp., 1984, Columnist Stockton Art League's newsletter, The Collagraph, 1984-86, 3 2d Place awards, Hon. Mention for sculpture, 1985; 1st prize Stockton Symphony program cover competition, 1984; Order of Pacific award U. of Pacific, 1980; honorable mention Spring Wine Show Art Exhibition, Lodi, Calif., 1986; honorable mention No. Calif. Arts, Inc. Open Exhbn., 1986; judge's choice 16th annual Nat. Small Painting Show, Albuquerque, N.Mex., 1987, 18th annual, 1989, hon. mention 4th Nat. N.C. Miniature Painting Show, 1988; purchase prize for sculpture 37th Ann. Art Exhibition, 1988; Haggin Mus., 1988. Shell grantee, 1960. Life fellow International Inst. Arts and Letters, 1960. Mem. Coll. Art Assn. of Am., Pacific Arts Assn. (editor Journalette 1951-52; pres. No. Cal. sect. 1951-52), Stockton Art League (pres. 1952-53, 80-82), Nat. Art Edn. Assn. (nat. chmn. membership com. 1952-53), AAUP (v.p. local chpt. 1958-59), Navy League U.S. (dir. Stockton br. 1981-83), Phi Kappa Phi (pres.-elect 1980-81, emeritus), Delta Epsilon, Phi Sigma Kappa, Phi Delta Kappa (emeritus). Episcopalian. Richard H. Reynolds Gallery named in his honor U. Pacif, Stockton, 1986. Contbr. articles to art publs. Exhibitor paintings, sculptures. Home: 3400 Wagner Heights Rd # 321 Stockton CA 95209

REYNOLDS, RICHARD PAULSEN, computer scientist; b. Berkeley, Calif., Nov. 16, 1946; s. Theodore Robert and Mary Louise (Green) R.; m. Barbara Jean Trent, Jan 21, 1967; 1 child, Debra Jean. AA, Chabot Coll., 1972; BA, Calif. State U., Hayward, 1973. Computer scientist AT&T, Pleasanton, Calif., 1973—. With U.S. Army, 1967-69, Vietnam. Mem. Engring. Achievement Soc. (Outstanding Achievement award 1988, 90, 91, 92), Internat. Platform Assn., Nat. Trust for Hist. Preservation. Republican. Home: 5504 Jasmine Ct Castro Valley CA 94552-1721 Office: AT&T 4440 Rosewood Dr Pleasanton CA 94588

REYNOLDS, ROBERT HARRISON, export company executive; b. Mpls., Sept. 6, 1913; s. Clarence H. and Helen (Doyle) R.; m. Gladys Marie Gaster, Apr. 7, 1934; 1 child, Shirley Anne (Mrs. Frank S. Potestio); m. Viola E. Shimel, June 26, 1982. Export sales mgr., rolled products sales mgr. Colo. Fuel & Iron Corp., Denver, 1938-46; pres. Rocky Mountain Export Co., Inc., Denver, 1941—. Mem. Denver Club. Home: 13850 E Marina Dr Aurora CO 80014-3707 Office: Rocky Mountain Export 12331 E Cornell Ave Aurora CO 80014-3323

REYNOLDS, STEPHEN PHILIP, utility company executive; b. Berkeley, Calif., Jan. 5, 1948; s. Philip Elmore and Annette (Medefind) R.; m. Sharon Ann Rudd, Sept. 6, 1969; 1 child, Matthew. BA in Econs., U. Calif., Berkeley, 1970; MBA in Prodn. Mgmt., U. Oreg., 1972. Various mktg./rate positions Pacific Gas and Electric Co., San Francisco, 1967-75, sr. rate engr., 1975-77, supervising rate engr., 1977-80, mgr. rate dept., 1980-84, v.p. rates, 1984-87; pres., chief exec. officer Pacific Gas Transmission Co. (subs. Pacific Gas and Electric), 1987—; bd. dirs. Pacific Gas Transmission, Interstate Gas of Am., Interstate Gas of Am. Found., Assn. of Northwest Gas Utilities. Contbr. numerous articles to trade publs. and profl. symposiums on rate issues. Served with Calif. Army N.G., 1970-76. Mem. Pacific Coast Gas Assn., Nat. Planning Assn. (Canadian-American Com.), Calif. Found. on Environment & Economy, San Francisco World Affairs Coun., San Francisco Engrs. Club, Commonwealth Club, World Trade Club.

REYNOLDS, STEVEN LEE, elementary school educator, minister; b. L.A., Sept. 22, 1952; s. Howard Lee and Berneita (Bagley) R.; m. Cynthia Pauline Ramsey, June 10, 1978; children: Jason Lee, Nathaniel Steven, Andrea Christine. BA, Biola Coll., 1974; MA, Talbot Sem., 1977; BS, Donsbach U., 1988. Ordained to ministry Ojai Valley Community Ch., 1979. Owner, dir. Reynolds' Personal Enrichment Resources, Porterville, Calif., 1976—; instrl. asst. Richland High Sch., Orange, Calif., 1977-78; tchr. Deep Valley Christian Sch., Redwood Valley, Calif., 1980-81, 84-85; tchr. instrumental music Anderson Valley (Calif.) Schs., 1983-84, St. Mary's Sch., Ukiah, Calif., 1983-84; tchr. summer sch. Willits (Calif.) Migrant Edn., 1985; tchr. Ctr. for Ind. Studies, Willits, 1985-86; tchr. project devel. Porterville (Calif.) Pub. Schs., 1986-90; tchr. Sunnyside Sch., Strathmore, Calif., 1990-92; developer, dir. So. Tulare County Practical Arts High Sch., 1993—; with Christian Printing Svc., Fulleton, Calif., 1973-78; assoc. pastor Ojai (Calif.) Valley Community Ch., 1978-80; interim pastor Springville (Calif.) Evang. Free Ch., 1989. Developer sch. framework Christian Inst. in Graphic Arts, 1977, Practical Arts High Sch., 1985. Publs. officer USCG Aux., Orange County, Calif., 1975-78; alt. Rep. Ctrl. Com., Mendocino County, Calif., 1986. Recipient Achievement-Music award Bank of Am., 1970. Mem. Am. Sci. Affiliation, Internat. Coll. Nutrition and Preventive Medicine, Christian Instrumental Dirs. Assn., Christian Community Health Fellowship, Christian Community Devel. Assn. Office: Reynolds' Personal Enrichment Resources Porterville CA 93257-1319

REYNOLDS, WILLIAM CRAIG, mechanical engineer, educator; b. Berkeley, Calif., Mar. 16, 1933; s. Merrill and Patricia Pope (Galt) R.; m. Janice Erma, Sept. 18, 1953; children—Russell, Peter, Margery. B.S. in Mech. Engring., Stanford U., 1954, M.S. in Mech. Engring., 1955, Ph.D. in Mech. Engring., 1957. Faculty mech. engring. Stanford U., 1957—, chmn. dept. mech. engring., 1972-82, 89—, Donald Whittier prof. mech. engring., 1986—, chmn.Inst. for Energy Studies, 1974-81; staff scientist NASA/Ames Rsch. Ctr., 1987—. Author: books, including Energy Thermodynamics, 2d edit, 1976; contbr. numerous articles to profl. jours. NSF sr. scientist fellow Eng., 1964. Fellow ASME, Am. Phys. Soc.; mem. AAUP, AIAA, Nat. Acad. Engring. Stanford Integrated Mfg. Assn. (co-chmn. 1990—), Sigma Xi, Tau Beta Pi. Office: Stanford U Dept Mech Engring Bldg 500 Stanford CA 94305

REZNICK, CHARLOTTE, educational psychologist, consultant; b. Bklyn., July 27, 1950; d. Louis and Irene (Sazinsky) R. BA, CUNY, 1971; MS, U. So. Calif., 1974, PhD, 1985. Sch. psychologist L.A. Unifed Sch. Dist., 1979—; pvt. practice L.A., 1984—; clin. supr. dept. psychology Grad. Sch. UCLA, 1991—; cons., creator Imagery for Kids, various cities, 1984—. Contbg. author: Divorce and Family Instability, 1984; contbr. articles to profl. jours. Subccom. mem. alcohol and drug abuse L.A. Task Force on Self-Esteem and Personal and Social Responsibility, 1988-89; mem. Nat. Coun. for Self-Esteem. Mem. Calif. Assn. Sch. Psychologists, L.A. Assn. Sch. Psychologists (Outstanding Psychologist award 1987), Nat. Assn. Sch. Psychologists, Assn. Humanistic Psychology, Assn. Transpersonal Psychology. Democrat. Jewish. Home: 11660 Chenault St Los Angeles CA 90049 Office: Santa Monica Family Cons 2510 Main St Ste 201 Santa Monica CA 90405

RHEA, ANN CRAWFORD, interior designer; b. Somerville, Tenn., Oct. 30, 1940; d. James Samuel and Annie Marie (Crawford) R. BA in Art Edn., U. Miss., 1962; BFA, Memphis Coll. Arts, 1967; postgrad., Scottsdale Community Coll., 1975-85, Gateway C.C., 1991. Cert. Nat. Council Interior Design. Interior designer Dottie Sanders Interiors, Memphis, 1968-70; designer Holiday Inns Inc., Memphis, 1970-72, Ramada Inns Inc., Phoenix, 1972-78; assoc. Continental Design, Scottsdale, Ariz., 1978-80, Hauser Designs, Scottsdale, 1980-82; prin. Design Criteria Group, Scottsdale, 1983—; cons. Embassy Suites Hotels Inc., 1985, 87, 89; substitute tchr. Sch. Dist. Phoenix, 1989—, Glendale High Sch. Dist.; art instr. Human Svcs. Divsn. City of Phoenix. Mem. Smithsonian Assn., 1970-92, Nat. Trust Hist. Preservation, 1970-89; art director Art Evening's Peoria Boys & Girls Club, 1990-92. Recipient outstanding sub-tchr. cert. Fowler Sch. Dist., 1989. Mem. NAFE, Ariz. Hotel Motel Assn. (com. for hospitality show 1987-89, com. allied membership 1987-91, Taste of Hospitality com. 1989, Svc. award 1989), Nat. Mus. Women in the Arts. Methodist. Home and Office: PO Box 60841 Phoenix AZ 85082-0841

RHEINISH, ROBERT KENT, university administrator; b. Mt. Vernon, N.Y., Oct. 27, 1934; s. Walter Washington and Doris Elizabeth (Standard) R.; m. Dorothy Ellen Steadman, May 3, 1957 (div. 1976); children: Robert Scott, Joel Nelson; m. Shirley Marie Suter, Aug. 1, 1976. BA, U. South Fla., 1963; MS, Ind. U., 1971, EdD, 1973. Staff engr. Armed Forces Radio & TV Svc., Anchorage, 1960-61; trainee Nat. Park Svc. Tng. Ctr., Grand Canyon, Ariz., 1965; historian Home of F.D.R., Nat. Historic Site, Hyde Park, N.Y., 1964-65, Sagamore Hill Nat. Hist. Site, Oyster Bay, N.Y., 1965-66; asst. coord. nat. environ. edn. devel. program Dept. of Interior, Washington, 1968; supervisory historian Lincoln Boyhood Nat. Meml., Lincoln City, Ind., 1966-68; dir. learning resources ctr. Whittier (Calif.) Coll., 1971-73; dir. media and learning resources Calif. State U., Long Beach, 1973-88; chmn. media dirs. The Calif. State Univs., Long Beach, 1975-76; radio announcer Sta. WTCX-FM, St. Petersburg, Fla., 1961-63; co-host with David Horowitz (2 broadcasts) On Campus, Sta. KNBC-TV, L.A., 1972-73; guest lectr. 6th Army Intelligence Sch., Los Alamitos Armed Forces Res. Ctr., 1987. Coord. multi-media program: In Search of Yourself, 1975 (Silver award Internat. Film and TV Festival of N.Y.), The House that Memory Built, 1981 (Cindy award Info. Film Producers of Am.), The Indochinese and Their Cultures, 1985 (Silver award Internat. Film & TV Festival of N.Y.). With RCAF, 1954-55, USAF, 1957-61. U.S. Office of Edn. grad. fellow, 1971-73; recipient Learning Resources Ctr. Fund Devel. award Pepsico, Sears, Prentice-Hall, et al, 1973; Nat. Def. Edn. Act grantee, 1974-76. Mem. Lake Havasu Yacht Club. Republican. Home: 1975 Gold Dust Dr Lake Havasu City AZ 86403

RHINE, ROBLEY DICK, communication educator; b. Winfield, Kans., Dec. 30, 1930; s. Richard Martin and Fern O. (Easterday) R.; m. Peggy Ann Luck, Sept. 7, 1958. BA, Southwestern Coll., Winfield, 1953; MA, U. Colo., 1957; PhD, U. Wis., 1967. Instr. Southwestern Coll., 1956-58; instr. communication U. Colo., Boulder, 1958-61, asst. prof., 1964-67; from assoc. prof. to prof. communication U. Colo., Denver, 1967—; parliamentarian, bd. regents U. Colo., Boulder, 1972—. Co-author: Speechmaking: Handbook. Mem. NEA (life), Speech Commun. Assn. (life), Internat. Commun. Assn. (life), Am. Commun. Adminstrs. (pres. 1978-79), Colo. Drama Speech Assn. (pres. 1979-80), Colo. Speech Commun. Assn. (Svc. award 1990). Democrat. Methodist. Home: 2810 Vassar Dr Boulder CO 80303 Office: U Colo PO Box 173364 Denver CO 80217

RHOADS, DEAN ALLAN, state senator, cattle rancher; b. Tonasket, Wash., Oct. 5, 1935; s. Clyde Chester and Mamie Katerine (Kennedy) R.; m. Sharon Lois Packer, Jan. 8, 1964; children: Shamria, Chandra. BS in Agrl. Bus. Mgmt., Calif. State Poly. Coll., San Luis Obispo, 1963. Mgr. Calif. Livestock Mktg. Assn., Visalia, 1963-66; cow-calf operator Tuscarora, Nev., 1966—; assemblyman Nev. State Legislature, Carson City, 1976-82, senator, 1988—. Past pres., bd. dirs. Pub. Lands Coun., Washington, 1970-91. Mem. Nev. Tax Payers Assn. (bd. dirs. 1982-91), Nev. Cattlemen's Assn. (bd. dirs. 1968-91, Cattleman of Yr. 1980), Rotary. Republican. Presbyterian. Home: Tuscarora NV 89834

RHODE, EDWARD ALBERT, veterinary medicine educator, veterinary cardiologist, university dean; b. Amsterdam, N.Y., July 25, 1926; s. Edward A. and Katherine (Webb) R.; m. Dolores Bangert, 1955; children: David E., Peter R., Paul W., Robert M., Catherine E. DVM, Cornell U., 1947. Diplomate Am. Coll. Veterinary Internal Medicine. Prof. vet. medicine U. Calif., Davis, 1964—, chmn. dept. vet. medicine, 1968-71, assoc. dean instrn. Sch. Vet. Medicine, 1971-77, 78-81, dean sch. Vet. Medicine, 1982-91. Mem. AAAS, Nat. Acad. Practices, Am. Coll. Vet. Internal Medicine, Am. Vet. Medicine Assn., Basic Sci. Coun., Am. Heart Assn., Am. Acad. Vet. Cardiology, Am. Physiol. Soc., Calif. Vet. Medicine Assn. Office: U Calif Sch Vet Medicine Davis CA 95616

RHODES, GERALD LEE, newspaper reporter, writer; b. Redding, Calif., June 18, 1954; s. Howard Gordon and Rosalie (Lowell) R.; m. Sue Ann Williams, April 28, 1990; 1 child, Erin Nicole Fossum. BA in Journalism and Native Am. Ethnic Studies, Calif. State U., Sacramento, 1976; MS in Interdisciplinary Studies, U. Oregon, 1984. Reporter The Springfield (Oreg.) News, 1984-90; writer bus. and sci. The Columbian, Vancouver, Wash., 1990—; fire fighter U.S. Forest Svc., Redding, Calif., 1971-73, U.S. Bureau Land Mgmt., Anchorage, 1975-78; fire mgmt. tng. instr., adminstr. U.S. Bureau Land Mgmt., Alaska Fire Svc., Fairbanks, 1979-84; free lance writer Comm. Works, Springfield, 1989-90; self employed editor, Vancouver, 1990-92; v.p. Lane Press Club, Eugene, 1990. Reporter, photographer: (newspaper series) Future Forests, 1987 (Bus. Reporting Award for Non-Daily Newspapers, Associated Oregon Industries, 1988). vol. evergreen chpt. Habitat for Humanity, Vancouver, 1992. Fellow Sci. Writers Workshop, Am. Chem. Soc., Washington, 1991; New Horizons fellow, Coun. for the Advancement of Sci. Writing, 1992; recipient 1st Gen. Column Writing award Soc. Profl. Journalists, Oreg., 1988, 1st Sci. and Environ. Reporting award, Pacific N.W., 1993. Mem. Nat. Assn. Sci. Writers. Lutheran. Office: The Columbian 801 W 8th St Vancouver WA 98660

RHODES, JAMES LAMAR, JR. (GRIZZLY BEAR), educator, research historian; b. Montgomery, Ala., May 3, 1948; s. James Lamar Rhodes and Mae Ellen (Childers) Holley; divorced; 1 child, Sharon Michelle Rhodes Carswell; m. Saturnina Alvarado Avina, Feb. 14, 1977; children: James Lamar III, Aaron Abraham, David Isaiah. AA in English Lit., Coll. of Marin, 1972; BS in Criminal Justice Adminstrn., Calif. State U., San Jose, 1977; AA in Law Enforcement, Canada Coll., Redwood City, Calif., 1978; MA in Bus. Mgmt., Webster U., St. Louis, 1988. Cert. peace officer, Calif.; cert. detention and corrections officer, Ariz. Communications technician Pacific Telephone Co., Calif., 1970-83; detention officer Yuma County, Yuma, Ariz., 1984-86; correctional svc. officer State of Ariz., Yuma, 1986-88; tchr. Immaculate Conception Sch., Yuma, 1988-91; writer Yuma, 1991—; 1st Am. tchr. with students touring Socialist Republic of Vietnam, 1990; rschr. agent orange/herbicidal poisoning, Saigon, summer 1992; conductor seminars field.

Author detention and correctional handbooks; author: (with others) Where Dreams Begin, 1993; co-editor: Legacy of the American Indian: Lessons for the Classroom, 1989. Mem. Milpitas (Calif.) San. Dist. Bd., 1978-80; bd. dirs. Ctr. for Employment and Tng., Yuma, 1986—; founder no-fee counseling svcs. for Vietnam vets., Yuma; mem. Agt. Orange Adv. Com.; union organizer Communication Workers Am., Calif., 1972-80. Sgt. USAF, 1967-69, Vietnam. Recipient Citizen of Honor award Vietnamese Community, Santa Clara County, Calif., 1983, appreciation award Cath. Social Svc., Santa Clara County, 1983, Luth. Soc. Svc., Santa Clara County, 1983, Am. Legion, Indpls., 1983, AMVETS, Yuma, 1986. Mem. Vietnam Combat Vets (nat. chmn. 1981—), Justice for Vet. Victims of VA (v.p. 1988—), DAV, U.S. Chess Fedn., AFSCME, World Federalist Assn., Vietnam Helicopter Crew Mems. Assn., Ariz. Indian Vietnam Vets. Assn., Am. Legion (post comdr. 1983), AMVETS (state judge advocate Ariz. chpt. 1986). Mem. Baha'i Faith. Home: 1740 W 24th Ln Yuma AZ 85364

RHODES, JAMES MAURAN, JR., retired air force officer; b. Santa Monica, Calif., June 21, 1937; s. James M. and Sybil (Wescott) R.; m. Catherine H. Rhodes, June 4, 1959 (div. Oct. 1971); m. Sylvia E. Dunlevy, Dec. 7, 1977; children: James Mauran IV, Joan Rhodes Webb, Jeffrey Michael. BS in Mil. Sci., USAF Acad., Colo., 1959; MS in System Mgmt., U. So. Calif., L.A., 1970, cert. in info. systems, 1988. Commd. 2nd lt. USAF, 1959, advanced through grades to brig. gen., 1985, fighter pilot, 1960-65; student USAF Aerospace Rsch., Edwards AFB, Calif., 1966; flying, acad. & space simulation inst. USAF Aerospace Rsch., Edwards AFB, 1967-70; flight cmdr. 8th Spec Ops Sqdn, Bien Hoa AB, Republic of South Vietnam, 1970-71; staff planning officer HQ USAF, Washington, 1972-76; cmdr. 10th Tac Recon Wing, RAF Alconbury, UK, 1982-84; command dir. HQ Norad, Colorado Springs, Colo., 1985-86; cmdr. 23rd Air Div./Norad Region/SE Air Def. Sector, Tyndall AFB, Fla., 1986-88; ret., 1988; dir. Clearbrook Co., Ltd., 1989—; v.p. Garjak Rsch., Inc., 1991-92, cons., 1992—. Author: Aircraft Dynamics (USAF Aeospace research pilot sch. text) 1969. Mem. Order of Daedalians (flight capt. 1986-88), Red River Valley Fighter Pilots Assn. (pres. 1992—). Republican. Home: 1208 Masterpiece Dr Oceanside CA 92057-7806

RHODES, JEFFREY IVER, courier service executive; b. N.Y.C., Nov. 14, 1954; s. David and Leona Rhodes; m. Kathleen B. Figley, Jan. 26, 1980; 1 child, Evan. BS, U. So. Calif., 1977. Pres. Express Svc. Mgmt. Group Inc., Now Courier, L.A., 1977—; past pres. Air Courier Conf. Am. Mem. Assn. of Messenger and Courier Svcs. (bd. dirs. 1987—), Assn. Messenger and Courier Svcs. (exec. bd. dirs.). Office: Now Courier 619 S New Hampshire Ave Los Angeles CA 90005

RHODES, KENT BERTIS, therapist, minister; b. Portales, N.Mex., May 26, 1958; s. H. Kenneth and Jean Carolyn (Poston) R. BA, Lubbock (Tex.) Christian U., 1979; MA, Tex. Tech U., 1981; EdD, Pepperdine U., 1990. Ordained to ministry Christian Ch., 1976. Dir. student recruitment Lubbock Christian U., 1981-83; youth minister Broadway Ch. of Christ, Lubbock, 1983-87; dir. christian devel. Western Christian Ministries, Laguna Niguel, Calif., 1988—; campus min. Long Beach (Calif.) Ch. of Christ, 1989-90; pres., founder. Inst. Intergenerational Resources, West Los Angeles, 1990—; group therapist Pat Boone Rapha Recovery Ctr., Van Nuys, Calif., 1990—; bd. dirs. Internat. Inst. for Adolescence Studies, Abilene, Tex., Manna Internat., Redwood City, Calif. Author: Life That Shines, 1988. Vol. L.A. AIDS Project, 1990. Office: Affinity Resources 9733 Venice Blvd Los Angeles CA 90034

RIACH, DOUGLAS ALEXANDER, marketing and sales executive; b. Victoria, B.C., Can., Oct. 8, 1919; s. Alex and Gladys (Provis) R.; came to U.S., 1925, naturalized, 1942; BA, UCLA, 1948; postgrad. in mktg. Fenn Coll., 1959, Grad. Sch. Sales Mgmt. and Mktg., 1960, U.S. Army Command and Gen. Staff Coll., 1966, Armed Forces Staff Coll., 1968, Indsl. Coll. of the Armed Forces, 1970-71; m. Eleanor Montague, Mar. 28, 1942; 1 dau., Sandra Jean. With Gen. Foods Corp., 1948-80, terr. sales mgr., San Francisco, 1962-80; with Food Brokers, San Francisco Bay area, 1980-90; exec. v.p. Visual Market Plans Inc., Novato, Calif., 1984-87; with Ibbotson, Berri, DeNola Brokerage, Inc., Emeryville, Calif., 1990—. Served to capt. inf. AUS, 1941-46, ETO; to col. inf. USAR, 1946-79, from comdr. 2d inf. brigade Calif. State mil. res., 1984-87 to brigadier gen. (ret.) 1990. Decorated Legion of Merit, Bronze Star with V device and oak leaf cluster, Purple Heart, Combat Infantry Badge, Croix de Guerre avec Palme (France), Medaille de la France Liberee (France), Croix de Voluntaire (France), Medaille Commemorative Francais (France), Royal Commemorative War Cross (Yugoslavia), Medaille de la Reconnaissance (Belgium), Commemorative War Medal (Belgium), Medaille du Voluntaire (Belgium), Grand Cross of Homage (Ardennes), Cross of Freedom (Poland), Medaille Commemorative de la Campaigne d' Italia (Italy); named knight Order of the Compassionate Heart (internat.); knight commdr. Sovereign Mil. Order, Temple of Jerusalem (knights templar), Commandery of Calif. (knights templar); knight commdr. sovereign Order of St. John of Jerusalem (knights hospitaller), knight commdr. Polonia Restituta; named to U.S. Army Inf. Hall of Fame, 1982; recipient Calif. Medal of Merit and cluster, Commendation medal. Mem. Long Beach Food Sales Assn. (pres. 1950), Assn. Grocers Mfrs. Reps. (dir. 1955), Am. Security Council (nat. adv. bd. 1975—), Res. Officers Assn. (San Francisco Presidio pres. 1974-76, v.p. 1977-82, v.p. dept. Calif. 1979, exec. v.p. 1980, pres. 1981, nat. councilman 1981-82), Exchange Club (v.p. Long Beach 1955), St. Andrews Soc. Queens Club San Francisco, Combat Infantry Assn., Assn. U.S. Army, Assn. Former Intelligence Officers, Presidio Soc., Navy League, Ret. Officers Assn., Mil. Order Purple Heart, DAV, Psychol. Ops. Assn., Nat. Guard Assn. Calif., State Def. Force Assn. Calif., Merchandising Execs. San Francisco (dir. 1970-75, sec. 1976-77, v.p. 1978-79, pres. 1980, bd. dirs. 1981-89), Commonwealth of Club Calif. (nat. def. sect. vice chmn. 1964-66, chmn. 1967-72), Elks, F & AM(lodge 400), . Republican. Presbyterian. Home: 2609 Trousdale Dr Burlingame CA 94010-5706

RIANHARD, CARL JORY, venture capitalist; b. Santiago, Chile, July 8, 1959; s. Davis Lincoln and Carol Lee (Jory) R. BS in Indsl. Engring., Stanford U., 1981; MBA, Harvard U., 1985. Mktg. dir. GE Co., N.Y., Calif. and Tex., 1981-83; devel. mgr. Koll Co., Newport Beach, Calif., 1985-87; dir. acquisitions Homart Devel. Co., Newport Beach, 1987-88; v.p. acquisitions Signal Landmark, Newport Beach, 1988-90; pres. CalaFia Group, Newport Beach, 1990—; cons. BEI Real Estate, Simi Valley, Calif., 1991; seminar leader Harvard Bus. Sch., 1992. Contbr. articles to profl. pubs. Treas., bd. dirs. Princeton Mgmt. Assocs., Irvine, Calif., 1991; bd. dirs. Stop Gap, Costa Mesa, Calif., 1989. Mem. Internat. Forum for Corp. Dirs., World Affairs Coun., Univ. Club. Office: CalaFia Group 4220 Van Karman Ave Ste 100 Newport Beach CA 92660

RIBAK, CHARLES ERIC, anatomy educator; b. Albany, N.Y., July 19, 1950; s. Marcus and Adele (Blank) R.; m. Julia Marianne Wendruck, Jan. 2, 1977; children—Marc Aaron, William Michael. B.S., SUNY-Albany, 1971; Ph.D., Boston U., 1975. Assoc. research scientist City of Hope Med. Ctr., Duarte, Calif., 1975-78; asst. prof. U. Calif.-Irvine, 1978-83, assoc. prof., 1983-90, prof., 1990—. NIH NLS-2 Study Sect., 1989-92. Assoc. editor Jour. Neurocytology, London, 1984-88, Epilepsy Research, 1986—, Brain Research, 1988—, Jour. Mind and Behavior, 1988-, Anatomy and Embryology, 1992-, Jour. Hirnforschung, 1993-, Archives of Med. Rsch., 1993—; contbr. over ninety articles on brain research to profl. jours. NSF Grants, Washington, 1981-84, 87-91; Klingenstein fellow, 1983; research grantee NIH, 1979, 83, 86, 90; recipient Michael prize 1987, Citation Classic award 1987, Javits award 1990. Mem. AAAS, Am. Assn. Anatomists, Soc. Neurosci., N.Y. Acad. Scis., Internat. Brain Research Orgn. Office: U Calif Dept of Anatomy and Neurobiology Irvine CA 92717

RIBERA, ANTHONY D., protective services official. Police chief San Francisco Police Dept. Office: San Francisco Police Commn Hall of Justice Rm 505 850 Bryant St San Francisco CA 94103*

RICARDI, LEON JOSEPH, electrical engineer; b. Brockton, Mass., Mar. 21, 1924; s. Philip Julius and Eva Isabel (DuBois) R.; m. Angelena Marie Giorgio, Jan. 19, 1947; children: Eva Marie, John Philip, Richard Christopher. B.S. in Elec. Engring, Northeastern U., 1949, M.S., 1952, Ph.D., 1969. Engr. Andrew Alford Cons. Engrs., Boston, 1950-51; project engr. Gabirel Labs., Needham, Mass., 1951-54; group leader, head Tech. Adv. Office, MIT-Lincoln Lab., Lexington, Mass., 1954-84; pres. L.J. Ricardi, Inc., El Segundo, Calif., 1985—; part-time tchr. Northeastern U., Boston, 1969-80; cons. U.S. Air Force, 1965-85. Served with USAF, 1943-45. Fellow IEEE. Roman Catholic. Office: L J Ricardi Inc 360 N Sepulveda Blvd Ste 2030 El Segundo CA 90245

RICARDO-CAMPBELL, RITA, economist, educator; b. Boston, Mar. 16, 1920; d. David and Elizabeth (Jones) Ricardo; m. Wesley Glenn Campbell, Sept. 15, 1946; children: Barbara Lee, Diane Rita, Nancy Elizabeth. BS, Simmons Coll., 1941; MA, Harvard U., 1945, PhD, 1946. Instr. Harvard U., Cambridge, Mass., 1946-48; asst. prof. Tufts U., Medford, Mass., 1948-51; labor economist U.S. Wage Stabilization Bd., 1951-53; economist Ways and Means Com. U.S. Ho. of Reps., 1953; cons. economist, 1957-60; vis. prof. San Jose State Coll., 1960-61; sr. fellow Hoover Instn. on War, Revolution, and Peace, Stanford, Calif., 1968—; lectr. health svc. adminstrn. Stanford U. Med. Sch., 1973-78; bd. dirs. Watkins-Johnson Co., Palo Alto, Calif., Gillette Co., Boston; mgmt. bd. Samaritan Med. Ctr., San Jose, Calif. Author: Voluntary Health Insurance in the U.S., 1960, Economics of Health and Public Policy, 1971, Food Safety Regulation: Use and Limitations of Cost-Benefit Analysis, 1974, Drug Lag: Federal Government Decision Making, 1976, Social Security: Promise and Reality, 1977, The Economics and Politics of Health, 1982, 2d edit., 1985; co-editor: Below-Replacement Fertility in Industrial Societies, 1987, Issues in Contemporary Retirement, 1988; contbr. articles to profl. jours. Commr. Western Interstate Commn. for Higher Edn. Calif., 1967-75, chmn., 1970-71; mem. Pres. Nixon's Adv. Coun. on Status Women, 1969-76; mem. task force on taxation Pres.'s Coun. on Environ. Quality, 1970-72; mem. Pres.'s Com. Health Services Industry, 1971-73, FDA Nat. Adv. Drug Com., 1972-75; mem. Econ. Policy Adv. Bd., 1981-90, Pres. Reagan's Nat. Coun. on Humanities, 1982-89, Pres. Nat. Medal of Sci. com., 1988—; bd. dirs. Ind. Colls. No. Calif., 1971-87, Mt. Pelerin Soc., 1988—; mem. com. assessment of safety, benefits, risks Citizens Commn. Sci., Law and Food Supply, Rockefeller U., 1973-75; mem. adv. com. Ctr. Health Policy Rsch., Am. Enterprise Inst. Pub. Policy Rsch., Washington, 1974-80; mem. adv. coun. on social security Social Security Adminstrn., 1974-75; bd. dirs. Simmons Coll. Corp., Boston, 1975-80; mem. adv. coun. bd. assocs. Stanford Librs., 1975-78; mem. coun. SRI Internat., Menlo Park, Calif., 1977-90. Mem. Am. Econ. Assn., Mont Pelerin Soc. (bd. dirs. 1988—, v.p. 1992—), Harvard Grad. Soc. (coun. 1991), Phi Beta Kappa. Home: 26915 Alejandro Dr Los Altos Hills CA 94022 Office: Stanford U Hoover Instn Stanford CA 94305-6010

RICCARDI, VINCENT MICHAEL, pediatrician, researcher, educator; b. Bklyn., Oct. 14, 1940; s. Gabriel John and Frances Mary (Novak) R.; m. Susan Leona Bogda, July 27, 1967; children: Angela M., Ursula M., Mikah F. AB, UCLA, 1962; MD, Georgetown U., 1966; MBA, U. LaVerne, 1993. Intern, resident in medicine U. Pitts., 1966-68; fellow in genetics Harvard Med. Sch., Boston, 1968-70, 72; asst. prof. medicine U. Colo. Med. Ctr., Denver, 1973-75; assoc. prof. medicine, pediatrics Med. Coll. Wis., Milw., 1975-77; prof. medicine, pediatrics Baylor Coll. Medicine, Houston, 1977-90; med. dir. The Genetics Inst., Pasadena, Calif., 1990-92; clin. prof. pediatrics UCLA, 1991—; founder, CEO Am. Med. Consumers, La Crescenta, 1992; dir. The Neurofibromatosis Inst., La Crescenta, Calif., 1985—. Author: Genetic Approach to Human Disease, 1977, Communication and Counseling in Health Care, 1983, Neurofibromatosis, 1986, rev. edit., 1992. Maj. U.S. Army, 1970-71. Fellow AAAS, Am. Coll. Physicians; mem. Am. Soc. Human Genetics, Am. Coll. Physician Execs. Home: 5415 Briggs Ave La Crescenta CA 91214 Office: The Neurofibromatosis Inst 5415 Briggs Ave La Crescenta CA 91214

RICCO, RAYMOND JOSEPH, JR., computer systems engineer; b. Tullahoma, Tenn., Aug. 7, 1948; s. Raymond Joseph and Betty Jean (Collins) R.; m. Susan Rae Frey, Mar. 30, 1985. BS, Mid. Tenn. State U., 1971; MS, U. Tenn., Tullahoma, 1976. Rsch. asst. U. Tenn. Space Inst., Tullahoma, 1972-76; prin. analyst Teledyne Brown Engring., Huntsville, Ala., 1976-78; sr. analyst Sci. Applications Internat., Huntsville, 1978-82; project dir. Bell Tech. Ops., Sierra Vista, Ariz., 1982-90; sr. mem. tech. staff Mitre Corp., Colorado Springs, Colo., 1982-83; sr. engr. analyst Sci. Applications Internat., Huntsville, 1983-84; project mgr. Systems Devel. Corp., Dayton, Ohio, 1984-85; bus. assoc. Booz Allen & Hamilton Inc., Dayton, 1985-87; ptnr. Ricco-Thompson Cons. Engrs., Sierra Vista, 1990-92, Gazelle Affiliates, Sierra Vista, 1992—; sr. engr., scientist SAIC, Sierra Vista, 1992—; mem. adv. bd. Am. Security Coun., Arlington, Va., 1981—. Contbr. articles to profl. jours. Mem. NRA, IEEE, IEEE Computer Soc., Am. Def. Preparedness Assn., Armed Forces Comm. and Electronics Assn., Air Force Assn. Home: PO Box 3672 Sierra Vista AZ 85636-3672 Office: SAIC 333 W Wilcox Ste 200 Sierra Vista AZ 85635 also: Gazelle Affiliates 3323 E Willow Dr Sierra Vista AZ 85635

RICE, BARBARA POLLAK, advertising and marketing executive; b. Ft. Scott, Kans., Nov. 11, 1937; d. Olin N. and Jeanette E. (Essen) Brigman; m. Stanley Rice, Apr. 28, 1978; 1 child, Beverly Johnson. Student N. Central Coll., 1955, Elmhurst Coll., 1956; BA in Communications, Calif. State U., Fullerton, 1982. Art dir. Gonterman & Assos., St. Louis, 1968-71; advt. mgr. Passpoint Corp., St. Louis, 1971-73; advt., pub. relations mgr. Permaneer Corp., St. Louis, 1973-74; advt. cons., advt. mgr. Hydro-Air Engring., Inc., St. Louis, 1974-76; mgr. mktg. services Hollytex Carpet Mills subs. U.S. Gypsum Co., City of Industry, Calif., 1976-79; pres. B.P. Rice & Co., Inc., Ceritos, Calif., 1979—; press affiliate Inst. Bus. Designers. Recipient Designer Best Exhibit award Nat. Farm Builders Trade Show, Creative Challenge Mead Top 60 award L.A. Bus. Profl. Advt. Assn. Mem. Am. Advt. Fedn. (dist. officer), Los Angeles Advt. Women (pres., dir., LULU award), Bus. Profl. Advt. Assn., Calif. State U.-Fullerton Sch. Communications Alumni Assn. (bd. dirs.), Beta Sigma Phi (past pres., outstanding mem.). Author: Truss Construction Manual, 1975. Home: 1721 N Redwillow Rd Fullerton CA 92633-1433 Office: 12951 166th St Artesia CA 90701-2104

RICE, DENIS TIMLIN, lawyer; b. Milw., July 11, 1932; s. Cyrus Francis and Kathleen (Timlin) R.; children: James Connelly, Tracy Ellen. A.B., Princeton U., 1954; J.D., U. Mich., 1959. Bar: Calif. 1960. Practiced in San Francisco, 1959—; assoc. firm Pillsbury, Madison & Sutro, 1959-61, Howard & Prim, 1961-63; prin. firm Howard, Rice, Nemerovski, Canady, Robertson & Falk, 1964—; dir. Gensler & Assocs., Inc., San Francisco; chmn., mng. com. San Francisco Inst. Fin. Svcs., 1983-92. Councilman, City of Tiburon, Calif., 1968-72, mayor, 1970-72, dir., Marin County Transit Dist., 1970-72, 77-81, chmn., 1979-80; supr. Marin County, 1977-81, chmn., 1979-80; commr. Marin Housing Authority, 1977-81; mem. San Francisco Bay Conservation and Devel. Commn., 1977-83; bd. dirs. Planning and Conservation League, 1981—, Marin Symphony, 1984-92, Marin Theatre Co., 1987—; mem. Met. Transp. Commn., 1980-83; mem. bd. visitors U. Mich. Law Sch. Served to 1st lt. AUS, 1955-57. Recipient Freedom Found. medal, 1956. Fellow Am. Bar Found.; mem. State Bar Calif. (vice chmn. exec. com. bus. law sect.), ABA (fed. regulation of securities com.), San Francisco Bar Assn., Am. Judicature Soc., Bankers Club, Tiburon Peninsula Club, Nassau Club, Olympic Club, Order of Coif, Phi Beta Kappa, Phi Delta Phi. Home: 1850 Mountain View Dr Belvedere Tiburon CA 94920-1810 Office: Suite 700 3 Embarcadero Ctr Ste 700 San Francisco CA 94111-4010

RICE, DEVEREUX DUNLAP, marketing executive; b. Johnson City, Tenn., Jan. 28, 1952; s. Charles Bailey and Hazel Hunt (Donaldson) R.; m. Marcia Diane Fish, Mar. 20, 1980; 1 child, Melissa Susanne. BEE, Ga. Inst. Tech., 1974; MBA, U. Santa Clara, 1979. Engr. Motorola Semicondr., Phoenix, 1974-75, McDonnell Douglas Co., St. Louis, 1975-76; mktg. mgr. Fairchild Semicondr., Mountain View, Calif., 1976-80; pres. N.W. Mktg., Bellevue, Wash., 1980—. Contbr. articles to mags. Office: NW Mktg Assocs Inc 12835 Bel Red Rd Ste 330N Bellevue WA 98005-2625

RICE, EDWARD WILLIAM, medical management consultant; b. Great Falls, Mont., July 24, 1911; s. Robert W. and Laura Sebina (Martin) R.; m. Patricia Arnold, July 27, 1940; children: Barbara Beth Rice Wescott, Catherine Marie Rice Green. BS in Econs., U. Kans., 1935; LLB, Kans. U., Lawrence, 1938, JD (hon.), 1953. Bar: Kans. 1938. Collector Internat. Harvester Co., Topeka, Kans., 1941-43; sr. price specialist U.S. Office Price Adminstrn., Boise, Idaho, 1941-43; pres. Profl. Adjustment Co., Boise, Idaho, 1947-84, Drs. Bus. Bur., Boise, Idaho, 1953—; cons. and lectr. in field. Editorial cons. Physician's Mgmt. mag., 1962—. Mem. city coun. City of Boise, 1954-59, pres., 1959; mem. State of Idaho Ho. of Reps., 1959-67. With USN, 1943-46, PTO, comdr. USNR. Mem. ABA, Idaho Collectors Assn. (pres. 1948-50), Nat. Med.-Dental Hosp. Burs. Am. (pres. 1959-61), Better Bus. Bur., Kiwanis, Shriners, Masons. Republican. Baptist. Home: 1214 Johnson St Boise ID 83705-6022

RICE, JERRY LEE, professional football player; b. Starkville, Miss., Oct. 13, 1962; m. Jackie Rice; 1 child, Jaqui. Student, Miss. State Valley U. Football player San Francisco 49ers, 1985—. Named Most Valuable Player, Super Bowl XXIII, 1989, Sporting News NFL Player of Yr., 1987, 90; named to Sporting News Coll. All-Am. team, 1984, Sporting News All-Pro team, 1986-90, Pro Bowl team, 1986-91; holder NFL single season rec. most touchdown receptions. Office: care San Francisco 49ers 4949 Centennial Blvd Santa Clara CA 95054

RICE, JONATHAN C., educational television executive; b. St. Louis, Feb. 19, 1916; s. Charles M. and May R. (Goldman) R.; m. Kathleen Feiblman, Aug. 6, 1946 (dec. June 1964); children: Jefferson Charles, Kit (dec.), May Nanette. AB, Stanford U., 1938. War photographer, reporter Acme Newspix/NEA Svc., PTO of WWII, 1941-43; picture book editor Look Mag., N.Y.C., 1947-48; news/spl. events dir. Sta. KTLA-TV, L.A., 1948-53; program mgr. Sta. KQED-TV, San Francisco, 1953-67, dir. program ops., 1967-78, asst. to pres., 1978-90, bd. dirs., 1990—; cons. NET, PBS, Corp. for Pub. Broadcasting, Ford Found., TV Lima Peru, Sta. WGBH-TV, Boston, Sta. WNET-TV, N.Y.C., French TV, Europe Eastern Edn. TV, Dept. Justice, 1955-90; lectr. Stanford U., 1958-77. Editor: Look at America, The South, Official Picture Story of the FBI, 1947. Bd. dirs. NATAS, San Francisco, Planned Parenthood, San Francisco and Marin County, Calif. Maj. USMC, 1943-47, PTO. Recipient George Foster Peabody award, 1956, Thomas Alva Edison award for best station, N.Y.C., 1960, Gov.'s award NATAS, 1972-73, Ralph Lowell award Corp. for Pub. Broadcasting, 1972; Jonathan Rice Studio named in his honor, 1986. Home: 1 Russian Hill Pl San Francisco CA 94133

RICE, JULIAN CASAVANT, lawyer; b. Miami, Fla., Jan. 1, 1924; s. Sylvan J. and Maybelle (Casavant) R.; m. Dorothy Mae Haynes, Feb. 14, 1958; children—Scott B., Craig M. (dec.), Julianne C., Linda D., Janette M. Student, U. San Francisco, 1941-43; JD cum laude, Gonzaga U., 1950. Bar: Wash. 1950, Alaska 1959, U.S. Tax Ct. 1988. Pvt. practice law Spokane, 1950-56, Fairbanks, Alaska, 1959—; prin. Law Office Julian C. Rice (and predecessor firms), Fairbanks, 1959; bd. dirs. Key Bank of Alaska, Anchorage, Key Trust Co. Alaska; founder, gen. counsel Mt. McKinley Mut. Savs. Bank, Fairbanks, 1965—, chmn. bd., 1979-80; v.p., bd. dirs., gen. counsel Skimmers, Inc., Anchorage, 1966-67; gen. counsel Alaska Carriers Assn., Anchorage, 1960-71, Alaska Transp. Conf., 1960-67. Mayor City of Fairbanks, 1970-72. Served to maj. USNG and USAR, 1943-58. Decorated Bronze Star, combat Infantryman's badge. Fellow Am. Bar Found. (life); mem. ABA, Wash. Bar Assn., Alaska Bar Assn., Am. Judicature Soc., Transp. Lawyers Assn., Spokane Exchange Club (pres. 1956). Office: Rice Bldg 330 Wendell St Ste A Fairbanks AK 99701-4896 also: PO Box 70516 Fairbanks AK 99707

RICE, KRAIG JOSIAH, truck driver; b. Hallettsville, Tex., Nov. 21, 1945; s. H. M. and Emily Ann (Schmidt) R.; m. Bonnie L. Babcock, Mar. 15, 1980; children: Brent, Kristen, Scott. AA, Santa Rosa (Calif.) Jr. Coll., 1965; BS, Bethany Bible Coll., 1972. Ordained evangelist, 1984. Pres. Current Evangelism Ministries, Cloverdale, Calif., 1967—; treas. Current Charities, Lodi, Calif., 1989-92; truck driver car, Calif., 1989. Author: The Gospel Afloat, 1990. With USN, 1965-67. Mem. Sons of the Rep. of Tex., First Families of Ohio. Office: Current Evangelism Ministri 91 Church Ln Cloverdale CA 95425-4201

RICE, MICHAEL LEWIS, business educator; b. Ann Arbor, Mich., Jan. 7, 1943; s. Edwin Stevens and Elaine (Ivey) R.; m. Eileen Lynn Barnard, July 7, 1961. BS, Fla. State U., 1971, MBA, 1972; PhD, U. N.C., 1975. Asst. prof. U. N.C., Chapel Hill, 1974-80; assoc. prof. Wake Forest U., Winston-Salem, N.C., 1980-83; prof., dean U. Alaska, Fairbanks, 1983-91, vice chancellor adminstrv. svcs., 1991—. Contbr. numerous articles on fin. topics. Pres. United Way of Tanana Valley, Fairbanks, 1986-91. Mem. Am. Mgmt. Assn., Am. Mktg. Assn., Am. Econs. Assn., Am. Assembly Collegiate Schs. Bus., Western Assn. Collegiate Schs. Bus. (sec.-treas.), Rotary (bd. officer Fairbanks 1986-92, pres. 1992—). Office: U Alaska Vice Chancellor Adminstrv Svcs Fairbanks AK 99775

RICE, NORMAN, mayor; b. 1943. With govt. City of Seattle, 1978—, city councilman, 1978-89, mayor, 1990—. Office: Office of the Mayor Municipal Bldg 12th Fl 600 4th Ave Seattle WA 98104-1873

RICE, PATRICIA ANN, consulting director; b. Aldrich, Mo., Aug. 24, 1946; d. William Wayne and Wilda Mae (Lowery) Rice; children: Jessica Jean Rice, Clifford Wayne Rice, Jacqueline Marie Rice, Alicia JoAnne Rice. AA, Southwest Baptist U., Bolivar, Mo., 1966; BA, Southwest Mo. State U.; postgrad. Calif. State U.-Fullerton. Office mgr. Patscheck-Veiga Constrn. Co., Tustin, Calif., 1972-75; asst. to controller Richards West Co., Newport Beach, Calif., 1976-78; acctg. supr. Warner Lambert Co., Anaheim, Calif., 1978-80, supr. fin. analysis and planning, 1980; mgr. fin. control Pepsi Cola, Torrance, Calif., 1980-82; sr. fin. cons. Microdata Corp., (name changed to McDonnell Douglas Computer Systems Co.), Newport Beach, Calif., 1982-86, corp. acct. mgr. Printronix, Irvine, Calif., 1986-88; sr. cons. Deloitte & Touche, Costa Mesa, Calif., 1988-91; project mgr. Dun & Bradstreet Software, L.A., 1991, cons. dir., 1991-93; ptnr. in charge Partners In Excellence, Agoura Calif., 1993—. Leader, life time mem. Girl Scouts U.S.; bd. dirs. Real Reasons Homes for Abused Children; v.p. Parent Faculty Assn. Mem. AAUW, NAFE, NOW (chpt. program chmn. 1977), Am. Prodn. and Inventory Control Soc., Am. Mgmt. Assn., LaLeche League (chpt. publicity chmn. 1972-73). Democrat. Roman Catholic. Home and Office: 638 Lindero Canyon Rd Ste 343 Oak Park CA 91301

RICE, RICHARD LEE, JR., minister, office manager; b. Hillsboro, Oreg., Mar. 29, 1967; s. Richard Lee Rice and Nanci Carol (Losli) Skriiko. AA in Biblical Studies, Multnomah Sch. of the Bible, Portland, 1988. Youth dir. Rock Creek Foursquare Ch., Portland, 1984-86; assoc. pastor Valley Full Gospel Ch., Hillsboro, 1986-88; min. Congl. Bible Chs., Inc., Hillsboro, 1988—, bishop, 1988-90; office mgr. Alliance Properties, Inc., Aloha, Oreg., 1990—. Author: A Study in Acts, 1986, Systematic Theology, 1988; editor (newsletter) Pentecostal Fire Crusader. Committeeperson Rep. Cen. Com., Hillsboro, 1992—; mem. Oreg. Right to Life Com., Hillsboro, 1990—, Portland City Club, 1993—. Mem. NRA, Nat. Rep. Senatorial Com., Rep. Nat. Com., Rep. Presdl. Task Force, Nat. Congl. Club, Federalist Soc. Home: 2395 NE Poynter St Hillsboro OR 97124

RICE, STEVEN DALE, electronics educator; b. Valparaiso, Ind., Aug. 11, 1947; s. Lloyd Dale and Mary Helen (Breen) R.; m. Reyanna Danti, Mar. 4, 1972; children: Joshua, Breanna. AAS, Valparaiso Tech. Inst., 1969; BS Health Sci., Ball State U., 1973; BSEE, Valparaiso Tech. Inst., 1973; MS in Vocat. Edn., No. Mont. Coll., 1991. Electronics technician Heavy Mil. Electronic Systems GE, Syracuse, N.Y., 1969-70; electronics technician Ball State U., Muncie, Ind., 1974-75; with electronic sales Tandy Corp., Valparaiso, 1976-77; electronics technician Missoula (Mont.) Community Hosp., 1977-84; instr. electronics Missoula Vocat. Tech. Ctr., 1984-88, instr., chmn. dept., 1988—. Book reviewer Merrill Pub., 1988—. Bd. dirs. Victor (Mont.) Sch. Bd., 1989—, chmn. bd., 1992—. Mem. IEEE, Instrument Soc. Am., Mont. Fedn. Tchrs. Office: Missoula Vocat Tech Ctr 909 South Ave W Missoula MT 59801-7910

RICE, THOMAS R., venture capitalist; b. Oakland, Calif., Oct. 20, 1945; s. George A. Jr. and Jeanne (Barry) R.; m. Ann Haney, June, 17, 1967 (div. Mar. 1987); children: Elizabeth, Mary, Ann; m. Deborah Coburn, Apr. 21, 1990. BSME, Stanford U., 1967; MSME, MIT, 1968; PhD, Stanford U., 1975. With Cornerstone Ventures, Menlo Park, Calif.; chmn. Worldview Corp., San Francisco, 1990—; bd. dirs. Photonics Corp., Campbell, Calif., Rasna Corp., San Jose. Mem. Phi Beta Kappa, Tau Beta Pi, Sigma Zi. Office: Cornerstone Mgmt 2420 Sandhill Rd # 202 Menlo Park CA 94025-6942

RICE, WALLACE WILLIAM, secondary education educator; b. Basin, Wyo., May 3, 1936; s. William Peace Jr. and Emma Anne (Wahl) R.; m. Rozella Peterson, June 23, 1962; children: Steven C., Kevin E. BS in Geology, U. Wyo., 1959, MS in Natural Sci., 1967. Oil well logger Anders Well Logging, Fort Collins, Colo., 1959-61; office mgr. Wyo. Hwy Dept., Cheyenne, Wyo., 1962; adminstrv. asst. Sch. Dist. #1, Cheyenne, 1962-63; sci. tchr. Johnson High Sch., Cheyenne, 1963-65; earth sci. tchr. Cen. High Sch., Cheyenne, 1966—; athletic ticket mgr. Cen. High Sch., Cheyenne, 1968—. Sec., treas. Laramie County Rheumatic Fever Prevention Soc., Cheyenne, 1962—; leader Boy Scouts Am.; v.p. Trinity Luth. Ch., 1978, 79, King of Glory Luth. Ch., 1989, 90, 91. With USNG, 1954-62. Nomniated Tchr. of Yr., State of Wyo., 1975; recipient Buckeroo award, Silver Beaver award Boy Scouts Am., 1985, Commr. award 1988. Mem. Nat. Sci. Tchr. Assn. (regional meeting dir. 1972), Wyo. Math. Sci. Assn., Am. Fedn. Tchrs. (pres. 1978, 79, 82, sec. 1982—). Home: 222 E 2nd Ave Cheyenne WY 82001-1406 Office: Cen High Sch 5500 Education Dr Cheyenne WY 82009-4098

RICE, WILLIAM CLEM, psychotherapist, educator; b. Westwood, Calif., Jan. 5, 1937; s. William Edward and Margaret Isabelle (Berrett) R.; m. Joan Cannon, Aug. 26, 1960; children: Christen Joan, Berrett William, Shannon Lee, Jeremy Cannon. BS, Brigham Young U., 1962, PhD, 1971; MS, Pa. State U., 1966. Employment counselor Calif. State Dept. Employment, Oroville, 1962; pers. mgr. Libby, McNeil & Libby, Sacramento, 1962-63; social worker Sacramento County, 1963-65; asst. prof. Brigham Young U., Provo, Utah, 1966-70; consulting psychologist Milford County (Utah) Sch. Dist., 1967-70, Clovis (Calif.) Sch. Dist., 1971-73; prof. Calif. State U., Fresno, 1970—; pvt. practice psychotherapy Fresno, 1970—; commentator Sta. KJEO-TV, Fresno, 1972-73. Author: (textbook) Interpersonal Emotions, 1972, (poetry) Notes from Happily Ever After, 1989; host, prodr. edn. series Sta. KVPT-TV, Fresno, 1987—. Active Utah PTA, 1968—. With U.S. Army, 1956-58, Germany. Fellow Acad. Scientific Hypnosis; clin. mem. Am. Assn. of Marriage and Family Therapists, Am. Soc. for Clin. and Experimental Hypnosis, Calif. Assn. Marriage and Family Therapists. Republican. Mem. LDS Ch. Office: Ctr Counseling and Therapy Ste 106 6245 N Fresno Fresno CA 93710

RICH, ADRIENNE, writer; b. Balt., May 16, 1929; d. Arnold Rice and Helen Elizabeth (Jones) R.; m. Alfred H. Conrad (dec. 1970); children: David, Paul, Jacob. AB, Radcliffe Coll., 1951; LittD (hon.), Wheaton Coll., 1967, Smith Coll., 1979, Brandeis U., 1987, Coll. Wooster, Ohio, 1988, CCNY, Harvard U., 1990, Swarthmore Coll., 1992. Tchr. workshop YM-WHA Poetry Center, N.Y.C., 1966-67; vis. lectr. Swarthmore Coll., 1967-69; adj. prof. writing divsn. Columbia U., 1967-69; lectr. CCNY, 1968-70, instr., 1970-71, asst. prof. English, 1971-72, 74-75; Fannie Hurst vis. prof. creative lit. Brandeis U., 1972-73; prof. English Douglass Coll., Rutgers U., 1976-79; Clark lectr., disting. vis. prof. Scripps Coll., 1983-84; A.D. White prof.-at-large Cornell U., 1981-87; disting. vis. prof. San Jose State U., 1984-85; prof. English and feminist studies Stanford U., 1986-93; Marjorie Kovler vis. lectr. U. Chgo., 1989. Author: A Change of World, 1951, The Diamond Cutters and Other Poems, 1955, Snapshots of a Daughter-in-Law, 1963, Necessities of Life: Poems, 1962-65, 1966, Leaflets, Poems, 1965-68, Necessities of Life: Poems, 1965-68, 1969, The Will to Change, 1971, Diving into the Wreck, 1973, Poems Selected and New, 1950-74, 1975, Of Woman Born: Motherhood as Experience and Institution, 1976, 10th anniversary ed., 1986, The Dream of a Common Language: Poems, 1974-1977, 1978, On Lies, Secrets and Silence: Selected Prose, 1966-1978, 1979, A Wild Patience Has Taken Me This Far: Poems, 1978-81, 1981, The Fact of a Doorframe: Poems 1978-81, 1979; Your Native Land, Your Life: Poems, 1986, Blood, Bread and Poetry: Selected Prose, 1986, Time's Power: Poems 1985-88, 1989, An Atlas of the Difficult World: Poems 1988-91, 1991, What Is Found There: Notebooks on Poetry and Politics, 1993; co-editor: Sinister Wisdom, 1980-84; editorial bd. Bridges, 1989-93; contbr. to numerous anthologies; contbr. numerous articles, revs. to jours. and mags. Mem. nat. adv. bd. Bridges Boston Women's Fund, Sisterhood in Support of Sisters in South Africa. Recipient Yale Series of Younger Poets award, 1951, Ridgely Torrence Meml. award Poetry Soc. Am., 1955, Nat. Inst. Arts and Letters award poetry, 1961, Bess Hokin prize Poetry mag., 1963, Eunice Tietjens Meml. prize, 1968, Shelley Meml. award, 1971, Nat. Book award, 1974, Fund for Human Dignity award Nat. Gay Task Force, 1981, Ruth Lilly Poetry prize, 1986, Brandeis U. Creative Arts medal for Poetry, 1987, Nat. Poetry Assn. award, 1989, Elmer Holmes Bobst award arts and letters NYU, 1989, Commonwealth award in Lit., 1991, Frost Silver medal Poetry Soc. Am., 1992, L.A. Times Book award for poetry, 1992, Lenore Marshall/Nation award, 1992, William Whitehead award, 1992, Lambda Book award, 1992, The Poets' prize, 1993; Guggenheim fellow, 1952, 61; Amy Lowell traveling fellow, 1962; Bollingen Found. translation grantee, 1962; Nat. Translation Center grantee, 1968; Nat. Endowment for Arts grantee, 1970; Ingram Merrill Found. grantee, 1973-74; Lucy Martin Donnelly fellow Bryn Mawr Coll., 1975; hon. fellow MLA; Acad. Am. Poets fellowship, 1992. Mem. PEN, Am. Acad. and Inst. Arts and Letters (dept. of lit. 1990—), Nat. Writers Union, The Authors' Guild, Am. Academy Arts and Scis. Office: care W W Norton Co 500 5th Ave New York NY 10110-0002

RICH, ALAN, music critic, editor, author; b. Boston, June 17, 1924; s. Edward and Helen (Hirshberg) R. A.B., Harvard, 1945; M.A., U. Calif.-Berkeley, 1952. Alfred Hertz Meml. Traveling fellow in music Vienna, Austria, 1952-53; Asst. music critic Boston Herald, 1944-45, N.Y. Sun, 1947-48; contbr. Am. Record Guide, 1947-61, Saturday Rev., 1952-53, Mus. Am., 1955-61, Mus. Quar., 1957-58; tchr. music U. Calif. at Berkeley, 1950-58; program and music dir. Pacifica Found., FM radio, 1953-61; asst. music critic N.Y. Times, 1961-63; chief music critic, editor N.Y. Herald Tribune, 1963-66; music critic, editor N.Y. World Jour. Tribune, 1966-67; contbg. editor Time mag., 1967-68; music and drama critic, arts editor N.Y. mag., 1968-81, contbg. editor, 1981-83; music critic, arts editor Calif. (formerly New West mag.), 1979-83, contbg. editor, 1983-85; gen. editor Newsweek mag., N.Y.C., 1983-87; music critic L.A. Herald Examiner, 1987-89, L.A. Daily News, 1989-92, L.A. Weekly, 1992—; tchr. New Sch. for Social Rsch., 1972-75, 77-79, U. So. Calif. Sch. Journalism, 1980-82, Calif. Inst. Arts, 1982—, UCLA, 1990-91; artist-in-residence Davis Ctr. for Performing Arts CUNY, 1975-76. Author: Careers and Opportunities in Music, 1964, Music: Mirror of the Arts, 1969, Listeners Guides to Classical Music, Opera, Jazz, 3 vols., 1980, The Lincoln Center Story, 1984; author interactive CD-ROM computer programs: Schubert's Trout Quintet, 1991, So I've Heard: Bach and Before, 1992, So I've Heard: The Classical Ideal, 1993, So I've Heard: Beethoven and Beyond, 1993; contbr. articles to entertainment mags. Recipient Deems Taylor award ASCAP, 1970, 73, 74. Mem. Music Critics Circle N.Y. (sec. 1961-63, chmn. 1963-64), N.Y. Drama Critics Circle, Am. Theatre Critics Assn., Music Critics Assn., PEN. Home: 2925 Greenfield Ave Los Angeles CA 90064-4019

RICH, BEN ARTHUR, lawyer, university official; b. Springfield, Ill., Mar. 27, 1947; s. Ben Morris and Betty Lorraine (Ingalls) R.; m. Caroline Rose Castle, Oct. 4, 1984 (div. Nov. 1988). Student, U. St. Andrews, Scotland, 1967-68; BA, DePauw U., 1969; JD, Washington U., 1973; postgrad., U. Colo. Bar: Ill. 1973, N.C. 1975, Colo. 1984. Rsch. assoc. U. Ill. Coll. Law, Urbana, 1973-74; staff atty. Nat. Assn. Attys. Gen., Raleigh, N.C., 1974-76; prin. Hollowell, Silverstein, Rich & Brady, Raleigh, 1976-80; dep. commr. N.C. Indsl. Commn., Raleigh, 1980-81; counsel N.C. Meml. Hosp., Chapel Hill, 1981-84; assoc. univ. counsel U. Colo. Health Scis. Ctr., Denver, 1984-86; gen. counsel U. Colo., Boulder, 1986-89, spl. counsel to the regents, 1989-90; asst. prof. attendent U. Colo. Sch. Med., 1986-91, asst. clin. prof. 1992—, adj. instr. Sch. Law, 1988—, vis. assoc. prof., 1990-91, lectr. U. Denver Coll. Law. Contbr. articles to jours., chpt. to book. Mem. Nat. Assn. Coll. and Univ. Attys. (sect. co-chair 1966-91), Am. Coll. Legal Medicine (assoc.-in-law 1987—), Am. Soc. Law, Medicine and Ethics (health law tchrs. sect.), Am. Philos. Assn., Toastmasters Internat. (pres. Raleigh chpt. 1978). Unitarian. Home: 71 Ridge Dr Boulder CO 80304-0447 Office: U Colo Sch Law Box 401 Denver CO 80309

RICH, DAVID BARRY, city official, auditor, accountant; b. Bronx, N.Y., July 3, 1952; s. Steven and Gizella (Kornfeld) R.; m. Mindy Hope, Aug. 3, 1983; 1 child, Suzanne Stephanie. BS in Health Adminstrn., Ithaca Coll., 1976; postgrad. in acctg., Bryant and Stratton Coll., Buffalo, 1977. Office mgr. Rubin Gorewitz, CPA, N.Y.C., 1977-78; auditor State of Ariz., Phoenix, 1979-83; internal auditor City of Phoenix, 1983-84; sales use tax auditor City of Mesa (Ariz.), 1984—; pres. Clovis Acctg. Inc., Mesa, 1980—; rep. H.D. Vest Investment Inc., Irving, Tex., 1985—; owner D.B. Rich Enterprises Import/Export, Mesa, 1992—. Treas., bd. dirs. Missing Mutts Inc., Tempe, Ariz., 1986-88. With USAF, 1971-76. Fellow Nat. Assn. Tax Preparers; mem. Toastmasters (treas. Mesa 1986-87), Phi Beta Kappa. Office: Clovis Accounting Inc PO Box 5391 Mesa AZ 85211-5391

RICH, ELIZABETH MARIE, nursing educator; b. Bklyn., Nov. 20, 1949; d. Oren Edward and Catherine (Raffaele) R. ADN, Grossmont Coll., El Cajon, Calif., 1983; BSN, U. Phoenix, 1988; MS, Nat. U., San Diego, 1991. Cert. pub. health nurse, gerontol. nurse. ICU-CCU staff nurse Villa View, San Diego, 1983-85, AMI Valley Hosp., El Cajon, 1985-86; nurse Nursing Registries, 1986-87; charge nurse, supr. nights Beverly Manor Convalescent Home, Escondido, Calif., 1987-88; dir. staff devel. Beverly Manor Convalescent Home, Escondido, 1988-90; DON, nurse educator cons. Vista Del Mar Care Ctr., San Diego, 1990; instr. vocat. nursing Maric Coll. Med. Careers, San Marcos, Calif., 1991—, curriculum coord., placement coord. Mem. Calif. Vocat. Nurse Educators. Home: 872 Venice Gln Escondido CA 92026-3165

RICH, FRANCES LUTHER, sculptor; b. Spokane, Wash., Jan. 8, 1910; d. Elvo Elcourt Deffenbaugh and Irene (Luther Deffenbaugh) Rich. BA, Smith Coll., 1931; art student, Paris studios, 1933-35, Boston Mus. Sch. Art, 1935-36, Cranbrook Acad. Art, Bloomfield Hills, Mich., 1937-40, Claremont (Calif.) Coll., 1946-47, Columbia U., 1946-47; pupil of, Malvina Hoffman, Carl Milles, Alexandre Iacovleff. Dir. pub. relations Smith Coll., 1947-50; with pvt. studios Rome, 1950-52, Paris, 1960-62. Pub. and pvt. marble sculpture include Army-Navy-Air Force Nurses Arlington Nat. Cemetery, Washington, 1938, St. Joseph, Benedictine Abbey Chapel, Mt. Angel, Oreg., 1954, Bronze Pelican, Earle C. Anthony Bldg., U. Berkeley, Calif., 1958, St. Joseph, Guadelupe Coll., Los Gatos, Calif., 1966; series St. Francis of Assisi, 4' St. Francis, Little Austria Terrace, Millesgården, Lidingö, Sweden, 1960; 6'7" St. Francis, St. Margaret's Episcopal Ch., Palm Desert, Calif., 1970, 7'6" Pierce-Deree Coll., Mt. Hymettus, Athens, Greece, 1970, 7'6" St. Francis, Pres.'s Garden Smith Coll., Northampton, Mass., 1978, 4'4" bronze Cranbrook Acad. Art Mus., Bloomfield Hills, Mich., 1983, 10' bronze "Our Lady of Combermere" grounds, The Madonna House Apolstolate Tng. Ctr., Combermere, Ont., Can., 1960, 19" bronze "Our Lady of Combermere", Madonna House Chapel, Edmonton, Can., medals of Our Lady of Combermere and 22" bronze "St. Catherine of Siena" (Santa Catalina Sch., Monterey, Calif.), 1968, and at Madonna House, Combermere, Ont., Can., 1989, 8 " Crucifix, The Madonna Chapel, Grace Cathedral, San Francisco, 1972, 30" bronze crucifix St. Margaret's Episcopal Ch., Palm Desert, Calif., 1990, bronze "The Healer", David L. Reeves Meml. Libr., Cottage Hosp., Santa Barbara, Calif., 1973, 15 bronze "Birds in Flight", Living Desert Reserve, Palm Desert, Calif., 1978; reliefs include: 6 nine ' stone panels Union Bldg., Purdue U., Lafayette, Ind., 1939; bronze 4'x 6' panel "Nunc Dimittis", St. Peter's Episcopal Ch., Redwood City, Calif., 1957; 8' "Our Lady Seat of Wisdom", St. Cecelia Ch., Stanwood, Wash., 1965; 8' bronze "Christ of the Sacred Heart", St. Sebastian's Ch., West Los Angeles, Calif. 1972; portraits include: Margaret Sanger, 1957 and Pres. Herbert Davis, 1950, Nielson Libr., Smith Coll., Northampton, Mass., Prof. Henry Russel Hitchcock, marble bust Alice Stone Blackwell, Boston Pub. Library, 1961; 3'6" terra cotta figure Katharine Hepburn, Shakespeare Mus., 1962 and bronze bust of Hepburn, 1961, both as Cleopatra, at Am. Shakespeare Theatre, Stratford, Conn.; also bronze head Lawrence Langner, Shakespeare Theater Foyer, 1963; bronze head Virgil Thomson, Virgil Thomson Room, NYU, 1977; Smith Coll. Mus. Art collection includes bronze portraits of Katharine Hepburn as Cleopatra, Lotte Lehman, Diego Rivera, 1978, terra cotta portraits of Margaret Sanger, bronze portrait of Pres. Herbert Davis and bronze bas relief of Laura Scales; further sculpture collections Smith Coll. Mus. Art and Cranbrook Acad. Art, 1981; one man shows: Art Ctr., Phoenix, 1954, Santa Barbara Mus. Art, 1955, Calif. Palace Legion of Honor, San Francisco, 1955, Laguna Blanca Sch., Santa Barbara, 1955, Palm Springs Desert Mus., 1969, 77, Smith Coll Mus. Art, 1981, Cranbrook Acad. Art Mus., 1983; group exhbns.: Am. Art Exhibit, World's Fair, N.Y., 1939, First Nat. Biennale Contemporary Religious Art, Set Hall Coll., Pa., 1953, Denver Liturgical Art Show, 1952, De Young Mus., Calif Liturgical Artists, 1952, Grace Cathedral, San Francisco, 1957, Knoedler's Gallery, N.Y.C., 1962, Members Exhibit, Archtl. League, N.Y.C., 1962, Boston Pub. Libr.; 10 bronzes Nat. Liturgical Art Week, Seattle World's Fair, 1962; 8 bronzes "Students of Carl Milles" Exhibit, Millesgården, Lidingö, summer 1986; Milles as Mentor: The Work of Cranbrook Sculptors, 1931-51, 5 bronzes Cranbrook Acad. Art, Bloomfield Hills, Mich., summer, 1990;12 1/2" bronzes of Our Lady of Combermere in each of 27 small Madonna House Small Lay Apostolates Worldwide, 1989, 4'5" bronze St. Francis of Assisi, Botanic Garden Ctr., Fort Worth. 1990; 15" bronze of St. Margaret of Scotland St. Margaret's Episcopal Ch., Palm Desert, 1990, Canongate Kirk, Edinburgh, 1990, 91; 18" bronze crucifix Canongate Kirk Manse; life size bronze bust Dr. George Bass, underwater archaeologies, 1993; numerous portraits, fountains, small bronzes and silvers for pvt. collectors. Served to lt. comdr. USNR, 1942-46. Mem. Archtl. League N.Y.C., Smith Coll. Alumnae Assn., Cosmpolitan Club (N.Y.C.). Home and Studio: 1208 E Bolivar St Payson AZ 85541 also: 4385 Marina Dr Santa Barbara CA 93110

RICH, GARETH EDWARD, financial planner; b. Gainesville, Fla., Feb. 28, 1961. Assoc. in Bus. Adminstrn., Gainesville Coll., 1981; BBA, U. Ga., 1983; postgrad., Coll. for Fin. Planning, Denver, 1986-88. Cert. fin. planner. Acct. exec. Gallo Wine Co., L.A., 1983-84; ins. and investment broker Fin. Design Group, Inc., Woodland Hills, Calif., 1984-92; ins. and investment broker, dir. equities and investments Calif. Fin. Advisors, Inc., Sherman Oaks, Calif., 1992—. Vol. City of Hope, L.A.; referee Am. Youth Soccer Orgn., Conejo Valley, Calif.; umpire Little League Baseball, Conejo Valley. Mem. San Fernando Valley Underwriters Assn., Internat. Assn. Fin. Planning. Republican. Home: 5626 Fairview Pl Agoura Hills CA 91301-2228 Office: 15260 Ventura Blvd #200 Sherman Oaks CA 91403

RICH, JOSEPH ASH, academic administrator, consultant, educator; b. Butler, Pa., May 13, 1943; s. Sanford A. and Lucille M. (Spinneweber) R.; m. Barbara M. Houpt (div. Oct. 1985); children: Joseph P., Nancy L., Michael K., Jennifer L.; m. Nancy A. Maxwell, Nov. 22, 1986. BSBA, Calif. State U., Sacramento, 1966, MA in Speech Arts, 1968; PhD in Edn., Oreg. State U., 1984. Cert. tchr., Calif. Instr. in speech and English Yuba Coll., Marysville, Calif., 1968-69; instr. in speech and English Butte Coll., Oroville, Calif., 1969-77, chair div. lang. and fine arts, humanities, 1977-82, asst. to supt., pres., 1982-84; dean of instruction Walla Walla (Wash.) C.C., 1984-90; pres. Spokane (Wash.) C.C., 1990—; chmn. Wash. Instruction Commn., 1990. Author: An Analysis of Oral Communication, 1968, An Examination of...Morale..., 1984. Mem. Alternative Edn. Com., Walla Walla, 1985; asst. scoutmaster Boy Scouts Am., Chico, Calif., 1976; bd. dirs. Omni Arts, Chico, 1978, Bravo, Chico, 1979. Mem. Nat. Coun. Instrnl. Adminstrs. (state rep. 1986-90), Nat. Coun. Occupational Educators, N.W. Assn. Schs. and Colls. (liaison officer Wash. chpt. 1984-90), Wash. Assn. Community & Tech. Coll. Pres., Spokane C. of C., Rotary. Democrat. Methodist. Office: Spokane C Coll 1810 N Greene St Spokane WA 99207-5399

RICH, ROBERT STEPHEN, lawyer; b. N.Y.C., Apr. 30, 1938; s. Maurice H. and Natalie (Priess) R.; m. Myra N. Lakoff, May 31, 1964; children: David, Rebecca, Sarah. AB, Cornell U., 1959; JD, Yale U., 1963. Bar: N.Y. 1964, Colo. 1973, U.S. Tax Ct. 1966, U.S. Supreme Ct. 1967, U.S. Ct. Claims 1968, U.S. Dist. Ct. (so. dist.) N.Y. 1965, U.S. Dist. Ct. (ea. dist.) N.Y. 1965, U.S. Dist. Ct. Colo. 1980, U.S. Ct. Appeals (2d cir.) 1964, U.S. Ct. Appeals (10th cir.) 1978; conseil juridique, Paris, 1968. Assoc. Shearman & Sterling, N.Y.C., Paris, London, 1963-72; ptnr. Davis, Graham & Stubbs, Denver, 1973—; adj. faculty U. Denver Law Sch., 1977—; adv. bd. U. Denver Ann. Tax Inst., 1985—; adv. bd. global bus. and culture divsn. U. Denver, 1992—; bd. dirs. Clos du Val Wine Co. Ltd., Danskin Cattle Co., Areti Wines , Ltd., Taltarni Vineyards, Christy Sports, Copper Valley Assn., pres.; bd. dirs. several other corps.; mem. Colo. Internat. Trade Adv. Coun., 1985—, tax adv. com. U.S. Senator Hank Brown; mem. Rocky Mountain Dist. Export Coun. U.S. Dept. Commerce, 1993—. Author treatises on internat. taxation; contbr. articles to profl. jours. Bd. dirs. Denver Internat. Film Festival, 1978-79, Alliance Française, 1977—; actor, musician N.Y. Shakespeare Festival, 1960; sponsor Am. Tax Policy inst., 1991—; trustee, sec. Denver Art Mus., 1982—. Capt., AUS, 1959-60. Fellow Am. Coll. Tax Counsel (bd. regents 10th cir. 1992—); mem. ABA, Internat. Bar Assn., Colo. Bar Assn., N.Y. State Bar Assn., Assn. of Bar of City of N.Y., Asia-Pacific Lawyers Assn., Union Internationale des Avocats, Internat. Fiscal Assn. (pres. Rocky Mt. br. 1992—, U.S. regional v.p. 1988—), Japan-Am. Soc. Colo. (bd. dirs., 1989—, pres. 1991—), Confrerie des Chevaliers du Tastevin, Meadowood Club, Denver Club, Cactus Club Denver, Yale Club, Denver Tennis Club. Office: Davis Graham & Stubbs PO Box 185 370 17th St Denver CO 80201

RICH, ROLLA ROSS, science, political science and economics educator; b. Atlantic City, N.J., Nov. 2, 1945; s. Clarence Edgar and Muriel Gertrude (Sullivan) R.; children: Damon Ronan, Diahn Renet, Daniel Reuel, Debra Ruth, Denise Rachel. BA in Phys. Chemistry, Cen. Wash. U., 1969; MS in Adminstrn. of Sci./Tech., George Washington U., 1977; JD, Western Sierra U., 1993. Cert. internat. healthcare profl., internat. product safety mgr., internat. hazard control mgr., others. Enlisted U.S. Army, Ft. Lewis, Wash., 1969; advanced through ranks to capt. U.S. Army, 1974; sgt. Basic Tng. Sch. U.S. Army, Ft. Lewis, 1969-70; various to chief, asst. head radiobiochemistry Walter Reed Army Inst. Rsch., Washington, 1970-72; head biol. chemistry USA Environ. Hygiene Agy., Edgewood Arsenal, Md., 1973-75; health physicist Aberdeen Proving Ground, Md., 1976-66; chief, health physics Letterman Army Med. Ctr., San Francisco, 1977-79; health physicist White Sands (N.Mex.) Missile Range, 1980-81; resigned U.S. Army, 1981; pres., chief exec. officer Western Artists Am., Las Cruces, N.Mex. and, San Diego, 1981—; dir. San Diego and Imperial Counties Legal Svcs.; cons. U.S. Army Inspector Gen., Washington, 1975-81, U.S. Army Health Svcs. Command IG/San Antonio, 1973-81, Calif. Dept. Indsl. Hygiene, Sacramento, 1977-80, Imperial Joint Powers Authority, El Centro, Calif., 1991; tchr. history, econs. Calexico (Calif.) High Sch., 1991-92. Inventor/author nuclear reactor monitoring devices, 1970-81, animal rsch. restraining devices; contbr. articles to profl. jours. and newspapers. Candidate for judge, Rep. Party, Las Cruces, 1986; city artist, Las Cruces, 1989; Rep. candidate Calif. Legislature, dist. 80, 1992. Recipient MAT fellowship U. Idaho, Moscow, 1969; named Citizen of Yr. U.S. Army, San Francisco, 1979. Mem. Internat. Healthcare Profls. Mgmt. Assn. (cert. master), Internat. Product Safety Mgrs. Assn. (cert. master), Am. Indsl. Hygiene Assn., Health Physics Soc., Am. Assn. Physicists in Medicine, Res. Officers Assn., Alexander Art Corp. (cert. instr.), Internat. Hazard Control Officers (cert. master), Hazardous Material Transp. Assn., Disabled Paralegals Group (sr. v.p. 1993), others. Republican. Pentecostal. Office: Western Artists of Am PO Box 7 Imperial CA 92251-0007

RICHARD, ANITA LOUISE, entrepreneur, managing principal; b. Willard, N.Y., June 22, 1951; d. Marvin Gerald and Illene (Rosenberg) Isaacson. Student, U. Fla., 1969-70, CUNY, Bklyn., 1972-74, Barnard Baruch U., 1974-76; BA magna cum laude, Golden Gate U., 1981. Mktg. mgr. Exxon Office Systems, N.Y.C., 1976-77; program mgr. Exxon Office Systems, Dallas, 1977-78; br. mgr. Exxon Office Systems, Pasadena, Calif., 1978-79; br. sales mgr. Exxon Office Systems, Century City, Calif., 1979; mgr. regional sales program Exxon Office Systems, Marina Del Rey, Calif., 1979-81; mktg. mgr. Exxon Office Systems, San Francisco, 1981-82; product mgr. Wells Fargo Bank, San Francisco, 1984; mng. dir. J. Richard and Co., Montara, Calif., 1984-92; prin. A. Richard & Assocs., Montara, 1993—. Mem. Am. Mgmt. Assn., Am. Compensation Assn. (cert. compensation specialist), Group Health Assn. Am., No. Calif. Human Resources Coun., Practicing Law Inst., L.A. Athletic Club. Republican. Jewish. Office: 1661 Main St PO Box 779 Montara CA 94037

RICHARD, MARTY, fire chief; b. N.Y.C., Oct. 15, 1940; s. Jerry and Esther Richard; m. Liz F. Little, July 21, 1963; children: Victoria, Mervyn, Charles. AA in Fire Sci., Western Nev. C.C., Reno, 1974, AA in Law Enforcement, 1975. Cert. exec. fire officer Nat. Fire Acad. Firefighter Reno Fire Dept., 1964-73, fire inspector, 1973-74, capt. investigations, 1974-78, fire marshal, 1978-90, fire chief, 1990—. Mem. Washoe County Child Care Adv. Bd., Reno, 1978—, past pres.; mem. State Emergency Response Commn., Carson City, Nev., 1992; pres. Kerak Temple Band, 1980-81. With USAF, 1959-63. Recipient Firefighter of Yr. award Am. Legion, 1976. Mem. Nat. Fire Protection Assn., Internat. Fire Chiefs Assn., Reno Rodeo Assn. (assoc.), Fire Marshals N.Am. (pres. 1986). Home: 915 Maple Creek Ct Reno NV 89511 Office: Reno Fire Dept 200 Evans Ave Reno NV 89501

RICHARD, ROBERT JOHN, library director; b. Oakland, Calif., Sept. 20, 1947; s. John Argyle and Vern Elizabeth (Bauer) R.; m. Anne Elizabeth Terrell, June 8, 1968 (div. 1982); children: Jennifer Lynn, Laura Ellen, Constance Anne, Andrea Lee. Student, Fullerton Coll., 1965-67; B.A. in Biology, Chapman Coll., Orange (Calif.), 1972; M.S.L.S., Calif. State U.-Fullerton, 1973. Cert. county librarian, Calif. Audiovisual specialist Fullerton Pub. Libr., 1969-72, asst. to city librarian, 1972-73, librarian, 1973-76; br. librarian Orange County Pub. Libr., Orange, 1976-78; regional adminstr. Orange County Pub. Libr., 1979-80; assoc. dir. Long Beach Pub. Libr., Calif., 1980-81; dir. Sacramento Pub. Libr., 1981-86, Santa Ana (Calif.) Pub. Libr., 1986—. Mem. ALA, Pub. Library Execs. Assn So. Calif., Calif. Library Assn., Library Adminstrn. and Mgmt. Assn., Library Info. and Tech. Assn., Pub. Library Assn. Office: Santa Ana Pub Libr 26 Civic Ctr PO Box 1988 Santa Ana CA 92702-1988*

RICHARDS, CHRISTOS, executive search and personnel consultant; b. Athens, Greece, Aug. 13, 1957; came to U.S., 1960; s. Arthur Terry Richards and Katrina (Nikita) Winsor; m. Pia Erismann, Sept. 23, 1977. B Guest Svc. Mgmt., Swiss Wirteschule, 1979. Mgr. Hotel Europe Express Restaurant, Davos, Switzerland, 1978-80; mng. dir. Jakobshorn Club, Davos, 1980-82; exec. v.p. Winsor-Richards & Assocs., Westlake Village, Calif., 1982-86; pres. Richards Cons., Thousand Oaks, Calif., 1986—; CEO Career Connection Bio/Pharm. & Environ. Sci. Job Fairs, 1990; founder, CEO The Nexium Cos., 1991—. Charter mem. Rep. Presdl. Task Force, Washington, 1982. Mem. L.A. World Affairs Coun., So. Calif. Golf Assn. Office: 468 Pennsfield Pl Sts 101 and 105 Thousand Oaks CA 91360

RICHARDS, DALE SCOTT, management consultant; b. Salt Lake City, Oct. 28, 1952; s. Ray Longstroth and Minnie (Garff) R.; m. Linda Jeanne Merrick, Sept. 19, 1971; children: Emily, Natalie, Keri, Bradley Dale, Andrea. BS in Chem. Engring. cum laude, U. Utah, 1975; MBA, Brigham Young U., 1986. Engr. in tng., Idaho. Br. lab. mgr. Monroc Corp., Salt Lake City, 1971-75; process engr. FMC Corp., Pocatello, Idaho, 1975-78; quality engr., chem. lab. supr. FMC Corp., Middleport, N.Y., 1978-81; chem. lab. supr. Utah Power and Light Co., Castle Dale, 1981-83; engring. project mgr. Utah Power and Light Co., Salt Lake City, 1983-86, mktg. dir. bus. devel., 1986-88, dir. econ. devel., 1988-89, mktg. dir. new products and svcs., 1989-90; mgmt. cons., prin. Excel Mgmt. Systems, Centerville, Utah, 1990—; part time dir. sales orgn. Amsoil, Inc., S.E. Idaho and Utah, 1975-81; co-owner Excel Energy, SMI, Electronic Cottage, Salt Lake City, 1991—; presenter in field. Bd. dirs. Medina (N.Y.) Red Cross, 1979-81; chmn. U.S. Savs. Bond Dr., 1985; chmn. tech. com. Utah Mfg. Assn., Salt Lake City, 1988-90; mem. Utah Partnership Edn., Salt Lake City, 1989-92; com. leader Utah Pioneer Partnership. Staff sgt. USAF, 1971-77. Recipient Eagle Scout, Order of Arrow, Boy Scouts Am., Salt Lake City, 1965. Mem. Mountain West Venture Group (v.p. 1986-91, pres. 1991), Pocatello (Idaho) Toastmasters Internat. (v.p. 1977-78), Univ. Utah AIChE Chpt. (pres. 1974-75), Phi Kappa Phi, Tau Beta Pi (sec. 1974-75). Church of Jesus Christ of Latter-Day Saints. Home: 164 West 1600 North Centerville UT 84014 Office: Excel Mgmt Systems 164 W Ricks Creek Way Centerville UT 84014

RICHARDS, ERIC ALBERT STEPHAN, lawyer; b. Detroit, Jan. 1, 1965; s. June Hill. BA, Yale Coll., 1986; JD, Harvard U., 1989. Assoc. O'Melveny & Myers, L.A., 1989—. Office: 400 S Hope St 15th Pl Los Angeles CA 90071

RICHARDS, GERALD THOMAS, lawyer, consultant; b. Monrovia, Calif., Mar. 17, 1933; s. Louis Jacquelyn Richards and Inez Vivian (Richardson) Hall; children: Patricia M. Richards Grauf, Laura J., Dag Hammarskjold; m. Mary Lou Richards, Dec. 27, 1986. BS magna cum laude, Lafayette Coll., 1957; MS, Purdue U., 1963; JD, Golden Gate U., 1976. Bar: Calif. 1976, U.S. Dist. Ct. (no. dist.) Calif. 1977, U.S. Patent Office 1981, U.S. Ct. Appeals (9th cir.) 1984, U.S. Supreme Ct. 1984. Computational physicist Lawrence Livermore (Calif.) Nat. Lab., 1967-73, planning staff lawyer, 1979, mgr. tech. transfer office, 1980-83, asst. lab. counsel, 1984—; sole practice, Livermore, 1976-78; mem. exec. com., policy advisor Fed. Lab. Consortium for Tech. Transfer, 1980-88; panelist, del. White House Conf. on Productivity, Washington, 1983; del. Nat. Conf. on Tech. and Aging, Wingspread,

Wis., 1981. Commr. Housing Authority, City of Livermore, 1977, vice chairperson, 1978, chairperson, 1979; pres. Housing Choices, Inc., Livermore, 1980-84; bd. dirs. Valley Vol. Ctr., Pleasanton, Calif., 1983, pres., 1984-86. Recipient Engring. award Gen. Electric Co., 1956. Maj. U.S. Army, 1959-67. Mem. ABA, Calif. State Bar (conv. alt. del. 1990-92), Alameda County Bar Assn., Eastern Alameda County Bar Assn. (sec. 1978, bd. dirs. 1991-92, chair lawyers referral com. 1992-93), Phi Beta Kappa, Tau Beta Pi, Sigma Pi Sigma. Home: 1070 Shady Creek Pl Danville CA 94526-4355 Office: Lawrence Livermore Nat Lab PO Box 808 Livermore CA 94551-0808

RICHARDS, HERBERT EAST, minister emeritus, commentator; b. Hazleton, Pa., Dec. 30, 1919; s. Herbert E. and Mabel (Vannaucker) R.; m. Lois Marcey, Jan. 1, 1942; children: Herbert Charles, Marcey Lynn, Robyn Lois, Fredrick East, Mark Allen. AB, Dickinson Coll., 1941; BD, Drew U., 1944; MA, Columbia, 1944; DD, Coll. of Ida., 1953; postgrad., Union Theol. Sem., 1941-48, Bucknell U., 1943-44. Accredited news reporter Nat. Assn. Broadcasters. Ordained to ministry Methodist Ch., 1944; pastor in Boiling Springs, Pa., 1937-40, Westchester, Pa., 1940-41, Basking Ridge, N.J., 1941-47; mem. faculty Drew U. and Theol. Sem., 1944-51, asso. prof. homiletics and Christian criticism, chmn. dept., asst. dean, 1947-51; spl. lectr. religion Howard U., 1947; minister 1st Meth. Cathedral, Boise, Idaho, 1951-69, 1st United Meth. Ch., Eugene, Oreg., 1969-78, Tabor Heights United Meth. Ch., Portland, Oreg., 1978-86; minister emeritus Tabor Heights United Meth. Ch., 1986—; weekly radio broadcaster Sta. KBOI, Sta. KIDO, 1941—; weekly TV broadcaster CBS, 1945—, ABC, 1969—, NBC, 1973; pres. Inspiration, Inc., TV Found., 1965—, TV Ecology, 1973; producer Life TV series ABC, 1974-75; also BBC, Eng., Suise Romande, Geneva, Switzerland; Chmn. Idaho bd. ministerial tng. Meth. Conf., 1954-60; chmn. TV, Radio and Film Commn., 1954-62, Oreg. Council Public Broadcasting, 1973; del. Idaho Conf. Meth. Gen. Conf., 1956, Jurisdictional Conf., 1956, World Meth. Council, 1957, 81, World Meth. Conf., 1981; mem. Gen. Conf., 1956-60, Jurisdictional Conf., 1956, 60; meml. chaplain Idaho Supreme Ct., 1960; chaplain Idaho Senate, 1960-68; mem. Task Force on TV and Ch., 1983. Author: In Time of Need, 1986; contbr. articles to religious publs.; composer: oratorios Prophet Unwilling, 1966, Meet Martin Luther, 1968, Dear Jesus Boy, 1973. Mem. Commn. on Centennial Celebration for Idaho, 1962-63; committeeman Boy Scouts Am. Bd.; dirs. Eugene chpt. ARC, 1954-73; trustee Willamette U., Cascade Manor Homes; adv. bd. Medic-Alert Found. Recipient Alumni citation in religious edn. Dickinson Coll., 1948, Golden Plate award Am. Acad. Achievement, 1965, Jason Lee Mass Media TV award, 1983; named Clergyman of Yr. Religious Heritage Am., 1964. Mem. AAUP, CAP (chaplain Idaho wing, lt. col.), Am. Acad. Achievement (bd. govs. 1967—), Am. Found. Religion and Psychiatry (charter gov.), Greater Boise Ministerial Assn. (pres.), Eugene Ministerial Assn. (pres. 1978), Masons (32 degree, editor Pike's Peak Albert That Is), Shriners, Elks, Rotary (editor Key and Cog, pres. dist. 510 Pioneer Club), Kappa Sigma (Grand Master of Beta Pi). Home: 10172 SE 99th Dr Portland OR 97266-7227 Office: Tabor Heights United Meth Ch 6161 SE Stark St Portland OR 97215-1935

RICHARDS, JAMES WILLIAM, electromechanical engineer; b. Portland, Oreg., Oct. 24, 1921; s. Jarvis William and Thelma Helen (Eoff) R.; m. Violet Victor Ray, Oct. 9, 1946; children: Betty, Sandra, Diane, William. Student, Nat. Tech. Sch., 1942, Nat. Radio Inst., 1948, Internat. Corr. Sch., 1955; AA, Pierce Coll., 1968. Mgr. Western Design, Santa Barbara, Calif., 1948-55; sr. engr. Bendix Corp., North Hollywood, Calif., 1955-66; v.p. Talley Corp., Newbury Park, Calif., 1966-75, dir. engring., 1982-87; pvt. practice electromech. engr., Eugene, Oreg., 1975-82, 87-89; pres. Western Design, Eugene, Oreg., 1990—. Mem. Masons. Republican. Baptist. Home: PO Box 5498 Eugene OR 97405-0498 Office: Western Design 28983 Fox Hollow Rd PO Box 5549 Eugene OR 97405

RICHARDS, JOHN M., wood and paper products company executive; b. 1937. BA, Stanford U., 1959; MBA, Harvard U., 1961. With Fernwood Tie Co., 1962-64, v.p.; with St. Maries Plywood Co., 1964-69, v.p., gen. mgr.; with Potlatch Corp., San Francisco, 1969—, sales mgr., wood products group mktg. div., 1970-72, v.p., wood products group western div., 1972-76, sr. v.p. fin., 1976-83, sr. v.p. fin. adminstrn., 1983-87, exec. v.p. fin. adminstrn., 1987-89, pres., chief oper. officer, 1989—. Office: Potlatch Corp PO Box 3591 1 Maritime Plz San Francisco CA 94111-3404*

RICHARDS, KENNETH EDWIN, management consultant; b. N.J., Oct. 9, 1917; s. Kenneth G. and Laura (Benson) R.; m. Evelyn Henderson, Dec. 12, 1942 (div. June 16, 1963); children: Kenneth A., Grant B., Kyle E., Diane L. Parmley, Kathleen E. Hilton, Kim E. Jackson, Cynthia G. Burger, Cheri O. Figueroa, Steven E. Benedict.; m. Sylvia Marie Benedict, Nov. 1979. BA, Wesleyan U., 1939. Asst. buyer J.C. Penney Co., 1945-48, buyer, 1948-55, dept. head women's & girl's sportswear apparel, 1955-58; from v.p., mdse. mgr. to dir. S.H. Kress Co., 1958-60; v.p. mdse. and sales Firth Carpet Co., 1960-62, dir., 1961-62; spl. cons. to pres. Mohasco Industries Inc., 1962-63; v.p., dir. Yorkshire Terrace Motel Corp., 1963-66; ptnr. Roxbury Hollow Farm, Cloverack, N.Y., 1955-66; sr. ptnr. Mgmt. Assocs., 1963—; pres. Western Dept. Stores, L.A., 1968-70; v.p. merchandising Rapid Merchandising, Costa Mesa, Calif., 1970-72; exec. v.p., gen. mgr. Skor-Mor Products, Santa Barbara, Calif., 1972-75; pres., chief exec. officer Resort to Life, Inc., Calabasas, Calif., 1980-84; exec. dir. Retirement Jobs of Idaho, Boise, 1985-87; pres. Seniors, Inc., Boise, 1987—. Mem. adv. editorial bd. Surgeon Gen. U.S. Army, 1948-55; co-developer no-iron cotton; developer women's wear "skort"; pioneer use of mix and match sportswear. Lt. col. AUS, 1940-45. Decorated for action against enemy in Normandy, France, 1944. Mem. Chi Psi. Methodist. Office: 6287 Morris Hill Rd Boise ID 83704-9352

RICHARDS, KENT HAROLD, religion educator; b. Midland, Tex., July 6, 1939; s. Eva E. Richards; m. Kristen A. Becker, Dec. 30, 1960; children: Lisken Lynn, Lisanne Elizabeth. BA, Calif. State U., 1961; MTh., Claremont Sch. Theology, 1964; PhD, Claremont Grad. Sch., 1969. Rsch. assoc. Inst. for Antiquities & Christianity, Claremont, Calif., 1967-68; asst. prof. Old Testament U. Dayton (Ohio), 1968-72; prof. Old Testament Iliff Sch. Theology, Denver, 1972—; vis. prof. Sch. of Theology/Grad. Sch., Claremont, 1969; mem. bd. of ordained ministry UMC, Rocky Mt. Conf., Denver, 1976-82, bd. of diaconal ministry, 1976-78. Editor: Biblical Scholarship in North America, 16 vols., 1981—, Writings in the Ancient World, (with David Peterson) Interpreting Hebrew Poetry, 1992. Chmn. Colo. Gov.'s award in Edn. Com., Denver, 1989-91, Vision 2020: A Study of the Colo. Cts.; jud. adv. coun. Colo. Supreme Ct., 1993—; bd. dirs. Colo. Jud. Inst., 1991—. Rsch. grantee NEH, 1985-91, Lilly Found., 1985-86. Mem. Internat. Meeting Program (chair 1973-92), Cath. Bibl. Assn. (program com. 1976-80), Soc. Bibl. Lit. (exec. sec. 1981-87), Am. Coun. Learned Socs. (coun. sec. 1981-87), Profl. Ski Instrs. Am. Office: Iliff Sch of Theology 2201 S University Blvd Denver CO 80210-4798

RICHARDS, MARILYN JEANETTE, newspaper editor; b. Kotzebue, Alaska, Aug. 1, 1957; d. Thomas and Dorothy (Reich) R.; 1 child, Christopher Thomas. BA in Journalism, U. Alaska, Fairbanks, 1976; postgrad., U. Alaska, Anchorage, 1978, Pratt Inst. Copywriter KFAR, 1974-75; editor River Times, Fairbanks, 1976-77; news-anchor, co-host Alaska Native Mag., Fairbanks, 1975; mng. editor Tundra Times, Fairbanks, 1977, Anchorage, 1977, 92—; editor Arctic Sounder, Kotzebue, 1986; coord. N.W. Arctic Borough Sch. Dist., Kotzebue, 1988-89; bd. dirs. Tundra Times; writer, corr. Daily News-Miner, Fairbanks, 1981-85, Northland News, Fairbanks, 1981-85. Editor: Alaska Native Land Claims, 1976, Forget-Me-Not, 1977, Inupiaq Studies, 1988, The King of Kotzebue, The Story of Archie Ferguson, 1992. Mem. secondary lang. arts curriculum com. Anchorage Sch. Dist., 1991-92; vol. Abbott-O-Rabbit Little League, St. Francis Xavier Mission, PTSA, Am. Legion Aux., 1988—. Named Miss Arctic Circle, Arctic Circle C. of C., 1970; Emily Ivanoff Brown scholar, 1971; Howard Rock fellow, 1973. Mem. ALA, Alaska Broadcasters Assn., PEN, Alaska State C. of C., Arctic Circle C. of C., Alaska State Press Club (Community Svc. award 1983), Alaska Press Women (award 1975). Roman Catholic. Office: 3400 Spenard Ste 4 PO Box 92247 Anchorage AK 99509-2247

RICHARDS, MORRIS DICK, social work administrator, environmental analyst; b. Los Angeles, Aug. 20, 1939; s. Morris Dick Richards and Annette (Fox) Briggs; m. Leslie Sondra Lefkowitz, Mar. 22, 1975. BA cum laude, Claremont Men's Coll., 1962; MA, U. Chgo., 1964; M in Pub. Adminstrn., U. So. Calif., 1965; LLB, La Salle Ext. U., 1971; MS in Hygiene, PhD in Social Work, U. Pitts., 1973; MBA, Chapman Coll., 1987. Diplomate Acad. Cert. Social Workers. Asst. dep. dir. children and youth services Orange County (Calif.) Dept. Mental Health, 1973-77; gen. mgr., indsl. therapist Paragon West, Anaheim, Calif., 1977-83; acting dir. alcohol and drug program Horizon Health Corp., Newport Beach, Calif., 1983; editor, pub. relations rep., sr. social worker Orange County Social Services Agy., 1983-85; staff analyst Environ. Mgmt. Agy., Orange County, 1985-90; exec. asst. to dir. planning Orange County, 1990-92; staff analyst Orange County Social Svc. Agy., 1992—; adj. clin. prof. Chapman Coll., Orange, Calif., 1974-85; instr. Calif. Grad. Inst., 1988-93; instr. U. Phoenix, 1992; program analyst, head child welfare worker L.A. County Pub. Social Svcs., 1967-71; psychiat. clin. specialist Jewish Big Bros., L.A. County, 1964-67; med. social work cons. Whittier (Calif.) Presbyn. Hosp., 1973-76; pvt. practice psychotherapy, Tustin, Calif., 1975-77. Editor newsletter Orange County Adv., 1984-85, Planning Perspective, 1990-91, Broadmoor Community News, 1992—; contbr. articles to profl. jours. Past bd. dirs. Orange County chpt. Am. Jewish Com., 1982-88, Broadmore Community Assn., Anaheim Hills, Calif., 1981-83, sec., 1990—; mem. Orange County Mental Health Adv. Bd., 1981-88, sec., bd. dirs.; mem. bd. dirs. Orange County Mental Health Assn., 1988-91; mem. Juvenile Diversion Task Force of Orange County, 1977. Served with USAR, 1958-64. Fellow U. Chgo., 1962, NIMH, 1962, 72; Haynes scholar U. So. Calif. Sch. Pub. Adminstrn., 1964; grantee Faulk Program in Urban Mental Health, U. Pitts., 1973. Mem. ACLU (Orange County chpt.), Nat. Assn. Social Workers (mental health liaison, v.p. local chpt. 1975-88, Social Worker of Yr. award Orange County chpt. 1987), Acad. Cert. Social Workers (lic. clin. social worker and marriage, family, child counselor), Registry Clin. Social Workers (diplomate in clin. social work), Orange County Mental Health Assn. (past sec.). Home: 6506 E Via Estrada Anaheim CA 92807-4227 Office: County of Orange Social Svcs Agy 1055 N Main Santa Ana CA 92701-9999

RICHARDS, PAUL A., lawyer; b. Oakland, Calif., May 27, 1927; s. Donnell C. and Theresa (Pasquale) R.; m. Ann Morgans, May 20, 1948 (dec. 1984); 1 child, Paul M. BA, U. Pacific, 1950; JD, U. San Francisco, 1953. Bar: Nev. 1953, U.S. Dist. Ct. Nev. 1953, U.S. Supreme Ct. 1964, U.S. Ct. Claims 1976, U.S. Ct. Appeals (9th cir.) 1982. Pvt. practice, Reno, 1953—, prin. Paul A. Richards, Ltd.; prof. environ. law Sierra Nevada Coll., 1970-80. Mem. Washoe Dem. Central Com., 1959-74, chmn., 1964-66, vice chmn., 1966-68; trustee Sierra Nevada Coll., 1970-82, Ducks Unltd., 1964-72; trustee emeritus, 1974—; mem. Fed. Land Law Commn., Nev., 1973-80; bd. dirs. Reno Rodeo Assn., 1963, pres., 1979. Served with U.S. Navy, 1945-46. Recipient Pres.'s Buckle and award Reno Rodeo Assn., 1979. Mem. Nev. Bar Assn., Washoe County Bar Assn. Democrat. Roman Catholic. Club: Press. Lodge: Elks. Office: 248 S Sierra St Richards Bldg Ste 1 Reno NV 89501

RICHARDS, PAUL LINFORD, physics educator, researcher; b. Ithaca, N.Y., June 4, 1934; s. Lorenzo Adolph and Zilla (Linford) R.; m. Audrey Jarratt , Aug. 24, 1965; children: Elizabeth Anne, Mary-Ann. AB, Harvard U., 1956; PhD, U. Calif., Berkeley, 1960. Postdoctoral fellow U. Cambridge (Eng.), 1959-60; mem. tech. staff Bell Telephone Labs., Murray Hill, N.J., 1960-66; prof. physics U. Calif., Berkeley, 1966—, Faculty Rsch. lectr., 1990-91; faculty sr. scientist Lawrence Berkeley Lab., 1966—; advisor NASA, 1975-92, Conductus Inc., Mountain View, Calif., 1988—; hon. prof. Miller Inst. Rsch. in Phys. Scis., Berkeley, 1969-70, 87-88; vis. prof. Ecole Normale Superieure, Paris, 1984, 92; vis. astronomer Paris Obs., 1984. Contbr. over 300 articles to profl. jours. Guggenheim Meml. Found. fellow, Cambridge, Eng., 1973-74; named Calif. Scientist of Yr., Mus. Sci., L.A., 1981; recipient sr. scientist award Alexander von Humboldt Found., Stuttgart, Fed. Republic Germany, 1982. Fellow NAS, Am. Phys. Soc., Am. Acad. Arts and Scis. Office: U Calif Dept Physics Berkeley CA 94720

RICHARDS, SANDRA LOUISE, research company executive; b. Montour Falls, N.Y., July 18, 1934; d. Arthur Harrison II and Elizabeth (Carpenter) R.; m. Delmont E. Goodine, May 5, 1952 (div. July 1986); children: John, Laura, Elise, Lue Anne, Linda, Jeffrey, Devon Goodine. AS, Corning (N.Y.) C.C., 1980. Reporter, photographer Watkins Rev. & Express, Watkins Glen, N.Y., 1963-65; assoc. editor Watkins Glen Rev. & Express, 1965-73; adminstrv. sec. dept. consumer econs. Cornell U., Ithaca, N.Y., 1973-78, adminstrv. aide Video Lab., 1980-84; tech. coord. Access Rsch. Corp., San Diego, 1984-89, supr. tng. and documentation, 1990-91, mgr. tng. and documentation, 1991—; cons. grant writing and tng. program for numerous orgns., corps. and charitable groups, 1980-92. Vol. AIDS Found. San Diego, 1990-92. Named Vol. of Yr. in Adminstrn. AIDS Found. San Diego, 1991. Mem. Nat. Soc. Performance Instrn., San Diego Career Women. Episcopalian. Home: 3610 Crown Point Dr San Diego CA 92109 Office: Access Rsch Corp 9655 Towne Centre Dr San Diego CA 92121

RICHARDS, VINCENT PHILIP HASLEWOOD, librarian; b. Sutton Bonington, Nottinghamshire, Eng., Aug. 1, 1933; emigrated to Can., 1956, naturalized, 1961; s. Philip Haslewood and Alice Hilda (Moore) R.; m. Ann Beardshall, Apr. 3, 1961; children: Mark, Christopher, Erika. A.L.A., Ealing Coll., London, 1954; B.L.S. with distinction, U. Okla., 1966. Cert. profl. librarian, B.C. Joined Third Order Mt. Carmel, Roman Catholic Ch., 1976; with Brentford and Chiswick Pub. Libraries, London, 1949-56; asst. librarian B.C. (Can.) Pub. Library Commn., Dawson Creek, 1956-57; asst. dir. Fraser Valley Regional Library, Abbotsford, B.C., 1957-67; chief librarian Red Deer (Alta., Can.) Coll., 1967-77; dir. libraries Edmonton (Alta.) Pub. Library, 1977-89; libr. and book industry cons. Ganges, Can., 1990—; pres. Faculty Assn. Red Deer Coll., 1971-72, bd. govs., 1972-73. Contbr. articles to profl. jours., 1954—. Vice pres. Jeunesses Musicales, Red Deer, 1969-70; bd. dirs. Red Deer TV Authority, 1975-76, Alta. Found. Lit. Arts, 1984-86; mem. Reform Party Can. Served with Royal Army Ednl. Corps, 1951-53. Mem. Reform Party Can.

RICHARDSON, ARTHUR BERTHOLIN LARSEN, marketing professional; b. Schenectady, N.Y., Apr. 22, 1935; s. Arthur L.B. and Marjory (Bush) R.; m. Heidrun Borgwardt, Nov. 3, 1966 (div. Sept. 1971); 1 child, Eric Arthur; m. Gayle L. Hong, Dec. 3, 1990. BS in History, Fordham Coll., 1958; cert. internat. mgmt., U. Hawaii, 1988. Asst. new products mgr. Colgate Palmolive Co., N.Y.C., 1958-61; advt. mgr. Hathaway Shirt Co., Waterville, Maine, 1961-65; internat. mktg. dir. Turner Jones Co., N.Y.C., Tokyo, 1965-70; sr. v.p., ptnr. Mayfield, Smith, Park Advt., Honolulu, 1974-85; sr. v.p. DDB Needham Worldwide, Honolulu, 1985-88; pres. Market Strategies, Honolulu, 1988-91; v.p. Sellers Advt., 1991—. Mem. Am. Mktg. Assn. (v.p. 1975-76), Japan Am. Soc., Advt. Agy. Assn. Hwaii (pres. 1984). Home: 3755 Pukalani Pl Honolulu HI 96816-3813 Office: Sellers Advt 745 Fort Street Mall Ste 204 Honolulu HI 96813-3801

RICHARDSON, A(RTHUR) LESLIE, medical group consultant; b. Ramsgate, Kent, Eng., Feb. 21, 1910; s. John William and Emily Lilian (Wilkins) R.; came to U.S., 1930, naturalized, 1937; student spl. courses U. So. Calif., 1933-35; m. B. Kathleen Sargent, Oct. 15, 1937. Mgr., Tower Theater, Los Angeles, 1931-33; accountant Felix-Krueper Co., Los Angeles, 1933-35; indsl. engr. Pettengill, Inc., Los Angeles, 1935-37; purchasing agt. Gen. Petroleum Corp. Los Angeles, 1937-46; adminstr. Beaver Med. Clinic, Redlands, Calif., 1946-72, exec. cons. 1972-75; sec.-treas. Fern Properties, Inc., Redlands, 1955-75, Redelco, Inc., Redlands, 1960-67; pres. Buinco, Inc., Redlands, 1956-65; vice chmn. Redlands adv. bd. Bank of Am., 1973-80; exec. cons. Med. Adminstrs. Calif., 1975-83. Pres., Redlands Area Community Chest, 1953; volunteer exec. Internat. Exec. Service Corps; mem. San Bernardino County (Calif.) Grand Jury, 1952-53. Bd. dirs. Beaver Med. Clinic Found., Redlands, 1961—, sec.-treas., 1961-74, pres., 1974-75, chmn. bd. dirs. 1992—. Served to lt. Med. Adminstrv. Corps., AUS, 1942-45. Recipient Redlands Civic award Elks, 1953. Fellow Am. Coll. Med Group Adminstrs. (life, disting. fellow 1980, pres. 1965-66, dir.); mem. Med. Group Mgmt. Assn. (hon. life; mem. nat. long range planning com. 1963-68, pres. western sect. 1960), Kiwanis (pres. 1951), Masons. Episcopalian. Home: 1 Verlie Dr Redlands CA 92373-6943

RICHARDSON, ARTHUR WILHELM, lawyer; b. Glendale, Calif., Apr. 3, 1963; s. Douglas Fielding and Leni (Tempelaar-Lietz) R. AB, Occidental Coll., 1985; student, London Sch. Econs., 1983; JD, Harvard U., 1988. Bar: Calif. 1989. Assoc. Morgan, Lewis and Bockius, L.A., 1988-90; staff lawyer U.S. SEC, L.A., 1990-92, br. chief, 1992—. Contbr. Harvard Civil Rights/Civil Liberties Law Rev. Mem. ABA, Calif. Bar Assn., Harvard/Radcliffe Club So. Calif., Town Hall Calif., L.A. World Affairs Coun., Phi Beta Kappa. Presbyterian. Home: 2615 Canada Blvd Apt 208 Glendale CA 91208-2077 Office: US SEC 11th Fl 5670 Wilshire Blvd Los Angeles CA 90036-3648

RICHARDSON, CAROLYN JANE, social worker; b. Dayton, Ohio, Nov. 23, 1943; d. John Robert and Elizabeth (Kuhns) Eck; m. Robert Allen Richardson, Dec. 9, 1967. BA, Denison U., Granville, Ohio, 1965; MS in Social Work, Case Western Res. U., 1967. Lic. ind. social worker, Ohio. Group worker and coord. vols. West Side Community House, Cleve., 1967-70; social worker family care prog. Univ. Hosps. of Cleve./Case Western Res. U. Sch. Medicine, 1970-80, social work coord. family care program, 1980-89; social worker Hospic Maui, Wailuku, Hawaii, 1991—. Sec. Mental Health Assn., Maui, Hawaii, 1989-92, v.p., 1993. Mem. Nat. Assn. Social Workers, Assn. Cert. Social Workers, Registry of Clin. Social Workers.

RICHARDSON, CHARLES LAWRENCE, non-profit association director; b. Georgetown, Ky., Jan. 15, 1935; s. William Ernest and Opal Chilton (Riddle) R.; m. Mary-Elisabeth Davenport, June 5, 1956 (div. 1981); chilren: Dawn Elisabeth Byloff, Brian Geoffrey Lawrence; m. Heather Holbrook Diamond, July 10, 1984. BA, Mich. State U., 1958; MA, Yale U., 1959. Instr. Yale U., New Haven, 1958-62; sr. intelligence officer CIA, Washington, 1962-84; ops. mgr. Assn. Mgmt. Group, Inc., Phoenix, 1984-87; exec. dir. Profl. Ins. Agts. Assn., Phoenix, 1987-89, Nat. Environ. Tng. Assn., Phoenix, 1989—; mem. Nat. Adv. Coun. on Environ. Policy and Tech., 1990-92. Contbr. articles to profl. jours. Mem. Ariz. Commn. on the Environ., Phoenix, 1992—; mem. numerous bds. and adv. couns. for environ. and tech. edn. orgns. With USAF, 1954-57. Fulbright fellow Taiwan Nat. U., 1959-60, Woodrow Wilson fellow, 1958-62. Mem. Am. Water Works Assn., Water Environ. Fedn., Assn. of Bds. of Cert. Republican. Office: Nat Environ Tng Assn Ste 185 2930 E Camelback Rd Phoenix AZ 85016-4412

RICHARDSON, GARLAND DALE, packaging products company executive; b. Emporia, Kans., Jan. 27, 1931; s. Samual Carl and Martha Delphine (Stout) R.; m. Jeanne Spencer, Nov. 5, 1955; children: Anne, Brock, Sarah. BBA, Washburn U., 1954; BS, Kans. U., 1959, MS, 1960. Engr. Union Carbide, Speedway, Ind., 1960-63; tech. sales Union Carbide, Atlanta, 1963-66; metallurgist Ball Bros., Muncie, Ind., 1966-71; materials processor Ball Packaging Products Group, Westminster, Colo., 1971-78, mgr. rsch. and devel., 1978-84, dir. rsch. and devel., 1984-87, dir. licensing technology, 1987—. Patentee in field; contbr. articles to profl. jours. Capt. USAF, 1954-57. Mem. Nat. Metal Decorators Assn. (sec./treas. 1988-89, v.p. 1989-91, pres. 1991-92), Master Brewers of Ams., Am. Soc. Metals (chpt. treas. 1970), Early Am. Indsl. Assn., Affiliation Rocky Mountain Tool Collectors (pres. 1980-81), Kiwanis (pres. Applewood chpt. 1983-84). Republican. Methodist. Home: 10849 West 30th Ave Lakewood CO 80215 Office: Ball Corp 9300 W 108th Cir Westminster CO 80021

RICHARDSON, JAMES TROY, sociology educator, consultant; b. Charleston, S.C., Aug. 25, 1941; s. Lylse Vega and Vera Veda (King) R.; m. Sept. 2, 1966; 1 child, Tamatha Lea. BA in Sociology, Tex. Tech U., 1964, MA in Sociology, 1965; PhD in Sociology, Wash. State U., Pullman, 1968; JD, Old Coll. Law Sch., 1986. Bar: Nev. 1986. Instr. Tex. Tech U., Lubbock, 1965-66; NIMH fellow Wash. State U., 1966-68; asst. prof. sociology U. Nev., Reno, 1968-71, assoc. prof. sociology, 1971-76, prof. sociology, 1976-88, prof. sociology and jud. studies, 1988—, dir. Master of Jud. Studies Degree Program, 1988—, dir. Ctr. Justice Studies, 1992—; pres. Litigation Techs., Reno, 1986—; prof. U. Nev.-Reno Found., 1989; visitor London Sch. Econs., 1974-75. Author: Conversions Careers, 1978, Organized Miracles, 1979, The Brainwashing/Deprogramming Controversy, 1983, Money and Power in the New Religion, 1988, The Satanism Scare, 1991; contbr. numerous articles to profl. jours. Chair Washoe County Dems., 1976-78, State Group Ins. Com., Nev., 1984-90. Fulbright fellow The Netherlands, 1981. Mem. ABA, Nev. Bar Assn., Assn. for Sociology of Religion (pres. 1985-86), Am. Sociol. Assn., Soc. for Sci. Study of Religion, Internat. Soc. for Sociology of Religion (coun. mem. 1989—). Home: 2075 Marlette Ave Reno NV 89503-1441 Office: U Nev Dept of Sociology Reno NV 89557

RICHARDSON, JOHN CHARLES, corporate executive; b. Santa Barbara, Calif., Oct. 17, 1953; s. Maynard Newton and Janis Nadine (Nelson) R.; children: Philippe John, Raphael Leah Screiberg-Richardson. BA, U. Calif., Santa Barbara, 1979; JD, Golden State U., 1982. Bar: D.C., 1984. Rsch. analyst Calif. Dept. Indsl. Rels., San Francisco, 1979-80; spl. program coord. So. Calif. Dist. Coun. Carpenters, L.A., 1990-92; pres. Labor Rsch. Group, Inc., Beverly Hills, Calif., 1983—; rsch. analyst Svc. Employees Internat. Union, L.A., 1992—. Author: (manual) Public Works, 1989. Sec. Burbank (Calif.) Labor Coalition, 1992. Staff sgt. USAF, 1972-76. Democrat.

RICHARDSON, JOHN EDMON, marketing educator; b. Whittier, Calif., Oct. 22, 1942; s. John Edmon and Mildred Alice (Miller) R.; m. Dianne Elaine Ewald, July 15, 1967; 1 child, Sara Beth. BS, Calif. State U., Long Beach, 1964; MBA, U. So. Calif., 1966; MDiv, Fuller Theol. Sem., 1969, D of Ministry, 1981. Assoc. prof. mktg. Sch. Bus. and Mgmt. Pepperdine U., Malibu, Calif., 1969—. Author: (leader's guides) Caring Enough to Confront, 1984, The Measure of a Man, 1985; editor: Ann. Editions: Marketing, 1987—, Bus. Ethics, 1990—. Lay counselor La Canada (Calif.) Presbyn. Ch., 1978-84, mem. lay counseling task force, 1982-84. Mem. Am. Mgmt. Assn., Soc. Bus. Ethics, Christian Writers Guild, Fuller Sem. Alumni Cabinet (pres. 1982-85), Am. Mktg. Assn., Beta Gamma Sigma. Office: Pepperdine U Sch Bus and Mgmt 400 Corporate Pt Culver City CA 90230-7615

RICHARDSON, JOHN VINSON, JR., educator; b. Columbus, Ohio, Dec. 27, 1949; s. John Vinson Sr. and Hope Irene (Smith) R.; m. Nancy Lee Brown, Aug. 22, 1971. BA, Ohio State U., 1971; MLS, Vanderbilt U., 1972; PhD, Ind. U., 1978. Asst. prof. UCLA, 1978-83, assoc. prof., 1983—; fellow Advanced Rsch. Inst. U. Ill., 1991; pres. Info. Transfer, Inglewood, Calif., 1988—; mem. edit. bd. Reference Svcs. Rev., Ann Arbor, Mich., 1991—, Gov. Pubs. Rev., Oxford, Eng., 1975—, Index to Current Urban Documents, Westport, Conn., 1987—, U. Calif. Press Catalogues and Bibliographies series, 1993—; vis. fellow Charles Sturt U. NSW Australia, 1990; chmn. Calif. Pacific Ann. Conf. Comm. on Archives and History, 1992—. Author: Spirit of Inquiry, 1982, Gospel of Scholarship, 1992. Mem. UCLA Grad. Coun., 1992—, systemwide coordinating com. on grad. affairs, 1993; pres. Wesley Found., L.A., 1981-87; lay del. Cal-Pac Conf. United Meth. Ch., 1985, 86, 92—. Recipient numerous rsch. grants Coun. on Libr. Resources, 1985, 90; Harold Lancour scholar Beta Phi Mu, 1986. Fellow Newberry Libr.; mem. ALA (Justin Winsor prize 1990, RASD Outstanding Paper award 1992), Assn. Libr. and Info. Sci. Educators (rsch. paper prize 1986, 91), Am. Statis. Assn., Assn. for Computing Machinery, Sigma Xi. Democrat. Office: UCLA GSLIS 300 Circle Dr N Ste 204 Los Angeles CA 90024-1520

RICHARDSON, KENNETH T., JR., psychotherapist, consultant, educator, author; b. Santa Monica, Calif., Sept. 16, 1948; s. Kenneth T. Richardson and Florence (Wheeler) Neal; m. Mary L. Nutter, Dec. 31, 1983; children: Kenneth T. III, Russell A., Shad Martin, Cheralyn Martin. BA, Prescott (Ariz.) Coll., 1985; postgrad., Antioch (Ohio) Coll., 1987-88. Cert. addictions counselor, Ariz.; nat. cert. NCRC/ADOA. Program dir. Calvary Rehab. Ctr., Phoenix, 1979-82; clin. dir. Friendship House Comprehensive Recovery Ctr., San Francisco, 1982-84; dir. treatment The Meadows, Wickenburg, Ariz., 1984-87; co-founder, dir. The Orion Found., Phoenix, 1989—; owner, dir. Phoenix Cons. and Counseling Assocs., 1987—; cons. Addictions Svcs., The Hopi Tribe, Kykotsmoni, Ariz., 1989—, Baywood Hosp., Houston, 1988-89; advisor Nat. Coun. on Co-Dependence, Phoenix, 1990—, Recourse Found., Phoenix, 1989—; faculty instr. Rio Salado C.C., Phoenix, 1987-90, The Recovery Source, Houston, 1989-90; co-chair Nat. Conv. of Men., Relationships and Recovery, Phoenix, 1990, 91. Creator, presenter 3 audio tape series, 1989. Mem. Nat. Assn. Alcoholism and Drug Counselors, Am. Counseling Assn., Am. Mental Health Counselors Assn. Office: Phoenix Cons and Counseling Ste A202 5333 N 7th St Phoenix AZ 85014

RICHARDSON, LESTER EDWIN, engineer; b. Shreveport, La., Sept. 7, 1961; s. Elias and Larna (Washington) R. AAS, ITT Tech. Inst., Arlington, Tex., 1988; BA in Applied Sci., ITT Tech. Inst., West Covina, Calif., 1990. Puller Piggly Wiggly Inc., Shreveport, 1981-83; assemblyman Volkswagen Am., Ft. Worth, 1984-85; inventory control clk. Graphic Arts, Inc., Ft. Worth, 1985-88; quality control clk., test engr., test technician Propietary Controls, Rancho Dominguez, Calif., 1989—; cameraman Ever Increasing Faith TV, L.A., 1990—. Inventor craft lamps. Mem. Soc. Mfg. Engrs. Home: 3805 Cimarron St Los Angeles CA 90062-1025

RICHARDSON, LINFORD LAWSON, protective services official; b. Glendale, Calif., Dec. 31, 1941; s. Linford Lawson and Phillis Anette (German) R.; m. Nancy Jane White, Apr. 9, 1961; 1 child, Robin Anette. AA, Riverside Community Coll., 1972; BA, Calif. Bapt. Coll., 1976. Fireman Riverside (Calif.) Fire Dept., 1964-67; police officer Riverside Police Dept., 1967-82, police chief, 1982—; chmn. adv. bd. POST Basic Acad., Riverside County, 1985; chmn. Law Enforcement Adminstrn., Riverside County, 1985. Mem. adv. com. Calif. Bapt. Coll., Riverside, 1985—; advisor Riverside County Coalition for Alternatives to Domestic Violence, 1983—; chmn. Salvation Army, Riverside, 1985; bd. dirs. Riverside Employee Credit Union, 1984—. Served with U.S. Army, 1960-63. Republican. Baptist. Lodge: Rotary (bd. dirs. Riverside club 1985). Office: City of Riverside Police Dept 4102 N Orange St Riverside CA 92501-3671*

RICHARDSON, RICHARD COLBY, JR., higher education educator, researcher; b. Burlington, Vt., Sept. 10, 1933; s. Richard Colby and Florence May (Barlow) R.; m. Patricia Ann Barnhart, Dec. 21, 1954; children—Richard Colby III, Michael Donald, Christopher Robin. B.S., Castleton State Coll., 1954; M.A., Mich. State U., 1958; Ph.D., U. Tex., 1963; Litt.D. (hon.), Lafayette Coll., 1973. Instr., counselor Vt. Coll., Montpelier, 1958-61; dean instrn. Forest Park Community Coll., St. Louis, 1963-67; pres. Northampton County Area Community Coll., Bethelehem, Pa., 1967-77; chmn. dept. higher edn. and adult edn. Ariz. State U., Tempe, 1977-84, prof. edn. leadership and policy studies, 1984—. Jr. author: The Two Year College: A Social Synthesis, 1965; sr. author: Governance for the Two-Year College, 1972, Functional Literacy in the College Setting, 1981, Literacy in the Open Access College, 1983, Fostering Minority Acess and Achievement in Higher Education, 1987, Achieving Quality and Diversity, 1991. Bd. dirs. Easton Hosp., 1973-77, v.p., 1975-77; exec. council Minsi Trails council Boy Scouts Am., Bethelehem, 1973-77. Named Disting. Grad., Coll. Edn., U. Tex., Austin, 1982; recipient Outstanding Research Publ. award Council Univ. and Colls.-Am. Assn. Community and Jr. Colls., 1983, Disting. Service award, 1984. Mem. Am. Assn. Higher Edn. (charter life, dir. 1970-73), AAUP, Assn. for Study of Higher Edn. (bd. dirs. 1984), Am. Assn. Community and Jr. Colls. (dir. 1980-83). Democrat. Home: 5654 E Wilshire Dr Scottsdale AZ 85257-1950 Office: Ariz State U Tempe AZ 85287

RICHARDSON, RORY FLEMING, counselor; b. Tokyo, June 12, 1953; came to U.S., 1953; s. Paul Wilson and Louise (Fleming) R.; m. Patricia Lynn Schimming, July 11, 1989; children by previous marriage: Berny Paul, Nicholas Edward, Rachelle Rene, Katie Joy. BA, Calif. State Coll. Sonoma, 1973; MA, Goddard Coll., 1974; postgrad., Fielding Inst., 1974-75; diploma in psychodrama, Moreno Inst., 1975. Lic. counselor, mental health examiner, Oreg. Pvt. practice counselling various locations, Oreg., 1977-84; co-owner, mgr. Richardson and Richardson, Eagle Creek, Oreg., 1982-85; therapist Tillamook (Oreg.) Counseling, Inc., 1986-88, alcohol/drug abuse program mgr., 1988-89, clin. dir., 1989—; mental health examiner Tillamook County, 1989—; instr. psychology Tillamook Bay Community Coll., 1988—; lectr., trainer in field. Exec. bd. Oreg. Community Mental Health Providers Assn., Salem, 1989—. Mem. Am. Assn. Counseling and Devel., Internat. Assn. Eating Disorders Profls. (edn. coun. 1990—), Am. Mental Health Counselors Assn., Assn. Supervision and Counselor Edn., Am. Soc. Psychodrama, Sociometry and Group Psychotherapy. Home: 613 Williams Ave Tillamook OR 97141-2751 Office: Tillamook Counseling Inc 2405 5th St Tillamook OR 97141-2426

RICHARDSON, SHEILA J., market development consultant; b. Richland, Wash., Sept. 4, 1948; d. Jackson Childress and Jeanne (Pike) R. BA, U. Wash., 1970. Founder Marakesh Handcraft Coop, Seattle, 1970-74; investor, mktg. dir. Powder Mag., Aspen, Colo., 1974-78; owner Aspen Welcome Distbn., 1977-81; pub. rels. rep. Aspen Skiing Corp., 1978-81; founder Richardson-Hurshell Pub. Rels., Inc., Seattle, 1982-92. Del. White House Conf. on Small Bus., Washington, 1986; exec. com. Gov.'s Conf. on Small Bus., 1987; founding mem. Seattle Ski Alliance, 1985—; mem. Procurement Commn. Poncho, 1984—. Mem. Pub. Rels. Soc. Am., Pacific N.W. Ballet League, U. Wash. Alumni Assn., Princeton Athletic Club, United Daughters of Confederacy, Phi Beta Kappa, Alpha Delta Pi. Office: Market Devel Cons 2350 10th Ave E # 223 Seattle WA 98102

RICHARDSON, THOMAS WILSON, small business owner; b. Buffalo, May 30, 1940; s. Robert Winsor and Mary Virginia (Wilson) R.; m. Keven Farley, Feb. 13, 1965; children: Andrew Wilson, John Carter. BA in Econs., Coll. of William & Mary, 1963. Salesperson O'Malley Realty & Devel., Phoenix, 1970-73; sales mgr. Grubb & Ellis Comml. Real Estate, Phoenix, 1973-74; mktg. mgr. Lincoln Property Co., Phoenix, 1974-75; exec. v.p., gen. mgr. O'Malley Realty & Devel., Phoenix, 1975-80; v.p., mgr. Russ Lyon Realty Co.-Comml., Phoenix, 1980-87; mng. gen. ptnr. Lyon Comml. Brokerage Co., Phoenix, 1987-92; pres. Colliers, MacCaulay, Nicolls (Ariz.), Inc., Phoenix, 1992—; vice chmn. Colliers Internat. Property Cons., Boston, 1989-92. Mem. editorial adv. bd. S.W. Real Estate News, 1978—. Mem. Commn. on the Economy, City of Phoenix, 1991-92; trustee Phoenix Art Mus., 1976-81, 1991—; trustee, v.p. Phoenix Country Day Sch., 1984-86. Capt. inf. U.S. Army, 1963-69, Korea, Vietnam. Mem. Ariz. Aasn. Indsl. Devel., Ariz. Town Hall, Phoenix C. of C. (chmn. 1991-92), Lambda Alpha. Republican. Episcopalian. Office: Colliers MacCaulay Nicolls Az Inc Ste 200 2036 E Camelback Rd Phoenix AZ 85016-4724

RICHARDSON, WILLIAM BLAINE, congressman; b. Pasadena, Calif., Nov. 15, 1947; m. Barbara Flavin, 1972. BA, Tufts U., Medford, Mass., 1970; MA, Fletcher Sch. Law and Diplomacy, 1971. Mem. staff U.S. Ho. of Reps., 1971-72, Dept. State, 1973-75; mem. staff fgn. relations com. U.S. Senate, 1975-78; exec. dir. N. Mex. State Democratic Com., 1978, Bernalillo County Democratic Com., 1978; businessman Santa Fe, N. Mex., 1978-82; mem. 98th-103rd Congresses from 3rd N.Mex. dist., Washington, 1982—; chief dep. majority whip 103d Congress. Vice chair Dem. Nat. Com.; active Big Bros.-Big Sisters, Santa Fe. Mem. Santa Fe Hispanic C. of C., Santa Fe C. of C., Council Fgn. Relations, NATO 2000 Bd., Congl. Hispanic Caucus, Am. G.I. Forum. Office: 2349 Rayburn House Office Bldg Washington DC 20515*

RICHARDSON, WILLIAM YORK, III, securities broker and analyst; b. Birmingham, Ala., Oct. 23, 1952; s. William York II and Jean Marie (McGlenn) R.; m. Sherri Lynn Reid, July 19, 1975; children: Mychal McGlenn, Paul Loren. BS, Oreg. State U., 1975. Registered rep. Dean Witter, Portland, Oreg., 1975-82, Paine Webber, Portland, 1982—. Cub master Cub Scouts of Am., Portland, 1990-91, pack master, 1989, 92; basketball coach Tualatin Hills Park and Recreation, Beaverton, Oreg., 1990—. Mem. Alumni Assn. of Beta Theta Pi (pres. 1988-90, treas. 1989—). Home: 9207 SW Taylor Portland OR 97225 Office: Paine Webber 111 SW 5th Ave # 1200 Portland OR 97204

RICHENS, GREG P., custom fit training director; b. Ogden, Utah, Sept. 10, 1959; s. Merlin and Kaye (Protzman) R.; m. Cherly L. Manning, July 19, 1985; 1 child, G. Adam. BS in Polit. Sci., Weber State U., 1985; MS in Pub. Adminstrn., Utah State U., 1992. Acad. advisor Weber State U., Ogden, 1982-84; sales cons. Wiser's, Ogden, 1986-88; coord. custom tng. for econ. growth Ogden Weber Applied Tech. Ctr., Ogden, 1988-90; dir. custom tng. for econ. growth Davis Applied Tech. Ctr., Kaysville, Utah, 1990—; congl. intern U.S. Congress, Washington, 1983. Exec. mem. Weber State U. Young Alumni Coun., Ogden, 1987-91; voter registrar Weber County, Utah, 1990; fin. chmn. Protzman Campaign, Weber County, 1990; state del. Rep. Party, Utah, 1992; mem., senate pres. Utah Intercollegiate Assembly, 1984. Recipient Outstanding Activities award Assoc. Students of Weber State Coll., 1983; named to Outstanding Young Men of Am., 1987. Mem. ASTD, Am. Polit. Sci. Assn., N.Am. Hunting Club, Pi Sigma Alpha, Pi Gamma Mu. LDS. Home: 842 E 5300 S Ogden UT 84405 Office: Davis Applied Tech Ctr 550 E 300 S Kaysville UT 84037

RICHENS, MURIEL WHITTAKER, counselor, educator; b. Prineville, Oreg.; d. John Reginald and Victoria Cecilia (Pascale) Whittaker; children: Karen, John, Candice, Stephanie, Rebecca. BS, Oreg. State U.; MA, San Francisco State U., 1962; postgrad., U. Calif., Berkeley, 1967-69, U. Birmingham, Eng., 1973, U. Soria, Spain, 1981. Lic. sch. adminstr., tchr. 7-12, pupil personnel specialist, Calif., marriage, child and family counselor, Calif. Instr. Springfield (Oreg.) High Sch., San Francisco State U.; instr., counselor Coll. San Mateo, Calif., San Mateo High Sch. Dist., 1963-86; therapist AIDS health project AIDS Health Project, U. Calif., San Francisco, 1988—; pvt. practice MFCC San Mateo; guest West German-European Acad. seminar, Berlin, 1975. Lifeguard, ARC. postgrad. student Ctr. for Human Communications, Los Gatos, Calif., 1974, U. P.R., 1977, U. Guadalajara (Mex.), 1978, U. Durango (Mex.), 1980, U. Guanajuato (Mex.) 1982. Mem. U. Calif. Berkeley Alumni Assn., Am. Contract Bridge League (life master, cert. instr., tournament dir.), Women in Communications, Computer-Using Educators, Commonwealth Club, Pi Lambda Theta, Delta Pi Epsilon. Roman Catholic. Home and Office: 847 N Humboldt St Condo 309 San Mateo CA 94401-1451

RICHES, KENNETH WILLIAM, nuclear regulatory engineer; b. Long Beach, Calif., Oct. 23, 1962; s. William Murray Riches and Carlene Katherine (Simmons) Anderson; m. Susan Ruth Flagg, Aug. 11, 1990; 1 child, Benjamin William Bancroft Riches. BSEE, U. Ill., 1984; MS in Engring. Mgmt., Santa Clara U., 1989. Registered profl. engr., Calif. Engr. Pacific Gas & Electric Co., San Luis Obispo, Calif., 1984-88, elec. engr., 1988—; prin. K.W. Riches & Assocs., Arroyo Grande, Calif., 1988—; owner The Peaberry Coffee Pub, Arroyo Grande, Calif., 1991-92. Mem. Rep. Nat. Com., 1986—; active Corp. Action in Pub. Schs., San Francisco, 1987, 88, World Wildlife Fund. Univs. Rsch. Assn. scholar, 1980. Mem. NSPE, IEEE (chpt. chmn. 1986-87, sect. dir. 1988-90), Power Engring. Soc. of IEEE (mem. nat. chpts. coun. 1988-92), Pacific Coast Engring. Assn., Nature Conservancy, Order of DeMolay (master counselor Paul Revere chpt. 1979). Methodist. Home: 775 Ridgemont Way Arroyo Grande CA 93420 Office: PG&E Diablo Canyon Power Plant PO Box 117 M/S 104/5/21A Avila Beach CA 93424

RICHESON, JAMES GRADY, environmental engineering executive; b. Atlanta, July 20, 1928; s. Marvin Grady and Frances Regina (Moore) R.; m. Mary Ann Neubeck, Apr. 11, 1953; 1 child, James G. Jr. BSCE, U. Notre Dame, 1952; MBA, St. Louis U., 1972. Registered profl. engr., Ont., Can. Dist. mgr. Carborundum Co., Kirkwood, Mo., 1952-72; div. mgr. Carborundum WErke, GmbH, Dusseldorf, Germany, 1972-74; gen. sales mgr. Carborundum Environ. Systems, Toronto, Ont., 1975-78; regional sales mgr. Standard Oil of Ohio, Newport Beach, Calif., 1979-89; pres. Richeson Environ. Engring., Newport Beach, 1990—. Sgt. U.S. Army, 1946-48, Japan. Mem. Air Pollution Control Assn. (pres. 1968-72), Am. Foundrymen's Soc. (pres. 1962-72). Roman Catholic. Office: Richeson Environ Engring PO Box 8358 Newport Beach CA 92658

RICHEY, EVERETT ELDON, religion educator; b. Claremont, Ill., Nov. 1, 1923; s. Hugh Arthur and Elosia Emma (Longnecker) R.; m. Mary Elizabeth Reynolds, Apr. 9, 1944; children: Eldon Arthur, Clive Everett, Loretta Arlene, Charles Estel. ThB, Anderson U., 1946; MDiv, Sch. Theology, Anderson, Ind., 1956; ThD, Iliff Sch. of Theology, Denver, 1960. Pastor Ch. of God, Bremen, Ind., 1946-47, Laurel, Miss., 1947-48; pastor First Ch. of God, Fordyce, Ark., 1948-52; prof. Arlington Coll., Long Beach, Calif., 1961-68; pastor Cherry Ave. Ch. of God, Long Beach, 1964-68; prof. Azusa Pacific U., Azusa, Calif., 1968—; mem. Greater L.A. Sunday Sch. Assn., 1968—; mem., chmn. Commn. on Christian Higher Edn./Ch. of God, 1982—; pres. Ch. Growth Investors, Inc., 1981—. Author: ednl. manual Church Periodical--Curriculum, 1971-83. Mem. Nat. Assn. Profs. Christian Edn., Assn. Profs. and Rschrs. of Religious Edn., Gen. Assembly (mins. of the Ch. of God). Republican. Home: 413 N Valencia St Glendora CA 91740 Office: Azusa Pacific U Grad Sch of Theology Azusa CA 91702

RICHINS, BARRY LANE, English language educator; b. Ogden, Utah, Apr. 29, 1941; s. Edward Moroni and Dessa LaVon (Brough) R.; m. Linda Louise Favour, June 14, 1974 (div. 1984); children: Barry Lane Jr., Lori Julia; m. Barbara Ellsworth, Nov. 20, 1987. BS in Edn. and Spanish, No. Ariz. U., 1968; MA in English, Ill. State U., 1973. Cert. reading specialist, community coll. instr. of English, reading, Spanish, Ariz. Spanish trainer Peace Corps-Ecuador, Bozeman, Mont., 1966-67; grad. asst. Spanish U. Iowa, Iowa City, 1968-69, Brigham Young U., Provo, Utah, 1969-71; Spanish tchr. Superior (Ariz.) High Sch., 1971-72; English instr. Ill. Cen. Coll., Peoria, 1973; English/bilingual reading tchr. Phoenix (Ariz.) Union High Sch. Dist., 1974-75; English/reading instr. Northland Pioneer Coll., Holbrook, Ariz., 1975—, chmn. English dept., 1982-93; chmn. Ariz. Edn. Articulation Com., 1987-90; faculty advisor local chpt. Phi Theta Kappa, Holbrook, 1989-93; radio talk show host Northland Pioneer Coll., KDJI Radio, Holbrook, 1981-93. Author: Wood, Time and Stone, 1982; producer, interviewer Oral History of Navajo County, 1976-77. EPDA fellow, 1972-73. Mem. Western Assn. Community Coll. English Tchrs., Rocky Mountain MLA, Nat. Coun. Tchrs. English, Rotary (sec. Holbrook chpt. 1983-84, v.p. 1984-85, pres. 1990-91), Delta Sigma Pi.

RICHKIND, MELVYN, veterinarian, endocrinologist; b. Cleve., Sept. 3, 1939; s. Morris Richkind and Blanche (Weiderhorn) Malone; m. Kathleen Edna Kauffman, Aug. 22, 1970 (div. 1985); children: Mia Olivia, Fara Morgan. AA, Pierce Coll., 1960; BS, Calif. State U., Fresno, 1965; MSc, U. Calif., Davis, 1966, DVM, 1970. Diplomate in endocrinology Swedish Royal Vet. Coll. Postdoctoral fellow Swedish Royal Vet. Coll., Stockholm, 1972; adj. instr. UCLA Sch. Medicine, Westwood, 1973-74, adj. asst. prof., 1974; rsch. assoc. UCLA Harbor Med. Ctr., Torrance, 1980; vis. assoc. prof. UCLA Sch. Medicine, Westwood, 1980; cons. veterinarian and endocrinologist L.A., 1982; adj. prof. vet. medicine Coll. Santa Fe, 1984; with Lab. Animal Medicine VA Med. Ctr., Sepulveda, Calif., 1975-90, chief vet. medicine officer, 1989; chief exec. officer, dir. Pet Family Planning Inc., Northridge, Calif., 1989—; vet. surgeon Animal Birth Control, Culver City, Calif., 1986-90; vet. rsch. assoc VA Med. Ctr., 1992; bd. dirs. Longwood Prodns., 1993; apprentice to Miguel Angel Ruiz, M D Ctr. of 6th Sun; condr. seminare in field. Contbr. articles to sci. jours. With USN, 1963-71. Recipient Humanity medal ARC, L.A., 1966; rsch. grantee U. Calif., Davis, 1968. Mem. NAS, So. Calif. Vet. Medicine Assn., N.Y. Acad. Scis., Sigma Xi. Office: Pet Family Planning 8256 Louise Ave Northridge CA 91325-4450

RICHMAN, ANTHONY E., textile rental company executive; b. Los Angeles, Dec. 13, 1941; s. Irving M. and Helen V. (Muchnic) R.; m. Judy Harriet Richman, Dec. 19, 1964; children: Lisa Michele, Jennifer Beth. BS, U. So. Calif., 1964. With Reliable Textile Rental Svcs., Los Angeles, 1964—, svc. mgr., 1969, sales and svc. mgr., 1970-73, plant mgr., 1973-75, gen. mgr., bd. dirs., 1975-78, chief exec. officer, 1978-82, v.p., sec.-treas., 1975-82, exec. v.p., chief exec. officer, 1982-84, pres., chief exec. officer, 1984—. Bd. dirs. Guild for Children, 1979—, Valley Guild for Cystic Fibrosis, 1974—, Cystic Fibrosis Found. of L.A. and Orange Counties, 1989—; pres. Textile Svcs. Promotion Coun., 1991—. Recipient cert. of Achievement Linen Supply Assn. Am., 1979. Mem. Textile Rental Svcs. Assn. Am. (pres. 1993-95). Office: Reliable Textile Rental Svcs 3200 N Figueroa St Los Angeles CA 90065-1596

RICHMAN, DAVID BRUCE, entomologist, educator; b. Dunkirk, N.Y., Nov. 6, 1942; s. Melvin Stanley and Florence Irene (Nottis) R.; m. Olive Lynda Goin, June 18, 1977; children: Julia Anne, Rebecca Leonna. AA, Ariz. Western Coll., 1968; BS, U. Ariz., 1970, MS, 1973; PhD, U. Fla., 1977. Grad. asst., then asst. curator U. Ariz., Tucson, 1970-73; grad. asst., then rsch. assoc. U. Fla., Gainesville, 1973-78, 81-82; rsch. assoc./asst. prof. N.Mex. State U., Las Cruces, 1978-81, rsch. assoc., 1983-85, coll. asst. prof., 1985-90, sci. specialist dept. entomology-plant pathology-weed sci., 1990—; rsch. assoc. Fla. State Collection Arthropods, Gainesville, 1978—. Contbr. articles to sci. jours. Mem. Am. Arachological Soc., Brit. Arachological Soc., Entomol. Soc. Am. (chmn. resolutions com. southwestern br. 1990-91), Assn. Systematic Collections, Ctr. Internat. Documentation Arachologique, Cambridge Entomol. Club, Entomol. Collections Network, Southwestern Entomol. Soc., Sigma Xi. Democrat. Mem. Soc. of Friends. Office: N Mex State U Dept Entomology-Plant Pathogy-Weed Sci Las Cruces NM 88003

RICHMAN, MARVIN JORDAN, real estate developer; b. N.Y.C., July 13, 1939; s. Morris and Minnie (Graubart) R.; m. Amy Paula Rubin, July 31, 1966; children: Mark Jason, Keith Hayden, Susanne Elizabeth, Jessica Paige. BArch, MIT, 1962; M Urban Planning, N.Y. U., 1966, postgrad., 1967-69; MBA, U. Chgo., 1977; U.S. Dept. State fellow U. Chile, 1960. Architect, planner Skidmore, Owings & Merrill, N.Y.C., 1964, Conklin & Rossant, N.Y.C., 1965-67; ptnr. Vizbaras & Ptnrs., N.Y.C., 1968-69; v.p. Urban Investment & Devel. Co., Chgo., 1969-79, sr. v.p., 1979; pres. First City Devels. Corp., Beverly Hills, Calif., 1979-80, Olympia & York (U.S.) Devel. (West), 1987-89, Olympia & York Calif. Equities Corp., L.A., 1981-87, Olympia & York Calif. Devel. Corp., 1981-87, Olympia & York Hope St. Mgmt. Corp., 1982-87, Olympia & York Homes Corp., 1983-89, Olympia & York Calif. Constrn. Corp., 1986-89, The Richman Co., L.A., 1989—; lectr. NYU, 1967-69, UCLA, 1989-90, Nat. Humanities Inst., other univs. Adv. Nat. Endowment for Arts. Bd. advisors UCLA Ctr. Fin. and Real Estate. With USAF, 1963-64. Registered architect; lic. real estate broker. Mem. AIA, Am Planning Assn.,Internat. Coun. Shopping Ctrs., L.A. World Affairs Coun., Urban Land Inst., Nat. Assn. Office and Indsl. Parks, Chief Exec.'s Round Table, Air Force Assn., Lambda Alpha.

RICHMAN, PETER SPEER, surgeon; b. Encino, Calif., July 26, 1957; s. Walter Powell and Marjorie (Speer) R.; m. Marie Martel, Aug. 5, 1990. BA, Amherst Coll., 1979; MD, UCLA, 1985. Resident Harbor-UCLA Med. Ctr., Torrance, 1985-91; surgeon Facey Med. Group, Missions Hills, Calif., 1991—. Author: (book chpt.) Current Therapy in Vascular Surgery, 1991. Fellow Am. Coll. Surgeons (assoc.); mem. AMA, Sigma Xi. Office: Facey Med Group 11211 Sepulveda Blvd Mission Hills CA 91345

RICHMOND, GERALD MARTIN, geologist, researcher; b. Providence, July 30, 1914; s. Gerald Martin Sr. and Isobel Stewart (Bryan) Richmond-Bullitt; m. Margaret Emerson (div.); children: Gerald Martin Jr., Marjorie, Tucker, Ann; m. Amelie Z. Reynolds. BA in Biology, Brown U., 1936; MA in Geology, Harvard U., 1938; PhD in Geology, U. Colo., 1954. Jr. geologist Panama Canal Commn., Diablo Heights, 1940-41; jr. geologist U.S. Geol. Survey, Washington, 1942-43, geologist, 1943-44; geologist U.S. Geol. Survey, Denver, 1944—. Contbr. articles to profl. jours. Recipient Silver Beaver award Boy Scouts Am., 1962, Albrecht Penck medal Deutsches Quartärvereinigung, 1978. Fellow Geol. Soc. of Am. (sr., Kirk Bryan award 1965); mem. Internat. Union for Quaternary Rsch. (pres. 1965-69), Am. Assn. for Quaternary Rsch., Friends of the Pleistocene. Office: US Geol Survey MS913 PO Box 25046 Denver CO 80225-0046

RICHMOND, PETER GRAHAM, marketing consultancy executive; b. Eastbourne, Surrey, U.K., Dec. 26, 1951; came to U.S., 1983; s. Anthony Desmond and Vera (Ratcliff) R.; m. Katherine Alice Pearson, Dec. 22, 1974. Higher Nat. degree in Elec. Engring., South Bank Poly., London, 1972; MS in Computer Sci., Ctrl. London Poly., 1975. Design engr. Marconi Space & Def., Frimley, U.K., 1974-75, Air-Log, Aldershot, U.K., 1975-77; mktg. mgr. Tex. Instruments, Bedford, U.K., 1977-79; mktg. dir. Mitel Semiconductor, Kanata, Ont., 1979-83, United Techs.-Mostek, Carrolton, Tex., 1983-85, GE-Semiconductor, Research Triangle Park, N.C., 1985-87, Gould-AMI, Santa Clara, Calif., 1987-88; mgr. corp. mktg. Advanced Micro Devices, Sunnyvale, Calif., 1988-90; founder, prin. Richmond Group Internat., Saratoga, Calif., 1990—. Contbr. articles to profl. jours. Office: Richmond Group Internat 13838 Espada Ct Saratoga CA 95070

RICHMOND, THOMAS G., chemistry educator; b. Buffalo, Jan. 4, 1957; s. George E. and Joan S. (Steinmiller) R.; m. Cynthia Squire, Aug. 31, 1989. ScB, Brown U., 1979; MS, Northwestern U., 1980, PhD, 1984. Bantrell fellow Calif. Inst. Tech., Pasadena, 1983-85; asst. prof. chemistry U. Utah, Salt Lake City, 1985-91, assoc. prof., 1991—; presdl. young investigator NSF, 1989—. Contbr. articles to profl. publs. NSF fellow, 1980-83, Alfred P. Sloan Rsch. fellow, 1991—; Camille and Henry Dreyfus Found. grantee, 1985. Mem. Am. Chem. Soc. Office: U Utah Dept Chemistry Salt Lake City UT 84112

RICHTER, BURTON, physicist, educator; b. N.Y.C., Mar. 22, 1931; s. Abraham and Fanny (Pollack) R.; m. Laurose Becker, July 1, 1960; children: Elizabeth, Matthew. B.S., MIT, 1952, Ph.D., 1956. Research assoc. Stanford U., 1956-60, asst. prof. physics, 1960-63, assoc. prof., 1963-67, prof., 1967—, Paul Pigott prof. phys. sci., 1980—, tech. dir. Linear Accelerator Ctr., 1982-84, dir. Linear Accelerator Ctr., 1984—; cons. NSF, Dept. Energy; dir. Varian Corp., Litel Instruments; Loeb lectr. Harvard U., 1974; DeShalit lectr. Weizmann Inst., 1975. Contbr. over 300 articles to profl. publs. Recipient E.O. Lawrence medal Dept. Energy, 1975; Nobel prize in physics, 1976. Fellow Am. Phys. Soc. (pres.-elect 1993), AAAS; mem. NAS, Am. Acad. Arts and Scis. Office: SLAC PO Box 4349 Palo Alto CA 94309

RICHTER, DENISE ANN, journal editor; b. Taylor, Tex., Mar. 29, 1961; d. Albert Frederick and Minnie Louise (Jensen) R. BS, Tex. A&M U., 1983. Reporter The Brazosport Facts, Clute, Tex., 1983-85; copy editor The Clarion Ledger, Jackson, Miss., 1985-86; asst. news editor Fort Worth Star Telegram, 1986-90; copy editor St. Petersburg (Fla.) Times, 1990-91; news editor Statesman Jour., Salem, Oreg., 1991-93, asst. mng. editor, 1993—. Bd. dirs. Willamette chpt. ARC, Salem, 1992. Honoree YWCA Tribute to Outstanding Women, 1993. Mem. AAUW, Soc. Newspaper Design.

RICHTER, JEAN LOUISE, educator; b. Chgo., Feb. 22, 1953; d. George Joseph and Delores R.; m. Johnnie Ray Vint (div.); 1 child, Jeremy; m. Michael Price, Aug. 15, 1992. BS in Botany, Plant Sci., U. Calif., Riverside, 1978; teaching credential, Calif. State U., San Bernardino, 1982. Cert. tchr., Calif. Tchr. Moreno Valley (Calif.) Unified Sch. Dist., 1982-91, mentor tchr., 1988-91; facilitator inland area sci. project Calif. State U. at San Bernardino- U. Calif. at Riverside, 1992—. Adult vol. local Boy Scouts Am., 1985—. Home: 32106 Rd 221 North Fork CA 93643

RICKE, P. SCOTT, obstetrician, gynecologist; b. Indpls., June 28, 1948; s. Joseph and Betty (Rae) R.; divorced; 1 child, Alaina Michelle. BA, Ind. U., 1970; MD, Ind. U. Sch. of Medicine, 1974. Bd. cert. ob-gyn., 1981. Intern St. Lukes Hosp., Denver, 1975; resident U. Calif. at Irvine, Orange, 1977-79; pvt. practice Ob-Gyn Tucson, 1981—. Inventor (med. instrument) Vaginal Retractor, 1989. Bd. dirs. City of Hope, Tucson, 1981-85, Am. Cancer Soc., Tucson, 1981-83. Fellow Am. Bd. Ob-Gyn. Home: 3755 N Tanuri Dr Tucson AZ 85715-1939 Office: 5501 N Oracle Rd Ste D Tucson AZ 85704-3850

RICKER, JEFFREY PAUL, investment strategist, researcher, consultant; b. Ft. Lauderdale, Fla., Sept. 12, 1957; s. Harold Herbert and Joanne (DiBello) R. BA, Vanderbilt U., 1979; MBA, U. Chgo., 1981. CFA. Investment researcher Wells Fargo/Nikko Investment Advisors, San Francisco, 1981-84; cons. in pvt. practice San Francisco, 1984—; chmn. audit com. Security Analysts of San Francisco, 1989—. Mem. Assn. for Invesment Mgmt. and Rsch., U. Chgo. Grad. Sch. Bus. Bay Area Alumni Assn. (chair 1991—). Office: 1730 Filbert St # 105 San Francisco CA 94123

RICKER, JOANNE DANETTE, systems engineer; b. Van Nuys, Calif., Jan. 31, 1965; d. Merton Edward and Jean Edith (O'Brien) R. BS in Engring., Calif. State U., Northridge, 1987. Software cons. Litton Data Systems, Agoura, Calif., 1985; systems engr. Hughes Space & Com., El Segundo, Calif., 1987—. Volunteer Sunnyvale Women Committed to Bus., 1991—. Mem. IEEE, NAFE, Am. Mensa Ltd. Republican. Office: Hughes Com Sys PO Box 92919 Los Angeles CA 90009

RICKEY, JUNE EVELYN MILLION, retired educator; b. Joliet, Ill., Oct. 15, 1923; d. Lawrence Ernest and Ethel Alden (Ringler) Million; m. Paul Rickey, June 29, 1944; children: William, Mary Ann, John, James. BS in Edn., Ill. State U., 1946; MA in Journalism, Adams State Coll., 1970. Cert. tchr., Colo. Tchr. English Ottawa (Ill.) Twp. High Sch., 1946-47, Alamosa (Colo.) High Sch., 1953-55, 59-77, Evans Jr. High Sch., Alamosa, 1956-59; tchr. drama McAllen (Tex.) High Sch., 1955-56. Publicity chmn. Women's Citizenship Club, Alamosa, 1978, Am. Cancer Soc., bd. dirs., 1986—; editorial staff San Luis Valley Hist. Soc., Alamosa, 1985—, Ethnic heritage

Project, 1977-78; trustee Creede (Colo.) Repertory Theatre, 1987, sec.-treas., 1987-90. Wall St. Jour. grantee, 1964. Mem. AAUW (sec. 1983-87), Adams State Coll. Alumni Assn. (bd. dirs.), PEO Sisterhood, DAR. Democrat. Presbyterian. Home: 16365 County Rd Bb Alamosa CO 81101-8702

RICKLEY, DAVID ARTHUR, communications systems manager; b. Lawrence, Mass., Jan. 11, 1956; s. Arthur Anthony and Shirley Ann (Ryan) R. Student, Rio Hondo Coll., 1976, L.A. Trade Tech. Coll. Photomech. engr. L.A. Times, 1974-82, lead color operator, 1982-86, color lab. supr., 1986-89, prepress graphics supt., 1989-91, tech. systems mgr., 1991-92, prodn. editor, 1992—. Office: Los Angeles Times Times Mirror Sq Los Angeles CA 90012-3816

RICKS, J. BRENT, lawyer, book publisher; b. Chgo., Nov. 11, 1949; s. Paul Brent R. and Marthe (Forte) Tremaine; m. Louise Perry (div. 1988); 1 child, Benjamin Brent; m. Valerie Swearingen, July 28, 1957; 1 child, Abigail Dawn. BA, Johns Hopkins U., 1971; JD, U. N.Mex., 1974. Bar: N.Mex. 1974, U.S. Dist. Ct. N.Mex. 1974, U.S. Supreme Ct. 1979. Pvt. practice atty. Albuquerque, 1974—; gallery dir. Adobe Gallery, Albuquerque, 1984-87; book pub. Avanyu Pub. Inc., Albuquerque, 1984—; mft. Southwest Composites Inc., Albuquerque, 1989—. Magistrate judge cand. Dem. Party, Albuquerque, 1978. Democrat. Home: 1407 Florida NE Albuquerque NM 87110 Office: P O Box 27134 Albuquerque NM 87125

RICKS, MARY FRANCES, university administrator, anthropologist; b. Portland, Oreg., July 6, 1939; d. Leo and Frances Helen (Corcoran) Samuel; m. Robert Stanley Ricks, Jan. 7, 1961; children: Michael Stanley, Allen Gilbert. BA, Whitman Coll., 1961; MA, Portland State U., 1977, MPA, 1981. Asst. to dir. auxiliary services Portland State U., 1975-79, instnl. researcher, 1979-85, dir. instnl. research and planning, 1985—. Contbr. articles and presentations to profl. socs. Vol. archeologist BLM-USDI, Lakeview, Oreg., 1983—. Fellow Soc. Applied Anthropology; mem. Soc. Am. Archaeology, Soc. Coll. and U. Planning, Pacific N.W. Assn. Instnl. Rsch. and Planning (pres. 1990-91), City Club of Portland, Assn. Oreg. Archaeologists (v.p. 1988-90), City Club of Portland, Sigma Xi. Home: 5466 SW Dover Loop Portland OR 97225-1033 Office: Portland State U Office Instnl Rsch/Planning PO Box 751 Portland OR 97207-0751

RIDDELL, ROBERT JAMES, JR., retired physicist; b. Peoria, Ill., June 25, 1923; s. Robert James and Hazel (Gwathmey) R.; m. Kathryn Gamble, Aug. 12, 1950; children: Cynthia Riddell Dunham, James Duncan R. BS, Carnegie-Mellon U., 1944; MS, U. Mich., 1947, PhD, 1951. Asst. prof. physics U. Calif., Berkeley, 1951-55; sr. physicist Lawrence Berkeley Lab., 1951-82; ret., 1982; scientist AEC, Washington, 1958-60; adv. bd. Coll. Nat. Resources, U. Calif. Trustee Pacific Sch. Religion, Berkeley, 1970—, chmn. bd., 1979-84; trustee Grad. Theol. Union, Berkeley, 1982—, chmn. bd., 1990—; pres. Friends U. Calif. Bot. Garden, 1984—. Lt. (j.g.) USNR, 1944-46. Home: 1095 Arlington Blvd El Cerrito CA 94530-2754

RIDDELL, ROBERT MCALPIN, graphic artist, sales promotion executive; b. Hanford Kings County, Calif., June 18, 1919; s. Edwin Belmont and Vesta Mercer (Baker) R.; m. Glengene Samis (div. 1960); children: Gloria Jean, William Bruce, Robert Glen, Edwin Belmont. Grad. high sch., Covina, Calif. Graphic artist pvt. practice, Stockton, Calif., 1989—. Artist: (books) Mosaic of Memory, 1990, Naked Woods, 1990. Mem. alcohol adv. bd. San Joaquin County, 1989—; pres. Alamo Club. Mem. Masons. Home and Office: Riddell Graphics 2367 Vail Ave Stockton CA 95205

RIDDER, DANIEL HICKEY, newspaper publisher; b. N.Y.C., May 3, 1922; s. Bernard Herman and Nell (Hickey) R.; m. Frani Cooper Ackerman, Oct. 13, 1971; children by previous marriage: Daniel Hickey, Randy Helen, Richard J. AB, Princeton U., 1943. Reporter N.Y. Jour. Commerce, Grand Forks (N.D.) Herald; pub. St. Paul Dispatch and Pioneer-Press, 1952-58; co-pub. Long Beach (Calif.) Ind. Press-Telegram, 1958-69, pub., 1969-88; chmn. Long Beach (Calif.) Ind. Press-Telegram, Long Beach, Calif., 1988-90; mem. operating com. Knight-Ridder, Inc., Long Beach, Calif., 1989—; bd. dirs. AP, 1975-84; v.p. Knight-Ridder, Inc., 1975-89. Chmn. bd. St. Mary Med. Ctr., 1987-92; past bd. dirs. Sta. KCET, L.A. United Way, Newspaper Advt. Bur., L.A. County Mus. Art, Calif., 1974-84; past chmn. bd. trustees Calif. State U. and Colls.; trustee Long Beach Mus. Art; vice chmn. bd. govs. Calif. Community Found. Lt. (j.g.) USN, 1942-46, ETO, PTO. Clubs: Virginia Country (Long Beach, Calif.); El Dorado Country (Palm Springs, C(life); L.A. Country; Cypress Point (Pebble Beach, Calif.). Home: 5531 Bryant Dr E Long Beach CA 90815-4111 Office: Knight-Ridder Inc 604 Pine Ave Long Beach CA 90844-0001

RIDDER, WILLIAM HENRY, III, optometry educator; b. Alton, Ill., Jan. 25, 1957; s. Mary (Atwood) R.; m. Karine Tam, July 29, 1990; 1 child, Stephen. BA in Biology, So. Ill. U., 1978, MS in Electrophysiology, 1985; BS in Vision Sci., Ill. Coll. Optometry, 1982, OD, 1984. Cert. optometrist, Ill., Mo., Tex. Calif. With dept. neuro-ophthalmology Michael Reese Hosp., Chgo., 1983-84; staff dr. depts. pediatrics, geriatrics, primary care U. Houston, 1984-86, Nat. Eye Inst. postdoctoral rschr., 1986-89; part-time pvt. practice with Dr. Moes Nasser Houston, 1985-89; assoc. prof. So. Calif. Coll. Optometry, Fullerton, 1989—; mem. faculty rsch. com. Southern Calif. Coll. Optometry, 1990—, chmn. faculty recruitment com., 1990—; dir. faculty exec. coun. So. Calif. Coll. Optometry, 1991—, mem. animal care com., 1991—, rsch. lectr. Faculty Inst., 1990-91. Editorial referee Optometry and Vision Sci., 1991; contbr. articles to profl. jours. Staff dr. Project Concern Vision Screenings, 1989—; cons. Blind Childrens Ctr., 1989—; judge 12th Ann. Sr. Rsch. Symposium. Bd. dirs. scholar, 1983. Fellow Am. Acad. Optometry; mem. Assn. for Rsch. in Vision and Ophthalmology, Beta Sigma Kappa. Home: 1142 Creekside Ln Corona CA 91720 Office: So Calif Coll Optometry 2575 Yorba Linda Blvd Fullerton CA 92631

RIDDIFORD, LYNN MOORHEAD, zoologist, educator; b. Knoxville, Tenn., Oct. 18, 1936; d. James Eli and Virginia Amalia (Berry) Moorhead; m. Alan Wistar Riddiford, June 20, 1959 (div. 1966); m. James William Truman, July 28, 1970. AB magna cum laude, Radcliffe Coll., 1958; PhD, Cornell U., 1961. Rsch. fellow in biology Harvard U., Cambridge, Mass., 1961-63, 65-66, asst. prof. biology, 1966-71, assoc. prof., 1971-73; instr. biology Wellesley (Mass.) Coll., 1963-65; assoc. prof. zoology, U. Wash., Seattle, 1973-75, prof., 1975—; mem. study sect. tropical medicine and parasitology NIH, Bethesda, Md., 1974-78; mem. Competitive Grants panel USDA, Arlington, Va., 1979, 89; mem. regulatory biology panel NSF, Washington, 1984-88; mem. governing coun. Internat. Ctr. for Insect Physiology and Ecology, 1985-91, chmn. program com., 1989-91; chmn. adv. com. SeriBiotech, Bangalore, India, 1989; mem. bio. adv. com. NSF, 1992—. Contbr. articles to profl. jours. Mem. editorial bd. profl. jours. NSF fellow, 1958-60, 61-63; grantee NSF, 1964—, NIH, 1975—, Rockefeller Found., 1970-79, USDA, 1978-82, 89—; fellow John S. Guggenheim, 1979-80, NIH, 1986-87. Fellow AAAS, Am. Acad. Arts and Scis., Royal Entomol. Soc.; mem. Am. Soc. Zoologists (pres. 1991), Am. Soc. Biochem. and Molecular Biology, Entomol. Soc. Am., Am. Soc. Cell Biology, Soc. Devel. Biology. Methodist. Home: 16324 51st Ave SE Bothell WA 98012-6140 Office: U Wash Dept Zoology Seattle WA 98195

RIDDLE, MATTHEW C(ASEY), educator, physician; b. Portland, Oreg., Dec. 9, 1938; s. Matthew Casey and Katharine Hope (Kerr) R.; children from previous marriage: Matthew Casey III, Ann E., James K., Sarah A. BA in English magna cum laude, Yale U., 1960; MD, Harvard U., 1964. Diplomate Am. Bd. Internal Medicine. Resident in medicine Rush-Presbyn. St. Luke Hosp., Chgo., 1968-69, fellow endocrinology, 1969-70; fellow endocrinology U. Wash., Seattle, 1971-73; asst. prof. medicine Oreg. Health Scis. U., Portland, 1973-82, assoc. prof. medicine, 1982—, head diabetes sect., 1975—. Contbr. articles to profl. jours. Capt. U.S. Army, 1966-68, Vietnam. Mem. Am. Diabetes Assn. (bd. dirs., pres., chmn. bd. Oreg. affiliate), Am. Fedn. Clin. Rsch., Endocrine Soc. Office: Oreg Health Scis U 3181 SW Sam Jackson Park Rd Portland OR 97201-3011

RIDDOCH, GREGORY LEE, professional baseball manager; b. Greeley, Colo., July 17, 1945; s. William Perry and Ruth C. (Gregory) R.; m. Linda Marcella Andre, Mar. 2, 1968; children: Rory David, Raliegh Davin. BBA, U. No. Colo., 1968; MA in Ednl. Adminstrn., Colo. State U., 1983. Minor league baseball player Cin. Reds, 1967-71, minor league mgr., 1973-80; scout Cin. Reds, Colo., Kans., Nebr., Wyo., 1981-83; asst. dir. player devel. and scouting Cin. Reds, 1984, dir. minor leagues, 1985; dir. instrn. San Diego Padres, 1986, coach, 1987-90, mgr., 1990—; substitute tchr. Greeley (Colo.) Sch. Dist., 1971-83; speaker in field. Writer videotapes: Tony Gwynn Fielding, 1989, Tony Gwynn Hitting, 1989. Vol. March of Dimes, Greeley, 1970—, Children's Hosp., San Diego, 1986—, Say No to Drugs, 1986—; fundraiser UNICEF, Greeley, 1970—. Named Mgr. of Yr., N.W. League, 1975-78; mgr. winning team State Spl. Olympics Boys Basketball Champions, 1975. Mem. Profl. Baseball Players Assn., NEA. Home: 1711 Glen Meadows Dr Greeley CO 80631-6831 Office: San Diego Padres PO Box 2000 San Diego CA 92112-2000

RIDDOCH, HILDA JOHNSON, accountant; b. Salt Lake City, July 25, 1923; d. John and Ivy Alma (Wallis) Johnson; m. Leland Asa Riddoch, Nov. 22, 1942; children: Ivy Lee, Leland Mark. Vocal student, Ben Henry Smith, Seattle; student, Art Instrn. Schs. Sales clk., marking rm. dist. office Sears, Roebuck & Co., Seattle, 1940-42; with billing dept., receptionist C.M. Lovsted & Co., Inc., Seattle, 1942-51; acct., exec. sec. Viking Equipment Co., Inc., Seattle, 1951-54; acct., office mgr. Charles Waynor Collection Agy., Seattle, 1955-57; pvt. practice, 1957—; acct., office mgr. Argus Mag., Seattle, 1962-67; acct. Law Offices Krutch, Lindell, Donnelly, Dempsey & Lageschulte, Seattle, 1967-72, Law Offices Sindell, Haley, Estep, et al, Seattle, 1972-77; co-founder, acct. Bus. Svc., Inc. and Diversified Design and Mktg., Federal Way and Auburn, Wash., 1975—; co-founder L & H Advt. and Distbg. Co., Orting, Wash., 1992—; sec.-treas., dir. Jim Evans Realty, Inc., Seattle, 1973-87; agt. Wise Island Water Co., P.U.D., Victoria, B.C., 1973-88, Estate Executrix, Seattle, 1987—. Author: Ticking Time on a Metronome, 1989-90; writer, dir. hist. play Presidents of Relief Society Thru Ages; writer, dir. teenager activation video, 1984; pub., editor Extended Family Newsletter, 1983—. Dir. speech and drama LDS Ch., 1938-88, ward pres. young women's orgn., mem. ward and stake choirs, 1983-85, stake genealogy libr., Federal Way, 1983-85, ward and stake newsletter editors various areas, West Settle, Seattle, Renton, Auburn, 1950-90, 1st counselor in presidency, tchr. various courses Ladies' Relief Soc. Orgn., 1965, 89; co-dir., organizer 1st Silver Saints Group, 1990-92; interviewer LDS Ch. Employee Svcs., 1992-93. Recipient Letter of Recognition, Howard W. Hunter, Gen. Authority, Latter-day Saints Ch. Home: PO Box 1300 Orting WA 98360-1300

RIDER, JANE LOUISE, artist, educator; b. Brownfield, Tex., Sept. 11, 1919; d. Oscar Thomas and Florence Myrtle (Bliss) Halley; m. Rolla Wilson Rider Jr., Mar. 26, 1944 (dec. July 1992); 1 child, Dorothy Jo Neil. BA, UCLA, Westwood, 1943; Diploma in Secondary Art, Chgo. Art Inst., 1945; postgrad., Chouinards, L.A., U. Oreg., Scripps, Claremont, Calif. Art supr., elem. and jr. high art tchr. Tulare (Calif.) City Schs. Dist., 1943-44, 44-45; art tchr. Beverly Hills (Calif.) High Sch., 1946-47; art tchr. jr. high gen. art and ceramics Santa Barbara City Schs., Goleta, Calif., 1964-66; head art dept., tchr. Morro Bay (Calif.) Jr.-Sr. High Sch. Dist., 1967-70; pvt. practice studio potter Cambria, Calif., 1961-85; pvt. practice painter Santa Rosa, Calif., 1985—; founder, dir., tchr. La Canada (Calif.) Youth House, 1953-60; dir. Pinedorado Art Show, Allied Arts Assn., Cambria, 1970-80. Exhibited in group shows Wine Country Artist's Spring Show, 1991, 92, 93, Gualala Art in Redwoods, 1986, 87, 88. Mem. Santa Rosa Art Guild (rec. sec. 1989), Cen. Coast Watercolor Soc. (charter mem. 1977), Oakmont Art Assn. Republican. Home: 7019 Overlook Dr Santa Rosa CA 95409

RIDGE, MARTIN, historian, educator; b. Chgo., May 7, 1923; s. John and Ann (Lew) R.; m. Marcella Jane VerHoef, Mar. 17, 1948; children: John Andrew, Judith Lee, Curtis Cordell, Wallace Karsten. AB, Chgo. State U., 1943; AM, Northwestern U., 1949, PhD, 1951. Asst. prof. history Westminster Coll., New Wilmington, Pa., 1951-55; from asst. prof. to prof. San Diego State Coll., 1955-66; prof. history Ind. U., Bloomington, 1966-79, Calif. Inst. Tech., 1980—; vis. prof. UCLA, summer 1963, Northwestern U., summer 1959; editor Jour. Am. History, 1966-77; sr. research assoc. Huntington Library, 1977—; bd. dirs. Calif. Hist. Landmarks Commn., 1954-64; cons. in field; Tanner lectr. Mormon Hist. Assn., 1991; Whitsett Meml. lectr., Calif. State U., 1992. Author: Ignatius Donnelly: Portrait of a Politician, 1962, 91, The New Bilingualism: An American Dilemma, 1981, Frederick Jackson Turner: Wisconsin's Historian of the Frontier, 1986, Atlas of American Fronteirs, 1992; co-author: California Work and Workers, 1963, The American Adventure, 1964, America's Frontier Story, 1969, Liberty and Union, 1973, American History after 1865, 1981, Westward Expansion, 1982; editor: Children of Ol'Man River, 1988, Westward Journeys, 1989. Served with U.S. Maritime Service, 1943-45. William Randolph Hearst fellow, 1950; fellow Social Sci. Research Council, 1952; fellow Guggenheim Found., 1965; fellow Am. Council Learned Socs., 1960; Newberry fellow, 1964; Huntington fellow, 1974; Annenberg scholar U. So. Calif., 1979-80; recipient Best Book award Phi Alpha Theta, 1963, Gilberto Espinos prize N.Mex. Historical Review, 1989, Ray Allan Billington prize Western History Assn., 1991. Mem. Am. Hist. Assn. (Best Book award Pacific Coast br. 1963), Orgn. Am. Historians, Western History Assn. (v.p. 1985-86, pres. 1986-87), So. History Assn., Agrl. History Soc., Social Sci. History Soc. Democrat. Address: Huntington Library San Marino CA 91108

RIDGWAY, DAVID WENZEL, educational film producer, director; b. Los Angeles, Dec. 12, 1904; s. David Nelson and Marie (Wenzel) R.; AB UCLA, 1926; MBA, Harvard U., 1928; m. Rochelle Devine, June 22, 1955. With RKO Studios, Hollywood, Calif., 1930-42; motion picture specialist WPB, Washington, 1942-43; prodn. mgr., producer Ency. Brit. Films, Wilmette, Ill., 1946-60; dir. film activities, exec. dir. Chem. Edn. Material Study, U. Calif. at Berkeley, 1960-90, dir., 1990—; producer, on-screen interviewer Am. Chem. Soc. TV series Eminent Chemists, 1981; advisor TV project Mech. Universe, Calif. Inst. Tech., 1985 also Am. Inst. Biol. Scis.; introduced CHEM study films to People's Republic of China, 1983. Lt. comdr. USNR, 1943-46. Recipient Chris award for prodn. CHEM Study Ednl. Films in Chemistry, Film Coun. Greater Columbus, 1962-63; Bronze medal, Padua, Italy, 1963; CINE Golden Eagle awards, 1962-64, 73; Gold Camera award for film Wondering About Things, U.S. Indsl. Film Festival, 1971; diploma of honour Internat. Sci. Film Assn. Festival, Cairo, 1st prize Am. Biol. Photog. Assn. for film MARS: Chemistry Looks for Life, 1978. Mem. Soc. Motion Pictures and TV Engrs. (chmn. San Francisco sect. 1970-72), Am. Chem. Soc., Am. Sci. Film Assn. (trustee 1974-81), Delta Upsilon, Alpha Kappa Psi. Clubs: Faculty (U. Calif.), Bohemian (San Francisco). Author: (with Richard J. Merrill) The CHEM Study Story, 1969; also articles in ednl. jours. Home: 1735 Highland Pl Berkeley CA 94709-1074 Office: U Calif Lawrence Hall of Sci Berkeley CA 94720

RIDLAND, JOHN MURRAY, poet, educator; b. London, July 4, 1933; came to U.S., 1936; s. John Galbraith and Margaret (Baird Murray) R.; m. Muriel Thomas, Apr. 18, 1957; children: John Forbes (dec.), Jenny Margaret, Michael Thomas. BA with honors, Swarthmore Coll., 1953; MA, U. Calif., Berkeley, 1958; PhD, Claremont Grad. Sch., 1964. Instr., asst. to assoc. prof. U. Calif., Santa Barbara, 1961-75, prof. English, 1975—; vis. prof. U. Colo., Boulder, 1967-68, U. Melbourne, Australia, 1993; lectr. in lit. Coll. Creative Studies U. Calif., Santa Barbara, 1985—; advisor Spectrum, Santa Barbara, 1979-93; dir. edn. abroad program U. Calif., Australia, 1994—; vis. prof. U. Melbourne, Australia, 1993. Author: (poems) Ode on Violence, 1969, Elegy for My Aunt, 1981, In the Shadowless Light, 1978, (with Muriel Ridland) And Say What He Is, 1975, Palms, 1993; translator: John the Valiant (from Hungarian of Sándor Petöfi), 1993; editor: The Little Square Review, Santa Barbara, 1966-72. With U.S. Army, 1954-55. Mem. Santa Barbara Swim Club, Robert Frost Soc., Huntington Lake Assn. Office: U Calif Coll Creative Studies Santa Barbara CA 93106

RIEBE, CYNTHIA MORRIS, interior designer; b. Mpls., Mar. 20, 1946; d. Arthur Marvin and Virginia (Swanke) Morris; m. Frederick Charles Riebe, Jan. 22, 1972; children: Uli Youn-Ho, Ilse Ae-Yoon. BA, U. Minn., 1969. Staff interior designer Gabberts, Inc., Mpls., 1970-72; chief interior designer HGA, Architects Inc., Mpls., 1974-75; prin. Cynthia Riebe Interior Design, Mpls., Tokyo and Carmel, Calif., 1975—; cons. interior designer for Minn. gov.'s residence, St. Paul, 1983; mem. Nat. Coun. for Interior Design Qualification, 1981. Mem. Leadership Monterey Peninsula, 1986-87; docent Monterey History and Art Assn., 1986-93. Recipient cert. of honor Design Internat, 1981, Monterey Bay mag. Grand Prize award Design Competition, 1992, winner Halo Lighting Design Competition, 1981; Scalamandre grantee, 1982. Mem. Am. Soc. Interior Designers (dir. significant interiors survey 1982-84, chmn. historic preservation 1984, corr. mem. nat. com. hist. preservation 1989—, bd. dirs. Minn. chpt. 1984, President's citation 1982, 83), Nat. Trust for Historic Preservation, Calif. Preservation Found. Republican. Episcopalian. Office: Lincoln at Ocean Box 4724 Carmel CA 93921

RIEDEL, CHARLES ALAN, finance company executive; b. Hartford, Conn., Feb. 13, 1949; s. Joe M. and Dorothy (Buckland) R.; m. Deborah Ann Riedel, Apr. 26, 1975; children: Schuyler, Heather. BS in Econs., U. Mich., 1971. CLU; ChFC. Ins. agt. Equitable Life, Denver, 1977-79, Conn. Mutual, Denver, 1979-81; cons. Conn. Mutual, Hartford, 1981-83; advanced sales dir. Conn. Mutual, Roseland, N.J., 1983-87; asst. gen. agt. C.M. Assocs. of Colo., Denver, 1987-92; co-owner, v.p. Eagle Fin. Resources, Evergreen, Colo., 1992; instr. Am. Coll., Denver, 1988—; owner Riedel Software Inc., 1986-90. Mem. Am. Soc. of CLU, Denver Assn. of Life Underwriters.

RIEDEL, RICHARD A., orthodontist, professor emeritus; b. Milw., Feb. 26, 1922; s. Otto Louis and Julia Christina (Kub) R.; m. Marie Emma Myers, Apr. 7, 1945; children: Richard, Thomas, Corinne, Carol. DDS, Marquette U., 1945; MSD, Northwestern U., 1948. Diplomate Am. Bd. Orthodontics. Instr., Northwestern U. Dental Sch., Chgo., 1948-49; instr. U. Wash. Dental Sch., Seattle, 1949-54, assoc. prof., 1958-64, prof., 1964-81, prof. emeritus, 1981—, acting dean, 1979-80; pvt. practice orthodontics, Seattle, 1949-84, Bainbridge Island, Wash., 1982—; pres. Am. Bd. Orthodontics, 1978-79; George Grieve Meml. lectr., 1976, Richard Bartlett Meml. lectr., 1976, Alton Moore Meml. lectr., 1984; lectr. Moyers Symposium, 1977, Denver Seminar, 1986. Author: Vistas in Orthodontics, 1967. Contbr. chpts. to Advanced Orthodontic Technics, 1970, 76, 84. Served to lt. (j.g.) Dental Corps, USN, 1945-47. Recipient Outstanding Rsch. award St. Louis U., 1977, Outstanding Dental Alumnus award Northwestern U. Dental Sch., 1983; grantee Japan Sci. Soc., 1979. Fellow Am. Coll. Dentists; mem. Am. Assn. Orthodontists (Albert Ketcham Meml. award 1983), Angle Soc. Orthodontists (pres. 1976-77), Federation Dentaire Internationale, Fedn. Orthodontists Cen. Am. and Panama (hon.), U. Wash. Alumni Assn., Sigma Xi, Omicron Kappa Upsilon, Delta Sigma Delta. First and only orthodontist to serve a rotation aboard ship HOPE, Maceio, Brazil, 1973. Avocations: photography, gardening. Home: 33 Nesika Bay Rd Poulsbo WA 98370-8633

RIEDER, RONALD FREDERICK, public relations executive; b. Oshawa, Ont., Can., Nov. 10, 1932; s. Joseph Samuel and Minnie (Collis) R.; m. Pauline Feldman, Sept. 22, 1957; children: Mitchell, Stephen, Robert. BA, Sir George Williams U., Montreal, 1955; BJ, Carleton U., Ottawa, 1956. Reporter Montreal Star, 1956-57; night city editor Valley News, Van Nuys, Calif., 1957-66; v.p. Hal Phillips & Assocs., Beverly Hills, Calif., 1966-71; dir. communications Daylin Inc., Beverly Hills, 1971-76; ptnr. The Phillips Group, Beverly Hills, 1976-87; dir. pub. affairs Jewish Fedn. Coun. Greater L.A., 1987-92; pres., prin. Ron Rieder and Assocs., Sherman Oaks, Calif., 1992—. Mem. Soc. Profl. Journalists, Pub. Rels. Soc. Am. Jewish. Home and Office: Ron Rieder and Assocs 5420 Sylmar Ave # 322 Sherman Oaks CA 91401

RIEDLSPERGER, MAX ERNST, history educator; b. San Luis Obispo, Calif., July 7, 1937; s. Helmuth Georg and Jean (Bennett) R.; m. Deanna Beckmann, Feb. 12, 1966; 1 child, Gretchen. AB, Wabash Coll., 1959; MA, U. Mich., 1961; PhD, U. Colo., 1969. Tchr. Eastern High Sch., Detroit, 1961-63, Day de Noc Community Coll., Escanaba, Mich., 1963-66; teaching assoc. U. Colo., Denver, 1966-67; instr. Colo. Women's Coll., Denver, 1967-68; asst. prof. Calif. Poly. State U., San Luis Obispo, 1969-72, assoc. prof., 1972-77, prof., 1977—, chmn. history dept., 1985—; dir. internat. programs Calif. State U., Heidelberg, Fed. Republic Germany, 1983-84. Author: Lingering Shadow of Nazism, 1978; contbr. articles to profl. publs., chpts. to books. Bd. dirs. San Luis Obispo Mozart Festival, 1979-83, 84-85, v.p., 1985-86. Austrian Ministry of Edn. fellow, 1968-69; grantee Am. Coun. Learned Socs., 1972, NEH, 1976, U.S. Dept. Edn., 1986-88. Mem. Am. Hist. Assn., German Studies Assn., Assn. Borderlands Scholars, Assn. for Study of Politics and Soc. in Germany, Austria and Switzerland. Democrat. Office: Calif Poly State U Dept History San Luis Obispo CA 93407

RIEGEL, BYRON WILLIAM, ophthalmologist, educator; b. Evanston, Ill., Jan. 19, 1938; s. Byron and Belle Mae (Huot) R.; B.S., Stanford U., 1960; M.D., Cornell U., 1964; m. Marilyn Hills, May 18, 1968; children—Marc William, Ryan Marie, Andrea Elizabeth. Intern, King County Hosp., Seattle, 1964-65; asst. resident in surgery U. Wash., Seattle, 1965; resident in ophthalmology U. Fla., 1968-71; pvt. practice medicine specializing in ophthalmology, Sierra Eye Med. Group, Inc., Visalia, Calif., 1972—; mem. staff Kaweah Delta Dist. Hosp., chief of staff, 1978-79; mem. staff Visalia Community Hosp.; asst. clin. prof. ophthalmology U. Calif., San Francisco, 1981-92. Bd. dirs., asst. sec. Kaweah Delta Dist. Hosp., 1983-90. Served as flight surgeon USN, 1966-68. Co-recipient Fight-for-Sight citation for research in retinal dystrophy, 1970. Diplomate Am. Bd. Ophthalmology, Nat. Bd. Med. Examiners. Fellow A.C.S., Am. Acad. Ophthalmology; mem. Calif. Med. Assn. (del. 1978-79), Med. Assn., Tulare County Med. Assns., Calif. Assn. Ophthalmology, Am. Soc. Cataract and Refractive Surgery, Internat. Phacoemulsification and Cataract Methodology Soc. Roman Catholic. Club: Rotary (Visalia). Home: 3027 W Keogh Ct Visalia CA 93291-4228 Office: 2830 W Main St Visalia CA 93291-4300

RIEGER, ELAINE JUNE, nursing consultant; b. Lebanon, Pa., June 7, 1937; d. Frank and Florence (Hitz) Plasterer; m. Jere LeFever Longenecker, Sept. 13, 1958 (div. 1968); children: Julie Lynn Porto, Jere Lee Longenecker; m. Bernhard Rieger, Oct. 12, 1971. Nursing diploma, Coatesville (Pa.) Hosp. Sch. of Nursing, 1958; BA, U. Redlands, 1976; MS in Healthcare Mgmt., Calif. State U., L.A., 1984. Cert. nursing adminstr. From staff nurse to clin. supr. to dir. of nurses St. Johns Regional Med. Ctr., Oxnard, Calif., 1966-86; dir. of nurses Motion Picture and TV Hosp., Woodland Hills, Calif., 1987-89; with Care West, Nothridge-Reseda, Calif., 1989-90; dist. nurse mgr. Hillhaven Corp., Newbury Park, Calif., 1990-91; quality assurance cons. Beverly Enterprises, Rancho Cordova, Calif., 1991—. Home: 1817 Shady Brook Dr Thousand Oaks CA 91362-1335 Office: Beverly Enterprises 10969 Trade Center Dr # 106 Rancho Cordova CA 95670

RIEGER, STEVEN ARTHUR, state legislator, business consultant; b. Pullman, Wash., May 14, 1952; s. Samuel and Olga (Skoblikoff) R.; m. Karen Jean Gibson, July 5, 1992. AB, Harvard U., 1974, MBA, 1976. Asst. to v.p. Crowley Maritime Corp., Seattle, 1976-79; asst. v.p. Seattle-Northwest Securities Corp., Anchorage, 1980-81; spl. asst. Alaska State Legislature, Juneau, 1981-82; v.p. William Kent Co., Anchorage, 1983-84; mem. Alaska Ho. Reps., Juneau, 1985-91; pres. S. Rieger & Co., Anchorage, 1991-92; mem. Alaska State Senate, Juneau, 1993—; dir. AJCH, Inc., Anchorage, 1991—. Republican. Office: Alaska State Legislature Box V Capitol Juneau AK 99811

RIEGERT, RAYMOND IRWIN, publisher, author; b. Dobbs Ferry, N.Y., Mar. 11, 1947; s. Arthur James Riegert and Gertrude (Irwin) Gibbons; m. Leslie Jean Henriques, Apr. 11, 1981; children: Keith Sebastian Henriques Riegert, Alice Rose Henriques Riegert. BA in English, U. N.Mex., 1971. Staff writer Daily Californian, Berkeley, 1974-75; editor, gen. mgr. Internat. News Keyus, Inc., Berkeley, 1975-79; gen. mgr. Sebago, Inc., Emeryville, Calif., 1980-84; pub., pres., author Ulysses Press, Berkeley, 1982—. Author: Hidden Hawaii, 1979, Ultimate California, 5 others; editor 20 books; contbr. over 100 articles to profl. jours. Bd. dirs. Sierra Sch., El Cerrito, Calif., 1993—. Recipient Best Guidebook award Hawaii Visitors Bur., Honolulu, 1991. Mem. Soc. Am. Travel Writers (Lowell Thomas awards 1986, 89), Calif. Alumni Assn., Berkeley Citizens Action. Democrat. Office: Ulysses Press 3286 Adeline St Ste 1 Berkeley CA 94703

RIEGLE, LINDA B., federal judge; b. 1948. BS, Shepherd Coll., Shepherdstown, W.Va.; JD, Union U., Albany, N.Y. Admitted to bar, 1978. Bankruptcy judge U.S. Dist. Ct. Nev., Las Vegas. Office: US Dist Ct 300 Las Vegas Blvd S Las Vegas NV 89101-5812

RIEKE, RICHARD DAVIS, communication educator; b. Alton, Ill., June 13, 1935; s. Herbert Louis and Evelyn Marie (Davis) R.; m. Regina Miller, June 14, 1959 (div. 1978); children: Linda, Alan, Brian; m. Mary Louise Willbrand, June 23, 1979. BS, So. Ill. U., 1957; MA, Ohio State U., 1958,

PhD, 1964. Instr. Dept. Speech, Ohio State U., Columbus, 1958-64; asst. prof. Dept. Speech, Ohio State U., 1964-67, assoc. prof., 1967-70; prof. dept. communication U. Utah, Salt Lake City, 1970—; chmn. dept. communication U. Utah, 1970-80; dir. dispute resolution cert. prog., U. Utah, 1988—; communication cons. Evans & Sutherland Computer Corp., Salt Lake City, 1987—. Co-author: Communication in Legal Advocacy, 1991, An Introduction to Reasoning, 1984, Argumentation and the Decision Making Process, 1984, Teaching Oral Communication in Elementary Schools, 1983. Adv. com. Am. Arbitration Assn., Utah, 1989—. Recipient Award for Teaching Excellence, Romona Cannon Com., U. Utah, 1989; Disput Resolution grantee, Thomas Dee Com., U. Utah, 1989, NEH grantee, 1983, others. Mem. Speech Communication Assn., Am. Forensic Assn., Soc. of Profls. in Dispute Resolution. Home: 1485 Sigsbee Ave Salt Lake City UT 84103-4476 Office: U Utah Dept Communication Salt Lake City UT 84112

RIEL, ROBERT JOSEPH, communications executive; b. Woonsocket, R.I., June 19, 1961; s. Robert R. Riel and Ellen (Parfitt) Bourget. BA in History and Polit. Sci., SUNY, Albany, 1991. Journalist Woonsocket (R.I.) Call Newspaper, 1981-83; promotion coord. Up With People, Tucson, 1984-86, edn. program mgr., 1987-88, corp. comm. mgr., 1989—. Office: Up With People 3103 N Campbell Ave Tucson AZ 85719

RIENNER, LYNNE CAROL, publisher; b. Pitts., Aug. 3, 1945; d. David and Molly (Rice) R. B.A., U. Pa., 1967. Exec. v.p., assoc. publisher, editorial dir. Westview Press Inc., Boulder, Colo., 1975-84; pres. Lynne Rienner Pub. Inc., Boulder, Colo., 1984—; pub. cons. various orgns.; lectr. U. Denver Pub. Inst., 1981-84, 93; panelist nat. meetings. Bd. dirs. Boulder Breast Cancer Coalition, 1993—. Mem. Soc. Scholarly Pub., Assn. Am. Pubs. (bd. dirs. 1992—). Office: Lynne Rienner Pub Inc 1800 30th St Ste 314 Boulder CO 80301-1026

RIENZI, THOMAS MATTHEW MICHAEL, retired army officer; b. Phila., Feb. 5, 1919; s. Luigi and Ethel (Johnston) R.; m. Claire M. Moore, Aug. 11, 1945; children: Thomas Matthew, Claire Mary. Student mech. engring., Lehigh U., 1937-38; BS in Mil. Sci., U.S. Mil. Acad., 1942; MEE, U. Ill., 1948; cert. in mgmt., U. Pitts., 1965; MA in Internat. Affairs, George Washington U., 1966. Commd. 2d lt. U.S. Army, 1942, advanced through grades to lt. gen., 1965; chief supply and maintenance div. signal sect. U.S. Army Pacific Hawaii, 1961; signal officer XVIII Airgorne Corps Ft. Bragg, N.C., 1961-63; exec. officer to chief signal officer, chief communications-electronics Washington, 1963-65, chief Combat Surveillance Office, Material Command, 1965-66; comdg. gen., comdt. Signal Center and Sch. Ft. Monmouth, N.J., 1966-68; comdg. gen., dep. comdg. gen 1st Signal Brigade S.E. Asia, Vietnam/Thailand/Laos, 1968-70; also dep. chief staff communications-electronics U.S. Army, Vietnam; comdg. gen Strategic Communications Command Pacific; also dep. chief of staff communications-electronics U.S. Army Pacific, 1970-72; dir. telecommunications and command and control Dept. Army, Washington, 1972-77; dep. dir. gen. NATO Integrated Communications System Mgmt. Agy., Brussels, 1977-79. Author: History of Communications-Electronics in Vietnam War, 1972; also articles. Permanent deacon Roman Catholic Ch., 1979—. Decorated D.S.M. with oak leaf cluster, Legion of Merit with oak leaf cluster, Bronze Star with oak leaf cluster, Air medal with 5 oak leaf clusters U.S.; Breast Order of Yun Hui Ribbon Nationalist China; Chung Mu Order of Merit Korea; Nat. Order Vietnam Knight Vietnam; recipient Papal award, 1970. Mem. Assn. U.S. Army (ann. mem.), Armed Forces Communications-Electronics Assn. (nat. officer 1972-77); life mem. Assn. Grads. U.S. Mil. Acad.; mem. U. Lehigh Alumni Assn., U. Ill. Alumni Assn., George Washington U. Alumni Assn., Rotary (hon. mem. Pearl Harbor chpt.). Home: 676 Elepaio St Honolulu HI 96816-4779

RIES, BARBARA ELLEN, alcohol and drug abuse services professional; b. Chgo., Oct. 27, 1952; d. Laurence B. and Genieveve (Wasiek) R. AAS in Human Svcs., Coll. of DuPage, Glen Ellyn, Ill., 1973; BA in Social Work, Sangamon State U., Springfield, Ill., 1978; postgrad., U. Mo., 1987-88, U. Tex., Arlington, 1991—. Cert. social therapist; nat. cert. alcohol and drug counselor; qualified chem. dependency counselor. Counselor Ray Graham Assn. for Handicapped, Addison, Ill., 1975-76; child abuse counselor Ill. Dept. Children and Family Svcs., Springfield, 1977-78; alcoholism counselor non-med. detoxification program S.H.A.R.E., Villa Park, Ill., 1978-80; outpatient therapist Ingalls Meml. Hosp., Harvey, Ill., 1980-83; dir. aftercare Lifeline Program, Chgo., 1984-85; case mgr. Lifecenter Program, Kansas City, Mo., 1985-87; counselor, acting clin. coord. Lakeside Hosp., Kansas City, 1988-89; program mgr., dir. chem. recovery programs Two Rivers Psychiat. Hosp., Kansas City, 1989-90; dir. day program and chem. dependency program SW Hosp./Citadel, Dallas, 1990—; dir. Flexcare program Dallas Meml. Hosp., 1990-91; pvt. practice Federal Way, Wash., 1991—. Recipient commendation Ingalls Hosp., 1983. Mem. Nat. Assn. Drug and Alcohol Counselors (cert.), Nat. Assn. for Relapse Prevention Counselors, Learning Disabilities Assn. Wash., Wash. Assocs. Alcoholism & Addictions Programs, Wash. Advs. Mentally Ill, Employee Assistance Profls. Am., Coalition Drug and Alcohol Leaders, Wash. Assn. Alcoholism and Drug Abuse Counselors, Nat. Assn. of Alcoholism and Drug Counselors (NCAC II), Am. Mktg. Assn., Dual Diagnosis Com. Republican.

RIESE, ARTHUR CARL, environmental engineering company executive, consultant; b. St. Albans, N.Y., Jan. 2, 1955; s. Walter Herman and Katherine Ellen (Moore) R. BS in Geology, N.Mex. Inst. Mining and Tech., 1976, MS in Chemistry, 1978; PhD in Geochemistry, Colo. Sch. Mines, 1982. Lic. geologist, N.C.; registered profl. geologist, N.C., S.C., Ark., Fla., Tenn., Wyo. Asst. petroleum geologist N.Mex. Bur. Mines and Mineral Resources, Socorro, 1973-76; geologist Nord Resources, Inc., Albuquerque, 1975; rsch. asst. N.Mex. Inst. Mining and Tech., Socorro, 1976-78; vis. faculty Colo. Sch. Mines, 1978-81; rsch. geochemist Gulf R & D Co., Houston, 1982-84; sr. planning analyst/mgr. tech. planning Atlantic Richfield Co., L.A., 1984-87; sr. v.p. Harding Lawson Assocs., Denver, 1987—; mem. affiliate faculty U. Tex., Austin, 1983—; speaker, conf. chmn. in field. Numerous patents in field. Panel participant N.Mex. First, Gallup, 1990. Mem. Am. Inst. Hydrology (cert. profl. hydrogeologist 1988), Am. Inst. Profl. Geologists (cert. geol. scientist 1988). Office: Harding Lawson Assocs 2400 Arco Tower 707 Seventeenth St Denver CO 80202

RIESEN, AUSTIN HERBERT, psychologist, researcher; b. Newton, Kans., July 1, 1913; s. Emil Richert and Rachel (Penner) R.; m. Helen Haglin, July 29, 1939; children: Carol, Kent. AB, U. Ariz., 1935; PhD, Yale, 1939; DSc (hon.), U. Ariz., 1981. Rsch. assoc. Yale U., New Haven, Conn., 1939; asst. prof. psychobiology Yerkes Labs. Primate Biology, Orange Park, Fla., 1939-49; assoc. prof. U. Chgo., 1949-56, prof. psychology, 1956-62; prof. psychology U. Calif., Riverside, 1962-80, also chmn., 1962-68, prof. emeritus psychology, 1980—; vis. rsch. prof. U. Rochester, 1951-53; researcher in psychiatry NIMH Found., Bethesda, Md., 1964-69; mem. vision rsch. com. NIH, 1959-63; rsch. lectr. Sigma Xi, U. Ariz., 1961, U. Calif., Riverside, 1975. Author: Development of Infant Chimpanzees, 1952; author, editor: Developmental Neuropsychology of Sensory Deprivation, 1975; editor: Advances in Psychobiology, 1972-76; contbr. numerous articles on visual development. Capt. USAF, 1943-46. Mem. Am. Psychol. Assn. (pres. divsn. 6 1965-67), Phi Beta Kappa, Phi Kappa Phi, Sigma Xi. Congregationalist. Office: Univ Calif Dept Psychology Riverside CA 92521

RIESENFELD, STEFAN ALBRECHT, law educator, consultant; b. Breslau, Ger., June 8, 1908; came to U.S., 1934, naturalized, 1940; s. Conrad Ernst and Margarethe (Landecker) R.; m. Phyllis B. Thogrimson, Dec. 23, 1943; children—Peter William, Stefan Conrad. J.U.D., U. Breslau, 1932, U. Milan, 1934; LL.B., U. Calif.-Berkeley, 1937; S.J.D., Harvard U., 1940; B.S., U. Minn., 1943; D.h.c., U. Cologne (Ger.), 1970. Bar: Minn. 1939, U.S. Supreme Ct. 1978. Prof. law U. Minn., Mpls., 1938-52; prof. law U. Calif.-Berkeley, 1952—, Emanuel S. Heller prof., 1954-75, prof. emeritus, 1975—; prof. law U. Calif., Hastings Coll. Law, San Francisco, 1975—; cons. to U.S. Bd. Econ. Warfare, 1942, UN ad hoc com., 1952; counselor on internat. law Dept. Def., 1955, Dept. State, 1977-82; mem. Adv. Com. on Bankruptcy Rules, 1961-72; vis. prof. various U.S. and fgn. univs.; cons. Calif. law revision comm., 1970-81, Legal Ref. Bur. of Hawaii, 1968-74. Served with USN, 1943-46. Recipient Silver medal Dept. State, 1979, 84; Verdienstkreuz, Fed. Republic of Germany, 1975. Mem. ABA, Nat. Bankruptcy Conf., Am. Acad. Arts and Scis., Am. Soc. Internat. Law, Internat. Law Assn. (Am. br.), Soc. Legal History. Lutheran. Author: Protection of Fisheries Under International Law, 1943, Modern Social Legislation, 1950, (with Hetland, Maxwell and Warren) California Secured Land Transactions, 4th edit., 1992, Creditors' Remedies and Debtors' Protection, 4th edit., 1986. Home: 1129 Amador Ave Berkeley CA 94707-2632 Office: U Calif Berkeley Law Sch Boalt Hall Berkeley CA 94720

RIETVELD, THOMAS ALAN, clergyman, small business owner; b. Harvey, Ill., Sept. 28, 1951; s. Glenn and Caryl Thelma (Kamstra) R.; m. Diane Wynn Garfield, June 9, 1973; 1 child, Jori Katherine. BA, Wheaton Coll., 1973; MRE, Trinity Evangel. Divinity Sch., 1976. Ordained to ministry Wheaton Bible Ch., 1980; ordained deacon So. Calif. Conf. Free Meth. Ch., 1992. Dir. Christian edn. No. Suburban Evangel. Free Ch., Deerfield, Ill., 1975-78; assoc. pastor Wheaton (Ill.) Bible Ch., 1978-82, Scottsdale (Ariz.) Bible Ch., 1984-88; mng. editor Gospel Light Pub. Co., Ventura, Calif., 1982-84, cons., 1984-88; owner, pres. Diamond Comml. Svcs., Phoenix, 1988-92; sr. pastor Mountain View Free Meth. Ch., Upland, Calif., 1992—; dir. Internat. Ctr. for Learning, Ventura, 1983-84; cons. So. Calif. Free Meth. Conf., Azusa, Calif., 1992—. Producer, dir. video tng. seminars; editor ch. sch. curriculum Living World Curriculum, 1982, Vanguard newsletter, 1984. Pres. Number 2, Wheaton, 1981; founder, pres. Children's Ministry Fellowship, Phoenix, 1987-88; bd. dirs. Greater Phoenix Sunday Sch. Conv., 1988; mem. Dad's Club of Scottsdale Christian Acad., 1988-90; mem. Better Bus. Bur., hoenix, 1991-92; treas. Upland Community Coord. Coun., 1993. Republican. Home: 1669 Erin Ave Upland CA 91786 Office: Mountain View Free Meth Ch 1020 W 8th St Upland CA 91786

RIGBY, MARTIN L., designer, computer consultant; b. Pocatello, Idaho, Nov. 19, 1964; s. Sherman Lee and Virginia Louise (Johnson) R. BA in Design, Brigham Young U., 1992. Owner, pres. Rigby Design Cons., Provo, Utah, 1990—. Missionary, immigrations sec. Ch. of Jesus Christ of Latter Day Saints, Tegucigalpa, Honduras, 1984-86. Office: Rigby Design Cons 590 S 100 West Ste 11 PO Box 235 Provo UT 84603

RIGGLEMAN, JAMES DAVID, professional baseball team manager; b. Ft. Dix, N.J., Dec. 9, 1952. Degree in Physical Edn., Frostburg State U. Minor league baseball player, 1974-81, minor league baseball mgr., 1982-88, 91-92; dir. player devel., then coach St. Louis Cardinals, 1988-90; mgr. San Diego Padres, 1993—. Office: San Diego Padres PO Box 2000 San Diego CA 92112-2000

RIGGS, CONRAD ALBERT, lawyer; b. Lausanne, Nov. 1, 1963; s. Richard Allen Riggs and Roswitha Margarete (Goeppert) Woolley. BS in Applied Maths., U. Calif., L.A., 1986; JD, Northwestern U., 1989. Bar: Calif. 1989. Assoc. Lillick & McHose, San Diego and L.A., 1989-90, Pillsbury, Madison & Sutro, San Diego and L.A., 1990—. Mem. ABA, Calif. Bar Assn. Home: PO Box 12 Rancho Santa Fe CA 92067-0012 Office: Pillsbury Madison & Sutro 101 W Broadway Fl 18 San Diego CA 92101-8201

RIGGS, HENRY EARLE, engineering management educator, academic administrator; b. Chgo., Feb. 25, 1935; s. Joseph Agnew and Gretchen (Walser) R.; m. Gayle Carson, May 17, 1958; children: Elizabeth, Peter, Catharine. BS, Stanford U., 1957; MBA, Harvard U., 1960. Indsl. economist SRI Internat., Menlo Park, Calif., 1960-63; v.p. Icore Industries, Sunnyvale, Calif., 1963-67, pres., 1967-70; v.p. fin. Measurex Corp., Cupertino, Calif., 1970-74; prof. engring. mgmt. Stanford U., Calif., 1974-88, Ford prof., 1986-88, v.p. for devel., 1983-88; pres. Harvey Mudd Coll., Claremont, Calif., 1988—; bd. dirs. Mutual Funds of Capital Rsch. Group. Author: Accounting: A Survey, 1981, Managing High-Tech Companies, 1983; contbr. articles to Harvard Bus. Rev. Bd. dirs. Stanford Area coun. Boy Scouts Am., 1986-88, Palo Alto YMCA, 1977-79, Mt. Baldy coun., 1993—. Baker scholar Harvard Bus. Sch., Boston, 1959; recipient Gores Teaching award Stanford U., 1980. Mem. Stanford Alumni Assn. (bd. dirs. 1990—, chmn. 1993), Phi Beta Kappa, Tau Beta Pi. Congregationalist. Club: California. Office: Harvey Mudd Coll Kingston Hall 201 Claremont CA 91711

RIGGS, JOHN FORREST, naval officer; b. McPherson, Kans., Mar. 3, 1959; s. Walter Landon and Alyce Mamie (Wedding) R.; m. Linda Wisniewski, Nov. 30, 1985. BA in Astronomy, U. Kans., 1982; postgrad., Naval Postgrad. Sch., Monterey, Calif., 1991—. Commd. ensign USN, 1982, advanced through grades to lt. comdr.; jet pilot Fleet Composite Squadron 5, Cubi Point, The Philippines, 1984-86, Air Antisubmarine Squadron 37, San Diego, 1987-91; fleet liaison officer Operation Desert Shield, Riyadh, Saudi Arabia, 1991. Mem. AIAA, Planetary Soc., Nat. Space Soc., U.S. Naval Inst., U.S. Space Found. Home: 10215 Centinella Dr La Mesa CA 91941 Office: Naval Postgrad Sch Code 31 Monterey CA 93943

RIGGS, PAULA DETMER, author; b. Hamilton, Ohio, Jan. 9, 1944; d. Paul Vermoyne and Nell Jeanease (Bohlander) Detmer; m. Charles Arthur Riggs, Feb. 21, 1965; children: Matthew, Alexander. BS, Miami U., Oxford, Ohio, 1965. faculty writing San Diego State U., Long Beach (Calif.) State U., Irvine (Calif.) State U., 1991. Author 16 novels. Recipient award for best Intimate Moments Romantic Times Mag., 1989, 90, Best Innovative Series, 1990. Mem. Romance Writers of Am., Novelists Inc., Douglas County Hist. Soc., Altrusa Internat.

RIGGS, ROBERT EDWON, law and political science educator; b. Mesa, Ariz, June 24, 1927; s. Lyle Alton and Goldie Esther (Motzkus) R.; m. Hazel Dawn Macdonald, Sept. 1, 1949; children: Robert, Richard, Russel, Rodney, Raymond, Reisa, Preston. BA, U. Ariz., 1952, MA, 1953, LLB, 1963; PhD in Polit. Sci., U. Ill., 1955. Bar: Ariz. 1963. Instr., then asst. prof. polit. sci. Brigham Young U., Provo, Utah, 1955-60, prof. J. Reuben Clark Law Sch., 1975-91, Guy Anderson prof. law, 1991-92; rsch. specialist Bur. Bus. and Pub. Rsch., U. Ariz., 1960-63; assoc. Riggs & Riggs, Tempe, Ariz., 1963-64; mem. faculty U. Minn., 1964-75, prof. polit. sci., 1968-75, dir. Harold Scott Quigley Center Internat. Studies, 1968-70. Author: Politics in the United Nations, 1958, reprinted 1984, The Movement for Administrative Reorganization in Arizona, rev. edit, 1964, (with Jack C. Plano) Forging World Order, 1967, Dictionary of Political Analysis, 1973, 2d edit. (with Jack C. Plano and Helenan S. Robin), 1982, US/UN: Foreign Policy and International Organization, 1971, (with Plano and others) Political Science Dictionary, 1973, (with I. J. Mykletun) Beyond Functionalism: Attitudes toward International Organization in Norway and the U.S, 1979, (with Jack C. Plano) The United Nations, 1988, 2d edit. 1994. Dem. precinct chmn., 1970-72, 76-80, 84-86; mem. Utah Dem. State Ctrl. Com., 1978-82; mayor Golden Valley, Minn., 1972-75; Dem. candidate for U.S. Congress from Minn. 3d dist., 1974; bd. dirs. Minn. UN Assn., 1967-74, Utah Legal Svcs. Corp., 1978-81; chmn. Utah State Adv. Com. to U.S. Commn. on Civil Rights, 1988-92. With AUS, 1945-47. Rotary Found. fellow Oxford (Eng.) U., 1952-53; James W. Garner fellow U. Ill., 1953-55; Rockefeller rsch. fellow Columbia U., 1957-58; NEH rsch. grantee, U. Minn., Brigham Young U. Mem. Phi Beta Kappa, Order of Coif, Phi Kappa Phi, Delta Sigma Rho, Phi Alpha Delta. Mem. Ch. of Jesus Christ of Latter-day Saints (missionary in Eng. 1947-49, in Ariz. 1993-94). Home: 1158 S 350 W Orem UT 84058-6730

RIIKOLA, MICHAEL EDWARD, lawyer; b. Phoenix, July 5, 1951; s. Merlin Jacob and Kathleen Mary (Hanrahan) R. BA, U. Ariz., 1975, JD, 1978. Bar: Ariz. 1978, U.S. Dist. Ct. Ariz. 1979, U.S. Ct. Appeals (9th cir.) 1979. Law clk. to presiding justice Ariz. Supreme Ct., Phoenix, 1978-79; assoc. to ptnr. Shimmel, Hill, Bishop and Gruender, P.C., Phoenix, 1979-85; ptnr. Shimmel, Hill, Bishop and Gruender, P.C., 1985-86; pvt. practice Phoenix, 1986—; cooperating atty. Christic Inst., Washington, 1986—. Contbr. articles to profl. jours. Spl. counsel Com. To Elect John J. Rhodes Gov., Ariz., 1988; issues dir. campaign com. Grant Woods for Ariz. Atty. Gen., 1990; issues dir. exploratory com. Bill Mundell for Congress, 1992. Mem. Trial Lawyers Pub. Justice, Phi Alpha Delta. Democrat. Roman Catholic. Office: 3030 N Central Ave Ste 1000 Phoenix AZ 85012-2717

RIKELMAN, HERMAN, psychologist; b. N.Y.C., July 25, 1911; s. Max and Jennie (LeShak) R.; m. Augusta Komarow, Oct. 27, 1934; 1 child, Herbert F. BS, Fordham U., 1934; MA, Columbia U., 1936; cert., N.Y. Sch. Social Work, 1940. Lic. clin. psychologist, N.Y. Asst. supr. Jewish Family Svc., N.Y.C., 1938-43; dir. community svcs. Jewish Bd. Guardians, N.Y.C., 1944-55; exec. dir. Karen Horney Clinic, N.Y.C., 1955-64, Family Agent Program, Santa Monica, Calif., 1964-68; hypnotist pvt. practice, Newport Beach, Calif., 1968—, clin. psychologist, 1968—, marriage family therapist, 1968—; Examiner Civl Svc. Commn., N.Y.C., 1955-57, chmn. Community Mental Health Svcs., N.Y.C., 1955-60, mem. Mental Health Com. Govt. Affairs, N.Y.C., 1960-62, Mental Health Workshop Cunard steamship, N.Y.C., Caribbean, 1963. Hon. designee Judea Hall of Fame, 1956. Home: 3010 Park Newport Apt 315 Newport Beach CA 92660-5838

RIKER, JOSEPH THADDEUS, III, resource manager, community development director; b. Klamath Falls, Oreg., Oct. 24, 1940; s. Joseph Thaddeus and Joyce Lucille (Packard) R.; m. Barbara Day Morris (div. Oct. 1973); children: Annette Lee, Michelle Louise, Nicole Marie; m. Joan Faith Marsh, Jan. 11, 1974; 1 child, Justina Dale. BS, Oreg. State U., 1962, MS, 1964; PhD, Purdue U., 1966; grad. in pub. adminstrn., U. Oreg., 1978. Asst. prof. U. N.H., Durham, 1966-69, Colo. State U., Ft. Collins., 1969-71; assoc. prof. Oreg. Inst. Tech., Klamath Falls, 1972-82; adult edn. dir. Orgn. of the Forgotten Am., Klamath Falls, 1983-84; planning dir. City of Klamath Falls, 1984-89, community devel. dir., 1989—; co-owner Klamath Cons. Svcs. Inc., Klamath Falls, 1977—. Writer nutrition news column Herald & News newspaper, 1983-87; contbr. articles to profl. jours. Chmn. Klamath County Rep. Cen. Com., 1976; pres. Westminster Found.-Campus Ministries of Oreg., 1984; dir. Klamath Soil & Water Conservation Dist., 1980-90. Recipient Goodyear Conservation award Goodyear Co., 1988. Mem. Am. Planning Assn., Oreg. City Planning Dirs. Assn. (bd. dirs. 1989—), N.Am. Lake Mgmt. Assn., Oreg. Lake Mgmt. Assn. (bd. dirs. 1990—), Pacific Fisheries Biologists, Klamath County C. of C. (bd. dirs. 1984—), Klamath Falls Kiwanis (bd. dirs. 1990—). Presbyterian. Home: 5127 Hwy 39 Klamath Falls OR 97603-9613 Office: City of Klamath Falls 226 S 5th St Klamath Falls OR 97601-6106

RILES, WILSON CAMANZA, educational consultant; b. Alexandria, La., June 27, 1917; m. Mary Louise Phillips, Nov. 13, 1941; children: Michael, Narvia Riles Bostick, Wilson, Phillip. B.A., No. Ariz. U., 1940; M.A., 1947, LL.D., 1976; LL.D., Pepperdine Coll., 1965, Claremont Grad. Sch., 1972, U. So. Calif., 1975, U. Akron, 1976, Golden Gate U., 1981; L.H.D., St. Mary's Coll., 1971, U. Pacific, 1971, U. Judaism, 1972. Tchr. elem. schs., adminstr. pub. schs. Ariz., 1940-54; exec. sec. Pacific Coast region Fellowship of Reconciliation, Los Angeles, 1954-58; with Calif. Dept. Edn., 1958-83, dep. supt. pub. instrn., 1965-70, supt. pub. instruction, 1971-83; pres. Wilson Riles & Assocs., Inc.; dir. emeritus Wells Fargo Bank, Wells Fargo Co. Past mem. editorial adv. bd.: Early Years mag. Ex-officio mem. bd. regents U. Calif., 1971-82; ex-officio trustee Calif. State Univs. and Colls., 1971-82; nat. adv. council Nat. Schs. Vol. Program; former mem. council Stanford Research Inst.; former mem. adv. council Stanford U. Sch. Bus.; former mem. adv. bd. Calif. Congress Parents and Tchrs.; former trustee Am. Coll. Testing Program; former mem. Edn. Commn. of States; past 2d v.p. Nat. PTA.; former trustee Found. Teaching Econs.; former mem. Joint Council Econ. Edn.; former mem. Nat. Council for Children and TV. With USAF, 1943-46. Recipient Spingarn medal NAACP, 1973. Mem. Assn. Calif. Sch. Adminstrs., Cleve. Conf., NAACP (Spingarn medal 1973), Nat. Acad. Pub. Adminstrn., Phi Beta Kappa. Office: 400 Capitol Mall Ste 1540 Sacramento CA 95814

RILEY, ANN L., management professional; b. Mineola, N.Y., July 25, 1950. BA in Ecology, Polit. Sci., Cornell Coll., 1972; M of Landscape Architecture, U. Calif., Berkeley, 1977, PhD in Environ. Planning, 1987. Lobbyist Sierra Club, Washington, 1971; environ. platform researcher, speech writer Senator Dick Clark of Iowa, 1971-72; researcher U.S. Dept. Interior, Washington, 1972; community organizer Hawkeye Area Community Action Program, Cedar Rapids, Iowa, 1972; dir. land use planning program Johnson County Health Dept., Iowa City, 1973-74; field worker U.S. Geol. Survey and Wyo. Geol. Survey, 1975; producer environ. projects reports Upper Green River Basin, Wyo., 1975-77; chmn. Nat. Environ. Health Assn. Land Use Com., Calif., 1975-76; developed landscape planning and water conservation program Calif. Dept. Water Resources, Sacramento, 1976-91; program mgr. integrated pest mgmt. program Calif. Dept. Water Resources, 1977-83, staff environ. planner, 1979-82, project mgr. summary report on San Francisco delta, 1983-84, program mgr. statewide stream restoration and flood control program, 1985-88, chief fin. assistance and environ. rev. br., 1988-91; exec. dir. Golden State Wildlife Fedn., Berkeley, 1991—; instr. Vista Coll., 1980-81, U.S. Army C.E. Waterways Experiment Sta., Vicksburg, Miss., 1986, 89. Founder, leader Orgn. of Women in Landscape, 1976-86; founder Yeast Bay Brewers, 1977-79; founder, mem. steering com. Women's Environ. Network, 1979-85; founder Urban Creeks Coun., 1982—; mem. steering com. Andy Cohen for East Bay Mcpl. Utility Dist. Bd., 1990—. Beatrix Farrand Grad. scholar, 1974-75, Nat. Environ. Health Assn. scholar, 1974-75; recipient award for involvement in Wildcat-San Pablo Creek Flood Control Project, 1986, Ann. award East Bay Lesbian/Gay Dem. Club, 1987, Highest Svc. award Urban Creeks Coun., 1989, Honor award Calif. Coun. Landscape Architects, 1989, award fro role in promotion of River Greenways in U.S. from Audubon Soc., 1991; named one of 20 San Francisco Bay Area East Bay Citizens Who Made a Difference by East Bay Express, 1987. Office: Golden State Wildlife Fedn 1250 Addison St Ste 107 Berkeley CA 94702

RILEY, BENJAMIN KNEELAND, lawyer; b. Pompton Plains, N.J., June 3, 1957; s. Christopher Sibley and Katharine Louise (Piper) R.; m. Janet Welch McCormick, Sept. 15, 1984; children: Keith McCormick, Jamin McCormick. AB, Dartmouth Coll., 1979; JD, U. Calif., Berkeley, 1983. Bar: Calif. 1983, U.S. Dist. Ct. (no. dist.) Calif. 1983, U.S. Ct. Appeals (9th cir.) 1983, U.S. Dist. Ct. (ea. dist.) Calif. 1985, U.S. Dist. Ct. (cen. dist.) Calif. 1987. Assoc. McCutchen, Doyle, Brown & Enerson, San Francisco, 1983-84; ptnr. Cooley, Godward, Castro, Huddleson, & Tatum, San Francisco, 1984—; lectr. Boalt Hall Sch. Law, 1989; mem. San Francisco Legal Services Clinic, 1983—. Assoc. editor Calif. Law Rev. Spl. asst. dist. atty., San Francisco, 1988; commr. Orinda Parks & Recreation Commn., 1992—; mem. City Orinda Gateway Task Force, 1990-92; bd. dirs. Children's Garden, 1987-92; v.p., mem. Orinda Assn., chmn. Orinda's 4th of July celebration. ABA, Calif. Bar Assn., San Francisco Bar Assn. Democrat. Club: Barrister of San Francisco. Office: Cooley Godward Huddleson & Tatum 1 Maritime Pla 20th Fl San Francisco CA 94111

RILEY, CARROLL LAVERN, anthropology educator; b. Summersville, Mo., Apr. 18, 1923; s. Benjamin F. and Minnie B. (Smith) R.; m. Brent Robinson Locke, Mar. 25, 1948; children: Benjamin Locke, Victoria Smith Evans, Cynthia Winningham. A.B., U. N.Mex., 1948, Ph.D., 1952; M.A., UCLA, 1950. Instr. U. Colo., Boulder, 1953-54; asst. prof. U. N.C., Chapel Hill, 1954-55; asst. prof. So. Ill. U., Carbondale, 1955-60, assoc. prof., 1960-67, prof., 1967-86, Disting. prof., 1986-87, Disting. prof. emeritus, 1987—, chmn. dept., 1979-82, dir. mus., 1972-74; rsch. assoc. lab. anthropology Mus. N.Mex., 1987-90, sr. rsch. assoc., 1990—; rsch. collaborator Smithsonian Instn., 1988—; adj. prof. N.Mex. Highlands U., 1989—. Author: The Origins of Civilization, 1969, The Frontier People, 1982, expanded edit., 1987; editor: Man Across the Sea, 1971, Southwestern Journals of Adolph F. Bandelier, 4 vols., 1966, 70, 75, 84, Across the Chichimec Sea, 1978; others; contbr. numerous articles to profl. jours. Served in USAAF, 1942-45. Decorated 4 battle stars; grantee Social Sci. Research Council, NIH, Am. Philos. Soc., Am. Council Learned Socs., NEH, others. Home: 1106 6th St Las Vegas NM 87701-4311

RILEY, CHARLES LOGAN (REX RILEY), hospital administrator; b. Toledo, Jan. 20, 1946; s. Charles Allen and Phyllis Mary (Logan) R.; m. Rosemarie Jeanette Webster, Apr. 10, 1971; children: Paul Anthony, Ross Evan. BA, U. Mich., 1968; MHA, U. New South Wales, 1976. Indsl. engr. Internat. Harvester, Melbourne, Victoria, Australia, 1972-74; with Royal Women's Hosp., Melbourne, 1974-79; chief operating officer Preston (Victoria) & Northcote Community Hosp., 1979-84, Valley Children's Hosp., Fresno, Calif., 1989—; chief exec. officer Geelong (Victoria) Hosp., 1984-89. Mem. Leadership Fresno, 1990-91; mem. exec. com. Combined Health Appeal, 1989-90; active Ronald McDonald House, Fresno, 1990-92. With USMC, 1968-72. Decorated Navy Commendation medal; scholar Buehler Found., 1964, Health Dept. Victoria, 1973. Fellow Australian Coll. Healthsvc. Execs. (registrar 1983-85, v.p. 1985-87, pres. 1987-88); mem. Am. Coll. Healthcare Execs., Rotary. Home: 2287 W Pinedale Ave Fresno CA 93711-7109 Office: Valley Children's Hosp 3151 N Millbrook Ave Fresno CA 93703-1497

RILEY, DAVID RICHARD, consultant, retired military officer; b. Spokane, Wash., Mar. 28, 1940; s. Lee James and Louise Elizabeth (Duncan) R.; m. Anna Maria Formigoni, July 6, 1963; children: David Scott, Michelle Andrea. BS in Naval Sci., USN Acad., 1963; MS in Applied Math., USN Post Grad. Sch., 1972; postgrad., Armed Forces Staff Coll., 1975. Ensign USN, 1963, advanced through grades to capt., 1984; antisubmarine warfare/antisubmarine rocket officer USN, Mayport, Fla., 1963-65; pilot trainee USN, Pensacola, Fla., 1965-67; designated naval pilot USN, San Diego, 1967, with antisubmarine/antiair warfare, 1967-74, maintenace officer, 1976-78; officer in charge USN, Nerra Naples, Italy, 1978-81; exec. officer Naval Aviation Depot, Alameda, Calif., 1981-84; comdg. officer Naval Aviation Depot, Pensacola, 1987-90; aviation depot program mgr. Navairsyscom Hdqrs., Washington, 1984-87; ret., 1990; cons. bus. planning and organizational devel. Chula Vista, Calif. Mem. Assn. Naval Aviation, Ret. Officers Assn., Am. Legion, Naval Helicopter Assn. Republican. Presbyterian. Home and Office: 609 E J St Chula Vista CA 91910-6528

RILEY, GERALD WAYNE, rehabilitation counselor; b. St. Joseph, Mich., Mar. 31, 1950; s. Gerald George and Doris (Louise) R.; m. Barbara Jane Usas, Dec. 27, 1973 (div. Aug. 1980); m. Jill Lucile Jezek, June 6, 1981; children: Sean A. Goings, Marc A. Goings. BS in Criminal Justice, Mich. State U., 1972; MS in Rehab. Counseling, Wright State U., 1977. Cert. rehab. counselor. Vocat. evaluator Goodwill Industries, Dayton, Ohio, 1974-76; rehab. counselor Goodwill Industries, Colorado Springs, Colo., 1976-81; mental health therapist Rehab. Cons., Colorado Springs, Colo., 1981-84; rehab. counselor Rehab. Svcs., Colorado Springs, Colo., 1984-89; rehab. counselor II Rehab. Svcs., Canon City, Colo., 1989-91; sr. rehab. counselor Rehab. Svcs., Colorado Springs, Colo., 1991—. Mem. Colorado Springs Epilepsy Assn. (bd. dirs., chmn. 1977-79), Great Plains Vocat. Evaluation and Work Adjustment Assn. (pres. 1979-80), Colo. Rehab. Assn. (bd. dirs. 1980-82, 89—, pres. 1993), Colo. Vocat. Evaluation and Work Adjustment Assn. (pres. 1978-79). Baptist. Office: Colorado Rehab Services 1322 Academy Blvd Colorado Springs CO 80909-3314

RILEY, HERBERT JAMES, trade association executive; b. Manila, Philippines, Aug. 11, 1925; s. Herbert James and Mary Berniece (Roach) R.; m. Marion Muriel Welbourn, Dec. 21, 1962; children: James Edward, Michael Jeffrey. BS, U. So. Calif., 1949. Asst. supt. C. Brewer & Co., Honolulu, 1950-55; personnel dir. Pacific Chem. & Fertilizer Co., Honolulu, 1955-60; indsl. rels. dir. Dillingham Corp., Honolulu, 1960-68; v.p. labor rels. Am. Pres. Lines, San Francisco, 1968-78; exec. dir. Printing Industries of No. Calif., San Francisco, 1978—; chmn., bd. trustees San Francisco Lithographers Pension Fund, 1979—; trustee Graphic Arts Ind. Joint Pension Fund, Washington, 1980—. POW, Manila, 1942-45, pvt. Infantry, 1945-46. Named Man of Yr., Internat. Assn. Printing House Craftsmen, 1989; recipient Haywood Hunt award. Office: Printing Industries 665 3rd St San Francisco CA 94107-1901

RILEY, JOHN FRANCIS, chemist, chemical researcher; b. New Bedford, Mass., Mar. 23, 1927; s. Charles Leo and Mary Theresa (Donaghy) R.; m. Grace Frances Tripp, Nov. 25, 1948; children: Patricia, John Francis III, Paula, Penelope, Brian, Timothy, Jane. BS magna cum laude, Providence Coll., 1951; MS, Yale U., 1952, PhD, 1954. Rsch. scientist Union Carbide, Tonawanda, N.Y., 1954-60, Oak Ridge (Tenn.) Nat. Lab., 1960-66; cons. scientist Lockheed Palo Alto (Calif.) Rsch. Lab., 1966-93; sr. mem. rsch. lab. Lockheed Missiles & Space Co., Palo Alto, 1981-93; cons. Palo Alto, 1993—. Contbr. articles to profl. jours. With USN, 1944-46. Named Outstanding Young Man of Yr. N.Y. State C. of C., 1959. Fellow Am. Inst. Chemists; mem. Am. Chem. Soc. (councilor 1982—, chmn. divsn. of chemistry and the law 1991). Roman Catholic. Home: 1842 Edgewood Dr Palo Alto CA 94303-3015 Office: Lockheed R & D Divsn 3251 Hanover St Palo Alto CA 94304-1121

RILEY, MICHAEL EUGENE, wireless communications engineer; b. Quantico, Va., Dec. 8, 1952; s. Peter Eugene and Patrice (Lindahl) R. Assoc. Sci. and Electronics Tech., Olympic Coll., 1984; BSEE, Seattle U., 1988. Freelance stage technician, 1980-88; sr. technician Broadway Performance Hall, Seattle, 1984-88; cellular system engr. McCaw Cellular Comms., Seattle, 1988-90; instr. electronics Olympic Coll., Bremerton, Wash., 1988-89; sr. RF engr. PacTel Internat., Stuttgart, Germany, 1990-92; mgr. systems engr. PacTel Internat., Walnut Creek, Calif., Nagoya, Japan, 1992-93, project mgr., 1993—; industry-acad. interface McCaw Cellular/Seattle U., 1988-90. Tech. aide African Famine Relief, Seattle, 1986. Bennett Meml. scholar Kiwanis, 1983, 84. Mem. IEEE (prs. Seattle U. br. 1987-88, Larry K. Wilson award 1988). Buddhist. Office: PacTel Internat 390 N Wiget Ln Ste 400 Walnut Creek CA 94598

RINEARSON, PETER MARK, journalist, author, software developer; b. Seattle, Aug. 4, 1954; s. Peter Morley and Jeannette Irene (Love) R.; m. Jill Chan, Sept. 15, 1991. Student, U. Wash., 1972-78. Editor Sammamish Valley News, Redmond, Wash., 1975-76; reporter Seattle Times, 1976-78, govt. and polit. reporter, 1979-81, aerospace reporter, 1982-84, Asian corr., 1985-86; pres. Alki Software Corp., Seattle, 1990—. Author: Word Processing Power with Microsoft Word (4th edit. Running Microsoft Word 5.5, 1991), Microsoft Word Style Sheets, 1987, Quick Reference Guide to Microsoft Word, 1988, Microsoft Word Companion Disk, 1988, Masterword, 1990, 91, 92. Recipient Spl. Paul Myhre award-series Penney-Mo. Newspaper awards, 1983, Disting. Writing award Am. Soc. Newspaper Editors, 1984, Pulitzer prize for feature writing, 1984, Lowell Thomas Travel Writing award, 1984, John Hancock award,1985, semi-finalist NASA Journalist-in-Space Project, 1986; U.S.-Japan Leadership Program fellow Japan Soc., 1988. Office: 300 Queen Anne Ave N # 410 Seattle WA 98109

RINEHART, CHARLES R., savings and loan association executive; b. San Francisco, Jan. 31, 1947; s. Robert Eugene and Rita Mary Rinehart; married; children: Joseph B., Kimberly D., Michael P., Scott. BS, U. San Francisco, 1968. Exec. v.p. Fireman's Fund Ins. Cos., Novato, Calif., 1969-83; pres., chief exec. officer Avco Fin. Services, Irvine, Calif., 1983-89; pres., chief oper. officer, dir. H.F. Ahmanson & Co., Irwindale, Calif., 1989—; vice chmn., chief oper. officer Home Savs. of Am., Irwindale. Trustee U. San Francisco. Served to 2d lt. U.S. Army, 1968-69. Fellow Casualty Actuarial Soc.; mem. Am. Mgmt. Assn., Am. Acad. Actuaries, Young Pres. Orgn. (Calif. Coast chpt.), Calif. Bus. Roundtable. Repubican. Roman Catholic. Office: Home Savs of Am 4900 Rivergrade Rd Baldwin Park CA 91706-1438

RINEHART, FREDERICK ROBERTS, publisher; b. N.Y.C., Sept. 30, 1953; s. George Henry Doran R. and Sharon Kerley (Bonner) Caulfield; m. Kim Bennett, Aug. 28, 1976; 1 child, Alexander Vaughan. BS with highest honors, U. Calif., Santa Barbara, 1977. Asst. dir. U. Press of Colo., Boulder, 1977-87; pres. Roberts Rinehart Pubs., Niwot, Colo., 1987—; pubs. bd. mem. Denver Mus. Natural History, 1989—. Editor: Chronicles of Colorado, 1984. Recipient Design awards Rocky Mountain Book Pubs. Assn., 1987, 88, 90, 91, 92, Merit award Am. Soc. of Landscape Architects, 1992. Mem. Kent Sch. Boat Club. Home: 12281 N 63rd St Longmont CO 80503 Office: Roberts Rinehart Pub 121 Second Ave Niwot CO 80544

RINEHART, NITA, state senator; b. Tex. BA, So. Meth. U.; JD. U. Wash. Mem. Wash. State Ho. of Reps., 1979-82; mem. Wash. State Senate, 1983—, vice chmn. edn. com., mem. rules, ways and means, govtl. ops. coms. Bd. dirs. Planned Parenthood of Seattle. Mem. LWV, Bus. and Profl. Women. Democrat. Office: State Senate State Capitol Olympia WA 98504 Home: 4515 51st Ave NE Seattle WA 98105-3830

RINEK, LARRY MOFFETT, business and technology consultant; b. Hartford, Conn., Sept. 3, 1947; s. John Ayers and Rheta Marion (Coulombe) R.; m. Bridget Lilian Beuning, July 19, 1975; 1 child, Heidi April. BS, UCLA, 1969, MBA, 1971. Cons. SRI Internat., Menlo Park, Calif., 1974—. Contbr. articles to profl. jours. 1st lt. USAF, 1971-74. Mem. SAE, Soc. Automotive Engrs. Internat. (vice chair mid-Calif. sect. 1993-94), San Jose Swim & Racquet Club (interclub capt. 1985—), Lambda Chi Alpha. Republican. Roman Catholic. Home: 80 Gilbert Ave Santa Clara CA 95051

RINGEN, SONJA GAY, chemist, consultant; b. Worland, Wyo., Apr. 10, 1953; d. Bruce Hoverson and Frances Emily (Berg) R.; m. Timothy Lovell Hale, June 10, 1977. AS, Casper (Wyo.) Coll., 1973; BS, U. Wyo., 1975. Cert. hazardous materials mgr. Chemist U.S. Dept. Energy, Laramie, Wyo., 1974-81; lab. mgr. Wyo. Analytical Labs., Laramie, 1981-89; chem. safety officer U. Wyo., Laramie, 1989—; cons. in field. Co-author: (tng. manual) The Total Quality Management Team Training Program, 1991; contbr. articles to profl. jours. Maine Laramie Rifle Range, 1989-93; Sunday sch. tchr. Zion Luth. Ch., 1989-93; chmn. Laramie/Albany County Environ. Commn., 1988-90; v.p. Laramie Collection Day, Inc. Mem. Am. Chem. Soc. (officer div. chem. health and safety), Maine Inst. Hazardous Materials Mgrs., Laramie Area Safety Assn., Campus Safety Assn. Lutheran. Home: 815 Mitchell St Laramie WY 82070-2150 Office: U Wyo 312 Merica Hall Laramie WY 82071-3413

RINGUETTE, DAVID AARON, agriculture educator; b. Hartford, Conn., Sept. 22, 1958; s. Joseph and Annette (Butkus) R. BS, Johnson (Vt.) State Coll., 1980; MS, Calif. Poly. Inst., 1985. Owner, operator Ringuette Roadside Stand, Suffield, Conn., 1969-71; farm laborer Markowski Farms, Suffield, 1971-77; vol. U.S. Peace Corps, Azrou, Morocco, 1980-82; cons. U.S. Agy. for Internat. Devel., Washington, 1984; instr. agriculture Maui Community Coll., Hoolehua, Hawaii, 1985-86; coord. agriculture Windward Community Coll., Kaneohe, Hawaii, 1986—; dir. Soil and Water Conservation Dist., Honolulu, 1989—; cons. Northshore Career Tng., Kahuku, Hawaii, 1986—. Author: Aquaculture in Morocco, 1981. Mem. Nat. Assn. Coll. Tchrs. in Agriculture, Coun. Agriculture, Sci. and Tech., Hawaii Farm Bur., Landscape Coun. Hawaii. Office: Windward Community Coll 45-720 Keaahala Rd Kaneohe HI 96744

RINNE, MARK DOUGLAS, dentist; b. Lincoln, Nebr., Mar. 10, 1952; s. Vernon W. and Mildred (Williamson) R.; m. Sarah W. Thorne, Oct. 2, 1976 (div.); children: Sarah, Katherine, Amy, Frederick III. DDS, U. Nebr., 1976. Pvt. practice Cheyenne, Wyo., 1986—; mem. dental adv. bd. Laramie County Community Coll., Cheyenne, 1989-92; mem. Wyo. State peer Rev. Bd., 1984-91, chmn., 1991. Mem. Nat. Congress of State Games Exec. Bd., Boston, 1988-90; sport liason U.S. Olympic Com., Oklahoma City, 1989, Olympic Festival, Mpls., 1990, L.A., 1991; councilman Cheyenne City Coun., 1989—, pres., 1990-91; founder Cowboy State Games, Cheyenne, 1986, v.p., 1992—; mem. Cheyenne Downtown Devel. Authority Bd., 1990—, treas., 1992; trustee Laramie County Community Coll., Cheyne, 1980-83, pres., 1983; chmn. Cowboy State Games Organizing Com., Casper, Wyo., 1988—. Mem. S.E. Dist. Dental Soc. (pres. 1983), Cheyenne C. of C. (steering com. 1990—, Forum 1999). Home: 2847 Foothills Rd Cheyenne WY 82009-4536 Office: 3116 Acacia Dr Cheyenne WY 82001-5804

RINSCH, CHARLES EMIL, insurance company executive; b. Vincennes, Ind., June 28, 1932; s. Emil and Vera Pearl (White) R.; m. Maryann Elizabeth Hitchcock, June 18, 1964; children: Christopher, Daniel, Carl. BS in Stats., Ind. U., 1953; MS in Bus., Butler U., 1959; MBA, Stanford U., 1960. Budget analyst Chrysler Corp., Indpls., 1955-57; sr. fin. analyst Ford Motor Co., Indpls., 1957-59; budget dir. Nat. Forge Co., Warren, Pa., 1960-61; div. controller and asst. to v.p., fin. Norris Industries, L.A., 1961-65; v.p., treas., sec. Teledyne Inc, L.A., 1965-88; pres., chief exec. officer Argonaut Group Inc., L.A., 1988—. Cubmaster Pack 721, Boy Scouts Am., L.A., 1987-88, treas. 1981-87; mem. dean's adv. coun. Ind. U. Sch. Bus. 1st lt. U.S. Army, 1953-55. Mem. Acad. Alumni Fellows Ind. U. Sch. Bus., L.A. Treas.'s Club. Home: 19849 Greenbriar Dr Tarzana CA 91356-5428 Office: Argonaut Group Inc Ste 1175 1800 Ave of the Stars Los Angeles CA 90067

RINSCH, MARYANN ELIZABETH, occupational therapist; b. L.A., Aug. 8, 1939; d. Harry William and Thora Analine (Langlie) Hitchcock; m. Charles Emil Rinsch, June 18, 1964; children: Christopher, Daniel, Carl. BS, U. Minn., 1961. Registered occupational therapist, Calif. Staff occupational therapist Hastings (Minn.) State Hosp., 1961-62, Neuropsychiat. Inst., L.A., 1962-64; staff and sr. occupational therapist Calif. Children's Svcs., L.A., 1964-66, head occupational therapist, 1966-68; researcher A. Jean Ayres, U. So. Calif., L.A., 1968-69; pvt. practice neurodevel. and sensory integraton Tarzana, Calif., 1969-74; pediat. occupational therapist neurodevel. & sensory integration St. Johns Hosp., Santa Monica, Calif., 1991—. Mem. alliance bd. Natural History Mus., L.A. County, 1983—; cub scouts den mother Boy Scouts Am., Sherman Oaks, Calif., 1986-88, advancement chair Boy Scout Troop 474, Boy Scouts Am., 1989—; bd. dirs. Valley Women's Ctr., 1990-91; project chmn. Vol. League San Fernando Valley, Van Nuys, Calif., 1986—; trustee Viewpoint Sch., Calabasas, Calif., 1987-90. Mem. Am. Occupational Therapy Assn., Calif. Occupational Therapy Assn. Home: 19849 Greenbriar Dr Tarzana CA 91356-5428

RIORDAN, JOHN STEPHEN, air force officer; b. Kearny, N.J., July 23, 1965; s. John Joseph and Annie (Minogue) R.; m. Shawn Lynn McGowen, June 8, 1991. BA, Montclair State Coll., 1987; postgrad., Colo. State U., 1989-91; MBA with honors, Regis U., Denver, 1993. Cert. tchr., instr. USAF. Supr. customer svc. BJ's Wholesale Club, East Rutherford, N.J., 1987-88; commd. 2d lt. USAF, 1988, advanced through grades to capt., 1991; combat crew instr. ops. tng. div. 90th Missile Wing, Cheyenne, Wyo., 1988-89, sr. crew instr., 1989-90, missile combat crew comdr. 319th missile squadron, 1990-91, chief programs sect. and quality control sect., 1991-92; instrnl. systems mgr., dir. total quality 90th ops. group 90th Ops. Support Squadron, Cheyenne, Wyo., 1992—; owner, COO Wolf Productivity Mgmt. Vice chmn. Warren Boosters Assn., Cheyenne, 1992. Mem. Am. Soc. Quality Control, Air Force Assn., Toastmasters. Home: PO Box 9504 FE Warren AFB WY 82003-9504 Office: 90th Ops Support Squadron D05 Bldg 1292 FE Warren AFB WY 82001

RIORDAN, WILLIAM F., lawyer; b. Wichita, Kans., Mar. 26, 1941. B.B.A., U. N.Mex., 1965, J.D., 1968. Bar: N.Mex. 1968, U.S. Tax Ct. 1972, U.S. Supreme Ct. 1971. Legal aid atty. Albuquerque, 1968-69; asst. atty. gen. N.Mex., 1969; asst. dist. atty. Bernalillo County, N.Mex., 1969-72; judge 2d Jud. Dist. of N.Mex., Albuquerque, 1972-80; justice N.Mex. Supreme Ct., Santa Fe, 1980-85; chief justice N.Mex. Supreme Ct., 1986-87; pvt. practice law Albuquerque, 1987—. Office: 20 First Pla Ste 402 Albuquerque NM 87102-5302

RIOS, ALBERTO ALVARO, English educator; b. Nogales, Ariz., Sept. 18, 1952; s. Alberto Alvaro and Agnes (Fogg) R.; m. Maria Guadalupe Barron, Sept. 8, 1979; 1 child, Joaquin. BA in Lit. & Creative Writing with honor, U. Ariz., 1974, BA in Psychology with honors, 1975, MFA in Creative Writing, 1979. Asst. prof. English Ariz. State U., Tempe, 1982-85, assoc. prof., 1985-89, prof., 1989—, dir. creative writing program, 1986-89, 92—; mem. editorial bd. New Chicano Writing, 1990—; corr. editor Manoa, 1989—; bd. dirs. Libr. of Congress/Ariz. Ctr. for the Book, 1988—, vice chair, 1989—. Author: Elk Heads on the Wall, 1979, Sleeping on Fists, 1981, Whispering to Fool the Wind, 1982, The Iguana Killer, 1984, Five Indiscretions, 1985, The Lime Orchard Woman, 1988, The Warrington Poems, 1989, Teodoro Luna's Two Kisses, 1990 (Pulitzer prize nomination); editor Ploughshares, 1991-92, advisory editor, 1992—; poetry editor Colorado Review, 1993; editorial bd. New Chicana/Chicano Writing, 1990—, Equinox, 1992—; contbr. poems and stories to numerous jours. and anthologies. Guggenheim fellow, 1988-89; recipient Western States Book award for Fiction, Walt Whitman award Acad. Am. Poets, Pushcart Prize, 1986, 88, 89, 93, Community Appreciation award Chicanos Por La Causa, 1988, Gov.'s Arts award State of Ariz., 1991; named Author of Yr. Mountain Plains Libr. Assn., 1991; NEA fellow; Ariz. State U. grantee. Office: Ariz State U Dept English Tempe AZ 85287-0302

RIOS, DIEGO MARCIAL, artist, educator; b. Frenso, Calif., Jan. 28, 1962; s. Herminio and Rosa (Aredondo) R. BA, U. Calif., Berkeley, 1985; MA, U. Wis., 1987, MFA, 1989; Cert. Paralegal, U. San Francisco, 1993. Instr. art Nat. Art Inst. and Disabilities, Richmond, Calif., 1989—, Mission Cultural Ctr., San Francisco, 1989, Richmond (Calif.) Art Ctr., 1992, Via Skills Ctr., Richmond, Calif., 1992; artist in residence Fresno (Calif.) Art Mus., 1991, Armory Ctr. Arts, Pasadena, Calif., 1992; mem. art dept. Just Publ., Berkeley, Calif., 1978-80; head art illustrator V.I.D.A. Internat., San Francisco, 1992. Active United Farmworkers, 1968-79. Recipient Purchase award Madison (Wis.) Print Club, 1988, Phelan award Phelan Soc., 1989, Purchase award, Nat. Works on Paper/Mo., 1991; named Best in Polit. Show of 80s U. Wyo. Art Mus., 1989. Mem. L.A. Printmakers, Calif. Etching Soc., Coll. Art Assn., U. Calif. Libr. Soc., San Francisco Bar Assn. Home: 869 Marin Rd El Sobrante CA 94803

RIPICH, STEFAN JOHN, nurse practitioner; b. Cleve., Jan. 27, 1957; s. Stephen John and Olga June (Douvris) R.; life ptnr. James Clair Franklin, May 5, 1986; children: James Caleb Franklin, Jamon Sullivan Franklin. Diploma in Nursing, Luth. Med. Ctr., Cleve., 1983; MSn, Case Western Res. U., 1992. Advanced clin. nurse Univ. Hosps. of Cleve., 1984-88; project dir. AIDS rsch. Case Western Res. U., Cleve., 1988-91; nurse practitioner infectious diseases Dept. Vet. Affairs Med. Ctr., Palo Alto, Calif., 1992—. Contbr. articles to profl. jours., chpt. to book. Nurse practitioner Free Clinic of Cleve., 1990-91; adv. bd. The Living Room, Cleve., 1989—. Recipient Elayne Martin award for Writing, Ohio Nurse's Assn., 1990. Mem. ANA, Ohio Nurse's Assn. (mem. human rights com.), Calif. Nurse's Assn., Am. Acad. Nurse Practitioners. Home: 1130 Welch Rd Apt 331 Palo Alto CA 94304 Office: Palo Alto Vet's Med Ctr 3801 Miranda Ave Palo Alto CA 94304

RIPINSKY-NAXON, MICHAEL, archaeologist, art historian, ethnologist; b. Kutaisi, USSR, Mar. 23, 1944; s. Pinkus and Maria (Kokielov) R.; m. Agata Dutkiewicz; 1 child, Tariel. AB in Anthropology with honors, U. Calif.-Berkeley, 1966, PhD in Archeology and Art History, 1979. Rsch. asst. Am. Mus. Natural History, N.Y.C., 1964, U. Calif.-Berkeley, 1964-66; mem. faculty dept. anthropology and geography of Near East, Calif. State U.-Hayward, 1966-67; asst. prof. Calif. State U.-Northridge, 1974-75; researcher, assoc. UCLA, 1974-75, sr. rsch. anthropologist Hebrew U., Hadassah Med. Sch., Jerusalem, 1970-71; curator Anthropos Gallery of Ancient Art, Beverly Hills, Calif., 1976-78; chief rsch. scientist Archaeometric Data Labs., Beverly Hills, 1976-78; dir. Ancient Artworld Corp., Beverly Hills, 1979-82; dir. prehistoric studies Mediterranean Rsch. Ctr., Athens, 1989-91; prof. Pedagogical U., Kielce, Poland; conducted excavations Israel, Egypt, Jordan, Mesopotamia, Mexico, Cen. Am; specialist in the development of early religions and shamanism, phenomenon of origins of domestication and camel ancestry; expert on art works from French Impressionists to ancient Egypt and classical world. Author: The Nature of Shamanism, 1993; contbr. articles to sci. and scholarly jours. dir. Cen. Am. Inst. Prehistoric and Traditional Cultures, Belize; chmn. bd. Am. Found. for Cultural Studies. Recipient Cert. of Merit for Sci. Endeavour, Dictionary of Internat. Biography, 1974. Mem. Archaeol. Inst. Am. (life), Soc. for Am. Archaeology, Am. Anthropol. Assn., Royal Anthropol. Inst., Am. Ethnol. Soc., History of Sci. Soc., Am. Chem. Soc., Assn. for Transpersonal Psychology, Soc. Ethnobiology, Soc. Archeol. Scis. (life), New England Appraisers Assns. Home: PO Box 2088 Cathedral City CA 92235-2088 Office: Pedagogical U, ul Żeromsjiego 5, 25-369 Kielce Poland

RIPLEY, EARLE ALLISON, meteorology educator; b. Sydney, N.S., Can., June 29, 1933; s. Edward E. and Hazel M. (Stephens) R.; m. Jean Helen McCrae, May 28, 1966; 1 child, Stephen H. BS, Dalhousie U., Halifax, N.S., Can., 1953; MA, U. Toronto (Can.), 1955. Meteorologist Can. Dept. Transport, Halifax, 1955-60, Nigerian Meteorol. Svc., Lagos, Nigeria, 1960-62; agrometeorologist East African Agr. and Forestry Rsch. Orgn., Nairobi, Kenya, 1962-67; rsch. assoc. U. Sask., Saskatoon, Can., 1968-74; prof. U. Saskatchewan, Saskatoon, Can., 1974—. Author: Environmental Impact of Mining in Canada, 1978. Fellow Royal Meteorol. Soc.; mem. Can. Meteorol. and Oceanographic Soc., Am. Meteorol. Soc. (profl.). Office: U Saskatchewan, Dept Crop Sci & Plant Ecology, Saskatoon, SK Canada S7N 0W0

RIPLEY, STUART MCKINNON, real estate consultant; b. St. Louis, July 28, 1930; s. Rob Roy and Nina Pearl (Young) R.; B.A., U. Redlands, 1952; M.B.A., U. Calif., Berkeley, 1959; m. Marilyn Haerr MacDiarmid, Dec. 28, 1964; children—Jill, Bruce, Kent. Vice pres., dir. J.H. Hedrick & Co., Santa Barbara and San Diego, 1958-63; v.p. mktg. Cavanaugh Devel. Co., San Gabriel, Calif., 1963-65; v.p. mktg. dir. Calabasas Park, Bechtel Corp., Calabasas, Calif., 1967-69; v.p. mktg. Avco Community Developers, Inc., La Jolla, Calif., 1969-74; mktg. dir. U.S. Home Corp., Fla. Div., Clearwater, 1974-75; pres., dir. Howard's Camper Country, Inc., National City, Calif., 1975-77; v.p., mktg. dir. Valcas Internat. Corp., San Diego, 1976-77, pres., 1977-79; pres. Stuart M. Ripley, Inc., 1977—, Sunview Realty, Inc., a Watt Industries Co., Santa Monica, Calif., 1979-80; owner Everett Stunz Co., Ltd., La Jolla, 1981—; exec. v.p. Harriman-Ripley Co., Fallbrook, Calif.; avocado/floraculture rancher, subdivider, Fallbrook, 1978—; lectr. UCLA, 1961. Served with USN, 1952-55. U. Redlands fellow, 1960—. Mem. Nat. Assn. Homebuilders, Sales and Mktg. Council, Sales and Mktg. Execs., Pi Chi. Republican. Episcopalian. Club: Elks. Home: 13180 Portofino Dr Del Mar CA 92014-3828 Office: 7644 Girard Ave La Jolla CA 92037-4420

RIPPER, RITA JO (JODY RIPPER), financial executive; b. Goldfield, Iowa, May 8, 1950; d. Carl Phillip and Lucille Mae (Stewart) Ripper; B.A., U. Iowa, 1972; M.B.A., N.Y.U., 1978. Contracts and fin. staff Control Data Corp., Mpls., 1974-78; regional mgr. Raytheon Corp., Irvine, Calif., 1978-83; v.p. Caljo Corp., Des Moines, Iowa, 1980-84; asst. v.p. Bank of Am., San Francisco, 1984-88; pres. The Northhaven Co., 1988—; pres. The Boardroom Adv. Group, 1990—. Vol. and alt. del. Rep. Party, Edina, Minn., N.Y.C., 1974—; vol. Cancer, Heart, Lung Assns., Edina, N.Y.C., Calif., 1974-78, 84—, Lita, 1986-90. Mem. Amnesty Internat., Internat. Mktg. Assn., World Trade Ctr. Assn., Acctg. Soc. (pres. 1975-76), Engrs. Club of San Francisco, Mensa, Beta Alpha Psi (chmn. 1977-78), Phi Gamma Nu (v.p. 1971-72) Presbyterian. Clubs: Corinthian Yacht, Mt. Tamalpais Racquet. Home and Office: 501 Oak Ln West Des Moines IA 50265 also: The Boardroom Adv Group 537 Newport Center Dr # 277 Newport Beach CA 92660-6900

RIPPEY, CLAYTON, artist; b. LaGrande, Oreg., Apr. 24, 1923; s. Harry and Inez (Clark) R.; m. Marcia Leona Sanford, June 12, 1946; children: John, Barbara. Student, Northwestern U., Evanston, Ill., 1941-42, Whitworth Coll., Spokane, 1946-47; BA/MA, Stanford U., 1949; postgrad., Instituto Allende, San Miguel Allende, Mex., 1955. Prof. art Bakersfield (Calif.) Coll., 1949-67, 68-80, chmn. dept. art, 1968-72; prof. art Maui Community Coll., Hawaii, 1967-68; owner Rippey Gallery, Bakersfield, 1955, Sea Spirit Gallery, Kapaa, Kauai, Hawaii, 1980-82; dir. exhibits Cunningham Mus., Bakersifled, 1953. One man shows include Lucian Labaudt, San Francisco, Circulo de Belles Artes, Majorca, Spain, Pioneer and Hagen Mus., Stockton, Calif., Hilo Libr., Wailuku Libr., Sea Spirit Gallery, Kauai, Ea. Oreg. Coll. Gallery, The Lighthouse, Hermosa Beach, Calif., Yves Joubent Gallery, Paris, Bakersfield Mus., Calif. State Madigan Gallery, Bakersfield, Babuino Gallery, Rome, Galleria Penanti, Florence, Italy, Galleria Mario Valente, Milan; others; annual one-man show Cezanne Internat., Bakersfield, 1967—; contbr. articles to profl. jours. Mem. Wilderness Soc., Common Cause, Habitat for Humanities, Nature Conservancy, Greenpeace, World Wildlife Fund, Nat. Wildlife Soc. Home and Office: 1908 Creekside Pl Anacortes WA 98221

RIPPLE, WILLIAM JOHN, forestry researcher, educator; b. Yankton, S.D., Mar. 10, 1952; s. John Franklin and Margaret (Sondergroth) R. BS, S.D. State U., 1974; MS, U. Idaho, 1978; PhD, Oreg. State U., 1984. Geographer S.D. State Planning Bur., Pierre, 1977-81; rsch. assoc. Oreg. State U., Corvallis, 1984-88; asst. prof. Forest Resources Dept. Oreg. State U., Corvallis, 1988-92; assoc. prof. forest resources dept. Oreg. State U., Corvallis, 1992—; dir. Environ. Remote Sensing Applications Lab. Oreg. State U., Corvallis, 1988—; cons. U.S. GAO, Washington, 1989. Editor: GIS for Resource Management, 1987, Fundamentals of GIS, 1989; contbr. articles to profl. jour. Active Corvallis Folklore Soc., treas., 1988-91. Mem. Am. Soc. for Photogrammetry and Remote Sensing (Presdl. Citation for Meritorious Svc. 1987, 88, 90), Columbia River Region (treas. 1987-88, v.p. 1988-89, pres. 1989-90). Home: 24549 Evergreen Rd Philomath OR 97370-9565 Office: Oreg State U Dept Forest Resources Corvallis OR 97331

RIRIE, CRAIG MARTIN, periodontist; b. Lewiston, Utah, Apr. 17, 1943; s. Martin Clarence and VaLera (Dixon) R.; m. Becky Ann Ririe, Sept. 17, 1982; children: Paige, Seth, Theron, Kendall, Nathan, Derek, Brian, Amber, Kristen. AA, San Bernadino Valley Coll., 1966; DDS, Creighton U., 1972; MSD, Loma Linda U., 1978. Staff mem. Flagstaff (Ariz.) Med. Ctr., 1974—; pvt. practice dentistry specializing in periodontics Flagstaff, 1974—; assoc. prof. periodontics No. Ariz. U., Flagstaff, 1979—, chmn. dept. dental hygiene, 1980-81; med. research cons. W.L. Gore, Flagstaff, 1983—. Contbr. articles to profl. jours. V.p. bd. dirs. Grand Canyon coun. Boy Scouts Am.,

1991—. Health professions scholarship Creighton U., Omaha, 1969-71; recipient Mosby award Mosby Pub. Co., 1972; research fellowship U. Bergen, Norway, 1978-79. Mem. ADA, Am. Acad. Periodontology (cert.), Western Soc. Periodontology (chmn. com. on research 1982—, bd. dirs. 1983—), No. Ariz. Dental Soc., Am. Acad. Oral Implantologists, Internat. Congress Oral Implantologists, Ariz. Dental Assn., Am. Cancer Soc. (bd. dirs.), Flagstaff C. of C., Rotary. Republican. Mem. LDS Ch. Home: 1320 N Aztec St Flagstaff AZ 86001-3004 Office: 1050 N San Francisco St Flagstaff AZ 86001-3259

RISCHIN, MOSES, historian, educator, history center director; b. N.Y.C., Oct. 16, 1925; s. Meer and Rachel (Nelson) R.; m. Ruth Solomon, Aug. 16, 1959; children: Sarah, Abigail, Rebecca. AB, Bklyn. Coll., 1947; AM, Harvard U., 1948, PhD, 1957. Lectr. UCLA, 1962-64; prof. history San Francisco State U., 1964—; dir. Western Jewish History Ctr. of Judah Magnes Mus., Berkeley, Calif., 1967—; mem. nat. adv. bd. Immigration History Rsch. Ctr., St. Paul, 1974—, Harvard Ency. of Am. Ethnic Groups, 1974-78. Author: The Promised City, 1962 (nominated for Pulitzer prize 1963); editor The American Gospel of Success, 1965, Immigration and the American Tradition, 1976, The Jews of the West: The Metropolitan Years, 1979, The Modern Jewish Experience, 59 vols., 1975, Grandma Never Lived in America: The New Journalism of Abraham Cahan, 1985, The Jews of North America, 1987, Like All the Nations? The Life and Legacy of Judah L. Magnes, 1987, Jews of the American West, 1991, The Jewish Legacy and the German Conscience, 1991; mem. editorial bd. Pacific Hist. Rev., 1974-77, Studies in Am. Jewish Lit., 1975—, Jour. Am. Ethnic History, 1981—. Mem. San Francisco Am. Issues Forum Com., NEH, 1974-76; mem. hist. com. Statue of Liberty-Ellis Island Bicentennial Commn., 1983—. Fellowship Am. Coun. Learned Socs., 1966, Guggenheim Found., 1968, NEH, 1977-78, Fulbright-Hays Commn., 1969, Rockefeller Found., 1984-85. Mem. Immigration History Soc. (pres. 1976-79, exec. bd.), Am. Hist. Assn., Orgn. Am. Historians, Am. Jewish Hist. Soc. Democrat. Jewish. Home: 350 Arballo Dr San Francisco CA 94132-2170 Office: San Francisco State Univ 1600 Holloway Ave San Francisco CA 94132-1722

RISCHIOTTO, ANN MARIE, sales and marketing professional; b. Vancouver, Wash., Dec. 19, 1957; d. Achille and Marie (Vinciquerra) R. BA, U. Portland, 1980. Mktg. intern Liberty Cable TV, Portland, Oreg., 1980-81; sales coord. Columbia Products, Portland, 1981-84; sales rep. Allnet Communications, Portland, 1984-86; asst. v.p. Amtech Communications, Portland, 1986-87; sales mgr. Pace Video Ctr., Portland, 1987-88; sales rep. Diner & Allied Film and Video Svcs., San Francisco, 1988-90; pvt. cons. San Francisco, 1990-92; accounts mgr. EDP Contract Svcs., San Francisco, 1992—. Mem. Delta Epsilon Sigma. Office: 685 Market St Ste 470 San Francisco CA 94105

RISCHITELLI, DONALD GARY, physician; b. Charleroi, Pa., Aug. 19, 1961; s. Dominic Henry and Dorothy Jean (Given) R.; m. Debra Lynn Schrader, June 18, 1988. BA with highest honors, St. Vincent Coll., Latrobe, Pa., 1983; MD, Baylor U., 1987. Intern Emanuel Hosp. and Health Ctr., Portland, Oreg., 1987-88; staff physician Good Samaritan Immediate Care Ctrs., Portland, 1989-92; staff physician Legacy Immediate Care Ctr., Gresham, Oreg., 1989-92, med. dir., 1990-91; med. dir. Mt. Hood Occupational Med. Clinic, Gresham, 1990-92; staff physician Ctr. for Occupational Health Providence Med. Ctr., Portland, 1992—. Mem. Portland Mountain Rescue, 1990. Mem. Am. Coll. Occupational and Environ. Medicine, N.W. Assn. Occupational Medicine, Multnomah County Med. Soc., Oreg. Med. Assn., Am. Pub. Health Assn., Am. Coll. Legal Medicine, ABA, MAZAMAS (rsch. com.), Profl. Assn. Diving Instrs. (divemaster 1987—). Home: 4824 SW Hamilton Ct Portland OR 97221-3059 Office: Providence Med Ctr Ctr for Occupational Health 5050 NE Hoyt Ste 626 Portland OR 97213

RISEBROUGH, DOUG, professional hockey team executive; b. 1954; m. Marilyn Risenbrough; children: Allison, Lindsay. Former player Montreal (Que.) Canadiens, for 8 years; former player Calgary (Alta., Can.) Flames, for 5 years, former asst. coach, 1987-89, asst. gen. mgr., 1989-90, head coach, 1990-92; General Manager Calgary (Alt., Can.) Flames, 1992—. Office: Calgary Flames, PO Box 1540, Calgary, AB Canada T2P 3B9*

RISENHOOVER, TERRY JACK, II, foundation executive, lawyer; b. Oklahoma City, Oct. 30, 1965; s. Terry Jack and Nancy Ellen (Maas) R. BS, Pepperdine U., 1987; MBA, U. Okla., 1988; JD, Vanderbilt U., 1993. Dir. The Crimson Group, Norman, Okla., 1987-88; mgn. dir. Black Marlin Capital, Nashville, 1993—; fin. cons. Merrill Lynch, Oklahoma City, 1988-89; prof. bus. Pepperdine U., Malibu, Calif., 1989-91; dir. fin. Found. 2000, Calabasas, Calif., 1990-91; summer assoc. Day, Hewett & Federman, Oklahoma City, 1993, McKinney, Stringer & Webster, 1992, Gullett, Sanford, Robinson & Martin, Nashville, 1992. League dir. Westlake Athletic Assn., Westlake Village, Calif., 1985-87; mgr. City of Norman Baseball, 1987-89; mem. exec. bd. Coll. Bus. Adminstrn., U. Okla., Norman, 1988-90. Republican. Mem. Ch. of Christ.

RISKAS, MIKE, physical education educator, coach, actor; b. Ely, Nev., June 22, 1934; s. Nicholas Vasiliou and Helen (Massouris) Riskas; m. Barbara Lou Watson, July 16, 1960; children: Michelle Dee Johnston, Steven Dean. BS, U. Calif., L.A., 1958, MS, 1967. Coach football and baseball U. Calif., L.A., 1958-59; freelance actor Hollywood, Calif., 1959—; coach football Alhambra (Calif.) High Sch., 1960; prof. Pomona Coll., Claremont, Calif., 1961—, coach football, 1961-85, coach baseball, 1963-86; course advisor, editor Azusa (Calif.) Pacific Coll., 1972-73; curriculum advisor, editor U. LaVerne, Calif., 1974-79; coach baseball U. Calif., L.A., 1980; baseball clinician Am. Baseball Assn./European Dept. of State, 1970, Am. Baseball Assn./U.S. Olympic Com., Colombia, S.A., 1984, U.S. Baseball Fedn., Eng., 1987; head baseball Coach French Nat. Team, France, 1988; instr. major league baseball envoq, France, 1993. Mem. Am. Football Coaches Assn., Am. Baseball Coaches Assn., Nat. Athletic Intercollegiate Assn. (chmn. div. III 1967, chmn. western region 1985-86), U.S. Baseball Fedn., Internat. Baseball Assn., UCLA 10th Player. Democrat. Greek Orthodox. Office: Pomona Coll 220 E 6th St Claremont CA 91711-6346

RISKIN, ADRIAN BOREAS, mathematician, educator, researcher; b. Westwood, Calif., July 11, 1963; s. William Butler Yeats and Samantha Lynn (Parrish) R.; m. Andrea Laureen Abraham, Nov. 24, 1986; children: Scarlett Rose, Stella Ray. BA, U. Calif., Davis, 1984, MA, 1985, PhD, 1989. Lect. U. Calif., Davis, 1989-90; asst. prof. No. Ariz. U., Flagstaff, 1990—. Contbr. articles to profl. jours. Mem. Math. Assn. Am., Am. Math. Soc. Democrat. Jesuit. Office: No Ariz U Dept Math Flagstaff AZ 86011-5717

RISLEY, LARRY L., air transportation executive. CEO Mesa Airlines. Office: Mesa Airlines 2325 E 30th St Farmington NM 87401

RISLEY, RALPH G., management consultant; b. Carmel, Calif., Mar. 15, 1937; s. Ralph G. and Margaret Mary (Davis) R.; m. Sava Glos, Sept. 29, 1962; children: Eric, Randall, Justin. BS, Columbia U., 1959; MS, U. Wyoming, 1961. Geologist Panhandle Eastern Pipeline Co., 1958-62; engr. Natural Gas Pipeline, 1962-64; sales engr. Norton Co., 1964-68; mgr. Gen. Electric Co., 1968-75; pres. Maine Wood Fuel, 1975-76; asst. to pres., founding shareholder Calif. Energy Co., 1976-81; pres. CUMA Internat., 1981—; dir., adv. Aquatech Svcs. Waste Water processing and volume reduction; pres. shareholder Calif. Transjet; shareholder, adv. Redwood Sanitary Svcs., Calif. Energy Commn., Calif. Pub. Utilities Commn.; chmn., bd. dirs., adv. Pacific Sanitary Svc.; project mgr. Williams Assocs.; counselor Vulcan Power Co.; speaker, advocate in field. active Calif. Air Quality Mgmt. Bd. and Local Dists. Mem. Calif. State Senate Select Com. on Small Bus. Enterprise, State of Maine Economic Devel. Bd., Sonoma County Solid Waste Mgmt. Bd. Republican. Episcopalian. Office: PO Box 724 Santa Rosa CA 95402

RISLEY, TODD ROBERT, educator, scientist; b. Palmer, Alaska, Sept. 8, 1937; s. Robert and Eva Lou (Todd) R.; 1 child, Todd Michael. A.B. with distinction in Psychology, San Diego State Coll., 1960; M.S., U. Wash., 1963, Ph.D., 1966. Asst. prof. psychology Fla. State U., Tallahassee, 1964-65; research assoc. Bur. Child Research, U. Kans., Lawrence, 1965-77, sr. scientist, 1977—, asst. prof. dept. human devel., 1967-69, assoc. prof., 1969-73, prof., 1973-84; prof. psychology U. Alaska, Anchorage, 1982—; pres. Ctr. for Applied Behavior Analysis, 1970-82; dir. Johnny Cake Child Study Ctr., Mansfield, Ark., 1973-74; vis. prof. U. Auckland (N.Z.), 1978; acting dir. Western Carolina Ctr., Morgantown, N.C., 1981; dir. Alaska Div. Mental Health and Devel. Disabilities, 1988-91; cons. in field to numerous orgns. and instns. Co-author: The Infant Center, 1977, Shopping with Children: Advice for Parents, 1978, The Toddler Center, 1979; editor: Jour. Applied Behavior Analysis, 1971-74; mng. editor: Behavior Therapy, The Behavior Therapist, Behavioral Assessment, 1977-80; mem. editorial bds. of numerous profl. jours.; contbr. revs. and numerous articles. Co-chmn. Fla. task force on use of behavioral procedures in state programs for retarded, 1974—; mem. resident abuse investigating com. div. retardation Fla. Dept. Health and Rehab. Services, 1972—; mem. adv. com. Social Research Inst., U. Utah, 1977—; mem. Alaska Gov.'s Council on Handicapped and Gifted, 1983-88, NIH Mental Retardation Research Com., 1987-88, Alaska Mental Health Bd., 1988. Grantee NIMH, 1971-72, 72-73; research grantee Nat. Ctr. Health Services, 1976-79; grantee Nat. Inst. Edn., 1973, NIH, 1967—. Fellow Am. Psychol. Assn. (coun. of reps. 1982-85, pres. div. 25, 1989); mem. AAAS, Am. Psychol. Soc., Am. Assn. Mental Deficiency, Assn. Advancement of Behavior Therapy (dir. 1975-80, pres. 1976-77, chmn. profl. rev. com. 1977—, series editor Readings in Behavior Therapy 1977—), Soc. Behavioral Medicine, Assn. Behavior Analysis, Sigma Xi. Office: U Alaska-Anchorage Dept Psychology 3211 Providence Dr Anchorage AK 99508-4614

RISSEEUW, JOHN LEWIS, art educator; b. Sheboygan, Wis., June 5, 1945; s. Lewis Abraham and Augusta Marie (DeMaster) R.; m. Linda Lee McDonald, July 5, 1969; children: Katherine Melissa, Laura Gabrielle. BS in Art with honors, U. Wis., 1968, MA in Art, 1972, MFA in Art, 1973. Tchr. art and printing Washington Jr. High Sch., Kenosha, Wis., 1968-71; instr. art U. S.D., Vermillion, 1975-78, asst. prof., 1979-80; vis. asst. prof. U. Wis., Madison, 1978-79; asst. prof. Ariz. State U., Tempe, 1980-85, assoc. prof., 1985—, mem. adv. bd. Visual Arts Rsch. Studios, 1984—; propr. Cabbagehead Press, Tempe, 1972—; bd. dirs. Pryacantha Press, Tempe; condr. works, lectr., in field. One-man shows include Tyler Sch. Art, Phila., 1977, Lawrence Gallery, Kansas City, Mo., 1979, U. Wis. Union, 1980, Ariz. State U. Art Mus., 1992, Knoxville (Tenn.) Mus. Art Factory Gallery, 1992; exhibited in numerous group shows, 1972—; represented in permanent collections Ariz. State U. Art Mus., Artpool, Budapest Hungary, Ctr. for Book Arts, N.Y.C., House of Humour & Satire, Gabrovo, Bulgaria, Mpls. Inst. Art, Nat. Baseball Hall of Fame, Brit. Libr., Libr. of Congress, Fudan U., Shanghai, Yale U., Newberry Libr., Chgo., Folger Shakespeare Libr., Bodleian Libr., Oxford, Eng., also numerous others. Recipient Best of Show award Sheboygan Festival Arts, 1971, award for prints Wausau Festival Arts, 1971, Milw. Lakefront Arts Festival, 1973, purchase award Northwestern U., 1979, award of excellence Virginia Beach Arts Ctr., 1979, Best Broadside award Small Press Art Exhbn., 1981, hon. mention San Diego Art Inst., 1991, also others; Vilas fellow U. Wis., 1972-73; rsch. grantee U. S.D., 1977-78; grantee S.D. Arts Coun., 1980, Ariz. State U., 1982, Ariz. Commn. on Arts, 1989; also others. Mem. Am. Printing History Assn., Am. Typecasting Fellowship, Assn. Book Arts Programs, Can. Bookbinders and Book Artists Guild, Ctr. for Book Arts, Educators for Social Responsibility, Internat. Assn. Hand Papermakers and Paper Artists, Pacific Ctr. for Book Arts, Friends Dard Hunter. Home: 1272 E Loma Vista Dr Tempe AZ 85282-2516 Office: Ariz State U Sch Art Tempe AZ 85287-1505

RISSLER, NIEL JUNIOR, publishing executive; b. Manchester, Iowa, Sept. 25, 1923; s. Oscar Raymond and Bessie Olivette (Hogren) R.; m. Dolores Wadene Clevenger, July 18, 1943 (div. 1967); children: Nancy Dee, Niel Dennis, Kim Alan; m. Jessie Harlene Scott, Nov. 11, 1968 (div. Jan. 1985). Grad. high sch., Moline, Ill. Sales rep. McElroy and Prewitt-Food Brokers, Iowa, 1948-52; ptnr., owner, operator Poor Farm/Dinner Club and Deli, Davenport, Iowa, 1952-56; field sales engr. R & R Welding Supply, Des Moines, 1956-62; field sales engr. for Midwest Vasco, 1962-68; ind. broker mobile home fin. various locations, 1968-80; ind. resale broker mobile homes, 1980-86; ptnr., sales coord. Creative Alchohol Awareness Program, Phoenix, 1986-88; owner, editor, pub. Brickwall Bulletin Newsletter, Scottsdale, Ariz., 1988-92; organizer 12-step programs, Ariz. With USAF, 1942-47, ETO. Decorated Air medal. Mem. Alcoholics Anonymous, Sci., Edn., Arts, Rsch. and Complete Health. Lutheran. Office: Brick Wall Pub PO Box 10308 Scottsdale AZ 85271-0308

RISSLING, ROY GERARD, state parole agent; b. Inglewood, Calif., Feb. 10, 1957; s. Ervin Barth and Ruth Helen (Guzinski) R. AA, Crafton Hills Coll., 1977; BA in Criminal Justice, Calif. State U., San Bernardino, 1979, MA in Ednl. Counseling, 1986. Group counselor County of San Bernardino, 1981-89, county probation officer, 1989-90; parole agt. State of Calif., North Hollywood, 1990-92; correctional counselor Calif. Correctional Ctr., Susanville, 1992—. Mem. Calif. Correctional Peace Officer Assn. Democrat. Roman Catholic. Office: Calif Correctional Ctr Susanville CA 96130

RISSO, PATRICIA ANN, history educator. AB, Bryn Mawr (Pa.) Coll., 1972; MA, McGill U., 1976, PhD, 1982. Asst. prof. history Ill. State U., Normal, 1984-86; assoc. prof. history U. N.Mex., Albuquerque, 1986—; chair Asian studies program U. N.Mex., Albuquerque, 1987-92. Mem. Assn. for Asian Studies, Mid. East Studies Assn. Office: U NMex Dept History Albuquerque NM 87131

RISTOW, BRUNO, plastic surgeon; b. Brusque, Brazil, Oct. 18, 1940; came to U.S., 1967, naturalized, 1981; s. Arno and Ally Odette (von Buettner) R.; student Coll. Sinodal, Brazil, 1956-57, Coll. Julio de Castilhos, Brazil, 1957-58; M.D. magna cum laude, U. Brazil, 1966; m. Urania Carrasquilla Gutierrez, Nov. 10, 1979; children by previous marriage: Christian Kilian, Trevor Roland. Intern in surgery Hosp. dos Estrangeiros, Rio de Janeiro, Brazil, 1965, Hospital Estadual Miguel Couto, Brazil, 1965-66, Instituto Aposentadoria Pensão Comerciarios Hosp. for Gen. Surgery, 1966; resident in plastic and reconstructive surgery, Dr. Ivo Pitanguy Hosp. Santa Casa de Misericordia, Rio de Janeiro, 1967; fellow Inst. of Reconstructive Plastic Surgery, N.Y. U. Med. Center, N.Y.C., 1967-68, jr. resident, 1971-72, sr. and chief resident, 1972-73; practice medicine specializing in plastic surgery, Rio de Janeiro, 1967, N.Y.C., 1968-73, San Francisco, 1973—; asst. surgeon N.Y. Hosp., Cornell Med. Center, N.Y.C., 1968-71; clin. instr. surgery N.Y. U. Sch. of Medicine, 1972-73; chmn. plastic and reconstructive surgery div. Presbyn. Hosp., Pacific Med. Center, San Francisco, 1974-92, chmn. emeritus, 1992—. Served with M.C., Brazilian Army Res., 1959-60. Decorated knight Venerable Order of St. Hubertus; Knight Order St. John of Jerusalem; fellow in surgery Cornell Med. Sch., 1968-71; diplomate Am. Bd. Plastic and Reconstructive Surgery. Fellow A.C.S., Internat. Coll. Surgeons; mem. Am. Soc. Aesthetic Plastic Surgery (chmn. edn.), Am. Soc. Plastic and Reconstructive Surgeons, Internat. Soc. Aesthetic Plastic Surgeons, Calif. Soc. Plastic Surgeons, AMA (Physician's Recognition award 1971-83), Calif. Med. Assn., San Francisco Med. Assn. Republican. Mem. Evang. Lutheran Ch. Club: San Francisco Olympic. Contbg. author: Cancer of the Hand, 1975; contbr. articles on plastic surgery to profl. publs. Office: Calif Pacific Med Ctr Pacific Profl Bldg 2100 Webster St Ste 502 San Francisco CA 94115-2381

RITCHEY, SAMUEL DONLEY, JR., retired retail store executive; b. Derry Twp., Pa., July 16, 1933; s. Samuel Donley and Florence Catherine (Litsch) R.; m. Sharon Marie Anderson, Apr. 6, 1956; children: Michael Donley, Tamara Louise, Shawn Christopher. B.S., San Diego State U., 1955, M.S., 1963; postgrad., Stanford U., 1964. With Lucky Stores Inc., 1951-61, 64-86, pres., chief operating officer, 1978-80, pres., chief exec. officer, 1980-81, chmn., chief exec. officer, 1981-85, chmn. bd., 1981-86; bd. dirs. Pacific Telesis, McClatchey Newspapers, De La Salle Inst., Rosenberg, FDT, Hughes Mkts., East Bay Community FDT; grad. mgr. San Diego State U., 1961-63; lectr. in field; adv. coun. grad. sch. bus. Stanford U. Sloan Found. fellow. Mem. Mex. Am. Legal Def. and Edn. Fund, Western Assn. Food Chains (bd. dirs., pres.), Food Mktg. Inst. (bd. dirs., vice chmn.), Sloan Alumni Assn. (adv. bd., pres.). Office: 485 Hartz Ave Ste 105 Danville CA 94526-3416

RITCHIE, BEEDY TATLOW, institute executive; b. Washington, Dec. 14, 1936; d. Richard Henry and Annette (Hart) Tatlow; m. C. Jackson Ritchie, Feb. 20, 1960 (div. 1984); children: Charles Jackson III, Henry Tatlow, Laura Beedy. BS in Bus., U. Colo., 1958; postgrad., Am. U. Asst. to exec. office Presidential Inaugural Com., 1981; exec. dir. Presidential Inaugural Trust, 1981-83; exec. asst. to pres. Wick Fin. Corp., 1981-89; spl. cons. The Am. Film Inst., L.A., 1990, dir. spl. events and community rels., 1991—; hospitality com., spl. events Presidential Com., 1981; asst. to dir. Coalition for a New Begining, 1981; regional dir. ad campaign for Pres. Reagan's Tax Bill, 1981; market rsch. analyst Colgate Palmolive Co., N.Y.C.. Trustee Internat. Visitors Coun. L.A.; mem. nat. alumni admission assistance program U. Colo.; co-chmn. Washington Antiques Show, 1970-89; bd. lady visitors Childrens Hosp. Nat. Med. Ctr., Washington, 1972-88. Mem. U. Colo. L.A. Alumni (dir.), L.A. Athletic Club, Chevy Chase Club, Sulgrave Club, Little Falls Swim Club, Colonial Dames of Am., Delta Gamma, Jr. League L.A. Home: 2102 Century Park Ln Los Angeles CA 90067 Office: The Am Film Inst 2021 N Western Ave Los Angeles CA 90027

RITCHIE, DANIEL LEE, university administrator; b. Springfield, Ill., Sept. 19, 1931; s. Daniel Felix and Jessie Dee (Binney) R. B.A., Harvard U., 1954, M.B.A., 1956. Exec. v.p. MCA, Inc., Los Angeles, 1967-70; pres. Archon Pure Products Co., Los Angeles, 1970-73; exec. v.p. Westinghouse Electric Corp., Pitts., 1975-78; pres. corp. staff and strategic planning Westinghouse Broadcasting Co., 1978-79, pres., chief exec. officer, 1979-81, chmn., chief exec. officer; chmn., chief exec. officer Westinghouse Broadcasting & Cable, Inc., 1981-87; owner Grand River Ranch, Kremmling, Colo., 1977—, Rancho Cielo, Montecito, Calif., 1977—; chancellor U. Denver, 1989—. With U.S. Army, 1956-58. Office: U Denver Office of the Chancellor University Park Denver CO 80208

RITCHIE, ERIC ROBERT DAVID, manufacturing engineering executive; b. Belfast, No. Ireland, Jan. 11, 1942; came to U.S., 1968; BME, Gen. Motors Inst., 1967; MSME, Union Coll., 1972. Registered profl. engr. Iowa, N.Y., Oreg. Process engr. GM of Can. Ltd., 1964-68; mgr. plant engring. GE, Schenectady, N.Y., 1968-73, mgr. internat. facilities, 1973-78; mgr. plant engring. services John Deere Waterloo Works, Waterloo, Iowa, 1978-85; mgr. materials engring. John Deere Component Works, Waterloo, 1985-89; ops. mgr. Garrett Products Automotrices, Mexicali, Mexico, 1989-90; corp. mfg. engring. mgr. Sulzer Bingham Pumps Inc.,, Portland, Oreg., 1990—. Active planning and allocation com. Cedar Valley United Way, Waterloo, 1986-89; elder, session leader, State St. Presbyn. Ch., Schenectady, 1972-78, Immanuel Presbyn. Ch., Waterloo, 1979-82, First Presbyn. Ch., Portland, Oreg., 1993—; mem. Mayors Commn. Mcpl. Power, Waterloo, 1987-88. Mem. ASHRAE, Soc. Automotive Engrs., Am. Soc. Metals. Republican. Office: Sulzer Bingham Pumps Inc 2800 NW Front Ave PO Box 10247 Portland OR 97210

RITCHIE, JOHN BENNETT, real estate executive; b. West Point, N.Y., Sept. 23, 1924; s. Isaac and Charlotte (Bennett) R.; B.A., Yale, 1946; postgrad. student George Washington U., 1946-47, U. Wash. Law Sch., 1948-50; m. Suzanne Raisin, Dec. 27, 1952; children—Randolph, Charlotte, Mark, Victoria. Pres. Ritchie & Ritchie Corp., indsl. and comml. realtors, San Francisco, Oakland, San Jose, Sacramento, Walnut Creek, Calif., Ritchie & Ritchie Ins. Brokers, Inc.; v.p. Cotton-Ritchie Corp., San Diego, Ritchie MacFarland Corp., Portland, Oreg.; owner, trustee Ritchie-Chancery Bldg., Barrett-Ritchie Block, Ritchie & Ritchie Devel. Co., Ritchie Western Mortgage Corp., Ritchie Western Equities Co.; past mem. San Francisco Planning Commn.; past mem. San Francisco Landmarks Bd.; hon. counsul Uruguay. With AUS. Mem. Soc. Indsl. Realtors, Calif. Assn. of Realtors (v.p. 1967), San Francisco (pres. 1966), Oakland, San Jose real estate bds., Calif. Hist. Soc. (pres. 1973), Japan Soc. San Francisco (pres. 1976). Republican. Mem. Ch. of Jesus Christ of Latter-day Saints (elder). Clubs: Presidio Golf (San Francisco); Tahoe Yacht (Lake Tahoe); Alta (Salt Lake City); Brook (N.Y.); Caledonian (London); Outrigger Canoe (Honolulu). Home: 2 Presidio Ter San Francisco CA 94118-1411 also: 209 S Meadow Rd Glenbrook NV 89413 also: 989 Rutherford Cross Rd Rutherford CA 94573 also: Penthouse Niihau Apts 247 Beachwalk Waikiki Honolulu HI 96815 Office: 41 Sutter St 200 Ritchie Chancery Bldg San Francisco CA 94104 also: 401 15th St Oakland CA 94612 also: 34 W Santa Clara St San Jose CA 95113 also: 233 A St Ste 1400 San Diego CA 92101 also: 133 SW 2d Ave Portland OR 97204

RITCHIE, MARK ELLIS, ecology educator; b. San Antonio, Aug. 26, 1960; s. Kenneth Marvin and Amy Beth (Sterling) R.; m. Estelle Davis, July 5, 1992. AB, Ind. U., 1981; MS, U. Mich., 1983, PhD in Natural Resources, 1987. Rackham fellow U. Mich., Ann Arbor, 1987, vis. lectr., 1988-89; postdoctoral rsch. assoc. U. Minn., Mpls., 1989-90; asst. prof. Utah State U., Logan, 1991—; mem. rsch. com. Sch. Natural Resources, U. Mich., Ann Arbor, 1987; mem. undergrad. curriculum com. Utah State U., Logan, 1991—. Author: (with others) Wildlife 2001: Populations, 1992; reviewer jour. articles and books Jour. Mammalogy, Decologia, Quar. Rev. Biology; contbr. articles to profl. jours. Mem., contbr. Emotions Anonymous, Blaine, Minn., 1989-90. Grantee NSF, 1990, Utah Agrl. Exptl. Sta., 1992—. Mem. Wildlife Soc., Ecol. Soc. Am., Soc. Am. Naturalists, AAAS, Soc. for the Study of Evolution, Orthopterists' Soc., Cache Velo Bicycling Club. Home: 705 Park Dr Hyrum UT 84321 Office: Dept Fisheries and Wildlife Dept Fisheries and Wildlife Utah State U Logan UT 84322-5210

RITCHIE, ROBERT OLIVER, materials science educator; b. Plymouth, Devon, U.K., Jan. 2, 1948; came to U.S., 1974; s. Kenneth Ian and Kathleen Joyce (Sims) R.; m. Connie Olesen (div. 1978); 1 child, James Oliver. BA with honors, U. Cambridge, Eng., 1969, MA, PhD, 1973, ScD, 1990. Cert. engr. Goldsmith's rsch. fellow Churchill Coll. U. Cambridge, 1972-74; Miller fellow in basic rsch. sci. U. Calif., Berkeley, 1974-76; assoc. prof. mech. engring. MIT, Cambridge, 1977-81; prof. U. Calif., Berkeley, 1981—; dir. Ctr. for Advanced Materials Lawrence Berkeley Lab., Cambridge, 1987—; dep. dir. materials sci. div. Lawrence Berkeley Lab., Berkeley, 1990—; cons. Alcan, Chevron, Exxon, GE, Grumman, Instron, Northrop, Rockwell, Westinghouse, Baxter, Carbonmedics, Carbon Implants, Med. Inc., Shiley, St. Jude Med. Editor six books; contbr. over 200 articles to profl. jours. Recipient Curtis W. McGraw Rsch. award Am. Soc. Engring. Educators, 1987, Mathewson Gold medal Minerals, Materials, Metals, Soc., 1985; named one of Top 100 Scientists, Sci. Digest mag., 1984. Fellow Inst. Materials (London), Am. Soc. Metals Internat., Internat. Congress on Fracture (hon., v.p.); mem. Minerals, Materials and Metals Soc., Am. Orchid Soc. Home: 590 Grizzly Peak Blvd Berkeley CA 94708-1238 Office: Lawrence Berkeley Lab MS-66-247 One Cyclotron Rd Berkeley CA 94720

RITCHIE, THOMAS HARALD, game company executive; b. Whittier, Calif., Aug. 4, 1962; s. William Leroy and Deborah (Magdelena) R.; m. Christine Francis Albrycht, June 22, 1991. BS in Math., U. Utah, 1986. CEO Classified Info., Salt Lake City, 1987—. Author: (game) Belter, 1990. Office: Classified Info PO Box 39 Sandy UT 84091

RITER, EMANUEL, retailer, consultant; b. N.Y.C., Oct. 19, 1927; s. Samuel and Eva (Malin) R.; m. Barbara Damast, Aug. 24, 1958; children: Evan, Jill. BBA, Columbia U., 1950; MS, NYU, 1953. Br. mgr. B. Gertz, N.Y.C., 1950-55; asst. gen. br. mgr. Lansburgh's, Washington, 1955-60; div. mgr. Winkelman's, Detroit, 1960-67, Lane Bryant, N.Y.C., 1967-72; pres., owner, mgr. Adorable Shops, San Diego, 1972-84; gen. mdse. mgr. Pacific Eyes, San Diego, 1985; gen. br. mgr. The Union, Columbus, Ohio, 1986-87; mdse. controller Weekend Exercise Co., San Diego, 1988-89, Clothestime, Anaheim, Calif., 1990-92; cons. in field. Bd. dirs. Mission Valley Mdse. Assn., San Diego, 1973-76; bd. dir. North Park Merchants Assn., San Diego, 1972-84; mem. Westchester Symphony, N.Y., 1967-72. Recipient N.Y. State scholarship, 1950-52. Mem. Masons.

RITMAN, BARBARA ELLEN, counselor; b. L.A., Oct. 19, 1946; d. Jack and June Harriett (Marcus) R. AA, Long Beach City Coll., 1969; BA (magna cum laude), Calif. State U., Long Beach, 1974; MA, Chapman Coll., 1976. Lic. marriage, family and child counselor. Instr. Mt. San Antonio Coll., Walnut, Calif., 1976-78; mental health worker Orange County (Calif.) Mental Health, 1978-80; therapist Family Svc., Long Beach, Calif., 1980-82; clin. dir. Neighborhood Youth Assn., Wilmington, Calif., 1981-88; head psychology svcs. Bellflower (Calif.) Med. Group, 1988-89; chem. dependency counselor Kaiser Permanente, Anaheim, Calif., 1990—; cons. Child Abuse Info. Ctr., L.A., 1976-78, Action Seminars for Progress, Santa Monica, Calif., 1976-82. Fellow mem. Calif. Assn. Marriage & Family Therapists. Office: Kaiser Permanente Chem Dependency Recovery Program 4201 W Chapman Ave Orange CA 92668

RITSCHARD, HANS VICTOR, clinical psychologist; b. Mt. Holly, N.J., Nov. 28, 1961; s. John Arnold and Carol Elise (Raymond) R.; m. Carolyn Marie McAlpin, Oct. 4, 1986; children: John Erik, Paul Victor. BS in Chemistry, Rensselaer Polytech Inst., 1985; MA in Theology, Fuller Theol. Sem., 1992. Assoc. staff chemist GE Corp. Rsch. & Devel. Ctr., Schenectady, N.Y., 1985-88; staff asst. Relational Dynamics Inst., Sierra Madre, Calif., 1989-91; med. psychology intern Huntington Meml. Hosp., Pasadena, Calif., 1991-92; commd. capt. USAF, Biomedical Health Sci. Corp., 1993—; cons. in field. Contbr. to books and articles to profl. jours.; patentee in field. Co-founder Enabling the Missionary, Pasadena, 1989. Headington Meml. scholar, 1991; recipient Stauffer fellow award Fuller Theol. Sem., 1992, Travis award Fuller Theol. Sem., 1991. Mem. Am. Psychol. Assn. (student affiliate), Am. Assn. Christian Counselors, Christian Assn. Psychol. Studies (student affiliate), Western Psychol. Assn. (student affiliate). Republican. Presbyterian. Home: 597 E Claremont St Pasadena CA 91104 Office: Fuller Theol Sem 134 N Oakland Ave Pasadena CA 91101

RITTENBACH, GAIL SYLVIA, education educator; b. Walla Walla, Wash., Mar. 16, 1948; d. Vernon Lee and Imogene (Davis) Perry; m. Gary James Rittenbach, July 5, 1970; children: Jon Vernon, Suzanne Dee, Alexander Philip. BA in English, Pacific Union Coll., 1970; MEd, U. Wash., Seattle, 1979, PhD in Edn., 1986. Tchr. Monterey Bay Acad., Watsonville, Calif., 1973-76, Auburn (Wash.) Acad., 1976-86; prof. edn. Walla Walla Coll., College Place, Wash., 1986—; chair rank and tenure com. Walla Walla Coll. Author short stories and poetry. Actor in corp. giving video Office of Devel., Walla Walla Coll., 1990—; bd. dirs. Kind-Hearts Children's Village, Ethiopia, Project Read, Walla Walla. Mem. Internat. Reading Assn., ASCE, Nat. Coun. of Tchrs. of Sci. Home: 240 Newtown Rd Walla Walla WA 99362 Office: Walla Walla Coll 208 Smith College Place WA 99324-1449

RITTENBERG, MARC A., sales and marketing executive; b. Cambridge, Mass., Jan. 27, 1945; s. Nathan J. and Dorothy (Gertman) R.; m. Terry A. Learner, Aug. 18, 1968 (div. 1971); 1 child, Mathew A.; m. Susan M. Aupperle, Aug. 31, 1990. BA, Northeastern U., 1968. Mgmt. trainee The Learner Co., Inc., Oakland, Calif., 1968-70; pers. rep. Hunt-Wesson Foods, Hayward, Calif., 1971-72; salesman Trans Oceanic Shipping, Oakland, Calif., 1973-74; owner, mgr. The Icecream Man's Pvt. Stock, Willits, Calif., 1976-80; sales rep. Dunlap Electronics, Sacramento, 1980-82, Dynasty Industries, San Jose, Calif., 1984-86; sales trainer Cal-Pac Roofing Inc., San Jose, 1987-88; corp. dir. mktg. and sales Western Sierra Indsl. Group Inc., Fremont, Calif., 1988-90; v.p. sales and mktg. Superior Systems, San Jose, Calif., 1990-91; v.p. sales & mktg. Fidelity-Pacific Inc., Santa Clara, Calif., 1991; pres., CEO Canadian Pacific Roofing Inc., San Jose, 1992—; cons. Cal Pac L.A., 1987-88. Editor Western Sierra Sentinel, newsletter, 1989. With USCG, 1967-68. Home: 1666 Trona Way San Jose CA 95125-5056 Office: Candadian Pacific Roofing Inc 1750 Meridian Ave Ste 5914 San Jose CA 95150

RITTENHOUSE, CARL HARRIS, psychologist; b. Garden City, S.D., Feb. 17, 1922; s. Carl Harris and Helen Alice (Doxrude) R.; m. Marilyn Jeanne Hawkins, Sept. 24, 1947; children—Eric Carl, Christine Amanda. B.A., Stanford U., 1947, M.A., 1949, Ph.D., 1951. Lic. psychologist, Calif. Research psychologist U.S. Air Force, Lowry AFB Colo., 1951-53; research scientist Human Resources, Monterey, Calif., 1953-58; head tng. group Philco Western Devel. Labs., Palo Alto, Calif., 1958-59; research psychologist Stanford Research Inst., 1959-66; asst. dir. edn. dept. SRI Internat. Menlo Park, Calif., 1966-78; cons. Oreg. Shakespeare Festival Assn., 1978-79; Rockwell-Patterson, Palo Alto, 1978-79; mng. ptnr. Roth-Kolker-Rittenhouse Assocs., 1979-82. Contbr. articles to profl. jours. Mem. Am Psychol. Assn., Phi Beta Kappa, Sigma Xi. Democrat. Lutheran.

RITTENHOUSE, DONNA JEAN, small business owner; b. Henlawson, W.Va., July 10, 1934; d. John Jasper Henry and Anna (Zekany) Allee; m. Donald Wilson Lynch Jr., Dec. 23, 1952 (div. Dec. 18, 1968); children: Guy Joseph, Kim Elizabeth Cross; m. Reginald Roy Rittenhouse, July 7, 1973; children: Dwanda Leah O'Connor, Donald LeRoy Rittenhouse. Student, Cypress Jr. Coll., 1965-66; EMT, Clark County Community Coll., Las Vegas, 1985. Heraldry shop owner Rittenhouse Family Coat of Arms, 1964-87; heraldry columnist Nev. Times News Paper, Las Vegas, 1991-92; pvt. investigator freelance Las Vegas, 1982-87; res. dep. sheriff Nye County Sheriffs Dept., Pahrump, Nev., 1985-86; EMT Pahrump Vol. Fire Dept., 1986-87, vol. firefighter, 1985-87; investigative reporter, columnist Gateway Gazette Newspaper, Pahrump, 1987-89; owner Rittenhouse Family Coats-of-Arm, Las Vegas, 1990—; cons. in field. Contbr. articles to profl. jours. Historian Pahrump Valley PTA, 1985. Office: Rittenhouse Coat of Arms 1190 S Mojave Rd #306 Las Vegas NV 89104

RITTER, DALE F., geologist, research association administrator; b. Allentown, Pa., Nov. 13, 1932; s. C. Century and Elizabeth (Bowden) R.; m. Jacqueline Leh, Aug. 15, 1953 (div. Jan. 1961); children: Duane, Darryl, Glen; m. Esta Virginia Lewis, Nov. 23, 1962; 1 child, Lisa Diane. BA in Edn., Franklin and Marshall Coll., 1955, BS in Geology, 1959; MS in Geology, Princeton U., 1963, PhD in Geology, 1964. From asst. to assoc. prof. geology Franklin and Marshall Coll., Lancaster, Pa., 1964-72; prof. geology So. Ill. U., Carbondale, 1972-90; exec. dir. Quaternary Sci. Ctr. Desert Rsch. Inst., Reno, Nev., 1990—. Author: Process Geomorphology, 2d edit., 1986. Fellow NSF, 1968-69; recipient Lindback award Disting. Teaching, Lindback Found., 1970, Outstanding Teaching award Amoco Found., 1979. Fellow Geological Soc. Am. (chmn. quaternary geology divsn. 1988-890; mem. Am. Quaternary Assn., Assn. Am. Geographers, Yellowstone-Big Horn Rsch. Assn. (pres. 1983-85). Office: Quaternary Sci Ctr Desert Rsch Inst 7010 Dandini Blvd Reno NV 89512

RITTER, DALE WILLIAM, obstetrician, gynecologist; b. Jersey Shore, Pa., June 17, 1919; s. Lyman W. and Weltha B. (Packard) Ritter; m. Winnie Mae Bryant, Nov. 13, 1976; children—Eric, Lyman, Michael, Gwendolyn, Daniel. A.B., UCLA, 1942; M.D., U. So. Calif., 1946. Diplomate Am. Bd. Obstetrics and Gynecology. Intern Los Angeles County Hosp., L.A., 1945-46, resident, 1949-52, admitting room resident, 1948-52; pvt. practice medicine specializing in obstetrics and gynecology, Chico, Calif., 1952—; founder, mem. staff, past chmn. bd. dirs. Chico Community Meml. Hosp.; guest lectr. Chico State Coll., 1956—; mem. staffs Enole Hosp., Chico, 1952—, Glenn Gen. Hosp., Willows, Calif., 1953—, Gridley Meml. Hosp., Calif., 1953-80; spl. cons. obstetrics Calif. Dept. Pub. Health, No. Calif., 1958-70. Contbr. articles to med. and archeol. jours. Bd. dirs. No. dist. Children's Home Soc., Chico, 1954-70. Served with AUS, 1943-45, with M.C., AUS, 1946-48. Paul Harris fellow Rotary Internat. 1989. Fellow ACS, Am. Coll. Obstetrics and Gynecology; mem. AMA, Calif. Med. Assn., Internat. Soc. Hypnosis, Am. Soc. Clin. Hypnosis, Am. Fertility Soc., Pacific Coast Fertility Soc., Assn. Am. Physicians and Surgeons, Pvt. Drs. of Am., Butte-Glenn County Med. Soc. (past pres.), Am. Cancer Soc. (former bd. dirs. Butte County), AAAS, Christian Med. Soc., Am. Assn. Pro-Life Obstetricians and Gynecologists, Butte-Glenn County Tumor Bd., Anthrop. Assn. Am., Archaeol. Inst. Am., Soc. Calif. Archaeology, Oreg. Archaeology Soc., Archeol. Survey Assn., Southwestern Anthrop. Soc., Am. Rock Art Rsch. Assn., Australian Rock Art Rsch. Assn., Internat. Assn. for Study of Prehistoric and Ethnologic Religions, Fretted Instrument Guild Am. (dir. Banjo Kats 'n Jammers), North Valley Banjo Band, Am. Philatelic Soc., Am. Horse Council, Am. Horse Shows Assn., Internat. Peruvian Horse Assn., Peruvian Paso Horse Registry of N.Am.., Assn. Owners Breeders Peruvian Paso Horses, Phi Chi, Lambda Sigma, Zeta Beta Sigma. Republican. Lodge: Rotary. Office: 572 Rio Lindo Ave Chico CA 95926-1851

RITTER, DIANNE MARIE, immunologist, researcher; b. Buffalo, Apr. 5, 1959; d. John Alan and Martha Jane (Simons) R.; m. Donald Bruce Hawthorne, Oct. 7, 1989; 1 child, Meghan Elizabeth Hawthorne. BS, SUNY, Fredonia, 1981; MS, U. Akron, 1984; PhD, Wake Forest U., 1988. Rsch. technician Sloan Kettering, Rye, N.Y., 1983-84; postdoctoral fellow Stanford U., Palo Alto, Calif., 1988-90, U. Calif., San Francisco, 1991—. Contbr. articles to profl. jours. NIH grantee, 1988-91; Sigma Xi grantee, 1987. Mem. Am. Assn. Immunologists, Am. Soc. Parasitologists, Am. Soc. Tropical Medicine and Hygiene, No. Calif. Soc. Parasitologists, Southeastern Soc. Parasitologists, Sigma Xi. Office: U Calif at San Francisco Bldg 2 Rm 360 4150 Clement Ave MC 113B San Francisco CA 94121

RITTER, RUSSELL JOSEPH, mayor, college official; b. Helena, Mont., July 22, 1932; s. Walter A. and Sally C. (Mellen) R.; m. Linaire Wells, Aug. 4, 1956; children—Michael, Leslie, Teresa, Gregory, Daniel. Student Carroll Coll., Helena, 1950-53; A.B. in History, U. Mont.-Missoula, 1957, M.A. in History and Polit. Sci., 1962, postgrad. in History, 1963. Salesman, Capital Ford, 1953-54, 56-57; tchr., coach Billings (Mont.) Central High Sch., 1957-58, Loyola High Sch., Missoula, 1958-62, Flathead High Sch., Kalispell, Mont., 1962-69; dir. devel. and community relations Carroll Coll., Helena, 1969-76, v.p. for coll. relations, 1976-91; dir. Goot Corp.- Rels. Washington Corp., 1991—; commr. City of Helena, 1977-80, mayor pro-tem, 1980, mayor, 1981—; exec. sec.-treas. Carroll Coll. Found., Inc.; owner Danny's Drive In, Kalispell, 1965-69; ptnr. R-B Enterprises, Inc., Kalispell, 1967-71; bd. dirs. Brubaker & Assos., Inc., Kalispell, 1971-74; v.p. Capital Investment, Inc. (KMTX Radio), Helena, 1973-80; pres. Swinging Door Art Gallery, Inc., Helena, 1973—; bd. dirs. Norwest Bank of Helena. Bd. dirs. All Am. Indian Hall of Fame, 1972-78, Jr. Achievement, 1975-79, Mont. Physicians Service, 1984-86, Blue Cross/Blue Shield Mont., 1986—, Mont. C. of C., chmn., Mont. Community Fin. Corp., 1986; bd. govs. Montt. Spl. Olympics, 1984-86; mem. Citizen's Adv. Council, 1975-76; chmn. City-County Bldg., Inc., 1978; mem. Mont. Friendship Force; co-chmn. Mont. Centenial Celebration. Served with USMC, 1953-56. Mem. Helena C. of C. (dir. 1972-75, v.p. 1973, pres. 1974, Ambassador's Club 1976—, chmn. 1978), Mont. Ofcls. Assn., Mont. Ambassadors (Ambassador of Yr. 1986, bd. dirs. 1989, 2d v.p. 1989, pres. 1991). Club: Montana. Lodge: K.C. (4th degree). Office: PO Box 5476 Helena MT 59604-5476

RITTMANN, PAUL DOUGLAS, health physicist; b. Mpls., Nov. 5, 1949; s. Donald Clarence and Jeanette Alice (Pearce) R.; m. Barbara Ann Behrmann, Oct. 16, 1976; children: Daniel Albert Rittmann, Erika Beth Rittmann. BA in Physics, U. Wis., 1971; MS in Physics, Purdue U., 1973, PhD in Theoretical Physics, 1976. Am. Bd. Health Physics, 1984. Instr. U.S. Naval Nuclear Power Sch., Orlando, Fla., 1976-80; radiological engr. Rockwell Hanford Co., Richland, Wash., 1980-87; prin. engr. Westinghouse Hanford Co., Richland, Wash., 1987—. contbr. articles to profl. jours. Mem. IBM and Compatible PC User's Group, Kennewick, 1989. Lt. Naval Res., 1976-80. Mem. Health Physics Soc. Republican. Home: 5001 W Skagit Ave Kennewick WA 99336 Office: Westinghouse Hanford Co PO Box 1970 Richland WA 99352

RIVENBURG, ROY, journalist; b. Phoenix, June 1, 1958; s. Roy P. and Mary Ann (Bishop) R. BA in Comm., Calif. State U., 1981; MS in Journalism, Columbia U., 1985. Contbg. editor Orange Coast Mag., Irvine, Calif., 1981-84; editor The Beacon, Dana Point, Calif., 1982-83; copy editor The Press-Enterprise, Riverside, Calif., 1986, The Orange County Register, Santa Ana, Calif., 1986-88; reporter Times Advocate, Escondido, Calif., 1988-91; freelance writer, 1991-92; reporter L.A. Times, 1992—. Author: (with others) Fearfully, Wonderfully, Weird-The Wittenburg Door's Greatest Hits, 1990. Recipient 1st Pl. Investigative Reporting, Soc. Profl. Journalists, 1988, 3d Pl. Feature Writing, 1989. Roman Catholic.

RIVERA, ARMANDO REMONTE, utilities engineer; b. Oas, Albay, Philippines, Jan. 27, 1940; came to U.S., 1969; s. Venanclo Rey Rivera and Eugenia (Raneses) Remonte; m. Carmelita Lim Chan, Dec. 11, 1971. BSME, U. of the Philippines, Quezon City, 1962; MBA, U. of the Philippines, Manila, 1967; postgrad., U. So. Calif., L.A., 1972. Registered profl. engr., Calif. Engr. Fluor Corp., L.A., 1969-71; energy svcs. engr. So. Calif. Edison Co., Rosemead, Calif., 1972-76; project engr. Aramco Overseas Co., Hague, Netherlands, 1976-82, London, 1982-84; sr. project engr. electric systems Anaheim (Calif.) Pub. Utilities, 1984—. EPA grantee U. So. Calif., 1972. Mem. ASME, Am. Assn. Cost Engrs., Nat. Soc. Profl. Engrs. Democrat. Roman Catholic. Home: 1523 N Pacific Ave Glendale CA 91202-1213 Office: Anaheim Pub Utilities 201 S Anaheim Blvd Anaheim CA 92805-9999

RIVERA, VICTOR MANUEL, retired bishop; b. Penuelas, P.R., Oct. 30, 1916; s. Victor and Filomena (Toro) R.; m. Barbara Ross Starbuck, Dec. 1944; 3 children. Student, Modern Bus. Coll. P.R., 1937, DuBose Meml. Ch. Tng. Sch., 1938; B.D., Ch. Div. Sch. Pacific, 1944, D.D., 1965; postgrad., St. Augustine Coll., Eng., 1957. Ordained deacon Episcopal Ch., 1943, priest, 1944; curate St. John's Cathedral, Santurce, P.R., 1944; rector St. Paul's Ch., Visalia, Calif., 1945-68; bishop San Joaquin, Fresno, Calif., 1968-88.

RIVERMAN, RYLLA CLAIRE, nurse, sales executive, health association administrator; b. Brewster, Wash., Apr. 16, 1955; d. Francis William and Helen Edna (Caldwell) Hicks; m. Brian Matthew Riverman, Nov. 2, 1985. BS in Nursing, Walla Walla Coll., 1978. RN. Nurse Portland (Oreg.) Adventist Med. Ctr., 1978-80; dir. pub. affairs Seaside (Oreg.) Gen. Hosp., 1980-82; pub. affairs assoc. Providence Child Ctr., Portland, 1982-83; utilization rev. coordinator St. Vincent Hosp., Portland, 1983-88; dir. internal ops. Metrocare Adminstrv. Svcs., Beaverton, Oreg., 1988-89; v.p. ETHIX Corp., Beaverton, Oreg., 1989—; lectr. Portland Community Coll., 1983—, Walla Walla Coll., 1983-85, 87, Portland Bus. Group on Health, 1987. Contbr. articles to profl. jours. Mem. Pacific St. Neighbor Watch, Portland, 1986—, Mansfield (Wash.) Grange # 883, 1976—, World Forestry Ctr., Portland, 1986—; chairperson employee fundraising United Way, 1986-87. Recipient Merit award St. Vincent Med. Found., Portland, 1986, U.S. flag for community service, U.S. Senate, Washington, 1982. Mem. Am. Bd. Quality Assurance and Utilization Rev. (diplomate), NW Healthcare Roundtable (v.p. 1984-85, pres. 1985-87, bd. dirs. 1987—, Merit award 1988). Republican. Home: 612 NE 144th Ave Vancouver WA 98684-8018 Office: ETHIX Corp 12655 SW Center St Beaverton OR 97005-1601

RIVERS, LAWRENCE ALAN, marketing professional; b. Sulphur, La., Mar. 26, 1956; s. Lawrence Harrison Jr. and Lois (Miller) R.; m. Roberta Choat, Oct. 7, 1978. B in Law Enforcement, La. State U., 1978; MS, Troy State U., 1982; JD, Tulane U., 1985. Bar: Colo., Calif., Tex. Assoc. Organ, Bell & Tucker, Beaumont, Tex., 1985-87, Benton, Orr, Duval & Buckingham, Ventura, Calif., 1987-88; mktg. mgr. Santa Barbara Rsch. Ctr./Hughes Aircraft, Goleta, Calif., 1988—; instr. U. LaVerne, 1992—. Mem. Gen. Plan Adv. Com., Lompoc, Calif., 1991-92, Cable TV Com., Lompoc, 1991—. With U.S. Army, 1978-82; maj. USAR, 1982—. Named Outstanding Young Man in Am., 1987. Mem. Calif. State Bar, Tex. State Bar, Colo. State Bar. Republican. Baptist. Home: 1216 Iris Ct Lompoc CA 93436 Office: SBRC 75 Coromar Dr Goleta CA 93117

RIVERS, RICHARD DOUGLAS, JR., political scientist; b. Louisville, Ky., June 7, 1956; s. Richard Douglas and Martha (Terstegge) R.; m. Sarah Simons, June 25, 1983. BA, Columbia U., 1977; PhD, Harvard U., 1981. Asst. prof. polit. sci. Harvard U., Cambridge, Mass., 1980-83; asst. prof. Calif. Inst. Tech., Pasadena, Calif., 1983-87; assoc. prof. UCLA, 1987-89; prof. Stanford (Calif.) U., 1989—; mem. bd. overseers Nat. Election Studies, Ann Arbor, Mich., 1987—. Contbr. numerous articles to profl. jours. Fellow Ctr. for Advanced Studies in Behavioral Scis., Stamford, 1992-93. Democrat. Office: Stanford U Dept Polit Sci Stanford CA 94305

RIVETT, ROBERT WYMAN, retired pharmaceutical company executive; b. Omaha, Jan. 20, 1921; s. Paul S. and Frances E. (Wyman) R.; m. Myra Jean Bevins, Oct. 18, 1940; children: Suzanne, Teresa, Paul. BS, U. Nebr., 1942, MS, 1943; PhD, U. Wis., 1946. Rsch. microbiologist Abbott Labs., North Chicago, Ill., 1946-48, sect. head antibiotic devel., 1948-57, asst. dir. devel., 1958-59, dir. devel., 1960-64, dir. rsch. adminstrn., 1964-71, dir. corp. quality assurance, 1971-76, dir. quality assurance agr. vet. div., 1976-77; dir. quality assurance Abbott sci. products divsn. Abbott Labs., L.A., 1977-78; v.p. quality assurance Alpha Therapeutic Corp., L.A., 1978-81; cons. chem. and chem. engring. RWR Cons., San Gabriel, Calif., 1982-88. Mem. Waukegan (Ill.) Sch. Bd., 1955-60; former warden Ch. of Our Saviour, San Gabriel. Mem. Am. Chem. Soc., Elk. Republican. Address: 3303 Taos Ct Deming NM 88030

RIZVI, TANZEEM R., electrical engineer; b. Lahore, Pakistan, July 9, 1949; came to U.S., 1975; s. Syed Rafiq Hassan and Haseena Rizvi; m. Hina KSardar, Feb. 9, 1982; children: Shan, Asad. BSEE, U. Peshawar, Pakistan, 1970; MSEE, U. So. Calif., 1977. Registered profl. engr., Calif., Alaska, Oreg. Asst. exec. engr. Karachi (Pakistan) Electric Supply Corp., 1971-75; field designer Fischback and Moore Inc., L.A., 1975-77; project engr. Crews MacInnes and Hoffman/Vitro Inc., Anchorage, 1977-80; project mgr., lead engr. Standard Oil Co. Inc., Anchorage, 1980-85; project mgr. Alaska Power Authority, Anchorage, 1985-88; prin. Engring. Cons. Internat., Tustin, Calif., 1988—. Mem. IEEE (chmn. Alaska sect. 1980-81, mem. nat. engrs. week edn. com. 1986), Alaska Profl. Design Council (bd. dirs. 1979-81), Nat. Soc. Profl. Engrs., Power Engrs. Soc., Communication Soc., Nordic Ski Club, Bridge Club. Home and Office: PO Box 3263 Tustin CA 92680

RIZZI, TERESA MARIE, bilingual speech and language pathologist; b. Denver, Aug. 8, 1964; d. Theophilus Marcus and Maudie Marie (Pitts) R. BA in Speech Pathology, U. Denver, 1986, BA in Spanish, 1986; MS in Speech Pathology, Vanderbilt U., 1988. Pediatric speech-lang. pathologist Rose Med. Ctr., Denver, 1988-90; pvt. practice Denver, 1990—; Spanish tchr. Temple Emanuel, Denver, 1992—; owner, operator Niños De Colo., Denver; Spanish tutor and interpreter, Denver, 1988—. G'arin grantee Ctl. Agency Jewish Edn., 1993. Mem. Am. Speech-Lang.-Hearing Assn. (Continuing Edn. award 1991), Colo. Speech-Lang.-Hearing Assn., Internat. Assn. Orofacial Myology, Phi Sigma Iota. Office: Teresa M Rizzi MS CCC 695 S Colorado Blvd Ste 410 Denver CO 80222

RIZZOTTO, KATHLEEN MARIE, lawyer; b. Santa Ana, Calif., Mar. 3, 1959; d. Martin Kenneth and Jacqueline June (Anderson) Galaway; m. David Wayne Rizzotto, Aug. 29, 1987. BA in Communications, Calif. State U., Fullerton, 1982; JD, Western State U., Fullerton, 1986. Bar: Calif. 1987. Assoc. Zonni, Ginocchio & Taylor, Santa Ana, 1987—. Mem. Calif. State Bar, L.A. County Bar Assn., Workers Compensation Def. Atty.'s Assn., Orange County Bar Assn., Zeta Tau Alpha, Delta Theta Phi. Republican. Home: 17501 Via Lindo Tustin CA 92680-9131 Office: Zonni Ginocchio & Taylor 450 W 4th St Santa Ana CA 92701-4562

RIZZUTO, CARMELA RITA, nursing administrator; b. Waterbury, Conn., Aug. 26, 1942; d. Joseph Anthony and Carmella Rosa R.; m. Thomas Lee Chernesky, Aug. 28, 1982. BS, St. Joseph Coll., 1965; MS, Boston Coll., 1971; EdD, Sch. Edn., UCLA, 1983. RN, Calif. Nursing instr. Samaritan Hosp. Sch. Nursing, Troy, N.Y., 1969; med. nursing coord., clin. specialist Harvard Community Health Plan, Boston, 1971-72; instr. inservice edn. Tufts-New Eng. Med. Ctr., Boston, 1972-73; instr. inservice edn. St. John's Hosp. and Health Ctr., Santa Monica, Calif., 1974-76; asst. clin. prof. Sch. Nursing, UCLA, 1976-79; assoc. dir. nursing edn. St. Francis Hosp. of Santa Barbara, 1981-83; asst. dir. nursing edn. and rsch. Stanford U. Hosp., 1983-90, dir. geriatric patient care grant, 1990-93, grantee USPHS, NIH, DHHS, USPHS nurse trainee, 1969-71; recipient Chancellor's Patent Fund, UCLA, 1972-73. Contbr. articles to profl. publs. Office: Stanford U Hosp Nursing Adminstrn Stanford CA 94305

ROACH, JOHN D. C., manufacturing company executive; b. West Palm Beach, Fla., Dec. 3, 1943; s. Benjamin Browning and Margaret (York) R.; m. Pam Flebbe, Dec. 29, 1967 (div. Aug. 1981); children: Vanessa, Alexandra; m. Elizabeth Louise Phillips, Aug. 28, 1982; children: Bruce Phillips, Bryce Phillips, Brian Phillips. BS in Indsl. Mgmt., MIT, 1965; MBA, Stanford U., 1967. Dir. mgmt. acctg. and info. systems Ventura div. Northrop Corp., Thousand Oaks, Calif., 1967-70; co-founder, mgr. Northrop Venture Capital, Century City, Calif., 1970-71; v.p., dir. Boston Consulting Group, Boston and Menlo Park, Calif., 1971-80; v.p., world-wide strategic mgmt. practice mng. officer Booz, Allen, Hamilton, San Francisco, 1980-82; world-wide strategic mgmt. practice mng. officer Houston, 1982-83; vice chmn., mng. dir. Braxton Assocs., Houston, 1983-87; sr. v.p., chief fin. officer Manville Corp., Denver, 1987-88, exec. v.p. ops., 1988-91; pres. Manville Sales Corp., Denver, 1988-90, Manville Mining and Minerals Group, Denver, 1990-91, Celite Corp., Denver, 1990-91; chmn., pres., chief exec. officer Fibreboard Corp., Concord, Calif., 1991—; bd. dirs. Thermal Ceramics, Inc. Author: Strategic Management Handbook, 1983; contbr. articles to profl. jours. Chmn. 65 Roses Sports Club Houston, 1986-87; bd. dirs. Am. Leukemia Soc., Houston, 1986, Opera Colo., Denver, 1987-91, Alta Bates Hosp. Found.; bd. dirs., mem. exec. com. San Francisco Opera Assn.; bd. dirs. Bay Area Coun., San Francisco. Mem. N.Am. Soc. Strategy Planners, Greater Denver C. of C. (bd. dirs.), Geol. Energy and Minerals Assn. (bd. dirs.), Colo. Forum, Soc. Corp. Planners (charter), Fin. Execs. Inst. (mem. planning forum), Stanford Grad. Sch. Bus. Club, MIT Alumni Club, Met. Racquet Club (Houston), Denver Athletic Club, Petroleum Club, Met. Club (Denver), Contra Costa Country Club (San Francisco, Claremont Country Club (San Francisco). Home: 125 Guilford Rd Piedmont CA 94611 Office: Fibreboard Corp 1000 Burnett Ave Concord CA 94520

ROACH, JOHN MICHAEL, gastroenterologist; b. Walla Walla, Wash., Feb. 28, 1947; s. John Francis and Johanna Patricia (Sullivan) R.; m. Nancy Marie Mudd, Mar. 31, 1973; children: Shannon, John, Luke, Patrick, William, Bartholomew, Michelle. BS, Seattle U., 1969; MD, U. Wash., 1973. Diplomate Am. Bd. Internal Medicine. Intern st. medicine Maricopa County Gen. Hosp., Phoenix, 1974, resident internal medicine, 1975-76, gastroenterology fellow, 1976-78; pvt. practice gastroenterology Kennewick, Wash., 1978—; pres. med. staff Kennewick Gen. Hosp., 1985. Contbr. articles to Gastrointestinal Endoscopy. Mem. Tri-City Renaissance Com., Pasco, Wash., 1987-91. Mem. ACP, Am. Soc. Gastrointestinal Endoscopy, Am. Gastroent. Assn., Am. Coll. Gastroenterology, Benton-Franklin County Med. Soc. (chmn. continuing med. edn. 1987-88, pres. 1989), Wash. State Med. Assn., Pacific NW Endoscopy Soc. Republican. Roman Catholic. Office: 811 S Auburn Kennewick WA 99336-5682

ROACH, ROBERT CORWINE, JR., research physiologist; b. Springfield, Ill., May 14, 1956; s. Robert Corwine and Rose Marie (Buchmann) R. BS, The Evergreen St. Coll., Olympia, Wash., 1979; MS, Cornell U., Ithaca, N.Y., 1985. Rsch. sci. Op. Everest II, U.S. Army Rsch. Inst. of Environ. Medicine, Natick, Mass., 1985, High Altitude Natives Rsch. Project, Ollague, Chile, 1986; assoc. dir. Denali Med. Rsch. Project U. of AK, Anchorage, 1982—; rsch. assoc. Lovelace Med. Found., Albuquerque, 1990—; mem., rsch. com., Colo. Altitude Rsch. Inst., Keystone, Colo.; assoc. dir. Siberian-Alaskan Med. Rsch. Exch., Novosibirsk, Siberia; editorial reviewer Jour. of Wilderness Medicine, Nashville. Author: High Altitude Pulmonary Edema, 1990, High Altitude Medical Problems, 1988, Bibliography of High Altitufe Medicine, 1989. Expdn. Leader Siberia AK Geographic and Mountaineering Exchange; mem. Sierra Club, World Wildlife Fund. Mem. Wilderness Med. Soc., Am. Alpine Club. Office: Lovelace Med Found 2425 Ridgecrest Dr SE Albuquerque NM 87108-5127

ROACHE, PATRICK JOHN, corporate professional; b. Detroit, Sept. 15, 1938; s. Emmet Joseph and Amelia (Schmiehowski) R.; m. Catharine Buchanan Stewart, June 1, 1963; children: Amelia, Anne (dec.), James, Elizabeth, Emmet. BS, U. Notre Dame, 1960, MS, 1962, PhD, 1967. Instr. U. Detroit, 1962-64; asst. prof. U. N.D., Grand Forks, 1964-65; rsch. aerodynamicist Sandia Labs., Albuquerque, 1968-73; sr. scientist Sci. Applications, Inc., Albuquerque, 1973-75; pres. Ecodynamics Rsch. Assocs., Albuquerque, 1975—; vis. prof. U. Ky., Lexington, 1970, N.C. State U., Raleigh, 1978, U. Calif., Davis, 1985, U. N.Mex., Albuquerque, 1968-87. Author: Computational Fluid Dynamics, 1972; contbr. more than 70 articles to profl. jours.; assoc. editor Jour. Fluids Engring., 1985-88. Ward chmn. Rep. Party of N.Mex., 1972; campaign mgr. Herb Hughes for Mayor, Albuquerque, 1974, Gov.'s Com. on Mcpl. Financing, Albuquerque, 1976. Mem. AIAA, Am. Phys. Soc., Am. Soc. Engring. Edn., ASME, Am. Geophys. Union, Soc. for Indsl. and Applied Math. Roman Catholic. Office: Ecodynamics PO Box 9229 Albuquerque NM 87119

ROARK, DENIS DAREL, college dean; b. Greensboro, N.C., Sept. 10, 1943; s. Russell William Gouge and Edith Marie (Servatius) Roark; m. Glenna Denise Sprakman, Aug. 6, 1973; children: Brian, Staci. BS, Tex. Tech. U., 1966; MS, East Tex. State U., 1969; EdD, U. Ariz., 1985. Libr. Spur (Tex.) Sch. Dist., 1966-67, Dallas (Tex.) Pub. Schs., 1967-68; dir. Learning Resource Ctr. Eastern N.Mex. U., Roswell, N.Mex., 1968-85, asst. dean of instrl. support, 1986-88, dean of instrn., 1988—. Contbr. articles to profl. jours. Mem. Assn. for the Study of Higher Edn. (adv. com. N.Mex. commn.), N. Mex. Libr. Assn. (past sec., membership chmn., local arrangements chmn., publs. and mailing chmn., conf. site chmn., treas.), N.Mex. Learning Resource Ctr. Coun., Rotary Internat. Home: 1102 Monterrey Dr Roswell NM 88201-8339 Office: Ea NMex U 58 University Roswell NM 88202-6000

ROARK, TERRY PAUL, university president; b. Okeene, Okla., June 11, 1938; s. Paul J. and Erma K. (Morrison) R.; m. Beverly Brown, Sept. 7, 1963; 1 child, David. C. BA in Physics, Oklahoma City U., 1960; MS in Astronomy, Rensselaer Poly. Inst., 1962, PhD in Astronomy, 1966. Asst. provost for curricula Ohio State U., Columbus, 1977-79, assoc. provost for instrn., 1979-83; prof. physics Kent (Ohio) State U., 1983-87, v.p. acad. and student affairs, 1983-87, provost, 1985-87; pres. U. Wyo., Laramie, 1987—; bd. dirs. Rocky Mountain Fed. Savs. Bank, chmn. audit com., 1989—; commr. Western Interstate Commn. for Higher Edn., 1987—, chmn., 1991; bd. dirs. Associated Western Univs., 1987—, chmn., 1991; mem. adv. bd. Wyo. Geol. Survey, 1987—; mem. Warren AFB Civilian Adv. Coun., 1987—; mem. exec. com. Wyo. State Math. Coalition. Mem., treas. Ctr. for Pub. Edn., Columbus, 1980-83; mem. fin. adv. com. LWV, Kent, 1986; mem. long range planning com. Cleve. Urban League, 1985-86; mem. adv. com. Battelle youth sci. program Columbus and Ohio Pub. Schs., 1982; bd. dirs. Ivinson Hosp. Found., 1987—. Mem. Am. Astron. Soc., Astron. Soc. Pacific, Internat. Astron. Union, AAUP, Am. Assn. for Higher Edn., Sigma Xi, Phi Kappa Phi, Omicron Delta Kappa. Home: 1306 E Ivinson Ave Laramie WY 82070-4161 Office: U Wyo Office of Pres PO Box 3434 Laramie WY 82071-3434*

ROATH, STEPHEN D., pharmaceutical company executive; b. 1941. With Long's Drug Stores Corp., 1964—, exec. v.p. store ops., 1988-91, pres., 1991—. Office: Longs Drug Stores Corp 141 N Civic Dr Walnut Creek CA 94596-3858*

ROBBINS, ANNE FRANCIS See REAGAN, NANCY DAVIS

ROBBINS, CHARLES DUDLEY, III, manufacturing executive; b. Montclair, N.J., Sept. 21, 1943; s. Charles Dudley Robbins Jr. and Elaine (Siebert) Stark; m. Rebecca Lucille Bender; children: Seth A., Evan F., Gwendolyn M., Catherine E., Christopher W. BS in Bus. Adminstrn., U. Phoenix, Irvine, Calif., 1982; MBA, U. Phoenix, Salt Lake City, 1986. Cert. mfg. engr., robotics. Project engr. Mead Paper Corp., Atlanta, 1969-73; engr. McGaw Labs., Glendale, Calif., 1973-75; mgr. tool engring. Weiser Lock Co., South Gate, Calif., 1975-77; chief engr. Bivans Corp., L.A., 1977-79; sr. project engr. Charls Wyle Engring. Corp., Torrance, Calif., 1979-80; automation specialist Mattel Toys Inc., Hawthorne, Calif., 1980-83; dir. automation engring. Deseret Med., Warner Lambert, Sandy, Utah, 1983-88; dir. mfg. Deseret Med., Becton Dickinson, Sandy, 1988—; dir. bus. devel. and strategic planning Deseret Med., Becton Dickinson Co., Franklin Lakes, N.J., 1988. Patentee in field. Dist. chmn. Utah Dem. party, Sandy, 1987-88. With U.S. Army, 1961-64. Mem. U. Phoenix Alumni Assn., L.A. Aquarium Soc. (pres. 1980-82, dir. 1982-83), Sandy C. of C. (bd. dirs. 1990). Democrat. Episcopalian. Home: 11 S Wolcott St Salt Lake City UT 84102 Office: Deseret Med 9450 State St Sandy UT 84070-3234

ROBBINS, CONRAD W., naval architect; b. N.Y.C., Oct. 11, 1921; s. Girard David and Ethyl Rae (Bergman) R.; m. Danae Gray McCartney, Jan. 8, 1923 (dec. Jan. 1971); children: Lorraine, Linton, Jennifer; m. Melissa Jahn, Apr. 15, 1971 (dec. Mar. 1992). BSE, U. Mich., 1942. Estimator Pacific Electric Co., Seattle, 1946-47; pres. Straus-Dupanquet, Lyons, Alpha, Albert Pick, N.Y.C. and Chgo., 1947-67, C.W. Robbins, Inc., Carefree, Ariz., 1967—; cons. in field. Capt. floating drydock USN, 1942-46. Home: PO Box 2208 Carefree AZ 85377-2208 Office: CW Robbins Inc 7500 Stevens Rd Carefree AZ 85377

ROBBINS, JACK HOWARD, lawyer; b. L.A., May 16, 1957; s. Albert M. and Helen (Karabenick) R.;m. Cindy L. Cannon, Jan. 7, 1990. BA in Polit. Sci. cum laude, Calif. State U., Northridge, 1979; JD, Loyola U., L.A., 1982. Bar: Calif. 1982, U.S. Dist. Ct. (cen., so. and ea. dists.) Calif. 1982. Assoc. Cooper & Brown, Pasadena, Calif., 1983-85, Wilson, Kenna & Borys, L.A., 1985-88, Bottum & Feliton, L.A., 1988-90, Law Office of Gary L. Hall, Rancho Cordova, Calif., 1990-91; pvt. practice Sacramento, 1991—; mem. arbitration panel Sacramento County Superior Ct., 1990—; mem. Sacramento Mediation Ctr., 1993—. Chmn. Fair Oaks (Calif.) Community Planning Adv. Coun., 1992—; mem. adv. com. Culver City City Hall, 1988-89; mem. cen. com. Sacramento County Dem. Party, 1990-92. Mem. ABA, Sacramento County Bar Assn. (mem. atty. client rels. commn.), Assn. Def. Counsel No. Calif., Def. Rsch. Inst. Jewish. Home: 8605 Jaytee Way Fair Oaks CA 95628-2976 Office: 1900 Point West Way Ste 248 Sacramento CA 95815-4704

ROBBINS, JAMES EDWARD, electrical engineer; b. Renovo, Pa., May 11, 1931; s. James Edward and Marguerite Neva (Cleary) R.; m. Elizabeth Anne Caton, 1959 (div. July 1971); children: James, Katherine, Ellen; m. Dorothy Raye Bell, July 23, 1971; stepchildren: Mark, Lori. BEE, Pa. State U., 1958; MS in Math., San Diego State U., 1961. Registered profl. engr., Calif., Ariz. Rsch. engr. Astronautics div. Gen. Dynamics Co., San Diego, 1961-62; mgr. tech. ops. Electronics div. Gen. Dynamics Co., Yuma, Ariz., 1976-82; sr. engr. Kearfott div. Gen. Precision Co., San Marcos, Calif., 1962-65; systems engring. specialist Teledyne Ryan Aerospace Co., San Diego, 1965-76; v.p. Cibola Info. Systems, Yuma, 1982-84; cons. engr. Robbins Engring. Co., Yuma, 1984-85; sr. engring. specialist Gen. Dynamics Svcs. Co., Yuma, Ariz., 1985-90; systems engr. Trimble Navigation, Sunnyvale, Calif., 1990—. Contbr. articles to profl. jours. With USN, 1951-55, Korea. Mem. Inst. Navigation, Nat. Soc. Profl. Engrs., Ariz. Soc. Profl. Engrs. (pres. western div. 1986), Am. Legion, VFW (post comdr. 1963-65), Tau Beta Pi. Home: 704 Lemans Way Half Moon Bay CA 94019-1437 Office: Trimble Navigation 585 N Mary Ave Sunnyvale CA 94086-2931

ROBBINS, LENORE RASMUSSEN, home economics educator; b. Preston, Idaho, Dec. 21, 1939; d. Woodrow Ivan and Carolyn Ruth (Frey) R.; children: Danalee Ruth Johnson McDermott, James Lane Johnson, Woodrow Tyler Johnson, Laralyn Dee Johnson; m. Charles Burtis Robbins, Jan. 18, 1992. BS, Utah State U., 1978; MS, Brigham Young U., 1984; PhD, Utah State U., 1993. Home econs. tchr. Tooele Sch. Dist., Dugway, Utah, 1979-82; instr. Dixie Coll., St. George, Utah, 1982-83; tchr. Star Valley High Sch., Afton, Wyo., 1983-84; asst. prof. So. Utah State Coll., Cedar City, 1984-90, chmn. dept., 1987-90; asst. prof. Utah State U. Extension Home Econs., Centerville, 1990—; mem. state adv. com. Voc. Home Econs. Edn., Salt Lake City, 1987—; sci. rep. Faculty Senate, Cedar City, 1985-87; historian Faculty/Staff Women's Assn., 1989-90; keynote speaker several profl. women's orgn. meetings, 1985-90; adv. Wyo. Dist. III Future Homemakers of Am. (adv. to pres. 1983-84). Mem. Gov.'s Conf. on Strengthening Families, 1989—; facilitator Families Alive Conf. Telecast, Cedar City, 1989; bd. dirs. Nat. Com. (Utah chpt.) for Prevention of Child Abuse, 1987-88; mem. program com. Utah chpt. Prevention of Child Abuse, 1988—. Mem. Am. Vocat. Assn., Am. Home Econs. Assn., Utah Vocat. Assn. (pub. rels. chair 1982-83), Utah Home Econs. Assn. (pub. rels. co-chair 1987-90, chair nominating com. 1991-93). Republican. Mormon. Home: 362 E 100 N Centerville UT 84014 Office: Utah State U Extension Home Econs 125 S Main St PO Box 618 Farmington UT 84025

ROBBINS, NEVILLE, mathematics educator; b. Brussels, Belgium, June 4, 1938; came to U.S. 1941; s. Harry and Lianne (Biala) R. AB, Columbia U., 1958; AM, Harvard U., 1965; PhD, Poly. U. Bklyn., 1972. Lectr. Beloit (Wis.) Coll., 1976; asst. prof. math. U. San Francisco, 1978-79; lectr. math. Baruch Coll., CUNY, N.Y.C., 1979-80, Calif. State U., San Bernardino, 1980-82; prof. math. San Francisco State U., 1982—. Contbr. articles to profl. jours.; asst. editor Fibonacci Quar. Jour., 1990—. Mem. Am. Math. Soc., Math. Assn. Am., Assn. for Women in Math., Fibonacci Assn. Office: San Francisco State Univ 1600 Holloway Ave San Francisco CA 94132-1722

ROBBINS, PETER NORMAN, psychologist, marriage and family counselor; b. Göppingen, Fed. Republic Germany, May 12, 1955; came to U.S., 1961; s. Renate Charlotte (Grossman) R.; m. Gloria Denise Erwin, Dec. 16, 1978; children: Jordan Vincent, Erika Charlotte, Whitney Charise, Austin Gayle. BA in Psychology, So. Calif. Coll., 1979; MA in Marriage and Family Counseling, Fuller Theol. Sem., Pasadena, Calif., 1981; PhD in Psychology, Cambridge Grad. Sch. Psychology, L.A., 1989. Cert. community coll. psychology and religion instr., counselor, Calif; ordained to ministry Evangelical Ch. Alliance, 1984. Emergency room cons. Diamond Bar (Calif.) Mental Health Assocs., 1983-89; trainer state bd. orals Pasadena Counseling Group Seminars, 1983-90; founder, exec. dir. Turning Point Counseling, Diamond Bar, 1983—; host Journey of the Heart, Sta. KKLA-FM, North Hollywood, Calif., 1990—; mem. therapy program adv. bd. Horizon Hosp., Pomona, Calif., 1988-90, v.p. marriage and family counseling dept., 1988; cons. emergency room Chino (Calif.) Hosp.; speaker on mental health and theology to workshops and seminars, 1983—. Mem. bd., deacon Glengrove Assembly of God Ch., La Puente, Calif., 1981-88. With U.S. Army, 1974-76. Mem. Am. Assn. for Marriage and Family Therapy (cert., approved supr.), Diamond Bar C. of C. Republican. Office: Turning Point Counseling 620B N Diamond Bar Blvd Diamond Bar CA 91765-1037

ROBBINS, SARAH ANN, preschool educator; b. Malad, Idaho, Oct. 26, 1955; d. George Lynn and May (Wren) Carter; m. Rex Grant Robbins, Nov. 3, 1977; children: Jared Rex, Bryce Merlin, Stacey Ann, Brady Lynn. BS, Idaho State U., 1979. Rsch. asst. dept. consumer econs. Idaho State U., Pocatello, 1978-80; ednl. cons. Discovery Toys, Malad, 1983-85; tchr. home econs. Oneida County Sch. Dist., Malad, 1985-87; tchr. presch. Rainbows and Rymes Presch., Malad, 1988—; state officer advisor Future Homemakers Am., Idaho, 1986-87. Tchr. LDS Ch., Malad and Pocatello, 1972—; den leader, asst. trainer, cub master Boy Scouts Am., Malad, 1987—; city coord. girls' softball Oneida Recreation, Malad, 1988—; com. mem. Young Woman of Yr., Malad, 1988—; sec. PTO, Malad, 1991—. Home econs. grantee State Bd. Vocat. Edn., 1986. Fellow Theater Guild, Phi Kappa Phi, Pi Upsilon Omicron. Home: 59 W Hwy 38 Malad ID 83252

ROBBINS, STEPHEN J. M., lawyer; b. Seattle, Apr. 13, 1942; s. Robert Mads and Aneita Elbert (West) R.; m. Nina Winifred Tanner, Aug. 11, 1967; children: Sarah E.T., Alicia S.T. AB, UCLA, 1964; JD, Yale U., 1971. Bar: D.C. 1973, U.S. Dist. Ct. D.C. 1973, U.S. Ct. Appeals (D.C. cir.) 1973, U.S. Ct. Appeals (3d cir.) 1973, U.S. Dist. Ct. (ea. and no. dists.) Calif. 1982, U.S. Dist. Ct. (cen. dist.) Calif. 1983. Pres. U.S. Nat. Student Assn., Washington, 1964-65; assoc. Steptoe & Johnson, Washington, 1972-75; chief counsel spl. inquiry com. on nutrition U.S. Senate, Washington, 1975-76; v.p., gen. counsel Straight Arrow Pubs., San Francisco, 1976-78; regional counsel U.S. SBA, San Francisco, 1978-80; spl. counsel Warner-Amex Cable Communications, Sacramento, 1981-82; ptnr. McDonough, Holland and Allen, Sacramento, 1982-84; v.p. Straight Arrow Pubs., N.Y.C., 1984-86; ptnr. Robbins & Livingston, Sacramento, 1986—. Staff sgt. U.S. Army, 1966-68. Mem. D.C. Bar, State Bar of Calif., ABA (sect. of urban, state and local govt. law-land use, planning and zoning com., sect. of real property, probate and trust law, sect. natural resources energy, environ. law, forum com. on affordable housing and community devel.), Urban Land Inst. (assoc.), Am. Planning Assn. (planning and law divsn., internat. divsn.), Internat. New Town Assn. Unitarian. Office: Robbins & Livingston 3300 Douglas Blvd Roseville CA 95661

ROBBLEE, RICHARD HOWARD, lawyer; b. Seattle, Apr. 18, 1952; s. John Henry and Florence Lynn (Palmer) R.; m. Nancy Elizabeth Durand, May 15, 1982; children: Elizabeth, Megan. BA magna cum laude, Harvard Coll., 1975; JD cum laude, U. Wash. Law Sch., 1978. Bar: Wash. 1978, U.S. Dist. Ct. (we. dist.) Wash. 1978, U.S. Dist. Ct. (ea. dist.) Wash. 1981, U.S. Ct. Appeals (9th cir.) 1981, U.S. Supreme Ct. 1985. Assoc. Hafer, Cassidy & Price, Seattle, 1978-81; ptnr. Hafer, Price, Rinehart & Schwerin, Seattle, 1982-91, Hafer, Price, Rinehart & Robblee, Seattle, 1992—. Contbr. law rev. comment to profl. jour. Dir. Conway Sch. Dist., Mount Vernon, Wash., 1988—. Named to Order of the Coif, U. Wash., 1978. Mem. Wash. State Bar Assn. Office: Hafer Price Rinehart et al 1100 Olive Way Ste 1600 Seattle WA 98101

ROBECK, CECIL MELVIN, JR., religious studies educator; b. San Jose, Calif., Mar. 16, 1945; s. Cecil Melvin and Berdetta Mae (Manley) R.; m. Patsy Jolene Gibbs, June 14, 1969; children: Jason Lloyd, John Mark, Peter Scott, Nathan Eric. AA, San Jose City Coll., 1967; BS, Bethany Bible Coll., Santa Cruz, Calif., 1970; MDiv, Fuller Theol. Seminary, Pasadena, Calif., 1973, PhD, 1985. Ordained to ministry Assemblies of God, 1973. Instr. religion So. Calif. Coll., Costa Mesa, 1973-74; adminstrv. asst. to dean Fuller Theol. Sem., 1974-77, acting dir. admissions, 1975-77, dir. admissions and records, 1977-79, dir. student svcs., 1979-83, dir. acad. svcs., 1983-85, asst. dean, asst. prof. ch. history, 1985-88, assoc. dean, assoc. prof. ch. history, 1988-92, adj. instr. hist. theology, 1981-85, prof. ch. history ecumenics, 1992—; trustee Bethany Bible Coll., 1985-88, mem. exec. com., 1986-88; mem. exec. com. Internat. Roman Cath. and Pentecostal Dialogue, 1986-92, co-chair, 1992—; mem. Commn. on Faith and Order, Nat. Coun. Chs., 1984—; Pentecostal advisor World Coun. Chs., 1989, mem. Commn. on Faith and Order, 1991—; mem. L.A. Evang. and Roman Cath. Com., 1987-92, co-chair, 1992—. Author: Prophecy in Carthage, Perpetua, Tertullian and Cyprian, 1992; editor: Charismatic Experiences in History, 1985; contbr. articles to profl. jours. Joseph L. Gerhart scholar, 1969; Assn. Theol. Schs. grantee, 1977. Fellow Wesleyan Holiness Studies Ctr.; mem. Soc. for Pentecostal Studies (1st v.p. 1981-82, pres. 1982-83, editor Pneuma 1984-92), N.Am. Acad. Ecumenists (exec. com. 1989—). Republican. Home: 1140 N Catalina Ave Pasadena CA 91104-3807 Office: Fuller Theol Sem 135 N Oakland Ave Pasadena CA 91182-0001

ROBERSON, JAMES EDWARD, marketing company executive; b. Atlanta, Oct. 31, 1944; s. James and Tiller (Johnson) R. BA cum laude, UCLA, 1972, MPA, 1977. Cert. econ. developer. Pub. affairs mgr. Xerox Computer Mktg., El Segundo, Calif., 1972-75; economist Econs. Rsch. Assocs., L.A., 1978-81; pres. James Roberson and Assoc., L.A., 1981-88, Pro-Am Mktg., Pasadena, Calif., 1988—; mktg. cons. Nations of Liberia and Nigeria, 1981, City of Pasadena, Calif., 1992-93, Pasadena Tournament of Roses Assn., 1993; mktg. dir. City of Pasadena Black History Festival; bd. dirs., co-founder N.W. Econ. Devel. Corp. Author: Marketing and Economic Development, 1983, High School Players' Guide to College Football Scholarships, 1985. Office: Pro Am Mktg 113 E Pine St Altadena CA 91001

ROBERT, RICHARD, federal criminal investigator; b. Bronx, N.Y., May 13, 1961; s. Hilario and Lydia (Tirado) R.; m. Suzanne Velvet Manacmul, Feb. 13, 1981; children: Jennifer, Veronique, Richard II. AA, Saddleback Coll., 1983; BA, Chapman U., 1985; MA, Nat. U., 1987. Commd. USMC, 1979, advanced through grades to staff sgt., 1986, ret., 1987; safety engr. Highlands Ins. Co., Irvine, Calif., 1987-89; reserve dep. sheriff Orange County (Calif.) Sheriff's Dept., 1988-89; immigration insp. Immigration & Naturalization Svc., L.A., 1988-89; criminal investigator IRS, Laguna Niguel, Calif., 1989-90; spl. agent Bur. Alcohol, Tobacco & Firearms, Long Beach, Calif., 1990—. Mem. Am. Soc. Safety Engrs. (pres.'s club 1989), Fed. Law Enforcement Officers Assn., Nat. U. Alumni Assn., Chapman U. Alumni Assn. (bd. dirs. 1993—). Office: Bur Alcohol Tobacco & Firearms 501 W Ocean Blvd Ste 7300 Long Beach CA 90802

ROBERT, SCOTT MATTHEW, restaurateur, consultant; b. Warwick, R.I., July 26, 1962; s. Samuel O. Robert and Jeanne L. (Valliere) Buckley. AOS in Culinary Arts, Culinary Inst. Am., Hyde Park, N.Y., 1982. Cert. working chef. Head cook Sambos, Poway, Calif., 1978-81; sous chef Fairchilds, Baton Rouge, 1982-83, La Maison du Lac, Carlsbad, Calif., 1983; exec. chef La Jolla (Calif.) Village Inn, 1984-89; owner, chef Heart Beat Cafe, Poway, 1989—; cons. Calif. Restaurant Cons., San Diego, 1987-89. Recipient Best Seafood Entree, Best Dessert and Grand Prize awards Taste of San Diego, 1984, Best Healthy Food Restaurant award North County Entertainer, 1989, Superior Coffee Svc. award Superior Coffee Co., 1990. Mem. Am. Culinary Fedn., Chefs de Cuisine Assn. San Diego, Elks. Republican. Roman Catholic. Home: PO Box 489 Poway CA 92074-0489 Office: Heart Beat Cafe 13385 Poway Rd Poway CA 92064-4625

ROBERTS, ALAN SILVERMAN, orthopedic surgeon; b. N.Y.C., Apr. 20, 1939; s. Joseph William and Fannie (Margolies) S.; BA, Conn. Wesleyan U., 1960; MD, Jefferson Med. Coll., 1966; children: Michael Eric, Daniel Ian. Rotating intern, Lankenau Hosp., Phila., 1966-67; resident orthopaedics Tulane U. Med. Coll., 1967-71; pvt. practice medicine, specializing in orthopedics and hand surgery, Los Angeles, 1971—; mem. clin. faculty UCLA Med. Coll., 1971-76. Served with AUS, 1961. Recipient Riordan Hand fellowship, 1969; Boyes Hand fellowship, 1971. Mem. Riordan Hand Soc., Western Orthopaedic Assn., A.C.S., AMA, Calif., Los Angeles County Med. Assns., Am. Acad. Orthopaedic Surgeons. Republican. Jewish. Contbr. articles to profl. jours.

ROBERTS, AMANDA, clinical psychologist, researcher, consultant; b. Zomba, Malawi, Africa, Feb. 13, 1958; came to U.S., 1976; d. Denys and Brenda (Marsh) R. BA in Polit. Sci., U. Calif., Berkeley, 1981; MA in Family Therapy, U. San Francisco, 1986; PhD, Calif. Inst. Integral Studies, 1993. Lic. marriage, family and child counselor. Counselor Sequoia Hosp., Redwood City, Calif., 1986-88; family program specialist Stanford (Calif.) Drug and Alcohol Ctr., 1988-89; assessment specialist Belmont (Calif.) Hills Hosp., 1990-91; pvt. practice Menlo Park, Calif., 1990—; fellow Stanford (Calif.) U., 1991-92; intern San Mateo County Outpatient Mental Health, Redwood City, 1992-93.

ROBERTS, ARCHIBALD EDWARD, retired army officer, author; b. Cheboygan, Mich., Mar. 21, 1915; s. Archibald Lancaster and Madeline Ruth (Smith) R.; grad. Command and Gen. Staff Coll., 1952; student U.S. Armed Forces Inst., 1953, U. Md., 1958; m. Florence Snure, Sept. 25, 1940 (div. Feb. 1950); children—Michael James, John Douglas; m. 2d, Doris Elfriede White, June 23, 1951; children—Guy Archer, Charles Lancaster, Christopher Corwin. Enlisted U.S. Army, 1939, advanced through grades to lt. col., 1960; served in Far East Command, 1942, 1953-55, ETO, 1943-45, 57-60; tech. info. officer Office Surgeon Gen., Dept. Army, Washington, 1950, Ft. Campbell, Ky., 1952-53, info. officer, Camp Chicamauga, Japan, Ft. Bragg, N.C., Ft. Campbell, Ky., 1953-56, Ft. Campbell, 1956-57, Ft. Benning, Ga., Wurzburg, Germany, 1957-58, spl. projects officer Augsburg, Germany, 1959-60, U.S. Army Info. Office, N.Y.C., 1960-61; writer program precipitating Senate Armed Services Hearings, 1962; ret., 1965; mgr., salesman Nu-Enamel Stores, Ashville, N.C., 1937-38; co-owner, dir. Roberts & Roberts Advt. Agy., Denver, 1946-49; pres. Found. for Edn., Scholarship, Patriotism and Americanism, Inc.; founder, nat. bd. dirs. Com. to Restore Constn., Inc., 1965—. Recipient award of merit Am. Acad. Pub. Affairs, 1967; Good Citizenship medal SAR, 1968; Liberty award Congress of Freedom, 1969; Man of Yr. awards Women for Constl. Govt., 1970, Wis. Legislative and Research Com., 1971; medal of merit Am. Legion, 1972; Speaker of Year award We, The People, 1973; Col. Arch Roberts Week named for him City of Danville, Ill., 1974; recipient Spl. Tribute State of Mich., 1979. Mem. Res. Officers Assn., Airborne Assn., SAR, Sons Am. Colonists. Author: Rakkasan, 1955; Screaming Eagles, 1956; The Marne Division, 1957; Victory Denied, 1966; The Anatomy of a Revolution, 1968; Peace: By the Wonderful People Who Brought You Korea and Viet Nam, 1972; The Republic: Decline and Future Promise, 1975; The Crisis of Federal Regionalism: A Solution, 1976; Emerging Struggle for State Sovereignty, 1979; How to Organize for Survival, 1982; The Most Secret Science, 1984; also numerous pamphlets and articles. Home: 2218 W Prospect PO Box 986 Fort Collins CO 80522-0986

ROBERTS, BARBARA, governor; b. Corvallis, Oreg., Dec. 21, 1936; m. Frank Roberts, 1974; children—Mark, Michael. Mem. Multnomah County Bd. Commrs., Oreg., 1978; mem. Oreg. Ho. of Reps., 1981-85; sec. of state State of Oreg., 1985-90, gov., 1990—. Mem. Parkrose Sch. Bd., 1973-83. Office: State Capitol Office of Gov Rm 254 Salem OR 97310*

ROBERTS, CHARLES MORGAN, optometry educator; b. Roswell, N.Mex., June 13, 1932; s. Clemence Arthur and Annie Lorene (Perkins) R.; m. Gloria Vivian Lasagna, Feb. 21, 1962; children: Mike, Janis. AA in Engring., Mt. San Antonio Community Coll., 1958; BA in Organic Chemistry, U. La Verne, 1962, MA in Organic Chemistry, 1968; BS in Pysiologic Optics, So. Calif. Coll. Optometry, 1972, OD, 1974. Diplomate Am. Acad. Optometry (cornea and contact lens); cert. in contact lenses. Eng. electronic system Aetron, Aerojet Gen., Covina, Calif., 1956-65; rsch. chemist Sunkist Orange Products Div., Ontario, Calif., 1965-70; cons. doctor USPHS, 1974-77; prof. optometry So. Calif. Coll. Optometry, Fullerton, Calif., 1974—; pvt. prac. San Juan Capistrano, Calif., 1975—. Author: Mathematics of Contact Lenses, 1976, Clinical Contact Lens Fitting and Modification, 1981; (with others) Dictionary of Visual Science, 1988, Special Contact Lens Fitting, 1992. With USN, 1951-55. Recipient Outstanding Achievement award Bausch and Lomb, 1974, Optometric Recognition award, 1991, Clin. Investigation Achievement award, 1990, 91, Membership Svc. award Rotary, 1990-91; named Rotarian of Yr., 1977-78; Rsch. fellow NSF, 1968, Bausch & Lomb, 1974. Mem. Rotary (bd. dirs. 1986, pres. 1986), Elks. Republican. Lutheran. Office: 32282 Camino Capistrano Ste B San Juan Capistrano CA 92675-3791

ROBERTS, CHARLES S., software engineer; b. Newark, Sept. 25, 1937; s. Ben and Sara (Fasten) R.; m. Wendy Shadlen, June 8, 1959; children: Lauren Roberts Gold, Tamara G. Roberts. BS in Chemistry, Carnegie-Mellon U., 1959; PhD in Physics, MIT, 1963. MTS, radiation physics rsch. AT&T Bell Labs., Murray Hill, N.J., 1963-68, head info. processing rsch., 1968-73, head interactive computer systems rsch., 1973-82; head, advanced systems dept. AT&T Bell Labs., Denver, 1982-87; head software architecture planning dept. AT&T Bell Labs., Holmdel, N.J., 1987-88; R&D mgr., system architecture lab. Hewlett-Packard Co., Cupertino, Calif., 1988-90, R&D mgr. univ. rsch. grants, 1990-92; prin. lab. scientist measurement systems architecture Hewlett-Packard Labs., Palo Alto, Calif., 1992—. Contbr. articles to profl. jours. Westinghouse scholar Carnegie Mellon U., 1955-59; NSF fellow MIT, 1959-63. Mem. IEEE, Assn. for Computing Machinery, Am. Phys. Soc., Sigma Xi, Tau Beta Pi, Phi Kappa Phi. Home: 210 Manresa Ct Los Altos CA 94022-4646 Office: Hewlett-Packard Labs 3500 Deer Creek Rd PO Box 10350 Palo Alto CA 94303

ROBERTS, DAVID LOWELL, journalist; b. Lusk, Wyo., Jan. 12, 1954; s. Leslie James and LaVerne Elizabeth (Johns) R. BA, U. Ariz., 1979; postgrad., U. Nebr., 1992—. Founder, editor, publisher Medicine Bow (Wyo.) Post, 1977-88; journalism instr. U. Wyo., Laramie, 1987-92; adviser U. Wyo. Student Publs., Laramie, 1987-92; exch. reporter The Washington Post, 1982; free lance reporter Casper (Wyo.) Star-Tribune, 1978-83, various publs. Co-author: (book) The Wyoming Almanac, 1988, 90; author: (book) Sage Street, 1991; columnist Sage Street, 1989-92. Chmn. Medicine Bow Film Commn., 1984; treas. Friends of the Medicine Bow Mus., 1984-88; pres. Medicine Bow Area C. of C., 1984; dir. Habitat for Humanity of Albany County, Laramie, 1991-92. Recipient Nat. Newspaper Assn. awards, over 40 Wyo. Press. Assn. awards, Five Editorial awards U. Wyo., Citizen of Yr. award People of Medicine Bow, 1986, Student Publs. awards U. Wyo., 1990, 92. Mem. Friends of Medicine Bow Mus., Habitat for Humanity of Albany County. Democrat. Methodist. Home: 2119 Grand Ave No 2 Laramie WY 82070

ROBERTS, DENNIS WILLIAM, association executive; b. Chgo., Jan. 7, 1943; s. William Owen and Florence Harriet (Denman) R.; BA, U. N.Mex., 1968; MA, Antioch U., 1982, St. John's Coll., 1984. Cert. assn. exec. Gen. assignment reporter Albuquerque Pub. Co., 1964, sports writer, 1960-64, advt. and display salesman, 1967-68; dir. info. N.Mex. bldg. br. Asso. Gen. Contractors Am., Albuquerque, 1968-79, asst. exec. dir., 1979-82, dir., 1982—. Active United Way, Albuquerque, 1969-78; chmn. Albuquerque Crime Prevention Council, 1982. Recipient Pub. Relations Achievement award Assoc. Gen. Contractors Am., 1975, 78. Mem. N.Mex. Pub. Relations Conf. (chmn. 1975, 82-83), Pub. Relations Soc. Am. (accredited, pres. N.Mex. chpt. 1981, chmn. S.W. dist. 1984, chmn. sect. 1988), Am. Soc. Assn. Execs. (cert.), Contrn. Specifications Inst. (Outstanding Industry Mem. 1974, Outstanding Com. Chmn. 1978), Sigma Delta Chi (pres. N.Mex. chpt. 1969). Republican. Lutheran. Clubs: Toastmasters (dist. gov. 1977-78, Disting. Dist. award 1978, Toastmaster of Year 1979-80), Masons, Shriners, Elks. Home: 1709 Hiawatha St NE Albuquerque NM 87112-4519 Office: Assn Gen Contractors 1615 University Blvd NE Albuquerque NM 87102-1717

ROBERTS, DWIGHT LOREN, management executive, novelist; b. San Diego, June 3, 1949; s. James Albert and Cleva Lorraine (Conn) R.; B.A., U. San Diego, 1976, M.A., 1979; m. Phyllis Ann Adair, Mar. 29, 1969; children: Aimee Renee, Michael Loren, Daniel Alexandr. Engring. aide Benton Engring. Inc., San Diego, 1968-73; pres. Robert's Tech. Research Co., also subs. Marine Technique Ltd., San Diego, 1973-76; pres. Research Technique Internat., 1978—; freelance writer, 1979—; owner Agrl. Analysis, 1985-88; constrn. mgr. Homestead Land Devel. Corp., 1988—. Served with U.S. Army, 1969-71. Mem. ASTM, AAAS, Nat. Inst. Sci., N.Y. Acad. Scis., Nat. Inst. Cert. in Engring. Techs., Soil and Found. Engr. Assn., Phi Alpha Theta. Baptist. Author: Geological Exploration of Alaska, 1898-1924, Alfred Hulse Brooks, Alaskan Trailblazer, Papaveraceae of the World, Demarchism, Arid Regions Gardening, Visions of Dame Kind: Dreams, Imagination and

Reality, Antal's Theory of the Solar System, Science Fair-A Teacher's Manual, Common Ground: Similarities of the World Religions, Black Sheep-Scientific Discoveries From the Fringe; contbr. articles to profl. jours. Office: 3111 E Victoria Dr Alpine CA 91901-3679

ROBERTS, EDWARD VERNE, institute administrator; b. San Mateo, Calif., Jan. 23, 1939; s. Verne Walter and Zona Lee (Harvey) R.; m. Catherine Dugan, Sept. 11, 1976 (div. 1983); 1 child, Lee. AA, Coll. San Mateo, 1962; BA, U. Calif., Berkeley, 1964, MA with distinction, 1966, postgrad.; LHD (hon.), Wright Inst., Berkeley, 1981. Teaching assoc. polit. sci. U. Calif., Berkeley, 1964-67, asst. to dean students, specialist removal of attitudinal and archtl. barriers, 1968-69; dir. project handicapped opportunity program for edn. U. Calif., Riverside, 1970-71; cons. student spl. svc. program U.S. Office Edn., Washington, 1969-70; co-founder, instr. Nairobi Coll., East Palo Alto, Calif., 1969-70; prof., dean students Common College, Woodside, Calif., 1971; exec. dir., co-founder Ctr. Ind. Living, Berkeley, 1972-75; dir. State Dept. Rehab., Sacramento, 1975-83; pres. World Inst. Disability, Oakland, Calif., 1983—; trainer Ptnrs. in Policymaking, 1989—, Ptnrs. in Leadership Advanced Tng., Mpls., 1992; trustee Common Coll., 1981—; co-founder, bd. dirs. Wright Inst.; bd. dirs. World Inst. Disability, Internat. Initiative Against Avoidable Disablement, East Sussex, Eng., and Geneva, Project Interdependence. Contbr. articles to profl. jours. Mem. adv. com. pathways to independence United Cerebral Palsy Alameda/Contra Costa County, 1990—, Richmond Unified Sch. Dist. Tech. Task Force, 1991—. Recipient N. Neal Pike prize Boston U., 1990, Disting. Svc. award Pres. U.S., 1991, Just Do It award Devel. Disabilities Commrs., 1991; fellow John D. & Catherine T. MacArthur Fedn., 1985-89. Mem. Disabled People's Internat.-USA (treas., vice chair 1982—), Through the Looking Glass (bd. dirs. 1983—), World Interdependence Fund (bd. dirs. 1990—), Greenlining Coalition, Assn. Severly Handicapped (bd. dirs. 1990—), Assn. Preservation Presdl. Yacht Potomac (bd. govs. 1991—). Democrat. Office: World Inst Disability 510-16th St Ste 100 Oakland CA 94612

ROBERTS, ELTON NEAL, school system administrator; b. Annabella, Utah, June 7, 1928; s. Elton Clynn and Clara (Savage) R.; m. Lorelei O'Halloran, May 31, 1946; children: Jan, Sue, Patricia. BS, Brigham Young U., 1950; MA, Claremont Coll., 1962; EdD, U. So. Calif., 1975. Elem. tchr. Richfield (Utah) Sch. Dist., 1950-53; elem. tchr. San Bernardino (Calif.) City Schs., 1954-61, adminstrv. asst., 1961-62, elem. sch. prin., 1962-66, dir. elem. and secondary edn. act, 1966-72, dir. compensatory edn., 1971-72, asst. to supt. desegregation programs, 1972-78, asst. to supt. instructional divsn., K-6, 1975-77, asst. supt. program mgmt., 1978-81, supt., 1982—; cons. in field, 1982—; prof. U. Redlands, Calif., 1990—; mem. Children's Network Policy Coun. Active YMCA, San Bernardino Edn. Round Table, San Bernardino Community Against Drugs. Recipient Certification of Appreciation, Exch. Club Uptown-San Bernardino, 1983, Cert. of Appreciation, Masonic Lodge, 1983, Calif. Inland Empire coun. Boy Scouts Am., 1985, Leadership and Devotion San Bernardino City Schs. award Masons, 1986, Citizen of Achievement award LWV, 1986, People Helping People award Arrowhead United Way, 1988, Friends of Children award Camp Fire, 1990; named Bus. Assoc. of Yr., Arrowhead chpt. Am. Bus. Women Assn., 1986. Mem. San Bernardino Sch. Mgrs., C. of C., Kiwanis. Home: 3895 Pepper Tree Ln San Bernardino CA 92404 Office: San Bernardino City Unified Sch Dist 777 N F St San Bernardino CA 92410

ROBERTS, GEORGE CHRISTOPHER, manufacturing executive; b. Ridley Park, Pa., May 27, 1936; s. George H. and Marion C. (Smullen) R.; m. Adriana Toribio, July 19, 1966; children: Tupac A., Capac Y. PhD, Frederico Villareal Nat. U., Lima, Peru, 1989, Inca Garcilosa de la Vega U., Lima, 1992. Sr. engr. ITT, Paramus, N.J., 1960-65; program mgr. Arde Rsch., Mawah, N.J., 1965-67; Space-Life Sci. program mgr., rsch. div. GATX, 1967-69; dir. rsch. and devel. Monogram Industries, L.A., 1969-71; chmn. Inca Mfg. Corp. 1970-72; pres. Inca-One Corp., Hawthorne, Calif., 1972—; pres. Environ. Protection Ctr., Inc., L.A., 1970-76. Bd. dirs., trustee Fairborn Obs.; founder Culver Nat. Bank, 1983; trustee Calif. Mus. Sci. and Industry, 1988-92; trustee Internat. Am. Profl. Photoelectric Photometrists, 1983—, Buckley Sch., 1984-92, Belair Prep Sch., 1992—; chmn. solar and stellar physics Mt. Wilson Rsch. Corp., 1984-87; bd. dirs. Peruvian Found. 1981, pres. 1986-89, chmn. 1989-91, appt. rep. govt. of Peru in L.A., 1988-91; chmn. Santa Monica Coll. Astronomy Ctr. Found., 1993—. Decorated Grade of Amauta Govt. Peru, 1989. Mem. Am. Astron. Soc., Astron. Soc. Pacific. Patentee advanced waste treatment systems, automotive safety systems. Office: 13030 Cerise Ave Hawthorne CA 90250-5523

ROBERTS, GEORGE R., venture capital company executive; married; 3 children. JD, U. Calif., San Francisco. With Bears, Stearns, New York, until 1976; now ptnr. Kohlberg, Kravis, Roberts, San Francisco; dir. Beatrice Co., Chgo., Houdaille Industries Inc., Northbrook, Ill., Malone and Hyde, Memphis, Union Tex. Petroleum Holdings Inc., Houston. Office: Kohlberg Kravis Roberts & Co 101 California St San Francisco CA 94111-5802

ROBERTS, HOWARD NICK, electrical engineer, research and development executive; b. Corpus Christi, Tex., Oct. 21, 1939; s. Henry Niel and Frankie Mae (Jones) R.; m. Patricia Gail Clark, June 10, 1961; children: Joanna Christine, Jordan Prescott. BSEE, U. Tex., 1963, MSEE, 1965, PhD in Engring and Physics, 1968. Teaching assoc. U. Tex., Austin, 1961-63, rsch. assoc., 1963-68; prin. engr. Radiation, Inc. divsn. Harris Corp., Melbourne, Fla., 1968-78; dir. engring. Harris Corp., Melbourne, 1978-80; dir. printer engring. Datapoint Corp., San Antonio, 1980-85; v.p. rsch. and devel. Spectra-Physics Scanning Systems, Inc., Eugene, Oreg., 1985—; adj. prof. Fla. Inst. Tech., Melbourne, 1974-76. Contbr. tech. papers in field; patents include: data storage and retrieval method and apparatus; Digital optical recorder/reproducer system; auto package label scanner; bar-code scanner with asterisk scan pattern; a scanning system of preferentially aligning a package in an optical scanning plane for decoding a bar code label. Mem. IEEE, Optical Soc. Am., Friar Soc., Phi Theta Kappa, Tau Beta Phi, Eta Kappa Nu, Omnicron Delta Kappa, Phi Kappa Phi. Republican. Office: Spectra-Physics 959 Terry St Eugene OR 97402

ROBERTS, JAMES CARL, communications executive, engineer; b. Orlando, Fla., May 6, 1953; s. James Ira and Avis Jean (Marg) R.; m. Lynne K. Lovvorn, Sept. 29, 1980; children: William D, Christine N., Jameson S., Michael B. BSEE, U. Miss., 1974; MBA, Newport (Calif.) U., 1988, DBA, 1992. Registered profl. engr., Kans. Pres. Accent Communications, Lakeland, Fla., 1977-80; engring. mgr. Motorola Corp., Foster City, Claif., 1980-83; regional mgr. MCI, Washington, 1983-84; dir. McCaw Communications, Denver, 1984-86; pres., chief exec. officer Communications Group Internat., Denver, 1986—; chief exec. officer Metro Page of Fla., Boca Raton, 1988—, Metrotek Ariz., Phoenix, 1988—; chief operating br. Tri-Pro, Denver, 1988—, CGI, Inc., Denver, 1986—, Metro, Inc., Ft. Meyers, Fla., 1988—, CGI, Denver, 1992—, Albania, 1992—; bd. dirs. Malta Cellular, Valeta; chmn., gen. dir. CGI-MT of Serbia, Yugoslavia, 1990-92; gen. dirs., chmn. Serbia Cellular, 1989-92. Author: Cellular for Malta, 1987. Staff sgt. USAF, 1969-77. Mem. Cellular Telephone Industry Assn., Telocator, Colo. Arabian Assn., Intercircle, Internat. Arabian Assn., Met. Club, St. James Club. Republican. Baptist. Office: CGI Inc 5555 Dtc Pky Ste 2000 Englewood CO 80111-3002

ROBERTS, JAMES MCGREGOR, retired professional association executive; b. Moncton, N.B., Can., Nov. 24, 1923; came to U.S., 1949, naturalized, 1956; s. Roland M. and Edith M. (Shields) R.; m. Thelma E. Williams, May 6, 1944; 1 dau., Jana M. B.Commerce, U. Toronto, Ont., Can., 1949. Auditor Citizens Bank, Los Angeles, 1949-54; auditor Acad. Motion Picture Arts and Scis., Hollywood, Calif., 1954—; controller Acad. Motion Picture Arts and Scis., 1956-71, exec. dir., 1971-89, exec. sec. acad. found., 1971-89; exec. cons. Acad. Motion Picture Arts and Scis., Hollywood, Calif., 1989-92. Served as pilot Royal Can. Air Force, World War II. Home: 450 S Maple Dr Beverly Hills CA 90212-4758 Office: Acad Motion Pictures Arts Scis 8949 Wilshire Blvd Beverly Hills CA 90211-1972

ROBERTS, JEAN REED, lawyer; b. Washington, Dec. 19, 1939; d. Paul Allen and Esther (Kishter) Reed; m. Thomas Gene Roberts, Nov. 26, 1958; children: Amy, Rebecca, Nathanial. AB in Journalism, U. N.C., 1966; JD, Ariz. State U., 1973. Bar: Ariz. 1974. Sole practice, Scottsdale, Ariz., 1975-84; founding ptnr. Reeves & Roberts, 1985—; legal dir., advisor to gov. Ariz.-Mex. Commn., 1980-89; judge pro tem Superior Ct., Maricopa County, Ariz., 1979-92; chmn. Bd. of Adjustment, Town of Paradise Valley, 1984-91; bd. dirs. YWCA, Maricopa County. Mem. ABA, Charter 100 of Phoenix, Nat. Acad. Elder Law, Scottsdale Bar Assn., Ariz. Bar Assn. Democrat. Jewish. Office: Reeves & Roberts 7110 E Mcdonald Dr Ste 1A Scottsdale AZ 85253-5426

ROBERTS, JOHN D., chemist, educator; b. Los Angeles, June 8, 1918; s. Allen Andrew and Flora (Dombrowski) R.; m. Edith Mary Johnson, July 11, 1942; children: Anne Christine, Donald William, John Paul, Allen Walter. A.B., UCLA, 1941, Ph.D., 1944; Dr. rer. nat. h.c., U. Munich, 1962; D.Sc. (hon.), Temple U., 1964, Notre Dame U., 1993, U. Wales, 1993. Instr. chemistry U. Calif. at Los Angeles, 1944-45; NRC fellow chemistry Harvard, 1945-46, instr. chemistry, 1946; instr. chemistry Mass. Inst. Tech., 1946, asst. prof., 1947-50, asso. prof., 1950-52; vis. prof. Ohio State U., 1952, Stanford U., 1973-74; prof. organic chemistry Calif. Inst. Tech., 1953-72, Inst. prof. chemistry, 1972-88, Inst. prof. chemistry emeritus, 1988—, dean of faculty, v.p., provost, 1980-83, lectr., 1988—, chmn. div. chemistry and chem. engring., 1963-68, acting chmn., 1972-73; Foster lectr. U. Buffalo, 1956; Mack Meml. lectr. Ohio State U., 1957; Falk-Plaut lectr. Columbia U., 1957; Reynaud Found. lectr. Mich. State U., 1958; Bachmann Meml. lectr. U. Mich., 1958; vis. prof. Harvard, 1958-59, M. Tishler lectr., 1965; Reilly lectr. Notre Dame U., 1960; Am.-Swiss Found. lectr., 1960; O.M. Smith lectr. Okla. State U., 1962; M.S. Kharasch Meml. lectr. U. Chgo., 1962; K. Folkers lectr. U. Ill., 1962; Phillips lectr. Haverford Coll., 1963; vis. prof. U. Munich, 1962; Sloan lectr. U. Alaska, 1967; Disting. vis. prof. U. Iowa, 1967; Sprague lectr. U. Wis., 1967; Kilpatrick lectr. Ill. Inst. Tech., 1969; Pacific Northwest lectr., 1969; E.F. Smith lectr. U. Pa., 1970; vis. prof. chemistry Stanford U., 1973-74; S.C. Lind lectr. U. Tenn.; Arapahoe lectr. U. Colo., 1976; Mary E. Kapp lectr. Va. Commonwealth U., 1976; R.T. Major lectr. U. Conn., 1977; Nebr. lectr. Am. Chem. Soc., 1977; Leermakers lectr. Wesleyan U., 1980; Iddles Meml. lectr. U. N.H., 1981; Arapahoe lectr. Colo. State U., 1981; Winstein lectr. UCLA, 1981; Gilman lectr. Iowa State U., 1982; Marvel lectr. U. Ill., 1982; vis. lectr. Inst. Photog. Chemistry, Beijing, People's Republic of China, 1983, King lectr. Kans. State U., 1984, Lanzhou U., People's Republic of China, 1985, Davis lectr. U. New Orleans, 1986, Du Pont lectr. Harvey Mudd Coll., 1987, 3M vis. lectr. St. Olaf Coll., 1987, Swift lectr. Calif. Inst. Tech., 1987, Berliner lectr. Bryn Mawr Coll., 1988; Friend E. Clark lectr. W. Va. U., 1990; George H. Büchi lectr. MIT, 1991; Henry Kuivala lectr. SUNY Albany, 1991, Fuson lect. U. Nev., 1992; dir., cons. editor W.A. Benjamin, Inc., 1961-67; cons. E.I. du Pont Co., 1950—; mem. adv. panel chemistry NSF, 1958-60, chmn., 1959-60, chmn. divisional com. math., phys. engring. scis., 1962-64, mem. math. and phys. sci. div. com., 1964-66; chemistry adv. panel Air Force Office Sci. Research, 1959-61; chmn. chemistry sect. Nat. Acad. Scis., 1968-71; chmn. Nat. Acad. Scis. (Class I), 1976-78, councillor, 1980-83, nominating com., 1992; dir. Organic Syntheses, Inc. Author: Basic Organic Chemistry, Part I, 1955, Nuclear Magnetic Resonance, 1958, Spin-Spin Splitting in High-Resolution Nuclear Magnetic Resonance Spectra, 1961, Molecular Orbital Calculations, 1961, (with M.C. Caserio) Basic Principles of Organic Chemistry, 1964, 2d edit., 1977, Modern Organic Chemistry, 1967, (with R. Stewart and M.C. Caserio) Organic Chemistry-Methane To Macromolecules, 1971; (autobiography) At The Right Place at the Right Time, 1990; cons. editor: McGraw-Hill Series in Advanced Chemistry, 1957-60; editor in chief Organic Syntheses, vol. 41; mem. editorial bd. Spectroscopy, Organic Magnetic Resonance in Chemistry, Asymmetry, Tetrahedron Computer Methodology. Trustee L.S.B. Leakey Found., 1983-92; bd. dirs. Huntington Med. Rsch. Insts., Organic Syntheses Inc., Coleman Chamber Music Assn.; mem. Calif. Competitive Tech. adv. com., 1989—. Recipient Alumni Profl. Achievement award UCLA, 1967; Guggenheim fellow, 1952-53, 55-56; recipient Am. Chem. Soc. award pure chemistry, 1954; Harrison Howe award, 1957, Roger Adams award in organic chemistry, 967, Alumni Achievement award UCLA, 1967, Nichols medal, 1972, Tolman medal, 1975, Michelson-Morley award, 1976, Norris award, 1978, Pauling award, 1980, Theodore Wm. Richards medal, 1982, Willard Gibbs Gold medal, 1983, Golden Plate award Am. Acad. Achievement, 1983, Priestley medal, 1987, Madison Marshall award, 1989, (with W. v.E. Doering) Robert A. Welch award, 1990, Nat. Medal Sci. 1990, Glenn T. Seaborg medal, 1991, Award in nuclear magnetic resource, 1991, Svc. to Chemistry award, 1991; named hon. alumnus Calif. Inst. Tech., 1990, SURF dedicatee, 1992. Mem. NAS (com. sci. and engring. pub. policy 1983-87), AAAS (councillor 1992—), Am. Chem. Soc. (chmn. organic chemistry div. 1956-57, exec. com. organic div. 1953-57), Am. Philos. Soc. (coun. 1983-86), Am. Acad. Arts and Scis., Am. Assn. Adv. Sci. (councillor 1992—), Sigma Xi, Phi Lambda Upsilon, Alpha Chi Sigma. Office: Calif Inst Tech Div of Chem 164-30 CR Pasadena CA 91125

ROBERTS, JOHN DERHAM, lawyer; b. Orlando, Fla., Nov. 1, 1942; s. Junius P. and Mary E. (Limerick) R.; m. Malinda K. Swineford, June 11, 1965; 1 child, Kimberlyn Amanda. Cert., Richmond (Va.) Bus. Coll., 1960; BS, Hampden-Sydney (Va.) Coll., 1964; LLB, Washington & Lee U., 1968. Bar: Va. 1968, Fla. 1969, U.S. Supreme Ct. 1969, U.S. Ct. Customs and Patent Appeals 1970, U.S. Tax Ct. 1970, U.S. Ct. Appeals (5th cir.) 1970, U.S. Ct. Appeals (9th cir.) 1974, U.S. Supreme Ct. 1969. Law clk. U.S. Dist. Ct., Jacksonville, Fla., 1968-69; assoc. Phillips, Kendrick, Gearhart & Aylor, Arlington, Va., 1969-70; asst. U.S. Atty. mid. dist. Fla. U.S. Dept. Justice, Jacksonville, 1970-74; asst. U.S. Atty. Dist. of Alaska, Anchorage, 1974-77, U.S. magistrate judge, 1977—. Bd. dirs. Teen Challenge Alaska, Anchorage, 1984-93; chmn. Eagle Scout Rev. Bd., 1993—; bd. dirs. Alaska Youth for Christ, 1993—. Recipient Citizenship award DAR, Anchorage, 1984, plaque, U.S. Navy, Citizen Day, Adak, Alaska, 1980. Mem. ABA, Nat. Conf. Spl. Ct. Judges (exec. bd. 1985-92), 9th Cir. Conf. Magistrates (exec. bd. 1982-85, chmn. 1984-85), Alaska Bar Assn., Anchorage Bar Assn., Chi Phi, Psi Chi, Phi Alpha Delta. Republican. Office: US Magistrate 222 W 7th Ave # 46 Anchorage AK 99513-7563

ROBERTS, JOHN WILLIAM (BILL ROBERTS), glass company owner; b. Omaha, Dec. 11, 1925; s. John William and Mary Jane (Hastings) R.; m. Mary Elizebeth Myer, Sept. 2, 1950 (div. Sept. 1965); children: John W., Phillip, Ted. Student, Nebr. U., 1948; 1st class radio lic., Radio Sch., 1970. Salesman, installer Ruscoe Window, Lincoln, Nebr., 1947-48; foreman Van Sykle Glass, Lincoln, 1948-49; owner Roberts Glass, Lincoln, 1949-50; glazier Cobbledick & Kibbie, Oakland, Calif., 1952-53, North Hollywood (Calif.) Glass, 1953-56; owner Roberts Glass, Canoga Park, Calif., 1956-90, Bill Roberts Enterprises, Lakewood, Colo., 1990—; band leader Jelly Roll Jazz Soc., L.A. 1975—; photographer, writer Mile High News, Denver, 1991—; stringer Broncos Star Broadcasting Boston, Denver, 1992; drummer all star band 4th of July celebration, Madison Sq. Garden, 1986; reporter Colo. U. Basketball, Boulder, Colo.; broadcasting reporter Sports Final Network. Author: Bill's Beat, 1992; contbr. articles to jazz mags. With USN, 1943-52. Named Baseball Mgr. of Yr. Chatsworth (Calif.) Jr. Baseball, 1965. Mem. Denver Jazz Club (bd. dirs. 1992—, pres. 1993), Kiwanis Club. Democrat. Office: 610 Garrison U-109 Denver CO 80215

ROBERTS, LARRY PAUL, broadcasting executive; b. Marengo, Iowa, June 17, 1950; s. Paul V. and Marcheta Jean (Moore) R.; m. Sheryl Irene Delamarter, Aug. 18, 1973; children: Jason, Stacey, Adam. Student, Northwestern U., 1968-69; BS, U. Minn., 1972. Ops. mgr. Sta. WPEO Radio, Peoria, Ill., 1969-70, Sta. WAYL Radio, Mpls., 1970-76; program dir. Sta. KXL and KXL-FM, Portland, Oreg., 1976-82; pres. Sunbrook Broadcasting, Inc. and Sunbrook Communications Corp., licensee of Stas. KDXT and KGRZ, Missoula, Mont., Stas. KQUY, KAAR-FM, KXTL, Butte, Mont., Stas. KBLG, KRKX, KYYA-FM Billings, Mont.,, 1982—, stas. KAAK, KXGF, Great Falls, Mont., 1982—; licensee of Sta. KEEH-FM, Spokane, Wash., Sta. KYSN-FM, East Wenatchee, Wash., Sta. KXAA-FM, Rock Island, Wash. Past pres. bd. dirs. Salvation Army, Pueblo Co.; v.p. United Way, Pueble; bd. dirs. Rocky Mountain coun. Boy Scouts Am., Wayside Cross Rescue Mission, Pueblo; trustee Western Evang. Sem.; mem. ministerial appointments com., bd. evangelism Columbia River Conf. of the Free Meth. Ch., chmn. fin. com., mem. official bd. of opportunity, lay minister. Recipient Outstanding Radio Broadcaster award So. Colo. Press Club, 1986; named Radio Copywriter of Yr., Mont. Broadcasters Assn., 1983, Editorial Writer of Yr., Sigma Delta Chi, 1979, one of Outstanding Young Men in Am., Jaycees, 1980, 85. Mem. Nat. Assn. Broadcasters (medium-market com.), Lions (past, v.p. Portland club 1982), Rotary (v.p. Pueblo club). Republican. Home: 7922 E Woodview Dr Spokane WA 99212-1615 Office: North 1212 Washington Ste 124 Spokane WA 99201

ROBERTS, LIONA RUSSELL, JR., electronic engineer; b. Sheffield, Ala., Apr. 9, 1928; s. Liona Russell Sr. and Julia Phillipia (Harrison) R.; m. Norma Jean Roberts, Mar. 15, 1952 (div. 1972); children: Laura Lee, Boyd Harrison, John King, Jenna Lynne; m. Carole Jeanne Hedges, 1973. BS in Physics, U. Miss., 1958; MS in Electronics, Navy Postgrad. Sch., Monterey, Calif., 1961; PhD in Mech. Engring., Cath. U. Am., 1977. Cert. amateur radio oper. Commd. ensign USN, 1945, advanced through grades to capt., 1967, ret., 1970; chief scientist Interstate Electronics Corp., Anaheim, Calif., 1970-83; v.p. Enigmatics, Inc., LaHabra, Calif., 1983—. Author: Signal Processing Techniques, 1977; patentee in field, 1987. Mem. IEEE (sr.), Rsch. Soc. Am., Sigma Xi. Home: 1885 Kashlan Rd La Habra CA 90631-8423

ROBERTS, LORIN WATSON, botanist, educator; b. Clarksdale, Mo., June 28, 1923; s. Lorin Cornelius and Irene (Watson) R.; m. Florence Ruth Greathouse, July 10, 1967; children: Michael Hamlin, Daniel Hamlin, Margaret Susan. B.A., U. Mo.-Columbia, 1948, M.A., 1950, Ph.D. in Botany, 1952. Asst. prof., then assoc. prof. botany Agnes Scott Coll., Decaur, Ga., 1952-57; vis. asst. prof. Emory U., 1952-55; mem. faculty U. Idaho, 1957—, prof. botany, 1967-91, prof. botany emeritus, 1991—; Fulbright research prof. Kyoto (Japan) U., 1967-68; research fellow U. Bari, Italy, 1968; Cabot fellow Harvard, 1974; Fulbright teaching fellow North-Eastern Hill U., Shillong, Meghalaya, India, 1977; Fulbright sr. scholar and fellow Australian Nat. U., Canberra, 1980; sr. researcher U. London, 1984; pres. botany sect. 1st Internat. Congress Histochemistry and Cytochemistry, Paris, 1960; Alexander von Humboldt vis. fellow Australian Nat. U., 1992. Author: Cytodifferentiation in Plants, 1976, (with J.H. Dodds) Experiments in Plant Tissue Culture, 1982, 2d edit., 1985, (with P.B. Gahan and R. Aloni) Vascular Differentiation and Plant Growth Regulators, 1988; contbr. articles to profl. jours. Served with USAAF, 1943-46. Alexander van Humboldt fellow, 1992; Decorated chevalier de l'Ordre du Merite Agricole France, 1961. Fellow AAAS; mem. N.W. Sci. Assn. (pres. 1970-71), Bot. Soc. Am., Am. Soc. Plant Physiologists, Internat. Assn. Plant Tissue Culture, Internat. Soc. Plant Morphologists, Am. Inst. Biol. Scis., Idaho Acad. Scis., Sigma Xi, Phi Kappa Phi, Phi Sigma. Home: 920 Mabelle Ave Moscow ID 83843-3834

ROBERTS, MARIE DYER, computer systems specialist; b. Statesboro, Ga., Feb. 19, 1943; d. Byron and Martha (Evans) Dyer; BS, U. Ga., 1966; student Am. U., 1972; cert. systems profl., cert. in data processing; m. Hugh V. Roberts, Jr., Oct. 6, 1973. Mathematician, computer specialist U.S. Naval Oceanographic Office, Washington, 1966-73; systems analyst, programmer Sperry Microwave Electronics, Clearwater, Fla., 1973-75; data processing mgr., asst. bus. mgr. Trenam, Simmons, Kemker et al, Tampa, Fla., 1975-77; mathematician, computer specialist U.S. Army C.E., Savannah, Ga., 1977-81, 83-85, Frankfurt, W. Ger., 1981-83; ops. rsch. analyst U.S. Army Contrn. Rsch. Lab., Champaign, Ill., 1985-87; data base adminstr., computer systems programmer, chief info. integration and implementation div. U.S. Army Corps of Engrs., South Pacific div., San Francisco, 1987—; instr. computer scis. City Coll. of Chgo. in Franfurt, 1982-83. Recipient Sustained Superior Performance award Dept. Army, 1983. Mem. Am. Soc. Hist. Preservation, Data Processing Mgmt. Assn., Assn. of Inst. for Cert. Computer Profls., Assn. Women in Computing, Assn. Women in Sci., NAFE, Am. Film Inst., U. Ga. Alumni Assn., Sigma Kappa, Soc. Am. Mil. Engrs. Author: Harris Computer Users Manual, 1983.

ROBERTS, MARK SCOTT, lawyer; b. Fullerton, Calif., Dec. 31, 1951; s. Emil Seidel and Theda (Wymer) R.; m. Sheri Lyn Smith, Sept. 23, 1977; children: Matthew Scott, Meredith Lyn, Benjamin Price. BA in Theater, Pepperdine U., 1975; JD, Western State U., 1979; cert. civil trial advocacy program, U. Calif., San Francisco, 1985; cert. program of instrn. for lawyers, Harvard U., 1990. Bar: Calif. 1980, U.S. Dist. Ct. (cen. dist.) Calif. 1980, U.S. Supreme Ct. 1989, U.S. Ct. Mil. Appeals 1989, U.S. Tax Ct. 1990. Concert mgr. Universal Studios, Hollywood, Calif., 1973-74; tchr. Anaheim (Calif.) Union Sch Dist., 1979-80; prin. Mark Roberts & Assocs., Fullerton, Calif., 1980—; instr. bus. law Biola U., La Mirada, Calif., 1980-84; judge pro tem Orange County Mcpl. Ct., Fullerton, 1988—, Orange County Superior Ct., Santa Ana, 1989—. Mem. Calif. State Bar Assn., Orange County Bar Assn. Office: Mark Roberts & Assocs 285 E Imperial Hwy Ste 107 Fullerton CA 92635-1048

ROBERTS, NATHAN JAY, retired lawyer, educator; b. N.Y.C., Aug. 1, 1906; s. Bernard and Jennie Zelda (Zatulove) R.; m. Margaret Jacobson, Aug. 27, 1950. AB, Syracuse U., 1926; JD, U. Fla., 1929; LLM, George Washington U., 1949. Bar: Fla. 1929, N.C. 1929, Calif. 1964, U.S. Supreme Ct. 1940. Pvt. practice Jacksonville, Fla., 1929-40; commd. capt. U.S. Army, 1937, advanced through grades to brig. gen., 1961; with Regular Army in JAGC, 1940-63; asst. judge advocate gen. for civil law U.S. Army, 1961-63, ret., 1963; prof. law Loyola U., L.A., 1966-77; ret., 1977. Co-author: Contemporary Business Law, Business and the Law. Pres. Exch. Club, Jacksonville, 1939-40. Decorated Legion of Merit with 1 oak leaf cluster. Home: 123 Conejo Rd Santa Barbara CA 93103-1637

ROBERTS, NORMAN FRANK, English composition educator; b. Guilford, Maine, Aug. 18, 1931; s. John Francis and Pearl Estelle (Crozier) R.; m. Shoko Kawasaki, Sept. 18, 1959; children: Norman F. Jr., Kenneth K., Kathryn M. BA, U. Hawaii, 1960, MA, 1963, cert. in linguistics, 1972. Instr. ESL, U. Hawaii, Honolulu, 1962-68; prof. English, linguistics Leeward Community Coll., Pearl City, Hawaii, 1968—, chmn. divsn. lang. arts, 1975-81, 1992—; cons. Nat. Council Tchrs. of English, 1972—. Author: Model Essay Booklet, 1989; co-author: Community College Library Instruction, 1979; contbr. articles to profl. jours. V.p. Pacific Palisades Community Assn., Pearl City, pres., 1973-74; mem. Aloha coun. Boy Scouts Am., Honolulu, 1972—, dir wood badge course, 1985, chmn. camping promotions, 1989-92. Recipient Dist. award of Merit Boy Scouts Am., 1986. Mem. Nat. Council Tchrs. of English, Hawaii Council Tchrs. of English (program chmn. 1974), Am. Dialect Soc. (program chmn. Honolulu conf. 1977), Linguistic Soc. Am. Office: Leeward Community Coll Lang Arts Div 96-045 Ala Ike Pearl City HI 96782

ROBERTS, P. ELAINE, biology and entomology educator; b. Mt. Clements, Mich., Feb. 18, 1944; d. Roger and Rose Olive (Sober) R. BA, Western Mich. U., 1967; PhDin Cell Biology, U. Ill., 1976. Postdoctoral fellow Mayo Clinic, Rochester, Minn., 1976-78; NIH postdoctoral fellow Queens U., Kingston, Ont., Can., 1978-79; asst. prof. Colo. State U., Ft. Collins, 1979-86, assoc. prof., 1986-91, prof. entomology, 1991—; coord. student retention Coll. Agrl. Scis., Colo. State U., Ft. Collins, 1991-92. Co-editor Regulation of Insect Gene Expression by Juvenile Hormone and Ecdysone, 1986; contbr. articles to profl. jours. Mem. AAAS, Entomol. Soc. Am., Am. Soc. Zoologists, Assn. Women in Sci., Sigma Xi. Home: 509 E Plum Fort Collins CO 80524 Office: Colo State U Dept Entomology Fort Collins CO 80523

ROBERTS, PETER CHRISTOPHER TUDOR, engineering executive; b. Georgetown, Demerara, Brit. Guiana, Oct. 12, 1945; came to U.S., 1979; s. Albert Edward and Dorothy Jean (Innis) R.; m. Julia Elizabeth Warner, Nov. 10, 1984; children: Kirsta Anne, Serena Amanda, Angelee Julia, Zephanie Elizabeth, Fiona Ann, Emrys Tudor, Peter Christopher Tudor Roberts II. BSc with honors, Southampton (Eng.) U., 1969, PhD in Microelectronics, 1975. Rsch. fellow dept. electronics Southampton U., 1974-77; prof. microcircuit dept. electronics INAOE, Tonantzintla, Mexico, 1977-79; staff scientist Honeywell Systems & Rsch. Ctr., Mpls., 1979-84; dir. advanced tech. Q-Dot Inc. R&D, Colorado Springs, Colo., 1984-86; program mgr. Honeywell Opto-Electronics, Richardson, Tex., 1986; vis. prof. U. N.Mex. CHTM, Albuquerque, 1987; supr. engring. Loral Inc. (formerly Honeywell), Lexington, Mass., 1988-90; mgr. engring. Litton Systems Inc., Tempe, Ariz., 1990—; cons. engr. Q-Dot, Inc. R&D, Colorado Springs, 1982—, pvt. stockholder, 1984—. Author: (with P.C.T. Roberts) Charge-Coupled Devices and Their Applications, 1980; contbr. articles to Boletin del INAOE, IEEE Transactions on Electron Devices, Procs. of the IEEE (U.K.), Procs. of the INTERNEPCON, Internat. Jour. Electronics, IEEE Electron Device Letters, Electronics Letters, Solid State and Electron Devices, IEEE Jour. Solid State Circuits, others. Republican. Christian. Home: 1017 W Peninsula Dr Gilbert AZ 85234-8903 Office: Litton Systems 1215 S 52d St Tempe AZ 85281

ROBERTS, PHILIP JOHN, history educator; b. Lusk, Wyo., July 8, 1948; s. Leslie J. and LaVerne Elizabeth (Johns) R. BA, U. Wyo., 1973, JD, 1977; PhD, U. Wash., 1990. Bar: Wyo. 1977. Editor Lake Powell Chronicle, Page, Ariz., 1972-73; co-founder, co-pub. Medicine Bow (Wyo.) Post, 1977; pvt. practice in law Carbon and Laramie County, Wyo., 1977-84; historian Wyo. State Hist. Dept., Cheyenne, 1979-84; editor Annals of Wyo., Cheyenne, 1980-84; owner, pub. Capitol Times, Cheyenne, 1982-84, Skyline West Press, Seattle, 1985-90; asst. prof. history U. Wyo., Laramie, 1990—; evaluator Wyo. Coun. for the Humanities, Laramie, 1990—; indexer Osborne McGraw-Hill, Berkeley, 1988—; organizing dir. U. Wyo. Press, 1993. Author: Wyoming Almanac, 1989 (pub. annually), Buffalo Bones: Stories from Wyoming's Past, 1979, 82, 84; contbr. articles to profl. jours. Bd. dirs. Wyo. Territorial Park, Laramie, 1991. With USMC, 1970-72. Mem. Wyo. State Hist. Soc. (life), Wyo. State Bar, Pacific N.W. Historians' Guild, 9th Judicial Cir. Hist. Soc., Western History Assn., Am. Hist. Assn., Orgn. of Am. Historians. Democrat. Office: U Wyo Dept History Laramie WY 82071

ROBERTS, ROBERT CANTWELL, technical college president; b. Butte, Mont., Aug. 28, 1935; s. Ellis Vaughn and Alice (Cantwell) R.; m. Sheila Hanley, Sept. 30, 1954; children: Evan, Deborah, Katherine, Elizabeth. BS in Edn., Western Mont. Coll., 1957, MS in Edn., 1962; EdD, U. Mont., 1970. Tchr., counselor Butte Sch. Dist. 1, 1957-65; edn. rsch. coord. Mont. Dept. Pub. Inst., Helena, 1965-67; adminstrv. asst. Missoula County High Schs., Missoula, Mont., 1967-71; asst. supt. Renton (Wash.) Sch. Dist. 403, 1971-91; dir. Renton Vocat. Tech. Inst., 1971-91; pres. Renton Tech. Coll., 1991—; tchr. trainer, Seattle U., Seattle Pacific U., U. Wash., So. Ill. U., Carbondale, 1975-92; presenter in field. Contbr. articles to profl. jours. Mem. Nat. Def. Exec. Res., U.S. Dept. Def., Pvt.-Industry Coun., Seattle-King County. Recipient Outstanding Svc. award Wash. Coun. on Vacat. Edn., 1987, individual award Wash. Human Devel., 1990; named Outstanding Adminstr., Wash. Coun. Local Adminstrn., 1984. Mem. Am. Assn. Adult and Continuing Edn., Am. Assn. Community Colls., Community Coll. Pers. Assn., Nat. Wash. Coun. for Occupational Edn., Wash. Assn. Community and Tech. Colls. (pres.), Internat. Soc. Gen. Semantics, N.W. Adult Edn., Renton C. of C., Seattle C. of C., Rotary, Phi Delta Kappa. Roman Catholic. Home: 20466 SE 159th St Renton WA 98059-9012 Office: Ranton Tech Coll 3000 NE 4th St Renton WA 98056

ROBERTS, WILLIAM HARRISON, aerospace engineer, consultant, researcher; b. Cin., Sept. 4, 1921; s. William Harrison and Hazel Gail (Prather) R.; m. Elisabeth Marie Jensen, May 26, 1973 (div. 1989); children: William, Christopher, Roy, Jon. Grad. in Aero. Engring., U. Cin., 1943; MS in Engring., UCLA, 1953; postgrad., Columbia Pacific U., 1991—. Dynamics specialist North Am. Aviation, L.A., 1943-58; chief dynamics and loads, mgr. structures rsch. Northrop, Hawthorne, Calif., 1958-63; chief structures Martin, Orlando, Fla., 1963-72; space shuttle dynamics mgr. Rockwell, Downey, Calif., 1972-74; preliminary design, structure dynamics Northrop, Hawthorne, 1974-77; space shuttle payload integration Hughes Aircraft Space and Communications, El Segundo, Calif., 1977-80; sr. cons. Sturctural Dynamics Consl., Inglewood, Calif., 1980-81; structural dynamics engr. Byron Jackson, Carson, Calif., 1981-82; sr. dynamics specialist FAA Airframes, Long Beach, Calif., 1982—; spl. assignment to Naval Rsch. Lab.; AIAA structural adv. com. to NASA Langley; invited papers to Acoustic Soc., USAF Symposium on Dynamic Models. Creator computer programs to optimize vehicle design; design and test wind tunnel models; developed capability to measure, describe and simulate dynamic environments; contbr. articles to profl. jours. Engr. to local group to stabilize homes due to massive landslides, Portuguese Bend, Calif., 1980-84. With USN, 1944-46. Fellow AIAA (assoc.); mem. Aerospace Flutter and Dynamics Coun., SAE (sub-com. shock and vibration 1980—), Tau Beta Pi, Phi Eta Sigma. Home: 2 Figtree Portuguese Bend CA 90274 Office: FAA 3229 E Spring St Long Beach CA 90806

ROBERTS, WILLIAM RICHARD, electronics company official; b. Portland, Oreg., Oct. 16, 1936; s. William Ward and Mary Louise (Kistler) R. BSChemE, Oreg. State U., 1958, postgrad., 1959. Registered engr.-in-tng., Calif. Devel. engr. Aerojet-Gen. Corp., Sacramento, 1959-64; field support specialist computer dept. GE, Sunnyvale and L.A., Calif., 1964-70; field support mgr. Honeywell Info. Systems, L.A., 1970-78; product mgr. Bull HN Info. Systems, Phoenix, 1978—. Home: 2901 W Altadena Ave Phoenix AZ 85029 Office: Group Bull POBox 8000-A92 Phoenix AZ 85066

ROBERTS-DEGENNARO, MARIA, social work educator; b. Austin, Minn., Oct. 10, 1947; d. Clinton M. and Laura E. (DeMets) Becker; m. Paul DeGennaro, July 7, 1984; 1 child, Matthew. B of Social Work, U. Minn., 1970, MSW, 1976; PhD, U. Tex., 1981. Family counselor Hennepin County Welfare Dept., Mpls., 1970-73; coord. YMCA, Mpls., 1973-74; dist. project coord. Child Abuse and Neglect Project, Phoenix, 1976-77; prof. San Diego State U., 1980—; dir. Interdisciplinary Ctr., San Diego State U., 1987-90; dir. Interdisciplinary Program on Early Intervention San Diego State U., 1989—. Contbr. articles to profl. jours. Mem. Assn. on Community Orgn. and Social Adminstrn., Nat. Assn. Social Workers, Coun. on Social Work Edn. Office: San Diego State U Sch Social Work San Diego CA 92182

ROBERTS-LINDSEY, CAROL ANNETTE, nursing educator, perinatal nurse consultant; b. L.A., Nov. 4, 1958; d. Carl Victor and Ernestine (King) Roberts; m. Ruben Lindsey, Apr. 6, 1991. BSN, Howard U., 1982. RN, Calif. Supervising nurse I, Martin Luther King Hosp., L.A., 1982-85; staff nurse Columbia Hosp. for Women, Washington, 1986; coord. utilization rev. Calif. Med. Rev. Inc., Torrance, 1986-88; instr. nursing Pacific Coast Coll., L.A., 1989—, asst. DON,, 1989-90; instr. nursing Maxine Waters Employment Preparation Ctr., L.A., 1992—; ind. contractor Calif. Med. Audit, L.A., 1987-90; instr. med. careers Bus. Industry Sch., L.A., 1988-90, instr. nursing, 1990-91; perinatal nurse cons. South Bay Perinatal Access Project, Torrance, 1992—. Mem. Bus. Women's Network, Sigma Theta Tau, Chi Eta Phi.

ROBERTSON, ALEXANDER, IV, lawyer; b. L.A., Dec. 27, 1959; s. Alex Jr. and Stephanie (Searles) R.; children: Alexander V, Jessica Neal. BSBA, Pepperdine U., 1982, JD, 1986. Bar: Calif. 1986, U.S. Dist. Ct. (cen. dist.) Calif. 1986, U.S. Claims Ct. 1986, U.S. Ct. Appeals (9th cir.) 1988, U.S. Dist. Ct. (ea., no., and so. dists.) Calif. 1989. Asst. gen. mgr. Alex Robertson Co., 1978-83; assoc. Acret & Perrochet, L.A., 1986-87; ptnr. Negele, Knopfler, Pierson & Robertson, Universal City, Calif., 1987—. Pres., bd. dirs. Calabasas Hills Community Assn., 1989-90, sec., 1990-91; bd. dirs. Calabasas Park Homeowners Assn., 1990-92, v.p., 1991-92. Mem. ABA (forum on constrn. industry), Los Angeles County Bar, Beverly Hills Bar Assn., Cowboy Lawyers Assn., Assoc. Gen. Contractors Calif. (underground constrn. com.), Pepperdine Univ. Assocs. (alumni bd. 1987-90), San Fernando Valley Bar Assn., Bldg. Industry Assn., So. Calif. Contractors Assn., Engring. Contractors Assn., Community Assn. Inst., The Beavers. Office: Negele Knopfler Pierson & Robertson 10 Universal City Plz Ste 1500 Universal City CA 91608-1002

ROBERTSON, C. ALTON, liberal studies educator; b. Brawley, Calif., Feb. 7, 1933; s. Clarence Asher and Leona (Lilly) R.; m. Shirley Joy Nowlin, Mar. 10, 1961 (div. 1974); children: Eric Alton, Elliott Ward. BA, U. Redlands, 1954; M in Div., Berkeley Bapt. Divinity Sch., 1957; MIA, Columbia U., 1967, MPhil, 1971. Dir. Commn. on World Mission Nat. Student Christian Fedn., N.Y.C., 1960-65; fraternal sec. Waseda Hoshien Student Christian Ctr., Tokyo, 1957-60, 67-69; dir. Overseas Pers. Recruitment Office, N.Y.C., 1970-72; office clk. System 99 Truck Line, Pico Rivera, Calif., 1974-82; mem. faculty U. Redlands, Calif., 1982—, asst. to dean, 1982-86, dir. weekend courses, 1986-89, assoc. prof. dept. liberal studies, 1989—; faculty dir. Year-in-Japan study program Calif. Pvt. Univs. and Colls. Consortium, 1990-91. Author: Is God Still Here?, 1968; columnist local newspaper, 1988, 90-91; contbr. articles to religious publs. Mem. Redlands Sister City Com., 1985—. Grantee Danforth Found., 1965-66, 69-70; Alice Stetton fellow Columbia U., 1966-67. Democrat. Episcopalian. Home: 224 Lillac Ct Redlands CA 92373 Office: U Redlands PO Box 3080 Redlands CA 92373

ROBERTSON, DANIEL CARLTON, museum director; b. Portland, Oreg., Sept. 17, 1951; s. Jerold Dean and Elsie Mae (Keck) R.; m. Emily A. Dana, June 17, 1979 (div. Apr. 1985); 1 child, Katherine Elizabeth; m. Shannon Lee Applegate, Aug. 17, 1985; children: Jessica, Colin, Ione, Max, Edane. BA, Portland State U., 1975. Intern curator Clatsop County Hist. Soc., Astoria, Oreg., 1979-80; dir. hist. services Benton County Hist. Soc., Corvallis, Oreg., 1980-83; dir. Douglas County Mus. of History and Nat. History, Roseburg, Oreg., 1983—. Mem. Roseburg City Coun., 1987-90; vice chmn. Roseburg Visitors and Conv. Bur., 1986-88; bd. dirs. Eliot Inst., 1989-92; pres. Umpqua Community Devel. Corp., 1991—; candidate for Oreg. Ho. of Reps. from dist. 45, 1992; chair Douglas County Dem. Ctrl. Com., 1992—; del. Oreg. Dem. Party Ctrl. Com., 1992—; exec. com. Oreg. Dem. Com., 1992—. With USN, 1969-71. Mem. Am. Assn. for State and Local History (awards chmn. region 11 1987-89, nat. chmn. awards com. 1990-92), Southwestern Oreg. Vis. Assn. (pres. 1989-90), Oreg. Mus. Assn. (pres. 1982-84, editor Dispatch 1980-82), Clatsop County Hist. Soc. (life). Democrat. Unitarian. Home: PO Box 441 Roseburg OR 97470-4827 Office: Douglas County Mus History & Natural History PO Box 1550 Roseburg OR 97470-0363

ROBERTSON, HUGH DUFF, lawyer; b. Grosse Pointe, Mich., Mar. 14, 1957; s. Hugh Robertson and Louise (Grey) Bollinger; m. Lynn Ann Wicker, June 10, 1978. BBA in Fin., U. Wis., Whitewater, 1978; JD, Whittier Coll., 1982. Bar: Calif. 1983, U.S. Tax Ct. 1984. Pres., chief exec. officer A. Morgan Maree Jr. & Assocs., Inc., L.A., 1979—; NFLPA mem. contract advisor, 1991—. Mem. ABA (forum com. on entertainment 1982—, forum com. on constrn. industry 1989), State Calif., L.A. County Bar Assn., Beverly Hills Bar Assn., Acad. TV Arts and Scis., Am. Film Inst., Phi ALpha Delta. Republican. Episcopalian. Office: A Morgan Maree Jr & Assocs 6363 Wilshire Blvd Ste 600 Los Angeles CA 90048

ROBERTSON, JACQUELINE LEE, entomologist; b. Petaluma, Calif., July 9, 1947; d. John Lyman and Nina Pauline (Klemenok) Schwartz; m. Joseph Alexander, Sept. 12, 1970 (div. Jan. 1978). BA, U. Calif., Berkeley, 1969, PhD, 1973. Registered profl. entomologist. Research entomologist USDA Forest Service, Berkeley, 1970—. Editor: Jour. Econ. Entomology, 1982—, Can. Entomologist, 1992—; author: Pesticide Bioassays with Arthropods, 1992; contbr. articles to profl. jours.; patentee lab. device, 1982. Mem. Entomol. Soc. Am., Entomol. Soc. Can., AAAS. Democrat. Office: US Forest Svc PSW Sta PO Box 245 Berkeley CA 94701

ROBERTSON, KAREN LEE, county official, acoustical consultant; b. Whittier, Calif., Mar. 21, 1955; d. Lethal Greenhaw Robertson and Lloydine Ann (Pierce) Robertson-Reese; children: Kimberlee Ann Kubski, Krista Linn Robertson. Student Calif. State U. Acoustical technician Hilliard & Bricken, Santa Ana, Calif., 1977-79, John J. Van Houten, Anaheim, Calif., 1979; prin. Robertson & Assocs., Boulder, Colo., 1980; acoustical technician David Adams & Assocs., Denver, 1980; v.p. engring. John Hilliard & Assocs., Tustin, Calif., 1985—; acoustical specialist County of Orange, Santa Ana, 1980-87; airline access, noise officer John Wayne Airport Adminstrn. of Orange County, 1987-92; chair Noise Abatement Com., 1992; sr. noise compatibility planner Dallas/Ft. Worth Internat. Airport, 1992—. Co-author Land Use/Noise Compatibility Manual, 1984; editor Noise Element of General Plan, 1984. Speaker in field. Mem. acoustical adv. bd. Orange County, 1985—; mem. Calif. Noise Officers Forum, 1987—. Recipient Achievement award Nat. Assn. Counties, 1986, 90, 91, Orange County Achievement award, 1990, Woman Achievement award, 1991. Mem. Acoustical Soc. Am. (bd. dirs. 1985-86), Transp. Research Bd. (tech. mem. 1985—), Nat. Assn. Noise Control Ofcls., Community/Indsl. Noise Control Assn., Inst. Noise Control Engring. (affiliate), Calif. Assn. Window Mfrs. (STC Task Group 1985). Republican. Home: 1804 Sandalwood Ln Grapevine TX 76051 Office: Dallas/Ft Worth Internat Airport PO Drawer DFW Dallas TX 75261

ROBERTSON, LAWRENCE MARSHALL, JR., neurosurgeon; b. Denver, Feb. 4, 1932; s. Lawrence M. and Mildred Eleanor (Blackwood) R.; m. Joan T. White, May 13, 1958 (div. Oct. 1973); children: Colette M., Michele E., Laurienne J., Lawrence M. III; m. Lee Ann Crawford, Sept. 24, 1982; one child, William M. BA, U. Colo., 1954; MD, U. Colo., Denver, 1957; postgrad., U. Denver, 1981-85. Diplomate Am. Bd. Med.-Legal Analysis in Medicine and Surgery, Am. Bd. Clin. Neurol. Surgery. Intern Kings County Hosp., Bklyn., 1957-58; resident in gen. surgery St. Joseph Hosp., Denver, 1958-59; resident in neurology U. Colo., Denver, 1959-60; resident in neurosurgery Boston City Hosp., 1960-64; fellow in neurosurgery Lahey Clinic, Boston, 1963; practice medicine specializing in neurosurgery Denver, 1964—; arbitrator Am. Arbitration Assn., 1983—. Contbr. articles on malpractice to legal jours. Capt. USNR, 1979-83, 85. Recipient Continuing Edn. Cert., Am. Assn. Neurol. Surgeons and Cong. Neurol. Surgeons, 1976, 1980-83, Physicians Recognition award AMA 1976-79, 80-83, 84-87. Fellow Am. Acad. Neurosurg. and Orthopedic Surgeons; mem. AAAS, Am. Coll. Legal Medicine, Colo. Neurosurg. Soc., N.Y. Acad. Scis., Nat. Rwy. Hist. Soc., Assn. Mil. Surgeons, U.S. Naval Res. Assn., Res. Officers Assn., U.S. Naval Inst., Interurban Neurosurg. Soc., Rocky Mountain Traumatologic Soc., Phi Alpha Delta. Office: Colo Neurosurgery PC 1635 Gilpin St Denver CO 80218-1632

ROBERTSON, MARIAN ELLA (MARIAN ELLA HALL), small business owner, handwriting analyst; b. Edmonton, Alta., Can., Mar. 3, 1920; d. Orville Arthur and Lucy Hon (Osborn) Hall; m. Howard Chester Robertson, Feb. 7, 1942; children: Elaine, Richard. Student, Willamette U., 1937-39; BS, Western Oreg. State U., 1955. Cert. elem., jr. high. tchr., supt. (life) Oreg.; cert. graphoanalyst. Tchr. pub. schs. Mill City, Albany, Scio and Hillsboro, Oreg., 1940-72; cons. Zaner-Bloser Inc., Columbus, Ohio, 1972-85, assoc. cons., 1985-89; pres. Write-Keys, Scio, 1980-90; owner Lifelines, Jefferson, Oreg., 1991—; tchr. Internat. Graphoanalysis Soc., Chgo., 1979; instr. Linn-Benton Community Coll., 1985-89. Sr. intern 5th Congl. Dist. Oreg., Washington, 1984, mem. sr. adv. coun.; precinct com. mem. Rep. Cen. Com., Linn County, 1986, alt. vice-chair, 1986, parliamentarian, 1988—; candidate Oreg. State Legis., Salem, 1986; del. Northwest Friends Yearly Meeting, Newberg, Oreg., 1990, 91, 92; master gardener vol. Marion County, Oreg. State U. Extension Svc., 1992; floriculture judge Marion County Fair, 1992; master gardener clinic Oreg. State Fair, 1992; clerk Marion Friends Monthly Meeting, 1992-93. Mem. Altrusa Internat. (internat. chmn. 1985-86, chmn. pub. rels. 1989—, corr. sec. 1990-91), Internat. Platform Assn. Republican. Mem. Soc. of Friends. Home: 37929 Kelly Rd Scio OR 97374-9710 Office: Lifelines PO Box 54 Jefferson OR 97352-0054

ROBERTSON, MONICA S., contractor; b. Indpls., Aug. 14, 1965; d. William Clarence Robertson and Patricia Luana (Robbins) Elder. BS, Ind. U., 1988. Account exec. Internat. Trading Group, Honolulu, 1989-90; gen. contractor GTE Hawaiian Telephone, Honolulu, 1990—. Vol. Project Respect, Honolulu, 1990—. Mem. Bldg. Industry Assn. (guest mem. of GTE Hawaiian Telephone). Office: GTE Hawaiian Telephone Mobile Communication 320 Ward Ave # 210 Honolulu HI 96815

ROBIN, DAVID ARTHUR, pastor; b. Walnut Creek, Calif., Dec. 7, 1960; s. Richard Allen and Dorothy Nell (Sharp) R.; m. Dollie Terena Armstrong, Aug. 21, 1982; children: Leah Danielle, Sarah Elizabeth, Rebecca Nahshon, Jonathon David. BA, Simpson Coll., 1985; MDiv, San Francisco Theol. Sem., 1989. Ordained to ministry Presbyn. Ch., 1991. Machinist Berglin Mfg. Corp., Hayward, Calif., 1978-83; unloader UPS, San Francisco, 1984; mover Baker Moving and Storage, Tiburon, Calif., 1985-88; assoc. pastor Gateway Presbyn. Ch., The Dalles, Oreg., 1989—; pres. Ch. Basketball League, The Dalles, 1989-90; treas. The Dalles Ministerial Assn., 1990-91. Bd. dirs. The Stronghold Cafe, The Dalles, 1990, Mid-Columbia Child and Family Ctr., The Dalles, 1991-92. Republican. Presbyterian. Home: 1415 Nevada The Dalles OR 97058 Office: Gateway Presbyn Ch 1111 Dry Hollow The Dalles OR 97058

ROBINETT, ANN, music educator; b. Soda Springs, Idaho, Aug. 27, 1949; d. Perry and Marcia Elaine (Finlayson) Warner; m. Ronald Roy Robinett, Sept. 12, 1968; children: Jeannine, Randy, Sean. Student, U. Idaho, 1967-68, Idaho State U., 1968. Tchr. music McCammon, Idaho, 1973—. Dir. choir LDS Ch., 1971-92, chmn. music, 1976—, organist, 1989-92; dir. community mus., 1975-86; dir. children's chorus, 1980-86; mem. parent adv. coun. Mt. View Sch. and Lewis and Clark Sch., Pocatello and McCammon, Idaho, 1981-89; bd. mem. Lewis and Clark Sch. PTA, Pocatello and McCammon, 1981-89; pres. Lewis and Clark Sch. PTA, Pocatello, 1984-85; bd. dirs. Pocatello Arts Coun., 1989—. Mem. Idaho Fedn. Music Clubs (pres. 1991-93), Pocatello Music Club (bd. dirs. 1982-92, pres. 1986-89). Republican.

ROBINS, ANN-LORRAINE, special events producer, meeting planner; b. San Diego, Mar. 15, 1958; d. Charles Luther and Gloria Nell (Bruce) R. BSBA, Nat. U.-U. San Diego, 1981; grad. cert. in European hospitality, Ecole Hoteliere, Lausanne, Switzerland, 1983; BS in Hotel and Restaurant mgmt., U. Nev., Las Vegas, 1984. Ops. mgr. Svc. Corp. Internat., San Diego, 1973-81; mgr. catering and bar Coll. Hotel Adminstrn., Las Vegas, 1982-84; dir. catering for U.S. western region Marriott Corp., Rancho Mirage, Calif., 1984-89; dir. ops. Advance Prodns., Internat., San Diego, 1989-93, A.L. Robins & Assocs., San Diego, 1993—; prodr. Jerry Brown Presdl. Campaign, So. Calif., 1992. Bd. dirs. San Diego Conv. and Visitors Bur., 1989—, Family Svc. Assn., San Diego, 1990—; fundraising dir. St. Paul's Retirement Manor; assoc. bd. dirs. San Diego Blood Bank, 1991; coord. San Diego Dist. Women's Club. Recipient merit award San Diego Conv. and Visitors Bur., 1990, award of merit Spl. Event mag., 1991. Mem. Internat. Spl. Events Soc. (v.p., bd. dirs. San Diego 1991—, honor award 1992), Nat. Assn. Catering Execs. (merit award 1990), Meeting Planners Internat., San Diego Hotel Sales and Mktg. assn., San Diego C. of C. Republican. Roman Catholic. Home: 4577 Barnhurst Pl San Diego CA 92117

ROBINS, RONALD DAVID, aerospace marketing and proposal management specialist; b. Palo Alto, Calif., Dec. 2, 1957; s. John Richard and Arlene (Murison) R.; m. Mary Johanna Stretmater, Jan. 11, 1986; children: Daniel Murison, Matthew Richard, Claire Alexandra. BS of Bus. in Mktg. and Fin., U. Md., 1979, MBA, 1983. Auditor Ford Motor Credit Corp., Balt., 1980-81; teaching asst. U. Md., College Park, 1981-83; bus. strategist Satellite Bus. Systems, Tyson Corner, Va., 1983-84; resource analyst Fed. Systems Div. IBM, Bethesda, Md., 1984-85, planning strategist, 1985-86; exec. asst. Fed. Systems Div. IBM, Boulder, Colo., 1987-88, mktg. rep., 1988-89; mktg. rep. Systems Integration Div. IBM, Boulder, Colo., 1989-91, mktg. and proposal mgmt., 1991—. Contbr. editorials to newspapers. Vol. United We Stand, Am., Boulder, 1992; vol., activist PTO, Boulder, 1992; active United Way of Boulder County, 1987-92, exec. mktg., 1988-91; bd. dirs. Flatirons Ctr. for Arts, Boulder, 1990-91. Mem. Soc. of Logistics Engrs., Armed Forces Communications and Electronics Assn., Air Force Assn., Am. Astronautical Soc., Nat. Security Indsl. Assn., Charles J. Givens Orgn. Roman Catholic. Home: 1550 Sumac Ave Boulder CO 80304 Office: IBM Fed Systems Co 6300 Diagonal Hwy Boulder CO 80301

ROBINSON, ALAN HADLEY, nuclear engineering educator; b. Phila., Oct. 25, 1934; s. Walter Hadley and Mariana (Webster) R.; m. Grace Greenwood Norton, Oct. 5, 1957 (div. 1972); children: Alan Hadley Jr., William Norton; m. Gail Patricia Skyrman, Apr. 8, 1972. BSME, Swarthmore Coll., 1956; MS in Nuclear Engring., Stanford U., 1961, PhD in Nuclear Engring., 1965. Registered profl. engr., Oreg. Assoc. prof. dept. nuclear engring. Oreg. State U., Corvallis, 1966-74; prof. Oreg. State U., 1974—, acting head dept. nuclear engring., 1986-87, head dept. nuclear engring., 1987—; cons. nuclear divsn. Siemens Power Corp., Richland, Wash., 1970—, Portland (Oreg.) GE Co., 1972-88, Westinghouse Hanford Corp., Richland, 1981—. Contbr. over 50 articles to profl. jours.; author conf. proceedings, reports. Capt. USMC, 1956-60. AEC fellow, 1961-64; recipient Lloyd Carter teaching award, Oreg. State U., 1979. Mem. Am. Nuclear Soc., Sigma Xi, Tau beta Pi. Office: Oreg State Univ Radiation Ctr C 116 Corvallis OR 97331-5902

ROBINSON, ANNETTMARIE, entrepreneur; b. Fayetteville, Ark., Jan. 31, 1940; d. Christopher Jacy and Lorena (Johnson) Simmons; m. Roy Robinson, June 17, 1966; children: Steven, Sammy, Doug, Pamela, Olen. BA, Edison Tech. U., 1958; BA in Bus., Seattle Community Coll., 1959. Dir. perss. Country Kitchen Restaurants, Inc., Anchorage, 1966-71; investor Anchorage, 1971—; cons. Pioneer Investments, Anchorage, 1983—, M'RAL, Inc. Retail Dry Goods, Anchorage, 1985. Mem. Rep. Presdl. Task Force, Washington, 1984—, Reps. of Alaska, Anchorage, 1987; mem. chmn. round table YMCA, Anchorage, 1986—; active Sta. KWN2, KQLO, Reno, Nev.; active in child abuse issues and prosecution. Named Woman of Yr. Lions, Anchorage, 1989, marksman first class Nat. Rifle Assn., 1953. Mem. NAFE, Spenard Lion's Aux. (past pres.).

ROBINSON, ARNOLD, manufacturing executive; b. N.Y.C., Oct. 27, 1929; s. Louis and Anna (Cohen) R.; m. Gertrude Leah Needleman, Nov. 14, 1954; children: Barry David, Lisa Robinson McConnell, Sanford. BS in Aero. Engring., Poly. Inst. Bklyn., 1951; MS in Aero. Engring., Drexel Inst. Tech., 1955. Registered profl. engr., N.Y., Pa., Fla. Engr. aircraft structures U.S. Naval Aircraft Devel. Ctr., Johnsville, Pa., 1951-54, U.S. Naval Aircraft Factory, Phila., 1954-55; group engr. aircraft structures missiles div. Republic Aviation Corp., Farmingdale, N.Y., 1955-57; asst. chief engr. Omega Aircraft Corp., New Bedford, Mass., 1957-59; v.p., engr., prin. DeVore Aviation Corp. Am., Albuquerque, 1960-91, pres., 1991—. Named Exporter of Yr. NMSBA, 1990; recipient Productivity award N.Mex. Sen. Bingaman, 1989. Mem. AIAA, Am. Helicopter Soc., Internat. Soc. Air Safety Investigators, N.Mex. Entrepreneurs Assn. (treas. 1988-89, pres., 1990—). Office: DeVore Aviation Corp Am 6104B Jefferson St NE Albuquerque NM 87109-3410

ROBINSON, BARBARA JÕN, librarian; b. Beatrice, Nebr., Feb. 28, 1944; d. Beryl William and Beulah Rose (Burgess) Potter; m. J. Cordell Robinson, Aug. 12, 1967 (div. 1987); children: Lisa Maria, Hilton Clifton. BA, Smith Coll., 1966; MA, Ind. U., 1967, MLS, 1969. Libr. Universidad de Los Andes, Bogotá, Colombia, 1969-70, Ind. U., Bloomington, 1970-71, U. Calif., Riverside, 1974-85, U. So. Calif., L.A., 1985—. Author: The Mexican American: A Critical Guide to Research Aids, 1980; editor: Artistic Representation of Latin American Diversity: Sources and Collections, 1993. Fellow Gulbenkian Found., 1966, Ford Found., 1967, Fgn. Area fellow, 1968-69. Mem. Seminar Acquisition Latin Am. Libr. Materials (pres. 1988-89), Phi Beta Delta. Methodist. Office: U So Calif Doheny Libr Univ Park Campus Los Angeles CA 90089-0182

ROBINSON, BERNARD LEO, retired lawyer; b. Kalamazoo, Feb. 13, 1924; s. Louis Harvey and Sue Mary (Starr) R.; m. Betsy Nadell, May 30, 1947; children: Robert Bruce, Patricia Anne, Jean Carol. BS, U. Ill., 1947, MS, 1958, postgrad. in structural dynamics, 1959; JD, U. N.Mex., 1973. Rsch. engr. Assn. Am. Railroads, 1947-49; instr. architecture Rensselaer Poly. Inst., 1949-51; commd. 2d lt. Corps Engrs., U.S. Army, 1945, advanced through grades to lt. col., 1965, ret., 1968; engr. Nuclear Def. Rsch. Corp., Albuquerque, 1968-71; admitted to N.Mex. bar, 1973, U.S. Supreme Ct. bar, 1976; practiced in Albuquerque, 1973-85, Silver City, N.Mex., 1985-89, Green Valley, Ariz., 1989-90, Sierra Vista, Ariz., 1990-91; pres. Robinson Fin. Svcs., 1993. Dist. commr. Boy Scouts Am., 1960-62. Vice chmn. Rep. Dist. Com., 1968-70. Decorated Air medal, Combat Infantry badge. Mem. ASCE, ABA, Ret. Officers Assn., DAV, Assn. U.S. Army, Am. Legion, VFW. Home: 3009 E San Juan Capistrano Dr Sierra Vista AZ 85635-9393

ROBINSON, CAROLE ANN, insurance executive; b. Omaha, Dec. 21, 1935; d. Harry B. and Mildred (Daley) Baker; widowed Mar. 1989; 1 child, Pamela Fleming. Clk. BlueCross/Blue Shield Colo., Denver, 1969-70; mgr. BlueCross/Blue Shield Colo., 1970-72, asst. to treas., 1972-74, dir., 1974-79, treas., 1980-86, sr. v.p., treas., 1986-90; v.p., treas., chief investment officer Rocky Mountain Health Care (Holding Co.), Denver, 1991—, sr. v.p., chief investment officer, chief fin. officer, 1986—; bd. dirs. Rocky Mountain Life Ins. Co., Denver, Occupational Health Mgmt. Svcs., Denver, HMO Colo., Denver, Colo. Compensation Ins. Authority, Denver, Combined Health Appeal, Denver. Mem. investment com. City and County of Denver, 1988. Mem. Colo. Cash Mgmt. Assn., Nat. Cash Mgmt. Assn., Life Office Mgmt. Assn. (treasury ops. com. 1985—). Republican. Office: Rocky Mountain Health Care Ste 990 700 Broadway Denver CO 80273-0001

ROBINSON, CHARLES PAUL, scientist, diplomat, business executive; b. Detroit, Oct. 9, 1941; s. Edward Leonard and Mary Opal (Edmondson) R.; m. Barbara Thomas Woodard, Dec., 1992; children by previous marriage: Paula S., Colin C. BS in Physics, Christian Bros. U., 1963; PhD in Physics, Fla. State U., 1967. Mem. nuclear test staff Los Alamos (N.Mex.) Nat. Lab., 1967-69, chief test operator, 1969-70, mem. advanced concepts staff, 1971-72, assoc. div. leader, lasers, 1972-76, div. leader, 1976-79, assoc. dir., 1980-85; sr. v.p., bd. dirs. Ebasco Services Inc. subs. Enserch Corp., N.Y.C., 1985-88; ambass. to nuclear testing talks U.S. Dept. State, Geneva, 1988-90; v.p. Sandia Nat. Labs., Albuquerque, 1990—; mem. sci. adv. group Def.

Nuclear Agy., Washington, 1981—; mem. nat. security bd. Los Alamos Nat. Lab., 1985—; chmn. Presdl. Tech. Adv. Bd., 1991; mem. U.S. Strategic Command Adv. Bd. Pres. Student Concerts Inc., Los Alamos, 1972-74; instr. U. N.Mex., Los Alamos, 1974-76. Mem. AAAS, Am. Phys. Soc., Am. Nuclear Soc., Rotary Internat. Office: Sandia Nat Labs Orgn 4000 PO Box 5800 Albuquerque NM 87185

ROBINSON, CHARLES SHERWOOD, consulting geologist; b. East Lansing, Mich., June 23, 1920; s. Charles Summers and Florence (Sherwood) R.; m. Elizabeth Hale, Feb. 10, 1950; children: Virginia C., Charles H., Peter S., Robert S. BS in Chemistry, Mich. Coll. Mines and Tech., 1942; PhD in Geology, U. Colo., 1956. Cert. prof. engr., Colo., Wyo., Mont., Nev., Iowa. Rsch. geologist U.S. Geol. Survey, Denver, 1948-65; pres. Charles S. Robinson & Assocs., Golden, Colo., 1965-80; v.p. Convers Ward Davis Dixion, Golden, 1980-81; gen. mgr. Mineral Systems, Inc., Golden, 1981-90; cons. geol. engr. M.A. Balcar & Assocs., Inc., Denver, 1990-91; gen. mgr. Mineral Systems, Inc., Golden, Colo., 1991—. Author numerous profl. publs.; mem. editorial bd. engring. geology Elsevier Pub., Amsterdam, 1964—. Dir. Urban Drainage and Flood Control Dist., Denver, 1968-76. Lt. USN, 1942-46. Fellow Geol. Soc. Am.; mem. Soc. for Mining, Metallurgy and Exploration of AIME, Internat. Assn. Engring. Geologists, Soc. Econ. Geologists, Assn. Engring. Geologists. Home: 5265 Mcintyre St Golden CO 80403-1244 Office: Mineral Systems Inc 5265 Mcintyre St Golden CO 80403-1244

ROBINSON, CHARLES WESLEY, energy company executive; b. Long Beach, Calif., Sept. 7, 1919; s. Franklin Willard and Anna Hope (Gould) R.; m. Tamara Lindovna, Mar. 8, 1957; children: Heather Lynne, Lisa Anne, Wendy Paige. AB cum laude in Econs., U. Calif., Berkeley, 1941; MBA, Stanford U., 1947. Asst. mgr. mfg. Golden State Dairy Products Co., San Francisco, 1947-49; v.p., then pres. Marcona Corp., San Francisco, 1952-74; undersec. of state for econ. affairs Dept. State, Washington, 1974-75, dep. sec. of state, 1976-77; sr. mng. partner Kuhn Loeb & Co., N.Y.C., 1977-78; vice chmn. Blyth Eastman Dillon & Co., N.Y.C., 1978-79; chmn. Energy Transition Corp., Santa Fe and Washington, 1979-82; pres. Robinson & Assocs., Inc., Santa Fe, 1982—; pres. Dyna-Yacht, Inc., Lajolla, Calif., 1982—; bd. dirs. The Allen Group, Northrop Corp., NIKE, Inc. Patentee slurry transport., Brookings Instn., Washington, 1977—. Served to lt. USN, 1941-46. Recipient Disting. Honor award Dept. State, 1977. Mem. Council on Fgn. Relations N.Y.C. Republican. Methodist. Office: Robinson & Assocs Inc PO Box 2224 Santa Fe NM 87504-2224

ROBINSON, CLARK ZACHARY, computer company executive; b. Sumter, S.C., Mar. 23, 1961; s. Fredrick Marlin and Joy Mildred May (Parks) R. BSME, Stanford U., 1983; MBA, UCLA, 1987. Mech. design engr. Shugart Corp., Sunnyvale, Calif., 1983-85; bus. planner Tandem Computers Inc., Cupertino, Calif., 1987-91; v.p. mktg. Atalla Corp., San Jose, Calif., 1991—. Author: Top Dollars for Technical Scholars, 1987; contbr. articles to profl. publs. GM scholar, 1981. Republican. Home: 1273 Crescent Ter Sunnyvale CA 94087 Office: Atalla Corp 2304 Zanker Rd San Jose CA 95131

ROBINSON, DAVID BROOKS, naval officer; b. Alexandria, La., Oct. 26, 1939; s. Donald and Marion (Holloman) R.; m. Gene Kirkpatrick, Aug. 1, 1964; children: Kirk, David. Student, Tex. A&M U., 1958-59; BS, U.S. Naval Acad., 1963; MS in Physics, Naval Postgrad. Sch., Monterey, Calif., 1969. Commd. ensign USN, 1963, advanced through grades to vice admiral, 1993; comdg. officer USS Canon and USS Ready, Guam, 1969-71; adminstrv. aide to Chmn. Joint Chiefs Staff, Washington, 1971-74; comdg. officer USS Luce, Mayport, Fla., 1976-78; mem. Fgn. Service Inst. Exec. Seminar, Washington, 1982; comdg. officer USS Richmond K. Turner, Charleston, S.C., 1983-84; chief of staff, comdr. Naval Surface Force, Atlantic Fleet, Norfolk, Va., 1984; exec. asst. and sr. aide to vice chief Naval Ops., Washington, 1985, dir. Manpower and Tng. div., 1986, dir. Surface Warfare div., 1987-88; cmdr. cruiser destroyer group 8, 1988-89; vice dir. and subsequently dir. operational plans and inter-operability directorate Joint Staff, Washington, 1989-91; dep., chief of staff to comdr. U.S. Pacific Fleet, 1991-93, comdr. naval surface force, 1993—. Decorated Navy Cross, Def. D.S.M., D.S.M., Legion of Merit with 4 gold stars, Bronze Star. Methodist. Lodge: Optimist (pres. Oakton, Va. 1986-87). Office: COMNAVSURFPAC 2421 Vella LaVella Rd San Diego CA 92135

ROBINSON, DAVID ROGER, infosystems specialist; b. Coshocton, Ohio, Aug. 10, 1951; s. Roger Linzey and Hazel Lucille (Snedeker) R.; m. Kathleen Margaret Carpenter, Aug. 12, 1972; children: Kristina Rose, Kimberley Gayle. BS in Math., BS in Physics, Ohio U., 1973; MS Indsl. Engring., U. Wis., Madison, 1975. Cert. systems profl. Systems analyst Burroughs Corp., Detroit, 1975-77, project leader, 1977-80, mgr. data networks, 1980-83, mgr. tech. services, 1983-85; mgr. data communications Joseph & Cogan, Woodland Hills, Calif., 1985-86; project mgr. network integration Burroughs and Sperry Corp., Woodland Hills, 1986-87; mgr. tech. svcs. Joseph & Cogan, Westlake Village, Calif., 1987-88, mgr. software devel., 1989; sr. staff software engr. Unisys Corp., Mission Viejo, Calif., 1990—; adjunct lectr. U. Mich., Ann Arbor, 1985; guest lectr. U. Detroit, 1985. Author: (software) Bitnet, 1979. Mem. GTE Telenet Users Group (pres. 1982-84, 84-86, sec. 1981-82). Republican. Methodist.

ROBINSON, DOROTHY MOKUREN, computer software engineer; b. Erie, Pa., June 28, 1951; d. Charles Gould and Beatrice Pauline (Lillie) R. Student, Allegheny Coll., 1969-72; BA in Biology cum laude, Mercyhurst Coll., 1975. Lab. technician Hammermill Papers, Erie, Pa., 1976-79, Neurol. Scis. Inst. of Good Samaritan Hosp., Portland, Oreg., 1979-84; engr. libr. support Computervision, Beaverton, Oreg., 1984-93; symbal interation engr. Analogy, Inc., Beaverton, Oreg., 1993—. Co-author: Buddhist America, 1988. Lay min. Dharma Rain Zen Ctr., Portland, 1987—; corp. sec. N.W. Zen Sangha, Portland, 1991-93. Mem. Internat. Soc. Folk Harpers and Craftsmen. Buddhist. Office: Analogy Inc 9205 Gemini Dr Beaverton OR 97005

ROBINSON, ERIC LARMUTH, minister, writer; b. London, Eng., May 4, 1912; came to U.S., 1959; s. William Larmuth and Maud Margaret (Birt) R.; m. Margaret Bailey, Jan. 8, 1949; children: Susan Mary Carlton, Ann Elizabeth Robinson. Diploma in theology, London U., 1937. Ordained to ministry Meth. Ch. Missionary Meth. Missionary Soc., India, 1937-46, Sri Lanka, 1946-53; min. Meth. Ch., Eng., 1953-59; pastor Meth. Ch., Portland, Oreg., 1959-65; radio broadcaster Nat. Coun. Chs., numerous world locations, 1965-66; peace and justice worker Fellowship of Reconciliation, Oreg., 1967-74; pastor United Meth. Ch., Cornelius, Oreg., 1974-77; broadcaster Brit. Broadcasting Corp., 1948-59; mem. Fellowship of Reconciliations, 1936—. Contbr. numerous articles to various jours. Vietnam protest leader, Portland, 1967-74. Mem. Nat. Writers Club. Democrat. Home: 1642 SW Squaw Creek Pl Corvallis OR 97333-1559

ROBINSON, FRANK ROBERT, radio station executive; b. Hollywood, Calif., Sept. 17, 1938; s. Frank Robert and Helen Macdonnel (James) R.; m. Ann Katherine Carman, Apr. 24, 1965 (div. 1984); children: Geoffrey Scott, Hilary Ann; m. Dian Winget, July 19, 1991. BS, Westminster Coll., 1967. Gen. mgr. Sta. KLUB and Sta. KISN, Salt Lake City, 1970-85; sta. mgr. KUER, 1986-90; western sales mgr. Custom Bus. Systems, Inc.

ROBINSON, GARY DALE, aerospace company executive; b. Colcord, W.Va., Sept. 9, 1938; s. Samuel Claytor and Madge (Fraley) R. Jr.; m. Lorelei Mary Christl, June 25, 1967; children: John Claytor, Kirk Dean. BA in Latin Am. Econ. History, So. Ill. U., 1964; PhD in Orgn. Behavior, Case Western Res. U., 1977. Program tng. chief The Peace Corps, Washington, 1969-71; cons. self-employed Ohio, 1971-76; health planning advisor USAID, San Salvador, El Salvador, 1976; project dir. Cen. Am. Inst. for Pub. Adminstrn. and Ministry of Health, San Jose, Costa Rica, 1977-78; mgmt. advisor Agy. for Internat. Devel., Santo Domingo, Dominican Republic, 1978-79; indsl. rels. mgr. Boeing Comml. Airplane Co., Everett, Wash., 1979-83; human resource mgr. Boeing Marine Systems, Renton, Wash., 1983-85; indsl. rels. mgr. The Boeing Co., Seattle, 1985-86, internal audit mgr., asst. to v.p. controller, 1986-90, 90—; cons. in field; adj. prof. Cen. Wash. U., Ellensburg, 1984—; mem. adv. bd. Drake, Beam & Moran, Seattle, 1991—; mem. adv. bd. and faculty Sch. of Advanced Studies in Orgnl. Cons., Santiago, chile, 1992—. Contbg. author: International Organizational Behavior, 1986. chmn. Metrocenter YMCA, Seattle, 1990-91; mem. Peace Corps Nat. Adv. Coun., Wash., 1988-89; founding mem. Pacific N.W. Orgn. Devel. Network, Seattle, 1982-86; bd. advisors Nat. Found. for Study Religion & Edn., Greensboro, N.C., 1984-87; mem. edn. com. World Affairs Coun., Seattle, 1987-88; sec., treas. The Edmonds Inst., Lynnwood, Wash., 1989-90; mem. Internat. Rels. Com. Named Paul Harris fellow Rotary Internat., 1989. Mem. AIAA, The Wash. Ctr. for Mgmt. and Leadership (founder, bd. dirs.), Inst. for Internal Auditors (co-editor Pistas newsletter 1991—), Nat. Orgnl. Devel. Network, Acad. of Mgmt., Earth Svcs. Corps (adv. bd.). Office: The Boeing Co PO Box 3707 M/S 11-KA Seattle WA 98124-2207

ROBINSON, GORDON PRINGLE, forester; b. Vancouver, B.C., Can., Apr. 7, 1911; came to U.S., 1920; s. Laforest George and Sarah Lawrence (Mitchie) R.; m. Adina Wiens, Feb. 7, 1943; children: Charlotte Wiens, Daniel Gordon, Lawrence Pringle. Student, J.C. Marin Jr. Coll., Kentfield, Calif., 1934; BS in Forestry, U. Calif., Berkeley, 1937. Forester So. Pacific Transp. Co., 1939-66; staff forester Sierra Club, 1966-79; cons. Tiburon, Calif., 1966—. Author: The Forest and the Trees: a guide to Excellent Forestry, 1988. Democrat. Unitarian. Home and Office: 16 Apollo Rd Tiburon CA 94920

ROBINSON, HERBERT HENRY, III, educator, therapist; b. Leavenworth, Wash., May 31, 1933; s. Herbert Henry II and Alberta (Sperber) R.; m. Georgia Murial Jones, Nov. 24, 1954 (div. 1974); children: Cheri Dean Asbury, David Kent, Peri Elizabeth Layton, Tanda Rene Graff, Gaila Daire. Grad. of Theology, Bapt. Bible Coll., 1959; BA in Philosophy/Greek, Whitworth Coll., 1968; MA in Coll. Teaching, Ea. Wash. U., 1976; postgrad., Gonzaga U., 1980—. Choir dir. Twin City Bapt. Temple, Mishawaka, Ind., 1959-61; min. Inland Empire Bapt. Ch., Spokane, 1961-73; tchr. philosophy Spokane (Wash.) C.C., 1969-72; dir. Alternatives to Violence, Women in Crisis, Fairbanks, Alaska, 1985-87; tchr. pub. rels. U. Alaska, Fairbanks, 1986-87; dir. Alternatives to Violence Men Inc., Juneau, 1988-89; tchr. leadership mgmt. U. Alaska S.E., Juneau, 1988-89; min. Sci. of Mind Ctr., Sandpoint, Idaho, 1989-92; dir., therapist Tapio Counseling Ctr., Spokane, 1991-93; cons. Lilac Blind/Alpha Inc./Marshall Coll., Spokane, 1975-85, Alaska Placer Mining Co., Fairbanks, 1987; tchr. Spokane Falls C.C., Spokane, 1979-85; seminar, presenter Human Resource Devel., Spokane and Seattle, Wash., Pa., 1980; guest trainer United Way/Kellogg Found. Inst. for Volunteerism, Spokane, 1983. First trombone Spokane (Wash.) Symphony, 1961; bd. dirs. Planned Parenthood, Spokane, 1984, Tanani Learning Ctr., Fairbanks, 1987; consensus bldg. team Sci. of Mind Ctr., Sandpoint, 1989-92. Cpl. USMC, 1953-56. Mem. ACA, Assn. for Humanistic Edn. and Devel., Assn. for Religious Values in Counseling, Internat. Assn. Addictions and Offender Counselors, Internat. Assn. Marriage and Family Counselors, Am. Assn. Profl. Hypnotherapists. Home: 11611 E Maxwell Spokane WA 99206 Office: Tapio Counseling Svcs Yellow Flag Bldg #109 104 S Freya Tapio Ctr Spokane WA 99202

ROBINSON, HERBERT WILLIAM, corporate executive, economist; b. Hull, Yorkshire, Eng., Jan. 2, 1914; came to U.S., 1943, naturalized, 1948; s. Herbert and Mary Elizabeth (Ellis) R.; m. Elsie Caroline Roenfeldt, May 8, 1948; children—Denise Patricia, Keith Brian. BSc in Econs. with 1st class honors, U. Coll. Hull, Eng., 1935; PhD, London Sch. Econs., 1937; DPhil, Oxford U., 1939; DSc in Econs. (hon.), U. Hull, 1992. Sr. lectr. math. statistics, econ. theory, trade cycle theory, indsl. orgn. U. Coll., Hull, 1939; asst. to Lord Cherwell, Prime Minister's Pvt. Office, 1939-42; asst. to Lord Layton, Ministry Prodn., 1942-43; Brit. staff mem. Combined Prodn. and Resources Bd., U.S., U.K., Can., 1943-44; dep. dir. statistics, econ. and statistics div. Ministry Agr. and Fisheries, 1945; chief econ. trends VA, 1946; chief operational analysis div. UNRRA Mission to Poland, 1946-47; loan and econs. depts. World Bank, 1947-51; dep. div. dir. Office Program and Requirements, Def. Prodn. Adminstrn., 1951-53; pres. Council Econ. and Industry Research, Inc., Washington, 1954-57; pres. renamed corp. C-E-I-R, Inc., 1958-67, chmn. bd., 1954-67; v.p. Control Data Corp., 1968-70; chmn. Internat. Mgmt. Systems Corp., 1970—. Author: Economics of Building, 1989, Election Issues, 1976; Challenge to Government: Management of a Capitalist Economy, 1991; author articles and reports on econ. subjects. Fellow Assn. Inc. Statisticians (chartered statistician), Royal Statis. Soc. (mem. coun. 1943-44); mem. Am. Soc. for Cybernetics (dir. 1967-75), Am. Econ. Assn., Inst. Mgmt. Scis., Am. Statis. Assn., Ops. Rsch. Soc., Econometric Soc., Cosmos Club (Washington), Fountain Hills (Ariz.) Club, Lambda Alpha, Alpha Kappa Psi. Home: 8320 Turnberry Ct Potomac MD 20854

ROBINSON, HURLEY, surgeon; b. L.A., Feb. 25, 1925; s. Edgar Ray and Nina Madge (Hurley) R.; m. Mary Anne Rusche, Mar. 14, 1953; children: Kathleen Ann Robinson Petschke, Mary Elizabeth, Lynda Jean Robinson Lamb, William Hurley, Patricia Kay Robinson Hardy, Paul Edgar. Student, U. Calif., Berkeley, 1943, U. Calif., Santa Barbara, 1946-48; BS, Northwestern U., 1950, MD, 1952. Diplomate Am. Bd. Surgery. Intern Wesley Meml. Hosp., Chgo., 1952-53; resident Milw. County Hosp., 1953-57; surgeon Abbott Med. Group, Ontario, Calif., 1957-59; pvt. practice Upland, Calif., 1959-64; ptnr. Robinson & Schechter Surg. Med. Group, Upland, 1964-92; sr. surg. staff San Antonio Community Hosp., Upland, 1958—, trustee, 1979-81, pres. med. staff, 1980; mem. staff Pomona (Calif.) Valley Med. Ctr., Dr.'s Hosp. Montclair, Calif., Ontatio Community Hosp.; exec. com. San Bernardino (Calif.) County Med. Ctr., 1974, adv. bd., 1974; clin. asst. vascular surgery London Hosp., Eng., 1973; cons. in field. Co-contbr. articles to Wis. Med. Jour. Chmn. troop com., camp dr. Boy Scouts Am., Upland, 1970-72. With U.S. Army, 1943-46. Fellow ACS, Am. Coll. Chest Physicians, Am. Coll. Angiology; mem. AMA, Am. Med. Soc. Vienna, Calif. Med. Assn., N.Y. Acad. Scis., San Bernardino County Med. Soc., Tri-County Surg. Soc. So. Calif. (pres.), Pan-Pacific Surgical Assn., Soc. Clin. Vascular Surgery, Royal Soc. Medicine. Republican. Presbyterian. Office: 415 W 16th St Upland CA 91786

ROBINSON, JOHN ALEXANDER, college football coach; b. Chgo., July 25, 1935; s. Matthew and Ethlyn (Alexander) R.; m. Barbara Lee Amirkhan, July 31, 1960; children: Teresa, Lynn, David, Christopher. B.S., U. Oreg., 1958. Asst. football coach U. Oreg., Eugene, 1960-71, U. So. Calif., Los Angeles, 1971-74, Oakland (Calif.) Raiders, 1975; head fooball coach U. So. Calif., 1976-82, 93—, v.p., 1982-83; head coach Los Angeles Rams Football Team, 1983—; coached winning Rose Bowl teams, 1977, 79, 80. Served with U.S. Army, 1958-59. Named Nat. Football Conf. Coach of Yr., UPI, 1983-84 season. Roman Catholic. Office: care Univ of So Calif University Park Los Angeles CA 90089-0602

ROBINSON, MARK LEIGHTON, oil company executive, petroleum geologist, horse farm owner; b. San Bernadino, Calif., Aug. 4, 1927; s. Ernest Guy and Florence Iola (Lemmon) R.; m. Jean Marie Ries, Feb. 8, 1954; children: Francis Willis, Mark Ries, Paul Leighton. AB cum laude in Geology, Princeton U., 1950; postgrad. Stanford U., 1950-51. Geologist Shell Oil Co., Billings, Mont., Rapid City, S.D., Denver, Midland, Tex., 1951-56, dist. geologist, Roswell, N.Mex., 1957-60, div. mgr., Roswell, N.Mex., 1961-63, Jackson, Miss., 1964-65, Bakersfield, Calif., 1967-68, mgr. exploration econs., N.Y.C., 1969; mgmt. advisor BIPM (Royal Dutch Shell Oil Co.), The Hague, The Netherlands, 1966; pres., chmn. bd. dirs. Robinson Resource Devel. Co., Inc., Roswell, 1970—. Campaign chmn. Chaves County Republican Com., Roswell, 1962; mem. alumni schs. com. Princeton U., 1980—. Served with USNR, 1945-46. Mem. Roswell Geol. Soc. (trustee 1972), Am. Assn. Petroleum Geologists, Stanford U. Earth Scientists Assn., Yellowstone Bighorn Research Assn., Am. Horse Shows Assn., SAR, Sigma Xi. Episcopalian. Discovered Lake Como oil field, Miss., 1971, McNeal oil field, Miss., 1973, North Deer Creek Gas Field, Mont., 1983, Bloomfield East Oil Field, Mont., 1986. Home: 1508 Oljeto Dr RR 2 Roswell NM 88201-9801 Office: Robinson Resource Devel Co Inc PO Box 1227 Roswell NM 88202-1227

ROBINSON, MARY SUSAN, nurse, administrator; b. San Luis Obispo, Calif., July 3, 1951; d. Allen Marion Diamond and Ella Geraldine (Eidson) Oatman; m. Richard Eugene Robinson, Apr. 21, 1991. AAS in Nursing, Casper Coll., 1982. RN, Colo. Staff nurse, charge nurse Meml. Hosp., Colorado Springs, Colo., 1983-88; staff nurse Colonial Columns Health Care Ctr., Colorado Springs, 1988, coord. staff devel., 1989, DON, 1990; supr. night shift Laurel Manor Care Ctr., Colorado Springs, 1990-91; staff nurse Lincoln Community Hosp. and Nursing Home, Hugo, Colo., 1991, nursing svc. adminstr., 1991—. Mem. Am. Soc. Long-Term Care Nurses. Republican. Episcopalian. Office: Lincoln Community Hosp and Nursing Home 111 6th St Hugo CO 80821

ROBINSON, PETER, paleontology educator, consultant; b. N.Y.C., N.Y., July 19, 1932; s. Edward and Carol Nye (Rhoades) R.; m. Patricia Ellen Fisher, Sept. 11, 1954 (div. Mar. 1980); children: Diane Elizabeth, Nathan; m. Paola D'Amelio Villa, Dec. 8, 1984. BS, Yale U., 1954, MS, 1958, PhD, 1960. Instr. Harpur Coll. SUNY, Binghamton, 1955-57; rsch. assoc. Yale Peabody Mus., New Haven, 1960-61; curator geology U. Colo. Mus., Boulder, 1961—, asst. prof. natural history, 1961-67, assoc. prof., 1967-71, prof., 1971—, dir. mus., 1971-82, prof. geol. sci., 1971—; geologist Colo. Nubian Expdn., Sudan, 1962-66; chief Colo. Paleontol. Expdn., Tunisia, 1967—; mem. geol. adv. group Colo. Bur. Land Mgmt., Denver, 1983—. Mem. AAAS, Soc. Vertebrate Paleontology (pres. 1977-78), Australian Mammal Soc., Soc. Española Paleontologia, Sigma Xi. Democrat. Home (summer): 5110 Williams Fork Trail 204 Boulder CO 80301 Office: Mus U Colo Campus Box 315 Boulder CO 80309

ROBINSON, RAPHAEL MITCHEL, mathematics educator; b. National City, Calif., Nov. 2, 1911; s. Bertram H. and Bessie B. (Stevenson) R.; m. Julia H. Bowman, Dec. 22, 1941 (dec. 1985). AB, U. Calif., Berkeley, 1932, MA, 1933, PhD, 1935. Instr. Brown U., Providence, 1935-37; from instr. to prof. U. Calif., Berkeley, 1937-73, prof. emeritus, 1973—. Contbr. articles to profl. jours. Mem. Am. Math. Soc., Math. Assn. Am. Office: Univ Calif Dept Math Berkeley CA 94720

ROBINSON, RICHARD ALLEN, JR., human resources development trainer, consultant; b. Ellensburg, Wash., Aug. 21, 1936; s. Richard Allen and Rosa Adele (Oswald) R.; m. R. Elaine Whitham, Sept. 8, 1956; children—Sharon E. Robinson Losey, Richard Allen, René L. B.A., U. Wash., 1958; postgrad. U.S. Army Command and Gen. Staff Coll., 1969-70; M.A., U. Mo., 1971. Commd. 2d lt. U.S. Army, 1958, advanced through grades to lt. col., 1972, various infantry assignments including command, 1958-72, research and devel. assignments including dep. dir. test of behavioral sci., dep. commandant U.S.A. Organizational Effectiveness, 1975-77, ret., 1979; chief office orgn. and employee devel. Wash. Dept. Social and Health Services, Olympia, 1979—; pvt. practice orgn. and mgmt. devel. cons./trainer, 1979—. Decorated Legion of Merit with oak leaf cluster, Bronze Star. Mem. Am. Soc. Tng. and Devel., Organizational Devel. Network, Internat. Platform Assn., Mass. Hort. Soc. Contbg. author: Games Trainers Play, vol. II, 1983. Office: DSHS Mail 8425 27th St W Tacoma WA 98466-2722

ROBINSON, RICK LEE, social services administrator; b. Denver, July 19, 1952; s. William Albert and Mary Jane (Olver) R.; m. Victoria Marie Vetter, July 5, 1986; children: Heather Marie, Christopher William. BA, U. No. Colo., 1974, MA, 1976. Drug abuse prevention specialist Weld Mental Health Ctr., Greeley, Colo., 1974-75; exec. dir. Cheyenne (Wyo.) Community Drug Abuse Treatment Coun., Inc., 1977—. Contbr. articles to newspapers. Mem. Gov.'s Statewide Drug Policy Bd. Mem. NACD, Nat. Rural Alcohol and Drug Abuse Network, Nat. Assn. Alcoholism and Drug Abuse Counselors, Wyo. Assn. Mental Health and Substance Abuse Ctrs., Wyo. Corrections Assn., Wyo Assn. Addiction Specialists, Wyo. Assn. Counseling and Devel., Larami County Coun. Community Svcs. Home: 5308 Liberty St Cheyenne WY 82001-2223 Office: 803 W 21st St Cheyenne WY 82001-3413

ROBINSON, ROBERT BLACQUE, association executive; b. Long Beach, Calif., Apr. 24, 1927; s. Joseph LeRoi and Frances Hansel R.; m. Susan Amelia Thomas, Jan. 21, 1960; children: Victoria, Shelly, Blake, Sarah. Student, Oreg. State Coll., 1946; BA, UCLA, 1950; student, U. Hawaii. Partner, Pritchard Assocs. (Mgmt. Cons.), Honolulu, 1956-58; asst. dir. Econ. Planning and Coordination Authority, Hawaii, 1959; dep. dir. dept. econ. devel. State of Hawaii, 1960-63; asst. mgr. Pacific Concrete and Rock Co., Ltd., Honolulu, 1963-66, exec. v.p. and gen. mgr., 1966-68, pres. and gen. mgr., 1968-75; chmn. Pacific Concrete and Rock Co., Ltd., 1976-77; pres. C. of C. of Hawaii, Honolulu, 1977—. Bd. govs. Hawaii Employers Coun., 1969-74, mem. exec. com., 1969-74, vice chmn., 1973-74; bd. dirs. Pacific Aerospace Mus., 1982-86; mem. Hawaii Tourism Conf., 1977, chmn., 1981-82; bd. dirs. Aloha United Fund, 1970-76, sec., 1972, v.p., 1973-76; bd. dirs. Oahu Devel. Conf., 1970-75; treas., bd. dirs. Crime Stoppers Hawaii, 1981—; mem. Hawaii Joint Coun. on Econ. Edn., 1985—; bd. dirs. Jr. Achievement Hawaii, 1967-73, pres., 1969; bd. dirs. Hawaii Ednl. Coun., 1974-75, Health and Community Services Coun. Hawaii, 1982-84; mem. exec. com. Hawaii Conv. Ctr. Coun., 1984—, Interagency Energy Conservation Coun., State of Hawaii, 1978—; trustee Cen. Union Ch., 1983-86; bd. dirs. Waikiki Improvement Assn. Inc., 1986—; mem. Ctr. for Tropical and Subtropical Aquaculture industry Adv. Coun., 1987—; chmn. Mayor's Adv. Com. on Pacific Nations Ctr., 1988-89. Lt. comdr. USNR, 1945-46, ret. Mem. Japan-Am. Conf. of Mayors and C. of C. Pres. (mem. Am. exec. com. 1974—), Am. Soc. Assn. Execs. (past dir. Hawaii chpt.), Hawaii Execs. Coun. (found. , Young Pres. Assn. (past mem.), Aloha Soc. Assn. Execs., C. of C. Hawaii (dir. 1972-75, chmn. 1975), Coun. of Profit Sharing Industries (past dir. Hawaii sect.), Cement and Concrete Products Industry of Hawaii (pres. 1968), Hawaii Mfrs. Assn. (past dir.), Navy League of U.S. (Hawaii council), Engring. Assn. Hawaii, Pacific Club, Rotary, Sigma Chi. Home: 1437 Kalaepohaku St Honolulu HI 96816-1804 Office: C of C Hawaii Ste 220 735 Bishop St Honolulu HI 96813-4817

ROBINSON, RONALD ALAN, oil company executive; b. Louisville, Mar. 23, 1952; s. J. Kenneth and Juanita M. (Crosier) R.; B.S., Ga. Inst. Tech., 1974; M.B.A. with honors, Harvard U., 1978. Staff engr., asst. to exec. v.p. ops. Dual Drilling Co., Wichita Falls, Tex., 1978-80; v.p. Dreco, Inc., Houston, 1980-84, pres., dir. subs. Triflo Industries Internat. Inc.; pres., chief operating officer Ramteck Systems, Inc., 1984-87; chmn. and chief exec. officer Denver Techs. Inc., 1988—. Recipient Optimist Internat. Citizenship award, 1970; Gardiner Symonds fellow, 1977. Mem. Harvard Alumni Assn. Home: 4815 Newstead Pl Colorado Springs CO 80906-5935 Office: 621 S Sierra Madre St Colorado Springs CO 80903-4096

ROBINSON, SAMUEL WILLIS, JR., information sciences specialist; b. Charlotte, N.C., Aug. 6, 1927; s. Samuel Willis and Gladys Pamelia (DeArmon) R.; m. Ramona Del Hatfield, Jan. 27, 1951; children: Sharon, Michael, Susan, Lorraine. BS in Physics, Davidson Coll., 1949; MS in Physics, Clemson U., 1951. Aerospace rsch. scientist Nat. Com. for Aeronautics, Langley AFB, Va., 1951-53; aerospace engr., mgr. Lockheed Ga. Co., Marietta, 1953-70; info. specialist Lockheed Calif. Co., Burbank, 1970-90, computer cost analyst Info. Svcs. div., 1982-90; ret., 1990; regional dir. Simulation Couns., Atlanta, 1960-70; cons. Computer Usage Billing, Burbank, 1987-90. Patentee in field. With USNR, 1945-46. Mem. Idyllwild Golf Assn. (corr. sec. 1991—), Phi Beta Kappa (Davidson chpt.), Sigma Pi Sigma. Presbyterian. Home: PO Box 1581 Idyllwild CA 92549

ROBINSON, SHANNON, state legislator. BA, JD, U. N.Mex. Atty.; mem. N.Mex. State Senate. Democrat. Home: 716 Indiana St SE Albuquerque NM 87108-3813 Office: NM State Senate State Capitol Santa Fe NM 85703

ROBINSON, SHERMAN, agricultural economics educator; b. Washington, June 2, 1942; s. L. Noble and Barbara (Gray) R.; m. Barbara Metzger; 1 child, Matthew Noble. BA, Harvard U., 1965, MA, 1969, PhD, 1970. Lectr. London Sch. Econs., 1969-71; asst. prof. econs. Princeton (N.J.) U., 1971-77; economist The World Bank, Washington, 1977-82, div. chief, 1982-83; assoc. prof. U. Calif., Berkeley, 1983-85, prof., 1985—; vis. prof. Georgetown U., Washington, 1981; vis. lectr. Johns Hopkins U., Balt., 1979; cons. The World Bank, 1983—, USAID, Washington, 1971-72, 76-78, USDA, 1987-89; vis. scholar Congl. Budget Office, 1992-93; mem. internat. adv. bd. policy econs. group KPMG Peat Marwick, 1990-91. Co-author: Income Distribution Policy in Developing Countries, 1978, General Equilibrium Models for Development Policy, 1982, Industrialization and Growth, 1986; mem. editorial bd. Jour. Econ. Lit., 1982-84, 91—, Jour. Devel. Econs., 1985-90, Rev. Econs. and Stats., 1993—. Bd. dirs. Berkeley Montessori Sch., 1986-91. Fellow Woodrow Wilson Found., Princeton, 1965-66, NSF, Washington, 1968-69. Mem. Am. Econ. Assn., Econometric Soc., Am. Agrl. Econs. Assn. Office: U Calif 207 Giannini Hall Berkeley CA 94720

ROBINSON, WILLIAM EARLE, outreach consultant secondary education; b. Morton, Miss., Nov. 18, 1940; s. P. B. and Gladys (Tuggles) R.; children: Jacqueline, William E. Student, Miss. Valley State U., 1958-59. Councilman City of North Las Vegas, 1983—; pres. Nev. League of Cities, 1988-89, pub. ofcl. of yr., 1990, com. and econ. steering com. devel., 1992; mem. gaming policy com. State of Nev., 1974-79. Named Jaycee of Yr., North Las Vegas, Nev., 1974, Outstanding Young Man of Am. Mem. Nevada Jaycees (pres. 1974, nat. dir.). Democrat. Methodist. Home: 2815 Bassler St North Las Vegas NV 89030 Office: City of North Las Vegas 2200 Civic Center Dr North Las Vegas NV 89030

ROBINSON, WILLIAM JAMES, engineering executive; b. La Jolla, Calif., June 26, 1953; s. Clarence Barss and Irene Florence (MacDonald) R.; m. Catherine Easterly, Sept. 22, 1979. AS in Electronics Tech., Grossmont Coll., 1974; student, Calif. State U., San Diego, 1975-77; BS cum laude, Nat. U., 1985. Instr. in electronic design engring. Dyn-Aura Engring. Labs., 1975-77; electronics test engr. Doric Sci., 1978-82; with R.A. Gray Inc., 1984-85; in-house teaching engr., v.p. engring. Metrox Inc., San Diego, 1985-92; dep. div. mgr. Sparta Inc., San Diego, 1992—. Recipient Picket Slide Rule award IEEE and ASME, 1971. Mem. IEEE. Home: 1127 Dawnridge Ave El Cajon CA 92021-3307 Office: Sparta Inc 9455 Towne Centre Dr San Diego CA 92121-1964

ROBITAILLE, LUC, professional hockey player; b. Montreal, P.Q., Can., Feb. 17, 1966. Hockey player Hull Olympiques Major Jr. Hockey League, Que., 1983-86, Los Angeles Kings, 1986—. Recipient Calder Meml. trophy, NHL Rookie of Yr., 1987; named to NHL All-Star team, 1988, 89, 90. Office: Los Angeles Kings PO Box 17013 3900 W Manchester Blvd Inglewood CA 90306

ROBLES, ROSALIE MIRANDA, educator; b. L.A., Oct. 30, 1942; d. Richard and Carmen (Garcia) Miranda; m. Ralph Rex Robles, July 12, 1986; children: Gregory, Eric, Karen. BA, Calif. State Coll., L.A., 1964; postgrad., Northridge State Coll. Playground supr. L.A. City Schs., 1961-64; elem. tchr. Montebello (Calif.) Unified Schs., 1964—; rep. Montebello Credit Union, 1973-75, Bilingual Com., 1983-88; mem. Sch. Site Coun., 1989-92, chmn. 1980-83. Chmn. Monterey Park Christmas Food Baskets, 1973-91; mem., boys coord., girls coord. Am. Youth Soccer; chmn. Boy Scouts Am., 1980-85; mem. exec. bd. PTA, 1978, 80, 85, 87, 1992—, pres. 1990-92, sec. St. Paul Parent Group, 1992-93, palimentarian, 1993—. Recipient Hon. Svc. award PTA, 1979, Hon. Svc. Continuing award PTA, 1982. Roman Catholic.

ROBROCK, JAMES LAWRENCE, plastic surgeon; b. Cleve., Aug. 21, 1956; s. Richard Barker and Joan Louise (Peers) R. BA, Kenyon Coll., Gambier, Ohio, 1978; MD, Ohio State U., 1981; cert. in liposuction surgery, Ea. Va. Med. Sch., 1985. Diplomate Am. Bd. Plastic Surgery. Intern in gen. surgery Northwestern U., Chgo., 1981-82, resident in gen. surgery, 1981-84; resident in plastic surgery Rush-Presbyn. St. Luke's Med. Ctr., Chgo., 1984-86; fellow in plastic surgery Maricopa Med. Ctr., Phoenix, 1986-87; pvt. practice Chandler and Phoenix, Ariz., 1987—; instr., attending surgeon Maricopa Med. Ctr., Phoenix, 1988—. Named Humanitarian of Yr., Chgo. Hosp. Coun., 1983, Chandler Vol. of Yr., Am. Cancer Soc., Rotary, Chandler cos., 1990-91, All-Am. in Swimming, NCAA, 1976, 77, 78. Fellow ACS (assoc.); mem. AMA, Ariz. Soc. Plastic and Reconstructive Surgeons, Ariz. Med. Assn., Am. Soc. Plastic and Reconstructive Surgeons, Maricopa County Med. Soc., Maricopa County Plastic Surgery Soc., Delta Tau Delta. Office: 485 S Dobson Rd Ste 205 Chandler AZ 85224-5604 also: 4950 E Elliot Rd Phoenix AZ 85044

ROBSON, SYBIL ANN, film producer; b. Tulsa, Dec. 8, 1956; d. John Nicholas and Alma Robson. BFA, So. Meth. U., 1979. Anchor, reporter Sta. WRR-AM Radio, Dallas, 1976-78; researcher Sta. WFAA-TV, Dallas, 1977-78; polit. researcher ABC News, Paris, 1978-79; anchor, reporter Sta. KOLR-TV, Springfield, Mo., 1979-80, Sta. WFMY-TV, Greensboro, N.C., 1980-83, Paramount Pictures, L.A., 1983-86; investor Robson Investments, L.A., 1982—; film producer Bernhard/Robson Entertainment, L.A., 1987-91; pres., film producer Robson Entertainment, Beverly Hills, Calif., 1992—. Mem. Earth Communications Office; mem. Hollywood Women's Political Com. Mem. Am. Film Inst., Ind. Feature Project, Women in Film, Environ. Media Assn., Sigma Delta Chi.

ROCCA, JAMES VICTOR, political science educator; b. Spokane, Wash., Mar. 22, 1930; s. Victer Joseph and Pierina (Balzaretti) R.; m. Hilda Kalchhauser, Jan. 16, 1966. BBA, Gonzaga U., 1952; Absolutorium, U. Vienna, Austria, 1962; Doctorate, U. Vienna, 1964. Claims mgr. Gen. Electric, Oakland, Calif., 1956-58; prof. polit. sci. and polit. econ. N.Mex. Highlands Univ., Las Vegas, N.Mex., 1965—; pres. AAUP, Las Vegas, N.Mex., 1968-70. Author: Imunitaet Von Lokaler Strafgerichtsbarkeit, 1965, Ius Humanitas, 1980; contbr. articles to profl. jours. With U.S. Army, 1952-55. Mem. AAUP (pres. N.Mex. state chpt.), Benevolent Order of Elks.

ROCCA, NICHOLAS FRANCIS, social worker, psychotherapist, consultant; b. Orange, N.J., Feb. 9, 1955; s. Thomas Joseph and Stella Theresa (Colavito) R. BA in Psychology, Seton Hall U., 1978; MSW, St. Louis U., 1980. Lic. clin. social worker, Calif. Psychotherapist Bond County Health Dept., Greenville, Ill., 1981-83; med. social worker Vis. Nurses Assn. L.A., 1983-86, Kaiser Found. Hosps., L.A., 1986-92, Assisted Home Recovery, Granada Hills, Calif., 1991—; mental health coord., clin. social worker, psychotherapist Northeast Valley Health Corp., Pacoima, Calif., 1992—; social worker Cancervive, Inc., L.A., 1984—; dir. clin. svcs. Children's Fight for Life, Inc., Van Nuys, Calif., 1991—; presenter workshops on HIV and AIDS, grief and loss; med. adv. bd. RN Home Care Plus, Woodland Hills, Calif., 1992; mem. San Fernando AIDS/HIV Consortium, North Hollywood, Calif., 1992. Sec.-treas. Terra Villa Homeowners Assn., Panorama City, Calif., 1990. Mem. NASW, Oncology Social Workers San Fernando Valley. Roman Catholic. Home: 14400 Tupper St Apt A Van Nuys CA 91402

ROCH, JEAN-MARC, biologist; b. Lausanne, Switzerland, Feb. 20, 1960; came to U.S., 1988; s. Claude and Janine (Rod) R.; m. Anne-Catherine Levecq, Aug. 20, 1983; 1 child, Stéphane. BSc, U. Lausanne, 1982, PhD, 1988; MSc, U. Geneva, 1983. Asst. rsch. neurosci. U. Calif., San Diego, 1992—. Recipient Combe award U. Lausanne, 1988; Swiss Nat. Sci. Found. grantee, 1988-89, 90-92; postdoctoral fellow U. Calif., San Diego, 1988-92. Mem. Am. Soc. Neurochemistry, Internat. Soc. Neurochemistry, Soc. Neuroscis. Home: 8202 Regents Rd Apt 201 San Diego CA 92122-1376 Office: U Calif Dept Neurosci 0624 La Jolla CA 92093

ROCHA, GUY LOUIS, archivist, historian; b. Long Beach, Calif., Sept. 23, 1951; s. Ernest Louis and Charlotte (Sobus) R. BA in Social Studies and Edn., Syracuse U., 1973; MA in Am. Studies, San Diego State U., 1975; postgrad., U. Nev., 1975—. Cert. archivist Am. Acad. Cert. Archivists. Tchr., Washoe County Sch. Dist., Reno, Nev., 1975-76; history instr. Western Nev. Community Coll., Carson City, 1976; curator manuscripts Nev. Hist. Soc., Reno, 1976-81, interim asst. dir., 1980, interim dir., 1980-81; state administr. archives and records Nev. State Libr. and Archives, Carson City, 1981—; hist. cons. Janus Assocs., Tempe, Ariz., 1980, Rainshadow Assocs., Carson City, 1983—; mem. State Bd. Geographic Names. Co-author The Ignoble Conspiracy: Radicalism on Trial in Nevada, 1986, The Earp's Last Frontier: Wyatt and Virgil Earp in Nevada 1902-1905, 1988; contbr. to book and govt. study; host weekly radio talk show Sta. KPTL, Carson City, 1988—. Ex-officio mem. Nev. Commn. Bicentennial U.S. Constitution, 1986-91. Mem. Washoe Heritage Council, Reno, 1983-85; editorial bd. Nev. Hist. Soc., Reno, 1983—; mem. Washoe County Democratic Central Com., Reno, 1984-87. Mem. Conf. Intermountain Archivists (Council mem 1979-87, v.p. 1984-85, pres. 1985-86), No. Nev. Pub. Administrs. Group (pres. 1986-87, S.W. Labor Studies Administrs., State Hist. Records Adv. Bd. (dep. coordinator 1984-86, coordinator 1986—), Westerners Internat. Nev. Corral (dep. sheriff 1980-81, sheriff 1984-85, mem. state coordinators steering com. 1985-87, vice chmn. 1986-87), Soc. Am. Archivists, Western History Assn., Nat. Assn. Govt. Archives and Records Adminstrs, Nat. Assn. Govt. Archives and Records Adminstrs., Orgn. Am. Historians. Democrat. Home: 1824 Pyrenees St Carson City NV 89703-2331 Office: Nev State Libr & Archives 100 Stewart St Carson City NV 89710-0001

ROCHESTER, DAVID JOHN, investment banker, consultant; b. Newcastle, Eng., Oct. 29, 1939; s. Edward and Ann Edna (Raine) R.; m. Ann Ganter, Sept. 2, 1961 (div. 1987); children: Lisa, Susan; m. Shannon Clements, Dec. 31, 1987; children: Raine Elizabeth, Hailey Clements. Student, Reigate, Eng., 1957, Sorbonne, Paris. cert. stock broker. Various positions Cazenove & Co., London, Sydney, Australia, Hong Kong, 1961-75; pres. Cazenove Inc., N.Y.C., 1975-81, Wedd Durlacher Inc., N.Y.C., 1981-83; v.p. Merrill Lynch, N.Y.C., 1983-85; mng. dir. Merrill Lynch Europe, London, 1985-89; dir. Private Fund Mgrs. Ltd., London, 1990—; pres. Private Fund Mgrs, Inc., Ketchum, Idaho, 1992—. Mem. City of London Club, Royal Sydney Golf, Union Club Sydney. Home: PO Box 739 Ketchum ID 83340

ROCHLIS, JEFFREY AARON, new entertainment product and business developer; b. Phila., May 11, 1945; s. James Joseph Rochlis; m. Ellen Margaret Dondorf (div.); 1 child, Jennifer Lisa. BA in Theatre Arts, Bard Coll., 1967. Account exec. Benton & Bowles, N.Y.C., 1970-72; account supr. McCann-Erickson, N.Y.C., 1972-73; v.p. mktg. Aurora Products, Corp., West Hempstead, N.Y., 1973-76; pres. Mattel Electronics, Hawthorne, Calif., 1976-80; pres., chief exec. officer IXO, Inc., Culver City, Calif., 1980-83; pres., COO, dir. Sega Enterprises, Inc., Paramount Pictures, L.A., 1983-85; exec. v.p. Walt Disney Studios, Burbank, Calif., 1985-87, Walt Disney Imagineering, Glendale, Calif., 1987-89; pres. King World Enterprises, L.A., 1990; pres., COO Rockann Enterprises, Inc., Beverly Hills, Calif., 1990—. 1st lt. U.S. Army, 1967-70. Office: Rockann Enterprises Inc 301 N Canon Dr Ste 315 Beverly Hills CA 90210-4725

ROCKSTROH, DENNIS JOHN, journalist; b. Hermosa Beach, Calif., Feb. 1, 1942; s. Philip Herman and Alicia (Rubio) R.; m. Le Thi Que Huong, May 2, 1970; children: Bryan Benjamin, Paula Kim-Mai. Student, San Luis Rey Coll., 1960-61, El Camino Coll., 1961-62, San Fernando Valley State Coll., 1965-67. Reporter Thousand Oaks (Calif.) News Chronicle, 1966-67; tchr. Girls' High Sch., Qui Nhon, Vietnam, 1967-70; instr. Dalat U./Vietnamese Mil. Acad., 1970-71, Ohlone Coll., Fremont, Calif., 1984—; freelance war corr. Dispatch News Svc., Vietnam, 1967-71; city editor Santa Paula (Calif.) Daily Chronicle, 1972-73; reporter San Jose (Calif.) Mercury News, 1973-90, columnist, 1990—; guest lectr. U. Calif., Berkeley, 1987-91. Vol. Internat. Vol. Svcs., Vietnam, 1967-71; bd. dirs. San Jose unit ARC, 1978, Hope Rehab., San Jose, 1976-77. With U.S. Army, 1962-65, Vietnam. Co-recipient Pulitzer prize for Loma Prieta earthquake coverage, 1989; decorated Army Commendation Medal for Valor, 1965. Mem. Soc. Profl. Journalists, St. Anthony's Sem. Alumni Assn. Roman Catholic. Home: 3573 Tankerland Ct San Jose CA 95121-1244 Office: San Jose Mercury News 39355 California St Ste 301 Fremont CA 94538-1447

ROCKWELL, DON ARTHUR, psychiatrist; b. Wheatland, Wyo., Apr. 24, 1938; s. Orson Arthur and Kathleen Emily (Richards) R.; m. Frances Pepitone-Arreola, Dec. 23, 1965; children: Grant, Chad. BA, Wash. U., 1959; MD, U. Okla., 1963; MA in Sociology, U. Calif., Berkeley, 1967. Diplomate Am. Bd. Psychiatry and Neurology. Intern in surgery San Francisco Gen. Hosp., 1963-64; resident in psychiatry Langley-Porter Neuropsychiatric Inst. U. Calif. Med. Ctr., San Francisco, 1964-67; instr. dept. psychiatry U. Calif. Sch. Medicine, Davis, 1969-70, asst. prof., 1970-74, assoc. prof., 1974-80, acting. assoc., dean curricular affiars, 1979-80, acting assoc. dean student affairs, 1980, assoc. dean student affairs, 1980-82, prof., 1980-84; career tchr. NIMH, 1970-72; assoc. psychiatrist Sacramento Med. Ctr.; med. dir. U. Calif. Med. Ctr., Davis, 1982-84; prof., vice chmn. dept. psychiatry and biobehavioral scis. UCLA, 1984—, dir. univ. Neuropsychiat. Hosp., 1984—, exec. assoc. dir. univ. Neuropsychiat. Inst., 1984—; chief of profl. staff Neuropsychiat. Inst., UCLA, 1984-85; chmn. U. Calif. Hosp. Dirs. Council, 1988-89; cons. Nat. Commn. on Marijuana, Washington, 1971-73. Co-author: Psychiatric Disorders, 1982; contbr. chpts. to books; articles to profl. jours. Bd. dirs. Bereavement Outreach, Sacramento, 1974-84, Suicide Prevention, Yolo County, 1969-84; bd. visitors U. Okla. Sch. Medicine; chmn. hosp. dirs. coun. U. Calif. Hosp.; governing coun. AHA Psychiat. Hosp. Fellow Am. Psychiat. Assn., Am. Coll. Psychiatrists, Am. Coll. Mental Health Adminstrs.; mem. AMA (gov. coun. psych. hosp.), Am. Sociologic Assn., Cen. Calif. Psychiat. Assn. (sec.-pres. 1977-78), U. Okla. Alumni Assn. (trustee 1981-86), Alpha Omega Alpha. Home: 1061 Palisair Pl Pacific Palisades CA 90272-2459

ROCKWELL, ROBERT GOODE, electrical engineer; b. La Junta, Colo., Aug. 20, 1922; s. Leroy Elwood and Laura Belle (Mc Clain) R.; m. Betty Jean Crawford, Dec. 29, 1945 (div. July 1960); children: Laura Amundsen, Melanie Vizenor; m. Norma Jean Fosnaugh, Mar. 25, 1961; children: Michael, Robyn Rockwell-Elkins. BSEE, U. Colo., 1944; MSEE, Stanford U., 1948, Engr., 1949. Mem. tech. staff Hughes Aircraft Corp., Culver City, Calif., 1949-52, Los Angeles, 1969-70; sect. mgr. Varian Assocs., Palo Alto, Calif., 1952-66; mem. tech. staff Fairchild Semiconductor, Palo Alto, 1966-68; mgr. tube tech. Zenith Radio Corp., Glenview, Ill., 1971-82; prin. engr. Rank Electronic Tubes, Scotts Valley, Calif., 1982-86; CRT dispenser cathode cons. Ceradyne Electron Sources, Costa Mesa, Calif., 1986-87; design engr. Electro-Scan, Inc., Garfield, N.J., 1988-89; sr. design engr. Litton Electron Devices, Tempe, Ariz., 1989-90; ret., 1991. Contbr. articles to profl. jours.; patentee in field. Pres. Manakin Huguenots, Calif., 1986-88; mem. Huguenot Soc. of Founders of Manakin in the Colony of Va. Served as lt. (j.g.) USNR, 1942-45. Mem. SAR, IEEE (life, sr. Centennial medal 1984), Soc. Info. Display (life), Am. Legion, Colo. Terr. Family, Bucks and Does Sq. Dance Club (Elk Grove Village, Ill., pres. 1979-80), Ahwatukee (Ariz.) Woodworking Club, Ahwatukee Sq. Dance Club, Ahwatukee Lawn Bowling Club (pres. 1993—), Masons, Sigma Xi, Tau Beta Pi, Eta Kappa Nu. Democrat. Christian Ch. Home: 4826 E Winnebago St Phoenix AZ 85044-2127

ROCKWELL, STEVEN ALBERT, personnel director, educator; b. Colorado Springs, Colo., Sept. 2, 1941; s. Clarence Albert and Margery Elizabeth (Boman) R.; m. Grace LaNell Sabin (div. Feb. 1986); 1 child, Richard Steven; m. Judith Ann Watkins, Aug. 20, 1989. BA, U. So. Colo., Pueblo, 1966; MPA, U. Colo., Denver, 1977, D of Pub. Adminstrn., 1980. Labor rels. USAF Acad., Colorado Springs, 1967-78, dir. civilian pers., 1978—; bd. dirs. Fed. Pers. Coun., Denver, USAFA AERO Club, Colo.; panel mem. USAF Blue Ribbon Panel, Washington, 1988—; mem. Fed. Exec. Bd., Denver, 1986—. Author: Equity and Discretion: A Study of Discipline, 1980. Mem. Air Force Assn. Home: 6874 Duke Dr Colorado Springs CO 80918-1007

ROCQUE, REBECCA HOMEDEW, mathematics educator; b. Monticello, Utah, July 6, 1954; d. Charles Daniel and Barbara Lucille (Petersen) Homedew; m. Kevin William Rocque, July 22, 1977; children: Heather, Ryan, Brandon, Brent, Dana. BA, Brigham Young U., 1992. Cert. secondary educator, level 4 math and computer sci. endorsement. Substitute tchr. Alpine Sch. Dist., Am. Fork, Utah, 1984-91; pre-sch. tchr. Discovery Days Presch., Lehi, Utah, 1981-91; dir. Sunshine Generation of No. Utah County, Lehi, Utah, 1989-92; tchr. math. Am. Fork (Utah) High Sch., 1991—, Young Mothers' High Sch., Pleasant Grove, Utah, 1991-92; yearbook adviser Am. Fork High Sch., 1992—, swim coach, 1992—. Girl scout leader Girl Scouts of Am., Lehi, 1986-89; rm. mother PTA, Lehi, 1982-91; soccer coach Lehi Youth Recreation, 1989-90, swim team coach, 1992—; tchr. Community Sch., Lehi, 1983-91. Named one of Outstanding Women of Am., 1991. Mem. NEA, Nat. Coun. Tchrs. Math., Utah Edn. Assn. Republican. LDS. Home: 755 W 240 S Lehi UT 84043 Office: Am Fork High Sch 510 N 600 E American Fork UT 84003

RODABAUGH, DAVID JOSEPH, engineer, mathematics educator; b. Kansas City, Mo., Jan. 14, 1938; s. Joseph Forrest and Minnie May (Mehl) R.; m. Marlene Jean Hinze, Sept. 19, 1959; children: Kenneth, Dale, Terrance. BS, U. Chgo., 1959, MS, 1960; PhD, Ill. Inst. Tech., 1963. Instr. Ill. Inst. Tech., Chgo., 1962-63; asst. prof. Vanderbilt U., Nashville, 1963-65; prof. U. Mo., Columbia, 1965-82; R&D engr. Lockheed, Burbank, Calif., 1981—; cons. NASA, Huntsville, Ala., 1965-66; lectr. in elec. engring., computer sci. and math. Calif. State U., Northridge, 1981-92, Masters Coll., 1993. Contbr. numerous articles to profl. jours. NSF fellow, 1959-60. Mem. IEEE, Soc. for Indsl. and Applied Maths., Assn. for Computer Machinery. Home: 2760 Bitternut Cir Simi Valley CA 93065-1315 Office: Lockheed Dept 25-52 Burbank CA 91520

RODDICK, DAVID BRUCE, construction company executive; b. Oakland, Calif., Oct. 31, 1948; s. Bruce Ergo and Hortensia Cabo (Castedo) R.; m. Sharon Ann Belan, May 25, 1975; children: Heather Marie, Christina Dee-Ann. BSCE, U. Calif., Davis, 1971. Engr. Bechtel Corp., San Francisco, 1971-77, contract specialist, 1977-78; subcontract adminstr. Boecon Corp., Richland, Wash., 1978-79; constrn. mgr. BE&C Engrs., Inc., Vancouver, Wash., 1979-81; contracts mgr. Boecon Corp., Tukwila, Wash., 1981-83; sr. constrn. mgr. BE&C Engrs., Inc., Wichita, Kans., 1983-84; v.p. ops. Carl Holvick Co., Sunnyvale, Calif., 1984-88, also sec. bd. dirs.; v.p., gen. mgr. Brookman Co. div. B.T. Mancini Co., Inc., Milpitas, Calif., 1988-92; v.p., sec., CFO B.T. Mancini Co., Inc., 1992—. Mem. devel. com. San Jose (Calif.) Mus. Assn.; pres. Reed Sch. PTA, San Jose, 1986-88, San Jose Coun. PTA's, 1988-89; trustee Heart of Valley Bapt. Ch.; bd. dirs. Vinehill Homeowners Assn., 1975-77. Maj. C.E., USAR, 1969—. Decorated Army Achievement medal, 1988, Commendation medal, 1991; recipient Calif. State PTA Hon. Svc. award, 1988. Mem. ASCE, Res. Officers Assn., Am. Arbitration Assn. (mem. panel arbitrators), Engr. Regimental Assn., Calif. Aggie Alumni Assn., Army Engr. Assn., Constrn. Fin. Mgmt. Assn., U. Calif.-Davis Century Club, Elks, Sigma Nu. Republican. Office: B T Mancini Co Inc 876 S Milpitas Blvd Milpitas CA 95035-6311

RODEFFER, STEPHANIE LYNN HOLSCHLAG, archaeologist, government official; b. Newark, Ohio, Oct. 5, 1947; d. Jerry Bernard and Joan Elizabeth (Dasher) Holschlag; m. Michael Joe Rodeffer, Sept. 11, 1971. BA, U. Ky., 1968; PhD, Wash. State U., 1975. Instr., then asst. prof. anthropology Lander Coll., Greenwood, S.C., 1974-77; archaeologist interagy. archaeol. svcs. Nat. Park Svc./Heritage Conservation and Recreation Svc., Atlanta, 1977-80; archaeologist div. cultural programs Nat. Park Svc., Albuquerque, 1980-82, Santa Fe, N.Mex., 1981-82; archaeologist, acting chief preservation planning br. Nat. Park Svc., Phila., 1982-86; chief interagy. archaeol. svcs. br. div. nat. register programs Nat. Park Svc., San Francisco, 1986-90; chief mus. collections repository Western Archaeol. and Conservation Ctr. Nat. Park Svc., Tucson, 1990—. Muster Chmn. Star Ft. Hist. Com., Ninety Six, S.C., 1975. Recipient spl. achievement award Nat. Park Svc., 1980, 82, mgmt. award So. Ariz. Fed. Execs. Assn., 1992; Woodrow Wilson fellow, 1969. Mem. Soc. for Hist. Archeology (membership chmn. 1976-78, sec.-treas. 1978—), Soc. for Am. Archaeology, Soc. Profl. Archaeologists. Roman Catholic. Office: Nat Park Svc Western Archaeol-Conservation Ctr 1415 N 6th Ave Tucson AZ 85705

RODELL, TIMOTHY CLARKE, pharmaceutical company executive, physician; b. L.A., Mar. 1, 1951; s. John and Mary Louise (Matteson) R.; m. Marjorie Miles McMillan, June 17, 1972; 1 child, Simon Alexander. AB, U. N.C., 1975, MD, 1980. Diplomate Am. Bd. Internal Medicine, Am. Bd. Pulmonary Medicine. Intern in internal medicine U. Colo. Health Scis. Ctr., Denver, 1980-81, resident in internal medicine, 1981-83; fellow in pulmonary & critical care medicine U. Colo. Health Scis. Ctr., Webb-Waring Lung Inst., Denver, 1983-86; asst. prof. medicine Health Sci. Ctr. U. Colo., Denver, 1987-88, clin. asst. prof. medicine, 1988—; v.p. Cortech, Inc., Denver, 1987—. Contbr. articles to profl. jours. Office: Cortech Inc 6840 Broadway Denver CO 80221-2852

RODEN, JOHANNA WAHL, German educator; b. Kassel, Germany, Dec. 3, 1928; d. Johannes and Dina (Rode) Wahl; m. Hans Wilhelm Roden, July 28, 1962; 1 son, Martin Eric. B.A. in Sociology, Calif. State U.-Long Beach, 1961, M.A. in Social Sci., 1962, M.A. in German, U. So. Calif., 1966, Ph.D. in German, 1970. Field dir. Long Beach (Calif.) council Girl Scouts U.S.A., 1953-56; instr. Long Beach City Coll., 1961-62; prof. German, Calif. State U.-Long Beach, 1962-91, prof. emeritus, 1991—, chmn. dept. German, Russian and Classics, 1969-85. Pres., United Ch. Retirement Home, 1978-80. Mem. UN Assn. (pres. Long Beach chpt. 1980-82), Am. Assn. Tchrs. German, Soc. Exile Studies, Internat. Arthur Schnitzler Rsch. Assn., German Studies Assn. Contbr. articles on German exile writers in U.S. to profl. jours and books. Office: Calif State U Long Beach CA 90840

RODEY, PATRICK MICHAEL, state senator; b. San Francisco, Jan. 22, 1943; s. James and Martha Leora (Phillips) R.; B.Ed., U. Alaska, 1966; J.D., U. Ariz., 1973; m. Barbara Jean Coffey, June 25, 1976. With Safeway Corp., 1963-66, U. Alaska, 1968-69, Peter Kiewits Sons, 1969-74; admitted to Alaska bar, 1973; ptnr. firm Abbott, Lynch & Farney, and predecessor firm, Anchorage, 1975-83, Aglietti, Pennington and Rodey, 1983-89, Aglietti, Rodey and Offret, 1990—; mem. Alaska Senate, 1974-93 (chmn. senate judiciary com., banking com., comm. and reg. affairs com.), chmn. code revision commn., 1976-78, Senate majority leader, 1980-82, 88-90 . Mem. Am., Alaska bar assns., Phi Alpha Delta. Democrat. Episcopalian. Home: 2335 Lord Baranof Dr Anchorage AK 99517-1261

RODGERS, BUCK (ROBERT LEROY RODGERS), professional baseball team manager; b. Delaware, Ohio, Aug. 16, 1938; m. Judi Long; children: Lori, Lisa, Jan and Jill (twins). Student, Ohio Wesleyan U, Ohio No. U. Player various minor league teams, 1956-61, 75, 77, L.A. Angels (now Calif. Angels), 1961-69; coach Minn. Twins, 1970-74; mgr. minor league team Calif. Angels, 1975, 77; coach San Francisco Giants, 1976; coach Milw. Brewers, 1978-80, mgr., 1980-82; mgr. minor league team Montreal Expos orgn., 1984; mgr. Montreal Expos, 1985-91, Calif. Angels, 1991—. Named Minor League Mgr. of Yr. Sporting News, 1984, Nat. League Mgr. of Yr. Baseball Writers' Assn. Am., 1987, Sporting News, 1987, Baseball Am., 1987, USA Today, 1987, Sports Illus., 1987, UPI, 1987. Office: care Calif Angels PO Box 2000 Anaheim CA 92803-2000*

RODGERS, FREDERIC BARKER, judge; b. Albany, N.Y., Sept. 29, 1940; s. Prentice Johnson and Jane (Weed) R.; m. Valerie McNaughton, Oct. 8, 1988; 1 child: Gabriel Moore. AB, Amherst Coll., 1963; JD, Union U., 1966. Bar: N.Y. 1966, U.S. Ct. Mil. Appeals 1968, Colo. 1972, U.S. Supreme Ct. 1974, U.S. Ct. Appeals (10th cir.) 1981. Chief dep. dist. atty., Denver, 1972-73; commr. Denver Juvenile Ct., 1973-79; mem. Mulligan Reeves Teasley & Joyce, P.C., Denver, 1979-80; pres. Frederic B. Rodgers, P.C., Breckenridge, Colo., 1980-89; ptnr. McNaughton & Rodgers, Central City, Colo., 1989-91; county ct. judge County of Gilpin, 1987—; presiding mcpl. judge cities of Breckenridge, Blue River, Black Hawk, Central City, Edgewater, Empire, Idaho Springs and Westminster, Colo., 1979—; chmn. com. on mcpl. ct. rules of procedure Colo. Supreme Ct., 1984—; mem. gen. faculty Nat. Jud. Coll. U. Nev., Reno, 1990—. Author: (with Dilweg, Fretz, Murphy and Wicker) Modern Judicial Ethics, 1992; contbr. articles to profl. jours. Mem. Colo. Commn. on Children, 1982-85, Colo. Youth Devel. Coun., 1989—. Served with JAGC, U.S. Army, 1967-72; to maj. USAR, 1972-88. Decorated Bronze Star with oak leaf cluster, Air medal. Recipient Outstanding County Judge award Colo. 17th Judicial Dist. Victim Adv. Coalition, 1991; Spl. Community Service award Colo. Am. Legion, 1979. Mem. ABA (jud. adminstrn. div. exec. coun. 1989—), Colo. Bar Assn. (bd. govs. 1986-88, 90-92), Denver Bar Assn. (bd. trustees 1979-82), First Jud. Dist. Bar Assn., Nat. Conf. Spl. Ct. Judges (chmn. 1989-90), Colo. Mcpl. Judges Assn. (pres. 1986-87), Denver Law Club (pres. 1981-82), Colo. Women's Bar Assn., Am. Judicature Soc., Nat. Coun. Juvenile and Family Ct. Judges, Univ. Club (Denver), Arlberg Club (Winter Park), Marines Meml. Club (San Francisco). Episcopalian. Home: 108 Casey St Central City CO 80427-0398 Office: Gilpin County Courthouse 142 Lawrence St Central City CO 80427

RODGERS, LA SANDRA, modeling company executive; b. L.A., June 20, 1950; d. James Armstead and Bobera D. (Goff) Brown; 1 child, Malcolm Jerome Tyson. Student, U. Calif., Irvine, 1968-69, L.A. Trade Tech., 1969-71. Clothing designer Simply Sandy Designs, Lynwood, Calif., 1965—; operator Pacific Telephone & Telegraph, Bel, Calif., 1969-74; svc. rep. Pacific Telephone & Telegraph, Compton, Calif., 1974-79; computer trainer Pacific Bell, Calif., 1985-86; mgr. Pacific Bell, L.A., 1979-91; exec. dir. Ubitquitdus Modeling Co., L.A., 1986-90; pres., CEO NuVison Modeling & Entertainment, L.A., 1991—; modeling instr. various cos., L.A., 1982-92. Area commr. Boy Scouts Am., Lynwood, 1985-86; troop leader Girl Scouts U.S., Lynwood, 1973-75; PTF pres. New Life Bapt. Sch., Lynwood, 1981-86; bd. dirs. Unity-N-Bus., L.A., 1981-84. Recipient various awards; named to Outstanding Young Women of Am., 1986. Office: NuVision Modeling PO Box 67 Lynwood CA 90262

RODMAN, ALPINE CLARENCE, arts and crafts company executive; b. Roswell, N.Mex., June 23, 1952; s. Robert Elsworth and Verna Mae (Means)

R.; m. Sue Arlene Lawson, Dec. 13, 1970; 1 child, Connie Lynn. Student, Colo. State U., 1970-71, U. No. Colo. Ptnr. Pinel Silver Shop, Loveland, Colo., 1965-68, salesman, 1968-71; real estate salesman Loveland, 1971-73; mgr. Traveling Traders, Phoenix, 1974-75; co-owner Deer Track Traders, Loveland, 1975-85; pres. Deer Track Traders, Ltd., 1985—. Author: The Vanishing Indian: Fact or Fiction?, 1985. Mem. Civil Air Patrol, 1965-72, 87-92, dep. comdr. for cadets, 1988-90; cadet comdr. Ft. Collins, Colo., 1968, 70, Colo. rep. to youth tng. program, 1969, U.S. youth rep. to Japan, 1970. Mem. Bur. Wholesale Sales Reps., We. and English Salesmen's Assn. (bd. dirs. 1990), Internat. Platform Assn., Indian Arts and Crafts Assn. (bd. dirs. 1988—, exec. com. 1989-92, v.p. 1990, pres. 1991, market chmn. 1992), Crazy Horse Grass Roots Club. Republican. Office: Deer Track Traders Ltd PO Box 448 Loveland CO 80539-0448

RODMAN, SUE ARLENE, wholesale Indian crafts company executive, artist; b. Fort Collins, Colo., Oct. 1, 1951; d. Marvin F. and Barbara I. (Miller) Lawson; m. Alpine C. Rodman, Dec. 13, 1970; 1 child, Connie Lynn. Student Colo. State U., 1970-73. Silversmith Pinel Silver Shop, Loveland, Colo., 1970-71; asst. mgr. Traveling Traders, Phoenix, 1974-75; co-owner, co-mgr. Deer Track Traders, Ltd., Loveland, 1975-85, exec. v.p., 1985—. Author: The Book of Contemporary Indian Arts and Crafts, 1985. Mem. U.S. Senatorial Club, 1982-87, Rep. Presdl. Task Force, 1984-90; mem. Civil Air Patrol, 1969-73, 87-90, pers. officer, 1988-90. Mem. NAFE, Internat. Platform Assn., Indian Arts and Crafts Assn., Native Am. Art Studies Assn., Inc., Western and English Sales Assn., Crazy Horse Grass Roots Club. Baptist. Avocations: museums, recreation research, fashion design, reading, flying. Office: Deer Track Traders Ltd PO Box 448 Loveland CO 80539-0448

RODNUNSKY, SIDNEY, lawyer, educator, Prince of Kiev, Prince of Trabzon, Duke of Chernigov, Count of Riga, Count of St. John of Alexandria, Baron of Vai; b. Edmonton, Alta., Can., Feb. 3, 1946; s. H. and I. Rodnunsky; m. Teresita Asuncion; children: Naomi, Shawna, Rachel, Tevie, Claire, Donna. BEd, U. Alberta, 1966, LLB, 1973; MEd, U. Calgary, 1969, grad. diploma, 1990; BS, U. of State of N.Y., 1988; MBA, Greenwich U., 1990. Served as regional counsel to Her Majesty the Queen in Right of the Dominion of Can.; former gov. Grande Prairie Regional Coll.; now prin. legal counsel Can.; past pres. Grande Prairie and Dist. Bar Assn. Author: Breathalyzer Casebook. Decorated Knight Grand Cross Sovereign and Royal Order of Piast, Knight Grand Cross Order of St. John the Baptist; knight Hospitaller Order St. John of Jerusalem; named to Honorable Order of Ky. Colonels; named adm. State of Tex.; recipient Presidential Legion of Merit. Mem. Law Soc. Alta., Law Soc. Sask., Canadian Bar Assn., Inst. Can. Mgmt. Address: Box 53, Smith, AB Canada T0G 2B0

RODRIGUE, CHRISTINE M., geography educator, business consultant; b. Los Angeles, Oct. 27, 1952; d. John-Paul and Josephine Genevieve (Gorsky) R. AA in French, German, Los Angeles Pierce Coll., 1972; BA in Geography summa cum laude, Calif. State U., Northridge, 1973, MA in Geography, 1976; PhD in Geography, Clark U., 1987. Computer analyst Jet Propulsion Labs., Pasadena, Calif., 1977; teaching asst. Clark U., Worcester, Mass., 1976-79, research asst., 1977-78; instr. geography Los Angeles Pierce Coll., Woodland Hills, Calif., 1981—; cons. Area Location Systems, Northridge, 1984—, tech. writer, 1990—; asst. prof. urban studies and geography Calif. State U., Northridge, 1980-89; asst. prof. geography and planning Calif. State U., Chico, 1989—, faculty senator, 1990-92, grad. geog. adviser, 1992—; owner Carmel (Calif.) Poster Gallery. Recipient Meritorious Performance and Profl. Promise award Calif. State U., 1987, 88, 89, Calif. State U. summer scholar grant, 1990, 92. Mem. NOW, AAAS, Assn. Am. Geographers (chmn. specialty group 1983-84), Capitalism Nature Socialism (editorial bd. 1991—), Los Angeles Geog. Soc. (v.p. 1987, pres. 1988, editor 1981-84), Union Concerned Scientists, The Planetary Soc., Sierra Club, Internat. Arabian Horse Assn., Arabian Horse Registry. Democrat. Office: Calif State U Dept Geography and Planning Chico CA 95929-0425

RODRIGUES, ALFRED BENJAMIN KAMEEIAMOKU, marketing consultant: b. Honolulu, Jan. 23, 1947; s. Alfred Benjamin Kameeiamoku and Ruth Shiegeko (Kameda) R. BA, U. San Francisco, 1969; postgrad. U. Wis., 1977. Pub. info. mgr. Hawaiian Tel.-GTE, Honolulu, 1979-80, pub. affairs program mgr., 1980-84, dir. pub. affairs, 1984-85, dir. mktg. communications, 1986-87, dir. mktg. communications and svcs., 1987-89 sr. v.p., Milici, Valenti and Gabriel Advt., Inc., 1989-91, exec. v.p., 1991-92; pres. Al Rodrigues & Assocs., 1992—. Bd. dirs., pub. rels. chmn. Am. Lung Assn., 1981-88; trustee, v.p. Hawaii Army Mus. Soc., 1982—; bd. dirs. ARC Hawaii, 1983-85; budget com. Aloha United Way. Maj. USAR, 1969-89. Decorated Bronze Star with three oak leaf clusters, Meritorious Svc. medal with oak leaf cluster, Army Commendation medal with 2 oak leaf clusters, Purple Heart with oak leaf cluster, Air medal with oak leaf cluster. Mem. Am. Mktg. Assn. (bd. dirs. Hawaii chpt.), Am. Advt. Fedn., Hawaii Advt. Fedn. (bd. dirs., pres., Advt. Man of Yr., 1989), Pub. Rels. Soc. Am. (pres. Hawaii), Res. Officers Assn., Hawaii C. of C., Rotary. Republican. Roman Catholic.

RODRIGUES, MARK, financial executive, manpower consultant; b. Jhansi, India, Oct. 7, 1948; came to U.S., 1983; s. Basil and Monica (Dasgupta) R.; m. Sandra Williams, Mar. 27, 1976; children: Sarah, Daniel. BTech, Loughborough U., Leicester, Eng., 1970; MBA, Strathclyde U., Glasgow, Scotland, 1971. Cert. Acct., Eng. Fin. analyst Ford Europe, Inc., London, 1971-73; mgmt. cons., London mgr. Mann Judd Mgmt. Cons., 1973-78; pres. Bur. and Industry Svcs. Ltd., London, 1978-81; mng. dir. Indsl. Engring. Svcs., London, 1981-83; v.p. Internat. Staffing Cons., Newport Beach, Calif., 1983-88; pres. Brit. Workforce, Inc., Mission Viejo, Calif., 1988—, Euro Swiss Inc., San Diego, Calif., 1991—; ptnr. Euro Precision, Laguna Hills, Calif., 1992—. Fellow Assn. Cert. Accts.; mem. Royal Oriental Club. Office: Brit Workforce Inc 26002 Marguerite Pkwy Ste 433 Mission Viejo CA 92692

RODRIGUEZ, ANTHONY ELLIS, lawyer, consultant; b. Frankfurt, Germany, June 10, 1961. BA with honors, U. Okla., 1983; JD, Georgetown U., 1987; U. Melbourne, Australia, 1985. Bar: Calif. 1990, Tex. 1987. Law clk. U.S. Dist. Ct., Houston, 1987-89; assoc. Dewey Ballantine, L.A., 1989-91; v.p. Rodriguez & Assocs., Las Palmas, Spain, 1991-93; ptnr. Stein Perlman, L.A., 1993—. Rotary scholar, 1985. Office: Stein Perlman 9000 Sunset Blvd Ste 500 Los Angeles CA 90069

RODRIGUEZ, JAY, foundation executive; b. La Verne, Calif., Jan. 15, 1928; s. Eliseo and Concha (Estrada) R.; m. Patricia Ann Giese, Aug. 26, 1961 (dec.); children: Kate, John, Paul, David, Steven. Student, Mt. San Antonio Coll., Walnut, Calif., 1946-48. Dir. spl. edit. Pomona (Calif.) Progress Bull., 1949-63; owner, mgr. restaurant chain, Pomona, Cucamonga, Calif., 1963-69; mgr. Sta. KNBC-TV, Burbank, Calif., 1969-79; v.p. NBC, Burbank, 1979-89; pres. Hafif Family Found., Claremont, Calif., 1989—. Chmn. Peace Officers Standards and Tng., Sacramento, 1983; bd. dirs. ARC, L.A., 1989-92, NCCJ, 1986-92; bd. trustees Univ. LaVene. Named Outstanding Young Man, Pomona Jaycees, 1963, Alumni of Yr., Calif. C.C., Sacramento, 1982, Outstanding Alumni, 1987; recipient Spotlight award ARC, 1991. Mem. Greater L.A. Press Club (pres. 1988-89), Nat. Latino Comm. Ctr. (chmn.). Democrat. Presbyterian. Office: Hafif Family Found 265 W Bonita Ave Claremont CA 91711

RODRIGUEZ, JOSE FRANCISCO, financial consultant; b. Highland Park, Mich., Mar. 3, 1942; s. Jose Alexander and Elvira Helen (Csillagh) R.; m. Doris Helen Sandoval, July 7, 1977; 1 child, Tamara Sue. BA, Northrop Inst. of Tech., 1967. Prodn. supr. AiResearch div. Garrett Corp., L.A., 1963-69; corp. staff Bestline Products, Inc., San Jose, Calif., 1969-73; dist. mgr. Avis Rent-A-Car, Palm Springs, Calif., 1974-77; owner, operator Giant Rock Airport, Landers, Calif., 1977-80; pres., chief exec. officer Jose Rodriguez & Assocs., Las Vegas, 1981—. Recipient Pres. Award for Edn., Office of the Pres. of U.S., 1967. Mem. United Smokers Assn. (founder, chmn.). Republican. Office: Jose Rodriguez & Assocs 1859 Helm Dr Las Vegas NV 89119-3911

RODRIGUEZ, LEONARD, public and private sector administrator; b. Phoenix, Jan. 27, 1944; s. Jesus H. and Manuela (Razo) R.; m. Jo Ann Gama, Jan. 16, 1965 ; 1 child, Lena Teresa. BS in Mktg., Ariz. State U., 1981. Cert. tchr., Ariz. Adminstrv. svcs. officer Title XX Adminstrn., Phoenix, 1979-81, Block Grants Adminstrn., Phoenix, 1981-84; property mgmt. mgr. State of Ariz., Phoenix, 1984-86; pres. LTR Mgmt. Svcs., Phoenix, 1986—; dir. PALS computer literacy program N.W. Resources and Learning Ctr., 1989-91; program cons. City of El Mirage, 1989-91; master tchr. Rio Salado C.C., 1989-91; project dir., exec. dir. Westside Coalition for Substance Abuse Prevention, 1990-91; adj. clin. instr., faculty assoc. Ariz. State U., 1979-89; cons. Applied Econs. Curriculum, Jr. Achievement of Cen. Ariz., Inc., 1987. Chmn. community rels. minority recruitment program Ariz. State U., Tempe, 1985-86; bd. dirs. Concilio Latino de Salud, Inc., vice chmn. Friendly House, Inc., Phoenix, 1982, chmn., 1993, pres., 1987; mem. community problem solving coordinating com. Valley of the Sun United Way, 1988; alliance chmn. Gov.'s Office of Drug Policy, mem. statewide exec. com., 1991; program cons. Cada Uno, Inc., 1990-91. Mem. Ariz. Adminstrs. Assn., Counterparts (founder 1986), Hispanic C. of C., Vesta Club (chmn. scholarship com. 1983), Rotary (pres. 1987-88, voting del. internat. conv. 1987). Home: 7650 S 14th St Phoenix AZ 85040-6711

RODRIGUEZ, NICHOLAS GEORGE, lawyer; b. Washington, Feb. 9, 1953; s. Nicholas and Mollie (Rodriguez) George; m. Eva Ferreira, Nov. 26, 1956 (div.); children: Elisa, Nicholas. BA, Cornell U., 1974; JD, U. Calif., Berkeley, 1977. Bar: Calif. 1977, U.S. Dist. Ct. (no. dist.) Calif. 1977, U.D. Dist. Ct. (ctrl. dist.) Calif. 1983. Staff atty. El Centro de Accion Social, Pasadena, Calif., 1977-84; assoc. Gronemeier, Barker & Huerta, Pasadena, 1985-89, ptnr., 1989—; dep. city atty. City of Pasadena, 1989-92, asst. city atty., 1992—. Mem. Blue Ribbon Com./Affordable Housing, Pasadena, 1982, Charter Study Com., Pasadena, 1987; mem. Pasadena Planning Commn., 1987-89, vice chmn., 1989. Recipient award Berkeley Law Found., 1978, Mover and Shaker award L.A. mag., 1982, also numerous others, including Pasadena Neighborhood Housing Svcs., Inc., Foothill Area Community Svcs., Urban League, El Centro de Accion. Mem. ABA, Mexican Am. Bar Assn. (treas. 1983), Tournament of Roses Assn. (provisional). Roman Catholic. Home: 537 N Chester Ave Pasadena CA 91106 Office: City of Pasadena 100 N Garfield Rm 228 Pasadena CA 91109

RODRIGUEZ, ROMAN, physician, child psychiatrist, educator; b. N.Y.C., Jan. 21, 1951; s. Roman Rodriguez and Margarita (Castillo) Torres. BS in Biology, St. Mary's Coll. of Calif., 1972; MD, U. Calif.-San Francisco, 1976. Diplomate Nat. Bd. Med. Examiners, Am. Bd. Psychiatry and Neurology-Gen. Psychiatry, Am. Bd. Psychiatry and Neurology-Child and Adolescent Psychiatry. Resident in gen. psychiatry Menninger Found., Topeka, 1976-79, fellow in child psychiatry, 1978-80; resident physician Topeka VA Med. Ctr., 1976-79; dir. psychiat. services Youth Ctr. Topeka, 1979-80; assoc. med. dir. Mission/SE Adolescent Day Treatment Ctr., San Francisco, 1980-81; staff psychiatrist, med. advisor Youth Guidance Ctr., San Francisco, 1980-82; clin. dir. Growing Mind Corp., San Rafael, Calif., 1980-85; pvt. practice child psychiatry, San Francisco and San Rafael, Calif., 1980-85; child team leader dept. psychiatry Kaiser Permanente Med. Ctr., South San Francisco, 1985—, physician well being com., 1990—; med. staff Children's Hosp., San Francisco, 1980-85; St. Luke's Hosp., San Francisco, 1981-85; Marin Gen. Hosp., Greenbrae, Calif., 1983-87; asst. clin. prof. U. Calif., San Francisco, 1981—, mem. admissions com. Sch. Medicine, 1980-85; examiner Am. Bd Psychiatry and Neurology, Inc., 1992—. Bd. dirs. Canal Community Alliance, San Rafael, 1985-86, Community Health Ctr. Marin, Fairfax, Calif., 1985-86, Bahia de Rafael Fourplex, San Rafael, 1986, Village in the Park Homeowners Assn., Daly City, 1991—. Mem. Am. Psychiat. Assn., Am. Soc. for Adolescent Psychiatry, Am. Acad. Child and Adolescent Psychiatry, No. Calif. Psychiat. Soc., Calif. Med. Assn., San Mateo County Med. Soc. Republican. Roman Catholic. Home: 116 City View Dr Daly City CA 94014-3446 Office: Kaiser Permanente Med Ctr Dept Psychiatry 1200 El Camino Real South San Francisco CA 94080-3299

RODROGUES, DONALD FRANK, landscape horticulture educator; b. Merced, Calid., Aug. 27, 1938; s. Anthony S. and Mary (Gorge) R.; m. Beverly Thomas, Apr. 24, 1940 (div.); children: Kimberly, Michael, Denise. BS, Fresno State U., 1963; MA, Calif. Polytech U., 1966. Prof. Ventura (Calif.) C.C., 1965—, Calif. Polytech U., San Luis Obispo, 1978-79, UCLA, 1985-88; pres. Delta-Pacific Hort., Ventura, 1980-90; prin. Pacific Hort. Cons., Ventura, 1990-92; cons. World Bank AID Program, Bangkok, Thailand, 1979-82, USN Western Div., 1980-92. Author of 3 books; contbr. articles to profl. jours. Pres. Turf & Landscape Coun., Ventura, 1985-87; advisor U. Calif. Coop. Extension Svc., Ventura County, 1987-92; mem. City of Ventura Hort. Review Bd., 1988-90. Rsch. grantee Ventura Community Coll., 1990. Mem. Internat. Soc. Hort. (mag. editor 1983-84), Calif. Assn. Nurserymen. Ca;of. Landscape Contractors Assn., Lions Club. Republican. Roman Catholic. Office: Pacific Hort Cons 3352 Loma Bista Rd Ventura CA 93003

ROE, BENSON BERTHEAU, surgeon, educator; b. L.A., July 7, 1918; s. Hall and Helene Louise (Bertheau) R.; m. Jane Faulkner St. John, Jan. 20, 1945; children: David B., Virginia St. John. AB, U. Calif., Berkeley, 1939; MD cum laude, Harvard U., 1943. Diplomate Am. Bd. Surgery, Am. Bd. Thoracic Surgery (dir. 1971-83, chmn. bd. 1981-83, chmn. exam. com. 1978, chmn. long-range planning com. 1980, chmn. program com. 1977). Intern Mass. Gen. Hosp., Boston, 1943-44, resident, 1946-50; nat. rsch. fellow dept. physiology Med. Sch., Harvard U., Boston, Mass., 1947, instr. surgery, 1950; Moseley Traveling fellow Harvard. U. at U. Edinburgh, Scotland, 1951; asst. clin. prof. surgery U. Calif., San Francisco, 1951-58, chief cardiothoracic surgery, 1958-76, prof. surgery, 1966-89, emeritus prof., 1989—; pvt. practice medicine specializing in cardiothoracic surgery San Francisco, 1952-85; cons. thoracic surgery VA Hosp., San Francisco Gen. Hosp., Letterman Army Hosp., St. Lukes Hosp., Blue Shield of Calif., Baxter Labs., Ethicon, Inc.; bd. dirs. Control Laser Corp.; vis. prof. U. Utah, U. Ky., U. Gdansk, Poland, Nat. Heart Hosp., London, U. Ibadan, Nigeria, Sanger Clinic, Charlotte, Rush-Presbyn. Hosp., Chgo., Penrose Hosp., Colorado Springs; bd. dirs. Internat. Bioethics Inst. Mem. editorial bd. Annals of Thoracic Surgery, 1969-82, Pharos; editor 2 med. texts; author 21 textbook chpts.; contbr. 172 articles to profl. jours. Bd. dirs. United Bay Area Crusade, 1958-70, mem. exec. com., 1964-65; bd. dirs. chmn. exec. com. San Francisco chpt. Am. Cancer Soc., 1955-57; bd. dirs. San Francisco Heart Assn., 1964-72, pres., 1964-65, chmn. rsch. com., 1966-71; mem. various coms. Am. Heart Assn., 1967-70; pres. Miranda Lux Found.; trustee Avery Fuller Found.; bd. dirs. Internat. Bioethics Inst., Point Reyes Bird Observatory. Served with Med. Svc. Corps, USNR, 1944-46. Fellow Am. Coll. Cardiology, ACS (chmn. adv. coun. thoracic surgery, program chmn. thoracic surgery, cardiovascular com.), Polish Surg. Assn. (hon.); mem. Am. Assn. Thoracis Surgery (chmn. memberhsip com. 1974-75), AMA (residency rev. com. for thoracic surgery), Am. Surg. Assn., Pacific Coast Surg. Assn., Calif. Acad. Medicine (pres. 1974), Calif. Med. Assn., Soc. Univ. Surgeons, Soc. Thoracic Surgeons (pres. 1972, chmn. standards and ethics com.), Soc. Vascular Surgery (v.p.). Clubs: Cruising of Am, Pacific Union, St. Francis Yacht, Calif. Tennis. Office: U Calif Div Cardiothoracic Surgery U Calif M593 San Francisco CA 94143-0118

ROE, CHARLES RICHARD, baritone; b. Cleve., May 24, 1940; s. Andrews Rogers and Margaret (Dalton) R.; children by previous marriage—Charles Andrews, Richard Nevins, Robert Arthur; m. Jo Ann Marie Belli, May 21, 1988. B.Mus., Baldwin-Wallace Coll., 1963; M.Mus., U. Ill., 1964. Instr. in music Tex. Tech. U., 1964-68; asst. prof. music Eastern Mich. U., 1968-74; vis. assoc. prof. U. So. Calif., L.A., 1976-77, assoc. prof., 1979-84, prof., 1984-89; prof. U. Ariz., Tucson, 1989—; vis. prof. and artist in residence Western Mich. U., 1978-79; faculty Music Acad. of the West, 1981, 82. Leading singer, N.Y.C. Opera, 1974-81; appeared in leading roles with, Mich. Opera Theater, Sacramento Opera, San Antonio Opera, Ft. Worth Opera, Ky. Opera, Conn. Opera, Utah Opera, Cleve. Opera, Miss. Opera, Lake George Opera, Shreveport Opera, Toledo Opera; appeared with, symphonies: Phila., Cleve., Detroit, Toledo, Wichita, Duluth. Mem. Am. Guild Musical Artists, Actors Equity, Nat. Assn. Tchrs. Singing (S.W. region Singer of Year 1966), AAUP. Office: care U Ariz Sch Music Tucson AZ 85721

ROE, WILLIAM THOMAS, behaviorial engineer, educator; b. N.Y.C., July 7, 1944; s. William T. and Harriet E. (Higgins) R.; m. Susan C. Kane, Aug. 30, 1972. BA in Enginlg./Indsl. Psychology, Calif. State U.-Northridge, 1971, MA in Human Factors and Applied Exptl. Psychology, 1978; post-grad., Walden U. Rsch. asst. XYZYX Info. Corp., Canoga Park, Calif., 1973-74; mem. psychol. staff Manned Systems Scis. Inc., Northridge, 1974-75; rsch. psychologist Inst. Safety and Systems Mgmt., U. So. Calif., L.A., 1975-76; mgr., acct. exec. systems and data processing Mgmt. Recruiters So. Calif., Encino, 1976-79; resource evaluation analyst Samaritan Health Svc., Phoenix, 1979; sr. methods analyst Valley Nat. Bank, Phoenix, 1979-81; indsl. engr. City of Scottsdale, Ariz., 1981-84; prof. psychology Phoenix Coll., 1984—; editorial reviewer numerous major text publs. Author: Ergonomic Models of Human Performance: Source Materials for the Analyst, 1975, Behavioral Engineering: Paradigm for Human Transformation, 1988; contbr. articles to profl. jours. With USN, 1961-67, Vietnam. Recipient Recognition certs. San Fernando Valley chpt. Data Processing Mgmt. Assn., 1978, Phoenix chpt. 1983. Mem. APA (divsn. 2), AACD, Am. Inst. Indsl. Engrs., Human Factors Soc., World Future Soc., Western Psychol. Assn., Ariz. Counselors Assn., Ariz. Mental Health Counselors Assn., Am. Assn. Profl. Hypnotherapists. Office: Phoenix Coll 1202 W Thomas Rd Phoenix AZ 85013-4234

ROEDER, CHARLES WILLIAM, structural engineering educator; b. Hershey, Pa., Oct. 12, 1942; s. Francis William and Myrtle Marie (Garrison) R.; m. Nancy Lee Newman, June 14, 1969; 1 child, Michael Thomas. BSCE, U. Colo., 1969; MSCE, U. Ill., 1971; PhD, U. Calif., Berkeley, 1977. Mem. gen. constrn. crew Shaffer and Son, Palmyra, Pa., 1960-66; structural engr. J. Ray McDermott, New Orleans, 1971-74; prof. of civil engr. U. Wash., Seattle, 1977—; cons. in field. Editor: Composite and Mixed Construction, 1985; contbr. articles to profl. pubs. Chmn. com. Transp. Rsch. Bd., Washington, 1990—. With U.S. Army, 1964-66, Vietnam. Mem. ASCE (chmn. 4 tech. coms., J. James R. Croes medal 1979, Raymond C. Reese Rsch. prize 1984), Am. Inst. Steel Constrn., Am. Welding Soc., Earthquake Engring. Rsch. Inst., Wilderness Soc., Sierra Club. Home: 5300 NE 67th St Seattle WA 98115-7755 Office: U Wash 233 B More Hall FX-10 Seattle WA 98195

ROEDER, STEPHEN BERNHARD WALTER, chemistry and physics educator; b. Dover, N.J., Aug. 26, 1939; s. Walter Martin and Katherine E.R. (Holz) R.; m. Phoebe E. Barber, June 28, 1969; children: Adrienne H.K., Roland K.W. B.A., Dartmouth Coll., 1961; Ph.D., U. Wis., 1965. Postdoctoral fellow Bell Telephone Labs., Murray Hill, N.J., 1965-66; lectr. physics U. Oreg., Eugene, 1966-68; asst. prof. chemistry and physics San Diego State U., 1968-72, assoc. prof., 1972-75, prof., 1975—, chmn. dept. physics, 1975-78, chmn. dept. chemistry, 1979-86, acting dir. Master of Liberal Arts Program, 1987, 89, chmn. dept. physics, 1991—; vis. staff mem. Los Alamos Nat. Labs., 1974—; vis. assoc. prof. chemistry U. B.C., Vancouver, Can., 1974-75; vis. prof. physics Tex A&M U., College Station, 1982; cons. Lovelace Med. Found., 1985—. Author: (with others) Experimental Pulse NMR, 1981. Recipient Outstanding Teaching award San Diego State U., 1971, Outstanding Prof. award San Diego State U., 1992; grantee Rsch. Corp., 1968, 71, 72. Mem. AAAS, Am. Chem. Soc., Am. Phys. Soc. Republican. Home: 6789 Alamo Way La Mesa CA 91941-5807 Office: San Diego State U San Diego CA 92182

ROEHL, WESLEY SCOTT, hotel administration educator; b. Atlantic City, N.J., June 1, 1959; s. Joseph William Roehl and Barbara (Vaughn) Simpkins; m. Joann Lee Krauss, Sept. 24, 1983 (div. Sept. 1991). BA, Trenton State Coll., 1981; MS, So. Illinois U., 1984; PhD, Tex. A&M U., 1988. Asst. prof. hotel adminstrn. U. Nev., Las Vegas, 1988—; co-chmn. Mus. and Attractions in Nev., Las Vegas, 1991. Book review editor: Jour. of Travel and Tourism Mktg.; contbr. articles to profl. jours. Mem. Coun. on Hotel, Restaurant and Institutional Edn., Travel and Tourism Rsch. Assn., Assn. of Am. Geographers, Nat. Recreation and Park Assn. Democrat. Office: Univ Nev Las Vegas 4805 Maryland Pkwy Las Vegas NV 89154

ROEHRS, ROBERT CHRISTIAN, exploration company executive, geologist; b. Graniteville, Mo., May 6, 1931; s. Paul Martin and Margaret Marie (Dinger) R.; m. Shirley Lucille McHenry, Mar. 30, 1956; children: Lizabeth Anne, Robert Christian Jr., Louis Fulton. BA, U. Mo., 1957, MA, 1958. Geologist Shell Oil Co., Casper, Wyo. and Denver, 1958-65; exploration geologist Davis Oil Co., Denver, 1965-68; ptnr. Lotus Petroleum Co., Denver, 1968-69; v.p., dir. Westgate Oil Co., Inc., Denver, 1969-71; pvt. practice in geology Denver, 1971-79; pres. ROMAC Exploration Co., Inc., Denver, 1979—, also bd. dirs. With USAF, 1948-52. Recipient Betty McWhorter Meml. award Desk and Derrick Club, 1980. Mem. Am. Assn. Petroleum Geologists, Rocky Mountain Assn. Geologists, Wyo. Geol. Assn., Ind. Petroleum Assn. Am. (bd. dirs. 1982—, v.p. Mountain States chpt. 1978, pres. 1979, bd. dirs. 1979—), Petroleum Pioneers Club. Republican. Lutheran. Home: 4 Waring Ln Greenwood Village Littleton CO 80121 Office: ROMAC Exploration Co Inc 4 Waring Ln Littleton CO 80121-1625

ROELKE, ADA (ELLEN), psychotherapist, consultant; b. Cumberland, Md., Aug. 24, 1928; d. George William Knock and Mary Emma (Roelke) Eichelberger; children: Karen Bahnsen, Steven Leveen. BA, Syracuse U., 1950; MSW, San Diego State U., 1967; PhD, Profl. Sch. of Psychol. Studies, 1986. Diplomate Am. Bd. Psychotherapy; bd. cert. social worker; lic. clin. social worker, Calif. Tchr. pub. schs., Syracuse, N.Y., 1960-61; social worker Dept. Pub. Welfare, San Diego, 1964-66; psychiat. social worker State of Calif., Bakersfield, 1967-68; child protection worker Dept. Social Service, San Diego, 1968-77; pvt. practice psychotherapy La Mesa, Calif., 1969-93; coordinator, psychotherapist, Chronic Program Grantville Day Treatment Ctr., San Diego, 1977-81; chief social services Edgemoor Geriatric Hosp., Santee, Calif., 1981-88. Fellow Nat. Assn. Social Workers; mem. Marriage Family and Child Counselors Assn., Lic. Clin. Social Workers Assn. Unitarian. Home: 919 Arrowhead Carson City NV 89701

ROEMER, EDWARD PIER, neurologist; b. Milw., Feb. 10, 1908; s. John Henry and Caroline Hamilton (Pier) R.; m. Helen Ann Fraser, Mar. 28, 1935 (dec.); children: Kate Pier, Caroline Pier; m. Marion Clare Zimmer, May 24, 1980. BA, U. Wis., 1930; MD, Cornell U., 1934. Diplomate Am. Bd. Neurology. Intern Yale-New Haven Hosp., 1934-36; resident internal medicine N.Y. Hosp., 1936; resident neurology Bellevue Hosp., N.Y.C., 1936-38; instr. Med. Sch. Yale U., New Haven, 1935-36; asst. prof. neurology Cornell U., N.Y.C., 1936-41; prof. neurology U. Wis., Madison, 1946-64; chief of neurology Huntington Meml. Hosp., Pasadena, Calif., 1964-78; pvt. practice Capistrano Beach, Calif., 1978—; founder, dir. Wis. Neurol. FDN, Madison, 1946-64; dir. Wis. Multiple Sclerosis Clinic, Madison, 1946-64; adv. bd. Inst. Antiquities and Christianity, Claremont Grad. Sch., 1970—; dir. found. Univ Good Hope, S.Africa. Contbr. rsch. articles on multiple sclerosis, neuropathies to profl. jours. Lt. col. med. corps U.S. Army, 1941-46, ETO. Fellow ACP, Royal Coll. Medicine, L.S.B. Leakey Found.; mem. Rotary Internat., Annandale Golf Club, El Niguel Country Club, Nu Sigma Nu, Phi Delta Theta. Republican. Home: 35651 Beach Rd Capo Beach CA 92624-1710

ROEMER, JOHN E., economics educator; b. Washington, Feb. 1, 1945; s. Milton I. and Ruth J. (Rosenbaum) R.; m. Carla N. Muldavin, 1968. BA, Harvard U., 1966; PhD, U. Calif., Berkeley, 1974. Prof. econs. U. Calif., Davis, 1974—. Author: General Theory of Exploitation & Class, 1982, Egalitarian Perspectives, 1993, A Future for Socialism, 1993. Guggenheim Found. fellow, 1980, Econometric Soc. fellow, 1986. Office: U Calif Dept Econs Davis CA 95616

ROEMMELE, BRIAN KARL, electronics, publishing, financial and real estate executive; b. Newark, Oct. 4, 1961; s. Bernard Joseph and Paula M. Roemmele. Grad. high sch., Flemington, N.J. Registered profl. engr., N.J. Design engr. BKR Techs., Flemington, N.J., 1980-81; acoustical engr. Open Reel Studios, Flemington, 1980-82; pres. Ariel Corp., Flemington, 1983-84, Ariel Computer Corp., Flemington, 1984-89; pres., chief exec. officer Ariel Fin. Devel. Corp., N.Y.C., 1987-91; pres., CEO Avalon Am. Corp., Temecula, Calif., 1990—; CEO United ATM Credit Acceptance, Beverly Hills; pres., CEO Coupon Book Ltd., 1987-89, Value Hunter Mags., Ltd., AEON Cons. Group, Beverly Hills, Calif.; bd. dirs. Waterman Internat., Whitehouse Station, N.J., United Credit Card Acceptance Corp., Temecula; electronic design and software cons., L.A., 1980—. Pub., editor-in-chief: Computer Importer News, 1987—. Organizer Internat. Space Week or Day, 1978-83; lectr. Trenton State Mus., N.J., 1983; chmn. Safe Water Internat., Paris. Mem. AAAS, AIAA, IEEE, Boston Computer Soc., Ford/Hall Forum, Am. Soc. Notaries, Planetary Soc. Office: Avalon Am Corp PO Box 1615 Temecula CA 92593-1615

ROESCH, WARREN DALE, customer service and management information systems executive; b. Oakland, Calif., Aug. 8, 1945; s. George Oscar and Dorothy Wenifred (Smith) R.; AA, Coll. of San Mateo, 1966; BA, Calif. State U., 1968; MBA, John F. Kennedy U., 1990. m. Marguerite Mary Whitman, Aug. 1, 1970; 1 son, Warren Whitman. Programmer, operator Western Title Ins. Co., San Francisco, 1973-74, mgr. data processing, 1974; mgr. data processing E. Bay Regional Park Dist., Oakland, 1974-78, Jacuzzi Whirlpool Bath, Walnut Creek, Calif., 1978-82; sr. bus. programmer Bechtel Corp., San Francisco, 1978; cons. systems analyst Packaging div. Crown Zellerbach, San Francisco, 1979, project mgr. MIS installations, 1980; founder, chief exec. officer Total Resource Group, Inc., San Mateo, Calif., 1982-84; project mgr. Point-of-Sale and Svc., 1984-86, mgr. svc. MIS, 1986-89, dir. svc. ops., 1989-90—, Businessland, San Jose, Calif.; dir. customer satifcation Supermac Tech., Sunnyvale, Calif., 1990-92; dir. cust. satisfaction Sigma Designs, Fremont, Calif., 1993—. Home: 646 Alhambra Rd San Mateo CA 94402-2258 Office: Sigma Designs 47900 Bayside Pkwy Fremont CA 94538

ROESELER, WILLIAM GENE, aerospace engineer, entrepreneur; b. Rockford, Ill., Feb. 17, 1943; s. Ernest F. and Grace B. (Cain) R.; m. Molly Hoberman, Jan. 1, 1966 (div. July 1976); children: Charles, Kristi, Cory; m. Brook Burnell, Dec. 31, 1978; children: Midge, Mark, Eric. BS, MIT, 1965, MS, 1966. Registered profl. engr. Engr. Boeing, Seattle, 1966-88; sect. head United Techs., San Diego, 1988-92; v.p. engring. and mfg. Kiteski Inc., 1992—; cons. America 3, San Diego, 1992, Ron Jones Marine, Kent, Wash., 1986—. Inventor composite spring, Kiteski, and hydrofoil hinge. Mem. AIAA, Sigma Xi, Tau Beta Pi. Home: 955 Harbor Island Dr Ste 145 San Diego CA 92101-1036 Office: Kiteski Inc 5555 Santa Fe St # E San Diego CA 92109

ROESSIG, JOHN ROBERT, financial consultant; b. Omaha, Apr. 14, 1947; s. Allen W. and Frances J. (Evans) R.; m. Barbara L. Schmitz, Aug. 8, 1970; children: Stephanie L., Scott A., Salena M. BS in Pharmacy, Creighton U. Coll. Pharmacy, 1970. CFP. Pharmacist Allen's Self Svc., Grand Island, Nebr., 1970-71; pharmacist U. Nebr. Med. Ctr. Hosp., Omaha, 1971-76, resident in hosp. pharmacy, 1975-76; asst. instr. Coll. Pharmacy U. Nebr., Omaha, 1973-76; pharmacist North Colo. Med. Ctr. Hosp., Greeley, 1976-86; fin. planner Master's Fin. Group, Greeley, 1985—, owner, v.p., 1989—; Facilitator Life Underwrites tng. Coun., Greeley, 1992. Author slide and tape series IV-Admixture technique, 1976. Chmn. Adolescent Health Care Com., Greeley, 1991-92; mem., chmn. nurturing com. Habitat for Humanity, Greeley, 1991—. Mem. Am. Health Ins. Agts. (founder), Greeley Pharmacy Assn. (pres. 1979-80), Kiwanis (sec., bd. dir. Rockies club 1991—, Appreciation award 1991). Republican. Roman Catholic. Office: Master s Fin Group Inc 1521 10th Ave Greeley CO 80631

ROGAWAY, BETTY JANE, school system administrator, social worker; b. San Francisco, Sept. 8, 1921; d. Irvine and Dorothy (Nathan) Hyman; m. Roderick Matthew Rogaway, Jan. 16, 1945 (dec. Aug. 1964); children: Stephen, Kathryn Rogaway Farrell. BA, U. Calif., Berkeley, 1942; MA, Calif. State U., San Jose, 1968. Lic. social worker, Calif. Social worker Travelers Aid, 1942, Child Welfare Svcs. Sutter County, Calif., 1945, ARC, 1942-45; juvenile welfare officer Palo Alto (Calif.) Police Dept., 1945-49; tchr., cons., coord. Palo Alto Unified Sch. Dist., 1958-82, ret., 1982; cons. HeadStart, San Francisco, 1966, Calif. State Dept. of Edn., Sacramento, 1982. Mem. City of Palo Alto Task Force on Child Care, 1973; mem. County Task Force on Reasonable Efforts for Child Abuse Protection, San Jose, 1988-90; mem., pres. Palo Alto Hist. Assn., 1989-92; v.p. Calif. Child Devel. Adminstrs. Assn., Sacramento, 1981-82; pres., mem. Children's Shelter Assn. of Santa Clara County, San Jose, 1983—. Home: 1302 Greenwood Ave Palo Alto CA 94301-3414

ROGERS, ARTHUR REX, drilling company executive, geologist; b. Roswell, N.Mex., Oct. 21, 1931; s. Melvin F. and Pansy (Evertt) R.; m. Margaret N. Holseapple, Dec. 25, 1953; children: Alice Evonne, Beth Eileen, Alan Lee. BS in Geology, U. Wyo., 1957. Registered profl. geologist, Wyo. Staff geologist Belco Petroleum, Big Piney, Wyo., 1958-59; instrument man Wyo. Hwy. Dept., Rawlins, 1959-60; staff geologist Western Nuclear, Jeffrey City, Wyo., 1960-62, 1965-66; staff engr. ACOO subs. U.S. Steel, Lander, Wyo.; chief geologist U.S. Energy Co., Riverton, Wyo., 1966-70; mng. ptnr. Rough Country Drilling, Riverton, 1970—. Cpl. U.S. Army, 1950-51. Mem. AIME (chmn. Wyo. mining and metals sect. SME 1964), Elks. Republican. Home and Office: Rough Country Drilling 1010 Mary Anne Dr Riverton WY 82501-2926

ROGERS, BARBARA ANN, educator; b. Frackville, Pa., Aug. 25, 1941; d. John R. and Clara M. (Chudzwick) R. BA in Edn., Millersville State Coll., 1963; MA in Chemistry, Bowling Green State U., 1968. Cert. tchr. Scis. tchr. N. Penn High Sch., Lansdale, Pa., 1963-68; sci. tchr. McKinley High Sch., Honolulu, 1968—, chair sci. dept., 1989—; mem. adv. com. Hawaii State Sci. and Engring. Fair, 1983-85, chmn. sci. tour com., 1979-87; coord. Dreyfus Chemistry Workshop, State of Hawaii, 1984-85, ECIA Chpt. 2 Devel. Grant, 1988-89; mem. staff Ann. Student Symposium on Marine Affairs, 1983-90; advanced placement chemistry workshop leader Hawaii Bd. Edn., Col. Bd., 1979, 85; mem. Presdl. Award Selection Com., 1986-90. Mem. Ellison Onizuka Scholarship Com., State of Hawaii, 1986—. Named Sci. Tchr. of Yr., Hawaii Acad. Sci., 1980; recipient NW Regional award High Sch. Chem. Teaching, Am. Chem. Soc., 1987, Presdl. award for Excellence in Sci. and Math. Teaching, Pres. of U.S., 1985, Dedication to Teaching Sci. and Encouragement of Research award Sigma Xi, 1983, Teaching Excellence award Nat. Marine Educators Assn., 1984, 85, 86; grantee NSF, Dreyfus Found. Mem. Am. Chem. Soc. (sec. Hawaii sect. 1982-84, chair 1984-86, numerous subcoms., grants, awards), Acad. Alliance in Chemistry (dir. Hawaii chpt. 1987-89), Nat. Sci. Tchrs. Assn., Hawaii State Sci. Tchrs. Assn., NEA, Hawaii State Tchrs. Assn., Smithsonian, Honolulu Acad. Arts. Democrat. Home: 425 Ena Rd # 606C Honolulu HI 96815-1745 Office: McKinley High Sch Sci Dept 1039 S King St Honolulu HI 96814-2164

ROGERS, BRADLEY BARNEY, engineering educator; b. Billings, Mont., June 29, 1957; s. Henry Thomas and Frances Audrey (Malone) R.; m. Mary Teresa Dunbar, Feb. 22, 1960; children: Caleb William, Lucas Murray, Lindsay Marie. BSME, Mont. State U., 1979, MSME, 1981, PhD in Mech. Engring., 1992. Scientist Mont. States Energy, Butte, 1981-84, 86; faculty mem. Ariz. State U., Tempe, 1984—; engr. McDonald Douglas Helicopter Co., Mesa, Ariz., 1985. Roman Catholic. Home: 1045 W Watson Dr Tempe AZ 85283-2640 Office: Ariz State U Dept Aeronautical Tech Tempe AZ 85287

ROGERS, BRIAN DOUGLAS, university administrator; b. Blue Hill, Maine, July 25, 1950; s. A. Raymond Jr. and Joan A. (Smith) R.; m. Sherry L. Modrow, Sept. 1, 1979; children: Christopher, Tracy. MPA, Harvard U., 1984. Asst. sgt.-at-arms Alaska Ho. of Reps., Juneau, 1975, legis. info. officer, 1975-76, adminstr. asst., 1976-77, state legislator, 1979-83; prin. Brian Rogers and Assocs., Fairbanks, Alaska, 1975-84; asst. dir. Taft Seminar, Fairbanks, 1985—; budget dir. U. Alaska, Fairbanks, 1984-87, v.p. fin., 1988—; treas. U. Alaska Found., Fairbanks, 1988—, Martin Luther King Found., Fairbanks, 1989—, Eight Stars Pub. Inc., Fairbanks, 1989-91; mem. Soc. of Coll. and Univ. Planners, 1990—; bd. trustees Internat. Pedagogical Univ., Magadan, Russia, 1992—. Contbr. articles to profl. jours. Pres. Fairbanks Community Food Bank, 1990—; conv. chair Alaska State Dem. Conv., Anchorage, 1982; vice chair Gov.-Elect's Budget Transition Team, Juneau, 1986; mem. Dem. State Ctrl. Com., Alaska, 1984-87, Alaska Statehood Commn., 1980-83; asst. scoutmaster Boy Scouts Am. Lucius Littauer fellow Harvard U., 1984. Mem. Rotary Club of Fairbanks, Acad. of Polit. Sci. Office: U Alaska 207D Butrovich Fairbanks AK 99775

ROGERS, CHRISTOPHER BRUCE, pathologist; b. Lafayette, Ind., Mar. 14, 1958; s. Bruce J. and Margaret R. R. BS, MS, Calif. Inst. Tech., 1979; MD, U. Calif., San Diego, 1984. Diplomate Am. Bd. of Pathology. Resident L.A. County, 1984-89; dep. med. examiner L.A. County Coroner, 1988—, chief forensic medicine, 1992—. Fellow Coll. Am. Pathologists, Am. Acad. of Forensic Scis. Office: LA County Coroner 1104 N Mission Rd Los Angeles CA 90033-1096

ROGERS, DAVID HALE, civil engineer, retired; b. Portland, Oreg., May 18, 1918; s. Walter and Mary Louise (Burns) R.; m. Edythe Ellen Sprague, Mar. 22, 1942; children: Steven David, Sylvia Kathryn Rogers Benzler. BS in Wood Products, Oreg. State U., 1948. Registered civil engr., Calif. Commd. 2d lt. US Army, 1941; advanced through grades to lt. col. USAF, 1955, ret., 1978; aerial navigator, bombardier, radar operator/ Tng. Commd. USAF, various, 1940-56; engring. asst. Calif. Dept. Transp., Sacramento, 1954-63, assoc. highway engr., 1963-78. Decorated Air medal with 6 oak leaf clusters, DFC. Presbyterian. Home: 3333 Sierra View Ln Sacramento CA 95821-2538

ROGERS, DWANE LESLIE, management consultant; b. Maywood, Calif., Oct. 6, 1943; s. Lloyd Donald and Della (McAlister) R.; B.S., Ariz. State U., 1967; M.S., Bucknell U., 1968; m. Doris L. Fantel, Aug. 22, 1970; 1 dau., Valerie Lynn. Successively mktg. research coordinator, customer service analyst, merchandising mgr., product planning mgr., order processing mgr. Samsonite Corp., Denver, 1968-74; dir. adminstrn. WISCO Equipment Co., Inc., Phoenix, 1974-75; dir. discontinued ops. Bowmar Instrument Corp., Phoenix, 1975-77; mgmt. cons., dir. Ariz. ops. Mariscal & Co., Phoenix, 1977-80; mgmt. cons. Ariz. Small Bus. Devel. Center, 1980-81; dir. accounts payable, accounts receivable, crude and finished product acctg. Giant Industries, Phoenix, 1981-92; instr. Maricopa County Community Coll., 1979-83; controller Hawaii Pacific Air, 1993—. Mem. Am. Mktg. Assn., Mass Retailing Inst. Republican. Episcopalian. Home: 441 Lewers St # 502 Honolulu HI 96815-2449

ROGERS, EARL LESLIE, artist, educator; b. Oakland, Calif., July 8, 1918; s. Robert Ray and Addie Myrtle (Dice) R.; m. Eileen Estelle MacKenzie, Apr. 9, 1945; children: Leslie Eileen, Brian Donald (dec.). Student, L.A. Valley Coll., 1949-52, Northridge State U., 1958-59, UCLA Extension, 1967, Sergei Bongart Sch. Art, 1967-68; AA, Pierce Coll., 1958. Cert. tchr., Calif. Various positions City of L.A., Van Nuys, Calif., 1948-55, Reseda, Calif., 1955-68; pvt. practice Canoga Park, Calif., 1948-68; art tchr. Mariposa (Calif.) County High Sch., 1969-70; art instr. Merced (Calif.) County Coll., 1970—; instr. Earl Rogers Studio Workshop, Mariposa, Calif., 1969—; art dir. Yosemite Nat. Park, Calif., 1973; art instr. Asilomar Conf. Grounds, Pacific Grove, Calif., 1980; juror various art orgns., 1971-93; demonstrator Clovis (Calif.) Art Guild, 1971, 89, Sierra Artists, Mariposa, 1972, 81, 82, 84, 91, Merced Art League, 1976, Yosemite Western Artists, Oakhurst, Calif., 1973, Madera (Calif.) Art Assn., 1978, Chowchilla (Calif.) Art Guild, 1983, 86, 87, 89, 91, Soc. We. Artists, 1981, 89, 93. One-man shows include L.A. City Hall, 1968, Merced Coll., 1969, Mariposa Title Co. Bldg., 1969, Coffee's Gallery, 1970, others; exhibited in group shows include West Valley Artists Assn., 1966-68, L.A. City Hall, 1967, Yosemite Nat. Park, 1973, Soc. Western Artists, 1977-78, Cannon Bldg. Rotunda, Washington, 1982, Mother Lode Gallery, Columbia, Calif., 1977, 78, Arbor Gallery, Merced, 1988, Gold Country Gallery, 1990, 91, Merced Coll., 1969-92, others; represented in permanent collections include John C. Freemont Hosp., Mariposa, Mariposa Family Med. Bldg., Bear Valley (Calif.) Mus., Mariposa County Libr., Mariposa County Arts Coun., Mariposa Mus. and History Ctr. Asst. scout master Boy Scouts of Am., Canoga Park, Calif., 1956-58; art instr. L.A. Recreation Corps, L.A. Parks and Recreation Dept., 1967. Mem. Soc. Western Artists (Neva Hall Meml. award 1978), Mariposa Mus. and Hist. Ctr. (life). Home and Office: 5323 Hwy 49 North Mariposa CA 95338

ROGERS, GILLUM HARRIS, archaeologist, consultant; b. Richmond, Va., May 15, 1947; s. John Henry and Beth (Harris) R.; m. Nancy Myers, Aug. 1970; 1 child, Donald. BS, Am. U., 1969; MA, U. So. Calif., 1972, PhD, 1975. Rschr. CIA, Washington, 1975-80; cons. UN, N.Y.C., 1980-85; cons. Sphinx Group Internat., Beverly Hills, Calif., 1985—, also bd. dirs. Author: China in Crisis, 1980, Russian Economy, 1981. Cons. Com. To Re-elect Pres., Washington, 1972; vice chmn. Reagan for Pres., Washington, 1980. Mem. Archaeologists Found., Beverly Hills Country Club, Rotary. Republican. Office: The Sphinx Group 270 N Canon Dr Apt 1517 Beverly Hills CA 90210

ROGERS, JACK DAVID, plant pathologist; b. Point Pleasant, W.Va., Sept. 3, 1937; s. Jack and Thelma Grace (Coon) R.; m. Belle C. Spencer, June 7, 1958. BS in Biology, Davis and Elkins Coll., 1960; MF, Duke U., 1960; PhD, U. Wis., 1963. From asst. prof. to assoc. prof. Wash. State U., Pullman, 1963-72, prof., chmn. dept. plant pathology, 1972—. Contbr. articles to profl. jours. mem. Mycological Soc. of Am. (pres., 1977-78), Am. Phytopathol. Soc., Botanical Soc. Am., British Mycological Soc.

ROGERS, MELINDA JANE, process engineer; b. London, Jan. 3, 1964; came to U.S., 1987; d. Keith Arthur Bertram and Gloria Ann (Leyden) R. MA in Metallurgy with honors, Oxford U., Eng., 1985. Grad. trainee Consol. Gold Fields PLC, London, 1985-86; metallurgist Goldsworthy Mining Ltd., Australia, 1986-87; asst. to mng. dir. Consol. Gold Fields PLC, London, 1987; metallurgist Gold Fields Chimney Creek, Winnemucca, Nev., 1987-89; mill metallurgist Barrick Goldstrike Mines, Inc., Elko, Nev., 1989-90, sr. process engr., 1990—. Recipient Strakosch scholarship, Oxford U., 1984. Mem. AIME, Inst. Mining and Metallurgy, Western Mill Maintenance Assn. (v.p.), London Bus. Sch. Alumni Assn., Oxford U. Alumni Assn. Office: Barrick Goldstrike Mines PO Box 29 Elko NV 89801-0029

ROGERS, MICHAEL ALAN, writer; b. Santa Monica, Calif., Nov. 29, 1950; s. Don Easterday and Mary Othilda (Gilbertson) R. BA in Creative Writing, Stanford U., 1972. Assoc. editor Rolling Stone Mag., San Francisco, 1972-76; editor-at-large Outside mag., San Francisco, 1976-78; sr. writer Newsweek mag., San Francisco, 1983—; mng. editor Newsweek Interactive, San Francisco, 1993—; vis. lectr. fiction U. Calif., Davis, 1980. Author: Mindfogger, 1973, Biohazard, 1977, Do Not Worry About The Bear, 1979, Silicon Valley, 1982, Forbidden Sequence, 1988; contbr. articles to mags., newspapers. Recipient Disting. Sci. Writing award AAAS, 1976, Best Feature Articles award Computer Press Assn., 1987. Mem. Author Guild, Sierra Club. Office: Newsweek 388 Market St Ste 1650 San Francisco CA 94111-5317

ROGERS, MICHAEL HOLMES, corporate planner, naval pilot; b. Natick, Mass., Nov. 1, 1949; s. Harrison Holmes and Amelia Mary (Remidies) R.; m. Carole Rose Anderson, Mar. 27, 1976 (div. Dec. 1981); m. Melanie Marie Carl, July 28, 1984 (div. Dec., 1991); 1 child. BS in Indsl. Tech., Calif. State Poly. U., 1972; MBA Fin. San Francisco State U., 1988. Lic. helicopter pilot. Food service clk. United Airlines, San Francisco, 1972-73; configuration analyst Kaiser Electronics, San Jose, Calif., 1980-81; corp. sr. planner U.S. Sprint, Burlingame, Calif., 1981-87; stockbroker Baraban Securities, San Bruno, Calif., 1988—; project mgmt. systems coord. United Airlines, San Francisco, 1988—. Served to comdr. USN, 1973-79, USNR, 1980—. Mem. Res. Officers Assn., Naval Reserve Assn., Naval Helicopter Assn., Am. Legion. Democrat. Office: United Airlines San Francisco Internat Airport San Francisco CA 94128

ROGERS, MICHELE DENISE, investment consultant; b. Kwang-Ju, South Korea, Aug. 4, 1945; m. Merle Nmi Rogers, Feb. 25, 1970. BA in English, Dankook U., Korea, 1969; BS in Bus. Mgmt., N.H. Coll., 1979. Fin. analyst Raytheon Co., Andover, Mass., 1977-81; fin. cons. Tucker, Anthony, Lawrence, Mass., 1983-88, Sutro, Sacramento, 1988-89; dir., owner Col. Fin. Aid Planners, Woodland, Calif., 1990—; fin. cons. Linsco/Pvt. Ledger, Woodland, Calif., 1990—. Home and Office: 812 Ashley Ave Woodland CA 95695-6809

ROGERS, MILTON BARDSTOWN, sales executive, consultant; b. Quantico, Va., Apr. 11, 1939; s. Milton B. and Emily Louise (Robbins) R.; m. Linda Ruth Dale, June 9, 1962 (div. Sept. 1983); 1 child, Stephen Dale Saalfield; m. Sheryl Kaye Gordon, Oct. 6, 1984. BA in Polit. Sci., U. Colo., 1961. Nat. account mgr. IBM, Washington and Tucson, 1967-82; gen. mgr. computer sales div. AT&T, Denver and Washington, 1982-87; pres., chief exec. officer Scope Mfg., Inc., Louisville, 1987; dir. of sales Micro Decisionware, Inc., Boulder, Colo., 1988-91; sr. account exec. Novell, Inc., Boulder, 1991—; cons. Blue Cross of Calif., 1989. Mem. Greater Washington Bd. of Trade, 1983-84; chmn. A&S Devel. Coun., U. Colo., Boulder, 1984-87. Capt. USMC, 1961-67, col. USMCR, 1967—. mem. Res. Officers Assn., Marine Corps Res. Officers Assn. Democrat. Roman Catholic. Home: 4975 Clubhouse Cir Boulder CO 80301-3725

ROGERS, RICHARD GREGORY, sociology educator; b. Albuquerque, Sept. 14, 1955; s. Calvin B. and Eloise (Wood) R.; m. Cynthia P. Raglin, June 14, 1980; children: Mary, Molly, Stacy. BA, U. N.Mex., 1978; MA, U. Tex., 1982, PhD, 1985. Programmer Cancer Rsch. and Treatment Ctr., Albuquerque, 1979-80; NIH population trainee NIH, Austin, 1981-84; asst. dir. tng. Population Prog., U. Colo., Boulder, 1985—; asst. prof. sociology Population Prog., U. Colo., 1985-92, assoc. prof., 1992—. Contbr. articles to profl. jours.; assoc. editor Jour. Health & Social Behavior, 1989-92. Mem. Am. Pub. Health Assn., Am. Sociol. Assn., Pacific Sociol. Assn., Population Assn. Am., Soc. for Study of Social Biology, So. Demographic Assn. (bd. dirs. 1989-91, v.p. 1991-92), Southwestern Social Sci. Assn., Western Social Sci. Assn. Office: Univ Colo Dept Sociology Campus Box 327 Boulder CO 80309-0327

ROGERS, RICK ALAN, private investigations company executive; b. Columbus, Ohio, Jan. 29, 1953; s. Thomas Rogers and Corinne J. (Muncie) R.; m. Kathleen Lynn Anderson, Feb. 28, 1981 (div.); children: Andrew Michael, Shane Alan, Blake Alan. AS in Criminal Justice, Columbus Tech. Inst., 1978. Lic. pvt. investigator, Calif. Pvt. investigator Krout & Scheinder, Inc., L.A., 1978-81, Haynes Investigations, Pomona, Calif., 1981-82, Gt. Western Investigations, Fullerton, Calif., 1982-83, J.H.R.I./I.R.S.C., Fullerton, 1983-84, Helios Investigations, Santa Ana, Calif., 1984-86, Ludwig & Assocs., Sacramento, 1986-89; owner, mgr. Spyglass Investigations, Sacramento, 1989—. Sgt. USAF, 1972-75. Recipient commendation U.S. Atty. Gen.'s Office, L.A., 1981, 13 awards Nat. Assn. Investigative Specialists, 1989. Mem. Valley Indsl. Claims Assn., U. S. C. of C., Citrus Heights C. of C. Republican. Office: Spyglass Investigations 7250 Auburn Blvd Ste 134 Citrus Heights CA 95610-3826

ROGERS, ROBERT REED, manufacturing company executive; b. Oak Park, Ill., Feb. 22, 1929; s. Glen Charles and Lucile (Reed) R.; m. Barbara June Fain, Feb. 22, 1951 (div.); children: Robin, Janeen, Kevin. BS in Chemistry, Berea Coll., 1951; MBA, Ill. Inst. Tech., 1958, postgrad., 1959-62. Asst. mgr. metallurgy research dept. Armour Research Found., Ill. Inst. Tech., 1955-56, mem. faculty, econs. dept., 1956-62; cons. McKinsey & Co., Inc., 1962-64; mgr. devel. planning, profl. group Litton Industries, Inc., 1964-67; pres. N.Am. subs. Muirhead & Co., Ltd., 1967-68; group v.p. Am. Electric Inc. subs. City Investing Co., 1968-70; pres. Cleartight Corp., 1971-73; pres. Newport Internat. Metals Corp., 1973-76; pres. Kensington Assocs., Inc., Newport Beach, Calif., 1976-83; pres., chmn. bd. Proteus Group, Inc., Newport Beach, 1981-83, pres., chmn. bd. Comparator Systems Corp., Irvine, Calif., 1983—. Officer USN, 1951-55. Decorated Knight of Grace Sovereign Order St. John; Machinery and Allied Products Inst. fellow, 1956-62; Berea Coll. grantee, 1947-51. Mem. Navy League, Mensa, Intertel, Ferrari Owners Club, Lido Isle Yacht Club. Republican. Mem. Ch. of Religious Sci. Home: 621 Lido Park Dr F-1 Newport Beach CA 92663-2676 Office: Comparator Systems Corp 92 Corporate Park Ste G-314 Irvine CA 92714-5023

ROGERS, TERESA, broadcast executive; b. Oklahoma City, May 26, 1956; d. William Guy and Virginia D. (Hicks) R.; m. Michael E. Worrall, Sept. 27, 1980. BS in Broadcasting, Ariz. State U., 1974-78. News anchor Sta. KRUX-AM, Phoenix, 1978-79, Sta. KARZ-AM, Phoenix, 1979-80; asst. news dir. Sta. KMJJ-AM, Las Vegas, Nev., 1980-84; news dir. Sta. KNPR-FM, Las Vegas, Nev., 1984-88; owner/mgr. Sta. KCMT-FM, Chester, Calif., 1988-90; news dir. Sta. KXBS-FM, Ventura, Calif., 1991; gen. mgr. Sta. KCSN-FM, Northridge, Calif., 1991—. Vol. publicist Sunset Symphony Orch., Las Vegas, Nev., 1986-88; cons. Am. String Tchrs. Assn., Athens, Ga.; bd. dirs. Plumas County Arts Commn., 1988-90, San Fernando Valley Arts Coun., 1992—; vol. Ventura Arts Coun., 1990; dir. Fine Arts for Youth, Camarillo, Ca, 1991.

ROGERS, THOMAS HARDIN, geologist; b. Washington, June 10, 1932; s. Harold Benjamin and Olive Caroline (Hardin) R.; m. Verna Jean Carlsen, Mar. 12, 1971. BA, Conn. Wesleyan U., 1954; MA, U. Calif., Berkeley, 1957. Registered geologist, Calif., registered engring. geologist, Calif., registered environ. assessor, Calif. Exploration geologist Standard Oil Co. of Calif., Bakersfield and Salt Lake City, 1957-60; sr. draftsman So. Pacific Mineral Survey, San Francisco, 1961-63; from jr. to assoc. geologist Div. Mines & Geology State of Calif., 1963-74; sr. project geologist Woodward-Clyde Cons., Oakland, Calif., 1974-92, Woodward-Clyde Fed. Svcs., Rockville, Md., 1992—; instr. U. Calif. Extension, Berkeley, 1972, Santa Cruz, 1970-74, Monterey (Calif.) Peninsula Coll., 1970-73. Fellow Geol. Soc. Am.; mem. Assn. Engring. Geologists, Am. Assn. Petroleum Geologists, Seismological Soc. Am., Earthquake Engring. Rsch. Inst.

ROGERS, VERN CHILD, engineering company executive; b. Salt Lake City, Aug. 28, 1941; s. Vern S. and Ruth (Child) R.; m. Patricia Powell, Dec. 14, 1962. BS, U. Utah, 1965, MS, 1965; PhD, MIT, 1969. Registered profl. engr. Assoc. prof. Brigham Young U., Provo, Utah, 1969-73; vis. assoc. prof. Lowell Tech. Inst., 1970-71; mgr. IRT Corp., San Diego, 1973-76; v.p. Ford, Bacon & Davis, Salt Lake City, 1976-80; pres. Rogers & Assocs. Engring. Corp., Salt Lake City, 1980—. Contbr. articles to profl. jours. Mem. Health Physics Soc., Am. Soc. Profl. Engrs., Am. Nuclear Soc., Am. Chem. Soc. Mormon. Office: Rogers & Assocs Engring Corp PO Box 330 Salt Lake City UT 84110-0330

ROGERS, WILLIAM CORDELL, financial executive; b. Louisville, Apr. 16, 1943; s. Delbert Clifton and Nelle Frances (Grimsley) R.; m. Elaine Elizabeth Nicolay, Apr. 10, 1966; children: William C. II, Erin D., Nicole M., Shannon D. AA, Lincoln Coll., 1969; BS, Ill. State U., 1971; MBA, U. Phoenix, 1993. Exec. Ill. Dept. Revenue, Springfield, 1972-74; fin. dir. Old Heritage Life Ins. Co., Lincoln, Ill., 1974-77; corp. fin. cons. DEN, Inc. CPAs, Tempe, Ariz., 1977-83; v.p., treas. Dahlberg Industries, Scottsdale, Ariz., 1983-91; cons. Act II Printed Cirs. Inc., Tempe, Ariz., 1991--; cons., Scottsdale, 1977—; instr. econ. Lincoln Coll., 1972-77, real estate taxation, 1978-80. With U.S. Army, 1964-67, Vietnam. Recipient Dow Jones award Dow Jones-Wall St. Jour., 1969. Mem. Nat. Assn. Pub. Accts., Ariz. Soc. Pub. Accts., Rotary (bd. dirs. Scottsdale club 1986—, pres., Paul Harris fellow 1985—). Republican. Home: 8549 E Turney Ave Scottsdale AZ 85251-2831 Office: Act II Printed Cirs Inc 3207 S Hardy Tempe AZ 85282

ROGERS, WILLIAM SHIELDS, JR., architect; b. Evanston, Ill., Aug. 1, 1943; s. William Shields Sr. and Eleanor (Males) R.; m. Sally Kay Buckmaster, June 3, 1967; children: Theresa Lynell, James Larson, Jayna Marie. BArch, U. Nebr., 1968. Registered architect, Nebr., Ill., Colo., Iowa, Mont., Ohio, Mo., Okla., Wyo. Architect ARE, Omaha, 1971-73, Hastings and Chivetta, Denver, 1973-74; architect, dir. constrn. CM Corp., Souix City, Iowa, 1974-76; architect, office mgr. Eugene Wright and Assocs., Lincoln, Nebr., 1976-77; architect Woodworth Assocs., Lakewood, Colo., 1977-81, Lee & Associated, Lakewood, 1981-84, 84-85; pvt. bus. Will Rogers Architect, Denver, 1985-88; architect, v.p. Am. Healthcare Designers, Ltd., Denver, 1988—. Sec., Holy Shepard Lutheran Ch., Denver, 1981-83, pres., 1984. Mem. Kiwanis (Bear Valley chpt., sec. 1981, 85). Republican. Office: Am Healthcare Designers Ltd Bldg 2 Ste 400 6000 E Evans Ave Denver CO 80222-5419

ROGGE, RICHARD DANIEL, former government executive, security consultant, investigator; b. N.Y.C., July 5, 1926; s. Daniel Richard and Bertha (Sarner) R.; m. Josephine Mary Kowalewska, June 6, 1948; children: Veronica Leigh Rogge-Erbeznik, Richard Daniel, Christopher Ames, Meredith Ann Rogge-Pierce. BS in Bus. Adminstrn., NYU, 1952. Cert. profl. investigator. Clerical worker FBI, N.Y.C., 1947-52, spl. agt., Phila., 1952-54, Washington, 1954-58, supr., 1958-65, asst. spl. agt. in charge, Richmond, Va., 1965-66, Phila., 1966-67, L.A., 1967-69, inspector, 1969, spl. agt. in charge, Honolulu, 1969-72, Richmond, 1972-74, Buffalo, 1974-77, now security cons., investigator, Calif.; police tng. instr.; writer, lectr. in field. With USMC, 1944-46; PTO. Recipient Order of Arrow award Boy Scouts Am., 1943, Svc. to Law Enforcement awards Va. Assn. Chiefs Police, 1975, N.Y. State Assn. Chiefs Police, 1977, others. Mem. Am. Soc. Indsl. Security, Calif. Assn. Lic. Investigators, Calif. Peace Officers Assn. Los Angeles County, World Assn. Detectives, Inc., Soc. Former Agts. FBI, Inc., Am. Legion, K.C., Elks. Republican. Roman Catholic. Home and Office: 32010 Watergate Ct Westlake Village CA 91361-4022

ROGGERO, MIGUEL LEONARDO (MIKE ROGGERO), motion picture company executive, consultant; b. San Diego, May 17, 1962; s. Roland Victor and Dinorah S. (Lopez) R. BS, U. So. Calif., 1984; MBA, U. Pa., 1989. Lic. real estate broker, Calif. Project analyst Stephen J. Cannell Prodns., L.A., 1984-85; sr. analyst Paramount Pictures Corp., L.A., 1985-87; pres., co-founder Prolube, Inc., L.A., 1989—; mgr. fin. projects Pepsico/Pizza Hut, Inc., 1990-92; mgr. fin. Walt Disney Co., 1992—; cons. Oto-Telick Inc., Sherman Oaks, Calif., 1987-88, Mgmt. Info. Network Inc., L.A., 1987-88. Recipient Calif. Masonic Found. scholarship, 1982. Mem. Smithsonian Assocs., U. So. Calif. Alumni Assn., U. So. Calif. Sch. Bus. Alumni Assn., Wharton Club, So. Calif., N.Y. , Sigma Alpha Mu, Beta Gamma Sigma (life mem.). Republican. Home: 4338 Oak Glen St Calabasas CA 91302-1978

ROHDE, JAMES VINCENT, software systems company executive; b. O'Neill, Nebr., Jan. 25, 1939; s. Ambrose Vincent and Loretta Cecilia R.; children: Maria, Sonja, Daniele. BCS, Seattle U., 1962. Chmn. bd. dirs., pres., Applied Telephone Tech., Oakland, 1974; v.p. sales and mktg. Automation Electronics Corp., Oakland, 1975-82; pres., chief exec. officer, chmn. bd. dirs. Am. Telecorp, Inc., 1982—; bd. dirs. Energlogica, Inc., 1989-91. Chmn. exec. com., chmn. emeritus Pres.'s Coun. Heritage Coll., Toppenish, Wash., 1985—; chmn. No. Calif. chpt. Coun. of Growing Cos., 1990-93; bd. dirs. Ind. Colls. No. Calif., 1991—. Mem. Am. Electronics Assn. (bd. dirs. 1992—, vice chmn. No. Calif. coun. 1992-93, chmn. 1993—). Republican. Roman Catholic. Office: Am Telecorp Inc 100 Marine Parkway Redwood City CA 94065

ROHE, JERE LOUIS, sales professional; b. Exeter, Calif., Dec. 25, 1945; s. Theodore Schultz and Etta Almira (Rutherford) R.; m. Lynda Moore; 1 child, Ryan Dwayne; m. Katherine Romeo, Mar. 1, 1975 (div. 1983); 1 child, Theodore Darrin; m. Doris Maxine Agers, Oct. 4, 1987. AA in Indsl. Arts, West Hills Jr. Coll., Coalinga, Calif., 1966; BBA Bus. Adminstrn. adn Indsl. Mgmt., Ea. N.Mex. U., 1971; postgrad., U. N.Mex., 1976-77; diploma, sales, Dale Carnegie, 1972, diploma, mgmt., 1973. Assoc. broker Hootem/Stahl Realtors, Albuquerque, 1971-72; sales mgr. Marberry Realtors, Albuquerque, 1972-73; account mgr. A to Z Tire Co., Albuquerque, 1973-76; ins. agt./owner Farmers Ins. Group, Albuquerque, 1976-82; ind. agt. Jere Rohe Agy., Albuquerque, 1982-85; agt. K-Mart Ins. Group, Albuquerque, 1985-87; ins. agt. Nat. Farmers Union Ins. Co., Albuquerque, 1987-89; sales rep. FHP Health Care, Albuquerque, 1989—; creator/promoter Home Trade Makers Corp., Albuquerque, 1972-73. Organizer Rio Grande Alumni Club of Delta Sigma Pi, Santa Fe, N.Mex., 1970's; mem. Heights Optimist Club, Albuquerque, 1972; v.p. Delta Sigma Pi Profl. Bus. Frat., Portales, N.Mex., 1971; speaker Albuquerque Spokeman Club/Albuquerque Grad. Club, 1978—. With USAF, 1966-70. Mem. Albuquerque Grad. Spokesman Club (v.p. 1990-91). Home: 3405 Garcia NE Albuquerque NM 87111

ROHILA, PRITAM KUMAR, clinical neuropsychologist; b. Jagadhari, Haryana, India, Sept. 25, 1935; s. Krishna Chandra and Champa Wati Rohila; m. Kundan Doshi, Nov. 17, 1983; children: Arun Rohila, Vineeta Andrews, Snehal Shah, Shilpa Gorajia. BA, Panjab U., India, 1954, B. Teaching, 1957, MA, 1960; MA, U. Oreg., 1968, PhD, 1969. Cert. psychologist, Oreg., Wash. Elem. sch. tchr. Directorate Pub. Instrn. PEPSU, India, 1955-56; secondary sch. tchr. Directorate Edn., Delhi, India, 1958-61; from rsch. asst. to counselor-lectr. Nat. Inst. Edn., Delhi, 1962-67; grad. rsch. asst. U. Oreg., Eugene, 1967-69; psychologist Western State Hosp., Ft. Steilacoom, Wash., 1969-73; pvt. practice clin. psychology Tacoma, Wash., 1973-79; neuropsychologist Oreg. State Hosp., Salem, 1979-85, sr. clin. psychologist (geropsychology), 1983-85; neuropsychologist Salem Hosp., 1986-87; pvt. practice neuropsychology Salem, 1982—; cons. Disability Determination Svc., Salem, 1985-91; psychologist Oreg. Women's Correctional Ctr., Salem, 1985-86, Clover Park Sch. Dist., Lakewood, Wash., 1978-79, involuntary treatment team Overlake Hosp., Bellevue, Wash., 1977. Author: Handbook of Training Facilities & Career Opportunities for School Leavers in Delhi, 1965; co-author: Officers in the Making, 1964, Guidance Services in Schools, 1964, Careers in Social Service Occupations, 1967. Bd. dirs. Mid-Valley Arts Coun., Salem, 1983-84, Unity of Salem, 1983-84, Mid-Willamette chpt. Alzheimers Assn., Salem, 1993— ; chair human resouce group Pierce County Growth Coun., Tacoma, 1977-78; mem. legis. com. Puget Health System Agy., Tacoma, 1976-77; pres. Assn. Communal Harmony in Asia, 1993. Mem. Internat. Neuropsychol. Soc., Nat. Acad. Neuropsychology, Am. Psychol. Assn., Oreg. Psychol. Assn. (chmn. bd. profl. affairs 1983-85), Wash. Psychol. Assn., South Sound Psychol. Assn. (pres. 1975-76). Office: 831 Lancaster Dr NE Ste 214 Salem OR 97301-2930

ROHLFING, FREDERICK WILLIAM, lawyer, judge; b. Honolulu, Nov. 2, 1928; s. Romayne Raymond and Kathryn (Coe) R.; m. Joan Halford, Nov. 15, 1952 (div. Sept. 1982); children: Frederick W., Karl A., Brad (dec.); m. Patricia Ann Santos, Aug. 23, 1983. BA, Yale U., 1950; JD, George Washington U., 1955. Bar: Hawaii 1955, Am. Samoa 1978. Assoc. Moore, Torkidson & Rice, Honolulu, 1955-60; ptnr. Rohlfing, Nakamura & Low, Honolulu, 1963-68, Hughes, Steiner & Rohlfing, Honolulu, 1968-71, Rohlfing, Smith & Coates, Honolulu, 1981-84; sole practice Honolulu, 1960-63, 71-81, Maui County, 1988—; dep. corp. counsel County of Maui, Wailuku, Hawaii, 1984-87, corp. counsel, 1987-88; land and legal counsel Maui Open Space Trust, Wailuku, 1992—; magistrate judge U.S. Dist. Ct. Hawaii. Mem. Hawaii Ho. Reps., 1959-65, 80-84; Hawaii State Senate, 1966-75; U.S. alt. rep. So. Pacific Commn., Noumea, New Caledonia, 1975-77, 1982-84. Capt. USNR, 1951-87. Mem. Hawaii Bar Assn., Am. Samoa Bar Assn. Home and Office: RR #1 Box 398 Kekaulike Ave Kula HI 96790

ROHN, GORDON FREDERICK, religious organization administrator, minister, missionary, lawyer; b. Fond du Lac, Wis., Feb. 4, 1939; s. Gordon F. and Janet (Reed) R.; m. Judith Amber Ciscel, June 11, 1960; children: Brian, Kevin, Grady, Nathan. MA in Mgmt., Webster Coll., 1981; BS in Polit. Sci., U. Wis., 1962, JD, 1965; MDiv, Trinity Evangel. Div. Sch., 1984. Bar: Wis., 1965; ordained to ministry Bapt. Ch., 1986. Commd. 2d lt. U.S. Army, 1962, advanced through grades to lt. col., ret., 1982; minister adminstrn. Fair Oaks Bapt. Ch., Concord, Calif., 1985-87; dir. internat. bur. Frontiers, Pasadena, Calif., 1988-90, dir. ch. rels., 1990-92, dir. ch. ministry, 1992—; pub. speaker in field; mgmt. cons. in field; tchr. comparative religious mission conf. speaker; founding bd. dirs. Tyndale Theol. Sem., Amsterdam, The Netherlands, 1983-85. Contbr. articles to profl. jours. Pres. Environ. Impact Assessment Group 1991—. Mem. Wis. Bar Assn., Officers Christian Fellowship (area coord. 1981-82), Christian Ministry Mgmt. Assn., Wycliffe Assocs. Republican. Baptist. Office: Frontiers 1605 Elizabeth Pasadena CA 91104

ROHRABACHER, DANA, congressman; b. June 21, 1947; s. Donald and Doris Rohrabacher. Student, L.A. Harbor Coll., 1965-67; BA in History, Long Beach State Coll., 1969; MA in Am. Studies, U. So. Calif., 1976. Reporter City News Svc./Radio West, L.A., 4 yrs.; editorial writer Orange County Register, 1979-80; asst. press. sec. Reagan for Pres. Campaign, 1976, 80; speechwriter, spl. asst. to Pres. Reagan White House, Washington, 1981-88; mem. 101st-103rd Congresses from 45th Calif. dist., 1989-92, 103d Congress from 45th dist. Calif., 1993—; U.S. del. Young Polit. Leaders Conf., USSR; disting. lectr. Internat. Terrorism Conf., Paris, 1985. Recipient Disting. Alumnus award L.A. Harbor Coll., 1987. Office: US Ho of Reps Longworth Bldg 1027 Washington DC 20515-0545

ROHRBACK, MICHAEL DAVID, federal government administrator; b. Adrian, Mich., Apr. 30, 1954; s. David Norman and Sara Joyce (Lehman) R.; m. Laura L. Buchan. BA in Econ. with honors, U. Mich., 1980, M of Pub. Policy, 1983, postgrad. Researcher Gt. Lakes Commn., Ann Arbor, Mich., 1982-83; econ. analyst U.S. Dept. State, Washington, 1983; audit mgr. U.S. GAO, Detroit, 1983-89; audit mgr. Far East Office U.S. GAO, Honolulu, 1989—. With USMC, 1972-76. Lutheran. Home: 1561 Pensacola St Honolulu HI 96822-3893 Office: US Gen Acctg Office PO Box 50187 Honolulu HI 96850-0001

ROHRBERG, RODERICK GEORGE, consultant; b. Minneola, Iowa, Sept. 26, 1925; s. Charles H. and Emma (Minsen) R.; BS in Naval Sci., Marquette U., 1946; BSCE, Iowa State U., 1949; m. Genevieve Mary Sogard, June 19, 1949; children—Karla (Mrs. George H. Witz, Jr.), Roderick K., Cheries, Timothy, Christopher. Bridge design engr. Alaska Rd. Commn., U.S. Dept. Interior, 1949-51; sr. tech. specialist North Am. Rockwell, research, Los Angeles, 1951-69; pres. Creative Pathways, Inc., advanced welding services, Torrance, Calif., 1969—; pvt. practice as cons. advanced welding process, micropro mgmt. controls for SPF/DB semiconductor fab., equipment design and devel., Torrance, Calif., 1972—. Served with USNR, 1944-46. Recipient 1st nat. Airco Welding award, 1966, commendation NASA, 1965, Engring. Profl. Achievement citation Iowa State U., 1973, 3d pl. Von Karman Meml. Grand award, 1974. Registered profl. engr., Calif. Mem. Am. Welding Soc. Lutheran. Patentee in field. Home: 2742 W 234th St Torrance CA 90505-3118 Office: Creative Pathways Inc 3121 Fujita St Torrance CA 90505-4080

ROHRBOUGH, KEITH JAMES, lawyer; b. Albany, Oreg., Feb. 13, 1949; s. Max Hawley and Frances Helen (Patterson) R.; m. Karen Louise Bopp, June 30, 1973 (div. Nov. 1986); children: Courtney Beth, Kevin James; m. Gaylyn Backman, Dec. 31, 1988 (div. April 1993). BS, Oreg. State U., 1971; JD, U. of the Pacific, 1974. Bar: Nev. 1974, U.S. Dist. Ct. Nev. 1974, Oreg. 1975, U.S. Dist. Ct. Oreg. 1978. Dep. pub. defender Washoe County Pub. Defender's Office, Reno, 1974—; pvt. practice Albany, Oreg., 1977—; mayor City of Albany, 1989-92. Bd. dirs. United Way, Albany, 1978. Mem. Linn County Bar Assn. (sec. 1987-88, pres. 1989-90), Oreg. Criminal Def. Lawyers Assn., Elks, Eagles, Rotary (pres. Albany chpt. 1980). Republican. Presbyterian. Home: 310 7th Ave SW Albany OR 97321 Office: 425 2D Ave SW Albany OR 97321

ROIG, RANDY ALLEN, environmental engineer, consultant; b. Berea, Ohio, June 5, 1949; s. Lester Clarence and Mildred Elaine (Lent) R.; m. Roberta Alice Berkman, Dec. 30, 1973; children: Jonathan Edward, Avi Webster. BS, U. Md., 1971; MA, Harvard U., 1972, PhD, 1975. Rsch. prof. U. Toronto, Can., 1975-77; dir. of impact assessment Md. Power Plant System, Annapolis, 1977-81; dir. Md. Power Plant System, 1981-84; dir. environ. info. Martin Marietta Environ. Systems, Columbia, Md., 1984-86; dir. mgmt. consulting ERM, Inc., Exton, Pa., 1986-89; prin. ERM West, Walnut Creek, Calif., 1989—; mem. governing bd. Calif. Registered Environ. Assessment Program, Sacramento, 1991—, U. Calif. Environ. Programs, Davis, 1990—, U. Calif. Environ. Programs, Berkeley, 1991—. Contbr. articles to profl. jours. Mem. bd. dirs. Hillsmere Assn., Annapolis, Md., 1981-83. Mem. Optical Soc. Am., Environ. Audit Round Table, Environ. Audit Forum. Office: ERM West 1777 Botelho Dr Walnut Creek CA 94596

ROITBLAT, HERBERT LAWRENCE, psychology educator; b. Milw., Apr. 2, 1952; s. Jack and Renee (Seigel) R.; m. Debra Jean Bortel, Aug. 24, 1975; 1 child, Benjamin. BA, Reed Coll., 1974; PhD, U. Calif., 1978. Asst. prof. Columbia U., N.Y.C., 1978-85; prof. U. Hawaii, Honolulu, 1985—. Author: Introduction to Comparative Cognition, 1987; editor: Animal Cognition, 1984, From Animals to Animals 2, 1993, Languages and Communication: Comparative Perspectives, 1993; contbr. articles to profl. jours. NSF fellow, 1978. Mem. Am. Psychol. Assn., Internat. Neural Network Soc., Psychonomic Soc. Office: U Hawaii Dept Psychology 2430 Campus Rd Honolulu HI 96822

ROIZ, MYRIAM, foreign trade executive; b. Managua, Nicaragua, Jan. 21, 1938; came to U.S., 1949; d. Francisco Octavio and Maria Herminia (Briones) R.; m. Nicholas M. Orphanopoulos, Jan. 21, 1957 (div.); children: Jacqueline Doggwiler, Gene E. Orphanopoulos, George A. Orphanopoulos. BA in Interdisciplinary Social Sci. cum laude, San Francisco State U., 1980. Lic. ins. agt. Sales rep. Met. Life Ins. Co., San Francisco, 1977-79; mktg. dir. Europe/Latin Am., Allied Canners & Packers, San Francisco, 1979-83, M-C Internat., San Francisco, 1983-88; v.p. mktg. Atlantic Brokers, Inc., Kinard Foods, Inc., Bayamon, P.R., 1988-92; pres. Aquarius Enterprises Internat., San Mateo, Calif., 1992—. Mem. Common Cause, World Affairs Coun.; coord. Robert F. Kennedy Presdl. campaign, Millbrae, San Mateo County, local mayoral campaign, Millbrae, 1975; bd. dir., organizer fund-raising campaign for earthquake-devastated Nicaragua; active World Hunger Program Brown U., Covenant House, Childhelp USA. Named Outstanding Employee of Yr. Hillsborough City Sch. Dist., 1973; recipient Sales award Met. Life Ins. Co., 1977. Mem. Nat. Assn. Female Execs., World Affairs Coun., Commonwealth Club San Francisco. Democrat. Roman Catholic. Office: Atlantic Brokers Inc PO Box 372 San Mateo CA 94401

ROJAS, WALDEMAR, school superintendent. Supt. schs. San Francisco Sch. Dist. Office: San Francisco Bd Edn 135 Van Ness Ave Ste 120 San Francisco CA 94102*

ROKOS, JOHN PAUL, marketing professional; b. L.A., July 21, 1952; s. John C. and Violet Mae R. BS, Wis. U., 1974. Programmer NCR, San Diego, Calif., 1974-76, Ford Motors Co., Mountain View, Calif., 1976-78; mgr. Zentec, Mountain View, 1978-82, Wyse Tech., San Jose, Calif., 1982—. Mem. Assn. Computing Machinery, IEEE. Office: Wyse Technology San Jose CA 95121

ROLAN, PHIDALIA LYNN, financial planner; b. Artesia, N.Mex., May 14, 1961; d. Johnny Charles and Velma Dean (Hughes) Brannan; m. Larry Lee Rolan, Nov. 3, 1979; children: Joshua Aaron, Caleb Andrew, Chayimel Cai. Student, U. Hawaii, 1979. CLU, ChFC. Fin. planner J.C. Brannan, CLU, ChFC & Assocs., Artesia, 1981—. Mem. Eddy County Assn. Underwriters (sec. 1985-86, v.p. 1987-88, pres. 1988-89, chmn. health ins. com. 1990-91, 1990-93). Mem. Assembly of God Ch. Home: 4214 W Main St Artesia NM 88210-9533 Office: 702 W Main St Artesia NM 88210-1961

ROLETTA, RICHARD PETER, education administrator; b. L.A., Sept. 19, 1939; s. Pietro Cellini and Rose Mary (Bavero) R.; m. Lucretia Ann Streechon, Apr. 1, 1977. BA in History, U. So. Calif., L.A., 1962; MA in Instructional Media, Calif. State U., Long Beach, 1971. Cert. secondary edn., gen. adminstrn. GATE coord. Dapplegray Intermediate, 1972-82, tchr., 1962-82, asst. prin., 1982-85; asst. prin. Ridgecrest Intermediate, Rancho Palos Verdes, Calif., 1985-87, Rancho Palos Verdes, 1987-91; prin. Dapplegray Intermediate, 1987, Soleado Elem. Sch., Rancho Palos Verdes, 1991—. Dist. membership rep., SASS rep. ACSA; pres. P.V.A.A., 1988-89. Recipient Vol. of Yr. award PTA, 1990, Hon. Svc. award PTA, 1982, Continuing Svc. award PTA, 1990, Golden Apple award PTA, 1982, Calif. pin PTA, 1993, Calif. Silver Bar award 1993.

ROLFES, HERMAN HAROLD, Canadian government official; b. Humboldt, Bask, Sask., Can., July 13, 1936; s. Joseph and Josephine (Heckmann) R.; m. Myrna Josephine Hopfner, Apr. 4, 1961; children: Debora Lynne, Brian Joseph. Student, St. Peter's Coll., Muenster, Sask., Tchrs. Coll. Sask., 1955-56; BA, U. Sask., 1961, BEd, 1965, MEd, 1971. Cert. tchr., Can. Mem. legis. assembly Saskatoon Nutana South, 1971-82, 86—, min. social svcs., 1975—, min. continuing edn., 1978—, now spkr. legis assembly.; min. health Sask., 1979-82. Mem. Sask. Elem. Tchrs. Assn. (past pres.), St. Thomas Moore Alumni Assn., KC. Roman Catholic. Home: 2802 Calder Ave, Saskatoon, SK Canada S7J 1W1 Office: Speaker, Legislative Bldg Rm 129, Regina, SK Canada S4S 0B3

ROLL, BARBARA HONEYMAN, anthropologist; b. Portland, Oreg., Apr. 4, 1910; d. Arthur and Carlotta (Parker) Honeyman; m. Scott Alexander Heath, Dec. 23, 1953 (dec. July 1974); m. George Frederick Roll, Mar. 5, 1977. BA, Smith Coll., 1932, LHD (hon.), 1989. Exec. sec. Const. Lab. P&S Med. Ctr., N.Y., 1948-51; rsch. assoc. U. Oreg. Med. Sch., Portland, Oreg., 1951-53; cons. Dr. H. H. Clarke U. Oreg., Eugene, 1957-68; cons. Dr. Margaret Mead AMNH, N.Y., 1966-75; rsch. assoc. U. Pa. Mus., Phila., 1975—; instr. anthropology Community Coll., Monterey, Calif., 1966-74; vis. scholar Inst. Anthropology, Moscow, 1967, 1975. Author: (with J.E.L. Carter) Somatotyping - Development and Applications, 1990; contbr. articles to profl. jours. Fellow AAAS, Am. Assn. Anthropology, NY Acad. Scis.; mem. Coun. Human Biol., Am. Assn. Phys. Anthropology, Inst. Intercultural Studies (sec. 1980-83). Home: 26030 Rotunda Dr Carmel CA 93923-8923

ROLL, JOHN MCCARTHY, lawyer; b. Pitts., Feb. 8, 1947; s. Paul Herbert and Esther Marie (McCarthy) R.; m. Maureen O'Connor, Jan. 24, 1970; children: Robert McCarthy, Patrick Michael, Christopher John. B.A., U. Ariz., 1969, J.D., 1972, LLM U. Va., 1990. Bar: Ariz. 1972, U.S. Dist. Ct. Ariz. 1974, U.S. Ct. Appeals (9th cir.) 1980, U.S. Supreme Ct. 1977. Asst. pros. atty. City of Tucson, 1973; dep. county atty. Pima County (Ariz.), 1973-80; asst. U.S. atty. U.S. Atty.'s Office, Tucson, 1980-87; judge Ariz. Ct. Appeals, 1987-91, U.S. Dist. Ct. Ariz., 1991—; lectr. Nat. Coll. Dist. Attys. U. Houston, 1976-87; mem. criminal justice mental health standards project ABA, 1980-83. Contbr. to Trial Techniques Compendium, 1978, 82, 84, Merit Selection: The Arizona Experience, Arizona State Law Journal, 1991. Coach, Frontier Baseball Little League, Tucson, 1979-84; mem. parish coun. Sts. Peter and Paul Roman Catholic Ch., Tucson, 1983-91, chmn., 1986-91; mem. Roman Cath. Diocese of Tucson Sch. Bd., 1986-90. Recipient Disting. Faculty award Nat. Coll. Dist. Attys., U. Houston, 1979. Mem. Am. Judicature Soc., Fed. Judges Assn., Pima County Bar Assn. Republican. Lodge: K.C. (adv. coun. 10441). Office: US Dist Ct 55 E Broadway Tucson AZ 85701

ROLLAND, ERIK, management information systems educator; b. Bergen, Norway, June 23, 1961; came to U.S., 1987; s. Ruth M. (Aamodt) R.; m. Denise M. Brennan; 1 child, Sonia. MSc, Norway Inst. of Tech., Trondheim, 1986; BS in Computer Info. Systems, Ohio State U., 1986, MA, 1989, PhD, 1991. Software specialist Digital Equipment Corp., Oslo, Norway, 1986-87; rsch. fellow Norwegian Rsch. Coun., Norway, 1987-90; teaching assoc. Ohio State U., Columbus, 1988-91; asst. prof. U. Calif., Riverside, 1991—; columnist Inland Empire Bus. Jour., Ontario, Calif., 1991—. Contbr. articles to profl. jours. Officer Royal Norwegian Army, 1980-84. Scholarship Am.-Scandinavian Found., 1990. Mem. IEEE, Ops. Rsch. Soc. of Am., Inst. of Mgmt. Scis., Assn. for Computing Machinery, Am. Assn. for Artificial Intelligence, The Decision Sci. Inst., Phi Beta Delta. Office: U Calif Grad Sch Mgmt Riverside CA 92521

ROLLE, BRIDGETTE DEANNE, academic advisor; b. Nassau, Mar. 9, 1964; d. James Rolle and Helen Hutcherson. AA in Hotel Mgmt., Bahamas Hotel Tng. Coll., Nassau, 1983; BA in Communications, St. Augustine's Coll., Raleigh, N.C., 1987; MS in Higher Edn., Iowa State U., 1989; PhD in Ednl. Adminstrn., U. Ariz. Acad. counselor Iowa State U., Ames, 1987-89; acad. advisor U. Ariz., Tucson, 1989—. Presenter in field. Mem. Far West Philosophy of Edn. Soc., Nat. Acad. Advising Assn., Univ. Profl. Advisors Assn., Phi Delta Kappa, Delta Sigma Theta (1st v.p. 1988-89). Roman Catholic. Home: 4601 N Via Entrada # 1009 Tucson AZ 85718 Office: U Ariz Coll Arts and Scis 347 Modern Languages Tucson AZ 85721

ROLLE, MYRA MOSS (MYRA E. MOSS), philosophy educator, author, translator; b. L.A., Mar. 22, 1937; d. Roscoe and Edith (Wheeler) Moss; m. Andrew Rolle, Nov. 5, 1983. BA, Pomona Coll., 1958; PhD, John Hopkins U., 1965. Asst. prof. U. Santa Clara, Calif., 1970-74; tutor philosophy Claremont (Calif.) McKenna Coll., 1975-82, adj. assoc. prof., 1982-88, adj. prof., 1988-89, prof., 1990—, chairperson, 1993—. Author: Benedetto Croce Reconsidered, 1987; transl.: Benedetto Croce's Essays on Literature, 1990; contbr. articles, essays, book revs. to profl. jours. and books. Dir. Flintridge Riding Club, Flintridge-LaCañada, Calif., 1990-91. Mem. AAUP, Am. Philos. Assn., Am. Soc. for Aesthetics, Am. Soc. for Social Philosophy (bd. dirs. 1983-90, asst. edit. 1988), Am. Soc. for Value Inquiry (assoc. editor jour. 1990—, assoc. editor book series 1990—). Office: Claremont McKenna Coll Dept Philosophy Claremont CA 91711

ROLLER, SUSAN LORRAYNE, industrial communications specialist, consultant; b. Portsmouth, Va., Sept. 13, 1954; d. Gilbert John Roller and Lois Carolyn (Moore) Logan. BS in Med. Scis., U. Wash., 1976, BA, 1980. Dir. med. programming Omnia Corp., Mpls., 1980-82; program developer Golle & Holmes, Mpls., 1982-83; dir. mktg. Santal Corp., St. Louis, 1983; pres. Fine Line, Ltd., Reno, Nev., 1984—; ind. film prodr., writer. Mem. Reno C. of C., Kappa Kappa Gamma. Republican. Episcopalian.

ROLLINS, JACK JAMES, mechanical engineer; b. Cottonwood Falls, Kans., July 30, 1922; s. James Clarence and Beulah Vivan (Colton) R.; m. Frances Elva Ernst, Aug. 5, 1945 (dec. 1986); children: Mark Steven, Marilyn Sue Rollins-Drucker. BS in Mech. Engring., Kans. State U., 1949. Registered profl. engr., Kans., Oreg. Chief engr. Ehrsam Mfg. Co., Enterprise, Kans., 1949-60, Fegles Constrn. Co., Mpls., 1960-69; dir. engring. Weitz-Hettelsater Co., Kansas City, Mo., 1969-73; pres. Watson Engrs., Overland Park, Kans., 1973-78; project mgr. Sandwell Internat. Harris Group, Portland, Oreg., 1978-92. Police judge City of Enterprise, 1955-57. Staff sgt. U.S. Army, 1942-45. Home: 17617 SW Arbor Ln Lake Oswego OR 97035

ROLLINS, JAMES GREGORY, air force officer; b. Vandenberg AFB, Calif., Apr. 6, 1963; s. Clarence Leslie and Mary Ethel (Brooks) R. BS in Bus. Adminstrn., San Jose State U., 1985; MSA in Gen. Adminstrn., Ctrl. Mich. U., 1992; MBA in Aviation Mgmt., Embry-Riddle Aero. U., 1992. Commd. 2d lt. USAF, 1985, advanced through grades to capt., 1989; minuteman intercontinental ballistic missile dep. crew comdr. USAF, Grand Forks AFB, N.D., 1985-86, minuteman intercontinental ballistic missile instr. dep. crew comdr., 1986-87, minuteman intercontinental ballistic missile evaluator dep. crew comdr., 1987-88, strategic air command missile combat competition instr., 1987-88, intercontinental ballistic missile crew comdr., 1988-89, scheduling br. chief ops., 1989-90, order tng. officer emergency war, 1990-91, intercontinental ballistic missile ops. plans officer, 1991-92; acquisition info. mgr. USAF, L.A. AFB, 1992—. Editor (newsletters) Families First, 1991, Vol. Network, 1990-91. Asst. project officer Project Sandbox fundraiser, 1986; founder Above and Beyond Vol. Tutoring, 1988, cons., 1988—; vol. staff Youth Ctr., Grand Forks AFB, 1988-91, Rebuild L.A. Edn. and Job Tng. Task Force; base project officer Rob's Coats for Kids, 1990, 91; vol. Grand Forks United Way Community Svcs., 1990-91; mem. Nat. Vol. Ctr., 1991—, Minn. Office Vol. Svcs., 1991—. Decorated Air Force Achievement medal, 1990, Air Force Commendation medal, 1992; named Vol. of Yr., 321st Strategic Missile Wing, 42d Air Divsn., 8th Air Force, Strategic Air Command, 1990. Mem. Air Force Assn., Assn. Vol. Adminstrs. Home: 4451 Pacific Coast Hwy Apt H304 Torrance CA 90505 Office: USAF SMC/MCPC Los Angeles CA 90009

ROLLINS, JAMES RICHARD, engineer; b. Iowa Falls, Iowa, Nov. 17, 1939; s. Richard Paley and Eleanor Blanche (Peterson) R.; m. Lyntha Carolyn Colby, June 3, 1962 (div. Mar. 1971). BSME, U. Iowa, 1961; MSME, U. Calif., Berkeley, 1966. Test engr. Gen. Dynamics, San Diego, 1961-65; lead engr. Rocketdyne, Canoga Park, Calif., 1966-77, Gen. Electric, San Jose, Calif., 1977-79; engring. supr. Lockheed Missiles & Space Co., Sunnyvale, Calif., 1980-85, engring. mgr., 1985—. Contbr. articles to profl. jours. Home: 814 Saratoga Ave Apt 305J San Jose CA 95129-2543 Office: Lockheed Missiles & Space 1111 Lockheed Way Bldg 159 Sunnyvale CA 94089-1212

ROLPHE, BEN RICHARD, JR., publishing company executive; b. L.A., June 19, 1932; s. Ben R. and Ruth LaVern (Bronson) R.; m. Shirley G. Foote, Mar. 21, 1951 (wid. Aug. 1976); children: Hope Anderson, B. Randy, Pennie Sanders; m. Anna Marie Swan, Feb. 14, 1980. Student, U. Santa Clara, 1953-59. Owner Calif. Meter Svc., San Jose, 1955-62, Western Svc. Systems, Portland, Oreg., 1962-71; pub. Glacier Herald Newspaper, Kalispell, Mont., 1971-76; pres. Century Pub. Co., Coeur d'Alene, Idaho, 1976—; instr. Oreg. Real Estate Commn., Salem, 1978-82; cons. Mini-Maid Systems, Inc., Salem, 1971-80, Wishing Star Found., Coeur d'Alene, 1985-89; del. U.S.-China Joint Session on Ind., Beijing, 1988. Author: How to Make Advertising Pay, 1980. Bd. dirs. Pan Am. Hwy. Commn., Yakima, Wash., 1968-69, Youth Help Line, 1991, Pacific Travel Assn., Bend, Oreg., 1970-71, Boy Scouts Am., Panhandle Coun., 1992, North Idaho Coll. Found., 1992-93. Lt. USAF, 1949-53. Named Best Original Editorial, Nat. Assn. Pub., 1976; recipient Employer of Yr. Am. Legion, 1989, Vets. of Fgn. Wars, 1990. Mem. Am. Pres. Assn., Masons, Shriners, Coeur d'Alene C. of C. (bd. dirs. 1990-93). Republican. Baptist. Home: 12582 Strahorn Rd Hayden ID 83835-9303 Office: Century Pub Co 5710 E Seltice Way Post Falls ID 83854-9703

ROLSTON, HOLMES, III, theologian, educator, philosopher; b. Staunton, Va., Nov. 19, 1932; s. Holmes and Mary Winifred (Long) R.; m. Jane Irving Wilson, June 1, 1956; children: Shonny Hunter, Giles Campbell. BS, Davidson Coll., 1953; BD, Union Theol. Sem., Richmond, Va., 1956; MA in Philosophy of Sci., U. Pitts., 1968; PhD in Theology, U. Edinburgh, Scotland, 1958. Ordained to ministry Presbyn. Ch. (USA), 1956. Asst. prof. philosophy Colo. State U., Ft. Collins, 1968-71, assoc. prof., 1971-76, prof., 1976—; vis. scholar Ctr. Study of World Religions, Harvard U., 1974-75;

lectr. Yale U., Vanderbilt U., others; official observer UNCED, Rio de Janiero, 1992. Author: Religious Inquiry: Participation and Detachment, 1985, Philosophy Gone Wild, 1986, Science and Religion: A Critical Survey, 1987, Environmental Ethics, 1988; assoc. editor Environ. Ethics, 1979—; mem. editorial bd. Oxford Series in Environ. Philosophy and Pub. Policy, Zygon: Jour. of Religion and Sci.; contbr. chpts. to books, articles to profl. jours. Recipient Oliver P. Penock Disting. Svc. award Colo. State U., 1983, Coll. Award for Excellence, 1991, Univ. Disting. Prof., 1992; Disting. Russell fellow Grad. Theol. Union, 1991, Disting. Lectr. Chinese Acad. of Social Scis., 1991, Disting. Lectr. Nobel Conf. XXVII. Mem. AAAS, Am. Acad. Religion, Soc. Bibl. Lit. (pres. Rocky Mountain-Gt. Plains region), Am. Philos. Assn., Internat. Soc. for Environ. Ethics (pres. 1989—), Phi Beta Kappa. Home: 1712 Concord Dr Fort Collins CO 80526-1602 Office: Colo State U Dept Philosophy Fort Collins CO 80523

ROLSTON, ROBERT LEE, cattle association executive; b. Sheridan, Wyo., July 1, 1936; s. Donald H. and Florence J. (Jelinek) R.; m. Colleen R. Larson, Mar. 28, 1958; children: Christi R., Jeffrey, Mary K. BS, U. Wyo., 1959. Dir. Wyo. Farm Bur. Fedn., Laramie, 1966-68, Wyo. Stock Growers Assn., Cheyenne, 1968-73, Am. Nat. Cattlemen's Assn., Denver, 1973-76; mgr. Calif. Beef Coun., Burlingame, 1976-80; dir. Am. Sheep Prodrs. Coun., Denver, 1983-86; exec. v.p. Colo. Cattlemen's Assn., Denver, 1986-89, Am. Salers Assn., Englewood, Colo., 1989—; mem. adv. com. Nat. Livestock & Meat Bd., Chgo., 1977-80; mem. selection com. Calif. State Commerce, Sacramento, 1977-80; dir. Jr. Grant Nat. Livestock Show, Cow Palace, 1977-80, Colo. Hwy. Users Conf., Denver, 1986-89. Mem. Nat. Cattleman's Assn. (exec. com. 1993). Republican. Home: 6185 S Jasmine Englewood CO 80111 Office: Am Salers Assn 5600 S Quebec Ste 220A Englewood CO 80111

ROMANELLI, PETER NICHOLAS, real estate developer; b. Bklyn., May 28, 1948; s. Otto Charles and Dorothy (Hicks) R.; m. Deborah Nuse, May 13, 1978 (div. 1984); m. Barbara Lee Roberts, Dec. 20, 1986 (div. 1987). BA in Cinema, SUNY, Binghamton, 1978; MA in Geography, Columbia U., 1984. Assoc. prod. MRC Films McLaughlin Enterprises, Ltd., N.Y.C., 1978-83; v.p. Minturn (Colo.) Realty subchpt. McLaughlin Ptnrs., 1984—; freelance writer, photographer, cinematographer. Mem. Avon/Beaver Creek Resort Assn. (bd. dirs. 1988—, v.p. 1991, pres. 1992). Home and Office: PO Box 130 Minturn CO 81645-0130

ROMANO, CLIFFORD SAMUEL, engineer, investigator; b. Jersey City, May 16, 1951; s. Samuel and Dolores (Fitzsimons) R.; m. Victoria Jean Lederer, Sept. 10, 1977; children: Brandon Timothy, Michelle Renee. BS in Transp. Engring., Calif. Poly. State U., San Luis Obispo, 1979. Profl. engr., Calif. Dir. photography Minicars Inc., Santa Barbara, Calif., 1971-72; comml. diver Underwater Svc. & Supply, Santa Barbara, 1972-73; transp. planner Calif. Dept. Transp., San Luis Obispo, 1978-79; bridge engr. office structure constrn. Calif. Dept. Transp., Sacramento, 1979-82; resident engr. Calif. Dept. Transp., Redding, 1982-88; pvt. practice profl. engr. Madera, Calif., 1984—; sr. transp. engr. office traffic engring. Calif. Dept. Transp., Sacramento, 1988-92; investigating engr. Calif. Hwy. Patrol Multidisciplinary Accident Investigation Team, Fresno, 1988-92; constrn. engr. Calif. Dept. Transp., Fresno, 1992—; instr., accident investigation instr. Calif. Hwy. Patrol Acad., Sacramento, 1990—; reconstrn. team engr. Calif. Hwy. Patrol San Francisco Earthquake Investigation, San Francisco, 1989-90; profl. underwater photographer, 1991—. Home: 514 Fairview Ave Madera CA 93637-4302

ROMANO, JOHN JOSEPH, JR., executive chef; b. Springfield, Mass., Aug. 20, 1947; s. John Joseph and Evelyn N. (Tardo) R.; m. Diana Marie Benal, Nov. 27, 1976. A. in Bus., U. Mass., 1967; AS, Culinary Inst. Am., Hyde Park, N.Y., 1969. Broiler cook Hamburger Haven, Hyannis, Mass., 1966; vegetable cook Colony Hotel, Kennebunkport, Maine, 1967; chef tournante Harborside Inn, Edgartown, Mass., 1968; food supr. SAGA Food Svc., Boston Coll., 1969-72; chef Pentagon/Gen. Long, Washington, 1970-71; owner Gallery Restaurant, Monterey, Calif., 1972-77; exec. chef Holiday Inn, Carmel, Calif., 1977-79, Beach and Tennis Club, Pebble Beach, Calif., 1979-91, Monterey Peninsula Country Club, Pebble Beach, 1991—. Advisor Culinary Inst.-West, Napa, Calif., 1992—; fundraiser L.A. Olympics, 1984, Monterey Sch. Dist., 1979—; judge fundraiser March of Dimes, Monterey, 1986—. With U.S. Army, 1969-71. Recipient Bronze medal Am. Culinary Fedn., 1985, cert. proficiency Nat. Restaurant Assn.; named Chef of Yr., am. Culinary Fedn., 1986. Mem. Les Touques Blanches, Monterey Chefs Assn. (bd. dirs. 1980—), Am. Culinary Fedn. (cert. exec. chef), Chaine de Rutisseine. Democrat. Roman Catholic. Home: 1120 Austin Ave Pacific Grove CA 93950 Office: Monterey Peninsula Country Club 3000 Club Rd Pebble Beach CA 93953

ROMANOS, NABIL ELIAS, healthcare systems company official; b. Roumie, Metn, Lebanon, June 3, 1965; came to U.S., 1982; s. Elias Rachid and Kamale (Salame) R. BA in Econs. and History magna cum laude, Georgetown U., 1986; postgrad., Hautes Etudes Commerciales, France, 1989; MBA, U. Calif., Berkeley, 1989. Rsch. assoc. Am. Fin. Svcs. Assn., Washington, 1986-87; fin. analyst Varian Assocs., Palo Alto, Calif., 1988, sr. fin. analyst, 1989-91; mgr. fin. mkt. analysis Varian Oncology Systems, Palo Alto, 1991-92; mgr. bus. devel. Varian Health Care Systems, Palo Alto, 1992—. Author: Finance Facts Yearbook, 1987. Vol. tutor for refugees Community Action Coalition, Washington, 1985-86; vol. interpreter emergency room Georgetown U., Washington, 1984-86; internat. vol. Internat. House U. Calif., Berkeley, 1987-89. Scholar Georgetown U., 1985-86, U. Calif., Berkeley, 1987-89. Mem. Phi Alpha Theta. Maronite Catholic. Home: 837 Cowper St Apt F Palo Alto CA 94301-2817

ROMANOW, ROY JOHN, provincial government official, barrister, solicitor; S. Michael and Tekla R. Educated at Univ. of Sask. Mem. Sask. Legislature, 1967-82, 1986—, provincial sec., 1971-72, atty. gen. of province, 1971-82, minister of intergovernmental affairs, 1979-82, leader, Sask. New Dem. Party, 1987—, leader of the opposition, 1987-91, leader of the majority, 1991—, premier, 1991—. Office: Legislative Assembly, 2405 Legislative Dr, Regina, SK Canada S4S 0B3

ROMBAUER, MARJORIE LORRAINE, law educator; b. Jamestown, N.D., May 11, 1927; d. Jasper John and Ellen Mary (Kline) Dick; m. Edgar Roderick Rombauer, May 13, 1954. BA, U. Wash., 1958, JD, 1960. Bar: Wash. 1960. Instr. U. Wash., Seattle, 1960-64, asst. prof., 1964-67, assoc. prof., 1967-71, prof., 1971—; bd. dirs. Legal Writing Inst., 1991—; vis. prof. Nat. Taiwan U., 1990; chairperson Wash. Law Revision Commn., 1990—. Author: Legal Problem Solving, 5th edit., 1991; (with L. Squires) Legal Writing in a Nutshell, 1982. Recipient Outstanding Achievement award, Wash. Law Review, 1992. Mem. ABA, Wash. State Bar Assn. (spl. merit award 1987), Legal Writing Inst. (bd. dirs. 1991—), Order of Coif, Scribes, Phi Beta Kappa. Office: U Wash Law Sch 1100 NE Campus Pky Seattle WA 98105-6617

ROMER, ROY R., governor; b. Garden City, Kans., Oct. 31, 1928; s. Irving Rudolph and Margaret Elizabeth (Snyder) R.; m. Beatrice Miller, June 10, 1952; children: Paul, Mark, Mary, Christopher, Timothy, Thomas, Elizabeth. B.S. in Agrl. Econs., Colo. State U., 1950; LL.B., U. Colo., 1952; postgrad., Yale U. Bar: Colo. 1952. Engaged in farming in Colo., 1942-52; ind. practice law Denver, 1955-66; mem. Colo. Ho. of Reps., 1958-62, Colo. Senate, 1962-66; owner, operator Arapahoe Aviation Co., Colo. Flying Acad., Geneva Basin Ski Area; engaged in home site devel.; owner chain farm implement and indsl. equipment stores Colo.; commr. agr. State of Colo., 1975, chief staff, exec. asst. to gov., 1975-77, 83-84, state treas., 1977-86, gov., 1987—; chmn. Gov. Colo. Blue Ribbon Panel, Gov. Colo. Small Bus. Council; mem. agrl. adv. com. Colo. Bd. Agr. Bd. editors Colo. U. Law Rev., 1960-62. Past trustee Iliff Sch. Theology, Denver; mem., past chmn. Nat. Edn. Goals Panel; co-chmn. Nat. Coun. on Standards and Testing. With USAF, 1952-53. Mem. Dem. Govs.' Assn. (chmn.), Nat. Govs.' Assn. (vice chmn., chmn.-elect), Colo. Bar Assn., Order of Coif. Democrat. Presbyterian. Office: Office of Gov State Capital Denver CO 80203*

ROMERO, PHILIP JOSEPH, economics and policy analyst; b. Abington, Pa., Mar. 22, 1957; s. Joseph John and Mildred Edith (Laundis) R.; m. Lita Grace Flores, Oct. 6, 1984. BA in Econs. and Polit. Sci., Cornell U., 1979; PhD in Policy Analysts, Rand Grad. Sch., 1988. Asst. to mayor Twp. of East Brunswick, N.J., 1977-78; policy analyst Sci. Applications Internat. Corp., Washington, 1980-83; rsch. assoc. RAND Corp., Santa Monica, Calif., 1983-88, assoc. economist, 1988-90; dir. strategic planning United Technologies/Carrier, Hartford, Conn., 1990-91; chief econ. adviser Gov.'s Office, Sacramento, Calif., 1991—; cons. Office of Tech. Assessment, Washington, 1989-90, RAND Corp., Washington, 1990-91, Sec. of Air Forces Sci. Adv. Bd., Washington, 1980-83, Undersecretary of Def., Washington, 1985-86. Co-author: (book) The Deescalation of Nuclear Crises, 1992; contbr. numerous reports and papers to profl. publs. Pres. RAND Grad. Sch. Alumni Assn., Santa Monica, 1989—; founder Adopt-A-School Honors Program, Pacific Palisades, Calif., 1986. Recipient Internat. Affairs fellowship Coun. on Fgn. Rels., N.Y.C., 1989. Mem. The Planning Forum, Am. Econ. Assn., Am. Polit. Sci. Assn., Ops. Rsch. Soc. of Am., Acad. Public Policy Analysts and Mgmt., Inst. Mgmt. Sci. Home: 1587 Barnett Circle Carmichael CA 95608 Office: Gov's Office 1400 Tenth St Sacramento CA 95814

ROMERO, SCOTT JOSEPH, promotions company executive; b. Syracuse, N.Y., Apr. 5, 1956; s. Donald Joseph and Cecelia (Koster) R.; m. Carol Carrico, Nov. 22, 1986. BS, Jacksonville U., Fla., 1978. Fin. cons. Bache & Co., Encino, Calif., 1978-83, Shearson/Am. Express, Woodland Hills, Calif., 1983-88; exec. v.p. T.J. Shephard & Assocs., Newport Beach, Calif., 1988—. Mem. Rotary (officer 1985—). Roman Catholic. Home: PO Box 5271 Newport Beach CA 92662 Office: TJ Shephard & Assoc 4590 MacArthur Blvd # 550 Newport Beach CA 92662

ROMJUE, JANE MURPHY (JANE M. VERDUGO), secondary education educator; b. Hyannis, Mass., May 20, 1944; d. Edward Aloysius and Effie (Hampton) Murphy; m. Benny Verdugo. BA in English, Smith Coll., 1966; MA in English, U. Hawaii, 1972. Cert. pvt. sch. tchr. English tchr. Punahou Sch., Honolulu, 1966-71, Maryknoll Sch., Honolulu, 1971-90, Hawaii Pacific U., Honolulu, 1983-90, Iolani Sch., Honolulu, 1990—; treas. Hawaii Speech League, Honolulu, 1981-83; judge Hawaii State Spelling Bee, Honolulu, 1988. Asst. editor quar. jour. Iolani Bull., 1992—. Sec. bd. dirs. Kapiolani Royale, Honolulu, 1988-92, pres., 1992—. Hawaii Writing Project fellow U. Hawaii, 1985. Mem. Nat. Coun. Tchrs. English, Hawaii Coun. Tchrs. English. Office: Iolani Sch 563 Kamoku St Honolulu HI 96826

ROMNEY, JOSEPH BARNARD, educator, administrator; b. Salt Lake City, July 20, 1935; s. Junius Stowell and Ruth (Stewart) R.; m. Florence Black, May 1, 1959; children: Matthew Joseph, Suzanne, Aaron Stewart. BS, U. Utah, 1960, MA, 1967, JD, 1963, PhD, 1969. Bar: Utah 1963. Commd. 2d lt. U.S. Army, 1960, advanced through grades to capt., ret., 1968; assoc. Romney and Boyer, Salt Lake City, 1963-68; asst. atty. gen. State of Utah, Salt Lake City, 1964-65; prof. history, assoc. dean Calif. Polytech. State U., San Luis Obispo, 1969-80; prof., assoc. dir. honors program, cello instr. Ricks Coll., Rexburg, Idaho, 1980—, dir. honors program, 1992—; cellist Utah Symphony Orch., Salt Lake City, 1954-56, 59-60, 66-68; pres. Millhollow Frozen Yogurt, Inc., Rexburg, 1982—. Author: A Research Guide to the History of San Luis Obispo County, California, 1983. Scoutmaster, dist. chmn. Boy Scouts Am., Utah, Calif. and Idaho, 1955-91. Recipient Dist. Merit award Boy Scouts Am., 1978. Mem. Utah State Bar Assn., Idaho Hist. Soc. (bd. editors 1988—), Mormon History Assn. (bd. editors 1979-81), Soc. Christian Philosophers. Republican. LDS. Home: 53 S Mill Hollow Rd Rexburg ID 83440-2030 Office: Ricks Coll Dept Religion Rexburg ID 83460

ROMNEY, RICHARD MILES, magazine editor; b. Salt Lake City, June 7, 1952; s. Richard Paul and Mary Lou (Stone) R.; m. Julene Larsen, Mar. 3, 1983; children: Taylor Larsen, Miles Anderson, Brittany Ann, McKay Manwill. Student, U. Utah, 1970-71; BA in Journalism magna cum laude, Brigham Young U., 1977, MPA with distinction magna cum laude, 1991. Cert. airplane mechanic; cert scuba diver. Editorial staff mem. Daily Utah Chronicle, Salt Lake City, 1970-71; reporter, editor Deseret News, Salt Lake City, 1970-72, 74, 76; editor, mng. editor Daily Universe, Provo, Utah, 1975-77; assoc. editor Utah Journalism Rev., Provo and Logan, 1982-83; editorial assoc., asst. and assoc. editor, asst. mng. editor New Era Mag., Salt Lake City, 1977-89, mng. editor, 1989—; Utah corr. Bur. Nat. Affairs, Washington, 1977-80; guest lectr. U. Utah, Salt Lake City, 1980—, Brigham Young U., Provo, 1983—; speaker Reader's Digest writer's workshops, Utah State U., Logan, Dixie Coll., St. George, 1984, 89. Contbr. articles to profl. jours. and encys. Missionary LDS Ch., Paris, 1972-74, bishop, Centerville, Utah, 1984-86; Good Will tour Soc. Profl. Journalists, Soviet Union, 1979-80; bd. dirs. Assoc. Latter-Day Media Artists, Salt Lake City, 1978-80; interpreter, mem. exch. team Rotary Club Vocat. Exch. Team, France, 1988. Sgt. Air Nat. Guard, 1970-78. Mem. Beta Gamma Sigma, Phi Kappa Phi. Home: 3463 S 2940 E Salt Lake City UT 84109-3163 Office: New Era Mag 50 E North Temple Salt Lake City UT 84150-0001

ROMOSER, SALLY BETH, public relations executive; b. Cleve., Aug. 6, 1958; d. William Carl and Marjorie Ethel (Harrison) R. BA in Journalism, Ohio State U., 1980. Asst. dir. pub. rels. Watts Lamb Inc., Cleve., 1981-83; v.p. pub. rels. J. Remington & Assocs., Cleve., 1983-86; dir. pub. rels. Chapman/Warick, San Diego, 1986-87; exec. v.p. Roni Hicks & Assocs., Inc., San Diego, 1987-92; pres. Harrison Graham Pub. Rels., 1992—; mem. Art in Pub. Places Com., San Diego City Commn. for Arts & Cultures; dir., sec. Earth Vision Prodns.; bd. mem. Friends of Downtown; co-chair Newsmakers-San Diego Press Club. Mem. Jr. League San Diego, 1986-90; mem. pub. rels. com. San Diego Oceans Found., 1987-90; mem. host com. San Diego Conv. and Visitors Bur., 1986—; pub. rels. liaison San Diego Super Bown Task Force, 1987-88. Mem. Pub. Rels. Soc. Am. (bd. dirs. 1987—, sec. 1989-90, v.p. 1990-91), dir.-at-large). Republican. United Methodist. Home: 3753 Balboa Ter Apt A San Diego CA 92117-5417

RONAN, TIMOTHY DWYER, lawyer; b. New Brusnwick, N.J., Sept. 19, 1959; s. John Joseph and Elizabeth Catherine (Corbin) R.; m. Victoria Catherine Lamb, Dec. 6, 1982; 1 child, Caolán McKenna. BA in Philosophy and Polit. Sci., Loyola Marymount U., L.A., 1981; JD, Georgetown U., 1984. Bar: Ariz. 1984. Assoc. Squire, Sanders & Dempsey, Phoenix, 1984-87, O'Connor Cavanagh, Phoenix, 1987-89, Killian, Nicholas & Fischer, Mesa, Ariz., 1989—; atty. Phoenix Shanti Group, 1986—. Mem. Mesa Human Svcs. Adv. Bd., 1989-91; bd. dirs., treas. Maricopa County Sports Authority, Phoenix, 1989—; bd. dirs. Mesa Conv. and Visitors Bur., 1990—. Mem. ABA, Ariz. Bar Assn. (Ltd. Liability Co. Act com. 1991-92). Republican. Roman Catholic. Office: Killian Nicholas & Fischer 40 N Center St Mesa AZ 85201

RONCA-BATTISTA, MELINDA JANE, health physicist; b. Lawrence, Kans., Mar. 18, 1959; d. Luciano Bruno and Jane Areta (Thorne) Ronca-Washburn; m. Frederick Anthony Battista, July 16, 1983; children: Frederick Luciano Ronca, Lorna Jane Ronca. BS, U. Mich., 1981, MS, 1984. Lab. asst. Physics dept. U. Mich., Ann Arbor, 1980-81; lab. tech. Radiation Control Svcs., U. Mich., Ann Arbor, 1982; tech. mgr. Environ. Rsch. Group, Inc., Ann Arbor, 1981-82; dosimetry staff asst. Enrico Fermi Atomic Power Plant Unit 2, Newport, Mich., 1983; project mgr. U.S. EPA, Washington, 1984-89; ind. cons. to radon measurement and rsch. firms Naperville, Ill., 1989—; rsch. mgr. Sci. X Comml. Systems Corp., Alexandria, Va., 1989—; contbr./speaker internat. workshops on radon, Italy, Portugal, 1987, 92. Contbr. articles to profl. jours. Vol. Parent and Child Edn. Soc., Naperville, 1991-92. Recipient Gold Medal for Exceptional Svc. U.S. EPA, 1986, Spl. Achievement award, 1985, 86. Mem. Health Physics Soc. Home: 14642 S 25th Pl Phoenix AZ 85044

RONDEAU, DORIS JEAN, entrepreneur, consultant; b. Winston-Salem, N.C., Nov. 25, 1941; d. John Delbert and Eldora Virginia (Klutz) Robinson; m. Robert Breen Corrente, Sept. 4, 1965 (div. 1970); m. Wilfrid Dolor Rondeau, June 3, 1972. Student Syracuse U., 1959-62, Fullerton Jr. Coll., 1974-75; BA in Philosophy, Calif. State U.-Fullerton, 1976, postgrad., 1976-80. Ordained to ministry The Spirit of Divine Love, 1974. Trust real estate clk. Security First Nat. Bank, Riverside, Calif., 1965-68; entertainer Talent, Inc., Hollywood, Calif., 1969-72; co-founder, dir. Spirit of Divine Love, Capistrano Beach, Calif., 1974—; pub., co-founder Passing Through, Inc., Capistrano Beach, 1983—; instr. Learning Activity, Anaheim, Calif., 1984—; chmn. bd., prin. D.J. Rondeau, Entrepreneur, Inc., Capistrano Beach, 1984—; co-founder, dir. Spiritual Positive Attitude, Inc., Moon In Pisces, Inc., Vibrations By Rondeau, Inc., Divine Consciousness, Expressed, Inc., Capistrano Beach, Doris Wilfrid Rondeau, Inc., Huntington Beach, Calif. Author, editor: A Short Introduction To The Spirit of Divine Love, 1984; writer, producer, dir. performer spiritual vignettes for NBS Radio Network, KWVE-FM, 1982-84; author: Spiritual Meditations to Uplift the Soul, 1988. Served with USAF, 1963-65. Recipient Pop Vocalist First Place award USAF Talent Show, 1964, Sigma chpt. Epsilon Delta Chi, 1985, others. Mem. Hamel Bus. Grads., Smithsonian Assocs., Am. Mgmt. Assn., Nat. Assn. Female Execs. Avocations: long-distance running, body fitness, arts and crafts, snorkeling, musical composition.

RONEY, JOHN HARVEY, lawyer; b. Los Angeles, June 12, 1932; s. Harvey and Mildred Puckett (Cargill) R.; m. Joan Ruth Allen, Dec. 27, 1954; children: Pam Peterson, J. Harvey, Karen Louise Hanke, Cynthia Allen Harmon. Student, Pomona Coll., 1950-51; B.A., Occidental Coll., 1954; LL.B., UCLA, 1959. Bar: Calif. 1960, D.C. 1976. Assoc. O'Melveny & Myers, Los Angeles, 1959-67, ptnr., 1967—; gen. counsel Pa. Co., 1970-78, Baldwin United Corp., 1983-84; dir. Coldwell Banker & Co., 1969-81, Brentwood Savs. & Loan Assn., 1968-80; spl. advisor to dep. Rehab. of Mut. Benefit Life Ins. Co., 1991—. Served to 1st lt. USMCR, 1954-56. Mem. ABA, Calif. Bar Assn. (chmn. ins. law com. 1993-94), L.A. County Bar Assn., San Francisco Bar Assn., D.C. Bar Assn., Coun. Fgn. Rels. N.Y., L.A. Com. on Fgn. Rels., Conf. Ins. Counsel. Republican. Clubs: California (Los Angeles); Sky (N.Y.C.). Home: The Strand Hermosa Beach CA 90254 Office: O'Melveny & Myers 400 S Hope St Los Angeles CA 90071-2899

RONSMAN, WAYNE JOHN, insurance company executive; b. Milw., Jan. 21, 1938; s. Harry Martin and Martha Elizabeth (Popp) R.; m. Joan P. Murphy-Mays, Nov. 30, 1974; children: Allison, Alanna; children by previous marriage: Rosemary, Harry, Martha. Student Marquette U., 1955-58, U. San Francisco, 1960-66. CLU, chartered fin. cons.; cert. fin. planner; registered fin. planner. Acct. Otis McAllister & Co., 1960-62; acct., salesman of data processing Statis. Tabulation Corp., San Francisco, 1962-66; chief acct., gen. mgr. Dillingham Bros. Ltd., Honolulu, 1966-67; ins. salesman Mut. Benefit Life Ins. Co., 1968—, gen. agt., Hawaii and Alaska, 1991; v.p. Brenno Assos., Honolulu, 1972-80; prin. Ronsman-Brenno, Anchorage, Alaska, 1980-90; owner Ronsman, Hammond & Assocs., 1991—; bd. dirs. Aloha Nat. Bank, Kihei, Maui; guest lectr. Chaminade U. Law Sch., Honolulu. Mem. Gov's Task Force to Program Correctional Facilities Land, 1970-72; mem. State Bd. Paroles and Pardons, 1972-75; treas. Spl. Edn. Center of Oahu, 1969-78; pres. Ballet Alaska, 1986-87, Maui Balet Co. Ltd., 1992—; dir. Make A Wish Found Hawaii, 1992—. Served with USMCR, 1958-60. Mem. Nat. Assn. Accts. (pres. Anchorage chpt. 1989-90), Am. Soc. CLUs, Internat. Assn. Registered Fin. Planning, Inst. Cert. Fin. Planners, Anchorage Estate Planning Council, Honolulu Assn. Life Underwriters (million dollar round table 1973—), Hawaii (state editor 1970-71, nat. dir. 1972-73), Kailua (pres. 1968-69) Jaycees, Hawaii C. of C., Nat. Assn. Securities Dealers, Kailua C. of C. (pres. 1977-78). Roman Catholic. Home: Ronsman-Hammond & Assocs 787 Maalahi St Wailuku HI 96793 Office: PO Box 336 Honolulu HI 96809-0336

ROOKS, JUDITH PENCE, family planning, maternal health care, midwifery consultant; b. Spokane, Wash., Aug. 18, 1941; d. Lawrence Cyrus and Christine Atrice (Snow) Pence; m. Peter Geoffrey Bourne, Mar. 1972 (div.); m. Charles Stanley Rooks, Sept. 21, 1975; 1 child, Christopher Robert. BS, U. Wash., 1963; MS, Cath. U. Am., 1967; MPH, Johns Hopkins U., 1974. Cert. edpidemiology, nursing, nurse-midwife, mediator. Staff nurse The Clin. Ctr., NIH, Bethesda, Md., 1965; asst. prof. nursing dept. San Jose (Calif.) State Coll., 1967-69; edpidemiologist Ctrs. for Disease Control, Atlanta, 1970-72, 74-78; asst. prof. dept. ob-gyn. Oreg. Health Sci. U., Portland, 1978-79; expert Office of the Surgeon Gen., Dept. HHS, Washington, 1979-80; project officer U.S. AID, Washington, 1980-82; prin. investigator Columbia U. Sch. Pub. Health, N.Y.C., 1988-89; cons. Portland, 1982—; mem. tech. adv. com. Family Health Internat., Research Triangle Park, N.C., 1986—; mem. editorial adv. com. population info. program Johns Hopkins U., Balt., 1984—; mem. com. Inst. of Medicine NAS, Washington, 1983-85. Co-author: Nurse-Midwifery in America, 1986; contbr. articles to profl. jours. Bd. overseers World Affairs Coun. Oreg., Portland, 1987—; bd. dirs. Planned Parenthood of the Columbia/Willamette, Portland, 1987-90; chmn. Ga. Citizens for Hosp. Abortion, Atlanta, 1969-70. Mem. APHA (chair com. on women's rights 1982-83, governing coun. 1976-77, 79-82), Am. Coll. Nurse-Midwifes (life, pres. 1983-85). Home and Office: 2706 SW English Ct Portland OR 97201

ROOP, JOSEPH MCLEOD, economist; b. Montgomery, Ala., Sept. 29, 1941; s. Joseph Ezra and Mae Elizabeth (McLeod) R.; B.S., Central Mo. State U., Warrensburg, 1963; Ph.D., Wash. State U., Pullman, 1973; m. Betty Jane Reed, Sept. 4, 1965; 1 dau., Elizabeth Rachael. Economist, Econ. Research Service, U.S. Dept. Agr., Washington, 1975-79; sr. economist Evans Econs., Inc., Washington, 1979-81; sr. research economist Battelle Pacific N.W. Labs., Richland, Wash., 1981—; instr. dept. econs. Wash. State U., 1969-71; with Internat. Energy Agy., Paris, 1990-91. Contbr. tech. articles to profl. jours. Served with U.S. Army, 1966-68. Dept. Agr. Coop. State Research Service research grantee, 1971-73. Mem. Am. Econ. Assn., Econometric Soc., Internat. Assn. Energy Economists. Home: 715 S Taft Kennewick WA 99336 Office: PO Box 999 Richland WA 99352

ROOS, DAVID BERNARD, surgeon; b. Decatur, Ill., Nov. 11, 1928; s. Edmund Carl and Frances (Kuny) R.; m. Edith Julia Edwards, June 10, 1954; children: Steven David, Gary Marshall, Wendy Jeanne, Linda Jennifer, Lisa Alison. AB, Harvard U., 1950; MD, Washinington U., St. Louis, 1954. Diplomate Am. Bd. Surgery. Intern in surgery Cin. Gen. Hosp., 1954-55; fellow in surg. pathology Washington U., St. Louis, 1955; resident in surgery U. Colo. Med. Ctr. and VA Hosp., Denver, 1957-61; pvt. practice Denver, 1962—; instr. in surgery U. Colo. Med. Ctr., Denver, 1960-65, asst. clin. prof. surgery, 1965-75, assoc. clin. prof. surgery, 1975-85, clin. prof. surgery, 1985—. Contbr. chpts. to surg. textbooks, articles to profl. jours. Capt. USAF, 1955-57. Fulbright scholar London, 1959-60. Fellow ACS, Belgian Soc. Surgery (hon.), Soc. Clin. Vascular Surgery (hon.); mem. AMA, Am. Coll. Chest Physicians, Internat. Cardiovascular Surg. Soc., Southwestern Surg. Congress, Soc. for Vascular Surgery, Western Vascular Soc. (founding mem.), Western Surg. Assn. Presbyterian. Office: Ste 206 1721 E 19th Ave Denver CO 80218-1239

ROOS, GEORGE WILLIAM, physicist; b. Yonkers, N.Y., July 1, 1932; s. George William Jr. and Corinne Elizabeth (Kelly) R.; m. Grace Lennon, Oct. 4, 1958; children: George, John, Edward, Daniel. BS in Physics, Iona Coll., 1953. Physicist Naval Rsch. Lab., Washington, 1953-54; program mgr. electric boat divsn. Gen. Dynamics Co., Groton, Conn., 1957-68, mgr. chg. control, 1968-72, dir. indsl. rels. and mgmt. engring., 1972-77; dir. resource mgmt. Gen. Dynamics Co., Ft. Worth, 1977-79; dir. integrated logistic support Convair divsn. Gen. Dynamics Co., San Diego, 1979-86, v.p. human resources Convair divsn., 1986-92; gen. mgr. Hughes Unmanned Strike System, San Diego, 1992—. Bd. dirs. ARC, San Diego, 1987—. Lt. USNR, 1953-57, Korea. Recipient A.A. Loftus award Iona Coll., 1974. Mem. Calif. Mgrs. Assn. (bd. dirs. 1988—, mem. exec. com. 1990—), U.S. Naval Inst., Navy League, Escondido Country Club. Republican. Roman Catholic. Home: 10726 Vista Valle Dr San Diego CA 92131

ROOS, NESTOR ROBERT, publisher; b. St. Louis, Aug. 19, 1925; s. Maurice and Fannie (Friedman) R.; m. Fay Weil, July 8, 1951; children: Marilyn Roos Hall, Eileen Roos Ruddell, Robert F. BBA, Washington U., St. Louis, 1948; MSBA, Washington U., 1949; D of Bus. Adminstrn., Ind. U., 1959. Instr. bus. La. State U., Baton Rouge, 1949-51; teaching fellow Ind. U., Bloomington, 1951-53; asst. prof. Ga. State U., Atlanta, 1953-55; prof. U. Ariz., Tucson, 1955-86, prof. emeritus, 1986; pres. Risk Mgmt. Pub. Co., Tucson, 1976-90, cons. editor, 1990—; cons., expert witness in field; bd. dirs. Blue Cross-Blue Shield Ariz., sec., 1993—; mem. Ins. Dirs.' Adv. Com., Phoenix, 1987—, Reverse Mortgage Adv. Com., Tucson, 1988-90. Author: (with others) Multiple Line Insurers, 1970, Governmental Risk Management Manual, 1976, Industrial Accident Prevention, 1980. Bd. dirs. Handmaker Geriatric Ctr., Tucson, 1987-92; pres. Temple Emanu-El, Tucson, 1981-83. With U.S. Army, 1943-45, ETO. Grantee Nat. Inst. Occupational Safety and Health, 1975. Mem. Risk and Ins. Mgmt. Soc., Western Risk and Ins. Assn. (pres. 1972-73), Public Risk and Ins. Mgmt. Assn. (dir. edn. and tng. 1982-89). Democrat. Jewish. Home: 7311 E Camino De Cima Tucson AZ

85715-2212 Office: Risk Mgmt Pub Co 2030 E Broadway Blvd Ste 106 Tucson AZ 85719-5908

ROOT, CHARLES JOSEPH, JR., finance executive, consultant; b. Pierre, S.D., July 26, 1940; s. Charles Joseph and Hazel Ann (Messenger) R.; 1 child, Roseann Marie Root. Student, San Francisco Jr. Coll., 1963-65, La Salle Extension U., 1970-71, Coll. of Marin, 1971-72, Am. Coll. Life Underwriters, 1978-82. Registered investment advisor; charter fin. cons.; cert. fin. planner. Estate planner Bankers Life Co., San Francisco, 1966-78; fin. planner Planned Estates Assocs., Corte Madera, Calif., 1978-81; mng. dir. Double Eagle Fin. Corp., Santa Rosa, Calif., 1981—, investment advisor, 1983—; personal bus. mgr., 1987—. V.p. Big Bros. of Am., San Rafael, Calif., 1976-80; treas. com. to elect William Filante, San Rafael, 1978, Community Health Ctrs. of Marin, Fairfax, Calif., 1982-83, Wellspring Found., Philo, Calif., 1981-85; treas., bd. dirs. Ctr. for Attitudinal Healing, Tiburon, Calif., 1989-92; bd. dirs. Pickle Family Circus, San Francisco, 1988, United Way Sondms Lake, Mendocino Counties, 1993—, Redwood Empire Estate Planning Coun., Santa Rosa, Calif., 1992—, sec., 1993. Mem. Internat. Assn. Fin. Planners, Coll. Fin. Planning (cert. fin. planner 1988), Registry of fin. Planning, Nat. Assn. Life Underwriters, Marin County Assn. Life Underwriters (v.p. 1971-76, editor newsletter 1976-80), Rotary (Paul Harris Fellow 1980). Republican. Office: Double Eagle Fin Corp 2300 Bethards Dr Ste R PO Box 2790 Santa Rosa CA 95405

ROOT, DORIS SMILEY, art director; b. Ann Arbor, Mich., June 28, 1924; d. George O. and Hazel (smith) Smiley. Student, Art Inst. of Chgo., 1943-45, N.Y. Sch. Design, 1976-77, Calif. Art Inst., 1984-85. Creative dir. All Mayco's, L.A., 1962-63; advt. sales pro. dir. Seibu, L.A., 1963-64; v.p. Walgers & Assoc., L.A., 1964-70; owner, designer At The Root of Things, L.A., 1970-73; adv. sales pro. dir. Ho. of Nine, L.A., 1973-74; asst. designer MGM Grand, Reno, Nev., 1974-76; designer, office mgr. Von Hausen Studio, L.A., 1976-82; ABC libr. ABC/Cap Cities, L.A., 1982-89; portrait artist Dorian Art Studio, L.A., 1982—. One-man shows include Cookeville, Tenn., 1989, Beverly Hills, Calif., 1991; artist in residence, Cookeville, 1989-90. Republican. Presbyterian.

ROOT, NILE, photographer, educator; b. Denver, Dec. 11, 1926; s. Victor Nile and Ella May (Holaway) R.; student U. Denver, 1968; MS in Instructional Tech., Rochester Inst. Tech., 1978; m. Abigail Barton Brown, Feb. 5, 1960; 1 child, James Michael. Microphotographer, U.S. Dept. Commerce, Fed. Republic Germany, 1946-48; free-lance photographer, 1949-51; pres. Photography Workshop, Inc., Denver, 1952-60; dir. dept. biophotography and med. illustration Gen. Rose Meml. Hosp., Denver, 1960-70; dir. med. illustration dept. Children's Hosp., Denver, 1970-71; dir. Photography for Sci., Denver, 1971-72; prof. biomed. photog. communications Rochester Inst. Tech. (N.Y.), 1972-86 , chmn. dept., 1974-86, prof. emeritus, 1986—; travel writer, photographer, Japan, China, S.E. Asia, 1986-89; writer, photographer, Tucson, 1989—. dir. HEW project for devel. of field, 1974-77. Served with USN, 1945-46. Recipient numerous awards for sci. photographs; Eisenhart Outstanding Tchr. award Rochester Inst. Tech., 1986; 1st Ann. Faculty fellow Sch. Photog. Arts and Scis., Rochester Inst. Tech., 1979. Fellow Biol. Photog. Assn. (registered, bd. govs. 1977-79, Louis Schmidt award 1986); mem. Ctr. Creative Photography, Friends of Photography, Internat. Mus. Photography. Democrat. Contbr. illustrations to med. textbooks; represented in numerous mus. photog. exhibits. Home and Office: 314 N Banff Ave Tucson AZ 85748-3311

ROOT, RICHARD KAY, medical educator; b. N.Y.C., Dec. 1, 1937; s. Raymond Willard and Carolyne Mary (Kay) R.; m. Marilyn Parletta, Mar. 19, 1960; children: Richard Allen, David Lawrence, Daniel Christopher. BA, Wesleyan U., 1959; MD, Johns Hopkins U., 1963; MA, U. Pa., 1973, Yale U., 1975. Resident Mass. Gen. Hosp., Boston, 1963-65, U. Wash., Seattle, 1968-69; sr. investigator Nat. Inst. Allergy and Infectious Disease, NIH, Bethesda, Md., 1969-71; asst. to assoc. prof. medicine U. Pa. Sch. Medicine, Phila., 1971-75; prof. medicine Yale U. Sch. Medicine, New Haven, Conn., 1975-82; prof. medicine U. Wash. Sch. Medicine, Seattle, 1982-85, 91—, vice chair medicine, 1991—; prof. medicine U. Calif., San Francisco, 1985-91; chief of medicine Seattle (Wash.) VA Med. Ctr., 1982-85, Harborview Med. Ctr., Seattle, 1991—; chair of medicine U. Calif. Sch. Medicine, San Francisco, 1985-89, assoc. dean, 1989-91. Editor: (textbook) Harrisony Principles of Internal Medicine, 1990; contbr. chpts. to books and articles to profl. jours. Mem. med. com., bd. dirs. Yale China Assn., New Haven, 1979-82; bd. dirs. Conn. Hospice, Branford, 1981-82. Comdr. USPHS, 1965-69. Recipient Rsch. Career Devel. award NIH, 1975-78. Fellow ACP, Infectious Diseases Soc. Am.; mem. Am. Fedn. Clin. Rsch. (pres. Ea. sect. 1978-79), Am. Soc. Clin. Investigation, Assn. Am. Physicians, Western Assn. Physicians (councilor 1986-89), Soc. Gen. Internal Medicine, Alpha Omega Alpha, Phi Beta Kappa. Home: 6035 78th Ave SE Mercer Island WA 98040 Office: Harborview Med Ctr 325 9th Ave Seattle WA 98104

ROOT, WAYNE ALLYN, television anchor/host; b. Mt. Vernon, N.Y., July 20, 1961; s. David and Stella (Reis) R.; m. Victoria Payne, Sept. 9, 1986 (div. 1990); m. Debra Parks, Aug. 3, 1991; 1 child, Dakota Skye. BA, Columbia U., 1983. Pres. Wayne A. Root & Assocs., Real Estate, White Plains, N.Y., 1983-86; account exec. Bixler Real Estate, Katonah, N.Y., 1986-88; owner Pure Profit Sport Analysis & Handicapping, White Plains, 1987-89; radio host NBC Source Radio Network, N.Y.C., 1988; TV anchorman Fin. News Network, L.A., 1989-91; author, pres. The Universal Frontier, Las Vegas, Nev., 1991—. Author: Root on Risk, 1989; contbg. sports editor Robb Report Mag., 1989-91. Republican. Office: The Universal Frontier Ste 107 6130 West Flamingo Rd Las Vegas NV 89103

ROOT, WILLIAM DIXON, construction company executive; b. Medford, Oreg., July 27, 1951; s. Earl Merrit and Helen Edith (Dixon) R.; m. Catherine Jeanine Smiraglia, July 10, 1981; children: Stacie Marie, Shawn Dixon. BSBA, U. Nev., Reno, 1978. Contr., sec.-treas. Jensen Elec., Inc., Reno, 1977-82; v.p., sec.-treas. Clark & Sullivan, Inc., Reno, 1982—; v.p., asst. sec. G & S Gen. Inc., Reno, 1986—; v.p., sec., treas. Westech Devel., Reno, 1986—, also bd. dirs.; cons. Micro-Tech., Reno, 1984-90. Mem. Am. Coun. for Constrn. Edn., Assn. Systems Mgrs. Constrn. Fin. Mgrs. Assn. (v.p. 1986-88, pres., 1988-90. chmn. 1990—, nat. bd. dirs., nat. chmn. chpt. formation com., exec. com., vice chmn. conf. planning com.), Assn. Gen. Contractors, Sierra Nevada IBM users, Sertoma Club (treas. 1983-88, Centurian award, 1986, Tribune award 1989, Disting Svc. award 1989), Rotary (sgt. arms) Sierra Challenge Athletics Assn.. (treas.). Republican. Home: 2505 Homeland Dr Reno NV 89511-9269 Office: Clark & Sullivan Inc 905 Industrial Way Sparks NV 89431-6009

ROPER, BIRDIE ALEXANDER, social sciences educator; b. New Orleans; d. Earl and Ethel (Charmer) Alexander; m. Morris F. Roper; 1 child, Andree Marie Driskell. BS, U. Dayton, 1949; MA, Azusa Pacific U., 1971, Claremont Grad. Sch., 1978; PhD, Claremont Grad. Sch., 1980. DON Flint Goodridge Hosp., New Orleans, 1954, 55; sch. nurse, health educator, classroom tchr. L.A. Unified Sch. Dist., 1963-91; extended day prof. social scis. dept. Pasadena City Coll., 1972—; clin. instr. dept. nursing Calif. State U., San Bernardino, 1993—; researcher, author, cons. in gerontology. Editor: (newsletter Calif. Nurses Assn.) Vital Signs. Mem. ANA, Am. Soc. Univ. Profs., Am. Soc. on Aging, Inst. for Rsch. on Aging, Nat. Coun. on Aging, Nat. Gerontol. Nursing Assn., Phi Delta Kappa (bd. mem. San Antonio chpt. 1981-92), Alpha Kappa Alpha. Home: 1657 W Sunnyview Dr Rialto CA 92376-1572 Office: Calif State U Dept Nursing San Bernardino CA 92404

ROPER, WALTER WILLIAM, grain cooperative executive; b. American Falls, Idaho, Mar. 31, 1945; s. Allen Dwight and Evelyn Ruth (Schneider) R.; B.A. in Journalism, U. Idaho, 1968; m. Patrica Jo Morgan, June 20, 1970; children—Valorie Jo, Jason William, Alison Evon. Part time elevator operator, Power County Grain Growers, American Falls, summers 1963-68, bookkeeper, 1970, asst. mgr., 1971-76, mgr., sec., treas., 1976-91, sec., treas., 1991—; city, county news reporter, Moscow (Idaho) Daily Idahonian, 1968, Rexburg (Idaho) Standard and Jour., 1969, part time Power County Press, American Falls, 1970-71. Co-chmn. Concerned Citizens for Clean Growth, 1977; VOCA vol., Saratov, Russia, 1993; trustee Am Falls Sch. Dist. #381, 1987-93, chmn., 1991-93. Mem. Grain Elevator and Processors Soc. (v.p. Intermountain chpt. 1982-83, pres. 1983-84), Idaho Feed and Grain Assn. (bd. dirs. Eastern dist. 1982—, bull. editor 1986—, exec. bd. 1987-91, pres. 1990), Farmers Grain Coop. Mgrs. Orgn. (sec., treas. 1976-85, pres. 1985-87, spl. projects mgr. 1991—). Democrat. Methodist. Clubs: American Falls Toastmasters (sec., treas. 1976-77), Tuesday Nighters Bowling League (pres. 1975-76, 76-77, sec., treas. 1977-78, 78-79). Home: 3054 Sunbeam Rd American Falls ID 83211-5415 Office: 138 Elevator Ave American Falls ID 83211

RORK, PETER ERNEST, orthopaedic surgeon; b. Paterson, N.J., May 15, 1953; s. Paul William and Ruth Anna (Buller) R.; m. Squirrel Ciavarella, July 5, 1991; children: Heidi, Cummings, Buller. BA, Rutgers Coll., 1974; MD, U. Md., 1979. Diplomate Am. Bd. Orthopaedic Surgeons. Intern, resident U. N.Mex., 1979-84; orthopaedic surgeon U.S. Ski Team, Jackson Hole, Wyo., 1992—. Hand surgery fellow Good Samaritan Hosp., Phoenix, 1984, knee surgery and aports medicine fellow So. Lake Tahoe, Calif., 1985. Home and Office: PO Box 3537 Jackson WY 83001

ROSA, FREDRIC DAVID, insurance and stockbrokerage executive; b. Monroe, Wis., Oct. 31, 1946; s. Fredric Carl and Irene (Sommers) R.; m. Melanie A. Downs, May 31, 1986; children: Mark, Katherine. BBA in Mktg., U. Wis., 1968. Dir. mktg. Swiss Colony Stores, Inc., Monroe, 1968-80; pres. Videotape Indsl. Prodns., Inc., Madison, Wis., 1980-82; agt. VR Bus. Brokers, Colorado Springs, Colo., 1982-83; sales rep. NCR Corp., Denver, 1983-85; prin. F. D. Rosa & Assocs., Denver and Eagle, Colo., 1985-89; pres. Peak Benefit Cons., Colorado Springs, 1989—; registered prin. Nexus Fin. Programs, Inc., Colorado Springs, Colo., 1990-92, Nutmeg Securities Ltd., Colorado Springs, 1992—; cons. Kolb-Lena Cheese Co., Lena, Ill., 1983-85; instr. The Am. Coll., Bryn Mawr, Pa., 1990-91; owner Rosa Constrn., Colorado Springs, 1990—. Contbr. articles to trade publs. and newspapers. Mem. Am. Soc. CLU and Chartered Fin. Cons., Mensa, Internat. Legion of Intelligence, Delta Sigma Pi (life). Methodist. Home and Office: Peak Benefit Cons and Rosa Constrn 901 Crown Ridge Dr Colorado Springs CO 80904-1733 also: Nutmeg Securities Ltd 405 S Cascade Ave # 102 Colorado Springs CO 80903-9999

ROSALES, DANIEL J., telephone company executive; b. Albuquerque, Sept. 24, 1945; s. Joseph F. and Irene (Garcia) R.; m. Patricia R. Rosales, May 24, 1975; children: Nancy, Ted, George, Kathy. Grad. parochial sch., Albuquerque. Machinist ACF Industries, Albuquerque, 1964-66, Sandia Corp., Albuquerque, 1966-67, Boeing Aircraft, Seattle, 1967-70; technician Mountain Bell, Albuquerque, 1970-75, account exec., 1975-77; product mgr. Mountain Bell, Denver, 1977-82; sales mgr. AT&T, Denver, 1982-86; pres. Nat. Bus. Comm., Denver, 1986-90, Northstar Tel. Systems Inc., Littleton, Colo., 1991—. Career speaker Lincoln High Sch., Denver, 1991—, Jr. Achievement counselor, 1992; del. Colo. Rep. Com., 1992; chmn. signs com. Golden (Colo.) Rep. Com. Mem. Hispanic C. of C., Kiwanis. Home: 6384 S Allison St Littleton CO 80123 Office: Northstar Tel Systems Inc 8250 Coal Mine Ste 13 Littleton CO 80123

ROSANDER, ARLYN CUSTER, mathematical statistician, management consultant; b. Mason County, Mich., Oct. 7, 1903; s. John Carl and Nellie May (Palmer) R.; m. Beatrice White, Aug. 26, 1933 (div.); children: Nancy Rosander Peck, Robert Richard Roger (dec.); m. Margaret Ruth Guest, Aug. 15, 1964. BS, U. Mich. 1925; MA, U. Wis., 1928; PhD, U. Chgo., 1933; postgrad. Dept. Agr., 1937-39. Rsch. asst. U. Chgo., 1933-34; rsch. fellow Gen. Edn. Bd. Tech. dir. Am. Youth Commn., Balt. and Washington, 1935-37; chief statistician urban study U.S. Bur. Labor Stats., Washington, 1937-39; sect. and br. chief War Prodn. Bd., Washington, 1940-45; chief statistician IRS, Washington, 1945-61; chief math. and stats. sect. ICC, Washington, 1961-69; cons. Pres.'s Commn. on Fed. Stats., Washington, 1970-71; cons., Loveland, Colo.; lectr. stats. George Washington U., 1946-52. Recipient Civilian War Service award War Prodn. Bd., 1945; Spl. Performance award Dept. Treasury, 1961. Fellow AAAS, Am. Soc. Quality Control (25 yr. honor award 1980, Howard Jones Meml. award 1984, chmn. emeritus svc. industries divsn. 1991); mem. Am. Statis. Assn. Author: Elementary Principles of Statistics, 1951; Statistical Quality Control in Tax Operations, IRS, 1958; Case Studies in Sample Design, 1977; Application of Quality Control to Service Industries, 1985, Washington Story 1985, The Quest for Quality in Services, 1989, Deming's 14 Points Applied to Services, 1991. Home and Office: 4330 Franklin Ave Loveland CO 80538-1715

ROSBOROUGH, BRADLEY JAMES, health care company executive; b. Long Beach, Calif., Mar. 12, 1958; s. James Fears Jr. and Norma Jean (Branscum) R.; m. Elyse Renee Shapiro, May 24, 1987. BA, Johns Hopkins U., 1980; M in Mgmt., Northwestern U., 1983. Cons. Md. Individual Practice Assn., Inc., Rockville, Md., 1980-81; sr. cons. Ernst & Whinney, Chgo., 1983-84; mgr. Arthur Young, L.A., 1984-88; dir. fin. analysis FHP, Inc., Fountain Valley, Calif., 1988-92, assoc. v.p. analysis and devel., 1992—. Mem. Healthcare Fin. Mgmt. Assn., Am. Hosp. Assn. Presbyterian. Office: FHP Internat 9900 Talbert Ave Fountain Valley CA 92708-5153

ROSE, DAVID WILLIAM, psychologist, consultant; b. Denver, Oct. 14, 1930; s. Clarence William and Marjorie (Skiff) R.; m. Ruth MacDonald, Dec. 27, 1957 (div. Jan. 1967); children: Scott David, Frederick William, Catharine Jean Hayes; m. Lorretta Espinosa, Oct. 5, 1973; 1 child, Janet Kathleen. BA, U. Colo., 1953; MS, U. Oreg., 1959, PhD, 1964. Lic. clin. psychologist, Colo. Psychologist trainee VA, Roseburg, Oreg., 1958-59, Vancouver, Wash., 1960-61; rsch. asst. U. Oreg., Eugene, 1961-62; clin. trainee USPHS, Eugene, 1962-63; from clin. psychologist to chief psychologist forensic div. Colo. State Hosp., Pueblo, 1963-90; ret., 1990, pvt. practice, , 1990—. Mem. APA, Colo. Psychol. Assn., Rocky Mountain Psychol. Assn., Am. Psychology-Law Soc., Am. Soc. Criminology, Am. Correctional Assn., Orgn. for Program Evaluation in Colo. Home: 627 Westacres St Pueblo CO 81005-1748 Office: 502 Jackson St Pueblo CO 81004-1834

ROSE, GREGORY MANCEL, neurobiologist; b. Eugene, Oreg., Feb. 3, 1953; s. Mancel Lee and Ilione (Schenk) R.; m. Kathleen Ann Frye, June 30, 1979; 1 child, Julian Mancel. BS cum laude, U. Calif., Irvine, 1975, PhD, 1980. Research fellow M.P.I. for Psychiatry, Munich, 1976; rsch. assoc. Miescher Labor, M.P.I., Tuebingen, Republic of Germany, 1980-81; regular fellow dept. pharmacology U. Colo. Health Sci. Ctr., Denver, 1981-84, asst. prof., 1984-89, assoc. prof., 1989—; rsch. biologist VA Med. Ctr., Denver, 1981—, co-dir. neurosci. tng. program, 1986-89, assoc. rsch. career scientist, 1989—. Achievements include discovery of importance of stimulus patterning for induction of hippocampal synaptic plasticity. Bd. dirs. Greater Park Hill Community, 1987-90. VA Rsch. Svc. grantee, 1984, 86, 89, 93, NSF grantee, 1988, 90, NIMH grantee, 1989, NIA grantee, 1991. Mem. AAAS, Am. Aging Assn., Soc. Neurosci., Am. Psychol. Soc., Internat. Brain Rsch. Orgn., Soc. Neurosci., N.Y. Acad. Sci. Democrat. Episcopalian. Office: VA Med Ctr Rsch Svc 1055 Clermont St # 151 Denver CO 80220-3873

ROSE, JERALD LYLE, truck repair shop owner; b. Reedsport, Oreg., June 1, 1935; s. Murle Leo and Esther M. (Brandon) R.; m. Dora Mae Brooks, Sept. 9, 1956; children: Traci Lee, Trina Dee. BS, Linfield Coll., McMinnville, Oreg., 1960. Owner, v.p. Mid Lane Truck & Equipment Repair, Eugene, Oreg., 1985—. With U.S. Army, 1954-56, Germany. Office: Mid Lane Truck & Equipment Repair 4237 W 5th Ave Eugene OR 97402

ROSE, LAURA POWELL, author; b. San Francisco, Aug. 9, 1942; d. Francis DeValera Belton and Barbara Jean (Malloch) Hahn; m. Arthur Gilbert Powell, Jan. 1, 1990; 1 child, David Belton Powell. BA summa cum laude, San Francisco State U., 1965; BS, U. Oreg., 1987. Life credential elem. educator, adminstr. Tchr. Laguna Salada Sch. Dist., Pacifica, Calif., 1966-67, Ferndale (Calif.) Elem. Sch., 1967-68; instr. Humboldt State U., Arcata, Calif., 1985—; teaching methods instr. Humboldt County Office of Edn., Eureka, Calif., 1983—; tchr. Pacific Union Elem. Sch., Arcata, 1968-91; edn. cons. in English. Author: (tchr. manual) Picture This, 1989, Picture This for Beginning Readers, 1991, Folktales, 1992, Write to Read and Spell, 1993. Youth choir leader Christ Episcopal Ch., Eureka, 1980-92; music dir. Humbold Redwood Cursillo, Eureka, 1990-92. Mem. Delta Kappa Gamma. Home and Office: 11 Randolph St Eureka CA 95503

ROSE, ROBERT E., state supreme court justice; b. Orange, N.J., Oct. 7, 1939. B.A., Juniata Coll., Huntingdon, Pa., 1961; LL.B., NYU, 1964. Bar: Nev. 1965. Dist. atty. Washoe County, 1971-75; lt. gov. State of Nev., 1975-79; judge Nev. Dist. Ct., 8th Jud. Dist., Las Vegas, 1986-88; justice Nev. Supreme Ct., Carson City, 1989—, chief justice, 1993—. Office: Nev Supreme Ct 100 N Carson St Carson City NV 89710-0001

ROSE, ROBERT LEON, retired geology educator; b. San Francisco, Sept. 3, 1920; s. Leon Guy and Jenny May (Maude) R.; m. Hazel Bernice Richardson, July 12, 1942; children: David Alan, Judith Lynne, Donald Eugene. AB, U. Calif., Berkeley, 1948, MA, 1949, PhD, 1957. Geologist Shell Oil Co., Calif., 1949-53; assoc. in geology U. Calif., Berkeley, 1953-56; acting asst. prof. geology Stanford (Calif.) U., 1956-57; asst. econ. geologist Nev. Bur. of Mine, Reno, 1957-59; from asst. prof. to prof. geology San Jose (Calif.) State U., 1959-84, emeritus prof. geology, 1984—; geologist U.S. Forest Svc., Calif., 1962-72, Abbot Hanks, Inc., San Francisco, 1962-65, Hales Testing Labs., Oakland, Calif., 1966-82, Bechtel Corp, San Francisco, 1971-80, Chevron Oil, San Francisco, 1973-79. Fellow Geol. Soc. Am.; mem. Am. Assn. Petroleum Geologists, Mineral. Soc. Am., Nat. Assn. Geology Tchrs. Home: 1080 Los Viboras Rd Hollister CA 95023-9416

ROSE, ROBERT PAUL, writer, composer; b. Galveston, Tex., June 28, 1966; s. David E. and Lilias K. (Kincaid) R.; m. Nancy Elizabeth Hyer, Dec. 4, 1992. Student, No. Tex. State U., 1984-86, U. Dallas, 1986-87. Composer Dallas Theatre Orgn., 1985-87; writer/composer various orgns., L.A., 1987—. Author: (play) My Time, 1989, MM, 1991, An Evening of Short Play, 1992. Republican.

ROSE, ROBERT R., JR., lawyer; b. Evanston, Ill., Nov. 1, 1915; s. Robert R. and Eleanor B. R.; m. Kathryn Lorraine Warner, June 14, 1948; children: Robert R. III, Cynthia Ann. JD, U. Wyo., 1941. Bar: Wyo. bar 1941. Atty. Dept. Justice, 1941; with UNRRA, China; asst. sec. Dept. Interior, 1951-52; sr. partner firm Rose, Spence, Dobos and Duncan, Casper, Wyo., 1968-75; justice Wyo. Supreme Ct., 1975-85, chief justice, 1981-82; assoc. Spence, Moriarity and Schuster, Cheyenne, Wyo., 1985—; organizer, past pres., chmn. bd. Title Guaranty Co. Wyo; faculty Nat. Coll. Criminal Def., 1977-90; founder, instr. Western Trial Advocacy Inst., 1977-93; vis. prof. trial practice U. Wyo. Coll. Law, 1985-86; Milward Simpson chair in polit. sci. U. Wyo., 1985-86; founder Western Trial Advocacy Inst., 1977—. Author legal articles. Past chmn. fund drive Casper Community Chest, Am. Cancer Soc.; mem. Wyo. Ho. of Reps., 1949-51; mayor of, Casper, 1950-51; past trustee Casper Coll. Served with USAAF, World War II. Recipient Jud. Achievement award Nat. Assn. Criminal Def. Lawyers, 1983. Mem. Am. Law Inst., Order of the Coif (hon.), Land and Water L. Rev. (bd. advs.). Episcopalian. Address: PO Box 1006 Cheyenne WY 82003

ROSEHNAL, MARY ANN, educational administrator; b. Bklyn., July 25, 1943; d. Frank Joseph and Mary Anna (Corso) R.; 1 child, Scott Stoddart. BA in Sociology, San Francisco State U., 1968; M in Sch. Bus. Adminstrn., No. Ariz. U., 1985. Lic. substitute tchr., Ariz.; lic. vocat. nurse, Calif.; cert. sch. bus. mgr., Ariz. Deliquency counselor, Calif., 1969-73; office mgr. Nurses Central Registry, Sun City, Ariz., 1973-75; bus. mgr. Nadaburg sch. dist., Wittmann, Ariz., 1975-78, Morristown (Ariz.) sch. dist., 1978—; served on 1st Assessment Handbook editing task force, Fair Employment Practices Handbook task force, 1979-80. Columnist Wickenburg Sun, 1975—. Clk. Morristown sch. bd., 1974-76; pres. Morristown PTA, 1977-78; sec. Wickenburg area bd., 1979; bd. dirs. Future Frontiers, 1979-81; rep. HUD block grant adv. com., 1979-85; active Wickenburg Friends of Music, 1984—, sec. of bd. dirs., 1986-92; sec. Wickenburg Regional Health Care Found., 1989-92, trustee, 1988—. Named to Ariz. Sch. Bd. Assn. Honor Roll, 1976; named Morristown Area Vol. of Yr., 1988. Mem. Assn. Govt. Accts., Ariz. Assn. Sch. Bus. Ofcls. (fin. dir., bd. dirs. 1985-91, v.p. 1991, pres. elect 1992-93, pres. 1993-94, Gold awards 1986, 87, 88, 90, 91, 92, Silver award 1989), Assn. Sch. Bus. Ofcls. Internat., Morristown Federated Women's Club (edn. chair 1990-93, Wickenburg scenic corridor com. 1990-92), Ariz. Theatre Guild, Wickenberg C. of C. (assoc.). Roman Catholic. Office: PO Box 98 Morristown AZ 85342-0098

ROSELL, SHARON LYNN, physics and chemistry educator, researcher; b. Wichita, Kans., Jan. 6, 1948; d. John E. and Mildred C. (Binder) R. BA, Loretto Heights Coll., 1970; postgrad., Marshall U., 1973; MS in Edn., Ind. U., 1977; MS, U. Wash., 1988. Cert. profl. educator, Wash. Assoc. instr. Ind. U., Bloomington, 1973-74; instr. Pierce Coll. (name formerly Ft. Steilacoom (Wash.) Community Coll.), 1976-79, 82, Olympic Coll., Bremerton, Wash., 1977-78; instr. physics, math. and chemistry Tacoma (Wash.) Community Coll., 1979-89; instr. physics and chemistry Green River Community Coll., Auburn, Wash., 1983-86; researcher Nuclear Physics Lab., U. Wash., Seattle, 1986-88; asst. prof. physics Cen. Wash. U., Ellensburg, 1989—. Mem. Math. Assn. Am., Am. Assn. Physics Tchrs. (rep. com. on physics for 2-yr. colls. Wash. chpt. 1986-87, v.p. 1987-88, pres. 1988-89), Am. Chem. Soc., Internat. Union Pure and Applied Chemistry (affiliate). Democrat. Roman Catholic. Home: RR 5 Box 880 Ellensburg WA 98926-9379 Office: Cen Wash U Physics Dept Ellensburg WA 98926

ROSEMAN, CHARLES SANFORD, lawyer; b. Jersey City, Feb. 26, 1945; s. Leon and Edith (Neidorf) R.; m. Jodyne Florence Snyder, July 3, 1967; children: Rochelle Lynn, Loren Scott. BA, Calif. State U., 1968; JD, U. San Diego, 1971. Bar: Calif. 1972, U.S. Dist. Ct. (so. dist.) Calif. 1972, U.S. Dist. Ct. (cen. dist.) Calif. 1975, U.S. Supreme Ct. 1980, U.S. Ct. Fed. Claims, 1990. Assoc. Greer, Popko, Nickoloff & Miller, San Diego, 1972-73; ptnr. Roseman & Roseman, San Diego, 1973-78, Roseman & Small, San Diego, 1978-82, Frank, Roseman, Freedus & Mann, San Diego, 1982-86; Roseman and Mann, 1986-92, Law Offices Charles S. Roseman & Assocs., San Diego, 1992—; judge pro tem San Diego County Mcpl. Ct., 1975—; San Diego County Superior Ct., 1977—; also arbitrator. Pres. Tifereth Israel Synagogue, San Diego, 1981-83; bd. dirs. Glenn Aire Community Devel. Assn., San Diego, 1972-73, Big Bros. San Diego County, 1973-81; bd. dirs. San Diego County Anti-Defamation League, 1981-83, chmn. exec. com., 1984-85, assoc. nat. commr., 1991—; bd. dirs. San Diego County Legal Aid Soc., 1988-89, Tifereth Israel Synagogue (pres. 1982-84). Mem. Assn. Trial Lawyers Am., ABA, Calif. Trial Lawyers Assn. (Recognition of Experience award 1984—), Calif. Bar Assn., Am. Arbitration Assn. (arbitrator, panel 1980—), San Diego Bar Assn., San Diego Trial Lawyers Assn. (bd. dirs. 1982-84), U. San Diego Sch. Law Alumni Assn. (bd. dirs. 1972-73). Democrat. Lodge: B'nai B'rith (pres. 1978). Office: Law Offices Charles S Roseman & Assocs 401 W A St Ste 2350 San Diego CA 92101-7999

ROSEN, ALEXANDER CARL, psychologist, consultant; b. L.A., Feb. 2, 1923; s. Benjamin and Pauline (Katz) R.; m. Florence Friedman, Mar. 18, 1951 (div. Nov. 1973); children: Diane, Judith; m. Susan Margaret Gersbacher, Nov. 4, 1973; 1 child, Rebecca. AA, U. Calif., L.A., 1943; AB, U. Calif., Berkeley, 1946, PhD, 1953. Diplomate clin. psychology Am. Bd. Profl. Psychology; lic. psychologist. Psychologist Contra Costa County, Martinez, Calif., 1953-56; asst. rsch. psychologist Office Naval Rsch. and San Francisco State Coll., 1953-56, UCLA-Neuropsychiat. Inst., L.A., 1956-57; asst. prof. to prof. psychiatry and behavioral sci. UCLA Sch. Medicine, L.A., 1956-89; chief psychology UCLA Neuropsychiatric Inst., L.A., 1958-89; prof. emeritus UCLA Sch. Medicine, L.A., 1989—; pvt. practice psychology cons. L.A., 1973—; instr. San Francisco State Coll., 1955; instr. psychology Calif. Inst. Tech., Pasadena, 1969; staff assoc. Nat. Tng. Lab. Inst. Applied Behavioral Sci., 1962—; cons. tng. U.S. Veteran's Assn., Sepulveda (Calif.) Hosp., 1966—; bd. mem. L.A. Group Psychotherapy Tng. Inst., 1972-75; bd. mem., trustee Calif. Sch. Profl. Psychology, 1974-76, 78; nat. bd., regional bd. Cert. Cons. Internat. Cons. Cons. editor: Jour. Genetic Psychology and Genetic Psychology Monograph, 1984—; contbr. articles to profl. jours. Mem. gov. bd. Hillel Coun., So. Calif.; cons. San Fernando Valley Counseling Ctr., 1991-92, Pacific Ctr. for AIDS, L.A., 1991—. Fellow APA, AAAS; mem. Calif. State Psychology Assn. (pres. 1977-78), Western Psychol. Assn. Home: 3625 Beverly Ridge Dr Sherman Oaks CA 91423 Office: Ste 408 4419 Van Nuys Blvd Sherman Oaks CA 91403

ROSEN, DAVID ALLEN, manufacturing executive; b. Anchorage, Aug. 4, 1955; s. Harold E. and Marlene (Allen) R.; m. Phyllis A. Romans, Aug. 19, 1980; children: Stephanie, Kevin, Stanford, Alex, Samuel, Kimberly. BS in Bus., Brigham Young U., 1980; MBA, U. Utah, 1990. Coord. Youth Devel. Enterprises, Salt Lake City, 1978-79; instr. Brigham Young U., Provo, 1980; v.p., loan officer Key Bank of Utah, Salt Lake City, 1980-92; dir. of mfg. Larson-Davis Labs., Provo, 1992—. Mem. fin. com. Greater Salt Lake City Area, YMCA, 1987-91. Mem. Brigham Young U. Mgmt. Soc., Kiwanis (pres. 1990-91). Mem. LDS Ch. Home: 124 E 3800 N Provo UT 84604 Office: Larson Davis Labs 1681 W 820 N Provo UT 84601

ROSEN, GEORGE M., aircraft rental company executive; b. 1936. BS, U. Ill., 1958; JD, Northwestern U., 1961; LLM, Georgetown U., 1967. With IRS; formerly exec. v.p. Mc Donnell Douglas Fin. Corp., Long Beach, Calif., now pres. With AUS, 1961-67. Office: McDonnell Douglas Fin Corp 340 Golden Shore St Long Beach CA 90802-4249

ROSEN, JEFFREY ARNOLD, accountant; b. Van Nuys, Calif., Nov. 28, 1961; s. Alan M. and Linda B. (Gellman) R. BS in Acctg. Theory and Practice, Calif. State U., Northridge, 1983, MS in Acctg. with distinction, 1985. CPA, Calif. Sr. mgr. Ernst & Young, L.A., 1985—. Mem. AICPA, Calif. Soc. CPAs, Calif. State U. Northridge Acctg. Alumni Assn. (pres. 1991-93), Beta Alpha Psi (pres. Calif. State U. Northridge chpt. 1984, exec. advisor 1985). Office: Ernst & Young # 2100 1999 Ave of the Stars Los Angeles CA 90067

ROSEN, JON HOWARD, lawyer; b. Bklyn., May 20, 1943; s. Eli and Vera (Horowitz) R.; m. Georgeanne Evans, 1993; children of a previous marriage: Jason Marc, Hope Terry. BA, Hobart Coll., 1965; JD, St. John's U., 1968; postgrad. Bernard Baruch Sch. Bus., CCNY, 1969-71. Bar: N.Y. 1969, Calif. 1975, Wash. 1977. Atty. FAA, N.Y.C., 1968-71; regional atty., contract adminstr. Air Line Pilots Assn., N.Y.C., Chgo., L.A., San Francisco, 1971-77; pvt. practice Seattle, 1977-80; ptnr. Frank and Rosen, Seattle, 1981—; instr. labor studies Shoreline Community Coll., 1978—. Mem. ABA (union co-chmn. com. on Employee Rights and Responsibilities, regional EEOC liaison, union co-chmn. employee rights and responsibilities com.), Am. Fedn. Tchrs., Seattle-King County Bar Assn. (past chmn. aviation and space law sect., past chmn. Pacific Coast Labor Law Conf., past chmn. labor law sect.), Nat. Employment Lawyers Assn. (state co-chair), Nat. Transp. Safety Bd. Bar Assn. Home: 335 Ward St Seattle WA 98109 Office: Frank & Rosen 705 2d Ave # 1200 Seattle WA 98104

ROSEN, MARTIN JACK, lawyer; b. L.A., Sept. 9, 1931; s. Irving and Sylvia (Savad) R.; B.A., UCLA, 1953; J.D., U. Calif.-Berkeley, 1956; m. Joan D. Meyersieck, Oct. 22, 1954; children—Dirk Rosen, Marika. Bar: Calif. 1957. Pvt. practice, Merced, Calif., 1960-62, San Francisco, 1962-82; mem. Silver, Rosen, Fischer & Stecher, P.C., San Francisco, 1964—. Pres. Trust for Pub. Land, 1979—. Served with USAF, 1958-60. Fellow internat. legal studies U. Calif. Law Sch./Inst. Social Studies, The Hague, 1956-57.

ROSEN, MARVIN JEROLD, communications and computer educator; b. L.A., Sept. 11, 1929; s. Joseph and Gertrude (Rhodeside) R.; m. Ruth Seagal, Apr. 14, 1955; children: Stephen Dennis, Jennifer Lynn, Joseph Allan. Student, U. Chgo., 1946-47; BS, U. Minn., 1951; MA, UCLA, 1958, EdD, 1968. Dir. Kansas City (Mo.) Resident Theater, 1956-58; dir. cultural arts U.S. Army, Nurnberg, Fed. Republic Germany, 1958-61; dir. Circle Arts Theater, San Diego, 1961-63; prof., adminstr. U. Calif., Santa Cruz and L.A., 1965-70; prof. communications Calif. State U., Fullerton, 1970—; instr. computer sci. Calif. Community Coll., Mission Viejo and Santa Ana, 1985—; vis. lectr. Towson (Md.) State U., 1976-77; vis. prof. Western Australian Inst. Tech., Perth, 1978-80; cons. Australian Commonwealth Schs. Commn., Perth, 1978-80; sole proprietor Omega Microwave Svcs., San Juan Capistrano, Calif., 1980—. Author: Introduction to Photography, 1974, 5th edit., 1993, (software) Basic Writing Skills, 1984; contbr. articles to profl. jours. Sgt. USAF, 1951-52. Rsch. grantee U.S. Dhew Office Edn., 1968. Mem. Phi Delta Kappa. Office: Calif State U Dept Communications Fullerton CA 92631

ROSEN, MOISHE, religious organization administrator; b. Kansas City, Mo., Apr. 12, 1932; s. Ben and Rose (Baker) R.; m. Ceil Starr, Aug. 18, 1950; children: Lyn Rosen Bond, Ruth. Diploma, Northeastern Bible Coll., 1957; DD, Western Conservative Bapt. Sem., 1986. Ordained to ministry Bapt. Ch., 1957. Missionary Am. Bd. Missions to the Jews, N.Y.C., 1956; minister in charge Beth Sar Shalom Am. Bd. Missions to the Jews, Los Angeles, 1957-67; dir. recruiting and tng. Am. Bd. Missions to the Jews, N.Y.C., 1967-70; leader Jews for Jesus Movement, San Francisco, 1970-73, exec. dir., 1973—, founder, chmn., 1973—; speaker in field. Author: Saying of Chairman Moishe, 1972, Jews for Jesus, 1974, Share the New Life with a Jew, 1976, Christ in the Passover, 1977, Y'shua, The Jewish Way to Say Jesus, 1982, Overture to Armageddon, 1991, The Universe is Broken: Who on Earth Can Fix It?, 1991, Demystifying Personal Evangelism, 1992. Trustee Western Conservative Bapt. Sem., Portland, Oreg., 1979-85, 86-91, Bibl. Internat. Coun. on Bibl. Inerrancy, Oakland, Calif., 1979-89; bd. dirs. Christian Advs. Serving Evangelism, 1987-91. Office: Jews for Jesus 60 Haight St San Francisco CA 94102-5895

ROSEN, SANFORD JAY, lawyer; b. N.Y.C., Dec. 19, 1937; s. Alexander Charles and Viola S. (Grad) R.; m. Catherine Picard, June 22, 1958; children: Caren E. Andrews, R. Durelle Schacter, Ian D., Melissa S. AB, Cornell U., 1959; LLB, Yale U., 1962. Bar: Conn. 1962, U.S. Supreme Ct. 1966, D.C. 1973, Calif. 1974. Law clk. to Hon. Simon E. Sobeloff U.S. Ct. Appeals, Balt., 1962-63; prof. sch. law U. Md., Balt., 1963-71; assoc. dir. Coun. on Legal Edn. Opportunity, Atlanta, 1969-70; vis. prof. law U. Tex., Austin, 1970-71; asst. legal dir. ACLU, N.Y.C., 1971-73; legal dir. Mex.-Am. Legal Def. Fund, San Francisco, 1973-75; ptnr. Rosen, Remcho & Henderson, San Francisco, 1976-80, Rosen & Remcho, San Francisco, 1980-82; prin. Law Offices of Sanford Jay Rosen, San Francisco, 1982-86; sr. ptnr. Rosen & Phillips, San Francisco, 1986-89; prin. Rosen & Assocs., San Francisco, 1990; sr. ptnr. Rosen, Bien & Asaro, San Francisco, 1991—; commr. Balt. Community Rels. Commn., 1966-69; mem. com. Patuxent Instn., Balt., 1967-69; ad hoc adminstrv. judge Calif. Agrl. Labor Rels. Bd., San Francisco, 1975-80; interim monitor U.S. Dist. Ct. (no. dist.) Calif., San Francisco, 1989. Contbr. articles to profl. jours. Mem. Com. on Adminstrn. of Criminal Justice, Balt., 1968; mem. adv. com. HEW, Washington, 1974-75; early neutral evaluator U.S. Dist. Ct. (no. dist.) Calif., San Francisco, 1987—; judge pro tem San Francisco Superior Ct., 1991—; lectr. Balt. State Attys., 1965. Mem. ABA, ATLA (Calif.), D.C. Bar Assn., Calif. Bar Assn., Bar Assn. of San Francisco, Calif. Attys. for Criminal Justice. Office: Rosen Bien & Asaro 155 Montgomery St Fl 8 San Francisco CA 94104-4105

ROSENBAUM, JEAN, fitness physician, health association executive; b. Cottondale, Fla., Mar. 27, 1927; s. Isaac and Lena (Braxton) R.; m. Veryl Ellis, Oct. 1961; 1 child, Marc. BA cum laude, Wayne State U., 1950, MD cum laude, 1954; PSA, Goddard Coll., Plainfield, Vt., 1960; DD, Universal Life Ch., Modesto, Calif., 1965. Cert. fitness and aerobic instr.; bd. cert. psychoanalyst. Intern, then resident Detroit Meml. Hosp., 1954-55; resident Detroit Receiving Hosp., 1955-58; rsch. asst. dept. neurophysiology Wayne State U. Coll. Medicine, Detroit, 1951-54, instr., 1957-63; ret., 1980; dir. Am. Aerobic Assn., Durango, Colo., 1980-90, Am. Fitness Assn., Durango, 1987—; pvt. practice Mich., N.Mex., Colo., 1955-80; mem. field faculty Goddard Coll., 1973-77; liaison President's Coun. on Phys. Fitness and Sports, 1982—; lectr. aerobic confs., workshops, seminars, and colls. through U.S.; cons. in field; mem. adv. bd. The Aerobic Way, Aerobic Pipeline, Princeton Aerobic Program; advisor team aerobic dance devel. com. AAU, 1987; tech. advisor Women's Sports and Fitness mag. Author 18 books; contbr. over 500 articles to profl. jours.; contbg. editor Profl. Nurse's Quar. With USNR, 1944-46, PTO. Recipient rsch. award Wayne State U. Alumni Assn., 1955, Max Thorek award for invention cardiac pacemaker, 1955; his artificial cardiac pacemaker in permanent collection Smithsonian Instn.; fellow Nat. Polio Found., 1952-53. Mem. ASTM (chmn. task force for aerobic footwear 1985-90, task force for aerobic surfaces 1988-90). Home: 6317 Florida Rd Durango CO 81301-8414

ROSENBAUM, MICHAEL FRANCIS, securities dealer; b. N.Y.C., Feb. 9, 1959; s. Francis Fels Jr. and Joyce (Keefer) R.; m. Elika Sosnick, Mar. 8, 1986; children: Erin Sosnick, Sarah Greer. AB, Princeton U., 1981. Cert. Nat. Assn. Securities Dealers. Product mgr. Sutro & Co., Inc., San Francisco, 1981-84; v.p. sales Pacific Securities, San Francisco, 1984-89; v.p., br. mgr. Rauscher Pierce Resfnes, San Francisco, 1989-92; v.p. sales Smith Mitchell Investment Group, San Francisco, 1992—; bd. dirs. S.G. Rosenbaum Found., N.Y.C. Patroller Nat. Ski Patrol, Northstar, Calif., 1988. Democrat. Jewish. Home: PO Box 1104 Ross CA 94957-1104

ROSENBERG, ALEX, mathematician, educator; b. Berlin, Germany, Dec. 5, 1926; came to U.S., 1949, naturalized, 1959; s. Theodore and Rela (Banet) R.; m. Beatrice Gershenson, Aug. 24, 1952 (div. Apr. 1985); children: Theodore Joseph, David Michael, Daniel Alex; m. Brunhilde Angun, June 14, 1985. B.A., U. Toronto, 1948, M.A., 1949; Ph.D., U. Chgo., 1951. From instr. to assoc. prof. math. Northwestern U., 1952-61; prof. math. Cornell U., Ithaca, N.Y., 1961-88; chmn. dept. Cornell U., 1966-69; prof., chmn. dept. U Calif., Santa Barbara, 1986-87, prof., 1987—; mem. com. undergrad. program math. Math Assn. Am., 1966-76; mem. Inst. Advanced Study, 1955-57; vis. prof. U. Calif., Berkely, 1961, 1979, U. Calif., Los Angeles, 1969-70, 82, U. London, Queen Mary Coll., 1963-64, U. Munich, 1975-76, E.T.H Zurich, 1976, U. Dortmund, 1984-85; trustee Am. Math Soc., 1973-83. Editor: Proc. Am. Math. Soc., 1960-66, Am. Math. Monthly, 1974-77; Contbr. articles to profl. jours. Recipient Humboldt Stiftung Sr. U.S. Scientist award U. Munich, 1975-76, U. Dortmund, 1981. Mem. Math. Assn. Am. Home: 1225 Plaza del Monte Santa Barbara CA 93101 Office: U Calif Dept Math South Hall Santa Barbara CA 93101

ROSENBERG, DAN YALE, retired plant pathologist; b. Stockton, Calif., Jan. 8, 1922; s. Meyer and Bertha (Naliboff) R.; A.A., Stockton Jr. Coll., 1942; A.B., Coll. Pacific, 1949; M.S., U. Calif. at Davis, 1952; m. Marilyn Kohn, Dec. 5, 1954; 1 son, Morton Karl. Jr. plant pathologist Calif. Dept. Agr., Riverside, 1952-55, asst. plant pathologist, 1955-59, assoc. plant pathologist, 1959-60, pathologist IV, 1960-63, program supr., 1963-71, chief exclusion and detection, div. plant industry, 1971-76, chief nursery and seed services div. plant industry, 1976-82, spl. asst. div. plant industry, 1982-87; pres. Health, Inc., 1972-73; agrl. cons., 1988—; mem. Gov.'s Interagy. Task Force on Biotech., 1986—; bd. dirs. Health Inc., Sacramento, 1967, pres., 1971-72, 79-81, 81-83. Served with AUS, 1942-46; ETO. Mem. Am. Phytopath. Soc. (fgn. and regulatory com. 1975—, grape diseases sect. 1977-79, grape pests sect. 1979-84), Calif. State Employees Assn. (pres. 1967-69). Contbr. articles to profl. jours. Home and Office: 2328 Swarthmore Dr Sacramento CA 95825-6867

ROSENBERG, EVA, taxation professional; b. Budapest, Hungary, Mar. 5, 1953; came to U.S., 1962; d. Tibor and Irene (Aranka) R. Student, UCLA, 1971-72; BA in Acctg., Calif. State U., Fullerton, 1977, MBA in Internat. Bus., 1982. Acct. Ernst and Whinney, CPAs, Newport Beach, Calif., 1978, Lester Witte and Co. CPAs, Newport Beach, 1978-79; contr. Huntington Investments, Huntington Beach, Calif., 1980-84; dir. Ind. Rsch. Svcs., Irvine, Calif., 1980-92, House Guests USA, Inc., Huntington Beach, 1983-92; tax mgr. Demetriou, Montano & Assoc., Tax Problem Specialists, Santa Monica, Calif., 1990—; isntr. IRS spl. exam. rev. course UCLA Ext., 1992—. Author: Tax Anxiety Experience, 1985; co-author: Tax Guide for Educators, 1986; contbr. to profl. publs. Treas. Friends of L.A. Commn. on Status of Women, 1987-92. Mem. NAFE (dir. 1985-92), South Coast Assn. Female Execs. (pres. 1985-92), Calif. Soc. Enrolled Agents (state dir. 1990-91, 92-93), bd. dirs. San Fernando Valley chpt. 1987-93), Book Publicists Soc. Calif. Jewish. Office: Ind Rsch Svc PO Box 2426 Van Nuys CA 91404-2426

ROSENBERG, HOWARD ALAN, manufacturing executive; b. N.Y.C., Nov. 2, 1927; s. Nathan and Anna (Bernstein) R.; m. Carol Hirsch, Feb. 21, 1951; children: Ellen Sue, Robin Jill, Ira Scott. BS, L.I. U., 1949; MA, NYU, 1951. Registered profl. engr. Jr. engr. Wright Aeronaut. Corp., Woodridge, N.J., 1950-52; quality engr. Fairchild Engine Div., Farmingdale, N.Y., 1952-55; quality control mgr. Burndy Corp., Norwalk, Conn., 1955-60; reliability mgr. LFE Corp., Boston, 1960-64; reliability dir. AIL-Cutler Hammer, Comack, N.Y., 1964-69; pres. Western Tech. Assocs., Anaheim, Calif., 1969-80, chief exec. officer, chmn. bd., 1980—; chmn. Printed Cir. Inst. Irvine Valley Coll.; cons. in field; instr. at various colls. Contbr. articles to profl. jours. Chmn. Anti-Defamation League, Santa Ana, Calif., 1984-86, nat. commr.; pres. Orange County Jewish Community Ctr., 1989. 1st lt. infantry USNG, 1949-54. Recipient ADL Civic Commitment award, 1991. Mem. Am. Soc. Quality Control, Calif. Circuits Assn. (bd. dirs. 1970-75), Am. Electroplaters Soc., Am. Legion, Jewish War Vets, Israel Bond Com. (co-chair), Jewish Nat. Fund (com. mem.), B'nai B'rith (mem. youth orgn.). Home: 13592 Carroll Way Tustin CA 92680-1805 Office: Western Tech Assocs 2897 E La Cresta Ave Anaheim CA 92806-1817

ROSENBERG, NEIL LLOYD, neurologist; b. Chgo., July 1, 1954; s. Charles B. and Helen (Deitchman) R.; m. Laura J. Watt, Sept. 17, 1977; children: Philip, Rachel. BS in Physiol. Psychology, U. Ill., 1976; MD, Chgo. Med. Sch., 1978. Intern and resident in internal medicine Cook County Hosp., Chgo., 1978-79; resident in neurology Oreg. Health Scis. U., Portland, 1979-82; fellow neuromuscular diseases U. Colo. Sch. Medicine, Denver, 1982-83, asst. prof., 1983-89; neurologist Denver Gen. Hosp., 1983-86; from assoc. investigator to rsch. assoc. VA Med. Ctr., Denver, 1983-89; med. dir. Ctr. for Occupational Neurology & Neurotoxicology Colo. Neurolog. Inst., Englewood, 1989—; med. dir. Neuromuscular Disease Program, 1989—, med. dir. Neuroimmunology Program, 1989—; exec. med. dir. Inst. for Occupational and Environ. Medicine, Englewood, 1989—, Internat. Inst. for Inhalant Abuse, Englewood, 1991—; chmn. rsch. com. Colo. Neruol. Inst., 1990—; vis. prof. Albert Einstein Coll. Medicine, Bronx, N.Y., 1989—; asst. clin. prof. U. Colo. Sch. Med., Denver, 1989—. Author: Frontiers of Neurotoxicology, 1992, Update on Neuroimmunology, 1993, Occupational and Environmental Neurology, 1993; contbr. articles to profl. jours. Recipient Bruno Epstein Intern Achievement award Cook County Hosp., 1979, Rsch. Assoc. award VA, 1986; postdoctoral fellow Muscular Dystrophy Assn., 1982. Mem. AAAS, AMA, Am. Soc. for Neurol. Investigation (pres. 1989-91), Am. Acad. Neurology, Am. Coll. Occupational and Environ. Medicine, Am. Assn. Electrodiagnostic Medicine, N.Y. Acad. Medicine. Avocations: bicycling, cross training, writing, public speaking, astronomy. Office: Colo Neurological Inst 799 E Hampden Ave Ste 500 Englewood CO 80110

ROSENBERG, RICHARD MORRIS, banker; b. Fall River, Mass., Apr. 11, 1930; s. Charles and Betty (Peck) R.; m. Barbara K. Cohen, Oct. 21, 1956; children: Michael, Peter. B.S., Suffolk U., 1952; M.B.A., Golden Gate Coll., 1962, LL.B., 1966. Publicity asst. Crocker-Anglo Bank, San Francisco, 1959-62; banking services officer Wells Fargo Bank, N.A., San Francisco, 1962-65; asst. v.p. Wells Fargo Bank, N.A., 1965-68, v.p. mktg. dept., 1968, v.p., dir. mktg., 1969, sr. v.p. mktg. and advt. div., 1970-75, exec. v.p., from 1975, vice chmn., 1980-83; vice chmn. Crocker Nat. Corp., 1983-85; pres., chief operating officer Seafirst Corp., 1986-87, also dir.; pres., chief operating officer Seattle First Nat. Bank, 1985-87; vice chmn. bd. BankAm. Corp., San Francisco, 1987-90, chmn., chief exec. officer, 1990—; dir. Airborne Express, Potlatch Corp., Northrop Corp; past chmn. Mastercard Internat. Bd. dirs. Marin Ecumenical Housing Assn.; trustee Golden Gate U., Calif. Inst. Tech. Served from ensign to comdr. USNR, 1953-59. Mem. Hillcrest Club, Rainier Club. Jewish. Office: BankAm Corp PO Box 37000 555 California St 40th Fl San Francisco CA 94104-1502

ROSENBLATT, ABRAM B., psychologist; b. Tucson, Dec. 1, 1960; s. Paul and Joan Barbara (Shufro) R.; m. Kathryn Ann Phillips, May 19, 1991. BA, U. Calif., San Diego, 1982; MA in Psychology, U. Ariz., 1986, PhD, 1988. Intern Kaiser Pecmanente Med. Ctr., L.A., 1987-88; fellow NIMH, U. Calif., San Francisco, 1988-91; asst. rsch. scientist U. Calif., San Francisco, 1991—; investigator Western Consortium for Pub. Health, Inst. for Mental Health Svcs. Rsch., San. Francisco, 1990—; rsch. cons. Portland (Oreg.) State U., 1989—; adv. panel Calif. Dept. Mental Health, Sacramento, 1992—; assoc. dir. Calif. AB377 Evaluation Project, San Francisco, 1989—; clin. svcs. rsch. panel NIMH, Washington, 1989-91, spl. review com. Assoc. editor: Jour. Child and Family Studies, 1992; contbr. articles to profl. jours. NIMH fellow, 1989. Mem. APHA, Am. Psychol. Soc., Am. Evaluation Assn. (evaluation stds. task force com.), N.Y. Acad. Sci. Office: U Calif 401 Parnassus Box CPT San Francisco CA 94143

ROSENBLATT, MURRAY, mathematics educator; b. N.Y.C., Sept. 7, 1926; s. Hyman and Esther R.; m. Adylin Lipson, 1949; children—Karin, Daniel. B.S., CCNY, 1946; M.S., Cornell U., 1947, Ph.D. in Math., 1949. Asst. prof. statistics U. Chgo., 1950-55; assoc. prof. math. Ind. U., 1956-59; prof. probability and statistics Brown U., 1959-64; prof. math. U. Calif., San Diego, 1964—; vis. fellow U. Stockholm, 1953; vis. asst. prof. Columbia U., 1955; guest scientist Brookhaven Nat. Lab., 1959; vis. fellow U. Coll., London, 1965-66, Imperial Coll. and Univ. Coll., London, 1972-73, Australian Nat. U., 1976, 79; overseas fellow Churchill Coll., Cambridge U., Eng., 1979; Wald lectr., 1970; vis. scholar Stanford U., 1982. Author: (with U. Grenander) Statistical Analysis of Stationary Time Series, 1957, Random Processes, 1962, (2d edit), 1974, Markov Processes, Structure and Asymptotic Behavior, 1971, Studies in Probability Theory, 1978, Stationary Sequences and Random Fields, 1985, Stochastic Curve Estimation, 1991; editor: The North Holland Series in Probability and Statistics, 1980; mem. editorial bd. Jour. Theoretical Probability. Recipient Bronze medal U. Helsinki, 1978; Guggenheim fellow, 1965-66, 71-72. Fellow Inst. Math Statistics, AAAS; mem. Internat. Statis. Inst., Nat. Acad. Scis. Office: U Calif Dept Math La Jolla CA 92093

ROSENBLATT, PAUL GERHARDT, federal judge. AB, U. Ariz., 1958, JD, 1963. Asst. atty. gen. State of Ariz., 1963-66; adminstrv. asst. to U.S. Rep., 1967-72; sole practice, Prescott, 1971-73; judge Yavapai County Superior Ct., Prescott, 1973-84; judge, U.S. Dist. Ct. Ariz., Phoenix, 1984—. Office: US Dist Ct US Courthouse & Fed Bldg 230 N 1st Ave Ste 7012 Phoenix AZ 85025-0007

ROSENBLUM, CARLA NADINE, travel agent, retirement community executive; b. Seattle, Apr. 25, 1937; d. Carl August and Nadine Chaffa (Schwartz) Mahne; m. A. Leon Rosenblum, Feb. 28, 1965; 1 child, Sara Lynnette. BS, Mills Coll., Oakland, Calif., 1959. Buyer, stationery City of Paris Dept. Store, San Francisco, 1959-63, Diamond's Dept. Store, Phoenix, 1963-65; corp. buyer Arkwright Corp., L.A., 1965-66; mgr. various travel agys. San Jose, Calif., 1977-84; supr. Incentive Journeys, San Jose, Calif., 1984-86, Internat. Passages, Santa Clara, Calif., 1986—; ptnr. Willow Glen Villa, San Jose; with Marisan Travel, Santa Clara, 1989-92; vacation svcs. coord. Wagons-Lits Traves, U.S.A., 1992—. Mem. San Jose Pacific Area Travel Assn., Travelarians San Jose, Assn. Retail Travel Agts. Democrat. Jewish. Home: 15999 Bohlman Rd Saratoga CA 95070-6340 Office: Willow Glen Villa 1660 Gaton Dr San Jose CA 95125-4534

ROSENBLUM, RICHARD MARK, utility executive; b. N.Y.C., Apr. 28, 1950; s. Victor Sigmund and Julia (Kessler) R.; m. Michele E. Cartier, Aug. 30, 1979; children: Gialisa, Jeremy Scott. BS, MS, Rensselaer Poly. Inst., 1973. Registered profl. engr., Calif. Startup engr. Combustion Engring. Inc., Windsor, Conn., 1973-76; engr. So. Calif. Edison Co., Rosemead, 1976-82, project mgr. San Onofre Nuclear Generating Sta., 1982-83, tech. mgr., 1983-84, nuclear safety mgr., 1984-86, mgr. quality assurance, 1986-89, mgr. nuclear regulatory affairs, 1989—. N.Y. State Regents scholar, 1968-73. Office: 2244 Walnut Grove Rosemead CA 91770

ROSENFELD, LESLIE KAREN, oceanographer, educator; b. N.Y.C., Oct. 4, 1955; d. Gabriel Ira and Louise Elsa (Passerman) R. AS, Fla. Inst. Tech., 1976; BS, U. Wash., 1978; PhD, MIT/Woods Hole Oceanographic Inst., 1987. Oceanographer U.S. Naval Oceanographic Office, Bay St. Louis, Mo., 1978; asst. staff oceanographer Chesapeake Bay Inst., Balt., 1979; postdoctoral assoc. cooperative inst. for marine & atmospheric studies U. Miami, Fla., 1987-89; asst. scientist Monterey Bay Aquarium Rsch. Inst., Pacific Grove, Calif., 1989—; adj. prof. Naval Postgrad. Sch., Monterey, Calif., 1989—; sec. Ea. Pacific Ocean Conf., 1989-92. Contbr. articles to profl. jours. Mem. Am. Meteorol. Soc., Am. Geophys. Union, Oceanography Soc., Sigma Xi.

ROSENFELD, MARTIN, accountant; b. Chgo., May 27, 1932; s. Meyer and Bessie (Kite) R.; m. Beatrice Premazon, Mar. 21, 1954; children: Elysa Lynn, Sherri Miriam, David Michael. Student, Calif. State U., L.A., 1957; BS, UCLA, 1959. CPA, Calif. Supr. Lefkowitz & Berk, Beverly Hills, Calif., 1957-63; chief fin. officer KRHM Broadcasting, L.A., 1963-69; mng. ptnr. Rosenfeld and Bueno, L.A., 1969—; dir. Connector Distribution Corp.; pres. Automated Bookkeeping Control, L.A., 1980—. Author: Engagement Letters, Going Into Business in L.A.; editor: (jour.) Inst. Mgmt. Accountants; contbr. acctg. articles to profl. jours. Bd. dirs. L.A. City Coll. Found. With U.S. Army, 1954-56. Mem. AICPA, Calif. Soc. CPAs (past pres.), L.A. Soc. Calif. Accts., Nat. Assn. Accts, Coun. for Accountancy (citation of merit 1979, named accountant of the Yr. 1981, founders award 1989, outstanding CPA 1991). Democrat. Jewish. Office: Rosenfeld and Bueno 642 N Larchmont Blvd Los Angeles CA 90004-1308

ROSENFELD, RON GERSHON, pediatrics educator; b. N.Y.C., June 22, 1946; s. Stanley I. and Deborah (Levin) R.; m. Valerie Rae Spitz, June 16, 1968; children: Amy, Jeffrey. BA, Columbia U., 1968; MD, Stanford U., 1973. Intern Stanford (Calif.) U. Med. Ctr., 1973-74, resident in pediatrics, 1974-75, chief resident pediatrics, 1975-76; pvt. practice Santa Barbara, Calif., 1976-77; postdoctoral fellow Stanford U. Sch. Medicine, 1977-80, from asst. to assoc. prof. pediatrics, 1980-89, prof. pediatrics, 1989-93; chmn., prof. pediatrics Oreg. Health Scis. U., 1993—; physician-in-chief Doernbecher Children's Hosp., 1993—; cons. Genentech, Inc., South San Francisco, 1980—, Kabi Pharmacia, Inc., Stockholm, 1990—, Novo Nordisk, Inc., Copenhagen, 1991—, Diagnostic Systems Labs., Webster, Tex., 1991—, Serono Labs., Inc., 1993—. Editor: Growth Abnormalities, 1985, Turner Syndrome, 1987, Turner Syndrome: Growth, 1990, Growth Regulation; editorial bd.: Jour. Clin. Endocrinology and Metabolism, Growth Factors, Clin. Pediatric Endocrinology, Growth and Growth Factors, Growth Regulation. Recipient Ross Rsch. award Ross Laboratories, 1985. Mem. Endocrine Soc., Soc. for Pediatric Rsch., Lawson Wilkins Pediatric Endocrine Soc., European Soc. for Pediatric Endocrinology, Diabetes Soc. Office: Oreg Health Scis U Dept Pediatrics 3181 SW Sam Jackson Park Blvd Portland OR 97201-3098

ROSENFIELD, JAMES STEVEN, real estate developer; b. L.A., June 22, 1962; s. Robert Allan and Elyse Harriet (Bernstein) R. BA in Polit. Sci., U. Calif., Berkeley, 1984. Polit. cons. Senator John Tunney, L.A., 1985—; assoc. Cloverleaf Group, Inc., L.A., 1985-87; pres. J.S. Rosenfield & Co., L.A., 1987—; ptnr. John V. Tunney & Assocs., L.A., 1991—; developer Sears Roebuck & Co. stores, Fresno and Modesto, Calif. Coro Found. fellow, 1985. Mem. Internat. Coun. Shopping Ctrs., Univ. Art Mus. at Berkeley. Democrat. Jewish. Office: Ste 1750 11111 Santa Monica Blvd Los Angeles CA 90025-3348

ROSENKILDE, CARL EDWARD, physicist; b. Yakima, Wash., Mar. 16, 1937; s. Elmer Edward and Doris Edith (Fitzgerald) R.; m. Bernadine Doris Blumenstine, June 22, 1963 (div. Apr. 1991); children: Karen Louise, Paul Eric; m. Wendy Maureen Ellison, May 24, 1992. BS in Physics, Wash. State Coll., 1959; MS in Physics, U. Chgo., 1960, PhD in Physics, 1966. Postdoctoral fellow Argonne (Ill.) Nat. Lab., 1966-68; asst. prof. math. NYU, 1968-70; asst. prof. physics Kans. State U., Manhattan, 1970-76, assoc. prof., 1976-79; physicist Lawrence Livermore (Calif.) Nat. Lab., 1979—, cons., 1974-79. Contbr. articles on physics to profl. jours. Woodrow Wilson fellow, 1959, 60. Mem. Am. Phys. Soc., Am. Astron. Soc., Soc. for Indsl. and Applied Math., Am. Geophys. Union, Acoustical Soc. Am., Phi Beta Kappa, Phi Kappa Phi, Phi Eta Sigma, Sigma Xi. Republican. Presbyterian. Club: Tubists Universal Brotherhood Assn. (TUBA). Current Work: Nonlinear wave propagation in complex media. Subspecialties: Theoretical physics; Fluid dynamics.

ROSENKRANS, KENNETH RAY, financial services; b. Waterloo, Iowa, Feb. 6, 1951; s. Frank Preston and Winona Marie (DeVore) R.; m. Francene Annette Maniscalco, June 23, 1989; children: Erin, Matthew, Melissa, Jennifer. BS in Mktg., U. No. Iowa, 1974. V.p. Norwest Mortgage, Waterloo, Iowa, 1977-82, Ticor Realty Tax Svcs., Chgo., 1982-87; sr. v.p. mktg. TRTS Data Svcs., L.A., 1987-92; sr. v.p. regional mgr. First Am. REal Estate Tax Svc., L.A., 1992—. With U.S. Army, 1976-79. Mem. Mortgage Bankers Assn. of Am., Orange County Mortgage Bankers Assn. Office: First Am Real Estate Tax Ste 450 1873 S Bellaire St Ste 510 Denver CO 80222

ROSENKRANTZ, LINDA, writer; b. N.Y.C., May 26, 1934; d. Samuel H. and Frances (Sillman) R.; m. Christopher Finch, Feb. 2, 1973; 1 child, Chloe. BA, U. Mich., 1955. Founding editor Auction Mag., N.Y.C., 1967-72; columnist Copley News Svc., San Diego, 1986—. Author: Talk, 1968; co-author: Gone Hollywood, 1979, SoHo, 1981, Beyond Jennifer and Jason, 1988, Beyond Charles and Diana, 1992, Beyond Shannon and Sean, 1992, Beyond Sarah and Sam, 1992.

ROSENMAN, HOWARD ZUI, motion picture executive/producer; b. N.Y.C., Feb. 1, 1945; s. Morris Joseph and Sima (Rosenfeld)

Rosenman. BA, Bklyn. Coll., 1965. Producer Benton & Bowles, N.Y.C., 1968-73, ABC, L.A., 1973-74; pres. RSO Films, L.A., 1974-78; producer Warner Bros., Universal, Paramount, L.A., 1978-83, Embassy, Orion, L.A., 1984-85, Disney (Touchstone), L.A., 1985-87; co-pres. Sandollar, L.A., 1987-93; pres. motion picture div. Brillstein-Grey Entertainment, L.A., 1993—. Prodr.: (TV) Isn't It Shocking?, 1974, Death Scream, 1975, Virginia Hill, 1975, All Together Now, 1976, Killer Bees, 1977, Tidy Endings, 1987, Common Threads: Stories of the Quilt, 1990, (film) Sparkle, 1978, Main Event, 1979, Resurrection, 1980, Lost Angels, 1989, Gross Anatomy, 1989, True Identity, 1990, Father of the Bride, 1991, Shining Through, 1991, Straight Talk, 1992, A Stranger Among Us, 1992, Buffy the Vampire Slayer, 1992. Mem. Acad. Motion Picture Arts and Scis., Design Industries for Fighting AIDS, Project Angel Food. Democrat. Jewish. Office: Brillstein Grey Entertainment Los Angeles CA 90069

ROSENSTEIN, ALLEN BERTRAM, electrical engineering educator; b. Balt., Aug. 25, 1920; s. Morton and Mary (Epstein) R.; m. Betty Lebell; children: Jerry Tyler, Lisa Nan, Adam Mark. B.S. with high distinction, U. Ariz., 1940; M.S., UCLA, 1950, Ph.D., 1958. Elec. engr. Consol. Vultee Aircraft, San Diego, 1940-41; sr. elec. engr. Lockheed Aircraft Corp., Burbank, Calif., 1941-42; chief plant engr. Utility Fan Corp., Los Angeles, 1942-44; prof. engring. UCLA, 1946—; founder, chmn. bd. Inet, Inc., 1947-53, cons. engr., 1954—; founder, chmn. bd. dirs. Pioneer Magnetics, Inc., Pioneer Research Inc., Anadex Instruments Inc.; dir. Internat. Transformer Co., Inc., Fgn. Resource Services; cons. ednl. planning UNESCO, Venezuela, 1974-76. Author: (with others) Engineering Communications, 1965, A Study of a Profession and Professional Education, 1968; contbr. articles to profl. jours.; patentee in field. Bd. dirs. Vista Hill Psychiat. Found. Served with USNR, 1944-46. Fellow IEEE (com. on compeitivenes); mem. AAAS, NSPE, Am. Soc. Engring. Edn., N.Y. Acad. Scis., Am. Electronics Assn. (domestic policy com., coun. on competitiveness), Sigma Xi, Phi Kappa Phi, Delta Phi Sigma, Tau Beta Pi. Home: 314 S Rockingham Ave Los Angeles CA 90049-3638

ROSENTHAL, DONNA, broadcast producer; b. El Paso, Tex., Jan. 6, 1950; d. Morris and Elinor (Greene) R.; m. Joe Lurie, 1986. BA, U. Calif., Berkeley, 1969; MSc, London Sch. Econs., 1977. Lectr. Sophia U., Tokyo, 1970-71; prodr. Israel TV, Jerusalem, 1972-74, Veronica TV, The Netherlands, 1979-85, Sta. KRON-TV, San Francisco, 1986; journalist The Atlantic, Newsweek, The L.A. Times, The Washington Post, The Boston Globe, 1986—; reporter The New York Daily News, 1986. Author: (screenplay) Dead Wrong, 1992. Mem. NATAS, Soc. Profl. Journalists. Office: Studio 9 1736 Stockton St San Francisco CA 94133

ROSENTHAL, JACK, broadcasting executive; b. Chgo., Aug. 7, 1930; s. Samuel J. and Celia (Weinberg) R.; m. Elaine Lois Brill, May 2, 1954; children: Michael Bruce, Robert Joseph, Richard Scott. BA in History, U. Wyo., 1952, LLD (hon.), 1993. Sec., treas. Buffalo Theatre Corp., 1952-57, No. Wyo. Broadcasting Corp., 1957-64; v.p., gen. mgr. Sta. KTWO Radio and TV, Casper, Wyo., 1964-69; exec. v.p. Harriscope Broadcasting Corp., 1969-77; pres. broadcast div. Harriscope Broadcasting Corp., Los Angeles, 1977-87; pres. Wyo. Radio Network, 1987—, Clear Channel Radio, Inc., 1988—; chmn. Wyo. industry adv. com. FCC; dir. Wyo. Nat. Bank, Affiliated Bank Corp. of Wyo.; dir. TV Info. Office, 1984; designer U.S. Postage stamps 15 cent Buffalo Bill Cody, 1988, 25 cent Wyo. Centennial Commemorative, 1990, 29 cent Oreg. Trail Commemorative, 1993; mem. ct. of honor World Stamp Expo '89, ct. of honor, Granada, Spain, 1992. Producer (TV film) Conrad Schwiering-Mountain Painter (Western Heritage award 1974). Mem. Wyo. Travel Commn., 1969-71, Wyo. Land and Water Commn., 1965-66, Yellowstone Nat. Park Centennial Commn., 1972, Wyo. Coun. Arts, 1969, City of Casper Art Fund, 1979-80; bd. dirs. Milward Simpson Endowment, U. Wyo. Found., 1970—; adv. Nat. Park Svc. Dept. Interior, 1974-76; mem. jud. planning com. Wyo. Supreme Ct., 1976-77; mem. citizens stamp adv. com. U.S. Postal Svc., 1985-89, chmn. 1990-92; trustee The Philatelic Found.; advisor, Nat. Postal Mus. Smithsonian Inst., 1993—. Served to 1st lt. U.S. Army, 1952-54, Korea. Recipient Alfred I. DuPont Found. award broadcast journalism, 1965, U.S. Conf. Mayors award for outstanding community service, 1966, Disting. Alumnus award U. Wyo., 1982, Commendation Casper C. of C., 1984, Disting. Alumnus award Coll. Arts and Scis., U. Wyo., 1991; named hon. mem. Shoshoni and Arapahoe Indian Tribes, 1965. Mem. Nat. Assn. Broadcasters (nat. chmn. TV and radio polit. action com. 1977-79, Grover C. Cobb meml. award 1983), Wyo. Assn. Broadcasters (pres. 1963), Fedn. Rocky Mountain States Ednl. TV Com. Office: 150 Nichols Ave Casper WY 82601-1816

ROSENTHAL, JOHN DAVID, dentist; b. Portland, Oreg., Feb. 26, 1950; s. Lawrence A. and H. Bertha (Klein) R.; m. Barbara J. Loomis, Apr. 1, 1977; children: Kristin, Benjamin. BS, U. Oreg., 1973; DMD, U. Oreg. Health Sci. U., 1976. Dentist Rosenthal & Rosenthal, DMD, Portland, 1976-79; pvt. practice Portland, 1979—. Dental chmn. United Way of Oreg., Portland, 1985; mem. membership com. Temple Beth Israel, Portland, 1984-87; mem. adv. com. Robison Retirement Home, Portland, 1986—. Fellow Am. Coll. Dentists, Acad. Gen. Dentistry, Acad. Dentistry Internat.; mem. Oreg. Soc. Dentistry for Children, Western Soc. Periodontology, Multnomah Dental Soc. (bd. dirs. 1979-81, pres. 1986), Oreg. Dental Assn. (membership chmn. 1984-88, chmn. mem. svcs. coun. 1988-91, Svc. award 1991), Oreg. Acad. Gen. Dentistry (bd. dirs. 1986-90, sec.-treas. 1990-91, pres. 1991-92), Oreg. Health Sci. U. Sch. Dentistry Alumni Assn. (bd. dirs. 1987-90), Theta Chi. Home: 6565 SW 88th Pl Portland OR 97223-7273 Office: 1110 SW Salmon St Portland OR 97205-2093

ROSENTHAL, PHILIP, gastroenterologist; b. Bayshore, N.Y., Oct. 18, 1949; m. Sherrin Jean Packer; children: Seth, Aaron. BS, SUNY, Albany, 1971; MD, SUNY, Bklyn., 1975. Asst. prof. pediatrics Coll. of Physicians and Surgeons Columbia U., N.Y.C., 1981-83; asst. prof. pediatrics U. So. Calif., L.A., 1983-89, tenured assoc. prof. pediatrics, 1989; dir. pediatrics and nutrition, med. dir. pediatric liver transplant program Cedars-Sinai Med. Ctr., L.A., 1989—; assoc. prof. UCLA, 1989—; asst. attending physician Presbyn. Hosp./Vanderbilt Clinic, N.Y.C., 1981-83, Babies Hosp./Columbia U., 1981-83, Children's Hosp. of L.A., 1983-89; with Vanderbilt Clinic/Columbia U., 1981-83; attending physician Harlem Hosp. and Med. Ctr., N.Y.C., 1981-83, L.A. County/U. So. Calif. Med. Ctr., 1988-89. Vol. City of L.A. Marathon, 1989-90; v.p. Westside Jewish Community Ctr., L.A., 1989-92, bd. dirs. program com., 1987, Children's Liver Found., 1986; mem adv. bd. Jewish Activities Mus., 1990—. Nat. Inst. Arthritis grantee, 1978-81, Children's Hosp. of L.A. grantee, 1984-86, 86-87, Abbott Labs. grantee, 1984-85, Children's Liver Found. grantee, 1985-86. Mem. Am. Acad. Pediatrics, N.Am. Soc. Pediatric Gastroenterology and Nutrition. Office: Cedars-Sinai Med Ctr 8700 Beverly Blvd # 4310 West Hollywood CA 90048-1865

ROSENTHAL, SOL, lawyer; b. Balt., Oct. 17, 1934; s. Louis and Hattie (Getz) R.; m. Diane Myra Sackler, June 11, 1961; children: Karen Abby, Pamela Margaret, Robert Joel. AB, Princeton U., 1956; JD, Harvard U., 1959. Bar: Md. 1959, Calif. 1961. Law clk. to chief judge U.S. Ct. Appeals, 4th cir., Balt., 1959-60; assoc. Kaplan, Livingston, Goodwin, Berkowitz & Selvin, Beverly Hills, Calif., 1960-66, ptnr., 1966-74; ptnr. Buchalter, Nemer, Fields & Younger, L.A., 1974—; bd. dirs. Playboy Enterprises, Inc., Chgo.; arbitrator Dirs. Guild Am., L.A., 1976—, Writers Guild Am., L.A., 1976—, Am. Film Mktg. Assn., 1989—; negotiator Writers Guild-Assn. Talent Agts., L.A., 1978—. Founder Camp Ronald McDonald for Good Times, L.A., 1985; charter founder Mus. Contemporary Art, L.A., 1988. Mem. ABA, Calif. Bar Assn., L.A. County Bar Assn. (trustee 1981-82), L.A. Copyright Soc. (pres. 1973-74), Acad. TV Arts and Scis. (bd. govs. 1990-92), Beverly Hills Bar Assn. (pres. 1982-83), Phi Beta Kappa. Office: Buchalter Nemer et al Ste 1500 2029 Century Park E Los Angeles CA 90067-3002

ROSENZWEIG, DAVID, newspaper editor; b. Jersey City, Feb. 17, 1940; s. Herbert and Ethel (Hinkes) Rosenzweig. B.A. in History, Rutgers U., 1961. Reporter Newark Star Ledger, N.J., 1962-63, Newark Evening News, N.J., 1963-64, AP, 1964-71; reporter L.A. Times, 1971-79, asst. met. editor, 1979-83, met. editor, 1983-89, asst. mng. editor, 1989—. Office: Los Angeles Times Times Mirror Sq Los Angeles CA 90012-3816

ROSENZWEIG, MARK RICHARD, psychology educator; b. Rochester, N.Y., Sept. 12, 1922; s. Jacob and Pearl (Grossman) R.; m. Janine S.A. Chappat, Aug. 1, 1947; children: Anne Janine, Suzanne Jacqueline, Philip Mark. B.A., U. Rochester, 1943, M.A., 1944; Ph.D., Harvard U., 1949; hon. doctorate, U. René Descartes, Sorbonne, 1980. Postdoctoral research fellow Harvard U., 1949-51; asst. prof. U. Calif., Berkeley, 1951-56; assoc. prof. U. Calif., 1956-60, prof. psychology, 1960-91, assoc. research prof., 1958-59, research prof., 1965-66, prof. emeritus, 1991—; vis. prof. biology Sorbonne, Paris, 1973-74; mem. exec. com. Internat. Union Psychol. Sci., 1972—, v.p., 1980-84, pres., 1988-92; chmn. U.S. Nat. Com. for Internat. Union Psychol. Sci., NRC-Nat. Acad. Sci., 1985-88, mem., 1988—. Author: Biologie de la Mémoire, 1976, (with A.L. Leiman) Physiological Psychology, 1982, 2d edit., 1989, (with D. Sinha) La Recherche en Psychologie Scientifique; editor: (with P. Mussen) Psychology: An Introduction, 1973, 2d edit., 1977, (with E.L. Bennett) Neural Mechanisms of Learning and Memory, 1976, International Psychological Science: Progress, Problems, and Prospects, 1992; co-editor (with L. Porter) Ann. Rev. of Psychology, 1968—, (with M.J. Renner) Enriched and Impoverished Environments: Effects on Brain and Behavior, 1987; contbr. articles to profl. jours. Served with USN, 1944-46. Recipient Disting. Alumnus award U. Rochester; Fulbright research fellow; faculty research fellow Social Sci. Research Council, 1960-61; research grantee NSF, USPHS, Easter Seal Found., Nat. Inst. Drug Abuse. Fellow AAAS, APA (Disting. Sci. Contbn. award 1982), Am. Psychol. Soc.; mem. NAS, NAACP (life), Am. Physiol. Soc., Am. Psychol. Soc., Internat. Brain Rsch. Orgn., Soc. Exptl. Psychologists, Soc. for Neuroscience, Société Française de Psychologie, Sierra Club (life), Common Cause, Phi Beta Kappa, Sigma Xi. Office: U Calif Dept Psychology 3210 Tolman Hall Berkeley CA 94720

ROSENZWEIG, RICHARD STUART, publishing company executive; b. Appleton, Wis., Aug. 8, 1935; s. Walter J. and Rose (Bahcall) R. B.S., Northwestern U., 1957; postgrad. Advanced Mgmt. Program, Harvard U., 1975. Credit rep. Dun & Bradstreet, Inc., 1958; with Playboy Enterprises, Inc., 1958—, exec. asst. to pres., 1963-73, sr. v.p., dir., 1973—, dir. mktg., 1974—, exec. v.p. publs. group, 1975-77, exec. v.p., head West Coast ops., 1977-80; exec. v.p. corp. affairs Playboy Enterprises, Inc., Los Angeles, 1980-82; exec. v.p., chmn. emeritus Playboy Enterprises, Inc., 1982—; dir. I. Bahcall Industries, Appleton. trustee Los Angeles Film Expn.; mem. 2d decade council Am. Film Inst.; bd. dirs. Mus. Contemporary Art, Chgo., Periodical and Book Assn. Am., Internat. Inst. Kidney Diseases of UCLA, Children of Night, Maple Ctr. Beverly Hills; mem., chmn. bd. UCLA Legis. Network, Town Hall of Calif.; adv. bd. West Hollywood Mktg. Corp., 1985—; bd. dirs. So. Calif. ACLU, 1985—; pres. Playboy Jazz Festivals; mem. L.A. County Mus.; apptd. to blue ribbon com. project West Coast Gateway. Served with AUS, 1957. Recipient Do-ers award, 1988. Mem. Am. Mktg. Assn., Los Angeles Pub. Affairs Officers Assn., UCLA Chancellor's Assocs., Pres.'s Cir., Beverly Hills C. of C. (bd. dirs., visitors' bur., v.p.), Beverly Hills Fine Arts Commn., Beverly Hills Econ. Devel. Coun., Founders Circle of Music Center, Pub. Affairs Council, Craft and Folk Art Mus., Pres.'s Council and Contemporary Arts Council of Los Angeles Mus. Contemporary Art, The Am. Cinematheque (groundbreaker). Club: Variety of So. Calif. (bd. dirs.). Office: Playboy Enterprises 9242 Beverly Blvd Beverly Hills CA 90210

ROSETT, ANN DOYLE, librarian; b. Valdosta, Ga., Jan. 9, 1955; d. David Spencer Doyle and Lois Annette Gray; m. Robert Allen Richardson, Aug. 1, 1976 (div. June 1981); children: Caitlin Ann, Brendan Wesley; m. John David Rosett, Aug. 6, 1983. Student, Kenyon Coll., 1972-75, U. Dayton, 1974, U. Ala., Birmingham, 1978; BA, Shepherd Coll., 1982; MLS, U. Wash., 1988. Cert. profl. libr., Wash. College libr. Northwest Coll., Kirkland, Wash., 1988—. Mem. ALA, Assn. Christian Librs. (dir.-at-large 1992-93), Assn. Coll. and Rsch. Librs., Am. Theol. Lib. Assn., N.W. Assn. Christian Librs. (treas. 1989-91, pres. 1991-93). Democrat. Mem. Assemblies of God Ch. Office: NW Coll DV Hurst Libr PO Box 579 5520 108th Ave NE Kirkland WA 98083-0579

ROSETT, ARTHUR IRWIN, lawyer, educator; b. N.Y.C., July 5, 1934; s. Milton B. and Bertha (Werner) R.; m. Rhonda K. Lawrence; children: David Benjamin, Martha Jean, Daniel Joseph. A.B., Columbia U., 1955, LL.B., 1959. Bar: Calif. 1968, N.Y. State 1960, U.S. Supreme Ct. 1963. Law clk. U.S. Supreme Ct., 1959-60; asst. U.S. atty. So. Dist. N.Y., 1960-63; practice law N.Y.C., 1963-65; assoc. dir. Pres.'s Commn. on Law Enforcement and Adminstrn. Justice, 1965-67; acting prof. law UCLA, 1967-70, prof., 1970—. Author: Contract Law and Its Application, 1971, 4th, rev. edit., 1988; (with D. Cressey) Justice by Consent, 1976; (with E. Dorff) A Living Tree, 1987. Served with USN, 1956-58. Mem. Am. Law Inst. Home: 641 S Saltair Ave Los Angeles CA 90049-4134 Office: UCLA Law Sch 405 Hilgard Ave Los Angeles CA 90024-1476

ROSICH, RAYNER KARL, physicist; b. Joliet, Ill., Aug. 28, 1940; s. Joseph F. and Gretchen (Cox) R.; BS in Physics cum laude with honors, U. Mich., 1962, MS in Physics, 1963; PhD, U. Colo., 1977; MBA, U. Denver, 1982; m. Judy Louise Jackson, Aug. 20, 1966; children: Heidi Ann, Kimberly Ann, Dawn Ann. Teaching fellow and research asst. U. Mich., Ann Arbor, 1962-67; staff, Argonne (Ill.) Nat. Lab. Applied Math. Div., summers 1961-63; physicist, project leader Inst. for Telecommunication Sci., U.S. Dept. Commerce, Boulder, Colo., 1967-80; sr. scientist and program mgr. Electro Magnetic Applications, Inc., Denver, 1980-82; applications mgr. Energy Systems Tech., Inc., Denver, 1982-83, mgr. R&D, 1983; prin. scientist, program mgr. Contel Info. Systems, Inc., Denver, 1983-84, dir. tech. audits, 1985, dir. basic and applied R&D, 1986; lab. scientist for systems engring. lab. Hughes Aircraft Co., Denver, 1986, lab. scientist for data systems lab, 1986-90, lab. scientist for systems lab., 1990-92; prin. engr., Advanced Systems Techs., Inc., Denver, 1992—; instr. math. Arapahoe Community Coll., 1987—. Vol. judo instr., county recreation dist., 1976-77. Recipient Spl. Achievement award U.S. Dept. Commerce, 1974, Outstanding Performance award, 1978, Sustained Superior Performance award, 1979; Libbey-Owens-Ford Glass Co./U. Mich. Phoenix Meml. fellow, 1964-66; NSF Summer fellow, 1965. Mem. Am. Phys. Soc., AAAS, IEEE, Assn. Computing Machinery, Applied Computational Electromagnetics Soc., Soc. Computer Stimulation, Sigma Xi, Phi Kappa Phi. Home: 7932 W Nichols Ave Littleton CO 80123-5558 Office: Advanced System Techs Inc 12200 E Briarwood Ave Ste 260 Englewood CO 80112-6702

ROSKY, BURTON SEYMOUR, lawyer; b. Chgo., May 28, 1927; s. David T. and Mary W. (Zelkin) R.; m. Leatrice J. Darrow, June 16, 1951; children: David Scott, Bruce Alan. Student, Ill. Inst. Tech., 1944-45; BS, UCLA, 1948; JD, Loyola U., L.A., 1953. Bar: Calif. 1954, U.S. Supreme Ct 1964, U.S. Tax Ct 1964; C.P.A., Calif. Auditor City of L.A., 1948- 51; with Beidner, Temkin & Ziskin (C.P.A.s), L.A., 1951-52; supervising auditor Army Audit Agy., 1952-53; practiced law L.A., Beverly Hills, 1954—; partner Duskin & Rosky, 1972-82, Rosky, Landau & Fox, 1982—; lectr. on tax and bus. problems; judge pro tem Beverly Hills Mcpl. Ct., L.A. Superior Ct.; mem. L.A. Mayor's Community Adv. Council. Contbr. profl. publs. Charter supporting mem. Los Angeles County Mus. Arts; contbg. mem. Assocs. of Smithsonian Instn.; charter mem. Air and Space Mus; mem. Am. Mus. Natural History, L.A. Zoo; supporting mem. L.A. Mus. Natural History; mem. exec. bd. So. Calif. coun. Nat. Fedn. Temple Brotherhoods, mem. nat. exec. bd. With USNR, 1945-46. Walter Henry Cook fellow Loyola Law Sch. Fellow Jewish Chautauqua Soc. (life mem.); mem. Am. Arbitration Assn. (nat. panel arbitrators), Am. Assn. Attys.-CPAs (charter mem. pres. 1968), Calif. Assn. Attys.-CPAs (charter mem., pres. 1963), Calif. Soc. CPAs, Calif., Beverly Hills, Century City, Los Angeles County bar assns., Am. Judicature Soc., Chancellors Assocs. UCLA, Tau Delta Phi, Phi Alpha Delta.; mem. B'nai B'rith. Jewish (mem. exec. bd., pres. temple, pres. brotherhood). Club: Mason. Office: 8383 Wilshire Blvd Beverly Hills CA 90211-2400

ROSNER, ROBERT ALLAN, advocate; b. Lincoln Park, N.J., Nov. 2, 1956; s. Henry and Katherine (Kravitt) R.; m. Robin Simons, May 20, 1989. BS, U. Puget Sound, 1980; MBA, U. Wash., 1992. Restaurant mgr. Eatery, Phila., 1976-78; pub. rels. mgr. Big Brothers/Sisters, Tacoma, Wash., 1979; pub. affairs dir. Sta. KNBQ, Tacoma, 1980; exec. dir. Safety Assistance from the Elderly, Seattle, 1981-82, Smoking Policy Inst., Seattle, 1982—; bd. dirs., chmn. bd. Giraffe Project, Langley, Wash., 1989, Coming of Age in Am., Seattle, 1989; adj. prof. Heritage Inst./Antioch, Seattle, 1988, Seattle Pacific U. Grad. Sch. Bus., 1993. Author: U.S. Environmental Protection, 1990, Guide to Workplace Smoking Policies, 1990; contbr. articles to profl. jours. Bd. dirs. Salvation Army, Seattle, 1992. Recipient Gen. News Reporting award, Soc. Profl. Journalists, 1980, Emerald award Internat. TV and Video Assn., Seattle, 1986, Surgeon Gen.'s medallion, 1988. Mem. Seattle Downtown Rotary. Office: Smoking Policy Inst PO Box 20271 Seattle WA 98102-5760

ROSS, ALVIN, manufacturing executive; b. Minot, N.D., Apr. 4, 1922; s. Samuel and Goldie (Perlin) R.; m. Barbie Wechsler, Apr. 14, 1946; children: Talby W., Gelb, Elyse M. Piper, Mark W. Ross. BA, U. Wash., 1946, Master degree, 1958. Sales mgr. midwest H.D. Lee Co., Mission, Kans., 1963-72; v.p. Wrangler Boys div. Midwest Blue Bell Corp. (Wrangler Co.), Greensboro, N.C., 1972-85; pres. Opportunity Mktg., City of Industry, Calif., 1990—; v.p mktg. U.S. Polo Club Industries, Rancho Cucamonga, Calif., 1993—, A-Line Trading Corp. Casual Isle Sportsware, City of Industry, Calif., 1993—; pres. opportunity mktg. consulting Apparel Industry, Palm Desert, Calif., 1991; v.p. mktg. U.S. Polo Club Industries, Inc./Monroe Sports Wear. Office: US Polo Club Industries 9047 Bridgeport Pl Rancho Cucamonga CA 91730 also: Opportunity Mktg Co 108 Chelsea Circle Palm Desert CA 92260 Office: 11110 NE 41st Dr # 44 Maple Valley WA 98038

ROSS, BETTIE LOUISE, musician, composer, songwriter; b. L.A., May 12, 1948; d. Jack Wayland Ross and Margaret Cregar (Stryker) McCartney; divorced; children: Noelle Bezart Simeon, Margaux Andrea Simeon; stepchildren: Leslie Syniec, Omer Theodore Simeon III, Eric Albert Simeon. Student, Trinity Coll., London, L.A., 1953-60, Calif. State U., Northridge, 1966-68, 69-71, Jamie Faunt Sch. Creative Music, 1979-81, 86-87; studies with Dr. Philip Springer, Eddy L. Manson, L.A., 1973-74; studies with Mario Feninger, 1990. Keyboardist various bands, musicals, and plays; tchr. piano, pipe organ, organ, synthesizers, music theory; accompanist various sch. orchestras, choral groups; owner Kameon Prodns.; keyboardist Melissa Manchester U.S. Tour, 1980, Bellamy Bros. U.S. Tour, 1976; conductor Bellamy Bros. Fifth Ann. Tokyo Music Festival, 1976; pipe organist various So. Calif. chs., 1963—; organist Encino Community Ch., 1990—; choir conductor/pianist Temple Shir Chadash, 1993—. Composed, played, recorded, performed music for Vogue 2000, 1986-87, (films) Have a Banana, 1985, Galaxy Express 999, 1985, Closing Night, 1984, (plays) Neon (A Vaudeville of Obsession), 1983, The Melville Boys, 1988; produced solo albums, The Alon Series, 1980, Romance Suite, 1982; composed original score for In Search of Fellini, 1992. Vol. 1st and 2nd ann. Baby Golf Classic for newborn intensive care unit Cedars-Sinai Med. Ctr., L.A., 1984, 85. Named Donna Delle Fave Meml. scholar, 1970-71; recipient Frederick Chopin Piano award, 1966, Bank of Am. Music award, 1966, Grand Prize and 3 awards Music City Song Festival, 1988. Mem. ASCAP, NARAS, Songwriters and Composers Assn. (pres. 1986-91), Am. Guild Organists, Music Assn. (pres. 1991-92), Musicians Union, Nat. Acad. Songwriters, L.A. Women in Music (bd. dirs. 1991—). Democrat.

ROSS, CAROL JOYCE WALLER, librarian; b. Farmerville, La., Dec. 6, 1942; d. Herbert B. and Avis (Kennedy) Waller; m. Joseph E. Ross, Nov. 28, 1964; children: Kayla Ann, Sharilynne. BA, La. Tech. U., 1963; MS, La. State U., 1972. Serials libr. La. State U., Baton Rouge, 1963-64; humanities libr. La. Tech. U., Ruston, La., 1964-65; libr., tchr. East Baton Rouge Parish, Baton Rouge, 1974-87; dir., co-owner Yours Truly Video, Baton Rouge, 1984-87; mgr. client tng. Follett Software Co., McHenry, Ill., 1987-90; user svcs. libr. NOTIS Systems Inc., Evanston, Ill., 1990-91; libr. automation rep. Dynix Scholar, Provo, Utah, 1991—. Troop leader Camp Fire Girls, Baton Rouge, 1973-77; mem. adminstrv. bd. United Meth. Ch., Baton Rouge, 1980-82. Mem. ALA, ASTD. Presbyterian. Home: 1015 Landing Rd Naperville IL 60540-5242 Office: Dynix Scholar 151 E 1700 S Provo UT 60201

ROSS, FRANCES MARGARET, medical technologist, artist; b. Brockport, N.Y., Nov. 20, 1950; d. Benjamin Berlin and Marjorie Lou (Wilder) R.; m. Dennis John Dolan, Aug. 27, 1983. BA in Bacteriology, U. Calif., L.A., 1976. Cert. med. technologist. Med. technologist Oreg. Med. Labs, Eugene, 1978—. Artist numerous watercolor paintings, 1991—. Recipient Grumbacher Bronze medal N.W. Watercolor Soc., 1992, Award of Excellence, Sacramento Fine Arts Ctr. Nat. Open Exhibit, 1991, People's Choice award Beaverton Arts Commn., 1991, Best in Show and Judge's Choice award Lane County Fair, 1990, 92. Mem. Watercolor Soc. Oreg. (Bronze Merit award 1992, Silver Merit award 1993), Eugene Concert Choir (graphic artist, Spl. Recognition award 1991, 92), Very Little Theatre. Home: 170 E 33d Ave Eugene OR 97405

ROSS, GLYNN, opera administrator; b. Omaha, Dec. 15, 1914; s. Herman and Ida (Carlson) R.; m. Angelamaria Solimene, Nov. 15, 1946; children: Stephanie, Claudia, Melanie, Anthony. Student, Leland Powers Sch. Theater, Boston, 1937-39. bd. dirs. O.P.E.R.A. Am., Nat. Opera Inst., Soc. for Germanic Music Culture; founder, dir. Pacific N.W. Festival, 1975—. Opera stage dir., U.S., Can., 1939-63, debut, San Francisco Opera, 1948, gen. dir., Seattle Opera Assn., Inc., 1963-83, dir., Ariz. Opera, 1983—. Served to 1st lt. AUS, 1942-47. Office: Ariz Opera Assn 3501 N Mountain Ave Tucson AZ 85719-1925

ROSS, HOWARD PERSING, geophysicist, consultant; b. Stockbridge, Mass., Oct. 26, 1935; s. Carroll Ara and Berniece Thelma (Banfill) R.; m. Barbara Marion Lewis, June 28, 1958; children: Steven Dana, Krista Sue, Kimber Ann. B.A. in Geology, U. N.H., 1957; M.S. in Geophysics, Pa. State U., 1963, Ph.D. in Geophysics, 1965. Seismic computer United Geophys. Corp., Pasadena, Calif., 1958-60; gen. phys. scientist Air Force Cambridge Research Labs., Bedford, Mass., 1965-67; sr. geophysicist Kennecott Exploration Inc., Salt Lake City, 1967-76, Bear Creek Mining Co., Salt Lake City, 1976-77; sect. head geophysics U. Utah Research Inst., Salt Lake City, 1977—; geophys. cons. Battelle Meml. Inst., Columbus, Ohio, 1979-87, Dept. Energy, Richland, Wash., 1979-83, Thermal Power Co., San Francisco, 1982-86; Orgn. Latinoamericana De Energia, Quito, Ecuador, 1985-86. Contbr. articles to profl. jours. Patentee spectrophotometer reflection attachment. Served with U.S. Army, 1957-58. Co-investigator Appllo Application Program, NASA, 1965-67. Mem. Soc. Exploration Geophysicists, Am. Geophys. Union, European Assn. Exploration Geophysicists, Am. Assn. Petroleum Geologists, Geothermal Resources Coun., Utah Geol. Assn., The Nature Conservancy, The Wilderness Soc. Clubs: Wasatch Mountain (Salt Lake City). Home: 7089 S Pinecone St Salt Lake City UT 84121-4311 Office: U Utah Rsch Inst Earth Sci Lab 391 Chipeta Way Ste C Salt Lake City UT 84108-1296

ROSS, HUGH COURTNEY, electrical engineer; b. Dec. 31, 1923; s. Clare W. and Jeanne F. Ross; m. Sarah A. Gordon (dec.); m. Patricia A. Malloy; children: John C., James G., Robert W. Student, Calif. Inst. Tech., 1942, San Jose State U., 1946-47; BSEE, Stanford U., 1950, postgrad., 1954. Registered profl. elec. engr., Calif. Instr. San Benito (Calif.) High Sch. and Jr. Coll., 1950-51; chief engr. vacuum power switches Jennings Radio Mfg. Corp., San Jose, Calif., 1951-62; chief engr. ITT Jennings, San Jose, Calif., 1962-64; pres. Ross Engring. Corp., Campbell, Calif., 1964—. Contbr. articles to tech. jours.; patentee in field. Fellow IEEE (life) (chmn. Santa Clara Valley subsect. 1960-61); mem. Am. Vacuum Soc., Am. Soc. Metals. Office: 540 Westchester Dr Campbell CA 95008-5012

ROSS, IAN KENNETH, biology educator, mycology consultant; b. London, May 22, 1930; came to U.S., 1945; s. Ronald Paton and Emmaline Elizabeth (Finch) R.; m. Muriel Elizabeth Mayhew, June 2, 1956; children: Karen Ann, Keith Alan. BS, George Washington U., 1952, MS, 1953; PhD, McGill U., Montreal, Que., Can., 1957. Postdoctoral assoc. U. Wis., Madison, 1957-58; instr. Yale U., New Haven, 1958-59, asst. prof., 1959-64; asst. prof. biology U. Calif., Santa Barbara, 1964-65, assoc. prof., 1965-71, prof., 1971—, vice chmn. dept. biol. scis., 1987-89; cons., 1991—. Author: Biology of the Fungi, 1979. Rsch. fellow Brit. Petroleum Venture Rsch. Unit, London, 1988-92. Mem. AAAS, Am. Soc. Microbiology, Mycol. Soc. Am. (exec. com. 1990-92), Internat. Mycol. Assn. (exec. com. 1991—). Office: U Calif Dept Biol Scis Santa Barbara CA 93106

ROSS, JACK CLIFFORD, city official; b. Vermillion, Alta., Jan. 11, 1945; m. Colette Ross; 4 children. BA in Psychology, U. Calgary, 1982. With traffic dept. City of Calgary, Alta., 1963-66, firefighter, 1966-82, fire lt., 1982-84; administrv. asst. City of Calvary Office of Commr., 1984-86, dep. chief administrn., 1986-88, fire chief, 1988—, acting asst. commr., 1991; bd.

dirs. Disaster Svcs., 1988. bd. dirs. Burns Meml. Fire Fund, 1988. Mem. Internat. Assn. Fire Chiefs, Can. Assn. Fire Chiefs, Alta. Fire Chiefs Assn. Office: Calgary Fire Dept, 4124 11th St SE, Calgary, AB Canada T2G 3H2

ROSS, JANET, retired English language educator; b. Duluth, Minn., Apr. 19, 1914; d. Guy Whittier Chadbourn and Helen (Mason) Ross. Student, Carleton Coll., 1931-32; BA, U. Minn., 1935, MA, 1940; PhD, U. Iowa, 1960. Asst. prof. English Fla. State U., Tallahassee, 1949-52, Macalester Coll., St. Paul, 1957-60; instr. English U. Iowa, Iowa City, 1952-54, 55-57, U. B.C. (Can.), Vancouver, 1960-62; prof. English, coord. MA teaching English as fgn. lang. Ball State U., Muncie, Ind., 1961-80; prof. emeritus Ball State U., Muncie, 1980—; vis. prof. U. Colo., Boulder, summers 1956-58, 60, 71-72, 83-85, Pontificia U. Rio Grande do Sol, Porto Alegre, Brazil, 1973; guest lectr. Montgomery (Md.) Community Coll., 1977, U. Saga (Japan), 1980, U. Panama, Panama City, 1981. Co-author: Language and Life in the U.S.A., 1961, 4th edit., 1982, To Write English, 1965, 3rd edit., 1984; author: Understanding English, 1982. Fulbright fellow, Netherlands, 1954-55; Danforth Found. grantee U. Mich., 1964; Nat. Assn. Fgn. Student Affairs travel study grantee Yale U., 1962, travel grantee, France, 1966. Mem. Tchrs. English to Speakers Other Langs. (regional sec. 1976-80), Colo. Authors League (sec. 1987—). Home: 500 Mohawk Dr Apt 606 Boulder CO 80303-3757

ROSS, JOHN, physical chemist; b. Vienna, Austria, Oct. 2, 1926; came to U.S., 1940; s. Mark and Anna (Krecmar) R.; m. Virginia Franklin (div.); children: Elizabeth A., Robert K.; m. Eva Madarasz. BS, Queens Coll., 1948; PhD, MIT, 1951; D (hon.), Weizmann Inst. Sci., Rehovot, Israel, 1984, Queens Coll., SUNY, 1987, U. Bordeaux, France, 1987. Prof. chemistry Brown U., Providence, 1953-66; prof. chemistry MIT, Cambridge, 1966-80, chmn. dept., 1966-71; chmn. faculty of Inst. MIT, 1975-77; prof. Stanford (Calif.) U., 1980—, chmn. dept., 1983-89; cons. to industries, 1979—; mem. bd. govs. Weizmann Inst., 1971—. Author: Physical Chemistry, 1980; editor Molecular Beams, 1966; contbr. articles to profl. jours. Served as 2d lt. U.S. Army, 1944-46. Recipient medal Coll. de France, Paris. Fellow AAAS, Am. Phys. Soc.; mem. NAS, Am. Acad. Arts and Scis., Am. Chem. Soc. (Irving Langmuir award 1992, Dean's award for Disting. Teaching 1992-93). Home: 738 Mayfield Ave Palo Alto CA 94305-1044 Office: Stanford U Dept Chemistry Stanford CA 94305-2060

ROSS, JOSEPH FOSTER, physician, educator; b. Azusa, Calif., Oct. 11, 1910; s. Verne Ralph and Isabel Mills (Bumgarner) R.; m. Eileen Sullivan, Dec. 19, 1942; children: Louisa, Elisabeth, Joseph, Jeanne, Marianne. A.B., Leland Stanford Jr. U., 1933; M.D., Harvard U., 1936. Diplomate Am. Bd. Internal Medicine (mem. 1973-83), Am. Bd. Nuclear Medicine (founding, sec. 1971-72, 79, chmn. 1973-77, pres., chief exec. officer 1980—). Asst. topographical anatomy Harvard U. Sch. Medicine, 1934-37, research fellow biochemistry, 1943-46; med. house officer Harvard cancer commn. Huntington Meml. Hosp., 1934-35; Palmer Meml., New Eng. Deaconess hosps., 1935-36; resident pathology Mallory Inst. Pathology, 1936-37; intern Harvard Med. Svc. Boston City Hosp., 1937-39; asst. pathology U. Rochester Sch. Medicine, 1939-40; resident pathology Strong Meml. Hosp., Rochester, N.Y., 1939-40; physician, dir. hematology and radioisotope divs. Mass. Meml. Hosp., 1940-54; instr., asst. prof., assoc. prof. medicine Boston U., 1940-54; dir. radioisotope unit Cushing VA, Boston VA hosps., 1948-54; prof. medicine UCLA, 1954—, prof. radiobiology, 1954-59, assoc. dean, 1954-58, chmn. dept. nuclear med. and radiation biology, 1958-60, dir. Lab. Nuclear Med. and Radiation Biology, 1958-65, prof., chmn. dept. biophysics and nuclear medicine, 1960-65, chief div. hematology, 1969-76; chief staff U. Calif. Hosp., Los Angeles, 1954-58; attending physician U. Calif. Hosp., 1954—; U.S. del. Internat. Conf. Peaceful Uses Atomic Energy, Geneva, 1955; mem. U.S. Atoms for Peace mission to Latin Am., 1956, U.S. AEC Life Scis. Mission to, Greece, Turkey, 1961; radiation biology Mission to USSR, 1965; mem. Calif. Adv. Council on Cancer, 1959-84, chmn., 1963-66, 74-77; mem. CENTO Sci. Mission Iran, Turkey, Pakistan, 1963; mem. nat. adv. cancer council Nat. Cancer Inst., 1956-60; Research preservation whole blood OSRD, World War II. Editorial bd.: Blood, Jour. Hematology, 1946-76, Annals Internal Medicine, 1960-70, Jour. Nuclear Medicine, 1968; med. book div., Little Brown Co., 1958-68, med. book series, U. Calif. Press, 1962-70; Contbr. articles to profl. jours. Recipient certificate of merit Pres. U.S., 1948; Van Meter award Am. Goiter Soc., 1953; Wilson medalist, lectr. Am. Clin. and Climatol. Assn., 1964; disting. fellow Am. Coll. Nuclear Physicians, 1993. Disting. Fellow Am. Coll. Nuclear Medicine; mem. ACP, AMA, Am. Soc. Exptl. Pathology, Am. Soc. Clin. Investigation, Assn. Am. Physicians, Am. Acad. Arts and Scis., Biophys. Soc., Radiation Research Soc. (council 1964-65), Internat. Soc. Hematology, Am. Soc. Hematology (pres. 1961-62), Western Assn. Physicians (pres. 1962-63), Am. Bd. Nuclear Medicine (co-founder 1972, sec. 1972-75, chmn., pres. 1975-78, exec. dir. 1978-79, pres. 1980—), Soc. Nuclear Med. (trustee 1962-72, pres. So. Calif. chpt. 1964-65, Nuclear Pioneer lectr. 1971, 77, Disting. Scientist award Western. sect. 1977, Disting. Svc. award 1984, Spl. Presdl. Recognition award 1991), L.A. County Med. Assn. (dist. v.p. 1976-77, 78-79, del. to Calif. Med. Assn. 1978-79), Am. Bd. Med. Spltys. (exec. com. 1982-84), Council Med. Splty. Socs. (sec. 1981-82, dir. 1980-82), World Fedn. Nuclear Medicine and Biology (chmn. statutes com. 1980-84), Phi Beta Kappa, Sigma Xi, Alpha Omega Alpha, Theta Xi, Nu Sigma Nu. Presbyterian (exec. com. Westminster Found. So. Calif. 1962-72, pres. 1968). Clubs: Harvard (Boston); Cosmos (Washington). Home: 11246 Cashmere St Los Angeles CA 90049-3503 Office: Am Bd Nuclear Medicine 900 Veteran Ave Room 12-200 Los Angeles CA 90024-1786

ROSS, KATHLEEN ANNE, college president; b. Palo Alto, Calif., July 1, 1941; d. William Andrew and Mary Alberta (Wilburn) R. BA, Ft. Wright Coll., 1964; MA, Georgetown U., 1971; PhD, Claremont Grad. Sch., 1979; LLD (hon.) Alverno Coll. Milw., 1990, Dartmouth Coll., 1991, Seattle U., 1992; LHD (hon.) Whitworth Coll., 1992, LLD (hon.) Pomona Coll., 1993. Cert. tchr., Wash. Secondary tchr. Holy Names Acad., Spokane, Wash., 1964-70; dir. rsch. and planning Province Holy Names, Wash. State, 1972-73; v.p. acads. Ft. Wright Coll., Spokane, 1973-81; rsch. asst. to dean Claremont Grad. Sch., Calif., 1977-78; assoc. faculty mem. Harvard U., Cambridge, Mass., 1981; pres. Heritage Coll., Toppenish, Wash., 1981—; cons. Wash. State Holy Names Schs., 1971-73; coll. accrediting assn. evaluator N.W. Assn. Schs. and Colls., Seattle, 1975—; dir. Holy Names Coll., Oakland, Calif., 1979—; cons. Yakima Indian Nation, Toppenish, 1975—; speaker, cons. in field. Author: (with others) Multicultural Pre-School Curriculum, 1977, A Crucial Agenda: Improving Minority Student Success, 1989; Cultural Factors in Success of American Indian Students in Higher Education, 1978. Chmn. Internat. 5-Yr. Convocation of Sisters of Holy Names, Montreal, Que., Can., 1981; TV Talk show host Spokane Council of Chs., 1974-76. Recipient E.K. and Lillian F. Bishop Founds. Youth Leader of Yr. award, 1986, Golden Aztez award Washington Human Devel., 1989, Harold W. McGraw Edn. prize, 1989, John Carroll award Georgetown U., 1991; Holy Names medal Ft. Wright Coll., 1981; Disting. Citizenship Alumna award Claremont Grad. Sch., 1986; named Yakima Herald Rep. Person of Yr. 1987, First Annual Leadership award Region VIII Coun. Advancement and Support Edn., 1993; numerous grants for projects in multicultural higher edn., 1974—. Mem. Nat. Assn. Ind. Colls. and Univs., Am. Assn. Higher Edn., Soc. Intercultural Edn., Tng. and Research, Sisters of Holy Names of Jesus and Mary. Roman Catholic. Office: Heritage Coll Office of Pres 3240 Fort Rd Toppenish WA 98948-9599

ROSS, KERRY LYNN, theatre educator; b. Augsburg, Germany, Mar. 25, 1960; came to U.S., 1960; d. James Kyle and Janet (Bean) Parker; m. Brent Derek Ross, Dec. 31, 1981; children: Parker Andrew, Garett Corbin. BFA, Ea. N.Mex. U., 1981, U. Tex., 1984; postgrad., Ea. N.Mex. U., 1987-89. Cert. tchr., Tex., N.Mex., Colo. Tchr. theatre Midland (Tex.) Freshman High Sch., 1982-86; theatre dir. Clovis (N.Mex.) High Sch., 1986-90; theatre tchr. Eaglecrest High Sch., Aurora, Colo., 1990—; cons. Clovis High Sch. Student Assistance Team, 1987-90, chairperson Clovis Schs. Curriculum Guide, 1987-90; mem. EHS assessment team; co-chair Cherry Creek Schs. Fine Arts Curriculum review com., 1992—; mem. Eaglecrest High Sch. Needs Assesment Com., 1992—, Proficiency Com., 1993—. Vol. Am. Cancer Soc., Midland, 1984, Clovis, 1988; block chairperson March of Dimes, Midland, 1983; bd. dirs. Cen. Christian Ch., Clovis, 1988-90; jr. church coord. S.E. Christian Ch., Englewood, Colo., 1992—. Mem. NEA, Internat. Platform Assn., Alliance for Colo. Theatre, Ednl. Theatre Assn., Beta Sigma Phi (Delta Epsilon chpt., sec. Clovis chpt. 1987-89), Colo. Alliance Theatre Educators, Colo. Edn. Assn. Republican. Home: 6312 S Emporia Circle Englewood CO 80111

ROSS, LANSON CLIFFORD, JR., broadcaster, author, consultant; b. Killdeer, N.D., June 23, 1936; s. Lanson Charles and Mabel (Smith) R.; children: David F., Lanson III. BA in Biblical Studies, Seattle Pacific U., 1960; M. Sacred Theology, Internat. Coll., 1984; D of Ministries, 1986. v.p. PAC RIM Coll; founder Planned Living Seminars, Seattle, 1978—. Club: Seattle Yacht. Author: Total Life Prosperity, 1983; Give Your Children a Target, 1985, Take Charge of Your Life, 1986, The Bubble Burst, 1987; producer 5 vol. video seminar A Planned Life Style, 1986, and film A Time to Grow (J.C. Mc Pheeters award 1988). Office: 112 N Lincoln PO Box 2777 Port Angeles WA 98362

ROSS, LEON THOMAS, public administrator, African American history lecturer; b. Jersey City, June 6, 1931; s. Leon Cooper and Gladys (Merritt) R.; children from previous marriage: Dave, Leo, Pamela, Teresa, Christopher; m. Sandra Kathleen LaDue, Nov. 21, 1982; 1 child, Traci LaDue. B in Gen. Edn., U. Nebr., 1966; MPA, Calif. State U., 1979; postgrad., U. So. Calif., 1981. Commd. 2d lt. USAF, 1952; advanced through grades to maj., 1972; assoc. dir. pers. San Joaquin County, Stockton, Calif., 1973-74, manpower tng. cons., 1974-75, affirmative action officer, 1975-86, dep. county administr., 1986-92; lectr. African-Am. Hist. variousorgns., 1979-92; lectr. Calif. State U., Stanislaus, Turlock, Calif., 1980-87; lectr. African-Am. Hist. U. Pacific, Stockton, Calif., 1980-92. Co-author: African American Almanac, 1992; contbr. articles to profl. jours. Bd. dirs. San Joaquin Concert Ballet, Stockton, 1978-82, Boys and Girls Club of Stockton, 1980-92,. Mem. NAACP (life), Am. Soc. Pub. Administrn. (pres. 1981-82), Stockton Esquire Club (sec. 1984-92), Rotary (chair com.).

ROSS, MARILYN ANN, publishing consulting company executive, author, speaker; b. San Diego, Nov. 3, 1939; d. Glenn James and Dorothy (Scudder) Markham; m. Theodore Heimberg (div.); m. Tom Mulvane Ross, May 25, 1977; children: Scott, Steve, Kevin, Laurie. Student San Diego State Coll., 1958-59. Writer, tchr., advt. and pub. cons., 1974-78; v.p. About Books, Inc., Buena Vista, Colo., 1978—; pres. Communication Creativity Corp., Buena Vista, 1978—. Author: Creative Loafing (Press Women award 1978), 1978; Discover Your Roots, 1978; The Encyclopedia of Self-Publishing, 1979 (Press Women award 1979); The Complete Guide to Self-Publishing, 1985, revised edition, 1989, How to Make Big Profits Publishing City and Regional Books, 1986, Big Marketing Ideas for Small Businesses, 1990, Country Bound: Trading Business Suit Blues for Blue Jean Dreams, 1992. Co-founder San Diego Women in Bus., 1980; bd. dirs. Ch. of Religious Sci., San Diego, 1979. Recipient award for restoration of historic hotel San Luis Valley Hist. Soc., Saguache, 1981. Mem. NAFE, Author's Guild, Am. Soc. Journalists and Authors (bd. dirs. 1991—), Nat. Speakers Assn., Internat. Assn. Ind. Pubs. (chmn. 1988-89), Com. Small Mag. Editors and Pubs. Republican. Club: Toastmistress (pres. local club). Home: 209 Church St Buena Vista CO 81211 Office: About Books Inc PO Box 1500 Buena Vista CO 81211-1500

ROSS, MOLLY OWINGS, gold and silversmith, jewelry designer, small business owner; b. Ft. Worth, Feb. 5, 1954; d. James Robertson and Lucy (Owings) R. BFA, Colo. State U., 1976; postgrad., U. Denver, 1978-79. Graphic designer Amber Sky Illustrators and Sta. KCNC TV-Channel 4, Denver, 1977-79; art dir. Mercy Med. Ctr., Denver, 1979-83, Molly Ross Design, Denver, 1983-84; co-owner Deltex Royalty Co., Inc., Colorado Springs, Colo., 1981—, LMA Royalties, Ltd., Colorado Springs, 1993—; art dir., account mgr. Schwing/Walsh Advt., Mktg. and Pub. Rels., Denver, 1984-87, prodn. mgr., 1987-88; jewelry designer Molly O. Ross, Gold and Silversmith, Denver, 1988—. Pres. Four Mile Hist. Pk. Vol. Bd., Denver, 1985-87; bd. dirs. Four Mile Hist. Pk. Assn., Denver, 1985-86, Hist. Denver, Inc., 1986-87, Denver Emergency Housing Coalition, 1989-90; coun. mem. feminization of poverty critical needs area coun. Jr. League Denver, 1989-90, chair children in crisis/edn. critical needs area, 1990-91, project devel., 1991-92, bd. dirs. Jr. League, Denver, 1993—; co-chair Done in a Day Community Project 75th Anniversary Celebration, 1991-93; v.p. community projects Jr. League Denver, 1993—. Named Vol. of Month (March), Jr. League Denver, 1990, Vol. of Yr., Four Mile Hist. Pk., 1988; recipient Gold Peak Mktg. award-team design Am. Mktg. Assn., 1986, Silver Peak Mktg. award-team design Am. Mktg. Assn., 1986, Gold Pick award-art dir. Pub. Rels. Soc. Am., 1980-81. Mem. Natural Resources Def. Coun., Physicians for Social Responsibility, Am. Farmland Trust, Nat. Trust for Hist. Preservation, Sierra Club, Environ. Def. Fund.

ROSS, ROBERT JOSEPH, head professional football coach; b. Richmond, Va., Dec. 23, 1936; s. Leonard Aloysius and Martha Isabelle (MMiller) R.; m. Alice Louise Bucker, June 13, 1959; children: Chris, Mary Catherine, Teresa, Kevin, Robbie. BA, Va. Mil. Inst., 1959. Tchr., head football coach Benedictine High Sch., Richmond, 1959-60; tchr., coach Colonial Heights (Va.) High Sch., 1962-65; asst. football coach Va. Mil. Inst., Lexington, 1965-67, Coll. William and Mary, Williamsburg, Va., 1967-71, Rice U., Houston, 1971-72, U. Md., College Park, 1972-73; head football coach The Citadel, Charleston, S.C., 1973-77; head coach U. Md., College Park, 1982-87; head football coach Ga. Inst. Tech., Atlanta, 1987-91; asst. coach Kansas City (Mo.) Chiefs, 1978-82; head coach San Diego Chargers, 1992—. 1st lt. U.S. Army, 1960-62. Named Coach of Yr., Washington Touchdown Club, 1982, Kodak Coach of Yr., 1990, Bobby Dodd Coach of Yr., 1990, Bear Bryant Coach of Yr., 1990, Scripps-Howard Coach of Yr., 1990, Nat. Coach of Yr., CBS Sports, 1990, Coach of Yr., Walter Camp Football Found., 1990, NFL Coach of Yr. UPI, 1992, Pro Football Weekly, 1992, Pro Football Writers' Assn., 1992, Football News, 1992, Football Digest, 1992, Maxwell Football Club, 1992, AFC Coach of Yr. Kansas City 101 Banquet. Mem. Am. Football Coaches Assn., Coll. Football Assn. (coaching com. 1988-92). Roman Catholic.

ROSS, ROBERT KING, retired educator; b. Manti, Utah, Jan. 27, 1927; s. Clarence King Ross and Annamae Plant Nielson; m. Patsy Ruth Tattu, Dec. 25, 1947 (dec. 1988); children: Scott, Barbara, Richard, Michael. BA in Secondary Edn., Ea. Wash. Coll. Edn., 1951. Cert. master tchr., Wash. Tchr. Reardon (Wash.) High Sch., 1951-52; microphotography specialist U.S. Atomic Energy Commn., Richland, Wash., 1952-54; mgr. St. Paul br. Dakota Microfilm Svc., 1954-61; system specialist 3M Co., Seattle, 1961-64; prin., tchr. U.S. Bur. Indian Affairs, Shungnak, Alaska, 1964-68; tchr. Port Angeles (Wash.) Sch. Dist., 1968-89; ret.; mem. Wash. State Newspaper in Edn. Com., Tacoma, 1970-92; instr. record ann. tchrs. seminars. Contbr. articles to profl. jours. With USMC, 1945-47. Recipient Cert. of Appreciation Seattle P.I. Newspaper, 1980. Fellow Elks; mem. DAV, VFW. Home: 324 E 11th St Port Angeles WA 99362-7932

ROSS, RUSSELL, pathologist, educator; b. St. Augustine, Fla., May 25, 1929; s. Samuel and Minnie (DuBoff) R.; m. Jean Long Teller, Feb. 22, 1956; children: Valerie Regina, Douglas Teller. A.B., Cornell U., 1951; D.D.S., Columbia U., 1955; Ph.D., U. Wash., 1962; DSc (hon.P, Med. Coll. of Pa., 1987. Intern Columbia-Presbyn. Med. Ctr., 1955-56, USPHS Hosp., Seattle, 1956-58; spl. research fellow pathology sch. medicine U. Wash., Seattle, 1958-62, asst. prof. pathology and oral biology sch. medicine and denistry, 1962-65, assoc. prof. pathology Sch. Medicine, 1965-69, prof. Sch. Medicine, 1969—, adj. prof. biochemistry Sch. Medicine, 1978—, assoc. dean for sci. affairs sch. medicine, 1971-78, chmn. dept. pathology sch. medicine, 1982—; vis. scientist Strangeways Research Lab., Cambridge, Eng.; mem. research com. Am. Heart Assn.; mem. adv. bd. Found. Cardiologique Princess Liliane, Brussels, Belgium; life fellow Clare Hall, Cambridge U.; mem. adv. council Nat. Heart, Lung and Blood Inst., NIH, 1978-81; vis. prof. Royal Soc. Medicine, U.K., 1987. Editorial bd. Procs. Exptl. Biology and Medicine, 1971-86, Jour. Cell Biology, 1972-74, Exptl. Cell Rsch., 1982-92, Jour. Exptl. Medicine, Growth Factors, Am. Jour. Pathology, Internat. Cell Biology Jour.; assoc. editor Arteriosclerosis, 1982-92, Jour. Cellular Physiology, Jour. Cellular Biochemistry; reviewing editorial bd. Sci. mag., 1987-90; contbr. articles to profl. jours. Trustee Seattle Symphony Orch. Recipient Birnberg Research award Columbia U., 1975, Nat. Rsch. Achievement award Am. Heart Assn., 1990; Gordon Wilson medal Am. Clin. and Climatol. Assn., 1981; named to Inst. Medicine, Nat. Acad. Scis.; Japan Soc. Promotion of Sci. fellow, 1985, Guggenheim fellow, 1966-67. Fellow AAAS, Am. Acad. Arts and Scis.; mem. Am. Soc. Cell Biology, Tissue Culture Assn., Am. Assn. Pathologists (Rous-Whipple award 1992), Internat. Soc. Cell Biology, Electron Microscope Soc. Am., Am. Heart Assn. (fellow Coun. on Arteriosclerosis, Nat. Rsch. Achievement award 1990), Royal Micros. Soc., Harvey Soc. (hon.), Am. Soc. Biochemistry and Molecular Biology, Royal Belgian Acad. Scis. (fgn. corr. mem.), Sigma Xi. Home: 4811 NE 42d St Seattle WA 98105 Office: U Wash Sch Medicine 1959 NE Pacific St Seattle WA 98195-0001

ROSS, STEVEN CHARLES, business administration educator, consultant; b. Salem, Oreg., Jan. 14, 1947; s. Charles Reed and Edythe Marie (Calvin) R.; m. Meredith Lynn Buholts, June 15, 1969; children: Kelly Lynn, Shannon Marie. BS, Oreg. State U., 1969; MS, U. Utah, 1976, PhD, 1980. Cons. IRS Tng. Staff, Ogden, Utah, 1977-80; asst. prof. Marquette U., Milw., 1980-88; assoc. prof. Mont. State U., Bozeman, 1988-89, Western Washington U., Bellingham, 1989—; govt. and industry cons.; cons. editor microcomputing series West Pub. Co. Author 25 books and several articles in computer systems field. Mem. adv. com. Milwaukee County Mgmt., 1981-85, Port of Bellingham, 1990—. Capt. U.S. Army, 1969-75. Recipient rsch. fellowship, U. Utah, 1977-79, Marquette U., 1981-84. Mem. Acad. Mgmt., Decision Scis. Inst., Inst. Mgmt. Scis., Assn. for Computing Machinery, Assn. Computer Educators, Bellingham Yacht Club (trustee 1992—). Office: Western Wash U Coll Bus and Econs Bellingham WA 98225

ROSS, TERENCE WILLIAM, architect; b. Saginaw, Mich., Sept. 27, 1935; s. Oran Lewis and Drucilla (Chadman) R.; BArch, U. Mich., 1958; m. Patricia Ann Marshall, Sept. 27, 1974; children by previous marriage: Deborah, David. Designer, Roger W. Peters Constrn. Co., Fond du Lac, Wis., 1958-62; draftsman Kenneth Clark, Architect, Santa Fe, N.Mex., 1962-63, Holien & Buckley, Architects, Santa Fe, 1963-64; office mgr. Philippe Register, Architect, Santa Fe, 1964-68; prin. Register, Ross, & Brunet architects, engrs., Santa Fe, 1968-71, Luna-Ross & Assoc., 1971-77; staff CNWC Architects, Tucson, to 1981, ADP Architects, 1981-89; sr. architect U. Calif., 1989—. Vice chmn. N.Mex. R.R. Authority, 1969-74, sec., 1970-72. Bd. dirs. Colo., N.Mex. Soc. Preservation of Narrow Gauge. Recipient award for hist. preservation N.Mex. Arts Commn., 1971, award for outstanding svcs.to community Santa Fe Press Club, 1972; named col. aide-de-camp State of N.Mex., 1968, hon. mem. staff atty. gen. Mem. AIA (chpt. pres. 1970, dir.), Constrn. Specifications Inst., N.Mex. Soc. Architects (dir. 1972), Ariz. Soc. Architects, N.Mex. R.R. Authorities (chmn. joint exec. com. 1970-74), Sacramento Valley Garden Ry. Soc. (pres. 1993), San Gabriel Hist. Soc. (hon.), Alpha Rho Chi, Sashay Rounders Sq. Dance Club (pres. 1974), Diamond Squares Sq. Dance Club, Railroad Club (pres. N.Mex. 1969, 70, dir.). Author: Track of the Cats. Home and Office: 2813 57th St Sacramento CA 95817-2403

ROSS, TERRY JOSEPH, real estate broker; b. Hungtington Park, Calif., Nov. 14, 1952; s. Atha Joseph and Mary Lucille (Smith) R.; m. Shirley Joan, July 27,, 1991. BA, U. So. Calif., L.A., 1974. Lic. real estate broker, Calif. Dir. pub. rels. L.A. Aztecs, Redondo Beach, Calif., 1975-76; sports info. dir. Calif. State U., Long Beach, 1976-84; v.p. mktg. Pacific Coast Realty, Long Beach, 1984-86; sales assoc. Realty World/SW Properties, Long Beach, 1986-89; broker-owner TR Properties, Long Beach, 1989—. Real estate columnist L.A. Herald Examiner, 1986-89, syndicated real estate columnist Realty Views, 1986—. Mem. Nat. Assn. Realtors, Calif. Assn. Realtors, Long Beach Dist. Bd. Realtors, Nat. Assn. Real Estate Editors, Coto de Caza Country Club. Office: TR Properties 371-C Redondo Ave Long Beach CA 90814

ROSS, TOM M., marketing consultant, author; b. St. John, Kans., Aug. 24, 1933; s. Charley M. and Alice Agnes (Culp) R.; m. Marilyn Ann Markham, May 25, 1977; children: Scott, Steve, Kevin, Mark. BSEE, Pacific Coll., 1973. Registered profl. mktg. cons. Engring. mgr. Vanguard Electronics, Englewood, Calif., 1972-74; operational mgr. Martin Wolf, Inc., San Diego, 1974-76; chief exec. officer, bd. chmn. Rsch. Electronics, San Diego, 1976-77; engring. mgr. TRW Electronics, San Diego, 1977-78; v.p., chief fin. officer Communication Creativity Corp., Buena Vista, Colo., 1978—; pres., chief exec. officer About Books, Inc., Buena Vista, 1978—, also bd. dirs., 1978—; bd. dirs. Communication Creativity Corp., Buena Vista, Paradise Valley Ranch Inc., Buena Vista. Author: Country Bound!, 1992; co-author: Encyclopedia/Self-Publishing, 1979 (Best Book award 1979), Complete Guide/Self-Publishing, 1985, Marketing Your Books, 1990 (Best Book award 1990), Big Marketing Ideas, 1990; editor: Creative Loafing, 1978 (Best Book award 1978). Bd. dirs. Paradise Valley Community Ch., Buena Vista, 1984—; work experience employer Buena Vista High Sch., 1990. Recipient Commendation for Community Svc. award Mayor's Office San Diego, 1978. Mem. Internat. Assn. Ind. Pubs. (COSMEP) (bd. dirs. 1991—), Am. Mgmt. Assn., Nat. Speakers Assn., Author's Guild, Pubs. Mktg. Assn., Buena Vista C. of C. (bd. dirs. 1990-92). Republican. Home: 209 Church St Buena Vista CO 81211 Office: About Books Inc 425 Cedar St Buena Vista CO 81211-1500

ROSS, VICTOR JULIUS, school superintendent; b. Salina, Kans., Mar. 2, 1935; s. Victor J. and Lola Ruth (Sloop) R.; m. Anna Marie Berger, June 15, 1957; children: Victor III, Diane E., Linda M. BA, U. Denver, 1958, MA, 1964; EdD, U. Colo., 1978. Tchr. English Littleton (Colo.) Schs., 1958-65; prin. Littleton Jr. High Sch., 1965-69, Moline (Ill.) High Sch., 1969-72, Lakewood (Colo.) High Sch., 1972-76; asst. supt. Bettendorf (Iowa) Community Sch. Dist., 1976-81; supt. Aurora (Colo.) Pub. Sch., 1981—. Author: The Forbidden Apple, 1985, Bite the Wall, 1986; contbr. articles to profl. jours. City councilman City of Littleton, 1964-68. Named Pub. Servant of Yr., Littleton Ind., 1965. Mem. Nat. Sch. Bds. Assn. (jour. conf. faculty 1982—, named one of 100 Top Exec. Educators, 1984), Collegial Assn. Devel. and Renewal Educators (jour. editor 1982—), Phi Delta Kappa. Episcopalian. Lodge: Rotary. Home: 15890 E 8th Cir Aurora CO 80011-7304 Office: Aurora Pub Schs 1085 Peoria St Aurora CO 80011-6297•

ROSS, VONIA PEARL, insurance agent; b. Taylorville, Ill., Dec. 4, 1942; d. Alvin Clyde and Lois Eva (Weller) Brown; m. Wyatt Gene Ross, Nov. 11, 1962 (Div. Nov. 1986); children: Craig Allen Ross, Cayle Allen Ross. Student, So. Ill. U., 1962-64, Palomar Coll., 1986-88, San Diego State U., 1988-90. Real estate agt. Joe Foster Agy., Collinsville, Ill., 1964-69; office mgr. real estate Bank of St. Louis, 1969-73; real estate agt. Palmer-Stelman, San Diego, 1986-89; office mgr. real estate McMillin Realty, San Diego, 1989-90; mgr., ins. agt. Calif. Plus Ins., San Diego, 1990—; mem. Calif. Assn. Real Estate, Sacramento, 1986—, San Diego Bd. Realtors, 1986—, Health Underwriters, 1991—. Mem. NOW, San Diego, 1988; mem. activist Barbara Boxer Campaign, San Diego, 1992, Susan Golding Campaign, San Diego, 1992. Recipient Ill. State Assembly scholarship, 1962. Mem. Soroptimist Rancho Bernardo, Rancho Bernardo C. of C. Methodist. Home: 18284 Fernando Way San Diego CA 92128

ROSS, WARREN HOWARD, rancher; b. Havre, Mont., Apr. 14, 1927; s. Thomas Alexander and Ella Marcy (Angell) R.; m. Betty Don McMillan, Nov. 25, 1950; children: Donald, Linda, John, Hugh. BS in Gen. Agriculture, Mont. State Coll., 1950. Ptnr. Ross Ranch, Chinook, Mont., 1950-68; pres. Ross 8 Bar 7 Ranch, Inc., Chinook, Mont., 1968—; dir. Helena (Mont.) br. Minn. Fed. Res. Bank, 1986-89; mem. Mont. Bd. Oil and Gas Conservation, Helena, 1986-94, chmn., 1990-94. Dir. Northern Mont. Health Care, Inc., Havre, 1983—, Western Bank, N.A., Chinook, 1990—, Mont. Community Found., Helena, 1990—. With USN, 1945-46, North Africa. Mem. Mont. Stockgrowers Assn., Am. Legion, Grand Lodge Mont. AF&AM (grand master 1984-85). Republican. Presbyterian. Home and Office: Rte 71 Box 17 Chinook MT 59523

ROSS, WILLIAM H., accountant; b. Meridian, Miss., Aug. 19, 1946; s. Bertrand Grady and Mary (McDonald) R.; m. Kitty Wesley, June 7, 1969; children: Julie, Grady. BS, U. Ala., 1969; MBA, U. Ala., Birmingham, 1984. Acct. Ernst & Whinney, Birmingham, 1972-82, Cleve., 1982-86; ptnr. Ernst & Whinney, Los Angeles, 1986—. Capt. U.S. Army, 1969-72. Mem. Am. Inst. CPA's. Office: Ernst & Whinney 515 S Flower St Ste 2800 Los Angeles CA 90071-2283

ROSSER, JAMES MILTON, university president; b. East St. Louis, Ill., Apr. 16, 1939; s. William M. and Mary E. (Bass) R.; m. Carmen Rosita Colby, Dec. 27, 1962; 1 son, Terrence. B.A., So. Ill. U., 1962, M.A., 1963, Ph.D., 1969. Diagnostic bacteriologist Holden Hosp., Carbondale, Ill., 1961-63; research bacteriologist Eli Lilly & Co., Indpls., 1963-66; coordinator Black Am. studies, instr. health edn. So. Ill. U., Carbondale, 1968-69; asst.

prof. Black Am. studies dir. So. Ill. U., 1969-70, asst. to chancellor, 1970; asso. vice chancellor for acad. affairs U. Kans., Lawrence, 1970-74; assoc. prof. edn., pharmacology and toxicology U. Kans., 1971-74; vice chancellor dept. higher edn. State of N.J., Trenton, 1974-79; acting chancellor State of N.J., 1977; pres., prof. health care mgmt. Calif. State U., Los Angeles, 1979—; mem. tech. resource panel Ctr. for Research and Devel. in Higher Edn., U. Calif., Berkeley, 1974-76; mem. health maintenance orgn. com. Health Planning Coun., State of N.J., 1975-79; mem. standing com. on research and devel. bd. trustees Ednl. Testing Service, 1976-77; mem. steering com. and task force on retention of minorities in engring. Assembly of Engring. NRC, 1975-78; mem. Bd. Med. Examiners, State of N.J., 1978-79; vis. faculty mem. Inst. Mgmt. of Lifelong Edn., Grad. Sch. Edn., Harvard U., 1979; mem. Calif. State U. Trustees Spl. Long Range Fin. Planning Com., 1982-87; mem. Am. Coun. on Edn., 1979—, AFL/CIO Labor Higher Edn. Coun., 1983—, Nat. Commn. Higher Edn. Issues, 1981-82; mem. The Calif. Achievement Coun., 1983-89, strategic adv. counc. Coll. and Univs. Systems Exchange, 1988-91; bd. dirs. Am. Humanities Coun., So. Calif. Am. Humanics, Inc. Coun., Sanwa Bank Calif., 1993—, Edison, Fedco, Inc. Author: An Analysis of Health Care Delivery, 1977. Mem. exec. bd., chmn. varsity scouting program Los Angeles Area council Boy Scouts Am., 1980—; bd. dirs. Hispanic Urban Ctr., Los Angeles, 1979—, Los Angeles Urban League, 1982—, Community TV of So. Calif., Sta. KCET, 1980-89, United Way, Los Angeles, 1980-91, Orthopaedic Hosp., 1983-86; mem. Citizen's Adv. Council Congl. Caucus Sci. and Tech., 1983—; bd. dirs. Los Angeles Philharm. Assn., 1986—; mem. performing arts council/edn. council Music Ctr., 1984—; mem. minority bus. task force Pacific Bell, 1985-86; mem. bd. of govs Nat. ARC, 1986-91, Mayor's Blue Ribbon Task Force on Drugs City of L.A., 1988; Nat. Adv. Council on Aging, 1989-93. NSF fellow, 1961; NDEA fellow, 1967-68; recipient award of recognition in Edn. Involvement for Young Achievers, 1981, Pioneer of Black Hist. Achievement award Brotherhood Crusade, 1981, Alumni Achievement award So. Ill. U., 1982, Friend of Youth award Am. Humanics, Inc., 1985, Leadership award Dept of Higher Edn. Ednl. Equal Opportunity Fund Program, 1989; Medal of Excellence Golden State Minority Found., 1990. Mem. Calif. C. of C. (bd. dirs.), Alhambra C. of C. (bd. dirs. 1979—), Los Angeles C. of C. (bd. dirs. 1985-90), Am. Assn. State Colls. and Univs., Kappa Delta Pi, Phi Kappa Phi. Roman Catholic. Office: Calif State U LA Office of the Pres 5151 State University Dr Los Angeles CA 90032-8500

ROSSI, AMADEO JOSEPH, chemist; b. Seattle, Sept. 23, 1954; s. Amadeo Joseph and Maria Asilia (Chinella) R.; m. Frances Marie Stotts, Sept. 19, 1981; children: Anthony Joseph, Matthew Christopher, Brian Michael. BS in Wood and Fiber Sci., U. Wash., 1979, MS in wood chemistry, 1987. Research aide U. Wash., Seattle, 1978-79; environ. engr. Georgia-Pacific Corp., Eugene, Oreg., 1980; engr., dir. hazardous waste remediation projects Ebasco Environ., Seattle, 1981—. Contbr. articles to profl. jours. Mem. Am. Chem. Soc., Air Pollution Control Assn., Forest Products Rsch. Soc., Xi Sigma Pi, Sigma Xi. Office: EBASCO Svcs Inc 10900 NE 8th St Bellevue WA 98004-4405

ROSSI, GUY ANTHONY, publishing executive; b. Binghamton, N.Y., Aug. 12, 1952; s. Anthony J. and Mary L. (Cannavino) R. Assoc. Liberal Arts, Broome Community Coll., 1973; BA, N.Mex. State U., 1977. Chief exec. officer, owner Inter Gen. Pub., Mesilla, N.Mex., 1977—; pub. Mesilla Valley Courier, 1977-81; graphic artist Las Cruces (N.Mex.) Sun News, 1981-85; owner Rossi's Cinderellas, Mesilla, 1985—; art dir. Hynes Advt., Las Cruces, 1986-89; graphic artist, printing and duplicating N.Mex. State U., Las Cruces, 1977-77; graphic artist Larry Edwards Advt., Las Cruces, 1991-92; head artist Las Cruces Sun News, 1992—; print media cons. N.Mex. Farm and Ranch Mag., Las Cruces, 1980-89. Pub., editor historic map: The Mesilla Map, 1977-81; artist commemorative envelopes and U.S. Postal Svc. postmarks, 1977—. Fellow Am. Philatelic Soc., Am. Revenue Assn., Am. Topical Assn., Cinderella Stamp Club of Eng., N.Mex. Philatelic Assn.; mem. Mesilla Valley Stamp Club (charter mem., pres., bd. dirs., 1990-91, graphic and print media cons., 1977—). Democrat. Office: Rossi's Cinderellas Inter Gen Pub PO Box 367 Mesilla NM 88046-0367

ROSSI, RICHARD JOSEPH, statistics educator; b. Long Beach, Calif., Mar. 13, 1956; s. Calvin Joseph and Alberta Elizabeth (Casier) R.; m. Debra Jo Schons, Jan. 2, 1987. BA, Sacramento State U., 1978; MS, Iowa State U., 1980; PhD, Oreg. State U., 1988. Fly tyer Scarlet Ibis Fly Shop, Corvallis, Oreg., 1982-88; statis. cons. Intelledex, Inc., Corvallis, 1984; instr. stats. Oreg. State U., Corvallis, 1985-88; prof. stats. Mont. State U., Bozeman, 1988-91, Calif. Poly. State U., San Luis Obispo, 1991—; agrl. cons. Mont. State U., 1988-92; statis. cons. Intelledex, Inc., 1984, Calif. Poly. State U., 1991-92; statis. referee Annals of Stats., 1991. Contbr. articles, book revs. to profl. publs. Fellow Sigma Xi.; mem. Am. Statis. Assn., Inst. Math. Stats., Mont. Statis. Assn. (sec.-treas. 1990-91), Phi Kappa Phi. Democrat. Home: 1417 14th St Los Osos CA 93402 Office: Calif Poly State U San Luis Obispo CA 93407

ROSSIN, HERBERT YALE, television broadcaster; b. Phila., May 15, 1936; s. Jack Rossin and Edna Wolinsky; m. Shirley Ann Heineman, Oct. 15, 1960 (div. Jan. 1964); m. Meryl Ann Barsky, Nov. 15, 1965; children: Abby Rae, Shane J.P. Student, Spring Garden Inst., Phila., 1956, Temple U., 1958. Gen. mgr. KIKU TV/13, Honolulu, 1968-70; br. mgr. Columbia Pictures, Las Vegas, 1970-74; pntr. Internat. TV Concepts, Las Vegas, 1974-78; sta. mgr. KUAM AM/FM/TV, Agana, Guam, 1978-80; v.p. Tag Mktg. and Advt., Cherry Hill, N.J., 1981-83; gen. mgr. WLXI-TV/61, Greensboro, N.C., 1983-85; v.p., gen. mgr. WHLL-TV/27, Boston, 1986-87; v.p. Home Shopping Network, L.A., 1987-88; owner A.S.A.P. Multi-Corp., Las Vegas, 1988—; broadcast cons. Fashion Channel-Video Mall, L.A., 1987-88; scriptwriter Four Star Pictures, L.A., 1988-89; network cons. Las Vegas TV Network, 1992; pres. Video Music TV Stas. Am., 1984-88, named Broadcaster of Yr., 1985. Producer motion picture Miss Conduct, 1957; creator TV show New Millionaires; editor Israel Mag., 1960. Producer telethon Heart Fund Am., Las Vegas, 1972, Albert Einstein Sch., Las Vegas, 1974; capt. CAP. With U.S. Air N.G., 1954-58. Recipient Edn. award Albert Einstein Hebrew Acad., 1974, People Law Sch. award Nev. Trial Lawyers, 1992 Citizenship award Govt. of Guam, 1979, others. Mem. Nat. Assn. TV Program Execs., Nat. Assn. Broadcasters, Am. Assn. Ret. People, Soc. for Prevention of Cruelty to Animals. Democrat. Jewish. Home and Office: ASAP Multi Corp 7704 Musical Ln Las Vegas NV 89128

ROSSO, LOUIS T., scientific instrument manufacturing company executive; b. San Francisco, 1933; married. A.B., San Francisco State Coll., 1955; M.B.A., U. Santa Clara, 1967. Product specialist Spinco div. Beckman Instruments, Fullerton, Calif., 1959-63, mktg. mgr., 1963-69, mgr. Spinco div., 1969-70, mgr. clin. instruments div., 1970-74, corp. v.p., mgr. analytical instruments group, 1974-80, corp. sr. v.p., 1980-83, pres., 1983—, now also chmn., chief exec. officer; also bd. dirs. Beckman Instruments, Inc.; v.p. SmithKline Beckman Corp., Phila. Office: Beckman Instruments Inc 2500 N Harbor Blvd Fullerton CA 92635-2600*

ROST, THOMAS LOWELL, botany educator; b. St. Paul, Dec. 28, 1941; s. Lowell Henry Rost and Agnes Marie (Wojtowicz) Jurek; m. Ann Marie Ruhland, Aug. 31, 1963; children: Christopher, Timothy, Jacquelyn. BS, St. John's U., Collegeville, Minn., 1963; MA, Mankato State U., 1965; PhD, Iowa State U., 1970. Postdoctoral fellow Brookhaven Nat. Lab., Upton, N.Y., 1970-72; prof. botany U. Calif., Davis, 1972—; cons. faculty of agronomy U. Uruguay, 1979, 89; vis. fellow Rsch. Soc. Biol. Sci., Canberra, Australia, 1979-80; vis. prof. U. Wroclaw, Poland, 1987, U. Exeter, 1993. Co-author: Botany: A Brief Introduction to Plant Biology, 1979, Botany: An Introduction on Plant Biology, 1982; co-editor: Mechanisms and Control of Cell Division, 1977; also numerous articles to profl. jours. Served to capt. U.S. Army, 1965-67. Fellow Royal Microscopy Soc., Japan Soc. Promotion of Sci.; mem. Bot. Soc. Am., Soc. Exptl. Biology, Soc. Devel. Biology, Am. Inst. Biol. Sci. Democrat. Roman Catholic. Office: U Calif Dept Botany Davis CA 95616-8537

ROSTAD, KENNETH LEIF, provincial government official; b. Yorkton, Sask., Can., Sept. 7, 1941; s. Leif and Mary Katherine (McLennan) R.; m. Shirley Gail Tien, May 19, 1979; children: Kyle, Kelsy, Karsten. B Commerce, U. Saskatoon, Sask., 1967, LLB, 1979. With Royal Bank Can., 1959-60, Shell Can. Ltd., 1967-69, Sears Can. Inc., 1969-76; ptnr. Gaede Fielding Rostad & Syed, Camrose, Alta., Can., 1979-86; solicitor gen. Govt. Alta., Edmonton, 1986-88, min. responsible for housing, 1987-88, min. responsible for native affairs, 1987-91, atty. gen., 1988—, apptd. min. justice and atty. gen., 1993-. Alderman City of Camrose, 1985-86; mem. legis. assembly Province Alta., 1986—. Mem. Law Soc. Alta. (hon. bencher), Can. Bar Assn., Lions Internat. (pres.). Progressive Conservative. Lutheran. Office: Atty Gen, Legislature Bldg Rm 423, Edmonton, AB Canada T5K 2E8

ROSTVOLD, GERHARD NORMAN, economist, consultant; b. Nashwauk, Minn., Oct. 15, 1919; s. Arndt and Olive Mathilda (Ness) R.; m. Virginia Fay Faubion, Feb. 3, 1945; children—Roger Mark, Laura Ann, Christine Marie, Ellen Alicia. A.B. in Econs.-Accountancy with great distinction, Stanford, 1948, M.A. in Econs, 1949, Ph.D. in Econs, 1955. Instr. Stanford U., 1949-51; prof. econs. and acctg. Pomona Coll., Claremont, Calif., 1952-66; cons. Urbanomics Rsch. Assoc., Laguna Hills, Calif., 1966—; adj. prof. econs. Pepperdine U.; econ. newscaster Sta. KHJ-TV, L.A., 1978-82; econ. cons. to govt., industry; trustee Mortgage & Realty Trust. Author: The Southern California Metropolis—1980, 1960, Financing California Government, 1967, The Economics of Energy, 1975, Economics and the Environment, 1975, The Economics of the Public Utility Enterprise, 1976, Understanding How the Economic System Works, 1976, Teacher's Instructional Program for Understanding How the Economic System Works, 1976, Charting Your Path to Economic and Financial Survival in the 1980's, 1979, How to Stretch your Dollars to Cope with the Inflation of the 1980's, 1981; co-author: California Local Finance, 1960, Garcia-Rostvold Work Experience Education Series, 1974, (with Thomas J. Dudley) Congressional report, New Perspectives on Grazing Fees and Public Land Management in the 1990s, 1992; social sci. editor: Stone/Leswing Social Sci. Series; editor: Rostvold Econ. Outlook and Personal Money Mgmt. Newsletter; contbr. articles to profl jours. Chmn. nat. adv. bd. Coun. Pub. Lands; mem. Calif. advisory bd., mem. Calif. Coun. Econ. Edn. Served with USAAF, 1942-45. NSF fellow Stanford U., 1965-66; recipient Wig Disting. Professorship award Pomona Coll., 1962; Conservation award Dept. Interior, 1975. Mem. Am. Econ. Assn., Western Econ. Assn. (pres. 1966-67), Nat. Tax Assn. (pres.), Lambda Alpha. Home: #4 Montpellier Laguna Niguel CA 92677 Office: Urbanomics Rsch 23276 S Pointe Dr Laguna Hills CA 92653-1432

ROSZAK, JOE GERARD, psychiatric treatment center administrator; b. Sheboygan, Wis., Nov. 4, 1958; s. Kenneth John and Mary Jane (Kuhn) R. BA, U. Wis., 1981; MA, So. Ill. U., 1987. Head resident Office of Student Housing, Whitewater, Wis., 1978-80; behavior modification technician Rock County Mental Health, Janesville, Wis., 1979-82; instr. So. Ill. U., Carbondale, 1982-83; resident mgr. Brehm Preparatory Sch., Carbondale, 1982-83, program coord., 1983-84, instr., 1984; community counselor Youth Options Project, Marion, Ill., 1984-85; div. dir. Inst. Logopedics, Wichita, Kans., 1985-88; exec. dir. Adolescent Day Treatment Ctr., Winston, Oreg., 1988—; bd. dirs. Oreg. Youth/Child Care Workers, Kans. Child Care Workers Assn.; pres. Interagy. Coun. Coach Spl. Olympics, Douglas County, Oreg., 1989—; vol. Salvation Army, Douglas County, 1989—, Jaycees, Douglas County, 1989—, Umpqua Wildlife Rescue, Douglas County, 1990—; state v.p. Job Svc. Employers Com., 1992—, chair Roseburg Area com., 1992—, So. Oreg. Regional dir., 1991-92, mem. 1990—; active Douglas County Domestic Violence Task Force. Mem. AAAS, NOW, Community Devel. Soc., Oreg. Assn. of Treatment Ctrs. (chmn. profl. devel., sec., treas. chair orgnl. devel.), Coun. for Exceptional Children, N.Y. Acad. Scis., Am. Sociogical Assn., Umpqua Coalition for Human Concerns, WInston Econ. Devel. Com., Child/Youth Issues Com., Project Leadership (chair 1993—), Diamond Lake Ski Patrol, Roseburg Area C. of C. (mem. bus. devel. and edn., bus. ptnrship coms.), Velo Club, Whitewater Club, Edelweiss Club, Phi Eta Sigma, Alpha Kappa Delta, Psi Chi, Phi Kappa Phi. Office: Adolescent Day Treatment 671 SW Main PO Box # 2033 Winston OR 97496

ROTBART, HEIDI LEE, personal entertainment manager; b. Cleve., Oct. 10, 1957; d. Alan Jerome and Yetta (Ringer) R. BS, Bradley U., 1979. Pub. rels. dir. Carousel Dinner Theatre, Ravenna, Ohio, 1979-80; tour mgr. to Phyllis Diller Phil Dil Prodns., L.A., 1981-86; entertainment personal mgr. Heidi Rotbart Mgmt., L.A., 1986—; comedy cons., L.A., 1986—. Author: Inside Hollywood, 1990. Named one of Men and Women of Distinction, F Same, Cambridge, Eng., 1990. Democrat. Jewish. Office: Heidi Rotbart Mgmt 1810 Malcolm Ave Los Angeles CA 90025-4704

ROTH, GARY WAYNE, electronic instrument company executive; b. Spokane, Wash., Feb. 13, 1947; s. William G. and Lillie (Wessell) R.; m. Karen B. Flowers, Aug. 28, 1948; children: Tenaya, Nathanial. BS in Physics, Seattle Pacific U., 1969. Chief engr. nuclear physics lab. U. Wash., Seattle, 1969-78; prin. rsch. engr. Spectra Tech., Bellevue, Wash., 1978-83; engr. mgr. Opcon, Everett, Wash., 1983-84; sr. engr. Eldec Corp., Lynnwood, Wash., 1984-86; owner, gen. mgr. SensorLink Corp., Acme, Wash., 1986—; cons. Seattle City Light, 1983. Contbr. articles to profl. jours.; inventor, patentee in field. Office: SensorLink Corp 5687 Doren Rd Acme WA 98220

ROTH, HADDEN WING, lawyer; b. Oakland, Calif., Feb. 10, 1930; s. Mark and Jane (Haley) R.; m. Alice Becker, Aug., 1987; 1 child, Elizabeth Wing. AA, Coll. Marin, 1949; BA, U. Calif., Berkeley, 1951; JD, U. Calif., San Francisco, 1957. Bar: Calif. 1958, U.S. Dist. Ct. (no. dist.) Calif. 1958, U.S. Ct. Appeals (9th cir.) 1958, U.S. Supreme Ct. 1966. Ptnr. Bagshaw, Weissich, Martinelli & Jordan, San Rafael, 1957-63; pvt. practice San Rafael, 1963—; dep. city atty. City of San Rafael, 1958-60, City of Sausalito and Mill Valley, Calif., 1964-66; dep. dist. atty. County of Marin, 1960-63; judge Marin County Mcpl. Ct., 1966-70; spl. cons. Marin Muni Water Dist., Corte Madera, Calif., County of Marin; atty. Bolinas Pub. Utility Dist., Ross Valley Fire Svc., Ross Valley Paramedics, Town of Ross and San Anselmo, Calif.; lectr. law Golden Gate Coll. Law, San Francisco, 1971-73. Chmn. Marin County prison task force, 1973;bd. dirs. Marin Gen. Hosp., 1964-66. With U.S. Army, 1952-54. Named Outstanding Citizen of Yr., Coll. Marin, 1972. Mem. ABA, Calif. Bar Assn., Marin County Bar Assn. Home: 343 Fairhills Dr San Rafael CA 94901-1110 Office: 1050 Northgate Dr San Rafael CA 94903-2544

ROTH, JOE, motion picture company executive; b. 1948. Prodn. assistant various commls. and feature films, San Francisco; also lighting dir. Pitchel Players, San Francisco; then producer Pitchel Players, L.A.; co-founder Morgan Creek Prodns., L.A., 1987-89; chmn. Fox Film Corp., L.A., 1989-92; founder Caravan Pictures, L.A., 1992—. Producer numerous films including Tunnelvision, Cracking Up, Americathon, Our Winning Season, The Final Terror, The Stone Boy, Where the River Runs Black, Bachelor Party, Off Beat, Streets of Gold (dir. debut), Revenge of the Nerds II (also dir.); exec. producer Young Guns, Dead Ringers, Skin Deep, Major League, Renegades, Coupe de Ville (also dir.), Enemies: A Love Story. Office: Caravan Pictures 500 S Buena Vista St Burbank CA 91521-1700

ROTH, LEONARD JEROME, financial consultant, insurance agent; b. Gary, Ind., Jan. 26, 1935; s. Milton James and Theresa (Kohn) R.; m. Betty Lou Bannerman (div.); children: Luanne, William, Rosemarie, Brad; m. Jo Ann Sandra Livingston, Mar. 11, 1978. BA, UCLA, 1957; MBA, Mich. State U., 1963. CLU. Chartered fin. cons. Century Benefit Cons., Encino, Calif., 1976-89; fin. planner Integrated Fin., Encino, Calif., 1989-90; chartered fin. cons. Fin. Mgmt. Svc., Inc., Reseda, Calif., 1990—; mem. Warner Ctr. Estate Planners Coun. Mem. Rep. Elen Gallegly Congl. Support Group, L.A., 1989—; bd. dirs. San Fernando Valley Men's ORT. With U.S. Army, 1957-58. Named Man of Yr. Nat. Fedn. Jewish Mens Clubs, 1975. Mem. San Fernando Valley CLU, San Fernando Valley Estate Planners, UCLA Alumni Assn. Jewish. Office: Roth Fin Svcs 17750 Sherman Way # 104 Reseda CA 91335-3380

ROTH, MOIRA, art historian; b. London, July 24, 1933; d. Herbert Austin and Gertrude Shannon. BA, NYU, 1959; MA, U. Calif., Berkeley, 1966, PhD, 1974. Various lectr. positions Calif., 1973-76; vis. assoc. prof. Hayward (Calif.) State U., 1979-80; Whitney Halstead vis. prof. Sch. Art Inst. of Chgo., 1981; asst. prof. visual arts dept. to assoc. prof. U. Calif. at San Diego, La Jolla, 1974-86; dir. U. Calif. San Diego Mandeville Art Gallery, 1974-76; dir. visual arts dept. grad. program U. Calif. at San Diego, 1978-79; vis. prof. Trefethen chair in art history Mills. Coll., Oakland, 1985-86, Trefethen prof. of art history, 1986—, head art dept., 1987-90; cons. and lectr. in field. Editor, contbr. The Amazing Decade: Women and Performance Art in America, 1970-80, 1983, Connecting Conversations: Interviews with 28 Bay Area Women Artists, 1988. Ednl. com. Mission Cultural Ctr., San Francisco, 1988-90; exhbs. com. Galeria de la Raza, San Francisco, 1989-91; mem. adv. bd. Headlands Ctr. for the Arts, Sausalito, Calif., 1989-91; mem. exhbn. com. Am. Indian Contemporary Art Gallery, San Francisco, 1990—. Recipient Second Ann. Vestal award Woman's Bldg., 1983, Midcareer Art History award Women's Caucus for Art, 1989. Mem. Internat. Assn. of Art Critics (Am. sect.), Asian Am. Women's Artists Assn., Korean-Am. Women Artists & Writers Assn. (adv. com. 1989), Coll. Art Assn. (bd. dirs. 1992—). Office: Art Dept Mills Coll 5000 MacArthrur Blvd Oakland CA 94613

ROTH, NORMAN, advertising executive; b. N.Y.C., Nov. 8, 1937; s. Frank and Zena (Kagan) R.; m. Irene Herbert, Oct. 15, 1961; children: Lawrence W., Michelle V. BBA, CCNY, 1960. Dist. sales mgr. Burroughs Wellcome & Co. (USA), Inc., Greensboro, N.C., 1960-69; exec. v.p. sales and mktg. Instore Advt., Inc., Passaic, N.J., 1969-81; account exec. Serigraphics Displays, La Mirada, Calif., 1981-82; sr. account exec. Republic Corp. Dauman Displays/Continental Graphics, L.A., 1982-87; pres., ceo Norman Roth and Assocs., Calabasas, Calif., 1987—. Mem. Pi Sigma Epsilon. Jewish. Home: 3969 Bon Homme Rd Calabasas CA 91302

ROTH, SANFORD HAROLD, rheumatologist, health care administrator, educator; b. Akron, Ohio, June 12, 1934; s. Charles and Rose Marie (Zelman) R.; m. Marcia Ann, June 9, 1957; children: Shana Beth, Sari Luanne. B.Sc., Ohio State U., 1955, M.D., 1959. Intern Mt. Carmel, Columbus, Ohio, 1959-60; fellow Mayo Grad. Sch. Medicine, 1962-65; pvt. practice medicine specializing in rheumatology Phoenix, 1965—; med. dir. Arthritis Ctr., Ltd., Phoenix, 1983—; dir. Arthritis Program Healthwest Regional Medical Ctr., Phoenix, 1987-89; med. dir. Arthritis/Orthopedic Ctr. for Excellence Humana Hosp., Phoenix, 1989—; dir. arthritis rehab. program St. Luke's Hosp., Phoenix, 1978-87; med. research dir. Harrington Arthritis Research Ctr., Phoenix, 1984-88; prof., dir. aging and arthritis program Coll. Grad. Program, Ariz. State U., Tempe, 1984—; dir. medicine Ariz. Insts., Phoenix, 1985—; past state chmn. Gov.'s Conf. on Arthritis in Ariz., 1967; cons., rep. arthritis adv. com. FDA, 1982—, chmn. anti-rheumatic new drug guidelines, 1984—; cons. Ciba-Geigy, 1983—, Upjohn, 1985-87, Pennwalt, 1985-88, Arthritis Found. Clinics, 3M-Riker Labs, Inc., 1981-89, VA, 1970-87, FTC, 1980—, Boots Pharm. Co., 1980-87, Greenwich Pharm., 1986-87, Hoffman-LaRoche, 1986—, FDA Office Compliance, 1987—, G.D. Searle, 1987—; prin. investigator Coop. Systematic Studies of Rheumatic Diseases; vis. scholar in rheumatology Beijing Med. Coll., People's Republic China, 1982; proctor, vis. scholar program U.S.-China Edn. Inst., 1982—; med. research dir., exec. bd., trustee Harrington Arthritis Research Ctr., 1983-88; co-chair PANLAR Collaborative Clin. Epidemiol. Group, 1989—; mem. com. on revision U.S. Pharmacopeial Conv., 1990—; mem. antirheumatic drug task force WHO-Internat. League Against Rheumatism, 1991—. Author: New Directions in Arthritis Therapy, 1980; Handbook of Drug Therapy in Rheumatoloy, 1985; med. contbg. editor RISS, Hosp. Physician, 1960-68, Current Prescribing, 1976-80; hon. internat. cons. editor Drugs, 1977—; editor in chief Arthron, 1982-85; editor, contbg. author: Rheumatic Therapeutics, 1985; med. cons. editor Update: Rheumatism, 1985, AMA Drug Evaluations, 6th edit., 1986, 7th edit., 1990; mem. editorial bd. VA Practitioner, 1985—, Comprehensive Therapy, 1987; mem. internat. editorial bd. Jour. Drug Devel., 1988—, Practical Gastroenterology, 1989—; contbr. numerous articles to profl. jours., chpts. to books. Fellow Am. Coll. Rheumatology (founding, liaison com. to regional med. program 1974-76, co-dir. med. info. system ARAMIS, computer com., chmn. antiinflammatory drug study club 1974—, com. on clubs and councils 1977-80, western regional co-chmn. 1977—, therapeutic and drug com. 1979—, glossary com. 1981-83, ad hoc com. on future meeting sites 1983); mem. AMA, ACP (regional program com., ann. Philip S. Hench lectureship chmn. 1978-79), Arthritis Found. (dir. central Ariz. chpt. 1982-83, past chmn. med. and sci. com. 1967-72), Lupus Found. Am. (bd. 1981—), Internat. Soc. Rheumatic Therapy (sec.-gen. 1990—, bd. dirs. 1987—, pres. 1992—), Maricopa County Med. Soc. (rehab. com.), Am. Soc. Clin. Rheumatology (past pres. exec. council), Am. Coll. Clin. Pharmacology, Soc. Internal Medicine, Mayo Clinic Alumni Assn., Mayo Clinic Fellows Assn. (sec. 1964-65), Argentine Rheumatology Soc. (hon.), Mayo Clinic Fellows Rheumatology Soc. (pres. 1964-65), Mayo Clinic Film Soc. (bd. dirs. 1964-65), Pan Am. League Against Rheumatism (chmn. clin. trials com. 1987—). Office: Arthritis Ctr Ltd 3330 N 2d St #601 Phoenix AZ 85012

ROTHAUS, BARRY, history educator; b. N.Y.C., Jan. 31, 1936; s. Harry Eli and Gertrude (Cooper) R.; m. Margaret Ann Galdonyi, Dec. 18, 1966; children: Eric, Elizabeth, Leslie. BA, CUNY, 1957; MS in History, U. Wis., 1960, PhD in History, 1968. Instr. Wayne State U., Detroit, 1962-66; asst. prof. Colo. State Coll., Greeley, 1966-69, assoc. prof., 1970-75; chair U. No. Colo., Greeley, 1969-75, 86—, prof., 1975—, asst. dean, 1981-83; vis. prof. Colo. State U., Ft. Collins., 1983; cons. Greenwood Press, Westport, Conn., 1989-90, NEH, Washington, 1987. Co-editor: (book) Historical Dictionary of the French Revolution, 1985; contbr. articles to profl. jours. Dem. precinct capt., 1990, 92. Grantee NEH, 1989, Am. Philos. Soc., 1972, U. No. Colo., 1990. Mem. French Hist. Studies, Western. Soc. French History (pres. 1982-83, coun. 1987-90), Consortium on Revolutionary Europe. Office: U No Colo Dept History Greeley CO 80639

ROTHBERG, JOEL ANTHONY, state official; b. Phila., Apr. 5, 1951; s. Herman J. and Dorothy S. R. BA, U. Md., 1973; JD, Georgetown U., 1976. Bar: Md. 1977, Alaska 1978, D.C. 1979. Atty. Alaska Legal Svcs. Corp., Anchorage, 1977-84, Alaska Consumer Advocacy Program, Anchorage, 1985-89; investigator Alaska State Commn. for Human Rights, Anchorage, 1990—. Mem. Phi Beta Kappa. Home: 3433 Tarwater # 2 Anchorage AK 99508 Office: Alaska State Commn for Human Rights Anchorage AK 99501

ROTHENBERG, ALAN I., lawyer, professional sports executive; b. Detroit, Apr. 10, 1939; m. Georgina Rothenberg; 3 children. B.A., U. Mich., 1960, J.D., 1963. Bar: Calif. 1964. Assoc. O'Melveny & Myers, Los Angeles, 1963-66; ptnr. Manatt Phelps Rothenberg & Phillips, Los Angeles, 1968-90, Latham & Watkins, Los Angeles, 1990—; instr. sports law U. So. Calif., 1969, 76, 84, Whittier Coll. Law, 1980, 84; pres., gen. counsel L.A. Clippers Basketball Team, 1982-89; pres. U.S. Soccer Fedn., Chgo., 1990—; chmn. World Cup USA '94 Orgn. Com., 1990—. Mem. soccer commn. 1984 Olympic Games, Equal Edn. Opportunities Commn. State Calif. Bd. Edn., 1972-75; chmn., pres., chief exec. officer 1994 World Cup organizing com., 1991—. Mem. ABA, State Bar of Calif. (pres. 1989-90), local and county bar assns., Nat. Basketball Assn. (bd. govs. 1971-79, 82—, N.Am. Soccer League (bd. govs. 1977-80), Constitutional Rights Found. (dir., pres. 1987-90), Order of Coif. Office: Latham & Watkins 633 W 5th St Ste 4000 Los Angeles CA 90071

ROTHENBERG, ELLEN, biologist; b. Northhampton, Mass., Apr. 22, 1952; d. Jerome and Winifred (Barr) R. AB summa cum laude, Harvard U., 1972; PhD, MIT, 1977. Postdoctoral fellow Meml. Sloan-Kettering Cancer Ctr., N.Y.C., 1977-79; asst. rsch. prof. The Salk Inst. for Biol. Studies, LaJolla, Calif., 1979-82; asst. prof. Calif. Inst. of Tech., Pasadena, 1982-88, assoc. prof., 1988—; Co-editor: Mechanisms of Lymphocyte Activation and Immune Regulation III, 1991; contbr. articles to profl. jours. Assoc. editor Jour. of Molecular and Cellular Immunology, 1984—, Jour. of Immunology, 1986-91, Molecular Reproduction and Development, 1987—. Scientific adv. bd. Hereditary Disease Found., 1991-94; mem. immunol. scis. study sect., div. of rsch. grants, NIH, Pub. Health Svc., 1988-92; rev. com. Calif. div., postdoctoral fellowship program, Am. Cancer Soc., 1982-85, 92—. Jane Coffin Childs Meml. fellowship, 1977-79. Mem. AAAS, Am. Assn. of Immunologists, Am. Soc. for Microbiology, Phi Beta Kappa. Office: Calif Inst Tech Biology Divsn 1201 E California Blvd Pasadena CA 91125-0001

ROTHENBERG, HARVEY DAVID, educational administrator; b. Fort Madison, Iowa, May 31, 1937; s. Max and Cecelia Rothenberg; A.A., Wentworth Mil. Acad., 1957; B.B.A., State U. Iowa, 1960; M.A., U. No. Colo., 1961; postgrad. Harris Tchrs. Coll., 1962-63, St. Louis U., 1962-63; Ph.D., Colo. State U., 1972; m. Audrey Darlynne Roseman, July 5, 1964; children—David Michael, Mark Daniel. Distributive edn. tchr. Roosevelt High Sch., St. Louis, 1961-63, Proviso West High Sch., Hillside, Ill., 1963-64, Longmont (Colo.) Sr. High Sch., 1964-69, 70-71; supr. research and spl. programs St. Vrain Valley Sch. Dist., Longmont, Colo., 1971-72; chmn. bus.

div. Arapahoe Community Coll., Littleton, Colo., 1972-75; dir. vocat., career and adult edn. Arapahoe County Sch. Dist. 6, Littleton, 1975—; instr. Met. State Coll., Denver, part-time, 1975—, Arapahoe Community Coll., Littleton, 1975—, Regis Coll., 1979—; vis. prof. U. Ala., Tuscaloosa, summer 1972; dir. Chatfield Bank, Littleton, 1974-83, Yaak River Mines Ltd., Amusement Personified Inc.; pres. Kuytia Inc., Littleton, 1975—; co-owner Albuquerque Lasers, profl. volleyball team. Mem. City of Longmont Long-Range Planning Commn., 1971-72, pres. Homeowners Bd., 1978-80. Recipient Outstanding Young Educator award St. Vrain Valley Sch. Dist., 1967, Outstanding Vocational Educator, Colo. 1992, We. Region U.S., 1993. Mem. Am., Colo. (mem. exec. com. 1966-68, treas. 1972-73) vocat. assns., Littleton C. of C., Colo. Assn. Vocat. Adminstrs, Colo. Educators For and About Bus., Delta Sigma Pi, Delta Pi Epsilon, Nat. Assn. Local Sch. Adminstrs., Colo. Council Local Sch. Adminstrs. Clubs: Elks, Masons, Shriners. Home: 7461 S Sheridan Ct Littleton CO 80123-7084 Office: Arapahoe County Sch Dist 6 5776 S Crocker St Littleton CO 80120-2094

ROTHENBERG, STEPHEN, computer software company executive; b. N.Y.C., Feb. 3, 1941; s. Charles and Dorothy (Schreier) R. BS, Carnegie Tech., 1962; PhD, U. Wash., 1966. Mgr. tech. svcs. Univ. Computing Co., Palo Alto, Calif., 1968-70; v.p. Info. Systems Design, Oakland, Calif., 1971-76; pres. Rothenberg Computing Systems, Santa Clara, Calif., 1976—. Contbr. articles to profl. jours. Office: Rothenberg Computer Systems 2975 Scott Blvd Ste 100 Santa Clara CA 95054

ROTHERHAM, LARRY CHARLES, insurance executive; b. Council Bluffs, Iowa, Oct. 22, 1940; s. Charles Sylvester and Edna Mary (Sylvanus) R.; m. Florene F. Black, May 29, 1965; children: Christopher Charles, Phillip Larry, Kathleen Florene. Student, Creighton U., 1959-61; BSBA, U. Nebr., 1965; postgrad., Am. Coll., Bryn Mawr, Pa., 1985, '87. CPCU, CLU, ARM. Claims rep. and underwriter Safeco Ins. Co., Albuquerque, New Mex., 1965-69; br. mgr. Ohio Casualty Group, Albuquerque, 1969—; assoc. in risk mgmt. Ins. Inst. Am., 1976—. Mem. PTA Collet Park Elem. Sch., Albuquerque, 1963-82, Freedom High Sch., Albuquerque, 1982-86. Mem. New Mex. Soc. Chartered Property & Casualty Underwriters (charter mem., pres. 1975-77), New Mex. Soc. Chartered Life Underwriters, New Mex. Ins. Assn. Democrat. Roman Catholic. Home: 2112 Gretta St NE Albuquerque NM 87112 Office: Ohio Casualty Group 10400 Academy Rd NE Ste 200 Albuquerque NM 87111

ROTHERMEL, SAMUEL ROYDEN, hydrogeologist, geochemist; b. Wyomissing, Pa., May 24, 1957; s. Walter Albert and Erika (Kapp) R. BS, Ohio U., Athens, 1980; MS, U. Ark., 1984. Cert. ground water profl.; registered environ. assessor; registered and cert. prof. geologist. Hydrogeol. cons. Ozark Geol. Svcs., Fayetteville, Ark., 1980-82; asst. hydrogeologist Edwards Aquifer Rsch. & Data Ctr., San Marcos, Tex., 1982-84; project hydrogeologist IT Corp., Baton Rouge, 1984-85, The MARK Group, Las Vegas, 1985-86; environ. engr., sr. hydrogeologist Century Environ. Scis., Portland, 1986, SRH Environ. Mgmt., Portland, 1986-89; sr. geologist Emcon Assocs., Phoenix, 1989-91; sr. hydrogeologist The Earth Tech. Corp., San Bernardino, 1991—; office mgr. The Earth Tech. Corp., Sacramento, Calif., 1992—. Co-author: Hydrogeological and Hydrochemical Investigation of the Edwards Aquifer in the San Marcos Area, Hays County, Texas, 1986, Hydrochemical Investigation of the Comal and Hueco Spring Systems, Comal County, Texas, 1987; contbr. articles to profl. jours. Mem. Nat. Groundwater Assn., Am. Inst. Profl. Geologists, Am. Water Resources Assn., Am. Geophysical Union (hydrology sect.), Groundwater Resources Assn. Calif., Society of Am. Mil. Engrs., Sigma Gamma Epsilon. Lutheran. Home: 1140 Tribune St Apt A Redlands CA 92374 Office: The Earth Tech Corp Ste 150 601 University Ave Sacramento CA 95825

ROTHHAAR, DENNIS K., lawyer; b. Ft. Wayne, Ind., June 8, 1944; s. Rollin L. and Martha L. (Bechdolt) R.; m. Miriam Steinbock, Sept. 14, 1973; 1 child, Jessica. AB in Sociology, Stanford U., 1966; JD, Harvard U., 1972. Bar: Calif. 1972; cert. specialist in family law. Pvt. practice Oakland, Calif., 1972—. Mem. Calif. Bar, Alameda County Bar Assn. (bd. dirs. 1982-84), Alameda Family Law Asns. (bd. dirs. 1989—, chair 1991—). Democrat. Office: 436 14th St Ste 1417 Oakland CA 94612

ROTHHAMMER, CRAIG ROBERT, social worker, consultant; b. San Francisco, May 17, 1954; s. Robert Charles and Gloria Lee (Molloy) R.; m. Dawn Alicia Alvarez, 1988. BA, U. Calif., Santa Barbara, 1976; MSW, San Diego State U., 1979. Lic. clin. social worker, Calif. Social work asst. Mercy Hosp., San Diego, 1977; psychiat. social worker Lanterman State Hosp., Pomona, Calif., 1979-83, Sonoma State Hosp., Eldridge, Calif., 1983-84; children's social worker County Adoption Service, San Bernardino, Calif., 1984-86; psychiatric social worker Patton State Hosp., 1987-88; psychiat. soc. worker II Crisis Outpatient Services Riverside (Calif.) County Mental Health, 1988-90; mental health svcs. supr. Interagy. Svcs. for Families, Riverside County Mental Health, 1990—; expert examiner Behavioral Sci. Examiners, Calif.; pvt. practice (part time) social work Redlands, Calif., 1986-89; field instr. MSW program Calif. State U., San Bernardino, 1989—, marriage, family & child counselor program Loma Linda (Calif.) U., 1993. Vol. Social Advs. for Youth, Santa Barbara, Calif., 1974-76, Am. Diabetes Assn., San Diego, 1978-79, San Diego Assn. For Retarded, 1978-80; liason Adoptive Family Assn., San Bernardino, 1986. Mem. Nat. Assn. Social Workers, Acad. Cert. Social Workers. Democrat. Office: Interagy Svcs for Families 9990 County Farm Rd Ste 1 Riverside CA 92503-3518

ROTHMAN, HAL K., history educator; b. Baton Rouge, Aug. 11, 1958; s. Neal Jules and Rozann (Cole) R.; m. Lauralee Rachel Paige, Aug. 13, 1989; 1 child, Talia. BA, U. Ill., 1980; MA, U. Tex., 1982, PhD, 1985. Asst. prof. Wichita (Kans.) State U., 1987-92; assoc. prof. U. Nev., Las Vegas, 1992—. Author: Preserving Different Past, 1989, On Rims and Ridges, 1992; book rev. editor: Environ. History Rev., 1989-92, editor, 1992—; newsletter editor: Am. Soc. for Environ. History, 1990—; contbr. articles to jours. Office: U Nevada Dept History 4505 Maryland Pkwy Las Vegas NV 89154-5020

ROTHMAN, JUDITH ELLEN, associate dean; b. Bklyn., Sept. 12, 1946; d. Benjamin and Shirley (Finkelstein) Siegel; m. Elliott charles Rothman, Jan. 1, 1983; children by previous marriage: Reed Adam Slatas, Kimberly Joy Slatas. BS in Acctg., Fairleigh Dickinson U., 1976, postgrad., 1976-77; postgrad., UCLA, 1986-87. Acct. Interpace Corp., Parsippany, N.J., 1976-77; mgr. fin. planning Blue Cross So. Calif., Woodland Hills, 1977-82; asst. dir. fin. Cedars-Sinai Med. Ctr., L.A., 1982-87; assoc. dean fin. and bus. affairs UCLA Sch. Medicine, Westwood, 1987—. Mem. Calif. Abortion Rights Action League, Friends of Calif. Spl. Olympics. Mem. NAFE, Assn. Am. Med. Colls. (region sec. 1992, region pres. 1993), Med. Group Mgmt. Assn., UCLA Alumni Assn. Office: UCLA Sch Medicine 12-138CHS 10833 Le Conte Ave Los Angeles CA 90024

ROTHMAN, JULIUS LAWRENCE, retired English language educator; b. N.Y.C., Sept. 22, 1920; s. Samuel and Bessie (Kantor) R.; m. Stella Lambert, June 23, 1948. BSS, CCNY, 1941; MA, Columbia U., 1947, PhD, 1954. Lectr. Hunter Coll., N.Y.C., 1947-50, Rutgers U., New Brunswick, N.J., 1950-53; tech. writer Olympic Radio & TV, L.I. City, N.Y., 1951-61; prof. English Nassau Community Coll., Garden City, N.Y., 1962-86; prof. emeritus Nassau Community Coll., Garden City, 1986—; broadcaster, talk show host weekly program Sta. WHPC, 1974-82; deputy dir. gen. Internat. Biographical Ctr., Cambridge, England, 1992—. Editor, contbg. author The Cabellian, 1968-72; contbr. sects. to books on folklore and legend; contbr. articles to profl. jours. Mem. Nat. Com. to Preserve Social Security and Medicare, Arthritis Found.; mem. adv. bd. 9th Senatorial Dist. N.Y., 1984-88; seat sponsor Ariz. State U. Sundome Performing Arts Assn. Named Internat. Man of Year 1991-92, Internat. Biographical Ctr., Cambridge. Mem. Cabell Soc. (founder 1967, exec. v.p. 1968-72), Ret. Pub. Employees Assn., Nat. Wildlife Fedn., Nat. Ret. Tchrs. Assn., Columbia U. Alumni Assn. Methodist.

ROTHMAN, PAUL ALAN, publisher; b. Bklyn., June 26, 1940; s. Fred B. and Dorothy (Regosin) R.; m. Mary Ann Dalson, July 28, 1966 (div. 1992); children: Deborah, Diana. BA, Swarthmore Coll., 1962; JD, U. Mich., 1965; LLM in Taxation, NYU, 1966. Bar: N.Y. 1965. Assoc. Dewey, Ballentine, Busby, Palmer & Wood, N.Y.C., 1965-67; v.p. Fred B. Rothman & Co., Littleton, Colo., 1967-85, pres., 1985—; chmn. bd. Colo. Plasticard, Littleton, 1983—. Editor Mich. Law Rev., 1963-65. Home: 25437 Stanley Park Rd Evergreen CO 80439-5512 Office: Fred B Rothman & Co 10368 W Centennial Rd Littleton CO 80127

ROTHMAN, STEVEN ISAIAH, oil explorationist, consultant; b. Greenwich, Conn., Dec. 23, 1947; s. Sidney and Florence Ann (Russakoff) R.; m. Barbara Jane Grower, June 29, 1969. BSEE in Computer Sci., Rensselaer Polytech. U., 1969; MSEM in Ops. Rsch., Northeasten U., 1972. Mem. tech. staff. Lincoln Labs. The MITRE Corp., Bedford, Mass., 1969-72; mem. tech. staff. NASA The MITRE Corp., Houston, 1972-74; mem. tech. staff. NORAD The MITRE Corp., Colorado Springs, 1974-75; mem. tech. staff. Energy Rsch. Devel. Adminstn. The MITRE Corp., Washington, 1975-76; v.p. Kilovolt Corp., Hackensack, N.J., 1976-79; owner Copper Creek Systems, Glenwood, N.Mex., 1979—; chmn. of bd. Bravo Resources, Glenwood, 1982—; bd. dirs. Zavanna Corp., Denver, 1992—; cons. Innuit Indians, Goose Bay, Labrador Canada, 1990-91. Author in field. Chmn. Sonic Booms Citizens Com., Glenwood, 1979—; tech. adv. Western N.Mex. U. Math. Dept., Silver City, N.Mex., 1980-81; part owner Catron County Courier, Reserve, N.Mex., 1987-90. Recipient Plaque of Appreciation award Catron County Govt., Reserve, 1985. Mem. N.Mex. Ornithol. Soc., Nature Conservancy, Amnesty Internat., Childreach. Jewish. Office: Bravo Resources Inc 1000 Catwalk Rd Glenwood NM 88039

ROTHMAN, STEWART NEIL, photographer; b. Rochester, N.Y., Dec. 27, 1930; s. Morris Zeus and Rose Mary (Cotler) R.; student Wayne State U., 1952-54; m. Shirley Mae Derry, Sept. 12, 1957; children—Leslie Paula, Karen Pat. Free-lance photographer, Detroit, 1952-57; photographer NASA, Gilmore Creek, Alaska, 1965-68; writer, photographer Jessen's Daily, Fairbanks, Alaska, 1968-69; propr. The Lens Unlimited, Fairbanks, 1959—; staff photographer Gen. Mac Arthur's Hdqrs., Tokyo, 1948-50; pres., chmn. bd. Arctic Publs., 1968-72; pres. Public Relations Specialists Co., 1973—; editor Arctic Oil Jour., 1968-72, This Month in Fairbanks, 1974--85; pub. The Fairbanks Mag., 1985—. Publicity adviser to mayor of Fairbanks; pres. Tanana-Yukon Hist. Soc. Served with U.S. Army, 1948-52, Korea, then USAF, 1957-65. Decorated Purple Heart with oak leaf cluster. Fellow Master Photographers Assn. Gt. Britain; mem. European Council Photographers, Fairbanks C. of C. Club: Farthest North Press. Lodges: Lions (pres.), Elks. Author: Nudes of Sixteen Lands, 1971; Hobo and Dangerous Dan McGrew, 1975; The Lens is My Brush, 1977; China, The Opening Door, 1980; Pope John Paul II's First Visit to Alaska, 1981; Window on Life, 1982; The Pope and the President, 1984, Alaska and the World, 1993. Home and Office: 921 Woodway St Fairbanks AK 99709

ROTHSCHILD, DEBORAH AVIVA, editor; b. Syracuse, N.Y., Apr. 11, 1964; d. Bertram Harold and Marilyn (Wachs) R. BA in English, U. Denver, 1985; MFA in Creative Writing, Emerson Coll., 1989. Clk. Barrett Elem. Sch., Denver, 1985-86; data processor cardiovascular divsn. Boston U. Sch. Medicine, 1987; asst. editor Am. Reference Books Annual Libraries Unltd., Englewood, Colo., 1991—; copy editor Libraries Unltd., Englewood, 1989—, with promotions, 1991—. Reviewer: (jour.) Acad. Libr. Book Rev., 1991—, (annual books) Science Fiction and Fantasy Book Review Annual, 1990—, American Reference Books Annual, 1989—. Vol. Rocky Mountain Skeptics, Boulder, Colo., 1983—. Nat. Merit scholar, 1981. Mem. Rocky Mountain Skeptics, Good Day Sunshine, Marharbour Writers' Group, Nat. Writers Club. Jewish. Home: 2343 S Vaughn Way # 3-309 Aurora CO 80014 Office: Libraries Unltd 6931 S Yosemite Englewood CO 80112

ROTHSCHILD, MICHAEL, economics educator; b. Chgo., Aug. 2, 1942; s. Edwin Alfred and Ann (Meyer) R.; m. Linda Preiss, Sept. 7, 1969 (div. 1991); children—David, Daniel. B.A., Reed Coll., 1963; M.A., Yale U., 1965; Ph.D., MIT, 1969. Asst. prof. econs. Harvard U., 1969-73; lectr. Princeton U., 1972-74, assoc. prof., 1974-75, prof., 1975-76; then prof. U. Wis., Madison, 1976-83; prof. U. Calif.-San Diego, 1983—, divisional dean social scis., 1985—. Editor: (with Peter Diamond) Uncertainty in Economics, 1978, (with Charles T. Clotfelder) Studies of Supply and Demand in Higher Education, 1993. Guggenheim fellow, 1978-79. Fellow Econometric Soc.; mem. Am. Econ. Assn. Home: 9554 La Jolla Farms Rd La Jolla CA 92037-1129 Office: U Calif-San Diego Econs Dept La Jolla CA 92037

ROTHSCHILD, MICHAEL LEE, writer; b. Schenectady, N.Y., Aug. 6, 1952; s. Max Theodore and Harriet Louise (Friedman) Feigenheimer; m. Leigh Sharon Marriner, Sept. 1, 1985; children: Adam Winston, Emma Eleanor. BA, SUNY, Binghamton, 1974; JD, Harvard U., 1978, MBA, 1978. Cons. Boston Consulting Group, 1978-80; v.p. Sequoia Group, Larkspur, Calif., 1980-81; dir. MicroPro Internat., San Rafael, Calif., 1982-84; prin. Cambridge Meridian Group, San Rafael, 1984-90; pres. Bionomics Inst., San Rafael, 1991—; bd. dirs. Animalens, Inc., Wellesley, Mass.; sr. fellow Found. for Rsch. on Econ. and the Environ., Seattle, 1991; sci. adv. bd. Synaptics, Inc., San Jose, Calif.; columnist Forbes ASAP, Upside. Author: Bionomics, 1990. Mem. Phi Beta Kappa. Jewish. Office: Bionomics Inst 2173 Francisco Blvd E San Rafael CA 94901-5523

ROTHSTEIN, BARBARA JACOBS, federal judge; b. Brooklyn, N.Y., Feb. 3, 1939; d. Solomon and Pauline Jacobs; m. Ted L. Rothstein, Dec. 28, 1968; 1 child, Daniel. B.A., Cornell U., 1960; LL.B., Harvard U., 1966. Bar: Mass. 1966, Wash. 1969, U.S. Ct. Appeals (9th cir.) 1977, U.S. Dist. Ct. (we. dist.) Wash. 1971, U.S. Supreme Ct. 1975. Pvt. practice law Boston, 1966-68; asst. atty. gen. State of Wash., 1968-77; judge Superior Ct., Seattle, 1977-80; judge Fed. Dist. Ct. Western Wash., Seattle, 1980-87, chief judge, 1987—; faculty Law Sch. U. Wash., 1975-77, Hastings Inst. Trial Advocacy, 1977, N.W. Inst. Trial Advocacy, 1979—. Recipient Matrix Table Women of Yr. award Women in Communication, Judge of the Yr. award Fed. Bar Assn., 1989. Mem. ABA (jud. sect.), Am. Judicature Soc., Nat. Assn. Women Judges, Fellows of the Am. Bar, Wash. State Bar Assn., Phi Beta Kappa, Phi Kappa Phi. Office: US Dist Ct 705 US Courthouse 1010 5th Ave Seattle WA 98104-1130

ROTHSTEIN, BARRY STEVEN, sales executive; b. Chgo., Sept. 5, 1953; s. Martin and Shirley Rothstein; m. Betsy Martin, July 26, 1981; children: Nathan, Madelyn, Jesse. BA, U. Calif., San Diego, 1975; MA, Western Mich. U., 1979. Resource contr. Boeing Co., Seattle, 1978-81; programmer, cons. Programs That Work, San Marcos, Calif., 1981-86; v.p. computer ops./sales Jet Abrasives, Inc., Vernon, Calif., 1986—. Coach Long Beach (Calif.) Little League.

ROTHSTEIN, CY, accountant; b. N.Y.C., June 26, 1934; s. Samuel and Rose (Werner) R.; m. Annalee Toblinsky, June 23, 1951 (div. 1965); children: Norman, Susan; m. Diane J. Colwell, 1967 (div. 1984); children: Jill Samantha, Amy Melissa. BBA, CCNY, 1956; MBA, NYU, N.Y.C., 1959. Staff acct. David Berdon & Co., CPAs, N.Y.C., 1958-61; sr. acct. Friedman, Alperin & Green, N.Y.C., 1961-65; asst. treas., controller Trans Beacon Corp., Beverly Hills, Calif., 1965-68, Nat. Gen. Corp., L.A., 1968-72; audit mgr., ptnr. Clarence Rainess & Co., CPAs, L.A., 1972-74; pvt. practice L.A., 1974-82, Mercer Island, Wash., 1982-90, Kirkland, Wash., 1990—; instr. Bklyn. Community Coll., 1958-59; mem. King County Com. Taxation, Seattle, 1982-83; mem. Fin. Acctg. Standards Bd., L.A., 1974. Mem. AICPA, Wash. State Soc. CPAs. Democrat.

ROTHSTEIN, MORTON, historian; b. Omaha, Jan. 8, 1926; s. Joseph Isadore and Rose (Landman) R.; m. Frances Irene Lustig, Nov. 18, 1950; children: Laurence, Eric, David. Student, Bklyn. Coll., 1952-54; Ph.D., Cornell U., 1960; postgrad., London Sch. Econs., 1956-57. Instr. U. Del., 1958-61; asst. prof. U. Wis.-Madison, 1961-65, assoc. prof., 1965-69, prof. history and agrl. econs., 1969-84, chmn. history dept., 1969-72; prof. history U. Calif., Davis, 1984—; vis. prof. London Sch. Econs., 1977; mem. acad. adv. bd. Eleutherian Mills-Hagley Found., 1970-74; mem. Wis. Humanities Com., 1978-84, chmn., 1980-82, Calif. Coun. Humanities, 1985-90, chmn. 1988-90. Editor: Explorations in Economic History, 1970-73, Agrl. History, 1984—; contbr. articles to profl. jours. Social Sci. Research Council fellow, 1956-57, 67-68; NEH fellow, 1976-77, 83. Mem. Orgn. Am. Historians, Agrl. History Soc. (pres. 1975-76), Bus. History Conf. (pres. 1985-86), Econ. History Assn., Econ. History Soc. (U.K.), So. Hist. Assn., Am. Hist. Assn., Western History Assn., Calif. Hist. Soc. (trustee 1989-90), Social Sci. History Assn. Jewish. Home: 3417 Seabright Ave Davis CA 95616-5641 Office: U Calif Dept History Voorhies Hall Davis CA 95616

ROTHWELL, ROBERT ALAN, investing and consulting company executive, writer; b. Newark, May 13, 1939; s. Albert Robert and Rose Gloria (Cundari) R. BA, St. Francis Coll., Loretto, Pa., 1961; MA, Seton Hall U., 1962; MS, Georgetown U. Sch. Fgn. Svc., 1963; PhD, Duquesne U., 1967; DHL, Georgetown U., 1967; D. Social Scis. with honors, Fribourgh U., Switzerland, 1969. Prof. psychology U. Steubenville, Ohio, 1966-73; dir. Edn. Dynamics, Las Vegas, 1973-76; pres. Robert's Investing and Cons., Las Vegas, 1976—; pres. Muscle & Power Talent Mgmt., Inc., Las Vegas, 1988—; v.p. Great Basin Mgmt. and Cons.,Inc., Las Vegas, 1991—; v.p. Telluride (Colo.) Mktg. and Distbn., 1992—; U.S. govt. cons. on Russian affairs, Washington, 1976—; spl. UN observer to various countries, 1966-81; mem. Nev. Gov.'s Commn. on Higher Edn., 1978-82; mem. Pres. Commn. on Psychol. Warfare, Washington, 1977-82. Author: (textbook) Existential Psychology, 1972; The Origin of Consciouness, 1974, The Bicameral Mind, 1976, Code Name: Grizzly, 1986. Capt. USMC, 1962-66. Decorated Navy D.S.M., Navy and Marine Corps Medal for Heroism, Bronze Star. Recipient Disting. Service award U.S. Def. Dept., 1966, Superior Service Nat. Security award U.S. Def. Dept., 1968; named Mr. Nev. Masters Bodybldg. Champion, 1985, Mr. Silver State Masters Bodybldg. Champion, 1985, Mr. U.S.A. Masters Bodybldg. Champion, 1986. Mem. AAUP, Nat. Assn. Sch. Psychologists, Assn. Advancement Psychology, Nat. Physique Com. (co-chmn. Nev. chpt.), Internat. Assn. Psychologists, Am. Psychologists Assn. Democrat. Roman Catholic. Office: 2449 Pickwick Dr Henderson NV 89014-3754

ROTKIN, MICHAEL ERIC, community studies educator, city official; b. N.Y.C., Sept. 17, 1945; s. Irving Jacob and Esther (Repps) R.; m. Karen Frost Rian, June 15, 1968 (div. Aug. 1983); m. Madelyn Suzanne McCaul, Sept. 17, 1989. BA summa cum laude, Cornell U., 1969; PhD in History of Consciousness, U. Calif., Santa Cruz, 1992. Vol. VISTA, Fla., 1965-66; teaching asst. U. Calif., Santa Cruz, 1969-73, lectr. community studies 1973—, dir. field studies, 1977—; mem. Santa Cruz City Council, 1979-88, 92—, mayor, 1981-82, 85-86. Co-author: Revolutionary Theory, 1983. Editor Socialist Rev., 1970-79. Contbr. numerous articles to mags. and newspapers. Mem. nat. com. New Am. Movement, Chgo., 1978-79; bd. dirs. Met. Transit Dist., Santa Cruz, 1979-88, 92—, chmn. bd., 1983, 88; chief negotiator UC-AFT, 1989—; bd. dir. Food and Nutrition, Inc., 1988-92, Santa Cruz Community Credit Union, 1988-92; chair Santa Cruz Action Network, 1988-92. Woodrow Wilson fellow, 1969. Democrat. Jewish. Office: U Calif Santa Cruz CA 95064

ROTMAN, DOUGLAS ALLEN, sales and leasing executive; b. Cawker City, Kans., Dec. 24, 1942; s. Antone Allen and Gladys Elisabeth (Deters) R.; m. Nancy Lee Anderson, Apr. 3, 1971; children: Julie, John, David. BS in Engring. Sci., U.S. Air Force Acad., 1964; MBA, Harvard U., 1973. Commd. 2d lt. USAF, 1964, advanced through grades to capt., 1987, resigned, 1971; gen. mgr. Danuser div. Hesston Corp., Claremore, Okla., 1973-74; product mgr. hydraulic crane div. FMC, Cedar Rapids, Iowa, 1976-79; v.p. mktg. Kewanee (Ill.) Machinery Co., 1979-81; mktg. svcs. mgr. Steiger Tractor Inc., Fargo, N.D., 1981-84; v.p. mktg. farm equipment div. Lear Siegler, Inc., Wahpeton, N.D., 1984-86; gen. mgr. Kioti Tractor Inc., Portland, Oreg., 1986-89; v.p., gen. mgr. L.B. Sales and Leasing, Inc., Boise, Idaho, 1989—. Deacon, treas. Christian Reformed Ch. Decorated DFC (2), Air medal (11). Mem. Wings Gymnastics Club Booster Club (pres.). Republican. Home: 11301 W Hickory Hill Ct Boise ID 83704-2468 Office: L B Sales and Leasing Inc 10830 Executive Dr Boise ID 83704-8938

ROTTER, PAUL TALBOTT, retired insurance executive; b. Parsons, Kans., Feb. 21, 1918; s. J. and LaNora (Talbott) R.; m. Virginia Sutherlin Barksdale, July 17, 1943; children—Carolyn Sutherlin, Diane Talbott. B.S. summa cum laude, Harvard U., 1937. Asst. mathematician Prudential Ins. Co. of Am., Newark, 1938-46; with Mut. Benefit Life Ins. Co., Newark, 1946—; successively asst. mathematician, asso. mathematician, mathematician Mut. Benefit Life Ins. Co., 1946-59, v.p., 1959-69, exec. v.p., 1969-80, ret., 1980. Mem. Madison Bd. Edn., 1958-64, pres., 1959-64; Trustee, mem. budget com. United Campaign of Madison, 1951-55; mem. bd., chmn. advancement com. Robert Treat council Boy Scouts Am., 1959-64. Fellow Soc. Actuaries (bd. govs. 1965-68, gen. chmn. edn. and exam. com. 1963-66, chmn. adv. com. edn. and exam. 1969-72); mem. Brit. Inst. Actuaries (asso.), Am. Acad. Actuaries (v.p. 1968-70, bd. dirs., chmn. edn. and exam. com. 1965-66, chmn. rev. and evaluation com. 1968-74), Asso. Harvard Alumni (regional dir. 1965-69), Actuaries Club N.Y. (pres. 1967-68), Harvard Alumni Assn. (v.p. 1964-66),Am. Lawn Bowls Assn. (pres. SW div.), Phi Beta Kappa Assos., Phi Beta Kappa. Clubs: Harvard N.J. (pres. 1956-57); Harvard (N.Y.C.); Morris County Golf (Convent, N.J.); Joslyn-Lake Hodges Lawn Bowling (pres. 1989-90). Home: 18278 Canfield Pl San Diego CA 92128-1002

ROTTSCHAEFER, WILLIAM ANDREW, philosophy educator; b. Tulsa, June 20, 1933; s. Dirk and Clara (Linsmeyer) R.; m. Marie Therese Schickel. BA, St. Louis U., 1956, MA, 1957, Licentiate in Sacred Theol., 1966; MS, U. Ill., 1969; PhD, Boston U., 1973. Asst. prof. philosophy SUNY, Oswego, 1972-73, Plattsburgh, 1973-75; asst. prof. philosophy Lewis & Clark Coll., Portland, Oreg., 1975-79, assoc. prof. philosophy, 1979-85, prof. philosophy, 1985—. Contbr. articles and revs. to profl. jours.; referee for several scholarly periodicals. Mem. Philosophy of Sci. Assn., Am. Philos. Assn., Inst. for Religion in an Age of Sci., Ctr. for Theology and the Natural Scis. (assoc.), Am. Acad. Religion. Office: Lewis and Clark Coll Dept Philosophy Portland OR 97219

ROUBAL, WILLIAM THEODORE, biophysicist, educator; b. Eugene, Oreg., Dec. 20, 1930; s. Frank J. and Irene I. (Ellenberger) R.; m. Carol Jean, Sept. 6, 1953; children: Diane Jeanette Roubal Daniel, Linda Ann Roubal Myrick, Sandra Mae Roubal, Cathy Roubal Hoover. BS, Oreg. State U., 1954, MS, 1959; PhD, U. Calif.-Davis, 1965. Chemist dept. entomology Oreg. State U., Corvallis, 1958-60; rsch. chemist Pioneer Rsch. Lab., Dept. Interior, Seattle, 1960-70; rsch. scientist Dept. Commerce, Seattle, 1970-75; sr. scientist NOAA, NMFS, Seattle, 1976—; biophysicist Environ. Conservation div. Nat. Marine Fisheries Svc., Seattle, 1968-75; assoc. prof. Sch. Fisheries, U. Wash., Seattle, 1976—; ednl. specialist Seattle Central Community Coll., 1974-85; instr., lectr. in field. Head usher Haller Lake United Methodist Ch., Seattle, 1974-89; workshop dir. Seattle YMCA Summer Family Camp, Seabeck, Wash., 1979—. Served as 1st lt. U.S. Army, 1954-56. Recipient award Seattle Central Community Coll., 1980. Mem. Am. Chem. Soc., Am. Oil Chemists' Soc. (A.E. MacGee award 1964), Am. Sci. Glassblowers Soc. (abstracts chmn. 1964-65), Claire Hammonds Guild, Sigma Xi. Home: 17840 Wayne Ave N Seattle WA 98133-5142 Office: NOAA NMFS EC Div 2725 Montlake Blvd E Seattle WA 98112-2097

ROUGEAU, LYNNE MARIE, computer software company executive; b. Winnipeg, Man., Can., Aug. 16; d. Gilbert Joseph and Jessie Evelyn (Wise) R.; m. Guy Edward Rougeau, Aug. 13, 1983; children: Lisa Kathleen, Michael Kenneth. B of Math. in Computer Sci., U. Waterloo, Ont., Can., 1983. Systems engr. IBM, Toronto, Ont., 1978-82; programmer A.C. Nielsen, Toronto, 1983; tech. specialist TSR, L.A., 1983-84; sr. software specialist Cognos, L.A., 1984-87; from sales cons., sales cons. mgr. to dir. tech. svcs. Oracle, L.A., 1987—. Home: 20011 Colgate Cir Huntington Beach CA 92646

ROUILLARD, ZELDA JEANNE, English language educator; b. Kearney, Nebr., June 6, 1929; d. Calvin Taylor and Marie (Bristow) Ryan; m. Theodore Chase Rouillard, June 23, 1959; 1 child, Gregory William. AB, U. Nebr., Kearney, 1951; postgrad., UCSW of Eng., 1951-52; MA, U. Wyo., 1953; PhD, U. Colo., 1959. Supply instr. U. Wyo., Laramie, 1953-54; instr. U. Colo., Boulder, 1959-60; tchr. English North High Sch., Denver, 1960-65, East High Sch., Denver, 1967, Nederland (Colo.) Jr.-Sr. High Sch., 1967-69; assoc. prof. Western State Coll., Gunnison, Colo., 1969-72, prof., 1972—, chmn. dept. modern languages, 1988—. Contbr. articles to profl. jours. Fulbright scholar, 1951-52; AAUW fellow, 1958-59. Mem. Colo. Lang. Arts Soc. (auditor 1974-76), Nat. Coun. Tchrs. English, Rocky Mountain MLA, MLA, Am. Folklore Soc., Calif. Folklore Soc., Popular Culture Assn., Xi Phi. Democrat. Methodist. Office: Western State Coll Gunnison CO 81231

ROULAC, STEPHEN E., real estate consultant; b. San Francisco, Aug. 15, 1945; s. Phil Williams and Elizabeth (Young) R.; children: Arthur, Fiona. BA, Pomona Coll., 1967; MBA with distinction, Harvard Grad. Sch.

Bus. Administrn., 1970; JD, U. Calif., Berkeley, 1976; PhD, Stanford U., 1978. CPA, Hawaii. Asst. constrn. supt., foreman, adminstr. Roulac Constrn. Co., Pasadena, Calif., 1963-66; rsch. asst. Econs. Rsch. Assocs., L.A., 1966-67; assoc. economist Urbanomics Rsch. Assocs., Claremont, Calif., 1967; acquisition auditor Litton Industries Inc., Chgo., Beverly Hills, 1967-68; tax cons. Lybrand, Ross Bros. and Montgomery, L.A., 1968; cons. to constrn. group and corp. planning dept. Owens-Corning Fiberglas Corp., Toledo, 1969-70; CEO Questor Assocs., San Francisco, 1972-83; chmn. nat. mgmt. adv. svcs. Kenneth Leventhal & Co., 1983-84; CEO Roulac Group, Kentfield, Calif., 1984—; expert witness, preparer econ. analyses for legal matters including civil trial of Irvine Co., Jewell et al. v. Bank of Am., Calif. Legis., Calif. Corps. Dept., Midwest Securities Commrs. Assn., Nat. Assn. Securities Dealers., Securities and Exch. Commn.; advisor to investment arm of Asian country, Calif. Pub. Employees Retirement System, U.S. Dept. Labor, numerous others; adj. prof. Tex. A&M U., 1986, U. Chgo., 1985, UCLA, 1983-84, Stanford Grad. Sch. Bus., 1970-79, Pacific Coast Banking Sch., 1978, Hastings Coll. Law, 1977-78, U. Calif. at Berkeley, 1972-77, Calif. State U., 1970-71, Northeastern U., 1969-70.; keynote speaker, instr. continuing edn. sessions, program chmn. corps., orgns. Author: (with Sherman Maisel) Real Estate Investment and Finance, 1976 (1976 Bus. Book of Yr. The Libr. Jour.); editor in chief, pub. Calif. Bicyclist, 1988—, Tex. Bicyclist, 1989—, Roulac's Strategic Real Estate, 1979-89; columnist Forbes, 1983, 84, 87, 92; mem. editorial adv. bd. Am. Real Estate and Urban Econs. Assn. Jour., 1977-81, Housing Devel. Reporter, 1978-80, Fin. Edn. Jour., 1976-70; contbg. editor Real Estate Law Jour., 1973-78, Real Estate Rev., 1973-75; spl. issue editor Calif. Mgmt. Rev., 1976; editor Real Estate Syndication Digest, 1971-72; contbr. articles to profl. jours., newspapers; cassettes; frequent appearer on TV shows including MacNeil/Lehrer Newshour, 1986, Cable News Network, 1987, ABC TV, 1987, KCBS Radio, 1986, WABC Radio, Dallas, 1986. Mem. real estate adv. com. to Calif. Commr. Corps., 1973, Calif. Corp. Commr.'s Blue Ribbon Com. on Projections and Track Records, 1973-74; mem. adv. bd. Nat. Bicycle Month, League of Am. Wheelmen, Ctr. for Real Estate Rsch. Kellogg Grad. Sch. Mgmt., Northwestern U. Named Highest Instr. Student Teaching Evaluations, Schs. Bus. Adminstrn., U. Calif., Berkeley, 1975-76; named to Pomona Coll. Athletic Hall of Fame, 1981; W.T. Grant fellow Harvard U., 1969-70,; George F. Baker scholar Harvard Grad. Sch. Bus. Adminstrn., 1970; Stanford U. Grad. Sch. Bus. fellow, 1970-71. Mem. Strategic Mgmt. Soc., Acad. Mgmt., Am. Real Estate Soc., Am. Real Estate and Urban Econs. Assn., World Future Soc., Am. Econ. Assn., Harvard Club N.Y., L.A. Adventurers Club. Office: Roulac Group 2 Tamal Vista La Kentfield CA 94904

ROUNDS, DONALD MICHAEL, public relations executive; b. Centralia, Ill., May 9, 1941; s. Donald Merritt and Alice Josephine (Soulsby) R.; m. Alma Genevieve Beyer, Dec. 13, 1975. BS in History, Polit. Sci., Colo. State U., 1963. Police reporter, night city editor The Rocky Mountain News, Denver, 1960-70; mgr. Don M. Rounds Co., Denver, 1970-75; sr. editor Western Oil Reporter, Denver, 1975-80; energy writer The Rocky Mountain News, Denver, 1980-87; sr. media rels. advisor Cyprus Minerals Co., Englewood, Colo., 1987-92, media and community rels. mgr., 1992—; adv. bd Colo. State Minerals, Energy, and Geology (appointed by gov.), 1992—. Contbr. articles to mags. and newspapers. Sec. covenant com. Ken Caryl Ranch Master Assn., Littleton, Colo., 1980-84. Recipient 1st place spl. news series AP, 1987, 1st place news sweepstakes, 1987, Margolin award U. Denver Coll. Bus., 1986, Betty McWhorter Commendation of Honor Desk & Derrick Club of Denver, 1987, Journalism award Rocky Mountain Assn. Geologists, 1985, Citizen Svc. award Denver Police Dept., 1969, Pub. Svc. award Englewood Police Dept., 1967. Mem. Nat. Coal Assn. (pub. rels. com.), Soc. Profl. Journalists, Sigma Delta Chi, Denver Press Club (bd. dirs. 1987). Republican. Methodist. Home: 8220 San Juan Range Rd Littleton CO 80127 Office: Cyprus Minerals Co 9100 E Mineral Cir Englewood CO 80112

ROUNTREE, RUTHANN LOUISE, social worker, lecturer; b. Denver, Mar. 18, 1950; d. Charles Lindy and Marian Louise (Jenkins) R. BSW, U. Nebr., 1972; MSW, Denver U., 1973; MDiv, Fuller Theol. Sem., 1988; postgrad., U. So. Calif., 1993—. Lic. clin. social worker; lic. preacher African Meth. Episc. Ch. Asst. dir. Denver br. Virginia Neal Blue Resource Ctr. for Colo. Women, Denver, 1973-76; cons, edn. coord. Aurora (Colo.) Community Mental Health Ctr., 1976-78; program evaluator Castle Substance Abuse Program, L.A., 1978-81; program ops. mgr. Nat. Coun. on Aging, L.A., 1981-85; program mgr. gerontology out-patient facility Fuller Theol. Sem., Pasadena, Calif., 1985-89; mem. faculty, dir. of admissions, dept. social work Calif. State U., Long Beach, 1989—; vice chair San Gabriel Valley Elder Abuse Task Force, Pasadena, Calif., 1987-88; bd. dirs. Living at Home Project, Pasadena, 1988-89; mem. Black Aging Network, L.A., 1990-92. Facilitator Diakanas-Inner Healing Workshops, Pasadena, 1987-88; adv. YWCA Rape Hotline, Pasadena, 1987-89; dir. westside counseling and tng. ctr., pastoral counselor Westminster Presbyn. Ch., 1991-93; trainer lay counselor and peer counselor. Recipient Gov.'s award State of Calif., 1987; named Outstanding Young Women of Am., 1987. Mem. NASW, Nat. Assn. Christian Social Workers, Assoc. Gerontology and Human Devel. Council on Social Work Education. Office: Calif State U Dept Social Work Long Beach CA 90840-0902

ROUSE, MARGARET OTHMER, bank officer; b. Ames, Iowa, Jan. 29, 1953; d. Richard Thomas and Betty Margaret (Will) Othmer; m. Michael John Rouse, Oct. 4, 1980; 1 child, Melinda Michelle. BS in Home Econs., Tex. Tech U., 1976; postgrad., U. N.Mex., 1976-88. Sales asst. Merrill Lynch Pierce Fenner & Smith, Albuquerque, 1976-82; ops. supr. Sunwest Bank of Albuquerque NA, 1982—. Sunwest Bank br. rep. United Way, Albuquerque, 1984-87; mem. Our Lady of Annunciation Cath. Ch., Albuquerque, 1987-92. Mem. Jr. League of Albuquerque (Com. Chmn. award 1988, 91). Republican. Roman Catholic. Home: 5504 Chelwood Pk NE Albuquerque NM 87111 Office: Sunwest Bank Albuquerque NA 11201 Montgomery Blvd NE Albuquerque NM 87111

ROUTER, PAUL GETTY, accountant, financial planner; b. Holland, Mich., Nov. 22, 1942; s. Dennis Worldly and Margarete (Schuler-Hotaling) R.; children: Paula, Rebecca, Roberta. Student, Cordon Bleu, Paris, 1962; M in Taxation, U. Mich., 1964. CFO SWR/Getty Corp., Malibu, Calif., 1964-83; pvt. practice L.A. and San Dimas, Calif., 1983—. with U.S. Army, 1968-70, Vietnam, col. USAR, 1970—. Recipient Black Hatt award Chaine Des Rotesseurs, 1970. Mem. LeTip, L.A. Athletic Club, Magic Castle, Union Rescue Mission. Democrat. Roman Catholic. Office: Pub Acctg and Tax Firm 667 Cliffside Dr San Dimas CA 91773

ROVIRA, LUIS DARIO, state supreme court justice; b. San Juan, P.R., Sept. 8, 1923; s. Peter S. and Mae (Morris) R.; m. Lois Ann Thau, June 25, 1966; children—Douglas, Merilyn. B.A., U. Colo., 1948, LL.B., 1950. Bar: Colo. 1950. Now chief justice Colo. Supreme Ct., Denver.; mem. Pres.'s Com. on Mental Retardation, 1970-71; chmn. State Health Facilities Council, 1967-76. Bd. dirs. YMCA, 1969-78; pres. Lowe Found. Served with AUS, 1943-46. Mem. ABA, Colo. Bar Assn., Denver Bar Assn. (pres. 1970-71), Colo. Assn. Retarded Children (pres. 1968-70), Alpha Tau Omega, Phi Alpha Delta. Clubs: Athletic (Denver), Country (Denver). Home: 4810 E 6th Ave Denver CO 80220-5137 Office: Colo Supreme Ct 2 E 14th Ave Denver CO 80203-2116

ROWAN, RONALD THOMAS, lawyer; b. Bozeman, Mont., Nov. 6, 1941; s. Lawrence Eugene and Florence M.; m. Katherine Terrell Sponenberg, Sept. 4, 1964; children: Heather, Nicholaus, Matthew. BA, Wichita U., 1964; JD, U. Denver, 1969. Bar: Colo. 1969, U.S. Dist. Ct. Colo. 1969. Asst. city atty. City of Colorado Springs, Colo., 1969-71; asst. dist. atty. 4th Jud. Dist., Colorado Springs, 1971-79; gen. counsel U.S. Olympic Com., Colorado Springs, 1979—. Chmn. CSC, Colorado Springs, 1975—; chmn. Criminal Justice Adv. Bd., 1983—; chmn. El Paso Criminal Justice Adv. Com.; bd. dirs. Crimestoppers, 1982-87, past pres. 1985-87, Internat. Anti-counterfeiting Coalition; chmn. Community Corrections Bd., 1981, 86, 87. Mem. ABA, Colo. Bar Assn., El Paso County Trial Lawyers (pres. 1972), El Paso County Bar Assn., U. Denver Law Alumni (chmn.), Colo. Trial Lawyers Assn., Pikes Peak or Bust Rodeo Assn. (Ramrod 1989). Republican. Roman Catholic. Home: 2915 Nevermind Ln Colorado Springs CO 80917-3544 Office: US Olympic Com 1750 E Boulder St Colorado Springs CO 80909-5746

ROWE, CARL OSBORN, municipal offical; b. Colorado Springs, Colo., Feb. 3, 1944; s. Prentiss Eldon and Jo Ann (Osborn) R.; m. Dale Robin Oren, Apr. 12, 1984; 1 child, Stefanie Osborn. BA in Govt. cum laude, George Mason U., 1972; M Urban Affairs, Va. Poly. Inst. and State U., 1976. Cert. pub. housing mgr. Spl. clk. FBI, Washington, 1968-71; mgmt. analyst ICC, Washington, 1972-75; dir. policy and mgmt. U.S. Bur. Reclamation, Washington, 1975-82; pres. Rowe Bus. Consulting, Las Vegas, Nev., 1982-90; exec. dir. City of Las Vegas Housing Authority, 1990—; bd. dirs. Flowtronics, Inc., Phoenix, Sportstech, Inc., Scottsdale, Ariz., MSP Systems, Inc., Scottsdale, LLV '93 Found. Columnist Las Vegas Bus. Press, 1989-90. Vice chmn. So. Nev. Reinvestment and Affordable Housing Com.; founding bd. dirs. Family Cabinet of So. Nev., Affordable Housing Inst. So. Nev.; active So. Nev. Homeless Coalition; mem. exec. bd. Nat. Assn. Housing and Redevel. Officials, Pacific S.W. Regional Conf., Oasis So. Nev. Community Svc. Guild, Las Vegas Community Empowerment Commn., No. Calif./Nev. Exec. Dirs. Assn., Pub. Housing Authorities Dirs. Assn. Decorated USAF Commendation medal. Mem. Am. Soc. Pub. Adminstrn. (governing coun.), Leadership Las Vegas, Las Vegas C. of C., Phi Theta Kappa. Office: Las Vegas Housing Authority 420 N 10th St Las Vegas NV 89101-3196

ROWE, GAIL STUART, history educator; b. L.A., Dec. 2, 1936; s. Lester G. and Alma Virginia (Abbott) R.; m. Mary Jordan, Sept. 7, 1957; children: Jennifer, Justin. BA, Fresno State U., 1959; MA, Stanford U., 1960, PhD, 1969. Tchr. James Logan High Sch., Union City, Calif., 1960-64, Mission San Jose (Calif.) High Sch., 1964-66; asst. prof. U. No. Colo., Greeley, 1969-73, assoc. prof., 1973-77, prof., 1977—. Author: Thomas McKean, 1978, Embattled Bench, 1993; contbr. articles to profl. publs. Mem. Orgn. Am. History, Inst. Early Am. History and Culture, Pa. Hist. Soc., Soc. for Historians of Early Am. Republic. Home: 1201 25th Ave Greeley CO 80631-3525 Office: U No Colo Dept History Greeley CO 80639

ROWE, MARJORIE DOUGLAS, retired social services administrator; b. Bklyn., July 29, 1912; d. Herbert Lynn and Mary Manson (Hall) Douglas; m. Richard Daniel Rowe, July 29, 1937; 1 child, Richard Douglas. AB cum laude, Whitman Coll., 1933; MS in Social Adminstrn., Case Western Res. U., 1936. Caseworker Children's Svcs., Cleve., 1933-36, supr., 1937-39; dir. Adoption Svc. Bur., Cleve., 1940-41; social work supr., psychiat. social work cons. Ea. State Hosp., Medical Lake, Wash., 1962-67; dir. social svcs. Interlake Sch.for Developmentally Disabled, Medical Lake, 1967-74, supt., 1975-82. Pres. chpt. R.P.E.O., Spokane, Wash., 1949, Spokane Alumnae chpt. Delta Delta Delta, 1955-57; chpt. mem. ARC, Orofino, Idaho, 1941-45, Orofino chpt. chmn., 1945-46; sec. Idaho state chpt. AAUW, 1945-46. Mem. Am. Assn. for Mental Deficiency (region I chmn. 1976-77, social work chmn. 1971-73), NASW (gold card mem.), P.E.O. (pres. Spokane Reciprocity 1950), Acad. Cert. Social Workers, Spokane Women of Rotary (pres.), Phi Beta Kappa, Delta Sigma Rho, Mortar Bd. Episcopalian. Home: 946 E Thurston Ave Spokane WA 99203-2948

ROWE, MARY SUE, accounting executive; b. Melrose, Kans., Aug. 31, 1940; d. Gene and Carmen (Glidewell) Woffard; m. Edward Rowe, Nov. 27, 1985; children from previous marriage: Denise, Dynell, Dalene, Denette. Student, MTI Bus. Coll., 1968, Calif. State U., Fullerton, 1969, Broome (N.Y.) Community Coll., 1974-76; cert. Sch. Bus. Mgmt., Calif. State U., San Bernardino, 1986; student, Calif. Coast U., 1991—. Variou bookkeeping and secretarial, 1968-76; asst. mgr., acct. RM Dean Contracting, Chenango Forks, N.Y., 1976-80; acctg. asst. Hemet (Calif.) Unified Sch. Dist., 1981-86; dir. acctg. Desert Sands Unified Sch. Dist., Indio, Calif., 1986-91; bus. svcs. cons. ednl. div. Vicenti, Lloyd & Stutzman, CPA, La Verne, Calif., 1991—. Bd. dirs. Family Svcs. Assn., Hemet, 1982-83. Mem. NAFE, Calif. Assn. Bus. Ofcls. (acctg. com., R & D com., vice chmn. 1988-90, chmn. 1990-91, state acctg. adv. com. 1990-92), Riverside Assn. Chief Accts. (co-chmn. 1986-88). Republican. Home: 2668 Grand Teton Hemet CA 92544 Office: Vicenti Lloyd & Stutzman 2100A E Foothill Blvd La Verne CA 91750-2996

ROWE, ROBERT HETSLEY, lawyer, consultant; b. Rockport, Ky., Sept. 1, 1929; s. Hetsley and Bessie K. (Acton) R.; m. Patricia Lew Swett, Mar. 5, 1983. BA, Mich. State U., East Lansing, 1980; JD, Cooley Law Sch., Lansing, Mich., 1981. Bar: Mich. 1981, U.S. Dist. Ct. (ea. and we. dists.) Mich. 1981. Chief dep. commr. Ins. Bur. State of Mich., Lansing, 1971-76; sr. v.p. League Life Ins. Co., Southfield, Mich., 1976-81; pvt. practice law Farmington Hills, Mich., 1981-84; treas., sec. Western Security Life Ins. Co., Phoenix, 1984-93; ret., 1993. Sgt. USMC, 1946-48, 51-52. Fellow Fin. Analysts Fedn., Life Office Mgmt. Inst.; mem. Mich. Bar Assn.

ROWE, WILLIAM WESTEL, cardiologist; b. Zurich, Switzerland, May 27, 1953; came to U.S., 1956; s. John Westel and Mary Dorothy (Lowenstein) R.; m. Faith Denise Szafranski, Apr. 26, 1986. BS, MIT, 1975; MD, U. Wis., 1979. Resident internal medicine U. Ill. Hosp., Chgo., 1979-82; staff internist USAF Hosp. Elmendorf AFB, Anchorage, 1982-85; cardiology fellow Meml. Hosp., U. N.C., Chapel Hill, 1985-88; cardiologist Pacific Northwest Cardiology, Inc., Mt. Vernon, Wash., 1988—. Major USAF, 1982-85. Fellow Am. Coll. Cardiology; mem. ACP, AMA, Wash. State Med. Assn., Am. Heart Assn., Skagit-Island County Med. Soc. Office: Pacific NW Cardiology 111 S 12th St Mount Vernon WA 98273

ROWEN, MARSHALL, radiologist; b. Chgo.; s. Harry and Dorothy (Kasnow) R.; m. Helen Lee Friedman, Apr. 5, 1952; children: Eric, Scott, Mark. AB in Chemistry with highest honors, U. Ill., Urbana, 1951; MD with honors, U. Ill., Chgo., 1954, MS in Internal Medicine, 1954. Diplomate Am. Bd. Radiology. Intern Long Beach (Calif.) VA Hosp., 1955; resident in radiology Los Angeles VA Hosp., 1955-58; practice medicine specializing in radiology Orange, Calif., 1960—; chmn. bd. dirs. Moran, Rowen and Dorsey, Inc., Radiologists, 1969—; asst. radiologist L.A. Children's Hosp., 1958; assoc. radiologist Valley Presbyn. Hosp., Van Nuys, Calif., 1960; dir. dept. radiology St. Joseph Hosp., Orange, 1961—, v.p. staff, 1972; dir. dept. radiology Children's Hosp. Orange County, 1964—, chief staff, 1977-78, v.p., 1978-83; asst. clin. prof. radiology U. Calif., Irvine, 1967-70, assoc. clin. prof., 1979-72, clin. prof. radiology and pediatrics, 1976, pres. clin faculty assn., 1980-81, v.p., trustee Children's Hosp. Orange County, 1990-91; trustee Choc. Padrinos; sec. Choco Health Svcs., 1987-89, v.p., 1990-93; trustee Found. Med. Care Orange County, 1972-76, Calif. Commn. Adminstrn. Svcs. Hosp., 1975-79, Profl. Practice Systems, 1990-92, Med. Specialty Mgrs., 1990-92, St. Joseph Med. Corp., 1993—; v.p. Found Med. Care Children's Hosp., 1988-89; v.p., bd. dirs. St. Joseph Med. Corp. IPA. Mem. editorial bd. Western Jour. Medicine; contbr. articles to med. jours. Founder Orange County Performing Arts Ctr., mem. Laguna Art Mus., Laguna Festival of Arts, Opera Pacific, S. Coast Reportory, Am. Ballet Theater, World Affairs Council. Served to capt. M.C., U.S. Army, 1958-60. Recipient Rea sr. med. prize U. Ill, 1953; William Cook scholar U. Ill., 1951. Fellow Am. Coll. Radiology; mem. AMA, Am. Heart Assn., Soc. Nuclear Medicine (trustee 1961-62), Orange County Radiol. Soc. (pres. 1968-69), Calif. Radiol. Soc. (pres. 1978-79), Radiol. Soc. So. Calif. (pres. 1976), Pacific Coast Pediatric Radiologists Assn. (pres. 1971), Soc. Pediatric Radiology, Calif. Med. Assn. (chmn. sect. on radiology 1978-79), Orange County Med. Assn. (chmn. UCI liason com. 1976-78), Cardioradiology Soc. So. Calif., Radiol. Soc. N.Am., Am. Roentgen Ray Soc., Am. Coll. Physician Execs., Soc. Chmn. Radiologists Children Hosp., Rams Booster Club, Center Club, Sequoia Athletic Club, Phi Beta Kappa, Phi Eta Sigma, Omega Beta Phi, Alpha Omega Alpha. Office: 1201 W La Veta Ave Orange CA 92668-4213

ROWLAND, FRANK SHERWOOD, chemistry educator; b. Delaware, Ohio, June 28, 1927; m. Joan Lundberg, 1952; children: Ingrid Drake, Jeffrey Sherwood. AB, Ohio Wesleyan U., 1948; MS, U. Chgo., 1951, PhD, 1952, DSc (hon.), 1989; DSc (hon.), Duke U., 1989, Whittier Coll., 1989, Princeton U., 1990, Haverford Coll., 1992; LLD (hon.), Ohio Wesleyan U., 1989, Simon Fraser U., 1991. Instr. chemistry Princeton (N.J.) U., 1952-56; asst. prof. chemistry U. Kans., 1956-58, assoc. prof. chemistry, 1958-63, prof. chemistry, 1963-64; prof. chemistry U. Calif., Irvine, 1964—, dept. chmn., 1964-70, Aldrich prof. chemistry, 1985-89, Bren prof. chemistry, 1989—; Humboldt sr. scientist, Fed. Republic of Germany, 1981; chmn. Dahlem (Fed. Republic of Germany) Conf. on Changing Atmosphere, 1987; vis. scientist Japan Soc. for Promotion Sci., 1980; co-dir. western region Nat. Inst. of Globe Environ. Change; lectr., cons. in field. Contbr. numerous articles to profl. jours. Mem. ozone commn. Internat. Assn. Meteorology and Atmospheric Physics, 1980-88, mem. commn. on atmospheric chemistry and global pollution, 1979-91; mem. acid rain peer rev. panel U.S. Office of Sci. and Tech., Exec. Office of White House, 1982-84; mem. vis. com. Max Planck Insts., Heidelberg and Mainz, Fed. Republic Germany; ozone trends panel mem. NASA, 1986-88; chmn. Gordon Conf. Environ. Scis.-Air, 1987; mem. Calif. Coun. Sci. Tech., 1989—. Recipient numerous awards including John Wiley Jones award Rochester Inst. of Tech., 1975, Disting. Faculty Rsch. award U. Calif., Irvine, 1976, Profl. Achievement award U. Chgo., 1977, Billard award N.Y. Acad. Sci., 1977, Tyler World Prize in Environment Achievement, 1983, Global 500 Roll of Honor for Environ. Achievement UN Environment Program, 1988, Dana award for Pioneering Achievements in Health, 1987, Silver medal Royal Inst. Chemistry, U.K., 1989, Wadsworth award N.Y. State Dept. Health, 1989, medal U. Calif., Irvine, 1989, Japan prize in Environ. Sci., 1989, Dickson prize Carnegie-Mellon U., 1991; Guggenheim fellow, 1962, 74. Fellow AAAS (pres. elect 1991, pres. 1992, chmn. bd. dirs. 1993), Am. Phys. Soc. (Leo Szilard award for Physics in Pub. Interest 1979), Am. Geophys. Union; mem. NAS (bd. environ. studies and toxicology 1986-91, com. on atmospheric chemistry 1987-89, com. atmospheric scis., solar-terrestial com. 1979-83, co-DATA com. 1977-82, sci. com. on problems environment 1986-89, Infinite Voyage film com. 1988-92, Robertson Meml. lectr. 1993, chmn. com. on internat. orgns. and programs 1993—), Am. Acad. Arts and Scis., Am. Chem. Soc. (chmn. div. nuclear sci. and tech. 1973-74, chmn. div. phys. chemistry 1974-75, Tolman medal 1976, Zimmermann award 1980, E.F. Smith lectureship 1980, Environ. Sci. and Tech. award 1983, Esselen award 1987, Peter Debye award 1993). Home: 4807 Dorchester Rd Corona Del Mar CA 92625-2718 Office: U Calif Irvine Dept of Chemistry 571 PS1 Irvine CA 92717

ROWLAND, RUTH GAILEY, hospital official; b. Salt Lake City, Dec. 7, 1922; d. Frederick George and Lucy Jane (Hill) N.; m. Joseph David Gailey, Apr. 9, 1942 (dec. July 1984); children: Sherylynne Harris-Roth, Joseph David Jr., Robert Nelson; m. Joseph Brigham Rowland, Oct. 14, 1986. Student, Felt-Tarrant Community Coll., Salt Lake City, 1941-42, U. Utah. Dir. vol. svcs., pub. rels. dir. Lakeview Hosp., Bountiful, Utah, 1961-92. Mem. com. Women's State Legis. Coun., Salt Lake City, 1970-92; mem. legis. com. Utah Comprehensive Planning Agy., Salt Lake City; mem. Farmington (Utah) Bd. Health, 1979-85; mem. Davis County Adv. Bd. Volunteerism; mem. social svcs. com. LDS Ch. Recipient Total Citizen award Utah C. of C., 1992. Mem. Assn. Dirs. Vol. Svcs. of Am. Hosp. Assn., Utah Assn. Vol. Auxs. (pres.), Utah Dirs. Vol. Svcs. (pres.), Salt Lake Dental Aux. (pres.), Bountiful C. of C. (bd. dirs. 1975-80), Sorompimists. Republican. Home: 871 South 750 East Bountiful UT 84010 Office: Lakeview Hosp 630 E Med Dr Bountiful UT 84010

ROWLAND, SUSAN BLAKE, English language educator; b. Balt., Feb. 9, 1946; d. Walter True and Susan Elizabeth (Stoll) B.; m. Bertram I. Rowland, Nov. 30, 1974; stepchildren: Shawn, Celia, Kevin. BA, Western Coll., Oxford, Ohio, 1968; postgrad., Columbia U., 1968; MA, San Francisco State U., 1976. Instr. Am. Lang. Inst., San Francisco, 1975-76; tchr. Burlingame (Calif.) Adult Sch., 1976-77; sr. lectr. English, Coll. of Notre Dame, Belmont, Calif., 1977—; substitute tchr. San Mateo (Calif.) Adult Sch., 1977—. Co-author: Academic Reading and Study Skills for International Students, 1985. Vol. de Young Mus., San Francisco, 1988—, San Mateo Pub. Libr. Mem. Tchrs. English to Speakers Other Langs., Calif. Assn. Tchrs. English to Speakers Other Langs. Home: 1420 Southdown Rd Hillsborough CA 94010-7252 Office: Coll of Notre Dame 1500 Ralston Ave Belmont CA 94002-1908

ROWLEY, PETER DEWITT, geologist; b. Providence, Dec. 6, 1942; s. Arthur Carroll and Barbara Jean (DeWitt) R.; m. Karen Lynn Eickleberry, June 16, 1969 (div. Mar. 1979); m. Adrienne Barbara Anderson, Nov. 26, 1981 (div. Feb. 1986); m. Mary Ann Siders, June 2, 1987; children: Scott Edward, Jill Elizabeth. BA, Carleton Coll., 1964; PhD, U. Tex., 1968. Temp. instr. geology Kent (Ohio) State U., 1968-69; asst. prof. Carleton Coll., Northfield, Minn., 1969-70; geologist U.S. Geol. Survey, Denver, 1970—; leader/co-leader/dep. leader five expeditions to remote, unexplored areas in Antarctica. Author, co-author and editor various books including Geology of Antarctica, Mt. St. Helens, Utah, Nevada, Colorado; contbr. articles to profl. jours. Alt. mem. Lakewood (Colo.) Planning Commn., 1973-79; active Green Mountain Homeowners Assn., Lakewood, 1970-75. Recipient Meritorious Svc. award Dept. of Interior, Antarctic Svc. medal; Rowley Massif, Antarctica, named feature/U.S. Bd. on Geographic Names; grantee NSF, 1971-86. Fellow Geol. Soc. Am. (Penrose Bequest grantee 1967-68), Explorers Club; mem. Am. Geol. Inst., Am. Geophys. Union, Soc. Econ. Geologists, Colo. Sci. Soc. (chmn. membership com. 1975-77), Rocky Mountain Assn. Geologists. Home: 5894 S Meadow Dr Morrison CO 80465-2632 Office: US Geol Survey MS 913 PO Box 25046 Denver CO 80225-0046

ROWLEY, WILLIAM DEAN, history educator; b. Chariton, Iowa, Aug. 4, 1939; s. Ernest W. and Rachel (Davis) R. B.A., U. Puget Sound., 1961; M.A., U. Nebr., 1963, Ph.D., 1966. Asst. prof. U. Nebr., 1966-67; asst. prof. U. Nev.-Reno, 1967-71, assoc. prof. Am. history, 1971-85, prof., 1986— ; cultural resource contractor U.S. Forest Service. Mem. Am. Soc. Environ. History, Forest History Soc., Western History Assn. (exec. sec. 1974-90). Author: M.L. Wilson and the Campaign for the Domestic Allotment, 1970; Reno: Hub of the Washoe Country, 1983, U.S. Forest Service Grazing and Rangelands: A History, 1985; editor Nev. Hist. Soc. Quar., 1991—. Office: U Nev Dept History Reno NV 89557

ROWLEY, WILLIAM ROBERT, surgeon; b. Omaha, June 7, 1943; s. Robert Kuhlmeyer and Dorothy Eleanor (Larson) R.; m. Eileen Ruth Murray, Aug. 11, 1968; children: Bill II, Jeff, Jill. BA in Psychology, U. Minn., 1966, MD, 1970. Diplomate Am. Bd. Surgery. Commd. lt. USN, 1972, advanced through grades to capt., 1985; intern U. Calif., San Diego, 1970-71, gen. surgery resident, 1971-72; gen. surgery resident Naval Regional Med. Ctr., Phila., 1973-76; peripheral vascular surgery fellow Naval Regional Med. Ctr., San Diego, 1977-78; staff surgeon Naval Regional Med. Ctr., Phila., 1977; staff vascular surgeon Naval Regional Med. Ctr., San Diego, 1978-85, chmn. dept. surgery, 1985-88, dir. surg. svcs., 1987-88; asst. chief of staff for plans and ops. Naval Med. Command S.W. Region, San Diego, 1988-89; dep. comdr. Nat. Naval Med. Ctr., Bethesda, Md., 1989-91; comdg. officer Naval Hospital, Camp Pendleton, Calif., 1991—; program dir. vascular surgery fellowship Naval Hosp., San Diego, 1980-85, gen. surgery residency, 1985-89; assoc. prof. surgery Uniformed Svcs. U. for Health Scis., Bethesda, 1985—. High adventure leader Boy Scouts Am. Fellow ACS; mem. AMA, Am. Coll. Physician Execs., Internat. Soc. Cardiovascular Surgery. Home: Qtrs 1152 14th St Oceanside CA 92054 Office: Naval Hosp Box 555191 Camp Pendleton CA 92055-5191

ROY, CATHERINE ELIZABETH, physical therapist; b. Tucson, Jan. 16, 1948; d. Francis Albert and Dorothy Orme (Thomas) R.; m. Richard M. Johnson, Aug. 31, 1968 (div. 1978); children: Kimberly Anne, Troy Michael. BA in Social Sci. magna cum laude, San Diego State U., 1980; MS in Phys. Therapy, U. So. Calif., 1984. Staff therapist Sharp Meml. Hosp., San Diego, 1984-89, chairperson patient and family edn. com., 1986-87, chairperson sex edn. and counselling com., 1987-89, chairperson adv. bd. for phys. therapy, asst. for edn. program, 1987-89; mgr. rehab. phys. therapy San Diego Rehab. Inst., Alvarado Hosp., 1989-91; dir. therapeutic svcs. VA Med. Ctr., San Diego, 1991—; lectr. patient edn., family edn., peer edn.; mem. curriculum rev. com. U. So. Calif. Phys. Therapy Dept., 1982; bd. dirs. Ctr. for Edn. in Health; writer, reviewer licensure examination items for phys. therapy Profl. Examination Services.. Tennis coach at clinics Rancho Penasquitos Swim and Tennis Club, San Diego, 1980-81; active Polit. Activities Network, 1985; counselor EEO, 1992-93. Mem. Am. Phys. Therapy Assn. (research presenter nat. conf. 1985, del. nat. conf. 1986-93, rep. state conf. 1987-89, 92-93, Mary McMillan student award 1984, mem. exec. bd. San Diego dist. 1985-88, 92-93), AAUW, NAFE, Am. Coll. Sports Medicine, Am. Congress Rehab. Medicine, Phi Beta Kappa, Phi Kappa Phi, Chi Omega. Home: 5067 Park West Ave San Diego CA 92117-1048 Office: San Diego VA Med Ctr Spinal Cord Injury Svc 3350 La Jolla Village Dr San Diego CA 92161

ROY, CHUNILAL, psychiatrist; b. Digboi, India, Jan. 1, 1935; came to Can., 1967, naturalized, 1975; s. Atikay Bandhu and Nirupama (Devi) R.; m. Elizabeth Ainscow, Apr. 15, 1967; children: Nicholas, Phillip, Charles. MB, BS, Calcutta Med. Coll., India, 1959; diploma in psychol. medicine, Kings

Coll., Newcastle-upon-Tyne, Eng., 1963. Intern Middlesborough Gen. Hosp., Eng., 1960-61; jr. hosp. officer St. Luke's Hosp., Middlesborough, Eng., 1961-64, sr. registrar, 1964; sr. hosp. med. officer Parkside Hosp., Macclesfield, Eng., 1964-66; sr. registrar Moorehaven Hosp., Ivybridge, Eng., 1966; reader, head dept. psychiatry Maulana Azad Med. Coll., New Delhi, 1966; sr. med. officer Republic of Ireland, County Louth, 1966; sr. psychiatrist Sask. Dept. Psychiat. Services, Can., 1967-68; regional dir. Swift Current, Can., 1968-71; practice medicine specializing in psychiatry Regina, Sask., Can., 1971-72; founding dir., med. dir. Regional Psychiat. Ctr., Abbotsford, B.C., Can., 1972-82; with dept. psychiatry Vancouver Gen. Hosp., 1987—; cons. to prison adminstrs.; hon. lectr. psychology and clin. prof. dept. psychiatry U. B.C.; ex-officio mem. Nat. Adv. Com. on Health Care of Prisoners in Can.; cons. psychiatrist Vancouver Hosp.; advisor Asian chpt. Psychosomatic Medicine, World Congress of Law and Medicine, New Delhi, 1985. Author: (with D.J. West and F.L. Nichols) Understanding Sexual Attacks, 1978; co-author: Oath of Athens, 1979; mem. editorial rev. bd. Evaluation, 1977—; assoc. editor Internat. Jour. Offender Therapy and Comparative Criminology, 1978—; mem. Bd. Internat. Law Medicine, 1979—; field editor Jour. of Medicine and Law; contbr. articles to profl. jours. Recipient merit award Dept. Health, Republic of Ireland, 1966, merit award Can. Penitentiary Svc., 1974, merit award Correctional Svcs. Can., 1983, citation by pres. U. B.C., 1983; knighted by Order of St. John Ecumenical Found., 1993; Hon. Consul designate Burkina Faso. Fellow Royal Coll. Psychiatry (Can.), Royal Coll. Psychiatry (Eng.), Pacific Rim Coll. Psychiatrists (a founder); mem. World Psychiat. Assn. (sec. sect. forensic psychiatry 1983), World Fedn. Mental Health, Internat. Coun. Prison Med. Services (founding sec.-gen. 1977), Can. Med. Assn., Can. Psychiat. Assn., Amnesty Internat., Internat. Acad. Legal Medicine and Social Medicine, Indian Psychiat. Assn. (life), Can. Assn. Profl. Treatment Offenders (founding dir. 1975), Assn. Physicians & Surgeons Who Work in Can. Prisons (founding pres. 1974), Internat. Found. for Tng. in Penitentiary Medicine and Forensic Psychiatry (founding pres. 1980, vice-chmn., sec.), World Psychiatry Assn., Australian Acad. Forensic Sci. (corr.), Can. Physicians Interested in South Asia (v.p. 1989, pres. 1990), Internat. Coll. Psychosomatic Med. (adv. Asian Chapt.), Internat. Conf. of Health, Culture, & Contemporary Soc. (chief advisor Bombay, India 1989, v.p. 1989, pres. 1990), Internat. Coun. Peniteniary Medicine (founding sec., bd. dirs.), World Psychiat. Assn. (vice chmn. forensic psychiat. sect. 1989), Order of St. John (knight 1992—), mem. bd. dirs., Vancouver Multi Cultural Soc. Home: 2439 Trinity St, Vancouver, BC Canada V5K 1C9 Office: 1417-750 W Broadway, Vancouver, BC Canada V5Z 1J4

ROY, HAROLD EDWARD, research chemist; b. Stratford, Conn., June 2, 1921; s. Ludger Homer and Meta (Jepsen) R.; B.A., Duke U., 1950; m. Joyce E. Enslin, Oct. 9, 1946 (div. 1975); children—Glenn E., Barbara Anne, Suzanne Elizabeth; m. Gail LaVer Jensen, Feb. 11, 1983. Chemist research div. Lockheed Propulsion Co., Redlands, Calif., 1957-61; sec., treas. The Halgene Corp., Riverside, Calif., 1961-63; self-employed chemist, Glendora, Calif., 1963-64; chief engr. propellant devel. Rocket Power, Inc., Mesa, Ariz., 1964-65; cons., Glendora, 1965-66; engring. specialist Northrop Corp., Anaheim, Calif., 1966-69; pres. Argus Tech., Beverly Hills, 1969-70, dir. Harold E. Roy & Assos., Glendora, 1969—. Served to lt. (j.g.) USNR, 1943-46. Mem. Exptl. Aircraft Assn., Am. Ordnance Assn., Am. Inst. Aeros. and Astronautics, Internat. Platform Assn., Acad. Parapsychology and Medicine, Calif. Profl. Hypnotists Assn., World Future Soc. Republican. Home: 143 Warren Rd PO Box 414 Selma OR 97538

ROY, RAMENDRA PRASAD, mechanical engineering educator; b. Dhanbad, Bihar, India, Nov. 26, 1942; came to U.S., 1965; s. Suresh Chandra and Pritikana Roy; m. Suchitra Mitra, Jan. 16, 1978; children: Rupali, Shilpi. BS in Physics, Presidency Coll. Calcutta U., India, 1960; BSME, Jadavpur (India) U., 1964; MS, U. Wash., 1966; MSc, U. Calif., Berkeley, 1971, PhD, 1975. Engr. Kuljian Corp., Calcutta, India, 1964-65, Bechtel Corp., San Francisco, 1966-71; Am. Chem. Soc. fellow U. Calif., 1972-75; asst. prof. nuclear engring. dept. U. Ill., Urbana, 1975-81; assoc. prof. mech. engring. Ariz. State U., Tempe, 1981-86, prof., 1986—; cons. Argonne (Ill.) Nat. Lab., 1978-83, Ariz. Pub. Svc. Co., Phoenix, 1988—. Contbr. articles to profl. jours. Mem. ASME, Asian Am. Faculty and Staff Assn. (pres. 1990-91), Sigma Xi. Democrat. Office: Ariz State U Dept Mech and Aerospace Engring Tempe AZ 85287

ROY, RAYMOND, bishop; b. Man., Can., May 3, 1919; s. Charles-Borromé e and Zephirina (Milette) R. B.A. in Philosophy and Theology, U. Man., 1942; student, Philos. Sem., Montreal, 1942-43, Major Sem., Montreal, 1943-46, Major Sem. St. Boniface, 1946-47. Ordained priest Roman Catholic Ch. 1947. Asst. pastor, then pastor chs. in Man., 1947-50, 53-66; chaplain St. Boniface (Man.) Hosp., 1950-53; superior Minor Sem., St. Boniface, 1966-69; pastor Cathedral Parish, St. Boniface, 1969-72; ordained bishop, 1972; bishop of St. Paul, Alta., Can., 1972—. Club: K.C. Address: 4410 51st Ave Box 339, Saint Paul, AB Canada T0A 3A0*

ROY, RAYMOND ALBERT, JR., pharmacist; b. Matewan, W.Va., Mar. 3, 1954; s. Raymond Albert and Mary (Howerton) R. B.S. in Pharmacy, W.Va. U., 1977. Registered pharmacist, Va., W.Va., N.C., S.C., Nev. Pharmacist Strosnider Drug Co., Williamson, W.Va., 1977-78; pharmacy mgr. Rite Aid Pharmacy, Morgantown, W.Va., 1978-80; pharmacist in charge, pharmacy mgr. K Mart Pharmacy, Lynchburg, Va., 1980-88, Las Vegas, 1988—; elder care and child care pharmacist Park-Davis Pharms., Morris Plains, N.J., 1985—. Recipient Pharmacy Edn. Program award Burroughs Wellcome Co., 1982. Mem. Am. Pharm. Assn., Nev. Pharmacist Assn. Roman Catholic. Home: 2713 St Clair Dr Las Vegas NV 89128-7296 Office: K Mart Pharmacy 3680 3760 E Sunset Rd Las Vegas NV 89120-3233

ROY, RONALD AURELE, research physicist, educator; b. Lewiston, Maine, Dec. 10, 1956; s. Aurele Joseph and Lucienne (Albert) R.; m. Nancy Stone, May 31, 1980; children: Caitlyn Stone, Sydney Elizabeth. BS in Physics summa cum laude, U. Maine, 1981; MS in Physics, U. Miss., 1984; MPhil in Mech. Engring., Yale U., 1985, PhD in Mech. Engring., 1987. Rsch. assoc., instr. Yale U., New Haven, Conn., 1987-88; dir. R & D Apfel Enterprises, New Haven, 1987-88; rsch. asst. prof. engring. U. Miss., Oxford, 1988-91; rsch. scientist Nat. Ctr. for Phys. Acoustics, Oxford, 1988-91; rsch. physicist Applied Physics Lab., U. Wash., Seattle, 1991—; cons. Internat. Paper Co., Mobile, Ala., 1989-91, Electro-Med Systems SA, Geneva, Switzerland, 1990-91, Dean Tech., Inc., Hanover, N.H., 1990-91; adj. asst. prof. physics U. Miss., Oxford, 1992—; presenter in field. Contbr. articles to profl. jours. Recipient NSF Undergrad. Rsch. fellowship NSF, 1980, Grad. fellowship Office Naval Rsch., 1982-87. Fellow Acoustical Soc. Am.; mem. Am. Inst. Ultrasound in Medicine, Am. Phys. Soc., European Soc. Sonochemistry, Sigma Xi, Tau Beta Pi, Sigma Pi Sigma, Phi Kappa Phi. Democrat. Roman Catholic. Home: 11305 117th Pl NE Kirkland WA 98034 Office: U Wash Applied Physics Lag 1013 NE 40th St Seattle WA 98105

ROYBAL-ALLARD, LUCILLE, congresswoman; b. Boyle Heights, Calif., June 12, 1941; d. Edward Roybal; married; 4 children. BA, Calif. State U., L.A. Former mem. Calif. State Assembly; mem. 103rd Congress from 33rd Calif. dist., 1993—. Office: House of Representatives Washington DC 20515

ROY-BURMAN, PRADIP, molecular biology and virology educator; b. Comilla, Bengal, India, Nov. 12, 1938; came to U.S., 1963; s. Prafulla Nath and Mrinalini (Barman) Roy-Burman; m. Sumitra Ghosh, Nov. 26, 1963. BSc. with honors, Calcutta (India) U., 1956, MSc., 1958, PhD, 1963. Rsch. assoc. dept. biochemistry Sch. of Medicine U. So. Calif., L.A., 1963-66, Dernham sr. rsch. fellow in oncology Am. Cancer Soc., 1966-71, asst. prof. dept. biochemistry, 1967-72, assoc. prof. dept. pathology and biochemistry, 1972-78, prof. dept. pathology and biochemistry, 1978—, vice chmn. dept. pathology, 1987—; ad hoc mem. pathology B study sect. NIH, Bethesda, Md., 1988-89, mem. pathology B study sect., 1990—, mem. spl. review com. Nat. Inst. Neurol. Disorders and Stroke extramural rsch. program, 1992-93; chmn. biomed. rsch. support grant com. U. So. Calif. Sch. Medicine, 1984—, instl. biosafety com., 1989—, univ. com. on appointments, promotions and tenure, health sci., 1989-92. Author (with others) books; contbr. articles to profl. jours.; book reviewer; inventor novel transcription regulatory elements for gene transfer vectors; mem. editorial bd. Hematological Oncology, 1987—. Mem. U. So. Calif./Bravo Magnate High Sch. partnership adv. com, 1992—, Bengali Assn. of So. Calif., greater L.A. area, 1970. Rsch. grantee Am. Cancer Soc., NIH, Am. Diabetes Assn., Wright Found. Mem. Am. Soc. for Microbiology, Am. Soc. for Biol. Chemists & Molecular Biology, Am. Soc. Virology, Internat. Assn. for Comparative Rsch. on Leukemia & Related Diseases. Democrat. Hindu. Office: U So Calif Sch of Medicine 2011 Zonal Ave HMR 204 Los Angeles CA 90033

ROYCE, EDWARD R. (ED ROYCE), congressman; b. Los Angeles, Oct. 12, 1951; m. Marie Porter. BA, Calif. State U. Tax mgr. Southwestern Portland Cement Co.; U.S senator from Calif. 93rd-103rd Congresses from 32d Calif. dist., 1983-93; mem. 103rd Congress from 39th dist. Calif., 1993—; chmn. Constl. Amenedments Com.; vice chmn. Public Employment and Retirement Com.; mem. Bus. and Profs. com., Health and Human Svcs. com., Indsl. Rels. com.; legis. author, campaign co-chmn. Proposition 15 Crime Victims/Speedy Trial Initiative; author nation's 1st felony stalking law, bill creating Foster Family Home Ins. Fund, legis. creating foster parent recruitment and tng. program. Named Legis. of Yr. Orange County Rep. Com., 1986, Child Adv. of Yr. Calif. Assn. Svc. for Children, 1987. Mem. Anaheim C. of C. Republican. Office: US Ho of Reps Office of Ho Mems Washington DC 20515 also: 4053 State Capitol Sacramento CA 95814

ROYCE, MARIE THERESE PORTER, environmental quality manager, sales executive; b. Upland, Calif., May 20, 1961; d. Ronald Herbert and Mary Barbara (O'Neil) Porter; m. Edward R. Royce, Nov. 9, 1985. BS in Mktg. Mgmt., Calif. Polytechnic U., 1984. Account mgr. sales The Procter & Gamble Co., Irvine, Calif., 1988—; sales cons. The Procter & Gamble Co., Orange, Calif., 1984-88; intern lead market trainer The Procter & Gamble Co., Irvine, Calif., 1992—; environ. quality mgr. The Procter & Gamble Co., Cinn., 1992—; co-owner Gloria Jean's Coffee Bean, Laguna Hills, Calif., 1990—, Costa Mesa, Calif., 1992—, Thousand Oaks, Calif., 1989—. Vol. chmn. Royce for Congress, Fullerton, Calif., 1991-92, campaign treas., 1989-91; mem. Young Reps., Costa Mesa, Calif., 1987—, Rep. Federated Women, Anaheim and Fullerton, 1988—. Named Mktg. Student of Yr. Sales and Mktg. Execs., 1983. Mem. Calif. Polytechnic Alumni Assn. (v.p. 1988-89, pres. bus. 1989-90, Dist. award 1990, Mktg. Alumni award 1992), Pi Sigma Epsilon (nat. sec. 1988, v.p. 1989, Top Alumni award 1988). Republican. Roman Catholic. Office: The Procter & Gamble Co 2 Procter & Gamble Pla Cincinnati OH 45202

ROYSTON, H. JAMES, forensic engineer, structural engineer; b. Carson City, Mich., Jan. 19, 1951; s. Harold James and Mary Ella (Tester) R.; m. Mary Evelyn Amend, Aug. 4, 1973; children: Hilary Ann, Ashley Brook. BA in Edn., Mich. State U., 1974; MS in Engring., U. Wyo., 1978. Registered profl. engr., Colo., Wyo. Rsch. engr. Rsch.-Cottrell/Custodis, Terre Haute, Ind., 1978-81; sr. cons. Knott Lab., Denver, 1981-90; pres., sr. cons. Analytical Engring., Inc., Denver, 1990—. Mem. Bd. Adjustment and Appeals, City of Aurora, Colo., 1990—; mem. coun. Mountain View Community Ch., Aurora, 1992—; cons. Habitat for Humanity, Denver, 1992; team coach Odyssey of the Mind, Cherry Creek Schs., Colo., 1987-89. Mem. ASCE, NSPE, ASTM, Nat. Acad. Forensic Engrs. (sr.), Colo. Soc. for Natural Hazards Rsch. (pres. 1986-87, bd. dirs. 1987-90), Internat. Conf. Bldg. Ofcls. (profl. mem.), Nat. Soc. Archtl. Engrs., Am. Concrete Inst., Nat. Inst. Bldg. Sci. Democrat. Office: Analytical Engring Inc 2180 S Ivanhoe St Ste 7 Denver CO 80222

ROZEMA, HAROLD ALDEN (HAL ROZEMA), artist, interior designer; b. Grand Rapids, Mich., Nov. 10, 1929; s. Harold Andrew and Minnie G. (Baas) R.; m. Janet M. Christensen, May 4, 1949 (div. May 1974); children: Timothy H., Merri Beth; m. Jacklyn Anne Bellamy Hoffman, Dec. 14, 1991. Student, Internat. Corr. Schs., 1963; AA, Grand Rapids Jr. Coll., 1976; BSBA, Aquinas Coll., Grand Rapids, 1976; postgrad., Univ. Coll., London, 1979. Cert. project mgr., Archtl. Woodworking Inst. Designer Am. Seating Co., Grand Rapids, 1948-54; designer, estimator Store Fronts Inc., Grand Rapids, 1954-59; engring. illustrator Lear Inc., Grand Rapids, 1959-65; ptnr. United Structural Laminated Sales, Grand Rapids, 1965-72; owner, mgr. Samson Marine West Mich., Grand Rapids, 1968-74, Harmyne Homes, Grand Rapids, 1970-80; artist Artists' Touring Assocs., Orlando, Fla., 1979-84; owner, CEO, The H A R Corp., artists mktg. and cons. svcs., Phoenix, 1984—; cons. Restaura Engring. and Design Group, Dial Corp., Phoenix, 1991-92. Illustrator: China Airlift—The Hump; over 200 commns. Mem. Ariz. Coun. on Arts, Phoenix, 1992—. Mem. Am. Soc. Aviation Artists (chmn. ethics com. 1988—), Guild Aviation Artists U.K., USAF Artists Assn. Office: The H A R Corp PO Box 15180 Phoenix AZ 85060

ROZENMAN, LIOR, recreation leader; b. Chgo., Aug. 20, 1968; s. Tzvi and Elena Kay (Radley) R. BA in Lit. and Writing, U. Calif. San Diego, 1990. Staff writer intern San Diego Rev. of Film, 1989-90; staff writer U. Calif. San Diego Daily, 1989-90; writer Robert Calhoun, L.A., 1990-92; recreation leader III Beverly Hills (Calif.) Recreation and Pks., 1990—. Home: 426 S Doheny Dr Beverly Hills CA 90211-3511

RUBAYI, SALAH, surgeon, educator; b. Baghdad, Iraq, Oct. 1, 1942; came to U.S., 1981; s. Abdulla Mossa Rubayi and Fatma (Ibriham) Al-Jarah; m. Cecile-Rose, June 23, 1985. MD, U. Baghdad, Iraq, 1966; LRCP and LRCS, Royal Coll. Surgeons and Physicians, Scotland, 1974. Lic. physician and surgeon, Calif. Surgeon burn and reconstructive surgery Birmingham Accident Hosp., Eng., 1978-81; fellow burn unit Los Angeles County/U. So. Calif. Med. Ctr., 1981-82; fellow plastic surgery Rancho Los Amigos Med. Ctr., Downey, Calif., 1982-85, mem. attending staff in plastic and reconstructive surgery, chief pressure ulcer mgmt. service, 1985—; chmn. Laser Safety Com. Rancho Los Amigos Med. Ctr., 1985—; asst. prof. surgery U. So. Calif. Contbr. articles to profl. jours. Fellow ACS, Internat. Coll. Surgeons, Am. Soc. Laser Medicine and Surgery; mem. Internat. Soc. Burn Injury, Am. Burn Assn., Internat. Soc. Paraplegia. Office: Rancho Los Amigos Med Ctr HB121 7601 Imperial Hwy Downey CA 90242-3496

RUBELI, PAUL E., gaming company executive; b. 1943; married. BS, U. Notre Dame; MBA, Columbia U., 1967. Assoc. A.T. Kearney Inc., Chgo., 1969-73; v.p., gen. mgr. Bunker-Ramo Corp., 1973-76; group v.p. Baker Industries, Parsippany, N.J., 1976-79; exec. v.p. and pres. Ramada Inns Inc., Phoenix, 1979-89; pres., CEO Aztar Corp., Phoenix, 1989—; chmn. Aztar Corp., 1991—. Served to 1st lt. AUS, 1967-69. Office: Aztar Corp 2390 E Camelback Rd Ste 400 Phoenix AZ 85016-3491

RUBENDALL, RICHARD ARTHUR, civil engineer; b. Pierre, S.D., Sept. 24, 1957; s. Quentin Theodore and Doris (Noe) R.; m. Sandra Mae Kovacich, June 8, 1985. BSCE, S.D. Sch. Mines & Tech., 1979; MSCE, U. N.Mex., 1993. Registered profl. engr., Mont., Ariz. Field engr. USPHS/Indian Health Svc., Lame Deer, Mont., 1979-86; sr. field engr. USPHS/Indian Health Svc., Many Farms, Ariz., 1986-89; sr. field engr. USPHS/Indian Health Svc., Sells, Ariz., 1989-90, dist. engr., 1990—. Comdr. USPHS, 1979—. Recipient USPHS Isolated Hardship award, 1980, 84, 88, 91, USPHS Hazardous Duty award 1984, USPHS Citation with plaque, 1990, USPHS Achievement medal, 1985; named Indian Health Svc. Engr. of Yr., Tucson area, 1990. Mem. ASCE, Am. Water Works Assn., Water Environment Fedn., USPHS Commd. Officer Assn. (pres. Tucson chpt. 1993—), Res. Officers Assn., Assn. Mil. Surgeons of the U.S. Home: 6944 E 42d St Tucson AZ 85730 Office: USPHS PO Box 548 Sells AZ 85634-0548

RUBENSTEIN, LEONARD SAMUEL, communications executive, ceramist, painter, sculptor, photographer; b. Rochester, N.Y., Sept. 22, 1918; s. Jacob S. and Zelda H. (Gordon) R.; widowed May 28, 1983; children—Carolinda, Eric, Harley. B.F.A. cum laude, Alfred U., 1939; student Western Reserve, 1938; postgrad. U. Rochester, 1940-41. Creative dir. Henry Hempstead Advt. Agy., Chgo., 1949-55; v.p., exec. art dir. Clinton E. Frank Advt. Agy., Chgo., 1955-63; v.p., nat. creative dir. Foster & Kleiser div. Metromedia, Inc., Los Angeles, 1967-73, v.p. corp. creative cons., Metromedia, Inc., Los Angeles, 1973-88; guest lectr. U. Chgo.; instr. Columbia Coll., Chgo.; past. pres. Art Dirs. Club Chgo. (spl. citation); instr. Fashion Inst., Los Angeles; lectr. in field. Mem. Soc. Typog. Arts (past dir.), Am. Ceramic Soc. (design chpt.), Am. Craft Coun., Inst. Outdoor Advt. (past plans bd.), Los Angeles County Mus. Art, Mus. Contemporary Art of L.A. (charter), Palos Verdes (Calif.) Art Ctr., Phi Epsilon Pi. Lodge: B'nai B'rith. Author: (with Charles Hardison) Outdoor Advertising; contbr. articles in field to profl. publs. One-man show: Calif. Mus. Sci. and Industry, 1970; two-person exhibition of porcelains, Palos Verdes Art Ctr., 1987; numerous juried nat. and regional group shows; creator concept for Smithsonian exhibition Images of China: East and West, 1982; writer-producer (ednl. video) Paul Soldner, Thoughts on Creativity, 1989; porcelains in permanent collections of 3 mus., 1992. Home and Office: 30616 Ganado Dr Palos Verdes Peninsula CA 90274-6223

RUBIN, DANIEL LEE, accountant; b. Denver, Apr. 20, 1955; s. Leon and Esther Shirley (Kaufman) R.; m. Susan Ann Elmblad, Aug. 27, 1978; children: Hilary, David. BA cum laude, Colo. Coll., 1977; MBA, U. Wash., 1981, JD, 1982. CPA, Colo. Staff acct. Arthur Andersen & Co., Denver, 1982-84; mem. firm, shareholder Ian D. Gardenswartz & Assoc., Denver, 1984—. Mem. AICPA, Colo. Soc. CPAs. Office: Ian D Gardenswartz & Assocs 6825 E Tennessee Ave # 235 Denver CO 80224-1606

RUBIN, JOEL DAVID, marketing executive; b. L.A., May 22, 1959; s. Matthew and Esther (Steinman) R.; m. Katherine Anne Lamken, Apr. 17, 1988. BA, U. Ariz., 1981. Sales rep. E&J Gallo Winery, Modesto, Calif., 1981-83; account mgr. Bacardi Imports, Inc., Miami, Fla., 1983-85; regional mgr. ETAK, Inc., Menlo Park, Calif., 1985-88; trade mktg. mgr. WD-40 Co., Valencia, Calif., 1988—. Office: WD-40 Co 123 Hodencamp Rd # 201 Thousand Oaks CA 91360-5825

RUBIN, LAWRENCE IRA, podiatrist; b. Buffalo, Dec. 19, 1945; s. Harold Philip and Rose (Kaiser) R.; m. Janis Bernstein, Sept. 12, 1970 (div. Apr. 1986); children: Alison Meredith, Stacy Heather; m. Linda Sleeth, Apr. 30, 1989. Student, Am. U., 1963-65; D of Podiatric Medicine, N.Y. Coll. of Podiatric Medicine, 1969. Diplomate Am. Bd. Podiatric Surgery. Resident in podiatry Kensington Hosp., Phila., 1970; pvt. practice medicine specializing in podiatry Clarence, N.Y., 1970-76; chief podiatric surgery and medicine Meml. Hosp. of Gardena, Calif., 1977—; cons. South Bay Free Clinic, Gardena, 1979—; bd. dirs. alumni and assocs. Calif. Coll. of Podiatric Medicine. Fellow Am. Coll. Foot Surgeons, Am. Coll. Podiatric Med. Rev.; mem. Calif. Podiatric Med. Assn. (peer review com., chmn. patient and ins. relations com. 1993—), L.A. County Podiatric Med. Soc. (pres. 1983-84, parliamentarian 1985-91, chmn. seminar com. 1980-82, 87-90, Pres.'s award 1984), Am. Acad. Podiatric Sports Medicine (assoc.). Democrat. Jewish. Lodge: Masons (master mason 1974—). Office: Gardena Podiatrist's Group 1141 W Redondo Beach Blvd Gardena CA 90247-3586 also: 4201 Torrance # 360 Torrance CA 90503

RUBIN, MICHAEL HOWARD, postsecondary education specialist; b. L.A., June 1, 1962; s. Eugene Samuel and Judith (Grossman) R. BA, UCLA, 1983; MA, U. Toronto (Can.), 1984; postgrad., Stanford U., 1992—. Dept. mgr. Sears Roebuck, North Hollywood, Calif., 1979-83; rsch. asst. psychology dept. UCLA, L.A., 1981-83, therapist young autism project, 1982-83; teaching assoc. U. Toronto, 1983-84; mgmt. exec. May Co. Calif., North Hollywood, 1984-86; sr. rsch. assoc. Western Psychol. Svcs., L.A., 1986-87; dir. ednl. studies Evaluation & Tng. Inst., L.A., 1987—; cons. Calif. Dept. Edn., Sacramento, 1987—, Calif. Community Colls., Sacramento, 1987, Chancellor's Office, Calif. State U., 1987—, Calif. State Libr., Sacramento, 1989—. Editor (newsletter) Calif. Connection, 1989—. Mem. gen. adv. bd. Santa Monica (Calif.) Coll., 1988—; office mgr. UCLA Charity Mardi Gras, L.A., 1982, bus. mgr., 1983; contbr. Calif. Dem. Party, 1988—; mem. Scholarship Com. UCLA Alumni, 1990—. Armco scholar Armco Found., 1980-84, Connaught scholar U. Toronto, 1983, Byron Holland scholar UCLA, 1980, Ontario Grad. scholar Govt. of Ont., Can., 1983-85. Mem. ALA, Am. Edn. Rsch. Assn., Am. Vocat. Assn., Phi Beta Kappa, Psi Chi, Pi Gamma Mu. Democrat. Home: 312 Fair Oaks St San Francisco CA 94110 Office: Evaluation & Tng Inst Ste 420 12300 Wilshire Blvd Los Angeles CA 90025-1073

RUBINSTEIN, CHARLOTTE STREIFER, author, lecturer, art historian; b. N.Y.C., Dec. 14, 1921; d. Aaron and Lillian (Kaufman) Streifer; m. William Rubinstein, May 30, 1941 (dec. Apr. 1991); children: Arthur, Joan, Elaine. BA, Bklyn. Coll., 1941; MA, Columbia U., 1946; MFA, Otis-Parsons Art Inst., 1969. Instr. West L.A. Coll., Fullerton Coll., Saddleback Coll., 1969-84. Author American Women Sculptors, 1990, American Women Artists, 1992 (Best Humanities Book of 1982 award); contbr. articles to art jours. Recipient Individual Rsch. grant AAUW, 1984. Mem. Coll. Art Assn., Women's Caucus for Art (nat. honor 1984), Assn. Am. Art Historians. Home and Office: 2680 Victoria Dr Laguna Beach CA 92651

RUBY, CHARLES LEROY, law educator, lawyer, civic leader; b. Carthage, Ind., Dec. 28, 1900; s. Edgar Valentine and Mary Emma (Butler) R.; certificate Ball State U., 1921-22; AB, Cen. Normal Coll., 1924, LLB, 1926, BS, 1931, BPE, 1932; MA, Stanford, 1929; JD, Pacific Coll. of Law, 1931; PhD, Olympic U., 1933; m. Rachael Elizabeth Martindale, Aug. 30, 1925; children: Phyllis Arline (Mrs. Norman Braskat), Charles L., Martin Dale. Prin., Pine Village (Ind.) High Sch., 1923-25; Glenwood (Ind.) Pub. Schs., 1925-26; tchr. El Centro (Calif.) Pub. Sch., 1926-27, Fresno Cen. (Calif.) Union High Sch., 1927-29; prof. law Fullerton Coll., 1929-66; prof. edn. Armstrong Coll., summer 1935, Cen. Normal Coll., summers 1929-33; admitted to Ind. bar, 1926, U.S. Supreme Ct. bar, 1970; pres. Ret. Service Vol. Program, North Orange County, Calif., 1973-76, 83-84; dir. North Orange County Vol. Bur., Fullerton Sr. Citizens Task Force. Life trustee, co-founder Continuing Learning Experiences program Calif. State U., Fullerton, hon. chmn. fund com. Gerontology Bldg; founder, dir. Fullerton Pub. Forum, 1929-39; founder Elks Nat. Found.; co-founder, benefactor Gerontology Ctr. Calif. State U., Fullerton; pres. Fullerton Rotary, 1939-40, hon. mem., 1983—; mem. U.S. Assay Commn., 1968—; mem. Orange County Dem. Cen. Com., 1962-78; bd. dirs. Fullerton Sr. Multi-purpose Ctr., 1981—; bd. dirs. Orange County Sr. Citizens Adv. Council; mem. pres.'s com. Calif. State U., Fullerton. Recipient Medal of Merit, Am. Numis. Assn., 1954, Spl. Commendation Calif. State Assembly, 1966, 88, Calif. State Senate, 1978, 86, Commendation Ind. Sec. of State, 1984, Commendation Bd. Suprs. Orange County, 1985, Commendation Fullerton City Council, 1986, 88, Commendation Orange County Bd. Supervisors, 1986, Commendation Calif. State Senate, 1986, Commendation Exec. Com. Pres. Calif. State U., Fullerton, 1986, Commendation Calif. gov., 1988; Charles L. and Rachael E. Ruby Gerontology Ctr. named in his and late wife's honor, Calif. State U., Fullerton. Fellow Ind. Bar Found.; mem. Pres. Assocs. Calif. State U. Fullerton, Fullerton Coll. Assocs. (named Spl. Retiree of Yr. 1986, Commendation 1986), Calif. (life, pres. So. sect. 1962-63, treas. 1964-65, pres. 1960-61, dir. 1956-65), pres. Fullerton Secondary Tchrs. Assn., Orange County Tchrs. Assn. (pres. 1953-55), Fullerton Coll. (pres. 1958-60) Tchrs. Assn., NEA (life), Ind. Bar Assn., Stanford U. Law Soc., Calif. State Council Edn., Am. Numismatic Assn. (gov. 1951-53, life adv. bd.), Ind. Bar Assn. (hon. life, Golden Career award 1983), Calif. Bus. Educators Assn. (hon. life), Calif. Assn. Univ. Profs., Pacific S.W. Bus. Law Assn. (pres. 1969-70, life), Numismatic Assn. So. Calif. (life, pres. 1961), Calif. Numis. Assn., Indpls. Coin Club (hon. life), Los Angeles Coin Club (hon. life), U.S. Supreme Ct. Hist. Soc., Calif. Town Hall, North Orange County Mus. Assn. (life, benefactor dir.), Stanford U. Alumni Assn. (life), Old Timers Assay Commn. (life), Fullerton Archeology (hon. life, benefactor dir.). Methodist. Clubs: Elks, Fullerton Coll. Vets. (hon. life). Contbr. articles in field to profl. jours. Home: 308 N Marwood Ave Fullerton CA 92632-1139

RUBY, LAWRENCE, nuclear science educator, engineer; b. Detroit, July 25, 1925; s. Irving Morris and Rose Ruby; m. Judith Ruby, Apr. 8, 1951; children: Jill, Peter, Frederick. AB in Physics, UCLA, 1945, MA in Physics, 1947, PhD in Physics, 1951. Registered profl. engr., Calif. Physicist Lawrence Berkeley (Calif.) Lab., 1950-87; lectr. in nuclear engring. U. Calif., Berkeley, 1959-61, assoc. prof. nuclear engring., 1961-66, prof. nuclear engring., 1966-87; prof. nuclear sci. Reed Coll., Portland, 1987-91; adj. profl. applied physics & elec. engring. Oreg. Grad. Inst. Sci. & Tech., Portland, 1991—; cons. Lawrence Livermore (Calif.) Nat. Lab., 1955-87. Mem. Am. Phys. Soc., Am. Assn. Physics Tchrs., Am. Nuclear Soc., Sigma Xi. Home: 663 Carrera Ln Lake Oswego OR 97034-1674 Office: Oreg Grad Inst Sci and Tech PO Box 91000 20000 NW Walker Rd Portland OR 97291-1000

RUCH, CHARLES P., university official; b. Longbranch, N.J., Mar. 25, 1938; s. Claud C. and Marcella (Pierce) R.; m. Sally Joan Brandenburg, June 18, 1960; children: Cheryl, Charles, Christopher, Cathleen. BA, Coll. of Wooster, 1959; MA, Northwestern U., 1960, PhD, 1966. Counselor, tchr. Evanston (Ill.) Twp. High Sch., 1960-66; asst. prof. U. Pitts., 1966-70, assoc. prof., dept. chmn., 1970-74; assoc. dean sch. edn. Va. Commonwealth U., Richmond, 1974-76, dean sch. edn., 1976-85, interim provost, v.p., 1985-86, provost, v.p., 1986-93; pres. Boise (Idaho) State U., 1993—; cons. various univs., govtl. agys., ednl. founds. Author or co-author over 50 articles, revs., tech. reports. Mem. Am. Psychol. Assn., Am. Ednl. Research Assn., Am. Assn. Counseling and Devel., Phi Delta Kappa. Office: Boise State U 1910 University Dr Boise ID 83725

RUCH, WAYNE EUGENE, microlithography engineer; b. Sewickly, Pa., Nov. 24, 1946; s. Eugene Herbert and Marian Adelle (Moreth) R. BS in Chemistry, Carnegie Mellon U., Pitts., 1968; MS in Chemistry, U. Fla., 1975. Sr. engr. Harris Corp., Palm Bay, Fla., 1975-80, lead engr., 1980-85, staff engr., 1985-91; microlithography inspection staff engr., cons. KLA Instruments, San Jose, Calif., 1991—; adj. prof. chemistry Fla. Inst. Tech., Melbourne, Fla., 1979-85. Contbr. articles to profl. jours. With U.S. Army, 1969-71. Decorated Bronze Star with oak leaf cluster. Mem. N.Y. Acad. Scis., Am. Chem. Soc. Home: 15100 Fern Ave Boulder Creek CA 95006-9776

RUCINSKI, ROBERT D., environmental company executive; b. Wisconsin Rapids, Wis., Apr. 22, 1943; s. Donald C. and Bertha M. (Krueger) R.; married; children: Christopher, Vicki. BS, U. Wis., Stevens Point, 1972; MPA, Brigham Young U., 1978. Cert. profl. contract mgr. Procurement intern U.S. Army Aviation Systems, St. Louis, 1972-73; supr. contracts U.S. Army Tooele (Utah) Army Depot, 1973-78; contract mgr. U.S. Corps of Engrs., Winchester, Va., 1978-79; mgr. acquisitions U.S. Dept. Energy, Laramie (Wyo.) Energy Tech. Ctr., 1979-83; v.p. U. Wyo. Rsch. Corp., Western Rsch. Inst., Laramie, 1983-88; pres., chmn. Resource Tech. Corp., Laramie, 1988—; mem. supervisory com. Univ. Wyo. Credit Union, Laramie, 1987—; mem. Am. Chem. Soc. adv. com. for Environ. Buyers Guide. Mem. com. State Rep. Party, Laramie, 1990. With USN, 1964-68. Mem. VFW (life), Am. Legion, DAV (life), Nat. Ski Patrol (dir. 1983-84), Elks. Roman Catholic. Home: 1814 Arnold St Laramie WY 82070-5423 Office: R T Corp PO Box 1346 Laramie WY 82070-1346

RUCKER, DANIEL EDWARD, development officer; b. Augusta, Ga., Oct. 17, 1956; s. Edward Joseph and Joyce Marie (Morgan) R.; m. Alison Louise Hager, July 24, 1982; children: Matthew James, Lisa Nicole. BS in Human Rels. and Orgn. Behavior, U. San Francisco, 1982. Dir. human resources, progs. and devel. Maryvale/The L.A. Orphan Asylum, Rosemead, Calif., 1985-87; assoc. dir. L.A. Orthopedic Hosp. and Found., 1987-89; dir. devel. Inland Counties/Am. Lung Assn., San Bernardino, Calif., 1990—. Mem. Nat. Soc. Fundraising Execs. Republican. Roman Catholic. Office: American Lung Assn 441 Mackay Dr San Bernardino CA 92408-3230

RUCKER, MICHAEL DAVID, electrical engineer; b. Mobile, Ala., Dec. 22, 1960; s. Lucian Maxwell and Betty Jean (Boswell) R.; m. Rosalynn Leigh Crook, Jul. 2, 1986; 1 child, Jessica. BEE, Ga. Inst. Tech., 1983. Engr. Motorola, Scottsdale, Ariz., 1984-87, GTE Communication Systems, Phoenix, 1987-90, AG Communication Systems, Phoenix, 1991—. Music leader Scottsdale Wesleyan Ch., 1986—. Republican. Home: 15627 E Chicory Fountain Hills AZ 85268

RUCKER, THOMAS DOUGLAS, purchasing executive; b. Ottumwa, Iowa, Aug. 30, 1926; s. Everett Henry and Harriett Mary (Evans) R.; A.B., Loyola U., 1951; postgrad. St. Patrick's Coll., 1950-52; m. Rita Mary Rommelfanger, Apr. 18, 1953; children—David, Theresa, Martin, Paul. Asst. purchasing agt. Radio TV Supply, Los Angeles, 1952-53; buyer Consol. Western Steel div. U.S. Steel, Commerce, Calif., 1953-64, S.W. Welding & Mfg. Co., Alhambra, Calif., 1964-70; dir. purchasing Southwestern Engring., Commerce, Calif., 1970-87, ret. Served with USAAF, 1945-46. Home: 10642 Abisko Dr Whittier CA 90604-2403 Office: Southwestern Engring 5701 S Eastern Ave Ste 300 Los Angeles CA 90040-2934

RUCKMAN, JO ANN, history educator, researcher; b. Des Moines, Dec. 27, 1938; d. William H. and Frances (Nies) Schrampfer; m. Paul Edward Ruckman, Feb. 27, 1965 (div. 1969); m. Peter Machotka, 1988. Student, Goucher Coll., 1956-57; BS, Iowa State U., 1960; MA, U. Chgo., 1963; PhD, No. Ill. U., 1975. Instr., N.W. Mo. State Coll., Maryville, 1963-64, Fort Hays Kans. State Coll., Hays, 1964-69, No. Ill. U., DeKalb, 1969-70; prof. Idaho State U., Pocatello, 1974—, chmn. dept. history, 1983-89. Trustee Idaho State Hist. Soc., 1990—. Author: The Moscow Business Elite, 1984. Contbr. articles to profl. publs. Sr. fellow Russian Inst., Columbia U., 1981. Mem. Am. Assn. Advancement Slavic Studies, N.W. Women's Studies Assn., Nat. Women's Studies Assn., Coalition for Western Women's History, Idaho State U. Profl. Women. Home: 327 S 12th Ave Pocatello ID 83201-4846 Office: Idaho State U Dept History Pocatello ID 83209

RUCKMAN, STANLEY NEAL, library director; b. Scottsbluff, Nebr., Jan. 16, 1936; s. John Perry and Violet Valentine (Runyan) R.; m. Jeanne Delano, Aug. 11, 1957 (div. 1977); m. Carol Ann Saulsberry, Aug. 26, 1978. BA in Edn., U. Oreg., 1957; MA in Librarianship, U. Denver, 1958. Libr. Oreg. City High Sch., 1958-61, Vandenberg Jr. High Sch., Lompoc, Calif., 1961-63; reference libr. Libr. Assn. Portland, Oreg., 1963-64, Coll. of Idaho, Caldwell, 1964-70; dir. reference Oreg. State Libr., Salem, 1970-72; libr. dir. Linn-Benton Community Coll., Albany, Oreg., 1972-86, N.Mex. State U., Alamogordo, 1986—. Bd. dirs. Libra Found., Inc. Mem. ALA (councilor 1977-81), Oreg. Libr. Assn. (pres. 1983-84), N.Mex. Libr. Assn. (bd. dirs. 1987-88), N.Mex. Acad. and Rsch. Librs. (pres. 1988-89), N.Mex. Coll., Univ. and Spl. LIbrs. (pres. 1987-88), Rotary. Democrat. Methodist. Home: 3034 Del Prado Alamogordo NM 88310-3960 Office: NMex State U at Alamogordo 2400 N Scenic PO Box 477 Alamogordo NM 88311-0477

RUDD, ELDON, retired congressman; b. Camp Verde, Ariz.; m. Ann Merritt. B.A., Ariz. State U., 1947; J.D., U. Ariz., 1950. Bar: Ariz. 1949, U.S. Supreme Ct. 1953. Pvt. practice Tucson, 1950; spl. agt.-diplomatic assignment principally Latin Am. FBI, 1950-70; pvt. practice law Tucson, 1950; mem. Maricopa County (Ariz.) Bd. Suprs., 1972-76; bd. dirs. Ariz.-Mex. Commn., 1972-92; with U.S.-Mex. Interparliamentary Com., 1976-84; mem. 95th-99th Congresses from 4th Dist. Ariz., 1976-87; of counsel Shimmel, Hill, Bishop & Gruender, P.C., Phoenix, 1987-93; prin. Eldon Rudd Consultancy, Scottsdale, Ariz.; pvt. practice, 1993—; bd. dirs. So. Pacific Transp. Co., 1987-88, Salt River Project, 1988—. Author: World Communism-Threat to Freedom, 1987. Mem. numerous pub. svc. orgns., including energy and water, mil. and internat. affairs. Fighter pilot USMCR, 1942-46. Mem. Fed. Bar Assn. (chpt. pres. 1976), Ariz. Bar Assn., Maricopa County Bar Assn., Scottsdale Bar Assn., Paradise Valley Country Club (bd. dirs. 1989-92), Phi Delta Phi, Blue Key. Republican. Roman Catholic. Home: PO Box 873 Scottsdale AZ 85252 Office: 6909 Main St Scottsdale AZ 85251

RUDD, HYNDA L., city official; b. Salt Lake City, May 20, 1936; d. Morris and Irene (Feldman) Aronovich; m. Eugene B. Chernick, Nov. 26, 1954 (div. Aug. 1955); 1 child, Jeffrey Allen; m. Hyman Z. Rudd, Mar. 7, 1956 (div.); 1 child, Melinda Renee Rudd Feldman. BS, U. Utah, 1974, MS, 1978; MLS, U. So. Calif., L.A., 1981. Co-owner Salt Lake Sanitation Co., Salt Lake City, 1961-73; librarian Marriott Library, U. Utah, Salt Lake City, 1970-74; records mgmt. specialist U. Utah, Salt Lake City, 1974-78; archivist City of L.A., 1980-85, records mgmt. officer, 1985—; established Jewish archives U. Utah, 1976; speaker records program City of L.A., So. Calif., 1980—; cons. Info. Mgmt., Glendale, Calif., 1986—. Author: Mountain West Pioneer Jewry: An Historical and Genealogical Source Book, 1980; project dir., compiler: Los Angeles and its Environs in the Twentieth Century: A Bibliography of a Metropolis--Part II, 1970-1990. Pres. Homeowner's Assn., Glendale, 1983-90; campaigner polit. offices, L.A. and Glendale, 1985—. Mem. L.A. City Hist. Soc. (bd. dirs. 1984—, pres. 1986-87), So. Calif. Jewish Hist. Soc. (bd. dirs. 1981—, v.p. 1985-87, 91—), Assn. Records Mgmt. and Adminstrs. (edn. chair 1988-90), Soc. Am. Archivists (cert. archivist 1989), Soc. Calif. Archivists, Great Books and Reading Discussion Group. Home: 107 W Mountain Ave Unit G Glendale CA 91202-1927 Office: City of LA 555 Ramirez St # 320 Los Angeles CA 90012-2974

RUDDELL, ALYSA ANN, clinical psychologist; b. Ellensburg, Wash., Nov. 11, 1949; d. Clyde Ruddell and Helen May (Ponath) Bostrom; m. Abdelmajid Azzedine, Sept. 15, 1989; children: Mostefa Azzedine. BA, Western Wash. U., 1972; MA, U.S. Internat. U., 1982, PhD, 1986. Counselor Salvation Army, Door of Hope, San Diego, 1982-84; psychology intern Cuyamaca Outpatient Clinic, San Diego, 1984, Southwood Adolescent Psychiat., San Diego, 1985; counselor Community Rsch. Found., San Diego, 1984-87; sexual assault counselor Women's Resource Ctr., San Luis Rey, Calif., 1986-87; mental health specialist Evergreen Counseling Ctr., Aberdeen, Wash., 1987-88; clin. psychologist Ruddell & Assocs., Aberdeen, 1988—, Federal Way, Wash., 1988—; clin. cons. health dept. St. Joseph Hosp. Aberdeen, 1987-90; clin. supr. Cath. Community Svcs., Tacoma, Wash., 1992—; expert witness Tech. Adv. Svc. for Attys., 1988—; guest radio talk shows, 1987-90. Dir. Camps Farthest Out, Wash., 1990; pres. of bd. Grays Harbor Rape Crisis, Aberdeen, 1987-90. Named for Spl. Contbns., Bellingham (Wash.) C. of C., 1979, for Outstanding Svc., YWCA, Bellingham, 1974. Mem. Wash. State Psychol. Assn., APA. Home: 6222 25th St NE Tacoma WA 98422 Office: Ruddell & Assocs 402 S 333 St Federal Way WA 98003

RUDDICK, STEPHEN RICHARD, state representative, lawyer, political consultant; b. Denver, Nov. 6, 1954; s. Paul Richard and Myra Jane (Brooks) R.; m. Ana Maria Peters, June 16, 1984. B.A., Met. State U., Denver, 1977; J.D., U. Denver, 1980. Bar: Colo. 1980, U.S. Dist. Ct. Colo. 1980, U.S. Ct. Appeals (10th cir.) 1980. Steward, Internat. Brotherhood of Teamsters, Denver, 1979; law clk., later assoc. law firm Anderson, Calder & Lembke, P.C., Aurora, Colo., 1979-80; sole practice law, Aurora, Colo., 1980-81; asst. city atty. City Atty.'s Office, Aurora, Colo., 1981—; state rep. Colo. Gen. Assembly, 1987—. Chmn., 18th Jud. Dist. Dem. Cen. Com., 1983—; vice-chmn. Arapahoe County Dem. Com., 1983-85; mem. Colo. Common Cause, Arapahoe-Denver NOW. Mem. Aurora Bar Assn. (sec.-treas. 1983-84, v.p. 1984-85, pres. 1985-86), Colo. Bar Assn. Democrat. Roman Catholic. Club: Aurora East Lions. Lodge: Masons (master 1983—). Home: 1031 Sable Blvd Aurora CO 80011-6813 Office: City Atty Office 15001 E Alameda Dr Aurora CO 80012-1547

RUDEE, MERVYN LEA, university dean, researcher; b. Palo Alto, Calif., Oct. 4, 1935; s. Mervyn C. and Hannah (Mathews) R.; m. Elizabeth Eager, June 20, 1958; children: Elizabeth Diane, David Benjamin. BS, Stanford U., 1958, MS, 1962, PhD, 1965. Asst. prof. Rice U., Houston, 1964-68, assoc. prof., 1968-72, prof., 1972-74; prof. U. Calif., San Diego, 1974—; provost Warren Coll., U. Calif.-San Diego, La Jolla, 1974-82, dean engring., 1982—; vis. scholar Corpus Christi Coll., Cambridge, Eng., 1971-72; vis. scientist IBM Thomas J. Watson Research Ctr., Yorktown Heights, N.Y., 1987. Served to lt. (j.g.) USN, 1958-61. Guggenheim fellow, 1971-72. Mem. Electron Microscope Soc. Am., Materials Rsch. Soc., Am. Physics Soc., Tex. Soc. Electron Microscopy (hon., pres. 1966), Sigma Xi, Tau Beta Pi. Home: 1745 Kearsarge Rd La Jolla CA 92037-3829 Office: U Calif San Diego La Jolla CA 92093-0403

RUDER, MELVIN HARVEY, retired newspaper editor; b. Manning, N.D., Jan. 19, 1915; s. Moris M. and Rebecca (Friedman) R.; m. Ruth Bergan, Feb. 10, 1950; 1 dau., Patricia E. Morton. B.A., U. N.D., 1937, M.A., 1941; grad. student, Northwestern U., 1940. Asst. prof. journalism U. N.D., 1940; indsl. relations specialist Westinghouse Electric Co., Sharon, Pa., 1940-41; pub. relations with Am. Machine & Foundry Co., N.Y.C., 1946; founder, editor Hungry Horse News, Columbia Falls, Mont., 1946-78; editor emeritus Hungry Horse News, 1978—. Chmn. adv. coun. Flathead Nat. Forest, Dist. 6 Sch. Bd., 1967-70. Served to lt. (s.g.) USNR, 1942-45. Recipient Pulitzer prize for gen. local reporting, 1965. Mem. Mont. Press Assn. (pres. 1957), Flathead Associated C. of C. (pres. 1971), Glacier Natural History Assn. (pres. 1983). Home: PO Box 1389 303 3rd Ave E Columbia Falls MT 59912

RUDGE, WILLIAM EDWIN, IV, computational physicist; b. New Haven, June 14, 1939; s. William Edwin III and Abigail (Hazen) R.; m. Georgiana Ludmila Kopal, June 24, 1962; children: Julia R. Gulbransen, Marian K., William E. V. BS in Physics, Yale U., 1960; PhD in Physics, MIT, 1968. Physicist IBM Corp., Poughkeepsie, N.Y., 1960-63; rsch. staff mem. IBM Corp., San Jose, Calif., 1968—. Contbr. to Phys. Rev., Phys. Rev. Letters, Nature. Mem. Am. Phys. Soc., Sigma Xi. Home: 1187 Washoe Dr San Jose CA 95120-5542 Office: IBM Almaden Rsch Ctr 650 Harry Rd San Jose CA 95120-6099

RUDIN, ANNE NOTO, former mayor, nurse; b. Passaic, N.J., Jan. 27, 1924; m. Edward Rudin, June 6, 1948; 4 children. BS in Edn., Temple U., 1945, RN, 1946; MPA, U. So. Calif., 1983; LLD (hon.), Golden Gate U., 1990. RN, Calif. Mem. faculty Temple U. Sch. Nursing, Phila., 1946-48; mem. nursing faculty Mt. Zion Hosp., San Francisco, 1948-49; mem. Sacramento City Council, 1971-83; mayor City of Sacramento, 1983-92; mem. World Conf. of Mayors for Peace. Pres. LWV, Riverside, 1957, Sacramento, 1961, Calif. Elected Women's Assn., 1973-89; mem. Calif. bd. dirs. Common Cause; bd. dirs. Sacramento Philharm., Sacramento Theatre Co. Recipient Women in Govt. award U.S. Jaycee Women, 1984; Woman of Distinction award Sacramento Area Soroptimist Clubs, 1985, Civic Contbn. award LWV Sacramento, 1989, Woman of Courage award Sacramento History Ctr., 1989, Peacemaker of Yr. award Sacramento Mediation Ctr., 1992; named Girl Scouts Am. Role Model, 1989.

RUDINSKY, ALEXANDER JOHN, artist; b. Corvallis, Oreg., Feb. 4, 1957; s. Julius Alexander and Norma (Leigh) R.; m. Catherine Joy Leedy; children: Anna Kikue, Julia Amaya. Student, Oreg. State U., 1975-76, U. Mass., 1976-77; BFA in Studio Arts, Syracuse U., 1979; MFA in Studio Arts, U. Calif., Irvine, 1989. instr. Pacific N.W. Coll. of Art, Portland, Oreg., 1986-87; teaching asst. studio art dept. U. Calif., Irvine, 1987-89; instr. Newport Harbor Art Mus., Newport Beach, Calif., 1988. Illustrator: Seven Slovak Stories, 1980, Jozef Mak, 1985; one-man shows include U. Calif. Irvine Fine Arts Gallery, 1988, 89; group shows include Laura Russo Gallery, Portland, 1990, John Thomas Gallery, Santa Monica, 1990, Berkeley (Calif.) Art Ctr., 1990, Transamerica Galleries, L.A., 1991, L.A. Contemporary Exhbns., 1991, Long Beach (Calif.) Arts, 1992. Bd. dirs. Hollywood Loz Feliz Jewish Community Ctr., L.A., 1992-93; facilitator All Saints Men's Group, Pasadena, 1992, Zen Ctr., L.A., 1993. Recipient two scholarships Ford Found., Syracuse U., 1978-79, multi-arts grant Met. Arts Comm., Portland, 1982, Regent's fellowship, tuition scholarship U. Calif., Irvine, 1987-88, two fine arts rsch. grants U. Calif., Irvine, 1989. Democrat. Zen-Episcopalian. Home: 1342 Westerly Terr Los Angeles CA 90026

RUDISILL, RICHARD, museum curator, educator; b. Butte, Mont., Jan. 17, 1932; s. Darl Cole and Margaret (White) R. A.A., Sierra Coll., 1950; B.A. in English, Sacramento State Coll., 1952, M.A. in English, 1957; Ph.D. in Am. Studies, U. Minn., 1967. Instr., Am. studies and English U. Minn., Mpls., 1959-67, research grantee grad. sch., 1964-65; prof. art U. N.Mex., Albuquerque, 1968-71, adj. prof. art and art history, 1987—; research assoc., vis. specialist photog. history Mus. N.Mex., Santa Fe, 1971-73; curator photog. history Mus. N.Mex., 1974—; prof. photog. studies Art Inst. Chgo., 1973-74. Author: Mirror Image: The Influence of the Daguerreotype on American Society, 1971, Photographers of the New Mexico Territory 1854-1912, 1973, Directories of Photographers: An Annotated World Bibliography, 1991; contbr. articles on photog. history to profl. jours. Served with AUS, 1953-55. Recipient McKnight Humanities award Am. History, 1967; Nat. Endowment Arts vis. specialist grantee, 1972-73. Democrat. Lutheran. Address: Mus of NMex Photo Archives PO Box 2087 Santa Fe NM 87504

RUDOLPH, RONALD ALVIN, human resources executive; b. Berwyn, Ill., May 12, 1949; s. Alvin J. and Gloria S. (Nicoletti) R. BA, U. Calif., Santa Cruz, 1971. Sr. cons. De Anza Assocs., San Jose, Calif., 1971-73; pers. adminstr. McDonnell Douglas Corp., Cupertino, Calif., 1974-75; employment rep. Fairchild Semiconductor, Mountain View, Calif., 1973-74, 75; compensation analyst Sperry Univac, Santa Clara, Calif., 1975-78; mgr. exempt compensation div. Intel Corp., Santa Clara, 1978-79, compensation mgr., 1979-82; dir. corp. compensation Intel Corp., 1982-85; v.p. human resources UNISYS Corp., San Jose, 1985-91, ASK Group Inc., Mountain View, Calif., 1991—; cons. Rudolph Assocs., Cupertino, 1982—; bd. dirs. Dynamic Temp. Svcs., Sunnyvale, Calif. Mem. Spl. Com. for Parolee Employment, Sacramento, 1973-75; bd. dirs. Jr. Achievement, San Jose, 1987-88. Mem. Am. Soc. Pers. Adminstrs., Am. Compensation Assn., No. Calif. Human Resources Coun. Office: ASK Computer Systems Inc PO Box 7640 2440 W El Camino Real Mountain View CA 94039-7640

RUDOLPH, THOMAS KEITH, aerospace engineer; b. Jamestown, N.D., Oct. 4, 1961; s. Arthur John and Melinda Magdelina (Nehlich) R. BS in Aerospace Engring., Iowa State U., 1983. Registered profl. engr., Wash. Engr. Boeing Advanced Systems, Seattle, 1984-88, sr. engr., 1988-90; sr. engr. Boeing Comml. Airplanes, Seattle, 1990-91, specialist engr., 1991—; chmn. weight improvement program Boeing B-2 Program, Seattle, 1986-88. Mem. AIAA, Soc. Allied Weight Engrs. (sr., chmn. activities com. 1985-86, treas. 1986-87, facilities chmn. internat. conf. 1987, v.p. 1987-88, pres. 1991-92), Iowa State U. Alumni Assn., Marston Club (life). Republican. Methodist. Office: Boeing Comml Airplanes PO Box 3707 M/S 02-34 Seattle WA 98124

RUDOLPH, WALTER BURNHAM, general manager public radio; b. Lovell, Wyo., Mar. 15, 1946; s. Walter A. and Delora (Burnham) R.; m. Marilyn Cloward, May 27, 1970; children: Walter Cloward, Stacia Anne, Erich Cloward, Vladimir Andrew Cloward. BA, Brigham Young U., 1970, MA, 1973. Spl. instr. Brigham Young U., Provo, Utah, 1973-79; instr. music U. Minn., Morris, 1973-74; chorister Lyric Opera, Chgo., 1975-77; singer Music of the Baroque, Chgo., 1975-77; program dir. KBYU-FM, Provo, 1977-81, station mgr., 1981—. Writer, producer: (radio documentaries) Birds of an Operatic Feather, 1978, Tribute to Jussi Bjorling, 1980, Giorgio Tozzi, Am. Basso, 1980, Bayreuth Festival, 1988, Hans Hotter Tribute, 1989. Recipient Excellence in Journalism award Soc. Prol. Journalists, Salt Lake City, 1988, UBEE, Utah Broadcasters, 1989 (2f), 92. Mem. Coll. of Fine Arts and Comm. (Adminstrv. Excellence award 1988), Rocky Mt. Pub. Radio Assn. (v.p. 1982-83). Mem. LDS ch. Office: Broadcast Svcs KBYU-FM C-302 HFAC Provo UT 84602

RUDOLPH, WALTER PAUL, engineering research company executive; b. Binghamton, N.Y., Aug. 17, 1937; s. Walter Paul and Frieda Lena (Hennemann) R.; m. Leila Ortencia Romero, Dec. 18, 1960; children: Jonathan, Jana, Catherine. BEE, Rensselaer Poly. Inst., 1959; MSBA, San Diego State U., 1964. Elec. engr. Gen. Dynamics/Astronautics, San Diego, 1959-62; ops. research analyst Navy Electronics Lab., San Diego, 1962-64; mem. profl. staff Gen. Electric Tempo, Honolulu, 1964-70, Ctr. for Naval Analysis, Arlington, Va., 1970-77; pres. La Jolla (Calif.) Research Corp., 1977—. Served to Capt. USNR, 1959-92. Republican. Presbyterian. Home: 1559 El Paso Real La Jolla CA 92037-6303 Office: La Jolla Rsch Corp PO Box 1207 La Jolla CA 92038-1207

RUDY, THOMAS JAMES, retired air force officer, civilian employee; b. Syracuse, N.Y., Sept. 6, 1948; s. Joseph Eugene and Bernice Marie (Walenia) R.; m. Carol Jean Chisenski, July 30, 1976. BS in Aerospace Engring., Ind. Inst. Tech., 1971; MS in Engring. Mgmt. with distinction, Golden Gate U., 1988. Commd. 2d lt. USAF, 1971, advanced through grades to maj., 1983; KC-135 program dir. 93d Bombardment Wing, Castle AFB, Calif., 1981-85; chief B-1 engring. 31 Test and Evaluation Squadron, Edwards AFB, Calif., 1985-86, dir. engring., 1986-88; dir. acquisition and test 31 Test and Evaluation Squadron, Castle AFB, 1988-91, tech. dir., 1991-93; tech. dir. 29 Tng. Systems Squadron, Castle AFB, 1993—; assoc. mem. Acquisition/Support Issues Group, Washington. Mem. Soc. Flight Test Engrs., Castle Air Mus. Found., Sigma Pi. Home: 300 E Marvis Dr Atwater CA 95301-3808 Office: Det 3 29 TSS Castle AFB CA 95342-5000

RUEBE, BAMBI LYNN, interior, environmental designer; b. Huntington Park, Calif., Nov. 13, 1957; d. Leonard John Ruebe and Vaudis Marie Powell. BS, UCLA, 1988. Millwright asst. Kaiser Steel Corp., Fontana, Calif., 1976-79; electrician Fleetwood Enterprises, Riverside, Calif., 1977; fashion model internat., 1977-85; free-lance draftsman, 1982-83; project coord. Philip J. Sicola Inc., Culver City, Calif., 1982-83; prin. designer Ruebe Inclusive Design, Highland, Calif., 1983-89, Ventura, Calif., 1990—; cons. mfg. design Burlington Homes New Eng. Inc., Oxford, Maine, 1987-90, DeRose Industries, Chambersburg, Pa., 1984, Skyline Corp., Redlands, Calif., 1982-84; cons. lighting Lightways Corp., L.A., 1984-87; mem. design rev. bd. San Bernardino (Calif.) Downtown Main St. Redevel. Com., 1987-89. Mem. World Affairs Coun., Inland So. Calif., 1986—; mem. Citizens adv. com. Highland Calif. Gen. Plan, 1988-90; co-chmn. civil rights com. AFL-CIO, Fontana, 1978-79. Recipient Cert. Merit Scholastic Art award Scholastic Mags. Inc., Southeastern Calif., 1974, Dirs. Incentive award for Archtl. Design City of Ventura, Calif., 1990. Mem. Nat. Trust for Hist. Preservation. Democrat. Office: Ruebe Inclusive Design 50 N Oak St Ventura CA 93001-2631

RUEDA, ALFONSO, physics researcher, educator; b. B/manga, Santander, Colombia, Apr. 17, 1940; came to U.S., 1989; s. Genaro and Emma (Acevedo) R.; m. Silvia Gaviria, Aug. 15, 1970; children: Cristina, Andres, Monica. BEE, MIT, 1963, MEE, 1963; MA in Applied Physics, Cornell U., 1968, PhD in Applied Math., 1973. Instr. U. de los Andes, Bogota, Colombia, 1963-66; OAS fellow Cornell U., Ithaca, N.Y., 1970-72; chmn. Physics Dept. U. de los Andes, Bogota, Colombia, 1974-76; dean Arts and Scis. U. de los Andes, Bogota, 1980-82, prof., researcher, 1973-84; assoc. prof., prof. U. Puerto Rico, Humacao, 1984-89; assoc. prof. Calif. State U., Long Beach, 1989-93; prof. Calif. State U., 1993—. Contbr. articles in profl. jours. Recipient associateship, sr. associateship Internat. Ctr. for Theoretical Physics, Trieste, Italy, 1980-86, 1987-93. Mem. IEEE, Am. Phys. Soc., N.Y. Acad. Scis., Planetary Soc., Bogota Gun Club, Eta Kappa Nu, Tau Beta Pi, Phi Kappa Phi. Office: Calif State U Dept Elec Engring ECS 561 1250 Bellflower Blvd Long Beach CA 90840-0001

RUEGG, CURTIS LANDON, research biochemist; b. L.A., May 19, 1962; s. Gary Haynes and Joyce Louise (Ferguson) R.; m. Pamela Marie Sudano, Feb. 22, 1992. BS in Toxicology, U. Calif., Davis, 1985; PhD in Pharmacology, Johns Hopkins U., 1990. Predoctoral fellow Johns Hopkins U. Sch. Medicine, Balt., 1985-90; postdoctoral fellow Stanford (Calif.) U. Sch. Medicine, 1990—. Contbr. articles to sci. jours. Predoctoral fellow NIH, 1985-88, postdoctoral fellow Cancer Rsch. Inst., 1991—. Mem. Phi Kappa Phi. Office: Stanford U Blood Ctr 800 Welch Rd Palo Alto CA 94304

RUEHL, FRANKLIN ROBERT, JR., television producer and host; b. Phila.; s. Franklin Robert and Florence Lucille (Grant) R. BS, UCLA, 1965, MS, 1967, PhD in Theoretical Nuclear Physics, 1970. Lectr. dept. physics UCLA, 1970; dir. Ctr. for Investigation of Extraterrestrial Life, Glendale, Calif., 1971—; lectr. Whole Life Expo, Santa Monica, Calif., 1988—; columnist Ruehl Syndicate, Glendale, 1991—; TV host MCA-TV, Universal City, Calif., 1992—; UFO investigator Internat. UFO Bur., Oklahoma City, 1973—. Author: The Universe is Teeming With Life, 1987, Life: Common Denominator of the Cosmic Backdrop, 1989; prodr. Mysteries From Beyond the Other Dominion, 1992—. Mem. AFTRA, Mensa, Dark Shadows Ofcl. Fan Club. Office: PO Box 847 Glendale CA 91209

RUEPPEL, MERRILL CLEMENT, museum director; b. Haddonfield, N.J., May 7, 1925; s. George Henry and Nellie Lester Rueppel; m. Joan Storberg, Sept. 15, 1956; children: Philip Cameron, Sarah Githens. BA, Beloit Coll., 1949; MA, U. Wis., 1952, PhD, 1955. Rsch. asst. Mpls. Inst. of Arts, 1956-57, asst. to dir., 1957-59, asst. dir., 1959-61; asst. dir. City Art Mus. St. Louis, 1961-64; dir. Dallas Mus. Fine Arts, 1964-73, Mus. Fine Arts, Boston, 1973-75, Contemporary Mus., Honolulu, 1991—; cons. Ford Found., N.Y.C., 1963-76, IRS, Washington, 1970-74, Rockefeller Bros. Fund, N.Y.C., 1978; assoc. prof. art history Washington U., St. Louis, 1963. Author exhbn. catalogues, 1961-72. With U.S. Army, 1942-45. Mem. Somerset Club Boston, Club of Odd Volumes (sec.-treas. 1984-91), Rotary, Phi Beta Kappa. Home and Office: Contemporary Mus 2411 Makiki Heights Dr Honolulu HI 96822

RUESCH, STEPHEN W., respiratory therapist, educator; b. Merrill, Wis., July 11, 1951; s. Edwin F. and Florence M. (Johnson) R. AAS, Milw. Area Tech. Coll., 1975; BS, Loma Linda (Calif.) U., 1979; MBA, Pepperdine U., 1984. Registered respiratory therapist. Clin. supr. Med. Ctr. Loma Linda U., 1979—, asst. prof., 1987—, adminstrv. dir. restorative svcs. Med. Ctr., 1987-88; expert witness Med. Bd. Calif., Sacramento, 1984-88; cons. various med. mfrs., 1979—; lectr., speaker and writer in field. Mem. editorial bd. (jour.) The Respiratory Practitioner, 1985-88, coordinating editor, 1987-88; contbr. articles to profl. publs. on respiratory, pulmonary and med. health topics. Rep. nominee Calif. State Assembly, 1964, 66; bd. dirs. Am. Lung Assn. of Inland Counties, 1987—, chair program com., 1989-90, v.p., 1989-90, pres. elect, 1990-91, pres., 1991-92; bd. dirs. Am. Lung Assn. Calif., Oakland, 1990—. Recipient commendation resolution award State of Calif.

Legislature, 1989; name Outstanding Young Man of Am., 1988, 89. Mem. Calif. Soc. Respiratory Care (life mem., treas. 1981-83, pres. elect 1983-84, pres. 1984-85), Nat. Bd. Respiratory Care, Calif. Thoracic Soc., Am. Soc. Laser Medicine, Undersea and Hyperbaric Medicine Soc., Am. Assn. Respiratory Care (chmn. state credentialing com. 1989-91), Phi Theta Kappa.

RUFF, HOWARD JOSEPH, editor, writer; b. Berkeley, Calif., Dec. 27, 1930; s. Wilson Rex and Rena Mayberry (Braley) R.; m. Kay Franc Felt, Apr. 18, 1955; children: Lawrence, Eric, David, Pamela, Sharon, Patty, Tim, Debbie, Terri Lynn. Student, Brigham Young U., 1950-54. Stockbroker, 1955-60, owner speed-reading franchises, No. Calif., 1960-68, distbr. food supplements, 1971-75; chmn. bd. Target Pubs., 1971—, The Main Street Alliance, 1990—; editor The Ruff Times. Author: How to Prosper during the Coming Bad Years, 1979, Howard Ruff from A to Z, 1980, Survive and Win in the Inflationary Eighties, 1981, Making Money, 1984. Served with USAF, 1955-59. Mem. Ch. Jesus Christ of Latter-day Saints. Office: PO Box 31 Springville UT 84663-0031

RUFFALO, ALAN MICHAEL, electrical distribution executive; b. Youngstown, Ohio, June 13, 1943; s. Don Michael and Helen Marie (Hewitt) R.; m. Karen Elizabeth Miller, Feb. 15, 1964 (div. 1972); 1 child, Sheryl Lynn; m. Sandra Ann Stupin, July 21, 1975; 1 stepchild, Andrea. Student, East L.A. City Coll., 1962, Cerritos (Calif.) City Coll., 1963. Salesman Bell (Calif.) Wholesale Electric Co., 1963-64; sales mgr. Bell (Calif.) Wholesale Electric Co., Santa Fe Springs, Calif., 1964-65, Superior Wholesale Electric Co., Santa Fe Springs, 1966-71, Sunlight Electric Supply Co., Santa Fe Springs, 1971-75; sales mgr. TFI Cos., Inc., Garden Grove, Calif., 1976-77, div. mgr., 1977-79; v.p. All City Electric Supply, Inc., Artesia, Calif., 1979-86, exec. v.p., 1986—; sales cons. RS&E Co., Brea, Calif., 1973-77, Teamco Co., Whittier, Calif., 1973-77, Bieber Lighting Co., Inglewood, Calif., 1973-77. With USAFR, 1966-72. Mem. Cal-24 Yacht Club (pres. 1967-69), South Bay Yacht Racing Club, Pacers Long Distance Running Club, Catalina 30 Yacht Club, Runners High Track Club, Norwalk Road Runners, Otterbien Mountain Runners. Republican. Roman Catholic. Home: 15004 Weeks Dr La Mirada CA 90638-1243 Office: Consol Elec Distbr Inc 16711 Parkside Ave Cerritos CA 90701

RUFOLO, ANTHONY MICHAEL, economics educator; b. Newark, Aug. 9, 1948; s. Philip and Marie Antoinette (Petrillo) R.; m. Patricia Jeanne Lickorai, Aug. 29, 1970; children: Amy, Laura, Christine. BS in Econs., MIT, 1970; PhD in Econs., UCLA, 1975. Cons. Appraisal Rsch. Assocs., Thousand Oaks, Calif., 1971-72; adj. asst. prof. Temple U., Phila., 1976-79; economist Fed. Res. Bank Phila., 1974-78, sr. economist, 1978-80; adj. assoc. prof. U. Pa., Phila., 1978-80; assoc. prof. Portland (Oreg.) State U., 1980-85, prof. urban studies and planning, 1985—; vis. prof. Jilin U. Tech., People's Republic of China, 1984, UCLA, 1984, 85, 88. Co-author: Public Finance and Expenditure In A Federal System, 1990; co-editor: Economics of Municipal Labor, 1983. Mem. Pub. Works Adv. Coun., Washington County, Oreg., 1981-84; mem. budget com. City of Beaverton, Oreg., 1989—, chair, 1992—; mem. Gov.'s Coun. Econ. Adv., Oreg., 1983—; mem. Citizen's Adv. Coun. on Budget, Tri-Met, 1991—; mem. investment adv. coun. City of Portland, Oreg., 1992—. Rsch. grantee Urban Mass Transp. Adminstrn., 1984, Portland State U., 1986, 87, Ford Found., 1988, U.S. Dept. Transp., 1991, 92, Urban Mass Transp. Adminstrn. tng. grantee, 1986. Mem. Am. Econ. Assn., Nat. Tax Assn., Soc. Oreg. Economists, Oreg. Acad. Scis. Home: 13255 SW Saratoga Ln Beaverton OR 97005-7607 Office: Portland State U PO Box 751 Portland OR 97207-0751

RUGE, NEIL MARSHALL, retired law educator; b. Washington, Dec. 28, 1913; s. Oscar Gustave and Ruth (Jones) R.; m. Madeleine Filhol, Jan. 1942 (dec. May 1944); m. Helga Maria Kley, July 23, 1949; children: Carl, Madeleine. Student, Calif. Inst. Tech., 1931-33; A.B., Stanford U., 1935; J.D., U. Calif. at Berkeley, 1938; postgrad., Harvard U. Grad. Sch. Bus. Adminstrn., 1946-47. Bar: Calif. 1938, U.S. Supreme Ct. 1962. Practiced law in Tulare, Calif., until 1941; joined U.S. fgn. service, 1947; assigned to Palermo, Italy, 1947-49, Casablanca, 1950-55, London, 1956, Cardiff, 1956-58; security and personnel officer State Dept., 1958-62; dep. prin. officer Munich, 1962-68; 1st sec. Am. embassy Guatemala, 1968-69; prof. law Calif. State U., Chico, 1969-80. Contbr. articles to profl. jours. Served to maj. AUS, 1941-46; colonel res. Mem. Sierra Club, Phi Beta Kappa. Home: 936 Bryant Ave Chico CA 95926-2818

RUGENSTEIN, ROBERT WAYNE, clothing designer; b. Indpls., Dec. 4, 1921; s. August Carl and Dorothy Jane (Wuellner) R.; m. Ida May Vazzano; children: Mark, Dominick, Warren, Connie, Kathryn. Lineman Alaska Hwy. telephone line Miller Constrn. Co., 1942-43; designer Ft. Wayne (Ind.) Tailors Co., 1946-63, Craddock Uniform Co., Kansas City, Mo., 1963-67, Hayes Garment Co., Nashville, 1967-69, Fechheimer Co., Cin., 1969-70, Campus Sweater and Sportswear, Paramus, N.Y., 1970-78; v.p. prodn., design Cherokee Apparel Corp., Venice, Calif., 1978-82; internat. clothing cons. Rugida Apparel Svc., Orovilla, Calif., 1982—. Patentee adjustable die cutter, solar energy home, solar energy builders; author: Revelation House, 1992. With U.S. Army, 1943-46, India. Recipient award Nat. Inventor's Soc., 1962, David Rockefeller Spirit of Svc. award Internat. Exec. Svc. Corp., 1992. Mem. Internat. Exec. Svc. Corp. (vol. exec.), Vols. in Tech. Assistance' Mensa, Shriners. Republican. Home and Office: 3229 Rugida Rd Oroville CA 95965-9762

RUGGE, SUE, information broker; b. Oakland, Calif., Mar. 7, 1941; d. William Warren and Marjorie (Sherman) Callow; m. Wayne Dee McKinney, Sept. 21, 1958 (dec. Dec. 1964); children: James Philip, William Warren ; m. Henry F. Rugge, Dec. 27, 1967. Libr. Physic Internat., San Leandro, Calif., 1963-66, Dalmo Victor, Belmont, Calif., 1966-69, Singer Bus. Machines, San Leandro, 1969-71; co-founder Info. Unltd., Berkeley, Calif., 1971-78; founder, pres. Info. on Demand, Berkeley, 1979-85; founder Innkeeper's Respite, Berkeley, 1985-87; founder The Rugge Group, Oakland, Calif., 1987-92, bd. dirs.; founder Information Profls. Inst., Oakland, 1993—. Co-author: Information Broker's Handbook, 1992—; contbr. numerous articles to profl. jours. Mem. Assn. for Ind. Info. Profls. (pres. 1987-88), Spl. Librs. Assn. Office: Info Profls Inst 46 Hiller Dr Oakland CA 94618

RUGGERI, ZAVERIO MARCELLO, medical researcher; b. Bergamo, Italy, Jan. 7, 1945; came to U.S., 1978; s. Giovanni and Anna (Dolci) R.; m. Rosamaria Carrara, June 12, 1971. MD magna cum laude, U. Milan, 1970; degree in Clin. and Exptl. Hematology magna cum laude, U. Pavia, Italy, 1973, degree in Internal Medicine magna cum laude, 1981. Asst. clin. prof. hematology U. Milan, 1972-80; assoc. dir. hemophilia ctr. Policlinico Hosp., Milan, 1980-82; vis. investigator Scripps Clinic and Research Found., La Jolla, Calif., 1978-80, asst. mem., 1982-85; assoc. mem. Scripps Clinic and Rsch. Found., La Jolla, Calif., 1985—; dir. Roon Ctr. for Arteriosclerosis and Thrombosis, 1989—; head div. Exptl. Thrombosis and Hemostasis, 1989—; vis. investigator St. Thomas/St. Bartholomews Hosps., London, 1974-76. Editor: Clinics in Haematology, 1985; mem. editorial bds. Blood, 1988-92, Peptide Research, 1988—, Haematologica, 1990—, Jour. Biological Chemistry, 1993—; contbr. articles to profl. jours., chpts. to books. Research scholar Italian Ministry of Edn., 1970, Italian Hemophilia Found., 1970-72. Mem. AAAS, Italian Hemophilia Found., Am. Soc. Clin. Investigation, Italian Soc. Thrombosis and Hemostasis, Internat. Soc. Thrombosis and Hemostasis, Am. Heart Assn. (council on thrombosis), World Fedn. Hemophilia, Am. Fedn. Clin. Research, N.Y. Acad. Scis., Am. Soc. Hematology. Office: Scripps Rsch Inst 10666 N Torrey Pines Rd La Jolla CA 92037

RUGGILL, SOLOMON P., psychologist; b. N.Y.C., Sept. 29, 1906; s. Abraham and Sarah (Silverberg) R.; m. Sophie Stock, June 8, 1938; children: Robert Zachary, Peter Alan. BS, CCNY, 1927; MA in Edn., Columbia U., 1930, PhD in Psychology, 1934. Lic. psychologist, N.Y. Tchr. elem. and jr. high sch. Bd. of Edn. of N.Y.C., 1929-59, psychologist, Bur. of Child Guidance, 1959-62; psychologist Baro Civic Ctr. Clinic, Bklyn., 1961-62; assoc. prof. L.I. U., Bklyn., 1962-69, prof., 1969-79, prof. emeritus, 1979—, acting chmn. dept. guidance and counseling, 1972-73; dir. Flatback Progressive Sch., Bklyn., 1943-45, Camp Kinderwelt, Fraternal Order Farband, N.Y.C., 1959-60; lectr. in gerontology to various orgns., Tucson, 1980—, Keeping Mentally Alert classes Sr. Day Ctrs., 1985—. Pres. Chancy Meml. Found., N.Y.C., 1961-63; mem. adv. council Pima Council on Aging, Tucson, 1987—. Mem. N.Y. Acad. Pub. Edn., N.Y. State Guidance Assn., Jewish Tchrs. Assn. (life). Jewish. Home: 425 W Paseo Redondo Apt 7E Tucson AZ 85701-8262

RUGGLES, CATHERINE JOAN, computer software engineer; b. New Haven, Sept. 2, 1953; d. Richard and Nancy (Dunlap) R. BA, Yale U., 1978. Dir. R & D, Sofistry, Inc., Irvine, Calif., 1984-85; pres. Prospect Rsch. Corp., North Hollywood, Calif., 1986-90; dir. internal devel. Symantec Corp., Santa Monica, Calif., 1990—. Home: 2012 Glencoe Ave Venice CA 90291 Office: Symantec 2500 Broadway Santa Monica CA 90200

RUHL, ROGER DONALD, JR., minister; b. Pasadena, Calif., Dec. 1, 1957; s. Roger Donald Ruhl and Sandra Colleen (French) Hills; m. Kerri Lee Handy, Feb. 25, 1978; children: Traci, Stephanie, Melissa. Min. Ch. of Christ, Long Beach, Calif., 1980-83, Klamath Falls, Oreg., 1983—. Editor: Balance of Truth and Freedom, 1987; author, editor The Bible Meditator mag., 1990—; contbr. articles to religious publs. Republican. Home: 5710 Bryant Ave Klamath Falls OR 97603 Office: Ch of Christ 2521 Nile St Klamath Falls OR 97603

RUHLMAN, TERRELL LOUIS, business executive; b. Warren, Pa., Nov. 13, 1926; s. Ross L. and Gertrude R.; m. Phyllis E., Jan. 15, 1951; children—Robyn Ruhlman Dempsey, Randall L., Heather Ruhlman Martin, Mark A. B.S., Pa. State U., 1949; J.D., George Washington U., 1954; postgrad., Duquesne U. Grad. Bus. Sch., 1966-68. Bar: D.C. bar. Patent counsel Joy Mfg. Co., Pitts., 1954-59; gen. counsel Joy Mfg. Co., 1959-62, asst. to pres., 1962-69; v.p. oilfield ops. Joy Mfg. Co., Houston, 1969-73; gen. mgr. Reed Tool Co., Houston, 1973-74; pres., chief operating officer Reed Tool Co., 1974-76, dir., 1975-76; v.p., dir. Baker Internat. Corp., 1975-76, pres. mining group, 1976; pres., chief exec. officer, dir. Ansul Co., Marinette, Wis., 1976-80; pres. Wormald Americas, Inc., Scottsdale, Ariz., 1980-88; chmn., chief exec. officer Cade Industries, Inc., Scottsdale, 1988—, also bd. dirs.; bd. dirs. Sonitrol Corp., Environ. Engring. Concepts Inc. Served with USAF. Home: 9710 E La Posada Cir Scottsdale AZ 85255-3716 Office: # 114 8711 E Pinnacle Peak Rd Scottsdale AZ 85255

RUHWEDEL, ROBIN LINNEA, dietitian, education consultant; b. Seattle, Aug. 14, 1958; d. Ray Allen Bovee and Mary Helena (Bekebrede) Bovee-Chesnut; m. John Henry Ruhwedel, Sept. 10, 1983; children: Evan Leilani, Chad James. BS in Nutrition Sci., U. Calif., Davis, 1980. Dietetic intern Rush-Presbyn.-St. Luke's Med. ctr., Chgo., 1981; clin. dietitian Fresno (Calif.) Community Hosp., 1981-82; nutrition edn. cons. Dairy Coun. Calif., Fresno and Oakland, 1982-85; program dir. Am. Heart Assn., Honolulu, 1985-88, Reno, 1988-89; program dir. Optifast at St. Mary's, Reno, 1989-91; issues mgr. Dairy Coun. Calif., San Diego, 1991—; nutrition advisor Scolaris/St. Mary's Commun. Edn. Program, Reno, 1990-91; nutrition cons. AHA Heart Ball, 1990-91. Contbr. articles to profl. jours. Sec., newsletter editor Enlisted Wives Club, USMC, San Diego, 1992. Named to Outstanding Young Women of Am., 1991. Mem. Am. Dietetic Assn., Calif. Dietetic Assn., San Diego Dist. Dietetic Assn., No. Nev. Dietetic Assn. (pres. 1990-91), Am. Running and Fitness Assn., U.S. Parachute Assn. Republican. Christian. Home: 8846 Pagoda Way San Diego CA 92126

RUIZ, JOSE GARCIA, public administrator; b. Ferriday, La., Mar. 18, 1947; s. Carlos and Maria Pascuala (Garcia) R.; m. Susan Marie Mortensen, Oct. 25, 1986. AA, Big Bend Coll., 1969; BA, Evergreen State Coll., 1973. Employment interviewer Wash. State Employment Security, Moses Lake, 1969-71; labor market analyst Wash. State Employment Security, Olympia, 1971-72, employment program coordinator, 1972-74; employment office mgr. Wash. State Employment Security, Yakima, 1974-77, Mt. Vernon, 1977—; owner The Ruiz Co., Anacortes, Wash., 1991—. Active Valley Mus. of Northwest Art; trustee United Way, Mt. Vernon, 1979-82, Skagit Valley Coll., Mt. Vernon, 1987—; bd. dirs. Self Help Housing, Mt. Vernon, 1985-87, Community Action Agy., 1981—. Mem. Econ. Devel. Assn., Mt. Vernon C. of C. (bd. dirs. 1978-82). Roman Catholic. Office: Wash Employment Security 320 Pacific Pl Mount Vernon WA 98273-5427

RUIZ, VICKI LYNN, history educator; b. Atlanta, Georgia, May 21, 1955; d. Robert Paul and Erminia Pablita (Ruiz) Mercer; m. Jerry Joseph Ruiz, Sept. 1, 1979 (div. Jan. 1990); children: Miguel, Daniel; m. Victor Becerra, Aug. 14, 1992. AS in Social Studies, Gulf Coast Community Coll., 1975; BA in Social Sci., Fla. State, 1977; MA in History, Stanford U., 1978, PhD in History, 1982. Asst. prof. U. Tex., El Paso, 1982-85; asst. prof. U. Calif., Davis, 1985-87, assoc. prof., 1987-92; Andrew W. Mellon prof. Claremont (Calif.) Grad. Sch., 1992—, chmn. history dept., 1993—; dir. Inst. of Oral History, U. Tex., El Paso, 1983-85, minority undergrad. rsch. program U. Calif., Davis, 1988—. Author: Cannery Women, Cannery Lives, 1987; co-editor: Women on U.S.-Mexican Border, 1987, Western Women, 1988, Unequal Sisters, 1990. Vice-chair Calif. Council for the Humanities. Fellow Univ. Calif. Davis Humanities Inst., 1990-91, Am. Coun. of Learned Socs., 1986, Danforth Found., 1977. Mem. Orgn. Am. Historians (chair com. on the status of minority history 1989—, nominating com. 1987-88), Immigration History Soc. (exec. bd. 1989—), Phi Beta Kappa. Democrat. Roman Catholic. Office: Dept History Claremont Grad Sch Claremont CA 91711

RULE, DANIEL RHODES, opera company executive; b. L.A., Aug. 25, 1940; s. Rhodes Elmore and Maud Justice (Edwards) R. BA, Occidental Coll., 1962. Asst. music adminstr. N.Y.C. Opera, 1965-70, assoc. mng. dir., 1970-79, mng. dir., 1980-83; gen. mgr. Central City Opera, Denver, 1984—; cons. Ohio State Arts Coun., Columbus, 1984, 86. Bd. dirs. Colo. Children's Chorale, Denver, Colo. Lawyers for Arts. Ford Found. fellow, N.Y., 1966-68. Mem. Am. Guild Mus. Artists (employer chmn. pension and health fund), Denver Athletic Club. Republican. Mem. Christian Ch. (Disciples of Christ). Office: Central City Opera House Assn 621 17th St Ste 1601 Denver CO 80293-1601

RULEY, STANLEY EUGENE, cost analyst; b. Akron, Ohio, Jan. 24, 1934; s. Royal Lovell and Opal Lenora (McDougall) R.; m. Annie Adam Patterson, Dec. 15, 1962; children: Cheryl Ann, Janice Lynn. Student, Kent State U., 1951-53; BSBA, Ohio State U., 1955. Registered profl. engr., Calif. Indsl. engr. Gaffers & Satler Inc., Hawthorne, Calif., 1961-62; mfg. engr. data systems div. Litton Industries Inc., Van Nuys, Calif., 1962-65; contract price analyst Naval Plant Rep. Office Lockheed, Burbank, Calif., 1966-72; contract negotiator Naval Regional Procurement, Long Beach, Calif., 1972-75; cost/price analyst Def. Contract Adminstrn. Services, Van Nuys, 1975-82; chief of contract pricing, dir. contracting Air Force Flight Test Ctr., Edwards AFB, Calif., 1982-89; cons. engr., Northridge, Calif., 1971—. Served as sgt. U.S. Army, 1956-59. Recipient Sustained Superior Performance award Air Force Flight Test Ctr., 1984, Excellent Performance award Air Force Flight Test Ctr., 1982-83, Outstanding Performance award NAVPRO Lockheed, 1970. Mem. Am. Inst. Indsl. Engrs., IBM Computer User Group (Madison, Wis., Conn., San Fernando Valley), Air Force Assn. (life), Nat. Contract Mgmt. Assn. Republican. Presbyterian. Clubs: Lockheed Employee Recreation (treas. Gem and Mineral 1976, pres. 1976), Camper (Burbank) (pres. 1974). Lodge: Masons (past master, 1992). Home: 18751 Vintage St Northridge CA 91324-1529 Office: Indsl Engring Svcs 18751 Vintage St Northridge CA 91324-1529

RULIFSON, JOHNS FREDERICK, computer company executive, computer scientist; b. Bellefontaine, Ohio, Aug. 20, 1941; s. Erwin Charles and Virginia Helen (Johns) R.; m. Janet Irving, June 8, 1963; children: Eric Johns, Ingrid Catharine. BS in Math., U. Wash., 1966; PhD in Computer Sci., Stanford U., 1973. Mathematician SRI, Internat., Menlo Park, Calif., 1966-73; scientist Xerox Rsch., Palo Alto, Calif., 1973-80; mgr. ROLM, Santa Clara, Calif., 1980-85; scientist Syntelligence, Sunnyvale, Calif., 1985-87; exec. Sun Microsystems, Mountain View, Calif., 1987—. Mem. IEEE, Assn. for Computing Machinery (System Software award 1990). Home: 3785 El Centro Palo Alto CA 94306 Office: Sun Microsystems 2550 Garcia Ave Mountain View CA 94043

RULIFSON, PAUL JOHN, computer systems consultant; b. Seattle, Feb. 4, 1958; s. John Robert and Nancy Agnes (Brown) Rulifson; m. Helen Andrie Steen, July 2, 1989; 1 child, Marta. BS in History, So. Oreg. State Coll., 1982. Systems analysts Western Computer Systems, Grants Pass, 1978-80; programmer analyst Courier Pub. Co., Grants Pass, 1980-83; computer systems mgr. Courier Pub. Co., Grants Pass, Oreg., 1985-90; pres. Cascade Computer Systems, Grants Pass, 1983-85; cons. Sierra Geophysics (Divsn. of Halliburton), Kirkland, Wash., 1990-91, Computer Task Group, Bellevue, Wash., 1991; software engr. Sierra Geophysics, Kirkland, Wash., 1992—; cons. computer task force, Bellevue, Wash., 1991-92. Mem. Atex Newspaper Users Group (chmn. composition com. 1987-89). Home: 4012 212th St SW Apt C201 Mountlake Terrace WA 98043-3569

RULON, PHILIP REED, history educator; b. Delaware, Iowa, Feb. 20, 1934; m. Annette Catherine (Kohlmeier) Rulon, Jan. 2, 1976; children: Yvonne, Ann Marie, William, Scott, Douglas. BA in History, Washburn U., Topeka, 1963; MA in History, Emporia (Kans.) State U., 1965; PhD in History and Higher Edn., Okla. State U., 1968. Instr. of history Okla. State U., Stillwater, 1965-67; asst. prof. of history No. Ariz. U., Flagstaff, 1967, assoc. prof. of history, 1971-80, prof. of history, 1980—; asst. prof. in history NDEA Inst. in Am. History, summer 1967; dir. (with Edgar Bruce Wesley) First Ann. No. Ariz. U. History of Edn. Inst., summer 1969, 2d, 3d, 4th and 5th ann. No. Ariz. U. History of Edn. Inst., summers 1970-73; postdoctoral visitor U. Tex. dept. Cultural Founds. of Edn. and Community Coll. Leadership Program, fall 1974; dir. Indian Edn. Oral History Project, 1976-77; dir. Coll. Bd. Workshop in Am. History No. Ariz. U., summer 1980, dir. Rsch. Ctr. Excellence in Edn., 1984-86; founding mem. Univ. Senate; mem. Publs. Com., Tchr. Edn. Com., South Acad. Ctr. Planning Com., Com. to Examine Holistic Grading for English Proficiency Test, History and Polit. Sci. Grad. Selection Com., Univ. Evaluation Com., Com. to Create Bachelor in Gen. Studies Com., Univ. Transition Com., Internat. Studies Com., Com. on Internat. Edn., Adv. Bd. for Internat. Studies; chmn. Coll. Arts and Scis. Com. to Evaluate Freshman Advising, Dept. of History and Polit. Sci. Grad. Asst. Com., Task Force on Lang. Immersion Rsch., Membership Com. for Ariz., Utah, Nev. and Idaho; evaluator NEG; humanist Ariz. Coun. on the Humanities and Pub. Policy; reader Forum Press for the Forum Series; mem. nat. adv. bd. Com. on History in the Classroom, adv. bd. Buffalo Soldiers Mus.; visitor North Cen. Assn. Evaluation Teams; regional dir. Nat. History Day, Apr. 1981, Mar. 1982; trustee Mus. No. Ariz., Flagstaff; founder Ariz. Alliance for Math., Sci. and Tech. Edn., Blue Ribbon Lecture Series; chmn., editorTaskforce Subcom. on Ctr. for Excellence in Edn. Orgnl. Structure Pers.; lectr. in field. Author: Oklahoma State University, 1975, Compassionate Samaritan: The Life of Lyndon Baines Johnson, 1981, Letters from the Hill Country: The Correspondence of Rebekah and Lyndon Baines Johnson, 1983, (with William H. Lyon) Speaking Out: An Oral History of the American Past, vol. I, 1981, (with Richard Jensen) rev. edit., (with Gladwell Richardson) Navajo Trader, 1986, (with Lou Bader) In the Shadow of San Francisco Peaks, 1988, Keeping-Christmas: The Celebration of an American Holiday, 1990; editor: At the Crossroads: A Presidential Task Force on Cross-Cultural Education; contbr. numerous articles to profl. jours. Mem. Ariz. Cancer Soc.; sr. warden Ch. of the Epiphany; trustee Community Episcopal Svcs. Served with U.S. Army. Recipient Statue of Victory World Culture Prize Academia Italia, 1985; grantee No. Ariz. State U., Lyndon Baines Johnson Found., Coll. Bd., Ariz. Humanities Coun., Am. Hist. Assn. Mem. Internat. Biog. Assn., Am. Biog. Inst. (nat. bd. advisors), Ctr. for Study of the Presidency, Orgn. Am. Historians, Am. Hist. Assn. (dir. svc. ctr. regional conf. teaching history 1970), Elks, Rotary Internat., Phi Kappa Phi (corr.sec. local chpt. 1982-83, chmn. com. select new faculty initiates, pres.-elect), Phi Alpha Theta (paper awards com. internat. chpt. 1969-74, internat. coun. 1979-81, internat. adv. bd. 1981-85, co-advisor, Best Chpt. award 1978). Democrat. Home: PO Box 22400 Flagstaff AZ 86002-2400 Office: No Ariz U PO Box 5725 Flagstaff AZ 86011-0001

RUMFORD, DOUGLAS JAMES, pastor; b. Detroit, June 25, 1953; s. Robert and Lillian R.; m. Sarah Moore, July 13, 1974; children: Kristen, Matthew, Timothy, Peter. BA, Miami U., 1975; MDiv, Gordon-Conwell Theol. Sem., 1978; D in Ministry, Fuller Theol. Sem., 1992. Asst. pastor Presbyn. Ch., Old Greenwich, Conn., 1978-79; assoc. pastor Presbyn. Ch., Old Greenwich, 1979-82; pastor First Presbyn. Ch., Fairfield, Conn., 1983-88, Fresno, Calif., 1988—. Contbr. articles to profl. jours. Mem. nat. steering com., program com. The Presbyn. Congress on Renewal, Dallas, 1982-85; vice-moderator Presbytery of So. England, 1986-87; mem. Evangelism and Pers. Coms., San Joaquin Presbytery, 1988—; chmn. Evangelicals for Social Action, LOVE Inc., 1993; bd. dirs. Fresno Leadership Found. Mem. Fresno Rotary Club (song leader 1988—). Office: First Presbyn Ch 1540 M St Fresno CA 93721

RUMMERFIELD, PHILIP SHERIDAN, medical physicist; b. Raton, N. Mex., Feb. 27, 1922; s. Lawrence Lewis and Helen Antoinette (Roper) R.; m. Mary Evelyn Kubick, Dec. 29, 1979; children: Casey Regan, Dana Jay. BSME, Healds Coll., 1954; MSc, U. Cin., 1964, DSc, 1965. Registered profl. engr., safety, nuclear, Calif. Piping engr. Morrison Knudsen Co., Surabaja, E. Java, 1956-57; civil engr. State of Calif., San Francisco, 1957-59, constn. and radiation engr., 1959-63; hosp. physicist and radiation safety officer U. Calif., San Diego, 1966-73; prin. Applied Radiation Protection Svc., Encinitas, Calif., 1973—. Contbr. articles to Science, Bull. Atomic Scientists, Occupational Health Nursing, Health Physics Jour., Internat. Jour. Applied Radiation & Isotopes. Candidate for City Coun., Carlsbad, Calif., 1984. Grantee Teaching grant NSF, 1969-71. Mem. Am. Nuclear Soc., Calif. Soc. Profl. Engrs., Am. Indsl. Hygiene Assn., Am. Assn. Physicists in Medicine (pres. So. Calif. chpt. 1971-72), Calif. Soc. Profl. Engrs., Health Physics Soc. (pres. So. Calif. chpt. 1973-74). Democrat. Home: 3303 Dorado Pl Carlsbad CA 92009-7706 Office: Applied Radiation Protective Svcs 700 2nd St Ste C Encinitas CA 92024-4459

RUNICE, ROBERT E., retired corporate executive; b. Fargo, N.D., Aug. 20, 1929; s. E.M. and Ruth (Soule) R.; m. Geraldine Kharas, June 26, 1954; children: Michael, Christopher, Paul, Karen. B.S., N.D. State U., 1951. Sr. v.p. Northwestern Bell Tel. Co., Omaha, Nebr., 1945-81; v.p. Am. Tel. & Tel. Co.-Info. Systems, Morristown, N.J., 1981-83; v.p., pres. comml. devel. div. US West, Inc., Englewood, Colo., 1983-91; bd. dirs. Bombay Co., Ft. Worth, Tandy Brands Accessories, Arlington, Tex., Utilx Corp., Kent, Wash. Trustee Colo. Symphony Assn. Republican. Episcopalian. Home: Box 503 10940 S Parker Rd Parker CO 80134-7440 Office: 9785 Maroon Cir Ste 332 Englewood CO 80112-5918

RUNNELLS, DONALD DEMAR, geochemistry educator; b. Eureka, Utah, Dec. 30, 1936; s. Raymond DeMar and Cleo Cecil (Beckstead) R.; m. Erika Anna Bahe, Sept. 3, 1958; children: Timothy, Suzanne. BS with high honors, U. Utah, 1958; MA, Harvard U., 1960, PhD, 1963. Rsch. geochemist Shell Devel. Co., Houston and Miami, 1963-67; asst. prof. U. Calif.-Santa Barbara, 1967-69; assoc. prof. geochemistry U. Colo., Boulder, 1969-75, prof., 1975-92, chair dept. geol. sci., 1990-92; pres. Shepherd Miller, Inc., Ft. Collins, Colo., 1993—. cons. geochemistry to cos., and govt. agys. Mem. water sci. and tech. bd. NRC/NAS, 1989-92. Contbr. articles to profl. publs. NSF fellow, 1958-62. Fellow Geol. Soc. Am.; mem. Assn. Exploration Geologists (pres. 1990-91), Soc. Econ. Paleontologists and Mineralogists, Assn. Ground-water Scientists and Engrs., Phi Kappa Phi. Home: 8032 Allott Ave Fort Collins CO 80525 Office: Shepherd Miller Inc 1600 Specht Point Dr Ste F Fort Collins CO 80525

RUNNICLES, DONALD, conductor; b. Edinburgh, Scotland, Nov. 16, 1954. Student, Edinburgh U., Cambridge U., London Opera Ctr. Repetiteur Mannheim, Germany, Nat. theater, from 1980, Kapellmeister, from 1984; prin. condr. Hanover, from 1987; numerous appearances with Hamburg Staatsoper; now chief condr. Stadtische Buhnen, Freiburg/Breisgau; mus. dir. San Francisco Opera, 1992—; appearances with Met. Opera include Lulu, 1988, The Flying Dutchman, 1990, The Magic Flute; has conducted at Vienna Staatsoper from 1990-91 season; debut at Glyndebourne with Don Giovanni, 1991; also numerous symphonic engagements. Office: San Francisco Opera War Meml Opera House San Francisco CA 94102 also: Stadtische Buhnen, Bertoldstr 46, W-7800 Freiburg/Breisgau Federal Republic of Germany

RUNYON, RICHARD PORTER, author; b. N.Y.C., June 1, 1925; s. Harold Porter and Fleeta Marie (Richardson) R.; m. Lois Ann Lesinger, Sept. 28, 1947; children: Amy, Richard, Nancy, Thomas, Maribeth. BA, Drew U., 1950; MS, Yale U., 1952, PhD, 1954. From asst. prof. to prof. psychology C.W. Post Coll., L.I. U., Greenvale, N.Y., 1954-74, chmn. dept., 1954-67, dean sci. dir., 1967-73. Co-author: The Energy Crisis, 1972, Fundamentals Behavioral Statistics, 1967, 7th edit., 1991; author: Winning with Statistics, 1977, How Numbers and Statistics Lie, 1981. With U.S. Army, 1943-46, ETO. Mem. APA. Home: 11455 E Speedway Blvd Tucson AZ 85748-2012

RUOHO, DAVID OLIVER, educational administrator; b. Apache Junction, Ariz., May 14, 1949; s. Oliver William and Irja (Sarkki) R.; m. Edye Louise Tucker, Apr. 3, 1971; children: Bradley, Joshua. BEd, Ariz. State U., Tempe, 1974; MEd, Nova U., 1982. Tchr. 1st and 4th grades Apache Junction Unified Sch. Dist., 1975-81; tchr. 6th grade Globe (Ariz.) Unified Sch. Dist., 1984-85; tchr. 6th grade Coolidge (Ariz.) Unified Sch. Dist., 1985-90, dean of students, 1990-91, asst. prin., 1991-92; pres., dir. New Covenant Ministries Counseling and Tng. Ctr., Mesa, Ariz., 1992—; cons. Ariz. Prevention Resource Ctr., Tempe, 1991—; facilitator Student Assistance Program, Phoenix, 19916; mentor Ariz. Residency Program, Phoenix, 1990—; trainer in peer mediation, 1990. Tchr., Broadway Christian Ch., Mesa, 1991; firefighter Apache Junction Fire Dist., 1985—. Named to Outstanding Young Men of Am., 1989. Mem. ASCD. Christian. Home: 1060E Estevan Apache Junction AZ 85219

RUOTSALA, JAMES ALFRED, historian, writer; b. Juneau, Alaska, Feb. 17, 1934; s. Bert Alfred and Eva (Karppi) E.; m. Janet Ann Whelan, July 31, 1987; stepchildren: Theresa Cowden, Douglas Whelan, Peggy MacInnis, Michael Whelan, Bruce Whelan. Student, U. Md., 1960-61, Basic Officers Sch., Maxwell AFB, 1964, Air U., Maxwell AFB, 1984; AA, U. Alaska, Kenai, 1990. Asst. div. mgr. Macmillan Pub. Co., 1964-80; mgr. Denny's Restaurants, 1980-82; dir. mktg. and sales Air Alaska, 1982-89; state security super. Knightwatch Security, Juneau, Alaska, 1990—; archival dir. Alaska Aviation Heritage Mus., 1987-90. Author: Lockheed Vegas in Southeast Alaska, 1980, We Stand Ready, 1986, Eielson, Father of Alaskan Aviation, 1986; Alaska's Aviation Heritage Air Alaska newspaper; contbr. articles to profl. jours. Journalist 1st cl. USN, 1951-56; master sgt. U.S. Army, 1958-64; lt. col. ASDR, 1985—. Decorated Korean Svc. medal with 2 combat stars, Korean Presdl. unit citation, UN Svc. medal, Nat. Def. Svc. medal; recipient USAF Brewer Aerospace award, Grover Loening award, Paul E. Garber award, 1984-85, State of Alaska Gov.'s Cert. Appreciation, 1983, Mayor's Pub. Svc. award, Anchorage, 1985, Commendation from Gov., 1993. Mem. VFW, Res. Officers Assn. (pub. affairs officer 1985—), U.S. Naval Inst., Aviation and Space Writers Assn., Gastineau Philatelic Soc., Am. Aviation Hist. Soc., Am. Legion, Pioneers of Alaska (sec. 1988, v.p. 1989, pres. 1990, Igloo 33, Cert. Appreciation 1988), Rotary. Methodist. Home: 2723 John St Juneau AK 99801 Office: Knightwatch Security PO Box 33251 Juneau AK 99803

RUPERT, DAVID ANDREW, religious organization superintendent, minister; b. Oil City, Pa., Aug. 16, 1940; s. John Reuben and Wealtha Audrey (Smoyer) R.; m. Lois Martha Annable, June 30, 1962; children: Glenn David, Martha Jean. BA, Roberts Wesleyan Coll., 1962; BD, Western Evang. Sem., 1967, MDiv, 1972; D Ministry, Fuller Theol. Sem., 1980. Asst. pastor Free Meth. Ch., Herkimer, N.Y., 1962-63, Portland, Oreg., 1963-64, Salem, Oreg., 1964-67; pastor Free Meth. Ch., Redmond, Oreg., 1967-71; sr. pastor Willow Vale Community Ch.-Free Meth., San Jose, Calif., 1971-79; sr. pastor Free Meth. Ch., Sacramento, 1979-84, conf. supt., 1984—; Lifo cons., trainer Stuart Atkins, Inc., Beverly Hills, Calif., 1981; del., mem. Gen. Conf. Free Meth. Ch., Winona Lake, Ind. and Seattle, 1985, 89, mem., sec. youth conf., Winona Lake, 1969, Gen. Bd. Adminstrn./Adminstrn. Com., Indpls., 1989—; trustee Seattle Pacific U., 1987—; trustee Western Evang. Sem., Portland, 1985—. Editor: Celebrating one Hundred Years, 1983. Member adminstrv. and exec. coms. Greater Sacramento Billy Graham Crusade, co-chair fin. com., 1983; pres. Redmond Ministerial, 1968-69, Greater Sacramento Assn. of Evangs., 1981-83; founder, pres. Greater San Jose Assn. of Evangs., 1974-78; bd. dirs. Redmond United Way Fund, 1969-71. Mem. Calif. Coun. on Alcohol Problems, Northern Calif. Assn. Evangs. (v.p. 1986-88, pres. 1988-91), Rotary (editor bull. Redmond chpt. 1969-71, 2d Pres.' award 1971). Republican. Home: 9241 Linda Rio Dr Sacramento CA 95826-2209 Office: Calif Conf Free Meth Ch # 212 9750 Business Park Dr Sacramento CA 95827-1716

RUPP, JEAN LOUISE, communications executive; b. Portland, Oreg., Aug. 29, 1943; d. Edward Howard and Dorothy Eugenia (Ross) Brown; m. Herbert Gustav Rupp, July 4, 1987. BA in English, Portland State U., 1965. Cert. tchr., Oreg. Tchr., dept. head Beaverton (Oreg.) Sch. Dist., 1967-88; pres., founder Write Communications, Portland, 1988—; adj. faculty Portland C.C., Clackamas C.C., Concordia Coll.; nat. trainer State of Oreg., City of Portland, Nike, Inc., Oreg. Health Scis. U., Oreg. Military Acad., Oreg. Fin. Instns. Assn., others, 1988—; speaker Tektronix, Fred Meyer, Pacific Power, Am. Inst. of Banking, Utah Power, Pacific Telecom, Inc., NIKE, Inc., others; writing dir. U.S. Army Corps of Engrs., USDA Forest Svcs., PacifiCare, others, 1988-90. Creator of the Grammar Gremlin; T.V. appearances include Sta. KATU-TV and Sta. KGW-TV. Vol. Dove Lewis Emergency Veterinary Clinic, Portland, 1989—, Doerbecher Childrens Hosp. Mem. Oreg. Speakers Assn. (program chair, bd. dirs. 1991—), Oreg. Ind. Cons. and Trainers (bd. dirs. 1989), Am. Soc. Tng. and Devel. Republican. Office: Write Comm 8885 SW Canyon Rd # 201 Portland OR 97225-3455

RUPPEL, EDWARD THOMPSON, geologist; b. Ft. Morgan, Colo., Oct. 26, 1925; s. Henry George and Gladys Myrtle (Thompson) R.; m. Phyllis Beale Tanner, June 17, 1956; children: Lisa, David, Douglas, Kristin. BA, U. Mont., 1948; MA, U. Wyo., 1950; PhD, Yale U., 1958. Cert. profl. geologist. Geologist U.S. Geol. Survey, Washington and Denver, 1948-86; chief cen. regional br. U.S. Geol. Survey, Denver, 1971-75, geologist, 1975-86; dir., state geologist Mont. Bur. Mines and Geology, Butte, 1986—. Contbr. about 40 articles to profl. jours. With USNR, 1943-46. Fellow Geol. Soc. Am., Soc. Econ. Geologists; mem. Am. Inst. Profl. Geologists, Mont. Geol. Soc., Assn. Am. State Geologists, Tobacco Root Geol. Soc., Rotary. Office: Mont Bur Mines & Geology West Park St Butte MT 59701

RUSCONI, LOUIS JOSEPH, marine engineer; b. San Diego, Calif., Oct. 10, 1926; s. Louis Edward and Laura Ethelyn (Salazar) R.; m. Virginia Caroline Bruce, Jan. 1, 1972. BA in Engring. Tech., Pacific Western U., 1981, MA in Marine Engring. Tech., 1982; PhD in Marine Engring. Mgmt., Clayton U., 1986. Cert. nuclear ship propulsion plant operator, surface and submarine. Enlisted USN, 1944, electrician's mate chief, 1944-65, retired, 1965; marine electrician planner U.S. Naval Shipyard, Vallejo, Calif., 1965-72; marine elec. technician Imperial Iranian Navy, Bandar Abbas, Iran, 1974-79; marine shipyard planner Royal Saudi Navy, Al-Jubail, Saudi Arabia, 1980-86; cons. in marine engring., 1986—. Author: Shipyards Operations manual, 1980, poetry (Golden Poet award 1989, Silver Poet award 1990). Mem. Rep. Presdl. Task Force, Washington, 1989-90, trustee, 1991. Mem. IEEE, U.S. Naval Inst., Soc. of Naval Architects and Marine Engrs. (assoc. mem.), Fleet Res., Nat. Geographic Soc. Home: 949 Myra Ave Chula Vista CA 91911-2315

RUSH, ANDREW WILSON, artist; b. Detroit, Sept. 24, 1931; s. Harvey Ditman and Mary Louise (Stalker) R.; m. Jean Cochran, Apr., 1957; children: Benjamin, Samuel, Joseph, Margaret; m. Ann Woodin, Oct., 1978. B.F.A. with honors, U. Ill., 1953; M.F.A., U. Iowa, 1958. Asso. prof. art U. Ariz., 1959-69; co-dir. Rockefeller Found. Indian Arts Project, 1960-64; vis. artist, artist-in-residence Ohio State U., 1970, U. Ark., 1972, Colo. Coll., 1973-74; resident mem. Rancho Linda Vista, Community of the Arts, Oracle, Ariz., 1969—. One-man shows include Carlin Galleries, Ft. Worth, 1973, Graphics Gallery, Tucson, 1972, 75, Tucson Art Inst., 1984; exhibited in group shows at World's Fair, N.Y.C., 1964, USIS exhbns., Europe, Latin Am., 1960-65; represented in permanent collections Libr. of Congress, Uffizzi Mus., Dallas Mus., Ft. Worth Mus., Seattle Mus., Free Libr., Phila.; illustrator: Andrew Rush on Oliver Wendell Holmes, 1973, Rule of Two (Ann Woodin), 1984, Voice Crying in the Wilderness (Edward Abbey), 1990, Ask Marilyn, 1992. Served with USMC, 1953-55. Fulbright grantee, 1958-59. Address: Rancho Linda Vista O M Star Rte 2360 Oracle AZ 85623

RUSH, ANNA LAURA (ANN RUSH), non-profit organization administrator; b. Kansas City, Mo., Jan. 30, 1917; d. Alva F. and Mary (Rees) Trueblood; m. Maurice McDonald, Oct. 20, 1939 (div. 1943); m. John Miles Ruth, June 24, 1945; children: Heath Rush, Freda Rush, Erica Pfister. Student, U. Nebr., 1936, U. Mich., 1938. Dress model Dept. Stores, Kansas City; nurses aide N.H.; pres. Friends of Peace Pilgrim, Hemet, 1985—. Co-compiler, pub. (book) Peace Pilgrim, Her Life and Works in Her Own Words, 1983. Recipient Loomis Peace award Si Mata Internat. Yoga and Health Inst., 1991. Mem. Soc. Friedns. Home: 43480 Cedar Ave Hemet CA 92544

RUSH, DOMENICA MARIE, health facilities administrator; b. Gallup, N.Mex., Apr. 10, 1937; d. Bernardo G. and Guadalupe (Milan) Iorio; m. W. E. Rush, Jan. 5, 1967. Diploma, Regina Sch. Nursing, Albuquerque, 1958. RN N.Mex.; lic. nursing home adminstr. Charge nurse, house supr. St. Joseph Hosp., Albuquerque, 1958-63; dir. nursing Cibola Hosp., Grants, 1960-64; supr. operating room, dir. med. seminars Carrie Tingley Crippled Children's Hosp., Truth or Consequences, N.Mex., 1964-73; adminstr. Sierra Vista Hosp., Truth or Consequences, 1974-88, pres., 1980-89; clin. nursing mgr. U. N.Mex. Hosp., 1989-90; adminstr. Nor-Lea Hosp., Lovington, N.Mex., 1990—; with Presbyn. Healthcare Svcs., Albuquerque, 1990—; bd. dirs. N.Mex. Blue Cross/Blue Shield, 1977-88, chmn. hosp. relations com., 1983-85, exec. com. 1983—; bd. dirs. Region II Emergency Med. Svcs. Originating bd. SW Mental Health Ctr., Sierra County, N.Mex., 1975; chmn. Sierra County Personnel Bd., 1983—. Mem. Am. Coll. Health Care Adminstrs., Sierra County C. of C. (bd. dirs. 1972, 75-76, svc. award 1973, Businesswoman of the Yr. 1973-74), N.Mex. Hosp. Assn. (bd. dirs., sec.-treas., pres.-elect, com. chmn., 1977-88, pres. 1980-81, exec. com., 1980-83, 84-85, recipient meritorius svc. award 1988), N.Mex. So. Hosp. Coun. (sec. 1980-81, pres. 1981-82), Am. Hosp. Assn. (N.Mex. del. 1984-88, regional adv. bd. 1984-88). Republican. Roman Catholic. Home: RR 2 Box 5B Lovington NM 88260-9804

RUSH, FRED WILLIARD, educational administrator; b. New Smyrna, Fla., Mar. 28, 1929; s. Scott and Gladys Lillian (Rush) Landon; m. Beverly Joan Bibler, Oct. 14, 1950; children: Linda, Lee, Deborah, Mark, Bret. BS in Biology, Calif. State Poly. Coll., 1957, MA in Edn., 1962. Tchr. biology Ceres (Calif.) Union High Sch., 1958-61; tchr. Sylvan Union Sch. Dist., Modesto, Calif., 1961-63, San Ardo (Calif.) Union Sch. Dist., 1963-71; resource specialist McSwain Union Sch. Dist., Merced, Calif., 1973-89; founder, dir. Rush Reading Clinic, Merced, Calif., 1976—. Author: A Time Management System for Rapid Development of Reading Fluency, 1981; author self-teaching videos: Rush Reading Tutor Videos, 1990. Chaplain Calif. Penal Instns., Merced and Fresno Counties, 1984—; mem. Rep. Task Force; active Habitat for Humanity. With USAF, 1948-52. Mem. Defenders of Wildlife (life). Republican. Christian Scientist. Office: Rush Reading Clinic 1071 Hansen Ave Merced CA 95340

RUSH, GARY ALFRED, agriculturist; b. Baker, Oreg., Sept. 26, 1935; s. John R. and Wilda L. (Trimble) R.; m. Joan Wolfe (div. 1969); children: Michael A., Patrick A.; m. Anna S. Smith, Sept. 4, 1969. Student, Ea. Oreg. Coll., 1953-54; BS, Oreg. State U., 1957; postgrad., Sacramento State U., 1960-61; MS, U. Nev., 1975, postgrad., 1981-82. Rsch. asst. U. Nev., Reno, 1969-71, lectr., 1971-72; extension agt. U. Calif., Alturas, 1973-83, Quincy, 1983-87; county dir. U. Calif., Hayfork, 1987-90; county dir. U. Calif., Redding, 1990-92, area extension agt., 1992—; pres. U. Calif. Youth Advisors Com., Davis, 1982-83; mem. Coop. Ext. Assembly Coun., Davis, 1982-83; bd. dirs. Green Thumb Inc., Great Northern Corp. Author various bulletins, booklets. Pres. Modoc C. of C., Alturas, Calif., 1978-80; mem. Community Devel. Soc., Coop. Ext. Rural Housing Task Force, Boy Scouts of Am. (comm. leader). With U.S. Army, 1957-60. Recipient Blue Ribbon award Western Fairs Assn., 1977, Svc. award March of Dimes, 1965, Affirmative Action award U. Calif., 1990; named Outstanding Citizen Modoc C. of C., 1974. Mem. Western Agrl. Econs. Assn., Assn. Evolutionary Econ., Calif. Cattlemens Assn., Shasta County Farm Bur., Rotary, Elks, Gamma Sigma Delta. Republican. Office: Coop Extension 3179 Bechelli Ln Ste 206 Redding CA 96002-2041

RUSH, HERMAN E., television executive; b. Phila., June 20, 1929; s. Eugene and Bella (Sacks) R.; m. Joan Silberman, Mar. 18, 1951; children: James Harrison, Mandie Susan. BBA, Temple U., 1950. With Ofcl. Films, 1951-57; owner Flamingo Films, 1957-60; with Creative Mgmt. Assos., N.Y.C., 1960-71; pres. TV div. Creative Mgmt. Assos., 1964-71, exec. v.p. parent co., dir., 1964-71; ind. producer, 1971-75; producer Wolper Orgn., 1975-76; pres. Herman Rush Assos., Inc. (Rush-Flaherty Agy. subs.), 1977-78, Marble Arch TV, Los Angeles, 1979-80, Columbia Pictures TV, Burbank, Calif., 1980-87; chmn., chief exec. officer Coca-Cola Telecommunications, 1987-88, Rush Assocs., Inc., Burbank, 1988—, Katz/Rush Entertainment, Beverly Hills, Calif., 1990—; chmn. Entertainment Industries Council. Trustee Sugar Ray Robinson Youth Found., 1967-75; pres. Retarded Infant Services, N.Y.C., 1957-63; bd. dirs. U.S. Marshall's Service Found., Just Say No Found.; conferee White House Conf. for a Drug Free America, 1987, 88. Mem. Acad. TV Arts and Scis., Hollywood Radio and TV Soc., Producers Caucus. Clubs: Friars, Filmex. Office: Katz/Rush Entertainment Ste 205 345 N Maple Dr Beverly Hills CA 90210

RUSH, HUBERT MICHAEL (MICK), broadcast engineer; b. Madera, Calif., May 31, 1946; s. Charles Thomas and LaVerne (Elliot) Casterline; m. Marilyn J. Dalton, Dec. 9, 1967 (div.); children: Charles, Joseph; m. Lucinda M. Taylor, June 12, 1990; 1 child, Woodrow. Student, Fresno State U., 1966, Golden West U., 1972. Maintenance engr. Sta. KGLM Radio, Avalon, Calif., 1967-71; maintenance engr. Sta. KBIG Radio, L.A., 1971-76, supr. engring., 1976-81; dir. engring. Sta. KOIT Radio, San Francisco, 1981-89; chief engr. Sta. KXOA Radio, Sacramento, Calif., 1989—. Scoutmaster Boy Scouts Am., Walnut Creek, Calif., 1985-86. Mem. Nat. Assn. Radio and Telecommunications Engrs. (sr.), Audio Engring. Soc. Home: 8020 Branson Ct Sacramento CA 95842 Office: Sta KXOA Radio 280 Commerce Circle Sacramento CA 95815

RUSHER, DAVID LYNN, electronics engineer; b. Scottsbluff, Nebr., Oct. 19, 1939; s. James Franklin and Alta Joy (Samuelson) R.; m. Louise May Jones, July 27, 1968; children: Kimberly S., Julia P. BSEE, Colo. State U., 1961; MSEE, U. So. Calif., 1966. Sr. reliability engr. Rockwell Internat., Anaheim, Calif., 1961, sr. rsch. engr., 1966-68, mem. tech. staff, 1968-83, rsch. engring. mgr., 1983-89, sr. engring. specialist, 1989—. Inventor radiation hardened bistable logic circuit, 1991. Recipient Scholarship Texaco, 1957. Mem. IEEE, Nat. Mgmt. Assn. Republican. Home: 2983 Mindanao Dr Costa Mesa CA 92626 Office: Rockwell Internat 3370 Miraloma Ave Anaheim CA 92803

RUSHFORTH, BRENDA LEA, human resources professional; b. Albert Lea, Minn., Sept. 27, 1960; d. A. William and Verles Elaine (Hauge) Emry; m. Gary Gordon Rushforth, Apr. 11, 1992. BS, Brigham Young U., 1983. Cert. profl. in human resources, notary pub. Coord. corp. devel. Osmond Found., Salt Lake City, 1983-84; pers. asst. William Morris Agy., Beverly Hills, Calif., 1984-86; agt., counselor Friedman Pers. Agy., L.A., 1986-87; pers. rep. The Fashion Channel, Carson, Calif., 1987-88; pers. dir. Pantron I Corp., L.A., 1988-90; dir. human resources and tng. L.A. County Med. Assn., 1990—. Pres. Studio City First Ward Relief Soc., North Hollywood, Calif., 1986-87; asst. supr. L.A. Mormon Temple, 1985-90, supr., 1990-92. Mem. NAFE, ASTD, Pers. and Indsl. Rels. Assn., Nat. Notary Assn., Soc. Human Resources Mgmt., Brigham Young U. Mgmt. Soc. Republican. Mem. LDS Ch. Office: LA County Med Assn 1925 Wilshire Blvd Los Angeles CA 90057

RUSHMER, ESTELLA (DIXIE) VIRGINIA, artist; b. Sullivan, Ind., Oct. 17, 1919; d. William Porter Jessop and Roxie Gertrude (Johnson) D.; m. Robert Frazer Rushmer, Apr. 5, 1942; children: Donald Scott, Anne, Elizabeth. BS, Purdue U., 1940. cert. Am. Dietetic Assn. Author, artist: Whidbey Island Sketchbook, 1985; one-woman shows include Good Years Gallery, Edmonds, Wash., 1975, 75, 77, Stillwater Gallery, Seattle, 1979, Artists Gallery Northwest, 1979, 82, 83, Stonington Gallery, Seattle, 1985, Port Angeles (Wash.) Fine Arts Ctr., 1988; group shows include Bellevue (Wash.)Art Mus., 1979, 82, 84, 86-90, Peter Kirk Gallery, Kirkland, Wash., 1985-90, Frye Mus., Seattle, 1979, Frederick and Nelson Gallery, Seattle, 1980, 82, Fremont Fine Art Gallery, Seattle, 1987, Black Swan Gallery, Seattle, 1989, Portico Gallery, Kobe, Japan, 1987, Meguro Mus., Tokyo, Japan, 1987, Columbia Art Ctr., Vancouver, Wash., 1990, Nat. Watercolor Soc. Show, Muckenthaler Cultural Ctr., Fullerton, Calif., 1990.

RUSKIN, MARY KATHY, cable television executive; b. Chgo., Jan. 17, 1953; d. Alfred R. and Jane (Earle) Piskorski; m. Frederic L. Ruskin, Apr. 28, 1991. BS, So. Ill. U., 1974; MBA, NYU, 1979. Mgr. Teleprompter Corp., N.Y.C., 1979-81; dir. Post-Newsweek Cable, Inc., Phoenix, 1981-90, v.p., 1990—. Bd. dirs. Ariz First Amendment Coalition, 1990-91, treas. 1992. Mem. Ariz. Cable Assn. (bd. dirs. 1989-90, sec.-treas. 1990, v.p. 1991, pres. 1992), Ariz. Cable Forum (bd. dirs. 1987-90, pres. 1987). Home: 6111 N 20th St Phoenix AZ 85016-1911 Office: Post-Newsweek Cable Inc Ste 270 4742 N 24th St Phoenix AZ 85016-4207

RUSS, DANIEL CHRISTOPHER, small business owner; b. Seattle, Aug. 10, 1961; s. John Bernard and Fumiko (Takemori) R. BBA, U. Wash., 1983; postgrad., U. Puget Sound, 1989—. Mktg. rep. Xerox Corp., Tukwila, Wash., 1983-85; co-founder Students, Ink, Seattle, 1984—; spl. asst. to dir., info. system svcs. divsn. Dept. Social & Health Svcs., Olympia, Wash., 1990—, sr. mis mgr., info. system svcs. divsn., 1992—. Editor: Healthcare Integrated Info. System Newsletter, Ft. Steilacoom, Wash., 1990-92; Contbr. articles to profl. jours. Capt. USAFR, 1985—. Gov's Exec. fellow, 1990-92. Mem. Air Force Assn., Nat. Eagle Scout Assn., Nat. Geographic Soc., Christian Legal Fellowship Soc., Res. Officers Assn. Roman Catholic. Home: 8714 Oxford Ct SE Olympia WA 98503-4188 Office: Dept Social and Health Svcs PO Box 45880 Olympia WA 98504-5880

RUSSELL, ANGELA V., state legislator, social worker; b. Crow Agency, Mont., Aug. 25, 1943; d. William A. and Josephine (Pease) R. BA, U. Mont., 1965; MSW, Tulane U., 1974. Lic. social wroker Mont. Field rep. United Scholar Svc., Denver, 1965-67; child welfare worker Yellowstone County Pub. Welfare, Billings, Mont., 1968-72; counselor Rocky Mt. Coll., Billings, Mont., 1972-73; com. organizer Crow Tribe Office of Coal Rsch., Crow Agency, Mont., 1975-76; cons. pvt. practice, Lodge Grass, Mont., 1976-77; project dir. Denver U. Social Rsch., 1977-78; med. social wroker U.S. Pub. Health Svc., Brow Agency, 1978-85; psychotherapist, cons. pvt. practice, Billings, 1985—. coord. Hist. Crow Calender, 1978—. Chmn. Mt. Rhodes Scholar Com., Missoula, Mont., 1990—, Nat. Assn. Native Am. Legis., Denver, 1991—; mem. adv. bd. Mont. Inst. Mortality in Infants, Helena, Mont., 1991—; rep. Mont. House Reps., Helena, 1987—; state adv. com. U.S. Civil Rights Commn. Rocky Mt. Region, Denver, 1976-83; trustee Lodge Grass Schs., 1981-84. Named to Salute to Women YWCA, Billings, 1990. Mem. NASW, Nat. Assn. Indian Social Workers (treas. 1986-88), Indian Law Resource Ctr. (bd. dirs. 1992—). Democrat. Baptist. Home: PO Box 333 Lodge Grass MT 59050 Office: 104 Broadway Billings MT 59101

RUSSELL, BILL, professional basketball team executive; b. Monroe, La., Feb. 12, 1934. Grad., San Francisco State Coll., 1956. Player, NBA Boston Celtics Profl. Basketball Club, 1956-69, coach, 1966-69; sportscaster ABC-TV, 1969-80, CBS-TV, 1980-83; coach NBA Seattle Supersonics, 1973-77; coach NBA Sacramento Kings, 1987-88, v.p. basketball ops., then exec. v.p., 1988-89; mem. U.S. Olympic Basketball Team (Gold medal), 1956. Appeared in: TV series Cowboy in Africa; also commls.; co-host: The Superstars, ABC-TV, 1978-79; Author: Second Wind: Memoirs of an Opinionated Man, 1979. Inducted into Basketball Hall of Fame, 1974; mem. 11 NBA championship teams. Office: Sacramento Kings 1 Sports Pky Sacramento CA 95834-2301

RUSSELL, CAROL ANN, personnel service company executive; b. Detroit, Dec. 14, 1943; d. Billy and Iris (Driver) Koud; m. Victor Rojas (div.). BA in English, Hunter Coll., 1993. Registered employment cons. Various positions in temp. help cos. N.Y.C., 1964-74; v.p. Wollborg-Michelson, San Francisco, 1974-82; co-owner, pres. Russell Personnel Svcs. Inc., San Francisco and Marin, 1983—; media guest, speaker, workshop and seminar leader in field. Pub. Workplace Newsline; contbr. articles to profl. publs. Named to the Inc. 500, 1989, 90. Mem. Internat. Platform Assn., No. Calif. Human Resources Coun., Soc. Human Resource Mgmt., Calif. Assn. Pers. Cons. (pres. Golden Gate chpt. 1984-85), Calif. Assn. Temp. Svcs., Bay Area Pers. Assn. (pres. 1983-84), Pers. Assn. Sonoma County. Office: Russell Pers Svcs Inc 120 Montgomery St San Francisco CA 94104-4302

RUSSELL, CHRISTOPHER THOMAS, geophysics educator; b. St. Albans, Eng., May 9, 1943; came to U.S., 1964; s. Thomas Daniel and Teresa Ada Susan (Mary) R.; m. Arlene Ann Thompson, June 25, 1966; children: Jennifer Ann, Danielle Suzanne. BS in Physics, U. Toronto, Ont., Can., 1964; PhD in Space Physics, UCLA, 1968. Research geophysicist Inst. Geophysics UCLA, 1969-81, prof. geophysics dept. earth and space sci., Inst. Geophysics, 1982—; chmn. com. on data mgmt. and computation Nat. Acad. Scis. Space Sci. Bd., 1985-88, commn. D. Com. on Space Research., 1982-86; Harold Jeffreys lectr. Royal Astron. Soc., 1987. Editor: Solar Wind Three, 1974, Auroral Processes, 1979, Active Experiments in Space Plasmas, 1981, The IMS Source Book, 1982, Solar Wind Interactions, 1986, Multipoint Magnetospheric Measurements, 1988, Physics of Magnetic Flux Ropes, 1990, Venus Aeronomy, 1991, Galileo Mission, 1992; contbr. over 600 articles to profl. jours. and books. Fellow AAAS, Am. Geophys. Union (pres. solar planetary relations sect. 1988-90, Macelwane award 1977); mem. Planetary Scis. div. Am. Astron. Soc., European Geophys. Soc. Office: UCLA Inst Geophysics & Planetary Physics Los Angeles CA 90024

RUSSELL, DANA, small business operator; b. Tuba City, Ariz., Aug. 2, 1949; s. Rudolph and Peggy (Sangster) R.; m. Caroline Ann Harrison; children: Grey Noel, Brian Haley-Allen, Grant David, Stephen Bradley. BBA, Cen. State U., 1972. Adminstr. community edn. Navajo Nation, Window Rock, Ariz., 1973-78; adminstr. higher edn. Navajo Community Coll., Tsaile, Ariz., 1978-90; pres., operator West Canyon Boiler, Inc., Flagstaff, Ariz., 1990-93; pres., owner Canyon Tng. and Sales, Flagstaff, 1993—; coun. mem. Navajo Nation - Pvt. Industry Coun., Window Rock, 1986-90. Office: Canyon Tng & Sales 2710 N Fremont Blvd Flagstaff AZ 86002

RUSSELL, DAVID E., judge; b. Chicago Heights, Ill., Mar. 19, 1935; s. Robert W. and Nellie (Petkus) R.; m. Denise A. Hurst, Apr. 1, 1968 (div. 1978); children: Dirk, Kent, Laura, Rachel; m. Sandra M. Niemeyer, Oct. 31, 1982. BS in Acctg., U. Calif., Berkeley, 1957, LLB, 1960. Bar: Calif. 1961, U.S. Dist. Ct. (no. dist.) Calif. 1961, U.S. Tax Ct. 1967; CPA, Calif. Staff acct. Lybrand, Ross Bros. & Montgomery, San Francisco, 1960-64; assoc. Robert C. Burnstein, Esquire, Oakland, Calif., 1964-65; ptnr. Russell & Humphreys, Sacramento, 1965; ptnr. Russell, Humphreys & Estabrook, Sacramento, 1966-70, prin., 1971-73; shareholder Russell, Jarvis, Estabrook & Dashiell, Sacramento, 1974-86; bankruptcy judge U.S. Dist. Ct. for Ea. Dist. Calif., Sacramento, 1986—. Office: US Bankruptcy Ct Rm 8038 650 Capitol Mall Sacramento CA 95814

RUSSELL, EDWARD CHARLES, computer software consultant; b. Detroit, May 12, 1938; s. Edward Charles and Blanche Murith (Johnson) R.; m. Lorna Louise Trefry, July 5, 1969; children: Courtney Lynn, Allison Leigh. BSEE, Wayne State U., 1960; MS in Engring., UCLA, 1963, PhD in Engring., 1969. Jr. engr. IBM, Endicott, N.Y., 1960-61; rsch. engr. UCLA, 1961-69; vis. scholar Inst. de Recherche d'Informatique & d'Automatique, Paris, 1969-71; sr. assoc. CACI, L.A., 1971-83, v.p., 1983-88; vis. lectr. bus. and engring. UCLA, 1972—; owner Russell Software Tech., Santa Monica, Calif., 1988—. Author: Building Simulation Models with Simscript II.5, 1983; coauthor Simscript II.5 computer lang. Bd. dirs. Larson Sound Ctr., Burbank, Calif., 1988—; general chair Winter Simulation Conf., L.A., 1993; trustee Berkeley Hall Sch., L.A., 1986—, Christian Sci. Orgn., UCLA, 1981—. Mem. Masons, Tau Beta Pi, Eta Kappa Nu, Sigma Xi. Republican. Home: 2369 Nalin Dr Los Angeles CA 90077 Office: Russell Software Tech 1735 Stewart St Santa Monica CA 90404

RUSSELL, FINDLAY EWING, physician; b. San Francisco, Sept. 1, 1919; s. William and Mary Jane (Findlay) R.; m. Marilyn Ruth Jenkins, Apr. 12, 1975; children—Christa Ann, Sharon Jane, Robin Emily, Constance Susan, Mark Findlay. BA, Walla Walla (Wash.) Coll., 1941; MD, Loma Linda (Calif.) U., 1950; postgrad. (fellow), Calif. Inst. Tech., 1951-53; PhD, U. Santa Barbara, Calif., 1974, LLD (hon.), 1989. Intern White Meml. Hosp., Los Angeles, 1950-51; practice medicine specializing in toxinology and toxicology Los Angeles, 1953—; mem. staff Los Angeles County-U. So. Calif. Med. Center, Loma Linda U. Med. Center, U. Ariz. Med. Ctr.; physiologist Huntington Inst. Med. Research, 1953-55; dir. lab. neurol. research Los Angeles County-U. So. Calif. Med. Center, 1955-80; mem. faculty Loma Linda U. Med. Sch., 1955—; prof. neurology, physiology and biology U. So.

Calif. Med. Sch., 1966-81; prof. pharmacology and toxicology U. Ariz., 1981—; cons. USPHS, NSF, Office Naval Research, WHO. Author: Marine Toxins and Venomous and Poisonous Marine Animals, 1965, Poisonous Marine Animals, 1971, Snake Venom Poisoning, 1980; co-author: Bibliography of Snake Venoms and Venomous Snakes, 1964, Animal Toxins, 1967, Poisonous Snakes of The World, 1968, Snake Venom Poisoning, 1983, Bibliography of Venomous and Poisonous Marine Animals and Their Toxins, 1984; editor: Toxicon, 1962-70. Served with AUS, 1942-46. Decorated Purple Heart, Bronze Star; recipient award Los Angeles County Bd. Suprs., 1960; award Acad. Medicine Buenos Aires, 1966; Skylab Achievement award, 1974; Jozef Stefan medal Yugoslavia, 1978. Fellow A.C.P., Am. Coll. Cardiology, Royal Soc. Tropical Medicine, N.Y. Acad. Scis.; mem. Internat. Soc. Toxinology (pres. 1962-66, Francisco Redi medal 1967), Royal Soc. Medicine, Am. Soc. Physiology, Western Soc. Pharmacology (pres. 1973). Office: U Ariz Coll Pharmacy Tucson AZ 85721

RUSSELL, FRANCIA, ballet director, educator; b. Los Angeles, Jan. 10, 1938; d. W. Frank and Marion (Whitney) R.; m. Kent Stowell, Nov. 19, 1965; children: Christopher, Darren, Ethan. Studies with, George Balanchine, Vera Volkova, Felia Doubrouska, Antonina Tumkovsky, Benjamin Harkarvy; student, NYU, Columbia U. Dancer, soloist N.Y.C. Ballet, 1956-62, ballet mistress, 1965-70; dancer Ballets USA/Jerome Robbins, N.Y.C., 1962; tchr. ballet Sch. Am. Ballet, N.Y.C., 1963-64; dir. staging over 90 George Balanchine ballet prodns. including Soviet Union and Peoples Republic of China for the first time., throughout N.Am., Europe and Asia, 1964—; co-dir. Frankfurt (Fed. Republic Germany) Opera Ballet, 1976-77; dir., co-artistic dir. Pacific N.W. Ballet, Seattle, 1977—; affiliate prof. of dance U. Wash. Named Woman of Achievement, Matrix Table, Women in Communications, Seattle, 1987, Gov.'s Arts award, 1989. Mem. Internat. Women's Forum. Home: 2833 Broadway E Seattle WA 98102-3935 Office: Pacific NW Ballet 301 Mercer St Seattle WA 98109

RUSSELL, GARY, broadcast executive; b. Winnepeg, Man., Can., Dec. 17, 1948; s. Raymond Anthony Wakefield and Florence Margret (Willson) Vidler; m. Deborah Kim Finnson, Oct. 10, 1984; children: Amanda, Charles. Grad., Kelvin High Sch., Winnepeg, 1967. Radio announcer Sta. CHLO, St. Thomas, Ont., 1967, Sta. CKOM, Saskatoon, Sask., 1968-69, Sta. CJMU, Regina, Sask., 1969, Sta. CKLU, Windsor, Ont., 1970; radio announcer Sta. CKLG, Vancouver, B.C., 1970-73, program dir., 1975-85; program dir. Sta. CKY, Winnepeg, 1973-75; nat. program dir. Moffat Comm., Winnepeg, 1986-89; v.p., gen. mgr. 54 Rock, Ottawa, 1990-92, Sta. CJAY, Calgary, Alta., 1992—. Office: Standard Radio Inc, Box 2750 Station M, Calgary, AB Canada TZP 4P8

RUSSELL, GARY E., minister; b. Detroit, Feb. 10, 1950; s. Billy Eugene Russell and Betty Mae (Harden) Berzley; m. Diane L. Rendel, Aug. 9, 1970; children: Chad M., Kurt L., Tara N., Bret M. BA in Theology, Andrews U., 1972, MDiv, 1974; MPH, Loma Linda U., 1981; DMin, Andrews U., 1993. Ordained to ministry Seventh-day Adventist Ch., 1979. Assoc. min. Fla. Conf. of Seventh-day Adventists, Winter Park, 1975-77; min. Fla. Conf. of Seventh-day Adventists, Okeechobee, 1977-79, Vero Beach, 1977-81; min. Mich. Conf. of Seventh-day Adventists, Boyne City, 1981-85, Traverse City, 1985-88, Dowagiac, 1988-93; min. S. Calif. Conf. of Seventh-day Adventists, Alhambra, 1993—; chaplain Cass County (Mich.) Sheriff's Dept., 1990-93, Dowagiac Police Dept., 1990-93, Wayne Twp. Vol. Fire Dept., 1991-93. Asst. editor (newsletter) Adventist Baby Boomer Awareness, 1991-92, editor, 1992—; contbr. articles to profl. jours. Active Cass County Coalition Against Domestic Violence, 1989 ; edn. dir. World Vision/Crop Walk for Hunger, Dowagiac, 1989. Named Man Who Affirms Women, Assn. of Adventist Women, Berrien Springs, 1990; recipient Recognition of Honor, Cass County Civitans, 1990, 93. Mem. Internat. Conf. Police Chaplains, Mich. Police Chaplains Assn., Dowagiac Ministerial Assn. (vice chair 1989-90, chmn. 1990-93), Theta Alpha Kappa (v.p. 1991—). Home: 10410 Live Oak Ave Arcadia CA 91007

RUSSELL, GAY MARTIN, television and film educator; b. Alpine, Tex., June 3, 1933; d. St. John and Ada (Harris) Martin; m. Harley E. Russell (div. 1981); children: Melodie Gay Russell McAhren, Howard Wesley Russell. AS, Arlington (Tex.) State U., 1952; BA, San Diego State U., 1967, MA, 1969. Cert. lifetime community coll. instr., Calif. Grad. asst. San Diego State U., 1967-69; prof. TV and film Grossmont Coll., El Cajon, Calif., 1969—, chmn. dept. TV and film, 1984—, chair of council of chairs, 1985-87; dir. several satellite teleconfs., 1988—. Writer, producer, dir., editor, advisor several videos and film: Who? Me, In College, 1969, Expressions of Love-James Hubbell, 1982, Half of Heaven-The New China, 1983-84, Empowering Children Against Molestation-No, It's My Body, 1985, A Montage of Preschool Days, 1985, Cooking With Preschoolers, 1985, A Directed Movement, 1985, Registration, 1987, Our Goal Is Your Success, 1988. Pres. Murray Hill Homeowners Assn., La Mesa, Calif., 1985-87. Mem. NEA, Calif. Tchrs. Assn., Community Coll. Assn. (treas. 1987-91, exec. bd. 1979—, communication liaison, caucus chmn. region IV, state council 1986—), Broadcast Edn. Assn. (bd. dirs. dist. VII 1991—), Am. Film Inst. Democrat. Home: 7200 Melody Ln Apt 76 La Mesa CA 91942-1409 Office: Grossmont Coll 8800 Grossmont College Dr El Cajon CA 92020-1765

RUSSELL, JAMES SARGENT, retired naval officer; b. Tacoma, Mar. 22, 1903; s. Ambrose J. and Loella Janet (Sargent) R.; m. Dorothy Irene Johnson, Apr. 13, 1929 (dec. Apr. 1965); children: Donald Johnson, Kenneth McDonald; m. 2d, Geraldine Haus Rahn, July 12, 1966. BS, U.S. Naval Acad., 1926; MS, Calif. Inst. Tech., 1935. Served with U.S. Mcht. Marine, 1918-22; commd. ensign U.S. Navy, 1926, advanced through grades to adm., 1958; naval aviator, 1929-65; comdg. officer aircraft sqdn. VP 42, Aleutians and Alaska, 1941-42; chief of staff to comdr. Carrier Div. Two, Pacific campaigns of Palau, P.I., Iwo Jima, Okinawa, 1944-45; bombing survey, Japan, 1945; comdg. officer U.S.S., Bairoko, 1946-47, U.S.S. Coral Sea, 1951-52; with aircraft carrier desk Bur. Aero., 1939-41, dir. mil. requirements, 1943-44; dept. dir. mil. application AEC, 1947-51; dir. air warfare div. Office Chief Naval Ops., 1952-54; comdr. carrier div. 17 & 5, Pacific Fleet, 1954-55, chief Bur. of Aero., 1955-57; dep. comdr. Atlantic Fleet, 1957-58, vice chief Naval Ops., 1958-61; comdr. NATO forces in So. Europe, 1962-65, ret., 1965; recalled to active duty, 1967, 68; mem. various Navy adv. bds.; cons. Boeing Co., 1965-79. Decorated D.S.M. with oak leaf cluster, Legion of Merit with two oak leaf clusters, D.F.C., Air medal (U.S.); grand cross Royal Order King George I (Greece); Grand Ofcl. Order Republic of Italy; comdr. Legion of Honor (France); Gt. Cross Peruvian Cross of Naval Merit; Grand Officer Order of Naval Merit (Brazil); recipient Collier-Trophy, 1956, Russell Trophy Order of Daedalians; named to Nat. Mus. of Naval Aviation Hall of Honor, 1990. Fellow AIAA. Home: 7734 Walnut Ave SW Tacoma WA 98498-5223

RUSSELL, KEN MARK, accountant, financial planner, consultant; b. Bryn Mawr, Pa., Aug. 14, 1956; s. Tim and Ruth E. (McComas) R. BA in Bus. and Acctg., U. Wash., 1980. CPA; CFP. Sr. Arthur Anderson, Seattle, 1980-82; acctg. officer Seafirst Bank, Seattle, 1982-84; avp Wells Fargo Bank, San Francisco, 1984-85; fin. cons. Merrill Lynch, Seattle, 1985-91; pres. Pacific N.W. Profl. Cons., Seattle, 1991—. Home: PO Box 1713 Seattle WA 98111 Office: Pacific NW Professional Cons 1818 Westlake Ave N Seattle WA 98109

RUSSELL, MARLOU, psychologist; b. Tucson, June 2, 1956; d. William Herman and Carole Eleanor (Musgrove) McBratney; m. Jan Christopher Russell, Sept. 9, 1989. BA U. Ariz., 1981; MA Calif. Grad. Inst., 1983, PhD, 1987. Lic. psychologist, marriage, family and child counselor. Asst. to pres. Western Psychol. Svcs., L.A., 1978-81; crisis counselor Cedars-Sinai Med. Ctr., L.A., 1980-84; counselor South Bay Therapeutic Clinic, Hawthorne, Calif., 1982-84; psychotherapist PMC Treatment Systems, L.A., 1984-85, Beverly Hills Counseling Ctr., 1984-85, Comprehensive Care Corp., L.A., 1985-86; pvt. practice, L.A., 1986—; counselor Brotman Med. Ctr., L.A., 1982-83, Julia Ann Singer Ctr., Los Angeles, 1984; bd. dirs. Los Angeles Commn. Assualts Against Women, 1987-89. Mem. Internat. Assn. Eating Disorders Profls, Women in Health, Women's Referral Svc., Am. Anorexia-Bulimia Assn., Calif. State Psychol. Assn., Calif. Assn. Marriage & Family Therapists. Democrat. Office: 1452 26th St Ste 103 Santa Monica CA 90404-3042

RUSSELL, NEWTON REQUA, state senator; b. L.A., June 25, 1927; s. John Henry and Amy (Requa) R.; m. Diane Henderson, Feb. 12, 1953; children—Stephen, Sharon, Julia. Postgrad., UCLA, Georgetown U.; BS, U. So. Calif., 1951. Spl. agt. Northwestern Mut. Life Ins. Co., Calif., 1954-64; mem. Calif. State Assembly, 1964-74, Calif. Senate, 1974—; vice-chmn. com. on energy and pub. utilities, mem. com. on local govt., vice chmn. com. on banking and commerce, internat. trade, mem. com. on transp., joint com. on rules, joint com. on state's economy, task force on legis. efficiency., joint com. on energy regulation and the environ., joint com. on mental health rsch. select com. on Calif.'s wine industry, select com. on children and youth, select com. on pacific rim, senate spl. com. on devel. disabilities and mental health. Mem. Rep. State Central Com. Served with USN, 1945-46. Recipient Outstanding Legislator award Calif. Rep. Assembly, 1968, 76, 81, Mayor's commendation City of Burbank, 1978, Disting. Service award County Suprs. Assn. Calif., 1980, Nat. Rep. Legislator of Yr., 1981, Legislator of Yr. award Los Angeles County Fedn. Rep. Women, 1982, Legislator of Yr. award Calif. Credit Union League, 1983, numerous honors from community orgns. and instns. Mem. Delta Tau Delta, Alpha Kappa Phi. Mem. Church on the Way. Office: Office of State Senate 401 N Brand Blvd #424 Glendale CA 91203

RUSSELL, PATRICK JAMES, priest; b. Boise, Idaho, May 10, 1959; s. Glenn Edward and Doralea (Trumble) R. BA, Boise U., 1982; MDiv, St. Patrick's Sem., 1986. Ordained priest Roman Catholic Ch., 1986. Assoc. pastor St. Marks Cath. Ch., Boise, 1986-91; now chaplain Chateau de Boise, 1991—. Named Outstanding Young Man of Am. 1983, 84, 86, 87, Outstanding Youth in Achievement, Cambridge, U.K. Mem. Am. Film Inst., Amnesty Internat., Internat. Biog. Ctr., Right to Life/Spl. Olympics, Sigma Phi Epsilon. Democrat. Office: St Marks Cath Ch 7503 Northview St Boise ID 83704-7235

RUSSELL, PAUL EDGAR, electrical engineering educator; b. Roswell, N.Mex., Oct. 10, 1924; s. Rueben Matthias and Mary (Parsons) R.; m. Lorna Margaret Clayshulte, Aug. 29, 1943; children: Carol Potter, Janice Russell Gregory, Gregory. BSEE, N.Mex. State U., 1946, BSME, 1947; MSEE, U. Wis., 1950, PhDEE, 1951. Registered elec. engr., Ariz. From instr. to asst. prof. elec. engrng. U. Wis., Madison, 1947-52; sr. engr., design specialist Gen. Dynamics Corp., San Diego, 1952-54; from prof. to chmn. elec. engrng. dept. U. Ariz., Tucson, 1954-63; dean engring. Kans. State U., Manhattan, 1963-67; prof. Ariz. State U., Tempe, 1967-90; dir. engrng. Ariz. State U. West, Phoenix, 1985-88; dir. Sch. Constrn. and Tech. Ariz. State U., Tempe, 1988-90; cons. in field, 1954—; programs evaluator, mem. engrng. commn. Accreditation Bd. for Engrng. and Tech., N.Y.C., 1968-81. Contbr. articles to jours. and chpts. to books. Served as sgt. U.S. Army, 1944-46. Recipient Disting. Service award N.Mex. State U., 1965. Fellow IEEE (life, chmn. Ariz. sect. 1960), Accreditation Bd. Engring. and Tech.; mem. Am. Soc. Engrng. Educators. Home: 5902 E Caballo Ln Paradise Valley AZ 85253-2216

RUSSELL, RICHARD WAYNE, artist; b. Salida, Colo., July 2, 1955; s. Charles Leonard and Elsie Kay (Roatcap) R.; m. Karen Denise Thompson, June 9, 1979; 1 child, Jennifer Nicole. Student, Mesa Coll., 1973-74. Cover illustrator (mag.) Ski the Summit, Frisco, Colo., 1991-92; watercolors exhibited Great Things West Art Gallery, Breckenridge, Colo., Grand Junction, Colo., 1992, Glenwood Springs, Colo., 1991, Colo. Mountain Coll., Breckenridge, 1991, Pueblo, Colo., 1991, Keystone, Colo., 1991-92, Mont. Workshop Cowboy Artists of Am. Mus., 1993; represented in over 10 pvt. collections. Treas. Summit County Arts Coun., Breckenridge, 1991—; v.p. Art for Silverthorne, Colo., 1986-87. Named Grand Champion, Local Mountain Community Fair Juried Art Exhibit, 1989-91, Advanced Grand Champion, Regional Juried Fall Art Festival, Glenwood Springs, 1991, Reserve Grand Champion, 1st Place Popular Choice, Brush & Pallete Club Regional Juried Exhibit, Grand Junction, Colo., 1992. Home: PO Box 381 Dillon CO 80435 Office: Designs West II PO Box 381 Dillon CO 80435 also: Great Things West Gallery PO Box 4150 224 S Main St Breckenridge CO 80424

RUSSELL, THOMAS ARTHUR, lawyer; b. Corona, Calif., Aug. 2, 1953; s. Larry Arthur Russell and Patricia Helena (Collins) Heath; m. Mary Ellen Leach, June 20, 1992. BS, U. Calif., Berkeley, 1976; JD, U. So. Calif., 1982. Bar: Calif. 1983, U.S. Dist. Ct. (cen. dist.) Calif. 1983, U.S. Ct. Appeals (9th cir.) 1986, U.S. Supreme Ct. 1988. Law clk. Calif. Ct. Appeal, L.A., 1981; assoc. Graham & James, Long Beach, Calif., 1982-88; ptnr. Williams Woolley Cogswell Nakazawa & Russell, Long Beach, 1988—; speaker, panelist Nat. Marine Bankers Assn., Chgo. 1987—; mem. adv. bd. U. So. Calif. Environ. Law, L.A., 1985—; bd. dirs., Ctr. Internat. Comml. Arbitration; bd. dirs., exec. v.p. Internat. Bus. Assn. of So. Calif., 1989—; lectr. Pacific Admiralty Seminar, 1992. Author: (with others) Recreational Boating Law, 1992; co-founder U. So. Calif. Jour. Law and Environment. Mem. ABA (Bronze Key award 1982, chmn. subcom. yacht fin. 1993—), Maritime Law Assn. U.S. (proctor, fin. and recreational boating coms., chmn. subcom. on recreational boating edn. 1991—), Calif. Bar Assn., L.A. County Bar Assn., Long Beach Bar Assn., Legion of Lex Am. Inn of Ct. (barrister). Republican. Roman Catholic. Home: 7 Mustang Rd Rancho Palos Verdes CA 90274 Office: Williams Woolley Cogswell Nakazawa & Russell 200 Oceangate Ste 700 Long Beach CA 90802-4333

RUSSIN, ROBERT ISAIAH, sculptor, educator; b. N.Y.C., Aug. 26, 1914; s. Uriel and Olga (Winnett) R.; m. Adele Mutchnick, May 21, 1937; children: Joseph Mark, Lincoln David, Uriel Robin. BA, CCNY, 1933, MS, 1935; postgrad. (Inst. fellow), Beaux Arts Inst. Design, 1935-36. Tchr. sculpture Copper Union Art Inst., N.Y.C., 1944-47; prof. art U. Wyo., Laramie, 1947-86; prof., artist-in-residence U. Wyo., 1976-85, Disting. prof. emeritus, 1985—. One-man shows Tucson Fine Arts Ctr., 1966, Colorado Springs (Colo.) Fine Arts Ctr., 1967, Palm Springs (Calif.) Desert Mus., Chas. G. Bowers Meml. Mus., Judah L. Magnes Meml. Mus., Berkeley, Calif.; retrospective one-man exhbn. Nat. Gallery Modern Art, Santo Domingo, Dominican Republic, 1976, Tubac Ctr. of the Arts, Ariz., 1987, Riggins Gallery, Scottsdale, Ariz., 1989, Fine Arts Mus., U. Wyo., 1991; sculpture commns. include 2 8-foot metal figures, Evanston (Ill.) Post Office, 1939, three life-size carved figures, Conshohocken (Pa.) Post Office, 1940, Benjamin Franklin Monument, U. Wyo., 1957, Bust of Lincoln, Lincoln Mus., Washington, (now in Gettysburg Mus.), 1959, Lincoln Monument atop summit Lincoln Hwy. Wyo, 1959, monumental bas-relief bronze Cheyenne (Wyo.) Fed. Bldg, 1966, two carved wood walls, Denver Fed. Bldg., 1966, monumental fountain, City of Hope Med. Ctr., Los Angeles, 1966-67, statue, Brookhaven (N.Y.) Nat. Lab., 1968, life-size bronze sculpture fountain, Pomona Coll., 1969, monumental bronze sculpture Prometheus Natrona County (Wyo.) Pub. Library, 1974, Man and Energy, Casper (Wyo.) C. of C., 1974, 12-foot marble carving Menorah Med. Ctr., Kansas City, Mo., 1975, Einstein and Gershwin medals Magnes Meml. Mus, Berkeley, Nat. Mus. Art, Santo Domingo, Dominican Republic, 1975, monumental fountain, Galleria d'Arte Moderna, Santo Domingo, 1977, Duarte Monument, Santo Domingo, 1977, 30 foot steel and water fountain monument City Hall, Casper, 1980, marble and bronze monument, Lincoln Centre, Dallas, 1982, acrylic steel and bronze monument, Herschler State Office Bldg., Cheyenne, 1984, marble monument, U. Wyo., Laramie, 1985, portrait head Charles Bluhdorn, chmn. Gulf & Western, 1975, portrait bust Pres. J. Balaguer of Dominican Republic, 1975, portrait head G. Wilson Knight, Shakespearean actor and scholar, 1975, 2 12-foot bronze figures The Greeting and the Gift for Bicentennial Commn., Cheyenne, 1976, monumental marble head of Juan Pablo Duarte liberator Dominican Republic, Santo Domingo, 1976, marble sculpture Trio, U. Wyo., 1985, Isaac B. Singer medal for Magnes Mus., 1983, monumental Holocaust Figure Tucson Jewish Community Ctr., 1989, granite monument Chthonodynamis, Dept. Energy Bldg., Washington, 1992, bust Hon. Milward Simpson, 1993, bust James Forest U. Wis., 1993; contbr. articles to profl. jours. Recipient awards sec. fine arts U.S. Treasury, 1939, 40, Lincoln medal U.S. Congress, 1959, Alfred G.B. Steel award Pa. Acad. Fine Arts, 1961, medal of Order of Duarte Sanchez y Mella, Dominican Republic, 1977; Ford Found. fellow, 1953. Mem. Nat. Sculpture Conf. (exec. bd.), Sculptors Guild, Nat. Sculpture Soc., AIA, AAUP, Coll. Art Internat. Inst. Arts and Letters, Phi Beta Kappa (hon.). Home: 61 N Frk Rd Centennial WY 82055 also: 1160 Placita Salubre Green Valley AZ 85614

RUSSO, ALVIN LEON, obstetrician, gynecologist; b. Buffalo, Dec. 2, 1924; s. Anthony Joseph and Sarah (Leone) R.; m. Mary Rose Hehir, Sept. 19, 1953; children: Mary B., Sally A. Silvestri, Daniel J., Jeanne Wotherspoon, Margaret Battaile, Terri A., Anthony A. Student, Baylor U., Waco, Tex., 1943-44, U. Iowa, 1944; MD, U. Kans., Kansas City, 1949. Diplomate Am. Bd. Obstetrics and Gynecology. Intern, then resident E. J. Meyer Meml. Hosp., Buffalo, 1949-55; Fellow in gynocological oncology Roswell Park Meml. Inst., Buffalo, 1955; pvt. practice ob/gyn. San Bernardino, Calif., 1955-89; med. dir. San Bernardino Community Hosp., 1989-92; ret., 1992; bd. dirs. San Bernardino Community Hosp., 1982-89, chmn. bd., 1982-85. Pres. San Bernardino unit Am. Cancer Soc., 1961-62; bd. dirs. More Attractive Community Found. Capt. USAF, 1951-53. Knight, St. John of Jerusalem, 1986--; recipient Distinguished Member award Boy Scouts Am., 1987. Fellow Am. Coll. Ob-Gyns.; mem. AMA, Calif. Med. Assn., N.Y. Acad. Scis., S.W. Ob-Gyn. Soc. (coun. mem. 1989—, v.p. 1992), San Bernardino-Riverside Ob-Gyn. Soc. (pres. 1966), Lions Internat. (dep. dist. gov. 1962-63), Serra Club (pres. San Bernardino chpt.), Arrowhead Country Club (bd. dirs., pres.). Republican. Roman Catholic. Home: 3070 Pepper Tree Ln San Bernardino CA 92404-2313

RUSSO, LAURA, gallery director; b. Waterbury, Conn., Mar. 7, 1943; d. Lawrence and Lillian A. (Russo) Kaplan; m. John I. Lawrence, May 6, 1962 (div. 1974); children: Maia Giosi, Dylan Russo. Cert., Pacific N.W. Coll. Art, 1975. Art instr. Tucker Maxon Oral Sch., Portland, Oreg., 1970-74, Pacific N.W. Coll. of Art, Portland, 1977-78; assoc. dir. Fountain Fine Arts, Seattle, 1981-82; asst. dir. The Fountain Gallery of Art, Portland, 1975-86; owner, dir. The Laura Russo Gallery, Portland, 1986—; lectr. Seattle Art Mus., 1987, Portland State Coll., 1992; juror Oreg. Sch. Design, Portland, 1988, Western Oreg. State Coll. 1992, Beaverton Arts Commn., 1992; com. mem. Oreg. Com. for Nat. Mus. Women in Arts, 1988; lectr. Oregon Hist. Soc., 1990. Mem. com. award and grants Met. Arts Commn., Portland, 1988, 89; mem. P.N.C.A.; juror Art in Pub. Schs. Program, 1990. Mem. Alumni Friends, Contemporary Arts Coun. (program chmn., v.p. 1989-91), Oreg. Art Inst., Friends Print Soc., Oreg. Art Inst., L.A. Mus. Contemporary Art, Seattle Art Mus. Democrat. Office: Laura Russo Gallery 805 NW 21st Ave Portland OR 97209-1408

RUSSO, SALVATORE FRANKLIN, chemistry educator; b. Hartford, Conn., Feb. 6, 1938; s. Sebastiano and Serafina (Corpaci) R.; m. Betty McConaughy, July 3, 1964 (div. Feb. 1967); m. Judy Lee Watke, Aug. 19, 1967; children: Amy Kathryn, Alan Sebastian. BA, Wesleyan U., Middletown, Conn., 1960; PhD, Northwestern U., 1964. Lectr. Northwestern U., Evanston, Ill., 1963-64; research assoc. U. Wash., Seattle, 1964-67; asst. prof. Sacramento State Coll., 1967-68, Western Wash. State Coll., Bellingham, 1968-72; assoc. prof. Western Wash. U., Bellingham, 1972-83; prof. West Wash. U., Bellingham, 1983—; vis. faculty U. Colo., Boulder, 1977-78, 1984-85, Wash. State U., Pullman, summer 1980; vis. scientist COBE Labs., Lakewood, Colo., summer 1981. Editorial bd. Environmental Scis., 1990—; contbr. numerous articles to profl. jours. NIH fellow 1965-66, 66-67; grantee Research Corp. 1968, Western Wash. State Coll., 1969, COBE Labs., 1983. Mem. AAUP, Am. Chem. Soc., Protein Soc., Sigma Xi (local v.p. 1991-92, local pres. 1992-93). Presbyterian. Home: 2100 Niagara St Bellingham WA 98226-5912 Office: Western Wash U Chemistry Dept MS # 9058 Bellingham WA 98225

RUSSOM, JAMES RAYFORD, minister; b. Memphis, Dec. 9, 1949; s. Rayford Pinkney and Leola Jane (Briley) R.; m. Susan Theresa Smith, June 1, 1968; 1 child, Mark Stephen. AA in Biblical Lit., Nazarene Bible Coll., 1971; BA in Religion and Philosophy, Bethany Nazarene Coll., 1982; M Ministry, So. Nazarene U., 1988; postgrad., Western Sem., 1989. Ordained to ministry Ch. of the Nazarene, 1975. Youth minister Los Altos Ch. of Nazarene, Albuquerque, 1971-72; youth/assoc. pastor Buena park (Calif.) First Ch. of Nazarene, 1972-74; sr. pastor Long Beach (Calif.) Westside Ch. of Nazarene, 1974-78, Metroplex Fellow Ch. of Nazarene, Oklahoma City, 1978-86, Flagstaff (Ariz.) Ch. of Nazarene, 1986-92, San Jose (Calif.) Ch. of Nazarene, 1992—; pres. Celebration At Sea, Inc., Oklahoma City, 1982-86; regional pres. S. Cen. Regional Nazarene Youth Internat., Oklahoma City, 1981-86; dist. pres. N.W. Okla. Nazarene Youth Internat., Oklahoma City, 1981-83; cons., pres. Eagle Bus. Cons., 1982—. Author: God's Plan for Marital Success, 1990, also youth program and curriculum in field. Founder Helping Hands, Oklahoma City, 1983. Mem. Eastside Businessmen's Alliance. Republican.

RUST, LIBBY KAREN, fundraising counselor; b. York, Maine, Feb. 8, 1951; d. Myron Davis and Meta Mildred (Libby) R.; BA, Wheaton Coll., 1973; MS, Columbia U., 1977. Day care field asst. Childhood Ednl. Enrichment Program, Waterville, Maine, 1974-75; cons. Ctr. for Community Planning and Cons., N.Y.C., 1975-76; intern Morgan Guaranty Trust Co., N.Y.C., 1976; staff asst. subcom. on mental health Task Force on N.Y.C. Fiscal Crisis, 1976-77; auditor AT&T, N.Y.C., 1977; budget examiner Legis. Office of Budget Rev., N.Y.C., 1977-78; exec. dir. Strafford County Human Svcs., Dover, N.H., 1978-79; dir. allocations and agy. rels. United Way, Inc., Portland, Maine, 1979-82, planning and allocations div. dir., 1982-84; exec. dir. Seacoast United Way, Portsmouth, N.H., 1984-87; dir. devel. Am. Cancer Soc., L.A., 1987-88; assoc. dir. St. Vincent Med. Ctr., L.A., 1988-89; dir. ann. giving St. Joseph Hosp. Found., Orange, Calif., 1989-91, asst. dir. devel., 1991—. Mem. budget com. Town of York, 1979-80; trustee Kents Hill Sch. Mem. Jr. League Orange County, Kents Hill Sch. Alumni Assn. (pres.). Republican.

RUST, LYNN EUGENE, geologist; b. York, Nebr., Apr. 1, 1952; s. Dale E. and Wilma J. (Wetzel) R.; m. C. Olander, Aug. 1974 (div. May 1979); m. Kristie L. Graham, Sept. 19, 1987. BA in Geology and History, U. Colo., 1975, postgrad., 1976-77; postgrad., Casper Coll., 1979-80. Registered Profl. Geologist, Wyo. Solar observer NOAA/Environ. Rsch. Labs./Space Environ. Svcs. Ctr., Boulder, Colo., 1970-75; phys. sci. tech. Geol. div. U.S. Geol. Survey, Lakewood, Colo., 1976-77; dist. environ. scientist Conservation div. U.S. Geol. Survey, Billings, Mont., 1977-78; regional environ. scientist Conservaton div. U.S. Geol. Survey Minerals Mgmt. Svc., Casper, Wyo., 1978-82; asst. dist. supr. Minerals Mgmt. Svc., Casper, 1982-83; geologist/fluids specialist U.S. Bur. Land Mgmt., Cheyenne, Wyo., 1983-90; chief, br. solid minerals U.S. Bur. Land Mgmt., Cheyenne, 1990—; lectr., seminar presenter; panel leader, mem., moderator on numerous panels for fed. and industry mineral workshops and confs.; mem. 5 nat. task forces on fed. mineral regulation, 1982—. Mem. Cheyenne (Wyo.) Symphony Orch., 1989—, patron, 1991—. Recipient Individual Skylab award NASA, 1976, Unit citation NOAA, 1976. Mem. AAAS, Am. Geol. Inst., Geol. Soc. Am., Am. Mensa (Wyo. Proctor coord. 1988—). Methodist. Home: 6828 Bomar Dr Cheyenne WY 82009-2632 Office: US Bur of Land Mgmt 2515 Warren Ave Cheyenne WY 82001-3198

RUST, NICHOLAS CREGG, training executive, consultant; b. Idaho Falls, Idaho, May 31, 1946; s. Henry Dean and Marion (Maughan) R.; m. Pamela Westerberg, June 13, 1968; children: Cassandra Nichola, Nicholas Peter. Student, Utah State U., 1964-65, 67-68; BA, U. Pacific, 1970; MA, U. Ariz., 1972. Dir. Lodi Woodbridge Ctr., Calif., 1973-75; tng. specialist Idaho 1st Nat. Bank, Boise, 1978-80; asst. v.p., mgr. tng. Bank Idaho, 1st Interstate Bank, Boise, 1981-82; pres. Environ. Systems Inc., Boise, 1982—; tng. officer Bank Stockton, Calif., 1982-87; prin. The Tng. Advantage, 1986—; cons., 1981-82. Mem. Stockton City Coun., 1990—, Eagle Scout 1960, San Joaquin County Coun. of Gov's., adv. coun. Boy Scouts of Am. # 52, San Joaquin Republican Ctrl. Com. Mem. ASTD. Republican. Mem. LDS Ch. Office: City of Stockton 425 N El Dorado St Stockton CA 95202-1997

RUTAN, DOUGLAS EDWIN, administrator; b. Boise, Idaho, Apr. 24, 1949; s. Leonard Lyle and nancy (Etta) R.; m. Nancy Elizabeth Cooksey, June 9, 1973; children: Jessica, Sarah, Kathryn. BS in Edn., Northern Az. U., 1971; MS in Edn., U. Az., 1975; Ednl. Specialist, U. Idaho, 1990. Tchr. Yuma (Az.) Sch. Dist., 1971-76; tchr. Meridian (Idaho) Sch. Dist., 1976-77, sch. prin., 1977-91, dir. spl. svcs., 1991—. Sec. Meridian (Idaho) Rotary Club, 1988-93, pres. elect, 1993; mem. Idaho State Centennial Commn., 1990, Meridian Centennial Commn., 1992-93. Recipient Idaho Gem award Idaho Assn. Elem. Prin., Boise, 1986, Excellence in Edn. award nat. Assn. Elem. Prin., Washington, 1991; named Adminstr. of Yr., Ada County Edn. Office Personnel, Boise, 1991. Mem. Coun. for Exceptional Children, Idaho Assn. Sch. Adminstrs., Meridian C. of C. Republican. Presbyterian. Home:

10421 Dason Dr Boise ID 83704 Office: Meridian Sch Dist 911 Meridian St Meridian ID 83642

RUTAN, RICHARD GLENN (DICK RUTAN), aircraft company executive; b. Loma Linda, Calif., July 1, 1938; s. George and Irene Rutan. BS, Am. Tech. U., 1975; D Sci. and Tech. (hon.), Cen. New Eng. Coll., 1987; HHD (hon.), Lewis U., 1989. Commd. 2d lt. USAF, 1959, advanced through grades to lt. col., 1976, ret., 1978; prodn. mgr., chief test pilot Rutan Aircraft Factory, Mojave, Calif., 1978-81; pres. Voyager Aircraft Inc., Mojave, 1981—; mng. dir. Bob Pond Race Team. Rep. nomination to 42d Congrl. Dist. (Calif.), 1992. Decorated Silver Star, D.F.C. with silver oak leaf cluster, Purple Heart, Air medals (16); recipient Louis Bleroit medal Fedn. Aeronautique Internationale, 1982, Collier trophy Nat. Aviation Club, 1986, Presdl. Citizen's Medal of Honor, 1986, Godfrey L. Cabot award Aero Club New Eng., 1987, Patriot of Yr. award, 1987, Newsmaker of Yr. award Aviation Writers Am., 1987, Daedalian Disting. Achievement award, 1987, Lindbergh Eagle award San Diego Aerospace Mus., 1987, Iven C. Kincheloe award Soc. Exptl. Test Pilots, 1987, Gold medal Royal Aero Club, Grande Medallion, Medalle de Ville Paris Paris Aero Club, World Record for 1st closed circuit, great circle distance around-the-world, non-stop, non-refueled flight, numerous others. Office: Voyager Aircraft Inc Hangar 77 1260 Flight Line Mojave CA 93501

RUTHERFORD, JAMES CHARLES, science and computer educator; b. Oakland, Calif., Aug. 27, 1946; s. Charles Kenneth and Elinor Margaret (Frazier) R.; m. Diane Edith Hammond, Mar. 15, 1983 (div. 1990). BS in Biology, Calif. State U., Hayward, 1968; MS in Zoology, U. Calif., Berkeley, 1971, PhD in Zoology, 1975. Asst. prof. zoology Oreg. State U., Corvallis, 1975-76; asst. prof. biology U. Hawaii, Hilo, 1976-80; salesperson Bowman Distbr., Kamuela, Hawaii, 1980-84; sci. tchr. Hawaii Preparatory Acad., Kamuela, 1984-86, Parker Sch., Kamuela, 1986—. Contbr. chpt. to book and articles to profl. jours. Treas. Bodega Marine Scis. Assn., Bodega Bay, Calif., 1971-75; bd. dirs. Kawaihae (Hawaii) Canoe Club, 1988-90. Recipient Rsch. grant NSF, 1971-75. Home: PO Box 725 Kamuela HI 96743 Office: Parker Sch Box 429 Kamuela HI 96743

RUTHSODOTTER, MARY ESTHER, project administrator; b. Fairfield, Iowa, Oct. 14, 1944; d. Ernest Edward and Ruth Eleanor (Moyer) Pegau; m. David E. Crawford, Aug. 29, 1964; 1 child, Alice Elizabeth. BA, UCLA, 1973. Adminstrv. analyst UCLA, 1971-77; projects dir. Nat. Women's History Project, Windsor, Calif., 1980—; chair Commn. on the Status of Women, Santa Rosa, Calif., 1978-79; cons. Calif. State Dept. of Edn., Sacramento, 1980-88; founder Women's Support Network, Santa Rosa, 1979; co-founder Nat. Women's History Project, Santa Rosa, 1980. Co-producer (video series) Women in American Life, 1990 (video) Las Mujeres, 1992. Co-chair Cherry St. Neighborhood Assn., Santa Rosa, 1990-92; vol. numerous progressive political campaigns, Sonoma County, Calif., 1977—. Named Woman of Yr. YWCA, 1980. Mem. NOW, Orgn. of Am. Historians, Nat. Coalition for Sex Equity in Edn., Women's Heritage Mus., Nat. Women's Polit. Caucus. Office: Nat Women's History Project 7738 Bell Rd Windsor CA 95492

RUTKOFF, ANANDA C., financial consultant; b. N.Y.C., Dec. 19, 1956; s. Murray and Tinette (Sherman) R. BS summa cum laude, Boston U., 1977. Chmn. Associated Media, Beverly Hills, Calif. Author: Global Leadership Perspecitves, 1993. Office: Associated Media Ste 404 8530 Wilshire Blvd Beverly Hills CA 90211

RUTLEDGE, D. MASON, youth minister, speaker; b. Seattle, Dec. 3, 1964; s. Donald Mervin and Louise Helen Ann (Berggren) R.; m. Brenda Grace Thuring, Nov. 9, 1991. BA in Comm., Wash. State U., 1988. Corp. comm. coord. Egghead Discount Software, Issaquah, Wash., 1988-90; area dir. Young Life, Edmonds, Wash., 1990—. Mem. faculty Rocky Mountain Greek Conf., Moscow, Idaho, 1989; trustee The Benefit Gang, Seattle, 1988-91. Mem. Pub. Rels. Soc. Am., Phi Kappa Tau (mem. faculty Leadership Acad. 1988-90, guest lectr. nat. conv. 1989). Lutheran. Office: Young Life PO Box 11 Lynnwood WA 98046-0011

RUTLEDGE, DAVID WAYNE, lawyer, distribution company executive; b. Lexington, Ky., Dec. 28, 1952; s. Farris and Irene (True) R.; m. Dana Nelson, Aug. 16, 1980; children: Brian, Austin. BS, U. Ky., 1974, JD, 1977; MBA, Vanderbilt U., 1985. Bar: Ky. 1977. Staff atty. Ashland (Ky.) Oil Inc., 1977-79; assoc. Woodward, Hobson & Fulton, Louisville, 1979; staff atty. Ingram Industries Inc., Nashville, 1979-83, asst. sec., 1981-86, assoc. counsel, 1983-86, v.p., gen. counsel, sec., 1986-91; sr. v.p. adminstrn. Ingram Micro Inc., Santa Ana, Calif., 1991—. Mem. ABA, Tenn. Bar Assn., Ky. Bar Assn.

RUTLEDGE, THOMAS ALEXANDER, prosecutor; b. Erie, Pa., Aug. 29, 1947; s. Thomas Alexander and Muriel Jeanette (Norris) R.; m. Carol Ann Wheaton, May 26, 1973; children: Bryan Lee, Sean Michael, Corrie Elizabeth. BA, U. N.Mex., 1970, JD, 1975. Bar: N.Mex. 1975, U.S. Dist. Ct. N.Mex. 1975, U.S. Ct. Appeals (10th cir.) 1979, U.S. Supreme Ct. 1980. Assoc. Martin & Hilton, P.A., Albuquerque, 1975-77; dep. dist. atty. Fifth Jud. Dist. Atty., Carlsbad, N.Mex., 1977-84, dist. atty., 1985—; pvt. practice Carlsbad, 1984; dist. atty. rep. N.Mex. Sentencing Guidelines Commn., Santa Fe, 1989—. Com. mem. Western States Hazardous Waste Project, Phoenix, 1989—; pres. Boys and Girls Club of Carlsbad, 1984-85; treas. Boy Scouts Am., 1990. With U.S. Army, 1970-72. Recipient Govt. Leader Against Drunk Drivers award MADD, Albuquerque, 1988, 1990. Mem. Nat. Dist. Attys. Assn., N.Mex. Dist. Attys. Assn. (pres. 1989-90), N.Mex. State Bar (prosecutor's sect. 1991—), Eddy County Bar Assn. (pres. 1991—), Elks. Republican. Methodist. Office: Dist Atty 5th Jud Dist PO Box 1448 Carlsbad NM 88221-1448

RUTLEDGE, WILLIAM P., manufacturing company executive; b. 1942. BS, Lafayette Coll., 1963; MS, George Washington U., 1967. With Bethlehem Steel Corp., 1963-68, foreman; with Stamco Sales Co., 1968-71, sales engr.; successively bus. planner, works mgr., dir. planning, div. mgr. FMC Corp., 1971-86; with Teledyne Inc., 1986—, group exec., v.p., 1987-88, sr. v.p., 1988-90, pres., 1990-91, pres., CEO, 1991—, also bd. dirs. Office: Teledyne Inc 1901 Avenue Of The Stars Los Angeles CA 90067-6001*

RUTSALA, VERN A., poet, English language educator, writer; b. Feb. 5, 1934; s. Ray Edwin and Virginia Mae (Brady) R.; m. Joan Merle Colby, Apr. 6, 1957; children: Matthew, David, Kirsten. BA, Reed Coll., 1956; MFA, U. Iowa, 1960. Instr. Lewis and Clark Coll., Portland, 1961-64, asst. prof., 1964-69, assoc. prof., 1969-76, prof., 1976—; vis. prof. U. Minn., Mpls., 1968-69, Bowling Green (Ohio) State U., 1970; writer-in-residence U. Idaho, Moscow, 1988, Redlands (Calif.) U., 1979; chair English dept. Lewis and Clark, Portland, 1986-89. Author: The Window, 1964, Laments, 1975, The Journey Begins, 1976, Paragraphs, 1978, Walking Home from the Icehouse, 1981, Backtracking, 1985, Ruined Cities, 1987, Selected Poems, 1991. With U.S. Army, 1956-58. Guggenheim Found. fellow, 1982-83, NEA fellow, 1975, 79, Masters fellow Oreg. Arts Commn., 1990; recipient Carolyn Kizer prize Western Oreg. State Coll., 1988, N.W. Poets prize N.W. Rev., 1975, Hazel Hall award Oreg. Inst. Lit. Arts, 1992, Juniper prize U. Mass. Press, 1993. Mem. AAUP, PEN, Poetry Soc. Am. Office: Lewis and Clark Coll Dept English Portland OR 97212

RUTTENBERG, HERBERT DAVID, pediatric cardiologist, pediatrics educator; b. Phila., June 14, 1930; s. Edward Harold and Goldene (Moss) R.; m. Diane Claire Hanson, July 30, 1955; children: Julia Ann, Kathleen Claire, Carolyn Jeanne, Loretta Lynne; m. Susan Rucker Ruttenberg, Aug. 17, 1979; children: Tamara Waller, Christian Waller, Carter Waller. BA, UCLA, 1952, MD, 1956. Intern San Francisco County Hosp., U. Calif., San Francisco, 1956-57; resident in pediatrics U. Minn., Mpls., 1957-58, 60-61, fellow in pediatric cardiology, 1961-63; rsch. fellow, dept. physiology and biophysics U. Wash., Seattle, 1963-64; asst. prof. pediatrics UCLA, 1964-69; chief, div. pediatric cardiology U. Utah Sch. Medicine, Salt Lake City, 1969-84, prof. pediatrics and pathology, 1984—; chief pediatrics USAF, Myrtle Beach AFB, S.C., 1958-60;. Author: (book chpts.) Corrected Transposition and Splenic Syndrome, Preventive Cardiology in Children, 1992. Bd. dirs. Park City (Utah) Chamber Music Soc., 1989—; mem. Wasatch Community Symphony, Salt Lake City, 1990—. Capt. USAF, 1958-60. Fellow Am. Acad. Pediatrics (chpt. pres. 1978), Am. Coll. Cardiology (gov. Utah 1970); mem. Am. Heart Assn. (regional v.p. 1987-88), Am. Pediatric Soc., Phi Beta Kappa. Home: 4981 N Silver Springs Rd Park City UT 84060-5908 Office: Univ Utah Sch of Medicine 100 N Medical Dr Salt Lake City UT 84113-1100

RUTTENBERG, JOHN JOSEPH, career officer; b. Redondo Beach, Calif., July 27, 1963; s. Bradley Jay and Karen Raye (Krake) R.; m. Nancy Repalda Gajes, May 16, 1991. BS in English, U.S. Naval Acad., 1985. Lic. naval aviator, comml. pilot, 1988. Commd. ensign USN, 1985, advanced through grades to lt., 1989; with detachment ops. HSL-37 Barbers Point, Hawaii, 1989, adminstrv. officer, 1990, with detachment maintenance, 1990-91, ops. officer, 1991; detachment officer-in-charge, HSL-41 North Island, Calif., 1991-92; flight instr. USS Robert E. Peary, 1989, USS Oldendorf, 1990-91, USS Brewton, 1991-92. Contbr. articles to profl. jours. Mem. Operation Handclasp, Western Pacific, 1989-91, Greenpeace, Hawaii, 1988—. Decorated 3 Air medals, 1991. Mem. Navy Helicopter Assn., Naval Inst., Cousteau Soc. Roman Catholic.

RUTTER, DEBORAH FRANCES, orchestra administrator; b. Pottstown, Pa., Sept. 30, 1956; d. Marshall Anthony and Winifred (Hitz) R. BA, Stanford U., 1978; MBA, U. So. Calif., 1985. Orch. mgr. L.A. Philharm., 1978-86; exec. dir. L.A. Chamber Orch., 1986-92, Seattle Symphony, 1992—. Bd. dirs. AIDS project L.A., 1985-92; active Jr. League L.A., 1982-92. Mem. Am. Symphony Orch. League, Assn. Calif. Symphony Orchs. (pres. 1988-91), Assn. N.W. Symphony Orchs. (bd. dirs. 1993—), Chamber Music Soc. L.A. (bd. dirs. 1987-92), Ojai Festival (pres.'s coun.). Democrat. Episcopalian. Office: Seattle Symphony Ctr House 305 Harrison St 4th Fl Seattle WA 98109

RUTTER, THOMAS ALBERT, electrical engineer, consultant; b. Havanna, Cuba, Mar. 23, 1931; came to U.S., 1932; s. Elry Lee and Anne Marie (Clausen) R.; m. Lavern Isobel Nelson, Feb. 14, 1952; children: Vernon, David, Kerry, Thomas II, Shanne. BSEE, Gonzaga U., 1963. Techn. Bonnville Power Adminstrn., Spokane, Wash., 1959-63; aerospace tech. NASA, Waliops Island, Va., 1963-65; engr. Motorola Aerospace Ctr., Phoenix, 1965-67, Unidynamics Phoenix, Litchfield Park, Ariz., 1967-68, Carr Inlet Acoustic Range, Bremerton, Wash., 1968-83, NAUSEADET (PERA-CV), Bremerton, 1983—; cons. Rutter and Sons., Bremerton, 1978—. Active Spokane (Wash.) Coun. Boy Scouts Am., 1958-59, Sci. Fair Bd., Bremerton, 1971-72. Mem. Nat. Soc. Tax Preparers. Church of Jesus Christ of Latter Day Saints. Home: 7525 Navajo Trail Bremerton WA 98310 Office: NAUSEADET (Pera-CV) 1305 Ironsides Ave Bremerton WA 98310

RUTZ, JAMES HENRY, writer; b. Aruba, Sept. 21, 1938; came to U.S., 1942; s. Jack Harold and Ruth (Thorpe) R. AA, Fullerton Jr. Coll., Fullerton, 1959; student, UCLA, 1960, L.A. State U., 1960; BA, San Francisco State U., 1961, MA, 1964. Direct distbr. Amway, Whittier, Calif., 1965-77; freelance writer Colorado Springs, Colo., 1973—; chmn. bd. dirs. Campus-by-the-Sea, Catalina Island, Calif., 1972-75; founder Strategic Careers Project, Colorado Springs, 1991—. Author: Come Run with Me, 1979, The Open Church, 1992; contbr. articles to mags. Founder Open Ch. Ministries, Colorado Springs, 1990—. With Calif. Nat. Guard, 1957-63. Mem. Nat. Assn. Evangelists. Republican. Office: PO Box 38519 Colorado Springs CO 80937

RUYBALID, LOUIS ARTHUR, social worker, community development consultant; b. Allison, Colo., Apr. 6, 1925; s. Mike Joseph and Helen Mary (Rodriguez) R.; m. Seraphima Alexander, June 12, 1949; children: Mariana, John. BA, U. Denver, 1946-49, MSW, 1951; PhD, U. Calif., Berkeley, 1970; Professor Ad-Honorem (hon.), Nat. U., Caracas, Venezuela, 1964. Social worker Ariz., Calif., Colo., 1951-62; advisor community devel. Unitarian Service Com., Caracas, 1962-64, U.S. Agy. for Internat. Devel., Rio de Janeiro, Brazil, 1964-66; area coordinator U.S. Office Econ. Opportunity, San Francisco, 1966-68; prof., dept. head U. So. Colo., Pueblo, 1974-80; licensing analyst State of Calif., Campbell, 1984—; prof. sch. of social work Highlands U., Las Vegas, N.Mex., 1988-89; cons. UN, Caracas, 1978, Brazilian Govt., Brazilia, 1966-67, Venezuelan Govt., Caracas, 1962-64. Author: (books) Favela, 1970, Glossary for Hominology, 1978, (research instrument) The Conglomerate Hom., 1976. Mem. exec. com. Pueblo (Colo.) Regional Planning Com., 1974-79, Nat. Advisory com. The Program Agy. United Presbyn. Ch., 1978-79. Served with USN, 1944-46. Recipient Pro Mundo Beneficio medal Brazilian Acad. Human Sci., Sao Paulo, 1976; United Def. Fund fellow U. Calif., Berkeley, 1961-62, Cert. World Leadership Internat. Leaders of Achievement, 1988-89. Mem. NASW (cert.), Ethnic Minority Commn., IMAGE (nat. edn. chair), Am. Hominol. Assn. (nat. pres. 1975-79), U. Calif. Alumni Assn., AARP (minority spokesperson), Phi Beta Kappa, Phi Sigma Iota. Democrat. Home and Office: Ruybalid Assoc Inc 129 Calle Don Jose Santa Fe NM 85701

RUYTER, NANCY LEE CHALFA, dance educator; b. Phila., May 23, 1933; d. Andrew Benedict Chalfa and Lois Elizabeth (Strode) McClary; m. Ralph Markson (div.); m. Hans C. Ruyter, Dec. 7, 1968. BA in History, U. Calif., Riverside, 1964; PhD in History, Claremont Grad. Sch., 1970. Tchr. theater dept. Pomona Coll., 1965-72; instr. dance program U. Calif., Riverside, 1972-76, acting chair dance program, 1974-75; instr. dance dept. UCLA, 1976; instr. phys. edn. dept. Orange Coast Coll., 1976-77; asst. prof. dept. phys. edn. and dance Tufts U., 1977-78; asst. prof. phys. edn. dept. Calif. State U., Northridge, 1978-82; asst. prof., then assoc. prof. dance dept. U. Calif., Irvine, 1982—, assoc. dean Sch. Fine Arts, 1984-88, chair dept. dance, 1989-91; presenter in field. Appeared with Jasna Planina Folk Ensemble, 1972-77, 78-79, Di Falco and Co., 1955-57; choreographer, dir. numerous coll. dance prodns.; contbr. articles, revs. to profl. publs.; author: Reformers and Visionaries: The Americanization of the Art of Dance, 1979. Mem. Am. Soc. Theatre Rsch., Bulgarian Studies Assn., Congress on Rsch. in Dance (bd. dirs. 1977-80, pres. 1981-85), Dance Critics Assn., Folk Dance Fedn., Internat. Fedn. Theatre Rsch., Soc. Dance Rsch., Soc. Ethnomusicology, Soc. Dance History Scholars (steering com. 1980-81), Spanish Dance Soc., Theatre Libr. Assn. Office: U Calif-Irvine Dept Dance Irvine CA 92717

RYAN, ALDEN HOOVER, electronic physicist, author; b. Scutari, Turkey, July 26, 1913; s. Arthur Clayton and Edith (Hoover) R.; m Sarah Mildred Haines, June 14, 1941; 1 child, Richard C. PhD, Iowa State U., 1939. Div. supt. Naval Rsch. Lab., Washington, 1943-56; mgr. microwave lab. GE, Palo Alto, Calif., 1956-59; pres. Emtec, Palo Alto, Calif., 1960-62; cons. various aerospace cos., 1963—; Author sci. and outdoor books, 1970—; contbr. articles to profl. jours. Roman Catholic. Home: PO Box 3909 West Sedona AZ 86340

RYAN, ARTHUR NORMAN, movie company executive; b. Gloucester, Mass., Dec. 22, 1938; s. Arthur Stanley and Mary (Ross) R.; children: Maya, Mark. B.S. in Polit. Sci, Suffolk U., Boston, 1962. Sr. acct. Price Waterhouse & Co., N.Y.C., 1962-66; asst. treas. Paramount Pictures, N.Y.C., 1966-67; dir. adminstrn. and bus. affairs Paramount Pictures, L.A., 1967-70, v.p. prodn. adminstrn., 1970-75, sr. v.p. prodn. ops., 1975-76; pres., chief operating officer Technicolor, Inc., L.A., 1976-83, vice chmn., chief exec. officer, 1983-84, chmn., chief exec. officer, 1985-91; chmn. bd., chief exec. officer Compact Video Svcs., Inc., 1984-87; chmn. exec. com. Four Star Internat. Inc., 1984-87. Bd. dirs. Hollywood Canteen Found., trustee Calif. Inst. Arts, vice chmn., 1985—. Served with inf. U.S. Army, 1963. Mem. Acad. Motion Picture Arts and Scis., Acad. TV Arts and Scis.

RYAN, CATHRINE SMITH, publisher; b. Calif.; d. Owen W. and Margarette D. Griffin; A.A., Bellevue Jr. Coll., Denver, 1948; grad. Barnes Sch. Commerce, Denver, 1950; student N.Y. Ballet Acad., 1954. Dir. Ballet Workshop, Enumclaw, Wash., 1958-64; dir. confs. and seminars San Francisco Theol. Sem., 1977-80; pres., dir. Cathi, Ltd., pub. and cons. office orgn. and mgmt., San Francisco, 1980—; freelance travel photographer, 1968-80; guest instr. in field; guest lectr. on German rsch. Recipient various certs. of recognition. Republican. Mormon. Author: Face Lifting Exercises, 1980, Sullivan's Chain, 1986; contbr. articles to procedure and policy manuals, geneal. rsch., family histories; translator old German script. Avocation: scuba diving.

RYAN, CLARENCE AUGUSTINE, JR., biochemistry educator; b. Butte, Mont., Sept. 29, 1931; s. Clarence A. Sr. and Agnes L. (Duckham) R.; m. Patricia Louise Meunier, Feb. 8, 1936; children: Jamie Arlette, Steven Michael (dec.), Janice Marie, Joseph Patrick (dec.). BA in Chemistry, Carroll Coll., 1953; MS in Chemistry, Mont. State U., 1956, PhD in Chemistry, 1959. Postdoctoral fellow in biochemistry Oreg. State U., Corvallis, 1959-61, U.S. Western Regional Lab., Albany, Calif., 1961-63; chemist U.S. Western Regional Lab., Berkeley, Calif., 1963-64; asst. prof. biochemistry Wash. State U., Pullman, 1964-68, assoc. prof., 1968-72, prof., 1972—, Charlotte Y. Martin disting. prof., 1991—, chmn. dept. agrl. chemistry, 1977-80, fellow Inst. Biol. Chemistry, 1980—; faculty athletics rep. to PAC-10 & NCAA Wash. State U., 1991—; vis. scientist dept. biochemistry U. Wash., 1981, Harvard U. Med. Sch., 1982; cons. Kemin Industries, Des Moines, 1981—, Plant Genetics, Davis, Calif., 1987-89; research adv. bd. Frito-Lay, Inc., Dallas, 1982, Plant Genetic Engring. Lab., N.M. State U., Las Cruces, 1986-89; mem. adv. rev. bd. Plant Gene Exptl. Ctr., Albany, Calif., 1990-93; mgr. biol. stress program USDA Competitve Grants Program, Washington, 1983-84; former mem. adv. panels for H. McKnight Found., Internat. Potato Ctr., Lima, Peru, Internat. Ctr. Genetic Engring. and Biotech., New Delhi, Internat. Ctr. Tropical Agr., Cali, Columbia, Internat. Tropical Agr., Ibandan, Africa; mem. grant rev. panels NSF, USDA, DOE, NIH; co-organizer Internat. Telecommunications Symposium on Plant Biotech. Mem. edit. bd. several biochem. and plant physiology jours.; contbr. articles to profl. publs., chpts. to books; co-editor 2 books. Grantee USDA, NSF, NIH, Rockefeller Found., McKnight Foun.; recipient Merch award for grad. research Mont. State U., 1959, career devel. awards NIH, 1964-74, Alumni Achievement award Carroll Coll., 1986, Pres.'s Faculty Excellence award in research Wash. State U., 1986; named to Carroll Coll. Alumni Hall Fame, 1981; Carroll Coll. Basketball Hall Fame, 1982. Mem. AAAS, Nat. Acad. Scis. (elected 1986), Am. Chem. Soc. (Kenneth A. Spencer award 1993), Am. Soc. Plant Physiology (Steven Hales Prize 1992), Am. Soc. Exptl.Biology, Biochem. Soc., Internat. Soc. Chem. Ecology, Internat. Soc. Plant Molecular Biology (bd. dirs.), Phytochem. Soc. N.Am., Nat. U. Continuing Assn. (Creative Programming award 1991), Phi Kappa Phi (Recognition award 1976, selected 1 of 100 centennial disting. alumni Mont. State U. 1993). Democrat. Office: Wash State Univ Inst Biol Chemistry Pullman WA 99164

RYAN, FREDERICK JOSEPH, JR., lawyer, public official; b. Tampa, Fla., Apr. 12, 1955; s. Frederick Joseph and Cordelia Beth (Hartman) R.; m. Genevieve Ann McSweeney, Dec. 28, 1985; 1 child, Genevieve Madeline. BA, U. So. Calif., 1977, JD, 1980. Bar: Calif. 1980, D.C. 1986. Assoc. Hill, Farrer and Burrill, Los Angeles, 1980-82; dep. dir. then dir. presdl. appointments and scheduling The White House, Washington, 1982-87, dir. pvt. sector initiatives, 1985-87, asst. to the Pres., 1987-89; chief of staff Office of Ronald Reagan, L.A., 1989—; mem. staff Reagan-Bush Campaign, Los Angeles, 1980; dir. Internat. Conf. on Pvt. Sector Initiatives, Paris, 1986, Italian-Am. Conf. on Pvt. Sector Initiatives, 1987, Brit.-Am. Conf. on Pvt. Sector Initiatives, 1988. Author (column) Legal Briefs, 1980-82. Chmn. Monterey Pk. (Calif.) Community Relations Commn., 1977-78. Recipient Presdl. Commendation for pvt. sector initiatives Pres. Ronald Reagan, 1986, Medal of Arts and Letters, Govt. of France, 1986, Golden Ambrosiana medal of Milan, Italy, 1987, The Lion of Venice medal, Italy, 1987, Medal of Order of Merit of Republic of Italy, 1992. Mem. ABA. Presbyterian. Office: Office of Ronald Reagan 34th Fl 2121 Ave of the Stars Los Angeles CA 90067

RYAN, HAROLD L., federal judge; b. Weiser, Idaho, June 17, 1923; s. Frank D.R. and Luella Neibling R.; m. Ann Dagres, Feb. 17, 1961; children: Michael C., Timothy F., Thomas P. Student, U. Idaho, 1941-43, U. Wash., 1943-44, U. Notre Dame, 1944; LL.B., U. Idaho, 1950. Bar: Idaho. Atty., 1950—; pros. atty. Washington County, Idaho, 1951-52; mem. Idaho State Senate, 1962-66; judge U.S. Dist Ct. Idaho, 1981—, chief judge, 1988-92, sr. judge, 1992—. Mem. Am. Bd. Trial Advocates, Idaho Bar Assn., Idaho Assn. Def. Counsel, Idaho Trial Lawyers Assn. Office: US Dist Ct Federal Bldg Box 040 550 W Fort St Boise ID 83724

RYAN, JOHN EDWARD, federal judge; b. Boston, Jan. 22, 1941; s. Howard Frederick and Mary (Burke) R.; m. Terri Reynolds; children: Valerie, Jennifer, Keely. BSEE, U.S. Naval Acad., 1963; LLB, Georgetown U., 1972; MS, Pacific Christian U., 1979. Assoc. Hale and Dorr, Boston, 1972-76, C.F. Braun, Alhambra, Calif., 1976-77; gen. counsel Altec Corp., Anaheim, Calif., 1977-79; v.p., sr. atty. Oak Industries, San Diego, 1979-82; sr. v.p. Oak Media, San Diego, 1982-84; ptnr. Dale and Lloyd, La Jolla, Calif., 1984-85, Jennings, Engstrand and Henrikson, San Diego, 1985-86; bankruptcy judge U.S. Bankruptcy Ct., Santa Ana, Calif., 1986—; ex officio dir. Orange County Bankruptcy Forum, chmn. spl. projects com. With USN, 1963-69. Mem. Mass. Bar Assn., Calif. Bar Assn., Orange County Bar Assn., Bankruptcy Judges Assn. Republican. Roman Catholic. Home: 3155 Summit Dr Escondido CA 92025-7529 Office: US Bankruptcy Ct PO Box 12600 Santa Ana CA 92712-2600

RYAN, MARK STEPHEN, coast guard officer; b. Methuen, Mass., Mar. 4, 1958; s. Francis James and Marion Ruth (Young) R.; m. Cornelia Lea Marin, Aug. 30, 1986; children: John Francis, Michael Sharkey. BS in Tech. Studies, SUNY, Albany, 1987. Helicopter pilot U.S. Army, Ft. Ord, Calif., 1984-88; rescue helicopter pilot USCG Air Sta., Cape Cod, Mass., 1988-91, Kodiak, Alaska, 1991—. Contbr. search and rescue stories to AP, Anchorage, 1991. Coach, adminstr. Kodiak Youth Baseball League, 1992. Lt. USCG, 1984—. Recipient Sikorsky Rescue award Sikorsky Aircraft Corp., Stratford, Conn., 1984, Army Commendation medal., 1985, 88. Home: PO Box 190628 Kodiak AK 99619 Office: CGAS Kodiak PO Box 33 Kodiak AK 99619

RYAN, MARY ELIZABETH, writer, editor, business owner; b. Seattle, Aug. 19, 1953; d. Leo Thomas Jr. and Lorraine Doris (Joseph) R.; m. Brent D. Youlden, Feb. 4, 1989. Cert., London Film Sch., 1974; BFA in Film/TV, NYU, 1977; MA in English, U. Wash., 1987. Copywriter Catalano and Gornick, N.Y.C., 1977-78; adminstr. The New Yorker Mag., N.Y.C., 1978-80; staff Coldwell Banker Residential, San Francisco, 1980-81; editorial cons. Andrews and Robb Lit. Agy., Seattle, 1983-85; student records coord. MPA dept. Seattle U., 1984; grant writer N.W. Renewable Resources, Seattle, 1984-85; adminstrv. asst. Bogle and Gates Law Firm, Seattle, 1985-88; legal asst. Helsell and Fetterman, Seattle, 1988-89; owner WordCrafters N.W., Seattle, 1989—. Author: Dance a Step Closer, 1984 (U. Iowa Outstanding Book 1985), I'd Rather Be Dancing, 1989, My Sister is Driving Me Crazy, 1991 (N.Y. Pub. Libr. Best List 1992), Me, My Sister and I, 1992 (N.Y. Pub. Libr. Best List 1993). Judge Bumbershoot Lit. Competition, Seattle, 1981; featured speaker Young Writers Conf., Ea. Wash. U., Cheney, Wash., 1985; speaker Wash. Communications Conf., Seattle, 1985; honoree Nat. Coun. Tchrs. of English, Seattle, 1991. Recipient Stegner fellowship Stanford U., 1982-83, Hoynes fellowship U. Va., 1982, grant Carnegie Fund for Writers, 1984, 85, grant PEN Am. Ctr., 1985. Mem. AFTRA, Authors Guild/Authors League (award 1985), Poets and Writers, Pacific N.W. Writers. Democrat. Unitarian. Office: WordCrafters NW # 202 4137 University Way NE Seattle WA 98105

RYAN, MARY GENE, military officer; b. Corona, Calif., Sept. 11, 1953; d. Robert James and Genevieve Louise (Kubilis) Guzinski; m. Robert Eldon Ryan III, June 9, 1979; children: Michael Warren, Jessica Gene, Matthew James. BSN, So. Conn. State Coll., 1975; MPH, U. Tex., 1980. Commd. 2d lt. USAF, 1976, advanced through grades to maj., 1987; staff nurse obstetrics U. Conn. Med. Ctr., Farmington, 1975-76; med.-surgical staff nurse Williams AFB (Ariz.) Hosp., 1976-77; flight nurse instr. 2d Aeromed. Evacuation Squadron, Rhein Main, Fed. Republic of Germany, 1977-79; officer in charge environ. health Wilford Hall Med. Ctr., Lackland AFB, Tex., 1980-84; chief environ. health AFSC Hosp., Edwards AFB, Calif., 1984-88; dir. occupational health Peterson Med. Clinic, Oxnard, Calif., 1988-89; mgr. health and safety County of Ventura (Calif.)/Gen. Svcs. Agy., 1989—; cons. environ. health L.A. AFB, 1984-88; chief nurse Calif. Air Nat. Guard 146 TAC Hosp., 1992—. Contbr. articles to profl. jours. Mem. choir, soloist, lay eucharistic minister Edwards AFB Cath. Chapel, 1984-88, mem. religious edn. com., 1984-85, lectr., commentator, 1986-87; AIDS educator, Edwards AFB, 1986-88. Recipient Meritorious Svc. medals USAF, Clin. award Am. Assn. Occupational Health Nurses, 1991. Mem. Am. Pub. Health Assn. (occupational health sect.), Am. Assn. Occupational Health Nurses, Calif. Assn. Occupational Health Nurses, Calif. Ctrl. Coast

Occupational Health Nurses Assn. (pres. 1993—), Ventura County Med. Aux. Office: County of Ventura/Gen Svcs Agy 800 S Victoria Ave Ventura CA 93009-0001

RYAN, MICHAEL LOUIS, controller; b. Corning, Iowa, Feb. 22, 1945; s. Leo Vincent and Elda May (Lawrence) R. AAS in Constrn. Tech., Iowa State U., 1965; BS in Acctg., Drake U., 1972. CPA, Iowa, Wyo. Acct. Ernst & Ernst, Des Moines, 1972-75, Becker, Herrick & Co., Pueblo, Colo., 1975-78; pvt. practice acctg. Gillette, Wyo., 1978-81; acct. Karen M. Moody, CPAs, Sheridan, Wyo., 1981-85; contr. T-C Investments, Inc., Sheridan, 1985—; ptnr. WHG Partnership, Sheridan, 1991—. With spl. forces U.S. Army, 1966-68, Vietnam. Mem. AICPA (tax div.), Wyo. Soc. CPAs, Am. Legion (fin. officer 1977-81), Lodge (sec. Sheridan club 1982-90, pres. 1989), Phi Kappa Phi, Beta Alpha Psi, Beta Gamma Sigma. Democrat. Roman Catholic. Home: 735 Canby St Sheridan WY 82801-4907 Office: T-C Investments Inc 856 Coffeen Ave Sheridan WY 82801-5318

RYAN, RALPH JAMES, auditing executive; b. Aurora, Ill., Aug. 3, 1931; s. Leo J. and Edna (Hall) R.; m. Lois M. Ryan, Aug. 16, 1955; children: James, Mark, Robert, Carl, Constance, Frank, Laura. BS in Edn., No. Ill. U., 1959, MS in Bus. Adminstrn., 1975. CPA, Calif.; CPCU, CLU, ChFC. Various positions Farmers Ins. Group, 1954-85; dir. regional auditing Farmers Ins. Group, L.A., 1985—. Mem. Chartered Casualty and Property Underwriters, CA. Soc. CPA's, Chartered Life Underwriter, Cert. Fraud Examiner, Chartered Fin. Cons. Office: Farmers Ins Group 4680 Wilshire Blvd Los Angeles CA 90010

RYAN, RANDEL EDWARD, JR., airline captain; b. N.Y.C., Jan. 11, 1940; s. Randel Edward and Ann Augusta (Horwath) R.; m. Pamela Michael Wiley, May 12, 1962; children: Katherine, Gregory. BS in Sci., Trinity Coll., 1961. Quality control supr. Ideal Toy Corp., Jamaica, N.Y., 1961-62; airline pilot United Airlines, San Francisco, 1967—. Editor: The Lowdown, 1980-83. Pres., Highlands Community Assn., San Mateo, Calif., 1975; chmn. Com. to Re-elect County Supr., San Mateo, 1976; mediator San Mateo County, 1986—; arbitrator Better Bus. Bureau, 1988—; rep. Highlands Community Assn., San Mateo, 1970-86; coach Little League and Babe Ruth Baseball, San Mateo, 1979-83. Served to capt. USAF, 1962-68. Recipient Vandor award San Mateo PTA, 1976, awards of merit United Airlines, San Francisco, 1975, 79. Mem. Air Line Pilots Assn. (chmn. speakers panel 1983—, community rels com. 1983—, bd. dirs. 1986-89, 91—, chmn. coun. 34 1991—, vice-chmn. 1986-89, editor newspaper The Bayliner 1984-86, mem. contract study com. 1984—, vice-chmn. grievance com. 1989-91—).Democrat. Club: Highland Tennis (San Mateo). Home: 1768 Lexington Ave San Mateo CA 94402-4025 Office: United Airlines San Francisco Internat Airport San Francisco CA 94128

RYAN, READE HAINES, JR., lawyer; b. Plainfield, N.J., Jan. 4, 1937; s. Reade Haines and Anne Mary (Moment) R.; m. Joan Louise Larson, June 16, 1966; children: Reade Haines III, Rebecca Marie. AB, Princeton U., 1959; LLB, Harvard U., 1965. Bar: N.Y. 1966, Calif. 1985. Assoc. Shearman & Sterling, N.Y.C., 1965-73; ptnr. Shearman & Sterling, 1973—; lectr. Practicing Law Inst., 1977-88, Am. Law Inst.-ABA, 1979-91. Trustee, elder Pacific Palisades Presbyn. Ch. Lt. USN, 1959-62. Mem. ABA, Internat. Bar Assn., Calif. State Bar, N.Y. State Bar Assn., Assn. of Bar of City of N.Y., L.A. County Bar Assn., Beverly Hills Bar Assn., L.A. County Bar Found. (trustee), Fin. Lawyers Conf. (trustee), The Calif. Club. Republican. Home: 201 Homewood Rd Los Angeles CA 90049-2709 Office: Shearman & Sterling 725 S Figueroa St 21st Fl Los Angeles CA 90017-5430 also: Shearman & Sterling 599 Lexington Ave at 53d St New York NY 10022

RYAN, STEPHEN JOSEPH, JR., ophthalmology educator, university dean; b. Honolulu, Mar. 20, 1940; s. S.J. and Mildred Elizabeth (Farrer) F.; m. Anne Christine Mullady, Sept. 25, 1965; 1 dau., Patricia Anne. A.B., Providence Coll., 1961; M.D., Johns Hopkins U., 1965. Intern Bellevue Hosp., N.Y.C., 1965-66; resident Wilmer Inst. Ophthalmology, Johns Hopkins Hosp., Balt., 1966-69, chief resident, 1969-70; fellow Armed Force Inst. Pathology, Washington, 1970-71; instr. ophthalmology Johns Hopkins U., Balt., 1970-71, asst. prof., 1971-72, assoc. prof., 1972-74; prof., chmn. dept. ophthalmology Los Angeles County-U. So. Calif. Med. Ctr., L.A., 1974—; acting head ophthalmology div., dept. surgery Children's Hosp., L.A., 1975-77; med. dir. Doheny Eye Inst. (formerly Estelle Doheny Eye Found.), L.A., 1977—; chief of staff Doheny Eye Hosp., L.A., 1985-88; dean U. So. Calif. Sch. Medicine, L.A., 1993—; mem. advisory panel Calif. Med. Assn., 1974—. Editor: (with M.D. Andrews) A Survey of Ophthalmology—Manual for Medical Students, 1970, (with R.E. Smith) Selected Topics in the Eye in Systemic Disease, 1974, (with Dawson and Little) Retinal Diseases, 1985, (with others) Retina, 1989; assoc. editor: Ophthalmol. Surgery, 1974—; mem. editorial bd.: Am. Jour. Ophthalmology, 1981—, EYESAT, 1981—, Internat. Ophthalmology, 1982—, Retina, 1983—, Graefes Archives, 1984—; contbr. articles to med. jours. Recipient cert. of merit AMA, 1971; Louis B. Mayer Scholar award Research to Prevent Blindness, 1973; Rear Adm. William Campbell Chambliss USN award, 1982. Mem. Wilmer Ophthal. Inst. Residents Assn., Am. Acad. Ophthalmology and Otolaryngology (award of Merit 1975), Am. Ophthal. Soc., Pan-Am. Assn. Ophthalmology, Assn. Univ. Profs. of Ophthalmology, Los Angeles Soc. Ophthalmology, AMA, Calif. Med. Soc., Los Angeles County Med. Assn., Pacific Coast Oto-Ophthal. Soc., Los Angeles County Acad. Medicine, Pan Am. Assn. Microsurgery, Macula Soc., Retina Soc., Nat. Eye Care Project, Research Study Club, Jules Gonin Club, Soc. of Scholars of Johns Hopkins U. (life). Office: Estelle Doheny Eye Found 1450 San Pablo St Los Angeles CA 90033-4681

RYAN, SUSAN MARY, art gallery owner, artist; b. Milw., May 29, 1938; d. John Patrick and Mary Catherine (Yakel) DeLance; m. Thomas Grant Ryan, June 21, 1972. BA, Clark Coll., 1960. Interior designer Forrer Interiors, Milw., 1960-62, EBSCO Industries, San Francisco, 1962-65, Kellog Bros., San Francisco, 1965-69, Interior Techniques, Portland, Oreg., 1970-74; free-lance artist Lake Oswego, Oreg., 1975-82, Atlanta, 1982-86; gallery owner Ryan Gallery, Lincoln City, Oreg., 1986—. Home: 29 Indian Shores Lincoln City OR 97367 Office: Ryan Gallery 4270 N Hwy 101 Lincoln City OR 97367

RYAN, SYLVESTER D., bishop; b. Catalina Island, Calif., Mar. 3, 1930. Grad., St. John's Sem., Camarillo, Calif. Ordained priest Roman Cath. Ch., 1957, titular bishop of Remesiana. Aux. bishop L.A., 1990-92; bishop Monterey, Calif., 1992—. Office: Chancery Office PO Box 2048 580 Fremont St Monterey CA 93940*

RYAN, WILLIAM MATTHEW, lineman, state legislator; b. Great Falls, Mont., June 28, 1955; s. William Duncan and Jeanette Rosette (Merrill) R.; m. Elaine Louise Brastrup, Jan. 19, 1974; children: Jennifer, Kelli, Katie. Grad., Great Falls. Cert. journeyman, lineman. Meter reader Mont. Power Co., Great Falls, 1973, head meter reader, 1974, dispatcher, 1975, groundman, 1976-79, apprentice, 1979-82, lineman, 1982—; mem. Ho. of Reps. Mont. State Legislature, Helena, 1993—; instr. Mont. Power Apprentice Program, 1982—. Mem. NAACP, Internat. Brotherhood Elec. Workers (local 44, unit v.p. 1984—, officer exam bd. 1988—, sec. Joint Apprenticeship Tng. Com. 1988—), Rocky Mountain Coord. Assn., Russell Country Sportsman, Walleyes Unlimited. Democrat. Roman Catholic. Home: 8 18th Ave S Great Falls MT 59405 Office: Mont Power Co 100 1st Ave N Great Falls MT 59404

RYDE, MAGNUS OLOF WALDEMAR, semiconductor equipment executive; b. Stockholm, Jan. 7, 1956; came to U.S., 1979; s. Torsten and Kerstin E. (Backe) R.;m. Nancy Ross, Mar. 4, 1989. BSIE, Anglian Regional Mgmt. Ctr., Danbury, Eng., 1979, Linköping (Sweden) U., 1979; MSIE, Stanford U., 1980. Prodn. control mgr. KLA Instruments Corp., Santa Clara, Calif., 1980-81, materials mgr., 1981-82, prodn. mgr., 1982-84, mfg. mgr., 1984-85, product mktg. mgr., 1985-87, dir. mktg., 1987-89; dir. Emmi bus. KLA Instruments Corp., San Jose, Calif., 1989-90, v.p. ops., 1992, v.p., gen. mgr., 1993; dir. KLA Instruments GmbH, Munich, 1990-91. Sgr. Swedish Army, 1974-75.

RYDELL, AMNELL ROY, artist, landscape architect; b. Mpls., Sept. 17, 1915; s. John S. and Josephine Henrietta (King) R.; m. Frances Cooksey, Jan. 24, 1942. BFA, U. So. Calif., 1937; postgrad., Atelier 17, Paris, 1938, U. Calif., Berkeley, 1939-40, U. Calif., Santa Cruz, 1988. Instr. engring. Douglas Aircraft, El Segundo, Calif., 1940-46; ind. artist, designer San Francisco, 1946-48; ind. artist, designer Santa Cruz, 1948—, ind. landscape architect, 1958-91. Author, cons.: Low Maintenance Gardening, 1974. Pres. Santa Cruz Hist. Soc., 1978-79, Rural Bonny Doon Assn., 1955-56, Santa Cruz Orgn. for Progress and Euthenics, 1977-78; mem. vision bd. City of Santa Cruz, 1991-92; mem. task force Ctr. for Art and History, 1986-93; bd. dirs. Santa Cruz Hist. Trust, 1978—, Art Mus. Santa Cruz County, 1982—. Mem. William James Assn. (vice chair bd. 1979—), Art Forum (chair 1983-90), Art League. Home: 201 Pine Flat Rd Santa Cruz CA 95060

RYDER, HAL, theatre educator, director; b. Evanston, Ill., Aug. 21, 1950; s. Lee Sigmund and Katherine (Philipsborn) Rosenblatt; m. Caroline Margaret Ogden, Nov. 17, 1976 (div. 1991). Student, U. Ariz., 1968-72, U. Miami, summer 1971; cert. in drama, Drama Studio London, 1973; BA in Drama, U. Wash., 1987. Drama specialist Rough Rock (Ariz.) Demonstration Sch., 1971-72; artistic dir. Mercury Theatre, London, 1973-75, Fringe Theatre, Orlando, Fla., 1976-79; dir. Drama Studio London, 1980-82, interim adminstrv. dir., 1985; artistic dir. Alaska Arts Fine Arts Camp, Sitka, 1987, Shakespeare Plus, Seattle, 1983—; instr. Cornish Coll. Arts, Seattle, 1982—, producer theatre, 1987—, acting-chmn. theatre dept., 1990; artistic dir. Open Door Theatre, 1992-93, Snoqualmie Falls Forest Theatre, 1992-93; creative cons. Sea World Fla., Orlando, 1979; lit. mgr. Pioneer Square Theatre, Seattle, 1983; space mgr. Seattle Mime Theatre, 1986-87. Author: Carmilla, 1976, (with others) Marvelous Christmas Mystery, 1978; editor: Will Noble Blood Die, 1987, The New Emperor's New Cloths, 1988, The Shakespeare Monologue Premier, 1990; dir. over 100 stage plays; appeared in over 40 prodns. Recipient Faculty Excellence award Seafirst Bank, Seattle, 1988. Mem. SAG, AFTRA, Am. Fedn. Tchrs. (Cornish chpt.). Democrat. Jewish. Home: 1012 NE 62d St Seattle WA 98115 Office: Cornish Coll Arts 710 E Roy St Seattle WA 98102-4696

RYDER, MALCOLM ELIOT, management information systems consultant; b. Norfolk, Va., Aug. 30, 1954; s. Noah Francis and Georgia May (Atkins) R.; m. Carolyn Mary Bradley, Sept. 12, 1992. BA, Princeton U., 1976. Photographer, sole owner Ryder Picture, N.Y.C., 1977—; visual arts sr. arts program specialist Nat. Endowment for the Arts, Washington, 1979-84; assoc. dir. artists fellowship grants program N.Y. Found. for the Arts, N.Y.C., 1984-85; dir. microsystems mgmt. info. N.Y. State Coun. on the Arts, N.Y.C., 1985-89; dir. client svcs., sr. cons. software divsn. Hammersly Tech. Ptnrs., San Francisco, 1990—; arts mgmt. cons., U.S., 1979—; cons. Family Crisis Ctr., San Francisco, 1992. Photographer exhbns. Urban Landscapes 1986-90, 1990, Va. Landscapes, 1984, Suburban Landscapes 1979-82, 1982. Bd. dirs. Paul Robeson Community Ctr., Princeton, N.J., 1977-79, Mid-Atlantic Arts Found., Balt., 1986-87, Ctr. for Critical Architecture, San Francisco, 1989-91. Mem. City Without Walls Artists Collective, The Art and Architecture Exhbn. Space. Home: Apt 6 1555 Oak St San Francisco CA 94117 Office: Hammersly Tech Ptnrs Ste 710 250 Montgomery St San Francisco CA 94104

RYDER, OLIVER ALLISON, geneticist, conservation biologist, educator; b. Alexandria, Va., Dec. 27, 1946; s. Oliver A. Ryder and Elizabeth R. (Semans) Paine; m. Cynthia Ryan, Dec. 5, 1970; children: Kerry, Ryan. BA, U. Calif., Riverside, 1968; PhD, U. Calif., San Diego, 1975. Postdoctoral fellow U. Calif., San Diego, 1975-78; geneticist San Diego Zoo, 1978-86, Kleberg genetics chair, 1986—; assoc. adj. prof. biology U. Calif., San Diego, 1988—. Editor: One Medicine, 1984, Jour. Heredity, 1989—, Conservation Biology, 1993—; contbr. over 130 articles on genetics and endangered species conservation to profl. jours. Species coord. Asian Wild Horse Species Surival Plan, San Diego, 1979. Med. rsch. fellow Bank Am.-Giannini Found., 1976; grantee Pew Charitable Trusts, 1989—, NIH, 1976-88; named 91 San Diegans to Watch, 1991. Fellow N.Y. Zool. Soc. (sci.), San Diego Soc. for Natural History; mem. Am. Assn. Zool. Parks, Am. Soc. Mammalogists, Am. Genetics Assn. (coun. 1990—), Soc. for Conservation Biology (founding), Soc. for Systematic Zoology, Soc. for Study Evolution, Am. Soc. for Microbiology. Office: San Diego Zoo Ctr for Reprodn Endangered Species PO Box 551 San Diego CA 92112-0551

RYE, DAVID BLAKE, television director; b. Norfolk, Va., Oct. 4, 1943; s. C. Glenn and Shirley Jean (Frye) R.; m. Gay Ann Darkenwald, Apr. 17, 1971; 1 child, Ian Glenn. BA in English, U. Mont., 1970. On-air personality Sta. KLTZ, Glasgow, Mont., 1969, Sta. KYLT, Missoula, Mont., 1970-71, Sta. KKGF, Great Falls, Mont., 1971-72, Sta. KGRC-FM, Hannibal, Mo., 1972, Sta. KUDI, Great Falls, 1972-74, Sta. KEIN, Great Falls, 1974; news dir. Sta. KFBB-TV, Great Falls, 1974-78; spl. asst. U.S. Hou. Rep. Ron Marlenee, Washington, 1978-80; news dir. Sta. KULR-TV, Billings, Mont., 1980—. Pres. City of Billings Animal Control Bd., 1987; bd. dirs. Horizon Home for the Sexually Abused, Billings, 1987. Served as sgt. U.S. Army, 1967-69, Vietnam. Named Newsperson of Yr. Billings Jaycees, 1985. Mem. Mont. Assn. Press Broadcasters (pres. 1985-87, Radio Programmer of Yr. 1972, TV Broadcaster of Yr. 1984, 86), Radio and TV News Dirs. Assn. Republican. Lutheran. Club: Hilands Golf (Billings). Lodges: Order of DeMolay, Kiwanis (v.p. Billings chpt. 1986-87). Home: 2211 Oak St Billings MT 59102-2558 Office: Sta KULR-TV 2045 Overland Ave Billings MT 59102-6454

RYEN, RICHARD HARLAN, financial consultant; b. Mpls., Mar. 27, 1933; s. Halvor and Elizabeth (Savage) R.; m. Ann A. Smith, Apr. 4, 1953 (div. 1976); children: Dawn, Richard, Rhea, Susan; m. Lillian Kay Rogalski, Oct. 22, 1977; children: Christopher, Daniel, Elizabeth. Student, U. Wis., 1951-52, Am. Coll., Bryn Mawr, Pa., 1991—. CLU, ChFC, cert. fin. planner. Loan analyst Pacific Nat. Bank, Seattle, 1957-63; agt. Equitable of Iowa, Seattle, 1963-67; ins. broker Ins. Svc. Inc., Seattle, 1967-71; mgr. Met. Life, Seattle, 1971-72; agt. Phoenix Mut., Seattle, 1972-74; gen. agt. Nat. Life, Seattle, 1975-90; agt. Nat. Life/Ryen & Assocs., Seattle, 1990—. Pres. Stevens Hosp. Found., Edmonds, Wash., 1990-91; chmn. fin. com. Seattle U. Albers Sch. Bus., Seattle, 1990—; bd. dirs. Vis. Nurse of Wash., Bellingham, 1991—, Am. Heart Assn. Wash., Seattle, 1971-75. Sgt. U.S. Army, 1949-51, Korea. Mem. CLUs (Seattle chpt., profl. mem., pres. 1990-91), Seattle Life Underwriters Assn. (pres. 1974-75, Inspirational award 1975), Res. Officers Assn., Sons of Norway (pres. 1966-68), Rotary. Republican. Roman Catholic. Office: Ryen & Assocs Inc 2200 6th Ave # 530 Seattle WA 98121

RYGIEWICZ, PAUL THADDEUS, plant ecologist; b. Chgo., Feb. 19, 1952; s. Sigismund Thaddeus and Regina (Korpalski) R. BS in Forestry, U. Ill., 1974; MS in Wood Sci., U. Calif., Berkeley, 1976; PhD in Forest Resources, U. Wash., 1983. Research wood technologist ITT Rayonier, Inc., Shelton, Wash., 1977; research assoc. Centre National de Recherches Forestières, Nancy, France, 1983-84; research soil microbiologist U. Calif., Berkeley, 1984-85; research ecologist EPA, Corvallis, Oreg., 1985—; asst. prof. dept. forest sci. Oreg. State U., 1987—. Contbr. articles to profl. jours.; rsch. on reforestation of tropical forests in Brazil, global climate changes on forests. Vol. Big Bros. of Am., Urbana, Ill., 1972-74. Fellow Regents U. Calif., Berkeley, 1973-74, Weyerhaeuser U. Calif., Berkeley, 1978-79, Inst. Nat. de la Recherche Agronomique, France, 1983-84, French Ministry of Fgn. Affairs, 1983-84. Mem. Ecol. Soc. Am., Am. Soc. Plant Physiologists, Soil Ecology Soc., Am. Inst. Biol. Scis., Forestry Club (Urbana and Berkeley), Sigma Xi, Gamma Sigma Delta, Xi Sigma Pi (officer 1973-74). Clubs: Portland Wheelmen Touring; Forestry (Urbana and Berkeley). Office: EPA 200 SW 35th St Corvallis OR 97333-4901

RYLANDER, ROBERT ALLAN, financial service executive; b. Bremerton, Wash., Apr. 8, 1947; s. Richard Algot and Marian Ethelyn (Peterson) R.; m. Donna Jean Marks, June 28, 1984; children: Kate, Josh, Erik, Meagan. BA in Fin., U. Wash., 1969; postgrad., U. Alaska, 1972-74. Controller Alaska USA Fed. Credit Union, Anchorage, 1974-77, mgr. ops., 1977-80, asst. gen. mgr., 1980-83, exec. v.p., chief operating officer, 1983—; chmn. Alaska Home Mortgage, Inc., Anchorage, 1992—; treas. Alaska Option Svcs. Corp., Anchorage, 1983—; bd. dirs. Alaska USA Ins., Inc., Anchorage. Served to capt. USAF, 1969-74. Mem. Credit Union Execs. Soc., Shared Networks Exec. Assn. Home: 6514 Lakeway Dr Anchorage AK 99502-1949 Office: Alaska USA Fed Credit Union PO Box 196613 Anchorage AK 99519-6613

RYLES, GERALD FAY, private investor, consultant; b. Walla Walla, Wash., Apr. 3, 1936; s. L. F. and Janie Geraldine (Bassett) R.; m. Ann Jane Birkenmeyer, June 12, 1959; children—Grant, Mark, Kelly. B.A., U. Wash., 1958; M.B.A., Harvard U., 1962. With Gen. Foods Corp., White Plains, N.Y., 1962-65, Purex Corp., Ltd., Lakewood, Calif., 1966-68; cons. McKinsey & Co., Inc., Los Angeles, 1968-71; with Fibreboard Corp., San Francisco, 1971-79, v.p., 1973-75, group v.p., 1975-79; with Consol. Fibres, Inc., San Francisco, 1979-88, exec. v.p., 1979-81, pres., dir., 1981-86, chief exec. officer, 1986-88; cons. Orinda, Calif., 1988-90; with Interchecks Inc., 1990-92, pres., CEO, 1990-92; cons., pvt. investor, 1992—. Mem. adv. com. entrepreneur and innovation program U. Wash. Bus. Sch. Served to capt. U.S. Army, 1958-66. Mem. Harvard Bus. Sch. Assn., Univ. Wash. Alumni Assn., World Trade Club (San Francisco), Orinda Country Club, Wash. Athletic Club. Republican. Episcopalian. Home: 2625 90th Ave NE Bellevue WA 98004-1601

RYMER, JUDITH MARQUIS, university administrator; b. Independence, Mo., Oct. 24, 1940; d. Francis Norwood and Leta Gertrude (Ryland) Marquis; m. Glenn George Rymer, Apr. 2, 1971. BS in Edn., Miami U., Oxford, Ohio, 1961; MA in Spanish, U. Kans., 1966; PhD in Spanish, Ohio State U., 1970. Tchr. English various schs., Colombia, S.Am., 1961-63; tchr. Spanish Rochester (N.Y.) City Sch., 1963-64; asst. instr. U. Kans., Lawrence, 1964-67; teaching asst. Ohio State U., 1967-69; asst. prof. Calif. State U., San Bernardino, 1970-74; assoc. prof. Calif. State U., 1974-79, prof. secondary edn., 1979—, exec. dean, 1984-88, v.p. for univ. rels., 1988—; cons. in field; dir. Coun. for Advancement and Support of Edn., 1988-90. Chmn. bd. Arrowhead United Way, San Bernardino, 1990; dir. Nat. Orange Show, San Bernardino, 1988—, pres., 1992—; elder 1st Presbyn. Ch., San Bernardino. Ctr. for Medieval & Renaissance Studies fellow, 1969-70; recipient Achievement in Edn. award, U. Redlands Town and Gown, 1987; named Woman of Achievement, Inland Bus. Mag., 1993. Mem. San Bernardino C. of C. (v.p. 1985-88, Athena award 1987), PEO, Gamma Phi Beta. Democrat. Presbyterian. Home: 2405 Shasta Dr San Bernardino CA 92404-3112 Office: California State Univ 5500 University Pky San Bernardino CA 92407-2318

RYMER, PAMELA ANN, federal judge; b. Knoxville, Tenn., Jan. 6, 1941. AB, Vassar Coll., 1961; LLB, Stanford U., 1964; LLD (hon.), Pepperdine U., 1988. Bar: Calif. 1966, U.S. Ct. Appeals (9th cir.) 1966, U.S. Ct. Appeals (10th cir.), U.S. Supreme Ct. Assoc. Lillick McHose & Charles, L.A., 1966-72, ptnr., 1973-75; ptnr. Toy and Rymer, L.A., 1975-83; judge U.S. Dist. Ct. (cen. dist.) Calif., L.A., 1983-89, U.S. Ct. Appeals (9th cir.), L.A., 1989—; faculty The Nat. Jud. Coll., 1986. Mem. Calif. Postsecondary Edn. Commn., 1974—, chmn., 1980-84; mem. Los Angeles Olympic Citizens Adv. Commn.; bd. visitors Stanford U. Law Sch., 1986—, Pepperdine U. Law Sch., 1987; mem. Edn. Commn. of States Task Force on State Policy and Ind. Higher Edn., 1987; bd. dirs. Constl. Rights Found., 1985—. Mem. ABA, Los Angeles County Bar Assn. (chmn. antitrust sect. 1981-82), Assn. of Bus. Trial Lawyers, Stanford Alumni Assn., Stanford Law Soc. So. Calif., Vassar Club So. Calif. (past pres.). Office: US Ct Appeals 9th Circuit 125 S Grand Ave Ste 304 Pasadena CA 91105-1652

RYNEAR, NINA COX, retired registered nurse, author, artist; b. Cochranville, Pa., July 11, 1916; d. Fredrick Allen and Nina Natalie (Drane) Cox; m. Charles Spencer Rynear, Aug. 22, 1934 (dec. May 1941); children: Charles Joseph, Stanley Spencer. RN, Coatesville Hosp. Sch. Nursing, 1945; BS in Nursing Edn., U. Pa., 1954. Interviewer Nat. Opinion Rsch. Ctr., U. Denver, Colo., 1942-47; sch. nurse West Goshen Elem. Sch., West Chester, Pa., 1946-47; pub. health nurse Pa. Dept. Health Bur. Pub. Health Nursing, Harrisburg, 1947-51; staff nurse V.A. Hosp., Coatesville, Pa., 1951-54; staff nurse, asst. head nurse V.A. Hosp., Menlo Park, Calif., 1954-56; asst. chief nursing svc. V.A. Hosp., Palo Alto, Menlo Park, Calif., 1956-76; self employed Reno, Nev., 1976—. Author: (poems, musical compositions) Old Glory and the U.S.A., 1989, Mister Snowman, 1988, Dawn Shadow of Lenape, 1988, (poem and song compilation) This Side of Forever, 1990; (musical compositions) Blessed Are Those Who Listen, What Can I Leave, The Hobo's Promise; paintings represented in numerous pvt. collections. Pres. Chester County Pub. Health Nurses Assn., 1950. Staff nurse Cadet Corps, 1944-45. Mem. VFW Aux. (patriotic instr. 1989-90, chmn. safety div. Silver State #3396 chpt. 1990-91), New Century Rebekah Lodge #244. Methodist. Home and Office: 7655 Hillview Dr Reno NV 89506-8670

RYNIKER, BRUCE WALTER DURLAND, industrial designer, manufacturing executive; b. Billings, Mont., Mar. 23, 1940; s. Walter Henry and Alice Margaret (Durland) R.; B. Profl. Arts in Transp. Design (Ford scholar), Art Ctr. Coll. Design, Los Angeles, 1963; grad. specialized tech. engring. program Gen. Motors Inst., 1964; m. Marilee Ann Vincent, July 8, 1961; children: Kevin Walter, Steven Durland. Automotive designer Gen. Motors Corp., Warren, Mich., 1963-66; mgmt. staff automotive designer Chrysler Corp., Highland Park, Mich., 1966-72; pres., dir. design Transform Corp., Birmingham, Mich., 1969-72; indsl. designer, art dir. James R. Powers and Assocs., Los Angeles, 1972-75; sr. design products mgr. Mattel Inc., El Segundo, Calif., 1975—; dir. design and devel. Microword Industries, Inc., Los Angeles, 1977-80, also dir.; exec. mem. Modern Plastics Adv. Council, 1976-80; elegance judge LeCercle Concours D'Elegance, 1976-77; mem. nat. adv. bd. Am. Security Council, 1980; cons. automotive design, 1972—. Served with USMC, 1957-60. Mem. Soc. Art Ctr. Alumni (life), Mattel Mgmt. Assn., Second Amendment Found., Am. Def. Preparedness Assn., Nat. Rifle Assn. Designer numerous exptl. automobiles, electric powered vehicles, sports and racing cars, also med. equipment, electronic teaching machines, ride-on toys. Home: 21329 Marjorie Ave Torrance CA 90503-5443 Office: 333 Continental Blvd El Segundo CA 90245-5012

RYPKA, EUGENE WESTON, microbiologist; b. Owatonna, Minn., May 6, 1925; s. Charles Frederick and Ethel Marie (Ellerman) R.; m. Rosemary Speeker, June 1, 1967. Student, Carleton Coll., 1946-47; BA, Stanford U., 1950, PhD, 1958. Prof. microbiology, systems, cybernetics U. N.Mex., Albuquerque, 1957-62; bacteriologist Leonard Wood Meml. Lab. Johns Hopkins U., Balt., 1962-63; sr. scientist Lovelace Med. Ctr., Albuquerque, 1963-71, chief microbiologist, 1971—; adj. prof. U. N.Mex., 1973—; cons. Hoffmann-LaRoche Inc., 1974—, Airline Pilots Assn., Washington, 1976, Pasco Lab., Denver, 1983—; advisor Nat. Com. Clinic Lab. Standards, Pa., 1980-84. Contbr. articles to profl. jours. and chpts. in books. Served with USNR, USMC 1943-46. Fellow AAAS; mem. IEEE, Internat. Soc. Systems Sci. Republican. Presbyterian. Home: 8345 Highland Sta Albuquerque NM 87198

SAAD, JOSEPH KANAN, lawyer; b. Clarksdale, Miss., Oct. 28, 1948; s. Joseph Saad and Jeanette (Farris) Chilli. BBA, U. Miss., 1970, JD, 1973. Bar: Miss. 1973, U.S. Dist. Ct. (no. dist.) Miss. 1973. Account exec. Dean Witter & Co., Memphis, 1973-75, Reynolds Securities, Houston, 1974, Lincoln Nat. Life Ins. Co., Houston, 1974-75; claims atty. Fidelity & Deposit Co. Md., Balt., New Orleans, Cleve. and Miami, 1975-80; bond claims atty. Transam Ins. Co., L.A., 1980-83, mgr. surety claims, 1983-84, asst. v.p. bonds, 1984-86, v.p. splty. claims, 1986-89; sr. v.p. splty. claims Transam Ins Co., L.A., 1989—; claims counsel Transam Ins. Co., L.A., 1988—; asst. v.p. Trans Premier Ins. Co., L.A., 1987—, Fairmont Ins. Co., L.A., 1987—, Chilton Ins. Co., Dallas, 1987—; pres. Rusco Svcs. Inc., 1990—. Mem. ABA (fidelity and Surety com. 1976—), Miss. Bar Assn., Fedn. Ins. and Corp. Counsel, Internat. Assn. Def. Counsel, Def. Rsch. Inst., So. Calif. Surety Assn. Office: Transam Ins Co 6300 Canoga Ave Woodland Hills CA 91367-2555

SAADANE, FABIENNE DENISE, food processing company executive; b. Aix, France, Jan. 13, 1958; came to U.S., 1992; d. Maurice and Ginette (Maurin) S. Naval engr. grad., Genie Naritine, Paris, 1977-80; MBA, Essec, 1980-82. Export engr. GEC Alsthom, Paris, 1982-84; mktg. mgr. ISA Riber, Paris, 1984-89; bus. mgr. ELF Sanofi, Paris, 1989-92; gen. mgr. ACP (ELF Sanofi group), Anaheim, Calif., 1992—. Mem. Inst. Food Tech. Roman Catholic. Home: 5380 Silver Canyon Rd 9F Anaheim CA 92687 Office: Anaheim Citrus Products 421E Commercial St Anaheim CA 92803

SAADEH, ABRAHAM, computer company executive; b. Jordan, June 19, 1955; s. Zaki S. BA, Syracuse U., 1980; MA, Calif. State U., Long Beach, 1986. Pres. Caldata Computer, Long Beach, Calif., 1987—. Office: Caldata Computer 3399 E 19th St Long Beach CA 90804

SAAR, FREDERICK ARTHUR, data processing executive; b. Scranton, Pa., Aug. 30, 1946; s. Frederick Arthur and Mary (Gray) S. Sr. programmer Fed. Reserve Bank, Charlotte, 1967-74; EDP auditor First Commerce Corp., New Orleans, 1974-76; audit dir. First Interstate Bancorp, Phoenix, 1976-84; mgr. info. resource mgmt. First Interstate Bank, Phoenix, 1984-90, cons. systemd devel. div., 1990-91; project mgr. First Interstate Bank of Oreg. div. First Interstate Bancorp, Portland, 1991—; pres. Hogan Users Group, Dallas, 1983-84. Served with U.S. Army, 1964-67, Vietnam. Named Auditor of Yr. Inst. Internal Auditors, Phoenix chpt., 1981-82. Mem. EDP Auditors Assn. (cert. info. systems auditor, pres. Phoenix chpt. 1985), Inst. Cert. Computer Profls. (cert. systems profl.). Republican. Episcopalian. Office: First Interstate Bank 1330 SW 5th Ave Portland OR 97201-5602

SAARI, ALBIN TOIVO, electronic engineer; b. Rochester, Wash., Mar. 16, 1930; s. Toivo Nickoli and Gertrude Johanna (Hill) S.; m. Patricia Ramona Rudig, Feb. 1, 1958; children: Kenneth, Katherine, Steven, Marlene, Bruce. Student, Centralia Community Coll., Wash., 1950-51; AS in Electronic Tech., Wash. Tech. Inst., Seattle, 1958; BA in Communications, Evergreen State Coll., Olympia, Wash., 1977. Electronic technician Boeing Co., Seattle, 1956-59; field engr. RCA, Van Nuys, Calif., 1959-61; tv engr. Gen. Dynamics, San Diego, 1961-65, Boeing Co., Seattle, 1965-70; chief media engr. Evergreen State Coll., Olympia, Wash., 1970—; adv. bd. KAOS-FM Radio, Olympia, 1979-82, New Mkt. Vocat. Skills Ctr., Tumwater, Wash., 1985—. Soccer coach King County Boys Club, Federal Way, Wash., 1968-70, Thurston County Youth Soccer, Olympia, 1973-78. With USAF, 1951-55. Recipient Merit award for electronic systems design Evergreen State Coll., 1978. Mem. Soc. Broadcast Engrs. (chmn. 1975-77), Soc. of Motion Picture and TV Engrs., IEEE, Audio Engring. Soc., Tele-Communications Assn., Assoc. Pub. Safety Communications Officers. Lutheran. Home: 6617 Husky Way SE Olympia WA 98503-1433 Office: Evergreen State Coll Media Engring L1309 Olympia WA 98505

SAARI, RUSSELL EDWARD, linguist; b. Caldwell, Idaho; s. Jack Ernest and Louella May (Hysell) S.; m. Teresa Lynn Maughan, Sept. 19, 1986; children: Cassandra Timbre Alexis, Wesley Devon. BS in Psychology, U. Md., 1991; AS in Avionics Electronics, Community Coll. USAF, Germany, 1991. Commd. airman 1st class USAF, 1985, advanced through grades to staff sgt., 1992; avionics technician USAF, Luke AFB, Ariz., 1986-88; avionics technician USAF, Ramstein AFB, Germany, 1988-89, with prodn. control, 1989-91; cryptologic linguist USAF Air Guard, Salt Lake City, 1991—; safety noncommd. officer USAF, Ramstein AFB, 1988-91, unit ARC instr., 1991. Decorated Achievement medal. Mem. Phi Kappa Phi. Republican. Mormon.

SAAVEDRA, CARLOS RAÚL, computer programmer, systems analyst; b. Rio Piedras, P.R., Jan. 17, 1961; came to U.S., 1985; s. Raúl and Helvia (Gonzalez) S. BS in Computer Sci., U. Sacred Heart, Santurce, P.R., 1984. Tutor computer programming U. Sacred Heart, Santurce, 1983-84; computer systems analyst, programmer San Mateo (Calif.) Postal Data Ctr., 1990—; mem. quality com. San Mateo Postal Data Ctr., 1991—. Mem. San Francisco Pub. Libr., 1986, San Mateo Postal Data Ctr. Campaign Dr., 1991; grad. Lifespring Leadership, San Francisco, 1991. With U.S. Army, 1985-90. Mem. Nat. Eagle Scout Assn., Fed. Hispanic Program Mgrs., Latin Am. Postal Employees, Bay Delta Hispanic Program (coord.), IMAGE de San Francisco, U.S. Postal Svc. San Mateo Postal Data Ctr. Affirmative Action/Equal Employment Opportunity Com. Roman Catholic. Home: PO Box 2471 Daly City CA 94015-2471 Office: San Mateo Postal Data Ctr 2700 Campus Dr San Mateo CA 94497-9100

SAAVEDRA, LOUIS E., mayor; b. Tokay, N.Mex., Mar. 18, 1933; s. Jose Ignacio and Nepumucena (Gabaldon) S.; m. Gail Griffith, Dec. 26, 1958; children: Ralph, Laura, Barbara. BA, MA, Eastern N.Mex. U., 1960, LLD (hon.), 1989; A of Humane Letters (hon.), Albuquerque Tech.-Vocat. Inst., 1989. Pres. Albuquerque Tech.-Vocat. Inst., 1964-89; mayor City of Albuquerque, 1989—. Commr. City Commn., Albuquerque, 1967-74. With U.S. Army, 1954-56. Recipient N.Mex. Disting. Pub. Svc. award State of N.Mex., 1977. Mem. Rotary. Democrat. Office: City of Albuquerque 1 Civic Ctr PO Box 1293 Albuquerque NM 87102*

SAAVEDRA, RO, communications director; b. Albuquerque, Sept. 20, 1952; d. Ben and Josephine (Martinel) S.; m. Gary D. Doll, Aug. 25, 1973 (div. 1979). B Univ. Studies, U. N.Mex., 1981, MA in Communications, 1983. Dir. communications KPMG Peat Marwick, Albuquerque, 1984—. Bd. dirs. Sr. Citizen Aid Found., Albuquerque, 1986-87; mem. U. N.Mex. Pub. Rels. and Centennial Campaign Com., 1991, mem. pub. rels. com.; account exec. 1990 campaign United Way Greater Albuquerque. Mem. Women in Communications (editor newsletter 1984-85, v.p. 1985-86, pres. 1986-87), Pub. Rels. Soc. Am. (chmn. El Conquistadors award com. 1992), N.Mex. Press Women (bd. dirs. 1991-92, 93), Albuquerque C. of C. (diplomats com. 1987-89). Office: KPMG Peat Marwick 6565 Americas Pky NE # 700 Albuquerque NM 87110-8119

SABA, NORMAN MORRIS, pediatrician; b. Phoenix, July 20, 1954; s. Morris Solomon and Mary Thomas (Habib) S.; m. Pamela Easton, May 21, 1983; children: Daniel Norman, Matthew Gregory, Rachel Katherine. BSc in Chemistry, U. Ariz., 1976; MD, Johns Hopkins U., 1980. Intern, then resident Johns Hopkins Hosp., 1980-83; attending staff pediatrician St. Joseph's Hosp., Phoenix, 1983-88, assoc. dir., pediatric residence program, 1986-88; pediatrician Pediatric Med. Assocs., Mesa, Ariz., 1988—. Mem. East Valley Pediatric Soc. (pres. 1990-94). Office: Pediatric Med Assocs PC 1520 S Dobson Rd # 203 Mesa AZ 85202

SABATINI, LAWRENCE, bishop; b. Chgo., May 15, 1930; s. Dominic and Ada (Piloi) S. Ph.L., Gregorian U., Rome, 1953, S.T.L., 1957, J.C.D., 1960; M.S. in Edn., Iona Coll., 1968. Ordained priest, Roman Catholic Ch., 1957, bishop, 1978. Prof. canon law St. Charles Sem., S.I., N.Y., 1960-71; pastor St. Stephen's Parish, North Vancouver, B.C., Canada, 1970-78; provincial superior Missionaries of St. Charles, Oak Park, Ill., 1978; aux. bishop Archdiocese Vancouver, B.C., Can., 1978-82; bishop Diocese Kamloops, B.C., Can., 1982—; procurator, adviser Matrimonial Tribunal, N.Y.C., 1964-71; founder, dir. RAP Youth Counseling Service, S.I., N.Y., 1969-71; vice ofcl. Regional Matrimonial tribunal of Diocese Kamloops, 1978-82; chmn. Kamloops Cath. Pub. Schs., 1982—. Named Man of Yr. Confratellanza Italo-Canadese, 1979. Mem. Can. Canon Law Soc., Canon Law Soc. Am., Can. Conf. Cath. Bishops. Office: Diocese of Kamloops, 635A Tranquille Rd, Kamloops, BC Canada V2B 3H5*

SABATO, GEORGE FRANK, educator, educational consultant, writer; b. Portsmouth, Va., Dec. 21, 1947; s. Frank Vincent and Mary Elizabeth (Carey) S.; m. Kathie Kay Beacom, June 21, 1975; children: Jennifer, Jillian. BA, Stanford U., 1970, MA, 1971. Tchr. Sequoia Union High Sch. Dist., San Mateo, Calif., 1971-73; tchr. Placerville (Calif.) Elem. Sch. Dist., 1974—, coach football and wrestling, 1979-93, dir. Gifted and Talented program, 1980-93; test author Ednl. Testing Svc., Berkeley, Calif., 1972; tchr., trainer El Dorado County Office of Edn., Placerville, 1991; cons. El Dorado County, 1988-91, Monterey (Calif.) Sch. Dist., 1990, Pollock Pines (Calif.) Elem. Sch. Dist., 1990, Calif. Waste Mgmt. Bd., 1992; speaker Calif. Assn. Middle Schs., Calif. Sch. Administrs., 1993. Assoc. editor, columnist Social Studies Rev., 1990-93; developer computer programs Micro-Ed, Inc. Campaign worker Dem. Party, Placerville, 1986-93; coach Placerville Bobby Sox League, 1989-90. Grantee NSF, 1989, Kraft Environ. Inst., Chgo., 1991; Honored for Archaelogical find Royal Jour. of Antiquaries, Ireland, 1989. Mem. NEA, Calif. Coun. for Social Studies (assoc. editor 1990—), Placerville Edn. Assn. (pres. 1985-86), Calif. Tchrs. Assn. Home: 222 Judy Dr Placerville CA 95667-3325 Office: Edwin Markham Middle Sch 2800 Moulton Dr Placerville CA 95667-4334

SABEY, J(OHN) WAYNE, academic administrator, consultant; b. Murray, Utah, Dec. 10, 1939; s. Alfred John and Bertha (Lind) S.; m. Marie Bringhurst, Sept. 10, 1964; children: Clark Wayne, Colleen, Carolyn, Natasha Lynne. BA in Asian Studies, Brigham Young U., 1964, MA in Asian History, 1965; PhD in East Asian History, U. Mich., 1972. Teaching asst. Brigham Young U., Salt Lake City, 1964-65, rsch. asst., 1965, adj. prof. history, 1988-89; rsch. asst. U. Mich., Ann Arbor, 1966; from instr. to asst. prof. history U. Utah, Salt Lake City, 1970-80; v.p. Western Am. Lang. Inst., Salt Lake City, 1980-84, dir., 1984-86, pres., 1986—; exec. v.p. Pacific Rim Bus. Coords., Salt Lake City, 1993—, also bd. dirs., 1993—; assoc. dir. exch. program between U. Utah and Nagoya Broadcasting Network of Japan, 1973-79; lectr. in field, Superior award in extemporaneous speaking, 1956. Author essay, contbr. articles to ency. Chmn. bd. trustees Western Am. Lang. Inst., 1986—, sec. to bd. trustees, 1980-86; chmn. bd. trustees Found. for Internat. Understanding, 1982—; mem. internat. adv. coun. Salt Lake C.C., 1988—; mem. bd. advisors Consortium for Internat. Edn., 1972-77. Horace H. Rackham Sch. grad. studies fellow, 1969-70, Fulbright-Hays rsch. fellow (Japan), 1968-69, U.S. Nat. Def. fgn. lang. fellow, 1965-68. Mem. Assn. for Asian Studies (gen. chairperson, chairperson local arrangements western conf. 1970-72), Phi Kappa Phi. Home: 1142 E First S Salt Lake City UT 84102-1640 Office: Western Am Lang Inst 4700 S 900 E Ste 41-E Salt Lake City UT 84117

SABHARWAL, RANJIT SINGH, mathematician; b. Dhudial, India, Dec. 11, 1925; came to U.S., 1958, naturalized, 1981; s. Krishan Ch and Devti (An) S.; m. Pritam Kaur Chadha, Mar. 5, 1948; children—Rajinderpal, Amarjit, Jasbir. B.A. with honors, Punjab U., 1944, M.A., 1948; M.A. U. Calif, Berkeley, 1962; Ph.D., Wash. State U., 1966. Lectr. math. Khalsa Coll., Bombay, India, 1951-58; teaching asst. U. Calif., Berkeley, 1958-62; instr. math. Portland (Oreg.) State U., 1962-63, Wash. State U., 1963-66; asst. prof. Kans. State U., 1966-68; mem. faculty Calif. State Hayward, 1968—, prof. math., 1974—. Author papers on non-Desarguesian planes. Mem. Am. Math. Soc., Math. Assn. Am., Sigma Xi. Address: 27892 Adobe Ct Hayward CA 94542

SABIN, JACK CHARLES, engineering and construction firm executive; b. Phoenix, June 29, 1921; s. Jack Byron and Rena (Lewis) S.; B.S., U. Ariz., 1943; B in Chem. Engring., U. Minn., 1947; m. Frances Jane McIntyre, Mar. 27, 1950; children—Karen Lee, Robert William, Dorothy Ann, Tracy Ellen. With Standard Oil Co. of Calif., 1947-66, sr. engr., 1966—; pres., dir. Indsl. Control & Engring., Inc., Redondo Beach, Calif., 1966—; owner/mgr. Jack C. Sabin, Engr.-Contractor, Redondo Beach, 1968—; staff engr. Pacific Molasses Co., San Francisco, 1975-77; project mgr. E & L Assocs., Long Beach, Calif., 1977-79; dir. Alaska Pacific Petroleum, Inc., 1968—, Marlex Petroleum, Inc., 1970, 71—. Served with U.S. Army, 1942-46; capt. Chem. Corps, Res., 1949-56. Registered profl. engr., Calif., Alaska; lic. gen. engring. contractor, Ariz., Calif. Mem. Nat. Soc. Profl. Engrs., Ind. Liquid Terminals Assn., Conservative Caucus, Calif. Tax Reduction Com., Tau Beta Pi, Phi Lambda Upsilon, Phi Sigma Kappa. Republican. Clubs: Elks; Town Hall of Calif. Address: 151 Camino de las Colinas Redondo Beach CA 90277

SABSAY, DAVID, library consultant; b. Waltham, Mass., Sept. 12, 1931; s. Wiegard Isaac and Ruth (Weinstein) S.; m. Helen Glenna Tolliver, Sept. 24,1 966. AB, Harvard U., 1953; BLS, U. Calif., Berkeley, 1955. Circulation dept. supr. Richmond (Calif.) Pub. Library, 1955-56; librarian Santa Rosa (Calif.) Pub. Library, 1956-65; dir. Sonoma County Library, Santa Rosa, 1965-92; libr. cons., 1992—; coordinator North Bay Coop. Library System, Santa Rosa, 1960-64; cons. in field, Sebastopol, Calif., 1968—. Contbr. articles to profl. jours. Commendation, Calif. Assn. Library Trustees and Commrs., 1984. Mem. Calif. Library Assn. (pres. 1971, cert. appreciation 1971, 80), ALA. Club: Harvard (San Francisco). Home and Office: 667 Montgomery Rd Sebastopol CA 95472-3020

SACCHETTI, ADELE IRENE, scientist, robotics and material handling consultant; b. Grangeville, Idaho, Sept. 27, 1931; d. Oscar Palmer and Esther Ruth (Mathies) Odden, m. Alfred L. Gregg, Jr. (div. 1973); children: Lynn Ellen, Eric Lawrence, Christopher Derek; m. Angelo Victorio Sacchetti, May 10, 1975; 1 child, Timothy Mario. BS in Chemistry, U. Alta., Edmonton, 1955; PhD in Engring. Physics, McGill U., Montreal, 1959. robotics cons. Metals & Controls Corp., U.S., Servomechanisms and Servosystems for the auto industry, Japan. Laser rsch. analyst Naval Ordinance Test Sta., China Lake, Calif., 1966-68; dir. loan mgmt. AR Ogden Venture Capital Mfrs. Fin., Beverly Hills, Calif., 1972-80; robotics cons. Lutheran. Home: 2024 Tibbetts Dr Longview WA 98632

SACKTON, FRANK JOSEPH, university official, lecturer, retired army officer; b. Chgo., Aug. 11, 1912; m. June Dorothy Raymond, Sept. 21, 1940. Student, Northwestern U., 1936, Yale, 1946, U. Md., 1951-52; B.S., U. Md., 1970; grad., Army Inf. Sch., 1941, Command and Gen. Staff Coll., 1942, Armed Forces Staff Coll., 1949, Nat. War Coll., 1954; M.Pub. Adminstrn., Ariz. State U., 1976. Mem. 131st Inf. Regt., Ill. N.G., 1929-40; commd. 2d lt. U.S. Army, 1934, advanced through grades to lt. gen., 1967; brigade plans and ops. officer (33d Inf. Div.), 1941, PTO, 1943-45; div. signal officer, 1942-43, div. intelligence officer, 1944, div. plans and ops. officer, 1945; sec. to gen. staff for Gen. MacArthur Tokyo, 1947-48; bn. comdr. 30th Inf. Regt., 1949-50; mem. spl. staff Dept. Army, 1951; plans and ops. officer Joint Task Force 132, PTO, 1952; comdr. Joint Task Force 7, Marshall Islands, 1953; mem. gen. staff Dept. Army, 1954-55; with Office Sec. Def., 1956; comdr. 18th Inf. Regt., 1957-58; chief staff 1st Inf. Div., 1959; chief army Mil. Mission to Turkey, 1960-62; comdr. XIV Army Corps, 1963; dep. dir. plans Joint Chiefs Staff, 1964-66; army general staff mil. ops., 1966-67, comptroller of the army, 1967-70, ret., 1970; spl. asst. for fed./state relations Gov. Ariz., 1971-75; chmn. Ariz. Programming and Coordinating Com. for Fed. Programs, 1971-75; lectr. Am. Grad. Sch. Internat. Mgmt., 1973-77; vis. asst. prof., lectr. public affairs Ariz. State U., Tempe, 1976-78; dean Ariz. State U. Coll. Public Programs, 1979-80; prof. public affairs Ariz. State U., 1980—, v.p. bus. affairs, 1981-83, dep. dir. intercollegiate athletics, 1984-85. Contbr. articles to public affairs and mil. jours. Mem. Ariz. Steering Com. for Restoration of the State Capitol, 1974-75, Ariz. State Personnel Bd., 1978-83, Ariz. Regulatory Council, 1981—. Decorated D.S.M., Silver Star, also Legion of Merit with 4 oak leaf clusters, Bronze Star with 2 oak leaf clusters, Air medal, Army Commendation medal with 1 oak leaf cluster, Combat Inf. badge. Mem. Ariz. Acad. Public Adminstrn., Pi Alpha Alpha (pres. chpt. 1976-82). Clubs: Army-Navy (Washington); Arizona (Phoenix). Home: 12000 N 90th St Apt 2071 Scottsdale AZ 85260-8604 Office: Ariz State U Sch Pub Affairs Tempe AZ 85287-0603

SADAVA, DAVID ERIC, biology educator; b. Ottawa, Ont., Can., Mar. 14, 1946; came to U.S., 1967; s. Samuel and Ruth (Bloom) S.; m. Angeline Douvas, June 15, 1972; 1 child, Dana Louise. BS, Carleton U., Ottawa, 1967; PhD, U. Calif. San Diego, La Jolla, 1971. Prof. biology Scripps Coll., Claremont, Calif., 1972—, chmn. Joint Sci. Program, 1980—; vis. prof. dept. pediatrics U. Colo., Denver, 1979—, dept. molecular biology, 1981—. Author: Cell Biology: Organelle Structure and Function, 1993; Co-author: Plants, Food, People, 1977; contbr. articles to profl. jours. Woodrow Wilson Found. fellow, 1968. Office: Claremont McKenna Coll Joint Sci Dept Claremont CA 91711

SADEGHI, ALI, architectural planner; b. Tehran, Iran, May 10, 1955; came to U.S., 1973; s. Mohammad Sadeghi and Homay Sadeghi-Nejad; m. Mitra Afsaneh Farokhpay, Apr. 18, 1980; children: Sanam Elika, Arya Farokh. BS in Architecture, Ohio State U., 1978, MArch, M in City and Regional Planning, 1981. Registered profl. architect, Ohio, Calif. Phys. planner Karlsberger Cos., Columbus, Ohio, 1981-83; med. planner Rochlin & Baran Assocs., L.A., 1983-84; facility planner Am. Med. Internat., L.A., 1984-86; dir. planning URS Corp, L.A., 1986-92; prin. API Cons., Irvine, Calif., 1992—. Mem. AIA, Calif. Council Architects, L.A. Inst. Architects. Office: API Cons 17744 Sykpark Circle Ste 180 Irvine CA 92714

SADEGHI, NASSER, architect; b. Tehran, Iran, Apr. 21, 1934; came to U.S., 1957; s. Mort and Roughie (Medikhan) S.; m. Apr. 19, 1976 (div. July 1982); 1 child, Sabrina Darya. BArch, U. Colo., 1963; M in Urban Design, Archtl. Assn. Sch. of Archt., London, England, 1971. Registered profl. architect Ariz., La., Colo. Architect Associated Design Forum, Aspen, Colo., 1969-74; vis. lectr. U. Colo. Sch. Environ. Design, Boulder, Colo., 1971-72; asst. prof. U. Colo. Sch. Environ. Design, Boulder, 1972-73; architect, interior designer Sadeghi Assocs., Aspen, 1973—; Trustee Internat. Wine & Food Soc., Aspen, 1978—; sec., treas. Plaza Devel. Corp., Salt Lake City, 1985—. Mem. AIA Am. Soc. Interior Designers, U. Colo. Alumni Assn., Archtl. Assn. (London), Nat. Trust for Hist. Preservation. Home: PO Box 1411 470 Red Mountain Rd Aspen CO 81612 Office: Sadeghi Assocs Architects 520 Cooper Ave Aspen CO 81611

SADER, ROBERT MAYO, lawyer, state assemblyman; b. Compton, Calif., Aug. 12, 1948; m. Candice K. Lofthouse, Nov. 30, 1980; children: Mae Lee, Clayton Mayo. BA in History, Stanford U., 1970; diploma in Russian, Def. Language Inst., 1971; LLD, Georgetown Law Ctr., 1977. Pvt. practice Reno, 1978—; assemblyman Nev. Legis., Carson City, Nev., 1980—; vice-chmn. ways and means com. Nev. State Assembly, Chgo., 1983-84, chmn. jud. com., 1987—, commr. uniform state law commn., 1983—, majority whip Nev. State Assembly, 1987—. Author: (book) Practicing Lawyer's Guide to 1989 Legislation, 1987. Mem. bd. dirs. RSVP, Reno, 1983—; pres. Stanford Reno (Nev.) Alumni Club, 1983, Sparks (Nev.) YMCA, 1986-87. With U.S. Army, 1970-73. Democrat. Office: 462 Court St Reno NV 89501-1778

SADILEK, VLADIMIR, architect; b. Czechoslovakia, June 27, 1933; came to U.S., 1967, naturalized, 1973; s. Oldrich and Antoine (Zlamal) S.; Ph.D. summa cum laude in City Planning and Architecture, Tech. U. Prague, 1957; m. Jana Kadlec, Mar. 25, 1960; 1 son, Vladimir, Jr. Chief architect State Office for City Planning, Prague, 1958-67; architect, designer Bank Bldg. Corp., St. Louis, 1967-70, assoc. architect, San Francisco, 1970-74; owner, chief exec. officer Bank Design Cons., San Mateo, Calif., 1974-81, West Coast Development Co., San Mateo, 1975—; pres., chief exec. officer Orbis Devel. Corp., San Mateo, 1981—. Served with Inf. of Czechoslovakia, 1958. Recipient awards of excellence from Bank Building Corp. and AIA for planning and design of fin. instns. in Hawaii, Calif. (1971), Ariz., N.Mex., Tex. (1972), Colo., Wyo. (1973), Idaho, Oreg., Washington (1974); lic. architect, 28 states. Republican. Roman Catholic. Home: 80 Orange Ct Burlingame CA 94010-6516 Office: 1777 Borel Pl San Mateo CA 94402-3509

SADLER, DICK SHERMAN, state official; b. Hawarden, Iowa, Sept. 10, 1928; s. Edward A. and Elsie J. (Sherman) S.; m. Mary A. Dusterhoft, Feb. 2, 1952; children—Edward, Richard, Connie. Roundhouse foreman C&NW R.R., Casper, Wyo., 1962-82; exec. dir. Wyo. Employment Security Commn., Casper, 1982—; mem. Wyo. Ho. of Reps., 1971-74, Wyo. Senate, 1975-82. Served with USN, 1946-49, PTO. Named Legislator of Yr., Wyo. Wildlife Fedn., 1981, Wyo. Wildlife Soc., 1982. Democrat. Roman Catholic. Home: 2311 Lee Ln Casper WY 82604-2795 Office: Wyo Employment Security Commn PO Box 2760 Casper WY 82602

SADLER, LOUIS RAY, history educator; b. Newton, Miss., Feb. 5, 1937; s. Bill B. and Katie Mae (Sansing) S.; m. Mary Elizabeth Miller, June 24, 1961; children: Lesley Ann, William Foxworth. BA, Miss. State U., Starkville, 1963, MA, 1965; PhD, U. S.C., 1971. Instr. dept. history U. S.C., Columbia, 1969; asst. prof. dept. history N.Mex. State U., Las Cruces, 1969—, assoc. prof. dept. history, 1972, chmn. dept. history, 1975-78, dir. Joint Border Rsch. Inst., 1978-89, dir. Ctr. Latin Am. Studies, 1979-89, with dept. history, 1989—; cons. U.S.-Mex. Border; sec.-treas. Rocky Mtn. Coun. Latin-Am. Studies, 1980-89; chmn. commr. N. Mex. Border Commn., 1981-89; bd. dirs. consortium of U.S. Rsch. Programs for Mex., treas., 1985-89; exec. sec. Conf. Latin Am. History, 1989-91. Co-author: The Border and the Revolution, 1988, rev. edit., 1990. Chmn. Dona Ana County Dem. Party, Las Cruces, 1975-79; mem. Cultural Properties Rev. Com., Santa Fe, 1979-86; mem. N.Mex. Dem. State Ctrl. Com., 1989—; mem. State treas. investment com. 1991—; fin. com. N.Mex. Border Authority, 1991-92. With USNG, 1959-65. Named co-winner H. Bailey Carroll prize Tex. State Hist. Assn., 1980; Andrew Mellon fellow Inst. Latin Am. Studies, U. Tex., 1983, Hall of Fame award Dona Ana County Hist. Soc., 1992. Mem. Rocky Mountain Coun. Latin Am. Studies (Charles Nason Disting. Svc. award 1990), Sigma Chi, Phi Alpha Theta, Phi Kappa Phi. Methodist. Office: N Mex State U Dept History PO Box 3 White Sands NM 88002-0019

SADLER, SALLIE INGLIS, social worker; b. Phila., Nov. 16, 1941; d. H. Barton Off and Janet (Miller) Nelson; m. William A. Sadler, Jr., Apr. 23, 1977; children: Bill, Lisa, Nelson, Ashley, Kirsten. BA, Rollins Coll., Winter Park, Fla., 1964; MSW with high acad. achievement, Rutgers U., 1979; postgrad., Pa. State U., 1986-89. Cert. social worker. Caseworker II, dir. group work Family and Children's Svc. West Essex, Caldwell, N.J., 1979-81; dir. Single Parent Ctr. West Essex, Montclair, N.J., 1981-85; pvt. practice Upper Montclair, N.J., 1981-85; chief clin. svcs. Family Svc. Ctr., U.S. Naval Air Base, Alameda, Calif., 1990—; adj. instr. div. social scis. Bloomfield (N.J.) Coll., 1979-81, N.J. Inst. Tech., 1984-85; instr. psychology dept. Lock Haven (Pa.) U., 1985-90. Mem. NASW, APA, Assn. Women Faculty in Higher Edn. Office: Family Svc Ctr Naval Air Sta Bldg 613 Alameda CA 94501-5068

SADLER, WILLIAM ALAN, JR., educational adminstrator, sociology educator; b. Evanston, Ill., Mar. 2, 1931; s. William Alan and Marjorie Elizabeth (Eason) S.; m. Sallie I. Off, 1977; children: William Alan III, Lisa, Kirsten. BA, U. Mich., 1953; ThM, Gen. Sem., 1956, Harvard U., 1957; PhD, Harvard U., 1962. Parish worker Episcopal Diocese N.Y., 1960-64; asst. prof. Bishop's U., Lennoxville, Que., Can., 1964-68; assoc. prof. Bates Coll., Lewiston, Maine, 1968-72; prof. sociology, head interdisciplinary studies and freshman core program Bloomfield (N.J.) Coll., 1972-85; disting. scholar Chapman Coll., Calif., 1981; exec. dir. acad. planning and devel., dean Coll. Arts and Scis., prof. sociology Lock Haven (Pa.) U., 1985-89; dean academic affairs Holy Names Coll., Oakland, Calif., 1990-92, prof. sociology, 1990—; dir. programs NEH, 1975-77; cons. in field. Author: Master Sermons Through the Ages, 1963, Existence and Love, 1969, Personality and Religion, 1970; contbr. articles to profl. jours. Mem. adv. bd. Outward Bound. Frederick Sheldon traveling fellow Harvard U., 1958-59; postdoctoral fellow Soc. for Values in Higher Edn., 1973, Danforth Assoc., 1976; grantee NEH, 1972, 75, 76, 77, Kittredge Found., 1988. Mem. Am. Sociol. Assn., Am. Assn. Higher Edn., Soc. Values in Higher Edn. Democrat. Episcopalian. Home: 34 Turtle Creek Oakland CA 94605 Office: Holy Names Coll 3500 Mountain Blvd Oakland CA 94619-1699

SADOWSKI, GEORGE, industrial safety engineer; b. Ewa Beach, Hawaii, Apr. 8, 1950; s. Ludwik and Wilda Poipe (Mahoe) S.; m. Linda Taylor, Aug. 20, 1974; children: Michael Napela, Sonia Leilani, Matthew George, Garrett Taylor. BS, BYU-Hawaii, 1976; MBA, U. Phoenix, 1986. Prototype developer Hercules, Inc., Magna, Utah, 1981-82, tech. asst., 1982-84, safety tng. rep., 1984, lead safety tng. rep., 1984-88, safety engr. plant safety and loss prevention, 1988-91, supr. safety and loss prevention, 1991—; chmn. bd. Central Valley Water Reclamation, Salt Lake City, 1988, cons. bd. safety com., 1990; chmn. bd. Kearns Improvement Dist., 1990. Mem. Am. Soc. Safety Engrs. (sec. 1990), Am. Water Works Assn. Republican. Mem. LDS Ch. Home: 5801 Copper City Dr Salt Lake City UT 84118-7708 Office: Hercules Advanced Materials Co PO Box 98-8119 Magna UT 84044

SADUN, ALFREDO ARRIGO, neuro-ophthalmologist educator; b. New Orleans, Oct. 23, 1950; s. Elvio H. and Lina (Ottoleghi) S.; m. Debra Leigh Rice, Mar. 18, 1978; children: Rebecca Eli, Elvio Aaron, Benjamin Maxwell. BS, MIT, 1972; PhD, Albert Einstein Med. Sch., Bronx, N.Y., 1976, MD, 1978. Intern Huntington Meml. Hosp. U. So. Calif., Pasadena, 1978-79; resident Harvard U. Med. Sch., Boston, 1979-82, HEED Found. fellow in neuro-ophthalmology Mass. Eye and Ear Inst., 1982-83, instr. ophthalmology, 1983, asst. prof. ophthalmology, 1984; dir. residential tng. U. So. Calif. Dept. Ophthalmology, L.A., 1984-85; asst. prof. ophthalmology and neurosurgery U. So. Calif., L.A., 1984-87, assoc. prof., 1987-90; full prof. U. So. Calif., 1990—; prin. investigator Howe Lab. Harvard U., Boston, 1981-84, E. Doheny Eye Inst., L.A., 1984—; examiner Am. Bd. Ophthalmology; mem. internal rev. bd. U. So. Calif. Author: Optics for Opthalmologists, 1988, New Methods of Sensory Visual Testing, 1989; contbr. articles to profl. jours. and chpts. to books. James Adams scholar; recipient Pecan D. award, 1988-92. Fellow Am. Acad. Ophthalmology, Neuro-Ophthalmologists; mem. NIH (Med. Scientist Tng. award 1972-78), Am. Assn. Anatomists, Am. Univ. Prof. Orgn. (assoc.), Soc. to Prevent Blindness, Nat. Eye Inst. (New Investigator Rsch. award 1983-86), Soc. Neurosci., Assn. Rsch. in Vision and Ophthalmology, N.Am. Neuro-Ophthal. Soc. (chmn. membership com. 1990—). Home: 2478 Adair St San Marino CA 91108-2610 Office: U So Calif E Doheny Eye Inst 1450 San Pablo St Los Angeles CA 90033-4581

SAFERITE, LINDA LEE, library director; b. Santa Barbara, Calif., Mar. 25, 1947; d. Elwyn C. and Polly (Frazer) S.; m. Andre Doyon, July 16, 1985. BA, Calif. State U., Chico, 1969; MS in Library Sci., U. So. Calif., 1970; cert. in Indsl. Relations, UCLA, 1976; MBA, Pepperdine U., 1979. Librarian-in-charge, reference librarian Los Angeles County Pub. Libr. System, 1970-73, regional reference librarian, 1973-75, sr. librarian-in-charge,

1975-78, regional adminstr., 1978-80; library dir. Scottsdale (Ariz.) Pub. Libr. System, 1980—; task force del. White House Conf. on Libr. and Info. Svcs., 1992—, rep. Region V, 1982-94. Bd. dirs. Scottsdale-Paradise Valley YMCA, 1981-86, Ariz. Libr. Friends, 1990-92; bd. dirs. AMIGOS, 1990, chmn., 1992-93; mem. Class 5, Scottsdale Leavership, 1991. Recipient Cert. Recognition for efforts in civil rights Ariz. Atty. Gen.'s Office, 1985, Libr. award Ariz. Libr. Friends, 1988, Women of Distinction award for Edn., 1989; named State Libr. of Yr., 1990. Mem. ALA, Ariz. State Libr. Assn. (pres. 1987-88), Ariz. Women's Town Hall AlumniAssn., Met. Bus. and Profl. Women (Scottsdale, pres. 1986-87), Soroptimist (pres. 1981-83). Republican. Office: Scottsdale Pub Libr 3839 N Civic Center Blvd Scottsdale AZ 85251-4467

SAFFELL, MICHAEL HERBERT, construction company executive; b. L.A., Feb. 24, 1946; s. Herbert Ray and Arlene Muriel (Thompson) S.; m. Patricia L. Reynolds; children: Michael, Thomas, David. BA, Calif. State U., Long Beach, 1973, MPA, 1976. Adminstrv. asst. Daniel Freeman Meml. Hosp., Inglewood, Calif., 1973-78, asst. adminstr., 1978-81; corp. dir. facilities Freeman Health Svcs., Culver City, Calif., 1981-88; project mgr. health facilities D.W. McNeil Constrn. Co., L.A., 1988-89; pres. M.H. Saffell & Assocs., Torrance, Calif., 1989—. Mem. Calif. Hosp. Polit. Action Com. With USN, 1963-67. Named Outstanding Young Man of the Yr. U.S. Jaycees, 1976. Mem. Nat. Fire Protection Assn., Calif. Soc. Hosp. Engring., Am. Hosp. Assn., Ctr. for Pub. Policy and Adminstrn. Alumni Assn., Lions, Phi Alpha Alpha. Baptist. Office: M H Saffell & Assocs PO Box 11217 Torrance CA 90510

SAFFO, MARY BETH, research biologist; b. Inglewood, Calif., Apr. 8, 1948; d. Paul Laurence and Joan (Wilson) S.; 1 child, Nathan Alexander Whitehorn. BA, U. Calif., Santa Cruz., 1969; PhD, Stanford U., 1977. Miller research fellow U. Calif., Berkeley, 1976-78; asst. prof. Swarthmore (Pa.) Coll., 1978-85; ind. investigator Marine Biol. Lab., Woods Hole, Mass., 1979-84; assoc. research marine biologist U. Calif., Santa Cruz, 1985—, lectr., 1988—; vis. scholar U. Wash., Seattle, 1982. Grantee Rsch. Corp., 1980, 84, Am. Philos. Soc., 1980, 83, NSF, 1981, 84, 85, 92, NIH, 1992, Whitehall Found., 1984; Woodrow Wilson fellow, 1969-70, Steps Toward Independence fellow, 1979, AAUW fellow U. Calif., Berkeley, 1981-82. Fellow AAAS (electorate nominating com. sect. G 1989-92, chair 1991-92); mem. Am. Soc. Zoologists (program officer div. invertebrate zoology 1985-87, mem. com. to ensure equal opportunity 1988-90), Mycological Soc. Am., Internat. Soc. Endocytobiology, Soc. Study of Evolution, Ecol. Soc. Am. Democrat. Office: U Calif Inst Marine Scis Santa Cruz CA 95064

SAFFORD, FLORENCE VIRAY SUNGA, travel agent and consultant; b. Masantol, Luzon, Philippines, Mar. 19, 1929; came to U.S., 1953; d. Filomeno Garcia and Dominga (Viray) Sunga; m. Francis Ingersoll Safford, Aug. 4, 1979; children: H. Robert, Erlinda Ann, Ruben Michael. BS in Edn., Adamson U., Manila, 1952; student Hotel Mgnt., Political Sci., Kapiolani C.C., Honolulu, 1975; student, Am. Travel Sch., Honolulu, 1977. Tchr. Cecilio Apostolic Elem. Sch., Manila, 1949-51, St. Michael Acad., Masantol, 1951-52; social worker Cath. Social Svc., Honolulu, 1970-77; cons. Travel Cons. of the Pacific, Honolulu, 1977—. Named Most Outstanding Leader of the Community, Filipino Jaycees of Honolulu, 1976. Mem. Women's Community Action League of Hawaii (pres. 1972-93, Oustanding Pres. 1992), Filipino C. of C. of Hawaii (treas., Outstanding award 1991-92), Aloha Bus. and Profl. Women's Club (treas., Outstanding award 1981-89). Republican. Roman Catholic. Office: Women's Community Action PO Box 1238 Honolulu HI 96807

SAFIR, KATHLYN MARY, metaphysicologist, metapsychologist, novelist; b. Oakland, Calif., Oct. 24, 1948; d. Jay Leonard and Vera Margarette (McDaniel) Swaim; m. Robert Arn, May 11, 1979 (div. 1982). AS in Computer Sci. summa cum laude, Westland Coll., 1985; AS in Electronics summa cum laude, Santa Rosa Jr. Coll., 1989; DD, Universal Life Ch. of Calif., 1991, PhD in Religious Sci. magna cum laude, 1992. Income tax analyst Safir Svcs., L.A., 1968-74; sci. of the mind counselor Fresno and Santa Rosa, Calif., 1977—; metaphysicologist, metapsychologist Santa Rosa, 1985—. Author: (novel) Dreamtime, 1988; contbr. Mik'ael's Point of View series of articles to Free Spirit mag. Mem. NAFE, Internat. Platform Assn. Address: PO Box 246 Santa Rosa CA 95402-0246

SAFRAN, DANIEL, educator, consultant; b. N.Y.C., Feb. 3, 1939; s. Saul and Hannah (Israel) S.; m. Naomi Ruth Lowinsky, July 1, 1979; children: Lisa, Debra, Adam, Aaron, Tamar, Shanti. BA, CUNY, 1960; MSW, Bryn Mawr Coll., 1963; PhD, U. Calif., Berkeley, 1979. Community organizer, human svcs. trainer, 1963-68; prof. U. Md., 1969-70; dir. tng. Peace Corps, Kenya, 1970-72; dir. Ctr. for Study Parent Involvement, Orinda, Calif., 1978; prof., chair cons. psychology John F. Kennedy U., Orinda, 1988—; cons., Orinda, 1965—. Office: Ctr for Study Parent Involvement 370 Camino Pablo Orinda CA 94563

SAGAN, GREGORY THADDEUS, management consultant; b. Sewickley, Pa., Oct. 19, 1947; s. Joseph and Rosemary (Norton) Kumpan; m. Heather Kathleen Gardner, July 3, 1969; children: Bryan, Natasha, Benjamin. BA, West Tex. State U., 1970; MBA, U. Colo., 1977; postgrad., U. Tex., 1978-80. Agt. N.Y. Life Ins. Co., Colorado Springs, Colo., 1973-74; office mgr. Dye Constrn. Co., Colorado Springs, 1974-75; dir. exec. devel. Joske's of Tex., San Antonio, 1977-78; v.p. Senn-Delaney Group, Long Beach, Calif., 1984-93; owner Sigma Scholarship Info. Svcs., 1993—, Sagan & Assocs., 1993—. Lt. comdr. USN, 1970-73, 80-84. Mem. Am. Nuclear Soc.

SAGAWA, YONEO, horticulturist, educator; b. Olaa, Hawaii, Oct. 11, 1926; s. Chikatada and Mume (Kuno) S.; m. Masayo Yamamoto, May 24, 1962 (dec. Apr. 1988); children: Penelope Toshiko, Irene Teruko. AB, Washington U., St. Louis, 1950, MS, 1952; PhD, U. Conn., 1956. Postdoctoral research assoc. biology Brookhaven Nat. Lab., Upton, N.Y., 1955-57; guest in biology Brookhaven Nat. Lab., 1958; asst. prof., then assoc. prof. U. Fla., 1957-64; dir. undergrad. sci. ednl. research participation program NSF, 1964; cons. biosatellite project NASA, 1966-67; prof. horticulture U. Hawaii, 1964—; dir. Lyon Arboretum, 1967-91; assoc. dir. Hawaiian Sci. Fair, 1966-67, dir., 1967-68; research assoc. in biology U. Calif., Berkeley, 1970-71; rsch. assoc. Bishop Mus., Honolulu, 1992—; mem. Internat. Orchid Commn. on Classification, Nomenclature and Registration; fellow Inst. voor Toepassing van Atoomenegerie in de Landbouw, U. Agr., Waginingen, The Netherlands, 1979-80; mem. sci. adv. bd. Nat. Tropical Bot. Garden, 1975—; councilor Las Cruces Bot. Garden, Costa Rica; cons. FAO, Singapore, 1971; dir. Hawaii Tropical Bot. Garden. Editor: Hawaii Orchid Jour, 1972—, Pacific Orchid Soc. Bull, 1966-71; editorial bd.: Allertonia, 1976; contbr. numerous articles to profl. jours. Trustee Friends of Foster Garden, 1973—. With AUS, 1945-47. Recipient Disting. Svc. award South Fla. Orchid Soc., 1968; grantee Am. Orchid Soc., AEC, NIH, HEW, IMS, Stanley Smith Hort. Trust, Honolulu Orchid Soc., 1958—. Mem. AAAS, Internat. Assn. Hort. Sci., Internat. Assn. Plant Tissure Culture, Internat. Palm Soc., Am. Anthurium Soc. (hon., life), Am. Orchid Soc. (hon., life), Bot. Soc. Am., Am. Soc. Hort. Sci., Kaimuki Orchid Soc. (hon., life), Honolulu Orchid Soc. (hon., life), Lyon Arboretum Assn. (trustee 1974-91), Garden Club Honolulu (hon., life), Phi Kappa Phi (past chpt. pres., v.p., councilor). Democrat. Club: Aloha Bonsai (Honolulu). Office: U Hawaii Horticulture Rm 102 3190 Maile Way Honolulu HI 96822

SAGE, RODERICK DUNCAN, dermatologist, educator; b. Iowa City, Iowa, Feb. 13, 1926; s. Erwin Carlton and Katherine (Miles) S.; m. Jacquelin Irene Price, June 14, 1952; children: Jonathan S., Jefferson D., Rowan F., Andrew E. BA, U. Iowa, 1949; MD, Stanford U., 1954. Diplomate Am. Bd. Dermatology. Intern Med. Coll. Va., Richmond, 1953-54; med. resident Dartmouth Coll., Hanover, N.H., 1954-55; resident in dermatology Stanford Hosp., San Francisco, 1955-58; pvt. practice Reno, Nev., 1958—; prof. U. Nev. Med. Sch., Reno, 1971—; lectr. Stanford (Calif.) Med. Sch., 1966—; lectr., cons. in field. Contbr. articles to profl. publs. With USN, 1943-46. Office: 975 Ryland St Reno NV 89520-0113

SAGE, WILLIAM MATTHEW, lawyer, physician; b. N.Y.C., Oct. 8, 1960; s. Harold Hubert and Grace (Kent) S. AB, Harvard U., 1982; JD, Stanford U., 1988, MD, 1988. Bar: CAlif. 1990, D.C. 1991. Intern Mercy Hosp. Med. Ctr., San Diego, 1988-89; resident in anesthesiology The Johns Hopkins Hosp., Balt., 1989-90; assoc. O'Melveny & Myers, L.A., 1990—; vol. faculty Med. Sch., UCLA, 1990—, U. So. Calif., L.A., 1990—. Contbr. articles to profl. jours. Mem. AMA, ABA, Am. Soc. Law and Medicine, Calif. Soc. Healthcare Attys., Phi Beta Kappa, Order of the Coif.

SAGER, DONALD ALLEN, insurance company executive; b. Cleve., Sept. 13, 1930; s. Albert Allen and Dolores Vera (Stone) S.; m. Shirley T. Sager, Dec. 23, 1951; children: Donald A. II, David Allen. BA, U. Md., 1958; postgrad., U. Md. Law Sch., 1958-60. Sr. underwriter Monumental Life Ins. Co., Balt., 1958-64; v.p. Am. Health & Life Ins. Co., Balt., 1964-77; asst. v.p. Univ. Life Ins. Co., Indpls., 1977-81; v.p. Vulcan Life Ins. Co., Birmingham, Ala., 1981-84, Modern Pioneers' Life Ins. Co., Phoenix, 1984-87, Old Reliance Ins. Co., Phoenix, 1987—. Dir. Hearing and Speech Agy., Balt., 1974-77; treas. Essex Recreational Coun., Balt., 1966-73; bd. dirs. Arthritis Found., Phoenix, 1988-91; precinct capt. Rep. Party, Phoenix, 1990—. With U.S. Army, 1951-53, Korea. Decorated Bronze Star. Mem. Assn. Health Underwriters (legis. com. 1991-93), Masons, Moose, Elks, Order of De Molay (cert., N.D. gov. 1988-90). Lutheran. Home: 5429 E Charter Oak Rd Scottsdale AZ 85254 Office: Old Reliance Ins Co 1433 N 3d Ave Phoenix AZ 85003

SAGHATELIAN, SUSANN MARIE, management consultant; b. Fresno, Calif., May 23, 1958; d. Herman and Joanna Mary (D'Angelo) S. BS in Finance magna cum laude, Calif. State U., Fresno, 1980, MBA, 1986. Comml. loan officer Bank of Fresno, 1980-82; chief fin. officer Valley Bakery, Inc., Fresno, 1982-88; mktg. mgr. U.C. Devel., Fresno, 1989-90; owner, operator Saghatelian & Co., Fresno, 1990—; mktg. advisor Missionary Sisters of Holy Rosary, Phila., 1991; bd. dirs. Valley Bakery, Inc., 1983-88. Author: (poetry) Loving, 1992, Conversations, 1991. Mem. fundraising com. Richardson Campaign, Fresno, 1990. Mem. Kiwani, Beta Gamma Sigma (v.p. 1979-80), Phi Kappa Phi (v.p. 1978-79), Golden Key. Republican. Roman Catholic. Home: 3473 E Ashlan Ave Fresno CA 93726 Office: Saghatelian & Co 3473 E Ashlan Fresno CA 93726

SAGMEISTER, EDWARD FRANK, business owner; b. N.Y.C., Dec. 10, 1939; s. Frank and Anna (Unger) S.; m. Anne Marie Ducker, Aug. 18, 1962; children: Cynthia Anne, Laura Marie, Cheryl Suzanne, Eric Edward. BS, U. San Francisco, 1962; MBA, Syracuse U., 1968; postgrad., Air Command and Staff Coll., 1977, Air War Coll., 1981. Commd. 2d lt. USAF, 1963, advanced through grades to lt. col., ret., 1984; dir. devel. Am. Cancer Soc., Riverside, Calif., 1984-87; cons. Redlands, Calif., 1987-92; pres., chief exec. officer Hospitality Pub and Grub, Inc., San Bernadino, Calif., 1992—; ptnr., owner Midway Med. Ctr., San Bernadino, 1990-91; instr. Am. Internat. U., L.A., 1987; program dir. Am. Radio Network, L.A., 1987. Foreman pro tem San Bernadino County Grand Jury, 1990-91; active Redlands 2000 Com., 1988; campaign cabinet mem. Arrowhead United Way, San Bernadino, 1986-87, loaned exec., 1985; exec. dir. Crafton Hills Coll. Found., Yucaipa, Calif., 1988; vol. San Bernadino County Dept. Probation; active Redlands Community Chorus. Mem. San Bernadino C. of C., Ret. Officers Assn., Nat. Soc. Fundraising Execs. (dir. Inland empire chpt. 1987-88), Empire Singers (v.p. 1987). Republican. Roman Catholic. Home: 503 Sunnyside Ave Redlands CA 92373 Office: Hospitality Pub and Grub 1987 S Diners Ct San Bernardino CA 92408

SAGO, PAUL EDWARD, college administrator; b. Mo., July 5, 1931; s. John and Mabel S.; m. Donna; children: Bruce, Brad. Student, Mineral Area Coll., 1949-51; BS, Findlay Coll., 1953; postgrad., Winebrenner Theol. Sem., 1953-55; MS, St. Francis Coll., 1964; PhD, Walden U., 1976. Dir. devel. Findlay (Ohio) Coll., 1964-67, Hiram (Ohio) Coll., 1967-68; v.p. fin. affairs, treas. Anderson (Ind.) Coll., 1968-76; pres. Azusa Pacific U., Azusa, Calif., 1976-90, Woodbury U., Burbank, Calif., 1990—; participant seminars and insts. Trustee Findlay Coll., 1958-64; mem. Ind. adv. council SBA, 1972-76. Mem. Assn. Governing Bds. (pres.'s coun.), Internat. Platform Assn., Coun. for Advancement and Support Edn., Nat. Assn. Ind. Colls. and Univs., Assn. Ind. Calif. Colls. and Univs., Rotary. Office: Woodbury U 7500 N Glenoaks Blvd Burbank CA 91504-1099

SAHARA, ROBERT FUMIO, veterinarian; b. Ogden, Utah, Mar. 13, 1942; s. William Hiroshi and Chiyo (Shimada) S.; m. Joyce Michiko Sanwo, July 23, 1967; 1 child, Jennifer Yuki. AA in Zoology, Santa Monica City Coll., 1962; AB in Zoology, U. Calif., Davis, 1965, MS in Animal Physiology, 1967, DVM, 1972. Lab. technician I chronic acceleration rsch. unit, U. Calif., Davis, 1962-66; lab. technician II Zoology dept., U. Calif., L.A., 1966-68; lab. technician II chronic acceleration rsch. unit animal physiology group, U. Calif., Davis, 1968-72; staff veterinarian, Romie Lane Vet. Hosp., Salinas, Calif., 1972-73, Bay Pet Hosp., Monterey, Calif., 1972-73, Midtown Animal Hosp., Sacramento, 1973-74; chief of staff Sacramento Emergency Vet. Clinic, 1974-76; co-owner, veterinarian Greenhaven Vet. Hosp., Sacramento, 1976-91, sole owner, 1991—; reserve warden Calif. Dept. Fish and Game, 1985—; bd. vistors U. Calif. Sch. Vet. Medicine, 1989-92. Bd. dirs. Jan Ken Po Gakko, Sacramento, 1981-84; chmn. Sacramentans for Hope-No on Measure L, 1989. Mem. AVMA, Calif. Vet. Med. Assn. (bd. govs. dist V, 1983-89, pres. 1989, co-chair environ. and pub. health com., Pres. award 1991), Sacramento Valley Vet. Med. Assn. (exec. bd. 1978-81, pres. 1980, chmn. membership com.), Monterey Bay Vet. Assn. Republican. Buddhist. Avocations: woodworking, photography, hunting, fishing, skeet shooting, pistol shooting. Office: Greenhaven Veterinary Hosp 1 Valine Ct Sacramento CA 95831

SAHLIN, ANNIE MALORY, bookkeeping professional, photographer; b. Princeton, N.J., June 14, 1948; d. John. C. and Malory (Campbell) Ausland; m. Richard Sahlin, Sept. 1977 (div. Dec. 1985). BA in Anthropology, U. Md., 1971; MA in Guidance and Counseling, U. N.Mex., 1977; postgrad., Gallaudet U., 1987. Counselor various youth agys. Albuquerque, Santa Fe, 1976-80; bookkeeper Agua Fria Nursery, Santa Fe, 1980-83, James Reid Ltd., Santa Fe, 1984-88; prin. Annie's In Bus., Santa Fe, 1989—; photographer Nat. Mus. Am. History-Smithsonian Instn., Washington, 1991—. Photographs appear in Am. Encounters exhibit Smithsonian Instn., 1992—, numerous books and articles; participant group exhbns., Santa Fe, 1988—. Big sister N.Mex. Sch. for Deaf, Santa Fe, 1986-92. Mem. Phi Beta Kappa.

SAICHEK, ALAN B., software test engineer; b. Milw., Mar. 13, 1946; s. Al and Corra Ruth (Nichols) S. BA, U. Wis., Madison, 1972; MS in Edn., U. Wis., Whitewater, 1974. Elem. tchr. pub. schs., Racine, Marinette, Menominee, Wis., 1974-77; field svc. instr. Astronautics Corp., Milw., 1979-81; tech. support specialist Benson-Varian, Inc., Mountain View, Calif., 1979-81; engr. in software quality assurance The Systems Group, Santa Clara, Calif., 1981-82; sr. graphics programmer Benson, Inc., Mountain View, 1982-84; sr. software test engr. Sytek, Inc., Mountain View, 1984-87; mgr. systems engring. DocuPro, Inc., Mountain View, 1987-89; systems adminstr. Omni Solutions/Interphase, Mountain View, 1989-90; software devel. kit test team leader GO Corp., Fremont, Calif., 1990—. With U.S. Army, 1964-68, Korea, Thailand. Mem. Assn. for Computing Machinery, Planetary Soc., Nat. Parks and Conservation Assn., Environ. Def. Fund. Home: PO Box S-3204 Carmel CA 93921

SAID, HAMID M., physiologist, educator; b. Baghdad, Dec. 23, 1954; came to U.S., 1981; s. Mohammed Said and Karema Abbas; m. Christy Lynn Lowe, Dec. 23, 1988; 1 child, Hannah Layla. PharmD, U. Baghdad, 1977; PhD, U. Aston, Birmingham, Eng., 1981. Postdoctoral rsch. fellow Scripps Clinic and Rsch. Found., La Jolla, Calif., 1981-82; asst. rsch. physiologist Sch. Medicine U. Calif., Irvine, 1982-84; co-dir. Intestinal Transport Rsch. Core, Nashville, 1984-88; dir. Nutrition Rsch. Lab., Nashville, 1984-88; asst. prof. Sch. Medicine Vanderbilt U., Nashville, 1984-88; assoc. prof. Sch. Medicine U. Calif., Irvine, 1988—; grant reviewer VA, USDA; reviewer numerous sci. jours. Contbr. 85 rsch. articles, 50 med. abstracts to profl. publs. Grantee NIH, 1988—, 89, NSF, 1989, VA, 1991—. Mem. Am. Physiol. Soc., Am. Gastroenterology Assn., Am. Inst. Nutrition, Am. Soc. Clin. Nutrition. Office: VA Med Ctr Med Rsch Svcs 151 Long Beach CA 90822

SAIER, MILTON H, JR., biology educator; b. Palo Alto, Calif., July 30, 1941; s. Milton H. and Lucelia (Bates) S.; m. Jeanne K. Woodhams; children: Hans H., Anila J., Amanda L. BS, U. Calif., Berkeley, 1964, PhD, 1968. Prof. biology U. Calif., Berkeley, 1959-68, Johns Hopkins U., Balt., 1968-72, U. Calif., San Diego, 1972—; cons. Merck, Eli Lilly. Author 4 books; contbr. 200 sci. articles to profl. jours. U.S. Pub. Health Svc. grantee NIH. Mem. Am. Soc. Microbiology, Am. Soc. Biochemistry and Molecular Biology. Home: 666 Quail Gardens Dr Encinitas CA 92024 Office: U Calif San Diego Dept Bio 0116 La Jolla CA 92093-0116

SAINES, MARVIN, hydrogeologist; b. Bronx, N.Y., Feb. 14, 1942. BS, Bklyn. Coll., 1963; MS, Miami U., Oxford, Ohio, 1966; PhD, U. Mass., 1973. Registered profl. engring. geologist, Oreg., hydrogeologist Am. Inst. Hydrology; cert. environ. mgr., Nev. Hydrogeologist Roy F. Weston Inc., West Chester, Pa., 1969-71, Harza Engring. Co., Chgo., 1971-80; sr. hydrogeologist Harza Engring. Co., Las Vegas, Nev., 1989-92, Woodard-Clyde, Chgo., 1980-81, Tetra Tech Internat., Arlington, Va., 1981-86; pres. Land & Water Co., Chgo., 1986-87; sr. hydrogeologist Donohue and Assocs., Chgo., 1987-89, Kleinfelden, Las Vegas, 1992; pvt. practice cons. Las Vegas, 1993—. Contbr. numerous articles to profl. jours. Mem. Assn. Engring. Geologists (founder Las Vegas chpt., chmn. 1990-93), Geol. Soc. Am., Nat. Groundwater Assn., Internat. Assn. Hydrology.

ST. AMAND, PIERRE, geophysicist; b. Tacoma, Wash., Feb. 4, 1920; s. Cyrias Z. and Mable (Berg) St. A.; m. Marie Pöss, Dec. 5, 1945; children: Gene, Barbara, Denali, David. BS in Physics, U. Alaska, 1948; MS in Geophysics, Calif. Inst. Tech., 1951, PhD in Geophysics and Geology, 1953; Dr. honoris causa, U. De Los Altos, Tepatitlan, Mex., 1992. Asst. dir. Geophys. Lab., U. Alaska, also head ionospheric and seismologic investigations, 1946-49; physicist U.S. Naval Ordnance Test Sta., China Lake, Calif., 1950-54; head optics br. U.S. Ordnance Test Sta., 1955-58, head earth and planetary sci. div., 1961-88, now cons. to tech. dir., head spl. projects office; fgn. service with ICA as prof. geol. and geophys. Sch. Earth Scis., U. Chile, 1958-60; originator theory rotational displacement Pacific Ocean Basin; pres. Saint-Amand Sci. Services; adj. prof. McKay Sch. Mines, U. Nev., U. N.D.; v.p., dir. Covillea Corp.; v.p., dir. Mutual Corp.; cons. World Bank, Calif. Div. Water Resources, Am. Potash & Chem. Co., OAS; mem. U.S. Army airways communications system, Alaska and Can., 1942-46; cons. Mexican, Chilean, Argentine, Philipines, Can. govts.; mem. Calif. Gov.'s Com. Geol. Hazards; mem. com. magnetic instruments Internat. Union Geodesy and Geophys., 1954-59, Disaster Preparation Commn. for Los Angeles; charter mem. Sr. Exec. Service. Adv. bd. GeoScience News; contbr. 100 articles to scientific jours. Chmn. bd. dirs. Ridgecrest Community Hosp.; chmn. bd. dirs. Indian Wells Valley Airport Dist.; v.p. bd. dirs. Kern County Acad. Decathlon. Decorated knight Mark Twain, Mark Twain Jour.; recipient cert. of merit OSRD, 1945, cert. of merit USAAF, 1946, letter of commendation USAAF, 1948, Spl. award Philippine Air Force, 1969, Diploma de Honor Sociedad Geologica de Chile, Disting. Civilian Svc. medal USN, 1968, L.T.E. Thompson medal, 1973, Thunderbird award Weather Modification Assn., 1974, Disting. Pub. Svc. award Fed. Exec. Inst., 1976, Meritorious Svc. medal USN, 1988, Disting. Alumnus award U. Alaska, 1990; Fulbright rsch. fellow France, 1954-55. Fellow AAAS, Geol. Soc. Am., Eathquake Engr. Rsch. Inst.; mem. Am. Geophys. Union, Weather Modification Assn., Am. Seismol. Soc., Sister Cities (Ridgecrest-Tepatitlan) Assn. (pres.), Rotary (past pres., Paul Harris fellow), Footprinters Internat. (mem. grand bd., pres.), Sigma Xi. Home: 1748 W Las Flores Ave Ridgecrest CA 93555-9672

ST. CLAIR, CARL, conductor, music director. Music dir. Pacific Symphony Orch., Santa Ana, Calif., 1990—. Office: Pacific Symphony Orch 1231 E Dyer Rd Santa Ana CA 92705-5606

ST. CLAIR, VERNON GAROLD, real estate broker; b. Catesby, Okla., May 21, 1930; s. Arthur Wilmas and Ruth Marie (O'Hair) St.C.; m. Barbara Maurath, 1956 (div. 1973); children: Cindy, Marianne, Sharon, Kevin, Dana, Keith; m. Anne Murphy, Aug. 23, 1975; children: Matthew, Christina. BS in Engring., West Coast Coll. Engring., 1957. Cert. property mgr.; cert. comml. investment mem. Prin. St. Clair Realty, Torrance, Calif., 1965-78; owner, pres., CEO St. Clair Investments, Inc. and St. Clair Property Mgmt., Redondo Beach, Calif., 1978—; lectr. and instr. in field. Contbr. articles to trade mags. With USN, 1950-58. Mem. We. Mobilehome Assn. (bd. dirs. 1982-87, chpt. pres. 1985-90, pres. 1991-92), Calif. Manufactured Housing Industry, Calif. Travel Parks Assn., Nat. Campground Owners Assn., Rotary Internat. (pres. 1977-78). Republican. Office: St Clair Investments Inc Ste 110 435 N Pacific Coast Hwy Redondo Beach CA 90277

ST. DENNIS, JERRY A., banker; b. Tacoma, WA, 1942. BA, UCLA, 1965, MA, 1967. V.p. Claremont Econs. Inst., 1978-81; chief fin. officer, exec. v.p., dir. CalFed Inc., L.A., 1981-89, pres., COO, 1989-90, chmn., pres., CEO, 1990—; chmn. bd. dirs. Calif. Fed. Bank (subs. CalFed Inc.), L.A., 1990—. Office: Calif Fed Bank 5700 Wilshire Blvd Los Angeles CA 90036-3659*

SAINT-ERNE, NICHOLAS JOHN DE, veterinarian; b. Wichita, Kans., Dec. 12, 1958; s. Philip George and Gladys May (Fitzgerald) de Saint-E. BS, Kans. State U., 1982, DVM, 1984. Magician Stevens Magic Emporium, Wichita, 1975-82, Midtown Manhattan, Kans., 1982-84; vet. Lake Mead Animal Hosp., Las Vegas, Nev., 1984-87, Exotic Pet Hosp., Las Vegas, 1987-89, Animal Med. Hosp., Las Vegas, 1989-92, Park Animal Hosp., Las Vegas, 1992—; bd. dirs. Wild Wing Project, Las Vegas, 1988-90. Author: The Chinese Linking Rings, 1981, The Berg Book, 1983. Mem. Internat. Assn. Aquatic Animal Medicine, Am. Vet. Med. Assn., Internat. Brotherhood of Magicians (ring pres. 1985-87), Soc. Aquatic Vet. Medicine, Las Vegas Avicultural Soc. (bd. dirs. 1986-87), Las Aquarium Soc. (pres. 1987-88), Assn. Avian Vets. Republican. Roman Catholic. Home: 441 Inglewood Cir Las Vegas NV 89123 Office: Park Animal Hosp 7380 S Eastern Ave Las Vegas NV 89123

SAINT-JACQUES, BERNARD, linguistics educator; b. Montreal, Que., Can., Apr. 26, 1928; s. Albert and Germaine (Lefebvre) Saint-J.; m. Marguerite Fauquenoy. M.A., Sophia U., Tokyo, 1962; M.S., Georgetown U., 1964; Doctorat es Lettres and Scis. Humaines, Paris U., 1975. Asst. prof. linguistics U. B.C., Vancouver, 1967-69; assoc. prof. U. B.C., 1969-78, prof., 1978-90, prof. emeritus, 1991—; prof. Aichi U., Japan, 1990—; mem. U.S. Citizen Amb. Program. Author: Structural Analysis of Modern Japanese, 1971, Aspects sociolinguistiques du bilinguisme canadien, 1976, Language and Ethnic Relations, 1979, Japanese Studies in Canada, 1985. Leave fellow Can. Council, 1974; profl. fellow Japan Found., 1981; research fellow French Govt., 1982, Ohira Programme, Japan, 1983. Fellow Royal Soc. Can. Acad.; mem. Sociolinguistic Assn. (co-editor), Linguistic Soc. Am., Can. Soc. Asian Studies, Can. Linguistics Assn. Office: U BC, Dept Linguistics, Vancouver, BC Canada V6T 1Z1 also: Aichi ShuKutoKu U., Katahira NagaKute, NagaKute-cho Aichi-gun Aichi 480-11, Japan

ST. JEAN, GARRY, professional basketball coach; m. Mary Jane St. Jean; children: Emily, Gregory. B in Phys. Edn., Springfield (Mass.) Coll., 1973, M in Phys. Edn., postgrad. cert. Head coach Chicopee (Mass.) High Sch., 1973-80; coll. scout, asst. bench coach, asst. dir. player pers. Milw. Bucks, 1980-86; asst. coach, asst. player pers. dir. N.J. Nets, 1986-88; asst. coach Golden State Warriors, 1988-92; head coach Sacramento Kings, 1992—. Office: Sacramento Kings One Sports Pkwy Sacramento CA 95834

ST. JOHN, EUGENE LOGAN, labor union director; b. Everett, Wash., Dec. 2, 1947; s. Huston Hopkins and Rena (Guillette) St. John; m. Carolyn Sue Crabb, July 15, 1978; children: Jeannine, Jordan, Michael, Matthew. BA, Western Wash. U., 1970; postgrad., U. Wash., 1978. VISTA vol. U.S. Govt. OEO, Ft. Lauderdale, Fla., 1970-71; organizer Internat. Fedn. Profl. and Tech. Engrs. Local 17 AFL-CIO, Seattle, 1972-74, bus. rep., 1974-80, program dir., 1980-82; exec. dir. Wash. Pub. Employees Assn., Olympia, 1982—. Bd. dirs. Evergreen State Coll. Labor Ctr., Olympia, 1988-90; mem. Pub. Employees Retirement System Adv. Com., Olympia, 1984-86; bd. dirs. Wash. Citizen Action, Seattle, 1990-92, People For Fair Taxes, Olympia, 1986-90, Thurston County Child Care Action Coun., Olympia, 1988-90. Mem. Wash. Soc. Assn. Execs., Indsl. Rels. Rsch. Assn., Wash. State Grange, Third House Lobbyist Orgn. Democrat. Office: Wash Pub Employees Assn 124 10th Ave SW Olympia WA 89501

ST. JOHN, PAUL MARION, lawyer; b. Le Mars, Iowa, Jan. 8, 1948; s. Marion E. and Audrey (Salas) St. J.; m. Caitlin Williams, Mar. 13, 1982; 1 child, Susan M. BA, Stanford U., 1970; MA, Washington U., St. Louis, 1972; JD, U. Calif., San Francisco, 1976. Bar: Calif. 1976. Dep. county counsel Contra Costa County, Martinez, Calif., 1977-78; atty. in pvt. practice San Francisco, 1978-85; dep. counsel San Bernardino County, San Bernardino, Calif., 1985—. Mem. bishop's com. St. Hilary's Episcopal Ch., Hesperia, Calif., 1992. Fulbright Swiss-Am. Exch. fellow, U. Neuchatel, 1970-71. Mem. State Bar Calif., Greater Inland Empire Bar Assn., Am. Radio Relay League. Democrat. Home: 13583 Buena Vista Dr Hesperia CA 92345 Office: San Bernardino County Counsel 385 N Arrowhead Ave 4th Fl San Bernardino CA 92415-0140

SAITO, FRANK KIYOJI, import-export firm executive; b. Tokyo, Feb. 28, 1945; s. Kaoru and Chiyoko S.; LL.B., Kokugakuin U., 1967; m. Elaine Tamami Karasawa, Feb. 22, 1975; children—Roderic Kouki, Lorine Erika. With import dept. Trois Co. Ltd., Tokyo, Japan, 1967-68; founder import/export dept. Three Bond Co., Ltd., Tokyo, 1968-71; sales mgr. Kobe Mercantile, Inc., San Diego, 1971-76; pres. K & S Internat. Corp., San Diego, 1976—. Office: K & S Internat Corp K & S Bldg 8015 Silverton Ave San Diego CA 92126-6383

SAITO, THEODORE T., physicist; b. Poston, Ariz., Sept. 9, 1942; s. Frank Hideo and Akiko Saito; m. Diane Gail Signorino, Aug. 31, 1968; children: Jennifer, Paul. BS, USAF Acad., 1964; SM, MIT, 1966; PhD, Pa. State U., 1970. Project officer, group leader Air Force Weapons Lab., Albuquerque, 1970-74; leader Lawrence Livermore (Calif.) Nat. Lab., 1974-77, dep. program leader precision engring. program, 1984-87, dept. dept. head, 1987-88, group leader, 1988-92, acting leader precision engring. program, 1993—; dir. mgmt. tech. Air Force Materials Lab., Wright Patterson AFB, Ohio, 1977-79, tech. area mgr., 1979-80; from dir. to comdr. F. J. Seiler Rsch. Lab. USAF Acad., Colo., 1980-84; Livermore Nat. Lab., Calif., 1992—. Contbr. articles to profl. jours. Mem., v.p. Japanese-Am. Citizen League, Plesanton, Calif., 1985—. Fellow Optical Soc. Am., Soc. Photo-Optical Instrumentation Engrs. (sec. No. Calif. chpt. 1989-90, sec. 1990, v.p. 1991, pres. 1992, immediate past pres. 1993), Am. Soc. Precision Engrs., Assn. Fed. Tech. Transfer Execs. (bd. dirs. 1993—). Office: Livermore Nat Lab PO Box 808 L-644 Livermore CA 94551-0808

SAITO, WILLIAM HIROYUKI, software company executive; b. L.A., Mar. 23, 1971; s. Toshiyuki and Yoko (Onago) S. BS in Biochemistry, BA in Polit. Sci., U. Calif., Riverside, 1992. Cert. EMT. Programmer Merrill Lynch, Burbank, Calif., 1985-86; instr. Calif. Poly. U., Pomona, 1985-87; staff cons. computer sci. dept. U. Calif., Rancho Cucamonga, Tokyo, 1988-92; ptnr. I/O Software, Walnut, Calif., 1987-90; pres. I/O Software, Riverside, Calif., 1990-91; pres., CEO, I/O Software, Inc., Cucamonga, Calif., 1991—; CEO, I/O Software Japan, Tokyo, 1991—; cons. IBM, Riverside, 1986-87, Japan IBM, Tokyo, 1988-90, Japan NEC, Tokyo, 1987-89, ASCII, Tokyo, 1988-90. Republican. Roman Catholic. Office: I/O Software Inc 10970 Arrow Rt Ste 202 Cucamonga CA 91730

SAKAMOTO, NORMAN LLOYD, civil engineer; b. Honolulu, May 22, 1947; s. Shuichi and Fusa (Hayashi) S.; m. Penelope A. Hayasaka, July 12, 1970; children: David H., Gregory F., Katherine E. BSCE, U. Hawaii, 1969; MSCE, U. Ill., 1970. Registered profl. engr., Calif., Hawaii; lic. spl. inspector, Hawaii. Engr. storm drain City of L.A., 1970-71, engr. streets and frwys., 1972-73; engr. hydrology C.E., 1971-72; v.p. S & M Sakamoto, Inc., Honolulu, 1973-85; pres. SC Pacific Corp., Ewa Beach, Hawaii, 1985—; bd. dirs. Bldg. Industry Assn., Honolulu, spl. appointee, 1991-92, pres.-elect, 1993; bd. dirs. City Contractors Assn., Honolulu. Scoutmaster Honolulu area Boy Scouts Am., 1989-92. Named Remodeler of Month Bldg. Industry Assn., 1990, 91, Remodeler of Yr., 1991. Mem. ASCE, Internat. Fellowship Christian Businessmen, Constrn. Industry Legis. Assn., C. of C. Evangelical. Office: SC Pacific Corp 91-178 Kalaeloa Blvd Kapolei HI 96707

SAKKAL, MAMOUN, interior designer; b. Damascus, Syria, Dec. 31, 1950; came to U.S., 1978; s. Lutfi Sakkal and Dourieh Khatib; m. Seta K. Sakkal, Mar. 13, 1980; children: Aida, Kindah. BArch with honors, U. Aleppo, Syria, 1974; MArch, U. Wash., 1982, cert. urban design, 1982. Registered architect, Syria; lic. interior designer, U.S. Archtl. designer MCE, Damascus, 1974-75; dir. design MCE, Aleppo, 1975-76; prin. Sakkal & Assocs., Aleppo, 1976-78; archtl. designer Arch. Assocs., Seattle, 1978-82; sr. designer RD&S, Bellevue, Wash., 1982-84; prin. Restaurant/Hotel Design, Seattle, 1984—, Sakkal Design, Bothell, 1991—; lectr. U. Aleppo, 1974-75, Applied Arts Inst., 1977-78, affiliate instr. U. Wash., 1990—. Author: Geometry of Muqarnas in Islamic Architecture, 1981; designer Oct. Mus., Damascus, Syria, 1977 (1st prize Syrian Ministry Dev.); one man shows include Nat. Mus. Aleppo, Syria, 1969, U. Aleppo, 1984, U. Wash., 1979, 80, 90, 91, U. Cambridge, Eng., 1990; contbr. articles to profl. jours. Recipient Best Logo Design award Arab Union Sports, 1976, Best Project Design award Aleppo Ministry of Culture, 1975, Best Moderization Project award Holiday Inns. System, 1986, Best Lounge Renovation award Bowlers Jour. Annual Design Contest, 1987. Office: Sakkal Design 1523 175th Pl SE Bothell WA 98012-6460

SAKSEN, LOUIS CARL, hospital administrator, architect; b. Washington, Dec. 30, 1946; s. Louis Karl and Sara Flower (Farr) S.; m. Elizabeth Helen Wilson, June 24, 1972; children: Alexander, Katie, Micheal. BArch, Cath. U. Am., 1969; MArch, Va. Poly. Inst. and State U., 1974; MS in Psychology, Old Dominion U., 1975. Registered architect, Va., Calif., NCARB. Mgr. planning, instl. rsch. and planning Va. Commonwealth U., Richmond, 1975-78, dir. facilities planning and constrn., 1978-81, asst. v.p. facilities mgmt. div., 1981-85; dep. v.p. health scis. facilities Columbia U., N.Y.C., 1986-88; v.p. for facilities Presbyn. Hosp. in the City of N.Y., 1988-90, sr. v.p., gen. mgr. facilities and svcs., 1990-91; assoc. hosp. dir., environ. and support svcs. Stanford (Calif.) Hosp., 1991—. Pres. parish coun. St. Peters Roman Cath. Ch., 1981-82; mem. Mayor's Com. on Handicapped, 1982; chmn. property com. ARC, 1982; chmn. ops. com. Port of Richmond Commn., 1983-84; mem. adv. bd. Hosp. Hospitality House, 1984-85; mem. Bd. Recreation, Essex Fells, N.J., 1988-92; mem. Archtl. Rev. Com., Half Moon Bay, Calif., 1992—. With USN, 1971-74. Recipient Letters of Appreciation, Supreme Allied Comdr. Atlantic; Letter of Commendation from comdr. U.S. Naval Communication Sta., Londonderry, No. Ireland, 1972; winner design competition for urban park Smithsonian Inst., Washington, 1968; named to Outstanding Young Mem. of Am., 1981. Mem. AIA (chpt. pres. 1982), Assn. Univ. Architects, Assn. Phys. Plant Adminstrs., Am. Hosp. Assn., Univ. Hosp. Consortium, Rotary Internat. Republican. Roman Catholic. Office: Stanford U Hosp 300 Pasteur Dr Stanford CA 94305

SAKUMA, THOMAS TAMOTSU, business executive, real estate broker; b. Okinawa, Japan, Feb. 11, 1947; came to U.S., 1984.; s. Seitoku and Chiyo (Machida) S.; m. Kazuko Sakuma, July 12, 1969; children: Makoto, Airi, Atau, Yumi M., Elika C. BA, Okinawa U., 1970; MPA, Brigham Young U., 1980. Instr. U. Md., Okinawa, 1983; fin. analyst Fotomat Corp., St. Petersburg, Fla., 1984-85; mem. staff The Bank of Tokyo, Seattle, 1986; agt. Bruch & Vedrich, Real Estate, Seattle, 1987-89; pres. Sakuma & Sjolund, Inc., Seattle, 1990; pres., v.p. SAM Japan & Assocs., Inc., Seattle, 1990-91; owner Karaoke Land, Edmonds, Wash., 1992—, Video Nippon, Edmonds, Wash., 1988—, Sakuma & Co., Internat., Edmonds, Wash., 1988—; pres. Kaythom Dynamics Corp., Edmonds, Wash., 1990—; bd. dirs. A&J Internat., Edmonds, pres. 1993—. Mem. high coun. Lynnwood (Wash.) Stake of LDS Ch., 1990—. Recipient scholarship U.S. Govt., Okinawa, 1968, Brigham Young U., Hawaii, 1977. Mem. Okinawan Club of Wash. State (pres. 1991—), Brigham Young U. Mgmt. Soc. (Seattle chpt.). Home: 8525 224th St SW Edmonds WA 98026 Office: 22315 Hwy 99 Ste J Edmonds WA 98026

SALAITA, GEORGE NICOLA, physicist; b. Madaba, Jordan, Apr. 22, 1931; came to U.S., 1954; s. Nicola J. and Azizeh (Shamas) S.; m. Linda Masou, July 30, 1959; children: Nicholas, John, Nadya. BS in Physics, Millikin U., 1957; MS in Physics, Tex. A&M, 1959; PhD, Va. Polytech. Inst. & State U., 1966. Rsch. tech. Mobil Rsch., Dallas, 1959-62; asst. prof., assoc. prof., prof. So. Meth. U., Dallas, 1966-81; sr. rsch. assoc. Chevron Oil Field Rsch. Co., LaHabra, Calif., 1981—; cons. Gearhart Inc., Ft. Worth, 1970-80; chmn. numerous IEEE, Soc. Petroleum Engrs. and Soc. Profl. Well Log Analysts symposia. Editor: The Log Analyst, 1988-89; contbr. tech. articles to profl. jours. Mem. Soc. Petroleum Engrs., Soc. Profl. Well Log Analysts, Am. Nuclear Soc., Sigma Xi. Office: Chevron Pet Tech Co 1300 S Beach Blvd La Habra CA 90631-6374

SALAMON, MIKLOS DEZSO GYORGY, mining educator; b. Balkany, Hungary, May 20, 1933; came to U.S., 1986; s. Miklos and Sarolta (Obetko) S.; m. Agota Maria Meszaros, July 11, 1953; children: Miklos, Gabor. Diploma in Engring., Polytech U., Sopron, Hungary, 1956; PhD, U. Durham, Newcastle, England, 1962; doctorem honoris causa, U. Miskolc, Hungary, 1990. Research asst. dept. mining engring. U. Durham, 1959-63; dir. research Coal Mining Research Controlling Council, Johannesburg, South Africa, 1963-66; dir. collieries research lab Chamber of Mines of South Africa, Johannesburg, 1966-74, dir. gen. research org., 1974-86; disting. prof., dir. Ctr. for Advanced Mining Systems, Colo. Sch. Mines, Golden, 1986—, head dept. mining engring., 1986-90, dir. Colo. Mining and Mineral Resources Rsch. Inst., 1990—; 22d Sir Julius Wernher Meml. lectr., 1988; hon. prof. U. Witwatersrand, Johannesburg, 1979-86; vis. prof. U. Minn., Mpls., 1981, U. Tex., Austin, 1982, U. NSW, Sydney, Australia, 1990, 91—. Co-author: Rock Mechanics Applied to the Study of Rockbursts, 1966, Rock Mechanics in Coal Mining, 1976; contbr. articles to profl. jours. Mem. Pres.'s Sci. Adv. Council, Cape Town, South Africa, 1984-86, Nat. Sci. Priorities Com., Pretoria, South Africa, 1984-86. Recipient Nat. award Assn. Scis. and Tech. Socs., South Africa, 1971. Fellow South African Inst. Mining and Metallurgy (hon. life, v.p. 1974-76, pres. 1976-77, gold medal 1964, 85, Stokes award 1986, silver medal 1991), Inst. Mining and Metallurgy (London); mem. AIME, Internat. Soc. Rock Mechanics. Roman Catholic. Office: Colo Sch of Mines Dept of Mining Engring Golden CO 80401

SALAND, LINDA CAROL, anatomy educator, researcher; b. N.Y.C., Oct. 24, 1942; d. Charles and Esther (Weingarten) Gewirtz; m. Joel S. Saland, Aug. 16, 1964; children—Kenneth, Jeffrey. B.S., CCNY, 1963, Ph.D. in Biology, 1968; M.A. in Zoology, Columbia U., 1965. Research assoc. dept. anatomy Columbia U. Coll. Physicians and Surgeons, N.Y.C., 1968-69; sr. research assoc. dept. anatomy Sch. Medicine, U. N.Mex., Albuquerque, 1971-78, asst. prof., 1978-83, assoc. prof., 1983-89, prof., 1989—. Mem. editorial bd. Anat. Record, 1980—; contbr. articles to profl. jours. Predoctoral fellow NDEA, 1966-68; research grantee Nat. Inst. on Drug Abuse, 1979-83, NIH Minority Biomed. Research Support Program, 1980—; NIH research grantee, 1986—. Mem. Am. Assn. Anatomists, Soc. for Neurosci., Women in Neuroscience (chair steering comm. 1991-93), Am. Soc. Cell Biology, Am. Soc. Zoologists, AAAS, Sigma Xi. Office: U NMex Sch Medicine Dept Anatomy Basic Med Sci Bldg Albuquerque NM 87131

SALAZAR, LUIS ADOLFO, architect; b. New Orleans, Sept. 17, 1944; s. Gustavo Adolfo and Luz Maria (Florez) S.; m. Sandra Kay Bucklew, May 30, 1969 (div. Jan. 1984); 1 child, Staci Dahnal. AA, Harbor Coll., 1966; BArch, Ariz. State U., 1971. Registered architect, Ariz., Calif., N.Mex. Area architect Peace Corps, Sierra Leone, 1971-73; project architect Van Sittert Assocs., Phoenix, 1973-77; pres., owner Salazar Assoc. Architects, Ltd., Phoenix, Inc., Inc., 1977—; Prin. works include bldg. design Kenema Cathedral, Kenema, Sierra Leone, West Africa, 1980. Bd. dirs. Community Behavioral Services, Phoenix, 1983-85; Phoenix Meml. Hosp., 1984—, Terraco Properties. mem. Subcom. on Bond Election, Phoenix, 1984; mem. Visual Improvement Awards Com., City of Phoenix, 1985-88. Mem. AIA (chmn. program com., honor award Ariz. chpt. 1984, visual improvement awards coms. 1985, 86), Soc. Am. Value Engrs., Inst. Architects. Roman Catholic. Office: Salazar Assocs Architects Ltd 2645 N 7th Ave Phoenix AZ 85007-1101

SALCUDEAN, MARTHA EVA, mechanical engineer, educator; b. Cluj, Romania, Feb. 26, 1934; emigrated to Can., 1976, naturalized, 1979; d. Edmund and Sarolta (Hirsch) Abel. B.Eng., U. Cluj, 1956; postgrad., 1962; PhD, U. Brasov (Romania), 1969; PhD (hon.), U. Ottawa, 1993 ; m. George Salcudean, May 28, 1955; 1 child, Septimiv E. (Tim). Mech. engr. Armatura, Cluj, 1956-63; sr. rsch. officer Nat. Rsch. Inst. Metallurgy, Bucharest, 1963-75; part-time lectr. Inst. Poly., Bucharest, 1967-75; sessional lectr. U. Ottawa (Ont., Can.), 1976-77, asst. prof., 1977-79, assoc. prof., 1979-81, prof., 1981-85; prof., head dept. mech. engring. U. B.C., 1985—; mem. grant selection com. for mech. engring. Natural Scis. and Engring. Rsch. Coun. Can.; mem. Nat. Adv. Panel to Min. Sci. and Tech. on advanced indsl. materials, Can., 1990; mem. governing coun. Nat. Rsch. Coun. Recipient Gold medal B.C. Sci. Coun., Killam Rsch. prize U. B.C. Rsch. Coun. Can. grantee, 1978—, Commemorative Medal 125th anniversary Can. Confederation, 1993. Fellow Can. Acad. Engring.; mem. Assn. Profl. Engrs. Ont., ASME. Contbr. numerous articles to profl. jours.; patentee in field. Home: 1938 Western Pkwy, Vancouver, BC Canada V6T 1W5

SALDICH, ROBERT JOSEPH, electronics company executive; b. N.Y.C., June 7, 1933; s. Alexander and Bertha (Kasakove) S.; m. Anne Rawley, July 21, 1963 (div. Nov. 1979); 1 child, Alan; m. Virginia Vaughan, Sept. 4, 1983; stepchildren: Tad Thomas, Stan Thomas, Melinda Thomas, Margaret Thomas. BSChemE, Rice U., 1956; MBA, Harvard U., 1961. Mfg. mgr. Procter & Gamble Mfg. Co., Dallas, Kansas City, Kans., 1956-59; rsch. asst. Harvard Bus. Sch., Boston, 1961-62; asst. to pres. Kaiser Aluminum & Chem. Corp., Oakland, Calif., 1962-64; mgr. fin. and pers., then gen. mgr. various divs. Raychem Corp., Menlo Park, Calif., 1964-83, with office of pres., 1983-87, sr. v.p. telecommunications and tech., 1988-90, pres., chief exec. officer, 1990—; pres. Raynet Corp. subs. Raychem Corp., 1987-88; chair mfg. com. of adv. bd. Leavy Sch. Bus. and Adminstrn., Santa Clara U. Chair mfg. com. adv. bd. Leavy Sch. Bus. and Adminstrn., Santa Clara U. Mem. Calif. Roundtable (dir. Bay Area Coun.), San Francisco Com. on Fgn. Rels. Jewish. Office: Raychem Corp Mailstop 120/7815 300 Constitution Dr Menlo Park CA 94025

SALE, GEORGE EDGAR, physician; b. Missoula, Mont., Apr. 18, 1941; s. George Goble and Ruth Edna (Polleys) S.; m. Joan M. Sutliff, 1989; children: George Gregory Colby, Teo Marie Jonsson. AB, Harvard U., 1963; MD, Stanford U., 1968. Intern U. Oreg., Portland, 1968-69; sr. asst. surgeon USPHS, Albuquerque, 1969-71; resident in pathology U. Wash., Seattle, 1971-75, instr. pathology, 1975-78, asst. prof., 1978-81, assoc. prof., 1981-88, prof., 1988—; mem. faculty dept. oncology Hutchinson Cancer Ctr., Seattle, 1975-88, assoc. prof., 1988-91, prof., 1991—. Author, editor: Pathology of Bone Marrow Transplantation, 1984, Pathology of Transplantation, 1990. Mem. AAAS, Internat. Acad. Pathology, Coll. Am. Pathologists, Am. Assn. Pathologists, Physicians for Social Responsibility. Home: 12146 Sunrise Dr NE Bainbridge Is WA 98110-4304 Office: Fred Hutchinson Cancer Rsh Ctr 1124 Columbia Pathology Seattle WA 98104

SALERNO, JOSEPH MICHAEL, air cargo company executive; b. Port Washington, N.Y., Jan. 12, 1917; s. Angelo and Anna Marie (Fasano) S.; m. Edith Evangeline Fields, Apr. 2, 1949; children: Linda Marie, Bruce Charles, Paul Michael, David Brian. BS, Tri-State Coll., 1943. Flight engr. Pan Am. World Airways, Inc., San Francisco, 1943-77; owner, pres. Salair, Inc., Seattle, 1980—, also bd. dirs. Pres. Horizon View Community, Bellevue, Wash., 1958-63; mem. Bellevue Citizens Sch. Adv. Coun., 1964; pres. Eastgate Elem. Sch. PTA, Bellevue, 1963. Republican. Roman Catholic. Home: 14560 SE 51st St Bellevue WA 98006-3510 Office: Salair Inc Spokane Internat Airport Hanger 745 Spokane WA 99204

SALESKY, WILLIAM JEFFREY, manufacturing company executive; b. Boston, June 12, 1957; s. Harry Michael Salesky and Eleanor Faith (Stutman) Spater; m. Cherri Lynne DeGreek, Nov. 27, 1982; 1 child, Joshua Steven. BS, U. Calif., Davis, 1978; MS, U. Calif., Berkeley, 1980, PhD, 1982. Co-op engr. Bechtel Corp. Inc., San Francisco, 1977-78; engr. U. Calif., Davis, 1978-79; rsch. assoc. Lawrence Berkeley Lab., 1979-82; project mgr. Smith Internat., Irvine, Calif., 1982-89; dir. engring. & quality assurance Mark Controls, Long Beach, Calif., 1989—; cons. Printnonix Corp., Irvine, Calif., 1988, Metal Alloys Inc., Irving, 1986-88, Ceracon Inc., Irvine, 1984-86; chmn. L.A. Conf. on Fugitive Emissions from Valves, 1993. Patentee in field. Mgr. Irvine Baseball Assn., 1990; grad. assembly rep. U. Calif., Berkeley, 1980-81; mem. race com. Internat. Am.'s Cup Class World Championship; mem. Am.'s Cup Race Com., 1992. Recipient meritorious award Petroleum Engr. mag., 1988. Mem. ASTM, Am. Soc. Metals Internat. (bd. dirs. 1988-90, Earl Parker fellow 1981), Soc. Petroleum Engrs., Am. Petroleum Inst., South Shore Yacht Club (CFO 1989-91, bd. dirs. 1991-93). Office: Pacific Valves 3201 Walnut Ave Long Beach CA 90807-5296

SALINAS, SIMON, special education services professional; b. Slayton, Tex., Oct. 8, 1955; s. Julian and Octavia (Reyes) S. BA in Polit. Sci., Latin Am. Studies, Claremont McKenna Coll., 1978; cert. in edn., San Jose State U., 1981; JD, Santa Clara Law Sch., 1984. Tchr. Alisal Sch. Dist., Salinas, Calif., 1984-89; ESL instr. Hartnell Coll., Salinas, 1989—. Mem. Salinas City Coun., 1989-93, mayor pro tem, 1991-93. Mem. League of Latin Am. Citizens (recipient Courage award 1989), Alisal Better Govt. Com., Jaycees. Home: 34 Argentine Pl Salinas CA 93905-3007 Office: Hartnell Community Coll 156 Homestead Ave Salinas CA 93901-1628

SALISBURY, DAVID FRANCIS, newspaper, television science writer; b. Seattle, Feb. 24, 1947; s. Vernon H. and Lurabelle (Kline) S. BS, U. Wash., 1969. Sci. editor Christian Sci. Monitor, Boston, 1972-76; correspondent Christian Sci. Monitor, Los Angeles, Boulder (Colo.) and San Francisco, 1976-85; sci. and tech. writer U. Calif., Santa Barbara, 1985—; mem. research adv. com. Pub. Service Electric and Gas Co., Newark, N.J., 1979-83. Author: Money Matters, 1982. contbr. many articles to popular mags. and tech. jours. Recipient sci. writing awards, NSPE, 1978, Aviation Space Writers Assn., 1981, Grand Gold medal and Bronze medal Coun. for Advancement and Support of Edn., 1988. Mem. AAAS (sci. writing award 1976), Nat. Assn. Sci. Writers (Sci-in-Soc. award 1974). Christian Scientist. Office: U Calif Pub Affairs 1124 Cheadle Hall Santa Barbara CA 93106

SALK, JONAS EDWARD, physician, scientist; b. N.Y.C., Oct. 28, 1914; s. Daniel B. and Dora (Press) S.; m. Donna Lindsay, June 8, 1939; children: Peter Lindsay, Darrell John, Jonathan Daniel; m. Francoise Gilot, June 29, 1970. BS, CCNY, 1934, LLD (hon.), 1955; MD, NYU, 1939, ScD (hon.), 1955; LLD (hon.), U. Pitts., 1955; PhD (hon.), Hebrew U., 1959; LLD (hon.), Roosevelt U., 1955; ScD (hon.), Turin U., 1957, U. Leeds, 1959, Hahnemann Med. Coll., 1959, Franklin and Marshall U., 1960; DHL (hon.), Yeshiva U., 1959; LLD (hon.), Tuskegee Inst., 1964. Fellow in chemistry NYU, 1935-37, fellow in exptl. surgery, 1937-38, fellow in bacteriology, 1939-40; Intern Mt. Sinai Hosp., N.Y.C., 1940-42; NRC fellow Sch. Pub. Health, U. Mich., 1942-43, research fellow epidemiology, 1943-44, research asso., 1944-46, asst. prof. epidemiology, 1946-47; asso. research prof. bacteriology Sch. Medicine, U. Pitts., 1947-49, dir. virus research lab., 1947-63, research prof. bacteriology, 1949-55, Commonwealth prof. preventive medicine, 1955-57, Commonwealth prof. exptl. medicine, 1957-63; dir. Salk Inst. Biol. Studies, 1963-75, resident fellow, 1963-84, founding dir., 1976—, disting. prof. internat. health scis., 1984—; developed vaccine, preventive of poliomyelitis, 1955, cons. epidemic diseases sec. war, 1944-47, sec. army, 1947-54; mem. commn. on influenza Army Epidemiol. Bd., 1944-54, acting dir. commn. on influenza, 1944; mem. expert adv. panel on virus diseases WHO; adj. prof. health scis., depts. psychiatry, community medicine and medicine U. Calif., San Diego, 1970—. Author: Man Unfolding, 1972, The Survival of the Wisest, 1973, (with Jonathan Salk) World Population and Human Values: A New Reality, 1981, Anatomy of Reality, 1983; Contbr. sci. articles to jours. Decorated chevalier Legion of Honor France, 1955, officer, 1976; recipient Criss award, 1955, Lasker award, 1956, Gold medal of Congress and presdl. citation, 1955, Howard Ricketts award, 1957, Robert Koch medal, 1963, Mellon Inst. award, 1969, Presdl. medal of Freedom, 1977, Jawaharlal Nehru award for internat. understanding, 1976. Fellow AAAS, Am. Pub. Health Assn., Am. Acad. Pediatrics (hon., assoc.); mem. Am. Coll. Preventive Medicine, Am. Acad. Neurology, Assn. Am. Physicians., Soc. Exptl. Biology and Medicine, Inst. Medicine (sr.), Phi Beta Kappa, Alpha Omega Alpha, Delta Omega. Office: Salk Inst Biol Studies PO Box 85800 San Diego CA 92186-5800

SALKIN, DAVID, physician; b. Khorol, Ukraine, USSR, Aug. 8, 1906; came to U.S., 1929; s. Samuel and Eva (Sturman) S.; m. Bess Marguerite Adelman, Sept. 12, 1934; 1 child, Barbara Ruth. MD, U. Toronto, Ont., Can., 1929. Intern St. Mary's Hosp., Detroit, 1929-30; pvt. practice Detroit, 1930-32; fellow Herman Kiefer Hosp., Detroit, 1932-33; pathologist Mich. State Sanatorium, Howell, Mich., 1933-34; med. dir., supt. Hopemont (W.Va.) Sanatorium, 1934-48; chief staff, dir. VA Hosp., San Fernando, Calif., 1948-71; mem. staff LaVina Hosp., Altadena, Calif., 1971-84; pvt. practice, rsch. Huntington med. Rsch. inst., Pasadena, Calif., 1984—; mem. faulcty U. Calif., L.A., 1951-61, U. Loma Linda, 1960—, U. Southern Calif., 1964—. Contbr. articles to profl. jours. Mem. Am. Lung Assn. Recipient L.A. County award Am. Lung Assn., 1989. Mem. Calif. Thoracic Soc. (Gold medal 1972), L.A. Med. Assn. (Trudeau award 1986), Am. Acad. TB Physicians (awards 1958, 62), Am. Coll. Chest Physicians (Disting. Svc. award 1973, Contbn. award 1984), Internat. Coccidioidomycosis Symposium. Home: 1820 Linda Vista Ave Pasadena CA 91103-1149 Office: Huntington Med Rsch Inst 660 S Fair Oaks Ave Pasadena CA 91105-2686

SALKIN, SAMUEL JOSEPH, retail executive; b. Greenville, Pa., Apr. 23, 1950; s. Herman Joel and Harriet (Mermelstein) S.; m. Frances Whitman, Sept. 13, 1981; children: Sarah Rose Whitman-Salkin, Leah Rivka Whitman-Salkin. BS, Cornell U., 1972, MS, 1979. Lectr. Human Affairs Program Cornell U., Ithaca, N.Y., 1971-74; pub. Ithaca New Times, 1975-76; lectr. Hobart & William Smith, Geneva, N.Y., 1978-79; planning coord. Puget Consumers' Co-op, Seattle, 1979-80; sr. planner Nat. Coop. Bank, Washington, 1980-83; v.p. planning Alaska Comml. Co., Anchorage, 1983-85, pres., CEO, 1985-91; sr. v.p. Smith & Hawken, Ltd., Mill Valley, Calif., 1991-92, exec. v.p., 1992—; founding dir. Nutra Source, Seattle, 1984-86; bd. advisor Frontier Coop. Herbs, Norway, Iowa, 1984—. Bd. dirs. Alaska Pub. Radio Network, Anchorage, 1989—, Alaska Coun. on Econ. Edn., Anchorage, 1988-91; vice chmn. Internat. No. Regions Conf., Anchorage, 1990. Democrat. Jewish. Office: Smith & Hawken Ltd 25 Corte Madera Mill Valley CA 94941

SALLEE, WESLEY W(ILLIAM), nuclear chemist; b. Perry, Okla., June 5, 1951; s. Jimmie Richard and Nadine A. (Barnes) S.; m. Exine Mamie Clark, Mar. 21, 1979; children: Rachel Nadine, Daniel Mason. BS in Chemistry, Okla. State U., 1974; PhD in Chemistry, U. Ark., 1983. Commd. 1st lt. USAF, 1976, advanced through grades to capt., 1978, resigned, 1979; nuclear physicist U.S. Army White Sands Missile Range, 1983—. Author technical reports and symposium papers; contbr. articles to profl. jours. Mem. ASTM. Republican. Home: 1515 Dorothy Cir Las Cruces NM 88001-1625 Office: Nuclear Effects Lab PO Box 333 White Sands NM 88002-0333

SALMON, MATTHEW JAMES, state legislator, public relations specialist; b. Salt Lake City, Jan. 21, 1958; s. Robert James and Gloria (Aagard) S.; m. Nancy Huish, June, 1979; children: Lara, Jacob, Katie, Matthew. BA in English Lit., Ariz. State U., 1981; MA in Pub. Adminstrn., Brigham Young U., 1986. Mgr. constrn. Mountain Bell, Tucson, 1982-83; claims adjuster Mountain Bell, Salt Lake City, 1983-85; area risk mgr. Mountain Bell, Phoenix, Ariz., 1985-88; mgr. pub. affairs U.S. West, Phoenix, 1988—; mem. Ariz. Senate, Mesa, 1990—, asst. majority leader, 1993. Bd. dirs. Mesa United Way, 1990—, Ariz. Sci. Mus., 1992—. Recipient Outstanding Svc. award Ariz. Citizens with Disabilities, 1991, Excellence in Govt. award Tempe Ctr. for Handicapped, 1992; named Outstanding Young Phoenician, Phelps Dodge/Phoenix Jaycees, 1990, Outstanding Legislator, Mesa United Way, 1991. Republican. Mormon. Home: 5021 E Evergreen Mesa AZ 85205 Office: Ariz State Senate 1700 W Washington Phoenix AZ 85007

SALMON, MERLYN LEIGH, laboratory executive; b. Macksville, Kans., June 24, 1924; s. Kenneth Elbert and Inez Melba (Prose) S.; student U. Kans., 1943-44; BS, U. Denver, 1951, MS, 1952; m. Flora Charlotte Sievers, Mar. 20, 1948; children: Charla Lee, Merlyn Leigh. Rsch. engr. Denver Rsch. Inst., U. Denver, 1951-56; owner-operator Fluo-X-Spec Lab., Denver, 1956-92; ret. 1992; cons. in field. With AUS, 1943-45, 45-47. Mem. Am. Chem. Soc., Soc. for Applied Spectroscopy (Outstanding Svc. award 1970), Am. Soc. Metals, Sigma Xi, Tau Beta Pi, Phi Lambda Upsilon. Omicron Delta Kappa. Democrat. Contbr. articles to profl. jours. Address: 718 Sherman St Denver CO 80203

SALMON, WILLIAM IRWIN, writer; b. Washington, Jan. 20, 1942; s. Harry Irwin and Corinne (Wall) S.; m. Lydia Susan Smith, Aug. 25, 1962; 1 child, Edward Lee. BS in Chemistry, Coll. of William and Mary, 1963; PhD in Phys. Chemistry, Iowa State U., 1971. Owner The Photographic Lab., Salt Lake City, 1974-81; sec.-treas. Light Source, Inc., Salt Lake City, 1980-83; instr. computer sci. dept. U. Utah, Salt Lake City, 1981-85, adj. asst. prof. computer sci. dept., 1985-91; pres. Interactive Ednl. Systems, Salt Lake City, 1990—; adj. assoc. prof. computer sci. dept. U. Utah, Salt Lake City, 1991—; cons. on computing various sch. dists. in Utah, Salt Lake City, Park City, 1986—. Co-author: Computing for Engineers and Scientists with

FORTRAN 77, 1988, A Second Course in Computer Science with Modula-2, 1987; author: Structures and Abstractions, 1991, The Structures and Abstractions Labs, 1992. Mem. IEEE, Assn. for Computing Machinery, Sigma Xi, Phi Beta Kappa, Phi Kappa Phi. Home and office: Interactive Ednl Systems 2135 S Wellington St Salt Lake City UT 84106-4116

SALONEN, ESA-PEKKA, conductor; b. Helsinki, Finland, June 30, 1958. Student, Sibelius Acad., Helsinki; studies with Rautavarra and Panula. Condr. Finnish Radio Symphony, 1979; guest condr. orchs., London, Berlin, Paris, L.A., Toronto, Ont., Can., Phila., Minn.; prin. condr. Swedish Radio Symphony Orch., 1985—; condr. Philharmonia Orch., London, 1983, prin. guest condr., 1984—; prin. guest condr. Oslo Philharm. Orch., 1985-90; artistic advisor Stockholm Chamber Orch., 1986—; music dir. L.A. Philharm. Orch., 1992—. Office: VanWalsum Mgmt, 26 Wadham Rd, London SW15 2LR, England also: Los Angeles Philharm Orch 135 N Grand Ave Los Angeles CA 90012 also: Swedish Radio Symphony, Sveriges Radio, S-105 10 Stockholm Sweden

SALSIG, DOYEN, photographer, photography studio owner; b. San Diego, Jan. 17, 1923; d. Felix and Fay (Doyen) Johnson; m. Budd Salsig, June 11, 1943; children: Winter, Kristin, Fay, Ben. AA, San Diego City Coll., 1965; BA in Biology, U. Calif., San Diego, 1970. Owner West Wind Studio, Flagstaff, Ariz., 1972—; photo workshop leader Mus. of No. Ariz., Flagstaff, 1978—. Author: Parole: Quebec; Counter-sign: Ticonderoga, 1980 (grand prize Coconino County Women of the Arts 1985); contbr., photographer articles and photographic essays to profl. jours. Bd. dirs., v.p. Grand Canyon (Ariz.) Natural History Assn., 1988—; v.p. Coconino County Rep. Ctrl. Com., Flagstaff, 1990—; pres. Rep. Women's Club, Flagstaff, 1989-91; docent Mus. No. Ariz., Flagstaff, 1975-82; mem. Ariz. Humanities Coun., 1991—. Republican. Home and Office: 428 E Birch Ave Flagstaff AZ 86001-5226

SALTA, STEVEN ANTHONY, infosystems executive; b. Portland, Oreg., Oct. 10, 1955; s. Joseph L. and Juanita M. (Sharp) S.; m. Martha Greer Katayama, Aug. 10, 1991. BA, Portland State U., 1978. Systems specialist Multnomah County Edn. Service Dist., Portland, 1978-79; team leader Tektronix, Inc., Beaverton, Oreg., 1979-81, project mgr., 1981-83, systems devel. mgr., 1983-85, infosystems mgr., 1985-89; mgr. sales automation Sequent Computer Systems, Inc., Beaverton, 1989-90, mgr. application systems, 1990-93; program mgr. Microsoft Corp., Redmond, Wash., 1993—; cons. Custom Software Systems, San Francisco, 1980-85; bd. dirs. Mindnet, Inc., 1988-93. Contbr. articles to profl. jours. Mem. adv. bd. Boy Scouts Am., 1974, presently active; mem. computer sci. adv. bd. Portland Pub. Schs., 1980; mem. steering com. Oregon Mus. of Sci. and Industry, 1988; bd. dirs. The Excellence Found., Portland, 1991-92. Recipient Eagle Scout award Boy Scouts Am., 1969, William T. Hornaday award Boy Scouts Am., 1973. Mem. Data Processing Mgmt. Assn., Assn. Systems Mgmt. (Spl. Achievement award 1984), Assn. Computing Machinery, Computer Soc. of IEEE, Computer Profls. for Social Responsibility. Office: Microsoft Corp 1 Microsoft Way Beaverton OR 98052-6024

SALTENBERGER, PAMELA GUAY, insurance executive; b. Berkeley, Calif., Apr. 17, 1944; d. Lawrence Edward Guay and Gladys (Walther) Marek; m. Peter Owen Brown, Dec. 27, 1967 (div.); m. Otto Henry Saltenberger, Oct. 14, 1978. BS, U. Oreg., 1966. CLU. Supr. adminstrn. Westland Life Ins. Co., San Francisco, 1967-69; v.p. adminstrn. Pacific Standard Life Ins. Co., Davis, Calif., 1972-85, CalFarm Life Ins. Co., Sacramento, 1985—. Bd. dirs. Tierra del Oro coun. Girl Scouts U.S., Sacramento, 1991—, sec., 1993—. Mem. Sacramento CLU Chpt. (pres. 1991-92). Office: CalFarm Life Ins Co 1601 Exposition Blvd Sacramento CA 95815

SALTER, PATRICK MORRIS, JR., trucking executive; b. Pasadena, Calif., Nov. 20, 1952; s. Patrick Morris and Jo (Pinkham) S.; m. Connie Jo Converse, Dec. 7, 1974; children: Bridget, Sean. Student, Los Angeles Valley Coll., 1970-72, 85, Los Angeles Pierce Coll., 1974; BS, U. Redlands, 1992. With United Parcel Svc., Van Nuys, Calif., 1974—, on-rd. supr., 1987; preload supr. United Parcel Svc., Lancaster, Calif., 1988-89, ctr. supr., 1989-92, loss prevention investigator, 1992—. Republican.

SALTMAN, SHELDON ARTHUR, telecommunications executive; b. Boston, Aug. 17, 1933; s. Nathan Herbert and Rose (Governman) S.; m. Mollie Heifetz, Aug. 26, 1956; children: Steven Gary, Lisa Faye. BA, U. Mass., 1953; MS in Communications Arts, Boston U., 1954. Pres., chief exec. officer sports div. 20th Century Fox; exec. v.p., gen. mgr. 20th Century Fox-Telecommunications; exec. v.p. Calif. Sports (Lakers, Kings, Forum); v.p. advt., promotion, mktg. and pub. rels. MCA-TV; pres. Saltman Assocs.; v.p. spl. projects Lorimar Telepictures; pres. Cinetex '88, Encino, Calif.; pres., CEO SS Telecom, Encino, Calif.; bd. dirs. Prism Entertainment, Phila., Hollywood Home Theatre, N.Y.C., Fanfare Pay TV, Houston, Choice Channel, L.A.; mktg. cons. World Cup Soccer, 1985; guest lectr., instr. mktg., promotion mgmt. and TV prodn. U. Mass., U. Ariz., Calif. State U., Northridge, 1970—; keynote speaker Internat. Sports Summit, Monte Carlo, 1977, Nat. High Sch. Fedn., Cambridge, Mass.; entertainment cons. Sands Hotel, vice chmn. ICT; chmn. ICT Bulgaria; pres., chief exec. officer SS Telecom. Autor: Evel Knievel on Tour, 1977; producer Olympic Salute Week, 1980. Event-TV cons. adv. bd. Nat. Fitness Inst. of President's Coun. on Phys. Fitness, 1980-; vol. TV coord., asst. commr. for boxing, 1984 Olympics. Recipient Outstanding Trade Promotion-Mktg. award Broadcast Promotion Assn., 1964, Broadcast Promotion Man of Yr. award, 1965; named one of 5 men who did most for women in sports in 1970's, Women's Sports mag., 1979. Mem. NATAS (blue ribbon panel 1966), AFTRA, SAG, Am. Film Inst. Jewish.

SALTZMAN, JOSEPH, journalist, producer, educator; b. L.A., Oct. 28, 1939; s. Morris and Ruth (Weiss) S.; m. Barbara Dale Epstein, July 1, 1962; children: Michael Stephen Ulysses, David Charles Laertes. BA, U. So. Calif., 1961; MS, Columbia U., 1962. Freelance writer, reporter, producer, 1960—; reporter Valley Times Today, Los Angeles, CA, 1962-64; editor Pacific Palisades Palisadian Post, 1964; sr. writer-producer CBS-KNXT TV, Los Angeles, 1964-74; freelance broadcast cons. Los Angeles, 1974—; sr. producer investigative unit Entertainment Tonight, 1983; supervising producer Feeling Fine Prodns., Los Angeles, 1984—; prof. journalism U. So. Calif., Los Angeles, 1974—. Documentaries include Black on Black, 1968, The Unhappy Hunting Ground, 1971, The Junior High School, 1971, The Very Personal Death of Elizabeth Schell-Holt-Hartford, 1972, Rape, 1972, Why Me?, 1974; spl. producer: Entertainment Tonight, 1983; supervising producer med. films, video, audio, 1984—; assoc. mass media editor, columnist USA Today, 1983—; syndicated columnist: King Features Syndicate, 1983-92; contbg. editor Emmy Mag., 1986—, Roberts Reviewing Service, 1964—; others. Recipient AP certificates of excellence and merit, 1968, 72, 73, 74, 75, Edward R. Murrow awards for distinguished achievements in broadcast journalism, 1969, 72, Alfred I. duPont-Columbia U. award in broadcast journalism, 1973-74, Silver Gavel award Am. Bar Assn., 1973, Ohio State award Am. Exhbn. Ednl. Radio-Television Programs and Inst. for Edn. by Radio-Television Telecommunications Center, 1974, Broadcast Media awards San Francisco State U., 1974, 75; Media award for excellence in communications Am. Cancer Soc., 1976; awards for teaching excellence U. So. Calif., 1977, 88, 90; Disting. Alumni award U. So. Calif., 1992; Seymour Berkson fellow, 1961; Robert E. Sherwood fellow, 1962; alt. Pulitzer traveling fellow, 1962-63. Mem. Radio-Television News Assn. (Golden Mike awards 1969, 71, 73, 75), Nat. Acad. Television Arts and Scis. (regional Emmy awards 1965, 68, 74, 75), Writers Guild Am., Greater Los Angeles Press Club (awards 1968, 74, 75), Columbia U., U. So. Calif. alumni assns., Skull and Dagger, Blue Key, Phi Beta Kappa, Sigma Delta Chi, Pi Sigma Alpha, Alpha Epsilon Rho. Home: 2116 Via Estudillo Palos Verdes Peninsula CA 90274-1931 Office: U So Calif Sch Journalism Univ Park Los Angeles CA 90089

SALTZMAN, ROBERT PAUL, insurance company executive; b. Chgo., Oct. 25, 1942; s. Al and Viola (Grossman) S.; m. Diane Maureen Schulman, Apr. 10, 1964; children: Amy, Adam, Suzanne. BA in Math., Northwestern U., 1964. Mgr. Continental Casualty Co., Chgo., 1964-69; sr. v.p. Colonial Penn Group, Phila., 1969-83; pres., chief exec. officer Sun Life Ins. of Am., Atlanta, 1985—; exec. v.p. mktg. Kaufman & Broad (now Broad, Inc.), Los Angeles, 1987—; bd. dirs. Sun Life Group, Atlanta, Anchor Nat. Fin. Services and Anchor Nat. Life Ins. Co., Phoenix. Office: Sun Life Insur Co of Am 11601 Wilshire Blvd Los Angeles CA 90025

SALVATIERRA, RICHARD CABALLERO, educational administrator; b. Tucson, July 29, 1920; s. Roberto C. and Julia (Caballero) S.; m. Clara Roseboro, Aug. 15, 1942; children: Richard, George and Yolanda (twins), Maria Cristina and Maria Elena (twins). BA, U. Ariz., 1943, MA, 1975. With U.S. Fgn. Svc., 1945-72; dep. dir. for Latin Am. USIA, 1960-62; dir. Latin Am. area studies Fgn. Svc. Inst., 1969-72; editorial writer Tucson Citizen, 1972-82, internat. affairs columnist, 1972—; spl. asst. to pres. U. Ariz., Tucson, 1982-92. Mem. Pima County Trial Cts. Appointments Commn.; bd. dirs. Hispanic Profl. Action Com., Tucson; mem. state bd. Ariz. Hist. Soc. Lt. U.S. Army, 1943-45. Recipient Recognition award Ariz. State Bar, 1989-91. Mem. Tucson Literary Club. Republican. Roman Catholic. Home: 2051 E Hawthorne St Tucson AZ 85719

SALVO, GINGER CALHOUN, horse trainer, sculptor; b. Columbia, S.C., June 20, 1947; d. George Clifton Salvo and Eugenia Calhoun (Gerald) Landon; divorced; 1 child, Tiffany Ann. Student, Rollins Coll., 1965. Horse trainer Mountain Home, Idaho, 1965—; designer Mountain Home, 1975—; instr. Wyo. Barrel Racing Club, Jackson, 1980, Idaho High Sch. Rodeo Assn., 1985. Leader 4-H Club, Mountain Home, 1975; founder, pres. Idaho High Sch. Rodeo Club, Mountain Home High Sch.; chmn. Idaho Barrel Racing Futurity Horse Sale, 1991, 93; founder Wilderness Barrel Racing Futurities Award, Idaho, Nev., Utah, 1991. Recipient several awards for sculptures Nat. Cowgirl Hall of Fame, numerous championships Idaho Cowboys Assn., Idaho Barrel Racing Futurity Assn. (including All-Around champion 1993), Am. Quarter Horse Assn., Utah Barrel Racing Futurity, Eastern Idaho Barrel Racing Futurity, Golden Spike Barrel Racing Futurity, Sweetwater Barrel Futurity, Idaho Quarter Horse Breeders Assn. Mem. NW Barrel Futurities Assn., Idaho Barrel Racing Futurity Assn. (bd. dirs. 1981-83, champion 1979, 83), Idaho Cowboys Assn. (bd. dirs. 1974-75, res. champion 1984), Ea. Idaho Rodeo Assn. (clinic instr. horsemanship, judge open house shows 1993), United Daus. of the Confederacy (Charleston, S.C.). Home and Office: RR 1 Box 756A Mountain Home ID 83647-9801

SALZARULO-MCGUIGAN, ANN MARIE, Latin American economic development specialist; b. Pittsfield, Mass., Sept. 25, 1958; d. Thomas Vincent and Jean Elaine (Castronova) Salzarulo; m. Michael Paul McGuigan, May 27, 1979. BA, Adelphi U., 1980; MA in Internat. Policy, Monterey Inst Internat Studies, Monterey, Calif., 1984; B in Latin Am. Studies, Tex. Christian U., U. de Sevilla, Spain. On-site rural devel. coord. Am. Friends Svc. Com., 1983-86; dir. Cen. Am. Scholarship Program, Mass., 1986-88; recruitment/selection coord. Cen. Am. and the Caribbean, Washington, 1988-89; internat. liaison Georgetown U., Washington, 1989-90; pres. Internat. Program Devel., San Diego, 1990—; dir. Interfaith Task Force on Cen. Am., San Diego, 1991-92; cons. sustainable economic devel. programs Internat. Program Devel. Latin Am. and the Caribbean, San Diego, 1990—. Contbr. articles to profl. jours. V.p. UN Assn., San Diego, 1991-92; chair Haiti Task Force, 1992; vol. Polit. Asylum Project, Tijuana, San Diego, 1990-92; symposium planner Binat. Mex.-U.S. Dialogue, Tijuana, San Diego, 1992. Mem. Inter Action Non-Govtl. Orgns., Soc. for Internat. Devel. (pres., founder 1991—), Interfaith Task Force on Cen. Am., Sons of Italy (Pittsfield, affiliate), United Nations Assn., Women's Equity Coun. (founding mem), Terra Segura. Democrat. Roman Catholic. Home: 4450 41st St San Diego CA 92116 Office: Internat Program Devel 4450 41st St San Diego CA 92116

SALZMAN, ANNE MEYERSBURG, psychologist; b. N.Y.C., Feb. 25, 1928; d. Reuben and Dorothy (Steinberg) Meyersburg; m. Paul Salzman, Sept. 11, 1952; children: Harold, Richard. BA, U. N.Mex., 1949; MA, NYU, 1950. Lic. psychologist. Psychologist, field instr. UCLA Psychology Clinic Sch., L.A., 1952-55; psychologist Temple Beth Am, L.A., 1956-60; psychologist, co-dir. Acad. Guidance Svcs., L.A., 1960-76; psychologist, dir. The Guidance Ctr., Santa Monica, Calif., 1976—. Mem. Am. Psychol. Assn., Fedn. Am. Scientists, Calif. State Psychol. Assn., L.A. County Psychol. Assn., Greenpeace. Democrat. Jewish. Office: The Guidance Ctr 1150 Yale St Ste 1 Santa Monica CA 90403-4738

SALZMAN, GARY CLYDE, biophysicist; b. Palo Alto, Calif., May 25, 1942; s. Harvey Austin and Amy Alfreda (Davis) S.; m. Joan Carolyn Hoyer, Jan. 30, 1965; children: Sonja, Eric. BA, U. Calif., Berkeley, 1965; MS, U. Oreg., 1968, PhD, 1972. Tchr. U.S. Peace Corps, Asankrangwa, Ghana, 1965-67; postdoctoral researcher physics divsn. Los Alamos (N.Mex.) Nat. Lab., 1972-73, staff mem. life scis. divsn., 1973—; owner Software Resource Co., Los Alamos, 1990—. Editor: Proceedings of SPIE Conference, 1989, 90; inventor, patentee biol. particle identification apparatus. Disting. Patent Award grantee Nat. Cancer Inst., 1990. Mem. AAAS, Soc. for Analytical Cytology (councilor 1993—). Home: 108 Sierra Vista Dr Los Alamos NM 87544 Office: Los Alamos Nat Lab Mail Stop M888 Los Alamos NM 87545

SAM, DAVID, federal judge; b. Hobart, Ind., Aug. 12, 1933; s. Andrew and Flora (Toma) S.; m. Betty Jean Brennan, Feb. 1, 1957; children: Betty Jean, David Dwight, Daniel Scott, Tamara Lynn, Pamela Rae, Daryl Paul, Angie, Sheyla. BS, Brigham Young U., 1957; JD, Utah U., 1960. Bar: Utah 1960, U.S. Dist. Ct. Utah 1966. Sole practice Duchesne, Utah, 1963-76; dist. judge State of Utah, 1976-85; judge U.S. Dist. Ct. Utah, Salt Lake City, 1985—; atty. City of Duchesne, 1963-72, Duchesne County, 1966-72; commr. Duchesne County, 1972-74; mem. adv. com. Codes of Conduct of Jud. Conf. U.S., 1987-91, Jud. Coun. of 10th Cir., 1991—; mem. U.S. Del. to Romania, Aug. 1991. Chmn. Jud. Nomination Com. for Cir. Ct. Judge, Provo, Utah, 1983; bd. dirs. Water Resources, Salt Lake City, 1973-76. Served to capt. JAGC, USAF, 1961-63. Mem. Utah State Bar Assn., Am. Judicature Soc., Am. Inns of Ct. VII (counselor 1986-89), A. Sherman Christensen Am. Inn of Ct. I (counselor 1989—), Utah Jud. Conf. (chmn. 1982—), Utah Dist. Judges Assn. (pres. 1982-83). Mem. LDS Ch. Office: US Dist Ct 148 US Courthouse 350 S Main St Salt Lake City UT 84101

SAMANIEGO, PAMELA SUSAN, executive producer; b. San Mateo, Calif., Nov. 29, 1952; d. Armando C. and Harriott Susan (Croot) S. Student, UCLA, 1972, Los Angeles Valley Coll., 1970-72. Asst. new accts. supr. Beverly Hills Fed. Savings, 1970-72; asst. controller Bio-Science Enterprises, Van Nuys, Calif., 1972-74; adminstr. asst. Avery/Tirce Prodns., Hollywood, Calif., 1974-78; sr. estimator N. Lee Lacy and Assocs., Hollywood, 1978-81; head of prodn. Film Consortium, Hollywood, 1981-82; exec. producer EUE/Screen Gems Ltd., Burbank, Calif., 1982-88; advt. agency dir. Barrett & Assocs., Las Vegas, Nev., 1988-90; exec. producer Laguna/Take One, Las Vegas, 1990—. Author: Millimeter & Backstage, 1982-88. Emergency room vol. San Mateo (Calif.) County Hosp., 1968-70; Sunday sch. tchr. Hillsdale Meth. Ch., San Mateo, 1968-70; vol. worker Hillsdale Meth. Ch. Outreach, San Francisco, 1967-70. Recipient CLIO award CLIO Awards, Inc., 1985, ADDY award Las Vegas Advt. Fedn., 1988. Mem. Dirs. Guild Am. (2nd asst. dir. 1987-88), Assn. Ind. Comml. Producers, Am. Horse Show Assn., Internat. Arabian Horse Assn., AHASFV (sec. 1978-79), AHASC (sec. 1978-88). Democrat. Methodist. Home: 803 Osprey Dr Post Falls ID 83854 Office: Laguna/Take One 2708 S Highland Dr Las Vegas NV 89109-1004

SAMARAS, MARY STENNING, educator, video producer, entrepreneur; b. Detroit, June 19, 1928; d. Walter Jeffrey and Laura Eugenia (Karas) Stenning; m. Thomas T. Samaras, June 1962 (div. 1982); children: William T. Jones, Daniel V. Jones. BA, Wayne State U., 1949, MA, 1952; EdD, U. So. Calif., 1974. Speech therapist Mich. and Calif. Pub. Schs., 1951-70; dir. Claremont (Calif.) Speech & Reading Lab., 1965-70; tchr. Calif. Pub. Schs., 1965-75; instr. Southwestern Coll., Chula Vista, Calif., 1975-90; pres. Nuvo, Ltd., Chula Vista, 1988—; apptd. by Gov. of Calif., State Bd. on Devel. Disabilities, 1980-84. Producer (videos) The Art of Table Napkin Folding, 1989, Fold-Along Napkin Art, 1991, Read English Today, 1993; inventor ornamental fingertip prosthesis; contbr. articles to profl. jours. Fellow in spl. edn. U.S. Office Edn., 1971, 72. Mem. Nat. Soc. Autistic Citizens, Sierra Club. Unitarian. Home and Office: 157 Theresa Way Chula Vista CA 91911-3518

SAMARDICH, VAL, dentist; b. Bisbee, Ariz., Oct. 7, 1928; s. George and Eva (Dabovich) S.; m. Bonnie Lynn Anderson, Dec. 12, 1959 (div. 1973); children: Tina, Shelly. BA, U. Ariz., 1950; DDS, St. Louis U., 1957. Pvt. practice Tucson, Ariz., 1957—. Active DeMolays Boys Orgn., Tucson, 1943-46, Boy Scouts Am., Tucson, 1943-44. 1st lt. USAF, 1950-53. Mem. Masons. Republican.

SAMET, MARC KRANE, pharmacologist; b. Chgo., Apr. 30, 1950; s. Herman and Nora (Krane) S. BS, No. Ill. U., 1973; MS, Northwestern U., 1975; PhD, Kans. U., 1983. Mem. faculty U. Calif., Berkeley/San Francisco, 1983-85; with Applied Immune Scis., Menlo Park, Calif., 1985-87, Glenwood Mgmt., Menlo Park, 1987; cons. Vitaphore Corp., Menlo Park, 1988-90, Van Med Venture Capital, Palo Alto, Calif., 1990; prin. strategic planning and mktg. firm, 1991, Merck & Co., 1992. Contbr. articles to profl. jours. NIH fellow, 1983-84, 84-85. Mem. N.Y. Acad. Sci., Am. Assn. Immunologists, Controlled Release Soc., Am. Assn. Pharm. Scientists. Jewish. Home: 923 Menlo Ave # 1 Menlo Park CA 94025-4623 Office: PO Box 1428 Menlo Park CA 94026-1428

SAMO, AMANDO, bishop; b. Moch Island, Federated States of Micronesia, Aug. 16, 1948; s. Benito and Esiper Samo. BA in Psychology, Chaminade U., 1973; diploma in religious edn., EAPI, Manila, Philippines, 1982. Ordained priest Roman Cath. Ch. Parish priest Cath. Ch., Truk, Federated States of Micronesia, 1977-87; bishop Diocese of the Carolines and Marshalls, Truk, 1987—; founder, bd. dirs. Marriage Encounter-Carolines-Marshalls, Truk, 1982-88; dir. ch. leadership tng. programs, Truk, 1986—. Home: PO Box 250, Truk 96942, Federated States Micronesia

SAMOFF, JOEL, educator, researcher, consultant; b. Phila., Nov. 27, 1943; s. Bernard Leon and Zelda (Semser) S.; m. Rachel Samoff, Mar. 30, 1967; children: Erika, Kara. BA in History, Antioch Coll., 1965; MA in Polit. Sci., U. Wis., 1967, PhD, 1972. Asst. prof. U. Mich., Ann Arbor, 1970-80; lectr. U. Zambia, Lusaka, 1973-75; vis. assoc. prof. U. Calif., Santa Barbara, Calif., 1989-90; assoc. prof. Stanford (Calif.) U., 1980-88, vis. scholar, 1988—; vis. asst. prof. Inst. Law and Devel. U. Wis., 1972; rsch. assoc. U. Dar es Salaam, Tanzania, 1968-69, 73-74, 83-85; dir. Ctr. African Studies U. Stanford, 1984-85; cons. Swedish Internat. Devel. Authority, Stockholm, 1987—, UNESCO, ILO, Paris and Geneva, 1989—; vis. prof. UCLA, 1993. Author: South Africa at Stanford, 1989; co-author: Swedish Public Administration Assistance in Tanzania, 1988, Education and Social Transition in the Third World, 1990, Microcomputers in African Development: Critical Perspectives, 1992; contbr. 33 articles to profl. jours., chpts. and revs. Bd. dirs. Ann Arbor Transp. Authority, 1974-77. Fellow Fgn. Area Fellow Program, Africa, 1968-70; grantee Spencer Found., 1980-81, 86-88, Social Sci. Rsch. Coun. Mem. African Assn. Polit. Sci., African Studies Assn. (bd. dirs. 1982-85), Assn. Concerned Africa Scholars (bd. dirs. 1979—), Am. Polit. Sci. Assn., Comparative and Internat. Edn. Soc., Internat. Polit. Sci. Assn. Home: 3527 S Court St Palo Alto CA 94306-4221 Office: Stanford U Ctr African Studies Encina Hall Rm 200 Stanford CA 94305

SAMPEDRO, YVETTE YRMA, English language educator; b. El Paso, Tex., June 25, 1966; d. Rafael and Lucy S. BA in English, Ariz. State U., 1988, MEd in Sec. Edn., 1991. English tchr. Mesa (Ariz.) Pub. Schs., 1988—, sch. Culture Club and Cheerleading sponsor, 1989—; English tchr. Maricopa Community Colls. Mem. NEA, Ariz. Reading Assn., Kappa Delta Pi. Roman Catholic.

SAMPIAS, ERNEST JOSEPH, communications executive; b. Evergreen Park, Ill., Mar. 4, 1951; s. Ernest Edward and Wilma (Egyed) S.; m. Susan Marie Repka, Oct. 20, 1973; children: Matthew, Michael, Marrisa. BS in Bus. with distinction, Ind. U., 1973; MBA, DePaul U., 1979. CPA. Div. contr. Lasalle Steel Co., Hammond, Ind., 1973-79; dir. fin. planning Aerojet Gen. Corp., Sacramento, 1979-85; v.p. fin. U.S. West Communications, Mpls., 1985—; Republican. Roman Catholic. Bd. dirs. Urban Coalition, Mpls. Mem. AICPA, SBDM Com., Tech. Com., Tech. Action Team, Strategic Planning Com. Home: 18990 E Geddes Ave Aurora CO 80016-2142

SAMPL, SCOTT ANDREW, marketing official; b. Hartford, Conn., Apr. 26, 1956; s. Frank R. and Barbara J. (Studney) S.; m. Lynne Marie Alessandrelli, Nov. 27, 1982; children: Lauren A., Emily A. BSEE, U. Rochester, 1978, MBA in Fin. and Econs., 1979. Product mktg. engr. Hewlett-Packard Co., Loveland, Colo., 1979-84, mgr. applications support, 1984-85, product mgr., 1985-88, mgr. field support, 1988-90, mem. data acquisition bus. team, 1990-91, mgr. product mktg., 1991—. Chmn. bd. dirs. Larimer County Ptnrs., Ft. Collins, Colo., 1991—. Alumni scholar U. Rochester, 1974. Office: Hewlett-Packard Co PO Box 301 Loveland CO 80539

SAMPLE, JOSEPH SCANLON, broadcasting consultant; b. Chgo., Mar. 15, 1923; s. John Glen and Helen (Scanlon) S.; m. Patricia M. Law, Dec. 22, 1942 (div.); children: Michael Scanlon, David Forrest, Patrick Glen; m. Miriam Tyler Willing, Nov. 19, 1965. B.A., Yale U., 1947. Trainee, media analyst, media dir. Dancer-Fitzgerald-Sample, Inc., advt. agy., Chgo., 1947-50; v.p., media dir. Dancer-Fitzgerald-Sample, Inc., advt. agy., 1952-53; pres. Mont. Television Network KTVQ, Billings, KXLF-AM-TV, Butte, Mont., KRTV, Great Falls, Mont., KPAX-TV, Missoula, Mont., 1955-84; cons., 1984—. Pres. Greater Mont. Found., 1986—; chmn. Wheeler Ctr. Mont State U., 1988—. Served with AUS, 1943-46. With U.S. Army, 1950-52. Clubs: Yellowstone Country, Rotary, Port Royal, Hole in the Wall Golf, Hilands Golf. Home: 606 Highland Park Dr Billings MT 59102-1909 Office: 14 N 24th St Billings MT 59101-2422

SAMPLE, STEVEN BROWNING, university president; b. St. Louis, Nov. 29, 1940; s. Howard and Dorothy (Cunningham) S.; m. Kathryn Brunkow, Jan. 28, 1961; children: Michelle Sample Smith, Melissa Ann. BS, U. Ill., 1962, MS, 1963, PhD, 1965; D.Hu.L. (hon.), Canisius Coll., 1989, LHD (hon.), 1989; LLD (hon.), U. Sheffield, Eng., 1991. Sr. scientist Melpar Inc., Falls Church, Va., 1965-66; assoc. prof. elec. engring. Purdue U., Lafayette, Ind., 1966-73; dep. dir. Ill. Bd. Higher Edn., Springfield, 1971-74; exec. v.p. acad. affairs, dean Grad. Coll. U. Nebr., Lincoln, 1974-82; prof. elec. and computer engring. SUNY, Buffalo, 1982-91, pres., 1982-91; pres. U. So. Calif., L.A., 1991—, prof. elec. engring., 1991—; bd. dirs. Ind., Moog, Inc., East Aurora, N.Y., First Interstate Bancorp, L.A., Presley Cos, Newport Beach, Calif., Bancorp., Beverly Hills, Calif., Litton Industries, Inc., Beverly Hills, Calif.; vice chmn., bd. dirs. Western N.Y. Tech. Devel. Ctr., Buffalo, 1982-91; chmn. bd. dirs. Calspan-UB Rsch. Ctr., Inc., Buffalo, 1983-91; mem. Calif. Coun. Sci. and Tech., Irvine, Calif.; cons. in field. Contbr. articles to profl. jours.; patentee in field. Timpanist St. Louis Philharm. Orch., 1955-58; chmn. Western N.Y. Regional Econ. Devel. Coun., 1984-91; trustee U. at Buffalo Found., 1982-91, Studio Arena Theatre, Buffalo, 1983-91, Western N.Y. Pub. Broadcasting Assn., 1985-91, L.A. Edn. Alliance for Restructuring Now; bd. dirs. Buffalo Philharm. Orch., 1982-91, Regenstrief Med. Found., Indpls., 1982-91, Rsch. Found. SUNY, 1987-91; chmn. Gov.'s Conf. on Sci. and Engring. Edn., Rsch. and Devel., 1989-91; bd. dirs. L.A. chpt. World Affairs Coun., Hughes Galaxy Inst. Edn., L.A., Rebuild L.A. Commn., Regenstrief Inst., Indpls., Coalition of 100 Club of L.A., Norris Cancer Ctr.; trustee L.A. Ednl. Alliance for Restructuring Now. Recipient Disting. Alumnus award Dept. Elec. Engring. U. Ill., 1980; citation award Buffalo Coun. on World Affairs, 1986, Engr. of Yr. award N.Y. State Soc. Profl. Engrs., 1985; Alumni Honor award Coll. Engring., U. Ill., 1985; Sloan Found. fellow, 1962-63, NSF Graduate fellow, 1963-65, Am. Coun. on Edn. fellow, Purdue U., 1970-71; NSF Rsch. grantee, 1968-73. Mem. AAAU, IEEE (Outstanding Paper award 1976), Nat. Assn. State Univs. and Land-Grant Colls. (ednl. telecommunications com., 1982-83, chmn. coun. of pres. 1985-86, edn. and tech. com. 1986-87, exec. com. 1987-89), Coun. on Fgn. Rels., Sigma Xi. Episcopalian. Home: 1550 Oak Grove Ave San Marino CA 91108 Office: U So Calif Office of the Pres University Park ADM 110 Los Angeles CA 90089-0012

SAMPLINER, LINDA HODES, psychologist, consultant; b. Cleve., Sept. 25, 1945; d. Walter J. and Caroline Jean (Klein) Hodes; m. Richard Evan Sampliner, July 31, 1966; children: Robert David, Steven Jay. BS, Western Res. U., Cleve., 1967; EdM, Boston U., 1972, EdD, 1975. Lic. psychologist, Ariz. Counselor The Family Life Ctr., Columbia, Md., 1976-80; psychologist Psychology & Rehab. Assocs., Tucson, 1981-85; pvt. practice Tucson, 1985—; cons., psychologist div. econ. security Child and Family Svcs., Tucson, 1985—; cons. SHARE, Tucson, 1985—; mem. allied staff Sonora Desert Hosp., Tucson, 1990-92. Bd. dirs. Adapt Inc., Tucson, 1985—, pres.,

1990-91. Mem. APA, Assn. Death Edn. and Counseling, So. Ariz. Psychol. Assn. Home and Office: 1760 E River Rd Tucson AZ 85718-5878

SAMPSON, BRYAN DIRK, lawyer; b. Columbus, Ohio; s. E. David and Elisabeth A. (Bryan) S.; m. Peggy S. Stark, Nov. 2, 1985. BS, U.S. Mil. Acad., 1981; JD, U. San Diego, 1989. Bar: Calif., 1989. Assoc. Walton, Ottesen, Meads & Koler, San Diego, 1989—. Contbr. articles to profl. jours. Pres. University Heights Community Assn., San Diego, 1990-91; sec. Uptown Planners, San Diego, 1990-91. Capt. U.S. Army, 1981-87. Mem. ABA, Calif. Bar Assn., San Diego County Bar Assn. (Bankruptcy & Bus. Law sects.). Office: Walton Ottesen Meads Koler 225 Broadway Ste 800 San Diego CA 92101

SAMPSON, DOUGLAS ANDREW, trucking executive; b. Denver, May 20, 1958; s. Ira Norman and Gloria Rhoda (Castle) S. BS, U. No. Colo., 1980. Cert. Prodn. Inventory Mgr. Time study analyst Imperial Distbn. Svcs., Denver, 1980-83, mktg. mgr., 1983-86, v.p. ops., 1986-89; v.p. L.J.R. distbn. co. Acme Distbn. Ctrs., Denver, 1989-91, v.p. corp. svcs., 1991—; owner All Ways Trucking, Inc., Denver, 1986-92; bd. dirs. Sampson Sports, Denver, 1987—. Author: (computer software) Time Study System for Warehouse Handling Analysis, 1986. Bd. dirs. Denver Margarita Soc., 1988—, Coalition for the Homeless, Denver, 1991. Mem. Warehouse Edn. and Rsch. Coun., Coun. of Logistic Mgmt., Am. Prodn. and Inventory Control Soc, Greater Denver C. of C. (ambassador, 1990, 91, 92), Denver Transp. Club., Delta Nu Alpha Transp. Fraternity. Office: Acme Distbn Co 18101 E Colfax Ave Aurora CO 80011

SAMPSON, ELLANIE SUE, library director; b. Ft. Monmouth, N.J., July 30, 1953; d. Arnold Ingvold and Edith Louise (Johnston) Sampson; m. Henry Clark Baisdon, Aug. 23, 1987. BA in Fine Arts, U. N.Mex., 1974; MLS, U. Okla., 1975. Slide libr. Sch. Art Okla. U., Norman, 1975-78; adminstr. Northeast Mo. Libr. Svc., Kahoka, 1978-79; libr., dir. Truth or Consequences Pub. Libr. (N.Mex.), 1979—; cons. depts. history, English, architecture, Norman, 1975-78, Herron Sch. Art, Purdue U., Indpls., 1977. Mng. editor Dry Country News, 1983-85; compiler/calligrapher/editor: Salad Out with Jazzworks, 1983. Mem. Truth or Consequences, 1983-91; organizer Stephen King Day, Truth or Consequences, 1983, Bibliofile Users Group N.Mex., PETA, Fund for Animals. Mem. ALA, N.Mex. Libr. Assn., U. Okla. Sch. Libr. Sci. Alumni Assn., Am. Bus. Women's Assn. Home: 918 Kopra St Truth Or Consequences NM 87901-1656 Office: Truth or Consequences Pub Libr 325 Library Ln Truth Or Consequences NM 87901-2375

SAMPSON, J. FRANK, artist, educator; b. Edmore, N.D., Mar. 24, 1928; s. Silas Abner and Mabel Elizabeth (Trimble) S. BA, Concordia Coll., Moorhead, Minn., 1950; MFA, U. Iowa, 1952, postgrad., 1956-59. Asst. prof. fine arts U. Colo., Boulder, 1961-67; assoc. prof. fine arts U. Colo., 1968-72, prof. fine arts, 1972-90, prof. emeritus fine arts, 1990—. One man shows at Walker Art Ctr., Mpls., 1954, Denver Art Mus., 1975; represented in permanent collections at Colo. Springs Fine Arts Ctr., Des Moines Art Ctr., Dulin Gallery of Art, Knoxville, Joslyn Art Mus., Omaha, Libr. of Congress, Littleton (Colo.) Hist. Mus., Minn. Mus. Art, St. Paul, Mulvane Art Ctr., Washburn U., Topeka, Kans., Sheldon Meml. Art Ctr., U. Nebr., Lincoln, Springfield (Mo.) Art Mus., Walker Art Mus., Mpls., Boston Pub. Libr., Nelson Gallery-Atkins Mus., Kansas City, Mo. With U.S. Army, 1954-56. Fulbright fellow, 1959-60. Lutheran. Home: 1912 Columbine Ave Boulder CO 80302-7919

SAMPSON, MICHAEL J., chemical engineer; b. Freeport, Tex., Jan. 26, 1944; s. Jack and Maxine Mildred (Merrell) S.; m. Delora Sue Cook, Nov. 21, 1971; children: Galen Patrick, Douglas Michael. BSChE, U. Tex., 1967. Registered profl. engr., Calif., Alaska. Chem. engr. Dow Badische Co., Anderson, S.C., 1967-69, Kelco div. Merck, San Diego, 1970-74; prodn. supt. Stauffer Chem. Co., Visalia, Calif., 1974-76; cons. Visalia, 1976-78; mgr. process engring. Davy McKee Corp., San Ramon, Calif., 1978-86; v.p. process devel. Ocean Genetics, Inc., Santa Cruz, Calif., 1986-87; founder, prin. Sampson Engring., Inc., Watsonville, Calif., 1987—; mem. tech. adv. bd. Monterey Bay Unified Air Pollution Control Dist. Mem. AICE, ASTM, Am. Inst. Plant Engrs. (pres. Monterey Bay chpt. 1989-90). Office: 6 Hangar Way Ste C Watsonville CA 95076-2456

SAMPSON, RICHARD ARNIM, security professional; b. New Haven, June 9, 1927; s. Richard Arnim Sampson and Ora Viola (Reese) Jackson; m. Marilyn Jo Gardner, June 10, 1950 (div. 1962); children: Gary, Susan; m. Janet Margaret Battaglia, Jan. 26, 1963 (div. 1987); children: Cynthia, David; m. Alice Annette Whitfield, July 23, 1988; stepchildren: Shareasa, Anthony, Erika. BS, Mich. State U., 1951; MPA, Auburn U., 1972; grad., Air War Coll., 1972. Exec. CIA, Washington, 1951-76; mgr. spl. projects Hughes Aircraft Co., El Segundo, Calif., 1976-80; mgr. security Advanced Systems div. Northrop Aircraft Co., Pico Rivera, Calif., 1980-83, Electronics div. Gen. Dynamics Corp., San Diego, 1983-92; dir. security GDE Systems, Inc., SanDiego, 1992—; instr., Southwest L.A. Coll., 1979-80; adj. faculty mem. Webster U., San Diego, 1991; advisor on security mgmt. curriculum Calif. State U., San Marcos. Author: Excessive Bureaucracy-Causes and Cures, 1972; author spl. projects indsl. security manual, 1965. Active Boy Scouts Am., McLean, Va., 1974, Palos Verdes, Calif., 1978; trustee 1st Congl. Ch. of Escondido, Calif., 1990-93; mem. adv. com. to leadership and mgmt. program in security Sch. of Criminal Justice, Mich. State U. Mem. Am. Soc. Indsl. Security (chmn. 1958-59), Signa Soc., CIA Retirees Assn. (treas. 1986-87), Nat. Mgmt. Assn., Indsl. Security Working Group (bd. dirs. 1987-88), Ops. Security Profls. Soc., Contractor Spl. Access Required/Spl. Access Programs Working Group, Security Affairs Support Assn., Aerospace Industries Assn. (security com.), Rsch. Security Assocs. Republican. Home: 1408 Westwood Pl Escondido CA 92026-1752

SAMSELL, LEWIS PATRICK, municipal finance executive; b. Morgantown, Va., Feb. 20, 1943; s. Lewis Hildreth and Harriet Elizabeth (Gidley) S.; m. Linda Joyce Hewitt, July19, 1967. BSBA in Acctg., W.Va. U., 1970; MBA in Acctg., George Washington U., 1975. CPA, V.I.; cert. mgmt. acct. Auditor GAO, Washington, 1971-79, Office of the U.S. Govt. Controller, St. Thomas, V.I., 1979-82; fin. officer City of Merced, Calif., 1982-86; dir. fin. City of Stockton, Calif., 1986—; bd. dirs. Stockton Coun. U.S. Navy League, 1993—; mem. state controllers task force on single audit, Calif. CAP Composite Squadron 147 Sr. Programs Officer, Merced, 1985; resource allocation team leader United Way of San Joaquin County; bd. dirs. United Way San Joaquin County. With USN, 1964-67. Recipient Cert. of Achievement Service Corps of Retired Execs., St. Thomas, 1982. Mem. Calif. Soc. LMcpl. Fin. Officers (profl. and tech. standards com. 1983—), Govt. Fin. Officers Assn., Nat. Assn. Accts. (pres. MPG chpt 1979, nat. bd. dirs. 1989-91), Calif. Mcpl. Treas. Assn., Am. Mgmt. Assn., Kiwanis, Rotary, Elks. Home: 7034 Bridgeport Cir Stockton CA 95207-2359 Office: City of Stockton 425 N El Dorado St Stockton CA 95202

SAMUDIO, JEFFREY BRYAN, architect, planner, educator; b. San Gabriel, Calif., Oct. 3, 1966; s. Grace (Alvarez) S. BArch, U. So. Calif., 1990, postgrad., 1990—. V.p. N.E. Design and Devel. Group, Glendale, Calif., 1989-90; instr. archtl. tech. L.A. Commun. Coll. Dist., 1989—; ptnr. Design AID, Architects & Planners, L.A., 1987—; asst. dir. U. So. Calif. Sch. Architecture , L.A. Co-author monograph; editor newsletter. Mem. planning adv. com. City of L.A. Planning Dept., 1988-91; founding bd. dirs. Eagle Rock Assn./TERA Inc., 1987—; bd. dirs. Richard J. Neutra Centennial Commn., L.A., 1991—; chmn. Main St. Community Renewal Program, Highland Pk. Calif. Freeman House fellow Graham Found., L.A., 1990-91; recipient Cert. of Appreciation for Commun. Svc., City of L.A., 1984, 89. Mem. AIA (Outstanding Svc. award 1990), Am. Planning Assn., Soc. Archtl. Historians, L.A. City Hist. Soc., Nat. Trust Forum-Nat. Trust for Historic Preservation, L.A. Conservancy, Archtl. Guild of U. So. Calif. Sch. Architecture.

SAMUDLO, JEFFREY BRYAN, architect, educator, planner, business owner; b. San Gabriel, Calif., Oct. 3, 1966; s. Lazaro and Grace (Alvarez) S. BArch, U. So. Calif., 1990. Ptnr. Design AID, Architects & Planners, L.A., 1987—; v.p. N.E. Design & Devel., Glendale, Calif., 1989-90; instr. L.A. Trade Tech. Coll., 1989—. Bd. dirs. Community Planning Adv. Bd., L.A., 1987-92; founding mem., bd. dirs. The Eagle Rock Assn., Inc., 1987—; co-chair Highland Park Main St. Urban Revitalization Com. Mem. AIA (assoc., vice chair preservation advocacy com.), Am. Planning Assn. (assoc.), Calif. Preservation Found., Arroyo Arts Collective, L.A. Conservancy, Soc. Archtl. Historians (life, So. Calif. chpt.), U. So. Calif. Archtl. Guild, L.A. City Hist. Soc. (life). Republican. Office: Design AID 2320 Langdale Ave Los Angeles CA 90041-2912

SAMUEL, GEORGE, healthcare information company executive; b. Tiruvalla, Kerala, India, May 25, 1958; came to U.S., 1980; s. VC and Elizabeth (Mammen) S. BS, Kerala U., 1979; AAS, Lehigh County Coll., 1980. Programmer, analyst Knowledge Data Systems, San Antonio, 1982-85, tech. mgr., 1985-87; dir. mgmt. info. system Knowledge Data Systems, Cin., 1987-88; v.p., acct. mgr. Knowledge Data Systems, Detroit, 1988-89; v.p., acct. mgr. Knowledge Data Systems, Larkspur, Calif., 1989-91, v.p., rsch. & devel. products div., 1991-93; pres., CEO Healthcare Media Enterprises Inc., Petaluma, Calif., 1993—. Vol. Project Open Hand, Oakland, Calif., 1992—. Mem. Am. Mgmt. Assn., Internat. Tandem Users Group, Info. Engring. Facility Users Group, Toastmasters Internat. Office: Healthcare Media Enterprises Inc 313 Westridge Pl Petaluma CA 94952

SAMUELS, ALLEN ROBERT, architect, electrical engineer; b. St. Petersburg, Fla., July 31, 1956; s. Allen Robert and Carol Rae (Morgenstein) S.; m. Mary Kathryn Hamm, May 26, 1984; children: Aaron Morgen, Rachel Marion. BSEE, Rice U., 1978. Sr. system programmer Burroughs County, Mission Viejo, Calif., 1978-80; sr. mem. tech. staff Harris Corp., Ft. Lauderdale, Fla., 1980-84; dir. I.C. Engring. Weitek Co., Sunnyvale, Calif., 1984—. Author several articles to mags. (award of excellence 1989). Mem. Internat. Assn. Elec. and Electronic Engrs., Assn. Computing Machinery.

SAMUELS, BARBARA ANN, planner, educator, information architect; b. Montreal, Quebec, Oct. 20, 1949; d. Louis and Frances Kalb; m. Keith Michael Samuels, Aug. 23, 1970; 1 child, Sumerlee Eden. BSc, U. Calgary, 1969; MEd, U. Oreg., 1973, PhD, 1978. Cert. profl. tchr., Alta. Tchr., asst. prin. Calgary (Alta.) Bd. Edn., 1971-79, planning specialist, 1980-83; asst. v.p. svcs. U. Calgary, 1983-84, dir. planning, 1986—; exec. dir. Can. Ctr. for Learning Systems, Calgary, 1984-86; prin. ptnr. Innovisions Cons. Group, Calgary, 1988—; pres. B.A. Samuels & Assocs., Calgary, 1985—. Author: Understanding Culture, 1985; developer, writer (video) New Faculty Recruitment, 1991; author, reseacher rsch. studies; author mag. articles. Trustee Calgary Zoo, 1989—, Akiva Acad. Sch. Bd., Calgary, 1986-87; dir. Banff-Cochrane Progressive Conservative Constituency Assn., 1989-91. F.J.C. Seymour fellow Alta. Tchrs'. Assn., 1977; recipient Women & Coop. Edn. grant Sec. of State, 1989, Centres of Excellence citation, 1984. Mem. Internat. Soc. for Planning and Strategic Mgmt., Can. Soc. for Study in Higher Edn., Kappa Delta Pi. Office: U Calgary Office of VP, 110 Administration Bldg, Calgary, AB Canada T2N 1N4

SAMUELS, JOSEPH, JR., police chief; b. 1949; m. Sabrina Samuels; 1 child, Joseph. BA in Psychology, Lincoln U.; MPA, Calif. State U., Hayward, 1988; student, Nat. Exec. Inst. Br. mgr. Household Fin. Corp.; with Oakland (Calif.) Police Dept., 1974-91, capt. patrol divsn., chief police, 1993—; police chief Fresno (Calif.) Police Dept., 1991-93; chair regional citizens adv. com. Calif. Youth Authority, 1986-91; former mem. Calif. State Commn. Crime, Juvenile Justice and Delinquency Prevention. Active YMCA, Oakland, East Oakland Youth Devel. Ctr., Oakland Citizens Com. Urban Renewal. Mem. Nat. Orgn. Black Law Enforcement Execs., Calif. Peace Officers Assn., Calif. Police Chiefs Assn., Internat. Assn. Chiefs Police, Police Exec. Rsch. Forum. Office: Police Headquarters 2323 Mariposa St Fresno CA 93721*

SAN AGUSTIN, JOE TAITANO, Guam senator, financial institution executive, management researcher; b. Agana, Guam, Oct. 15, 1930; s. Candido S. and Maria P. (Taitano) San A.; m. Carmen Santos Shimizu, June 18, 1955; children: Mary, Ann, Joe, John. BA, George Washington U., 1954, MA, 1965. Chief budget and mgmt. Office of Govt. Guam, Agana, 1966-68; dir. dept. adminstrn. Govt. Guam, Agana, 1968-74; senator Guam Legislature, Agana, 1976—, minority leader 16th Guam Legislature, 1981-82, vice-speaker 17th and 18th Guam Legislature, 1983-86, chmn. com. on ways and means 17th and 18th Guam Legislatures, 1983-86, chmn. com. on health, edn. and welfare 19th Guam Legislature, 1987, chmn. com. on edn., 1991; speaker 20th, 21st, and 22nd Guam Legislature, 1989—; bd. dirs. Bank of Guam, Agana. Democrat. Roman Catholic. Office: 155 Hessler Pl Agana GU 96910-5004

SANBORN, DONALD FRANCIS, software consultant; b. Tacoma, Wash., June 21, 1959; s. Francis Joseph Sanborn and Janet Jean (Lawrie) Taylor; m. Sharon Lee Fountain, May 14, 1983. BS in Agrl. Engring., Colo. State U., 1982, postgrad. Irrigation engr. Edaw, Ft. Collins, Colo., 1983-87; program analyst Systems & Applied Scis. Corp., SM System Rsch. Corp., Ft. Collins, 1987-89, Nat. Ctr. for Animal Health Info. Systems, Ft. Collins, 1987-89; owner, cons. Unique Solutions, Colorado Springs, Colo., 1989—; software cons. Aqua Engring Co., Ft. Collins, 1987—, Rain Bird Sales, Glendora, Calif., 1988—, USAF Acad., Colorado Springs, 1990—. Contbr. to profl. publs. Timing dir. Pikes Peak Auto Hill Climb, Manitou Springs, Colo., 1991-92, bd. dirs., 1993—; active Pikes Peak Hwy. Adv. Commn., Colorado Springs, 1993—. Mem. Assn. Computing Machinery, No. Colo. Autocad Users Group, Tau Beta Pi. Home and Office: Unique Solutions 392 Cobblestone Dr Colorado Springs CO 80906

SANCHEZ, DENNIS ROBERT, English language educator; b. East L.A., Sept. 21, 1956; s. Florentino and Carol Olympia (Moncivais) S.; m. Susan Louise Boggs, Dec. 14, 1985. AA, East L.A. Coll., 1981; BA, U. So. Calif., 1983; MA, San Francisco State U., 1986, Calif. State U., 1991. Cert. high sch. tchr., Calif.; lic. real estate agent, 1990. English tchr. El Camino Real High Sch., Woodland Hills, Calif., 1986-92; asst. English prof. East L.A. City Coll., Monterey Park, Calif., 1992—. Author short stories. Asst. coach Academic Decathlon, Woodland Hills, 1989-91; mem. Human Rels. Commn., L.A., 1987. Democrat. Roman Catholic. Home: 4141 Picasso Ave Woodland Hills CA 91364 Office: East LA City Coll 1301 Brooklyn Ave Monterey CA 91754

SANCHEZ, GILBERT, university president, microbiologist, researcher; b. Belen, N.Mex., May 7, 1938; s. Macedonio C. and Josephine H. Sanchez; m. Lorena T. Tabet, Aug. 26, 1961; children—Elizabeth, Phillip, Katherine. B.S. in Biology, N.Mex. State U., 1961; Ph.D. in Microbiology, U. Kans., 1967. Research asst. U. Kans., Lawrence, 1963-67; research assoc., postdoctoral fellow Rice U., Houston, 1967-68; prof. N.Mex. Inst. Tech., Socorro, 1968-79; dean grad. studies Eastern N.Mex. U., Portales, 1979-83; v.p. acad. affairs U. So. Colo., Pueblo, 1983-85; pres. N.Mex. Highlands U., Las Vegas, 1985—; cons. NIH, NSF, Solvex Corp., Albuquerque, 1979-83; bd. dirs. Fed. Res. Bank, Denver. Contbr. numerous articles to profl. jours. Patentee in field. Pres. Socorro Sch. Bd., 1974-79, Presbyn. Hosp. Bd., Socorro, 1977-79. Research grantee Dept. Army, 1976-79, N.Mex. Dept. Energy, 1979-83, NSF, 1979. Mem. Am. Soc. Microbiology, Am. Soc. Indsl. Microbiology, AAAS, Am. Assn. Univs. and Colls. (bd. dirs. 1988-90), Hispanic Assn. Univs. and Colls. (pres. 1986-89). Roman Catholic. Lodge: Rotary. Office: NMex Highlands U Las Vegas NM 87701

SANCHEZ, LEONEDES MONARRIZE WORTHINGTON, fashion designer; b. Flagstaff, Ariz., Mar. 15, 1951; s. Rafael Leonedes and Margaret (Monarrize) S. BS, No. Ariz. U., 1974; studied, Fashion Inst. Tech., N.Y.C., 1974-75; AA, Fashion Inst. D&M, L.A., 1975; lic., La Ecole de la Chambre Syndical de la Couture Parisian, Paris, 1976-78. Lic. in designing. Contract designer/asst. to head designer House of Bonnet, Paris, 1976—; dress designer-in-residence Flagstaff, 1978—; mem. faculty No. Ariz. U., Flagstaff, 1978-80; designer Ambiance, Inc., L.A., 1985—; designer Interiors by Leonedes subs. Studio of Leonedes Couturier, Ariz., 1977, Calif., 1978, London, Paris, 1978, Rome, 1987, Milan, Spain, 1989; designer Liturgical Vesture subs. Studio of Leonedes Couturier; owner, designer Studio of Leonedes, Ltd., London, Milan, Paris, Spain, Ambiance Ariz., Calif., Spain, Appolonian Costuming, Ariz., London, Milan, Paris; cons. House of Bonnet, Paris, 1976—, Bob Mackie, Studio City, Calif., 1974-75; art dir., art instr. St. Mary's Regional, 1987-90; owner, designer Studio of Leonedes, Ltd.; active Nat. Physique Com. Bd. dirs. Roman Cath. Social Svcs., 1985-86, Northland Crisis Nursery, 1985—; bd. dir., chmn. Pine Country Transit, 1986-88; pres. Chicanos for Edn.; active master's swim program ARC, Ariz., 1979—; eucharistic minister, mem. art and environ. com., designer liturgical vesture St. Pius X Cath. Ch.; vol. art tchr., instr. St. Mary's Regional Sch., Flagstaff, 1987-90, vol. art dir. Recipient Camellian Design award 1988, Atlanta. Mem. AAU, Am. Film Inst., Am. Assn. Hist. Preservation, Costume Soc. Am., Nat. Physique Com., Internat. Consortium Fashion Designers, Nat. Cath. Ednl. Assn., La Legion de Honour de la Mode Parisienne, Phi Alpha Theta (historian 1972-73, pres. 1973-74), Social Register Assn., Pi Kappa Delta (pres. 1972-73, historian 1973-74). Republican.

SANCHEZ, LORENZO, accounting educator; b. San Benito, Tex., May 17, 1943; s. Abelardo and Concepcion (Martin) S.; m. Debra Mae Sanchez, May 21, 1978; children: Michelle Loren, Lorenzo Dean. BA, North Tex. State U., Denton, 1965; MBA, Pan-Am. U., 1980. Athletic coord., head football coach Brownsville (Tex.) Ind. Sch. Dist., 1965-78; sales rep. Am. Founder's Ins., Brownsville, 1975-78; acctg. coord. Pan-Am. U., Brownsville, 1984-87; pvt. practice CPA Portales, N.Mex., 1978—; asst. prof. acctg. Ea. N.Mex. U., Portales, 1987—. Mem. implementation com. N.Mex. First Town Halls on Environ. Issues; mem. fund drive team United Way, 1989-90; bd. dirs. Bethany Sch. for Girls, 1984-87, Esperanza Sch. for Boys, 1984-87, Portales Campfire Girls, 1988-90; treas. Mental Health Resources Bd., 1989-90; pres. Community Svcs. Bd., 198-90. Mem. AICPAs, Am. Acctg. Assn., Tex. Soc. CPAs, N.Mex. Soc. CPAs. Democrat. Roman Catholic. Home: 755 Kathryn Ave Las Vegas NM 87701-4923 Office: Ea NMex U Portales NM 88130

SANCHEZ, MARLA RENA, controller; b. Espanola, N.Mex., Mar. 3, 1956; d. Tomas Guillermo and Rose (Trujillo) S.; m. Bradley D. Gaiser, Mar. 5, 1979. BA, Stanford U., 1979, MS, 1979; MBA, Santa Clara U., 1983. Rsch. biologist Syntex, Palo Alto, Calif., 1980-81; fin. analyst Advanced Micro Devices, Sunnyvale, Calif., 1983-85; fin. mgr. ultrasound divsn. Diasonics, Inc., Milpitas, Calif., 1985-86, contr. therapeutic products divsn., 1989-93, contr. internat. divsn., 1992-93; contr. Ridge Computers, Santa Clara, Calif., 1986-88. Home: 1234 Russell Ave Los Altos CA 94024-5541

SANCHEZ, RUBEN DARIO, minister, parochial school educator, writer; b. Buenos Aires, Feb. 13, 1943; s. Ramon Jose and Maria Concepcion (Pardino) S.; m. Lina Alcira Tabuenca, Feb. 7, 1966; children: Adrian Nelson, Vivian Ethel. BA, River Plate Coll., Puiggari, Argentina, 1969; postgrad., Andrews U., 1971-72, MA, 1975; PhD, Calif. Sch. Theology, 1979. Ordained to ministry Seventh-day Adventist Ch., 1976. Pastor, tchr. River Plate Coll., Puiggari, 1969; min. lit. So. Calif. Conf., Glendale, 1970-71, Ill. Conf., Brookfield, 1972-77, Oreg. Conf., Portland, 1977-80; dir. Bible sch., assoc. speaker Voice of Prophecy, Thousand Oaks, Calif., 1980-84; dir. devel. Written Telecast, 1985—; founder Pacific N.W. Christian Sch., Woodburn, Oreg., 1979; founder, dir. Instituto Biblico Christiano, 1979-80; dir. Escuela Radiopostal (Corr. Bible Sch.), 1980-84; mem. Religious Broadcasters. Editor: Antologia Poetica, 1976; author: (textbook) Apasionante Exploration de la Biblia, 1977, Introduction to the Old Testament, 1979; (doctrinal devotional) Hungary Heart, 1984; contbr. articles to publs. Recipient Outstanding Service to Spanish Community in Oreg. award Sta. KROW, 1980; Andrews U. scholar, 1972. Mem. Assn. Christian Counselors, Christian Mgmt. Assn. Home: 2983 Elinor Ct Newbury Park CA 91320-3061 Office: Adventist Media Ctr 1100 Rancho Conejo Blvd Newbury Park CA 91320-1401

SANCHEZ, VICTORIA WAGNER, science educator; b. Milw., Apr. 11, 1934; d. Arthur William and Lorraine Marguerite (Kocovsky) Wagner; m. Rozier Edmond Sanchez, June 23, 1956; children: Mary Elizabeth, Carol Anne, Robert Edmond, Catherine Marie, Linda Therese. BS cum laude, Mt. Mary Coll., 1955; MS, Marquette U., 1957; postgrad., U. N.Mex., 1979-86, U. Del., 1990. Cert. secondary tchr., N.Mex. Chemist Nat. Bur. Standards, Washington, 1958-60; tchr., chmn. sci. dept. Albuquerque Pub. Schs., 1979—; chmn. pub. info. area convention Nat. Sci. Tchrs. Assn., 1984, mem. sci. review com. Albuquerque Pub. Schs., 1985-86, 92-93. Bd. dirs. Encino House, Albuquerque, 1976-92, treas., 1977-79; leader Albuquerque troop Girl Scouts U.S., 1966-77. Named Outstanding Sci. Tchr., NW Regional Sci. Fair, Albuquerque, 1983, 88, 90; recipient St. George's award N.Mex. Cath. Scouting Com., 1978, Focus on Excellence award ASCD, Albuquerque, 1985, 89, Presdl. awards for excellence in sci. and math. Mem. AAUW (officer Albuquerque br. 1976-77, N.Mex. div. 1977-78), NSTA, N.Mex. Sci. Tchrs. Assn. (treas. 1988-90), Albuquerque Sci. Tchrs. Assn. (treas. 1984-85, v.p., pres.-elect 1986--87, pres. 1987-88), N.Mex. Acad. Sci., Am. Coun. on Edn. (math. and sci. edn. nat. com. 1990—), DuPont Honors Workshop for Tchrs., Albuquerque Rose Soc. (sec. 1962-63). Democrat. Roman Catholic. Home: 7612 Palo Duro Ave NE Albuquerque NM 87110-2315 Office: Van Buren Sch 700 Louisiana Blvd SE Albuquerque NM 87108-3898

SANCHEZ-H., JOSE, fine arts educator, producer, director, media consultant; b. Cochabamba, Bolivia, June 28, 1951; s. Victor Sanchez and Margarita Hermoso. MA, U. Mich., 1977, PhD, 1983. Media specialist High/Scope Edn. Rsch. Found., Ypsilanti, Mich., 1978-79; engring. technician NBC, WDIV/TV 4, Detroit, 1980-81; asst. prof. Univ. del Sagrado Corazon, P.R., 1984-88, Calif. State U., Long Beach, 1988—; actor Ninon Davalos Co., Cochabamba, 1969, Dept. of Fine Arts, Guadalajara, Mex., 1970-72; rsch. cons. U. Mich., Ann Arbor, 1984, media engr., 1982-83; photographer Mus. of Contemporary Art, L.A., 1989—; cons. Loyola Marymount U., L.A., 1989. Cinematographer (film) Chautauqua: Famous American Voices of 1914, 1984; still photography (film) Secret Honor, 1984; dir. (video) Pope John Paul II, 1984; producer/dir. (videos) The Carillon Concert, 1979, Yo No Entiendo a la Gente Grande, 1986, Platinotipo, 1988, Artificial Intelligence, 1989, Partners for Success, 1990, The L.A. Mexican Dance Co., 1990, Rudolf Arnheim: Theories of Art, 1991, Themes in Bicultural Education, 1991, Fue Cosa de Un Dia, 1992, (films) You and I, 1976, Who Cares About the Time?, 1977, Cartas de Dos Mujeres Solitarias, Inside Cuba: The Next Generation, 1990; writer, producer, dir. (film) La Paz, 1991; writer (play) La Paz, 1989. Mem. The Long Beach Mus. of Art, Hispanic Acad. of Arts, 1987-89. Recipient Exceptional Achievement award Coun. Advancement and Support of Edn., 1982, Rackham Dissertation award U. Mich., 1982, Rackham scholarship, 1980-83. Mem. NEA, Latin Am. Found., Am. Film Inst., Nosotros, Broadcast Edn. Assn., Profl. Photographers, Ptnrs. of the Ams. Office: Calif State U Long Beach Radio/TV/Film Dept 1250 N Bellflower Blvd Long Beach CA 90840-0001

SANDAGE, ALLAN REX, astronomer; b. Iowa City, June 18, 1926; s. Charles Harold and Dorothy (Briggs) S.; m. Mary Lois Connelley, June 8, 1959; children: David Allan, John Howard. AB, U. Ill., 1948, DSc (hon.), 1967; PhD, Calif. Inst. Tech., 1953; DSc (hon.), Yale U., 1966, U. Chgo., 1967, Miami U., Oxford, Ohio, 1974, Graceland Coll., Iowa, 1985; LLD (hon.), U. So. Calif., 1971; D Honoris Causa, U. Chile, 1992. Astronomer Mt. Wilson Obs., Palomar Obs., Carnegie Instn., Washington, 1952—; Peyton postdoctoral fellow Princeton U., 1952; asst. astronomer Hale Obs., Pasadena, Calif., 1952-56; astronomer Obs. Carnegie Instn., Pasadena, Calif., 1956—; sr. rsch. astronomer Space Telescope Sci. Inst. NASA, Balt., 1986—; Homewood Prof. of Physics Johns Hopkins U., Balt., 1987-89; vis. lectr. Harvard U., 1957; mem. astron. expdn. to South Africa, 1958; cons. NSF, 1961-64; Sigma Xi nat. lectr., 1966; vis. prof. Mt. Stromlo Obs., Australian Nat. U., 1968-69, ; vis. rsch. astronomer U. Basel, 1985-92; rsch. astronomer U. Calif., San Diego, 1985-86; vis. astronomer U. Hawaii, 1986; Lindsey lectr. NASA Goddard Space Flight Ctr., 1989; Jansky lectr. Nat. Radio Astron. Obs., 1991; Grubb-Parsons lectr. U. Durham, Eng., 1992. With USNR, 1944-45. Recipient Pope Pius XI gold medal Pontifical Acad. Sci., 1966, Rittenhouse medal, 1968, Presdl. Nat. Medal of Sci., 1971, Adon medal Obs. Nice, 1988, Crafoord prize Swedish Royal Acad. Scis., 1991, Tomalla Gravity prize Swiss Phys. Soc., 1992; Fulbright-Hays scholar, 1972. Mem. Lincei Nat. Acad. (Rome), Am. Astron. Soc. (Helen Warner prize 1960, Russell prize 1973), Royal Astron. Soc. (Eddington medal 1963, Gold medal 1967), Astron. Soc. Pacific (Gold medal 1975), Royal Astron. Soc. Can., Franklin Inst. (Elliott Cresson medal 1973), Phi Beta Kappa, Sigma Xi. Home: 8319 Josard Rd San Gabriel CA 91775-1003 Office: 813 Santa Barbara St Pasadena CA 91101-1232

SANDARS, LEIBERT JOVANOVICH, radiologist; b. Balt., Apr. 17, 1914; s. Michael and Katherine (Jovanovich) Skandarski; m. Annel Branch, 1947; children: Jill Bonifield, Judy Klaich. MD, U. Chgo., 1941. Diplomate Am. Bd. Radiology. Intern St. Lukes Hosp., San Francisco, 1941-42; resident in radiology U. Calif., San Francisco, 1949-52; dir., founder Dept. Radiology, Washoe Med. Ctr., Reno, Nev., 1952-88; dir., cons. radiologist VA Hosp.,

Reno, Nev., 1954-68; chmn. Reno Radiol. Assocs., 1958-88. Artist in watercolor and oils. Lt. (j.g.) USNR, 1941-43. Fellow Am. Coll. Radiology (Nev. councilor 1954-68); mem. No. Calif. Radiol. Soc. (pres. 1964), Washoe County Med. Soc. (pres. 1964), Prospectors Club. Republican. Home: 6178 Laurelwood Dr Reno NV 89509

SANDE, BARBARA, interior decorating consultant; b. Twin Falls, Idaho, May 5, 1939; d. Einar and Pearl M. (Olson) Sande; m. Ernest Reinhardt Hohener, Sept. 3, 1961 (div. Sept. 1971); children: Heidi Catherine, Eric Christian; m. Peter H. Forsham, Apr. 1990. BA, U. Idaho, 1961. Asst. mgr., buyer Home Yardage Inc., Oakland, Calif., 1972-76; cons. in antiques and antique valuation, Lafayette, Calif., 1977-78; interior designer Neighborhood Antiques and Interiors, Oakland, Calif., 1978-86; owner, Claremont Antiques and Interiors, Berkeley, Calif., 1987—; cons. Benefit Boutique Inc., Lafayette; cons., participant antique and art fair exhibits, Orinda and Piedmont, Calif., 1977—. Decorator Piedmont Christmas House Tour, 1983, 88, 89, Oakland Mus. Table Setting, 1984, 85, 86, Piedmont Showcase Family Room, 1986, Piedmont Showcase Music Room, 1986, Piedmont Kitchen House Tour, 1985, Santa Rosa Symphony Holiday Walk Benefit, 1986, Piedmont Benefit Guild Showcase Young Persons Room, 1987, Piedmont Showcase Library, 1988, Peidmont Showcase Solarium, 1989, Jr. League Table Setting, Oakland-East Bay, 1989, 90. Bd. dirs. San Leandro Coop. Nursery Sch., 1967; health coord. parent-faculty bd., Miramonte High Sch., Orinda, 1978, Acalanes Sch. Dist., Lafayette, Calif., 1978; bd. dirs. Orinda Community Ctr. Vols., 1979; originator Concerts in the Park, Orinda, 1979; cons. not-for-profit Benefit Boutigue, Inc., Lafayette, Calif, 1991. Mem. Am. Soc. Interior Design (assoc.), Am. Soc. Appraisers (assoc.), Am. Decorative Arts Forum, De Young Mus., Nat. Trust Historic Preservation, San Francisco Opera Guild, San Francisco Symphony Guild. Democrat. Avocations: travel, hiking.

SANDER, ALFRED DICK, history professor emeritus; b. Cin., Dec. 26, 1925; s. Alfred A. and Katherine Irene (Taylor) S.; m. Helen Doris Barnes, May 31, 1947; children: Robert W., Richard H. AB, Am. U., 1948; MA, Miami U., Oxford, Ohio, 1950; PhD, Am. U., 1955. Analyst Nat. Security Agy., Washington, 1951-62; prof. Purdue U., Hammond, Ind., 1962-90; dean Purdue U., Hammond, 1974-86. Author: A Staff for the President, 1989. Mayor New Carrolton, Md., 1960-62. Staff Sgt. U.S. Army, 1944-46, ETO. Ford Found. rsch. grantee, 1979. Home: 1169 E Crown Ridge Dr Tucson AZ 85737-8802

SANDER, ELLEN JANE, writer; b. N.Y.C., Jan. 7, 1949; d. Eitel and Faye (Schnee) S. Sr. tech. writer Quarterdeck Office Systems, Santa Monica, Calif., 1990. Author: Trips: Rock Life in the 60's, 1972, (with others) Tom Rettigs Foxpro Handbook, 1989, FoxPro 2: Self Teaching Guide, 1992; contbr. numerous articles to various jours. and publs. including Vogue, Saturday Rev., N.Y. Times, L.A. Times, others. Jewish.

SANDER, SUSAN BERRY, environmental planning engineering corporation executive; b. Walla Walla, Wash., Aug. 26, 1953; d. Alan Robert and Elizabeth Ann (Davenport) Berry; m. Dean Edward Sander, June 3, 1978. BS in Biology with honors, Western Wash. U., 1975; MBA with honors, U. Puget Sound, 1984. Biologist, graphic artist Shapiro & Assocs., Inc., Seattle, 1975-77, office mgr., 1977-79, v.p., 1979-84, pres., owner 1984—, also bd. dirs. Merit scholar Overlake Service League, Bellevue, Wash., 1971, Western Wash. U. scholar, Bellingham, 1974-75, U. Puget Sound scholar, 1984; named Employer of Yr. Soc. Mktg. Profl. Svcs. 1988, Small Bus. of Yr. City of Seattle, Environ. Cons. of Yr. King County. Mem. Seattle C. of C., Soroptimist Internat. (bd. dirs.). Avocations: swimming, hiking, traveling, painting. Office: Shapiro & Assocs Inc 1201 3d Ave Ste 1700 Seattle WA 98101

SANDERS, (CATHERINE) ADELLE, social worker; b. Huntsville, Ala., Dec. 22, 1946; d. Willie Marion and Harriet Catherine (Worley) S.; 1 child, Eric Daniel Jones. Student, Monterey Peninsula Coll., 1973-75; BS in Human Devel., U. Calif., Davis, 1977; MSW, Calif. State U., Sacramento, 1980; postgrad., U. So. Calif., 1992—. Social svcs. planner Placer County Human Rels. Commn., Auburn, Calif., 1980-81; Indian desk coord. Calif. Office Econ. Opportunity, Sacramento, 1981-82; cons. Robinson Rancheria, Clear Lake, Calif., 1980-87; community devel. coord. Sacramento Housing and Redevel. Agy., 1984-88; cons. Grey Eagle & Assocs., West Sacramento, Calif., 1989-90, Sacramento Regional Purchasing Coun., 1990-91, Solano-Napa Agy. on Aging, Vallejo, Calif., 1992; cons., owner Sanders & Assocs., Sacramento, 1980—; prof. social work Calif. State U., Sacramento, 1986—. Commr., vice chair Sacramento Human Rights/Fair Housing Commn., 1991—; commr. Sacramento History and Sci. Commn., 1992—; mem. Sacramento Cultural Competency and Sensitivity Task Force, 1992—, Sacramento Human Svcs. Cabinet, 1992—. Recipient Doctoral Incentive award Calif. State U., 1990. Home: Ste 360 2222 Gateway Oaks Dr Sacramento CA 95833 Office: Calif State U Dept Social Work 6000 J St Sacramento CA 95819

SANDERS, ADRIAN, educator; b. Paragould, Ark., Aug. 3, 1938; s. Herbert Charles and Florence Theresa (Becherer) S.; m. Molly Jean Zecher, Dec. 20, 1961. AA, Bakersfield Coll., 1959; BA, San Francisco State U., 1961; MA, San Jose State U., 1967. 7th grade tchr. Sharp Park Sch., Pacifica, Calif., 1961-62; 5th grade tchr. Mowry Sch., Fremont, Calif., 1962-64; sci. tchr. Blacow Sch., Fremont, Calif., 1964-76; 5th grade tchr. Warm Springs Sch., Fremont, 1977-87, 5th grade gifted and talented tchr., 1987—; history social sci. chair Warm Springs Sch., Fremont, 1992-93. Mem. San Jose Hist. Mus. Assn., 1980—, Nat. Geog. Soc., Washington, 1976—; vol. 7 km. Race for Alzheimer's Disease Willow Glen Founders Day, San Jose, 1988—. Named Outstanding Young Educator, Jr. C. of C., Fremont, Calif., 1965. Mem. NEA, Fremont Unified Dist. Tchrs. Assn., Calif. Tchrs. Assn. Home: 15791 Rica Vista Way San Jose CA 95127 Office: Warm Springs Sch 47370 Warm Springs Blvd Fremont CA 94539

SANDERS, AUGUSTA SWANN, retired nurse; b. Alexandria, La., July 22, 1932; d. James and Elizabeth (Thompson) Swann; m. James Robert Sanders, Jan. 12, 1962 (div. 1969). Student, Morgan State U., 1956. Pub. health nurse USPHS, Washington, 1963-64; mental health counselor Los Angeles County Sheriff's Dept., 1972-79; program coordinator Los Angeles County Dept. Mental Health, 1979-88; program dir. L.A. County Dept. Health Svcs., 1989-92; appointee by Calif. Gov. Jerry Brown to 11th Dist. Bd. Med. Quality Assurance, 1979-85. Mem. Assemblyman Mike Roo's Commn. on Women's Issues, 1981—, Senator Diane Watson's Commn. on Health Issues, 1979—; chmn. Commn. Sex. Equity Los Angeles Unified Sch. Dist., 1984-90. Mem. NAFE, L.A. County Employees Assn. (v.p. 1971-72), So. Calif. Black Nurses Assn. (founding mem.), Internat. Fedn. Bus. and Profl. Women (pres. L.A. Sunset dist. 1988-89, dist. officer 1982-89), Internat. Assn. Chemical Dependency Nurses (treas. 1990-92), Chi Eta Phi. Democrat. Methodist.

SANDERS, DAVID CLYDE, management and marketing consultant; b. Lubbock, Tex., Oct. 8, 1946; s. Jasper Clyde and Mary Jo (Baber) S.; m. Barbara Ann Huck 1976 (div. July 1983); m. Marcia Lynn Fik, Nov. 20, 1983; children: Ashton Harrison, Geoffrey Davidson. Student, U. Tex., 1964; BA, Tex. Tech. U., 1969; postgrad., So. Meth. U., 1969-70, U. Tex., 1970-71. Exec., auditor Ch. Scientology Tex., Austin, 1971-75; exec., cons. Expansion Consultants, L.A., 1975-77; cons. pub. relations Exec. Mgmt. Specialists, L.A., 1977-80; exec. dir. Inst. for Fin. Independence, Glendale, Calif., 1980-83; mktg. dir. Michael Baybak & Co., Beverly Hills, Calif., 1983-85; sr. cons., ptnr. Mgmt. Tech. Consultants, L.A., 1985-86; sr. cons. Sterling Mgmt. Systems, Glendale, 1986—, sr. v.p., 1988-89, exec. coun. mem., exec. establishment officer, 1988-89, advanced cons., 1989—; speaker, ptnr. JPR & Assocs., L.A., 1985-88; pres. Prosperity Assn., 1990—; direct distbr. Amway Corp., 1991—; sr. cons. Mgmt. Success, 1993—. Author, Sanders Newsletter, 1983-88. Co-founder, pres. Bus. Adv. Bur. So. Calif., Huntington Beach, 1977-79; mem., contbr. Citizen's Commn. on Human Rights, L.A., 1976—; co-founder Vol. Ministers L.A., 1977-78. Mem. World Inst. Scientology Enterprises (chartered), Internat. Hubbard Ecclesiastical League of Pastors, Citizens for Alternative Tax System (sustaining), Friends of Narconon Chilocoo New Life Ctr., Alpha Phi Omega (sec. Tex. Tech U. chpt. 1965-69). Libertarian. Home: 6246 Delfino St Tujunga CA 91042-2935 Office: 143 S Glendale Ave Glendale CA 91205

SANDERS, DOUGLAS LEE, aerospace industry executive; b. Lindsay, Calif., June 20, 1946; s. Lee Samuel Sanders and Ruth Virginia (Barnes) Earley; m. Nan Beyeler, June 10, 1977; children: Jane-Ann, Matthew. BA, Brigham Young U., 1968; MPA, U. Calif., 1973; MS, Am. Grad. U., 1977; postgrad., Claremont Grad Sch., 1990—. Editor Procurement Assocs. Inc., Covina, Calif., 1968-71, sr., rsch. assoc., 1973-79; staff researcher Jet Propulsion Lab., Pasadena, Calif., 1979-84, 87-91, mgr. subcontract review, 1984-87, ethics advisor, 1992—; prin. assoc. The Sanders Group, Azusa, Calif., 1988-92; cons. Ernst & Young, L.A., 1985-90. Creator, editor of newsletters; contbr. to textbooks. Trustee Nat. Assn. Pvt. Nontraditional Schs. & Colls., Grand Junction, Colo., 1980-86. Fellowship Claremont Grad. Sch. 1991-92. Fellow Nat. Contract Mgmt. Assn. Home: 1132 N Angeleno Ave Azusa CA 91702 Office: Jet Propulsion Lab 4800 Oak Grove Dr Pasadena CA 91109

SANDERS, ESTHER JEANNETTE, retired aerospace company executive; b. Ogden, Utah, Feb. 19, 1926; d. Warren Lynn and Esther Marguerite (Harris) Garner; B.A., U. Colo., 1948; m. Thomas Wesley Sanders, Jan. 10, 1946. With Calif., Inst., Tech. Coop. Wind Tunnel, Pasadena, 1948; with Sperry Gyroscope Co., Point Mugu, Calif., 1949-55; with Propulsion Research Corp., Santa Monica, Calif., 1955-57; with TRW, Redondo Beach, Calif., 1957-84, head engrng. test data analysis sect., retired. Author 1 pub. story, 12 pub. poems. Home: 15405 Callahan Ranch Rd Reno NV 89511-9048

SANDERS, JAMES ALVIN, minister, biblical studies educator; b. Memphis, Nov. 28, 1927; s. Robert E. and Sue (Black) S.; m. Dora Cargille, June 30, 1951; 1 son, Robin David. BA magna cum laude, Vanderbilt U., 1948, BD with honors, 1951; student, U. Paris, 1950-51; PhD, Hebrew Union Coll., 1955; DLitt, Acadia U., 1973; STD, U. Glasgow, 1975; DHL, Coe Coll., 1988, Hebrew Union Coll., 1988. Ordained teacher Presbyn. Ch., 1955; instr. French Vanderbilt U., 1948-49; faculty Colgate Rochester Div. Sch., 1954-65, assoc. prof., 1957-60, Joseph B. Hoyt prof. O.T. interpretation, 1960-65; prof. O.T. Union Theol. Sem., N.Y.C., 1965-70, Auburn prof. Bibl. studies, 1970-77; adj. prof. Columbia, N.Y.C., 1966-77; prof. Bibl. studies Sch. Theology and Grad. Sch., Claremont, Calif., 1977—; ann. prof. Jerusalem Sch. of Am. Schs. Oriental Research, 1961-62; fellow Ecumenical Inst., Jerusalem, 1972-73, 85; Ayer lectr., 1971, 79, Shaffer lectr., 1972, Fondren lectr., 1975, Currie lectr., 1976, McFadin lectr., 1979, Colwell lectr., 1979; guest lectr. U. Fribourg, Switzerland, 1981, 90, Hebrew Union Coll., 1982, 88, Oral Roberts U., 1982, Tulsa U., 1982, Ind. U., 1982, Coe Coll., 1983, Garrett Sem., 1984, Pepperdine U., 1985, Western Sem., 1985, Bethany Sem., 1986; lectr. Union Sem. Sesquicentennial, 1987, U. Wis., 1987, U. Chgo., 1987; Gray lectr. Duke U., 1988; guest lectr. Notre Dame U., Georgetown U., Tex. Christian U., 1989, Alexander Robertson lectr. U. Glasgow, 1990-91, lecturer U. Ariz., 1993, Calif. Lutheran U., 1993, Willamette U., 1993; assocs. program lectr. Smithsonian, 1990, Am. Bible Soc. Sesquicentennail, 1991, U. N.Mex., 1992, Am. Interfaith Inst., 1992, Georgetown U., 1992; Lily Rosmen lectr. Skirball Mus., 1992; vis. prof. U. N.Mex., 1992, Southwestern U., 1992, Calif. Luth. U., 1992, Willamette U., 1993; mem. internat. O.T. text critical com. United Bible Socs., 1969—; exec. officer Ancient Bibl. Manuscript Ctr. for Preservation and Research, 1977-80, pres., 1980—; Gustafson lectr. United Theol. Sem., 1991. Author: Suffering as Divine Discipline in the Old Testament and Post-Biblical Judaism, 1955, The Old Testament in the Cross, 1961, The Psalms Scroll of Qumran Cave 11, 1965, The Dead Sea Psalms Scroll, 1967, Near Eastern Archaeology in the Twentieth Century, 1970, Torah and Canon, 1972, 74, Identité de la Bible, 1975, God Has a Story Too, 1979, Canon and Community, 1984, From Sacred Story to Sacred Text, 1987; also numerous articles; mem. editorial bd. Jour. Bibl. Lit., 1970-76, Jour. for Study Judaism, Bibl. Theology Bull., Interpretation, 1973-78, New Rev. Standard Version Bible Com. Trustee Am. Schs. Oriental Research. Fulbright grantee, 1950-51, Lilly Endowment grantee, 1981, NEH grantee, 1980, 91-92; Lefkowitz and Rabinowitz interfaith fellow, 1951-53, Rockefeller fellow, 1953-54, 85, Guggenheim fellow, 1961-62, 72-73, Human Scis. Rsch. fellow, 1989. Mem. Soc. Bibl. Lit. and Exegesis (pres. 1977-78), Phi Beta Kappa, Phi Sigma Iota, Theta Chi Beta. Home: PO Box 593 Claremont CA 91711-0593 Office: Ancient Bible Manuscript Ctr PO Box 670 Claremont CA 91711-0670

SANDERS, JERRY CHARLES, import, export executive; b. Denver, June 18, 1942; s. Charles Hannas and Gladys Mary (Twiss) S. BA, U. Hawaii, 1966; MBA, Calif. Polytech Inst., 1969. From asst. to vice chancellor Calif. State U., L.A., 1966-74; creative asst. Playwrighting Team of Lawrence/Lee, Malibu, Calif., 1974-75; dist. adminstr. Philips of Holland, L.A., 1975-79; dir. edn. & admissions Appraisal Inst., Chgo., 1979-83; ptnr. Prostiege Internat. Mktg., Chgo., 1983-85, Supris Ltd., Chgo., 1985-88; owner Sanders Enterprises, Riverside, Calif., 1988—; trade rep. Danish Embassy, Chgo., 1984—; cons. African Trade Commn., Atlanta, 1989—, Tianjin (China) Arts & Crafts Corp., 1992—. Del. Dem. NAt. Com., N.Y.C., 1992; inspector Registrar of Voters, Riverside, 1989, 90, 91; judge Calif. Election Com., Riverside, 1992. Mem. Internat. Importers Assn., Soc. Real Estate Appraisors, Only Child Assn. (exec. dir. 1985—), Save the Whale, Mensa, Toastmasters, Braile Inst. Democrat. Roman Catholic. Home and Office: 9810 Magnolia Ave Riverside CA 92503

SANDERS, MARK STEVEN, city executive; b. Dallas, Nov. 28, 1959; s. Dale Frank and Irene (Rodriguez) S. BS in Computer Sci., Tex. A&M U., 1983, MS in Computer Sci., 1984. Mgr. computer svcs. Tex. Engrng. Experiment Sta., College Station, 1982-84; supr. office info. systems E-Systems, Inc., Garland, Tex., 1984-86; mgr. systems and support Texas Instruments, Inc., Dallas, 1986-87; dir. of MIS Environ. Systems Rsch. Inst., Redlands, Calif., 1987-92; dir. infor. svcs. City of Glendale, Calif., 1992—. Mem. Soc. for Info. Mgmt. (So. Calif. chpt.), IEEE Computer Soc., Assn. Computing Machinery, Assn. Info. Mgrs., Data Processing Mgmt. Assn., Assn. for Computer Ops. Mgmt., Computer Profls. for Social Responsibility, Assn. for Systems Mgmt. Office: City of Glendale 141 N Glendale Ave Glendale CA 91206-4997

SANDERS, WALTER JEREMIAH, III, electronics company executive; b. Chgo., Sept. 12, 1936; s. Walter J. and Kathleen (Finn) S.; m. Linda Lee Drobman, Nov. 13, 1965 (div. 1982); m. Tawny Lee Wutzke, June 3, 1990; children: Tracy Ellen, Lara Whitney, Alison Ashley. BEE, U. Ill., 1958. Design engr. Douglas Aircraft Co., Santa Monica, Calif., 1958-59; applications engr. Motorola, Inc., Phoenix, 1959-60; sales engr. Motorola, Inc., 1960-61; with Fairchild Camera & Instrument Co., 1961-69; dir. mktg. Fairchild Camera & Instrument Co., Mountain View, Calif., 1961-68, group dir. mktg. worldwide, 1968-69; pres. Advanced Micro Devices Inc., Sunnyvale, Calif., until 1987, chmn. bd., chief exec. officer, 1969—; dir. Donaldson, Lufkin & Jenrette. Mem. Semicondr. Industry Assn. (co-founder, dir.), Santa Clara County Mfg. Group (co-founder, dir.). Office: Advanced Micro Devices Inc PO Box 3453 901 Thompson Pl Sunnyvale CA 94086-4518

SANDERSON, DAVID R., physician; b. South Bend, Ind., Dec. 26, 1933; s. Robert Burns and Alpha (Rodenberger) S.; divorced, 1978; children: David, Kathryn, Robert, Lisa; m. Evelyn Louise Klunder, Sept. 20, 1980. BA, Northwestern U., 1955, MD, 1958. Cons. in medicine Mayo Clinic, Rochester, Minn., 1965-87, chmn. dept. Thoracic Disease, 1977-87; cons. in medicine Mayo Clinic Scottsdale, Ariz., 1987—, chmn. dept. internal medicine, 1988—, vice chmn. bd. govs., 1987—; assoc. dir. Mayo Lung Project, Nat. Cancer Inst., Rochester. Contbr. articles to profl. jours. Recipient Noble award, Mayo Found., Rochester, "Significant Sig" award, Sigma Chi Fraternity, Ill., 1989, Chevalier Jackson award, Am. Bronchoesophagologic Assn., Fla., 1990. Fellow Am. Coll. of Physicians (gov. for Minn. 1981-87), Am. Bronchoesophagologic Assn., World Assn. for Bronchology, Internat. Bronchoesophagologic Assn., Internat. Assn. Study of Lung Cancer, AMA. Presbyterian. Home: 10676 E Bella Vista Scottsdale AZ 85258-6086 Office: Mayo Clinic Scottsdale 13400 E Shea Blvd Scottsdale AZ 85259-5499

SANDHU, JATINDER SINGH, software engineer; b. Chandigarh, Punjab, India, Apr. 28, 1961; came to U.S., 1980; s. Anoop Singh and Ravinder Kaur (Berar) S.; m. Balwinder Kaur Hundal, Sept. 30, 1988. BA, SUNY, 1986, MA, 1988; PhD, Ohio State U., 1990. Software engr. in geographic info. systems Environ. Systems Rsch. Inst., Redlands, Calif., 1990—. Developer (software) OSU-MAP for the PC, 1988; contbr. articles to profl. jours. Mem. Assn. of Computing Machinery, Assn. of Am. Geographers.

SANDLER, HERBERT M., savings and loan association executive; b. N.Y.C., Nov. 16, 1931; s. William B. and Hilda (Schattan) S.; m. Marion Osher, Mar. 26, 1961. BSS, CCNY, 1951; JD, Columbia U., 1954. Bar: N.Y. 1956. Asst. counsel Waterfront Commn. N.Y. Harbor, 1956-59; partner firm Sandler & Sandler, N.Y.C., 1960-62; pres., dir., mem. exec. com. Golden West Savs. & Loan Assn. and Golden West Fin. Corp., Oakland, Calif., 1963-75; chmn. bd., chief exec. officer, dir., mem. exec. com. World Savs. & Loan Assn. and Golden West Fin. Corp., Oakland, 1975—; charter mem. Thrift Instns. Adv. Coun. to Fed. Res. Bd., Oakland, 1963-75; bd. dirs. Fed. Home Loan Bank, San Francisco; former chmn. legis. and regulation com. Calif. Savs. Loan Leage. Pres., trustee Calif. Neighborhood Services Found.; chmn. Urban Housing Inst.; mem. policy adv. bd. Ctr. for Real Estate and Urban Econs. U. Calif., Berkeley. With U.S. Army, 1954-56. Office: Golden W Fin Corp 1901 Harrison St Oakland CA 94612-3574*

SANDLER, MARION OSHER, savings and loan association executive; b. Biddeford, Maine, Oct. 17, 1930; d. Samuel and Leah (Lowe) Osher; m. Herbert M. Sandler, Mar. 26, 1961. BA, Wellesley Coll., 1952; postgrad., Harvard U.-Radcliffe Coll., 1953; MBA, NYU, 1958; LLD (hon.), Golden Gate U., 1987. Asst. buyer Bloomingdale's (dept. store), N.Y.C., 1953-55; security analyst Dominick & Dominick, N.Y.C., 1955-61; sr. fin. analyst Oppenheimer & Co., N.Y.C., 1961-63; sr. v.p., dir. Golden West Fin. Corp. and World Savs. & Loan Assn., Oakland, Calif., 1963-75, vice chmn. bd. dirs., CEO, mem. exec. com., dir., 1975-80, pres., co- chief exec. officer, dir., mem. exec. com., 1980-93, chmn. bd. dirs., CEO, mem. exec. com., 1993—; pres., chmn. bd. dirs., CEO Atlas Assets, Inc., Oakland, 1987—, Atlas Advisers, Inc., Oakland, 1987—, Atlas Securities, Inc., Oakland, 1987—. Mem. Pres.'s Mgmt. Improvement Coun., 1980, Thrift Insts. Adv. Coun. to Fed. Res. Bd., 1989-91, v.p., 1990, pres., 1991; mem. policy adv. bd. Ctr. for Real Estate and Urban Econs. U. Calif., Berkeley, 1981—, mem. exec. com. policy adv. bd., 1985—; mem. adv. coun. Fed. Nat. Mortgage Assn., 1983-84; mem. ad hoc com. to rev. Schs. Bus. Adminstrn. U. Calif., 1984-85; vice chmn. industry adv. com. Fed. Savs. and Loan Ins. Corp., 1987-88, Ins. Corp., 1987-88; bd. overseers NYU Schs. Bus., 1987-89; mem. Glass Ceiling Commn., 1992—. Mem. Phi Beta Kappa, Beta Gamma Sigma. Office: Golden W Fin Corp 1901 Harrison St Oakland CA 94612-3574

SANDLER, MAURICE, urologist; b. N.Y.C., Dec. 13, 1937; married; 3 children. BA, NYU, 1957; PhD, Emory U., 1961, MD, 1964. Diplomate Am. Bd. Urology. Intern in surgery Bronx Mcpl. Hosp. Ctr., Albert Einstein Coll. Medicine, 1964-65; jr. asst. resident in surgery Upstate Med. Ctr., Syracuse, N.Y., 1965-66, fr. asst. resident in urology, 1966-67, asst. resident in urology, 1967-68, chief resident in urology, 1968-69; assoc. attending physician Upstate Med. Ctr., Syracuse, 1969-72, Crouse-Irving Meml. Hosp., Syracuse, 1972; attending physician Brookside Hosp., San Pablo, Calif., 1972—, Dr.'s Hosp., Pinole, Calif., 1972, Richmond (Calif.) Hosp., 1972, Herrick Hosp., Berkeley, Calif., 1972; staff physician VA Hosp., Syracuse, 1972; chief of staff Dr.'s Hosp., chief surgery; chief surgery Brookside Hosp.; med. dir. West Contra Corto Urological Surg. Med. Group Inc.; adj. assoc. prof. dept. zoology Syracuse U., 1966; assoc. prof. dept. urology Upstate Med. Ctr., 1969-72; rsch. assoc. dept. anatomy Emory U., 1960-64; cons. in field. Fellow ACS, Internat. Coll. Angiology; mem. Soc. Univ. Urologists, Am. Urol. Assn., Am. Nephrology Soc., Internat. Soc. Nephrology, So. Anatomical Soc., Am. Anatomical Soc., Histochem. Soc., Sigma Xi. Office: 2089 Vale Rd 25 San Pablo CA 94806

SANDLIN, FRED ALLEN, JR., personnel analyst; b. Ft. Benning, Ga., Aug. 24, 1952; s. Fred Allen Sr. and Grace Buren (Strahan) S.; m. Sara Virginia Scott, Oct. 19, 1985. BS, U. Montevallo, 1981. Cert. pub. pers. adminstr. Pers. analyst Pers. Bd. Jefferson County, Birmingham, Ala., 1986-90; pers. analyst II Washoe County Pers. Div., Reno, Nev., 1990—. Mem. Internat. Pers. Mgmt. Assn., Phi Kappa Phi. Home: 10075 Timberwolf Dr Reno NV 89523 Office: Washoe County Pers Div 1001 E 9th St Reno NV 89520

SANDLIN, MARLON JOE, planned giving representative, financial planner; b. Berkeley, Calif., Jan. 14, 1953; s. Ernest L. and Eunice (Knouf) S.; m. Sheryll L. Ballard, July 14, 1979; children: Chelsea, Kelly. AA, Diablo Valley Coll., Pleasant Hill, Calif., 1973; BA, U. Calif., Berkeley, 1975; MDiv, Fuller Theol. Sem., 1979. Cert. fin. planner. Assoc. dir. ch. rels. Fuller Theol. Sem., Pasadena, 1979-81; dir. ch. rels. Fuller Theol. Sem., 1981-84; sr. planned giving rep. Compassion Internat., Colorado Springs, Colo., 1984—. Bd. dirs. San Gorgonio Girl Scout Coun. Mem. Christian Estate Planners of Calif., Planned Giving Roundtable of So. Calif., Inst. CFPs. Republican. Presbyterian. Home and Office: 9363 Shamouti Dr Riverside CA 92508-6463

SANDLIN, STEVEN MONROE, power company contracts executive; b. Lebanon, Ind., May 9, 1935; s. Alva Rogers and Bertha Marie (Spiedel) S.; m. Joann Dana Borke, Aug. 9, 1957; children: Suzann, Sharyln, Syndi, Steven. BS in Aero Enrging., Purdue U., 1957; MA in Edn., Roosevelt U., 1961; AA in Bus., De Anza Coll., 1977. Registered Profl. engr., Wash. Commd. ensign USN, 1957; naval constructor USN Civil Engr. Corps, 1957-67; contracts mgr. A.G. Schoonmaker Co., Sausalito, Calif., 1967-70; contracts and program mgr. Hewlett-Packard Co., Cupertino, Calif., 1970-78; bus. mgr. Wash. Pub. Power Supply System, Richland, 1978—; v.p. Reno Holiday Club, Cupertino, 1975-78; mktg. mgr. Pennywhistle Prodns., Richland, 1980-85. Author (pamphlet) U.S. Naval Institute Proceedings, 1965, U.S. Civil Engineer, 1960. Mem. Richland Planning Devel. Commn., 1986; chmn. Richland Libr. Bd., 1985. Fellow Nat. Mgmt. Assn. (v.p. 1984, pres. 1992); mem. Nat. Contract Mgmt. Assn. (chmn. 1990), Wash. Army N.G., Am. Mil. Insignia Collectors Club, Co. Mil. Historians, Am. Polar Soc. Republican. Home: 2250 Davison Ave Richland WA 99352-1919 Office: Wash Pub Power Supply 3000 George Washington Way Richland WA 99352-1617

SANDO, EPHRIAM, English language educator; b. Chgo., Mar. 1, 1934; s. Samuel Saul and Frieda Gardenia (Kolinsky) S. BA with highest honors, UCLA, 1956, MA, 1958, PhD, 1962. Asst. in English UCLA, 1958-62; asst. prof. U. Iowa, Iowa City, 1962-67; asst. prof. Calif. State U.-Dominguez Hills, Carson, 1967-68, assoc. prof., 1968-73, prof. English, 1973—; acting chair English Calif. State U., Dominguez Hills, Carson, 1971-72; dir. Susan E. Barrett Poetry award, Carson. Co-translator: The Alhambra, 1968, High Wedlock Then Be Honoured, 1970; contbr. criticism and poetry to profl. jours. Recipient Found. Rsch. award Found. Com., Carson, 1987, Meritorious Performance awards Awards Com., Carson, 1987-88. Democrat. Jewish. Home: 704 E Elsmere Dr Carson CA 90746-2317 Office: Calif State U 1000 E Victoria St Carson CA 90747-0005

SANDO, JAMES FRANK, collegiate retail executive; b. L.A., Dec. 15, 1954; s. Frank Joseph and Gertrude G. (Haky) S.; m. Sally Carpenter, May 26, 1979; children: David Joseph, Kevin Daniel. BA, Calif. State U., L.A., 1976. Mgr. shipping/receiving Trident Shops Calif. State U., L.A., 1973-78; book buyer El Camino C.C., Torrance, Calif., 1978-80; asst. gen. mgr. Franciscan Shops San Francisco State U., 1980-83; dir. comml. ops. Calif. State U. Fullerton Found., 1983—; dir., treas. Collegiate Stores Coop., Northridge, Calif., 1989-93, Oro Hermosa Corp., 1992. Mem. Nat. Assn. Coll. Stores, Calif. Assn. Coll. Stores. Democrat. Mem. Soc. of Friends. Home: 4472 Casa Oro Yorba Linda CA 92686 Office: Nonprofit Adv Group 761 West Kimberly Ave Placentia CA 92670

SANDOR, JOHN ABRAHAM, state agency administrator; b. Buckley, Wash.; m. Lenore Barbot, 1956; children: Mary, Janet. BA in Forestry, Wash. State U., 1950; MPA, Harvard U., 1959. Dep. regional forester U.S. Forest Svc., Milw., 1972-76; regional forester U.S. Forest Svc., Juneau, Alaska, 1976-84; cons. Alaska-Pacific Rim Enterprises, Juneau, 1984-88; exec. dir. Alliance Juneau's Future, Inc., 1988-90; commr. Alaska Dept. Environ. Conservation, Juneau, 1990—. 2d lt. M.C., U.S. Army, 1945-46. Named Conservationist of Yr., Alaska Wildlife Conservation and Sportsmen Coun., 1979; recipient Superior Svc. award U.S. Dept. Agriculture, 1983. Fellow Soc. Am. Foresters (coun. 1985-86). Methodist. Office: Alaska Dept Environ Conservation 410 Willoughby Ave Juneau AK 99801

SANDOVAL, VANESSA FOWLER, counselor; b. Morenci, Ariz., July 8, 1967; d. Harold Dean and Patricia (Romero) Fowler; m. Raul M. Sandoval, May 18, 1991. BA, U. Ariz., 1990; postgrad., No. Ariz. U., 1991—. Admissions counselor U. Ariz., Phoenix, 1990—; grad. asst. South Learning Assistance Ctr. No. Ariz. U., Flagstaff, 1993—. Treas. Mujer, Inc., 1990-92; mentor STAR Program, 1992—; vol. Chicanos for La Causa, 1991—; advisor Anytown Camp, 1991; mem. Ariz. Assn. Chicanos in Higher Edn., 1987-90. Named One of Outstanding Young Women of Am., 1991. Roman Catholic. Home: 6833 S Roosevelt St Tempe AZ 85283 Office: No Ariz U PO Box 15075 Flagstaff AZ 86011-5075

SANDQUIST, GARY MARLIN, engineering educator, researcher, consultant, author; b. Salt Lake City, Apr. 19, 1936; s. Donald August Sandquist and Lillian (Evaline) Dunn; m. Kristine Powell, Jan. 17, 1992; children from previous marriage: Titia, Julia, Taunia, Cynthia, Carl; stepchildren: David, Michael, Scott, Diane, Jeff. BSME, U. Utah, 1960, PhD in Mech. Engrng., 1964; MS in Engrng. Sci., U. Calif., Berkeley, 1961; postdoctoral student MIT, 1969-70. Registered profl. engr., Utah, Calif., Minn.; cert. health physicist. Staff mem. Los Alamos Sci. Lab. (N.Mex.), 1966; vis. scientist MIT, Cambridge, 1960-70; research prof. surgery Med. Sch., U. Utah, Salt Lake City, 1974—; prof., dir. nuclear engrng., mech. engrng. dept. U. Utah, Salt Lake City, 1975—, acting chmn. dept., 1984-85; expert in nuclear sci. IAEA, UN, 1980-82; chief scientist Rogers and Assocs. Engrng. Corp., Salt Lake City, 1980—; advisor rocket design Hercules, Inc., Bachus, Utah, 1962; sr. nuclear engr. Idaho Nat. Engrng. Lab., Idaho Falls, Idaho, 1963-65; cons. various cos.; cons. nuclear sci. State of Utah, 1982—. Author: Geothermal Energy, 1973; Introduction to System Science, 1984. Served to comdr. USNR, 1954-56, Korea. Recipient Glen Murphy award in nuclear engrng. Am. Soc. Engrng. Edn., 1984. Fellow ASME, Am. Nuclear Soc.; mem. Am. Soc. Quality Control, Am. Health Physics Soc., Alpha Nu Sigma of Am. Nuclear Soc., Sigma Xi, Tau Beta Pi, Pi Tau Sigma. Republican. Mormon. Home: 2564 Neffs Circle Salt Lake City UT 84109-4055 Office: U Utah 1205 Merrill Engrng Bldg Salt Lake City UT 84112

SANDS, LAWRENCE KEITH, public health physician; b. Detroit, Feb. 9, 1955; s. Eugene Nathan and Sylvia Sandra (Edison) S.; m. Edee Jeanne Ritten, Dec. 21, 1986; children: Talyah Michele, Margot Beth, Michaela Marti. BS in Zoology with honors, U. Mich., 1977, MPH, 1986; DO, Chgo. Coll. Osteo. Medicine, 1981. Diplomate Nat. Bd. Osteo. Med. Examiners, Am. Bd. Preventive Medicine. Intern Phoenix Gen. Hosp., 1981-82; resident in ophthalmology Pontiac (Mich.) Osteo. Hosp., 1982-83; pvt. practice gen. medicine Sands Family Clinic, P.C., Dearborn, Mich., 1983-86; resident in pub. health U. Mich. Sch. Pub. Health, Ann Arbor, 1985-87; med. cons. Ind. Bd. Health, Indpls., 1986-87; fellow in clin. adminstrn. Samaritan Health Ctr., Detroit, 1987-88; chief infectious disease svcs. Ariz. Dept. Health Svcs., Phoenix, 1988—, acting asst. dir. div. disease prevention, acting state epidemiologist, 1992-93, state infectious disease epidemiologist, 1988—, dep. state Tb control officer, 1988—. U.S. Dept. HHS grantee, 1985; Nat. Assn. Community Health Ctrs. fellow, 1987-88. Mem. APHA, Am. Osteo. Assn., Ariz. Osteo. Medicine Assn., Ariz. Pub. Health Assn., Ariz. Infectious Disease Soc. Office: Ariz Dept Health Svcs Disease Prevention Svcs 3815 N Black Canyon Hwy Phoenix AZ 85015

SANDS, MICHAEL STEPHEN, law educator; b. N.Y.C., Feb. 21, 1937; m. Marilyn L. Brubeck, June 25, 1966; children: Deborah, Mark, Scott. BS, U. Ariz., 1959; LLB, Stanford U., 1962. Bar: Calif. 1963, U.S. Supreme Ct. 1977. Intern Calif. Assembly, Sacramento, 1962-63; rsch. atty. Calif. Ct. Appeal, Sacramento, 1963-64; assoc. Archibalt M. Mull, Sacramento, 1964-65; asst. pub. defender Sacramento County, Sacramento, 1965-70; pvt. practice, Sacramento, 1970-91; prof. U. Pacific McGeorge Sch. Law, Sacramento, 1991—. Mem. Sacramento City Coun., 1970-77. Mem. Sacramento County Bar Assn. (prs. 1985), Sacramento Barristers Club (pres. 1969). Office: PO Box 22692 Sacramento CA 95822

SANDS, RUSSELL BERTRAM, insurance company executive; b. Santa Cruz, Calif., Feb. 14, 1940; s. Clarence Russell and Betty Ellyn (Weeks) S.; m. Jacquelyn Marie Hall, Sept. 9, 1960; children: Douglas Clarence, Gwendolyn Marie. Student, Wheaton Coll., 1957-59, U. Calif., Berkeley, 1960-61; BA, Western Ill. U., 1984. Mgr. CIGNA Corp., San Francisco, 1961-69; v.p. Bayly, Martin & Fay, San Francisco, 1969-76; chmn., CEO Frank B. Hall & Co., San Francisco, 1976-92; mng. gen. ptnr. Wendy Petroleum, San Carlos, Calif., 1980—; ptnr. Sanbro Properties, 1987—; pres. Rollins Hudig Hall No. Calif., San Francisco, 1992—; bd. dirs. Hammerwell Inc., Los Gatos, Calif.; prin. Sands Properties, San Carlos, Calif., 1972—; gen. ptnr. Sanbro Holdings I, 1987—. Bd. dirs. Fellowship Acad., San Francisco, 1985—, Young Life of San Francisco, 1981—, City Team Ins., San Jose, Calif., Fellowship Urban Outreach, 1987-93; mem. adv. coun. Mount Hermon Assn., Felton, Calif., 1984-90; moderator First Bapt. Ch., San Carlos, 1979-80. Mem. Ind. Ins. Brokers Assn. Republican. Presbyterian. Clubs: World Trade (San Francisco); Churchill (Palo Alto, Calif.). Office: Rollins Hudig Hall No Calif 1 Market Plz Ste 2100 San Francisco CA 94105-1189

SANDS, SHARON LOUISE, graphic design executive; b. Jacksonville, Fla., July 4, 1944; d. Clifford Harding Sands and Ruby May (Ray) MacDonald; m. Jonathan Michael Langford, Feb. 14, 1988. BFA, Cen. Washington U., 1968; postgrad, UCLA, 1968. Art dir. East West Network, Inc., L.A., 1973-78, Daisy Pub., L.A., 1978; prodn. dir. L.A. mag., 1979-80; owner, creative dir. Carmel Graphic Design, Carmel Valley, Calif., 1981-85; creative dir., v.p. The Video Sch. House, Monterey, Calif., 1985-88; graphic designer ConAgra, ConAgra, Nebr., 1988; owner, creative dir. Esprit de Fleurs, Ltd., Carmel, Calif., 1988—; lectr. Pub. Expo, L.A., 1979, panelist Women in Mgmt., L.A., 1979; redesign of local newspaper, Carmel, Calif., 1982. Contbr. articles to profl. mags. Designer corp. ID for Carmel Valley C. of C., 1981, 90, redesign local newspaper, Carmel, Calif., 1982. Recipient 7 design awards Soc. Pub. Designers, 1977, 78, Maggie award, L.A., 1977, 5 design awards The Ad Club of Monterey Peninsula, 1983, 85, 87, Design awards Print Mag. N.Y., 1986, Desi awards, N.Y., 1986, 88. Mem. NAFE, Soc. for Prevention of Cruelty to Animals, Greenpeace. Democrat. Home and Office: 37302 Tassajara Rd Carmel Valley CA 93924-9123

SANDS, WILLIAM ARTHUR, physiology educator; b. Madison, Wis., Feb. 8, 1953; s. Arthur Mathew and Joan Marie (Ehredt) S. BS in Phys. Edn. magna cum laude, U. Wis., Oshkosh, 1975; MS in Exercise Physiology, U. Utah, 1985, PhD in Exercise Physiology. Asst. coach Am. Acad. Gymnastics, Des Plaines, Ill., 1975-78; dir., founder Mid-America Twisters, Northbrook, Ill., 1978-83; dir. edn. and research U.S. Gymnastics Fedn., Ft. Worth, 1980-81; asst. gymnastics coach U. Utah, Salt Lake City, 1983—, assoc. prof. dept. exercise and sport sci., 1990—; cons. biomechanics Chgo. Sports Medicine, 1983—; mem. exercise physiology com., biomechanics com. U.S. Gymnastics Fedn., Indpls., chmn. sport sci. com., 1984—; asst. nat. coach U.S. Gymnastics Fedn. World Championships, 1979, coached U.S. team in various internat. tournaments. Author: Coaching Women's Gymnastics, 1984, Everybody's Gymnastic Book, 1984, Modern Women's Gymnastics, 1982, Beginning Gymnastics, 1981. Recipient Nat. Assn. Intercollegiate Athletics All-Am. Gymnastics award, 1974, 75; inducted U. Wis. Oshkosh Athletic Hall of Fame, 1989; named Outstanding Young Alumni, U. Wis. Oshkosh, 1987. Mem. Am. Coll. Sports Med., Phi Kappa Phi. Home: PO Box 8798 Salt Lake City UT 84108 Office: U Utah Coll Health Exercise and Sport Sci Salt Lake City UT 80158-4728

SANDSTROM, JOANNE WULF, academic publishing professional; b. Bklyn., June 23, 1938; d. William August and Florence Bertha (Lotz) W.; m. Donald Albert Sandstrom, Sept. 5, 1959; children: Donald David, Erik William. BA, U. Calif., Berkeley, 1959; MA, Calif. State U., 1967. Tchr. English Cen. High Sch., Mpls., 1960-61, El Cerrito (Calif.) High Sch., 1961-62; tchr., chair dept. English Costa Mesa (Calif.) High Sch., 1969-75; instr. English Saddleback Coll., Mission Viejo, Calif., 1971-75, Her Majesty's Govt., Larnaca, Cyprus, 1978-79; freelance writer, 1975-90; mng. editor Inst. East Asian Studies/U. Calif., Berkeley, 1980—; pub. Earendil Press; mem. chancellor's staff adv. com. U. Calif., Berkeley, 1990—. Author: There and Back Again, 1984; contbr. articles, essays to various publs. Mem. AAUW (chmn. internat. rels. 1987-88), LWV No. Calif. Book Publicists Assn. (prog. dir. 1987-88), Bookbuilders West, Calif. Writer's Club, Phi Beta Kappa. Office: Inst East Asian Studies 2223 Fulton St Fl 6 Berkeley CA 94720-0001

SANDSTROM, ROBERT EDWARD, physician, pathologist; b. Hull, Yorkshire, Eng., Apr. 4, 1946; came to U.S., 1946; s. Edward Joseph and Ena Joyce (Rilatt) S.; m. Regina Lois Charlebois (dec. May 1987); children: Karin, Ingrid, Erica. BSc, McGill U., Montreal, 1968; MD, U. Wash., 1971. Diplomate Am. Bd. Pathology, Am. Bd. Dermatopathology. Internship Toronto (Can.) Gen. Hosp., 1971-72; resident pathologist Mass. Gen. Hosp., Boston, 1974-78; clin. fellow Harvard U. Med. Sch., Boston, 1976-78; cons. King Faisel Hosp., Riyadh, Saudi Arabia, 1978; pathologist, dir. labs. St. John's Med. Ctr., Longview, Wash., 1978—; v.p. Intersect Systems Inc.; chmn. bd. Cowlitz Med. Svc., Longview, 1988; participant congl. sponsored seminar on AIDS, Wash., 1987. Script writer movie Blood Donation in Saudi Arabia, 1978; contbr. articles to profl. jours. Surgeon USPHS, 1972-74. Fellow Coll. Am. Pathologists, Royal Coll. Physicians; mem. Cowlitz-Wahkiakum County Med. Soc. (past pres.). Roman Catholic. Home: 49 View Ridge Ln Longview WA 98632-5556 Office: Lower Columbia Pathologists 1606 E Kessler Blvd Ste 100 Longview WA 98632-1841

SANDVEN, LARS ARILD, schools program coordinator, counselor; b. Norheimsund, Norway, Oct. 5, 1945; came to U.S., 1963; s. Haakon and Anna (Faerevaag) S.; m. Ann Louise McCutchan, July 5, 1974; children: Jan Alfred, Tor Haakon, Anna Kristina. BA, Augsburg Coll., 1969; grad. in English, U. Bergen, Norway, 1970; teaching degree, Sagene Tchrs. Coll., Oslo, Norway, 1974; MEd, Coll. Idaho, 1989. Spanish instr. People's U., Bergen, 1969-71; elem. sch. tchr. Oslo Sch. Bd., 1974-78, Raelingen Sch. Bd., Strommen, Norway, 1978-80; jr. high, elem. sch. tchr. Nampa (Idaho) Sch. District, 1982-89, drug free sch. coord., 1989-92; middle sch. counselor Meridian (Idaho) Sch. Dist., 1992—; English tchr. Royal Norwegian Airforce, Bodø, Norway, 1965-66; Norwegian instr. Augsburg Coll., Mpls., 1967-68; TV host, anchor, translator, announcer Sta. NRK-TV, Oslo, 1973-75, 79-80; mem. adv. bd. U. Idaho Extension Svc., Caldwell, 1991-92; chmn. COSAC, Southwestern Idaho, 1990-91. Diosesan refugee coord. Episcopal Ch., Idaho, 1983-89; cubmaster, leader Boy Scouts Am., Nampa, 1986-87; mem. adv. bd. Port of Hope Treatment Ctr., Nampa, 1991—; active edn. com. Gov.'s Commn. on Alcohol and Drug Abuse, 1992—; chair edn. com. Treasure Valley Alcohol and Drug Coalition, 1991-92. Mem. Nat. Edn. Assn. (building rep. 1987), Idaho Lung Assn. (adv. bd. 1990—), Idaho School Counselors Assn., Idaho Soc. Ind. Psychology. Democrat. Home: 1916 N 24th St Boise ID 83702-0203 Office: Lowell Scott Middle Sch 3400 E McMillan Rd Meridian ID 83642

SANDZA, YVONNE ANNE, microbiologist; b. Weehawken, N.J., Dec. 23, 1952; d. Norberto and Elliana Frances (Martinez) Marrero; m. Walter Sandza, Aug. 19, 1978; children: Katherine, Krystal. BS in Biology, U. P.R., Rio Piedras, 1974; BS in Chemistry, Cata U. Ponce, P.R., 1977; med. technologist, U. Del., 1980. Lic. microbiologist, Calif., med. technologist, Calif. Microbiology supr. Humana Hosps., Mountain View, Calif., 1981-88; microbiology supr., lab. info. systems coord. Community Hosp. Chula Vista, Calif., 1988-90; dir. lab., lab. info. systems coord. SHARP Chula Vista Med. Ctr., 1990—; cons. San Diego, 1991-92. Editor: (newsletter) Gate Program, 1990. Coach Poway (Calif.) Soccer Club, 1990-91; mgr. San Diego Soccer Club, 1991-92. Recipient Participation award P.R. Olympic Com., Calgary, 1988, Rsch. award Am. Chem. Soc., 1976. Mem. Am. Soc. Clin. Pathology (lic. technologist 1980—), Am. Soc. Microbiology (lic. microbiologist 1985—), Clin. Lab Mgrs. Assoc., Greenpeace. Democrat. Roman Catholic. Home: 13422 Ct Dawn Ln Poway CA 92064 Office: SHARP Chula Vista Med Ctr 751 Med Ctr Ct Chula Vista CA 91911

SANETO, RUSSELL PATRICK, neurobiologist; b. Burbank, Calif., Oct. 10, 1950; s. Arthur and Mitzi (Seddon) S. BS with honors, San Diego State U., 1972, MS, 1975; PhD, U. Tex. Med. Br., 1981. Teaching asst. San Diego State U. 1969-75; substitute tchr. Salt Lake City Sch. Dist., 1975; teaching and research asst. U. Tex. Med. Br., 1976-77, NIH predoctoral fellow, 1977-81, postdoctoral fellow, 1981; Jeanne B. Kempner postdoctoral fellow UCLA, 1981-82, NIH postdoctoral fellow, 1982-87; asst. prof. Oreg. Regional Primate Rsch. Ctr. div. Neurosci., Beaverton, 1987-89; asst. prof. dept. cell biology and anatomy Oreg. Health Scis. U., Portland, 1988-90, U. Osteo. Medicine & Surgery, 1991—; lectr. rsch. methods Grad. Sch., 1982; vis. scholar in ethics So. Baptist Theol. Sem., Louisville, 1981. Contbr. articles to profl. jours. Recipient Merit award Nat. March of Dimes, 1978; named one of Outstanding Young Men in Am., 1979, 81, Man of Significance, 1985. Mem. Bread for World, Save the Whales, Sierra Club, Am. Soc. Human Genetics, AAAS, Winter Confs. Brain Research, Neuroscis. Study Program, N.Y. Acad. Scis., Am. Soc. Neurochem., Soc. Neurosci., Am. Soc. Neurochemistry, Soc. Neurosci. Democrat. Mem. Evangelical Free Ch. Club: World Runners.

SANFORD, ALLAN ROBERT, research seismologist, educator; b. Pasadena, Calif., Apr. 25, 1927; s. Roscoe Frank and Mabel Aline (Dyer) S.; m. Alice Elaine Carlson, Aug. 31, 1956; children: Robert Allan, Colleen Ann. BA, Pomona, 1949; MS, Caltech, 1954, PhD, 1958. Asst. prof. New Mex. Tech., Socorro, N.M., 1957-64; assoc. prof. New Mex. Tech., Socorro, 1964-68, coord. Geophysics program, 1978—, prof., 1968—. Contbr. articles to profl. jours. With USN, 1945-46. Recipient Disting. Rsch. award New Mex. Tech., 1985. Mem. Am. Geophyscial Union, Am. Assn. Advancement Sci. (fellow 1964), Soc. Exploration Geophysicists, Seismological Soc. Am., Sigma Xi. Home: 1302 North Dr Socorro NM 87801-4442 Office: New Mex Tech Geoscience Dept Socorro NM 87801

SANFORD, GEORGE ROBERT, insurance broker; b. Brockton, Mass., Apr. 9, 1927; s. Cecil Nickerson and Rachel Dorothy (Riberdy) S.; m. Barbara Joan Hendrick, Nov. 25, 1950 (div. 1970); children: Arthur Hendrick, Jane Sanford Stabile, Brian Michael, Paul Sheldon; m. Joanne Marie Cesareo, July 18, 1970. BS in Engrings., Brown U., 1949. CPCU. Engr. Liberty Mut. Group, N.Y.C., 1949-54; resident engr. Factory Mut. Engring., Providence, 1954-60; sr. account exec. Arkwright Ins., Hartford, Conn., 1960-90; ins. broker, cons. San Diego, 1990—. Author: Simplified Water Supply Analysis, 1954. Mem. Soc. Fire Protection Engrs.

SANFORD, KATHLEEN DIANE, nursing administrator; b. San Diego, Oct. 4, 1952; d. Donald Brown and JoAlice (Robertson) Smith; m. William Mack Sanford, May 11, 1974; children: Jonathan Mack, Michael Andrew, Stephanie Alyse. BSN, U. Md., 1974; MA, Pepperdine U., 1977; MBA, Pacific Lutheran U., Tacoma, Wash., 1983; D in Bus. Administrn., Nova U., Ft. Lauderdale, Fla., 1993. Officer U.S. Army Nurse Corps, Ft. Belvoir, Va., 1974-78; supr. Eden Hosp., Castro Valley, Calif., 1978-80; clin. coord. St. Joseph Hosp., Tacoma, 1980-83; v.p. nursing Harrison Meml. Hosp., Bremerton, Wash., 1983—; tchr. Pacific Luth. U., 1982-90; bd. mem. Kitsap Health Planning Coun., Bremerton, 1984-92, Green Mountain Rehab. Ctr., Bremerton, 1987-92. Contbr. articles to profl. jours; columnist Community Style Newspaper. Mem. nursing adv. bd. Olympic Coll., Bremerton, 1988; bd. dirs. Kitsap County United Way; chairperson South Kitsap Cub Scouts, Olalla, Wash., 1988. Capt. U.S. Army, 1974-78; active Am. Heart Assn., bd. dirs., 1988. Walter Reed Army Inst. Nursing scholarship U.S. Army, 1970; named Am.'s New Traditional Homemaker Frozen Food Industry, N.Y.C., 1986. Mem. Am. Bus. Women's Assn. (Woman of Yr. 1988, 93), Nat. League for Nursing, Am. Orgn. Nurse Execs., Wash. Orgn. Nurse Execs. (pres. 1993). Republican. Methodist. Office: Harrison Meml Hosp 2520 Cherry Ave Bremerton WA 98310-4229

SANFORD, LEROY LEONARD, rancher; b. Sanford Ranch, Wyo., June 24, 1934; s. Claude Leonard and Herminnie May (Brockmeyer) S.; m. Barbara Jo Shackleford, June 15, 1965 (dec. Oct. 1965); stepchildren: Christina Dolan, Marlena McCollum, Diana Sumners; 1 foster child, Catherine Frost. Cert. satellite geodesy, Johns Hopkins U., 1971; cert. astron. geodecy, U.S. Geol. Survey-Branch R & D, 1971. Cert. Geodesic Surveyor. Rancher Sanford Ranch, Douglas, Wyo., 1952-57; topographer, photogrametrist U.S. Geol. Survey-Topog. Divsn.-Hdqs., Denver, 1957-81; rancher Sanford Ranch, Douglas, 1981—; speaker various schs. and community orgns. Congl. Svc. medal U.S. Congress, 1972. Mem. NRA (endowment), Antarctican Soc., Wyo. Farm Bur. Republican. Home: 400 Windy Ridge Rd Douglas WY 82633

SANFORD, RON, wildlife and travel photographer; b. Gridley, Calif., June 13, 1939; s. Keith David and Aileen (McIntyre) S.; m. Nancy Wallace, June 17, 1961; children: Michael D., Daniel E. BS, U. Calif., Berkeley, 1961. Corp. pres. Gridley (Calif.) Growers Inc., 1965-78; photographer Gridley, 1979—. Photographs exhibited at Palace of Fine Arts, San Francisco, Rockefeller Ctr., N.Y.C.; photographs pubished in various books and mags. Bd. mem. Gridley Union High Sch.; treas. Gridley-Biggs Meml. Hosp., 1976-90. Capt. U.S. Army, 1962-65. Named Wildlife Photographer of Yr., Calif. Dept. Fish and Game, Sacramento, 1984, Nature Series award World Press Photo, Amsterdam, 1988, 90, Paul Harris award Rotary Internat., 1988, award World Press, Holland Found., 1990; named to Alumni Hall of Fame, Gridley Union High Sch., 1986; named Wildlife Photographer of Yr., Calif. Fish and Game Commn. Mem. Am. Soc. Magazine Photographers, Audubon Soc., Nature Conservancy, Ducks Unltd., Gridley Rotary Club (pres. 1973-74). Office: PO Box 248 Gridley CA 95948-0248

SANFORD, SARAH J., nurse, health care executive; b. Seattle, July 20, 1949; d. Jerome G. and Mary L. (Laughlin) S. BS in Nursing, U. Wash., 1972, MA in Nursing, 1977. Cert. in advanced nursing adminstrn. Critical care staff nurse Valley Gen. Hosp., Renton, Wash., 1972-75, Evergreen Gen. Hosp., Kirkland, Wash., 1975-76; instr. nursing Seattle Pacific U., 1977-79; with Overlake Hosp. Med. Ctr., Bellevue, Wash., 1979-88, critical care coord., 1979-80, dir. acute care nursing, 1980-82, assoc. adminstr., 1982-83, sr. v.p. patient care, 1983-88; exec. dir. AACN, Newport Beach, Calif., 1988-90, chief exec. officer, 1990—; bd. dirs. Found. for Critical Care, Washington, 1989-91, Partnership for Organ Donation, Boston, 1990—. Co-editor: Standards for Nursing Care of the Critically Ill, 1989; contbr. articles to books and jours. Fellow Am. Acad. Nursing; mem. AACN (pres. 1984-85, bd. dirs. 1981-83), ANA, Soc. for Critical Care Medicine, Am. Orgn. Nurse Execs., Sigma Theta Tau. Office: AACN 101 Columbia Aliso Viejo CA 92656-1491

SANFORD, WALTER SCOTT, real estate broker; b. Pasadena, Calif., Mar. 5, 1956; s. Harry William and Nadine Ellen (Grayson) S. AA, Pasadena City Coll., 1976; BA, U. So. Calif., L.A., 1979. Owner Walter Sanford and Assocs., Arcadia, Calif., 1976-79; pres. N&S Enterprises, El Monte, Calif., 1977-80; broker J.T.M. Brokerage, Long Beach, Calif., 1980-87; pres. Sanford Group, Inc., Long Beach, 1987—; Ptnr. Pelican Pub., Long Beach, 1989—. Contbr. articles to profl. jours.; editor (newsletter) Mega Agent, 1990. Named Investment Counselor of Yr., Long Beach Investment and Exchange Group, 1986, 87, 88. Office: Sanford Group Inc 3700 E 7th St Long Beach CA 90804-5393

SANGUINETTI, EUGENE FRANK, art museum administrator, educator; b. Yuma, Ariz., May 12, 1917; s. Eugene F. and Lilah (Balsz) S.; children: Leslie, Gregory. BA, U. Santa Clara, 1939; postgrad., U. Ariz., 1960-62. Instr. art history U. Ariz., Tucson, 1960-64; dir. Tucson Mus. and Art Ctr., 1964-67, Utah Mus. Fine Arts, Salt Lake City, 1967—; adj. prof. art history U. Utah, Salt Lake City, 1967—. Contbr. articles to profl. jours. Served with USAAF, 1942-44, to capt. M.I., U.S. Army, 1944-46. Mem. Am. Assn. Museums, Am. Assn. Mus. Dirs., Am. Fedn. of Arts, Coll. Art Assn., Western Assn. Art Museums, Salt Lake City C. of C. Home: 30 S St Salt Lake City UT 84103-4133

SANKAR, SUBRAMANIAN VAIDYA, aerospace engineer; b. New Delhi, India, June 22, 1959; came to U.S. 1982; s. V.S.S. and Bala (Sankar) Narayanan; m. Asha Govindarajan, July 31, 1988; 1 child, Sitara Sankar. B.Tech., Indian Inst. Tech., Madras, 1982; MSAE, Ga. Inst. Tech., Atlanta, 1983; PhD, Ga. Inst. Tech., 1987. R & D dir. Aerometrics, Inc., Sunnyvale, Calif., 1987—. Contbr. articles to profl. jours. J.N. Tata scholar, India. Mem. AIAA, Nat. Geog. Soc., AAAS. Home: 34211 Petard Ter Fremont CA 94555-2611 Office: Aerometrics Inc 550 Del Rey Ave Unit A Sunnyvale CA 94086

SANKOVICH, JOSEPH BERNARD, cemetery management consultant; b. Johnstown, Pa., Feb. 6, 1944; s. Joseph George and Helen Mary (Kasprzyk) S. Student, St. Francis Sem., 1964-68; BA, St. Francis Coll., 1966; postgrad., St. John Provincial Sem., 1968-69; MA, U. Detroit, 1973. Cert. cemetery exec., cath. cemetery exec., profl. cons. Assoc. pastor St. Mary's Ch., Nanty Glo, Pa., 1970-71, Sacred Heart Ch., Dearborn, Mich., 1971-74; dir. Mt. Kelly Cemetery, Dearborn, 1972-84; admissions counselor U. Detroit, 1974-81; dir. religious edn. St. James Ch., Ferndale, Mich., 1981-84; exec. Diocesan Cemetery Cons., Wyoming, Pa., 1984-86; dir. cemeteries Archdiocese of Seattle, 1986-91; mgmt. cons., owner Joseph B. Sankovich & Assocs., Edmonds, Wash., 1991—; cons. Archdiocese St. Paul and Mpls., 1990—, Diocese San Diego, 1991—, Archdiocese Santa Fe, Albuquerque, 1991—, Diocese Tucson, 1991—. Author, editor Directory of Western Cath. Cemeteries, 1992; author mgmt. assessments, sales programs, market analyses, 1986—; contbr. articles to profl. jours. Mem. Am. Cemetery Assn., Nat. Cath. Cemetery Conf., Wash. Interment Assn. (bd. dirs. 1990-91), Cath. Cemeteries of the West (founder 1987, governancy com. 1987-90). Home and Office: Joseph B Sankovich & Assocs 24006 92d Ave W Edmonds WA 98026

SANKS, ROBERT LELAND, environmental engineer, emeritus educator; b. Pomona, Calif., Feb. 19, 1916; s. John B. and Nellie G. (Church) S.; m. Mary Louise Clement, May 16, 1946; children: Margaret Nadine, John Clement. Registered profl. engr., Mont. Draftsman City of La Habra Calif., 1940; asst. engr. Alex Morrison cons. engr., Fullerton, Calif., 1941; jr. engr. U.S. Army Engrs., Los Angeles, 1941-42; asst. research engr. dept. civil engrng. U. Calif.-Berkeley, 1942-45; structural engr. The Austin Co., Oakland, Calif., 1945-46; instr. dept. civil engrng. U. Utah, Salt Lake city, 1946-49; asst. prof. U. Utah, Salt Lake City, 1949-55, assoc. prof., 1955-58; structural engr. The Lang Co., Salt Lake City, 1950; instrument man Patti McDonald Co., Anchorage, 1951; checker Western Steel Co., Salt Lake City, 1952; structural engr. Moran, Proctor, Meuser and Rutledge, N.Y.C., 1953, F.C. Torkelson Co., Salt Lake City, 1955; soils engr. R.L. Sloane & Assocs., Salt Lake City, 1956; prof., chmn. dept. civil engrng. Gonzaga U., Spokane, Wash., 1958-61; prof. dept. civil engrng.-engrng. mechanics Mont. State U., Bozeman, 1966-82, prof. emeritus, 1982—; vis. prof. U. Tex.-Austin, 1974-75; part-time sr. engr. Christian, Spring, Sielbach & Assoc., Billings, Mont., 1974-82; cons. engr., 1945—; lectr. at pumping sta. design workshops, 1988—; assoc. specialist San. Engrng. Research Lab., 1963-65, research engr., 1966. Author: Statically Indeterminate Structural Analysis, 1961; co-author: (with Takashi Assano) Land Treatment and Disposal of Municipal and Industrial Wastewaters, 1976, Water Treatment Plant Design for the Practicing Engineer, 1978; editor-in-chief: Pumping Station Design, 1989 (award Excellence profl. & scholarly pub. div. Assn. Am. Pubs. 1989); contbr. articles on civil engring. to profl. publs. Named to Wall of Fame, Fullerton High Sch., 1987; NSF fellow, 1961-63. Fellow ASCE (chmn. local qualifications com. intermountain sect. 1950-56, pres. intermountain sect. 1957-58), Am. Acad. Environ. Engrs. (diplomate); mem. Am. Water Works Assn. (life, pres. Mont. sect. 1981-82 George Warren Fuller award), Mont. Water Pollution Control Fedn., Water Environment Fedn., Assn. Environ. Engrng. Profs., Sigma Xi, Chi Epsilon. Clubs: Rotary, Camera of Bozeman (pres. 1980-81). Home: 411 W Dickerson St Bozeman MT 59715-4538 Office: Mont State U Dept Civil and Agrl Engrng Bozeman MT 59717

SANNER, MONTY RAY, non-profit organization administrator; b. Riverside, Calif., Oct. 11, 1953; s. Russell Ray and Rose-Marie (Took) S.; m. Jackie Ora Damon, Sept. 11, 1976; children: Kristen, Adam, Kaci. BA in Sociology, Ea. Ky. U., 1976; MA in Communications, Regent U., 1989. With customer svc. United Airlines, Chgo., 1978-80; account exec. Evergreen Internat. Airlines, Chgo., 1980-81, Coca Cola, Lenexa, Kans., 1981-82; asst. dir. advt. Thomas Nelson Pubs., Nashville, 1984-85; dir fundraising Logoi Ministries, Miami, Fla., 1985-86; account exec. South Cen. Bell, Nashville, 1986-87; dir. customer svc. Compassion Internat., Colorado Springs, Colo., 1987—. Contbr. articles to profl. jours. Mem. Internat. Customer Svc. Assn., Am. Soc. Travel Agts., Internat. Platform Assn., Phi Kappa Alpha. Republican. Episcopalian. Home: 3461 Trenary Ln Colorado Springs CO 80918-7339 Office: Compassion Internat 3955 Cragwood Dr Colorado Springs CO 80918-7860

SANNER, ROBERT CHARLES, real estate mortgage broker, consultant; b. Frederick, Md., Nov. 16, 1945; s. Charles S.V. and Patricia F. Sanner; m. Barbara Moor, July 1, 1972; children: Daniel, Richard, Timothy. BA cum laude, Dartmouth Coll., 1967; MBA, Stanford U., 1969. CPA, Calif.; lic. real estate broker, Calif. Sr. accountant Arthur Andersen & Co., San Francisco, 1971-73; controller Bank of Montreal, San Francisco, 1973-76; asst. controller Arcata Corp., Menlo Park, Calif., 1976-80; chief fin. officer

Sutter Hill Ltd., Palo Alto, Calif., 1980-84; devel. assoc. Hare, Brewer & Kelley, Palo Alto, 1984-85; dir. mortgage fin. Damon Raike & Co., San Francisco, 1985—; lectr. econs. dept. Stanford U., Palo Alto, 1970-71. Dist. enrollment dir. Dartmouth Coll., San Francisco Peninsula, 1991—; pres. dist. 21 Am. Contract Bridge League, San Francisco area, 1974; treas. Mira Glen Homeowners Assn., San Francisco, 1975. Mem. AICPA, Bay Area Mortgage Assn., Calif. Soc. CPA's, Foothills Swim and Tennis Club. Home: 3925 El Cerrito Rd Palo Alto CA 94306-3113

SANNWALD, WILLIAM WALTER, librarian; b. Chgo., Sept. 12, 1940; s. William Frederick and Irene Virginia (Stanish) S.; children: Sara Ann, William Howard. B.A., Beloit Coll., 1963; M.A.L.S., Rosary Coll., River Forest, Ill., 1966; M.B.A., Loyola U., Chgo., 1974. Mktg. mgr. Xerox Univ. Microfilms, 1972-75; assoc. dir. Detroit Public Library, 1975-77; dir. Ventura (Calif.) County Library, 1977-79; city libr. San Diego Public Libr., 1979—; vis. instr. mktg. San Diego State U. Author: Checklist of Library Building Design Considerations, 2d edit., 1992; chairperson editorial adv. bd. Pub. Librs. Pres. Met. Libraries Sect., 1989. Recipient Outstanding Prof. award and Outstanding Mktg. Prof. award, 1985; Award of Merit AIA San Diego chpt., 1988. Mem. ALA, Calif. Library Authority for Systems and Services (pres. congress of mems. 1980), Calif. Library Assn. Roman Catholic. Home: 1201990 Calle De Medio El Cajon CA 92019-4905 Office: San Diego Pub Libr 820 E St San Diego CA 92101-6416

SANO, ROY I., bishop. Ordained to ministry United Meth. Ch., later consecrated bishop; appointed Bishop Rocky Mountain Conf., United Meth. Ch., Denver. Office: Rocky Mt Conf United Meth Ch 2200 S University Blvd Denver CO 80210-4797*

SANSOM, MATT RUDIGER, medical products executive; b. Hamburg, Fed. Republic of Germany, Feb. 14, 1950; came to U.S., 1953; s. Ken Sansom and Carla Schnibbe; m. Janice Hoyt, May 4, 1973; children: Amy, Stephen, Sara, Lindsay. BS, Brigham Young U., 1974. Salesman N.Y. Life Ins. Co., Phoenix, 1975-76, No Nonsense Fashions, Phoenix, 1976-78; assoc. Zimmer-Ross Corp., Phoenix, 1978-85; distbr. Depuy Inc., Salt Lake City; exec. v.p. Megadyne Med. Products Inc., Draper, Utah, 1984—, also bd. dirs.; ptnr. Orthodyne, Sandy, Utah, 1988—. Asst. scoutmaster Boy Scouts Am., Sandy, 1988. Mem. Sports Mall. Republican. Mormon. Office: Megadyne Med Products Inc 11506 S State St Draper UT 84020

SANSWEET, STEPHEN JAY, journalist, author; b. Phila., June 14, 1945; s. Jack Morris and Fannie (Axelrod) S. BS, Temple U., 1966. Reporter Phila. Inquirer, 1966-69; reporter Wall Street Jour., Phila., 1969-71, Montreal, Que, Can., 1971-73; reporter Wall Street Jour., L.A., 1973-84, dep. bur. chief, 1984-87, bur. chief, 1987—; lectr. bus. journalism U. So. Calif., L.A., 1984-87. Author: The Punishment Cure, 1976, Science Fiction Toys and Models, 1981, Star Wars: From Concept to Screen to Collectible, 1992; consulting editor: Star Wars Galaxy, 1993. Recipient award for best fire story Phila. Fire Dept., 1968, Pub. Svc.-Team Mem. award Sigma Delta Chi, 1977; finalist Loeb award, 1990. Mem. Soc. Profl. Journalists. Office: Wall Street Jour Ste 1500 6500 Wilshire Blvd Los Angeles CA 90048 also: The Wall Street Journal 200 Liberty St New York NY 10281

SANTARELLI, EUGENE DAVID, air force officer; b. Canton, Ohio, Aug. 14, 1944; s. Inez Louize Santarelli; m. Barbara Olsen, Aug. 1966 (div. 1974); m. Denniseen Kay Bright, Dec. 3, 1976. BBA, U. Notre Dame, 1966; M in Mil. Sci., U.S. Army Command and Staff Coll., Ft. Leavenworth, Kans., 1980; M in Adminstrn. and Mgmt., Troy (Ala.) State U., 1981. Commd. 2d lt. USAF, 1966, advanced through grades to maj. gen., 1993; staff officer Hdqrs. Tactical Air Command, Langley AFB, Va., 1980-81, asst. sr. officer matters, 1981-82; asst. dir. ops. 363d Tactical Fighter Wing, Shaw AFB, S.C., 1982-84; student Air War Coll., Maxwell AFB, Ala., 1984-85; dir. USAF Bd. Structure, Office Vice Chief of Staff, Washington, 1985-87; vice comdr., then comdr. 52d Tactical Fighter Wing, Spangdahlem Air Base, Fed. Republic Germany, 1987-89; exec. officer Office Chief of Staff, Washington, 1989-90; comdr. 836th Air Div., Davis-Monthan AFB, Ariz., 1990; comdr. 4404th Comp Wing USCENTAF Forward, Dhahran, Saudi Arabia, 1991; comdr. 355th Wing Davis-Monthan AFB, Ariz., 1992—. Co-chmn. Combined Fed. Campaign, Tucson, 1990-93. Mem. Air Force Assn., VFW, Order of Daedalians, Rotary. Roman Catholic. Home: 4173 S Hinden Blvd Tucson AZ 85708-1221 Office: 355th Wing Davis Monthan A F B AZ 85707

SANTEE, DALE WILLIAM, lawyer, air force officer; b. Washington, Pa., Mar. 28, 1953; s. Robert Erwin and Elsbeth Emma (Bantleon) S.; divorced; 1 child, Enri De'Von; m. Junko Mori, June 2, 1992. BA, Washington & Jefferson Coll., 1975; MA, U. No. Ariz., 1982; JD, U. Pitts., 1978. Bar: Pa. 1978, U.C. Ct. Mil. Appeals 1979, Calif. 1989. Floor mgr., commn. salesman J.C. Penney Co., Washington, Pa., 1971-76; asst. mgr. Rach Enterprises, Charleroi, Pa., 1977-78; legal intern Washington County Pub. Defender; commd. 2d lt. USAF, 1979, advanced through grades to major, 1989; from asst. staff judge advocate to area def. counsel Luke Air Force Base, Ariz., 1979-81; claims officer 343 Combat Support Group/Judge Advocate, Eielson AFB, Alaska, 1981-83; sr. staff legal adviser Dept. Vet. Affairs, Washington, 1983-89; asst. staff judge advocate Mil. Justice div. Air Force Judge Advocate Gen.'s Office, Washington, 1986-89, 63CSG/Judge Advocate, Norton Air Force Base, Calif., 1989-91; dep. pub. defender Juvenile div. San Diego County, 1990—; staff judge advocate 445MAW, Norton AFB, Calif., 1991—; v.p. Neuer Enterprises, Nanjemoy, Md., 1983-89; participant Mgmt. Devel. Seminar, 1988. Mem. San Diego County Rep. Party; pres., legis. com. co-chmn. PTA Zamorano Elem. Sch., San Diego, chmn. SITE com.; mem. San Diego County Child Abuse Coord. Coun., San Diego County Commn. on Children and Youth, San Diego County Juvenile Ct. Mental Health Task Force, San Diego County Unified Sch. Dist., Parent Adv. Coun. Decorated Air Force Commendation medal, 1981, 89, Air Force Meritorious Svc. medal, 1991; named Outstanding Young Man of Am., U.S. Jaycees, Montgomery, Ala., 1981; acad. scholar Washington & Jefferson Coll., 1971-75, Beta scholar Washington & Jefferson Coll., 1974, Pa. Senatorial scholar Pa. Senate, 1975, 76, 77, 78. Mem. Pa. Bar Assn., Calif. Bar Assn., San Diego County Bar Assn., San Diego County Psych-Law Soc. Home: 1110 Manzana Way San Diego CA 92139-1448

SANTIAGO, BENITO RIVERA, professional baseball player; b. Ponce, P.R., Mar. 9, 1965; m. Bianca Santiago; 1 child, Benny Beth. Catcher San Diego Padres, 1986-92, Florida Marlins, 1993—. Named Nat. League Rookie of Yr. Baseball Writers' Assn. Am., 1987, Sporting News, 1987, All-Star Team, 1989-92; recipient Gold Glove award, 1988-90, Silver Slugger award, 1987-88, 90-91; holder maj. league rookie record for most consecutive games batted safely. Office: Florida Marlins 2269 NW 199th St Miami FL 33056

SANTIAGO, DAWN TERESA, editor, historical consultant; b. Sherman, Tex., July 15, 1959; d. Doyle Leroy and Vera Mae (Jewitt) Moore; m. Mark Kenneth Santiago, July 2, 1983; children: Edward Stephan, Alexander Trajan and Justin Constantine (twins). BA, U. Ariz., 1981, MA, 1988. Editorial asst. U. Ariz., Tucson, 1981-83; clk. typist Ariz. Western Coll., Yuma, 1986-88; assoc. faculty Pima Community Coll., Tucson, 1990-91; curatorial aid Ariz. Hist. Soc., Tucson, 1989—; hist. cons. Mrs. Patricia Stephenson, Tucson, 1990-91; editorial asst. Jour. Ariz. Hist., Tuscon, 1992—. Contbr. articles to profl jours. Home: 726 S Camino Seco Tucson AZ 85710-6261 Office: 949 E 2nd St Tucson AZ 85719

SANTILLAN, ANTONIO, financial company executive; b. Buenos Aires, May 8, 1936; naturalized, 1966; s. Guillermo Spika and Raphaella C. (Abaladejo) S.; children: Andrea, Miguel, Marcos. Grad., Morgan Park Mil. Acad., Chgo., 1954; BS in Psychology, Coll. of William and Mary, 1958. Cert. real estate broker. Asst. in charge of prodn. Wilding Studios, Chgo., 1964; pres. Adams Fin. Services, Los Angeles, 1965—. Writer, producer, dir. (motion pictures) The Glass Cage, co-writer Dirty Mary/Crazy Harry, Viva Knievel; contbg. writer Once Upon a Time in America; TV panelist Window on Wall Street; contbr. articles to profl. fin. and real estate jours. Served with USNR, 1959. Recipient Am. Rep. award San Francisco Film Festival, Cork Ireland Film Fest, 1961. Mem. Writer's Guild Am., L.A. Bd. Realtors, Beverly Hills Bd. Realtors (income/investment divsn. steering com.), Westside Realty Bd. (bd. dirs.), L.A. Ventures Assn. (bd. dirs.), Jonathan Club (L.A.), Rotary, Roundtable, Toastmasters Internat. Office: Adams Fin Svcs Inc 425 N Alfred St West Hollywood CA 90048-2504

SANTILLAN, JOSÉ LEOPOLDO, equity fund manager; b. Chgo., Sept. 28, 1957; s. Leopoldo and Juana (Loosa) S.; m. Jazmin M. Lopez, Aug. 20, 1983. BS in Acctg., U. Ill., Chgo., 1980; MBA in Fin., De Paul U., 1984. Chartered fin. analyst, 1987. Mgmt. assoc., equity analyst, trust officer, asst. v.p., then v.p. La Salle Nat. Bank & Trust, Chgo., 1980-92; ptnr. Peña Investment Advisors, Inc., Denver, 1992--. Mem. Proviso Assn. Retarded Citizens, Chgo. Awarded Favorable Consideration Mechanical Drawing, Ill. Inst. Tech., 1973. Mem. Investment Analyst Soc. Chgo. (chmn. mem. com. 1988-91, bd. dirs. 1991-92), Denver Soc. Securities Analyst, Delta Mu Delta, Beta Gamma Sigma, U. Ill. Alumni Assn., De Paul U. Alumni Assn. Republican. Roman Catholic. Office: Peña Investment Advisor 1200 17th St Ste 1250 Denver CO 80202

SANTILLI, ALCIDE, electrical engineer; b. Providence, May 28, 1914; s. Camillo and Mary Santilli; m. Lois Margaret Lee, May 7, 1952. ScBEE, Brown U., 1936. Registered profl. engr., N.Mex. Design engr. Philco Radio, Phila., Detroit, 1938-40; ptnr., owner Meteorol. and Aero. Instrumentation, Cambridge, Mass., 1940-42; commd. U.S. Army, 1942, advanced through grades to lt. col., 1965, served with ordnance, meteorol., communications, physicist, ret., 1965; cons. in field; part-time designee flight instr. examiner FAA Designee Pilot Examiners-Gliders, Albuquerque, 1980—; competition dir. Littlefield (Tex.) Regional Soaring Contests, 1983-84; mem. contest staff, ops. Nat. Standard Class Championships, Hobbs, N.Mex., 1990. Patentee in field; vol. staff author monthly jour. Flying Rev., Albuquerque, 1976—. Mem. Am. Assn. Aero. and Astronautics, Am. Radio Relay League, Soaring Soc. Am. (Soaring Hall of Fame 1982), Albuquerque Soaring Club (ops. officer 1989-90, vol. flight instr. 1966—), Sigma Xi (assoc.), Tau Beta Pi.

SANTORO, CARMELO JAMES, electronics executive; b. Port Chester, N.Y., July 18, 1941; s. Frederick James and Celeste (Fraioli) S.; m. Elizabeth Higgins, June 23, 1963 (div. July 1980); m. Nancy Jo Kested, Sept. 6, 1980; children: Suzan, Patricia, Stephen, Steven. BS, Manhattan Coll., 1963; PhD, Rensselaer Poly. Inst., 1968. Ops. mgr. Motorola, Inc., Phoenix, 1968-76; v.p. mfg. Am. Micro Systems, Santa Clara, Calif., 1976-80; v.p. integrated cirs. RCA, Somerville, N.J., 1980-82; pres., chmn., chief exec. officer Silican Systems, Tustin, Calif., 1982—; bd. dirs. Ashton-Tate, Torrence, Calif., Dallas Semiconductor. Bd. dirs. Orange County Performing Arts Ctr., Newport Beach, Calif., 1989. Republican. Office: AST Research Inc PO Box 19658 Irvine CA 92713

SANTOS, E(NOS) FRANCIS (FRANK), agrochemical company executive; b. Crockett, Calif., May 24, 1933; m. Norma Lee Stone, Jan. 30, 1955; children: Gary Edward, Debra Lynn, Scott Anthony. Student, U. Calif., Berkeley, 1951-53, 56, ICS Schs., 1959, U. Del., 1969-70; BA, Calif. Western U., 1977, MBA, 1978. Rsch. engr. Chevron Rsch. Corp., Richmond, Calif., 1955-59; v.p., area mgr. Chevron Chem. Internat., Singapore, 1976-80; dir. Nippon Petroleum Detergent, Tokyo, 1978-80; mgr. affiliates Chevron Chem. Co., San Francisco, 1980-81; gen. mgr. Chevron Chem. Co., San Ramon, 1989-90; v.p. Chevron Chem. Internat., Inc., San Francisco, 1981-84; v.p., dir. Chevron do Brasil, Ltd., Sao Paulo, Brazil, 1984-88; v.p. Chevron Internat. Chemicals, Inc., San Ramon, Calif., 1988-90; pres., CEO, dir. Valent USA Corp. subs. Sumitomo Chem. Co., Walnut Creek, Calif., 1990—. Bd. dirs. Walnut Creek C. of C., 1992—. With U.S. Army, 1953-55, Italy. Mem. Nat. Agrl. Chem. Assn. (bd. dirs. 1989—), Nat. Future Farmers of Am. Sponsor's Bd. (bd. dirs. 1992—), Commonwealth Club Calif., Am. Mgmt. Assn. (guest faculty ops. enterprise), Blackhawk Country Club. Republican. Roman Catholic. Office: Valent USA Corp 1333 N California Blvd Walnut Creek CA 94596

SANTRY, BARBARA LEA, venture capitalist; b. Key West, Fla., Jan. 20, 1948; d. Jere Joseph and Frances Victoria (Appel) S. BS in Nursing, Georgetown U., 1969; MBA, Stanford U., 1978. Program analyst, br. chief U.S. Dept. HEW, Washington, 1973-76; mgr. cons. div. Arthur Andersen and Co., San Francisco, 1978-80; asst. v.p. Am. Med. Internat., Washington, 1980-83; v.p. Alex Brown and Sons, Inc., Balt., 1983-86; ptnr. Wessels, Arnold and Henderson, Mpls., 1986-88; v.p. Dain Bosworth Inc., Mpls., 1988-90, sr. v.p., 1990-91; ptnr. Pathfinder Venture Capital Funds, Menlo Park, Calif., 1991—. Served to lt. USNR, 1967-72. Office: 3000 Sand Hill Rd Bldg 3 Ste 255 Menlo Park CA 94025

SANWICK, JAMES ARTHUR, mining executive; b. Balt., Feb. 15, 1951; s. Alfred George and Catherine Anne (von Sas) S.; m. Brenda Julia Tietz, Sept. 20, 1980; children: Luke Graham, Sierra Catherine. AS, Catonsville (Md.) Community Coll., 1975; BS, U. No. Colo., 1976; M in Pub. Administn., U. Alaska S.E., 1985. Recreation therapist Md. Sch. for the Blind, Balt., 1974; dir. camp New Horizon United Cerebral Palsy Md., Balt., 1975; sub-dist. mgr. Nat. Park Svc., various, 1976-82; freelance mgmt. cons. Juneau, Alaska, 1982-84; regional mgr. div. labor standards Alaska Dept. Labor, Juneau, 1983-88; adj. faculty sch. bus. and pub. administrn. U. Alaska S.E., Juneau, 1985—; mgr. Alaska Productivity Improvement Ctr., Juneau, 1989-93; mgr. human resources and pub. affairs Greens Creek Mining Co., Juneau, 1989-93; mgr. human resources Denton-Rawhide Mining Co., Fallon, Nev., 1993—; bd. dirs. Gov.'s Com. on Employment Disabled Persons, Alaska Acad. Decathalon Inc.; chmn. Job Svc. Employer Com., Alaska, 1989-93; bd. advisors Inst. Mine Tng. U. Alaska S.E., 1989-93. Co-author: (info. phamphlet) Blue Water Paddling in Alaska, 1980; editor: (film) Green's Creek Project, 1990; photographic editor: Inside Passage Mag., 1982, 83; photographer: (book) Death Valley, 1977. Patrolman Nat. Ski Patrol System, Juneau, 1978-83; instr., trainer ARC, Alaska, Utah, Ariz., 1979-82; v.p. bd. dirs. Alaska Acad. Decathlon. Sgt. USMC, 1970-73. Recipient Nat. New Svc. award United Cerebral Palsey, 1975; named Candidate of Yr. Nat. Ski Patrol System, 1979. Mem. Soc. Human Resources Mgmt., Juneau Ski Club. Office: Denton Rawhide Mining Co PO Box 2070 Fallon NV 89406

SANZ, KATHLEEN MARIE, management consultant; b. L.A., Sept. 29, 1955; d. Jess Quevedo and Rosemary Helen (Debley) S. Student, Chabot Coll., 1975-76, City of Costa Mesa (Calif.), 1985. Lic. tax preparer, Calif. Admistrv. positions, 1973-80; office mgr. The Printery, Laguna Hills, Calif., 1980-83, Astro Vista, Inc., Irvine, Calif., 1983-85; adminstrv. dir. Orange County Pacific Symphony, Santa Ana, Calif., 1985-86, Image Printing, Irvine, 1986-88; adminstr. Conant Constrn. Corp., Corona Del Mar, Calif., 1988-90; owner, cons. KMS & Assocs., Mission Viejo, Calif., 1990—; nat. coord. PED Inc., Reno, Nev., 1985-86; cons. Forms Mgmt. Co., Reno, 1987-89. Author: (collection of poetry) In the Twighlight of Life, 1978; author acctg. system; contbr. articles to profl. jours. Mem. City Renovation Com., Santa Ana, 1985, Environ. Def. Fund, Washington, 1989—; team capt. San Clemente (Calif.) Triathalon, 1988; vol. Orange County Rep. Party Orgn., Santa Ana, 1989-90, United Way of Orange County, South County Region (coun. officer, sec. 1990—, logistics coord. Community Expo 1993). Named Outstanding Vol., Lake Forest Showboaters, 1988, South Orange County region United Way, 1993. Mem. NAFE, The Enterprising Woman, Lake Forest Showboaters (bd. govs. 1987-88), Nat. Conservatory, World Wildlife Found., Amnesty Internat., Saddleback C. of C., Greenpeace, Cousteau Soc. Presbyterian. Home and Office: KMS & Assocs 26196B Sanz Mission Viejo CA 92691-6822

SAPERSTEIN, SIDNEY, former nutritionist, biochemist; b. Bklyn., Apr. 2, 1923; s. Louis and Mary (Felsher) S.; m. Irene Pearl, June 21, 1947; children: Susan Beth, Karen Anne, Mark David. BA, Bklyn., 1947; MA, UCLA, 1948; PhD, U. Calif., Davis, 1953. Chemist Borden Spl. Products Co., N.Y.C., 1954-55; supr. microbiology div. Borden Spl. Products Co., Elgin, Ill., 1955-67; dir. for rsch. pharm. div. Borden Co., N.Y.C., 1967-71; dir. nutrition div. Syntex Labs., Inc., Palo Alto, Calif., 1971-72, asst. dir. nutrition lab., 1972-73, prin. scientist rsch. div., 1978-79, mgr. sci. affairs, 1979-81, assoc. dir. sci. affairs, 1981-93; prin. scienist Inst. Agrisci. and Nutrition, Palo Alto, 1972-78; mem. tech. adv. group to nutrition com. Am. Acad. Pediatrics, Evanston, Ill., 1967-72, 77-81; grants reviewer NSF, Washington, 1976. Contbr. numerous articles to profl. jours.; patentee in field. Active radio communications com. ARC Disaster Svcs., Palo Alto, 1984—, mem. damage assessment com. Staff sgt. U.S. Army, 1943-46, PTO. Recipient Outstanding Svc. Citation, Am. Acad. Pediatrics, 1981. Mem. AAAS, Am. Chem. Soc., Am. Dietetic Assn., Am. Inst. Nutrition, Am. Soc. Clin. Nutrition.

SAPOCH, JOHN CRIM, JR., management consultant; b. Allentown, Pa., Feb. 1, 1937; s. John Crim and Dorothy Salome (Rems) S.; m. Betty Katherine Wingert, Aug. 9, 1958 (div.); children: John Crim III, William Martin; m. Ava Helena Anttila, Jan. 9, 1991. AB, Princeton U., 1958; MBA, U. Pa., 1964. Tchr., coach, dean students Kent (Conn.) Sch., 1958-61; asst. to dean admissions U. Pa., Phila., 1961-62; sec. for alumni assns. Princeton (N.J.) U., 1962-65, dir. Princeton U. Conf., 1965-66; adminstrv. dir., treas., gen. mgr., exec. v.p. J.P. Cleaver Co., Inc., Princeton, 1966-78; also pres. subs., bd. dirs. J.P. Cleaver Co. Inc., Princeton, 1966-78; chmn., pres., treas., bd. dirs. SINC, Princeton, 1978—, Princeton Pacific Inc., Manhattan Beach, Calif., 1980—. Author tng. manuals. Vice pres., pres. class of 1958, Princeton U., 1958-68; bd. dirs., treas. Princeton Youth Ctr., 1966-70; founder, trustee Princeton Youth Fund, 1967-68; founder, bd. dirs. Princeton Midget Football League, 1968-73; chmn. Friends Princeton U. Football, 1974-78; founder, chmn. Friends Princeton High Sch. Athletics, 1978-80. Named hon. mem. Princeton High Sch. Class of 1980. Mem. Princeton U. Alumni Assn., Wharton Grad. Sch. Alumni Assn., Wharton Club of So. Calif., Princeton Alumni Club (founder, treas. 1965), U. Pa. Alumni Assn. So. Calif., Princeton Area Alumni Assn., Princeton Club (N.Y.C., So. Calif.), Ivy Club (Princeton), 200 Club (Trenton, N.J.), Torrequebrada Country Club. Home: 4003 The Strand Manhattan Beach CA 90266-0274 Office: Princeton Pacific Inc PO Box 279 Manhattan Beach CA 90266-0279

SAPONTZIS, STEVE F., philosophy educator, writer; b. N.Y.C., Feb. 9, 1945; s. Zissis Peter and Lea Marie (Vial) S.; m. Jeanne Marie Gocker, Dec. 25, 1992. BA, Rice U., 1967; postgrad., U. Paris, 1967-68; MPhil, Yale U., 1970, PhD, 1971. From asst. to full prof. philosophy Calif. State U., Hayward, 1971—; lectr. Stanford U., Palo Alto, Calif., 1986. Author: Morals Reason and Animals, 1987; co-editor: Between The Species Jour., 1984—; mem. bd. edit. advisors Am. Philosophical Quarterly, 1991—. Mem. animal welfare rsch. com. Lawrence Berkeley (Calif.) Lab., 1986-90; pres. Hayward Friends of Animals Humane Soc., 1985—; bd. dirs. Paw Pac Animal Welfare, Sacramento, 1984—. Fulbright fellow U.S. Govt., 1967-68, Woodrow Wilson Found. fellow Yale U., 1968-69; NEH grantee, 1976, Am. Coun. Learned Socs. grantee, 1988. Mem. Am. Philos. Assn., Internat. Soc. for Environ. Ethnics, Soc. for Study Ethics and Animals (bd. dirs. 1984—). Democrat. Office: Calif State U Dept of Philosophy Hayward CA 94542

SAPP, DONALD GENE, minister; b. Phoenix, Feb. 27, 1927; s. Guerry Byron and Lydia Elmeda (Snyder) S.; m. Anna Maydean Nevitt, July 10, 1952 (dec.); m. Joann Herrin Mountz, May 1, 1976; children: Gregory, Paula, Jeffrey, Mark, Melody, Cristine. AB in Edn., Ariz. State U., 1949; MDiv, Boston U., 1952, STM, 1960; D Ministry, Calif. Grad. Sch. Theology, 1975. Ordained to ministry Meth. Ch., 1950. Dir. youth activities Hyde Park (Mass.) Meth. Ch., 1950-52; minister 1st Meth. Ch., Peabody, Mass., 1952-54, Balboa Island (Calif.) Community Meth. Ch., 1954-57, Ch. of the Foothills Meth., Duarte, Calif., 1957-63; sr. minister Aldersgate United Meth. Ch., Tustin, Calif., 1963-70, Paradise Valley (Ariz.) United Meth. Ch., 1970-83; dist. supt. Cen. West Dist. of Desert S.W. Conf. United Meth. Ch., Phoenix, 1983-89. Editor Wide Horizons, 1983-89; contbr. articles to profl. jours. Chaplain City of Hope Med. Ctr., Duarte, 1957-63; trustee Plaza Community Ctr., L.A., 1967-70; corp. mem. Sch. Theology at Claremont, Calif., 1972-80; pres. Met. Phoenix Commn., 1983-85; del. Western Jurisdictional Conf. United Meth. Ch., 1984, 88; bd. dirs. Coun. Chs., L.A., 1963-67, Orange County (Calif.) Human Rels. Coun., 1967-70, Interfaith Counseling Svc. Found., 1982-89, Wesley Community Ctr., Phoenix, 1983-89; mem. gen. conf. United Meth. Ch., 1988. With USN, 1945-46. Mem. Ariz. Ecumenical Coun., Bishops and Exec. Roundtable, Rotary (pres.), Kappa Delta Pi, Tau Kappa Epsilon. Democrat. Home: 5225 E Road Runner Rd Paradise Valley AZ 85253-3306

SAPP, ROY G., clergy man; b. Wills Point, Tex., Sept. 13, 1928; s. Willis R. Sapp and Harriot (Telia) Girdley; m. Irene Odelle Cunningham, Sept. 1, 1948; 1 child, Sharon Diane Seaward. DD, Calif. Grad. Sch. Theology, 1975, BTh, 1982; DHL, So. Calif. Theol. Sem., 1992. Ordained to ministry Assembly of God, 1951. Pastor Ctrl. Assembly of God, Lubbock, Tex., 1948-49; kpastor First Assembly of God, Santa Ana, Calif., 1953-58; presbyter So. Calif. Dist. of Assemblies of God, Pasadena, Calif., 1955-58, youth dir., 1959-62; dir. youth missions Gen. Coun. Assemblies of God., Springfield, Mo., 1962-65; pastor First Assembly of God, Wilmington, Calif., 1965-76; gen. presbyter Gen. Coun. of the Assemblies of God, Springfield, 1969-76; presbyter So. Calif. Dist. Assemblies of God, Pasadena, 1968-76; pastor First Assembly of God, Honolulu, 1976—. Bd. dirs. So. Calif. Coll., Costa Mesa, 1955-58, Bethany Coll., Santa Cruz, Calif., 1980-83, King Manor Hosp., 1970-76, Bethany Retirement Home, Costa Mesa, 1970-76. Office: First Assembly of God 3400 Moanalua Rd Honolulu HI 96819

SAPSOWITZ, SIDNEY H., entertainment and media company executive; b. N.Y.C., June 29, 1936; s. Max and Annette (Rothstein) Sapsowitz; m. Phyllis Skopp, Nov. 27, 1957; children: Donna Dawn Chazen, Gloria Lynn Aaron, Marsha Helene Gleit. BBA summa cum laude, Paterson (N.J.) State Coll., 1980. Various fin. and oper. systems positions Metro Goldwyn Mayer, N.Y.C., 1957-68; exec. v.p. Penta Computer Assoc. Inc., N.Y.C., 1968-70, Cons. Actuaries Inc., Clifton, N.J., 1970-73, Am. Film Theatre, N.Y.C., 1974-76; exec. v.p., CFO Cinema Shares Internat. Distributors, N.Y.C., 1976-79; sr. cons. Solomon, Finger & Newman, N.Y.C., 1979-80; exec. v.p., chief fin. officer Metro Goldwyn Mayer, L.A., 1980-85; various positions leading to exec. v.p. fin. and adminstrn., CFO MGM/UA Entertainment Co., Culver City, Calif., 1985-86; also bd. dirs. MGM/UA Entertainment Co., L.A.; fin. v.p.; chief bus. and ops. officer, Office of Pres., dir. United Artists Corp., Beverly Hills, Calif., 1986-87; chmn. bd., CEO MGA/UA Telecommunications Corp., Beverly Hills, 1986-89; sr. exec. v.p., dir., mem. exec. com. MGA/UA Communications Co., 1986-89; chmn., CEO Sid Sapsowitz & Assocs., Inc., 1989—. Pres., Wayne Conservative Congregation, N.J., 1970-77. Mem. Am. Mgmt. Assn. (cons., lectr. 1967), Am. Film Inst., Acad. Motion Picture Arts and Scis., Fin. Exec. Inst., TV Acad. Arts and Scis., KP (chancellor comdr. 1970).

SARAF, DILIP GOVIND, electronics executive; b. Belgaum, India, Nov. 10, 1942; s. Govind Vithal and Indira Laxman (Divekar) S.; m. Mary Lou Arnold, July 25, 1970; 1 son, Rajesh Dilip. B. Tech with honors, Indian Inst. Tech., Bombay, 1965; M.S.E.E., Stanford U., 1969. Sr. mgmt. trainee Delhi Cloth and Gen. Mills Co. (India), 1965-68; sr. research engr. SRI Internat., Menlo Park, Calif., 1969-78; project dir. Kaiser Electronics, San Jose, Calif., 1978-87; sr. engring. mgr. Varian Assocs., Santa Clara, Calif., 1987-90, pres. TOTAL QUALITY, 1990— ; cons. teaching U. Santa Clara, 1972, 73. Bd. dirs. Peninsula Childrens' Ctr., Palo Alto, Calif. Mem. IEEE, Soc. Am. Inventors, Am. Soc. Quality Ctrl., Speakers' Bur. Contbr. articles to profl jours. Patentee in field. Club: Toastmasters. Home: 28050 Horseshoe Ln Los Altos CA 94022-1924 Office: 101 1st St # 203 Los Altos CA 94022-2706

SARAS, JAMES J., agricultural products, grain company executive; b. 1933. BA, Stanford U., 1955. Peach grower Modesto, Calif., 1955—; chmn. Tri-Valley Growers, 1979—, CEO, 1987—. Office: Tri-Valley Growers Inc 1255 Battery St San Francisco CA 94111-1101

SARATHY, PARTHA RAGAVACHARI RANGACHARI, financial executive; b. Amoor, India, May 15, 1952; came to U.S., 1983; s. Rangiachari Iyengar and Sakunthaca Rengachari; m. Priya Partha Sarathy, Feb. 5, 1987; 1 child, Amrit P. BS, Annamalai U., India. CPA, Calif. Chief acct. Pal Cons., Santa Clara, Calif., 1984-85; sr. acct. McDonnell Douglas, Cupertino, Calif., 1985-86; mgr. gen. acctg. Silvar-Lisco, Menlo Park, Calif., 1986-89; v.p. fin., chief fin. officer Solitec, Inc., Santa Clara, 1989—; sr. internal auditor Kothani Indsl. Corp., Madras, India, 1978-84. Instr. yoga West Valley Coll., Saratoga, Calif., 1985. Mem. Inst. Chartered Accts. India. Hindu. Home: 460 Cumulus Ave Sunnyvale CA 94087 Office: Solitec Inc 3901 Burton Dr Santa Clara CA 95054

SARAVO, ANNE COBBLE, clinical psychologist, mental health administrator; b. Atlanta, Feb. 23, 1938; d. William Edwin and Iris Benny (Norman) Cobble; m. James Vincent Saravo, June 13, 1958; children: Stacy Anne, Lisa Ames Furmanek. BA, Tex. Tech. U., 1959; MS, U. Mass., 1964, PhD, 1965; postgrad., Regional Health Authority, London, 1978-79, U. So. Calif., 1980-81. Lic. psychologist, Calif. Assoc. prof. psychology Antioch Coll., Yellow Springs, Ohio, 1966-69; cons. Winchester (Eng.) Day Treatment Nursery

Sch., 1971-73; sch. psychologist Muroc Unified Sch. Dist., Edwards AFB, Calif., 1974-75; clinical psychologist Antelope Valley Hosp., Lancaster, Calif., 1975-76, Farnborough Hosp., Kent, Eng., 1978-80, Orange County (Calif.) Mental Health Svc., 1981-84; pvt. practice clin. psychology Seal Beach, Calif., 1981—; chief adult out-patient svc. Orange County (Calif.) Mental Health Svc., 1984-87, chief adult inpatient svcs., 1987—; bd. dirs. High Hopes Neurological Recovery Group, Costa Mesa, Calif.; geriatric coord. ORange County Mental Health Svcs., 1985-87; chmn. profl. adv. bd. Orange County Caregiver Resource Ctr., 1989—. Contbr. articles to profl. jours. Chairperson Conf. Geriatric Mental Health, Asilomar, Calif., 1986, So. Calif. Geriatric Mental Health Coordinators, 1985-87. U.S. Pub. Health fellow Fels Research Inst., 1966-67. Mem. Am. Psychol. Assn., Calif. Psychol. Assn. (subcoms. 1990—), Nat. Acad. Neuropsychol. (grad.), Brit. Psychol. Soc. Office: Orange County Mental Health Svc 515 N Sycamore St Santa Ana CA 92701-4637 also: # 203 550 Pacific Coast Hwy Seal Beach CA 90740

SARGENT, DIANA RHEA, corporate executive; b. Cheyenne, Wyo., Feb. 20, 1939; d. Clarence and Edith (de Castro) Hayes; grad. high sch.; m. Charles Sargent, Apr. 17, 1975 (div. 1991); children: Rene A. Coburn, Rochelle A. Rollins, Clayton R. Weldy, Christopher J. IBM proof operator Bank Am., Stockton, Calif., 1956-58, gen. ledger bookkeeper, Modesto, Calif., 1963-66; office mgr., head bookkeeper Cen. Drug Store, Modesto, 1966-76; pres. Sargent & Coburn, Inc., Modesto, 1976—; ptnr. R.C.D. Farms (almond ranch), Just a Little Something (antique dolls and miniatures). Mem. Stanislaus Women's Ctr. Mem. NOW, San Francisco Mus. Soc., Modesto Women's Network. Office: 915 14th St Modesto CA 95354-1010

SARGENT, HARRY TOMPKINS, professional golfer; b. San Diego, Mar. 30, 1947; s. Marston Cleves and Grace Charlotte (Tompkins) S.; m. Debra Kay Sponnoble, Sept. 19, 1981; children: Katie Lynn, Lucas Jon, Samantha Ann. BA in French and History, San Diego State U., 1970. Asst. golf profl. Carlton Oaks Country Club, Santee, Calif., 1973-76; mini-tour player various golf tours, 1974-76; head golf profl. Yorba Linda (Calif.) Country Club, 1978—. Mem. PGA (v.p. 1991, v.p. So. Calif. sect. 1988-90, pres. 1993, jr. golf leader award 1983, 84, leader award 1989, 91, tchr. of yr. award So. Calif. sect. 1986, nat. jr. golf leader award 1989, Horton Smith award 1990 Golf Profl. of Yr. 1991), PGA Jr. Golf Assn. (pres. 1991, 92, 93, Bill Bryant award 1985). Home: 3805 Singingwood Dr Yorba Linda CA 92686-6909 Office: 19400 Mountain View Ave Yorba Linda CA 92686-5599

SARGENT, MURRAY, III, physicist, educator; b. N.Y.C., Aug. 18, 1941; s. Murray Jr. and Lucy (Garfield) S.; m. Helga Reineke, May 21, 1967; children: Nicole, Christine. BS in Physics, Yale U., 1963, MS, 1964, PhD, 1967. Postdoctoral researcher Yale U., New Haven, Conn., 1967; mem. tech. staff Bell Telephone Labs., Holmdel, N.J., 1967-69; prof. optical sci. U. Ariz., Tucson, 1969—; sr. software design engr. Microsoft, Redmond, Wash., 1992—; vis. prof. U. Stuttgart, 1975-76, Max Planck für Festkorperforschung, 1975-76, Max Planck für QuantenOptik, 1982-92, U. Toronto, 1991; pres. Scroll Systems, Inc., Tucson, 1981—. Author: Laser Physics, 1977, Interfacing Microcomputers, 1981, IBM PC from Inside Out, 1984, Elements of Quantum Optics, 1991. Recipient U.S. Sr. Scientist award Humboldt Stiftung, 1975. Fellow Optical Soc. Am.; mem. Am. Phys. Soc., Sigma Xi. Republican. Office: Microsoft One Microsoft Way Bldg 9 Redmond WA 98052

SARGENT, THOMAS REECE, III, coast guard officer; b. Woolwich, Eng., Dec. 20, 1914; s. Thomas Reece and Rose (Chapman) S. II; m. Lucy Agusta Berg; children: Thomas R. IV, Karl David, Diane E. Ryan. BS, USCG Acad., 1938; BCE, Rensselaer Poly., 1952. Line officer USCG Cutter Tahoe, 1938-39, USCG Cutter Modoc, 1939-42; commanding officer U.S.S. PC 469, 1942-43; officer USCG Duane, 1943-44; commanding officer U.S.S. Sandusky, 1944-45; instr., pub. works officer USCG Acad., New London, Conn., 1945-50; exec. officer USCG Cutter Bibb, 1950-51; dist. civil engr. 13th Coast Guard Dist., Seattle, 1952-54; commdg. officer USCG Winnebago, 1954-56; officer, chief civil engr., ops. officer, dist. comdr. various Coast Guard Hdqs. & Dists., 1954-74; retired vice commandant U.S. Coast Guard, 1974; cons. Ecological Systems, Inc., Lake San Marcos, Calif., 1989—; pres. Lake San Marcos Security Assn., Lake San Marcos Community Assn. Recipient Bronze Star medal USN, 1945, All Area Campaign medals USN, 1942-45, Am. Def. Svc. medal USN, 1945, Legion of Merit award, 1965, Viet Nam Svc. medal USCG, 1965, Coast Guard Commendation medal USCG, 1968, Exceptional Pub. Svc. award Dept. Transp., 1973, Disting. Svc. medal, 1974. Mem. Royal Nat. Lifeboat Inst. of Great Britain (hon. life gov.). Republican. Home: 1311 San Julian Dr Lake San Marcos CA 92069

SARGENT, WALLACE LESLIE WILLIAM, astronomer, educator; b. Elsham, Eng., Feb. 15, 1935; s. Leslie William and Eleanor (Dennis) S.; m. Anneila Isabel Cassells, Aug. 5, 1964; children: Lindsay Eleanor, Alison Clare. B.Sc., Manchester U., 1956, M.Sc., 1957, Ph.D., 1959. Research fellow Calif. Inst. Tech., 1959-62; sr. research fellow Royal Greenwich Obs., 1962-64; asst. prof. physics U. Calif., San Diego, 1964-66; mem. faculty dept. astronomy Calif. Inst. Tech., Pasadena, 1966—; prof. Calif. Inst. Tech., 1971-81, Ira S. Bowen prof. astronomy, 1981—. Contbr. articles to profl. jours. Alfred P. Sloan fellow, 1968-70. Fellow Am. Acad. Arts and Scis., Royal Soc. (London); mem. Am. Astron. Soc. (Helen B. Warner prize 1969, Dannie Heineman prize 1991), Royal Astron. Soc. (George Darwin lectr., 1987), Internat. Astron. Union. Club: Athenaeum (Pasadena). Home: 400 S Berkeley Ave Pasadena CA 91107-5062 Office: Calif Inst Tech Astronomy Dept 105-24 Pasadena CA 91125

SARIKAS, PHILIP CHARLES, electrical engineer; b. Decatur, Ill., Sept. 8, 1960; s. Robert Henry and Rita Marie (Heumann) S.; m. Diane Patricia Maher, Aug. 6, 1983; children: Ryan Phillip, Rebecca Christina Marie. BSEE, U. Ariz., 1983; MBA, Ariz. State U., 1991. Registered profl. engr., Ariz. Asst. engr. Mohave Electric Coop., Bullhead City, Ariz., 1982-83; Sr. engr. Salt River Project, Phoenix, 1984—. Mem. IEEE. Roman Catholic. Home: 11428 S Mandan St Phoenix AZ 85044-1813 Office: Salt River Project Phoenix AZ 85072

SARKANY, ANNA REGINA, software house executive; b. Oroszlany, Hungary, Dec. 13, 1946; came to U.S., 1976; d. Mihaly and Katalin (Simai) G.; m. Zoltan Sarkany, Dec. 19, 1966; children: Andrea, Victoria. With R.J. McDonald, Chgo., 1980-81; acct. VSS, Inc., Tempe, 1982-83; pres. Computerline, Inc., Tempe, 1983-88; v.p. CHMS, Inc., Tempe, 1988-90; pres. Sterling Computers, Ltd., Mesa, 1990—. Republican. Baptist. Office: Sterling Computers Ltd 540 W Iron Ave #108 Mesa AZ 85210

SARKANY, ZOLTAN, software house executive; b. Kelebia, Hungary, Dec. 17, 1948; came to U.S., 1969; s. Zoltan and Matilda (Gulyas) Borsos; m. Anna R. Gergely, Dec. 19, 1966; children: Andrea, Victoria. Mgr. Howard Johnson, L.A., 1970-79; dist. mgr. Berendsohn, Chgo., 1979-81; contr. VSS, Inc., Tempe, 1982-83; v.p.. Computerline, Inc., Tempe, 1983-88; pres. CHMS, Inc., Tempe, 1989-90; v.p. Sterling Computers, Ltd., Mesa, Ariz., 1990—; pres. Exotic Cars of USA, Mesa, 1991—. Republican. Baptist. Office: Sterling Computers Ltd 540 W Iron Ave #108 Mesa AZ 85210

SARKAR, DIPAK KUMAR, physiologist, educator; b. Calcutta, India, Aug. 25, 1950; came to U.S., 1980; s. Joydeb Chandra and Aruna (Mondal) S.; m. Shirley Ann Sanderson, May 4, 1984; children: Abby Joya, Sophie Dipti. BSc, Calcutta U., 1970, MSc, 1973, PhD, 1975; DPhil, Oxford (Eng.) U., 1979. Vis. postdoctoral assoc. Sch. of Medicine Yale U., New Haven, 1979; rsch. assoc. Mich. State U., East Lansing, 1980-83; asst. prof. U. Calif., San Diego, 1983-88; assoc. prof. Wash. State U., Pullman, 1988—, adj. assoc. prof. pharmacology and toxicology, 1989—, adj. assoc. prof. genetics and cell biology, 1989—; ad hoc grant reviewer NSF, Washington, 1987, 91; mem. rsch. rev. com. NIAAA/Pub. Health Svcs., Bethesda, Md., 1991—; invited speaker at nat. and internat. confs., various insts. Editorial bd. Endocrinology, 1989—, Neuroendocrinology, 1987-90; contbr. chpt. to Neuroendocrinology of Aging, 1983; contbr. articles, abstracts to profl. publs. Grantee Andrew Mellon Found., 1983-86, San Diego Reproductive Medicine Rsch. and Edn. Found., 1985-87, March of Dimes, 1985-87, NIH/NIA, 1985-89, NIH/NICHD, 1986-89, Wash. State U., 1988-91, NIH/NIAAA, 1991—. Mem. AAAS, N.Y. Acad. Scis., Soc. for Neurosci., Internat. Soc. Neuroendocrinology, Internat. Brain Rsch. Orgn., Soc. Endocrinology (U.K.), Endocrine Soc. Office: Wash State Univ 215 Wegner Pullman WA 99164-6520

SARKISIAN, JACK REUBEN, principal; b. Boston, Apr. 3, 1928; s. Reuben Hagop and Rose Vartanoush (Ohannessian) S.; m. Mildred Ann Ching, Mar. 25, 1966. AA, L.A. City Coll., 1955; BA, L.A. State Coll., 1957; MA, Calif. State Coll., L.A., 1968. Cert. ednl. adminstrn. elem. and sec., tchr. elem. and sec. Elem. tchr. L.A. Unified Sch. Dist., 1957-88, tng. tchr., 1961-68, asst. prin., 1971-76, prin., 1976-88; inst. U. So. Calif., L.A., 1983-88; dir. L.A. Tchrs. Credit Union, 1965—, vice chmn. bd., 1970-73, chmn., 1973-76, chief fin. officer, sec., 1987-91; dir. Nat. Assn. State Chartered Credit Unions, 1992—. Chmn. Associated Adminstrs. L.A. Region B, 1976-78, vice. chmn. Associated Adminstrs. L.A. Region C, 1972-73; mem. PTA. Mem. Calif. Retired Tchrs. Assn., Loyal Order Moose, Nat. Assn. of State Chartered Credit Unions (bd. dirs.), Phi Delta Kappa. Office: Los Angeles Tchrs Credit Union 420 Rosenell Ter Los Angeles CA 90026-4996

SARLES, LYNN REDMON, physicist; b. Grand Forks, N.D., Jan. 22, 1930; s. Lynn Redmon Sr. and Clara Sophie (Elken) S.; m. Lucretia Ione Zopf, Sept. 9, 1951; children: Laura Lyn, Jennifer Lenore, Jeffrey Peter Lynn, Christopher Lynn. AB, U. Calif., Berkeley, 1951; PhD, Stanford U., 1957. Mgr. geophysics rsch. Varian Assocs., Palo Alto, Calif., 1958-62, 63-67; head optical physics dept. Maser Optics-West, Palo Alto, 1962-63; v.p. adminstrn. Oreg. Grad. Ctr., Beaverton, 1967-73; cons. Portland, Oreg., 1973—; cofounder SciMaTech Corp., Palo Alto, 1971—. Contbr. articles to profl. jours.; inventor, patentee optical magnetometer and gradiometer. Chmn. Washington County Oreg. Comprehensive Health Planning Coun., 1971. Postdoctoral fellow in Physics, Alfred P. Sloan Found., 1957-58. Fellow AAAS. Home: PO Box 253 Keyport WA 98345

SARLEY, JOHN G., broadcast executive, writer; b. Cleve., Mar. 1, 1954; s. Edward James and Ann (Ropret) S. BA, Cleve. State U., 1977. Writer, producer Marschalk Co. Advt., Cleve., 1977-80, DOCSI Corp., Hollywood, Calif., 1980—; pres. Sarley, Bigg & Bedder Inc., Hollywood, 1981—. Mem. Broadcast Promotion and Mktg. Execs., Hollywood C. of C. Office: Sarley Bigg & Bedder Inc 1644 N Stanley Ave West Hollywood CA 90046-2713

SARSON, JOHN CHRISTOPHER, television producer, director, writer; b. London, Jan. 19, 1935; s. Arnold Wilfred and Annie Elizabeth (Wright) S.; m. Evelyn Patricia Kaye, Mar. 25, 1963; children: Katrina May, David Arnold. BA with honors, Trinity Coll., Cambridge, Eng., 1960, MA, 1963. Dir. Granada TV, Manchester, Eng., 1960-63; producer, dir. Sta. WGBH-TV, Boston, 1963-73; pres. Blue Penguin, Inc., Boulder, Colo., 1974—; v.p. TV programming Sta. WYNC-TV, N.Y.C., 1989-90; dir. Pub. Broadcasting Assocs., Newton, Mass.; cons. to numerous pub. TV stations. Creator, producer Masterpiece Theatre, PBS, 1970-73, Zoom, PBS, 1971-73; producer Live From the Met, PBS, 1977-79, Kid's Writes, Nickelodeon, 1982-83, American Treasure, a Smithsonian Journey, 1986, Spotlight Colorado, 1991. Served with Royal Navy, 1956-57. Recipient Emmy award, 1973, 74; Peabody award Ohio State U., 1978; Internat. Emmy award, 1983. Mem. Dirs. Guild Am., Nat. Acad. TV Arts and Scis. Home and Office: 3031 5th St Boulder CO 80304-2501

SASAKI, Y. TITO, business services company executive; b. Tokyo, Feb. 6, 1938; came to U.S., 1967, naturalized, 1983; s. Yoshinaga and Chiyoko (Imada) S.; m. Janet Louise Cline, June 27, 1963; 1 child, Heather N. BS, Chiba U., 1959; postgrad. Royal Coll. Art, London, 1961, U. Oslo, 1962; MS, Athens Tech. Inst., Greece, 1964; postgrad. U. Calif., Berkeley, 1969. Chief designer Aires Camera Industries Co., Tokyo, 1958-59; tech. officer London County Council, 1961-62; researcher Athens Ctr. Ekistics, 1964-66; sr. researcher Battelle Inst., Geneva, 1966-68; project engr. Marin County Transit Dist., San Rafael, Calif., 1968-69; chief planning, research Golden Gate Bridge Dist., San Francisco, 1969-74; pres. Visio Internat. Inc., Somona, Calif., 1973—; chmn. steering com. Kawada Industries Inc., Tokyo, 1974-82; chief exec. officer Quantum Mechanics Corp., Somona, 1981—; bd. dirs., v.p. Sonoma Skypark, Inc., 1986-89. Mem. ASME, Am. Soc. Testing and Materials, Am. Welding Soc., Helicopter Assn. Internat., AIAA, Am. Inst. Cert. Planners, World Soc. Ekistics, Am. Vacuum Soc., Aircraft Owners and Pilots Assn. Roman Catholic. Office: Visio Internat Inc PO Box 1888 Sonoma CA 95476-1888

SASS, JAMES ROBERTUS, international commodities trader; b. Bartlesville, Okla., Mar. 6, 1945; s. Andrew Michael and Norma Bea (Hegwer) S.; m. Diane Marie Quandt, July 12, 1979 (div. 1991); children: Charlene, John, Carridad. AA in Behavioral Sci., Coll. of Marin, 1974; BA, San Francisco State U., 1976. Devel. fin. mgr. Calif. Equity Investment Group, San Rafael, Calif., 1974-76; v.p. fin. Group 80, Inc., San Francisco, 1976-80; pres. Mass. Plan, Inc., Pittsfield, Mass., 1980-82, Republic Mortgage & Investment Corp., Cocoa Beach, Fla., 1982-86, InterAmerican Fin. & Trade Group, Miami, Fla., 1986-88, Ocean Star Internat. Corp., San Rafael, 1988-90; ptnr. Orchid Internat., San Rafael, 1990—; mng. ptnr. J.R. Sass and Assocs., San Rafael, 1988—; pres. InterAmerican Food Products, San Rafael, 1990-93; ptnr. Four C's Internat. Corp., San Rafael, 1991-93; gen. ptnr. Equity Ptnrs. IV, San Rafael, 1991—, Cencal Devel. Fund, San Rafael, 1991-92, Cencal Devel. Fund II, San Rafael, 1993; bd. dirs. Firebird Internat., Inc., Petaluma, Calif., Zelinsky Ctr. and Mus., Moscow, Cybertech Joint Venture, Minsk, Republic of Belarus, Land and Timber Holdings, Ltd., Belize City, Belize, Internat. Peninsular S.A. de C.V., Mex.; cons. Mitsui Trading Co., Georgetown, Grand Cayman, 1986—; chmn. U.S. Trade Adv. Bd., Washington, 1993—. Author: (pamphlet) Investing in Mexican Real Estate, 1988. Past chpt. pres. U.S. Jaycees, Vacaville, Calif., 1978; state v.p. Young Rep., Bishop, Tex., 1963-64; mem. Am. Vets. Alliance, San Rafael, 1990. Sgt. U.S. Army, 1966-72, Vietnam. Decorated two Bronze Stars, Purple Heart, others; recipient grant and scholarship NSF, Okla. State U., 1962, Tex. Chem. Coun. award, 1963. Mem. U.S. Coun. for Internat. Bus., Am. Assn. Exporters and Importers, U.S. C. of C., Am. Legion, Union Entrepreneurs Republic of Belarus, Mensa, World Trade Ctr. Club, Commonwealth Club Calif. (San Francisco). Office: 325 Fairhills Dr San Rafael CA 94901-1110

SASSOON, VIDAL, hair stylist; b. London, Eng., Jan. 17, 1928; s. Nathan and Betty (Bellin) S.; divorced 1980; children—Catya, Elan, Eden, David. Student, NYU. Founder, former chmn. bd. Vidal Sassoon, Inc. (beauty treatment products, appliances), Europe and Am.; pres. Vidal Sassoon Found.; lectr. in field. Author: autobiography A Year of Beauty and Health, 1976. Served with Palmach Israeli Army. Recipient award French Ministry of Culture, award for services rendered Harvard Bus. Sch.; Intercoiffure award Cartier, London, 1978; Hair Artists Internat. fellow. Clubs: Anabelle (London, Eng.), Ambassadeurs (London, Eng.), Claremont (London, Eng.); Le Club (N.Y.C.). Office: Vidal Sassoon Inc 2029 Century Park E Los Angeles CA 90067-2901

SATEREN, TERRY, theater technical production; b. Madison, Wis., Dec. 5, 1943; s. Leland Bernhard and Eldora (Johnson) S. BA, Augsburg Coll., 1968. Tech. prodn. dir. Guthrie Theatre, Mpls., 1974-78, dir. prodn., 1985-87; dir. exhibits Sci. Mus. Minn., St. Paul, 1978-85; tech. prodn. dir. Seattle Repertory Theatre, 1987—; cons. acad. and community theaters and museums, 1974—, U. Minn., 1992; Master class lectr. U. Wash., Seattle, 1989-91; adj. prof. U. Wash., 1991-92. Designer: (operas) Three Penny Opera, 1972, Newest Opera in the World, 1972, Don Giovanni, 1973; commd. sculptor numerous inds., chs. and acad. instns., 1966—. Pres.'s scholar Valparaiso (Ind.) U., 1967. Mem. U.S. Inst. Theatre Tech. Home: 7341 23d Ave NW Seattle WA 98117-5661 Office: Seattle Repertory Theatre 155 Mercer St Seattle WA 98109-4639

SATHER, GLEN CAMERON, professional hockey team coach and executive; b. High River, Alta., Canada, Sept. 2, 1943. Former professional hockey player; pres., gen. mgr. Edmonton Oilers, Nat. Hockey League, Alta., Can., coach, 1977-89, now alt. gov.; coach winning team in Stanley Cup competition, 1987. Recipient Jack Adams Award for NHL Coach of the Yr., 1986. Office: care Edmonton Oilers, Northlands Coliseum, Edmonton, AB Canada T5B 4M9*

SATO, IRVING SHIGEO, educational administrator; b. Honolulu, Sept. 4, 1933; s. Jusaku and Matsuyo (Uchida) S.; m. Helen Hatsuko, Aug. 18, 1956. B.Ed. with honors, U. Hawaii, 1955; M.S., U. So. Calif., 1962. Tchr. high sch., Honolulu, 1957-58; tchr., chmn. English and history Pasadena High Sch., Calif., 1958-66; cons. gifted and creative student programs Colo. Dept. Edn., Denver, 1966-68; cons. edn. mentally gifted Calif. Dept. Edn., Los Angeles, 1968-72; dir. Nat. State Leadership Tng. Inst. on Gifted and Talented, Los Angeles, 1972-93; instr. U. Denver, 1966-67, U. Colo., 1967-68, U. So. Calif., 1970-75, Widener U., Pa., 1981-91; cons. on gifted programs to numerous sch. dists., states, fgn. countries, 1966—; conf. speaker. Editor: (with James A. Gallagher and Sandra N. Kaplan) Promoting the Education of the Gifted/Talented: Strategies for Advocacy, 1983; co-editor (newsletter) The Gifted Pupil, 1968-72. Contbr. articles to profl. jours. Served to 1st lt. U.S. Army, 1955-57. Recipient cert. of recognition Office Gifted and Talented, U.S. Office Edn., 1974. Mem. Coun. State Dirs. Programs for Gifted (pres. 1969-71), Assn. for Gifted (exec. bd. 1972-79, pres. 1977-78), Nat. Assn. for Gifted Children (bd. govs. 1977-88, cert. of merit 1973, disting service award 1982), Calif. Assn. Gifted (Educator of Yr. award 1976), Assn. Supervision and Curriculum Devel., Phi Delta Kappa, Phi Kappa Phi. Home: 1744 Via Del Rey South Pasadena CA 91030-4128

SATO, MAMORU, art educator; b. El Paso, Tex., Apr. 15, 1937; s. Tetsuro and Mitsuye (Tashiro) S.; m. Lois Harumi Tani, Aug. 26, 1962 (div. 1974); 1 child, Tristen Anne; m. Kathleen Sunaye Nagata, Dec. 29, 1976; children: Jessica Kanani, Joshua Shogo. BA, U. Colo., 1963, MFA, 1965. Prof. art U. Hawaii, Honolulu, 1965—. Office: U Hawaii Dept of Art Honolulu HI 96822

SATO, MICHAEL KEI, sales and marketing executive; b. Lansing, Mich., June 30, 1958; s. Herbert Shuichi and Rae T. (Towata) S.; m. Cynthia M.H. Ho, June 11, 1988; children: Nicole Leilani, Noelani Rae. BBA, U. Hawaii, 1981. From store mgr. to dir. mktg. Chs. Fried Chicken, Honolulu, 1978-81; mgr. Castle Pk. Hawaii, Honolulu, 1981-82; from sales rep. to profl. sales Procter & Gamble Distbg. Co., Honolulu, 1983-86; account exec. The Ad Agy., Honolulu, 1986; sales rep. Aikane Mktg., Honolulu, 1987, Royal Hawaiian Perfumes, Honolulu, 1988-90; sales and mktg. mgr. Castle & Cooke Splty. Foods, Honolulu, 1990—. Founder, pres. Kaiser Key Club, Honolulu, 1974-76; judge Hugh O'Brian Youth Found. of Hawaii, 1989; bd. dirs. Pearl Horizon Owners Assn., Alea, Hawaii, 1990-92. Recipient Nat. Write Up award U.S. Jr. C. of C., 1988, Ho'oponopono svc. award Castle & Cooke Properties, 1990. Mem. West Oahu Jaycees (dir. 1986-87, v.p. 1987-88, pres. 1988-89, chmn. 1989-90), Hawaii Haycees (bd. dirs. 1989-91, v.p. 1989-90, program mgr. 1990-91, State Speak Up award 1988. Office: Castle & Cooke Splty Foods 650 Iwilei Rd Honolulu HI 96817-5086

SATO, NORIE, artist; b. Sendai, Japan, July 19, 1949; came to U.S. 1954; d. Hiroshi and Kyoko (Amemiya) Sato; m. Ralph Moore Berry, July 25, 1980; 1 child, Tomohiro Branik. BFA, U. Mich., 1971; MFA, U. Wash., 1974. Media/visual arts dir. And/Or Arts Center Seattle, 1976-81; instr. Cornish Coll. of the Arts, Seattle, 1978-81, 86-88, Western Wash. U., Bellingham, 1989; panelist Nat. Endowment for the Arts, Washington, 1977-83. One person shows include Vancouver (B.C.) Art Gallery, 1984, Seattle Art Mus., 1984, Elizabeth Leach Gallery, Portland, Oreg., 1989, 1991, Reed Coll., Portland, 1989, Linda Farris Gallery, Seattle, 1990, 1993; group shows include Guggenheim Mus., Bklyn. Mus., Modern Art Mus.; represented in permanent collections at Guggenheim Mus., Seattle Art Mus., Bklyn. Mus., City of Seattle; pub. art projects include Dallas Conv. Ctr. Expansion, Westside Light Rail Project, Portand. Commr. Seattle Arts Commn., 1975-79; trustee Western States Arts Fedn., Santa Fe, N.Mex., 1988-92; commr., v.p. Seattle Planning Commn., 1984-90. Recipient Gov.'s award, 1990; Wash. State Arts Commn. artist's fellow, 1990, Nat. Endowment for Arts fellow, 1981, Betty Bowen Meml. awardee, Seattle Art Mus., 1983, others. Mem. Ctr. on Contemporary Art, 9-1-1 Media Arts Ctr., Coll. Art Assn. Office: 619 Western Ave # 14 Seattle WA 98104-1440

SATO, RONALD MASAHIKO, health facility administrator; b. Honolulu, Dec. 29, 1944. BA in Chemistry summa cum laude, U. Hawaii, 1966; postgrad., Yale U., 1966-70. Diplomate Nat. Bd. Med. Examiners, Am. Bd. Plastic Surgery. Intern Stanford (Calif.) U. Med. Sch., 1970-71, resident in gen., plastic and reconstructive surgery, 1971-77, chief resident in plastic and reconstructive surgery, 1977-78; asst. prof. plastic and reconstructive surgery U. Tex. Health Sci. Ctr., Dallas, 1978-82, Stanford U. Med. Ctr., 1982-86; assoc. chief plastic and reconstructive surgery Santa Clara Valley Med. Ctr., San Jose, Calif., 1982-86, dir. burn ctr., 1982-86; dir. burn ctr. and outpatient clinic Brookside Hosp., San Pablo, Calif., 1986—, dir. wound ctr. and outpatient clinic, 1991—; clin. instr. in surgery Stanford U. Med. Ctr., 1980-82; adv. bd. Burn Traumas United, 1985-87; editorial staff Jour. Burn Care and Rehab., 1980-82; plastic surgery in-svc. exam com. Nat. Bd. Med. Examiners, 1980-82. Contbr. articles to profl. jours. Burn fellow U. Tex. Health Sci. Ctr., Dallas, 1976-77. Mem. AMA, Am. Assn. Tissue Banks, Am. Burn Assn. (ednl. com. 1980-82), Confederation de Trabujadores Cirugias Plasticas de Stanford, Internat. Soc. for Burn Injuries, Interplast (bd. dirs. 1978-79, faculty, 1986—), Zedplast. Office: Brookside Hospital 2000 Vale Rd San Pablo CA 94806

SATO, TADASHI, artist; b. Maui, Hawaii, Feb. 6, 1923. Student, Honolulu Sch. Art, Bklyn. Mus. Art Sch., New Sch. Soc. Rsch. Exhbns. include Guggenheim Mus., N.Y.C., 1954, Honolulu Acad. Arts, 1957, Pacific Heritage Exhibit, L.A., 1963, McRoberts and Tunnard Ltd., London, 1964, White House Festival of Arts, Washington, 1965, Berlin Art Festival, 1967; represented in permanent collections Albright-Knox Art Gallery, Buffalo, Guggenheim Mus., Whitney Mus. Am. Art, N.Y.C., Honolulu Acad. Arts, U. Art Gallery, Tucson, (mosaic) Hawaii State Capitol Bldg., State Libr. Aina Haina, Oahu, State Hosp., Kea-lakekua, Hawaii, Wailuku War Meml. Gymnasium, Maui, Krannert Art Mus., Ill., U. Nebr.; executed murals Halekulani Hotel, Honolulu, (mosaic) West Maui Recreation Ctr., (oil) Bay Club, Kapalua, Maui; retrospective Hui No Eau, Makawao, Maui, 1992. Office: PO Box 476 Lahaina HI 96767-0476

SATRE, RODRICK IVERSON, product development professional; b. Geneseo, N.Y., July 14, 1951; s. Roy Ingvold Jr. and Patricia Ruth (Holder) S.; m. Bonita Daley, Sept. 30, 1978. BS in Chem. Engring., Clarkson U., 1973; MBA in Internat. Bus., John F. Kennedy U., 1989. Plant engr., then operating asst. Chevron Chem. Co., Richmond, Calif., 1975-78, area supr., 1978-80, sr. analyst Chevron Chem. Co., San Francisco, 1980-85; group leader, then sr. rsch. engr. Chevron Chem. Co., Richmond, 1985-89; mgr. Internat. Tech. Corp., Martinez, Calif., 1990—; prin. SSD Consulting, Point Richmond, Calif., 1990-92; gen. mgr. Internat. Tech. Corp., Houston, 1992—; prin. assoc. Kertesz Internat., Inc., San Francisco, 1990—. Patentee in field. Sci. judge Richmond Unified Sch. Dist., 1985—. Mem. Berkeley Ski Club (v.p. 1978-79, pres. 1981-82). Republican.

SATTERFIELD, WADE JAMES, software engineer; b. Emporia, Kans., May 31, 1959; s. Leon James and Mary Ann (Bernard) S.; m. Joanne Lorraine Fish, Nov. 3, 1989; 1 Leslie. BS, Nebr. Wesleyan U., 1981; MS, U. Nebr., 1987, PhD, 1989. Software engr. Hewlett-Packard, Ft. Collins, Colo., 1989—. Contbr. articles to profl. jours. Precinct del. County Dem. Conv., 1984, County Rep. Conv., 1980. Mem. Assn. for Computing Machinery. Democrat. Office: Hewlett Packard 3400 E Harmony Rd Fort Collins CO 80525

SATTERWHITE, TERRY FRANK, lawyer; b. New Braunfels, Tex., Apr. 23, 1946; s. Elmer and Emilie (Graef) S.; m. Robin Ann Rabun, Apr. 27, 1974; children: Emilie Nora, Ellen Bess. BBA with highest honors, U. Tex., 1971, MPA, 1977; JD, U. Colo., 1980. Bar: Colo. 1981, U.S. Tax Ct. 1981, U.S. Dist. Ct. Colo. 1981; CPA, Colo., Tex. Tax acct. Touche Ross & Co., Austin, Tex., 1971-74; sr. tax acct. Deloitte Haskins & Sells, Colorado Springs, Colo., 1974-77; legal rsch. asst. regional office of appeals IRS, Denver, 1978-79; assoc. Spurgeon, Haney & Howbert, Colorado Springs, 1980-81; assoc. Berniger, Berg, Rioth & Diver, P.C., Colorado Springs, 1981-85, ptnr., 1985—. Editor column Colo. Lawyer; contbr. to Annual Survey of Colorado Law, 1991; mem. bd. editors U. Colo. Law Review, 1979-80. Bd. dirs. Care & Share, Colorado Springs, 1991—. Mem. ABA, AICPA, Colo. Bar Assn. (mem. exec. coun. tax sect. 1989—, chairperson-elect 1993-94), El Paso County Bar Assn. (mem. libr. adv. bd. 1983—, chairperson 1992-93), Colo. Soc. CPAs (chmn. tax tech. com. 1976), Tex. Soc. CPAs (program chmn. 1974), Order of Coif, Phi Kappa Phi, Beta Alpha Psi. Democrat. Lutheran. Home: 1414 Alamo Ave Colorado Springs CO 80907-7302 Office: Berniger Berg Rioth Diver PC 102 S Tejon St Ste 800 Colorado Springs CO 80903-2265

SATTIN, ALBERT, psychiatry and neuropharmacology educator; b. Cleve., Oct. 5, 1931; s. Sam and Edith (Stolarsky) S.; m. Renee Schnider, Dec. 16, 1962; children—Rebecca Lee, Michael M. B.S., Western Reserve U., 1953, M.D., 1957. Diplomate Am. Bd. Psychiatry and Neurology. Intern Washington U., St. Louis, 1957-58; resident in psychiatry Case-Western Reserve U., Cleve., 1958-62; fellow Dept. Biochemistry, U. London, 1965-66; instr., sr. instr. Case-Western Res. U. Sch. Medicine, 1965-1970, asst. prof. psychiatry and pharmacology, 1970-77; assoc. prof. psychiatry Ind. U. Sch. Medicine, Indpls., 1977-84, assoc. prof. psychiatry and neurobiology, Ind. U. Grad. Sch., 1984-91; assoc. clin. prof. psychiatry and behavioral scis. UCLA, 1991—; chief Antidepressant Neuropharmacology Lab, Sepulveda VA Med. Ctr., 1991—; psychiat. cons. Olive View L.A. County Med. Ctr., 1991—, Valley Hosp. Med. Ctr., 1991—. Contbr. articles to profl. jours. Grantee NIMH, NSF, VA; Am. Psychiat. Assn. fellow, 1969. Mem. Am. Psychiat. Assn., Soc. for Neurosci. Soc. Biol. Psychiatry, Internat. Soc. Neurochemistry. Office: 116 A/11 DVA Sepulveda Med Ctr 16111 Plummer St Sepulveda CA 91343-2036

SAUDE, LINDA KOCH ROBERTSON, visual arts educator, artist; b. San Francisco, Apr. 28, 1942; d. Frederick Charles and Winifred Marie (Holmes) Koch; m. Leonard Bruce Robertson, July 1, 1967 (div. Dec. 1980); children: Chad Michael, Brandt Richard; m. Stephen Joseph Saude, Jan. 28, 1990; stepchildren: India, Steve. BA, San Jose State U., 1965; MA, R.I. Sch. Design, 1990. Cert. tchr., Calif. Tchr. Campbell (Calif.) Sch. Dist., 1966-67, Orcult (Calif.) Sch. Dist., 1967-72, Hancock C.C., Santa Maria, Calif., 1974-78, Auberry (Calif.) Union Sch. Dist., 1978-89; art specialist Sierra Unified Sch. Dist., Auberry, 1989—, mentor tchr., 1993—; educator, cons. Calif. Arts Project, Calif. State Dept., 1986—; artist mem. Fig Tree Gallery, Fresno, Calif., 1990—; mem. mastery adv. coun. Sierra Unified Sch. Dist., 1992. Artist, Will Someone Please Teach Me a Dance?, 1992. Recipient Bank of Am. award Bank of Am., 1960, Tchr. as Artist Program fellowship Marie Walsh Sharpe Found., 1993. Fellow Calif. Arts Project; mem. Nat. Art Educators, Calif. Art Educators (Douc Langor award 1987), Alliance for Women Artists. Home: Box 345 Shaver Lake CA 93664 Office: Sierra Unified Sch Dist 31975 Lodge Rd Shaver Lake CA 93664

SAUER, CHRISTINE, economics educator; b. Schweinfurt, Germany, May 20, 1958; came to U.S., 1980; d. Hermann and Gisela Sauer. BA in Econs., Kiel (Germany) U., 1979; MA in Econs., Brown U., 1982, PhD in Econs., 1987. Lectr. econs. U. N.Mex., Albuquerque, 1985-87, asst. prof., 1987-93, assoc. prof., 1993—; mem. faculty German Summer Sch. U. N.Mex., Taos, 1988, 89; rsch. asst. World Bank, Washington, summer 1983. Author: Alternative Theories of Output, Unemployment and Inflation in Germany: 1960-1985, 1989; also articles. Exch. fellow Kiel and Brown Univs., 1980-81; travel grantee German Fulbright Commn., 1980-81; tuition scholar Brown U., 1983-84. Mem. Am. Econ. Assn. Midwest Econs. Assn. Office: U NMex Dept Econs 1915 Roma NE Albuquerque NM 87131

SAUL, ROGER STEPHEN, missionary, author, humorist; b. N.Y.C., Oct. 23, 1948; s. Warren Elmer and Jean Francis (Chamberlin) S.; child from previous marriage: Bonnie; m. Alma Salazar Aliviado; 1 child, James Roger. BS, SUNY, 1970. Founder Worldwide Interfaith Peace Mission, Albuquerque, 1988—. Author: How and Why to Settle an Unfair Contested Divorce in 30 Days Without Litigation, 1993, Divorce Without Court. Fellow U.S. Drug Free Powerlifting Assn., Worldwide Christian Divorced Fathers (founder). Home: 1429 Columbia Dr NE Albuquerque NM 87106-2632

SAUNDERS, DUNCAN REID, university administrator; b. Sioux City, Iowa, Mar. 21, 1948; s. Ernest William and Verina May (Rogers) S.; m. Judith Lynn Smith, Nov. 1, 1969; children: Sandra, Heather, Duncan Jr. BA in History, St. Leo Coll., 1980, BA in Mgmt., 1981; MS in Human Resources, Chapman U., 1991; M. Internat. Bus. Adminstrn., West Coast U., 1992. Cert. secondary edn., community coll. teaching. Enlisted USN, 1969, chief yeoman, 1969-88, retired, 1988; instr. Cen. Tex. Coll., San Diego, 1989; adminstr. West Coast U., San Diego, 1989-90, enrollment mgr., 1990-92; substitute tchr. Grossmont, Sweetwater and San Diego Sch. Dists., 1992-93; sec. SED programs San Diego Sch. Dist., 1993—. Leader Boy Scouts Am., advancement chair, 1989-91; mem. Otay Mesa C. of C., San Diego, 1991. Recipient Leadership award C. of C., San Diego, 1985; scholar Nat. U., 1985. Mem. ASTD. Republican. Methodist.

SAUNDERS, JAMES, management and training consultant; b. Chgo., Sept. 22, 1924; s. James Windam and Carrie Evelyn (Cox) S.; m. Gwendolyn Haithcox, Oct. 21, 1945 (dec. May 1971); children: Patricia Ann, Kathryn Lynn; m. Anita Joanne Laster, Sept. 16, 1972 (div. Oct. 1977); m. Bettye Jean Ricks, Apr. 18, 1981. BS in Math., Roosevelt U., 1953. Quality assurance rep. Dept. Army and Signal Corps., Chgo., 1945-63; dep. dir. quality assurance U.S. Naval Ordnance Plant, Forest Park, Ill., 1963-70; quality systems mgr. Gen. Foods Corp., Chgo., 1970-82; pres. Saunders and Assocs., Peoria, Ariz., 1982—; councilman, vice mayor City of Peoria, 1985-91. Bd. dirs., sec. Ariz. Retirement Ctrs., Peoria, 1984-85; mem. Peoria Personnel Bd., 1984-85; mem. Maricopa County Pvt. Industry Coun., 1984-89, chmn. bd. dirs., founder, Peoria Econ. Devel. Group, 1987-91, dir. emeritus, 1991—; mem. exec. com. Westside Transp. Coalition, Peoria, 1988-89. Recipient Black Achiever of Industry award Chgo. YMCA, 1977, Image Govt. award NAACP, 1989, also various other awards. Mem. Peoria C. of C. (v.p., bd. dirs. 1985), Westside Coalition Chambers Commerce, Lions (sec., v.p. Peoria chpt. 1983-86), Kiwanis, Masons, Alpha Phi Alpha. Home: 18847 N 88th Dr Peoria AZ 85382-8528 Office: Peoria City Hall 8401 W Monroe St Peoria AZ 85345-6560

SAUNDERS, JAMES HARWOOD, accountant; b. Carlsbad, N.Mex., Apr. 2, 1948; s. Eugene C. and Ruth (Powelson)S.; m. Kathleen Sue Matson, Jan. 26, 1974 (div. Apr. 1982); m. Bette Kim McCutcheon, Sept. 4, 1982; children: James C., Carl J., William K. AA in Adminstrn. Justice, Glendale Coll., Glendale, Ariz., 1975; BSBA, Ariz. State U., 1978. CPA, N.M., Ariz., Colo., Nev., Utah; lic. funeral dir. and embalmer; cert. fraud examiner. Embalmer Denton Funeral Home, Carlsbad, 1964-69; clk., trainee Sears & Roebuck Co., Dallas and Albuquerque, 1969-71, Phoenix, 1971-73; police sgt. spl. ops. Phoenix Police Dept., 1973-80; staff acct. various CPA firms, Carlsbad, 1980-83; owner James H. Saunders Acctg., Carlsbad, 1983-86; pvt. practice acctg. Eagar, Ariz., 1987—; auditor, mgmt. advisor to several Ariz. municipalities, 1987—; bd. dirs. Ariz. Lion Eye Bank. Vol. fireman Carlsbad Fire Dept., 1965-68; reserve dep. Bermallio County Sheriff Dept., Albuquerque, 1969-70. Mem. AICPA, Ariz. Soc. CPAs, N.Mex. Soc. CPAs, N.Mex. Assn. Funeral Dirs., Lions (sec. Carlsbad chpt. 1985-87, pres. Springerville, Ariz. chpt. 1987-91). Office: PO Box 1270 74 N Main Eagar AZ 85925

SAUNDERS, JOSEPH WOODROW, store owner; b. Grand Junction, Colo., Mar. 31, 1947; s. Woodrow Wilson and Laura Elizabeth (Potter) S.; m. Gail Ann Zanett, Nov. 19, 1972; children: Andrew Joseph, Denton Fredrick. Student, Mesa Coll., Grand Junction, 1965-67, Colo. State U., Ft. Collins, 1971-72. Owner, mgr. Village Shoes, Leadville, Colo., 1972-73; mgr. Flory's Shoes, Salida, Colo., 1973-74; owner 3-S Shoes, Montrose, Colo., 1974-75, Montrose Shoes, 1975-88, Montrose Shoes & Sports, 1975-88, The Coffee Shop, Delta, Colo., 1990-91, Sportsmans Surplus Liquidators, Montrose, 1991—. Coach youth soccer, Montrose, 1988—; tennis coach Colo. West Christian Sch., 1992, soccer coach, 1993; deacon Montrose Christian Ch., 1990—; mem. Small Bus. Adv. Bd., 1990-93. With U.S. Army, 1967-69, Vietnam. Mem. Scottish Rite, Masons, Elks, Order Ea. Star.

SAUNDERS, ROBERT MALLOUGH, engineering educator, college administrator; b. Winnipeg, Man., Can., Sept. 12, 1915; s. Robert and Mabel Grace (Mallough) S.; m. Elizabeth Lenander, June 24, 1943. BEE, U. Minn., 1938, MS, 1942; D.Eng., Tokyo Inst. Tech., 1971. Design engr. Electric Machinery Co., Mpls., part-time 1938-42; teaching asst. elec. engring. U. Minn., 1938-42, instr., 1942-44; faculty U. Calif., Berkeley, 1946-65, prof. elec. engring., 1957-65, chmn. dept., 1959-63; asst. to chancellor for engring. U. Calif., Irvine, 1964-65, prof. elec. engring., 1965—, dean Sch. Engring., 1965-73; vis. assoc. prof. MIT, 1954-55; cons. Gen. Motors Research Lab., Apollo Support Dept., Gen. Electric Co., Hughes Aircraft, Sundstrand, Aerospace Corp., Rohr Corp.; sec. Nat. Commn. for Elec. Engring. films, 1962-71; mem. ECPD Engring. Edn. and Accreditation Com., 1965-71, chmn., 1969-70, bd. dirs., 1971-75; mem. engring. adv. com. NSF, 1968-71; mem. Sec. Navy's Bd. Edn. and Tng., 1972-78. Co-author: Analysis of Feedback Control Systems, 1956; contbr.: Ency. Brit.; tech. jours. Bd. visitors U.S. Army Transp. Sch., 1970-73; mem. com. on edn. and utilization of engring. NRC, 1983-84. Served to lt. (j.g.) USNR, 1944-46. Simon fellow engring. Manchester U., Eng., 1960. Fellow AAAS, IEEE (chmn. ednl. activities bd. 1973-74, mem. exec. com., dir. 1973-79, v.p. regional activities 1975-76, pres. 1977, Centennial medal 1984, Haraden Pratt award 1990), Accrediting Bd. for Engring. and Tech.; mem. Am. Soc. Engring. Edn. (chmn. elec. div. 1965-66), Am. Assn. Engring. Socs. (organizing com. 1977-80, exec. com. 1982-84, chmn. bd. govs. 1983, chmn. awards com. 1984-85, nominating com. 1984-85), Rotary, Sigma Xi, Tau Beta Pi, Eta Kappa Nu. Office: U Calif Sch Engring Irvine CA 92717

SAUNDERS, RONALD STEPHEN, planetary geologist, researcher; b. Parsons, Kans., Oct. 8, 1940; s. Ronald Victor and Jeanne Ann (Dixon) S.; children: Stephen Victor, Paul Patterson, Robert Alexander. BS in Geology, U. Wis., 1963; MSc in Geology, Brown U., 1968, PhD in Geology, 1970. Geologist U.S. Peace Corps, Ghana, 1963-65, U.S. Geol. Survey, Flagstaff, Ariz., 1967-69; mem. tech. staff Jet Propulsion Lab., Pasadena, Calif., 1974-77, leader planetology devel. program, 1976-81, dir. regional planetary image facility, 1976—, supr. Earth and Planetary Sci. Group, 1977-79, mgr. planetology and oceanography sect., 1979-81, project scientist Magellan, 1981—, sr. rsch. scientist, 1985—. Contbr. articles to profl. jours. Trustee Altadena (Calif.) Libr., 1989—. Recipient Exceptional Svc. medal NASA, 1988, Exceptional Sci. Achievement medal, 1992. Mem. Rotary. Republican. Home: 616 Deodara Dr Altadena CA 91001-2308 Office: Jet Propulsion Lab Mail Stop 183-501 4800 Oak Grove Dr Pasadena CA 91109-8099

SAUSE, SAMUEL H., transportation professional; b. Stayton, Oreg., Nov. 30, 1936; s. Henry Richard Jr. and Martha Alice (Painton) S.; married; children: David (dec.), Paula, Carole. BBA, U. Oreg., 1961; MBA, Armstrong Coll., 1975; cert., Lasalle Sch. Traffic, Transp. Import traffic mgr. Montgomery Wards, Oakland, Calif., 1964-72; traffic mgr. Grand Auto Stores, Oakland, 1972-75, Marine Terminals, Oakland, 1975-77; sales rep. Kerr Steamship Co., San Francisco, 1977-85; owner, gen. mgr. Grand Transport Agy., Alameda, Calif., 1985—. With U.S. Army, 1959-61. Mem. Oakland World Trade Club (sec., dir.), Rotary (vocat. chair, program com. Alameda chpt.), Delta Nu Alpha. Democrat. Episcopalian. Office: Grand Transport Agy 816 Grand St Alameda CA 94501

SAUSSER, ROBERT GARY, army officer; b. St. Benedict, Pa., Apr. 6, 1941; s. Robert Jacob and Maxine Larue (Earley) S.; married Nov. 2, 1963; 1 child, Geoffrey Robert. BS, U.S. Mil. Acad., West Point, N.Y., 1963; MS, Ind. U., 1971. Commd. 2d lt. U.S. Army, 1963, advanced through grades to brig. gen., 1989; ops. officer 25th Div. Arty., Schofield Barracks, Hawaii, 1977-78; comdr. 1st Bn., 8th F.A., Schofield Barracks, 1978-80; pers. officer 7th Inf. Div., Ft. Ord, Calif., 1980-83; student U.S. Army War Coll., Carlisle Barracks, Pa., 1983-84; comdr. 25th Div. Arty., Schofield Barracks, 1984-86; exec. asst. to Comdr. in Chief, Combined Forces Command, Seoul, Republic of Korea, 1986-88; chief of staff U.S. Army I Corps, Ft. Lewis, Wash., 1988-89; chief U.S. Mil. Assistance Group, Manila, 1989-92; dep. comdr. U.S. Army Pacific, Ft. Shafter, Hawaii, 1992; asst. divsn. comdr. 6th Inf. Divsn. U.S. Army Pacific, Ft. Richardson, Alaska, 1992—; bd. dirs. Army, Air Force Exch. Svc., Dallas, 1992—. Decorated Bronze Star, Legion of Merit, Def. Superior Svc. medal. Mem. Assn. U.S. Army, U.S. Army F.A. Assn., West Point Alumni Assn. Republican. Office: US Army Pacific Asst Divsn Comdr 6th Inf. Divsn. Fort Richardson AK 99505

SAUTE, ROBERT EMILE, drug and cosmetic consultant; b. West Warwick, R.I., Aug. 18, 1929; s. Camille T. and Lea E. (Goffinet) S.; m. Arda T. Darnell, May 18, 1957; children: Richard R., Steven N., Allen K. BS, R.I. Coll. Pharmacy, 1950; MS, Purdue U., 1952, PhD, 1953. Registered pharmacist. Tech. asst. to pres. Lafayette (Ind.) Pharmacal, 1955-56; sr. rsch. and devel. chemist H.K. Wampole Denver Chem. Co., Phila., 1956-57; supt. Murray Hill (N.J.) plant Strong Cobb Arner Inc., 1957-60; adminstrv. dir. rsch. and devel. Avon Products Inc., Suffern, N.Y., 1960-68; dir. rsch. and devel. toiletries div. Gillette Co., Boston, 1968-71; group v.p. Dart Industries, L.A., 1972-75; pres. Saute Cons., Inc., L.A., 1975—; bd. dirs. Joico Labs., Inc., Cosmetics Enterprises, Ltd. Contbr. to books; patentee in field. With U.S. Army, 1953-55. Fellow Soc. Cosmetic Chemists (bd. dirs. 1987—, chmn. Calif. chpt. 1986); mem. N.Y. Acad. Scis., Soc. Investigative Dermatology, Am. Assn. Pharm. Scientists, AAAS, Sigma Xi, Rho Chi.

SAVAGE, TERRY RICHARD, information systems executive; b. St. Louis, Oct. 21, 1930; s. Terry Barco and Ada Vanetta (Cochran) S.; m. Gretchen Susan Wood, Sept. 26,1 964; children: Terry Curtis, Christopher William, Richard Theodore. AB, Washington U., St. Louis, 1951, MA, 1952; PhD, U. Pa., 1954. Mgr. system software IBM Rsch., Yorktown Heights, N.Y., 1956-63; dir. data processing Documentation Inc., Bethesda, Md., 1963-64; mgr. info. systems Control Data Corp., Rockville, Md., 1964-67; dir. rsch. Share Rsch. Corp., Santa Barbara, Calif., 1967-68; computer-aided acquisition and logistic support program mgr. TRW, Redondo Beach, Calif., 1968-92; ret., ind. cons. pvt. practice, 1992—; expert witness coms. U.S. Congress, 1981, 84, 88, 89; bd. dirs. Savage Info. Svcs., Inc. Contbr. articles to profl. jours. Bd. dirs. ABC-Clio Press, Santa Barbara, 1970-75, Help the Homeless Help Themselves, Rancho Palos Verdes, Calif., 1988—, ChorusLiners, Rancho Palos Verdes, 1983—. Mem. Cosmos Club. Home and Office: 30000 Cachan Pl Palos Verdes Peninsula CA 90274-5412

SAVIN, RONALD RICHARD, chemical company executive, inventor; b. Cleve., Oct. 16, 1926; s. Samuel and Ada (Silver) S.; m. Gloria Ann Hopkins, Apr. 21, 1962; children: Danielle Elizabeth, Andrea Lianne. Student, U. Cin., 1944-46; BA in Chemistry and Literature, U. Mich., 1948; postgrad., Columbia U., 1948-49, Sorbonne, Paris, 1949-50; grad., Air War Coll., 1975, Indsl. Coll. Armed Forces, 1976. Pres., owner Premium Finishes, Inc., Cin., 1957-91; cons. aerospace and anti-corrosive coatings; inventor Hunting Indsl. Coatings. Contbr. articles on aerospace, marine industry and transp. to profl. jours.; adv. coun. Chem. Week mag.; patentee in field of aerospace and anti-corrosion coatings; 8 patents. With USAF, 1948-55, World War II and Korea, col. Res. 1979, ret. 1986. Mem. Nat. Assn. Corrosion Engrs., Air Force Assn., Am. Internat. Club (Geneva), Res. Officers Assn. Home: L'Eden, Thonon-les-Bains France Office: PO Box 1169 Rancho Mirage CA 92270-1169

SAVONA, MICHAEL RICHARD, physician; b. N.Y.C., Oct. 21, 1947; s. Salvatore Joseph and Diana Grace (Menditto) S.; m. Dorothy O'Neill, Oct. 18, 1975. BS summa cum laude, Siena Coll., 1969; MD, SUNY, Buffalo, 1973. Diplomate Am. Bd. Internal Medicine. Intern in internal medicine Presbyn. Hosp. Columbia U., N.Y.C., 1973-74, resident in internal medicine, 1974-76; vis. fellow internal medicine Delafield Hosp./Columbia U. Coll. Physicians and Surgeons, N.Y.C., 1974-76; practice medicine specializing in internal medicine Maui Med. Group, Wailuku, Hawaii, 1976-87, gen. practice medicine, 1987—; dir. ICU, Maui Meml. Hosp., also dir. respiratory therapy, CCU., chmn. dept. medicine, 1980—; clin. faculty John A. Burns Sch. Medicine, U. Hawaii, asst. prof. medicine, 1985—, asst. rsch. prof., 1989—. Bd. dirs. Maui Heart Assn.; dir. profl. edn. Maui chpt. Am. Cancer Soc.; mem. Maui County Hosp. Adv. Commn.; mem. coun. Community Cancer Program of Hawaii. Recipient James A. Gibson Wayne J. Atwell award, 1970, physiology award, 1970, Ernest Whitebsky award, 1971, Roche Lab. award, 1972, Pfiser Lab. award, 1973, Phillip Sang award, 1973, Hans Lowenstein M.D. Meml. award, 1973. Mem. AMA, Am. Thoracic Soc., Hawaii Thoracic Soc., Maui County Med. Assn. (past pres.), Hawaii Med. Assn., Hawaii Oncology Group, ACP, SW Oncology Coop. Group, Alpha Omega Alpha, Delta Epsilon Sigma. Office: 1830 Wells St Wailuku HI 96793-2334

SAVRUN, ENDER, engineering executive, researcher, engineer; b. Adana, Turkey, July 29, 1953; came to U.S., 1978; s. Yusuf and Nemide Savrun; m. Canan Erdamar, Oct. 23, 1979; 1 child, Altay. BS, Istanbul (Turkey) Tech. U., 1976, MS, 1978; PhD, U. Wash., 1986. Rsch. engr. Charlton Industries, Redmond, Wash., 1984-85; rsch. scientist Flow Industries, Kent, Wash., 1985-87, Photon Scis., Bothell, Wash., 1987-88; mgr. rsch. Keramont Rsch. Corp., Tucson, 1988-89; v.p. R & D Keramont Corp., Tucson, 1989-92; founder, pres. Sienna Rsch., Inc., Tucson, 1992—. Contbr. articles to profl. jours.; patentee in field. Turkish Govt. scholar, 1979. Mem. ASME, Am. Soc. for Metals, Am. Ceramic Soc. Office: Sienna Rsch Inc 2810 E Plaza Encantada Tucson AZ 85718-1238

SAVVA, SAVELY L. (SAVELY L. ZHUKOBORSKY), researcher, executive director; b. Leningrad, USSR, June 12, 1932; came to U.S., 1978; s. Aaron M. Sterlin and Rakhil S. Zhukoborsky; m. Lyubov Z. Danilova, Jan. 19, 1965; children: Elena, Alexander. MSME, Leningrad Tech. Inst., 1955. Workshop engr., mgr. Leningrad Meat Packing Plant, 1955-58; budget prodn. mgr. Integrated Refrigeration Svc. Plant, Leningrad, 1958-59, chief designer, 1960-65; rsch. assoc. Leningrad Inst. Refrigeration Industry, 1965-71; sr. researcher All-Union Inst. Tech. Aesthetics, Leningrad, 1972-76; engr. I.A. Naman & Assoc., Inc., Houston, 1978-80; rsch. engr. Virginia KMP, Inc., Dallas, 1981-85; pres. SZ Consulting Co., Monterey, Calif., 1983—; Russian lang. instr. Def. Lang. Inst., Monterey, 1987—; exec. dir., founder Monterey Inst. Study Alt. Healing Arts, 1990—; founder, coord. Sci. Seminar, Leningrad, 1974-77; cons. Atmospheric Instrumentation Rsch., Boulder, Colo., 1988—. OTIS Engring., Inc., Dallas, 1985-86. Contbr. 30 articles to profl. jours. Mem. ASHRAE. Home and Office: Monterey Inst for Study Alt Healing Arts 400 Virgin St Monterey CA 93940-3862

SAWOSKI, JOHN ROBERT, keyboardist, composer; b. Phila., Nov. 23, 1962; s. Edward John and Mary D. Sawoski. BA, Stanford U., Palo Alto, Calif., 1985; postgrad., UCLA. Owner Sawoski Music Group, Beverly Hills, CA, 1985—. Composer, arranger, conductor How to Become a Legend in Your Own Mind, 1982-83; composer: Gaieties 83: Raiders of the Lost Axe, Gaieties 84: Cardinal Sins, 1983-84; pianist, music. dir. Sitmar Cruises Fairsea Show Band, 1987; music. dir., pianist Mable King's Christmas TV Special, 1988; keyboardist L.A. Gospel TV Show, 1989, Hard Rock Nightmare, 1989; composer, keyboardist, producer A Moment with Rozlyn, 1989, solo pianist, accompanist; keyboardist, composer, producer (christian rock albums) Psalms & Acclamations, 1991, Singing Morning & Evening Prayer, 1992, (film score) Hearing the Call, United Way, 1991; keyboardist, arranger (pop album) The Adam Yurman Project, 1990-91; keyboardist Broadway play, The Secret Garden (nat. tour), 1993. Recipient NAJE award for best jazz pianist Chaffey Coll. Jazz Festival, 1981. Mem. ASCAP, NARAS, Am. Fedn. Musicians, Pacific Composers Forum, L.A. Composers Guild. Home and Office: PO Box 7060 Beverly Hills CA 90212-7060

SAWYER, GRANT, lawyer; b. Twin Falls, Idaho, Dec. 14, 1918; s. Harry William and Bula Bell (Cameron) S.; m. Bette Norene Hoge, Aug. 1, 1946; 1 child, Gail. BA, Linfield Coll., 1939; student, U.Nev., Reno, 1940-44; JD, Georgetown U., 1948. Bar: Nev. 1948, D.C. 1948, U.S. Dist. Ct. Nev. 1967, U.S. Ct. Appeals (9th cir.) 1974, U.S. Supreme Ct. 1959. Pvt. practice Elko, Nev., 1948-50; dist. atty. Elko County, Nev., 1950-58; gov. State of Nev., 1959-67; sr. ptnr. Lionel Sawyer & Collins, Las Vegas, 1967—. Author books and articles on gaming. Mem. bd. regents U. Nev., 1957-58; Dem. nat. committeeman for Nev., 1968-88; chmn. Nev. Commn. on nuclear Projects, 1985—; mem. adv. bd. Aid for Aids of Nev., 1987—; trustee Bluecoats, Inc., 1987—; mem. exec. com. U. Nev. Las Vegas Found., 1988—; mem. nat. adv. coun. ACLU, 1988—; bd. dirs. Nat. Jud. Coll., 1991—. Pvt. to 1st lt. U.S. Army, 1942-46, PTO. Mem. ABA, Nev. Bar Assn., D.C. Bar Assn., Am. Judicature Soc., Phi Delta Phi. Office: Lionel Sawyer & Collins 300 S 4th St Stop 1700 Las Vegas NV 89101-6053

SAWYER, THOMAS EDGAR, management consultant; b. Homer, La., July 7, 1932; s. Sidney Edgar and Ruth (Bickham) S.; BS, UCLA, 1959; MA, Occidental Coll., 1969; PhD, Walden U., 1990; m. Joyce Mezzanatto, Aug. 22, 1954; children—Jeffrey T., Scott A., Robert J., Julie Anne. Project engr. Garrett Corp., L.A., 1954-60; mgr. devel. ops. TRW Systems, Redondo Beach, Calif., 1960-66; spl. asst. to gov. State of Calif., Sacramento, 1967-69; prin., gen. mgr. Planning Rsch. Corp., McLean, Va., 1969-72; dep. dir. OEO, Washington, 1972-74; assoc. prof. bus. mgmt. Brigham Young U., 1974-78; pres. Mesa Corp., Provo, 1978-82, chmn. bd., 1978-82; pres. and dir. Sage Inst. Internat., Inc., Provo, Utah, 1982-88; pres., chmn. bd. Pvt. Telecom Networks, Inc. (name changed to Nat. Applied Computer Techs., Inc.), Orem, Utah, 1988—; dir. Intechna Corp., HighTech Corp., Nat. Applied Computer Tech. Inc. (chmn.), Indian Affiliates, Inc. Chmn. Nat. Adv. Council Indian Affairs; chmn. Utah State Bd. Indian Affairs; mem. Utah Dist. Export Coun.; mem. Utah dist. SBA Council; chmn. So. Paiute Restoration Com.; mem. adv. coun. Nat. Bus. Assn.; mem. Utah Job Tng. Coordinating Coun. Served with USMC, 1950-53. Mem. Am. Mgmt. Assn., Am. Soc. Public Adminstrn., Utah Coun. Small Bus. (dir.). Republican. Mormon. Club: Masons. Author: Assimilation Versus Self-Indentity: A Modern Native American Perspective, 1976, Computer Assisted Instruction: An Inevitable Breakthrough, Current Challenges of Welfare: A Review of Public Assistance As Distributive Justice, 1989, Impact of Failure By Senior Executives to Receive Accurate Critical Feedback on Pervasive Change, 1990, The Promise of Funding a New Educational Initiative Using the Microcomputer, 1988, New Software Models for training and Education delivery, 1989, New Organizations: How They Deviate from Classical Models, 1989, Increasing Productivity in Organizations: The Paradox, 1989, An Introduction and Assessment of Strategic Decision Making Paradigms in Complex Organizations, 1989, The Influence of Critical Feedback and Organizational Climate on Managerial Decision Making, 1990, Future of Technology in Education, 1989. Home: 548 W 630 S Orem UT 84058-6154 Office: Nat Applied Computer Techs Inc 744 S 400 E Orem UT 84058-6322

SAWYER, THOMAS WILLIAM, air force officer; b. Turlock, Calif., Nov. 19, 1933; s. Everett Edward and Marie Georgine (Gunderson) S.; m. Faith Barry Martin, Feb. 16, 1957; children: William Everet, John Martin, Susan Quincy. BS in Mil. Sci., U. Nebr., 1965; MS in Internat. Rels., George Washington U., 1974. Enlisted U.S. Air Force, 1952, commd. and advanced through grades to maj. gen., 1983; comdr. 57th Fighter Squadron, Keflavik, Iceland, 1971-73; chief internat. relations div. Hdqrs. U.S. Air Force, Washington, 1974-77; vice comdr. 20th Air Div., Fort Lee, Va., 1977-78; mil. asst. to Sec. Air Force, 1978-80; comdr. 26th Air Div., Luke AFB, Ariz., 1980-82; dep. ops. NORAD and Space Command, Colorado Springs, Colo., 1982-86; retired USAF, 1986; founder, pres. Aerospace Network Inc., 1986. Bd. dirs. Pikes Peak chpt. ARC, Colo./Wyo. chpt. Am. Def. Preparedness Assn. Decorated Disting. Service medal, Def. Disting. Service medal, Legion of Merit with 2 oak leaf clusters, Silver Star (2). Mem. Phoenix C. of C. (bd. dirs. 1980-82), Colorado Springs C. of C. Home: 10 W Cheyenne Mountain Blvd Colorado Springs CO 80906-4335 Office: Aerospace Network Inc 10 W Cheyenne Mountain Blvd Colorado Springs CO 80906-4335

SAX, HERBERT, financial planner; b. N.Y.C., Nov. 5, 1929; s. Murray and Rose (Rifkin) S.; m. Carolyn Tambor, Jan. 20, 1952; children: Jeffrey F., Edward J. BA in Psychology, Bklyn. Coll., 1950; postgrad., Bernard Baruch Sch. Bus. Adminstrn., 1953-59, Coll. for Fin. Planning, 1986-88. CPA; cert. fin. planner; registered investment adviser. Asst. office mgr. Arrow Metal Products, N.Y., 1953-54; acct. Samuel Arlow & Co., N.Y., 1954-56, Morris R. Feinsod & Co., N.Y., 1956-60; contr., treas., v.p. fin. Ehrenreich Photo-Optical Industries and Nikon Inc., Garden City, N.Y., 1960-73, pres., chief exec. officer, 1973-84; exec. dir. Coalition to Preserve Integrity Am. Trademarks, Washington, 1984-85; pres. Herbert Sax & Assocs., Woodland Hills, Calif., 1986—; bd. dir. Internat. Photographic Coun., N.Y. Cpl. U.S. Army, 1951-53. Mem. AICPA, N.Y. State Soc. CPAs, Internat. Bd. Standards and Practices for Cert. Fin. Planners.

SAX, JOSEPH LAWRENCE, lawyer, educator; b. Chgo., Feb. 3, 1936; s. Benjamin Harry and Mary (Silverman) S.; m. Eleanor Charlotte Gettes, June 17, 1958; children—Katherine Elaine, Valerie Beth, Anne-Marie. AB, Harvard U., 1957; JD, U. Chgo., 1959; LLD (hon.), Ill. Inst. Tech., 1992. Bar: D.C. 1960, Mich., 1966, U.S. Supreme Ct. 1969. Atty. Dept. Justice, Washington, 1959-60; pvt. practice law Washington, 1960-62; prof. U. Colo., 1962-65, U. Mich., Ann Arbor, 1966-86; James H. House and Hiram H. Hurd prof. U. Calif., Berkeley, 1987—; vis. prof. U. Calif. Law Sch., Berkeley, 1965-66, 86, U. Paris I, 1981, 82, Stanford Law Sch., 1985; fellow Ctr. Advanced Study in Behavioral Scis., 1977-78; cons. U.S. Senate Com. on Pub. Works, 1970-71; mem. cons. council Conservation Foundation, 1969-73; mem. legal adv. com. Pres.'s Council on Environ. Quality, 1970-72; mem.

environ. studies bd. Nat. Acad. Sci., 1970-73; mem. Mich. Environ. Rev. Bd., 1973-74. Author: Waters and Water Rights, 1967, Water Law, Planning and Policy, 1968, Defending the Environment, 1971, Mountains Without Handrails, 1980, Legal Control of Water Resources, 1991. Bd. dirs. Environ. Law Inst., Washington, 1970-75; trustee Center for Law and Social Policy, 1970-76; regional gov. Internat. Coun. Environmental Law; gov.'s rep. Gt. Lakes Task Force, 1984-85. With USAF, 1960. Fellow AAAS; mem. University Club (San Francisco). Home: 850 Powell St Apt 106 San Francisco CA 94108-2036

SAXENA, AMOL, podiatrist, consultant; b. Palo Alto, Calif., June 5, 1962; s. Arjun Nath and Veera Saxena; m. Karen Ann Palermo, Aug. 11, 1985; children: Vijay, Tara Ann. Student, U. Calif., Davis, 1980-82; BA, Washington U., St. Louis, 1984; D in Podiatric Medicine, William Scholl Coll. Podiatric Medicine, 1988. Lic. podiatrist, Calif., Ill. Resident in podiatric surgery VA Westside Br., Chgo., 1988-89; cons. Puma U.S.A., Inc., Framingham, Mass., 1986—; pvt. practice Mountain View, Calif., 1989—; dir. Puma Sports Medicine, Framingham; mem. podiatry team St. Frances/Gunn Los Altos (Calif.) High Sch., Palo Alto, 1989—, Stanford (Calif.) U., 1989—; mem. med. staff El Camino Hosp., 1989—, team podiatrist Stanford U., 1989—. Contbr. articles to profl. jours. Vol. coach Gunn High Sch. Track and Cross County, Palo Alto, 1989—; podiatrist U.S. Olympic Track and Field Trials, New Orleans, 1992, 1993. Fellow Am. Acad. Podiatric Sports Medicine; mem. Am. Coll. Foot Surgeons (assoc.), Am. Podiatric Med. Assn., Calif. Podiatric Med. Assn., Am. Med. Soccer Assn., Aggie Running Club. Republican. Office: 2204 Grant Rd # 104 Mountain View CA 94040-3877

SAXENA, AVADH BEHARI, physicist, researcher; b. Jodhpur, Rajasthan, India, June 10, 1960; came to U.S., 1982; s. Anand Behari Lal and Sushila (Devi) S. BE in EE with honors, Birla Inst. Tech. and Sci., Pilani, India, 1982, MSc in Physics with honors, 1982; MA in Physics, Temple U., 1983, PhD in Physics, 1987. Univ. fellow, rsch. asst. Temple U., Phila., 1982-86; rsch. assoc. Pa. State U., University Park, 1986-89; cons., vis. scientist Los Alamos (N.Mex.) Nat. Lab., 1990-92, tech. staff mem., 1993—. Contbr. articles to profl. jours. Recipient scholarships; Lab. R&D grantee Los Alamos Nat. Lab., 1991-92. Mem. Am. Phys. Soc. (STEP grantee 1986), Materials Rsch. Soc., Indian Physics Assn., European Materials Rsch. Soc., Internat. Hindi Assn., Sigma Xi. Office: T-11 MS B262 Los Alamos Nat Lab Los Alamos NM 87545

SAXENA, NARENDRA K., marine research educator; b. Agra, India, Oct. 15, 1936; came to U.S., 1969; s. Brijbasi Lal and Sarbati Saxena; m. Cecilia H. Hsi, Mar. 21, 1970; Sarah Vasanti, Lorelle Sarita. Diploma Geodetic Engring., Tech. U., Hanover, Fed. Republic Germany, 1966; D in Tech Scis., Tech. U., Graz, Austria, 1972. Research assoc. geodetic sci. Ohio State U., Columbus, 1969-74; asst. prof. U. Ill., Urbana, 1974-78; asst. prof. U. Hawaii, Honolulu, 1978-81, assoc. prof., 1981-86, prof., 1986—; adj. research prof. Naval Postgrad. Sch., Monterey, Calif., 1984—; co-chmn. Pacific Congresses on Marine Tech., Honolulu, 1984, 86, 88; pres. Pacon Internat. Inc., 1987—. Editor Jour. Marine Geodesy, 1976—. Mem. Neighborhood Bd., Honolulu, 1984. Fellow Marine Tech. Soc. (various offices 1974—); mem. ASCE, Am. Geophys. Union, The Tsunami Soc. (sec. 1985—). Office: U Hawaii Dept Civil Engring Honolulu HI 96822

SAYANO, REIZO RAY, electrochemical engineer; b. Los Angeles, Dec. 15, 1937; s. George Keiichiro and Miyo (Nakao) S.; m. Tamiko Shintani, May 28, 1967; children—Kiyomi Coleen, Naomi Jennifer. A.A., Los Angeles Community Coll., 1958; B.S., UCLA, 1960, M.S., 1962, Ph.D., 1967. Research asst. electrochem. and shock tube research dept. engring. UCLA, 1961-66; mem. staff TRW Systems, corrosion and advanced battery research and devel. Redondo Beach, Calif., 1966-78; dir. engring. Intermedics Intraocular Inc., Pasadena, Calif., 1978-80, dir. research and devel., 1980-82, v.p. engring. devel. and research, 1982-84; v.p. research and devel. Interpore Internat. Inc., 1984-85; dir. research and devel., product process devel. IOLAB Corp. subs. Johnson & Johnson Co., Claremont, Calif., 1985-87, dir. new tech., research and devel., 1987-88; v.p., gen. mgr. Nidek Techs., Inc., Pasadena, Calif., 1988—. NASA predoctoral trainee, 1964-65. Mem. Electrochem. Soc., Nat. Assn. Corrosion Engrs., AAAS, Am. Mgmt. Assn., Sigma Xi. Office: 675 S Arroyo Pky Ste 330 Pasadena CA 91105-3264

SAYER, PAUL, surgeon; b. Trenton, Mo., June 8, 1938; s. James Rudolph and Dorothy Mae (Harris) S.; m. Melinda Rees Miller, 1966 (div. 1972); children: Elizabeth, Andrew, Timothy James; m. Francine Mary Russell, 1984. MD, U. Mo., 1964. Diplomate Am. Bd. Surgery. Intern USPHS, Seattle, 1964-65, resident gen. surgery, 1965-69, surgeon, 1964-69; dep. chief surgery BIA Hosp., USPHS, Anchorage, 1969-71; surgeon in pvt. practice Anchorage, 1971-79, Homer, Alaska, 1979—. Deacon, Faith Bapt. Ch., Homer, 1990-92. Lt. comdr. USPHS, 1964-70. Fellow ACS. Republican. Home and Office: Box 10 Homer AK 99603

SAYLES, MARTIN LUTHER, military officer; b. Montgomery, Ala., June 16, 1957; s. Morris and Lula (Baskin) S.; m. Sharon Billups, Aug. 15, 1981. BBA, Ala. State U., 1980; postgrad., Golden Gate U., 1986-87. Cert. in mgmt. and adminstrn. Commd. 2d lt. USAF, 1980, advanced through grades to maj., 1992; billeting officer USAF, Langley AFB, Va., 1980-81; exec. officer USAF, Langley AFB, 1981-82, squadron sect. commdr., 1982-83; chief of adminstrn. USAF, Gibbsboro AFB, N.J., 1983-84; squadron sect. commdr. USAF, Shaw AFB, S.C., 1985; hdqrs. squadron commdr. USAF, Shaw AFB, 1985-89; detachment commdr. USAF, Osan AFB, Republic of Korea, 1989-90; exec. officer USAF, Davis-Monthan AFB, 1990—; USCENTAF exec. officer Operation Desert Storm, 1991. Mem. unit adv. coun. Shaw AFB, advisor, 1985—; mem. squadron welfare coun. Gibbsboro AFB, chmn. 1983-84. Named one of Outstanding Young Men Am., 1983, 85, 87; recipient Disting. Achievement award Tactical Air Command. Mem. Kappa Alpha Psi (Acad. Achievement award 1979-80), Phi Beta Lambda (parliamentarian 1977-78). Democrat. Roman Catholic. Home: PSC 78 Box 2147 APO AP 96326 Office: Exec Officer 335th Support Group Davis Monthan A F B AZ 85707

SAYLOR, RICHARD SAMUEL, composer, conductor; b. Reading, Pa., Aug. 6, 1926; s. Samuel William S. and Miriam Adelaide (Swoyer) Santiago; m. Naomi Roth, May 6, 1950 (dec. 1983); children: Janine, Mark, David. BS, Ithaca Coll., 1950, MusB, 1955; MusM, U. Mich., 1958; DMA, Stanford U., 1966. Dir. music Boliver Sch., Bolivar, N.Y., 1952-55; instr. music Xavier U., New Orleans, 1958-59; asst. prof. St. Lawrence U., Canton, N.Y., 1959-69; prof. music, chair Calif. State U., San Bernardino, 1969-91, prof. emeritus, 1991—; conductor Ithaca Civic Opera, 1950-52, Riverside (Calif.) Opera Co., 1972-74, Palm Springs (Calif.) Symphony, 1973, San Bernardino Chamber Orch., 1969-91. Composed numerous musical compositions. With USN, 1944-46. Travelli Found. fellow, 1964-66; recipient award for adventuresome programming ASCAP, 1972. Fellow Smithsonian Inst., Am. Inst. Indian Studies; mem. Coll. Music Soc., Am. Fedn. Musicians (life), Schonberg Soc. Home: 2761 N Golden Ave # 13 San Bernardino CA 92404

SAYRE, EDWARD CHARLES, librarian; b. Longview, Wash., Aug. 15, 1923; s. Kenneth C. Sayre and Clare (Davis) Clingan; m. Virginia A. Hoy, June 9, 1951; children: Steven Anthony, Sabrina Karen. BA, Coll. of Gt. Falls, 1955; MA, U. Idaho, 1961; MLS, U. Md., 1968. Coordinator library services Thomas Nelson Community Coll., Hampton, Va., 1968-69; dir. Roswell Pub. Library, N.Mex., 1969-70; cons. N.Mex. State Library, Santa Fe, 1970-72; dir. Central Colo. Library System, Denver, 1972-78, Serra Coop. Library System, San Diego, 1978-79, Los Alamos County (N.Mex.) Library System, 1979-88; county adminstr. Los Alamos County, 1988-89; cons., 1976—, ret., 1989. Contbr. articles to profl. jours. Served to maj. USAF, 1951-67. HEA Title II fellow, 1968. Mem. ALA, N.Mex. Library Assn. (pres.-elect 1972), Beta Phi Mu (dir. 1973-74). Democrat. Unitarian. Home: 3 Timber Ridge Rd Los Alamos NM 87544

SAYRE, JOHN MARSHALL, lawyer, former government official; b. Boulder, Colo., Nov. 9, 1921; s. Henry Marshall and Lulu M. (Cooper) S.; m. Jean Miller, Aug. 22, 1943; children: Henry M., Charles Franklin, John Marshall Jr., Ann Elizabeth Sayre Taggart (dec.). B.A., U. Colo., 1943, J.D., 1948. Bar: Colo. 1948, U.S. Dist. Ct. Colo. 1952, U.S. Ct. Appeals (10th cir.) 1964. Law clk. trust dept. Denver Nat. Bank, 1948-49; asst. cashier, trust officer Nat. State Bank of Boulder, 1949-50; ptnr. Ryan, Sayre, Martin, Brotzman, Boulder, 1950-66, Davis, Graham & Stubbs, Denver, 1966-89, of counsel, 1993—; asst. sec. of the Interior for Water and Sci., 1989-93. Bd. dirs. Boulder Sch. Dist. 3, 1951-57; city atty. City of Boulder, 1952-55; gen. counsel Colo. Mcpl. League, 1956-63; counsel No. Colo. Water Conservancy Dist. and mcpl. subdist., 1964-87, spl. counsel, 1987, bd. dirs. dist., 1960-64; legal counsel Colo. Assn. Commerce and Industry. Lt. (j.g.) USNR, 1943-46. Decorated Purple Heart. Fellow Am. Bar. Found., Colo. Bar Found; mem. ABA, Colo. Bar Assn., Boulder County Bar Assn., Denver Bar Assn., Nat. Water Resources Assn. (Colo. dir. 1980-89, pres. 1984-86), Denver Country Club, Denver Club, Mile High Club, Phi Gamma Delta, Phi Beta Kappa. Republican. Episcopalian. Office: Davis Graham & Stubbs PO Box 185 Denver CO 80201-0185

SAYRE, NANCY K., marketing director; b. Southington, Conn., Mar. 19, 1955; d. Edward G. and Adeline (Maher) Kuchta; m. Christopher T. Sayre, May 28, 1988. BS in Chemistry, U. Conn., 1977; cert. Physician Asst., Cornell U., 1979; MA in Healthcare Mktg., U. Denver, 1990. Physician's asst. Cornell Med. Ctr., N.Y.C., 1980-83; clin. editor Surg. Care Publs., N.Y.C., 1981-85; editorial dir. Micromedex Inc., Denver, 1985-89, dir. mktg., 1989—. Author: (chpt.) CD-ROM: The New Papyrus, 1986. Big sister, Big Sisters of Am., Denver, 1990—. Mem. Am. Mktg. Assn., Am. Med. Writers Assn., Colo. Acad. Health Svcs. Mktg., Colo. Assn. Physician Assts. Home: 1380 S Lafayette Denver CO 80210

SBARBARO, JOHN ANTHONY, physician, educator; b. Chgo., Mar. 10, 1936; s. Anthony and Marie (Morici) S.; m. Marlene Ruth Kreiling, Aug. 26, 1961; children: John Andrew, Anthony James, AnneMarie. BA, St. Mary's Coll., Winona, Minn., 1958; MD, John Hopkins U., 1962; MPH, Harvard U., 1968. Diplomate Am. Bd. Preventive Medicine, Am. Coll. Chest Physicians. Dir. Denver Dept. Health, 1969-86; med. dir. Denver Gen. Hosp., 1972-86; v.p. St. Anthony Hosp. Systems, Denver, 1986-90; prof. medicine U. Colo., Denver, 1990—, vice chmn. dept. medicine, also med. dir. Univ. Physicisns, Inc.,; cons. Tb unit WHO, Geneva, 1990, Ctrs. for Disease Control, Atlanta, 1969-89; pres. Colo. Found. for Med. Care, 1993-94. Author books chpts.; contbr. articles to profl. jours. Past bd. dirs. United Way, Denver; nat. rep. Am. Lung Assn. Colo.; mem. adv. com. Elimination Tuberculosis Ctrs. for Disease Control, Air Quality Control Commn., Colo. Statewide Health Coord. Coun., Colo. Front Range Project, Colo. Physicians Coun. Primary Care. Col. USAR, 1983—. Mem. Colo. Med. Soc. (pres. 1990-91), Denver Med. Soc. (pres. 1987-88). Home: 2908 Pierson Way Lakewood CO 80215-7136

SCAFE, LINCOLN ROBERT, JR., sales executive; b. Cleve., July 28, 1922; s. Lincoln Robert and Charlotte (Hawkins) S.; student Cornell U., 1940-41; m. Mary Anne Wilkinson, Nov. 14, 1945; children—Amanda Katharine, Lincoln Robert III. Service mgr. Avery Engring. Co., Cleve., 1946-51; nat. service mgr. Trane Co., LaCrosse, Wis., 1951-57; service and installation mgr. Mech. Equipment Supply Co., Honolulu, 1957-58; chief engr. Sam P. Wallace of Pacific, Honolulu, 1958-62; pres. Air Conditioning Service Co., Inc., Honolulu, 1962-84; sales engr. G.J. Campbell & Assocs., Seattle, 1984-89. Served with USNR, 1942-45; PTO. Mem. ASHRAE, Alpha Delta Phi. Clubs: Cornell Hawaii (past pres.); Outrigger Canoe. Republican. Author tech. service lit. and parts manuals; contbr. articles to trade publs. Home: 10721 SW 112th St Vashon WA 98070-3044 Office: GJ Campbell and Assocs 11613 Rainier Ave S Seattle WA 98178-3945

SCAGLIONE, CECIL FRANK, marketing executive; b. North Bay, Ont., Can., Dec. 2, 1934; came to U.S., 1967, naturalized, 1982; s. Frank and Rose (Aubin) S.; m. Mary Margaret Stewart, Nov. 11, 1954 (div. 1982); children: Cris Ann, Michael Andrew, Patrick Andrew; m. Beverly Louise Rahn, Mar. 25, 1983; student North Bay Coll., 1947-52, Ryerson Tech. Inst., Toronto, Ont., 1955-56, San Diego State U. Inst. World Affairs, 1979. Fin. writer Toronto Telegram, 1955; reporter Sarnia (Ont.) Observer, 1956-57; reporter, editor Kitchener-Waterloo (Ont.) Record, 1957-61; reporter, editor, analyst Windsor (Ont.) Star, 1961-67; writer, editor, photo editor Detroit News, 1967-71; reporter, assoc. bus. editor San Diego Union, 1971-80; mgr. corp. communications Pacific Southwest Airlines, San Diego, 1981-83; sr. v.p. media rels. Berkman & Daniels, Inc., San Diego, 1984-87, prin. Scaglione Mktg. Communications, 1987— prin. Mature Life Features, 1990—, pres.; chmn., chief exec. officer Spl. Info. Svcs., Inc. Mem. adv. coun. SBA, Accredited Pub. Rels. Soc. Am. Recipient award B.F. Goodrich Can., Ltd., 1962, 66, Spl. Achievement award Nat. Assn. Recycling Industries, 1978, award SBA, 1980; Herbert J. Davenport fellow, 1977; Can. Centennial grantee, 1966. Mem. San Diego Press Club (hon. life, past pres.) awards 1978, 80, 84, Airline Editors Forum awards 1982, 83, Soc. Profl. Journalists. Roman Catholic. Founding editor-in-chief Aeromexico mag., 1973; contbr. articles, columns and photographs to various publs. Office: 3911 Kendall St San Diego CA 92109-6130

SCALA-WHITE, MICHELLE DIANE, communications specialist; b. Denver, Mar. 3, 1968; d. Joseph John and Diane Elizabeth (Perry) Scala; m. Darren John White, Sept. 28, 1991. BA in Comm., Mesa State Coll., 1990. Procedures specialist Pace Membership Warehouse Corp. Office, Englewood, Colo., 1991—; mktg. asst. Internat. Llama Assn., Denver, 1992—; writer/typesetter, Aurora, Colo., 1991. Editor newsletter Pacesetter, 1991—, Update, 1991-92; typesetter newsletter Focus, 1991—; author brochure: Helpful Hints, 1992. Recipient Excellence in News Coverage award Colo. Press Assn., 1990. Mem. Soc. Profl. Journalists (Outstanding Grad. in Journalism award 1990). Roman Catholic. Home: 1081 Fulton St Aurora CO 80010 Office: Pace Membership Warehouse 5680 Greenwood Plaza Blvd Englewood CO 80111

SCALBERG, DANIEL ALLEN, history educator; b. Medford, Oreg., Oct. 6, 1952; s. Wilbur Samuel and Martha Pearl (Tremblay) S. BA, So. Oreg. State Coll., 1975; MA, Wheaton (Ill.) Coll., 1977; PhD, U. Oreg., 1990. Instr. Multnomah Bible Coll., Portland, Oreg., 1977-79; teaching fellow U. Oreg., Eugene, 1979-80, asst. prof., 1980-88, assoc. prof., 1988-89, prof., 1990—; vis. prof. U. Oreg., 1990; chmn. gen. edn. dept. Multnomah Bible Coll., 1982-88. Author: Dictionary of Christianity in America, 1989, Fortified Towns in New France, 1989. Can. Embassy fellow, 1986; NEH grantee, 1988, 89. Mem. Western Soc. for French History, Fides et Historia (Conf. on Faith and History), French Colonial Hist. Soc., Am. Hist. Assn., Eagle and Child Reading Club. Evangelical. Office: Multnomah Bible Coll 8435 NE Glisan St Portland OR 97220-5898

SCALISE, FREDERICK WAYNE, environmental consultant; b. Springfield, Mass., Feb. 16, 1954; s. Frederick and Alma Doris (Wood) S.; m. Tamara Jane Pierce, June 21, 1984. BS, Pa. State U., 1976; MS, U. Oreg., 1982; PhD, Wesleyan U., Middletown, Conn., 1987. Cert. hazardous materials mgr. Ind. cons. hazardous materials Springfield, Mass., 1977-80; environ. biologist U. Oreg., Eugene, 1980-82; rsch. fellow, teaching asst. Wesleyan U., Middletown, 1982-86; cons. OMNIS Rsch. Cons., Middletown, 1983-86; pres., sr. cons. OMNICON Environ. Mgmt., Eugene, 1986—. Contbr. articles to profl. jours. Co-founder Associated Lane Emergency Response Teams, Lane County, Oreg., 1988—. Mem. Sigma Xi.

SCANLON, DERALEE ROSE, registered dietition, educator, author; b. Santa Monica, Calif., Aug. 16, 1946; d. Stanley Ralph and Demba (Runkle) S.; m. Alex Spataru, July 20, 1970 (div. 1974). AA, Santa Monica Coll., 1968; accred. med. record tech., East L.A. Coll., 1980; BS, U. Calif., L.A., 1984. Registered Dietitian. V.p. corp. sales, nutrition dir. LIfeTrends Corp., Carlsbad, Calif., 1984-86; dir. media, nutrition Irvine Ranch Farmers Markets, L.A., 1987-88; spokesperson for media Calif. Milk Adv. Bd., San Diego, 1986; nutrition reporter Med-NIWS, L.A., 1990-91; dietitian Sta. ABC-TV The Home Show, L.A., 1991—, Sta. NBC-TV David Horowitz Fight Back, L.A., 1991-92; media spokesperson Lifetime Food Co., Seaside, Calif., 1992—; contbr. writer L A. Parent Mag., Burbank, Calif., 1991—; syndicated nutrition reporter Live N'Well TV Series, Utah, 1992—; nutrition educator Emeritus Coll. Sr. Health, Santa Monica, 1990-92; nutrition lectr. Princess Cruises, L.A., 1987; nutrition video host AMA Campaign Against Cholesterol, 1989; media spokesperson Weight Watchers, 1993. Author: The Wellness Book of IBS, 1989, Diets That Work, 1991, revised edit., 1992, 93; newspaper columnist: Ask The Dietitian, 1990—; contbr. articles to profl. jours. Mem. Dietitians in Bus./Comms. (regional rep. 1990-92, So. Calif. chairperson 1991-92), Am. Dietetic Assn. (pub. rels. chair 1985-87), Calif. Dietetic Assn. (Dietitian of Yr. in Pvt. Practice, Bus. and Comm. 1993), Soc. for Nutrition Edn., Nat. Speakers Assn., AFTRA. Home and Office: 1569 1/2 Manning Ave Los Angeles CA 90024

SCANLON, PATRICK C., material control executive; b. Burbank, Calif., Sept. 25, 1949; s. Charles Edward and Clara Daily (Cook) S.; m. Marianne E. Metcalf, Apr. 14, 1973; children: Stephen, Michael. BA in Mktg. and Fin., Calif. State U., 1972. Sales engr. Litton Med. Products, Santa Fe Springs, Calif., 1972-75; prodn. control specialist Tylan Corp., Torrance, Calif., 1975-80; master scheduler, supr. Westech Gear, Lynwood, Calif., 1980-86; material control mgr. Am. Magnetics, Torrance, 1986-89, Rosemount Analytical, LaHabra, Calif., 1989—. Mem. Am. Prodn. and Inventory Control Soc. Democrat. Home: 16247 Janine Dr Whittier CA 90603 Office: Rosemount Analytical 600 S Harbor Blvd La Habra CA 90631

SCANNELL, WILLIAM EDWARD, aerospace company executive, consultant, educator; b. Muscatine, Iowa, Nov. 11, 1934; s. Mark Edward and Catharine Pearson (Fowler) S.; m. Barbara Ann Hoemann, Nov. 23, 1957; children: Cynthia Kay, Mark Edward, David Jerome, Terri Lynn, Stephen Patrick. BA in Gen. Edn., U. Nebr., 1961; BS in Engring., Ariz. State U., 1966; MS in Systems Engring., So. Meth. U., 1969; PhD, U.S. Internat. U., 1991. Commd. 2d lt. USAF, 1956, advanced through grades to lt. col., 1972; B-47 navigator-bombardier 98th Bomb Wing, Lincoln Air Force Base, Nebr., 1956-63; with Air Force Inst. of Tech., 1963-65, 68-69; chief mgmt. engring. team RAF Bentwaters, England, 1965-68; forward air contr. 20th Tactical Air Support Squadron USAF, Danang, Vietnam, 1970-71; program mgr. Hdqrs. USAF, Washington, 1971-74, staff asst. Office of Sec. Def., 1974-75, ret., 1975; account exec. Merrill Lynch, San Diego, 1975-77; program engring. chief Gen. Dynamics, San Diego, 1977-79, engring. chief, 1979-80, program mgr., 1980-83; mgr. integrated logistics support Northrop Corp., Hawthorne, Calif., 1984-88; mgr. B-2 program planning and scheduling Northrop Corp., Pico Rivera, Calif., 1988-91; pres. Scannell and Assocs., Borrego Springs, Calif., 1991—; mem. adj. faculty U.S. Internat. U., San Diego. Decorated DFC with three oak leaf clusters, Air medal with 11 oak leaf clusters. Mem. APA, Calif. Psychol. Assn., Soc. Indsl. and Orgnl. Psychology, Inst. Indsl. Engrs., Coronado Cays Yacht Club, Psi Chi. Republican. Roman Catholic. Home: PO Box 2392 717 Anza Park Trail Borrego Springs CA 92004 Office: Scannell and Assocs PO Box 2392 Borrego Springs CA 92004

SCARDINO, CHARLES ANTHONY, environmental engineer; b. N.Y.C., Feb. 8, 1949; s. Charles and Jean Scardino; m. Maureen Louisa Wright, May 27, 1984; 1 child, Dmitri Wright. BSCE, Northeastern U., 1972; MS in Pub. Health, U. N.C., 1974. Registered profl. engr., Va., Nev. Sr. air pollution control investigator City of Boston, 1970-71; rschr. on air pollution Northeastern U., Boston, 1972; EPA trainee U. N.C., Chapel Hill, 1973; staff environ. engr. TRW, McLean, Va., 1974-76; sr. environ. engr. Sci. Applications Internat. Corp., Las Vegas, Nev., 1977-92; environ. cons., 1992—; mem. environ. subcom. for high speed rail Transp. Rsch. Bd., NRC, 1990. Mem. Chi Epsilon. Office: 3864 Alice Ln Las Vegas NV 89103

SCATENA, LORRAINE BORBA, rancher, women's rights advocate; b. San Rafael, Calif., Feb. 18, 1924; d. Joseph and Eugenia (Simas) de Borba; m. Louis G. Scatena, Feb. 14, 1960; children: Louis Vincent, Eugenia Gayle. BA, Dominican Coll., San Rafael, 1945; postgrad., Calif. Sch. Fine Arts, 1948, U. Calif., Berkeley, 1956-57. Cert. elem. tchr., Calif. Tchr. Dominican Coll., 1946; tchr. of mentally handicapped San Anselmo (Calif.) Sch. Dist., 1946; tchr. Fairfax (Calif.) Pub. Elem. Sch., 1946-53; asst. to mayor Fairfax City Recreation, 1948-53; tchr., libr. U.S. Dependent Schs., Mainz am Rhine, Fed. Republic Germany, 1953-56; translator Portugal Travel Tours, Lisbon, 1954; bonding sec. Am. Fore Ins. Group, San Francisco, 1958-60; rancher, farmer Yerington, Nev., 1960—; hostess com. Caldecott and Newbury Authors' Awards, San Francisco, 1959; mem. Nev. State Legis. Commn., 1975; coord. Nevadans for Equal Rights Amendment, 1975-78, rural areas rep., 1976-78; testifier Nev. State Senate and Assembly, 1975, 77; mem. adv. com. Fleischmann Coll. Agr. U. Nev., 1977-80, 81-84; speaker Grants and Rsch. Projects, Bishop, Calif., 1977, Choices for Tomorrow's Women, Fallon, Nev., 1989. Trustee Wassuk Coll., Hawthorne, Nev., 1984-87; mem. Lyon County Friends of Libr., Yerington, 1971—, Lyon County Mus. Soc., 1978; sec., pub. info. chmn. Lyon County Rep. Women, 1968-73, v.p. programs, 1973-75; mem. Lyon County Rep. Cen. Com., 1973-74; mem. Marin County Soc. Artists, San Anselmo, Calif., 1948-53; charter mem. Eleanor Roosevelt Fund Women and Girls, 1990, sustaining mem., 1991—; Nev. rep. 1st White House Conf. Rural Am. Women, Washington, 1980; participant internat. reception, Washington, 1980; mem. pub. panel individual presentation Shakespeare's Treatment of Women Characters, Nev. Theatre for the Arts, Ashland, Oreg. Shakespearean Actors local performance, 1977. Recipient Outstanding Conservation Farmer award Mason Valley Conservation Dist., 1992, Soroptimist Internat. Women Helping women award 1983, invitation to first all-women delegation to U.S.A. from People's Republic china, U.S. House Reps., 1979; Public Forum Travel grantee Edn. Title IX, Oakland, Calif., 1977; fellow World Lit. Acad., 1993. Mem. Lyon County Ret. Tchrs. Assn. (unit pres. 1979-80, 84-86, v.p. 1986-88, Nev. div. Outstanding Svc. award 1981, state conv. gen. chmn. 1985), Rural Am. Women Inc., AAUW (br. pres. 1972-74, 74-76, edn. found. programs, 1983—, state convention gen. chmn. 1976, 87, state div. sec. 1970-72, state div. legis. program chmn. 1976-77, state div. chmn. internat. rels. 1979-81, state div. pres. 1981-83, br. travelship, discovering women in U.S. history Radcliffe Coll. Div. Humanities award 1975, Future Fund Nat. award 1983), Mason Valley Country Club, Italian Cath. Fedn. Club (pres. 1986-88), Uniao Portuguesa Estado da Calif. Roman Catholic. Home: 1275 Hwy 208 Yerington NV 89447

SCAVO, FRANK JAMES, scientist; b. Syracuse, N.Y., Mar. 5, 1959; s. Frank Patrick and Mary Rose (Susco) S.; m. Katherine Theresia Law, Apr. 13, 1986; children: Frank Anthony, Veronica Marie. BS, Rensselaer Poly. Inst., Troy, N.Y., 1981; MS, San Diego State U., 1985, U. Calif.-San Diego, 1990. Mem. tech. staff Hughes Aircraft Co., Culver City, Calif., 1981-83; scientist Mission Rsch. Corp., San Diego, 1985-86; sr. scientist Sci. Applications Internat. Corp., San Diego, 1987-91, McDonnell Douglas Technologies, Inc., San Diego, 1991—; chief engr. Scavo Engring., Lemon Grove, Calif., 1990—. Contbr. articles to profl. jours. N.Y. State Regent's Scholar, 1977. Mem. Soc. Photo-Optical Instrumentation Engrs., Optical Soc. Am. Home: 2230 St Croix Ct Lemon Grove CA 91945-3509 Office: McDonnell Douglas Technologies Inc 16761 Via Del Campo Ct San Diego CA 92127

SCHAAF, MIV, writer, business owner. Student, HSU. Columnist L.A. Times, 1972-87; owner Miv Schaaf Assocs., 1954—; seminar tchr. UCLA, U. Calif. Irvine, Scripps Coll., 1977—; del. White House Conf. Librs., 1979; judge Robert B. Campbell book collection UCLA, 1980; speaker in field. Author: Who Can Not Read About Crocodiles, 1988; Calif. State Libr. Found. writer North Coast Jour., 1993—. Pres. Archtl. Panel, L.A., 1951-59; founder Pasadena Cultural Heritage Commn., 1973; cello player Humboldt Symphony. Recipient Premier award Pasadena Heritage, 1977, Met. Coop. Libr. System and Calif. Libr. Assn. award, 1982, Gold Crown award Pasadena Arts Coun., 1983. Home: 83 Wilson Ln Fieldbrook CA 95521

SCHAAFSMA, CURTIS FORREST, archaeologist; b. Vallejo, Calif., Jan. 22, 1938; s. Harold Fye Schaafsma and Gertrude Alpha (Iverson) Offutt; m. Polly Avis Dix, Sept. 28, 1958; children: Hoski, Pieter. BA, U. Colo., 1962; MA, U. N.Mex., 1971. Archaeologist Ft. Burgwin Rsch. Ctr., Taos, N.Mex., 1964-65; park ranger U.S. Nat. Park Svc., Kayenta, Ariz., 1966; archaeologist U. Utah, Salt Lake City, 1970, State Planning Office, Santa Fe, 1971, MAPCO, Inc., Tulsa, 1972-73; survey archaeologist Colo. State Archaeologist, Boulder, 1974, U. N.Mex., Albuquerque, 1972; rsch. archaeologist Sch. Am. Rsch., Santa Fe, 1974-79; state archaeologist Mus. N.Mex., Santa Fe, 1979-92, curator anthropology, 1992—. With USN, 1956-58. Mem. Am. Soc. Conservation Archaeology (pres. 1984-88), Soc. Am. Archaeology, Nat. Assn. State Archaeologists (sec., treas. 1979-81), Archaeol. Soc. N.Mex. (bd. dirs. 1979—), N.Mex. Archaeol. Coun., N.Mex. Assn. Mus. Office: Mus NMex PO Box 2087 Santa Fe NM 87504-2087

SCHABER, DOUGLAS CRAIG, cardiologist, educator; b. Wheeling, W.Va., Feb. 7, 1950; s. Henry Herman and Dorothy Mae (Anderson) S.; children: Dustin, Megan. BS, Bethany (W.Va.) Coll., 1972; DO in Osteopathy, W.Va. Sch. Osteo. Medicine, 1978. ACLS, ATLS. Intern Detroit Osteo. Hosp., 1978-79; cardiology fellow Cleve. Clinic Found., 1981-82, 83-85; emergency room physician Doctors Svcs., Inc., Cleve., 1981; staff physician, emergency room Emergency Care, Inc., Cleve., 1982-83; flight physician Metro Life Flight/Metro Gen. Hosp., Cleve., 1984-85; invasive cardiologist Cardiology Cons., Tucson, 1985—; dir. med. edn. Tucson Gen. Hosp., 1986—; bd. dirs. Acad. Osteo. Dirs. of Med. Edn.; clin. instr. emergency medicine, Case Western Res. U., 1984-86; asst. prof. medicine, Coll. Osteo. Medicine of the Pacific, Pomona, Calif., 1986—; assoc. prof. medicine, Kirksville (Mo.) Coll. Osteo. Medicine, 1987—. Contbr. articles to profl. jours. Lt. col. USPHS, 1979-81. Mem. Am. Osteo. Assn., Ariz. Osteo. Med. Assn. Office: Cardiology Cons 3801 N Campbell Ave # E Tucson AZ 85719-1453

SCHABERG, BEN FRANKLIN, mining company executive; b. St. Louis, Sept. 11, 1916; s. Ben F. and Alice E. (Glass) S.; m. Helen M. Dorn, Dec. 28, 1948 (div. Sept. 1975); children: John, Jill, Linda, Grace; m. Harriett N. Schaberg, Aug. 22, 1980. BS in Econ. Geology and Geography, U. Mo., 1936. Prof. econ. geography and phys. edn., athletic coach Nat. U. China, Beijing, 1936-41; chief China div. Office Lend Lease Adminstrn., Washington, 1941-45; v.p. sales and trade devel. William Hunt & Co., Inc., N.Y.C., 1945-48; gen. mgr. Lawrence Johnson & Co., Phila., 1948-52; fgn. trade cons. Pennsalt Internat. Corp., Phila., 1952-56; export mgr. for Robbins Floor Products, Inc., Ben F. Schaberg Co., 1952-62; agt. Oglebay Norton Co., 1956-62; sales and raw material sources developer Kerschner Marshall & Co., Pitts., 1962-67; ind. broker ores and dminerals Seaforth Ore andd Mineral Co., Cleve., 1967-73; dir. numerous mining projects Ben F. Schaberg Inc./Mission Mining, various, 1973-84; pres. Mission Mining Inc., Las Cruces, N.Mex., 1984—; mem. Am.-Can. strategic minerals del. to South African Inst. Mining and Metallurgy, 1983. Home: 2055 San Acacio Las Cruces NM 88001 Office: Mission Mining Inc Box 455 Las Cruces NM 88004

SCHABOW, JOHN WILLIAM, accountant; b. Chgo., Mar. 30, 1937; s. William John and Mary V. (Brink) S.; m. Gail P. Ekren, Oct. 17, 1959; children: Robin, John R. Student, Davis Elkins Coll., 1955-58, Ariz. State U., 1972-74. Accredited tax advisor Accreditation Coun. for Accountancy & Taxation. Cost clk. G.D. Searle, Skokie, Ill., 1958-60; acct. Sugarcreek Foods, Chgo., 1960-63, Arlington Park Rack Track, Chgo., 1963-65, G. Heiss & Assocs., Chgo., 1965-69, Murray & Murray CPA's, Phoenix, 1969-70, Wm. R. Schulz & Assocs., Phoenix, 1970-73; pres., owner John W. Schabow, Ltd., Phoenix, 1973—; registered rep. H.D. Vest Investment Securities, Inc., Phoenix, 1985—, adv. bd. dirs. Mem. editorial adv. bd. Accounting Today, 1993—. Bd. dirs. Inst. for Partially Sighted, Phoenix, 1986-87. Served with U.S. Army, 1961-62. Mem. Ariz. Soc. Practicing Accts. (pres. 1987-88, co-founder), Nat. Soc. Pub. Accts. (state dir. 1983-87, bd. govs. 1988-92), Internat. Assn. Fin. Planners. Republican. Lutheran. Home: 4440 W Bluefield Ave Glendale AZ 85308-1613 Office: 11725 N 19th Ave Phoenix AZ 85029-3500

SCHACHMAN, HOWARD KAPNEK, molecular biologist, educator; b. Phila., Dec. 5, 1918; s. Morris H. and Rose (Kapnek) S.; m. Ethel H. Lazarus, Oct. 20, 1945; children—Marc, David. BSChemE, Mass. Inst. Tech., 1939; PhD in Phys. Chemistry, Princeton, 1948; DSc (hon.), Northwestern U., 1974; MD (hon.), U. Naples, 1990. Fellow NIH, 1946-48; instr., asst. prof. U. Calif., Berkeley, 1948-54, assoc. prof. biochemistry, 1954-59, prof. biochemistry and molecular biology, 1959-91; prof. emeritus, dept. molecular and cell biology U. Calif. at Berkeley, 1991—; chmn. dept. molecular biology, dir. virus lab. U. Calif., Berkeley, 1969-76, prof. emeritus, 1991—; mem. sci. coun. and sci. adv. bd. Stazione Zoologica, Naples, Italy, 1988—; cons. bd. sci. Meml. Sloan-Kettering Cancer Ctr., 1988—; mem. sci. adv. com. Rsch.! Am., 1990—; William Lloyd Evans lectr. Ohio State U., 1988. Author: Ultracentrifugation in Biochemistry, 1959. Mem. bd. sci. counselors Cancer Biology and Diagnosis div. Nat. Cancer Inst., 1989-92. Served from ensign to lt. USNR, 1945-47. Recipient John Scott award, 1964, Warren Triennial prize Mass. Gen. Hosp., 1965, Alexander von Humboldt award, 1990, Berkeley citation for disting. achievement and notable svc. U. Calif., 1993; Guggenheim Meml. fellow, 1956. Mem. AAAS, NAS (chmn. biochemistry sect. 1990-93, mem. panel on sci. responsibility and conduct of rsch. 1990-92), Am. Chem. Soc. (recipient award in chem. instrumentation 1962, Calif. sect. award 1958), Am. Soc. Biochemistry and Molecular Biology (pres. 1987-88, chmn. pub. affairs com. 1989-92, Merck award 1986), Am. Acad. Arts and Scis., Fedn. Am. Socs. for Exptl. Biology (pres. 1988-89), Sigma Xi. Office: U Calif Dept Molecular and Cell Biology Wendell M Stanley Hall Rm 229 Berkeley CA 94720

SCHACHT, CATHERINE ANN, classical violinist; b. Racine, Wis., Feb. 3, 1950; d. Wallis August and Doris (Carlson) S. MusB cum laude, U. N.Mex., 1983. chamber music coach Elder Hostel, Jemez Springs, N.Mex., 1991—; music faculty orch. and chorus Hummingbird Music Camp, Jemez Springs, 1991-92. Composer: (art song) Once in a Song, 1991, (choral) Prayer for Choristers, 1991, (chant) Eagle Poem, 1992; violinist with N.Mex. Symphony, Albuquerque, 1978-89, Opera Southwest, Albuquerque, 1982-89, San Juan Symphony, Durango, Colo., 1987—, Santa Fe (N.Mex.) Symphony, 1990—, New S.W. Symphony, Albuquerque, 1992, others; singer with N.Mex. Symphony Chorus, 1990-91, Santa Fe Symphony Chorus, 1991-92, others; alto soloist midnight mass Santa Fe Symphony Charpentier, 1992. Organist, pianist Rio Rancho Presbyn. Ch.; violinist Terzetto String Trio; singer, guitarist Desert Song. Mem. Am. Fedn. Musicians (sec. 1988-90), Chamber Music Am. Democrat. Home: 3939 Rio Grande NW Albuquerque NM 87107

SCHACHTER, BONNIE LYNN, publisher; b. Flushing, N.Y., Oct. 20, 1952; d. Irving Schachter and Yetta Wells. BA, Queens Coll., 1974. Pres. Multi-ling Tours, Ltd., Boston, 1976-77; owner Breakfast From Tiffany's, N.Y.C., Rent-An-Event, N.Y.C.; pres. Informative Amenities, Santa Monica, Calif., 1984—. Pub.: (jours.) Full Life Srs., Full Life Mens, Full LIfe Womens, Personal Fin. Jour., Pet Passport, All About Me (children's health jour.). Mem. Med. Mktg. Assn., Am. Mgmt. Assn., Promotion Mktg. Assn. Am., Fin. Women Internat. Office: Informative Amenities PO Box 1280 Santa Monica CA 90406

SCHACHTER, JAMES ROBERT, newspaper editor; b. Glendale, Calif., July 20, 1959; s. Stanley Herman and Margot (Lipiner) S.; m. Pamela Haag, May 19, 1985; children: Ariel Shira, Miriam Rachel. BA, Columbia U., 1980. Reporter Jacksonville (Fla.) Jour., 1980-82; reporter Kansas City (Mo.) Star, 1982-84, labor writer, 1984-85; reporter L.A. Times, San Diego, 1985-87; bus. writer L.A. Times, L.A., 1987-90, asst. bus. editor, 1990-93, Sunday bus. editor, 1993—. Recipient Bus. and Fin. Journalism award John Hancock Ins. Co., 1988, Best News Article award San Diego Press Club, 1987, Best Local News Reporting award Inland Daily Press Assn., Chgo., 1984. Mem. Investigative Reporters and Editors. Office: L A Times Times Mirror Sq Los Angeles CA 90053

SCHAD, CLAYTON LEWIS, newspaper publisher; b. Winston Salem, N.C., Aug. 27, 1952; s. Virgal Leonard and Floe Mary (Beam) S.; m. Lurinda Gail Stonoff, Mar. 17, 1984; children: Ashley, Jeremy. BA, U. Nebr., 1976. Editor Valley Newspapers, Inc., Phoenix, 1977-79; pub. Ahwatukee Foothills News, Phoenix, 1979—. Mem. Ariz. Newspaper Assn. Methodist. Office: Ahwatukee Foothills News 9831 S 51st St Ste C-116 Phoenix AZ 85044

SCHADE, GEORGE HENRY, obstetrician-gynecologist; b. Pitts., Apr. 20, 1936; s. George Henry and Jane (Welty) S.; m. Janice Cooley, Aug. 23, 1958; children: Jim, Ann, Kristin. BS in Chemistry, MIT, 1958; MD, U. Pitts., 1962. Diplomate Am. Bd. Ob-gyn.; lic. MD, Ariz., Pa., Ohio. Internship McKeesport (Pa.) Hosp., 1962-63; residency Good Samaritan Hosp., Phoenix, 1965-68; ob-gyn. pvt. practice Phoenix, 1968—; clin. instr. gynecology Maricopa Med. Ctr., 1968-84, Phoenix Bapt. Hosp., 1982-86; staff various hosps. Mem. Am. Fertility Soc., Am. Soc. for Coposocopy & Colpomicroscopy, Am. Soc. Gynecol. Laparoscopists, AAAS, Maricopa County Med. Soc., Ariz. Med. Soc., AMA. Am. Coll. Ob-Gyns. Office: George H Schade MD PC 50 E Dunlap Ave Phoenix AZ 85020-2877

SCHAEF, ANNE WILSON, writer; b. Siloam Springs, Ark., Mar. 22, 1934; d. Virgil Eustace and Manilla (Longan) Willey; m. Paul Wilson; 1 child, Beth Anne; m. Robert Schaef; 1 child, Rodney Walter. AB in psychology, Washington U., St. Louis, 1956, MA; PhD, Union Inst., 1986; HHD (hon.), Kenyon Coll., 1992. Pvt. practice psychologist Mo., Ill., 1960-68; pvt. practice psychotherapist Colo., 1968-84; pres. Wilson-Schaef Assoc., Boulder, Colo., 1984—; cons. drug & alcohol treatment ctrs., co-dependency treatment ctrs.; adj faculty San Francisco Theol. Sem.; lectr. in field. Author: Women's Reality, 1981, Co-dependence: Misunderstood/Mistreated, 1986, When Society Becomes an Addict, 1987, Escape From Intimacy/Untangling the Love Addictions: Sex, Romance, Relationships, 1989, Meditations for Women Who Do Too Much, 1990, Laugh, I Thought I'd Die... If I Didn't, 1990; Author: (with D. Fassel) The Addictive Organization, 1988, Beyond Therapy, Beyond Science: A New Model for Healing the Whole Person, 1992. Nat. Honor fellow Washington U., Danforth Grad. fellow, Danforth Spl. fellow, NIMH fellow; Spl. grantee Union Theol. Sem. Office: Wilson-Schaef Assoc Inc PO Box 18686 Boulder CO 80308

SCHAEFER, CHARLES ANDREW, psychologist; b. Norfolk, Va., Nov. 10, 1958; s. Thomas Aquinas and Nancy (Gallup) S. BS in Physics, Rensselaer Poly. Inst., Troy, N.Y., 1980; MSEE, Rensselaer Poly. Inst., 1981; MA in Theology, Fuller Theol. Sem., Pasadena, 1991; PhD in Clin. Psychology, Fuller Theol. Sem., 1992. Computer ctr. dir. Wycliffe Bible Translators, Togo, West Africa, 1984-85; sr. assoc. engr./scientist IBM, Burlington, Vt., 1981-87; computer cons. Pasadena, 1988—; psychological asst. Sacramento, Calif., 1992—; chmn. Enabling the Missionary Orgn., Pasadena, 1989-91; teaching asst. Wycliffe Quest Program, N.Z., 1989, 90; program asst. Personal Effectiveness Enhancement Quest, Angelus Oaks, Calif., 1988. Contbr. articles to profl. jours.; patentee in field. Youth leader Jericho Congl. Ch., Vt., 1983-87. With USCG, 1976-78. Recipient Clare W. Headinton Meml. award Fuller Theol. Sem., 1990, Lee Edward Travis award, 1990, 92, Delano M. Goehner Meml. award, 1992; John Stauffer fellow, 1991. Mem. APA, Western Psychol. Assn. Home: 6151 Shadow Ln Apt 132 Citrus Heights CA 95621

SCHAEFER, DAN L., congressman; b. Gutenberg, Iowa, Jan. 25, 1936; s. Alvin L. and Evelyn (Everson) S.; m. Mary Margaret Lenney, 1959; children: Danny, Darren, Joel, Jennifer. B.A., Niagara U., 1961, LLD (hon.), 1986; postgrad., Potsdam State U., 1961-64. Pub. relations cons., 1967-83; mem. Colo. Gen. Assembly, 1977-78; mem. Colo. Senate, 1979-83, pres. pro tem, 1981-82, majority whip, 1983; mem. 98th-103rd Congresses from 6th dist. Colo., Washington, 1983—; mem. house small bus. com., 1983, govt. ops. com., 1983, energy and commerce com., 1984-86 (subcom. on fossil and synthetic fuels; commerce, transp. and tourism; oversight/investigations), environ. and energy study com., 1987-90 (subcoms. on Transp. and Hazardous materials, Telecom. and Fin.), Energy and Commerce ranking Rep Oversight and Investigations, 1993—, Rep. study com.; mem. house sci. and high tech. task force, mil. reforms caucus, congl. grace caucus; mem. adv. com., com. of concern for Soviet Jewry. Pres. Foothills Recreation Bd., 1973-76; sec. Jefferson County Republican Party, Colo., 1975-76. Served with USMCR, 1955-57. Recipient Colo. Park and Recreation citation, 1976; named Elected Ofcl. of Yr., Lakewood/South Jeffco C. of C., 1986, 88, 90, Leadership award U.S. Congl. Adv. Bd., Am. Security Coun. Found.; Taxpayers Best Friend award Nat. Taxpayer's Union, 1985-86, 88, 90, 91, Golden Bulldog award Watchdog of Treasury, 1985-86, 86-87, 87-88, 88-89, 89-90, 91-92. Mem. C. of C., Beta Theta Pi. Roman Catholic. Lodge: Rotary. Office: House of Representatives 2448 Rayburn House Office Bldg Washington DC 20515*

SCHAEFER, GEORGE LOUIS, theatrical producer and director, educator; b. Wallingford, Conn., Dec. 16, 1920; s. Louis and Elsie (Otterbein) S.; m. Mildred Trares, Feb. 5, 1954. BA magna cum laude, Lafayette Coll., 1941, LittD, 1963; postgrad., Yale Drama Sch., 1942; LHD, Coker Coll., 1973. Producer, dir. TV series Hallmark Hall of Fame, 1955-68; freelance producer, dir., 1945—; assoc. dean sch. theater, film and TV UCLA, 1986-91; artistic dir. N.Y.C. Ctr. Theatre Co., 1949-52; dir. Dallas State Fair Musicals, 1952-58; pres. Compass Prodns., Inc., 1959-86. Dir. Broadway prodns. G.I. Hamlet, 1945, Man and Superman, 1947, The Linden Tree, 1948, The Heiress (revival), 1949, Idiot's Delight (revival), 1950, Southwest Corner, 1955, The Apple Cart, 1956, The Body Beautiful, 1958, Write Me a Murder, 1961, The Great Indoors, 1966, The Last of Mrs. Lincoln, 1972, Mixed Couples, 1980; co-producer Broadway and London prodns. The Teahouse of the August Moon, 1953; dir., co-producer Zenda for Los Angeles Civic Light Opera Co., 1963; producer To Broadway with Love for N.Y. World's Fair, 1964; producer, dir. TV spls. Do Not Go Gentle into That Good Night, 1967, A War of Children, Sandburg's Lincoln, 1974-76, In This House of Brede, 1975, Truman at Potsdam, Amelia Earhart, 1976, Our Town, 1977, First You Cry, Orchard Children, 1978, Blind Ambition, Mayflower, 1979, The Bunker, 1981, Jean Harris Trial, 1982, A Piano for Mrs. Cimino, 1982, Deadly Game, 1983, Answers, 1983, Right of Way, 1983, Children in the Crossfire, 1984, Stone Pillow, 1985, Mrs. Delafield Wants to Marry , 1986, Laura Lansing Slept Here, 1988, Let Me Hear You Whisper, 1990, The Man Upstairs, 1992; dir. films An Enemy of the People, Generation, Doctor's Wives, Pendulum, Macbeth; dir. Los Angeles prodn. Leave It To Jane, 1987. Mem. Nat. Council on the Arts, 1983-88. Recipient Emmy awards, 1959, 60, 61, 68, 73, Dirs. Guild Am. TV awards, 1961, 64, 67, 68, Dinneen award Nat. Cath. Theatre Conf., 1964; named Dir. of Yr. Radio-TV Daily, 1957, 60, 63, 65. Mem. Dirs. Guild Am. (v.p. 1961-79, pres. 1979-81), Phi Beta Kappa.

SCHAEFER, RICHARD ALAN, cardiologist; b. Corpus Christi, Tex., Sept. 27, 1943; s. Orvine Herbert and Ruth Louise (Bolken) S.; m. Janet Louise Shearer, May 15, 1966 (div. July 1978); children: Christopher, David; m. Sharon Lee McClure, June 19, 1982. BA, Stanford U., 1965; MD, U. Rochester, 1969. Diplomate Am. Bd. Internal Medicine and Cardiology. Intern medicine Strong Meml. Hosp., Rochester, N.Y., 1969-70, resident medicine, 1970-71; resident medicine Health Sci. Ctr. U. Oreg., Portland, 1971-72, fellow in cardiology, 1972-74; cardiologist Cardiology Cons., Medford, Oreg., 1974—. Contbr. articles to profl. jours. Bd. dirs. Rogue Valley YMCA, Medford, 1980-88. Mem. AMA, Oreg. Med. Assn. (exec. com. 1974—), N.W. Soc. Internal Medicine, Am. Coll. Cardiology (pres. Oreg. state chpt. 1992—). Home: 4288 E Barnett Rd Medford OR 97504 Office: Cardiology Cons 520 Medical Ctr Medford OR 97504

SCHAEFER, (ALBERT) RUSSELL, physicist; b. Oklahoma City, Oct. 13, 1944; s. Albert R. and Marcella (Russell) S.; m. Judith Ann Bracewell, Jan. 19, 1968; children: Amy M., Brandon M. BS in Physics, U. Okla., 1966, PhD in Atomic and Molecular Physics, 1970. Physicist Nat. Bur. Standards, Washington, 1970-86; chief scientist Western Rsch. Corp., San Diego, 1986-87; sr. scientist Sci. Applications Internat. Corp., San Diego, 1987—; adj. prof. physics Montgomery Coll., Rockville, Md., 1974-86; presenter in field. Contbr. articles to profl. jours. Co-founder, bd. dirs. Greater Laytonville (Md.) Civic Assn., 1975. Recipient Bronze medal U.S. Dept. Commerce, 1981; NSF fellow, 1966-70. Mem. Soc. Photo-Optical Instrumentation Engrs., Optical Soc. Am. (teller com. 1976), Phi Beta Kappa, Sigma Xi. Methodist. Office: Sci Application Internat 4161 Campus Point Ct San Diego CA 92121

SCHAEFFER, GARY N., mayor; b. York, Pa., May 8, 1948; s. Calvin William and Jane Rae (Desenberg) R.; m. Katherine Lyn Dowler, June 22, 1968; children: Andrew, Ryan. BS, York Coll. of Pa., 1973. Tchr. Upper Adams Sch. Dist., Biglerville, Pa., 1974-75, Dallastown (Pa.) Area Schs., 1975-79, Laramie County Sch. Dist., Cheyenne, Wyo., 1982-89; owner Auto Hosp., Cheyenne, 1979-82; mayor City of Cheyenne, 1989—. Author: Eat your Heart Out, 1979. Sgt. USAF, 1967-71. Mem. Cheyenne C. of C. (bd. dirs. 1989—), Leads (bd. dirs. 1989—), VFW, Am. Legion, Amvets, U.S. Conf. of Mayors (chmn. subcom. on water 1990). Home: 418 Lafayette Blvd Cheyenne WY 82009-2015 Office: City of Cheyenne 2101 O'Neil Ave Cheyenne WY 82001

SCHAEFFER, LEONARD DAVID, health care insurance executive; b. Chicago, Ill., July 28, 1945; s. David and Sarah (Levin) S.; m. Pamela Lee Sidford, Aug. 11, 1968; children: David, Jacqueline. BA, Princeton U., 1969. Mgmt. cons. Arthur Andersen & Co., 1969-73; dep. dir. mgmt. Ill. Mental Health/Devel. Disability, Springfield, 1973-75; dir. Ill. Bur. of Budget, Springfield, 1975-76; v.p. Citibank, N.A., N.Y.C., 1976-78; asst. sec. mgmt. and budget Health Care Financing Adminstr., Washington, 1978; adminstr. HCFA HHS, Washington, 1978-80; exec. v.p., COO Student Loan Mktg. Assn., Washington, 1980-82; pres., CEO Group Health, Inc., Mpls., 1983-86; chmn., CEO Blue Cross of Calif., Woodland Hills, 1986—, WellPoint Health Networks Inc., 1993—; bd. dirs. Tokos Med. Corp., Santa Ana; mem. Calif. Dept. Corps. Health Care Svc, Plan Adv. Com., 1992; bd. councilors U. So. Calif. Sch. Pub. Adminstrn., 1988—; bd. dirs., exec. com. Blue Cross/Blue Shield Assn., Chgo., 1986—; mem. Pew Health Professions Com., Phila., 1990—; mem. Congl. Prospective Payment Assessment Commn., 1987—; chmn. bd. trustees Nat. Health Found., L.A., 1992. Mem. editorial adv. bd. Managed Healthcare, 1989—. Bd. dirs. Valley Industry and Commerce, Woodland Hills, Calif., 1987—, The Cultural Found., Woodland Hills, 1987—; bd. govs. Town Hall of Calif., L.A., 1989—. Kellogg Found. fellow, 1981-89, King's Fund Coll., London, 1990; recipient Citation/Outstanding Svc., Am. Acad. Pediatrics, 1981, Corp. Social Responsibility award U. Calif., Berkeley, 1987, Disting. Pub. Svc. award HEW, Washington, 1980, Leadership in Health Affairs award Hosp. Coun. So. Calif., 1992. Mem. Cosmos Club, Princeton Club, Banker's Club San Francisco, Regency Club. Office: Blue Cross of Calif 21555 Oxnard St Woodland Hills CA 91367

SCHAEFFER, MONICA CLARE, nutrition scientist; b. St. Louis, Jan. 5, 1951; d. George Washington and Rita Ann (Mulhern) S.; m. Donald Bernard Hunt, May 10, 1987; 1 child, Timothy Carl. BA in Philosophy, St. Louis U., 1972; MPH in Nutrition, U. Mich., 1977; PhD in Nutrition, U. Calif., Davis, 1984. Rsch. nutrition scientist Western Human Nutrition Rsch. Ctr., Agrl. Rsch. Svc., USDA, San Francisco, 1984—. Contbr. articles to sci. publs. Anita S. Miller fellow AAUW, 1982, Jastro-Shields Nutrition fellow U. Calif., 1981. Mem. Am. Inst. Nutrition, Sigma Xi. Office: WHNRC USDA PO Box 29997 San Francisco CA 94129

SCHAEFFER, PETER MORITZ-FRIEDRICH, literature educator; b. Breslau, Germany, May 14, 1930; came to U.S., 1939; s. Rudolf Franz and Katharina (Krebs) S.; m. Brigitte Ehrler, Sept. 4, 1968. Lic. Theol., U. Ottawa, Ont., Can., 1959; PhD, Princeton U., 1971. Asst. prof. Princeton (N.J.) U., 1970-74; vis. lectr. U. Calif., Berkeley, 1974-76; assoc. prof. U. Calif., Davis, 1976-83, prof. German and comparative lit., 1983—. Editor, translator: De poetica (Vadianus), 1973-77, Aethiopica (Heliodor), 1984, Two Poems (Hans Sachs), 1990, De curriculo (Hoffmanswaldau), 1992. Grantee NEH, 1989, 91, 93. Mem. 16th Century Soc., Erasmus of Rotterdam Soc., Amis de la Bibliotheque Humaniste. Democrat. Jewish. Home: 1101 Alice St Davis CA 95616 Office: Dept German Univ Calif Davis CA 95616

SCHAEFFER, REINER HORST, air force officer, retired librarian, foreign language professional; b. Berlin, Lichterfelde, Fed. Republic Germany, Jan. 13, 1938; came to U.S., 1958; s. Immanuel Emil and Wilhelmine (Fahrni) Frei-S.; m. Cathy Anne Cormack, Apr. 6, 1966; 1 child, Brian Reiner. Nat. Cert., Bus. Sch., Thun, Switzerland, 1957; B.G.S. in Bus., U. Nebr., 1970; M.P.A. in Orgnl. Behavior, U. Mo., 1972; Ph.D. in Fgn. Lang. Edn., Ohio State U., 1979. Commd. officer USAF, 1958, advanced through grades to lt. col.; instr. German, French USAF Acad., Colorado Springs, Colo., 1975-77, assoc. prof., 1979-81, chmn. German, 1981, dir. librs., 1982-86, prof., 1986-92, dir. Acad. Librs., 1986—. Mem. People to People, Colorado Springs; bd. dirs. Friends of AF Acad. Librs. Named Disting. Grad. Air Force Inst. Tech, Wright-Patterson AFB, Ohio, 1979; recipient 5 Meritorious Service medals, 5 Air Force Commendation medals. Mem. Am. Assn. Tchrs. of German, Swiss Club (pres. Colorado Springs chpt. 1990—, chmn. Lewis Palmer High Sch. accountability com.), Pi Alpha Alpha, Alpha Sigma Alpha. Republican. Home: 515 Celtic Ct Colorado Springs CO 80921-1807 Office: Fgn Lang Ctr LLC 733 N Tejon St Colorado Springs CO 80903

SCHAFFER, ARTHUR FREDERICK, JR., lawyer; b. Bethlehem, Pa., Aug. 26, 1931; s. Arthur Frederick Schaffer and Jane Williams Billiard; children: Stephen, Elizabeth, Samara, Molly. BA in Internat. Rels., Lehigh U., 1956; JD, Ariz. State U., 1978. Sales rep./mktg. U.S. Steel Corp., Pitts. and N.Y.C., 1956-69; ptnr. Crichton & Co., N.Y.C., 1969-72; registered rep. Bache & Co., Phoenix, 1972-75; atty. Furth, Fahrner, Bluemle & Mason, Phoenix, 1976-80; atty., owner A.F. Schaffer & Assocs., P.C., Phoenix, 1981-91; atty., ptnr. Lerch, Schaffer, Mack & Henry, Phoenix, 1991—; pres. Real Estate Securities and Syndicate Inst., Phoenix, 1987-91. Mem. Phoenix Bond Adv. Com., 1981-82. sgt. lt. U.S. Army, 1949-52. Decorated Bronze Star for Valor (2), Combat Inf. badge. Mem. ABA, Ariz. State Bar Assn. (securities law coun. 1990—), Nat. Assn. Securities Dealers, Bd. Arbitrators. Republican. Presbyterian. Home: 2921 E Keim Dr Phoenix AZ 85016 Office: Lerch Shaffer et al 3300 N Central Ave # 2320 Phoenix AZ 85012

SCHAFFER, GREGORY LYNN, electronics executive; b. Glendale, Calif., Apr. 2, 1943; s. Francis Matthias and Lorraine Martha S.; m. Susan Mitchell Thackeray, Dec. 28, 1968. BSEE, MIT, 1965; MSEE, U. Calif., Berkeley, 1969; MS in Computer Sci., U. Ariz., 1971, secondary tchg. credentials in math, sci, 1966. Scientist NASA, Mountain View, Calif., 1966-69; design engr. Burr-Brown Rsch. Corp., Tucson, 1971-73; sr. design engr. Dana Labs., Irvine, Calif., 1973-75; staff engr. Doric Scientific, San Diego, 1975-81; I.C. design engr. Telmos, Inc., Sunnyvale, Calif., 1981-84; sr. IC design engr. Sierra Semiconductor, Milpitas, Calif., 1985-86; dir. I.C. design devel. Maxim Integrated Products, Sunnyvale, Calif., 1986 --; panelist Internat. Solid State Circuits Conf., 1984, 1990. Patentee 6 patents; contbr. articles to profl. jours. Active Trail Adv. Coun., Los Altos, CAlif., 1989-90; trail construction The Tra il Ctr, Los Altos, 1984-90; cons. Santa Clara County Parks and Recreation, San Jose, Calif., 1990. Recipient Harold E. Lobdell Disting. Svc. award MIT, 1979. Mem. IEEE, Sigma Xi.

SCHAFFER, JEFFREY LEE, non-profit organization executive; b. L.A., Oct. 28, 1958; s. Mervin Bernard and Zena Harriet (Lindsay) S.; m. Reina Maria Alonso, Sept. 9, 1989; 1 child, Philip Santos. BA, U. Calif., Berkeley, 1980; MPA, U. So. Calif., 1987. Field rep. Office Congressman A.C. Beilenson, Washington, L.A., 1980-82; mcpl. devel. advisor Peace Corps, Kosrae, Ea. Caroline Islands, 1982-84; staff asst. CARE, Washington, 1985; rsch. asst. Office Treasurer, State of Calif., Sacramento, 1986; account exec. Braun & Co., L.A., 1986-89; assoc. dir. Shelter Partnership, L.A., 1989—. Editor Homeless Reporter newsletter, 1989-90; exec. prodr. video Neighbors in Need, 1990. Group leader Operation Crossroads Africa, Kithumula Kenya, 1986; bd. dirs. Friends of Coro, L.A., 1990-91, Los Angeles Countywide Coalition for Homeless, L.A., 1991—; pres., bd. dirs. Peace Corps Svc. Coun., L.A., 1990-91; mem. met. bd. Jewish Fedn. Coun., L.A., 1990-92; participant New Leaders Project, L.A., 1992; chmn. Ams. with Disabilities Act com. L.A. Emergency Food and Shelter Local Bd., 1992—. Mem. U. Calif. Alumni Assn., UCLA Internship Assn., Friends of Micronesia, Sigma Delta Pi (life). Democrat. Office: Shelter Partnership 1010 S Flower Ste 400 Los Angeles CA 90015

SCHAFFER, JOEL LANCE, dentist; b. Bklyn., Oct. 18, 1945; s. Martin Alter and Irene Natalie (Shore) S.; m. Susan Anne Swearingen, Feb. 14, 1980 (div.); 1 child, Jericho Katherine. BS, L.I. U., 1967; DDS, Howard U., 1971. Dental intern Eastman Dental Ctr., Rochester, N.Y., 1971-72; gen. practice dentistry, Boulder, Colo., 1973—; evaluator Clin. Research Assocs.; lectr. in field, 1972—. Contbr. articles to dental jours; patentee in field. Mem. Boulder County Com. for Persons with Disabilities. Named outstanding clinician Boulder County Dental Forum, 1979. Mem. ADA, Am. Acad. Oral Implantology, Boulder County Dental Soc., Am. Soc. Dental Aesthetics. Jewish. Home: 3874 Campo Ct Boulder CO 80301-1793 Office: 2880 Folsom St Boulder CO 80304-3739

SCHAFFER, MARVIN BAKER, engineer scientist; b. N.Y.C., July 14, 1926; s. Joseph and Bessie (Baker) S.; m. Betty Borenstein, Sept. 4, 1948; children: Jody Ann Schaffer Jacobs, Leslie Elyse Schaffer Belay, Merri Susan Schaffer Toney. BChemE, Cooper Union, 1950; MSChemE, Newark Coll., 1956. Chem. engr. Kohn & Pechenick, Jersey City, N.J., 1950-52; ordnance design engr. Picatinny Arsenal, U.S. Army, Dover, N.J., 1952-60; engr. Lockheed Electronics Co., Bedminster, N.J., 1960-61; rsch. engr. Rand Corp., Santa Monica, Calif., 1961-71, R&D Assocs., Marina Del Rey, Calif., 1971-76, 83-85, Sci. Applications Inc., LaJolla, Calif., 1976-83; sr. scientist Rand Corp., Santa Monica, Calif., 1985—; cons. Expersoft, LaJolla, 1990—, EOS Corp., Santa Monica, 1985—, Lawrence Livermore Nat. Labs., 1992—; pres. Baker Schaffer Assocs., Inc., Pacific Palisades, Calif., 1987—. Inventor Novel small arms. With U.S. Army, 1944-46. Home: 911 Greentree Rd Pacific Palisades CA 90272-3913

SCHAFFER, ROBERT WARREN, state senator; b. Cin., July 24, 1962; s. Robert James and Florence Ann (Bednar) S.; m. Maureen Elizabeth Menke, Feb. 8, 1986; children: Jennifer, Emily, Justin. BA in Polit. Sci., U. Dayton, 1984. Legis. asst. State of Ohio, Columbus, 1985; majority adminstrv. asst. Colo. Senate, Denver, 1985-87; Colo. senator representing Dist. 14 Ft. Collins, 1987—; commr. Colo. Advanced Tech. Inst., 1988—; proprietor No. Front Range Mktg. and Distbn., Inc. Mem. Mental Health Bd. Larimer County, 1986-87, Bus. Affairs, Edn., Nat. Conf. State Legislatures Com. on Econ Devel. Commerce; campaign co-chair Arnold for Lt. Gov., Larimer and Weld Counties, 1986; head coach Ft. Collins Youth Baseball, 1986—; chmn. Senate Fin. Com. Mem. Colo. Press Assn., Colo. Press Club, Jaycees (Jaycee of the Month Ft. Collins chpt. 1987), KC. Republican. Roman Catholic. Home: 3284 Silverthorne Dr Fort Collins CO 80526 Office: The State Senate State Capitol Denver CO 80203

SCHAIDER, CYNTHIA DENISE, behavioral health consultant; b. Phoenix, July 6, 1957; d. Francis Earl McCann and Betty Jo (Turpin) Gutierrez; m. Stephen Edward Schaider, Nov. 15, 1980; 1 stepchild, Bree Therese. AA with distinction, Phoenix Coll., 1977; BA, U. Ariz., 1979. Cert. substance abuse counselor, Ariz. Counselor Behavioral Health Agy. Cen. Ariz., Casa Grande, 1980-89, coord. driving whilt intoxicated program, psychiat. mgr. to Pinal County Jail, coord. community svcss.; social svcs. planner Cen. Ariz. Assn. Govts., Florence, 1989-90; behavioral health cons., Casa Grande, 1990—; exec. asst. Behavioral Health Agy. Ctrl. Ariz., Casa Grande, 1992—; coord. Red Ribbon Drug Prevention Project, Casa Grande, 1988, 90; chmn. Adolescent Health Needs Task Force, Florence, 1988; instr. Ctrl. Ariz. Law Officers Tng. Acad. Lead singer Harvest Family Ch. Music Ministry, Casa Grande, 1985—; sec. Women's Aglow Christian Fellowship, Casa Grande, 1984-87; vol. leader Pinal County 4H Club, 1986-91; mem. Community Alliance Network, Casa Grande, 1988—, Gov's. Alliance Against Drugs, 1990-93; bd. dirs. Pinal County United Way, 1990—. Recipient Cert. of Appreciation Pres. of U.S., 1974, Outstanding Young Women of Am. award, 1983; Ednl. scholar Valley Nat. Bank Vaqueros. Mem. Phi Theta Kappa. Republican. Home: 1169 E Manor Dr Casa Grande AZ 85222-2911 Office: 120 W Main St Casa Grande AZ 85222

SCHALESTOCK, PETER KIRK, public relations consultant; b. N.Y.C., Sept. 11, 1967; s. Peter Fairfield Shelby and E. Ann (Williamson) Schalestock. Student, Cornell U., 1985-88; BA in Polit. Sci., U. Wash., 1992. Control analyst Keystone Group, Cambridge, Mass., 1986-89; acctg. and control supr. Investors Bank and Trust, Boston, 1989-90; cons. mut. funds Colum O'Brien Assocs., Boston, 1991; rsch. and issues dir. McDonald for Gov. Campaign, Redmond, Wash., 1991-92; communications dir. Wash. State Rep. Party, Bellevue, 1992—. Home: 2726 60th Ave # 205 Seattle WA 98116 Office: Wash State Rep Party 9 Lake Bellevue Dr Bellevue WA 98005

SCHALLER, JOANNE FRANCES, nursing consultant; b. Columbus, Ga., July 15, 1943; d. John Frank and Ethel Beatrice (Spring) Lanzendorfer; m. Robert Thomas Schaller, Jan. 22, 1977 (div. Aug. 1987); 1 child, Amy. BS, Pacific Luth. U., 1969; M in Nursing, U. Wash., 1971. House supr. UCLA Hosp., 1971-72; outpatient supr. Harborview Hosp., Seattle, 1973-75; outpatient clinic and emergency room supr. U. Wash. Hosp., Seattle, 1975-77; coauthor, researcher with Robert Schaller MD Seattle, 1977-87; prin. Nursing Expert-Standards of Care, Seattle, 1987—; cons. Wash. State Trial Lawyers, Wash. Assn. Criminal Def. Lawyers, 1989—; founder, chief exec. officer Present Perfect, Seattle, 1991—. Contbr., editor articles to profl. jours. Bd. dirs. Pacific Arts Ctr.,1992—; vol. guardian ad litem King County Juvenile Ct., 1978—; vol. Make a Wish Found. U.S. Bank, 1984—, Multiple Sclerosis Assn., 1986—, Am. Heart Assn., 1986—, Internat. Children's Festival, 1987—, Seattle Children's Festival, 1987—, Seattle Dept. Parks and Recreation Open Space Com., 1990—, Pacific N.W. Athletic Congress, 1991—, Wash. Fed. Garden Clubs Jr. Advisor, 1992—; mem. Photo Coun. Seattle Art Mus., 1986—, Native Am. Coun. Seattle Art Mus., 1989—, NAOO Coun., 1989—, Plestcheeff Inst. Decorative Arts, 1992—; mem, fundraiser Children's Hosp. Med. Ctr., 1977—. Mem. ANA, Wash. State Nurses Assn., U. Wash. Alumni Assn. Home and Office: 914 Randolph Ave Seattle WA 98122-5267

SCHANDER, EDWIN, law librarian; b. Harbin, China, Mar. 9, 1942; came to U.S., 1957; s. Robert and Olga (Linder) S.; m. Mary Lea, July 3, 1971. BA, Calif. State U., Northridge, 1969; postgrad., UCLA, 1969-72, MLS, 1973. Reference librarian Los Angeles County Law Library, 1973-79, sr. reference librarian, 1979-86, head reference services, 1986—, acting fgn. and internat. law libr., 1987-90; commr. Pasadena (Calif.) Pub. Libr., 1988-89; mem. steering com. METRONET, 1989-93; cons. Rand Corp., Santa Monica, Calif., 1975; bd. dirs. Pasadena Community Access Corp., 1990. Contbr. articles on law to profl. jours. Freelance TV producer Community Access Channel, City of Pasadena. Served with U.S. Army, 1964-66. Mem. Am. Assn. Law Libraries, So. Calif. Assn. Law Librs., Humane Soc. U.S., LWV. Club: Los Angeles Athletic. Home: 301 W 1st St Pasadena CA 91106 Office: LA County Law Libr 301 W First St Los Angeles CA 90012

SCHANDER, MARY LEA, police official; b. Bakersfield, Calif., June 11, 1947; d. Gerald John Lea and Marian Lea Coffman; B.A. (Augustana fellow) Calif. Luth. Coll., 1969; M.A., U. Calif., Los Angeles, 1970; m. Edwin Schander, July 3, 1971. Staff aide City of Anaheim (Calif.) Police Dept., 1970-72, staff asst., 1972-78, sr. staff asst., 1978-80; with Resource Mgmt. Dept., City of Anaheim, 1980-82; asst. to dir. Pub. Safety Agy., City of Pasadena Police Dept., 1982-85, spl. asst. to police chief, 1985-88, adminstrv. comdr., 1988-92, police comdr., 1992—; freelance musician, publisher Australian Traditional Songs, 1985; lectr. Calif. Luth. Coll.; cons. City of Lodz, Poland; assessor Nat. Commn. on Accreditation for Law Enforcement Agencies; speaker, panelist League of Calif. Cities, Pasadena Commn. on Status of Women. Producer (cable TV program) Traditional Music Showcase. Contbr. articles in field to profl. jours. Recipient Women at Work Medal of Excellence, 1988. Mem. Pasadena Arts Coun., L.A. County Peace Officers, LWV, Internat. Assn. Chiefs of Police. Home: PO Box 50151 Pasadena CA 91115 Office: Pasadena Police Dept 207 N Garfield Ave Pasadena CA 91101-1791

SCHANKMAN, ALAN ROBERT, ophthalmologist; b. Bklyn., Jan. 1, 1947; s. Barnet and Sylvia (Barken) S.; m. Vicky Barbara Gellman, Dec. 10, 1973; children—Dana, Lauren, Alison, Michael. B.S., Bklyn. Coll., 1968; M.D., Downstate Med. Sch., SUNY-Bklyn., 1972. Diplomate Am. Bd. Ophthalmology. Intern Beth Israel Med. Ctr., N.Y.C., 1973; resident in ophthalmology E.J. Meyer Meml. Hosp., Buffalo, 1973-76; pvt. practice, N.Y.C., 1976-78, Los Angeles, 1978—; co-founder, v.p. and sec. S & S Med. Office Systems, Inc.; clin. instr. Jules Stein Eye Inst., UCLA Med. Sch., 1980—; co-founder, v.p. S&S Med. Office Systems, Inc.; cons. Braille Inst. Developer refractive eye surgery, myopia, 1980; investigator Yag laser surgery, 1982. Fellow Am. Acad. Ophthalmology; mem. Internat. Assn. Ocular Surgeons, Calif. Assn. Ophthalmology, Los Angeles County Ophthal. Soc., Calif. Med. Soc., Los Angeles County Med. Assn., Internat. Glaucoma Congress, Am. Soc. Contemporary Ophthalmology, Am. Assn. Ophthalmology, Keratorefractive Soc., N.Y. Acad. Scis. Office: 12840 Riverside Dr North Hollywood CA 91607-3327

SCHAPANSKY, ELWOOD JAY, physics educator, author; b. Corn, Okla., Apr. 28, 1938; s. Ervin Isaac and Elizabeth (Friesen) S.; m. Dovie Dee Lee Meskimen, June 17, 11961 (div. 1972); m. Karen Elizabeth Lehman, Feb. 15, 1981. BA in Physics, Calif. State U., Fresno, 1961; MA in Physics, U. Calif., 1963; PhD in Physics, Colo. State U., Ft. Collins, 1972. Scientist, airline transport pilot Lockheed Aircraft Corp., Palo Alto, Calif., 1961-62; scientist Hoffman Electronics Corp., Santa Barbara, Calif., 1962-63; prof. physics Santa Barbara City Coll., 1963—; summer pilot Peninsula Airways, Anchorage, 1980—; chmn. physics dept. Santa Barbara City Coll., 1973-81, 88-89, faculty lectr., 1987. Author: Basic Airmanship, 1969, Thinking Physics with Vectors, 1990. Recipient Nat. Teaching Excellence award U. Tex., 1989; NSF fellow, 1969. Democrat. Home: 1414 Kenwood Rd Santa Barbara CA 93109-1225 Office: Santa Barbara City Coll 721 Cliff Dr Santa Barbara CA 93109-2394

SCHAPIRA, MOREY RAEL, electronics sales executive; b. Chgo., Jan. 4, 1949; s. Julius and Rose (Schwartz) S; m. Barbara Stein, May 29, 1977; children: Rachel, Deborah, Michael. BS in Physics cum laude, Case Western Res. U., 1970; MBA, Harvard U., 1977. Rsch. scientist rsch. div. Raytheon Co., Waltham, Mass., 1970-75; cons. scientist Lincoln Labs., MIT, Lexington, 1976; product mktg. engr. microwave semicondr. div. Hewlett Packard Co., San Jose, Calif., 1977-80; domestic sales mgr. optoelectronics div. Hewlett Packard Co., Palo Alto, Calif., 1980-81, distbr. mktg. mgr. optoelectronics div., 1981-83; corp. distbn. mgr. Hewlett Packard Components, San Jose, Calif., 1983-85; nat. distbr., sales mgr. Micro Power Systems, Santa Clara, Calif., 1985-87; nat. sales mgr. Network Gen. Corp., Menlo Park, Calif., 1987-89, v.p. worldwide sales, 1989-90, gen. mgr. Asia/Ams. sales, 1991—. Editor-in-chief, then pub. A Guide to Jewish Boston, 1974-77; pub., editor-in-chief HarBus News, 1976-77. gen. mgr. network gen. Asia, Ams. Div. chmn. United Way Campaign., 1978; nat. v.p. Union of Councils for Soviet Jews, 1979-84, nat. pres., 1984-86; pres. Bay Area Council on Soviet Jewry, San Francisco, 1980-84. Mem. Am. Mgmt. Assn., No. Calif. Venture Capital Assn., Harvard Bus. Sch. Assn. No. Calif., Am. Phys. Soc., Churchill Club. Home: 1154 Crespi Dr Sunnyvale CA 94086-7039 Office: Network Gen Corp 4200 Bohannon Dr Menlo Park CA 94025-1097

SCHAPP, REBECCA MARIA, museum director; b. Stuttgart, Fed. Republic Germany, Dec. 12, 1956; came to U.S., 1957; d. Randall Todd and Elfriede Carolina (Scheppan) Spradlin; m. Thomas James Schapp, May 29, 1979. AA, DeAnza Coll., 1977; BA in Art, San Jose State U., 1979, MA in Art Adminstrn., 1985. Adminstrv. dir. Union Gallery, San Jose, Calif., 1979-82; mus. coordinator de Saisset Mus. Santa Clara (Calif.) U., 1982-86, asst. dir., 1984, acting dir., 1986-87, asst. dir., 1987-89, dep. dir., 1989-92, dir., 1993—. Mem. San Francisco Mus. Modern Art; bd. dirs. Works of San Jose, v.p. 1983-85. Mem. Non-Profit Gallery Assn. (bd. dirs.). Democrat. Office: de Saisset Museum 500 El Camino Real Santa Clara CA 95053

SCHATZ, MONA CLAIRE STRUHSAKER, social worker, educator; b. Phila., Jan. 4, 1950; d. Milton and Josephine (Kivo) S.; m. James Fredrick Struhsaker, Dec. 31, 1979; 1 child, Thain Mackenzie. BA, Metro State Coll., 1976; postgrad., U. Minn., 1976; MSW, U. Denver, 1979; D in Social Work/Social Welfare, U. Pa., 1986. Teaching fellow U. Pa., Phila., 1981-82; asst. prof. S.W. Mo. State U., Springfield, 1982-85; researcher family & children policy, foster care & children svcs., generalist and advanced generalist practice Colo. State U., Ft. Collins, 1979—, assoc. prof., 1985—, field coord., 1986-88, project dir. Colo. foster care tng. program, 1987—, dir. youth agy. adminstrn. program Am. Humanics, 1988-90; cons. Mgmt. and Behavioral Sci. Ctr., The Wharton Sch. U. Pa., 1981-82; resource specialist So. N.J. Health Systems Agy., 1982; adj. faculty mem. U. Mo., Springfield, 1984; med. social worker Rehab. and Vis. Nurse Assn., 1985-90; mem. Colo. Child Welfare Adv. Com., Family Preservation Initiative. Contbr. articles to profl. jours. Cons., field rep. Big Bros./Big Sisters of Am., Phila., 1979-83; acting dir., asst. dir. Big Sisters of Colo., 1971-78; owner Polit. Cons. in Colo., Denver, 1978-79; active Food Co-op, Ft. Collins, Foster Parent, Denver, Capital Hill United Neighbors, Adams County (Denver) Social Planning Coun., Co., Colo. Justice Coun., Denver, Regional Girls Shelter, Springfield; bd. dirs. Crisis Helpline and Info. Svc. Scholar Lilly Endowment, Inc., 1976, Piton Found., 1978; recipient Spl. Recognition award Big Bros./Big Sisters of Am., 1983, Recognition award Am. Humanics Mgmt. Inst., 1990. Mem. Counsel Social Work Edn., Group for Study of Generalist Social Work, Social Welfare History Group, Nat. Assn. Social Workers (nominating chmn. Springfield chpt., state bd. dirs., No. Colo. rep.), Student Social Work Assn. of Colo. State U. (adv. 1986-89), Permanency Planning Coun. for Children and Youth, NOW (treas. Springfield chpt. 1984-85), Student Nuclear Awareness Group (advisor), Student Social Work Assn. (advisor), Har Shalom, Emissaries of Divine Light, Alpha Delta Mu. Democrat. Jewish. Office: Colo State U Social Work Dept Fort Collins CO 80523

SCHAUSS, ALEXANDER GEORGE, psychologist, researcher; b. Hamburg, Fed. Republic of Germany, July 20, 1948; came to U.S., 1953; s. Frank and Alla (Demjanov) S.; m. Laura Babin; children: Nova, Evan. BA, U. N.Mex., 1970, MA, 1972; PhD, Calif. Coast U., 1992. State probation/parole officer 2nd Judicial Dist. Ct., Albuquerque, 1969-73; criminal justice planner Albuquerque/Bernalillo County Criminal Justice Planning Com., 1973-75; state asst. adminstr. dept. corrections State of S.D., Pierre, 1975-77; dir. Pierce County Probation Dept., Tacoma, Wash., 1977-78; tng. officer IV Wash. State Criminal Justice Tng. Commn., Olympia, 1978-79; dir. Inst. Biosocial Rsch. City Univ. Grad. Sch., Seattle, 1979-80; exec. dir. Am. Inst. Biosocial Rsch. Inc., Tacoma, 1980-93, Am. Preventive Med. Assn., 1992—; mem., WHO Study Group on Health Promotion, Copenhagen, 1985; vis. lectr. pediatrics The John Radcliffe Hosp., Oxford U., England, summer 1985; sec. coun. on food policy Nat. Assn. Pub. Health Policy, 1990—; vis. scholar Kans. Community Coll. Consortium, 1982; vis. lectr. McCarrison Soc. Conf. at Oxford U., 1983. Author: Diet, Crime and Delinquency, 1980, rev., 1992, Nutrition and Behavior, 1986, Nutrition and Criminal Behavior, 1990; co-author: Zinc and Eating Disorders, 1989, Eating For A's, 1991; contbr. articles to profl. jours.; editor-in-chief Internat. Jour. Biosocial and Med. Rsch., 1979—; mem. editorial bd. 4 jours., 1979—. Master arbitrator Tacoma/Pierce County Better Bus. Bur., Tacoma, 1986—; mem. Pierce County N. Area Transp. Adv. Coun., Tacoma, 1991—; trustee Faith Homes Puget Sound Area Charity, 1991—; mem. Pierce County Pub. Safety Task Team, 1993. Recipient Rsch. award Wacker Found., 1983-85, 88; fellow Am. Coll. Nutrition, 1986-87. Fellow Am. Orthopsychiat. Assn.; mem. Brit. Soc. Nutritional Medicine (hon.), Am. Nutritionists Assn., Assn. Chemoreception Scis., Internat. Assn. Eating Disorders Profls., Am. Assn Correctional Psychologists, Am. Found. Preventative Medicine (treas. 1992), Acad. Criminal Justice Scis., Am. Soc. Criminology, Rotary (chmn. community scs. com. Tacoma chpt. 1989-90, chmn. civic affairs com. 1989-90, mem. Vladivostok com. 1991-93), N.Y. Acad. Scis. (emeritus.). Office: Am Inst Biosocial Rsch Inc Divsn Life Scis PO Box 1174 Tacoma WA 98401-1174

SCHAWLOW, ARTHUR LEONARD, physicist, educator; b. Mt. Vernon, N.Y., May 5, 1921; s. Arthur and Helen (Mason) S.; m. Aurelia Keith Townes, May 19, 1951; children: Arthur Keith, Helen Aurelia, Edith Ellen. BA, U. Toronto, Ont., Can., 1941, MA, 1942, PhD, 1949, LLD (hon.), 1970; DSc (hon.), U. Ghent, Belgium, 1968, U. Bradford, Eng., 1970, U. Ala., 1984, Trinity Coll., Dublin, Ireland, 1986; DTech (hon.), U. Lund, Sweden, 1987; SLD (hon.), Victoria U., Toronto, 1993. Postdoctoral fellow, research asso. Columbia, 1949-51; vis. assoc. prof. Columbia U., 1960; research physicist Bell Telephone Labs., 1951-61, cons., 1961-62; prof. physics Stanford U., 1961-91, also J.G. Jackson-C.J. Wood prof. physics, 1978, prof. emeritus, 1991—, exec. head dept. physics, 1966-70, acting chmn. dept., 1973-74. Author: (with C.H. Townes) Microwave Spectroscopy, 1955; Co-inventor (with C.H. Townes), optical maser or laser, 1958. Recipient Ballantine medal Franklin Inst., 1962, Thomas Young medal and prize Inst. Physics and Phys. Soc., London, 1963, Schawlow medal Laser Inst. Am., 1982, Nobel prize in physics, 1981, U.S. Nat. Medal of Sci., 1991; named Calif. Scientist of Yr., 1973, Marconi Internat. fellow, 1977. Fellow Am. Acad. Arts and Scis., Am. Phys. Soc. (coun. 1966-70, chmn. div. electron and atomic physics 1974, pres. 1981), Optical Soc. Am. (hon. mem. 1983, dir.-at-large 1966-68, pres. 1975, Frederick Ives medal 1976); mem. NAS, IEEE (Liebmann prize 1964), AAAS (chmn. physics sect. 1979), Am. Philos. Soc., Royal Irish Acad. (hon.). Office: Stanford U Dept Physics Stanford CA 94305-4060

SCHEA, HENRY EMILE, III, chemist; b. Boston, June 20, 1952; s. Henry Emile Jr. and Evangaline Marie (Debonise) S.; m. Lisa Gabrielle Dawson, Mar. 21, 1980; children: Jeremy White, Brian Emile, Isaac Henry. BS in Microbial Genetics, U. Mass., 1976. Rsch. technician Eunice Kennedy Shriver Med. Ctr., Waltham, Mass., 1976-79; lab. mgr. The Salk Inst., La Jolla, Calif., 1979-81; lab. supr. Amgen Inc., Thousand Oaks, Calif., 1981; rsch. scientist Hybritech Inc., San Diego, 1991—. Patentee in field. Webelos den leader Boy Scouts Am., Oxnard, Calif., 1989—, asst. cub master, 1991-92; team mgr. Sunset Little League, Oxnard; Sunday sch. tchr. Bible Fellowship Ch., Uta, Calif. Mem. AAAS. Republican. Office: Hybritech Inc PO Box 269006 San Diego CA 92196

SCHECHTER, MARTIN, mathematician, educator; b. Phila., Mar. 10, 1930; s. Joshua and Rose (Shames) S.; m. Naomi Deborah Kirzner, Dec. 23, 1957; children: Sharon Libby, Arthur Irving, Isaac David, Raphael Morris. BS, CCNY, 1953; MS, NYU, 1955, PhD, 1957. Instr. NYU, N.Y.C., 1957-59, from asst. prof. to assoc. prof., 1959-65, prof., 1965-66; prof. Yeshiva U., N.Y.C., 1966-83, U. Calif., Irvine, 1983—; vis. assoc. prof. U. Chgo., 1961; vis. prof. Hebrew U., Jerusalem, 1973, Autonomous U., Mexico City, 1979. Author: Principles of Functional Analysis, 1971, Spectra of Partial Differential Operators, 1971, 2d edit., 1986, Modern Methods in Partial Differential Equations, 1977, Operator Methods in Quantum Mechanics, 1981; contbr. more than 100 articles to profl. jours. Office: U Calif Math Dept Irvine CA 92717

SCHEER, JANET KATHY, mathematics educator; b. Bklyn., Apr. 22, 1947; d. Seymour and Hilda (Shoer) S. BA, Bklyn. Coll., 1968; MS, Syracuse (N.Y.) U., 1969; PhD, Ariz. State U., 1977. Cert. tchr., N.Y., Ariz.; cert. prin., Ariz. Math. tchr. Jamesville (N.Y.) DeWitt Middle Sch., 1969-72; math. tchr., middle sch. coordinator Am. Internat. Sch., Kfar Shmaryahu, Israel, 1972-74; from asst. prof. to assoc. prof. So. Ill. U., Carbondale, 1977-88; nat. product devel. specialist Scott, Foresman and Co., Glenview, Ill., 1989-90; dir. field svcs. for math. Scott, Foresman and Co., 1991; exec. dir. Create A Vision, Mountain View, Calif., 1992—; cons. in field, 1977—; sr. nat. math. cons. Holt, Rinehart & Winston, N.Y.C., 1986-89, Harcourt Brace-Jovanovich/Holt, 1989. Editor Ill. Math. Tchr. jour., 1980-83; author: Manipulatives in Mathematics Unlimited, 1987; contbr. to textbooks and profl. jours. Named one of Outstanding Young Women Am., 1978, 81-85, Outstanding Tchr. Yr. So. Ill. U., 1978-79; recipient numerous grants. Mem. Nat. Council Tchrs. Math., Research Council for Diagnostic and Prescriptive Math. (charter mem., v.p. 1984-86), Ill. Council Tchrs. Math. (various offices), Phi Delta Kappa, Kappa Delta Pi. Office: Create A Vision 1300 Villa St Mountain View CA 94041

SCHEIBEL, J(ERRY) AUSTIN, investment firm executive; b. Elwood City, Pa., May 24, 1950; s. Harry Louis Scheibel and Elizabeth Galombos Legan; m. Gael Ann Donegan, Apr. 21, 1972; children: Victoria Ashley, Summer Alyse. BBA, U. Hawaii, 1975; postgrad., N.Y. Inst. Fin., Ariz. State U., 1983. Cert. prin. of gen. securities and options prin. Chmn. of bd. Internat. Brokering Ltd., Reno, 1979-82; dir. rsch., v.p. product devel. Am. We. Securities, Reno, 1980-82; investment exec. Paine Webber Jackson Curtis, Phoenix, 1982-84; account exec. Shearson Am. Express, Scottsdale, Ariz., 1985; v.p. Wall St. West, Scottsdale, 1985-89; v.p. investments, v.p. corp. fin. Simmons & Bishop Co. Inc., Scottsdale, 1989—; cons. E.N. Phillips, Reseda, Caif., 1992—; pres. Design Visions, Bomehia, N.Y., 1991—. Author and/or editor rsch. reports in field. Participant UN, Honolulu, 1973-74; mem. Waikiki Redevel. Project, Honolulu, 1974; mem. Make a Wish Found., Scottsdale, 1985; active Rep. Nat. Steering Com., 1990. Recipient Travel award Hotel and Restaurant Assn., 1974; honored by UN, 1974. Republican. Home: 6501 E Caron Dr Paradise Valley Scottsdale AZ 85253 Office: Simmons & Bishop Co Inc 13402 N Scottsdale Rd Scottsdale AZ 85254

SCHEIBER, HARRY N., legal educator; b. N.Y.C., 1935. BA Columbia U., 1955; MA, Cornell U., 1957, PhD, 1961; MA (hon.), Dartmouth Coll., 1965. instr. to assoc. prof. history Dartmouth Coll., 1960-68, prof., 1968-71; prof. Am. history U. Calif., San Diego, 1971-80; prof. law Boalt Hall, U. Calif., Berkeley, 1980—, chmn. jurisprudence and social policy program, 1982-84, 90—, assoc. dean, 1990—; The Stefan Riesenfeld Prof., 1991—; Fulbright disting. sr. lectr., Australia, 1983, marine affairs coord. Calif. Sea Grant Coll. Program, 1989—. Chmn. Littleton Griswold Prize Legal History, 1985-88; pres. N.H. Civil Liberties Union, 1969-70; chmn. Project '87 Task Force on Pub. Programs, Washington, 1982-85; dir. Berkeley Seminar on Federalism, 1986—; cons. judiciary study U.S. Adv. Commn. Intergovernmental Rels., 1985-88; dir. NEH Inst. on Constitutionalism, U. Calif., Berkeley, 1986-87, 88-91. Recipient Sea Grant Colls. award, 1981-83, 84-85, 86—; fellow Ctr. Advanced Study in Behavioral Scis., Stanford Calif., 1967, 71; Guggenheim fellow, 1971, 88; Rockefeller Found. humanities fellow, 1979, NEH fellow, 1985-86; NSF grantee, 1979, 80, 88-89; Fellow U. Calif. Humanities Rsch. Inst., 1989. Mem. Am. Hist. Assn., Orgn. Am. Historians, Agrl. History Soc. (pres. 1978), Econ. History Assn. (trustee 1978-80), Law and Soc. Assn. (trustee 1979-81), Am. Soc. Legal History (dir. 1982-86, 90—), Am. Bar Found. (legal history fellowship com. 1982-86), Nat. Assessment History and Citizenship Edn. (chmn. nat. acad. 1986-87), Marine Affairs and Policy Assn. (bd. dirs. 1991—), Ocean Governance Study Group (steering com. 1991—), Internat. Coun. Environ. Law. Author numerous books including: (with L. Friedman) American Law and the Constitutional Order, 1978, 2d edit. 1988; contbr. articles to law revs., 1963—. Office: U Calif Berkeley Law Sch Boalt Hall Berkeley CA 94720

SCHEIDIG, PAUL A., environmental scientist, association administrator; b. Phila., Aug. 17, 1942; s. William C. and Helen S. (Whitkowski) S.; m. Diane E. Youtzy, Nov. 27, 1985; 1 child, Stephan A. BS in Forest Mgmt., Humboldt State U., Arcata, Calif., 1972; MBA, Ariz. State U., 1984. Dist. mgr. U.S. Forest Svc., Calif., Oreg., 1972-79; fed. timber mgr. Nat. Forest Products Assn., Washington, 1979-80; resource adminstr. S.W. Forst Industries, Phoenix, 1980-86; pres. Delphi Container Corp., Phoenix, 1986-87; ombudsman Ariz. Dept. Environ. Quality, Phoenix, 1987-90; mgr. environ. compliance Emcon Assocs., Phoenix, 1990; environ. and resource mgr. Nev. Mining Assn., Reno, 1990—. With U.S. Army, 1960-63. Mem. Ariz. Hazardous Waste Mgmt. Soc., Ariz. State U. Alumni Assn. (life), Forestry Honor Soc. (life). Republican. Office: Nev Mining Assn 3940 Spring Dr Ste 11 Reno NV 89502

SCHEID-RAYMOND, LINDA ANNE, property management professional; b. Rochester, N.Y., Aug. 13, 1953; d. Arthur F. and Anna M. Scheid; m. Dan Raymond, June 27, 1987. BFA, U. Colo., 1975. Leasing agt. Richard E. Rudolph, Boulder, Colo., 1975-77; adminstrv. asst., co-mgr. Harsh Investment Corp., Denver, 1977-83; property mgr. A.G. Spanos Mgmt., Colorado Springs, Colo., 1984-85, Carmel Devel. and Mgmt., Denver, 1985-88, Property Asset Mgmt., Denver, 1989—. Contbr. photographs to profl. mags.

SCHEINBAUM, DAVID, photography educator; b. Bklyn., Apr. 14, 1951; s. Louis and Rhoda (Feerman) S.; m. Vicki Golden, May 30, 1973 (div. 1975); m. Janet Ann Goldberg-Russek, Mar. 21, 1982; stepchildren: Jonathan Russek, Andra Russek; 1 child, Zachary. BA, CUNY, 1973. Instr. photography Pace U., N.Y.C., 1974-75, LaGuardia (N.Y.) Community Coll., 1975-78; assoc. prof. art Coll. Santa Fe, 1979-81, 82—, assoc. prof. of art photography, 1981—; printer, asst. to Beaumont Newhall, Santa Fe, 1980-93; printer to Eliot Porter, Santa Fe, 1980-90; co-dir. Scheinbaum & Russek, Ltd., Santa Fe, 1979—. Author: (photographs) Bisti, 1987, Miami Beach: Photographs of an American Dream, 1990; photography exhbns. include Pace U., 1974, Midtown Y Gallery, N.Y., 1977, Santa Fe Gallery for Photography, 1979, 81, The Armory for the Arts, Santa Fe, 1980, 1981, Sea Breeze Gallery, Block Island, R.I., 1982, Highlands U., Las Vegas, N.Mex., 1982, Gov's. Gallery, Santa Fe, 1982, Santa Fe Festival for the Arts, 1982, Coll. Santa Fe, 1983, Dem. Conv., San Francisco, 1984, Mus. Natural History, Albuquerque, Bisti/Miami Beach Photogroup Coral Gables, Fla., 1990, Ctr, Met. Studies U. Mo., St. Louis, 1988, Earthscope Expo '90 Photo Mus., Osaka, Japan, 1990, Jamestown CC, N.Y., 1990, Neikrug Gmiery Gallery Internat., Tokyo, 1987, Neikrug Gmiery Gallery, N.Y., 1987; in permanent collections Norton Gallery Mus., West Palm Beach, Fla, Amon Carter Mus., Ft. Worth, N.Mex. State U., Las Cruces, Ctr. Creative Photography, Tucson, Ariz., Mus. Fine Arts, Santa Fe, Bklyn. Mus., U. Okla., Norman, Bibliothèque Nationale France, Paris, Gernsheim Collection. U. Tex., Austin, Albuquerque Mus., Rockwell Mus., Corning, N.Y., Chase Manhattan Bank, N.Y. Pub. Libr., Fogg Art Mus., Harvard U., Met. Mus. Art, N.Y.C., Frito-Lay Collection, Kans. City, Expo 90 Photo Mus., Osaka. Mem. N.Mex. Coun. on Photography (founder, v.p., bd. dirs.), Santa Fe Ctr. Photography (bd. dirs. 1978-85). Jewish. Home: 328 S Guadalupe St Santa Fe NM 87501-1882 Office: Coll Santa Fe Saint Michaels Dr Santa Fe NM 87501

SCHEINMAN, LESLIE KASS, radio sales executive; b. Flushing, N.Y., Oct. 27, 1953; d. R. Robert and Geraldine N. (Rothberg) Kass; m. William T. Scott, III, May 25, 1975 (div. Oct. 1981); m. Gerald Lynn Scheinman, July 1, 1984; children: Lee Jacob (dec.), Rachel Lee, Carly Rebecca. Student Boston U.; BFA, U. R.I. Store mgr. McDonald's Corp., Raleigh, N.C., 1976-78; media dir. Martin J. Simmons Advt., Chgo., 1978-79; asst. dir. advt. Penta Investments, San Diego, 1979; account exec. Gemini II Advt., San Diego, 1980; media planner/buyer Cole & Weber, L.A., 1980-83; account exec. McGavren Guild Radio, L.A., 1983-88; v.p. sales, 1988-90—; v.p., dir. sales Schubert Radio Sales, 1991-92; v.p. The Interep Radio Store; cons. small advt. agys. Leader/organizer Young World Devel./Am.

Freedom from Hunger Found., 1971; patron Los Angeles County Mus. Art, 1984—. Boston U. scholar, 1971-72. Mem. NAFE, Advt. Industry Emergency Fund, Mortar Bd. Jewish. Avocations: crafts, sculpture, sports.

SCHELAR, VIRGINIA MAE, chemistry educator, consultant; b. Kenosha, Wis., Nov. 26, 1924; d. William and Blanche M. (Williams) S. BS, U. Wis., 1947, MS, 1953; MEd, Harvard U., 1962; PhD, U. Wis., 1969. Instr. U. Wis., Milw., 1947-51; info. specialist Abbott Labs., North Chgo., Ill., 1953-56; instr. Wright Jr. Coll., Chgo., 1957-58; asst. prof. No. Ill. U., DeKalb, 1958-63; prof. St. Petersburg (Fla.) Jr. Coll., 1965-67; asst. prof. Chgo. State Coll., 1967-68; prof. Grossmont Coll., El Cajon, Calif., 1968-80; cons. Calif., 1981—. Author: Kekule Centennial, 1965; contbr. articles to profl. jours. Active citizens adv. coun. DeKalb Consol. Sch. Bd.; voters svc. chair League Women Voters, del. to state and nat. convs., judicial chair, election laws chair. Standard Oil fellow, NSF grantee; recipient Lewis prize U. Wis. Fellow Am. Inst. Chemists; mem. Am. Chem. Soc. (membership affairs com., chmn. western councilor's caucus, exec. com., councilor, legis. counselor, chmn. edn. com., editor state and local bulletins). Office: 5702 Baltimore Dr Apt 282 La Mesa CA 91942-1665

SCHELL, FARREL LOY, transportation engineer; b. Amarillo, Tex., Dec. 14, 1931; s. Thomas Phillip and Lillian Agnes (McKee) S.; m. Shirley Anne Samuelson, Feb. 6, 1955; children: James Christopher, Maria Leslyn Schell Peter. BS, U. Kans., 1954; postgrad., Carnegie-Mellon U., 1974. Registered profl. engr., Calif., Colo. Resident engr. Sverdrup & Parcel, Denver, 1957-61; project engr. Bechtel Corp., San Francisco, 1961-62, Parsons, Brinckerhoff-Tudor-Bechtel, San Francisco, 1962-67; mgr. urban transp. dept. Kaiser Engrs., Oakland, Calif., 1967-78; program dir. San Francisco Mcpl. Rwy I.C., 1978-80; project mgr. Houston Transit Cons., 1980-83, Kaiser Transit Group, Miami, 1983-85; mgr. program devel. Kaiser Engrs., Oakland, 1985-87; project mgr. O'Brien-Kreitzberg & Assocs., San Francisco, 1987-89; sr. project mgr. Bay Area Rapid Transit Dist., Oakland, Calif., 1989—; dir. Schelter Devel. Corp., Piedmont, Calif., 1982—. Contbr. articles to profl. jours. Lt. (j.g.) USN, 1954-57, PTO. Mem. ASCE, ASME, Nat. Soc. Profl. Engrs., Nat. Coun. Engring. Examiners, Am. Planners Assn., Am. Pub. Transit Assn., Lakeview Club, Scarab Club, Pachacamac Club, Sigma Tau, Tau Beta Pi. Home: 24 York Dr Piedmont CA 94611-4123 Office: Bay Area Rapid Transit Dist 800 Madison St Oakland CA 94607-4730

SCHELLER, ERIN LINN, publishing company executive; b. Port Arthur, Tex., Dec. 25, 1942; d. Truman Edward Jr. and Margaret Jane (Imhoff) Linn; m. Herman Scheller, Oct. 19, 1983; 1 child, Christopher Wayne Levy. Student, Barat Coll., 1960-61; BS, U. Tex., 1964. Tchr. Cath. Sch. Dist., Houston, 1965-67; owner, pres. The Pub.'s Mark, Incline Village, Nev., 1982—; guest lectr. death edn. related orgns., U.S., 1982—. Author: Children Are Not Paper Dolls, 1982, I Know Just How You Feel, 1986, Dear Teacher, 1988, 150 Facts About Grieving Children, 1990, Premonitions, Visitations and Dreams, 1991. Advisor Mo. Bapt. Children's Group, St. Louis, 1980-81; chpt. leader The Compassionate Friends, Denver, 1980-81, Greeley, Colo., 1981-83; 2nd v.p. Republican Women's Club, Incline Village, 1987-90; mem. AAUW, Incline Village, 1987-89; pres. Teester's Ladies Golf Assn., Incline Village, 1987-90; mem. Assn. for Death. Edn. and Counseling, 1985—, Grief Edn. Inst., 1981—, The Compassionate Friends, 1980—. Named Honored Author, Ill. Libr. Exposition, 1985. Republican. Lutheran. Home and Office: The Publishers Mark PO Box 6300 Incline Village NV 89450-6300

SCHELLING, GERALD THOMAS, scientist, educator; b. Sterling, Ill., Mar. 24, 1941; s. Ralph Ernest and Phyllis (Lucille) S.; m. Margaret Ann Esterly, Aug. 18, 1963; children: John Matthew, Douglas Wesly. BS, U. Ill., 1963, MS, 1964, PhD, 1968. Rsch. sci. Smith, Kline Labs., Phila., 1968-70; asst. prof. and assoc. prof. U. Ky., Lexington, 1970-79; prof. Tex. A & M Univ., College Station, 1979-88; prof., dept. head U. Idaho, Moscow, 1988—; cons. in field. Contbr. articles to profl. jours. Mem. Internat. Congress of Nutrtion, Am. Soc. Animal Sci. (editorial bd., 1975-78, 82-85), Am. Inst. Nutrition. Home: 725 SW Staley Dr Pullman WA 99163 Office: U Idaho Dept Animal Sci Moscow ID 83843

SCHELLINGER, JAMES RAYMOND, advertising sales executive; b. Casper, Wyo., Apr. 18, 1963; s. William Joseph and Trina Louise (Cundall) S.; m. Cheryl Lynne Wentz, June 27, 1987; 1 child, Cody Lee. AAS, N.W. C.C., Powell, Wyo., 1984; BS, Black Hills State Coll., Spearfish, S.D., 1986. Operator, roustabout Valentine Constrn., Inc., Glenrock, Wyo., 1980-86; resident asst. N.W. C.C., 1982-84, Black Hills State Coll., 1984-86; sales mgr. Sta. KWIV and KATH, Douglas, Wyo., 1987-89; account exec. Sta. KROE, Sheridan, Wyo., 1989—. Bd. dirs. Am. Heart Assn., Douglas, 1987-89, Hugh O'Brian Youth Found.; info. coord. Am. Cancer Soc., Douglas, 1988-89; mem. Sheridan Youth Steering Com., 1990-91. Mem. U.S. Jr. C. of C. (bd. dirs. 1991-92, Hamilton award 1991, Frost award 1992), Wyo. Jaycees (regional bd. dirs. 1989-90, v.p. 1990-91, pres. 1991-92, Officer of Yr. award 1990, 91), Sheridan Area C. of C. (chmn. retail com. 1989-92), Phi Beta Lambda (state pres. 1985-86). Republican. Roman Catholic. Home: 735 Clarendon Ave Sheridan WY 82801 Office: Sta KROE 1716 KROE Ln Sheridan WY 82801

SCHEMMEL, TERENCE DEAN, physicist; b. Newport News, Va., Feb. 2, 1963; s. Ronald Joseph and Elizabeth Irene (McCord) S.; m. Laurel Ann Mitchell, Jan. 5, 1985. BS in Physics, Colo. State U., 1985. Mem. tech. staff Santa Barbara Rsch. Ctr., Goleta, Calif., 1986-88; thin film physicist Vec-Tec Systems, Inc., Boulder, Colo., 1988-89; thin film engr. Storage Tech. Corp., Louisville, Colo., 1989-92; sr. devel. engr. Rocky Mountain Magnetics, Louisville, 1992—. Mem. Am. Vacuum Soc. (chpt. chmn. 1991-92), Optical Soc. Am. Office: Rocky Mountain Magnetics Corp 2270 S 88th St Louisville CO 80028-8188

SCHENDEL, WINFRIED GEORGE, insurance company executive; b. Harpstedt, Germany, June 19, 1931; s. Willi Rudolf Max and Anna Margarete (Sassen) S.; came to U.S., 1952, naturalized, 1956; B.S. in Elect. and Indsl. Engring., Hannover-Stadthagen U., Hannover, W. Germany, 1952; m. Joanne Wiiest, Aug. 24, 1953; children—Victor Winfried, Bruce Lawrence, Rachelle Laureen. Elec. draftsman Houston Lighting & Power Co., 1954-57; elec. draftsman, corrosion technician Transcontinental Gas Pipeline Co., Houston, 1957-59; elec. engr. Ken R. White Cons. Engrs., Denver, 1959-61; sales engr. Weco div. Food Machinery & Chem. Corp., various locations, 1961-64; ins. field underwriter N.Y. Life Ins. Co., Denver, 1964-66, asst. mgr., 1966-70, mgmt. asst., 1970-71, gen. mgr., 1971-77, mgr., 1979-85, field underwriter, 1985—; ind. gen. agt., Denver, 1978-79. Instl. rep., advancement chmn. Denver Area council Boy Scouts Am., Lakewood, Colo., 1968-72; precinct chmn. Republican Party, Jefferson County, Colo., 1976, 78; founder, mem. (life) Sister City Program, Lakewood, Colo.; chmn. adv. bd. ARC, Jefferson County, Colo., 1986-88. Recipient Centurion award, 1966; Northwestern Region Leader Manpower Devel. award N.Y. Life Ins. Co., 1968, Salesman of Yr. award Jefferson County Salesman with a Purpose Club, 1983, Top awards ARC, 1988-89. Mem. Nat. Assn. Life Underwriters, Gen. Agents and Mgrs. Assn. (recipient Conf. Nat. Mgmt. award, 1975), Colo. Life Underwriters Assn. (reg. v.p. Denver Metro area 1989-90), Mile High Assn. Life Underwriters (pres. 1986-87, nat. com. 1988, 91), Lakewood C. of C. (pres. people-to-people, Trailblazer of Yr. award 1982, 83, Trail Boss of Yr. 1983). Presbyterian (elder). Clubs: Lions, Edelweiss, Internat. Order Rocky Mountain Goats, N.Y. Life Star (leading asst. mgr. Continental region 1980), Masons, Rotary, Shriners. Home: 13802 W 20th Pl Golden CO 80401-2104 Office: NY Life Ins Co 13802 W 20th Pl Golden CO 80401

SCHENK, LYNN, congresswoman; b. Bronx, N.Y.; m. C. Hugh Friedman. BA, UCLA; JD, U. San Diego; postgrad, London (Eng.) Sch. Econs. Dep. atty. gen. Calif. Atty. Gen.'s Office; atty. San Diego Gas & Electric Co.; spl. asst. v.ps. Nelson Rockefeller and Walter Mondale, Washington, 1976-77; sec. bus., transp. and housing State of Calif., 1980-83; mem. 103rd Congress from 49th Calif. dist., 1993—; founder San Diego Urban Corp, The Women's Bank, The Lawyer's Club. Vice chair bd. dirs. San Diego Unified Port Dist, commr., Ctr. for Nat. Policy, Washington; bd dirs. Edmund G "Pat" Brown Inst. Govt. Affairs, Calif. State U., L.A.; trustee Claremont U. Ctr. and Grad. Sch. Recipient Israel Peace medal; named Outstanding Young Citizen San Diego Jaycees. Office: US Ho of Reps Office of House Mems Washington DC 20515 also: 8340 Clairmont Mesa Blvd Ste 105 San Diego CA 92111

SCHENK, RAY M(ERLIN), electronics company executive; b. Logan, Utah, Dec. 18, 1946; s. Merlin F. and Thelma E. (Birch) S.; B.S. in Acctg. magna cum laude, Utah State U., 1969. C.P.A., Utah. Staff acct. Haskins and Sells, Phoenix, 1969, Salt Lake City, 1969-71; controller Kimball Electronics, Salt Lake City, 1971—. Recipient Scholastic Achievement cert. Phi Kappa Phi, 1967, 68; 1st Security Found. scholar, 1968; Alpha Kappa Psi scholarship award, 1969; C.P.A. medallion, 1970. Mem. Nat. Assn. Accts., Am. Acctg. Assn., Utah Assn. C.P.A.s, Am. Inst. C.P.A.s. Home: 5044 Boabab Dr Salt Lake City UT 84117-6807 Office: Kimball Electronics 350 Pierpont Ave Salt Lake City UT 84101-1788

SCHENKER, MARC BENET, medical educator; b. L.A., Aug. 25, 1947; s. Steve and Dosella Schenker; m. Heath Massey, Oct. 8; children: Yael, Phoebe, Hilary. BA, U. Calif., Berkeley, 1969; MD, U. Calif., San Francisco, 1973; MPH, Harvard U., Boston, 1980. Instr. medicine Harvard U., Boston, 1980-82; asst. prof. medicine U. Calif., Davis, 1982-86, assoc. prof., 1986-92, prof., 1992—. Fellow ACP; mem. Am. Coll. Occupational Medicine, Am. Thoracic Soc., Am. Pub. Health Assn., Soc. Epidemiologic Rsch., Am. Coll. Epidemiology, Phi Beta Kappa, Alpha Omega Alpha. Office: U Calif Divsn Occupational & Environ Medicine ITEH Davis CA 95616

SCHEPP, GEORGE PHILLIP, JR., incentive premium and promotions research consultant; b. L.A., Apr. 14, 1955; s. George Phillip and Mary Opal (Andrews) S. BSBA, El Camino Coll., Torrance, Calif., 1976. Mktg. cons. Rockwell Internat., L.A., 1977-79; with promotional sales and rsch. dept. N.W. Surplus, Inc., Seattle, 1979-81; v.p. incentive premium and promotions Bear Images Internat., Inglewood, Calif., 1981-91; sales promotions rsch. cons. Gifthouse Internat., Cypress, Calif., 1989—; spl. advisor internat. sales, mktg. promotional rsch. divsn. Wade Ceramics Ltd., Stohe-on-Trent, U.K., 1990—. Republican. Methodist. Office: Bear Images Internat PO Box 1578 Inglewood CA 90308-1578

SCHERER, RONALD CALLAWAY, voice scientist, educator; b. Akron, Ohio, Sept. 11, 1945; s. Belden Davis and Lois Ramona (Callaway) S.; m. Mary Ellen Angel, Aug. 14, 1971; children: Christopher, Maria. BS, Kent State U., 1968; MA, Ind. U., 1972; PhD, U. Iowa, 1981. Research asst. U. Iowa, Iowa City, 1979-81, asst. research scientist, 1981-83, adj. asst. prof., 1983-88, adj. assoc. prof., 1988—; adj. prof. U. Denver, 1984-86; asst. adj. prof. U. Colo., Boulder, 1984-93, adj. prof., 1993—; research scientist The Denver Ctr. for the Performing Arts, 1983-88, sr. scientist, 1988-93, sr. scientist & gen. mgr., 1993—; lectr. voice and speech sci. Nat. Theatre Conservatory, Denver, 1990—; asst. clin. prof. Sch. Medicine U. Colo., Denver, 1988—; mem. editorial bd. Journal of Voice, 1987—, sci. adv. bd., 1993—. Author: (with Dr. I. Titze) Vocal Fold Physiology: Biomechanics, Acoustics and Phonatory Control, 1983; contbr. articles to profl. jours. Nat. Inst. Dental Research fellow, 1972-76. Fellow Internat. Soc. Phonetic Scis. (auditor 1988-91); mem. Internat. Arts Medicine Assn., Am. Speech-Lang.-Hearing Assn., Acoustical Soc. Am., Internat. Assn. Logopedics and Phoniatrics, Am. Assn. Phonetic Scis. (nominating com. 1985-87), Pi Mu Epsilon, Sigma Xi. Office: Denver Ctr for Performing Arts 1245 Champa St Denver CO 80204-2104

SCHERICH, ERWIN THOMAS, civil engineer, consultant; b. Inland, Nebr., Dec. 6, 1918; s. Harry Erwin and Ella (Peterson) S.; student Hastings Coll., 1937-39, N.C. State Coll., 1943-44; B.S., U. Nebr., 1946-48; M.S., U. Colo., 1948-51; m. Jessie Mae Funk, Jan. 1, 1947; children—Janna Rae Scherich Thornton, Jerilyn Mae Scherich Dobson, Mark Thomas. Civil and design engr. U.S. Bur. Reclamation, Denver, 1948-84, chief spillways and outlets sect., 1974-75, chief dams br., div. design, 1975-78, chief tech. rev. staff, 1978-79, chief div. tech. rev. Office of Asst. Commr. Engring. and Rsch. Ctr., 1980-84; cons. civil engr., 1984—. Mem. U.S. Com. Internat. Commn. on Large Dams. Served with AUS, 1941-45. Registered profl. engr., Colo. Fellow ASCE; mem. NSPE (nat. dir. 1981-87, v.p. southwestern region 1991-93), Profl. Engrs. Colo. (pres. 1977-78), Wheat Ridge C. of C. Republican. Methodist. Home and Office: 3915 Balsam St Wheat Ridge CO 80033-4449

SCHERSON, ISAAC DAVID, computer systems design educator; b. Santiago, Chile, Feb. 12, 1952; s. Raul and Ester (Szpirman) S.; m. Y. Talma Gittler, Jan. 23, 1977; 1 child, Yaniv D. BS in Engring., Nat. U. of Mex., Mexico City, 1975, MSEE, 1977; PhD, Weizmann Inst., Rehovot, Israel, 1983. Asst. prof. U. Calif., Santa Barbara, 1983-87, Princeton (N.J.) U., 1988-90; assoc. prof. U. Calif., Irvine, 1990—. Patentee in field. Mem. IEEE, Assn. for Computing Machinery, Etta Kappa Nu. Office: U Calif Dept Info/Computer Sci Irvine CA 92717

SCHERSON, YONA TALMA, neurobiologist, educator, researcher; b. Tel-Aviv, Apr. 30, 1954; came to U.S., 1983; d. Elias and Raquel Gittler; m. Isaac David Scherson, Jan. 23, 1977; 1 child, Yaniv. BSc with honors, U. Nat. Autonoma de Mexico, Mexico City, 1977; PhD, Weizmann Inst. Sci., Rehovot, Israel, 1984. Rsch. assoc. U. Calif., San Francisco, 1983-87, Princeton (N.J.) U., 1988-90; asst. rsch. prof. neurobiology U. Calif., Irvine, 1991—. Contbr. articles to profl. jours. NIH grantee, 1983—, Am. Cancer Soc. grantee, 1983, Weizmann fellow. Mem. Am. Soc. for Cell Biology. Office: U Calif Irvine Irvine CA 92717

SCHEU, FRIEDRICH, engineer manager; b. New Berlin, Ukraine, Nov. 29, 1942; came to U.S., 1956; s. Friedrich and Magdalena (Kaefer) S.; m. Phyllis Lynn Johann, Dec. 2, 1967; children: Erika Christina, Rebecca Lynn, Brian Frederick. BSEE, U. Wis., 1966; MSEE, San Jose State U., 1975. Engr. General Motors, Milw., 1966-70, Fairchild Semiconductor, Mt. View, Calif., 1970-73; sr. engr. Hewlett Packard, Cupertino, Calif., 1973-80; sect. mgr. Hewlett Packard, Vancouver, Wash., 1980-83; dept. engring. mgr. Tektronix Inc., Beaverton, Oreg., 1983-86; div. engring. mgr. Tektronix Inc., Redmond, Oreg., 1986—. Patentee in field. Mem. IEEE, Internat. Soc. Hybrid Engrs. and Mfrs. Home: 1612 NW Promontory Dr Bend OR 97701 Office: 625 S E Salmon Redmond OR

SCHEUER, PAUL JOSEF, chemistry educator; b. Heilbronn, Germany, May 25, 1915; came to U.S., 1938, naturalized, 1944; s. Albert and Emma (Neu) S.; m. Alice Elizabeth Dash, Sept. 5, 1950; children: Elizabeth E., Deborah A., David A.L., Jonathan L.L. BS, Northeastern U., 1943; MA, Harvard U., 1947, PhD with high honors, 1950. Asst. prof. U. Hawaii, Honolulu, 1950-55; assoc. prof. U. Hawaii, 1955-61, prof. chemistry, 1961-85, prof. emeritus, 1985—, chmn. dept., 1959-62; vis. prof. U. Copenhagen, 1977, 89; prof. Toyo Suisan U., Tokyo, 1992; Barton lectr. U. Okla., 1967; J.F. Toole lectr. U. N.B., 1977; Lilly lectr. Kansas U., 1993. Author: Chemistry of Marine Natural Products, 1973; editor: Marine Natural Products: Chemical and Biological Perspectives, vols. 1-2, 1978, vol. 3, 1980, vol. 4, 1981, vol. 5, 1983, Bioorganic Marine Chemistry, vol. 1, 1987, vol. 2, 1988, vol. 3, 1989, vol. 4, 1991, vols. 5, 6, 1992; mem. editorial bd. Toxin Revs. Served with AUS, 1944-46. Recipient Regents' award for excellence in rsch. U. Hawaii, 1972, Outstanding Alumni award Northeastern U., 1984, inaugural Paul J. Scheuer award in marine natural projects, 1992. Mem. AAAS, Am. Chem. Soc., Swiss Chem. Soc., Royal Soc. Chemistry, Sigma Xi, Phi Kappa Phi. Home: 3271 Melemele Pl Honolulu HI 96822-1431 Office: U Hawaii 2545 The Mall Honolulu HI 96822

SCHIAVIO, FEDERICO, management consultant; b. Rome, Dec. 22, 1962; came to U.S., 1990; s. Giorgio Schiavio and Liliana de Martini. Diploma, Overseas Sch. Rome, 1981; postgrad., UCLA, 1990-91. Operator, programmer Incentive S.P.A., Rome, 1985-90; cons. Schiavio & Assocs., L.A., 1991—, Turner & Assocs., Chatsworth, Calif., 1991—; cons. Exec. Life Ins., 1991-92, Calif. Software Products, 1990-93, Barnes Wholesale, 1993—. Cpl. Italian Paratroops, 1987-88. Office: Schiavio & Assocs 25 Navy St # 16 Venice CA 90291

SCHICK, HAROLD RALPH, III, policy planner, consultant; b. Salem, Oreg., June 10, 1955; s. Harold Ralph Jr. and Jordis Adele (Benke) S. BS, U. Oreg., 1978; postgrad., U. Wash., 1979-80. Rschr. com. on land use Oreg. Ho. of Reps., Salem, 1978; asst. sgt.-at-arms Oreg. Senate, Salem, 1979; asst. program coord. Seattle City Light, 1979-80; policy analyst Bonneville Power Adminstrn., Portland, Oreg., 1980-83, team leader, 1983-86; sr. cons. Barakat & Chamberlin, Inc., Oakland, Calif., 1986-89; mgr. Barakat & Chamberlin, Inc., Portland, 1989—; conf. presenter in field. Co-author; Financing Energy Conservation, 1986. Office: Barakat & Camberlin Inc 1001 SW 5th Ave Ste 1000 Portland OR 97204

SCHIEL, JOHN MICHAEL, management consultant; b. Waterloo, Ont., Can., Nov. 28, 1937; s. Walter Frederick and Theresa Elizabeth (Donner) S.; m. Martha Church, Oct. 2, 1965; children: Andrea, Michael. BA with honors, U. Western Ont., 1961; MSc, McGill U., Montreal, Que., Can., 1965; MBA, York U., Toronto, Ont., 1970. Cert. mgmt. cons.; registered psychologist, Alta. Pers. adminstr. Domtar, Montreal, Que., 1961-65; prin. P. S. Ross & Ptnrs., Toronto, 1965-74; per. mgr. Torstar Corp., Toronto, 1974-78; dir. human resources Suncor, Edmonton, Alta., Can., 1978-79; dir., ptnr. Western Mgmt. Cons., Edmonton, 1979—; faculty adv. engring. U. Alta., Edmonton, 1980—. Bd. dirs., exec. Edmonton Symphony Orch., 1982, Edmonton Art Gallery, 1984. Fellow Inst. Cert. Mgmt. Cons. Can. (pres. Alta. bd. dirs. 1988, pres. Can. bd. dirs. 1992), Sigma Xi. Office: Western Mgmt Cons, #1500, 10250 - 101st St, Edmonton, AB Canada T5J 3P4

SCHIELDS, VICKIE MARIE, elementary educator; b. Hazen, N.D., July 9, 1957; d. Richard Carl and Leona Irene (Wetzel) S. BS in Elem. Edn. cum laude, Dickinson State U., 1979. Cert. tchr., Mont. Tchr. elem. sch. Lambert (Mont.) Pub. Schs., 1979—; negotiator Lambert Edn. Assn., 1984-85; judge Richland County Spelling Bee, Sidney, Mont, 1979—; chmn. I Love to Read program, Lambert, 1980-82, Grandparents Day program, 1987; coord. Book It program, 1988—; rep. OBE Conv., Rochester, Minn., 1992, Gifted & Talented Conf., Mpls., 1993; coord. travel group Nat. Finals Rodeo, 1990. Game chmn. Farmers Union, Golden Valley, N.D., 1978—; Bible sch. tchr. St. Paul's Luth. Ch., Dodge, N.D., 1978-83, organist, 1978—, ch. janitor, 1978—; judge Dunn County 4-H, Killdeer, N.D., 1979-85; crusader Am. Cancer Soc., 1980—; cook Lion's Den Teen Ctr., Lambert, 1991—. Named one of Outstanding Young Women of Am., 1987; recipient Outcome Based Edn. award, Lambert Pub. Sch. Mem. Mont. Edn. Assn., Lambert Edn. Assn., PTA, Lambert Domestic Club (sec. 1990—), Women of Moose, Guys and Gals Square Dance Club, Richey Rodeo Club. Lutheran. Home: PO Box 126 Lambert MT 59243 Office: Lambert Pub Sch PO Box 236 Lambert MT 59243

SCHIELE, PAUL ELLSWORTH, JR., educator, writer; b. Phila., Nov. 20, 1924; s. Paul Ellsworth Sr. and Maud (Barclay) S.; m. Sarah Irene Knauss, Aug. 20, 1946; children: Patricia Schiele Tiemann, Sandra Schiele Kicklighter, Deborah Schiele Hartigan. AT, Temple U., 1949; BA, LaVerne U., 1955; MA, Claremont Coll., 1961; PhD, U.S. Internat. U., San Diego, 1970. Cert. sec. tchr., Calif. 1961. Tchr. sci. and math. Lincoln High Sch., Phila., 1956-57, Ontario (Calif.) Sch. Dist., 1957-65; math. and sci. cons. Hacienda La Puente U. Sch. Dist., Calif., 1965-75; asst. prof. Calif. State U., Fullerton, 1975-83; pres., owner Creative Learning Environments and Resources, Glendora, Calif., 1983—, cons. sci. curriculum, 1985—; dir. title III project ESEA, 1974-75, cons. for project, 1975-77; cons. in field. Author: Primary Science, 1972, 2d edit., 1976; editor: A Living World, 1974, 2d edit., 1986; writer 9 sound filmstrips; writer model units for sci. and math. activity books; editor 21 sci. and math. activity books; writer, co-dir. TV show Marine Biology Series, 1970-71; designer in field. Apptd. adv. com. Sci. and Humanities Symposium Calif. Mus. Sci. and Industry, 1974; mem. State Sci. Permit Com., Tide Pools of Calif. Coast, 1974-75. Mem. Internat. Platform Assn., ABI Rsch. Assn. (bd. govs.), Calif. Music Theatre, Calif. Elem. Edn. Assn. (hon.), Nat. PTA (hon.), Calif. Inter-Sci. Coun. (pres., chmn. 1971), Elem. Sch. Scis. Assn. (past pres., bd. dirs.), Phi Delta Kappa (chartered). Republican. Lutheran. Home: 231 N Catherine Park Dr Glendora CA 91740-3018

SCHIELL, CHARLES RANDALL, leasing company executive; b. Aurora, Colo., Nov. 15, 1952; s. Charles and Audrey Mary (Parsons) S.; m. Janelle Marie Norris, Dec. 28, 1974; children: Charles Christopher, Angela Janelle. BA, U. Colo., 1975; MBA, Colo. State U., 1985. Br. mgr. Gen. Fin. Corp., Ft. Collins, Colo., 1977-78; collection mgr. 1st Nat. Bank, Ft. Collins, 1978-79; mgr. ops. Tri Continental Leasing Corp., Englewood, Colo., 1979-82; credit mgr. Colo. Nat. Leasing Corp., Golden, 1982-83, v.p. credit and ops., 1983-84; v.p. ops, treas. 1st Centennial Leasing Corp., Denver, 1984-89; v.p. ops., treas. 1st Concord Acceptance Corp., 1990-92, sr. v.p. ops., 1992—. Precinct committeeman Denver County Dem. Com., 1976, 77, Jefferson County Dem. Com., 1990—; precinct committeeman Arapahoe County Dem. Com., 1984-86, dist. capt., 1986-88; bd. dirs., treas. Lake Crest Met. Dist., 1990—; bd. dirs. Standley Lake Homeowners Assn., 1991—. Mem. Equipment Leasing Assn., Western Assn. Equipment Lessors. Presbyterian. Home: 12172 W 84th Pl Arvada CO 80005-5167 Office: 1st Concord Acceptance Corp 1515 Arapahoe St Ste 1095 Denver CO 80202-2110

SCHIERER, PAUL DUANE, lawyer; b. Peoria, Ill., Nov. 14, 1954; s. Arthur F. and Arlene M. (DuBois) S. BA, Ill. Benedictine Coll., 1979; JD, Vt. Law Sch., 1983. Bar: Wyo. 1984. Assoc. Pence and MacMillan, Laramie, Wyo., 1985-89, ptnr., 1989—; adj. prof. law U. Wyo., Laramie, 1990-93. Sec., spokesman Citizens Adv. Commn. Albany County Jail, Laramie, 1990-93. Mem. ABA, Wyo. State Bar Assn. (commr. 1992—, chair legal edn. com. 1989-92, by-laws com. 1992—), Albany County Bar Assn. (pres. 1989-92), Def. Rsch. Inst., Def. Lawyers Assn. Wyo., Wis. State Bar. Democrat. Office: Pence and MacMillan 501 Garfield Laramie WY 82070

SCHIERHOLZ, PAUL MILTON, computer company executive, software developer, chemical engineer; b. Postville, Iowa, Sept. 28, 1946; s. Milton Robert and Selma (Nelson) S.; children: Elizabeth, Stephanie, Patricia, Ryan, Andrew, Thomas. BSChemE, Iowa State U., 1968, MSChemE, 1969, D of Chem. Engring., 1974. Registered profl. engr. Engr. Du Pont, Beaumont, Tex., 1969-71; asst. prof. Mich. State U., East Lansing, 1973-75; assoc. prof. Colo. State U., Fort Collins, Colo., 1975-78; CEO Phoenix, Colorado Springs, 1979—. Contbr. over 20 articles to profl. jours. Recipient fellowship Nat. Def. Edn. Act, 1972. Mem. Phi Kappa Phi. Republican. Lutheran. Office: Phoenix 2132 W Colorado Ave Colorado Springs CO 80904

SCHIFF, ADAM BENNETT, lawyer; b. Framingham, Mass., June 22, 1960; s. Edward Maurice and Sherrill Ann (Glovsky) S. BA, Stanford U., 1982; JD, Harvard U., 1985. Bar: Calif. 1986. Assoc. Gibson, Dunn & Crutcher, L.A., 1986; asst. U.S. atty. U.S. Atty.'s Office, L.A., 1987—; spl. assignment to Czechoslovakia, Justice Dept., Bratislava, 1992. Contbr. articles to newspapers. Candidate State Assembly, 46th Dist., L.A., 1991. Mem. Calif. Bar (com. on environ. 1990-91). Office: US Attys Office 312 N Spring St Los Angeles CA 90012

SCHIFF, GUNTHER HANS, lawyer; b. Cologne, Germany, Aug. 19, 1927; came to U.S., 1936; s. Hans and Alice (Goldstein) S.; m. Katharine MacMillan, Jan. 27, 1950 (div. 1957); children: Eric Alan, Mary Alice; m. JoAnn R. Schiff; children: Jage, Hans Judson. B.S.F.S., Georgetown U., 1949, J.D., 1952. Bar: D.C. 1952, Calif. 1953. Assoc., ptnr. various firms, Beverly Hills, Calif., 1954—; sec. Los Angeles Copyright Soc., Beverly Hills, 1975-76. Contbr. articles to profl. jours. Pres. Beverly Hills Civil Svc. Commn., 1984-85, 88-89, Free Arts for Abused Children; chmn. Rent Control Rev. Bd., Beverly Hills, 1980-84; trustee Young Musicians Found. With USNR, 1945-46. Mem. Beverly Hills Bar Assn. (chmn. Resolutions Com. 1977-78), Los Angeles County Bar Assn., ABA, U.S. Copyright Soc., Los Angeles Copyright Soc. Clubs: Lake Arrowhead Country, Calif. Yacht. Home: 612 N Foothill Rd Beverly Hills CA 90210-3404 Office: Law Office Gunther H Schiff 9430 Olympic Blvd Beverly Hills CA 90210

SCHIFF, LAURIE, lawyer; b. Newark, Apr. 24, 1960; d. Norman Nathan and Claire Jane (Schott) S.; m. Ralph Conrad Shelton II, 1992. BS in Law, We. State U., Fullerton, Calif., 1987, JD, 1988. Bar: Calif. 1989. Ptnr. Schiff Mgmt., Newport Beach, Calif., 1983-89; pvt. practice Schiff & Assocs., Irvine, Calif., 1989-91; ptnr. Schiff & Shelton, 1991—; probation monitor State Bar Ct. Calif., 1991—. Producer: (record album) Boys Just Want to Have Sex, 1984. Mem. ABA, Orange County Bar Assn., Am. Mensa, Am. Polocrosse Assn., Saddlebrook Polocrosse (treas. 1991), Am. Quarterhouse

Assn. Democrat. Jewish. Office: 3 Hutton Centre Dr Ste 400 Santa Ana CA 92707

SCHIFF, STEVEN HARVEY, congressman, lawyer; b. Chicago, Ill., Mar. 18, 1947; s. Alan Jerome and Helen M. (Ripper) S.; m. Marcia Lewis, Nov. 8, 1968; children: Jaimi, Daniel. BA, U. Ill., Chgo., 1968; JD, U. N.Mex., 1972. Bar: N.Mex. 1972, U.S. Dist. Ct. N.Mex. 1972, U.S. Ct. Appeals (10th cir.) 1980. Asst. dist. atty. Dist. Atty.'s Office, Albuquerque, 1972-77, sole practice, 1977-79; asst. city atty. City of Albuquerque, 1979-81; dist. atty. State of N.Mex., Albuquerque, 1981-89; mem. 101st-103rd Congresses from 1st N.Mex. dist., Washington, D.C., 1989—; lectr. U. N.Mex., Albuquerque, 1981—. Chmn. Bernalillo County Rep. Party Conv., Albuquerque, 1984, 87, staff judge adv. N.Mex. Air N.G. Lt. Col., USAF Res. Recipient Law Enforcement Commendation medal SR, 1984. Mem. ABA, Albuquerque Bar Assn., N.Mex. Bar Assn. Republican. Jewish. Club: Civitan. Lodge: B'nai Brith (pres. 1976-78). Home: 804 Summit Ave NE Albuquerque NM 87106-2045 Office: House of Representatives 1009 Longworth Washington DC 20515 also: 625 Silver Ave SW Ste 140 Albuquerque NM 87102

SCHIFFELER, JOHN WILLIAM, sinologist; b. San Francisco, Sept. 21, 1940; s. Karl vom Stein and Marjorie Culver (Wintermute) S.; m. Katherine Yuan Chang, Dec. 21, 1963; 1 child, Chantal Suzanne. BA, San Francisco State U., 1964; MA, U. Hawaii, 1968; PhD, Ind. U., 1974; MA, U. Calif., 1979. Lectr. U. Calif., Berkeley, 1970-72, 93—, Dominican Coll. of San Rafael, Calif., 1972, 90—, San Francisco State U., 1974; rsch. coord. U. Calif., Berkeley, 1976-78. Author: The Legendary Creature of the Shan Hai Ching, 1978, An English-Chinese Dictionary of Geographical Terminology, 1976; contbr. articles to profl. jours. Bd. dirs. Tiburon (Calif.) Adv. Bd., 1970, Enterprise for High Sch. Students, San Francisco, 1975-76; pres. Pine Terrace Homeowners' Assn., Tiburon, 1971-72; v.p. Sea Cliff Homeowners' Assn., San Francisco, 1978-79. Lt. col. USAR. Earl C. Anthony History of Health Scis. fellow, U. Calif., San Francisco, 1976; recipient Monterey (Calif.) Rotary Club scholarship, 1964, Calif. State Colls. Internat. Prog. scholarship, San Francisco State U., 1966, Hon. Mention awards NSF, 1971, Asian Inst. of the Hague, The Netherlands, 1973, grants Pacific Cultural Found., Taipei, 1976, 77, 78, 84, 89. Mem. The Soc. of Cin. (pres. 1977-80, 88-91), Soc. of Mayflower Descendants (colony gov. 1980-81), Social Register Assn., Soc. for Asian Art (bd. dirs. 1975-81), China Soc., Soc. for Study of Early China, Internat. Assn. for Study of Traditional Asian Medicine, The Calif. Assn., The China Soc. Republican. Episcopalian. Home: 511 El Camino del Mar San Francisco CA 94121-1041 Office: Dominican Coll Dept History PO Box 8008 San Rafael CA 94912-8008

SCHIFFER, MICHAEL BRIAN, anthropologist, educator; b. Winnipeg, Man., Can., Oct. 4, 1947; came to U.S., 1953; s. Louie and Frances-Fera (Ludmer) S.; m. Annette Leve, Dec. 22, 1968; children: Adam Joseph, Jeremy Alan. BA in Anthropology summa cum laude, UCLA, 1969; MA, U. Ariz., 1972, PhD in Anthropology, 1973. Teaching asst. archaeol. field methods UCLA, spring 1969; student project supr. S.W. Expedition, Field Mus. Nat. History, summer 1969, rsch. asst., summer 1970, rsch. assoc., summer 1971; asst. prof. dept. anthropology U. Ark., 1973-75; teaching assoc. world prehistory U. Ariz., Tucson, 1972, teaching assoc. archaeol. interpretation, 1973, asst. prof. dept. anthropology, 1975-79, assoc. prof. dept. anthropology, 1979-82, prof., 1982—; dir. lab. traditional tech. dept. anthropology, 1984—; archaeologist Phoenix dist. Bur. Land Mgmt., summers, 1980-81; dir. various archaeol. surveys and projects; vis. disting. archaeologist U. S.C., summer, 1977; vis. assoc. prof. U. Wash., summer 1979; vis. disting. prof. Ariz. State U., fall, 1982; cons. in field. Author: Behavioral Archeology, 1976, Formation Processes of the Archaeological Record, 1987, The Portable Radio in American Life, 1991, Technological Perspectives on Behavioral Change, 1992; co-author (with W. L. Rathje) Archaeology, 1982; editor: Advances in Archaeological Method and Theory, Vols 1-11, 1978-87, Selections for Students from Vols. 1-4, 1982; Archaeological Method and Theory, Vols. 1-5, 1989-93; co-editor: (books) Archaeology of US, 1981, Hohokam and Patayan: Prehistory of Southwestern Arizona, 1982, others; contbr. articles to profl pubs. Woodrow Wilson fellow, 1969-70. Fellow AAAS, Am. Anthrop. Assn.; mem. Soc. Am. Archaeology, Soc. Hist. Archaeology, Soc. Archeol. Scis., Soc. Hist. Tech., Phi Beta Kappa. Democrat. Jewish. Home: 2718 E 10th St Tucson AZ 85716-4750 Office: Univ Ariz Dept Anthropology Tucson AZ 85721

SCHIFFNER, CHARLES ROBERT, architect; b. Reno, Sept. 2, 1948; s. Robert Charles and Evelyn (Keck) S.; m. Iovanna Lloyd Wright, Nov. 1971 (div. Sept. 1981); m. Adrienne Anita McAndrews, Jan. 20, 1983. Student, Sacramento Jr. Coll., 1967-68, Frank Lloyd Wright Sch. Architecture, 1968-77. Registered architect, Ariz., Nev., Wis. Architect Taliesin Associated Architects, Scottsdale, Ariz., 1977-83; pvt. practice architecture Phoenix, 1983—; instr. Ariz. State U., Tempe, 1983-87. Prin. works include Ahwatukee House of the Future (cert. distinction Am. Architecture 1985), addition to Richard Black Residence, Encanto Park, Ariz. (1st place J. Brock 1986), The Pottery House, Paradise Valley, Ariz., Seventh Day Adventist Exec. Hdqrs., Scottsdale, Condominium Project, Phoenix, SRPMIC Replacement Housing Program, Outer Loop Hwy., Scottsdale; author (poem) Yellowstone Stream (2d prize Winter Wheat contest 1986). Named one of 35 Most Promising Young Americans Under 35, US mag., 1979; recipient Restoration award Sunset Mag. Western Home, 1989, 91. Democrat. Roman Catholic. Home: 5202 E Osborn Rd Phoenix AZ 85018-6137 Office: Camelhead Office Ctr 2600 N 44th St # 208 Phoenix AZ 85008-1521

SCHIFFNER, JOAN LESSING, consultant; b. Hollywood, Calif., Nov. 26, 1944; d. Lessing Robert and Ruth Isabel (Chamberlain) Sattler; m. Ernest F. Schiffner: children: Robert Garrett, Gregory Garrett, Laura Garrett. BA, San Jose State U., 1970, postgrad.; postgrad., U. Calif. Cert. in non-profit orgn.mgmt. Cons. to health and human svc. govtl. and non-profit orgns. Civilian Pers. Office, Fort Ord, Calif., 1993—; bd. dirs. Growth and Opportunity, Inc; cons. Saving Our Libr.'s Excellence Com. 1992-93. Pub. info. officer San Benito County (Calif.) United Way, bd. dirs., 1988-90; founding mem. San Benito County Vol. Ctr. Task Force, San Benito County Cable Access Commn., 1987-90; co-founder San Benito County Action Team; vice chair San Benito County Voluntary Orgns. Active in Disasters, 1990-91; appointed to cen. com. ARC No. Calif. Earthquake Relief and Preparedness Project, 1991; pres. Network of San Benito, 1988-90; mem. San Benito County Econ. Group, Mex. Am. Com. on Edn., 1970—, Hollister Sister Cities Assn., 1989—; sec. bd. dirs. Econ. Devel. Corp.; exec. dir. San Benito County Interfaith, 1990-91; mem. adv. bd. San Benito Health Found., 1991—; pub. rels. chair San Benito County AIDS Project, 1992—; active numerous non-profit and civic orgns.; bd. dirs ARC. Mem. AAUW. Phi Alpha Theta, Psi Chi, Alpha Kappa Delta. Democrat. Roman Catholic. Home: 845 Helen Dr Hollister CA 95023-6613

SCHIFFRIN, MILTON JULIUS, physiologist; b. Rochester, N.Y., Mar. 23, 1914; s. William and Lillian (Harris) S.; m. Dorothy Euphemia Wharry, Oct. 10, 1942; children: David Wharry, Hilary Ann. AB, U. Rochester, 1937, MS, 1939; PhD cum laude, McGill U., 1941. Instr. physiology Northwestern U. Med. Sch., Evanston, Ill., 1941-45; lectr. pharmacology U. Ill. Med. Sch., 1947-57, clin. asst. prof. anesthesiology, 1957-61; with Hoffmann-La Roche, Inc., Nutley, N.J., 1946-79, dir. drug regulatory affairs, 1964-71, asst. v.p., 1971-79; pres. Wharry Rsch. Assn., Seattle, Wash., 1979—; chmn. Everglades Health Edn. Ctr., 1986-87. Author: (with E.G. Gross) Clinical Analgetics, 1955; editor: Management of Pain in Cancer, 1957. Capt. USAAF, 1942-46. Mem. Am. Med. Writers Assn. (bd. dirs. 1967—, pres. N.Y. chpt. 1967-68, nat. pres. 72-73), Am. Physiol. Soc., Internat. Coll. Surgeons, Am. Therapeutic Soc., Coll. Clin. Pharmacology and Therapeutics, Am. Chem. Soc. Home and Office: Unit 401 1001 2d Ave W Seattle WA 98119

SCHILBRACK, KAREN GAIL, system analyst; b. Tomahawk, Wis., Sept. 28; d. Edward Richard and Irene Angeline (Ligman) S. Student U. Calif.-Santa Barbara, 1967-69; B.A. in Anthropology, U. Calif.-Davis, 1971; postgrad. in Edn. and Archeology, Calif. State Poly. U., San Luis Obispo, 1971-72. Cert. tchr., computer specialist, data processing; lic. cosmetologist. Computer specialist Facilities Systems Office, Port Hueneme, Calif., 1975-78, sr. computer specialist, 1978-80, project mgr. U.S. Naval Constrn. Bn. Ctr., 1980-89, imaging systems computer specialist Comptr. Office, 1989-92; fiscal quality specialist D.D. Defense Finance and Acctg. Svc., DAO, Port Hurricane, 1992—; tng. cons. FACSO, 1981, 82; curriculum cons. Ventura Community Coll., Calif., 1981-89; instr. U.S. Navy, Port Hueneme, 1983, 91, Civil Service Commn., Port Hueneme, 1978-80. Author: AMALGAMAN Run Procedures, 1976; Cobol Programming Efficiencies, 1978, Imaging System UserManual, 1991; co-author, editor: Training Manual for Direct Data Entry System, 1983. Mem. Vols. for Camarillo State Hosp., Camarillo, 1978-88, coord. Ventura County, 1981; chmn. scholarship fund drive Ventura, Santa Barbara, Los Angeles, Counties, 1980. Named Young Career Woman of Yr., Calif. Bus. and Profl. Women, 1979. Mem. Young Ladies Inst. (pres. Santa Paula, dist. dep. Ventura/Santa Barbara Counties), Am. Biog. Inst. Research Assn. (lifetime dep. gov.). Lodge: Toastmistress. Home: 6993 Wheeler Canyon Rd Santa Paula CA 93060-9727 Office: Compt Office Code 243-A USNCBC Port Hueneme CA 93042

SCHILLER, DANIEL TOBY, communications educator; b. N.Y.C., July 10, 1951; s. Herbert Irving and Anita Louise (Rosenbaum) S.; m. Susan Gray Davis, July 23, 1978; children: Ethan Davis, Lucy Hazel. BA, U. Wis., 1972; MA, U. Pa., 1976, PhD, 1978. Rsch. scholar U. Leicester (Eng.) Ctr. for Mass Communication Rsch., 1978-79; asst. prof. radio-TV-film dept. Temple U., Phila., 1979-83, assoc. prof., 1983-86; assoc. prof. Grad. Sch. of Libr. and Info. Scis. UCLA, 1987-90; assoc. prof. communications dept. U. Calif., San Diego, 1990—. Author: Objectivity and the News, 1981, Telematics and Government, 1982. Gannett Ctr. for Media Studies fellow Columbia U., 1986-87. Office: U Calif San Diego Dept Comm San Diego CA 92093-0503

SCHILLER, JOHANNES AUGUST, clergyman, educator; b. Gaylord, Kans., June 17, 1923; s. Johann Carl and Adele Dorothea (Kirchoff) S.; m. Aleen B. Linhardt, Aug. 26, 1946; children: Paul Omar, Samuel Robert. BA, Capital U., 1945; cand. theology, Evangel. Luth. Theol. Sem., 1947; MA, U. Mo., 1959; PhD in Sociology, U. Wash., 1967. Ordained to ministry Am. Luth. Ch., 1947. Pastor Peace Luth. Ch., Sterling, Colo., 1947-49, Trinity-St. Paul Parish, Malcolm, Iowa, 1949-51, Immanuel Luth. Ch., Beatrice, Nebr., 1951-56, Salem Luth. Ch., Lenexa, Kans., 1956-58; asst. prof., assoc. prof., now prof. sociology Pacific Luth. U., Tacoma, Wash., 1958-91; prof. emeritus Pacific Luth. U., Tacoma, 1991—; regency prof. Pacific Luth. U., Tacoma, Wash., 1976—, chair dept. sociology, 1956-71, 86-88, dean div. social scis., 1969-76, 88-91, dir. grad. programs div. social scis., 1977-82, dir. Ctr. Social Rsch. and Pub. Policy, 1987-90; chaplain Beatrice State Home, 1953-56; adj. prof. San Francisco Theol. Sem., San Anselmo, Calif., 1978-89. Editor: The American Poor, 1982; contbr. articles to profl. publs. Mem. Am. Sociology Assn., Pacific Sociology Assn., Nat. Coun. Family Rels., Wash. State Sociol. Assn. Home: 1217 Wheeler St S Tacoma WA 98444-3843

SCHILLING, DEAN WILLIAM, manufacturing executive; b. Waverly, Iowa, Apr. 25, 1944; s. Alvin Louis and Etta Christine (Poppe) S.; m. Betty Ann (Homeister), Aug. 5, 1962; children: Angela Marie, Christine Ann. AS, Iowa State U., 1964, BS, 1969. Engr. Systems Genetics, Clarksville, Iowa, 1970-81; sr. tech. support Hewlett Packard, Sunnyvale, Calif., 1983-85; pres. Cryo Genetic Technology, Soquel, Calif., 1985—. Inventor biol. devices and methods to remedy human infertility; holder 3 patents. Mem. Am. Fertility Soc., Soc. Cryobiology, Iowa State Alumni. Lutheran. Lodge: Order of Knoll (founders club 1988).

SCHILLING, FREDERICK AUGUSTUS, JR., geologist, consultant; b. Phila., Apr. 12, 1931; s. Frederick Augustus and Emma Hope (Christoffer) S.; m. Ardis Ione Dovre, June 12, 1957 (div. 1987); children: Frederick Christopher, Jennifer Dovre. BS in Geology, Wash. State U., 1953; PhD in Geology, Stanford U., 1962. Computer geophysicist United Geophys. Corp., Pasadena, Calif., 1955-56; geologist various orgns., 1956-61, U.S. Geol. Survey, 1961-64; underground engr. Climax (Colo.) Molybdenum Co., 1966-68; geologist Keradamex Inc., Anaconda Co., M.P. Grace, Ranchers Exploration & Devel. Corp., Albuquerque and Grants, N.Mex., 1968-84, Hecla Mining Co., Coeur d'Alene, Idaho, 1984-86, various engrng. and environ. firms, Calif., 1986-91; prin. F. Schilling Cons., Canyon Lake, Calif., 1991—. Author: Bibliography of Uranium, 1976. Del. citizen amb. program People to People Internat., USSR, 1990-91. With U.S. Army, 1953-55. Fellow Explorers Club; mem. Geol. Soc. Am., Am. Assn. Petroleum Geologists, Soc. Mining Engrs., Internat. Platform Assn., Masons, Kiwanis, Sigma Xi, Sigma Gamma Epsilon. Republican. Presbyterian. Office: F Schilling Cons 30037 Steel Head Dr Canyon Lake CA 92587

SCHILLING, RICHARD JAMES, dentist; b. Lincoln, Nebr., Aug. 4, 1933; s. Dale Delbert and Gladys Viola (Renfro) S.; m. Marlene Alice Willie, Aug. 11, 1956; children: Bradley R., Jennifer J. Lock, Christopher. BS, U. Nebr., 1957, DDS, 1957. Pvt. practice Loveland, Colo., 1960—; staff mem. McKee Med. Ctr. Found., Loveland, bd. dirs. Artist numerous one-man shows and nat. art shows. Pres. Loveland-Berthoud United Fund, 1967-68. Sr. dental officer USPHS, 1956-60. Mem. ADA, Larimer County Dental Soc. (pres. 1963-64), Colo. State Dental Assn. Republican. Office: 1907 Boise Ave Loveland CO 80538-4291

SCHINDLER, ABBOTT MICHAEL, marketing consultant; b. L.A., Mar. 8, 1950; s. Milton and Hilma (Markowitz) S.; m. Sandra Wilks, Dec. 20, 1970 (div. May 1975). Rsch. biochemist VA Hosp., Sepulveda, Calif., 1967-78; engr. Burroughs Corp., Westlake Village, Calif., 1978-81; dir. engring Magnetic Info. Tech., Chatsworth, Calif., 1981-82; sr. engr. Apple Computer, Inc., Newbury Park, Calif., 1982-84; prin. engr. Digital Equipment Corp., Colorado Springs, Colo., 1984-90, product mktg. cons., 1990—; cons. in field. Author: Cycling Routes of Colorado Springs, 1989; patentee in field. Pres. Colorado Springs Atronom. Soc., 1985-87; guest instr. El Paso County Parks, Colorado Springs, 1989-90. Mem. Digital Equipment Users Soc., Interex, Colorado Springs Cycling Club (bd. dirs. 1989—). Office: Digital Equipment Corp 301 S Rockrimmon Blvd Colorado Springs CO 80919-2303

SCHINDLER, KEITH WILLIAM, software engineer; b. Selma, Calif., May 27, 1959; s. George Junior and Doris Angelynn (Young) S. BSEE in Computer Sci. with honors, U. Calif., Berkeley, 1982. Programmer Summit Group, Berkeley, 1979-81; jr. programmer Control Data, Inc., Sunnyvale, Calif., 1983; assoc. mem. tech. staff Symbolics, Inc., Chatsworth, Calif., 1987-88; sr. mem. tech. support Graphics div. Symbolics, L.A., 1988-90; software engr. Sidley, Wright & Assoc., Hollywood, Calif., 1990-92; cons. Out-Takes, Inc., L.A., 1992—; ptnr. Schindler Imaging, West Hollywood, Calif., 1992—; tech. dir. Sidley-Wright & Assoc., Hollywood, 1990-92, Movie Time Cable Channel, Hollywood, 1990, Video Image, Marina Del Rey, Calif., 1990; cert. developer Apple Computer, Inc., 1991—, Truevision, Inc., 1990—; developer software Out-Takes' Digital Photography System; creator The Matte Machine. Patentee in field. Mem. IEEE Computer Soc., Assn. for Computing Machinery (spl. interest group graphics), Tau Beta Pi. Democrat. Office: Schindler Imaging PO Box 69778 West Hollywood CA 90069

SCHINZINGER, ROLAND, electrical and computer engineering educator; b. Osaka, Japan, Nov. 22, 1926; s. Robert Karl Edmund and Annelise (Hebting) S.; m. Jane Harris, June 19, 1952; children: Stefan, Annelise, Barbara. BSEE, U. Calif., Berkeley, 1953, MSEE, 1954, PhD in Elec. Engring., 1966. Registered profl. engr., Calif. Mem. liaison staff Nippon Steel Tube Co., Tsurumi Shipyard, Japan, 1946-47; asst. mgr. Far Eastern Equip. Co., Ltd., Tokyo, 1947-48; lectr. U. Pitts., 1955-58; elec. engr. Westinghouse Elec. Corp., East Pittsburgh, 1954-58; asst./assoc. prof. Robert Coll., Istanbul, Turkey, 1958-63; mem. faculty dept. elec. and computer engring. and mgmt. U. Calif., Irvine, 1965-92, prof., assoc. dean, 1979-83, 85-86. Author: (with M. Martin) Ethics in Engineering, 1983, 2d edit., 1989, (with P.A. Laura) Conformal Mapping: Modern Applications and Methods, 1991; contbr. articles to profl. jours., chpts. to books. Sci. faculty fellow NSF, 1964. Fellow IEEE (Centennial medal 1983, award for Contbn. to Professionalism 1993), Inst. for Advancement Engring.; mem. AAAS, Ops. Rsch. Soc. Am., Am. Soc. for Engring. Edn., Soc. for Philosophy and Tech., Computer Scientists for Social Responsibility, Sigma Xi, Tau Beta Pi, Eta Kappa Nu. Office: Univ of Calif Elec and Computer Engring Irvine CA 92717

SCHIRMACHER, STANLEY L., retired industrial arts educator; b. Beaver Dam, Wis., Sept. 21, 1908; s. Charles William Fred and Martha Louise (Mittelstadt) S.; m. Ruth Ollye Arline Scales Horsley, Aug. 1935; 1 child, JimmyRuth Horsley LeTarte Vaughan. BA, Ariz. State U., 1935, MA, 1951. Carpenter apprentice Beaver Dam, Wis., 1926-29; doorman and carpenter State Theatre and Tempe Beach Theatre, Tempe, Ariz., 1933-35; shop tchr. Jordon Sch., Mesa, Ariz., 1935-36; coach, indsl. arts tchr. Clemenceau Jr. High Sch., Cottonwood, Ariz., 1936-42; indsl. arts instr. Tempe Union High Sch., 1942-46, Cottonwood (Ariz.) High Sch., 1946-55; indsl. arts instr. Papago Sch. Creighton Dist., Phoenix, 1955-75, ret., 1975; Navy E draftsman Goodyear Aircraft, summers 1942-45. Author: Slide Rule in A Nutshell, 1960; contbr. articles to profl. jours.; author newsletter. Sec. Sedona (Ariz.) Camera Club, 1955. Inducted into Living History Hall of Fame, 1991. Mem. Golden Circle Ariz. State U., Freedoms Found. at Valley Forge (Teacher's medal 1965), Internat. Freelance Photographers Orgn., Sons of Sherman's March to the Sea (founder, dir.), Civil War Shack (founder, dir.), Kingdom of Callaway, Mo. (knight). Baptist. Home: 1725 S Farmer Ave Tempe AZ 85281-6533

SCHKLAIR, GLORYA BELGRADE, accountant, business owner; b. Evansville, Ind., Dec. 4, 1931; d. Benjamin N. and Sarah (Cohen) Belgrade; m. Eugene Schklair, June 22, 1952; children: Steven Jay, Sanford Brian, Victoria Jean, Julia Karen. BA, U. Ill., Chgo., 1969. Asst. comptroller Robinson Bros. Steel Co., Inc., Chgo., 1960-62; clinic mgr. Elmhurst (Ill.) Dental Clinic, 1962-77, 79-84; law firm mgr. Gov. Dan Walker Law Offices, Oakbrook, Ill., 1977-79; owner, cons. The Practical Organizer, Thousand Oaks, Calif., 1986—; fins. cons. Regal Casualty Ins. Co., Inc., Westlake Village, Calif., 1988-91, Bergan Isle Ins. Co., Ltd., Tortola, B.V.I., 1988-91, KTS Mgmt. Co., Westlake Village, 1988-91. Author: Glorya's Gourmet Gallery, 1992. Bd. dirs. Work Tng., Inc., Woodland Hills, Calif., 1987-90; founder, pres. Lane Assn. for Retarded Citizens, Winnetka, Ill., 1975-80; legis. chmn. Glenkirk Assn. Handicapped Children, Northbrook, Ill., 1973-75; mem. exec. bd. Ray Graham Assn. Handicapped Children, Elmhurst, 1970-73; mem. steering com. Pub. TV Channel 11 Auction, Chgo., 1968-70. Recipient Daumier award for sculpture Armand Hammer Mus. Arts, L.A., 1990. Mem. NAFE, Nat. Orgn. Profl. Organizers, Am. Inst. Profl. Bookkeepers, Thousand Oaks Art Assn. Office: The Practical Organizer 3463 Indian Mesa Dr Thousand Oaks CA 91360

SCHLADOR, PAUL RAYMOND, JR., insurance agent; b. Riverside, Calif., Oct. 16, 1934; s. Paul Raymond Sr. Schlador and Lois Geraldine (Burrus) Kaeding; m. Evangeline Kathern, Aug. 19, 1955; children: Debora Lynn TeSam, Cheryl Jean Bastian, Bonnie Kay Tucker. Student, San Diego City Jr. Coll., 1954-55, Ins. Industry, San Diego, 1960-62, Am. Coll., San Diego, 1970-74. CLU. Agt. Bankers Life of Nebr., San Diego, 1959-63; agt./ mgr. Southwestern Life Ins. Co., San Diego, 1966-78; ind. agt. State Farm Ins. Co., San Diego, 1978—. With USNG, 1952-60. Mem. San Diego Assn. Life Underwriters (pres. 1989-90, legis. v.p. 1988), Kiwanis Club El Cajon Valley. Republican. Methodist. Home: 1267 Oakdale Ave # C El Cajon CA 92021-6454 Office: State Farm Ins 7800 University Ave # 1A La Mesa CA 91941-4928 also: BPOE Lodge # 1812 El Cajon CA 92021

SCHLAPAK, BENJAMIN RUDOLPH, state official, retired army officer; b. Winsted, Conn., Nov. 14, 1937; s. Rudolph and May Adelaide (Bradford) S.; divorced; children: Eric, Rudy, Sara; m. Helen Ann McCoy, Apr. 25, 1970; children: Tony, Lygia, Nicholas. BSME, Norwich U., 1959; BSCE, Tex. A&M U., 1964, MECE, 1965. Registered profl. engr., Vt., Tex., Hawaii. Commd. 2d lt. U.S. Army, 1959, advanced through grades to col., 1979; asst. div. engr., then dist. engr. U.S. Army Pacific Ocean Div., Ft. Shafter, Hawaii, 1976-80; dir. engring. U.S. Army So. Command, Corozal, Panama, 1980-83; command engr. U.S. Army Western Command, Ft. Shafter, 1983-85, dir., cons. family housing, 1985-89; ret., 1989; project mgr. M & E Pacific Inc., Honolulu, 1989-92; head planning engr. airports div. Hawaii Dept. Transp., Honolulu, 1992—; contracting officer U.S. Army C.E., Buffalo, 1968-69, Ft. Shafter, 1976-80. Contbr. articles to mil. publs. Mem. Hawaii Gov.'s Com. on Housing, 1988-89; mem. Rapid Transit Sta. Community Adv. Com., Honolulu, 1991-92. Decorated Legion of Merit, Bronze Star with 6 oak leaf clusters; recipient merit award Freedoms Found., 1969. Mem. NSPE, ASCE, Soc. Am. Mil. Engrs., Am. Pub. Works Assn. Home: 1545 Molina St Honolulu HI 96818 Office: Hawaii Dept Transp Airports Div Honolulu Internat Airport Honolulu HI 96819

SCHLEGEL, JOHN PETER, university president; b. Dubuque, Iowa, July 31, 1943; s. Aaron Joseph and Irma Joan (Hingtgen) S. BA, St. Louis U., 1969, MA, 1970; BDiv, U. London, 1973; DPhil, Oxford U., 1977. Joined Soc. of Jesus, 1963, ordained priest Roman Cath. Ch., 1973. From asst. prof. to assoc. prof. Creighton U., Omaha, 1976-79, asst. acad. v.p., 1978-82; dean Coll. Arts and Scis. Rockhurst Coll., Kansas City, Mo., 1982-84, Marquette U., Milw., 1984-88; exec. and acad. v.p. John Carroll U., Cleve., 1988-91; pres. U. San Francisco, 1991—; cons. Orgn. for Econ. Devel. and Cooperation, Paris, 1975-76. Author: Bilingualism and Canadian Policy in Africa, 1979; editor: Towards a Redefinition of Development, 1976; contbr. articles to profl. jours. Mem. Milw. County Arts Coun., 1986-88; mem. Mo. Coun. on Humanities, Kansas City, 1984; trustee St. Louis U., 1985-91, Loyola U., Chgo., 1988—, St. Ignatius High Sch., Cleve., 1990-91, Loyola Coll. in Md., 1992—; bd. dirs. San Francisco ARC. Oxford U. grantee, 1974-76; Govt. of Can. grantee, 1977-78. Mem. Am. Coun. on Edn., Canadian Studies in U.S., Olympic Club, Bohemian Club. Office: U San Francisco Office of Pres 2130 Fulton St San Francisco CA 94117-1080

SCHLEGEL, PAUL LOIS, JR., graphic arts firm executive, consultant; b. Kent, Ohio, Feb. 1, 1927; s. Paul Lois Sr. and Ruth (Bindley) S.; m. Shirley Ann Kipp, Jan. 1, 1947; children: Terrie Lynn Bagnuolo, Laurie Darlene Downey. Student, U. So. Calif., 1945-47, 55-60. Gen. mgr. McDuffey-Brown, L.A., 1947-49; salesperson Smart Supply Co. Inc., L.A., 1949-55, sales mgr., 1955-60, v.p. sales, bd. dirs., 1960-70, pres., 1970-75; founder, bd. dirs. # 1 Network, Chgo., 1974-75; div. pres. Hammermill Paper Co., L.A., 1975-77, semi-ret., 1977; prin. P.L. Schlegel & Assocs., Laguna Beach, Calif., 1983—; cons. Visual Graphics Corp., Tamarac, Fla., 1982—; mem. exec. com., cons. K. Wilson Co., Inc., San Francisco, 1986—; bd. dirs., cons. Sage Tech. subs. Polaroid, Rancho Bernardo, Calif., 1986-87. Pres. Laguna Beach Taxpayers Assn., Calif., 1984, 85, Calif. Rep. Assembly, Laguna Beach, 1986, 87; bd. dirs. North Laguna Community Assn., Laguna Beach, 1984-88, Orange County Rep. Assembly, Garden Grove, Calif., 1987, 88. With USN, 1944-45, World War II and Korea. Mem. Inst. for Sales Rsch. (pres. 1960's), Printing Industries of Am. (bd. dirs. Calif. chpt. 1976-77), Graphic Arts Equipment and Supply Dealers Assn. (charter, 1st v.p. 1976), Sales Execs. Club of L.A. Republican. Home: 23288 Pompeii Dr Dana Point CA 92629-3549 Office: PL Schlegel & Assocs PO Box 3367 Princeville HI 96722-3367

SCHLEH, EDWARD CARL, business analyst; b. St. Paul, Nov. 2, 1915; s. Edward G. and Augusta (Seltz) S.; m. Myra Adelle Oberschulte, June 7, 1941; children: Jeanne, John, Richard, Elizabeth, Robert. BBA, U. Minn., 1937. Placement officer U. Minn. Employment Office, Mpls., 1937-39, Ells Employment Svc., Mpls., 1939-40; mgr. personnel rsch. 3-M Co., St. Paul, 1940-48; pres. Schleh Assocs., Inc., Mpls. and Palo Alto, Calif., 1948—; U.S. del. to internat. mgmt. confs. in Chile, France, Germany, Australia, Japan; bd. Exec. Svc. Corps., San Francisco; adv. bd. Santa Clara U. Bus. Sch.; bd. dirs. Coun. Internat. Progress in Mgmt.; presenter seminars, speeches for profit orgns. U.S. and abroad. Author: Successful Executive Action, Management by Results, Effective Management of Personnel, The Management Tactician, How to Boost Your Return on Management; contbr. articles to profl. publs. Mem. Soc. Advancement of Mgmt. (Frederick Taylor Key award), Am. Mgmt. Assn. (wall of fame). Home: 368 Selby Ln Menlo Park CA 94027-3933 Office: 2600 El Camino Real Palo Alto CA 94306-1705

SCHLEI, NORBERT ANTHONY, lawyer; b. Dayton, Ohio, June 14, 1929; s. William Frank and Norma (Lindsley) S.; m. Jane Moore, Aug. 26, 1950 (div. 1963); children: Anne C. Buczynski, William K., Andrew M.; m. Barbara Lindemann, Mar. 7, 1965 (div. 1981); children: Bradford L., Graham L., Norbert L., Norma Blake, Elizabeth Eldridge. BA, Ohio State U., 1950; LLB magna cum laude, Yale U., 1956. Bar: Ohio 1956, Calif. 1958, D.C. 1963, U.S. Supreme Ct. 1963. Law clk. to Justice Harlan U.S. Supreme Ct., 1956-57; assoc. atty. O'Melveny & Myers, L.A., 1957-59; ptnr. Greenberg, Shafton & Schlei, L.A., 1959-62; asst. atty. gen. U.S. Dept. Justice, Washington, 1962-66; ptnr. Munger, Tolles, Hills & Rickershauser, 1968-70, Kane, Shulman & Schlei, Washington, 1968-70; ptnr.-in-charge Hughes Hubbard & Reed, L.A., 1972-89; pres., CEO Kahala Capital Corp.,

Santa Monica, Calif., 1983—; gen. counsel Clinicorp Inc., L.A., 1991—. Author: (with M.S. McDougal and others) Studies in World Public Order, 1961 (Am. Soc. Internat. Law ann. book award); State Regulation of Corporate Financial Practices, 1962; editor-in-chief Yale Law Jour., 1955-56. Dem. nominee for Calif. Assembly, 1962, for sec. of state Calif., 1966; bd. dirs. Constl. Rights Found., Japan-Am. Found., Inc. Mem. ABA, Fed. Bar Assn., Am. Judicature Soc., Am. Soc. Internat. Law, Calif. Bar, Los Angeles County Bar Assn., Yale Club So. Calif., Calif. Yacht Club (Marina del Rey, Calif.), Riviera Country Club (Pacific Palisades, Calif.), Plaza Club Honolulu. Office: 1875 Century Park E Ste 1360 Los Angeles CA 90067 also: 75-5751 Kuakini Hwy Ste 201 Kailua-Kona HI 96740

SCHLENKER, EDGAR ALBERT, educator, entrepreneur; b. Sacramento, June 4, 1961; s. Albert and Irmgard (Hess) S.; m. Adele Margaret Gibbons, Jan. 8, 1983 (div.); 1 child, Margaret Adele. BS in Pub. Affairs, Calif. State U., Sacramento, 1986; MBA, U. Calif., Berkeley, 1988. Founder Precious Gifts Ltd., Sacramento, 1983-86; prin. RSA Cons., Berkeley, 1986-88; assoc. Dowdell Investment Banking, San Rafael, Calif., 1988-89; dir. mktg. and sales Info Store, Inc., San Francisco, 1988-90; dir. Solano County Small Bus. Devel. Ctr., Suisun, Calif., 1990—; chmn. Internat. Reprint Corp., Berkeley, 1988—; pres. IRC Med. Pub., Benicia, Calif. chmn. Internat. Reprint Corp., Berkeley, 1988—; pres. IRC Med. Pub., Benicia, Calif. Elected to Solano County Bd. Suprs., 2d Dist., 1992. Fellow Inst. Dirs.; mem. U. Calif.-Berkeley Alumni Assn. Independent. Home: PO Box 12004 Vallejo CA 94590-9004 Office: Solano County Small Bus Devel Ctr 320 Campus Ln Suisun City CA 94585-1400

SCHLESINGER, DEBORAH LEE, librarian; b. Cambridge, Mass., Sept. 13, 1937; d. Edward M. and Edith D. (Schneider) Hershoff; divorced; children: Suzanne, Richard. BA, U. Mass., 1961; MS, Simmons Coll., 1974; postgrad., U. Pitts., 1983. Reference librarian Bently Coll., Waltham, Mass., 1964-65; dir. Carnegie Library, Swissvale, Pa., 1973-77, South Park Twp. Library, Library, Pa., 1977-81, Monessen (Pa.) Library, 1981-82, Lewis & Clark Library, Helena, Mont., 1983-88, 89—; state librarian Mont. State Library, Helena, Mont., 1988-89; vis. scholar Pitts. Regional Library Ctr., 1982-83. Editor Pa. Union List, 1982-83. Mem. exec. bd. Mont. Cultural Advocacy, 1983—. Mem. Mont. Library Assn. (chmn. legis. com. 1984-92, MLA lobbyist 1992—), Mont. Assn. Female Execs. (fin. com. 1986—), AAUW (exec. com. 1985-86). Democrat. Club: Montana (Helena). Home: 507 5th Ave Helena MT 59601-4359 Office: Lewis & Clark Libr 120 S Last Chance Mall Helena MT 59601

SCHLESINGER, RUDOLF BERTHOLD, lawyer, educator; b. Munich, Germany, Oct. 11, 1909; s. Morris and Emma (Aufhauser) S.; m. Ruth Hirschland, Sept. 4, 1942; children: Steven, June, Fay. Dr. Jur., U. Munich, 1933; LLB, Columbia U., 1942. Bar: N.Y. 1942, U.S. Supreme Ct. 1946. Law sec. to Chief Judge Irving Lehman, N.Y. Ct. Appeals, 1942-43; confidential law sec. Judges N.Y. Ct. Appeals, 1943- 44; asso. Milbank, Tweed, Hope & Hadley, N.Y.C., 1944-48; asso. prof. Cornell U., 1948-51, prof., 1951-75, William N. Cromwell prof. internat. and comparative law, 1956-75; prof. Hastings Coll. Law, U. Calif., 1975—, vis. prof., 1974; Cons. N.Y. State Law Rev. Commn., 1949—; mem. adv. com. internat. rules of jud. procedure, 1959-66; vis. prof. Columbia, 1952, Salzburg Seminar, 1964; Charles Inglis Thomson disting. vis. prof. U. Colo., summer 1976. Author: Cases, Text and Materials on Comparative Law, 2nd edit, 1959, 3d edit., 1970, 4th edit., 1980, 5th edit., 1988 (with Baade, Damaska & Herzog), Formation of Contracts: A Study of the Common Core of Legal Systems, 2 vols, 1968; others.; Editor-in-chief: Columbia Law Rev, 1941-42; bd. editors: Am. Jour. Comparative Law; contbr. articles on legal topics. Trustee Cornell U., 1961-66. Carnegie Corp. Reflective year fellowship, 1962-63. Mem. Am. Law Inst. (life), Am. Bar Assn., Internat. Acad. Comparative Law, Phi Beta Kappa, Order of Coif. Home: 2601 Vallejo St San Francisco CA 94123-4642 Office: Univ Calif Hastings Coll of Law 200 McAllister St San Francisco CA 94102-4976

SCHLIEKER, JANICE ELAINE JONES, campus minister; b. Omaha, Jan. 10, 1957; d. Robert W. and Greta Jane (Young) Jones; m. John F. Schlieker III, Sept. 12, 1981. BTh in New Testament, Ozark Bible Coll., 1980. Ordained to ministry Christian Ch., 1981. Cashier, bookkeeper Northampton 4 Theaters, Omaha, 1973-75; florist Higdon's Florist, Joplin, Mo., 1978-80; assoc. campus min. Koinonia Campus Ministry, Joplin, Mo., 1978-80; campus min. Colorado Christian Campus Ministries, Ft. Collins, 1980—. Mem. Day Spring Christian Ch., Ft. Collins, 1986—; local planning com. N.Am. Christian Conv., Cin., 1990-91. Mem. Nat. Assn. Christian Campus Ministries (sec.-treas. 1987—), Univ. Religious Dirs. Assn. (v.p. Ft. Collins chpt. 1986-87), Ft. Collins Running Club, No. Colo. Running Club. Office: Colo Christian Campus Ministry 1501 S Whitcomb Fort Collins CO 80521

SCHLIMPERT, CHARLES EDGAR, college president; b. Sydney, Nebr., Aug. 13, 1945; s. Edgar Theodore and Melba Marie (Schlesselman) S.; m. Patricia Burke, July 22, 1966; children: Scott, Justin. BA, Concordia Coll., 1968; MEd, U. Mo., 1971; PhD, U. So. Calif., L.A., 1980. Dir. Christian edn. Our Savior Luth. Ch., St. Charles, Mo., 1968-70; youth dir. Holy Cross Luth. Ch., Los Alamitos, Calif., 1970-73; guidance dir., tchr. Luth. High Sch., Orange, Calif., 1973-75, prin., 1975-81; exec. dir. Luth. High Sch. Assn., Orange, 1981-83; pres. Concordia Coll., Portland, Oreg., 1983—; bd. dirs. Luth. Edn. Conf. N.Am., Washington, 1988-90. Contbr. articles to profl. jours. Mem. Oreg. Ind. Coll. Assn. (bd. dirs. 1983—, pres. 1990-92). Republican. Office: Concordia Coll 2811 NE Holman St Portland OR 97211-6067

SCHLOSE, WILLIAM TIMOTHY, health care executive; b. West Lafayette, Ind., May 16, 1948; s. William Fredrick and Dora Irene (Chitwood) S.; m. Linda Lee Fletcher, June 29, 1968 (div. 1978); children: Vanessa Janine Schlose Hubert, Stephanie Lynn; m. Kelly Marie Martin, June 6, 1987; 1 child, Taylor Jean Martin-Schlose. Student, Bowling Green State U., 1966-68, Long Beach City Coll., 1972-75; teaching credential, UCLA, 1975. Staff respiratory therapist St. Vincent's Med. Ctr., L.A., 1972-75; cardio-pulmonary chief Temple Community Hosp., L.A., 1975-76; adminstrv. dir. spl. svcs. Santa Fe Meml. Hosp., L.A., 1976-79; mem. mktg. and pub. rels. staff Nat. Med. Homecare Corp., Orange, Calif., 1979-81, Medtech of Calif., Inc., Burbank, Calif., 1981-84; regional mgr. Mediq Health Care Group Svcs., Inc., Chatsworth, Calif., 1984-88; pres. Baby Watch Homecare, Whittier, Calif., 1988-90, Tim Schlose and Assocs., Anaheim, Calif., 1990—; staff instr., Montebello (Calif.) Adult Schs. Author: Fundamental Respiratory Therapy Equipment, 1977. With USN, 1968-72. Mem. Am. Assn. Respiratory Care, Calif. Soc. Respiratory Care (past officer), Nat. Bd. Respiratory Care, Nat. Assn. Apnea Profls., Am. Assn. Physicians Assts., L.A. Pediatric Soc., Calif. Perinatal Assn., Porsche Owners Club L.A., Porsche Club Am. Republican. Methodist. Office: Tim Schlose and Assocs 1290 E Katella Ave Anaheim CA 92805-6627

SCHLOSS, ERNEST PETER, healthcare facility administrator, planner; b. N.Y.C., Mar. 15, 1949; s. Gerd Tobias and Helene (Alberta) S.; m. Janice Gail Callender, Mar. 25, 1972 (div. 1977); 1 child, Jacob Alan; m. Marie Patricia Kearney, Apr. 20, 1985. BA in Anthropology, Prescott (Ariz.) Coll., 1971; MA in Anthropology, U. Ariz., 1973, PhD in Edn. Adminstrn., 1983. Exec. dir. Cochise County Comprehensive Health Planning Coun., Bisbee, Ariz., 1973-74; sr. data analyst Pima Health Systems, Tucson, 1974-76; project coord. Southwestern Ctr. for Behavioral Health Studies, Tucson, 1976; dir. planning Health Systems Agy. Southwestern Ariz., Tucson, 1976-79, exec. dir., 1980-81; exec. dir. community health programs Carondelet Health Svcs., Tucson, 1981-85, dir. planning and rsch., 1985-87; asst. dean of planning Coll. of Medicine U. Ariz., Tucson, 1987—; v.p. Univ. Med. Ctr., Tucson, 1987—; clin. lectr. dept. of family & community medicine, U. Ariz., 1980—, adj. asst. prof. dept. mgmt. and policy, 1985-86, chmn. preventive medicine com. Coll. of Medicine, U. Ariz., 1984—; faculty mem. U. Phoenix, 1983-87; mem. planning com. Healthcare Corp. of Sisters of St. Joseph of Carondelet, St. Louis, 1987; mem. mktg. coun. U. Hosp. Consortium, Chgo., 1987—, chair, 1993—. Author (chpt. in book) Health Risk Appraisal in Promoting Health Through Risk Reduction, 1982; contbr. articles to profl. jours. Bd. dirs. Pima Coun. on Aging, Tucson, 1980-86, United Way of Greater Tucson, 1986-89, Tucson Tomorrow, 1988-89. Mem. Am. Mktg. Assn., World Future Soc., Soc. for Hosp. Planning and Mktg., Internat. Health Futures Network. Democrat. Home: 5190 N Hillcrest Dr Tucson AZ 85704-5811 Office: Univ Med Ctr 1501 N Campbell Ave Tucson AZ 85724-0001

SCHMALENBERGER, JERRY LEW, pastor, seminary administrator; b. Greenville, Ohio, Jan. 23, 1934; s. Harry Henry and Lima Marie (Hormel) S.; m. Carol Ann Walthall, June 8, 1956; children: Stephen, Bethany Allison, Sarah Layton. BA, Wittenberg U., 1956, DDiv (hon.), 1984; MDiv, Hamma Sch. Theology, Springfield, Ohio, 1959, D of Ministry, 1976. Ordained to ministry Luth. Ch., 1959. Dir. Camp Mowana, Mansfield, Ohio, 1958-59; pastor 3d Luth. Ch., Springfield, 1959-61, 1st Luth. Ch., Bellefontaine, Ohio, 1961-66; sr. pastor 1st Luth. Ch., Tiffin, Ohio, 1966-70, Mansfield, 1970-79; sr. pastor St. John's Luth. Ch., Des Moines, 1979-88; pres., prof. parish ministry Pacific Luth. Theol. Sem., Berkeley, Calif., 1988—; co-dir. Iowa Luth. Hosp. Minister of Health Program, Des Moines, 1986-88; Roland Payne lectr. Gbarnga (Liberia) Sch. Theology, 1987. Author: Lutheran Christians' Beliefs Book One, 1984, Book Two, 1987, Iowa Parables and Iowa Psalms, 1984, Saints Who Shaped the Church, 1986, Stewards of Creation, 1987, Nights Worth Remembering, 1989, The Vine and the Branches, 1992, Call to Witness, 1993; columnist Rite Ideas, 1987-88. Bd. dirs. Grand View Coll., Des Moines, 1980-88, Wittenberg U., Springfield, Ohio, 1974-87, Luth. Social Services of Iowa, 1980-87, chmn. pre fund drive, 1988; bd. dirs. Planned Parenthood of Mid-Iowa, Des Moines, 1987-88; dir. Evang. Outreach/Luth. Ch. Am., 1983-85; mem. Iowa Luth. Hosp. Charitable Trust, 1986-88; chair Com. for Homeless Fund, Des Moines, 1986. Named Outstanding Alumni Wittenberg U., 1965, Young Man of Yr. Tiffin Jaycees, 1965, Man of Yr. Bellefontaine Jaycees, Disting. Alumni award Trinty Sem., Columbus, 1989. Mem. NAACP, Acad. Preachers, Acad. Evangelists (organizer 1986—), Kiwanis, Rotary. Home & Office: 2770 Marin Ave Berkeley CA 94708-1597

SCHMALTZ, ROY EDGAR, JR., artist, art educator; b. Belfield, N.D., Feb. 23, 1937; s. Roy and Mercedes (Martin) S.; m. Julia Mabel Swan, Feb. 1, 1958; children: Liese Marlene, Jennifer Lynn, Gregory Jason. Student Otis Art Inst., Los Angeles, 1959-60, U. Wash., 1960-61, Akademie der Bildenden Kunste, Munich, W. Ger., 1965-66; B.F.A., San Francisco Art Inst., 1963, M.F.A., 1965. Lectr. art Coll. of Notre Dame, Belmont, Calif., 1968-70, M. H. De Young Meml. Art Mus., San Francisco, 1968-70; prof. art St. Mary's Coll. of Calif., Moraga, 1969—, chmn. dept. art; mem. artists' bd. San Francisco Art Inst., 1989-92; exhbns. include: Seattle Art Mus., 1959, M. H. De Young Meml. Art Mus., 1969, Frye Art Mus., Seattle, 1957, San Francisco Mus. Modern Art, 1971, U. Calif.-Santa Cruz, 1977, Fine Arts Mus. of San Francisco, 1978, Oakland Art Mus., 1979, Rutgers U., Camden, N.J., 1979, Springfield (Mo.) Art Mus., 1980, Butler Inst. Am. Art, Youngstown, Ohio, 1981, Huntsville (Ala.) Mus. Art, 1982, Haggin Mus., Stockton, Calif., 1982, U. Hawaii-Hilo, 1983, Alaska State Mus., Juneau, 1981, Tex. State U., San Marcos, 1980, Crocker Art Mus., Sacramento, 1982, Hearst Art Gallery, 1986; group exhbns. include San Francisco Internat. Airport Gallery, 1987, Solano Coll., Fairfield, Calif., 1988, U. Del., Newark, 1988, San Francisco Art Inst., 1989, Natsoulas Gallery, Davis, Calif., 1989, Bedford Regional Ctr. Arts, Walnut Creek, Calif., 1989; represented in permanent collections: Richmond Art Ctr. (Calif.), U. Hawaii-Hilo, Las Vegas Art Mus. (Nev.), Hoyt Mus. and Inst. Fine Arts, New Castle, Pa., Frye Art Mus., San Francisco Art Inst., M. H. De Young Meml. Art Mus., Mills Coll., Oakland, Amerika-Haus, Munich, Contra Costa County Art Collection, Walnut Creek, Calif., Western Wash. U., Bellingham, Clemson U., S.C.; dir. Hearst Art Gallery, St. Mary's Coll.; vis. artist lectr. Academie Art Coll., San Francisco, 1971, grad. program Lone Mountain Coll., San Francisco, 1973-74. Coach Little League Baseball Team, Concord, Calif., 1982; mem. artist's bd. San Francisco Art Inst., 1989-93. Fulbright fellow, 1965-66; Frye Art Mus. traveling fellow, 1957; recipient Painting award All Calif. Ann., 1965; Nat. Watercolor award Chautauqua Inst., 1980; Seattle Art Assn. Painting award, 1957; San Francisco Art Inst. award, 1961; Otis Art Inst. award, 1959; Walnut Creek Civic Art Ctr. award, 1982, San Francisco Art Commn. award, 1985, Calif. State Fair Art award, 1985, Sears award for excellence in leadership, 1989-90. Mem. Coll. Art Assn., Fine Arts Mus. of San Francisco, AAUP, San Francisco Art Inst. Alumni Assn. Home: 1020 Whistler Dr Suisun City CA 94585-2929 Office: Saint Marys Coll Dept Art Moraga CA 94575

SCHMALZ, GREGORY DAVID, nuclear engineer; b. Covington, Ky., Dec. 9, 1952; s. William Earl Jr. and Madeline Kathryn (Jones) S.; m. Charlotte Ann Easter-Marschall, July 14, 1979; 1 child, Zachary William. BS in Nuclear Engring., U. Cin., 1976, MS in Nuclear Engring., 1976. Registered profl. engr., Ky., Colo., Ill., Calif. Mech. engr. Sargent & Lundy Engrs., Chgo., 1976-86; fire protection, program mgr. Pub. Svc. Co. Colo., Denver, 1986-92, decommissioning mgr., 1992—; cons., co-owner Mountain Magic Cons., Evergreen, Colo., 1989—. Patentee in field. Named to Hon. Order Ky. Cols., 1986. Mem. Edison Electric Inst., Nuclear Electric Ins. (mem. ltd. engring. adv. com.), Am. Nuclear Soc. Republican. Episcopalian. Home: 8751 S Grizzly Way Evergreen CO 80439-6231 Office: Pub Svc Co Colo PO Box 840 Denver CO 80202

SCHMELING, HELEN MARGARET, clinical social worker; b. Denver, Jan. 31, 1951; d. Herbert Henry and Lillian Anna (Meyer) Thimm; m. William Allan Schmeling, Jr., July 24, 1982 (div. Dec., 1992); children: Dustin William, Alexander Thimm. BA in Psychology, U. Colo., 1973; MSW, U. Denver, 1982. Lic. profl. social worker, Wyo. Peer counselor Met. Community Coll., Omaha, 1975-76; outreach worker South Omaha Crisis Ctr., 1976-77; child care worker Mt. St. Vincent's Youth Home, Denver, 1978-81; social work intern health scis. ctr. U. Colo., Denver, 1981-82; coord. crisis line Vol. Info. Referral Service, Rock Springs, Wyo., 1983-85; clin. social worker, coord. elderly svcs. S.W. Counseling Svc., Rock Springs, 1985-92; med. social worker Wyo. Home Health Care, Rock Springs, 1986—; pvt. practice, 1992—; facilitator Alzheimer's Family Support Group, Rock Springs, 1983-92; social work cons. Castle Rock Convalecent Ctr., Green River, Wyo., 1990, Sage View Care Ctr., 1992—; sch. counselor Desert View Sch., 1992—. Mem. Nat. Assn. Social Workers (regional rep. on bd. dirs. Wyo. chpt.). Democrat. Office: Desert View Elem Sweetwater Sch Dist # 1 PO Box 1089 Rock Springs WY 82902-1089

SCHMELZEL, JOHN EDWIN, chemist; b. Casper, Wyo., July 29, 1964; s. Walter Lee and Carol Rebecca (Sether) S. BS in Chemistry, U. Colo., 1986. Lab. technician Chem Assay, Golden, Colo., 1986-87; lab technician CSMRI, Golden, 1986-87, Chevron U.S.A., Denver, 1987-89; application sci. Thermo Jarrell Ash, Menlo Park, Calif., 1989—. Mem. Am. Chem. Soc., Soc. for Applied Spectroscopy. Office: Thermo Jarrell Ash 175 Jefferson Dr Menlo Park CA 94025-1114

SCHMID, HORST A., Canadian provincial administrator; b. Munich, Fed. Republic Germany; came to Can., 1952. LLD (hon.) U. Alta., 1986. Gold miner Yellowknife, 1952-56; chief exec. officer Internat. Export Corp., 1956-71; active in civic provincial and fed. polit. campaigns, 1960—; mem. Alta. Legis. Assembly from Edmonton-Avonmore, 1971-86, minister of culture, youth and recreation, 1971, minister govt. services and minister responsible for culture, 1975, minister of state for econ. devel. and internat. trade, 1979, minister internat. trade, 1982-86; commr. gen. trade and tourism Govt. Alta., 1986—; Alta. commr. for Spokane World's Fair; dir., adv. bd. Petroleum Inst. of Thailand. Recipient numerous awards from provincial, nat. and internat. orgns., including Silver Ribbon award City of Edmonton, Spl. award Nat. Music Council for Encouragement to Music in Alta. and Can., Disting. Service award Alta. Motion Picture Industries Assn.; inducted Edmonton Cultural Hall of Fame, 1987; recipient The Great Canadian award, 1989, The Star of Friendship Among Nations in Gold, 1989, Commanders Cross of the Order of Merit Fed. Republic of Germany, 1990, Golden Helm award Internat. Pub. Rels. Hotel Travel Agencies, 1991; named Hon. Indian Chief Flying Eagle, Man of Yr., Commonwealth Games Found. Office: Commr Gen Trade and Tourism, 1800 Royal Trust Tower, Edmonton Centre, Edmonton, AB Canada T5J 2Z2

SCHMID, PETER, biochemist; b. Signau, Bern, Switzerland, Sept. 5, 1927; came to U.S., 1955; s. Edwin A. and Julia (Trachsel) S.; m. Charlotte Staubli, July 3, 1954 (dec.); children: Peter A., Christine A. BS, Inst. Tech., Winterthur, Switzerland, 1952; MS, U. Calif., Berkeley, 1959; PhD, U. Calif., San Francisco, 1963. Investigator CIBA Pharm. Co., Basel, Switzerland, 1952-55; NIH fellow U. Calif., San Francisco, 1959-63; investigator in radio biology U.S. Naval Radiol. Def. Lab., San Francisco, 1964-67; sr. investigator, mgr. for Lasers in Skin Biology Letterman Army Inst. Rsch., San Francisco, 1967—; adviser Letterman Army Med. Ctr., San Francisco, 1970—; cons. officer rep. U.S. Army Med. Rsch. & Devel. Command, Frederick, Md., 1984—. Contbr. articles to profl. jours. Adviser Dixie Sch. Dist., San Rafael, Calif., 1970; co-organizer Open Space Bond Issue, San Rafael, 1972; tech. adviser Open Space Mgmt., San Rafael, 1976—; bd. dirs. Santa Margarita Home Owners Assn., San Rafael, 1972; bd. dirs., councilor Community Congregational Ch., meditation program mgr., 1980—. Mem. Am. Mgmt. Assn., N.Y. Acad. Sci., Am. Chem. Soc., AAAS, Sigma Xi. Home: 840 Montecillo Rd San Rafael CA 94903-3138 Office: Letterman Army Inst Rsch San Francisco CA 94929

SCHMID, RUDI (RUDOLF SCHMID), physician, educator, academic administrator, researcher; b. Switzerland, May 2, 1922; came to U.S., 1948, naturalized, 1954; s. Rudolf and Bertha (Schiesser) S.; m. Sonja D. Wild, Sept. 17, 1949; children: Isabelle S., Peter R. B.S., Gymnasium Zurich, 1941; M.D., U. Zurich, 1947; Ph.D., U. Minn., 1954. Intern U. Calif. Med. Center, San Francisco, 1948-49; resident medicine U. Minn., 1949-52, instr., 1952-54; research fellow biochemistry Columbia U., 1954-55; investigator NIH, Bethesda, Md., 1955-57; assoc. medicine Harvard U., 1957-59, asst. prof., 1959-62; prof. medicine U. Chgo., 1962-66; prof. medicine U. Calif., San Francisco, 1966-91, prof. emeritus, 1991—, dean Sch. Medicine, 1983-89, assoc. dean internat. relations, 1989—, prof. emeritus, 1991—; Cons. U.S. Army Surgeon Gen., USPHS, VA. Mem. editorial bd. Jour. Clin. Investigation, 1965-70, Blood, 1962-75, Gastroenterology, 1965-70, Jour. Investigative Dermatology, 1968-72, Annals Internal Medicine, 1975-79, Proceedings Soc. Exptl. Biology and Medicine, 1974-84, Chinese Jour. Clin. Scis., Jour. Lab. Clin. Medicine, 1991—, Hepatology Comm. Internat. (Japan), 1993—; cons. editor Gastroenterology, 1981-86. Served with Swiss Army, 1943-48. Fellow AAAS, N.Y. Acad. Scis., Royal Coll. Physicians; mem. NAS, Am. Acad. Arts and Scis., Assn. Am. Physicians (pres. 1986), Am. Soc. Clin. Investigation, ACP (master), Am. Soc. Biol. Chemists, Am. Soc. Hematology, Am. Gastroenterol. Assn., Am. Assn. Study Liver Disease (pres. 1965), Internat. Assn. Study Liver (pres. 1980), Leopoldina. Home: 211 Woodland Rd Kentfield CA 94904 Office: U of Calif Med Sch Office of Dean PO Box 0410 San Francisco CA 94143-0410

SCHMID, RUDOLF, botanist, educator; b. Springfield, Mass., Aug. 8, 1942; s. Fritz K. and Ruth (Wertz) S.; m. Marvin J. Taylor, Aug. 19, 1967 (div. 1976); 1 child, Acmena Maria; m. Janet Hildebrand, Aug. 9, 1989. BS, U. Calif., Davis, 1964, MA, 1965; MS, U. Mich., 1967, PhD, 1971. Smithsonian Fellow Smithsonian Inst., Washington, 1971-72; asst. prof. U. Calif., Berkeley, 1972-79, assoc. prof., 1979—; assoc. curator U. Herbarium, U. Calif., Berkeley, 1983—. Author: Diversity of Plants and Fungi, 1992; contbr. numerous articles to profl. jours. Chmn. Blake Estate Architectural Com., Kensington, Calif., 1988—. Fellow Linnean Soc. London; mem. Botanical Soc. Am. (officer 1977-80), Internat. Assn. for Plant Taxonomy (editor, reviews and notices of publs., Utrecht, Holland, 1986—), Internat. Assn. of Wood Anatomists, Calif. Botanical Soc. (officer 1976-79). Office: U Calif Dept Integrative Biology Berkeley CA 94720

SCHMIDT, ALAN FREDERICK, consulting cryogenic engineer; b. Chgo., Mar. 21, 1925; s. Ethan Warner and Lucille (Bouilly) S.; m. Jane Theresa Baker, Mar. 17, 1951; children: Rae Lynn, Liane. BSME, Ill. Inst. Tech., 1951; MSME, U. Colo., 1953. Project engr. Nat. Bur. Standards, Boulder, Colo., 1952-63, cons., 1963-76; prin. Alan F. Schmidt, cons., cryogenics engring., Boulder, 1976—. Co-author: Liquid Cryogens: Liquefaction, Storage and Handling, 1982; contbr. articles on cryogenic engring., chpt. to book. Staff sgt. inf. AUS, 1943-46, ETO. Fellow Tex. Co., 1951-52. Mem. ASME, Sci. Rsch. Soc. Am., Sigma Xi. Home and Office: 133 Elk Rd Lyons CO 80540-8149

SCHMIDT, CONNIE LU, small business owner, consultant; b. Mason City, Iowa, Apr. 8, 1949; d. Conrad Eugene and Lucie Dorathea (Apel) S.; m. Don Allen Walford, May 24, 1975 (div. Mar. 1978). AA, North Iowa Area Community Coll., 1971; BA, Ariz. State U., 1984. Teller, proof encoder, bookkeeper Am. State Bank, Mson City, 1970-72; vault teller Ariz. Bank, Tempe, 1973; utility clk. 1st Nat. Bank, Lincoln, Nebr., 1974-75, supr. account info., 1977-81; teller, bookkeeper, sec. Farmers Nat. Bank, Central City, Nebr., 1975-77; teller II Thunderbird Bank, Tempe, 1981-82; mktg. sec. Tri-Continental Leasing, Phoenix, 1982-83; saleswoman, dept. head Dillard's Dept. Stores, Mesa, Ariz., 1984-86; teller 1st Interstate Bank Ariz., Mesa, 1986-87; beauty cons., vip team leader Mary Kay Cosmetics, Inc., Mesa, 1979-89; office mgr., sales person Weisfield Jewelers/Sterling, Inc., Scottsdale, Ariz., 1989—; owner, mgr. dressmaking and alterations svc., Mesa, 1981—; ptnr. WISCH Promotions, Mesa, 1986—; interviewer Western Pers., Mesa, 1989-90. Mem. Ariz. State U. Alumni Assn., Nora Springs-Rocks Falls Alumni Assn., Am. Inst. Banking (basic cert.). Republican. Presbyterian. Home and Office: 5948 E Casper Rd Mesa AZ 85205-7412

SCHMIDT, DAVID KELSO, engineering educator; b. LaFayette, Ind., Mar. 4, 1943; s. Herbert R. and Barbara E. (Lipp) S.; m. Karalee Sue Krause, Nov. 24, 1979; children: Jeff, Kelly, Russ, Jeremy, Jillian, Kerry. BS in Aero. Engring., Purdue U., 1965; MS in Aero. Engring., U. So. Calif., L.A., 1968; PhD, Purdue U., 1972. Staff engr. McDonnell Douglas Astro Corp., Huntington Beach, Calif., 1965-69; rsch. staff Stanford Rsch. Inst., Menlo Park, Calif., 1972-74; prof. of engring. Purdue U., West Lafayette, Ind., 1974-88, Ariz. State U., Tempe, 1988-93; dir. Aerospace Rsch. Ctr. Ariz. State Univ., Tempe, 1990-92; chmn. Dept Aerospace Engring. Univ. Md., College Park, 1993—; cons. Northrop Aircraft, Hawthorne, Calif., 1985, Honeywell Systems Rsch. Ctr., Mpls., 1986, Systems Technology, Inc., Hawthorne, Calif., 1987. Contbr. numerous articles to profl. jours. Assoc. fellow Am. Inst. of Aeros. and Astronauts, Am. Soc. for Engring. Edn.; mem. IEEE.

SCHMIDT, ERIC EMERSON, computer company executive; b. Washington, Apr. 27, 1955; s. Wilson Emerson and Eleanor Schmidt; m. Wendy Susan Boyle, June 28, 1980; children: Virginia Alison, Sophie Elizabeth. BSEE, Princeton U., 1976; MS in Engring., U. Calif., Berkeley, 1979, PhD in Computer Sci., 1982. Research intern Xerox Parc, Palo Alto, Calif., 1979-80, mem. research staff, 1980-83; software mgr. Sun Microsystems, Mountain View, Calif., 1983-84, software dir., 1984-85, v.p., gen. mgr. software products div., 1985-88, v.p. gen. systems group, 1988-91; pres. Sun Tech. Enterprises, Inc., Mountain View, 1991—. Patentee in field. Mem. IEEE, Assn. Computing Machinery, Sigma Xi. Office: Sun Microsystems 2550 Garcia Ave Mountain View CA 94043-1100

SCHMIDT, FRANK BROAKER, executive recruiter; b. Shamokin, Pa., Aug. 8, 1939; s. Frank Wilhelm and Doris (Maurer) S.; children by previous marrage: Susan E., Tracie A.; m. Elizabeth Mallen, Mar. 18, 1989; children: Alexandra M., Frank W.M. BS, U. Pa., 1962; MBA, Case Western Res. U., 1969; cert. brewmaster, Siebel Inst. Brewing Tech., Chgo., 1964. With Carling Brewing Co., Cleve., 1964-69, mgr. sales and advt. div., brand mgr., 1969-70, advt. and merchandising mgr., 1970-71; dir. mktg. programs, then dir. mgmt. devel. The Pepsi-Cola Co., Purchase, N.Y., 1971-74; mgr. sales and mktg. The Olga Co., Van Nuys, Calif., 1974-75; pres. F.B. Schmidt, Internat., L.A., 1975—. Author: Draft Beer Manual, 1967, Assn. Nat. Advertisers Computerized Media System, 1970. Mem. Calif. Exec. Recruiters Assn., Wharton Alumni Assn., Personnel Cons. Am. (region chmn. 1981-83, 92—), Am. Mktg. Assn. Republican. Office: 30423 Canwood St Ste 239 Agoura Hills CA 91301-2082

SCHMIDT, JOSEPH DAVID, urologist; b. Chgo., July 29, 1937; s. Louis and Marian (Fleigel) S.; m. Andrea Maxine Herman, Oct. 28, 1962. BS in Medicine, U. Ill., 1959, MD, 1961. Diplomate Am. Bd. Urology. Rotating intern Presbyn. St. Luke's Hosp., Chgo., 1961-62, resident in surgery, 1962-63; resident in urology The Johns Hopkins Hosp., Balt., 1963-67; faculty U. Iowa Coll. Medicine, Iowa City, 1969-76; faculty U. Calif., San Diego, 1976—, prof., head div. urology, 1976—; cons. U.S. Dept. Navy, San Diego, 1976—; attending urologist Vets. Affairs Dept., San Diego, 1976—. Author, editor: Gynecological and Obstetric Urology, 1978, 82, 93. Capt. USAF, 1967-69. Recipient Francis Senear award. U. Ill., 1961. Fellow Am. Coll. of Surgeons; mem. AMA, Am. Urol. Assn. Inc., Alpha Omega Alpha. Office: U Calif San Diego Med Ctr Div Urology 200 W Arbor Dr San Diego CA 92103-8897

SCHMIDT, KAREN ANNE, travel company executive, state legislator; b. L.A., Nov. 27, 1945; d. Ernest Potter and Anne Ruth (Cieslar) Jacobi; m. Gary Manning Schmidt, Jan. 30, 1970 (div. Jan. 1984); children: Geoffrey, Gavin; m. Simeon Robert Wilson III, Mar. 20, 1993. Student, Ariz. State U., 1963-66. Stewardess TWA, Kansas City, Mo., 1966-67, Western Airlines, L.A., 1967-68; sales rep. Delta Airlines, Atlanta, 1968-70; owner Go Travel Svc., Bainbridge Island, Wash., 1971—; mem. Wash. Legislature, 1980—. Named Legislator of the Yr. Hwy. Users Found., 1992. Mem. Bainbridge Island C. of C. (dir. 1971-81, pres. 1976), Rotary (named Woman of the Yr. 1979). Office: Go Travel Svc 155 Madrone Ln Bainbridge Is WA 98110 also: Wash House of Reps Office of House Mems Olympia WA 98504

SCHMIDT, L(AIL) WILLIAM, JR., lawyer; b. Thomas, Okla., Nov. 22, 1936; s. Lail William and Violet Kathleen (Kuper) S.; m. Diana Gail (div. May 1986); children: Kimberly Ann, Andrea Michelle; m. Marilyn Sue, Aug. 11, 1990. BA in Psychology, U. Colo., 1959; JD, U. Mich., 1962. Bar: Colo. 1962, U.S. Dist. Ct. Colo. 1964, U.S. Tax Ct. 1971, U.S. Ct. Appeals (10th cir.) 1964. Ptnr. Holland & Hart, Denver, 1962-77, Schmidt, Elrod & Wills, Denver, 1977-85, Moye, Giles, O'Keefe, Vermeire & Gorrell, Denver, 1985-90; of counsel Mankoff, Hill, Held & Goldburg, Dallas, 1989—; pvt. practice law Denver, 1990—; lectr. profl. orgns. Author: How To Live--and Die--with Colorado Probate, 1985, A Practical Guide to the Revocable Living Trust, 1990; contbr. articles to legal jours. Pres. Luth. Med. Ctr. Found., Wheat Ridge, Colo., 1985-89; pres. Rocky Mountain Poison and Drug Found., Denver, 1986—; bd. dirs. Luth. Hosp., Wheat Ridge, 1988—; bd. dirs. Denver Planned Giving Roundtable. Fellow Am. Coll. Trust and Estate Counsel (Colo. chmn. 1981-86); mem. ABA, Am. Judicature Soc., Rocky Mtn. Estate Planning Coun. (founder, pres. 1970-71), Greater Denver Tax Counsel Assn., Am. Soc. Magicians, Denver Athletic Club, Phi Delta Phi. Republican. Baptist. Office: 1200 17th St 10th Fl Denver CO 80202-5835

SCHMIDT, MAARTEN, astronomy educator; b. Groningen, Netherlands, Dec. 28, 1929; came to U.S., 1959; s. Wilhelm and Antje (Haringhuizen S.; m. Cornelia Johanna Tom, Sept. 16, 1955; children—Elizabeth Tjimkje, Maryke Antje, Anne Wilhelmina. B.Sc., U. Groningen, 1949; Ph.D., Leiden U., Netherlands, 1956; Sc.D., Yale U., 1966. Sci. officer Leiden Obs., The Netherlands, 1953-59; postdoctoral fellow Mt. Wilson Obs., Pasadena, Calif., 1956-58; mem. faculty Calif. Inst. Tech., 1959—, prof. astronomy, 1964—, exec. officer for astronomy, 1972-75, chmn. div. physics, math. and astronomy, 1975-78; mem. staff Hale Obs., 1959-80, dir., 1978-80. Co-winner Calif. Scientist of Yr. award, 1964. Fellow Am. Acad. Arts and Scis. (Rumford award 1968); mem. Am. Astron. Soc. (Helen B. Warner prize 1964, Russell lecture award 1978), Nat. Acad. Scis. (fgn. assoc.) (recip. James Craig Watson Medal, 1991), Internat. Astron. Union, Royal Astron. Soc. (assoc., Gold medal 1980). Office: Calif Inst Tech 105 24 Robinson Lab 1201 E California Blvd Pasadena CA 91125

SCHMIDT, NANCY INGEBORG, sales executive; b. Chgo., Dec. 17, 1962; d. John and Ingeborg (Kopanke) S. AAS in Radio Broadcasting, Lewis & Clark Coll., 1985. Account exec. WCFL, Chgo., 1985-88; territory sales mgr. Arneson Products, San Diego, 1988-91; owner SonShine Pools, San Diego, 1991-92; bus. devel. mgr. First Am. Title Ins., San Diego, 1992—. Author instrn. book: Build Your Own Pool, 1991. Dist. 1 coord. Susan Golding for Mayor, San Diego, 1992; pub. rels. speaker U.S. Olympic Tng. Com., San Diego, 1991-92. Mem. San Diego Bd. Realtors (bd. dirs. 1992), Toastmasters (sec. bd. 1992, Disting. Svc. 1991). Republican. Presbyterian. Home: 750 State St San Diego CA 92101

SCHMIDT, PATRICIA FAIN, nurse educator; b. Chgo., June 17, 1941; d. Lawrence D. and Catherine B. (Schira) Fain; m. Donald W. Schmidt, July 16, 1966; children: Kathryn, Kristine, Michael. BSN, Coll. of St. Teresa, 1963; MSN, Marquette U., 1965; EdD, U.S. Internat. U., 1981. Instr. Coll. of St. Teresa, Winona, Minn.; asst. prof. San Diego State U.; assoc. prof. Palomar Coll., San Marcos, Calif. Mem. Sigma Theta Tau. Home: 12573 Utopia Way San Diego CA 92128-2229

SCHMIDT, ROBERT HOWARD, educator; b. Springfield, Ohio, June 15, 1954; s. Donald Paul and Lois Carolina (Grossenbacher) S.; m. Caroline Lee Shugart, Dec. 20, 1986; children: Katelin Leeann Puanani Shugart-Schmidt, Wesley Howard Ancil Shugart-Schmidt. BS, Ohio State U., 1976; MS, U. Nebr., 1981, U. Calif., Davis, 1985; PhD, U. Calif., Davis, 1986. Natural resource specialist Dept. Forestry and Resource Mgmt., U. Calif., Berkeley, 1986-91; asst. prof. Dept. Fisheries and Wildlife, Utah State U., Logan, 1991—. Co-editor: Predation Management in North Coastal California, 1990; contbr. numerous articles to profl. jours. Bd. dirs. Sacramento River Preservation Trust, Chico, Calif., 1984-85; mem. Forest Adv. Com., Ukiah, Calif., 1989-91; pres. Peregrin Audubon Soc., Ukiah, 1988-89. Recipient Group Study Exch. award Rotary Internat., 1986, Pub. Svc. award County of Mendocino, Calif., 1992. Mem. Wildlife Soc. (pres. western sect. 1989-90, Award of Recognition, 1990), Ecol. Soc. of Am. (chair western chpt. 1989-91), Nat. Animal Damage Control Assn. (exec. bd.), Soc. for Range Mgmt., Am. Soc. Mammalogists. Democrat. Home: 1665 E 1350 North Logan UT 84321 Office: Utah State U Dept Fisheries and Wildlife Logan UT 84322-5210

SCHMIDT, ROGER PHILLIP, English language educator; b. Seattle, Dec. 24, 1955; s. Richard Eugene and Mary Carol (Gardiner) S.; m. Paula Jean Hillis, Aug. 7, 1982; children: Camille Maria, Fletcher William. BA in English magna cum laude, U. Wash., 1980, MA, 1985, PhD in English, 1989. Instr. Inst. on North Am. Studies, Barcelona, Spain, 1982-83; teaching asst. U. Wash., Seattle, 1983-89; asst. prof. Idaho State U., Pocatello, 1989—. Reader, storyteller Wash. Elem. Sch., Pocatello, 1991—. U. Wash. Rsch. fellow Pembroke Coll. Cambridge (Eng.) U., 1987-88, McMurphy fellow U. Wash., Seattle, 1985-86. Mem. Nat. Coun. Tchrs. of English, Am. Soc. for 18th Cen. Studies. Democrat. Office: Idaho State U Box 8056 Pocatello ID 83209-0009

SCHMIDT, RUDOLPH DAVID, retired design engineer; b. Deshler, Nebr., Dec. 11, 1928; s. Rudolf and Myrtle (Imhoff) S.; m. Mary Elizabeth Seidlemann, Sept. 16, 1950; children: Karen Lee Schmidt Henry, Alan David. BS in Physics, San Diego State U., 1973; MS in Mgmt., U. LaVern (Calif.), 1982. Registered profl. engr., Calif.; cert. tchr., Calif. Electronic technician RCA Svc. Co., San Diego, 1955-65; broadcast engr. San Diego State U., 1965-70; elec. engring. mgr. Naval Aviation Depot, San Diego, 1973-93; instr. San Diego Community Coll. Dist., 1970-84. Sgt. USMC, 1946-48, 50-51, Korea. Mem. North Island Profl. Engrs. Assn., North Island Assn. (dept. rep. 1984-86), E. Clampus Vitus Hist. Soc. Republican. Lutheran. Home: 4236 Loma Del Sur La Mesa CA 91941-6916 Office: Naval Aviation Depot NAS North Island San Diego CA 92135

SCHMIDT, TERRY LANE, health care executive; b. Chgo., Nov. 28, 1943; s. LeRoy C. and Eunic P. S.; children: Christie Anne, Terry Lane II. B.S., Bowling Green State U., 1965; M.B.A. in Health Care Adminstrn, George Washington U., 1971. Resident in hosp. adminstrn. U. Pitts. Med. Center, VA Hosp., Pitts., 1968-69; adminstrv. asst. Mt. Sinai Med. Center, N.Y.C., 1969-70; asst. dir. Health Facilities Planning Council of Met. Washington, 1970-71; asst. dir. dept. govtl. relations A.M.A., Washington, 1971-74; pres. Terry L. Schmidt Inc. Physician Svcs. Group, San Diego, 1974—; exec. dir., chief operating officer Emergency Health Assocs. P.C., Phoenix, 1989-91, Charleston Emergency Physicians, S.C., 1990—, Joplin Emergency Physican Assocs., 1991-92, Big Valley Med. Group, 1991-92, Blue Ridge Emergency Physicians, P.C., 1992-93, Berkeley Emergency Physicians, P.C., 1992-93; pres. Med. Cons. Inc., 1983-84; v.p. Crisis Communications Corp. Ltd., 1982-90; pres. Washington Actions on Health, 1975-78; partner Washington counsel Medicine and Health, 1979-81; pres. Ambulance Corp. Am., La Jolla, Calif., 1984-87; chmn., pres. Univ. Inst., 1992—; lectr., part-time faculty dept. health care adminstrn. George Washington U., 1969-84, preceptor, 1971-84; asst. prof. Nat. Naval Sch. Health Care Adminstrn., 1971-73; mem. faculty CSC Legis. Insts., 1972-76, Am. Assn. State Colls. and Univs. Health Tng. Insts.; mem. adv. com. on ambulatory care standards Joint Commn. on Accreditation of Hosps., 1971-72. Author: Congress and Health: An Introduction to the Legislative Process and the Key Participants, 1976, A Directory of Federal Health Resources and Services for the Disadvantaged, 1976, Health Care Reimbursement: A Glossary, 1983; Mem. editorial adv. bd.: Nation's Health, 1971-73; Contbr. numerous articles to profl. jours. Bd. dirs. Nat. Eye Found., 1976-78. Mem. Am. Hosp. Assn., Med. Group Mgmt. Assn., Hosp. Fin. Mgmt. Assn., Med. Group Mgrs., Assn. Venture Capital Groups (bd. dirs. 1984-89), Med. Adminstrs. of Calif., San Diego Venture Group (chair 1984-87), U. Calif. San Diego Faculty Club, Alpha Phi Omega (pres. Bowling Green alumni chpt. 1967-70, sec.-treas. alumni assn. 1968-71). Clubs: George Washington University, Nat. Democratic (life), Nat. Republican (life), Capitol Hill. Office: Ste 360 9191 Towne Centre Dr San Diego CA 92122

SCHMIDT, WALDEMAR ADRIAN, pathologist, educator; b. L.A., Aug. 22, 1941; s. Waldemar Adrian and Mary Charlotte (Parker) S.; m. Karmen LaVer Bingham, Feb. 1, 1963; children: Rebecca, Sarah, Waldemar, Diedrich. BS, Oreg. State U., 1965; PhD, U. Oreg., 1969, MD, 1969. Intern U. Oreg. Hosps. and Clinics, Portland, 1969-70, resident, 1970-73; pathologist LDS Hosp., Salt Lake City, 1973-77; prof. pathology U. Tex. Med. Sch., Houston, 1977-91, Oreg. Health Sci. U. and VA Med. Ctr., Portland, 1991—. Author: Principles and Techniques of Surgical Pathology, 1982; editor Cytopathology Annual, 1991—. Asst. scoutmaster Boy Scouts Am., Houston, 1982-91. Maj. U.S. Army, 1970-76. Mem. Coll. Am. Pathologists (surg. pathology program 1988—), Sigma Xi, Alpha Omega Alpha. Office: VA Med Ctr 3710 SW US Veterans Hosp Rd Portland OR 97207

SCHMIDT, WILLIAM C., investment software developer; b. Cin., Nov. 7, 1940; s. William C. and Edna Marie (Baldwin) S. BA, Yale U., 1962; PhD, Columbia U., 1972. Pres. Tiger Investment Software Peerless Stock Market Timing, San Diego, Calif., 1981—, Tiger Investment Software, San Diego, 1981—. Author: (software) Peerless Stock Market Timing; pub., writer Peerless Forecasts jour., 1984—; editor: Santa Fe Seers, 1974-76; contbr. articles to profl. jours. Democrat. Home: PO Box 9491 San Diego CA 92169-0491 Office: Tiger Investment Software PO Box 9491 San Diego CA 92169-0491

SCHMIEDER, CARL, jeweler; b. Phoenix, Apr. 27, 1938; s. Otto and Ruby Mable (Harkey) S.; m. Carole Ann Roberts, June 13, 1959; children: Gail, Susan, Nancy, Amy. Student Bradley Horological Sch., Peoria, Ill., 1959-61; BA, Pomona Coll., 1961; Owner timepiece repair svc., Peoria, 1959-61; clock repairman Otto Schmieder & Son, Phoenix, 1961-65, v.p., 1965-70, pres., 1970—, chief exec. officer, 1970—. Mem. subcom. Leap Commn., 1966; area rep. Pomona Coll., 1972-76. Cert. jeweler; cert. gemologist, gemologist appraiser; recipient Design award Diamonds Internat., 1965, Cultured Pearl Design award, 1967, 68, Diamonds for Christmas award, 1970; winner Am. Diamond Jewelry Competition, 1973; bd. dirs. Lincoln Hosp., 1983—, Ariz. Mus., 1984-88; delegate White House Conf. on Small Bus., 1986; chmn. Gov.'s Conf. on Small Bus., 1988-91; col. Confederate Air Force. Mem. Am. Gem. Soc. (dir. 1973-86, nat. chmn. nomenclature com. 1975-77, chmn. membership com. 1977-81, officer 1981-86), Ariz. Jewelers Assn. (Man of Yr. 1974), Jewelers Security Alliance (dir. 1974-78), Jewelers Vigilance Com. (dir. 1981-87), Jewelry Industry Council (dir. 1982-88), 24 Karat Club So. Calif., Exptl. Aircraft Assn., Warbirds of Am. (dir. 1990—), Deer Valley (Ariz.) Airport Tenants Assn. (dir. 1980-90, pres. 1983-90), Ariz. C. of C. (bd. dirs. 1985-89), Small Bus. Council (bd. dirs. 1985-89, chmn. 1988, del. to White House Conf., 1986, chmn. Govs. Conf. on small bus. 1988-89), Nat. Small Bus. United (bd. dirs. 1990—), Kiwanis (pres. Valley of Sun chpt. 1975-76), Friends of Iberia, Rotary. Republican. Methodist. Home: 537 W Kaler Dr Phoenix AZ 85021-7244 Office: Park Ctrl Phoenix AZ 85013

SCHMITT, MARILYN LOW, foundation program manager, art historian; b. Chgo., May 24, 1939; d. Abraham A. and Mae (Willett) Low. BA, Lawrence U., 1960; MA, U. Calif., Berkeley, 1962; PhD, Yale U., 1972. Instr. Dickinson Coll., Carlisle, Pa., 1964-66; acting instr. Yale Univ., New Haven, 1969-70; asst. prof. So. Conn. State U., New Haven, 1970-75; assoc. prof. U. Miami, Coral Gables, Fla., 1976-82; program officer J. Paul Getty Trust, L.A., 1983-85; program mgr. Getty Art History Info. Program, Santa Monica, Calif., 1985—; bd. dirs. Internat. Ctr. of Medieval Art, N.Y.C.; ex-officio bd. dirs. Recovery, Inc., Chgo., 1971—; 1st v.p. Abraham A. Low Inst., Chgo., 1989—. Co-author: Object, Image, Inquiry: The Art Historian at Work, 1988; co-editor: Report on Data Processing Projects in Art, 1988. Recipient Woodrow Wilson fellowship, 1960-61, AAUW fellowship, 1968-69, NEH fellowship for ind. rsch., 1981-82. Mem. Coll. Art Assn. Am., Art Librs. Soc. N.Am., Phi Beta Kappa. Home: 1440 Veteran Ave #362 Los Angeles CA 90024 Office: Getty Art History Info Program 401 Wilshire Blvd #1100 Santa Monica CA 90401

SCHMITT, RICHARD GEORGE, industrial engineer; b. St. Cloud, Minn., June 18, 1948; s. George William and Viola Theresa (Mechenich) S.; m. Ligia Marie Pereira, Aug. 29, 1970; children: Christopher Michael, Scott Andrew. B in Indsl. Engring. with honors, Gen. Motors Inst., 1971. Indsl. engr. Gen. Motors, Fremont, Calif., 1966-78; sr. indsl. engr. Gen. Motors, Oklahoma City, 1978-80; indsl. engring. mgr. Shugart Assocs., Sunnyvale, Calif., 1980-81; mfg. tech. mgr. Magnex Corp., San Jose, Calif., 1981-82, prodn. mgr., 1982-83; facilities mgr. Apple Computer, Fremont, 1983, indsl. engring. mgr., 1984-85, robotics mgr., 1985-86, new product ops. mgr., 1987, Pacific logistics ops. mgr., 1988-92; Pacific phys. logistics mgr. Apple Computer, Cupertino, 1992—. Transp. chmn. Mt. Hamilton dist. Boy Scouts Am., 1984, asst. scoutmaster, 1986-92; chief YMCA Indian Guides, San Jose, 1977-83. Mem. Am. Assn. Indsl. Engrs. (sr.), Soc. Mfg. Engrs. (sr.), Coun. Logistics Mgmt., Am. Prodn. Inventory Control Soc., Lions (scholar 1966). Democrat. Roman Catholic. Home: 1963 Wave Pl San Jose CA 95133-1127 Office: Apple Computer 20330 Stevens Creek Blvd Cupertino CA 95014

SCHMITT, ROMAN AUGUSTINE, educator, researcher; b. Johnsburg, Ill., Nov. 13, 1925; s. Joseph Stephen and Mary B. (Freund) S.; m. Jean. M. Vertovec, Dec. 28, 1954; children: Joseph, Mary, Peter, Katherine. MS, U. Chgo., 1950, PhD, 1953. Postdoctoral fellow U. Ill., Champaign, 1953-56; scientist Gen. Atomic Inc., San Diego, 1956-66; prof. chemistry, oceanography, & geology Oreg. State U., Corvallis, 1966—. Assoc. editor Geochimica et Cosmochimica Acta, 1974—; contbr. numerous articles to profl. jours. With U.S. Army, 1944-46, ETO. Recipient George Merrill award NAS, 1972. Roman Catholic. Home: 1830 NW Hawthorn Pl Corvallis OR 97330-1835 Office: Oreg State U Radiation Ctr Corvallis OR 97331

SCHMITZ, CHARLES EDISON, evangelist; b. Mendota, Ill., July 18, 1919; s. Charles Francis Schmitz and Lucetta Margaret (Foulk) Schmitz Kaufmann; m. Eunice Magdalene Ewy, June 1, 1942; children: Charles Elwood, Jon Lee. Student, Wheaton Coll., 1936-37, 38, 39; BA, Wartburg Coll., Waverly, Iowa, 1940; BD, Wartburg Theol. Sem., Dubuque, Iowa, 1942, MDiv, 1977. Ordained to ministry Luth. Ch., 1942. Founding pastor Ascension Luth. Ch., L.A., 1942-48, Am. Evang. Luth. Ch., Phoenix, 1948-65; dir. intermountain missions, founding pastor 12 Evang. Luth. Parishes, Ariz., N.Mex., Fla., 1948-65; evangelist Am. Luth. Ch., Mpls., 1965-73; sr. pastor Peace Luth. Ch., Palm Bay, Fla., 1973-89; pastor-at-large Am. Evang. Luth. Ch., Phoenix, 1989—; charter mem. Navajo Luth. Mission, Rock Point, Ariz., 1960—; pastoral advisor Ariz. Luth. Outdoor Ministry Assn., Prescott, 1958-65, 89—; Kogudus Internat. Retreat master and chaplain, Fla., Berlin and Marbach, Germany, 1990; mem. transition team Fla. Synod Evang. Luth. Ch. Am., 1985-89. Author: Evangelism for the Seventies, 1970; co-author: ABC's of Life, 1968; assoc. editor Good News mag., 1965-71. Founder, chmn. Ariz. Ch. Conf. on Adult and Youth Problems, 1956-65; vice chmn. synod worship & ch. music com. Am. Luth. Ch., Mpls., 1960-66; chmn. Space Coast Luth. Retirement Ctr., Palm Bay, Fla., 1985-89; chaplain Ariz. chpt. Luth. Brotherhood, 1991—. Named Citizen of Yr., Palm Bay C. of C., 1979. Mem. Nat. Assn. Evangelicals, Nat. Chaplain German Am. Nat. Congress, Lions (officer Phoenix and Palm Bay clubs 1952—), Kiwanis (bd. dirs. L.A. chpt. 1942-48). Republican. Home: 12444 W Toreador Dr Sun City West AZ 85375-1926

SCHMITZ, DENNIS MATHEW, English language educator; b. Dubuque, Iowa, Aug. 11, 1937; s. Anthony Peter and Roselyn S.; m. Loretta D'Agostino, Aug. 20, 1960; children—Anne, Sara, Martha, Paul, Matthew. B.A., Loras Coll., 1959; M.A., U. Chgo., 1961. Instr. English Ill. Inst. Tech., Chgo., 1961-62, U. Wis., Milw., 1962-66; asst. prof. Calif. State U., Sacramento, 1966-69, assoc. prof., 1969-74, prof., 1974—; poet-in-residence, 1966—. Author: We Weep for Our Strangeness, 1969, Double Exposures, 1971, Goodwill, Inc., 1976, String, 1980, Singing, 1985, Eden, 1989, About Night: Selected and New Poems, 1993. Recipient Discovery award Poetry Center, N.Y.C., 1968; winner First Book Competition Follett Pub. Co., 1969; di Castagnola award Poetry Soc. Am., 1986; Shelley Meml. award Poetry Soc. Am., 1987; NEA fellow, 1976-77, 85-86, 92-93, Guggenheim fellow, 1978-79. Mem. PEN, Assoc. Writing Programs. Roman Catholic. Office: Calif State U Dept English 6000 Jay St Sacramento CA 95819

SCHMITZ, ROBERT LENZEN, academic administrator; b. Chgo., Mar. 29, 1951; s. Robert L. and Georgia (Kavanagh) S.; m. Jodi M. Ward, June 15, 1977; children: Matthew, Zachary, Whitney. BS, Regis Coll., 1973; MNM, Regis U., 1993. Alumni dir. Regis Coll., Denver, 1979-80; dir. devel. Ursuline Acad., Dallas, 1980-85; dir. devel. Law Sch. So. Meth. U., Dallas, 1986-87; v.p. for devel. and pub. affairs Regis U., Denver, 1987—; cons. Fairhill Sch., Dallas, 1985-86. Mem. pres.'s coun. Regis U. Mem. Nat. Soc. Fund Raising Execs., Coun. for Advancement and Support of Edn. (mentor region VI 1992), Denver Athletic Club. Roman Catholic. Office: Regis U 3333 Regis Blvd Denver CO 80221

SCHMITZ, VINCENT HERMAN, healthcare facility executive, finance executive; b. Bakersfield, Calif., Aug. 12, 1946; s. Walfred Nicholas and Mildred Telitha (Sparks) S.; m. Frances Conrad, Mar. 21, 1970 (div. Jan. 1980); children: Phoenix, Ingrid; m. Sondra Lynn Brown, Oct. 14, 1983; 1 child, Michael John. BA, U. Calif., Santa Barbara, 1968; MBA, Calif. State U., Sacramento, 1971. Acct. Tenneco, Bakersfield, 1971, Kern Union High Sch. Dist., Bakersfield, 1972; chief acct. Mercy Hosp., Bakersfield, 1972-73, chief fin. officer, 1973-87; exec. v.p., chief fin. officer Mercy Healthcare Sacramento, 1987—. Mem. Rotary Internat., Bakersfield, 1978-87, Paul Harris fellow, 1984. Mem. Am. Coll. Healthcare Execs., Health Care Fin. Mgmt. Assn. (pres. No. Calif. chpt. 1986), Rotary (Sacramento chpt.). Home: 3 Still Shore Ct Sacramento CA 95831-5567 Office: Mercy Health Care 10540 White Rock Rd Rancho Cordova CA 95670

SCHMUTZ, ARTHUR WALTER, lawyer; b. Akron, Ohio, Aug. 2, 1921; s. Paul Edward and Elizabeth (Williams) S.; m. Elizabeth Moore, June 17, 1951; children: David H., Stuart R., Jonathan M., Anne Marie. AB summa cum laude, Johns Hopkins U., 1949; LLB cum laude, Harvard U., 1952. Bar: Calif. 1953. Assoc. Gibson, Dunn & Crutcher, L.A., 1952-59, ptnr., 1960-69, sr. ptnr., 1969-86, adv. ptnr., 1987-90, adv. counsel, 1991—; bd. dirs. H.F. Ahmanson & Co. Home Savs. Am., L.A., Ducommun Inc., L.A., Data-Design Labs. Inc., Portland, Oreg. Trustee Orthopaedic Hosp., L.A.; mem. bd. govs. Cedar-Sinai Med. Ctr., L.A. With USAAF, 1942-45. Decorated Bronze Star. Fellow Am. Bar Found.; mem. Calif. Club, La Jolla Beach and Tennis Club, Lakeside Golf Club, Phi Beta Kappa. Office: 333 S Grand Ave Los Angeles CA 90071-1504

SCHNACK, GAYLE HEMINGWAY JEPSON (MRS. HAROLD CLIFFORD SCHNACK), corporate executive; b. Mpls., Aug. 14, 1926; d. Jasper Jay and Ursula (Hemingway) Jepson; student U. Hawaii, 1946; m. Harold Clifford Schnack, Mar. 22, 1947; children: Jerrald Jay, Georgina, Roberta, Michael Clifford. Skater, Shipstad & Johnson Ice Follies, 1944-46; v.p. Harcliff Corp., Honolulu, 1964—, Schnack Indsl. Corp., Honolulu, 1969—, Nuimeg Corp., Cedar Corp.; ltd. ptnr. Koa Corp. Mem. Internat. Platform Assn., Beta Sigma Phi (chpt. pres. 1955-56, pres. city council 1956-57). Established Ursula Hemingway Jepson art award, Carlton Coll., Ernest Hemingway creative writing award, U. Hawaii. Office: PO Box 3077 Honolulu HI 96802-3077 also: 1200 Riverside Dr Reno NV 89503

SCHNACKE, ROBERT HOWARD, judge; b. San Francisco, Oct. 8, 1913; s. Carl H. and Elfriede A. (Hanschen) S.; m. June Doris Borina, Sept. 7, 1956. Student, U. Calif. at Berkeley, 1930-32; J.D., Hastings Coll. of Law, 1938. Bar: Calif. 1938. Practiced in San Francisco, 1938-42, 51-53, 59-68; dep. commr. div. corps. San Francisco, State of Calif., 1947-51; chief criminal div. Office U.S. Atty., San Francisco, 1953-58; U.S. atty. No. Dist. Calif., San Francisco, 1958-59; judge Superior Ct., San Francisco, 1968-70, U.S. Dist. Ct. (no. dist.) Calif., San Francisco, 1970—; Chmn. uniform rules of evidence com. 9th Circuit Jud. Conf., 1963-76. Pres. Guide Dogs for Blind, 1959-62; bd. dirs. Fed. Jud. Ctr., 1975-79; mem. Jud. Panel on Multidist. Litigation, 1979-90. Served with AUS, 1942-46. Mem. Fed. Bar Assn., San Francisco Bar Assn., Am. Judicature Soc., Masons, Burlingame Country Club. Home: Hillsborough CA 94010 Office: US Dist Ct PO Box 36060 450 Golden Gate Ave San Francisco CA 94102

SCHNAPP, ROGER HERBERT, lawyer; b. N.Y.C., Mar. 17, 1946; s. Michael Jay and Beatrice Joan (Becker) S.; m. Candice Jacqueline Larson, Sept. 15, 1979; 1 child, Monica Alexis. BS, Cornell U., 1966; JD, Harvard U., 1969; postgrad. Pub. Utility Mgmt. Program, U. Mich., 1978. Bar: N.Y. 1970,, U.S. Ct. Appeals (2d cir.) 1970, U.S. Supreme, 1974, U.S. Dist. Ct. (so. dist.) N.Y. 1975, U.S. Ct. Appeals (4th and 6th cirs.) 1976, U.S. Ct. Appeals (7th cir.) 1977, U.S. Dist. Ct. (so. dist.) N.Y. 1975, U.S. Dist. Ct. (no. dist.) Calif. 1980, U.S. Ct. Appeals (8th cir.) 1980, Calif., 1982, U.S. Dist. Ct. (cen. dist.) Calif. 1982, U.S. Ct. Dist. (ea. dist.) Calif., 1984. Atty. CAB, Washington, 1969-70; labor atty. Western Electric Co., N.Y.C., 1970-71; mgr. employee rels. Am. Airlines, N.Y.C., 1971-74; labor counsel Am. Electric Power Svc. Corp., N.Y.C., 1974-78, sr. labor counsel, 1978-80; indsl. rels. counsel Trans World Airlines, N.Y.C., 1980-81; sr. assoc. Parker, Milliken, Clark & O'Hara, L.A., 1981-82; ptnr. Rutan & Tucker, Costa Mesa, Calif., 1983-84, Memel, Jacobs, Pierno, Gersh & Ellsworth, Newport Beach, Calif., 1985-86, Memel, Jacobs & Ellsworth, Newport Beach, 1986-87; pvt. practice, Newport Beach, 1987—; bd. dirs. Dynamic Constrn., Inc., Laguna Hills, Calif., 1986—,Chapman U., 1991—; commentator labor rels. Fin. News Network; commentator Sta. KOCN Radio, 1990-91; lectr. Calif. Western Law Sch., Calif. State U.-Fullerton, Calif. State Conf. Small Bus.; lectr. collective bargaining Pace U., N.Y.C.; lectr. on labor law Coun. on Edn. in Mgmt.; N.E. regional coord. Pressler for Pres., 1979-80. Mem. bus. rsch. adv. coun. U.S. Dept. Labor; trustee Chapman U., 1991—. Mem. Calif. Bar Assn., Am. Arbitration Assn. (adv. com. Orange County area, cons. collective bargaining com.), Conf. R.R. and Airline Labor Lawyers, Balboa Bay Club, The Ctr. Club. Republican. Jewish. Author: Arbitration Issues for the 1980s, 1981, A Look at Three Companies, 1982; editor-in-chief Indsl. and Labor Rels. Forum, 1964-66; columnist Orange County Bus. Jour., 1989-91; contbr. articles to profl. pubs. Office: PO Box 9049 Newport Beach CA 92658-1049

SCHNEBLY, F(RANCIS) DAVID, aerospace and electronics company executive; b. San Francisco, May 1, 1926; s. Frederick Dorsey and Mary Florence (Blake) S.; m. Miriam Louise Ford, Aug. 27, 1949; children: Mary Diane, Linda Marie, Anne Louise, David Albert, Kathleen Marie. BE in Areo. Engring., U. So. Calif., 1950; cert. advanced mgmt., Harvard U., 1970. Project engr. Hiller Aircraft Corp., Palo Alto, Calif., 1950-55, mgr. ops. rsch., 1955-58; mgr. ops. analysis Lockheed Missiles & Space Co., Sunnyvale, Calif., 1958-63, mgr. mil. programs, 1963-65, asst. dir. advanced programs, 1965-67, project mgr. advanced aircraft, 1967-70, dir. airborne systems, 1970-76, dir. remotely piloted vehicles, 1976-83; pres. F. David Assocs., Inc., Santa Rosa, Calif., 1983—; bd. dirs. Command Systems Group, Inc., Torrance, Calif.; mem. panel U.S. Army Sci. Adv. Bd., Washington, 1965-66; presenter seminars in field.. Author: Helicopter Performance Analysis Method, 1955. Pres. Hiller Mgmt. Club, Palo Alto, 1957; capt. Mounted Patrol San Mateo County, Woodside, Calif., 1976. Recipient award U.S. Army Aviation Rsch. and Tech. Labs. Mem. Am. Unmanned Systems Orgn., Am. Assn. Profl. Mgrs., Shack Riders (bd. dirs. 1983-87), Alpha Eta Rho (pres. Iota chpt. 1949). Republican. Home and Office: 453 Cahill Ln Santa Rosa CA 95401-5560

SCHNEEWEIS, HAROLD NATHAN, security specialist; b. N.Y.C., May 23, 1938; s. Theodore and Rae (Knopf) S.; m. Diane Lenore Ackerman, June 26, 1960; children: Scott Bryan, David Michael, Richard Alan, Beth Lynn. BA, NYU, 1959; postgrad., Brooklyn Law Sch., 1959-61; MA, Sam Houston State U., 1972; student, FBI Acad., 1974; Mgmt. degree, Nat. War Coll., 1980. Commd. U.S. Army, 1959, advanced through grades to col., 1980; commdg. officer U.S. Army Correctional Facility, Ft. Hood, Tex., 1972-73; staff officer hdqs. Dept. of Army, Washington, 1974-75; commdg. officer 519th Military Police Battalion, Washington, 1975-77; staff officer Joint Chiefs of Staff, Washington, 1977-79; dir. ops. hdqs. U.S. Army Criminal Investigation Com., Washington, 1980-82; commdg. officer 6th region U.S. Army Criminal Investigation Com., San Francisco, 1982-85; ret. U.S. Army, 1985; chief MILSTAR security Lockheed Space & Missle Co., Sunnydale, Calif., 1985-86; supervising security rep. Pacific Gas & Electric

Co., San Francisco, 1986—; ind. security cons., San Francisco, 1985—. Decorated Air medal, Bronze Star, Legion of Merit. Mem. Am. Soc. Indsl. Security, FBI Nat. Acad. Assocs., U.S. Army CID Agents Assn., Calif. Peace Officers Assn. Republican. Jewish. Home: 2528 Laguna Vista Dr Novato CA 94945 Office: Pacific Gas & Electric Co 123 Mission St San Francisco CA 94106

SCHNEIBEL, VICKI DARLENE, human resource liaison, office manager; b. Astoria, Oreg., Mar. 11, 1946; d. Howard Stanley and Sally (Thompson) Brandt; m. Lawrence Walter Schneibel, Mar. 18, 1967. AAS, Anchorage Community Coll., 1986; BA, Alaska Pacific U., 1991. Cert. profl. sec. Clk. typist The Oregonian, Portland, Oreg., 1964-67; statis. typist Rader Pneumatics, Inc., Portland, Oreg., 1967-71; sec., bookkeeper Larry's Custom Remodeling, Portland, Oreg., 1971-73; bookkeeper Tualatin Hills Pk. & Recreation Dist., Portland, Oreg., 1973-74; pvt. sec. Aloha (Oreg.) Community Bapt. Ch., 1974-79; exec. sec. Hyster Sales Co., Tigard, Oreg., 1979-83, 1st Nat. Bank of Anchorage, 1983-84; office mgr. Control Data Alaska, Anchorage, 1984-86; corp. office mgr. Westmark Hotels, Inc., Anchorage, 1986—. Mem. ASTD, Am. Mgmt. Assn., Adminstrv. Mgmt. Soc., Soc. for Human Resource Mgmt. Lutheran. Home: 6646 Cimarron Circle Anchorage AK 99504 Office: Westmark Hotels Inc 880 H St Ste #101 Anchorage AK 99501

SCHNEIDER, ANNI CHRISTINE, secondary science educator; b. Eau Claire, Wis., Dec. 16, 1952; d. Robert Ernest and Gail Ann (Curnow) S.; m. Thomas Bruce Bowers, Sept. 17, 1977 (div. Apr. 1987); m. David Michael McCormick, Aug. 11, 1990; 1 child, Connor John. BS in Secondary Sci. Edn. cum laude, Utah State U., 1975. Profl. ski patroller Solitude Ski Resort, Brighton, Utah, 1976-80; sci. educator Gilroy (Calif.) Unified Sch. Dist., 1981-85; helicopter ski guide Wasatch Powerbird Guides, Snowbird, Utah, 1985-89; earth sci. educator Park City (Utah) Sch. Dist., 1989—; bass player, musician Jarmen Kingston Quartet, Salt Lake City, 1987-91; dir. Earth Kids Environ. Group, Park City, 1989-92; advisor Community of Caring, Park City, 1990-92. Composer: (record album) The Frames, 1987. Pres. Sierra Club, Oshkosh, Wis., 1972-73; mem. Community Coalition, Park City, 1989-91; pres. Park City (Utah) Recycling Assn., 1992. Wetlands Rehab. grantee Park City (Utah) Sch. Bd., 1991, grant Tree, Utah, 1993; recipient Teaching award Amway/Newsweek Mag., 1993, Environ. Teaching award Sea World, 1993. Mem. Nat. Sci. Tchrs. Assn., Utah Sci. Tchrs. Assn., Utah Edn. Assn., Park City Edn. Assn. Democrat. Office: Treasure Mt Middle Sch PO Box 1920 Park City UT 84060-1920

SCHNEIDER, ARNOLD MARK, educational association executive; b. Boston, July 13, 1945; s. Meyer Joseph and Miriam (Leondar) S.; m. Linda C. Gallo, June 30, 1968 (div. 1986); children: Michael, Sarah; m. Linda M. Schlusberg, Nov. 6, 1988. BA in Polit. Sci., U. Mass., 1968, MS in Labor Rels., 1974. Tchr. Sudbury (Mass.) Pub. Schs., 1968-69; staff asst. U. Mass., Amherst, 1969-71; cons., organizer Mass. Tchrs. Assn., Boston, 1971-73; exec. dir. Inter Faculty Orgn., St. Paul, 1973-79; pres. Arnold M. Schneider, Importer, San Francisco, 1979-91; exec. dir. Am. Assn. Classified Sch. Employees, San Jose, Calif., 1991—. Mem. Am. Arbitration Assn. (arbitrator 1984—). Democrat. Jewish. Home: 14404 Outrigger Dr San Leandro CA 94577 Office: Am Assn Classified Sch Employees 2045 Lundy Ave PO Box 640 San Jose CA 95106

SCHNEIDER, BARRY CHARLES, superior court judge; b. Bronx, N.Y., Feb. 24, 1943; s. Morris David and Ann S.; m. Willa Terri Friedman, Aug. 20, 1967; children: Danna, Brian. BA, Harpur Coll., 1964; JD, St. John's U., 1968. Bar: Ariz. 1972. Staff atty. Bedford Stuyvesant Community Legal Svcs., Bklyn., 1968-69; assoc. Guzik & Boukstein, N.Y.C., 1969-71, Langerman, Begam, Lewis & Marks, Phoenix, 1972-77; ptnr. Rosen & Schneider, Phoenix, 1977-86; judge Superior Ct., Phoenix, 1986—, civil presiding judge, 1988-91. Mem. ABA, State Bar of Ariz., Maricopa County Bar Assn. Democrat. Jewish. Office: Superior Ct 201 W Jefferson St Phoenix AZ 85003-2205

SCHNEIDER, CALVIN, physician; b. N.Y.C., Oct. 23, 1924; s. Harry and Bertha (Green) S.; A.B., U. So. Calif., 1951, M.D., 1955; J.D., LaVerne (Calif.) Coll., 1973; m. Elizabeth Gayle Thomas, Dec. 27, 1967. Intern Los Angeles County Gen. Hosp., 1955-56, staff physician, 1956-57; practice medicine West Covina, Calif., 1957—; staff Inter-Community Med. Ctr., Covina, Calif. Cons. physician Charter Oak Found., Covina, 1960—. With USNR, 1943-47. Mem. AMA, Calif., L.A. County med. assns. Republican. Lutheran. Office: 224 W College St Covina CA 91723-1902

SCHNEIDER, CHARLES I., newspaper executive; b. Chgo., Apr. 6, 1923; s. Samuel Hiram and Eva (Smith) S.; m. Barbara Anne Krause, Oct. 27, 1963; children: Susan, Charles I. Jr., Kim, Karen, Traci. BS, Northwestern U., 1944. Indsl. engr., sales mgr., v.p. mktg. Curtis-Electro Lighting Corp., Chgo., 1945-54, pres., 1954-62; pres. Jefferson Electronics, Inc., Santa Barbara, Calif., 1962-64; pres. 3 sub., v.p., asst. to pres. Am. Bldg. Maintenance Industries, Los Angeles, 1964-66; group v.p. Times Mirror Co., Los Angeles, 1966-88; ret. Times Mirror Co.; pvt. investor and cons., 1988—; bd. dirs. Jeppesen Sanderson, Inc., Denver, Graphic Controls Corp., Buffalo, Regional Airports Improvement Corp. Bd. regents Northwestern U., Evanston, Ill.; trustee, past pres. Reiss-Davis Child Study Center, L.A.; bd. govs., past pres. The Music Ctr.; bd. visitors UCLA Grad. Sch. Edn.; trustee the Menninger Found. Served with AUS, 1942-44. Mem. Chief Execs. Orgn. (past pres., bd. dirs.). Clubs: Standard (Chgo.); Beverly Hills Tennis (Calif.); Big. Ten of So. Calif. Home: 522 N Beverly Dr Beverly Hills CA 90210-3318 Office: 1801 Ave of the Stars Ste 709 Los Angeles CA 90067-5802

SCHNEIDER, DONALD ERIK, computer engineer, contractor; b. Ann Arbor, Mich., May 15, 1965; s. Jan and Sandra (Wilson) S. BS, Cornell U., 1987. Computer programmer Ford Motor Credit Co., Dearborn, Mich., 1987-89; rsch. engr. Loral Aerospace, Santa Clara, Calif., 1989-91; computer contractor Apple Computers, Inc., Cupertino, Calif., 1992—. Mem. Palo Alto Run Club, Zeta Psi (pres. Psi chpt. 1987-88).

SCHNEIDER, EDWARD LEE, botanic garden administrator; b. Portland, Oreg., Sept. 14, 1947; s. Edward John and Elizabeth (Mathews) S.; m. Sandra Lee Alfarone, Aug. 2, 1968; children: Kenneth L., Cassandra L. BA, Cen. Wash. U., 1969, MS, 1971; PhD, U. Calif., Santa Barbara, 1974. From asst. to assoc. prof. botany S.W. Tex. State U., San Marcos, 1974-84, prof., 1984-93, chmn. biology dept., 1984-89, dean sci., 1989-92; dir. Santa Barbara (Calif.) Botanic Garden, 1992—. Co-author: Botanical World, 1994; contbr. articles to profl. jours. NSF grantee, 1980, 90; recipient Presdl. Rsch. award S.W. Tex. State U., 1985. Fellow Tex. Acad. Sci. (pres. 1992-93); mem. Internat. Water Lily Soc. (bd. dirs., sec. 1989—), Internat. Pollination Congress, Nat. Coun. Deans, Tex. Assn.Deans. Home: 1140 Tunnel Rd Santa Barbara CA 93105 Office: Santa Barbara Botanic Garden 1212 Mission Canyon Rd Santa Barbara CA 93105

SCHNEIDER, EDWARD LEWIS, academic administrator, research administrator; b. N.Y.C., June 22, 1940; s. Samuel and Ann (Soskin) S. BS, Rensselaer Poly. Inst., 1961; MD, Boston U., 1966. Intern and resident N.Y. Hosp.-Cornell U., N.Y.C., 1966-68; staff fellow Nat. Inst. Allergy and Infectious Diseases, Bethesda, Md., 1968-70; research fellow U. Calif., San Francisco, 1970-73; chief, sect. on cell aging Nat. Inst. Aging, Balt., 1973-79, assoc. dir., 1980-84, dep. dir., 1984-87; prof. medicine, dir. Davis Inst. on Aging U. Colo., Denver, 1979-80; dean Leonard Davis Sch. Gerontology U. So. Calif., L.A., 1986—, exec. dir. Ethel Percy Andrus Gerontology Ctr., 1986—, prof. medicine, 1987—, William and Sylvia Kugel prof. gerontology, 1989—; sci. dir. Buck Ctr. for Rsch. in Aging, 1989—; cons. MacArthur Found, Chgo., 1985—, R.W. Johnson Found., Princeton, N.J., 1982-87, Brookdale Found., N.Y.C., 1985-89. Editor: The Genetics of Aging, 1978, The Aging Reproductive System, 1978, Biological Markers of Aging, 1982, Handbook of the Biology of Aging, 1985, Interrelationship Among Aging Cancer & Differentiation, 1985, Teaching Nursing Home, 1985, Modern Biological Theories of Aging, 1987, The Black American Elderly, 1988, Elder Care and the Work Force, 1990. Med. dir. USPHS, 1968—. Recipient Roche award, 1964. Fellow Gerontology Soc., Am. Soc. Clin. Investigation; mem. Am. Assn. Retired Persons, U.S. Naval Acad. Sailing Squadron (coach 1980-86). Office: U So Calif Andrus Gerontology Center Los Angeles CA 90089-0191

SCHNEIDER, GENE W., cable television company executive, movie theater executive; b. Enid, Okla., Sept. 8, 1926; s. Harry W. and Gladys C. (Campbell) S.; m. Phyllis Gertrude Stelter, Jan. 23, 1954 (dec. 1975); children: Mark Lyle, Marta Gene Schneider Randell, Tina Michele, Carla Gene; m. Louise Huguette Rouillier, June 21, 1977; children: Michele Marie Seiver, Kim Marie Crosby, Carter John Price. BS in Engring., U. Tex., 1949. Registered profl. engr. With Continental Oil Co., 1949-51, Kwik Kafe Koffee Service, 1951-52, United Artists Entertainment Co. (and predecessors), 1952—; chmn. United Artists Entertainment Co. (and predecessors), Denver; bd. dirs. Turner Broadcasting, Atlanta, C-SPAN. Washington, Blockbuster Entertainment Corp., Ft. Lauderdale, Think Entertainment, Studio City, Calif.; chmn. United Internat. Holdings Inc., 1989—. Active Hope for the Children, St. Joseph's Hosp. Assn. Bd., others. Served with USN, 1944-46. Mem. Nat. Cable TV Assn. (bd. dirs.), Econ. Club Colo. (founding mem.). Republican. Clubs: Vintage (Indian Wells, Calif.); Cherry Hills Country (Englewood, Colo.), Glenmoor Country. Home: 6 Sunrise Dr Englewood CO 80110-4107 Office: United Artists 2930 E 3rd Ave Denver CO 80206-5014

SCHNEIDER, HOWARD BARRY, chiropractic physician; b. N.Y.C., Jan. 21, 1955; s. Irving and Ida (Schwartz) S.; m. Susan Mineo, May 17, 1980; children: Andrew, Bryan. BS in Biology, CUNY, 1976; D of Chiropractic, L.A. Coll. of Chiropractic, 1983. Cert. indsl. disability examiner, QME; cert. in ergonomics and injury prevention ARC. Rsch. asst. Albert Einstein Coll. of Medicine, Bronx, N.Y., 1976; rsch. animal biologist Am. Health Found., Valhalla, N.Y., 1976-78; mktg. rep. EM Industries, Elms Ford, N.Y., 1978-80; teaching assoc. L.A. Coll. of Chiropractic, Whittier, Calif., 1981-83; preceptor faculty L.A. Coll. Chiropractic, Whittier, Calif., 1981-83; intern Glendale (Calif.) Chiropractic Clinic, 83; pvt. practice Chiropractic Ctr. of Walnut Creek, Calif., 1984—. Contbr. articles to profl. jours. Bd. dirs. CitiArts/Theatre, Concord, Calif. Mem. Am. Chiropractic Assn., Calif. Chiropractic Assn., Nat. Bd. Chiropractic Examiners, Found. for Chiropractic Edn. and Rsch., Am. Heart Assn. (bd. dirs.), Nat. Ctr. Homeopathy, The Referral Source, Walnut Creek C. of C. (amb.) Sigma Chi Pi. Office: Chiropractic Ctr Walnut Crk 1874 Bonanza St Ste A Walnut Creek CA 94596

SCHNEIDER, HUBERT GEORGE, III, military officer; b. Washington, Oct. 19, 1958; s. Hubert George and Mary Victoria (Grass) S.; m. Peggy Darlene Beasley, June 5, 1982; children: Elizabeth Ann, Christopher John. BSEE, Va. Mil. Inst., 1980; MSEE, Air Force Inst. Tech., 1984. Commd. 2d lt. USAF, 1980, advanced through grades to maj., 1992; chief, minuteman Survival Power Br. Ballistic Systems div., Norton AFB San Bernardino, Calif., 1980-83; satellite systems engr. USAF, Omaha, 1985-88, chief, systems engring., 1988-89; asst. prof. USAF Acad., Colorado Springs, 1989—; dir. aeronautics lab. 5, Colorado Springs, 1992—; officer in charge USAF Acad. Student Grotto, 1989-92. Mem. Nat. Speleological Soc. Democrat. Roman Catholic. Office: USAF Acad Dept Aeronautics Aeronautics Lab Colorado Springs CO 80840

SCHNEIDER, JERRY ALLAN, pediatrics educator; b. Detroit, Nov. 14, 1937; s. Benjamin and Sarah (Dorfman) S.; m. Elaine Barbara Bergner, Dec. 8, 1963; children: Danielle, Jane. Student, U. Mich., 1955-58; BS, Northwestern U., 1959, MD, 1962. Intern, resident Johns Hopkins Hosp., Balt., 1962-65; postdoctoral fellow NIH, Bethesda, Md., 1965-69, CNRS, Gif-sur-Yvette, France, 1969-70; from asst. prof. to assoc. prof. Pediatrics U. Calif., San Diego, 1970-77, prof. Pediatrics, 1977—. Guggenheim fellow Imperial Cancer Rsch. Found., London, 1977-78, Fogarty Internat. fellow, 1983-84. Office: U Calif San Diego Pediatrics 0609-F La Jolla CA 92093-0609

SCHNEIDER, JOSEPH FRANCIS, journalism educator, editor; b. Louisville, Aug. 26, 1932; s. John M. and Sarah A. (Weatherly) S.; m. Lenore T. Sharpley, Nov. 14, 1953; children: Stephen, Thomas. BA, U. Louisville, 1955; MA, Sophia U., Tokyo, 1972. Sports editor Va.-Tennessean, Bristol, Va., 1955-56; law enforcement reporter Evansville (Ind.) Courier, 1956-57, Fla. Times-Union, Jacksonville, 1957-58; asst. state editor Greensboro (N.C.) Daily News, 1958-62; S.E. Asia/Vietnam bur. chief Pacific Stars & Stripes, Tokyo, 1962-66, asst. editorial/feature editor, 1968-73; asst. mil. editor Stars & Stripes, Darmstadt, Fed. Republic Germany, 1966-68; asst. city editor San Diego Union-Tribune, 1973—; instr. investigative reporting San Diego State U., 1975—; instr. journalism U. San Diego, 1992—. Mem. Soc. Profl. Journalists, Asian Am. Journalists Assn., San Diego Hist. Soc., Investigative Reporters and Editors, Kappa Tau Alpha, Pi Kappa Phi. Democrat. Roman Catholic. Office: San Diego Union-Tribune 350 Camino de la Reina San Diego CA 92112

SCHNEIDER, MEIER, industrial hygiene engineer, retired, consultant; b. Worcester, Mass.; s. Theresa Bell (Gershman) S.; children: Alan L., Leah S. Bergman, Diane F. BA in Chemistry and Biology, U. Rochester, 1940; MS in Occupational and Environ. Health, Calif. State U., Northridge, 1973; postgrad., Calif. State U., L.A. Registered profl. chem. and safety engr., Calif., environmental assessor, Calif.; cert. safety profl., indsl. hygienist, hazard control mgr., hazardous materials mgr. Commd. capt. U.S. Army, 1950, advanced through grades to lt. col., 1967, ret., 1971; sr. chemist L.A. County Air Pollution control Dist., 1948-52; rsch. specialist, L.A. div. Rockwell Internat., 1955-68; safety and indsl. hygiene coord. Lockheed-Calif. Co., Burbank, 1968-70; sr. indsl. hygiene engr. environ. health svcs. program Occupational Health sect. Calif. State Dept. Health, 1970-73; indsl. hygiene engr. dept. pers., med. svcs. div. City of L.A., 1973-81; chief, occupational safety and health Met. Water Dist. So. Calif., L.A., 1981-87; part-time assoc. then full prof. environ. and occupational health Calif. State U., Northridge, 1974-88; part-time field prof. U. So. Calif., Norton AFB Satellite Campus, 1976-86; part-time prof. dept. health sci. Calif. State U., L.A., 1981-88; served on State of Calif. Adv. COms. for noise control, revision of permissible exposure limits for airborne toxic substances and hazardous chem. labelling: cons. McGraw Hill Co., 1958-68, NAS; profl. rep. to Task Force on Applied Competitive Techs., 1989-90. Co-author: Occupational Safety and Health, 1989, An Attorney's Guide to Engineering; contbr. articles to profl. jours. Lt. col. U.S. Army. Mem. Am. Indsl. Hygiene Assn. (past pres. So. Calif. sect.), Am. Conf. Govtl. Indsl. Hygienists (Calif. indsl. hygiene rep. to the chem. agts. threshold limit value com.), Sigma Xi. Home: 1208 S Point View St Los Angeles CA 90035-2621

SCHNEIDER, RICHARD CLARENCE, psychology educator; b. Jefferson, Wis., Sept. 20, 1927; s. Carl F. and Adele G. (Gau) S. BA, Carthage Coll., 1948; MDiv, Luther-Northwestern Theol. Sem, 1951; MEd, U. Tex., 1955. Organizer Evang. Luth. Ch., Tex., 1951-55; mem. faculty, adminstrn. Carthage Coll., Carthage, Ill., 1955-56; mem. faculty Riverside (Calif.) Community Coll., 1956—; psychotherapist State of Calif., 1956—. Leader Sierra Club, Riverside, 1969—. Recipient NSF study grant Beloit (Wis.) Coll., 1964, U.S. Dept. Edn. study grant India, 1980, Egypt, 1981, Nigeria, 1982. Unitarian. Home: 24117 Fir Ave Moreno Valley CA 92553-3196 Office: Riverside Community Coll 4800 Magnolia Ave Riverside CA 92506-1242

SCHNEIDER, SANFORD, physician, educator; b. Tappan, N.Y., Feb. 4, 1937; s. Jacob and Ann Georgia (Ritz) S.; m. Joan Helene Schwitz, 1959; children: Lisa, Paul, Marc. B.A., U. Rochester, 1959; M.D., NYU, 1963. Diplomate Am. Bd. Psychiatry and Neurology, Am. Bd. Pediatrics. Intern Duke U., Durham, N.C.; resident in pediatrics and neurology Columbia-Presbyn. Med. Ctr., N.Y.C.; dir. child neurology Loma Linda U., Calif., 1971—, prof. pediatrics and neurology, 1979—; chmn. pediatrics Riverside Gen. Hosp., Calif., 1982-91. Served to capt. USAF, 1966-68. Fellow Am. Acad. Neurology, Am. Acad. Pediatrics. Office: Loma Linda U Child Neurology 11262 Campus St West Hall Rm 150 Loma Linda CA 92354

SCHNEIDER, THOMAS R(ICHARD), physicist; b. Newark, N.J., Nov. 14, 1945; s. Valentine William and Mary Bernadette (Scanlon) S.; m. Paula Doris Tulecko, June 8, 1968 (div. June 1984); 1 child, Laurie Ann. BS with high honors, Stevens Inst. Tech., Hoboken, N.J., 1967; PhD, U. Pa., 1971. Postdoctoral fellow U. Pa. Nat. Ctr. for Engergy Mgmt. and Power, Phila., 1971-72; prin. rsch. physicist Pub. Svc. Electric & Gas Co., Newark, 1972-77; various positions, dir. dept., exec. scientist Electric Power Rsch. Inst., Palo Alto, Calif., 1977—; pres. bd. dirs. Lighting Rsch. Inst., N.Y.C., 1990—; bd. dirs., chmn. energy task force Coun. on Superconductivity for Am. Competiveness, Washington, 1991—; coord. for Ad hoc Working Group Report on Power Applications of Superconductivity for Dept. Commerce, 1990-91. Mem. IEEE, AAAS, Am. Phys. Soc., Illuminating Engring. Soc., Am. Soc. Assn. Execs. Office: Electric Power Rsch Inst 3412 Hillview Ave PO Box 10412 Palo Alto CA 94303

SCHNEIDERMAN, WILLIAM, corporate executive; b. N.Y.C., Sept. 22, 1949; s. Morris and Beatrice (Bernstein) S.; m. Carla Marie Escher, July 16, 1977; children: Daniel Morris, Christopher Scott. AB with honors, Harvard, 1971; PhD, U. Mich., Ann Arbor, 1976; M in Bus. Adminstrn. with highest distinction, Dartmouth Coll., 1984. Asst. prof. Univ. Alberta, Edmonton, 1976-79, Marshall Univ., Huntington, W.V., 1979-82; mgr. IBM, Rochester, Minn., 1984-89, San Jose, Calif., 1989-91; ops. mgmt. cons. Pittiglio Rabin Todd and McGrath, Mountain View, Calif., 1991—; bd. dirs. Family Service Inc. Huntington, 1981-82. Contbr. articles to profl. jours. Recepient Gulf Oil Fellowship, 1983; Tuck scholar Dartmouth Coll.; rsch. grantee NSF, 1980-82. Mem. Trout Unltd., Sigma Xi.

SCHNEIDERS, SANDRA MARIE, religion educator; b. Chgo., Nov. 12, 1936; d. Alexander Aloysius and Glen Elizabeth (Ogle) S. BA, Marygrove Coll., 1960; MA, U. Detroit, 1967; S.T.L., Inst. Catholique, Paris, 1971; S.T.D., Pontifical Gregorian U., Rome, 1975. Joined Sisters, Servants of Immaculate Heart of Mary, Roman Cath. Ch., 1955. Tchr. various grade schs., 1958, 60-62; tchr. Immaculate Heart of Mary High Sch., Westchester, Ill., 1962-65; asst. prof. Marygrove Coll., Detroit, 1965-67; tchr. St. Mary High Sch., Akron, Ohio, 1967-68; asst. prof. Marygrove Coll., Detroit, 1971-72; prof. Jesuit Sch. of Theology, Berkeley, Calif., 1976—; Madeleva lectr. St. Mary's Coll., Notre Dame, Ind., 1986; disting. faculty lectr. Grad. Theol. Union, Berkeley, 1988. Author: New Wineskins, 1986, Women and the Word, 1986, Beyond Patching, 1991, The Revelatory Text, 1991; contbr. articles to profl. jours. Rsch. grantee Assn. Theol. Schs., 1979. Mem. Cath. Theol. Soc. Am., Cath. Bibl. Assn. Am., Soc. Bibl. Lit. (pres. western region 1988), Am. Acad. Religion, Pacific Coast Theol. Soc., Soc. for New Testament Studies. Democrat. Roman Catholic. Office: Jesuit Sch of Theology 1735 Le Roy Ave Berkeley CA 94709-1193

SCHNEITER, GEORGE MALAN, golfer, development company executive; b. Ogden, Utah, Aug. 12, 1931; s. George Henery and Bernice Slade (Malan) S.; B. Banking and Fin., U. Utah, 1955; m. JoAnn Deakin, Jan. 19, 1954; children: George, Gary, Dan, Steve, Elizabeth Ann, Michael. With 5th Army Championship Golf Team U.S. Army, 1955-56; assoc. golf pro Hidden Valley Golf Club, Salt Lake City, 1957; golf pro Lake Hills Golf Club, Billings, Mont., 1957-61, sec., 1957-61, pres., 1964—; pres. Schneiter Enterprises, Sandy, Utah, 1964—; developer Schneiter's golf course, 1973—, and subdiv., 1967—; player PGA tour 1961-77; sr. player PGA tour, 1981—. With U.S. Army, 1955-56. Winner Utah sect. Sr. Championship, Wyo. Open Super Sr. Championship, Salt Lake City Parks Tournament, Vernal Brigham Payson Open, Yuma Open, Ariz.; named U.S. Army Ft. Carson Post Golf Champ, 1955-56. Mem. PGA, Am. Mormon, Salt Lake City C. of C., Internat. Golf Course Supertaints Assn. Office: 8968 S 1300 E Sandy UT 84094 also: 4155 Vegas Valley Dr Las Vegas NV 89121

SCHNELL, ROGER THOMAS, retired military officer, state official; b. Wabasha, Minn., Dec. 11, 1936; s. Donald William and Eva Louise (Barton) S.; m. Barbara Ann McDonald, Dec. 18, 1959 (div. Mar. 1968); children: Thomas Allen, Scott Douglas; m. Young H. Kim, Sept. 25, 1987; children: Eunice, Candice. A in Mil. Sci., Command and Gen. Staff Coll., 1975; A in Bus. Administn., Wayland Bapt. U., 1987. Commd. 2d lt. Alaska N.G., 1959, advanced through grades to col., 1975; shop supt. Alaska N.G., Anchorage, 1965-71, personnel mgr., 1972-74, chief of staff, 1974-87, dir. logistics, 1987; electrician Alaska R.R., Anchorage, 1955-61, elec. foreman, 1962-64; dir. support personnel mgmt. Joint Staff Alaska N.G., 1988-92, ret.; personnel mgr. State of Alaska, 1992; asst. commr. dept. mil. and vets. affairs State of Alaska, Ft. Richardson, 1992—. Mem. Fed. Profl. Labor Relations Execs. (sec. 1974-75), Alaska N.G. Officers Assn. (pres. 1976-78, bd. dirs. 1988—), Am. Legion, Amvets. Republican. Methodist. Lodge: Elks. Home: 1814 Parkside Dr Anchorage AK 99501-5750 Office: Hdqrs Alaska NG Camp Denali PO Box 5800 Bldg # 4900 Ste C200 Fort Richardson AK 99505-0800

SCHNELL, RUSSELL CLIFFORD, atmospheric scientist, researcher; b. Castor, Alta., Can., Dec. 12, 1944; s. Henry Emmanuel and Anna (Traudt) S.; m. Suan Neo Tan, May 25, 1974; children: Alicia, Ryan. BSc with distinction, U. Alta. (Can.), Edmonton, 1967; BSc, Meml. U., St. John's, Nfld., Can., 1968; MSc, U. Wyo., 1971, PhD, 1974. Research scientist U. Wyo., Laramie, 1971-74, Nat. Ctr. Atmospheric Research and NOAA, Boulder, Colo., 1974-76; dir. Mt. Kenya study World Meteorol. Orgn. div. UN, Nairobi, Kenya, 1976-78; research scientist U. Colo., Boulder, 1979-82, dir. Arctic Gas and Aerosol Sampling Program, 1982-92, fellow Coop. Inst. Research in Environ. Scis., 1985-92; dir. Mauna Loa Observatory, Hilo, Hawaii, 1992—; mem. aerobiology com. Nat. Acad. Sci., 1976-79; cons. UN, Geneva, 1977-80, Shell Devel., Modesto, Calif., 1978-79, Holme, Roberts & Owen, 1990-92; mem. adv. bd. Frost Tech., Norwalk, Conn., 1983-85; bd. dirs. TRI-S Inc., Louisville, Colo., Magee Sci.,. Editor Geophys. Research Letters, Arctic Haze Edit., 1983-84; discovered bacteria ice nuclei, 1969; patentee in field; contbr. articles to profl. jours. Bd. dirs. Boulder Valley Christian Ch., 1978-91; chmn. Boulder Council Internat. Visitors, 1983-85. Rotary Internat. fellow, 1968-69. Mem. Am. Geophys. Union, AAAS, Am. Meteorol. Soc. (cert. cons. meteorologist), Internat. Assn. Aerobiology, Soc. Cryobiology, Sigma Xi, Sigma Tau. Home: 1 Kahoa St Hilo HI 96721 Office: Mauna Loa Observatory PO Box 275 Hilo HI 96721-0275

SCHNELLER, EUGENE S., sociology educator; b. Cornwall, N.Y., Apr. 9, 1943; s. Michael Nicholas and Anne Ruth (Gruner) S.; m. Ellen Stauber, Mar. 24, 1968; children: Andrew Jon, Lee Stauber. BA, L.I. U., 1967; AA, SUNY, Buffalo, 1965; PhD, NYU, 1973. Rsch. asst. dept. sociology NYU, N.Y.C., 1966-70; project dir. Montefiore Hosp. and Med. Ctr., Bronx, N.Y., 1970-72; asst. prof. Med. Ctr. and sociology Duke U., Durham, N.C., 1973-75; assoc. prof., chmn. dept. Union Coll., Schenectady, 1975-79, assoc. prof., dir. Health Studies Ctr., 1979-85; prof., dir. Sch. Health Adminstrn. and Policy, Ariz. State U., Tempe, 1985-91, assoc. dean rsch. and adminstrn. Coll. Bus., 1992—; dir. L. William Seidman Rsch. Ctr., Tempe, 1992—; vis. rsch. scholar Columbia U., N.Y.C., 1983-84; chmn. Western Network for Edn. in Health Adminstrn., Berkeley, Calif., 1987-92; mem. Ariz. Medicaid Adv. Bd., 1990-92, Ariz. Data Adv. Bd., 1989-91, Ariz. Health Care Group Adv. Bd., 1989; mem. health rsch. coun. N.Y. State Dept. Health, 1977-85; fellow Accrediting Commn. on Edn. for Health Svcs. Adminstrn., 1983-84. Author: The Physician's Assistant, 1980; mem. editorial bd. Work and Occupations, 1975-93, Hosps. and Health Svcs. Adminstrn., 1989-92, Health Adminstrn. Press, 1991—; contbr. articles to profl. jours., chpt. to book. Trustee Barrow Neurol. Inst., Phoenix, 1989—. Mem. APHA, Am. Sociol. Assn., Assn. Univ. Programs Health Adminstrn. (bd. dirs. 1990—). Home: 9906 E Cinnabar Ave Scottsdale AZ 85258-4738 Office: Ariz State Univ Office of Dean Coll Bus Tempe AZ 85287

SCHNITZER, ARLENE DIRECTOR, art dealer; b. Salem, Oreg., Jan. 10, 1929; d. Simon M. and Helen (Holtzman) Director; m. Harold J. Schnitzer, Sept. 11, 1949; 1 child, Jordan. Student, U. Wash., 1947-48; BFA (hon.) Pacific NW Coll. Art., 1988. Founder, pres. Fountain Gallery of Art, Portland, Oreg., 1951-86; sr. v.p. Harsch Investment Corp., 1951—. Apptd. to Oreg. State Bd. Higher Edn., 1987-88; bd. dirs. Oreg. Symphony Assn., v.p. Oreg. Symphony; bd. dirs. U.S. Dist. Ct. Hist. Soc.; bd. dirs. Boys and Girls Club, 1988—; mem. Gov.'s Expo '86 Commn., Oreg.; mem. exec. com., former bd. dirs. Artquake; mem. adv. bd. Our New Beginnings; bd. dirs. Artists Initiative for a Contemporary Art Collection; former trustee Reed Coll., 1982-88; exec. com. bd. dirs. Bus. Com. for Arts. Recipient Aubrey Watzek award Lewis and Clark Coll., 1981, Pioneer award U. Oreg., 1985, Met. Arts Commn. award, 1985, White Rose award March of Dimes, 1987, Disting. Svc. award Western Oreg. State Coll. 1988, Oreg. Urban League Equal Opportunity award 1988, Gov's. award for Arts, 1987, Woman of Achievement award YWCA, 1987, Disting. Svc. award U. Oreg., 1991; honored by Portland Art Assn., 1979. Mem. Univ. Club, Multnomah Athletic Club, Portland Golf Club. Office: Harsch Investment Corp 1121 SW Salmon St Portland OR 97205-2000

SCHNITZER, GARY ALLEN, steel company executive; b. Portland, Oreg., Jan. 29, 1942; s. Gilbert and Thelma Edith (Steinberg) S.; children: Andrea Beth, Gregory Nelson. BS, U. So. Calif., 1964. With Schnitzer Steel Products, Oakland, Calif., 1965—, exec. v.p., 1975—; dir. Lasco Shipping Co., Island Equipment Co. Chmn., 1st ann. Oakland Marathon, 1979; mem. planning commn., Piedmont, Calif., 1975, commr., 1975, 76, Orinda, Calif., 1977, 78; mem. Alameda County Solid Waste Commn., 1975-76, Alameda Pretrial Adv. Com., 1976; mem. vehicle theft legis. adv. com. Dept. Calif. Hwy. Patrol, 1975; vice chmn. fgn. trade com., Inst. Scrap Iron and Steel, 1974-77, pres. No. Calif. chpt., 1972-73, dir., 1972, 73, 77, 84. Bd. dirs., Oakland Mus. Assn., 1985—, Goodwill Industries, 1984—, nat. dir., West Coast rep., 1976, vice chmn. fgn. trade com., 1984; pres. Network (minority employment); bd. dirs. Big Bros. Am., 1976, 77, 78, 79, Seven Hills Sch., Child Assault Prevention; Mayor's Econ. Emergency Task Force City of Oakland, 1993. Mem. Oakland C. of C. (dir. 1977-81), Lake Merritt Breakfast Club, Silverado Country Club, Multnomah Club (Portland, Oreg.), Calif. Tennis Club, Berkeley Tennis Club, B'nai B'rith (bd. dirs. Anti-Defamation League 1977). Republican. Jewish. Office: Schnitzer Steel Products Foot of Adeline St PO Box 747 Oakland CA 94604

SCHOBER, ROBERT CHARLES, electrical engineer; b. Phila., Sept. 20, 1940; s. Rudolph Ernst and Kathryn Elizabeth (Ehrisman) S.; m. Mary Eve Kanuika, Jan. 14, 1961; children: Robert Charles, Stephen Scott, Susan Marya. BS in Engring. (Scott Award scholar), Widner U., 1965; postgrad., Bklyn. Poly. Extension at Gen. Electric Co., Valley Forge, Pa., 1965-67, U. Colo., 1968-69, Calif. State U.-Long Beach, 1969-75, U. So. Calif., 1983-84. Engr. Gen. Electric Co., Valley Forge, 1965-68, Martin Marietta Corp., Denver, 1968-69; sr. engr. Jet Propulsion Lab., Pasadena, Calif., 1969-73, sr. staff, 1986—; mem. tech. staff Hughes Semiconductor Co., Newport Beach, Calif., 1973-75; prin. engr. Am. Hosp. Supply Corp., Irvine, Calif., 1975-83; sr. staff engr. TRW Systems, Redondo Beach, Calif., 1983-84; cons. Biomed. LSI, Huntington Beach, Calif. Mem. IEEE (student br. pres. 1963-65), Soc. for Indsl. and Applied Math., Assn. for computing Machinery, Tau Beta Pi. Republican. Patentee cardiac pacemakers. Current Work: Develop large scale integrated circuits for computer, spacecraft, and military, as well as commercial applications; design high speed signal processing integrated circuits. Subspecialties: application specific microprocessor archtl. design; ultra low power analog and digital systems, integrated circuits; cardiology and other implantable medical devices. Office: Jet Propulsion Lab 4800 Oak Grove Dr Pasadena CA 91109-8099

SCHOCKEN, JOSEPH L., investment banker; b. Renton, Wash., Sept. 21, 1946; s. Henry and Ruth (Hamlet) S.; m. Judith A. Block, Sept. 10, 1969; children: Celina, Kara, Andrew, Trea. BA with honors, U. Wash., 1968; MBA, Harvard U., 1970. V.p. corp. fin. WITS, Inc., Seattle, 1970-72; v.p., pres. ENI Corp., Seattle, 1973-76; pres. Schocken Capital Corp., Seattle, 1977-79; v. chmn. Cralin & Co., Inc., Seattle, 1979-84; ptnr. Weatherly Pvt. Capital, Bellevue, Wash., 1984-86; pres. Broadmark Capital Corp., Seattle, Wash., 1987——; bd. dir. Bingham Communications Group, Royal Seafoods, Inc., Seattle, Alamar Biosciences Inc., Sacramento, Calif., Western Franchise Devel. Corp., Dublin, Calif.; chmn. bd. dirs. Freshmark Food Corp., Seattle, Wash. Mem. Jewish Fedn. Seattle (dir. 1980-84), Herzl Ner Tamid Synagogue (dir. 1978-82), Mercer Island, Wash., Wash. Athletic Club, Rainier Club, Columbia Tower Club, Lakes Club. Home: 5911 77th Ave SE Mercer Island WA 98040-4815

SCHOENDORF, JUDSON RAYMOND, allergist; b. New Orleans, Jan. 13, 1942; s. John Adam and Thelma Elizabeth (Verges) S. BA, Tulane U., 1962; MD, La. State U., 1966; MBA, Pepperdine U., 1992. Lic. physician, La., Calif.; cert. Am. Bd. Med. Mgmt. Intern Charity Hosp. of La., New Orleans, 1966-67; resident in pediatrics L.A. County/U. So. Calif. Med. Ctr., 1969-70; fellow UCLA/Harbor Gen. Hosp., 1970-72; allergist Russell T. Spears, M.D., Long Beach, 1972-76, The Harriman Jones Med. Group, Long Beach, 1976—; chief exec. officer The Harriman Jones Med. Group, 1989-91; staff Kaiser Hosp, Bellflower, 1970-72, Children's Hosp., Long Beach, 1972—, Bauer/St. Mary's Hosp., Long Beach, 1972—, UCLA Hosp., 1972—, Community Hosp., Long Beach, 1977—; faculty UCLA, 1972—, Harbor Gen. Hosp., 1972—, others. Contbr. articles to profl. jours. Bd. dirs. Long Beach Children's Clinic, 1976-81, pres., 1978-81; bd. dirs. Long Beach Symphony Orch., 1985-89; bd. dirs. Am. Lung Assn. Calif., 1985—, exec. com., 1988—; adv. coun. phys. edn. dept. Calif. State U., Long Beach, 1985—; mem. Civil Svc. Commn., City of Long Beach, 1981-89, pres., 1982-83, 85-86; bd. dirs. Long Beach Civic Light Opera, 1986-88; mem. Redevel. Agy., City of Long Beach, 1989—. To lt. USN, 1967-69, to capt. USNR, 1985—. Decorated Navy Achievement Medal, Republic of Viet Nam Campaign Medal, Vietnamese Cross of Gallantry, others. Mem. Calif. Med. Assn., L.A. County Med. Assn., Long Beach Med. Assn., Acad. Allergy, L.A. Soc. Allergy and Immunology, Am. Acad. Physician Execs. Office: Harriman Jones Med Group 2600 Redondo Ave Long Beach CA 90806-2328

SCHOENFELD, GARY HERMAN, banker; b. Seattle, Dec. 17, 1962; s. Walter E. and Esther S.; m. Michelle G., Oct. 29, 1988. BA in Econs., UCLA, 1984; MBA, Stanford Grad. Sch. Bus., 1988. Analyst David H. Murdock Devel. Co., L.A., 1984-86; sr. assoc. Goldman Sachs & Co., N.Y.C., 1987; ptnr. McCown De Leeuw & Co., Menlo Park, Calif., 1988—; dir. Century Fasteners Inc., L.A., 1990—, Hawaiian Airlines, 1992—. Office: McCown De Leeuw & Co 3000 Sand Hill Rd #3-290 Menlo Park CA 94025

SCHOENFELD, LAWRENCE JON, jewelry manufacturing company executive, travel industry consultant; b. Los Angeles, Nov. 30, 1945; s. Donald and Trudy (Libizer) S.; Carol Sue Gard, Aug. 24, 1969. AA, Los Angeles Valley Coll., Van Nuys, Calif., 1963; BBA, Wichita State U., 1969, MSBA, 1970; grad., US Army Command/Gen Staff Sch., Ft. Leavenworth, Kans., 1988. Cert. tchr., Calif.; lic. real estate broker, Calif. Asst. treas. Advance Mortgage, Los Angeles, 1970-72; v.p. ops. Unigem Internat., Los Angeles, 1972—; pres. L. & C. Schoenfeld Corp.; bd. dirs. The Schoenfeld Constrn. Co., Telcom Group, Uniorr Corp., Execucentre-West, Schoenfeld & Co., Customer Ground Handling Svc. Corp.; co-developer Bay-Osos Mini Storage Co., San Luis Obispo, Calif., El Mercadero World Trade Show, Guatemala, 1986, Santiago, 1987, Bahai, 1988, Paraguay, 1989, El Mercado, Costa Rica, 1990, Los Osos Mini Storage Co., Quito, 1991; pres. Accents on Beverly Hills. Mem. Improvement Commn., Hermosa Beach., Calif. 1976-78. Served to maj. US Army Med. Service Corps, 1970-72, lt. col. with res. 1972—. Mem. South Am. Travel Assn., World Trade Assn. (assoc.), Town Hall, Wichita State U. Alumni Assn. (nat. dist. rep.), Res. Officers Assn., Brit. Am. C. of C. Jewish. Office: Unigem Internat 350 S Beverly Dr Ste 350 Beverly Hills CA 90212-4817

SCHOENGARTH, R(OBERT) SCOTT, life insurance company executive; b. L.A., June 27, 1949; s. Bruce William and Barbara Agnes (Wiggins) S.; m. Margaret Kathleen Maguire, Nov. 29, 1986; children: Tobey, Mandy. Student, Glendale (Calif.) Coll., 1970; BA in Journalism, Calif. State U., Northridge, 1973. News and sports writer Sta. KFWB, Hollywood, Calif., 1971-72; sports writer Sta. KMPC, L.A., 1973-74; sr. writer, rsch. analyst, asst. dir. sales promotion Transam./Occidental Life Ins. Co., L.A., 1974-79; dir. mktg. svcs. Gt. Am. Life Ins. Co., Beverly Hills, Calif., 1979-81; asst. v.p., dir. mktg. communications Sunset Life Ins. Co., Olympia, Wash., 1981—; workshop host, meeting planner Olympia Visitors and Conv. Bur., 1989, 1st v.p., 1988. Pres. parish coun. Sacred Heart Ch., Lacey, Wash., 1980-85; chmn. credit com. Essell Credit Union, Olympia, 1987-93; lector, eucharistic min., choir leader St. Michael's Ch., Olympia, 1990—; chmn. Sunset Life's United Way Campaign; bd. dir. United Way Thurston County. Recipient Advt. Excellence award Nat. Underwriter Mag., 1992. Mem. Life Communicators Assn. (exec. com. 1989-90, chmn. ann. meeting 1989, media chmn. 1990-91, award of excellence 1986, 90, Best of Show award 1988, Morgan Crockford award 1989, Special Recognition award 1992, ann. meeting arrangements chmn. 1992), Ins. Conf. Planners Assn. Republican. Office: Sunset Life Ins Co 3200 Capitol Blvd S Olympia WA 98501-3396

SCHOENI, DOUGLAS EUGENE, wholesale distribution executive; b. Mt. Holly, N.J., Aug. 18, 1957; s. Donald Dean and Donna Eugene (Summers) S. Student, U. Kans., 1976-78. Asst. mgr. Rusty's IGA, Lawrence, Kans., 1978-82; dept. mgr. Willards IGA, Osawatomie, Kans., 1982-83; store mgr. Bonner Springs (Kans.) IGA, 1983-87; sales rep. Tombstone Pizza Corp., Medford, Wis., 1988-89; br. mgr. Saxton Inc., Denver, 1990—. Mem. Optimist, Bonner Springs, 1987; vol. United Way Big Brothers Program. Office: Saxton Inc 3950 Nome Unit H Denver CO 80239

SCHOENSTEIN, JOSEPH ROY, accountant; b. Jamaica, N.Y., Nov. 30, 1957; s. Leroy Joseph and Carolyn Nelda (Richrod) S.; m. Sherry Ann McMullen, Sept. 1 , 1979. BSBA, Ohio State U., 1979; MBA, U. Dayton, 1991. Staff acct., SCOA Industries, Inc., Columbus, Ohio, 1979-81, sr. acct., 1984-86; supr. acctg. SCA Internat., Inc., Columbus, Ohio, 1981-84; supr. gen. acctg. Warner Cable Communications, Dublin, Ohio, 1986-88, mgr. gen. acctg., 1988-92; v.p., fin. and contr. Bakersfield (Calif.) div. Time Warner Cable, 1992—; bd. dirs., treas. Kern County Econ. Opportunity Corp., 1993. Home: 2428 Moffitt Way Bakersfield CA 93309

SCHOEPPE, HANS JUERGEN, educator, management executive; b. Vienna, Austria, Dec. 2, 1937; came to U.S., 1969; s. Karl K. and Edith Schoeppe; m. Shari S. Zachar, June 1, 1973. Student, Welthandel, Vienna, 1961-62. Asst. mktg. dir. A.K.U. Netherlands, Vienna, 1962-65; ptnr. Eurotex/Import-Export, Innsbruck, Austria, 1965-67; asst. dir. advt. Mobil Oil Austria, Vienna, 1967-69; dir., CFO Comm. Decorating Svcs., Canoga Park, Calif., 1987—; dir., CFO, gen. mgr. South Beach Med. Inc., Lawndale, Calif., 1989—. Fundraiser Rep. Party, L.A., 1980, 84. Named Hon. Citizen L.A. by Mayor Sam Yorty, 1972. Mem. Am. Turnaround Mgmt. Assn. (com. mem. 1991—).

SCHOESLER, MARK GERALD, state legislator, farmer; b. Ritzville, Ga., Feb. 16, 1957; s. Gerald E. and Dorothy (Heinemann) S.; m. Ginger J. Van Aelst, Apr. 8, 1978; children: Veronica, Cody. AA, Spokane (Wash.) C.C., 1977. Mem. Wash. Ho. Reps. Pres. Wash. Friends Farms and Forests, 1991-92. Mem. Wash. Assn. Wheat Growers (dir. 1990-92). Republican. Mem. United. Ch. Christ. Home: Rte 1 Box 151 Ritzville WA 99169

SCHOETTGER, THEODORE LEO, city official; b. Burton, Nebr., Sept. 2, 1920; s. Frederick and Louise Cecelia (Gierau) S.; m. Kathlyn Marguerite Hughey, June 3, 1943; children—Gregory Paul, Julie Anne. B.S. in Bus. Adminstrn. with Distinction, U. Nebr., 1948. C.P.A., Calif. Sr. acct. Haskins & Sells, Los Angeles, 1948-55; controller Beckman Instruments, Inc., Fullerton, Calif., 1955-58; corp. chief acct. Beckman Instruments, Inc., 1958-60; treas. Documnun Inc., Los Angeles, 1960-77; fin. dir. City of Orange, Calif., 1977—. Mem. fin. com., treas., bd. dirs. Childrens Hosp. Served to lt. USNR, 1942-45. Mem. Calif. Soc. CPA's (nat. dir., v.p., past pres. Los Angeles chpt.), Fin. Execs. Inst., Mcpl. Fin. Officers Assn., Beta Gamma Sigma, Alpha Kappa Psi. Methodist. Clubs: Jonathan, Town Hall. Home: 9626 Shellyfield Rd Downey CA 90240-3418 Office: 300 E Chapman Ave Orange CA 92666-1591

SCHOETTLER, GAIL SINTON, state treasurer; b. Los Angeles, Oct. 21, 1943; d. James and Norma (McLellan) Sinton; children: Lee, Thomas, James; m. Donald L. Stevens, June 23, 1990. BA in Econs., Stanford U., 1965; MA in History, U. Calif., Santa Barbara, 1969, PhD in History, 1975. Businesswoman Denver, 1975-83; exec. dir. Colo. Dept. of Personnel, Denver, 1983-86; treas. State of Colo., Denver, 1987—; bd. dirs. Pub. Employees Retirement Assn., Denver, Nat. Jewish Hosp., Nat. Taxpayers' Union, Mi Casa Resource Ctr., Douglas County Edn. Found.; past bd. dirs. Women's Bank, Denver, Equitable Bankshares of Colo., Littleton, Equitable Bank. Mem. Douglas County Bd. Edn., Colo., 1979-87, pres., 1983-87; trustee U. No. Colo., Greeley, 1981-87; pres. Denver Children's Mus., 1975-85. Recipient Disting. Alumna award U. Calif. at Santa Barbara, 1987. Mem. Nat. Women's Forum (bd. dirs. 1981-89, pres. 1983-85), Women Execs. in State Govt. (bd. dirs. 1981-87, chmn. 1988), Leadership Denver Assn. (bd. dirs. 1987, named Outstanding Alumna 1985), Nat. Assn. State Treas., Stanford Alumni Assn. Democrat. *

SCHOFIELD, ANNETTE CECELIA, software publisher; b. Chgo., Mar. 26, 1957; d. Donald Rogers and Beverly Jean (Hollman) Gerth; m. Robert E. Schofield, July 7, 1991; children: Ryan, Riley. BA, U. Calif., Davis, 1979. Copywriter Sierra On-Line, Oakhurst, Calif., 1982-84, mgr. mktg. communications, 1984-86, mgr. customer svc., 1986-87, mgr. consumer mktg., 1987-88; dir. ops. CinemaWare, Westlake Village, Calif., 1988; v.p. mkg. Virgin Mastertronic, Irvine, Calif., 1988-91; pres. LivingSoft, Janesville, Calif., 1991—. Mem. Software Pubs. Assn. Democrat. Episcopalian. Office: Livingsoft PO Box 970 Janesville CA 96114

SCHOFIELD, JAMES ROY, computer programmer; b. Reedsburg, Wis., Aug. 16, 1953; s. G. C. Schofield and Margaret (Collies) Tverberg. BA, Carleton Coll., 1976. Programmer Brandon Applied Systems, San Francisco, 1977-78, Rand Info. Systems, San Francisco, 1979-83; systems programmer IBM, San Jose, Calif., 1983-91; programmer Office of Instnl. Rsch./U. Calif., Berkeley, 1991—. Mem. Assn. for Computing Machinery, Assn. for Computing Machinery Spl. Interest Group in Computers and Soc., Phi Beta Kappa. Home: PO Box 11755 Berkeley CA 94701-2755 Office: Office Instnl Rsch Univ Calif Berkeley CA 94720

SCHOFIELD, JOHN-DAVID MERCER, bishop; b. Somerville, Mass., Oct. 6, 1938; s. William David and Edith Putnam (Stockman) S. BA, Dartmouth Coll., 1960; MDiv, Gen. Theol. Sem., N.Y.C., 1963, DD (hon.), 1989. Joined Monks of Mt. Tabor, Byzantine Cath. Ch., 1978; ordained priest Episcopal Ch. Asst. priest Ch. of St. Mary the Virgin, San Francisco, 1963-65, Our Most Holy Redeemer Ch., London, 1965-69; rector, retreat master St. Columba's Ch. and Retreat House, Inverness, Calif., 1969-88; bishop Episcopal Diocese of San Joaquin, Fresno, Calif., 1988—; aggregate Holy Transfiguration Monastery, 1984—; bishop protector Order Agape and Reconciliation, Chemainus, B.C., Can., 1990—. Episcopal visitor to Community of Christian Family Ministry, Vista, Calif., 1991—; trustee Nashotah House Sem., Wis., 1991—. Mem. Episcopal Synod of Am. (founder 1989), Episcopalians United (bd. dirs. 1987—). Republican. Office: Diocese of San Joaquin 4159 E Dakota Ave Fresno CA 93726-5297

SCHOFIELD, WYVONNA L., academic administrator, educator; b. Portland, Oreg., Sept. 2, 1943; d. Harold S. and Frieda (Von Fintel) Wilson; m. Byron L. Swann (div.); children: John R., Richard A.; m. Jonathan G. Schofield, Oct. 7, 1980. AA, Laramie County Community Coll., 1978; BS, U. Wyo., 1980, MA, 1982. Dir. human resources tng. State of Wyo., Cheyenne, 1982-84; cons. Colorado Springs, Denver, 1984—; instr. Park Coll., Lowry AFB, Colo., 1985—, acad. dir., 1989-90, adminstr., 1990—. Author: Boards and You, 1982. Mem. Phi Delta Kappa. Republican. Roman Catholic. Home: 3232 S Hillerest Dr # 3 Denver CO 80237-1169 Office: Park Coll 3415 MSS A/MSE Bldg 375 Lowry AFB CO 80230

SCHOLES, PETER DICKSON, land conservation specialist; b. Berkeley, Calif., July 8, 1951; s. Robert Bruce and Catherine (Dickson) S.; m. Jacqueline Dee Frankfourth, Sept. 2, 1984; 1 child, Chloe Markley. BA, U. Calif., Santa Cruz, 1974. Field rep. The Wilderness Soc., Anchorage, 1976-77; Alaska program dir. The Wilderness Soc., Washington, 1977-80; heritage land bank mgr. Municipality of Anchorage, 1982-84, real estate div. dir., 1984-88; real property analyst City of Seattle, 1989; project mgr. Trust for Pub. Land, Seattle, 1990—; pres., bd. dirs. Alaska Ctr. for Environ., Anchorage, 1974-77; mem. citizens adv. com. Alaska Land Use Coun., Anchorage, 1983-84; mem. citizens adv. com. Seattle Open Space Program, 1991—. Mem. Washington Wildlife and Recreation Lands Mgmt. Task Force, 1992—. Office: Trust for Pub Land 506 2d Ave # 1510 Seattle WA 98504

SCHOLES, ROBERT THORNTON, physician, research administrator; b. Bushnell, Ill., June 24, 1919; s. Harlan Lawrence and Lura Zolene (Camp) S.; m. Kathryn Ada Tew, Sept. 3, 1948; 1 child, Delia. Student Knox Coll., 1937-38; BS, Mich. State U., 1941; MD, U. Rochester, 1950; postgrad. U. London, 1951-52, U. Chgo., 1953. Intern, Gorgas Hosp., Ancon, C.Z., 1950-51; lab. asst. dept. entomology Mich. State U., 1940-41; rsch. asst. Roselake Wildlife Exptl. Sta., 1941; rsch. assoc. Harvard U., 1953-57; served to med. dir. USPHS, 1954-71, med. officer, dep. chief health and sanitation div. U.S. Ops. Mission, Bolivia, 1954-57, chief health and sanitation div., Paraguay, 1957-60, internat. health rep. Office of Surgeon Gen., 1960-62; br. chief, research grants officer, acting assoc. dir. Nat. Inst. Allergy and Infectious Diseases, NIH, Bethesda, Md., 1962-71; co-founder, pres. The Bioresearch Ranch, Inc., Rodeo, N.Mex., 1977—; cons. Peace Corps, 1961, Hidalgo County Med. Services, Inc., 1979—, N.Mex. Health Systems Agy., 1980-86, N.Mex. Health Resources, Inc., 1981—, Hidalgo County Health Coun., 1993, Luna County Charitable Found., 1993. Served to capt. USAAF, 1942-45. Commonwealth Fund fellow, 1953. Mem. AAAS, Am. Soc. Tropical Medicine and Hygiene, N.Y. Acad. Sci., Am. Pub. Health Assn., Am. Ornithologists Union, Sembot Hon. Soc. Contbr. papers to profl. publs. Achievements include research, writing and field test of first health survey indices detailing anthopological parameters; institution of first country wide malaria control project in Paraguay. Home and Office: PO Box 117 Rodeo NM 88056-0117

SCHOLL, ALLAN HENRY, retired school system administrator, education consultant; b. Bklyn., May 6, 1935; s. Joseph Arnold and Edith (Epstein) S.; m. Marina Alexandra Mihailovich, July 3, 1960. BA, UCLA, 1957; MA, U. So. Calif., 1959, PhD in History, 1973. Lic. gen. secondary tchr. (life), administrv. svcs. (life), jr. coll. tchr. (life) Calif. Tchr. social studies L.A. Unified Sch. Dist., 1960-82, adviser social studies sr. high schs. div., 1982-84, dir. secondary social studies Office Instrn., 1984-91; instr. history L.A. City Coll., 1966-69, U. So. Calif., L.A., 1968-69, Community Coll., Rio Hondo, Calif., 1971-74, Cerritos (Calif.) Coll., 1973-74; dir. Almar Ednl. Cons., Rancho Mirage, Calif., 1991—; ednl. cons.; curriculum writer (interactive TV and computer programs). Co-author: History of the World, 1990, History of the World: The Modern Era, 1991; author: United States History and Art, 1992, 20th Century World History: The Modern Era, 1993; cons. high sch. govt. and U.S. history textbooks, 1987; contbr. articles to profl. jours. Bd. dirs. Pasadena Chamber Orch., 1977-78, Pasadena Symphony Orch., 1984-85, City of Pasadena Centennial Com., 1985, Martyrs Meml. and Mus. of Holocaust, 1992—; ednl. adv. bd. Gene Autry Western Heritage Mus., 1992—. With U.S. Army, 1958-59. NDEA fellow Russian lang. studies, 1962; Chouinard Art Inst. scholar, 1952. Mem. Am. Hist. Assn., Nat. Council Social Studies, Calif. Council Social Studies, So. Calif. Social Studies Assn. (bd. dirs. 1982-84), Assoc. Adminstrs. L.A. (legis. council 1984-86), Nat. Found. Ileitis and Colitis, Phi Alpha Theta. Office: Almar Ednl Cons 15 Sunrise Dr Rancho Mirage CA 92270

SCHOLTEN, PAUL, obstetrician-gynecologist, educator; b. San Francisco, Oct. 14, 1921; s. Henry Francis and Gladys (Lamborn) S.; m. Marion Lucy O'Neil, Feb. 7, 1948; children: Catherine Mary (dec.), Anne Marie, Pauline Marie, Joseph, Stephen, John. AB, San Francisco State U., 1943; postgrad., Stanford U., 1946-47; MD, U. Calif., San Francisco, 1951. Diplomate Am. Bd. Ob-Gyn. Intern San Francisco Gen. Hosp., 1951-52; resident in ob-gyn U. Calif., San Francisco, 1952-55; pvt. practice specializing in ob-gyn San Francisco, 1955-80; coll. physician Student Health Svc. San Francisco State U., 1956-80, dir. women's svcs. Student Health Svc., 1980-91; pvt. practice San Francisco, 1991—; part-time ship's surgeon Delta Lines, 1980-84; assoc. clin. prof. Med. Sch., U. Calif., San Francisco, 1955-92, assoc. clin. prof. Nursing Sch., 1987-92; preceptor Med. Sch., Stanford U., 1989-91; lectr. on health and wine at numerous univs., profl. groups. Contbr. articles to profl. publs., chpts. to books. Cons. U.S. Wine Inst.; sci. advisor Calif. State Adv. Bd. on Alcohol-Related Problems, 1980-86; bd. dirs. A.W.A.R.E., Century Coun. Sgt. U.S. Army, 1944-46. Mem. AMA, Calif. Med. Assn., Pan Am. Med. Assn., San Francisco Med. Soc. (editor 1971-92, historian), San Francisco Gynecol. Soc., Am. Coll. Ob-Gyn., Soc. Med. Friends of Wine (bd. dirs. 1955-92, past pres.), San Francisco Wine and Food Soc. (bd. dirs. 1960-92, past pres.), Internat. Wine and Food Soc. (gov. 1989-92, Bronze medal 1989), San Francisco State U. Alumni Assn. (bd. dirs. 1962-92), German Wine Soc., Sierra Club. Republican. Roman Catholic. Home and Office: 121 Granville Way San Francisco CA 94127-1133

SCHOLTZ, ROBERT ARNO, electrical engineering educator; b. Lebanon, Ohio, Jan. 26, 1936; s. William Paul and Erna Johanna (Weigel) S.; m. Laura Elizabeth McKeon, June 16, 1962; children: Michael William, Paul Andrew. B.S. in E.E., U. Cin., 1958; M.S. in E.E., U. So. Calif., 1960; Ph.D., Stanford U., 1964. Co-op student Sheffield Corp., Dayton, Ohio, 1953-58; M.S. and Ph.D. fellow Hughes Aircraft Co., Culver City, Calif., 1958-63, sr. staff engr., 1963-78; vis. prof. U. Hawaii, 1969, 78; prof. U. So. Calif., 1963—; cons. LinCom Corp., L.A., 1975-81, Axiomatix Inc., L.A., 1980-86, JPL, Pasadena, 1985, Tech. Group, 1987-89, TRW, 1989, Pulson Comm., 1992—. Co-author: Spread Spectrum Comm., 3 vols., 1984; contbr. numerous articles to profl. jours. (recipient Leonard G. Abraham Prize Paper award 1983, Donald G. Fink Prize award 1984, Signal Processing Soc. Sr. Paper award 1992). Pres., South Bay Community Concert Orgn., Redondo Beach, Calif., 1975-79. Fellow IEEE (bd. govs. info. theory group 1981-86, bd. govs. communication soc. 1981-83, chmn. fin. com. NTC 1977, program chmn. ISIT 1981). Office: U So Calif Comm Scis Inst Dept Elec Engring Los Angeles CA 90089

SCHON, ALAN WALLACE, lawyer; b. Mpls., Nov. 27, 1946; s. Hubert Adelbert and Jennie (Jamieson) S.; m. Linda Kay Long, June 14, 1969; 1 child, Cynthia Ann. BA, U. Minn., 1969; JD, William and Mary Coll., 1973. Bar: Minn. 1973, U.S. Dist. Ct. Minn., Alaska 1986, U.S. Dist. Ct. Alaska, U.S. Ct. Appeals (9th cir.) 1988. Prin. Schon Law Office, Fairbanks, Alaska, 1986—; owner, pub. Nordland Pub. Co., Fairbanks, Alaska, 1991—; nationwide environ. group mgr. Delphi Info. Network, Gen. Videotex Corp., Cambridge, Mass., 1991—. Author, pub. EnvironLaw, 1991—. Dir. Alaska State Fair, Fairbanks, 1987-91, Fairbanks Light Opera Theater, Fairbanks, 1991—; dir., sec. Riding for Am., Inc., 1993—; dir. Interior Ala. Econ. Devel. Ctr., 1993—. Maj. U.S. Army, 1974-86. Mem. Fairbanks C. of C. (chmn. environ. concerns com. 1992—). Home: 204 Sacia Ave Fairbanks AK 99712 Office: Schon Law Office 402 7th Ave Fairbanks AK 99701-4974

SCHONFELD, WILLIAM ROST, political science educator, researcher; b. N.Y.C., Aug. 28, 1942; s. William A. and Louise R. (Rost) S.; m. Elena Beortegui, Jan. 23, 1964; children: Natalie Beortegui, Elizabeth Lynn Beortegui. Student, Cornell U., 1960-61; B.A. cum laude with honors, NYU, 1964; M.A., Princeton U., 1968, Ph.D., 1970. Research asst. Princeton U., 1966-69, research assoc., 1969-70, vis. lectr., 1970; asst. prof. polit. sci. U. Calif.-Irvine, 1970-75, assoc. prof., 1975-81, prof., 1981—, dean Sch. Social Scis., 1982—; sr. lectr. Fond. Nat. de Sci. Politique, Paris, 1973-74; researcher Centre de Sociologie des Organisations, Paris, 1976-78. Author: Youth and Authority in France, 1971, Obedience and Revolt, 1976, Ethnographie du PS et du RPR, 1985. Recipient Disting. Teaching award U. Calif.-Irvine, 1984; Fulbright fellow Bordeaux, France, 1964-65; Danforth grad. fellow, 1964-69; Fulbright sr. lectr. Paris, 1973-74; NSF-CNRS Exchange of Scientists fellow Paris, 1976-78; Ford Found. grantee France, Spain, 1978-79; finalist Prof. Yr. Council for Advancement and Support of Edn., 1984. Mem. Am. Polit. Sci. Assn., Assoc. Francaise de Sci. Pol., Phi Beta Kappa. Office: U Calif Sch Social Scis Irvine CA 92717

SCHOOLEY, DAVID ALLAN, biochemistry educator; b. Denver, Apr. 17, 1943; s. Elmer Wayne and Gertrude (Rogers) S.; m. M. Eleanor Dobbins, Feb. 3, 1968; children: Christine M., Stephen T., Anna K. BS, N.Mex. Highlands U., Las Vegas, 1963; PhD, Stanford U., 1968; postgrad., U. Fla., 1968-69, Columbia U., N.Y.C., 1969-71. Sr. biochemist Zoecon Corp., Palo Alto, Calif., 1971-74; dir. biochem. rsch. Zoecon Corp. (name now Sandoz Crop Protection), 1974-88; prof. U. Nev. Dept. Biochemistry, Reno, 1988—; cons. Sandoz Crop Protection, 1988-91; mem. grant adv. panel Nat. Sci. Found., Washington, 1986-89. Contbr. articles to profl. jours. and chpts. to books. Asst. scoutmaster troop 5 Stanford Area Coun., Palo Alto, 1984-88; bd. editors 3 sci. jours. Mem. AAAS, Am. Chem. Soc. (Baxter, Burdick and Jackson award 1990), Am. Soc. for Biochemistry and Molecular Biology, Protein Soc. Office: U Nev Dept Biochemistry Reno NV 89557

SCHOOLLAND, LI ZHAO, fine arts company executive, teacher, consultant; b. Tianjin, China, Mar. 16, 1958; came to U.S., 1984; d. Robert Yunnian Chao and Qizhen Cao; m. Shiy Zhang, Aug., 1984 (div. 1987); m. Kenneth Lloyd Schoolland, Aug. 8, 1988; 1 child, Kenli Dulcinea. BA, Foreign Lang. Inst., Tianjin, China, 1983; MA, U. Minn., 1987; Mgmt. Sci. (Japanese), Japan-Am. Inst. Mgmt. Sci., Honolulu, 1988; MS in Japanes Bus. Study, Chaminade U., Honolulu, 1988. Steel mill worker Guang Xi, China, 1969-78; tchr. Liu-Zhou Steel Mill High Sch., Guang Xi, 1978; translator, researcher China Dept. Transp., Beijing, 1983-84; teaching asst. U. Minn., Mpls., 1985-87; intern trainee Tobu Dept. Store, Tokyo, Japan, 1988; pres. Schoolland Internat. Partnership, 1988—; sales mgr. trainee Duty Free

Shops, Honolulu, 1989; gen. mgr. Double-Eye Hawaii, Honolulu, 1989-92, 1989—. Editor: (newsletters) Double-Eye News, 1989-92, Libertarian Party Hawaii News, 1991-93. Chmn. membership com. U.S.-China People's Friendship Assn., 1988-89; mem. legis. com. Small Bus. Hawaii; bd. dirs. Libertarian Party Hawaii, 1992. Recipient Model Citizen award Mpls. Police Dept., 1992; named Outstanding Grad. Student, U. Minn., 1992. Mem. Am. Mktg. Assn. (bd. dirs.), Am. Soc. Interior Designers, Sales and Mktg. Execs. of Honolulu, Honolulu Japanese C. of C. (chair com.), Honolulu Acad. Art, Japan-Am. Assn. Hawaii, Assn. Hawaii Artists (corr. sec.), Chinese C. of C. Honolulu.

SCHOON, CHRIS VOHN, exobiologist, cryogenics theorist; b. Sioux Falls, S.D., Dec. 23, 1951; s. Daschel R. and Isolde (Kanaranzi) S.; m. Kathleen Mercedes, May 20, 1989. BS, U. Nebr., 1976; MS, U. Iowa, 1980; PhD, Staadts Technique, Vienna, Austria and Bonn, Germany, 1985. Technician radio telemetry ground sta. H.U.M.E.R.D.U., Wallaboroo, West Australia; sr. technician Copernicus Probe Design Com., L.A., Vienna, Bonn, 1982-84; cons. sci. officer New Planetary Exploration Assn., L.A., 1986—; head tech. com. New Planetary Exploration Assn., L.A., 1987—; chairperson exobiology conf. NAV-COM Gen. Assembly Conf., New Orleans, 1988. Author: Life and the Carbon-Base Paradigm, 1989. Mem. Ea. Cowl of the Raven (assignee). Presbyterian.

SCHOON, DOUGLAS DEAN, chemical consultant; b. Marshaltown, Iowa, June 7, 1954; s. Shirley Jean Elsey. BS in Chemistry, Long Beach State (Calif.) U.; MS, U. Calif., Irvine, 1984. Chief rsch. chemist Creative Nail Design Inc., Irvine, 1984-88; exec. dir. Chem. Awareness Tng. Svc., Newport Beach, Calif., 1988—; ind. litigation cons., polymer coatings cons., Newport Beach, 1989—; chem. cons. Am. Beauty Assn., Chgo., 1992—. Author: Chemistry and Structure of Hair, 1992, Classroom Experiments in Hair Structure and Chemistry, 1992, HIV/AIDS and Hepatitis in the Salon; author tng. videotape on chem. safety, 1990; contbr. articles on chem. safety to various publs. With U.S. Army, 1974-78. Mem. Am. Chem. Soc. Republican. Office: Chem Awareness Tng Svc PO Box 16383 Irvine CA 92013

SCHOONMAKER, ROBERT CADBURY, management consultant; b. Northampton, Mass., June 26, 1944; s. John Warder and Ann Pitkin (Palmer) S.; m. Kama Sue Conger, Jan. 22, 1968; children: Rachael, Melanie, Trista, Tara, Tania, Robert J., Trent, Benjamin, Joshua, Nicole, Jeremy. BS in History, Brigham Young U., 1968, M. Accountancy, 1973. Cert. in mgmt. acctg. Dir. regulatory affairs Gen. Telephone Co. of Ill., Bloomington, Ill., 1979-81; acctg. dir. Gen. Telephone Co. of Mich., Muskegon, 1981; contr. Gen. Telephone Co. of Ind., Ft. Wayne, 1981-82; v.p. revenue requirements Gen. Telephone Co. of the Midwest, Grinnell, Iowa, 1982-84; v.p. GVNW Inc./Mgmt., Colorado Springs, Colo., 1984-90; v.p. fin. Fidelity Comms., Sullivan, Mo., 1990-91; v.p. GVNW Inc./Mgmt., Colorado Springs, 1991—. With U.S. Army, 1969-72. Mem. LDS Church. Home: 5317 Miranda Rd Colorado Springs CO 80918 Office: GVNW Inc/Mgmt 2270 La Montana Way Colorado Springs CO 80918

SCHOPKE, CHRISTIAN RUDOLF, biologist, researcher; b. Bad Homburg, Hessen, Germany, Dec. 13, 1955; came to U.S., 1989; s. Lothar and Ursula (Hartmann) S.; m. Aura Estela Gonzalez Orellana, Sept. 5, 1986; children: Christian Alexander, Angela Mariana. MS, Johann Wolfgang Goethe U., Frankfurt, 1982; PhD, Johann Wolfgang Goethe U., 1989. Rsch. assoc. Washington U., St. Louis, 1989-91; sr. rsch. assoc. Scripps Rsch. Inst., La Jolla, Calif., 1991; charge de recherche inst. français de recherche scientifique pour le devel. en cooperation Scripps Rsch. Inst., 1992—; mem. Steering Com. for the Symposium Biotech. for Crop Improvement in Latin Am., La Jolla, Calif., 1992—. Author: (book) In vitro-Kultur bei Kaffee: Versuche zur Isolierung und Kultivierung von Protoplasten und zur Regeneration von Pflanzen, 1989; contbr. articles to profl. jours. Grantee fellowship Tropical Agrl. Rsch. and Tng. Ctr., Turrialba, Costa Rica, German Acad. Exch. Svc., 1983-85. Mem. Internat. Assn. for Plant Tissue Culture, Internat. Soc. for Plant Molecular Biology, Tissue Culture Assn, Gesellschaft Deutscher Naturforscher und Arzte. Home: 11331 Porreca Pt San Diego CA 92126 Office: Scripps Rsch Inst Dept Plant Biology MRC7 10666 N Torrey Pines Rd La Jolla CA 92037

SCHOPPA, ELROY, accountant, financial planner; b. Vernon, Tex., Aug. 25, 1922; s. Eddie A. and Ida (Foerster) S.; m. Juanita C. Young, Aug. 11, 1956 (div.); children: Karen Marie, Vickie Sue; m. Gail O. Evans Martin, May 12, 1984; stepchildren: Veronica, Vanessa. BBA, Tex. Tech U., 1943; postgrad. Law Sch., U. Tex., 1946-47; MA, Mich. State U., 1950. CPA, Tex., Calif.; cert. real estate broker; cert. ins. agt. Mem. faculty Tex. Tech U., Lubbock, 1943, U. Tex., Austin, 1946-47, Mich. State U., East Lansing, 1947-50; auditor Gen. Motors Corp., 1950-56; dir. systems and procedures Fansteel Metall. Corp., 1956-59; gen. auditor Consol. Electro Dynamics Corp., 1959-60; auditor, sr. tax acct. Beckman Inst. Inc., Fullerton, Calif., 1960-70; pres. Elroy Schoppa Acctg. Corp., La Habra, Calif., 1960—; fin. planner Nat. Assn. Stock Dealers; cons. to bus. Treas. La Habra Devel. Corp.; organizer, pres. 4-H Club, Vernon; adviser Jr. Achievement, Waukegan, Ill.; bd. dirs. Klein Ctr. for Prevention of Domestic Violence; asst. football and basketball coach, Manzanola, Colo.; coach Am. Girls Sport Assn., La Habra. Served with USN, 1942-46; USNR, 1946-62. Mem. Calif. Soc. CPA's, Alpha Phi Omega, Theta Xi. Republican. Lutheran. Club: Phoenix (Anaheim, Calif.). Avocations: hunting, fishing, camping. Office: 801 E La Habra Blvd La Habra CA 90631-5531

SCHORA, BARBRA ANN, programmer, analyst; b. Pawtucket, R.I., Apr. 15, 1957; d. Robert Howard Schora and Elizabeth (Manion) Costa. Apprentice mechanic Internat. Packaging, Pawtucket, R.I., 1975-78; data processing mgr. The N.J. of San Francisco, 1979-81, Pearl Cruises, San Francisco, 1981-84; programmer, analyst E.D.S., Oakland, Calif., 1985-86, Safeway Stores Inc., Oakland, 1987-88; sr. programmer, analyst Hamilton-Taft & Co., San Francisco, 1985-91; sr. programmer analyst Wells Fargo Bank, 1992—; cons. Lightning Express, San Francisco, 1988, Locke McCorkle Co., Mill Valley, Calif., 1988, Quality Motorcycle Repair, Mill Valley, 1990—, City of Berkeley, Calif., 1991, The Northface, Berkeley, 1991. Home: 220 Redwood Hwy # 31 Mill Valley CA 94941-3683

SCHORR, ALAN EDWARD, librarian, publisher; b. N.Y.C., Jan. 7, 1945; s. Herbert and Regina (Fingerman) S.; m. Debra Genner, June 11, 1967; 1 son, Zebediah. BA, CUNY, 1966; MA, Syracuse U., 1967; postgrad., U. Iowa, 1967-71; MLS, U. Tex., 1973. Tchr., rsch. asst. dept. history U. Iowa, 1967-70; govt. publs. and map libr., asst. prof. Elmer E. Rasmuson Library, U. Alaska, Fairbanks, 1973-78; assoc. prof., dir. library U. Alaska, Juneau, 1978-84; prof., univ. library dean Calif. State U., Fullerton, 1984-86; pres. The Denali Press, Juneau, Alaska, 1986—; free lance indexer and bibliographer; vis. lectr. Birmingham (Eng.) Poly., 1981; mem. Alaska Ednl. Del. to People's Republic China, 1975. Author: Alaska Place Names, 1974, 4th edit., 1991, Directory of Special Libraries in Alaska, 1975, Government Reference Books, 1974-75, 1976, 1976-77, 1978, Government Documents in the Library Literature 1909-1974, 1976, ALA RSBRC Manual, 1979, Federal Documents Librarianship 1879-1987, 1988, Hispanic Resource Directory, 1988, 2d edit., 1992, Refugee and Immigrant Resource Directory, 1990, 92; editor: The Sourdough, 1974-75, Directory of Services for Refugees and Immigrants, 1987, 3d edit., 1993, Guide to Smithsonian serial publs., 1987 ; book reviewer, columnist: S.E. Alaska Empire, 1979—, L.A. Times; contbr. articles to profl. jours. Mem. Auke Bay (Alaska) Vol. Fire Dept.; mem. Juneau Borough Cemetery Adv. Com., 1980-81, Am. Book Awards Com., 1980, Juneau Borough Library Adv. Com., 1981-82, Juneau Sch. Bd. Strategic Com., Juneau Bd. Edn., 1991—. Mem. ALA (reference and subscription books rev. com. 1975-86, reference and adult services div. publs. com. 1975-77, Nat. Assn. Hispanic Publications, Mudge citation commn. 1977-79, 84-86, Dartmouth Coll. Medal Commn., Governing Council 1977-84, Dewey medal com. 1984-85, Denali Press award), Alaska Library Assn. (exec. bd. 1974-75, nominating com. 1977-79), Pacific N.W. Library Assn. (rep. publs. com. 1973-75), Assn. Coll. and Research Libraries (publ. com. 1976-80), Spl. Libraries Assn. (assoc. editor geography and map div. bull. 1975-76), Soc. for Scholarly Pub., Internat. Assn. Ind. Pubs (bd. dirs. 1990—), Pub. Mktg. Assn., Alaska Assn. Small Presses, PEN Ctr. USA West, Amnesty Internat., Explorers Club N.Y. Office: PO Box 1535 Juneau AK 99802-0078

SCHORR, MARTIN MARK, forensic psychologist, educator, writer; b. Sept. 16, 1923; m. Dolores Gene Tyson, June 14, 1952; 1 child, Jeanne Ann. Student Balliol Coll., Oxford (Eng.) U., 1945-46; AB cum laude, Adelphi U., 1949; postgrad., U. Tex., 1949-50; MS, Purdue U., 1953; PhD, U. Denver, 1960; postgrad., U. Tex. Diplomate in psychology; lic. clin. pscyhologist. Chief clin. psychol. svcs. San Diego County Mental Hosp., 1963-67; clin. dir. human services San Diego County, 1963-76; pvt. practice, forensic specialist San Diego, 1962—; forensic examiner superior, fed. and mil. cts., San Diego, 1962—; prof. abnormal psychology San Diego State U., 1965-68; chief dept. psychology Center City (Calif.) Hosp., 1976-79; cons. Dept. Corrections State of Calif., Minnewawa, 1970-73, Disability Evaluation Dept. Health, 1972-75, Calif. State Indsl. Accident Commn., 1972-78, Calif. Criminal Justice Adminstrn., 1975-77, Vista Hill Found., Mercy Hosp. Mental Health, Foodmaker Corp., Convent Sacred Heart, El Cajon, FAA Examiner. Author: Death by Prescription, 1988; co-dir. Timberline Films, Inc. Recipient award for aid in developing Whistle Blower Law Calif. Assembly, 1986. Fellow Internat. Assn. Soc. Psychiatry; mem. AAAS, PEN, Am. Psychology Assn., Am. Acad. Forensic Scis., Qualified Med. Evaluator, Calif., 1993, Internat. Platform Assn., WOrld Mental Health Assn., Mystery Writers Am., Nat. Writers' Club., Mensa. Home and Office: 2970 Arnoldson Ave University City San Diego CA 92122-2114

SCHORZMAN, MARK HEWIT, industrial hygienist; b. Spokane, Wash., Sept. 6, 1937; s. Lester Richard and Esther Ann (Cowen) S.; m. Judy Kennett Lavender, Aug. 22, 1959; children: Mark Hewit, Douglas Wheeler. BS, U. Wash., 1961, MS in Pub. Health, 1975; grad. with honors, Army Command and Gen. Staff Coll., 1976; registered sanitarian, Wash.; diplomate Am. Acad. Sanitarians, Am. Acad. Indsl. Hygiene. Sanitarian, Thurston-Mason Health Dist., Wash., 1961-62; commd. 2d lt., U.S. Army, 1962, advanced through grades to maj., 1967, ret., 1982, chief environ. sanitation, N. Baveria Med. Dist., W. Germany, 1968-69, chief preventive medicine Madigan Gen. Hosp., Tacoma, 1970-74, preventive medicine cons. Comdr. U.S. Army Health Svcs. Command, Ft. Sam Houston, Tex., 1975-77, chief environ. sci. Fitzsimons Army Med. Center, Denver, 1977-82; risk mgmt. officer Adams County, Colo., 1982-84; cons. in indsl. hygiene Mark H. Schorzman and Assocs., Denver, 1984-90; sr. indsl. hygienist Stone & Webster Engring., Denver, 1990—; instr. Nat. Inst. for Food Svc. Industry, 1980-83. Scouting chmn. Centennial dist. Boy Scouts Am., 1977-79, mem. tng. com., 1977-82; instr. ARC. U.S. Army Med. Dept. scholar, 1974. Mem. Am. Indsl. Hygiene Assn., Nat. Environ. Health Assn., Automatic Merchandising Assn., Am. Conf. Govtl. Indsl. Hygienists, Royal Soc. Health U.K., Sigma Chi. Anglican Catholic. Contbr. articles to profl. jours. Home: 3419 S Nucla Way Aurora CO 80013-2074

SCHOTT, HAROLD CHARLES, II, veterinarian, equine medicine educator; b. Cin., Apr. 21, 1959; s. Walter Edward and Margaret (Henkel) S. BS, Cornell U., 1980; DVM, Ohio State U., 1984; PhD, Wash. State U., 1991. Diplomate Am. Bd. Vet. Internal Medicine. Assoc. veterinarian Santa Barbara Equine Practice, Goleta, Calif., 1984-87; resident dept. vet. clin. medicine and surgery Wash. State U., Pullman, 1987-91, instr., 1991-92, asst. prof. equine medicine, 1992—. Contbr. articles to profl. jours. Mem. AVMA, Am. Assn. Equine Practitioners, Am. Coll. Sports Medicine, Internat. Soc. for Vet. Perinatology, Am. Physiol. Soc., Assn. for Equine Sports Medicine (bd. dirs. 1992—). Roman Catholic. Office: Wash State U Dept Vet Clin Med and Surg Pullman WA 99164-6610

SCHOW, TERRY D., state official; b. Ogden, Utah, Dec. 14, 1948; s. Hugh Stuart Sloan and Minnie Aurelia (Ellis) Mohler; m. June Hansen, Feb. 14, 1973; children: Amy, Jason. Associates, Honolulu Community Coll., 1975; Bachelors, Chaminade U., 1975. Mgmr. cert. Utah. Spl. and criminal investigator State of Utah, Ogden, 1976-83, lead investigator, 1984-92; investigator Fed. Govt., Salt Lake City, Denver, 1983-84; mgr. State of Utah, Ogden, 1992—. Mem. Gov.'s Coun. on Vets. Issues, 1989—, chmn., 1990—; mem. State of Utah Privatization Policy Bd., 1989-92; chmn. 1st Congressional Dist. Utah Rep. Party, 1982-83, mem. state exec. com., 1982-83; chmn. legis. dist Weber County Rep. Party, Ogden, 1987-91, 93—; trustee Utah's Vietnam Meml., Salt Lake City, 1988—; leader Boy Scouts Am., Ogden, 1985—. Sgt. U.S. Army, 1967-70, 72-76; Vietnam. Decorated Bronze Star, 1970, Combat Inf. Badge, 1970; recipient Championship Team Trophy Pistol U.S. Army, 1975. Mem. DAV (life, jr. vice-comdr. Weber chpt. 4 1989-90, sr. vice-comdr. 1990—, comdr. 1993—, state 3d jr. vice commdr. 1992, state 2d jr. vice commdr. 1993—), NRA (life), VFW, Utah Peace Officers Assn., Utah Pub. Employees Assn. (bd. dirs. 1988-89, v.p. 1989-92, pres. 1992-93, chmn. Ogden Valley dist.), Kiwanis (bd. dirs. Ogden chpt. 1988—, v.p. 1990—, pres. 1992-93, pres. Layton chpt. 1985-86, named Kiwanian of Yr. 1982-83). Republican. Mormon. Home: 1540 Sunview Dr Ogden UT 84404-5344 Office: State of Utah Office Recoveries 2650 Washington Blvd Fl 4 Ogden UT 84401-3623

SCHOWE, SHERAL LEE SPEAKS, special education educator; b. San Francisco, June 14, 1953; d. Veral John and Myrtle Lee (Hunter) Speaks; m. Derryll Boyd Schowe, Aug. 7, 1982; 1 child, Devin. B degree, Brigham Young U., 1977, M degree, 1979; AA, Ricks Coll., Rexburg, Idaho, 1974; fellow, Gallaudet Coll., 1978. Lic. therapeutic recreation specialist; cert. spl. edn. instr. Asst. Calif. Jud. Edn. and Rsch., Berkeley; coord. Cottonwood Elem. Community Sch., Holladay, Utah; founder, coord. handicap svcs. Granite Dist. Community Edn., Salt Lake City; founder, coord. ind. living skills program Hartvigsen Community Sch., Salt Lake City; area dir., exec. dir. Utah Spl. Olympics, Sandy, Utah; fund raising cons. non-profit orgns.; spl. edn. instr. Granite Sch. Dist., Salt Lake City. Contbr. numerous articles to profl. jours. Mem. archtl. barriers com. Salt Lake 504 Coun., 1978-80; mem. Salt Lake County Community Devel. Citizens Adv. Coun., 1981, vice chair, 1982, chair, 1983; mem. panel Salt Lake County Title XX Adv. Coun., 1984-87; pres., moderator Presbyn. Women United Cottonwood Presbyn. Ch., 1992, 93; v.p. PTA Truman Elem. Sch., 1991, 92, 93, PTA rep. 1992, '93; rep. Granite Edn. Assn., 1992, '93. Named Edn. of Handicapped of Yr. Mental Retardation Assn., 1982, Woman of Yr. Salt Lake City JayCees, 1982; recipient Outstanding Contribution to Fitness award Utah Gov's. Coun. on Health & Physical Fitness, 1990. Mem. Utah Community Edn. Assn. (Profl. Community Educator of Yr. 1987), Nat. Assn. Spl. Olympics Profls. (bd. dirs. 1990), Coun. Exceptional Children, Zonta (svc. com. chair 1987, bd. dirs. 1988, pub. rels. chair 1990, '91, Soviet Art Exch.chair 1991, '92, '93), Exec. Women's Svc. Orgn., Russian Cultural Exch. Program (chair 1992, 93), Presbyn. Women's Assn. Democrat. Presbyterian. Home: 11454 High Mountain Dr Sandy UT 84092-5661 Office: Granite Sch Dist Dept Spl Edn 340 E 3545 S Salt Lake City UT 84115

SCHRADER, HARRY CHRISTIAN, JR., retired naval officer; b. Sheboygan, Wis., Aug. 4, 1932; s. Harry Christian and Edna Flora (Stubbe) S.; m. Carol Joan Gossman, June 23, 1956; 1 child, Mary Clare. B.S., U.S. Naval Acad., 1955; M.S., U.S. Naval Postgrad. Sch., 1963. Commd. ensign U.S. Navy, 1955, advanced through grades to vice adm., 1982; comdr. U.S.S. Tawasa, 1963-64, U.S.S. A. Hamilton, 1970-72, U.S.S. Jackson, 1972-73, U.S.S. Gilmore, 1973-75, U.S.S. Long Beach, 1975-78; dir. MLSF Amphibious, Mine Warfare and Advanced Vehicles div. Office Naval Ops., Washington, 1978-80; comdr. Cruiser Destroyer Group One, San Diego, 1980-82, Naval Surface Forces, U.S. Pacific Fleet, San Diego, 1982-85; ret., 1985; with Rockwell Internat., Anaheim, Calif., 1985-87; pres. Coronado (Calif.) Tech. Internat., 1987—. Mem. Am. Def. Preparedness Assn., San Diego Oceans Found. (adv. bd.), Sigma Xi. Office: Rancho Santa Fe Tech Corp 6574 Caminito Northland La Jolla CA 92037-5822

SCHRADER, LAWRENCE EDWIN, plant physiologist, educator; b. Atchison, Kans., Oct. 22, 1941; s. Edwin Carl and Jenna Kathryn (Tobiason) S.; m. Elfriede J. Massier, Mar. 14, 1981. BS, Kans. State U., 1963; PhD, U. Ill., 1967; grad., Inst. Ednl. Mgmt., Harvard U., 1991. Asst. prof. dept. agronomy U. Wis., Madison, 1969-72; assoc. prof. U. Wis., 1972-76, prof., 1976-84; prof., head dept. agronomy U. Ill., Urbana, 1985-89; dean Coll. Agr. and Home Econs. Wash. State U., Pullman, 1989—; chief competitive rsch. grants office Dept. Agr., Washington, 1980-81; trustee, treas. Agrl. Satellite Corp., 1991—. Contbr. chpts. to books, articles to profl. jours. Active Consortium for Internat. Devel., 1989—, chair fin. com., vice chair exec. com., 1990-92, trustee, 1989—; mem. exec. com. Coun. of Agrl. Heads of Agr., 1992—. Capt. U.S. Army, 1967-69. Recipient Soybean Researchers Recognition award 1983, Disting. Service award in Agriculture Kansas State U., 1987; Romnes Faculty fellow U. Wis., 1979. Fellow AAAS (mem. steering group, sect. agr.), Am. Soc. Agronomy, Crop Sci. Soc. Am.; mem. Am. Soc. Plant Physiologists (sec. 1983-85, pres. elect 1986, pres. 1987), Am. Chem. Soc., Wash. State Bd. Natural Resources, Sigma Xi, Gamma Sigma Delta, Phi Kappa Phi, Phi Eta Sigma, Blue Key, Alpha Zeta. Methodist. Home: NW 1425 Orion Pullman WA 99163-3331 Office: Wash State U Coll Agr and Home Econs 421 Hulbert Hall Pullman WA 99164-6242

SCHRAG, PETER, editor, writer; b. Karlsruhe, Germany, July 24, 1931; came to U.S., 1941, naturalized, 1953; s. Otto and Judith (Haas) S.; m. Melissa Jane Mowrer, June 9, 1953 (div. 1969); children: Mitzi, Erin Andrew; m. Diane Divoky, May 24, 1969 (div. 1981); children: David Divoky, Benaiah Divoky; m. Patricia Ternahan, Jan. 1, 1988. A.B. cum laude, Amherst Coll., 1953. Reporter El Paso (Tex.) Herald Post, 1953-55; asst. sec., asst. dir. publs. Amherst Coll., 1955-66, instr. Am. Studies, 1960-64; asso. edn. editor Sat. Rev., 1966-68, exec. editor, 1968-69; editor Change mag., 1969-70; editor at large Saturday Rev., 1969-72; contbg. editor Saturday Review/Education, 1972-73; editorial adv. bd. The Columbia Forum, 1972-75; editorial bd. Social Policy, 1971—; contbg. editor More, 1974-78, Inquiry, 1977-80; editorial page editor Sacramento Bee and McClatchy Newspapers, 1978—; vis. lectr. U. Mass. Sch. Edn., 1970-72; fellow in profl. journalism Stanford U., Palo Alto, Calif., 1973-74; lectr. U. Calif. at Berkeley, 1974-78, 90—; Pulitzer Prize juror, 1988-89. Author: Voices in the Classroom, 1965, Village School Downtown, 1967, Out of Place in America, 1971, The Decline of the Wasp, 1972, The End of the American Future, 1973, Test of Loyalty, 1974, (with Diane Divoky) The Myth of the Hyperactive Child, 1975, Mind Control, 1978; contbr. articles. Mem. adv. com. Student Rights Project, N.Y. Civil Liberties Union, 1970-72; mem. Com. Study History, 1958-72; Trustee Emma Willard Sch., 1967-69; bd. dirs. Park Sch., Oakland, Calif., 1976-77, Center for Investigative Reporting, 1979-81. Guggenheim fellow, 1971-72; Nat. Endowment for Arts fellow, 1976-77. Office: Sacramento Bee 21st and Q Sts Sacramento CA 95852

SCHRAMM, RAYMOND EUGENE, physicist; b. St. Charles, Mo., Aug. 11, 1941; s. Earl E. and Dorothy R. (Huber) S. B.S. in Math., Regis Coll., 1964; M.S. in Physics, Mich. Tech. U., 1965; postgrad. U. Colo., 1966-68. Jr. physicist Ames Lab., Iowa, 1965-66; teaching asst. physics dept. U. Colo., Boulder, 1966-67; physicist Nat. Inst. Standards and Tech. (formerly Nat. Bur. Standards), Boulder, 1967—. Contbr. articles to profl. jours. Mem. Am. Assn. Physics Tchrs., AAAS. Democrat. Roman Catholic. Home: 9814 Lane St Denver CO 80221-8030 Office: Nat Inst Standards & Tech/853 Materials Reliability Divsn 325 Broadway Boulder CO 80303

SCHREIBER, ANDREW, psychotherapist; b. Budapest, Hungary, Aug. 1, 1918; s. Alexander and Bella (Gruen) S.; m. Mona Schreiber, Aug. 6, 1950; children: Julie, Brad, Robin. BA, CCNY, 1941, MEd, 1943; MSW, Columbia U., 1949; PhD, Heed U., 1972. Diplomate Am. Bd. Sexology; lic. psychotherapist, Calif. Pvt. practice Belmont, Calif., 1970—; sales mgr. vibro ceramics dir. Gulton Industries, Metuchen, N.J., 1949-57; mktg. mgr. Weldotron Corp., Newark, 1957-63; head dept. spl. edn. San Mateo (Calif.) High Sch. Dist., 1964-70; mem. faculty Heed U., 1970-71, advisor to doctoral candidates on West Coast, 1971; lectr. spl. edn. U. Calif.-Berkeley, 1973. Art Students League of N.Y. scholar, 1933-35, San Francisco State U. grantee. Fellow Am. Acad. Clin. Sexology; mem. NEA, AACD, Learning Disabilities Assn., Am. Assn. Sex Educators, Counselors and Therapists, Calif. Assn. Marriage and Family Therapists, Calif. Tchrs. Assn. Home: 2817 San Ardo Way Belmont CA 94002-1341

SCHREIBER, EDWARD, computer scientist; b. Zagreb, Croatia, Mar. 17, 1943; came to U.S., 1956, naturalized, 1960; s. Hinko and Helen (Iskra) S.; m. Barbara Nelson, 1967 (div. 1969); m. Lea Lusia Hausler, Nov. 7, 1983. BSEE, U. Colo., Denver, 1970. Registered profl. engr. Colo.; cert. data processor. Sr. software scientist Autotrol, Denver, 1972-78; software engr. Sigma Design, Englewood, Colo, 1979-82; founder, v.p. Graphics, Info., Denver, 1982-86; chmn. Schrieber Instruments, 1987—; instr. computer sci. U. Colo., Denver, 1971-72, Colo. Women's Coll., Denver, 1972-73, U. Denver, 1983. Contbr. articles on computer graphics to profl. jours. Trustee 1st Universalist Ch., Denver, 1972-78; Dem. candidate for U.S. Ho. of Reps., 1980. Served with U.S. Army, 1960-66. Mem. IEEE, Assn. for Computing Machinery, Nat. Computer Graphics Assn., Mensa. Office: Schreiber Instruments Inc Ste # 250 4800 Happy Canyon Rd Denver CO 80237

SCHREIBER, EVERETT CHARLES, JR., chemist, educator; b. Amityville, N.Y., Nov. 13, 1953; s. Everett Charles Sr. and Mary Elizabeth (Johnston) S.; m. Jane Karen Sklenar, July 19, 1980. BS, Pace U., 1975; PhD, U. Nebr., 1980. Rsch. assoc. SUNY, Stony Brook, 1980-82; asst. dir. rsch. Muscular Dystrophy Assn., N.Y.C., 1983-84; rsch. assoc. SUNY, 1984-86; spectroscopist G.E. NMR Instruments, Fremont, Calif., 1986-87; quality assurance engr. Varian NMR Instruments, Palo Alto, Calif., 1987-89, tech. tng. specialist, 1989—. Author of tng. texts in engring. and computers. Vice pres. Old Bailey Place Home Owners Assn., Fremont, 1989, pres., 1990-93. Mem. Am. Chem. Soc., Biophys. Soc., N.Y. Acad. Sci., Soc. Magnetic Resonance in Medicine. Republican. Roman Catholic. Office: Varian NMR Instruments 3120 Hansen Way Palo Alto CA 94304-1015

SCHREIBER, OTTO WILLIAM, retired manufacturing company executive; b. Greenwood, Wis., July 4, 1922; s. Otto Waldemar and Meta Wilhelmina (Suemnicht) S. BSEE, U. Wis., Madison, 1944. Electroacoustic scientist Navy Electronics Lab., San Diego, 1980-91; electronics engr. then mgr. electronic engring. dept., ordnance div. Librascope, Sunnyvale, Calif., 1956-65; chief engr. Teledyne Indsl. Electronics Co., San Jose, Calif., 1965-68; exec. v.p. Marcom Corp., San Francisco, 1969; test mgr. MB Assocs., San Ramon, Calif., 1970-71; ops. mgr. Am. Svc. Products, Inc., Newhall, Calif., 1972-75; mfg. mgr. UTI, Inc., Sunnyvale, Calif., 1975-80; dir. mfg. Hi-Shear Ordnance/Electronics, Torrance, Calif., 1980-82; tech. writing supr. Marine div. Westinghouse, Sunnyvale, 1980-92; retired Sunnyvale, 1991. Lt. comdr. USNR, 1944-59. Mem. IEEE (life), Soc. Tech. Communication, Eta Kappa Nu, Kappa Eta Kappa. Republican. Lutheran. Home: 1623 New Brunswick Ave Sunnyvale CA 94087-4261

SCHREMPF, DAVID WILLIAM (BILL SCHREMPF), management consultant; b. Inglewood, Calif., Apr. 10, 1942; s. Frederick William Schrempf and Belva Mary (Mannix) Swanstrom; m. Katherine Marie Beckham, June 13, 1963; children: Heather Marie, David Owen. AB, Stanford U., 1963, MBA, 1967. Indsl. engr. U.S. Steel, Pittsburg, Calif., 1963-65; contr., div. pres. air conditioning div. Am. Standard, Elyria, Ohio, 1967-72; group pres. Tappan's Environ. Products Group, Elyria, 1973-76; exec. v.p. Bactomatic (Johnson & Johnson), Palo Alto, Calif., 1976-78; pres. CT div., Technicare-Johnson & Johnson, Solon, Ohio, 1979-80; exec. v.p. Ins. Co. N.Am., Phila., 1980-82; pres., chief exec. officer Cigna Worldwide Ins., Phila., 1982-85; pres. Casualty Ins. Group, Teledyne, L.A., 1985-86; pres., chief exec. officer Argonaut Gorup, Inc., L.A., 1986-88, The Schremof Group Inc., L.A., 1988—; White House fellow Dept. Def., Washington, 1972-73. Author: Challenges in International Marketing, 1987. Trustee Lorain County Community Coll., Elyria, 1973-76; trustee Mountain View (Calif.) Sch. Dist., 1977-79; regent Calif. Luth. U., Thousand Oaks, Calif., 1987-90. Office: The Schrempf Group Inc 4204 Mildred Ave Los Angeles CA 90066

SCHRODER, DIETER KARL, electrical engineering educator; b. Lübeck, Germany, June 18, 1935; came to U.S., 1964; s. Wilhelm and Martha (Werner) S.; m. Beverley Claire Parchment, Aug. 4, 1961; children: Mark, Derek. BSc, McGill U., Montreal, Que., Can., 1962, MSc, 1964; PhD, U. Ill., 1968. Sr. research and devel. sect. Westinghouse Electric Corp., Pitts., 1968-73, fellow engr., 1973-77, adv. engr., 1977-79, mgr., 1979-81; prof. elec. engring. Ariz. State U., Tempe, 1981—; researcher Inst. Solid-State Physics, Freiburg, Fed. Republic Germany, 1978-79. Author: Advanced MOS Devices, 1987, Semiconductor Material and Device Characterization, 1990; patentee in field; contbr. articles to profl. jours. Fellow IEEE; mem. Electrochem. Soc., Sigma Xi, Eta Kappa Nu. Baha'i. Home: 1927 E Bendix Dr Tempe AZ 85283-4203 Office: Ariz State U Dept Elec Engring Tempe AZ 85287-5706

SCHROEDER, ARNOLD LEON, mathematics educator; b. Honolulu, May 27, 1935; s. Arnold Leon and Wynelle (Russell) S.; BS in Math., Oreg. State U., 1960, MS in Stats., 1962; NSF Insts. at UCLA, 1964, U. So. Calif.,

1965; m. Maybelle Ruth Walker, Nov. 9, 1956; children: Steven, Michael, Wendy. Assoc. prof. math. Long Beach (Calif.) Community Coll., 1962—; computer cons. McDonnell-Douglas Corp., 1966-74, statis. researcher in med. and social sci., 1976-80; cons. statis. software including SPSS, BMDP, and Fortran, 1980—; dir. Schroeder's Statis. Svcs. Author: Statistics/Math Note's for Colleges, 1986—. Chmn. bd. elders Grace Bible Ch., South Gate, Calif., 1985-92. Served with USAF, 1953-57. Mem. Faculty Assn. Calif. Community Colls., Calif. Teaching Assn., Am. Bowlers Tour (life). Home: 5481 E Hill St Long Beach CA 90815-1923 Office: 4901 E Carson St Long Beach CA 90808-1706

SCHROEDER, BRYCE GREGORY, computer company executive; b. Portland, Oreg., Aug. 5, 1961; s. Charles Houston O'Neil and Ardis Jean (Anderson) S.; m. Angela Kay Milam, July 14, 1984; children: Allison Renee, Bethany Christine. BSEE, Oreg. State U., 1984, BS in Computer Sci., 1984, BS in Computer Engring., 1984; MS in Engring. Mgmt., Portland State U., 1993. Software engr. Quantitative Tech. Corp., Beaverton, Oreg., 1984-87, Cadic Inc., Beaverton, 1987; system adminstr., programmer Tektronix, Inc., Beaverton, 1987-90, computer resource group mgr., 1990-92, mgr. tech. computing, 1992—. Recipient Internat. Grad. Student Paper award Project Mgmt. Inst., 1990. Republican. Presbyterian. Home: 10040 SW 153rd Beaverton OR 97007 Office: Tektronix Inc PO Box 500 MS 47-622 Beaverton OR 97075

SCHROEDER, DOUGLAS ROBERT, engineering company executive; b. St. Petersburg, Fla., Mar. 10, 1943; s. Henry Carl and Sarah Frances (Roser) S.; m. Librada Labrador; children: Dawn R. Zimmerman, Teresa D. Pennick, Felicia Y., Douglas R. Jr., Anna Lisa. BSEE, Auburn U., 1968; MSEE, MIT, 1970; grad., USN Test Pilot Sch., 1973. Enlisted USAF, 1962, advanced through grades to maj., 1979; flight test engr. Armament Devel. Test Ctr. USAF, Eglin AFB, Fla., 1970-72; instr. test pilot sch. USAF, Edwards AFB, Calif., 1973-75; chief engr. combat sage USAF, Clark Air Base, Philippines, 1975-81; chief flight test engr. Air Force Wright Aero. Labs. USAF, Wright-Patterson AFB, Ohio, 1981-82; dep. program mgr. X-29 program office Flight Dynamics Lab. USAF, Wright-Patterson AFB, 1982-83; retired USAF, 1983; sr. engr. Comarco, Ridgecrest, Calif., 1984-85; chief engr. CTA, Inc., Ridgecrest, Calif., 1985-88; pres. Locust Dynamics, Inc., Ridgecrest, 1988—. Author articles, tech. reports. Mem. Ret. Officers Assn., Sigma Xi, Tau Beta Pi, Eta Kappa Nu, Phi Kappa Phi. Home and Office: Locust Dynamics Inc 301 S Locust St Ridgecrest CA 93555-4446

SCHROEDER, DUANE DAVID, pharmaceutical company executive; b. Newton, KS, Nov. 4, 1940; s. David Jasper and Hilda (Schmidt) S.; m. Lois Elizabeth Epp, Aug. 3, 1961; children: Kirsten, Darren, Allison. AB in Chemistry and Psychology, Bethel Coll., 1962; PhD in Biochemistry, Tulane U., 1967. Post doctoral fellow MIT, Cambridge, Mass., 1967-69; sr. rsch. biochemist Cutter Labs., Berkeley, Calif., 1969-71, biochem. rsch. supr., 1971-73, mgr. biochem. rsch., 1973-80; rsch. fellow Bayer AG, Wuppertal, Germany, 1975; assoc. dir. biochem. rsch. and devel. Cutter Biologicals/Miles Inc., Berkeley, 1980-87, assoc. dir. R & D planning and adminstrn., 1987—; adj. assoc. prof. medicine U. Rochester, 1984—. Republican. Mennonite. Office: Miles Inc PO Box 1986 4th and Parker St Berkeley CA 94701

SCHROEDER, EDISON BLAKE, computer product marketing manager, consultant; b. Miami, Fla., Mar. 22, 1935; s. John G. and Corrine (Sitton) S.; m. Lynne Reed, Apr. 25, 1958; children: Blake, Reed. BA, U. Chgo., 1955. Instr. IBM Corp., Chgo., 1960-67; bus. systems analyst Std. Oil, Chgo., 1967-68; v.p., founder Edutronics Systems Internat., L.A., 1968-75; v.p. mfg. Environ. Communications, Santa Ana, Calif., 1975-79; product mgr. ITEL/Xerox Corp., Newport Beach, Calif., 1979-84, Candle Corp., L.A., 1984-91; ptnr. Mgmt. and Funding Svcs., San Diego, 1991—. Author, prodr. EDP Edn. Films, 1973 (Cindy award 1973, 74, 75). Republican. Methodist. Home: 2567 Greyling Dr San Diego CA 92123

SCHROEDER, GARY J., business owner, state legislator, writer; b. Columbus, Wis., Nov. 8, 1944; s. Delbert Charles and Agnes Clara (Balzer) S.; m. Sharon A. Rodhain, Mar. 20, 1982; 1 child, Barrett Von Schroeder. BS, U. Wis., Superior, 1969; MS, U. Idaho, 1972. Mgr. far west Hudson's Bay & Annings, London, 1973-82; owner, mgr. Moscow (Idaho) Hide & Fur, 1973—; mem. Idaho Senate, 1992—. field editor Fur Fish Game, 1988—; pub. The Schroeder Report, 1987—. Pres. region 2 Idaho Wildlife Coun., 1991-92; mem. IDFG Black Bear Mgmt. Task Force, Boise, Idaho, 1991-92; mem. consensus 2000 Moscow Sch. Dist., 1992—. With USN, 1962-65. Mem. Farm Bur., Am. Legion. Republican. Home: 1289 Highland Moscow ID 83843 Office: Idaho Senate Box 8838 Moscow ID 83843

SCHROEDER, GLENN BURNETT, education administration educator; b. Dallas, July 12, 1927; s. Alfred Raymond and Vesta Abigail (Zumwalt) S.; m. Eileea Joan Enstad, Aug. 9, 1953 (div. Dec. 1961); m. Carolyn Jeanne Ledgerwood, Feb. 14, 1962; children: Jason Lee, Christopher Gray, Peary Whitman. BS, Western Oreg. State Coll., 1952; MEd, U. Oreg., 1957; PhD, U. N.Mex., 1969. Cert. elem./secondary prin. Secondary sch. tchr. Myrtle Creek (Oreg.) Schs., 1953-59; elem./secondary sch. tchr. U.S. Dept. Def., U.S. Forces, Fed. Republic Germany, 1959-66; asst. prof. Temple U., Phila., 1969-71; assoc. prof. U. No. Colo., Greeley, 1971-75, prof., 1975—; dept. chair U. No. Colo., Greeley, 1975-89; cons. Arabian Am. Oil Co., Dharahn, Saudi Arabia, 1984, U.S. Census Bur., Lakewood, Colo., 1990. Author: Management Decision Making, 1989, Writing Behavioral Objectives, 1969, (with others); author 14 cons. studies. Precinct chair Dem. Party, Greeley, 1974-86. With USN, 1945-51, Korea. Decorated Purple Heart. Mem. Colo. Sch. Exec. (bd. dirs. 1972-86, Disting. Svc. award 1987), Gen. Soc. Mayflower Descendants, Pilgrim John Howland Soc. Republican. Congregationalist. Home: 612 36th Ave Ct Greeley CO 80634

SCHROEDER, GLENN C., lawyer, educator; b. Ann Arbor, Mich., Mar. 21, 1953; s. Glenn A. Schroeder and Monnie C. (Hamling) Phillips; m. Janet S. Wong, Jan. 1, 1990. BA, U. Calif., L.A., 1975; MA, U. Ill., 1976; JD, Yale U., 1979. Bar: Calif. 1979. Assoc. Loeb and Loeb, L.A., 1979-86, ptnr., 1987; gen. counsel, sr. v.p. Sta. KCET Community TV of So. Calif., L.A., 1987—; adj. prof. Loyola U. Law Sch., L.A., 1982, Whittier Coll. Sch. of Law, L.A., 1988—. Bd. dirs. Asian Rehab. Svcs., L.A., 1989-90. Mem. L.A. County Bar Assn. (exec. com. of intellectual property sect. 1988-92), L.A. Copyright Soc. Office: Community TV of So Calif Sta KCET 4401 W Sunset Blvd Los Angeles CA 90027-6090

SCHROEDER, JEAN DARLENE, educator, researcher; b. Salem, S.D., Apr. 22, 1938; d. Lionel Wilfred Schroeder and Thelma (Ovedia) Brager; m. A. Taylor Anderson, Apr. 6, 1974. BA, Augustana Coll., 1960; AA, U. Calif., Davis, 1958, MA, 1963. From asst prof. to assoc. prof. in polit. sci. and German Napa Valley (Calif.) Coll., 1965-75, prof. in polit. sci. and German, 1975—; guest prof. U. Muenster (West Germany), 1972-73; rep. Calif. Community Coll. Faculty for the policy bds. of Calif. Internat. Studies Project, Calif. Foreign Lang. Project;. Fgn. policy editor Envee mag., 1991. Mem. World Affairs Coun. No. Calif. (trustee 1982—). Office: Napa Valley Coll 2277 Hapa Vallejo Hwy Napa CA 94558

SCHROEDER, MARY ESTHER, wood products executive; b. Dayton, Ohio, July 29, 1947; d. James Walter and Mary Agnes (Danzig) McIver; m. Reinhard Schroeder, Sept. 10, 1966 (div. Mar. 1989). BS in Forest Industries Mgmt., Ohio State U., 1978. Fiber supply supr. Crown Zellerbach, Inc., Port Townsend, Wash., 1978-83; fiber supply and transp. mgr. Port Townsend Paper Corp., Bainbridge Island, Wash., 1983-87; dir. Pacific Wood Fuels, Redding, Calif., 1987-90; fuel mgr. Wheelabrator Shasta Energy, Anderson, CA, 1990—; bd. dirs. Peninsula Devel. Assn., Port Angeles, Wash., 1985—; mgr. Wayfarer Bookstore. Screenwriter: As the Chips Fall, 1988; producer for TV Life Is A Classroom; prodr. Principles for Successful Living, 1991; pub. Jump Into Life, 1992; contbr. seminar Speaking from the Heart, 1992, workbook Hi-balling Your Life, 1993. Precinct committeeman Kitsap County Reps., Poulsbo, Wash., 1984-86; active Rep. Presdl. Task Force. Mem. Soc. Am. Foresters, Shasta Alliance for Resources and Environment, Am. Pulpwood Assn., Writers' Forum, Am. Film Inst., Calif. Forestry Assn. Home: PO Box 5480 Cottonwood CA 96022 Office: Wheelabrator Shasta Energy 20811 Industry Rd Anderson CA 96007-8703

SCHROEDER, MARY MURPHY, federal judge; b. Boulder, Colo., Dec. 4, 1940; d. Richard and Theresa (Kahn) Murphy; m. Milton R. Schroeder, Oct. 15, 1965; children: Caroline Theresa, Katherine Emily. B.A., Swarthmore Coll., 1962; J.D., U. Chgo., 1965. Bar: Ill. 1966, D.C. 1966, Ariz. 1970. Trial atty. Dept. Justice, Washington, 1965-69; law clk. Hon. Jesse Udall, Ariz. Supreme Ct., 1970; mem. firm Lewis and Roca, Phoenix, 1971-75; judge Ariz. Ct. Appeals, Phoenix, 1975-79, U.S. Ct. Appeals (9th cir.), Phoenix, 1979—; vis. instr. Ariz. State U. Coll. Law, 1976, 77, 78. Contbr. articles to profl. jours. Mem. Am. Bar Assn., Ariz. Bar Assn., Fed. Bar Assn., Am. Law Inst., Am. Judicature Soc. Democrat. Club: Soroptimists. Office: US Ct Appeals 9th Cir 6421 Courthouse & Fed Bldg 230 N 1st Ave Phoenix AZ 85025-0230*

SCHROEDER, PATRICIA SCOTT (MRS. JAMES WHITE SCHROEDER), congresswoman; b. Portland, Oreg., July 30, 1940; d. Lee Combs and Bernice (Lemoin) Scott; m. James White Schroeder, Aug. 18, 1962; children: Scott William, Jamie Christine. B.A. magna cum laude, U. Minn., 1961; J.D., Harvard U., 1964. Bar: Colo. 1964. Field atty. NLRB, Denver, 1964-66; practiced in Denver, 1966-72; hearing officer Colo. Dept. Personnel, 1971-72; mem. faculty U. Colo., 1969-72, Community Coll., Denver, 1969-70, Regis Coll., Denver, 1970-72; mem. 93d-103d Congresses from 1st Colo. dist., 1973—; co-chmn. Congl. Caucus for Women's Issues, 1976—; mem. Ho. of Reps. armed svcs. com., chair subcom. rsch. and tech., judiciary com., post office and civil svc. com. Congregationalist. Office: House of Representatives 2208 Rayburn House Office Bldg Washington DC 20515

SCHROEDER, PAUL CLEMENS, biologist, educator; b. Bklyn., Aug. 13, 1938; s. Henry Clemens and Gertrude Irene (Kenny) S.; m. Alice Louise Andersen, June 25, 1966; children: Lianne, Lisa. B.S., St. Peter's Coll., 1960; postgrad. U. Zurich, Switzerland, 1960-61; Ph.D., Stanford U., 1966. Postdoctoral fellow U. Calif.-Berkeley, 1966-68; asst. prof. zoology Wash. State U., Pullman, 1968-73, assoc. prof., 1973-82, prof., 1982—, assoc. chmn. dept. zoology, 1983-87, chmn. 1987-91; dir. Charles R. Conner Natural History Mus., 1992—. Co-author: Beetles and How They Live, 1978; editor: Jour. Exptl. Zoology, Marine Biology, 1989; contbr. articles on reprodn. in animals to profl. publs., 1964—. Pres. Rose Creek Preserve, Nature Conservancy, Pullman and Seattle, 1984-88. Alexander von-Humboldt Found. fellow U. Cologne, W.Ger., 1974-75; Fulbright research fellow USPHS Fogarty; Alex Von Humboldt fellow, Biocenter, U. Basel, Switzerland, 1989, Fogarty Internat. fellow U. Queensland, Australia, 1982. Fellow AAAS (coun. mem. 1990-92); mem. Am. Soc. Zoologists (div. sec. 1978-80), Internat. Soc. Invertebrate Reprodn. (exec. com., sec. 1988—), Home: 145 SW Arbor St Pullman WA 99163-2908 Office: Wash State U Dept Zoology Pullman WA 99164-4236

SCHROEDER, RICHARD JOHN, broadcast journalist; b. Mountain Lake, Minn., May 28, 1944; s. Menno David and Esther Elma (Ratzlaff) S.; m. Theora Faye Pauls, June 27, 1965; children: Myra, Michael. BA in History, Bethel Coll., 1966. Lic. radiotelephone operator 1st class. Profl. staff KRKS-AM Radio, Denver, 1969-76, sta. mgr., 1976-84; dir. news and pub. affairs KWBI-FM Radio, Denver, 1984—; network news dir. Colo. Christian U. Med. Network, Denver, 1992—. Author: (news commentary) The Cutting Edge, 1973-75. Vol. rsch. analyst Garden Pk. Ch., Denver, 1992; vol. probation counselor Jefferson County Ct. System, Golden, Colo., 1971. Recipient Pub. Svc. Commendation, Am. Radio Relay League, 1984, Svc. Recognition, Mile High Red Cross, 1983; named one of Outstanding Young Men of Am., 1973. Mem. Am. Radio Relay League. Mennonite. Home: 1513 S Cody St Lakewood CO 80232

SCHROEDER, RITA MOLTHEN, chiropractor; b. Savanna, Ill., Oct. 25, 1922; d. Frank J. and Ruth J. (McKenzie) Molthen; m. Richard H. Schroeder, Apr. 23, 1948 (div.); children—Richard, Andrew, Barbara, Thomas, Paul, Madeline. Student, Chem. Engring., Immaculate Heart Coll., 1940-41, UCLA, 1941, Palmer Sch. of Chiropractic, 1947-49; D. Chiropractic, Cleve. Coll. of Chiropractic, 1961. Engring.-tooling design data coordinator Douglas Aircraft Co., El Segundo, Santa Monica and Long Beach, Calif., 1941-47; pres. Schroeder Chiropractic, Inc., 1982—; dir. Pacific States Chiropractic Coll., 1978-80, pres. 1980-81. Recipient Palmer Coll. Ambassador award, 1973. Parker Chiropractic Research Found. Ambassador award, 1976, Coll. Ambassador award Life West Chiropractic Coll. Mem. Internat. Chiropractic Assn., Calif. Chiropractic Assn., Internat. Chiropractic Assn. Calif., Assn. Am. Chiropractic Coll. Presidents, Council Chiropractic Edn. (Pacific State Coll. rep.), Am. Pub. Health Assn., Royal Chiropractic Knights of the Round Table. Home: 9870 N Millbrook Ave Fresno CA 93720-1313 Office: Schroeder Chiropractic Inc 2535 N Fresno St Fresno CA 93703-1896

SCHROEDER, WILLIAM ROBERT, actor, entrepreneur; b. L.A., July 9, 1941; s. Robert Manville and Miriam Ruth (Sloop) S.; m. Marie Paule Fautrel, Sept. 7, 1963. BA, UCLA, 1964; BFA, Art Ctr. Coll. Design, Pasadena, Calif., 1971. Mailman U.S. Post Office, Santa Monica, Calif., 1967-71; art dir., producer N.W. Ayer/West, Los Angeles, 1971-75; pres., gen. mgr. Advt. Ctr., Los Angeles, 1976-77, Alouette Internat., Santa Monica, Calif., 1972—; free-lance woodcarver, Santa Monica, 1981—; free-lance actor, Hollywood, Calif., 1983—; appeared in feature films King of the Streets, 1983, The Forbidden Tome, 1984, The End of Innocence, 1985, Poltergeist II, 1986. Producer TV commercials, 1972-75; author, creator computerized lang. courses Mattel Intellivision, 1980-82; real estate developer, 1989—. Publicity mgr. Concerned Homeowners of Santa Monica, 1981-82. Recipient 1st Pl. award Belding award for Excellence in Advt., Los Angeles, 1974; Cert. of Merit, Art Dirs. Club Los Angeles, 1972. Mem. Am. Fedn. Radio and TV Artists, Santa Monica C. of C., Mensa (Los Angeles), Combat Pilots Assn., Orange County Squadron, Internat. Plastic Modelers Soc., The Found. Brain Research, Internat. Legion of Intelligence, Santa Monica Theatre Guild, The Air Mus. Libertarian. Office: Alouette Internat 1626 Montana Ave Santa Monica CA 90403-1808

SCHROFF, WILLIAM K., real estate professional, business consultant; b. N.Y.C., Mar. 1, 1947; s. William L. and Kathleen (McDonnell) S.; m. Karen M. Zeanah, June 1968 (div. 1977); children: Zachary, William. BBA, Stetson U., 1968, MBA, 1969. V.p. N. Donald & Co., Denver, 1981-82; pres., dir. Westfin Corp., Denver, 1982-83; chmn., exec. v.p., dir. Vantage Securities, Emglewood, Colo., 1983-85; pres., dir. Dunhill Investments Ltd., Englewood, 1985-88; assoc. Prudential Hampton Realtors, Palm Springs, Calif., 1989-90; prin., v.p. Empowerment Housing, Denver, 1992—; prin. Electra Holdings, Denver, 1991—; mng. dir. West World Properties, Palm Springs, 1990-92; dir. Computer Periph. Prods, Denver, 1985—; cons. Electra 2000, Denver, 1991-92; com. chmn. Palm Springs Bd. Realtors (top com. award 1992). Dir. GLAD, Cathedral City, Calif., 1991-92, Log Cabin Fedn. of Calif., Riverside County, 1991-92; del. LIFE Lobby Sacramento, 1992; mem. com. Colo. Coalition for Homeless. Mem. Nat. Assn. Realtors, Calif. Assn. Realtors, Colo. Assn. Realtors, Denver Profl. Men's Club, Log Cabin Club Colo. (founder). Office: Empowerment Housing 2370 Clermont St Denver CO 80207

SCHROY, CARTER BRETT, medical physicist; b. Lansdale, Pa., Apr. 5, 1947; s. Kermit Ambrose Harry and Mary Kathryn (McCammon) S. BS in Biophysics, Pa. State U., 1969, MS in Biophysics, 1974, PhD in Genetics, 1978. Diplomate therapeutic radiol. physics Am. Bd. Radiology. NIH fellow Case Western Res. U., Cleve., 1978-81; rsch. staff Cleve. Clin. Fedn., 1981-83, clin. staff, 1985-87; NIH fellow U. Ky. Med. Ctr., Lexington, 1983-85; asst. prof., profl. staff M.D. Anderson Cancer Ctr. U. Tex., Houston, 1987-91; chief med. physicist Scripps Clinic and Res. Found., La Jolla, Calif., 1991—. Contbr. sci. papers and abstracts to profl. jours. Mem. Young Profls. of Cleve., 1982-87. Named Outstanding Alumnus of Pa. State U., Ogontz Campus, 1983. Mem. Am. Soc. for Therapeutic Radiology and Oncology, Am. Assn. Physicists in Medicine, European Soc. for Therapeutic Radiology and Oncology, Radiation Rsch. Soc., Am. Coll. Med. Physics, Mensa. Office: PO Box 990 Del Mar CA 92014

SCHRYVER, BRUCE JOHN, safety engineer; b. Newark, Aug. 14, 1944; s. Francis Henry and Ann Laura (Hart) S.; m. Lorraine Patricia Simodis, Oct. 8, 1966; children: Holly Lynn, Wendy Marie. BA in Occupational Safety and Health, Western States U., 1984, MS in Safety Mgmt., 1989, PhD in Safety Mgmt., 1989. Cert. safety profl.; cert. products safety mgr.; cert. hazard control mgr.; cert. hazardous materials mgr.; cert. healthcare safety profl. Inspector Lansing B. Warner Inc., Chgo., 1968-69; engring. rep. Glens Falls Ins. Co., Newark, 1969; safety dir. Hillside Metal Products, Newark, 1969-70; loss prevention specialist Warner Ins. Group, Chgo., 1970-79, regional loss control mgr., 1979-82, nat. loss control coordinator, 1982-85; mgr., asst. v.p. loss control svcs. Ins. Co. of the West, San Diego, 1985-90; v.p. loss control svcs. Ins. Co. of the West, 1990—; v.p. mcpl. law enforcement svcs. Ins. Co. of the West, San Diego, 1992—. Inventor Emergency Light Mount, 1971. Mem. Town of Clay (N.Y.) Pub. Safety Com., 1976-78, Beacon Woods East Homeowners Assn., Hudson, Fla., 1979-85, Meadowridge Homeowners Assn., La Costa, Calif., 1986—; cons. Town of Clay Police Dept., 1975-78. With USCG, 1964-68. Recipient lettter of appreciation Town of Clay, 1977, cert. of appreciation DAV, 1968, Golden State award, 1990. Mem. Am. Soc. Safety Engrs., Soc. Fire Protection Engrs., Nat. Safety Mgmt. Soc., Vets. Safety, Nat. Fire Protection Assn., San Diego Safety Coun., Calif. Conf. Arson Investigators. Republican. Roman Catholic. Home: 3047 Camino Limero Carlsbad CA 92009-4525 Office: Ins Co of the West 10140 Campus Point Dr San Diego CA 92121-1592

SCHUBERT, RONALD HAYWARD, retired aerospace engineer; b. Bklyn., Aug. 25, 1932; s. John and Joan Sarah (Hayward) S.; m. Dorothy May Smith, Mar. 5, 1953 (div. 1961); children: Marcus H., Malcolm F., Ronald J. (dec.), Ann E.; m. Linda Jane van der Ploeg, Mar. 6, 1961 (div. 1988). BA cum laude, Ohio State U., 1956. Assoc. engr. Hughes Aircraft Co., Fullerton, Calif., 1957-61; physicist Nat. Cash Register Co., Dayton, Ohio, 1962-63; sr. research engr. Lockheed Missiles and Space Co., Sunnyvale, Calif., 1963-90. Served as sgt. USMC, 1951-54. Recipient Hon. mention Woodrow Wilson Fellowship Com. Mem. Phi Beta Kappa. Democrat. Roman Catholic. Home: #1023 201 W California Sunnyvale CA 94086

SCHUBERT, TODD ALAN, marketing professional; b. Torrance, Calif., Oct. 10, 1968; s. Lawrence James and Sheryl Kay (Yanken) S. BA in Social Ecology, U. Calif., Irvine, 1991. Mgmt. trainee Avco Fin. Svcs., Irvine, 1991-92; ins. svc. rep. Balboa Life & Casualty, Irvine, 1992, product mktg. coord., 1992—. Named to Outstanding Young Men of Am. Mem. Toastmasters Internat. (v.p. 1991-92, pres. 1992—), Order of Omega. Home: 5533 Sara Dr Torrance CA 90503

SCHUCK, CARL JOSEPH, lawyer; b. Phila., Nov. 21, 1915; s. Joseph and Christina (Schadl) S.; m. Mary Elizabeth Box, June 7, 1941; children: Mary Ann, John, James, Catherine, Christopher. BS, St. Mary's Coll., 1937; postgrad., U. So. Calif., 1937-38; JD, Georgetown U., 1941. Bar: D.C. 1940, Calif. 1943, U.S. Supreme Ct. 1952. Atty. Dept. Justice, Washington, 1940-42, Alien Property Custodian, San Francisco, 1942-44; mem. firm Overton, Lyman & Prince, L.A., 1947-79, profl. corp. mem. firm, 1979-85; lectr. Practising Law Inst., 1973; Del. 9th Cir. Jud. Conf., 1963-80, chmn. lawyer-dels. com., 1972, mem. exec. com., 1976-80, chmn. exec. com., 1977-78, mem. sr. adv. bd., 1989—; mem. disciplinary bd. State Bar Calif., 1970-71. Fellow Am. Coll. Trial Lawyers (chmn. com. on complex litigation 1979-81, regent 1981-85), L.A. County Bar Assn. (trustee 1974-76), Phi Alpha Delta. Club: Chancery (pres. 1984-85). Home and Office: 4723 Cordoba Way Oceanside CA 92056-5109

SCHUCK, JOYCE HABER, author; b. N.Y.C., Dec. 9, 1937; d. Francis F. and Florence (Smith) H.; m. Stephen Martin Schuck, June 15, 1958; children: William David, Thomas Allen, Ann Elizabeth. BA in Human Svcs. and Counseling, Loretto Hts. Coll., Denver, 1982. Counselor, tchr. Vision Quest, Colorado Springs, 1979-82; cons., program designer for govt. agys. Colorado Springs, 1982-85; author, 1987—; asst. to cons. Volusia County Dept. Corrections, Daytona Beach, Fla., 1982; cons. student svcs. program Pikes Peak C.C., Colorado Springs, 1982; cons., designer Juvenile Probation of El Paso County, Colorado Springs, 1982, 4th Jud. Dist./Dist. Atty.'s Office, Colorado Springs, 1984. Author: Political Wives, Veiled Lives, 1991. Co-founder Community Transitions, Colorado Springs, 1984; coord. El. Paso County Shape Up Program, 1982; v.p. Community Coun. of Pikes Peak Region, Colorado Springs, 1983, Women's Found. of Colo., Denver, 1987. Recipient Mayor's award for civic leadership City of Colorado Springs, 1983. Mem. Jr. League of Colorado Springs (sustaining), Salon de Femme (founding).

SCHUEGRAF, KLAUS KARL, company executive; b. Basel, Switzerland, Aug. 20, 1927; came to U.S. 1960; s. Karl M. and Auguste A. (Zametzer) S.; children: Susanne A., Andrea P., Klaus F. BS in Physics/Math., U. Tuebingen, Germany, 1951; MS in Physics, U. Tuebingen, 1954; PhD in Physics, Tech. U., Stuttgart, 1960. Devel. engr. Suedd. Aparate Fabrik/ITT, Nuremberg, Germany, 1954-56; rsch. asst. Tech. U. Stuttgart, 1956-60; staff engr. IBM Corp., Poughkeepsie, N.Y., 1960-62; fellow engr. Westinghouse Corp., Newbury Park, Calif., 1962-65; dir. devel. Telefunken, Nuremberg, 1965-66; sr. staff/section head TRW, Redondo Beach, Calif., 1966-71; dir. Northrop Corp., Hawthorne, Calif., 1971-78; v.p. Tylan Corp., Torrance, Calif., 1979-88; pres. Tystar Corp., Torrance, Calif., 1988—; faculty UCLA, 1968-90. Author/editor: Handbook Thin Film Deposition, 1988. Mem. Environ. com. Rancho Palos Verdes, Calif., 1974-80. Mem. Electrochem. Soc. Office: Tystar Corp 361 Van Ness Way Torrance CA 90501

SCHUELER, GEORGE FREDERICK, philosophy educator; b. Columbus, Ohio, Aug. 9, 1944; s. George Frederick and Edith (Pursley) S.; m. Karen Rebecca Spitler, June 18, 1966; children: Gregory W., Jason W. AB, Stanford U., 1966; MA, U. Calif., Berkeley, 1968, PhD in Philosophy, 1973. Asst. prof. U. N.Mex., Albuquerque, 1971-79, assoc. prof., 1979-90, prof., 1990—, dir. grad. studies in philosophy, 1980-89. Author: The Idea of a Reason for Acting, 1989; contbr. articles to profl. jours. Mem. Am. Philos. Assn. Office: U NM Philosophy Dept Albuquerque NM 87131

SCHUELER, JON CHRISTOPHER, television producer, consultant; b. Columbus, Ohio, Dec. 11, 1955; s. George Frederick and Edith Ester (Pursley) S.; m. Carol Marie Pierce, Oct. 2, 1982 (div. May 1992). BA in English, Drama, U. Pacific, 1978; MA in Directing, Playwriting, U. N.Mex., 1985. Show mgr. Up With People, Tucson, 1980-81; host, assoc. prodr. Sta. KGGM-TV, Albuquerque, 1981-89, anchor, prodr., 1989-90, exec. prodr. News 101, 1990—, exec. prodr. Nat. News 101, 1992—; pres. Play Right Prodns., Albuquerque, 1992—; dir. Ctr. for Edn., Social Policy and Media, Inst. Pub. Law, U. N.Mex., Albuquerque, 1991—; assoc. prodr. Eyes of the Children, New West Prodns., Albuquerque, 1992. Dir/prodr.: (nat. video release) A Company of Pilgrims; author: (play) Dandelion Wine, 1985; (musical) Earthstar, 1987. Playwright Healthcare for the Homeless, N.Mex., 1990—; mem. adv. bd. Living Through Cancer, N.Mex., 1991-93; bd. dirs. Hospice and Home Care, N.Mex., 1992. Recipient Rocky Mountain Emmy award NATAS, 1991, Innovator of Yr. award Nat. Broadcasters Assn. Community Affairs, 1991, Advancement of Learning Through Broadcasting award NEA, 1991, Excellence in Community Svc. award CBS TV Network, 1992, Nat. Iris award, 1993. Mem. U. N.Mex. Alumni Assn. (pres. 1993), Alpha Kappa Lambda (Alumni Support award 1979). Presbyterian. Office: Sta KRQE-TV 13 Broadcast Plz SW 13 Broadcast Plz SW Albuquerque NM 87103

SCHUENKE, JEFFREY ALLEN, engineering executive; b. Milw., Feb. 18, 1956; s. Kenneth Earl S. and Susan (Radmonovich) Hicks; m. Alexandra Heilweil Miller, (div.); 1 child, Daniel Justin. BS, U. Wis., 1978; MS, U. Calif., Berkeley, 1982. Design engr. MEA Assoc. Ltd., Oakland, Calif., 1982; design engr. NADY Systems, Oakland, 1982-87; asst. prof. U. Wis., Platteville, 1987-89; assoc. scientist Nat. Ctr. for Atmospheric Rsch., Boulder, Colo., 1989-92; mgr. Nat. Ctr. for Atmospheric Rsch., Boulder, 1989—. Lighting designer theatrical prodn. (Bay Area Critics Circle Best Design 1980-81). Office: NCAR 1850 Table Mesa Dr Boulder CO 80303-5602

SCHUETTE, KURT MICHAEL, sports coach; b. Santa Barbara, Calif., Mar. 25, 1962; s. Bruce Thomas and Patricia Schuette. BA in Communications, Pepperdine U., 1986. Pub. rels. intern Los Angeles Lakers, Inglewood, Calif., 1985-86; golf prof. Santa Barbara (Calif.) Golf Club, 1986-87, North Ranch Country Club, Westlake Village, Calif., 1987-88; head men's golf coach Pepperdine Univ., Malibu, Calif., 1988—; dir. Classic Golf Days, Westlake Village, 1990—. Named All Conf. Men's Golf, Western Athletic Conf., Santa Barbara City Coll., 1982-83, West Coast Athletic Conf., Pepperdine Univ., 1984-85. Mem. NCAA (Dist. VIII selection com. mem.

1991—, West Coast Conf. Coach of Yr. 1993), U.S. Golf Assn. (assoc.), Nat. Golf Found., Golf Coaches Assn. Am. Republican. Roman Catholic. Home: 56 Amador Ave Goleta CA 93117 Office: Pepperdine Univ Athletic Dept Malibu CA 90263

SCHUETZ, JOHN MICHAEL, sales executive; b. Chgo., Apr. 16, 1947; s. Henry Albert and Ann Delores (Kunst) S.; m. Jacqueline Claire Furneaux, Apr. 22, 1972; children: Michael Richard, Sean David. BS in Advt., Marquette U., Milw., 1969. Gen. field mgr. Ford Motor Co., San Jose, 1972-85; v.p. we. region IVECO Trucks of N.Am., Huntington Beach, Calif., 1985-91; nat. dealer mgr. Wynnoil Co., 1992—; bd. dirs. Forsyte Research Group, Santa Rosa, Calif., 1988—. Leader Boy Scouts Am., El Toro, Calif., 1988—; coach Am. Youth Soccer Orgn., Saddleback Valley. Lt. USN, 1969-72. Mem. Sun and Sail Club, Phi Theta Psi. Republican. Roman Catholic. Home: 21821 Ticonderoga Ln El Toro CA 92630

SCHULDT, EVERETT ARTHUR, engineer, consultant; b. Newark, Oct. 29, 1938; s. Arthur John and Ruby Ellen (Warner) S.; m. Georgiana Louise Benson, Sept. 24, 1960; children: David Arthur, Carl Everett. BSME, Rensselaer Poly. Inst., 1960. Lic. profl. engr., Ohio, Calif., Fla., Washington. Mfg. mgr. Procter & Gamble Co., N.Y.C., 1960-70; engr. Procter & Gamble Co., Cin., 1970-72, group leader, 1972-76, sr. engr., 1976-85, tech. section head, 1985-93; ret., 1993. Mem. Am. Soc. of Mech. Engrs., Am. Inst. of Chemical Engrs., Natl. Soc. of Profl. Engrs., Am. Welding Soc., Soc. of Naval Architects & Marine Engrs., Engrs. & Scientists Cin., Am. Boat & Yacht Coun., Nat. Marine Mfrs. Assn. Republican. Presbyterian. Home and Office: 8037 Brooklyn Ave NE Seattle WA 98115

SCHULLER, GUNTHER ALEXANDER, composer; b. N.Y.C., Nov. 22, 1925; s. Arthur E. and Elsie (Bernartz) S.; m. Marjorie Black, June 8, 1948; children—Edwin Gunther, George Alexander. Student, St. Thomas Choir Sch., N.Y.C.; MusD (hon.), Manhattan Sch. Music, 1987, Northeastern U., 1967, U. Ill., 1968, Colby Coll., 1969, Williams Coll., 1975, Cleve. Inst. Music, 1977, New Eng. Conservatory Music, 1978, Rutgers U., 1980, Manhattan Sch. Music, 1987, Oberlin Coll., 1989. tchr. Manhattan Sch. Music, 1950-63; head composition dept. Tanglewood, 1963-84; pres. New Eng. Conservatory of Music, 1967-77; artistic dir. Berkshire Music Center, Tanglewood, 1969-84, Festival at Sandpoint, 1985—; founder, pres. Margun Music Inc., 1975, GM Recs., 1980. French horn player, Ballet Theatre, then prin. horn player, Cin. Symphony Orch., 1943-45, prin. French horn, Met. Opera Orch., 1945-59, Concerto #1 for Horn, 1945; composer: Quartet for Four Double Basses, 1947, Fantasy for Unaccompanied Cello, 1951, Recitative and Rondo for Violin and Piano, 1953, Music for Violin, Piano and Percussion, 1957, Contours, 1958, Woodwind Quintet, 1958, Seven Studies on Themes of Paul Klee, 1959, Spectra, 1960, Six Renaissance Lyrics, 1962, String Quartet No. 2, 1965, Symphony, 1965, opera The Visitation 1966, opera Fisherman and His Wife, 1970, Capriccio Stravagante, 1972, The Power Within Us, 1972, Tre Invenzioni, 1972, Three Nocturnes, 1973, Four Soundscapes, 1974, Concerto No. 2 for Orch., 1975, Triplum II, 1975, Horn Concerto No. 2, 1976, Violin Concerto, 1976, Diptych for organ, 1976, Sonata Serenata, 1978, Contrabassoon Concerto, 1978, Deaï for 3 orchs., 1978, Trumpet Concerto, 1979, Octet, 1979, Eine Kleine Posaunenmusik, 1980, In Praise of Winds (Symphony for Large Wind Orch.), 1981, Symphony for Organ, 1982, Concerto Quaternio, 1983, Concerto for Bassoon and Orch., 1984, Farbenspiel (Concerto No. 3 for Orch.), 1985, On Light Wings (piano quartet), 1984; author: Horn Technique, 1962, Early Jazz: Its Roots and Development, 1968, Musings: The Musical Worlds of Gunther Schuller, 1985, The Swing Era, 1989; premiere of Symphony for Brass and Percussion, Cin., 1950, Salzburg Festival, 1957, Dramatic Overture, N.Y. Philharm., 1956, String Quartet, Number 1 Contemporary Arts Festival, U. Ill., 1957, String Quartet Number 3, 1986, Concertino for Jazz Quartet and Orch, Balt. Symphony Orch., 1959, Seven Studies on Themes of Paul Klee, Ford Found., commn., Minn. Symphony, 1959, Spectra, N.Y. Philharm. 1960, Music for Brass Quintet, Coolidge Found., Library of Congress, 1961, Concerto No. 1 for Orch, Chgo. Symphony Orch., 1966, Triplum, N.Y. Philharm. commd. Lincoln Center, 1967, Aphorisms for Flute and String Trio commd, Carlton Coll. Centennial, 1967, Eine Kleine Posaunenmusik, 1980, In Praise of Winds, 1983, Concerto Quaternio, N.Y. Philharm., 1983, Duologue for Violin and Piano, Library of Congress, 1984, Farbenspiel, Berlin Philharm., 1985, Concerto for Viola and Orch., 1985, String Quartet No. 3, 1986, Chimeric Images, 1988, Concerto for String Quartet and Orchestra, 1988, Concerto for Flute and Orchestra, 1988, On Winged Flight: A Divertimento for Band, 1989, Chamber Concerto, 1989, Concerto for Piano Three Hands, 1989, Phantasmata for Violin and Marinba, 1989, 5 Impromptus Eng. Horn and String Quartet, 1989, Impromptus and Cadeazas, 1990, Violin Concert No. 2, 1991, Sonata Fantasia for piano, 1992, Ritruica Melodia Armonia for orchestra, 1992. Recipient Creative Arts award Brandeis U., 1960, Deems Taylor award ASCAP, 1970, Alice M. Ditson Conducting award, 1970, Rodgers and Hammerstein award, 1971, Friedheim award, 1988, William Schuman award Columbia U., 1989; Guggenheim grantee, 1962, 63; McArthur fellow, 1991; recipient Down Beat Lifetime Achievement award, 1993. Mem. Nat. Inst. Arts and Letters, Am. Acad. Arts and Scis. Address: care Margun Music 167 Dudley Rd Newton Center MA 02159 also: care Festival at Sandpoint Box 695 Sandpoint ID 83864

SCHULLER, ROBERT HAROLD, clergyman, author; b. Alton, Iowa, Sept. 16, 1926; s. Anthony and Jennie (Beltman) S.; m. Arvella DeHaan, June 15, 1950; children: Sheila, Robert, Jeanne, Carol, Gretchen. B.A., Hope Coll., 1947, D.D., 1973; B.D., Western Theol. Sem., 1950; LL.D., Azusa Pacific Coll., 1970, Pepperdine U., 1976; Litt.D., Barrington Coll., 1977. Ordained to ministry Reformed Ch. in Am., 1950; pastor Ivanhoe Ref. Ch., Chgo., 1950-55; founder, sr. pastor Garden Grove (Calif.) Community Ch., 1955—; founder, pres. Hour of Power TV Ministry, Garden Grove, 1970—; founder, dir. Robert H. Schuller Inst. for Successful Ch. Leadership, Garden Grove, 1970—; chmn. nat. religious sponsor program Religion in Am. Life, N.Y.C., 1975—; bd. dirs. Freedom Found. Author: God's Way to the Good Life, 1963, Your Future Is Your Friend, 1964, Move Ahead with Possibility Thinking, 1967, Self Love, the Dynamic Force of Success, 1969, Power Ideas for a Happy Family, 1972, The Greatest Possibility Thinker That Ever Lived, 1973, Turn Your Scars into Stars, 1973, You Can Become the Person You Want To Be, 1973, Your Church Has Real Possibilities, 1974, Love or Loneliness— You Decide, 1974, Positive Prayers for Power-Filled Living, 1976, Keep on Believing, 1976, Reach Out for New Life, 1977, Peace of Mind Through Possibility Thinking, 1977, Turning Your Stress Into Strength, 1978, Daily Power Thoughts, 1978, The Peak to Peek Principle, 1981, Living Positively One Day at a Time, 1981, Self Esteem: The New Reformation, 1982, Tough Times Never Last, But, Tough People Do!, 1983, Tough Minded Faith for Tender hearted People, 1984, The Be-Happy Attitudes, 1985, Be Happy You Are Loved, 1986, Success is Never Ending, Failure is Never Final, 1988, Believe in the God Who Believes in You, 1989; co-author: The Courage of Carol, 1978. Bd. dirs. Religion in Am. Life; pres. bd. dirs. Christian Counseling Service; founder Robert H. Schuller Corr. Center for Possibility Thinkers, 1976. Recipient Disting. Alumnus award Hope Coll., 1970, Prin. award Freedoms Found., 1974; named Headliner of Year in Religion, Orange County, 1977, Clergyman of Year, Religious Heritage Am., 1977. Mem. Religious Guild Architects (hon.), AIA (bd. dirs. 1986—). Club: Rotary. Office: Religion in Am Life 12141 Lewis St Garden Grove CA 92640-4618

SCHULMAN, ELIZABETH WEINER, financial consultant; b. Tucson, Nov. 17, 1950; d. Leonard and Doris (Goldman) Weiner; m. Steven Andrew Schulman, Aug. 15, 1981. BA, Brandeis U., 1972; postgrad., U. Ariz., 1976-78. Office mgr. Assocs. in Periodontics and Endodontics, Tucson, 1973-78; campaign cons. various polit. campaigns Tucson, 1978-79; asst. v.p. Merrill Lynch Pvt. Client Group, Tucson, 1979—. Bd. dirs. Catalina coun. Boy Scouts of Am., Tucson, 1987-90, adv. coun., 1990-92; bd. dirs. Jewish Community Found., Tucson, 1989-91; mem. alumni admissions coun. Brandeis U., 1990—. Mem. Investment Mgmt. Cons. Assn. (bd. dirs. 1991—, chmn. cert. com. 1989—, treas. 1993—), Jr. League of Tucson (coun. sec. 1989-90), Hadassah (spl. gifts. chmn. 1989-91). Office: Merrill Lynch 5460 E Broadway Blvd Ste 350 Tucson AZ 85711-3728

SCHULMAN, MICHAEL ADLAI, marketing executive; b. Washington, Oct. 5, 1957; s. Joseph Robert and Joan (Weisberg) S.; m. Lori S. Schulman, Nov. 24, 1984; children: Jessica, Daniel. BS, Cornell U., 1979, MS, 1981. Assoc. engr. Lockheed Missiles and Space, Sunnyvale, Calif., 1981-84; rsch. engr. Ridge Computers, Santa Clara, Calif., 1984-86; sr. software designer Cemax, Inc., Santa Clara, 1986-87; mktg. mgr. Silicon Graphics, Mountain View, Calif., 1987—. Mem. IEEE, Assn. of Computing Machinery. Home: 1708 Carleton Ct Redwood City CA 94061

SCHULMAN, SEYMOUR, hospital administrator; b. N.Y.C., Apr. 5, 1926; s. Sol and Nancy (Klein) S.; m. Alizia Gur, Oct. 10, 1964 (div. 1980); 1 child, Michael. BS, U. Calif., Berkeley, 1950, MPH, 1952. Exec. dir. City of Hope Med. Ctr., Duarte, Calif., 1953-57, Cedars of Lebanon Hosp., L.A., 1957-62, Cedars-Sinai Med. Ctr., L.A., 1962-65, Los Robles Med. Ctr., Thousand Oaks, Calif., 1967-74; dir. European ops. Hosp. Corp. Am., London, 1974-76; exec. dir. Valley Hosp. Med. Ctr., Las Vegas, Nev., 1976-80, Spring Valley Hosp., Las Vegas, 1989—; pres. Las Vegas Surg. Ctr., 1981—. Staff sgt. Cavalry, U.S. Army, 1943-46, PTO. Home: 2673 S Decatur Blvd Apt 1121 Las Vegas NV 89102-8548 Office: Spring Valley Hosp PO Box 80726 Las Vegas NV 89180-0726

SCHULNER, LAWRENCE MAYER, lawyer; b. Chgo., Aug. 14, 1938; s. Harry and Ethel (Greenberg) S.; m. Diane Banchik, Sept. 1, 1962 (div. June 1970); children: Sherri Ellen, Keith Allen; m. 2d Sharalynn Stein, Aug. 15, 1970; 1 child, Matthew Loren. BSBA, Roosevelt U., 1959; JD, UCLA, 1963. Bar: Calif. 1964, U.S. Dist. Cts. (so. and cen. dists.) Calif. 1964, U.S. Ct. Appeals (9th cir.) 1964, U.S. Ct. Appeals (4th cir.) 1969. Tax acct. Pritkin, Finkel & Co., Beverly Hills, Calif., 1963-65; ptnr. Rudoff & Schulner, Los Angeles, 1965-67; pres. Fin. Concepts Inc., Los Angeles, 1967-73, Capital Concepts, Corp., Los Angeles, 1969—, L&L Distbrs., Inc., Los Angeles; v.p. Med.-Dental Bus. Service, Inc., Los Angeles, 1964-67; pres., dir. Complan Inc., Los Angeles, 1969—; chmn. bd. Nightwatch Corp., Los Angeles; pres. L.M. Schulner & Assocs., Camarillo, Calif., 1977—; ptnr. Schulner & Camarena, Camarillo, 1983—; faculty mem. Hastings Coll. Advocacy, 1986—, So. Calif. Inst. Law, UCLA extension, prin. educator Interactive Learning for Lawyers, 1992—; chmn. bd. Nat. Computer Car Network, Camarillo, 1982-85; judge pro tem Ventura Superior Ct., 1981-84, Ventura Mcpl. Ct., 1981-84. Dem. candidate for mayor Los Angeles, 1969, for U.S. Ho. Reps., 1969, chmn. Congressman Tom Rees campaign, 26th Dist., 1970; bd. dirs. Los Angeles West Side br. ARC, Temple Adat Elonim, 1992—; organizer Van DeKamp for Atty. Gen., Calif., 1983; chmn. com. United Jewish Fund, Los Angeles, 1980-82; Named to Outstanding Young Men Am., 1970. Mem. Fed. Bar Assn., Ventura Bar Assn., Los Angeles Trial Lawyers Assn., Ventura Trial Lawyers Assn., Calif. Bar Assn. Office: L M Schulner & Assocs. 360 Mobil Ave Camarillo CA 93010-6325

SCHULTE, HENRY GUSTAVE, college administrator; b. Seattle, Oct. 14, 1920; s. John Henry and Alma (Winter) S.; m. Joan Noel Burton, Aug. 20, 1949; children—Steven Craig, Scott John, Jane Martha. B.A. in Econs. and Bus., U. Wash., 1948. With D.K. MacDonald & Co., Seattle, 1952-67, asst. treas., 1957-60, treas., 1960-67; bus. mgr. legal firm Bogle, Gates, Dobrin, Wakefield & Long, Seattle, 1967; adminstr. Child Devel. and Mental Retardation Ctr. U. Wash., Seattle, 1968-86; mem. steering com. mental retardation research ctrs. group Nat. Inst. Child Health and Human Devel., 1971-85. Mem. exec. bd., treas. Assn. Univ. Affiliated Facilities, 1974-77. Served with AUS, 1940-45. Mem. Soc. Research Adminstrs. (mem. exec. com. 1971-72), Am. Assn. Mental Deficiency. Office: U Wash WJ-10 Seattle WA 98195

SCHULTE, WILLIAM HOBART, III, restaurateur; b. Phoenix, Oct. 4, 1962; s. William Hobart and Carolyn (Dunkin) D. BS in Advt., Ariz. State U., 1984. Pres. Left Field, Inc., Pinetop, Ariz., 1984-92; asst. restaurant mgr. Foodmaker, Inc., Scottsdale, Ariz., 1992—. Bd. dirs. Show Low Main St. Redevel. Project, 1990-92. Mem. Show Low C. of C. (bd. dirs. 1987-92). Democrat. Home: 12231 N 19th St # 145 Phoenix AZ 85022 Office: Foodmaker Inc 3737 N Scottsdale Rd Scottsdale AZ 85251-9999

SCHULTHEIS, PATRICK JOSEPH, lawyer; b. Spokane, Wash., Sept. 3, 1964; s. John Arthur and Catherine Christina (McCann) S. AB, Stanford U., 1986; JD, U. Chgo., 1989. Bar: Calif. 1989. Assoc. Wilson, Sonsini, Goodrich & Rosati, Palo Alto, Calif., 1989—. Mem. ABA (bus. law sect.), Federalist Soc., Buck Club, Kappa Sigma. Republican. Roman Catholic. Home: 2884 South Court Palo Alto CA 94306 Office: Wilson Sonsini Goodrich & Rosati Two Palo Alto Sq Palo Alto CA 94306

SCHULTZ, CAROLINE REEL, artist; b. Evansville, Ind., July 5, 1936; d. Howard and Helene (Engbert) Reel; m. Milton H. Schultz, Feb. 2, 1958; children: Paul, Jim. Student various including, Art Ctr. Coll. of Design, L.A., U. Ill., 1960-62, European Sch. of Art, Mallorca, Spain, 1962; Diploma of Merit (hon.), U. Arts, Parma, Italy, 1970. Dir. Spanish Village Art Ctr., San Diego, 1974; art dir. East African Wildlife Soc., Kenya; African safari organizer various spl. interest groups; art dir. Creative TV Prodns.; pres. Creel Fine Arts, Inc., San Diego, Calif., 1979—; owner African Impressions, San Diego, 1980—; dir. safari U.S. Internat. U., 1993—; lectr. on animal anatomy and art/Africa; participant spl. TV shows; travel writer, others. Major exhibits and one-woman shows include: San Diego Mus. of Art, 1960, Evansville, Ind. Mus. of Art, Exposition of Art, Urbana, Ill., 1960, Art Ctr. Gallery, St. Louis, Springfield, Ill. Art Assn., East African Wildlife Soc. Gallery, Mt. Kenya Safari Club, Nairobi, Kenya, 1991 (one award), Palm Springs Festival of Arts and Music, 1980 (three awards), San Diego County Exposition of Art (award), Whaletail, Nairobi, Kenya, 1991. Recipient Appreciation award Jean-Pierre Hallet/Pygmy Fund, 1980. Mem. Assn. for Promotion of Tourism to Africa, East African Wildlife Soc., Nat. Assn. Scuba Divers, Cen. Ill. Artist League, So. Calif. Presswomen. Home: 10405 Viacha Dr San Diego CA 92124-3412

SCHULTZ, GUSTAV HOBART, religious organization administrator; b. Foley, Ala., Sept. 23, 1935; s. Gustav H. and Anna H. (Coaker) Schultz; m. Flora Redd, June 16, 1958; children: Gustav Hobart III, Timothy Martin, Locke Elizabeth, Bettina Pauley. BD, Concordia Sem., 1961; MST, Luth. Sch. Theology, 1977. Pastor Holy Trinity Luth. Ch., Rome, Ga., 1961-65; asst. pastor Ascension Luth. Ch., Riverside, Ill., 1965-69; pastor U. Luth. Chapel, Berkeley, Calif., 1969—; dean of chapel Pacific Luth. Sem., Berkeley, 1977-78; aux. bishop Southwest Province Assn. Evang. Luth. Chs., 1979-87; chmn. Nat. Sanctuary Def. Fund, San Francisco, 1985—, Salvadoran Humanitarian Aid, Rsch. and Edn. Found., San Francisco, 1984—. Mem. Berkeley City Planning Commn., 1981-83; bd. dirs. Berkeley Emergency Food Project, 1983-92, No. Calif. Ecumenical Coun., San Francisco, 1984-87; founding mem. Internat. Com. for Peace and Reunification of Korea, 1989-92; founding mem. Bd. Stop Torture in Korea, 1992—. Recipient Annual Berkeley Peace Prize, Warwick and Assocs. and Mayor of Berkeley, 1985. Office: U Luth Chapel 2425 College Ave Berkeley CA 94704-2427

SCHULTZ, LESLIE BROWN, management executive; b. Fresno, Calif., Dec. 9, 1936; d. Albert Brown and Marion Jean (Riese) Brown-Propp; married, Jan. 20, 1957 (div. 1972); children: Susan, Steven, David, Thomas. BS, U. So. Calif., 1958. Office mgr. pvt. practice physician, Long Beach, Calif., 1971-73; cost acct. Panavision, Inc., Tarzana, Calif., 1974-76; exec. sec. Hartman Galleries, Beverly Hills, Calif., 1976-78; adminstrv. asst. Galanos Originals, L.A., 1978—. Mem. Alpha Epsilon Phi (nat. pres. 1985-89, trustee, sec. found. 1990-91, pres. found. 1991—). Republican. Jewish. Home: 1745 S Bentley Ave # 1 Los Angeles CA 90025-4307 Office: Galanos Originals 2254 S Sepulveda Blvd Los Angeles CA 90064-1887

SCHULTZ, ROBERT ALLEN, computer information systems educator; b. Ansonia, Conn., Oct. 2, 1942; s. Adam Benedict and Stella Ruth (Waleika) S.; m. Joanna Klaw, June 15, 1968 (div. Aug. 1981); children: Rebecca, Katie. AB, U. Chgo., 1963; AM, Harvard U., 1965, PhD, 1971. Asst. to assoc. prof. philosophy U. Pitts., 1968-75, Cornell U., Ithaca, N.Y., 1970-71, U. So. Calif., L.A., 1975-79; asst. to the pres. A-Mark Fin. Corp., Beverly Hills, Calif., 1979-80; data processing mgr. A-Mark Precious Metals, Beverly Hills, 1980-85; prof. computer info. systems, chair Woodbury U., Burbank, Calif., 1989—, dir. acad. computing, 1989—; adj. faculty U. San Francisco, 196-87, U. Calif., Santa Barbara, 1986-87, West Coast U., 1986-87; exec. bd. Acad. Excelerator Users Group, Cambridge, Mass., 1990-92; bd. advisors computer sci. dept. Glendale (Calif.) C.C., 1990—. Contbr. articles to profl. jours. Mem. Ojai Festival. Mem. Assn. Computing Machinery, Computer Measurement Group. Office: Woodbury U 7500 Glenoaks Blvd Burbank CA 91510

SCHULTZ, SUSAN MARTHA, English educator; b. Belleville, Ill., Oct. 10, 1958; d. Frederick William and Martha Jean (Keefe) S. BA in History, Yale U., 1980; MA in English, U. Va., 1984, PhD, 1989. Vis. asst. prof. English Coll. of William and Mary, Williamsburg, Va., 1989-90; asst. prof. English U. Hawaii, Honolulu, 1990—. Contbr. articles, revs. and poetry to profl. jours. Mem. Hawaii Lit. Arts Coun. (pres. 1992-93). Office: U Hawaii Dept English 1733 Donaghho Rd Honolulu HI 96822

SCHULTZ, THOMAS ROBERT, hydrogeologist; b. Van Wert, Ohio, July 2, 1946; s. Robert Roland and Mary Avanell (Davies) S.; m. Sandra Lee Pound, Aug. 29, 1968; children: Lindsay D., Zachary T. BS in Geology, Ohio State U., 1969, MS in Geology, 1972; Phd in Hydrology, U. Ariz., 1979. Cert. profl. hydrogeologist Am. Inst. Hydrology. Hydrologist Ariz. State Land Dept., Phoenix, 1977-79, U.S. Office Surface Mining, Denver, 1979-80; sr. hydrogeologist Wahler Assocs., Denver, 1980-82, Kaman Scis. Tempo, Denver, 1983-84; sr. project hydrogeologist Woodward Clyde Cons., Denver, 1984-87; sr. assoc. hydrogeologist Harding Lawson Assocs., Denver, 1987-92, Haley & Aldrich, 1992—; advisor Environ. Tech. Program, Colo. Mountain Coll., Leadville, 1985—, chmn. adv. bd., 1992-93. Contbr. articles to profl. jours. 2d lt. Ohio Nat. Guard, 1969-75. Mem. Nat. Water Well Assn., Colo. Ground Water Assn., Colo. Hazardous Waste Mgmt. Soc.

SCHULTZE, ERNST EUGENE, marketing communications executive; b. Columbia, Mo., Jan. 20, 1944; s. Andrew Byron and Jeanne V. (Homsley) S.; m. Marlene Diane Finke, June 7, 1964 (div. 1981); 1 child, Nicole Johanna Dove. BA, Nebr. Wesleyan U., 1968; MBA, San Diego State U., 1975; lifetime teaching credential, Calif. Community Colls. Mktg. coord. Ektelon Corp., San Diego, 1976-79, ops. project mgr., 1979-80; exec. v.p. Mktg. Group, San Diego, 1980-83; v.p. Jack Lewis Agy., San Diego, 1983-84; mktg. strategist Gable Agy., San Diego, 1984-85; pres. Schultze & Wilson, San Diego, 1985—; pres. Nat. Mgmt. Assn., 1979; mktg. com. Gaslamp Quarter Coun., San Diego, 1988-98; bd. dirs. MedEquip Ams., Inc. Contbr. articles to profl. jours. Counsel Schulze City Coun. campaign, San Diego, 1975, Killea City Coun. campagin, San Diego, 1981. Recipient Golden State award, 1989; named Big Hitter in Bus. City San Diego. Mem. Am. Mktg. Assn., Phi Kappa Tau. Republican. Office: 3111 Camino Del Rio N San Diego CA 92108-5720

SCHULZE, KEITH ALAN, urologist; b. Erie, Pa., Feb. 10, 1954; s. James Lee and Mollie Jean (Conner) S.; m. Terrie Lee Ward; 1 child, Gwendolyn Renee. Student, Wabash Coll., Crawfordshire, Ind., 1972-73; BS in Biology cum laude, Centre Coll., Danville, Ky., 1976; MD, U. Louisville, 1980. Diplomate Am. Bd. Urology. Gen. surg. intern U. Calif. Davis Med. Ctr., Sacramento, 1980-81, resident in gen. surgery, 1981-82; chief resident in urology VA Med. Ctr., Martinez, Calif., 1982-83; resident in urology U. Colo. Health Sci. Ctr., Denver, 1983-86; resident in extracorporeal shockwave lithotripsy U. Ariz., Tucson, 1987; pvt. practice urology Aberdeen, Wash., 1986-90, Kitsap Urology Assocs., Bremerton, Wash., 1990—. Contbr. articles to profl. jours. Mem. AMA, Am. Urology Assn., Wash. State Med. Assn., Kitsap County Med. Soc., Wash. State Urology Soc., Phi Beta Kappa. Office: Kitsap Urology Assocs 2500 Cherry Ave # 301 Bremerton WA 98310

SCHULZE, ROBERT CURREY, JR., pediatrician; b. Oakland, Calif., Nov. 3, 1942; s. Robert C. and Barbara Middleton (Buckley) S.; m. B. Jeanette Swanson, Dec. 28, 1968; children: Robert III, John Middleton. BA, Willamette U., 1964; MD, Tex. Tech. U., 1975. Diplomate Am. Bd. Pediatrics. Intern U. Calif. Davis, Sacramento, 1975-76, resident, 1976-79; pvt. practice pediatrician Davis, 1979—; chief pediatrics Woodland (Calif.) Meml. Hosp., 1988-90. Mem. Sacramento Pediatric Soc. Home: 3127 Shelter Cove Pl Davis CA 95616 Office: 765 Covell Blvd Davis CA 95616

SCHULZINGER, ROBERT DAVID, historian educator; b. Cin., Nov. 24, 1945; s. Maurice and Ann (Zusman) S.; m. Marie E. Manes, July 20, 1985; 1 child, Elizabeth Anne. BA, Columbia U., 1967; MPhil, Yale U., 1969, PhD, 1971. Vis. asst. prof. U. Denver, 1971-72; asst. prof. U. Ariz., Tucson, 1972-73, U. Denver, 1973-77; assoc. U. Colo., Boulder, 1977-84, prof., 1984—. Author: The Making of the Diplomatic Mind, 1975, The Wise Men of Foreign Affairs, 1984, American Diplomacy in 20th Century, 1989, 90, Henry Kissinger, 1989, Present Tense, 1992; exec. editor Peace and Change, 1987-93. Fellow Coun. on Fgn. Rels. 1982; grantee NEH 1977, 92. Mem. Soc. for Historians of Am. Fgn. Rels. (bd. dirs. 1989-92), Am. Hist. Assn., Orgn. Am. Historians. Office: U Colo Hist Dept CB 234 Boulder CO 80309-0234

SCHUMACHER, HENRY JEROLD, former army officer, business executive; b. Torrance, Calif., June 17, 1934; s. Henry John and Rene (Wilcox) S.; m. Barbara Howell, Aug. 24, 1958; children: Sheri Lynn, Henry Jerold II. Student, Stanford U., 1953; B.S., U.S. Mil. Acad., 1957; M.S., Northeastern U., Boston, 1965; M.B.A., Auburn U., 1977. Commd. lt. U.S. Army, 1958, advanced through grades to maj. gen., 1982; army attaché Moscow, 1969-71; chief communications ops. Vietnam, 1971-72; exec. officer Office Chief of Staff, 1972-75; comdr. U.S. Army Communications Command, Panama, 1977-79; dir. network integration, Office Asst. Chief of Staff Automation and Communications, Dept. Army, 1979-81; comdr. The White House Communications Agy., Washington, 1981-82; chief U.S. Army Signal Corps, 1981-83; ret., 1983; sr. v.p. Visa Internat., 1983-86; chief oper. officer Fuel Tech., Inc., Stamford, Conn., 1986-87; pres. IMM Systems, Phila., 1987-89; exec. v.p. Cylink Corp., Sunnyvale, Calif., 1990—. Decorated Def. D.S.M., D.S.M., Legion of Merit. Home: 156 Normandy Ct San Carlos CA 94070-1519 Office: Cylink Corp 300 N Mary Ave Sunnyvale CA 94086-4119

SCHUMER, GEORGE NORMAN, court reporting agency owner; b. N.Y.C., Apr. 29, 1949; s. Richard and Doris (Hirsch) S.; m. Catherine Reeves, June 4, 1976 (div. Nov. 1, 1985); m. Ana Fatima Costa, May 31, 1991; children: Alexander G. Krumland, Jacob Jon Schumer. AB in Econs., Bates Coll., 1970; Cert. Shorthand Reporter, Oakland Coll. of Ct. Reporting, 1976; M in Christian Studies, New Coll.-Berkeley, 1991. Cert. shorthand reporter, Calif. Ct. reporter freelance, Richmond, Calif., 1976-80; owner East Bay Reporting, Berkeley, Calif., 1980—; dir. transcription Holocaust Oral History Project, San Francisco, 1984-85. Contbr. articles to profl. jours. Pres. Liberty Toastmasters, Oakland, 1983-84; treas. Shepherd of the Hills Luth. Ch., Berkeley, 1989-91. Recipient Cert. as Tchr., Firewalking Inst., 1991. Mem. Nat. Ct. Reporters Assn., Calif. Ct. Reporters Assn. Libertarian. Office: East Bay Reporting 2140 Shattuck Ave #405 Berkeley CA 94704

SCHURLE, ROBERT RAY, small business owner; b. Manhattan, Kans., Nov. 25, 1936; s. George Ervin and Fannie Mille (Schwab) S.; m. Shirley Ann Regier, Feb. 24, 1957 (div. May, 1980); children: Steven, Ruth, Mark, Timothy, Rebecca, Deborah, Matthew. Grad. high sch., Keats, Kans. Certified plumber. Laborer, helper Beck & Hahn Plumbing, Van Nuys, Calif., 1957-59; counterman, estimator West Valley Plumbers of Woodland Hills, Calif., 1959-66; owner, pres. Pipe Plumbing Contractors of the Valley, Inc., Canoga Park, Calif., 1966—. Republican. Baptist. Home: 22201 Roscoe Blvd Canoga Park CA 91304-3344 Office: Pipe Plumbing Contractors 8757 Canoga Ave Canoga Park CA 91304-1599

SCHURMANN, GERARD, composer, conductor; b. Kertosono, Dutch East Indies, The Netherlands, Jan. 19, 1924; came to U.S., 1981; s. Johan Gerard and Elvire Stephanie Adeline (Dom) S.; m. Vivien Hind, Sept. 1949 (div. 1972); 1 child, Karen; m. Carolyn Mary Nott, May 26, 1973. Studied composition with Alan Rawsthorne (in Eng.), piano with Kathleen Long (in Eng.), and conducting with Franco Ferrara (in Italy). Cultural attaché Embassy of The Netherlands, London, 1945-48; resident conductor Dutch Radio, Hilversum, Holland, 1948-50; composer, conductor various orgns., London, 1950-81, L.A., 1981—. Music compositions include: (orchestral) Six Studies of Francis Bacon, 1968, Variants, 1970, Attack and Celebration, 1971, Piano Concerto, 1972-73, Violin Concerto, 1975-78, The Gardens of Exile, 1989-90; (chamber and instrumental) Bagatelles-for piano, 1945, Fantasia-for cello and piano, 1967, Sonatina-for flute and piano, 1968, Serenade-for violin solo, 1969, Contrasts-for piano, 1973, Leotaurus-for piano, 1975, Two Ballades-for piano, 1981-83, Duo-for violin and piano, 1983-84, Quartet for Piano and Strings, 1986, Ariel-oboe solo, 1987; (vocal and choral) Chuench'i-for high voice and piano, 1966, Chuench'i-for high voice and orchestra, 1967, Summer is Coming, 1970, The Double Heart, 1976,

Piers Plowman, 1979-80, Slovak Folk Songs-for high voice and piano, 1987, Slovak Folk Songs-for soprano, tenor and orchestra, 1988; composer of over 40 feature films which include: Not in Vain, The Third Key, The Long Arm, Man in the Sky, Lease of Life, Camp on Blood Island, The Two-Headed Spy, The Ruthless One, Horrors of the Black Musuem, Konga, The Headless Ghost, Cone of Silence, The Living Earth, Dr Syn, The Ceremony, The Bedford Incident, Attack on the Iron Coast, The Lost Continent, Claretta; orchestrator of films including: Lawrence of Arabia (Winner Academy Award), Exodus (Winner Academy Award), The Vikings, Cross of Iron; composed music for theatre including: The Old Vic Theatre, London (Shakespeare), La Comedie Francaise, Paris (Racine, Moliere), TNP, Paris (Shakespeare), Commedia Dell'arte, Rome (Pirandello, Shakespeare). Lt. Royal Air Force, Eng., 1941-45. NEA grantee, 1984, Bursary award British Arts Coun., 1973, Internat. Music awardBritish Coun., 1980, Vis. Fellowship award U.S. State Dept., 1980, National Endowment for the Arts grant, 1985-86. Mem. ASCAP, Acad. Motion Pictures, Arts and Scis., Brit. Acad. Film and TV Arts, Assn. Profl. Composers, Composers Guild of Great Britain, Performing Right Soc., Assn. Composers and Pub., Phyllis Court Club. Home: 3700 Multiview Dr Los Angeles CA 90068

SCHUSTER, DONALD GENE, collection agency executive; b. Modesto, Calif., Sept. 18, 1950; s. Ned Donald and Cecilia Marshal (Victorino) S. AA, Modesto C.C., 1971; postgrad., U. Calif. Stanislaus, Turlock, 1971-74. Lic. qualified mgr., Calif. Collector Stanislaus Credit Control, Modesto, 1974-75, mgr.-trainee, 1975-77; mgr. Delta Collection Svc., Stockton, Calif., 1978-89; v.p., divsn. mgr. Stanislaus Credit Control, Modesto, 1989—, bd. dirs. Republican. Methodist. Home: 313 Goldrun Dr Modesto CA 95354 Office: Stanislaus Credit Control 914 14th St Modesto CA 95354

SCHUSTER, JACK HERMAN, education educator; b. Shreveport, July 23, 1937; s. Morris Harry and Sallye (Abramson) S.; m. Diane Tickton, Jan. 1969; children: Jordana Ariel, Ariana Moriel. BA, Tulane U., 1959; JD, Harvard U., 1963; MA, Columbia U., 1969; PhD, U. Calif., Berkeley, 1977. Asst. dir. admissions Tulane U., New Orleans, 1963-66; legis./adminstrv. asst. to congressman U.S. Ho. of Reps., Washington, 1967-70; asst. to the chancellor, lectr. polit. sci. U. Calif., Berkeley, 1970-77; prof. edn. and pub. policy Claremont (Calif.) Grad. Sch., 1977—; vis. scholar U. Mich., Ann Arbor, 1985; guest scholar The Brookings Inst., Washington, 1988; vis. fellow, rsch. assoc. dept. ednl. studies Brasenose Coll. Oxford U., 1992; mem. grad. fellowship adv. com. Calif. Student Aid Commn., 1989—; mem. adv. bd. Coll. Bd., Washington, 1992—. Co-author: American Professors, 1986, Governing Tomorrow's Campus, 1989, Enhancing Faculty Careers, 1990; book reviewer; mem. adv. bd. Higher Edn. Abstracts, 1981—, Am. Jour. Edn., 1987-90; mem. editorial bd. Jour. Higher Edn., 1988—, chair editorial bd., 1991; mem. editorial bd. Rev. Higher Edn., 1981-87; mem. editorial rev. bd. Innovative Higher Edn., 1990—; contbr. articles to profl. jours. Trustee Temple Beth Israel, Pomona, Calif., 1980-91, pres. 1987-89; v.p. ea. region Jewish Fedn. Coun. of Greater L.A., 1984-87, bd. dirs. 1980-87; bd. dirs. L.A. Hillel Coun., 1982-89; v.p. Pacific Southwest Coun. Union Am. Hebrew Congregations, 1989-91; labor arbitrator Am. Arbitration Assn. Nat. Labor Panel, 1981—, roster of arbitrators Fed. Mediation and Conciliation Svc., 1982—; bd. dirs. Assn. for Study of Higher Edn., 1983-85. 1st Lt. USAR. Recipient Rsch. Achievement award Assn. for the Study of Higher Edn., 1989, F.W. Ness award Assn. Am. Colls., 1987, Disting. Achievement award Ednl. Press Assn. Am., 1983. Mem. Acad. Resources Network (bd. dirs. 1989—), Am. Coun. on Edn. (nat. leadership group 1985—), AAUP (mem. coun. 1988-91). Home: 1558 N Tulane Rd Claremont CA 91711-3424 Office: Claremont Grad Sch 150 E 10th St Claremont CA 91711-6160

SCHUSTER, PHILIP FREDERICK, II, lawyer; b. Denver, Aug. 26, 1945; s. Philip Frederick and Ruth Elizabeth (Robar) S.; m. Barbara Lynn Nordquist, June 7, 1975; children: Philip Christian, Matthew Dale. BA, U. Wash., 1967; JD, Willamette U., 1972. Bar: Oreg. 1972, U.S. Dist. Ct. Oreg. 1974, U.S. Ct. Appeals (9th cir.) 1986, U.S. Supreme Ct. 1986. Dep. dist. atty. Multnomah County, Portland, Oreg., 1972; title examiner Pioneer Nat. Title Co., Portland, 1973-74; assoc. Buss, Leichner et al, Portland, 1975-76; from assoc. to ptnr. Kitson & Bond, Portland, 1976-77; pvt. practice Portland, 1977—; arbitrator Multnomah County Arbitration Program, 1985—. Contbr. articles to profl. jours. Organizer Legal Aid Svcs. for Community Clinics, Salem, Oreg. and Seattle, 1969-73; Dem. committeeman, Seattle, 1965-70. Mem. ABA, Multnomah Bar Assn. (Vol. Lawyers Project), NAACP (exec. bd. 1979—), ACLU, Internat. Platform Assn., Alpha Phi Alpha. Office: 1500 NE Irving St Ste 540 Portland OR 97232-4209

SCHUSTER, RICHARD NELSON, educational association administrator, consultant; b. Pueblo, Colo., Nov. 21, 1941; s. Nelson and Alice Martha (Bristow) S.; m. Vassiliki Paschalides, Aug. 20, 1963 (div. 1974); 1 child, Clifford Nelson; m. Carolina Lee Monroy; 1 child, Richard Michael-Hewitt. BA, Ctrl. Mo. State U., 1964. Tchr. Francis Parker Sch., San Diego, 1963-66, Long Beach Schs., Long Beach, Lakewood, Calif., 1966-68; restaurant owner Foodmaker Corp., L.I., N.Y., 1968-70; tchr. El Centro Schs., El Centro, Calif., 1970-75; cons., bargainer Calif. Tchrs. Assn., El Centro, 1975-79, Chula Vista, 1979-81, Eureka, 1981-88, San Leandro, 1988—; election cons. Colo. Edn. Assn., Denver, 1978. Bd. mem. Boys Club, El Centro, 1973-74; cons. Tom Suitt Assembly Campaign, El Centro, 1974; mem. Dem. state ctrl. com., Calif., 1974-76. Democrat. Congregationalist. Home: 6389 Hansen Pleasanton CA 94566 Office: Calif Tchrs Assn 14895 E 14th St # 440 San Leandro CA 94578

SCHUSTER, ROBERT PARKS, lawyer; b. St. Louis, Oct. 25, 1945; s. William Thomas Schuster and Carolyn Cornforth (Daugherty) Hathaway; 1 child, Susan Michele. AB, Yale U., 1967; JD with honors, U. of Wyo., 1970; LLM, Harvard U., 1971. Bar: Wyo. 1971, U.S. Ct. Appeals (10th cir.) 1979, U.S. Supreme Ct. 1984, Utah 1990. Dep. county atty. County of Natrona, Casper, Wyo., 1971-73; pvt. practice law, Casper, 1973-76; assoc. Spence & Moriarty, Casper, 1976-78; ptnr. Spence, Moriarty & Schuster, Jackson, Wyo., 1978—. Trustee U. Wyo., 1985-89; polit. columnist Casper Star Tribune, 1987—. Ford Found. Urban Law fellow, 1970-71; pres. United Way of Natrona County, 1974; bd. dirs. Dancers Workshop, 1981-83; chair Wyo. selection com. Rhodes Scholarship, 1989—; mem. bd. visitors Coll. Arts and Scis., U. Wyo., 1991—; mem. planning com. Wyo. Dem. Party; mem. platform com. Dem. Nat. Conv. 1992—; mem. Dem. Nat. Com., 1992—; mem. Wyo. Public Policy Forum, 1992—; bd. dirs. Community Visual Art Assn. Mem. ABA, Assn. Trial Lawyers Am., Wyo. Trial Lawyers Assn. Home: PO Box 548 Jackson WY 83001-0548 Office: Spence Moriarty & Schuster 15 S Jackson St Jackson WY 83001

SCHÜTRUMPF, ECKART ERNST, classical languages and philosophy educator; b. Marburg, Hesse, Germany, Feb. 3, 1939; came to U.S., 1987; s. Hans Justus and Margarethe (Wetz) S.; m. MaryAnne Leaver, Dec. 21, 1971; children: Fleming, Caroline, Helene, Justin. PhD, Philipps U., Marburg, 1966, Habilitation, 1976. Lectr. Philipps U., Marburg, 1966-81; pvt. docent Philips U., Marburg, 1979-83; sr. lectr. U. Cape Town, 1983-85, prof., 1985-87; prof. classics, dept. chmn. U. Colo., Boulder, 1987—. Author: Die Bedeutung des Wortes ethos in der Poetik des Aristoteles, 1970, Die Analyse der polis durch Aristoteles, 1980, Xenophon Poroi, Vorschläge zur Beschaffung von Geldmitteln, 1982, Aristoteles Politik Buch I-III (2 vols.), 1991; contbr. 35 articles to profl. publs. Rsch. scholar Deutsche Forschungsgemeinschaft, 1973-75, Exch. scholar British Coun., 1979, Rsch. scholar Volkswagenwerk Found., 1981-83. Mem. APA, Classical Assn. Mid West and South, Mommsen Gesellschaft. Office: U Colo Classics Dept Campus Box 248 Boulder CO 80309

SCHUTZ, JOHN ADOLPH, historian, educator, university dean; b. Los Angeles, Apr. 10, 1919; s. Adolph J. and Augusta K. (Gluecker) S. AA, Bakersfield Coll., 1940; BA, UCLA, 1942, MA, 1943, PhD, 1945. Asst. prof. history Calif. Inst. Tech., Pasadena, 1945-53; assoc. prof. history Whittier (Calif.) Coll., 1953-56, prof., 1956-65; prof. Am. history U. So. Calif., L.A., 1965-91; chmn. dept. history U. So. Calif., 1974-76, dean social scis. and communication, 1976-82. Author: William Shirley: King's Governor of Massachusetts, 1961, Peter Oliver's Origin and Progress of the American Rebellion, 1967, The Promise of America, 1970, The American Republic, 1978, Dawning of America, 1981, Spur of Fame: Dialogues of John Adams and Benjamin Rush, 1980; editor: Boston's First City Directory 1789, 1989; joint editor: Golden State Series; contbg. author: Spain's Colonial Outpost, 1985, Generations and Change: Genealogical Perspectives in Social History, 1986, Making of America: Society and Culture of the United States, 1990, rev. edit., 1992. Trustee Citizens Rsch. Found., 1985—. NEH grantee, 1971; Sr. Faculty grantee, 1971-74. Mem. Am. Hist. Assn. (pres. Pacific Coast br. 1972-73), Am. Studies Assn. (pres. 1974-75), Mass. Hist. Soc. (corr.), New. Eng. Hist. Geneal. Soc. (trustee 1988—, editor, author intro. book Boston Merchant Census of 1789, 1989), Colonial Soc. Mass. (corr.). Home and Office: 1100 White Knoll Dr Los Angeles CA 90012-1353

SCHUTZKY, MARILYN HORSLEY, artist; b. Soda Springs, Idaho, July 13, 1936; d. Earl James and Alta (Bollwinkle) Horsley; m. Victor Sergay Schutzky, Oct. 11, 1957; children: Allen Victor, Sandra Kristin. Student, U. Calif., Berkeley, 1954-55, U. Utah, 1955-57. Free-lance artist, 1957—. One-woman shows include Design Concepts, Alamo, Calif., 1991, Harbor Studio Gallery, Gig Harbor, 1991, Back Bay Gardens Gallery, Corte Madera, Calif., 1988, St. Paul Towers, Oakland, Calif., 1988, Marin Arts Guild, Larkspur, Calif., 1986, Two Birds, Forest Knolls, Calif., 1983, Avoir Gallery, Kirkland, Wash., 1993; exhibited in groups shows at Waterworks '92, Seattle Conv. Ctr., Grand Exhbn. '92, Akron (Ohio) Soc. of Artists, Howard Mandeville Gallery, Kirkland, 1992, The Nut Tree, 1991, Kaiser Gallery, 1991 and others. Recipient 1st award Frye Art Mus., 1990, James Copley Purchase award San Diego Watercolor Soc., 1988. Mem. N.W. Watercolor Soc. (Past Pres.'s award 1992, Signature award 1992), Marin Soc. Artists, Oakland Art Assn. (Francis Coan award 1991), Eastbay Watercolor Soc. (Signature award 1989), Fedn. Can. Artists, Marin County Watercolor Soc., Watercolor West. Home and Studio: 8915 N Harborview Dr #103 Gig Harbor WA 98332 Also: Marilyn Schutzky Studio 7340 Turquoise Ave Scottsdale AZ 85258

SCHUYLER, GREGORY ALAN, interior design company executive; b. San Jose, Calif., June 16, 1940; s. George Alan and Helen Grace (Mishler) S.; m. Lynda Ruth East, June 17, 1962 (div. June 1974); children: Dawn Elizabeth Schuyler Estenson, Shawn Adam Alan; m. Sharon Rae Nelson, Feb. 16, 1986; 1 child, Sabrina Leigh. AA, Diablo Valley Coll., 1961; BS in Engring., U. Calif., Berkeley, 1964. Asst. Albert & Nancy Rubey Interiors, Alamo, Calif., 1958-64; designer Albert & Nancy Rubey Interiors, Alamo, 1964-75; v.p. Rubey Interiors, Alamo, 1976-89; exec. v.p. Rubey Interiors, San Ramon, Calif., 1989-90; owner, prin. Rubey Interiors, San Ramon, 1991—. Active local schs., Alamo, Danville, Calif., 1971-92, Alamo (Calif.) Music Festival, 1982-92; active Christmas festival Children's Home Soc., San Ramon, 1991; sponsor Children's Home Soc., 1991—. Mem. Bldg. Industry Assn. USA, Sales and Mktg. Coun. Bldg. Industry Assn., Rotary Club Alamo (pres. 1985-86, Paul Harris award 1990-91, Rotarian of Yr. 1990-91). Republican. Home: 2990 Limestone Rd Alamo CA 94507 Office: Rubey Interiors 2411 T Old Crow Canyon Rd San Ramon CA 94583

SCHUYLER, ROBERT LEN, investment company executive; b. Burwell, Nebr., Mar. 4, 1936; s. Norman S. and Ilva M. (Hoppes) S.; m. Mary Carol Huston, June 13, 1958; children: Kylie Anne, Nina Leigh, Melynn Kae, Gwyer Lenn. BS, U. Nebr., 1958; MBA, Harvard U., 1960. Asst. to treas. Potlatch Forests, Inc., Lewiston, Idaho, 1962-64; dir. corp. planning Potlatch Forests, Inc., San Francisco, 1964-66; mgr. fin. analysis Weyerhaeuser Co., Tacoma, 1966-68; mgr. investment evaluation dept. Weyerhaeuser Co., 1968-70, v.p. fin. and planning, 1970-72, sr. v.p. fin. and planning, 1972-85, exec. v.p., chief fin. officer, 1985-91; mng. ptnr. Nisqually Ptnrs., Tacoma, 1991—; chief exec. officer S&S Land & Cattle Co., Tacoma, 1985—; past mem. nat. adv. bd. Chem. Bank, U. Wash. MBA program, coun. fin. exec. Conf. Bd., Pvt. Sector Coun., exec. com. Am. Paper Inst.; bd. dirs. Multicare Health System, Paragon Trade Brands Inc. Trustee Weyerhaeuser Co. Found.; bd. dirs. Tacoma-Pierce County YMCA. Mem. Anglers Club. Home: 12101 Gravelly Lake Dr SW Tacoma WA 98499-1415 Office: Nisqually Ptnrs 820 S A St Ste 350 Tacoma WA 98402-5212

SCHUYLER, RONALD G., environmental engineer; b. Denver, Mar. 19, 1945; s. Maurice E. and Audry Bell (Pendell) S.; m. Sharon Kay Schmidt, June 9, 1968; children: Sydney Lynn, Shelby Ann. BSCE, Colo. State U., 1967, MS in Microbiology, 1970. Registered profl. engr., Colo. Dist. engr. water quality control div. Colo. Dept. Health, Denver, 1970-71; dist. engr. water qualaity control div. Colo. Dept. Health, Ft. Collins, 1971-75; chief tech. svcs. Colo. Dept. Health, Denver, 1976-82, dep. dir. div., 1982-85, chief permits and enforcement, 1985-87, chief field support, 1987-90; environ. engr. on loan EPA Region VIII, Denver, 1990-92; sr. project mgr. RTW, Denver, 1992—; owner Ronald G. Schuyler, PE, DEE, Ft. Lupton, Colo., 1977—, Something More, Ft. Lupton, 1977—. Deacon 1st Bapt. Ch., Ft. Lupton, 1976—. Recipient Arthur Sidney Bedell award Water Pollution Control Fedn., 1987, svc. award, 1990. Mem. Am. Acad. Environ. Engrs., Nat. Environ. Trainers Assn. (China del. participant 1983), Rocky Mountain Water Pollution Control Assn. (pres. 1985-86com. chmn. 1977-89, svc. award 1986). Republican. Office: RTW 1600 Stout Ste 1800 Denver CO 80202-3126

SCHWAB, ALICE MAE GWILLIAM, nursing educator; b. Park City, Utah, Feb. 10, 1938; d. James Llewellyn and Alice (Lefler) Gwilliam; diploma L.A. County (Calif. Gen. Hosp. Sch. Nursing, 1959; BA, U. Redlands, 1975, MA, 1978; m. Harry Loren Holbrook, Aug. 19, 1960 (dec.); children: Jimmy Edward, William Loren, Mary Alice, Daniel Raymond; m. Donald E. Schwab, June 1988. Nurse, VA Hosp., Long Beach, Calif., 1959-61; supervising nurse U. Calif., Irvine Med. Ctr., 1964-74; patient care coord. Fountain Valley (Calif.) Community Hosp., 1975-78; supervising nurse Hoag Meml. Hosp., Newport Beach, Calif., 1978-79; dir. nursing svc. Los Banos (Calif.) Community Hosp., 1979-81, ; dir. nursing Sonoma Valley Dist. Hosp., 1981-83; nursing edn. Rancho Arroyo Vocat. Tech. Inst., Sacramento, 1985-88; instr. North Orange County Community Coll. Dist., 1976-79, Merced Community Coll.; cons. human resources devel. and personal growth, 1988—; nursing edn. cons. Calif. Bd. of Registered Nursing, 1989—. Mem. AAUW, Dirs. Nursing Council. Home: 620 Jones Way Sacramento CA 95818-3312

SCHWAB, CHARLES R., brokerage house executive; b. Sacramento, 1937; m. Helen O'Neill; 5 children. Stanford U., 1959, Postgrad., 1961. Formerly mut. fund mgr. Marin County, Calif.; founder brokerage San Francisco, 1971; now chmn., CEO Charles Schwab & Co., Inc. Author: How to be Your Own Stockbroker, 1984. Republican. Office: Charles Schwab & Co Inc 101 Montgomery St San Francisco CA 94104*

SCHWAB, HOWARD JOEL, judge; b. Charleston, W.Va., Feb. 13, 1943; s. Joseph Simon and Gertrude (Hadas) S.; m. Michelle Roberts, July 4, 1970; children: Joshua Raphael, Bethany Alexis. BA in History with honors, UCLA, 1964, JD, 1967. Bar: Calif. 1968, U.S. Dist. Ct. (cen. dist.) Calif. 1968, U.S. Ct. Appeals (9th cir.) 1970, U.S. Supreme Ct. 1972. Clk. legal adminstrn. Litton Industries, L.A., 1967-68; dep. city atty. L.A., 1968-69; dep. atty. gen. State of Calif., L.A., 1969-84; judge Mcpl. Ct. L.A. Jud. Dist., 1984-85; judge Superior Ct. Superior Ct. L.A. County, L.A., 1985—; mem. faculty Berkeley (Calif.) Judicial Coll., 1987—. Contbr. articles to profl. jours. Recipient CDAA William E. James award Calif. Dist. Atty.'s Assn., 1981. Mem. San Fernando Valley Bar Assn., Inn of Ct., Calif. Judges Assn., Constl. Rights Found., Phi Alpha Delta. Democrat. Jewish. Office: LA Superior Ct 6230 Sylmar Ave Van Nuys CA 91401

SCHWABE, PETER ALEXANDER, JR., judge; b. Portland, Oreg., July 23, 1935; s. Peter Alexander and Evelyn (Zingleman) S.; A.B., Stanford, 1958; J.D., Willamette U., 1960; m. Bonnie Jean LeBaron, June 21, 1958; children—Mark, Karen, Diane, Patricia, Kurt. Admitted to Oreg. bar, 1960; pvt. practice, Portland, 1960-76; fed. adminstrv. law judge, 1976—. Del. nat. policy council Office of Hearings and Appeals, Social Security Adminstrn., Dept. Health and Human Services, 1980—. Mem. ABA, Oreg. State Bar Assn., Beta Theta Pi, Phi Delta Phi. Home: 4366 Dorking Ct Sacramento CA 95864-6150 Office: 2031 Howe Ave Sacramento CA 95825-0176

SCHWANTES, CARLOS ARNALDO, history educator, consultant; b. Wilmington, N.C., Mar. 7, 1945; s. Arnaldo and Frances (Casteen) S.; m. Mary Alice Dassenko, Sept. 4, 1966; children: Benjamin, Matthew. BA, Andrews U., 1967; MA, U. Mich., 1968, PhD, 1976. From instr. to prof. Walla Walla Coll., College Place, Wash., 1969-85; prof. history U. Idaho, Moscow, 1984—; cons. TV History of Idaho, 1981-88. Author: Coxey's Army: An American Odyssey, 1985, The Pacific Northwest: An Interpretive History, 1989, In Mountain Shadows: A History of Idaho, 1991, also author or editor 8 other books; mem. editorial bd. Pacific N.W. Quar., 1982—, Idaho Yesterdays, 1987—, Forest and Conservation History, 1988—, Pacific Hist. Review, 1991—; contbr. articles to profl. jours. Mem. Latah County Hist. Preservation Com., Moscow, 1990-92. NEH fellow, 1982-83, rsch. fellow Idaho Humanities Coun., 1989-90; Idaho State Bd. Edn. rsch. grantee, 1990-91. Mem. Orgn. Am. Historians, Western History Assn., Mining History Assn. (coun. 1990—), Lexington Soc., Idaho State Hist. Soc. Republican. Seventh-day Adventist. Office: U Idaho Dept History Moscow ID 83843

SCHWARTZ, ARTHUR SOLOMON, research psychologist; b. N.Y.C., June 12, 1924; s. Aaron and Elsie (Silverstein) S.; m. Eileen Hannigan, June 2, 1951; children—Amy, Andrew, Jainah, Beth, Nancy. B.A., NYU, 1950; Ph.D., U. Buffalo, 1957, postdoctoral fellow, UCLA, 1956-58. Research psychologist NIH, Washington, 1958-62, Barrow Neurol. Inst., Phoenix, 1962—; adj. assoc. prof. Ariz. State U., Tempe, 1962—; cons. in field. Contbr. articles to profl. jours. Served with U.S. Army, 1943-46. Grantee NIH, NSF. Mem. Assn., Soc. Neorosci., Internat. Neuropsychology Soc., Democrat. Jewish. Office: Barrow Neurol Inst 350 W Thomas Rd Phoenix AZ 85013-4496

SCHWARTZ, CHERIE ANNE KARO, storyteller; b. Miami, Fla., Feb. 24, 1951; d. William Howard and Dorothy (Olesh) Karo; m. Lawrence Schwartz, Aug. 12, 1979. BA in Lit., The Colo. Coll., 1973; MA in Devel. Theater, U. Colo., 1977. Tchr. English, drame, mime, creative writing, speech coach South High Sch., Pueblo, Colo., 1973-76; tchr. drama St. Mary's Acad., Denver, 1979-81; tchr. English and drama Rocky Mountain Hebrew Acad., Denver, 1981-83; full-time profl. storyteller throughout N.Am., 1982—; storyteller, docent, tchr. tng., mus. outreach Denver Mus. Natural History, 1982—; trainer, cons., performer, lectr, keynote speaker various orgns., instns., agys., confs. throughout the country, 1982—; chairperson Omanim b'Yachad: Artists Together, Nat. Conf. Celebrating Storytelling, Drama, Music and Dance in Jewish Edn., Denver, 1993. Storyteller: (audio casette tapes) Cherie Karo Schwartz Tells Stories of Hanukkah From Kar-Ben Books, 1986, Cherie Karo Schwartz Tells Stories of Passover From Kar-Ben Books, 1986, Miriam's Tambourine, 1988, Worldwide Jewish Stories of Wishes and Wisdom, 1988; storyteller, actor: (video tape) The Wonderful World of Recycle, 1989, author: (book) The Biggest Latke in the World, 1993. Title III grantee State of Colo. Edn., Pueblo, 1975-76. Mem. Coalition for Advancement Jewish Edn. (coord. Jewish Storytelling Conf. 1989—), Nat. Assn. for Preservation and Perpetuation of Storytelling, Rocky Mountain Storytelling Guild. Democrat. Jewish. Home: 996 S Florence St Denver CO 80231

SCHWARTZ, EDWARD J., federal judge. Judge Mcpl. Ct. and Superior Ct., San Diego; judge U.S. Dist. Ct. for So. Dist. Calif., former chief judge, now sr. judge. Office: US Dist Ct 940 Front St San Diego CA 92189-0010

SCHWARTZ, FRED HAROLD, environmentalist, consultant; b. Montreal, Que., Can., Apr. 25, 1949; came to U.S., 1990; s. Jack and Elsie Hilda (Salomons) S.; children: Emma, Charles. BEd, McGill U., Montreal, 1970; M Environ. Studies, York U., Toronto, Ont., Can., 1973. Teaching scholar York U., 1971, 72; pres. Scenario Cons., Toronto, 1973-81, 87-88; mgr. Ministry Energy, Toronto, 1981-87; exec. v.p. Powerx Energy Corp., Toronto, 1988-89; program coord. Pacific Gas & Electric Co., San Francisco, 1990—; cons. Environ. Can., Ottawa, Ont., 1977-80, Thrust Tube Propulsion, Vancouver, B.C., Can., 1988—, Green Solutions, Vancouver, 1991—, Trinity Flywheels, San Francisco, 1993—. Cons. Nat. Geog., 1980. Recipient Challenge award for environ. and conservation Pres. of U.S., 1991. Mem. Can.-Am. C. of C. Home: 77 Brentwood Dr San Rafael CA 94901 Office: Pacific Gas & Electric Co 444 Market St San Francisco CA 94177

SCHWARTZ, GEORGE EDWIN, paper company executive; b. Nampa, Idaho, May 28, 1924; s. Arthur Earl and Alpha Mable (White) S.; m. Marjorie May Allen, Apr. 1, 1944; children: Kathryn Dee Schwartz Schroeder, Thomas George, Steven George. BA in Econs. and Bus., U. Wash., 1948. Sr. acct. Price Waterhouse & Co., Portland, Oreg., 1948-53; instr. acctg. Multnomah Coll., Portland, 1952-53; successively asst. treas., sec., treas., v.p. fin., v.p. adminstrn. Longview (Wash.) Fibre Co., 1953-75, v.p. prodn., asst. sec., 1975-86, exec. v.p., asst. sec., 1986-92; also bd. dirs., 1958—. Trustee through pres. Monticello Med. Ctr., Longview, 1959-84, The Health Care Found., Longview; mem. hosp. and med. facilities adv. council Dept. Soc. and Health Services, State of Wash., Tacoma, 1968-74. Served to cpl. AUS, 1943-46, ETO. Mem. Northwest Pulp and Paper Assn. (pres. 1979-80), Wash. Pulp and Paper Found. (pres. 1985-87), Paper Industry Mgmt. Assn., TAPPI, Oreg. Soc. CPA's. Methodist. Lodges: Lions (Longview), Masons. Office: Longview Fibre Co PO Box 639 Longview WA 98632-7411

SCHWARTZ, HARVEY ROY, electronic engineer; b. Chgo., Apr. 24, 1943; s. Samuel Franklin and Mary Schwartz; m. Charlotte Ann Valparaiso, Oct. 1, 1981. AA, Pasadena City Coll., 1984; student, Calif. State U., L.A., 1986-90. Engr. Motown Record Corp., Detroit, 1966-69; engring. cons. L.A., 1969-79; engr. KTLA/Golden West Broadcasters, L.A., 1978-79; asst. engr. Jet Propulsion Lab., Pasadena, 1979-81, engr., 1985—; test engr. Mattel Electronics, Hawthorne, Calif., 1981-82; design engr. Resdel Engring. Corp., Arcadia, Calif., 1982-85; computer cons. Harvey Design, Sierra Madre, Calif., 1991-92, video/animation artist, 1992—. Contbr. articles to profl. jours. Mem. Assn. of Computing Machinery, IEEE Computer Soc. Office: Harvey Design PO Box 1065 Sierra Madre CA 91025

SCHWARTZ, HENRY JESSE CALVIN, internist, naval officer; b. Minocqua, Wis., June 15, 1941; s. Sam Schwartz and Eleanor Isadore (Brothers) Larmon; m. Linda Johnson, July 28, 1967; children: David, Nancy, Michael. BS in Zoology, U. Wis., 1961, MD, 1965. Diplomate Am. Bd. Internal Medicine. Resident in internal medicine Med. Coll. Wis., Milw., 1969-72; commd. capt. U.S. Navy, 1966; med. officer U.S. Navy, Charleston, S.C., 1966-69; physician Lakeland Med. Assocs., Woodruff, Wis., 1972-81; med. officer U.S. Navy, Panama City, Fla., Honolulu, 1981—; cons. in internal medicine Howard Young Med. Ctr., Woodruff, 1972-81; force med. officer Submarine Force, U.S. Pacific Fleet, Honolulu, 1990—. Author rsch. reports of diving rsch. at Navy Exptl. Diving Unit, 1981-90. Mem. AMA, Undersea and Hyperbaric Med. Assn. Home: 11B Makalapa Dr Honolulu HI 96818 Office: Submarine Force US Pacific Fleet Pearl Harbor HI 96860

SCHWARTZ, JOAN LAM, computer graphics consultant, writer, artist; b. Phila., Dec. 19, 1928; d. Alfred C. and Sara (Maybaum) Lam; m. Arthur J. Schwartz, Sept. 17, 1952; children: Charles, Dona. BArch, U. Pa., 1951; MA in Adminstrn., Antioch U., 1983; postgrad., Northrop U., 1984. Cert. community coll. instr., Calif. Archtl. designer Pullinger, Stevens, Bruder and Assocs., Phila., 1951-52; pvt. practice Phila., 1952-75; acct. exec. Fahnestock and Co., N.Y. Stock Exch., Phila., 1975-80; rsch. cons. The Rand Corp., Santa Monica, Calif., 1982-83; rsch. analyst Info. Displays, Inc., L.A., 1984-85, Info. Internat., Inc., Culver City, Calif., 1985; computer graphics cons. L.A., 1985—. One man shows Barzansky Galleries, N.Y.C., 1966, 68; represented in mus. collections; contbr. articles to profl. jours. Recipient nat. 3d prize Beaux Arts Inst. Design, 1949, Benedictine award, 1967, Honorable mention Corel Draw Internat. Design Contest, 1991. Mem. N.Y. Artists Equity, Nat. Computer Graphics Assn., L.A. Computer Soc., Assn. Computing Machinery. Democrat. Home and Office: 13107 Mindanao Way # 4 Marina Del Rey CA 90292

SCHWARTZ, JOHN ANDREW, surgeon; b. Lorain, Ohio, June 19, 1952; s. William Marvin and Joan Marie (Nellis) S.; 1 child, Lauren Caroline. BS, Xavier U., 1974; MD, U. Cin., 1978. Diplomate Am. Bd. Surgery. Internship gen. surgery U. Ill., 1978-79, residency in gen. surgery, 1979-84; fellowship vascular surgery N.C. Meml. Hosp., 1984-86; asst. prof. U. South Fla., Tampa, 1986-89; surgeon Medford (Oreg.) Clinic, 1989—; instr. surgery U. Ill., Chgo., 1980-84; clin. instr. surgery U. N.C., Chapel Hill, 1984-86; attending surgeon Ashland Community Hosp., Providence Hosp., Rogue Valley Med. Ctr., 1990; co-dir. vascular lab. U. South Fla. Med. Clinic, 1986-89; chmn. Surg. ICU Com., James A. Haley VA Hosp., 1986-89. Contbr. numerous articles to profl. jours. Recipient The Peter B. Samuels Essay award, 1986. Fellow Am. Coll. Surgeons; mem. Assn. for Acad. Surgery, Nathan A. Womack Surg. Soc., Woutheastern Surg. Congress, The Warren H. Cole Soc., So. Assn. for Vascular Surgery, Oreg. Med. Assn.,

Jackson County Med. Soc. Office: Medford Clinic 555 Black Oak Dr Medford OR 97504-8311

SCHWARTZ, JOHN CHARLES, chemical engineer; b. Seattle, Apr. 30, 1939; s. Charles and Elizabeth Mercy (Dougherty) S.; m. Sandra Helene Waroff, Aug. 20, 1960 (div. Sept. 1982); children: Barry, Allan, Craig. BS in Chemistry, U. Okla., 1960; MS in Chemistry, Rutgers U., 1968. Research chemist FMC Corp., Carteret and Princeton, N.J., 1962-74; sr. process engr. FMC Corp., Green River, Wyo., 1974—, technologist phosphorous chem. div., 1989—; lab. stockroom operator U. Okla., Norman, 1956-60. Contbr. articles to prof. jours.; patentee in field. Co-founder Cong. Beth Israel of Sweetwater County, Wyo.; active New Jewish Agenda; sec. Wyo. chpt. Nat. Alliance for Mentally Ill, pres. Sweetwater County, Wyo. chpt. Capt. Chem. Corps, U.S. Army, 1960-66. Mem. VFW, Am. Legion, Am. Chem. Soc. (pres. U. Okla. chpt. 1957), Nat. Mental Health Consumer's Assn., Alpha Epsilon Pi, Alpha Chi Sigma, Phi Lambda Upsilon, Phi Eta Sigma. Democrat. Jewish. Lodge: Eagles. Home: PO Box 648 Green River WY 82935-0648 Office: FMC Wyo Corp PO Box 872 Green River WY 82935-0872

SCHWARTZ, JOHN LEONARD, publishing executive, psychiatrist; b. Washington, Jan. 2, 1946; s. Harry and Ruth (Blumner) S.; divorced; children: David, Mark. Student, MIT, 1962-64; BA, Columbia Coll., 1966; MD, N.Y. U., 1970. Diplomate Am. Bd. Psychiatry. Chmn., psychiatry Children's Hosp., Orange, Calif., 1976-84; chmn., psychiatry Western Med. Ctr., Santa Ana, Calif., 1975-86, pres., med. staff, 1980-82; psychiatrist-in-chief Western Med. Ctr., Anaheim, Calif., 1981-84, United Western Med. Ctr., Santa Ana, 1980-86; chief exec. officer Continuing Med. Edn., Inc., Santa Ana, 1978—; editor-in-chief The Psychiatric Times, Santa Ana, 1984—. Fellow Am. Psychiat. Assn., Am. Assn. for Social Psychiatry, Am. Acad. Child Psychiatrists. Republican. Jewish. Avocations: jogging, bike riding, automobile collecting. Office: Continuing Med Edn Inc 1924 E Deere Ave Santa Ana CA 92705-5723

SCHWARTZ, KIMBERLY ANN, public relations professional; b. Chgo., Apr. 10, 1959; d. John Lowell and Carol Celene (Hajicek) Bender; m. Stanley Elliot, Feb. 13, 1988. BA in Communications, Wartburg Coll., 1981; postgrad., U. No. Iowa, 1986-87, Calif. State U., Fullerton, 1991-92. PM anchor, reporter Sta. WYBR-FM, Rockford, Ill., 1980; reporter, editor, dir. Sta. KIMT-TV, Mason City, Iowa, 1981; PM anchor/reporter Sta. KXEL-AM/KCNB-FM, Waterloo, Iowa, 1981-83; dir., media/publs. ARC Hawkeye Chpt. Blood Region, Waterloo, 1983-87; dir. pub. info. and fin. devel. ARC San Bernardino (Calif.) County Chpt., 1987-88; dir., mktg. com. ARC Greater Long Beach (Calif.) Chpt., 1988—. Contbg. author: Red Cross Communications During a Crisis, 1991, Crisis Communications, 1992. Loaned exec. United Way of L.A., 1989, other positions. Mem. Pub. Rels. Soc. Am. (accredited), Soc. Collegiate Journalists, Nat. Honor Soc. Office: ARC 3150 E 29th St Long Beach CA 90806-2397

SCHWARTZ, LAWRENCE, aeronautical engineer; b. N.Y.C., Nov. 30, 1935; s. Harry and Fanny (Steiner) S.; m. Cherie Anne Karo, Aug. 12, 1979; children: Ronda, Daran. SB in Aero. Engring., MIT, 1958, SM in Aero. Engring., 1958; postgrad. Ohio State U., 1960, U. Dayton, 1962-63; PhD in Engring., UCLA, 1966. Electronics design engr. MIT. Instrumentation Lab., Cambridge, 1959; aerospace engr., Wright-Patterson AFB, Ohio, 1962-63; mem. tech. staff Hughes Aircraft Co., Culver City, Calif., 1963-65, staff engr., 1965-67, sr. staff engr., 1967-72, sr. scientist, 1972-79, chief scientist lab., 1979-93, tech. mgr. 1985-87; chmn., tech. adv. bd., 1987-88, prin. scientist/engr. 1993—; cons., tchr. in field. With USAF, 1959-62. Registered profl. engr., Colo., Calif. Mem. IEEE, AAAS, Sigma Xi, Sigma Gamma Tau, Tau Beta Pi. Contbr. articles to profl. jours. Home: 996 S Florence St Denver CO 80231-1952 Office: 16800 E Centretech Pky Aurora CO 80011-9046

SCHWARTZ, LOUIS, radiologist; b. N.Y.C., Sept. 19, 1940; s. Abraham and Paula (Hojmon) S.; m. Marilyn Carole Altman, Aug. 28, 1965; children: Debra, Steven, Susan. BS magna cum laude, Adelphi Coll., 1961; MD, Albert Einstein Coll. Medicine, 1965. Radiologist Riverside (Calif.) Gen. Hosp., 1971—; radiologist Parkview Community Hosp., Riverside, 1972—, chief radiology, 1979—; pres. Arlington Radiol. Med. Group Inc., Riverside, 1982—; chief of staff Parkview Community Hosp., Riverside, 1990-91. Mem. AMA, Am. Coll. Radiology, Calif. Radiol. Soc., Inland Radiol. Soc. (pres. 1979), Riverside County Med. Assn. Office: Arlington Radiol Med Group Inc 3900 Sherman Dr Riverside CA 92503-4005

SCHWARTZ, MILTON LEWIS, federal judge; b. Oakland, Calif., Jan. 20, 1920; s. Colman and Selma (Lavenson) S.; m. Barbara Ann Moore, May 15, 1942; children: Dirk L., Tracy Ann, Damon M., Brooke. A.B., U. Calif. at Berkeley, 1941, J.D., 1948. Bar: Calif. bar 1949. Research asst. 3d Dist. Ct. Appeal, Sacramento, 1948; dep. dist. atty., 1949-51; practice in Sacramento, 1951-79; partner McDonough, Holland, Schwartz & Allen, 1953-79; U.S. dist. judge Eastern Dist. Calif., 1979—; prof. law McGeorge Coll. Law, Sacramento, 1952-55; Mem. Com. Bar Examiners Calif., 1971-75. Pres. Bd. Edn. Sacramento City Sch. Dist., 1961; v.p. Calif. Bd. Edn., 1967-68; Trustee Sutterville Heights Sch. Dist. Served to maj. 40th Inf. Div. AUS, 1942-46, PTO. Named Sacramento County Judge of Yr., 1990. Fellow Am. Coll. Trial Lawyers; mem. State Bar Calif., Am. Bar Assn., Am. Bd. Trial Advocates, Anthony M. Kennedy Am. Inn of Ct. (pres. 1988-90, pres. emeritus 1990—). Office: US Dist Ct 1060 US Courthouse 650 Capitol Mall Sacramento CA 95814-4708

SCHWARTZ, MODEST EUPHEMIA, real estate company executive; b. Chgo., Dec. 14, 1915; d. Giles E. and Evelyn (Tomczak) Ratkowski; m. Edward Joseph Schwartz, Feb. 9, 1946 (dec. July 1979); children: Kathryn Ann, Edward Thomas. BA, UCLA, 1936, MA, 1938; libr. credential, Immaculate Heart Coll., L.A., 1958. Cert. tchr., libr., Calif. Tchr. Alhambra (Calif.) City Schs., 1938-58, libr., 1958-72; v.p. Fremont Svc., Alhambra, 1959-83, pres., 1983-86; v.p. Moulding Supply Co., Alhambra, 1967-83, pres., 1983-85; v.p., bd. dirs. Sequoia Mgmt. Co., Alhambra, 1969-86; mng. ptnr. SRSH Realty Ptnrs., Alhambra, 1986-89. Bd. dirs. Found. for Cardiovascular Rsch., Pasadena, Calif., 1973-85, Progressive Savs., Alhambra, 1979-85; mem. Ret. Sr. Vol. Program, Alhambra, 1979—, Alhambra Community Hosps. Aux., 1987—, med. libr., 1990—; mem. Friends Alhambra Pub. Libr., 1981—; pres. bd. trustees Alhambra Pub. Libr., 1981-83, 89-91, mem., 1976-83, 85-93; pres. Alhambra Pub. Libr. Found., 1990-93, L.A. County Art Mus., Met. Mus., N.Y. Mem. ALA, NEA, AAUW (life, Edn. Found. grant in her name 1988, br. treas. 1986-88, 89-91, corr. and rec. sec. 1992-93), Calif. Ret. Tchrs. Assn. (co-chair hospitality 1991—, membership chmn.), UCLA Alumni Assn., Women's City Club. Home: 1117 N Stoneman Apt K Alhambra CA 91801

SCHWARTZ, STEPHAN ANDREW, entrepreneur; b. Cin., Jan. 10, 1942; s. Abraham Leon and Bertha Culbertson (Watson) S.; m. Katherine Rowland, Jan. 6, 1965 (div. 1979); 1 child, Catherine Rowland; m. Hayden Oliver Gates, July 10, 1982; 1 stepchild, Lea Daniel Meyers. Student, U. Va. Founder, chmn., rsch. dir. The Mobius Soc., L.A., 1977—; pres. S. A. Schwartz & Assocs., L.A., 1992—; chmn. Clearlight TV Prodns., L.A.; former vis. prof. John F. Kennedy U.; adv. bd. PHOENIX: New Directions in the Study of Man; sr. fellow Philos. Rsch. Soc.; cons. to oceanographer USN; spl. asst. rsch. and analysis Chief Naval Ops.; gen. ptnr. U-Partners, Inc.; cons. in field. Editor: Seapower Magazine; author: The Secret Vaults of Time, 1978, The Alexandria Project, 1980, 1983, Psychic Detectives, 1987; author: (with others) Stories From Omni, 1984; contbr. over 47 publications to profl. jours.; screenwriter spl. presentations and documentaries. Bd. dirs. World Children's Transplant Found., 1992—. Fellow Royal Geog. Soc.; mem. Internat. Soc. for Subtle Energies and Energy Medicine (bd. dirs., editor Subtle Energies Jour.), Soc. for the Anthropology of Consciousness (past pres., founding mem.), Soc. for Hist. Archaeology, Calif.-Russia Trade Assn. (bd. dirs.), Explorer's club. N.Y. Home: 2243 Ronda Vista Dr Los Angeles CA 90027-4641 Office: Schwartz & Assocs 4470-107 Sunset Blvd Ste 339 Los Angeles CA 90027 other: Ste 339 4470-107 Sunset Blvd Los Angeles CA 90027

SCHWARTZ, SUSAN, property management professional. BBA in Real Estate, Nat. U., 1979, MS in Edn., 1982, MBA, 1984. Assoc. dean of students Nat. U., San Diego, 1980-86; pres. Am. Property Mgmt., San Diego, 1986—. Mem. CAI.

SCHWARTZMAN, ARNOLD MARTIN, film director, graphic designer; b. London, England, Jan. 6, 1936; came to U.S., 1978; s. David and Rose S.; m. Isolde, Oct. 17, 1980; 1 child, Hannah. Student, Canterbury Coll. Art, 1953, Nat. Diploma in Design, 1955. Sr. designer Associated Rediffusion TV, London, England, 1959-65; concept planning exec. Erwin-Wasey Advt., London, England, 1965-68; dir. Conran Design Group, London, England, 1968-69; prin. Designers Film Unit, London, England, 1969-78; film dir. The Directors Studio, London, England, 1969-78; design dir. Saul Bass and Assoc. Inc., L.A., 1978-79; pres. Arnold Schwartzman Prod., L.A., 1979—; dir. design Olympic Games, L.A., 1982-83. Author, photographer: Graven Images, 1993; author: Phono-Graphics, 1993; co-author: Airshipwreck, 1978. Recipient Oscar Acad. award, Acad. Motion Picture Arts and Scis., 1982, Silver award, Designers and Art Dirs. Assn. London, 1969, 71, 75. Mem. Acad. Motion Picture Arts and Scis. (documentary exec. com.), Alliance Graphique Internationale, Brit. Acad. Film and TV Arts (bd. dirs.), Am. Inst. Graphic Arts (mem. adv. bd.). Home: 317 1/2 N Sycamore Ave Los Angeles CA 90036-2689

SCHWARY, RICHARD JOSEPH, investment company executive; b. L.A., Dec. 7, 1944; s. Joseph Louis and Mary (Koury) S.; m. Rose Ann Martin, June 10, 1978; children: Kristen Rose, Brandon Richard. BS, Calif. State U., Long Beach, 1973. With. Hughes Aircraft, El Segundo, Calif., 1973-76; v.p. JCI Inc., Ingelwood, Calif., 1976-80; pres. Calif. Numis. Investments, Inc., Redondo Beach, Calif., 1980—; chmn. bd. Am. Numis. Exch., Newport Beach, Calif., 1988—; expert witness FTC, FBI, L.A., 1988—. Contbr. author United States Pattern: Experimental and Trial Pieces, 7th edit., 1982, A Guide Book of United States Coins, 44th edit. With USAF, 1965-69. Mem. Profl. Numismatists Guild. Republican. Roman Catholic. Office: Calif Numis Investments Inc 1712 S Pacific Coast Hwy Redondo Beach CA 90277-5902

SCHWARZ, GERARD RALPH, conductor, musician; b. Weehawken, N.J., Aug. 19, 1947; s. John and Gerta (Weiss) S.; B.S., MA, Juilliard Sch., 1972; D.M.A. (hon.), DFA (hon.). m. Jody Greitzer, June 23, 1984; children: Alysandra, Daniel, Gabriella, Julian. Trumpet player Am. Symphony Orch., 1965-72, Am. Brass Quintet, 1965-73, N.Y. Philharm., 1973-77; trumpet player, guest condr. Aspen Music Festival, 1969-75, bd. dirs., 1973-75; music dir. Erick Hawkins Dance Co., 1967-72, SoHo Ensemble, 1969-75, Eliot Feld Ballet Co.; music dir., condr. N.Y. Chamber Symphony, 1977—, Los Angeles Chamber Orch., 1978-86, White Mountains (N.H.) Music Festival, 1978-80, Music Today, 1981-89, Mostly Mozart Festival, Lincoln Ctr., 1982—; prin. condr. Waterloo Festival, 1975—, Music Sch. Princeton U.; music dir. Seattle Symphony, 1983—; mem. faculty Juilliard Sch., 1975-83, Mannes Coll. Music, 1973-79, Montclair State Coll., 1975-80; rec. artist Columbia, Nonesuch, Vox, MMO, Desto, Angel, Delos records; guest condr. various orchs. including Phila. Orch., L.A. Philharmonic, St. Louis, Buffalo, Detroit, San Francisco, Atlanta, Houston, Pitts., Minn., Jerusalem Symphony, Israel Chamber Orch., Moscow Philharmonic, Moscow Radio Orch., Orchestra National de France, London Symphony Orch., Frankfurt Radio, Stockholm Radio, Helsinki Philharm., Ensemble InterContemporain, Monte Carlo Philharm., Nat. Orch. Spain, English Chamber Orch., London Symphony, Scottish Chamber Orch., City of Birmingham Symphony, Orchestre National Paris, Nouvel Orchestre Philharmonique, Sydney Symphony, Melbourne Symphony, Orchestre National de Lyon, France, Orchestre Philharm. de Montpellier, Wash. Opera, Da Capo Chamber Players, 20th Century Chamber Orch., Montclair State Coll., Chamber Music Soc. Lincoln Ctr., Washington Opera, San Francisco Opera, Seattle Opera, Orchestre Nationale de France. Bd. dirs. Naumburg Found., 1975—. Recipient award for concert artists Ford Found., 1973, Ditson Condrs. award, 1989; Grammy award nominee. Office: NY Chamber Symphony 1395 Lexington Ave New York NY 10128

SCHWARZ, HENRY G., East Asian studies educator; b. Berlin, Dec. 14, 1928; came to U.S., 1929; s. Eugene Alfred and Gertrude Maria (Vogel) S.; widowed; 1 child, Kenji Eugene. BA, U. Wis., 1954, MA, 1958, PhD, 1962. Asst. prof. Marquette U., Milw., 1963-64, U. Wash., Seattle, 1965-69; vis. prof. U. Philippines, Manila, 1964-65, Asia U., Tokyo, 1980-81, 84-85; prof. East Asian studies Western Wash. U., Bellingham, 1969—. Editor: Ctr. for East Asian Studies, Western Wash. U., 1971—, Reminiscences, 1983, Chinese Medicine on the Golden Mountain, 1984, An Uyghur-English Dictionary, 1993; author: Leadership Patterns in China's Frontier Regions, 1964, China: Three Facets of a Giant, 1966, Mongolian Short Stories, 1974, Bibliotheca Mongolica, 1978, The Minorities of Northern China: A Survey, 1984, Mongolia and the Mongols, 1993; contbr. articles to profl. publs., chpts. to books. With U.S. Army, 1954-56. Office: Western Wash U Ctr for East Asian Studies Bellingham WA 98225-9056

SCHWARZ, JOSEPH RICHARD, engineering manager; b. Pomona, Calif., Dec. 7, 1954; s. Robert Joseph and Edith M. (Varian) S.; m. Pamela Anne Galligan, Apr. 8, 1978 (div. June 1983). BSEE magna cum laude, Calif. State Polytech. U., Pomona, 1977. Digital systems engr. Metron Corp., Upland, Calif., 1977-78; installation mgr. Hughes Aircraft, Denmark, Hawaii and Fed. Republic Germany, 1978-88; co-owner Penrose Gallery, Big Bear Lake, Calif., 1988-90; system engr. Gen. Dynamics, Pomona, Calif., 1989-91; ops. mgr. Amacron/Cycad Corp., Placentia, Calif., 1991—. Telephone counselor Garden Grove (Calif.) Community Ch., 1984-90. Mem. ACLU, L.A. Music Ctr., Sierra Club, Toastmasters, Eta Kappa Nu, Tau Beta Pi. Republican. Home: 611 Opal Ct Upland CA 91786-6525

SCHWARZ, MICHAEL, lawyer; b. Brookline, Mass., Oct. 19, 1952; s. Jules Lewis and Estelle (Kosberg) S. BA magna cum laude, U. No. Colo., 1975; postgrad. U. N.Mex., 1977, JD, 1980; Rsch. reader in Negligence Law, Oxford U., 1978; diploma in Legal Studies, Cambridge U., 1981. Bar: N.Mex. 1980, U.S. Dist. Ct. N.Mex. 1980, U.S. Ct. Appeals (10th, D.C., and Fed. cirs.) 1982, U.S. Ct. Internat. Trade, 1982, U.S. Tax Ct. 1982, U.S. Supreme Ct. 1983, N.Y. 1987. VISTA vol., Albuquerque, 1975-77; rsch. fellow N.Mex. Legal Support Project, Albuquerque, 1978-79; supr. law Cambridge (Eng.) U., 1980-81; law clk. to chief justice Supreme Ct. N.Mex., Santa Fe, 1981-82; pvt. practice law, Santa Fe, 1982—; spl. prosecutor City of Santa Fe, 1985; spl. asst. atty. gen., 1986-88; mem. editorial adv. com. Social Security Reporting Svc. Author: New Mexico Appellate Manual, 1990; contbr. articles to profl. jours. Vice dir. Colo. Pub. Interest Rsch. Group, 1974; scoutmaster Great S.W. Area coun. Boy Scouts Am., 1977-79; mem. N.Mex. Acupuncture Licensing Bd., 1983. Recipient Cert. of Appreciation Cambridge U., 1981, Nathan Burkan Meml. award, 1980, N.Mex. Supreme Ct. Cert. Recognition, 1992. Mem. ABA (litigation com. on profl. responsibility, litigation com. on pretrial practice and discovery), Assn. Trial Lawyers Am., State Bar N.Y., N.Mex. State Bar (bd. dirs. employment law sect. 1990-92, chair employment law sect. 1991-92), N.Y. Bar Assn., First Jud. Dist. Bar Assn. (treas. 1987-88, sec. 1988-89, v.p. 1989-1990, pres. 1990-91, local rules com. mem. 1989-92), N.Mex. Supreme Ct. (standing com. on profl. conduct 1990—), Sierra Club, Amnesty Internat. Home and Office: PO Box 1656 Santa Fe NM 87504-1656

SCHWARZBACK, CHARLES, III, medical educator, columnist; b. N.Y.C., Dec. 21, 1945; m. Mary Lee Peters; 2 children. AB, Kenyon Coll., 1967; EdM, Boston U., 1970; MS, Harvard U., 1971; PhD, U. Tex., 1976. Cert. child psychoanalysis. Staff psychologist Mass. Gen. Hosp., Boston, 1970-72; with med. sch. faculty George Washington U., Washington, 1979-82, Georgetown U., Washington, 1983-86; mem. faculty Washington (D.C.) Sch. Psychiatry, 1980-89; columnist Children Today, Washington, 1985—; mem. faculty med. sch. U. Wash., Seattle, 1989—, U. B.C., Vancouver, 1992—. Fellow NIMH, 1972-75, scientific fellow Tavisticle Ctr., London, 1976-79. Home: 1422 E Valley St Seattle WA 98112

SCHWARZER, WILLIAM W, federal judge; b. Berlin, Apr. 30, 1925; came to U.S., 1938, naturalized, 1944; s. John F. and Edith M. (Daniel) S.; m. Anne Halbersleben, Feb. 2, 1951; children: Jane Elizabeth, Andrew William. A.B. cum laude, U. So. Calif., 1948; LL.B. cum laude, Harvard U., 1951. Bar: Calif. 1953, U.S. Supreme Ct. 1967. Teaching fellow Harvard U. Law Sch., 1951-52; asso. firm McCutchen, Doyle, Brown & Enersen, San Francisco, 1952-60; ptnr. McCutchen, Doyle, Brown & Enersen, 1960-76; judge U.S. Dist. Ct (no. dist.) Calif., San Francisco, 1976—; dir. Fed. Jud. Ctr., Washington, 1990—; sr. counsel Pres.'s Commn. on CIA Activities Within the U.S., 1975; chmn. U.S. Jud. Conf. Com. Fed.-State Jurisdiction, 1987-90; mem. faculty Nat. Inst. Trial Advocacy, Fed. Jud. Ctr., Ali-ABA, U.S.-Can. Legal Exch., 1987, Salzburg Seminar on Am. Studies; adj. prof. Georgetown Law Ctr. Author: Managing Antitrust and Other Complex Litigation, 1982, Civil Discovery, 1988, Federal Civil Procedure Before Trial, 1989; contbr. articles to legal publs., aviation jours. Trustee World Affairs Coun. No. Calif., 1961-88; chmn. bd. trustees Marin Country Day Sch., 1963-66; chmn. Marin County Aviation Commn., 1969-76; mem. vis. com. Harvard Law Sch., 1981-86. Served with Intelligence, U.S. Army, 1943-46. Fellow Am. Coll. Trial Lawyers (S. Gates award 1992), Am. Bar Found.; mem. ABA, Am. Law Inst., San Francisco Bar Assn., State Bar Calif., Coun. Fgn. Rels. Office: Fed Jud Ctr 1 Columbus Circle NE Washington DC 20002

SCHWEIGERT, LYNETTE AILEEN, interior designer, consultant; b. Sacramento, July 6, 1949; d. Marvin Gerhardt and Aileen Helen (Velcoff) S.; m. Alan H. Randolph, May 1, 1976; 1 child, Tyler Mason Randolph. BS in Design, U. Calif., Davis, 1971. Display designer Weinstock's, Sacramento, 1971-72, Roos-Atkins, Sacramento, 1972-73; prin., project designer Randolph-Schweigert & Co., Reno, 1975—; prin. Design Ctr. Cons., Reno, 1982—, ptnr., project designer Hospitality Design Group, Reno, 1985—; cons. interior design Dan Carne AIA, Reno, 1980—, Paul Huss AIA, Reno, 1985—, U.S. West Investments, Reno, 1984—; cons. space planning Family Counseling Service of No. Nev., Reno, 1986—. Named one of Top 60 Restaurant Designers, Contract Mag., 1985; recipient Finalist prize Sierra Arts Found., Reno, 1980, Cert. Recognition for Participation in Preprofessional Internship Program U. Nev., 1987. Mem. Inst. Bus. Designers (affiliate).

SCHWEIKERT, DANIEL GEORGE, electrical engineer, administrator; b. Bemidji, Minn., June 15, 1937; s. George and Viola (Brecht) S.; m. Judith Butler Johnson, Aug. 12, 1961; children: Eric, Karl, Kristen. B of Engring., Yale U., 1959; PhD, Brown U., 1966. Group head Gen. Dynamics/Electric Boat, Groton, Conn., 1961-64; supr. Bell Telephone Labs., Murray Hill, N.J., 1966-80; dir. United Techs. Microelectronics Ctr., Colorado Springs, Colo., 1980-88, Cadence Design Systems, San Jose, Calif., 1988—; gen. chair Design Automation Conf., Anaheim, Calif., 1992, mem. exec. com., 1986—; speaker in field. Contbr. articles to profl. jours. Mem. Berkeley Heights (N.J.) Planning Bd., 1974-80. Fellow IEEE; mem. Assn. for Computing Machinery. Home: 1578 Eddington Pl San Jose CA 95129 Office: Cadence Design Systems 555 River Oaks Pkwy 4A2 San Jose CA 95134

SCHWEITZER, RAYMOND D., city manager, author; b. Dodge City, Kans., Jan. 16, 1936; s. Howard R. and Mary Mildred (Montgomery) S.; m. Jean Barker, May 30, 1966. AA, Dodge City Jr. Coll., 1961; AB in Polit. Sci., Ft. Hays (Kans.) State U., 1963; postgrad., Kans. U., 1964-66. Asst. city mgr. City of Oak Ridge, Tenn., 1965-68; city mgr. City of Alcoa, Tenn., 1968-71, City of Prescott, Ariz., 1971-72; adminstr. City of Morristown, Tenn., 1972-76; city mgr. City of North Las Vegas, Nev., 1976-82; dep./city adminstr. City of San Bernardino, Calif., 1982-88; freelance author, 1988-89; city mgr. City of Banning, Calif., 1989—. Author: (novel) The Elder's Avenger, 1989, Tattletale Heart, 1990, The Elder's Avenger Part II, 1991. Mem. Internat. City Mgrs. Assn., Banning C. of C. (bd. dirs. 1989-92), Kiwanis. Home: 1319 Fairway Oaks Ave Banning CA 92220-6417

SCHWENK, TODD WILLIAM, small business owner; b. Allentown, Pa., May 18, 1962; s. Galen John and Patricia Ann (Folk) S.; m. Stephanie Palajac, July 4, 1991. BA in Mass Communication, Calif. State U., Hayward, 1991. Co-founder, CEO Eye-On Alarm, San Leandro, Calif., 1986—; freelance journalist. Author, dir., prodr. live TV satire Crystal Mirage, 1984-87 (Best Live Prodn. award Nat. Fedn. Local Cable Programmers). Democrat. Office: Eye-On Alarm 2256 Placer Dr San Leandro CA 94578

SCHWICHTENBERG, DARYL ROBERT, drilling engineer; b. nr. Tulare, S.D., Nov. 8, 1929; s. Robert Carl and Lillian Rose (Hardie) S.; m. Helen M. Spencer, 1955 (div. Jan. 1971); children: Helayne, Randall, Hyalyn, Halcyon, Rustan; m. Helen Elizabeth Doehring, Nov. 11, 1971 (div. May 1982); 1 child, Suzanne. Student, U. Wyo., 1954-55; BSME, S.D. Sch. Mines and Tech., 1957; postgrad., Alexander Hamilton Inst., N.Y.C., 1962-63. Lic. pilot, rated AMEL. Office engr. Ingersoll-Rand Co., Mpls., 1957-58; sub br. mgr. Ingersoll-Rand Co., Duluth, Minn., 1959-60; product engr. Ingersoll-Rand Co., N.Y.C., 1960-63, devel. engr., 1964; sales mgr. Ingersoll-Rand Co., Phillipsburg, N.J., 1965; pres., founder Daryl Drilling Co., Inc., Flagstaff, Ariz., 1965-82; pres. Silent Rose Mining Co., Fallon, Nev., 1982-85; sr. design engr. Nev. Test Site Fenix & Scisson, 1985-90; sr. project engr. Raytheon Svcs. Nev., Nevada Test Site, 1990—; co-owner, mgr. Dead Shot Ranch, Bondurant, Wyo., 1977-82. Inventor electronic subtitling for opera patrons. 1st lt. U.S. Army, 1950-54, Korea. Decorated Bronze Star. Mem. ASME, NRA, Inst. Shaft Drilling Tech. (speaker, instr. 1986—), Mensa. Republican. Office: Raytheon Svcs Nev PO Box 328 Mercury NV 89023-0328

SCHWIESOW, RONALD LEE, research engineer; b. Pitts., May 22, 1940; s. Philip Heinrich and Esther Emma (Zeckser) S.; m. Nancy Claire Olson, Dec. 29, 1962; children—Erich John, Paul Albert, Sara Lynn. B.S. with distinction, Purdue U., 1962; Ph.D., Johns Hopkins U., 1968; M.S., Pa. State U., 1975. Cert. cons. meteorologist. Farmer, Johnson County, Kans., 1954-58; chem. engr. E. I. DuPont, Buffalo, 1962; instr. physics Johns Hopkins U., Balt., 1962-67; physicist NOAA, Boulder, Colo., 1968-84; research engr. Nat. Ctr. Atmospheric Research, Boulder, 1984—. guest scientist Risø Nat. Lab., Roskilde, Denmark, 1978-79; vis. scientist DFVLR, Oberpfaffenhofen, W. Ger., 1982-83. Contbr. articles to profl. publs.; patentee in field. Recipient Spl. Achievement award ERL/NOAA, 1975, Sustained Superior Performance award, 1984; ESSA postdoctoral fellow, NRC, 1968-70; Gilman fellow, 1962-67. Mem. Optical Soc. Am., Am. Meteorol. Soc., U.S. Power Squadrons, Am. Scientific Affiliation, Sigma Xi. Lutheran. Home: 1440 Elder Ave Boulder CO 80304-2628 Office: NCAR PO Box 3000 Boulder CO 80307-3000

SCHWINDEN, TED, former governor of Montana; b. Wolf Point, Mont., Aug. 31, 1925; s. Michael James and Mary (Preble) S.; m. B. Jean Christianson, Dec. 21, 1946; children: Mike, Chrys, Dore. Student, Mont. Sch. Mines, 1946-47; B.A., U. Mont., 1949, M.A., 1950; postgrad., U. Minn., 1950-54. Owner grain farm Roosevelt County, Mont., 1954—; land commr. State of Mont., 1969-76, lt. gov., 1977-80, gov., 1981-89; disting. prof. pub. affairs, 1989—; mem. U.S. Wheat Trade Mission to Asia, 1968. Chmn. Mont. Bicentennial Adv. Council, 1973-76; mem. Mont. Ho. of Reps., 1959, 61, Legis. Council, 1959-61, Wolf Point Sch. Bd., 1966-69, Pub. Employees Retirement System Bd., 1969-74. Served with inf. AUS, 1943-46. Decorated Combat Inf. badge. Mem. Mont. Grain Growers (pres. 1965-67), Western Wheat Assos. (dir.). Democrat. Lutheran. Clubs: Masons, Elks. Home: 1335 Highland St Helena MT 59601-5242

SCHWINGER, JULIAN, physicist, educator; b. N.Y.C., Feb. 12, 1918; s. Benjamin and Belle (Rosenfeld) S.; m. Clarice Carrol, 1947. A.B., Columbia U., 1936, Ph.D., 1939, D.Sc., 1966; D.Sc. (hon.), Purdue U., 1961, Harvard U., 1962, Brandeis U., 1973, Gustavus Adolphus Coll., 1975; LL.D., CCNY, 1972; D Honoris Causa, U. Paris, 1990. NRC fellow, 1939-40; research assoc. U. Calif.-Berkeley, 1940-41; instr., then asst. prof. Purdue U., 1941-43; staff mem. Radiation Lab., MIT, 1943-46; staff Metall. Lab., U. Chgo., 1943; asso. prof. Harvard U., 1945-47, prof., 1947-72, Higgins prof. physics, 1966-72; prof. physics UCLA, 1972-80, Univ. prof., 1980—; mem. bd. sponsors Bull. Atomic Sci.; sponsor Fedn. Am. Scientists; J.W. Gibbs hon. lectr. Am. Math. Soc., 1960. Author: Particles and Sources, 1969, (with D. Saxon) Discontinuities in Wave Guides, 1968, Particles, Sources and Fields, 1970, Vol. II, 1973, Vol. III, 1989, Quantum Kinematics and Dynamics, 1970, Einstein's Legacy, 1985; editor: Quantum Electrodynamics, 1958. Recipient C. L. Mayer nature of light award, 1949, univ. medal Columbia U., 1951, 1st Einstein prize award, 1951; Nat. Medal of Sci. award for physics, 1964; co-recipient Nobel prize in Physics, 1965; recipient Humboldt award, 1981, Monie A. Fest Sigma Xi award, 1986, Castiglione di Sicilia award, 1986, Am. Acad. of Achievement award, 1987; Guggenheim fellow, 1970. Mem. AAAS, ACLU, Nat. Acad. Scis., Am. Acad. Arts and Scis., N.Y. Acad. Scis. Office: U Calif Dept Physics 405 Higard Ave Los Angeles CA 90024*

SCHWORTZ, BARRIE MARSHALL, video/film producer; b. Pitts., Sept. 12, 1946; s. Nathan Schwortz and FLorence T. (Rosenfeld) Black; m. Erin J.

Gallant, Sept. 11, 1971 (div.); 1 child, David Henry. BA, Brooks Inst., Santa Barbara, 1971. Owner Barrie Schwortz Studios, Santa Barbara, 1971-85; pres., founder Ednl. Video, Inc., Santa Barbara, 1978-88; owner Barrie Schwortz Prodns., L.A., 1985—; imaging cons. Cedars-Sinai Med. Ctr., L.A., 1990—; documenting photographer Shroud of Turin Rsch. Project, 1978-88; faculty mem. Brooks Inst. Photography, Santa Barbara, 1975-85. Producer: (videotape program) Shroud of Turin Symposium, 1984; writer, producer: (videotape program) The Complete Birth, 1985, New Tools For an Ageold Task, 1989. With USN, 1965-69. Recipient Merit awards Art Direction Mag., 1979, 81, 84, San Francisco Art Dirs., 1984, 87, N.Y. Art Dirs. Club, 1982, 87, 88. Mem. Santa Barbara Video Assn. (pres., founder 1984). Jewish. Home and Office: Barrie Schwortz Prodns 3003 Glendale Blvd Los Angeles CA 90039

SCHWYN, CHARLES EDWARD, accountant; b. Muncie, Ind., Oct. 12, 1932; s. John and Lela Mae (Oliver) S.; m. Mary Helen Nickey, May 25, 1952; children: Douglas, Craig, Beth. BS, Ball State U., 1957. CPA, Calif., D.C. With Haskins, Sells & Orlando, Chgo., Orlando, Fla., 1958-67; mgr. Deloitte, Haskins & Sells, Milan, Italy, 1967-70, San Francisco, 1970-80; with Deloitte, Haskins & Sells (now Deloitte & Touche), Oakland, Calif., 1972-80, ptnr. in charge, 1980-92, ret., 1992; bd. dirs. Summit Med. Ctr. (formerly Merritt Peralta Med. Ctr.). Bd. dirs. Jr. Ctr. of Art and Sci., 1982-89, pres., 1987-88; bd. dirs., trustees Oakland Symphony, 1982-86, 89-91; bd. dirs. Oakland Met. YMCA, 1984-89, Oakland Police Activities League, 1981-91, Joe Morgan Youth Found., 1982-91, Marcus A. Foster Ednl. Inst., 1986—, pres., 1991-93; mem. adv. bd. Festival of the Lake, 1984-89; mem. adv. bd. U. Oakland Met. Forum, 1992—, co-chmn. Commn. for Positive Change in Oakland Pub. Schs.; mem. campaign cabinet United Way of Bay Area, 1989. With USN, 1952-56. Recipient Cert. Recognition Calif. Legis. Assembly, 1988, Ctr. for Ind. Living award, Oakland Bus. Arts award for outstanding bus. leader Oakland C. of C., 1992; date of job retirement honored in his name by Oakland mayor. Mem. AICPA (coun. 1987-90), Oakland C. of C. (chmn. bd. dirs. 1987-88, exec. com. 1982-89), Calif. Soc. CPAs (bd. dirs. 1979-81, 83-84, 85-87, pres. San Francisco chpt. 1983-84), Nat. Assn. Accts. (pres. Fla. chpt. 1967), Round Hill Golf and Country Club, Claremont Country Club (treas., bd. dirs. 1989—), Lakeview Club (bd. govs. 1987-92), Rotary (bd. dirs. Oakland club 1986-88, 91-92, treas. 1984-86, pres. 1991-92). Office: Deloitte & Touche 2101 Webster St 20th Fl Oakland CA 94612

SCIAME, DONALD RICHARD, computer systems analyst, dentist, magician, locksmith; b. Bklyn., Sept. 10, 1945; s. Mario and Ruth Marie (Kozell) S.; m. Kathy Ann Thamann, Mar. 17, 1987. AB, Rutgers U., 1967; DMD, N.J. Coll. Medicine & Dentistry, 1971; MAPA, U. N.Mex., 1984; cert. locksmith, electronic security, NRI Schs., 1988. Dep. chief svc. unit dental program USPHS Indian Hosp., Whiteriver, Ariz., 1971-73; chief svc. unit dental program USPHS Indian Hosp., Sacaton, Ariz., 1973-76, Santa Fe, 1976-88; systems analyst USPHS Area Office, Albuquerque, 1988-90; dir. div. info. mgmt. svcs. USPHS-IHS Area Office, Albuquerque, 1990—. Contbr. articles to profl. jours. Mem. IHS Dental Profl. Specialty Group, IHS Dental Computer Users Group, ADA, Internat. Coll. Dentists, Psi Omega Dental Fraternity, N.J. Dental Sch. Alumni Assn., USPHS Commn. Officers Assn., Albuquerque Area Dental Soc. Indian Health Svcs., Mumps User's Group, Soc. Am. Magicians. Home: 1914 Conejo Dr Santa Fe NM 87501-4917 Office: IHS Area Office 505 Marquette Ave NW Ste 1506 Albuquerque NM 87102-2163

SCIAMMAS, JACQUES DANIEL, financial services executive, controller; b. Cairo, Jan. 9, 1956; came to U.S., 1968; s. Ben and Jenny (Massuda) Shammas. BA, Bowdoin Coll., 1975; MBA, Rutgers U., 1979. Fin. analyst TransWorld Airlines, Inc., N.Y.C., 1979-81, sr. fin. analyst, 1981-82, mgr., 1982-84, dir., 1985-86; group contr. McGraw-Hill, Inc., N.Y.C., 1987-88, contr., 1988-91; dir. fin. planning and analysis Charles Schwab & Co. Inc., San Francisco, 1991—. Treas. Fin. Exec. Inst., San Francisco. Recipient Book prize Harvard U., 1970, Man of Future citation Mayor Kevin White, Boston, 1970, full academic scholarship Bowdoin Coll., 1971-75. Mem. Rutgers U. Alumni Assn. (chmn. class of 1970s). Home: 2 Fallon Pl Apt 31 San Francisco CA 94133-3626 Office: Charles Schwab & Co Inc 101 Montgomery St San Francisco CA 94104-4122

SCIOLARO, CHARLES MICHAEL, cardiac surgeon; b. Kansas City, Kans., July 5, 1958; s. Gerald Michael and Charleen Gwen (Walter) S.; m. Vicki Lynn Mizell, Sept. 29, 1984; children: Rachel Diane, Lynsey Michelle, Ryan Michael. BA, Mid Am. Nazarene Coll., 1980; MD, U. Kans., Kansas City, 1984. Resident in surgery U. Ariz., Tucson, 1984-90; cardiothoracic fellow Loma Linda U. Med. Ctr., 1990—; emergency rm. physician, cons. Nat. Emergency Corp., Tucson, 1986—. Author: (manuscripts) Aortic Coarctation in Infants, 1991. Cardiothoracic Rsch. fellow U. Ariz., Tucson, 1986. Republican. Home: 5135 Windermere Blvd Alexandria LA 71303 Office: Mac Arthur Surgical Clinic Doctors Bldg Ste 200 3311 Prescott Rd Alexandria LA 71301

SCIUTTO, JOSEPH A., dentist; b. Salinas, Calif., Oct. 19, 1906; s. Charles and Louise (Moiso) S.; M. Dorothy Louise Gale, June 30, 1934; children: Robert James, Barbara Blunden. DDS, U. Calif. Med. Ctr., 1928. Dental surgeon Cowell Meml. Hosp. U. Calif., Berkeley, 1928-37; gen. practice Berkeley, 1928-83; clin. instr. U. Calif. Med. Ctr., San Francisco, 1958-75; lectr. continuing dental edn. U. Calif. Sch. of Dentistry, San Francisco, 1955, mem. prosthetic clin. and investigative group, 1970; chmn. 5th Internat. Dental Seminars, Tokyo, Kyoto, Bangkok, Bogota, Lima, Santiago, Buenos Aires, Rio de Janeiro, 14th World Dental Congress, Paris. Named Disting. Alumnus, U. Calif., 1991. Fellow Am. Coll. Dentists, Internat. Coll. Dentists; mem. ADA, Berkeley Dental Soc. (pres.), Calif. Dental Assn. (gen. chmn., ann. meeting), Pacific Dental Conf. (v.p.), U. Calif. San Francisco Dental Alumni Assn. (pres.), Fedn. Dentaire Internat., Am. Prosthodontic Soc., Internat. Prosthodontic Conf., U. Calif. Alumni Assn. (life mem.), Rotary (pres., Paul Harris fellow), Claremont Country Club, Xi Psi Phi. Home: 1860 Tice Creek Blvd # 1433 Walnut Creek CA 94595

SCLAROW, MARSHALL HILLEL, lawyer; b. Duluth, Minn., Mar. 15, 1930; s. Abe M. and Bessie (Levine) S.; m. Dov Baer, Dec. 27, 1959; children: Halden L., Kendra Moshe. Student, Iowa State U., 1948-50; BA, U. Iowa, 1953, JD, 1955. Bar: Colo. 1955. Pvt. practice Denver, 1957; ins. agt. various ins. cos., Boulder, Colo., 1957-73; pvt. practice Boulder, 1973-86, 87-89; prin. Denver, 1989—; owner, with Joy and Ease unlimited. Pres. Har Ha Shem Congregation, Boulder, 1971-72, 83, Boulder County Estate Planning Coun., 1983. Lt. col. USAF, 1955-57, USAFR, 1957-78. Home: 3540 S Pearl St # 208 Englewood CO 80110-3872

SCOFIELD, DAVID WILLSON, lawyer; b. Hartford, Conn., Oct. 17, 1957; s. Leslie Willson and Daphne Winifred (York) S. AB, Cornell U., 1979; JD, U. Utah, 1983. Bar: Utah 1983, U.S. Dist. Ct. Utah 1983, U.S. Ct. Appeals (10th cir.) 1990. Assoc. Parsons & Crowther, Salt Lake City, 1983-87; assoc. Callister, Duncan & Nebeker, Salt Lake City, 1987-89, ptnr., 1989-92; one of founding ptnrs. Parsons, Davies, Kinghorn & Peters, Salt Lake City, 1992—. Author: Trial Handbook for Utah Lawyers, 1993; mem. Utah Law Rev., 1981-83; contbr. articles to legal jours. Named to Outstanding Young Men of Am., 1986. Mem. ABA, Assn. Trial Lawyers Am., Utah Trial Lawyers Assn., Salt Lake County Bar Assn., Zeta Psi. Congregationalist. Home: 4427 S 3065 E Salt Lake City UT 84124-3785 Office: Parsons, Davies, Kinghorn & Peters Ste 1100 310 S Main St Salt Lake City UT 84101

SCOFIELD, LARRY ALLAN, civil engineer; b. Niskyuna, N.Y., Mar. 23, 1952; s. Jack Dewayne and Edythe Mae (Van Wie) S.; m. Apr. 3, 1981 (div. Aug. 1982). BSE, Ariz. State U., 1975, MSE. Registered profl. engr., Ariz. Engr.-in-tng. Ariz. Dept. of Transp., Phoenix, 1976-78, constrn. project engr., 1978-80, pavement design engr., 1980-81, resident engr., 1981-82, geologic and found. invest. engr., 1982-84, transp. engr. supr., 1984-90, mgr. transp. rsch., 1990—; mem. panel Nat. Coop. Hwy. Rsch. Program, Washington, 1986—; mem. Transp. Rsch. Bd. Com., Washington, 1990—; mem. expert task group Strategic Hwy. Rsch. Program, Washington, 1989—; mem. adv. panel Fed. Hwy. Adminstrn., Washington, 1986—. Contbr. articles to profl. jours. Mem. ASCE, ASTM, Asphalt Paving Technologists. Republican. Baptist. Home: 807 W Keating Ave Mesa AZ 85210-7611

SCOLLARD, JEANNETTE REDDISH, entrepreneur, lecturer, author; b. Nashville; d. Andrew Johnson and Ruby Jewel (Wheeler) Mabry; m. Garrett F. Scollard, July 4, 1979 (div. 1988). BA, Vanderbilt U., 1966. Editor Wall Street Transcript, N.Y.C., 1971-73; sr. editor Fin. World mag., N.Y.C., 1973-78; v.p. Chesebrough-Pond's, Greenwich, Conn., 1978-79; fin. cons. MMT Sales, N.Y.C., 1979-82, vice chmn., 1983-88; chmn. SCS Comm., N.Y.C., 1986-89, Costa Resort Properties, Carlsbad, Calif., 1989—, SCS Mktg., Carlsbad, 1989—; Fin.Vid.Proj., 1992—; advisor Entrepreneurial Ctr., Manhattenville Coll., Purchase, N.Y.; columnist Entrepreneur Mag. Author: No Nonsense Management Tips, 1984, The Self-Employed Woman, 1986, Risk to Win, 1989. Bd. dirs. Milestone House, 1992—; trustee Internat. Radio and TV Found., 1988-91; trustee Am. Women in Radio and TV Found., 1986-91, fundraising chair, 1990—; mem. adv. coun. Entrepreneurial Ctr., Manhattanville, N.Y., 1988-92; mem. adv. com. Mentor program SBA, 1990—; advocate San Diego SBA, 1992. Woodrow Wilson Found. teaching fellow. Mem. N.Y. Fin. Writers (trustee 1978-79), Com. of 200, San Diego Backgammon Club, San Diego Women in Bus. Home: 28 Castillos del Mar, Rosarito Beach, Baja California Norte Mexico Office: SCS Mktg 2070 Caleta Ct Carlsbad CA 92009-6117

SCORA, RAINER WALTER, botanist; b. Mokre, Silesia, Poland, Dec. 5, 1928; came to U.S., 1951; s. Paul Wendelin and Helene (Nester) S.; m. Christa Maria Fiala, June 24, 1971; children: George Alexander, Katharina Monarda, Peter Evan. BS, DePaul U., 1955; MS, U. Mich., 1958, PhD, 1964. From asst. prof. to prof. botany U. Calif., Riverside, 1964—. Author over 100 sci. pubs. With U.S. Army, 2d Div., Signal Corps, 1955-57. Alfred P. Sloan fellow, 1959; recipient Cooley award Am. Inst. Biological Scis., 1968. Mem. Am. Inst. Biol. Scis., Botanical Soc. Am., Phytochem. Soc. N.Am., Internat. Assn. Plant Taxonomists, Internat. Orgn. Plant Biosystematists, Gamma Sigma Delta, Sigma Xi. Republican. Roman Catholic. Office: Univ Calif Dept Botany & Plant Scis Riverside CA 92521

SCORSINE, JOHN MAGNUS, lawyer; b. Rochester, N.Y., Dec. 3, 1957; s. Frank and Karin (Frennby) S.; m. Susan Nauss, May 31, 1980 (div.); m. Theresa A. Burke, Dec. 17, 1988; 1 child, Jennifer E. BS, Rochester Inst. Tech., 1980; JD, U. Wyo., 1984. Bar: Wyo. 1984, U.S. Dist. Ct. Wyo. 1984, U.S. Ct. Appeals (10th cir.) 1989. Part-time deputy sheriff Monroe County (N.Y.), 1978-80; police officer Casper (Wyo.) Police Dept., 1980-81; intern U.S. Atty. Office, Cheyenne, Wyo., 1983-84; sole practice Rock Springs, Wyo., 1984-85; ptnr. Scorsine and Flynn, Rock Springs, 1986; owner Scorsine Law Office, Rock Springs, 1986—; ptnr. Sunset Advt., 1987-89; chmn. bd. dirs. Youth Home Inc., Rock Springs, 1987-88; treas. Sweetwater County Community Corrections Bd., 1990—; mem. Nat. Ski Patrol, 1976—. Leader Medicine Bow Ski Patrol, Laramie, Wyo., 1983; legal advisor Rocky Mountain div. Nat. Ski Patrol, 1984; asst. patrol leader White Pine Ski Area, Pinedale, Wyo., 1986; avalanche advisor Jackson Hole Snow King Ski Patrol, 1987—; sect. chief Teton sect. Nat. Ski Patrol, 1991—; mem. Sweetwater County Search and Rescue, 1989—; mem. Sweetwater County Emergency Dive Team, 1990—, mem. Sweetwater County Fire Dept., 1992-93; mem. Am. N. Peary Land Expdn., 1989; scoutmaster Boy Scouts Am., 1987-93; pres. Sweetwater County Vol. Fire Assn., 1993—. 1st lt. JAG, USAR, 1991—. Mem. Wyo. State Bar, ABA, Wyo. Trial Lawyers Assn., Assn. Am. Trial Lawyers, Res. Officers Assn. (1st v.p., nat. del. Wyo. 1993—), Rock Springs C. of C. Democrat. Lutheran. Lodge: Rotary. Home: 519 Wasatch Cir Rock Springs WY 82901-4586 Office: Scorsine Law Office 1400 Dewar Dr Rock Springs WY 82901-5813

SCOTT, CHARLES KENNARD, state senator, cattle rancher; b. Oreg., Aug. 19, 1945; s. Oliver Kennard and Deborah Ann (Hubbard) S.; m. Elaine Fenton, Dec. 20, 1975; children—Daniel, Abigail. A.B., Harvard Coll., 1967; M.B.A., Harvard U., 1969. Analyst, HEW and EPA, 1969-74; v.p., mgr. Bates Creek Cattle Co., Casper, Wyo., 1974—; mem. Wyo. Ho. of Reps., 1979-82; mem. Wyo. Senate, 1982—; v.p. Senate, chmn. Labor, Health and Social Svc. Com.

SCOTT, DAVID BYTOVETZSKI, dental research and forensic odontology consultant; b. Providence, May 8, 1919; 4 children. A.B., Brown U., 1939; D.D.S., U. Md., 1943; M.S., U. Rochester, 1944; Sc.D. (hon.), Med. and Dental Coll. N.J., 1979, U. Louis Pasteur, Strasbourg, France, 1981. Commd. officer, advanced through grades to asst. surgeon gen. USPHS, 1944-65, 75-81; Staff Nat. Inst. Dental Research, NIH, Bethesda, Md., 1944-56; chief lab. histology and pathology Nat. Inst. Dental Research, NIH, 1956-65, dir. inst., 1976-82; now pvt. cons. dental research and forensic odontology; faculty Case Western Res. U., Cleve., 1965-76; Thomas J. Hill Distinguished prof. phys. biology Sch. Dentistry, prof. anatomy Sch. Medicine Case Western Res. U., 1965-76, dean Sch. Dentistry, 1969-76. Recipient Arthur S. Flemming award, 1955; award for Rsch. in Mineralization Internat. Assn. Dental Rsch., 1968; Rsch. Achievement award Mass. Dental Soc., 1978; Fred Birnberg Dental Rsch. medal Columbia U., 1978; Callahan Meml. award Ohio Dental Assn., 1985; named to Hall of Fame Sch. Dentistry U. Md., 1990; decorated Order Rising Sun Japanese Govt., 1983. Mem. ADA, Am. Acad. Forensic Sci. (forensic odontology award 1981), Electron Micros. Soc. Am., Internat., Am. colls. dentists, Internat. Assn. Dental Research, Royal Soc. Medicine (hon.), Am. Bd. Forensic Odontology (cert.). Office: 10448 Wheatridge Dr Sun City AZ 85373-1906

SCOTT, DAVID IRVIN, resident manager; b. Yakima, Wash., Dec. 5, 1947; s. Jack Phillip and Betty Lucille (Paronto) S.; m. Jill Louise Baker, June 23, 1982 (div. May 1991). AA, Monterey Peninsula Coll., Calif., 1975. Accredited resident mgr., Inst. Real Estate Mgmt., 1987. Courier Gallery Hawaii, Inc., Honolulu, 1981; acting resident mgr. Fairway Gardens, Honolulu, 1981; resident mgr. Waimalu Park, Honolulu, 1981-83, Waikiki Skyliner, Honolulu, 1983-84, Bishop Gardens, Honolulu, 1985-86, Plaza Landmark, Honolulu, 1986-88, Westlake Apts., Honolulu, 1988, Fairway Gardens, Honolulu, 1988—; condo mgmt. cons. Mem. Honolulu Bd. Realtors, Inst. Real Estate Mgmt., Alpha Gamma Sigma. Libertarian. Office: Choices USA 1290D Maunakea St # 201 Honolulu HI 96817-4120

SCOTT, DONALD MICHAEL, educational association administrator, educator; b. Los Angeles, Sept. 26, 1943; s. Bernard Hendry and Barbara (Lannin) S.; m. Patricia Ilene Pancoast, Oct. 24, 1964 (div. June 1971); children: William Bernard, Kenneth George. BA, San Francisco State U., 1965, MA, 1986. Cert. tchr. Calif. Tchr. Mercy High Sch., San Francisco, 1968-71; park ranger Calif. State Park System, Half Moon Bay, 1968-77; tchr. adult div. Jefferson Union High Sch. Dist., Daly City, Calif., 1973-87; dir. NASA-NPS Project Wider Focus, Daly City, 1983-90; dir. Geo. S. Spl. Projects Wider Focus, San Francisco, 1990—; also bd. dirs. Wider Focus, Daly City; nat. park ranger/naturalist Grant-Kohrs Ranch Nat. Hist. Site, Deer Lodge, Mont., 1987-88; nat. park ranger pub. affairs fire team Yellowstone Nat. Park, 1988; nat. park ranger Golden Gate Recreation Area, 1988-92; research subject NASA, Mountain View, Calif., 1986, 90; guest artist Yosemite (Calif.) Nat. Park, 1986; nat. park ranger Golden Gate Nat. Recreation Area, Nat. Park Svc., San Francisco, 1986, nat. park svc. history cons. to Bay Dist., 1988—; adj. asst. prof. Skyline Coll., 1989—, Coll. San Mateo, 1992—. Contbr. articles, photographs to profl. jours., mags. Pres. Youth for Kennedy, Lafayette, Calif., 1960; panelist Community Bds. of San Francisco, 1978-87; city chair Yes on A Com., So. San Francisco, San Mateo County, Calif., 1986; active CONTACT Orgn. ednl. com., 1991—, Libr. Co. of Phila. Mem. Yosemite Assn. (life), Smithsonian Air & Space, Wider Focus. Democrat. Home: care 95 Paul Ave Brisbane CA 94005 Office: Wider Focus PO Box 280456 San Francisco CA 94128-0456

SCOTT, DONALD WALTER, labor relations consultant; b. St. Paul, Mar. 15, 1945; s. Albert Lee and Gladys May (Moreside) S.; m. Sally Ann Landt, Dec. 26, 1971 (div. Mar. 1988); children: Brian Patrick, Tasha Ann. BS in Psychology, Oreg. State U., 1968. Capt. U.S. Army, Ft. Lewis, Wash., 1968-71; labor rels. asst. King County, Seattle, 1971-74; sr. cons. Local Govt. Personnel Inst., Salem, Oreg., 1974-79; labor rels. cons. Scott & Assocs., Salem, Oreg., 1979—. Contbg. author: New Dimesnions in Dispute Resolution, 1976. Budget com. City of Salem, 1991—. Mem. Soc. Bargainers. Republican. Home and Office: Scott & Assocs 2565 Myrtle Ave NE Salem OR 97303

SCOTT, FREDDIE, JR., career officer; b. Rock Island, Ill., Jan. 1, 1955; s. Freddie Sr. and Mertha Mae (Colvin) S.; m. Peggy Lorraine Jackson, June 5, 1974; children: Geoffrey Neal, Shannon Danae, Kevin Cordell, Michael Tyler. BS, U. Md., 1987; MBA cum laude, Okla. City Univ., 1988. Enlised U.S. Army, 1979, advanced through grades to sgt., 1981, advanced through grades to staff sgt., 1991; coord. day camp Martin Luther King Ctr., Rock Island, 1977-79; pharmacy specialist U.S. Army, Ft. Wainwright, Alaska, 1988—; adj. prof. Wayland Bapt. U., Fort Wainwright, 1989—, U. Alaska, Fairbanks, 1993—. Republican. Home: 1203 Bainbridge Blvd Fairbanks AK 99701-2731 Office: US Army-Alaska care Pharmacy Svc Fort Wainwright AK 99703

SCOTT, GORDON LEE, finance executive; b. Holyoke, Colo., Nov. 13, 1948; s. George B. and Vivian Lois (Glover) S.; m. Patricia Lee Zettle, June 15, 1974. AA in Physics, Northeastern Jr. Coll., 1968; BS in Math. with high honors, Colo. State U., 1970, MS in Math., 1973. CLU, ChFC. Various actuarial positions Western Farm Bur. Life Ins. Co., Denver, 1974-83, asst. v.p., 1985-90; cons. actuary Lewis & Ellis Cons. Actuaries, Overland Park, Kans., 1983-85; sr. v.p. fin., treas. Western Farm Bur. Mgmt. Co., Denver, 1990—. Fellow Soc. of Actuaries, Casualty Actuarial Soc., Life Office Mgmt. Assn.; mem. Am. Acad. Actuaries, Mensa, Phi Kappa Phi, Phi Theta Kappa, Kappa Mu Epsilon. Office: Western Farm Bur Mgmt Co 1200 Lincoln St Denver CO 80203-2121

SCOTT, GREGORY KELLAM, judge; b. San Francisco, July 30, 1943; s. Robert and Althea Delores Scott; m. Carolyn Weatherly, Apr. 10, 1971; children: Joshua Weatherly, Elijah Kellam. BS in Environ. Sci., Rutgers U., 1970, EdM in Urban Studies, 1971; JD cum laude, Ind. U., Indpls., 1977. Asst. dean resident instrn. Cook Coll. Rutgers U., 1972-75; trail atty. U.S. SEC, Denver, 1977-79; gen. counsel Blinder, Robinson & Co., Inc., Denver, 1979-80; asst. prof. coll. law U. Denver, 1980-85, assoc. prof., 1985-93, assoc. prof. emeritus, 1993—, chair bus. planning program, 1986-89, 92-93; justice Colo. Supreme Ct., Denver, 1993—; of counsel Smith & Radford, Indpls., 1987-92; v.p., gen. counsel Comml. Energies, Inc., 1990-91; presenter in field. Author: (with others) Structuring Mergers and Acquisitions in Colorado, 1985, Airport Law and Regulation, 1991, Racism and Underclass in America, 1991; contbr. articles to profl. jours. Mem. ABA, Nat. Bar Assn., Nat. Assn. Securities Dealers, Inc., Nat. Arbitration Panel (arbitrator), Colo. Bar Found., Sam Cary Bar Assn., Am. Inn Ct. (founding mem. Judge Alfred A. Arraj inn).

SCOTT, J. BRIAN, sales executive; b. Chgo., Dec. 12, 1963; s. Joe and Marilyn (Fant) S.; m. Sandra L. McGinnis, Sept. 5, 1987. BS in Engring., U. Ill., 1985; MBA, City U., Bellevue, Wash., 1993. Applications engr. Grasso, Inc., Evansville, Ind., 1985; sales rep. Grasso, Inc., Grand Rapids, Mich., 1985; applications engr. FMC Corp., Hoopeston, Ill., 1987-89; dist. sales mgr. FMC Corp., Columbus, Wis., 1989-90; area sales mgr. FMC Corp., Vancouver, Wash., 1990-93. Mem. Midwest Food Processors, Assn. Allied Industries (exec. treas. 1990), N.W. Food Processors Assn.

SCOTT, JAMES WILLIAM, educator; b. Liverpool, Lancashire, Eng., Sept. 30, 1925; s. James Arthur and Edith (Hall) S.; m. Barta Sibrechta Devrij, Apr. 30, 1955; 1 child, Antoinetta Edith. BA with honors, Cambridge U., Eng., 1949; MA, Cambridge U., 1952; PhD, Ind. U., 1971. Sch. tchr. Eng., Can., and Argentina, 1950-63; asst. prof. Western Washington U., Bellingham, 1966-71, assoc. prof., 1971-82, prof., 1982—; dir. Ctr. Pacific Northwest studies Western Wash. U., 1971—. Author: Social Science Research Handbook, 1974, Historical Atlas of Washington, 1987, Washington: A Centennial Atlas, 1990; contbr. articles and revs. Mem. Wash. State Hist. Record Bd., 1977—. Mem. Pacific Coast Geographers (pres. 1991-92, editor yearbood 1979-87). Democrat. Home: 1812 24th St Bellingham WA 98225 Office: Western Wash U Bellingham WA 98225

SCOTT, JOHN CARLYLE, gynecologist, oncologist; b. Mpls., Sept. 24, 1933; s. Horace Golden and Grace (Melges) S.; m. Beth Krause, 1958 (div. 1977); m. Paola Maria Martini, Feb. 8, 1986; children: Jeff, David, Suzanne, Danielle. AB, Princeton U., 1956; BS, MD, U. Minn., 1961. Intern Sch. Medicine Marquette U., Milw., 1961-62, resident Sch. Medicine, 1962-66; resident Harvard Med. Sch., Boston, 1965; Am. Cancer fellow Marquette Med. Sch., Milw., 1966-67, instr. ob-gyn., 1966-67; clin. instr. ob-gyn. U. Wash. Med. Sch., Seattle, 1968-75, clin. asst. prof., 1975-85, clin. assoc. prof., 1985—; mem. faculty adv. com. dept. ob-gyn. U. Wash., Seattle, 1973-92. Author: First Aid for N.W. Boaters, 1977; author Am. Jour. Ob-Gyn., 1970, 75, 77. Bd. dirs. Renton (Wash.) Handicapped Ctr., 1968-70, March of Dimes, 1974-79; bd. dirs. enabling systmes U. Hawaii, Honolulu, 1977-80. Capt. U.S. Army, 1950-52, Korea. Fellow Am. Coll. Ob-Gyn. (diplomate), Internat. Coll. Surgeons (v.p. 1988—); mem. AMA, Pan Am. Ob-Gyn. Soc. (diplomate), S.W. Oncology Group, N.W. Oncology Group, Puget Sound Oncology Group, Seattle Gynecol. Soc. (pres. 1978), Sigma Xi, Baker Channing Soc. Home: 726 16th Ave E Seattle WA 98112 Office: 9730 4th Ave NE Ste 101 Seattle WA 98115

SCOTT, JOHN FRANCIS, biology educator; b. New Orleans, July 29, 1944; s. Cecil John and Leonora Frances (Speer) S.; m. Helena Roselle Watts, June 15, 1965 (div. 1976); 1 child, John Michael; m. Deborah Lynn Seybert, Dec. 19, 1987; 1 child, Kaimi Nohea. BS in Chemistry, U. Calif., Berkeley, 1974; PhD in Biochemistry, Stanford U., 1979. Stock clk. Bullocks Westwood, L.A., 1962; computer operator Measurex Corp., Cupertino, Calif., 1971-78; lab. instr. Foothill Coll. Biology, Los Altos Hills, Calif., 1973-74; rsch. asst. prof. U. Calif., L.A., 1979-81; asst. prof. U. Ill., Campaign-Urbana, 1981-86; assoc. prof. U. Hawaii, Hilo, 1986—, Manoa, 1988—; program dir. U. Hawaii Hilo Minority Biomed. Rsch. Support Program, 1988—. Author: (with others) Met. Res. Indust. Yeasts, 1987, others; contbr. articles to profl. jours. Mem. assistance adv. coun. USN Recruiting Dist. With USN, 1964-71. Rsch. grantee NIH, 1979-81, 81-83, 83-87, 88-92, 92-96, NSF, 1983-86. Mem. AAAS, Am. Chem. Soc., Am. Soc. Cell Biology, Am. Soc. Microbiology, Genetics Soc. Am., Stanford Alumni Assn., Stanford Club of Hawaii, USN League, Sigma Xi (pres. U. Hawaii Hilo club 1989-90). Office: U Hawaii Dept Biology 523 W Lanikaula St Hilo HI 96720-4000

SCOTT, JONATHAN LAVON, retail executive; b. Nampa, Idaho, Feb. 2, 1930; s. Buell Bonnie and Jewel Pearl (Horn) S.; children: Joseph Buell, Anthony Robert (dec.), Richard Teles, Daniel Ross. BA magna cum laude, Coll. Idaho, 1951; grad., Advanced Mgmt. Program, Harvard U., 1968, 69. With Albertson's Inc., Boise, Idaho, 1955-75; vice chmn. bd., chief exec. officer Albertson's Inc., 1972-75; vice chmn. bd. Gt. Atlantic & Pacific Tea Co., Inc., Montvale, N.J., 1975; chmn. bd., chief exec. officer Gt. Atlantic & Pacific Tea Co., Inc., 1975-80, J.L. Scott Enterprises Inc., Irving, Tex., 1980-86; chmn., chief exec. officer Am. Superstores Inc., Wilmington, Del., 1987-89; pres., chief exec. officer Am. Stores Co., Salt Lake City, 1990-92; bd. dirs. Morrison-Knudsen Co., Trus Joist Corp. Trustee Com. Econ. Devel. Served to 1st lt. USAF, 1953-55. Home: 3898 Thousand Oaks Cir Salt Lake City UT 84124-3960

SCOTT, LEANNE BROOKS, developmental biology researcher; b. Ellensburg, Wash., May 13, 1961; d. Terry Nels Brooks and Carole Joanne (Read) Applebaum; m. Sam Shea Scott, July 1, 1984; 1 child, Sarah Alana. BA, Rice U., 1983; PhD, U. Tex., 1989. Recipient Profl. Staff Cert. Dept. of Edn. State of Hawaii. Rsch. asst. M.D. Anderson Cancer Ctr., Houston, 1984-89; assoc. investigator Howard Hughes Med. Inst., Baylor Coll. Medicine, Houston, 1989-91; mem. faculty Punahou Sch., Honolulu, 1991-92. Fund drive sec. St. Clement's Episcopal Ch., Honolulu, 1992. Flatable Denton Briggs scholar Rice U., 1979-83; Rosalie B. Hite fellow U. Tex., 1985-88. Mem. AAAS, Union Concerned Scientists. Home: 1621 Dole St Honolulu HI 96822

SCOTT, MICHAEL DENNIS, lawyer; b. Mpls., Nov. 6, 1945; s. Frank Walton and Donna Julia (Howard) S.; m. Blanca Josefina Palacios, Dec. 12, 1981; children: Michael Dennis, Cindal Marie, Derek Walton. B.S., MIT, 1967; J.D., UCLA, 1974. Bar: Calif. 1974, U.S. Dist. Ct. (no., so. and cen. dists.) Calif. 1974, U.S. Patent Office 1974, U.S. Ct. Appeals (9th cir.) 1974, U.S. Supreme Ct. 1978, U.S. Ct. Appeals (fed. cir.) 1989. Systems programmer NASA Electronics Research Lab., Cambridge, Mass., 1967-69, Computer Sciences Corp., El Segundo, Calif., 1969-71, Univac, Valencia, Calif., 1971; from assoc. to ptnr. Smaltz & Neelley, Los Angeles, 1974-81; sole practice Los Angeles, 1981-86, 88-89; ptnr. Scott & Roxborough, Los Angeles, 1986-88, Graham & James, 1989—; exec. dir. Ctr. for Computer/Law, Los Angeles, 1977—; pres. Law and Tech. Press, 1981—; adj. assoc.

prof. law Southwestern U., L.A., 1975-80; chmn. World Computer Law Congress, L.A., 1991, 93. Author: (with David S. Yen) Computer Law Bibliography, 1979, The Scott Report, 1981-86, Computer Law, 1984, Scott on Computer Law, 1991, Multimedia: Law and Practice, 1993; editor in chief: Computer/Law Jour., 1978—, Software Protection, 1982-92, Software Law Jour., 1985—, Internat. Computer Law Adviser, 1986-92. Mem. ABA, Calif. State Bar Assn. (co-chiar standing com. on computer law), Internat. Bar Assn. (vice chmn. com. 1985-88), L.A. County Car Assn., Computer LAw Assn., Licensing Exec. Soc. Office: Graham & James 801 S Figueroa St 14th FL Los Angeles CA 90017

SCOTT, MORRIS DOUGLAS, ecologist; b. Mason City, Iowa, Sept. 8, 1945; s. Morris William and Maxine Imogene (Eppard) S.; m. Suvi Annikki Lehtinen, Aug. 12, 1983. BS, Iowa State U., 1967; PhD, Auburn U., 1971. Instr. zoology Auburn U., Ala., 1971-72; asst. prof. So. Ill. U., Carbondale, 1972-74; sr. ecologist Amax Coal Co., Indpls., 1974-75, environ. mgr., Billings, Mont., 1975-77; rsch. assoc. Mont. State U., Bozeman, 1977-80, dir. Inst. Natural Resources, 1980-86; biologist, rsch. div. Yellowstone Nat. Park, Wyo., 1986—; cons. mining industry. Author: Heritage from the Wild, Familiar Land and Sea Mammals of the Northwest. Editor Conf. Proceedings Plains Aquatic Research, 1983. Contbr. articles to profl. jours. Bd. dirs. Bridger Canyon Property Owners Assn., Bozeman, 1984—. Auburn U. fellow, 1970. Mem. Ecol. Soc. Am., Wildlife Soc., Animal Behavior Soc., Gamma Sigma Delta. Current work: Land use planning systems for microcomputers; wildlife mgmt. on reclaimed surface mines; behavioral ecology of feral dogs; ecology of waterfowl and grouse; biology of pronghorn antelope. Home: 16257 Bridger Canyon Rd Bozeman MT 59715-8286

SCOTT, OTTO, writer; b. N.Y.C., May 26, 1918; s. Otto Felix and Katherine (McGivney) S.; m. Rose Massing (div. 1952); children: Katherine, Nellie Mouradian, Mary, Philipa; m. Anna Barney Scott, Apr. 29, 1963; 1 child, Ann Elizabeth. MA in Polit. Sci., Valley Christian U., Fresno, Calif., 1985. Mem. staff United Features Syndicate, N.Y.C., 1939-40; v.p. Globaltronix de Venezuela, Caracas, 1954-56, Mohr Assocs., N.Y.C., 1957-59, Becker, Scott & Assocs., N.Y.C., 1960-63; editor Bill Bros., N.Y.C., 1964-67; asst. to chmn. Ashland (Ky.) Oil, Inc., 1968, 69; edn. writer, reviewer San Diego Union Tribune, 1970; sr. writer Chalcedon Found., Vallecito, Calif., 1982—; cons. Ashland Oil, Inc., 1972—; editor, pub. Otto Scott's Compass, Murphys, Calif., 1990—. Author: History Ashland Oil (The Exception) 1968, Robespierre: Voice of Virtue (History French Revolution), 1974, The Professional: Biography of J.B. Saunders, 1976, The Creative Ordeal: History of Raytheon Corporation, 1976, James I: The Fool as King, 1976, 86, Other End of the Lifeboat (History of South Africa), 1985, Buried Treasure: The Story of Arch Mineral, 1987, The Secret Six: The Fool as Martyr, 1987, The Great Christian Revolution, 1991. With U.S. Merchant Marine, 1941-47. Mem. Author's Guild, Overseas Press Club, Calif. State Sheriff's Assn. (assoc.), Com. for Nat. Policy, Com. for Monetary Rsch. and Edn. Presbyterian. Home: 1437 Wingdam Rd Murphys CA 95247 Office: Otto Scotts Compass Box 1769 Murphys CA 95247

SCOTT, PETER BRYAN, lawyer; b. St. Louis, Nov. 11, 1947; s. Gilbert Franklin and Besse Jean (Fudge) S.; m. Suzanne Rosalee Wallace, Oct. 19, 1974; children: Lindsay W., Sarah W., Peter B. Jr. A.B., Drury Coll., 1969; J.D., Washington U., St. Louis, 1972, LL.M., 1980. Bar: Mo. 1972, Colo. 1980; diplomate Ct. Practice Inst. Sole practice, St. Louis, 1972-80; assoc. firm McKie and Assocs., Denver, 1980-81; ptnr. firm Scott and Chesteen, P.C., Denver, 1981-84, Veto & Scott, Denver, 1984-92; pvt. practice atty., Denver, 1992—; tchr. Denver Paralegal Inst., Red Rocks Community Coll. Mem. Evergreen Christian Ch., Disciples of Christ. Capt. USAR, 1971-79. Mem. ABA, Mo. Bar Assn., Colo. Bar Assn., Denver Bar Assn. Republican. Home: 26262 Wolverine Trl Evergreen CO 80439-6203 Office: Peter B Scott PC 6595 W 14th Ave Denver CO 80214-1998

SCOTT, RICHARD WALTER, biology educator, botany and ecology researcher; b. Modesto, Calif., June 30, 1941; s. Frank Houseman and Dorothy Isabel (Betz) S.; m. Beverly Jean Wilson, Sept. 9, 1961; children: Suzanne Elaine, Kevin Richard. BS, U. Wyo., 1964, MS, 1966; MA, U. Mich., 1969, PhD, 1972. Asst. prof. biology Albion (Mich.) Coll., 1969-75; instr. Cen. Wyo. Coll., Riverton, 1975-85, prof., 1985—. Contbr. articles to profl. jours. NDEA fellow U. Mich., 1966-69. Mem. Am. Polar Soc., Mont. Native Plant Soc., Wyo. Native Plant Soc., Sigma Xi, Phi Delta Kappa. Home: 841 Christy Dr Riverton WY 82501-3019 Office: Cen Wyo Coll Dept Biology Riverton WY 82501

SCOTT, STANLEY VANAKEN, marketing educator, consultant; b. Lakeworth, Fla., Apr. 20, 1943; s. Stanley VanAken and Julia Mae (Pitcock) S.; m. Tatiana E. Scott; children: Shellie Ann, Tobie Lou, Kristopher Kent, Jennifer Ann. BBA, U. Alaska, 1981; MA, Ohio State U., 1985, PhD, 1986. Mapper U.S. Geol. Survey, Denver, 1966-70; contract mgr. Plains Builders, Abilene, Tex., 1970-73; owner, mgr. Allens Park (Colo.) Stables, 1973-77; photomapper Boulder County, Boulder, Colo., 1975-77; mgr. Ambuco Alaska, Anchorage, 1977-79; asst. to dean Coll. Bus. U. Alaska, Anchorage, 1979-81, assoc. prof. mktg., 1990—; grad. asst. Ohio State U., Columbus, 1982-85; asst. prof. mktg. Boise (Idaho) State U., 1985-90, mem. faculty senate Coll. Bus., 1987-88, 88-89; assoc. with Alaska Ctr. Internat. Bus., 1992-93; cons. NPT com. SBDC, 1992, Idaho State Lottery, 1990, Idaho NPT EMD, 1989, Kellog Idaho Gondola, 1988; mem. Idaho Gov.'s Market Plan, 1987;. Author Idaho Innovations, 1987-88, Jour. Internat. CNSR Behavior, 1989, Jour. Marketing for Higher Education, 1989, Great Ideas in Teaching Marketing, 1990. Rsch. grantee U.S. West Commn., 1989, Idaho Nat. Engrng. Lab, 1988. Fellow Acad. Mktg. Sci.; mem. Am. Mktg. Assn., Ak. Youth Parents Fedn. (bd. dirs.), Internat. Acad. Mktg. and Mgmt., Acad. Bus. Adminstrn., U. Alaska Anchorage Mktg. Mgmt. Club (adv. 1990—), Beta Gamma Sigma, Pi Sigma Epsilon (advisor 1985—, Favorite Mktg. Tchr. award 1986, 87, 88). Office: U Alaska Anchorage 3211 Providence Dr Anchorage AK 99508-4614

SCOTT, WILLIAM ARTHUR, III, treasurer, swami; b. L.A., Apr. 10, 1949; s. William Arthur Jr. and Mary Lyndal (Dutton) S. BA, Occidental Coll., 1971; MA, Stanford (Calif.) U., 1972; postgrad., UCLA, 1973-76. Cert. tchr., Calif. Tchr. Quartz Hill (Calif.) High Sch., 1972-78; treas. Vedanta Soc. of So. Calif., Hollywood, 1984—; swami Ramakrishna Order of India, Belur, Calcutta, 1990—. Composer operetta Claudia & Alexander. Nat. Merit scholar, 1967. Mem. Calif. Rare Fruit Growers, So. Calif. Iris Soc., Am. Iris Soc., Aril Soc. Internat. (pres. 1979-89), Phi Beta Kappa, Phi Mu Alpha Sinfonia (pres. Eta Kappa chpt. 1969-71). Republican. Home: 1946 Vedanta Pl Los Angeles CA 90068-3996

SCOTT, WILLIAM CORYELL, medical executive; b. Sterling, Colo., Nov. 22, 1920; s. James Franklin and Edna Ann (Schillig) S.; m. Jean Marie English, Dec. 23, 1944 (div. 1975); children: Kathryn, James, Margaret; m. Carolyn Florence Hill, June 21, 1975; children: Scott, Amy Jo, Robert. AB, Dartmouth Coll., 1942; MD, U. Colo., 1944, MS in OB/GYN, 1951. Cert. Am. Bd. Ob-Gyn., 1956, 79, Am. Bd. Med. Mgmt., 1991. Intern USN Hosp., Great Lakes, Ill., 1945-46, Denver Gen. Hosp., 1946-47; resident Ob-Gyn St. Joseph's Hosp., Colo. Gen. Hosp., Denver, 1946-51; practice medicine specializing in Ob-Gyn Tucson, 1951-71; clin. assoc. prof. U. Ariz. Med. Sch., Tucson, 1971—; v.p. med. affairs U. Med. Ctr., Tucson, 1984—. Contbr. articles to med. jours. and chpt. to book. Pres. United Way, Tucson, 1979-80, HSA of Southeastern Ariz., Tucson, 1985-87; chmn. Ariz. Health Facilities Authority, Phoenix, 1974-83. Served to capt. USNR, 1956-58. Recipient Man of Yr. award, Tucson, 1975. Fellow ACS, Am. Coll. Ob-Gyn, Pacific Coast Ob-Gyn Soc., Ctrl. Assn. of Ob-Gyn; mem. AMA (coun. on sci. affairs 1984-93, chmn. 1989-91), Am. Coll. Physician Execs., Am. Coll. Health Care Execs., Ariz. Med. Assn., La Paloma Country Club. Republican. Episcopalian. Home: 335 Country Club Rd Tucson AZ 85716 Office: Univ Med Ctr 1501 N Campbell Ave Tucson AZ 85724-0001

SCOTT, WILLIAM EDWARD, agricultural services executive, economist; b. Denver, July 16, 1953; s. Alexander Danforth and Elinor (Olsen) S.; m. Amy Ann Osterholm, Dec. 30, 1982; 1 child, Alexander Richard. Student, Coll. de Sion, Valais, Switzerland, 1971-72; cert., Inst. d'Etudes Politques, Paris, 1975; BA in History, Stanford (Calif.) U., 1977, MA in Agrl. Econs., 1979. Agrl. economist U.S. Agy. for Internat. Devel., Yaoundé, Cameroon, 1979-81; analyst Calif. Coastal Commn., San Francisco, 1981-83; agrl. economist Elliott Berg Assocs., Arlington, Va., 1983-85, Louis Berger, Internat., E. Orange, N.J., 1985-86; v.p. Agland Investment Svcs., Inc., Larkspur, Calif., 1986—; cons. U.S. Agy. for Internat. Devel., Niger, 1983, World Bank, Belize, 1985, Asian Devel. Bank, Pakistan, 1987, African Devel. Bank, Cameroon, Tanzania, 1988—, U.S. Agy. Internat. Develop., Morocco, 1992-93, Internat. Fin. Corp., Russia, 1993. Mem. Stanford Choir, Chorale and Chorus, 1972-78, Agricultural Caucus, Calif. Agricultural Leadership Program; Pacific region rep. YMCA Internat. Div., No. Calif., 1971-74; pres. Calif. Bach Soc., San Francisco, 1981-84; chmn. Stanford U. Rsch. Liaison Office, 1977-79. Recipient Achievement award Bank of Am., 1971; Am. Field Svc. scholar Switzerland, 1971; U.S. Endowment for Humanities grantee, 1977; U.S. Govt. fellow, 1978-79. Mem. Am. Assn. Agrl. Economists, Am. Econs. Assn., Am. Soc. Agrl. Cons., Calif. Agrl. Leadership Program, San Francisco Farmers Club (v.p.), Commonwealth Club (vice chair agrl. section). Democrat. Methodist. Home: 96 Kingston Rd Kensington CA 94707-1334 Office: Agland Investment Svcs Inc 900 Larkspur Landing Cir Larkspur CA 94939-1757

SCOTTI, FRANK ANTHONY, ophthalmologist; b. Brooklyn, N.J., Aug. 23, 1952; s. Anthony Emil and Christine (Imburgia) S. BS, Rutgers U., 1973, MS, 1974; MD, N.J. Coll. Medicine, 1978. Diplomate Am. Acad. Ophthalmology. Ophthalmologist Navy Hosp., San Diego, 1980-83; chief ophthalmology Navy Hosp., Okinawa, 1983-85; ophthalmologist Navy Hosp., Camp Pendleton, Calif., 1985-87; pvt. practice ophthalmology Encinitas, Calif., 1987—. Fellow Am. Acad. Ophthalmology, San Diego Zool. Sic.; mem. Calif. Med. Assn., S.D. County Med. Soc., Mericos Eye Inst., Rotary. Roman Catholic. Office: 320 Santa Fe Dr Ste 104 Encinitas CA 92024

SCOWCROFT, JOHN MAJOR, petroleum refinery process development executive; b. Ogden, Utah, June 19, 1924; s. John William and Charlene (Major) S.; m. Barbara Marie Caine, Mar. 12, 1951; children: Charlene, John Arthur, Barbara Ann, Sally Caine. BS, U. Utah, 1951; MBA, Northwestern U., 1952. Various mgmt. positions Standard Oil Co. (Ind.), Chgo., N.Y.C., 1952-74; gen. mgr. Deseret Mgmt. Corp., Salt Lake City, 1974-84; founder Utah Tech. Fin. Corp., Salt Lake City, 1984; exec. v.p. Utah Innovation Ctr., Salt Lake City, 1984-86; founder Utah Ventures, Salt Lake City, 1985; pres. Process Innovators, Inc., Salt Lake City, 1986—, bd. dirs.; cons. small bus. devel. various orgns., Salt Lake City, 1984—; bd. dirs. Maverik Country Stores, Afton, Wyo., IMPETUS, Inc., Spl. Ltd. Ptnr. of Utah Ventures; mem. Salt Lake bd. 1st Security Bank Utah, Salt Lake City. Mem. nat. adv. coun. David Eccles Sch. Bus., U. Utah; bd. trustees Salt Lake Conv. and Visitors Bur.; chmn. Mountain West Venture Group; chmn. ednl. sub-com. Salt Lake Conv. Ctr. Modernization Com.; advisor Beta Theta Pi, U. Utah; mem. fin. com. candidate for U.S. Ho. of Reps. Sgt. U.S. Army, 1943-46, MTO. Cash Rsch. grantee U.S. Dept. Energy, 1989, Utah Dept. Energy, 1990, Utah Ctrs. of Excellence, 1989, Utah Tech. Fin. Corp., 1989. Mem. Salt Lake Area C. of C. (chmn. 1983), Rotary Club Salt Lake (treas. 1988-89, pres. 1993-94). Republican. Mem. LDS Church. Home: 1292 Federal Heights Dr Salt Lake City UT 84103 Office: Utah Ventures 419 Wakara Way # 206 Salt Lake City UT 84108

SCRIBNER, DOROTHY NESBITT, community relations executive, consultant; b. San Francisco, June 21, 1938; d. John and Freda (Keller) Nesbitt; children: Diana Lynne Vaughn, Karen Elizabeth Weber, Matthew Joseph Duffy. Exec. sec. East Bay Zool. Soc., Oakland, Calif., 1968-73; field coord. San Francisco Bay Girl Scout Coun., San Leandro, Calif., 1975-77; owner, operator Specialty Svcs., Pleasanton, Calif., 1972-85, Design Works Ltd., Pleasanton, 1980-82, Star Coffee Svc., Pleasanton, 1985-86; exec. dir. Danville (Calif.) Area C. of C., 1985-86; mgr. downtown project Town of Danville, 1986-89; event coord. Valley Vol. Ctr., Pleasanton, 1990; investor, bus. owner Pleasanton, 1990-93. Contbg. editor (newsletters) Zoo's News, 1969-73, Progress, 1985-86. Chmn. Evergreen br. Children's Hosp., 1979-80, treas., 1991; bd. dirs., treas. Children's Hosp., Oakland, 1982-85; chmn. Downtown Assn. Heritage Days Celebration, Pleasanton, 1990-91; mem. Alameda County Libr. Commn., Oakland, 1991; vice mayor City of Pleasanton, 1992—. Mem. Pleasanton C. of C. (com. econ. devel. 1991), Stockwatchers Club, Nat. Trust Hist. Preservation.

SCRIBNER, JAMES BRUCE, financial planner; b. Connersville, Ind., Sept. 19, 1937; s. Clayton Wilson and Elizabeth Patrick (Tippy) S.; m. Eadean Sandra Stark, June 3, 1960; children: Jon, Mark, Tamsen. BA, U. Redlands, 1959; MS, Calif. State U., Long Beach, 1971; Chartered Life Underwriter, Am. Coll., 1979; Cert. Fin. Planner, Coll. for Fin. Planning, Denver, 1987. Credit rep. Standard Oil Co., L.A., 1962-63; bank loan officer Union Bank, L.A., 1963-71; bank v.p. Riverside (Calif.) Nat. Bank, 1971-73; life ins. salesman various cos., Riverside, 1973-82; fin. planner Scribner & Assocs., Riverside, 1982—; instr. Univ. Calif./Extension, Riverside, 1985—; bd. dirs. Parkview Community Hosp., Riverside. Pres., founder Friday Morning Club, Riverside, 1984; treas. All Saints Episcopal Ch., Riverside, 1985-90. Lt. (j.g.) USNR, 1959-62, Japan. Mem. Rotary (pres. Magnolia Ctr. 1991-92), CLU and Chartered Fin. Cons. (pres. Arrowhead Chpt. 1991-92), Riverside County Assn. Life Underwriters (pres. 1984-85), Toastmasters Internat. (past are gov. 1980-81), Riverside County Estate Planning Coun., Internat. Assn. for Fin. Planning, Masons. Republican. Home: 1220 Via Vallarta Riverside CA 92506 Office: Scribner & Assocs Ste 104 6833 Indiana Ave Riverside CA 92506

SCRIMSHAW, GEORGE CURRIE, retired plastic surgeon; b. Canajoharie, N.Y., Nov. 10, 1925; s. George and Margaret Eleanor (Salkeld) S.; m. Erna Christine Adam, Sept. 20, 1957 (div. 1982); m. Helen Irene Mott, Dec. 4, 1982; children: Katherine, Kristen, Kirby, Tracy. BA, Harvard U., 1948; MD cum laude, Tufts U., 1952. Diplomate Am. Bd. Plastic Surgery. Intern N.Y. Hosp./Cornell Med. Ctr., N.Y.C., 1952-53, resident in surgery, 1953-54; resident in surgery New England Med. Ctr., Boston, 1954-55; resident in plastic surgery Franklin Hosp./U. Calif., San Francisco, 1955-57; pvt. practice Fresno, Calif., 1957-58, Quincy, Mass., 1958-62; chief dept. plastic surgery Permanente Med. Group, Oakland, Calif., 1962-88, ret., 1988; cons., attending plastic surgeon Faulkner Hosp., Southshore Hosp., Quincy Hosp., 1959-62. Contbr. articles to profl. jours. With U.S. Army, 1944-46. Mem. ASC (life), Am. Cleft Palate Assn. (life), Am. Soc. of Plastic and Reconstructive Surgery (life), Calif. Soc. fo Plastic Surgeons (life), Am. Soc. of Aesthetic Surgery (life), Alpha Omega Alpha (life).

SCRITSMIER, JEROME LORENZO, light fixture manufacturing company executive; b. Eau Claire, Wis., July 1, 1925; s. Fredrick Lorenzo and Alvera Mary (Schwab) S.; B.S., Northwestern U., 1950; m. Mildred Joan Lloyd, June 27, 1947; children—Dawn, Lloyd, Janet. Salesman, Sylvania Elec. Products, Los Angeles, 1951-69; chmn. Cameron Properties Inc.; chief fin. officer Environ. Lighting for Architecture Co., Los Angeles, 1973—. Served with USAAF, 1943-46. Mem. Apt. Assn. (pres., dir. Los Angeles County). Republican. Club: Jonathan (Los Angeles). Home: 2454 N Cameron Ave Covina CA 91724-3921 Office: 17891 Arenth St City of Industry CA 91748

SCRIVER, ROBERT MACFIE, sculptor; b. Browning, Mont., Aug. 15, 1914; s. Thaddeus Emery and Ellison Scriver; m. Mary Helen Strachan, Nov. 27, 1966 (div. Nov. 1970); m. Lorraine, Aug. 15, 1972. Student, Dickinson State Tchr's Coll., N.D., 2 years; Bachelor's degree, Vandercook Sch. Music, Chgo., 1935, Master's degree, 1941; postgrad., Northwestern Univ., summer 1937, U. Wash., summer 1938; D.Arts hon., Carroll Coll. mem. C.M. Russell Adv. Bd., Great Falls, Mont., 1983—. Group of works include No More Buffalo, 1983 (gold medals 1983), An Honest Try (gold medals), Bob Scriver Hall of Bronze Mus. Mont. Wildlife, 1989; author: No More Buffalo, 1983 (pub. awards 1983), An Honest Try (pub. awards), The Blackfeet, Artists of the Northern Plains, 1990 (pub. awards). Justice of the peace Glacer County, Mont.; city magistrate City of Browning. Served to sgt. USAAF, 1940. Recipient Gold and Silver medals Cowboy Artists Am., Phoenix, Gold and Silver medals Nat. Acad. Western Arts, Oklahoma City, Mont. State Gov.'s award, 1990; honoree Bob Scriver Day State Mont., Helena. Mem. Nat. Sculpture Soc., Nat. Acad. Western Art, Soc. Animal Artists, Browning C. of C. (pres.); mem. emeritus Cowboy Artists Am. Republican. Native American. Lodge: Masons. Office: Museum Mont Wildlife Junction Hwvs 2 and 89 Browning MT 59417

SCROGGS, DEBBIE LEE, communications professional; b. Norton, Va., Sept. 27, 1953; d. Jennings Eugene and Edith Marie (Harris) S.; m. John L. Price, Apr. 1, 1984. AAS in Acctg., C.C. of Denver, 1981; BSBA magna cum laude, Regis Coll., 1987; MSS in Applied Comms., U. Denver, 1992. Bookkeeper Am./Trayer, Inc., Bristol, Va., 1972-74; assessment transcriber Dept. of Interior, Bristol, 1974-78; supr. computer asst. Dept. of Labor, Mine Safety and Health Adminstrn., Lakewood, Colo., 1978-82; lead tech. writer OAO Corp., Lakewood, 1982-83; tech. writer, editor Tele-Communications, Inc., Denver, 1984-85, Integrated Svcs., Inc., Aurora, Colo., 1985-87; sr. documentation specialist AT&T Document Devel. Orgn., Denver, 1988-89, sr. project mgr., 1989—. Contbr. articles to profl. jours., publs. Vol. Art Reach of Denver, 1988—, Channel 6 TV, Denver, 1989—. Mem. Assn. Computing Machinery (assoc.), Soc. for Tech. Communication (sr. mem., Achievement award for User Manual, 1986, Achievement award for Mktg. Brochure, 1986, Merit award for User Manual, 1988, moderator and co-prester, 1991, networking lunch coord./nat. conf., 1992). Office: AT&T 7979 E Tufts Ave Denver CO 80237

SCUDDER, DAVID BENJAMIN, economist, foundation administrator; b. Evanston, Ill., July 30, 1923; s. Guy and Ruth Marilla (Benjamin) S.; m. Marjorie Adell Buckland, Dec. 27, 1946; children: David Foster, Rexford Guy. BS, Bowling Green State U., 1948; AM, U. Chgo., 1950, postgrad., 1950-51. Economist CIA, Washington, 1951-81, econ. cons., 1981-84; editor, co-pub. World Amateur Dancer, McLean, Va., 1982-84; treas. The Scudder Assn., Inc., Arlington, Va., 1990—. Editor quarterly newsletter The Scudder Assn. Inc, 1989—; contbr. articles and reports to jours. Active Springfield Civic Assn., Fairfax County, Va., 1956-61. With USAF, 1943-45, ETO. Home: 1031 Strawberry Ln Boise ID 83712

SCUDDER, JACK HOWARD, newspaper editor; b. Mpls., Nov. 23, 1919; s. Clarence and Ethel Elizabeth (Johnson) S.; m. Josephine Louise Woodward, Feb. 26, 1944; children: Janet Louise, James Howard, David Woodward, John Douglas. BA cum laude, U. Minn., 1942. Editor Idaho Free Press, Nampa, 1955-66; pub. Daily-Record Gazette, Banning and Beaumont, Calif., 1966-68; dir. rsch. Scripps League of Newspapers, Seattle, 1968-75, J.G. Scripps Newspapers, Seattle, 1975-86; pres. Scudder/Western Rsch., Inc., Nampa, Idaho, 1986-89. Pres. Community Concert Assn., Little Falls, Minn., 1954, Banning C. of C., 1967; bd. dirs. Nampa Area United Way, 1964-66, Idaho Press Club, Boise, 1964-66, Rotary, Banning, 1968; pres. Nampa Civic Ctr. Aux., 1991-93, Nampa Civic Ctr. Commn., 1991—. Mem. Soc. Profl. Journalists. Methodist. Home: 384 Holland Dr Nampa ID 83651-2059

SCULLEY, JOHN, computer company executive; b. N.Y.C., Apr. 6, 1939; s. John and Margaret Blackburn (Smith) S.; m. Carol Lee Adams, Mar. 7, 1978; children: Margaret Ann, John Blackburn, Laura Lee. Student, R.I. Sch. Design, 1960; BArch, Brown U., 1961; MBA, U. Pa., 1963. Asst. account exec. Marschalk Co., N.Y.C., 1963-64, account exec., 1964-65, account supr., 1965-67; dir. mktg. Pepsi-Cola Co., Purchase, N.Y., 1967-69, v.p. mktg., 1970-71, sr. v.p. mktg., 1971-74, pres., chief exec. officer, 1977-83; pres. PepsiCo Foods, Purchase, 1974-77; pres., chief exec. officer Apple Computer Inc., Cupertino, Calif., 1983-1993, chmn., tech. officer, 1986—; bd. dirs. Comsat Corp. Chmn. Wharton Grad. Exec. Bd., 1980; mem. art adv. com. Brown U., 1980; bd. dirs. Keep Am. Beautiful.; mem. bd. overseers Wharton Sch., U. Pa. Mem. U.S. C. of C. Clubs: Indian Harbor, N.Y. Athletic; Coral Beach (Bermuda); Wharton Bus. Sch. of N.Y. (bd. dirs.); Camden (Maine) Yacht. Office: Apple Computer Inc 20525 Mariani Ave Cupertino CA 95014-6201*

SCULLY, JOHN KENNETH, engineering executive, consultant; b. N.Y.C., Nov. 19, 1935; s. Francis Joseph and Dorothy Bonita (Cadley) S.; m. Roxanne Allison Glaser, Feb. 12, 1966; children: Roxanne Allison, Rebecca Suzanne. BS in Physics, Hofstra U., 1959; MS in Engrng., UCLA, 1962; postgrad., Poly. Grad. Ctr., Farmingdale, N.Y., 1962-64. Engr. Sperry Corp., Great Neck, N.Y., 1956-60; sr. engr. Northrop Corp., Anaheim, Calif., 1960-62; dept. mgr. Harris Corp., Syosset, N.Y., 1962-72; sr. mem. tech. staff Litton Industries, Woodland Hills, Calif., 1972-80; pres. JKS Systems Ltd., Westlake Village, Calif., 1980—; spl. asst. to pres. GTT Industries, Inc., Westlake Village, 1991—; mng. dir. Adam-Tech. Group, Geneva, 1991—; chmn. R&D subtask Industry/Joint Svcs., 1979. Contbr. over 30 tech. papers to prof. jours. Mem. IEEE. Office: JKS Systems Ltd Lindero Corp Ctr 5701 Lindero Cyn #1-201 Westlake Village CA 91362

SCULLY, SAMUEL EDWARD, classics educator, university official; b. Manchester, Eng., Sept. 30, 1942; arrived in Can., 1966; s. James and Edith (Pyatt) S.; m. Jennifer Grace Parker Lewis, Oct. 13, 1965; 1 child, Samantha Helen. BA with honours, U. Bristol, Eng., 1964, MLitt, 1967; PhD, U. Toronto, Ont., Can., 1973. Teaching asst. dept. classics U. Bristol, 1965-66, U. Toronto, 1967-69; lectr., asst. prof. U. Victoria, B.C., Can., 1969-81, assoc. prof., 1981—, acting chmn. dept., 1975-76, chmn., 1977-82, assoc. dean for humanities, 1981-83, dean, 1983-87, dean Faculty Arts and Scis., 1984-85, v.p. acad., 1988-91, v.p. acad., provost, 1991—; pub. orator, 1991—; instr. Trinity Coll. Co-editor Echos du Monde Classique/Classical Views, 1990—. Treas. Vancouver Island (B.C.) Rugby Union, 1986-88. Mem. Classical Assn., Soc. for Promotion Hellenic Studies, Classical Assn. Can. (coun. 1977-79), Classical Assn. Pacific NW (exec. mem. 1975-76, v.p. 1981-82, pres. 1982-83), Classical Assn. Vancouver Island (sec.-treas. 1973-75, pres. 1987-88). Home: 1795 Brymea Ln, Victoria, BC Canada V8N 6B7

SEABORG, GLENN THEODORE, chemistry educator; b. Ishpeming, Mich., Apr. 19, 1912; s. H. Theodore and Selma (Erickson) S.; m. Helen Griggs, June 6, 1942; children: Peter, Lynne Seaborg Cobb, David, Stephen, John Eric, Dianne. AB, UCLA, 1934; PhD, U. Calif.-Berkeley, 1937; numerous hon. degrees; LLD, U. Mich., 1958, Rutgers U., 1970; DSc, Northwestern U., 1954, U. Notre Dame, 1961, John Carroll U., Duquesne U., 1968, Ind. State U., 1969, U. Utah, 1970, Rockford Coll., 1975, Kent State U., 1975; LHD, No. Mich. Coll., 1962; DPS, George Washington U., 1962; DPA, U. Puget Sound, 1963; LittD, Lafayette Coll., 1966; DEng, Mich. Technol. U., 1970; ScD, U. Bucharest, 1971, Manhattan Coll., 1976; PhD, U. Pa., 1983. Rsch. chemist U. Calif., Berkeley, 1937-39, instr. dept. chemistry, 1939-41, asst. prof., 1941-45, prof., 1945-71, univ. prof., 1971—, leave of absence, 1942-46, 61-71, dir. nuclear chem. research, 1946-58, 72-75, asso. dir. Lawrence Berkeley Lab., 1954-61, 71—; chancellor Univ. (U. Calif.-Berkeley), 1958-61; dir. Lawrence Hall of Sci., U. Calif., Berkeley, 1982-84, chmn. Lawrence Hall of Sci., 1984—; sect. chief metall. lab. U. Chgo., 1942-46; chmn. AEC, 1961-71, gen. adv. com., 1946-50; research nuclear chemistry and physics, transuranium elements.; chmn. bd. Kevex Corp., Burlingame, Calif., 1972-87, Advance Physics Corp., Santa Barbara, Calif., 1988—; mem. Pres.'s Sci. Adv. Com., 1959-61; mem. nat. sci. bd. NSF, 1960-61; mem. Pres.'s Com. on Equal Employment Opportunity, 1961-65, Fed. Radiation Council, 1961-69, Nat. Aeros. and Space Council, 1961-71, Fed. Council Sci. and Tech., 1961-71, Nat. Com. Am.'s Goals and Resources, 1962-64, Pres.'s Com. Manpower, 1964-69, Nat. Council Marine Resources and Engrng. Devel., 1966-71; chmn. Chem. Edn. Material Study, 1959-74, Nat. Programming Council for Pub. TV, 1970-72; dir. Ednl. TV and Radio Center, Ann Arbor, Mich., 1958-64, 67-70; pres. 4th UN Internat. Conf. Peaceful Uses Atomic Energy, Geneva, 1971, also chmn. U.S. del., 1964, 71; U.S. rep. 5th-15th gen. confs. IAEA, chmn., 1961-71; chmn. U.S. del. to USSR for signing Memorandum Cooperation Field Utilization Atomic Energy Peaceful Purposes, 1963; mem. U.S. del. for signing Limited Test Ban Treaty, 1963; mem. commn. on humanities Am. Council Learned Socs., 1962-65; mem. sci. adv. bd. Robert A. Welch Found., 1957—; mem. Internat. Orgn. for Chem. Scis. in Devel., UNESCO, 1981-92, pres. emeritus, 1992—; mem. Nat. Commn. on Excellence in Edn., Dept. Edn., 1981-83; co-discoverer elements 94-102 and 106: plutonium, 1940, americium, 1944-45, curium, 1944, berkelium, 1949, californium, 1950, einsteinium, 1952, fermium, 1953, mendelevium, 1955, nobelium, 1958, element 106, 1974; co-discoverer nuclear energy isotopes Pu-239, U-233, Np-237, other isotopes including I-131, Fe-59, Te-99m, Co-60; originator actinide concept for placing heaviest elements in periodic system. Author: (with Joseph J. Katz) The Actinide Elements, 1954 , The Chemistry of the Actinide Elements, 1957, (with Joseph J. Katz and Lester R. Morse) 2d ed. Vols. I & II, 1986, The Transuranium Elements, 1958, (with E.G. Valens) Elements of the Universe, 1958 (winner Thomas Alva Edison Found. award), Man-Made Transuranium Elements, 1963, (with D.M. Wilkes) Education and the Atom, 1964, (with E.K. Hyde, I. Perlman) Nuclear Properties of the Heavy Elements, 1964, (with others) Oppenheimer, 1969, (with Ben Loeb) Stemming the Tide, 1987, (with W.R. Corliss) Man and Atom, 1971, Nuclear Milestones, 1972, (with Ben Loeb) Kennedy, Khruschev and the Test Ban, 1981, (with Walt Loveland) Eements beyond Uranium, 1990; editor: (with Ben Loeb) The Atomic Energy Commission Under Nixon, 1992, Transuranium Elements: Products of Modern Alchemy, 1978, (with W. Loveland) Nuclear Chemistry, 1982; assoc. editor Jour. Chem. Physics, 1948-50; mem. editorial adv. bd. Jour. Inorganic and Nuclear Chemistry, 1954-82, Indsl. Rsch., Inc, 1967-75; mem. adv. bd. Chem. and Engring. News, 1957-59; mem. editorial bd. Jour. Am Chem. Soc, 1950-59, Ency. Chem. Tech., 1975—, Revs. in Inorganic Chemistry, 1977—; mem. hon. editorial adv. bd. Internat. Ency. Phys. Chemistry and Chem. Physics, 1957—, Nuclear Sci. and Techniques, Chinese Nuclear Soc.; mem. panel Golden Picture Ency. for Children, 1957-61; mem. cons. and adv. bd. Funk and Wagnalls Universal Standard Ency, 1957-61; mem.: Am. Heritage Dictionary Panel Usage Cons., 1964—; contbr. articles to profl. jours. Trustee Pacific Sci. Center Found., 1962-77; trustee Sci. Service, 1965—, pres., 1966-88, chmn. 1988—; trustee Am.-Scandinavian Found., 1968—, Ednl. Broadcasting Corp., 1970-72; bd. dirs. Swedish Council Am., 1976—, chmn. bd. dirs., 1978-82; bd. dirs. World Future Soc., 1969—, Calif. Council for Environ. and Econ. Balance, 1974—; bd. govs. Am. Swedish Hist. Found., 1972—. Recipient John Ericsson Gold medal Am. Soc. Swedish Engrs., 1948; Nobel prize for Chemistry (with E.M. McMillan), 1951; John Scott award and medal City of Phila., 1953; Perkin medal Am. sect. Soc. Chem. Industry, 1957; U.S. AEC Enrico Fermi award, 1959; Joseph Priestley Meml. award Dickinson Coll., 1960; Sci. and Engring. award Fedn. Engring. Socs., Drexel Inst. Tech., Phila., 1962; named Swedish Am. of Year, Vasa Order of Am., 1962; Franklin medal Franklin Inst., 1963; 1st Spirit of St. Louis award, 1964; Leif Erikson Found. award, 1964; Washington award Western Soc. Engrs., 1965; Arches of Sci. award Pacific Sci. Center, 1968; Internat. Platform Assn. award, 1969; Prometheus award Nat. Elec. Mfrs. Assn., 1969; Nuclear Pioneer award Soc. Nuclear Medicine, 1971; Oliver Townsend award Atomic Indsl. Forum, 1971; Disting. Honor award U.S. Dept. State, 1971; Golden Plate award Am. Acad. Achievement, 1972; John R. Kuebler award Alpha Chi Sigma, 1978; Founders medal Hebrew U. Jerusalem, 1981; Henry DeWolf-Smyth award Am. Nuclear Soc., 1982, Great Swedish Heritage award, 1984, Ellis Island Medal of Honor, 1986, Vannevar Bush award NSF, 1988, Nat. Medal of Sci. 1991, Royal Order of the Polar Star Sweden, 1992; decorated officier Legion of Honor France; Daniel Webster medal, 1976. Fellow Am. Phys. Soc., Am. Inst. Chemists (Pioneer award 1968, Gold medal award 1973), Chem. Soc. London (hon.), Royal Soc. Edinburgh (hon.), Am. Nuclear Soc., Calif., N.Y., Washington acads. scis., AAAS (pres. 1972, chmn. bd. 1973), Royal Soc. Arts (Eng.); mem. Am. Chem. Soc. (award in pure chemistry 1947, William H. Nichols medal N.Y. sect. 1948, Charles L. Parsons award 1964, Gibbs medal Chgo. sect. 1966, Madison Marshall award No. Ala. sect. 1972, Priestley medal 1979, pres. 1976), Am. Philos. Soc., Royal Swedish Acad. Engring. Scis. (adv. council 1980), Am. Nat., Argentine Nat., Bavarian, Polish, Royal Swedish, USSR acads. scis., Royal Acad. Exact, Phys. and Natural Scis. Spain (acad. fgn. corr.), Soc. Nuclear Medicine (hon.), World Assn. World Federalists (v.p. 1980), Fedn. Am. Scientists (bd. sponsors 1980), Deutsche Akademie der Naturforscher Leopoldina (East Germany), Nat. Acad. Pub. Adminstrn., Internat. Platform Assn. (pres. 1981-86), Am. Hiking Soc. (bd. dirs. 1979-84, v.p. 1980, adv. com. 1984—), Phi Beta Kappa, Sigma Xi, Pi Mu Epsilon, Alpha Chi Sigma (John R. Kuebler award 1978), Phi Lambda Upsilon (hon.); fgn. mem. Royal Soc. London, Chem. Soc. Japan, Serbian Acad. Sci. and Arts. Clubs: Bohemian (San Francisco); Chemists (N.Y.C.); Cosmos (Washington), University (Washington); Faculty (Berkeley). Office: U Calif Lawrence Berkeley Lab Bldg 70A RM 3307 Berkeley CA 94720*

SEAGRAVES, MARY ANN, meteorologist; b. Hobbs, N. Mex., Dec. 29, 1939; d. Robert Samuel and Ruth (Scott) Blymn; m. Squire B. Seagraves, June 9, 1960; children: William, Roger. BS in Math., N. Mex. Inst. Mining & Tech., Socorro, 1961; MS in Math., N. Mex. State U., 1963; PhD in Atmospheric Sci., Colo. State U., 1983. Mathematician Nat. Range Ops. U.S. Army, White Sands Missile Range, N. Mex., 1963-66; mathematician Atmospheric Scis. Lab. U.S. Army, White Sands Missile Range, 1966-80, meteorologist, 1980-92; meteorologist Rsch. Lab. Army Rsch. Lab., White Sands Missile Range, 1992—; dir. Battle Weather Data Divsn., U.S. Army Rsch. Lab., White Sands Missile Range, N. Mex., 1991-92. Contbr. articles to profl. jours. Named Outstanding Centennial Alumna, N. Mex. State U., Las Cruces, 1988. Mem. Am. Meteorol. Soc., Optical Soc. Am., Mil. Ops. Rsch. Soc., Sigma Xi. Office: US Army Rsch Lab Attn AMSRL-BE White Sands Missle Range NM 88002

SEAGREN, DANIEL ROBERT, minister; b. Chgo., Oct. 31, 1927; s. Elmer Fredrick and Selma Agusta (Hill) S.; m. Barbara Anne Johnson, Mar. 21, 1959; children: Laurie Lee Holmquist, Scott Robert. BA, U. Minn., 1950; Diploma, North Park Seminary, Chgo., 1953; MA, U. So. Calif., L.A., 1959; Cert. in Counseling, U. Calif., Santa Barbara, 1988. Ordained to ministry Evang. Covenant Ch. Faulty and adminstr. Azusa (Calif.) Pacific U., 1959-62, North Park Coll., Chgo., 1962-66; assoc. pastor First Covenant Ch., Mpls., 1966-69; fundraiser Northwest Covenant Conf., Mpls., 1969; pastor Covenant Ch., Berkeley, Calif., 1970-74; internat. pastor Evang. Covenant Ch., Stockholm, 1974-77; pastor Forest Park Covenant Ch., Muskegon, Mich., 1977-82; internat. pastor Evang. Covenant Ch., Mexico City, 1982-84; chaplain Samarkand Retirement Community, Santa Barbara, 1985—; columnist Berkeley Gazette, 1971-74; anchorman cable TV sta., Muskegon, Mich., 1977-82; bd. dirs., sec. Morning Song radio broadcast. Author nine books in field. With USN, 1946, PTO. Mem. Am. Soc. on Aging, Nat. Coun. on Aging, Rotary, Kiwanis. Home: 2843 Miradero Dr Santa Barbara CA 93105 Office: Samarkand Retirement Comm 2550 Treasure Dr Santa Barbara CA 93105

SEAL, MERLIN IRENEUS, pastor, retired; b. Sisseton, S.D., Feb. 12, 1921; s. Martin and Ida Irene (Storbraaten) S.; m. Muriel Annette Helen Strand, Jan. 2, 1946; children: Robert Peter, Barbara Ann Seal Ogle-Reid, JoAnn Elizabeth Seal Lincoln. BA, St. Olaf Coll., 1943; Candidate of Theology, Luther Theol. Sem., 1949. Ordained to ministry Lutheran Ch., 1949. Pastor Luther Meml. Ch., Gays Mills, Wis., 1949-52, Our Savior's Luth. Ch., Soldiers Grove, Wis., 1949-52, Park View Luth. Ch., Chgo., 1952-55; co-pastor First Luth. Ch., Duluth, Minn., 1955-59; pastor Holy Cross Luth Ch., Wheaton, Ill., 1959-65; assoc. pastor Grace Luth. Ch., Palo Alto, Calif., 1965-72; sr. pastor St. Peter Luth. Ch., Mesa, Ariz., 1972-78; sr. pastor Trinity Luth. Ch., Hawthorne, Calif., 1978-83, pastor emeritus, 1983—; pastor emeritus Am. Luth. Ch., Mpls., 1983—; dean Peninsula Conf. of Am. Luth. Ch., Palo Alto, 1969-72; pres. Wheaton Ministerial Assn., 1962-63. 2d lt. USMCR, 1941-45. Mem. Kiwanis (bd. dirs.). Home: 1919 Forest Hill Dr SE Olympia WA 98501-3738

SEALE, ROBERT L., state treasurer; b. Inglewood, Calif., Oct. 4, 1941; m. Judy Seale (dec.). BSA, Calif. Poly. U. Former contr. and sr. fin. officer Rockwell Internat.; sr. accountant Ernst & Ernst, L.A.; mng. ptnr. Pangborn & Co., Ltd. CPA's, 1985-88; now state treas. State of Nev.; trustee, chmn. fin. com. Desert Rsch. Inst. Bd. dirs. Nev. Mus. Art; former treas. Nev. Rep. Party. Office: Office of State Treas Capital Complex Carson City NV 89710

SEALE, ROBERT MCMILLAN, office services company executive; b. Birmingham, Ala., Feb. 1, 1938; s. Robert McMillan and Margaret Sutherland (Miller) S.; B.A., Emory U., 1959. With N.Y. Life Ins. Co., San Francisco, 1960-67; with Dictaphone Office Services div. Dictaphone Corp., San Francisco, 1967-69; pres. Am. Profl. Service, Inc., Dictation West, Miss Jones' Word Processing, San Francisco, Pleasant Hill, South San Francisco, Calif., Los Angeles, Beverly Hills, Riverside, Portland, Phoenix, Las Vegas, Orange County, Calif. and Denver, 1969-93, Environments West, 1980-86, Los Arcos Properties, 1980—; founder Seale Orgn., 1993; bd. dirs. The Rose Resnic Ctr. for Blind and Handicapped; med. word processing cons. to hosps., health care insts., office equipment mfrs.; lectr. in field. Contbr. articles in field to profl. jours. Chmn. San Francisco Mayor's Com. for Employment of Handicapped, 1971-73; mem. Calif. Gov.'s Planning and Adv. Com. for Vocat. Rehab. Planning, 1968-69; pres. Calif. League for Handicapped, 1968-70, bd. dirs., 1966-73, 84-89, adv. council, 1973-77; v.p. Stebbins Found., 1980—89; pres Stebbins Housing Corp., 1980-89; assoc. St. Francis Hosp. Found., 1990—. Recipient Spoke and Spark award U.S. Jr. C. of C., 1967; KABL Outstanding Citizen's award, 1965, 71. Mem. Am. Med. Records Assn., Adminstrv. Mgmt. Soc., Sales and Mktg. Execs. Assn., Am. Assn. Med. Transcription (rep. to Computer-Based Patient Record Inst., Disting. Service award 1985), Med. Transcription Industry Alliance, Emory U. Alumni Assn., Emory Lamplighters Soc., Internat. Word Processing Inst., U.S. C. of C., Olympic Athletic Club, Delta Tau Delta. Republican. Office: 1177 Mission Rd S San Francisco CA 94080

SEAMAN, ARLENE ANNA, musician, educator; b. Pontiac, Mich., Jan. 21, 1918; d. Roy Russell and Mabel Louise (Heffron) S. BS, life cert., Ea. Mich. U., 1939; MMus, Wayne State U., 1951; postgrad., Colo. Coll., 1951-52, Acad. Music, Zermatt Switzerland, 1954, 58, U. Mich. guest conductor Shepherds and Angels, Symphonie Concertante, 1951; asst. conductor Detroit Women's Symphony, 1960-68; adjudicator Mich. State Band and Orch. Festivals, Solo and Ensemble Festivals, 1950-70, Detroit Fiddler's Band Auditions, 1948-52, Mich. Fedn. Music Clubs, 1948-55; tchr. Ea. Mich. U., 1939-42, Hartland Sch. Music, 1939-42, Pontiac (Mich.) Pub. Schs., 1942-45, Detroit Pub. Schs., 1945-73, pvt. studio, 1973-90. Performer cello South Oakland Symphony, 1958-65, Detroit Women's Symphony, 1951-68, Riviera Theatre Orch., 1959, 60, Masonic Auditorium Opera, Ballet Seasons, 1959-65, Toledo Ohio Symphony, 1963-70, others; performer trumpet Detroit Brass Quartet, 1974-78; piano accompanist various auditions, recitals, solo and ensemble festivals; composer: Let There Be Music, 1949, Fantasy for French Horn and Symphonic Band, 1951. Mem. Quota Internat., Delta Omicron. Home: 14650 N Alamo Canyon Dr Tucson AZ 85737-8812

SEAMAN, MICHAEL RAY, investment company executive; b. Tacoma, Wash., Nov. 15, 1951; s. Frank F. and Louise Mae (Nichols) S.; m. Janice Stevenson Hoffmann, July 4, 1983; children: Anne Louise, Carolyn Mershon. Student, Waseda U., Japan, 1972; BA, Occidental Coll., 1974; MBA in Real Estate Fin., Claremont Grad Sch., 1977; MBA in Econs., U. So. Calif., 1978, postgrad., 1978-80. Mgmt. cons. Arthur Anderson, CPA, L.A., 1977-78; prin. Seaman & Assocs., Astroria, Oreg., 1980-87; broker comml. real estate Matlow-Kennedy, Torrance, Calif., 1987-89; v.p., gen. mgr. Shuwa Investments Corp., L.A., 1989-90; v.p., gen. mgr. Kibel, Green Inc., Santa Monica, 1991—, bd. dirs.; Bd. dirs. Turnaround Mgmt. Assn., L.A. Rsch. author: Work and Health, 1980. Active L.A. County Art Mus. Grad. fellow State of Calif., 1975-79. Mem. Japan Am. Soc., Waseda U. Alumni Assn., Occidental Coll. Alumni Assn., U. So. Calif. Bus. Sch. Alumni Assn., Claremont Grad Sch. Alumni Assn. Office: Kibel Green Inc Ste 420 2001 Wilshire Blvd Santa Monica CA 90402

SEAMANS, DAVID ALVIN, engineering educator; b. Lawrence, Kans., June 13, 1927; s. Robert Liddel and Ruth (Fisher) S.; m. Saralou Mather, Apr. 6, 1957 (dec. July, 1990); children: John Christian, Ruth Elizabeth. BEE, U. Kans., 1950, MEE, 1956; PhD, Oregon Stte U., Corvallis, 1968. Jr. engr. Black and Veatch, Kansas City, Mo., 1950-52; asst. U. Kans., Lawrence, 1952-54; asst. prof. Wash. State U., Pullman, 1954-62; assoc. prof. Washington State U., Pullman, 1962-92, ret., 1992. With USNR, 1945-46. Mem. IEEE (sr. mem., student branch advisor 1988-91), Am. Soc. for Engring. Edn. (campus rep. 1984-91). Republican. Episcopalian. Home: 1405 NW Orion Dr Pullman WA 99163-3331 Office: Wash State U Sch Elec Engring & Comp Sci Pullman WA 99164-2752

SEARIGHT, PATRICIA ADELAIDE, retired radio and television executive; b. Rochester, N.Y.; d. William Hammond and Irma (Winters) S. BA, Ohio State U. Program dir. Radio Sta. WTOP, Washington, 1952-63, gen. mgr. info., 1964; radio and TV cons., 1964-84; ret., 1984; producer, dir. many radio and TV programs; spl. fgn. news corr. French Govt., 1956; v.p. Micro Beads, Inc., 1955-59; sec., dir. Dennis-Inches, Corp., 1955-59; exec. dir. Am. Women in Radio and TV, 1969-74; fgn. service officer U.S. Dept. State, AEC, ret. Mem. pres.'s coun. Toledo Mus. Art. Recipient Kappa Kappa Gamma Alumna achievement award. Mem. Am. Women in Radio and TV (program chmn.; corrs. sec.; dir. Washington chpt.; pres. 1958-60, nat. membership chmn. 1962-63, nat. chmn. Industry Info. Digest 1963-64, Mid-Eastern v.p. 1964-66), Soc. Am. Travel Writers (treas. 1957-58, v.p. 1958-59), Nat. Acad. TV Arts and Scis., Women's Advt. Club (Washington, pres. 1959-60), Nat. Press Club, Soroptimist, Kappa Kappa Gamma. Episcopalian. Home: 9498 E Via Montoya Dr Scottsdale AZ 85255-5074

SEARING, LEE RICHARD, manufacturing executive; b. Inglewood, Calif., Mar. 15, 1948; s. Richard Lee Searing and Eileen Theresa Sullivan; m. Susan Mattie Brown, Feb. 25, 1972; children: Christina, Richard, Katherine. BA, LaVerne Coll., 1970. Plant mgr. State Awning, Montebello, Calif., 1970-72, Bernard Epps & Co., Vernon, Calif., 1972-85; co-owner, exec. v.p. Searing Industries, Rancho Cucamonga, Calif., 1985—. Pres. West Arcadia (Calif.) Pony League, 1990, bd. dirs., 1992—. Republican. Home: 60 W Wistaria Ave Arcadia CA 91007

SEARS, JAMES DONALD, environmental planner, writer; b. Fort Knox, Ky., Sept. 1, 1922; s. Charles Henry and Vivian (Fosdick) S.; m. Dorothy Rue, Oct. 4, 1947; children Jamie Bechtold, Christopher H., Matthew F. BS in Forestry, U. Mich., 1943; postgrad. in wildlife conservation, U. Mo., 1946-47. Registered forester, Calif. Instr. forestry U. Mo., Columbia, 1946; recreation planner Mo. Dept. Resources and Devel., Jefferson City, Mo., 1947-50; park landscape architect Nat. Park Svc., Santa Fe, N.Mex., 1950-54; engr. U.S. Forest Svc., Fresno, Calif., 1954-56; landscape architect U.S. Forest Svc., San Francisco, 1956-61; chief recreation sect. U.S. Army Corps of Engrs., San Francisco, Calif., 1961-66; chief environ. rsch. div. U.S. Army Corps of Engrs., San Francisco, 1966-88; writer, environ. cons. pvt. practice, Walnut Creek, Calif., 1988—; exec. com. Nat. Safety Coun., Chgo., 1975-87, bd. dirs., 1979-83, v.p. 1983-87; sr. environ. advisor U.S. Army, Norton AFB, 1981-82; vis. lectr. U. Calif., Berkeley, Davis, Tex. A&M. Author: Guide-Environmental Policy, 1991. Sgt. U.S. Army, 1944-46, Mideast. Mem. Calif. Writers Club (bd. dirs. 1991), Nat. Assn. Ret. Fed. Employees, Sons in Retirement, Sigma Alpha Epsilon. Episcopalian. Home: 1784 Alvarado Walnut Creek CA 94596

SEARS, LOWELL EDWARD, financial executive; b. Seattle, Feb. 27, 1951; s. Rolland Eugene and Doris Ann (Davidson) S.; m. Cynthia Ann Cox, Dec. 31, 1977; 1 child, Ian. BA in Econs., Claremont McKenna Coll., 1973; MBA, Stanford U., 1976. Funding analyst Chem. Bank, London, 1973-74; analyst, then sr. analyst Atlantic Richfield Co., L.A., 1976-78, financing mgr., 1978-80, mgr. ops. analysis, 1983-84, mgr. control and analysis, 1984-86; chief fin. officer Ventures div. Atlantic Richfield Co., Woodland Hills, Calif., 1980-83; treas. Amgen, Inc., Thousand Oaks, Calif., 1986-88, v.p., chief fin. officer, 1988-92; sr. v.p. Asia Pacific, 1992—. Office: Amgen Inc Amgen Ctr Thousand Oaks CA 91362

SEARS, STEVEN LEE, screenwriter, consultant; b. Ft. Gordon, Ga., Dec. 23, 1957; s. Richard Bruce Sr. and Marian (Dean) S. AA, U. Fla., 1976; BA in Theater cum laude, Fla. State U., 1980. Writer Stephen J. Cannell Prodns., Hollywood, Calif., 1984-88, story editor, 1987-88; story editor VI-ACOM/Hargrove/Silverman Prodns., 1988; writer A. Shane Prodns., Superboy Prodns., 1989; exec. story cons. Highwayman Glen Larson/New West Prodns., Universal City, Calif., 1988; writer TV pilots Columbia Pictures Television, 1990. Writer (TV shows) Riptide, 1984-86, Hadcastle & McCormick, 1985, The A-Team, 1986-87, Stingray, 1987, Jesse Hawkes, 1989, Superboy, 1989, Grand Slam, 1989, Hardball, 1989, Who Gets Harry?, 1989, (TV pilots) Harry O'Fell-Detective from Hell, 1990, The Inquisitor, 1990, (screenplay) Endangered Species; story editor TV shows J.J. Starbuck, 1987-88, The Father Dowling Mysteries, 1988; co-producer (TV show) Swamp Thing, 1991; producer (TV show) Raven, 1992-93. Mem. AFTRA, SAG, Writers Guild Am. Democrat.

SEASTONE, BRIAN ARTHUR, protective services official, consultant; b. Boulder, Colo., May 27, 1957; s. Walter Gene and Elizabeth Joyce (Cronland) S. BA, U. Phoenix, 1987. Dep. sheriff, evidence technician Boulder (Colo.) County Sheriff's Dept., 1974-80; officer U. Ariz. Police Dept., Tucson, 1980-84, pub. info. officer, cpl., 1984-87, sgt., 1987-89, adminstrv. sgt., 1989—; faculty senator U. Ariz., 1990-92. Tech. advisor (video) Date Rape What Could Happen?, 1988 (Cert. of merit 1989). Recipient Outstanding Citizen award Boulder C. of C., 1973, Greek Achievement award Western Regional Greek Conf., 1992; named Ariz. Crime Prevention Officer of Yr., Ariz. Crime Prevention Assn., 1987, 88. Mem. Internat. Assn. Campus Law Enforcement Adminstrs. (assoc.), Ariz. Accreditation PAC, So. Ariz. Alumni Assn. (v.p. 1989-90, pres. 1990-93), Kappa Alpha (advisor). Democrat. Roman Catholic. Office: U Ariz Police Dept 1200 E Lowell Tucson AZ 85721

SEATON, MICHAEL DAVID, personnel executive; b. Laramie, Wyo., Apr. 3, 1950; s. Ralph David Seaton and Evelyn Marie (Kelly) Holderness; m. Susan Carol Runyon, Feb. 14, 1971 (div. 1992); 1 child, Sean Michael. D-raftsman Lutz Mfg. Inc., Laramie, 1972-77; shop foreman Wyo. Constrn. Co., Laramie, 1977-86; purchasing mgr. Mountain Cement Co., Laramie, 1986-91, dir. pers./safety, 1991—. With USN, 1968-72, Vietnam. Recipient Cert. of Merit, ARC, 1990. Home: 707 E Bradley St Laramie WY 82070-3225 Office: Mountain Cement Co 5 Sand Creek Rd # 339 Laramie WY 82070-6865

SEAU, TIAINA, JR. (JUNIOR SEAU), professional football player; b. Samoa, Jan. 19, 1969. Student, U. So. Calif. Linebacker San Diego Chargers, 1990—. Office: San Diego Chargers PO Box 609609 San Diego CA 92120

SEAVER, BRYAN RONDEAU, sports marketing company executive; b. Brookline, Mass., July 27, 1956; s. Donald Brown and Joanne (Rondeau) S.; m. Christine Patricia Carranza, July 11, 1987; children: Alexander Rondeau, Ryan Gilbert. BS, Syracuse U., 1978. Account exec. Carson-Shepherd Advt., Houston, 1978-79; ops. mgr. One World, Inc., San Diego, 1980; restaurant mgr. T.G.I. Fridays, Buffalo, 1981-82; commd. sales person San Diego Padres, 1983, promotions asst., 1984-85, promotions mgr., 1985-86, dir. promotions, 1986-90; v.p. Fastastic Sports Promotions, San Diego, 1990—; mem. steering com. ann. bus. meetings Major League Baseball, N.Y.C., 1989-90. Bd. dirs. San Diego Downtown Lions Club annual charity 10K and fun run. Republican. Office: Fantastic Sports Promotions 3760 Convoy St Fl 3D San Diego CA 92111-3742

SEAWELL, DONALD RAY, lawyer, publisher, arts center executive, producer; b. Jonesboro, N.C., Aug. 1, 1912; s. A.A.F. and Bertha (Smith) S.; m. Eugenia Rawls, Apr. 5, 1941; children: Brook Ashley, Donald Brockman. A.B., U. N.C., 1933, J.D., 1936, D.Litt., 1980; L.H.D., U. No. Colo., 1978. Bar: N.C. 1936, N.Y. 1947. With SEC, 1939-41, 45-47, Dept. Justice, 1942-43; chmn. bd., dir., pub., pres. Denver Post, 1966-81; chmn. bd., dir. Gravure West, L.A., 1966-81; dir. Swan Prodns., London; of counsel firm Bernstein, Seawell, Kove & Maltin, N.Y.C., 1979—; chmn. bd., chief exec. officer Denver Ctr. for Performing Arts, 1972—; ptnr. Bonfils-Seawell Enterprises, N.Y.C.; bd. vis. UNC Sch. of the Arts. Chmn. bd. ANTA, 1965—; mem. theatre panel Nat. Coun. Arts, 1970-74; bd. govs. Royal Shakespeare Theatre, Eng.; trustee Am. Acad. Dramatic Arts, 1967—, Hofstra U., 1968-69, Cen. City Opera Assn., Denver Symphony; bd. dirs., chmn. exec. com. Air Force Acad. Found., Nat. Ints. Outdoor Drama, Walter Hampden Meml. Library, Hammond Mus.; pres. Helen G. Bonfils Found., Denver Opera Found.; dir. Found. for Denver Ctr. for Performing Arts Complex, Population Crisis Com.; bd. dirs. Family Health Internat., Found. for Internat. Family Health; bd. visitors N.C. Sch. Arts, 1992—. With U.S. Army, WW II. Recipient Am. Acad. Achievement award, 1980, Tony award for producing On Your Toes, 1983, Voice Research and Awareness award Voice Found., 1983. Clubs: Bucks (London); Players, Dutch Treat (N.Y.C.); Denver Country, Denver, Cherry Hills Country, Mile High (Denver); Garden of Gods (Colorado Springs, Colo.). Office: Denver Ctr for Performing Arts 1050 13th St Denver CO 80204-2157

SEBALD, HANS, sociology educator; b. Selb, Bavaria, Germany, Feb. 22, 1929; came to U.S., 1954; s. Georg and Anna (Blank) S. BA, Manchester (Ind.) Coll., 1958; MS, Ohio State U., 1960, PhD, 1963. Rsch. asst. Ohio State U., Columbus, 1959-60, asst. instr., 1960-63; asst. prof. to prof. sociology Ariz. State U., Tempe, 1963—. Author: Momism-The Silent Disease of America, 1976, Witchcraft-The Heritage of a Heresy, 1978, Hexen damals-und heute?, 1989, Adolescence-A Social Psychological Analysis, 4 edits., 1968-92, Der Hexenjunge: Fallstudie eines Inquisitionsprozesses, 1992. Recipient Rsch. Stipends Ariz. State U., Tempe, 1975-91; Deutscher Akademischer Austauschdienst, Bonn, Germany. Mem. Phoenix Skeptics, Sierra Club.

SEBASTIAN, STEVEN BRYSON, investment banker; b. Lake Forest, Ill., July 23, 1954; s. Rex Arden and Dorothy (Bryson) S.; m. Ann Heidt, Apr. 28, 1984; children: Jonathan Rex, Katherine Ann. BA, Northwestern U., 1975, JD, 1979, MBA, 1979. Bar: Tex. 1979, N.Y. 1980. Law clk. to Chief Judge John R. Brown U.S. Ct. Appeals for 5th Circuit, Houston, 1979-80; assoc. Sullivan & Cromwell, N.Y.C., 1980-83; investment banker E.F. Hutton & Co., N.Y.C., 1983-85, Kidder, Peabody & Co., N.Y.C., 1985-89, Drexel Burnham Lambert, Beverly Hills, Calif., 1989-90; mng. dir. BT Securities Corp. sub. Bankers Trust N.Y. Corp., L.A., 1990—. Mem. Calif. Club, L.A. Country Club. Office: BT Securities Corp 300 S Grand Ave Los Angeles CA 90071

SEBASTIANI, DONALD AUGUST, winery executive. Former Calif. state assemblyman; chmn., chief exec. officer Sebastiani Vineyards, Sonoma, Calif. Office: Sebastiani Vineyards PO Box Aa Sonoma CA 95476-1219

SECKINGER, GERALD EDWIN, investor; b. Manchester, Mich., May 28, 1925; s. Joseph Edward and Myrta Mae (Weber) S.; widowed; children: Marianne Leitereg, Mark Bernard, Margo Lynn Guzman, Martin Neil, Martha Jean Toffol, Michael John, Matthew Joseph. BA, Mich. State U., 1950. Gen. mgr. Del Mar Hotel, Sault Ste. Marie, Mich., 1950-52; food svc. dir. Montgomery Ward & Co., Chgo., 1952-82; food svc. cons., pres. Seckinger Assocs., Glenview, Ill., 1982-87; pvt. investor Gerald Seckinger, Scottsdale, Ariz., 1987—. Civil defense officer U.S. Govt., Glenview, 1962-64. 1st lt. U.S. Army Air Corps, 1943-46. Mem. McCormick Ranch, POA, K of C, AM. Legion. Republican. Roman Catholic. Home: 7806 E Via De La Entrada Scottsdale AZ 85258

SECORD, RONALD LEE, computer engineer; b. Pontiac, Mich., June 23, 1937; s. Ralph Earl and Claudia Marie (Hill) S.; m. Carol Marie Inness, May 7, 1987. BSEE, U. Mich., 1963; MS in Computer Sci., Bradley U., 1970. Cert. data processor. Computer programmer GE, Bloomington, Ill., 1963-84; computer engr. Bull HN, Phoenix, 1984—. With USN, 1955-59. Mem. IEEE, Assn. of Computing Machinery. Home: 6901 W Stockman Glendale AZ 85308 Office: Bull HN Thunderbird & Black Canyon Phoenix AZ 85066

SEDARES, JAMES L., conductor; b. Chgo., Jan. 15, 1956. BMusEd, Webster U., 1977; MMusEd, Washington U., St. Louis, 1979. Assoc. condr. San Antonio Symphony, 1979-89; music dir. Phoenix Symphony Orch., 1989—. Office: Phoenix Symphony Orch Symphony Hall 3707 N 7th St Ste 107 Phoenix AZ 85014-5094

SEDLOCK, JOY, psychiatric social worker; b. Memphis, Jan. 23, 1958; d. George Rudolph Sedlock and Mary Robson; m. Thomas Robert Jones, Aug. 8, 1983. AA, Ventura (Calif.) Jr. Coll., 1978; BS in Psychology, Calif. Luth. U., 1980; MS in Counseling and Psychology, U. LaVerne, 1983; MSW, Calif. State U., Sacramento, 1986. Research asst. Camarillo (Calif.) State Hosp., 1981, tchr.'s aide, 1982; sub. tchr. asst. Vertura County Sch. Dist., 1981; teaching asst. Ventura Jr. Coll., 1980-82, tchr. adult edn., 1980-84; psychiatric social worker Yolo County Day Treatment Ctr., Broderick, Calif., 1986, Napa (Calif.) State Hosp., 1986—. Bd. dirs. Napa County Humane Soc. Mem. NOW. Home: PO Box 1095 Yountville CA 94599-1095 Office: Napa State Hosp Napa/Vallejo Hgwy Napa CA 49558

SEDORY, PAUL EDWARD, engineer; b. Oak Park, Ill., Feb. 11, 1963; s. Edward Thomas and Barbra (Reinecke) S. BS in Chem. Engring., U. Ill., Chgo., 1987; MS in Civil Engring., UCLA, 1992. Engr. in Tng., Calif. Lab technician Allied-Signal Engring. Materials Rsch. Ctr., Des Plaines, Ill., 1985-86; engr. mgr. pilot and equipment svc. sect. James M. Montgomery Cons. Engrs., Inc., Pasadena, Calif., 1987—; lectr. Joint Instrumentation Conf., Santa Ana, Calif., 1990, '91. Contbr. articles to profl. jours. Mem. AICHE, Am. Water Works Assn. Office: Montgomery Engrs 250 N Madison Ave Pasadena CA 91101

SEDWICK, JOHN WEETER, federal judge; b. Kittanning, Pa., Mar. 13, 1946; s. Jack D. and Marion (Hilton) S.; m. Deborah Brown, Aug. 22, 1966; children: Jack D. II, Whitney Marie. BA summa cum laude, Dartmouth Coll., 1968; JD cum laude, Harvard U., 1972. Bar: Alaska 1972, U.S. Dist. Ct. Alaska 1972, U.S. Ct. Appeals (9th cir.) 1973. Lawyer Burr, Pease and Kurtz, Anchorage, 1972-81, 1982-92; dir. div. lands State of Alaska,

Anchorage, 1981-82; sole practice Anchorage, 1983; judge U.S. Dist. Ct. Alaska, Anchorage, 1992—. Mem. membership com. Commonwealth North, Anchorage, 1985; bd. dirs. South Addition Alaska R.R. Com., Anchorage, 1984. Served to sgt. USNG, 1969-72. Mem. ABA, Alaska Bar Assn. (chmn. environ. law sect. 1984, law examiners com. 1986-89, civil rules com. 1990-92, fee arbitration com. 1991-92), Anchorage Bar Assn. Episcopalian. Home: 1112 S St Anchorage AK 99501-4230 Office: Box 32 222 W 7th Ave Anchorage AK 99513

SEE, RONALD EUGENE, neuroscientist; b. Portland, Oreg., July 15, 1961; s. Donald Harlan and Bernice (Jurovich) S.; m. Diane Brenda Griffith, July 26, 1986; children: Amanda, Andrew. BA, U. Calif., Berkeley, 1984; MA, UCLA, 1985, PhD, 1989. Rsch. assoc. UCLA, 1984-89; asst. prof. neurosci. Wash. State U., Pullman, 1989—. Contbr. articles to profl. jours. Recipient NIH First award, 1991, Young Investigator award Am. Coll. Neuropsychopharmacology, 1991. Mem. AAAS, Am. Sci. Affiliation, Soc. for Neurosci. Baptist. Office: Wash State Univ Dept Psychology Pullman WA 99164-4820

SEEBA, HINRICH CLAASSEN, language educator; b. Hannover, Germany, Feb. 5, 1940; came to U.S., 1967; s. Hinrich and Irmgard (Witte) S. Student, Göttingen, Zürich, Tübingen univs., 1960-67; staatsexamen, U. Tübingen, Fed. Republic of Germany, 1966, PhD, 1967. Asst. prof. German U. Calif., Berkeley, 1968-72, assoc. prof., 1972-76, prof., 1976—, chmn. dept. German, 1977-81, 89-91; vis. prof. Free U. Berlin, 1992. Author: Kritik des ästehtischen Menschen, 1970, Die Liebe zur Sache, 1973; author, editor: Kleist: Dramen I, 1987, II, 1991; co-editor Politzefs, 1975, Brinkmanfs, 1981; contbr. scholarly papers on German lit. to jours.; editorial bd. Lessing Yearbook, 1979—, Eighteenth Century Studies, 1982-85, The German Quar., 1988-92; adv. bd. German Studies Rev., 1990—. Studienstiftung fellow, 1963-68, Guggenheim Found. fellow, 1970-71. Mem. MLA, Am. Assn. Tchrs. German, German Studies Assn., Philol. Assn. of Pacific, Lessing Soc. (pres. 1985-87), Heine Soc., Grillparzer Gesellschaft, Herder Gesellschaft. Lutheran. Office: U Calif Dept German Berkeley CA 94720

SEEBASS, ALFRED RICHARD, III, aerospace engineer, educator, university dean; b. Denver, Mar. 27, 1936; s. Alfred Richard and Marie Estelle (Wright) S.; m. Nancy Jane Palm, June 20, 1958; children: Erik Peter, Scott Gregory. B.S.E. magna cum laude, Princeton U., 1958, M.S.E. (Guggenheim fellow), 1961; Ph.D. (Woodrow Wilson fellow), Cornell U., 1962. Asst. prof. Cornell U., 1962-64, assoc. prof., 1964-72, prof., 1972-75, assoc. dean, 1972-75; prof. aerospace and mech. engring., prof. math. U. Ariz., Tucson, 1975-81; dean Coll. Engring. and Applied Sci., U. Colo., Boulder, 1981—; cons. in field; mem. coms. NAE, NAS, NRC, NASA, Dept. Transp., sci. adv. bd. Air Force, Aeros. and Space Engring. Bd., Los Alamos Nat. Lab; grant investigator NASA, Office Naval Rsch., Air Force Office Sci. Rsch., 1966—. Editor: Sonic Boom Research, 1967, Nonlinear Waves 1974; mem. editorial bd. Ann. Rev. Fluid Mechanics, Phys. Fluids, AIAA Jour.; editor-in-chief Progress Astro. and Aeronatuics; contbg. author: Handbook of Applied Mathematics, 1974; contbr. articles to profl. jours. Recipient (with H. Sobieczky) Max Planck Rsch. prize, Germany, 1991. Fellow AIAA, AAAS; mem. NAE, Tau Beta Pi. Office: Univ Colo Coll Engring and Applied Sci Boulder CO 80309

SEEDS, DALE STIMMEL, retired career military officer; b. Spokane, Wash., Jan. 12, 1918; s. Albert Roscoe and Margaret Olive (Stimmel) S.; m. Eleanor Grace Sutton, Oct. 21. 1946; 1 child, Barbara. BA, U. Wash., 1940. Cert. command pilot. Commd. 2d lt. USAF, 1941, advanced through grades to col., ret., 1970; instr. pilot USAAF, Tex. and La., 1941-43; base commdr. USAAF, Roberts Field, Liberia, Dhahran, Saudi Arabia, and Gunter AFB, Ala., 1946-51; with A-3 55th bomb wing 15th AF, Italy, 1944-45; ops. officer CIA, 1952-55; ops. officer joint staff O/JCS, 1955-59; ops. officer USAF and USAF Security Svc. (later Air Force Electronic Security Command), 1959-65, Defense Intelligence Agy., 1965-66, Nat. Security Agy., 1966-70. Charter mem. Hist. Hawaii Found., Honolulu, 1974—, Rep. Presdl. Task Force, Washington, 1982—. Decorated Disting. Flying Cross USAAF, Air medals (2) USAAF. Mem. Hawaiian Philatelic Soc. (life), U. Wash. Alumni Assn. (life), Ret. Officers Assn. (life), Nat. Eagle Scout Assn. of Boy Scouts Am. (life), Seattle Yacht Club (life). Republican. Home: 67323 Kiapoko Pl Waialua HI 96791-9533

SEEGALL, MANFRED ISMAR LUDWIG, retired physicist, educator, real estate executive; b. Berlin, Germany, Dec. 23, 1929; s. Leonhard and Vera Antonie (Vodackova) S.; came to U.S., 1952, naturalized, 1957; m. Alma R. Sterner Clarke; 2 stepchildren: James, Mark. BS magna cum laude, Loyola Coll., 1957; MS, Brown U., 1960; PhD, Stuttgart (Germany) Tech. U., 1965. Research engr. Autonetics Corp. div. N.Am. Aviation, Downey, Calif., 1959-61; physicist Astronautics div. Gen. Dynamics, Inc., San Diego, 1961-62; research scientist Max Planck Inst., Stuttgart, 1962-65; instr. stats. and algebra San Diego City Coll., 1966; sr. research engr. Solar div. Internat. Harvester Co., San Diego, 1967-73; research cons. in energy and pollution, San Diego, 1974-83; part-time evening instr. Mesa Coll., San Diego, 1980-81; instr. Grossmont Coll., El Cajon, Calif., 1981; sr. scientist Evaluation Research Corp., San Diego, 1981-82, RCS analyst Teledyne Micronetics, San Diego, 1983-84, sr. design specialist Alcoa Defense Systems, San Diego, 1984-87, cons. phys scis., 1987-89; ind. contractor in tech. writing, engring. rsch. and real estate, 1990-92, freelance writer, 1993—. Mem. IEEE (sr.), Internat. Platform Assn., Calif. Parapsychology Found. (sec. research com.), Cottage of Czechoslovakia of House of Pacific Relations, Rosicrucian Order, Loyola Coll., Brown U. alumni assns. Republican. Club: San Diego Lodge AMORC. Contbr. articles on acoustics, pollution and temp. measurement methods to tech. jours.; patentee in field. Address: 8735 Blue Lake Dr San Diego CA 92119

SEEGER, SONDRA JOAN, artist; b. L.A., May 27, 1942; d. Reinhold Josheph and Bertha Catherine (Monese) S.; m. Richard John Pahl, Aug. 18, 1961 (div. 1974); children: Catherine Marie, Douglas Richard, Angela Gay, Susan Joan; m. David Ernest Matteson, Apr. 25, 1990. Student, Marylhurst Coll., 1960. Pvt. practice musician various locations, 1973-81; security guard MGM Hotel, Las Vegas, 1981-82; real estate salesperson Century 21, Kent, Wash., 1983-85; mgr. Viera Land & Cattle, Inc., La Grande, Oreg., 1984-92; self employed artist La Grande, 1991-92; ptnr. Old West Saddle Shop, La Grande, 1989—; com. mem. Oreg. State Forest Practices Com., N.E. Region, 1990-91. Named Union Co. Tree Farmer of Yr., Am. Tree Farm System, 1987. Mem. NRA, Mont. Miniature Art Soc., Small Woodlands Assn., Knickerbocker Artists (assoc.), United Pastelists of Am., The Art League, Miniature Art Soc. Fla. Republican. Home and Office: Old West Saddle Shop 55503 Oregon Hwy #244 La Grande OR 97850

SEEGMILLER, DONALD GLEN, artist; b. Provo, Utah, Sept. 24, 1955; s. David William and Jean (Black) S.; m. Marta Lynn Zawacki, Jan. 17, 1977; children: Jennifer Ann, Nicole Lynn, Andrew James. BFA, Brigham Young U., 1979. Graphic designer David O. McKay Inst. Edn., Provo, 1979-81; fine artist represented by Wadle Galleries Ltd., Santa Fe, 1981—; pvt. practice human figure painting instr., Orem, Utah, 1988-92. Represented in permanent collection Springville Mus. Art, numerous other pub. and pvt. collections; contbr. articles to profl. jours. Vol. Boy Scouts Am., Orem, 1988-91, Orem (Utah) Pub. Libr., 1988-92. Republican. Church of Jesus Christ Latter Day Saints. Home: 1665 N Main St Orem UT 84057

SEELENFREUND, ALAN, distribution company executive; b. N.Y.C., Oct. 22, 1936; s. Max and Gertrude (Roth) S.; m. Ellyn Bolt; 1 child, Eric. BME, Cornell U., 1959, M. in Indsl. Engring., 1960; PhD in Mgmt. Sci., Stanford U., 1967. Asst. prof. bus. adminstrn. Grad. Sch. Bus. Stanford U., Palo Alto, Calif., 1966-71; mgmt. cons. Strong, Wishart and Assocs., San Francisco, 1971-75; various mgmt. positions McKesson Corp., San Francisco, 1975-84, v.p., chief fin. officer, 1984-86, exec. v.p., chief fin. officer, 1986-89, chmn., chief exec. officer, 1989—, also bd. dirs.; bd. dirs. Armor All Products Corp. Trustee Golden Gate Nat. Park Assn. Mem. World Affairs Coun. No. Calif., Bus. Roundtable, San Francisco C. of C. (bd. dirs.), Calif. Bus. Roundtable, Bankers Club, St. Francis Yacht Club, Villa Taverna Club. Office: McKesson Corp 1 Post St San Francisco CA 94104-5203

SEELEY, ERIC EUGENE, electronics engineer; b. Seattle, Aug. 5, 1966; s. Eugene B. and Darlene E. (Watts) S.; m. Traci S. Davis, July 23, 1989. BSEE, Wash. State U., 1989. Electronics engr. Naval Air Warfare Ctr., China Lake, Calif., 1989—.

SEELEY, GILBERT STEWART, musician, educator, conductor; b. Evanston, Ill., June 9, 1938; s. Ralph Sherwood and Ethel (Stewart) S.; m. Elaine Fenimore, June 27, 1964 (div. 1981); children: Karen, Diane; m. Janet Schaeffer, Dec. 27, 1981; 1 child, Nicole. BM, Oberlin Conservatory of Music, Ohio, 1961; MM, U. So. Calif., 1966, DMA, 1969. Instr. U. Calif., Santa Cruz, 1967-70; asst. prof. music Calif. Inst. of the Arts, Valencia, 1970-75; assoc. prof. music Lewis & Clark Coll., Portland, Oreg., 1975-81; prof. music Lewis & Clark Coll., 1981—, chair dept music., 1992—; faculty Aspen Choral Inst., Colo., 1971-75; dir. Oreg. Repertory Singers, 1976—; mem. choral grants panel Nat. Endowment for Arts, Washington, 1986-88; guest conductor; conductor workshops in field. Album: (with Oregon Repertory Singers) The Glory of Christmas, 1992, Lou Harrison: Mass to St. Anthony Arvo Pårt: Berliner Messe, 1993. Mem. Am. Choral Dirs. Assn. Republican. Episcopalian. Home: 7054 SE 35th Ave Portland OR 97202-8314 Office: Lewis & Clark Coll 615 SW Palatine Hill Rd Portland OR 97219-7899

SEELEY, RODERICK ELI, cruise travel executive; b. L.A., Jan. 21, 1946; s. Walter Eli and Nancy Jane (Staples) S.; m. June Frei, Aug. 17, 1972; children: Evan, Jennifer. Student, Santa Barbara City Coll., 1965-67, 71, Mitchell Coll., 1969-71. Cert. cruise counselor. Advt. prodn. specialist J.C. Penney Co., Huntington Beach, Calif., 1971-72; advt. prodn. mgr. Associated Valley Publs., Encino, Calif., 1972-73; v.p., creative dir. Abonnir Advt., Northridge, Calif., 1973-76, Santa Barbara, Calif., 1976-78; v.p. ops. Barlin Pub., Encino, 1978-80; dir. mktg. ExperWorld/ExperCruise, Van Nuys, Calif., 1980-83; pres., chief exec. officer Cruise Pro Inc., Thousand Oaks, Calif., 1983—; dir. mktg. adv. bd. Norwegian Cruise Line, 1985—; dir. cruise adv. bd. Sunset Mag., 1987—. With USN, 1967-70. Recipient Cert. Appreciation Travel Trade Publs., 1987. Mem. Santa Barbara Advt. Fedn. (dir. 1975-78, pres. 1976-77, 4 profl. awards), Am. Advt. Fedn. L.A. (chmn. student ad competition dist. 15 1976-78), Nat. Assn. Cruise Only Agys. (charter/founding 1985, dir. 1985-88, treas. 1988-89, 91-92, 1st v.p. 1989-90, v.p. communications 1990-91), Internat. Platform Assn., Agoura Valley C. of C. Office: Cruise Pro Inc 99 Long Ct Ste 200 Thousand Oaks CA 91360-6066

SEELMEYER, JOHN MARVIN, newspaper editor; b. Sidney, Nebr., Mar. 28, 1951; s. George M. and Irene R. (Jantzen) S.; m. Shelley A. Costigan, June 14, 1977 (div. 1987); m. Barbara K. Marquand, May 19, 1990. BA, U. No. Colo., 1974. Reporter The Tribune, Greeley, Colo., 1974-84; freelance writer Greeley, 1984-88; asst. city editor The Tribune, Greeley, 1988-89; mng. editor Oroville (Calif.) Mercury-Register, 1989-90, The Union, Grass Valley, Calif., 1990—; instr. U. No. Colo., Greeley, 1974-88. Author: Quick! Call A Cop!, 1977; contbr. over 400 articles to profl. jours. Recipient Forum award Atomic Indsl. Forum 1982, Best Bus. Story award Nat. Newspaper Assn. 1989, Outstanding Svc. award Colo. Press Assn. 1982. Mem. Sun. Painting Club. Home: 321 Buena Vista Grass Valley CA 95945 Office: The Union 11464 Sutton Way Grass Valley CA 95945

SEETHALER, WILLIAM CHARLES, international business executive, consultant; b. N.Y.C., Dec. 4, 1937; s. William Charles and Catherine Frances (Flaherty) S. Student, Quinnipiac Coll., Conn., 1955-56, Ohio State U., 1956-58; BSBA, U. San Francisco, 1977; MBA, Pepperdine U., 1982. Asst. to v.p. sales T. Sendzimir, Inc., Waterbury, Conn. and Paris, 1960-66; mgr. internat. ops. Dempsey Indsl. Furnace Co., E. Longmeadow, Mass., 1966-67; mgr. internat. sales Yoder Co., Cleve., 1967-74; mng. dir., owner Seethaler & Assocs., Palo Alto, Calif.; owner, chief exec. officer Seethaler Internat. Ltd., Palo Alto, Calif., 1974—; ptnr. DFS Computer Assocs., San Jose, Calif., 1976-87. Bd. dirs. Palo Alto Fund, 1979—, chmn., 1986-88; community rels. advisor Stanford U., 1986—. Mem. Inst. Indsl. Engrs. (sr., v.p. profl. rels. Peninsula chpt. 1988-90, del. to Silicon Valley Engring. Coun. 1991-92, bd. dirs.), Joint Venture: Silicon Valley (bd. dirs. 1992—), Assn. Iron and Steel Engrs., Am. Mgmt. Assn., Assn. MBA EXecs., Palo Alto C. of C. (v.p. orgn. affairs 1976-77, pres. 1977-78, bd. dirs. 1975-79), U. San Francisco Alumni Assn., Stanford U. Alumni Assn., Pepperdine U. Alumni Assn., Stanford Buck Club, Stanford Cardinal Cage Club, Stanford Diamond Club. Office: 701 Welch Rd Ste 323 Palo Alto CA 94304-1705

SEFERIAN, EDWARD, symphony conductor; b. Cleve., Mar. 23, 1931; s. Loutfeg and Berjhewie (Kouzouian) S.; m. Jan Barbara Spears, June 11, 1955; children: Susan, Linda, Marc. BS in Violin, Juilliard Sch. Music, N.Y.C., 1957; MS, Juilliard Sch. Music, 1958. Prof. music U. Louisville, 1958-59, U. Puget Sound, Tacoma, 1959—; asst. concertmaster Seattle Symphony, 1960-66; condr., mus. dir. Tacoma Symphony, 1959—; with USMC band; dir. Winterim program U. Puget Sound, 1973-74. Violinist U. Puget Sound Faculty Trio, Tacoma Symphony String Quartet; first performance of William Bergsma's Concerto for Violin and Orchestra, 1966, Leroy Ostransky's Concerto for Violin and Orchestra, 1980. Sgt. USMC, 1951-54. Invited by Pablo Casals to Casals Festival, P.R., 1959-69; recipient Nat. award for Cultural Achievement, Steinway Piano Co., 1967, Faculty Recognition award U. Sound Alumni Assn., 1972, Tacoma Arts Commn. Achievement in the Arts award, 1983, James H. Binns Disting. Svc. award Friends of Tacoma Community Coll. Libr., 1988, Wash. String Tchrs. Assn. award for outstanding string teaching in higher edn., 1992. Mem. Music Educators Nat. Conf. Home: 2714 N Vista View Dr Tacoma WA 98407-1017 Office: U Puget Sound 1500 N Warner St Tacoma WA 98416-0001

SEFTOR, RICHARD EDWARD BARNET, biochemist; b. Van Nuys, Calif., July 13, 1952; s. Gerald Michael and Hilda (Cohen) S.; m. Elisabeth Ann Rabinek, Aug. 30, 1972; 1 child, Rebecca Merle. BS, U. Calif., Berkeley, 1977; PhD, U. Calif., L.A., 1983. Postdoctoral rsch. assoc. in biochemistry U. Ariz., Tucson, 1983-86, postdoctoral rsch. assoc. in anatomy, 1986-90, rsch. asst. prof., 1990—; presenter papers in field. Author: (with R.G. Jensen) chpt. in Model Building in Plant Physiology/Biochemistry, 1987, (with others) chpt. in Progress in Photosynthesis Research, 1987, (with J.P. Thornber and others) chpt. in Advances in Photosynthesis Research, 1984; contbr. articles to profl. jours. Scolarship Marine Biol. Lab., 1980; Teaching fellowship U. Calif., 1978-82, NIH Cancer Biology Tng. Grant fellow U. Ariz., 1986-89; grantee NIH, U. Ariz., UpJohn Co., Instl. Am. Cancer Soc., Ariz. Disease Control Rsch. Commn. Mem. AAAS, Am. Soc. for Cell Biology, Metastasis Rsch. Soc. Jewish. Home: 2234 E Water St Tucson AZ 85719-3439 Office: U Ariz Dept Anatomy 1501 N Campbell Ave Tucson AZ 85724-0001

SEGAL, D. ROBERT, publishing and broadcast company executive; b. Oshkosh, Wis., Oct. 30, 1920; s. Morris Henry and Ida (Belond) S.; m. Kathryn McKenzie; children: Jonathan McKenzie, Janet Elizabeth Crane. Currently pres., chief exec. officer, dir. Freedom Newspapers, Inc., Irvine, Calif.; pres. Freedom Communications, Inc., Orange County Cable News, Kinston (N.C.) Free-Press, New Bern (N.C.) Sun Jour., Burlington (N.C.) Times-News, Jacksonville (N.C.) Daily News, WLNE-TV, New Bedford, Mass. and Providence, KFDM-TV, Beaumont, Tex., WTVC-TV, Chattanooga, WRGB-TV, Schenectady, Freedom Newspapers of Fla., Inc., Crawfordsville Jour.-Rev. (Ind.), Greenville (Miss.) Delta Dem. Pub. Co., Dothan (Ala.) Progress; mng. ptnr. Clovis News-Jour. (N.Mex.), Rio Grande Valley Newspaper Group (Tex.), Gastonia Gazette (N.C.), Lima News (Ohio), Odessa Am. (Tex.), Pampa Daily News (Tex.), Orange County Cablenews Network. Trustee Children's Hosp of Orange County, Calif., Boy Scout Council of Orange County. Served with USAAF, 1942-45. Office: Freedom Newspapers Inc 17666 Fitch Irvine CA 92714-6022

SEGAL, STEVEN PAUL, social work educator; b. Bklyn., Jan. 13, 1943; married, 2 children. BA, Hunter Coll., Bronx, 1965; MSW, U. Mich., 1967; PhD, U. Wis., 1972. Caseworker N.Y. Bur. Child Welfare, N.Y.C., 1965; social group worker Windsor Group Therapy Project, Ont., 1965-66; unit supr. Fresh Air Soc., Detroit, 1966; caseworkr Lansing (Mich.) Cons. Ctr., 1966-67, Jewish Family & Children's Svcs., Detroit, 1967; asst. to assoc. prof. and rsch. social worker U. Calif., Berkeley, 1972-88; prin. investigator Inst. Sci. Analysis, Berkeley, 1982—; assoc. dir. Ctr. for Rsch. on Orgn. and Financing, Western Consortium, Berkeley, 1988-92; dir. Mental Health and Social Welfare Rsch. Group U. Calif., Berkeley, 1973—; prof. sch. social welfare and pub. health U. Calif., 1988—; dir. Ctr. Self Help Rsch., 1990—; lectr. in field; conductor workshops in field. Contbr. numerous articles to profl. jours. Recipient Medal of Brescia, Italy, 1987, Western European Regional Rsch. Fulbright award, 1986-87; NIMH traineeships, 1965, 66, 67, 68, 69, 70-72; N.Y. State Rsch. fellow in psychiat. epidemiology, 1969-71, others. Mem. NASW, APHA, Am. Sociol. Assn., Am. Psychol. Assn. Home: 733 Santa Barbara Rd Berkeley CA 94707-2045 Office: Sch Social Welfare 120 Haviland Hall U of Calif Berkeley CA 94720

SEGALL, MARK M., physician, colon and rectal surgeon; b. Far Rockaway, N.Y., Jan. 20, 1948; s. Solomon Kief and Sylvia Tina (Stangel) S.; m. Nikki Forbes, Feb. 18, 1978; children: Jeremy, Eli, Leah, Noah. Student, Wayne State U., 1965-66, U. Mich., 1966-68; MD, U. Mich., 1972. Diplomate Am. Bd. Surgery, Am. Bd. Colon and Rectal Surgery. Intern in surgery UCLA, 1972-73; physician Kaiser, W. L.A., 1973-75; resident in surgery William Beaumont Hosp., Royal Oak, Mich., 1975-79; colon and rectal surgery fellow U. Minn., Mpls., 1979-80; pvt. practice surgeon Southfield, Mich., 1980-83, Los Gatos, Calif., 1983—; clin. instr. Wayne State U. Sch. Medicine, Detroit, 1980-84, Stanford U. Sch. Medicine, Palo Alto, Calif., 1984—; clin. asst. prof. Dept. Surgery Stanford U. Sch. Medicine, 1990—. Contbr. articles to profl. jours. Active Little Learners, 1986—. Recipient Profl. Vol. of Yr. award Am. Cancer Soc., 1988. Fellow Southwestern Surg. Cong., Am. Coll. Surgeons, Am. Soc. Colon and Rectal Surgeons (Ohio Valley Proctologic Soc. award); mem. Soc. Am. Gastrointestinal Endoscopic Surgeons, San Jose Surg. Soc., Santa Clara Surg. Soc., N.W. Soc. Colon and Rectal Surgeons, No. Calif. Soc. Colon and Rectal Surgeons, Santa Clara County Med. Soc., Calif. Med. Assn., Am. Med. Assn. Democrat. Jewish. Office: 15195 National Ave # 202 Los Gatos CA 95032-2631

SEGEL, KAREN LYNN JOSEPH, tax professional, lawyer; b. Youngstown, Ohio, Jan. 15, 1947; d. Samuel Dennis and Helen Anita Joseph; m. Alvin Gerald Segel, June 9, 1968 (div. Sept. 1976); 1 child, Adam James. BA in Soviet and East European Studies, Boston U., 1968; JD, Southwestern U., 1975. Adminstrv. asst. Olds Brunel & Co., N.Y.C., 1968-69, U.S. Banknote Corp., N.Y.C., 1969-70; tax acct. S.N. Chilkov & Co. CPA's, Beverly Hills, Calif., 1971-74; intern Calif. Corps. Commr., 1975; tax. sr. Oppenheim Appel & Dixon CPA's, L.A., 1978, Fox, Westheimer & Co. CPA's, L.A., 1978, Zebrak, Levine & Mepos CPA's, L.A., 1979; ind. cons. acctg., taxation specialist Beverly Hills, 1980—; bd. dirs. World Wide Motion Pictures Corp., L.A. Editorial adv. bd. Am. Biog. Inst. High sch. amb. to Europe People-to-People Orgn., 1963. Named 1991, 93 Woman of Yr., Am. Biog. Inst. Mem. Nat. Soc. Tax Profls., Nat. Trust for Hist. Preservation, Am. Mus. Natural History, Winterthur Guild, Women's Inner Circle of Achievement.

SEGGER, MARTIN JOSEPH, museum director, art history educator; b. Felixtowe, Eng., Nov. 22, 1946; s. Gerald Joseph and Lillian Joan (Barker-Emery) S.; m. Angele Cordonier, Oct. 4, 1968; children: Cara Michelle, Marie-Claire, Margaret Ellen. B.A., U. Victoria, 1969, Diploma in Edn., 1970; M. in Philosophy, U. London, 1973. Prof. art history U. Victoria, B.C., 1970-74; museologist Royal B.C. Mus., Victoria, 1974-77; dir. Maltwood Art Mus., prof. art history U. Victoria, B.C., 1977—; cons. Nat. Mus. Corp., Ottawa, 1977, UNESCO, O.E.A., Cairo, 1983. Author: exhbn. catalogue House Beautiful, 1975, Arts of the Forgotten Pioneers, 1971, Victoria: An Architectural History, 1979, (commendation Am. Assn. State and Local History 1980), This Old House, 1975, This Old Town, 1979, British Columbia Parliament Buildings, 1979, The Heritage of Canada, 1981, Samuel Maclure: In Search of Appropriate Form, 1986 (Hallmark award 1987), (a guide) St. Andrew's Cathedral, 1990, The Development of Gordon Head Campus, 1988, An Introduction to Museum Studies, 1989, An Introduction to Heritage Conservation, 1990. Bd. govs. Heritage Can. Found., 1979-83; chmn. City of Victoria Heritage Adv. Com., 1975-79; bd. dirs. B.D. Heritage Trust, 1977-86, B.C. Touring Coun.; mem. B.C. Heritage Adv. Bd., 1973-83; councillor City of Victoria, 1987—, Provincial Capital Commn., 1991—; bd. dirs. B.C. Govt. House Found., 1987-93; pres. Assn. Vancouver Island Municipalities, 1993—. Recipient award Heritage Can. Communications, 1976, Heritage Conservation award Lt. Gov. B.C., 1989. Fellow Royal Soc. Arts; mem. Can. Mus. Assn. (counsellor 1975-77), Internat. Coun. Mus. (exec.), Internat. Coun. Monuments and Sites (bd. dirs. 1980-92), Soc. Study Architecture Can. (bd. dirs. 1979-81), Authors Club (London), Can. Mus. Dirs. Orgn., Canarvon Club. Roman Catholic. Home: 1035 Sutlej St, Victoria, BC Canada V8V 2V9 Office: U Victoria, PO Box 1700, Victoria, BC Canada V8W 2Y2

SEGNA, DON ROBERT, federal government administrator; b. Fontana, Calif., June 3, 1932; s. Dominick and Sylvia (Orion) S.; m. Joan Frances Mottoh, Oct. 17, 1959; children: Keri Robin, Jan Marie, Todd Dominick. AA, Chaffey Jr. Coll., Ontario, Calif., 1952; BS in Aero., Calif. State Poly. U., 1958. Flight test engr. Gen. Dynamics Corp., San Diego, 1958-60, lead test engr., 1960-62; mission requirements mgr. NASA-Johnson Space Ctr., Houston, 1963-75, launch criteria mgr., 1967-79, shuttle requirements mgr., 1975-77; R&D adminstr. Dept. of Energy, Richland, Wash., 1979—; mission staff engr. Apollo 16, Johnson Space Ctr., Houston, 1971-72; experiment mgr. Apollo/Soyous, Johnson Space Ctr., 1974; synthesis group mem. space exploration com. NASA, Crystal City, Va., 1991; instr. energy U. Houston, 1976. Author (aerospace confs.) Nuclear Rocket Reliability, 1991, Nuclear Electric Reliability, 1992. V.p., engr. Water and Sewer Dist. 50, Seabrook, Tex., 1969-71; pres. El Cary Civic Orgn., Seabrook, 1975; v.p. Seabrook Soccer Club, Seabrook, 1978-79; chmn. Nuclear Medicine Working Group. JC Man of Yr., Jr. C. of C., Clear Lake City, Tex., 1968. Mem. AIAA, ASHRAE (v.p. 1984-85, pres. 1985-86, chmn. regional meeting 1986, Outstanding award 1986). Office: Dept of Energy Richland Field Office MS A5-90 PO Box 550 Richland WA 99352

SEIBEL, ERWIN, oceanographer, educator; b. Schwientochlowitz, Germany, Apr. 29, 1942; came to U.S., 1952. BS, CCNY, 1965; MS, U. Mich., 1966, PhD, 1972. Asst. research oceanographer U. Mich., Ann Arbor, 1972-75, assoc. research oceanographer, 1975-78, asst. dir. sea grant, 1975-78; environ. lab dir. San Francisco State U., 1978-81, chmn. dept. geoscis., 1981-88, dean undergraduate studies, 1988—; sr. scientist cruises U. Mich., 1971-78; mem. sea grant site rev. teams Nat. Sea Grant Program, Washington, 1978—; bd. govs. Moss Landing Marine Labs., Calif., 1981—; mem. adv. com. Ctr. Advancement Mercantile Spacefaring; coord. Biology Forum Calif. Acad. Scis., 1988-89; exec. sec. Oceans 83 Marine Tech. Soc., IEEE, San Francisco, 1982-83; coord. Symposium for Pacific AAAS El Nino Effect, 1983-84; dir. environ. monitoring nuclear power plant, 1972-78; mem. sci. adv. panel Calif. Commn. Tchr. Credentialing, 1988-93; mem. steering com. Pacific Basin Studies Ctr., 1990—. Contbr. articles to profl. jours.; developer photogrammetric technique for continuous shoreline monitoring. Advisor MESA program for Minority Students, San Francisco area, 1981-88; vol. San Francisco Bay Area council Girl Scouts U.S., 1982-86. Served to capt. U.S. Army, 1967-71, Vietnam. Grantee Am. Electric Power Co., 1972-78, Gt. Lakes Basin Commn., 1975-76, Calif. Div. Mines and Geology, 1986-88, Am. Coun. Edn. and Ford Found., 1990—. Recipient Exceptional Merit Service award San Francisco State U., 1984. Fellow AAAS, Calif. Acad. Scis., Geol. Soc. Am.; mem. N.Y. Acad. Scis., Am. Geophys. Union, Marine Tech. Soc. (pres. San Francisco Bay chpt. 1982-83), U. Mich. Alumni Assn., Gold Key (hon.), Sigma XI (pres. San Francisco State U. chpt. 1982-84, 90-92, Chautauqua coord, 1989—, faculty athletic rep. NCAA, NCAC, 1991—). Office: San Francisco State U Dean of Undergrad Studies 1600 Holloway Ave San Francisco CA 94132-1722

SEIDE, MARILYN BERNSTEIN, mental health administrator; b. Bklyn., Dec. 25, 1930; d. Louis and Hannah Rose (Bistrong) Bernstein; m. Ray Seide, Nov. 20, 1960; children: Jared David, Liam Evan. BA, Bennington Coll., 1952; MA, New Sch. Social Rsch., 1973; PhD, Union Inst., 1981. Mental health specialist, rsch. assoc. Juvenile Justice Inst., N.Y.C., 1973-79; supr. compliance monitoring Div. Criminal Justice Svcs., N.Y.C., 1979-80; assoc. dir. North Cen. Bronx (N.Y.) Hosp., 1980-87; program dir. Psychiatric Pavillion Bergen Pines City Hosp., Paramus, N.J., 1988-91; mgr. adult svcs. Riverside (Calif.) County Dept. Mental Health, 1991—. Contbr. articles to profl. jours. Pres. bd. vis. Manhattan Children's Psychiat. Ctr., 1977-91; adv. bd. Commn. on Quality Care, 1977-90; mem. Mental Health Advocacy Group for Children and Youth, 1984-91; pres. bd. trustees Walden Sch., 1988-90. Fellow Am. Orthopsychiatric Assn.; mem. APHA, Am. Coll. Healthcare Execs., Assn. Mental Health Adminstrs. Office: Riverside County Dept Mental Health 4095 County Circle Dr Riverside CA 92503

SEIDEL, EUGENE MAURICE, entrepreneur; b. Ft. Wayne, Ind., Mar. 18; s. Emil Richard and Tona Therese (Aden) S.; m. Nancy Ward Biddle, Sept. 2, 1950; children: Amy Aden Seidel Marks, Betsy Roberts Seidel Martin. BS in Chemistry, Bus. Adminstrn., Ind. U., 1944. Tech. service chemist Eberbach & Son Co., Ann Arbor, Mich., 1945-46; with tech. purchasing dept. W.A. Sheaffer Pen Co., Ft. Madison, Iowa, 1946-48; dir. chem. labs. Ind. U., Bloomington, 1948-53; mktg. and comml. developer Comml. Solvents Corp., Terre Haute, Ind., 1953-57; mgr. bus. exploration Crown Zellerbach Co., Camas, Wash., 1957-82; pres. Eugene M. Seidel Assocs., Inc. (including EMSA, Inc.), Gleneden Beach, Oreg., 1982-88, 1988—. Elder First Presbyn. Ch., Vancouver; mem. Clark County (Wash.) Comprehensive Health Planning Com., 1984 Ad Hoc com.; founder, bd. dirs. Columbia Bus. Community for the Arts, Vancouver, 1980-86, pres. 1984-86, v.p., 1987—; bd. dirs. Clark Coll. Found., Vancouver, 1983-88, Clark County Arts Council; trustee Neskowin (Oreg.) Valley Sch.; apptd. by gov. to 4 yr. term Health Coordination Council; past pres. Southwest Wash. Health Systems Agy., Shorewood West Condominium Owners Assn. Mem. AAAS, Am. Econ. Assn., Am. Mktg. Assn. (past bd. dirs.), Am. Chem. Soc. (past bd. dirs.), Chem. Mgmt. & Rsch. Assn. (life), Tech. Assn. Pulp and Paper Industry, Salishan Leaseholders, Inc. (chmn. bd. dirs., mem. archtl. com.). Lodge: Rotary. Home: 142 Salishan Dr PO Box 709 Gleneden Beach OR 97388 Office: The Marketplace at Shalishan PO Box 495 Gleneden Beach OR 97388

SEIDEL, GEORGE ELIAS, JR., animal scientist, educator; b. Reading, Pa., July 13, 1943; s. George E. Sr. and Grace Esther (Heinly) S.; m. Sarah Beth Moore, May 28, 1970; 1 child, Andrew. BS, Pa. State U., 1965; MS, Cornell U., 1968, PhD, 1970; postgrad., Harvard U. Med. Sch., Boston, 1970-71. Asst. prof. physiology Colo. State U., Ft. Collins, 1971-75, assoc. prof., 1975-83, prof., 1983—; vis. scientist Yale U., 1978-79, M.I.T., 1986-87. Co-editor: New Technologies in Animal Breeding, 1981; contbr. articles to profl. jours. Recipient Alexander Von Humboldt award, N.Y.C., 1983, Animal Breeding Research award Nat. Assn. Animal Breeders, Columbia, Mo., 1983, Clark award Colo. State U., 1982, Upjohn Physiology award, 1986; Gov's. award for Sci. and Tech., Colo., 1986. Mem. AAAS, NAS, Am. Dairy Sci. Assn., Am. Soc. Animal Sci. (Young Animal Scientist award 1983), Soc. for Study of Reprodn., Internat. Embryo Transfer Soc. (pres. 1979). Home: 3101 Arrowhead Rd Laporte CO 80535-9374 Office: Colo State U Animal Reprodn Lab Fort Collins CO 80523

SEIDEL, JOAN BROUDE, stockbroker, investment advisor; b. Chgo., Aug. 16, 1933; d. Ned and Betty (Treiger) Broude; m. Arnold Seidel, Aug. 18, 1957; children: David, Craig. BA, UCLA, 1954; postgrad., N.Y. Inst. Fin. Registered prin., investment advisor Morton Seidel & Co. Inc., L.A., 1970-74, v.p., 1974—, also bd. dirs.; instr. UCLA Extension, 1979-84. Treas. City of Beverly Hills, Calif., 1990—, chmn. rent adjustment bd., 1989-90, mem., 1983-89; mem. investment com. YWCA, L.A., 1987—, chmn. bd. dirs., 1989—, treas. Greater L.A., 1992—; bd. dirs. Discovery Fund for Eye Rsch., L.A., 1987—. Named Citizen of Yr. Beverly Hills C. of C., 1993. Fellow Assn. for Investment Mgmt. and Rsch.; mem. Nat. Assn. Security Dealers (bus. com. dist. 2S 1993—), L.A. Soc. Fin. Analysts, Orgn. Women Execs., Women in Bus., City Club, Phi Sigma Alpha. Home: 809 N Bedford Dr Beverly Hills CA 90210-3023 Office: Morton Seidel & Co Inc 350 S Figueroa St Bldg 499 Los Angeles CA 90071-1203

SEIDEL, ROBERT WAYNE, museum administrator, science historian; b. Kansas City, Mo., June 9, 1945; s. Wayne Herman and Harriet Anita (Day) S.; m. Judy Irene Sharp, Dec. 28, 1966 (div. 1969); m. Alison Publicover, Aug. 26, 1972 (div. 1989); 1 child, Mary Ruth;m. Patricia Mary Wing, Sept. 16, 1989 (div. 1990). BA, Westmar Coll., 1967; MA, U. Calif., Berkeley, 1968, PhD, 1978. Exhibit designer Lawrence Hall Sci., Berkeley, 1970-72; specialist Poland 4-city tour USIA, Warsaw, 1971-72; grad. rsch. and teaching asst. U. Calif., 1972-78; asst. prof. Tex. Tech U., Lubbock, 1978-83, dir. rsch., 1979-83; rsch. historian U. Calif., Berkeley, 1980-82, Laser History Project, Albany, Calif., 1983-85; adminstr. Bradbury Sci. Mus., Los Alamos, N.Mex., 1985-90, project leader, 1990-92; sr. staff mem. Ctr. Nat. Security Studies, Los Alamos, N.Mex., 1992—; cons. Office Naval Rsch., Washington, 1984—. Author: Lawrence and His Laboratory: A History of the Lawrence Berkeley Laboratory, 1989. Mem. Lubbock Heritage Soc., 1983, N.Mex. Sci. Ctr. Commn., 1989—; mem. adv. com. County Cultural Ctr., Los Alamos, 1986-89. Woodrow Wilson fellow, 1967, U. Calif. Regent's fellow, 1968, German Marshall Fund fellow, Grenoble, France, 1975. Mem. History Sci. Soc., Soc. for History Tech., Am. Hist. Assn., Soc. for Philosophy Tech., N.Mex. Acad. Scis. Democrat. Home: 505 Oppenheimer Dr Los Alamos NM 87544-2358 Office: Ctr Nat Security Studies MS A112 Los Alamos NM 87545

SEIDENSTICKER, EDWARD GEORGE, Japanese language and literature educator; b. Castle Rock, Colo., Feb. 11, 1921; s. Edward George and Mary Elizabeth (Dillon) S. B.A., U. Colo., 1942; M.A., Columbia U., 1947; postgrad., Harvard U., 1947-48; LittD (hon.), U. Md., 1991. With U.S. Fgn. Service, Dept. State, Japan, 1947-50; mem. faculty Stanford U., 1962-66, prof., 1964-66; prof. dept. Far Eastern langs. and lit. U. Mich., Ann Arbor, 1966-77; prof. Japanese Columbia U., 1977-85, prof. emeritus, 1986—. Author: Kafu The Scribbler, 1965, Japan, 1961, Low City, High City, 1983, Tokyo Rising, 1990; Translator: (by Murasaki Shikibu) The Tale of Genji, 1976. Served with USMCR, 1942-46. Decorated Order of Rising Sun Japan; recipient Nat. Book award, 1970; citation Japanese Ministry Edn., 1971; Kikuchi Kan prize, 1977; Goto Miyoko prize, 1982; Japan Found. prize, 1984; Tokyo Cultural award, 1985; Yamagata Banto prize, 1992.

SEIDMAN, MATTHEW SANFORD, psychotherapist; b. N.Y.C., June 4, 1934; s. David Saul and Anne (Greenblatt) S.; m. Micheline Conquy, May 18, 1967 (div. Dec. 29, 1978); 1 child, Anthony Paul; m. Kimberly Ann Kirkland, Dec. 30, 1982. BS, Syracuse U., 1955; MA, Azusa Pacific U., 1977; PhD, U. So. Calif., 1989. Licensed marriage and family therapist. News editor Radio-TV Daily, N.Y.C., 1955-57; acct. exec. Lee Kirkland Group Travel, N.Y.C., 1957-66; west coast v.p. Lee Kirkland Group Travel, L.A., 1966-75; fundraiser City of Hope Nat. Med. Ctr., L.A., 1971-87; columnist Valley Mag., Van Nuys, Calif., 1990-91; affiliate Valley Med. Ctr., Van Nuys, Calif., 1991—; psychotherapist pvt. practice L.A., 1981—; guest speaker in field. Appeared on Broadway in A Gift of Time, 1962, in various TV series, 1966-75 and feature films as Guy Danfort. Speaker Am. Parkinson Disease Assn., So. Calif., 1991—; vol. therapist Pacific Ctr. for Counseling & Psychotherapy, 1991—. Mem. Calif. Assn. Marriage and Family Therapists, Group Psychotherapy Assn. So. Calif. (pres. elect). Jewish. Home and Office: 13384 Contour Dr Sherman Oaks CA 91423-4802

SEIFERT, GEORGE, professional football coach; b. San Francisco, Jan. 22, 1940; m. Linda Seifert; children: Eve, Jason. Grad., U. Utah, 1963. Asst. football coach U. Utah, 1964; head coach Westminster Coll., 1965; asst. coach U. Iowa, 1966, U. Oreg., 1966-71; secondary coach Stanford U., 1972-74; head coach Cornell U., 1975-76; from secondary coach to defensive coord. San Francisco 49ers, 1980-89, head coach, 1989—. With AUS, 1963. Office: San Francisco 49ers 4949 Centennial Blvd Santa Clara CA 95054-1254*

SEIFERT, JOSEF, chemist, educator; b. Prague, Czech Republic, Sept. 21, 1942; came to U.S., 1977; s. Josef and Marta (Nova) S.; m. Yukari Takeuchi, Dec. 26, 1988; 1 child, Daniela. MSc, Prague Inst. Chem. Tech., 1964, PhD, 1973; postgrad., U. Calif., Berkeley, 1977-78. Rsch. specialist Prague Inst. Chem. Tech., 1973-77; from asst. to assoc. rsch. specialist pesticide chemistry and toxicology lab. U. Calif., Berkeley, 1978-85; prof., pesticide chemist dept. environ. biochemistry U. Hawaii, Honolulu, 1986—; adj. prof. Coll. Agr., Prague, 1976; vis. assoc. prof., chemist U. Calif., Davis, 1992-93; speaker in field, 1971—. Contbr. 52 articles to profl. jours. Grantee USDA, 1987, 1988-92. Mem. Am. Chem. Soc. (divsn. agrochemicals, program com. 1987—, exec. com. 1992—), U.S. Tennis Assn., Soc. Toxicology, Soc. Neuroscience (Hawaii state chpt.). Home: 1545 Nehoa # 401 Honolulu HI 96822 Office: U Hawaii Dept Environ Biochemistry 1800 E-W Honolulu HI 96822

SEIFTER, HARVEY, theater director, consultant; b. Cleve., Jan. 20, 1954; s. Benjamin and Betty (Levinsky) S. BA with high honors, Brandeis U., 1976. Exec. dir. Theater for the New City, N.Y.C., 1981-87; mng. dir. Magic Theatre, San Francisco, 1988—; panelist Nat. Endowment for the Arts, 1982-83; cons. Nat. Inst. for Archtl. Edn., N.Y.C., 1987-88, N.Y. State Council on the Arts, 1987-88; guest lectures on theatre include Harvard U., NYU, Ecole Nat., Paris. Translator play Scrapers in the Sky, 1985. Recipient 11 Obie awards, 1981-87. Democrat. Jewish. Office: Magic Theatre Fort Mason Ctr Bldg D San Francisco CA 94123

SEIGAL, BERNARD ROBERT (BUDDY BLUE), musician, writer; b. Syracuse, N.Y., Dec. 30, 1957; s. Clarence and Suzanne (Burrell) S. AA, Grossmont Coll., San Diego, 1982. Self employed musician and writer San Diego, 1981—, talent buyer, 1986—. Rec. artist Tales of the New West, 1984, Glad 'n' Greasy, 1985, Van Go, 1985, Jacks Are Wild, 1988, Guttersnipes 'n' Zealots, 1991; music journalist, contbr. articles to newspapers and mags. Recipient Best Arts Story award San Diego Press Club, 1991. Mem. Sigma Delta Chi (scholar 1982). Democrat. Office: PO Box 3763 La Mesa CA 91944

SEIGEL, DANIEL A., retail executive. With Thrifty Corp., pres., COO, 1990, then pres., CEO, now pres.; also exec. v.p. Pacific Enterprises. Office: Thrifty Corp 3424 Wilshire Blvd Los Angeles CA 90010

SEIGENTHALER, JOHN M(ICHAEL), television news reporter; b. Nashville, Dec. 21, 1955; s. John Lawrence and Dolores (Watson) S.; m. Kerry Lynn Brock, Jan. 4, 1992. BA in Pub. Policy, Duke U., 1978. Reporter Nashville Tennesean, 1978-79; advance rep. Kennedy for Pres., Washington, 1979-80; writer WDCN-TV, Nashville, 1980; producer WNGE-TV, Nashville, 1980-81; reporter, anchor WSMV-TV, Nashville, 1981-90, KOMO-TV, Seattle, 1990—. Reporter, producer documentaries: An Eye for An Eye, 1984 (ABA award), Reflections in Black and White, 1986 (Robert F. Kennedy Journalism award), Breaking Down the Barriers, 1990 (Pres.'s Com. on Employment for Disabled award); reporter, producer pub. affairs programs: Prison Riots, 1985 (Am. assn. TV Program Execs. award). Recipient 2 local Emmy awards, 1986. Mem. NATAS, Soc. Profl. Journalists. Roman Catholic. Office: KOMO TV 100 4th Ave N Seattle WA 98109

SEILER, FRITZ ARNOLD, physicist; b. Basel, Switzerland, Dec. 20, 1931; came to U.S., 1980; s. Friedrich and Marie (Maibach) S.; m. Mary Catherine Coster, Dec. 22, 1964; children: Monica, Simone, Daniel. BA in Econs., Basel Sch. of Econs., 1951; PhD in Physics, U. Basel, 1962. Rsch. assoc. U. Wis., Madison, 1962-63; scientific assoc. U. Basel, 1963-69, privat dozent, 1969-75, dozent, 1975-80; sr. scientist Lovelace Inhalation Toxicology Inst., Albuquerque, 1980-90; sr. tech. assoc. IT Corp., Albuquerque, 1990-92, disting. tech. assoc., 1992—; cons. Swiss Dept. Def., 1968-74; vis. scientist Lawrence Berkeley Labs., 1974-75. Contbr. numerous articles to profl. jours. With Swiss Army staff, 1964-75. Fellow Am. Phys. Soc., Health Physics Soc., Soc. for Risk Analysis, Fachverband fuer Strahlenschutz, Am. Stats. Assn., Am. Nat. Stds. Inst. (mgmt. coun. 1987—, com. N14 1986—). Office: Internat Tech Corp Ste 700 5301 Central Ave NE Albuquerque NM 87108

SEIP, TOM DECKER, securities executive; b. St. Louis, Feb. 15, 1950; s. Norman Walter and Margaret Ann (Decker) S.; m. Linda Shinabarger, Sept. 1976 (div. 1987); children: Parker, Jared; m. Alexa Clay Giddings, Mar. 24, 1990. BA in Psychology, Pa. State U., 1972; postgrad., U. Mich., 1972-74. Regional human resources mgr. Merrill, Lynch, Pierce Fenner and Smith, Inc., N.Y.C., San Francisco, 1975-77; v.p., ptnr. Korn/Ferry Internat., Palo Alto, Calif., 1977-83; v.p. human resources Charles Schwag & Co., Inc., San Francisco, 1983-85; sr. v.p., nat. sales programs Charles Schwab & Co., Inc., San Francisco, 1985-86, sr. v.p. specialized bus., 1986-88, sr. v.p. ea. div., 1988-91; pres., COO Charles Schwab Investment Mgmt., Inc., San Francisco, 1991—; exec. v.p. The Charles Schwab Corp., San Francisco, 1992—; dir. Ridgefield Devel. Corp., Erie, Pa. Office: Charles Schwab & Co Inc 101 Montgomery St San Francisco CA 94104

SEITELMAN, JEFFREY KEVIN, psychoanalyst, psychiatrist; b. N.Y.C., Aug. 28, 1952; s. Max and Margot (Bravman) S.; m. Susan Debra Gimovsky, Mar. 21, 1976 (div. Nov. 1981); 1 child, Robert Matthew; m. Judith June Gilden, Nov. 18, 1984. BA in Chemistry, Williams Coll., 1973; MD, SUNY, Buffalo, 1977; PhD in Psychoanalysis, So. Calif. Psychoanal. Inst., 1993. Diplomate in gen. psychiatry and child psychiatry Am. Bd. Psychiatry and Neurology; diplomate Nat. Bd. Med. Examiners. Resident in psychiatry U. Calif. Irvine Med. Ctr., Orange, 1977-79; resident in psychiatry Los Angeles County-U. So. Calif. Med. Ctr., L.A., 1979-80, fellow in child psychiatry, 1980-83; clin. assoc. So. Calif. Psychoanalytic Inst., Beverly Hills, 1986-91, advanced clin. assoc., 1991-93, faculty psychotherapy div., 1990—; psychiatrist, psychoanalyst in pvt. practice Long Beach, Calif., 1983-89, Seal Beach, Calif., 1989—; asst. clin. prof. dept. psychiatry U. Calif. Irvine Med. Ctr., 1986—, Harbor-UCLA, Torrance, 1984—. Mem. Jewish Community Ctr., Long Beach, 1977—, Temple Beth David, Westminster, Calif., 1990—. Capt. USAFR, 1973-83. Herbert H. Lehman fellow, Pfizer fellow Williams Coll., 1971-73. Fellow Am. Orthopsychiat. Assn.; mem. Am. Psychoanalytic Assn. (affiliate), Am. Acad. Psychoanalysis, Am. Psychiat. Assn., Orange County Psychiat. Assn., So. Calif. Soc. for Child and Adolescent Psychiatry. Democrat. Office: # 345 13991 Seal Beach Blvd Seal Beach CA 90740-2753

SEITZ, WALTER STANLEY, cardiovascular research consultant; b. L.A., May 10, 1937; s. Walter and Frances Janette (Schleef) S. BS in Physics and Math., U. Calif., Berkeley, 1959; PhD in Biophysics, U. Vienna, 1981, MD, 1982. Health physicist U. Calif. Radiation Lab., 1959-61; rsch. assoc. NIH at Pacific Union Coll., 1961-63; physicist Lockheed Rsch. Labs., Palo Alto, Calif., 1961-63; staff scientist Xerox Corp., Pasadena, Calif., 1963-66; sr. scientist Applied Physics Cons., Palo Alto, 1966-75; instr. clin. sci. U. Ill Coll. Medicine, Urbana, 1983-84; cons. cardiology Cardiovascular Rsch. Inst. U. Calif. Sch. Medicine, San Francisco, 1987—; sr. scientist Inst. Med. Analysis and Rsch., Berkeley, 1987—. Contbr. articles to profl. jours. Postdoctoral Rsch. fellow, U. Calif. San Francisco, 1984. Fellow Am. Coll. Angiography; mem. AAAS, Royal Soc. Medicine London, N.Y. Acad. Scis., Physicians for Social Responsibility. Office: IMAR Cons Inc 38 Panoramic Way Berkeley CA 94704

SEKAYUMPTEWA, LOREN, social worker; b. Winslow, Ariz., Mar. 23, 1950; s. Dayton Aquilla and Myra (Nez) S.; m. Mary A. Billiman (dec.); children: Lorie L., Carrie L., Christina L., Tracey M., Shaandiin C.; m. Marilyn J. Gishie; 1 child, Andrea L. AA, Brigham Young U., 1971, BS, 1973; MSW, U. Utah, 1981-83, postgrad. Cert. social worker, Utah. Social svc. rep. Bur. Indian Affairs, Keams Canyon, Ariz., 1973-74; dir. social svcs. Hopi Ctr. for Human Devel., Second Mesa, Ariz., 1975-76, human svcs. cons., 1974-75; counselor Navajo Community Coll., Tsaile, Ariz., 1975-76, dir. counseling, 1975-76, dean of students, 1977-81; chief adminstr. Hotevilla (Ariz.)-Bacavi Community Sch., 1983-84; exec. dir. Dine Ctr. for Human Svcs., Tsaile, 1984-87; clin. dir. Toyei Industries, Inc., Ganado, Ariz., 1987-91; exec. dir. Navajo Nation Pub. Sch. Bd. Assn., Window Rock, Ariz., 1991—; cons. linguistics anthropology dept. U. Utah, Salt Lake City, 1973-74; cons. edn. Toyei Industries, Inc., Ganado, Ariz., 1985-87, Utah Navajo Devel. Corp., Blanding, 1985-87; mem. bd. rev. Western Region Indian Alcoholism Ctr., Salt Lake City, 1974-75. Chairperson Gov.'s Coun. on Devel. Disabilities, State of Ariz., Phoenix; pres. No. Ariz. Health Edn. Ctr., Flagstaff, 1985-90; vice chmn. Ariz. Mental Health Planning Coun., Phoenix, 1986-90; pres. Native Am. Rsch. and Tng. Ctr., U. Ariz., Tucson, 1984-90. NIMH scholar, 1973-75. Navajo. Office: Navajo Nation Pub Sch Bds Assn Box 1909 Saint Michaels AZ 86511

SELBY, JANET S. GROSHART, retired elementary educator; b. La Junta, Colo., Mar. 15, 1927; d. Oscar Doyle and Helen Rucker (Gard) Groshart; m. Meredith H. Stice, June 28, 1946 (dec. 1964); children: Barry W., Mitchell R., Tracy S., Meredith G., Aaron M.; m. Andrew G. Sligar, Jan. 2, 1982 (div. 1992). BA in Elem. Edn., U. Ariz., 1965; MA in Early Childhood Edn., U. LaVerne, Calif., 1975, MS in Sch. Counseling, 1983. Cert. in elem. edn., high sch. counseling. Elem. educator Santa Ana (Calif.) Unified Schs., 1966-68, Capistrano Unified Sch. Dist., San Juan Capistrano, Calif., 1968-85. Mem. AAUW (arts chair 1989-90), Women's Nat. Polit. Caucus. Episcopalian. Home: 462 Ulumalu Rd Haiku HI 96708

SELBY, JEROME M., mayor; b. Wheatland, Wyo., Sept. 4, 1948; s. John Franklin and Claudia Meredith (Hudson) S.; m. Gloria Jean Nelson, June 14, 1969; children: Tyan, Cameronn, Kalen. BS in Math., Coll. Idaho, 1969, MA in Ednl. Adminstrn., 1974; MPA, Boise State U., 1978. Assoc. engr. Boeing Co., Seattle, 1969-71; dir. evaluation WICHE Mountain States Regional Med. Program, Boise, 1971-74; dir. rsch., evaluation Mountain States Health Corp., Boise, 1974-76, with health policy analysis and accountability, 1976-78; dir. health Kodiak (Alaska) Area Native Assn., 1978-83; mgr. Kodiak Island Borough, 1984-85, mayor, 1985—; proprietor Kodiak Tax Svc., 1978—, Registered Guide, Kodiak, 1987—; cons. Nat. Cancer Inst., Washington, 1973-78, others. Contbr. articles to profl. jours. Treas., bd. dirs. ARC, Kodiak, 1978—, chmn. 1989-90, mem. western ops. hdqrs. adv. bd., 1986-92, mem. group IV and V nat. adv. com., 1986-89, nat. bd. govs., 1989—; pres. S.W. Alaska Mcpl. Conf., Anchorage, 1988-89, v.p., 1986-87, pres., Alaska Mcpl. League Investment Pool, Inc., 1992—; v.p. Alaska Mcpl. League, 1988-90, pres., 1990-91, bd. dirs. 1988—; mem. Alaska Resource Devel. Coun., 1987—, exec. com., 1989—; mem. policy com. of outer continental shelf adv. bd. U.S. Dept. Interior, 1990—; mem. Nat. Assn. Counties, Community and Econ. Devel. Steering Com., 1990—, Alaska govtl. roles task force, 1991-92; chmn. Kodiak Island Exxon Valdez Restoration com., 1991—; dir. Kodiak Health Care Found., 1992—. Paul Harris fellow, 1987, 88, 91, 92. Mem. Alaska Conf. Mayors, Nat. Soc. Tax Profls., Acad. Polit. Sci., Alaska Mcpl. Mgrs. Assn., Kodiak C. of C. (dir. 1983—), Rotary. Office: Kodiak Island Borough 710 Mill Bay Rd Kodiak AK 99615-6398

SELDERS, CRAIG STEPHEN, employee and business mobility professional; b. Kansas City, Mo., June 12, 1953; s. Daniel Burr and Mildred Iola (McConville) S.; m. Deborah June Demeter, Oct. 30, 1982; children: Derek James, Brooke Danielle. BS in Bus., U. Conn., 1975; MBA, U. Chgo., 1990. Field coord. PHH Homequity, Inc., Chgo., 1977-78; field mgr. PHH Homequity, Inc., Binghamton, N.Y., 1978-80; mgr. ops. PHH Homequity, Inc., Danbury, Conn., 1980-84; sales mgr. PHH Homequity, Inc., Oak Brook, Ill., 1984-86; dir. ops. PHH Capital Resources, Oak Brook, 1986-87; sr. cons. PHH Fantus Corp., Chgo., 1987-88; nat. accounts mgr. Prudential Relocation Mgmt., Schaumburg, Ill., 1988-90; v.p. Moran, Stahl & Boyer Internat., Boulder, Colo., 1990-92; v.p. client svcs. Prudential Relocation Mgmt., Houston, 1992—; quality improvement leader Prudential Relocation Mgmt., Valhalla, N.Y., 1990—. Chmn. civic com. University Heights Homeowners Assn., Naperville, Ill., 1985-86.

SELIGMAN, THOMAS KNOWLES, museum administrator; b. Santa Barbara, Calif., Jan. 1, 1944; s. Joseph L. and Peggy (Van Horne) S.; children: Christopher, Timothy, Dylan. BA, Stanford U., 1965; BFA with honors, San Francisco Acad. Art, 1967; MFA, Sch. Visual Art, N.Y.C., 1968. Tchr., mus. dir. Peace Corps, Liberia, 1968-70; curator dept. Africa, Oceania and Ams. Fine Arts Museums, San Francisco, 1971-88; dep. dir. edn. and exhbns. Fine Arts Museums, 1972-88, dep. dir. ops. and planning, 1988-91; dir. Stanford (Calif.) U. Mus. Art, 1991—; mem. cultural property adv. com. USIA, 1988-92. Author mus. catalogues, articles in field. Trustee Internat. Coun. Museums/Am. Assn. Museums, Am. Fedn. Arts; mem. adv. coun. Acad. of Art Coll. Grad. Program. Fellow Nat. Endowment Arts, 1974-75, 87. Mem. Am. Assn. Museums, Leaky Found. Address: Stanford U Mus Art Stanford CA 94305-5060

SELING, THEODORE VICTOR, engineer, radio astronomy designer; b. Lansing, Mich., Mar. 27, 1928; s. Ernest and Alice Helen (Venzke) S.; m. Gwendolyn Ludwig, Dec. 6, 1952; children: Stanley Ernest, Suart Alan. BS in Elec. Engring., Mich. State U., 1949; MS in Engring., U. Mich., 1960, PhD in Elec. Engring., 1969. Pub. utilites engr. Mich. Pub. Svc. Commn., Lansing, 1949-50; ionosphere data analyst U.S. Army Signal Corps, Ft. Monmouth, Adak, Alaska, 1950-52; project engr. AC Spark Plug div. GMC, Flint, 1952-56; sr. project engr. AC Spark Plug and Def. Systems div. GMC, Milw. and Santa Barbara, Calif., 1956-62; rsch. scientist U. Mich., Ann Arbor, 1962-82; chief engr. radio astronomy Calif. Inst. Tech., Pasadena, 1982—; cons. Erim, Ann Arbor, 1978-81, Spacek Labs, San Barbara, 1980-82. Author several pubs. on microwave instrumentation and radio astronomy; inventor several on microwave radiometry. Mem. IEEE (sr. 1959—), Am. Astron. Soc. Home: 165 S Lima Ave Sierra Madre CA 91024-2348 Office: Calif Inst of Tech 359 S Hollister Ave Pasadena CA 91125-0001

SELINGER, PATRICIA GRIFFITHS, computer science professional; b. Cleve., Oct. 15, 1949; d. Fred Robert and Olive Mae (Brewster) Priest; m. James Alan Griffiths, Aug. 29, 1970 (div. 1973); m. Robert David Selinger, July 22, 1978; children: David Robert, Thomas Robert. AB, Harvard U., 1971, MS, 1972, PhD, 1975. Rsch. staff IBM Rsch. Lab, San Jose, Calif., 1975-78, mgr., 1978-83, mgr. computer sci., 1983-86, program dir. Database Technology Inst., 1986—. Patentee in field; co-author numerous tech. papers. Recipient YWCA Tribute to Women in Industry award, 1989. Mem. Assn. for Computing Machinery (System Software award 1989, former vice-chmn. spl. interest group for mgmt. data). Office: IBM Rsch K01/801 650 Harry Rd San Jose CA 95120-6099

SELL, ROBERT EMERSON, electrical engineer; b. Freeport, Ill., Apr. 23, 1929; s. Cecil Leroy and Ona Arletta (Stevens) S.; m. Ora Lucile Colton, Nov. 7, 1970. B.S., U. Nebr., 1962. Registered profl. engr., Nebr., Mo., Ill., Ind., Ohio, W.Va., Ky., Ark., Tex., Oreg., Wash., Calif. Chief draftsman Dempster Mill Mfg. Co., Beatrice, Nebr., 1949-53; designer-engr. U. Neb., Lincoln, 1955-65; elec. design engr. Kirkham, Michael & Assocs., Omaha, 1965-67; elec. design engr. Leo A. Daly Co., Omaha, St. Louis, 1967-69; mech. design engr. Hellmuth, Obata, Kassabaum, St. Louis, 1969-70; chief elec. engr. Biagi-Hannan & Assos., Inc., Evansville, Ind., 1971-74; elec. project engr. H.L. Yoh Co., under contract to Monsanto Co., Creve Coeur, Mo., 1974-77; elec. project engr. Dhillon Engrs., Inc., Portland, Oreg., 1978-85; project coordinator Brown-Zammit-Enyeart Engring., Inc., San Diego, 1985-88; elec. engr. Morgen Design, Inc., San Diego, 1988; lead elec. engr. Popov Engrs., Inc., San Diego, 1988-89; mech. and elect. specialist Am. Engring. Labs., Inc. div. Prof. Svc. Industries, Inc., San Diego, 1990—; instr. Basic Inst. Tech., St. Louis, 1971. Mem. ASHRAE, IEEE. Home: PO Box 261578 San Diego CA 92196-1578 Office: AEL/PSI 7940 Arjons Dr Ste A San Diego CA 92126-6303

SELMAR, KATHERINE L., elementary school educator; b. Seattle, July 5, 1956; d. John William and Lois (Schneider) S. BA, Pacific U., 1979, MEd, 1985. Tchr. 1st and 2d grade Harvey Clarke Elem. Sch., Forest Grove, Oreg., 1979-90; scholar Auckland (New Zealand) Coll. Edn., 1990; tchr. 3d and 4th grade Cornelius (Oreg.) Elem. Sch., 1991-93, tchr. chpt. one reading, 1993—. Mem. United Ch. of Christ, Forest Grove, 1979—, mem. outreach commn., 1992—; mem. Theater in the Grove, 1980—, Forest Grove Libr. Commn., 1985-86; chmn. Forest Grove Negotiations Team, Forest Grove, 1992. Scholar P.E.O., 1985. Mem. Forest Grove Edn. Assn. (v.p. 1986-87, pres. 1987-88), Rotary (scholar 1990), Delta Kappa Gamma. Democrat.

SELOVER, WILLIAM CHARLTON, corporate communications executive; b. Long Beach, Calif., Dec. 12, 1938; s. John Jesse and Myrtis Charlton (Holmes) S.; m. Mary-Louise Hutchins, Jan. 5, 1963 (div. 1985); children: Victoria, Edward. BA, Principia Coll., 1960; MA, U. Va., 1962. Mem. editorial staff Christian Sci. Monitor, from Congl. corr. to diplomatic corr.; spl. asst. to sec. of the navy USN; mem. White House Coun. on Internat. Econ. Policy, Washington; history and archives divsn. chief Cost of Living Coun., Exec. Office of the Pres., Washington; asst. to adminstr. U.S. EPA, Washington; staff mem. White House Domestic Coun., Washington; speechwriter Pres. Gerald R. Ford, Washington; pub. affairs exec. Ford Motor Co., Detroit; pub. affairs mgr. diversified products ops. Ford Motor Co.; regional pub. affairs mgr. Ford Motor Co., L.A., 1988-91; v.p. corp. comms. U.S. Leasing Internat. Inc. (subs. Ford Fin. Svcs. Group), 1991—. Speechwriter for Pres. Gerald R. Ford. Helen Dwight Reid Found. fellow, Carnegie Found./Maxwell Grad. Overseas fellow, 1962. Mem. Conference Bd. (coun. corp. comm. exec.), Nat. Press Club, Press Club Detroit, Press Club L.A., Motor Press Guild, Internat. Motor Press Assn., Leadership Detroit Alumni Assn., Am. Polit. Sci. Assn. Home: 1257 Union St San Francisco CA 94109 Office: US Leasing Inc 733 Front St San Francisco CA 94111

SELVEY, MARYLIN ROSE LUNDSTROM, labor union administrator; b. Phoenix, Aug. 31, 1954; d. Norris Esley and Mary Louise (Slater) Selvey; m. Roger W. Lundstrom, (div. 1986). CLU, Am. Coll., 1981, Chartered Fin. Cons., 1983. Sales/mktg. rep. Gen. Ins., Phoenix, 1974-79; life/health mgr. Anderson Reeve & Assocs., Scottsdale, Ariz., 1979-81; v.p. Colo. Life Ins. Co./Pioneer Holding Co., Denver and Phoenix, 1981-85; mktg. cons. The Blessman Co., Denver, 1985-87; asst. trader J.W. Gant & Assocs., Denver,

1987-88; dir. L.A. County Employees Assn. S.E.I.U. AFL-CIO, 1988—; guest speaker in field; instr. CLU, Phoenix, 1981-83. Author health and benefits newsletter. Econs. instr. Jr. Achievement, Denver, 1986; advisor Six Sixty Srs. Assn., L.A., 1988—; mem. pub. policy commn. Vision Plan of Am., L.A.; del. Congress of Calif. Srs. Mem. Bus. and Profl. Women (Young Career Woman of Yr. 1984), Greater Phoenix Assn. Life Underwriters (bd. dirs. 1975-84), Scottsdale C. of C., Denver C. of C. Office: SEIU Local 660 AFL-CIO 950 W Washington Blvd Los Angeles CA 90015

SELVIN, NANCY, artist, art educator; b. L.A., Aug. 19, 1943; d. Gus. O. and Marcia (Cohen) Brown; m. Steve Selvin, Jan. 30, 1965; 1 child, Elizabeth. B.A., U. Calif.-Berkeley, 1969, M.A., 1970. Instr. ceramics SUNY-Albany, 1970-72, Laney Coll., Oakland, Calif., 1973—; instr. color theory Fashion Inst. of Design, San Francisco, 1973; dir. ceramics Walnut Creek Art Ctr., Calif., 1974-75; lectr. ceramics numerous art schs. in Eng. and Wales, 1982-83; mem. Pub. Art Adv. Commn., Oakland, Calif., 1990—. One-woman shows include: Anhalt Gallery, Los Angeles, 1981, Calif. Crafts Mus., Palo Alto, 1982, Oxford Gallery, Eng., 1983, The Elements, N.Y.C., 1984, Grossmont Coll., Calif., 1990, Looking Through Glass, Berkeley, 1991, Sybaris Gallery, 1992, Maveety Gallery, 1993; work included in numerous publs. including New York Times, L.A. Times, Ceramics Monthly mag., Am. Craft mag., Artweek. Vol. Albany Home, N.Y., 1971-72, Cragmont Pub. Sch., Berkeley, 1984. Nat. Endowment for The Arts fellow, 1980, 88; chair adv. com. Oakland Pub. Art, 1991-93; recipient Craftsmen Merit award Calif. Craftsmen Assn., 1978, Purchase award Westwood Ceramics, 1980. Mem. Am. Crafts Coun., Pro Arts Oakland (bd. dirs. 1989—, pres. 1989-90, exec. dir. 1989-91), Nat. Coun. Edn. Ceramic Arts, British Crafts Coun.

SELZ, PETER HOWARD, art historian, educator; b. Munich, Germany, Mar. 27, 1919; came to U.S., 1936, naturalized, 1942; s. Eugene and Edith S.; m. Thalia Cheronis, June 10, 1948 (div. 1965); children: Tanya Nicole Eugenia, Diana Gabrielle Hamlin; m. Carole Schemmerling, Dec. 18, 1983. Student, Columbia U., U. Paris; MA, U. Chgo., 1949, PhD, 1954; DFA, Calif. Coll. Arts and Crafts, 1967. Instr. U. Chgo., 1951-56; asst. prof. art history, head art edn. dept. Inst. Design, Ill. Inst. Tech., Chgo., 1949-55; chmn. art dept., dir. art gallery Pomona Coll., 1955-58; curator dept. painting and sculpture exhbns. Mus. Modern Art, 1958-65; dir. univ. art mus. U. Calif., Berkeley, 1965-73, prof. history of art, 1965—; Zaks prof. Hebrew U., Jerusalem, 1976; vis. prof. CUNY, 1987; mem. pres.'s council on art and architecture Yale U., 1971-76; trustee Am. Craft Coun., 1983-88. Author: German Expressionist Painting, 1957, New Images of Man, 1959, Art Nouveau, 1960, Mark Rothko, 1961, Fifteen Polish Painters, 1961, The Art of Jean Dubuffet, 1962, Emil Nolde, 1963, Max Beckmann, 1964, Alberto Giacometti, 1965, Directions in Kinetic Sculpture, 1966, Funk, 1967, Harold Paris, 1972, Ferdinand Holder, 1972, Sam Francis, 1975, The American Presidency in Political Cartoons, 1976, Art in Our Times, 1981, Art in a Turbulent Era, 1985, Chillida, 1986, Twelve Artists from the GDR, 1989, Max Beckmann: The Self Portraits, 1992, William Congdon, 1992; editor: Art in Am., 1967—, Art Quar., 1969-75, Arts, 1981-92; contbr. articles to art publs. Trustee Am. Crafts Coun., 1985-89, Creators Equity Found., 1980—; pres. Berkeley Art Project, 1988-93; mem. adv. coun. archives Am. Art, 1971—; project dir. Christo's Running Fence, 1973-76; commr. Alameda County Art Commn, 1990—; mem. acquisitions com. Fine Arts Mus. San Francisco, 1993—. With OSS AUS, 1941-46. Decorated Order of Merit Fed. Republic Germany; Fulbright grantee Paris, 1949-50; fellow Belgian-Am. Ednl. Found.; sr. fellow Nat. Endowment for Humanities, 1972. Mem. Coll. Art Assn. Am. (dir. 1959-64, 67-71), AAUP, Internat. Art Critics Assn. Office: U Calif Dept Art History Berkeley CA 94720

SEMMER, ROBERT CLEMENT, media company executive; b. Pitts., June 27, 1961; m. Sharon Ann Lowe, Dec. 21, 1985; children: Caroline, Elizabeth. BS in Polit. Sci., St. Joseph's, 1983. Admissions dir. St. Joseph Coll., Collegeville, Ind., 1983-84; acct. exec. Kroy, Inc., Chgo., 1984-85, Airborne Express, Chgo., 1985-86, Mediatech, Chgo., 1986-88, Mediatech West, Hollywood, Calif., 1988; regional sales mgr. Mediatech West, Hollywood, 1988-89, v.p., gen. mgr., 1989-91; v.p., gen. mgr. Mediatech, Hollywood, Chgo., 1991-92, sr. v.p. sales and customer svc., 1992—. Mem. Internat. TV & Video, Internat. Teleprodn. Soc., Hollywood C. of C., L.A. Ad Club, Chgo. Ad Club. Office: Mediatech West 1640 N Gower St Los Angeles CA 90028-9800

SEMRUD-CLIKEMAN, MARGARET ELAINE, psychologist, educator; b. Albany, Oreg., July 9, 1950; d. Ray Allen and Margaret Elaine (Schoppenhurst) S.; m. John Charles Clikeman, Oct. 10, 1979. BA, Concordia Coll., 1972; MS, U. Wis., 1975; PhD, U. Ga., 1990. Lic. psychologist, Wash., Wis. Sch. psychologist III Portage (Wis.) Pub. Schs., 1974-75, Mequon (Wis.)-Thiensville Pub. Schs., 1975-86; asst. dir. Ctr. Clin. and Devel. Neuropsychology U. Ga., Athens, 1988-89; electrophysiological fellow U. Jyvaskyla, Finland, 1988; neuropsychology intern U. Ga., Athens, 1988-89; sch. psychology intern Jasper County Schs., Monticello, Ga., 1988-89; psychology intern Mass. Gen. Hosp., Boston, 1989-90, post-doctoral fellow in neurosci., 1990-91; asst. prof. U. Wash., Seattle, 1991; clin. fellow in psychology Mass. Gen. Hosp., 1989-91. Contbr. articles to numerous profl. jours. Mem. Jr. Women's Club, Grafton, Wis., 1982-86. Myrtle Baker scholar Women's Clubs of Wis., 1986-87, Merit scholar U. Ga., 1987-89; NIH Tng. fellow Harvard U., 1991; recipient Outstanding Dissertation award Orton Dyslexia Soc., 1991. Mem. APA, Nat. Assn. Sch. Psychologists, Internat. Neuropsychology Soc. Lutheran. Office: U Wash 322 Miller Hall DQ-12 Seattle WA 98195

SENENSIEB, NORBERT LOUIS, management consultant; b. Hamburg, Germany, May 31, 1930; s. Max Herman and Friede (Rubinger) S.; came to U.S., 1947, naturalized, 1952; student L.A. City Coll., 1948-49; BS, UCLA, 1951, MBA (Walter Loewy grad. fellow), 1953; m. Mildred Zuckerman, Feb. 2, 1952; children: Miryam Senensieb Brewer, David. Indsl. engring. statistician Bendix Aviation Corp., North Hollywood, Calif., 1956-57; mgr. methods and procedures Electro Data div. Burroughs Corp., Pasadena, Calif., 1957-58; systems analyst Rocketdyne div. Rockwell Internat. Corp., Canoga Park, Calif., 1958-59; sr. systems analyst, head systems and procedures of communications div. Hughes Aircraft Corp., Culver City, Calif., 1959-60; systems and procedures adminstr. West Coast Missile div. Radio Corp. Am., Van Nuys, Calif., 1960-61; mgr. integrated data processing systems dept. TRW Systems, Inc., Redondo Beach, Calif., 1961-64; v.p. systems Automation Svcs. Corp., L.A., 1965-66; v.p. Universal Data Systems, Inc., L.A., 1966-68; v.p., dir. Western div. Computer Methods Corp., L.A. and White Plains, N.Y., 1968-70; v.p. Gottfried Cons. Inc., L.A., 1970-78; mgmt. cons., 1978-79; pres. CES Cons., Inc., cons. to mgmt., 1979-91; instr. bus. systems L.A. Pierce Coll., 1961-63, UCLA Bus. Adminstrn. Extension, 1963-64. Area chmn. L.A. United Jewish Fund, 1975-81; bd. dirs. San Fernando Valley Region, Jewish Fedn. Coun. Greater L.A., 1979—, mem. exec. com., 1983-92, co-chmn. Planning and Budgeting com., 1984-87, v.p., 1983-84, bd. dirs. Cen. Fedn., 1983-88, 92—, chmn. computer adv. com., 1985-86; bd. dirs. and exec. com. Bur. Jewish Edn., 1983-93, vice-chmn., 1985-93; pres. L.A. Labor Zionist Alliance, 1990—. With AUS, 1953-55. Cert. data processor 1965. Mem. Assn. Systems Mgmt. (life, internat. pres. 1963-64, internat. dir. 1961-67, disting. svc. award 1967), Inst. Mgmt. Cons. (cert. mgmt. cons. 1973), Assn. Systems Mgmt. (cert. systems profl. 1985), Am. Philatelic Soc., Soc. Israel Philatelists (pres. L.A. chpt. 1975-79), UCLA Alumni Assn. Jewish. Mem. editorial adv. bd. Jour. Systems Mgmt., 1966-69. Contbr. chpts. to books, articles to Ency. Mgmt. and profl. jours. Home: 15032 Acre St Sepulveda CA 91343-5503

SEN GUPTA, RATAN, utility company executive; b. Calcutta, West Bengal, India, May 22, 1947; s. Ranendra Lal and Anjali (Dutta Choudhury) Sen G.; m. Shikha Choudhury, Feb. 19, 1976; 1 child, Indranil. BTech with honors, Indian Inst. Tech., Kharagpur, West Bengal, 1969; MS, U. Cin., 1971; MBA, Syracuse U., 1973. Sr. project estimator The Ralph M. Parson Co., Pasadena, Calif., 1980-81; supr., project cost engr., estimator Bechtel Petroleum Inc., San Francisco, 1981-83; supr. cost estimating sect. Pacific Gas & Electric Co., San Francisco, 1983—. Mem. Expt. in Internat. Living, Putney, Vt., 1969-76; treas. Bay Area Prabasi, San Francisco, 1985-86, mem. bd. 1987-89. Mem. ASCE, Am. Assn. Cost Engrs. (treas. 1986-88, v.p. 1988-89, pres. 1989-90 San Francisco Bay Area chpt.). Hindu. Home: 45216 Elk Ct Fremont CA 94539-6039 Office: Pacific Gas & Electric Co Rm582F/201 Mission San Francisco CA 94106-0001

SENNETT, FRANK RONALD, JR., editor, columnist, public relations consultant; b. Missoula, Mont., Feb. 16, 1968; s. Frank Ronald S. and Leslie Denise (Crowe) McClintock. BS in Journalism, Northwestern U., 1990; postgrad., U. Mont. pub. rels. cons. Chgo. Conv. and Tourism Bur., 1988—. Asst. editor, columnist: Relax, 1990-91; columnist: Woman's World, 1991-92, Tradeshow Week, 1990—, contbg. editor, 1990—; contbg. author: London's Best-Kept Secrets, 1991. Democrat. Office: 324 W Sussex Missoula MT 59801

SENTER, THOMAS PAUL, dermatologist; b. Oakland, Calif., Oct. 15, 1946; s. Vance Edward and Alice Virginia (Hanson); m. Susan La Von Crane, Oct. 3, 1983; children: Katherine Alice, Samuel Edward. BA in English Lit., Fla. State U., 1967; MD, U. Nebr. Coll of Medicine, 1971. Diplomate Am. Acad. Dermatology, 1981. Rotating intern U. Calif.-Davis, Sacramento Med. Ctr., 1971-72; resident in dermatology U. Calif.-San Diego, 1975-78; chief of dermatology Permanente Med. Assn. of Tex., 1980-81; pvt. practice dermatology Anchorage and Fairbanks, Alaska, 1981—; vice-chmn. Gov.'s Interim Commn. on Health Care, Anchorage and Juneau, Alaska, 1987-89; mem. nat. adv. ctr. Robert Wood Johnson Improving the Health of Native Ams. Prog., Princeton, N.J., 1988—; med. cons. Alaska Native Health Ctr., Anchorage, 1981—. Contbr. articles to profl. jours. Pres. Alaskare, Anchorage, 1989-90; mem. adv. bd. dirs. Head Start chpt. KIDS Corpsof Anchorage, 1989—. With USN, 1972-75. VA clin. scholar Stanford/U. Calif. San Francisco/Robert Wood Johnson combined program, 1978-80. Mem. AMA, Anchorage Med. Soc. (pres. 1985-86), Alaska State Med. Soc. (councilor 1984—), Assn. for the Preservation of Civil War Sites, Assn. for Health Svcs. Rsch., Alpha Omega Alpha. Office: 636 Barrow St Anchorage AK 99501-3631

SENUNGETUK, VIVIAN RUTH, lawyer; b. Syracuse, N.Y., Sept. 27, 1948; d. George Albert and Ethel Margaret (Hearl) Bender; children: Adam George Moore, William Guugzhuk Senungetuk. BA, SUNY, Binghamton, 1968; MAT, U. Alaska, 1972; JD, Boston U., 1984. Bar: Alaska 1985, Mass. 1985, U.S. Dist. Ct. Alaska 1985. Adminstr. Indian Edn., Sitka, Alaska, 1974-76, Cook Inlet Native Assn., Anchorage, 1977-80; assoc. Erwin, Smith & Garnett, Anchorage, 1984-86; sole practice Anchorage, 1986—; adj. prof. constitutional law U. Alaska, Anchorage, 1986-88. Author: A Place for Winter, 1987. Mem. Am. Arbitration Assn., Assn. Trial Lawyers Am., Alaska Acad. Trial Lawyers. Democrat. Methodist. Office: 425 G St Ste 850 Anchorage AK 99501-2139

SEOANE, EMILIO, accountant; b. Havana, Cuba, Oct. 13, 1944; came to U.S., 1960; s. Emilio M. and Carmen Seoane; m. Angeles Gonzalez, Sept. 13, 1988; children: Heidi, Ledu. Acct., Havana U., 1959. Acct. Seoane Bookkeeping Svc., Miami, Fla., 1964-66, L.A., 1967-79; acct. Empresa Svcs. Hispanos, Anaheim, Calif., 1980-88, Latinos Enterprise, Inc., Santa Ana, Calif., 1988—. Mem. Nat. Soc. Pub. Accts., Nat. Notary Assn., Am. Soc. Notaries, Nat. Assn. Tax Cons., Nat. Soc. Tax Profls. Republican. Roman Catholic. Office: Latinos Enterprise Inc 1017 S Fairview St Santa Ana CA 92704

SEOANE, MARTA HEBE, demographer, social scientist; b. Canelones, Uruguay, May 11, 1943; came to U.S., 1964; d. Joaquin Raul and Felipa Josefa (Scaglione) S.; m. Kingsley Davis, Nov. 5, 1985; 1 child, Austin Alexander Seoane Davis. BA in Sociology, Calif. State U., Northridge, 1976; MA in Sociology, U. So. Calif., 1983, PhD in Sociology, 1988. Cons. Demographic Rsch., Stanford, Calif., 1989—; sr. demographer Hispanic Market Connections, Inc., Los Altos, Calif., 1992—; rsch. assoc. Knight and Leavitt Assocs., Inc., Las Vegas, Nev., 1991—; ctr. assoc. Internat. Population Ctr., U. Calif., San Diego, 1991—; adj. prof. San Diego State U., 1992—. Recipient Hubert B. Herring Meml. award for best dissertation Pacific Coast Coun. on Latin Am. Studies, 1989. Mem. Assn. Acad. Programs in Latin Am. and the Caribbean, Am. Sociol. Assn., Latin Am. Assn., Population Assn. Am., Calif. Sociol. Assn., Pacific Coast Coun. on Latin Am. Studies. Home: 975 Wing Pl Stanford CA 94305 Office: Hispanic Market Connections Ste D-11 5150 El Camino Real Los Altos CA 94022

SEPEHR, MANSOUR, hydrologist, president; b. Maragheh, Azarbaijan, Iran, Feb. 1, 1948; came to U.S., 1977; s. Ahmad and Sakineh (Vargandeh) S. BS in Soil Sci., Tehran U., 1970; MS in Irrigation Engring., Utah State U., 1981, PhD in Civil and Environ. Engring., 1984. Registered civil engr., Calif. Project hydrologist Dames & Moore, Salt Lake City, 1985-86; sr. hydrologist McLanen Environ. Engring., Sacramento, 1986-87; sr. assoc. hydrologist Levine & Fricke, Emeryville, Calif., 1987-91; pres. SOMA Environ. Engring., Oakland, Calif., 1991—. Contbr. articles to profl. jours. Home: 200 Pioneer Ct El Sobrante CA 94803-2648

SEPESI, JOHN DAVID, artist; b. Monessen, Pa., Aug. 12, 1931; s. John Lloyd and Gizella Elizabeth (Gnip) S. AA, San Bernardino Valley Coll., 1957; BA, Mexico City Coll., 1958. One-man shows include Washoe County Libr., 1987, Reno City Hall Gallery, 1990, Town Ctr. Gallery, 1992; exhibited in group shows at Wilbur D. May Mus., Reno, 1986, Reno City Hall Gallery, 1987, 88, Shoppers Sq., Reno, 1990-91, Brewery Art Ctr., Carson City, 1991-93, Las Vegas Hist. Soc. Mus., 1990, El Wiegand Mus., Reno, 1990, Town Ctr. Gallery, 1992-93; contbr. articles to profl. jours. Staff sgt. USAF, 1952-56. Mem. Nev. Artists Assn. (v.p. 1990—, exec. bd. 1991—), Sierra Watercolor Soc., Sierra Arts Found., Nev. Mus. Art, Nev. State Coun. on the Arts, Nev. Alliance for the Arts. Republican. Home and Office: 280 Island Ave 1007 Reno NV 89501

SEPPI, EDWARD JOSEPH, physicist; b. Price, Utah, Dec. 16, 1930; s. Joseph and Fortunata S.; m. Betty Stowell, Aug. 25, 1953; children: Duane Joseph, Kevin Darrell, Cynthia Rae. BS, Brigham Young U., 1952; MS, U. Idaho, 1956; PhD, Calif. Inst. Tech., 1962. Staff physicist Gen. Electric Co., Richland, Wash., 1952-58; rsch. fellow Calif. Inst. Tech., Pasadena, 1962; staff physicist Inst. for Def. Analysis, Washington, 1962-64; rsch. area dept. head SLAC, Stanford, Calif., 1966-68, head exptl. facility dept., 1968-74; mgr. med. diagnosis Varian Assocs., Palo Alto, Calif., 1974-76, sr. scientist, 1980-90; sr. scientist Superconducting Super Collider, Dallas, 1990-91; with Varian Assocs., Palo Alto, Calif., 1991—. Author (with others) The Stanford Two-Mile Accelerator, 1968; contbr. articles to sci.jours.; patentee med. instrumentation. Asst. scoutmaster Boy Scouts Am., Menlo Park, Calif., 1969-75; bd. dirs. Ladera Community Assn., 1988-90. Mem. Am. Phys. Soc. Home: 320 Dedalera Dr Portola Valley CA 94028

SEQUEST, RICHARD CARL, research institute administrator; b. Saco, Maine, Jan. 15, 1944; s. Carl Axel and Ida (Rowe) S.; m. Nancy Williams, Apr. 18, 1987; 1 child, Adam Luis. BA in Psychology and Bus. Administrn., Calif. State U., Chico, 1971, MA in Psychology, 1973. Cert. energy mgr. Assn. Energy Engrs.; life C.C. teaching credential, Calif. Asst. planner Superior Calif. Comprehensive Health Planning, Chico, 1972-73; project dir. No. Calif. Emergency Med. Care Coun., Redding, 1973-76; asst. exec. dir. Am. Heart Assn. Greater Miami, Fla., 1976-79; pres. Energy Rsch. Info. Svcs., Mountain View, Calif., 1979-81; dir. tng. Calif. Labor Mgmt. Energy Coun., Sacramento, 1981-82; dir. mktg. Energy Mgmt. Inst. Calif., Sacramento, 1982-84, state dir., 1984-85; regional dir. Nat. Energy Mgmt. Inst., Sacramento, 1985—. Editor: Energy Independence: Consequences for Huuman Health, 1980; editor, pub. Energy Mgrs. Newsletter, 1980-81; contbr. numerous articles to various publs. Regional dir. Combined Health Agys. Drive, Sacramento, 1980-81; mem. Clean Air Task Force, Sacramento, 1990. Staff sgt. USAF, 1954-69. Recipient Energy Futures award Responsive Energy Tech. Symposium Internat. Exposition, 1989; rsch. grantee Calif. State U., 1971, grantee Calif. Regional Med. Programs, 1973, So. Health Found., 1977. Mem. Assn. Energy Mgrs. (founding pres. Sacramento chpt. 1980-81). Home: 4046 Hillswood Dr Sacramento CA 95821 Office: Nat Energy Mgmt Inst 4441 Auburn Blvd Ste 0 Sacramento CA 95841

SERA, NATALIE ALDERMAN, secondary educator; b. Great Falls, Mont., Mar. 7, 1948; d. Samuel I. and Ruth E. (Minkoff) Alderman; 1 child, Joshua I. Sera. BA, UCLA, 1970; MA, Calif. State U., Northridge, 1979. Cert. secondary educator, Nev. Tchr. Scottsbluff (Nev.) Schs., 1979-82, Lyon County (Nev.) Elem. Sch., 1982-84; case worker No. Nev. Ctr. for Ind. Living, Reno, 1984-85; instr. Western Nev. Community Coll., Carson City, 1983-85; singer Trinity Episcopal Ch., Reno, 1989—; instr. U. Nev. Reno, 1983-85; tchr. Reno High Sch., 1985—; pres., founder Nev. Inform Centro pri Esperanto, Reno, 1990—; dir. Nev. Barefoot Consort, Reno, 1983—. Recipient scholarship Esperanto League for North Am., 1990, Viola da Gamba Soc. Am., 1988. Mem. Esperanto League for North Am., Viola da Gamba Soc. Am., Universal Esperanto Assn. Democrat. Jewish. Office: Nev Info Ctr pri Esperanto PO Box 50113 Reno NV 89513-0113

SERAFIN, ROBERT JOSEPH, science center administrator, electrical engineer; b. Chgo., Apr. 22, 1936; s. Joseph Albert and Antoinette (Gazda) S.; m. Betsy Furgerson, Mar. 4, 1961; children: Katherine, Jenifer, Robert Joseph Jr., Elizabeth. BSEE, U. Notre Dame, 1958; MSEE, Northwestern U., 1961; PhDEE, Ill. Inst. Tech., 1972. Engr. Hazeltine Rsch. Corp. Ill. Inst. Tech. Rsch. Inst., 1960-62; assoc. engr., rsch. engr., sr. rsch. engr. Nat. Ctr. for Atmospheric Rsch., Bouulder, Colo., 1962-73, mgr. field observing facility, 1973-80, dir. atmospheric tech. div., 1981-89, dir. ctr., 1989—. Author: Revised Radar Handbook, 1989; also numerous articles; editorial founder Jour. Atmospheric and Oceanic Tech.; patentee in field. Chmn. Citizens Adv. Com., Boulder; speaker various civic groups in U.S. and internationally. Mem. NAS (coms.), IEEE (sr.), Am. Meteorol. Soc. (exec. com.), Boulder C. of C. Office: Nat Ctr Atmospheric Rsch PO Box 3000 1850 Table Mesa Dr Boulder CO 80303

SERAFINI, VICTOR RENATO, aerospace engineer; b. Chgo., June 9, 1934; s. Renato Victor and Stella (Koch) S. BS in Aero. Engring., U. Ill., 1957, postgrad., 1957-65; postgrad., UCLA, 1957-65. Research and project engr. Rocketdyne Div. N.Am. Aviation, Canoga Park, Calif., 1957-67; program/project mgr. TRW Inc., Redondo Beach, Calif., 1967-78; dir. spacecraft engring. Communications Satellite Corp., El Segundo, Calif., 1978—; bd. dirs. Autobahn West, Westlake Village, Calif.; mgmt. cons. Westoaks Realty, Westlake Village, 1975—; pres. STD Assocs., Rancho Palos Verdes, Calif., 1965—. Recipient award of Recognition, TRW Inc., 1965, Recognition of Outstanding Effort award NASA and TRW, 1963-64. Mem. AIAA (liquid rocket tech. com. 1985-86). Mem. Christian Ch. Home: PO Box 2665 Palos Verdes Peninsula CA 90274-8665 Office: Communications Satellite Corp 2250 E Imperial Hwy Ste 720 El Segundo CA 90245-3547

SERBEIN, OSCAR NICHOLAS, business educator, consultant; b. Collins, Iowa, Mar. 31, 1919; s. Oscar Nicholas and Clara Matilda (Shearer) S.; m. Alice Marie Bigger, Sept. 16, 1952; children: Mary Llewellyn Serbein Parker, John Gregory. BA with highest distinction, U. Iowa, 1940, MS, 1941; PhD, Columbia U., 1951. Grad. asst. math. U. Iowa, Iowa City, 1940-41; clk. Met. Life Ins. Co., N.Y.C., 1941-42; lectr. U. Calif., Berkeley, summer 1948, 50; lectr., asst. prof., assoc. prof. Columbia U., N.Y.C., 1947-59; prof. ins. Stanford (Calif.) U., 1959-89, prof. emeritus ins., 1989—; cons. Ins. Info. Inst., N.Y.C., 1971-78, N.Am. Re-Assurance Life Service Co., Palo Alto, 1973, SRI Internat., Menlo Park, Calif., 1980-81, other bus.; cons., expert witness various law firms. Author: Paying for Medical Care in the U.S., 1953, Educational Activities of Business, 1961; co-author: Property and Liability Insurance, 4 ed., 1967, Risk Management: Text and Cases, 2 ed., 1983; also articles. Bd. dirs. Sr. Citizens Coord. Coun., Palo Alto, 1986-89, dir. emeritus, 1990—. Decorated Bronze Star, 1944. Mem. Am. Risk and Ins. Assn., Western Risk and Ins. Assn., Phi Beta Kappa, Sigma Xi, Beta Gamma Sigma. Democrat. Methodist. Club: Stanford Faculty. Home: 731 San Rafael Pl Stanford CA 94305-1007 Office: Stanford U Grad Sch Bus Stanford CA 94305

SEREDA, ROBERT EMANUEL, II, accountant; b. Oakland, Calif., June 17, 1954; s. Robert Emanuel and Beverly Ann (Lagorio) S.; m. Laura Lorraine Dalrymple, June 28, 1975; children: Lisa Michelle, Michelle Nicole. BS in Bus. Adminstrn., Calif. State U., Hayward, 1977. CPA, Calif., 1979. Staff position up to mgr. Dubney Accountancy Corp., Hayward, 1977-83; CPA, ptnr. Sereda & McAvoy, CPAs, Castro Valley, Calif., 1983-88; CPA, pres. Sereda Accountancy Corp., Castro Valley, 1988—. Mem. AICPA, Calif. Soc. CPA, Delta Sigma Pi. Republican. Roman Catholic. Office: Sereda Accountancy Corp 22025 Center St Castro Valley CA 94546-6707

SERFAS, RICHARD THOMAS, county official, educator; b. Reading, Pa., Nov. 24, 1952; s. Clifford Donald and Helen Catherine (McGovern) S. Student, Jacksonville U., 1970-72; BA, Colo. State U., 1974; MPA, Pa. State U., 1977. Project coord. ACTION Peace Corps, VISTA, Gary, Ind., 1974-75; city adminstr. City of Beverly Hills, Mo., 1975; grad. rsch. asst. dept. pub. adminstrn. Pa. State U., Middletown, 1976-77; community planner St. Louis County Dept. Planning, 1977-78; mgmt. analyst Clark County Sanitation Dist., Las Vegas, Nev., 1978-79; environ. planner Clark County Dept. Comprehensive Planning, Las Vegas, 1979-80, prin. planner, 1980-84, asst. coord. planning, 1984-85, coord. advance planning, 1985-89, asst. dir., 1989—; instr. U. Nev. Sch. Architecture, Las Vegas, 1989—; student advisor Las Vegas chpt. AIA, 1989—. Staff advisor Clark County Comprehensive Plan Steering Com., 1980—, Environ. Task Force, Las Vegas, 1984—, Archtl. Design Task Force, Las Vegas, 1984—, Devel. Sector Task Force, Las Vegas, 1984—; mem. Transit Tech. Com., Las Vegas, 1989—. Recipient achievement award Nat. Assn. Counties, 1983-90. Mem. Am. Inst. Cert. Planners, Urban Land Ins., Am. Planning Assn. (treas. Nev. chpt. 1979-91, pres. 1992—, Appreciation award 1981, 83, 85, 87, 89, 91, Outstanding Pub. Sector Planning Accomplishment award 1987, 88, 90, 91), Community Assns. Inst. So. Nev. (bd. dirs. 1990-92, sec. 1993—). Democrat. Roman Catholic. Home: 2713 Brookstone Ct Las Vegas NV 89117-2442 Office: Clark County Dept Comprehensive Planning 225 Bridger Ave Las Vegas NV 89155-0001

SERIZAWA, MARTHA GUERRA (MARTI), urban planner, educator; b. San Marcos, Tex., Jan. 8, 1943; d. Francisco Walls and Linda (Aguirre) Guerra; m. Sheldon L. Maram, 1967 (div. 1985); 1 child, David Alexander; m. Thomas T. Serizawa, June 4, 1988. BA in English Lit., U. Calif., Santa Barbara, 1969; MA in Communs., Calif. State U., Fullerton, 1980. Cert. C.C. teaching credential in comm. and basic edn., Calif.; cert. in land use planning and devel., hazardous waste mgmt. Prodr., host bilingual Spanish and English programs Sta. KOCE-TV, 1974-75; producer, host bilingual programs Radio KSBR, Mission Viejo, Calif., 1975-76; asst. dir. Orange County Fair Housing Coun., 1976; planner Orange County Housing/Community Dept., 1978-84, County of Orange, Coastal/Community Planning, 1984-87, County of Orange, Zoning Adminstrn., 1987-92, County of Orange, Environ. Resources and Water Pollution, Anaheim, Calif., 1992-93; planner devel. svcs., implementer clean water act Orange County, Santa Ana, 1993—; instr. ESL, Instituto-Brazil Estados Unidos, Rio de Janeiro, 1970-71, Rancho Santiago C.C., 1989—; cons., presenter in field. Prodr., writer documentary slide show on Am. group visit to Nicaragua, 1984; contbr. articles to profl. jours. Mem. ACLU, AAUW, MADRE, Calif. Assn. Tchrs. English to Speakers Other Langs. (bd. dirs. 1992—), Amnesty Internat., Nat. Parks and Conservation Assn., Nature Conservancy, Environ. Def. Fund, Pub. Citizen, People for Am. Way. Home: 3119 Oregon Ave Long Beach CA 90806 Office: Orange County Devel Svcs Drainage Sect NPDES 300 N Flower Rm 210 Santa Ana CA 92702-4048

SERN, JONJEN SAMUEL, computer engineer; b. Taitung, Taiwan, Republic of China, Apr. 11, 1959; came to U.S., 1988; s. Chun-Chan and Yin-Mei (Liu) S. BSEE, Tamkang U., Taipei, 1983; MSEE, U. N.C., Charlotte, 1991. Info. analyst Sci. Tech. Info. Ctr., Nat. Sci. Coun., Taipei, 1985-87; CAD engr. Philips Semiconductors/Signetics Co., Sunnyvale, Calif., 1991—. Mem. Rep. Presdl. Task Force, Washington, 1989—, Nat. Rep. Senatorial Com., Washington, 1992—. With Taiwanese Army, 1983-85. Mem. Am. Assn. Individual Investors, Chinese Software Profl. Assn., PAC-Bay Investment Club. Home: 1722 Holin St San Jose CA 95131 Office: Philips Semiconductors 811 E Arques Ave Sunnyvale CA 94088

SERTNER, ROBERT MARK, producer; b. Phila., Oct. 7, 1955; s. Morton I. Sertner and Laurie (Hymes) Blicker. BBA, U. Tex., 1977. Ptnr. von Zerneck/Sertner Films, Los Angeles, 1985—. Producer over 50 TV movies including Hostage Flight, Too Young To Die? (INH Best Movie award), The Courtmartial of Jackie Robinson, Combat High, To Heal A Nation, 1987 (Best Picture Internat. TV Movie awards), Trouble in the City of Angels, Celebration Family, Proud Men, Gore Vidal's Billy the Kid (winner Houston Film Festival), Man Against the Mob, Maybe Baby; co-producer (mini series) The Big One: The Great Los Angeles Earthquake, Queenie, Jackie Collins' Lady Boss, TNT's Native American Miniseries, 1993. Mem. Acad. TV Arts and Scis., Hollywood Radio and TV Soc., Nat. Acad. Cable

Programming, Mus. of Broadcasting Creative Coun., Caucus for Producers, Writers and Dirs. Office: von Zerneck/Sertner Films 12001 Ventura Pl # 400 Studio City CA 91604-2626

SESHACHARI, NEILA C., English language educator, literary critic, writer, editor; b. Belgaum, India, Aug. 8, 1934; came to U.S., 1969; d. Dinker D. and Indira (Shirali) Idgunji; m. Candadai Seshachari; children: Roopa S. Hashimoto, Ruthi Priya, Ranjit. BA with honors, Poona (India) U., 1953; MA, Gujarat (India) U., 1960; PhD, U. Utah, 1975. Asst. lect. in English Gujarat U., Ahmedabad, 1960-61; lectr. Osmania U., Hyderabad, India, 1961-69; mem. faculty Weber State U., Ogden, Utah, 1973—, prof. English, 1982—, editor Weber Studies: An Interdisciplinary Humanities Jour., 1987—; vis. scholar Stanford U., Palo Alto, Calif., 1984-85; cons. editor Coll. Teaching, Washington, 1979—; faculty assoc. Danforth Found., 1976-84. Author: Great Debates and Ethical Issues, 1989; contbr. articles to profl. jours. Utah del. White House Conf. on Librs. and Info. Svcs., Washington, 1979—; mem. civil leaders' tours USAF, Hill AFB, Utah, 1979, 90; mem. devel. com. Weber County Libr., Ogden, 1988-90; mem. Ogden Symphony Ballet Assn., 1985—; bd. dirs. Utah Humanities Coun., Salt Lake City, 1985-91, vice chmn., 1990-91; mem. lit. arts panel Utah Arts Coun., Salt Lake City, 1990-93. Named Woman of Yr. Your Community Connection, 1989. Mem. AAUW (regonal coord., humanities scholar, pres. Utah div. 1982-84, Woman of Yr. 1979), MLA, Utah Acad. Scis., Arts and Letters (chair letters div. 1977-81, pres.-elect 1993—), Western Social Sci. Assn. (exec. coun. 1988-91, v.p. 1992-93), Rocky Mountain MLA (exec. coun. 1991-93), Phi Kappa Phi (pres. chpt. 119 1986-87). Hindu. Home: 4763 Monroe Blvd Ogden UT 84403-3042 Office: Weber State U Ogden UT 84408-1201

SESSLER, ANDREW MARIENHOFF, physicist; b. Bklyn., Dec. 11, 1928; s. David and Mary (Baron) S.; m. Gladys Lerner, Sept. 23, 1951; children: Danial Ira, Jonathan Lawrence, Ruth. BA in Math. cum laude, Harvard U., 1949; MA in Theoretical Physics, Columbia U., 1951, PhD in Theoretical Physics, 1953. NSF fellow Cornell U., N.Y., 1953-54; asst. prof. Ohio State U., Columbus, 1954, assoc. prof., 1960; on leave Midwestern Univs. Research, 1955-56; vis. physicist Lawrence Rediation Lab., 1959-60, Niels Bohr Inst., Copenhagen, summer 1961; researcher theoretical physics U. Calif. Lawrence Berkeley Lab., Berkeley, 1961-73, researcher energy and environment, 1971-73, dir., 1973-80, sr. scientist plasma physics, 1980—; U.S. advisor Panjab U. Physics Inst., Chandigarh, India; mem. U.S.-India Coop. Program for Improvement Sci. Edn. in India, 1966, high energy physics adv. panel to U.S. AEC, 1969-72, adv. com. Lawrence Hall Sci., 1974-78; chmn. Stanford Synchrotron Radiation Project Sci. Policy Bd., 1974-77, EPRI Advanced Fuels Adv. Com., 1978-81, BNL External Adv. Com. on Isabelle, 1980-82; mem. sci. pol. bd. Stanford Synchrotron Radiation Lab., 1991-92; L.J. Haworth dist. scientist Brookhaven Nat. Lab., 1991—. Mem. editorial bd. Nuclear Instruments and Methods, 1969—; correspondent Comments on Modern Physics, 1969-71; contbr. articles in field to profl. jours. Mem. hon. adv. bd. Inst. Advanced Phys. Studies, LaJolla Internat. Sch. Physics, 1991—; mem. Superconducting Super Collider Sci. Policy Com., 1991-94. Recipient E.O. Lawrence award U.S. Atomic Energy Commn., 1970, U.S. Particle Accelerator Sch. prize, 1988; fellow Japan Soc. for Promotion Sci. at KEK, 1985. Fellow AAAS (nominating com. 1984-87), Am. Phys. Soc. (chmn. com. internat. freedom scientist 1982, study of directed energy weapons panel 1985-87, chmn. panel pub. affairs 1988, chmn. div. physics of beams 1990, chmn. com. applications of physics 1993); mem. NAS, IEEE, Fedn. Am. Scientists Coun. (vice chmn. 1987-88, chmn. 1988-92), N.Y. Acad. Sci., Assoc. Univ. Inc. (bd. dirs. 1991-94). Home: 225 Clifton St Apt 201 Oakland CA 94618-1478 Office: U Calif Lawrence Berkeley Lab 1 Cyclotron Rd Berkeley CA 94720

SESTINI, VIRGIL ANDREW, biology educator; b. Las Vegas, Nov. 24, 1936; s. Santi and Merceda Francesca (Borla) S. BS in Edn., U. Nev., 1959; postgrad., Oreg. State U., 1963-64; MNS, U. Idaho, 1965; postgrad., Ariz. State U., 1967, No. Ariz. U., 1969; cert. tchr., Nev. Tchr. biology Rancho High Sch., 1960-76; sci. chmn., tchr. biology Bonanza High Sch., Las Vegas, 1976-90; ret., 1990; part time tchr. Meadows Sch., 1987—. Served with USAR, 1959-65. Recipient Rotary Internat. Honor Tchr. award, 1965, Region VIII Outstanding Biology Tchr. award, 1970, Nev. Outstanding Biology Tchr. award Nat. Assn. Biology Tchrs., 1970, Nat. Assn. Sci. Tchrs., Am. Gas Assn. Sci. Teaching Achievement Recognition award, 1976, 1980, Gustov Ohaus award, 1980, Presdl. Honor Sci. Tchr. award, 1983; Excellence in Edn. award Nev. Dept. Edn., 1983; Presdl. award excellence in math. and sci. teaching, 1984, Celebration of Excellence award Nev. Com. on Excellence in Edn., 1986, Hall of Fame award Clark County Sch. Dist., 1988, Excellence in Edn. award, Clark County Sch. Dist., 1987, 88, Spl. Edn. award Clark County Sch. Dist., 1988, NSEA Mini-grants, 1988, 89, 92, World Decoration of Excellence medallion World Inst. Achievement, 1989, Cert. Spl. Congl. Recognition, 1989, Senatorial Recognition , 1989, minigrant Jr. League Las Vegas., 1989, Excellence in Edn. award, Clark Country Sch. Dist., 1989; named Nev. Educator of Yr., Milken Family Found./Nev. State Dept. Edn., 1989; grantee Nev. State Bd. Edn., 1988, 89, Nev. State Edn. Assn., 1988-89. Author: Lab Investigations For High School Honors Biology, 1989, Microbiology: A Manual for High School Biology, 1992, Laboratory Investigations in Microbiology, 1992; co-author: A Biology Lab Manual For Cooperative Learning, 1989, Metrics and Science Methods: A Manual of Lab Experiments for Home Schoolers, 1990; contbr. articles to profl. jours. Mem. NEA, Nat. Sci. Tchrs. Assn. (Nev. State chpt. 1968-70), Nat. Assn. Biology Tchrs. (OBTA dir. Nev. State 1991—), Am. Soc. Microbiology, Coun. for Exceptional Children, Am. Biographic Inst. (rsch. bd. advisors 1988), Nat. Audubon Assn., Nat. Sci. Suprs. Assn., Am. Inst. Biol. Scis.

SETCHKO, EDWARD STEPHEN, minister, theology educator; b. Yonkers, N.Y., Apr. 27, 1926; s. Stephen John and Mary Elizabeth (Dulak) S.; m. Penelope Sayre, Nov. 18, 1950; children—Marc Edward, Kip Sherman, Robin Elizabeth, Jan Sayre, Dirk Stephen. B.S., Union Coll., 1948; M.Div. cum laude, Andover Newton Theol. Sch., 1953, S.T.M., 1954; Th.D., Pacific Sch. Religion, 1962. Ordained to ministry United Ch. of Christ, 1954; cert. profl. hosp. chaplain. Psychometrician, Union Coll. Character Research Project, Schenectady, N.Y., 1947-50; asst. pastor Eliot Ch., Newton, Mass., 1950-54; clin. tng. supr. Boston City Hosp., 1951-54; intern, chaplain Boston State Mental Hosp., 1953-54; univ. campus minister U. Wash., Seattle, 1954-58; Danforth grantee, 1958-59; grad. fellow in psychotherapy Pacific Sch. Religion, Berkeley, Calif., 1959-60, instr. dept. pastoral psychology, 1960-61, grad. fellow, lectr. theology and psychology, 1961-62, asst. prof. psychology and counseling, 1962-63, dir. continuing theol. edn., 1962-63; field research sec. laity div. United Ch. Christ, Berkeley, Calif. and N.Y.C., 1963-68; vis. prof. psychology Starr King Ctr. for Religious Leadership, Berkeley, 1967-69; assoc. prof. religion and soc. Starr King Ctr., Grad. Theol. Union, Berkeley, Calif., 1969-71, prof., 1971-83; career counselor The Ctr. for Ministry, Oakland, Calif., 1986-89; mem. faculty, chmn. curriculum and faculty com. Layman's Sch. Religion, Berkeley, 1960-67; cons. and lectr. in field. Mem. Peace Del., Mid-East, 1983; lectr. Internat. Conf. on the Holocaust and Genocide, Tel Aviv, 1982, Nuclear Disarmament Conf., W.Ger., 1980, 81, 82, Internat. Ctr. for Peace in the Middle East, Resource Ctr. for Non-Violence, Clergy & Laity Concerned, Ecumenical Peace Inst., Internat. Peace Acad.; World Policy Inst., Inst. Peace and World Order, Am. Friends Service Com. (bd. dirs.), Ristad Found., Am. Friends Golan Heights, Elmwood Coll. Criminal Justice; dir. The Project for Peace and Reconciliation in the Middle East (non-profit Calif. Found. 1983-89); vol. South Berkeley hunger project Alta Bates Hospice. Lt. (j.g.) USNR, 1944-46, WW II. Mem. Am. Psychol. Assn. (cert.), Calif. State Psychol. Assn., Assn. Clin. Pastoral Edn., World Future Soc., Soc. Sci. Study of Religion, Inst. Noetic Scis., Com. for Protection Human Subjects (U. Calif.-Berkeley). Democrat. Contbr. articles to profl. jours.; condr. seminars: Futurology; Intricacies of Being Human, Images of Women and Men; Changing Values in Roles Between the Sexes in a Technological Society, Cybernetics and Humanization of Man; developer curriculum: Peace and Conflict Studies (U. Calif., Berkeley).

SETEROFF, SVIATOSLAV STEVE, management and logistics information systems consultant; b. Shanghai, People's Republic of China, Oct. 6, 1937; came to U.S., 1949; s. Leo G. an Olga D. (Pankova) S.; m. Deanna Catherine Rogers (div. 1964); children: Steven James, Richard Aubrey; m. Joyce Eileen Schieldge, Feb. 22, 1965; children: Barbara Lynn Seteroff Anderson, Leanne Marie Seteroff. AA, Chapman Coll., 1974, BA cum laude, 1975; MBA, U. Puget Sound, 1983. Enlisted USN, 1955-75, commd. warrant officer, 1976-85; sr. analyst McDonnell Douglas Astronautics Co., Rockville, Md., 1985-87; program mgr. Anadac, Inc., Arlington, Va., 1987; v.p. Systems Mgmt. Am. Corp., San Diego, 1987-89; project mgr. info. systems, logistics, sr. ops. analyst MERIT Systems, Inc., Bremerton, Wash., 1989-91; founder, owner Mgmt. and Logistics Assocs., 1990—; instr. Residence Edn. Ctr., Chapman Coll., Bangor, Wash., 1985. Developer Scrivener Masonic Lodge Mgmt. Program, 1992; current work on LDS2B logistics database for U.S. mil. support. Mem. Am. Soc. Naval Engrs. (nat. chmn. logistics symposium 1991-93, Pres. award 1993), Am. Soc. Logistics Engrs. (symposium presenter), Ret. Officers Assn., Masons. Office: 12890 Old Military Rd NE Poulsbo WA 98370-7972

SETH, OLIVER, judge; b. Albuquerque, May 30, 1915; s. Julien Orem and Bernice (Grefe) S.; m. Jean MacGillivray, Sept. 25, 1946; children: Sandra Bernice, Laurel Jean. A.B., Stanford U., 1937; LL.B., Yale U., 1940. Bar: N.Mex. 1940. Practice law Santa Fe, 1940, 46-62; judge U.S. Ct. Appeals 10th Circuit, 1962—, chief judge, from 1976, now senior judge; dir. Santa Fe Nat. Bank, 1949-62; chmn. legal com. N.Mex. Oil and Gas Assn., 1956-59, mem. regulatory practices com., 1960-62; counsel N.Mex. Cattlegrowers Assn., 1950-62, N.Mex. Bankers Assn., 1952-62; govt. appeal agent SSS, 1948-52. Mem. bd. regents Mus. of N.Mex., 1956-60; Bd. dirs. Boys Club, Santa Fe, 1948-49, New Mex. Land Resources Assn., 1956-60, Ghost Ranch Mus., 1962—; mng. bd. Sch. Am. Research, 1950—. Served from pvt. to maj. AUS, 1940-45, ETO. Decorated Croix de Guerre (France). Mem. Santa Fe C. of C. (dir.), N.Mex., Santa Fe County bar assns., Phi Beta Kappa. Presbyterian. Office: US Ct Appeals10th Circuit PO Drawer I Santa Fe NM 87504

SETH, PHILIP DOYLE, college administrator; b. Lawton, Okla., Aug. 14, 1958; s. Gerald Doyle and Viginia Edna (Hart) S.; m. Lynn Marchant Doidge, Aug. 5, 1981; 1 child, Emma Jo Lynn. BA in Math/Bus., Linfield Coll., 1980. Systems analyst Linfield Coll., McMinnville, Oreg., 1980-81; programmer, analyst Linfield Coll., McMinnville, 1981—; adminstr. Lynn Marchant Acad. of Ballet, McMinnville, 1981-92; sec., treas., bd. dirs. Marchant Dance Corp., McMinnville, 1992—. Bd. dirs., gen. mgr., treas. Oreg. Children's Ballet Theatre, McMinnville, 1984-89. Mem. IEEE (Computer Soc.), Assn. for Computing Machinery, U.S. Chess Fedn. (life). Republican. Office: Marchant Dance Corp PO Box 793 McMinnville OR 97128

SETO, JOSEPH TOBEY, virologist, educator; b. Tacoma, Aug. 3, 1924; s. Toraichi and Kiyo Morita Seto; m. Grace K. Nakano, Aug. 9, 1959; children: Susan L., Steven F. BS, U. Minn., 1949; MS, U. Wis., 1955, PhD, 1957. Postdoctoral fellow UCLA, 1958-59; asst. prof. San Francisco State U., 1959-60; prof. microbiology Calif. State U., L.A., 1960-88, prof. emeritus, 1988; cons. U.S. Naval Biology Lab., Oakland, Calif., 1959-61; vis. prof. Inst. Virology, Giessen, Fed. Republic Germany, 1965-66, 72-73, 79-80, 86-87, NATO sr. scientist, 1972, WHO Exchange Worker, 1972. Sgt. U.S. Army, 1945-46. United Health Found. fellow, 1965; recipient Humboldt Found. award 1972, 86, Humboldt Found. medal 1991. Fellow Am. Soc. Microbiology; mem. AAAS, Electron Microscope Soc., Sigma Xi. Office: Calif State U Dept Microbiology Los Angeles CA 90032

SETZER, KAREN LEE, nurse; b. Spring Valley, Ill., Jan. 16, 1944; d. Ivan Elmer and Shirle Mae (Harker) Anderson; m. Fred Teufel Setzer, Aug. 15, 1965; children: Damon Anderson, Tania Charise. Student, Bethany Coll., Lindsborg, Kans., 1961-62; BS in Nursing, U. Colo., 1966; postgrad., Lesley Coll., Cambridge, Mass., 1986, Red Rocks Coll., Golden, Colo., 1992, Lesley Coll., 1993. RN, Colo.; type E spl. svcs. cert. Staff nurse, asst. head nurse, head nurse Colo. Psychiat. Hosp., Denver, 1966-68; mgr. InterLuth. Inst. Worship and Music, Loretto Heights Coll., Denver, 1980; nurse Golden (Colo.) Med. Clinic, 1984—; trainer, developer for Hospice Am. Luth. Ch., Denver, 1979-80; fund raising chair, counselor Nat. Youth Gathering, Evang. Luth. Ch. Am., San Antonio, 1988, mem. synod coun. Rocky Mountain Synod, 1991—, mem. exec. com., 1992—, v.p. Rocky Mountain Synod Women of Evang. Luth. Ch. Am., 1987-88, pres. Denver Conf., 1978-80; presenter Search Bible Study pilot program, 1982. Author: (plays) I Get No Respect, 1984, A Day in the Life of Darwin Disaster, 1992 (state PTA award 1992); dir. cherub choir, 1972-82. Worship chmn. Faith Luth. Ch., Golden, 1977-79, pres. of women's orgn., 1974-76; mem., sec. steering com. Denver House of Studies, Wartburg Sem., Denver, 1977-79; publicity co-chair InterLuth. Renaissance Festival, Denver, 1978; mem. Colo. Chorale, Denver, 1979-85; program chair, safety chair Mitchell Elem. PTA, Golden, 1982-84.

SEVER, LOWELL ENYEART, epidemiologist; b. Yakima, Wash., Sept. 22, 1939; s. Ralph Wesley and Virginia Love (Enyeart) S.; m. Susan Curry Carter, Dec. 18, 1965; children: Jeremy Carter, Alison Mary. AA, Wenatchee Valley Coll., 1959; BA, U. Wash., 1966; MA, U. Wis., Milw., 1968; PhD, U. Wash., 1973. Rsch. assoc. U. Wash., Seattle, 1972-74; asst. prof. U. Calif., L.A., 1974-79; sr. rsch. scientist Battelle Pacific Northwest Labs., Richland, Wash., 1979-84; asst. dir. for sci. div. of birth defects Ctrs. for Disease Control, Atlanta, 1984-89; staff scientist Battelle Pacific Northwest Labs., Richland, 1989—; summer faculty New England Epidemiology Inst., Medford, Mass., 1985—; affiliate prof. U. Wash. Sch. of Pub. Health, Seattle, 1990—. Contbr. articles to profl. jours. Exec. com. March of Dimes Birth Defects Found., Richland, 1980-84, Atlanta, 1985-89, Seattle, 1990—. Recipient Spl. Recognition award USPHS, 1988. Fellow Am. Coll. Epidemiology; mem. Soc. for Pediatric Epidemiologic Rsch. (pres. 1989-90), Am. Epidemiol. Soc., Soc. for Epidemiologic Rsch., Am. Pub. Health Assn., Teratology Soc. Office: Battelle Seattle Rsch Ctr 4000 NE 41st St Seattle WA 98105

SEVERINO, ROBERT ANTHONY, aerospace company executive; b. El Paso, Tex., June 19, 1954; s. Murrie Albert and Ann Elizabeth (Croce) S. BS in Engring., Harvey Mudd Coll., Claremont, Calif., 1977; MBA with honors, Pepperdine U., Malibu, Calif., 1986; postgrad., Claremont Grad. Sch., 1989—. Program mgr. Hughes Aircraft Co., Fullerton, Calif., 1977-84, Tracor Flight Systems, Mojave, Calif., 1984—. Recipient Elks award, 1972. Mem. Am. Def. Preparedness Assn., Assn. Old Crows. Home: 5 Los Gatos Irvine CA 92715-2982 Office: Tracor Flight Systems 6500 Tracor Ln Austin TX 78725

SEVERINSEN, DOC (CARL H. SEVERINSEN), conductor, musician; b. Arlington, Oreg., July 7, 1927; m. Emily Marshall, 1980; children—Nancy, Judy, Cindy, Robin, Allen. Ptnr. Severinsen-Akwright Co. Mem., Ted Fio Rito Band, 1945, Charlie Barnet Band, 1947-49, then with, Tommy Dorsey, Benny Goodman, Norro Morales, Vaughn Monroe; soloist network band: Steven Allen Show, NBC-TV, 1954-55; mem., NBC Orch. Tonight Show, 1962-67 , music dir., 1967-92 ; past host of: NBC-TV show The Midnight Special; recs., RCA Records, including; albums: Brass Roots, 1971, Facets, 1988, The Tonight Show Band, Night Journey. Address: care NBC Press Dept KNBC 3000 W Alameda Ave Burbank CA 91523

SEVERSON, KIM MARIE, reporter; b. Eau Claire, Wis., Sept. 12, 1961; d. James Howard and Anne Marie (Zappa) S. Student, Mich. State U., 1979-83, U. Wash., 1984. Reporter Seattle Post Intelligencer, 1983; reporter, copy editor The Weekly, Seattle, 1984-85; reporter, editor The Lynnwood (Wash.) Enterprise, 1984-85; reporter The Oregonian, Portland, 1985-86, The Morning News Tribune, Tacoma, 1986-91, Anchorage Daily News, 1991—. Mem. Nat. Lesbian and Gay Journalist Assn. (chpt. coord. 1992—), Soc. Profl. Journalists. Home: 125-1/2 E Manor Anchorage AK 99501 Office: Anchorage Daily News 1001 Northway Dr Anchorage AK 99514

SEVEY, ROBERT WARREN, broadcast journalist; b. Mpls., Dec. 6, 1927; s. Benjamin Warren and Helen Margaret (Benham) S.; m. Rosalie Fergueson Thomas, Jan. 28, 1950; children: Michael Warren, David Ellis. BA, U. Calif., Santa Barbara, 1951. Announcer, newscaster WOI and KASI, Ames, Iowa, 1947-49; sports dir. KIST, Santa Barbara, 1949-51; prodn. asst. CBS-TV, Hollywood, Calif., 1951-52; producer, announcer KPHO-TV, Phoenix, 1952-54; prodn. mgr. KULA-TV, Honolulu, 1954-57; prodn. mgr. radio-TV Holst & Male Inc., Honolulu, 1957-59; sta. mgr. KGMB-TV, Honolulu, 1959-61; news dir. Sta. KHVH-TV, Honolulu, 1961-65, Sta. KGMB-TV, Honolulu, 1966-86; v.p. news/corporate affairs Heftel Broadcasting Co., Honolulu, 1987-90; with Heftel Broadcasting Co., L.A., 1990-91; ret., 1991. S/sgt. U.S. Army, 1945-47. Mem. Radio-TV News Dirs. Assn., Honolulu Press Club (pres. 1969-70, mem. Hall of Fame 1987—).

SEVILLA, CARLOS A., bishop; b. San Francisco, Aug. 9, 1935. Ed., Gonzaga U., Santa Clara U., Jesuiten Kolleg, Innsbruck, Austria, Cath. Inst. Paris. Ordained priest Roman Cath. Ch., 1966, bishop, 1989. Titular bishop Mina, 1989—; aux. bishop San Francisco, 1989—. Office: Archdiocese San Francisco 445 Church St San Francisco CA 94114-1720*

SEWELL, CHARLES ROBERTSON, geologist, exploration company executive, investor; b. Malvern, Ark., Feb. 7, 1927; s. Charles Louis and Elizabeth (Robertson) S.; m. Margaret Helen Wilson, Dec. 26, 1953 (dec. July 1985); children: Michael Stuart, Charles Wilson, Marion Elizabeth; m. Louise T. Worthington, Nov. 29, 1985; 1 child, Ginger B. BS, U. Ark.-Fayetteville, 1950; MA, U. Tex.-Austin, 1955, postgrad., 1961-64. Registered geologist, Calif., Ariz. Well logging engr. Baroid, Houston, 1950; asst. metallurgist Magcobar, Malvern, Ark., 1951; geologist Socony-Mobil Petroleum Co., Roswell, N.Mex., 1955; sr. geologist Dow Chem. Co., Freeport, Tex., 1956-61; spl. instr. U. Tex., Austin, 1962-65; pvt. practice cons. geologist, Austin, 1962-65; dist. geologist, mgr. Callahan Mining Corp., Tucson, 1965-68; owner, cons. geologist Sewell Mineral Exploration, worldwide, 1968—, extensive work USSR-CIS, 1988—. Contbr. articles to profl. jours. Elder, Presbyn. Ch., Tucson, 1973—. With USN, 1944-46, 51-53. NSF grantee, 1962-64, 63. Mem. AIME, Ariz. Geol. Soc., Mining Club Southwest (bd. govs. 1982-86, 90—, pres. 1984). Republican. Lodge: Masons. Discoverer/co-discoverer numerous metallic and non-metallic ore deposits. Home and Office: 260 S Sewell Pl Tucson AZ 85748-6700

SEWELL, WILLIAM R., real estate company executive; b. Barstow, Tex., Nov. 13, 1926; s. William Floyd Sewell and Mamie (Reeves) Sewell Moon; m. Verna Mae Shaw, Jan. 24, 1960; children: William Shaw, Michele Elaine, Scott R. AA, Visalia (Calif.) Jr. Coll., 1948; BS, UCLA, 1950. Staff officer Matson Nav. Co., San Francisco, 1950-59; ptnr. Palms Constrn., Honolulu, 1960-62; pres., owner Waialae Builders, Inc., Honolulu, 1962-88, Sewell Assocs., Inc., Honolulu, 1972-85, Spencer/Sewell Realty, Honolulu, 1985-89; pres. Home Inspections, Inc., Honolulu, 1988—; dir. specialized residences Century 21-Kahala Hale, Honolulu, 1992—; realtor various cos., Honolulu, 1967-72. Mem. Neighborhood Bd. 3, Honolulu, 1982-84, Neighborhood Bd. 2, 1986-88. With U.S. Army, 1944-46. Mem. Nat. Assn. Realtors, Nat. Assn. Home Builders, Bldg. Industry Assn. (past pres.), Honolulu Bd. Realtors (bd. dirs. 1986-88), Mercury Bus. Club (past pres.), Outrigger Canoe Club (com. 1990-92), Rotary, Elks. Home: 1635 Kalaniiki St Honolulu HI 96821

SEXAUER, ROXANNE DENISE, artist, educator; b. N.Y.C., Nov. 24, 1952; d. Roland Dietrich and Ann Margaret (Pacsuta) S.; m. David Robert Joseph, Nov. 24, 1982. BFA, U. Iowa, 1979; MFA, SUNY, Purchase, 1989. Instr. City of Iowa City, 1976-86, Iowa Arts Coun., Washington & Williamsburg, 1978; lectr. SUNY-Purchase, 1989; lectr. Calif. State U., Long Beach, 1989-90, asst. prof., 1990—; ind. artist, 1974—; guest curator Neuberger Mus., Purchase, 1988-89. Illustrator (books) Charles Olson: Early Poems, 1978, Robert the Devil, 1981, Blood Harvest, 1986; one-woman shows include Hiram (Ohio) Coll., 1989, MiraCosta Coll., Oceanside, Calif., 1992; numerous other solo, group exhbns. Artist dialogue South Bay Contemporary Mus. Art, Torrance, Calif., 1992; panel mem. Mus. of Art Calif. State U.-Long Beach, 1990. Resident The Hambidge Ctr., Rabun Gap, Ga., 1992, Palenville (N.Y.) InterArts, 1991; recipient touring citation Mid-Am. Arts Alliance, 1990. Mem. Calif. Women in Higher Edn., Coll. Art Assn., L.A. Printmaking Soc., Phila. Print Club, U. Iowa Alumni Assn., Women's Caucus for Arts. Democrat. Home: 2822 Freckles Rd Lakewood CA 90712-4017 Office: Calif State U Long Beach Art Dept 1250 Bellflower Blvd Long Beach CA 90840

SEXTON, JAMES DEAN, anthropology educator, author; b. Sept. 1, 1942; s. Marion S. and Violet J. (Towery) S.; m. Marilyn Rex, Dec. 26, 1966; 1 child, Randall Rex. BA, UCLA, 1967, MA, 1971, PhD, 1973. From teaching asst. to assoc. UCLA, 1970-72; asst. prof. anthropology No. Ariz. U., Flagstaff, 1973-84, prof. anthropology, 1984-91, regents' prof., 1991—. Author: Son of Tecún Umán, Campesino, Ignacio and Mayan Folktales, 1992, Education and Innovation in a Guatemalan Community. With U.S. Army, 1968-69, Vietnam. U.S. AID grantee UCLA, 1972-73, Am. Philos. Soc. grantee, 1988; recipient NAU Prs. award, 1982. Fellow Am. Anthropol. Assn.; mem. Southwestern Anthropol. Assn. (exec. bd. 1986-88, v.p., pres. 1992-93), Am. Ethnological Soc., Soc. for Latin-Am. Anthropology, Phi Kappa Phi. Office: No Ariz U Dept Anthropology Box 15200 Flagstaff AZ 86011

SEYBOLD, STEVEN JON, entomologist; b. Madison, Wis., Oct. 14, 1959; s. Robert Russel and Patricia Jane (Sovinec) S.; m. Jeni Ann Hartmann, Dec. 22, 1984. BS in Forestry, U. Wis., 1983; PhD in Entomology, U. Calif., Berkeley, 1992. Nat. resources asst. Forest Pest Mgmt. Unit Wis. Dept. Natural Resources, Madison, 1982; forest practitioner Swedish Forest Svc., Hedemora, Sweden, 1983; grad. rsch. asst. Dept. Entomol. Scis., U. Calif., Berkeley, 1984-92; postdoctoral rsch. entomologist Forest Svc., USDA, Albany, Calif., 1992—. Literacy tutor Marin County Literacy Project, 1986-87; van pool coord. Larkspur Vanpool, Marin County, 1989-93; mem. Dept. Entomol. Scis. Grad. Adv. Com., Berkeley, 1987, Bioscis. Libr. Adv. Com., U. Calif., Berkeley, 1988-92. NSF grantee, 1990; NSF fellow, 1985-88; Phi Beta Kappa merit scholar, 1989. Mem. Entomol. Soc. Am., Internat. Soc. Chem. Ecology, Am. Chem. Soc., Sigma Xi, Phi Beta Kappa, Gamma Sigma Delta, Xi Sigma Pi, Phi Kappa Phi. Office: USDA Forest Svc Pacific SW Rsch Sta 800 Buchanan St PO Box 245 Berkeley CA 94710

SEYFERT, HOWARD BENTLEY, JR., podiatrist; b. Clifton Heights, Pa., July 10, 1918; s. Howard Bentley and Mabel (Ashenbach) S.; m. Anna Mary van Roden, June 26, 1942; 1 child, Joanna Mary Irwin. D of Podiatric Medicine, Temple U., 1940. Cert. Nat. Bd. Podiatry Examiners (past pres.), Ariz. State Bd. Podiatry Examiners (past pres.). Pvt. practice podiatry Phoenix, 1950-82, Sedona, Ariz., 1982—; mem. med. staff Marcus J. Lawrence Meml. Hosp., Cottonwood, Ariz. Served to capt. USAAF, 1942-46, ETO, lt. col. Res. ret. Decorated Bronze Star. Fellow Acad. Ambulatory Foot Surgery, Am. Coll. Foot Surgeons; mem. Ariz. Podiatric Med. Assn. (past pres.), Am. Podiatric Med. Assn. Republican. Presbyterian. Clubs: OakCreek Country (Sedona); Fairfield Flagstaff Country (Flagstaff, Ariz.). Home: 370 Oakcreek Dr Sedona AZ 86336-7734 Office: Roadrunner Profl Pla 105 Roadrunner Dr Sedona AZ 86336-3767

SEYFERTH, HAROLD HOMER, real estate appraising company executive, educator; b. Stockton, Calif., Jan. 22, 1922; s. Lester L. and Bernice (Perkins) S.; m. Betty Jean Stanley, Apr. 12, 1943; children: Mary B., Laurence P. BA, San Jose State U., 1948; MBA, Ph.D., Pacific Western U., 1981. Locomotive engr. Western Pacific R.R., 1939-50; asst. planner City of San Jose, 1950-54; mgr. City of Hollister (Calif.), 1959-63; property mgr. City of Salinas (Calif.), 1963-68; redevel. chief land officer City of Seaside (Calif.), 1968-69; pres. H. Seyferth Assocs., Monterey, Calif., 1969—; lectr. in field. Chmn., bd. dirs. Carmel Riviera Mut. Water Co.; bd. dirs. Boy's City Boy's Club, San Jose, Am. Cancer Soc., San Jose; trustee Enterprise Sch. Dist., Hollister, Calif. With USN, 1942-45. Coro fellow, 1950. Mem. Am. Assn. Cert. Appraisers (cert.), Am. Planning Assn., Am. Assn. Retired Persons (pres. Monterey Peninsula chpt. 97), Calif. Assn. Real Estate Tchrs., Internat. Coll. Real Estate Cons. Profls., Internat. Inst. Valuers, Internat. Orgn. Real Estate Appraisers, Internat. Right of Way Assn., Nat. Assn. Cert. Real Property Appraisers, Nat. Assn. Rev. Appraisers, Real Estate Educators Assn., Urban Land Inst. Office: 734 Lighthouse Ave Pacific Grove CA 93950-2522

SEYMOUR, JEFFREY ALAN, governmental relations consultant; b. L.A., Aug. 31, 1950; s. Daniel and Evelyn (Schwartz) S.; m. Valerie Joan Parker, Dec. 2, 1973; 1 child, Jessica Lynne. AA in Social Sci., Santa Monica Coll., 1971; BA in Polit. Sci., UCLA, 1973, M Pub Adminstrn., 1977. Councilmanic aide L.A. City Coun., 1972-74; county supervisor's sr. dep. L.A. Bd. Suprs., 1974-82; v.p. Bank of L.A., 1982-83; prin. Jeffrey Seymour & Assocs., L.A., 1983-84; ptnr. Morey/Seymour & Assocs., 1984—; mem. comml. panel Am. Arbitration Assn., 1984—. Chmn. West Hollywood Parking Adv. Com., L.A., 1983-84; chmn. social action com. Temple Emanuel of Beverly Hills, 1986-89, bd. dirs. 1988—, v.p., 1990-93; mem. Pan

Pacific Park Citizens Adv. Com., L.A., 1982-85; bd. dirs. William O'Douglas Outdoor Classroom, L.A., 1981-88; exec. sec. Calif. Fedn. Young Dems., 1971; mem. Calif. Dem. Cen. Com., 1979-82; pres. Beverlywood-Cheviot Hills Dem. Club, L.A., 1978-81; co-chmn. Westside Chancellor's Assocs. UCLA, 1986-88; mem. L.A. Olympic Citizens Adv. Com.; mem. liaison adv. commn. with city and county govt. for 1984 Olympics, 1984; v.p. community rels. metro region, Jewish Fedn. Coun. of L.A., 1985-87, co-chmn. urban affairs commn., 1987-89, vice chmn., 1989-90, subcom. chmn. local govt. law and legislation commn., 1990—; mem. adv. bd. Nat. Jewish Ctr. for Immunology & Respiratory Medicine, 1991—; bd. dirs. Hillel Coun. of L.A., 1991—; mem. platform on world peace and internat. rels. Calif. Dems., 1983; pres. 43d Assembly Dist. Dem. Council, 1975-79; arbitrator Better Bus. Bur., 1984—; trustee UCLA Found., 1989—; pres. UCLA Jewish Alumni, 1992—. Recipient Plaques for services rendered Beverlywood Cheviot Hills Dem. Club, L.A., 1981, Jewish Fedn. Coun. Greater L.A., 1983; Certs. of Appreciation, L.A. Olympic Organizing Com., 1984, County of L.A., 1984, City of L.A., 1987; commendatory resolutions, rules com. Calif. State Senate, 1987, Calif. State Assembly, 1987, County of L.A., 1987, City of L.A., 1987. Mem. Am. Soc. Pub. Adminstrn., Am. Acad. Polit. and Social Scis., Town Hall of Calif., So. Calif. Planning Congress, Urban Land Inst., UCLA Alumni Assn. (govtl. affairs steering com. 1983—). Office: Morey/Seymour and Assocs 233 Wilshire Blvd Ste 290 Santa Monica CA 90401

SEYMOUR, PETER MARK, psychiatrist; b. Rochester, N.Y., Apr. 13, 1948; s. Holland Parker and Rozel Louise (Whitenack) S.; m. Sherry Ann Almquist, Apr. 21, 1985; 1 child, Andrew Mark. AB in History, Stanford U., 1970; MS in Rehab. Counseling, San Diego State U., 1975; MD, Boston U., 1981. Diplomate Nat. Bd. Med. Examiners; cert. Am. Bd. Psychiatry & Neurology. Psychiatrist Columbia (Tenn.) Area Mental Health Ctr., 1985-87; pvt. practice psychiatry Columbia, 1987-90, San Diego, 1990—; med. dir. Harbor View Partial Hospitalization Program, La Mesa, Calif., 1992—; mem. clin. faculty dept. psychiatry U. Calif. San Diego Sch. Medicine, La Jolla, 1991—. Recipient Regional Adminstrs. award Nat. Health Svc. Corps, 1987. Mem. Am. Psychiat. Assn., Am. Assn. Psychiatry & Law, Calif. Med. Assn., Calif. Soc. for Indsl. Medicine & Surgery, San Diego Soc. Psychiat. Physicians, San Diego County Med. Soc. Office: 2780 Cardinal Rd Ste A San Diego CA 92123

SFERRAZZA, PETER JOSEPH, mayor, lawyer; b. N.Y.C., Apr. 30, 1945; s. Peter Joseph and Jane S. (Terry) S.; m. Vivian Ann Canty, 1968 (div.); children—Jessica, Joey. BA, Mich. State U., 1967; JD, U. Wis., 1972. Bar: Wis. 1972, Nev. 1977. Legal intern Wis. Judicare, Madison, 1971-72; staff atty. Wis. Judicare, Wausau, 1972-75, Dane County Legal Services, Wausau, 1972; sole practice Wausau, 1975-76; dir. Nev. Indian Legal Service, Carson City, 1976-79; ptnr. Howard, Cavallera & Sferrazza, Reno, 1979-81; sole practice Reno, 1981—; mayor City of Reno, 1983—; tribal judge Washoe Tribe, Carson City, 1979-80. Alderman city of Wausau, 1976; councilman City of Reno, 1981-83; del. Nat. Democratic conv., 1984; chmn. Nev. Dem. Conv., 1984. Roman Catholic. Office: City of Reno Office of Mayor 490 S Center St Reno NV 89501-2191*

SHACKELFORD, GORDON LEE, JR., educator; b. South Bend, Ind., Apr. 7, 1948; s. Gordon Lee and Leatha Mae (Andrews) S.; m. Janis Elizabeth Mead, Apr. 6, 1974. BS in Physics, San Diego State U., 1970, MS in Radiol. Physics, 1974. Electronic designer for physics dept. San Diego State U., 1969-70; electronic engr. Naval Electronics Lab., Point Loma, Calif., 1970; electronic engr. product design Info. Machine Corps., Santee, Calif., 1970-71; lectr. physics San Diego State U., 1971—, asst. dir. alumni and devel. Coll. of Scis., 1980-81, assoc. dean scis., external rels., 1981—, project mgr. Biomass Power Plant, 1984-87, 89—; project mgr. SDSU 100 Telescope, 1989—, Tijuana River Tidal Wetlands Restoration Project. Mem. quality life bd. City of San Diego; chmn. Lakeside Community Planning Group. Home: 9716 Red Pony Ln El Cajon CA 92021-2343 Office: San Diego State U Physics Dept San Diego CA 92182

SHACTER, DAVID MERVYN, lawyer; b. Toronto, Ont., Can., Jan. 17, 1941; s. Nathan and Tillie Anne (Schwartz) S. BA, U. Toronto, 1963; JD, Southwestern U., 1967. Bar: Calif. 1968, U.S. Ct. Appeals (9th cir.) 1969, U.S. Supreme Ct. 1982. Law clk., staff atty. Legal Aid Found., Long Beach, Calif., 1967-70; asst. city atty. City of Beverly Hills, Calif., 1970; ptnr. Shacter & Berg, Beverly Hills, 1971-83, Capalbo, Lowenthal & Shacter Profl. Law Corp., 1984—; del. State Bar Conf. Dels., 1976—; lectr. Calif. Continuing Edn. of Bar, 1977, 82, 83, 86; judge pro tem L.A. and Beverly Hills mcpl. cts.; arbitrator L.A. Superior Ct., 1983—, also judge pro tem; disciplinary examiner Calif. State Bar, 1986. Bd. dirs. and pres. Los Angeles Soc. Prevention Cruelty to Animals, 1979-89. Mem. Beverly Hills Bar Assn. (bd. govs. 1985—, editor-in-chief jour., sec. 1987-88, treas. 1988-89, v.p. 1989-90, pres.-elect 1990-91, pres. 1991-92), Los Angeles County Bar Assn., Am. Arbitration Assn. (nat. panel arbitrators), City of Hope Med. Ctr. Aux., Wilshire C. of C. (bd. dirs., gen. counsel 1985-87). Office: 3580 Wilshire Blvd Ste 1510 Los Angeles CA 90010

SHADDOCK, PAUL FRANKLIN, SR., human resources director; b. Buffalo, Apr. 7, 1950; s. William Edmund and Rhea (Riester) S.; m. Linda Jeannine Bauer, July 19, 1980; children: Paul Jr., Jessica. BS, State U. Coll. N.Y., Buffalo, 1973; MBA, SUNY, Binghamton, 1975. Warehouse mgr. Ralston Purina Co., Denver, 1976-77; prodn. supr. Samsonite Corp., Denver, 1978-79, labor rels. rep., 1979-83; dir. human resources NBI, Inc., Denver, 1984-89, United Techs. Corp., Colorado Springs, Colo., 1990—. Mem. Colo. Alliance of Bus., Denver, 1983-85, 90—, exec. com. U. Colo., Colorado Springs, 1990—. Mem. Assn. of Quality Participation, Am. Personnel Assn., Colo. Human Resource Assn., Human Resource Electronics Group, Mountain States Employers Coun., Rocky Mountain Human Resources Group, Colorado Springs C. of C. Republican. Roman Catholic. Home: 2360 Shiprock Way Colorado Springs CO 80919

SHADMEHRI, BAHRAM, materials management executive; b. Tehran, Iran, July 26, 1952; came to U.S., 1978; s. Hassan Shadmehri and Keshvar Afshari; m. Ziba Khodadadi, July 14, 1989. B in Gen. Bus., Tehran Bus. Coll., 1974; MBA, U. Ariz. 1980. Prodn. control supr. Digital Equipment Corp., Phoenix, 1981-85; prodn. and inventory mgr. Micom Systems, Sun Valley, Calif., 1985-87; dir. materials Systems Industries, Milpitas, Calif., 1987—. Office: Systems Industries 1855 Barber Ln Milpitas CA 95035

SHAEFFER, CHARLIE WILLARD, JR., cardiologist; b. Phila., Feb. 8, 1938; s. Charlie Willard and Lucy Virginia (Chambliss) S.; m. Claire Brightwell, Feb. 24, 1959; children: Charlie Willard III, James Robert. BS, Fla. State U., 1960; MD, Washington U., St. Louis, 1964. Diplomate Am. Bd. Internal Medicine, Am. Bd. Cardiovascular Disease, Am. Bd. Critical Care Medicine. Rotating intern Naval Hosp., Bethesda, Md., 1964-65; resident in internal medicine Naval Hosp., Oakland, Calif., 1965-68; fellow cardiology Naval Hosp., Bethesda, 1968-70; staff cardiology Naval Hosp., Portsmouth, Va., 1970-71, chief, cardiology, 1971-74; cardiologist, corp. sec. Desert Cardiology Cons., Med. Group, Inc., Rancho Mirage, Calif., 1974—; cons. Naval Hosp., San Diego, 1974-75; head cardiology Eisenhower Med. Ctr., Rancho Mirage, Calif., 1976-78, pres., med. staff, 1982-83; instr. Advanced Cadiopulmonary Life Support, Am. Heart Assn., Dallas, 1983—. Contbr. articles to profl. jours. Pres. Riverside (Calif.) County Heart Assn., 1978-79, Calif. affiliate Am. Heart Assn., Burlingame, Calif., 1984-85, Desert div., Palm Desert, Calif., 1989-90; chair-elect S.W. Region Am. Heart Assn., 1991—; bd. dirs. Eisenhower Med. Ctr., Rancho Mirage, 1990-93, Eisenhower Meml. Hosp., Rancho Mirage, 1990-93. Recipient Bronze Svc. award Calif. affiliate Am. Heart Assn., 1982, Silver Svc. award 1983, 85, 87, Gold Svc. award 1988, named Physician Vol. of Yr., 1989. Fellow Clin. Cardiology Am. Heart Assn., Am. Coll. Cardiology, Am. Coll. Physicians, Am. Coll. Chest Physicians. Office: Desert Cardiology Cons 39000 Bob Hope Dr Rancho Mirage CA 92270

SHAEUMIN, MINAYA, customer service representative; b. San Francisco, July 11, 1928; d. John Jesse and Helen Elizabeth (Forsyth) McNeil; m. Maurice Loren Turner, July 28, 1949 (div. Nov. 1955); 1 child, Colleen Ann; m. Rayee Shaeumin, Feb. 13, 1973. Student, Santa Rosa (Calif.) Jr. Coll., 1958-60; AA, Tanana Valley C.C., Fairbanks, Ark., 1987; BS in Anthropology, Oreg. State U., 1992. Lic. life ins. agt., health and accident agt. Intern tchr. 2d grade Primrose Elem. Sch., Santa Rosa, 1961-62; floor clk. surg. wing Santa Rosa Meml. Hosp., 1962; lab. technician Optical Coating Labs., Santa Rosa, 1962-63; live-in practical nurse, housekeeper, sch. tchr. Healsburg, Calif., 1963-65; saleslady, mgr. cosmetic dept. Empire Drug Store, Santa Rosa, 1965-67; community ctr. aide, coord. Community Ctr., Ukiah, Calif., 1968-69; picture framer New Horizons Art Gallery, Fairbanks, Alaska, 1985; seed analyst Oreg. State U. Seed Lab., Corvallis, 1988; owner, operator Best Publs., 1991-92. Inventor matchbook holder-dispensor; inventor-designer free standing mag. rack; writer songs. Active mem. Pro-Choice Orgn., 1991—; mem. The Planetary Soc., 1989-91, Nat. Space Soc., 1990-91; mem. gold club North Shore Animal League, N.Y., 1985—. Recipient Benefactor award North Shore Animal League, 1991, Cert. of Appreciation, Nat. Cm. to Preserve Social Security and Medicare, 1991. Mem. Amnesty Internat. U.S.A., Ams. to Limit Congl. Terms, Am. Policy Inst. "We the People", World Future Soc., NAFE, LWV, Srs. Coalition, So. Poverty Law Ctr., Nat. Com. to Preserve Social Security and Medicare. Home: 205 NW 11th St # 2 Corvallis OR 97330-6048

SHAFER, DALLAS EUGENE, psychology-gerontology educator, minister; b. Holyoke, Colo., Jan. 26, 1936; s. Howard C. and Mary M. (Legg) S.; m. Opal Iline Bruner, Aug. 22, 1954; children: Kim, Jana, Amy. BA, Nebr. Christian, 1958; postgrad., U. Colo., Colorado Springs, 1968-72, U. So. Calif., L.A., 1973; PhD, Walden U., 1978. Cert. clin. pastoral counseling; ordained to ministry Christian Ch., 1958. Minister Christian Ch., Colorado Springs, 1960-62, Julesburg, Colo., 1962-67; instr. of honors program U. Colo., Colorado Springs, 1974, 75; instr. psychology-gerontology Coll. of St. Francis, Colorado Springs, 1982, 84; adj. grad. faculty U. Colo., Colorado Springs, 1992; sr. minister counseling Christian Ch., Security, Colo., 1967—; instr./coord. psychology gerontology Pikes Peak C.C., Colorado Springs, 1969—; vice chair devel. team Westley White Rehab. Ctr., Julesburg, 1966-67; trainer-cons. Pikes Peak Hospice, Colorado Springs, 1980-81; cons. St. Thomas Moore Hospice, Canon City, Colo., 1982, Sante Christo Hospice, Pueblo, Colo., 1983-84. Author: Approaches to Palliative Care, 1978, 92, Delphi-80-Study of Ministry, 1981; contbr. articles to Christian Standard. Bd. dirs. Colo. State Bd. Examiner for Nursing Home, Denver, 1977-83, chmn., 1981-83; moderator Conf. on Prevention of Violence-Sch. Dist. #3, Security, 1992. Office: Pikes Peak CC 5675 S Academy Blvd Colorado Springs CO 80906

SHAFER, JAMES ALBERT, health care administrator; b. Chgo., Aug. 26, 1924; s. James Earl and Kathleen (Sutterland) S.; m. Irene Jeanne Yurcega, June 20, 1948; children: Kathleen Mary, Patricia Ann. Technician Zenith Radio Corp., Chgo., 1946-47; owner, operator Eastgate Electronics, Chgo., 1947-61; applications engr. Perfection Mica Co., Bensenville, Ill., 1961-71; pres. Electronics Unltd., Northbrook, Ill., 1972-73, Ariz. Geriatric Enterprises Inc., Safford, 1974-86; bd. dirs. Mt. Graham Community Hosp., Safford. Republican. Roman Catholic. Home: Skyline Ranch Pima AZ 85543-0630 Office: Saguaro Care Inc PO Drawer H Pima AZ 85543

SHAFF, BEVERLY GERARD, educational administrator; b. Oak Park, Ill., Aug. 16, 1925; d. Carl Tanner and Mary Frances (Gerard) Wilson; m. Maurice A. Shaff, Jr., Dec. 20, 1951 (dec. June 1967); children: Carol Maureen, David Gerrard, Mark Albert. MA, U. Ill., 1951; postgrad., Colo. Coll., 1966, 73, Lewis and Clark Coll., 1982, Portland State U., 1975-82. Tchr. Haley Sch., Berwyn, Ill., 1948-51; assoc. prof. English, Huntingdon Coll., Montgomery, Ala., 1961-62; tchr. English, William Palmer High Sch., Colorado Springs, Colo., 1964-67, 72-76, dir., 1967-72; tchr. English, Burns (Oreg.) High Sch., 1976-78; tchr. English as 2d lang. Multnomah County Ednl. Svc. Dist., Portland, Oreg., 1979-85; coord. gen. studies Portland Jewish Acad., 1984-90; with Indian Edn. Prog./Student Tng. Edn. Prog. (STEP) Portland Pub. Schs., 1990-92; tchr. St. Thomas More Sch., Portland, 1992—. Del. Colorado Springs Dem. Com., 1968, 72; active Rainbow Coalition, Portland. Mem. Nat. Assn. Admnstrs., Nat. Assn. Schs. and Colls., Nat. Coun. Tchrs. Math., Nat. Coun. Tchrs. English. Home: 4676 SW Comus Pl Portland OR 97219-7273

SHAFFER, GARY MORRIS, anthropology and archaeology educator, researcher; b. Logan, Utah, Oct. 19, 1940; s. Ellis and Vanona (Morris) S.; m. Kathryn Spendlove, Nov. 23, 1979; children: Adrienne, Garrison, Wendy, Michelle, Martin, Jeffrey. BS, Utah State U., Logan, 1967; MS, Utah State U., Logan, 1969; postgrad., Ariz. State U., 1970-72. Pvt. practice cons. on Native Am. cultures S.W., 1972—; archaeologist, ethnology researcher, linguist Navajo lang., applied anthropologist Scottsdale (Ariz.) Community Coll., 1972—; archaeol. researcher Recon, San Diego, 1988—; cons. S.W. Studies Inst., Scottsdale, 1980—. Supporter Boy Scouts Am., Phoenix, 1980—; vol. Ft. McDowell Yavapai/Apache Community, 1992—. Home: 8514 E Valley Vista Dr Scottsdale AZ 85250-5828 Office: Scottsdale Community Coll 9000 E Chaparral Rd Scottsdale AZ 85250-2699

SHAFFER, HEIDI JO, secretary, receptionist; b. Elgin, Ill., Oct. 12, 1956; d. Harry George Bendtsen and Shirley Ilene (Windau) Brown; m. Brian Kent Shaffer, Sept. 21, 1983; children: David, Westin, Thomas. Student, Kishwaukee Coll., 1973-74, 76; AA, Ricks Coll., 1976; student, Utah State U., 1982, 83. Sec. DeKalb (Ill.) Ag Rsch., 1973-74, lithographer, 1976-77; lithographer Thiokol Chem. Corp., Brigham City, Utah, 1979-81; sec., receptionist Harris Truck & Equipment, Tremonton, Utah, 1981—. Historian, fin. sec. New Freedom Singers, Rexburg, Idaho, 1974-76; instr. first aid and CPR Am. Red Cross, DeKalb County, Ill., 1976-77, Box Elder Co., Brigham City, 1980-86; rev. dir. Am. Field Svc., Sycamore, Ill., 1977; chpt. vice-chmn. Am. Red Cross, Box Elder Co., Brigham City, 1982-84 (chpt. sec. 1985-90); bike-a-thon chmn. St. Jude's Children Rsch., 1983. Mem. Church of Latter-day Saints.

SHAFFER, KATHRYN MARSH, artist, architect, consultant; b. Wichita, Kans., Nov. 29, 1961; d. Robert Leroy and Marion Elliot (Barnes) Marsh; m. William Bradley Shaffer, Nov. 10, 1984. B Interior Architecture, Kans. State U., 1984; BArch, La. Tech U., 1988. Registered architect, Calif., Conn.; cert. Nat. Coun. Archtl. Registration Bds. Archtl. illustrator Mike W. Lin, Manhattan, Kans., 1981; grad. asst. La. Tech U. Sch. Art and Architecture, Ruston, 1987; design architect Dal Pos Assocs. Architects, Syracuse, N.Y., 1988-90; prin. K.M. Shaffer Architect, Sausalito, Calif., 1990—; cons. Pacific Gas & Electric Co., San Francisco. Patentee chair; exhibited in numerous group shows, including Fairfield (Calif.) Regional Juried Art Show, 1990, 91, Contract Design Ctr., San Francisco, 1991, Visions Gallery, Reedley, Calif., 1991, Artisans Gallery, Mill Valley, Calif., 1991, AIA Gallery, San Francisco, 1991, World Trade Ctr., New Orleans, 1992, Haggin Mus., Stockton, Calif., 1992, Cassandra Kersting Gallery, Sausalito, 1992—; works represented in Ency. Living Artists in Am., 1992, also others. Recipient award Napa Town and Country Fair Fine Art Show, Coastal Art League, 1990. Mem. AIA, Mus. Soc. San Francisco. Home and Office: 33 Cazneau Ave Sausalito CA 94965

SHAFFER, MARY LOUISE, art educator; b. Blufton, Ind., Nov. 23, 1927; d. Gail H. and Mary J. (Graves) S. AB, Northwest Nazerene Coll., 1950; MA, Ball State Tchrs. Coll., 1955; EdD, MS, Ind. U., 1964. Art and music tchr. Kuna (Ind.) High Sch., 1950-55; asst. prof. art Northwest Nazerene Coll., Nampa, Idaho, 1955-56, head art dept., 1971—; asst. prof. art Pasadena (Calif.) Coll., 1956-61; prof. art Olivet Nazerene Coll., Kankakee, Ill., 1964-71; dir. music Kankakee Congl. Ch., 1964-71, Nampa Christian Ch., 1971-76, Nampa Meth. Ch., 1976-81; speaker various civic clubs and confs., 1965-81. Participant European Images Art Show, 1989. E.I. Lilly grantee, 1961-62; women's singles tennis champion Boise (Idaho) Racquet and Swim Club, 1973; Idaho Sr. Tennis champion Sun Valley, 1984. Mem. Nat. Art Edn. Assn., Idaho Arts Edn. Assn. Home: 4755 E Victory Rd Meridian ID 83642-7011 Office: NW Nazerene Coll Holley at Dewey Nampa ID 83651

SHAFFER, RICHARD JAMES, lawyer, former manufacturing company executive; b. Pe Ell, Wash., Jan. 26, 1931; s. Richard Humphrys and Laura Rose (Faas) S.; m. Donna M. Smith, May 13, 1956; children: Leslie Lauren Shaffer and Stephanie Jane Athenton. B.A., U. Wash.; LL.B., Southwestern U. Bar: Calif. Vice pres., gen. counsel, sec. NI, Inc., Long Beach, Calif., 1974-89; gen. counsel Masco Bldg. Products Corp., Long Beach, 1985-89; pvt. practice Huntington Beach, Calif., 1989—. Trustee Ocean View Sch. Dist., 1965-73, pres., 1966, 73; mem. fin. adv. com. Orange Coast Coll., 1966; mem. Long Beach Local Devel. Corp., 1978-89, Calif. Senate Commn. on Corp. Governance, Shareholders' Rights and Securities Transactions, chmn. drafting com. ltd. liability co. act, 1991—. With USN, 1954-57. Mem. ABA, Nat. Assn. Securities Dealers (bd. arbitrators), Calif. Bar Assn. (exec. com. corp. law dept. com. bus. sect. 1981-88), Orange County Bar Assn., Huntington Harbour Yacht Club, Wanderlust Skiers of Huntington Harbour, Huntington Harbour Ski Club. Office: 16412 Sundancer Ln Huntington Beach CA 92649-2553

SHAFFER, THOMAS ALBERT, museum director, rancher; b. Thermopolis, Wyo., June 28, 1933; s. Roy Albert and Irene Wilson (Meahl) S.; m. Eileen Naylor, Nov. 20, 1965; children: Wade Thomas, Leslie Ann Shinaver, Chad Eric. BS in Animal Prodn., U. Wyo., 1960. Asst. county agt. U. Wyo., Basin, 1960-62; ranch hand Basin Ranch, Thermopolis, 1962-67; park attendant Wyo. Recreation Commn., Thermopolis, 1967-68; park supt. Wyo. Recreation Commn., South Pass City, 1968-71; hist. sites adminstr. Wyo. Recreation Commn., Cheyenne, 1971-73, chief systems planning div., 1973-78, dep. dir., 1978-79; ranch mgr. Double K Ranch, McFadden, Wyo., 1979-83; dir. Hot Springs Hist. Mus., Thermopolis, 1983—. Author: (with others) Independence Rock, 1973 (Bicentennial Commn. award 1974), Wyoming, A Guide to Historic Sites, 1976. Mem. planning com. McFadden Sch., 1981-83; deacon North Cheyenne Bapt. Ch., 1974-77; bd. dirs. South Cheyenne Sewer & Water Bd., 1978-79, Old Thermopolis, Inc., 1989—; chmn. scout com. Troop 53 Boy Scouts Am., 1984—; mem. R.R. Days Com., 1985. With USAF, 1953-56. Mem. NRA, VFW, Colo. Wyo. Assn. Mus. (bd. dirs. 1987—), Wyo. Trails Coun., U. Wyo. Alumni Assn., C. of C. (tourism com. 1983-86), Mountain Plains Mus. Assn. Republican. Home: 515 S 9th St Thermopolis WY 82443-3046 Office: Hot Springs Hist Mus 700 Broadway St Thermopolis WY 82443-2722

SHAGAM, MARVIN HÜCKEL-BERRI, educator; b. Monongalia, W.Va.; s. Lewis and Clara (Shagam) S. AB magna cum laude, Washington and Jefferson Coll., 1947; postgrad., Harvard Law Sch., 1947-48, Oxford (Eng.) U., 1948-51. Tchr. Mount House Sch., Tavistock, Eng., 1951-53, Williston Jr. Sch., Easthampton, Mass., 1953-55, Westtown (Pa.) Sch., 1955-58, The Thacher Sch., Ojai, Calif., 1958—; dept. head Kurasimi Internat. Edn. Centre, Dar-es-Salaam, Tanzania, 1966-67, Nkumbi Internat. Coll., Kabwe, Zambia, 1967-68; vol. visitor Prisons in Calif., 1980—, Calif. Youth Authority, 1983—; sr. youth crisis counsellor InterFace, 1984—. 1st lt. M.I. res. U.S. Army, 1943-56. Danforth Found. fellow, 1942; Coun. for the Humanities fellow, Tufts U., 1983; Marvin Shagam Ann. Scholarship award named in his honor, 1992. Mem. Western Assn. Schs. and Colls. (accreditation com., Cooke Chair in Great Teaching 1977—, Marvin Shagam scholarship named in his honor 1989—), Phi Beta Kappa, Delta Sigma Rho, Cum Laude Soc. Republican.

SHAH, DEVANG KUNDANLAL, software engineer; b. Mombasa, Kenya, Oct. 2, 1963; s. Kundan B. and Saryu K. (Mehta) S. BTech Electronics Engring. with honors, Inst. Tech. Banaras Hindu U., Varanasi, India, 1985; MA in Computer Sci., U. Tex., 1989. Software engr. Tata Consultancy Svcs., Bombay, India, 1985-86; mem. tech. staff SunSoft, Inc. subs. Sun Microsystems, Inc., Mountain View, Calif., 1990—; Sun Microsystems rep. to Unix Internat. multiprocessor working group, Parsippany, N.J., 1990. Author tech. papers in field. Mem. IEEE (tech. com. on oper. systems & stds. 1990-91, stds. com. on threads ext. for portable oper. systems), Assn. for Computing Machinery. Home: 1031 Foster City Blvd # B Foster City CA 94404-2328 Office: SunSoft Inc 2550 Garcia Ave M/S 5-40 Mountain View CA 94043

SHAH, GIRISH POPATLAL, data processing services company executive; b. Junagadh, India, Apr. 11, 1942; came to U.S., 1963; s. Popatlal Gulabchand and Lalitaben Popatlas (Kamdar) S.; m. Devmani Manilal Jhaveri, June 18, 1968; children: Nivisha, Munjal, Bhavin. B in Tech., Indian Inst. Tech., Bombay, 1963; MS, U. Calif., Berkeley, 1965. Project analyst IBM Corp., Palo Alto, Calif., 1965-67; v.p. Optimun Systems, Inc., Palo Alto, 1967-72; pres. Banking Systems Internat. Corp., Jakarta, Indonesia and Campbell, Calif., 1972-76; dir. software services Tymshare Transactions Services, San Francisco, 1980-83; sr. scientist McDonnell Douglas Corp., Fremont, Calif., 1984-86; dir. corp. devel. Sysorex Internat., Inc., Cupertino, Calif., 1986-87; v.p. Sysorex Internat., Inc., Mountain View, Calif., 1987—; sr. v.p. Sysorex Info. Systems Inc., Mountain View, 1987-91. Mem. adv. bd. Goodwill Industries, San Francisco; bd. dirs. Gujarate Cultural Assn., 1982; chmn. temple bd. Jain Ctr., 1990—; co-chmn. Jaina Conv., 1991; city gov. Fedn. Indo-Am. Assns., Fremont, Calif., 1991—. J.N. Tata Trust nat. scholar, 1963. Mem. Ops. Research Soc. Am., Assn. Indians in Am. (v.p. 1980). Democrat. Home: 4048 Twyla Ln Campbell CA 95008-3721 Office: Sysorex Info Systems Inc 335 E Middlefield Rd Mountain View CA 94043-4028

SHAH, SURESH CHANDRA, anesthesiologist; b. India, June 1, 1951; m. Vishaka Shah; children: Shalini, Amy, Neal. MD, U. Gujarat, Ahmedabad, India, 1973. Diplomate Am. Bd. Anesthesiology. Intern V.S. Gen. Hosp., Ahmedabad, India, 1973-74; resident dept. surgery St. Catherine's Hosp., Tralee, Ireland, 1974-75; jr. resident dept. anesthesiology West-Wales (Eng.) Gen. Hosp., Carmathen, 1976-77; sr. resident dept. anesthesiology North Middlesex Hosp., London, 1976-77; resident in anesthesiology and pain mgmt. Temple U. Hosp., Phila., 1977-79; assoc. anesthesiologist Mercy Hosp., Wilkes-Barre, Pa., 1979-83; attending anesthesiologist Hollywood Presbyn. Hosp., L.A., 1983—, John F. Kennedy Meml. Hosp., Indio, Calif., 1984—; med. dir. S.W. Pain Control and Sports Therapy Ctr., Palm Desert, Calif., 1986—. Mem. Am. Congress Rehab. Medicine, Am. Assn. for Study of Headaches, Calif. Med. Assn., Riverside County Med. Soc., Am. Acad. Pain Medicine, Internat. Assn. for Study of Pain, Am. Pain Soc., Calif. Soc. Anesthesiologists, Am. Heart Assn. (bd. dirs. 1980—), Am. Soc. Regional Anesthesia, Am. Soc. Anesthesiologists, Internat. Anesthesia Rsch. Soc. Home: 40-530 Morningstar Rd Rancho Mirage CA 92270 Office: SW Pain Control 73-345 Hwy 111 Palm Desert CA 92260

SHAHIN, THOMAS JOHN, drycleaning wholesale supply company executive; b. Buffalo, July 30, 1943; s. Thomas Mark and Marie (Colletto) S.; m. Laraine Edna Clements, Feb. 25, 1967; 1 child, Lori Lynn. BSBA, Calif. State U., L.A., 1966. Asst. v.p. stock brokerage div. United Calif. Bank, L.A., 1969-76; v.p., gen. mgr., treas. Newhouse Splty. Co. Inc., Santa Ana, Calif., 1976—, also bd. dirs. Patentee belt buckle. Officer USN, 1966-69, Vietnam. Mem. Textile Care Allied Trade Assn., Laundry and Drycleaners Suppliers, Internat. Fabricare Inst., Internat. Drycleaners Congress, Calif. Fabricare Inst., Beta Gamma Sigma. Republican. Roman Catholic. Office: Newhouse Splty Co Inc 2619 S Oak St Santa Ana CA 92707

SHAHRUZ, SHAHRAM MOJADDAD, electrical engineer; b. Abadan, Iran, Oct. 20, 1955; came to U.S. 1980; s. Kamal Mojaddad Shahruz and Sedigha Izadpanah. BS, Sharif U. Tech., Tehran, 1979; MS, Ariz. State U., 1982; MA, U. Calif.-Berkeley, 1987, PhD, 1988. Rsch. assoc. U. Calif.-Berkeley, 1984-88, teaching assoc., 1987; postdoctoral fellow U. Calif.-Davis, 1988; rsch. scientist Berkeley Engring. Rsch. Inst., Berkeley, 1989—. Contbr. articles to profl. jours. Mem. Am. Math. Soc., IEEE, ASME.

SHAIMA, MARY LEE, minister of music; b. San Diego, Oct. 20, 1960; d. Lee Frederick and Joan Marie (Kleine) Weikum; m. Michael Leo Shaima, June 24, 1989. BA in Drama, U. Calif. San Diego, 1983. Purchasing agt. McKellar Homes, San Diego, 1983-86, IBE Investments, San Diego, 1986-88; innkeeper West Adams Bed & Breakfast Inn, L.A., 1988-89; devel. cons. Barratt Am., Carlsbad, Calif., 1989—; minister of music Bethlehem Luth. Ch., Encinitas, Calif., 1986—; cons. West Adams Bed & Breakfast Inn, L.A., 1989-91; freelance crafts person supply to various retailers, San Diego, L.A., 1988—. Editor: (book) Songs of Faith, 1991. Mem. West Adams Hist. Assn., L.A., 1988—. Recipient Continuing Edn. grant Bethlehem Luth. Ch., 1992. Mem. Nat. Assn. Pastoral Musicians, North San Diego County Inter-Faith Ministerial Assn. Lutheran. Home: 1561 E Mission Rd Fallbrook CA 92028

SHAKELY, JOHN BOWER (JACK SHAKELY), foundation executive; b. Hays, Kans., Jan. 9, 1940; s. John B. and Martha Jean (Gaston) S.; 1 child, Benton. BA, U. Okla., 1962. Vol. Peace Corps., Costa Rica, 1963-64; editor publs. Dept. Def., 1967-68; dir. devel. U. Okla., 1968-70, Resthaven Mental Health Ctr., L.A., 1970-74; pres. Jack Shakely Assocs., L.A., 1974-75; sr. adv. Grantsmanship Ctr., L.A., 1975-79, Coun. on Founds., Washington, 1979; pres. Calif. Community Found., L.A., 1980—; lectr. in field. Bd. dirs. Emergency Loan and Assistance Fund, 1985—, chairperson bd. dirs.,

1988—; bd. dirs. Coro Found., L.A., 1982-85, So. Calif. Assn. Philanthropy, 1980—, Calif. Hist. Soc., 1985-88, Comic Relief, 1987—. 1st lt. U.S. Army, 1965-68. Decorated Army Commendation medal; named Nat. Philanthropy Day Outstanding Exec., L.A. Com. Nat. Philanthropy Day, 1989. Office: Calif Community Found Ste 2400 606 S Olive St Los Angeles CA 90014-1526

SHAM, LU JEU, physics educator; b. Hong Kong, Apr. 28, 1938; s. T.S. and Cecilia Maria (Siu) Shen; m. Georgina Bien, Apr. 25, 1965; children: Kevin Shen, Alisa Shen. GCE, Portsmouth Coll., Eng., 1957; BS, Imperial Coll., London U., Eng., 1960; PhD in Physics, Cambridge U., Eng., 1963. Asst. rsch. physicist U. Calif. at San Diego, La Jolla, 1963-66, assoc. prof., 1968-76, prof., 1975—, dean div. natural scis., 1985-89; asst. prof. physics U. Calif. at Irvine, 1966-67; rsch. physicist IBM Corp., Yorktown Heights, N.Y., 1974-75; reader Queen Mary Coll. U. of London, 1967-68; summer visitor neutron physics Chalk River Nuclear Lab. AEC Inst., Can., 1969; cons. Bell Tel. Labs., Murray Hill, N.J., 1968, Bellcore, Redbank, N.J., 1988-90. Contbr. sci. papers. to profl. jours. Recipient Churchill Coll. studentship, Eng., 1960-63, Sr. U.S. Scientist award Humboldt Found., Stuttgart, Germany, 1978; fellow Guggenheim Found., 1984. Fellow Am. Phys. Soc.; mem. AAAS. Democrat. Office: U Calif San Diego Dept Physics 0319 La Jolla CA 92093-0319

SHAMANSKY, SHERRY LEE, nursing administrator, educator; b. Columbus, Ohio, Sept. 30, 1943; d. Isaac Shamansky and Ethel Marilyn (Feinstein) Dragics; m. Wallace A. Wing, 1991. BS, Simmons Coll., 1966; MSN, Yale U., 1969, D of Pub. Health, 1977. Staff nurse Ohio State U. Hosp., Columbus, 1966; dir. of nursing Hill Health Ctr., New Haven, 1969-71; asst. prof. Sch. Nursing Fairfield (Conn.) U., 1974-78, U. Wash., Seattle, 1978-80; Robert Wood Johnson postdoctoral fellow in primary care Indpls., 1980-81; chair, assoc. prof. Sch. Nursing Yale U., New Haven, 1981-85; v.p. ops. Nat. Ctr. for Homecare Edn. and Rsch., N.Y.C., 1986-88; v.p. for nursing Group Health Coop., Seattle, 1988—; cons. in field. Co-editor: Public Health Nursing. Bd. dirs. Operation Child Care, New Haven, 1968-71, Parents of Stillborns, Seattle, 1979-80, Albertus Magnus Coll. Nursing, Hamden, Conn., 1981-84, Tower One/Tower East, New Haven, 1983-85. Fellow Am. Acad. Nursing; mem. Nat. Orgn. Nurse Practitioner Faculties (pres. 1984-85), Sigma Theta Tau (pres. Psi chpt. 1990-91). Democrat. Jewish.

SHAMBAUGH, STEPHEN WARD, lawyer; b. South Bend, Ind., Aug. 4, 1920; s. Marion Clyde and Anna Violet (Stephens) S.; m. Marilyn Louise Pyle; children: Susan Wynne Shambaugh Hinkle, Kathleen Louise Shambaugh Thompson. Student San Jose State Tchrs. Coll., 1938-40, U. Ark., 1951; LLB, U. Tulsa, 1954. Bar: Okla. 1954, Colo. 1964. Mem. staff Reading & Bates, Inc., Tulsa, 1951-54; v.p., gen. mgr., legal counsel Reading & Bates Drilling Co. Ltd., Calgary, Alta., Can., 1954-61; sr. ptnr. Bowman, Shambaugh, Geissinger & Wright, Denver, 1964-81; sole practice, Denver, 1981—; dir., fin. counsel various corps. Col. USAF ret. Mem. ABA, Fed. Bar Assn., Colo. Bar Assn., Okla. Bar Assn., Denver Bar Assn., P-51 Mustang Pilots Assn., Masons, Shriners, Elks, Spokane Club, Petroleum Club of Bakersfield, Phi Alpha Delta.

SHANAFELT, NANCY SUE, organizational development specialist; b. Northampton, Mass., Nov. 21, 1947; m. John D. Shanafelt; children: Amy, Nicholas. BS, U. Mass., 1969; MAin Human Resources/Orgn. Devel., USF, 1991. Tchr. Southwick (Mass.) Pub. Schs., 1969-70; acctg. asst. Maricopa County Schs., Phoenix, Ariz., 1973-74; tax auditor to br. chief IRS, San Jose, 1974-89; enrolled agt., 1984-85; OD specialist IRS, Phoenix, 1991—; creator IRS Women's Network, San Francisco, 1981—. Leader Girl Scouts U.S., Santa Clara, 1980-81, cons., 1981-82, svc. mgr., 1982-84, trainer, 1982-84; facilitator Unwed Parents Anonymous, 1992—; master catechist Diocese of San Jose, 1992—. Mem. Bus. and Profl. Women (sec. 1983-84), AAUW, NAFE, Commonwealth Club, Am. Soc. Tng. and Devel., Italian Cath. Fedn. (sec. 1991—), Bay Area OD Network, Medugorje PGL. Office: IRS 55 S Market St Ste 812 San Jose CA 95113-2326

SHANAHAN, MICHAEL GEORGE, police officer; b. Seattle, Oct. 14, 1940; s. Raymond Roderick and Carletta (Anderson) S.; m. Jo-Anne Genevieve David, Sept. 16, 1961; children: Patrick, Matthew, Raymond. BA in Psychology, Stanford U., 1962. Asst. police chief U. Wash., Seattle, 1970-71, police chief, 1971—; mem. law enforcement task force interim mcpl. com. Wash. State Legis., 1970-71, campus law enforcement task force-higher edn. com., 1970-71; co-chmn. Wash. Law Enforcement Standards Task Force; founding chmn. Washington Law Enforcement Exec. Forum, 1981; others. Author: Private Enterprise and the Public Police: The Professionalizing Effects of a New Partnership, 1985; contbr. articles to profl. jours. Mem. nat. exploring com. Boy Scouts Am., 1977, exec. bd., chief Seattle council, 1984-88; mem. Blanchet High Sch. Bd., Seattle, 1978-79, Gov.'s Coun. on Criminal Justice, 1980-81, Gov.'s Coun. Food Assistance, 1983-86. Major U.S. Army, 1963-70, Vietnam. Decorated Bronze Star; recipient award for pub. svc. U.S. Dept. Transp., 1984, Humanitarian award Seattle chpt. NCCJ, 1985, Silver Beaver award Boy Scouts Am., 1986, St. Matthew award Northwest Harvest, 1987, Paul J. Breslin award Internat. Security Mgrs. Assn., 1990, Criminal Justice award of excellence Wash. State U., 1989. Mem. FBI Nat. Acad. Assocs., Nat. Inst. Justice (peer rev. program), Internat. Assn. Chiefs of Police (bd. officers 1983-84, gen. chmn. divsn. state assns. 1983-84, co-chair strategic planning com., vice chair campus police sect., co-chmn. pvt. sector liaison com.), Police Exec. Rsch. Forum, Wash. Assn. Sheriffs and Police Chiefs, Rotary Internat. (pres. Univ. Rotary Club Seattle 1985-86, founding chmn. Rotary Op. First Harvest, Svc. Above Self award 1988). Roman Catholic. Lodge: Rotary (pres. Univ. club. Seattle 1985-86). Office: U Wash Police Dept 1117 NE Boat St Seattle WA 98105-6797

SHANAMAN, FRED CHARLES, JR., business consultant; b. Tacoma, June 21, 1933; s. Fred Charles and Marjorie Blanch (Jeffries) S.; m. Jane Francis Aram, July 7, 1962; children: Fred C. III, Mara Shanaman Burke. BA, Dartmouth Coll., 1957; postgrad., U. B.C., Vancouver, 1958. presdl. appointment to commerce sec. Elliot Richardson's Regional REp. in N.W.; sec. of commerce spokesman and prin. liaison; mem. Commerce Depts. rep. Fed. Regional Coun. and the Pacific N.W. River Basins Commn., 1975-77. Sales rep. Air Reduction Co., San Francisco, 1958-62; pres. Bulk Distbrs., Tacoma, 1962-75, Pyrodyne Corp., Tacoma, 1964-75, Toys Galore, Tacoma, 1964-75, Youth Entrepreneurship Corp., Tacoma, 1978-86; pres., owner Rainier Mgmt. Corp., Tacoma, 1970—; bd. dirs. Puget Sound Bancorp., Tacoma, Bellingham (Wash.) Nat. Key Bank of Wash., Tacoma Rockets Hockey Club, Puget Sound Hockey Ctrs. Author: 101 Money Making Ideas for Young Adults 10 to 18 Year of Age, 1980, The First Official Moneymaking Book for Kids of All Ages, 1983, The Best is Yet to Come: Retirement A Second Career, 1984. Chmn. NCAA Womens Final Four, Tacoma, 1988-89; commr. Ice Hockey Goodwill Games, Seattle, 1990; past bd. dirs. Annie Wright Sch., Faith Home, United Way, Tacoma Symphony, Bellarmine Preparatory Sch., Greater Lakes Mental Health Clinic, Tacoma Actors Guild, Assn. of Washington Bus., Mary Bridge Hosp., Tacoma Leukemia Soc., Vt. Acad., and others. Mem. Tacoma Country Club, Canterwood Country Club, Elks, Lakes Club, Gyro Club, Le Mirador (Switzerland). Republican. Epsicopalian. Office: Tacoma Rockets Ste 104 222 E 26th St Tacoma WA 98421

SHANE, MARK ROBERT, chiropractor; b. Hayward, Calif., Jan. 30, 1956; s. Philip Elrod and Dorthey (Goodman) S.; m. Michell Angela Bailey, Nov. 15, 1981; children: Ciel-Nicole, Brett, Logan, Thea. B in Chemistry, Brigham Young U., 1981; D of Chiropractic, Life Chiropractic Coll., 1985. Pres. Wyo. State Bd. Chiropractic Examiners, 1990—. Asst. scoutmaster Boy Scout Am., Cody, Wyo., 1986-89; bd. dirs. Big Horn chpt. Trout Unltd., Cody, 1987—. Mem. Rotary Club (Cody). Republican. LDS. Home: 1401 24th St Cody WY 82414 Office: Cody Chiropractic Ctr 1708 Stampede Ave Cody WY 82414

SHANK, GREGORY LLOYD, journal editor; b. Vallejo, Calif., Dec. 5, 1948; s. Clifford Lewis Shank and Barbara Lee (Metzger) Finstrom; m. Jennifer Suzanne Dod, Oct. 28, 1977 (div. 1987); 1 child, Renee Andrea. BA in Sociology, U. Calif., Berkeley, 1974, BA in Criminology, 1974, MA in Sociology and Edn., 1977. Mng. editor Crime and Social Justice, Berkeley, 1974-85, Social Justice, San Francisco, 1986—; dir. rsch. Ctr. for Study of Crime and Social Justice, San Francisco, 1984-88; bd. dirs. Global Options, San Francisco, 1987—. Editorial adv. bd. Law in Context, Victoria, Australia, 1986—; editor: Power, Politics and Order in the 1990s, 1992, South Africa in Transition, 1991; contbr. articles to profl. jours. Participant Friends of Urban Forest project, San Francisco, 1992. Mem. ACLU, Criminal Justice Editors Rsch. Group, East-West Project, World Affairs Coun., Phi Beta Kappa. Home: 2766 23d St San Francisco CA 94110 Office: Social Justice PO Box 40601 San Francisco CA 94140

SHANK, MAURICE EDWIN, aerospace engineering executive, consultant; b. N.Y.C., Apr. 22, 1921; s. Edwin A. and Viola (Lewis) S.; m. Virginia Lee King, Sept. 25, 1948; children: Christopher K., Hilary L. Shank-Kuhl, Diana L. Boehm. B.S. in Mech. Engring., Carnegie-Mellon U., 1942; D.Sc., MIT, 1949. Registered profl. engr., Mass. Assoc. prof. mech. engring. MIT, Cambridge, 1949-60; with Pratt & Whitney, East Hartford, Conn., 1960-87, dir. engine design and structures engring., 1980-81, dir. engring. tech., 1981-85, dir. engring. tech. assessment, 1985-86; v.p. Pratt Whitney of China, Inc., East Hartford, 1986-87; pvt. exec. cons. to industry and govt., 1987—; cons. editor McGraw-Hill Book Co., N.Y.C., 1960-80; adv. com. to mechanics div. Nat. Bur. Standards, Washington, 1964-69; vis. com. dept. mech. engring. Carnegie-Mellon U., Pitts., 1968-78; corp. vis. coms. depts. materials sci. and engring., dept. aeros. and astronautics MIT, 1968-74, 79-92; mem. rsch. and tech. adv. coun. com. on aero. propulsion NASA, Washington, 1973-77, mem. aero. adv. com., 1978-86; mem. aero. and space engring. bd. NRC, 1989-92; lectr. in field. Contbr. articles to profl. jours. Served to maj. U.S. Army, 1942-46. Fellow AIAA, ASME, AIME, Am. Soc. Metals; mem. Nat. Acad. Engring., Conn. Acad. Sci. and Engring. Episcopalian. Club: Cosmos.

SHANK, RUSSELL, librarian, educator; b. Spokane, Wash., Sept. 2, 1925; s. Harry and Sadie S.; m. Doris Louise Hempfer, Nov. 9, 1951 (div.); children: Susan Marie, Peter Michael, Judith Louise. B.S., U. Wash., 1946, B.A., 1949; M.B.A., U. Wis., 1952; Dr.L.S., Columbia U., 1966. Reference libr. U. Wash., Seattle, 1949; asst. engring. libr. U. Wis.-Madison, 1949-52; chief pers. Milw. Pub. Libr., 1952; engring.-phys. scis. libr. Columbia U., N.Y.C., 1953-59; sr. lectr. Columbia U., 1964-66, assoc. prof., 1966-67; asst. univ. libr. U. Calif.-Berkeley, 1959-64; dir. sci. libr. N.Y. Met. Reference and Rsch., 1966-68; dir. librs. Smithsonian Instn., Washington, 1967-77; univ. libr. prof. UCLA, 1977-89, asst. vice chancellor for libr. and info. svcs. planning, 1989-91, univ. libr., prof. emeritus, 1991—; cons. Indonesian Inst. Sci., 1970; bd. cons. Pahlavi Nat. Library, Iran, 1975-76; pres. U.S. Book Exchange, 1975; bd. trustees Freedom to Read Found., 1989—. Trustee OCLC, Inc., 1978-84, 87, chmn., 1984; mem. library del. People's Republic of China, 1979; bd. dirs. Am. Council on Edn., 1980-81. Served with USNR, 1943-46. Recipient Disting. Alumnus award U. Wash. Sch. Librarianship, 1968, Role of Honor award Freedom to Read Found., 1990, Disting. Alumnus award Columbia U. Sch. Libr. Sci., 1992; fellow Coun. on Libr. Resources, 1973-74. Fellow AAAS; mem. ALA (pres. 1978-79, coun. 1961-65, 74-82, exec. bd. 1975-80, chmn. internat. rels. com. 1980-83, pres. info. sci. and automation div. 1968-69), Assn. Coll. and Rsch. Librs. (pres. 1972-73, Hugh Atkinson award 1990), Assn. Rsch. Librs. (bd. dirs. 1974-77), Am. Soc. Info. Sci. Home: 12919 Montana Ave Apt 101 Los Angeles CA 90049

SHANK, THOM LEWIS, real estate executive, entertainment consultant; b. Butler, Pa., Apr. 23, 1953; s. Berdyne Delmont and Florence Elizabeth (Glasser) S. BA in Sociology, U. Pa., 1974; MBA, Pepperdine U., 1981. Negotiator Worldmark Travel, N.Y.C. and Phila., 1971-76; retail ops. mgr. Just Plants, Inc., Roxborough, Pa., 1973-79; founder, mgr. The Best-direct mail sales, Edgemoor, Del., 1974-79; property mgr. Moss and Co., Westwood, Calif., 1977-82; talent mgr. Thom Shank Assocs., Brentwood, Calif., 1979-84; pres., founder The Great Am. Amusement Co., Palm Desert, Calif., 1979-84; sales exec. Fred Sands Realtors, Brentwood, 1981-85; sales and mktg. dir. Coldwell Banker, Newport Beach, Calif., 1985-86; dist. and regional mgr. E.R.A. Real Estate, Pasadena, Calif., 1986; owner Century 21 Realtors, Tarzana, Calif., 1987-89. Lutheran. Home: 4 Skyline Dr Burbank CA 91501 Office: Great Western Ranches 101 S First St # 1200 Burbank CA 91502

SHANNEY, WILLIAM I., retired aerospace engineer; b. N.Y.C., Jan. 25, 1925; s. William I. and Rose Anne (Quinnan) S.; m. Edith Irene Rushmore, Aug. 5, 1949 ; children: Anne, George, Joseph, Colleen, Robert; m. Louise Daggett, Aug. 11, 1979. BEE, Manhattan Coll., 1948; postgrad., Stevens U., 1950-55, Columbia U., 1954-55. Armament engr. Arma Corp., Bklyn., 1948-52; system engr. Maxson Corp., N.Y.C., 1952-56; dep. project mgr. Republic Aviation Corp., Farmingdale, N.Y., 1956-66; mgr. space test safety and ops. Aerospace Corp., El Segundo and Sunnyvale, Calif., 1966-91; ret., 1991; cons. in field., 1991—. Author tech. papers in field. With USN, 1943-46. Mem. Ingenieurs et Scientifiques de France. Home: 3626 South Ct Palo Alto CA 94306

SHANNON, RICHARD JOHN, dentist; b. LaCrescent, Minn., July 11, 1949; s. Charles Thomas and Mary Mercedes (Logan) S.; children: Heather Mary, Richard John II. BS, St. John's U., Collegeville, Minn., 1971, U. Minn., 1975; DDS, U. Minn., 1975; M in Counseling, Ariz. State U., 1993. Dentist Nat. Health Svc. Corps. U.S. Pub. Health Svc. Ctr., N.D., 1975-77; pvt. practive dentistry Bismarck, N.D., 1977-86, Phoenix, Ariz., 1986—; counselor doctor's health program Ariz. Med. Assn., Phoenix, 1991; cons. Ariz. State Bd. Dental Examiners, 1992—. Bd. dir. N.D. Hypertension Control Program Adv. com. State Health Dept., Bismarck, 1985-86; vol. speaker Heartview Found. Treatment Ctr., Mandan, N.D., 1980-86; vol. Prairie Publ Radio, Bismarck, 1979-86. Recipient Nat. Bd. cert. Coun. of Nat. Bd. of Dental Examiners, 1975, cert. Cen. Regional Dental Testing Svc., 1975, Western Regional Examining Bd., 1986; named Eagle Scout, Boy Scouts of Am., 1963. Mem. ADA, Cen. Ariz. Dental Soc., Ariz. Dental Assn. Home: 1957 E Sunburst Ln Tempe AZ 85284-1762

SHANNON, RICHARD STOLL, III, financial executive; b. N.Y.C., Mar. 22, 1943; s. Richard Stoll Jr. and Margaret (Cather) S.; m. Ann Wright Schmidt, June 14, 1965; children: Clea Cather, Kathryne Baltzelle, Arianna Wright. BA, Stanford U., 1966, MA, 1969; PhD, Harvard U., 1973. Asst. prof. U. Mich., Ann Arbor, 1973-78; mgr., trustee, gen. ptnr. various family trusts, partnerships and corps. Englewood, Colo., 1978-84; pres. Shannon Mgmt. Corp., Englewood, 1985—; bd. dirs. Escalante Internat. Corp., Denver. Author: The Arms of Achilles, 1975; editor (with others) Oral Literature and The Formula, 1976. Bd. dirs. Cherryvale Sanitation Dist., Englewood, 1984—, pres., 1986-93; regional chmn. Stanford Ann. Fund/Keystone Project, 1985—. Teaching fellow Harvard U., 1970-73. Mem. Am. Philol. Assn., Denver C. of C., Cherry Creek Commerce Assn., Cherry Hills Country Club, Denver Petroleum Club, Phi Beta Kappa. Office: Shannon Mgmt Corp 3098 S Pennsylvania St Englewood CO 80110-1699

SHANNON, ROBERT RENNIE, optical sciences center administrator, educator; b. Mt. Vernon, N.Y., Oct. 3, 1932; s. Howard A. and Harriebell (Rennie) S.; m. Helen Lang, Feb. 13, 1954; children: Elizabeth, Barbara, Jennifer, Amy, John, Robert. B.S., U. Rochester, 1954, M.A., 1957. Dir. Optics Lab., ITEK Corp., Lexington, Mass., 1959-69; prof. Optical Scis. Ctr., U. Ariz., 1969—, dir., 1983-92, prof. emeritus, 1992—; cons. Lawrence Livermore Lab., 1980-90; mem. commn. next generation currency, 1992—; trustee Aerospace Corp., 1985—; mem. Air Force Sci. Adv. Bd., 1986-90; mem. NRC Commn. on Next Generation Currency, 1992—; mem. com. on def. space tech. Air Force Studies Bd., 1989—, Hubble Telescope recovery panel, 1990; bd. dirs. Precision Optics Corp., Schott Glass Techs. Editor: Applied Optics and Optical Engineering, Vol. 7, 1980, Vol. 8, 1981, Vol. 9, 1983, Vol. 10, 1987, Vol. 11, 1992. Fellow Optical Soc. Am. (pres. 1985, mem. engring. coun. 1989-91), Soc. Photo-Optical Instrumentation Engrs. (pres. 1979-80, recipient Goddard award 1982); mem. NAE, Tucson Soaring Club (past pres.), Sigma Xi. Home: 7040 E Taos Pl Tucson AZ 85715-3344 Office: U Ariz Optical Scis Ctr Tucson AZ 85721

SHANNON, THOMAS F., German educator; b. Cambridge, Mass., Mar. 16, 1948; m. Christine D. Höner. BA in German summa cum laude, Boston Coll., 1969; MA in German Lit., SUNY, Albany, 1973; MA in Thero. Linguistice, Ind. U., 1975, PhD in Germanic Linguistics, 1982. Instr. in German Boston Coll., 1969-70; teaching fellow in German SUNY, albany, 1971-73; univ. fellow Ind. U., Bloomington, 1973-74, assoc. instr., 1974-76, 1979-80; acting asst. prof. in Germanic linguistics U. Calif., Berkeley, 1980-82, asst. prof., 1987—, dir. lang. lab., 1989—; cons., presenter, speaker in field; mem. editorial adv. bd. Am. Jour. Germanic Linguistics and Lits., 1988—. Contbr. articles to profl. publs. With USAR, 1970-76. Grantee U. Calif.-Berkeley, 1983-84, Am. Coun. Learned Socs., 1987, Internat. Assn. Netherlandic Studies, 1988, Fulbright Found., 1979; NDEA fellow, 1969. Mem. Am. Assn. Netherlandic Studies, Am. Assn. Tchrs. German, Assn. Computers and Humanities, Internat. Assn. Netherlandic Studies, Internat. Assn. Germanstik, Internat. Soc. Hist. Linguistics, Linguistic Soc. Am., MLA, Netherlands Am. Univ. League, Philol. Assn. Pacific Coast., European Linguistic Soc., Alpha Sigma Nu. Home: 770 Rose Dr Benicia CA 94510-3709 Office: U Calif Dept German 5317 Dwinelle Hall Berkeley CA 94720

SHANOR, CLARENCE RICHARD, clergyman; b. Butler, Pa., Dec. 26, 1924; s. Paul L. and Marion (McCandless) S.; B.A., Allegheny Coll., 1948; S.T.B., Boston U., 1951, Ph.D., 1958; m. Anna Lou Watts, June 23, 1948; 1 son, Richard Watts. Ordained to ministry Methodist Ch., 1950; pastor Meth. Ch., South Hamilton, Mass., 1951-54; research asso. Union Coll., Schenectady, 1954-55; prof. Christian edn. Nat. Coll., Kansas City, Mo., 1956-58; asso. minister First United Meth. Ch., St. Petersburg, Fla., 1958-61, First United Meth. Ch., Fullerton, Calif., 1961-66; coord. Metro dept. San Diego dist. United Meth. Union, San Diego, 1966-87, ret., 1987; pres. Human Svcs. Corp., 1972-77. Treas. San Diego County Ecumenical Conf., 1970-71, pres., 1975-77; chmn. Coalition Urban Ministries, 1970-71, Cultural and Religious Task Force Rancho San Diego, 1970-74; chmn. western jurisdiction Urban Network United Meth. Ch., 1978. Chmn. San Diego Citizens Com. Against Hunger, 1969-72; bd. dirs. Interfaith Housing Found., chmn., 1979, pres. 1988—; v.p. North County Interfaith Coun., 1987—; mem. Gaslamp Quarter Project Area Com., San Diego, 1978, mem. coun., 1980-84; chmn. bd. Horton House Corp., 1978; mem. Mayor's Task Force on the Homeless, 1983-84; chmn. Downtown Coordinating Coun., 1983-84; mem. regional Task Force on Homeless, 1986-87; vice-chmn. Community Congress, 1987, ret., 1987. Recipient San Diego Inst. for Creativity award, 1969, Boss of Yr. award Am. Bus. Women's Assn., 1972, Christian Unity award Diocesan Ecumenical Commn., 1984, Congl. Disting. Svc. award, 1984, Helen Beardsley Human Rights award, 1986, Mayor O'Connor's Seahorse award 1989, Ecumenical Conf. award San Diego County, 1991, Vol. Extraordinaire award No. County Interfaith Coun., 1993. Author: (with Anna Lou Shanor) Kindergartner Meet Your World, 1966. Home: 1636 Desert Gln Escondido CA 92026-1849

SHANSTROM, JACK D., federal judge; b. Hewitt, Minn., Nov. 30, 1932; s. Harold A. and Willian (Wendorf) S.; m. June 22, 1957; children: Scott S., Susan K. BA in Law, U. Mont., 1956, BS in Bus., 1957, LLB, 1957. Atty. Park County, Livingston, Mont., 1960-65; judge 6th Jud. Dist. Livingston, 1965-82; U.S. magistrate Billings, Mont., 1983-90, U.S. Dist. judge, 1990—. Capt. USAF, 1957-60. Office: US Dist Ct PO Box 985 Billings MT 59103-0985

SHAPELL, NATHAN, financial and real estate executive; b. Poland, Mar. 6, 1922; s. Benjamin and Hela S.; m. Lilly Szenes, July 17, 1948; children: Vera Shapell Guerin, Benjamin (dec.). Co-founder Shapell Industries, Inc., Beverly Hills, Calif., 1955; now chmn. bd. Shapell Industries, Inc.; mem. adv. bd. Union Bank, Beverly Hills; mem. residential bldgs. adv. com. Calif. Energy Resources Conservation and Devel. Commn.; speaker in field. Mem. Calif. Commn. Govt. Reform, 1978; Atty. Gen. Calif. Adv. Council, Dist. Atty. Los Angeles County Adv. Council; chmn. Calif. Govt. Commn. Orgn. and Economy, 1975—, Gov.'s Task Force on Affordable Housing, 1980—; mem. adv. council Pres.'s Commn. on the Holocaust, 1979; pres. Am. Acad. Achievement, 1975—; mem. deans council UCLA Sch. Architecture and Urban Planning, 1976—. Author: Witness to the Truth, 1974. Trustee U. Santa Clara, Calif., 1976—; bd. councillors U. So. Calif. Med. Sch., 1973—. Recipient Golden Plate award Am. Acad. Achievement, 1974, Fin. World award, 1977. Jewish. Club: Hillcrest Country (Los Angeles). Address: Shapell Industries Inc 8383 Wilshire Blvd Ste 700 Beverly Hills CA 90211

SHAPERO, HARRIS JOEL, pediatrician; b. Winona, Minn., Nov. 22, 1930; s. Charles and Minnie Sara (Ehrlichman) S.; m. Byong Soon Yu, Nov. 6, 1983; children by previous marriage: Laura, Bradley, James, Charles. A.A., UCLA, 1953; B.S., Northwestern U., 1954, M.D., 1957. Diplomate and cert. specialist occupational medicine Am. Bd. Preventive Medicine; cert. aviation medicine FAA. Intern, Los Angeles County Harbor Gen. Hosp., 1957-58, resident in pediatrics, 1958-60, staff physician, 1960-64; attending physician Perceptually Handicapped Children's Clinic, 1960-63; disease control officer for tuberculosis, L.A. County Health Dept., 1962-64; pvt. practice medicine specializing in pediatrics and occupational medicine, Cypress, Calif., 1965-85; pediatric cons. L.A. Health Dept., 1963-85, disease control officer sexually transmitted diseases, 1984-85; emergency room dir. AMI, Anaheim, Calif., 1968-78; mem. med. staff Anaheim Gen. Hosp., Beach Community Hosp., Norwalk Community Hosp.; courtesy staff Palm Harbor Gen. Hosp., Bellflower City Hosp.; pediatric staff Hosp. de General, Ensenada, Mex., 1978—; primary care clinician Sacramento County Health, 1987-88; pvt. practice medico-legal evaluation, 1986-92; founder Calif. Legal Evaluation Med. Group; apptd. med. examiner in preventive and occupational medicine State of Calif. Dept. of Indsl. Rels., 1989; health care provider, advisor City of Anaheim, City of Buena Park, City of Cypress, City of Garden Grove, Cypress Sch. Dist., Magnolia Sch. Dist., Savanna Sch. Dist., Anaheim Unified Sch. Dist., Orange County Dept. Edn.; pediatric and tuberculosis cons. numerous other orgns.; FAA med. examiner, founder Pan Am. Childrens Mission. Author: The Silent Epidemic, 1979. Named Headliner in Medicine Orange County Press Club, 1978. Fellow Am. Coll. Preventive Medicine; mem. L.A. County Med. Assn., L.A. County Indsl. Med. Assn., Am. Pub. Health Assn., Mex.-Am. Border Health Assn. Republican. Jewish. Avocations: antique books and manuscripts, photography, graphics, beekeeper. Home: PO Box 228 Wilton CA 95693-0228

SHAPIRO, ALAN ISAIAH, endocrinologist; b. Far Rockaway, N.Y., Apr. 17, 1951; s. Norman Israel and Elouise Ida (Greenbaum) S.; m. Sallie Sandra Berlowe, June 24, 1972; children: Jeffrey A., Lisa R. BA in Chemistry, U. Ariz., 1973, MD, 1975. Diplomate Am. Bd. Obstetrics and Gynecology. Resident physician Maricopa County Gen. Hosp., Phoenix, 1975-79; physician The Reproductive Inst. of Tucson, 1989—. Comdr. USN, 1979-88. Fellow Am. Coll. Obstetricians and Gynecologists; mem. Am. Fertility Soc., Soc. Reproductive Endocrinologists, Pacific Coast Fertility Soc. Jewish. Office: The Reproductive Inst 1200 N El Dorado Pl Bldg G Tucson AZ 85715

SHAPIRO, BARRY, toy company executive; b. Bklyn., Apr. 18, 1942; s. Sidney and Anne (Sokol) S.; m.. Frances Rosenfeld, Apr. 5, 1970 (div. Mar. 1993); children: David Scott, Sean Jonathan. BA in English, Rutgers U., 1963. Asst. buyer J.C. Penney Co., N.Y.C., 1966-69; dir. product planning and internat. ops. Gabriel Industries, Inc., N.Y.C., 1969-78; exec. v.p. Lakeside Games div. Leisure Dynamics, Inc., Mpls., 1978-79, pres., 1979-80; exec. v.p. Toy Game & Hobby Group div. Leisure Dynamics, Inc., Mpls., 1980-81; exec. v.p., gen. mgr., chief exec. officer Wham-O, San Gabriel, Calif., 1981-83; exec. v.p., gen. mgr. Imagineering, Inc., Phoenix, 1984-91; pres. Packing Specialist Inc. SW, Phoenix, Ariz., 1991—; cons. to various toy cos. Vol. Jewish Big Bros., 1964-78, vice chmn. Big Bros. of N.Y., 1976-78; coach Little League, Mpls., Arcadia, Calif., 1979—; v.p. Temple Shaarei Tikvah, Arcadia, 1982-84; bd. dirs. Har Zion Synagogue, 1988-90, v.p. 1989-90. Recipient Army Commendation medal. Mem. Assn. Toy Mfg. Am. Jewish. Home: 8165 Via De La Escuela Scottsdale AZ 85258

SHAPIRO, DAVID, psychologist; b. N.Y.C., July 20, 1924; s. Benjamin and Sarah (Kramer) S.; m. Shirley Jean Walrath, Dec. 31, 1951;. AB, U. Ill., 1948, AM, U. Mich., 1950, PhD, 1953. Lic. psychologist, Calif. Lectr. to assoc. prof. Harvard U., Cambridge, Mass., 1953-74; prof. U. Calif., L.A., 1974—; con. NSF, Jour. of Personality and Social Psychology, 1966—, Sci., 1969—, NIMH, 1972—, Psychol. Bull., 1973—, IEEE, 1974—, Plenum Pub. Corp., 1974—, Biol. Psychology, 1974—, Jour. of Cons. and Clin. Psychology, 1975—, Behavior Therapy, 1975—, Nat. Heart, Lung, & Blood Inst., 1975—, McGill U. Grad. Sch. Psychology, Can., 1975—, Internat. Jour. of Clin. and Exptl. Hypnosis, 1976—, Acad. Press, 1978—, New Eng. Jour. Medicine, 1980—, Biol. Psychology, 1981—, and many others. Contbr. numerous articles to profl. jours. With U.S. Army, 1943-46. Recipient Disting. Contbns. to Biofeedback, Biofeedback Soc. Am., 1989;

numerous grants. Fellow AAAS, Acad. of Behavioral Medicine Rsch., Am. Psychol. Assn., Soc. of Behavioral Medicine; mem. Am. Psychosomatic Soc. (program com. 1991—), Soc. for Psychophysiol. Rsch. (com. for early career contbn. award 1988—, chair archives com. 1986—, pub. bd. 1978-86, chair ethics com. 1971-74, Disting. Contbs. to Psychophysiology, 1988), Assn. for Applied Psychophysiology and Biofeedback, Biofeedback Soc. of Calif., Sigma Xi, Phi Beta Kappa. Office: Dept Psychiatry UCLA 760 Westwood Pla Los Angeles CA 90024

SHAPIRO, JEROME LEE, engineering company executive; b. N.Y.C., Feb. 13, 1932; s. George Israel and Dora (Richman) S.; m. Shirley Stutman, Jan. 24, 1954; children: Leah Beth, Kenneth Jay. BME, CCNY, 1954; MSE in Nuclear Engrng., U. Mich., 1955, PhD in Nuclear Engrng., 1960. Registered profl. engr., Calif. Nuclear engr. Bendix Rsch. Lab., Southfield, Mich., 1956-57; instr. U. Mich., Ann Arbor, 1957-60; supr. Atomics Internat., Canoga Park, Calif., 1960-61; rsch. fellow, assoc. prof. Calif. Inst. Tech., Pasadena, 1961-70; chief nuclear and environ. engr. Bechtel Power Corp., L.A., 1970-83; mgr., energy R&D Bechtel Power Corp., San Francisco, 1983-86; pres. Cardinal Group, Menlo Park, Calif., 1987-89, Age Hazardous Waste Mgmt., Campbell, Calif., 1988-89; v.p. Indsl. Environ. Svcs. Co., Palo Alto, Calif., 1989—; cons. various utilities and constrn. cos., San Francisco, 1986—; bd. dirs. Pacific Concord Corp., Hong Kong. Contbr. articles to profl. jours. Mem. ASME, AAAS, Am. for Energy Ind. (founder, pres. 1979-80), N.Y. Acad. Sci., Am. Nuclear Soc., Hazardous Materials Control Rsch. Inst., Sigma Xi, Pi Tau Sigma. Office: IESCO 701 Welch Rd Bldg 323 Palo Alto CA 94304-1705

SHAPIRO, REID ALLAN, athletic footwear company strategic planner; b. Newport Beach, Calif., June 14, 1965; s. Haskell Shapiro and Patricia (Chamberlain) Herzog. BA in Internat. Affairs cum laude, George Washington U., 1988; M. of Pacific Internat. Affairs, U. Calif., San Diego, 1990. Staff employee Congressman Jerry Patterson, Washington, 1983-84; gen. mgr. Dynasty Enterprises, Beijing, 1987; staff employee Select Com. on Secret Mil. Assistance to Iran, U.S. Senate, Washington, 1987; researcher U. Calif. San Diego, Hong Kong, 1989; bus. analyst Dun & Bradstreet, Santa Ana, Calif., 1990; strategic planner L.A. Gear, Inc., L.A., 1990—. Regent's fellow U. Calif. Regents, 1989. Democrat. Home: 287 Evening Canyon Rd Corona del Mar CA 92625 Office: LA Gear Inc 2850 Ocean Park Blvd Santa Monica CA 90405

SHAPIRO, RICHARD STANLEY, physician; b. Moline, Ill., June 11, 1925; s. Herbert and Esther Dian (Grant) S.; B.S., St. Ambrose Coll., 1947; B.S. in Pharmacy, U. Iowa, 1951, M.S. in Preventive Medicine and Environ. Health, 1951, M.D., 1957; m. Arlene Blum, June 12, 1949; children—Michele Pamela, Bruce Grant, Gary Lawrence; m. 2d, Merry Lou Cook, Oct. 11, 1971. Pharmacist, Rock Island, Ill., 1951-53; research asst. U. Iowa Coll. Medicine, Iowa City, 1950-51, 53-57; practice medicine specializing in allergy, Beverly Hills, Calif., 1958-62, Lynwood, Calif., 1962—; attending physician Good Hope Found. Allergy Clinic, Los Angeles, 1958-62, Cedars of Lebanon Hosp., Hollywood, Calif., 1959-68, U. So. Calif.-Los Angeles County Med. Center, 1962—; physician St. Francis Hosp., Lynwood, 1962—; assoc. clin. prof. medicine U. So. Calif., 1978-84, emeritus, 1984—. Bd. dirs. Westside Jewish Community Center, 1961-65, Camp JCA, 1964-65. Served with USNR, 1943-45; PTO. Diplomate Am. Bd. Allergy and Immunology. Fellow Am. Geriatric Soc., Am. Coll. Allergy, Am. Assn. Clin. Immunology and Allergy; mem. Am. Soc. Tropical Medicine and Hygiene, Am. Acad. Allergy, Los Angeles Allergy Soc., AMA, Calif., Los Angeles County med. assns., West Coast Allergy Soc., AAAS, Am., Calif. socs. internal medicine, Calif. Soc. Allergy, Am. Heart Assn., Sierra Club, Sigma Xi. Jewish. Mason; mem. B'nai B'rith. Contbr. articles to profl. jours. Office: 11411 Brookshire Ave Downey CA 90241-5003

SHAPLEY, LLOYD STOWELL, mathematics and economics educator; b. Cambridge, Mass., June 2, 1923; s. Harlow and Martha (Betz) S.; m. Marian Ludolph, Aug. 19, 1955; children—Peter, Christopher. A.B., Harvard U., 1948; Ph.D., Princeton U., 1953; PhD (hon.), Hebrew U., Jerusalem, 1986. Mathematician Rand Corp., Santa Monica, Calif., 1948-50; 54-81; prof. depts. math. and econs. UCLA, 1981—; instr. Princeton U., 1952-54; sr. research fellow Calif. Inst. Tech., 1955-56; fellow Inst. Advanced Studies, Hebrew U., Jerusalem, 1979-80; mem. faculty Rand Grad. Inst. for Policy Studies, 1970—. Author: (with S. Karlin) Geometry of Moment Spaces, 1953, (with R. Aumann) Values of Non-Atomic Games, 1974; editor: (with others) Advances in Game Theory, 1964; mem. editorial bd. Internat. Jour. Game Theory, 1970—, Math. Programming, 1971-80, Jour. Math. Econs, 1973—, Math. Ops. Research, 1975—, Games and Econ. Behavior, 1988—. Served with AC U.S. Army, 1943-45. Decorated Bronze Star. Fellow Econometric Soc., Am. Acad. Arts and Scis.; mem. Nat. Acad. Scis., Ops. Research Soc. Am., Am. Math. Soc., Math. Programming Soc. Office: UCLA Dept Math Los Angeles CA 90024

SHARIAT, HORMOZ, pastor; b. Teheran, Iran, Sept. 9, 1955; came to U.S., 1979; s. Javad and Shamsi (Rastegar) S.; m. Donnell Jean Roper, Oct. 23, 1977; children: Hanniel Mina, Jonathan Navid, Michelle Mojdeh. BSEE, Arya Mehr U., Tehran, Iran, 1978; MSEE, U. So. Calif., 1981, PhD, 1986; BS, San Jose Christian Coll., 1993. Ordained minister Iranian Christian Ch., 1991. Mem. technical staff Rockwell Internat., Seal Beach, Calif., 1981-87; rsch. scientist Lockheed Artificial Intelligence Ctr., Menlo Park, Calif., 1987-91; pastor Iranian Christian Ch., San Jose, Calif., 1991—. Author: (with others) Motion Understanding: Robot and Human Vision 1988; contbr. articles profl. jours. Sec. to bd. dirs. Radio Voice of Christ, Portland, Oreg., 1983-88; lectr. Fellowship of Iranian Christians, L.A., 1983-87; asst. pastor Iranian Christian Ch., San Jose, 1991—; mem. exec. bd. The Worldwide Alliance of Iranian Christian Orgns., Chs. and Groups, 1988—, pres., 1991. Home: 1026 Whitebick Dr San Jose CA 95129-3049 Office: Iranian Christian Ch 4265 Kirk Rd San Jose CA 95124-4816

SHARIFF, ASGHAR J., geologist; b. Haft Kel, Iran, July 28, 1941; came to U.S., 1964, naturalized, 1978; s. Abdulwahab and Sakineh (Kamiab) S.; m. Kay L. Schoenwald, Aug. 9, 1969; 1 child, Shaun. B.Sc., Calif. State U., Northridge, 1971, M.Sc., 1983. Cert. profl. geologist, Va., Wyo. Petroleum geologist Iranian Oil Exploration and Producing Co., Ahwaz, 1971-74; geol. cons. D.R.L., Inc., Bakersfield, Calif., 1974-76, Strata-log, Inc., 1976-79, Energy Log, Inc., Sacramento, 1979-80; geologist U.S. Dept. Energy, Washington, 1980-81, Bur. Land Mgmt. Dept. Interior, Washington, 1981-89, asst. dist. mgr., Rawlins, Wyo., 1989—. Contbr. articles to profl. jours. Mem. Am. Assn. Petroleum Geologists, Soc. Profl. Well Log Analysts, Soc. Petroleum Engrs.

SHARKEY, RICHARD DAVID, product designer; b. Columbus, Ohio, May 8, 1957; s. John David and Beatrice Diane (Ziesler) S.; m. Melissa Duke Smith, Dec. 21, 1980; children: Flax Allistair Linden, Ambrosia Rose Ashley. Student, U. No. Colo., 1975-77, Emporia State U., 1977-78, U. Denver, 1978-81. Music tchr., pvt. studio, piano, cello, composition theory Evergreen, Colo., 1978-82; pvt. bus., period residential restoration Sharkey and Assocs., Evergreen and Denver, 1978-86; stair apprentice Denver Stair Co., 1985-86; stair master Heidelberg Stair Co., Evergreen, 1986; pvt. bus., designer period staircases, millwork O'Searcaigh, Ltd., Evergreen and Denver, 1986—; cons. stair and millwork design, Heidelberg Stair, Evergreen, Frank's Woodworking, Lyons, Colo., numerous manufacturers, contractors, architecture, design firms, 1987—. Composer/music: numerous piano compositions, 1972—; designer: numerous architecture, millwork and interior designs; inventor: woodworking tools and accessories, and building products, 1986—. Recipient scholarship Outward Bound Colo., Optimist Club of Evergreen, 1973, music grant, U. No. Colo., Greeley, 1975-76, Emporia (Kans.) U., 1977. Mem. Internat. Soc. Archtl. Artisans (pres., founder 1988—), Denver Cherry Creek Club (charter mem.), Rotary. Mem. Christian Science Ch. Home: PO Box 280856 Lakewood CO 80228-0856 Office: O'Searcaigh Ltd PO Box 280593 Lakewood CO 80228-0593

SHARMA, ARJUN DUTTA, cardiologist; b. Bombay, June 2, 1953; came to U.S., 1981; s. Hari D. and Gudrun (Axelsson) S.; m. Carolyn D. Burleigh, May 9, 1981; children: Allira, Eric, Harison. BSc, U. Waterloo, Ont., Can., 1972; MD, U. Toronto, Ont., 1976. Intern Toronto Gen. Hosp., 1976-77, resident in medicine, 1978-80; resident in medicine St. Michael's Hosp., Toronto, 1980-81; residency medicine Toronto Gen. Hosp., 1977-78; Rsch. assoc. Washington U., St. Louis, 1981-83; asst. prof. pharmacy and toxicology U. Western Ont., London, 1985-89, asst. prof. medicine, 1983-89, assoc. prof. medicine, 1989-90; dir. interventional electrophysiology Sutter Meml. Hosp., Sacramento, 1990—; abstract reviewer, faculty of ann. scientific sessions North Am. Soc. for Pacing and Electrophysiology, 1993; assoc. clin. prof. U. Calif., Davis, 1990—; cons. Medtronic Inc., Mpls., 1985-89, Telectronics Pacing Systems, Inc., 1990—; mem. rsch. com. Sutier Inst. Med. Rsch.; mem. exec. com. Sutter Heart Inst. Reviewer profl. jours., including Circulation, Am. Jour. Cardiology; contbr. articles to profl. publs. Mem. coun. for basic sci. Am. Heart Assn., chmn. ann. sci. session, 1989; active Crocker Art Mus. Recipient John Melady award, 1972, Dr. C.S. Wainwright award, 1973-75, Rsch. prize Toronto Gen. Hosp., 1979, 80, Ont. Career Scientist award Ont. Ministry of Health, 1983-89; Med. Rsch. Coun. Can. fellow, 1981-83. Office: 3941 J St Ste 260 Sacramento CA 95819

SHARMA, SANJAYA, electrical engineer; b. Jodhpur, Rajasthan, India, Mar. 3, 1962; s. Ambika Prasad and Vimla (Violet) S. BSEE, Ohio U., 1983, MSEE, 1987. Rsch. asst. Avionics Engrng. Ctr., Ohio U., Athens, 1985-87; rsch. engr. UPS/II Morrow, Inc., Salem, Oreg., 1988—. Recipient William E. Jackson award Radio Tech. Commn. for Aeronautics, Washington, 1987. Mem. Inst. of Navigation, Wild Goose Assn. Office: II Morrow Inc/UPS 2345 Turner Rd SE Salem OR 97302

SHARMA, SATISH, academic administrator, social worker; b. Batala, Punjab, India, Apr. 2, 1941; came to U.S., 1971; s. Shiv Dass and Kaushalya Sharma; m. Asha Sharma, July 8, 1967; children: Ashish, Anu. MA, Panjab (India) U., 1964; PhD, Ohio State U., Columbus, 1974; MSW, U. Iowa, 1980. Asst. prof. Punjab Agrl. U., Ludhiana, India, 1966-71, U. No. Iowa, Cedar Falls, 1974-81; assoc. prof. U. Nev., Las Vegas, 1982-86, dir., pres. social work, 1986—; cons. Clark County Social Svcs., Las Vegas, 1982-84, Nathan Adelson Hospice, Las Vegas, 1983-86. Author: Gandhi, Women and Social Development, 1982, Modernism and Planned Change, 1982, (monograph) Migratory Workers, 1964; assoc. editor: Internat. Jour. Contemporary Sociology, 1988—. Mem. adv. bd. Nathan Adelson Hospice, Las Vegas, 1983-89; mem. allocations bd. United Way, Las Vegas, 1984-88; mem. faculty senate U. Nev., Las Vegas, 1988—. Barrick scholar, 1988. Fellow Asian Rsch. Svc. Hong Kong; mem. NASW, Internat. Devel. Consortium (v.p. 1990), Coun. on Social Work Edn., Indian Sociol. Soc., Am. Rural Sociol. Soc., Internat. Assn. Schs. Social Work, Inter-Univ. Consortium for Internat. Social Devel. Office: U Nev Dept Social Work Las Vegas NV 89154

SHARMA, SURENDRA PRASAD, aerospace engineer, scientist; b. Gorakhpur, India, Feb. 3, 1943; came to U.S., 1971; s. Suresh Dutt and Dhanpati (Devi) S.; m. Prabha Durgapal; 1 child, Seema. BS, U. Gorakhpur, 1962; MS in Engrng., Peoples' Friendship U., Moscow, USSR, 1968; PhD, MIT, 1978. Scientist Scientists' Pool, Coun. of Sci. and Indsl. Rsch., New Delhi, 1968-70; lectr., Dept. of Aeronautics Indian Inst. Tech., Bombay, India, 1970-71; rsch. asst. MIT, Cambridge, Mass., 1972-78; adj. rsch. prof. aeronautics Naval Postgrad. Sch., Monterey, Calif., 1979; rsch. engr. U. Tenn. Space Inst., Tullahoma, Tenn., 1979-81; sr. engr. Brown & Root, Inc., Houston, 1981-82, Sii Drilco, Smith Internat., Houston, 1982-85; rsch. scientist NASA Ames Rsch. Ctr., Moffett Field, Calif., 1986—. Contbr. articles profl. jours. Mem. PTA, Cupertino, Calif. Assoc. fellow Am. Inst. Aeronautics and Astronautics; mem. Soc. Petroleum Engrs., IEEE, Sigma Xi (MIT chpt.). Office: MS 230-2 NASA Ames Rsch Ctr Moffett Field CA 94035-1000

SHARMA, VINOD KUMAR, chemical engineer; b. Bombay, India, July 10, 1946; came to the U.S., 1970; s. Devendra and Rama (Sharma) S.; m. Manjula Tyagi, Jan. 18, 1976; children: Udit Kumar, Nidhi. ISc, Aara Coll., India, 1961; BSChE, Agra Coll., 1966; MS, Worcester Poly. Inst., 1973. EIT, Pa. Chem. engr. Starit Engrng. Co. Pvt. Ltd., Bombay, 1966-68, Esco Engrs., Bombay, 1969-70; project engr. Bechtel Inc., N.Y.C., 1973-74; project specialist Permutit Co., Paramus, N.J., 1974-79; sr. process engr. Pa. Engrng. Co., Pitts., 1979-86; process engr. Ogden Projects Inc., Fairfield, N.J., 1986-91; mgr. project coordination Emcon Assocs., San Jose, Calif., 1991—. Mem. Am. Inst. Chem. Engrs. Office: Emcon Assocs 1921 Ringwood Ave San Jose CA 95131

SHARMAN, WILLIAM, basketball executive; b. Abilene, Tex., May 25, 1926; m. Joyce Sharman; children by previous marriage: Jerry, Nancy, Janice, Tom. Student, U. So. Calif. Basketball player Washington Capitols, 1950-51, Boston Celtics, 1951-61; coach Los Angeles/Utah Stars, 1968-71; coach Los Angeles Lakers, 1971-76, gen. mgr., 1976-82, pres., 1982-88, spl. cons., 1991—. Author: Sharman on Basketball Shooting, 1965. Named to Nat. Basketball Assn. All Star First Team, 1956-59, 2d Team, 1953, 55, 60, All League Team, 7 times; named Coach of Year Nat. Basketball Assn., 1972, Naismith Basketball Hall of Fame, 1976. Address: 4511 Roma Ct Marina Del Rey CA 90292

SHARON, TIMOTHY MICHAEL, physicist; b. Portsmouth, Va., Aug. 21, 1948; s. Lester Clark and Ruth May (Banister) S.; student Santa Ana Coll., 1966-68; B.A., U. Calif.-Irvine 1970, M.A., 1972, Ph.D., 1976; m. Carla Deon Colley, Dec. 17, 1977. Jr. specialist solid state theory U. Calif.-Irvine, 1976, research asst. radiation physics Med. Center and Sch. Medicine, 1976-77, cons. to attending staff Research and Edn. Found., 1976-77; mktg. physicist Varian Assos., Irvine, 1977-78; prin. engr., program mgr. Spectra Research Systems, Newport Beach, Calif., 1977-82; v.p. Brewer-Sharon Corp., Newport Beach, 1981-86, Micor Instruments, Inc., Irvine, Calif., 1983-86; pres., chief exec. officer Medelec Instruments Co., Inc., Newport Beach, 1986-88; pres. Pacific Crest Enterprises, El Toro, Calif., 1988-91; pres., chief exec. officer Novus Group NA, Irvine, Calif., 1991—; adj. faculty physics and engrng. Columbia Pacific U., San Rafael, Calif., 1981-87; dean Sch. Engrng., Newport U., Newport Beach, Calif., 1983-87; mem. adv. panel on pub. Am. Inst. Physics, 1974-75. Brython P. Davis univ. fellow, 1973-74. Mem. AAAS, Am. Phys. Soc., Brit. Interplanetary Soc. (asso. fellow), Am. Assn. Physicists in Medicine, IEEE, Assn. Advancement Med. Instrumentation, Smithsonian Instn., Am. Film Inst., Nat. Hist. Soc., Nat. Geog. Soc., Festival of Arts Laguna Beach, Mensa, Intertel, Sigma Pi Sigma, Phi Theta Kappa, Alpha Gamma Sigma. Clubs: Acad. Magical Arts, Club 33. Contbr. articles to profl. jours.

SHARP, DAVID LEE, advertising executive, consultant; b. Chgo., Apr. 18, 1952; s. Homer Glenn and Jo Ann (Harbour) S.; m. Christine Rowe, Oct. 18, 1975; children: Tara Ann, Erica Dana. B.S., Bradley U., 1974; M.S., U. Ill., 1975. Advt. exec. Caterpillar Tractor, Peoria, Ill., 1975-76; sales promotion supr. Armstrong Cork Co., Lancaster, Pa., 1976-78; sr. account exec. Kraft Smith Advt., Seattle, 1978-80; pres. Sharp, Hartwig Advt., Inc., Seattle, 1980—; chmn. Response Mktg., Inc., Seattle, 1982-91; instr. Cornish Inst., 1980; cons. Simpson Timber Co., Port of Seattle. Trustee, Eastside Community Mental Health Ctr., 1983—. Trustee Phila. String Quartet, 1989—; chmn. advt. and pub. rels. div. United Way of King County, 1989—; active Seattle Allied Arts, 1988—. Mem. Bus. Profl. Advt. Assn. (v.p. 1982-83), Intermarket Assn. Advt. Agy., Am. Assn. Advt. Agy. (gov. 1984—, vice chmn. 1984-85, chmn. 1986-87), Mutual Advt. Agy. Network (v.p. programs 1988-90), Seattle Advt. Fedn., Wash. Athletic Club, Juanita Bay Athletic Club, Univ. Rotary Club (program chmn. 1982-83). Republican. Methodist. Home: 11647 73d Pl NE Kirkland WA 98034 Office: 100 W Harrison Pla S Tower Ste 500 Seattle WA 98119

SHARP, GARY DUANE, oceanographer, consultant; b. Lubbock, Tex., Feb. 22, 1944; s. J.E. and Dorothy Lillian (Christian) S.; m. Kathleen Teresa Dorsey, Oct. 31, 1981. BS in Zoology, San Diego State U., 1967, MS in Biology, 1968; PhD in Marine Biology, U. Calif. San Diego, 1972. Sr. scientist Inter-Am. Tropical Tuna Commn., La Jolla, Calif., 1969-78; fisheries resources officer Food & Agriculture Orgn., Rome, 1978-83; cons. Ctr. for Climate/Ocean Resources Study, Gainesville, Fla., 1983-88; vis. scientist NOAA Ctr. for Ocean Analysis and Prediction, Monterey, Calif., 1989-91; scientific dir. Coop. Inst. for Rsch. in Integrated Ocean Scis., Monterey, Calif., 1991—. Author, editor: The Physiological Ecology of Tunas, 1978; editor: FAO Atlas of Living Resources of the Sea, 1980; co-editor: Procs. and Report of th Expert Consultation of the Changes in Distribution, Abundance and Species Composition of Neritic Fish Resources, 1983. Mem. Am. Soc. Limnology and Oceanography, Am. Geophys. Union, Am. Soc. Advancement of Sci., Oceanography Soc. Office: CIRIOS 2560 Garden Rd Monterey CA 93940

SHARP, GERALD WHITE, scientist; b. Salt Lake City, Oct. 8, 1930; s. James Cannon and Ruth (White) S.; m. Marilyn Nordberg, Sept. 2, 1932; children: LeAnne, Lorilynn, Susan, Jonathan, Michael. BA, U. Utah, 1952; MS, U. Wis., 1954, PhD, 1957. Rsch. physicist Stanford Rsch. Inst., Menlo Park, Calif., 1957-58; sr. staff scientist Lockheed Missiles & Space Co., Palo Alto, Calif., 1958-72; asst. for space and applications Nat. Aeronautics and Space Coun., Washington, 1972-73; chief spacelab sci. payloads NASA, Washington, 1973-76; chief spacelab projects NASA, Kennedy Space Center, Fla., 1976-84; asst. to pres. Eyring Rsch. Inst., Inc., Provo, Utah, 1984-86; staff engr. TRW Space and Tech. Group, Ogden, Utah, 1986—; cons. NASA Goddard Space Flight Ctr., Greenbelt, Md., 1986-90. Co-editor: Shuttle Environment Handbook, 1988; contbr. articles to profl. publs. Chmn. Mountain View (Calif.) Planning Commn., 1969; mem. adv. coun. State Ctrs. of Excellence Program, Salt Lake City, 1987—. Mem. Phi Beta Kappa, Sigma Xi, Phi Kappa Phi, Sigma Pi Sigma. Home: 141 Edgecombe Dr Salt Lake City UT 84103 Office: TRW Ogden Engrng Ops 1104 Country Hills Dr Ogden UT 84403

SHARP, JANE ELLYN, deputy operations director; b. Chgo., Jan. 5, 1934; d. Truman V. and Mildred L. (Sweitzer) Lasswell; m. David H. Sharp, July 24, 1965 (div. Aug. 1979); children: Michelle Lynn, Lisa Elizabeth. BBA, Coll. Santa Fe, 1985, MBA, 1988. Adminstrv. asst. San Diego State U., 1956-58; dir. classified personnel Grossmont (Calif.) Union High Sch. and Jr. Coll. Dist., 1959-62; legal asst. Stockly & Boone, Attys., Los Alamos, N.Mex., 1974-75; with adminstrn. Los Alamos (N.Mex.) Nat. Lab., 1976-78, pub. rels. specialist, 1978-81, asst. group leader, 1981-82, dep. group leader, 1982-83, asst. div. leader, 1983-84, office dir. protocol, 1984-89, dep. assoc. dir. for ops., 1989—. Mem. adv. bd. Youth Working for Youth, Los Alamos, 1985—; mem. Adults Working for Youth, Los Alamos, Santa Fe Rail Link Task Force, 1987-90, Los Alamos Community Devel. Com., 1989—; bd. dirs. Los Alamos Econ. Devel. Corp., 1989—, Los Alamos United Way, 1992—. Recipient Woman at Work award Coun. on Working Women, 1984. Mem. Tri Area Assn. for Econ. Devel., Los Alamos Nat. Lab. Community Coun. (rep. exec. bd. 1986—), Los Alamos C. of C. (bd. dirs. 1991—). Democrat. Office: Los Alamos Nat Lab PO Box 1663 Los Alamos NM 87544-0010

SHARP, KERRY LANCASTER, business development manager; b. Omaha, Jan. 24, 1949; s. Kermit Hobson and Alice Lucille (Lancaster) S.; m. Marilyn Kay Galbraith, Dec. 9, 1972; children: Brian, Catherine, Christopher. BS in Civil Engrng. with high honors, Mich. State U., 1971; MBA, Harvard U., 1977. Engr.-in-tng., Mich. Methods engr. So. Pacific Transp. Co., San Francisco, 1977-78; asst. to mgr. banking and credit Boise (Idaho) Cascade Corp., 1978-81, mgr. fin. adminstrn., 1981-85; bus. devel. mgr. Boise (Idaho) Cascade Corp., Portland, Oreg., 1985-87, St. Helens, Oreg., 1987—. Officer Oreg. Air Nat. Guard, Portland, 1986—; steering com. mem. Leadership Lake Oswego, Oreg., 1988-90; adv. group mem. The Oreg. Quality Initiative, State Oreg., 1992—. Capt. USAF, 1971-75. Mem. Nat. Guard Assn. Oreg. (dir. 1988—), Harvard Bus. Sch. Assn. Oreg. (dir. 1987—), The Am. Legion.

SHARP, PAMELA ANN, mining engineer; b. Pullman, Wash., Dec. 20, 1950; d. Robert Melvin and Vivian Lois (Steele) Olson; m. David William Sharp, June 16, 1973; children: Jaime David, Erik Scott. Student, Big Bend C.C., Moses Lake, Wash., 1969-70; BS in Zoology, Wash. State U., 1973; postgrad., Portland State U., 1976. Lab. technician The Carter Mining Co., Gillette, Wyo., 1977-79, lab. supr., 1979-80, quality control supr., 1980-81, engrng. analyst, 1982-88; engr. quality control The Carter Mining Co., Gillette, 1988-89; owner Sharp Consulting, Gillette, 1989—; leader auditor tng. ISO 9000; obedience dog tng. instr., 1990—. Supt. Campbell County Fair, Gillette, 1985-87. Mem. AIME, ASTM (proximate analysis chmn. 1985—, chmn. on-line analysis com.), Am. Water Ski Assn. (regular judge 1974-91, eastern regional water ski trick record 1975, 3d nat. trick title 1962, state champion in tricks Wash., Idaho, Mont. 1961-73, 2d 1987 Western region women's III tricks). Republican. Presbyterian. Office: Sharp Consulting PO Box 2302 Gillette WY 82717-2302

SHARP, PEGGY AGOSTINO, education educator, consultant; b. Portland, May 4, 1950; d. Ernest E. and Vra Juanita (Work) A.; m. John Lester Chamberlain; children: David, Catherine L. BA, U. Oreg., 1973, MA, 1974; MA, Columbia U., 1991, EdD, 1993. Library media specialist Fern Ridge Pub. Schs., Veneta, Oreg., 1973-75, Lake Oswego (Oreg.) Pub. Schs., 1975-80; asst. prof. edn. Portland State U., 1981—; cons. Bur. of Edn. and Rsch., Bellevue, Wash., 1985—; also numerous sch. dists. Author: ABC of Children's Book Activities, 1983, Sharing Your Good Ideas, 1993, Exploring the Pacific States, 1993; contbr. articles to profl. jours. Named Outstanding Young Educator, Fern Ridge Pub. Schs., 1975; recipient Evelyn Sibley Lampman award, Oreg. Library Assn. Mem. Internat. Reading Assn. (bd. dirs. 1985-88), Nat. Staff Devel. Assn., Oreg. Staff Devel. Coun. (bd. dirs. 1988-89), Oreg. Ednl. Media Assn. Democrat. Office: Designs for Learning PO Box 29078 Portland OR 97229-0078

SHARP, ROBERT PHILLIP, geology educator, researcher; b. Oxnard, Calif., June 24, 1911; s. Julian Hebner Sharp and Alice Sharp Darling; m. Jean Prescott Todd, Sept. 7, 1938; adopted children—Kristin Todd, Bruce Todd. B.S., Calif. Inst. Tech., Pasadena, 1934, M.S., 1935; M.A., Harvard U., Cambridge, Mass., 1936, Ph.D., 1938. Asst. prof. U. Ill., Urbana, 1938-43; prof. U. Minn., Mpls., 1946-47; prof. Calif. Inst. Tech., Pasadena, 1947-79, chmn., 1952-67, prof. emeritus, 1979—. Author: Glaciers, 1960, Field Guide-Southern California, 1972, Field Guide-Coastal Southern California, 1978, Living Ice-Understanding Glaciers and Glaciation, 1988, (with A.F. Glazner) Geology Under Foot in Southern California, 1993. Served to capt. USAF, 1943-46. Recipient Exceptional Sci. Achievement medal NASA, 1971, Nat. Medal Sci., 1989, Chas. P. Daly medal Am. Geog. Soc., 1991; Robert P. Sharp professorship Calif. Inst. Tech., 1978. Fellow Geol. Soc. Am. (councillor, Kirk Bryan award 1964, Penrose medal 1977), Am. Geophys. Union; hon. fellow Internat. Glaciological Soc.; mem. NAS. Republican. Home: 1901 Gibraltar Rd Santa Barbara CA 93105-2326 Office: Calif Inst Tech 1200 E California Blvd Pasadena CA 91125-0001

SHARP, WILLIAM CHARLES, system engineer; b. Cambridge, N.Y., Dec. 2, 1953; s. William Leland and Phyllis Evelyn (Burns) S.; children: William Welsey Leland, Natasha Nicole Nativa. BS in System Engrng., Rensselaer Poly. Inst., 1976. Engr. Applicon, Burlington, Mass., 1976-78, Xylogics, Burlington, 1978, McDon, Long Beach, Calif., 1978-81, Hughes Aircraft Co., Fullerton, Calif., 1981-82; engrng. mgr. Able Computer, Irvine, Calif., 1982-84; engr. Sierra Cybernetics, Brea, Calif., 1984-86, Midcom Corp., Anaheim Hills, Calif., 1986-91, Jet Propulsion Lab., Pasadena, Calif., 1986-91; pres. Glacier Blue, Rancho Santa Margarita, Calif., 1986—. Mem. Armed Forces Comm. and Electronics Assn., Digital Equipment Corp. User's Soc., Order of DeMolay (adult advisor, chevalier). Libertarian. Home and Office: 1 San Pablo Rancho Santa Margarita CA 92688-2518

SHARPE, ROLAND LEONARD, retired engineering company executive, earthquake and structural engineering consultant; b. Shakopee, Minn., Dec. 18, 1923; s. Alfred Leonard and Ruth Helen (Carter) S.; m. Jane Esther Steele, Dec. 28, 1946; children: Douglas Rolfe, Deborah Lynn, Sheryl Anne. B.S. in Civil Engring., U. Mich., 1947, M.S.E., 1949. Registered civil engr. and structural engr., Calif. Designer, Cummins & Barnard, Inc., Ann Arbor, Mich., 1947-48; instr. engring. U. Mich., 1948-50; exec. v.p. John A. Blume & Assocs., engrs., San Francisco, 1950-73; chmn., founder Engring. Decision Analysis Co., Inc., Cupertino, 1974-87; cons. earthquake engr., 1987—; mng. dir. EDAC, GmBH, Frankfurt, Germany, 1974-82; dir. EDAC; pres. Calif. Devel. & Engring. Co., Inc., Las Vegas, Nev., 1973-81; mem. nat. earthquake hazard reduction program adv. com. overviewing Fed. Emergency Mgmt. Agy., U.S. Geol. Survey, NSF and Nat. Inst. Standards and Tech. Author: (with J. Blume, E.G. Kost) Earthquake Engineering for Nuclear Facilities, 1971. Mem. Planning Commn., Palo Alto, 1955-60; mng. dir. Applied Tech. Council, Palo Alto, 1973-83; dir. Earthquake Engrng. Research Inst., 1972-75, now mem.; project dir., editor Tentative Provisions for Devel. of Seismic Regulations for Buildings, 1978; tech. mgr., contbr., editor Data Processing Facilities: Guidelines for Earthquake Hazard Mitigation, 1987. Served with USMC, 1942-46. Author, co-author over 200 engrng. papers and reports. Fellow ASCE (life mem., chmn. dynamic effects com., 1978-80, exec. com. structural div. 1980-84, 89-93, chmn. 1983, mgmt. group B 1989-93); mem. Japan Structural Cons. Assn. (hon. mem. 1992), Structural Engrs. Assn.

Calif. (dir. 1971-73, chmn. seismology com. 1972-74), Structural Engrs. No. Calif. (dir. 1969-71), Am. Concrete Inst. Recipient citation for contbn. to constrn. industry Engring. News Record, 1978-79, 86-87; chmn. U.S. Joint Com. on Earthquake Engring., 1982-88. Home: 10320 Rolly Rd Los Altos CA 94024-6520

SHARPE, RONALD MARTIN, small business owner; b. L.A., Nov. 23, 1950; s. Martin Joseph and Kathleen (O'Sullivan) S. BS in Acctg., Calif. State U., L.A., 1975, BS in Fin., 1972; AA, Pasadena City Coll., 1970. Lic. real estate broker, Calif. Real estate broker Sinnette Realtors, Pasadena, 1978-81; tax preparer Ed McGinley,CPA, San Marino, Calif., 1981; v.p. fin. Newport Investment Mgmt. Corp., Newport Beach, Calif., 1981; prin. Internat. Investors Devel. Corp., Newport Beach, Calif., 1981; gen. mgr., controller Mgmt. Svcs. Group, Huntington Beach, Calif., 1981-82; fin. adminstr. Marina Cove Ltd./HMR Ltd., Redondo Beach, Calif., 1982-83; pres., CEO Universal Concepts, Inc., Chehalis, Wash., 1984—, Cook Lumber, Inc., Chehalis, Wash., 1984-87, Sharpe Cedar Products, Chehalis, Wash., 1985—. Mem. Nat. Fedn. Ind. Bus. Roman Catholic. Office: Universal Concepts Inc PO Box 681 Chehalis WA 98532

SHARPE, WILLIAM FORSYTH, economics educator; b. Cambridge, Mass., June 16, 1934; s. Russell Thornley Sharpe and Evelyn Forsyth (Jillson) Maloy; m. Roberta Ruth Branton, July 2, 1954 (div. Feb. 1986); children: Deborah Ann, Jonathan Forsyth; m. Kathryn Dorothy Peck, Apr. 5, 1986. AB, UCLA, 1955, MA, 1956, PhD, 1961. Economist Rand Corp., 1957-61; asst. prof. econs. U. Wash., 1961-63, assoc. prof., 1963-67, prof., 1967-68; prof. U. Calif., Irvine, 1968-70; Timken prof. fin. Stanford U., 1970-89, Timken prof. emeritus, 1989-92; prin. William F. Sharpe Assocs., 1986-92; prof.fin. Stanford U., 1993—. Author: The Economics of Computers, 1969, Portfolio Theory and Capital Markets, 1970, Fundamentals of Investments, 1989, Investments, 4th edit., 1989. With U.S. Army, 1956-57. Recipient Graham and Dodd award Fin Analysts' Fedn., 1972, '73, '86-88. Nicholas Molodovsky award, 1989. Nobel prize in econ. scis., 1990. Mem. Am. Fin. Assn. (v.p. 1979, pres. 1980), Western Fin. Assn. (Enduring Contbn. award 1989), Ea. Fin. Assn. (Disting. Scholar award 1991), Am. Econ. Assn., Phi Beta Kappa.

SHARPTON, THOMAS, physician; b. Augusta, Ga., July 15, 1949; s. Thomas and Elizabeth (Dozier) S. BA, Northwestern U., 1971; MS, Stanford U., 1973, MD, 1977. Intern Martinez (Calif.) VAMC, 1977-78, resident, 1978-80; mem. staff Kaiser Permanente Med. Group, Oakland, Calif., 1980—; cons. Berkeley (Calif.) Free Clinic, 1977—; chmn. peer review Kaiser Permanente Med. Group, Oakland, 1985-86; clin. mem. faculty U. Calif., San Francisco, 1992. Mem. Alameda County Profl. Adv. Com., Oakland, 1984-88, Alameda County AIDS Task Force, Oakland, 1985-88. Fellow ACP; mem. Calif. Med. Assn., Alameda-Contra Costa Med. Assn., Mensa, Sigma Pi Sigma, Phi Beta Kappa. Democrat. Club: Phi Beta Kappa of No. Calif. Office: Kaiser PMG 280 W Macarthur Blvd Piedmont CA 94611-5693

SHASTRI, AMITA, political scientist, educator, researcher; b. Kanpur, India, Apr. 23, 1956; came to U.S., 1981; d. Raghunath Sahai Gupta and Kumud (Rastogi) Sahai; m. Nilabh Shastri, Oct. 20, 1977; 1 child, Avantika. BA, U. Delhi, India, 1975; MA, Jawaharlal Nehru U., India, 1977, MPhil, 1980, PhD, 1985. Rsch. fellow Calif. Inst. Tech., Pasadena, 1984-85; vis. scholar U. Calif., L.A., 1985-87; rsch. assoc. U. Calif., Berkeley, 1987-89; lectr. San Francisco State U., 1988-89, asst. prof., 1989-93, assoc. prof., 1993—; vis. fellow Internat. Ctr. for Ethnic Studies, Colombo, Sri Lanka, summer 1991. Contbr. articles to profl. jours. Recipient Pew Faculty fellowship in Internat. Affairs, John F. Kennedy Sch. Govt., 1990-91, Faculty Affirmative Action award San Francisco State U., 1989, Jr. and Sr. Rsch. fellowships Univ. Grants Commn., India, 1977-81. Mem. Am. Polit. Sci. Assn., Assn. for Asian Studies, Internat. Studies Assn., Internat. Polit. Sci. Assn. Home: 6219 Plymouth Ave Richmond CA 94805 Office: San Francisco State Univ 1600 Holloway Ave San Francisco CA 94132

SHATNEY, CLAYTON HENRY, surgeon; b. Bangor, Maine, Nov. 4, 1943; s. Clayton Lewis and Regina (Cossette) S.; m. Deborah Gaye Hansen, Apr. 5, 1977; children: Tony, Andy. BA, Bowdoin Coll., 1965; MD, Tufts U., 1969. Asst. prof. surgery U. Md. Hosp., Balt., 1979-82; assoc. prof. U. Fla. Sch. Medicine, Jacksonville, 1982-87; clin. assoc. prof. Stanford (Calif.) U. Sch. Medicine, 1987—; dir. traumatology Md. Inst. Emergency Med. Svcs., Balt., 1979-82; dir. trauma U. Hosp., Jacksonville, 1982-85; assoc. dir. trauma Santa Clara Valley Med. Ctr., 1992—; cons. VA Coop. Studies Program, Washington, 1980—. Editorial bd. Circulatory Shock, 1989—, Shock Research, 1993—; writer, actor med. movie. Maj. U.S. Army, 1977-79. State of Maine scholar Bowdoin Coll., 1961-65. Fellow ACS, Southeastern Surg. Congress, Southwestern Surg. Congress, Soc. Surg. Alimentary Tract, Am. Assn. Surg. Trauma, Soc. Critial Care Med., Societe Internat. de Chirurgie, Phi Kappa Phi. Home: 900 Larsen Rd Aptos CA 95003-2605 Office: Dept Surgery Valley Med Ctr 751 S Bascom Ave San Jose CA 95128-2604

SHATTUCK, DANIEL VERN, producer, radio; b. San Mateo, Calif., July 13, 1948; s. Charles Adolphus and Pearl Ione (Bohnett) S.; m. Laura Anne Janneck, May 17, 1975 (div. July 1986); children: Ashley, Christopher, Michael. AA in History, Grossmont Coll., 1969; BA in History, U. Calif., Irvine, 1971; BA in Philosophy, U. Calif., 1971. Lic. radio operator class 3. Mgmt. trainee Montgomery Ward, Grossmont, Calif., 1967-71; mgmt. res. Montgomery Ward, Anchorage, 1971-74; assoc. producer All Night TV, Anchorage, 1971-79; advt. mgr. Montgomery Ward, Anchorage, 1979-82; promotion dir. Northern Television, Anchorage, 1982-86; program dir. KCSY Radio, Soldotna, Alaska, 1986-91, KSLD Radio, Soldotna, Alaska, 1991—; v.p. Alaska Magic Circle, Anchorage, 1982; art tutor in field; announcer Alaska Martial Arts Demonstration, Anchorage, 1984; dialect coach in various theaters, San Diego, 1969-70. Author: (tape series) Your Creative Mind, 1989. Bd. dirs. Alaska Spl. Olympics, Anchorage, 1983; vol. Kenai Peninsula Food Bank, Soldotna, 1989-92. Recipient Goldie award Alaska Broadcasters Assn., 1988, 89, 90, 92. Mem. Kenai Performers. Methodist. Home: 35837 Rassmussens Ct Soldotna AK 99669 Office: KSLD Radio 374 Lovers Ln Soldotna AK 99669

SHATTUCK, PETER HAMILTON, history educator; b. Mass., July 11, 1935; s. Roger Whipple and Emily Mayo (Sutton) S.; m. Elizabeth Johnson Horr, Aug. 27, 1960; children: Arthur Hamilton, John Whitney. BA, Yale U., 1956; MA, U. Calif., Berkeley, 1960. Lectr. U. Calif., Davis, 1964-65; asst. prof. history Calif. State U., Sacramento, 1965-69, assoc. prof., 1969-74, prof., 1974—; chmn. acad. senate Calif. State U., Sacramento, 1973-74, 84-87, sec. statewide acad. senate, 1987-88. Trustee Sacramento History Mus., 1988—. With U.S. Army, 1957-59, Korea. Travel grantee Calif. State U., Sacramento, Europe, 1985, Can. Govt., 1989; recipient Resolution of Commendation, Calif. State Legislature, 1988. Mem. Am. Hist. Assn., Calif. Coun. for Social Studies, Poplar Forest Assn., Nat. Trust Hist. Preservation, Sacramento Club. Democrat. Office: Calif State U Dept History Sacramento CA 95819

SHATTUCK, RALPH EDWARD, metal products executive; b. Cleve., July 28, 1929; s. Ralph Eugene and Lucille (Kulas) S.; m. Nancy Rowley, Oct. 10, 1953; children: Nancy Elizabeth, Richard Hale. Salesman Republic Steel, Ferndale, Mich., 1955-75; sales mgr. Connors-Steel, Birmingham, Ala., 1975-80; owner Luger Pistol-Sales, 1980—. Assoc. editor: Man At Arms, 1985. Republican. Home and Office: 19044 N 98th Ln Peoria AZ 85382-2666

SHAU, HUNGYI, immunologist; b. Chanhua, Taiwan, Sept. 25, 1952; came to U.S., 1977; s. Ming-Je and Ton-Kuei (Lin) S.; m. Ching-Ching Lin, Sept. 13, 1956; children: Carol, Calvin. BS, Nat. Taiwan U., 1975; PhD, Duke U., 1982. Postdoctoral fellow Duke U., Durham, N.C., 1982-83, UCLA, 1983-85; rsch. asst. prof. U. So. Calif., L.A., 1985-86; asst. rsch. oncologist UCLA, 1986-88, adj. asst. prof., 1988-91, asst. prof., 1991—. Contbr. articles to profl. jours., chpts. to books. Mem. Am. Assn. Immunologists, Am. Assn. Cancer Rsch. Office: Div Surg Oncology UCLA Sch Medicine 54-140 CHS Los Angeles CA 90024-1782

SHAW, CHARLES ALDEN, engineering executive; b. Detroit, June 8, 1925; s. Fred Alden and Amy (Ellis) S.; m. Barbara Loveland, Mar. 9, 1963 (div. 1979); children: Amy Elizabeth, Polly Nicole; m. Jeanne Steves Partridge, Apr. 22, 1989. BS, Harvard U., 1945; MSEE, Syracuse U., 1958. Test and design engr. G.E., Syracuse-Schenectady, N.Y., 1947-51; chief engr. Onondaga Pottery Co., Syracuse, 1951-60; mgr. semiconductor div. G.E., Syracuse-Schenectady, 1960-66; cons. to gen. dir. Bull-G.E., Paris, 1966-69; mgr. CAD sect. integrated cir. product dept. G.E., Syracuse, 1969-71, mgr. CAD ctr. solid state applied ops., 1971-78, mgr. computer support solid state applied ops., 1978-81; dir. CAD G.E. Intersil, Cupertino, Calif., 1981-88; cons. in field Cupertino, 1988-89; mgr. tech. program Cadence Design Systems, Santa Clara, Calif., 1989—. Trustee Hidden Villa, Los Altos Hills, Calif., 1986-92; vol. tech. KTEH Channel 54 pub. TV, 1984—. With USN, 1942-45, PTO. Mem. IEEE, Assn. Computing Machinery (chmn. spl. interest group SIGDA 1986-91), Design Automation Conf. (exec. bd. 1985—), Harvard Club of Peninsula. Democrat. Unitarian. Home: 4925 Monaco Dr Pleasanton CA 94566-7671 Office: 555 River Oaks Pky San Jose CA 95134-1937

SHAW, DAVID ALLEN, magazine publisher; b. Lafayette, Ind., Oct. 24, 1959; s. Stanley Allen and Patricia (Ford) S.; m. Marjorie E.L. Shaw, Jan. 1, 1982 (div.); m. Rene Sue Redfield, Sept. 26, 1992. BA with honors, U. Calif., Irvine, 1981; cert., Mgmt. Action Program, 1988; cert. Pub. Mgmt. Inst., Kellogg Grad. Sch. Mgmt., 1989. Mng. editor Brentwood Pub. Corp., L.A., 1981-82, Hester Communications, Irvine, 1982-84; editor east coast HBJ Publs., N.Y.C., 1985-86; dir. market rsch. HBJ Publs., Irvine, 1986-88; pub. Edgell Communications, Irvine, 1988-91; pub. dir. Edgell Communications (name changed to Advanstar Comms., 1992), Irvine, 1991-93; group pub. Advanstar Comm., Santa Ana, 1993—; awards chmn. N.Y. Bus. Press Editors, 1985-86. Contbr. articles to profl. jours. Mem. Am. Bus. Press, World Futurists Soc., Western Pubs. Assn. (17 Maggie nominations, 1 Maggie award), Video Software Dealers Assn. Democrat. Office: Advanstar Comm 1700 E Dyer Rd Ste 250 Santa Ana CA 92705-5716

SHAW, DAVID LYLE, journalist, author; b. Dayton, Ohio, Jan. 4, 1943; s. Harry and Lillian (Walton) S.; m. Alice Louise Eck, Apr. 11, 1965 (div. Sept. 1974); m. Ellen Torgerson, July 17, 1979 (dec.); stepchildren: Christopher, Jordan; m. Lucy Stille, Apr. 14, 1988; 1 child, Lucas. BA in English, UCLA, 1965. Reporter Huntington Park Signal (Calif.), 1963-66, Long Beach Independent (Calif.), 1966-68; reporter L.A. Times, 1968-74, media critic, 1974—. Author: WILT: Just Like Any Other 7-Foot, Black Millionaire Who Lives Next Door, 1973, The Levy Caper, 1974, Journalism Today, 1977, Press Watch, 1984; contbr. numerous articles to mags. including Gentlemen's Quar., Esquire, TV Guide, New York. Recipient Mellet Fund Nat. award, 1983, PEN West award, 1990, Calif. Bar Assn. Gold Medallion, 1990, Pulitzer Prize for Disting. Criticism, 1991. Office: LA Times Times Mirror Sq Los Angeles CA 90012-3816

SHAW, EDWIN LAWRENCE, religious leader, educator; b. Emmett, Idaho, Nov. 17, 1938; s. Harold Wetherby Shaw and Genevieve T. (Knight) Shaffer; m. Marcella Mae Beecher, June 11, 1960; children: Rebecca, Pamela, Dawn. BA, Bob Jones U., 1961; MA, Mich. State U., 1964. Ordained to ministry Bapt. Ch.; cert. tchr., adminstr. Supt. Nampa (Idaho) Christian Schs., 1963-70; headmaster King's Schs., Seattle, 1970-74; asst. pastor Esperance Bapt. Ch., Edmonds, Wash., 1974-77; sr. pastor Grace Conservative Bapt. Ch., Seattle, 1977-89; gen. dir. S.W. Conservative Bapt. Assn., Phoenix, 1989—; co-owner Stas. KBGN/KBXL Radio, Boise, Idaho, 1976-90; speaker various confs., workshops, retreats, radio programs, 1963—. Bd. dirs. Southwestern Coll., Phoenix, 1989—; trustee Western Sem., Portland, Oreg., 1979-85. Home: 19013 N 90th Way Scottsdale AZ 85255-9287 Office: SWCBA 2535 E Cactus Rd Phoenix AZ 85032-7098

SHAW, GEORGE ARTHUR, JR., electronics executive; b. Lorain, Ohio, Oct. 1, 1948; s. George Arthur and Lucia (Gutierrez) S.; m. Pamela Anne Bowen, July 27, 1968; children: Chris, Aaron. BS in Mech. Engring., Calif. Poly. U., 1974. Package engr. Nat. Semiconductor, Santa Clara, Calif., 1974-78; mng. dir. Nat. Semiconductor, Bandung, Indonesia, 1981-84, Bangkok, 1984-88; v.p. package engring. Nat. Semiconductor, Santa Clara, 1988-90; package engr. Precision Monolithics inc., Santa Clara, 1978-79; engring. dir. Dynetics Inc., Manila, 1979-81; v.p. ops. Aptix Corp., San Jose, Calif., 1990—. Staff sgt. USAF, 1967-71. Office: Aptix Corp 2890 N 1st St San Jose CA 95134

SHAW, JAMES WILLIAM, minister; b. Chgo., June 18, 1940; s. Walter Leroy S. and Antoinette Marie (Reingruber) Krajacki; m. Shirley Fay LeCureux, Dec. 8, 1962; children: Cynthia, James III, Susan, Sandra, John, Joel. BA, Pillsbury Bible Coll., 1962; PhD, Calif. Grad. Sch. Theol., 1991. Pastor, youth Ashburn Bapt. Ch., Chgo., 1962-75; pastor Emmanuel Ch., Bellevue, 1975-92; pres. Emmanuel Sch. of the Bible, Bellevue, 1975-92; pastor Faith Bapt. Ch. Skagit Valley, Burlington, Wash., 1992—; prof. Cascade Bible Coll., Bellevue, 1976-92, prof., coord. Seattle Extention-Calif. Grad. Sch. Theol., Bellevue, 1987—. Author: What's With This Kid?, 1970, Ending the Travelague Syndrome: A Balaneed Strategem of Bible Study Methods, 1991. Coord. ski swap, Newport PTSA, Bellevue, 1982-90. Mem. Bellevue Ski Club (pres. 1979—). Office: Faith Baptist Ch 800 Rio Vista Ave Burlington WA 98233

SHAW, JERRY MICHAEL, sales executive, marketing, computer consultant; b. Pasadena, Calif., Nov. 8, 1945; s. Daniel Ernest and Elise Elizabeth (Thebérge) S.; m. Clara Louise Powers, Mar. 18, 1968 (div. Nov. 1974); children: Daniel Edward, Jennifer Nicole; m. Gail Lynn Losee, Dec. 1, 1990. Student, L.A. City Coll., 1964-65, Pasadena City Coll., 1967; grad., Life Underwriters Tng. Course, 1972. Agent Prudential Ins. Co., L.A., 1969-71, sales mgr., 1972-81; dist. mgr. Prudential Ins. Co., Pasadena, 1982-83; tng. cons. Prudential Ins. Co., Honolulu, 1984; dist. mgr. Prudential Ins. Co., San Dimas, Calif., 1984-86; sales mgr. Prudential Ins. Co., San Luis Obispo, Calif., 1986-91; sales mgr., mktg. cons. Prudential Ins. Co., Honolulu, 1992—. Mem. Nat. Assn. Life Underwriters (pres. 1974, nat. quality award 1974), Am. Soc. CLU and CHFC, Hawaii Assn. Life Underwriters, Million Dollar Round Table. Republican. Home: 1362 Akiahala Pl Kailua HI 96734 Office: Prudential Ins Co Penthouse 677 Ala Moana Blvd Honolulu HI 96813

SHAW, JOHN FIRTH, orchestra administrator; b. Chesterfield, U.K., June 28, 1948; s. Jack Firth and Mary Stuart (MacPherson) S.; m. Julia Valette Phillips, Dec. 29, 1973; children: Mary Valette, Mark Firth, Andrew Nicholas. Licentiate Royal Acad. Music, 1968; grad. Royal Schs. of Music, 1970. Freelance musician, 1966-70; prin. musician Calgary Phil. Orch., 1970-77, asst. mgr., 1977-78, asst. gen. mgr., 1978-79, gen. mgr., 1979-93. Bd. dirs. Calgary Philharm. Soc., 1974-77, Calgary Centre for Performing Arts, 1980-85, Choral Music Assn. Calgary, 1991-92; mem. adv. com. Mount Royal coll Conservatoryof Music, 1990—. Recipient Alta. Achievement award, 1991. Mem. Assn. Can. Orchs. (dir. 1982-84, 86—, pres. 1988-92, dir. 1992—). Office: Box 19, Site 38 RR # 12, Calgary, AB Canada T3W 6W3

SHAW, LILLIE MARIE KING, vocalist; b. Indpls., Nov. 27, 1915; d. Earl William and Bertha Louise (Groth) King; m. Philip Harlow Shaw, June 26, 1940. Student, Jordan Conservatory Music, Indpls., 1940-43; BA, Ariz. State U., 1959; MA, Denver U., 1962; pvt. vocal study, 1944-70. Educator, libr. Glendale (Ariz.) Schs., 1959-67; lectr. libr. sci. Ariz. State U., Tempe, 1962-68. Concertizing, oratorio, symphonic soloist, light opera, 1965—; soloist First Ch. of Christ Scientist, Sun City West, Ariz., 1980—. Monthly lectr. Christian Women's Fellowship, Phoenix, 1989—; World Conf. del. Soc. of Friends, 1967. Mem. Nat. Soc. Arts and Letters (sec. 1990—, nat. del. 1992), Am. Philatelic Assn. (life), Am. Topical Assn., Phoenix Philatelic Soc., Auditions Guild Ariz. (sec. 1989—), Phoenix Opera League, Phoenix Symphony Guild (bd. mem. youth activities 1986—), Sigma Alpha Iota Alumnae (life, treas. 1988, Sword of Honor 1972, Rose of Honor 1982). Republican. Home: 6802 N 37th Ave Phoenix AZ 85019-1103

SHAW, MARK HOWARD, lawyer, business owner, entrepreneur; b. Albuquerque, Aug. 26, 1944; s. Brad Oliver and Barbara Rae (Mencke) S.; m. Ann Marie Brookreson, June 29, 1968 (div. 1976); adopted children: Daniel Paul, Kathleen Ann, Brian Andrew; m. Roslyn Jane Ashton, Oct. 9, 1976; children: Rebecca Rae, Amanda Leith. BA, U. N.Mex., 1967, JD, 1969. Bar, N.Mex. 1969. Law clk. to presiding justice N.Mex. Supreme Ct., Santa Fe, 1969-70; ptnr. Gallagher & Ruud, Albuquerque, 1970-74, Schmidt & Shaw, Albuquerque, 1974-75; sr. mem. Shaw, Thompson & Sullivan P.A., Albuquerque, 1975-82; chief exec. officer United Ch. Religious Sci. and Sci. Mind Publs., L.A., 1982-91; atty., bus. owner, entrepreneur Santa Fe, N.Mex., 1991—. Trustee 1st Ch. Religious Sci., Albuquerque, 1974-77, pres. 1977; trustee Sandia Ch. Religious Sci., Albuquerque, 1980-82, pres. 1981-82; trustee United Ch. Religious Sci., Los Angeles, 1981-82, chmn. 1982; trustee Long Beach (Calif.) Ch. Religious Sci., 1983-86, chmn. 1983-86; chmn. Bernalillo County Bd. Ethics, Albuquerque, 1979-82. Served as sgt. USMCR, 1961-69. Mem. N.Mex. Bar Assn., Pres.'s Assn., Am. Mgmt. Assn. Home and Office: 2724 Puerto Bonito Santa Fe NM 87505-6534

SHAW, MORGAN ALBERT, architect, consultant; b. Ogden, Utah, Dec. 3, 1916; s. William Henry and Elizabeth (Johns) S.; m. Ramona Story, Sept. 28, 1940 (dec. Apr. 1990). Student, Corcoran Art Sch., Washington, 1937-39; cert., Art Students' League, N.Y.C., 1939-41; BArchwith honors, U. Calif., Berkeley, 1949. Lic. architect. Designer, draftsman Walter Wagner, Architect and Engr., Fresno, Calif., 1949-50, Skidmore, Owings & Merrill, San Francisco, 1950-51; job capt. Falk & Booth, San Francisco, 1951-52; owner, prin. Morgan Shaw, Architect, Berkeley, 1953—; instr. U. Calif., San Francisco, 1966-67. Contbr. articles to profl. jours. 1st lt. USAF, 1942-45, ETO. Mem. Phi Beta Kappa. Home: 2500 Hillegass Ave # 15 Berkeley CA 94704

SHAW, ROSS FRANKLIN, biologist, educator; b. Fillmore, Minn., May 12, 1930; s. Franklin B. and Mary G. (Newhall) S.; children: Franklin, Ronald, Jeffrey, Bradley, Kimberly. BS in Chemistry, Seattle Pacific Coll., 1952; MA in Zoology, U. S.D., 1958; PhD in Zoology, U. Iowa, 1961. Instr. Wessington Springs (S.D.) Coll., 1952-56; prof. biology Greenville (Ill.) Coll., 1961-65; prof. biology, dir. Blakely campus Seattle Pacific U., 1965—. NSF fellow, 1960-61. Mem. AAAS, Soc. Protozoologists. Mem. Free Methodist Ch. Home: 824 W Argand St Seattle WA 98119-1518 Office: Seattle Pacific Univ Seattle WA 98119

SHAW, SCOTT, actor, film maker, writer; b. L.A., Sept. 23, 1958. AA, L.A. Pierce Coll., 1979; BA, Calif. State U., Northridge, 1982; MA, Calif. State U., L.A., 1981, Emerson Coll. Herbology, 1983; PhD, Northwestern U., 1987. Cert. Grand master Tae Kwon Do, Master instr. Hap Ki Do. Chief instr. Shaw's Taekwondo, Reseda, Calif., 1976-85; pres. Asian Studies Ltd., Manhattan Beach, Calif., 1987—; CEO Buddha Rose Internat., Hermosa Beach, Calif., 1987—; adv. Calif. Martial Arts Assn., L.A., 1980—; founder Kawa Do Internat., 1982. Author 29 books, prodr. 8 films, dir. 5 films.; actor, star in 17 films. Fellow Am. Coll. Herbology; mem. Screen Actors Guild (actor), World Tae Kwon Do Fedn. (marital artist), Am. Tae Kwon Do Fedn. (martial artist). Home: P O Box 548 Hermosa Beach CA 90254 Office: Budda Rose Internat PO Box 548 Hermosa Beach CA 90254

SHAW, SCOTT RICHARD, entomologist, educator; b. Detroit, Sept. 29, 1955; s. Edward B. and Vesta G. (McKay) S.; m. Marilyn Rieden, July 13, 1979; children: Robert, Matthew, Michael. BS in Entomology, Mich. State U., 1977; MS, U. Md., 1981, PhD, 1984. Biol. lab. technician Systematic Entomology Lab., Washington, 1982-84; curatorial assoc. Mus. Comparative Zoology, Harvard U., Cambridge, Mass., 1984-89; asst. prof. entomology U. Wyo., Laramie, 1989—; asso. Mus. Comparative Zoology, Harvard U., 1990-92; cooperating scientist Ctr. for Insect Identification, Cin., 1988-93. Author, organizer mus. exhbn. Beetlemania, 1987; contbg. author: Hymenoptera of Costa Rica, 1992. Recipient Cert. of Merit USDA, 1984; Am. Philos. Soc. rsch. grantee, 1989, Nat. Park Svc. rsch. grantee, 1990. Mem. Entomol. Soc. Am. (Snodgrass award 1983, Pres.'s prize 1984), Entomol. Soc. Washington, Willi Hennig Soc., Internat. Soc. Hymenopterists, Ptnrs. of the Ams., Xerces Soc., Sigma Xi, Gamma Sigma Delta. Office: Dept Plant Soil Insect Sci U Wyo Laramie WY 82071-3354

SHAW, SUZANNE ALIX, law office manager; b. Jamaica, N.Y., Mar. 12, 1945; d. Arthur Tennyson and Dorothy Katherine (Pagano) S.; m. James L. Morrison III, July 25, 1964 (div. Dec. 1981). Student, Bklyn. Coll., 1963-64, Pierce Coll., 1970-72, UCLA, 1990-92. Advt. sec. Kinney Shoe Corp., N.Y.C., 1964-69; office mgr. Mfrs. Hanover Factors, L.A., 1969-72; bus. mgr. S.A. Shaw & Co., L.A., 1972-82; office mgr. Fest & Williams, Attys., Canoga Pk., Calif., 1982—. Author: (game invention) Dotz, 1972. Dir. Woodland Hills (Calif.) Homeowners Orgn., 1988—; mem. Pet Rescue, Glendale, Calif., 1980—; vol. Pacific Lodge Boys' Home, Woodland Hills; mem. Amanda Found., Beverly Hills, Calif.; deacon Woodland Hills Community Ch., 1992-95. Recipient Pres.'s award Woodland Hills Homeowners ORgn., 1988. Presbyterian. Home: 5625 Mason Ave Woodland Hills CA 91367

SHAW, TOBEY KENT, special education educator; b. Detroit, Dec. 1, 1952; d. Lewis and Helen (Babbush) Kent; m. Gary N. Shaw, Apr. 19, 1979; children: Jennifer Alexis, Ari Matthew. BA, Calif. State U., Northridge, 1976; postgrad., Calif. State U., 1991—. Spl. edn. tchr. L.A.R.C. Ranch, Saugus, Calif., 1976-78; tchrs. asst. L.A. Unified Sch. Dist., 1978-79; tchr. 5th grade Award Acad., Canoga Park, Calif., 1979-81; owner, pres. Learning Lab. Software, Northridge, 1984-91; exec. v.p. Learning Lab. Pub., Northridge, 1987—; spl. edn. tchr. Ventura County/Simi Valley Unified Sch. Dist., Simi Valley, Calif., 1991-92, L.A. Unified Sch. Dist., 1992-93; learning disabilities and tech. specialist The Frostig Ctr., Pasadena, Calif., 1993—; ednl. therapist in pvt. practice, Northridge, 1982—; advaptive tech. specialist, Moorpark, Calif., 1984—; instr. continuing edn. Calif. Luth. U., Thousand Oaks, Calif., 1992—; dir. projects Spl. Awareness Computer Ctr., Simi Valley, 1991—; mem. adv. bd. Computer Access Ctr., Santa Monica, Calif., 1988—. Author, pub. software; contbr. articles to profl. jours. Vol., Tri-Valley Spl. Olympics, Burbank, Calif., 1977—, chmn. bd., 1980-81. Mem. Coun. for Exceptional Children, Computer Using Educators. Democrat. Jewish. Home: 12008 Rivergrove Moorpark CA 93021

SHAW, WILLIAM JAY, public finance specialist; b. San Francisco, Jan. 14, 1962; s. William Cooper and Mary Elizabeth (Wolfe) S.; m. Kimberly Ann Kolman, Aug. 21, 1991; 1 child, William Henry. BS, U. of Pacific, 1984; M Pub. Adminstrn., U. So. Calif., 1989. Market analyst Fin. Corp. Am., Stockton, Calif., 1984-85; builder account mgr. Bank Am., San Francisco, 1985-88; housing fin. officer Community Devel. Commn. County of Los Angeles, Monterey Park, Calif., 1990—. Mem. Soc. Calif. Pioneers, Soc. Colonial Wars, Soc. Mayflower Descendants, Delta Sigma Pi (founding pres. Lambda Mu chpt. 1983-84). Republican. Methodist. Home and Office: 20780 Cottonwood Rd Yorba Linda CA 92687

SHAW, WILLIAM WEI-LIEN, plastic surgeon; b. Kwei-Yang, China, Mar. 12, 1942; came to U.S., 1957; s. Emil and Rosemarie (Lam) S.; m. Nan Zhang. BS, UCLA, 1964, MD, 1968. Intern, Albert Einstein Med. Coll. Bronx Mcpl. Hosp., N.Y., 1968-69; gen. surg. residency UCLA, 1969-75, Johns Hopkins Hosp., 1972; plastic surgery resident, Inst. Reconstructive Plastic Surgery NYU, 1975-77; assoc. prof. surgery NYU Med. Ctr., N.Y.C., 1977-89; chief of plastic surgery Bellevue Hosp., N.Y.C., 1977-89; prof., chmn. plastic surgery UCLA Med. Ctr., 1989—. Author: Microsurgery in Trauma, 1987. Maj. U.S. Army, 1970-72. Named hon. surgeon N.Y.C. Police Dept., 1979, hon. prof. Chinese Acad. Med. Sci., Beijing, 1986. Fellow ACS, Am. Soc. Plastic and Reconstructive Surgery, Internat. Soc. Reconstructive Microsurgery. Office: UCLA Div Plastic Surgery 10833 Le Conte Ave Los Angeles CA 90024

SHAY, ROSHANI CARI, political science educator; b. Milw., Oct. 5, 1942; d. Walter John and Dorothee May (Dahnke) O'Donnell; 1 child, Mark Sather. Student, Willamette U., 1960-63; BA, U. Oreg., 1968, MA, 1971, PhD, 1974. Adminstrv. asst. Dept. of Youth Svcs., Lubbock, Tex., 1963; teaching asst., instr. U. Oreg., Eugene, 1969-72; vis. asst. prof. Oreg. State U., Corvallis, 1973-74, Willamette U., Salem, Oreg., 1973-79, Lewis and Clark Coll., Portland, Oreg., 1976, 78; from asst. prof. to prof. Western Oreg. State Coll., Monmouth, 1979—, chair history, polit. sci., pub. adminstrn. dept., 1991-93. Author: (with others) The People of Rajneeshpuram, 1990, (simulation) European Unity Project, 1982. Co-founder, v.p. Ind. Opportunities Unltd., Salem, 1986—; co-founder, sec. Inst. for Justice and Human Rights, San Francisco, 1988—; bd. dirs. Oreg. UN Assn., Portland, 1982—, Salem UN Assn., 1982-91; v.p., pres., bd. dirs. Garten Found. for Disabled, Salem, 1989—; pres. Assn. Oreg. Faculties, 1989-91; mem. adv. bd. Connections Program for Disabled Deaf, Salem,

1989—; pres., bd. dirs. Model UN of the Far West, San Deigo, 1981-84, 86-88; mem. Oreg. Women's Polit. Caucus. Danforth Found. fellow, 1968-74; named Woman of Achievement YWCA Tribute, Salem, 1990. Mem. Am. Fedn. Tchrs. (v.p. and legis. officer local 2278 1982-88), Western Polit. Sci. Assn., Communal Studies Assn., Global Connections (west coast coord. acad. sect.), Internat. Assn. Parents of the Deaf, Mental Health Assn. Oreg., Oreg. Acad. Sci., Oreg. Internat. Coun., Phi Kappa Phi (hon.). Democrat. Home: 348 S Main St Falls City OR 97344-9763 Office: Western Oreg State Coll 345 Monmouth Ave N Monmouth OR 97361-1314

SHCOLNIK, ROBERT MILTON, insurance company executive; b. South Bend, Ind., Aug. 21, 1938; s. Harry and Esther (Baim) S.; m. Linda K. Egleberry, Aug. 10, 1972; children: Scott, Keith, Carin. BS in Bus., Ariz. State U., 1960; student, Am. Savings & Loan Inst., 1961; diploma in ins., Hartford Ins. Group Ins. Group, 1965. Loan officer, branch mgr., asst. to the pres. Home Savings & Loan Assn., 1959-61; pres. Harris/Shcolnik & Assocs., Inc., Phoenix, 1961—; ptnr. Harris/Shcolnik Properties; v.p., bd. dirs. My Florist, Inc., 1970—; guest lectr. in ins. Phoenix Coll.; speaker Nat. Assn. Independent Ins. Agts. Nat. Conv. Contbr. articles to profl. jours.; designer interface mini-computer concept. Mem. nat. presidents circle Cen. Mutual Ins. Co., inter-circle, 1975-76, Ariz. Jonathan Trumbull Coun., Hartford Ins., 1979-80, Nat. Great Am. Ins. Agts. Adv. Coun., 1979-81, chmn. 1979, Pacer (agts. coun.) CNA Group, agts. coun. Cigna Ins.; former mem. Key Club, Continental Assurance Co.; past pres. Am. Savings and Loan Inst., Ariz.; bd. dirs. Jewish Community Ctr., 1980-86, v.p., exec. com., 1983-85; mem. combined ops. coun. Jewish Ctrs. Greater Phoenix, 1987-88. Named Outstanding Agt. of Yr. Maricopa County Assn. Independent Ins. Agts., 1973, 76-78; recipient Jewish Community Ctr. Disting. Svc. award, 1981, 83, 85. Mem. Ind. Ins. Agts. Ariz. (pres. 1985). Republican. Jewish. Office: Harris Shcolnik & Assocs 4808 N Central Ave Phoenix AZ 85012-1714

SHEA, MICHAEL ALAN, lawyer; b. Iowa City, Oct. 9, 1946; s. Robert Wallace and Florence (Foley) S.; m. La Donna Reiner, Mar. 3, 1979. BA, U. Iowa, 1968, JD, 1974; BLitt, Oxford U., England, 1973. Bar: Hawaii 1974, U.S Tax Ct. 1974, U.S. Dist. Ct. Hawaii 1974, U.S. Ct. Appeals (9th cir.) 1974, U.S. Supreme Ct. 1983. From assoc. to ptnr. Cades, Schutte, Fleming & Wright, Honolulu, 1974-83; ptnr. Goodsill, Anderson, Quinn & Stifel, Honolulu, 1983—. Mem. Gov.'s adv. com. on adoption of Tax Reform Act, 1986; bd. dirs. Arts Coun. Hawaii, Honolulu, 1975-89, Honolulu Community Theatre, 1976-82. Mem. ABA (exempt orgns. com. tax sect.), Hawaii Bar Assn. (chmn. tax sect. com. 1986, chmn. tax sect. 1988-89), Honolulu C. of C. (chmn. tax com. 1985—, pub. health com., bd. dirs. 1987-93). Clubs: Honolulu, Hawaii Yacht (Honolulu). Home: 12 Prospect St Honolulu HI 96813-1742 Office: Goodsill Anderson Quinn & Stifel PO Box 3196 Honolulu HI 96801-3196

SHEA, ROBERT STANTON, academic dean; b. Quincy, Mass., Oct. 15, 1928; s. Arthur Joseph and Isabella (Crowley) S.; m. Ruth Eva Summers, May 30, 1952; children: Robert S. Jr., Stephen D., Lisa A., Louise M., David R. BS in Math., Boston Coll., 1952; MBA, Calif. State U., Fullerton, 1969. CLU, Chartered Fin. Cons. Test equipment engr. Hughes Aircraft Co., El Segundo, Calif., 1952-56; rsch. engr., project engr. Rockwell Internat., Anaheim, Calif., 1956-70; acctg. systems analyst Safeguard Bus. Systems, Van Nuys, Calif., 1971-76; cons. Am. Grad. U., Covina, Calif., 1987—; registered rep. Mut. of N.Y., Anaheim, Calif., 1976-84; fin. cons. Empcom Ins. Svcs., Inc., Long Beach, Calif., 1984—, also bd. dirs.; dean Coll. of Bus. Adminstrn. Pacific States U., L.A., 1972—. Track and field official The Athletics Congress, L.A., 1958-88; mem. Anaheim East chpt. Rotary Internat., Anaheim, 1973-85, pres. 1980; patrol leader Boy Scouts Am., Anaheim, 1964-75. With USN, 1946-48. Recipient Merit award Rotary Internat., 1978, Award of Merit, The Athletics Congress, 1977. Mem. Beta Gamma Sigma. Republican. Roman Catholic. Home: 204 N Royal Pl Anaheim CA 92806-3232 Office: Pacific States U 1516 S Western Ave Los Angeles CA 90006-4234

SHEA, THEODORE WILLIAM, obstetrician, gynecologist; b. L.A., Feb. 14, 1960; s. William Henry and Karen Ruth (Olsen) S. BS, Andrews U., 1982; MD, Loma Linda U., 1987. Resident physician Glendale (Calif.) Adventist Med. Ctr., 1987-91; pvt. practice Vallejo, Calif., 1991—. Mem. AMA, Am. Coll. Ob/Gyn., Am. Assn. Gyn. Laparoscopists, Calif. Med. Assn., Solano County Med. Soc. Republican. Office: Bay View Med Ctr 127 Hospital Dr Vallejo CA 94589-2562

SHEA, WILLIAM FRANCIS, air transportation executive; b. White Plains, N.Y., 1930; m. Carol; 5 children. BA, U. N.H., 1954; MEd, Mass. State Coll., 1958; EdD (hon.), Hawthorne Coll., 1962. Dir. U. Nebr. at Omaha Aviation Inst., to 1992; pres. Shea Aviation Assocs., Seaside, Oreg., 1992—; commr. transp. Broome County, N.Y., 1974-76; spl. cons. Aviation Inst.; chief Calif. Divsn. Aeronautics; assoc. adminstr. airports, FAA; dir. aviation Port of Portland; chmn. dept. aviation U. N.D.; pres. World Aerospace Edn. Orgn., 1992-93; mem. Seaside Airport Com., 1993. Col. Civil Air Patrol. With USAF, 1946-49. Recipient Crown Circle award outstanding leadership aerospace edn. Nat. Aerospace Congress, 1992. Mem. N.Y. Airport Mgrs. Assn. (founder, 1st pres.), Internat. Aviation Coun. Office: Shea Aviation Assocs 1315 Ave A Seaside OR 97138

SHEAFFER, RICHARD ALLEN, electrical engineer; b. Bronxville, N.Y., May 30, 1950; s. Harold Aumond and Carol Lois (Henry) Sweet; children: Alan Michael Sheaffer, Russell Logan Sheaffer, Neil Andrew Sheaffer; m. Pamela Christine Clark, May 23, 1987. BSEE, Pa. State U., 1972; MSEE, U. So. Calif., 1975. Registered profl. engr., Calif., Fla. Elec. engr. So. Calif. Edison Co., Rosemead, 1973-79, 80-90, Harris Controls div., Melbourne, Fla., 1979-80; cons. to elec. utility industry, 1990-91; sr. engr. San Diego Gas & Electric, 1991—; project leader nomogram study for Pacific and S.W. transfer subcom. Western Systems Coordinating Coun., 1988, 91. Author: 1984 West-of-the-River Operating Study, 1985, December 22, 1982 Disturbance Study, 1983. Mem. IEEE (Power Engring. Soc., Engring. Mgmt. Soc.), Phi Eta Sigma. Episcopalian.

SHEAFOR, STEPHEN JAMES, engineering executive; b. Topeka, Kans., Dec. 15, 1949; s. Harold Norman and Margaret Mize (Strawn) S.; m. Cindy Jo Lindsay, May 13, 1972. BA, MEE, Rice U., 1972; PhD in Elec. Engring., U. Ill., 1974; MBA, U. Santa Clara (Calif.), 1980. Mem. tech. staff Hewlett Packard, Cupertino, Calif., 1974-6, project mgr., 1976-79, section mgr., 1979-81; hardware mgr. Dialogic Systems Corp., San Jose, Calif., 1981-84, engring. dir., 1984-85; engring. dir. Chronon Computers, Mountain View, Calif., 1985-86; founder, dir. v.p. engring. Cornerstone Imaging, San Jose, 1986—. Patentee in field. Office: Cornerstone Imaging 1990 Concourse Dr San Jose CA 95131

SHEALY, MIRIAM SCHUMPERT, accountant; b. Charleston, S.C., Dec. 20, 1959; d. Milton Wyse and Patricia Ann (Kirkland) Schumpert; m. David Andrew Shealy, Feb. 24, 1990. BS, U. S.C., 1986. CPA, S.C., Calif. Sr. auditor S.C. State Auditor's Office, Columbia, S.C., 1986-90; controller D.L. Olsen & Assocs., Inc., San Diego, 1990-92; pvt. practice acctg. San Diego, 1992—. Republican. Lutheran. Home: 4429 Del Mar Ave San Diego CA 92107

SHEARER, CAROLYN JUANITA, educator; b. Heber Springs, Ark., May 20, 1944; d. James A. and Juanita Ruth (Wallace) S. BS, U. Colo., Boulder, 1966, MA, 1972. Cert. tchr., Colo. Tchr. Aurora (Colo.) Pub. Schs., reading resource tchr.; presenter writing process workshops. Author curriculum materials. Mem. PTA. Mem. NEA, ASCD, Colo. Edn. Assn., Aurora Edn. Assn. (bd. dirs., bargaining support team), Internat. Reading Assn., Colo. Reading Assn., Aurora Reading Assn., Pi Lambda Theta. Democrat. Methodist. Office: West Mid Sch 10100 E 13th Ave Aurora CO 80010-3302

SHEARING, MIRIAM, judge; b. Waverly, N.Y., Feb. 24, 1935. BA, Cornell U., 1956; JD, Boston U., 1964. Bar: Calif. 1965, Nev. 1969. Justice of peace Las Vegas Justice Ct., 1977-81; judge Nev. Dist. Ct., 1983-86, chief judge, 1986—; alt. referee Juvenile Ct., Clark County, 1975-76. Mem. ABA, Am. Judicature Soc., Nev. Judges Assn. (sec. 1978), Nev. Dist. Ct. Judges Assn. (sec. 1984-85, pres. 1986-87), State Bar Nev., State Bar Calif., Clark County Bar Assn. Democrat. *

SHEASGREEN, BETTY, interior designer, painter, sculptor; b. Thief River Falls, Minn., May 16, 1920; d. Harry Weiser and Genevieve (Schutt) Protzeller; m. Otto Frederick Stoehr, June 3, 1951 (div. June 1964); 1 child, Cynthia Jane Stoehr Arenander; m. Francis Barrett Sheasgreen, Nov. 28, 1978. AA, Stephens Coll., 1940; student, U. Minn., 1940-42, Maharishi Internat. U., 1989-90, Clatsop C.C., Astoria, Oreg., 1990—. Designer Conrae Interiors, Reno, Nev., 1963-65; owner, designer Studio West, Reno, 1965-75; interior designer McQueen's Interiors, Lahaina, Hawaii, 1975-82; owner Compass-Rose Travel Agy., Portland, Oreg., 1982-85; ind. artist Seaside, Oreg., 1990—; designer interiors condominium projects Maui, Hawaii. Interior designs include Middlefork Lodge, Harrah's Clubs. With USN, 1942-45. Mem. N.W. Watercolor Soc., Watercolor Soc. Oreg., Trails End Art Assn. (pres. 1992). Mem. Natural Law Party. Transcendental Meditationist. Home and Studio: PO Box 838 2460 Ocean Vista Dr Seaside OR 97138

SHEBS, STANLEY TODD, computer scientist; b. Oakland, Calif., July 8, 1960; s. William Todd and Delis Irene (Christensen) S.; m. Natalie Shebs, Sept. 27, 1992. BS, Tex. A&M U., 1981; PhD, U. Utah, 1988. Software engr. Boeing Aerospace, Seattle, 1981-83; computer scientist Apple Computer Inc., Cupertino, Calif., 1988—; reviewer Computing Revs., N.Y.C., 1985—, Sci. and Tech. Annual Reference Rev., Chgo., 1990—. Author: Portable Common Lisp Subset, 1986, Implementing Primitive Datatypes for Higher-Level Languages, 1988, Macintosh Port of Gnu "C" Compiler, 1990. Recipient fellowship Amoco Found., 1983. Mem. Assn. Computing Machinery. Democrat. Home: 3663 Cabernet Vineyards Cir San Jose CA 95117 Office: Apple Computer Inc 20525 Mariani Ave Cupertino CA 95014-6201

SHECKLER, DALE ALAN, publisher; b. Inglewood, Calif., May 23, 1957; s. Ronald Laverne and Ella May (Hickman) S.; m. Kim Ann Reed, Dec. 4, 1982; children: Christopher, Reed, Eric. AA, El Camino Coll., Torrance, Calif., 1977. Diver Ocean Systems, Houston, 1978-84; producer Scuba, The Dive Show, Torrance, Calif.; pubr. Calif. Diving News, Torrance, Calif.; pres. St. Brendan Corp., Torrance, Calif. Author: Under Water Hunting, 1991; co-author: Southern California Best Beach Dives, 1991, Diving and Snorkeling Guide to Southern California, 1987, Diving and Snorkeling Guide to the Channel Islands, 1987. Mem. Divers Alert Network, Catalina Conservancy Divers (dir. 1991—), Greater L.A. Coun. of Divers (dir. 1990-92). Republican. Christian Ch. Office: St Brendan Corp PO Box 11231 Torrance CA 90510

SHEDENHELM, WILLIAM REX CHARLES, writer; b. L.A., Mar. 18, 1924; s. Charles Walter and Jeanne DeEarl (Williamson) S.; m. Geri Fleming, 1959 (div. 1960); m. Shirley Joan Sayers, July 30, 1965; 1 child, Richard Scott. AA, L.A. City Coll., 1948; BS, Columbia U., 1952; MA, Calif. State U., Dominquez Hills, 1985. Seismic chief computer Western Geophys. Co., 1954-55; petroleum geologist Tex. Petroleum, Venezuela, 1956-58; mng. editor Trailer Life Mag., L.A., 1959, MotoRacing, L.A., 1959-61, Sports Car Graphic Mag., L.A., 1961-68; sr. editor Rock & Gem Mag., Ventura, Calif., 1970-93; geology tchr. Elderhostel, Ventura, Calif., 1990-93. Author ten books on auto repair, backpacking, rockhounding, stained glass work, travel. With U.S. Army, 1943-46, ETO, S.W. PTO. Mem. AAAS, Nat. Rifle Assn., E Clampus Vitus. Office: 5260 Elmhurst St Ventura CA 93003

SHEEAN, CAROL A., social worker, consultant, psychotherapist; b. Tacoma, Dec. 28, 1941; d. Mark H. and Lorraine M. (Steen) Canterbury; m. David V. Sheean, Aug. 25, 1961; children: Ketner, Arden, Mitchell. BA cum laude, Pacific Luth. U., 1978; MSW, U. Wash., Seattle, 1980; postgrad., Seattle Inst. for Psychoanalysis, 1993. Diplomate Am. Bd. Examiners, Nat. Assn. Social Work. Psychotherapist, educator Cath. Community Svcs., Tacoma, 1980-82; br. coord., program adminstr. Tacoma Dept. Family Counseling, 1982-84; assessment coord. Maschhoff, Barr & Assoc., Tacoma, 1984-89; human resource cons. R & Assoc. Logicon, Tacoma, 1984-89, Exec. Effectiveness, San Diego, 1989—; psychotherapist Commencement Day Assn., Tacoma, 1989—; pvt. practice Tacoma, 1993—; instr. Pacific Luth. U., Tacoma, 1983-85, U. Wash., Seattle, 1983-85; cons. program for family living CPVII, Tacoma, 1984—. Sustainer, Jr. League, Tacoma, 1970—; founding mem. City Club of Tacoma, 1985; mem. YMCA, 1989; bd. dirs. program for family living Clouer Park Vocat./Tech. Inst., Tacoma, 1985—; bd. dirs. Greater Lakes Mental Health Found., Tacoma, 1988—. Mem. NASW, N.W. Alliance for Psychoanalytic Study (assoc.), Tacoma Country and Golf Club, Lakewood Racquet Club. Republican. Office: Commencement Bay Assn 2412 N 30th Ste 202 Tacoma WA 98407

SHEEHAN, LAWRENCE JAMES, lawyer; b. San Francisco, July 23, 1932. AB, Stanford U., 1957, LLB, 1959. Bar: Calif. 1960. Law clk. to chief judge U.S. Ct. Appeals 2d Cir., N.Y.C., 1959-60; assoc. O'Melveny & Myers, L.A., 1960-68, ptnr., 1969—; bd. dirs. Am. Capital Mutual Funds, FPA Mutual Funds, TCW Convertible Securities Fund Inc., Source Capital, Inc. Mem. ABA, Los Angeles County Bar Assn., Calif. Bar Assn., Order of Coif. Office: O'Melveny & Myers 1999 Avenue Of The Stars Los Angeles CA 90067-6022 also: O'Melveny & Myers 400 S Hope St Los Angeles CA 90071-2899

SHEEHAN, THOMAS HENRY, JR., management consultant; b. Detroit, Dec. 28, 1935; s. Thomas H. Sheehan and Ethel Knechtel. BS in Mech. Engring., U. Mich., 1959; MBA in Prodn. and Mktg., U. Chgo., 1963; PhD in Mineral Econ., Colo. Sch. Mines, 1976. Engr. Reliable Electric Co., Chgo., 1959-60; mgmt. systems specialist Lockheed Aircraft Corp., Marietta, Ga., 1960-64; mgmt. cons. Touche Ross & Co., N.Y.C., 1965-69, ptnr., Madrid and N.Y.C., 1969-72; mgmt. cons. Spencer Stuart, Chgo., 1972-74; exec. dir. Colo. Dept. Adminstrn., Denver, 1976-78; pres. Sheehan Internat., Golden, Colo., 1979-85, 89—; prin. mgmt. cons. SRI Internat., Menlo Park, Calif., 1985-89; prof. internat. bus. Internat. U. Am., S.F., 1993—. Served with USMC, 1960, with Res., 1961-66. Mem. N.Am. Soc. for Corp. Planning (exec. v.p. 1984-85), U. Chgo. Alumni Assn. San Francisco Area (pres. 1986—). Office: Sheehan Internat Palo Alto CA 94301

SHEELEY, ELLEN RAE, marketing consultant; b. Charles City, Iowa, Oct. 15, 1956; d. William D. and Patricia M. (Britt) S. BA in Psychology, Wright State U., 1978; MBA, Colo. State U., 1982. Product mgr. Ctrl. Bank of Denver, 1982-83; mktg. cons. Devel. Bank of Western Samoa, Apia, Western Samoa, South Pacific, 1983-86; sr. ops. mgr. Bank of Am., San Francisco, 1986-89; pres. Nob Hill Consulting, San Francisco, 1989—; adj. faculty U. San Francisco, 1989, Golden Gate U., 1992, San Francisco State U., 1991—. Contbr. numerous articles to profl. jours. Mem. Sierra Club, San Francisco, 1991—, NOW, San Francisco, 1991—; legis. intern U.S. Ho. of Reps., Washington, 1975. Recipient Exceptional Performance award Bank of Am., 1988, 89; grantee, 1974-82. Mem. Commonwealth Club, World Affairs Coun. Republican. Roman Catholic. Office: Nob Hill Consulting 795 Pine St #43 San Francisco CA 94108

SHEEN, PORTIA YUNN-LING, retired physician; b. Republic of China, Jan. 13, 1919; came to U.S., 1988; d. Y. C. and A. Y. (Chow) Sheen; m. Kuo, 1944 (dec. 1970); children: William, Ida, Alexander, David, Mimi. MD, Nat. Med. Coll. Shanghai, 1943. Intern, then resident Cen. Hosp., Chungking, Szechuan, China, 1943; with Hong Kong Govt. Med. and Health Dept., 1948-76; med. supt. Kowloon Hosp., Kowloon, Hong Kong, 1948-63, Queen Elizabeth Hosp., Kowloon, Hong Kong, 1963-73, Med. and Health Hdqrs. and Health Ctr., Kowloon, Hong Kong, 1973-76, Yan Chai Hosp., New Territories, Hong Kong, 1976-87. Fellow Hong Kong Coll. Gen. Practitioners; mem. AAAS, British Med. Assn., Hong Kong Med. Assn., Hong Kong Pediatric Soc., N.Y. Acad. Sci. Methodist. Home: 1315 Walnut St Berkeley CA 94709-1408

SHEETS, EDWARD WENDELL, science administrator; b. Missoula, Mont., Oct. 7, 1949; s. Lowell Allen Sheets and Dorothy Marie (Craig) Trent; m. Ronda Skubi, Mar. 28, 1981; children: Andrew, Elizabeth. BA, Brown U., 1972; MA, U. Wash., 1975. Gen. mgr. Sta. WBRU-FM, Providence, 1970-71; rsch. asst. Inst. for Environ. Studies, U. Wash., Seattle, 1973-75, dir. energy info. project, 1975-77; spl. asst. to Senator Warren G. Magnuson, U.S. Senate, Washington, 1977-81; dir. Wash. State Energy Office, Olympia, 1981; exec. dir. N.W. Power Planning Coun., Portland, Oreg., 1981—; mem. state and regional planning panel NAS, Washington, 1988-89; bd. dirs. Am. Coun. for Energy Efficient Economy, Washington, 1989—; cons. on nat. energy strategy Dept. Energy, Washington. Mem. editorial bd. N.W. Energy News mag., 1981—; prodr. TV documentary Washington's Waters, 1975, Oil and Water: Do They Mix?, 1975 (Best of West award 1975). Chmn. energy and environ. com. Portland Ctrl. City Plan, 1988-89; chmn. budget rev. com. Portland Pub. Schs., 1989—. HEW grantee U. Wash., 1975-77. Home: 3055 NW Cumberland Rd Portland OR 97210 Office: NW Power Planning Coun 851 SW 6th Ave Ste 1100 Portland OR 97204

SHEETS, JOHN WESLEY, JR., research scientist; b. Jacksonville, Fla., Sept. 17, 1953; s. John Wesley and Alice Marie (Hagen) S.; m. Robin Adair Ritchie, June 27, 1987. BS in Zoology, U. Fla., 1975, MS in Materials Sci., 1978, PhD in Materials Sci., 1983. Grad. rsch. asst. U. Fla., Gainesville, 1976-78, grad. rsch. assoc., 1978-82; biomaterials engr. Intermedics Intraocular, Pasadena, Calif., 1982-84, mgr. biomaterials rsch., 1984-87; dir. rsch. Pharmacia Ophthalmics, Pasadena, 1987-88; dir. new product and process devel. IOLAB Corp. Johnson & Johnson, Claremont, Calif., 1988—; lectr. Calif. State Poly. U., Pomona, 1984; evaluator, chmn. subcom. Am. Nat. Standards Inst. Z80.7, Accreditation Bd. for Engring. and Tech. Contbr. articles to profl. jours. Mem. AAAS, Accreditation Bd. for Engring. and Technology, Am. Chem. Soc., Soc. Plastics Engrs., Soc. Biomaterials, Mensa, Sigma Xi, Tau Beta Pi, Alpha Sigma Mu. Home: 2241 Brigden Rd Pasadena CA 91104-3304 Office: IOLAB Corp A Johnson & Johnson Co 500 W Iolab Dr Claremont CA 91711-4881

SHEFFIELD, WILLIAM JENNINGS, former governor; b. Spokane, Wash., June 26, 1928; s. William J. and Hazel L. (Kraudelt) S.; m. Lorraine T. Demler. Student, Broadcast Engring. Sch., Chgo., 1949-51. With svc. dept. Sears, Roebuck & Co., Seattle, 1951-53; with sales and svc. depts. Sears, Roebuck & Co., Anchorage, 1953-60; owner, mgr. Sheffield Hotels, Anchorage, 1960-82; gov. State of Alaska, Juneau, 1982-86; bd. dirs. Commonwealth North, Martech USA. Regent Alaska Pacific U.; past chmn. Easter Seal Telethon, Anchorage; past pres. March of Dimes, Anchorage; mem. planning commn. City of Anchorage, 1960-63. With USAAF, 1946-49. Mem. Alaska C. of C. (past pres.), Alaska Visitors Assn. (past pres., VFW, Am. Legion, Rotary, Lions, Elks. Democrat. Presbyterian.

SHEFT, DOUGLAS JOEL, radiologist; b. Orange, N.J., Nov. 22, 1935; s. David K. and Lillian (Hodes) S.; m. Carole Sahn, Feb. 22, 1959; children: Lauren, Andrea, Mark. AB, Cornell U., 1957; MD, Harvard U., 1961. Diplomate Am. Bd. Radiology. Resident, diagnostic radiology Thomas Jefferson U. Hosp., Phila., 1962-65; chief, diagnostic radiology U.S. Army Letterman Gen. Hosp., San Francisco, 1965-66; chief, radiology 12th Evacuation Hosp., Cu Chi, Vietnam, 1966-67; asst. prof. radiology U. Calif., San Francisco, 1967-74, assoc. clin. prof., 1974-85, clin. prof. radiology, 1985—; attending radiologist St. Francis Meml. Hosp., San Francisco, 1971—, chmn. radiology dept., 1971-74, 80-83, chmn. dept. spl. svcs., 1984-87; cons. U.S. Pub. Health Svc. Hosp., San Francisco, 1970-72, San Francisco Gen. Hosp., 1969-80, VA Hosp., San Francisco, 1969-82. Contbg. author: Diagnostic Radiology: A Companion to Harrison's XNT Medicine, 1970, Computer Tomography, Ultrasound and X-Ray, 1980; contbg. editor: What's New in Cancer Care, 1973-83; contbr. articles to profl. jours. Mem. admissions com. Cornell U., Marin County, Calif., 1975—; mem. U.S. Com. on Mil. Curriculum, Washington, 1988-90. Capt. U.S. Army, 1965-67, Vietnam. Fellow Am. Cancer Soc., Phila., 1964. Fellow Am. Coll. Radiology (councilor 1978-84); mem. San Francisco Radiol. Soc. (pres. 1981-82), Calif. Radiol. Soc. (exec. coun. 1978-84), Radiol. Soc. North Am., AMA, Calif. Med. Assn., San Francisco Med. Assn. Office: St Francis Meml Hosp 900 Hyde St San Francisco CA 94109

SHEKHAR, STEPHEN S., obstetrician, gynecologist; b. New Delhi, India, Jan. 13, 1944; s. S.P. Jain and Shakuntala Mithal; m. Claudette Dorita, Jan. 6, 1978; children—Sasha, Stephen. M.B., B.S., Govt. Med. Coll., Punjabi U., Patiala, 1966. Came to U.S., 1972. Intern, Columbia U. Coll. Phys. and Surgeons-Roosevelt Hosp. N.Y.C., 1972-73; surgeon, Nat. Health Service U.K., 1966-72; resident in ob-gyn St. Clare's Hosp.-Margaret Hauge Maternity Hosp., N.Y.C. and N.J., 1973-76, Columbia U., Harlem Hosp., N.Y.C., 1976-77; practice medicine specializing in ob-gyn, North Hollywood, Calif., 1977—; mem. staff Los Angeles County-U. So. Calif. Med. Sch.; assoc. prof. clin. Ob-Gyn L.A. county U. So. Calif. Sch. Medicine. Fellow Am. Coll. Ob-Gyn, ACS, Los Angeles Soc. Ob-Gyn; mem. Calif. Med. Assn., Los Angeles County Med. Assn., AMA. Jain. Office: 12626 Riverside Dr Ste 403 Studio City CA 91607

SHEKTER, WILLIAM BERNARD, ophthalmologist; b. Jamaica, N.Y., Jan. 20, 1928; s. Adela Breakstone (Fisher) S. BA, Tufts U., 1947; MD, NYU, 1950. Diplomate Am. Bd. Ophthalmology. Chief dept. ophthalmology Kaiser-Permanente Med. Ctr., San Francisco, 1960-93; mem. exec. com. ophthalmology dept. Calif. Pacific Med. Ctr., San Francisco, 1980-93, assoc. prof. ophthalmology , co-chair. Bd. dirs. Baphr Found., San Francisco, 1991—, Lighthouse for the Blind & Visually Disabled, San Francisco, 1988—. Lt. comdr. USNR, 1955-60, PTO. Fellow Am. Acad. Ophthalmology, ACS; mem. Pacific Coast Oto-Ophthalmol. Soc. Office: Kaiser Permanente Med Offices 1635 Divisadero St San Francisco CA 94115-3000

SHELBY, THOMAS STANLEY, construction manager; b. Lafayette, Ind., Nov. 21, 1958; s. Charles Francis and Martha Jo (Bentley) S.; m. Linda Catherine Traczyk, Oct. 6, 1990. BS, Purdue U., 1981; MBA in Econs., Ariz. State U., 1989, MS in Decision Info. Systems, 1989. Sr. engr. Bechtel Power Corp., San Francisco, 1981-89; constrn. mgr. Kiewit Pacific Co., Santa Fe Springs, Calif., 1991—; project engr. Brinderson Corp., Irvine, Calif., 1990-91. Mem. Assn. Systems Mgmt., Assn. Gen. Contractors, Purdue Alumni Assn, Ariz. State Alumni Assn. Republican. Home: 26981 La Flores Mission Viejo CA 92691-2860

SHELDON, GARY, conductor, music director; b. Bay Shore, N.Y., Jan. 21, 1953. Student, Wash. U., St. Louis, 1972; BMus, Juilliard Sch. Music, 1974; diploma, Inst. Hautes Etudes Musicales, Montreux, Switzerland, 1975. Prin. condr. Opera Theater, Syracuse, 1976-77; asst. condr. Syracuse Symphony Orch., 1976-77, New Orleans Symphony Orch., 1977-80; assoc. condr. Columbus (Ohio) Symphony Orch., 1982-89. Composer: A Theme of Handel, 1984, Mississippi River (for documentary film at Miss. River Mus.), Memphis; rec. performances include Beauty and the Beast (with Frank DiGiacomo), 1977, Ballet Class with Karen Herbert, 1982. Recipient New Orleans Music and Drama Found. award, 1982, Third prize Rupert BBC Symphony Found., London, 1982. Mem. Am. Symphony Orch. League (youth orch. div. bd. dirs. 1980—). Office: Marin Symphony Orchestra Marin Center Aud 4340 Redwood Hwy San Rafael CA 94903

SHELDON, MARK SCOTT, research engineer; b. Orange, Calif., May 19, 1959; s. Howard Lezurn and Vida Louise (Winegar) S.; m. Marti Reisman, Aug. 8, 1986. BS in Engring. and Applied Sci., Calif. Inst. Tech., 1981; MSME, Cornell U., 1985. Rsch. engr. Energy and Environ. Rsch. Corp., Irvine, Calif., 1985-91, sr. rsch. engr., 1991—. Mem. ASME (assoc.). Mem. Reorganized LDS Ch. Office: Energy and Environ Rsch Corp 18 Mason Irvine CA 92718-2798

SHELDON, MARTI REISMAN, software engineer; b. Miami, Fla., Sept. 28, 1961; d. Murray and Eleanor (Orton) Reisman; m. Mark Scott Sheldon, Aug. 8, 1986. BS in Computer Sci., Cornell U., 1983; MS in Computer Sci., UCLA, 1989. Sr. staff engr. Hughes Aircraft Co., L.A., 1981—. Mem. IEEE, Assn. Computer Machinery, Tau Beta Pi, Alpha Phi Omega. Democrat. Jewish. Office: Hughes Aircraft Co PO Box 92919 S64/C410 Los Angeles CA 90009

SHELDON, THOMAS ANDREW, radio personality; b. Grand Junction, Colo., May 21, 1964; s. Richard Hinkle and Beatrice Ann (Turner) S.; m. Lori Ann Suminski, Apr. 20, 1991. Student, Mesa State Coll., 1982-84. Air personality Jan-di Broadcasting, Fruita, Colo., 1984-86; music dir. Jan-di

Broadcasting, Grand Junction, Colo., 1986-93; program dir. KOOL 107.9 FM, Grand Junction, 1993—. Author: Music Notes, 1990—. Celebrity auctioneer Ptnrs. of Mesa County, Grand Junction, 1989-92. Mem. Acad. Country Music. Office: KBKL-FM 315 Kennedy Grand Junction CO 81501

SHELDON, WARREN CORYDON, school principal; b. Oakland, Calif., June 9, 1936; s. Ward Corydon and Azelle (Barton) S.; m. Carolyn Jean Williams, Apr. 9, 1960; children: Carren, Elizabeth, Martha. BA in Music, San Jose State, 1958, MA in Sch. Adminstrn., 1965. Classroom tchr. Vacaville (Calif.) Union Sch. Dist., 1958-66; prin. Elmira (Calif.) Sch., 1966-69, Monte Vista Sch., Vacaville, 1969-71, Alamo Sch., Vacaville, 1971-85, Sierra Vista Sch., Vacaville, 1985—; participant Inst. Prin. and Sch. Improvement, Harvard U., Cambridge, Mass., 1985. Author: History of Grace Church 1867-1992, 1992. Mem. Native Sons of the Golden West. Mem. ASCD, Scottish Rite Bodies (Oakland, Calif.), Masons (Master Suisun lodge no. 55 1982, Hiram award 1992, Educator of Yr. 1990, Mason of Yr. 1985). Republican. Episcopalian. Home: Box 433 Vacaville CA 95696 Office: Sierra Vista Sch 301 Bel Air Dr Vacaville CA 95687

SHELL, ART, professional football coach; b. Charleston, S.C.; m. Janice Shell; 2 children. Student, Md. State Coll. Player L.A. Raiders, 1968-83, coach, 1983-89, head coach, 1989—. Inducted into Pro Football Hall of Fame, 1989; recipient, Jackie Robinson Award for Athletics (Ebony mag.), 1990; named N.F.L. Coach of Yr., 1991. Office: Los Angeles Raiders 332 Center St El Segundo CA 90245-4098*

SHELL, DEBRA MAYHEW, clinical laboratory scientist; b. Lincoln, Nebr., Dec. 7, 1949; d. Donald Edward and Helene Caroline (Ebberson) Mayhew; m. James Warren French, Dec. 13, 1969 (div. Nov. 1980); children: Mark James, Ryan Lee; m. David Murphy Shell, May 11, 1990. BS in Microbiology, Idaho State U., 1977, BS in Med. Tech., 1978. Cert. med. technologist and Specialist in Microbiology, Am. Soc. Clin. Pathologist; cert. clin. lab. scientist and clin. lab. dir. Nat. Cert. Agy. for Med. Lab. Personnel. Clin. chemistry staff technologist Bannock Regional Med. Ctr. Lab., Pocatello, Idaho, 1978-79, 82-85, clin. microbiology staff technologist, 1979-82, supr. clin. microbiology, 1985—, mem. Coll. Am. Pathologists inspection team, 1990, 92; mem. coordinating com. Intermountain States Seminar, 1985—, chmn., 1992-93, exhibits chmn. Idaho planning com., 1991-92; presenter in field. Div. commr. Gate City Youth Soccer League, Pocatello, 1983; mem. parent adv. coun. Highland High Sch., Pocatello, 1985-89, treas. Band Boosters, 1987-88; mem. Adopt-A-Hwy. Team, Pocatello, 1991-93. Named Med. Technologist of Yr., Intermountain States Seminar, 1983, 92. Mem. Am. Soc. for Med. Tech. (bd. dirs. region VIII 1989—, Omicron Sigma award 1981-93), Idaho Soc. for Med. Tech. (bd. dirs. 1987-93, Mem. of Yr. award 1992), Pyramid Club, Alpha Mu Tau. Home: 5812 Buckskin Rd Pocatello ID 83201 Office: Bannock Regional Med Ctr Memorial Dr Pocatello ID 83201

SHELLEY, MARLIN CARL, manufacturing executive; b. American Fork, Utah, May 30, 1948; s. Carl Thomas and Edna (Ryskamp) S.; m. Kathryn Rae Johnson, Aug. 5, 1975. BEE, U. Utah, 1972, M of Engrin. Adminstrn., 1974, MBA, 1976. Elec. engr. UNIVAC (name now UNISYS), Salt Lake City, 1972-78; v.p. engring. Micro Peripherals Inc., Salt Lake City, 1978-85; pres. Cirris Systems Corp., Salt Lake City, 1985—. Patentee cable tester. Mem. ASTD, Am. Soc. Quality Control. Office: Cirris Systems Corp 1991 W Parkway Blvd Salt Lake City UT 84119-2026

SHELTON, CAROLYN ZANDRA, small business owner; b. Inglewood, Calif., Aug. 26, 1956; d. Joe and Faye Roth; m. James Loyd Shelton, Oct. 27, 1990. BS, U. Calif., Davis, 1979. Freelance environ. writer and photographer, Denver, 1986-88; interpretive planner Bur. Land Mgmt., Oreg., Colo., Calif., 1976-90; interpretive planner, cons. Raven Comms., Sultan, Wash., 1990—. Contbr. over 60 articles on environ. issues and investigative journalism to nat. mags. Mem. Outdoor Writers Assn. Am., Nat. Assn. for Interpretation, N.W. Outdoor Writers Assn., Fedn. Flyfishers (officer Oreg. and Wash), Trout Unltd. (officer Oreg. and Wash.). Home and Office: 13416 Kellogg Lake Rd Sultan WA 98294

SHELTON, CHARLITA LUCILLE, college placement director; b. Chgo., Oct. 5, 1958; d. James Wesley and Mary Edna (Davis) S. BS in Communications, Western Mich. U., 1980; postgrad., Nat. U., 1993—. Mgr., supr. Inst. for Def. Analyses, Alexandria, Va., 1986-87; sales rep. United Bus. Machines, Lorton, Va., 1987-88; field admissions rep. Nat. Tech. Schs., San Diego, 1989; account exec. Metromedia ITT, San Diego, 1990—; placement dir. Kelsey Jenney Bus. Coll., San Diego. Served with USMC, 1982-86. Mem. Met. Bus. Assn., Exec. Women Internat., San Diego Soc. for Human Resource Mgmt., Non-Commd. Officers Assn., Delta Sigma Theta. Democrat. Home: 7560 Charmant Dr Apt 1528 San Diego CA 92122-5060 Office: Kelsey Jenney Bus Coll 201 A St San Diego CA 92101-4003

SHELTON, JOEL EDWARD, clinical psychologist; b. Havre, Mont., Feb. 7, 1928; s. John Granvil and Roselma Fahy (Ervin) S.; m. Maybelle Platzek, Dec. 17, 1945; 1 child, Sophia. AB, Chico (Calif.) State Coll., 1951; MA, Ohio State U., 1958, PhD, 1960. Psychologist Sutter County Schs., Yuba City, Calif., 1952-53; tchr., vice prin. Lassen View Sch., Los Molinos, Calif., 1953-55; tchr. S.W. Licking Schs., Pataskala, Ohio, 1955-56; child psychologist Franklin Village, Grove City, Ohio, 1957; clin. psychologist Marion (Ohio) Health Clinic, 1958; intern Children's Mental Health Ctr., Columbus, Ohio, 1958-59; acting chief research psychologist Children's Psychiat. Hosp., Columbus, 1959-60; cons. to supt. schs. Sacramento County, Calif., 1960-63; mem. faculty Sacramento State Coll., 1961-69; clin. psychologist DeWitt State Hosp., Auburn, Calif., 1965; exec. dir. Children's Ctr. Sacramento, Citrus Heights, Calif., 1963-70, Gold Bar Ranch, Garden Valley, Calif., 1964-72; clin. psychologist El Dorado County Mental Health Ctr., Placerville, Calif., 1968-70, Butte County Mental Health Dept., Oroville, Chico, Calif., 1970—; dir. dept. consultation, edn. and community services Butte County Mental Health Ctr., Chico, 1974-85, outpatient supr., 1985-86; MIS cons., 1986—; mgmt. cons., 1972—; advisor to pres. Protaca Industries, Chico, 1974-80; exec. sec. Protaca Agrl. Rsch., 1974-80; small bus. cons., 1983—; cons. on coll. scholarships and funding, 1991-92. Mem. APA, Western Psychol. Assn. Home: 1845 Veatch St Oroville CA 95965-4742 Office: Butte County Mental Health 18C County Center Dr Oroville CA 95965-3317

SHELTON, ROBERT CHARLES, electronics engineer; b. L.A., July 31, 1934; s. Weir Mitchell and Martalena (Scavarda); BSEE, Calif. State Poly. U., 1961; divorced; 1 son, Kevin Lyle. Ops. mgr. Halcyon, Palo Alto, Calif., 1971-74; mfg. mgr. Programmed Power, Menlo Park, Calif., 1974-78; pres. Shelton Electronics, Menlo Park, 1976—. Bd. dirs. Herbert Hoover Boys Club, Menlo Park; vol. Peninsula Meml. Blood Bank, St. Anthony Padua Dining Rm. Served with USN, 1952-56. Mem. IEEE, Profl. and Tech. Cons. Assn. Clubs: Elks (chmn. Palo Alto public relations); Rotary (bd. dirs., pres. 1981-82) (Menlo Park). Roman Catholic. Rsch. and publs. in telecommunication microwave and high energy physics, small computer systems and data communications; patentee various cryogenic and computer devices. Address: PO Box 2573 Menlo Park CA 94026 Office: 1259-351 El Camino Real Menlo Park CA 94025

SHEN, HSIEH WEN, civil engineer, consultant, educator; b. Peking, China, July 13, 1931; s. Tsung Lien and Bick Men (Jeme) S.; m. Clare Tseng, Oct. 20, 1956; children—Eveline, Anthony. B.S., U. Mich., 1953, M.S., 1954; Ph.D., U. Calif.-Berkeley, 1961. Hydraulic engr. Harza Engring. Co., Chgo., 1961-63; mem. faculty Colo. State U., Ft. Collins, 1964-86; prof. civil engring. U. Calif., Berkeley, 1986—; cons. World Bank, UN, Harza, Stone & Webster, U.S. Army C.E. Author, editor: River Mechanics 1971; Sedimentation, 1973; Modeling of Rivers, 1979. Recipient AGU Horton award, 1976, Guggenheim Found. fellow, 1974. Mem. Internat. Assn. Hydraulic Research (pres. fluvial hydraulics 1984-86), ASCE (Freeman scholar 1966, chmn. probability approach 1983-84). Office: U Calif 412 O'Brien Hall Berkeley CA 94720

SHEN, JUN, scientist; b. Wuhan, Hubei, People's Republic of China, Jan. 26, 1959; came to U.S., 1982; s. Yi Li Shen and Guo Ying Liu; m. Jie Si, July 27, 1988. BS, South China Inst. Tech., Guangzhou, 1982; MS, Tex. Tech U., 1984; PhD, U. Notre Dame, 1990. Sr. staff scientist Motorola Inc., Tempe, Ariz., 1990—; grad. teaching, rsch. asst. Tex. Tech U., Lubbock, 1982-84; grad. rsch. asst. U. Notre Dame, Ind., 1984-90. contbr. numerous articles to profl. jours. Mem. IEEE, Am. Phys. Soc. Office: Motorola Inc 2100 E Elliot Rd # EL508 Tempe AZ 85284-1801

SHEN, MASON MING-SUN, pain and stress management center administrator; b. Shanghai, Jiang Su, China, Mar. 30, 1945; came to U.S., 1969; s. John Kaung-Hao and Mai-Chu (Sun) S.; m. Nancy Hsia-Hsian Shieh, Aug. 7, 1976; children: Teresa Tao-Yee, Darren Tao-Ru. BS in Chemistry, Taiwan Normal U., 1963-67; MS in Chemistry, S.D. State U., 1971; PhD in Biochemistry, Cornell U., 1977; MS in Chinese Medicine, China Acad., Taipei, Taiwan, 1982; OMD, San Francisco Coll Acupuncture, 1984. Diplomate Nat. Commn. for Cert. of Accupuncturists; lic. acupuncturist. Rsch. assoc. Lawrence Livermore (Calif.) Lab., 1979-80; assoc. prof. Nat. Def. Med. Coll., Taipei, 1980-82; prof. Inst. of Chinese Medicine China Acad., Taipei, 1981-82, San Francisco Coll. Acupuncture, 1983-85; chief acupuncturist Acupuncture Ctr. of Livermore, Calif., 1982-93; prof. Acad. Chinese Culture & Health Scis., Oakland, Calif., 1985-86; chief acupuncturist Acupuncture Ctr. of Danville, Calif., 1985-89; dir. Pain & Stress Mgmt. Ctr., Danville, Calif., 1989-90; chmn. adminstrn. subcom., 1991-92, acupuncture com. State of Calif., 1988-92. Contbr. articles to profl. jours. Rep. Rep. Party, Danville, 1988—; bd. dirs. Asian Rep. Assembly, 1989—. 2d lt. Rep. of China Army, 1966-69. Recipient Nat. Rsch. Svc. award NIH, 1977. Mem. AAAS, N.Y. Acad. Sci., Calif. Cert. Acupuncturists Assn. (bd. dirs. 1984-88, pres. 1984-85), Acupuncture Assn. Am. (bd. dirs. 1986-90, v.p. 1987-89), Am. Assn. Acupuncture and Oriental Medicine (bd. dirs. 1987-92, pres. 1989-90), Nat. Acupuncture Detoxification Assn. (cons. 1987—), Presdl. Round Table (presdl. adv. com.), Hong Kong and Kowloon Chinese Med. Assn. (hon. life pres. 1985). Republican. Home: 3240 Touriga Dr Pleasanton CA 94566-6966 Office: Pain and Stress Mgmt Ctr 185 Front Ste 207 Danville CA 94526-3323

SHEN, NELSON MU-CHING, fiber optics communications scientist; b. Taiwan, Sept. 2, 1946; came to U.S., 1971; s. Mao-Chang and Ching (Chang) S.; m. Jane Chu; children: Helen Diana, Basil Francis. BS in Physics, Chung Yuan Christian U., Taiwan, 1969; MS in Physics, North Western State U., La., 1972; PhD in Physics, U. Tex., Dallas, 1977. Rsch. assoc. U. So. Calif., L.A., 1977-79; chief scientist, dir. techs. Kaptron corp., Palo Alto, Calif., 1979-81; sr. engr. GTE Corp., Mountain View, Calif., 1981-82; sr. scientist Raychem Corp., Menlo Park, Calif., 1982—. Patentee in fiber optics; contbr. papers to profl. publs. Chmn. bd. trustee, Canaan Ch., Mountain View, 1986—. Mem. Optical Soc. Am., Internat. Soc. for Optical Engring. Home: 3138 Louis Rd Palo Alto CA 94303-3954 Office: Raychem Corp 181 Constitution Dr Menlo Park CA 94025-1181

SHEN, SAMUEL SHANPU, mathematics educator; b. Huoshan, Anhui, China, Aug. 12, 1960; came to U.S., 1983; BS, East China Engring. Inst., 1982; MA, U. Wis., 1985, PhD, 1987. Vis. asst. prof. math. Tex. A&M U., College Station, 1987-89; asst. prof. math. U. Sask., Saskatoon, 1989-91; asst. prof. math. U. Alta., Edmonton, 1991-93, assoc. prof. math., 1993—. Office: U Alta Math Dept, Edmonton, AB Canada T6G 2G1

SHEN, YUEN-RON, physics educator; b. Shanghai, China, Mar. 25, 1935; came to U.S.,; BS, Nat. Taiwan U., 1956; MS, Stanford U., 1959; PhD, Harvard U., 1963. Rsch. asst. Hewlett-Packard Co., Palo Alto, Calif., 1959; rsch. fellow Harvard U., Cambridge, Mass., 1963-64; asst. prof. U. Calif., Berkeley, 1964-67, assoc. prof., 1967-70, full prof., 1970—; prin. investigator Lawrence Berkeley Lab., 1964—. Author: The Principles of Nonlinear Optics, 1984. Sloan fellow, 1966-68; recipient Guggenheim Found. fellowship, 1972-73, Charles Hard Townes award, 1986, Arthur L. Schawlow prize Am. Phys. Soc., 1992, Alexander von Humboldt award, 1984. Fellow Am. Phys. Soc., Optical Soc. Am.; mem. Am. Acad. Arts and Scis., Academic Sinica. Office: U Calif Berkeley Dept Physics Berkeley CA 94720

SHEP, ROBERT LEE, editor, publisher, textile book researcher; b. Los Angeles, Feb. 27, 1933; s. Milton and Ruth (Miller) Polen S. B.A., U. Calif.-Berkeley, 1955; student Royal Acad. Dramatic Art, London, 1956; B.Fgn. Trade, Am. Inst. Fgn. Trade, 1960. Asst. area mgr. fgn. dept. Max Factor, Hollywood, Calif., 1960-65; editor, pub. The Textile Booklist, Lopez Island, Wash., 1980-84; free-lance writer, book reviewer, library appraiser, book repairer. Author: Cleaning and Repairing Books, 1980, Cleaning and Care for Books, 1983, Bhutan - Fibre Forum, 1984; co-author: (annotated edit.) The Costume or Annals of Fashion, 1986, Dress and Cloak Cutter: Womens Costume 1877-1882, 1987; editor: The Handbook of Practical Cutting, 2d rev. edit., 1986; pub. Ladies' Guide to Needle Work, 1986, Edwardian Ladies' Tailoring, 1990. Art of Cutting and History of English Costume, 1987; editor, pub. Tailoring of the Belle Epoque, 1991, Late Georgian Costume, 1991, Civil War Cooking, 1992, Art in Dress, 1993, Minister's Complete Guide to Practical Cutting, 1993, Freaks of Fashion, 1993; pub. Civil War Era Etiquette, 1988, Ladies Self Instr., 1988; mem. editorial rev. bd. The Cutter's Rsch. Jour. Bd. dirs AIDS Care and Edn. Svcs., Pacific Textiles. Mem. Costume Soc. (London), Costume Soc. Am. (bd. dirs. 1985-87), Costume Soc. Ont., Mendocino County HIV Consortium (mem. sterring com.), Australian Costume and Textile Soc., U.S. Inst. Theatre Tech. Home: PO Box 668 Mendocino CA 95460-0668

SHEPARD, EARL ALDEN, retired government official; b. Aurora, Ill., Sept. 30, 1932; s. Ralph George and Marcia Louise (Phelps) S.; m. Carolyn Mae Borman, Sept. 1, 1959; 1 son, Ralph Lyle. AS magna cum laude in Bus. Adminstrn., Southeastern U., 1967, BSBA magna cum laude, 1969; MBA, U. Chgo., 1974. Chief program budget div. U.S. Army Munitions Command., Joliet, Ill., 1971-73; comptr., dir. adminstrn. U.S. Navy Pub. Works Ctr., Gt. Lakes, Ill., 1973-77; dep. comptr. U.S. Army Electronics Command/U.S. Army Communications Electronics Materiel Readiness Command, Ft. Monmouth, N.J., 1977-79; dir. resource mgmt., comptr., dir. programs U.S. Army, White Sands Missile Range, N.Mex., 1979-92; bd. dirs. 1st Nat. Bank of Dona Ana County, 1987—; mem. adv. com. Rio Grande Bancshares/First Nat. Bank of Dona Ana County, 1983-84. Bd. govs., Southeastern Univ. Ednl. Found., 1969-71; chmn. fin. com. No. Va. Assn. for Children with Learning Disabilities, 1966-67, treas., 1968-70; pres. West Long Branch (N.J.) Sports Assn., 1979. Fed. and local govt. employee scholar, 1967, Ammunition Procurement Supply Agy. fellow, 1974. Republican. Home: 2712 Topley Ave Las Cruces NM 88005

SHEPARD, KYLE MARK, aerospace engineer; b. Abilene, Tex., Mar. 4, 1963; s. John Courtland and Carol S. BS in Aero. Engring., Calif. Poly. State U., San Luis Obispo, 1988. Design engr. Lockeed Missile & Space Co., Sunnyvale, Calif., 1987-88; lead engr. advanced propulsion systems, program coord. nuclear propulsion program, 1989-92; mem. design group, sr. engr. launch vehicle engring. Gen. Dynamics Space Systems, San Diego, 1992—. Mem. AIAA (chmn. nuclear thermal propulsion tech. com., coauthor space propulsion analysis and design), Nat. Space Soc., Delta Sigma Phi. Republican. Home: 1491 S Orange Ave El Cajon CA 92020-7417 Office: Gen Dynamics Space Systems Div PO Box 85990 San Diego CA 92186-5990

SHEPARD, MARIDEAN MANSFIELD (MARI), data processing executive, advocate for rights for the disabled; b. Enid, Okla., Jan. 20, 1952; d. Howard Ernest and Nadine (Miller) Mansfield; m. Kent Lee Shepard, June 25, 1977. Student, Ventura Coll., 1969-72, Mission Coll., 1979-81, 93, Learning Tree U., 1990-92. Spl. edn. aide, Braille transcriber, Spanish interpreter Hueneme Sch. Dist., Port Hueneme, Calif., 1970-76; entertainer, musician, 1972-87; spl. edn. tchr. Found. for Jr. Blind, L.A., 1977-78; music tchr. Pinecrest Sch., Northridge, Calif., 1978-79; libr./textbook clk. Burbank (Calif.) Sch. Dist., 1980-81; receptionist, sec. Van Nuys (Calif.) Coll. Bus., 1981-84; bookkeeper, computer operator, sec. Pacific Coast Tech. Inst., Van Nuys, 1984-85; sec. tng. dept., computer operator, transcriber Braille, interpreter sign lang. Internat. Guiding Eyes, Sylmar, Calif., 1985-86; computer operator, bookkeeper Engelhard Corp., Sylmar, 1989—; founder, disABILITIES Info. Svcs., at Quantum, 1986, at Am. OnLine, 1990, at GEnie, 1989—; producer, host disABILITIES Roundtable and Equal Access Cafe BBS, 1990—; speaker World Inst. on Disabilities, Oakland, Calif., 1990, Abilities Expo, Anaheim, 1992, Calif. State U. Northridge Conf. Tech. and Disabilities, 1993; session chair Accessing Tech. Through Online Svcs., ADA Conf., Washington, 1993. Co-author: (computer database program) Johns Hopkins Technology Search Regional Finals, 1991. Vol. voter registration LWV, Ventura County, Calif., 1978; vol. tchr. Pleasant Valley Convalescent Hosp., Port Hueneme, 1971; vol. transcriber Ventura County Braille Transcribers Assn., 1963-76; volunteer relay/interpreter Greater L.A. Coun. on Deafness, Van Nuys, 1980-82; vol. writer, decorator Ventura County USO, Oxnard, 1969-71; Sunday sch. tchr. 1st Presbyn. Ch., Oxnard, 1973-74. Scholar Ventura County Bus. and Profl. Women, 1973; recipient 1st place mixed media Ventura County Fair, 1970. Office: disABILITIES Info Svc 9840 Stanwin Ave Arleta CA 91331-5303

SHEPARD, ROBERT CARLTON, English language educator; b. Akron, Ohio, Dec. 20, 1933; s. Robert and Mildred Lucille (Stewart) S.; m. Marjorie Alma Mackey, June 9, 1956; children: Robert Lincoln, Donald Ward. BA, U. Oreg., 1970, MA, 1971; postgrad., England, 1979, 1991. Prof. English Southwestern Oreg. Community Coll., Coos Bay, 1971—, chair divsn. English, 1976-78; liaison Oreg. com. for Humanities, 1985-86; judge statewide writing contests Nat. Coun. Tchrs. English, Urbana, Ill, 1987-88; founder Willamette Valley Vineyards, Turner, Oreg., 1991. Author, photographer, producer: (multi-image show) Christmas Fiestas of Oaxaca (Mexico), 1985. With USMCR, 1954-58. Grad. Teaching fellow U. Oreg., 1970-71. Democrat. Office: Southwestern Oreg C C 1988 Newmark Ave Coos Bay OR 97420-2911

SHEPHERD, GREGG REID, school counselor; b. Phila., May 9, 1953; s. Robert D. and Thelma Marie (Maddock) S.; m. Teresa Franklin, Dec. 1, 1954; children: Mario, Venessa. BS in Edn., Millersville State U., 1975; postgrad., Temple U., 1976; MS in Counseling, Human Rels., Villanova U., 1980; postgrad., Calif. Inst. Integral Studies, 1984-86. Cert. spl. edn. tchr., Ariz. Asst. dir. aquatics Boy Scouts Am., Lancaster County, Pa., 1975; tchr. manual arts Delta Sch., Phila., 1975-76, classrm. tchr., 1976-77; testment, evaluator Career Devel. and Tng. Ctr., Upland, Pa., 1979, mgr. learning, 1979-80; therapist outdoor rsch. Inst. for Outdoor Awareness, Swarthmore, Pa., 1981; sch. counselor Dilkon (Ariz.) Boarding Sch., Navajo Nation, 1982-87; substance abuse prevention specialist Office of Indian Edn. Programs, Navajo Nation, 1987-91; sch. counselor Seba Dalkai Sch., Teesto, Ariz., 1991—; grant writer, cons. Tsezhintah Community Improvement and Devel. Office, Teesto, 1991—; dir., founder Leadership Tng. and Counseling Ctr., Teesto, 1991—. Prodn. asst. Citizens Against Ruining Our Environ. video (Best Documentary award Native Am. Film Festival 1989). Vol. counselor Phila. Dept. Adult Edn., 1976-77, Berkeley (Calif.) Alcohol and Drug Svcs., 1985-86; scout leader Boy Scouts Am., Dilkon, 1982-83; founder, treas. Citizens Against Ruining Our Environ, Dilkon, 1988—; adult sponsor Teesto Organized Youth, 1992—. Mem. Ariz. Counselor's Assn., Teesto Navajo Housing Authority Resident Housing Orgn. (v.p. 1992—), Kappa Delta Pi. Home: Seba Dalkai Sch Star Rte # 1 Winslow AZ 86047 Office: PO Box 7236 Teesto CPU Winslow AZ 86047

SHEPHERD, JANET EILEEN, physician; b. Cin., May 13, 1950; d. Harold Edward and Anna Mary (Huber) S.; m. Richard Anthony Behler, Jan. 29, 1982. BS summa cum laude, U. Dayton, 1971; MD, Northwestern U., Chgo., 1975. Diplomate Am. Bd. Ob-Gyn., Nat. Bd. Med. Examiners. Resident in ob-gyn. U. Cin., 1975-79; pvt. practice Cin., 1979-85; fellowship in reproductive endocrinology U. South Ala., Mobile, 1985-86; staff gynecologist Penny Wise Budoff Women's Med. Ctr., Bethpage, N.Y., 1986-87, Boulder Valley Women's Health Ctr., 1988-91; clin. instr. Dept. Ob-Gyn., U. Cin., 1980-85; instr. Dept. Ob-Gyn., U. South Ala., Mobile, 1985-86; clin. asst. prof. Dept. Ob-Gyn., SUNY, Stony Brook, 1986-87; contract ob-gyn. Boulder Maternity Program, Rocky Mountain Planned Parenthood, Longmont, Colo., 1992—; course dir. Nat. conf. for Women Physicians, Breckenridge, Colo., 1991; speaker in field. Editor Balance, 1990-91; editorial bd. Athena, Relax, 1992—; contbr. articles to profl. pubs. Co-chair Alice Paul Ho., Battered Women's Shelter, Cin., 1984-85, bd. dirs. 1982-85, Boulder Valley Women's Health Ctr., 1991-92, Cin. Husband-Coached Natural Childbirth Assn., Cin., 1981-85. Fellow Am. Coll. Ob-Gyn. Home: 2020 B 5th St Boulder CO 80302

SHEPHERD, KAREN, congresswoman; b. Silver City, N.Mex., July 5, 1940; m. Vincent P. Shepherd. BA, U. Utah, 1962; MA, Brigham Young U., 1963. Former mem Utah Senate; mem 103rd Congress from 2nd Utah dist., Washington, D.C., 1993—. Recipient Women in Bus. award U.S. Small Bus. Assn. Home: 1261 2nd Ave Salt Lake City UT 84103 Office: US Ho Reps 414 Cannon Washington DC 20515-4402

SHEPHERD, PAUL H., elementary school educator; b. Salt Lake City, Sept. 6, 1955; s. Richard Lawrence and Janis (Hoskings) S.; m. Marlene Wade, Aug. 31, 1978; children: Janice, Faith, Matthew, Andrew, Luke. BS in Elem. Edn., U. Utah, 1981, MEd, 1985. Cert. elem. tchr., Utah. Printer Transamerica Film Svc., Salt Lake City, 1978-81; tchr. Granite Sch. Dist., Salt Lake City, 1981—; pres. Granite Fedn. Tchrs., 1985-87, treas., 1990-92. Bishop LDS Ch., West Jordan, Utah, 1988; mem. Oquivrh Shadows Community Coun., West Jordan, 1987; chmn. rels. com. Boy Scouts Am., 1972—. Recipient Outstanding Tchr. award Excel Found., 1985, Elem. Tchr. of Yr. award Utah Fedn. Tchrs., 1991. Mem. ASCD, Utah Assn Gifted Children. Democrat. Home and Office: 6644 S 5095 W West Jordan UT 84084

SHEPHERD, R. F., retired bishop; b. July 15, 1926; s. Herbert George and Muriel (Grant) S.; m. Ann Alayne Dundas, 1952; 6 children. BA with honors, U. B.C., 1948; postgrad., King's Coll., London; DD (hon.), St. John's Coll., Winnipeg, 1988. Curate St. Stephen's, London, 1952-57; rector St. Paul's, Glanford, Ont., 1957-59, All Sts., Winnipeg, 1959-65; dean, rector All Sts. Cathedral, Edmonton, Alta., 1965-69, Christ Ch. Cathedral, Montreal, 1970-83; rector St. Matthias, Victoria, B.C., 1983-84; Anglican Bishop of B.C., 1985-92. Fellow Coll. of Preachers. Home: RR4 Fairway C-74 Granges, Salt Spring Island, BC Canada VOS IEO

SHEPHERD, THOMAS IRVIN, mining specialist, electrical engineer; b. Riverton, Wyo., Feb. 11, 1953; s. Marion Thomas and Berethe Patricia (Bergstrom) S.; m. Carol Ann Fuoss, Aug. 12, 1978; children: Sara Elaine, Andrew Thomas. BSEE, U. Wyo., 1976. With elec. maintenance dept. AMAX Coal Co./Belle Ayr Mine, Gillette, Wyo., 1976-79, AMAX Coal Co./Eagle Butte Mine, Gillette, 1979-80; elec. engr. scales dept. We. div. AMAX Coal Co., Gillette, 1980-89, dryer supr., 1989—. Co-inventor electronic coupled-in-motion railroad track scale. Sponsor Luth. Youth Fellowship, Gillette, 1977; den leader Boy Scouts Am., Gillette, 1990-92, asst. scout master, 1992—; coach Little League Baseball, Gillette, 1990-92. Mem. IEEE, Indsl. Computing Soc., Luth. Layman's League, Instrument Soc. Am. Republican. Home: 1217 Shipwheel Ln Gillette WY 82716-4828 Office: AMAX Coal Co Belle Ayr Mine PO Box 3005 Gillette WY 82717-3005

SHEPHERD, WILLIAM C., pharmaceutical company executive; b. 1939. With Allergan Inc., Irvine, Calif., 1964—, pres., chief oper. officer, 1984—, pres., CEO, 1992—, bd. dirs. Office: Allergan Inc PO Box 19534 2525 Dupont Dr Irvine CA 92715-1599

SHEPIC, JOHN ANTHONY, mechanical metallurgist, consultant; b. Pueblo, Colo., Dec. 5, 1948; s. John and Ann Frances (Panion) S.; m. Charlotte L. Thomas, Sept. 20, 1980; 1 child, Samuel. BS, Colo. Sch. of Mines, 1971. Staff engr. Martin Marietta, Denver, 1971-91; consulting metallurgist Lakewood, Colo., 1991—. Recipient New Tech. award NASA, 1977, Tech. Innovator award, 1986. Mem. Am. Soc. Metals. Roman Catholic. Home and Office: John Shepic Co 14031 W Exposition Dr Lakewood CO 80228

SHEPPARD, HOWARD REECE, accountant; b. Monmouth, Ill., Mar. 1, 1926; s. Loren Ernest and Ruby Pearl (Magee) S.; m. Mary Kathryn Hofstetter, June 8, 1951 (div.); children: Stephen, Peter, Jean Elizabeth; m. Maxine Dolores Johnson, Nov. 28, 1974. BSBA, Northwestern U., Evanston, Ill., 1946. CPA, Calif. Chief cost acct. Sunkist Growers Plant, Corona, Calif., 1946-52; fiscal officer U.S. Guided Missile Test Ctr., Pt. Mugu, Calif., 1952-54; internal auditor Sunkist Growers Plant, Corona, Calif., 1954-58; auditor Eadie & Payne CPAs, San Bernardino, Calif., 1958-61; pvt. practice Corona, 1961-63, 87—; ptnr. Sheppard, Reynolds & Sholl, Corona, 1963-85, Sheppard, Reynolds & Green, Corona, 1985-87; faculty expert Hastings Law Sch., U. Calif., San Francisco, 1986—; lectr. Dept. Water and Power, L.A., 1986. Author: Litigation Services Resource Directory, 1989, 3rd rev. edit., 1993; co-author: Litigation Services Handbook, 1990. Lt. USN. Mem. AICPA, Calif. Soc. CPAs, Assn. Govt. Accts., Far Western chpt. Nat. Soc. Accts. for Coops., Am. Arbitration Assn. (panel of arbitrators), Kiwanis, Corona C. of C. (bd. dirs.). Home: 6370 Percival Dr Riverside CA 92506-5139 Office: Howard Reece Sheppard 675 S Main St Corona CA 91720-3402

SHEPPARD, JACK W., retired air force officer; b. Parkersburg, W.Va., Aug. 8, 1931; s. James Lee and Audrey Irene (Heiney) S.; m. Norma Ann Stutler, Sept. 4, 1953; children—Bradley, Gregory. B.A.C., U. Akron, Ohio, 1955; M.A. in Pub. Adminstrn., George Washington U., 1965. Commd. lt. U.S. Air Force, 1955, advanced through grades to maj. gen.; vice comdr. 60 Mil. Airlift Wing, USAF, Travis AFB, Calif., 1977-79; comdr. 1606 Air Base Wing, USAF, Kirtland AFB, N.Mex., 1979-81; dir. internat. staff Inter Am. Def. Bd., USAF, Washington, 1981-82; dep. chief staff for personnel USAF Mil. Airlift Command, Scott AFB, Ill., 1982-83, chief of staff, 1983-85; comdr. Twenty First Air Force, McGuire AFB, N.J., 1985-87; asst. dep. chief staff programs and resources Hdqrs. USAF, Washington, 1987-88, ret., 1988. Mem. Order of Daedalians, Air Force Assn., Airlift Assn., Theta Chi. Presbyterian. Home: PO Box 908 21 Beaver Ln Cedar Crest NM 87008

SHEPPARD, ROGER DAVIES, design engineer; b. Oakland, Calif., Oct. 30, 1949; s. Robert Tyler and Barbara Huntoon (Davies) S.; m. Sandra Elaine Raynal, Feb. 27, 1987; 1 child, Katrina Roxanne. BSEE, U. Calif., Berkeley, 1976, MSEE, 1977. Design engr. Hewlett Packard Co., Santa Clara, Calif., 1977-81, Santa Rosa, Calif., 1981—; design engring. cons. Sierra Design, Santa Rosa, 1985-86. Co-inventor in field. Office: Hewlett Packard Co 1400 Fountaingrove Pkwy Santa Rosa CA 95403

SHEPPERSON, WILBUR STANLEY, history educator; b. Arbela, Mo., May 23, 1919; s. Clinton Artis and Ruby (Dietrich) S.; m. Margaret Loraine Dietze, Feb. 17, 1945; children—Stanley Carlyle, Tara Loraine. B.S., N.E. Mo. State Coll., 1941; M.A., U. Denver, 1947; Ph.D., Western Res. U., 1951; postgrad., Johns Hopkins, 1941-42, U. London, 1948-49. Pers. cons. Glen L. Martin Aircraft Co., Balt., 1941-42; interviewer USES, Denver, 1947-48; instr. Western State Coll., 1947-48; instr., asst. prof., asso. prof. U. Nev., Reno, 1951-63, prof., 1963-91, chmn. dept. history, 1966-74, 79-91; dir. U. Nev. Press, 1965-66; Fulbright prof. U. Liverpool, Eng., 1967-68; historian rsch. div. U.S. Dept. State, Washington, 1952; Grace A. Griffin chair in history U. Nev., Reno, 1987-91; vis. lectr. U. Wales, 1954-55; apl. agt. U.S. Bur. Census, Reno, 1963-66; cons. U.S. Dept. Interior, 1958-60. Author: British Emigration to North America, 1957, Samuel Roberts, A Welsh Colonizer in Tennessee, 1961, Emigration and Disenchantment, 1965, Retreat to Nevada: A Socialist Colony During World War I, 1966, Restless Strangers: Nevada's Immigrants, 1970, Questions from the Past, 1973, Hardscrabble: A Narrative of the California Hill Country, 1975, East of Eden-West of Zion: Essays on Nevada, 1989, Sagebrush Urbanity: Nevada Humanities, 1990, Mirage Land: Images of Nevada, 1992; History and Humanities, 1989, Festschrift in honor of Wilbur S. Shepperson; News editor Historian, 1951-53; editor: Nev. Studies in History and Polit. Sci, 1960-91, Nevada Historical Society Quarterly, 1970-73, Halcyon: A Journal of Humanities, 1978; contbr. numerous articles to profl. jours. Chmn. Nev. Humanities Com., 1973-91. Served with USAAF, 1942-46. Fellow Hon. Soc. Cymmrodorion; mem. Nat. Hon. History Soc. (nat. councillor 1958-62). Home: 2490 Pioneer Dr Reno NV 89509-5143

SHER, BYRON D., legal educator; b. 1928. BSBA, Washington U., St. Louis, 1949; JD, Harvard U., 1952. Bar: Mass. 1952. Sole practice, Boston, 1952-54; teaching fellow Harvard U., Cambridge, Mass., 1954-55; asst. prof. law So. Methodist U., Dallas, 1955-57; asst. prof. Stanford (Calif.) U. Law Sch., 1957-59, assoc. prof., 1959-62, prof., 1962—; cons. Fulbright research scholar Victoria U., Wellington, N.Z., 1964. Mem. Nat. Conf. Commrs. Uniform State Laws. Author: (with others) Law and Society, 1960. Office: The House of Representatives 74 Peter Coutts Circle Stanford CA 94305

SHERBURN, EARL FRANKLIN, community arts director, tour consultant; b. Van Wert, Ohio, May 28, 1943; s. Carl Edwin and Esther Edith (Rager) S. MusB, U. Mich., 1965, MusM, 1970; D in Mus. Arts, U. So. Calif., 1984. Pvt. instr. music Van Wert City Schs., summers 1962-64; dir. music Virginia City (Mont.) Players, summer 1965, Burroughs High Sch., Ridgecrest, Calif., 1965-69; dir. vocal music Bakersfield Jr. Coll., Ridgecrest, 1967-69; teaching asst. U. Mich., Ann Arbor, 1969-70; dir. instrumental music Palmdale (Calif.) High Sch., 1970-86; teaching asst. U. So. Calif., L.A., 1977-78; dir. art ctr. Dept. Cultural Affairs, L.A., 1986-90, dir. community arts, 1990—; cons. Tours of L.A. Area, Glendale, Calif., 1986—; v.p. Glendale Regional Arts Coun., 1990-92. Arranger various jazz ensemble compositions. Prin. percussionist Antelope Valley Symphony Orch., Lancaster, Calif., 1970-86; city councilman City of Palmdale, 1978-86; mem. arts com., community com. Calif. Contact Cities Assn., El Monte, 1978-86; founding chair Antelope Valley Found., Palmdale, 1984-86; asst. dir. Founders Cathedral Choir, L.A., 1986-90; mem. L.A. County Mus. Art, Mus. Contemporary Art, Natural History Mus. Mem. U. So. Calif. Alumni Assn., U. Mich. Alumni Club (L.A. chpt.), Phi Delta Kappa, Pi Kappa Lambda, Kappa Kappa Psi. Democrat. Mem. Ch. Religious Sci. Office: Dept Cultural Affairs 433 S Spring St 10th Fl Los Angeles CA 90013

SHERF, HARRIET N., book publishing consultant; b. Chgo., Dec. 31, 1934; d. Mortimer and Beatrice Rose (Flamm) S. BA in Journalism, U. Calif., Berkeley, 1956, BA, 1957. Women's editor The WAVE Newspapers, L.A., 1956-57; publicity dir. Stiller, Rouse & Hunt, Inc., Beverly Hills, Calif., 1957; pub. rels. dir. Motor Hotels div. Hyatt Corp. Am., Sepulveda, Calif., 1962-64; pub. rels. dir. Julian Kay Advt., Inc., Van Nuys, Calif., 1964-66; pres. Terry Sherf Assocs., Sherman Oaks, Calif., 1966-76; exec. v.p. Banner Books Internat., Sherman Oaks, 1976-78; pres. All-Media Svcs., Sherman Oaks, 1978—. Writer (TV show) Queen for a Day, 1958-60; syndicated columnist, 1959-62. Mem. Am. Publicists Guild (founder, pres. 1976-80), Cons. in Pub. (pres. 1979-80).

SHERFESEE, JOHN, academic administrator, air force officer; b. Portsmouth, N.H., Feb. 29, 1948; s. Louis Jr. and Anna (Latham) S.; m. Pamela J. Williams, Feb. 16, 1980. BSME, BS in Aero. Engring., U. Ariz., 1971, MS in Aero. Engring., 1972. Commd. 2d lt. USAF, 1973, advanced through grades to lt. col., 1988; with USAF Acad. USAF, Colorado Springs, Colo., 1979—, asst. prof. aero. engring., 1981-84, assoc. registrar, 1982-88, assoc. prof. aero. engring., 1984—, asst. dean faculty, 1988—. Named Hon. Citizen Gulfport (Miss.) C. of C., 1981. Mem. Air Force Assn., Am. Assn. Higher Edn., Am. Assn. Collegiate Registrars and Admissions Officers, Am. Alpine Club. Roman Catholic. Home: 5752 Tuckerman Ln Colorado Springs CO 80918-1939

SHERIDAN, GEORGE EDWARD, manufacturing company executive; b. Emporia, Kans., July 4, 1915; s. George and Josephine Frances (Benson) S.; m. Edith Joye Card, July 4, 1940; 1 dau., Phyllis Lynne. Liberal arts student Coll. of Emporia, 1934-36; engring. student Nat. Schs., 1936-37, Los Angeles City Jr. Coll., 1937-38. Cert. mfg. engr.; registered profl. engr., Calif. With Douglas Aircraft, Santa Monica, Calif., 1939-40, Northrop Aircraft, Hawthorn, Calif., 1940-45; pres. Sheridan Products, Inc., Inglewood, Calif., 1940—. Active, YMCA, Inglewood, 1960—. Mem. Soc. Mfg. Engrs. (life, award 1979-80, Industrialist of Yr. 1982 past chmn.), U.S. Power Squadron, Am. Ordnance Def. Preparedness Assn., Nat. Rifle Assn., Smithsonian Assos., Cutting Tool Mfg. Assn., Nat. Fedn. Ind. Bus., Mech. Bank Collectors Am., Antique Toy Collectors Am. Republican. Quaker. Patentee double edge scraper. Home and Office: Sheridan Products Inc 27692 Via Rodrigo San Juan Capistrano CA 92692-2019

SHERIDAN, WILMA FROMAN, dean; b. Ashland, Oreg., Jan. 31, 1926; d. Carl Edwin and Mary Charlotte (Evans) Froman; m. Robert Jackson Sheridan, May 24, 1946; children: Sarah Ruth, Richard Carl, Scott Daniel. MusB, Willamette U., 1945; MusM in Edn., Lewis and Clark Coll., 1955; PhD, U. Oreg., 1979. Secondary choral music tchr. Ashland Pub. Schs., 1945-46; instr. in piano Wash. State U., Pullman, 1946-47; comml. tchr. Everett (Wash.) High Sch., 1949-50, Ashland High Sch., 1950-51; elem. music tchr. Portland (Oreg.) Pub. Schs., 1954-60; from instr. to prof. in music Portland State U., 1969-85, head music dept., 1980-85, dean Sch. Fine and Performing Arts, 1985—; instr. in music Lewis and Clark Coll., Portland, 1956-65. Composer, arranger various mus. works, including How Blest Are They, Christmas Bells; author: The Oregon Plan for Mainstreaming in Music, 1978. Bd. dirs., mem. music com. Ecumenical Ministries, Portland, 1965-68; bd. dirs. Portland Symphonic Choir, 1972-76, Community Music Ctr., Portland, 1984—. Mem. Music Educators Nat. Conf. (mem. nat. com. for handicapped learners 1978-81), Multhomah Athletic Club, Mu Phi Epsilon (chpt. Mem. of Yr. 1989, award for music therapy 1982, 85). Home: 2400 NW 92d Ave Portland OR 97220 Office: Portland State U PO Box 751 Portland OR 97207

SHERK, WARREN ARTHUR, counselor, educator; b. Buffalo, July 12, 1916; s. Warren E. and Jennie (Taylor) S.; m. Martha Jean Kritzer, June 11, 1954; children: Elena E., Adra K., Lydian M., Warren M., Wilson E. Student Hiram Coll., 1934-35, U. Rangoon, Burma, 1938-39, Duke U., 1939-40; AB, Allegheny Coll., 1938; BD, Berkeley Bapt. Div. Sch., 1945, ThM, 1952; STD, Burton Sem., 1958. Minister, Meth. chs. in western N.Y., 1941-43; Protestant chaplain Ariz. State Prison, 1971-72; vis. prof. Iliff Sch. Theology, U. Denver, 1945-47; field sec. to Pearl S. Buck, 1948-49; minister edn., Indiana, Pa., 1949-51; minister Waitsburg Meth. Ch., Washington, 1951-52, Community Ch., Watertown, Mass., 1955-58, Savanna, Ill., 1958-59, Nogales (Ariz.) United Ch., 1960-61; exec. Dynamics Found., Tucson, 1962—; personal counselor, 1962—; faculty Phoenix Coll., 1963-66, Mesa Community Coll., Eastern Ariz. Coll., Pima Coll., 1963-78, Western International U., 1984-90, Portland (Oreg.) State U., 1991-93, LinnBenton C.C., 1993—; cons. spl. seminars Pepsi Cola Mgmt. Inst., 1967-68; dir. bus. and profl. seminars for execs., 1968-90; lectr. U. Durham (Eng.), summer 1981, Iliff Sch. Theology, summer 1982, Elder Hostels, N.Y., summer 1983,, St. Deinels Libr, Wales, summer 1985, S.S. Rotterdam N.Y.C. to South Africa, 1984; founder, exec. sec. Valley of Sun Forum, Phoenix, 1963-67; coordinator Assoc. Bus. Execs. Phoenix, 1963-67. Author: Wider Horizons, 1941, Agnes Moorehead: A Biography, 1976, Pearl Buck, 1987; contbr. numerous articles to mags. Chmn. spl. gifts div. Maricopa County Heart Fund. Corporate mem. Perkins Sch. for the Blind; bd. dirs. Boston World Affairs Council, N.E. Assn. UN; hon. bd. govs., bd. dirs. Pearl S. Buck Found. Fellow Am. Acad. Polit. Sci., Am. Geog. Soc.; mem. NCCJ, AAUP, Thoreau Soc., Emerson Soc., Watertown Hist. Soc., Pimeria Alta Hist. Soc., Maricopa Mental Health Assn., Internat. Winston Churchill Soc., English Speaking Union, Theodore Roosevelt Assn., Execs. Internat. (founder, exec. dir. 1967-90), Nat. Assn. Approved Morticians (exec. sec. 1967-69), Internat. Platform Assn., Tucson Com. Fgn. Rels., Phoenix Com. Fgn. Relations, Portland World Affairs Coun., Oreg. Writers Colony, P.E.N. Northwest, Northwest China Coun., The Newcomen Soc., Ariz. Club, Univ. Club, Kiva Club, Theta Chi. Republican. Address: 33125 White Oak # 4 Corvallis OR 97333

SHERMAN, BRADLEY JAMES, state official, lawyer, accountant; b. L.A., Oct. 24, 1954; s. Maurice H. and Lane (Moss) S. BA summa cum laude, UCLA, 1974; JD magna cum laude, Harvard U., 1979. Bar: Calif. 1979; CPA, Calif. Pvt. practice, L.A., 1980-91; mem. Calif. Bd. Equalization, Sacramento, 1991—, chmn., 1991—; lectr. on tax law and policy; mem. Calif. Franchise Tax Bd. Contbr. articles to legal jours. Bd. dirs., rep. on tax issues Calif. Common Cause, 1984-89; mem. exec. com. Calif. Dem. Com., 1991—. Mem. Calif. State Bar. Jewish. Office: Calif Bd Equalization 901 Wilshire Blvd Ste 210 Santa Monica CA 90401

SHERMAN, DAVID MATTHEW, consulting engineer; b. Burien, Wash., Dec. 18, 1959; s. Donald E. and Rose M. (Kiss) S. BSEE, U. Wash., 1981, MSEE, 1982. Lic. profl. engr., Wash. Assoc. design engr. John Fluke Mfg. Co., Inc., Everett, Wash., 1982-85, design engr., 1985-86; electronic engr. Intermec, Inc., Everett, 1986-89; pres. David Sherman Engring. Co., Everett, 1989—. Inventor, patentee in field; contbr. articles on design to trade publs.

SHERMAN, DEBORAH, psychologist; b. Batesville, Ind., Aug. 22, 1951; d. Paul Frederick and Ruth Margaret Bland; m. David Keith Sherman, Jan. 24, 1953. BS in Psychology, Sociology, Purdue U., 1972; MEd in Student Pers., Ind. U., 1975; MA in Clin. Psychology, Western Sem., 1984, PhD in Clin. Psychology, 1986. Lic. psychologist, Idaho, Oreg. Res. dir. U. Calif., Davis, 1975-77; counselor IDAK Career Consultants, Portland, Oreg., 1980-83; asst. prof. Western Evang. Sem., Portland, 1988, Western Bapt. Sem., Portland, 1986-88; psychology resident Willamette Therapy, Woodland Park Hosp., Portland, 1986-89, Western Psychol. and Counseling, Portland, 1986-89; prof. Warner Pacific Coll., Portland, 1989, U. Idaho, Coeur d'Alene, Idaho, 1992; pvt. practice psychology Coeur d'Alene, 1989—. Mem. APA, Oreg. Psychol. Assn., Idaho Psychol. Assn., Wash. Psychol. Assn. Office: # 200 2251 Ironwood Center Dr Coeur D Alene ID 83814-2697

SHERMAN, DONALD H., civil engineer; b. Jackson, Wyo., May 14, 1932; s. Howard M. and Dorothy (Turner) S.; m. Myrle J. Jenkins, Jan. 25, 1962 (div. Mar., 1987); children: D. John, Cynthia Lynn Sherman Pierceall, Richard L., Sheila L. Bufmack; m. Patricia A. Hoffman, June 26, 1993. AA in Engring., Fullerton Jr. Coll., 1953; diploma in surveying and mapping, I.C.S., 1955; BS in Geology, U. Wyo., 1960, BS in Civil Engring., 1968. Registered profl. engr., Wyo., Colo. Geophysicist Texaco Geophysical, Casper, Wyo. and Billings, Mont., 1960-63; surveyor Wyo. Hwy. Dept., Jackson, 1963-64; engring. geologist Wyo. Hwy. Dept., Cheyenne, 1964-66, hydraulics engr., 1968-72; civil engr., rotation trainee U.S. Bur. Reclamation, Denver, 1972-73; civil engr. D.M.J.M.-Phillips-Reister-Haley, Denver, 1973-79, Stearns Roger, Inc., Glendale, Colo., 1980-82, Centennial Engring., Arvada, Colo., 1983-85; civil engr. land devel. York Assocs., Denver, 1986-87; civil engr. City of Colo. Springs, 1987-92; owner Valley View Trailer Park, Jackson, 1965-92; advisor to U.S. Sen. Clifford Hansen on Black 14 incident, 1969. Recipient Presdl. Legion of Merit Rep. Nat. Com., 1992, Presdl. Commn., Rep. Nat. Com., 1992, Cert. of Award Presdl. Adv. Commn., 1991-92. Republican. Home: 2015A Lelaray Colorado Springs CO 80909 Office: City Engring Rm 403 CAB 30 S Nevada Ave Colorado Springs CO 80901

SHERMAN, ERIC, director, writer, educator; b. Santa Monica, Calif., June 29, 1947; s. Vincent and Hedda (Comorau) S.; m. Eugenia Blackiston Dillard, Apr. 1, 1978; children: Cosimo, Rocky. BA cum laude, Yale U., 1968. Film producer, dir., writer, photographer and editor; films include: Charles Lloyd-Journey Within, 1968; Paul Weiss-a Philosopher in Process, 1972; Waltz, 1980; Inside Out, 1982; Measure of America, 1983; Michael Reagan's Assault on Great Lakes, 1983, Futures, 1990 (Peabody Broadcast award 1990); represented in film festivals N.Y.C. Cine Golden Eagle, Melbourne, Australia, Bilbao, Spain, others; books include: (with others) The Director's Event, 1970; Directing the Film, 1976; Frame by Frame, 1987, Selling Your Film, 1990; pres. Film Transform; film tchr. Art Ctr. Coll. Design, Pepperdine U., UCLA; guest lectr. Yale, Calif. Inst. Tech., U. So. Calif.; Andrew Mellon lectr. on arts Calif. Inst. Tech., 1977; contbr. numerous articles to film publs. and distbn. catalogues, book dedication; works include three oral histories for Am. Film Inst. under Louis B. Mayer Found. grant. Trustee Am. Cinematheque; bd. dir. Film Forum. Mem. Soc. Motion Picture and TV Engrs. (asso.), Assn. Ind. Video and Filmmakers, Univ. Film Assn., Assn. Visual Communicators, Nat. Alliance Media Arts Ctrs. Home and Office: 2427 Park Oak Dr Los Angeles CA 90068-2539

SHERMAN, FRANCES ADAMS, placement service company executive; b. Bklyn., Dec. 8, 1934; d. James Lee and Frances Evelyn (Gann) Adams; m. James Thomas Kneeshaw, Jan. 14, 1956 (div. July 1979); children: Holly Elizabeth, Wendy Patricia, James Adams, Kelly Frances; m. Jerry Bernard Sherman, Oct. 8, 1983. BS in Edn., SUNY, Plattsburg, 1956. Lic. tchr., N.Y.; cert. personnel cons. Elem. tchr. Trumansbury (N.Y.) Cen. Sch., 1956-57, Bolton Cen. Sch., Bolton Landing, N.Y., 1962-65, Queensbury Cen. Sch., Glens Falls, N.Y., 1965-69, Glens Falls (N.Y.) Schs., 1969-78; employment cons. Key Personnel, Phoenix, 1983-85; pres. TOP/Personnel, Phoenix, 1985—; tchr. CPC Program, Phoenix, 1987-89; cons. Dept. of Econs. Security Job Svc. Coun., 1990. Guide Hyde Mus., Glens Falls, 1978-83; chairperson Hosp. Guild, Glens Falls, 1978-83; vol. United Way Meals on Wheels, Glens Falls, 1980. Mem. Ariz. Assn. Personnel Cons. (bd. mem. 1988-89, sec. 1989-90, pres. 1990—, pres. Phoenix br. 1987-88, John M. Balla award 1987, cert. personnel cons. award 1987), Nat. Assn. Personnel Cons. (Ariz. state chairperson cert. personnel cons. program, 1987-90), Leads Exchange Assn. Phoenix, Better Bus. Bur., Phoenix C. of C. Republican. Presbyterian. Office: TOP Personnel Inc 4647 N 16th St Ste 240 Phoenix AZ 85016-5153

SHERMAN, GERALD, financial planner, insurance broker, physicist; b. Bklyn., Sept. 7, 1938; s. Saul and Claire S.; m. Annette Ellen Drasin, Aug. 29, 1965; children: Rochelle Heidi, Sondra Nicole. BA in Physics, UCLA, 1960, MS in Nuclear Physics, 1962, postgrad., 1962-64; PhD in Physics, Columbia Pacific U., 1985. Physics instr., lower divsn. Lab. UCLA, 1960-62, physics instr. upper divsn. nuclear physics, 1961-62; physicist, principle investigator Northrop Space Sci. Lab., Hawthorne, Calif., 1966-70; pres. Sherman Ins. Agy., Inc., L.A., 1970-84; pres., CEO Sherman Fin. Svcs., Inc., Thousand Oaks, Calif., 1984—. Contbr. numerous articles to scientific jours. Recipient Top Prodr. Nationwide award U.S. Life Ins. Co. Calif., 1978, Leading Disability Prodr. Nationwide award Chubb Life Ins. Co. Am., 1984-85, 90, Leading Combined Life and Disability Prodr. award Chubb, 1987, Leading Combined Life and Disability Agy. award Chubb, 1989. Mem. Calif. Assn. Life Underwriters, Westlake Art Guild, Sigma Pi Sigma. Office: Sherman Financial Svcs Inc 2158 Calle Riscoso Thousand Oaks CA 91362

SHERMAN, KENNETH, educational corporate executive, educator, electrical engineer; b. Bklyn., June 24, 1936; s. Louis and Frances (Savran) S.; m. Susan Rona Silverman, Feb. 1, 1958; children: Gayle Ilene, Mark Jason, Samantha Jayne. BEE, Rensselaer Poly. Inst., 1957; MSEE, U. So. Calif., 1960; PhD, Columbia Pacific U., 1986. Sr. engr. Northrop Corp., Hawthorne, Calif., 1957-61; project/program mgr. ITT Corp., Paramus, N.J., 1961-67; program mgr. Marshall Communications, Santa Ana, Calif., 1967-69; various exec. positions Cordura Corp., L.A., 1969-75; pres. K. Sherman and Assocs., Villa Park, Calif., 1975-78, InfoComm Inc., Villa Park, Calif., 1978—; exec. dir. Ctr. for Advanced Profl. Devel., Santa Ana, 1982—; instr. U. Calif., Irvine, 1987—. Author: Auditext, 1977, Data Communications: A Users Guide, 1981, 3d edit. 1990; author tech. jour. Data Communications, 1983. Office: Ctr for Advanced Profl Devel 1820 E Garry St Ste 110 Santa Ana CA 92705

SHERMAN, MALCOLM CHARLES, business consultant; b. Boston, Aug. 19, 1931; s. Benjamin and Kay (Sheff) S.; m. Jill Barbara Tawil, Dec. 6, 1970; children: Isaac, Martin. JD, Boston U., 1955. Registered profl. engr., Calif.; bar: Mass. 1955. Contract mgr. Curtiss-Wright, Quehanna, Pa., 1956-58, Litton Industries, L.A., 1958-64; program mgr. Hughes Aircraft Co., L.A., 1964-68; v.p. devel. Planning Rsch. Corp., L.A., 1971-74; sr. v.p. Info. Gen., L.A., 1968-69; pres., CEO, Meridian Group Internat., L.A., 1974-83; pres. KDT Systems, L.A., 1983-89; exec. cons. Rockwell Internat., L.A., 1989-91; bus. cons., El Segundo, Calif., 1991—; adj. prof. U. So. Calif., L.A., 1965-77, UCLA, 1965-77; lectr. NSF, Bangkok, 1989; cons. Asian-Am. Enterprise, L.A., 1992—. Contbr. articles to profl. publs. Recipient recognition and appreciation award Samsung Industries, Republic of Korea, 1989, NRC, 1990, Office Sci. Tech., Thailand, 1990. Mem. L.A. Execs. Club (v.p. 1983-84). Office: 17 Waldrup Trace Fletcher NC 28732

SHERMAN, ROBERT, communications executive, producer; b. N.Y.C., Jan. 9, 1950; s. Allan Sherman and Dolores Miriam (Chackes) Golden. Student, San Fernando Valley State Coll., 1968, UCLA, 1969, Brandeis U., 1970. pres., founder The TV Co., 1970—, See Other Page, 1987—, Hollywood Interactive, 1989—, Robert Sherman Prodns., 1989—; pres., co-owner Curtain Call Prodns., 1973—. Producer, co-creator Spellbinders, 1978, The Better Sex, 1977-78, Puzzlers, 1980, Blockbusters, 1980-82, 87, Star Words, 1983; assoc. producer Tattletales, 1974-78, co-producer, 1982; writer, assoc. producer Match Game, 1973-81; producer Password Plus, 1979-82 (Daytime Emmy as Outstanding Game Show 1981-82), That's My Dog!, 1991-92; exec. producer Match Game/Hollywood Sqs. Hour, 1983-84, Super Password, 1984-89, That's My Dog!, 1993—; exec. producer, creator Body Language, 1984-86, Baby Races, 1993—; producer, creator Oddball, 1986; contbr. articles to profl. jours.; inventor dimmer control system. Mem. NATAS (Emmy award 1971-72), Writers Guild Am., Mensa. Home: 1555 Rising Glen Rd West Hollywood CA 90069-1225 Office: 9028 W Sunset Blvd Ste 200 West Hollywood CA 90069-1830

SHERMAN, ROBERT B(ERNARD), composer, lyricist, screenwriter; b. N.Y.C., Dec. 19, 1925; s. Al and Rosa (Dancis) S.; student UCLA, 1943; BA, Bard Coll., 1949; MusD (hon.) Lincoln U., 1990; m. Joyce Ruth Sasner, Sept. 27, 1953; children: Laurie Shane, Jeffrey Craig, Andrea Tracy, Robert Jason. Popular songwriter, 1950-60, including Tall Paul, Pineapple Princess, You're Sixteen (Gold Record); songwriter Walt Disney Prodns., Beverly Hills, Calif., 1960-68, for 29 films including The Parent Trap, 1961, Summer Magic, 1963, Mary Poppins, 1964, That Darn Cat, 1965, Winnie The Pooh, 1965, Jungle Book, 1967, Bedknobs and Broomsticks, 1971; co-composer song It's A Small World, theme of Disneyland and Walt Disney World, Fla.; composer, lyricist United Artists, Beverly Hills, 1969—, songs for film Chitty, Chitty, Bang, Bang, 1969, Snoopy, Come Home!, 1972; song score Charlotte's Web, 1972; composer for Walt Disney's Wonderful World of Color, TV, 1961—; co-producer NBC-TV spl. Goldilocks, 1970; v.p. Musi-Classics, Inc.; co-producer, composer, lyricist stage musical Victory Canteen, 1971; composer-lyricist Broadway show Over Here, 1975; screenplay and song score Tom Sawyer, United Artists, 1972, Huckleberry Finn, 1974, The Slipper and the Rose, 1977, The Magic of Lassie, 1978. Served with inf. AUS, 1943-45; ETO. Decorated Purple Heart; recipient 2 Acad. awards best score for Mary Poppins, 1964, best song for Chim Chim Cheree, 1964; Grammy award, 1965; Christopher medal, 1965, 74; nine Acad. award nominations; Acad. award nomination for song score Bedknobs and Broomsticks, 1971, for best song The Age of Not Believing, 1971, others; 16 golden, 4 platinum and one diamond record album, 1965-83; first prize best composer song score Tom Sawyer, Moscow Film Festival, 1973, B.M.I. Pioneer award, 1977; Golden Cassette awards for Mary Poppins, Jungle Book, Bed Knobs and Broomsticks, 1983, Mouscar award Disney Studios, Disney Legend award, 1990, BMI Richard Kirk Achievment award, 1991. Mem. Acad. Motion Picture Arts and Scis. (exec. bd. music br. 12 yrs.), AFTRA, Nat. Acad. Rec. Arts and Scis., Composers and Lyricists Guild (exec. bd.), Writers Guild Am., Dramatists Guild, Authors League. Office: 9030 Harratt St West Hollywood CA 90069-3858

SHERMAN, ROBERT DEWAYNE, radiologic technologist; b. Concord, Calif., May 31, 1949; s. Chester Josiah and Bette Louise (Elrod) S.; m. Cora Sue Donahue, June 15, 1968 (div. 1973); 1 child, Eric James; m. Virginia Marie Mayer, July 27, 1975 (div. 1988); 1 child, Jana Marie. AA, Foothill Coll., Los Altos, Calif., 1970. Cert. radiol. technologist, Calif. Staff technologist Palo Alto (Calif.) Med. Found., 1971-74, CT technologist, 1974-76, CT supr., 1976—, angiography team, 1982—, MRI staff, 1989—. Office: Palo Alto Med Found 300 Homer Ave Palo Alto CA 94301

SHERMAN, SIGNE LIDFELDT, securities analyst; b. Rochester, N.Y., Nov. 11, 1913; d. Carl Leonard Broström and Herta Elvira Maria (Thern) Lidfeldt; m. Joseph V. Sherman, Nov. 18, 1944 (dec. Oct. 1984). BA, U. Rochester, 1935, MS, 1937. Chief chemist Lab. Indsl. Medicine and Toxicology Eastman Kodak Co., Rochester, 1937-43; chief rsch. chemist Chesebrough-Pond's Inc., Clinton, Conn., 1943-44; ptnr. Joseph V. Sherman Cons., N.Y.C., 1944-84; advisor Signe L. Sherman Cons., Troy, Mont., 1984—. Author: The New Fibers, 1946. Fellow Am. Inst. Chemists; mem. AAAS, AAUW (life), Am. Chem. Soc., Am. Econ. Assn., Am. Assn. Ind. Investors (life), Fedn. Am. Scientists (life), Union Concerned Scientists (life), Western Econ. Assn. Internat., Earthquake Engring. Rsch. Inst., Nat. Ctr. for Earthquake Engring. Rsch., N.Y. Acad. Scis. (life), Cabinet View Country Club. Office: Signe L Sherman Cons Angel Island 648 Halo Dr Troy MT 59935-9415

SHERMAN, ZELDA CHARLOTTE, artist; b. L.A., June 18, 1924; d. Jacob and Celia (Knopow) Pynoos; m. Lawrence James Sherman, Dec. 17, 1943; children—Susan Meyers, Daniel Michael. Student UCLA, 1945-47, Otis Art Inst., Los Angeles, 1947-50, Kann Art Inst., Los Angeles, 1950-52. Exhibited in group shows at Sao Paulo Biennial, Brazil, 1961, Heritage Gallery, Los Angeles, 1963-91, D'Allesio Gallery, N.Y.C., 1965-66, Grand Prix Internat. de Deauville, Paris, 1972, Priz de Rome, Palais des Beaux Artes, Rome, 1973, Heritage Gallery, Los Angeles, 1992; represented in permanent collections Mcpl. Art Gallery, Los Angeles, Palm Springs Mus., Winthrop Rockefeller Found., Laguna Mus. Art, Calif., Container Corp. Am. Recipient award Phelan Found., 1961, Pasadena Mus., 1961, All City Exhbn. award Barnsdale, 1963, 65. Mem. Nat. Watercolor Soc. Home: 1300 Chautauqua Blvd Pacific Palisades CA 90272-2606 Office: Heritage Gallery 718 N La Cienega Blvd Los Angeles CA 90272

SHERRARD, RAYMOND HENRY, government official; b. Chgo., Mar. 8, 1944; s. Henry Loren and Minnie Valeria (Elrod) S.; m. Marsha L. McDermid, 1967 (div. 1971). AA, Long Beach City Coll., 1965; BA, Calif. State U., 1967; grad., Treasury Dept. Law Enforcement, Washington, 1970. Spl. dep. U.S. Marshal, L.A., 1970; pres. RHS Enterprises, Cypress, Calif., 1981—; criminal investigator criminal investigation div. IRS, Santa Ana, Calif., 1969—; story cons. Charles Fries Prodns., Hollywood, Calif., 1976—; instr. Fed. Law Enforcement Tng. Ctr., Glynco, Ga., 1977—; screenwriter Orion TV, Century City, Calif., 1984—; tech. advisor Paramount Pictures, Hollywood, 1987—; dir. speaker panel IRS, Laguna Niguel, Calif., 1984-92. Author: Federal Law Enforcement Patches, 1983, vol. 2, 1987, About Badges, 1987, Badges of the United Marshals, 1990; contbr. articles to profl. jours. Recipient Presidential Commendation, Pres. U.S.A., Washington, 1980, Spl. Act award U.S. Treasury Dept., L.A., 1978, 87. Mem. Fed. Criminal Investigators Assn. (life, regional v.p. 1978-80), Assn. Fed. Investigators, Fed. Law Enforcement Officers Assn., Calif. Narcotic Officers Assn. (life, sec. 1974). Republican. Home: PO Box 5779 Garden Grove CA 92645-0779

SHERRATT, GERALD ROBERT, college president; b. Los Angeles, Nov. 6, 1931; s. Lowell Heyborne and Elva Genevieve (Lamb) S. B.S. in Edn., Utah State U., 1953, M.S. in Edn. Adminstrn., 1954; Ph.D. in Adminstrn. Higher Edn., Mich. State U., 1975. Staff assoc. U. Utah, Salt Lake City, 1961-62; dir. high sch. relations Utah State U., Logan, 1962-64, asst. to pres., 1964-77, v.p. for univ. relations, 1977-81; pres. So. Utah U., Cedar City, 1982—; dir. Honeyville Grain Inc., Utah; mem. council pres. Utah System Higher Edn., 1982—; chmn. bd. Utah Summer Games, Cedar City, 1984—; chmn. pres.'s council Rocky Mountain Athletic Conf., Denver, 1984-85. Author hist. pageant: The West: America's Odyssey, 1973 (George Washington Honor medal 1973). Chmn. Festival of Am. West, Logan, Utah, 1972-81; chmn. bd. Utah Shakespearean Festival, Cedar City, 1982-86; mem. bd. dirs. Salt Lake City Branch of the Federal Reserve Bank of San Francisco. Served to 1st. lt. USAF, 1954-57. Recipient Editing award Indsl. Editors Assn., 1962, Robins award Utah State U., 1967, Disting. Alumnus award Utah State U., 1974, So. Utah U., 1991, Total Citizen award Cedar City C. of C., 1993; named to Utah Tourism Hall of Fame, 1989. Mem. Am. Assn. State Colls. and Univs., Cache C. of C. (bd. dirs. 1980-82), Phi Kappa Phi, Phi Delta Kappa, Sigma Nu (regent 1976-78). Mem. LDS Ch. Lodge: Rotary. Home: 331 W 200 S Cedar City UT 84720-3101 Office: So Utah U 351 W Center St Cedar City UT 84720-2498

SHERRELL, LYNN MARGARET, lawyer, educator; b. Rochester, N.Y., Nov. 2, 1940; d. Leo P. and Elsie Beeman (Trickey) S.; m. Arthur B. Kessner, Apr. 17, 1962 (div. Dec. 1974); 1 child, Gawain. BA, U. Calif., Berkeley, 1963; MA, San Francisco State U., 1978; JD, Golden Gate U., 1983. Bar: Calif. 1983, U.S. Dist. Ct. (no. dist.) Calif. 1983, U.S. Ct. Appeals (9th cir.) 1984. Tchr. Berkeley Unified Sch. Dist., 1966-77; assoc. Law Offices J.J. Duryea, San Francisco, 1983-86, Law Offices Weltin, Van Dam & Flores, San Francisco, Calif., 1986-90, Law Office David Hirshik, Walnut Creek, Calif., 1991, Law Office Brayton, Gisvald & Harley, Novato, Calif., 1992—; instr. Russian Berkeley Adult Sch., 1975-78; adj. prof. Golden Gate U., San Francisco, 1983-85. Editor (poetry) The Laurentian, 1960-61; writer numerous poems. Candidate workers' compensation law Calif. Bd. Legal Specialization. Mem. Lawyers Against War, Queens Bench, Calif. Applicants Attys. Assn., Toastmasters Internat., Phi Delta Epsilon. Club: Olympic Circle Sailing. Home: 2411 Emerson St Berkeley CA 94705-1812 Office: Law Office Brayton, Grisvald & Harley 900 Grant Ave Novato CA 94948

SHERRIFFS, RONALD EVERETT, communications and film educator; b. Salem, Oreg., Apr. 10, 1934; s. Robert William and Margaret Kathleen (Tutt) S.; m. Mary Lona West, July 9, 1960; children: Ellen, Matthew. BA, San Jose State U., 1955, MA, 1957; PhD, U. So. Calif., 1964. Instr. theater Mich. State U., East Lansing, 1960-61; asst. prof. broadcasting Tex. Tech U., Lubbock, 1964-65; asst. prof. speech U. Oreg., Eugene, 1965-70, assoc. prof., 1970-79, prof. telecommunications and film, 1979-92, chmn. dept. speech, 1978-84, 88-90, prof. journalism and comm., 1993—. Author: (with others) Speech Communication via Radio and Television, 1971, TV Lighting Handbook, 1977, Small Format Television Production, 1985, 3d edit. 1993; producer, dir. TV programs, 1965—. Mem. Oreg. Pub. Broadcasting Policy Adv. Bd., 1980-88. Served to lt. comdr. USNR, 1957-68, PTO. Faculty enrichment program grantee Can., 1984, 91. Mem. Speech Communication Assn. Am., AAUP, Western States Communication Assn. Clubs: Oreg. Track; McKenzie Flyfishers (Eugene). Office: U Oreg Eugene OR 97403

SHERROW, GREG HUNTER, cameraman, writer; b. Harrodsburg, Ky., Nov. 27, 1953; s. Robert Lee and Jane Allen (Hunter) S.; m. Marva Juel Parker, Nov. 23, 1979. AA, San Diego City Coll., 1984; student, San Diego State U., 1985. Camerman San Diego and L.A., 1980-88; cameraman Network NBC-TV, Burbank, 1988-89, Network CBS-TV, L.A., 1989—. Author: The Sandman, 1984; author short stories; contbr. articles to profl. publs. Mem. Internat. Brotherhood of Elec. Workers, Nat. Assn. of Broadcast Engrs. and Technicians. Methodist. Office: CBS-TV 7800 Beverly Blvd Ste 67 Los Angeles CA 90036

SHERRY, KENNETH EDWARD, telecommunications engineering consultant; b. Porterville, Calif., Sept. 7, 1939; s. Lester Edward and Emmalouise (Clatte) S.; m. Hermalee Wiseman, June 9, 1962; children: Edward, Melanie, Steve. BSEE, BSME, Fresno State U., 1963. Dist. mgr. Pacific Telephone Co., Sacramento, Calif., 1963-82; dir. mktg. L.L.B. & E. Architects, Sacramento, 1983-85; dir. engring. Vector Telecom, Inc., Sacramento, 1985-86; gen. mgr. S & S Telecom, Inc., Sacramento, 1986; v.p. Advanced Fiberoptics Corp., Phoenix, Ariz., 1986-87; pvt. practice cons. Scottsdale, Ariz., 1987-88, 89—; mgr. engring. Tesnic, Inc., Phoenix, 1988-89. With USMC, 1959-64. Home: 5343 E Grandview Rd Scottsdale AZ 85254

SHERWOOD, ALLEN JOSEPH, lawyer; b. Salt Lake City, Sept. 26, 1909; s. Charles Samuel and Sarah (Abramson) Shapiro; m. Edith Ziff, Jan. 19, 1941; children—Mary (Mrs. John Marshall), Arthur Lawrence. Student, UCLA, 1927-30; AB, U. So. Calif., 1933, LLB, 1933. Bar: Calif. 1933, U.S. Supreme Ct. 1944. Pvt. practice law L.A., 1933-54, Beverly Hills, 1954—; legal counsel Internat. Family Planning Rsch. Assn., Inc., 1970-76; bd. dirs. Family Planning Ctrs. Greater L.A., Inc., 1968-84, pres., 1973-76. Mem. editorial bd. So. Calif. Law Rev., 1932-33. Contbr. articles to profl. jours. Mem. Calif. Atty. Gen.'s Vol. Adv. Coun. and its legis. subcom., 1972-78. Mem. Med.-Legal Soc. So. Calif. (bd. dirs. 1966-74), ABA, L.A. County Bar Assn., Beverly Hills Bar Assn., State Bar of Calif., Am. Arbitration Assn. (nat. panel arbitrators 1965—), Order of Coif, Tau Delta Phi, Brentwood Country Club (L.A.), Masons. Home: 575 Moreno Ave Los Angeles CA 90049-4840 Office: 12424 Wilshire Blvd Bldg 900 Los Angeles CA 90025-1043

SHERWOOD, LAWRENCE LEIGHTON, non-proft administrator; b. Rochester, N.Y., Dec. 13, 1954; s. Wade Wellington and Virginia (Smith) S. AB, Dartmouth Coll., 1977. Assoc. dir. N.E. Solar Energy Assn., Brattleboro, Vt., 1979-85, exec. dir., 1985-88; exec. dir. Am. Solar Energy Assn., Boulder, Colo., 1988—. County coord. campaign Kunin for Gov., Montpelier, Vt., 1986. Mem. Am. Soc. Assn. Execs., Colo. Soc. Assn. Execs., Sierra (chair Burlington, Vt. chpt., exec. com. Colo. chpt. 1990—, Boston chpt.). Office: Am Solar Energy Soc 2400 Central Ave # 1G Boulder CO 80301-2843

SHERWOOD, ROBERT PETERSEN, retired sociology educator; b. Black Diamond, Wash., May 17, 1932; s. James Brazier and Zina (Petersen) S.; m. Merlene Burningham, Nov. 21, 1951; children: Robert Lawrence, Richard William, Rolene, RaNae. BS, U. Utah, 1956, MS, 1957; EdD, U. Calif., Berkeley, 1965. Tchr. Arden-Carmichael Sch. Dist., Carmichael, Calif., 1957-59; vice prin. jr. high Arden-Carmichael Sch. Dist., 1960-61, prin. jr. high, 1962-65; v.p., prin. San Juan Unified Sch. Dist., Sacramento, 1966-70; assoc. prof. Calif. State U., Sacramento, 1966-71; dir. outreach progs. Am. River Coll., Sacramento, 1971-73; acting assoc. dean of instrn. Am. River Coll., 1973-74, prof. sociology, 1970-92; retired, 1992; chmn. sociology/anthropology dept. Am. River Coll., 1980-86; pres. acad. senate Am. River Coll., 1990-91. With USN, 1953-55. Recipient Merit Recognition award, Boy Scouts Am., 1989. Mem. NEA, Calif. Tchrs. Assn., Faculty Assn. Calif. Community Colls., Western Assn. Schs. and Colls., Calif. Fedn. Coll. Profs., Phi Delta Kappa (life). Mem. LDS Ch. Home: 4053 Esperanza Dr Sacramento CA 95864-3069

SHETTEL, DON LANDIS, JR., geochemist, consultant; b. Balt., Oct. 21, 1949; s. Don Landis and Frances (Fager) S.; m. Cheryl Rebecca Wieg, July 2, 1971. BSc in Geology with honors, U. Mich., 1971; MSc, Pa. State U., 1974, PhD, 1978. Asst. field geologist Humble Oil & Refining Co., Bangor, Maine, 1971; rsch. asst. dept. geoscis. Pa. State U., University Park, 1971-77; faculty rsch. assoc. dept. chemistry Ariz. State U., Tempe, 1977-78; staff geoscientist Bendix Field Engring. Corp., Grand Junction, Colo., 1978-82; sr. rsch. geochemist Exxon Prodn. Rsch. Co., Houston, 1982-86; sr. geochemist Mifflin & Assocs., Inc., Las Vegas, Nev., 1986-91; v.p. Geoscis. Mgmt. Inst., Inc., Boulder City, Nev., 1991—; owner, cons. GeoData Systems, Boulder City, 1991—; treas. Mifflin & Assocs., Inc., 1986-91; cons. Geoware, Boulder City, 1988-91. Sec. Nev. Community Cardiac Rehab., Inc., Las Vegas, 1988-91. Mem. AAAS, Am. Geophys. Union, Apple Programmers and Developers Assn., Computer Oriented Geol. Soc., Geochem. Soc., Internat. Assn. Geochemistry and Cosmochemistry, Internat. Assn. Math. Geologists, Assn. Eng. Geol., Assn. Expl. Geochem. Home: 1564 Inverness Ct Boulder City NV 89005-3620 Office: GMI Inc & GeoData Systems 1000 Nevada Hwy Ste 106 Boulder City NV 89005-1828

SHICHOR, DAVID, sociology educator; b. Budapest, Hungary, Mar. 17, 1933; came to U.S. 1975; s. Jacob and Malvin (Goldman) Suranyi; m. Pnina Pearl Shankman, Dec. 20, 1964; children: Nadav, Nomi. BA, Hebrew U., Jerusalem, Israel, 1962; MA, Calif. State U., L.A., 1966; PhD, U. So. Calif., 1970. Lectr. Tel-Aviv (Israel) U., 1970-75; lectr. to prof. criminal justice Calif. State U., San Bernardin, 1976—. Co-editor: Critical Issues in Delinquency, 1980; co-author: Victimization and Urban Structure, 1982; contbr. articles to profl. jours. Bd. dirs. Jewish Fedn. Coun., Orange County, Calif., 1989—. Mem. Am. Soc. Criminology, Am. Sociol. Assn., Pacific Sociol. Assn. Jewish. Office: Calif State U 5500 University Pky San Bernardino CA 92407-2397

SHICKLE, PAUL EUGENE, educator; b. Bloomington, Ill., Aug. 29, 1927; s. Benjamin Wilson and Eathel Delores (Rowe) S. B.S., Ill. State U., 1949. Cert. secondary tchr., Calif. Tchr. San Marino Unified Sch. Dist., Calif., 1956—, head fgn. lang. dept., 1967—. Mem. performing arts council Music Ctr. Los Angeles County. Mem. ACLU, NAACP, Soc. Indian Pioneers, Filson Club, Calif. Classical Assn. (pres. so. sect. 1981-82), Modern and Classical Assn. So. Calif., Am. Council Study Fgn. Lang., Calif. Humanities Assn., Am. Acad. Religion, Nat. Tchrs. Assn., Calif. Tchrs. Assn., Assn. for Supervision and Curriculum Devel., Am. Classical Assn., , Am. Acad. Polit. Sci., Am. Acad. Polit. & Social Sci., Am. Council for Arts, Ams. United for Separation Ch. and State, Ind. Hist. Soc., Bibl. Archaeology Soc., Calif. Assn. Supervision and Curriculum Devel., Am. Film Inst., Va. Geneal. Soc., Ky. Geneal. Soc., N.Am. Conf. Brit. Studies, History Sci. Soc., Nelson County (Ky.) Hist. Soc., Smithsonian Assocs., Nat. Trust for Historic Preservation, Met. Mus. Art (nat. assoc.), Met. Opera Guild, Asia Soc., Zionist Orgn. Am., Ctr. for Study of Presidency, Friends of the Quilt, L.A. World Affairs Coun., Clan Fraser Soc. North Am., Archeol. Inst. Am., Va. Country Civil War Soc., Nat. Park and Conservation Assn., UN Assn. of U.S., Soc. French Hist. Studies, Am. Conf. for Irish Studies, Irish Cultural Ctr., Nat. Coun. Social Studies, Conf. Group for Cen. European History. Republican. Roman Catholic. Home: 2115 Leafwood Ln Arcadia CA 91007-8126 Office: San Marino Unified Sch Dist 2701 Huntington Dr San Marino CA 91108-2295

SHIELDS, LORA MANGUM, biology educator emeritus, radioecology researcher; b. Choctaw, Okla., Mar. 13, 1912; d. William Lee and Ethel Florence (Talbott) S.; m. Clarence Leslie Mangum, Oct. 1932; 1 child, William Kay. BS in Edn. and Biology, U. N.Mex., 1940, MS in Biology, 1942; PhD in Botany, U. Iowa, 1947. Tchr., adminstr. pub. schs., McKinley, N.Mex., 1932-43; teaching asst. U. Iowa, Iowa City, 1943-47; prof., chair dept. biology N.Mex. Highlands U., Las Vegas, 1947-77, prof. emeritus, 1977—; prof., dir. rsch. Navajo Community Coll., Shiprock, N.Mex., 1978-88, prof. emeritus, 1988—. Contbr. over 90 articles to profl. publs. Recipient numerous grants NIH, NSF, AEC. Fellow AAAS (mem. com. on arid lands 1973-83, exec. officer SW/RM div. 1978-79, cert. of merit 1979); mem. Ecol. Soc. Am. (v.p. 1962-63), Nat. Assn. Acads. Sci. (pres. 1975-77), N.Mex. Acad. Sci. (v.p., pres. 1959-61, editor jour. 1971-77). Mem. LDS Ch. Home: 4825 W 9th St Greeley CO 80634-2030

SHIELDS, L(ORAN) DONALD, state agency administrator, former university president; b. San Diego, Sept. 18, 1936; s. Clifford L. and Malta S.; m. Patricia Ann Baldwin, Sept. 1, 1957; children: Ronald, Steven, Cynthia, Laurie. B.A., U. Calif. at Riverside, 1959; postgrad. (grad. asst. teaching fellow), U. Ill., 1959, U. So. Calif., 1959, U. Calif. at Los Angeles, 1959; Ph.D. (duPont teaching fellow), U. Calif. at Los Angeles, 1964. Asst. prof. chemistry Calif. State U., Fullerton, 1963-66; assoc. prof. Calif. State U., 1966-67, prof., 1967—, v.p. for adminstrn., 1967-70, acting pres., 1970-71, pres., 1971-80; pres. So. Meth. U., Dallas, 1980-86; exec. dir., coord. project Calif. Calif. Coun. on Sci. and Tech., 1989—; vis. prof. chemistry UCLA, summers, 1964-67; Cons. NSF, 1970—; mem. Nat. Sci. Bd., 1974-80. Author: Analytical Methods of Organic and Biochemistry, 1968, 76, Modern Methods of Chemical Analysis, 1968, 2d edit., 1976; Contbr. articles to profl. jours. Trustee Nat. Commn. Coop. Edn., 1977-84; bd. dirs. Dallas Citizens Council, 1986-87. Recipient Calif. State Legislature Distinguished Teaching award, 1965; named one of Five Outstanding Young Men Calif. Jr. C. of C., 1971; du Pont fellow, 1961-62. Mem. AAAS, Am. Chem. Soc., Am. Coll. Pub. Relations Assn., Am. Inst. Chemists (Honor Scroll award 1980), Orange County C. of C., Tex. Lyceum, Dallas Assembly, Town Hall Calif., Sigma Xi, Phi Lambda Upsilon. Office: Calif Coun Science & Technology 100 Academy Dr Irvine CA 92715

SHIELDS, WALTER W., management consultant; b. Spokane, Wash., Oct. 18, 1935; s. John S. and Mary L. (Wiley) S.; m. Shizuko Saito, Apr. 2, 1958 (div. 1978); children: Linda I., Theresa Ann, William Wiley, John William; m. Betty Ann Fetterhoff, Dec. 24, 1983 (div. 1992). Student, Santa Ana Community Coll., 1954-55; student in Bus. Adminstrn., Wash. State U., 1961-64. Dist. mgr. Universal Motor Club, Spokane, 1958-59; wholesale salesperson Berliner's, Spokane, 1959-60; dist. supr. Greyhound Lines, Inc., Phoenix, 1960-79; cons. Transp. Specialist, Spokane, 1979-80; transp. mgr. spl. svcs. Saudi Pub. Transport Co., Riyadh, Saudi Arabia, 1980-82; pvt. practice Spokane, 1982—; prin. Mgmt. Analysis, Spokane, 1987—; Ea. province transp. coord. Saudi Pub. Transport Co., 1981. Mem. citizen adv. com. on transp. for Spokane County, 1979-80; mem. adv. bd. Multiple-Sclerosis, Spokane, 1983-84. Sgt. USMC, 1953-58, Korea. Recipient cert. of appreciation for contbn. to devel. of Saudi Pub. Transp. Co., 1982. Mem. U.S. Assn. for Small Bus. and Entrepreneurs, Internat. Coun. for Small Bus. Office: Mgmt Analysis N 6105 Elm Spokane WA 99205

SHIER, DANIEL EDWARD, oil company executive; b. Columbus, Ohio, Oct. 22, 1939; s. George R. and Marie S. (Shouse) S.; m. Clare F. Cichowski, June 26, 1940; children: Lisa Marie, Sarah Suzanne, Dana Helene, Alexander Craig. BA, Rice U., 1961; PhD, Fla. State U., 1965. Geologist Shell Oil Co., Houston, 1965-69, New Orleans, 1969-74; mgr. Scientific Software Corp., Denver, 1974-81; cons. geologist Golden, Colo., 1981-89; pres. Energy Data Svcs., Englewood, Colo., 1989—; tchr. several courses/seminars in field, 1976—. Author several pub. domain PC progs. for geologists; contbr. articles to profl. jours. Mem. Mitchel Sch. Improvement Com., Golden, 1988-90. Mem. Computer Oriented Geol. Soc. (sec. 1982), Am. Assn. Petroleum Geologists, Soc. Profl. Well Log Analysts (field trip leader 1989, publs. com. 1980-91), Rocky Mountain Assn. Geologists. Republican. Office: Energy Data Svcs 98 Inverness Dr E Ste 170 Englewood CO 80112-5108

SHIFFER, JAMES DAVID, utility executive; b. San Diego, Mar. 24, 1938; s. Kenneth Frederick and Thelma Lucille (Good) S.; m. Margaret Edith Rightmyer, Sept. 5, 1959 (div. July 1986); children: James II, Elizabeth Warren, Russell; m. Esther Zamora, Sept. 13, 1986; stepchildren: Bryan Boots, Jeremy Hellier, Marisol Boots. BS ChemE, Stanford U., 1960, MS ChemE, 1961. Registered profl. engr., Calif. Nuclear engr. Pacific Gas & Electric Co., Humboldt Bay Power Plant, Eureka, Calif., 1961-71; tech. mgr. Pacific Gas & Electric. Co., Diablo Canyon Power Plant, Avila Beach, Calif., 1971-80; mgr. nuclear ops. Pacific Gas & Electric Co., San Francisco, 1980-84, v.p. nuclear power generation, 1984-90, sr. v.p., gen. mgr. nuclear power generation bus. unit, 1990-91, exec. v.p. elec. supply, nuclear power generation bus. units, 1991—, also bd. dirs; bd. dirs. PG and E Enterprises, Western Energy and Comm. Assn. Mem. Am. Inst. Chem. Engrs., Am. Nuclear Soc., Commonwealth Club of Calif. (bd. govs.), Pacific Coast Elec. Assn. (bd. dirs.). Republican. Episcopalian. Home: 2550 Royal Oaks Dr Alamo CA 94507-2227 Office: Pacific Gas & Electric Co PO Box 770000 77 Beale St B32 San Francisco CA 94177

SHIFFMAN, MAX, mathematician, educator; b. N.Y.C., Oct. 30, 1914; s. Nathan and Eva (Krasilchick) S.; m. Bella Manel (div. 1957); children: Bernard, David. BS, CCNY, 1935; MS, NYU, 1936, PhD, 1938. Instr. math. St. John's U., N.Y.C., 1938-39, CCNY, 1938-42; researcher Dept. Navy, NYU, 1942-45; asst. prof. math. NYU, 1945-49; prof. math. Stanford U., Palo Alto, Calif., 1949-66; prof. Calif. State U., Hayward, 1967-81; owner, mathematician Mathematico, Hayward and San Francisco, 1970—. Contbr. articles to profl. jours. Blumenthal fellow, 1935-38. Mem. Am. Math. Soc., Math. Assn. Am., Soc. Indsl. and Applied Math. Home and Office: 16913 Meekland Ave Apt 7 Hayward CA 94541-1300

SHIFFMAN, MELVIN ARTHUR, surgeon, oncologist; b. Bklyn., Aug. 23, 1931; s. Albert and Eva (Krieger) S.; m. Pearl Asher, Aug. 28, 1955; children: Scott, Karen, Denise. BS in Biochemistry, Union Coll., 1949; student dental medicine, Harvard U., 1953-54; MD, Northwestern U., 1957; JD, Western State U., 1976. Bd. cert. surgeon. Intern Los Angeles County Hosp., 1957-58; resident VA Hosp., Long Beach, Calif., 1960-64; pvt. practice oncologic surgery, cosmetic and reconstructive surgery Anaheim, Calif., 1964; chief of surgery Anaheim Gen. Hosp., 1969; chief of surgery Tustin (Calif.) Community Hosp., 1974, also chief of staff, bd. dirs., 1974; pvt. practice med.-legal cons. Tustin, 1976; prof. surgery and oncology, St. Lucia (West Indies) Health Scis. U., 1982-84; past chmn. bd. dirs. Monte Park Hosp., El Monte, Calif., 1975. Editor-in-chief Am. Jour. Cosmetic Surgery, 1993—; contbr. articles to med. jours. With USPHS, 1958-60. Fellow Internat. Biographical Assn., Internat. Coll. Surgeons, Am. Coll. Legal Medicine, Am. Soc. Cosmetic Breast Surgery, Inst. Bloodless Medicine and Surgery; mem. Soc. Head and Neck Surgeons, Am. Soc. Clin. Oncology, So. Calif. Acad. Clin. Oncology, Soc. Abdominal Surgeons, Am. Acad. Cosmetic Surgery, Soc. Liposuction Surgery, Internat. Soc. Cosmetic Surgery, Am. Soc. Law, Medicine and Ethics, Orange County Oncologic Soc. (founder, pres. 1970), Am. Cancer Soc. (pres. Orange County chpt. 1971-73), Union Am. Physicians and Dentists (bd. dirs. Orange County chpt. 1988, pres. 1982-88, bd. dirs. Calif. Fedn. 1982-88), Safari Club. Office: 1101 Bryan Ave # G Tustin CA 92680

SHIFRIN, BRUCE CARL, electrical engineer; b. Balt., June 14, 1947; s. Joseph Lewis and Sylvia (Spuntoff) S. BSEE, Poly. Inst. Bklyn., 1968; MSEE, Northeastern U., 1972, MSEM, 1976; m. Caryn Barbara Nadler, June 29, 1969; children: Jason Adam, Ian Todd. Engr. equipment devel. labs. Raytheon Co., Wayland and Sudbury, Mass., 1968-72, 73-77, systems engring. mgr. Sudbury, 1977-81; mgr. project mgmt. Iotron Corp., Bedford, Mass., 1982; program mgr. ATEX/EPPS inc. subs. Eastman Kodak Corp, 1982-84, dir. systems rsch. and engring., 1984-88; program mgr. R&D Linotype Co., Hauppage, N.Y., 1988-89; cons., Ashland, Mass., 1990; staff engr. C.S. Draper Lab. MIT, Cambridge, 1972-73; sr. cons. Dainippon Screen C.R.A., Inc., Brea, Calif., 1990—. Mem. IEEE Computer Soc. (chmn. Cen. New Eng. chpt. 1978-81), ACM, NCGA. Home: 10 Dion Laguna Niguel CA 92677-8619 Office: 3230 E Imperial Hwy Brea CA 92621

SHIH, BENEDICT CHESANG, investment company executive; b. Taipei, Taiwan, Jan. 3, 1935; s. Yun Ping and Chyu Ying (Shih) Chiu; m. Sophia Sufu Wu, Oct. 12, 1960; children: Vivian F. Shih Hauer, Peggy F., Phoebe F. Shih Sharp, Jonathan T. BA, Nat. Taiwan U., 1957. Pres. NOEC Corp., Taipei, 1973-78, KTT Corp., Irvine, Calif., 1983, Nat. Investment Corp., Taipei, 1983—, Nat. Investment Co. (U.S.) Corp., Issaquah, Wash., 1990—, Shih Corp., Issaquah, Wash., 1990—; cons. NCR Corp., Dayton, Ohio, 1979-83; ptnr. Blue Heron Assocs., Seabeck, Wash., 1989—; also bd. dirs. NOEC Corp., Taipei, Nat. Investment Corp., Taipei; bd. dirs. Shih Corp. Mem. TRW Credentials Svc., 1989—. Mem. Taiwan C. of C. of Seattle, Taiwan Chiaw Chi Country Club, Taiwan First Country Club, Taiwan Golf and Country Club, Bankers Club Taipei, Sahalee Country Club. Office: NIC (US) Corp 14800 SE 38th St Issaquah WA 98027-5727

SHIH, HONG, chemistry researcher; b. Qingdao, People's Republic of China, Dec. 2, 1945; came to U.S., 1981; s. Lin Shih and Yan Wang; m. Shaoping Chen, Oct. 1, 1976; 1 child, Alice (Yunyu). BS in Chemistry, Peking U., People's Republic of China, 1970; MS in Electrochemistry, Academia Sinica, People's Republic of China, 1981; PhD in Metallurgy, Pa. State U., 1986. Heat treat engr. Electric Power and Machinery Factory, Xian, People's Republic of China, 1970-73; analytical chemistry engr. Electric Power and Machinery Factory, Xian, 1973-78; rsch. engr. Academia Sinica, Xian, 1978-81; rsch. asst. Pa. State U., University Park, 1981-86; sr. rsch. scientist U. So. Calif., L.A., 1986-89, rsch. asst. prof., 1989-91; sr. scientist GM Rsch. Lab, Warren, Mich., 1991-92; corrosion engr. FMC Corp. Tech. Ctr., San Jose, Calif., 1992; pres., chief rsch. scientist Cortech Corp. Co., L.A., 1992—; cons. Leviton Mfg. Co., Inc., L.A., 1991-93, Schlumberger Tech., Inc., 1992-93, Applied Materials, San Jose, 1992-93, BASF Corp., Wyandotte, Mich., 1992-93, GM Rsch. Lab., Warren, 1993—; mem. planning com. 6th Pa. State U. Read Conf. on Electrodeposition, 1985; guest prof. corrosion sci. inst. Academia Sinica. Contbr. over 65 articles to profl. jours. including Jour. Electrochem., Jour. Environ. Enging., Electrochemica Acta, Corrosion Sci., Corrosion. Named 1st place winner grad. student poster contest Nat. Assn. Corrosion Engrs., 1984. Mem. AAAS, Am. Soc. of Testing Machines, Nat. Assn. Corrosion Engrs., The Electrochemical Soc. Home: 19030 Garnet Way Walnut CA 91789-4728 Office: 14145 Proctor Ave Ste 14 La Puente CA 91746

SHIKIAR, RICHARD, research center administrator; b. N.Y.C., Apr. 4, 1946; s. Benny and Rachel (Arestie) S.; m. Barbara Beverly Wexler, Aug. 19, 1967; children: Daniel Benjamin, Andrew Brett. BS, CCNY, 1967; MA, U. Ill., 1970, PhD, 1972. Asst. prof. Colo. State U., Ft. Collins, 1971-76, assoc. prof., 1976-79; rsch. scientist Battelle Human Affairs Rsch. Ctrs., Seattle, 1979-81; dir. Human Affairs Rsch. Ctrs. Social Change Study Ctr., Seattle, 1981-84, Battelle HARC, Seattle, 1984—, Battelle Seattle Rsch. Ctr., 1988—; mem. NAS/NRC Com. on Human Factors Rsch. Needs in Nuclear Industry, Washington, 1986-88. Contbr. articles to profl. jours. Bd. dirs. Seattle Symphony Orch., 1989—, Japan-Am. Soc. Wash., Seattle, 1991—. Mem. Am. Psychol. Soc., Nat. Acad. Mgmt., Soc. Indsl. and Orgnl. Psychology, Rocky Mt. Psychol. Assn. (sec. 1976-79), Rotary Club Seattle. Office: Battelle Seattle Rsch Ctr 4000 NE 41st St Seattle WA 98105-5428

SHILLATO, ROBERT WILLIAM, software quality executive; b. Granite City, Ill., July 16, 1940; s. Robert H. and Helen M. (Hawkins) S.; m. Sharon M. Doneen, Oct. 24, 1964; children: Sean M., Christina M. BS in Internat. Rels., Purdue U., 1962; AA in Bus., Sacramento City Coll., 1977. Cert. quality analyst. Support analyst RCA Corp., Sacramento, 1969-71; programmer City of Sacramento/County of Napa, Sacramento, 1971-72; programmer State of Calif., Sacramento, 1972-74, supr., 1974-76, analyst/mgr., 1976-80; project mgr. Wash. State U., Pullman, 1980-82; software quality analyst, cons. NCR Corp., San Diego, 1982-89; mgr. systems quality assurance Emerald Systems, Inc., San Diego, 1989-90; mgr. DDP Financials quality assurance Internat. Bill. Svcs., El Dorado Hills, Calif., 1991—. Capt. USAF, 1962-69. Recipient Award of Merit, Boy Scouts Am., 1990. Mem. Soc. for Software Quality (1st v.p. 1987-93), Quality Assurance Inst. (certification bd.), IEEE. Roman Catholic. Office: Internat Billing Svc 5220 R J Mathews Pkwy El Dorado Hills CA 95630-5712

SHIM, MIKE LEE, facilities, operations executive, consultant; b. San Francisco, Feb. 15, 1956; s. William E. and Rosalee Almol (Lee) Shim. BCE, U. Calif., Berkeley, 1978. Cert. plant engr., Calif. Switching engr. Pacific Telephone, San Jose, Calif., 1977-78; project engr., mgr. Procter & Gamble, Modesto, Calif., 1978-81; assoc. engr. Best Foods div. CPC Internat., San Francisco, 1981-82; corp. project engr. Ogden Food Products, Stockton, Calif., 1982-83; project mgr. Stamping Tech. Corp., Milpitas, Calif., 1983-88, dir. facilities ops., 1988-90; dir. facilities ops. Dyna-Craft Inc., Milpitas, Calif., 1990—; affirmative action instr. Procter & Gamble,

Modesto, 1979-81; co. energy rep. Calif. League Food Processors, Sacramento, 1982-83; exec. recruiter Shima's Pers. Svcs., Modesto, 1983-86; coop. dir. San Jose State U., 1984-87. 1st Big Brother Big Bros. & Big Sisters, Stockton, 1982-85. Recipient Energy Achievement award Pacific Gas & Electric Co., San Francisco, 1982, Water Pollution award Calif. Water Pollution Assn., San Jose, 1986, 88, 89, 90, Best Maintenance Orgn. award Maintenance Tech. Mag., Chgo, 1989, Safety award Calif. Safety Coun. Inc., Sacramento, 1989. Mem. Am. Inst. Plant Engrs. Office: Dyna Cratr Inc 2919 San Ysidro Way Santa Clara CA 95051-0683

SHIMABUKURO, ELTON ICHIO, sales professional; b. Hilo, Hawaii, Oct. 26, 1950; s. Hideo and Chieko (Hanashiro) S.; m. Lily Yuriko Fujimoto, May 3, 1980; 1 child, Kelli. BEd, U. Hawaii, Honolulu, 1974. CLU; chartered fin. cons. Sales pres. Sun Fin. Group, Honolulu, 1974-79, sales mgr., 1979—. Pres. Greenview Condominium Assn. of Apt. Owners, Honolulu, 1980-82; bd. dirs. Honolulu Japanese Jr. C. of C., 1983-84, Hawaii Lupus Found., Inc., 1990. With USAR, 1968-77. Mem. Am. Soc. CLUs and Chartered Fin. Cons., Internat. Assn. Fin. Planners, Gen. Agts. and Mgrs. Conf., West Honolulu Assn. Life Underwriters (bd. dirs. Honolulu chpt. 1984-86, treas. 1986-88, Life Ins. Profl. of Yr. 1989), Hawaii State Assn. Life Underwriters (chair membership com. Honolulu chpt. 1979-80, chmn. pub. rels. com. 1981-82), Kiwanis. Office: Sun Fin Group 711 Kapiolani Blvd Ste 1100 Honolulu HI 96813-5286

SHIMEK, DEAN TROY, mechanical engineer; b. Austin, Tex., Nov. 4, 1948; s. George Dean and Mary Ellen (White) S. AAS, Austin Community Coll., 1978, AS, 1978; BS in Mech. Engring., U. Tex., 1982; MS in Systems Mgmt., U. So. Calif., 1990. Mech. engr. USN Gage and Standards Ctr., Pomona, Calif., 1983-87; engring. data mgr. gov.-industry data exch. program USN Warfare Assessment Ctr., Corona, Calif., 1987—. Chmn. Gage and Standards Ctr. savings bond drive USN, 1986; mgr. Navy Twilight Golf League, Pomona, 1985. Mem. Navy League (local chpt. program com. 1984), Precision Measurements Assn. (treas. 1987-88), Air and Space Smithsonian (charter), U. S.C. Alumni Assn., Ex-Student's Assn. U. Tex., Smithsonian Inst. (assoc.). Methodist. Home: 6846 Plum Way Rancho Cucamonga CA 91739-1528 Office: USN NWAC C Code QA50 Corona CA 91718-8000

SHIMER, DONALD ALBERT, foundation administrator; b. Easton, Pa., Dec. 5, 1929; s. Arthur Charles and Dora (Alice) S.; m. Virginia Ries (div. Dec. 1969); m. Patricia Nan Worthington, Apr. 12, 1970; children: Donald Albert Jr., Peter Arthur, W. Ralph Lammers III. AB, Lafayette Coll., 1951; postgrad., Springfield Coll., 1954, U. Oreg., 1966, JFK Univ., 1978. Exec. YMCA, Worcester, Mass., Orange, N.J., Asbury Park, N.J., Portland, Oreg., 1951-69; v.p. J. Panas & Ptnrs., Chgo., 1969-74; pres. Shimer & Sons, Walnut Creek, Calif., 1974-84; exec. dir. Marin Gen. Hosp. Found., Greenbrae, Calif., 1984-89; exec. v.p. Gandhi Found., Orinda, Calif., 1989—; pres. Dollberger & Worthington Inc., 1991—; cons. USN, 1981, Security Pacific Bank, L.A., 1984, Moscow State Tech. U., 1989-91. Vice chmn. Calif. YMCA Youth and Govt., San Mateo; mem. San Francisco YMCA planning and ops. com.; lay eucharistic minister St. Paul's Episcopal Ch., Walnut Creek, Calif. Mem. Nat. Assn. Hosp. Devel. (accredited/cert.). Republican. Home: 1510 Arkell Rd Walnut Creek CA 94598-1207 Office: Gandhi Found 4 Bates Blvd Orinda CA 94563-2804

SHIMIZU, TAISUKE, bank executive; b. Osaka, Japan, Apr. 8, 1936; m. Tomoko Shimizu; children: Yumi, Toru, Megumi. BF, U. Tokyo. With Bank Tokyo, 1959-85, gen. mgr. Brussels office, 1982, gen. mgr. Europe and Africa div., 1984-85; exec. v.p., chief fin. officer Calif. First Bank, San Francisco, 1985-87; gen. mgr. overseas div. Bank Tokyo, 1987-88; vice chmn., dir. Calif. First Bank, Union Bank, San Francisco, 1988-90; pres., chief exec. officer Union Bank, San Francisco, 1990—. Office: Union Bank 350 California St San Francisco CA 94104-1402

SHIMPFKY, RICHARD L., bishop. Formerly rector Christ Ch. Ridgewood, N.J.; Episc. bishop, Diocese of El Camino Real Monterey, Calif., 1990—. Office: Diocese of El Camino Real PO Box 1903 Monterey CA 93942-1903*

SHIN, ERNEST EUN-HO, physicist, research institute executive; b. Chindo, Republic of Korea, Dec. 31, 1935; came to U.S., 1953; s. Hyung Sik and Ok Bin (Lim) S.; m. Shin-Ai Park, July 27, 1963; children: Irene, Juliet, Mariette, Michelle. BS in Physics, Carnegie Inst. Tech., 1957; AM in Physics, Harvard U., 1959, PhD in Physics, 1961. Rsch. fellow Cyclotron Lab., Harvard U., Cambridge, Mass., 1957-58, teaching fellow physics dept., 1958-59; rsch. assoc. Arthur D. Little, Inc., Cambridge, 1960-62; rsch. assoc. Francis Bitter Nat. Magnet Lab., MIT, Cambridge, 1962-66; prof. physics U. Miami, Coral Gables, Fla., 1966-72, founder, dir. Solid State Physics Lab., 1969-72; dir. Nieman Inst., Dallas, 1972-73; vis. scientist Korea Atomic Energy Rsch. Inst., Seoul, 1973-74; chmn., chief exec. officer Yulsan Am., Inc., San Francisco, 1974-89; dir. Chestnut Hill Inst., Napa, Calif., 1984—; co-founder Yulsan Group Cos., Seoul, 1974. Contbr. over 100 articles on biophysics, math. physics and elem. particle physics, superconduuctivity, optical properties of metals to profl. jours. Woodrow Wilson fellow Harvard U., 1959. Mem. AAAS, Am. Phys. Soc. (life), N.Y. Acad. Scis. Home: 3400 Redwood Rd Napa CA 94558-9706 Office: Chestnut Hill Inst PO Box 3510 Napa CA 94558-0350

SHIN, PAULL H., investment company executive; b. Kumchon, Korea, Sept. 27, 1935; came to U.S., 1955; adopted s. Ray and Eloise (Siddoway) Paull; m. Donn June Skaggs, June 12, 1963; children: Paull Y., Alisa M. BA, Brigham Young U., 1962; MPIA, U. Pitts., 1964; MA, U. Wash., 1972, PhD, 1978. Asst. prof. Brigham Young U., Laie, Hawaii, 1964-67; prof. Shoreline Coll., Seattle, 1969-72; pres. A.P.S. Investment Co., Seattle, 1982—; chmn. T.T.I. Telecom. Inc., Bellevue, Wash., 1992—; rep. Wash. State, Olympia; commr., chmn. Office of Pres. Korea, Seoul, 1985-88. Mission pres. LDS Ch., Seoul, 1988-91; bd. dirs. Asian-Ams. for Political Action, Seattle, 1982-84, United Way, Snohomish County, 1992—; advisor internat. trade Office Gov., Wash. State, 1983-88, Boy Scouts Am., 1986-88. With U.S. Army, 1958-60. Recipient Outstanding Svc. award Pres. Korea, 1985. Mem. Wash. State Korean Assn. (pres. 1983-84, Community Svc. award 1983), Rotary Club. Home: 8910 189th Pl SW Edmonds WA 98026 Office: 405 John O'Brien Bldg Olympia WA 98504

SHIN, SUK-HAN, geography educator, director Korean-American affairs; b. Seoul, Korea, Aug. 28, 1930; came to U.S., 1964; s. Kee Duk and Jung Sook (Shin) S.; m. Myung Jah Kim, Dec. 30, 1958; children: Yong Wook, Soo Hyun. BA, Seoul Nat. U., 1954; MA, Clark U., 1967; PhD, U. Pitts., 1975. Tchr. Jin Myung Girls Sr. High Sch., Seoul, 1954-61; urban planner Chonghab Architect Rsch. Ctr., Seoul, 1961-62; asst. planner S.W. Pa. Regional Planning Commn., Pitts., 1968; rsch. fellow Korea Rsch. Inst. of Human Settlements, Seoul, 1980; environ. cons. Engring.-Sci., Inc., Pasadena, Calif., 1982; prof. geography Ea. Wash. U., Cheney, 1969-92, prof. emeritus, 1992—; dir. Inst. Korean-Am. Affairs, Ea. Wash. U., Spokane, Wash. Author: Journal of Environmental Conservation, 1977, Impact of Industrial Development, 1980, Environment: Conservation Management and B/C, 1983; (chpt. in book) Themes and Research Methods, 1983. Mem. Adv. Coun. on Peaceful Unification of Republic of Korea, Seoul, 1982-87, 91—, Spokane Internat. Coordinating Coun., Spokane, 1986-88; pres. Spokane Korean Assn., 1978-84, Spokane Korean-Am. Citizens Assn., 1989—; chmn. Seoul Olympic Supporting Com. of Spokane, 1986-88. Donnelly fellow Clark U., 1965-66; grantee Korea Rsch. Found.; recipient City Medal of Seoul, 1980, Disting. Korean Scientist Abroad, Min. Sci. and Tech., ROK, 1980, Cert. of Appreciation Korea Rsch. Inst. Human Settlements, 1981, Minister of Environ., Republic of Korea, 1983, Cert. of Achievement, Korean Consul Gen., 1986. Mem. Assn. Am. Geographers (session chmn., 1983, '84, '91), Assn. Pacific Coast Geographers (session chmn. 1984), N.W. Sci. Assn. (chmn. soc. sci. 1975-76), Western Regional Sci. Assn. (session chmn. 1983, '84), Korean Geog. Soc., Korean Sci. and Engring. Assn., Am. Regional Sci. Assn. Office: East Washington U. Dept Geography Cheney WA 99004

SHINGLER, ARTHUR LEWIS, college official; b. Donalsonville, Ga., Mar. 8, 1941; s. A. Lewis and Bertha (Gunn) S.; m. Ginger Brady, July 28, 1961; children: Elizabeth, Arthur Lewis III, Brad, Jon. BA, Pasadena/Point Loma Coll., San Diego, 1962; MBA in Fin., U. So. Calif., 1965. CPA, Calif. Acct., cons. Peat, Marwick, Mitchell, L.A. and Denver, 1965-74; pres. Western Empire Fin., Denver, 1974-75; v.p. fin. Cen. Fed. Savs. & Loan, San Diego, 1976-80; v.p., then pres. Am. Savs., Stockton, Calif., 1980-85; broker, owner La Jolla (Calif.) Pacific Realty, 1986-91; v.p. fin. Point Loma Nazarene Coll., San Diego, 1991—. Recipient Disting. Alumnus award U. So. Calif., 1985. Mem. Christian Exec. Officers, Rotary (Paul Harris fellow 1989). Republican. Mem. Nazarene Ch. Home: 11514 Alba Rosa Dr Lakeside CA 92040 Office: Point Loma Nazarene Coll 3900 Lomaland Dr San Diego CA 92106

SHINN, DUANE K., music publisher; b. Auburn, Calif., Nov. 13, 1938; s. Archie W. and Iola E. (Eisley) S.; m. Beverly J. Luman; children: Kurt, Kendra, Garin, Garth. BS, So. Oreg. State Coll., 1970, MS, 1977. Prin. Keyboard Workshop/Duane Shinn Pubs., Medford, Oreg., 1965—. Author, pub. instructional audio and video cassettes on piano playing, including: Piano Improvising, 1985, How to Dress Up Naked Music, 1988, Keyboard by Chords, 1982, Piano Tricks: author: Will Herk Go to Hell for Biting the Avon Lady, 1980. Office: Duane Shinn Publs PO Box 700 Medford OR 97501-0047

SHIOTA, TAKAO, telecommunication research company executive; b. Tokyo, Feb. 16, 1950; s. Takeo and Masako (Matsusita) S.; m. Keiko Anna Akagi, March 15, 1981; children: Kentaro, Shinjiro, Sachiko. BS, Chiba U., Japan, 1972. Engr. Japan Distillation Industry, Inc., Chiba, 1972-73; engr. R & D Fujikura Ltd., Tokyo, 1973-83; mgr. R & D Fujikura Ltd., Chiba, 1983-91; group leader Optical Tech. Rsch. Corp. Noll Rsch. Group, Tsukuba, Japan, 1987-91; pres. Fujikura Tech. Am. Corp., Sunnyvale, Calif., 1991—. Author: Fundamentals and Application of MicroOptics, 1987, Handbook of Advanced Electronics Material, 1990; editor: Japan Jour. of Applied Physics, 1988-91. Mem. Optical Soc. of Am., Internat. Soc. for Optical Engring., Soc. Cable TV En grs. Office: Fujikura Tech Am Corp 743 Pastoria Ave Sunnyvale CA 94086

SHIPBAUGH, CALVIN LEROY, physicist; b. Huntington, Ind., Aug. 28, 1958; s. Paul and Marguerite (Pinkerton) S. BA, Rice U., 1980; PhD, U. Ill., 1988. Rsch. asst. U. Ill., Champaign-Urbana, 1981-88; analyst RAND Corp., Santa Monica, Calif., 1988—; space and surface power panel mem. Rand Support to NASA Project Outreach, Santa Monica, 1990; vis. scientist Fermilab, Batavia, Ill., 1982-85; workshop leader biotechnology Group, RAND; team mem. POET, Arlington, Va., 1989-92. Contbr. articles to Phys. Rev. Letters, Physics Letters and RAND Pub. Series. Mem. AIAA, Am. Phys. Soc. Office: The RAND Corp 1700 Main St Santa Monica CA 90401-3297

SHIPLEY, JAMES PARISH, JR., technology manager; b. Clovis, N.Mex., Jan. 3, 1945; s. James Parish and Cleta (Alexander) S.; m. Carolyn Gail Hall, June 29, 1962; children: Gary Don, Martin Everett, James Collin. BSEE, N.Mex. State U., 1966; MSEE, U. N.Mex., 1969, PhDEE, 1973. Program mgr. safeguards and security Los Alamos (N.Mex.) Nat. Lab., 1982-87, program mgr. for treaty verification, 1989—91, program dir. environ. mgmt., 1991—; sr. advisor to ambassador-at-large for non-proliferation policy U.S. Dept. State, Washington, 1987-89; pres. JP Systems, Inc., Los Alamos, 1991—. Mem. editorial bd. Rev. of Sci. Instruments, 1974-78; author, editor over 50 published works in the tech. field. Mem. Def. Sci. Bd./Summer Study Drugs and Terrorism, Washington, 1987; bd. dirs. Los Alamos Econ. Devel. Corp., 1985-87. Mem. IEEE, Am. Nuclear Soc., Inst. Nuclear Materials Mgmt. (exec. com. 1985-87), Kiwanis (pres. Los Alamos chpt. 1981-82). Home: 1646 Camino Uva Los Alamos NM 87544-2727

SHIPMAN, KEITH BRYAN, sportscaster; b. Puyallup, Wash., Apr. 26, 1961; s. Richard James and Carol Esther (Christianson) S.; m. Julie Anne Poppe, June 30, 1984; 1 child, Alicia Bryanne. BA in Comms., Wash. State U., 1983. Sportscaster/producer KOMO Radio/TV, Seattle, 1983-85; sports/pub. affairs dir. KCPQ TV, Tacoma-Seattle, 1986—; AM drive sports host KJR Radio, Seattle, 1991-93; disc jockey KPUG AM/KNWR FM Radio, Bellingham, Wash., 1978-81; play-by-play announcer Tri-Cities Triplets Baseball, KAFR-FM Radio, Richland, Wash., 1985; baseball guide track announcer Turner Broadcasting System, Atlanta, 1990; host/producer "The Chuck Knox Show", Anderson/Baer Prodns., Bainbridge Island, Wash., 1987-88; host "The Chuck Knox Show", Andersen Ent., Bellevue, Wash., 1985-88, various other free-lance work. Pres. bd. dirs. Plaza Hall, Tacoma, Wash., 1989—; exec. com. Muscular Dystrophy Assn., Seattle, 1989-91; vol. Boys and Girls Club of King County, Seattle and Whatcom County, Bellingham, 1988—. Named Sportscaster of the Yr. for Wash., Nat. Sportscasters and Sportswriters Assn., 1986, 87, 88; recipient Emmy award Nat. Acad. TV Arts and Scis., 1990, 92. Mem. Nat. Sportscasters and Sportswriters Assn. (bd. dirs. 1989—, 2nd v.p.), Nat. Acad. TV Arts and Scis., Radio TV News Dirs. Assn. Office: KCPQ TV 4400 Steilacoom Blvd SW Tacoma WA 98499

SHIPMAN, MICHAEL SCOTT, wildlife biologist; b. Topeka, Mar. 12, 1963; s. Donald Eugene and Judith Kae (Henry) S. Student, U. Nebr., Omaha, 1982-83, Arapahoe C.C., 1987-88, Lincoln U., 1989; BS in Wildlife Biology, Colo. State U., 1992. Seasonal ranger Colo. Div. Parks and Outdoor Recreation, Franktown, summer 1988; seasonal ranger Colo. Div. Parks and Outdoor Recreation, Littleton, summer 1990, interpretive ranger, summer 1992; technician Colo. Div. Wildlife, Ft. Collins, 1990, Colo. State U., Ft. Collins, 1990-91; curatorial asst. Denver Mus. Natural History, 1991—, biol. technician, spring 1992; biol. technician Nat. Ecology Rsch. Ctr., U.S. Fish and Wildlife Svc., Ft. Collins, 1991-92; hawk watch coord. Denver Mus. Nat. History, spring 1993; Denver rep. Operation Raleigh, U.S.A., Denver, 1986-88. Asst. scoutmaster Boy Scouts Am., Bellevue, Nebr., 1981, Eagle Scout, 1981. Recipient Cert. of Appreciation, Hugh O'Brian Youth Found., 1986, HRH Prince Charles, 1987. Mem. Cousteau Soc., Wildlife Soc. Home: 6355 W Frost Dr Littleton CO 80123

SHIPP, JOSEPH CALVIN, physician, educator; b. Northport, Ala., Feb. 10, 1927; s. Ezra Jonah and Norah (Earnest) S.; m. Marjorie Madelline Morris, Nov. 25, 1961; children: Joseph Calvin, Sherise, Dana, Michele. BS, U. Ala., 1948; MD, Columbia U., 1952. Diplomate Am. Bd. Internal Medicine. Asst. prof. medicine Harvard Med. Sch., Boston, 1958-60; rsch. scientist Oxford U., Eng., 1958-59; assoc. prof. medicine U. Fla., Gainesville, 1960-65; prof. medicine U. Fla., 1965-70; prof. and chmn. dept. medicine U. Nebr., Omaha, 1970-80; regent's disting. prof. medicine U. Nebr., 1980-86; prof. medicine U. Calif. San Francisco, Fresno, 1986—; cons. NIH, 1965-85, Fulbright-Hayes Internat. Medicine, 1976—. Contbr. over 200 articles to profl. jours. in field of diabetes and medicine. With USN, 1944-46. Fulbright-Hayes awardee, 1977. Fellow ACP; mem. Am. Diabetes Assn., Endocrine Soc., Am. Soc. Clin. Investigation, Assn. Am. Physicians, Rotary (chmn. internat. activities com. 1988-89), Alpha Omega Alpha, Phi Beta Kappa, Masons, Elks. Republican. Roman Catholic. Home: 7463 N Laguna Vista Ave Fresno CA 93711-0231 Office: U Calif San Francisco 445 S Cedar Ave Fresno CA 93702-2907

SHIPPER, FRANK MARTIN, management educator, consultant, author; b. Martinsburg, W.Va., June 27, 1945; s. Paul Bishop and Lillian Foreman (Flagg) S.; m. Frances Irene Clarke, Dec. 19, 1981; children: Christopher Clarke, James Ford, Jay Martin. BSME, W. Va. Univ., 1968; MBA, U. Utah, 1973, PhD, 1978. Asst. prof. Ariz. State U., Tempe, 1977-81, assoc. prof., 1982-91; prof. mgmt. Salisbury (Md.) State U., 1991—; coord. Purdue Sch. Rsch., 1991—; human productivity cons., U.S. Navy, Washington, 1980-81; cons. Dushoff & Sacks, Phoenix, 1979-80, 1984-86, Streich, Lang, Weeks & Cardon, Phoenix, 1981-85, De Concini, McDonald, Brammer, Yetwin & Lacy, Tucson, 1982-91, Penton Learning Systems, N.Y.C., 1986-87, Booth-Wright Mgmt. Systems, Boulder, Colo., 1986-87, City of Phoenix, 1987, Phoenix VA, 1987, Holsum Bakeries, 1987, prin. investigator VA, Phoenix, 1986-89, Intel, 1990, Clark Wilson Group, 1991—. Author: Business Strategy for the Political Arena, 1984, Avoiding and Surviving Lawsuits: The Executive Guide to Strategic Legal Planning, 1988, Task Cycle Management: A Competency-Based Course for Operating Managers, 1990; contbr. numerous articles to profl. jours. Co-founder, pres. Data Based Organizational Research Group, Tempe, 1979-80; bd. dirs. East Valley Big Bros., 1983; mem. exec. com. Ariz. State U., 1984-85; mem. State Bd. of Edn., 1990-91. Served to capt. USAF, 1968-72. Faculty grantee Ariz. State U., 1979, 82, 90; Fed. Faculty fellow Am. Assembly of Collegiate Schs. of Bus., 1980-81. Mem. Am. Psychol. Assn., Acad. Mgmt., Assn. for Quality and Participation, Assn. for Quality and Participation (bd. dirs. chpt. 1983-85, pres. 1984-85), Nat. Ctr. for Employee Ownership, Internat. Assn. for Bus. and Soc. (founding mem.). Republican. Presbyterian. Avocations: skiing, cycling, swimming.

SHIPPER, TODD JEFFREY, communications executive; b. Detroit, Nov. 18, 1946; s. Norman N. Shipper and Evaline (Spring) Krasner; m. Sherry E. Brown, May 30, 1968 (div. 1969). AA, L.A. Valley Coll., 1970; student, Calif. State U., Northridge, 1970-72. Announcer various radio stas., 1967-73; salesman, mgr. Standard Shoes, Encino, Calif., 1973-76; asst. mgr. K-Mart, Westminster, Calif., 1976-77; salesman Contractors Lic. Sch., Van Nuys, Calif., 1977-80; dir. mktg. Columbia Sch. Broadcasting, Hollywood, Calif., 1980-84; owner, operator Nat. Broadcasting Sch., Sacramento, Portland, Seattle, 1984-92, Las Vegas, 1984—; owner, operator NBS Travel Tng. Sch., 1989-92, Nat. Career Tng. Ctr., Las Vegas, 1992—; prin. Nat. Advt. Agy., Las Vegas, 1986—, Nat. Ednl. Cons., Las Vegas, 1986—. With USAF, 1965-67. Mem. Nat. Assn. Trade and Tech. Schs., Assn. Broadcasters. Democrat. Jewish. Office: Nat Career Tng Ctr 1771 E Flamingo Rd Las Vegas NV 89119-5155

SHIPPEY, SANDRA LEE, lawyer; b. Casper, Wyo., June 24, 1957; d. Virgil Carr and Doris Louise (Conklin) McC.; m. Ojars Herberts Ozols, Sept. 2, 1978 (div.); children: Michael Ojars, Sara Ann, Brian Christopher; m. James Robert Shippey, Jan. 13, 1991. BA with distinction, U. Colo., 1978; JD magna cum laude, Boston U., 1982. Bar: Colo. 1982, U.S. Dist. Ct. Colo. 1985. Assoc. Cohen, Brame & Smith, Denver, 1983-84, Parcel, Meyer, Schwartz, Ruttum & Mauro, Denver, 1984-85, Mayer, Brown & Platt, Denver, 1985-87; counsel western ops. GE Capital Corp., San Diego, 1987—. Mem. Phi Beta Kappa, Phi Delta Phi. Republican. Mem. Ch. of Christ. Home: 11878 Glenhope Rd San Diego CA 92128-5002 Office: GE Capital Corp 10251 Vista Sorrento Pky San Diego CA 92121-2715

SHIRAI, SCOTT, communications executive; b. Honolulu, June 5, 1942; s. George Yoshio and Thelma Takeko (Tominaga) M.; children: Todd, Kimberly, Lance, Lyle. MusB, U. Hawaii, 1983; exec. dir. news, reporter Sta. KHON-TV, Honolulu, 1974-81; asst. gen. mgr. Vanguard Investments, Berkeley, Calif., 1976-79; newscaster Sta. KPOI, Honolulu, 1979-80; news dir. Sta. KGU, Honolulu, 1981-82; owner Visual Perspectives, 1981—; dir. pub. rels. Hawaiian Electric Co., Honolulu, 1982-90; dir. community rels., Hawaiian Electric Industries, 1990—. Bd. dirs., sec. Hawaii Com. For Freedom of Press, 1982—; bd. dirs. Mental Health Assn. in Hawaii, 1981—, Moanalua Gardens Found., 1981-84, Health and Community Services Council, 1982-86, Pohakupu Community Assn., 1984—, Friends of Father Damien, 1986; v.p. Mele Nani Singers, 1986—; mem. Mayors Adv. Com. on Mcpl. TV, 1987, Office of Hawaiian Affairs Pub. Rels. Adv. Com., 1987, (all Honolulu); sec., dir. Pro Geothermal Alliance, 1990-91. Recipient Jefferson award Honolulu Advertiser, 1985, Gold award Audio-Visual Producers Assn. Am., 1985, Audio-Visual Dept. of Yr. award Videography mag., 1986, Award of Excellence Nat. Hospice Orgn., 1987, Intre award Inst. Teleradial Atica Puerto Rico, Inc., 1988. Mem. Internat. TV Assn. (pres. 1983—), Am. Soc. Tng. and Devel., Am. Film Inst., AFTRA (bd. dirs. 1980-83), Pub. Relations Soc. Am. (pres.-elect 1993), Hawaii Speakers Assn., Hawaii Film Bd., Honolulu Community Media Council, Hawaii Community TV Assn. (pres. 1990—), Honolulu Community TV Prodrs. Assn. (pres. 1991—). Clubs: Honolulu Press (bd. dirs. 1984—), Hui Luna (bd. dirs. 1986-90) (Honolulu). Avocation: martial arts. Office: Hawaiian Electric Industries PO Box 730 1001 Bishop St Ste 811 Honolulu HI 96808

SHIRASAWA, RICHARD MASAO, systems analyst and coordinator; b. Cleve., Jan. 18, 1948. BS, Mich. State U., 1970; MPA, U. So. Calif., 1992. Lab. technician Litton Bionetics, Bethesda, Md., 1971-73; biologist NIH, Washington, 1973-79; mgmt. intern Dept. HHS, Washington, 1979-81; systems coord. Health Care Financing Adminstrn., San Francisco, 1981—. Mem. Toastmasters Internat. (named Competent Toastmaster 1988). Office: Health Care Fin Adminstrn 75 Hawthorne St San Francisco CA 94105

SHIRE, HAROLD RAYMOND, legal educator, author, social scientist; b. Denver, Nov. 23, 1910; s. Samuel Newport and Rose Betty (Herman) S.; m. Cecilia Goldhaar, May 9, 1973; children: David, Darcy, Esti. MBA, Pepperdine U., 1972; LLD (hon.), 1975; JD, Southwestern U., L.A., 1974; M in Liberal Arts, U. So. Calif., 1977; PhD in Human Behavior, U.S. Internat. U., San Diego, 1980. Bar: Calif. 1937, U.S. Dist. Ct. (so. dist.) Calif. 1939, U.S. Supreme Ct. 1978. Dep. dist. atty. L.A. County, Calif., 1937-38; asst. U.S. atty. So. Dist. Calif., L.A. and San Diego, 1939-42; pvt. practice, L.A., 1946-56; pres., chmn. bd. Gen. Connectors Corp., U.S. and Eng., 1956-73; prof. mgmt. and law Pepperdine U., Malibu, Calif., 1974-75, U.S. Internat. U., San Diego, 1980-83; dir. Bestobell Aviation, Eng., 1970-74. Advisor U. S.C. Gerentology, Andrus Ctr., pre-retirement tng., 1976-80; bd. dirs. Pepperdine U., 1974-80; nat. bd. govs. Union Orthodox Jewish Congregations Am., 1973—. With U.S. Army, 1942-46. Author: Cha No Yu and Symbolic Interactionism: Method of Predicting Japanese Behavior, 1980; The Tea Ceremony, 1984. Patentee aerospace pneumatics; invented flexible connectors. Pres. Jewish Nat. Fund Legion of Honor, 1991—; mem. Presdl. Roundtable, Washington, 1989-93. Decorated chevalier du vieux moulin (France); companion Royal Aero. Soc. (U.K.); recipient Tea Name Grand Master Soshitsu Sen XV Urasenke Sch., Kyoto, Japan, 1976, Medal of Honor Jewish Nat. Fund, 1991, Legion of Honor, 1991. Mem. Am. Legion (svc. officer China #1), Masons (32 degree), Royal Arch, Shrine. Republican. Office: PO Box 1352 Beverly Hills CA 90213-1352

SHIREMAN, JOAN FOSTER, social work educator; b. Cleve., Oct. 28, 1933; d. Louis Omar and Genevieve (Duguid) Foster; m. Charles Howard Shireman, Mar. 18, 1967; 1 child, David Louis. BA, Radcliffe Coll., 1956; MA, U. Chgo., 1959, PhD, 1968. Caseworker N.H. Children's Aid Soc., Manchester, 1959-61; dir. research Chgo. Child Care Soc., 1968-72; assoc. prof. U. Ill., Chgo., 1972-85; prof. Portland (Oreg.) State U., 1985—; research cons. child welfare orgns., Ill., 1968-85, Oreg. 1985—; lectr. U. Chgo., 1968-72. Co-author: Care and Commitment: Foster Parent Adoption Decisions, 1985; mem. editorial bd. Jour. Sch. Social Work, 1978-81, Social Work Rsch. and Abstracts, Children and Youth Svcs. Rev., Jour. of Social Work Edn., 1990—; contbr. chpts. to books and articles to profl. jours. Bd. dirs. Oreg. chpt. Nat. Assn. for Prevention of Child Abuse, 1985-87, Friendly Houns, Portland, 1992—; mem. adv. com. Children's Svcs. div. State of Oreg., 1985—. Grantee HEW, 1980-82, Chgo. Community Trust, 1982-86, Oreg. Children's Trust Fund, 1991—. Mem. Nat. Assn. Social Workers, AAUP, Citizens for Children, Acad. Cert. Social Workers, Council on Social Work Edn., Phi Beta Kappa. Home: 2535 SW Sherwood Dr Portland OR 97201-1679 Office: Portland State U Grad Sch Social Work PO Box 751 Portland OR 97207-0751

SHIRILAU, JEFFERY MICHEAL, engineering executive; b. Honolulu, Aug. 30, 1953; s. Cornelius Afai Lauliiuokalani and Dolores Bennett (Bezanson) Lau; life ptnr. Mark Steven Shirey. Cert. data processing, ITT Peterson, Seattle, 1982; AS, Rancho Santiago, Santa Ana, Calif., 1984. Ordained deacon The Ecumenical Cath. Ch., Sept. 23, 1984. Owner Lau & Assocs., Seattle, 1979-82; div. mgr. M.S.E., Santa Ana, 1982-86; supr. U.S. Postal Svc., Alhambra, Calif., 1986-87; pres., CEO Aloha Systems, Inc., Villa Grande, Calif., 1987—, also bd. dirs. With airborne rangers and Green Beret U.S. Army, 1971-74. Charter mem. Assn. of Demand-Side Mgmt. Profls.; mem. IEEE, Ainahau Hawaiian Orange County, Calif. Civic Club, Pacific Bears Leather Motorcycle Club. Republican. Home: 20200 River Blvd Monte Rio CA 95462 Office: Aloha Systems Inc PO Box 32 Villa Grande CA 95486-0032

SHIRLEY, DAVID ARTHUR, chemistry educator, science administrator; b. North Conway, N.H., Mar. 30, 1934; m. Virginia Schultz, June 23, 1956; children: David N., Diane, Michael, Eric, Gail. BS, U. Maine, 1955, ScD (hon.), 1978; PhD in Chemistry, U. Calif.-Berkeley, 1959; D honoris causa, Free U. Berlin, 1987. With Lawrence Radiation Lab. (now Lawrence Berkeley Lab.), U. Calif., Berkeley, 1958-92, assoc. dir., head materials and molecular research div., 1975-80, dir., 1980-89, lectr. chemistry, 1959-60, asst. prof., 1960-64, assoc. prof., 1964-67, prof., 1967-92, vice chmn. dept. chemistry, 1968-71, chmn. dept. chemistry, 1971-75; sr. v.p. rsch., dean grad. sch. Pa. State U., University Park, 1992—. Contbr. over 350 rsch. articles. NSF fellow, 1955-58, 66-67, 70; recipient Ernest O. Lawrence award AEC, 1972, Humboldt award (sr. U.S. scientist); listed by Sci. Citation Index as one of the world's 300 most cited scientists for work published during 1965-78. Fellow Am. Phys. Soc.; mem. Nat. Acad. Scis., Am. Chem. Soc., AAAS, Am. Acad. Arts and Scis., Sigma Xi, Tau Beta Pi, Sigma Pi Sigma, Phi Kappa Phi.

SHIRLEY, GEORGE PFEIFFER, lawyer, educational consultant; b. Algood, Tenn., Dec. 12, 1939; s. Howard Dunbar and Maryhils Lewis (Pfeiffer) S.; m. Mary Ann Clawson, May 24, 1958 (div.); m. Susan Hawkins, July 24, 1971 (div.); m. Laura Gail Salmonsen, Feb. 29, 1992; children: Kathleen Underwood, Bryan. BA, U. Denver, 1962, MA, 1963, JD, 1966. Tchr. various high schs., coll. and law schs., 1964—; adminstr. Pan Am Petrol, Denver, 1966-68; lobbyist Sacramento and Washington, 1968-72; lawyer, exec. dir. legal svcs. Calif., Fla. and Minn., 1972-83; pvt. ednl. cons. San Jose, Calif., 1986—; bd. dirs. Cal-Micro, Inc., San Jose, Am. Grinding Co., San Jose; lectr. various univs., 1986—. Campaign coord. Dem. Party, Sacramento, 1972. 1st lt. ROTC, USMC 1957-66. Mem. Internat. Platform Assn., Order of Coif, Pi Gamma Mu. Methodist. Home: 1721 Gladstone Ave San Jose CA 95124

SHIRLEY, JOHN JEFFERY, manufacturing executive; b. Dallas, Jan. 28, 1955; s. John Albert Jr. and Margaret Louise (Webb) S.; m. Kathe Wright Hildreth, Sept. 20, 1978. BS in Computer Sci., Nat. U., 1987, MS in Software Engring., 1989. Engr. 3M Co., San Diego, 1973-82; sr. engr. Grumman Aerospace, Virginia Beach, Va., 1982-85; computer specialist Grumman Aerospace, San Diego, 1985-89, dir. computer ops. Western area, 1989—; owner Digital Concepts, San Diego, 1978—; instr. P.D. Pruden Votech, Chesapeake, Va., 1982-83; assoc. prof. Nat. U., San Diego, 1989—; instr. U. Calif., San Diego, 1989—. Republican. Office: Grumman Aircraft Svcs PO Box 366 San Diego CA 92112-0366

SHIRLEY, MICHAEL JAMES, ski area executive; b. Flagstaff, Ariz., Oct. 25, 1941; s. James Watson and Lorraine Elizabeth (Thomson) S.; m. Gloria Marie Bruni, Aug. 20, 1966; children: Brian Michael, Cynthia Marie. BS, No. Ariz. U., Flagstaff, 1969; MBA, U. Ariz., 1970. Sr. acct. Morrison-Knudsen Co., Inc., Boise, Idaho, 1970-72; asst. treas. Morrison-Knudsen Co., Inc., 1972-74, corp. treas., 1974-75, v.p. adminstrn., 1975-85; v.p. adminstrn. Morrison Knudsen Corp., 1985-89, v.p. fin., treas., 1989-91; gen. mgr. Bogus Basin Ski Area, Idaho, 1991—. Bd. dirs. United Way Ada County, 1975-81; bd. dirs. Jr. Achievement of S.W. Idaho, 1978-86, pres., 1983-86; mem. Idaho Coun. Econ. Edn., 1978—; bd. dirs. Boise Philharm. Assn., 1982-85, Bogus Basin Recreation Assn., 1984—. Staff sgt. USAF, 1963-67. Recipient Wall St. Jour. award No. Ariz. U., 1969, Alumni Achievement award, 1978. Mem. Boise Area C. of C. (bd. dirs. 1985-89). Republican.

SHIRLEY, ROBERT BRYCE, lawyer; b. Morehead City, N.C., Feb. 5, 1951; s. Robert Wayne Shirley and JoAnne Elaine (Shook) S.; m. Marilyn Jeanette Roy, June 30, 1973; children: Robert Wayne, James Roy, Emma Kate. BA, Stanford U., 1973, MBA, 1977, JD, 1977. Bar: Calif. 1977, Ohio 1981, U.S. Dist. Ct. (cen. dist.) Calif., 1978, U.S. Dist. Ct. (no. dist.) Ohio 1984, U.S. Dist. Ct. (so. dist.) Ohio 1985. Assoc. McKenna & Fitting, Los Angeles, 1977-79; gen. counsel The Way Internat., New Knoxville, Ohio, 1980-85; ptnr. Morrison & Shirley, Irvine, Calif., 1985-87; sr. real estate atty., Taco Bell Corp., Irvine, 1988-92; corp. counsel PepsiCo, Inc., Irvine, 1993—. Mem. ABA, Calif. Bar Assn., Orange County Bar Assn. Republican. Avocations: skiing, tennis, golf. Home: 13692 Andede Way Irvine CA 92720-3201 Office: Taco Bell Corp 17901 Von Karman Blvd Irvine CA 92714

SHIRLEY, ROBERT CLARK, university president, strategic planning consultant, educator; b. Jacksonville, Tex., July 1, 1943; s. James Cullen and Mary Jim (Clark) S.; m. Terrie Thomas, June 17, 1967; children: Robin, Deron. B.B.A., U. Houston, 1965, M.B.A., 1967; Ph.D., Northwestern U., 1972. Asst. dean faculties U. Houston, 1974-76; asst. to pres. SUNY-Albany, 1976-77, assoc. v.p. acad. affairs, 1977-79; assoc. prof. Central U. Iowa, Pella, 1979-81; prof. Trinity U., San Antonio, 1981-84; pres. U. So. Colo., Pueblo, 1984—; cons. on strategic planning and mgmt. to numerous colls. and univs. Author: Strategy and Policy Formation, 1981; contbr. articles to profl. publs. Mem. Pueblo Econ. Devel. Bd. Bill Laufman Meml. scholar U. Houston, 1965-66; Northwestern U. fellow, 1969-71; HEW research asst. grantee, 1971, 72; La. State U. Found. grantee, 1972, 73. Mem. Acad. Mgmt., Soc. Coll. and Univ. Planning, Pueblo C. of C. Presbyterian. Lodge: Rotary. Office: U So Colo 2200 Bonforte Blvd Pueblo CO 81001-4990

SHIRROD, TERRY S., mechanical engineer; b. La Jolla, Calif., Nov. 22, 1946; s. William Byron and Barbara Nadie (Wake) S.; m. Barbara Lynn Grince, June 19, 1976; children: Christina, Kimberley. BS with honors, U. Calif., Davis, 1969; MS, UCLA, 1971. Engr. Hughes Aircraft Co., El Segundo, Calif., 1969—. Patentee in field. Pres. St. Luke Luth. Ch., Albuquerque, 1991—.

SHIRTCLIFF, JOHN DELZELL, business owner, oil jobber; b. Roseburg, Oreg., Mar. 2, 1948; s. Henry Marion and Sheila Nell (Delzell) S.; m. Connie Lee Cantrell, June 13, 1975; children: Darcie, Danielle, Andrew. BS, Oregon State U., 1970. Pres. Shirtcliff Oil Co., Myrtle Creek, Oreg., 1971—. Engr. Myrtle Creek (Oreg.) Vol. Fire Dept., 1971—, emergency technician, 1981—; mem. Rep. Cen. Com., Roseburg, Oreg., 1982-88; chmn. Umpqua Community Coll. Budget Com., Roseburg, 1983—; bd. dirs. Mercy Hospice, Roseburg, 1988—. 2nd lt. U.S. Army, 1970-71. Named Citizen of Year, Myrtle Creek City, 1986, Vol. of Year, Douglas County C. of C., 1987. Mem. Petroleum Marketers Assn. Am. (dir. Oreg. 1988), Oreg. Petroleum Marketers Assn. (v.p. legis. chmn. 1986, pres. 1987, PMAA dir. 1988), Pacific Oil Conf. (bd. dirs.), Lions, Elks, Masons, Shriners. Republican. Office: Shirtcliff Oil Co 283 SW Western Ave PO Box 6003 Myrtle Creek OR 97457

SHIRTS, RANDALL BRENT, chemistry educator, researcher; b. Mt. Pleasant, Utah, Apr. 28, 1950; s. Morris Alpine and Dorothy Maxine (Baird) S.; m. Kathryn Adele Hanson, June 12, 1974; children: Michael, Brian, Caitlin, Peter, Kristen, Erica. BS in Chemistry, Brigham Young U., 1973; AM in Physics, Harvard U., 1978, PhD in Chem. Physics, 1979. Postdoctoral assoc. JILA, Boulder, Colo., 1979-81; asst. prof. chemistry Georgetown U., Washington, 1981-82; asst. prof. chemistry U. Utah, Salt Lake City, 1982-88, vis. assoc. prof. chemistry, 1990-91; vis. assoc. prof. chemistry Brigham Young U., 1991; scientific specialist EG & G Idaho, Inc., Idaho Falls, 1987-91; assoc. prof. chemistry Brigham Young U., Provo, 1991—; prin. investigator INEL theoretical chemistry initiative, 1987-91. Contbr. articles to profl. jours. Grantee Nat. Sci. Found., 1985-88, Research Corp., 1982-84, Petroleum Research Fund, 1982-84. Mem. Am. Chem. Soc., Am. Phys. Soc., Sigmi Xi. Mormon. Office: Brigham Young Univ Dept Chemistry Provo UT 84602

SHISHIDO, CALVIN M., protective services administrator; b. Honolulu, Aug. 24, 1933; s. Isamu and Kane (Seto) S.; children: Dale, Neala. BS, Florence State, 1961. Spl. agt. IRS, Pitts., 1962-65, FBI, Washington, 1965-84; pvt. investigator Honolulu, 1987-88; spl. asst. to deputy dir. Harbors Div Dept. of Transp., Hawaii, 1988-90; sheriff State of Hawaii, 1990-91, spl. projects mgr. dept. pub. safety, 1991—. Sgt. USAF, 1952-57. Mem. Soc. Former Spl. Agts. of FBI (chpt. chmn. Honolulu 1987-88), Lions (program chmn. San Francisco 1970-71), Jr. C. of C.

SHISHIDO, FUMITAKE, cruise company executive; b. Tokyo, Mar. 3, 1960; came to U.S., 1985; s. Osamu and Miyoko (Sugiue) S.; m. Kayoko Matsubara, June 21, 1986. BA, Waseda U., Tokyo, 1982; MBA, Columbia U., N.Y.C., 1987. Line mgr. Nippon Yusen Kaisha, Tokyo, 1982-84, investment analyst, 1984-85, project team mem., 1987-88; dir. fin. and asst. sec. Crystal Cruises, Inc., L.A., 1988-92, v.p., treas., 1993—. Mem. Town Hall of So. Calif., Columbia Bus. Sch. Club Japan, Beta Gamma Sigma (N.Y.). Office: Crystal Cruises 2121 Avenue Of The Stars Los Angeles CA 90067-5010

SHISSLER, STEVEN ALAN, insurance representative; b. Denver, Mar. 29, 1962; s. Franklin William Shissler and Corentha Ann Nevins Briles. BS, Metro. State U., Denver, 1987. Bodily injury claims rep. State Farm Ins., Westlake Village, Calif., 1988—. With U.S. Army, 1980-83. Recipient Humanitarian Svc. award U.S. Army, 1981, Golden Key, 1987. Episcopalian. Home: 2080 W Hillcrest Dr Newbury Park CA 91320 Office: State Farm Ins 31303 Agoura Rd Westlake CA 91363

SHIVELY, JOHN TERRY, business executive; b. Middletown, N.Y., July 1, 1943; s. Marvin Rathfelder and Esther (Manning) Westervelt; adopted child, Harold Eugene Shively; B.A., U. N.C., 1965. Vol. worker VISTA, Bethel, Yakutat, and Fairbanks, Alaska, 1965-68; health planner Greater Anchorage Area Community Action Agy., 1968-69; health cons. Alaska Fedn. Natives, Anchorage, 1969; dep. dir. Rural Alaska Community Action Program, Anchorage, 1969-70, exec. dir., 1971-72; exec. v.p. Alaska Fedn. Natives, Anchorage, 1972-75; v.p. ops. NANA Regional Corp., Kotzebue, Alaska, 1975-77, NANA Devel. Corp., Anchorage, 1977-82, sr. v.p., 1982-83; chief of staff to gov. of Alaska, 1983-85; cons. bus. and govt., 1985-86; sr. v.p. NANA Regional Corp., Inc., 1986-92, pres. NANA Devel. Corp. 1992—; chmn., chief exec. officer United Bar Corp., United Bank Alaska, 1987-88; chmn. Alaska State Bd. Game, 1983-84. dir. Unicorp. Inc., United Bank of Alaska. Mem. Greater Anchorage Area Comprehensive Health Plan Council, 1969-75, chmn., 1969-75; founding mem. bd. dirs. Alaska Pub. Interest Research Group, 1974-75, 86-90, chmn. 1987-90; mem. Gov.'s Rural Affairs Council, 1971-76, Gov.'s Manpower Commn., 1971, Greater Anchorage Health Bd., 1969-75, Alaska Pipeline Edn. Com., 1973-74; bd. regents U. Alaska, 1979-83. Democrat. Episcopalian. Home: PO Box 101758 Anchorage AK 99510-1758 Office: NANA Devel Corp 1001 E Benson Blvd Anchorage AK 99508-4256

SHIVELY, RUSSELL ALAN, international product operations executive; b. Long Beach, Calif., Dec. 27, 1940; s. James Latimer and Billie Louise (Cox) S.; m. JoAnn Holland, Dec. 15, 1961; children: Rodney David, Vicki Diane. Student, Long Beach City Coll., 1959-66; AA in Bus. Adminstrn., Yavapai Coll., 1982; BSBA, Ariz. State U., 1986; postgrad., U. Mo., 1988. Product engr. U.S. Elec. Motors Co., Los Angeles, 1961-67; supr. engring. U.S. Elec. Motors Co., Mena, Ark., 1968-70, supr. prodn. control, 1970-72, mgr. materials, 1972-74; sr. project engr. U.S. Elec. Motors Co., Milford, Conn., 1974-76; project mgr. U.S. Elec. Motors Co., Prescott, Ariz., 1976-87; internat. mgmt. cons. ops. Emerson Motor Co. (formerly U.S. Elec. Motors Co.), St. Louis, 1987-88; v.p. ops. Ebara Internat. Corp., Sacramento, 1989. Co-author: Electric Power Supply and System Considerations, 1987; contbr. articles to profl. jours. Chmn. bd. deacons Dallas Ave Bapt. Ch., Mena, 1974; chmn. bd. deacons 1st So. Bapt. Ch., Prescott, 1980, trustee, 1981-82; judge Saguaro Internat. Photographic Exhibition, Phoenix, 1981. Mem. Am. Mgmt. Assn., Sigma Iota Epsilon, Beta Gamma Sigma. Republican. Club: Prescott Camera (pres. 1979-81). Lodge: Masons. Home: 260 Crestridge La Folsom CA 95630 Office: Ebara Internat Corp 51 Main Ave Sacramento CA 95838

SHKOLNIK, SELWYN, internist; b. Chgo., Sept. 14, 1931; s. Samuel and Bessie Muriel (Goldstein) S.; m. Dolores Chenkin, June 27, 1953; children: Steven, Laurie Robin, Michael David, Leslie Susan. MD, U. Ill., 1956. Diplomate Am. Bd. Internal Medicine. Rotating intern San Francisco Gen. Hosp-U. Calif., 1956-57, resident in internal medicine, 1957-59; USPHS postdoctoral fellow Am. Heart Inst., 1961-62; pvt. practice L.A., 1962—; clin. chief pulmonary disease svc. Cedars-Sinai Med. Ctr., 1974-76. Capt. USAF, 1957-59. Fellow ACP; mem. AMA, Calif. Med. Assn., L.A. Med. Assn. Republican. Jewish. Office: 8733 Beverly Blvd Los Angeles CA 90048

SHKURKIN, EKATERINA VLADIMIROVNA (KATIA SHKURKIN), social worker; b. Berkeley, Calif., Nov. 20, 1955; d. Vladimir Vladimirovich and Olga Ivanovna (Lisenko) S. Student, U. San Francisco, 1972-73; BA, U. Calif., Berkeley, 1974-77; MSW, Columbia U., 1977-79; postgrad., Union Grad. Sch., 1986. Cert. police instr. domestic violence, Alaska. Social worker Tolstoy Found., N.Y.C., 1978-79, adminstr., 1979-80; program supr. Rehab. Mental Health Ctr., San Jose, Calif., 1980-81; dir. service counselor Kodiak (Alaska) Crisis Ctr., 1981-82; domestic violence counselor Abused Women's Aid in Crisis, Anchorage, 1982-85; pvt. practice social work specializing in feminist therapy Susitna Therapy Ctr., Anchorage, 1985—; pvt. practice, 1985-89; field instr. Abused Women's Aid in Crisis, Anchorage, 1983-88, State of Alaska, Div. of Family and Youth Svcs., 1989-91, South Cen. Found.-Dena A. Coy Prematernal Alcohol Treatment Ctr., 1991-92; expert witness Anchorage Mcpl. Cts. 1982—; interim faculty U. Alaska, Anchorage, summer, 1985, fall, 1988—, LaVerne U., Anchorage, spring, 1986—, fall, 1987, summer, 1988, winter, 1988—. Coordinator Orthodox Christian Fellowship, San Francisco, 1972-76; pub. speaker Abused Women's Aid in Crisis, Anchorage, 1982—; active nat. and local election campaigns, 1968—. Mem. Nat. Assn. Social Workers (cert.). Democrat. Russian Orthodox. Home and Office: 3605 Arctic Blvd # 768 Anchorage AK 99503-5789

SHMAEFF, ROBERT T., banker, pharmacist; b. L.A., June 11, 1939; s. Hyman and Betty Shmaeff; m. Osie Shmaeff, June 18, 1987; children: Michael, Erinn, David. BS, U. N.Mex., 1961; MPA, U. So. Calif., 1979. Pharmacist Thrifty Drug Store, L.A., 1961, Gavin Herbert Pharmacy, L.A., 1961-63; mgr., pharmacist Bennett Pharmacy, L.A., 1963-65; owner, pharmacist Crescent Med. Pharmacy, L.A., 1965-77; pres. Pioneer Pharmacy Enterprises, Studio City, Calif., 1969-82, owner, 1982—; chmn. Western United Nat. Bank, L.A., 1985—. Bd. dirs. Q.S.A.D., L.A., Guardians, L.A. Recipient resolution Los Angeles County, 1981, 87, City of L.A., 1981, 87, State of Calif., 1987, congl. insert U.S. Ho. of Reps., 1989. Office: Pioneer Pharmacy Enterprises 13135 Ventura Blvd Ste 206 Studio City CA 91604-2219

SHNEOUR, ELIE ALEXIS, biochemist; b. Neuilly-sur-Seine, France, Dec. 11, 1926; came to U.S., 1941, naturalized, 1945; s. Zalman and Salomea (Landau) S.; m. Polly M. Henderson, 7 Sept. 1990; children from previous marriage: Mark Zalman, Alan Brewster. B.A., Columbia U., 1947, DSc (hon.), 1969; M.A., U. Calif., Berkeley, 1955; Ph.D., U. Calif., L.A., 1958. Teaching., research fellowship U. Calif., Berkeley, 1953-55, Am. Heart Assn. research fellow, 1958-62; teaching., research fellowship U. Calif., L.A., 1958; research fellow Nat. Cancer Inst., 1956-57; Am. Heart Assn. research fellow N.Y.U., 1958-59; research assoc. genetics Stanford U., 1962-65; assoc. prof. biology and neurosciences U. Utah, 1965-69; research neurochemist City of Hope Nat. Med. Ctr., Duarte, Calif., 1969-71; dir. rsch. Calbiochem., 1971-75; pres. Biosystems Insts., Inc., 1975—; dir. Biosystems Rsch. Inst., 1979—; mem. exec. com. Nat. Acad. Sci. Study Group on Biology and the Exploration of Mars, 1964; chmn. Western Regional coun. Rsch. in Basic Bioscis. for Manned Orbiting Missions, Am. Inst. Biol. Scis., NASA, 1966-69. Author: Extraterrestrial Life, 1965, (with S. Moffat) Life Beyond the Earth, 1966, The Malnourished Mind, 1974; Contbr. numerous articles to sci. and lay jours. Chmn. citizens adv. coun. San Diego Pub. Schs., 1971-72; mem. adv. coun. Cousteau Soc., 1977—; bd. dirs. Am.-Ukranian Trade Coun., 1991-93. With U.S. Army, 1944-45, World War II. Recipient William Lockwood prize, 1947. Mem. IEEE, AAAS (chmn. So. Calif. Skeptics soc. Pacific divsn. 1988-90), Am. Chem. Soc., N.Y. Acad. Scis., Am. Inst. Biol. Scis., Am. Soc. for Biochemistry and Molecular Biology (chmn. sci. advisors program 1973-75, mem. com. on pub. policy 1974-76), Am. Soc. Neurochemistry (mem. coun. 1971-73), Soc. Neurosci., Internat. Soc. Neurochemistry, U.S. C. of C. (bd. dirs. 1993—), Sigma Xi, Phi Sigma. Office: Biosystems Rsch Inst Naiman Tech Ctr CDM-608 700 Front St San Diego CA 92101-6009

SHOAI, ELINOR JOSEPHINE KELLY, elementary school educator; b. Atlanta, June 30, 1943; d. Neal Kelly and Kathryn Brown-Kelly; m. Morteza Shoai, Dec. 13, 1973; 1 child, Shirin Elma. AA, Merritt Coll, 1962; BA, San Francisco State U., 1964. Cert. elem. tchr., Calif. Elem. tchr. Oakland (Calif.) Pub. Schs., 1967—. Founder, editor: The West Oakland Gryphon, 1981-82 (Marcus Foster award 1981-82). Grantee Marcus Foster Inst., 1982. Mem. Oakland Ednl. Assn., Toastmasters (3 first place awards 1989-90). Democrat. Roman Catholic. Home: 707 33rd St Oakland CA 94609 Office: Prescott Elem Sch 920 Campbell St Oakland CA 94607

SHOCTOR, JOSEPH HARVEY, barrister, producer, civic worker; b. Edmonton, Alta., Can., Aug. 18, 1922. BA, LLB, U. Alta., 1946, LLD (hon.), 1981; diploma in theatre adminstrn. (hon.), Grant McEwan Coll., 1986. Named to Queens Counsel, 1960. Barrister, solicitor, sr. ptnr. Shoctor & Ferguson, Edmonton; bd. dirs. Saxony Motor Hotel Ltd., Westward Motor Inn, Citadel Mortgage Corp. Ltd.; pres., exec. officer Harvey Holdings Ltd. Producer Broadway plays including Peter Pan, 1965, Henry, Sweet Henry, 1967, Billy, 1969, Hamlet, 1969; founder, pres., exec. producer, bldg. chmn., campaign chmn. Citadel Theater; producer Circle 8 Theatre, Civic Opera, Red Cross Entertainment; panelist pub. affairs talk show and sports forum. Active United Community Fund, 1968—; chmn. Downtown Devel. Corp., Edmonton, 1986; mem. Edmonton Jewish Welfare Bd.; past pres. Edmonton Jewish Community Council; past nat. sec. Federated Zionist Orgn.; past nat. v.p. United Israel Appeal, Inc.; past bd. dirs. Can. Council Jewish Welfare Funds; chmn. div. Brit. Commonwealth Games Found., 1978; bd. govs. Nat. Theatre Sch. of Can., officer Order of Can., 1986. Inducted into Cultural Hall of Fame, 1987; named Man of Hr., Sta. CFRN-TV, 1966, Citizen of Yr., B'nai B'rith, 1966, one of Twelve Top Albertans of the 70's, The Alberta Report; recipient Performing Arts award City of Edmonton, 1972, Theatre Arts Achievement award Province of Alta., 1975, Prime Minister's medal State of Israel, 1978, Builder of Community award City of Edmonton, 1979, Queen's Silver Jubilee medal, 1977, City of Edmonton Silver Ribbon award, 1985, Great Canadian award, 1992, Commemorative medal for 125th Anniversary Canadian Confederation, 1992; The Shoctor Theatre named in his honor, 1976; Alta. Order of Excellence. Mem. Edmonton C. of C. Clubs: The Edmonton, The Centre, Eskimo Football (founder, past sec.-mgr.). Office: Shoctor & Ferguson, 1501 Toronto-Dominion Tower, Edmonton, AB Canada T5J 2Z1

SHOE, STEPHEN CHARLES, marketing professional; b. Kansas City, Mo., Oct. 12, 1935; s. Charles Arthur and Mary Margaret (Skaggs) S.; m. Patricia Carmen Williams, Mar. 9, 1958; children: David Mark, Peggy Jo, Rebecca Lynn. BA, U. North Colo., 1958, MA, 1961. Tchr. art & advt. Borah (Idaho) High Sch., 1960-66; account exec. KEST Radio, Boise, Idaho, 1966-68, KBIO & KGDN Radio, Seattle, 1968-70; dir. sch. svcs. Nat. Assn. Christian Sch., Wheaton, Ill., 1970-73, dir., 1973-74; pub. rels. dir. Wheaton (Ill.) Christian High Sch., 1974-75; pub. relations dir. Rockmont Coll. (now Colo. Christian U.), Lakewood, 1975-78; cons. Lakewood, 1978—; pres. Railroad Promotions, 1990—; pub. rels. Georgetown Loop Railroad, 1984—. Contbr. articles to profl. jours. Mem. Model R.R. Industry Assn. (exec. dir. 1987—), South Lakewood Optimist Club (past pres.), Seattle Optimist Club (past pres.). Republican. Home: 12235 W Texas Dr Lakewood CO 80228-3619

SHOECRAFT, WILLARD RENDELL, owner, manager radio stations; b. Kansas City, Mo., Jan. 22, 1921; s. Emerson Strong and Ella Sarah (Rendell) S.; m. Wilma Ruth White (dec. 1977); children: Paul, John, Robert; m. Ruth Annette Jennings, June 5, 1979. Owner, mgr. Radio Station KIKO, Globe, Ariz., 1958—, Radio Station KATO, Stafford, Ariz., 1961-68, Radio Station KINO, Winslow, Ariz., 1968-71; owner, mgr. Radio Station KIKO FM, Globe, 1976-86, Miami, Ariz., 1991—. Vice mayor City of Globe, 1956-60; pres. Gila Gen. Hosp. Bd., Globe, 1991. Mem. Ariz. Broadcasters Assn. (Hall of Fame Inductee 1992), Globe Elks (life), Lions (Ariz. sec. 1961-62). Democrat. Office: Radio Station KIKO AM/FM 401 Broadway Miami AZ 85539

SHOEMAKER, BILL (WILLIAM LEE SHOEMAKER), retired jockey; b. Fabens, Tex., Aug. 19, 1931; s. B. B. and Ruby (Call) S.; m. Cynthia Barnes, Mar. 7, 1978; 1 dau., Amanda Elisabeth. Jockey, 1949-90, ret., 1990, trainer, 1990—. Office: Care Vincent Andrews Mgmt 315 S Beverly Dr Ste 216 Beverly Hills CA 90212

SHOEMAKER, CAMERON DAVID JAMES, dean, educator; b. Honolulu, Dec. 15, 1940; s. John James and Belle Bird (Kellogg) S.; m. Catherine LaMoyne Prevost, May 23, 1966 (div. 1969); 1 child, David James; m. Leona Martha Wohlwend, May 18, 1972; 1 child, Jennifer Lee. BA in Polit. Sci., The Citadel, 1963; MA in History, San Jose State U., 1973; EdD, U. San Francisco, 1990. Commd. 2d lt. U.S. Army, 1963, advanced through grades to maj., 1971; fgn. area officer U.S. Army, U.S., Korea, Germany and Vietnam, 1972-84; ret. U.S. Army, 1984; mgmt. analyst Def. Lang. Inst., Monterey, Calif., 1985; ednl. tech. project mgr. Def. Lang. Inst., Monterey, 1985-86, dir. info. resources mgmt., 1986-90; evening coll. adminstr., instnl. researcher Monterey Peninsula Coll., 1990-92; dean of bus. Sacramento (Calif.) City Coll.; instr., Chapman Coll., Monterey, 1982-84, Monterey Inst., 1987; chmn. Asian Employment Program Com., Monterey, 1983-84; guest lectr., Naval Postgrad. Sch., Monterey, 1986-87; mem. Handicapped Individual Program Com., Monterey, 1986—, treas., 1989-90. Contbr. articles to various publs. Pres., Creekside Community Assn., Salinas, Calif., 1985-86; mem. County Svc. Area Adv. Bd., Salinas, 1985-87, Flood Control Dist. Planning Com., Salinas, 1986-87; active Leadership Monterey Peninsula, grad., 1992. Decorated Silver Star medal; recipient Comdrs. award for Civilian Svc. Dept. of Army, 1990; Carl D. Perkins fellow, 1993. Mem. Royal Asiatic Soc., Monterey Peninsula Scottish Soc. (treas. 1986-92), Phi Delta Kappa. Republican. Roman Catholic. Home: 22315 Capote Dr Salinas CA 93908-1006 Office: Sacramento City Coll 3835 Freeport Blvd Sacramento CA 95822

SHOEMAKER, EUGENE MERLE, geologist; b. Los Angeles, Apr. 28, 1928; s. George Estel and Muriel May (Scott) S.; m. Carolyn Jean Spellmann, Aug. 18, 1951; children: Christine Carol, Patrick Gene, Linda Susan. B.S., Calif. Inst. Tech., 1947, M.S., 1948; M.A., Princeton U., 1954, Ph.D., 1960; Sc.D., Ariz. State Coll., 1965, Temple U., 1967, U. Ariz., 1984. Geologist U.S. Geol. Survey, 1948, exploration uranium deposits and investigation salt structures Colo. and Utah, 1948-50, regional investigations geochemistry, vulcanology and structure Colorado Plateau, 1951-56, research on structure and mechanics of meteorite impact and nuclear explosion craters, 1957-60, with E.C.T. Chao, discovered coesite, Meteor Crater, Ariz., 1960, investigation structure and history of moon, 1960-73, established lunar geol. time scale, methods of geol. mapping of moon, 1960, application TV systems to investigation extra-terrestrial geology, 1961—, geology and paleomagnetism, Colo. Plateau, 1969—, systematic search for planet-crossing asteroids and comets, 1973—, Trojan asteroids, 1985—, geology of satellites of Jupiter, Saturn, Uranus and Neptune, 1978—, investigating role of large body impacts in evolution of life, 1981—; impact craters of Australia, 1983—; organized br. of astrogeology U.S. Geol. Survey, 1961; co-investigator TV expt. Project Ranger, 1961-65; chief scientist, center of astrogeology U.S. Geol. Survey, 1966-68, research geologist, 1976—; prin. investigator geol. field investigations in Apollo lunar landing, 1965-70, also television expt. Project Surveyor, 1963-68; prof. geology Calif. Inst. Tech., 1969-85, chmn. div. geol. and planetary scis., 1969-72. Recipient (with E.C.T. Chao) Wetherill medal Franklin Inst., 1965; Arthur S. Flemming award, 1966; NASA medal for exceptional sci. achievement, 1967; honor award for meritorious service U.S. Dept. Interior, 1973; Disting. Service award, 1980; Disting. Alumni award Calif. Inst. Tech., 1986, co-recipient Rittenhouse medal, 1988; Nat. Medal of Sci., 1992. Mem. NAS, Geol. Soc. Am. (Day medal 1982, Gilbert award 1983), Mineral Soc. Am., Soc. Econ. Geologists, Geochem. Soc., Am. Assn. Petroleum Geologists, Am. Geophys. Union, Am. Astron. Soc. (Kuiper prize 1984), Internat. Astron. Union, Meteoritical Soc. (Barringer award 1984, Leonard medal 1985). Home: PO Box 984 Flagstaff AZ 86002-0984 Office: US Geol Survey 2255 N Gemini Dr Flagstaff AZ 86001-1698

SHOEMAKER, FORREST HILTON, JR., marketing and sales executive, consultant; b. Waycross, Ga., Sept. 2, 1953; s. Forrest Hilton Sr. and Flora Kay (Jacobs) S.; married 1974 (div. 1985) children: Thomas, Myriah; m. Corazon Betty Kendall, Dec. 18, 1982; children: Stephanie, Ryan. BA, Armstrong State Coll., 1975. Pres., mng. ptnr. Shoemaker Cons. Inc., Savannah, Ga., 1981-85, Hawaii Juice Co., Honolulu, 1986-87; gen. mgr. Island Liquid Sunshine, Honolulu, 1985-86, Barry Hall Sales/Banana Boat Hawaii, Honolulu, 1988-91; v.p. sales Practice Mgmt. Svcs., Honolulu, 1987-88; dir. mktg. and sales Webco Hawaii Inc.-Schering-Plough Healthcare Divsn., Honolulu, 1991—; v.p., mgmt. cons. Artistic Table Lighting Hawaii, 1992—. Home: 959 18th Ave Honolulu HI 96816 Office: Webco Hawaii Inc 2840 Mokumoa St Honolulu HI 96814

SHOEMAKER, HAROLD LLOYD, infosystem specialist; b. Danville, Ky., Jan. 3, 1923; s. Eugene Clay and Amy (Wilson) S.; A.B., Berea Coll., 1944; postgrad. State U. Ia., 1943-44, George Washington U., 1949-50, N.Y. U., 1950-52; m. Dorothy M. Maddox, May 11, 1947 (dec. Feb. 1991). Research physicist State U., Ia., 1944-45, Frankford Arsenal, Pa., 1945-47; research engr. N.Am. Aviation, Los Angeles, 1947-49, Jacobs Instrument Co.,

Bethesda, 1949-50; asso. head systems devel. group The Teleregister Corp., N.Y.C., 1950-53; mgr. electronic equipment devel. sect., head planning for indsl. systems div. Hughes Aircraft Co., Los Angeles, 1953-58; dir. command and control systems lab. Bunker-Ramo Corp., Los Angeles, 1958-68, v.p. Data Systems, 1968-69, corp. dir. data processing, 1969-75; tech. staff R & D Assocs., Marina Del Rey, Calif., 1975-85; info. systems cons., 1985—. Served with AUS, 1945-46. Mem. IEEE. Patentee elec. digital computer. Home: PO Box 3385 Granada Hills CA 91394-0385

SHOEMAKER, RALPH WARREN, measurement systems engineer, consultant; b. Portland, Oreg., Nov. 19, 1941; s. Robert Comly and Ann Wood (Okie) S.; m. Kenda Kay Sorter, June 9, 1964; children: Kay Warren, Mark Oberly. Student, U. Pa., 1959-60, U. Colo., 1964-66; BS in Applied Sci. and Engring., Portland State U., 1969, MS in Applied Sci. and Engring., 1974. Registered profl. engr., Oreg. Assoc. engr. Western Electric Co., Denver, 1964-66, Electro Sci. Industries, Portland, 1967-69; chief engr. Monitek Corp., Multnomah, Oreg., 1974-75; electronics engr. Bonneville Power Adminstrn., Portland, 1969-79; sect. chief Bonneville Power Adminstrn., Vancouver, Wash., 1980-85, sr. measurement systems engr., 1985—; med. electronics and energy conservation systems cons. Contbg. author: Engineering Fundamentals, 1978; co-patentee sonic distance measurement system; co-inventor lightning resistant system. Com. mem. citizens adv. bd. Mt. Hood C.C., Portland, 1976-79; vol. tchr. Talented and Gifted Students Program, Portland, 1978-80; com. chmn. Cub Scouts, Boy Scouts Am., Portland, 1981-83, com. chmn. troop 592, 1986-89. With USAF, 1961-63. Recipient letters of appreciation Beaverton (Oreg.) Sch. Dist. 48, Vancouver Sch. Dist., Mt. Hood C.C., certs. of commendation U.S. Dept. Energy. Mem. NSPE, IEEE (sr.), Instrument Soc. Am. (sr.), Profl. Engrs. Oreg. Republican. Office: Bonneville Power Adminstrn 5411 NE Hwy 99 Vancouver WA 98663

SHOEMAKER, ROBERT COMLY, JR., state senator, lawyer; b. Boston, Feb. 22, 1932; s. Robert Comly Sr. and Ann Wood (Okie) S.; m. Beverly Sluyter, Feb. 27, 1953; children: Robert C. III, Warren G., David L., Richardson O. II. BS in Polit. Sci., Lewis and Clark Coll., 1953; LLB, Harvard U., 1958. Assoc. Wood, Wood, Tatum, Mosser and Brooke, Portland, Oreg., 1958-61, Black and Apicella, Portland, 1961-68; ptnr. Shoemaker, Coleman, Bartlett and Saverude, Portland, 1968-71, Lindsay, Hart, Neil and Weigler, Portland, 1971-90; of counsel Ater, Wynne, Hewitt, Dodson and Skerritt, Portland, 1990-92; state senator Oreg.; chmn. Health Care and Bioethics Com.; vice chmn., mem. Jud., Agriculture and Natural Resources; asst. clin. prof. Oreg. Health Scis. Univ. Chmn. Multnomah County Planning Commn.; former bd. pres. Oreg. Sch. of Arts and Crafts, First Unitarian Ch., Schs. for the City, The Nature Conservancy, Chamber Music N.W.; bd. dirs. local Alzheimer's Assn., Wash. County Community Action Orgn.; former chmn. Multnomah County Oreg. Planning Commn. Mem. ABA, Oreg. State Bar, Multnomah County Bar Assn., Portland City Club (former bd. pres.). Democrat. Unitarian. Home: 4837 W Burnside Rd Portland OR 97210-1087 Office: Oreg Health Scis Univ 3181 SW Sam Jackson Park Rd Portland OR 97201

SHOEMAKER, SCOTT DAVID, network engineer, educator; b. Milw., Oct. 28, 1958; s. Alan Kent and Barbara Jean (Pepe) S.; m. Glenda Faye Coates, June 8, 1985; children: Brock, Paige, Leah. BA in Secondary Edn., Purdue U., West Lafayette, Ind., 1982; MEd, Ariz. State U., 1987; MS in Computer Sci. Edn., U. Evansville, Ind., 1988. Tchr. Monument Valley High Sch., Kayenta, Ariz., 1982-86; instr. computer sci. Grand Canyon U., Phoenix, 1986-90; systems analyst Bull NH Info. Systems, Phoenix, 1990-92; network engr. Honeywell IAC, Phoenix, 1992—; seminar instr. PCAI mag. Hands-On Seminars, Phoenix, 1985-90. Contbr. articles to profl. mags. Elder, Metro Presbyn. Ch., Glendale, Ariz., 1992—. Mem. Assn. Computing Machinery (sponsor student chpt. 1988-90), IEEE (soc. affiliate). Republican. Presbyterian. Home: 8738 W Indianola Ave Phoenix AZ 85037-2338 Office: Honeywell IAC 16404 N Black Canyon Hwy MS AZ15/IE11 Phoenix AZ 85023

SHOKEIR, MOHAMED HASSAN KAMEL, medical geneticist, educator; b. Mansoura, Egypt, July 2, 1938; emigrated to Can., 1969, naturalized, 1974; s. Hassan Sayed and Lolia Nora (Kira) S.; m. Donna Jean Nugent, Feb. 27, 1968; children: Marc Omar, Vanessa May. MB, BCh in Medicine and Surgery, Cairo U., 1960, ChD, 1963, ChD in Orthopedics, 1964; MS, U. Mich., 1965, PhD, 1969. Intern Cairo U. Hosps., 1960-61, resident, 1961-64; Fulbright rsch. scholar dept. human genetics U. Mich., 1964-69; asst. prof. pediatrics U. Sask., Saskatoon, 1969-71, assoc. prof., 1971-73, prof., 1977—, dir. div. med. genetics, 1975—, head dept. pediatrics, 1979—; head sect. clin. genetics U. Man., Winnipeg, 1973-75; mem. staffs Univ. Hosp., Saskatoon City Hosp., St. Paul's Hosp.; cons. Winnipeg Health Scis. Centre, Regina Gen. Hosp. Contbr. articles to profl publs. Mem. Acad. Freedom and Tenure Com., Ottawa, Ont., Can., 1980-90, Queen Elizabeth II scientist, 1969-75. Med. Rsch. Coun. grantee, 1970-79; Canadian Coll. Med. Geneticists Found. fellow, 1975—. Fellow Can. Coll. Med. Geneticists, Can. Soc. Clin. Investigation (councillor 1974-76), Can. Med. Assn. (chmn., mem. adv. com. 1987—); mem. Assn. Med. Sch. Pediatric Dept. Chairmen, Assn. Canadian Univ. Dept. Chairmen, Am. Pediatric Soc., Soc. Pediatric Research, N.Y. Acad. Scis., Am. Geriatrics Soc., Am. Fedn. Clin. Research, Mid-Western Soc. Pediatric Research, Western Pediatric Soc., Am. Soc. Human Genetics, Genetics Soc. Am., Genetics Soc. Can., Am. Genetic Assn., Am. Pub. Health Assn. Home: 108 Riel Crescent, Saskatoon, SK Canada S7J 2W6 Office: U Sask, Dept Pediatrics, Saskatoon, SK Canada S7N 0X0

SHOLIN, TERRY MICHAEL, adult education educator; b. Jamestown, N.Y., Nov. 26, 1957; s. Adolph Reinhold and Beverly Leola (Morgan) S. BA in English, Colo. State U., 1981, BS in Tech. Journalism, 1984. News editor, reporter Collegian, Fort Collins, Colo., 1981-84; reportr, editor Hobbs (New Mex.) Daily News-Sun, 1984—; GED Instr. N. Mex. Jr. Coll., Hobbs, 1988—. Past mem. bd. dirs. Hobbs Jaycees, 1990; vol. Hobbs Beautiful, 1990-92. Recipient cert. of appreciation (2) New Mex. Adult Basic Edn. Program, Santa Fe, 1991-92, cert. of appreciation New Mex. Human Svcs. , Santa Fe, 1991. Mem. New Mex. Press Assn. Home: 1106 N Gulf Hobbs NM 88240

SHOLLY, STEVEN CRAIG, environmental risk analyst, consultant; b. Mechanicsburg, Pa., Feb. 21, 1953; s. John Franklin and Beverly Lucille (Spahr) S.; m. Juana Faye Gore, Dec. 21, 1975; children: Kendra Gail, Geoffrey Scott. BS in Edn., Shippensburg (Pa.) State U., 1975. Cert. secondary tchr., wastewater treatment plant mgr., Pa. Tchr. Carlisle (Pa.) Area Sch. Dist., 1975-76, West Shore Sch. Dist., Camp Hill, Pa., 1976-77; operator Borough of Lemoyne, Pa., 1977-78, Derry Twp. Mcpl. Authority, Hershey, Pa., 1978-80; project dir. Three Mile Island Pub. Interest Rsch. Ctr., Harrisburg, Pa., 1980-81; risk analyst Union Concerned Scientists, Washington, 1981-86; sr. cons. MHB Tech. Assocs., San Jose, Calif., 1986—. Co-author: The Source Term Debate, 1986. Democrat. Office: MHB Tech Assocs 1723 Hamilton Ave Ste K San Jose CA 95125

SHOLTIS, JOSEPH ARNOLD, JR., nuclear engineer, retired military officer; b. Monongahela, Pa., Nov. 28, 1948; s. Joseph and Gladys (Frye) S.; m. Cheryl Anita Senchur, Dec. 19, 1970; children: Christian Joseph, Carole Lynne. BS in Nuclear Engring. (Disting. Mil. Grad.), Pa. State U., 1970; diplomas Air Univ., 1975, 78; MS in Nuclear Engring., U. N.Mex., 1977, postgrad., 1978-80. Lic. sr. reactor operator NRC, 1980-84. Mathematician, statistician, mine safety analyst U.S. Bur. Mines, Pitts., 1968-70; commd. 2d lt. USAF, 1970, advanced through grades to lt. col. 1988, ret., 1993; nuclear rsch. officer Fgn. Tech. Div., USAF, Wright-Patterson AFB, Ohio, 1971-74; chief space nuclear system safety sect. Air Force Weapons Lab., Kirtland AFB, N.Mex., 1974-78; mil. mem. tech. staff, project officer Sandia Nat. Labs., Albuquerque, 1978-80; chief radiation sources div., reactor facility dir. Armed Forces Radiobiology Rsch. Inst., Bethesda, Md., 1980-84; program mgr. SP-100 space reactor power system tech. devel. program Air Force Element U.S. Dept. Energy, Germantown, Md., 1984-87; chief analysis and evaluation br., 1988-91, chief nuclear power and sources div., 1991-92, chief nuclear energy systems Air Force Safety Agency, Kirtland AFB, N.Mex., 1987-93; sr. v.p., gen. mgr. we. ops. Oakton Internat. Corp., Va., 1993—; space shuttle nuclear payload safety assessment officer Air Force Weapons Lab., Kirtland AFB, 1976-78; instr. med. effects nuclear weapons Armed Forces Radiobiology Rsch. Inst., Bethesda, 1980-85, mem. reactor and radiation facility safety com., 1980-85; faculty, lectr. Uniformed Svcs. Univ. Health Scis., Bethesda, 1982-87; chmn. Power System Subpanel Interagency Nuclear Safety Rev. Panel risk assessments of Galileo, Ulysses, Cassini, and TOPAZ-II nuclear-powered space missions, 1987-92; Dept. of Def. chmn. Interagency Nuclear Safety Rev. Panel evaluation of Ulysses, Cassini and Topaz-II nuclear-powered space missions for the office of the pres.; instr. Inst. for Space Nuclear Power Studies U. N.Mex., 1987-91; U.S. del., tech. advisor UN Sci. and Tech. Subcom. and Legal Subcom. Working Group on Nuclear Power Sources in Outer Space, 1984-88; mem. U.S. contingent U.S. and U.S.S.R. discussions on nuclear space power system safety, 1989-90; mem. adv. com., tech. program com. Symposia on Space Nuclear Power and Propulsion, U. N.Mex., 1989—; mem. Multimegawatt Space Reactor Power Project safety working group, 1988-91; mem. SP-100 Space Reactor Project safety adv. com., 1990—; mem. space exploration initiative Nuclear Safety Policy Working Group, 1990-91; mem. Air Force Thermionic Space Power Program Safety com., 1990—; mem. safety com., 1990-93; mem. Strategic Def. Initiative Orgn. Ind. Evaluation Group, 1991-93; mem. U.S. Dept. Energy Ind. Safety Assessment of TOPAZ-II space reactor power system, 1993; mem. program com. Reactor Safety Divsn. Am. Nuclear Soc., 1992—; lectr. N.Mex. Acad. of Sci. Vis. Scientist Program, 1992—. Author: (with others) LMFBR Accident Delineation, 1980, Military Radiobiology, 1987, Power System Subpanel Report for Galileo Space Mission, 1989, Power System Subpanel Report for Ulysses Space Mission, 1990, Safety Evaluation Report for Ulysses Space Mission, 1990; contbr. articles, chpts. in books. Pres. Fort Detrick Cath. Parish Community, Md., 1984; charter mem. N.Mex. Edn. Outreach Com., 1989—; Decorated Def. Meritorious Service medal (2), Air Force Meritorious Svc. medal (2) Air Force Commendation medal (3), Nat. Def. Svc. medal (2), U.S. Army Reactor Comdr. Badge, U.S. Air Force Missileman Badge, Air Force Master Space Systems Badge, Nat. Aeronautics and Space Administration Achievement awards (2). Mem. Am. Nuclear Soc. (Best Paper 1977), ASME, AIAA, AAAS, N.Mex. Acad. Scis., Sigma Xi. Republican. Avocations: hunting, fishing, camping, golfing, motorcycle touring. Office: Oakton Internat Corp care 2 Oso Dr Tijeras NM 87059-7632

SHONFELD, EDWIN MARSHALL, internist; b. Pitts., Feb. 23, 1936; s. Irving and Ruth (Bolner) S.; m. Marcia Sue Shonfeld, Oct. 13, 1963; children: Dana, Victoria. AA, U. Calif.-Berkeley, 1955, BA, 1957; MD, U. Calif., San Francisco, 1960. Assoc. clin. prof. medicine and radiation oncology U. Calif. Med. Sch., San Francisco; rsch. assoc. Cancer Rsch. Inst., San Francisco; pvt. practice specializing in internal medicine/oncology San Francisco, 1966—; pres. The Cancer Care Found., San Francisco, 1975—. Contbr. articles to profl. jours. With USPHS, 1961-63. Mem. San Francisco Med. Soc., Calif. Med. Soc., Phi Beta Kappa, Alpha Omega Alpha, Phi Eta Sigma. Office: 45 Castro St # 337 San Francisco CA 94114-1010

SHONK, ALBERT DAVENPORT, JR., advertising executive; b. L.A., May 23, 1932; s. Albert Davenport and Jean Spence (Stannard) S.; BS in Bus. Adminstrn., U. So. Calif., 1954. Field rep. mktg. div. Los Angeles Examiner, 1954-55, asst. mgr. mktg. and field supr. mktg. div. 1955-56, mgr. mktg. div., 1956-57; account exec. Hearst Advt. Svc., Los Angeles, 1957-59; account exec., mgr. Keith H. Evans & Assos., San Francisco, 1959-65; owner, pres. Albert D. Shonk Co., L.A., 1965—; gen. ptnr. Shonk Land Co. LTD, Charleston, W.Va., 1989—; pres. Signet Circle Corp., Inc., 1977-81, dir., 1962-81, hon. life dir., 1981—, treas., 1989—. Bd. dirs. Crittenton Ctr. for Young Women and Infants, sec., 1978, 1st v.p., 1978-79, exec. v.p., 1979-81, pres., 1981-83, chmn. bd., 1983-85, hon. life dir., 1986—; co-chair centennial com., founding chmn. Crittenton Assocs. Recipient Medallion of Merit Phi Sigma Kappa, 1976, Founders award, 1961,NIC Interfraternal award, 1989 . Mem. Advt. Club Los Angeles, Bus. and Profl. Advt. Assn., Pubs. Rep. Assn. of So. Calif., Nat. Assn. Pubs. Reps. (past v.p. West Coast 1981-83), Jr. Advt. Club L.A. (hon. life, dir., treas., 1st v.p.), Trojan Club, Skull and Dagger, U. So. Calif., U. S.C. Commerce Assocs. (nat. bd. 1991—), Inter-Greek Soc. (co-founder, hon. life mem. and dir., v.p. 1976-79, pres. 1984-86), Phi Sigma Kappa (dir. grand council 1962-70, 77-79, grand pres. 1979-83, chancellor 1983-87, 90-91, v.p. meml. found. 1979-84, pres. 1984, trustee pres. Phi Sigma Kappa found. 1984—), Alpha Kappa Psi, Town Hall. Home: 3460 W 7th St Apt 806 Los Angeles CA 90005 Office: Albert Shonk Co 3156 Wilshire Blvd Ste 7 Los Angeles CA 90010-1209

SHOPP, GEORGE MILTON, JR., toxicologist; b. Harrisburg, Pa., May 21, 1955; s. George Milton Sr. and Carol Ardella (Culver) S. BS in Biology, Bucknell U., 1977; PhD in Toxicology, Med. Coll. Va., 1984. Postdoctoral fellow Inhalation Toxicology Rsch. Inst., Albuquerque, 1984-86; assoc. scientist II Lovelace Med. Found., Albuquerque, 1986-92; toxicologist Synergen Inc., Boudler, Colo., 1992—; grant proposal reviewer Health Effects Inst., Cambridge, Mass., 1990—; bd. dirs. Marine Environ. Rsch. Inst., Bluehill, Maine. Contbr. articles to profl. jours. Grantee NIH, 1989-92. Mem. Soc. of Toxicology, Am. Assn. of Immunologists, Am. Coll. Toxicology, Sierra Club and Def. Fund, ACLU, Wilderness Soc. Office: Synergen Inc 1885 33rd St Boulder CO 80466

SHORETT, ALICE JUDY, public policy and mediation consultant; b. Tacoma, Dec. 14, 1944; d. John William and Sara (Brown) Judy; m. David Shorett, Dec. 23, 1967; children: Mark, Peter. BA, Whitman Coll., 1967; MA, Tufts U., 1969. Vol. U.S. Peace Corps, Micronesia, 1968-70; planning dir. Seattle-King County Econ. Bd., Seattle, 1970-72; pub. svc. dir. Inst. Environ. Studies, U. Wash., Seattle, 1973-75; spl. asst. Office of Gov. of Wash., Olympia, 1975-76; mediator Office Environ. Mediation, U. Wash., Seattle, 1976-79; prin., owner Triangle Assoc., Seattle, 1979—. Author: Micronesian Background, 1970; co-author: The Pike Place Market, 1982, Negotiating Settlements, 1984. Mem. Am. Arbitration Assn. (mem. panel of arbitrators), Soc. Profls. in Dispute Resolution, Am. Pub. Works Assn., Seattle-King County C. of C. Office: Triangle Assoc 811 1st Ave # 255 Seattle WA 98104-1434

SHORT, C. BRANT, communications educator; b. Rupert, Idaho, Oct. 21, 1955; s. Calvin Short and Barbara Ann (Nussbaum) Stennett; m. Dayle C. Hardy, Aug. 6, 1983; children: Spencer Walter, Jeffery Keene. BA, Idaho State U., 1978, MA, 1980; PhD, Ind. U., 1985. Instr. Trinity U., San Antonio, 1984-85; asst. prof. SW Tex. State U., San Marcos, 1985-86; asst. prof. comm. dept. Idaho State U., Pocatello, 1986-91, assoc. prof., 1991—. Author: Ronald Reagan and the Public Lands, 1989; editor: Democratic Demise/Republican Ascendancy, 1988; contbr. articles to profl. jours. Dir. Pocatello Soup Kitchen, 1990-93. Mem. Speech Comm. Assn., Western Comm. Assn. (div. chair 1990-91). Episcopalian. Office: Idaho State U PO Box 8115 Pocatello ID 83209-8115

SHORT, KARLETON GENE, borough official; b. Oklahoma City, July 24, 1955; s. Gene W. Short and Barbara H. (Hopfinger) Hannah; m. Shirley Jean Strange, Dec. 14, 1986; children: David, Stacy, Angela, Jason. AA, N.Mex. Mil. Inst., Roswell, 1975; BS in Mktg., U. No. Colo., Greeley, 1979, BS in Acctg., 1980. Acct. City and County of Denver, 1980-83; acct. Kodiak Island Borough, Kodiak, Alaska, 1983-90, fin. dir., 1990—. Mem. Govt. Fin. Officers Assn. (budget reviewer 1990—, award of fin. reporting achievement 1991), Kodiak Island Sportsmen Assn. (pres. 1990—). Office: Kodiak Island Borough 710 Mill Bay Rd Kodiak AK 99615

SHORTLIFFE, EDWARD HANCE, internist, medical information science educator; b. Edmonton, Alta., Can., Aug. 28, 1947; s. Ernest Carl and Elizabeth Joan (Rankin) S.; m. Linda Marie Dairiki, June 21, 1970; children: Lindsay Ann, Lauren Leigh. AB, Harvard U., 1970; PhD, Stanford U., 1975, MD, 1976. Diplomate Am. Bd. Internal Medicine. Trainee NIH, 1971-76; intern Mass. Gen. Hosp., Boston, 1976-77; resident Stanford Hosp., Palo Alto, Calif., 1977-79; asst. prof. medicine Stanford U. Sch. Medicine, Palo Alto, 1979-85, assoc. prof., 1985-90, prof., 1990—, chief div. gen. internal medicine, 1988—; pres. SCAMC, Inc. (Symposium on Computer Applications in Med. Care), Washington, 1988-89; mem. tech. adv. bd. Teknowledge, Inc., Palo Alto, 1983-88; advisor Nat. Bd. Med. Examiners, Phila., 1987—; mem. Nat. Fed. Networking Adv. Coun., NSF, 1991-93; mem. computer sci. and telecommunications bd. NRC, 1991—. Editor: Rule-Based Expert Systems, 1984, Readings in Medical Artificial Intelligence, 1984, Medical Informatics: Computer Applications in Health Care, 1990; developer several medical computer programs including MYCIN, 1976 (Grace M. Hopper award Assn. Computing Machinery). Recipient Young Investigator award Western Soc. Clin. Investigation, 1987, rsch. career award Nat. Libr. of Medicine, 1979-84; scholar Kaiser Family Found., 1983-88. Mem. Am. Assn. Artificial Intelligence, Soc. for Med. Decision Making (pres. 1989-90), Inst. Medicine, Am. Soc. for Clin. Investigation, Am. Coll. Med. Informatics, Am. Med. Informatics Assn., Am. Clin. and Climatological Assn., Am. Assn. Physicians. Office: Stanford U Sch Medicine Sect on Med Informatics 300 Pasteur Dr Stanford CA 94305-5479

SHOTWELL, CHARLES BLAND, air force officer, lawyer; b. Tucson, Jan. 10, 1955; s. William Bedford and Pauline (Bainbridge) S.; m. Jeannene V. Brooks, Aug. 10, 1988. BA, U. Puget Sound, 1977, JD, 1980; LLM, Am. U., 1991. Bar: Hawaii 1980, U.S. Dist. Ct. Hawaii 1980, U.S. Ct. Mil. Appeals 1981, D.C. 1989, U.S. Ct. Appeals D.C. 1989. Commd. 2d lt. USAF, 1980, advanced through grades to maj., 1989; chief civil law USAF, K.I. Sawyer AFB, Mich., 1980-83; mil. justice reviewer USAF, Sembach Air Base, Fed. Republic Germany, 1983-84, area def. counsel, 1984-85; desk officer Internat. Negotiations Div. USAF, Ramstein Air Base, Fed. Republic Germany, 1985-88; chief legis. sect., dir. internat. programs Pentagon USAF, Washington, 1988-91; adj. instr. aviation law and ins. Embry-Riddle Aero. U., Ramstein Air Base, 1985-88; USAF Nat. Def. fellow Tufts U., 1991-92; instr. USAF Acad., 1992—. Newsletter editor; contbr. to profl. publs. Mem. ABA, Hawaii State Bar Assn., D.C. Bar Assn., Air Force Assn. Home: 19715 Top O' The Moor Dr Monument CO 80132 Office: Dept Polit Sci U S A F Academy CO 80840

SHOUP, TERRY EMERSON, university dean, engineering educator; b. Troy, Ohio, July 20, 1944; s. Dale Emerson and Betty Jean (Spoon) S.; m. Betsy Dinsmore, Dec. 18, 1966; children: Jennifer Jean, Matthew David. BME, Ohio State U., 1966, MS, 1967, PhD, 1969. Asst. prof. to assoc. prof. Rutgers U., New Brunswick, N.J., 1969-75; assoc. prof. to prof. U. Houston, 1975-80; asst. dean, prof. Tex. A&M U., College Sta., 1980-83; dean, prof. Fla. Atlantic U., Boca Raton, 1983-89; dean, Sobrato prof. Santa Clara (Calif.) U., 1989—; cons., software specialist Numerical Methods in Engring. Author: (books) A Practical Guide to Computer Methods for Engineers, 1979, Resheniye Ingenyernikh Zadach NA EVM Prakticheskoye rukovodstvo, 1982, Narichnik Po Izchislitelni Methodi Za Ingeneri, 1983, Numerical Methods for the Personal Computer, 1983, Applied Numerical Methods for the Microcomputer, 1984, (with L.S. Fletcher) Introduction to Engineering with FORTRAN Programming, 1978, Solutions Manual for Introduction to Engineering Including FORTRAN Programming, 1978, Introduccion a la ingenieria Incluyendo programacion FORTRAN, 1980, (with L.S. Fletcher and E.V. Mochel) Introduction to Design with Graphics and Design Projects, 1981, (with S.P. Goldstein and J. Waddell) Information Sources, 1984, (with Carl Hanser Verlag) Numerische Verfahren fur Arbeitsplatzrechner, 1985, (with F. Mistree) Optimization Methods with Applications for Personal Computers, 1987; (software) Numerical Methods for the Personal Computer-Software User's Guide, Version 2, 1983, Optimization Software for the Personal Computer, 1986; editor in chief Mechanism and Machine Theory, 1977—; contbr. more than 100 articles to profl. jours. Fellow ASME (chmn. Design Engring. div. 1987-88, Mech. Engring. div. 1980-81, Centennial medal 1980, Gustus Larson award 1981); mem. Am. Soc. for Engring. Edn. (Dow Outstanding Faculty award 1974, Western Electric award 1984), Fla. Engring. Soc. Home: 1310 Quali Creek Circle San Jose CA 95120 Office: Santa Clara Univ Coll of Engring Office of the Dean Santa Clara CA 95053

SHOWALTER, DENNIS EDWIN, history educator; b. Delano, Minn., Feb. 12, 1942; s. Edwin Thomas and Ann Francis (Jaunich) S.; m. Clara Anne McKenna, Nov. 27, 1965; children: Clara Kathleen, John. BA, St. John's U., Collegeville, Minn., 1963; MA, U. Minn., 1965, PhD, 1969. Prof. history Colo. Coll., Colorado Springs, 1969—; lectr. various civic and fraternal groups, Colorado Springs, 1969—, Colo. Endowment for the Humanities, Colorado Springs, 1989-90. Author: Railroads and Rifles, 1975, German Military History, 1983, Tannenberg: Clash of Empires, 1991; co-author: Voices from the 3rd Reich, 1989; contbr. articles to profl. jours. Trustee, v.p. Soc. Mil. History, 1981-89, 91—. Recipient Burlington Northern Faculty award, 1986, NEH Summer fellow, 1973, 84, Alexander V. Humboldt fellow, 1979-80. Office: Colo Coll Colorado Springs CO 80903

SHRADER, MARK JOEL, finance educator; b. Houston, Jan. 10, 1957; s. Harold Eugene Shrader and Dorothy Ann (Anderson) Shrader McGowen; m. Arleen catherine Parker, June 24, 1989; 1 child, Jacqueline Elaine. BBA, U. Tex., 1979; PhD, Tex. Tech. U., 1988. Instr. Tex. Tech., Lubbock, 1982-85, S.W. Tex. State U., San Marcos, 1986; asst. prof. Gonzaga U., Spokane, Wash., 1987—; investment cons., Spokane, Wash., 1987—. Contbr. articles to profl. jours. Faculty grantee Tex. Tech. U., 1984. Mem. Am. fin. Assn., So. Fin. Assn., S.W. Fin. Assn., Western Fin. Assn., Fin. Mgmt. Assn. Republican. Methodist. Office: Gonzaga U Sch of Bus Spokane WA 99258

SHRADER, RODNEY LEE, military officer, consultant; b. Nashville, Feb. 2, 1955; s. Reginald Woodrow and Freda Olene (Presley) S.; m. Josephine Mary Pratt; Apr. 25, 1981; children: Gregory, Laura, Rachel. BS, USAF Acad., 1977; MPA, Troy State U., 1988. Commd. 2d lt. USAF, 1977, advance through grades to lt. col., 1992; weapons officer, A-10 pilot 91, 76 and 510 Tactical Fighter Squads USAF, RAF Bentwaters, Eng., and Eng. AFB, La., 1979-84, 85-88; air ops. officer Hdqs. USAF The Pentagon, Washington, 1984-85; chief weapons, F-117 pilot 37 Fighter Wing Tonopah Test Range, Nev., 1989—; tng. systems engr. spl. programs USAF. Author: Multi-Command Manual 3-1, 1992; contbr. articles to profl. jours. Decorated DFC, Air medal. Mem. Red River Valley Fighter Pilots, Pi Alpha Alpha. Republican. Roman Catholic.

SHREEVE, JEAN'NE MARIE, chemist, educator; b. Deer Lodge, Mont., July 2, 1933; d. Charles William and Maryfrances (Briggeman) S. BA, U. Mont., 1953, DSc (hon.), 1982; MS, U. Minn., 1956; PhD, U. Wash., 1961; NSF postdoctoral fellow, U. Cambridge, Eng., 1967-68. Asst. prof. chemistry U. Idaho, Moscow, 1961-65; asso. prof. U. Idaho, 1965-67, prof., 1967-73, acting chmn. dept. chemistry, 1969-70, 1973, head dept., and prof., 1973-87, vice provost rsch. and grad. studies, prof. chemistry, 1987—; Lucy W. Pickett lectr. Mt. Holyoke Coll., 1976, George H. Cady lectr. U. Wash., 1993; mem. Nat. Com. Standards in Higher Edn., 1965-67, 69-73. Mem. editorial bd. Jour. Fluorine Chem., 1970—, Jour. Heteroatom Chemistry, 1988—, Accounts Chem. Rsch., 1973-75, Inorganic Synthesis, 1976—; contbr. articles to chem. jours. Bd. govs. Argonne Nat. Lab., 1992—. Recipient Disting. Alumni award U. Mont., 1970; named Hon. Alumnus, U. Idaho, 1972; recipient Outstanding Achievement award U. Minn., 1975, Sr. U.S. Scientist award Alexander Von Humboldt Found., 1978, Excellence in Teaching award Chem. Mfrs. Assn., 1980; U.S. hon. Ramsay fellow, 1967-68, Alfred P. Sloan fellow, 1970-72. Mem. AAUW (officer Moscow chpt. 1962-69), AAAS (bd. dirs. 1991—), Am. Chem. Soc. (bd. dirs. 1985—, chair Fluorine div. 1969-71, PRF adv. bd. 1975-77, women chemists com. 1972-77, Fluorine award 1978, Garvan medal 1972, Harry and Carol Mosher award Santa Clara Valley sect. 1992), Phi Beta Kappa, Sigma Xi, Phi Kappa Phi. Office: U Idaho Dept Chemistry 111 Morrill Hall Moscow ID 83843

SHREVE, PEG, educator; b. Spencer, Va., July 23, 1927; d. Hubert Smith and Pearl (Looney) Adams; m. Don Franklin Shreve, June 17, 1950 (dec. Sept. 1970); children: Donna, Jennifer, John, Don. BA, Glenville State U., 1948. Cert. elem. tchr., Va., Wyo. Reading tchr. Wood County Bd., Parkersburg, W.Va., 1948-50; elem. tchr. Mt. Solon, Va., 1950-52, Bridgewater, Va., 1952-53, Cody, Wyo., 1970-86. Pres. PEO AO, Cody, 1981-82; dir. Walden Cancer Found., Cheyenne, Wyo., 1985—; mem. scout council Girl Scouts Am., White Sulphur Springs, W.Va., 1962-65; chair com. Travel, Recreation and Wildlife, State House of Reps., Wyo., 1983—, majority whip; co-chair Legis. Exec. Conf., Wyo., 1987; mem. Nat. Con. State Legislatures, 1982—, Nat. Women Legislators, 1984—, Rep. Women, 1975—. Mem. AAUW (exec. bd.), Beta Sigma Phi (Lady of Yr. award 1986). Presbyterian. Lodge: Soroptimist (Women Helping Women award 1985). Home: PO Box 2257 Cody WY 82414-2257

SHREVE, THEODORE NORRIS, construction company executive; b. St. Louis, Feb. 14, 1919; s. Truxtun Benbridge and Beulah (Dyer) S.; m. Caroline Prouty, Jan. 7, 1943; children: Sara Ann Caile, Suzanne Foster Shreve, Theo Carol. BS, U. Colo., 1942. Sec., treas. Trautman & Shreve, Inc., Denver, 1946-68, pres., 1965-86, chmn. bd., 1984—; pres. 4030 Corp., 1984—. Mem. Colo. U. Found. Bd., 1988—; Rep. County Assembly, 1962. Served with USNR, 1942-45. Registered profl. engr., Colo. Mem. Mech.

Contractors Assn., Colo. Soc. Profl. Engrs., Rotary, Gyro Club, Denver Country Club, Sigma Phi Epsilon. Republican. Episcopalian. Home: 1510 E 10th Ave Apt 13W Denver CO 80218-3101 Office: Trautman & Shreve 4406 Race St Denver CO 80216-3818

SHRIVASTAVA, CHINMAYA ANAND, electrical engineer; b. Sagar, India, Oct. 17, 1951; came to U.S., 1984; s. Rewa Prasad and Bhagyavati Devi Shrivastava; m. Vanita Sinha, July 2, 1979; children: Sugandha, Aditi, Aparna. BEngring, Jabalpur (India) U., 1973; MEE, U. Utah, 1985, DEE, 1991. Sr. tech. officer Electronics Corp. of India Ltd., Hyderabad, 1973-84; project engr. Cordin Co., Salt Lake City, 1986—. Scholar State Govt. of Madhya Pradesh, Jabalpur, 1968-73. Fellow IETE, India; mem. IEEE (sr. mem., electron devices soc.). Hindu. Home: 1133 Roosevelt Ave Salt Lake City UT 84105-2539 Office: Cordin Co 2230 S 3270 W Salt Lake City UT 84119-1194

SHRONTZ, FRANK ANDERSON, airplane manufacturing executive; b. Boise, Idaho, Dec. 14, 1931; s. Thurlyn Howard and Florence Elizabeth (Anderson) S.; m. Harriet Ann Houghton, June 12, 1954; children: Craig Howard, Richard Whitaker, David Anderson. Student, George Washington U., 1953; LLB, U. Idaho, 1954; MBA, Harvard U., 1958; postgrad., Stanford U., 1969-70. Asst. contracts coordinator Boeing Co., Seattle, 1958-65, asst. dir. contract adminstrn., 1965-67, asst. to v.p. comml. airplane group, 1967-69, asst. dir. new airplane program, 1969-70, dir. comml. sales operations, 1970-73, v.p. planning and contracts, 1977-78; asst. sec. Dept. Air Force, Washington, 1973-76, Dept. Def., Washington, 1976-77; v.p., gen. mgr. 707/727/737 div. Boeing Comml. Airplane Co., Seattle, 1978-82, v.p. sales and mktg., 1982-84; pres. Comml. Airplane Co. Boeing Div., Seattle, 1986—; pres., chief exec. officer The Boeing Co., Seattle, 1986—, chmn., chief exec. officer, 1988—; bd. dirs. Ctr. for Strategic and Internat. Studies, 1986, Citicorp, Boise Cascade Corp., 3M Co.; mem. The Bus. Coun., 1987. Mem. Bus. Roundtable (policy com.). 1st lt. AUS, 1954-56. Mem. Phi Alpha Delta, Beta Theta Pi. Clubs: Overlake Golf and Country, Columbia Tower. Home: 8434 W Mercer Way Mercer Island WA 98040-5633 Office: Boeing Co PO Box 3707 7755 E Marginal Way S Seattle WA 98108-4002*

SHROPSHIRE, DONALD GRAY, hospital executive; b. Winston-Salem, N.C., Aug. 6, 1927; s. John Lee and Bess L. (Shouse) S.; m. Mary Ruth Bodenheimer, Aug. 19, 1950; children: Melanie Shropshire David, John Devin. B.S., U. N.C., 1950; Erickson fellow hosp. adminstrn., U. Chgo., 1958-59; LLD (hon.), U. Ariz., 1992. Personnel asst. Nat. Biscuit Co., Atlanta, 1950-52; asst. personnel mgr. Nat. Biscuit Co., Chgo., 1952-54; adminstr. Eastern State Hosp., Lexington, Ky., 1954-62; assoc. dir. U. Md. Hosp., Balt., 1962-67; adminstr. Tucson Med. Ctr., 1967-82, pres., 1982-92, pres. emeritus, 1992—; pres. Tucson Hosps. Med. Edn. Program, 1970-71, sec., 1971-86; pres. So. Ariz. Hosp. Council, 1968-69; bd. dirs. Ariz. Blue Cross, 1967-76, chmn. provider standards com., 1972-76; chmn. Healthways Inc., 1985-92; chmn. Healthways Inc., 1985-92; bd. dirs. First Interstate Bank of Ariz., Tucson Electric Power Co. Bd. dirs., exec. com. Health Planning Council Tucson, 1969-74; chmn. profl. div. United Way Tucson, 1969-70, vice chmn. campaign, 1988, Ariz. Health Facilities Authority, 1992—; chmn. dietary services com., vice chmn., 1988. Md. Hosp. Council, 1966-67; bd. dirs. Ky. Hosp. Assn., 1961-62, chmn. council profl. practice, 1960-61; past pres. Blue Grass Hosp. Council; trustee Assn. Western Hosps., 1974-81, pres., 1979-80; mem. accreditation Council for Continuing Med. Edn., 1982-87, chmn., 1986; bd. govs. Pima Community Coll., 1970-76, sec., 1973-74, chmn., 1975-76, bd. dirs. Found., 1978-82, Ariz. Bd. Regents, 1982-90, sec., 1983-86, pres. 1987-88; mem. Tucson Airport Authority, 1987—, bd. dirs., 1990— ; v.p. Tucson Econ. Devel. Corp., 1977-82; bd. dirs. Vol. Hosps. Am., 1977-88, treas., 1979-82; mem. Ariz. Adv. Health Coun. Dirs., 1976-78, Ariz. Health Facilities Authority Bd., 1992—; bd. dirs. Tucson Tomorrow, 1983-87, Tucson Downtown Devel. Corp., 1988—, Rincon Inst., 1992—; dir. Mus. No. Ariz., 1988—; nat. bd. advisors Coll. Bus. U. Ariz, 1992—, chmn. Dean's Bd. Fine Arts, 1992—. Named to Hon. Order Ky. Cols.; named Tucson Man of Yr. 1987; recipient Disting. Svc. award Anti-Defamation League B'nai B'rith, 1989, Salisbury award Ariz. Hosp. Assn. Mem. Am. Hosp. Assn. (nominating com. 1983-86, trustee 1975-78, ho. dels. 1972-78, chmn. coun. profl. svc. 1973-74, regional adv. bd. 1969-78, chmn. joint com. with Nat. Assn. Social Workers 1963-64, Disting. Svc. award 1989), Ariz. Hosp. Assn. (Salisbury award, bd. dirs. 1967-72, pres. 1970-71), Ariz. C. of C. (bd. dirs. 1988—), Assn. Am. Med. Colls. (mem. assembly 1974-77), Tucson C. of C. (bd. dirs. 1968-69), United Comml. Travelers, Nat. League Nursing, Ariz. Acad. (bd. dirs. 1982, treas. 1985), Pima County Acad. Decathlon Assn. (dir. 1983-85), Tucson Community Coun. Baptist (ch. moderator, chmn. finance com., deacon, ch. sch. supt., trustee, bd. dirs. ch. found.). Home: 6734 N Chapultepec Circle Tucson AZ 85715 Office: TM Care 2195 River Rd Ste 202 Tucson AZ 85718

SHROPSHIRE, HELEN MAE, historian; b. Prosser, Nebr., May 7, 1909; d. William Pearl and Dicy Belle (Myer) Stafford. Grad., Rogers Bus. Coll., Everett, Wash., 1928. Co-owner Camera Exchange, Pacific Grove, Calif., 1947-62; co-owner, photographer, writer Shropshire Film Prodns., Pacific Grove, 1950-76; pilot, co-owner Monarch Aviation, Monterey, Calif., 1962-63; co-founder, mgr. Calif. Heritage Guides, Monterey, Calif., 1971—. Mem. Ninety Nines Inc. (life). Republican. Home: 1623 Josselyn Canyon Rd Monterey CA 93940 Office: Calif Heritage Guides 10 Custom House Plz Monterey CA 93940-2430

SHRYOCK, BENJAMIN CHARLES, small business owner; b. Seattle, Aug. 13, 1962; s. Edwin Forrest Shryock and Marilyn Fay (Nelson) Martin; m. Lynelle Fay DeRoo, Aug. 3, 1986. BSBA, U. Calif., Berkeley, 1987. Cert. gen. bldg. contractor; lic. real estate sales. Owner Shower Walls of the Bay Area, Oakland, Calif., 1988—, Alpenbach of N.Am., Oakland. Mem. Better Bus. Bur., Oakland C. of C., U. Calif. Berkeley Alumni Assn., Golden Key Nat. Honor Soc. Office: Alpenbach NA 2601 Adeline St # 190 Oakland CA 94607-2407

SHUBART, DOROTHY LOUISE, artist, educator; b. Ft. Collins, Colo., Mar. 1, 1923; d. Adam Christian and Rose Virginia (Ayers) Tepfer; m. Robert Franz Shubart, Apr. 22, 1950; children: Richard, Lorenne. AA, Colo. Women's Coll., 1944; student, Western Res. U., 1947-48; BA, St. Thomas Aquinas Coll., 1974; MA, Coll. New Rochelle, 1978. Art tchr. Denver Mus., 1942-44, Cleve. Recreation Dept., 1944-50; ind. artist, portrait painter Colo., Cleve., N.Y., and N.Mex., 1944—; adult edn. art tchr. Nanuet (N.Y.) Pub. Schs., 1950-65, Pearl River (N.Y.) Adult Edn., 1950-51. Exhbns. include Hopper House, Rockland Ctr. for Arts, CWC, Cleve. Inst. Art, Coll. New Rochelle. Leader 4-H Club, Nanuet, 1960-80, Girl Scouts, Nanuet, 1961-68; mem. scholarship and gen. com. PTA, Nanuet, 1964-68. Gund scholar Cleve. Inst. Art, 1946. Mem. Delta Tau Kappa, Phi Delta Kappa. Democrat. Home: 8 Hidalgo Ct Eldorado Santa Fe NM 87505-8898

SHUBB, WILLIAM BARNET, lawyer; b. Oakland, Calif., May 28, 1938; s. Ben and Nellie Bernice (Fruechtenicht) S.; m. Sandra Ann Talarico, July 29, 1962; children: Alisa Marie, Carissa Ann, Victoria Ann. AB, U. Calif., Berkeley, 1960, JD, 1963. Bar: Calif., 1964, U.S. Ct. Internat. Trade 1981, U.S. Customs Ct. 1980, U.S. Ct. Appeals (9th cir.) 1964, U.S. Supreme Ct. 1972. Law clk. U.S. Dist. Ct., Sacramento, 1963-65; asst. U.S. atty., Sacramento, 1965-71; chief asst. U.S. atty. (ea. dist.) Calif., 1971-74; assoc. Diepenbrock, Wulff, Plant & Hannegan, Sacramento, 1974-77, ptnr., 1977-80, 81—; U.S. atty. Eastern Dist. Calif., 1980-81; judge U.S. Dist. Ct. (ea. dist.) Calif., 1990—; chmn. com. drafting of local criminal rules U.S. Dist. Ct. (ea. dist.) Calif., 1974, mem. speedy trial planning com., 1974-80; lawyer rep. 9th Cir. U.S. Jud. Conf., 1975-78; mem. faculty Fed. Practice Inst., 1978-80; instr. McGeorge Sch. Law, U. Pacific, 1964-66. Mem. ABA, Fed. Bar Assn. (pres. Sacramento chpt. 1977), Calif. Bar Assn., Assn. Def. Counsel, Am. Bd. Trial Advs., Sacramento County Bar Council. Office: US Courthouse 650 Capitol Mall Sacramento CA 95814-4708

SHUBIN, ELLIOT BRIAN, physician; b. Phila., Dec. 8, 1942; s. Harry and Celia (Fireman) S.; m. Sally Ann Sternau, July 1, 1967. BA, Wesleyan U., 1964; MD, Temple U., 1969. Surgeon USPHS, San Francisco, 1969-72; resident ob-gyn. Kaiser Found. Hosp., San Francisco, 1972-75; sr. shareholder Permanente Med. Group Inc., South San Francisco, 1975—. Fellow ACOG; mem. Am. Fertility Soc., San Mateo County Med. Assn. (com. mem. 1990—, alternate del. 1992-93). Office: Permanente Med Group Inc 1200 El Camino Real South San Francisco CA 94080

SHUBIN, TATIANA, mathematician, educator; b. Kharkov, Russia, Dec. 4, 1950; came to U.S. 1978; d. Igor A. and Lidia L. (Galperina) Sapozhnikov; m. Zachary Y. Deretsky, Jan. 17, 1975 (div. 1988); 1 child, Zinaida Deretsky; m. Sergei G. Shubin, Aug. 29, 1989; 1 child, Sergei Jr. BS in Math., Moscow U., 1972; MA in Math., Kazakh U., Russia, 1974, U. Calif.-Santa Barbara, 1980; PhD in Math., U. Calif.-Santa Barbara, 1983. Tchr. pub. schs., Leningrad, 1972-73; teaching asst. Kazakh U., Alma-Ata, Russia, 1973-75; rsch. mathematician Radio-Electronic Equip. Factory, Leningrad, 1975-77; teaching asst. U. Calif.-Santa Barbara, 1979-83; vis. lectr. U. Calif.-Davis, 1983-85; lectr. San Jose State U., 1985-86, asst. prof. math., 1986-88, assoc. prof. math., 1988—; lectr. in field. Contbr. articles to profl. jours.; reviewer Math. Rev., 1983—; referee various rsch. jours. Recipient Meritorious Performance and Profl. Promise award, San Jose State U., 1989. Mem. Am. Math. Soc., Math. Assn. Am., Santa Clara Valley Math. Assn., Soc. of Archimedes. Russian Orthodox. Office: San Jose State Univ Dept Math/Computer Sci San Jose CA 95192

SHUGART, ALAN F., electronic computing equipment company executive; b. L.A., Sept. 27, 1930. BS in Engring. and Physics, U. Redlands, 1951. Dir. engring. IBM, San Jose, Calif., 1952-69; v.p. Memorex Corp., Sunnyvale, Calif., 1969-73; pres. Shugart Assocs., 1973-78; chmn., chief exec. officer Seagate Tech., Scotts Valley, Calif., 1978—, also bd. dirs. Office: Seagate Tech 920 Disc Dr Scotts Valley CA 95066-4542*

SHUKAT, CHARLES PHILIP, video editor; b. Miami Beach, Fla., May 31, 1954; s. Abraham Herman and Miriam Estelle (Steiner) S.; m. Amy Susan Mayer, Mar. 6, 1983. AS cum laude, Miami Dade Jr. Coll., 1974; BA, U. Ctrl. Fla., 1976. Videographer, sr. video editor Instant Replay Video Mag., Coconut Grove, Fla., 1979-84; sr. video editor, prodn. mgr. Cable Mktg. Systems, Miami, Fla., 1984-86; on-line video editor Miami Video and Post/WBFS-TV, Miami, Fla., 1986-89; freelance video editor Video Press Pak, L.A., 1990, Despie & Miziker Prodn., L.A., 1990, Rhino Home Video, L.A., 1991; video editor Stanhaven Prodn., Agoura, Calif., 1992—, Associated TV Inc., 1992. Mem. Screen Actors Guild, Screen Actors Guild Casting Com. Home: 11640 Woodbridge St # 109 Studio City CA 91604 Office: Stanhaven Prodns 4930 Lewis Rd Agoura CA 91301

SHUKLA, PRADIP KANTILAL, academic administrator, educator, consultant; b. Ahmedabad, Gujarat, India, Sept. 7, 1956; came to U.S., 1961; s. Kantilal T. and Manju K. (Vyas) S.; m. Yatri P. Thaker, Jan. 6, 1983; children: Monica, Amy. BSc in Bus. Adminstrn., Calif. State U., Long Beach, 1978, BA in Econs., 1978, MBA, 1979; MSc in Bus. Adminstrn., U. So. Calif., 1983; MEd, UCLA, 1983, PhD in Ednl. Adminstrn., 1990. Cert. prodn. and inventory mgr. Coord. tutoring ctr. Compton (Calif.) Coll., 1976, instr. bus. and law, 1980-86, adminstrv. analyst, 1982-83, dir. instnl. rsch., 1986-88, asst. to pres., 1990—; night libr. Lynwood (Calif.) Adult Sch., 1974-78; lectr. in mgmt. Calif. State U., Long Beach, L.A., Northridge, 1978-91; mgmt. cons. P.K. Shukla & Assocs., Orange, Calif., 1979—; assoc. prof. mktg. and mgmt. Chapman U., Orange, 1985—; cons. various corps. and colls., Calif., 1979—; internat. cons. and speaker import/export ventures. Adv. bd. St. Francis Med. Ctr., Lynwood, Calif., 1979-81, Santa Ana (Calif) Zoo, 1988—; community breakfast chairperson City Lynwood, 1980; polit. cons. various candidates local and statewide, Calif., 1979—. Scholar Bank of Am., Soc. Calif. Edison Co., UCLA Grad. Sch. Mgmt.; grantee U.S. Dept. Edn., Compton Coll., Chapman U. Mem. Internat. Acad. Mgmt. Mktg., Internat. Acad. Bus. & Soc. (charter), Computer Using Instrs., Western Acad. Mgmt. (program reviewer, arrangements com., program com.), Western Mktg. Educators Assn. (program reviewer, session chmn.), Am. Mktg. Assn., Acad. Mgmt. (program reviewer). Republican. Home: 3148 N Hartman St Orange CA 92665-1215 Office: Chapman U 333 N Glassell St Orange CA 92666-1099

SHULER, ROBIN LANE, accountant; b. Medford, Oreg., Nov. 22, 1952; s. Garry Couie and Marian (Mitchell) S.; m. Ellen Tarr, Mar. 20, 1976; children: Ian Daniel, Darin Andrew. BA in Acctg., Seattle Pacific U., 1976; MBA in Fin., U. Puget Sound, 1980. CPA, Wash. Dir. acctg. URS Engrs., Seattle, 1976-86; contr. ESCA Corp., Bellevue, Wash., 1986-88; CFO St. Catherine's, North Bend, Oreg., 1989-90, W & H Pacific, Inc., Bellevue, 1990—; chmn. of bd. Mustard Seed Assocs., Seattle, 1990-93. Elder 1st Presbyn. Ch., Coos Bay, Oreg., 1989-90. Staff sgt. Oreg. Army N.G./USAF, 1972-78. Mem. AICPA, Wash. State Soc. CPA's, Inst. Mgmt. Accts., Fin. Mgrs.' Group. Office: W & H Pacific Inc 3025 112th Ave NE Bellevue WA 98009

SHULER, SALLY ANN SMITH, telecommunications, computer services and software company executive; b. Mt. Olive, N.C., June 11, 1934; d. Leon Joseph and Ludia Irene (Montague) Simmons; m. Henry Ralph Smith Jr., Mar. 1, 1957 (div. Jan. 1976); children: Molly Montague, Barbara Ellen, Sara Ann, Mary Kathryn; m. Harold Robert Shuler, Aug. 2, 1987. BA in Math., Duke U., 1956; spl. studies, U. Liège, Belgium, 1956-57; postgrad. in bus. econs., Claremont Grad Sch., 1970-72. Mgr. fed. systems GE Svcs. Co., Washington, 1976-78; mgr. mktg. support GE Svcs. Co., Rockville, Md., 1978-81; dir. bus. devel. info. tech. group div. Electronic Data Systems, Bethesda, Md., 1981-82; v.p. mktg. optimum systems div. Electronic Data Systems, Rockville, 1982-83; v.p. planning and communications Electronic Data Systems, Dallas, 1983-84; exec. dir. comml. devel. U.S. West Inc., Englewood, Colo., 1984-90; v.p. mktg. devel. Cin. Bell Info. Systems Inc., 1990-92; mgmt. cons. in M&A, mktg. and strategic planning Denver, 1992—. Recipient GE Centennial award, Rockville, 1978. Fellow Rotary Internat. Found.; mem. Phi Beta Kappa, Tau Psi Omega, Pi Mu Epsilon. Democrat. Presbyterian.

SHULGASSER, BARBARA, writer; b. Manhasset, N.Y., Apr. 10, 1954; d. Lew and Luba (Golante) S. Student, Sarah Lawrence Coll., 1973-74; BA magna cum laude, CUNY, 1977; MS, Columbia U., 1978. Feature writer Waterbury (Conn.) Rep., 1978-81; reporter, feature writer Chgo. Sun Times, 1981-84; film critic San Francisco Examiner, 1984—; freelance book critic N.Y. Times Book Rev., N.Y.C., 1983—; guest interviewer City Arts and lectures of San Francisco, 1990—. Freelance columnist-video N.Y. Times Sunday Arts & Leisure, N.Y.C., 1989, features for Mirabella and Premiere mags, short story Glamour mag., 1990. Office: San Francisco Examiner 110 5th St San Francisco CA 94103

SHULTZ, C. E. (CHUCK SCHULTZ), exploration and production company executive. Degree in Geological Engring., Colo. Sch. of Mines, 1961; postgrad, U. Va., 1980, Harvard Bus. Sch., 1984. With Tenneco Oil Co., divsn. Tenneco Inc., 1961; v.p., gen. mgr. Western Gulf of Mex. divsn. Tenneco Oil Co., Lafayette, La., 1980-85; v.p., corp. planning and devel., officer Tenneco Inc., Houston, 1985-88; sr. v.p. Tenneco Oil Co., Houston, 1988-1989; pres., chief oper. officer Gulf Canada Resources Ltd., Calgary, 1989, pres., chief exec. officer, 1990—, also bd. dirs.; bd. dirs. Home Oil Co. Ltd., Interprovincial Pipe Line Co. Chmn. U.S. Nat. Energy Policy Coun., Nat. Petroleum Coun., selected study com., Teche API Chpt. (So. La.), Colo. Sch. Mines, pres.'s coun.; gov. Can. Petroleum Assn., exec. com., Oilmen's; chmn. Can-USSR Bus. Coun. Energy Group. Office: Gulf Can Resources Ltd, 401 9th Ave SW PO Box 130, Calgary, AB Canada T2P 2H7

SHULTZ, EMMET LAVEL, marketing executive; b. Blackfoot, Idaho, Apr. 23, 1934; s. Emmet Franklin and Alba Elizabeth (Larsen) S.; children: Joanne M. Shultz Greaney, Jeanette G. Shultz Yanez. Asst. to pres. Flying Diamond Corp., Salt Lake City, 1973-74; pres., also bd. dirs. Shuhart Industries, Inc., Salt Lake City, 1974-75; v.p. Hunstman Chem. and Oil Corp., Salt Lake City, 1975-76; exec. v.p. Huntsman Coal Corp., Salt Lake City, 1975-76; pres., chmn. bd. Gulf Energy Corp., Salt Lake City, 1976-90, Channel Energy Corp., 1983—, Kita Corp., 1985—, Inst. for Adept Health Rsch., Inc., 1988-90; pres., chmn. bd. Ancestors, Inc. Bd. Dirs. Ballet West, 1980-83, Utah Symphony, 1980-83. With USN, 1952-56. Republican. Home: 20915 Fawn Ct # 42 West Linn OR 97068 Office: 19363 Willamette Dr Ste 121 West Linn OR 97068

SHULTZ, FRED TOWNSEND, geneticist, biologist; b. Grinnell, Iowa, Mar. 3, 1923; s. J. Gordon and Katharine Lucia (Townsend) S.; m. Carolyn Covell June 24, 1961; children: Trina, Rebecca, Daniel, Brian. AB in Biol. Sci., Stanford U., 1947; PhD in Genetics, U. Calif.-Berkeley, 1952. Geneticist, biologist Animal Breeding Cons., Sonoma, Calif., 1952—; pres. Avian Allure; chmn. bd. dirs. Biol. Frontiers Inst. Inventor new life forms and prodn. systems. Served to 2nd lt. USAF, 1942-45. Recipient Poultry Sci. Research award Poultry Sci. Assn., 1954. Mem. Genetic Soc. Am., Am. Genetics Assn., Genetic Soc. Can., Poultry Sci. Assn., World Poultry Sci., World Aquaculture Soc., Am. Fisheries Soc., Nat. Shellfisheries Assn., Calif. Acad. Sci., Am. Soc. Agrl. Cons. Republican. Home: 19443 Marna Ln Sonoma CA 95476-6309 Office: Animal Breeding Cons PO Box 313 Sonoma CA 95476

SHULTZ, GEORGE PRATT, former secretary of state, economics educator; b. N.Y.C., Dec. 13, 1920; s. Birl E. and Margaret Lennox (Pratt) S.; m. Helena M. O'Brien, Feb. 16, 1946; children: Margaret Ann Shultz Tilsworth, Kathleen Pratt Shultz Jorgensen, Peter Milton, Barbara Lennox Shultz White, Alexander George. BA in Econs., Princeton U., 1942; PhD in Indsl. Econs., MIT, 1949; hon. degrees, U. Notre Dame, Loyola U., U. Pa., U. Rochester, Princeton U., Carnegie-Mellon U., Baruch Coll., N.Y.C., Northwestern U., Yeshiva U., U. Tel Aviv, Technion-Israel Inst. Tech. Mem. faculty M.I.T., 1949-57; assoc. prof. indsl. relations MIT, 1955-57; prof. indsl. relations Grad. Sch. Bus., U. Chgo., 1957-68, dean sch., 1962-68; fellow Ctr. for Advanced Studies in Behavioral Scis., 1968-69; U.S. sec. labor, 1969-70; dir. Office Mgmt. and Budget, 1970-72; U.S. sec. treasury, also asst. to Pres., 1972-74; chmn. Council on Econ. Policy, East-West Trade Policy com.; exec. v.p. Bechtel Corp., San Francisco, 1974-75, pres., 1975-77; vice chmn. Bechtel Corp., 1977-81; also dir.; pres. Bechtel Group, Inc., 1981-82; prof. mgmt. and pub. policy Stanford U., 1974-82, prof. internat. econs., 1989-91, prof. emeritus, 1991—; chmn. Pres. Reagan's Econ. Policy Adv. Bd., 1981-82; U.S. sec. of state, 1982-89; disting. fellow Hoover Instn., Stanford, 1989—; bd. dirs. Bechtel Group, Inc.; mem. corp. adv. coun. GM, Gulfstream Aerospace Corp.; chmn. J.P. Morgan Internat. Coun., chmn. adv. coun. Inst. Internat. Studies, Gov.'s Econ. Policy Adv. Bd. State of Calif. Author: Pressures on Wage Decisions, 1951, (with Charles A. Myers) The Dynamics of a Labor Market, 1951, (with John R. Coleman) Labor Problems: Cases and Readings, 1953, (with T.L. Whisler) Management Organization and the Computer, 1960, (with Arnold R. Weber) Strategies for the Displaced Worker, 1966, (with Robert Z. Aliber) Guidelines, Informal Controls and the Market Place, 1966, (with Albert Rees) Workers and Wages in the Urban Labor Market, 1970, Leaders and Followers in an Age of Ambiguity, 1975, (with Kenneth W. Dam) Economic Policy Beyond the Headlines, 1977, Turmoil and Triumph: My Years as Secretary of State, 1993; also articles, chpts. in books, reports. Served to capt. USMCR, 1942-45. Mem. Am. Econ. Assn., Indsl. Relations Research Assn. (pres. 1968), Nat. Acad. Arbitrators. Office: Stanford U Hoover Instn Stanford CA 94305

SHULTZ, SILAS HAROLD, lawyer; b. Scribner, Nebr., Mar. 21, 1938; s. Harold Mohr and Arlene E. (Spath) S. BS, U. Pa., 1960; LLB, U. Ariz., 1966. Bar: Ariz. 1966, U.S. Supreme Ct. 1988; cert. specialist in personal injury and wrongful death, Ariz. Ptnr., dir. Fennemore, Craig, P.C., Phoenix, 1966-85; trial specialist Law Office of Richard Grand, Tucson, 1985-88; officer Shultz & Rollins, Ltd., Tucson, 1988—. 1st lt. U.S. Army Res., 1961-66. Mem. Am. Bd. Trial Advocates, Ariz. Trial Lawyers Assn. Office: Shultz & Rollins Ltd 4280 N Campbell Ave Ste 214 Tucson AZ 85718-6585

SHULTZ, TERRY DALE, educator, scientist; b. Caldwell, Idaho, July 26, 1947; s. Dean Wilfred and Donna Ray (Ritter) S.; m. Megan Ann Holdridge, May 20, 1973; children: Christopher, Melissa. BA in Biology/Chemistry, N.W. Nazarene Coll., 1969; MS in Mammlian Physiology, U. Idaho, 1973; PhD in Human Nutrition, Oreg. State U., 1980; postdoctorate, Mayo Clinic, Rochester, Minn., 1980-82. Registered dietitian. Supr. lipids dept. Internat. Chem. Nuclear, Portland, 1973-74; rsch. assoc. Mountain States Tumor Inst., Boise, 1974-76; rsch. fellow dept. endocrine rsch. Mayo Clinic, Rochester, 1980-82; asst. to assoc. prof. Dept. of Nutrition Sch. Pub. Health, Loma Linda (Calif.) U., 1982-89, Dept. Biochemistry Sch. Medicine, Loma Linda U., 1984-89; asst. prof., scientist Dept. Food Sci. and Human Nutrition, Wash. State U., Pullman, 1989—; cons. Nat. Cancer Inst., 1986, grant rev. mem., 1988, Am. Cancer Soc., 1990; speaker in field. contbr. chpts. to books and numerous articles to profl. jours. Reviewer Am. Jour. of Clin. Nutrition, 1989-91, Preventive Medicine, 1989, Brit. Jour. of Cancer, 1991, Nutritional Biochemistry, 1989, Am. Oil Chemists' Soc., 1991. With U.S. Army, 1969-71. Grantee NIH/NCI, 1983-86, Nat. Livestock and Meat Bd., 1990-91, Nat. Dairy Promotion and Rsch. Bd., 1992—, Wash. State Dairy Products Commn., 1992—. Mem. Ass. of Am. Med. Technologists, Am. Soc. for Bone and Mineral Rsch., The Endocrine Soc., Am. Inst. of Nutrition, Am. Soc. of Clin. Nutrition, Am. Dietetic Assn., Am. Assn. for Cancer Rsch., Internat. Assn. for Vitamin and Nutritional Oncology, Phi Kappa Phi, Phi Sigma, Omicron Nu, Delta Omega, Sigma Xi (pres. Loma Linda U. chpt. 1988-89). Office: Dept Food Sci & Human Nutrition Wash State U Pullman WA 99164-6376

SHUMAN, THOMAS ALAN, correctional operations executive, consultant; b. Fairmont, W.Va., Dec. 31, 1946. BA, N.Mex. State U., 1969, 73; postgrad., U. N.Mex., 1988. Mgr. Drum Appliance, Inc., Las Cruces, N.Mex., 1971-75; classification supr. N.Mex. Corrections Dept., Santa Fe, 1976-80, mgmt. analyst supr., 1981-83, dir. classification, 1983-84, dep. sec., 1984-87; pres. Correctional Data Systems, Santa Fe, 1987—; owner Desktop Publ. Co., Santa Fe, 1988—; dir. N.Mex. Corrections Tng. Acad., 1991—; pres. Silicon Wizard Corp., 1989—; cons. Nat. Inst. Corrections, Washington, 1988, Am. Correctional Assn., Md., 1987—. Mem. Smithsonian Inst., U.S. Naval Inst. Served to lt. U.S. Army, 1969-71, Vietnam. Decorated Bronze Star, Presdl. Commendation. Mem. NRA, N.Mex. State U. Alumni Assn. Republican. Presbyterian.

SHUMATE, CHARLES ALBERT, physician; b. San Francisco, Aug. 11, 1904; s. Thomas E. and Freda (Ortmann) S.; B.S., U. San Francisco, 1927, H.H.D., 1976; M.D., Creighton U., 1931. Pvt. practice dermatology, San Francisco, 1933-73, ret., 1973; asst. clin. prof. dermatology Stanford U., 1956-62; pres. E Clampus Vitus, Inc., 1963-64; hon. mem. staff St. Mary's Hosp. Mem. San Francisco Art Commn., 1964-67, Calif. Heritage Preservation Commn., 1963-67; regent Notre Dame Coll. at Belmont, 1965-78, trustee, 1977-93; pres. Conf. Calif. Hist. Socs., 1967; mem. San Francisco Landmarks Preservation Bd., 1967-78, pres., 1967-69; trustee St. Patrick's Coll. and Sem., 1970-86. Served as maj. USPHS, 1942-46. Decorated knight comdr. Order of Isabella (Spain); knight Order of the Holy Sepulchre, knight of St. Gregory, knight of Malta. Fellow Am. Acad. Dermatology; mem. U. San Francisco Alumni Assn. (pres. 1955), Calif. Book Club (pres. 1969-71), Calif. Hist. Soc. (trustee 1958-67, 68-78, pres. 1962-64), Soc. Calif. Pioneers (dir. 1979—). Clubs: Bohemian, Olympic, Roxburghe (pres. 1958-59) (San Francisco); Zamorano (Los Angeles). Author: Life of George Henry Goddard; The California of George Gordon, 1976, Jas. F. Curtis, Vigilante, 1988, Francisco Pacheco of Pacheco Pass, 1977; Life of Mariano Malarin, 1980; Boyhood Days: Y. Villegas Reminiscences of California 1850s, 1983, The Notorious I.C. Woods of the Adams Express, 1986, Rincon Hill and South Park, 1988, Captain A.A. Ritchie, Pioneer, 1991. Home: 1901 Scott St San Francisco CA 94115-2613 Office: 490 Post St San Francisco CA 94102-1401

SHUMWAY, NORMAN D., former congressman; b. Phoenix, July 28, 1934; m. Luana June Schow; children: Jennifer, Neal, Perry, Tyler, Stuart, Brenda. A.A., Stockton Coll., 1954; B.S., U. Utah, 1960; J.D., Hastings Coll. Law, U. Calif., 1963. Bar: Calif. 1964. Practice law Downey, Calif.; formerly partner firm Cavalero, Bray, Shumway & Geiger; mem. 96th-101th Congresses from 14th Calif. Dist., 1979-91; commr. Calif. Pub. Utilities Commn., 1991—. Mem. San Joaquin County Bd. Supvrs., 1974-78, chmn. bd., 1978; past chmn. Goodwill Industries of San Joaquin Valley, Inc., U.S. English, Inc,; bd. dirs. Legal Svcs. Corp., Goodwill Industries Am.; exec. bd. Nat. Assn. Regulatory Utility Commns.; bd. visitors Brigham Young U. Law Sch.; former bishop, missionary to Japan Ch. Jesus Christ of Latter-day Saints. Office: Calif Pub Utilities Commn 505 Van Ness Ave Rm 5213 San Francisco CA 94102-3214

SHURTLEFF, AKIKO AOYAGI, artist, consultant; b. Tokyo, Jan. 24, 1950; d. Kinjiro and Fumiyo (Sugata) Aoyagi; m. William Roy Shurtleff, Mar. 10, 1977; 1 child, Joseph Aoyagi. Grad., Women's Coll. Art, Tokyo, 1971; student, Acad. Art, San Francisco, 1991—. Fashion designer, illustrator Marimura Co. and Hayakawa Shoji, Inc., Tokyo, 1970-72; co-founder, art dir. Soyfoods Ctr. consulting svcs., Lafayette, Calif., 1976—; lectr. U.S. Internat. Christian U., Tokyo, 1977, Japanese Tofu Mfrs. Conv., Osaka, 1978; presenter cooking demonstrations, tchr. cooking classes. Co-author, illustrator: The Book of Tofu, 1975, The Book of Miso, 1975, The Book of Kudzu, 1977, Tofu and Soymilk Production, 1979, The Book of Tempeh, 1979, Miso Production, 1979, Tempeh Production, 1980; illustrator: Spirulina (by L. Switzer), 1982, The Book of Shiatsu-The Healing Art of Finger Pressure (by S. Goodman), 1990, Staying Healthy with Nutrition (by E. Haas), 1992, Culinary Treasures of Japan (by John and Jan Belleme), 1992. Office: Soyfoods Ctr PO Box 234 Lafayette CA 94549

SHUTLER, KENNETH EUGENE, lawyer; b. Wichita, Kans., Mar. 27, 1938; s. Walter Kenneth and Charlene Belle (Swearingen) S.; m. Jean E. Rohner, June 24, 1967 (div.); children: Samantha Elizabeth, Whitney Anne; m. Carol Spiegel, Nov. 27, 1987. A.B., U. Pa., 1960; LL.B., Yale U., 1963. Bar: Pa. 1965, Calif. 1971. Practiced in Phila., 1965-68; assoc. Stradley, Ronon, Stevens & Young, Phila.; v.p. Shareholders Mgmt. Co., Los Angeles, 1968-72; v.p., gen. counsel Republic Corp., Los Angeles, 1972-78; sr. v.p., gen. counsel Nat. Med. Enterprises, Inc., Los Angeles, 1978-79; v.p. law div. Continental Aircraft Services, Inc., subs. Continental Airlines, 1979-81; v.p., gen. counsel Caesars World, Inc., 1981-83; ptnr. Troy & Gould, Los Angeles, 1983-91; exec. v.p., gen. counsel MGM Grand, Inc., Las Vegas, Calif., 1991-92, Las Vegas, Nev., 1993—; bd. dirs. Project Control of Tex. Bd. dirs. Constl. Rights Found., L.A. coun. Girl Scouts U.S.A., 1980-82, L.A. Chamber Orch., 1983-85; trustee Nev. Symphony Orch., 1993; alumni trustee, Pres.'s coun., U. Pa. Capt. U.S. Army, 1963-65. Mem. ABA, Calif. Bar Assn., L.A. County Bar Assn., Yale Alumni Assn. (schs. com.), U. Pa. Alumni Assn. (pres. So. Calif. 1971-72), Venice Squash Club, Bel-Air Bay Club, Ctr. Cts. Club, Beefeaters Club., Green Valley Athletic Club. Clubs: Venice Squash, Bel-Air Bay, Ctr. Cts., Beefeaters, Green Valley Ath. Office: MGM Grand Inc 3155 W Harmon Las Vegas NV 89103

SHVYRKOV, VLADISLAV V., statistician, economist; b. Petropavlovsk, USSR, Oct. 12, 1931; came to U.S., 1978; s. Vasilij L. and Tanij N. (Kuchkovskaj) S.; m. Tamara Sirotkina, Sept. 20, 1956 (div. Oct. 1979); 1 child, Irina; m. Marie I. Zanzarov, Aug. 8, 1980. MS, Moscow Fin. Inst., 1956; PhD, Moscow Inst. Nat. Econ., 1959; DSc, Leningrad (USSR) U., 1969. Referent Sci. Inst. Labor and Wages, Moscow, 1956-59; asst. prof. Inst. Nat. Econ., Moscow, 1959-63; assoc. prof. Moscow State U., 1963-69; prof., chmn. Inst. Food Industry, Moscow, 1969-77; vis. prof. Helsinki U., Finland, 1977-78; rsch. scientist NYU, 1978-79; prof. Rider Coll., Trenton, N.J., 1979-84; vis. lectr. San Francisco State U., 1984-85; vis. prof. U. San Francisco, 1985-86; lectr. Sonoma State U., Rohnert Pk., Calif., 1986—; chief expert State Planning Com. USSR. Moscow, 1963-69; program chmn. Seminar, Sheffield, England, 1984; speaker numerous univs., colls. and orgns. Author of 21 books and workbooks in field; contbr. 150 articles to profl. jours. Recipient rsch. award Inst. Nat. Econ., USSR, 1958, achievement award Gosplan USSR, 1965, NSF achievement award, U. San Francisco, 1986. Mem. Internat. Soc. Statis. Sci. in Econs. (prof., chmn. 1982—), Internat. Statis. Inst., Am. Statis. Assn., Bernouilli Soc. for Math., Stats. and Probability. Office: IS-SSE 536 Oasis Dr Santa Rosa CA 95407-7717

SHWACHMAN, BEN, anesthesiologist, lawyer; b. July 20, 1937; s. Sam and Bella (Gilberg) S.; m. Elise E. Doss, Oct. 15, 1966; children: Amy, Arthur. BS in Pharmacy, U. Ill., 1955, MD, 1964; JD, Loyola U. L.A., 1969. Diplomate Nat. Bd. Med. Examiners, Am. Bds. Anesthesiology; Bar: Calif. Intern Milw. County Gen. Hosp., 1964; resident anesthesiology U. Ill. Rsch. and Edn. Hosps., Chgo., 1965-66, L.A. County Gen. Hosp., 1966-67; anesthesiologist Intercommunity Med. Ctr., Covina, Calif., chief of staff, 1992-93; anesthesiologist Valley Med., Covina, 1969—. Bd. dirs. Calif. Polit. Action Com. Officer U.S. Marine Corps, USN, 1967-69, Vietnam. Mem. AMA, ABA, Am. Soc. Anesthesiologists (profl. liability and bylaws coms.), Calif. Soc. Anesthesiologists (many offices including bd. dirs., chmn. liason com. with Calif. Dental Assn.), L.A. County Med. Assn. (many offices including treas., bd. dirs. polit. action com., pres. 1993—), Calif. Med. Assn. (bd. dirs., ho. dels., many coms.), Am. Soc. Cardiovascular Anesthesiologists, Am. Inst. Parliamentarians, Nat. Health Lawyers Assn., State Bar of Calif., others. Office: Valley Med 230 W College St Ste C Covina CA 91723

SIART, WILLIAM ERIC BAXTER, banker; b. Los Angeles, Dec. 25, 1946; s. William Ernest and Barbara Vesta (McPherson) Baxter; m. Noelle Ellen Reid, Sept. 17, 1966; children—Shayne Allison, Tiffany Ann. B.A. in Econs., U. Santa Clara, 1968; M.B.A., U. Calif., Berkeley, 1969. With Bank of Am., 1969-78; v.p. corp. banking Bank of Am., Brussels, 1977-78; sr. v.p. charge mktg. Western Bancorp, Los Angeles, 1978-81; pres., chief operating officer First Interstate Bank of Nev. N.A., Reno, 1981-82; pres., chief exec. officer First Interstate Bank of Nev. N.A., 1982-84, chmn. bd., pres., chief exec. officer, 1984; formerly chmn., pres., chief exec. officer First Interstate Bank Calif., L.A., also bd. dirs.; pres. First Interstate Bancorp, L.A., 1990—. Trustee U. Nev.-Reno Found.; bd. dirs. Sierra Arts Found. Mem. Am. Bankers Assn. (mem. govt. relations council), Reno-Sparks C. of C. (dir.). Republican. Roman Catholic. Office: First Interstate Bancorp 633 W 5th St Los Angeles CA 90017-3501*

SIBBIO, MICHAEL GREGORY, promoter, audio technical consultant; b. Akron, Ohio, Feb. 2, 1955; s. Dominic Rocco Sibbio and Elizabeth Mari (Sadler) Parsons. Grad. high sch., Akron. Job supt. UNS Constrn. Co., Phoenix, 1973-75; gen. mgr. Staff Music Co., Akron, 1975-79; pres., sole propr. Mike's Music, Inc., Akron, 1979-88; pres., exec. producer, audio technician Sibcon Prodns., Akron, 1985-88; exec. dir., freelance producer Fastrac Comml. div. Akron Music Ctrs., 1988; staff cons. Akron Music Ctrs., 1988; dir. of promotions Western Park Model and RV, Inc., Mesa, Ariz., 1990-91; dir. promotions AAA Park Models Inc., Mesa, Ariz., 1991-92; mktg. cons. Polychrome Inc., Akron, Ohio, 1991; dir. market Color Burst, Inc., Simi Valley, Calif., 1992—, P.I.C., Phoenix, 1992—; cons. Fangrabber, Inc., 1992—; pres. FASTRAC Communication, Mesa, Ariz., 1991—; dir. promotions Western RV, Inc., 1993—; cons. McDonald's Corp., North Royalton, Ohio, 1989, CMI Nashville, 1989, Motorola GEG, 1989, Pro Performance, 1992—, Second Story Concepts, Canton, Ohio, 1993—; exclusive ofcl. lic. holder Wilson Sporting Goods, Chgo., 1993, Sports Market '93, Pro Performance. Fundraiser Am. Heart Assn., Easter Seal Soc. Mem. Nat. Sound Contractors Assn. Home: 1362 N Roca Mesa AZ 85213-4200

SICKEL, JOAN SOTTILARE, foundation administrator; b. Jersey City, Dec. 29, 1941; d. Peter S. and Rose M. (Maresca) Sottilare; m. Walter F. Sickel Jr., Jan. 4, 1964 (div. July 1979); children: Walter F. III (dec.), Linda Hilaire. AB, Georgian Ct. Coll., 1963. Dir. ann. giving Tucson Med. Ctr. Found., 1980-87; dir. devel. and pub. rels. Ariz. Children's Home, Tucson, 1987—. Mem. women's studies adv. coun. U. Ariz. Mem. Nat. Soc. Fund Raising Execs., Nat. Assn. for Hosp. Devel., Pub. Rels. Soc. Am., Planned Giving Round Table of So. Ariz., AAUW, Ariz. Assn. for Hosp. Devel. (treas. 1986-88), U. Ariz. Presidents Club, U. Ariz. Wildcat Club, Soroptimists Internat. (chairperson fin. com. 1985). Home: 1060 W Camino Desierto Tucson AZ 85704-4507 Office: Ariz Childrens Home 2700 S 8th Ave Tucson AZ 85713-4790

SICKELS, WILLIAM LOYD, secondary educator; b. Porterville, Calif., Mar. 26, 1936; s. Roy Ernest and Lula Mae (Weaver) S.; m. Donna Louise Eilers; 1 child, Alan Michael. AA, Porterville (Calif.) Coll., 1956; BA, San Jose (Calif.) State U., 1960, MA, 1965. Tchr. Redwood High Sch., Visalia, Calif., 1962-68; instr. Victor Valley Coll., Victorville, Calif., 1968-70; athletic dir., tchr. Tulare (Calif.) Western High Sch., 1970—. Pres. Sequoia Lake Conf. of YMCA's (pres. 1990-91, bd. dirs. 1982—). With U.S. Army, 1960-62. Named to Hall of Fame Visalia YMCA, 1990, Man of Yr., 1984. Fellow Y's Men Internat. (pres. 1985—), Calif. State Athletic Dirs. Assn. (v.p. 1984—, Athletic Dir. Yr. 1981). Republican. Methodist. Home: 2723 W Country Ave Visalia CA 93277 Office: Tulare Western High Sch 824 W Maple Tulare CA 93274

SIDDOWAY, HENRY RALPH, company executive; b. Vernal, Utah, Sept. 10, 1905; s. William Henry and Emily Jane (Dunster) S.; m. Marsale Eunice Eaton, Apr. 24, 1921; children: William Ralph, Lynn Irwin, Charyl Anita. BS with honors, U. Utah, 1928, postgrad., 1963; postgrad., Brigham Young U., 1929-30. Cert. secondary tchr., music tchr., social svc. worker. Tchr. Uintah High Sch., Vernal, Utah, 1928-46, treas., 1928-44; acct., bus. mgr. Calder Motor Co.-S. Calder, Vernal, 1930-34; dir. of owners self interest 3000 sheep Utah, 1946-80; bus. mgr., dir. Vernal Milling Co., 1933-56; stockholder, dir., sec., treas. Ashley Coop. Merc. Inst., 1943—; office mgr., acct. Calder Bros. Creamers, Vernal, 1947-50; office mgr. Uintah Oil Refinery, 1950-54; dir. S. Raven Oil & Refining co., Rangely, Colo., 1960-65; mem. U.S. Bur. Land Mgmt., Uintah, Duchesne Dagget County, Utah, 1943-60, sec., 3 County, 1943-60, mem. adv. bd., 1957-60. Mem. Utah State Adv. Bd., Unitah County Bd. Edn., 1942, pres. 1944-45; mayor City of Vernal, 1958-62; dir. Uintah County Coun. on Aging, 1970-78, Area Agy. on Aging, 1978-89. Recipient Help Line Profl. Svc. award Dept. Social Svcs. Div. Alcohlism and Drugs, Salt Lake City, 1978. Mem. Lions Club. Republican. Mem. LDS Ch. Home: 673 N Vernal Ave Vernal UT 84078 Office: Ashley Coop Merc Inst 22 W Main St Vernal UT 84078

SIDHU, GURMEL SINGH, geneticist; b. Jullunder, India, May 23, 1943; came to U.S., 1980; s. Naranjan Singh and Kartar Kaur (Hoti) S.; m. Baljit Aulakh, Mar. 21, 1979; children: Vikram, Roop. BS, Punjab U., Chandigarh, India, 1960, MS, 1966; PhD, U. B.C., Can., 1974. Rsch. scientist SFU, Burnaby, 1973-80; asst. prof. Genetics U. Nebr., Lincoln, 1980-86; vis. prof. Calif. State U., Fresno, 1978, rsch. scientist, adj. prof., 1986—; plant pathologist, breeder Germaine's Inc., Fresno, 1989—. Editor: Genetics of Plant Pathogenic Fungi, 1988; assoc. Phytopathology, 1980-86, Crop Improvement, 1980-86. Mem. AAAS, Phytopathology Soc. Am., Genetics and Cytology Soc. of Can. Home: 1637 Gettysburg Ave Clovis CA 93611-4509 Office: Calif State U Shaw & Cedar Fresno CA 93740

SIDHU, MOHAN, anesthesiologist; b. India, June 15, 1950; came to U.S., 1975; s. Gurdial and Bachan S.; m. Gurpreet Brar, 1979; children: Simren, Jasmin, Sonya. MBBS, Christian Med. Sch., Ludhiana, India, 1973. Diplomate Am. Bd. Anesthesiology. Dir. outpatient anesthesia U. Calif. Irvine Med. Ctr., Orange, Calif., 1982-84; chief anesthesia Women's Hosp., Long Beach, Calif., 1987—; assoc. clin. prof. U. Calif. Irvine. Fellow Am. College Anesthesiologists. Office: Women's Hosp 2801 Allantic Long Beach CA 90801

SIDHU, VICTOR S., investment executive; b. Pitts., Nov. 23, 1938; s. S. S. and Mary Elizabeth (Homoney) S.; m. Nancy Dayton; 1 child, Mary Sidhu Pittman. Student, Princeton U., 1956-59; BA, U. Chgo., 1961; MA, U. Ill., 1967. Chartered fin. analyst. Asst. to chmn. of dept. U. Ill., Champaign, 1963-65; account exec. Dean Witter Co., Chgo., 1967-70; pres., founder RMI Corp., Winnetka, Ill., 1970-72; investment mgr. Lincoln Nat. Investment Advisors, Chgo., 1972-73; lectr. Northeastern Ill. U., Chgo., 1971-73; v.p., div. mgr. Harris Bank, Chgo., 1973-87; v.p., chief investment officer First Interstate Bank of Calif., L.A., 1987-90; sr. v.p. Capital Rsch. and Mgmt. Co., L.A., 1990—. Bd. advisors Salvation Army, Santa Monica, Calif., 1988—; bd. dirs. U. Chgo. Alumni Assn., L.A., 1989-90. Fellow Fin. Analysts Fedn.; mem. L.A. Soc. Fin. Analysts (pres. 1992-93, gov. 1989—), Investment Analysts Soc. Chgo. (bd. dirs.), Am. Fin. Assn. (life), Am. Mgmt. Assn., Inst. Chartered Fin. Analysts. Republican. Congregationalist. Home: 39 Sea Colony Dr Santa Monica CA 90405-5322 Office: Capital Rsch & Mgmt Co 333 S Hope St Los Angeles CA 90071-1406

SIDLEY, MICHAEL I., lawyer; b. L.A., July 23, 1961; s. Milton and Saralyn Irene (Gitlin) S. BA in Polit. Sci., U. Calif., Berkeley, 1983; JD, U. Pacific, 1988. Bar: Calif. 1989. Atty. Los Angeles County Pub. Defender's Office, L.A., 1989-90; pvt. practice, L.A., 1990—. Mem. nat. staff Mondale for Pres., Washington, 1984, Dukakis for Pres., Boston, 1988. Mem. Calif. Trial Lawyers Assn., Calif. Attys. for Criminal Justice, Criminal Cts. Bar Assn., Order of Coif. Democrat. Office: Ste 1350 2049 Century Park E Los Angeles CA 90067

SIDNAM, WILLIAM ROBERT, newspaper columnist; b. Anaheim, Calif., Oct. 28, 1934; s. Claude Charles and Beulah Elizabeth (Davis) S.; m. Judith Anne Fink, June 30, 1957; children: Elizabeth Anne, William Davis, Roberta Dorothy. BA, Calif. State U., Long Beach, 1957; MS, Calif. State U., Fullerton, 1972. Educator Calif. Schs., 1958-75; garden columnist L.A. Times, 1975—, Orange County (Calif.) Register, 1977—, Riverside (Calif.) Enterprise, 1979—, Westways Mag., So. Calif., 1989—. Recipient Calif. Environ. Merit award, 1975, 77, Presdl. Environ. Merit award, 1977, 81. Home: 2707 N Lyon Santa Ana CA 92701 Office: LA Times Times Mirror Square Los Angeles CA 90053

SIEBERT, DIANE DOLORES, author, poet; b. Chgo., Mar. 18, 1948; m. Robert William Siebert, Sept. 21, 1969. RN. Author: Truck Song, 1984 (Notable Children's Book award ALA, 1984, Sch. Libr. Jour. one of Best Books 1984, Outstanding Children's Book award N.Y. Times Book Rev. 1984, Reading Rainbow Selection book 1991), Mojave, 1988 (Children's Editor's Choice 1988, Internat. Reading Assn. Tchrs.' Choice award 1989, others), Heartland, 1989 (award Nat. Coun. for Social Studies/Children's Book Coun. 1989, on John Burroughs List Nature Book for Young Readers 1989, award Ohio Farm Bur. Women 1991), Train Song, 1990 (Notable Children's Book award ALA, 1990, Redbook Mag. one of Top Ten Picture Books 1990, one of Best Books award Sch. Libr. Jour. 1990, others), Sierra, 1991 (Outstanding Sci. Trade Book for Children award Nat. Sci. Tchrs.' Assn. 1991, Notable Children's Trade Book in Field Social Studies award Nat. Coun. Social Studies 1991, Beatty award Calif. Libr. Assn. 1992), Plane Song, 1993. Home: PO Box 758 Terrebonne OR 97760-0758

SIEBERT, STEPHANIE RAY, video production company executive; b. Phoenix, Sept. 17, 1949; d. Richard and Jacquelyn (Schmunk) S. AA, Yavapai Community Coll., 1967; BS, U. Minn., 1970. Acctg. mgr. Ski Mart of Newport Beach, Calif.; contr. Brown Jay Prodns., L.A.; gen. mgr. Video Tape Libr., Ltd., L.A.; pres. Film/Video Stock, Inc., L.A.; pres., chmn. Unfettered Mind, non-profit Calif. corp. Bd. dirs., officer Buddhist orgn. Mem. NAFE, NOW (past pres. Laguna Beach), Women's Bus. Enterprises, Assn. Women Entrepreneurial Developers, Am. Film Inst., Am. Mgmt. Assn., Am. Assn. Female Execs., Nat. Assn. Women Bus. Owners, Women in Film, Hollywood C. of C., Bus. and Profl. Women's Assn., Women in Show Bus. Office: 10700 Ventura Blvd # E Studio City CA 91604-3561

SIEBERTS, JAN KRISTIAN, bank executive; b. Portland, Oreg., Aug. 26, 1942; s. Ned Alworth and Solveig (Storkersen) S.; m. Gail Ann Smith, Dec. 28, 1971; children: Solveig Kara, Soren K. B.S., U. Oreg., 1967. Mgr. Master-Charge 1st Nat. Bank, Anchorage, 1968-75; sr. v.p. Nat. Bank of Alaska, Anchorage, 1975—. Bd. dirs. Anchorage Econ. Devel. Commn., 1990—, Anchorage Neighborhood Housing Svcs. Served with U.S. Army, 1962-64; Korea. Mem. Mortgage Bankers Assn., Anchorage C. of C. (bd. dirs.) Office: Nat Bank of Alaska 301 W Northern Lights Blvd Anchorage AK 99503

SIECK, GREG R., advertising executive; b. L.A., June 12, 1956; s. David Wieboldt and Ruth Helen (Rodgers) S.; m. Barbara Marcellyn Flanders, Oct. 29, 1989. BA, U. So. Calif., 1978. V.p. J. Walter Thompson, N.Y.C., 1982-89, San Francisco, 1989-91; v.p. Foote, Cone & Belding Advt., L.A., 1991—. Office: Foote Cone & Belding Advt PO Box 2505 Santa Ana CA 92707-0505

SIEGEL, BROCK MARTIN, chemist; b. Binghamton, N.Y., Aug. 25, 1947; s. Samuel Joseph and Clara Louise (Davenport) S.; m. Catherine Sandra Bloomfield, Dec. 19, 1978; children: Justin, Aaron, Rachael. BS, Syracuse U., 1969; PhD, U. Ill., 1974. Postdoctoral assoc. Columbia U., N.Y.C., 1974-76; asst. prof. U. Minn., Mpls., 1976-79; tech. dir. Henkel Corp., Mpls., 1979-86, Henkel Rsch. Corp., Santa Rosa, Calif., 1986-90; mgr. MilliGen/Biosearch, Novato, Calif., 1990-91; mgr., sr. scientist Applied Biosystems Inc., Foster City, Calif., 1991—. Author: Nucleic Acids, 1975; contbr. articles to profl. jours.; patentee vitamin E chemistry. Bd. dirs. Camp Chai, Santa Rosa, 1987-91. NIH fellow, 1972-74, NIH fellow, 1975, DuPont Found. fellow U. Minn., 1978. Mem. Am. Chem. Soc., N.Y. Acad. Sci. Office: Applied Biosystems Inc 850 Lincoln Centre Dr Foster City CA 94404-1128

SIEGEL, MICHAEL ELLIOT, nuclear medicine physician, educator; b. N.Y.C., May 13, 1942; s. Benjamin and Rose (Gilbert) S.; m. Marsha Rose Snower, Mar. 20, 1966; children: Herrick Jove, Meridith Ann. A.B., Cornell U., 1964; M.D., Chgo. Med. Sch., 1968. Diplomate Nat. Bd. Med. Examiners. Intern Cedars-Sinai Med. Ctr., L.A., 1968-69; resident in radiology, 1969-70; NIH fellow in radiology Temple U. Med. Ctr., Phila., 1970-71; NIH fellow in nuclear medicine Johns Hopkins U. Sch. Medicine, Balt., 1971-73, asst. prof. radiology, 1972-76; assoc. prof. radiology, medicine U. So. Calif., L.A., 1976—; prof. radiology, 1989—; dir. div. nuclear medicine, 1982—; dir. Sch. Nuclear Medicine, L.A. County-U. So. Calif. Med. Ctr., 1976—; dir. div. nuclear medicine Kenneth Norris Cancer Hosp. and Rsch. Ctr., L.A., 1983—; dir. nuclear medicine Orthopaedic Hosp., L.A., 1981—, dir. dept. nuclear medicine Intercommunity Hosp., Covina, Calif., 1981—; cons. dept. nuclear medicine Rancho Los Amigos Hosp., Downey, Calif., 1976—. Author: Textbook of Nuclear Medicine, 1978, Vascular Surgery, 1983, 88, and numerous others textbooks; editor: Nuclear Cardiology, 1981, Vascular Disease: Nuclear Medicine, 1983. Mem. Maple Ctr., Beverly Hills. Served as maj. USAF, 1974-76. Recipient Outstanding Alumnus award Chgo. Med. Sch., 1991. Fellow Am. Coll. Nuclear Medicine (sci. investigator 1974, 76, nominations com. 1980, program com. 1983, bd. trustees 1993, disting. fellow, 1993, bd. reps., 1993—); mem. Soc. Nuclear Medicine (sci. exhbn. com. 1978-79, program com. 1979-80, Silver medal 1975), Calif. Med. Assn. (sci. adv. bd. 1987—), Radiol. Soc. N.Am., Soc. Nuclear Magnetic Resonance Imaging, Alpha Omega Alpha. Lodge: Friars So. Calif. Research on devel. of nuclear medicine techniques to: evaluate cardiovascular disease and diagnose and treat cancer, clinical utilization of video digital displays in nuclear medicine development; inventor pneumatic radiologic pressure system. Office: U So Calif Med Ctr PO Box 693 1200 N State St Los Angeles CA 90033

SIEGEL, MO J., beverage company executive; b. Salida, Colo., Nov. 21, 1949; s. Joe E. and Betty Siegel; children—Gabriel, Sarah, Megan, Kate, Luke. Founder Celestial Seasonings Herb Tea Co., Boulder, Colo.; pres., chief exec. officer Celestial Seasonings Herb Tea Co., until 1984, Celestial Seasonings div. Dart and Kraft, 1984-86; founder, pres. Earthwise Corp., 1990; pvt. investor, lectr., TV talk show guest; CEO Celestial Seasonings Herb Tea Co., 1991—; bd. dirs. numerous orgns. Author numerous articles. Founder, pres. Inst. Advancement Internat. Fedn. Democracies, Jesusonian Non Profit Found.; founder Coors Classic Bicycle Race (formerly Red Zinger Bicycle Classic). named One of Best of New Generation, Esquire Mag.; Celestial Seasonings named One of 100 Best Cos. to Work For. Mem. Young Pres.' Orgn.

SIEGEL, SHIRLEY JEAN, mental health client advocate; b. Seattle, June 16, 1925; d. Oliver C. and Maude Lillian (Anderson) Smith; m. Robert W. Siegel, Dec. 27, 1959; children: Steven W., John R. Grad. high sch., Seattle. Various secretarial positions, 1947-80; founder nat. client advocate group Stop Abuse By Counselors, Seattle, 1980—. Author: What To Do When Psychotherapy Goes Wrong, 1991; contbr. articles to publs. Mem. adv. com. counselor program review Wash. State Dept. Health, Olympia, Wash., 1988. Recipient Profl. Svc. award Wash. Mental Health Counselors Assn., 1986. Mem. ISBN, LCCN. Office: Stop Abuse By Counselors PO Box 68292 Seattle WA 98168-0292

SIEGFRIED, WILLIAM, chemist; b. Phila., July 4, 1925; s. Howard and Sadie L. (Wolverton) S.; m. Brenda M. Bowen, Jan. 2, 1948 (div. Jan. 1964); children: Patricia, Michael; m. Katherine Ann Delia, Feb. 29, 1964. BS in Chemistry, Bucknell U., 1950. Chemist Ohio Apex div. F.M.C. Corp, Nitro, W.Va., 1950-52; chief chemist Kindt-Collins Co., Cleve., 1952-58, 60-64; dir. rsch. Munray Product div. Fanner, Cleve., 1958-60, Victrylit Candle Co., Oshkosh, Wis., 1964-68; chief chemist Freeman Mfg. Co., Cleve., 1968-79; mng. dir. R&D Blended Waxes, Inc., Oshkosh, 1979-85; chief chemist J.F. McCaughin Co., Rosemead, Calif., 1985—. Patentee in field. With USN, 1943-46, PTO. Home: 1409 N Tamar Dr La Puente CA 91746-1123 Office: J F McCaughin 2628 River Ave Rosemead CA 91770-3395

SIEMENS, LOIS ANN, accountant; b. Riverside, Calif.; d. C. Bruce and Manette Tomlinson; m. Glenn A. Siemens, Oct. 1985; 1 child, Brian. AA, Riverside City Coll., 1978; BS, Calif. Poly. U., 1983. CPA, Calif. Acct. C.W. Jaehnig CPA, Riverside, Calif., 1978-82, Moss Adams CPAs, Costa Mesa, Calif., 1982-84; asst. contr. At Beepers Inc., Torrance, Calif., 1984-85; contr., CFO Magna Sales Inc., Santa Clara, Calif., 1985-89; CFO Advanced Systems Components, Santa Clara, 1988-89; pvt. practice Moreno Valley, Calif., 1989—. Bd. dirs., treas. Moreno Valley Meth. Ch., 1990—; founder, bd. dirs., bus. mgr. Riverside Summer Festival the Arts, 1978-82; vol. Habitat for Humanity, Riverside, 1990-92. Mem. The Bus. Network Internat. (treas. 1990), Moreno Valley C. of C., PEO (treas. 1990—, pres. 1983-85, reciprocity pres. 1993—). Office: Lois A Siemens CPA 24594 Sunnymead Ste H Moreno Valley CA 92553

SIEMENS, RICHARD ERNEST, metallurgy administrator, researcher; b. Coeur d'Alene, Idaho, July 7, 1938; s. John Charles and Ruth Eva (Schumaker) S.; m. Louise Irene Niehaus, June 21, 1959; children: Rhonda Kaye, Leann Marie. BS, Oreg. State U., 1960, postgrad., 1961-65, 70-71; postgrad., Linfield Coll., McMinnville, Oreg., 1960-61. Rsch. physicist Albany (Oreg.) Rsch. Ctr. U.S. Bur. Mines, 1961-77, metallurgist, 1977-80, group supr., 1980-84, rsch. supr., 1984-89; sr. tech. monitor, contract officers' rep. pilot plant U.S. Bur. Mines, Tucson, 1980-81; acting rsch. dir. Tuscaloosa (Ala.) Rsch. Ctr. U.S. Bur. Mines, 1988, rsch. dir. Reno Rsch. Ctr., 1989—; mem. adv. com. Profl. Coun. Fed. Scientists and Engrs., 1990—, MacKay Sch. Mines, U. Nev., Reno, 1991—; presenter numerous tech. mtgs. Contbr. over 50 articles to profl. jours. and internal publs. Pres. Fed. Metals Cen. Credit Union, Albany, 1976-89. Recipient Meritorious Svc. award U.S. Dept. Interior, 1981, Raiffeisen award Nat. Credit Union Assn., 1988; NDEA fellow Oreg. State U., 1960-63. Mem. AIME, Sigma Xi. Home: 39416 Hwy 62 Chiloquin OR 97624 Office: US Bur Mines 1605 Evans Ave Reno NV 89512-2295

SIEMON-BURGESON, MARILYN M., education administrator; b. Whittier, Calif., Nov. 15, 1934; d. John Roscoe and Louise Christina (Secoy) Mason; m. Carl J. Siemon, Aug. 18, 1956 (div. Oct. 1984); children: Timothy G., Melanie A. Siemon Imes; Troy M.; m. James K. Burgeson, Jan. 24, 1987. BA, U. Redlands, 1956; MA, Pacific Oaks Coll., 1975; postgrad., Point Loma Coll., 1979-80. Cert. elem. and early childhood tchr. Tchr., administr. Sierra Madre (Calif.) Community Nursery Sch., 1970-77; tchr. parent edn. and music Pasadena (Calif.) Unified Schs., 1977-79, project coordinator, 1980-82, tchr. curriculum resource dept., 1982-83, head tchr., Washington Children's Ctr., 1983—; endorsed trainer High Scope Found. Register, 1990—. Active Arcadia, Calif. Bicentennial Commn., 1974-76, policy coun. for community housing svcs. Pasadena Head Start, 1992—; life mem. Sierra Madre Sch. PTA, also chpt. liaison; chmn. Pasadena Foothill Consortium on Child Care, 1987—; mem. Child Care Coalition, Pasadena. Ednl. Professions Devel. fellow Pacific Oaks Coll., Pasadena, 1969. Mem. Nat. Assn. Edn. Young Children, So. Calif. Assn. Edn. Young Children (grantee 1970), Child Care Info. Service (bd. dirs., chmn. parent edn. and family affairs 1986—), Women Ednl. Leadership (asst. program v.p., past pres.), AAUW (co-chmn. Math.-Sci. Conf. 1983, chair Coll./Univ. Relations 1988—, grantee 1982, 83), Delta Kappa Gamma (pres. 1986-88, 92-94). Republican. Episcopalian. Home: 2266 Kinclair Dr Pasadena CA 91107-1022 Office: Washington Children's Ctr 130 E Penn St Pasadena CA 91103-1828

SIERCKS, RANDOLPH LAVERNE, computer science educator, administrator; b. Hollywood, Calif., Aug. 13, 1946; s. LaVerne George and Neva V. (Mitchell) S.; m. Nicia Lenore Weiss, Aug. 15, 1976; 1 child, Stephen Jeffrey. BS, Calif. State U., Pomona, 1969. Cert. tchr., Calif. Instr. L.A. Unified Schs., 1969-81; mgr. tech. edn. dept. MAI Basic Four, Inc., Tustin, Calif., 1981-85; div. mgr. edn. Sunar Hauserman, Inc., Cleve., 1985-87; dir. of student programs The Buckley Sch., L.A., 1987—; cons. The Oak Creek Ranch, Ojai, Calif., 1977-80. Vice pres. Casas Verdes, Palos Verdes, Calif., 1984, pres., 1985. Mem. ASTD, L.A. Agriculture Tchrs. Assn., Assn. Computer Tchrs., Computer Using Educators Calif., Oxford Country Club. Home: 18624 Cassandra St Tarzana CA 91356-4509 Office: The Buckley Sch 3900 Stansbury Ave Sherman Oaks CA 91423-4699

SIERRA, RUBEN ANGEL, professional baseball player; b. Rio Piedras, P.R., Oct. 6, 1965. Grad. high sch., Rio Piedras, P.R. Player Tex. Rangers, 1986-92; with Oakland Athletics, 1992—. Named Am. League Player of Yr., Sporting News, 1989, recipient Silver Slugger award, 1989; named to All-Star team, 1989, 91-92; Am. League RBI Leader, 1989. Home: Carolina PR Office: Oakland-Alameda County Coliseum 7000 Coliseum Way Oakland CA 94621-1918

SIFFORD, BENTON ALEXANDER, III, state official; b. Evanston, Ill., Sept. 20, 1955; s. Benton Alexander Jr. and Gail Byrd (Sollender) S.; m. Saralynn Baker, Nov. 6, 1982. BA in Geography, U. Calif., Santa Barbara, 1978; MS in Geography, U. Idaho, 1984. Mgr. Oak Tree Antiques, London, 1978-80; geothermal specialist Idaho Office Energy, Boise, 1980; sr. assoc. Eliot Allen & Assocs., Salem, Oreg., 1981-84; program mgr. Oreg. Dept. Energy, Salem, 1984—; pres. Wood Energy Coordination Group, Portland, 1988—. Author: Geothermal Resources Council Transactions, Vol. 7, 1984, Vol. 14, 1990, Bioenergy Conversion Opportunities, 1988; also articles. Pres. Neskowin (Oreg.) Community Assn., 1989—. Recipient cert. of appreciation USDA Forest Svc., 1988, 89, Lions Internat., Salem, 1990. Mem. Geothermal Resources Coun. (pres. Pacific N.W. sect. 1985-88, bd. dirs. 1988-90), Assn. Pacific Coast Geographers, Internat. Dist. Heating Assn. Home: Box 870 Neskowin OR 97149 Office: Oreg Dept Energy 625 Marion St NE Salem OR 97310

SIFFT, JOSIE MARIE, physical education educator; b. Canton, Ohio, Apr. 10, 1954; d. George and Pauline J. (Yurich) S. BA, Ohio Dominican Coll., 1976; MS, U. Wyo., 1978; PhD, U. Oreg., 1981. Grad. teaching fellow U. Wyo., Laramie, 1976-78; grad. teaching/rsch. fellow U. Oreg., Eugene, 1978-81; lectr. U. Wyo., Laramie, 1981-82; asst./assoc. prof. Calif. State Poly. U., Pomona, 1982—, Fort Lewis Coll., Durango, Colo.; cons. San Dimas, Calif., 1989-90. Contbr. articles profl. jours. Life mem. Sierra Club, 1987—, USTA, 1984—; mem. Tree People, 1988—. One of Outstanding Young Women of Am., 1984; recipient Emerging Profl. award Western Soc. for Phys. Edn. Coll. Women, 1988-89. Mem. Am. Alliance for Health, Phys. Edn., Recreation and Dance (rsch. chair for Southwest Dist. 1987-89), Calif. Assn. for Health, Phys. Edn., Recreation and Dance, Nat. Strength and Conditioning Assn. (assoc. editor for jour. 1983—); charter mem. Assn. for the Advancement of Applied Sport Psychol. Office: Fort Lewis Coll Durango CO 81301

SIGAL, SANFORD DAVID, real estate developer; b. L.A., Jan. 28, 1964; s. Martin Irving and Gloria (Blatter) S.; m. Cindy Sisino, Mar. 12, 1988; 1 child, Hayden Joshua. BS, UCLA, 1987. Dir. comml. devel. West Venture Devel., Encino, Calif., 1984—; developer Firestone Shopping Ctr., Norwalk, Calif., 1990, Norwalk Square Shopping Ctr., 1989, Azusa (Calif.) Promenade, 1989, La Mirada (Calif.) Ctr., 1988, Bonnie Brae Retail Shopping Ctr., L.A., 1987. Mem. Econ. Devel. Commn., Alusa. Mem. Internat. Coun. Shopping Ctrs., Pres'. Club. Republican. Jewish. Office: West Venture Devel 6345 Balboa Blvd Ste 225 Encino CA 91316-1522

SIGALA, RALPH, university administrator; b. Dexter, N.Mex., Aug. 16, 1942; s. Adolario and Veronica (Giron) S.; m. Mary Alice Sanchez, May 27, 1967; children: Jeanene, Michael, Cynthia. BA, Ea. N.Mex. U., Portales, 1965, MA, 1969; PhD, U. N.Mex., 1980. Psychologist N.Mex. Boys Sch./Camp Sierra Blanca, Ft. Stanton, 1966; exec. dir. Chavez County Community Action Program, 1967-68; dir. Home Edn. Livelihood Program, Portales, 1968; psychologist Counseling Ctr., Calif. State U., Fresno, 1969-74; counselor U. Albuquerque, 1975-76; asst. dir. Multicultural Edn. Ctr. U. N.Mex., Albuquerque, 1976-77, instr. guidance and counseling, 1985-87, spl. asst. to v.p., 1985-87, asst. dean students, 1978-90; dir. Valencia campus U. N.Mex., Los Lunas, 1990—; cons. Belen Pub. Schs. Bd. Edn., Santa Rosa Pub. Schs. Adminstrn. and Bd. Edn., Bernalillo County Sheriff's Dept. Promotion Bd., Bernalillo County Commn. Mgmt. Labor Arbitration Bd., North Ctrl. Assn. Colls. and Univs., West Las Vegas Sch. Dist., Bernalillo Sch. Dist., N.Mex. Mil. Inst., Latin Am. Projects in Edn., U. N.Mex., Westat Inc., Rockville, Md., S.W. Bilingual Edn. Tng./Resource Ctr., U. N.Mex., Native Am. Tech. Assistance Corp., Marion, Ind. Mem., pres., v.p., chmn. edn. com. Albuquerque Bd. Edn., 1981-87; mem. Valencia County Hosp. Com., 1991—; mem. Valencia County Econ. Devel. Forum, 1990—; bd. dirs. Valencia County Econ. Devel. Corp., 1990—; mem. Valencia County Cultural Com., 1990—; panelist N.Mex. Young Woman of Yr., 1989; mem. Albuquerque Bd. Edn., 1981-87, pres., 1985-86; mem. Albuquerque Goals Com., 1985; mem. Albuquerque Econ. Devel., Inc., 1984-86; ednl. div. chmn. United Way of Greater Albuquerque. Recipient Certs. of Appreciation United Way of Greater Albuquerque, 1983, Albuquerque Bd. Edn., 1987. Mem. Am. Assn. Community Colls., Hispanic Assn. Colls. and Univs., N.Mex. Assn. Community, Jr. and Tech. Colls. (sec.-treas. 1991-92, v.p., pres. elect 1991—), Phi Delta Kappa, Pi Eta Sigma. Office: U N Mex Valencia Campus 180 La Entrada Los Lunas NM 87031-7633

SIGLER, JOHN WILLIAM, fisheries, aquatic ecologist; b. Ames, Iowa, Dec. 20, 1946; s. William F. and Margaret Eleanor (Brotherton) S.; m. Betty Jean Sigler, July 3, 1976; children: James M. Simmons, William Adam, Stacey Michelle. BS in Wildlife/Fisheries Mgmt., Utah State U., 1969, MS in Wildlife/Water Quality, 1972; PhD in Fisheries Mgmt., U. Idaho, 1980. Rsch. asst. NSF Lake Powell rsch. project U. N.Mex., Albuquerque, 1975-76; grad. rsch. asst. U. Idaho, Moscow, 1977-80; aquatic ecologist W.F. Sigler & Assocs., Inc., 1980-86; mgr. environ. sci. and tech. group Spectrum Scis. and Software, Inc., Logan, Utah, 1986—. Co-author: Fishes of the Great Basin, 1987, Recreational Fisheries: Management, Theory and Applications, 1990; author: (with others) Wilderness Issues in the Arid Lands of the Western United States, 1992; contbr. articles to profl. publs. With USAF, 1972-75. Mem. Am. Fisheries Soc. (cert. fisheries scientist), Ecol. Soc. Am. (cert. sr. ecologist), Am. Inst. Fishery Rsch. Biologists, Pacific Fisheries Biologists, Audubon Soc. (bd. dirs. Bridgerland chpt. 1988-93), Utah State U. Coll. Natural Resources Alumni Assn. (pres. 1990), Pheasants Forever (pres. no. Utah chpt. 1989-91). Office: Spectrum Scis One Environ Ctr 980 West 1800 S Logan UT 84321-6220

SIGLER, WILLIAM FRANKLIN, environmental consultant; b. LeRoy, Ill., Feb. 17, 1909; s. John A. and Bettie (Homan) S.; m. Margaret Eleanor Brotherton, July 3, 1936; children: Elinor Jo, John William. B.S., Iowa State U., 1940, M.S., 1941, Ph.D., 1947; postdoctoral studies, UCLA, 1963. Conservationist Soil Conservation Service, Ill., 1935-37; cons. Central Engring. Co., Davenport, Iowa, 1940-41; research assoc. Iowa State U., 1941-42; 1945-47; asst. prof. wildlife sci. Utah State U., 1947-50, prof., head dept., 1950-74; pres. W.F. Sigler & Assocs. Inc., 1974-86; cons. U.S. Surgeon Gen., 1963-67, FAO, Argentina, 1968. Author: Theory and Method of Fish Life History Investigations, 1952, Wildlife Law Enforcement, 1956, 3d edit., 1980, Fishes of Utah, 1963; (with J.W. Sigler) Fishes of the Great Basin, 1987, Recreational Fisheries Management: Theory and Application, 1990; also numerous articles. Mem. Utah Water Pollution Control Bd., 1957-65, chmn., 1963-65. Served as lt. (j.g.) USNR, World War II. Named Wildlife Conservationist of Yr. Nat. Wildlife Fedn., 1970, Outstanding Educator of Year, 1971; recipient Disting. Service cert. recognition Iowa Coop. Wildlife Research Unit, 1982, Outstanding Service award Utah State U., 1986, Alumni Achievement award Coll. Natural Resources Utah State U., 1987, award of Merit Bonneville chpt. Am. Fisheries Soc., 1990. Fellow Internat. Acad. Fishery Scientists, AAAS; mem. Ecol. Soc. Am., Wildlife Soc. (hon.), Am. Fisheries Soc., AAUP, Outdoor Writers Am., Sigma Xi, Phi Kappa Phi. Home: 309 E 2d S Logan UT 84321

SIGMAN, MELVIN MONROE, psychiatrist; b. N.Y.C., Dec. 15, 1935; s. Irving and Lillian (Pearlman) S. BA, Columbia U., 1956; MD, SUNY, N.Y.C., 1960; postgrad., William Alanson White Analytic Inst., N.Y.C., 1969. Staff psychiatrist Hawthorne (N.Y.) Cedar Knolls Sch., 1966-68; pvt. practice psychiatry N.Y.C., 1966-72, Fresno, Calif., 1974-87; staff psychiatrist Fresno County Dept. of Health, 1974-87, Psychol. Svcs. for Adults, L.A., 1987—; attending staff psychiatry Bellevue Hosp., N.Y.C., 1966-68; cons. N.Y. Foundling Hosp., N.Y.C., 1966-72; assoc. attending staff Roosevelt Hosp., N.Y.C., 1967-72; asst. clin. prof U. Calif. San Francisco, Fresno, 1977; chmn. cen. Calif. com. Columbia Coll. Nat. Alumni Secondary Schs. Served to capt. USAF, 1961-63. Fellow Royal Soc. Health, Am. Orthopsychiat. Assn.; mem. Am. Psychiat. Assn., Hollywood Spa Calif. Fresno Racquet. Office: Psychol Svcs for Adults 11755 Wilshire Blvd Ste 1840 Los Angeles CA 90025

SIGNOR, PHILIP WHITE, paleobiology educator, researcher; b. Waterbury, Conn., July 2, 1950; s. Philip W. and Fern M. (Tracey) S.; m. Beth R. Onken, Dec. 28, 1988; children: Lara, Sarah, Emma. BA, U. Rochester, 1972, MS, 1978; MA, Johns Hopkins U., 1979, PhD, 1982. Sr. mus. scientist U. Calif., Davis, 1981-85, asst. prof., 1985-89, assoc. prof. of paleobiology, 1989—; assoc. rsch. geologist. Co-editor: Paleobiology Paleontol. Soc., 1987-91; contbr. articles to profl. jours. Lt. (j.g.) USN, 1972-76, capt. USNR. Grantee NSF, 1982, 85, 88, 91. Mem. Paleontol. Soc., Geol. Soc. Am., Am. Malacol. Union, Calif. Malacozool. Soc., Internat. Union Geol. Scientists (corr. mem. three coms.). Office: Dept Geology U Calif Davis CA 95616

SIKKA, SATISH, marketing executive; b. Jammu, India, June 7, 1945; came to U.S., 1967; s. Basheshar Nath and Rampyari (Soni) S.; m. Indu Sushma Jawa, June 24, 1974; 1 child, Simi Kavita. BSc in Engring., U. Delhi (India), 1967; M.A.Sc. in Mech. Engring., U. B.C., Vancouver, Can., 1969; MBA with high distinction, Harvard U., 1974. Systems analyst, project leader IBM Can., Toronto, Ont., 1969-72; bus. analyst Xerox Can., Toronto, 1974-76, mgr. demand and revenue planning, 1977-78, mgr. market planning and spl. projects, 1979, mgr. mktg. strategy and pricing, 1980-82; mgr. internat. ops. Xerox Corp., Dallas, 1982-84; mgr. internat. bus. and OEM/VAR mktg. Xerox Corp., Sunnyvale, Calif., Palo Alto, Calif., 1984-89; mgr. tng. and customer edn. Xerox Corp., Palo Alto, 1989—; bd. dirs. Nest Software, Inc., San Jose, Calif. Contbr. articles to profl. jours. Co-chmn. civil rights com. Fedn. of Indo-Ams., Fremont, Calif., 1991—. Baker scholar Baker Found., Harvard U., 1974. Mem. Harvard Bus. Sch. Assn. of No. Calif. Home: 45977 Paseo Padre Pkwy Fremont CA 94539 Office: Xerox Corp 3400 Hillview Ave Palo Alto CA 94303

SIKORA, JAMES ROBERT, educational business administrator; b. Sacramento, July 8, 1945; s. George Robert and Marian Frances (Fears) S.; m. Marie Lynore Nyarady, June 22, 1968. BEE, U. Santa Clara, 1967; postgrad., U. Calif.-Santa Cruz, 1979--. Electronic engr. GTE-Sylvania, Santa Cruz, 1967-69; systems analyst GTE-Sylvania, 1969-71; sr. support analyst GTE-Sylvania, Mt. View, Calif., 1971-73; bus. systems coordinator Santa Clara County Office Edn., San Jose, Calif., 1973-76; dir. dist. payroll, personnel svcs. Santa Clara County Office Edn., 1976-85, dir. dist. bus. svcs., 1985—; cons. records mgmt. County Santa Clara, San Jose, 1982; v. chair Edn. Mandated Cost Network Exec. Bd., 1991—; mem. Schs. Fin. Svcs. subcom. 1987—. Author, co-editor Howdy Rowdy Memorial, 1979. Sponsor San Jose/Cleveland Ballet, Santa Cruz County Symphony, Monterey Bay Aquarium Patrons Circle, Long Marine Lab., San Jose Repertory Theater, Ctr. Photographic Arts, Napa Valley Wine Libr. Mem. Assn. Records Mgrs. and Adminstrs. (v.p. 1983-86) , Pub. Agy. Risk Mgmt. Assn., Am. Diabetes Assn., Calif. Assn. Sch. Bus. Ofcls.. (subsection pres. 1984-85, sect. bd. dirs. 1987—, sect. pres. 1991-92, state bd. dirs. 1991-92), Norwegian Elkhound Assn. (pres. 1977-79), Wine Investigation for Novices and Oenephiles, U. Calif. Chancellors' Cir., Amnesty Internat., Am. Dog Owners Assn., Jaycees, Sierra Club (life member). Libertarian. Roman Catholic. Home: 400 Coon Heights Rd Ben Lomond CA 95005 Office: Santa Clara County Office Edn MC 252 100 Skyport Dr San Jose CA 95110

SIKORYAK, KIM EUGENE, national park service ranger; b. Long Island, N.Y., Feb. 17, 1949; s. Michael William and Olga S.; m. Jane Allegra Johnson, Oct. 31, 1975. BS cum laude, Rutgers U., 1971; postgrad., U. Alaska, 1971-75. Palynological technician Rutgers U., New Brunswick, N.J., 1969-70; instr. U. Alaska, Fairbanks, 1971-73; duty dir. Sta. KUAC-TV, PBS, Fairbanks, 1974, performer, 1975; instr. Community Coll. Denver, Golden, Colo., 1976-77; cartographer soil conservation svc. USDA, Portland, Oreg., 1979; chief interpreter John Day (Oreg.) Fossil Beds Nat. Monument, 1978-87; program analyst Nat. Park Svc., Washington, 1987; chief interpreter Haleakalā Nat. Park, Nat. Park Svc., Makawao, Hawaii, 1988-91; interpretive specialist S.W. region Nat. Park Svc., Santa Fe, 1991—; corrd. interpretive skills team Nat. Park Svc., Santa Fe, 1991—. Author: (with others) Conservation Biology in Hawaii, 1989, NPS Museum Handbook, 1985. Rsch. assoc. Ctr. for East-West Studies, Honolulu, 1990—; advisor Interpret Hawaii Adv. Com. U. Hawaii, Honolulu, 1990-91. Irene Ryan scholar Am. Coll. Theater Assn., 1973. Mem. Nat. Assn. Interpretation (founding), Hawaii Environ. Edn. Assn., Internat. Carnivorous Plant Soc. (charter). Office: PO Box 728 Santa Fe NM 87504-0728

SILBER, IRWIN, writer, editor; b. N.Y.C., Oct. 17, 1925; s. Bernard and Matilda (Gettinger) S.; m. Sylvia Kahn, Sept. 15, 1950 (div. 1974); children: Joshua, Fred, Nina; m. Barbara Spillman Dane, Dec. 23, 1976. BA, Bklyn. Coll., 1945. Exec. dir. People's Songs, N.Y.C., 1947-49; editor Sing Out!, N.Y.C., 1951-67; dir. prodn. Folkways Records, N.Y.C., 1958-65; co-owner, editor-in-chief Oak Publs., N.Y.C., 1959-67; cultural editor, exec. editor The Guardian, N.Y.C., 1968-71, 72-79; editor Frontline, Oakland, Calif., 1982-89; co-dir. Paredon Records, N.Y.C., Oakland, Calif., 1969-89; assoc. editor Crossroads, Oakland, 1990—. Author: Kampuchea-The Revolution Rescued, 1975, Songs of Civil War, 1960, Songs of Great American West, 1967, Songs America Voted By, 1971, 88, Songs of Independence, 1973; editor: Voices of National Liberation, 1970; co-editor: The Vietnam Songbook, 1970.

SILBERGELD, ARTHUR F., lawyer; b. St. Louis, June 1, 1942; s. David and Sabina (Silbergeld) S.; m. Carol Ann Schwartz, May 1, 1970; children: Diana Lauren, Julia Kay. BA, U. Mich., 1968; M City Planning, U. Pa., 1971; JD, Temple U., 1975. Bar: N.Y. 1976, Calif. 1978, D.C. 1983, U.S. Ct. Appeals (2d, 9th and D.C. cirs.). Assoc. Vladeck, Elias, Vladeck & Lewis, N.Y.C., 1975-77; field atty. NLRB, Los Angeles, 1977-78; ptnr., head employment law practice group McKenna, Conner & Cuneo, L.A., 1978-89; ptnr., head labor and employment law practice group Graham & James, L.A., 1990—; instr. extension div. UCLA, 1981—. Author: Doing Business in California: An Employment Law Handbook, 1989, Advising California Employers, 1990, 91, 93 supplements; contbr. articles to profl. jours. Founding mem. L.A. Mus. Contemporary Art; mem. Mus. Modern Art, N.Y., Art Inst. Chgo.; bd. dirs. Bay Cities unit Am. Cancer Soc., Calif., 1981-85, Jewish Family Svc. L.A., 1981-85, So. Calif. Employment Round Table, 1990—. Mem. ABA (com. on devel. law under NLRA 1975—), L.A. County Bar Assn. (exec. bd. labor law sect. 1984—). Office: Graham & James 801 S Figueroa St 14th fl Los Angeles CA 90017

SILBERMAN, IRWIN ALAN, public health physician; b. Newport News, Va., Sept. 1, 1932; s. Henry and Toby (Weiss) S.; m. Mitsue Fukuyama, May 7, 1964 (div. July 1984); children: Denise, Donn, Daniel, Dean, Dana. BA, U. Calif., Berkeley, 1953; MD, U. Calif., San Francisco, 1956; MS, U. No. Colo., 1980. Intern L.A. County Harbor Gen. Hosp., Torrance, Calif., 1956-57; resident in ob-gyn. L.A. County Harbor Gen. Hosp., Torrance, 1957-61; commd. USAF, 1961, advanced through grades to col., 1971; staff obstetrician-gynecologist Tachikawa (Japan) Air Base, 1963-65; chief ob-gyn. Mather Air Force Base, Sacramento, 1965-66; chief aeromed. services Yokota Air Base, Tokyo, 1966-68; dir. base med. services Itazuke Air Base, Fukuoka, Japan, 1968-70, Kirkland Air Force Base, Albuquerque, 1970-72; chief hosp. services USAF Hosp. Davis-Monthan, Tucson, 1972-81; ret. USAF, 1981; med. dir. CIGNA Healthplan of Fla., Tampa, 1981-83; chief women's clinic H.C. Hudson Comprehensive Health Ctr., L.A., 1983-85; dir. maternal health and family planning programs Los Angeles County Dept. Health Svcs., L.A., 1985-91, dir. family health programs, maternat and child health, 1991—; mil. cons. to surgeon-gen., USAF, Tucson, 1980-81; bd. dirs. Los Angeles Regional Family Planning Council, Perinatal Adv. Council of Los Angeles Communities. Chmn. health profls. adv. com. March of Dimes, Los Angeles, 1988; camp physician Boy Scouts Nat. Jamboree, Fort Hill, Va., 1985. Recipient Meritorious Service medal, USAF, 1972, 81, Air Force Commendation medal, 1980, Air medal, 1969. Fellow Am. Coll. Obstetricians and Gynecologists, Am. Coll. Physician Executives; mem. Am. Acad. Med. Dirs., Am. Pub. Health Assn., So. Calif. Pub. Health Assn. (governing council 1988—). Home: 3716 Beverly Ridge Dr Sherman Oaks CA 91423-4509 Office: LA County Dept Health Svcs 241 N Figueroa St Los Angeles CA 90012-2602

SILBERT, AMY FOXMAN, clinical art therapist; b. Augusta, Ga., July 11, 1953; d. Elliott and Anita Foxman; m. Philip Silbert, Sept. 6, 1987; children: Sean Kenneth, Karen Debra. BA in Design, UCLA, 1976; MA, Loyola Marymount U., 1990. Art dir., advt. mgr. Unico Am. Corp., L.A., 1976-78; freelance graphic artist, art specialist, tchr., 1979-82; vol. coord., tchr. Craft and Folk Art Mus., L.A., 1983-86; art specialist Art Reach, UCLA Calif. Arts Coun., 1983-84; editor in chief Grad. Achievement Preparation Svc., Santa Monica, Calif., 1985-87; tchr. coordinator art exhibit Hebrew Union Coll., Los Angeles, 1984; guest children's TV programs, 1970-84. Gov. intern U.S. Congress, Washington, 1973. Recipient 1st Place award traffic light design City Monterrey, Calif., 1973. Democrat. Jewish. Office: PO Box 2238 Culver City CA 90231-2238

SILCOX, ROY W., animal science educator; b. Riverton, Utah, Apr. 14, 1955; s. Jack W. and Myrl (Beckstead) S.; m. Cathy Meyers, Feb. 18, 1977; children: Jed W., Jack W., Matthew W. BS in Animal Science, Brigham Young U., 1981; MS in Physiology, N.C. State U., 1984, PhD, 1986. Lab asst. Brigham Young U., Provo, Utah, 1980-81, asst. prof., 1992—; teaching asst. N.C. State U., Raleigh, 1981-84, rsch. asst., 1984-86; rsch. fellow U. Mo., Columbia, 1986-88; asst. prof. U. Ga., Athens, 1988-92. Contbr. articles to profl. jours. Asst. scoutmaster Boy Scouts Am., Riverton, 1976-78, Raleigh, 1982-83, cubmaster, 1986-87, varsity scout coach, 1987-88; coach little league baseball, West Jordan, Utah, 1973-74. Rsch. grantee Provo Rotary Club, 1981, N.C. State U. Biomedical Rsch. Support, 1985, U. Ga. Faculty Rsch., 1989, Ga. Agrl. Commodity Commn., 1989, 90, 91. Mem. Am. Soc. Animal Science (2d place rsch. paper 1984), Am. Dairy Science Assn. (physiology com. 1992), Internat. Embryo Transfer Soc., Gamma Sigma Delta, Sigma Xi. Office: Brigham Young U 365 WIDB Provo UT 84602

SILENCE, SCOTT, physical chemist; b. Passaic, N.J., Mar. 11, 1964; s. Ronald and Mary Ann (Perry) S.; m. Jill Meixner, Aug. 19, 1989. BS in Chemistry, MS in Phys. Chemistry, U. Chgo., 1986; PhD in Physical Chemistry, MIT, 1991. Vis. scientist IBM Almedan Rsch. Ctr., San Jose, Calif., 1991—. Mem. Am. Phys. Soc. Office: IBM Almedan Rsch Ctr 650 Harry Rd San Jose CA 95120

SILK, MARSHALL BRUCE, emergency physician; b. Providence, Apr. 3, 1955; s. Marvin and Ruth Helen (Kenner) S. BA, Drake U., 1977; DO, Coll. Osteo. Medicine, 1981. Diplomate Am. Bd. Emergency Medicine. Pvt. practice, owner Silk Emergency Care, 1984—. Mem. Am. Coll. Emergency Physicians, Am. Osteo. Assn., N.Mex. Osteo. Med. Assn., Am. Assn. Osteo. Specialists. Home: Villa Muro Di Grani Star Rte 610 Placitas NM 87043

SILLIMAN, RON (RONALD GLENN SILLIMAN), writer, poet, marketing executive; b. Pasco, Wash., Aug. 5, 1946; s. Glenn Sherman and Patricia Ruth (Tansley) S.; m. Rochelle Myra Nameroff, Oct. 31, 1965 (div. 1972); m. Krishna Evans, Apr. 6, 1986; children: Colin Robert, Jesse Kyle. Student, Merritt Coll., 1965, 69, San Francisco State U., 1966-69, U. Calif., 1970-71. Dir. edn. Commn. Prisoner Humanity and Justice, San Rafael, Calif., 1972-76; project mgr. Tenderloin Ethnographic Rsch. Project, San Francisco, 1977-78; dir. outreach Ctrl. City Hospitality House, San Francisco, 1978-81; dir. pub. rels. devel. Calif. Inst. Integral Studies, San Francisco, 1982-86; exec. dir. Ctr. Social Rsch., Berkeley, Calif., 1986-89; svc. mktg. specialist ComputerLand Corp., Pleasanton, Calif., 1989—; tectr. creative writing San Francisco State U., 1981; vis lectr. lit. U. Calif., San Diego, 1982; writer in residence New Coll. Calif., 1982. Author: Crow, 1971, Ketjak, 1978, Sitting Up, Standing, Taking Steps, 1978, Tjanting, 1981, Bart, 1982, Paradise (Poetry Ctr. Book award 1985), Lit, 1987, What, 1988, Demo to Ink, 1992, Toner, 1992, others. Recipient Artist in Community award Calif. Arts Coun., 1979, 80. Mem. Nat. Writers Union, Modern Lang. Assn., Dem. Socialist Am. Home: 1819 Curtis St Berkeley CA 94702 Office: ComputerLand Corp Box 9012 MS J2-1A Pleasanton CA 94566

SILLS, DAVID GEORGE, judge; b. Peoria, Ill., Mar. 21, 1938; s. George Daniel and Mildred Mina (Luthy) S. BS, Bradley U., 1959; LLB, U. Ill., 1961. Bar: Calif. 1965. Counsel Ill. Nat. Bank & Trust Co., Rockford, Ill., 1961-62; pvt. practice in Orange, then Newport Beach, Calif., 1965-85; judge Superior Ct., 1985-90; presiding justice Calif. Ct. Appeal (4th dist.), 1990—. Mem. Irvine (Calif.) City Council, 1976-85; mayor City of Irvine, 1976-77, 79-80, 82-83, 84-85; mem. Rep. State Central Com. Calif., 1966-68; chmn. Rep. Assocs., Orange County, Calif., 1968-69, bd. dirs. 1967-71; mem. Orange County Sanitary Dist. Bd. Dirs., 1984-85; chmn. bd. dirs. Irvine Health Found., 1985—. Served to capt. USMC, 1962-65. Mem. Am. Judicature Soc., So. Calif. Assn. Governments (exec. com. 1984-85), Orange County Bar Assn., Phi Delta Phi, Pi Kappa Delta, Omicron Delta Kappa.

SILVA, ROBERT OWEN, retired protective service official; b. La Junta, Colo., Sept. 5, 1935; s. Owen Delbert and Gertrude H. (Kerr) S.; m. Meredith Ann Ginn, Dec. 18, 1953; children—Edward, Andrew, Colleen. Student Pueblo Jr. Coll., 1953, FBI Nat. Acad., 1975, Police Found. Exec. Program, 1979-80. Cert. peace officer, Colo. Police officer Pueblo Police Dept., Colo., 1958-66, sgt., 1966-72, capt., 1972-77, chief of police, 1977-92, dir. Colo. Police Officers Standards and Tng. Bd. dirs. Salvation Army, Pueblo, Easter Seals Soc., Pueblo, Community Corrections Bd., Pueblo, Served with U.S. Army, 1955-57; apptd. by gov. Colo. Crim. Justice Comsn., 1990. Mem. Pueblo Community Coll. Criminal Justice Adv. Bd., Leadership Pueblo Steering Com., Pikes Peak Community Coll. Criminal Justice Program (chmn. adv. bd. 1981), Organized Crime Strike Force (bd. dirs. 1977-84, chmn. 1982, 83, 84); Colo. Assn. Chiefs of Police (pres. 1984-85), Rocky Mountain Info. Network (chmn. bd. dirs. 1986—), Presbyterian (elder). Lodges: Kiwanis (bd. dirs. 1982-84), Elks. Office: Pueblo Police Dept 130 Central Main St Pueblo CO 81003-4294

SILVAS-OTTUMWA, SALLY, publishing executive; b. San Juan, P.R., May 1, 1950; d. Hector Juan and Eulencia Regina (Mariposa) S.; m. William Ottumwa, May 1, 1975 (div. 1989). BA, Vassar Coll., 1973; MA, Columbia U., 1978, MLS, 1985. Pub. asst. Random House, N.Y.C., 1973-76; editorial asst./assoc. Princeton U. Press, Princeton, N.J., 1978-82; assoc. editorial dir. Addison-Wesley Publs., Reading, Mass., 1985-87, The Denali Press, Juneau, Alaska, 1988—. Mem. Reading (Mass.) Human Rights Comm., 1987. Recipient Fleckman award, Columbia U., N.Y.C., 1978. Mem. Assn. Am. Publishers, Latinos in Publishing, Hispanic Women in the Media (sec. 1985-87, exec. bd. 1990-92). Office: The Denali Press Box 021535 Juneau AK 99802

SILVEIRA, RONALD LOUIS, video company executive; b. San Diego, Sept. 29, 1948; s. Oliver L. and Leoma E. (Singmaster) S.; m. Annaliz Durham, Nov. 17, 1984. BA in Biol. Scis., U. Calif., Berkeley, 1971; M of Mgmt., Willamette U., 1977. Adminstrv. mgr. Video Prodn. Services Inc., Berkeley, 1977-80; gen. mgr. Astin Zappia Post-Prodn., Los Angeles, 1980-84; sales mgr. Compact Video Services, Inc., Burbank, Calif., 1984-86; v.p. sales and mktg. Compact Video Services, Burbank, 1986-88; pres. Compact Video Svcs. & Image Transform, 1988-90; with Unitel Video, L.A.; chmn. Hollywood Radio and TV Soc., Internat. Broadcast Awards com., 1985, 86. Adminstrv. asst. to rep. Jay Haskell, Harrisburg, Pa., 1974. Mem. Internat. Teleprodn. Soc. (v.p. So. Calif. chpt. 1991-93), Acad. TV Arts and Scis.

SILVER, BARNARD STEWART, mechanical engineer, consultant; b. Salt Lake City, Mar. 9, 1933; s. Harold Farnes and Madelyn Cannon (Stewart) S.; m. Cherry Bushman, Aug. 12, 1963; children: Madelyn Stewart Palmer, Cannon Farnes, Brenda Picketts Call. BS in Mech. Engring., MIT, 1957; MS in Engring. Mechanics, Stanford U., 1958; grad. Advanced Mgmt. Program, Harvard U., 1977. Registered profl. engr., Colo. Engr. aircraft nuclear propulsion div. Gen. Electric Co., Evandale, Ohio, 1957; engr. Silver Engring. Works, Denver, 1959-66, mgr. sales, 1966-71; chief engr. Union Sugar div. Consol. Foods Co., Santa Maria, Calif., 1971-74; directeur du complexe SODESUCRE, Abidjan, Côte d'Ivoire, 1974-76; supt. engring. and maintenance U and I, Inc., Moses Lake, Wash., 1976-79; pres. Silver Enterprises, Moses Lake, 1971-88, Salt Lake, 1990—, Silver Energy Systems Corp., Moses Lake, 1980—, Salt Lake, 1990— ; pres., gen. mgr. Silver Chief Corp., 1983—; pres. Silver Corp., 1984-86, 93—; chmn. bd. Silver Pubs., Inc., 1986-87, 89—; v.p. Barnard J. Stewart Cousins Land Co., 1987-88, 92—; dir. Isle Piquant Sugar Found., 1993—; mem. steering com. World Botanical Inst., 1993—; instr. engring. Big Bend C.C., 1980-81. Explorer adviser Boy Scouts Am., 1965-66, 89-90, chmn. cub pack com., 1968-74, chmn. scout troop com., 1968-74, vice chmn. Columbia Basin Dist., 1986-87; pres. Silver Found., 1971-84, v.p., 1984—; ednl. counselor MIT, 1971-89; pres. Chief Moses Jr. High Sch. Parent Tchr. Student Assn., 1978-79; missionary Ch. of Jesus Christ of Latter-day Saints, Can., 1953-55, West Africa, 1988, Côte d'Ivoire, 1988-89, Zaire, 1989, Holladay Stake, 1991; 2d counselor Moses Lake Stake Presidency, 1980-88; bd. dirs. Columbia Basin Allied Arts, 1986-88; mem. Health Sci. Coun. U. Utah, 1991—; mem. Sunday sch.

gen. bd. Ch. of Jesus Christ of Latter-Day Saints, 1991—, com. for mems. with disabilities, 1992—. Served with Ordnance Corps, U.S. Army, 1958-59. Decorated chevalier Ordre National (Republic of Côte d'Ivoire). Mem. ASME, Assn. Energy Engrs., AAAS, Am. Soc. Sugar Beet Technologists, Internat. Soc. Sugar Cane Technologists, Am. Soc. Sugar Cane Technologists, Sugar Industry Technicians, Nat. Fedn. Ind. Bus.; Utah State Hist. Soc. (life), Mormon Hist. Assn., G.P. Chowder and Marching Soc., Western Hist. Assn., Univ. Archeol. Soc. (life), Kiwanis, Sigma Xi (life), Pi Tau Sigma, Sigma Chi, Alpha Phi Omega. Republican. Mormon. Home: 4391 Carol Jane Dr Salt Lake City UT 84124-3601 Office: Silver Energy Systems Corp 4390 S 2300 E Salt Lake City UT 84117 also: Silver Enterprises 4391 South 2275 East Salt Lake City UT 81424-3601 also: Silver Pubs Inc PO Box 17755 Salt Lake City UT 84117-0755

SILVER, DAVID FRANCIS, historical organization adminstrator; b. San Francisco, Jan. 26, 1957; s. Frank George and Marjorie Frances (Anderson) S.; m. Ramona Marie Dennis, Oct. 15, 1983. BA in Anthropology, San Francisco State U., 1981. Pres., CEO Internat. Photographic Hist. Orgn., San Francisco, 1982—. Office: Internat Photographic PO Box 16074 San Francisco CA 94116

SILVER, DONALD ALLAN, company executive, accountant; b. Detroit, July 15, 1941; s. Carl and Elaine (Sitneck) S.; m. Arlene Silver (div. 1989); m. Louise Silver, May 6, 1989; children: Mollie, Jerry, Robert, Don, Mike, Linda. AA, Phoenix Coll., 1970; BS, Ariz. State U., 1972, MPA, 1973. Pres. S.W. Recreation, Phoenix, 1972-84; chmn. Silver Star Cos., Grand Junction, Colo., 1984—; pres. Bowling Cons. Inc., Phoenix, 1984—; cons. Golden Bowl, San Diego, 1984-90. With USAF, 1960-64. Office: Bowling Cons Inc 15-2766 Papio St Pahoa HI 96778-8575

SILVER, JAMES ALLEN, former military physician; b. Tracy, Minn., Apr. 7, 1933; s. Bernard J. and Nora J. (Bustad) S.; m. Regina Alohanohea Lover, June 15, 1964; children: Maile, Moana, Gregory, Telu, James K. BA, St. John's U., 1955; BS, MD, U. Minn., 1958; MPH, U. Mich., 1973. Diplomate Am. Bd. Occupational Medicine. Asst. med. dir. Marathon Oil Co., Findlay, Ohio, 1973-74; commd. USAF, 1974, advanced through grades to col., 1976; chief preventive medicine HQPACAF, Hickam AFB, Hawaii, 1974-78; comdr. USAF Hosp., Kirtland AFB, N.Mex., 1978-83; dir. med. inspection div. HQAFISC, Norton AFB, Calif., 1983-85; dir. environ. health ops. HQAFLC, Wright-Patterson AFB, Ohio, 1985-88; with 15 Med GP/SG, Hickam AFB, Hawaii, 1988-93; ret., 1993. Fellow Am. Coll. Preventive Medicine; mem. Am. Acad. Occupational Medicine, Aerospace Med. Assn., Soc. Air Force Flight Surgeons. Republican. Roman Catholic. Lodge: ELks. Home: 2840 Cooper Creek Dr Henderson NV 89014

SILVER, JEAN, state legislator, accountant; b. Spokane, Wash., July 25, 1926; d. Harlow Eugene and Helen Grace (Merten) Merrill; m. Charles Wesley Silver; children: Douglas W., Mitchell C., Kipp E. BBA, Eastern Wash. U., 1975; postgrad., U. Wash., 1980-87. CPA, Wash. Prin. Jean Silver Acctg. Svc., Spokane, 1950—; acct. Coopers & Lybrand, Spokane, 1976-80; state legislator State of Wash., Olympia, 1983—; cons. econ. devel. financing City and County of Spokane, 1980-86; bd. dirs. Wash. Water Power Co.; chmn. govt. ops. and pension com. Nat. Conf. State Legislators, 1989—. Bd. dirs. Greater Spokane Bus. Devel. Assn., 1984—, Holy Names-Ft. George Wright, Spokane, 1984—; trustee Holy Family Hosp., Spokane, 1986-87, Jr. League, 1987—; mem. adv. bd. Spokane Incubator Assn., 1987-89. Named Legislator of Yr., Assn. Builders and Contractors, 1985, Outstanding Govt. Woman of Yr., YWCA, 1988, Hosp. and Health Care award 1989. Mem. Wash. CPAs Soc. Republican. Office: Wash State Legislature HOB # 413 State Capitol Olympia WA 98504

SILVER, MARK ALAN, endocrinologist; b. N.Y.C., Jan. 6, 1955; s. Julius and Sylvia (Brandmark) S.; m. Janet Joy Silbergeld, Mar. 15, 1992. BS, U. Mich., 1975; MD, U. Pa., 1979. Diplomate Am. Bd. Internal Medicine. Resident in internal medicine George Washington U., Washington, 1979-82, fellow in endocrinology, 1982-84; pvt. practice, Edmonds, Wash., 1984—. Mem. Endocrine Soc., Am. Diabetes Assn. Office: 21616 76th Ave W Ste 103 Edmonds WA 98026

SILVER, SCOTT ROGER, geophysicist, consultant; b. Rapid City, S.D., Sept. 15, 1953; s. Richard Roger and Elizabeth Ann (Whittlake) S.; m. Mary Kathryn Powell, Feb. 14, 1977; 1 child, Calvin Roger Powell Silver. BSc, No. Ill. U., 1980; MBA, Houston Bapt. U., 1990. Proration geophysicist Amoco Prodn. Co., Houston, 1980-82, tech. geophysicist, 1982-86, geophysicist Netherlands region, 1986-87, geophysicist Spain region, 1987-88, geophysicist Norway region, 1988-89, geophysicist Yugoslavia region, 1989-90; pvt. practice cons. geophysicist Boulder, Colo., 1990—; pres. S.R. Silver Assocs., Inc., Boulder. Contbr. articles to internat. profl. jours. Contbr. Malcolm P. Weiss Fund, No. Ill. U., DeKalb, 1984; mem. Friends of Libr., Colo. Sch. of Mines, 1990—. Mem. Am. Assn. Petroleum Geologists, Soc. Exploration Geophysicists. Mem. Christian Ch. Home: 4693 Carter Trl Boulder CO 80301-3811

SILVER, STEVE, producer, director, writer; b. San Francisco, Feb. 6, 1944; s. Louis J. and Claire (Bencich) S. BA in Graphic Design, San Jose State U., Calif., 1969. Asst. art dir. Harold and Maude film, 1970; assoc. dir. plays Am. Conservatory Theatre, San Francisco, 1971-72; producer, dir., writer, designer, orginator Beach Blanket Babylon, San Francisco, 1974—; dir. musical event honoring Queen Elizabeth and Prince Philip's visit to San Francisco, 1986; curator de Young mus. exhibit Beach Blanket Babylon costumes and hats., San Francisco, 1988. Funded pediatric playroom Children's Hosp., San Francisco, 1983, Child Devel. Ctr. Parent's Pl., San Francisco, 1987, Aids Outreach program Open Hand, San Francisco, 1987, AIDS rsch. grant U. Calif. San Francisco Med. Ctr., 1988. Named Most Outstanding Musical Prodn., Bay Area Theatre Critics, San Francisco, 1979, Most Outstanding Dir. Musical, 1979, Most Outstanding Costume Designer, 1979, dir. Most Outstanding Achievment, DramaLogue, 1980, prodn. Most Outstanding Achievment, 1980; recipient John L. Wasserman Meml. award for outstanding contbrn. to entertainment, 1983, Paine Knickerbocker award for Excellence, Bay Area Theatre Critics, 1985; cited by Sonoma (Calif.) League for Hist. Preservation, 1986, others. Mem. Dramatists Guild. Home and Office: 678 Green St San Francisco CA 94133-3802

SILVERBERG, ROBERT, author; b. N.Y.C., 1935; s. Michael and Helen (Baim) S.; m. Barbara Brown, 1956; m. Karen Haber, 1987. B.A., Columbia U., 1956. Author: novels Thorns, 1967, The Masks of Time, 1968, Hawksbill Station, 1968, Nightwings, 1969, To Live Again, 1969, Tower of Glass, 1970, The World Inside, 1971, Son of Man, 1971, A Time of Changes, 1971, Dying Inside, 1972, The Book of Skulls, 1972, Born With the Dead, 1974, Shadrach in the Furnace, 1976, Lord Valentine's Castle, 1980, Majipoor Chronicles, 1982, Lord of Darkness, 1983, Valentine Pontifex, 1983, Gilgamesh the King, 1984, Tom O'Bedlam, 1985, Star of Gypsies, 1986, At Winter's End, 1988, To the Land of the Living, 1989, The New Springtime, 1990, (with Isaac Asimov) Nightfall, 1990, The Face of the Waters, 1991, (with Isaac Asimov) The Ugly Little Boy, 1992, Kingdoms of the Wall, 1993, (with Isaac Asimov) The Positronic Man, 1993; non-fiction The Face of the Lost Cities and Vanished Civilizations, 1962, The Great Wall of China, 1965, The Old Ones: Indians of the American Southwest, 1965, Scientists and Scoundrels: A Book of Hoaxes, 1965, The Auk, the Dodo and the Oryx, 1966, The Morning of Mankind: Prehistoric Man in Europe, 1967, Mound Builders of Ancient America: The Archaeology of a Myth, 1968, If I Forget Thee, O Jerusalem: American Jews and the State of Israel, 1970, The Pueblo Revolt, 1970, The Realm of Prester John, 1971. Recipient Hugo award World Sci. Fiction Conv., 1956, 69, 87, 90; Nebula award Sci. Fiction Writers Am., 1970, 72, 75, 86. Mem. Sci. Fiction Writers Am. (pres. 1967-68). Address: Box 13160 Station E Oakland CA 94661

SILVERBERG, STUART OWEN, obstetrician, gynecologist; b. Denver, Oct. 14, 1931; s. Edward M. and Sara (Morris) S.; B.A., U. Colo., 1952, M.D., 1955; m. Joan E. Snyderman, June 19, 1954 (div. Apr. 1970); children: Debra Sue Owen, Eric Owen, Alan Kent; m. 2d, Kay Ellen Conklin, Oct. 18, 1970 (div. Apr. 1982); 1 son, Cris S.; m. 3d, Sandra Kay Miller, Jan., 1983. Intern Women's Hosp. Phila., 1955-56; resident Kings County Hosp., Bklyn., 1958-62; practice medicine specializing in obstetrics and gynecology, Denver, 1962—; mem. staff Luth. Hosp., Rose Med. Ctr., St. Josephs Hosp., Denver; mem. staff St. Anthony Hosp., chmn. dept. obstetrics and gynecology, 1976-77, 86-87, dir. Laser Ctr., 1990—; clin. instr. U. Colo. Sch. Medicine, Denver, 1962-72, asst. clin. prof., 1972-88, assoc. clin. prof., 1989—, dir. gynecol. endoscopy and laser surgery, 1988-90; v.p. Productos Alimenticos, La Ponderosa, S.A.; dir., chmn. bd. Wicker Works Video Prodns., Inc., 1983-91; cons. Ft. Logan Mental Health Ctr., Denver, 1964-70; mem. Gov.'s Panel Mental Retardation, 1966; med. adv. bd. Colo. Planned Parenthood, 1966-68, Am. Med. Ctr., Spivak, Colo., 1967-70. Mem. Colo. Emergency Resources Bd., Denver, 1965—. Served to maj. AUS, 1956-58; Germany. Diplomate Am. Bd. Obstetrics and Gynecology, Am. Bd. Laser Surgery. Fellow Am. Coll. Obstetricians and Gynecologists, Am. Soc. Laser Medicine and Surgery, ACS; mem. Am. Internat. fertility socs., Colo. Gynecologists and Obstetricians Soc., Hellman Obstet. and Gynecol. Soc., Colo. Med. Soc., Clear Creek Valley Med. Soc. (trustee 1978, 80, 87, 93—), Phi Sigma Delta, AMA, Flying Physicians Assn., Aircraft Owners and Pilots Assn., Nu Sigma Nu, Alpha Epsilon Delta. Jewish. Mem. editorial rev. bd. Colo. Women's Mag.; editor in chief First Image, Physicians Video Jour., 1984-86. Office: 4860 W 80th Ave Westminster CO 80030-4413

SILVERMAN, ALAN H., lawyer; b. N.Y.C., Feb. 18, 1954; s. Melvin H. and Florence (Green) S.; m. Gretchen E. Freeman, May 25, 1986. BA summa cum laude, Hamilton Coll., 1976; MBA, U. Pa., 1980, JD, 1980. Bar: N.Y. 1981, U.S. Dist. Ct. (so. and ea. dist.) N.Y. 1981, U.S. Ct. Internat. Trade 1981, D.C. 1986, U.S. Supreme Ct. 1990. Assoc. Hughes, Hubbard & Reed, N.Y.C., 1980-84; asst. counsel Newsweek, Inc., N.Y.C., 1984-86; v.p., gen. counsel, dir. adminstrn. Post-Newsweek Cable, Phoenix, 1986—. Contbr. articles to profl. jours. Mem. prevention adv. com. Gov. Pa. Justice Commn., 1975-79; bd. dirs. Lawyers' Alliance for N.Y., 1982-85, N.Y. Lawyers Pub. Interest, 1983-85, Bus. Vols. for Arts, Inc., Phoenix, 1989—, Nat. Assn. JD-MBA Profls., 1983-85; mem. Maricopa County Citizens Jud. Adv. Coun., 1990—. Mem. ABA, Assn. of Bar of City of N.Y., D.C. Bar Assn., Phi Beta Kappa. Home: 5222 N 34th Pl Phoenix AZ 85018-1521 Office: Post-Newsweek Cable 4742 N 24th Ste 270 Phoenix AZ 85016

SILVERMAN, RICHARD LEE, software engineer; b. L.A., Dec. 13, 1945; s. Harry and Francis (Rudman) S.; m. Linda Corcoran, June 3, 1979; children: Denise, Matthew, Deborah. AA, L.A. City Coll., 1967; BA, St. Mary's Coll., Moraga, Calif., 1993. Cert. system profl. Bus. systems cons. Pacific Bell, San Ramon, Calif., 1964—; project mgr. GUIDE, Chgo., 1988-91. Vice chair, commr. Community Svcs. Commn., Concord, Calif., 1989—; commr. Urban Resources Commn., Concord, 1984-86; res. police officer Concord Police Dept., 1974-86. With USN, 1964-76. Republican. Jewish. Office: Pacific Bell 2600 Camino Ramon 3W200B San Ramon CA 94583

SILVERN, LEONARD CHARLES, engineering executive; b. N.Y.C., May 20, 1919; s. Ralph and Augusta (Thaler) S.; m. Gloria Marantz, June 1948 (div. Jan. 1968); 1 child, Ronald; m. Elisabeth Beeny, Aug. 1969 (div. Oct. 1972); m. Gwen Taylor, Nov. 1985. BS in Physics, L.I. U., 1946; MA, Columbia U., 1948, EdD, 1952. Registered profl. consulting engr., Calif. Tng. supr. U.S. Dept. Navy, N.Y.C., 1939-49; tng. dir. exec. dept. N.Y. Div. Safety, Albany, 1949-55; resident engring. psychologist Lincoln Lab. MIT for Rand Corp., Lexington, 1955-56; engr., dir. edn., tng., rsch. labs. Hughes Aircraft Co., Culver City, Calif., 1956-62; dir. human performance engring. lab., cons. engring. psychologist to v.p. tech. Northrop Norair, Hawthorne, Calif., 1962-64; cons. engr., 1969—; prin. scientist, v.p., pres. Edn. and Tng. Cons. Co., L.A., 1964-80, Sedona, Ariz., 1980, pres. Systems Engring. Labs. div., 1980—; cons. hdqrs. Air Tng. Command USAF, Randolph AFB, Tex., 1964-68, Electronic Industries Assn., Washington, 1963-69, Edn. R and D Ctr., U. Hawaii, 1970-74, Ctr. Vocat. and Tech. Edn., Ohio State U., 1972-73, Coun. for Exceptional Children, 1973-74, Canadore Coll. Applied Arts and Tech., Ont., Can., 1974-76, Centro Nacional de Productividad, Mexico City, 1973-75, N.S. Dept. Edn., Halifax, 1975-79, Aeronutronic Ford-Ford Motor Co., 1975-76, Nat. Tng. Systems Inc., 1976-81, Nfld. Pub. Svc. Commn., 1978, Legis. Affairs Office USDA, 1980, Rocky Point Techs., 1986; adj. prof. edn., pub. adminstrn. U. So. Calif. Grad. Sch., 1957-65; vis. prof. computer scis. U. Calif. Extension Div., L.A., 1963-72. Dist. ops. officer, disaster communications svc. L.A. County Sheriff's Dept., 1973-75, dist. communications officer, 1975-76; bd. dirs. SEARCH, 1976—; mem. adv. com. West Sedona Community Plan of Yavapai County, 1986-88; councilman City of Sedona, 1988-92; rep. COCOPAI, 1988-89; vol. earth team Soil Conservation Svc., U.S. Dept Agr., 1989-92; Verde Resource Assn., 1988-90, Group on Water Logistics, 1989-90; chair publs. com. Ariz. Rural Recycling Conf., 1990. With USNR, 1944-46. Mem. IEEE (sr.), Am. Psychol. Assn., Am. Radio Relay League (life), Nat. Solid Waste Mgmt. Symposium (chmn. publs. com. 1988-89), Ariz. Rural Recycling Conf. (chair publs. com. 1990), Friendship Vets. Fire Engine Co. (hon.), Soc. Wireless Pioneers (life), Quarter Century Wireless Assn. (life), Sierra Club (treas. Sedona-Verde Valley Group 1991-93), Sedona Westerners., Assn. Bldg. Coms., Vox Pop (chmn. bd. dirs. Sedona, 1986-93, dir. 1993—), Nat. Parks and Conservation Assn., Wilderness Soc., Ariz. Ctr. Law in Pub. Interest. Contbg. editor Ednl. Tech., 1968-73, 81-85; reviewer Computing Revs., 1962-92. Contbr. numerous articles to profl. jours. Office: PO Box 2085 Sedona AZ 86339-2085

SILVERS, DONALD EUGENE, kitchen designer, writer, lecturer, chef, consultant; b. Chgo., Dec. 30, 1929; s. Milton and Ruth (Swartz) S.; m. Monica Silvers, 1960 (div. 1972); children: Michelle Andrea, Joshua Marc; m. Sally Kaye Silvers, Sept. 4, 1988. AA, L.A. Trade Tech. Sch., 1959; postgrad., UCLA, 1978-80. 1st cook Alberto's, Westwood, Calif., 1959-61; exec. chef Renaissance Restaurant, L.A., 1961-67; dir. food resources Synanon Found., Santa Monica, Calif., 1967-72; prin., designer, cons. Kitchens & Other Environments by Design, L.A., 1973—; cons. Good Stuff Natural Foods, L.A., 1972-74, A.R.A. Food Mgmt. Co., L.A., 1972-73, Le Campion Gourmet Food Club, San Francisco, 1974-78, Am. Food Processors, Culver City, Calif., 1975-78, United Design Assn., L.A., 1989—; mem. adv. bd. L.A. Mission Coll., Sylmar, Calif., 1992. Contbr. over 40 articles to profl. jours. and mags. Recipient Outstanding Leadership award Nat. Assn. Food Equipment Mfrs., 1971; named one of Top 10 Innovative Food Dirs. in the Country, Instn. Mag., 1969. Mem. AIA (assoc.), Nat. Kitchen and Bath Assn. (cert. kitchen designer, v.p. 1990-91, Outstanding Leadership award 1990-91), Chef De Cuisine, Food and Wine, So. Calif. Culinary Assn. (advisor, bd. dirs.), Internat. Soc. Interior Designers (assoc.), Soc. Cert. Kitchen Designers. Democrat.

SILVERS, E. RANDALL, computer system manager; b. Somerville, N.J., July 8, 1951; s. William Joseph Silvers Sr. and Edna Rebecca (Pysher) Silvers-Brennan; m. Cynthia Lee Mulch, Aug. 6, 1974; children: Benjamin Judah, Deborah Lynn. AA summa cum laude, Palomar Coll., 1979; ASBA, Thomas Nelson Coll., 1984, AAS in Data Processing, 1984; postgrad., Christopher Newport, Newport News, Va., 1984-85. Cert. nat. registry EMT. Maintenance chief Escondido (Calif.) Convalescent Ctr., 1977-79; registrar, instr. Profl. Med. Inst., Hampton, Va., 1980-81; corps asst. Salvation Army, Logansport, Ind., 1985-88; computer system mgr. Salvation Army Harbor Light, L.A., 1988—; rep. divisional computer bd. (MIS) Salvation Army So. Calif., L.A., 1991—. Arranger orchestration for cantata; composer march; author poem. Scoutmaster Boy Scouts Am., San Diego, 1972-75, Camp Pendleton, Calif., 1975-76, Hampton, Va., 1980-84, Huntington Park, Calif., 1990-92, Whittier, Calif, 1992—; commr., San Diego County, Calif., 1976-79; bandmaster Salvation Army, San Diego, 1970-71, 72-73, Escondido, 1974-77, Hampton, 1979-85, Logansport, 1985-88, Huntington Park, Calif., 1988-92; asst. dir., prin. euphonium Peninsula Community Band, Newport News, 1980-85; instr./trainer ARC, Langley AFB, Va., 1979-85, 1st aid/CPR chmn., 1981-84. Sgt. USMC, 1969-77, Vietnam. Named Vol. of Month and Yr., ARC, 1980; decorated Air Force Achievement medal. Mem. Students Vets. Assn. (pres. 1982-84), Am. Legion (sgt. at arms 1974, 2d vice comdr. 1972—), VFW, Alpha Micro Users Soc., Phi Beta Lambda (parliamentarian 1983-84). Republican. Office: Salvation Army Harbor Light 809 E 5th St Los Angeles CA 90013

SILVERSTEIN, JOSEPH HARRY, musician; b. Detroit, Mar. 21, 1932; s. Bernard and Ida (Katz) S.; m. Adrienne Shufro, Apr. 27; children—Bernice, Deborah, Marc. Student Curtis Inst. Music, 1945-50; hon. doctoral degrees Tufts U., 1971, Rhode Island U., 1980, Boston Coll., 1981, New Eng. Conservatory, 1986. Violinist, Houston Symphony Orch., Phila. Orch.; concertmaster Denver Symphony Orch., Boston Symphony Orch.; formerly chmn. string dept. New Eng. Conservatory Music; also chmn. faculty Berkshire Music Sch.; mem. faculty Boston U. Sch. Music, Yale U. Sch. Music; music dir. Boston Symphony Chamber Players, Boston U. Symphony Orch., Chautauqua (N.Y.) Instn., 1987—; interim music dir. Toledo Symphony Orch.; prin. guest condr. Balt. Symphony Orch., 1981; condr. Utah Symphony; mus. dir. Worcester Orch., Mass., until 1987. Recipient Silver medal Queen Elizabeth of Belgium Internat. contest, 1959, Naumberg found. award, 1960; named one of ten outstanding young men, Boston C. of C., 1962. Fellow Am. Acad. Arts and Scis. Office: care Utah Symphony Orch 123 W South Temple Salt Lake City UT 84101-1496

SILVERSTEIN, MARTIN ELLIOT, surgeon, author, consultant; b. N.Y.C., Sept. 6, 1922; s. Louis and Ethel (Statman) S.; m. Mabelle A. Cremer, Dec. 10, 1962. AB cum laude, Columbia U., 1945; MD, N.Y. Med. Coll., 1948. Instr. bacteriology N.Y. Med. Coll., 1953-57, asst. to dean for clin. scis., 1953-58, instr. surgery, 1953-55, asst. dean, 1958; asst. vis. surgeon Bird S. Coler Hosp., N.Y.C., 1953-57, assoc. vis. surgeon, 1957-60; asst. vis. surgeon Met. Hosp., N.Y.C., 1953-57, assoc. vis. surgeon, 1957-60; asst. attending surgeon Flower and 5th Ave. Hosps., N.Y.C., 1953-57; asst. attending surgeon Monorah Med. Ctr. U. Kans. Sch. Medicine, N.Y.C., 1963-65; exec. dir. Monorah Med. Ctr. U. Kans. Sch. Medicine, Kansas City, 1963-65; exec. dir. Danciger Inst. for Health Scis. U. Kans. Sch. Medicine, Kansas City, Mo., 1963-66; chmn. dept. exptl. surgery Danciger Inst. for Health Scis. U. Kans. Sch. Medicine, Kansas City, 1963-66; chmn. dept. Surgery Menorah Med. Ctr. U. Kans. Sch. Medicine Affiliate, Kansas City, 1963-66; assoc. clin. prof. surgery U. Kans. Sch. Medicine, Kansas City, 1966-67; surgeon courtesy staff N.Y. Infirmary, 1969; surgeon Grand Canyon Med. Group and Hosp., 1979-70; chief sect. on surgery of trauma, dept. surgery U. Ariz. Coll. Med., Tucson, 1974-80, adj. assoc. prof. optical scis., 1979-83, assoc. prof. surgery, 1974-84, dir. quality assurance Univ. Hosp., 1983-84, rsch. prof. family and community medicine, internat. medicine, 1984-85, rsch. prof. surgical biology, 1984-85; sr. fellow in sci. and tch. Ctr. for Strategic and Internat. Studies Georgetown U., Washington, 1983-87; bd. dirs. Claude Gips Found. Inc., N.Y.C.; disting. vis. prof. Uniformed Svcs. U. Health Scis., 1984, clin. prof. surgery F. Edward Hepert Sch. Medicine, 1984—; disting. vis. prof. Tulane U. Med. Sch., 1984; mem. internat. adv. bd. Univ. Microfilms Internat. Collections on Terrorism, 1987—. Author Disasters: Your Right to Survive, 1991; mem. editorial bd. Terrorism, 1976—, Jour. Prehosp. Care, 1984-85, Prehosp. and Disaster Medicine, 1989—; contbr. articles to profl. jours. With U.S. Army, 1943-45; lt. (j.g.) USNR, 1946-53. Recipient Pres.'s award NSF, 1977; Fgn. fellow NSF, 1974. Fellow ACS (chmn. Ariz. State com. of trauma 1979-84), Am. Assn. for Surgery of Trauma, Am. Coll. Emergency Physicians, Am. Coll. Gastroenterology, Am. Coll. Nuclear Med.; mem. Internat. Coun. for Computer Communications (bd. govs., v.p., 1972—), World Assn. for Emergency and Disaster Medicine (exec. com. 1987—). Republican.

SILVERSTEIN, STEVEN DAVID, commercial lender; b. Columbus, Ohio, Nov. 15, 1966; s. H. Robert Silverstein and Rosalind (Ribyat) Katz. BA, Columbia U., 1988. Credit analyst City Nat. Bank, Beverly Hills, Calif., 1988-92; comml. lender City Nat. Bank, L.A., 1992—. Republican. Jewish. Home: 320 N Palm Dr # 312 Beverly Hills CA 90210

SILVESTER, JOHN ANDREW, computer systems educator, consultant; b. Orpington, Kent, England, Apr. 26, 1950; came to U.S., 1971, s. Henry James and Alice Lillian (Shaw) S.; m. Maria Heloisa Penedo, Apr. 19, 1980. BA, Cambridge U., 1971; MA, 1975; MS, W.Va. U., 1973; PhD, UCLA, 1980. Rsch. asst. W.Va. U., Morgantown, 1971-73; UCLA, 1973-78; assoc. prof. U. So. Calif., L.A., 1979—; dir. cons. Tech. Transfer Inst., 1985-86; cons. Lockheed, L.A., 1979-80, U.S. Army, Ft. Monmouth, N.J., 1983, Jet Propulsion Lab., L.A., 1983-84, Tech. Transfer Inst., L.A., 1983—. Contbr. articles to profl. jours. Vice pres. Cellarmasters, L.A., 1983-84. Grantee, Naval Air Systems Command, 1983-85, Army Rsch. Office, 1984-90. Mem. Assn. computing Machinery, IEEE (chmn. Infocom. 1990), IEEE Communications Soc. (chmn. tech. com. on computer communications 1985-87), Tau Beta Pi. Office: Univ So Calif Dept EE Systems University Park Los Angeles CA 90089

SILVEY, LEN, training and development executive; b. Sacramento, Mar. 19, 1943; s. C. Joseph and Helen L. (Graham) S. BA, U. Calif., Davis, 1966; MS, Calif. State U., Sacramento, 1970. Budget officer State of Calif., Sacramento, 1961-63, fiscal mgmt. tng. cons., 1963-70, chief justice Advanced Tng. Ctr., 1970-77; exec. dir. Monterey Bay Area Regional Tng Ctr., Monterey, Calif., 1977-81; pres., chief exec. officer Len Silvey, Inc., Sacramento, 1981—; bd. sec. Jackson Ct., City Share Owners, San Francisco, 1986-92; instr. U. Calif.-Davis Extension, 1991—. Co-author: Systems Sense, 1988. Mem. Calif. Probation Parole and Corrections Officers Assn., Combined Correctional Assns. Calif. (exec. com. 1991-92). Democrat. Home and Office: PO Box 1744 Orangevale CA 95662

SILVIA, JOHN DAVID, fighter pilot, career officer; b. Melrose, Mass., Mar. 29, 1960; s. John and Lorraine (Pinheiro) S.; m. Sherry Anne Young, June 14, 1986; children: Sarah Elizabeth, Christopher David. BS in Computer Tech., USAF Acad., 1982; MS in Info. Systems, Golden Gate U., 1990. Capt. USAF, 1982; F-4E flight lead 68 Fighter Squadron USAF, Moody AFB, Ga., 1984-86; F-4E fighter 20 Fighter Squadron, weapons sch. instr. USAF, George AFB, Calif., 1986-91; F-117 weapons officer 416 Fighter Squadron USAF, Holloman AFB, Calif., 1991-93; major selectee ACSC USAF, Maxwell AFB, Ala. Pres. Cath. Parish Coun., George AFB, 1987-91, Cath. Choir, USAF Acad., 1982; chief squire Columbian Squires Cath. Youth, North Reading, Mass., 1978. Mem. IEEE, Assn. Computing Machinery, Air Force Assn. Home: 703 Eagle Dr Alamogordo NM 88310 Office: 416FS/DOW Holloman Air Force Base NM 88330

SILVIS, DONN EUGENE, communications educator, consultant; b. Greeley, Colo., May 6, 1942; s. William Arthur and Mildred Ruth (Lowe) S.; m. Sharon Cowles, Apr. 24, 1966; 1 child, Donn Bradley. AA, East L.A. Community Coll., 1962; BS in Journalism, Calif. State Poly Tech., San Luis Obispo, 1965; MA in Mass Communications, Calif. State U., Fullerton, 1988. Coord. employee communications Norris Industries, L.A., 1965-76; asst. v.p. mktg. communications Avco Fin. Svcs., Newport Beach, Calif., 1976-85; lectr. Calif. State U., Fullerton, 1982-88; asst. prof. Calif. State U., L.A., 1989; assoc. prof. communications, dept. chmn. Calif. State U., Dominguez Hills, 1990—; owner Silvis Communications, Cerritos, Calif., 1986—. Assoc. editor: Newport Beach '75; co-editor: Inside Organizational Communications, 1981; co-author: Public Relations Writing: Strategies and Skills, 1991. Advisor Juvenile Diversion Project, Cerritos, 1971-75; bd. dirs. South Orange County Vol. Ctr., Santa Ana, Calif., 1981-86; mem. press, pub. rels. and publications comm. 1984 Olympics, L.A., 1981-84. Capt. U.S. Army, 1965-68, Korea. Fellow Internat. Assn. Bus. Communicators (v.p. 1976-78); mem. Pub. Rels. Soc. Am. Office: Calif State U Dominguez Hills Comm Dept 1000 E Victoria St Carson CA 90747-0005

SIMA, EDWARD DONALD, international banker; b. Seattle, May 22, 1929; s. Edward Patrick and Leona Clara (Culver) S.; m. Carole Cecilia Sloane, Nov. 3, 1962; children: Christine Marie, Gerald Edward, Timothy John. Comml. banking major degree, Am. Inst. Banking, Seattle, 1954; BA, U. Wash., 1965. Various positions Seattle First Nat. Bank, 1947-58, credit issuance officer, 1958-88; internat. ops. specialist Bank Calif. N. Am., Seattle, 1988—. Treas. troop 319 Boy Scouts Am., Seattle, 1975-85; precinct committeeman Dem., Seattle, 1968-72; active mem. Parish of St. Mark, Seattle, Worldwide Marriage Encounter; bd. dirs. Park Place Condominium Homeowners Assn., 1992. Mem. U.S. Coun. Internat. Banking, Seattle-Tacoma Com. Letters of Credit, Seattle Coun. KC (James Shield Gen. Assembly 4th degree, past faithful navigator), Seattle Rose Soc., Park Place Condominium Owners Assn. (bd. dirs.). Democrat. Roman Catholic. Home: 18200 15th Ave NE #302 Seattle WA 98155

SIMAN, JAIME ERNESTO, plastic materials and processes engineer; b. San Salvador, El Salvador, Nov. 18, 1954; came to U.S., 1981; s. Jorge Jose and Margarita (Jacir) S.; m. Clara Isabel Crespo, May 1, 1979; children: Clara Isabel (Clarisa), Jaime Daniel. ChemE, U. C.Am. José Simeon Canas, San Salvador, 1976; M Chem. Engring., McGill U., Montreal, Can., 1978; postgrad., Columbia Bible Coll. and Sem., 1986-87. Acting prodn. mgr., asst. to gen. mgr., R & D mgr. Tecnoplasticos div. of Sigma, San Salvador, 1978-81; R & D, materials engr. Westinghouse Electric Corp., Athens, Ga., 1982-83, R & D project engr., 1983-86; R & D sr. staff engr. Baxter Healthcare Corp., Irvine, Calif., 1988-92, R & D project engr., 1992—; speaker on thermomechanical analysis-R & D applications, Ga., Pa., 1982, 83. Contbr. articles to profl. jours.; patentee electric induction apparatus; designer med. catheters; patent pending new polymer alloy for thermodilution catheters. Sr. mem. Soc. Plastics Engrs.

SIMBURG, EARL JOSEPH, psychiatrist; b. Vonda, Sask., Can., Mar. 21, 1915; came to U.S., 1941; s. Joseph E. and Liza (Yurovsky) S.; m. Virginia Ronan, Feb. 10, 1958; children by previous marriage: Arthur, Melvyn, Sharon. Cert. medicine, U. Sask., Saskatoon, 1935; MDCM, McGill U., Montreal, Que., Can., 1938; grad., San Francisco Psychoanal. Inst., 1959. Diplomate Am. Bd. Psychiatry and Neurology. Intern Royal Victoria Hosp., Montreal, 1938-39; sr. physician Brandon (Can.) Hosp. Mental Diseases, 1939-41; resident Grace New Haven Hosp., 1941-43; pvt. practice psychiatry Berkeley, Calif., 1947—; mem. faculty San Francisco Psychoanalytic Inst.; instr. psychiatry Yale U., New Haven, 1941-43, U. Calif., San Francisco, 1949-59; cons. Calif. Dept. Health, Berkeley, 1975-76; pres. med. staff Herrick Hosp. and Health Ctr., 1985. Contbr. articles to the Jour. of the Am. Psychoanalytic Assn. Served to major M.C. USAF, 1943-47. Fellow Am. Psychiat. Assn. (life), AAAS; mem. AMA, Am. Psychoanalytic Assn. (life, cert.), Calif. Med. Assn., Alameda Contra Costa County Med. Assn., Am. Geriatrics Soc., Am. Assn. for Geriatric Psychiatry. Home: 86 Tamalpais Rd Berkeley CA 94708-1949 Office: 2006 Dwight Way Berkeley CA 94704-2609

SIMINI, JOSEPH PETER, accountant, financial consultant, author, former educator; b. Buffalo, Feb. 15, 1921; s. Paul and Ida (Moro) S.; B.S., St. Bonaventure U., 1940, B.B.A., 1949; M.B.A., U. Calif.-Berkeley, 1957; D.B.A., Western Colo. U., 1981; m. Marcelline McDermott, Oct. 4, 1968. Insp. naval material Bur. Ordnance, Buffalo and Rochester, N.Y., 1941-44; mgr. Paul Simini Bakery, Buffalo, 1946-48; internal auditor DiGiorgio (Fruit) Corp., San Francisco, 1950-51; tax accountant Price Waterhouse & Co., San Francisco, 1953; sr. accountant Richard L. Hanlin, C.P.A., San Francisco, 1953-54; prof. accounting U. San Francisco, 1954-79, emeritus prof., 1983—; mem. rev. bd. Calif. Bd. Accountancy, 1964-68. Mem. council com. Boy Scouts Am., Buffalo, San Francisco, 1942-65, Scouters Key, San Francisco council; bd. dirs. Nat. Italian Am. Found., Washington, 1979—. Served to ensign USNR, 1944-46. Recipient Bacon-McLaughlin medal St. Bonaventure U., 1940, Laurel Key, 1940; Outstanding Tchr. award Coll. Bus. Adminstrn., U. San Francisco, 1973; Disting. Tchr. award U. San Francisco, 1975, Joseph Peter Simini award, 1977. Crown Zellerbach Found. fellow, 1968-69; Gold Medal Associazione Piemontese nel Mondo, Turin, Italy, 1984; decorated Knight Order of Merit, Republic of Italy, 1982. CPA, Calif. Mem. Am. Inst. C.P.A.s, Calif. Soc. C.P.A.s (past chmn. ednl. standards, student relations com. San Francisco chpt.), Inst. of Mgmt. Accts. (past pres. San Francisco chpt.), Am. Acctg. Assn., Am. Mgmt. Assn. (lectr. 1968-78), Am. Arbitration Assn. (comml. arbitrator), Delta Sigma Pi (past pres. San Francisco alumni club), Beta Gamma Sigma. Roman Catholic. Clubs: Serra (past pres. Golden Gate chpt.), Il Cenacolo (past pres.), Toastmasters (past pres. Magic Word). Lodges: K.C., Rotary. Author: Accounting Made Simple, 1967, 2d rev. edit., 1987, Cost Accounting Concepts for Nonfinancial Executives, 1976, Become Wealthy! Using Tax Savings and Real Estate Investments, 1982, Balance Sheet Basics for the Nonfinancial Managers, 1989, Petals of the Rose, 1990, Wealth-Building Basics Letter, 1990. Tech. editor, Accounting Essentials, 1972. Patentee Dial-A-Trig and Verbum Est card game. Home: 977 Duncan St San Francisco CA 94131-1800 Office: PO Box 31420 San Francisco CA 94131-0420

SIMINUK, MARK ANTHONY, manufacturing engineer, consultant; b. North Hollywood, Calif., Dec. 12, 1956; s. Mike James and Anne (Remple) S.; m. Sheilah Marie Pruitt, Sept. 28, 1991. BS in Biology, BS in Chemistry, Calif. State U., Hayward, 1979; AA in Engring., Saddleback Coll., 1982; MS in Engring., West Coast U., 1985. Cert. community coll. edn. Lab. tech. Vet. Reference Lab., San Leandro, Calif., 1979-80; mfg. engr. Shiley, Inc., Irvine, Calif., 1980-89; staff mfg. engr. Mentor, Inc., Goleta, Calif., 1989-90; cons. Shiley, Inc., Irvine, 1990-91; process engr. Advanced Interventional Systems, Irvine, 1991—.

SIMKINS, JOLENE MARIE, ceramic company executive, educator; b. Pine Bluffs, Wyo., July 22, 1945; d. Donald George and Lorraine Mae (Hanson) Phillips; m. Robert Eugene Simkins, Aug. 10, 1963; 1 child, Garth Robert. Student, U. Wyo., Laramie County Community Coll. Sec. various, Laramie, Wyo., 1963-67, State of Wyo., Evanston, 1968-72, various, Pine Bluffs, Wyo., 1977-79; owner Creations Unltd., Pine Bluffs, Wyo., 1979—. Councilwoman City Coun., Pine Bluffs, 1985-89; bd. dirs. Laramie County Joint Powers Tourism Bd., 1987—, lobbyist, 1991, 92, 93; bd. dirs. Pvt. Industry Coun., Wyo. Job Tng. Commn., 1992—; apptd. Wyo. Travel Comsn., 1993—; founder, bd. dirs. Tex. Trail Mus. Laramie County, Pine Bluffs, 1987-92; police commr. Town of Pine Bluffs, 1985-89; lobbyist Wyo. Restaurant and Lodging Assn., 1991, 92, 93. Mem. Ceramic Art Inst. (cert.), Sagebrush Ceramic Club (sec., treas., v.p., pres. 1981-87), C. of C. (founder, bd. dirs. 1985—). Democrat. Roman Catholic. Home: 503 Maple Pine Bluffs WY 82082-0667 Office: Creations Unltd 309 Elm Pine Bluffs WY 82082-0667

SIMMEL, EDWARD CLEMENS, psychology educator, consultant; b. Berlin, Jan. 30, 1932; s. Ernst and Herta Helen (Brüggemann) S.; m. Marilyn Simmel (div. July 1980), children: Gregg, Cassandra, Kristina; m. Wendy Taylor, Jan. 4, 1983. BA, U. Calif., Berkeley, 1955; PhD, Wash. State U., 1960. Asst. prof. Western Wash. U., Bellingham, 1960-62, Calif. State U., L.A., 1962-65; asst. prof. Miami U., Oxford, Ohio, 1965-67, assoc. prof., 1967-71, prof., 1971-90, prof. emeritus, 1990—; cons. Human Factors in Aviation Safety, Borrego Springs, Calif., 1990—; vis. investigator Jackson Lab., Bar Harbor, Maine, 1970, 73, 75, 81. Editor: Perspectives in Behavior Genetics, 1986; mem. editorial bd. Behavior Genetics Jour., 1980-90; contbr. numerous articles to profl. jours. With USAF, 1951-52. NSF grantee, 1972-73. Fellow Am. Psychol. Soc.; mem. Assn. Aviation Psychologists, Western Psychol. Assn., Aircraft Owners and Pilots Assn., Aerospace Med. Assn., Sigma Xi (pres. Miami U. chpt. 1971-72, Outstanding Rsch. award 1976). Home: PO Box 759 Borrego Springs CA 92004-0759

SIMMONS, BRADLEY WILLIAMS, pharmaceutical company executive; b. Paterson, N.J., Apr. 16, 1941; s. John Williams and Grace Law (Van Hassel) S.; m. Diane Louise Simmons, June 6, 1964 (div. May 1986); children: Susan, Elizabeth, Jonathan. AB, Columbia U., 1963, BSChemE, 1964; MBA, NYU, 1974. Chem. engr. Pfizer, Inc., N.Y.C., 1969-73, analyst, 1973-76, dir. planning, 1976-79; dir., bus. analysis Bristol-Myers, N.Y.C., 1979-82, v.p., 1982-85; pres. Oncogen subs. Bristol-Myers, Seattle, 1985-87, sr. v.p. adminstrn., 1987—; adj. prof. Farleigh Dickinson U., Teaneck, N.J., 1974-84; v.p. Empty Space Theatre, Seattle, 1991—, also bd. dirs.. Coun. mem. Borough of Allendale, N.J., 1977-82; mem. Bergen County (N.J.) Com., 1974-82; bd. dirs. Washington Exhibition Sci. and Tech., 1989—; v.p., bd. dirs. Empty Space Theatre, 1991—. Mem. Wash. State Biotech. Assn. (chmn. external rels. com. 1989-90, vice-chmn., bd. dirs. 1990-91), Wash. Exhbn. Sci. and Tech. (bd. dirs.). Republican. Mem. Unity Ch.

SIMMONS, GEORGE MICHAEL, educational administrator; b. Portland, Oreg., June 26, 1943; s. Vernon L. and Petra K. (Svenddal) S.; m. Mary Katherine Walker, June 27, 1970; 1 child, Alex George. BS in Chem. Engring., U. Idaho, 1965, MS in Chem. Engring., 1966; PhD in Chem. Engring., Stanford U., 1970. Registered profl. engr., Idaho. NASA postdoctoral trainee, then sr. engr. Jet Propulsion Lab., Pasadena, Calif., 1970-74; prof. chem. engring. U. Idaho, Moscow, 1975—, chmn. dept. chem. engring., 1982-85, dean Sch. Art and Architecture, 1990-92, assoc. v.p., 1985-91, vice provost, 1991—; coll. div. chmn. U. Idaho Centennial Campaign, 1985-89; adv. bd. North Idaho Bus. Technology Incubator, Moscow, 1989—. Contbr. articles to chem. engring. publs. Bd. dirs. St. Augustine's Found., Moscow, 1990—, Arts for Idaho, 1992—. Kellogg Found. fellow, 1987-90. Office: U Idaho Academic Affairs Moscow ID 83843

SIMMONS, HARRIS H., banker; b. Salt Lake City, June 25, 1954; s. Roy William and Elizabeth (Ellison) S. B.A. in Econs., U. Utah, 1977; M.B.A., Harvard U., 1980. Comml. loan officer Allied Bancshares, Houston, 1980-81; asst. v.p. Zions Bancorp, Salt Lake City, 1981, fin. v.p.., 1981-82; sr. v.p. fin. Zions Utah Bancorp, Salt Lake City, 1982-83, exec. v.p., sec., treas., 1984-86, pres., 1986—; pres. Zions Mortgage Co., 1987—; chief exec. officer Zions Bancorp, Salt Lake City, 1990—; pres., chief exec. officer Zions 1st Nat. Bank, 1990—; bd. dirs. Questar, Inc., Salt Lake City, Entrada Industries, Inc., Salt Lake City, Keystone Communications, Salt Lake City, S.F.I., Inc., Salt Lake City, Zions 1st Nat. Bank, Salt Lake City, Nev. State Bank, Las Vegas. Bd. dirs. United Way, Salt Lake City, 1983-89, Utah Symphony, 1986—, vice-chmn., 1990—; trustee IHC Salt Lake Valley Hosps., Salt Lake City, 1987—; v.p. fin. Great Salt Lake coun. Boys Scouts Am., 1991—; co-chair Greater Salt Lake Shelter-the-Homeless Com., 1986-89. Mem. Utah Bankers Assn. (bd. dirs. 1987—, chmn. 1990-91), Salt Lake Area C. of C. (bd. dirs. 1991—), Phi Beta Kappa. Mem. LDS Ch. Office: Zions Bancorp 1380 Kennecott Bldg Salt Lake City UT 84133

SIMMONS, MICHAEL PAUL, public relations and marketing executive; b. Angola, Ind., June 14, 1953; s. Paul Emery Simmons and Anna Lee (Hathaway) Moore; m. Kimberlee Sue Hoddap, Oct. 4, 1980 (div. July 1988); children: Christopher Robert, Adam Michael; m. Deborah Ann Stresing, July 4, 1989. Student, Ind. U., Ft. Wayne, 1971-76. Asst. mgr. Russell's Formal Wear, Ft. Wayne, Ind., 1974-77; mgr. Schuler's House of Weddings, Ft. Wayne, 1977-79; sales mgr. Midwest Baker Supply Co., Ft. Wayne, 1979-80; asst. mgr. Gordon Jewelry Corp., Ft. Wayne, 1980-82; ops. mgr. Gordon Jewelry Corp., Quincy, Ill., 1982-84; owner, operator Balloon-A-Grams, Quincy, 1983-91; sales rep. Profl. Displays, Inc., Quincy, 1990-92; mktg. and sales tng. cons. Forum-3 Weight Loss Ctrs., Quincy, 1991-92; mktg. and sales estimator Centerline Constrn., Blanchly, Oreg., 1992—; long term care specialist L.T.C. Inc., Kirkland, Wash., 1993—. Chmn. Riverfest grounds com. Quincy Soc. Fine Arts, 1982-92; active Big Bros.-Big Sisters, Quincy, 1985-90; sec. bd. dirs. Unity Ch. Quincy, 1985, v.p., 1986, pres. 1987; mem. Quincy Conv. and Visitors Bur., 1986-92; mem. Uptown Quincy Inc., 1986-92, promotions chmn., 1983-89, goodwill com., 1989-92, parking com., 1990-92, bd. dirs., 1989-92; grand juror Adams County Grand Jury, 1989—. Mem. Triangle Lake Grange. Republican. Home and Office: 91090 Nelson Mountain Rd Greenleaf OR 97445 Office: Balloon-A-Grams of Quincy 119 N 6th St Quincy IL 62301-2903

SIMMONS, NOEL ALEXANDER, human resources executive, consultant; b. San Francisco, Dec. 28, 1947; s. Clifford Edgar and Mildred (Malchow) S.; m. Elaine Diane Meyer, July 27, 1974; children: Carly Michelle, Rebecca Marie. BA, U. Calif., Berkeley, 1971; MBA, San Francisco State U., 1973. Regional acctg. mgr. ITT Continental Bakery, San Francisco, 1973-75; regional personnel mgr. VWR Sci. Corp., San Francisco, 1976-79; indsl. rels. mgr. Signetics Corp., Sunnyvale, Calif., 1979-81; human resources dir. Eaton Corp., Sunnyvale, 1981-89; human resources cons. The Simmons Group, Belmont, Calif., 1989—. Mem. No. Calif. Football Officials Assn., Calif., 1971-75; advisor Jr. Achievement, San Mateo County, Calif., 1976-79; sec. Redwood City (Calif.) Shores Homeowners Assn., 1983. Capt. USAF, 1973-79. Mem. Labor Adjustment Bd., Am. Soc. Personnel Adminstrs., No. Calif. Human Resources Coun., Calif. Unemployment Ins. Coun., Santa Clara (Calif.) Valley Personnel Assn., Peninsula Employee Rels. Coun. Home: 645 Spar Dr Redwood City CA 94065-1151 Office: Simmons Group 951-2 Old County Rd Ste 136 Belmont CA 94002

SIMMONS, PAULA JOAN, title company official; b. Long Beach, Calif., Dec. 1, 1961; d. Peter Steven Polchert and Joan Marilyn (Perrin) Rockwell; 1 child, Abby Marie; m. Christopher Laird Simmons, Jul. 25, 1992. Student, Calif. State U., 1979-81. Dist. mgr. sales Olan Mills, Inc., Scottsdale, Ariz., 1982-84; asst. mgr. retail merchandising Max Factor and Co., Hollywood, Calif., 1984-87; sr. account exec. Transworld Systems, Inc., Long Beach, Calif., 1987-89; mktg. cons. Sebastian Internat., Chatsworth, Calif., 1989-91; account exec. Paris Ace, City of Industry, Calif., 1992-93; account mgr. Western Cities Title, El Monte, Calif., 1993—. Mem. parent adv. coun. PTA, Long Beach, 1986—. Mem. NAFE, Cousteau Soc., Smithsonian Assocs., Amnesty Internat., Met. Mus. Art, World Wildlife Fund, Rain Forest Found. Democrat. Home: 822 E Carson St Long Beach CA 90807-2903 Office: Western Cities Title 9650 Flair Dr Ste 500 El Monte CA 91731

SIMMONS, ROBERT WAYNE, synthetics and coating manufacturing company executive; b. Sayre, Okla., July 1, 1946; s. Ova Wayne Simmons and Verna L. Simmons-Harris; m. Mari Melissa Reeves, Aug. 12, 1974; children—Tia Michelle, Ashley Megan. A.A., Bacone Jr. Coll., Muskogee, Okla., 1967; B.S. in Zoology, Northeastern Okla. State U., 1970. Drilling fluid engr. Baroid Engring. Co., Houston, 1970-71; sales rep. GAF Corp., Cape Girardeau, Mo., 1971-79, product engr., N.Y.C., 1979-80, assoc. prodn. mgr., 1980, mktg. mgr., 1980-81; midwest regional sales mgr. Gen. Tire & Rubber Co., Toledo, 1981-81, nat. sales mgr., bldg. products group mgr., 1983-85, dir. mktg. coated fabric group, 1985, 86; nat. mktg. mgr., gen. mgr. Pleko Products Corp., 1986-88; pres. chief exec. officer RW Simmons & Assocs., Inc. Served with USMC, 1968-69. Recipient Pres. Club award GAF Corp., 1976; named hon. capt. Girardeau Navy, 1979. Mem. Constrn. Specification Inst., Roofing Industry Ednl. Instn., Am. Mgmt. Assn., Phi Sigma Epsilon. Democrat. Lutheran. Lodges: Rotary (sec./treas. Cape Girardeau club 1978), Masons, Shriners, Elks. Author: Super System, Maintenance & Repair, Roofing Manual, 1981. Patentee roofing system application. Office: RW Simmons & Assocs Inc 31849 Pacific Hwy S Ste 159 Federal Way WA 98003-5400

SIMMONS, ROY WILLIAM, banker; b. Portland, Oreg., Jan. 24, 1916; s. Henry Clay and Ida (Mudd) S.; m. Elizabeth Ellison, Oct. 28, 1938; children—Julia Simmons Watkins, Matthew R., Laurence E., Elizabeth Jane Simmons Hoke, Harris H., David E. Asst. cashier First Nat. Bank Layton, Utah, 1944-49; Utah bank commr., 1949-51; exec. v.p. Bank of Utah, Ogden, 1951-53; pres. Lockhart Co., Salt Lake City, 1953-64, Zion's First Nat. Bank, Salt Lake City, 1964-81; chmn. bd. Zion's First Nat. Bank, 1965—; chmn., CEO Zion's Utah Bancorp, 1965-91, chmn. bd. 1991—; chmn. bd. Zion's Savs. & Loan Assn., 1961-69; pres. Lockhart Co., 1964-87; bd. dirs. Beneficial Life Ins. Co., Mountain Fuel Supply Co., Ellison Ranching Co. Chmn. Utah Bus. Devel. Corp., 1969-80; Mem. Utah State Bd. Regents, 1969-81. Mem. Salt Lake City C. of C. (treas. 1964-65), Sigma Pi. Republican. Mem. Ch. of Jesus Christ of Latter Day Saints. Home: 817 E Crestwood Rd Kaysville UT 84037-1712 Office: Zion's Utah Bancorp 1000 Kennecott Bldg Salt Lake City UT 84133

SIMMONS, TED CONRAD, writer; b. Seattle, Sept. 1, 1916; s. Conrad and Clara Evelyn (Beaudry) S.; m. Dorothy Pauline Maltese, June 1, 1942; children: lynn, Juliet. Student U. Wash., 1938-41, UCLA and Los Angeles State U., 1952-54, Oxford (Eng.) U., 1980. Drama critic Seattle Daily Times, 1942; indsl. writer, reporter-editor L.A. Daily News, 1948-51; contbr. Steel, Western Metals, Western Industry, 1951—; past poetry dir. Watts Writers Workshop; instr. Westside Poetry Center; asst. dir. Pacific Coast Writers Conf., Calif. State Coll. Los Angeles. Served with USAAF, 1942-46. Author: (poetry) Deadended, 1966; (novel) Middlearth, 1975; (drama) Greenhouse, 1977, Durable Chaucer, 1978, Rabelais and other plays, 1980, Dickeybird, 1981 (nominated TCG Plays-in-Progress award 1985), Alice and Eve, 1983, Deja Vu, Deja Vu, 1986, The Box, 1987, Ingrid Superstar, 1988, Three Quarks for Mr. Marks, 1989, Ingrid: Skier on the Slopes of Stromboli, 1990, A Midsummer's Hamlet, 1991, Hamlet Nintendo, After Hours, Dueling Banjoes, Viva el Presidente, Climate of the Sun, 1992, Nude Descending Jacob's Ladder, 1993; writer short story, radio verse; book reviewer Los Angeles Times; contbr. poetry to The Am. Poet, Prairie Wings, Antioch Rev., Year Two Anthology; editor: Venice Poetry Company Presents, 1972. Grantee Art Commn. King County, 1993.

SIMMONS, VICTOR J., real estate and insurance broker; b. Vallejo, Calif., June 17, 1945; s. Victor J. Simmons; children: Miriam Victoria, Jonathan Victor. BA, U. Nev., 1968. Bid coord. Dietary Products div. Am. Hosp. Supply Corp., Irvine, Calif., 1972-73; loan officer, appraiser Brentwood Savs., L.A., 1973-77; loan cons. Union Fed. Savs., L.A., 1978-79; mortgage broker Far West Mortgage, L.A., 1980-81; ins. agt. Met. Life Ins., L.A., 1981-84; mortgage, ins. broker Far West Mortgage, L.A., 1984-85; loan cons. Coast Savs., Beverly Hills, Calif., 1985-90; dist. agt., rep. Prudential Life Ins. Co., El Segundo, Calif., 1990-92; mortgage loan cons. Great Western Bank, Torrance, Calif., 1992—. Contbr. articles to profl. jours., 1967-71. 1st lt. USMCR, 1968-71. Democrat. Baptist. Home: 3503 W 85th St Inglewood CA 90305-1616 Office: Great Western Bank 3400 Torrance Blvd Torrance CA 90503-9999

SIMMONS, WARREN LEE, association administrator; b. Rochester, N.Y., Sept. 29, 1937; s. Arthur Burnell and Grace Margaret (Evans) S.; m. Leilani Ann Bell, Mar. 15, 1970; 1 child, Kevin Arthur. BS in Physics, Syracuse U., 1959; MS in Physics, Calif. Inst. Tech., Pasadena, 1961. Commd. 2d lt. USAF, 1959, advanced through grades to col., 1977; rsch. physicist Air Force Weapons Lab., Albuquerque, 1961-64; from instr. to assoc. prof. in Physics USAF Acad., Colorado Springs, Colo., 1964-83; dir. counseling and scheduling USAF Acad., Colorado Springs, 1968-76, dir. admissions, registrar, 1976-83, ret., 1983; edn. and tng. advisor Vietnamese Air Logistics Command, Bien Hoa AB, 1971-72; tournament dir. Denver Post Champions of Golf, Castle Rock, Colo., 1984-86; exec. dir. Colo. Golf Assn., Denver, 1987—; bd. dirs. Colo. Golf Found., 1983—, Colo. Golf Hall of Fame (pres. 1984-86); mem. U.S. Golf Assn. Handicap Procedure Com., Far Hills, N.J., 1987—, U.S. Golf Assn. Handicap Rsch. Team, 1984—. Bd. dirs. Pikes Peak YMCA/USO, Colorado Springs, 1974-88 (chmn. 1979-81); bd. dirs. Colo. Golf Assn., Denver, 1977-85 (pres. 1982-85); mem. Denver Park and Recreation Golf Adv. Com., 1986—. Named 1st Team All-Am., Golf Coaches Assn., Syracuse U., 1959, Sr. Player Yr. Colo. Golf Assn., 1990; inductee Colo. Golf Hall of Fame, 1988. Mem. Internat. Assn. Golf Adminstrs. (pres. 1993), Air Force Assn., Internat. Order Old Bastards, The Country Club at Castle Pines (bd. dirs. 1990-92), Lakewood Country Club (hon.), Fox Hollow Golf Club (hon.), Phi Beta Kappa. Republican. Methodist. Home: 332 Woodstock Ln Castle Rock CO 80104 Office: Colo Golf Assn 5655 S Yosemite Ste 101 Englewood CO 80111

SIMMS, MARIA ESTER, health services administrator; b. Bahia Blanca, Argentina, Nov. 19, 1938; came to U.S., 1963; d. Jose and Esther (Guays) Barberio Esandi; m. Michael Simms, July 15, 1973; children: Michelle Bonnie Lee Carla, Michael London Valentine, Matthew Brandon. Degree medicine, Facultad del Centenario, Rosario, Argentina, 1962; Physician Asst. Cert. (hon.), U. So. Calif., 1977. Medical diplomate. V.p. Midtown Svcs. Inc., L.A., 1973—. V.p., editor The Ebell of L.A., 1985-88; chmn. bd. dirs. America's Film Inst., Washington. Fellow Am. Acad. Physicians' Assts.; mem. Bus. for Law Enforcement (northeast div.), Physicians for Soc. Responsibility, Mercy Crusade Inc., Internat. Found. for Survival Rsch., Noetic Scis. Soc., Inst. Noetic Scis., So. Calif. Alliance for Survival, Supreme Emblem Club of U.S., Order of the Eastern Star, Flying Samaritans, Shriners.

SIMMS, MARIA KAY, publishing and computer services executive; b. Princeton, Ill., Nov. 18, 1940; d. Frank B. and Anna (Haurberg) S.; m. Neil F. Michelsen, Oct. 2, 1987 (dec. 1990); children: Shannon Sullivan Stillings, Molly A. Sullivan, Elizabeth Maria Jossick. BFA, Ill. Wesleyan U., 1962. cert. cons. profl. astrologer. Art tchr. elem. and jr. high pub. schs., Dundee, Northbrook, Ill., 1962-65; high sch. art tchr. Danbury, Conn., 1975-76; self employed gallery painter various cities, 1962-77, free-lance comml. illustrator, 1972-74, 86-87; shop, gallery, café owner Conn., 1976-79; art dir. ACS Pubs., Inc., San Diego, Calif., 1987-90; pres. Astro Comm. Svcs., Inc. (formerly ACS Pubs.), San Diego, 1990—; conf. lectr. United Astrology Congress, Washington, 1992, Am. Fedn. Astrologers Internat. Conv., Chgo., 1992. Author: Twelve Wings of the Eagle, 1988, Dial Detective, 1989; co-author: Search for the Christmas Star, 1989; contbr. numerous articles to mags. V.p. New Milford (Conn.) C. of C., 1977-78. Recipient numerous art awards. Mem. Nat. Assn. Women Bus. Owners, Nat. Coun. Geocosmic Rsch. Inc. (dir., pubs. dir. 1981-93, editor NCGR Jour. 1984-92), Am. Fedn. Astrologers, Internat. Soc. Astrol. Rsch., Mid City C. of C. San Diego, New Age Pubs. Assn., Alpha Gamma Delta. Office: Astro Comm Svcs Inc 408 Nutmeg St San Diego CA 92103

SIMMS, MARY MARGARET, counselor; b. Bklyn., May 19, 1952; d. Jack and Mary (Walker) Mitchell; m. Martin Luther Simms, Nov. 30, 1974; children: Mary Pauline, Martin L. IV. BA in Speech Communications, U. Ariz., 1974; MS in Pastoral Counseling, Trinity Coll., 1983, MA in Marriage, Family and Child Therapy, 1984. Lic. marriage and family counselor, Calif. Career counselor Calif. State U., Long Beach, 1977-84; marriage and career counselor Grace Counseling Svcs., Harbor City, Calif., 1986-92; founder, dir. Family Outreach Counseling, Long Beach, 1992—; pvt. cons. Mendes Cons. Svcs., L.A., 1984—; speaker in field. Contbr. articles to profl. jours. Named Outstanding Young Women of Am., 1984. Fellow Calif. Assn. Marriage and Family Therapist. Office: Family Outreach Counseling 4320 Atlantic Ave #125 Long Beach CA 90807

SIMMS, PRISCILLA CLAYTON, human resources consultant; b. San Francisco, Apr. 26, 1933; d. George and Genevieve (Dale) S. BS, U. Calif., Santa Barbara, 1955; MS, NYU, 1956. Job methods analyst Walker Scott Co., San Diego, 1956-59, ops. supt., 1960-63, store mgr., 1963-65, asst. dir. personnel, 1966-67, v.p. personnel, 1968-87; pres. Personnel/HUman Resources Cons. Services, San Diego, 1987—; bd. dirs. Walker-Scott Corp., San Diego, 1972-74. Chair Greater San Diego Industry Edn. Council, 1971-77, San Diego County Employee Relations Panel, 1976-80, San Diego Employers Health Cost Coalition, 1980—; pres., trustee Sr. Adult Services, San Diego, 1980—. Mem. Am. Soc. for Human Resources (chair dist. 1972-73, San Diego chpt. 1968—), Greater San Diego C. of C. (co-chair seminar com. 1987-90, small bus. 1991—), Sigma Kappa (dir. alumnae 1974-87, Bylaws chair 1992—). Republican. Episcopalian. Home: 4196 Falcon St San Diego CA 92103-1836 Office: Personnel/Human Resources Cons Services 701 B St Ste 1300 San Diego CA 92101-8194

SIMMS, STEVEN RODNEY, anthropology educator; b. Tujunga, Calif., Dec. 12, 1951; s. Rodney Melvin and Isabel Marie (Eastlack) S.; m. Marina Lorraine Hall, Dec. 6, 1989. BA, U. Utah, 1973, PhD, 1984; MA, U. Nev., 1976; postgrad., U. Pitts., 1978. Assoc. instr. U. Utah, Salt Lake City, 1981-84; asst. prof., dir. archaeol. technician program Weber State Coll., Ogden, Utah, 1985-87; asst. prof. Utah State U., Logan, 1988-90, assoc. prof., 1991—; cons. Dames & Moore, Salt Lake City, 1991—, Intermountain Rsch., Silver City, Nev., 1987-89; dir. archaeol. field schs. Weber State Coll., Utah State U., 1985-92; co-investigator Petra (Jordan) Ethnoarchaeol. Project, 1986-90. Author: Behavioral Ecology and Hunter-Gatherer Foraging, 1987; contbr. chpts. to books and articles to profl. jours. Mem. Antiquities Task Force, Salt Lake City, 1992, Utah Govs. Adv. Com. on Native Am. Burials, Salt Lake City, 1990-91, Utah Govs. Com. on Historic Preservation, Salt Lake City, 1984-85. Recipient numerous grants NSF and others, 1981—. Mem. Utah Profl. Archaeol. Coun. (pres. 1992—, v.p. 1989-91), Soc. for Am. Archaeology, Utah Statewide Archaeol. Soc. (Archaeology Preservation award 1988), Sigma Xi. Office: Dept Sociology Social Work & Anthropology Utah State U Logan UT 84322-0730

SIMON, DAVID HAROLD, retired public relations executive; b. Washington, Dec. 3, 1930; s. Isaac B. and Marjorie S. (Felstiner) S.; m. Ruth Lurie, Mar. 2, 1962; children: Rachel, Jessie. BEE, Cornell U., 1954. Mktg. engr. Sylvania Elec. Products, Inc., Boston, 1957-58; advt. mgr. Sylvania Elec. Products, Inc., Mountain View, Calif., 1958-60; regional sales engr. Sylvania Elec. Products, Inc., L.A., 1960-63; mgr. advt. and pub. rels. Electronic Splty. Co., L.A., 1963-66; corp. dir. advt. and pub. rels. Teledyne, Inc., L.A., 1966-67; pres. Simon/Pub. Rels., Inc., L.A., 1967-91. Contbr. articles on pub. rels. to various publs. Res. dep. sheriff L.A. Sheriff's Dept., 1973—; mem. L.A. Olympic Citizens' Adv. Commn., 1980-84; commr. City of L.A. Cultural Affairs Commn., 1987-92, pres., 1990-92; trustee Calif. Chamber Symphony, 1981-84; mem., founder L.A. Philharmonic, 1984—; mem. Philharmonic Men's Com., 1986—; bd. dirs. L.A. Mozart Orch., Odyssey Theater, L.A., 1992—. With USN, 1954-57. Mem. Pub. Rels. Soc. Am. (bd. mem. L.A. chpt.), Nat. Assn. Sci. Writers, Nat. Assn. Corp. Dirs. (founding pres. L.A. chpt.) Opera Buffs Inc. (bd. dirs. 1986-87), Mensa. Home: 13025 Weddington St Van Nuys CA 91401-6160

SIMON, ERIC MICHAEL, medical designer; b. Lansing, Mich., Nov. 16, 1959; s. Gerald Dave and Lois Hermine (Lefkowitz) S. Student, U. Mich., 1978-80; BS in Material Sci. & Engring., U. Utah, 1983, ME in Bioengring., 1985. Orderly E.W. Sparrow Hosp., Lansing, Mich., 1979; prodn. technician Eclipse, Inc., Ann Arbor, Mich., 1980; rsch. technician BME Ctr. for Polymer Implants, Salt Lake City, 1981-83; mfg. engr. Am. Med. Optics, Irvine, Calif., 1983; draftsperson Jacoby Engring., Ketchum, Idaho, 1985; biomaterials engr. Ctr. for Engring. Design, Salt Lake City, 1985-91; consulting engr. Dexterity Design & Devel. Svcs., Salt Lake City, 1991—; pres. Dexterity, Inc., Salt Lake City, 1991. Patentee implantable drug delivery system with piston activation, 1991, multiple vesicle implantable drug delivery system, 1992, disposable toothbrush cover, 1992. Vol. Tree Utah, Salt Lake City, 1992. Regents scholar U. Mich., 1978, Coll. Engring. scholar U. Utah, 1982. Mem. Profl. and Tech. Cons. Assn., Intermountain Biomed. Assn., Intermountain Soc. Inventors and Designers, Utah Soc. Biomaterials Rsch. (pres. 1985), Tau Beta Pi, Phi Kappa Phi. Home and Office: Dexterity Design and Devel Svcs/Dexterity Inc Salt Lake City UT 84108

SIMON, GERALD AUSTIN, management consultant; b. N.Y.C., Aug. 19, 1927; s. William and Ray (Goldberg) S.; m. Margaret Cornwall, Dec. 1979; 1 son by previous marriage, Dana Alexander; 6 stepchildren. BBA, CCNY, 1950; MBA, Harvard U., 1956, postgrad. rsch. fellow, 1956-58. With various advt. firms, Phila., N.Y.C., Providence, 1950-54; rsch. asst., Ford Found. doctoral rsch. fellow Bus. Sch. Harvard U., 1956-58; vis. lectr. Northwestern U., Evanston, Ill., 1958-59; mng. dir. Cambridge Rsch. Inst., 1959-79; pres. Gerald Simon & Assocs., Berkeley, Calif., 1979—. Co-editor: Chief Executives Handbook, 1976; chmn. editorial bd. Jour. Mgmt. Cons. Served with USNR, 1945-46. Fellow Cert. Mgmt. Cons., mem. Inst. Mgmt. Cons. (founding mem., past dir.); mem. Assn. Cons. Mgmt. Engrs. (past dir.), Harvard U. Bus. Sch. Assn. (exec. coun., past dir.), Harvard Univ. Alumni Assn. (past dir.), Assn. Corp. Growth, Harvard Club (N.Y.C., Boston), Harvard U. Faculty Club, U. Calif. at Berkeley Faculty Club, World Trade Club (San Francisco).

SIMON, RALPH E., electronics executive; b. Passaic, N.J., Oct. 20, 1930; s. Paul and Sophie (Epstein) S.; m. Elena Schiffman, June 22, 1952; children: Richard L., David P., Michael A. BA, Princeton U., 1952; PhD, Cornell U., 1959. Mem. tech. staff RCA Labs., Princeton, N.J., 1958-67, dir., 1967-69; mgr. RCA Electronic Components, Lancaster, Pa., 1969-75; v.p. RCA Solid State Div., Lancaster, 1975-80; v.p. optoelectronics div. Gen. Instrument Corp., Palo Alto, Calif., 1980-84; pres. Lytel Inc., Somerville, N.J., 1984-87; pres., chief exec. officer Quality Techs. Corp., Sunnyvale, Calif., 1989—; dir. Xsirius Scientific, Inc., Marina Del Rey, Calif., 1988-91, Applied Electron Corp., Santa Clara, Calif., 1987—. pres., mem. Lawrence Twp. Bd. Edn., Lawrenceville, N.J., 1964-69, Community Action Orgn., 1967-69. Recipient UK Zworykin prize IEEE, 1973. Office: Quality Techs Corp 610 N Mary Ave Sunnyvale CA 94086-2999

SIMON, RICHARD HEGE, lawyer; b. Englewood, Colo., Jan. 15, 1911, AB, U. Denver, 1934, JD, 1936. Bar: Colo. 1938, U.S. Supreme Ct. 1970. Pvt. practice, Englewood, 1941—; mem. Simon, Lee & Shivers and predecessors, 1942-49; ptnr. Simon, Kelley, Hoyt & Malone, 1967-69; ptnr. Simon, Eason, Hoyt & Malone, 1969-76; sole practice, 1977—; dist. atty. First Jud. Dist. Colo., 1941-49; dir. First Nat. Bank Englewood, 1961-80, Key Savs. and Loan Assn., 1961-81. Founder, pres., dir. Arapahoe County (Colo.) Fair Assn., 1946—; bd. dirs., pres. Sch. Dist 1, Arapahoe County; sec., pres., chmn. bd., gen. counsel Centennial Turf Club, Inc., 1949-83; bd. dirs., pres. Arapahoe Park, Inc., 1983—; trustee Denver Met. United Way; state and county chmn. Republican Central Com.; pres., trustee Iliff Sch. Theology, 1960-88; pres., dir. Arapahoe Mental Health Ctr., 1960-75, Arapahoe County Mile High United Way, 1958-74. Fellow Am. Bar Found.; mem. Arapahoe County Bar Assn. (rep. to bd. govs. Colo. Bar Assn. 1958-67) ABA, Colo. Bar Assn. (pres. 1969-70), Am. Judicature Soc. Clubs: Denver Athletic, Columbine Country.

SIMON, RICHARD LOUIS, meteorologist, consultant; b. Oakland, Calif., Dec. 1, 1950; s. Ralph and Norma Eileen (Brodine) S.; m. Katherine Lynn Burwell, June 1, 1985; children: Kyra Burwell Simon, Emylena Galaen Laferriere. BA in Geography, U. Calif., Berkeley, 1973; MS in Meteorology, San Jose State U., 1976. Meteorologist Nat. Environ. Satellite Svc., Redwood City, Calif., 1976; rsch. assoc. San Jose (Calif.) State U., 1975-78; pres. Global Weather Cons., Inc., Palo Alto, Calif., 1977-80; meteorologist Pcific Gas & Electric Co., San Francisco, 1980-82; sr. meteorologist Am. Energy Projects, Inc., Palo Alto, 1982-83; cons. meteorologist in pvt. practice Mill Valley, Calif., 1983—; Author monograph, conf. publ., jour. articles. Instr. Met. Adult Edn. Program, San Jose, 1977-78; guest lectr. East Bay Park Dist., Berkeley, 1984. Mem. Am. Meteorol. Soc., Am. Wind Energy Assn. Home and Office: 80 Alta Vista Ave Mill Valley CA 94941

SIMON, RONALD I., finance consultant; b. Cairo, Nov. 4, 1938; came to U.S., 1942; s. David and Helene (Zilkha) S.; m. Anne Faith Hartman, June 19, 1960; children: Cheryl, Eric, Daniel. BA, Harvard U., 1960; MA, Columbia U., 1962, PhD, 1968. V.p. Harpers Internat., N.Y.C., 1959-62; fin. analyst Amerace Corp., N.Y.C., 1965-66; v.p. Am. Foresight Inc., Phila., 1966-67; asst. to pres. Avco Corp., Greenwich, Conn., 1967-70; exec. v.p. Avco Community Developers Inc., La Jolla, Calif., 1970-73; pres. Ronald I. Simon Inc., La Jolla, 1973—, Delta Data Systems Corp., Phila., 1980-81; exec. v.p. Towner Petroleum Corp., Houston, 1983-85; mng. dir., chief fin. officer The Henley Group Inc., La Jolla, 1986-90; pvt. practice fin. cons. La Jolla, 1990—; chmn. Sonant Corp., San Diego; bd. dirs. Craig Corp., L.A., Reading Co., Phila. Bd. dirs. San Diego Opera Co., 1988-90; bd. dirs. Mandeville Art Gallery U. Calif., San Diego. Ford Found. fellow, 1963-65; recipient Ann. award Nat. Comml. Fin. Conf., 1963. Mem. University Club (N.Y.C.). Office: 1020 Prospect St Ste 410C La Jolla CA 92037-4148

SIMON, SHELDON WEISS, political science educator; b. St. Paul, Jan. 31, 1937; s. Blair S. and Jennie M. (Dim) S.; m. Charlann Lilwin Scheid, Apr. 27, 1962; 1 child, Alex Russell. BA summa cum laude, U. Minn., 1958, PhD, 1964; MPA, Princeton U., 1960; postgrad., U. Geneva, 1962-63. Asst. prof., then prof. U. Ky., 1966-75; prof. polit. sci. Ariz. State U., 1975—, chmn. dept., 1975-79, dir. Ctr. Asian Studies, 1980-88; vis. prof. George Washington U., 1965, U. B.C. Can., 1972-73, 79-80, Carleton U., 1976, Monterey Inst. Internat. Studies, 1991, Am. Grad. Sch. Internat. Mgmt., 1991-92; cons. USIA Rsch. Analysis Corp., Am. Enterprise Inst. Pub. Policy Rsch., Hoover Instn., Orkand Corp., Nat. Bur. Asian Rsch. Author: The ASEAN States and Regional Security, 1982, Asian Neutralism and U.S. Policy, 1975, The Future of Asian-Pacific Security Collaboration, 1988; editor: The Military and Security in the Third World, 1978, East Asian Security in the Past--Cold War Era, 1993, other books, rsch. articles; contbr. chpts. to books. Mem. Com. Fgn. Relations, Phoenix, 1976—; bd. dirs. Phoenix Little Theater, 1976-79. Grantee Am. Enterprise Inst., 1974, Earhart Found., 1979, 81, 82, 84, 88; Hoover Instn. fellow, 1980, 85. Mem. Am. Polit. Sci. Assn., Assn. Asian Studies, AAUP, Internat. Studies Assn. (profl. ethics com. 1987—, v.p. 1991—), Asia Soc. (contemporary affairs com. 1987—), Phi Beta Kappa. Democrat. Jewish. Home: 5630 S Rocky Point Rd Tempe AZ 85283-2134 Office: Ariz State U Polit Sci Dept Tempe AZ 85287

SIMON, STEVEN DAVID, transportation executive; b. N.Y.C., Oct. 8, 1936; s. Eugene Bernard and Rosalie Eleanor (Myers) S.; m. Lucille Hannah Mintz, Aug. 26, 1962; children: Suzanne Mara, Ronald Elliott, Gary Dean. BS in Engring. and Bus. Adminstrn., MIT, 1958. Staff asst. City of Long Beach, N.Y., 1956-57, N.Y. State Dept. Pub. Works, Albany, 1957-58; sr. facilities adminstr. Boeing Co., Seattle, 1958-70; pres. Bus. Mail Svc., 1970—, Limo I of Wash., 1983—. Mem. Seattle Jr. C. of C. (pageant chmn. 1960-64), MIT Club of Puget Sound (treas. 1962-65), Elks. Office: Wash Transport Group 500 S Lander PO Box 36 Seattle WA 98111

SIMON, WILLIAM LEONARD, film writer; b. Washington, Dec. 3, 1930; s. Isaac B. and Marjorie (Felsteiner) S.; m. Arynne Lucy Abeles, Sept. 18, 1966; 1 child, Victoria Marie; 1 stepson, Sheldon M. Bermont. BEE, Cornell U., 1954; MA in Ednl. Psychology, Golden State U., 1982, PhD in Communications, 1983. Writer features and TV movies, documentary and indsl. films, TV programs, 1958—; lectr. George Washington U., Washington, 1968-70; juror Coun. on Nontheatrical Events Film Festival, 1975-90, Cindy Festival Blue Ribbon Panel, 1985—; jury, chmn., bd. dirs. CINE film festival, 1990—. Writer over 600 produced works for motion pictures and TV, including (screenplays) Fair Woman Without Discretion, Majorca, Swindle, A Touch of Love, (teleplays and documentaries) From Information to Wisdom, Flight of Freedom II, Missing You, (home video) Star of India at Sea, Combat Vietnam series; writer, producer The Star of India: Setting Sail. Pres. Foggy Bottom Citizens Assn., 1963-65, mem. exec. bd., 1965-69; v.p. Shakespeare Summer Festival, 1966-67, trustee, 1965-70; mem. interview com. Cornell U., 1987-88. Lt. USN, 1954-58. Recipient 10 Golden Eagle awards Cine Film Festival, gold medal N.Y. Internat. Festival, gold medal Freedoms Found., IFPA Gold Cindy; awards Berlin, Belgrade and Venice film Festivals, numerous others. Mem. Nat. Acad. TV Arts and Scis. (gov. D.C. chpt. 1970-73), Writers Guild Am., Am. Film Inst., Internat. Documentary Assn., Rotary (bd. dirs., program chmn.), Eta Kappa Nu (chpt. pres. 1953-54), Tau Beta Pi. Republican. Home: 6151 Paseo Delicias PO Box 2048 Rancho Santa Fe CA 92067-2048

SIMONDS, JOHN EDWARD, newspaper editor; b. Boston, July 4, 1935; s. Alvin E. and Ruth Angeline (Rankin) S.; m. Rose B. Muller, Nov. 16, 1968; children—Maximillian P., Malia G.; children by previous marriage—Rachel F., John B. B.A., Bowdoin Coll., 1957. Reporter Daily Tribune, Seymour, Ind., 1957-58, UPI, Columbus, Ohio, 1958-60; reporter, asst. city editor Providence Jour. Bull., 1960-65, Washington Evening Star, 1965-66; corr. Gannett News Svc., Washington, 1966-75; mng. editor Honolulu Star Bull., 1975-80, exec. editor, 1980-87, sr. editor, editorial page editor, 1987-93; exec. Hawaii Newspaper Agy., Honolulu, 1993—. Served with U.S. Army, 1958. Mem. Am. Soc. Newspaper Editors, AP Mng. Editors, Soc. Profl. Journalists, Nat. Conf. Editorial Writers. Home: 5316 Nehu Pl Honolulu HI 96821-1942 Office: Hawaii Newspaper Agy 605 Kapiolani Blvd Honolulu HI 96813

SIMONS, BARBARA BLUESTEIN, computer scientist, researcher; b. Boston, Jan. 26, 1941; d. Richard Nathan and Eleanor (Getzug) Bluestein; m. James Harris Simons (div.); children: Elizabeth, Paul, Nathaniel. PhD, U. Calif., Berkeley, 1981. Mem. rsch. staff IBM Rsch. Lab, San Jose, Calif., 1980-92; mem. tech. staff IBM Santa Teresa Lab, San Jose, Calif., 1991—; co-organizer, chair steering com. Coalition for Sci. and Tech. in a New Era, nationwide, 1990-91. Author: Fault-Tolerant Distributed Computing, 1990; co-inventor clock synchronization; contbr. articles to profl. jours. Recipient Norbert Wiener award Computer Profls. Social Responsibility, 1992. Mem. Assn. for Computing Machinery (chair com. sci. freedom and human rights 1987-90, vice-chair Theoretical Computer Sci. Group 1983-90, chair sci. policy com. 1986-90, sec. 1990-92, chair pub. policy commn. 1992—). Office: IBM Santa Teresa Lab 555 Bailey Rd San Jose CA 95141

SIMONS, LYNN OSBORN, state education official; b. Havre, Mont., June 1, 1934; d. Robert Blair and Dorothy (Briggs) Osborn; BA, U. Colo., 1956; postgrad. U. Wyo., 1958-60; m. John Powell Simons, Jan. 19, 1957; children: Clayton Osborn, William Blair. Tchr., Midvale (Utah) Jr. High Sch., 1956-57, Sweetwater County Sch. Dist. 1, Rock Springs, Wyo., 1957-58, U. Wyo., Laramie, 1959-61, Natrona County Sch. Dist. 1, Casper, Wyo., 1963-64; credit mgr. Gallery 323, Casper, 1972-77; Wyo. state supt. public instrn., Cheyenne, 1979-91; mem. State Bds. Charities and Reform, Land Commrs., Farm Loan, 1979-91; mem. State Commns. Capitol Bldg., Liquor, 1979-91; Ex-officio mem. bd. trustees U. Wyo., 1979-91; ex-officio mem. Wyo. Community Coll. Commn., 1979-91; mem. steering com. Edn. Commn. of the States, 1988-90; mem. State Bd. Edn., 1971-77, chmn., 1976-77; advisor Nat. Trust for Hist. Preservation, 1980-86. Mem. LWV (pres. 1970-71). Democrat. Episcopalian.

SIMONS, MARLENE J., state legislator, rancher; b. Deadwood, S.D., July 1, 1935; d. Royal B. Mills and Elsie M. Snook; m. Frank Simons, Sept. 24, 1951; children: Greg, Linda, Sully. Grad. high sch., Sundance, Wyo. Pres. Outdoors Unltd., Kaysville, Utah; mem. Wyo. Ho. of Reps., 1979—, rules com., chair agr. com., appropriations com., western legis. state conf. com., water policy com.; vice chmn. Pub. Lands Adv. Coun., 1986—; stockgrower Farm Bur., Wyo., 1969-92; rancher, outfitter. Pres. Wyo. Multiple Use Coalition, Ranch A Restoration Found.; sec. Black Hills Multi-Use Coalition; mem. Madison water steering com. Black Hills Hydrology Study; leader 4-H. Republican. Home: Windy Acres Ranch PO Box 20 Beulah WY 82712-0221 Office: Outdoors Unltd PO Box 373 Kaysville UT 84037-0373

SIMONS, ROBERT WALTER, geneticist, educator; b. Rockford, Ill., Jan. 28, 1945; s. DeWayne Kimble and Helen Lucille (Bush) S.; m. Elizabeth Lindsay; children: Sarah Christina, Rebecca Ann. BS, U. Ill., 1972; PhD, U. Calif., Irvine, 1980. Staff rsch. biochemist U.Mex., Albuquerque, 1972-75, lectr. dept. biology, 1973-74; tutor, lectr. molecular biology Bd. Tutors Biochem. Scis./Harvard U., Cambridge, Mass., 1981-84; postdoctoral fellow dept. molecular biology Harvard U., 1980-85; mem. Jonsson Comprehensive Cancer Ctr./UCLA, 1985—; asst. prof. dept. microbiology and molecular genetics UCLA, 1985-90, assoc. prof., 1990—. Editor: Molecular Microbiology jour., 1990—; contbr. articles to profl. jours. With USN, 1965-69, Vietnam. Recipient Steinhaus award for Outstanding Grad. Tchr., U. Calif., Irvine, 1978, Nat. Rsch. Svc. award in Molecular Biology and Biochemistry, 1977-80, Postdoctoral Fellowship, Damon Runyon-Walter Winchell Cancer Fund, 1980-82, NIH, 1982-83, Leukemia Soc. of Am., 1983-85, Jr. Faculty Rsch. award Am. Cancer Soc., 1986-89, numerous grants in field. Mem. Am. Soc. Microbiology, AAAS, Genetics Soc. Am., Sigma Xi. Democrat. Office: Dept Microbiology and Molecular Genetics/UCLA 1602 Molecular Science Los Angeles CA 90024

SIMONS, STEPHEN, mathematics educator, researcher; b. London, Aug. 11, 1938; came to U.S., 1965; s. Jack Isidore Simons and Ethel Esther (Littman) Harris; m. Jacqueline Mania Berchadsky, Aug. 13, 1963; 1 son, Mark. BA, Cambridge U., Eng., 1959, PhD, 1962. Instr. U. B.C., Vancouver, Can., 1962-63; asst. prof. U. BC., Vancouver, Can., 1964-65; asst. prof. U. Calif., Santa Barbara, 1965-67, assoc. prof., 1967-73, prof., 1973—, chmn. dept., 1975-77, 88-89; trustee Math. Scis. Rsch. Inst., Berkeley, Calif., 1988—. Peterhouse rsch. fellow, Cambridge U., 1963-64. Mem. Am. Math. Soc., The Inst. Mgmt. Scis. Office: Univ Calif Dept Math Santa Barbara CA 93106

SIMONSON, KENNETH WAYNE, JR., restaurant financial executive; b. N.Y.C., July 5, 1955; s. Kenneth Wayne and Alyce (Baumgarten) S.; m. Ellen Andrea Meinzer, Sept. 17, 1983; children: Andrea Elizabeth, Jennifer Ashley. AA, Mesabi Community Coll., Virginia, Minn., 1977; BS in Bus., U. Minn., 1979. Field underwriter Mut. N.Y., Mpls., 1979-80; budget analyst Motel 6 Inc., Santa Barbara, Calif., 1980-81, field acctg. mgr., 1981-82; office mgr. Traister's Ethan Allen Gallery, Ventura, Calif., 1982-83; fin. analyst Carrows Restaurants, Inc., Santa Barbara, 1984-85; fin. reporting mgr. W.R. Grace Restaurant Co. Family Div. Carrows Restaurant, Santa Barbara, 1985-86, dir. fin. and acctg., 1987-88; pres. Adminstrv. Spltys., Inc. (dba Office Svcs. Unltd.), Santa Barbara, 1988-89; mgmt. svcs. officer extension div. Santa Barbara U. Calif., Goleta, 1989-90; v.p., contr. Nanco Restaurants, Inc., Santa Barbara, 1990-92, Elephant Bar Restaurants, Inc., Santa Barbara, 1990-92, Jeremiah's Restaurants, Inc., Santa Barbara, 1990-92; pres., gen. mgr. Virginia Hotel, Ltd., West Haley Properties, Inc., Santa Barbara, 1993—, Va. Hotel, Ltd., West Haley Properties, Inc. Republican. Jewish.

SIMONSON, MICHAEL, lawyer, judge; b. Franklin, N.J., Feb. 5, 1950; s. Robert and Eleanor (Weiss) S. BA, U. Ariz., 1973; JD, Southwestern U., Los Angeles, 1976; LLM in Taxation, Washington U., St. Louis, 1978. Bar: Ariz. 1977, U.S. Dist. Ct. Ariz. 1979, U.S. Tax Ct. 1978. Bailiff, law clk. Superior Ct. Maricopa County Div. 2, Phoenix, 1976-77; sole practice, Scottsdale, Ariz., 1978-79; ptnr. Simonson, Groh, & Lindteigen, Scottsdale, 1979-81, Simonson & Preston, Phoenix, 1984-86, Simonson, Preston & Arbetman, 1986-87, Simonson & Arbetman, 1987-89; judge pro tempore Mcpl. Ct., City of Phoenix, 1984—, City of Mesa, 1990—; judge pro tempore Maricopa County Superior Ct., 1991—; adj. prof. Ariz. State U Coll. Bus., Tempe, 1984—, Coll. for Fin. Planning, Denver, 1984—, Maricopa County Community Colls., 1984—, Western Internat. U., Phoenix, 1984—, Ottawa U., 1987—; prof. law Univ. Phoenix, 1985—, area chmn. legal studies, 1986-90, Keller Grad. Sch. Mgmt., 1990—. Mem. Maricopa County Foster Child Care Rev. Bd. No. 17, 1978-81; pres. Camelback Mountainview Estates Homeowners Assn., 1980-81, Congregation Tiphereth Israel, 1979-81; dir., sec. Fifth Ave Area Property Owners Assn., 1988-92. Co-author: Buying and Selling Closely Held Businesses in Arizona, 1986, 89, Commercial Real Estate Transactions, 1986. Fellow Ariz. Bar Found.; mem. ABA (taxation sect., various coms.), State Bar Ariz. (cert. specialist in tax law), Maricopa County Bar Assn., Cen. Ariz. Estate Planning Coun., Nucleus Club, Mensa, Shriner, Masons. Democrat. Jewish. Office: 6925 E 5th Ave Ste O Scottsdale AZ 85251-3804

SIMONSON, MILES KEVIN, real estate executive, professional speaker; b. Monmouth, Ill., May 25, 1950; s. John E. and Margaret Katherine (Huston) S. BA, No. Ill. U., 1972. Sgt. DeKalb County Sheriff's Police, Sycamore, Ill., 1972-75; owner Kishwaukee Realty, DeKalb, 1976-78; v.p and chief ops. officer Realty World, Oak Brook (Ill.), Tampa (Fla.), Phoenix, St. Louis, 1978-84; pres., chief exec. officer Realty 500, Inc., Reno, 1985-87, also bd. dirs.; founder, owner Simonson Seminars, Long Beach, Calif., 1987—. Author: Professional Sales, 1985, Professional Listing, 1985, How to Control your Mind and Time, 1990, High-Tech Selling, 1993. Office: Simonson Seminars 2180 Eucalyptus Ave Long Beach CA 90806-4519

SIMONSON, SUSAN KAY, hospital administrator; b. La Porte, Ind., Dec. 5, 1946; d. George Randolph and Myrtle Lucille (Opfel) Menkes; m. Richard Bruce Simonson, Aug. 25, 1973. BA with honors, Ind. U., 1969; MA, Washington U., St. Louis, 1972. Perinatal social worker Yakima Valley Meml. Hosp., Yakima, Wash., 1979-81, dir. patient support and hospice program, 1981—, dir. social svc., 1982—; instr. Spanish, ethnic studies, sociology Yakima Valley Coll., Yakima, Wash., 1981—; pres. Yakima Child Abuse Council, 1983-85; developer nat. patient support program, 1981. Contbr. articles to profl. jours. Mem. Jr. League, Yakima; mem. adv. council Robert Wood Johnson Found. Rural Infant Health Care Project, Yakima, 1980, Pregnancy Loss and Compassionate Friends Support Groups, Yakima, 1982—, Teen Outreach Program, Yakima, 1984—. Recipient NSF award, 1967, discharge planning program of yr. regional award Nat. Glasrock Home Health Care Discharge Planning Program, 1987; research grantee Ind. U., 1968, Fulbright grantee U.S. Dept. State, 1969-70; Nat. Def. Edn. Act fellowship, 1970-73. Mem. AAUW, Soc. Med. Anthropology, Soc. Hosp. Social Work Dirs. of Am. Hosp. Assn. (regional award 1989), Nat. Assn. Perinatal Social Workers, Nat. Assn. Social Workers, Phi Beta Kappa. Office: Yakima Valley Meml Hosp 2811 Tieton Dr Yakima WA 98902-3799

SIMONTON, ANN JOSEPHINE, activist, educator; b. Harlan, Ky., June 23, 1952; d. William Johnston Jr. and Josephine (Pittman) S.; m. Joseph Schultz, July 9, 1989; 1 child, Wiley. BA with honors, U. Calif., Santa Cruz, 1978. Profl. model Eileen Ford-Nina Blanchard, N.Y.C., L.A., Milan, 1968-75; dir. Media Watch, Santa Cruz, 1984—; univ. lectr., agt. K&S Speakers, Cambridge, Mass., 1986—; main organizer, coord. Miss Calif. Protest, Santa Cruz, San Diego, 1984-90; founder, dir. Media Watch: For Improving Women's Image in Media. Contbg. author: I Never Told Anyone, 1982, Her Wits About Her, 1986; author video scripts Warning: The Media..., 1990, Don't Be a TV..., 1992 (Silver Apple award Nat. Ednl. Film Festival 1993); appeared in documentary Miss or Myth, 1985-86; contbr. editorials to local and nat. newspapers. Named Humanist Heroine of Yr., Am. Humanist Soc., 1989. Office: Media Watch PO Box 618 Santa Cruz CA 95061-0618

SIMONTON, RICHARD ARNOLD, lawyer; b. Wahpeton, N.D., July 7, 1944; s. Arnold E. and Mary Ann (Benroth) S.; m. LaNette E. Ames, Mar. 4, 1989; children: Eric, Mark. AA, Dawson Community Coll., 1964; BS, N.D. State U., 1966; JD, U. Mont., 1971. Bar: Mont. 1971, N.D. 1981, U.S. Dist. Ct. Mont. 1971. Lawyer Simonton, Howe & Schneider, P.C., Glendive, Mont., 1971—; atty. Dawson County, Glendive, 1974-90, City of Glendive, 1975-78; dir., atty. Montana County, 1986-88; chmn. Mont. Bd. Social Work Examiners and Profl. Counselors. Chmn. bd. trustees Dawson C.C. Mem. ABA, Mont. Bar Assn., N.D. Bar Assn., Mont. Sch. Bd. Attys., Am. Trial Lawyer Assn. Office: Simonton Howe & Schneider Box 1250 Glendive MT 59330

SIMPLOT, JOHN R., agribusiness executive; b. Dubuque, Iowa, Jan. 4, 1909; m. Esther Becker; children: Richard, Don, Scott, Gay Simplot Otter. Founder, chmn. J.R. Simplot Co., Boise, Idaho, 1941—; bd. dirs. Micron Technology, First Security Corp., Continental Life and Accident Co., Morrison-Knudsen, Inc. Former chmn. bd. trustees Coll. Idaho. Avocations: skiing, horseback riding, hunting, fishing. Pioneer in commercial frozen french fries. Office: J R Simplot Co PO Box 27 1 Capitol Ctr Boise ID 83707

SIMPLOT, THOMAS MICHAEL, lawyer; b. Ottumwa, Iowa, Jan. 30, 1961; s. Allen Richard and Joanne Mae (Stark) S. BS, Ariz. State U., 1983; JD, U. Iowa, 1986. Bar: Ariz. 1986. Assoc. Lorona & Assocs., Mesa, Ariz., 1986-88, Hunter & Assocs., Phoenix, 1988-90; chief adminstr. Maricopa County Bd. Suprs., Phoenix, 1990—; instr. Ford Sch. Real Estate, Phoenix, 1989-90; trustee Maricopa County Bar Found., Phoenix, 1990—, Maricopa County Self Ins. Trust Fund, 1992—. Bd. dirs. Ariz. Young Reps., Phoenix, 1987-88, Friends of Compas, Phoenix, 1991—, Ariz. Rep. Caucus, Phoenix, 1992—; chmn. fund raising St. Mary's Sch. Found. Com., Phoenix, 1992—; mem. dean's bd. Ariz. State U., pres., 1989-91. Mem. ABA, State Bar Ariz., Maricopa County Bar Assn. (chmn. lawyer referral svc. 1989-92, Barristers Ball 1991-93, Law Week 1991, bd. dirs., treas. young lawyers div. 1991-92, Mem. of Month award 1992), Ariz. State U. Coll. Bus. Alumni Assn. (bd. dirs. 1987-92). Roman Catholic. Office: Maricopa County Bd Suprs 301 W Jefferson 10th Fl Phoenix AZ 85003

SIMPSON, ALAN KOOI, senator; b. Cody, Wyo., Sept. 2, 1931; s. Milward Lee and Lorna (Kooi) S.; m. Ann Schroll, June 21, 1954; children—William Lloyd, Colin Mackenzie, Susan Lorna. BS, U. Wyo., 1954, JD, 1958; LLD (hon.), Calif. Western Sch. of Law, 1983, Colo. Coll., 1986, Notre Dame U., 1987; JD (hon.), Am. U., 1989. Bar: Wyo. 1958, U.S. Supreme Ct. 1964. Asst. atty. gen. State of Wyo., 1959; city atty. City of Cody, 1959-69; partner firm Simpson, Kepler, and Simpson, Cody, Wyo., 1959-78; mem. Wyo. Ho. of Reps., 1964-77, majority whip, 1973-75, majority floor leader, 1975-77, speaker pro tem, 1977; legis. participant Eagleton Inst. Politics, Rutgers U., 1971; mem. U.S. Senate from Wyo., 1978—, asst. majority leader, 1985-87, asst. minority leader, 1987—, ranking minority mem. vets. affairs com., ranking minority mem. nuclear regulation subcom., ranking minority mem. subcom. on immigration and refugee policy; guest lectr. London exchange program Regent's Coll., London, 1987. Formerly v.p., trustee N.W. Community Coll., Powell, Wyo., 1968-76; trustee Buffalo Bill Hist. Ctr., Cody; trustee Grand Teton Music Festival, Gottsche Found. Rehab. Ctr., Thermopolis, Wyo.; del. Nat. Triennial Episcopal Ch. Conv., 1973, 76. With U.S. Army, 1954-56. Recipient Nat. Assn. Land Grant Colls. Centennial Alum award U. Wyo., 1987. Mem. Wyo. Bar Assn., Park County Bar Assn., Fifth Jud. Dist. Bar Assn., Am. Bar Assn., Assn. Trial Lawyers Am., U. Wyo. Alumni Assn. (pres. 1962, 63, Disting. Alumnus award 1985), VFW (life), Am. Legion, Amvets. (Silver Helmet award). Lodges: Eagles, Elks, Masons (33 deg.), Shriners, Rotary (pres. local club 1972-73). Office: US Senate 261 Dirksen Senate Bldg Washington DC 20510-5002*

SIMPSON, AMY MARCY, university administrator; b. Seattle, Apr. 26, 1963; d. Lewis Lombard and Amy (McEvoy) S.; m. R. Thomas Euler, Oct. 12, 1991. BS, Mont. State U., 1986; MA, Bowling Green (Ohio) State U., 1988; postgrad., U. Ariz., 1988—. Unit dir. Bowling Green State U., 1986-88; asst. dir. admissions and new student enrollment orientation U. Ariz., Tucson, 1988—. Mem. Nat. Orientation Dirs. Assn. (bd. dirs. 1990-93), Chi Omega (alumni advisor 1989-91). Home: 1702 E Lind Rd Tucson AZ 85719 Office: U Ariz Orientation Office Old Main 202 Tucson AZ 85721

SIMPSON, ANDREA LYNN, energy communication executive; b. Altadena, Calif., Feb. 10, 1948; d. Kenneth James and Barbara Faries Simpson; m. John R. Myrdal, Dec. 13, 1986; 1 child, Christopher Ryan Myrdal. BA, U. So. Calif., 1969, MS, 1983; postgrad. U. Colo., Boulder, 1977. Asst. cashier United Calif. Bank, L.A., 1969-73; asst. v.p. mktg. 1st Hawaiian Bank, Honolulu, 1973-78; v.p. corp. communications BHP Petroleum Americas, Inc. (formerly Pacific Resources, Inc.), Honolulu, 1978—. Bd. dirs. Arts Coun. Hawaii, 1977-81, Hawaii Heart Assn., 1978-83, Coun. Pacific Girl Scouts U.S., 1982-85, Child and Family Svcs., 1984-86, Honolulu Symphony Soc., 1985-91, Kapiolani Women's and Children's Hosp., 1988—, Sta. KHPR Hawaii Pub. Radio, 1988-92, Kapiolani Found., 1990—, Hanahaoli Sch., 1991—; trustee Hawaii Loa Coll., 1984-86, Hawaii Sch. For Girls at LaPietra, 1989-91; commr. Hawaii State Commn. on Status of Women, 1985-87, State Sesquecentennial of Pub. Schs. Commn., 1990-91; bd. dirs. Hawaii Strategic Devel. Corp., 1991—. Named Panhellenic Woman of Yr. Hawaii, 1979, Outstanding Woman in Bus. Hawaii YWCA, 1980, Outstanding Young Woman of Hawaii Girl Scouts Coun. of the Pacific, 1985, 86, Hawaii Legis., 1980. Mem. Am. Mktg. Assn., Pub. Rels. Soc. Am. (bd. dirs. Honolulu chpt. 1984-86, Silver Anvil award 1984, Pub. Rels. Profl. Yr. 1991), Pub. Utilities Communicators Assn. (Communicator of Yr. 1984), Honolulu Advt. Fedn. (Advt. Woman of Yr. 1984), U. So. Calif. Alumni Assn. (bd. dirs. Hawaii 1981-83), Outrigger Canoe Club, Pacific Club, Kaneohe Yacht Club, Rotary (pub. rels. chmn. 1988—, Honolulu chpt.), Alpha Phi (past pres., dir. Hawaii), Hawaii Jaycees (Outstanding Young

Person of Hawaii 1978). Office: BHP Petroleum Americas 733 Bishop St Ste 3100 Honolulu HI 96813-4025

SIMPSON, ANN MARCOUX, international marketing executive, transportation executive; b. Jackson, Mich., Oct. 12, 1954; d. William Joseph and Kae Marie Marcoux; m. David Ritchie Simpson, Jan. 4, 1975. BA, U. Mich., 1976. Dept. mgr. Jacobsons, Ann Arbor, Mich., 1976-78; mktg. Braniff, Dallas, 1978-79; customer rels. Dillards, Dallas, 1979-80; mktg. cons. Imagery, Seattle, 1980-85; pub. rels. Sundance Cruiseline, Seattle, 1985-86; account exec. Sammers & Conner, Seattle, 1986-88; dir. Airborne Express, Seattle, 1988—; pres. mktg. com. exec. internat., 1992-93; speaker in field. Contbr. articles to profl. jours. Campaign chair Rep. House, Mich., 1972-78; com. chair Poncho, Washington, 1980-90. Mem. Internat. Assn. Bus. Commn. (pres. 1986-87, 6th dist. dir. 1986-89), Internat. Com. Am. Electronics Assn. Office: Airborne Express 3101 Western Ave Seattle WA 98121

SIMPSON, C. DENE, clinical neuropsychologist, psychophysiologist; b. Ashland, Ky., Sept. 16, 1936; s. Curtis Zotto and Clarice Lorrine (McDavid) S.; m. Margaret Louise Cline, Aug. 17, 1956; children: René, Michelle, Yvonne. BA, Bethany Nazarene Coll., 1958; MA, U. Kans., 1962; PhD, U. Okla., Oklahoma City, 1974. Lic. psychologist, Idaho, Okla. Statis. analyst Ford Motor Co., Claycomo, Mo., 1959-63; prof. N.W. Nazarene Coll., Nampa, Idaho, 1963-66, head Dept. of Psychology, 1970-88; prof. Bethany (Okla.) Nazarene Coll., 1966-67; rsch. psychologist Okla. Med. Rsch. Found., Oklahoma City, 1967-68, Okla. Ctr. for Alcohol Related Studies, Oklahoma City, 1968-70; clin. neuropsychologist Boise, Idaho, 1976—; pres. Human Tech., Inc., Boise, 1985—; cons. VA Med. Ctr., Boise; vis. prof. U. St. Andrews, Scotland, 1988; cons. neuropsychologist Intermountain Hosp. of Boise, 1983—. Contbr. sci. articles to profl. jours. Mem. The Nature Conservancy, 1988—, The Perringrine Fund, Boise, 1988—, World Ctr. for Birds of Prey. Fellow NSF-U. Mo., 1967, Nat. Def. Edn. Act-U. Okla., 1968-70; equipment grantee Nat. Sci. Found.-N.W. Nazarene Coll., 1978-79. Fellow Idaho Psychol. Assn. (pres. 1974-77, exec. bd. 1988); mem. Am. Psychol. Assn., Western Psychol. Assn., Internat. Neuropsychology Soc., N.Y. Acad. Scis., Internat. Assn. for the Study of Traumatic Brain Injury, Assn. for Applied Psychophysiology and Biofeedback. Republican. Mem. Ch. of the Nazarene. Home: 979 Strawberry Ln Boise ID 83712-7724 Office: 317 Allumbaugh St Boise ID 83704-9208

SIMPSON, PETER KOOI, university official; b. Sheridan, Wyo., July 31, 1930; s. Milward Lee and Lorna Helen (Kooi) S.; m. Lynne Alice Livingston, June 18, 1960; children: Milward Allen, Margaret Ann, Peter Kooi Jr. BA, U. Wyo., 1953, MA, 1962; PhD, U. Oreg., 1973. Pres. Western Hills, Inc., Billings, Cody, Wyo., 1959-61; asst. prof. history Ea. Oreg. Coll., La Grande, Oreg., 1962-65, Lane Community Coll., Eugene, Oreg., 1968-69, 70-72; instr. U. Oreg., Eugene, 1969-70; asst. to pres. Casper (Wyo.) Coll., 1974-77, coord. U.Wyo.-Casper Coll. upper div., 1976-77; dean instrn. Sheridan Coll., 1977-83, asst. to pres. for devel., dean instrn., 1983-84; v.p. for devel., alumni and univ. rels., exec. dir. Found., U. Wyo., Laramie, 1984-89; v.p. for institutional advancement, 1989—; bd. dirs. lst Interstate Bank, Laramie. Author: The Community of Cattlemen, 1987; also articles. Mem. Wyo. Ho. of Reps., 1980-84; Rep. candidate for gov. of Wyo., 1986; bd. dirs. Wyo. Vol. Assistance Corp., Laramie, 1985—, Casper Troopers, 1988—. Lt. USN, 1954-60. Recipient award for signal contbn. to hist. preservation Wyo. Cons. Com., 1989; grantee Oreg. Edn. Coordinating Coun., 1971; named Outstanding Educator of Am. Fuller and Dees, 1975. Mem. SAG, Wyo. Hist. Soc., Cowboy Joe Club (exec. com. 1984—), Rotary (chmn. Found. 1990-92), Masons (32 degree, K.C.C.H.), Shriners, Jesters. Episcopalian. Home: 812 E Grand Ave Laramie WY 82070-3942 Office: U Wyo Found PO Box 3963 Laramie WY 82071-3963

SIMPSON, RICHARD JOHN, police officer, municipal official; b. Greensburg, Pa., Oct. 23, 1953; s. Henry Theodore and Marceline (Krempasky) S.; m. Gail Montgomery, Jan. 10, 1977 (div. May 1981); m. Jeri Anne Sheely, July 10, 1981. BA, Calif. U. Pa., 1976, 78; cert., Pa. Police Acad., 1978. Asst. security supt. Rouse Svc. Co., Greensburg, 1971-77; asst. police chief Ellsworth (Pa.) Borough Police Dept., 1977-78; police officer Fallowfield Twp. Police Dept., Charleroi, Pa., 1978-80; police detective, trainer, instr., coord. field tng. Rock Springs (Wyo.) Police Dept., 1980—; rsch. asst. centennial com. Rock Springs Police Dept.; police instr. State of Wyo, 1982—; actor, cons. tng. films series theater dept. Western Wyo. Coll., Rock Springs, 1987-88. Editor quar. newsletter Blue Knights News Wyo., 1986-92. Asst. basketball coach Spl. Olympics, Rock Springs, 1987. Recipient numerous commedations Rock Springs Police Dept., 1980—, Outstanding Law Enforcement Officer award, 1985, Disting. Svc. medal, 1987, Svc. medal 1988. Mem. Police Protective Assn. (v.p. 1984-85, treas. 1990—), Western Alliance Police Officers (v.p. 1985-87), Caluf. U. Pa. Alumni Assn., Intermountain World War II Reenactment Assn., Shooting Stars Motorcycle Club (pres. 1980-84), Blue Knights Internat. Law Enforcement Motorcycle Club (pres. Wyo. chpts. 1985-92, bd. dirs. Wyo. chpt. 1 1992—), High Desert Riders, Motorcycle Club (legis. officer, 1991—). Home: 103 Agate St Rock Springs WY 82901-6601 Office: Rock Springs Police Dept 221 C Rock Springs WY 82901

SIMPSON, VELMA SOUTHALL, insurance agent; b. Denver, Jan. 29, 1948; d. Herbert Eugene and Gladys Jane (Pasquale) Southall; m. Stephen Wayne Simpson, Aug. 24, 1968; children: Sarah, Anna, Benjamin. BA, Colo. State U., 1971; postgrad., U. Denver, 1975-76. Agt. Allstate Ins. Co., Longmont, Colo., 1983—. Bd. dirs. Family Extension Inn Between; active St. Vrain Hist. Soc., Longmont Theatre Co., Mountain Prairie coun. Girl Scouts U.S., 1st Congl. Ch. Democrat. Home: 13966 N 75th St Longmont CO 80503 Office: Allstate Ins Co 1600 Hover Rd # 3D Longmont CO 80501-2440

SIMPSON, WARREN CARL, information brokerage executive; b. Waukegan, Ill., Apr. 5, 1954; s. Barton Oliver and Irene Susan (Brockway) S.; m. Tina Marie Barney, Nov. 25, 1981 (div. Feb. 1989); children: Sara, Robert, Shawn; m. Debra Jeanne Graves, Sept. 30, 1990; 1 child, Harmony. Student, Tucson Bus. Coll., 1985; A. in Computer Scis., Pima Coll., 1987; postgrad., U. Ariz., 1988-90. With retail sales various cos. Waukegan, 1968-72; with mgmt. Donovan's Inc., Chgo., 1972-74; owner Master Photographers, Tucson, 1975-79; with mgmt. various cos. Tucson, 1979-84; records clk. State of Ariz., Tucson, 1985-90; pres., founder C.S. Svcs., Tucson, 1990—, chmn. bd. dirs., 1990—. Author: The New Power-Information, 1991, (handbook) Speaking to Hold, 1988. Pub. activist, Tucson, 1978—; coach Little League baseball, Tucson, 1986-87; ordained minister non-denominational ch. Mem. Toastmasters Internat. (Tucson, hon. life, pres. 1987, 88, Competent Toastmaster 1986, Parliamentarian 1987, Most New Mem. Drive 1987, Best Entertaining Speech 1989). Home: 7425 E 45th Tucson AZ 85730 Office: C S Svcs 445 N Pantano Ste 106 Tucson AZ 85710-2312

SIMPSON, WILLIAM ARTHUR, insurance company executive; b. Oakland, Calif., Feb. 2, 1939; s. Arthur Earl and Pauline (Mikalasic) S.; m. Nancy Ellen Simpson, Mar. 31, 1962; children—Sharon Elizabeth, Shelley Pauline. B.S., U. Calif.-Berkeley, 1961; postgrad. Exec. Mgmt. Program, Columbia U. C.L.U. V.p. agys. Occidental Life of Calif., L.A., 1976-79; v.p. mktg. Countrywide Life, L.A., 1973-76; pres., chief exec. officer Vol. State Life, Chattanooga, 1979-83; exec. v.p. Transam. Occidental Life Ins. Co., L.A., 1983-86, pres., 1986-88, pres., CEO, 1988-90, also bd. dirs.; dir. US-LIFE Corp., N.Y.C., Calif., 1990—; pres., CEO, All Am. Life Ins. Co., Pasadena, Calif., 1990—; bd. dirs. USLIFE, N.Y.C. Pres. Chattanooga coun. Boy Scouts Am., 1982, bd. dirs., L.A., 1983, v.p., 1983-85, vice-chmn L.A. area, 1989, chmn., 1989; pres. bd. councillors L.A. County Am. Cancer Soc.; trustee Verdugo Hills Hosp. Found. 1st lt. U.S. Army, 1961-64. Mem. Am. Soc. CLUs, Life Ins. Mktg. and Rsch. Assn. (bd. dirs. 1986-89). Republican. Presbyterian. Lodge: Rotary. Office: All Am Life Ins Co 99 S Lake St Pasadena CA 91101

SIMPSON, WILLIAM BRAND, economist, educator; b. Portland, Oreg., Nov. 30, 1919; s. John Alexander and Janet Christie (Brand) S.; m. Ruth Laura Decker, June 12, 1957. B.A. in Math., Reed Coll., 1942; M.A. in Stats., Columbia U., 1943; Ph.D. in Econs., Claremont Grad. Sch., 1971. Cons. Nat. Def. Mediation Bd., 1941-42, U.S. Dept. Interior, 1942, U.S. War Dept., Tokyo, 1947; head econ. sect. Counter-Intelligence Office, Manila, 1945; spl. rep. Supreme Commander Allied Powers, Japan, 1945-46; exec. dir. Cowles Commn. Research Econs., U. Chgo., 1948-53; co-founder, bd. dirs. Inst. Social and Personal Rels., Oakland, Calif., 1955-61; prof. econs. Calif. State U., L.A., 1958—; econs. cons. higher edn. Author: Cost Containment in Higher Education, 1991; mng. editor, co-editor Econometrica, 1948-53; contbr. articles to profl. jours. Fellow Nat. Social Sci. Rsch. Coun.; mem. ACLU; Econometric Soc. (internat. sec. 1948-52); AAUP (state pres. 1975-76, mem. com. econ. status acad. profession 1976-79, nat. council 1978-81, com. govt. rels. 1982-88, state chmn. com. issues and policy 1981—), Am. Econs. Assn. (chmn. panel polit. discrimination 1978-80), Am. Assn. Higher Edn., Congress Faculty Assns., United Scottish Socs. So. Calif., Sierra Club (L.A. chpt.), Phi Beta Kappa. Democrat. Home: PO Box 41526 Los Angeles CA 90041-0526 Office: Calif State U Los Angeles CA 90032

SIMS, PAUL KIBLER, geologist; b. Newton, Ill., Sept. 8, 1918; s. Dorris Lee and Vere (Kibler) S.; m. Dolores Carsell Thomas, Sept. 15, 1940; children: Thomas Courtney, Charlotte Ann. AB, U. Ill., 1940, MS, 1942; PhD, Princeton, 1950. Spl. asst. geologist Ill. Geol. Survey, 1942-43; geologist U.S. Geol. Survey, 1943-61; prof. geology, dir. Minn. Geol. survey U. Minn., 1961-73; research geologist U.S. Geol. Survey, 1973—; pres. Econ. Geology Pub. Co., 1979—; Bd. dirs. North Star Research and Devel. Inst., Mpls., 1966-73. Co-editor: Geology of Minnesota, 1972, 75th anniversary vol. Economic Geology. Adviser Minn. Outdoor Recreation Resources Commn., 1963-67. Served with USNR, 1943-46. Recipient Meritorious Service award U.S. Dept. Interior, 1984; Goldich medal Inst. on Lake Superior Geology, 1985, Disting. Svc. award U.S. Dept. Interior, 1991. Fellow Geol. Soc. Am., Soc. Econ. Geologists (councilor 1965-68, pres. 1975, Ralph W. Marsden award medal 1989); mem. Internat. Assn. on Genesis of Ore Deposits, Internat. Union Geol. Sci. (subcom. Precambrian stratigraphy, sec. 1976-84), Assn. Am. State Geologists (hon.), Colo. Sci. Soc. (hon.). Home: 1315 Overhill Rd Golden CO 80401-4238

SIMS, ROBERT CARL, university dean; b. Ft. Gibson, Okla., Dec. 26, 1936; s. Carl Raymond and Irene (Weatherford) S.; m. Elizabeth Ann Crow, June 3, 1963; children: Sarah, Barry, Todd. BA, Northeastern Okla. State Coll., 1963; MA, U. Okla., 1965; PhD, U. Colo., 1970. Asst. prof. history Boise State U., 1970-73, assoc. prof., 1973-79, prof., 1979—, dean Coll. Social Scis. and Pub. Affairs, 1985—. Author: Idaho's Governors, 1992; editorial bd. Idaho Yesterdays mag., 1980—; contbr. articles to mags. Commr. Boise City Planning and Zoning Commn., 1979-85, chmn., 1983-85; bd. dirs. Idaho Humanities Coun., 1980-86. With U.S. Army, 1958-61. Democrat. Home: 1636 E Holly Boise ID 83702-3442 Office: Boise State U Coll Social Sci-Pub Affairs 1910 University Dr Boise ID 83725-0001

SIMS, ROGER LAFE, employee benefits director, consultant; b. Salt Lake City, June 17, 1941; s. Lafayette Tuellor and Izola (Dunn) S.; m. Joyce Mary Petrus, Dec. 15, 1967; children: Kristina Sims Johnson, Laurel I. BBA, U. Wash., 1963, MBA, 1967. Cons. Johnson & Higgins, Seattle, 1969-76; dir. benefits and compensation Payn Save Corp., Seattle, 1976-87; dir. benefits N.Y. State Dept. Civil Svc., Albany, 1988-90; v.p. Risk Mgmt. Svcs., Inc., Seattle, 1991—; instr. U. Wash., Whatcom C.C, 1991—. With USAFR, 1963-69. Mem. We. Pension Conf., Self-Insurers Assn. (pres. 1983), Am. Coll. Life Underwriters, Internat. Fedn. Benefit Plans, Puget Sound Health Care Purchasers Assn. (founding mem. 1985), Puget Sound Health Systems Agy., Am. Arbitrators Assn. Democrat. Home: 23458 130th Ave SE Kent WA 98031-3689 Office: Risk Mgmt Svcs Inc PO Box 88124 Seattle WA 98138-2124

SIMUNICH, MARY ELIZABETH HEDRICK (MRS. WILLIAM A. SIMUNICH), public relations executive; b. Chgo.; d. Tubman Keene and Mary (McCamish) Hedrick; student Phoenix Coll., 1967-69, Met. Bus. Coll., 1938-40; m. William A. Simunich, Dec. 6, 1941. Exec. sec. sales mgr. KPHO radio, 1950-53; exec. sec. mgr. KPHO-TV, 1953-54; account exec. Tom Rippey & Assos., 1955-56; pub. rels. dir. Phoenix Symphony, 1956-62; co-founder, v.p. Paul J. Hughes Pub. Rels., Inc., 1960-65; owner Mary Simunich Pub. Rels., Phoenix, 1966-77; pub. rels. dir. Walter O. Boswell Meml. Hosp., Sun City, Ariz., 1969-85; pub. rels. cons., 1985—; instr. pub. rels. Phoenix Coll. Evening Sch., 1973-78. Bd. dirs. Anytown, Ariz., 1969-72; founder, sec. Friends Am. Geriatrics, 1977-86. Named Phoenix Advt. Woman of Year, Phoenix Jr. Advt. Club, 1962; recipient award Blue Cross, 1963; 1st Pl. award Ariz. Press Women, 1966. Mem. NAFE, Women in Communications, Internat. Assn. Bus. Communicators (pres. Ariz. chpt. 1970-71, dir.), Pub. Rels. Soc. Am. (sec., dir. 1976-78), Am. Soc. Hosp. Pub. Rels. (dir. Ariz. chpt. 1976-78), Nat., Ariz. Press Women. Home: 4133 N 34th Pl Phoenix AZ 85018-4771

SINCLAIR, GEORGE MICHAEL, marketing executive; b. San Francisco, Dec. 21, 1953; s. Kenneth F. and Carole J. (Lucas) S.; m. Martha Poppy, Mar. 24, 1990; 1 child, Gregory P. BA in Geography, San Jose State U., 1979. Mktg. mgr. Xetex, Inc., Sunnyvale, Calif., 1980—. Office: Xetex Inc 1275 Hammerwood Ave Sunnyvale CA 94089

SINCLAIR, HERBERT JOSEPH, sales executive; b. Jacksonville, Fla., Dec. 15, 1956; s. Abram Samuel and Christine (Robinson) S. BS, Morehouse Coll., Atlanta, 1980; BS in Indsl. Engring., Ga. Inst. Tech., 1980. Real Estate Broker's Lic., Calif. Facilities planner IBM, Lexington, Ky., 1981-82, strategic planner, 1982-84, project mgr., 1984-86; systems engr. IBM, San Francisco, 1986-87, Oakland, Calif., 1987-88; acct. systems engr. IBM, Walnut Creek, Calif., 1988-89; O.E.M. account rep. Santa Cruz (Calf.) Operation, Inc., 1989-91, sr. acct. rep., 1991-93, systems integrator, sr. account rep., 1993—; computer cons. Contra Costa Bd. Edn., Walnut Creek, Calif., 1987-89. Voter registrar Sam Nunn Senatorial Campaign, Fitzgerald, Ga., 1968, Jesse Jackson Presdl. Campaign, San Francisco, 1984, H. Ross Perot Presdl. Campaign, Santa Cruz, Calif., 1992; mem. diversity coun. Santa Cruz Operation, 1993. Mem. Toastmasters Internat., Morehouse Coll. Alumni Club, Ga. Tech. Alumni Club, Nat. Assn. Realtors, Profl. Assn. Dive Instrs. Episcopalian. Home: 175 Frederick St Santa Cruz CA 95062 Office: Santa Cruz Operation 400 Encinal St Box 1900 Santa Cruz CA 95061

SINCLAIR, JOSEPH TREBLE, III, real estate consultant, lawyer; b. Detroit, Nov. 17, 1940; s. Joseph Treble II and Miriam (Hoener) S.; m. Lani Jan Wallin, Oct. 4, 1986; 1 child, Brook. BA, U. Mich., 1964, JD, 1971; cert. in real estate, U. Colo., 1976. Bar: Mich. 1971, Colo. 1973, U.S. Dist. Ct. (ea. dist.) 1972, U.S. Dist. Ct. Colo. 1974, U.S. Ct. Appeals (6th cir.) 1972, U.S. Ct. Appeals (10th cir.) 1974. Assoc. Dyer Meek Rutsegger & Bullard, Detroit, 1972-74; ptnr. Harshman Sinclair & Brown, Grand Junction, Colo., 1975-77; broker Sinclair & Assocs., Grand Junction, 1978-83; cons. 1st Internat. Equities of Houston, 1984-85; acquisitions mgr. Calif. Fed. Syndications, L.A., 1986; cons. Sinclair & Assocs., Benicia, Calif., 1987—; cons. Fin. Internat. Corp., Durango, Colo., 1989—. Author: Real Numbers--Analyzing Income Properties for a Profitable Investment, 1993; contbr. articles to profl. jours. Bd. dirs. Sta. KPRN-Pub. Radio, Grand Junction, 1983-84. Lt. (j.g.) USNR, 1965-68, Vietnam. Mem. Comml. Investment Real Estate Inst. (cert. comml. investment mem., Marshall S. Sanders award 1991). Office: Sinclair & Assocs PO Box 1304 Benicia CA 94510

SINCLAIR, SARA VORIS, long term care facility administrator, nurse; b. Kansas City, Mo., Apr. 13, 1942; d. Franklin Defenbaugh and Inez Estelle (Figenbaum) Voris; m. James W. Sinclair, June 13, 1964; children: Thomas James, Elizabeth Kathleen, Joan Sara. BSN, UCLA, 1965. RN, Utah; lic. health care facility adminstr.; cert. health care adminstr. Staff nurse UCLA Med. Ctr. Hosp., 1964-65; charge nurse Boulder (Colo.) Meml. Hosp., 1966, Boulder (Colo.) Manor Nursing Home, 1974-75, Four Seasons Nursing Home, Joliet, Ill., 1975-76; dir. nursing Home Health Agy of Olympia Fields, Joliet, Ill., 1977-79; dir. nursing Sunshine Terr. Found., Inc., Logan, Utah, 1980, asst. adminstr., 1980-81, adminstr., 1981—; mem. long term care profl. and tech. adv. com. Joint Commn. on Accreditation of Healthcare Orgns., Chgo., 1987-91, chmn., 1990-91; adj. lectr. Utah State U., 1991—; adj. clin. faculty Weber State U., Ogden, Utah. Author: (chpt. in book) Associate Degree Nursing & the Nursing Home, 1988; moderator (radio program) Healthwise Sta. KUSU-FM, 1985—; speaker Nat. Coun. Aging, 1993, Alzheimer's Disease Assn. Ann. Conf., 1993. Mem. dean's adv. coun. Coll. Bus. Utah State U., Logan, 1989-91, mem. presdl. search com., 1991-92; chmn., co-founder Cache Community Health Coun., Logan, 1985; chmn. bd. Hospice of Cache Valley, Logan, 1986; mem. Utah State Adv. Coun. on Aging, 1986—; apptd. chmn. Utah Health Facilities Com., 1989—; mem. Utah Adv. Coun. on Aging, 1987—; chmn. Bear River Dist. Adv. Coun. on Aging, 1989-91. Recipient Disting. Svc. award Utah State U., 1989. Fellow Am. Coll. Health Care Adminstrs. (presenter 1992-93); mem. Am. Health-care Assn. (non-proprietary v.p. 1986-87, region v.p. 1987-89, presenter workshop convs. 1990—, exec. com. 1993—), Utah Health Care Assn. (pres. 1983-85, treas. 1991—, Disting. Svc. award 1991), Cache C. of C. (pres. 1991), Logan Bus. and Profl. Women's Club (pres. 1989, Woman of Achievement award 1982, Woman of Yr. 1982), Rotary (Logan chpt., chair community svc. com. 1989-90). Office: Sunshine Terr Found Inc 225 N 200 W Logan UT 84321-3805

SINCLAIR, WILLIAM DONALD, church official; b. L.A., Dec. 27, 1924; s. Arthur Livingston and Lillian May (Holt) S.; m. Barbara Jean Hughes, Aug. 9, 1952; children: Paul Scott, Victoria Sharon. BA cum laude, St. Martin's Coll., Olympia, Wash., 1975; postgrad. Emory U., 1978-79. Commd. 2d lt. USAAF, 1944, advanced through grades to col., USAF, 1970; served as pilot and navigator in Italy, Korea, Vietnam and Japan; ret., 1975; bus. adminstr. First United Methodist Ch., Colorado Springs, Colo., 1976-85; bus. adminstr. Village Seven Presbyn. Ch., 1985-87; bus. adminstr. Sunrise United Meth. Ch., 1987-89; vice-chmn. council fin. and adminstrn. Rocky Mountain conf. United Meth. Ch., U.S.A., 1979-83. Bd. dirs. Chins-Up Colorado Springs, 1983—; chmn. bd. dirs. Pikes Peak Performing Arts Ctr., 1985-92; pres. Pioneers Mus. Found., 1985—; Rep. candidate for Colo. State Chmn., 1992-93. Decorated Legion of Merit with oak leaf cluster, D.F.C. with oak leaf cluster, Air medal with 6 oak leaf cluster, Dept. Def. Meritorious Service medal, Vietnam Cross of Gallantry with Palms. Fellow Nat. Assn. Ch. Bus. Adminstrs. (nat. dir., regional v.p., v.p. 1983-85, pres. 1985-87; Ch. Bus. Adminstr. of Yr. award 1983), Colo. Assn. Ch. Bus. Adminstrs. (past pres.), United Meth., Assn. Ch. Bus. Admins. Adminstrs. (nat. sec. 1978-81), Christian Ministries Mgmt. Assn. (dir. 1983-85), USAF Acad. Athletic Assn. Clubs: Colorado Springs Country, Garden of the Gods, Met. (Denver), Winter Night Club. Lodge: Rotary (pres. Downtown Colorado Springs club 1985-86), Order of Daedalians. Home: 3007 Chelton Dr Colorado Springs CO 80909-1008

SINCOFF, STEVEN LAWRENCE, science administrator, scientist; b. N.Y.C., Apr. 17, 1948; s. Murray B. and Lillian (Goldberg) S.; m. Marcella Seay, June 12, 1993; children by previous marriage: Kristina Lynne, Carolyn Suzanne. BSChemE, N.J. Inst. Tech., 1969, MSChemE, 1972; PhD in Analytical Chemistry, Ohio State U., 1980. Commd. 2d lt. USAF, 1969, advanced through grades to lt. col., 1987, retired, 1991; fuels mgmt. officer USAF, Albuquerque and Galena, Alaska, 1970-74; chem. engr. Aero. Systems Div., Wright-Patterson AFB, Ohio, 1974-77; assoc. prof. chemistry USAF Acad., Colorado Springs, Colo., 1980-84, dir. continuing edn. dept. chemistry, 1982-84; chief gas analysis lab. McClellan (AFB) Cen. Lab., Calif., 1984-88; exec. officer to comdr. Tech. Ops. Div. McClellan AFB, Calif., 1988-89, chief info. officer, 1989-91; gen. mgr. ChemWest Analytical Lab., Sacramento, 1991-92; dir. ops. Barringer Labs., Inc., Golden, Colo., 1992—; reviewer chemistry textbooks Saunders Pub., Phila., 1983-84. Mem. Am. Chem. Soc., Air Force Assn. Jewish. Home: 9757 W Nova Ave Littleton CO 80127 Office: Barringer Labs 15000 W 6th Ave Ste 300 Golden CO 80401

SINEGAL, JAMES D., variety store wholesale business executive; b. 1936. With Fed-Mart Corp., 1954-77, exec. v.p.; v.p. Builders Enporium, 1977-78; exec. v.p. Price Co., 1978-79; with Sinegal/Chamberlin & Assocs., 1979-83; pres., chief oper. officer Costco Wholesale Corp., 1983—, chief exec. officer, 1988—, bd. dirs. Office: Costco Wholesale Corp 10809 120th Ave NE Kirkland WA 98033-5030

SINES, RANDY DWAIN, business executive; b. Spokane, Jan. 16, 1948; s. Myron Jones and Paula Inez (Walls) S.; student Wash. State U., 1966-67, U. Wash., 1968-69; m. Irene Cheng, Mar. 18, 1981. With Boeing Co., 1967; with Winchell's Donut House, Inc. , Seattle, 1968-71; owner, mgr. bakeries, Wash. and Mont., 1972-78; owner, mgr. Sonsine Inc., Great Falls, Mont., 1976-79; pres. Gardian Port Corp., Oxnard, Calif., 1980-82; pres., chmn. SNS Motor Imports, Inc., Oxnard, 1982-86; chmn. Karakal Corp. of Ams., Ventura, Calif., 1986-89; chief exec. officer, chmn. Steel Stix, U.S.A., 1990—; chmn. Mitt USA, 1991—. Recipient alumni grant Wash. State U., 1967; lic. water well contractor, Wash., Mont. Patentee sports apparatus, over 20 patents worldwide. Home and Office: S 4056 Madelia Spokane WA 99203

SINGER, BETH ANN, business owner; b. Buffalo, July 2, 1961; d. Haskell Abraham and Helene Lois (Newman) S.; m. Savannah S. Singer, Dec. 18, 1988. Grad. high sch., Amherst, N.Y. Owner Gay and Lesbian Community Traffic Sch., Costa Mesa, Calif., 1989, Think Pink Directory-Ofcl. Gay and Lesbian Community Directory of So. Calif., Santa Ana, 1992, Gone with the ERA Antiques and Collectibles, L.A., 1992. Photographer: (art show) Long Beach Ctr., 1990; (art exhibit) Long Beach Pride Festival, 1989; (photo contest) Long Beach Ctr., 1990 (3d pl.); (photo exhibit) Orange County Gay and Lesbian Pride Festival, 1989 (1st pl.). Protestor March on Sacramento, 1991. Democrat. Jewish. Office: Gay & Lesbian Community Traffic Sch 1533 Baker St # 6 Costa Mesa CA 92626

SINGER, EARL GARDNER, writer, publisher; b. Alameda, Calif., June 20, 1930; s. Chester Earl and Almeida Kendall (Gardner) S.; m. Marietta Louise Zaro, Mar. 17, 1951. BA in Philosophy, Calif. State U., San Jose, 1952; M of City and Regional Planning, U. Calif., Berkeley, 1959. Urban planner U.S. Dept. HUD, San Francisco, 1959-63, urban design advisor, 1963-67, community devel. officer, 1967-80; co-pub. Connoisseurs' Guide to Calif. Wine, Alameda, 1974—. Co-author: Connoisseurs' Handbook to California Wine, 1st edit., 1980. With U.S. Naval Air Res., 1952-54. Mem. Am. Soc. for Enology and Viticulture. Home: 2062 Lynwood Terr San Jose CA 95128

SINGER, ELYSE JOY, physician; b. N.Y.C., June 26, 1952; d. Herman and Charlotte (Grossman) S.; m. Bradley A. Manning, Sept. 17, 1989. BA, SUNY, Buffalo, 1973; MD, U. South Ala., 1978. Diplomate Am. Bd. Psychiatry and Neurology. Intern in internal medicine West LA VA Med. Ctr., resident in adult neurology; fellow UCLA Pain Mgmt. Ctr., 1982-84; med. staff fellow NIH, Bethesda, Md., 1984-86; rsch. physician West L.A. VA Med. Ctr., 1987—; asst. prof. UCLA Sch. Med., 1987—; neurology co-investigator L.A. Men Study, 1991—; neurologist UCLA AIDS Clinical Trials Group, 1987—. Mem. Internat. Assn. for the Study Pain, Am. Pain Soc., Am. Acad. Neurology. Office: West LA VA Medical Ctr Dept Neurology W127 Wilshire & Sawtelle Blvds Los Angeles CA 90073

SINGER, FRANK J., insurance executive; b. N.Y.C., Mar. 12, 1944; s. Frank James and Margaretta (Barnes) S.; m. Christine Heins, Feb. 14, 1987; children: Frank, Blake, Cole, Deborah, Victoria. BS, Calif. Western U., 1983, MBA, 1987. Cert. ins. counselor. Sales mgr. Liberty Mut. Ins. Co., Boston, 1963-74; v.p. Sentry Ins., Stevens Point, Wis., 1974-87; pres., CFO Comml. Acceptance Ins. Co., Sacramento, 1987—; owner Eve Ins. Co.; chmn. Pacific Bank of Commerce, Sacramento, 1990—, Pacific Mut. Ins. Co., Sacramento, 1990—. With U.S. Army, 1962-65. Mem. MENSA, Calif. Portuguese Soc. Republican. Office: Comml Acceptance Ins Co 4600 Northgate #110 Sacramento CA 95834

SINGER, JEFFREY ALAN, surgeon; b. Bklyn., Feb. 2, 1952; s. Harold and Hilda (Ginsburg) S.; m. Margaret Sue Gordon, May 23, 1976; children: Deborah Suzanne, Pamela Michelle. BA cum laude, Bklyn. Coll., 1973; MD, N.Y. Med. Coll., 1976. Diplomate Am. Bd. Surgery. Intern Maricopa County Gen. Hosp., Phoenix, 1976-77, resident, 1977-81, mem. teaching faculty, 1981—; trauma cons. John C. Lincoln Hosp., Phoenix, 1981-83; pvt. practice Phoenix, 1981-87; group pvt. practice Valley Surg. Clinics, Ltd., Phoenix, 1987—; sec.-treas. med. staff Humana Desert Valley Hosp., Phoenix, 1987-89, chief of surgery, 1985-87, 91—. Rep. precinct committeeman, Phoenix, 1986—. Fellow ACS, Internat. Coll. Surgeons, Southwestern Surg. Congress, Am. Soc. Abdominal Surgeons; mem. AMA, Ariz. Med. Assn. (bd. dirs. polit. com. 1985, chmn. 1991—, legis. com. 1986—), Alpha Omega Alpha. Office: Valley Surg Clinics Ltd 16601 N 40th St Ste 105 Phoenix AZ 85032

SINGER, KURT DEUTSCH, news commentator, author, publisher; b. Vienna, Austria, Aug. 10, 1911; came to U.S., 1940, naturalized, 1951; s.

Ignaz Deutsch and Irene (Singer) S.; m. Hilda Tradelius, Dec. 23, 1932: children: Marian Alice Brigit, Kenneth Walt; m. Jane Sherrod, Apr. 9, 1955 (div. Jan., 1985); m. Katherine Han, Apr. 8, 1989. Student, U. Zurich, Switzerland, 1930, Labor Coll., Stockholm, Sweden, 1936; Ph.D., Div. Coll. Metaphysics, Indpls., 1951. Escaped to Sweden, 1934; founder Ossietzky Com. (successful in release Ossietzky from concentration camp); corr. Swedish mag. Folket i Bild, 1935-40; founder Niemöller Com.; pub. biography Goring in Eng. (confiscated in Sweden), 1940; co-founder pro-Allied newspaper Trots Allt, 1939; corr. Swedish newspapers in, U.S., 1940; editor News Background, 1942; lectr. U. Minn., U. Kans., U. Wis., 1945-49; radio commentator WKAT, 1950; corr. N.Am. Newspaper Alliance, N.Y.C., 1953—; pres. Singer Media Corp., 1987—; dir. Oceanic Press Service, San Clemente, Calif. Author, editor: underground weekly Mitteilungsblätter, Berlin, Germany, 1933; author: The Coming War, 1934, (biog.) Carl von Ossietzky, 1936 (Nobel Peace prize), Germany's Secret Service in Central America, 1943, Spies and Saboteurs in Argentina, 1943, Duel for the Northland, 1943, White Book of the Church of Norway, 1944, Spies and Traitors of World War II, 1945, Who are the Communists in America, 1948, 3000 Years of Espionage, 1951, World's Greatest Women Spies, 1952, Kippie the Cow; juvenile, 1952, Gentlemen Spies, 1953, The Man in the Trojan Horse, 1954, World's Best Spy Stories, 1954, Charles Laughton Story; adapted TV, motion pictures, 1954, Spy Stories and Asia, 1955, More Spy Stories, 1955, My Greatest Crime Story, 1956, My Most Famous Case, 1957, The Danny Kaye Saga; My Strangest Case, 1958, Spy Omnibus, 1959, Spies for Democracy, 1960, Crime Omnibus Spies Who Changed History, 1961, Hemmingway-Life and Death of a Giant, 1961, True Adventures in Crime, Dr. Albert Schweitzer, Medical Missionary, 1962, Lyndon Baines Johnson-Man of Reason, 1964, Ho-i-man; juveniles, 1965; Kurt Singer's Ghost Omnibus, 1965; juvenile Kurt Singer's Horror Omnibus; The World's Greatest Stories of the Occult, The Unearthly, 1965, Mata Hari-Goddess of Sin, 1965, Lyndon Johnson-From Kennedy to Vietnam, 1966, Weird Tales Anthology, 1966, I Can't Sleep at Night, 1966, Weird Tales of Supernatural, 1967, Tales of Terror, 1967, Famous Short Stories, 1967, Folktales of the South Pacific, 1967, Tales of The Uncanny, 1968, Gothic Reader, 1968, Bloch and Bradbury, 1969, Folktales of Mexico, 1969, Tales of the Unknown, 1970, Tales of the Macabre, 1971, Ghouls and Ghosts, 1972, Satanic Omnibus, 1973, Gothic Horror Omnibus, 1974, Dictionary of Household Hints and Help, 1974, They are Possessed, 1976, True Adventures into the Unknown, 1980, I Spied—And Survived, 1980, First Target Book of Horror, 1984, 2d, 1984, 3d, 1985, 4th, 1985; editor: UN Calendar, 1959-58; contbr. articles to newspapers, popular mags., U.S., fgn. countries, all his books and papers in Boston U. Library-Spl. Collections. Mem. UN Speakers Research Com., UN Children's Emergency Fund, Menninger Found. Mem. Nat. Geog. Soc., Smithsonian Assos., Internat. Platform Assn. (v.p.), United Sch. Assemblies (pres.). Address: Singer Media Corp Seaview Business Pk 1030 Calle Cordillera # 106 San Clemente CA 92673

SINGER, MICHAEL HOWARD, lawyer; b. N.Y.C., Nov. 22, 1941; s. Jack and Etta (Appelbaum) S.; m. Saundra Jean Kupperman, June 1, 1962; children: Allison Jill, Pamela Faith. BS in Econs., U. Pa., 1962; JD, NYU, 1965, LLM in Taxation, 1968. Bar: N.Y. 1965, U.S. Ct. Claims 1968, U.S. Supreme Ct. 1969, U.S. Ct. Appeals (6th cir.) 1970, D.C. 1972, U.S. Tax Ct. 1972, Nev. 1973, U.S. Ct. Appeals (9th cir.) 1973. Law asst. Appellate Term Supreme Ct., N.Y.C., 1965-68; trial lawyer Ct. Claims Tax Div., Washington, 1968-72; tax lawyer Beckley, DeLanoy & Jemison, Las Vegas, 1972-74; ptnr. Oshins, Singer, Segal & Morris, Las Vegas, 1974-87; pvt. practice law Las Vegas, 1987; ptnr. Michael H. Singer Ltd., Las Vegas, 1987—. Pres. Las Vegas chpt. NCCJ, 1980-82. Mem. ABA, ABI, Nev. Bar Assn., Las Vegas Country Club. Democrat. Jewish. Home: 4458 Los Reyes Ct Las Vegas NV 89121-5341 Office: 520 S 4th St 2d Fl Las Vegas NV 89101

SINGER, SARAH BETH, poet; b. N.Y.C., July 4, 1915; d. Samuel and Rose (Dunetz) White; m. Leon Eugene Singer, Nov. 23, 1938; children: Jack, Rachel. B.A., NYU, 1934; postgrad., New Sch. Social Research, 1961-63. Tchr. creative writing Hillside Hosp., Queens, N.Y., 1964-75, Samuel Field YMCA, Queens, 1980-82. Author: Magic Casements, 1957, After the Beginning, 1975, Of Love and Shoes, 1987, The Gathering, 1992; contbr. poetry to anthologies, poetry mags. and quars. including American Women Poets, 1976, Yearbook of American Poetry, 1981, The Best of 1980, 1981, Filtered Images, 1992, The Croton Rev., The Lyric, Bitterroot, Judaism, Encore, The Jewish Frontier, Yankee, Hartford Courant, Poet Lore, N.Y. Times, Christian Sci. Monitor, Voices Internat., The Round Table, Orphic Lute, Brussels Sprout, Poetry and Medicine Column Jour. AMA; cons. editor Poet Lore, 1975-81. Recipient Stephen Vincent Benet award Poet Lore, 1968, 71, Dellbrook award Shenandoah Valley Acad. Lit. and Dellbrook-Shenandoah Coll. Writers' Conf., 1978, 79, C.W. Post poetry award, 1979, 80, award for best poem Lyric quar., 1981, biennial award for achievement in poetry Seattle Br. Nat. League of Am. Penwomen, 1988, award for traditional poetry Wash. Poets Assn., Cert. of Merit Muse Mag., 1990, Editor's Choice award for haiku Brussels Sprout, 1992, poem chosen for Metro Bus. Poetry Project Seattle, 1992. Mem. Nat. League Am. Penwomen (poetry chmn. L.I. br. 1957-87, publicity chmn. 1990, sec. Seattle br. 1990, pres. 1992—, publicity chmn. for State of Wash. 1992—, Marion Doyle Meml. award 1976, 1st prize nat. poetry contest 1976, Drama award 1977, Poetry award 1977, 1st prize for modern rhymed poetry 1978, Lectr. award 1980, Sonnet award Alexandria br. 1980, 81, Catherine Cushman Leach award 1982; poetry award Phoenix br. 1983, Pasadena br. 1984, Alexandria br. 1985, 1st prize award Portland br. 1990, structured verse award Spokane br. 1992), Poetry Soc. Am. (v.p. 1974-78, exec. dir. L.I. 1979-83, James Joyce award 1972, Consuelo Ford award 1973, Gustav Davidson award 1974, 1st prize award 1975, Celia Wagner award 1976), Poets and Writers. Address: 2360 43d Ave E Unit 415 Seattle WA 98112

SINGH, AMBUJ KUMAR, computer scientist; b. Daltonganj, Bihar, India, Apr. 21, 1959; came to U.S., 1982; s. Gaureshwar Narain and Shanti S.; m. Sapna Singh, June 18, 1987; 1 child, Rashi. BS in Computer Sci. & Engring., Indian Inst. Tech., 1982; MS in Computer Scis., Iowa State U., 1984; PhD in Computer Scis., U. Tex., 1989. Grad. rsch. asst. dept. computer scis. U. Tex., Austin, 1986-89; asst. prof. computer sci. U. Calif., Santa Barbara, 1989—. Contbr. articles to profl. jours. MCD fellow U. Tex., 1984-86. Mem. IEEE, Assn. for Computing Machinery, Phi Kappa Phi, Beta Alpha Phi. Office: Dept Computer Sci U Calif Santa Barbara CA 93106

SINGH, AVTAR, engineering educator, consultant; b. Panjab, India, June 2, 1947; came to U.S., 1972; s. Lal and Amar (Kaur) S.; m. Jaswant K. Singh, Dec. 26, 1976; children: Jasbir, Harjeet, Sharan. BSEE, Panjab U., Chandigarh, India, 1969; M Tech EE, Indian Inst. Tech., New Delhi, 1971; MEE, CCNY, 1974; PhD in Elec. Engineering, CUNY, 1982. Adj. lectr. CCNY, 1972-74, 78; asst. dir. Met. Tech. Inst., Saddlebrook, N.J., 1974-78; asst. prof. engineering County Coll. of Morris, Randolph, N.J., 1978-82; sect. head Nat. Semiconductor, Santa Clara, Calif., 1982-83; sr. elec. engr. Anderson Jacobson, San Jose, Calif., 1983-85; v.p. R & D Vivix Corp., Milpitas, Calif., 1985-87; assoc. prof. elec. engring. San Jose State U., 1987—, also bd. dirs.; cons. Vivix Corp., Milpitas, 1987-90. Author 9 books. Mem. IEEE. Office: San Jose State U Electrical Engineering Dept San Jose CA 95192

SINGH, HARINDER (HARRY), business executive, consultant; b. Patiala, Punjab, India, Dec. 23, 1941; came to U.S., 1960; s. Nihal and Lajwanti (Devi) S.; m. Harriet Mae Varnum, Dec. 31, 1963 (div. Jan. 1989); children: Sarita, Sushila, Sanjay, Samita. BA with honors, Punjab U., 1959; MS, U. N.C., 1962; PhD, St. Louis U., 1965. Rsch. geophysicist Mobil Oil/Exxon Corp., Dallas, 1965-70; cons., educator U. Tex., Arlington, 1970-79; sr. mgr. IBM Corp., Purchase, N.Y., 1979-91; ind cons., dir. Santa Clara, Calif., 1991—. Patentee office systems. Mem. Rotary Internat. Home: 1075 Crosspoint Ct San Jose CA 95120-1528

SINGH, MAHENDRA PRATAP, manufacturing executive; b. Allahabad, India, Aug. 23, 1950; came to U.S. 1971; s. Rajendra Prasad and Shanti Singh; m. Usha Rani Singh, July 16, 1977; children: Niharika, Namita, Deepti. BS, Indian Inst. Tech., Kanpur, 1971; MS, Case Western Res. U., 1974; MBA, U. Ill., 1976. Registered profl. engr., Wis. Research asst. Case Western Res. U., Cleve., 1971-73; rsch. asst. dept. econs., survey rsch. lab. U. Ill.-Champaign, 1974-75; mgr. application engring. AFL Industries, West Chicago, Ill., 1976-79; product mgr. Dana Corp., Elgin, Ill., 1979-80; product mgr. Reliance Electric Co., Greenville, S.C., 1980-88, gen. mgr., Seattle, 1988—. Tech. reviewer Am. Soc. Heating, Refrigerating and Air-Conditioning Engrs. Jour.; contbr. numerous articles to profl. lit.; patentee control for variable speed drives. NASA rsch. grantee, 1972-73; EPA rsch. grantee, 1974. Mem. ASHRAE, Am. Mktg. Assn., Toastmasters (past pres.). Home: 7809 SE 75th Pl Mercer Island WA 98040-5501 Office: Reliance Electric Co PO Box 81085 Seattle WA 98108-1085

SINGH, NARESH PRATAP, physician, pulmonary and critical care specialist; b. Calcutta, Sept. 3, 1959. BS in Psychobiology cum laude, UCLA, 1981; MD, U. Nev., 1985. Intern U. Med. Ctr. of So. Nev., Las Vegas, 1985-86; resident in internal medicine U. Med. Ctr. of So. Nev., 1986-88; fellow in pulmonary medicine Irvine Med. Ctr. U. (Orange) Calif. and Long Beach VA, Orange, 1988-90; fellow in critical care medicine Irvine Med. Ctr. U. Calif. and Long Beach VA, Long Beach, 1990-91; clin. instr. Dept. Internal Medicine U. Nev., 1987, Dept. Internal Medicine U. Calif. Irvine Med. Ctr., 1989. Contbr. med. articles to profl. jours. Fellow Am. Coll. Chest Physicians; mem. AMA (Physician's Recognition award in continuing med. edn.), ACS (assoc.), Am. Thoracic Soc. (assoc.), Calif. Thoracic Soc. (assoc.), Alpha Chi Sigma.

SINGH, TARA See TARA

SINGLEHURST, DONA GEISENHEYNER, horse farm owner; b. Tacoma, June 19, 1928; d. Herbert Russell and Rose Evelyn (Rubish) Geisenheyner; m. Thomas G. Singlehurst, May 16, 1959 (dec.); 1 child, Suanna Singlehurst Campbell. BA in Psychology, Whitman Coll., 1950. With pub. rels. and advt. staff Lane Wells, L.A., 1950-52; staff mem. in charge new bus. Bishop Trust Co., Honolulu, 1953-58; mgr. Town & Country Stables, Honolulu, 1958-62; co-owner, v.p. pub. rels. Carol & Mary, Ltd., Honolulu, 1964-84; owner Stanhope Farms, Waialua, Hawaii, 1969—; internat. dressage judge, sport horse breeding judge Am. Horse Shows Assn. Chmn. ways and means com. The Outdoor Cir., Hawaii, 1958-64, life mem.; pres. emeritus Morris Animal Found., Englewood, Colo., 1988—, pres., 1984-88. Recipient Best Friends award Honolulu Vt. Soc., 1986, Spl. Recognition award Am. Animal Hosp. Assn., 1988, Recognition award Am. Vet. Med. Assn., 1992. Mem. NAFE, Hawaii Horse Show Assn. (Harry Hutaff award 1985, past pres., bd. dirs.), Hawaii Combined Tng. Assn. (past pres. bd. dirs.), Calif. Dressage Soc., U.S. Dressage Fedn., U.S. Equestrian Team (area chmn. 1981-85), Delta Soc. (bd. dirs.), Hawaiian Human Soc. (life), U.S. Pony Clubs (dist. commr. 1970-75, nat. examiner 1970-75), Pacific Club, Outrigger Canoe Club. Republican. Episcopalian. Home and Office: Stanhope Farms Waialua HI 96791

SINGLETON, ALICE FAYE, health facility administrator, physician; b. N.Y.C.; d. Philip Herbert and Alma Mae (Donaldson) S. BA, NYU, 1964; MD, SUNY, N.Y.C., 1968; MPH, UCLA, 1976. Dir. ambulatory pediatrics King/Drew Med. Ctr., L.A., 1978—; assoc. prof. pediatrics Charles R. Drew U., L.A., 1985-91, asst. dean student affairs, 1987-89, assoc. dean student affairs, 1989-92, prof. pediatrics, 1991—; assoc. prof. pediatrics UCLA, 1986-92, asst. dean for student affairs sch. medicine, 1987—. Contbr. articles to profl. jours. Fellow Am. Acad. Pediatrics; mem. Ambulatory Pediatrics Assn., L.A. Pediatric Soc., Phi Beta Kappa. Office: King/Drew Med Ctr 12021 Wilmington Ave Los Angeles CA 90059-3099

SINGLETON, FRANCIS SETH, dean; b. Phila., July 13, 1940; s. William Francis and Anna A. (Setian) S.; m. Margaret Neff, June 14, 1962 (div. 1983); children: William, Andrew; m. Charlotte T. Kennedy, Jan. 16, 1988. AB, Harvard U., 1962; MA, Yale U., 1963, PhD, 1968. Budget examiner Bur. of Budget, Washington, 1964-65; dean Pearson Coll. Yale U., New Haven, 1966-69; lectr. U. Dares Salaam, Tanzania, 1969-70; asst. prof. U. Alta., Edmonton, Can., 1970-71; from assoc. prof. to prof., chair politics and govt. Ripon (Wis.) Coll., 1972-83; rsch. assoc. Russian Ctr., Harvard U., Cambridge, Mass., 1983-84; dean arts and scis. Pacific U., Forest Grove, Oreg., 1984-91, prof. govt., 1991—; ampart lectr. U.S.I.A., Africa, 1983, 90; bd. dirs. Oreg. Internat. Coun., Salem, 1986—; lectr. Ural U., Russia, 1991; cons. Russia Fedn. Govt., 1992. Author: Africa in Perspective, 1968; contbr. articles to profl. publs., chpts. to books. Bd. dirs. Com. Fgn. Rels., Portland, 1989—; mem. adv. com. Light Rail Tri-Met, Portland, Oreg., 1989—. Grantee Rockefeller Found., 1969-70, Nat. Coun. Soviet and E. Europe Rsch., 1983-84. Home: 3421 NW Thurman St Portland OR 97210-1228 Office: Pacific U 2043 College Way Forest Grove OR 97116

SINGLETON, HAROLD CRAIG, music educator; b. Decatur, Ala., Sept. 5, 1950; s. Harold Millard and Evelyn Marion (Lumpkin) S.; m. Margaret Elizabeth Stephenson, Feb. 22, 1974; children: Stephen Mark, William Craig. BA, Samford U., 1973; M in Ch. Music, So. Bapt. Sem., Louisville, 1976, D in Musical Arts, 1980; M in Music Edn., Holy Names Coll., 1990. Prof. ch. music Golden Gate Bapt. Sem., Mill Valley, Calif., 1980—; min. music Tiburon Bapt. Ch., Calif., 1985—; condr. Golden Gate Choral Soc., Mill Valley, 1987—. Mem. Nat. Assn. Tchrs. Singing, Hymn Soc. Am., Am. Choral Dirs. Assn., Orgn. Am. Kodály Educators, So. Bapt. Ch. Music Conf. (v.p. 1984—). Democrat. Office: Golden Gate Sem Strawberry Pt Mill Valley CA 94941

SINGLETON, HENRY EARL, industrialist; b. Haslet, Tex., Nov. 27, 1916; s. John Bartholomew and Victoria (Flores) S.; m. Caroline A. Wood, Nov. 30, 1942; children: Christina, John, William, James, Diana. S.B., S.M., Mass. Inst. Tech., 1940, Sc.D., 1950. V.p. Litton Industries, Inc., Beverly Hills, Calif., 1954-60; CEO Teledyne Inc., Los Angeles, 1960-86; chmn. Teledyne Inc., 1960-91, Singleton Group, Beverly Hills, Calif., 1988—; chmn. exec. com. Teledyne, Inc., L.A., 1991—. Home: RR 3 Box 32 Santa Fe NM 87505-9802 Office: 335 N Maple Dr Ste 177 Beverly Hills CA 90210-3858*

SINGLETON, JAMES KEITH, federal judge; b. Oakland, Calif., Jan. 27, 1939; s. James K. and Irene Elisabeth (Lilly) S.; m. Sandra Claire Hoskins, Oct. 15, 1966; children: Matthew David, Michael Keith. Student, U. Santa Clara, 1957-58; AB in Polit. Sci., U. Calif., Berkeley, 1961, LLB, 1964. Bar: Calif. 1965, Alaska, 1965. Assoc. Delaney Wiles Moore and Hayes, Anchorage, 1963, 65-68, Law Offices Roger Cremo, Anchorage, 1968-70; judge Alaska Superior Ct., Anchorage, 1970-80, Alaska Ct. Appeals, Anchorage, 1980-90, U.S. Dist. Ct. for Alaska, Anchorage, 1990—; chmn. Alaska Local Boundary Commn., Anchorage, 1966-69. Chmn. 3d Dist. Rep. Com., Anchorage, 1969-70. Mem. ABA, Alaska Bar Assn., Phi Delta Phi, Tau Kappa Epsilon. Office: US Dist Ct 222 W 7th Ave Anchorage AK 99513-7524

SINGLETON, WILLIAM DEAN, newspaper publisher; b. Graham, Tex., Aug. 1, 1951; s. William Hyde and Florence E. (Myrick) S.; m. Adrienne Casale, Dec. 31, 1983; children: William Dean II, Susan Paige. Student, Tyler (Tex.) Jr. Coll., El Centro Coll., Dallas, U. Tex., Arlington. Various positions with The Dallas Morning News, Tyler Morning Telegraph, Wichita Falls Record News, and others, 1966-78; various positions with Albritton Communications Co., 1976-78, pres. newspaper div., 1978-83; pres. Gloucester County Times, Inc., 1983-85; pres. MediaNews Group, Inc., 1985-88, vice chmn., chief exec. officer, 1988—; chmn., pres. The Houston Post, 1988—. Mem. Salvation Army, Am. Heart Assn. of Ft. Bend County. Mem. Am. Newspaper Assn., So. Newspapers Assn., New Eng. Newspaper Assn., N.J. Press Assn., Greater Houston Partnership Assn., Tex. Daily Newspaper Assn. Baptist. Office: The Houston Post PO Box 4747 4747 South Fwy Houston TX 77004-6063 also: Media News Group Loop Central One 4888 Loop Central Dr # 525 Houston TX 77081

SINHA, ALOK KUMAR, software design engineer; b. Hazaribagh, Bihar, India, Apr. 7, 1963; came to U.S., 1985; s. Ajit Kumar and Chinmoyee (Ghosh) S. B in Tech., Banaras Hindu U., 1984; MS in Mining Engring., U. Alaska, 1987, MS in Computer Sci., 1989. Systems engr. Computer Maintenance Corp., Calcutta, India, 1984-85; VAX systems adminstr. U. Alaska, Fairbanks, 1988-89; product support engr. Microsoft Corp., Redmond, Wash., 1989-90; software design engr. Microsoft Corp., Redmond, 1990—; X.500/Distributed File system test team lead Microsoft, Redmond, 1990—. Contbr. articles to profl. jours. Vol. Wash. Spl. Summer Olympics for Disabled Athletes, Wash., 1990—. Mem. Assn. for Computing Machinery (spl. invest group on computer comm.), Phi Kappa Phi. Office: Microsoft One Microsoft Pl Redmond WA 98053

SINHA, DIPENDRA KUMAR, engineering educator; b. Patna, Bihar, India, Feb. 18, 1945; came to U.S., 1984; s. Jogendra P. and Saraswati S.; m. Basanti Shrivastawa, July 30, 1971; children: Priyamvada, Udayan. BS, Patna U., 1967; postgrad. diploma in Bus. Mgmt., Xavier Inst., Jamshedpur, India, 1976; MS in Mechanical Engring., U. Manchester, Eng., 1978, PhD, 1981. Asst. design engr. TATA STEEL, Jamshedpur, India, 1970-74, devel. engr., 1974-76; asst. prof. U. Manitoba, Winnipeg, Man., Can., 1981-84, Va. Mil. Inst., Lexington, Va., 1984-85; assoc. prof. U. Wis., Platteville, 1985-87; assoc. prof. San Francisco State U., 1987-91, prof., 1991—; mem. Engring. Design Graphics Modernization Adv. Com., U. Tex., 1988-90. Author: Engineering Graphics with AutoCAD, 1990; co-author: Finite Element Analysis by Microcomputers, 1988, Advanced Machine Design by Microcomputers, 1989, Computer Aided Design: An Integrated Approach, 1992; contbr. articles profl. jours. Mem. Indo-U.S. Forum for Cooperative Rsch. and Technology Transfer, Morgantown, W.Va., 1989. Mem. ASME (assoc.), Am. Soc. Engring. Edn. Home: 515 Chesterton Ave Belmont CA 94002-2516 Office: San Francisco State U 1600 Holloway Ave San Francisco CA 94132-1722

SINISHTA, GJON, pastoral associate; b. Podgorica, Yugoslavia, Apr. 8, 1930; came to U.S., 1965; s. Prenk and Viktoria (Gjokaj) S.; m. Maria Theresa Amaya, Jan. 3, 1968; 1 child, Michael John. Degree in radio broadcasting-journalism, Journalist Broadcasting Sch., Belgrade, Yugoslavia, 1947; student, Colombiere Coll., Clarkston, Mich., 1966-67, John Carroll U., 1967-68, U. Santa Clara, 1973-74. Broadcaster, translator, writer Yugoslav Broadcasting Inst., Belgrade, 1947-56; imprisoned for anti-communist propaganda, 1956-61; acct. Zagreb (Croatia) Textile Co., 1961-63; escaped from Yugoslavia, in refugee camps in Italy, 1963-64; assembler Ford Motor Co., Wixom, Mich., 1965-66; pressman GM, Cleve., 1967-68; asst. food mgr. U. Santa Clara, Calif., 1968-71, dir. Mission Ch., 1971-77; pastoral assoc. St. Ignatius Ch., U. San Francisco, 1977—; exec. sec. Albanian Cath. Inst. Univ. San Francisco, 1970-93; editor Albanian Cath. Bull., San Francisco, 1980—. Author: The Fulfilled Promise: A documentary account on religious persecution in Albania, 1976; co-author: (booklet) Sacrafice for Albania, 1966, Mediaterranean Europe Phrasebook, 1992. Lt. Yugoslav Army, 1951-52. Mem. Amnesty Internat. Democrat. Roman Catholic. Home: 650 Parker Ave San Francisco CA 94118-4267 Office: U San Francisco St Ignatius Ch 2300 Fulton St San Francisco CA 94117-1080

SINNETTE, JOHN TOWNSEND, JR., research scientist, consultant; b. Rome, Ga., Nov. 4, 1909; s. John T. Sinnette and Katherine Alice Lyon. BS, Calif. Inst. Tech., 1931, MS, 1933. Chemist Met. Water Dist., Banning, Calif., 1937-39, Boulder City, Nev., 1939-40; physicist U.S. Bur. Reclamation, Boulder City, 1940-41; rsch. scientist Nat. Adv. Com. for Aeronautics, Langley Field, Va., 1941-43, Cleve., 1943-51; cons. physicist U.S. Naval Ordnance Test Sta., Pasadena, Calif., 1951-58, Cleve. Pneumatic Industries, El Segundo, Calif., 1958-60; tech. dir. Hydrosystems Co., El Segundo, 1960-62; physicist Thrust Systems Corp., Costa Mesa, Calif., 1963-64; lectr. compressor design Case Inst. Tech., 1946-48; cons. many firms in aeronautical and related industries, 1950-79. Contbr. papers to sci. meetings and confs. Vol. Am. Cancer Soc., Costa Mesa, Calif., 1976-80, Cancer Control Soc., 1979-82; contbr. Action on Smoking and Health, Washington, 1985-93. Mem. AAAS, Am. Statistical Assn., Am. Math Soc., Nat. Health Fed. Democrat. Home: 135 N B St Tustin CA 92680-3110

SINOTO, YOSIHIKO H., archaeologist, educator; b. Tokyo, Sept. 3, 1924; came to U.S., 1954; s. Yosito and Yosie (Yanagimoto) S.; m. Kazuko Sato, Apr. 24, 1949; 1 child, Akihiko. BA in Anthropology, U. Hawaii, 1958; DSc, U. Hokkaido, Sapporo, Japan, 1962. Archaeologist Archaeol. Inst. Japan, Chiba Prefecture, 1949-54; fellow in anthropology Bishop Mus., Honolulu, 1958-61, anthropologist, 1962-89, chmn. dept. anthropology, 1970-89, sr. anthropologist, Kenneth Pike Emory disting. chair, 1990—; affiliate faculty Grad. Sch. U. Hawaii, Honolulu, 1962—; cons. Marshall Islands Historic Places Rev. Bd., 1986—; mem. Hawaii Historic Places Rev. Bd., 1986—; assoc. Micronesia Area Rsch. Ctr., U. Guam, 1988—. Grantee Nat. Geographic Soc., 1973, 74, 79, Ter. Govt. French Polynesia, 1982, 84, 86, numerous others. Mem. Japanese Archaeol. Assn., Polynesian Soc., Soc. Am. Archaeology, Indo-Pacific Prehistory Assn., Soc. Oceanists. Office: Dept Anthropology Bishop Mus PO Box 19000A Honolulu HI 96817-0916

SINSIGALLI, ANDREW THOMAS, mutual fund wholesaler; b. Naha, Okinawa, Japan, May 14, 1967; came to U.S., 1967; s. Robert Author and Margaret Ann (O'Brien) S.; m. Else Marie Green, July 18, 1992. BA, U. Mass., 1990. Regional market rep. Wells Fargo Bank, San Francisco, 1990-91; regional mutual fund wholesaler Stephens Inc./Wells Fargo Bank, Laguna Niguel, Calif., 1991—. Mem. Am. Assn. Individual Investors. Roman Catholic. Home: 30902 Clubhouse Dr # 8H Laguna Niguel CA 92677

SINTON, WILLIAM MERZ, astronomer, educator; b. Balt., Apr. 11, 1925; s. Robert Nelson and Alma Merz (Summers) S.; m. Marjorie Anne Korner, June 4, 1960; children: Robert William, David Theodore, Alan Nelson. AB, Johns Hopkins U., 1949, PhD, 1953. Rsch. assoc. Johns Hopkins U., Balt., 1953-54; rsch. assoc., lectr. Harvard U., Cambridge, Mass., 1954-57; astronomer Lowell Obs., Flagstaff, Ariz., 1957-66; prof. physics and astronomy U. Hawaii, Honolulu, 1966-90; ret., 1990; adj. astronomer Lowell Obs., Flagstaff, Ariz., 1989—. Co-author: Tools of the Astronomer, 1961; contbr. articles to sci. jours. Sgt. U.S. Army, 1943-46, ETO. Fellow Optical Soc. Am. (Adolph Lomb medal 1954); mem. Am. Astron. Soc. (committeeman div. planetary sci. 1971-73), Am. Geophys. Union. Home: 850 E David Dr Flagstaff AZ 86001-4731

SIRI, JEAN BRANDENBURG, citizen advocate; b. Lakota, N.D., Mar. 11, 1920; d. Tunis Orville and Edith Marion (Molloy) Brandenburg; m. William E. Siri, Dec. 3, 1947; children—Lynn, Ann. B.S., Jamestown Coll., 1942; postgrad., U. Calif.-Berkeley, 1945-46, U. Calif., San Francisco, 1944. Biologist, Donner Lab., U. Calif., Berkeley, 1945-52. Clin coun. mem. State Solid Waste & Resource Recovery Adv. Coun., Sacramento, 1973-75; dir., chmn. Stege Sanitary Dist., El Cerrito, Calif., 1975-79; elected bd. dirs. ward 1 East Bay Regional Park, 1993—; coun. mem. El Cerrito City Coun., 1980-85, 87-91, mayor, 1982-83, 88-89. Mem. Save San Francisco Bay Assocs., Contra Costa Hazardous Waste Task Force, 1985-86, County Environ. Health Coordinating Council, 1985-88, County Hazardous Materials Commn., 1986-92, County Pub. and Environ. Health Adv. Bd., 1987—, Contra Costa Housing Trust Fund Task Force, 1991; founder, chmn. West County Toxics Coalition, 1986—; alternate solid waste West Contra Costa Joint Powers Authority, 1988-89. Served to lt. USNR, 1942-44. Recipient Sol Feinstone Environ. award U. Syracuse, 1977, Clean Air award Lung Assn. Santa Clara, 1976, Get Tough on Toxics Environ. award, 1986, Spl. award Homeless and Hungry Volunteers of Am., 1987. Mem. LWV, NAACP, Gray Panthers, Native Plant Soc., Sierra Club (city rep. to county homeless adv. com. 1988-93, Scope Environ. award 1986), Calif. State Local Emergency Planning Com. (rep. 1990-92), Audubon Soc., West Contra Costa Conservation League (pres.), League of Conservation Voters (dir 1978-79), West Contra Costa Transp. Joint Powers Authority. Democrat.

SIROTKIN, PHILLIP LEONARD, educational administrator; b. Moline, Ill., Aug. 2, 1923; s. Alexander and Molly (Berghaus) S.; m. Cecille Sylvia Gussack, May 1, 1945; children—Steven Marc, Laurie Anne. B.A. (McGregor Found. scholar), Wayne State U., 1945; M.A., U. Chgo., 1947, Ph.D. (Walgreen Found. scholar, Carnegie fellow), 1951. Lectr. U. Chgo., 1949-50; instr. Wellesley Coll., 1950-52, asst. prof. polit. sci., 1953-57; asso. dir. Western Interstate Commn. Higher Edn., Boulder, Colo., 1957-60; exec. asst. to dir. Calif. Dept. Mental Hygiene, Sacramento, 1960-63; asst. dir. NIMH, 1964-66, asso. dir., 1967-71, cons., 1971-73; exec. v.p., acad. v.p. State U. N.Y. at Albany, 1971-76; exec. dir. Western Interstate Commn. Higher Edn., Boulder, Colo., 1976-90, sr. adviser, 1990—; sr. adviser Midwestern Legis. Higher Edn. Steering Com., Boulder, Colo., 1990-91; sr. cons. Midwestern Higher Edn. Commn., 1991—; bd. dirs. Boulder County Mental Health Ctr., 1992—; mem. ovesight commn. Hispanic Agenda, Larasa, 1992—; mem. nat. adv. com. Soc. Coll. and Univ. Planning, 1976, adv. panel, rev. state system higher edn. in N.D., 1986, gov.'s com. on bi-state med. edn. plan for N.D. and S.D., 1988-90, Edn. Commn. States' Nat. Task Force for Minority Achievement in Higher Edn., 1989-91; cons. Bur. Health Manpower Edn., NIH, 1972-74, Nat. Ctr. Hlth Svcs. Rsch., 1975-85; spl. cons. AID, 1963-64; case writer Resources for the Future, 1954-55; mem.

1st U.S. Mission on Mental Health to USSR, 1967. Author: The Echo Park Dam Controversy and Upper Colorado River Development, 1959. Bd. dirs. Council Social Work Edn., 1959-60. Served to 1st lt. AUS, 1943-46. Recipient Superior Service award HEW, 1967; Wellesley Coll. Faculty Research award, 1956. Home: 299 Green Rock Dr Boulder CO 80302-4745 Office: PO Drawer P Boulder CO 80302

SISEMORE, CLAUDIA, producer-director educational films and videos; b. Salt Lake City, Sept. 16, 1937; d. Darrell Daniel and Alice Larril (Barton) S. BS in English, Brigham Young U., 1959; MFA in Filmmaking, U. Utah, 1976. Cert. secondary tchr., Utah. Tchr. English, drama and writing Salt Lake Sch. Dist., Salt Lake City, 1959-66; tchr. English Davis Sch. Dist., Bountiful, Utah, 1966-68; ind. filmmaker Salt Lake City, 1972—; filmmaker-in-residence Wyo. Coun. for Arts and Nat. Endowment for Arts, Dubois, Wyo., 1977-78; producer, dir. ednl. films Utah Office Edn., Salt Lake City, 1979—. Prodr., dir. Beginning of Winning, 1984 (film festival award 1984), Dancing through the Magic Eye, 1986, Se Hable Espanol, 1986-87; writer, dir., editor film Building on a Legacy, 1988, videos Energy Conservation, 1990, Alternative Energy Sources, 1990, Restructuring Learning, 1991, Kidsercise, 1991, Traditional Energy Sources, 1992, A State Government Team, 1992, Problem Solving Using Math Manipulatives, 1993; exhibited (abstract paintings) in group show Phillips Gallery; represented in numerous pvt. and pub. collections. Juror Park City (Utah) Arts Festival, 1982, Utah Arts Festival, Salt Lake City, 1982, Am. Film Festival, 1985-86, Best of West Film Festival, 1985-86; bd. dirs. Utah Media Ctr., Salt Lake City, 1981-87; mem. multi-disciplinary program Utah Arts Coun., Salt Lake City, 1983-87. Recipient award Utah Media Ctr., 1984, 85; Nat. Endowment for Arts grantee, 1978, Utah Arts Coun. grantee, 1980. Mormon. Office: Utah Office Edn 250 E 500 S Salt Lake City UT 84111-3204

SISKIND, LAWRENCE JAY, lawyer; b. Swampscott, Mass., July 4, 1952; s. Bernard Sumner and Selma (Lipsky) S.; m. Patricia Williams, Feb. 15, 1986; children: Leah, Cory. BA, Harvard U., 1974, JD, 1978. Bar: Calif. Assoc. McCutchen, Doyle, Brown & Enersen, San Francisco, 1979-81, Cooper, White & Cooper, San Francisco, 1981-85; ptnr. Cooper, White & Cooper, 1986-87, 89—; spl. counsel immigration-related unfair employment practices U.S. Dept. Justice, Washington, 1987-89; bd. dirs. Am. Jewish Com., San Francisco, 1984-87, 89—, Bus. Laws, Inc., Chesterland, Ohio, Internat. Inst., San Francisco. Contbr. numerous articles to profl. pubs. Mem. ABA, Calif. Bar Assn., San Francisco Barristers Club, Phi Beta Kappa. Republican. Office: Cooper White & Cooper 201 California St Piedmont CA 94611

SISSON, JOHN ROSS, marine engineer; b. Everett, Mass., July 25, 1926; s. John Barkley and Nellie (Gronevoudt) S.; m. Alice Christine Wilson, Apr. 23, 1950; children: John C., Robin C. Lynam, Raymond C. BS in Marine Engring., U.S. Merchant Marine Acad., 1946. Marine supt. U.S. Steel, Pitts., 1956-59, Puerto Ordaz, Venezuela, 1959-63; devel. engr. Brookhaven Nat. Lab., L.I., N.Y., 1963-67; marine supt. Exxon Internat., Florham Park, N.J., 1967-84; dir. engring. Mil. Sealift Command (Pacific Fleet), Oakland, Calif., 1984—; marine surveyor Am. Bur. Shipping Puerto Ordaz, 1960-63. Served to lt. cmdr. USN, 1949-54. Home: 271 Calle La Mesa Moraga CA 94556-1644 Office: Mil Sealift Command Pacific Bldg 310 Naval Supply Ctr Oakland CA 94625-5010

SITES, BETSI, small business owner; b. N.Y.C., Jan. 10, 1946; d. Kenneth Graham and Marjorie Christine (Smith) S.; 1 child, Tchikima. BA in Biology, Boston U., 1968. Master hypnotherapist. Electron microscopist Harvard Med. Sch., Boston, 1966-68; massage therapist Berkeley (Calif.) Sch. of Massage, 1969; secondary sch. tchr. sci., math., English Peace Corps Africa, Kananga/Lubumbashi/Kinshasa, Zaire, 1972-75; baker, vegetarian cook True Nature Health Foods, Boulder Creek, Calif., 1987-92; cross-cultural rels. coord. Campaign for the Earth, Boulder, Colo., 1991-93; music and entertainment coord. Campaign for the Earth, Earth Summit, Rio de Janeiro, 1992; asst. producer Boulder/Moscow Spacebridge Project, summer 1992; owner, mgr. Comfey Carrier, 1985-93; free-lance writer. Home: PO Box 447 Santa Cruz CA 95061

SITES, JAMES PHILIP, lawyer, consul; b. Detroit, Sept. 17, 1948; s. James Neil and Inger Marie (Krogh) S.; m. Barbara Teresa Mazurek, Apr. 9, 1978; children: Philip Erling, Teresa Elizabeth. Student, U. Oslo, Norway, 1968-69; BA, Haverford U., 1970; JD, Haverford Coll., 1973; ML in Taxation, Georgetown U., 1979. Bar: Md. 1973, D.C. 1974, U.S. Supreme Ct. 1978, Mont. 1984, U.S. Tax Ct. 1984, U.S. Dist. Ct. Mont. 1984, U.S. Ct. Appeals (9th cir.) 1988. Law clk. to judge James C. Morton, Jr. Ct. Spl. Appeals Md., Annapolis, 1974-75; law clk. to judge Orman W. Ketcham Superior Ct. D.C., Washington, 1975-76; gen. atty. U.S. Immigration & Naturalization Svc., Washington, 1976-77; trial atty. tax div. U.S. Dept. Justice, Washington, 1977-84; ptnr. Crowley, Haughey, Hanson, Toole & Dietrich, Billings, Mont., 1984—; consul for Govt. of Norway State of Mont., Billings, 1987—; instr. Norwegian Ea. Mont. Coll., 1987-88, Sons of Norway, 1989—; v.p. Scandinavian Studies Found., 1989—; bd. dirs. Billings Com. on Fgn. Rels., 1988—. State reporter Maxwell Macmillan State and Local Taxes Weekly, Englewood Cliffs, N.J., 1990—. Mem. local exec. bd. Ea. Mont. Coll., 1993—. U. Oslo scholar, 1969; recipient Peace Rsch. award Haverford Coll., 1970. Mem. Md. State Bar Assn., Mont. State Bar (co-chmn. com. on income and property taxes 1987-91, chair tax and probate sect. 1991-92, chair tax litigation subcom. 1992—), D.C. Bar, Continuing Legal Edn. Inst., Am. Immigration Lawyers Assn., Norwegian-Am. C. of C., Billings Petroleum Club, Hilands Golf Club, Kenwood Golf and Country Club, Billings Stamp Club, Elks, Masons. Office: Crowley Haughey Hanson Toole & Dietrich Consulate for Norway 490 N 31st PO Box 2529 Billings MT 59103-2529

SIVADAS, IRAJA (WILLIAM SHEPARD WATKINS), educator; b. Palo Alto, Calif., Aug. 6, 1950; s. Charles Edward and Wilma Barbara (Comstock) Watkins; m. Ophelia Nuñez, June 9, 1979. AS in Math., Cabrillo Community Coll., 1975; BA in Math., U. Calif., Santa Cruz, 1978, MA in Math., 1987; postgrad., San Jose State U., 1981-83. Prodn. head backward wave oscillator Watkins-Johnson, Scotts Valley, Calif., 1978-80; supr. final quality assurance Intel, Santa Cruz, Calif., 1980-81; instr. math. Cabrillo Community Coll., Aptos, Calif., 1983-87, Kauai Community Coll., Lihue, Hawaii, 1987—. Co-author: Hawaiian Profiles in Non-Violence, Kauai County Energy Self-Sufficiency Report. U.S. del. Finastras Peace Conf., San Salvador, El Salvador, 1985; mem. energy adv. bd. Kauai County, 1989—; mem. Spark Matsunaga Inst. Peace, 1988—, exec. com., 1989—; 28th Dist. Dem. sec., Calif., 1986-88; participant Vets. Fast for Life (fasted 23 days on water), 1986. With USN, 1969-72, Vietnam. Mem. Am. Math. Soc., Math. Assn. Am., Hawaiian Acad. Scis., U. Hawaii Profl. Assmebly, Naval Order, VFW (post 5888, liaison Nicaraguan Govt. 1984-86, Santa Cruz chmn. 1984-87, commdr. 1987, awards 1986, 87). Hindu. Home: PO Box 607 Hanapepe HI 96716-0607 Office: Kauai Community Coll 3-1901 Kaumualii Hwy Lihue HI 96766

SIVERSON, RANDOLPH MARTIN, political science educator; b. Los Angeles, July 29, 1940; s. Clifford Martin and Lorene (Sanders) S.; m. Mary Suzanne Strayer, Dec. 31, 1966; children: Andrew, Erica, Courtney. AB, San Francisco State U., 1962, MA, 1965; PhD, Stanford U., 1969. Lectr. polit. sci. Stanford U., Calif., 1967; asst. prof. U. Calif., Riverside, 1967-70; asst. prof. U. Calif., Davis, 1970-75, assoc. prof., 1975-81, prof., 1981—; Fulbright lectr. El Colegio de Mexico, Mexico City, 1974-75; vis. prof. Naval Postgrad. Sch., Monterey, Calif., 1980. Co-author: The Diffusion of War, 1991; editor: (with others) Change in the International System, 1980; editor Internat. Interactions, 1984-91; mem. editorial bd. Am. Polit. Sci. Rev., 1989-91. Mem. Internat. Studies Assn., Am. Polit. Sci. Assn., Western Polit. Sci. Assn. (pres. 1991), Midwest Polit. Sci. Assn. Roman Catholic. Office: U Calif Davis Dept Polit Sci Davis CA 95616

SIVERSON, SUSAN JO, credit union executive; b. Lexington, Ky., Nov. 6, 1960; d. Kenneth and Ruth Tollefson; m. David J. Siverson, June 8, 1985; children: Eric, Trent. BA, Seattle Pacific U., 1981; MBA, Baylor U., 1982. Info. systems mgr. Standard Autobody Supply, Seattle, 1983; mgr., treas. Seattle Pacific Credit Union, 1984—; bus. cons., Seattle, 1990—. Mem. nursing home ministry team Free Meth. Ch., 1974—, mem. music com., 1988, nursery co-coord., 1989. Office: Seattle Pacific Credit Union 2 Nickerson St Ste 102 Seattle WA 98109-1652

SIYAN, KARANJIT SAINT GERMAIN SINGH, software engineer; b. Mauranipur, India, Oct. 16, 1954; came to U.S., 1978; s. Ahal Singh and Tejinder Kaur (Virdi) S.; m. Dei Gayle Cooper, Apr. 8, 1987. B in Tech. Electronics, Indian Inst. Tech., 1976, M in Tech. Computer Sci., 1978; MS in Engring., U. Calif., Berkeley, 1980, postgrad in computer sci. Cert. enterprise netware engr.; cert. microsoft profl. Sr. mem. tech. staff Rolm Corp., San Jose, Calif., 1980-84; cons. Siyan Cons. Svcs., L.A., 1985-86, Emigrant, Mont., 1987—. Author, sr. instr.: Learning Tree Internat., L.A., 1985—; author: Network - The Professional Reference, 1992; co-author: Downsizing Netware, LAN Connectivity; author seminars on Novell Networking, TCP/IP networks, Windows NT, Solaris-PC Network Integration. Mem. IEEE, ACM, CNEPA, ECNE, Windos NT MCP, Kappa Omicron Phi.

SIZEMORE, HERMAN MASON, JR., newspaper executive; b. Halifax, Va., Apr. 15, 1941; s. Herman Mason and Hazel (Johnson) S.; m. Connie Catterton, June 22, 1963; children: Jill, Jennifer. AB in History, Coll. William and Mary, 1963; postgrad., U. Mo., 1965; MBA, U. Wash., 1985. Reporter Norfolk (Va.) Ledger-Star, summers 1961, 62, 63; copy editor Seattle Times, 1965-70, copy-desk chief, 1970-75, asst. mng. editor, 1975-77, mng. editor, 1977-81, prodn. dir., 1981-83, asst. gen. mgr., 1984, v.p., gen. mgr., 1985, pres., chief operating officer, 1985—; vis. instr. Sch. Comms. U. Wash., 1972-78; bd. dirs. Times Comms. Co., Walla Walla Union-Bull, Inc., Yakima Herald-Republic, Times Community Newspapers, Inc., Northwestern Mut. Life Ins. Co., 1993—, mem. policyowner examining com., 1985, chmn., 1986. Bd. dirs. Ctrl. Puget Sound Camp Fire Coun., 1985-91, pres., 1989-90, bd. dirs. Ptnrs. in Pub. Edn., 1987-88, Downtown Seattle Assn.; adv. coun. Puget Sound Blood Ctr. and Program. Named Seattle Newsmaker of Tomorrow, 1978. Mem. AP Mng. Editors, Soc. Profl. Journalists, Newspaper Assn. Am., Pacific N.W. Newspaper Assn., Allied Daily Newspapers Washington, Coll. William and Mary Alumni Assn. (bd. dirs.), Greater Seattle C. of C., U. Wash. Exec. MBA Alumni Assn. (pres. 1988, bd. dirs.), Wash. Athletic Club, Rainier Club, Rotary. Methodist. Home: 2054 NW Blue Ridge Dr Seattle WA 98177-5428 Office: Seattle Times PO Box 70 Seattle WA 98111-0070

SIZEMORE, NICKY LEE, computer scientist; b. N.Y.C., Feb. 13, 1946; d. Ralph Lee and Edith Ann (Wangler) S.; m. Frauke Julika Hoffmann, Oct. 31, 1974; 1 child, Jennifer Lee Sizemore; 1 stepchild, Mark Anthony Miracle. BS in Computer Sci., SUNY, 1989. Sgt. first class U.S. Army, 1964-68, 70-86; computer operator UNIVAC, Washington, 1968-69, programmer, 1969-70; programmer/analyst Ultra Systems, Inc., Sierra Vista, Ariz., 1986-87; computer scientist Comarco, Inc., Sierra Vista, 1987-92, ARC, Profl. Svcs. Group, Sierra Vista, 1992—; speaker numerous confs., seminars, symposia. Mem. Am. Assn. for Artificial Intelligence, Assn. for Computing Machinery, Computer Soc. of IEEE, Armed Forces Comms.-Electronics Assn., Am. Def. Preparedness Assn. Home: 880 Charles Dr Sierra Vista AZ 85635 Office: ARC Profl Svcs Group 1838 Paseo San Luis Sierra Vista AZ 85635

SJOEN, KENNETH DIOMED, protective services official; b. Haugesund, Karmoy, Norway, Nov. 13, 1948; came to U.S., 1949; s. Simon Jonas and Anastasia (Savvon) S.; m. Janet Rae Jacobson, Jan. 17, 1970 (div. Jan. 1988); children: Erik Simon, Leanne Deborah; m. Monica Ellen Wniegar, Feb. 14, 1988. AA, Santa Rosa (Calif.) Jr. Coll., 1972; BA, Golden Gate U., 1978; MS, Pepperdine U., 1986; cert., FBI Acad., 1992. Dep. sheriff Somona County Sheriff's Dept., Calif., 1972-74; lt. Rohnert Park Dept. of Public Safety, 1974-84; law enforcement specialist Nat. Sch. Safety Ctr., 1984-86, U.S. Dept. Justice, 1984-86; dir. of public safety Pepperdine U., Malibu, Calif., 1986-89; chief of police U. Nev. Police, Reno, 1989—; lectr. in field; instr. U.S. Dept. of Treasury; cons. Nat. Sch. Safety Ctr. Capt. USNG, 1979-85. Mem. Internat. Assn. of Chiefs of Police, Nev. Chiefs and Sheriffs Assn., Golden Gate U. Alumni Assn., Pepperdine U. Alumni Assn. Republican. Lutheran. Office: U Nevada Police 1305 Evans Ave Reno NV 89557

SJOGREN, CLIFFORD FRANK, JR., university dean, consultant; b. Detroit, June 30, 1928; s. Clifford Frank and Mabel Pauline (Gould) S.; m. Patricia Ruth Chick, June 20, 1953; children: Stephen Jon, Janice Sue, Sue Ann, Sigurd Franz. BS, Cen. Mich. U., Mt. Pleasant, 1954; MA, U. Mich., 1958, PhD, 1972. Tchr., counselor local high schs. Mich., 1954-60; admissions counselor Western Mich. U., Kalamazoo, 1960-64; asst. dir., dir. admissions U. Mich., Ann Arbor, 1964-72, dir. admissions, 1972-88; cons. admissions Coll. Prelims, Traverse City, Mich., 1988-89; dean admissions, fin. aid U. So. Calif., L.A., 1989—; trustee Internat. Baccalaureat, N.A., N.Y.C., 1973—. Contbr. articles to profl. publs. With USN, 1948-52. Mem. Am. Assn. Collegiate Registrars and Admissions Officers (hon., pres. 1981-82), Nat. Assn. Fgn. Student Affairs (hon.), Rotary Internat. Republican. Home: 788 E California Blvd Pasadena CA 91106-3844 Office: U So Calif Admissions Office University Park Los Angeles CA 90089-0911

SJOGREN, SANDRA LEE, lawyer; b. Wichita, Kans., Dec. 18, 1954; d. Philip Wendell and Mona Maxine (Wells) Corp. BA, Wichita State U., 1978; JD, U. Utah, 1984. Asst. atty. gen. State of Utah, Salt Lake City, 1984—. Mem. Utah State Bar (disciplinary hearing panel com. 1992—), Salt Lake County Bar. Office: Utah Atty Gen's Office 36 S State St 11th Fl Salt Lake City UT 84111

SJOHOLM, PAUL FREDRIC, optical engineer; b. Everett, Wash., Feb. 22, 1961; s. Frederic Pierre and Joanne Marie (Pearson) S.; m. Janet Diane Scherschligt, June 1, 1991. BS in Physics, Seattle Pacific U., Seattle, 1983; MS in Applied Math., U. Wash., 1989. Engr. Boeing Def. and Space Group, Seattle, 1984—; adj. prof. in physics Seattle Pacific U., 1992—. Office: The Boeing Co Mail Stop 8H-18 PO Box 3999 Seattle WA 98124

SJOLANDER, GARY WALFRED, physicist; b. Bagley, Minn., Dec. 5, 1942; s. Tage Walfred and Evelyn Mildred (Kaehn) S.; m. Joann Lorraine Tressler, June 18, 1966; 1 child, Toby Ryan. BS in Physics, U. Minn., 1970, MS in Physics, 1974, PhD in Physics, 1975. Rsch. assoc. U. Minn., Mpls., 1975-76; rsch. scientist Johns Hopkins U., Balt., 1977-78, sr. physicist, 1978-82; sr. engr. Westinghouse Electric Corp., Annapolis, Md., 1982-85; sr. group engr. Martin Marietta Astronautic Group, Denver, 1985—; pres. Cypress Improvement Assn., Inc., Severna Park, Md., 1984-85; advisor Inroads/Denver, Inc., 1986-88. Author numerous articles in field. With USAF, 1960-64. Mem. Am. Phys. Soc., Am. Geophys. Union, AIAA, The Planetary Soc. Lutheran. Home: 811 W Kettle Ave Littleton CO 80120-4443 Office: Martin Marietta Astronautics Group PO Box 179 Denver CO 80201-0179

SJOSTROM, JOAN SEVIER, travel consultant; b. Denver, Nov. 10, 1931; d. George Field and Martha Watson (Turnbull) Sevier; m. Rex William Sjostrom, Mar. 16, 1952; children: Sandra, Anne, John, Sharon. Student, Colo. State U., 1949-51. Bookkeeper U.S. Nat. Bank, Denver, 1951-52, First Nat. Bank, Ft. Collins, Colo., 1952, Larimer County Credit Assn., Ft. Collins, 1953-55, Fox Drug, Castle Rock, Colo., 1974-86; owner, mgr. Travel Haus Inc., Castle Rock, 1984—. Vol. Swedish Emergency Ctr., 1976-82, Douglas County Schs. Spl. Edn. Program, 1980-84; mem. Interfaith Task Forceboard, 1987-88; mem. Douglas County Bd. Edn., 1978-88; mem. Douglas County Placement Alternative Commn., Castle Rock, 1984—; mem. D.C. Schs. Sr. Program, Castle Rock, 1992. Mem. Castle Rock Rotary (v.p. 1992—, pres. 1993-94, dist. scholarship 1991, 92, 93). Republican. Lutheran. Home: 2072 W Wolfensberger Rd Castle Rock CO 80104 Office: Travel Haus Inc 741 Wilcox Castle Rock CO 80104

SJOSTROM, REX WILLIAM, aerospace executive, consultant; b. Norcross, Minn., July 8, 1930; s. William Andrew and Ruth Francis (Cushman) S.; m. Joan Sevier, Mar. 16, 1952; children: Sandra L., Anne M., John W., Sharon M. BSCE, Colo. St. U., 1952, MSEE, 1956. Registered profl. engr., Colo. Staff engr. Martin Marietta Corp., Denver, 1956-84; v.p. space systems div. Martin Marietta Corp., 1984-92; aerospace cons., 1992—; dir. engring. Dean's Adv. Bd., Colo. State U., Ft. Collins, 1983-86. Recipient Pub. Service award NASA, 1976. Mem. Sigma Xi. Republican. Lutheran. Home: 2072 W Wolfensberger Rd Castle Rock CO 80104-9635

SKAGEN, JAMES COLVIN, athletic director; b. Shelton, Wash., Mar. 5, 1931; s. James C. and Gudrun (Schultz) S.; m. Muriel I. Landon, Aug. 22, 1959; children: Lynn, Gwyn. BA in Edn., Cen. Wash. State U., 1953, MA in Edn., 1961; postgrad., U. Wash., 1960-61, Seattle Pacific U., 1964-65. Tchr., coach Carnation (Wash.) schs., 1957-61, Edmonds (Wash.) Sch. Dist., 1961-67, Kent (Wash.) Sch. Dist., 1967-71; athletic dir., phys. edn. tchr., varsity basketball coach Multnomah Sch. of the Bible, Portland, Oreg., 1971—. V.p. Edmonds PTA, 1965. Mam. Nat. LIttle Coll. Athletic Assn. (pres. 1975), Pacific N.W. Coll. Conf. (v.p. 1983, Coach of Yr. 1977-78, 80-81), Pacific N.W. Nat. Christian Coll. Athletic Assn. (pres. 1984-88). Home: 8435 NE Glisan Ct Portland OR 97220

SKAGGS, DAVID E., congressman; b. Cin., Feb. 22, 1943; s. Charles and Juanita Skaggs; m. Laura Locher, Jan. 3, 1987; 1 child, Matthew; stepchildren: Clare, Will. BA in Philosophy, Wesleyan U., 1964; student law, U. Va., 1964-65; LLB, Yale U., 1967. Bar: N.Y. 1968, Colo. 1971. Assoc. Newcomer & Douglass, Boulder, Colo., 1971-74, 77-78; prin. staff asst. Congressman Tim Wirth, Washington, 1975-77; ptnr. Skaggs, Stone & Sheehy, Boulder, 1978-86; mem. 100th-103rd Congresses from 2d Colo. dist., Washington, 1987—; mem. Appropriations com., subcoms. Commerce and Justice, D.C. Interior, Intelligence com.; mem. Colo. Ho. of Reps., Denver, 1980-86, minority leader 1982-85. Former bd. dirs. Rocky Mountain Planned Parenthood, Mental Health Assn. Colo., Boulder County United Way, Boulder Civic Opera. Served to capt. USMC, 1968-71, Vietnam; maj. USMCR, 1971-77. Mem. Colo. Bar Assn., Boulder County Bar Assn., Boulder C. of C. Democrat. Congregationalist. Office: US Ho of Reps 1124 Longworth Bldg Washington DC 20515-0602 also: 9101 Harlan St Ste 130 Westminster CO 80030*

SKAGGS, L. SAM, retail company executive; b. 1922; married. With Am. Stores Co., Salt Lake City, 1945—, chmn. bd., chief exec. officer, from 1966, pres., chief exec. officer, until 1988, now chmn., also bd. dirs.; chmn. Sav-On Drugs, Anaheim, Calif., bd. dirs. Served with USAAF, 1942-45. Office: Am Stores Co PO Box 27447 709 E South Temple Salt Lake City UT 84127 also: Am Stores Co 19100 Von Karman Ave Irvine CA 92715*

SKAGGS, SAMUEL ROBERT, materials scientist; b. Philipsburg, Pa., June 23, 1936; s. Samuel Ralph and Martha Amelia (Montes) S.; m. Barbara Jan Hurley, Apr. 7, 1958; children: Russell, Cheryl, Michael, Teresa, Katherine. BSME, N.Mex. A&MA, 1958; MS in Nuclear Engring., U. N.Mex., Los Alamos, 1967; PhDChemE and Materials Sci., U. N.Mex., Albuquerque, 1972. Mech. engr. Argonne (Ill.) Nat. Lab., 1958-60; staff mem. Los Alamos (N.Mex.) Nat. Lab., 1960-61, 62-67, 71—, program mgr. materials and fossil energy, 1982-86, program mgr. armor protective systems, 1986—; program mgr. U.S. Dept. Energy, Germantown, Md., 1981-82; cons. USAF, 1970-80. Author 30 tech. pubs. in high temperature ceramics. Field coordinator N.Mex. State Search and Rescue Operation, 1961-87, patrol leader and regional dir. Rocky Mountain div. Nat. Ski Patrol, 1978-84. Served to lt. U.S. Army 1961-62, capt. Res. Mem. Am. Ceramic Soc. (life), AAAS. Roman Catholic. Home: RR 11 Box 81E Santa Fe NM 87501-9810 Office: Los Alamos Nat Lab PO Box 1663 Los Alamos NM 87545-0001

SKAGGS, SANFORD MERLE, lawyer; b. Berkeley, Calif., Oct. 24, 1939; s. Sherman G. and Barbara Jewel (Stinson) S.; m. Sharon Ann Barnes, Sept. 3, 1976; children: Stephen, Paula, Barbara, Darren Peterson. B.A., U. Calif.-Berkeley, 1961, J.D., 1964. Bar: Calif. 1965. Atty. Pacific Gas and Electric Co., San Francisco, 1964-73; gen. counsel Pacific Gas Transmission Co., San Francisco, 1973-75; ptnr. firm Van Voorhis & Skaggs, Walnut Creek, Calif., 1975-85, McCutchen, Doyle, Brown & Enersen, San Francisco and Walnut Creek, 1985—; mem. Calif. Law Revision Commn., 1990—, vice chmn., 1992—; adv. council Lawrence Hall of Sci. U. Calif.-Berkeley, 1988—. Councilman City of Walnut Creek, 1972-78, mayor 1974-75, 76-77; bd. dirs. East Bay Mcpl. Utility Dist., 1978-90, pres. 1982-90; trustee Regional Arts Ctr., Inc., 1980-88, Contra Costa County Law Libr., 1978—. Mem. Calif. State Bar Assn., Contra Costa County Bar Assn., Urban Land Inst., Lambda Alpha, Alpha Delta Phi, Phi Delta Phi. Republican. Office: McCutchen Doyle Brown & Enersen 1331 N California Blvd PO Box V Walnut Creek CA 94596

SKALAGARD, HANS MARTIN, artist; b. Skuo, Faroe Islands, Feb. 7, 1924; s. Ole Johannes and Hanna Elisa (Fredriksen) S.; came to U.S., 1942, naturalized, 1955. Pupil Anton Otto Fisher, 1947; m. Mignon Diana Haack Haegland, Mar. 31, 1955; 1 child, Karen Solveig Sikes. Joined U.S. Mcht. Marine, 1942, advanced through grades to chief mate, 1945, ret., 1965; owner, operator Skalagard Sq., Rigger Art Gallery, Carmel, 1966—; libr. Mayo Hays O'Donnel Libr., Monterey, Calif., 1971-73; painter U.S. Naval Heritage series, 1973—; exhibited in numerous one-man shows including Palace Legion of Honor, San Francisco, 1960, J.F. Howland, 1963-65, Fairmont Hotel, San Francisco, 1963, Galerie de Tours, 1969, 72-73, Pebble Beach Gallery, 1968, Laguna Beach (Calif.) Gallery, 1969, Arden Gallery, Atlanta, 1970, Gilbert Gallery, San Francisco, Maritime Mus. of Monterey, Calif., 1993, Rigger Art Gallery, Carmel, Calif.; group shows: Am. Artists, Eugene, Oreg., Robert Louis Stevenson Exhibit, Carmel Valley Gallery, Biarritz and Paris, France, David Findley Galleries, N.Y.C. and Faroe Island, Europe, numerous others; represented in permanent collections; Naval Post Grad. Sch. and Libr., Allen Knight Maritime Mus., Salvation Army Bldg., Monterey, Calif., Robert Louis Stevenson Sch., Pebble Beach, Anenberg Art Galleries, Chestlibrook Ltd., Skalagard Art Gallery, Carmel, 1984; profiled in profl. jours.; lectr. Bd. dirs. Allen Knight Maritime Mus., 1973—, mem. adv. and acquisition coms., 1973-77. Recipient Silver medal Tommaso Campanella Internat. Acad. Arts, Letters and Scis., Rome, 1970, Gold medal, 1972, Gold medal and hon. life membership Academia Italia dell Arti e del Honoro, 1980, Gold medal for artistic merit Academia d'Italia. Mem. Navy League (bd. dir. Monterey), Internat. Platform Assn., Sons of Norway (cultural dir. 1974-75, 76-77). Subject of cover and article Palette Talk, 1980, Compass mag., 1980. Home: 25197 Canyon Dr Carmel CA 93923-8329 Office: PO Box 6611 Carmel CA 93921-6611 also: Dolores at 5th St Carmel CA 93921

SKARDA, RICHARD JOSEPH, clinical social worker; b. Santa Monica, Calif., Jan. 2, 1952; s. Robert Ralph and Cathryn Marie (Tourek) S. AA, Los Angeles Valley Coll., Van Nuys, Calif., 1976; BA, U. Calif., Berkeley, 1978; MSW, UCLA, 1980. Lic. clin. social worker, Calif.; Diplomate Am. Bd. Clin. Social Workers. Children's services worker Los Angeles County Dept. Children's Services, Panorama City, Calif., 1980-82; police service rep. Los Angeles Police Dept., 1982; psychiatric social worker Penny Lane, Sepulveda, Calif., 1983; children's services worker Ventura (Calif.) County Pub. Social Services Agy., 1983-85; head social work dept. Naval Med. Clinic, Port Hueneme, Calif., 1985—. Mem. dean's coun. UCLA Sch. Social Welfare. With USN, 1970-74. Fellow Calif. Soc. Clin. Social Work; mem. Nat. Assn. Social Workers (diplomate), Acad. Cert. Social Workers. Office: Naval Med Clinic Port Hueneme CA 93043

SKEEN, JOSEPH RICHARD, congressman; b. Roswell, N.Mex., June 30, 1927; s. Thomas Dudley and Ilah (Adamson) S.; m. Mary Helen Jones, Nov. 17, 1945; children: Mary Elisa, Mikell Lee. B.S., Tex. A&M U., 1950. Soil and water engr. Ramah Navajo and Zuni Indians, 1951; rancher Lincoln County, N.Mex., 1952—; mem. N.Mex. Senate, 1960-70, 97th-103rd Congresses from 2nd N.Mex. dist., Washington, D.C., 1981—; mem. appropriations com., subcom. agr., ranking mem. appropriations subcom. defense. Chmn. N.Mex. Republican Party, 1963-66. Served with USN, 1945-46; Served with USAFR, 1949-52. Mem. Nat. Woolgrowers Assn., Nat. Cattle Growers Assn., N.Mex. Woolgrowers Assn., N.Mex. Cattle Growers Assn., N.Mex. Farm and Livestock Bur. Republican. Roman Catholic. Clubs: Elks, Eagles. Office: House of Representatives Washington DC 20515

SKEEN, TODD RICHARD, financial executive; b. Ogden, Utah, May 28, 1950; s. Richard Ellison and Margaret (Badger) S.; m. Sandra Lee Larsen, Aug. 15, 1974; children: Tyler, Kimberlee, Jed, Jordan. BS in Bus. Adminstrn., Weber State Coll., Ogden, 1975. Asst. sales mgr. Bag Boy div. Browning, Morgan, Utah, 1976-79, regional credit mgr., 1979-81, collection mgr., 1981—; bd. dirs. Browning Employees Credit Union, 1984-89, McKay-Dee Credit Union, Ogden, 1991—. Advisor Jr. Achievement Program, Ogden, 1982-85. Named to Outstanding Young Men of Am., 1983. Republican. Mormon. Home: 114 East 5300 South Ogden UT 84405 Office: Browning 1 Browning Pl Morgan UT 84050

SKELTON, DAVID LEE, lawyer; b. Windom, Minn., Apr. 9, 1947; s. Donald P. and Lois L. (Olson) S. BA, U. Minn., 1969; JD, U. San Diego,

1980, LLM in Taxation, 1986. Bar: Calif. 1980. Instrnl. designer tng. courses Northrop Worldwide Aircraft Svcs., 1977-78; tng. analyst computer-assisted instrn. Control Data Corp., 1979-80; pvt. law practice, 1981; ptnr. Ashfield & Skelton, 1981-82; chpt. 13 trustee So. Dist. Calif., San Diego, 1982—. Lt. USN, 1969-76. Mem. Nat. Assn. Chpt. 13 Trustees, San Diego County Bar Assn. Office: Chpt 13 Trustee 620 C St Ste 413 San Diego CA 92101

SKELTON, GEORGE ALBERT, administrative assistant; b. Long Beach, Calif., Dec. 16, 1963; s. George Henry and Audrey Christina (Tucker) S. BA, U. Calif., Irvine, 1985; postgrad., Calif. State U., Fullerton, 1985-86; ABD, Calif. State U., Riverside, 1989, MA, 1991. Adminstrv. intern City of Garden Grove, Calif., 1985-90, adminstrv. analyst, 1990—. Friends scholar U. Calif., 1982, univ. scholar 82-85; Claude Lambe fellow Inst. for Humane Studies, 1988-90, Humane Studies Found. fellow, 1989. Mem. Am. Polit. Sci. Assn., Acad. Polit. Scis. (life), N.Y. Acad. Scis., So. Polit. Sci. Assn., Ctr. for the Study of the Presidency. Home: 12271 Fallingleaf St Garden Grove CA 92640-4208 Office: City of Garden Grove Adminstrv Svcs 11391 Acacia Pky Garden Grove CA 92640-5395

SKELTON, JOHN EDWARD, computer science educator, consultant; b. Amarillo, Tex., May 10, 1934; s. Floyd Wayne and Lucille Annabelle (Padduck) S.; m. Katherine Dow, Mar. 22, 1959; children: Laura Ann, Jeanette Kay, Jeffrey Edward. BA, U. Denver, 1956, MA, 1962, PhD, 1971. Mathematician U.S. Naval Ordnance Lab., Corona, Calif., 1956-59; various sales support and mktg. positions Burroughs Corp., Denver, Detroit, Pasadena, Calif., 1959-67; asst. prof. U. Denver, 1967-74; dir. Computer Ctr., U. Minn., Duluth, 1974-85; prof., dir. computing svcs. Oreg. State U., Corvallis, 1985—; cons. World Bank, China, 1988, Educom Cons. Group, 1985. Author: Introduction to the Basic Language, 1971; co-auhtor: Who Runs the Computer, 1975; also articles. Mem. Assn. for Computing Machinery (pres. Rocky Mountain chpt. 1971, faculty advisor U. Minn. 1980-82, peer rev. team 3 regions 1981-90), Assn. for Spl. Interest Group on Univ. Computing (bd. dirs. 1987-91), Rotary (dist. youth exch. com. 1991—), Sigma Xi (chpt. pres. 1983-84), Phi Kappa Phi (chpt. pres. 1989-90). Episcopalian. Office: Oreg State U Computer Ctr Corvallis OR 97331

SKEWES-COX, BENNET, accountant, educator; b. Valparaiso, Chile, Dec. 12, 1918; came to U.S., 1919, naturalized, 1943; s. Vernon and Edith Page (Smith) S-C.; B.A., U. Calif., Berkeley, 1940; M.A., Georgetown U., 1947; B.B.A., Golden Gate Coll., 1953; m. Mary Osborne Craig, Aug. 31, 1946; children: Anita Page McCann, Pamela Skewes-Cox Anderson, Amy Osborne Skewes-Cox (Mrs. Robert Twiss). Asst. to press officer Am. Embassy, Santiago, Chile, 1941-43; state exec. dir. United World Federalists of Calif., 1948-50; pvt. practice acctg., San Francisco, 1953—; asst. prof. internat. relations San Francisco State U., 1960-62; grad. researcher Stanford (Calif.) U., 1962-63, Georgetown U., Washington, 1963-65; pres. Acad. World Studies, San Francisco, 1969—; sec. Alpha Delta Phi Bldg. Co., San Francisco, 1957—; lectr. in field. Mem. Democratic state central com. Calif., 1958-60, fgn. policy chmn. Calif. Dem. Council, 1959-61, treas. Marin County Dem. Central Com., 1956-62; founder, 1st. chmn. Calif. Council for UN Univ., 1976—; compiler World Knowledge Bank; bd. dirs. Research on Abolition of War; treas. Marin Citizens for Energy Planning. Served as lt. (j.g.), USNR, 1943-46. Mem. Assn. for World Edn. (internat. council 1975—), Am. Soc. Internat. Law, Am. Polit. Sci. Assn., San Francisco Com. Fgn. Relations, Am. Acctg. Assn., Calif. State Univ. Profs., AAUP, Nat. Soc. Public Accts., Fedn. Am. Scientists, UN Assn., Internat. Polit. Sci. Assn. World Federalists Assn., World Govt. Orgns. Coalition (treas.). Clubs: University, Commonwealth of Calif., Lagunitas Country. Author: The Manifold Meanings of Peace, 1964; The United Nations from League to Government, 1965; Peace, Truce or War, 1967. Home: Monte Alegre PO Box 1145 Ross CA 94957-1145 Office: Acad World Studies 2806 Van Ness Ave San Francisco CA 94109-1426

SKIDMORE, DONALD EARL, JR., government official; b. Tacoma, Apr. 27, 1944; s. Donald E. and Ingeborg (Johnsrud) S.; BSc, Evangel Coll., 1968. With Dept. Social and Health Svcs., State of Wash., Yakima, 1967-74; quality rev. specialist Social Security Adminstrn., Seattle, 1974-76, program analyst, Balt., 1976-79, Seattle, 1979-81, quality assurance officer, mgr. Satellite office, Spokane, Wash., 1981-84, program analyst, Seattle, 1984-90, mgmt. analyst, 1990—. Pres., bd. dirs. Compton Court Condo Assn., 1980-81; v.p., trustee Norwood Village, 1987-90; vice chair ops. subcom., mem. citizen's adv. com. METRO, 1987-89; mem. citizen's adv. com. land use planning, Bellevue, Wash., 1988-90. Grad. Bellevue Police Citizen's Acad., 1992. Office: 2201 6th Ave M/S RX-55 Seattle WA 98121

SKIDMORE, ERIC ARTHUR, industrial engineer; b. Colville, Wash., Apr. 4, 1952; s. Donald Lee and P. Jean (Kifer) S.; m. Brenda Carol White, Mar. 22, 1975 (div. June 1981); children: Lynn Danae, Walter Neil; m. Susan Kae Dillon, Apr. 28, 1984. AS, Spokane Community Coll., Wash., 1973. Journeyman electrician Tower Electric, Spokane, 1973-75; panel wireman Electro-Power Corp., Spokane, 1975-76; roller mill operator Cominco American, Inc., Spokane, 1976-78; assembly supr. R.A. Pearson Co., Spokane, 1978-80; elec. designer Electro Engring., Spokane, 1981-82, R.A. Pearson Co., 1983-86; indsl. engr. ASC Machine Tools, Inc., Spokane, 1986-90; chief exec. officer, computer systems analyst Consol. Bus. Resources, Inc., Harrison, Idaho, 1990—; indsl. engr. Wagstaff Inc., Spokane, 1991—. Office: Consol Bus Resources Inc HC 2 Box 6 Harrison ID 83833-9601

SKIDMORE, ERIC DORR, information systems manager; b. Sangley Point Naval Base, Philippines, May 28, 1960; parents Am. citizens; s. Ellis Dee and Elaine Nadine (Hoffman) S.; married; two children. Student, Oreg. State U., 1978-80; BS in Bus. and Econs., Eastern Oreg. State Coll., LaGrande, 1983. Programmer JAHL Data Systems, Klamath Falls, Oreg., 1980-83, v.p. customer support, 1983-85; programming/support supr. Kennewick (Wash.) Indsl., 1985-86, data div. mgr., 1986-89; info. systems mgr. Bright Wood Corp., Madras, Oreg., 1989—; bd. dirs. Jefferson County Devel. Corp., Madras, 1992—; mem. bus. adv. coun., bus. dept. Madras Sr. High Sch., 1991—. Mem. Portland Area Novell Users Group, Phi Beta Lambda. Republican.

SKIDMORE, REX AUSTIN, social work educator; b. Salt Lake City, Dec. 31, 1914; s. Charles H. and Louise (Wangsgaard) S.; m. Knell Spencer, Aug. 31, 1939; children: Lee Spencer, Larry Rex. BA, U. Utah, 1938, MA, 1939; PhD, U. Pa., 1941. Instr. sociology U. Pa., 1940-41, Utah State Agrl. Coll., Logan, 1941-42; spl. agt. FBI, Miami, Fla., San Francisco, San Antonio, 1943-45; dir. bur. student counsel U. Utah, 1947-57, asso. prof., 1947-50, prof., 1950-85, dean Grad. Sch. Social Work, 1956-75. Author: Mormon Recreation: Theory and Practice, 1941, Building Your Marriage, 1951, 3d edit., 1964, Marriage Consulting, 1956, Introduction to Social Work, 1964, 5th edit., 1991, Introduction to Mental Health, 1979, Social Work Administration, 1983, 2d edit., 1990; contbr. articles to sociol. jours. Chmn. Western Mental Health Council, Western Interstate Commn. Higher Edn., 1964-65; mem. Nat. Adv. Council Nat. Manpower and Tng. Recipient distinguished service awards Community Service Council, Nat. Assn. Social Work, 1975, distinguished service awards Utah Conf. on Human Services, 1976. Mem. Coun. on Social Work Edn., Phi Kappa Phi, Pi Kappa Alpha, Pi Gamma Mu. Mem. Ch. of Jesus Christ Latter-Day Saints. Home: 1444 S 20th E Salt Lake City UT 84108

SKIELLER, CHRISTIAN, manufacturing executive; b. Copenhagen, Mar. 23, 1948; came to U.S., 1979; s. Erik C. and Vibeke (Tvilstegaard) S.; m. Kathleen E. Christman, Jan. 11, 1986; children: Claudia Christman, Christina Christman. MSc, Tech. U. Denmark, Copenhagen, 1971; MBA, Stanford U., Calif., 1981. Mgr. mfg. ops. Schou Mfg., Copenhagen, 1972-76; systems engr. IBM, Copenhagen, 1976-79; partner, gen. mgr. CSMC, Menlo Park, Calif., 1982-84; mfg. mgr. Oximetrix/Abbott Labs., Mountain View, Calif., 1984-87; prin. cons. Christian Skieller Cons., Menlo Park, 1987-90; v.p. ops. ABAXIS, Mountain View, 1990-91; v.p. mfg. Medtronic Cardio-Rhythm, San Jose, Calif., 1992—. Mem. Am. Prodn. and Inventory Control Soc. Home: 55 Black Fox Way Woodside CA 94062

SKILES, VIOLET DENICE, artist; b. Toppenish, Wash., Apr. 24, 1954; d. Clarence Herman and Hazel Emma (Middleton) Johnson; m. Randall Kent Skiles, Oct. 2, 1976; children: Brandon, Megan. Grad., Granview High Sch., Wash., 1972; studied with Judi Betts, Frank Webb, Barbara Nechls and Al Brouillette. One-woman show Edmonds (Wash.) Art Festival Mus., 1992; exhibited in group shows Allied Artists of Am. 73rd Internat. Show, N.Y.C., 1986, Am. Watercolor Soc. 120th Internat. Show, N.Y.C., 1987, Women Painters of Wash., Kobe, Japan, 1987, Toyko, 1987, Rhine, Germany, 1989, San Diego (Calif.) Watercolor Soc. Internat. Shows, 1989, 90, N.W. Watercolor Soc. Show, Kirkland, Wash., 1991, 93. Recipient Purchase award Seattle (Wash.) Telco Fed. Credit Union Competition, 1987, Pacific N.W. Arts and Crafts Fair award, Bellevue (Wash.) Art Mus., 1988, Watercolor West award San Diego Watercolor Soc. Internat. Exhbn., 1989, Painting Competition finalist Artist Mag., 1992. Mem. N.W. Watercolor Soc. (signature), Women Painters Wash. (Elizabeth Everett Meml. award 1988), Christians in the Visual Arts. Home: 3206 174th Ave NE Redmond WA 98052

SKILLIN, THERESE JENO, elementary school educator; b. San Jose, Calif., Feb. 16, 1956; d. Joseph John and Eloise Martha (Holden) Jeno; m. Robert Hance Skillin, Sept. 28, 1985; children: Paul Holden, Julia Rose. BA, San Francisco State U., 1978, MA, 1983. Cert. Calif. multiple subject life tchr. Tchr. Lost Hills (Calif.) Union Sch., 1979-81, Panama Unified Sch. Dist., Bakersfield, Calif., 1981-85, Santa Paula (Calif.) Sch. Dist., 1985-90; adult literacy tutor Family Literacy Aid to Reading Program, Bakersfield, 1986, 87; cons. Ventura (Calif.) County Farm Bus., 1987-88, Ventura County Supt. County Schs.; sci. specialist & chairperson Ventura County Environ. and Energy Edn. Coun., 1990; originator, presenter Farm Day, Kern and Ventura Counties; presenter Ventura County Creative Arts Seminar, 1990; tchr. agrl. seminar, Kern County, 1992, conservation in farming, Lori Brock Jr. Mus., 1993. Author children's books. Mem. AAUW (mem. Camarillo Creative Arts Workshop 1988), Ventura County Reading Assn., Northern Calif. Kindergarten Assn., Southern Calif. Assn. Sci. Specialists, Wasco Jr. Woman's Club (sec. 1982-83, v.p. 1983-84, dir. Annual Fun Run 1982-84, named Woman of Yr. 1982), Santa Barbara Cactus and Succulent Soc. (cons.). Democrat. Roman Catholic. Home and Office: 2901 22d St Bakersfield CA 93301

SKINNER, KNUTE RUMSEY, poet, English educator; b. St. Louis, Apr. 25, 1929; s. George Rumsey and Lidi (Skjoldvig) S.; m. Jeanne Pratt; 1953; divorced 1954; 1 child, Frank; m. Linda Kuhn, Mar. 30, 1961 (div. Sept. 1977); children: Dunstan, Morgan; m. Edna Kiel, Mar. 25, 1978. Student, Culver-Stockton Coll., 1947-49; B.A., U. No. Colo., 1951; M.A., Middlebury Coll., 1954; Ph.D., U. Iowa, 1958. Instr. English U. Iowa, Iowa City, 1955-56, 57-58, 60-61; asst. prof. English Okla. Coll. for Women, 1961-62; lectr. creative writing Western Wash. U., Bellingham, 1962-71; asso. prof. English Western Wash. U., 1971-73, prof. English, 1973—; pres. Signpost Press Inc., nonprofit corp., 1983—. Author: Stranger with a Watch, 1965, A Close Sky Over Killaspuglonane, 1968, 75, In Dinosaur Country, 1969, The Sorcerers: A Laotian Tale, 1972, Hearing of the Hard Times, 1981, The Flame Room, 1983, Selected Poems, 1985, Learning to Spell "Zucchini", 1988, The Bears and Other Poems, 1991; editor: Bellingham Rev., 1977-83, 93—; contbr. poetry, short stories to anthologies, textbooks, periodicals. Nat. Endowment for the Arts fellow, 1975. Mem. Am. Conf. Irish Studies, Wash. Poets Assn. Office: Western Washington U HU 323 Bellingham WA 98225-9055

SKINNER, MARILYN BERGLUND, Greek and Latin educator; b. Salt Lake City, Mar. 28, 1939; d. Edwin John and Marie Magdalene (Michalsky) Berglund; m. Ronald Frank Skinner, Mar. 22, 1969; 1 child, Daniel. BA in English, Seattle U., 1961; MA in Latin, U. Calif., Berkeley, 1964; PhD in Classics, Stanford U., 1977. Vis. asst. prof. Reed Coll., Portland, Oreg., 1976-77; lectr. UCLA, 1977-78; asst. prof. No. Ill. U., DeKalb, 1979-85, assoc. prof., chair dept., 1985-91; prof., head dept. classics U. Ariz., Tucson, 1991—; vis. assoc. prof. U. Tex., Austin, spring 1989, Colgate U., Hamilton, N.Y., fall 1989. Author: Catullus' Passer, 1981; editor jour. issue Rescuing Creusa, 1986; contbr. articles to scholarly publs. Fellow Whiting Found., 1975-76, NEH, 1982-83; ACLS travel grantee, 1987. Mem. Am. Philological Assn., Classical Assn. of Midwest and South, Ill. Classical Conf. (pres. 1984-86), Women's Classical Caucus (co-chair 1979-81), Vergilian Soc. (trustee 1984-87). Democrat. Office: U Ariz Dept Classics Modern Langs 371 Tucson AZ 85721

SKINNER, NANCY JO, recreation executive; b. Ogallala, Nebr., Nov. 5, 1956; d. Dale Warren Skinner and Beverly Jane (Fister) Berry. AA, Platte Community Coll., 1977; BS, U. Ariz., 1981; MBA, U. Phoenix, 1990; diploma, Nat. Exec. Devel. Sch., 1992. Sports specialist YWCA, Tucson, 1981, asst. dir. summer day camp, 1981, dir. health, phys. edn. and recreation, 1981-82; sr. recreation specialist Pima County Parks and Recreation Dept., Tucson, 1983, recreation program coord., 1983-90; recreation coord. III Phoenix Parks, Recreation and Libr. Dept., 1990—; labor mgmt. quality of work life rep. Pima County Govt., 1987; dist. coord. Atlantic Richfield Co. Jesse Owens Games, Tucson, 1986-89; adv. Pima County Health Dept. Better Health Through Self Awareness, 1982-83. Dir. tournament Sportsman Fund-Send a Kid to Camp, Tucson, 1984, 85, 86; mem. labor mgmt. quality of working life com. Pima County Govt., 1987; dist. coord. Nat. Health Screening Coun., Tucson, 1982-85; event coord. Tucson Women's Commn. Saguaro Classic, 1984; com. mem. United Way, Tucson, 1982-83; panelist Quality Conf. City of Phoenix, 1992. Musco/APRF Grad. scholar. Mem. Nat. Recreation and Parks Assn., Ariz. Parks and Recreation Assn. (cert., treas. dist. IV 1987, pres. 1988, 89, state treas. 1990, pub. rels. chair 1993, Tenderfoot award 1984), Delta Psi Kappa. Democrat. Methodist. Office: Phoenix Pks Recreation & Libr Dept 1802 W Encanto Blvd Phoenix AZ 85007

SKINNER, STANLEY THAYER, utility company executive, lawyer; b. Fort Smith, Ark., Aug. 18, 1937; s. John Willard and Irma Lee (Peters) S.; m. Margaret Olsen, Aug. 16, 1957; children—Steven Kent, Ronald Kevin. B.A. with honors, San Diego State U., 1960; M.A., U. Calif., Berkeley, 1961, J.D., 1964. Bar: Supreme Ct. Calif. bar 1965, U.S. Circuit Ct. Appeals for 9th Circuit bar 1965, 10th Circuit bar 1966. Atty. Pacific Gas and Electric Co., San Francisco, 1964-73; sr. counsel Pacific Gas and Electric Co., 1973, treas., 1974-76, v.p. fin., 1976, sr. v.p., 1977, exec. v.p., 1978-86, exec. v.p., chief fin. officer, 1982-85, vice chmn. bd., 1986-91, pres., chief oper. officer, 1991—; bd. dirs. Pacific Gas and Electric Co., Pacific Gas Transmission Co., Elec. Power Rsch. Inst. Bd. dirs. United Way of Bay Area, campaign chmn., 1992; trustee, former chmn. bd. dirs. Golden Gate U. Mem. San Francisco C. of C. (bd. dirs.), Calif. State Bar Assn., Pacific Coast Elec. Assn. (bd. dirs.), Pacific Coast Gas Assn., Calif. State C. of C. (bd. dirs.), Bankers Club San Francisco, Claremont Country Club. Republican. Presbyterian. Office: Pacific Gas & Electric Co 77 Beale St San Francisco CA 94111-5330

SKIPP, TRACY JOHN, legal support service company owner; b. Bourne, Mass., Feb. 10, 1966; s. Herbert Bucklin and Nanette Marie (Fisher) S.; m. Karyn Shayann Brennan, Nov. 24, 1986; children: Tracy John Jr., Brennan Ross Anthony. Student, Albuquerque Career Inst., 1989, U. N.Mex., 1992—. Med. asst. pvt. psychiat. practice, Albuquerque, 1987-89; owner Skipp's Legal Support Resources, Albuquerque, 1990—; rsch. scholar Dudley Wynn Honors Ctr., U. N.Mex., Albuquerque, 1992—. Supporter, activist Nat. League of Families of POW/MIAs in S.E. Asia, Albuquerque, 1987—; sustaining mem. Rep. Nat. Com., Washington, 1988-92. Mem. Am. Freedom Coalition, Nat. Notary Assn., Legal Assts. N.Mex., Nat. Fedn. Paralegal Assns. Republican. Methodist. Office: Skipp's Legal Support Resources 604 Dorado Pl SE Albuquerque NM 87123-3827

SKIRVIN, WILLIAM DAVID, artist, art director; b. Barstow, Calif., Mar. 8, 1952; s. Orval and Sylvia (Reynolds) S.; div.; children: Donovan Steven, Sarah Michelle, Dylan Thomas. Grad. high sch., Barstow. Tech. illustrator McDonnell Douglas Corp., Lemoore, Calif., 1973-80; freelance artist San Francisco, Calif., 1980—; fine artist, 1992—; art dir. Sierra On-Line, Inc., Oakhurst, Calif., 1987-91. Pvt. collections include USN, Hewlett Packard, Apple Computers, and others. Republican.

SKLADAL, ELIZABETH LEE, elementary school educator; b. N.Y.C., May 23, 1937; d. Angier Joseph and Julia May (Roberts) Gallo; m. George Wayne Skladal, Dec. 26, 1956; children: George Wayne Jr., Joseph Lee. BA, Sweet Briar Coll., 1958; EdM, U. Alaska, 1976. Choir dir. Main Chapel, Camp Zama, Japan, 1958-59, Ft. Lee, Va., 1963-65; choir dir. Main Chapel and Snowhawk, Ft. Richardson, Alaska, 1968-70; tchr. Anchorage (Alaska) Sch. Dist., 1970—. Active Citizens' Adv. Com. for Gifted and Talented, Anchorage, 1981-83, music com. Anchorage Sch. Dist., 1983-86; soloist Anchorage Opera Chorus, 1969—, Community Chorus, Anchorage, 1968-80; mem. choir First Presbyn. Ch., Anchorage, 1971—, deacon, 1988—; participant 1st cultural exch. from Anchorage to Magadan, Russia with Alaska Chamber Singers, 1992. Named Am. Coll. Theater Festival winner Amoco Oil Co., 1974. Mem. AAUW, Anchorage Concert Assn. Patron Soc. (assocs. coun. of dirs.), Alaska Chamber Singers, Am. Guild Organists (former dean, former treas.). Republican. Presbyterian. Home: 1841 S Salem Dr Anchorage AK 99508-5156

SKLANSKY, JACK, electrical and computer engineering educator, researcher; b. N.Y.C., Nov. 15, 1928; s. Abraham and Clara S.; m. Gloria Joy Weiss, Dec. 24, 1957; children: David Alan, Mark Steven, Jeffrey Paul. BEE, CCNY, 1950; MSEE, Purdue U., 1952; D in Engring. Sci., Columbia U., 1955. Research engr. RCA Labs., Princeton, N.J., 1955-65; mgr. Nat. Cash Register Co., Dayton, Ohio, 1965-66; prof. elec. and computer engring. U. Calif., Irvine, 1966—; pres. Scanicon Corp., Irvine, 1980-89. Author: (with others) Pattern Classifiers and Trainable Machines, 1981; editor: Pattern Recognition, 1973, (with others) Biomedical Images and Computers, 1982; editor-in-chief: Machine Vision and Applications, 1987. Recipient best paper award Jour. Pattern Recognition, 1977; rsch. grantee NIH, 1971-84, Army Rsch. Office, 1984-91, NSF, 1992—. Fellow IEEE; mem. Assn. Computing Machinery. Office: U Calif Dept Elec and Computer Engring Irvine CA 92717

SKLOVSKY, ROBERT JOEL, physician, educator; b. Bronx, N.Y., Nov. 19, 1952; s. Nathan and Esther (Steinberg) S.; m. Michelle Sklovsky-Welch, Dec. 21, 1985. BS, Bklyn Coll., 1975; MA in Sci. Edn., Columbia U., 1976; PharmD, U. of Pacific, 1977; D in Naturopathic Medicine, Nat. Coll. Naturopathic Medicine, 1983. Intern Tripler Army Med. Ctr., Honolulu, 1977; prof. pharmacology Nat. Coll. Naturopathic Medicine, Portland, Oreg., 1982-85; pvt. practice specializing in naturopathic medicine Milwaukie, Oreg., 1983—; cons. State Bd. Naturopathic Examiners, Oreg., Hawaii, Clackamas County Sherriff's Dept.; cons. Internat. Drug Info. Ctr., N.Y.C., 1983—; cons. Albert Roy Davis Scientific Research Lab, Orange Park, Fla. 1986. Recipient Bristol Labs. award, 1983. Fellow Am. Coll. Apothecaries; mem. N.Y. Acad. Sci., Soc. for Study of Biochem. Intolerance, Internat. Bio-oxidative Med. Found. Office: 6910 SE Lake Rd Portland OR 97267-2196

SKOGEN, HAVEN SHERMAN, oil company executive; b. Rochester, Minn., May 8, 1927; s. Joseph Harold and Elpha (Hemphill) S.; m. Beverly R. Baker, Feb. 19, 1949; 1 child, Scott H. BS, Iowa State U., 1950; MS, Rutgers U., 1954, PhD, 1955; MBA, U. Chgo., 1970. Registered profl. engr., Wis. Devel. engr. E.I. duPont, Wilmington, Del., 1955-57; prof. Elmhurst (Ill.) Coll., 1957-58; chief engr. Stackpole, St. Marys, Pa., 1958-62; plant mgr. Magnatronics, Elizabethtown, Ky., 1962-65; mgr. Allen-Bradley, Milw., 1965-70; v.p. Dill-Clithrow, Chgo., 1970-74; chief chemist Occidental Oil Co., Grand Junction, Colo., 1974—. Author: Synthetic Fuel Combustion, 1984; inventor radioactive retort doping, locus retorting zone. Naval Rsch. fellow, 1951-55. Fellow Am. Inst. Chemists; mem. Masons, Elks, Sigma Xi, Phi Beta Kappa, Phi Lambda Upsilon. Republican. Home: 3152 Primrose Ct Grand Junction CO 81506-4147 Office: PO Box 2399 Grand Junction CO 81502-2399

SKOOG, DOUGLAS ARVID, retired chemistry educator, writer; b. Willmar, Minn., May 4, 1918; s. Arvid C. and Hilma E. (Erickson) S.; m. Judith Bone, Oct. 10, 1942; children: James Arvid, Jon Douglas. BS, Oreg. State U., 1940; PhD, U. Ill., 1943. Research chemist Standard Oil Co. of Calif., Richmond, Calif., 1943-47; asst. prof. chemistry Stanford (Calif.) U., 1947-53, assoc. prof., 1953-62, prof., assoc. exec. head dept. chemistry, 1963-76, prof. emeritus, 1976—; writer Stanford, 1976—. Author: Fundamentals of Analytical Chemistry, 6th rev. edit., 1988, Principles of Instrumental Analysis, 1991, 4th rev. edit., 1992, Analytical Chemistry, 5th rev. edit., 1990; contbr. articles to profl. jours. Mem. Am. Chem. Soc. (pres. Santa Clara Valley sect. 1962), Sigma Xi, Phi Kappa Phi, Alpha Chi Sigma. Club: Bohemian (San Francisco). Home: 401 Webster St Palo Alto CA 94301-1242

SKOOG, WILLIAM ARTHUR, oncologist; b. Culver City, Calif., Apr. 10, 1925; s. John Lundeen and Allis Rose (Gatz) S.; A.A., UCLA, 1944; B.A. with gt. distinction, Stanford U., 1946, M.D., 1949; m. Ann Douglas, Sept. 17, 1949; children—Karen, William Arthur, James Douglas, Allison. Intern medicine Stanford Hosp., San Francisco, 1948-49, asst. resident medicine, 1949-50; asst. resident medicine N.Y. Hosp., N.Y.C., 1950-51; sr. resident medicine Wadsworth VA Hosp., Los Angeles, 1951, attending specialist internal medicine, 1962-68; practice medicine specializing in internal medicine, Los Altos, Calif., 1959-61; pvt. practice hematology and oncology Calif. Oncologic and Surg. Med. Group, Inc., Santa Monica, Calif., 1971-72; pvt. practice med. oncology, San Bernardino, Calif., 1972—; assoc. staff Palo Alto-Stanford (Calif.) Hosp. Center, 1959-61, U. Calif. Med. Center, San Francisco, 1959-61; asso. attending physician U. Calif. at Los Angeles Hosp. and Clinics, 1961-78; vis. physician internal medicine Harbor Gen. Hosp., Torrance, Calif., 1962-65, attending physician, 1965-71; cons. chemistry Clin. Lab., UCLA Hosp., 1963-68; affiliate cons. staff St. John's Hosp., Santa Monica, Calif., 1967-71, courtesy staff, 1971-72; courtesy attending med. staff Santa Monica Hosp., 1967-72; staff physician St. Bernardine (Calif.) Hosp., 1972—, San Bernardino Community Hosp., 1972-90, courtesy staff, 1990—; chief sect. oncology San Bernardino County Hosp., 1972-76; cons. staff Redlands (Calif.) Community Hosp., 1972-83, courtesy staff, 1983—; asst. in medicine Cornell Med. Coll., N.Y.C., 1950-51; jr. research physician UCLA Atomic Energy Project, 1954-55; instr. medicine, asst. research physician dept. medicine UCLA Med. Center, 1955-56, asst. prof. medicine, asst. research physician, 1956-59; clin. asso. hematology VA Center, Los Angeles, 1956-59; co-dir. metabolic research unit UCLA Center for Health Scis., 1955-59, 61-65; co-dir. Health Scis. Clin. Research Center, 1965-68, dir., 1968-72; clin. instr. medicine Stanford, 1959-61; asst. clin. prof. medicine, assoc. research physician U. Calif. Med. Center, San Francisco, 1959-61; lectr. medicine UCLA Sch. Medicine, 1961-62, assoc. prof. medicine, 1962-73, assoc. clin. prof. medicine, 1973—. Served with USNR, 1943-46, to lt. M.C., 1951-53. Fellow ACP; mem. Am., Calif. med. assns., So. Calif. Acad. Clin. Oncology, Western Soc. Clin. Research, Am. Fedn. Clin. Research, Los Angeles Acad. Medicine, San Bernardino County Med. Soc., Am. Soc. Clin. Oncology, Am. Soc. Internal Medicine, Calif. Soc. Internal Medicine, Inland Soc. Internal Medicine, Phi Beta Kappa, Alpha Omega Alpha, Sigma Xi, Alpha Kappa Kappa. Episcopalian (vestryman 1965-70). Club: Redlands Country. Contbr. articles to profl. jours. Home: 30831 Miradero Dr Redlands CA 92373-7429 Office: 401 E Highland Ave Ste 552 San Bernardino CA 92404-3801

SKOOR, JOHN BRIAN, art educator, art consultant; b. Mount Vernon, Wash., Dec. 14, 1939; s. George Nephi and Marie Elizabeth (Collins) S.; m. Susan Diane Waugh, June 17, 1972; children: Marie Elizabeth, Christine Elaine. AA in Edn., Graceland Coll., Lamoni, 1960; BA in Art, Cen. Wash. U., 1962, BA in Edn., 1965, MA in Art, 1969. Art instr. Delta (Mich.) Coll., Saginaw, 1977-79; instr. Renton (Wash.) Vocat. Tech. Inst., 1981-83; art instr. Green River (Wash.) Community Coll., Auburn, 1988—; cons. staff and development instr. various Seattle sch. dists., 1988—; art instr. Highline Community Coll., Seattle, 1990—; adj. faculty Cen. Wash. U., 1984—, Seattle Pacific U., 1986—; dir. sr. programs Highline C.C., 1992—; guest speaker Wash. Art Educators Assn. Conv., 1990. Illustrator of religious curriculum texts, 1978-80; exhibited acrylic theol. paintings show, Independence, Mo., 1980. Guest speaker Alma (Mich.) Art Dept., 1977, Nat. Camping Assn., Detroit, 1979, Wash. Art Tchrs. Assn., 1990; coord. sr. programs Highline C. of C., 1992—; elder Reorganized Ch. of Jesus Christ of Latter Day Saints, Seattle, 1966—, pastor, 1987—, bd. dirs. creative arts festival, Mich., 1977. Mem. Wash. Alliance for Arts Edn. (commn. chmn. 1987—), Richland Art Tchrs. Assn. (pres. 1965-66), Tri-City Art Tchrs. Assn. (pres. 1966-67), Nat. Art Educators Assn. Home and Studio: 4830 S Morgan St Seattle WA 98118

SKOPIL, OTTO RICHARD, JR., federal judge; b. Portland, Oreg., June 3, 1919; s. Otto Richard and Freda Martha (Boetticher) S.; m. Janet Rae Lundy, July 27, 1956; children: Otto Richard III, Casey Robert, Shannon Ida, Molly Jo. BA in Econs., Willamette U., 1941, LLB, 1946, LLD (hon.), 1983. Bar: Oreg. 1946, IRS, U.S. Treasury Dept., U.S. Dist. Ct. Oreg., U.S.

Ct. Appeals (9th cir.), U.S. Supreme Ct. 1946. Assoc. Skopil & Skopil, 1946-51; ptnr. Williams, Skopil, Miller & Beck (and predecessors); Salem, Oreg., 1951-72; judge U.S. Dist. Ct., Portland, 1972-79; chief judge U.S. Dist. Ct., 1976-79; judge U.S. Ct. Appeals (9th cir.), Portland, 1979—; chmn. com. adminstrn. of fed. magistrate system U.S. Jud. Conf., 1980-86; co-founder Oreg. chpt. Am. Leadership forum; chmn. 9th cir. Jud. Coun. magistrates adv. com., 1988-91; chmn. U.S. Jud. Conf. Long Range Planning Com., 1990—. Hi-Y adviser Salem YMCA, 1951-52; appeal agt. SSS, Marion County (Oreg.) Draft Bd., 1953-66; master of ceremonies 1st Gov.'s Prayer Breakfast for State Oreg., 1959; mem. citizens adv. com., City of Salem, 1970-71; chmn. Gov.'s Com. on Staffing Mental Instns., 1969-70; pres., bd. dirs. Marion County Tb and Health Assn., 1958-61; bd. dirs. Willamette Valley Camp Fire Girls, 1946-56, Internat. Christian Leadership, 1959, Fed. Jud. Ctr., 1979; trustee Willamette U., 1969-71; elder Mt. Park Ch., 1979-81. Served to lt. USNR, 1942-46. Recipient Oreg. Legal Citizen of Yr. award, 1986, Disting. Alumni award Willamette U. Sch. Law, 1988. Mem. ABA, Oreg. Bar Assn. (bd. govs.), Marion County Bar Assn., Am. Judicature Soc., Oreg. Assn. Def. Counsel (dir.), Def. Research Inst., Assn. Ins. Attys. U.S. and Can. (Oreg. rep. 1970), Internat. Soc. Barristers, Prayer Breakfast Movement (fellowship council). Clubs: Salem, Exchange (pres. 1947), Illahe Hills Country (pres., dir. 1964-67). Office: US Ct Appeals 232 Pioneer Courthouse 555 SW Yamhill St Portland OR 97204-1336

SKOTHEIM, ROBERT ALLEN, museum administrator; b. Seattle, Jan. 31, 1933; s. Sivert O. and Marjorie F. (Allen) S.; m. Nadine Vail, June 14, 1953; children—Marjorie, Kris, Julia. BA, U. Wash., 1955, MA, 1958, PhD, 1962; LLD (hon.), Hobart and William Smith Colls., Geneva, N.Y., 1975; LittD (hon.), Whitman Coll., 1988; LHD (hon.), Coll. Idaho, 1988, Occidental Coll., 1989, Ill. Wesleyan U., 1990; DFA (hon.), Willamette U., 1989. Prof. history U. Wash., 1962-63; prof. history Wayne State U., Detroit, 1963-66; prof. UCLA, 1966-67, U. Colo., Boulder, 1967-72; provost, dean faculty Hobart and William Smith Colls., 1972-75; pres. Whitman Coll., Walla Walla, Wash., 1975-88; pres. Huntington Library, art collections Bot. Gardens, San Marino, Calif., 1988—. Author: American Intellectual Histories and Historians, 1966, Totalitarianism and American Social Thought, 1971; Editor: The Historian and the Climate of Opinion, 1969; co-editor: American Social Thought: Sources and Interpretations, 2 vols, 1972. Guggenheim fellow, 1967-68. Mem. Phi Beta Kappa (hon.). Office: Huntington Libr Art Collections Bot Gardens 1151 Oxford Rd San Marino CA 91108-1299

SKRATEK, SYLVIA PAULETTE, mediator, arbitrator, state legislator; b. Detroit, Dec. 23, 1950; d. William Joseph and Helen (Meskauskas) S.; m. John Wayne Gullion, Dec. 21,1984. BS, Wayne State U., 1971; MLS, Western Mich. U., 1976; PhD, U. Mich., 1985. Media specialist Jackson (Mich.) Pub. Schs., 1971-79; contract specialist Jackson County Edn. Assn., 1976-79; field rep. Mich. Edn. Assn., E.Lansing, 1979-81; contract adminstr. Wash. Edn. Assn., Federal Way, 1981-85, regional coord., 1985-88, program adminstr., from 1988; dir. mediation svcs. Conflict Mgmt. Inst., Lake Oswego, Ore., 1986-87; exec. dir. N.W. Ctr. for Conciliation, 1987-88; elected to Wash. State Senate, 1990; tng. cons. City of Seattle, Wash., 1986—; trustee Group Health Cooperative of Puget Sound, Wash., 1984-87. Contbr. articles to legal jours. Vol. Brock Adams Senatorial campaign, Seattle, 1986. Mem. Soc. for Profls. in Dispute Resolution, Indsl. Relations Research Assn., Mediation Consortium of Wash.

SKROCKI, EDMUND STANLEY, II, health fair promoter, executive; b. Schenectady, N.Y., Sept. 6, 1953; s. Edmund Stanley I and Lorraine (Nocian) S.; m. Diane Carolyn Sittig, Sept. 6, 1976 (div. 1992); children: Carolyn, Michelle, Edmund III, Johnathan. AA, LaValley Coll., 1981; BA, Sonoma State U., 1982, MA, 1987; postgrad., Am. Inst. Hypnotherapy. Pres. Skrocki's Philos. Svc., Lakeview Terrace, Calif., 1971-81; pres., CEO Skrocki's Superior Svc., Lakeview Terrace, 1971-76; pres., chief exec. officer Skrocki's Superior Svc., Redding, Calif., 1976—; pres., CEO, promoter Redding (Calif.) Health Faire, 1991—. Named one of Outstanding Young Men Am., 1980. Mem. Shasta Submarine Soc. (pres. 1984—). Home and Office: 755 Quartz Hill Rd Redding CA 96003

SKYLSTAD, WILLIAM S., bishop; b. Omak, Wash., Mar. 2, 1934; s. Stephen Martin and Reneldes Elizzbeth (Danzl) S. Student, Pontifical Coll., Josephinum, Worthington, Ohio; M.Ed., Gonzaga U. Ordained priest Roman Catholic Ch., 1960; asst. pastor Pullman, Wash., 1960-62; tchr. Mater Cleri Sem., 1961-68, rector, 1968-74; pastor Assumption Parish, Spokane, 1974-76; chancellor Diocese of Spokane, 1976-77; ordained bishop, 1977; bishop of Yakima, Wash., 1977-90, Spokane, Wash., 1990—. Office: Diocese of Spokane PO Box 1453 1023 W Riverside Ave Spokane WA 99210-1453 Home: 1025 W Cleveland Spokane WA 99205*

SLACK, DONALD CARL, agricultural engineer, educator; b. Cody, Wyo., June 25, 1942; s. Clarence Ralbon and Clara May (Beightol) S.; m. Marion Arline Kimball, Dec. 19, 1964; children: Jonel Marie, Jennifer Michelle. BS in Agrl. Engring., U. Wyo., 1965; MS in Agrl. Engring., U. Ky., 1968, PhD in Agrl. Engring., 1975. Registered profl. engr., Ky., Ariz. Asst. civil engr. City of Los Angeles, 1965; research specialist U. Ky., Lexington, 1966-70; agrl. engring. advisor U. Ky., Tha Phra, Thailand, 1970-73; research asst. U. Ky., Lexington, 1973-75; from asst. prof. to assoc. prof. agrl. engring. U. Minn., St. Paul, 1975-84; prof. U. Ariz., Tucson, 1984—, head dept. agrl. and biosystems engring., 1991—; tech. advisor Ariz. Dept. Water Resources, Phoenix, 1985—; cons. Winrock Internat., Morrilton, Ark., 1984, Water Mgmt. Synthesis II, Logan, Utah, 1985, Desert Agrl. Tech. Systems, Tucson, 1985—, Portek, Hermosillo, Mex., 1989—, World Bank, Washington, 1992—; deputy program support mgr. Research Irrigation Support Project for Asia and the Near East, Arlington, Va., 1987—. Contbr. articles to profl. jours. Fellow ASCE (Outstanding Jour. paper award 1988); mem. Am. Soc. Agrl. Engrs., Am. Geophys. Union, Am. Soc. Agronomy, Soil Sci. Soc. Am., Am. Soc. Engring. Edn., Sigma Xi, Tau Beta Pi, Alpha Epsilon, Gamma Sigma Delta. Democrat. Lutheran. Home: 9230 E Visco Pl Tucson AZ 85710-3167 Office: U Ariz Agrl Biosystems Engring Dept 507 Shantz Bldg # 38 Tucson AZ 85721

SLADICH, HARRY HAMILL, university administrator; b. Anaconda, Mont., Jan. 9, 1938; s. Joseph Francis and Caroline (Hamill) S.; m. Marguerite Dill, June 18, 1960; children: Harry G., Jennifer M., Suzanne. B.B.A., Gonzaga U., 1959, M.B.A., 1967. Asst. prof. Gonzaga U., Spokane, Wash., 1963—, dir. adminstrv. services, 1962-71, asst. to pres., 1972-83, v.p. adminstrn. and planning, 1983—. Bd. dirs. ARC, Spokane, 1978—, chmn., 1981-83, adv. council western ops., Burlingame, Calif., 1983-86; mem. com. on nominations ARC, Washington, 1991-92; mem. exec. com. adv. bd. Wash. State Higher Edn. Bd., 1986-87; bd. dirs. Wash. State Catholic Conf., Seattle, 1980-84, Mus. Native Am. Culture, Spokane, 1989-92; chmn. edn. div. United Way, Spokane, 1983, bd. dirs. 1991—. Roman Catholic. Home: 1103 W 17th Ave Spokane WA 99203-1108 Office: Gonzaga U 502 E Boone Ave Spokane WA 99258-0001

SLAGLE, KERRY D., newspaper editor; b. Maryville, Mo., Nov. 26, 1948; s. W. Raymond and Elenora Agnes (Adwell) S.; m. Ellen Stone, Mar. 2, 1974. BJ, U. Mo., 1983. Editor features sect. Palm Beach Post, West Palm Beach, Fla., 1973-75; editor news sect. Trenton (N.J.) Times, 1975-76; editor mag. Dallas Times-Herald, 1976-77, mng. editor, 1980-87; editor sports sect. Chgo. Sun-Times, 1977-79; sr. editor Inside Sports/Newsweek, N.Y.C., 1979-80; mng. editor Sarasota (Fla.) Herald-Tribune, 1987-90, Seattle Post-Intelligencer, 1990—. Recipient Nat. Headliner award Nat. Headliners Club, 1981. Mem. AP Mng. Editors, Newspaper Features Coun. (bd. dirs. 1987—). Office: Seattle Post-Intelligencer 101 Elliott Ave W Seattle WA 98119-4220

SLANE, FREDERICK ALEXANDER, career officer; b. Portland, Oreg., Oct. 25, 1957; s. Charles Littleton and Kathleen Warner (Miller) S.; m. Jean Marie Howie, Apr. 18, 1985; children: Frederick Alexander Jr., John Ryan. BA in Physics and Math., Wilamette U., 1980; BS in Aero Engring., Air Force Inst. Tech., 1983; MS in Physics, U. N.Mex., 1993. Commd. lt. USAF, 1981, advanced through grades to major, 1992; associated researcher U. N.Mex., Albuquerque, 1990—. Contbr. articles to profl. jours. Dir. Sunday sch. Holy Trinity Epsicopal Ch., 1988-92. Mem. AIAA.

SLANSKY, RICHARD C., physicist; b. Oakland, Calif., Apr. 3, 1940; s. Cyril M. and Elvera (Tewell) S.; m. Lynne Hutton, Feb. 1, 1963 (dec. June 1974); children: Jill, Joseph; m. Helene Harlem, July 27, 1976. BA, Harvard U., 1962; PhD, U. Calif., Berkeley, 1967. Postdoctoral fellow Calif. Tech. Inst., Pasadena, 1967-69; from instr. to asst. prof. Yale U., New Haven, 1969-74; mem. staff, fellow Los Alamos (N.Mex.) Nat. Lab., 1974-89, div. leader, 1989—. Office: Los Alamos Nat Lab MSB210 T-DO Los Alamos NM 87574

SLATER, DAN, photooptical instrumentation engineer; b. Inglewood, Calif., Feb. 6, 1949; s. John and Eva (Zeitz) S. Student, Calif. State U., Fullerton, 1969-73. Chief engr. Magicam div. Paramount Pictures, Hollywood, Calif., 1972-79; v.p. Nearfield Systems, Inc., Carson, Calif., 1988—; cons. TRW, Redondo Beach, Calif., 1980—, TEI, Saratoga, Calif., 1980—. Author: Nearfield Antenna Measurements, 1991; patentee in field; contbr. articles to profl. publs. Recipient Tech. Achievement award Acad. Motion Picture Arts and Scis., 1980, Sci. and Engring. award Acad. Motion Picture Arts and Scis., 1989. Mem. AIAA (sr.), Soc. Photooptical Instrumentation Engrs., Steadicam Operators Assn. Home: 1352 Dorothea Rd La Habra CA 90631-8180 Office: Nearfield Systems Inc 1330 E 223d St #524 Carson CA 90745

SLATER, DON AUSTIN, shipyard executive, consultant; b. Bay City, Mich., May 27, 1938; s. William Stuart and Inez Fern (Hagen) S.; m. Sara Belva Sanford, Feb. 3, 1962; children: Shandra Sanford, Nathan Dorman. BS in Naval Architecture and Marine Engring., U. Mich. Naval architect Western Boat Bldg. Corp., Tacoma, 1964; exec. v.p. and gen. mgr. Star Marine Industries, Tacoma; gen. mgr. Shipyard div. Marine Iron Works, Tacoma; pres., CEO Marine Industry N.W., Inc., Tacoma, 1976—; cons. to various law firms, Wash. and N.J., 1975—; arbitrator Am. Arbitration Assn., 1985—. 1st v.p. Va. V Found., Seattlem 1986; bd. dirs. Puget Sound Marine Hist. Soc., 1978-80. Home: 30720 43d Ave SW Federal Way WA 98003 Office: Marine Industries NW Inc 313 E F St # 1275 Tacoma WA 98421-1821

SLATER, GRANT GAY, biochemist, consultant; b. Rochester, N.Y., Jan. 6, 1918; s. Lee Grand and Erma (Gay) S.; m. Roslyn Bernice Alfin, July 30, 1948; children: Robert,Joanne Catani. BS in Chemistry, U. Miami, Fla., 1940; MS in Biochemistry, U. So. Calif., L.A., 1950; PhD in Biochemistry, U. So. Calif., 1954. Chemist Keuffel & Esser, Hoboken, N.J., 1947-48; rsch. assoc. Rsch. Inst. Cedars Lebanon Hosp., L.A., 1954-55; instr. biochemistry U. So. Calif., L.A., 1954-59; rsch. biochemist Neurobiochemistry Vets. Adminstrn., L.A., 1961-68, Gateway Hosp., L.A., 1961-68; researcher Sch. Pub. Health, UCLA, 1972-80, researcher biochemist, 1980-83; cons. Slater Cons., L.A., 1988—; mem. nutrition com. Calif. Avocado Nutrition Bd., 1973-93; lectr. in field. Editorial bd. Biochem. Medicine and Metabolic Biology, 1980-93; contbr. articles to profl. jours.; patentee in field. Lt. col. U.S. Army, 1942-78. Grantee, State of Calif./USPHS, 1958-65, GAteways Hosp., 1971, USPHS, 1974, Am. Egg Bd., 1977, Nat. Dairy Coun., 1980. Mem. Am. Chem. Soc., Am. Physiol. Soc., Brain Rsch. Inst., The Endocrine Soc., Soc. of Neurosci., Am. Oil Chemists, Sigma Xi. Office: Slater Consultants 986 Somera Rd Los Angeles CA 90077-2624

SLATER, LEONARD, writer, editor; b. N.Y.C., July 15, 1920; s. Max and Jean (Lenobel) S.; m. Betty Moorsteen, 1946; children: Amy, Lucy. BA in Polit. Sci., U. Mich., 1941. Reporter, writer NBC News, Washington, 1941-44; corr. Washington bur. Time mag., 1945-47; assoc. editor Newsweek mag., N.Y.C., 1947-59, corr. Eastern Europe and Middle East; bur. chief Newsweek mag., Los Angeles; sr. editor, columnist McCalls' mag., N.Y. and Europe, 1960-63; free-lance writer, editor, 1963—. Author: Aly, 1965, The Pledge, 1970; contbr. articles to mags. Mem. Authors League of Am. Home: 4370 Arista Dr San Diego CA 92103-1029 also: Binicalaf Minorca, Balearic Islands Spain

SLATER, MANNING, broadcasting consultant; b. Springfield, Mass., Aug. 29, 1917; s. Ely and Sarah Deenah (Hurwitz) Slotnick; m. Anita Norman, July 1, 1977; children—Gary Edward, Richard Stuart. B.A., Am. Internat. Coll., 1939. Pres. Community Markets, Springfield, Mass., 1939-46; v.p., treas. Bridgeport Broadcasting Co., Conn., 1947-58; pres., chmn. bd. Hercules Broadcasting Co., Sacramento and Seattle, 1959—; also Slater Broadcasting Co.; pres. Slater Investment Co. Bd. govs. Mercy Hosp., Sacramento. Named Man of Yr. State of Israel Bonds, 1989. Mem. Nat. Assn. Broadcasters, Radio Advt. Bur., Sacramento C. of C., B'nai B'rith. Democrat. Jewish. Clubs: University, Comstock Club Sacramento. Home: 660 Lake Wilhaggin Dr Sacramento CA 95864-7227 also: 48 635 Sundrop Ct Palm Desert CA 92260 Office: 1337 Howe Ave Ste 110 Sacramento CA 95825-3361

SLATER, SHELLEY, engineering specialist; b. Ogden, Utah, June 26, 1959; d. Lynn Russell and Darlene (Allen) Slater; m. Dale Thomas Hansen, Jan. 26, 1977 (div. Feb. 1979); 1 child, Thomas Arthur; m. Eugene Allan DuVall, Mar. 8, 1981 (div. Dec. 1985); 1 child, Gregory Allan; m. Steven Blake Allender, June 9, 1990 (div. May 1993). BBA cum laude, Regis U., 1992, postgrad., 1992—. Installation, repair technician MT Bell, Clearfield, Utah, 1977-81; ctrl. office technician MT Bell, Salt Lake City, 1981-83, engring. specialist, 1983-86; engring. specialist U.S. West Comms., Englewood, Colo., 1986—; bus. cons. Jr. Achievement, Denver, 1988-89. Day capt. AZTEC Denver Mus. of Natural History, 1992; loaned exec. Mile High United Way, 1993. Mem. U.S. Women West, SOMOS/Hispanic Resource Network. Democrat. Home: 9618 Cordova Dr Highlands Ranch CO 80126 Office: US West Communications 6912 S Quentin St Englewood CO 80112

SLAUGHTER, JOHN BROOKS, university president; b. Topeka, Mar. 16, 1934; s. Reuben Brooks and Dora (Reeves) S.; m. Ida Bernice Johnson, Aug. 31, 1956; children: John Brooks, Jacqueline Michelle. Student, Washburn U., 1951-53; BSEE, Kans. State U., 1956, DSc (hon.), 1988; MS in Engring., UCLA, 1961; PhD in Engring. Scis, U. Calif., San Diego, 1971; D Engring. (hon.), Rensselaer Poly. Inst., 1981; DSc (hon.), U. So. Calif., 1981, Tuskegee Inst., 1981, U. Md., 1982, U. Notre Dame, 1982, U. Miami, 1983, U. Mass., 1983, Tex. So. U., 1984, U. Toledo, 1985, U. Ill., 1986, SUNY, 1986; LHD (hon.), Bowie State Coll., 1987; DSc (hon.), Morehouse Coll., 1988, Kans. State U., 1988; LLD (hon.), U. Pacific, 1989; DSc (hon.), Pomona Coll., 1989; LHD (hon.), Alfred U., 1991, Calif. Luth. U., 1991, Washburn U., 1992. Registered profl. engr., Wash. Electronics engr. Gen. Dynamics Convair, San Diego, 1956-60; with Naval Electronics Lab. Center, San Diego, 1960-75, div. head, 1965-71, dept. head, 1971-75; dir. applied physics lab. U. Wash., 1975-77; asst. dir. NSF, Washington, 1977-79; dir. NSF, 1980-82; acad. v.p., provost Wash. State U., 1979-80; chancellor U. Md., College Park, 1982-88; pres. Occidental Coll., Los Angeles, 1988—; bd. dirs., vice chmn. San Diego Transit Corp., 1968-75; mem. com. on minorities in engring. Nat. Rsch. Coun., 1976-79; mem. Commn. on Pre-Coll. Edn. in Math., Sci. and Tech. Nat. Sci. Bd., 1982-83; bd. dirs. Monsanto Co., ARCO, Avery Dennison Corp., IBM, Northrop Corp., Music Ctr. L.A. Country. Editor: Jour. Computers and Elec. Engring, 1972—. Bd. dirs. San Diego Urban League, 1962-66, pres., 1964-66; mem. Pres.'s Com. on Nat. Medal Sci., 1979-80; trustee Rensselaer Poly. Inst., 1982; chmn. Pres.'s Com. Nat. Collegiate Athletic Assn., 1986-88; bd. govs. Town Hall of Calif., 1990; bd. dirs. L.A. World Affairs Coun., 1990. Recipient Engring. Disting. Alumnus of Yr. award UCLA, 1978, UCLA medal, 1989, Roger Revelle award U. Calif. at San Diego, 1991; Disting. Svc. award NSF, 1979,. Svc. in Engring. award Kans. State U., 1981, Disting. Alumnus of Yr. award U. Calif., San Diego, 1982; Naval Electronics Lab. Ctr. fellow, 1969-70. Fellow IEEE (chmn. com. on minority affairs 1976-80), Am. Acad. Arts and Scis.; mem. NAE, Nat. Collegiate Athletic Assn. (chmn. pres. commn.), Tau Beta Pi, Eta Kappa Nu, Phi Beta Kappa (hon.). Office: Occidental Coll 1600 Campus Rd Los Angeles CA 90041-3314

SLEIGHT, ARTHUR WILLIAM, chemist; b. Ballston Spa, N.Y., Apr. 1, 1939; s. Hollis Decker and Elizabeth (Smith) S.; AB, Hamilton Coll., 1960; PhD, U. Conn., 1963; m. Betty F. Hilberg, Apr. 19, 1963; children—Jeffrey William, Jeannette Anne, Jason Arthur. Faculty, U. Stockholm, Sweden, 1963-64; with E.I. du Pont de Nemours & Co., Inc., Wilmington, Del., 1965-89, rsch. mgr. solid state/catalytic chemistry, 1981-89; Harris Chair prof. materials sci. Oreg. State U., Corvallis, 1989—; adj. prof. U. Del., 1978-89. Mem. Presdl. Commn. Superconductivity, 1989. Recipient Phila. chpt. Am. Inst.. Chemists award, 1988. Mem. Am. Chem. Soc. (award Del. sect. 1978). Assoc. editor Materials Rsch. Bull., 1977—; editorial bd. Inorganic Chemistry Rev., 1979—, Jour. Catalysis, 1986—, Applied Catalysis, 1987—, Solid State Scis., 1987—, Chemistry of Materials, 1988—, Materials Chemistry and Physics, 1988—, Jour. of Solid State Chemistry, 1988—; patentee in field; contbr. articles to profl. jours. Home: PO Box 907 Philomath OR 97370-0578 Office: Oreg State U Dept Chemistry Gilbert 153 Corvallis OR 97331-4003

SLENTZ, ANDREW PAUL, human resources executive; b. Rochester, N.Y., Oct. 20, 1961; s. Robert Donald and Pruedence (Holdridge) S.; m. Danielle Henderson, July 13, 1991. BS in Govt., Hamilton Coll., 1983; M in Indsl. Labor Rels., Cornell U., 1986. Human resourc advisor Exxon Co., Thousand Oaks, Calif., 1986-88; employee rels. rep. Mobil Chem. Co., Canandigua, N.Y., 1988-90; employee rels. mgr. Mobil Chem. Co., Bakersfield, Calif., 1990—. Mem. adv. coun. Bakersfield (Calif.) Adult Sch., 1991—. Office: Mobil Chem Co 2024 Norris Rd Bakersfield CA 93308

SLEVIN, MARGARITA H., computer accessories distributor; b. Buenos Aires, Nov. 23, 1953; came to U.S., 1963; d. Arthur and Jolan (Diettrich) Kovats; m. Richard S. Slevin, Dec. 24, 1972. BS in Indsl. Engring., SUNY, Buffalo, 1977. Indsl. engr. Carborundum, Niagara Falls, N.Y., 1977-78; sales engr. HG&P, Beaumont, Tex., 1978-80; prodn. control mgr. Amdahl Corp., Sunnyvale, Calif., 1980-84; prodn. control/customer svc. mgr. Raychem Corp., Menlo Park, Calif., 1984-86; materials mgr. Velobind, Inc., Fremont, Calif., 1986-89; dir. ops. Aesculap, Inc., South San Francisco, Calif., 1989-92, Kensington Microware Ltd., San Mateo, Calif., 1992—. Mem. Am. Prodn. and Inventory Control Soc. Office: Kensington Microware Ltd 2855 Campus Dr San Mateo CA 94403

SLIKER, TODD RICHARD, accountant, lawyer; b. Rochester, N.Y., Feb. 9, 1936; s. Harold Garland and Marion Ethel (Caps) S.; BS with honors (Ford Found. scholar), U. Wis., 1955; PhD, Cornell U., 1962; MBA, Harvard, 1970; JD, U. Denver, 1982; m. Gretchen Paula Zeiter, Dec. 27, 1963; children: Cynthia Garland, Kathryn Clifton. Bar: Colo. 1983. With Clevite Corp., Cleve., 1962-68, head applied physics sect., 1965-68; asst. to pres. Granville-Phillips Co., Boulder, Colo., 1970; v.p., gen. mgr. McDowell Electronics, Inc., Metuchen, N.J., 1970-71; pres. C.A. Compton, Inc., mfrs. audio-visual equipment, Boulder, 1971-77; chief acct. C&S Inc., Englewood, Colo., 1977-80, v.p., 1980-82; sole practice law, Boulder, 1983-88; mgmt. real estate, 1972—. Del., Colo. Rep. Assembly, 1974, 76; Rep. dist. fin. coordinator, 1974-75; precinct committeeman, 1974-86, 92—; chmn. Boulder County Rep. 1200 Club, 1975-79; mem. Colo. Rep. State Cen. Com., 1977-81, asst. treas., 1979-87; sect. corr. Harvard U., 1981—. Served to 1st lt. USAF, 1955-57. Recipient paper award vehicular communication group IEEE, 1966. Lic. real estate salesman, securities salesman; CPA, Colo. Mem. Colo. Soc. CPAs (govt. relations task force 1983-86), Colo. Bar Assn. (publs. com. 1982-84), Am. Phys. Soc., Optical Soc. Am. (referee Jour.), Sigma Xi, Phi Kappa Phi, Theta Chi, Beta Alpha Psi. Club: Historic Boulder, Rotary. Contbr. articles to profl. jours. Patentee in field. Home: 604 Tantra Dr Boulder CO 80303-6161

SLINKER, DAVID KENT, sculptor; b. Oakland, Calif., Mar. 2, 1952; s. Hubert and Beverly Jean (Conway) S. Student, Brooks Art Inst., 1971. Owner The Dinosaur Man, Ojai, Calif., 1972—. Recipient art scholarship, 1970. Mem. Internat. Calcite Collectors Assn. Office: The Dinosaur Man PO Box 1807 Ojai CA 93024

SLINKER, JOHN MICHAEL, academic director; b. Lafayette, Ind., Jan. 8, 1952; s. William Guy Mahan and Betty Lucille (Utterback) and Richard Earl Slinker; m. Pamela Jo Pickering, Mar. 15, 1975. BS, Ea. N.Mex. U., 1974, MA, 1979; EdD, No. Ariz. U., 1988. Asst. sports infor. dir., news writer Ea. N.Mex. U., Portales, 1970-74, news svcs. dir., sports info. dir., 1974-82; dir. univ. news and publs. No. Ariz. U., Flagstaff, 1982-86; dir. pub. affairs Humboldt State U., Arcata, Calif., 1988-92, dir. univ. rels., 1992—; cons. Calif. Dept. Parks and Recreation, Sacramento, 1989-90. Vol. Boy Scouts Am., Eureka, Calif., 1991—, dist. commr., 1991-92. Mem. Coun. for Advancement and Support of Edn. (Bronze medal), Sigma Nu (div. comdr. 1976-81, chpt. advisor, Outstanding Alumnus 1976, 79, 81, 82). Republican. Methodist. Home: 1221 West Ave # A Eureka CA 95501 Office: Humboldt State U Office Univ Rels Arcata CA 95521

SLOAN, EARLE DENDY, JR., chemical engineering educator; b. Seneca, S.C., Apr. 23, 1944; s. Earle Dendy and Sarah (Bellotte) S.; m. Marjorie Nilson, Sept. 7, 1968; children: Earle Dendy III, John Mark. BSChemE, Clemson U., 1965, MSChemE, 1972, PhD in Chem. Engring., 1974. Engr. Du Pont, Chattanooga, 1965-66, Seaford, Del., 1966-67; cons. Du Pont, Parkersburg, W.Va., 1967-68; sr. engr. Du Pont, Camden, S.C., 1968-70; postdoctoral fellow Rice U., 1975; prof. chem. engring. Colo. Sch. Mines, Golden, 1976—, Gaylord and Phyllis Weaver dist. prof. chem. engring., 1992—; pres. faculty senate, Colo. Sch. Mines, 1989-90. Author: Clathrate Hydrates of Natural Gases, 1990; chmn. pub. bd. Chem. Engring. Edn., 1990—. Scoutmaster local Cub Scouts; elder Presbyn. Ch., Golden, Colo., 1977-79, 92—. Mem. Am. Soc. for Engring. Edn. (chmn. ednl. rsch. methods div. 1983-85, chem. engring. div. 1985), Am. Inst. Chem. Engrs. (chmn. area Ia thermodynamics and transport 1990-93), Am. Chem. Soc. Home: 2121 Washington Ave Golden CO 80401-2377

SLOAN, JERRY (GERALD EUGENE SLOAN), professional basketball coach; b. Mar. 28, 1942; m. Bobbye; 3 children: Kathy, Brian, Holly. Student, Evansville Coll., Evansville, Ind. Professional basketball player, Baltimore, 1965-66, Chicago Bulls, NBA, 1966-76; head coach Chicago Bulls, 1979-82; scout Utah Jazz, NBA, Salt Lake City, 1983-84, asst. coach, 1984-88, head coach, 1988—; player 2 NBA All-Star games; named to NBA All-Defensive First Team, 1969, 72, 74, 75. Office: care Utah Jazz 5 Triad Ctr Ste 500 Salt Lake City UT 84180-1105*

SLOAN, L. LAWRENCE, publishing executive; b. N.Y.C., 1947. Grad., UCLA. Chmn. Price Stern Sloan, Inc., West Hollywood, Calif.; pres. Sloan Co. Office: Price Stern Sloan Inc 410 N La Cienega Blvd West Hollywood CA 90048-1907 also: Price Stern Sloan Inc 11150 Olympic Blvd Los Angeles CA 90064

SLOAN, LANNY GENE, municipal official; b. Denver, Aug. 30, 1945; s. Vincent Eugene and Leta Valma (Atwood) S.; m. Janet Cellen, July 5, 1968 (div. 1973); m. Patti Stucker, 1990. Student, U. Utah, 1963-68; BA in Bus. Mgmt., Lewis-Clark State Coll., 1990. Registered land surveyor, Idaho. Engr.'s technician Idaho Dept. Transp., Jerome, 1970-77; land surveyor Edwards-Howard-Martens, Engrs., Twin Falls, Idaho, 1977-80; project supt. J. Holley Constrn., Wells, Nev., 1981—; dir. pub. works City of Jerome, 1982-90, City of Coos Bay (Oreg.); mem. adv. bd. N.W. Tech. Transfer Ctr., Olympia, Wash. Chmn. bd. dirs. Jerome City Libr., 1986-90, bd. trustees Coos Bay Libr., 1991—; bd. dirs. Jerome City Airport, 1986-90, Bay Area Rehab., 1990—. Mem. Am. Pub. Works Assn., Am. Water Works Assn. (trustee intermountain sect. 1987—), Pacific N.W. Pollution Control Assn., Green Drake Soc. Office: City of Coos Bay 500 Central Ave Coos Bay OR 97420-1895

SLOAN, MARGARET MACKENZIE, minister; b. N.Y.C., June 15, 1918; d. Heaton Ives Treadway and Marguerite Jeanette (Kalt) Hawley; m. William Milligan Sloan, June 25, 1940 (div. 1972); children: William M. Jr., Margaret MacKenzie II, Stephen Elmendorf, Jonathan Treadway, Rosemary. BA, Vassar Coll., 1940; MA, Brown U., 1965; MDiv, Ch. Div. Sch. of the Pacific, 1982. Minister Christ Ch., Alameda, Calif., 1979-80, Ch. of Transfiguration, San Mateo, Calif., 1980-84, St. Andrew's Episc., Tucson, 1984-88, Grace Episc., Tucson, 1988-91; dir. A Place Apart, Tucson, 1984—; tchr. Episc. Ch., Providence, 1948-72, Tucson, Phoenix, Ariz., 1976-92; counsellor, 1955-92. Contbr. articles to profl. jours. Activist civil rights SCLC; dir. People Against Poverty, Providence. Recipient Purchase prize Valley Nat. Bank 1976, Nat. Painting 3rd place, 1976, 4th place awards Wanamaker, 1936; fellow Coolidge Colloquium, 1991. Mem. Ariz. Artist Guild, South Ariz. Watercolor Guild, Am. Counselling Assn., Mensa, Colonial Dames Am. Democrat.

SLOAN, MICHAEL DANA, information systems specialist; b. Santa Monica, Calif., Sept. 30, 1960; s. Avery and Beverly Rae (Krantz) S.; m. Barbara Rogers; 1 child, Ashley Harrison. BS in Bus. Adminstrn., Calif.

State U., Northridge, 1983; MBA, Pepperdine U., 1987. Programmer/analyst TICOR, Inc., L.A., 1979-80; data processing analyst Deluxe Check Printers, Inc., Chatsworth, Calif., 1980-83; fin. systems analyst Wismer & Assocs., Inc., Canoga Park, Calif., 1983-84; sr. systems analyst Coast Savs. & Loan, Granada Hills, Calif., 1984-86; microcomputer systems specialist Litton Industries, Woodland Hills, Calif., 1986-87; systems mgr., info. resources mgr. TRW, Inc.- Space and Def., Redondo Beach, Calif., 1987-93; project mgr. Health Net, Woodland Hills, 1993—; cons., Data Most, Inc., Chatsworth, 1982-83, Home Savs. & Loan, North Hollywood, Calif., 1987, Micro Tech, L.A., 1987. Mem. Salle Gascon Fencing Club, U.S. Fencing Assn., Delta Sigma Pi.

SLOAN, MICHAEL EUGENE, stockbroker; b. Pueblo, Colo., Jan. 30, 1943; s. Ralph Eugene and Utoka Wilma (Paden) S.; m. Nancy Lynn Hansen, Mar. 22, 1962 (div. June 1974); children: Deseri Lynn, Michael Wesley, Heather Shuibhne; m. Nancy Marie Horton, Dec. 5, 1974; children: Melanie Rae, Mark Harland, Michelle Adelle, Matthew Eugene. BA, Adams State Coll., 1965. Meat cutter Safeway Stores, Inc., Alamosa, Colo., 1961-71; tchr. Alamosa Pub. Schs., 1965-71; owner, operator McDermith Motors Inc., Alamosa, 1971-80; stockbroker Dain Bosworth Inc., Monte Vista, Colo., 1980-91, Edward D. Jones & Co., Monte Vista, 1991—; bd. dirs. Aspen Potato Co., Inc., Monte Vista. Treas. Splashland Inc., Alamosa, 1987—. Mem. San Luis Valley Running Club (pres. 1981—), Masons (past master 1975), Rotary (bd. dirs. Monte Vista club). Republican. Mormon. Office: Edward D Jones & Co 806 1st Ave Monte Vista CO 81144-1404

SLOANE, BEVERLY LEBOV, writer, consultant; b. N.Y.C., May 26, 1936; d. Benjamin S. and Anne (Weinberg) LeBov; m. Robert Malcolm Sloane, Sept. 27, 1959; 1 child, Alison Lori. AB, Vassar Coll., 1958; MA, Claremont Grad. Sch., 1975, doctoral study, 1975-76; cert. in exec. mgmt., UCLA, 1982, grad. exec. program., UCLA, 1982; grad. profl. pub. course, Stanford U., 1982; grad. intensive bioethics course Kennedy Inst. Ethics, Georgetown U., 1987, advanced bioethics course, 1988; grad. sem. in Health Care Ethics, U. Wash. Sch. Medicine, Seattle, summer 1988, 89, 90; grad. Summer Bioethics Inst. Loyola Marymount U., summer, 1990; grad. Annual Summer Inst. on Teaching of Writing, Columbia U. Tchrs. Coll., summer, 1990; cert. in ethics corps tng. program, Josephson Inst. of Ethics, 1991; ethics fellow Loma Linda U. Med. Ctr., 1989; cert. clin. intensive biomedical ethics, Loma Linda U., 1989. Circulation librarian Harvard Med. Library, Boston, 1958-59; social worker Conn. State Welfare, New Haven, 1960-61; tchr. English, Hebrew Day Sch., New Haven, 1961-64; instr. creative writing and English lit. Monmouth Coll., West Long Branch, N.J., 1967-69; freelance writer, Arcadia, Calif., 1970—; v.p. council grad. students, Claremont Grad. sch., 1971-72; mem. adv. council tech. and profl. writing Dept. English, Calif. State U., Long Beach, 1980-82; mem. adv. bd. Calif. Health Rev., 1982-83; mem. Foothill Health Dist. Adv. Council L.A. County Dept. Health Svcs., 1987—, pres., 1989-91, immediate past pres., 1991-92. Ann. Key Mem. award, 1990. Author: From Vassar to Kitchen, 1967, A Guide to Health Facilities: Personnel and Management, 1971, 2d edit., 1977, 3d edit., 1992. Mem. pub. relations bd. Monmouth County Mental Health Assn., 1968-69; mem. task force edn. and cultural activities, City of Duarte, 1987-88, strategic planning task force com., campaign com. for pre-eminence, Claremont Grad. Sch., 1986-87; Vassar Coll. Class rep. to Alumnae Assn. Fall Coun. Meeting, 1989,, class corr. Vassar Coll. Quarterly Alumnae Mag., 1993—; grad. AMA Ann. Health Reporting Conf., 1992, 93; mem. exec. program network UCLA Grad. Sch. Mgmt., 1987—; trustee Ctr. for Improvement of Child Caring, 1981-83; mem. League Crippled Children, 1982—, bd. dirs., 1988-91, treas. for gen. meetings, 1990-91, chair hostesses com., 1988-89, pub. rels. com., 1990-91; bd. dirs. L.A. Commn. on Assaults Against Women, 1983-84; v.p. Temple Beth David, 1983-86; mem. community relations com. Jewish Fedn. Council Greater Los Angeles, 1985-87; del. Task Force on Minorities in Newspaper Bus., 1987-89; community rep. County Health Ctrs. Network Tobacco Control Program, 1991. Recipient cert. of appreciation City of Duarte, 1988, County of L.A., 1988; Coro Found. fellow, 1979; named Calif. Press Woman Communicator of Achievement, Woman of Yr., 1992. Fellow Am. Med. Writers Assn. (dir. 1980—, Pacific S.W. del. to nat. bd. 1980-87, 89-91, chmn. various conv. coms., chmn. nat. book awards trade category 1982-83, chmn. Nat. Conv. Networking Luncheon 1983, 84, chmn. freelance and pub. relations coms. Nat. Midyr. Conf. 1983-84, workshop leader ann. conf. 1984-87, 90, 91, 92, nat. chmn. freelance sect. 1984-85, gen. chmn. 1985, Asilomar Western Regional Conf., gen. chmn. 1985, workshop leader 1985, program co-chmn. 1987, speaker 1985, 88-89, program co-chmn. 1989 nat. exec. bd. dirs. 1985-86, nat. adminstr. sects. 1985-86, pres.-elect Pacific S.W. chpt. 1985-87, pres. 1987-89, immediate past pres. 1989-91, bd. dirs., 1991—, moderator gen. session nat. conf. 1987, chair gen. session nat. conf., 1986-87, chair Walter C. Alvarez Meml. Found. award 1986-87, Appreciation award for outstanding leadership 1989, named to Workshop Leaders Honor Roll 1991); mem. Women in Comm. (dir. 1980-82, 89-90, v.p. community affairs 1981-82, N.E. area rep. 1980-81, chmn. awards banquet 1982, sem. leader, speaker ann. nat. profl. conf., 1985, program adv. com. L.A. chpt. 1987, v.p. activities 1989-90, chmn. Los Angeles chpt. 1st ans Underwood Freedom of Info. Awards Banquet 1982, recognition award 1983, nominating com. 1982, 83, com. Women of the Press Awards luncheon 1988, Women in Comm. awards luncheon 1988), Am. Assn. for Higher Edn., AAUW (legis. chmn. Arcadia br. 1976-77, books and plays chmn. Arcadia br. 1973-74, creative writing chmn. 1969-70, 1st v.p. 1975-76, networking chmn. 1981-82, chmn. task force promoting individual liberties 1987-88, Woman of Yr., Woman of Achievement award 1986, cert. of appreciation 1987), Coll. English Assn., Am. Pub. Health Assn., Am. Soc. Law and Medicine, Calif. Press Women (v.p. programs L.A. chpt. 1982-85, pres. 1985-87, state pres. 1987-89, past immediate past state pres. 1989-91, chmn. state speakers bur. 1989—, del nat. bd. 1989—, moderator ann. spring conv., 1990, 92, chmn. nominating com. 1990-91, Calif. lit. dir. 1990-92, dir. state lit. com. 1990-92, dir. family literary day Calif., 1990, Cert. of Appreciation, 1991, named Calif. Communicator of Achievement 1992), AAUP, Internat. Comm. Assn., N.Y. Acad. Scis., Ind. Writers So. Calif. (bd. dirs. 1989-90, dir. Specialized Groups 1989-90, dir. at large 1989-90, bd. dirs. corp. 1988-89, dir. Speech Writing Group, 1991-92), Hastings Inst., AAAS, Am. Med. Writers Assn. (pres. 1987-89, nat. adminstr. sects. 1985-86, nat. exec. bd. dirs. 1985-86, chmn. nominating com. Pacific S.W. chpt., 1987-89, workshop leader ann. conf. 1984-87, 90, 91, steering com. seminar on med. writing 1988, program planning com. for daylong program on med. writing in collaboration with Ind. Writers So. Calif., 1988-89, topic leader Nat. Conf. Networking Breakfast 1988, del. nat. bd. 1989-91, Appreciation award Outstanding Leadership, 1989, Presdl. award Pacific S.W. chpt. 1990, Am. Med. Writers Workshop Leaders Honor Roll 1991), Nat. Fedn. Press Women, (bd. dirs. 1987-89, nat. co-chmn. task force recruitment of minorities 1987-89, del. 1987-89, nat. dir. of speaker bur. 1989—, editor of speakers bur. directory 1991, cert. of appreciation, 1991, Plenary of Past Pres. state 1989—, workshop leader-speaker ann. nat. conf. 1990, chair state women of achievement com. 1986-87, editor Speakers Bur. Addendum Directory, 1992, editor Speakers Bur. Directory 1991, 92, named 1st runner up Nat. Communicator of Achievement 1992), AAUW (chpt. Woman of Achievement award 1986, chmn. task force promoting individual liberties 1987-88, speaker 1987, Cert. of Appreciation 1987, Woman of Achievement-Woman of Yr. 1986), Internat. Assn. Bus. Communicators, Soc. for Tech. Comm. (workshop leader, 1985, 86), Kennedy Inst. Ethics, Soc. Health and Human Values, Assoc. Writing Programs. Clubs: Women's City (Pasadena), Vassar of So. Calif., Claremont Colls. Faculty House, Petroleum (L.A.), Pasadena Athletic, Town Hall of Calif. Faculty (vice chair community affairs sect. 1982-87, speaker 1986, faculty-instr. Exec. Breakfast Inst. 1985-86, mem. study sect. council 1986-88). Lodge: Rotary (chair Duarte Rotary mag. 1988-89, mem. dist. friendship exch. com. 1988-89, mem. internat. svc. com. 1989-90, info. svc. com. 1989-90). Home and Office: 1301 N Santa Anita Ave Arcadia CA 91006-2419

SLOANE, ROBERT MALCOLM, hospital administrator; b. Boston, Feb. 11, 1933; s. Alvin and Florence (Goldberg) S.; m. Beverly LeBov, Sept. 27, 1959; 1 dau., Alison. A.B., Brown U., 1954; M.S., Columbia U., 1958. Adminstrv. resident Mt. Auburn Hosp., Cambridge, Mass., 1957-58; med. adminstr. AT&T, N.Y.C., 1959-60; asst. dir. Yale New Haven Hosp., 1961-67; assoc. adminstr. Monmouth Med. Center, Long Branch, N.J., 1967-69; adminstr. City of Hope Nat. Med. Center, Duarte, Calif., 1969-80; pres. Los Angeles Orthopedic Hosp., Los Angeles Orthopedic Found., 1980-86; pres., chief exec. officer Anaheim (Calif.) Meml. Hosp., 1986—; mem. faculty Columbia U. Sch. Medicine, 1958-59, Yale U. Sch. Medicine, 1963-67, Quinnipiac Coll., 1963-67, Pasadena City Coll., 1972-73, Calif. Inst. Tech., 1973-85, U. So. Calif., 1976-79, clin. prof., 1987—, UCLA, 1985-87; chmn. bd. Health Data Net, 1971-73; pres. Anaheim (Calif.) Meml. Hosp., 1986—, Anaheim Meml. Devel. Found., 1986—. Author: (with B. L. Sloane) A Guide to Health Facilities: Personnel and Management, 1971, 3d edit., 1992; mem. editorial and adv. bd. Health Devices, 1972-90; contbr. articles to hosp. jours. Bd. dirs. Health Systems Agy. Los Angeles County, 1977-78; bd. dirs. Calif. Hosp. Polit. Action Com., 1979-87, vice chmn., 1980-83, chmn., 1983-85. Served to lt. (j.g.) USNR, 1954-56. Fellow Am. Coll. Hosp. Adminstrs. (regent 1989-93); mem. Am. Hosp. Assn., Hosp. Council So. Calif. (bd. dirs., sec. 1982, treas. 1983, chmn. elect 1984, chmn. 1985, past chmn. 1986, 89), Calif. Hosp. Assn. (bd. dirs., exec. com. 1984-86, 89), Vol. Hosps. Am. (bd. dirs. west region 1986—, vice-chmn. 1990-93, chmn 1993—). Home: 1301 N Santa Anita Ave Arcadia CA 91006-2419 Office: PO Box 3005 1111 W LaPalma Ave Anaheim CA 92803

SLOMANSON, WILLIAM REED, law educator, legal writer; b. Johnstown, Pa., May 1, 1945; s. Aaron Jacob and Mary Jane (Reed) S.; m. Anna Maria Valladolid, June 24, 1972; children: Lorena, Michael, Paul, Christina. BA, U. Pitts., 1967; JD, Calif. Western U., 1974; LLM, Columbia U., N.Y.C., 1975. Bar: Calif. 1975. Assoc. Booth, Mitchel, Strange & Smith, L.A., 1975-77; prof. law Western State U., San Diego and Fullerton, Calif., 1977—; judge Provisional Dist. World Ct., L.A., 1990—; mem. bd. advisors San Diego Community Coll. Dist., 1989—. Author: (reference book) International Business Bibliography, 1989, (textbooks) Fundamental Perspectives on International Law, 1990, California Civil Procedure, 1991, California Civil Procedure in a Nutshell, 1992. Lt. USN, 1967-71, Vietnam. Mem. Am. Soc. Internat. Law (editor newsletter on UN decade of internat. law), San Diego County Bar Assn. (chair internat. sect. 1988—). Office: Western State U 2121 San Diego Ave San Diego CA 92110-2905

SLOSKY, LEONARD C., environmental consultant; b. Colo. Springs, Colo., Sept. 18, 1952; s. Harry and Shirley Mae (Hoffman) S. BA, U. Colo., 1975. Registered environ. assessor, Calif. Staff asst. Colo. Gov's. Office, Denver, 1975-77; staff dir. Intergovtl. Sci., Engrng. & Tech. Adv. Panel Natural Resources Task Force Exec. Office of the Pres., Washington, 1978-81; asst. to the Gov. Colo. Gov.'s Office, Denver, 1981-85; pres. Slosky & Co., Inc., Denver, 1985—; exec. dir. Rocky Mountain Low-Level Radioactive Waste Bd., Denver, 1983—; mem. Waste Isolation Pilot Plant blue ribbon com., Washington, 1989-91. Mem. Greater Denver C. of C. (co-chairperson, mem. environ. com. 1992). Office: Slosky & Co Inc 1675 Broadway #1400 Denver CO 80202

SLOUBER, JAMES KIRK, accountant; b. Chgo., Feb. 12, 1952; s. Robert James and Doris Marie (Olson) S.; m. Kerry Perry, Oct. 24, 1981; children: Erika, Kirsten, Bradon. BA in Acctg., Econs., and Bus., Augustana Coll., Rock Island, Ill., 1974; MS in Taxation, DePaul U., 1978. CPA, Calif., Ill. Acct. Procon, Inc., Des Plaines, Ill., 1974-75; tax supervising sr. Peat, Marwick, Mitchell & Co., Chgo., Newport Beach, Calif., 1977-80; tax mgr. Price Waterhouse, West Los Angeles, Calif., 1980-83; sr. tax mgr. Price Waterhouse, Washington, 1983-84; sr. mgr. in charge tax dept. Price Waterhouse, Riverside, Calif., 1984-89; tax ptnr. in charge Pannell Kerr Forster, L.A., 1989-91, Goldfarb, Whitman & Cohen, L.A., 1991—; mem. citizens univ. com. U. Calif., Riverside, 1985-89. Author: (booklet) Interest Expense Rules After Tax Reform, 1989; contbr. 7 articles to profl. jours. Bd. dirs. United Way Inland Valleys, Riverside, 1986-90, Luth. Sch. Foothills, 1993—. Mem. AICPA (tax divsn., tax exempt orgns. com.), Calif. Soc. CPA's, Ill. Soc. CPA's, L.A. City Hdqrs. Assn., Kiwanis, Canyon Crest Country Club. Republican. Lutheran. Home: 9426 Carlynn Pl Tujunga CA 91042-3319 Office: Goldfarb Whitman & Cohen 12233 W Olympic # 210 Los Angeles CA 90064

SLOVER, ARCHY F., chemist; b. Oshkosh, Wis., July 8, 1920; s. Archie F. and Josephine Petronella (Zindler); BA, UCLA, 1947; m. Mary Beatrice Corkill, May 25, 1946 (dec. June 17, 1987); 1 child, Mary Kay Slover Eckhardt. Devel. chemist Kelite Products Co., L.A., 1946-49; v.p., gen. mgr. Delco Chems. Inc., L.A., 1949-57; mgr. indsl. spltys. Pennwalt Corp., L.A., 1957-74; chemist Custom Chem. Formulators Inc., Cudahy, Calif., 1974—; mgr. Cherokee Chem. Co., Inc., Compton, Calif., 1976-89; cons. in field. Capt. U.S. Army, 1942-46. Fellow AAAS, Am. Inst. Chemists; mem. Nat. Assn. Corrosion Engrs., Am. Chem. Soc., Am. Electroplaters Soc., USAF Assn., Soc. Advancement Material Process Engrs., Res. Officers Assn., Sigma Alpha Epsilon, Ky. Cols. Patentee in field. Address: 21 Hacienda Dr Arcadia CA 91006

SLUSKY, JOSEPH, sculptor, educator; b. Phila., June 7, 1942; s. Nathan and Jean (Lorber) S.; m. Marjorie Ann Title, Sept. 2, 1967 (div. Nov. 1972). BArch., U. Calif., Berkeley, 1966, MA in Sculpture, 1968. Lectr. in sculpture U. Calif., Berkeley, 1968-70, 73, 77-80, lectr. in architecture, 1980—; instr. in art Ohlone Coll., Fremont, Calif., 1972-86, San Jose City Coll., Calif., 1972-77, Merritt Coll., Oakland, Calif., 1975; lectr. in sculpture San Francisco State U., 1978. One-man shows include Victor Fisher Galleries, Oakland, 1986, Dorothy Weiss Gallery, San Francisco, 1988, Holy Names Coll., Oakland, 1990, Smith Andersen Gallery, Paloato, calif., 1992, Barclay Simpson Gallery, Lafayette, Calif., 1992; group shows include Syntex Corp., Palo Alto, 1979-80, Sun Gallery, Hayward, Calif., 1980, Palo Alto Cultural Ctr., 1980, San Mateo County Arts Coun., Belmont, Calif., 1980, Sonoma State U., Rohnert Park, Calif., 1982, Kaiser Ctr., Oakland, 1982, Olive Hyde Art Ctr., Fremont, 1982, San Jose Inst. Contemporary Art, 1983, Wurster Hall Gallery, Coll. Environ. Design, U. Calif., Berkeley, 1983, Triton Mus. Art, Santa Clara, Calif., 1985 , The Haggin Mus., Stockton, Calif., 1988, Calif. State Fair, Sacramento, 1988, Gallery Concord, Calif., 1988, 89, Pla. of the Ams., Dallas, 1990, Berkeley Art Ctr., Berkeley, Calif., 1990, Vorpal Gallery, San Francisco, 1991, Bell Ross Gallery, Memphis, 1991, Richmond (Calif.) Art Ctr., 1992, Contract Design Ctr., San Francisco, 1992, John Natsoulas Gallery at L.A., 1992, Art Fair, L.A., 1992; represented in permanent collections City San Francisco, City of Hayward, City of Berkeley; prin. works include Calliope Berkeley Marina, 1980, Calypso in interior lobby San Francisco Dept. Water, 1984. Recipient 2d place award Calif. State Fair, Sacramento, 1985, Merit award, 1992, 1st place sculputre award Bay Arts Exhibition, San Mateo Arts Coun., 1987, Merit award, 1990, award of Excellence Calif. State Fair, 1988, 91, Sculpture award Gallery House, 1989; U. Calif., Berkeley edn. abroad grantee, Sweden, 1967-68. Democrat. Home: 2612A Regent St Berkeley CA 94704-3315 Office: U Calif Dept Architecture 232 Wurster Hall Berkeley CA 94720

SLUSSER, ROBERT WYMAN, aerospace company executive; b. Mineola, N.Y., May 10, 1938; s. John Leonard and Margaret McKenzie (Wyman) S.; BS, MIT, 1960; MBA, Wharton, 1962; ERC, Ft. Belvior Def. Systems Mgmt. Sch., 1977; AMP, Claremont, 1982; m. Linda Killeas, Aug. 3, 1968; children: Jonathan, Adam, Robert, Mariah. Assoc. adminstr.'s staff NASA Hdqrs., Washington, 1962-65; with Northrop Corp., Hawthorne, Calif., 1965—, adminstr. Space Labs., 1965-68, mgr. bus. and fin. Warnecke Electron Tubes Co. div., Chgo., 1968-71, controller Cobra Program Aircraft div., Hawthorne, 1971-72, mgr. bus. adminstrn. YF-17 Program, 1972-75, mgr. adminstrn. F-18/Cobra programs, also mgr. F-18 design to cost program, 1975-79, mgr. engrng. adminstrn., 1980-82, acting v.p. engrng., 1982, mgr. data processing, 1983-84, v.p. info. resources, 1985-91, mgr. long range planning, 1991—; CFO, bd. dirs. So. Calif. Hist. Aviation Found., 1987-90, chmn. of bd., pres., 1990—; bd. dirs., contracting officer, Inc., 1988-91; mem. dirs. adv. bd. S.C. Rsch. Authority, 1991—. Grumman Aircraft Engrng. scholar, 1956-60. Fellow AIAA (assoc.); mem. So. Calif. Soc. Info. Mgnt., (mem. exec. com. 1985-91), Northrop Mgmt. Club (bd. dirs. 1992-93, Man of Yr. 1991-92). Home: 7270 Berry Hill Dr Palos Verdes Peninsula CA 90274-4402 Office: Northrop Aircraft Div 1 Northrop Ave Hawthorne CA 90250-3236

SMALL, LAWRENCE FREDERICK, oceanography educator; b. St. Louis, Feb. 16, 1934; s. Frederick Ruse and Adele Naomi (Edwards) S.; m. Janice Ethel Hammersley; children: Karen Loraine, Stephen Lawrence, Suzanne Marie. AB, U. Mo., 1955; MS, Iowa State U., 1959, PhD, 1961. Asst. prof. oceanography Oreg. State U., Corvallis, 1961-67, assoc. prof., 1967-74, prof., 1974—, assoc. dean oceanography, 1983—; cons. IAEA, Monaco, 1971-72, 78, LaSpezia, Italy, 1990, Cuernavaca, Mex., 1992, Pacific Northwest River Basins Commn., Portland, Oreg., 1980-81, Columbia River Data Mgmt. Program, Astoria, Oreg., 1982. Contbr. articles to profl. jours. Served to 1st lt. arty. U.S. Army, 1955-57. Recipient Spl. Service awards IAEA, 1972, 78; grantee NOAA, NSF, Dept. Energy, Office Naval Research, EPA, 1962—. Mem. AAAS, Am. Soc. Limnology and Oceanography, Oceanography Soc., Sigma Xi, Beta Theta Pi. Office: Coll Oceanic-Atmos Scis Oreg State U Corvallis OR 97331

SMALLEY, TOPSY NEHER, librarian; b. Boston, Dec. 5, 1943; d. H. Victor and Sara Elizabeth (Yoder) Neher; 1 child, Brian. BA, Pomona Coll., 1966; MLS, UCLA, 1976; MA in Liberal Studies, SUNY, Plattsburgh, 1982. Head libr. Greenville (Pa.) Pub. Libr., 1967-70; asst. libr. Feinberg Libr. SUNY, 1970-76, assoc. libr., 1980-84; asst. dir. Clinton C.C. Libr., Plattsburgh, 1978-79; head pub. svcs. Monterey (Calif.) Peninsula Coll. Libr., 1984-88, Cabrillo Coll. Libr., Aptos, Calif., 1988—. Contbg. author: Theories of Bibliographic Education, 1982; also articles. Mem. ALA. Democrat. Home: 850 Rosedale Ave Apt 44 Capitola CA 95010 Office: Cabrillo Coll Libr 6500 Soquel Dr Aptos CA 95003

SMALLMAN, GAIL ELIZABETH, information systems manager; b. Buffalo, Mar. 24, 1953; d. Lemuel James and Beverly Ann (Waldron) S.; m. Ronald Hugh Strasser, 1974 (div. 1975). Student, Oreg. State U., 1971-72, Portland State, 1972-74, City U., Seattle, 1979. Word processor Atty. Gen.'s Consumer Protection, Portland, Oreg., 1974-75, Lane Powell Moss & Miller, Seattle, 1978-79; sec. Carney, Probst & Levak, Portland, 1975-76, Jones, Lang, Klein, et al., Portland, 1978; office mgr. Corl & Willis, Corvallis, Oreg., 1976-77; adminstrv. asst. Reed McClure Moceri et al., Seattle, 1978-80; systems mgr. Lane Powell Spears et al., Seattle, 1980—; v.p. Wang/Informatics special interest group VS Legal Users' Group, Sacramento, 1990-91. Active Residents Opposed to Aircraft ReRouting, 1991. Scholar Oregon State U., 1971. Mem. Am. Mgmt. Assn., LawNet, Inc. (v.p., dir. 1991—). Republican. Episcopal. Home: 10245 NE Sunrise Pl Bainbridge Is WA 98110 Office: Lane Powell Spears Lubersky 1420 5th Ave Ste 4100 Seattle WA 98101

SMALLWOOD, BETTY, lawyer; b. Eagle Pass, Tex., Nov. 27, 1946; d. Charles Augustus and Helen Elizabeth (Stanford) S. BA, U. Tex., 1968, BS, 1970; grad., Med. Tech. Sch., 1970; JD, U. San Diego, 1986. Bar: Tex. 1992, Nev. 1987; lic. real estate agt. Nev.; cert. med. technologist. Med. technologist VA Med Ctr., Denver and Houston, 1977-83; atty. Clark & Sacco, Las Vegas, Nev., 1987-88, Jeffrey Burr & Assocs., Las Vegas, 1988-91; pvt. practice Henderson, Nev., 1991—; instr., coord. U. Nev. Las Vegas Ctr. for Internat. Bus., 1992. Exec. editor U. San Diego Law Rev., 1985-86. Campaign worker Nev. U.S. Senator, 1988, Clark County Attys. for Nev. Atty. Gen., Las Vegas, 1990; girls day vol. Las Vegas Boys and Girls' Club, 1991; bd. dirs. United Cerebral Palsey of South Nev., 1992-93. Named Disting. Women So. Nev. Careline Inc., 1990, 91. Mem. ABA, So. Nev. Internat. Bus. Coun., Am. Bus. Women's Assn., So. Nev. Assn. of Women Attys. (sec. 1989-90), State Bar of Nev., State Bar of Tex., Henderson C. of C. (ambassador corps 1992-93). Office: Bldg 2 Ste 104 153 West Lake Mead Dr Henderson NV 89015

SMARANDACHE, FLORENTIN, mathematics researcher, poet; b. Balcesti-Vilcea, Romania, Dec. 10, 1954; came to U.S., 1990; s. Gheorghe and Maria (Mitroiescu) S.; m. Eleonora Niculescu; children: Mihai-Liviu, Silviu-Gabriel. MS, U. Craiova, 1979; postgrad., Ariz. State U., 1991. Mathematician I.U.G., Craiova, Romania, 1979-81; math. prof. Romanian Coll., 1981-82, 1984-86, 1988; math. tchr. Coop. Ministry, Morocco, 1982-84; French tutor pvt. practice, Turkey, 1988-90; software engr. Honeywell, Phoenix, 1990-93. Author: Nonpoems, 1990, Only Problems, Not Solutions, 1991, numerous other books; contbr. articles to profl. jours. Mem. U.S. Math. Assn., Romania Math. Assn., Zentralblatt fur Math. (reviewer). Home: PO Box 42561 Phoenix AZ 85080-2561

SMART, WILLIAM BUCKWALTER, newspaper and magazine editor; b. Provo, Utah, June 27, 1922; s. Thomas Laurence and Nellie (Buckwalter) S.; m. Donna Toland, July 15, 1945; children: William Toland, Melinda, Kristen, Thomas Toland, Alfred Lawrence. Student, U. Wyo., 1943-44, U. Utah, 1949-51; B.A., Reed Coll., 1948. Reporter Internat. News Service, Portland, Oreg., 1941-43; reporter The Oregonian, Portland, 1946-48, The Deseret News, Salt Lake City, 1948-52; chief editorial writer, editor The Deseret News, 1952-66, exec. editor, 1966-72, editor, gen. mgr., 1972-86, sr. editor, 1986-88; editor This People mag., 1988—. Author: Old Utah Trails, Messages For a Happier Life. Exec. com. Grand Canyon Trust; chmn. Sta. KUED; mem. nat. adv. bd. Snowbird Inst. for Arts and Humanities; chmn. Utah Innovation Found.; chmn. Inst. for Study of Humanities; exec. com. Coalition for Utah's Future. 1st lt. inf. AUS, 1943-46, PTO. Mem. Bonneville Knife and Fork Club (past pres.), Timpanogos Club (past pres.), Fort Douglas (Hidden Valley) Club, Aztec Club, Phi Beta Kappa, Sigma Delta Chi, Kappa Tau Alpha. Mem. Ch. of Jesus Christ of Latter-day Saints. Home: 55 Laurel St Salt Lake City UT 84103-4349

SMATHERS, JAMES BURTON, medical physicist, educator; b. Prairie du Chien, Wis., Aug. 26, 1935; s. James Levi and Irma Marie (Stindt) S.; m. Sylvia Lee Rath, Apr. 20, 1957; children—Kristine Kay, Kathryn Ann, James Scott, Ernest Kent. B.Nuclear Engrng., N.C. State Coll., 1957, M.S., 1959; Ph.D., U. Md., 1967. Diplomate Am. Bd. Radiology, Am. Bd. Med. Physics, Am. Bd. Radiation Oncology Physics; cert. in radiation oncology physics; registered profl. engr., D.C., Tex., Calif. Research engr. Atomics Internat., Canoga Park, Calif., 1959, Walter Reed Army Inst. Research, Washington, 1961-67; prof. nuclear engrng. Tex. A. and M. U., College Station, 1967-80; prof., head bioengrng. Tex. A. and M. U., 1976-80; prof., head med. physics, dept. radiation oncology UCLA, 1980—; cons. U.S. Army, Dept. Energy, also pvt.; industry. Served with U.S. Army, 1959-61. Recipient Excellence in Teaching award Gen. Dynamics, 1971; Excellence in Research award Tex. A. and M. U. Former Students Assn., 1976. Mem. Am. Nuclear Soc., Health Physics Soc., Am. Assn. Physcists in Medicine, Am. Soc. Engrng. Edn. (Outstanding Tchr. award in nuclear engrng. div. 1972), Radiation Research Soc., Nat. Soc. Profl. Engrs., Calif. Soc. Profl. Engrs., Sigma Xi, Sigma Pi Sigma, Phi Kappa Phi. Home: 18229 Minnehaha St Northridge CA 91326-3427 Office: UCLA Dept Radiation Oncology B265 200 UCLA Med Plz Los Angeles CA 90024

SMATKO, ANDREW JOHN, gynecologist, obstetrician; b. Fort Edward, N.Y., June 14, 1917; s. John George and Anna Mary (Matochik) S.; m. Shirley Jean; 1 child, Andrew John Jr. BA, Columbia Coll., 1937; MD, NYU, 1941. Rotating intern City Hosp., N.Y.C., 1941-43; resident in ob/gyn. Florence Crittenton Hosp., Detroit, 1943-45; pvt. practice Beverly Hills, Calif., 1945-52, Santa Monica, Calif., 1948—, L.A., 1951-52; sr. cons. in ob/gyn. St. Johns Hosp., Santa Monica, 1946—, Santa Monica Hosp., 1947—; cons. in field; lectr. in field. Contbr. articles to profl. jours.; author: Mountaineer's Guide to the High Sierra, 1972; inventor spl. gynecol. surg. instruments. Columbia Coll. scholar. Mem. L.A. County Med. Assn., Calif. Med. Assn., L.A. Obs. and Gynecol. Soc., Pan Pacific Surg. Assn., Beverly Hills Mens Club, Columbia Coll. Alumni Assn., NYU Alumni Assn. Republican. Roman Catholic. Office: 2001 Santa Monica Blvd Santa Monica CA 90404-2102

SMELICK, ROBERT MALCOLM, investment bank executive; b. Phoenix, Mar. 27, 1942; s. Valentine and Mary Helen (McDonald) S.; m. Gail Paine Sterling, Dec. 10, 1979; children: Christopher Paine, Alexandra McBryde, Gillian Sterling. BA, Stanford U., 1964; MBA, Harvard U., 1968; postgrad. U. Melbourne (Australia), 1965-66. v.p. Kidder Peabody & Co., Inc., N.Y.C. and San Francisco, 1968-79; mng. dir. First Boston Corp., San Francisco, 1979-89; mng. prin., founder Sterling Payot Company, San Francisco, 1989—; bd. dirs. Willamette Industries, Portland, Oreg., AdExpress Co., San Francisco; trustee Town Sch. for Boys, San Francisco. Republican. Episcopalian. Office: 222 Sutter St Fl 8 San Francisco CA 94108-4445

SMERDON, ERNEST THOMAS, academic administrator; b. Ritchey, Mo., Jan. 19, 1930; s. John Erle and Ada (Davidson) S.; m. Joanne Duck, June 9, 1951; children: Thomas, Katherine, Gary. BS in Engrng., U. Mo., 1951, MS in Engrng., 1956, PhD in Engrng., 1959. Registered profl. engr., Ariz. Chmn. dept. agrl. engrng. U. Fla., Gainesville, 1968-74, asst. dean for rsch., 1974-76; vice chancellor for acad. affairs U. Tex. System, Austin, 1976-82; dir. Ctr. for Rsch. in Water Resources U. Tex., 1982-88; dean Coll. Engrng. and Mines U. Ariz., Tucson, 1988-92; vice provost, dean Engrng

U. Ariz., 1992—; mem. bd. sci. and tech. for internat. devel. NRC, Washington, 1990—. Editor: Managing Water Related Conflicts: The Engineer's Role, 1989. Mem. Ariz. Gov.'s Sci. and Tech. Coun., 1989—; bd. dirs. Greater Tucson Econ. Coun., Tucson, 1990. Recipient Disting. Svc. in Engring. award U. Mo., 1982. Fellow AAAS, Am. Soc. Agrl. Engrs.; mem. ASCE (Outstanding Svc. award irrigation and drainage div. 1988, Royce Tipton award 1989), NAE (peer com. 1986—, acad. adv. bd. 1989-92, tech. policy options co. 1990-91), Am. Water Resources Assn. (Icko Iben award 1989), Am. Geophys. Union, Univ. Coun. on Water Resources, Ariz. Soc. Profl. Engrs. (Engr. of Yr. award 1990), Sigma Xi, Phi Kappa Phi, Tau Beta Pi, Pi Mu Epsilon. Office: University of Arizona Engineering Experiment Station 100 Civil Engineering Bldg Tucson AZ 85721

SMIDTH, KAREN CARABETTA, graphic designer; b. Aarhus, Denmark, Feb. 27, 1959; came to the U.S., 1985; d. Hans and Birgit J. (Petersen) Smidth; m. Michael J. Carabetta Jr., Oct. 4, 1986; children: Elsinore, Bendix. Student, Design Coll. Denmark, 1982. With graphic design studio Copenhagen, 1982-85; sr. designer Landor Assocs., San Francisco, 1985-89; pvt. practice San Francisco, Mill Valle, Calif., 1989—. Bd. dirs. Music in Schs. Today, San Francisco, 1990-92; cons. Opera Ptnrs., San Francisco, 1991-92. Office: 41 Catalpa Ave Mill Valley CA 94941

SMILEY, RICHARD WAYNE, research center administrator, researcher; b. Paso Robles, Calif., Aug. 17, 1943; s. Cecil Wallace and Elenore Louise (Hamm) S.; m. Marilyn Lois Wenning, June 24, 1967; 1 child, Shawn Elizabeth. BSc in Soil Sci., Calif. State Poly. U., San Luis Obispo, 1965; MSc in Soils, Wash. State U., 1969, PhD in Plant Pathology, 1972. Asst. soil scientist Agrl. Rsch. Svc., USDA, Pullman, Wash., 1966-69; rsch. asst. dept. plant pathology Wash. State U., Pullman, 1969-72; soil microbiologist Commonwealth Sci. and Indsl. Rsch. Orgn., Adelaide, Australia, 1972-73; rsch. assoc. dept. plant pathology Cornell U., Ithaca, N.Y., 1973-74, asst. prof., 1975-80, assoc. prof., 1980-85; supt. Columbia Basin Agr. Rsch. Ctr., prof. Oreg. State U., Pendleton, 1985—; vis. scientist Plant Rsch. Inst., Victoria Dept. Agr., Melbourne, Australia, 1982-83. Author: Compendium of Turfgrass Diseases, 1983, 2d edit., 1992; contbr. more than 200 articles to profl. jours.; author slide set illustrating diseases of turfgrasses. Postdoctoral fellow NATO, 1972. Mem. Am. Phytopath. Soc. (sr. editor APS Press 1984-87, editor-in-chief 1987-91), Am. Soc. Agronomy, Internat. Turfgrass Soc., Am. Sod Producers Assn. (hon. life), Coun. Agrl. Sci. and Tech., Rotary (Pendleton, pres. 1991-92). Office: Oreg State U Columbia Basin Agr Rsch Ctr PO Box 370 Pendleton OR 97801-0370

SMILEY, ROBERT WILLIAM, industrial engineer; b. Phila., Oct. 18, 1919; s. Albert James and Laura Emma (Hoiler) S.; children from previous marriage: Robert, James, Lauralee, Mary; m. Gloria Morais, Jun. 30, 1990; stepchildren: Deborah, Sheila, Vicki, James, Sonja, Michelle. Certificate in Indsl. Engring, Gen. Motors Inst., 1942; student, U. Rochester, 1948; student mgmt. program for execs., U. Pitts. Grad. Sch. Bus., 1968; student, San Jose State Coll., 1969; BSBA, Coll. Notre Dame, Belmont, Calif., 1972, MBA, 1974. Registered profl. engr., Calif. With A.S. Hamilton (cons. engrs.), Rochester, N.Y., 1946-48; commd. lt. USN, 1952, advanced through grades to comdr., 1960; engaged in tech. contract mgmt. (Poseidon/Polaris and Terrier Missile Programs), 1952-64; officer in charge (Polaris Missile Facility Pacific), Bremerton, Wash., 1964-66; resigned, 1966; mgr. product assurance Missile Systems div. Lockheed Missiles and Space Co., Sunnyvale, Calif., 1966-72; mgr. materiel Missile Systems div. Lockheed Missiles and Space Co., 1972-77; mgr. product assurance McDonnell Douglas Astronautics, 1977-78; dir. product assurance Aerojet Tactical Systems, Sacramento, 1978-83; dir. quality assurance Aerojet Solid Propulsion Co., Sacramento, 1984-92, Tahoe Surg. Instruments, Inc., 1992—; frequent guest lectr. at colls. on quality control and reliability; chmn. Polaris/Minuteman/Pershing Missile Nondestruct Test Com., 1958-64; quality control cons. Dragon Missile Program, U.S. Army, 1971. Contbr. articles to sci. jours., chpt. to Reliability Handbook, 1966, Reliability Engineering and Management, 1988. Served with USNR, 1942-46, 51-52; now capt. ret. Recipient letters of Commendation for work on Polaris/Poseidon Sec. of Navy, 1960, certificate of Honor Soc. for Nondestructive Testing, 1966. Fellow Am. Soc. Quality Control (chmn. San Francisco sect. 1969-70, exec. bd. 1966—, chmn. reliability div. 1971, 81, nat. v.p. 1984-85), SCORE seminars; mem. Aircraft Industries Assn. (chmn. quality assurance com.), Navy League, AAAS, Am. Mgmt. Assn. Home and Office: 9144 Green Ravine Ln Fair Oaks CA 95628-4110

SMIRNOFF, STEVE ROSS, telecommunications company official; b. Shanghai, China, Aug. 23, 1939; came to U.S., 1952; s. Vsevolod Nicolas Smirnoff; m. Cindy Cheney, Sept. 8, 1979. B.A. in Journalism, U. N.D., 1966; postgrad. U. Mont., 1968, U. Wis., 1969-70. Advt., sales specialist Gen. Electric Co., Chgo., 1966-68; dir. spl. communications U. Wis.-Oshkosh, 1970-71; dir. pub. relations Alaska Pacific U., Anchorage, 1971-74; sr. pub. affairs rep. Alascom, Inc., Anchorage, 1978-90, mgr. advt. & sales promotion, 1990-92; spl. asst. Internat. Rels. to Mayor of Anchorage, 1992—; cons. Soviets-U.S. joint ventures. Bd. dirs. Alaska Heart Assn., AMA, PRSA. Author: Doing Business with the Soviets During Perestroika, 1989; pub. (newsletter) Joint Venture News; contbr. articles to trade publs. on current Russian trends. Recipient citation for pioneering work with Russian Fedn. Alaska State Legis. Mem. Pub. Relations Soc. Am. (cert., dir. Alaka chpt., Inducted Counselors Acad. 1993—), Armed Forces Communications and Electronics Assn., Alaska Press Club, Alaska Advt. Fedn., Anchorage C. of C. Home: 3581 Kachemak Cir Anchorage AK 99515-2337 Office: 3001 C St Anchorage AK 99503

SMISSON, DAVID CLAYTON, physician; b. Ft. Valley, Ga., Oct. 23, 1933; s. Hugh Franklin Sr. and Emily Carolyn (Wright) S.; m. Joan Patricia Fox, Sept. 24, 1960; children: David Clayton Jr., Richard Michael, Anne Marie, Sharon Lynn, Angela Jane, Victoria Leah. BS in Pre-Medicine, The Citadel, 1954; MD, Johns Hopkins U., 1958. Intern Med. Ctr. U. Colo., Denver, 1958-59; resident in surgery Med. Ctr. U. Kans., Kansas City, 1959-61; resident in internal medicine Med. Coll. Ga., Augusta, 1963-65, fellow in cardiology, 1965-66; pvt. practice St. Joseph's Hosp., Minot, N.D., 1966-90; chief med. svc. VA Med. Ctr., Miles City, Mont., 1990—. Author: (monograph) Transvenous Pacemaker Implantation Techniques: Recommendations Based on 20 Years of Experience, 1989. Capt. U.S. Army, 1961-63. Fellow ACP, Am. Coll. Cardiology; mem. N.Am. Soc. Pacing and Electrophysiology. Roman Catholic. Home: 105 Lynam Dr Miles City MT 59301-4748 Office: VA Med Ctr 210 S Winchester Ave Miles City MT 59301

SMITH, ALAN JAY, computer science educator, consultant; b. N.Y.C., Apr. 10, 1949; s. Harry and Elsie (Mark) S. SB, MIT, 1971; MS, Stanford (Calif.) U., 1973, PhD in Computer Sci., 1974. From asst. prof. to full prof. U. Calif., Berkeley, 1974—; assoc. editor ACM Trans. on Computer Systems, 1982-93; vice-chmn. elec. engring. & computer sci. dept. U. Calif., Berkeley, 1982-84; nat. lectr. ACM, 1985-86; mem. editorial bd. Jour. Microprocessors and Microsystems, 1988—; subject area editor Jour. Parallel and Distbn. Computing, 1989—; mem. IFIP working group 7.3. Fellow IEEE (disting. visitor 1986-87); mem. Assn. for Computing Machinery (chmn. spl. interest group on computer architecture 1991-93, chmn. spl. interest group on ops. systems 1983-87, bd. dirs. spl. interest group on performance evaluation 1985-89, bd. dirs. spl. interest group on computer architecture 1993—), Computer Measurement Group. Office: U Calif Dept of Computer Sci Berkeley CA 94720

SMITH, ALBERT CROMWELL, JR., investments consultant; b. Norfolk, Va., Dec. 6, 1925; s. Albert Cromwell and Georgie (Foreman) S.; m. Laura Thaxton, Oct. 25, 1952; children: Albert, Elizabeth, Laura. BS in Civil Engring., Va. Mil. Inst., 1949; MS in Govtl. Adminstrn., George Washington U., 1965; MBA, Pepperdine U., 1975. Enlisted USMC, 1944, commd. 2d lt., 1949, advanced through grades to col., 1970; comdr. inf. platoons, companies, landing force; variously assigned staffs U.K. Joint Forces, U.S. Sec. Navy, Brit. Staff Coll., Marine Staff Coll.; adviser, analyst amphibious systems; ret., 1974; pres. A. Cromwell-Smith, Ltd., Charlottesville, Va., 1973, head broker, cons. A. Cromwell Smith, Investments, La Jolla and Coronado, Calif., 1975—. Bd. dirs. Reps. La Jolla, 1975-76; vestryman St. Martin's Episcopal Ch., 1971-73. Decorated Legion of Merit with oak leaf cluster with V device, Bronze Star with V device with oak leaf cluster, Air medal with 2 oak leaf clusters, Purple Heart. Mem. ASCE, Nat., Calif. assns. Realtors, San Diego, Coronado bds. Realtors, Stockbrokers Soc., So. Calif. Options Soc., SAR, Mil. Order Purple Heart. Club: Kona Kai. Author: The Individual Investor in Tomorrow's Stock Market, 1977, The Little Guy's Stock Market Survival Guide, 1979, Wake Up Detroit! The EVs Are Coming, 1982, The Little Guy's Tax Survival Guide, 1984, The Little Guy's Sailboat Success Guide, 1986, The Little Guy's Business Success Guide, 1988, Little Guy's Real Estate Success Guide, 1990, Little Guy's Stock Market Success Guide, 1992; contbr. articles to civilian and mil. publs. Office: 1001 B Ave Ste 319/320 PO Box 192 Coronado CA 92178

SMITH, ANDREW VAUGHN, telephone company executive; b. Roseburg, Oreg., July 17, 1924; s. Andrew Britt and Ella Mae (Vaughn) S.; m. Dorothy LaVonne Crabtree, Apr. 25, 1943; children: Janet L., James A. B.S. in Elec. Engring, Oreg. State U., 1950. Registered profl. engr., Oreg. With Pacific N.W. Bell Tel. Co., 1951-88; asst. v.p. ops. Pacific N.W. Bell Tel. Co., Seattle, 1965, v.p. ops., 1970-78; v.p., gen. mgr. Pacific N.W. Bell Tel. Co., Portland, Oreg., 1965-70; pres. Pacific N.W. Bell Tel. Co., Seattle, 1978-88; pres. ops. U.S. West Communications, 1988-89; exec. v.p. U.S. West Inc., 1989; pres. Telephone Pioneers of Am., 1989-90; ret. U.S. West Inc., 1989; bd. dirs. U.S. Bancorp, Portland, Unigard Mut. and Unigard Ins. Cos., Univar Corp., Seattle, Cascade Natural Gas, Seattle, Airborne Freight Corp., Seattle, Momentum Distbn., Bellevue, Wash., Aldus Corp., Seattle, Tektronix Inc., Portland. Hon. trustee Oreg. State U. Found., U. Wash. Grad. Sch. Bus., 1985, chmn. bd. trustees, 1984-85; gen. chmn. United Way of King County, 1980-81; mem. Wash. State Investment Com., Olympia, 1989-92; mem. bd. regents U. Wash., 1989—. With USNR, 1943-46. Mem. Seattle C. of C. (chmn. 1985-86). Mem. Wash. Athletic Club, Seattle Yacht Club, Rainier Club, Overlake Golf and Country Club, Multnomah Club (Portland), Columbia Tower Club (Seattle), Desert Island Country Club (Palm Desert, Calif.), Masons. Episcopalian. Office: 1600 Bell Pla Rm 1802 Seattle WA 98191

SMITH, ANTHONY YOUNGER, urologist, surgeon; b. Rochester, Minn., June 11, 1955; s. William George and Georgia Lee (Carter) S.; m. Sheila Jean Pym, July 4, 1982; children: Cameron Younger, Sheldon Laverick. B-SChemE, N.Mex. State U., 1977; MD, U. Tex., Dallas, 1981. Diplomate Am. Bd. Urology. Intern then resident in gen. surgery U. Louisville, 1981-83; resident in urology U. N.Mex., Albuquerque, 1983-86, asst. prof. surgery, 1987—; fellow in transplantation U. Tex., Houston, 1986-87; dir. urologic oncology U. N.Mex. Sch. Medicine, Albuquerque, 1987—. Author several chpts. in books; contbr. articles to profl. jours. Mem. Am. Soc. Transplant Surgery, Am. Soc. Transplant Physicians, Am. Urologic Assn., Urologic Soc. Transplantation & Vascular Surgery, S.W. Oncology Group (com. mem.), Western Assn. Transplant Surgeons. Republican. Methodist. Office: Univ N Mex Med Sch Div Urology Lomas Blvd # 2211 Albuquerque NM 87101

SMITH, ARTHUR KITTREDGE, JR., university official, political science educator; b. Derry, N.H., Aug. 15, 1937; s. Arthur Kittredge and Rena Belle (Roberts) S.; m. June Mary Dahar, Nov. 28, 1959; children: Arthur, Valerie, Meredith. B.S., U.S. Naval Acad., 1959; M.A., U. N.H., 1966; Ph.D., Cornell U., 1970. Vis. prof. El Colegio de Mexico, Mexico City, 1968-69; asst. prof. polit. sci. SUNY-Binghamton, 1970-74, assoc. prof., 1974-84, prof., 1984-88, provost for grad. studies and research, 1976-83, v.p. for adminstrn., 1982-88; prof. govt. and internat. studies U. S.C., Columbia, 1988-91, exec. v.p. for acad. affairs, provost, 1988-90, 91, interim pres., 1990-91; pres., prof. polit. sci. U. Utah, Salt Lake City, 1991—. Author: (with Claude E. Welch, Jr.) Military Role and Rule: Perspectives on Civil-Military Relations, 1975; contbr. articles to profl. jours. Active Am. Stores Co., First Security Corp. Served with USN, 1959-65. Lehman fellow, 1966-69, NDEA fellow, 1969-70. Mem. Am. Polit. Sci. Assn., Latin Am. Studies Assn., Inter-Univ. Sem. on Armed Forces and Society, Am. Coun. on Edn., World Affairs Coun. (pres. Binghamton 1975-76), Phi Beta Kappa, Pi Sigma Alpha, Omicron Delta Kappa, Phi Delta Kappa, Beta Gamma Sigma. Home: 1480 Military Way Salt Lake City UT 84103 Office: U Utah Office of the Pres 203 Park Bldg Salt Lake City UT 84112

SMITH, BARBARA BARNARD, music educator; b. Ventura, Calif., June 10, 1920; d. Fred W. and Grace (Hobson) S. B.A., Pomona Coll., 1942; Mus.M., U. Rochester, 1943, performer's cert., 1944. Mem. faculty piano and theory Eastman Sch. Music, U. Rochester, 1943-49; mem. faculty U. Hawaii, Honolulu, 1949—; assoc. prof. music U. Hawaii, 1953-62, prof., 1962-82, prof. emeritus, 1982—; sr. fellow East-West Center, 1973; lectr., recitals in Hawaiian and Asian music, U.S., Europe and Asia, 1956—; field researcher Asia, 1956, 60, 66, 71, 80, Micronesia, 1963, 70, 87, 88, 90, 91, Solomon Islands, 1976. Author publs. on ethnomusicology. Mem. Internat. Soc. Music Edn., Internat. Musicol. Soc., Am. Musicol. Soc., Soc. Ethnomusicology, Internat. Coun. for Traditional Music, Asia Soc., Am. Mus. Instrument Soc., Coll. Music Soc., Soc. for Asian Music, Music Educators Nat. Conf., Pacific Sci. Assn., Assn. for Chinese Music Rsch., Phi Beta Kappa, Mu Phi Epsilon. Home: 581 Kamoku St Apt 2004 Honolulu HI 96826-5210

SMITH, BENJAMIN ERIC, venture capitalist, executive; b. L.A., Mar. 22, 1915; s. Jesse Oliver and Clara Louise (Ferris) S.; m. Donelle Ray, Jan. 6, 1956 (div. 1971); children: Lee Fleming, Deidre Ray Folsom. BA, U. Redlands, 1937; postgrad., Yale U., 1938-39; MA, U. So. Calif., 1940. Mgr. Birch-Smith Storage Co., L.A., 1940-42; div. mgr. Bekins Van & Storage Co., L.A., 1946-50; nat. sales mgr. Meletron Corp., L.A., 1952-56; v.p. Leo G. MacLaughlin Co., Pasadena, Calif., 1956-57; sr. cons. Barry & Co., L.A., 1957-65; pres. Benjamin E. Smith & Assocs., L.A., 1965—, Lancer Pacific Inc., Carlsbad, Calif., 1973-79, Aries Group, San Diego, 1979—; dir. Corp. Fin. Coun., San Diego, 1976—; faculty mem. Southwestern U., L.A., 1941-42, U. So. Calif., 1959-60; mem. San Diego in the Global Economy Com., San Diego, 1990-91. Chmn. 57th Assembly Dist. Rep. Cen. Com., Hollywood, 1958-62; exec. dir. L.A. County Cen. Com., 1957. Lt. col. U.S. Army, 1942-46, 50-52. Republican. Episcopalian. Home: 3017 Azahar Ct Carlsbad CA 92009-8301 Office: Aries Group 5841 B Mission Gorge Rd San Diego CA 92120

SMITH, BERNALD STEPHEN, pilot, aviation consultant; b. Long Beach, Calif., Dec. 24, 1926; s. Donald Albert and Bernice Merrill (Stephens) S.; m. Marilyn Mae Spence, July 22, 1949; children: Lorraine Ann Smith Foute, Evelyn Donice Smith DeRoos, Mark Stephen, Diane April (dec.). Student, U. Calif., Berkeley, 1944-45, 50-51. Cert. airline transport pilot, flight engr., FAA. Capt. Transocean Air Lines, Oakland (Calif.) and Tokyo, 1951-53, Hartford, Conn., 1954-55; 1st officer United Air Lines, Seattle, 1955, San Francisco, 1956-68; tng. capt. United Air Lines, Denver and San Francisco, 1961-68; capt. United Air Lines, San Francisco, 1968—; founder, v.p. AviaAm., Palo Alto, Calif., 1970-72, AviaInternat., Palo Alto, 1972-74; cons. Caproni Vizzola, Milan, 1972-84; prin., cons. Internat. Aviation Cons. and Investments, Fremont, Calif., 1985—; instr. aviation Ohlone Coll., Fremont, 1976; founder Pacific Soaring Coun.; founder, trustee AirSailing, Inc., 1970—, Soaring Safety Found., 1985—. Author/editor: American Soaring Handbook, 1975, 80; contbr. articles to profl. jours. Trustee Nat. Soaring Mus., 1975—, pres. 1975-78. Comdr. USNR, 1944-75. Mem. AIAA (pub. bd. 1977—), Soaring Soc. Am. (pres. 1969-70, chmn. pub. bd. 1971-84, bd. dirs. 1963—, Warren Eaton Meml. Trophy 1977, Exceptional Svc. award 1970, 75, 82, 88, 91, named to Hall of Fame 1984), Soc. Automotive Engring., Nat. Aero. Assn., Exptl. Aircraft Assn., Aircraft Owners and Pilots Assn., Airline Pilots Assn., Seaplane Pilots Assn., Orgn. Scientifique et Technique Internat. du Vol a Voile (bd. dirs., U.S. del. 1981—), Fedn. Aeronatique Internat. (Paul Tissandier Diplome 1992), Commn. de Vol A Voile (U.S. del. 1970-71, 78, 85—, v.p. 1988—), U. Calif. Alumni Assn. (life). Democrat. Methodist. Office: Internat Aviation Cons Investments PO Box 3075 Fremont CA 94539-0307

SMITH, BERNARD JOSEPH CONNOLLY, civil engineer; b. Elizabeth, N.J., Mar. 11, 1930; s. Bernard Joseph and Julia Susan (Connolly) S.; B.S., U. Notre Dame, 1951; B.S. in Civil Engring., Tex. A&M U., 1957; M.B.A. in Fin., U. Calif.-Berkeley, 1976; m. Josephine Kerley, Dec. 20, 1971; children—Julia Susan Alice, Teresa Mary Josephine, Anne Marie Kathleen. Asst. Bernard J. Smith, cons. engr. office, Dallas, 1947-57; hydraulic engr. C.E., U.S. Army, San Francisco, 1957-59, St. Paul dist., 1959-60, Kansas City (Mo.) dist., 1960-63, Sacramento dist., 1963-65; engr. Fed. Energy Regulatory Commn., San Francisco Regional Office, 1965—. Served with U.S. Army, 1952-54. Registered profl. engr., Calif., Mo.; lic. real estate broker, Calif. Mem. ASCE (sec. power div. San Francisco sect. 1969), Soc. Am. Mil. Engrs. (treas. Kansas City post 1962), Am. Econ. Assn., Nat. Soc. Profl. Engrs., Res. Officers Assn. (chpt. pres. 1973). Club: Commonwealth of Calif. Home: 247 28th Ave San Francisco CA 94121-1001 Office: Fed Energy Regulatory Commn 901 Market St San Francisco CA 94103-1729

SMITH, BERNICE LAWSON, librarian; b. Delavan, Wis., May 9, 1917; d. Theodore Hale and Ada Byers S. Student, Northland Coll., 1936-38, U. Wis., 1938-39, Mizen Acad. Art, Chgo., 1939-40. Cert. ct. reporter, Ill. Precision inspector Dodge, Chgo., 1943-45, Ford Aircraft, Chgo., 1951-58, Ordnance Engring. Assocs., Chgo., 1959-60; ct. reporter Chgo. Mcpl. Cts., 1961-76; precision inspector Internat. Harvester, Chgo., 1977-80; libr. John C. Stevenson, Architect, San Diego, Calif., 1991—. Mem. Am. Assn. Individual Investors (life). Home: Apt 4-D 111 W Pennsylvania Ave San Diego CA 92103-4054

SMITH, BOBBIE EUGENE, alcohol treatment specialist; b. L.A., Dec. 26, 1933; s. John and Martha (Stewart) S.; m. Hyale Wall, Oct. 23, 1971; 1 child, Constance Irene Smith Redgrave. BSBA, UCLA, 1962. Cert. alcohol/drug evaluation specialist, marijuana evaluation specialist, Oreg. Counselor Cen. Oreg. Alcohol Coun., Bend, 1977-78; clin. social worker Deschutes County Mental Health Ctr., Bend, 1978-84; owner, counselor B.E. Smith Counseling Svcs., Bend, 1984—; bd. dirs. Oreg. Substance Abuse Profis. Assn., 1978-82. Co-founder Deschutes County chpt. MADD, Bend, 1980; bd. dirs. Bend Golf and Country Club, 1988-89; candidate Calif. State Senator, L.A., 1960, Deschutes County Commn., Bend, 1992; bd. dirs. Community Correction Adv. Bd., 1980—. Sgt. U.S. Army, 1950-53, Korea. Reciipent Outstanding Vol. Work award MADD, 1985. Mem. ACA, Rotary. Democrat. Methodist. Office: BE Smith Counseling Svcs 1012 NW Wall Ste 221 Bend OR 97701

SMITH, BRUCE NEPHI, university dean, educator; b. Logan, Utah, Apr. 3, 1934; s. Nephi Pratt and Laura (Peterson) S.; m. Ruth Olean Aamodt, Dec. 18, 1959; children: Rebecca, Trudy, Alan, Marilee, Edward, Samuel. B.S., U. Utah, 1959, M.S., 1962; Ph.D., U. Wash., 1964. Acting instr. U. Wash., Seattle, 1962-63; postdoctoral fellow UCLA, 1964-65; research fellow Calif. Inst. Tech., Pasadena, 1965-68; asst. prof. botany U. Tex.-Austin, 1968-74; assoc. prof. botany Brigham Young U., Provo, Utah, 1974-79, prof., 1979—, dean Biology and Agr. Coll., 1982-88. Contbr. articles to profl. jours. Recipient 2d Miler award Boy Scouts Am., 1978, Dist. award of Merit, 1980; named Silver Beaver, 1986. Mem. AAUP, Am. Soc. Plant Physiology (chmn.-elect western sect. 1984-85, chmn. 1985-88), Geochem. Soc., Japanese Soc. Plant Physiologists, Sigma Xi (sec. chpt. 1990-93), Phi Kappa Phi, Golden Key. Democrat. Mormon. Home: 411 W 530 S Orem UT 84058-6121 Office: Brigham Young U Coll Biology and Agr Dept of Botany and Range Scis Provo UT 84602

SMITH, BRUCE WARREN, photographer, writer; b. Myrtle Point, Oreg., Aug. 10, 1952; s. Warren Andrew and Enness Margaret (Hager) S.; m. Patricia Anne Thurston, Feb. 16, 1974. Student, Judson Baptist Coll., 1970-72, U. Oreg., 1982-84. Parts mgr. JI Case Co., sub-store, Coos Bay, Oreg., 1979-82; features editor Four Wheeler Mag., Canoga Park, Calif., 1984-85; tech. editor Four Wheeler Mag., Canoga Park, 1985-86, sr. editor, 1986-87, editorial dir., spl. publs. div., 1987-88, contbg. editor, 1988—; U.S. overseas editor 4x4 England, Brentwood, Eng., 1988-91; field editor American Hunter Mag., Herndon, Va., 1987—; freelance writer, photographer Lancaster, Calif., 1988—; mng. editor Off-Road, L.A., 1988-91; field editor Sports Afield, N.Y.C., 1990—; off-road racing press liaison GMC/Vista Group Pub. Rels., Van Nuys, Calif., 1989-90, GM Truck Motorsports Pub. Rels. Rep.; contract pub. rels. photographer Chevrolet Truck and Bus. Pub. Rels., Warren, Mich., 1988-90, Nissan Motorsports/Bob Thomas and Assocs., Redondo Beach, Calif., 1989-90. Editor: Monster Trucks: The Poster Book, 1986 (Maggie award 1987). With U.S. Army, 1972-75. Mem. Soc. Profl. Journalists. Democrat. Home and Office: 43612 Easy St Lancaster CA 93535-5600

SMITH, CARL ANTHONY, broadcast executive; b. Athens, Ala., July 5, 1954; s. Frank Johnson and Sally Faye (Tribble) S.; m. Teresa Gloria Jordan, Jan. 5, 1980; children: Jordan Anthony, Rebecca Ann. AA in Broadcasting, Fullerton Coll., 1983; BA in Comm., Calif. State, Fullerton, 1984. Sales exec. S.W. Ins. Co., Brea, Calif., 1985-90; nat. sales mgr. KATY-FM Radio, Hemet, Calif., 1990—. Cpl. USMC, 1977-81. Republican. Office: KATY-FM 43613 E Florida Ave Hemet CA 92544

SMITH, CAROL BABB, information systems analyst; b. Sacramento, Jan. 10, 1963; d. George Alonso and Ruth (Adams) Babb; m. Mitchell Kent Dryden, Apr. 16, 1988 (div. Aug. 1990); m. Randy Lee Smith, Oct. 10, 1992. Info. systems analyst Dept. Justice, Sacramento, 1982-92; assoc. info. systems analyst Calif. State Personnel Bd., Sacramento, 1992—; instr. software programs. Office: Calif State Personnel Bd 801 Capitol Mall MS-54 Sacramento CA 95814

SMITH, CARTER BLAKEMORE, broadcaster; b. San Francisco, Jan. 1, 1937; s. Donald V. and Charlotte M. (Nichols) S.; children: Carter Blakemore, Clayton M. AA, City Coll. San Francisco, 1958; BA, San Francisco State U., 1960; postgrad. N.Y. Inst. Finance, 1969-70; Assoc. in Fin. PLanning, Coll. for Fin. Planning, 1984. Announcer, Sta. KBLF, Red Bluff, Calif., 1954-56; personality Sta. KRE-KRE FM, Berkeley, Calif., 1958-63, Sta. KSFO, San Francisco, 1963-72, Sta. KNBR, San Francisco, 1972-83, Sta. KSFO, San Francisco, 1983-86, Sta. KFRC, San Francisco, 1986-91, 93—; mem. faculty radio-TV dept. San Francisco State U., 1960-61. Mem. adv. bd. Little Jim Club Children's Hosp., 1968-71; bd. dirs. Marin County Humane Soc., 1968-73, San Francisco Zool. Soc., 1980-90; trustee Family Svc. Agy. Marin, 1976-85; mem. alumni bd. Lowell High Sch. Recipient award San Francisco Press Club, 1965; named one of Outstanding Young Men in Am. U.S. Jaycees, 1972. Mem. Amateur Radio Relay League (life), Quarter Century Wireless Assn., Alpha Epsilon Rho. Office: Sta KFRC 500 Washington St San Francisco CA 94111-2906

SMITH, CATHLEEN LYNNE, psychology educator; b. Salt Lake City, Mar. 17, 1947; d. Dasil Clawson and Melba (Fairbourn) S. BA with honors, U. Utah, 1968, MA, 1972, PhD, 1976. Asst. prof. of psychology Portland (Oreg.) State U., 1975-79, assoc. prof. psychology, 1979-83, prof. psychology, 1983—. Contbr. articles to profl. jours. Chair Portland Foster Grandparent Program Adv. Coun., 1983-86. Mem. Am. Psychol. Assn., We. Psychol. Assn., Gerontol. Soc. Am., Soc. for Rsch. in Child Devel., Phi Beta Kappa, Phi Kappa Phi, Sigma Xi. Democrat. Home: 2518 SW Vista Portland OR 97201 Office: Dept Psychol Portland State U PO Box 751 Portland OR 97207

SMITH, CECIL RANDOLPH, JR., retired research chemist; b. Denver, May 31, 1924; s. Cecil Randolph and Elsie (Myers) S.; m. Donna Davies Sublette, Aug. 27, 1954; children: Stanley Edward, David Russell, Carolyn Elizabeth. BA, U. Colo., 1946, MS, 1948; PhD, Wayne State U., 1955. Rsch. chemist Northern Regional Rsch. Ctr. USDA, Peoria, Ill., 1956-85; rsch. leader Northern Regional Rsch. Ctr. USDA, Peoria, 1974-85; vis. scientist Inst. Nat. Product Chemistry, CNRS, Gif-sur-Yvette, France, 1985; asst. to dir. Cancer Rsch. Inst. Ariz. State U., Tempe, 1986-88; collaborator Western Cotton Rsch. Lab., USDA, Phoenix, 1988-92. Author: Sesbanimide and Use Thereof in Treating Leukemic Tumors, 1984; contbr. chpts. to books and sci. lit. articles to profl. jours; patentee in field. Mem. Am. Chem. Soc. (chmn. Peoria sect. 1983-84), Am. Oil Chemists' Soc. (recipient Alton E. Bailey medal, 1984), Am. Soc. Pharmacognosy, Sigma Xi. Quaker. Home: 514 E Colgate Dr Tempe AZ 85283-1906

SMITH, CHARLES ANTHONY, businessman; b. Santa Fe, Sept. 16, 1939; s. Frances (Mier) Vigil; student various adminstrv. and law courses; m. Paula Ann Thomas, June 26, 1965; 1 dau., Charlene Danielle. Circulation mgr. Daily Alaska Empire, 1960-63; agt. Mut. of N.Y. Life Ins. Co., Juneau, Alaska, 1964-65; mng. partner Future Investors in Alaska and Cinema Alaska, Juneau, 1961-62; SE Alaska rep. K & L Distbrs., 1966-68; mgr. Alaska Airlines Newspapers, SE Alaska, 1969; dep. Alaska Retirement System, Juneau, 1970-71; apptd. dir. hwy. safety, gov.'s hwy. safety rep., Juneau, 1971-83; pres. Valley Service Ctr., Inc., 1984—. Alaska pres. Muscular Dystrophy Assn. Am.; pres. SE Alaska Emergency Med. Services Council, 1965-72. Served to major Army N.G., 1964-88. Named Alaska

Safety Man of Yr., 1977. Mem. Am. Assn. Motor Vehicle Adminstrs., Alaska Peace Officers Assn., Nat. Assn. Gov.s' Hwy. Safety Reps., N.G. Assn., Internat. Platform Assn. Roman Catholic. Club: Elks (Juneau). Author various hwy. safety manuals and plans, 1971—. Home: PO Box 32856 Juneau AK 99803-2856 Office: Pouch N Juneau AK 99811

SMITH, CHARLES CONARD, refractory company executive; b. Mexico, Mo., Feb. 10, 1936; s. Charles Adelbert and Waldine (Barnes) S.; m. Constance Nagel, Oct. 6, 1962; children: Stewart Ashley, Graham Prior. BS in Ceramic Engring., Iowa State U., 1958; MBA, Stanford U., 1962. Process engr. Kaiser Refractory divsn. Kaiser Aluminum, Moss Landing, Calif., 1962-65; materials mgr. Kaiser Refractory divsn. Kaiser Aluminum, Mexico, Mo., 1965-67; divsn. planning Kaiser Refractory divsn. Kaiser Aluminum, Oakland, Calif., 1967-69; v.p., gen. mgr. Kaiser Refractories Argentina, Buenos Aires, 1969-74; with divsn. planning Kaiser Refractories divsn. Kaiser Aluminum, Oakland, 1974-77, mktg. mgr., 1977-80, gen. mgr. mfg., 1980-82, v.p., gen. mgr. refractories divsn., 1982-85; chmn., pres., CEO Nat. Refractories and Mineral Corp., Livermore, Calif., 1985—. Patentee in refractory field. Lt. USNR, 1958-60. Mem. Refractories Inst. (past chmn., exec. com.). Republican. Home: 63 Lincoln Ave Piedmont CA 94611

SMITH, CHARLES FRANCIS, project leader, nuclear chemist; b. Casper, Wyo., Aug. 8, 1936; s. Charles Francis and Olive Bernice (Williamson) S.; m. Ann Elaine Abbott, Aug. 20, 1960; children: Karen Ann, Sheryl Diane, Steven Charles. BS in Chemistry, Purdue U., 1958, MS in Physical and Inorganic Chemistry, 1961; PhD in Nuclear Chemistry, U. Calif., Berkeley, 1965. Chemist Lawrence Livermore (Calif.) Nat. Lab., 1964-74, project leader, 1974—; cons. Def. Nuclear Agy., Albuquerque, 1988—; chmn. Chemistry & Radiochemistry Working Corp. Def. Nuclear Agy., Albuquerque, 1988—. Trombonist Livermore/Amador Symphony, 1965—, Pleasanton (Calif.) Community Band, 1978—. Republican. Presbyterian. Home: 2884 Tahoe Dr Livermore CA 94550-6628 Office: Lawrence Livermore Nat Labs MS 231 PO Box 808 Livermore CA 94551-0808

SMITH, CHARLES LEWIS, retired naval officer and association executive; b. Clarkston, Ga., Oct. 27, 1920; s. Robert Clyde and Emelyn (Bloodworth) S.; m. Mildred Lee Stilley, Sept. 5, 1947; children: Jan, Robert Eugene. Student, Ga. Sch. Tech., 1938-39. Enlisted USN, 1937, advanced through grades to comdr., 1968; various assignments including comdg. officer USS Chickasaw (ATF 83), 1962-64; leadership devel. officer Amphibious Force U.S. Pacific Fleet, 1964-66; comdg. officer USS Tioga County (LST 1158), 1966-68; dept. head Amphibious Sch. U.S. Naval Amhibious Base, Coronado, Calif., 1968-70, ret., 1970; dir. pub. rels. and fin. San Diego County coun. Boy Scouts Am., 1971-80, dir. pub. rels., 1980-82, dir. planned giving, 1982-85, ret., 1985. Trustee God Bless Am. Week, Inc., 1972-80, pres., 1977-78, co-chmn. San Diego Bicentennial Pageant, 1976; mem. adv. bd. Commd. Officers Mess (Open) U.S. Naval Sta., 1973-89; bd. dirs. Boys Club Chula Vista, Calif., 1985-87; devel. com. Alvarado Health Found., Alvarado Hosp. Med. Ctr., 1986-87; charter rev. com. City of Chula Vista, 1986-88; mem. accolades com. City of San Diego, 1988-90; rsch. bd. advisors Am. Biog. Inst., 1988—; vol. Boy Scouts Am. 1935-71, 85—; scout commr. San Diego County coun. 1969-71, mem. internat. rels. com. 1985-92, scoutmaster 7th Nat. Jamboree, Farragut State park, Idaho, 1969, 13th World Jamboree, Japan, 1971, mem. nat. staff Nat. Jamboree, Ft. A.P. Hill, Va., 1986. Recipient svc. award Civitan Internat., 1968, Community Svc. resolution Calif. Senate, 1970, Southwestern Coll., 1973, Silver Beaver award Boy Scouts Am., 1965, Svc. to Youth resolution Calif. Senate, 1985, award Armed Forces YMCA Century Club, 1988, Appreciation award United Way San Diego, 1974-82, citation for heroism Sheriff of San Diego, 1991, Recognition award San Diego Rotary Club, 1991, citation for svc. City of San Diego Accolades Com. 1992.; Scouter Chuck Smith Day proclaimed by City of San Diego, 1985; flagpole dedicated to Scouter Chuck Smith San Diego County Coun. BSA, 1992; named to Honorable Order Ky. Cols., 1985. Mem. Nat. Soc. Fund Raising Execs. (bd. dirs. San Diego chpt., 1975-80, 84-85, hosp. com. 1984-85), UN Assns. (bd. dirs. San Diego chpt. 1972-85), Ret. Officers Assn. (bd. dirs. Sweetwater chpt. 1972—, pres. 1975, 81), Navy League U.S. (bd. dirs. 1984—, greeters 1983—, Appreciation award 1985, Cert. of Merit 1991), Mil. Order World Wars (comdr. 1989-90, nat. citations 1987, 91, 92, Outstanding Chpt. Comdr. award Dept. So. Calif. 1990), Am. Legion, VFW, Crazy Horse Meml. Found., Clarkston Civitan Club (founding bd. dirs.), Eagle Scout Alumni Assn. (founder 1973, bd. dirs. 1986-88, life mem. 1985—), Hammer Club San Diego, Kiwanis (bd. dirs. 1984-88, chmn. fellowship com. 1983-84, boys and girls com. 1984-85, planned giving com. 1988-89), Order of the Arrow (vigil, Cross Feathers award 1968), Masons, Shriners, Order of Ea. Star (life). Methodist.

SMITH, CHARLES RICHARD, marketing executive; b. Covington, Ohio, Nov. 5, 1932; s. Richard Weller and Harriet Rosalind (Minton) S.; m. Margaret Jean Porter, Aug. 7, 1954; children: David Paul, Kevin Richard, Jennifer Perlee, Melinda Jean. BA, Ohio Wesleyan U., Delaware, 1954; B Chem. Engring., Ohio State U., 1960. Product engr. Dow Corning Corp., Midland, Mich., 1960-63; tech. pub. rels. mgr. Clyde Williams & Co., Columbus, Ohio, 1963-66; dir. pub. rels. Chem. Abstracts Svc., Columbus, 1966-68; v.p. sales/mktg. Ventron Corp., materials div., Bradford, Pa., 1968-73; v.p. sales/svc. Applied Materials, Inc., Santa Clara, Calif., 1973-77; gen. mgr. Gyrex Corp., Santa Barbara, Calif., 1977-81; pres., CEO Auto/Recognition Systems, Santa Barbara, 1982-84; v.p. mktg./sales Tylan Corp., Torrance, Calif., 1984-85, Benzing Tech., Santa Clara, Calif., 1985-88; v.p. sales High Yield Tech., Sunnyvale, Calif., 1988-91; cons. Internat. Remote Imaging Systems, Chatsworth, Calif., 1981-82, Hakuto Co. Ltd., Tokyo, 1989—; dir. Micropulse Systems, Santa Barbara, Benzing Tech., Santa Clara; founder Action Pro Tem internat. bus. cons. co. Author: Plasma Jet Technology, 1962; contbr. articles to profl. jours. Mem. U.S. English, Washington, Citizens Against Waste, Washington. With USAF, 1955-57. Mem. Semiconductor Equipment and Materials Internat. (chmn. stds. group 1970-71, chmn. sales exec. coun. 1988-90, W.C. Benzing award 1990), Soc. Photo Optical Instrumentation Engrs., Churchill Club. Republican. Home: 107 Via Teresa Los Gatos CA 95030-1655 Office: Action Pro Tem PO Box 35681 Monte Sereno CA 95030-5681

SMITH, CHARLES ROGER, English language educator; b. Omaha, Sept. 8, 1941; s. Roger Charles and Mildred Marie Smith; m. Patricia Ann Bergstrom. BA with honors, U. Nebr., 1965, MA, 1966; PhD, Princeton (N.J.) U., 1972. Instr. Colo. State U., Ft. Collins, 1969-72, asst. prof., 1972-83, assoc. prof., 1983-88, prof., 1988—; cons. Jamestown Community Coll, Tarrytown, N.Y., 1984, USDA, Ft. Collins, 1986, Wayne State U., Detroit, 1986, WRITER (Conduit), Iowa City, 1986-89, Stevens Tech. Inst., Hoboken, N.J., 1987, IBM, Bethesda, Md., 1989. Asst. bd. dirs. Quality of Life Coalition, Ft. Collins, 1984. Mem. Nat. Coun. for Tchrs. of English, Assn. for Computers and Humanities, Assn. for Lit. and Linguistic Computing, Assn. for Computational Linguistics, Modern Lang. Assn. Helsinki, Medieval Acad. Am., New Chaucer Soc. Home: 624 S Loomis Ave Fort Collins CO 80521-3626 Office: Colo State U Dept of English Fort Collins CO 80523

SMITH, CHARLES VINTON, mayor, retired electrical engineer; b. Frankfort, Ohio, July 21, 1932; s. Vinton Jay and Bernice Louetta (Blue) S.; m. Nancy Carol Johnson, Apr. 9, 1960; children: Robin, Jeffrey, Stacy, Scott. BEE, Ohio State U., 1959. Mem. tech. staff Hughes Aircraft, Culver City, Calif., 1959-61; rsch. engr. N.Am. Aviation, Anaheim, Calif., 1961-63, sr. rsch. engr., 1963-65; engring. supr. N.Am.-Rockwell, Anaheim, Calif., 1965-76; project engr. Rockwell Internat., Anaheim, 1976-90, ret., 1990; mayor City of Westminster, Calif., 1988—; v.p., treas. Merit Micro Software Corp., Oklahoma City, 1983-87; v.p. SDS Land Corp., Chillicothe, Ohio, 1976-70; gen. ptnr. Caloh, a ltd. partnership, Westminster, Calif., 1969—; pres., broker S & A Realty and Investment, Garden Grove, Calif., 1978—. Planning commr. Westminster Planning Commn., Westminster, 1978-84; city councilman Westminster City Coun., 1984-88; life mem. Westminster Community Theater, 1979. Sgt. USMC, 1950-54. Mem. IEEE, Westminster Lions Club (pres. 1982-83), Masons (master mason 1960-90, Ohio chpt.), West Orange County Bd. of Realtors. Republican. Home: 8761 Tamarisk Cir Westminster CA 92683-6840 Office: City of Westminster 8200 Westminster Blvd Westminster CA 92683-3395

SMITH, CHARLES Z., state supreme court justice; b. Lakeland, Fla., Feb. 23, 1927; s. John R. and Eva (Love) S.; m. Eleanor Jane Martinez, Aug. 20, 1955; children: Carlos M., Michael O., Stephen P., Felica L. BS, Temple U., 1952; JD, U. Wash., 1955. Bar: Wash. 1955. Law clk. Wash. Supreme Ct., Olympia, 1955-56; dep. pros. atty., asst. chief criminal div. King County, Seattle, 1956-60; ptnr. Bianchi, Smith & Tobin, Seattle, 1960-61; spl. asst. to atty. gen. criminal div. U.S. Dept. Justice, Washington, 1961-64; judge criminal dept. Seattle Mcpl. Ct., 1965-66; judge Superior Ct. King County, 1966-73; former assoc. dean, prof. law U. Wash., 1973; now justice Wash. Supreme Ct., Olympia. Mem. adv. bd. NAACP, Seattle Urban League, Wash. State Literacy Coun., Boys Club, Wash. Citizens for Migrant Affairs, Medina Children's Svc., Children's Home Soc. Wash., Seattle Better Bus. Bur., Seattle Foundation, Seattle Symphony Orch., Seattle Opera Assn., Community Svc. Ctr. for Deaaf and Hard of Hearing, Seattle U., Seattle Sexual Assault Ctr., Seattle Psychoanalytic Inst., The Little Sch., Linfield Coll., Japanese Am. Citizens League, Kawabe Meml. Hous, Puget Counseling Ctr, Am. Cancer Soc., Hutchinson Cancer Rsch. Ctr., Robert Chinn Found.; pres. Am. Bapt. Chs. U.S.A., 1976-77, lt. col. ret. Mem. ABA, Am. Judicature Soc., Washington Bar Assn., Seattle-King County Bar Assn., Order of Coif., Phi Alpha Delta, Alpha Phi Alpha. Office: Wash Supreme Ct Temple of Justice Olympia WA 98504*

SMITH, CHESTER, broadcasting executive; b. Wade, Okla., Mar. 29, 1930; s. Louis L. and Effie (Brown) S.; m. Naomi L. Crenshaw, July 19, 1959; children: Lauri, Lorna, Roxanne. Country western performer on Capitol records, TV and radio, 1947-61; owner, mgr. Sta. KLOC, Ceres-Modesto, Calif., 1963-81, Sta. KCBA-TV, Salinas-Monterey, Calif., 1981-86; owner, gen. ptnr. Sta. KCSO-TV, Modesto-Stockton-Sacramento, Sta. KREN-TV, Reno, Nev., Sta. KCVU-TV, Paradise-Chico-Redding, Calif., Sta. KNSO-TV, Merced, Calif., Sta. KTA-TV, Santa Maria, Calif., Sta. KO9UF-TV, Morro Bay, Calif., 1986—; co-owner Sta. KBVU-TV, Eureka, Calif., 1990—; owner Sta. KNSO-TV, Merced-Fresno. Mem. Calif. Broadcasters Assn. Republican. Mem. Christian Ch. original rec. Wait A Little Longer Please Jesus; inducted Country Music Hall of Fame, Nashville, 1955, inductee Western Swing Hall of Fame, Sacramento, 1988.

SMITH, CHRISTOPHER CULVER, controller, electronics company executive; b. Spokane, Wash., Sept. 27, 1955; s. Christopher Culver and Jane (Tigha) S.; m. Linda Bloom, June 20, 1984; children: Bradley Clay, Jeffrey Kyle. BSBA, U. Puget Sound, 1977; MS in Indsl. Adminstrn., Purdue U., 1978. Fin. analyst Hewlett Packard-Loveland (Colo.) Instrument, 1978-81; cost acctg. mgr. Hewlett Packard-Lake Stevens Instrument, Everett, Wash., 1981-83; area bus. mgr. Hewlett Packard-N.W. Area Sales, Bellevue, Wash., 1988-90; divsn. contr. Hewlett Packard-Lake Stevens Instrument, Everett, Wash., 1983-87, 91—; campus recruiting mgr. U. Wash., Seattle, 1990—; loaned prof. Fla. A&M U., Tallahassee, 1988, campus recruiting mgr., 1988-90. Office: Hewlett Packard 8600 Soper Hill Rd Everett WA 98205-1298

SMITH, CHRISTOPHER DUNCAN, deputy sheriff; b. Oklahoma City, Jan. 19, 1950; s. Edwin Lewis and Judith M. (Morgan) S.; m. Mary Kathaleen MacDonald, Apr. 1, 1978; children: Tonya Maree, Sandra Kaye, Deborah Anne. B in Vocat. Edn. summa cum laude, Calif. State U., San Bernardino, 1989, MA in Edn., 1990. Mechanic Don Rice AMC, Glendale, Calif., 1968-69; sta. mgr. Crestline (Calif.) Arco, 1969-70; mechanic Jules Meyers Pontiac, L.A., 1970-71, asst. svc. mgr., 1971-72, used car sales mgr., 1972-73; svc. mgr. Midway Corp., Riverside, Calif., 1973-76; res. dep. sheriff San Bernardino (Calif.) County Sheriff, 1975-76; constable Bear Valley Jud. Dist., Big Bear Lake, Calif., 1976-78; dep. sheriff San Bernardino County Sheriff, 1978—. Mem. Sheriff's Employees Benefit Assn. (labor rels. negotiator 1983—, bd. dirs. 1978-79, 80-82, 87—, pres. 1990—), Info. Mgmt. Assn. (v.p. membership 1989—), Peace Officers Rsch. Assn. Calif., Assn. Police Planning and Rsch. Officers, Am. Vocat. Assn., Calif. Assn. Vocat. Edn., Phi Kappa Phi. Republican. Baptist. Office: San Bernardino County Sheriffs Office 655 E 3d St San Bernardino CA 92415

SMITH, CLARK CAVANAUGH, historian; b. L.A., Aug. 17, 1934. BA, U. Calif., Santa Barbara, 1956; PhD, U. Calif., Berkeley, 1972; MA, U. Wash., 1958. Prof. dept. rhetoric U. Calif., Berkeley, 1972-79; adj. prof. Coll. of Profl. Studies, U. San Francisco, 1981-89. Author: Brothers, Black Soldiers in the Nam, 1982, Oral History as Therapy in Strangers at Home, 1980, The Vietnam Map Book, 1981; editor (newspaper) The Ally, 1968-72; editor The Short-Times Jour., 1981-82. Co-chair Agent Orange Vets. Adv. Com., 1981-84; bd. dirs. Winter Soldier Archive, Berkeley, 1980-85, Oral History Inst., Berkeley, 1992—; pres. Internat. Agt. Orange Data Base Project, 1986-89.

SMITH, CLAY TAYLOR, geology educator; b. Omaha, June 30, 1917; s. Dean Taylor and Gertrude Maude (Taylor) S.; m. Sarah Gwendolyn Austin, May 19, 1940; children: Dean Austin, Stanley Dickinson. B.S. in Sci., Calif. Inst. Tech., 1938, M.S., 1940, Ph.D., 1943. Jr. geologist U.S. Geol. Survey, Washington, 1940-42; exploration geologist Con. Mining and Smelting, Trail, B.C., 1943; party chief Union Mines Devel. Corp., Grand Junction, Colo., 1943-46; field geologist U.S. Vanadium Corp., Winnemucca, Nev., 1946-47; prof., dean admissions N.Mex. Inst. Mines and Tech., Socorro, 1947-82, dir. alumni relations, 1983-86, prof. emeritus, 1986—; cons. geologist, 1947—. Contbr. articles to profl. jours. Named Outstanding Tchr. N.M., N.M. Acad. Sci., 1972; Golden Deeds award Exchange Club, 1983; Appreciation award N.Mex. Sci. Tchrs. Assn., 1972. Fellow AAAS, Geol. Soc. Am., Soc. Econ. Geologists; mem. N.Mex. Geol. Soc. (hon. mem., pres. 1956-57), Am. Inst. Profl. Geologists, Nat. Assn. Geology Tchrs. Republican. Presbyterian. Clubs: Lions (pres. 1956). Home: 1205 Vista Dr Socorro NM 87801-4445 Office: Geoscience Dept N Mex Inst Mining and Tech Socorro NM 87801

SMITH, CRAIG ALVIN, lawyer; b. Waterloo, Iowa, Mar. 9, 1945; s. Alvin Andrew and Marcella Elizabeth (Reichert) S.; m. Mary Alice Johnson, June 6, 1970; children: Christine E., Kathryn M. BS, U. Minn., 1967; JD, U. Mich., 1972. Law clk. Oreg. Supreme Ct., Salem, 1972-74; ptnr. Hershner, Hunter, Moulton, Andrews & Neill, Eugene, Oreg., 1974—. Precinct committeeman Rep. Party, Lane County Oreg. With U.S. Army, 1968-70. Mem. Oreg. State Bar (exec. com. bus. sect. 1984-89), Rotary. Office: Hershner Hunter Mouton et al 180 E 11th Ave Eugene OR 97401

SMITH, CRAIG C., mechanical engineer, educator; b. Provo, Utah, May 1, 1944; s. George Clinton and Metta (Crawford) S.; m. Illa Mae Horton, July 29, 1966; children: Hugh C., Mark H., Natalie, Matthew S. BES, Brigham Young U., 1969, MS, 1970; PhD, MIT, 1973. Profl. engr. Instr. Brigham Young U., Provo, 1969-70; rsch. asst. MIT, Cambridge, Mass., 1970-73; asst. prof. U. Tex., Austin, 1973-79, assoc. prof., 1979-80; assoc. prof. Brigham Young U., Provo, 1980—; assoc. editor Jour. Dynamic Systems Measurement & Control, N.Y.C., 1980-87. Author: Fourier and Spectral Analysis in Dynamic Systems, 1980; contbr. more than 20 articles to profl. jours. NSF fellow, 1970-73; recipient various rsch. grants. Mem. ASME (chair tech. panel dynamic systems & control div. 1977-83, honors com. chair 1988—, mem. div. exec. com. 1991—), Soc. Automotive Engrs. (Ralph R. Tector award 1975), Am. Soc. for Engring. Edn., Sigma Xi, Phi Kappa Phi, Tau Beta Pi. Mem. LDS Church. Home: 3110 Foothill Dr Provo UT 84604-4862 Office: Brigham Young U 242 CB Provo UT 84602

SMITH, DALE METZ, biological science educator, researcher; b. Portland, Ind., Dec. 23, 1928; s. Homer and Gertrude (Metz) S.; m. Ruth Wyne, Aug. 12, 1950; children: Teresa Lynn Smith Prather, Gayle Marie Smith Seymour. BS, Ind. U., 1950, PhD, 1957; MS, Purdue U., 1952. Instr. U. Ariz., Tucson, 1952-53; from instr. to assoc prof. U. Ky., Lexington, 1955-60; assoc. prof. U. Ill., Champaign, 1960-64; from assoc. prof. to prof. emeritus U. Calif., Santa Barbara, 1964—; cons. Environ. Cons. Firms, Santa Barbara, 1971-80. Author bot. rsch. papers. Recipient Cooley award Am. Soc. Plant Taxonomists, 1963. Fellow Linnean Soc. London; mem. numerous sci. socs. Home: Box 106 Deputy IN 47230-0106 Office: U Calif Santa Barbara CA 93106

SMITH, DANA KRUSE, real estate developer; b. Waterloo, Iowa, May 28, 1957; s. Richard Walter and Joanne (Kruse) S.; 1 child, Tara Nicole. AA, Orange Coast Coll., 1976. Dir. comml. devel. Barnett-Range Corp., Stockton, Calif., 1982-86; pres. Dannor Corp., Stockton, 1966-92, Baltic Land Corp., Stockton, 1992—. Mem. Stockton Sailing Club (winner various races), Yosemite Club, Ducks Unltd. Republican. Office: Baltic Land Corp PO Box 7815 Stockton CA 95267

SMITH, DANIEL HOYT, lawyer; b. Chgo., Jan. 20, 1944; s. Daniel C. and Louise (Hoyt) S.; m. Linda M. Turner, Dec. 22, 1971; 1 child, Suvarna. BA, U. Chgo., 1966; JD, U. Wash., 1969. Bar: Wash. 1969, U.S. Dist. Ct. (we. dist.) Wash. 1969, U.S. Ct. Appeals (9th cir.) 1970, U.S. Ct. Appeals (11th cir.) 1988, U.S. Supreme Ct. 1973. Atty. VISTA, Seattle, 1969-70; ptnr. Smith Kaplan and Withey, Seattle, 1970-82, Smith Midgley & Pumplin, Seattle, 1983-89, MacDonald Hoague & Bayless, Seattle, 1990—. Contbr. articles to profl. jours. Pres. bd. dirs. N.W. Immigrant Rights Project, Seattle, 1993; bd. dirs. Nat. Immigration Project. Recipient Civil Libertarian award ACLU Wash., 1986. Mem. Am. Immigration Lawyers Assn. (chair Wash. chpt. 1985-86), Wash. State Bar Assn., Nat. Lawyers Guild (pres. Seattle chpt. 1980). Office: 1500 Hoge Bldg 705 2d Ave Seattle WA 98104

SMITH, DAVID ALLEN, insurance company executive; b. Hunstsville, Ala., Aug. 1, 1943; s. Clarence Theodore and Bernice (Snell) Smith; m. Michelle Haviland McCaffrey, June 1, 1964; 1 child, Eric Michael. BA, Calif. State U., L.A., 1969. Mgr. Allstate Ins. Co., L.A., 1969-81; v.p. Nat. Am. Ins. Co., Long Beach, Calif., 1982-86, First Calif. Property & Casualty Ins., Calabasas, Calif., 1987-89; sr. v.p. Sterling Casualty Ins. Co., Van Nuys, Calif., 1989—; cons. various ins. cos. and law firms. Contbr. numerous environmental and outdoor articles. Vice chmn. Boy Scouts Am., L.A.; instr. ARC, Pasadena; vol. U.S. Forest Service, Angeles Nat. Forest, L.A. Recipient Silver Beaver award, Boy Scouts Am., L.A., 1986, award of merit, 1983, vigil honor, 1980; Vol. Service award, U.S. Forest Service, 1987. Mem. Blue Goose Internat., High Adventure Team. Republican. Presbyterian. Home: 961 Micheltorena St Los Angeles CA 90026-2721 Office: Sterling Casulaty Ins Co 6710 Kester Ave Van Nuys CA 91407

SMITH, DAVID ASHER, software consultant; b. Bklyn., Dec. 3, 1946; s. Samuel Harry and Adelle (Seftel) S.; m. Barbara Joan Suntup, Sept. 29, 1974 (div. May 1981); m. Rita Carol Patterson, Oct. 20, 1985 (div. Dec. 1992); 1 child, Sylvia Ganeet. BS in Psychology, CCNY, 1977; MBA, San Jose State U., 1988. Programmer/analyst Control Data Corp., Sunnyvale, Calif., 1978-80; owner, operator Pet Way, San Jose, 1980-82; mgr. software Heald Bus. Coll., San Jose, 1982; mgr. data processing ICORE, Sunnyvale, 1982-84; software analyst Fairchild Research Ctr., Mountain View, Calif., 1985-86; software project mgr. Oximetrix, Mountain View, Calif., 1987-88; founder, owner, operator IDS, Campbell, Calif., 1987-90; pres. Simvirons, Inc., 1990—; co-founder, treas. Bay Area Mapics Users Group, Sna Francisco, 1984-85; software cons., tax preparer. Youth leader Friends Outside, San Jose, 1978—; chmn. Bikkur Cholim, San Jose, 1987—. Republican. Jewish. Home and Office: 235 N 2nd St Campbell CA 95008-2027

SMITH, DAVID ELVIN, physician; b. Bakersfield, Calif., Feb. 7, 1939; s. Elvin W. and Dorothy (McGinnis) S.; m. Millicent Buxton; children: Julia, Suzanne, Christopher Buxton-Smith. Intern San Francisco Gen. Hosp., 1965; fellow pharmacology and toxicology U. Calif., San Francisco, 1965-67, assoc. clin. prof. occupational medicine, clin. toxicology, 1967—, dir. psychopharmacology study group, 1966-70; practice medicine specializing in toxicology and addiction San Francisco, 1965—; physician Presbyn. Alcoholic Clinic, 1965-67, Contra Cost Alcoholic Clinic, 1965-67; dir. alcohol and drug abuse screening unit San Francisco Gen. Hosp., 2967-68; co-dir. Calif drug abuse info. project U Calif Med. Ctr., 1967-72; founder, med. dir. Haight-Ashbury Free Med. Clinic, San Francisco, 1967—; research dir. Merritt Peralta Chem. Dependency Hosp., Oakland, Calif., 1984—; chmn. Nat. Drug Abuse Conf., 1977; mem. Calif. Gov's. Commn. on Narcotics and Drug Abuse, 1977—; nat. health adviser to former U.S. Pres. Jimmy Carter; mem. Pres. Clinton's Health Care Task Force on Addiction and Nat. Health Reform, 1993; dir. Benzodiazepine Research and Tng. Project, Substance Abuse and Sexual Concerns Project, PCP Research and Tng. Project; cons. numerous fed. drug abuse agys. Author: Love Needs Care, 1970, The New Social Drug: Cultural, Medical and Legal Perspectives on Marijuana, 1971, The Free Clinic: Community Approaches to Health Care and Drug Abuse, 1971, Treating the Cocaine Abuser, 1985, The Benzodiazepines: Current Standard Medical Practice, 1986, Physicians' Guide to Drug Abuse, 1987; co-author: It's So Good, Don't Even Try it Once: Heroin in Perspective, 1972, Uppers and Downers, 1973, Drugs in the Classroom, 1973, Barbiturate Use and Abuse, 1977, A Multicultural View of Drug Abuse, 1978, Amphetamine Use, Misuse and Abuse, 1979, PCP: Problems and Prevention, 1981, Sexological Aspects of Substance Use and Abuse, Treatment of the Cocaine Abuser, 1985, The Haight Ashbury Free Medical Clinic: Still Free After all these Years, Drug Free: Alternatives to Drug Abuse, 1987, Treatment of Opiate Dependence, Designer Drugs, 1988, Treatment of Cocaine Dependence, 1988, Treatment of Opiate Dependence, 1988, The New Drugs, 1989, Crack and Ice in the era of Smokeable Drugs, 1992, others; also drug edn. films; founder, editor Jour. Psychedelic Drugs (now Jour. Psychoactive Drugs), 1967—; contbr. over 100 articles to profl. jours. Pres. Youth Projects, Inc.; founder, chmn. bd., pres. Nat. Free Clin. Council, 1968-72. Recipient Rsch. award Borden Found., 1964, AMA Rsch. award, 1966, Community Svc. award U. Calif.-San Francisco, 1974, Calif. State Drug Abuse Treatment award 1984, Vernelle Fox Drug Abuse Treatment award, 1985, UCLA Sidney Cohen Addiction Medicine award, 1989. Mem. AMA (alt. del.), CMA (alt. del.), Am. Soc. on Addiction Medicine (bd. dirs., pres.-elect), San Francisco Med. Soc., Am. Pub. Health Assn., Calif. Soc. on Addiction Medicine (pres., bd. dirs.), Am. Soc. Addiction Medicine, Sigma Xi, Phi Beta Kappa. Methodist. Home: 289 Frederick St San Francisco CA 94117-4051 Office: 409 Clayton St San Francisco CA 94117-1998

SMITH, DAVID EUGENE, business administration educator; b. Boise, Idaho, Dec. 14, 1941; s. Roy Arthur and Anna Margaret (Fries) S.; m. Patricia Stroy, Aug. 4, 1973; 1 child, Zachary Adam. BS in Applied Stats., San Francisco State Coll., 1964, MS in Mgmt. Sci., 1966; MBA, PhD in Bus. Adminstrn., U. Santa Clara, 1969. Asst. to dir. mgmt ctr. Grad. Sch. Bus., U. Santa Clara, Calif., 1966-69, lectr. mktg., 1968; asst. prof. bus. adminstrn. Mktg./Quantitative Studies Dept., San Jose State U., Calif., 1969-71, assoc. prof. bus. adminstrn., 1971-76, prof. bus. adminstrn., 1976—, chmn. dept., 1986-89. Author: Quantitative Business Analysis, 1977, Internat. Edit., 1979, 1982; contbr. articles to profl. jours. Mem. Inst. Mgmt. Sci., Ops. Research Soc. Am., Decision Scis. Inst., Phi Kappa Phi, Beta Gamma Sigma. Republican. Home: 22448 Tim Tam Ct Los Gatos CA 95030-8521 Office: San Jose State Univ Mktg/Quantitative Studies One Washington Sq San Jose CA 95192

SMITH, DAVID KENNETH, geologist; b. Orange, N.J., Jan. 2, 1956; s. Sheridan Rome and Ruth (Riggs) S. AB in Geology, Hamilton Coll., 1979; MS in Geol. Sci., U. Calif., Riverside, 1982. Registered environ. assessor, geologist, Calif. Rsch. assoc. U. Calif., Riverside, 1982-84, Santa Cruz, 1984-87; geochemist Lawrence Livermore (Calif.) Nat. Lab., 1987—. Contbr. articles to profl. jours. Recipient Rogers Prize in Geology Hamilton Coll., 1979. Mem. Geol. Soc. Am., Am. Geophysical Union, Sigma Xi. Office: Nuclear Chemistry Div LLNL L-231 PO Box 808 Livermore CA 94550

SMITH, DAVID KING, publishing executive, newspaper; b. L.A., Oct. 12, 1963; s. Michael David and Dorothy Margaret (Mason) S.; m. Kirstin Andrea Gustafson, June 20, 1991; 1 child, Zachary David Smith. BA, UCLA, 1987. Salesperson, advt. exec. Calif. Newspaper Svc., 1989-91; leadership cons. Phi Gamma Delta Internat. Fraternity, Lexington, Ky. 1987-89. Republican. Episcopalian. Office: Daily Journal Co PO Box 54026 915 E First St Los Angeles CA 90012

SMITH, DAVID LAWSON, psychologist, education professional; b. Beckeley, W.Va., Aug. 4, 1951; s. Willard Lawson and Thelma Mae (Hurt) S.; m. Deborah Ann Kissler, July 6, 1974; children: Andrew Lawson, Virginia Ann. BA in Psychology with honors, Calif. State U., Fullerton, 1973; PhD in Social Psychology, U. Nev., 1987. Predoctoral trainee NIMH/U. Nev., Reno, 1974-77; mental health therapy behavioral coord. Lakes Crossing Ctr. for Mentally Disordered Offenders, Reno, 1977-78; instr. Western Nev. C.C., Carson City, 1981-86, Truckee Meadows C.C., Reno, 1980-87; coord. rsch. unit Nev. Dept. Edn., Carson City, 1988-91, evaluation cons., 1991—; affiliate faculty U. Nev., Reno, 1974-87; trainee Nat. Ctr. for Rsch. in Vocat. Edn., Columbus, Ohio, 1988; subcom. mem. com. on evaluation and info. systems Coun. of Chief State Sch. Officers, Washington, 1989-90; fellow Nat. Ctr. Edn. Stats., Washington, 1991. Contbr. articles to profl. jours.; reviewer Jour. for Theory of Social Behavior, 1989. Chair Commn. on Ch. and Soc., Reno; mem. Meth. Coun. Ministries, Reno; mem. data task force Nev.

Commn. Econ. Devel., Carson City, 1991; recruiter Reno/Sparks Interfaith Hunger Walk, 1992. Mem. Am. Ednl. Rsch. Assn., United Meth. Men's Orgn., Mackay Soc. U. Nev., Wolf Club U. Nev., Porsche Club Am. (bd. dirs. Sierra Nev. region), Sigma Xi, Phi Kappa Phi. Democrat. Office: Nev Dept Edn 400 W King St Carson City NV 89710

SMITH, DAVID ROLLIN, archivist; b. Pasadena, Calif., Oct. 13, 1940; s. Loy Herman and Felicia May (Eastman) S. A.A., Pasadena City Coll., 1960; B.A., U. Calif.-Berkeley, 1962, M.L.S., 1963. Librarian, Library of Congress, Washington, 1963-65, UCLA, Los Angeles, 1965-70; archivist Walt Disney Co., Burbank, Calif., 1970—; exec. dir. Manuscript Soc., Burbank, 1980—. Author: The Ultimate Disney Trivia Book, 1992; contbr. articles to profl. jours. Recipient Award of Distinction, Manuscript Soc., 1983; Service award Internat. Animated Film Soc. Fellow Manuscript Soc.; mem. Soc. Calif. Archivists (council), Soc. Am. Archivists (chmn. bus. archives com.). Republican. Mem. Christian Ch. (Disciples of Christ). Home: 350 N Niagara St Burbank CA 91505-3648 Office: Walt Disney Co 500 S Buena Vista St Burbank CA 91521-1200

SMITH, DAVID SIDNEY, food engineer; b. Oakland, Calif., Sept. 2, 1963; s. Sidney Emerson and Linda Ann (Stevenson) S.; m. Donna Lynn Friesen, June 22, 1985; 1 child: Kerri Melissa. BSChE, U. Calif., Davis, 1985. EIT. Loss prevention rep. Liberty Mut. Ins., Long Beach, Calif., 1985-86; process engr. Hunt-Wesson, Inc., Fullerton, Calif., 1986-91, sr. engr. R&D, 1991—. Chmn. adminstrn. South Bay Christian Ch., Redondo Beach, Calif., 1992. Mem. Am. Inst. Chem. Engrs. (assoc.), Pioneer 8's Dance Club. Democrat. Office: Hunt Wesson Inc R&D 1645 W Valencia Dr MS 501 Fullerton CA 92633

SMITH, DAVID WAYNE, psychologist; b. Ind., Apr. 16, 1927; s. Lowell Wayne and Ruth Elizabeth (Westphal) S.; m. Marcene B. Leever, Oct. 20, 1948; children: David Wayne, Laurreen Lea. B.S., Purdue U., 1949; M.S., Ind. U., 1953, Ph.D., 1955. Prof. rehab., dir. Rehab. Center; asso. dean, later asst. v.p. acad. affairs Ariz. Health Scis. Center, U. Ariz., Tucson, 1955-80; research prof. rehab., adj. prof. medicine, cons. in research S.W. Arthritis Center, Coll. Medicine, 1980-87; prof. rehab. and rheumatology, dept. medicine U. Ariz., 1987—; pres. allied health professions sect. Nat. Arthritis Found.; bd. dirs. Nat. Arthritis Found. (S.W. chpt.); nat. vice chmn. bd. dirs.; mem. NIH Nat. Arthritis Adv. Bd., 1977-84; also chmn. subcom. community programs and rehab.; mem. staff Ariz. Legislature Health Welfare, 1972-73; Mem. Gov.'s Council Dept. Econ. Security, 1978-85; pres., bd. dirs. Tucson Assn. for Blind, 1974-86; chmn. Gov.'s Council on Blind and Visually Impaired, 1987—; exec. sec. Gov.'s Council on Arthritis and Musculoskeletal Disease, 1987—. Author: Worksamples; contbr. chpts. to books and articles to profl. jours. Recipient Gov.'s awards for leadership in rehab., 1966, 69, 72, 73; awards for sci. and vol. services Nat. Arthritis Found., 1973, 75; 1st nat. Addie Thomas award Nat. Arthritis Found., 1983, Benson award, 1989, Govt. Affairs award, 1989; Arthritis Found. fellow, 1983. Mem. Am. Psychol. Assn. (div. 17 counseling psychology), Assn. Schs. Allied Health Professions, Nat. Rehab. Assn., Ariz. Psychol. Assn. Home: 5765 N Camino Real Tucson AZ 85718-4213 Office: U Ariz Ariz Health Scis Ctr Tucson AZ 85724

SMITH, DENNIS, professional football player; b. Santa Monica, Calif., Feb. 3, 1959. Student, U. So. Calif. Safety Denver Broncos, 1981—. Office: Denver Broncos 13655 Broncos Pkwy Englewood CO 80112

SMITH, DERRIN RAY, information systems company executive; b. Columbus, Ohio, Feb. 19, 1955; s. Ray Stanley Smith and Clara (Diddle) Craver; m. Catherine Marie Massey, Aug. 18, 1979; children: Shannon Cathleen, Allison Collette, Micayla Colleen, Nicole Catherine. BS, Regis U., 1981; MBA, U. Phoenix, 1984; PhD, U. Denver, 1991. Test lab. mgr. Ball Aerospace Systems, Ball Corp., Boulder, 1975-84; sr. systems engr. Martin Marietta Info. Systems, Denver, 1984-87; tech. cons. MITRE Fed. R & D Ctr., Colorado Springs, 1988-92; pres. DRS Scis., Inc., Denver, 1992—; tech. cons. U.S. Space Command--RAPIER, Colorado Springs, 1989-91, Unisys Corp., Greenwood Village, Colo., 1992; adj. prof. CIS dept. Univ. Coll., U. Denver, 1992; secretariat Corp. Planner's Roundtable, St. Louis, 1982-84; speaker in field. Author: Evolving the Mountain; Defense Acquisition Management of Strategic Command and Control System Procurements, 1991; contbr. articles to profl. jours. Res. police officer Federal Heights (Colo.) Police Dept., 1979-82. With USMC, 1978-84. Recipient Outstanding Achievement award Rocky Mountain News, 1981, Reservist of Yr. award Navy League U.S., 1981. Mem. Assn. Former Intelligence Officers (pres. Rocky Mountain chpt.). Roman Catholic. Home: 3746 E Easter Cir S Littleton CO 80122 Office: DRS Scis Inc Arco Tower Ste 2900 707 17th St Denver CO 80202

SMITH, DIANNE HARRIS, import/export company executive; b. Rock Hill, S.C., July 4, 1942; d. Stanhope Alexander and Dorothy Alma (Ray) Harris; widowed; children: Sandra, Daphne, Rodney. Student, Norwalk Coll., 1980. Clk. Ea. Products, Balt., 1959-60; model Terri Fashions, La Habra, Calif., 1963-64, bookkeeper, 1964-65; acct. Whittier, Calif., 1964-66; sec. Kirk Hill Rubber Co., Brea, Calif., 1968-74; rschr. ESA, Glendora, 1992—. Recipient Presdl. Sports award Sports Assn., 1979. Mem. NAFE, WWF, AnCloc County Santa Soc., United Srs. Assn., Sierra Club, The Colisteali Soc., The Nature Conservancy, Defenders of Wildlife, United Seniors Coalition. Democrat.

SMITH, DICK MARTIN, oil field service company executive-owner; b. Alamosa, Colo., Nov. 20, 1946; s. Jack and Mary (Turnbull) S.; m. Janyce Wood Smith, Jan. 5, 1971 (div. May 1975); 1 child, DAnna Marie; m. Patricia Ann Connors, June 5, 1987; stepchildren: Shawna Parker, Scott Parker. Student, U. Md., 1969-74, U. York, Harrogate, Eng., 1969-72, U. N.Mex., 1975-79. With spl. ops. Nat. Security Agy., U.S. Govt., Ft. Meade, Md., 1969-74; with engring. rsch. U. N.Mex., Albuquerque, 1974-78; engr. fluids Internat. Mincifl and Chem. Co., Houston, 1978-82; owner, pres., CEO Corrosions Monitoring Svcs. Inc., Capser, Wyo., 1981—; bd. dirs. Trenching Svcs., Casper, CMS Farms, Alamosa, Colo. With USN, 1964-68. Decorated Navy Unit Citation. Mem. Soc. Petroleum Engrs., Casper Wildcatters, Aircraft Owners Pilots Assn., DAV. Republican. Home: 4471 E 12th St Casper WY 82609 Office: CMS Inc PO Box 9826 Casper WY 82609

SMITH, DONALD E., broadcast engineer, manager; b. Salt Lake City, Sept. 10, 1930; s. Thurman A. and Louise (Cardall) S.; B.A. Columbia Coll., Chgo., 1955; B.S.; U. Utah, 1970; postgrad. U. So. Calif., U. Utah, PhD (hon.) Columbia Coll., 1985; m. Helen B. Lacy, 1978. Engr., Iowa State U., (WOI-TV), 1955-56; asst. chief engr. KLRJ-TV, Las Vegas, 1956-60; studio field engr. ABC, Hollywood, Cal., 1960; chief engr. Teletape, Inc., Salt Lake City, 1961; engring. supr. KUER, U. Utah, Salt Lake City, 1962-74, gen. mgr., 1975-85. Free lance cinematography, 1950—; cons. radio TV (mgmt. engr. and prodn.), 1965—. Mem. Soc. Motion Pictures and TV Engrs., Lambda Chi Alpha. Home: 963 Hollywood Ave Salt Lake City UT 84105-3347

SMITH, DONALD EVANS, library consultant; b. Shanendoah, Iowa, Dec. 2, 1915; s. William Wesley and Bess Alice (Evans) S.; student Ricks Coll., 1939-40; BA, Hastings Coll., 1946; MLS, U. Wash., 1964. Tchr. English, librarian Tenino (Wash.) High Sch., 1950-51, Rochester (Wash.) High Sch., 1954-59; librarian North Thurston High Sch., Lacey, Wash., 1959-67; head librarian, coord. instructional materials Lakes High Sch., Lakewood Ctr., Wash., 1967-80; library cons., 1980—. Mem. awards com. Wash. Library Commn., 1964-66. With Signal Corps, AUS, 1942-45; to 1st lt., M.I., U.S. Army, 1951-54; to col. Wash. State Guard, 1971-80, now ret. Mem. Wash. Assn. Sch. Librarians (com. chmn.), Clover Park Edn. Assn. (com. chmn. 1970-71), Am. Legion, Phi Delta Kappa (del. nat. confs.). Home and Office: 4530 26th Loop SE Lacey WA 98503

SMITH, DONALD KENDALL, communication educator; b. Portland, Oreg., Aug. 1, 1929; s. Leslie Frederick and Nina Christina (Coffee) S.; m. Faye Gladys Schick, June 25, 1950; children: Donald Vance, Julisa Faye. BS in Biology, U. Oreg., 1951, MS in Gen. Studies, 1952, MA with honors in Journalism, 1967, PhD, 1969. Cert. secondary edn. tchr. Lectr. Evang. Tchr. Tng. Coll., Vryheid, Natal, Union South Africa, 1952-55; dir., pub. Africa Christian Lit. Advance, Johannesburg, Transvaal, Union South Africa, 1956-63; editor-in-chief Our Africa monthly mag., Johannesburg, 1958-63; dir. Daystar Publs., Bulawayo, Zimbabwe, 1964-73; dir. Daystar Comm., Bulawayo, 1969-73, Nairobi, Kenya, 1974-79; founder Daystar U. Coll., Nairobi, 1979-81; dir. Inst. Internat. Christian Comm., Portland, Oreg., 1981—; prof. intercultural comm. Western Sem., Portland, 1981—; rsch. dir. Comm. for Devel. Project, Luth. World Fedn., Sudan, Cameroon, 1979-85; internat. rsch. dir. Living Bibles Internat., Wheaton, Ill., 1971-80. Author: Writing is Thinking - Plbslshd in Rhodesia, 1966, Make Haste Slowly, 1985, Creating Understanding, 1992; editor lit. materials in Ndebele and Shona: Rhodesia Chs. Nat. Lit. Project, 1965-69. NDEA fellow, U. Oreg., 1968. Mem. Internat. Comm. Assn., Am. Soc. Missiology, Evangelical Soc. of Missiology. Baptist. Home: 5235 SE Salmon St Portland OR 97215-2672 Office: Western Bapt Sem 5511 SE Hawthorne Blvd Portland OR 97215-3399

SMITH, DONALD RICHARD, editor, publisher; b. Stockton, Calif., Aug. 20, 1932; s. Robert Gordon and Gertrude (Schweitzer) S.; m. Darlene Ruth Thomas, May 7, 1961; children: Douglas Robert, Deborah Renae. Student, Coll. Pacific, 1951, Delta Coll., 1951-52. Editor, pub. Calif. Odd Fellow & Rebekah, Linden, 1950—; editor Elk Grove (Calif.) Citizen, 1953-55; asst. dir. U.N. Pilgrimage for Youth, N.Y.C., 1956-59; editor, pub. Linden (Calif.) Herald, 1959-86, Lockeford (Calif.)-Clements Post, 1960-62, Internat. Rebekah News, Linden, 1963-86, Internat. Odd Fellow & Rebekah, Linden, 1986—; dir. communications Sovereign Grand Lodge, Linden, 1990-92. Author: From Stagestop to Friendly Community, 1976, Leadership Manual, 1980, The Three Link Fraternity, 1993. Bd. dirs. Odd Fellow-Rebekah Youth Camp, Inc., Long Barn, Calif., 1959-61; chmn. Linden Rep. Com., 1962-66, Linden Centennial Observance, 1963, Linden Mcpl. Council, 1981-90. Recipient Legion of Honor Order of Demolay, 1961, John R. Williams award S.J. Tchrs. Assn., 1963, 87, Golden Key award Stockton Tchrs. Assn., 1971, Achievement award County Bd. Suprs., 1970, Citizen of Yr. award Lions Internat., 1982. Mem. IOOF Internat. Press Assn. (pres. 1962-63), Desktop Pub. Assn., Boston Computer Soc., Berkeley Macintosh Users Assn., Linden Peters C. of C. (pres. 1968-69), S.J. Hist. Soc. (trustee 1986-90). Methodist. Lodges: Lions, Odd Fellows (Calif.) (grand master 1958-59), Odd Fellows Internat. (sovereign grand master 1969-70), Internat. Coun. 100F (sec. 1990—). Home: 5350 Harrison St Linden CA 95236-9630 Office: Linden Publ 19033 E Main PO Box 129 Linden CA 95236-0129

SMITH, DONNA, mayor, small business owner; b. Upper Darby, Pa., July 19, 1954; d. Dave and Theresa (McAleer) Fekay; m. Robert Howard Smith Jr., Dec. 1, 1951; children: Robert H. III, Sean M., Terence J. Grad. high sch., Pomona, Calif., 1970. Mayor City of Pomona, 1987—; owner Pomona Generator Co., 1976—. Pres. Simons Jr. High Sch. PTA, 1983-85; pres., sec. Pomona Youth Sports Com., 1983-85; mem. City Coun. Dist. 3, Pomona, 1985-87; mem. Garey High Sch. Booster Club, 1985—; mem. Hispanic youth task force; mem. econ. and human devel. com. SCAG Community, 1985-87; mem. Pomona Cen. Bus. Dist.; mem. policy com. Rapid Transit Dist.; vice chairperson Tri-City Mental Health; mem. Pomona Valley handicapped and sr. citizens com.; mem. exec. bd. Teen Outreach, ARC; mem. Old Baldy Coun. Boy Scouts Am.; U.S. Olympic torch runner, 1991; mem. U.S. Conf. of Mayors, 1991, chmn. com. disaster preparedness, chair community devel. and housing com., mem. membership com., Lincoln Inst. of Land Policy; mem. adv. bd. Nat. Coalition Against Pornography; mem. U.S. Conf. Mayors; appointed to State of Calif. Rep. Ctrl. Com.; runner U.S. Olympic Torch; hon. chair March of Dimes, Lukemia Soc. Am.; mem. State Rep. Ctrl. Com. Named Women Achiever of 1985, Humanitarian of Yr., 1986, one of Five Outstanding Californians Calif. Jaycees, 1990; recipient PTA Honorary Service award 1985, PTA Honorary Lifetime Service award 1986. Mem. Calif. Elected Women's Assn., Pomona Bus. and Profl. Women's Assn., Pomona Hist. Soc., Pomona C. of C. (legis. action com., edn. com., city affairs com.), Pomona Valley Rep. Women Federated (v.p.), Pomona Jaycees (Disting. Svc. award 1988), Pomona Jaycees (hon. life 1991), Am. Bus. Women's Assn. (hon. life 1991), Nat. League of Cities, League of Calif. Cities (state adminstrv. policy con.), Kiwanis, Fraternal Order of Police, Women of Moose. Mem. Ch. of God. Office: City of Pomona Office of Mayor 1555 S Palomares St Pomona CA 91766-5312

SMITH, DONNA DEAN, nurse, educator, artist; b. Pearisburg, Va., Oct. 20, 1946; d. Russell E. and Elizabeth K. (Conley) Bivens; m. Eugene Baxter Smith Jr., Dec. 21, 1968; children: Christina Marie, Daniel Eugene. BSN, U. Tenn., 1969; postgrad., U. N.Mex., 1990—. Staff St. Mary's Hosp., Knoxville, Tenn., 1969, Bapt. Meml. Hosp., Memphis, 1969, McKinley Gen. Hosp., Gallup, N.Mex., 1970; DON McKinley Gen. Hosp., Gallup, 1970-71; RN refresher U. Albuquerque, N.Mex., 1981; sr. faculty U. N.Mex. Gallup (N.Mex.) Br. Nursing Program, 1982—. Exhibited in group show Gallup Art Coun. Show, 1982, pvt. show, 1987. Tchr. Bapt. Ch., Gallup, 1971-91, youth dir., 1975-77; pres. Bapt. Young Women, Gallup, 1974-77; sec. Tse Yaaniichii Promoters, Gallup, 1978-79. Mem. ANA, Nat. League for Nursing, N.Mex. League for Nursing. Home: 1416 Grandview Gallup NM 87301 Office: Univ N Mex Gallup Br 200 College Rd Gallup NM 87301

SMITH, DONNIE LOUISE, nurse; b. Mountain Home, Idaho, Aug. 14, 1952; d. Bernard Armour and Lillian Doris (Lazzari) S.; children: Daniel Taylor, Drew Thomas. AA in Nursing, Solano Community Coll., 1973. RN, Calif. Staff nurse Woodland (Calif.) Clinic Med. Group, 1973-74, 79; office nurse Gaing W. Chan, MD, West Sacramento, Calif., 1974-76; staff nurse med.-surg. and critical care unit Woodland Meml. Hosp., 1976-79; staff nurse Upjohn Healthcare, 1979; staff nurse coronary care unit Santa Barbara (Calif.) Cottage Hosp., 1979-80; charge nurse critical care unit Northbay Med. Ctr., Fairfield, Calif., 1981-83, endoscopy nurse specialist, 1983-87; dir. svcs. Sacramento Autologous Svc. Inc., Sacramento, 1987-90; endoscopy charge nurse North Bay Med. Ctr., Fairfield, Calif., 1990-92, continuity care coord., 1990-92, staff nurse post-anesthesia care unit, 1992—; owner Kelley Cooper Svcs., 1992—; staff nurse Nurse Focus, Napa, Calif., 1989-90. Mem. Rescue Now, Sacramento, 1985—. Recipient appreciation award Northbay Med. Ctr., 1987. Mem. Soc. Gastrointestinal Assts., Solano Community Coll. Profl. Registered Nurse Alumni (sec. 1986—). Democrat. Roman Catholic. Office: North Bay Med Ctr 1800 Pennsylvania Ave Fairfield CA 94533-3587

SMITH, DORSETT DAVID, pulmonologist; b. N.Y.C., Feb. 2, 1937; s. Harry Dorsett and Kathrin Lowe S.; m. Dorothy Louise Frank, June 12, 1962; children: Talbot St. John, Tiffany Louise, Sarah Carrington. BA, Colgate U., 1959; MD, U. Pa., 1963. Diplomate Am. Bd. Internal Medicine, Am. Bd. Pulmonary Disease. Pres. Most Devel. Inc., Chest Diseases Inc.; pres. N.W. Cardiopulmonary Panel; clin. prof. medicine U. Wash. Contbr. articles to profl. jours. Mem. Med. Disciplinary Bd. State of Wash.; pres. Physicians for Moral Responsibility. Fellow ACP, Am. Coll. Chest Physicians. Office: Chest Diseases Inc 4310 Colby Ave Everett WA 98203-2338

SMITH, DOUGLAS A., dermatologist; b. Grand Forks, N.D., Jan. 17, 1951; s. Herbert Phelps and Virginia Mae (Tannahill) S. BS, Loyola U., L.A., 1974; MPH, UCLA, 1975; MD, U. Okla., 1979. Diplomate Am. Bd. Dermatology, Nat. Bd. Med. Examiners, Dermatopathology Spl. Competetence. Intern St. Mary Med. Ctr., Long Beach, Calif., 1979-80; resident, fellow dermatology/dermatopathology U. Okla., Oklahoma City, 1980-83, 84, dermatology instr., 1983-84; pvt. practice dermatology Long Beach, 1984—; sect. chief dermatology St. Mary Med. Ctr., Long Beach, 1988—; dermatology cons. Meml. Med. Ctr., Long Beach, 1986—. Mem. Downtown Long Beach Assn., 1985—, St. Hedwig's Parents Assn., Los Alamitos, Calif., 1988-92; sponsor St. Hedwig Pony League Baseball, Los Alamitos, 1990-92, Los Alamitos AYSO soccer, 1990-92. Recipient Calif. State Grad. Fellowship, 1975, Singer Scholarship, U. Okla., 1976. Mem. AMA, Soc. Dermatologic Surgery and Oncology, Am. Acad. Dermatology, Internat. Soc. Dermatology, Physicians Who Care, Soc. for Laser Medicine and Surgery, Long Beach Dermagology Soc., Alpha Omega Alpha. Office: PO Box 90369 Long Beach CA 90809-0369

SMITH, DOUGLAS LYNN, lubrication engineer; b. Spokane, Wash., July 16, 1963; s. Lee Robinson and Dorothy (Rolls) S.; m. Allyson Beecher, Nov. 24, 1990. BS in Indsl. Engring., U. Tex., El Paso, 1987. Inds. engr. Photocircuits Atlanta, 1988-89; lubrication engr. Conoco Inc., Billings, Mont., 1989—. Mem. Soc. Automotive Engrs. Office: Conoco Inc Norwest Ctr 338 Hwy E 175 N 27 St 10th Fl Billings MT 59101

SMITH, DUANE ALLAN, history educator, researcher; b. San Diego, Apr. 20, 1937; s. Stanley W. and Ila B. (Bark) S.; m. Gay Woodruff, Aug. 20, 1960; 1 child, Laralee Ellen. BA, U. Colo., 1959, MA, 1961, PhD, 1964. Prof. history Ft. Lewis Coll., Durango, Colo., 1964—. Author: Horace Tabor, 1973 (Cert. of Commendation 1974), Mining America, 1987, Mesa Verde National Park, 1988, The Birth of Colorado, 1989, Rocky Mountain West, 1992. Chmn. La Plata County Dem. Com., Durango, 1984-85; mem. Colo. Centennial Commn., 1974-76, Durango Hist. Preservation Commn., 1989-91, Durango Hist. Preservation Bd., 1991—, Gary Hart Campaign La Plata County, 1974, 80, 84. Huntington (Calif.) Libr. fellow, 1968, 73, 78; recipient Fred H. Rosenstock award Denver Westerners, 1987; named Colo. Humanist of the Yr., Colo. Endowment for the Humanities, 1989, Colo. Prof. of the Yr. 1990, Rodman Paul award, 1992. Mem. Soc. for Am. Baseball Rsch., Mining History Assn. (presiding chmn. 1989-90), Western History Assn. (coun. 1985-88), Colo. Hist. Soc. Methodist. Home: 2911 Cedar Ave Durango CO 81301-4481 Office: Ft Lewis Coll Durango CO 81301

SMITH, DUNBAR WALLACE, retired physician, clergyman; b. Dunbar, Nebr., Oct. 17, 1910; s. Clarence Dunbar and Marie Christine (Eden) S.; m. Kathryn Avis Johnson, May 2, 1935; children: Dunbar Wesley, John Wallace. BSc, La Sierra Coll., Riverside, Calif., 1949; MD, Loma Linda U., 1950; DTM and Hygiene, Sch. of Tropical Med. London U., 1951; MPH, Columbia U., 1967. Diplomate Nat. Bd. Med. Examiners. Pastor 7th-day Adventist Chs., San Diego, Omaha, India, Ceylon, 1935-44; med. dir. 7th-Day Adventist Mission Hosps., India, 1951-056; adminstr. Battle Creek (Mich.) Sanitarium, 1957-62; med. dir. Bates Meml. Hosp., Yonkers, N.Y., 1962-67; dep. commr. health Nassau County, N.Y., 1967-69; dir. dept. health for Africa, 7th-day Adventist Ch., 1969-76; dir. dept. health for Far East, 7th-day Adventist Ch., Singapore, 1976-80; asst. prof. internat. health Loma Linda Univ., Calif., 1980-90; pres. Emerald Health and Edn. Found., Loma Linda, Calif., 1986-91; bd. dirs. Leprosy Rsch. Found., Loma Linda, Calif., 1980—. Author: (book) Report of CME (now Loma Linda U. Sch. Medicine) Research to Date, 1946; contbr. numerous articles to various publs. V.p. Emerald Health and Edn. Found., 1991—. Recipient Honored Alumnus award Loma Linda U. Sch. Medicine, 1975, Golden award La Sierra U. Alumni Soc., 1992. Fellow AMA, Am. Coll. Nutrition, Royal Soc. Tropical Medicine, Royal Soc. Health, SAR. Republican. Home: 408 Sandalwood Dr Calimesa CA 92320 Office: Emerald Health and Edn Found 11075 Benton St Loma Linda CA 92354

SMITH, EDWARD DAVID, entrepreneur; b. Toronto, Ont., Feb. 29, 1972; s. Mortimer S. and Aleene Jean S. BA in Philosophy, U. Calif., Berkeley, 1993; JD, Tulane U., 1993—. Founding chmn. World Affairs Can., Toronto, Ont., 1987-92; pres. Arbor Group, Toronto, Ont., 1988-90; chmn., CEO RT Ent., Pleasant Hill, Calif., 1989—; cons. New World Cons., Pleasant Hill, Calif., 1990—; dir. World Affairs Am., Berkeley, 1989-91; mem. editorial bd. World Affairs Can. Quar., 1990, The Inside Story, 1992—; dir. rsch. Inside Story Communications, 1992—. Author: (with others) Breeding Bird Atlas of Ontario, 1987. Dept. chair liaison Earth Day '90, Berkeley. Mem. Nar. Com. for Jews in Captive Lands (pres. 1993), Fedn. Ont. Naturalists, Toronto Field Naturalists. Office: Inside Story Communicator 190 El Cerrito Plz Ste 201 El Cerrito CA 94530

SMITH, EDWIN MILTON, law educator; b. Lexington, Ky., May 11, 1950; s. Edwin Milton and Camie Ernestine (Call) S.; m. Denelle Carlene Bentley, May 17, 1980; 1 child, Dylan Toussaint Bentley Smith. AB magna cum laude, Harvard U., 1972, JD, 1976. Bar: Calif. 1976. Assoc. Rosenfeld, Meyer & Susman, Beverly Hills, Calif., 1976-79; atty., adviser Nat. Oceanic & Atmosphere Adminstrn., Dept. Commerce, Seattle, 1979-80; asst. prof. law U. So. Calif. Law Ctr., L.A., 1980-82, assoc. prof. law, 1982-86, prof. law, 1986—; spl. counsel Senator Daniel Patrick Moynihan, Washington, 1987-88; prof. law and internat. rels. U. So. Calif., L.A., 1990—; vis. prof. law U. Pa., 1991-92; bd. dirs. Forum for U.S.-Soviet Dialogue, Washington, 1989-91. Author: (with others) First Use of Nuclear Weapons, 1987; contbr. articles to profl. jours. Internat. Affairs fellow Counsel on Fgn. Rels., Washington, 1987, fellow Oxford-U. So. Calif. Legal Theory Inst., Oxford U., 1990. Mem. Coun. on Fgn. Rels., Am. Soc. Internat. Law (exec. coun. 1989-92), UN Assn. U.S.(mem. nat. coun. 1991—), Acad. Coun. on UN System, Calif. Bar Assn. Office: U So Calif Law Ctr University Park Los Angeles CA 90089-0071

SMITH, ERNEST KETCHAM, electrical engineer; b. Peking, China, May 31, 1922; (parents Am. citizens); s. Ernest Ketcham and Grace (Goodrich) S.; m. Mary Louise Standish, June 23, 1950; children: Priscilla Varland, Nancy Smith, Cynthia Jackson. BA in Physics, Swarthmore Coll., 1944; MSEE, Cornell U., 1951, Ph.D., 1956. Chief plans and allocations engr. Mut. Broadcasting System, 1946-49; with Nat. Bur. Standards, 1951-65; chief ionosphere research sect. Nat. Bur. Standards, Boulder, Colo., 1957-60; div. chief Nat. Bur. Standards, 1960-65; dir. aeronomy lab. Environ. Sci. Services Adminstrn., Boulder, 1965-67; dir. Inst. Telecommunication Scis., 1968, dir. univ. relations, 1968-70; assoc. dir. Inst. Telecommunications Scis. Office of Telecommunications, Boulder, 1970-72, cons., 1972-76; mem. tech. staff Jet Propulsion Lab. Calif. Inst. Tech., Pasadena, 1976-87; adj. prof. dept. Elec. and Computer Enging. U. Colo., Boulder, 1987—; vis. fellow Coop. Inst. Research on Environ. Scis., 1968; assoc. Harvard U. Coll. Obs., 1965-75; adj. prof. U. Colo., 1969-78, 87—,; internat. vice-chmn. study group 6, Internat. Radio Consultative Com., 1958-70, chmn. U.S. study group, 1970-76; mem. U.S. comm. Internat. Sci. Radio Union, mem.-at-large U.S. nat. com., 1985-88. Author: Worldwide Occurrence of Sporadic E, 1957; (with S. Matsushita) Ionospheric Sporadic E, 1962. Contbr. numerous articles to profl. jours. Editor: Electromagnetic Probing of the Upper Atmosphere, 1969; assoc. editor for propagation IEEE Antennas and Propagation Mag., 1989—. Served with U.S. Army, 1944-45. Recipient Diploma d'honneur, Internat. Radio Consultative Com., Internat. Telecommunications Union, 1978. Fellow IEEE (fellow com. 1993), AAAS; mem. Am. Geophys. Union, Electromagnetics Acad., Svc. Club, Kiwanis. Mem. First Congregational Ch. Clubs: Harvard Faculty; University (Boulder); Athenaeum (Pasadena); Boulder Country. Home: 5159 Idylwild Trl Boulder CO 80301-3618 Office: U Colo Dept Elec and Computer Engring Campus Box 425 Boulder CO 80309

SMITH, E(WART) BRIAN, hazardous waste management executive; b. Poughkeepsie, N.Y., Jan. 31, 1938; s. Ewart Gladstone and Genevieve (Contois) S.; m. Betti LaVonne Stoddard, Mar. 26, 1966; children: Samantha, Georgina, Sara, Amanda, Justin. BSEE, Purdue U., 1960; MS in Fin. Mgmt., George Washington U., 1966. Registered civil engr., Calif., registered profl. engr., Ind. Staff civil engr. USNR, 1960-66; chief engr. Fluor, Thailand, 1966-68; project coordinator Bechtel Co., San Francisco, 1968-69; group v.p. Holmes & Narver, Inc., Orange, Calif., 1976-82; v.p., gen. mgr. Fluor Engrs., Inc., Irvine, Calif., 1982-84, sr. v.p., gen. mgr., 1984-85; pres. Fluor Venture Group, Irvine, 1985-86; sr. v.p. Internat. Tech., Torrance, Calif., 1986-90, pres., chief operating officer, 1990-92; CEO Smith Environ., Irvine, Calif., 1992—. Served to capt. USNR, 1989. Mem. Project Mgmt. Inst., IEEE, Am. Assn. Cost Engrs., Soc. Am. Mil. Engrs. Republican. Roman Catholic. Club: Beavers. Home: 51 Montecito Dr Corona Del Mar CA 92625-1017 Office: IT Corp 2355 Main St Ste 100 Irvine CA 92714-9999

SMITH, FERN M., judge; b. San Francisco, Nov. 7, 1933. A.A., Foothill Coll., 1970; B.A., Stanford U., 1972, J.D., 1975. Bar: Calif. 1975. Assoc. firm Bronson, Bronson & McKinnon, San Francisco, 1975-81, ptnr., 1982-86; judge San Francisco County Superior Ct., 1986-88, U.S. Dist. Ct. for Northern Dist. Calif., 1988—; mem. hiring, mgmt. and pers. coms., active recruiting various law schs. Contbr. articles to legal publ. Apptd. by Chief Justice Malcolm Lucas to the Calif. Jud. Coun.'s Adv. Task Force on Gender Bias in the Cts., 1987-89; bd. visitors Law Sch. Stanford U. Mem. ABA, Queen's Bench, Nat. Assn. Women Judges, Calif. Women Lawyers, Women's Forum West/Internat. Women's Forum, Bar Assn. of San Francisco, Fed. Judges Assn., 9th Cir. Dist. Judges Assn., Am. Judicature Soc., Calif. State Fed. Judicial Coun., Phi Beta Kappa.*

SMITH, FRED WESLEY, communications company executive; b. Arkoma, Okla., Jan. 1, 1934; s. Erma (Howard) Wells; m. Mary Blanche Moore, May 1961; children: Fred W. Jr., Jonathan Paul, Deborah Lee. Student, Ark. Poly. Tech. Coll. Classified advt. salesman S.W. Times Record, Ft. Smith, Ark., 1951-53; classified advt. mgr. Southwest Times Record, Ft. Smith,

Ark., 1953-55, nat. advt. mgr., 1956-59, advt. mgr., 1959-60, asst. gen. mgr., 1960-61; gen. mgr. Las Vegas Rev. Jour., 1961-66; v.p. western newspaper div. Donrey Media Group, Las Vegas, 1966-73, exec. v.p., 1973-87, pres., 1987—; bd. dirs. First Interstate Bank of Nev., Reno. Former bd. dirs. United Fund, Clark County Boys Club, Las Vegas; mem. exec. bd. Boy Scouts Am., Las Vegas; former mem., chmn. adv. bd. Salvation Army, Las Vegas; bd. trustees U. Nev. Las Vegas Found., U. of the Ozarks; nat. adv. bd. First Comml. nank, Little Rock. Mem. Sigma Delta Chi. Office: Donrey Media Group 601 N Hollywood Blvd Las Vegas NV 89110-4105 also: Las Vegas Review-Journal PO Box 70 1111 W Bonanza Las Vegas NV 89125-0070

SMITH, FREDERICK GERARD, engineering executive; b. Denver, Dec. 28, 1962; s. Thomas Benedict and Gerarda Lee (Klein) S.; m. Holly Ann Ottinger, Feb. 7, 1987. BS in Computer Sci., U. Mo., 1985; MSEE, Wash. U., St. Louis, 1989, MS in Computer Sci., 1989. Programmer, analyst CAD/CAM McDonnell Douglas, St. Louis, 1984, engr. flight simulation, 1985-88, tech. specialist quality processes, 1988-90, prin. investigator new aircraft products, 1990-91; sr. software developer Integrated Surg. Systems, Sacramento, Calif., 1991-92, mgr. imaging systems, 1992—. Contbr. articles to profl. jours. Mem. IEEE, Assn. for Computing Machinery, Phi Beta Kappa. Roman Catholic. Home: 9267 Laguna Knoll Ct Elk Grove CA 95758 Office: Integrated Surg Systems 829 W Stadium Ln Sacramento CA 95834

SMITH, GARY DOUGLAS, artist; b. San Francisco, July 29, 1948; s. Douglas Owen and Mercedes Maria (Moniz) S.; m. Cassandra Lee Durham, Nov. 14, 1973; children: Nalon Ennis, Oliver Ryan. BFA in Drawing and Printmaking with honors, Calif. Coll. Arts and Crafts, Oakland, 1971; studied with Richard Newlin, Houston, 1978-79; studied with S. W. Hayter and George Ball, Paris, 1979-80; studied with Yozo Hamaguchi, S.F., 1981-83. Lectr. in silverpoint Calif. Coll. Arts and Crafts, Oakland, 1987-88; lectr. in drawing, watercolor and silverpoint Inverness (Calif.) Studio, 1991-93; Solo exhbns. include U. Calif., Berkeley, 1965, 67, Designer's Gallery, Oakland, 1966, Vorpal Gallery, Chgo., 1977-79, Soho, N.Y.C., 1978-83, Laguna Beach, 1976, 82, 85, San Francisco, 1976, 77, 79, 81, 86, Ctr. Integrated Systems, Stanford U., Calif., 1993, Bolinas (Calif.) Mus., 1993, others; group shows include Gallery Route One, Calif., 1991, Caldwell Gallery, San Francisco, 1991, Waterworks Gallery, Wash., 1991, Friday Harbor, Wash., Bolinas Mus., 1991, Yamagataya Gallery, 1989-90, Claudia Chapline Gallery , Stinson Beach, Calif., 1988, 89, 91, 93, Syntex Corp. Gallery, Palo Alto, Calif., 1992, Yamagatoya Gallery, Japan, 1989-93, many others. Works in permanent collections at Achenbach Found. for Graphic Arts, Palace of the Legion of Honor, San Francisco, De Saisset Mus., U. Santa Clara, Calif., Palm Springs Desert Mus., Calif. Acad. Scis., San Francisco, Calif. Coll. Arts and Crafts, Vorpal Galleries, San Francisco, N.Y.C., Keiser Corp., Novato, Calif., Mirfax Assocs., Inc., Oakland, Houston Fine Art Press, Limestone Press, others. Office: The Inverness Studio Box 244 Inverness CA 94937

SMITH, GEORGE IRVING, geologist; b. Waterville, Maine, May 20, 1927; s. Joseph Coburn and Ervena (Goodale) S.; m. Patsy Jean Beckstead, Oct. 31, 1954 (div. May 1970); children: Randall G., Laura E.; m. Teruko Kuwada, Aug. 2, 1974; stepchildren: Michele M. Ono, Marla M. Ono, Mireya M. Ono. AB, Colby Coll., Waterville, Maine, 1949; MS, Calif. Inst. Tech., Pasadena, 1951, PhD, 1956. Instr. Occidental Coll., Eagle Rock, Calif., 1951-52; geologist U.S. Geol. Survey, Claremont, Calif., 1952-58, Menlo Park, Calif., 1958—. Contbr. articles to profl. jours. With USN, 1945-46. Fulbright sr. rsch. fellow, 1981. Fellow Geol. Soc., Am. Mineral Soc.; mem. Am. Quaternary Assn., Soc. Econ. Geologists, Geochem. Soc., Sigma Xi. Office: US Geol Survey 345 Middlefield Rd MS 902 Menlo Park CA 94025-3591

SMITH, GEORGE LARRY, analytical and environmental chemist; b. Beloit, Kans., Oct. 11, 1951; s. Richard Bailey and Vonda Ellene (Cox) S.; m. Charlene Janell Musgrove, Sept. 4, 1973; 1 child, Brian Lawrence. BA, Augustana Coll., 1973. Cert. grade 3 water treatment operator, Calif. Lab. technician Sanitary Dist. of Hammond, Ind., 1973; chemist Federated Metals Corp., Whiting, Ind., 1973-77; rsch. technician Air Pollution Technology, Inc., San Diego, 1978-80, environ. chemist, 1980-81, sr. tech. asst., 1981; staff chemist I Occidental Research Corp., Irvine, Calif., 1981-82, receiving chemist, 1982-84; processing chemist Chem. Waste Mgmt., Inc., Kettleman City, Calif., 1984-87, analytical chemist, 1987-89, wet analytical chemistry group leader, 1989-90, inorganic lab. supr., 1990—; lab. analyst for published article in environ. sci. and tech., 1981. bd. dirs. Apostolic Christian Missions, Inc., San Diego, 1978-82. Mem. Am. Chem. Soc., Assn. Rsch. and Enlightenment, Pan-Am. Indian Assn. Home: 205 E Merced St Avenal CA 93204-1251 Office: Chem Waste Mgmt Inc PO Box 471 Kettleman City CA 93239-0471

SMITH, GEORGIA FLOYD, molecular geneticist; b. Atlanta, Jan. 17, 1949; d. Acey LeRoy and Annette Floyd; m. Randall Allen Smith, Aug. 12, 1978; children: Kendall, Jessica. BA, U. Calif., Santa Barbara, 1972; MPH, U. Mich., 1974; PhD, U. Calif., Riverside, 1979. Postdoctoral fellow Yale U., New Haven, 1979-82; assoc. rsch. scientist Yale U., 1983-85; asst. prof. zoology Ariz. State U., Tempe, 1985-91, assoc. prof. zoology, molecular and cellular biology, 1991—. Contbr. articles to profl. jours. Grantee, NIH, 1988, Am. Cancer Soc., 1988, Ariz. Disease Control Rsch. Commn., 1987, 90, others. Mem. Am. Chem. Soc., Soc. for Biochemistry and Molecular Biol., Internat. Soc. Interferon Rsch. Methodist. Office: Dept Zoology Ariz State Univ Tempe AZ 85287-1501

SMITH, GORDON C., food products company executive; b. 1929. BS, Idaho State U., 1960. CPA. With J.R. Simplot Co., 1954—, v.p., contr., 1975-77, v.p. fin., 1977-82, sr. v.p., 1977-82, pres., chief exec. officer, 1982—. With U.S. Army, 1951-53. Office: J R Simplot Co PO Box 27 Boise ID 83707-0027

SMITH, GORDON EUGENE, pilot; b. Corpus Christi, Tex., Nov. 22, 1953; s. Orvis Alvin and Helen Lucille (Lockhart) A.; m. Crisanta Lacson Oqueriza, Jan. 5, 1979; children: Pia Marie, Helena Irita. AAS in Electronics, Riverside City Coll., 1985; BSEE, Calif. Polytech., 1987. Electronics technician Lear Siegler, Inc., Ontario, Calif., 1981-86, Rockwell Internat., Palmdale, Calif., 1986-87; pilot Orion Air Inc., Raleigh, N.C., 1987-90; pilot, dir. maintenance, asst. dir. ops. Nat. Air, Riverside, Calif., 1990—. With USAF, 1972-79, with Res. 1979—. Mem. Aircraft Owners and Pilots Assn., Team One (v.p. 1980—). Republican. Dunkard Brethren. Office: National Air 6871 Airport Dr Riverside CA 92504-1924

SMITH, GORDON PAUL, management consulting company executive; b. Salem, Mass., Dec. 25, 1916; s. Gordon and May (Vaughan) S.; m. Ramona Chamberlain, Sept. 27, 1969; children: Randall B., Roderick F. B.S. in Econs, U. Mass., 1947; M.S. in Govt. Mgmt, U. Denver (Sloan fellow), 1948; postgrad. in polit. sci, NYU, 1948-50. Economist Tax Found., Inc., N.Y.C., 1948-50; with Booz, Allen & Hamilton, 1951-70; partner Booz, Allen & Hamilton, San Francisco, 1959-62, v.p., 1962-67, mng. pntr. Western U.S., 1968-70; partner Harrod, Williams and Smith (real estate devel.), San Francisco, 1962-69; state dir. fin. State of Calif., 1967-68; pres. Gordon Paul Smith & Co., Mgmt. Cons., 1968—; pres., chief exec. officer Golconda Corp., 1972-74, chmn. bd., 1974-85; pres. Cermetek Corp., 1978-80; bd. dirs., exec. com. First Calif. Co., 1970-72, Groman Corp., 1976-85; bd. dirs. Madison Venture Capital Corp.; adviser task force def. procurement and contracting Hoover Commn., 1954-55; spl. asst. to pres. Republic Aviation Corp., 1954-55; cons., Hawaii, 1960-61, Alaska, 1963; cons. Wash. Hwy. Adminstrn., 1964, also 10 states and fed. agys., 1951-70, Am. Baseball League and Calif. Angels, 1960-62; advisor Monterey Coll. Law, 1991—; chmn. Ft. Ord Econ. Devel. Adv. Group, 1991; over 750 TV, radio and speaking appearances on econs., mgmt. and public issues. Author articles on govt., econs. and edn. Mem. 24 bds. and commns. State of Calif., 1967-72; mem. Calif. Select Com. on Master Plan for Edn., 1971-73; mem. alumni council U. Mass., 1950-54, bd. dirs. alumni assn., 1964-70; bd. dirs. Alumni Assn. Mt. Hermon Prep. Sch., 1963; bd. dirs. Stanford Med. Ctr., 1960-62, pres., chmn., 1962-66; chmn. West Coast Cancer Found., 1976-87 ; trustee, chmn. Monterey Inst. Internat. Studies, 1978—; trustee Northfield Mt. Hermon Sch., 1983—; mem. devel. council Community Hosp. of Monterey Peninsula, 1983—; bd. dirs. Friends of the Performing Arts, vice chmn., 1985—; chmn. The Stanton Ctr., 1988—; advisor Monterey Coll. Law, 1991—; chmn. Ft. Ord Econ. Redevel. Adv. Group, 1991. Served to 1st lt., cav. AUS, 1943-46, ETO. Recipient spl. commendation Hoover Commn., 1955; Alumni of Year award U. Mass., 1963; Trustee of Yr. award Monterey-Peninsula, 1991, Monterey-Peninsula Outstanding Citizen of Yr. award, 1992; Laura Bride Powers Heritage award, 1991; U.S. Congl. award, 1992; Calif. Senate and Assembly Outstanding Citizen award, 1992; Wisdom award of honor Wisdom Soc., 1992; permanent Gordon Paul Smith Disting. Chair for Internat. Study established at Monterey Inst. Internat. Studies; Gordon Paul Smith Scholarship Fund named in his honor Northfield Mt. Hermon Sch.; named to Honorable Order of Ky. Colonels. Mem. Monterey History and Art Assn. (bd. dirs., vice chmn. 1985-87, chmn. 1987—, chmn. The Stanton Ctr. Heritage Ctr., 1988—), Salvation Army (bd. dirs.), Monterey Peninsula Mus. Art, Carmel Valley (Calif.) Country Club, Monterey Peninsula Country Club, Old Capital Club. Home: 253 Del Mesa Carmel CA 93921

SMITH, GORDON STUART, materials scientist, researcher; b. St. Louis, June 10, 1928; s. Paul Howard and Blanche Etta (Root) S.; m. Renee Constance Corey, June 12, 1954; children: Kevin Marshall, Darren Gordon. AB, Washington U., St. Louis, 1952; PhD, Cornell U., 1957. Postdoctoral fellow Cornell U., Ithaca, N.Y., 1957-58; fellow Mellon Inst., Pitts., 1958-63; materials scientist Lawrence Livermore (Calif.) Nat. Lab., 1963—; life mem. joint com. Powder Diffraction Standards, Swarthmore, Pa., 1974—. contbr. rsch. articles to profl. jours. Co-founder del Valle Fine Arts Assn. Mem. Am. Crystallographic Assn. (various offices and coms. 1958—), Applied Crystallography Group (sec. 1982—), Sigma Xi. Home: 5262 Irene Way Livermore CA 94550-3508 Office: Lawrence Livermore Nat Lab PO Box 808 Livermore CA 94551-0808

SMITH, GRANT GILL, retired chemistry educator; b. Fielding, Utah, Sept. 25, 1921; s. Joseph Howe and Bertha (Jensen) S.; m. Phyllis Cook, Dec. 30, 1946; children: Meredith Lynn, Kathleen, Vivienne, Geoffrey Gill, Randall Cook, Roger Todd. BA, U. Utah, 1943; PhD, U. Minn., 1949. Instr. U. Minn., Mpls., 1948-49; from asst. to assoc. prof. chemistry Wash. State U., Pullman, 1949-61; prof. Utah State U., Logan, 1961-90; dir. Internat. Office of Water Edn. Utah State U., Logan, 1990-92; prof. U. Minn. (summer) 1967; vis. prof. Stanford (Calif.) U., 1969-70, Rsch. Sch. Chemistry Australian Nat. U., Camberra, 1982-83, Inst. for Atomic-Molecular Physics, Amsterdam, The Netherlands, 1983. Contbr. numerous articles to profl. jours. Recipient Faculty Honors lecture Utah State U., Logan, 1967, First prize Analytical and Applied Analysis Internat., Lund, Sweden, 1989. Mem. Am. Chem. Soc. (chmn. Wash.-Idaho border 1955-56, Salt Lake sect. 1965-66, Utah award 1977, 78), Utah Acad. Sci., Arts, Letters (pres. 1975-76). Republican LDS Ch. Home: 805 River Heights Blvd Logan UT 84321

SMITH, GREGORY ALLAN, lawyer; b. Washington, Dec. 9, 1945; s. Allan F. and Alene M. (Mullikin) S.; m. Barbara M. Mathews, Jan. 28, 1967; children: Michelle Anne Risch-Smith, Pamela Cheryl Smith. BA, Princeton (N.J.) U., 1968; JD, U. Wis., 1971. Bar: Wis. 1971, Calif. 1972. Assoc. Pillsbury, Madison & Sutro, San Francisco, 1971-78, ptnr., 1979-89; ptnr. Heller, Ehrman, White & McAuliffe, San Francisco, 1990—. Mem. ABA (tax sect.), Western Pension and Benefits Conf., Calif. State Bar (tax sect., empoyee benefits com., steering com. 1991—). Democrat. Office: Heller Ehrman White & McAuliffe 333 Bush St San Francisco CA 94104

SMITH, GREIG LOUIS, deputy councilman; b. South Pasadena, Calif., Nov. 26, 1948; s. John Harold and Gloria Mae (Pitre) S.; m. Christine Marie Crippen, Apr. 14, 1973; children: Krista Lynn, Matthew John. AA, Pierce Coll., 1978; cert. advt., UCLA, 1988. Area dir. Rep. Ctrl. Com., 1969-70; youth dir. Re-elect Senator Murphy, L.A., 1970-71; mktg. dir. V.I.V.A., L.A., 1971-72; exec. dir. Ams. for Agnew, Washington, 1972-73; owner Greig's Formal Wear, Northridge, Calif., 1973-81; chief dep. for Councilman Bernson City of L.A., 1979—; govt. rels. officer L.A. Olympic Organizing Com., 1984. Vice chmn. San Fernando Valley Breakfast Forum, 1975-78, C.I.V.I.C.C., San Fernando Valley, 1976-78; pres. North Hills Jaycees, Granada Hills, Calif., 1976-77; chmn. bd. North Valley YMCA, Mission Hills, Calif., 1979-80, 92—; founding mem. North Valley Rep. Assembly, 1992., founding mem. SOLID Foundation, commd. reserve police officer City of L.A., 1993. Named Citizen of Yr. Granada Hills C. of C., 1977, Vol. of Yr. North Valley YMCA, 1988, Citizen of Yr. Internat. Order of Foresters, 1990. Mem. Jr. Chamber Internat. (senator, life), Alpha Sigma Gamma. Office: City of LA Rm 237 City Hall 200 N Spring Los Angeles CA 90012

SMITH, GWENDOLYN MAKEDA, public relations executive; b. L.A., Jan. 6, 1961; d. Myles and Constance (Wilson) S.; children: Jasmine Imani, Asha Jaha. BS, Boston U., 1982; M, U. Southern Calif., 1985. Publicist Debra Baum Pub. Rels., L.A., 1985-87; assoc. dir. Hervey & Co., L.A., 1987-88; pres., owner Jazzmyne Pub. Rels., Burbank, Calif., 1988—.

SMITH, HAMILTON ALLEN, retired aerospace engineer, career officer, international marketing professional; b. Dothan, Ala., Oct. 22, 1923; s. Hugh Grice and Susan (Liddon) S.; m. Gloria Gene Rodene, July 10, 1954 (div. 1974); 1 child, Jeffrey Hamilton S. BS in Aero. Engring., Auburn U., 1947; student, Ga. Inst. Tech., 1943-44; cert. in engring., U. Wash., 1972; MBA, U. Puget Sound, 1980. Enlisted USN, 1942, advanced through grades to lt. comdr., 1956, served in various locations including PTO, aero. engring. officer, ret., 1965; aero. rsch. scientist Nat. Adv. Com. Aeronautics/Langley Aero. Lab., Hampton, Va., 1947-51; engring. mgr. Def. & Space Group, Aerospace & Electronics divsn. Boeing Co., Seattle, 1952-89; owner, mgr. Vanguard Internat. Mktg. Co., Seattle, 1971-91. Author several aerodynamics rsch. reports, numerous documents on mgmt. and ops. of missile and space projects. Mem. Sigma Nu. Home: 2704 W Dravus St Seattle WA 98199-2847

SMITH, HARRY MENDELL, JR., educator; b. Wichita, Kans., Aug. 19, 1943; s. H. Mendell and Sevilla Mae (Cooper) S.; m. Cecile Marie Adams, Sept. 19, 1964; children: Jeff, Shauna, Noelle. AA, Pasadena Coll., 1966; BA, Calif. State U., L.A., 1970; Vocat. Credential, UCLA, 1979. Tchr. Glendora (Calif.) Unified Schs., 1970-80; instr. Citrus Coll., Azusa, Calif., 1978-82; mgr. Christian Chapel, Walnut, Calif., 1980-82; pres. Whitmore Printing, Inc., La Puente, Calif., 1982-85; mgr. Evang. Free Ch., Fullerton, Calif., 1985-87; prof. Mt. San Antonio Coll., Walnut, 1985—, chair divsn. applied sci. and tech., 1993—; dir. Faculty Senate, Mt. San Antonio Coll., 1989-91. Chancellor's Office Electronic Tech. grantee, 1990. Mem. Nat. Assn. Radio and Telecommunications Engrs., Home Bldrs. Fellowship (pres. 1990-92), Calif. Indsl. Arts and Edn. Assn. Republican. Home: 951 S Idaho St Apt 70 La Habra CA 90631-6649 Office: Mount San Antonio College 1100 N Grand Ave Walnut CA 91789-1341

SMITH, HEATHER LYNN, psychotherapist, recreational therapist,; b. Modesto, Calif., May 31, 1956; d. Gary Fremont and Marilyn Rae (Brown) S. BS, Calif. State U., Fresno, 1979; MA, U. San Francisco, 1989. Recreational therapist Casa Colina Rehab. Hops., Pomona, Calif., 1979-82; evaluator developmentally delayed, coord. family edn. Cath. Charities, Modesto, 1982-87; bereavement counselor Hospice, Modesto, 1983-87; high risk youth counselor Ctr. Human Svcs., Modesto, 1987—, substance abuse coord., 1990—; pvt. practice, family therapist John Yost, Modesto, 1990—; coord. substance abuse Stanislaus County Juvenile Hall, 1990. Named Outstanding Young Woman of Stanislaus County, 1986, Citizen of Yr., Civitan, 1986. Mem. Calif. Assn. Marriage and Family Therapists, Kappa Kappa Gamma. Republican. Episcopalian. Home: 806 Claratina Ave Modesto CA 95356-9610 Office: Ctr Human Svcs 11B 1700 McHenry Village Way Modesto CA 95356

SMITH, HELENE SHEILA CARETTNAY, microbiologist; b. Phila., Feb. 13, 1941; d. Joseph Cohen; m. Allan Smith; 1 child, Joshua. BS in Edn. cum laude, U. Pa., 1962, PhD in Microbiology, 1967. Postdoctoral rsch. fellow Princeton U., 1967-69, Nat. Cancer Inst., 1969-71; asst. rsch. virologist cell culture lab. sch. pub. health U. Calif., Berkeley, 1971-75, assoc. rsch. virologist, 1975-77; staff Peralta Cancer Rsch. Inst., Oakland, Calif., 1975-89, asst. dir., 1980-85, assoc. dir., 1985-89; dir. Geraldine Brush Cancer Rsch. Inst., San Francisco, 1989—; lectr. sch. pub. health U. Calif., Berkeley, 1973-78; staff Donner Lab. Lawrence Berkeley Lab. U. Calif., 1977-82; grad. group in genetics U. Calif., 1979-82, adj. assoc. prof., San Francisco, 1984—; speaker in field; mem. spl. rev. com. Nat. Cancer Inst., 1991, reviewer metabolic pathology study sect., 1991, spl. rev. com. program project, 1988, ad hoc reviewer, 1988, 87; ad. com. oral contraceptives and breast cancer Inst. Medicine, 1989-90; mem. cell biology study sect. NSF, 1980-84. Contbr. numerous articles to profl. jours. Speaker Am. Cancer Soc., 1986. Recipient Award of Distinction Susan G. Komen Found., 1987, 89, 90, 91. Mem. Am. Assn. for Cancer Rsch., Am. Soc. for Cell Biology, Soc. for Analytic Cytology, Tissue Culture Assn. Office: Geraldine Brush Cancer Rsch Inst 2330 Clay St 2d Fl San Francisco CA 94115

SMITH, HENRY CHARLES, III, symphony orchestra conductor; b. Phila., Jan. 31, 1931; s. Henry Charles Jr. and Gertrude Ruth (Downs) S.; m. Mary Jane Dressner, Sept. 3, 1955; children—Katherine Anne, Pamela Jane, Henry Charles IV. BA, U. Pa., 1952; artist diploma, Curtis Inst. Music, Phila., 1955. Solo trombonist Phila. Orch., 1955-67; condr. Rochester (Minn.) Symphony Orch., 1967-68; assoc. prof. music Ind. U., Bloomington, 1968-71; resident condr., ednl. dir. Minn. Orch., Mpls., 1971-88; prof. music U. Tex., Austin, 1988-89, Frank C. Erwin Centennial Prof. of Opera, 1988-89; prof. music Ariz. State U., Tempe, 1989—; vis. prof. U. Tex., Austin, 1987-88; founding mem. Phila. Brass Ensemble, 1956—. Composer 5 books of solos for trombone including Solos for the Trombone Player, 1963, Hear Us As We Pray, 1963, First Solos for the Trombone Player, 1972, Easy Duets for Winds, 1972; editor 14 books 20th century symphonies lit. Music dir. S.D. Symphony, Sioux Falls, 1989—. Served to 1st lt. AUS, 1952-54. Recipient 3 Grammy nominations, 1967, 76, 1 Grammy award for best chamber music rec. with Phila. Brass Ensemble, 1969. Mem. Internat. Trombone Assn. (dir.), Am. Symphony Orch. League, Music Educators Nat. Conf., Am. Guild Organists, Am. Fedn. Musicians, Tubist Universal Brotherhood Assn., Acacia Fraternity. Republican. Congregationalist. Home: 1239 E Krista Way Tempe AZ 85284-1566 Office: Ariz State U Sch Music Tempe AZ 85287

SMITH, HOWARD, curator; b. Houston, May 29, 1956; s. Howard Sr. and Blanche Margaret (Phillips) S.;. BA, U. So. Miss., 1977; diploma, U. Dijon (France), 1978. Freelance photographer New Orleans, 1979-86; photographer, printer Stewart Croxton, Inc., L.A., 1986-88, asst. visual resources curator, 1988-91, visual resources curator, 1991—. Exhibited in group shows at Seven Western States Juried Exhbns., L.A., 1990 (1st place), Peacemaking in Action Exhbn., L.A., 1990 (1st place). Fulbright fellow, Bourdeaux, France, 1977. Mem. Art Librs., Visual Resources Assn., La. Ctr. Photographic Studies (auction com. 1991-92), Nat. Trust Hist. Preservation, Coll. Art Assn. Office: U So Calif WAH Rm 104 Los Angeles CA 90089-0292

SMITH, HOWARD RUSSELL, manufacturing company executive; b. Clark County, Ohio, Aug. 15, 1914; s. Lewis Hoskins and Eula (Elder) S.; m. Jeanne Rogers, June 27, 1942; children: Stewart Russell, Douglas Howard, Jeanne Ellen Smith Akins. A.B., Pomona Coll., 1936. Security analyst Kidder, Peabody & Co., N.Y.C., 1936-37; economist ILO, Geneva, 1937-40; asst. to pres. Blue Diamond Corp., Los Angeles, 1940-46; pres., dir. Avery Dennison Corp., Pasadena, Calif., 1946-75, chmn. bd., 1975-84, chmn. exec. com., 1984—; chmn. bd. Kinsmith Fin. Corp., San Marino, Calif., 1979—. Bd. dirs., past pres., chmn. Los Angeles Philharm. Assn.; chmn. emeritus, bd. trustees Pomona Coll., Claremont, Calif.; past chmn. bd. Children's Hosp. Los Angeles, Community TV of So. Calif. (Sta. KCET), Los Angeles. With USNR, 1943-46. Home: 1458 Hillcrest Ave Pasadena CA 91106-4503 Office: Avery Dennison Corp 150 N Orange Grove Blvd Pasadena CA 91103

SMITH, JACK CARTER (JOHN SMITH), business owner; b. L.A., Oct. 16, 1943; s. John Wilkons and Jane Marie (Carter) S.; m. Kay Marie Campbell, Aug. 25, 1963 (dec. Mar. 1980); children: Jay Edgar, Jana Kay; m. Barbara Ann Bramwell, Sept. 14, 1980. Student, Walla Walla Coll., 1962-64. Co-owner Barnes, Campbell & Smith, Redmond, Wash., 1966—, Campbell-Smith Enterprises, Fall City, Wash., 1966-86, SCS Enterprises, Mt. Vernon, Wash., 1968—; owner Smith Enterprises, Sandpoint, Idaho, 1968—; co-owner Smith & Clay Enterprises, Spokane, Wash., 1984—. Bd. dirs. Mont. Conf. Seventh Day Adventist Ch., Bozeman, 1980-83, Walla Walla Coll., College Place, Wash., 1983-88, Walla Walla Coll. Endowment Fund, 1986-92, Upper Columbian Acad., Spangle, Wash., 1986—; exec. com. elem. bd. edn., North Pacific Union Conf. Seventh Day Adventist Ch., 1991—. Seventh Day Adventist. Home and Office: 2900 Oden Bay Rd Sandpoint ID 83864-9494

SMITH, JACK LEE, bank executive; b. Yale, Okla., Feb. 2, 1948; s. George W. and Alta E. (Tilley) S.; m. Rose Mary Cantrell, Feb. 3, 1968 (div. Feb. 1980); children: Anissa Kay, Melany Elaine; m. Janice A. Houston, Aug. 2, 1981). BS, Okla. State U., 1972. Asst. v.p. Production Credit Assn., 1972-76; v.p., office mgr. Mountain Plains Prodn. Credit Assn., Ft. Collins, 1976-81; dist. mgr. Ralston Purina, St. Louis, 1981-83; 2d v.p. Omaha Nat. Bank, 1983-85; v.p., office mgr. FirsTier Bank, N.A., Omaha, Ft. Collins, 1985—; bd. dirs. Colo. Cattle Feeders Assn.; chmn. Allied Industry Coun. for Agr. Recipient Agr. Econs. Dept. Club scholarship, 1971. Mem. Am. Bankers Assn., Colo. Bankers Assn., Colo. Cattle Feeders (bd. dirs.), Nat. Cattlemen's Assn., Kans. Livestock Assn., Colo. Cattlemen's Assn., Ft. Collins C. of C., Elks. Republican. Home: 704 Knollwood Cir Fort Collins CO 80524-1585 Office: FirsTier Bank N A Omaha 323 S College Ave Ste 2 Fort Collins CO 80524-2845

SMITH, JAMES A., security consultant, private investigator; b. Tyler, Tex., Apr. 21, 1965; s. James William and Madonna Jean Smith. BA in Psychology, U. Tex., 1988, BS in Speech, 1988. Security officer Zimco Security Cons., Austin, Tex., 1987-90; security mgr. Colo. Security Systems, Boulder, 1990-91; owner, dir. Donovan Pers. Svcs., Boulder, 1991—; safety cons. Ideal Market, Boulder. Author: (screenplay) Mercy Streets, 1992, Bombay Revisited, 1992. Mem. Boulder C. of C. Office: Donovan Pers Svcs 1630 30th St Ste 150 Boulder CO 80301-1000

SMITH, JAMES ALEXANDER, metal processing executive; b. Harvey, N.D., Jan. 16, 1926; s. James Kay MacKenzie and Palma Theresa (Johnson) S.; m. Cleo Lorraine, Sept. 1, 1948 (div. 1962); children: Deborah Kay Smith Hooper, Daryl Lynn Smith O'Neill, Darcey Amelia Smith Ryan; m. Louise Mae Hammer, July 21, 1979. BS, U. Minn., 1951. Ptnr., v.p. VIP, Phoenix, 1960-78; founder Therm-O-Low Inc., Phoenix, 1978-84; v.p., gen. mgr., pres. 3XKryogenics, Phoenix, 1984-86; founder and pres. Cryogenics Internat., Inc., Tempe, Ariz., 1987—; lectr. and speaker in field. Patentee (U.S. and fgn.) in field. Staff sgt. U.S. Infantry, 1943-46, ETO, Japan. Mem. Soc. Mfg. Engrs. (Ariz. chpt. chmn. 1983, chmn. western states zone 1985, Pres.'s award 1984), Cryogenic Soc. Am., Am. Soc. Metals, VFW (life mem.). Republican. Lutheran. Home and Office: Cryogenic Consultants Co 4128 E Calle Redonda # 73 Phoenix AZ 85018-3760

SMITH, JAMES DEAN, research scientist and engineer; b. Albuquerque, Dec. 20, 1955; s. Schuyler George and Kathleen Reta (Tarling) S.; m. Capri Louise Corlis, Oct. 13, 1990. BS in Applied Math., N.Mex. Inst. Mining and Tech., 1977; MS in Nuclear Engring., U. N.Mex., 1983. Rsch. analyst Falcon R & D, Albuquerque, 1977-81; high power laser physicist Rockwell Internat./Rocketdyne, Albuquerque, 1981-82; rsch. engr., scientist VERAC subs. Ball Aerospace, Albuquerque, 1982-84; directed energy rsch. engr., scientist Kaman Scis. Corp., Albuquerque, 1984-90; sr. nuclear engr. GRAM, Inc., Albuquerque, 1992—; high speed spectroscopics Terminal Effects Rsch. and Analysis, N.Mex., 1973-77. Mem. Am. Math. Soc., Am. Nuclear Soc. (Trinity sect.), Nat. Assn. Radio and Telecommunications Engrs., KAFB Aero Club, Eagle Pointe Flying Club. Republican. Home: 5804 Alegria Rd NW Albuquerque NM 87114-4817 Office: GRAM Inc 8500 Menaul Blvd NE Albuquerque NM 87107

SMITH, JAMES LAWRENCE, research physicist; b. Detroit, Sept. 3, 1943; s. William Leo and Marjorie Marie (Underwood) S.; m. Carol Ann Adam, Mar. 27, 1965; children: David Adam, William Leo. BS, Wayne State U., 1965; PhD, Brown U., 1974. Mem. staff Los Alamos (N.Mex.) Nat. Lab., 1973-82, fellow, 1982-86, dir. ctr. materials sci., 1986-87, fellow, 1987—; chief scientist Superconductivity Tech. Ctr., 1988—. Co-editor Philos. Mag., 1990—; contbr. articles to profl. jours. Recipient E.O. Lawrence award, 1986. Fellow Am. Phys. Soc. (internat. prize for new materials 1990); mem. AAAS, Materials Rsch. Soc., Minerals Metals Materials Soc., Am. Crystallographic Assn. Office: Los Alamos Nat Lab Superconductivity Tech Ctr Mail Stop K763 Los Alamos NM 87545

SMITH, JAMES THOMAS, mathematician; b. Springfield, Ohio, Nov. 8, 1939; s. Earl Gearhart and Betty Mae (McCartney) S.; m. Helen Marie Patteson, Jan. 26, 1963; 1 son, Jedediah. A.B., Harvard U., 1961; M.A., San Francisco State U., 1964; M.S., Stanford U., 1967; Ph.D., U. Sask., Regina, Can., 1970. Mathematician U.S. Navy, San Francisco, 1962-67; asst. prof. math. San Francisco State U., 1969-72, assoc. prof., 1972-75, prof., 1975—; dir. software devel. Blaise Computing, Berkeley, 1984-85; vis. prof. Mills Coll., Oakland, Calif., 1982-83, U. Alaska-Fairbanks, 1983, Calif. State U.-Hayward, 1984, SUNY, 1988-89. Author tech. reports on mil. ops. analysis, 1963-67. Author: IBM PC/AT Programmer's Guide, 1986, Getting the Most from Turbo Pascal, 1987, Advanced Turbo C, 1989, C for Scientists and Engineers, 1991, C Applications Guide, 1992; contbr. papers on math. rsch. to profl. publs. Mem. schs. com. Harvard Club, San Francisco, 1978—, v.p. schs., 1989-93. Mem. Am. Math Soc., Math. Assn. Am. (chmn. north Calif. sect. 1992-93), Deutsche Mathematiker-Vereinigung. Home: 1363 27th Ave San Francisco CA 94122-1508 Office: San Francisco State U Math Dept San Francisco CA 98132

SMITH, JAN, management consultant; b. Oakland, Calif., Oct. 12, 1945; d. Howard J. and Emily E. (Lyon) S. BS in Bus., Mich. State U., 1967. Asst. sec., dir. planning Pacific Industries, Modesto, Calif., 1977-79; owner System Organizer, Modesto, 1979—; ptnr. Mr. Pool Guy, Modesto, 1991-92. Mem. Modesto City Planning Commn., 1988-92, chmn., 1992; dir. tng. United Way Ann. Fundraising Campaign, Modesto, 1990-91; bd. dirs. Modesto Civic Theater, 1981-82; costume mistress Shakespeare in the Park, 1981. Mem. Network of Exec. Women, Modesto C. of C. (bd. dirs. 1982-88, chair, trade show com., 75th anniversary com. Leadership Modesto 1980-88). Office: System Organizer 2443 Fair Oaks Blvd Sacramento CA 95825

SMITH, JAY MYRVEN, JR., accountant, educator; b. Denver, June 14, 1932; s. Jay Myrven and Relia (Cooley) S.; m. Jena Vee Cordon, Aug. 27, 1952; children: Michael, Blaine, Jaynie, Relia, Randall, Cynthia, Debra, Frank, David, Kevin, Kristy. AA, Boise (Idaho) Jr. Coll., 1951; BS, Brigham Young U., 1953, MS, 1960; PhD, Stanford U., 1965. CPA, Utah. Auditor Arthur Andersen & Co., L.A., 1953-54, 56-57; asst. prof. acctg. Brigham Young U., Provo, Utah, 1957-61; assoc. prof. U. Minn., Mpls., 1964-71; prof. acctg. Brigham Young U., 1971—; author South-Western Pub. Co., Cin., 1969—. Author: Intermediate Accounting, 1972, 5th edit., 1992; editor monograph; author articles. Mem. exec. com. Boy Scouts Am., Provo, 1982-84; stake pres. Ch. of Jesus Christ of Latter Day Saints, Mapleton, Utah, 1974-84. With U.S. Army, 1954-56. Recipient Outstanding Univ. Tchr. award Blue Key Frat., 1982, others. Mem. Am. Acctg. Assn. (com. chair, Auditing Svc. award 1992). Home: 1825 Oak Ln Provo UT 84604 Office: Brigham Young U Provo UT 84602

SMITH, JEAN, interior design firm executive; b. Oklahoma City; d. A. H. and Goldy K. (Engle) Hearn; m. W. D. Smith; children: Kaye Smith Hunt, Sidney P. Student Chgo. Sch. Interior Design, 1970. v.p. Billco-Aladdin Wholesale, Albuquerque, 1950-92, v.p. Billco Carpet One of Am, 1970. Pres. Albuquerque Opera, 1979-83, advisor to bd. dirs.; active Civic Chorus, Cen. Meth. Ch.; pres. Inez PTA, 1954-55, life mem.; hon. life mem. Albuquerque Little Theater, bd. dirs. Republican. Clubs: Albuquerque County, Four Hills Country, Daus. of the Nile (soloist Yucca Temple). Home: 1009 Santa Ana Ave SE Albuquerque NM 87123-4232 Office: Billco-Aladdin Wholesale 7617 Menaul Blvd NE Albuquerque NM 87110-4647

SMITH, JEFFREY R., military officer; b. Syracuse, N.Y., July 28, 1948; s. Robert Dwight and Elma Luella (Gerhardt) S.; divorced; children: Jolie Nicole, Jordan Zeno, Julia Monet. BS in Engring., U. Buffalo, 1971; MEd, Boston U. Ext., Naples, Italy, 1975; postgrad., Naval Postgrad. Sch., Monterey, Calif., 1986. Commd. ensign USN, 1971, advanced through grades to lt. comdr., 1984; pub. affairs officer USN Sigonelia, Catania, Sicily, 1977-78; logistics officer, chief pilot Naval Sta. Roosevelt Rds., Ceiba, P.R., 1978-83; exec. officer USNR, Norfolk, Va., 1983-86; coll. math. instr. Tidewater Coll., Virginia Beach, Va., 1983-85; high sch. math. tchr. Mavry High Sch., Norfolk, 1983-85; 1st officer Henson Airlines, Salisbury, N.Y., 1985-86; aviation safety/chief pilot USN Sigonelia, Catania, 1986-90; aviation safety officer USN Naval Air Sta., Alameda, Calif., 1990—. Editor Carrier newspaper, 1991. Pres. Geo. P. Miller Sch. PTA, Alameda, 1992; vol. Cub Scouts Pack 108, Alameda, 1992; math aide Geo. P. Miller Elem. Sch., Alameda, 1992. With USNR, 1983-86. Mem. ACLU, Amnesty Internat., Sierra Club, VR-24 Alumni Assn. (sec. 1992). Home: 109 Pearl Harbor Alameda CA 94501

SMITH, JEFFRY ALAN, public health administrator, physician, consultant; b. L.A., Dec. 8, 1943; s. Stanley W. and Marjorie E. S.; m. Jo Anne Hague. BA in Philosophy, UCLA, 1967, MPH, 1972; BA in Biology, Calif. State U., Northridge, 1971; MD, UACJ, 1977. Diplomate Am. Bd. Family Practice. Resident in family practice WAH, Takoma Park, Md., NIH, Bethesda, Md., Walter Reed Army Hosp., Washington, Children's Hosp. Nat. Med. Ctr., Washington, 1977-80; occupational physician Nev. Test Site, U.S. Dept. Energy, Las Vegas, 1981-82; dir. occupational medicine and environ. health Pacific Missile Test Ctr., Point Mugu, Calif., 1982-84; dist. health officer State Hawaii Dept. Health, Kauai, 1984-86; asst. dir. health County of Riverside (Calif.) Dept. Health, 1986-87; regional med. dir. Calif. Forensic Med. Group, Salines, 1987—; med. dir. Community Human Svcs. Project, Monterey, Calif., 1987—. Fellow Am. Acad. Family Physicians; mem. AMA, Am. Occupational Medicine Assn., Flying Physicians, Am. Pub. Health Assn. Home: 27575 Via Sereno Carmel CA 93923

SMITH, JO-AN RICHARDSON, goldsmith designer; b. Eugene, Oreg., Apr. 8, 1933; children: Greg, Jeff. BA in Art, U. Tex., El Paso, 1970; MA in Art, N.Mex. State U., Las Cruces, 1975; design cert., Am. Gemology Soc., Calif., 1977. Pvt. practice writer Las Cruces, 1972—, pvt. practice designer, 1975—; cons. Glenn Cutter Jewelers, Las Cruces, El Paso, 1976—; instr. N.Mex. State U., 1974-81. Designer Medallion in Stand (Roush award 1985—), Golden Chile Jewelry, 1983—; author: House Buying Guide, 1975. Recipient N.Mex. State U. Roush award, 1985. Mem. Dona Ana Arts Coun. (Treasure Trio 1985-89), Soc. N.Am. Goldsmiths (disting. mem., hon. mention 1976-77), Phi Kappa Phi. Office: Box 426 Dona Ana NM 88032

SMITH, JOBAN JONATHAN, recreational therapist; b. Albuquerque, New Mex., Mar. 7, 1962; s. William Oswalt and Lou Ella (Agan) Hernandez; 1 child, Connor Nigel Smith. Student, Pensacola Christian Coll., 1980-81, Bradley U., 1981-82; BA in Psychology, Fellowship U., 1985; AA in Alcohol and Drug Counseling, SIPI, Albuquerque, 1990. Underwater demolitions trainer Dept. Defense, Pensacola, Fla., 1980-81; courier, escort Dept. Defense, Peoria, Ill., 1982-86, U.S. Consulate, N.Y.C., 1987-88; security cons. Atlantic Record Co., L.A., 1988; recreation therapist Indian Health Svc., Iselta, New Mex., 1990-91, Manor Care Nursing Home, Albuquerque, 1991—; owner Joban Smith & Assocs., Albuquerque, 1990—; cons. S.W. Fun & Lesiure, Albuquerque, 1991—, McGartland & Assocs., 1991—. Mem. NRA, Nat. Assn. Security Cons., New Mex. Activities Assn.

SMITH, JOEY SPAULS, mental health nurse, biofeedback therapist, bodyworker, hypnotist; b. Washington, Oct. 9, 1944; d. Walter Jr. and Marian (Och) Spauls; children: Kelly, Sean. BSN, Med. Coll. Va., 1966; MA in Edn., U. Nebr., Lincoln, 1975. RNC, ANA; cert. psychiat. and mental health nurse; cert. massage practitioner, cert. hypnotist, cert. biofeedback therapist. Staff nurse Booth Meml. Hosp., Omaha, 1969-71; asst. house supr. Nebr. Meth. Hosp., Omaha, 1971-72; head nurse, clin. instr. U. Calif., Davis, 1976-78; staff nurse Atascadero State Hosp., Calif. Dept. Mental Health, 1978-79; nurse instr. psychiat. technician Atascadero State Hosp., 1979-84, insvc. tng. coord., 1984-86; nursing coord. chem. dependency recovery program French Hosp. Med. Ctr., San Luis Obispo, Calif., 1986-87; nurse instr., health svcs. staff devel. coord. Calif. Men's Colony, Dept. Corrections, San Luis Obispo, 1987-92; pvt. practice San Luis Obispo, Calif., 1990—; relief house supr. San Luis Obispo County Gen. Hosp., 1982-88, regional program assoc. statewide nursing program Consortium Calif. State U., 1986-88; clin. instr. nursing div. Cuesta Coll., 1988—. 1st lt. U.S. Army Nurse Corps., 1965-67. Mem. Assn. Applied Psychophysiology and Biofeedback, Am. Holistic Nurses Assn., Consol. Assn. Nurses in Substance Abuse (cert. chem. dependency nurse), Biofeedback Cert. Inst. Am. (cert. biofeedback therpaist, cert. stress mgr., stress mgmt. edn.), Alpha Sigma Chi, Phi Delta Gamma. Home: 1321 Cavalier Ln San Luis CA 93405-9999 Office: PO Box 4823 San Luis Obispo CA 93403-4823

SMITH, JOHN KERWIN, lawyer; b. Oakland, Calif., Oct. 18, 1926; 1 dau., Cynthia. BA, Stanford U.; LLB, Hastings Coll. Law, San Francisco. Ptnr., Haley, Purchio, Sakai & Smith, Hayward, Calif; bd. dirs. Berkeley Asphalt, Mission Valley Ready-Mix; gen. ptnr. Oak Hill Apts., City Ctr. Commercial, Creekwood I and Creekwood II Apts. Road Parks Commn., 1957, mem. city coun., 1959-66, mayor, 1966-70; chmn. Alameda County Mayors Conf., 1968; chmn. revenue taxation com. League Calif. Cities, 1968; vice-chmn. Oakland-Alameda County Coliseum Bd. Dirs.; bd. dirs. Coliseum Found., Mission Valley Rock, Rowell Ranch Rodeo; former pres. Hastings 1066 Found. (Vol. Svc. award 1990), Martin Kauffman 100 Club. Recipient Alumnus of Yr. award Hastings Coll. Law, 1989. Mem. ABA, Calif. Bar Assn., Alameda County Bar Assn., Am. Judicature Soc., Rotary. Office: 22320 Foothill Blvd #620 Hayward CA 94541

SMITH, JOSEPH BENJAMIN, communications company executive; b. Chelsea, Mass., Jan. 26, 1928; s. Philip and Lillian Esther (Schlafman) S.; m. Dione Greenstone, Aug. 25, 1957; children: Jeffrey Duke, Julie. B.A., Yale University., 1950. Radio broadcaster in Va., Pa. and Mass., 1950-61; with Warner Bros. Records, Burbank, Calif., 1961-75; pres. Warner Bros. Records, 1971-75; chmn. bd. Elektra/Asylum Records, 1975-83; pres., chief exec. officer Home Sports Entertainment div. Warner Amex Cable, 1983-84; pres. Unison Prodns., Inc., 1984-93, CEO, chmn., 1993-; pres., chief exec. officer Capitol-EMI Music Inc., 1987-93; dir. Capitol-EMI Music, Inc., GM Records, WEA Distbg. Co.; Pres. community relations for rec. industry, 1968—; pres., bd. dirs. Nat. Acad. Recording Arts and Scis., 1986-87; dir. Westwood One Productions, Rock and Roll Hall of Fame. Mem. Pres.'s Council on Phys. Fitness and Sports, 1977—; founder Los Angeles Music Center, Mus. Contemporary Art; mem. pres.'s adv. com. for music Yale U.; trustee Calif. Sch. of Arts; bd. govs. Cedar-Sinai Hosp.; trustee Calif. Inst. of the Arts; bd. dirs. T.J. Martell Found.; trustee Basketball Hall of Fame; bd. dirs. Magic Johnson Found. Served with AUS, 1945-47. Recipient Industry Exec. of Yr. award Nat. Assn. Record Merchandisers, 1975; Promotion Exec. of Yr. award Bill Gavin Report, 1963, 64, 65; named Man of Yr. Anti-Defamation League, 1973; Man of Yr. Record Industry Promotion Assn., 1969; Exec. of Yr. Radio Broadcasters, 1976, Humanitarian of Yr. City of Hope, 1988. Mem. Nat. Acad. Rec. Arts and Scis. (pres. 1986), Country Music Assn. (v.p.), Record Industry Assn. Am. (dir.). Clubs: Variety (dir.), Hillcrest Country, Malibu Riding and Tennis. Office: Unison Prodns Ste 2800 1999 Ave of the Stars Los Angeles CA 90067

SMITH, JULIA B., banker; b. Great Falls, Mont., May 25, 1953; d. George Clyde and Florence Ethelyn (Snyder) Baldwin; m. William Geoffrey Roberts, Mar. 31, 1973 (div. 1989); children: W. Jay, Zachary W.; m. Bronson B. Smith, Aug. 14, 1992. BA cum laude, U. Mont., 1977. Teller Valley Bank Kalispell, Mont., 1977-78, note window supr., 1978-81, money desk mgr., 1981-84, investment officer, 1984-87, investment and security officer, 1987—. Scorekeeper Pee Wee Baseball, Kalispell, 1989-91; vol. sect. chair United Way Flathead County, Kalispell, 1990-91. Mem. Fin. Women Internat. (v.p. Flathead Valley group 1987-88, pres. 1988-89, state awards and scholarship chmn. 1989-90, group pub. affairs chmn., 1990-91, group pres. 1992-93, state v.p. 1993-94). Office: Valley Bank Kalispell 41 3d St W Kalispell MT 59901

SMITH, KARL JOSEPH, mathematician, educator, author; b. Pasadena, Calif., Oct. 12, 1943; s. Karl B. Averill and Rosamond K. (Pellkofer) Foley; m. Linda Ann Sovndal, June 29, 1963; children: Melissa, Shannon. BA in Math., UCLA, 1965, MA in Math., 1967; PhD in Math. Edn., Southeastern La. U., 1979. Tchr. Culver City (Calif.) Jr. High Sch., 1965-67; instr. Whitworth Coll., Spokane, Wash., 1967-68; prof. Santa Rosa (Calif.) Jr. Coll., 1968—, chmn. dept. math., 1973-78; Invited speaker Internat. Congress on Math. Edn., Budapest, Hungary, 1988. Author: Introduction to Symbolic Logic, 1974, Analytic Geometry: A Refresher, 1974, Finite Mathematics: A Discrete Approach, 1975, Basic Mathematics, 1981, Arithmetic for College Students, 1981, Essentials of Trigonometry, 2d edit., 1986, Mathematics: Its Power and Utility, 3 edit., 1990, Precalculus Mathematics: A Functional Approach, 4th edit., 1990, The Nature of Mathematics, 5th edit., 1987, Trigonometry for College Students, 4th edit., 1987, Algebra and Trigonometry, 1987, Business Mathematics, 3d edit., 1992, Finite Mathematics, 3d edit., 1992, Applied Calculus, 1992, Mathematics and Calculus, 1988, Mathematics for Business, 1990; co-author: (with Pat Boyle) Algebra and Trigonometry, 1979, Study Guide for Elementary Algebra, 2d edit., 1980, Study Guide for Intermediate Algebra, 2d edit., 1985, College Algebra, 4th edit., 1989, Intermediate Algebra for College Students, 4th edit., 1989, Primer for College Algebra, 1990, Study Guide for Algebra, 1990, Beginning Algebra for College Students, 4th edit., 1990; mem. editorial com. UME Trends: News and Reports on Undergrad. Math. Edn., 1990—; contbr. articles to profl. jours. Recipient Outstanding Tchr. award Santa Rosa Jr. Coll., 1989. Mem. Am. Math. Assn. of Two-Yr. Colls. (founding editor Western AMATYC News 1979-83, mem. exec. bd. 1980—, v.p. western chpt. 1980-83, nat. sec. 1983-85, nat. pres. 1987-89, chairperson nominations and election com. 1990), Math. Assn. Am. (accreditation com. 1987-90, remediation com. 1987, two-yr. coll. com. 1987—), Coun. Sci. Soc. Pres. (math. and sci. edn. com. 1989—), Coll. Bd. Math. Scis. (exec. com. 1989-91), Calif. Math. Coun. for Community Colls. (mem. at large 1978-80). Lutheran. Office: Santa Rosa Jr Coll 1501 Mendocino Ave Santa Rosa CA 95401-4332

SMITH, KEITH LARUE, research company executive; b. Salida, Colo., Dec. 15, 1917; s. Leroy Holt and Verna Lea (Tunnell) S.; student Marion Coll., 1935-38; A.B. in Math., Ind. U., 1946; postgrad. DePauw U., 1946-47; M.A. in Internat. Affairs, Harvard U., 1955; M.P.A., Calif. State U.-Fullerton, 1979; m. Evelyn May De Bruler, Aug. 29, 1943; 1 son, Eric Douglas. Mil. intelligence research specialist Dept. of Army, Washington, 1951-60; staff engr. Librascope div. Gen. Precision, Inc., Glendale, Cal., 1960-61; sr. operations research analyst Space div. N.Am. Rockwell Corp., Downey, Cal., 1961-71; dir. research Am. Research Corp., Paramount, Calif., 1972—; instr. math. and polit. sci. DePauw U., 1946-47; cons. model bldg. and gaming techniques, 1960—; mgmt. cons., 1970—; instr. math. and sci. Verbum Dei High Sch., 1974-85 . Adult leader Boy Scouts Am., Long Beach, Calif., 1961-75. Treas., UN Council Harvard, 1947-49, Young Democratic Club, Arlington, Mass., 1949-50. Served to capt. USAAF, 1941-46; ETO. Recipient scholarship award Inst. World Affairs, 1947, Outstanding Efficiency award Dept. Army, 1960, Apollo 11 medallion NASA, 1970. Mem. Am. Mus. Natural History, Nat. Geog. Soc., Harvard Alumni Assn., Pi Sigma Alpha. Methodist. Mason. Research on lunar mission cartography, mil. operations research and war game model bldg. Home: 3451 E Curry St Long Beach CA 90805-3815

SMITH, KENNETH JAMES, hematologist; b. White Plains, N.Y., July 19, 1948; s. Henry James and Greta Elizabeth (Olson) S.; m. Catherine Horton, June 25, 1972; children: Patricia, Amy, David. AB, Fordham U., 1970; MD, Cornell U., 1974. Diplomate Am. Bd. Blood Banking, Am. Bd. Internal Medicine, sub-bds. Med. Oncology, Hematology. Intern then resident U. Pitts. Hosp., 1974-77, rsch. fellow in hematology/oncology, 1977-80; asst. prof. pathology and medicine U. N.Mex. Sch. Medicine, Albuquerque, 1980-86, assoc. prof., 1986-90; assoc. med. dir. United Blood Svcs., Albuquerque, 1980-90, med. dir., 1990—; prof. medicine and pathology. Contbr. articles to sci. jours.; patentee blood product, 1988. Mem. Gov.'s AIDS/HIV Task Force, 1990; v.p. Sangre de Oro (N.Mex.) Hemophilia Program. Rsch. fellow U. Wash., 1977-80; rsch. grantee Blood Systems Rsch. Found., Inc., Ellis Pharm. Cons., Ortho Pharm., Inc., Rorer, Inc., Am. Heart Assn. Mem. ACP (councillor N.Mex. chpt. 1990, pres.-elect N.Mex. chpt. 1991, pres. 1992-93), Am. Heart Assn. (vice chmn. rsch. com. N.Mex. affiliate 1991, rsch. grantee), Am. Soc.Hematology, Am. Fedn. Clin. Rsch., Am. Assn. Blood Banks. Democrat. Home: 1522 Wellesley Dr NE Albuquerque NM 87106-1137 Office: U NMex Sch Medicine Dept Pathology Albuquerque NM 87131

SMITH, KIRK ROBERT, environmental scientist, researcher; b. Calif., Jan. 19, 1947. MPH, U. Calif., Berkeley, PhD in Biomed. & Environ. Health Scis., 1977. Founder, leader energy program East-West Ctr., Honolulu, 1978-85, sr. fellow, program area coord. environ. risk, 1985—; educator U. Hawaii. Author: 7 books; contbr. numerous articles to profl. jours. Named One of Am.'s 100 Brightest Young Scientists, Sci. Digest, 1984, Alumnus of Yr., U. Calif. Sch. Pub. Health, 1989. Office: East-West Ctr 1777 East-West Rd Honolulu HI 96848

SMITH, LANE JEFFREY, automotive journalist, technical consultant; b. Honolulu, May 17, 1954; s. Gerald Hague and JoEllen (Lane) S.; m. Susan Elizabeth Gumm, May 24, 1980; children: Amber Elizabeth, Graham Hague. BS in Journalism, Iowa State U., 1978. Feature editor Car Craft mag. Peterson Pub., L.A., 1979—, tech. editor, sr. editor, editor Hot Rod Mag., 1987-92, exec. editor, 1993—; speaker in field. Home: 17646 Hamlin Van Nuys CA 91406 Office: Hot Rod Mag 6420 Wilshire Blvd Los Angeles CA 90048

SMITH, LAWRENCE HOWARD, vocational educator; b. Teledo, Oreg., Oct. 8, 1942; s. Howard George and Alice Elisabeth (Munhall) S.; m. Janele Beth Willford, June 19, 1964; children: Andrew, Nathaniel. BS, Oreg. State U., 1964, MEd, 1965; EdD, UCLA, 1976. Asst. dean Claremont (Calif.) McKenna Coll., 1969-71; dir. ednl. career svcs. UCLA, 1971-78, dir. MBA placement, 1978-80; dir. career planning and placement U. Oreg., Eugene, 1980—; chmn. telecommunications task force U. Oreg., 1987-88; v.p. Fenton & Lee Confections, Eugene, 1984—; cons. Advanced Sci. and Tech. Inst., Eugene, 1987—. Contbr. articles to profl. jours. Coach AYSO, Eugene, 1980-86. 1st lt. U.S. Army, 1966-69. Mem. Roundtable of Eugene (v.p. 1990, sec. 1989), Western Coll. Placement Assn. (co-chair annual conf. 1989-90), Northwest Assn. for Sch., Coll. and Univ. Staffing (pres. 1989-90). Office: U Oreg 244 Hendricks Hall Eugene OR 97403

SMITH, LE ROI MATTHEW-PIERRE, III, municipal administrator; b. Chgo., Jan. 11, 1946; s. Le Roy Matthew and Norma Buckner (McCamey) S.; 1 son, Le Roi Matthew Pierre. B.A. in Psychology, Idaho State U., 1969; Ph.D. in Psychology, Wash. State U., 1977. Instr. psychology Idaho State U., Pocatello, 1969-70, Wash. State U., Pullman, 1970-71; mem. faculty dept. psychology Evergreen State Coll., Olympia, 1971-81; dir. diversity program Port of Seattle, 1981—; cons. in field. Bd. dirs. Thurston-Mason County Community Mental Health Ctr., Olympia; v.p., Idaho State Human Rights Commn., Bannock County, Idaho, 1968-70. Office Edn. fellow, 1969-70; U.S. Dept. Labor grantee, 1968; NSF grantee, 1972; Lilly Found. fellow, 1980. Mem. Am. Psychol. Assn., Am. Personnel and Guidance Assn., Wash. State Black Econs. and Edn. Conf., Assn. Black Psychologists, Am. Assn. of Affirmative Action Officers, Phi Delta Kappa. Democrat. Roman Catholic. Home: 761 S 45th St Tacoma WA 98408-4962 Office: PO Box 1209 Seattle WA 98111

SMITH, LEE L., hotel executive; b. Long Beach, Calif., Oct. 15, 1936; s. Lowell Llake and Violet Margaret (Chrissman) S.; m. Sharon M.C. Lanahan, (div. 1977). AA, Long Beach City Coll., 1958; BA in Music, Chapman Coll., 1965; postgrad., Calif. State U., Long Beach, 1966-67, U. Calif., Santa Barbara, 1974. Cert. tchr. Calif.; lic. ins. agt., Calif. Owner, mgr. Lee's Land Cattle Ranch, Cuyama Valley, Calif., 1960—; tchr. Cuyama Valley Schs., New Cuyama, Calif., 1967-79; owner, mgr. Cuyama Buckhorn Restaurant & Motel, New Cuyama, 1979-83; owner Allstate Ins. Agy., Desert Hot Springs, Calif., 1987-91; owner, mgr. Caravan Resort Spa, Desert Hot Springs, 1983-91; owner S & S Printing, 1990—, Lee's Land Bed & Breakfast, 1992—. Violinist Bakersfield (Calif.) Symphony, 1967—, Brook String Quartet, Palm Springs, Calif., 1984-91; dir. Planning Commn., Desert Hot Springs, 1985-87; chmn. Environ. Rev., Desert Hot Springs, 1986-88; mem. Redevel. Com., Desert Hot Springs, 1983-88; mem. exec. bd. growth and devel. Boys and Girls Club; bd. dirs. Food Now Program, 1988-91. Mem. Am. Fedn. Musicians, Desert Hot Springs C. of C. (Bus. Person Yr. 1987), Breakfast Rotary (pres. 1987-88), Taft Rotary, Elks. Republican. Home: St Rte 1 Box 185B Maricopa CA 93252 Office: S & S Printing 623 Center St Taft CA 93268

SMITH, LESTER MARTIN, broadcasting executive; b. N.Y.C., Oct. 20, 1919; s. Alexander and Sadie S.; m. Bernice Reitz, Sept. 28, 1962; 1 child, Alexander. B.S. in Bus. Adminstrn, NYU, 1940. Chief exec. officer Alexander Broadcasting Co., radio stas. in, 1954—; gen. partner 700 Investment Co.; past dir. Seattle C. of C.; past chmn. dir. Radio Advt. Bur. Served to maj. U.S. Army, 1942-46. Decorated Bronze Star. Mem. Nat. Assn. Broadcasters (past dir.), Oreg. Assn. Broadcasters (past pres.), Broadcast Pioneers. Clubs: Rotary (Seattle), Rainer (Seattle), Wash. Athletic (Seattle). Address: 700 112th NE Bellevue WA 98004

SMITH, LEVERETT RALPH, chemistry educator. BA, U. Calif., Santa Cruz, 1970; MS, Cornell U., 1974, PhD, 1976. Postdoctoral fellow Cornell U., Ithaca, N.Y., 1976-77; postdoctoral assoc. SUNY Coll. Environ. Sci., Syracuse, 1977-78; asst. prof. chemistry Oberlin (Ohio) Coll., 1978-81; chemistry editor Academic Press, Inc., San Francisco, 1981-83; lab. mgr. Pacific Environ. Lab., San Francisco, 1983-91; instr. in chemistry Merritt Coll., Oakland, Calif., 1991—. Contbr. articles to profl. jours. Mem. Am. Chem. Soc., Sigma Xi. Office: Merritt Coll 12500 Campus Dr Oakland CA 94619

SMITH, LEVERING, retired naval officer; b. Joplin, Mo., Mar. 5, 1910; s. Aa Levering and Ethel McClellan (Bacon) S.; m. Beulah Lewis, Feb. 1, 1933. BS, U.S. Naval Acad., 1932; LLD, N.Mex. State U., 1962. Commd. ens. USN, 1932, advanced through grades to vice adm., 1977; head dept., dep. tech. dir. Naval Ordnance Test Sta., 1947-54; tech. dir. Polaris project Dept. Navy, Washington, 1956-65; comdg. officer U.S. Naval Missile Test Facility, White Sanda, N.Mex., 1954-56; dir. Polaris/Poseidon project Dept. Navy, Washington, 1965-77; retired, 1977; nat. security cons. U.S. Govt., 1977-92; mem. Pres. Com. on Strategic Forces, 1983. Decorated DSM with two stars; knight commdr. Order Brit. Empire; recipient C.N. Hickman award Am. Rocket Assn., 1957, Parsons award Navy League, 1961, Forrestal award Nat. Security Indsl. Assn., 1978. Fellow AIAA; mem. Nat. Acad. Engring., Am. Soc. Naval Engrs. (recipient Gold medal 1961), Sigma Xi. Home: 3306 Curlew St San Diego CA 92103-5541

SMITH, LINDA A., state legislator; d. Vern Smith; children: Sheri, Robi. Office mgr.; former mem. Wash. State Ho. of Reps.; now mem. Wash. State Senate. Republican. Home: 10009 NW Ridgecrest Ave Vancouver WA 98685-5159

SMITH, LOUIS, maintenance engineer; b. Shreveport, La., Nov. 2, 1934; s. Louis and Savannah (Durham) S.; m. Velma Smith, Jan. 1, 1961; 1 child, Gerald W. Student, Rancho Los Amigos, Downey, Calif., 1976. Maintenance engr. L.A. Dept. Water and Power, 1968—; chauffeur Cowboy Limosine Svc., Pasadena, Calif., 1988—; show horseman Com. for Altadena (Calif.) Old Fashioned-Day Parades; leading rider monty police Palm Spring Parade, 1991; 1st pl. Western singleman rider, Lancaster, 1991; featured rider Palm Springs, 1993. Mem. Tournament of Roses Com., Pasadena Coun. Parade of Roses. With U.S. Army, 1957-58. Recipient Trophies, Altadena Town Coun., 1982, Desert Circus, 1985, 86, Palm Springs C. of C., 1981, 87, City of Barstowe (Calif.), 1988, 89, Golden West Parader Assn., 1989, San Bernardino City Coun., 1990. Mem. Internat. Platform Assn., Golden West Parader Assn., Friends of the Friendless, First Travel Club. Democrat. Baptist. Home: 1980 Santa Rosa Ave Pasadena CA 91104-1127

SMITH, LYNWOOD STEPHEN, retired fisheries educator; b. Snohomish, Wash., Nov. 15, 1928; s. Stephen Johnson and Erna (von Lehe) S.; m. Betty Ann Mars, Sept. 15, 1951; children: Rebecca Jean, Peggy Lynn, Paul Kevin. BS in Biol. Edn., U. Wash., 1952, MS in Zoology, 1955, PhD in Zoology, 1962. Instr. biology Olympic Community Coll., Bremerton, Wash., 1955-60; asst. prof. zoology U. Victoria (B.C.), Can., 1962-65; from asst. prof. to prof. Sch. of Fisheries, U. Wash., Seattle, 1965-92, assoc. dir. instrn., 1986-91; vis. scientist Biol. Sta., Nanaimo, B.C., Can., 1963-65, Cath. U. of Valparaiso, Chile, 1970; resource devel. project P.I., U.S. Agy. for Internat. Devel., Jakarta, Ambon, Indonesia, 1979-84. Author: Introductory Fish Physiology, 1981, Living Shores, 1975, Seashore Animals, 1962; contbr. articles to profl. jours. Mem. Shorelines Hearing Bd., Bothell, Wash., 1975-86. Grantee Fed. Water Pollution Control Adminstrn., 1966-70, U.S. Agy. for Internat. Devel., 1979-83, Wash. Sea Grant, 1981-84. Mem. Exptl. Aircraft Assn. Office: U Wash Sch Fisheries Seattle WA 98195

SMITH, M. FRANCES, writer, photographer; b. Kansas City, Kans., Apr. 13, 1927; d. Joseph Vincent and Rachel Alma (Pennington) Van Cleve; m.

Daniel P. Baker, Apr. 1948 (div.); children: Diane, Patricia Lynn, Jerri Ann; m. Benjamin L. Smith, Dec. 1968. BA in Music and French, Middlebury Coll., 1948; MA in Music and French, U. Nev., 1968. Cert. (spl.) in music and French. Vocal coach, asst. tchr. U. Nev., Reno, 1961-85; with pub rels. Maytan Music Co., Reno, 1968; tchr. Alameda County, Hayward, Calif., 1968-70, Washoe County, Reno, 1961-79; writer layout Pahrump News, Beatty/Amargosa News, Pahrump, Nev., 1982-83; tax preparer Benjamin L. Smith, CPA, Pahrump, 1982—; writer, photographer Creative Pursuits, Pahrump, 1979—. Author: Hawaiian Holiday, 1989, Desert Creation, 1992; contbr. articles, poems, stories, and photographs to mags. Scholar U. Nev., Reno, 1962. Jehovah's Witness. Home: PO Box 1307 Pahrump NV 89041-1307

SMITH, MALCOLM GREVILLE, observatory administrator, researcher, educator; b. Tavistock, Devon, Eng., Apr. 17, 1941; came to U.S., 1985; s. Robert Charles and Edith Nancy Millicent (Copp) S.; m. Ana Maria Maraboli, Aug. 8, 1970; children: Paulina Vivian, Carol Allison. BSc with spl. honors, U. London, 1964; PhD, U. Manchester, Eng., 1967. Postdoctoral fellow Kitt Peak Nat. Obs., Tucson, 1967-69; assoc. astronomer Cerro Tololo Interam. Obs., La Serena, Chile, 1969-76; prin. rsch. scientist Anglo-Australia Obs., Sydney, 1976-79; tech. head Royal Obs., Edinburgh, Scotland, 1979-84; astronomer-in-charge U.K. Infrared Telescope, Hilo, Hawaii, 1985-87; dir. U.K.-Can.-Netherlands Joint Astronomy Ctr., Hilo, 1987-93, Cerro Tololo Interam. Obs., La Serena, Chile, 1993—; assoc. dir. observations U.S. Nat. Optical Astronomy, Tucson, 1993—; cons. Royal Greenwich Obs., Herstmonceux, Eng., 1973, Royal Obs., 1976; affiliate prof. U. Hawaii, Hilo, 1986-93; bd. dirs.-at-large A.U.R.A., Inc., Washington, 1987-93. Contbr. over 100 articles and revs. to rsch. jours. Advisor Ctr. for Astronomy and Space Sci. Edn., Hilo, 1988—. Fellow Royal Astron. Soc. (editor monthly notices 1984-85); mem. Am. Astron. Soc., Astron. Soc. Pacific, Internat. Aston. Union., Rotary Club of Hilo. Office: CTIO Casilla 603 La Serena HI 96720

SMITH, MARGO BRADSHAW, entrepreneur; b. Logan, Utah, May 26, 1950; d. Robert B. and Ila (Gessel) Bradshaw; m. T. Jackson Smith, Sept. 10, 1969; children: Jennifer, Diana, Thomas, Daniel, Sarah, Laura, Samuel, Jacob, Kate. BA magna cum laude, Weber State Coll., 1977. Motel owner Millstream Motel, Ogden, Utah, 1977—; Yellow Cab v.p. Smith Transp., Ogden, Utah, 1980-89, Yellow Cab sec., 1989—; ptnr. J & J Auto Body, Ogden, Utah, 1989—; apt. bldg. owner/mgr. Ogden, Utah, 1988—; self-storage unit mgr. Millstream Storage, Ogden, Utah, 1982—. Mem. Internat. Taxicab & Livery Assn., No. Utah Lodging Assn., Utah Hotel/Motel Assn., C. of C. Republican. LDS. Office: Millstream Motel 1450 Washington Blvd Ogden UT 84404

SMITH, MARIANNE (MARIANNE GOLDSMITH), communications executive; b. Waco, Tex., June 29, 1948; d. Elmer I. and Naomi (Chazanow) Smith; m. John Jekabson, Nov. 11, 1989; 1 child, Alida R. BA, Pitzer Coll., 1970; MA, San Francisco State U., 1975. Writer, curriculum developer Learning about Learning Found., San Antonio, 1968-71; writer, editor, publicist various locations, 1971-89; mgr. corp. comms. and pub. rels. The Harper Group, San Francisco, 1990-91; contract writer ComputerLand Corp., Pleasanton, Calif., 1991—; publicist interactive math. program NSF, Berkeley, Calif., 1992—. Author/editor: (anthology) For the Time Being, 1978; author short stories in Dark Horse Lit. quar., 1976-79; author reviews on lit. and arts, 1982-89. Mem. Internat. Assn. Bus. Comm., Amnesty Internat. Democrat. Jewish. Home: 577 62nd St Oakland CA 94609

SMITH, MARIE EDMONDS, real estate agent, property manager; b. Quapaw, Okla., Oct. 5, 1927; d. Thomas Joseph and Maud Ethel (Douglas) Edmonds; m. Robert Lee Smith, Aug. 14, 1966 (dec. 1983). Grad. vocat. nurse, Hoag Hosp., Costa Mesa, Calif., 1953; BA, So. Calif. Coll., 1955; MS, U. Alaska, 1963. Lic. vocat. nurse, Calif.; cert. sci. tchr., Alaska. Nurse Calif. Dept. Nurses, Costa Mesa, 1952-60; tchr. Alaska Dept. Edn., Aniak and Anchorage, 1955-60; tchr. sci. Garden Grove (Calif.) Sch. Dist., 1960-87; property mgr. Huntington Beach, Calif., 1970—; agent Sterling Realtors, Huntington Beach, 1988—. Author: Ocean Biology, 1969. Bd. dirs., tchr. Harbor Christian Fellowship, Costa Mesa, 1966-83; com. chmn. Garden Grove Unified Sch. Dist. PTA, 1977. NSF grantee, 1960-62. Mem. AAUW, So. Calif. Coll. Alumnae Assn. Republican. Home: 83ll Reilly Dr Huntington Beach CA 92646 Office: 18153 Brookhurst St Fountain Valley CA 92708

SMITH, MARILYN NOELTNER, science educator, consultant; b. Los Angeles, Feb. 14, 1933; d. Clarence Frederick and Gertrude Bertha (Smith) Noeltner; m. Edward Christopher Smith, Sept. 11, 1971. BA, Marymount Coll., 1957; MA, U. Notre Dame, 1966; MS, Boston Coll., 1969. Cert. tchr.; cert. community coll. tchr., Calif.; cert. adminstr., Calif. Tchr., chmn. sci. dept. Marymount High Sch., Santa Barbara, Calif., 1954-57, Los Angeles, 1957-58, 69-79; tchr., chmn. sci. and math. depts. Marymount High Sch., Palos Verdes, Calif., 1959-69; tchr., chmn. math. dept. Corvallis High Sch., Studio City, Calif., 1958-59; instr. tchr. tng. Marymount-Loyola U., Los Angeles, 1965-71, instr. freshman interdisciplinary program, 1970-71; tchr. math. Santa Monica (Calif.) High Sch., 1971-72; instr. math., chemistry, physics Santa Monica Coll., 1971—; tchr. sci. Beverly Vista Sch., Beverly Hills, Calif., 1972—; cons. Calif. State Sci. Framework Revision Com., Los Angeles, 1975; chmn. NASA Youth Sci. Congress, Pasadena, Calif., 1968-69, Hawaii, 1969-70; participant NASA Educators Conf. Jupiter Mission, Ames Research, San Francisco, 1973, NASA Educators Conf. Viking-Mars Ames Project, San Francisco, 1976-77, NASA Landsat Conf., Edward's AFB, Calif., 1978, NASA Uranus Mission, Pasadena, Calif., 1986, NASA Uranus-Voyager Mission, Pasadena, 1989, NASA Neptune-Voyager Mission, Pasadena, 1989; mem. State Calif. CAP test scoring com. U. Santa Barbara, 1992, writing com. State Calif. CAP Test Trainers Manuel, 1993. Author articles, books and computer progs. on space and physics including NASA Voyager-Uranus Sci. Symposium for Educators, 1989, NASA Voyager 2 Neptune Encounter Conf., 1989, others. Sponsor Social Svc. Club, Palos Verdes, 1959-69, moderator, sponsor ARC Youth Svc. Chmn., Beverly Hills, 1974-77, judge L.A. County Sci. Fair, 1969—, mem. blue ribbon com. Nat. Acad. TV Arts and Scis., 1971—; bd. dirs. Children First, Beverly Hills, Calif., 1990-91; vol. sch. initiative, Beverly Hills, 1989-90; others. Recipient Commendation in Teaching cert. Am. Soc. Microbiology, 1962, Salute to Edn. award So. Calif. Industry Edn. Council, 1962, Outstanding Teaching citationCons. Engrs. Assn. Calif., 1967, Cert. Honor, Silver Plaque Westinghouse Sci. Talent Search, 1963-68, Tchr. award Ford-Future Scientists of Am., 1968, Biomed. award Com. Advance Sci. Tng., 1971, Outstanding Tchr. award Los Angeles County Sci. Fair Com., 1975-76, Contbns. to Youth Service citation ARC, 1976-77, Outstanding Tchr. award Kiwanis Club Beverly Hills, 1987, NAST Pres'. award, 1990, Woman of Yr. award, 1990. Mem. We. Assn. Schs. and Colls. (vis. com. 1968, writing com. 1969—), Assn. Advancement Biomed. Edn. (pres. 1970-71), 1st Internat. Sci. Tchrs. Conf. (presider, evaluator 1977), Nat. Sci. Tchrs. Assn. (presider, evaluator 1976, chmn. contributed papers com. 1977-78, presenter 1990), Beverly Hills Edn. Assn.(pres. faculty coun. 1980-81, 85-86, sch. rep. 1990—), Chemist's Club, Calif. Statewide Math. Adv. Com., So. Calif. Industry Edn. Council, Calif. Assn. Chemistry Tchrs. (program chmn. 1960), Calif. Sci. Tchrs. Assn., Am. Chem. Soc., AAAS, South Bay Math. League (sec. 1967-68, pres. 1968-69, 72, 1969-70), Calif. Math. Council, Nat. Assn. Biology Tchrs. Republican. Roman Catholic. Home: 3934 Sapphire Dr Encino CA 91436-3635 Office: Beverly Vista Sch 200 S Elm Dr Beverly Hills CA 90212-4011

SMITH, MARION EDMONDS, research biochemist; b. Susanville, Calif., July 13, 1926; d. Marc Weston and Antoinette (Petersen) Edmonds; m. Kendric Charles Smith, Feb. 5, 1955; children—Nancy Carol, Martha Ellen. B.A., U. Calif.-Berkeley, 1952, M.A., 1954, Ph.D., 1956. Research assoc. Stanford U., Calif., 1956-70, sr. scientist, 1971-74, prof. neurology (research), 1974—; research biochemist VA Hosp., Palo Alto, Calif., 1961—; cons. NIH, Bethesda, Md., 1973-77, 80-84; mem. Nat. Multiple Sclerosis adv. com., N.Y.C., 1981-83, 84-86, merit rev. adv. com. VA, Washington, 1983-85. Contbr. numerous articles to sci. jours., chpts. to books. Mem. Am. Soc. for Neurochemistry (coun. 1975-79, 87-91, sec. 1981-83, 83-85, 85-87, , 93—, pres. 1991-93), Soc. for Neurosci., Internat. Soc. for Neurochemistry, Sierra Club. Democrat. Episcopalian. Home: 927 Mears Ct Palo Alto CA 94305-1041 Office: VA Med Ctr 3801 Miranda Ave Palo Alto CA 94304-1207

SMITH, MARK LEE, architect; b. L.A., Nov. 16, 1957; s. Selma (Moidel) Smith. BA in History of Architecture, UCLA, 1978, MA in Architecture, 1980. Registered architect Calif., 1983, Nev., Oreg., Wash., Tenn., 1986. Designer, drafter John B. Ferguson and Assocs., L.A., 1976-83, architect, 1983; pvt. practice architecture L.A., 1984—; mem. Los Angeles County Archtl. Evaluation Bd., 1990—. Contbr. articles to profl. jours. Regents scholar, U. Calif., Berkeley, UCLA, 1975-78; UCLA Grad. Sch. Architecture Rsch. fellow, 1979-80. Mem. AIA (treas. San Fernando Valley chpt. 1986, v.p. 1987, pres. 1988, Design award 1988, 89, 90, 91, bd. dirs. Calif. coun. 1989—, v.p. 1991—, chmn. continuing edn. 1991—, chmn. 1992 conf.). Office: 18340 Ventura Blvd Ste 225 Tarzana CA 91356-4256

SMITH, MARSHALL SAVIDGE, education educator, college dean, government official; b. East Orange, N.J., Sept. 16, 1937; s. Marshall Parsons and Ann Eileen (Zulauf) S.; m. Carol Goodspeed, June 25, 1960 (div. Aug. 1962); m. Louise Nixon Claiborn, Aug. 1964; children: Adam, Jennifer, Matthew, Megan. AB, Harvard U., 1960, EdM, 1963, EdD, 1970. Computer analyst and programmer Raytheon Corp., Andover, Mass., 1959-62; instr., assoc. prof. Harvard U., Cambridge, Mass., 1966-76; asst., assoc. dir. Nat. Inst. Edn., Washington, 1973-76; asst. commr. edn. HEW, Washington, 1976-79, chief of staff to dept. edn. sec., 1980; prof. U. Wis., Madison, 1980-86; prof., dean Sch. Edn. Stanford (Calif.) U., 1986—; under-sec. edn. U.S. Dept. Edn., 1993—; task force, chmn. Clinton Presdl. Transition Team, 1992-93; chmn. PEW Forum on Ednl. Reform; chmn. bd. internat. com. studies in edn. NAS, 1992—. Author: The General Inquirer, 1967, Inequality, 1972; contbr. several articles to profl. jours, chpts. to books. Pres. Madison West Hockey Assn., 1982-84. Mem. Am. Ednl. Rsch. Assn. (chmn. orgn. instl. affiliates 1985-86), Cleve. Conf., Nat. Acad. Edn. Democrat. Home: 1256 Forest Ave Palo Alto CA 94301-3034 Office: Under Sec Edn 400 Maryland Ave Sw Washington DC 20202 also: Stanford U Stanford CA 94305

SMITH, MARTIN BERNHARD, journalist; b. San Francisco, Apr. 20, 1930; s. John Edgar and Anna Sophie (Thorsen) S.; m. Joan Lovat Muller, Apr. 25, 1953; children: Catherine Joan, Karen Anne. AB, U. Calif., Berkeley, 1952, M Journalism, 1968. Reporter, city editor Modesto (Calif.) Bee, 1957-64; reporter, mng. editor Sacramento Bee, 1964-75; polit. editor, columnist McClatchy Newspapers, Sacramento, 1975-92; ret., 1992. Episcopalian.

SMITH, MARY LYNN, electrical engineer; b. Miami, Fla., Feb. 20, 1965; d. Charles Dibrell and Marylin May (Peterson) S. BEE, Ga. Inst. Tech., 1988. Engr. trainee NASA, Kennedy Space Ctr., Fla., 1983-87; mem. tech. staff Watkins-Johnson Co., San Jose, 1988—; lectr. in field. Recipient Cert. of Appreciation for participation in space shuttle Challenger's accident investigation, NASA, 1986. Mem. IEEE, Antenna and Propagation Soc., Microwave Theory and Techniques Soc., Assn. Old Crows. Republican. Methodist. Office: Watkins-Johnson Co 2525 N First St San Jose CA 95131-9999

SMITH, MAUREEN MCBRIDE, chemist; b. Santa Monica, Calif., Mar. 4, 1952; d. Clayton Laird McBride and Luella (Sullivan) Boudreau; step-father Henry A Boudreau; m. Gary Howard Cothran, July 27, 1974 (div. Apr. 1982); m. Guy Gordon Smith, Feb. 12, 1983; stepchildren: Keri Lynn, Scott Allen. BS magna cum laude, Calif. State Coll., San Bernardino, 1978, postgrad. Analytical chemist Chalco Engring., Edwards AFB, Calif., 1978-79, 82; microbiol. lab. tech. AVEK Water Agy., Quartz Hill, Calif., 1979-81, chemist, lab. mgr., 1982—; instr. Antelope Valley Coll., Lancaster Calif., 1980-82. Mem. AAAS, Am. Chem. Soc. Office: Antelope Valley E Kern Water Agy 6500 W Ave N PO Box 3176 Quartz Hill CA 93586

SMITH, MICHAEL A., engineer, meditation instructor; b. Gooding, Idaho, Aug. 25, 1949; s. Alan F. and Mary A. (Dixon) S.; m. Tracy A. L'Herisson, July 9, 1989. BSChemE, U. Idaho, 1971, MSChemE, 1973. Registered profl. engr., Idaho. Environ. engr. State of Idaho Dept. Health and Welfare, Boise, 1973-82, sr. water quality engr., 1983-91, supr. prevention and cert., 1992. Capt. USAR, 1973-81. Mem. Boise Transcendental Meditation Program (chmn. 1983—), Sigma Tau. Office: Idaho Dept Health Welfare 1420 N Hilton DEQ Boise ID 83706-1260

SMITH, MICHAEL STEVEN, data processing executive; b. San Antonio, May 7, 1956; s. Columbus and Mary Patricia (Leahy) S.; m. Lynda M. Gillen, July 30, 1992. Student, San Bernardino Valley (Calif.) Coll., 1974-76, AS in Computer Scis., 1983; student, L.A. Community Coll., 1978-79, U. Md., 1980-81, City Colls. Chgo., 1980-81. Communications cons. Telephone Products Corp., San Bernardino, 1974-76; student svcs. advisor computer scis. lab. San Bernardino Valley Coll., 1982-83; assoc. programmer Aerojet ElectroSystems Corp., Azusa, Calif., 1983-85; mgr. data processing. Bonita Unified Sch. Dist., San Dimas, Calif., 1985—, dir. computer info. svcs., 1989—; analyst computer mktg. Pentamation Enterprises, Bethelehem, Pa., 1987—; cons. computer systems San Dimas, 1985—. With USN, 1976-82. Mem. Assn. for Computing Machinery, Digital Equipment Computer Users Soc., Calif. Assn. Sch. Bus. Ofcls., Calif. Ednl. Data Processing Assn. Office: 115 W Allen Ave San Dimas CA 91773-1437

SMITH, MOISHE, printmaker; b. Chgo., Jan. 10, 1929; s. Louis and Esther (Zoob) S.; m. B. Maria Wollmar, July 27, 1964 (div. Aug. 1986); m. Carolyn Waller, June 15, 1991. BA, New Sch. Social Research, 1950; MFA, U. Iowa, 1953, Academica of Florence, Italy, 1959-61; studied with Giogio Morandi, 1959-61. Instr. printmaking So. Ill. U., 1955-59; asst. prof. Stout (Wis.) State U., 1965-66; vis. artist U. Wis., 1966-67, Ohio State U., 1971, U. Iowa, 1971, Utah State U., 1971, U. Calgary, Can., 1974; assoc. prof. U. Wis., Parkside, 1972-77; prof. printmaking Utah State U., Logan, 1977—. One-man exhbns. include R.M. Light and Co., Boston, 1960, 63, AAA Gallery, N.Y.C., 1965, 74, Jane Halsem Gallery, 1967, 74, 86, Brooks Meml. Art Gallery, Louisville, 1977, Madison Art Ctr., 1978; retrospective Salt Lake Art Ctr., Gayle Weyher Gallery, Salt Lake City, 1988, 90, Yvonne Rapp Gallery, Louisville, 1987, 89, Finch Lane Gallery, Salt Lake City, 1991; group exhbns. include Sao Paulo Internat., 1955, Print Coun. Am., 1959, 62, Bklyn. Mus., 1977, Cracow Internat. Biennale, 1978, 80, 84, 86, 88, Frechen Internat., 1980, 86, Ljubljana Internat., 1981, Grenchen Internat., 1982, Taiwan Internat., 1988; represented in major museums in U.S., Europe, Asia. Fulbright fellow 1959-61, Guggenheim fellow, 1967-68, Utah Arts Council fellow, 1988; grantee Utah State U., 1978-82. Mem. NAD (academician), Soc. Am. Graphic Artists, L.A. Printmaking Soc. Home: PO Box 747 260 S 400 E Hyde Park UT 84318 Office: Utah State U Art Dept UMC 4000 Logan UT 84322

SMITH, MONTE, craft store executive; b. Lehi, Utah, Apr. 30, 1938; m. Suzanne Kay Waldron, Dec. 13, 1982. BA in Bus. Adminstrn. magna cum laude, U. Utah, 1971; MA in Govt. summa cum laude, Cornell U., 1974, PhD with high honors, 1977. Spl. agt., then staff mgr. Prudential Ins. Co., Ogden, Utah, 1962-66; spl. agt. Lincoln Nat. Life, Salt Lake City, 1966-67; night mgr. Ramada Inns, Inc., Salt Lake City, 1969; counselor Human Resource Ctr., Salt Lake City, 1970-71; instr. Cornell U., Ithaca, N.Y., 1971-73; bus. mgr. Winnebago (Nebr.) Tribal Coun., 1974-75; dir. dept. social svcs. Winnebago Tribe Nebr., 1976-78; pres. Eaglecrafts, Inc., Ogden, 1977—, WestWind, Inc., Ogden, 1982—; prof. polit. sci. Nebr. Intertribal Coll., 1975-77. Author: A Different Drummer: A Case Study of Systemic Intrusion and Dysfunction, 1977, Techniques of North American Indian Beadwork, 1983, Quill and Beadwork of the North American Indian: A Sourcebook, 1984, Traditional Indian Crafts, 1987, Traditional Indian Bead and Leather Crafts, 1987, North American Indian Burial Customs, 1988; editor: Techniques of Beading Earrings, 1984, Crow Indian Beadwork, 1985, Making Indian Arrows, 1987, Making Indian Bows and Arrows, 1987; also others. Bd. dirs. Drug Crisis Ctr., Salt Lake City, 1970-73; mem. Winnebago City Coun., 1974-77. Woodrow Wilson fellow Cornell U., 1971-72, rsch. grantee, 1972; grantee Ctr. for Internat. Studies, 1973, Ford Found., 1973-74. Mem. Western Writers Am., English Setter Assn. Am., Porsche Club Am., Mt. Ogden Kennel Club (sec.-treas. 1987-88), Wolf Creek Country Club, Phi Beta Kappa, Pi Sigma Alpha, Phi Alpha Theta. Home: 6756 N Fork Rd Eden UT 84310 Office: 168 W 12th St Ogden UT 84404

SMITH, N. RANDY, lawyer; b. Logan, Utah, Aug. 11, 1949; s. Norman B. and Patricia (Mendenhall) S.; m. La Dean Egbert, Jan. 3, 1984. BS, Brigham Young U., 1974, JD magna cum laude, 1977. Bar: Idaho 1977. Instr. Brigham Young U., Provo, Utah, 1974-77; asst. gen. counsel J.R. Simplot Co., Boise, Idaho, 1977-82; ptnr. Merrill & Merrill, Pocatello, Idaho, 1983—; adj. prof. Boise State U., 1977-82; mem. vis. com. Idaho State Coll. Bus., 1990—; lawyer rep. U.S. Ct. Appeals for 9th Cir., 1990-92, Conf. Exec. Com., 1992—. Chmn. Iron Horse dist. Boy Scouts Am., Pocatello, 1990—; pres. Idaho Civic Symphony, Pocatello, 1990—; chmn. Bannock County Reps., 1991—; Idaho State Rep. Chmn., 1993—. Named Young Man of Yr., U.S. Jaycees, Boise, 1979. Mem. ABA (taxation com. 1991—), 6th Dist. Bar Assn. (sec. 1992-93, v.p. 1993—), Def. Rsch. Inst. (state del. 1991—), Idaho Def. Coun. Assn. (pres. 1992-93), Gate City Rotary (pres. 1992-93). Mem. LDS Ch. Office: Merrill & Merrill Chartered Center and Arthur PO Box 991 Pocatello ID 83204

SMITH, NATHAN MCKAY, library and information sciences educator; b. Wendell, Idaho, Apr. 22, 1935; s. M. Blair and Vaunda H. (Hawkes) S.; m. Joyce A. Carman, July 5, 1953; children: Nathan M., Jeffrey M., Pamela J., Russell A., Kristen E. B.S. in Secondary Edn., Eastern Oreg. Coll., 1961; M.S. in Gen. Sci., Oreg. State U., 1965; M.L.S., Brigham Young U., 1969, Ph.D. in Zoology, 1972. Tchr. sci. Dalles Jr. High Sch., The Dalles, Oreg., 1961-64; asst. sci. librarian Brigham Young U., Provo, Utah, 1968, life sci. librarian, 1970-73; prof. Sch. Library and Info. Sci., Brigham Young U., Provo, Utah, 1973-82, dir., 1982-93, life sci. libr., 1993—; cons. Weber County Library, Ogden, Utah, 1980—; back issues sec. Herpetologists League, 1976-81. Served to sgt. USAF, 1953-57. Yr. scholar NSF Acad., 1964; fellow NDEA Title IV, 1969; recipient research award Assn. Library and Info. Sci. Edn., 1983. Mem. ALA (councilor legis. council), Assn. Library Info. Sci. Edn., Mountain Plains Library Assn., Utah Library Assn. (exec. bd., pres.), N. Am. Soc. Adlerian Psychology, Phi Kappa Phi, Sigma Xi, Beta Phi Mu. Mem. LDS Ch. Home: 1606 Locust Ln Provo UT 84604-2806 Office: Brigham Young U Bean Mus 5042 Harold B Lee Libr Provo UT 84602

SMITH, OTTO J. M., electrical engineering educator; b. Urbana, Ill., Aug. 6, 1917; s. Otto Mitchell and Mary Catherine (Carr) S.; m. Phyllis P. Sterling, Sept. 3, 1941; children: Candace B., Otto J.A., Sterling M., Stanford D. BS in Chemistry, Okla. State U., 1938; BSEE, U. Okla., 1938; PhDEE, Stanford U., 1941. Registered profl. engr., Calif. Instr. elec. engring. Tufts U., Medford, Mass., 1941-43; asst. prof. elec. engring. Denver U., 1943-44; research engr. Westinghouse Research Labs., Forest Hills, Pa., 1944-46; sr. research fellow econs. Monash U., Melbourne, Australia, 1966-67; prof. elec. engr. U. Calif., Berkeley, 1947—; chief engr. Smith and Sun, Berkeley, 1976—. Author: Feedback Control Systems, 1958; contbr. articles to profl. jours.; patentee in field. Dist. commr. Boy Scouts Am., Berkeley, 1949-53; trustee South Campus Community Ministry, Berkeley, 1968-70, Wesley Found., Berkeley, 1969-72. Guggenheim fellow, 1960. Fellow AAAS, IEEE; mem. Soc. Social Responsibility Engring., Soc. Social Responsibility in Sci., Am. Solar Energy Soc., Internat. Solar Energy Soc., Am. Wind Energy Assn., Calif. Writer's Club (bd. dirs.). Democrat. Methodist. Club: Berkeley City Commons (pres. 1963). Home: 612 Euclid Ave Berkeley CA 94708-1332 Office: U Calif Dept Elec Engr & Computer Scis Berkeley CA 94720

SMITH, PATRICIA JACQULINE, marketing executive; b. Orange, N.J., June 13, 1944; d. Michael Joseph and Helen Francis (Costello) S. BS, U. Md., 1967. Field dir. Colgate Palmolive Co., N.Y.C., 1967-71; account exec. Foote Cone & Belding, N.Y.C., 1971-72; dir. regional sales, dir. ARA Services, Inc., Phila., 1973-76; dir. federally funded programs Ogden Food Service, Boston, 1976-79; v.p. Smith Tool Co., Manesquan, N.J., 1979-84; chmn., chief exec. officer Hygolet Metro, Inc., New Canaan, Conn., 1984-87; mktg. cons. Smith Mktg. Svcs., LaJolla, Calif., 1988—; bd. dirs. Smith Tool Co., Manesquan, N.J., Shore Precision, Inc., Manesquan, P.J. Smith Interiors, N.Y.C., Hygolet Metro Inc., New Canaan, Conn.; ptnr. La Jolla Playhouse. Bd. dirs., treas. Big Sister League, San Diego; mem. exec. com. Multiple Sclerosis Brunch Soc.; ptnr. LaJolla Playhouse. Mem. Women in Sales, Nat. Assn. Profl. Saleswomen, Bus. and Profl. Women's Club (N.Y.). Republican. Home: 5537 Bellevue Ave La Jolla CA 92037-7627

SMITH, PAUL ALEXANDER, engineering manager; b. Ann Arbor, Mich., Mar. 13, 1949; s. Chester Earl and Ruth (Wolfe) S.; m. Linda Kay Johnson, Aug. 18, 1979; children: Erin Marie, Alexis Ayn. BS in Engring. and Physics, U. Mich., 1971; MS in Physics, Mich. State U., 1974, PhD in Physics, 1976. Rsch. assoc. U. Colo., Boulder, 1976-80; engring. mgr. Stainless Equipment Co., Denver, 1980-82, exec. v.p., 1982-84; dir. Molitor Industries, Inc., Denver, 1982-84; product mgr. Cryenco, Inc., Denver, 1984-89; project mgr. Merrick and Co., Los Alamos, N.Mex., 1989—. Contbr. articles to tech. publs. Mem. Am. Glovebox Soc. (Founder award 1987). Republican. Presbyterian. Home: 262 Barranca Rd Los Alamos NM 87544-2410 Office: 600 6th St Los Alamos NM 87544-3948

SMITH, PAULA SUZANNE, public relations executive; b. Hastings, Nebr., Nov. 3, 1950; d. Paul Victor and Lois Elaine (Bartunek) Ritz; m. Michael Lynn Smith, June 13, 1970 (div. 1993); 1 child, Casey Michael Smith. BA, Kearney (Nebr.) State Coll., 1973; MS in Mgmt., Friends U., Wichita, Kans., 1988. Dir. creative svcs. KRGI Radio, Grand Island, Nebr., 1976-78; advt. mgr. Eakes Office Products, Inc., Grand Island, 1978-79; dir. pub. rels. St. Francis Med. Ctr., Grand Island, 1979-82; community club awds. dir. KFDI Radio Sta., Wichita, Kans., 1982-84; mktg. asst. LS Ind., Wichita, 1984; dir. pub. rels. Friends U., Wichita, 1984-87; communications specialist ARC, Tulsa, 1987-88; pub. rels. staff City of Mesa, Ariz., 1988-89; dir. community rels. Chandler (Ariz.) Unified Sch. Dist. No. 80, 1989—; cons. in field. Contbr. articles to profl. jours.; editor Tune-In mag., 1983, Focus mag., 1984-87. Mem. Parent Adv. Coun. Rhodes Jr. High, Mesa, 1990; vol. chmn. United Way, Chandler, 1990—, Regional United Way Coun., 1991—. Recipient March of Dimes State Vol. award 1982, Young Career Woman of Grand Island award 1979, Bus. and Profl. Women's Club award; named Outstanding Young Woman of Grand Island, Jaycettes, 1980. Mem. Pub. Rels. Soc. Am. (accreditation chmn. 1990—), Ariz. Sch. Pub. Rels. Assn., Nat. Sch. Pub. Rels. Assn., Chandler C. of C. Republican. Methodist. Office: Chandler Unified Sch Dist 1525 W Frye Rd Chandler AZ 85224-6112

SMITH, PHILIP WALTER, savings and loan association executive, real estate consultant; b. Cumberland, Md., Aug. 21, 1945; s. Charles David and Beatrice Estella (Lewis) S.; m. Evelyn Kay Baker, Aug. 7, 1965; 1 child, Valerie Leigh. AA, Strayer Coll., 1965; BS in Applied Econs., U. San Francisco, 1984; AS in Real Estate, Mt. San Antonio Coll., 1987; postgrad., Calif. Poly. Inst., 1991—. Lic. real estate broker. Supr. bookkeeping Montgomery Ward & Co., Wheaton, Md., 1967; controller, mgr. credit Nat. Jet., Inc., LaVale, Md., 1968; treas. Maine Raceways, Inc. (Ogden Corp.), Scarborough, 1969-72; gen. mgr. R/C Ventures, Scarborough, 1972-77; fin. cons. Scarborough, Walnut, Calif., 1977-83; major loan officer Encino (Calif.) Savs. and Loan, 1984; v.p., chief lending officer Huntington Savs. and Loan, Huntington Beach, Calif., 1985-90; fin. cons. Diamond Bar, Calif., 1990-91; sr. v.p., chief lending officer Universal Savs. Bank, Orange, Calif., 1991-92; asset mgr. Long Beach Bank, f.s.b., Orange, 1992—; dir., CFO McBo Corp., 1993—; speaker Internat. Coun. Shopping Ctrs., N.Y.C., 1973-75; tchr. real estate Mt. San Antonio Coll., Walnut, 1989—, Inst. Fin. Edn., L.A., 1991—; real estate broker Calif. Dept. Real Estate, Sacramento, 1987. Co-inventor method to convert sewerage sludge to gas and organic fertilizer. Founder Secondary Info. Network Group, 1985; mem. cable adv. bd. City of Walnut, 1986-91, mem. fin. com., 1987, mem. econ. devel. com., 1989; mem. real estate adv. com. Mt. San Antonio Coll., Walnut, 1991—. Strayer Coll. scholar, 1963. Mem. Calif. League Savs. Instns. (panelist/moderator 1986-92, secondary market com., real estate com., exec. lending com.), Calif. Real Estate Educators Assn., Real Estate Edn. Assn. Office: Long Beach Bank 1100 Town and Country Rd Orange CA 92668

SMITH, PHILLIP DALE, whey products marketing director; b. Louisville, Nov. 20, 1952; s. Phill and Hazel (Coe) S.; m. Linda A. Daigle, Feb. 10, 1979; children: Phillip Lindale, Leslie Ann, Alexis Lynn. BA in Chemistry, De Pauw U., 1974; postgrad., U. Louisville, 1974-75, 79-80. Quality control mgr. Streis Industries, Louisville, 1975-76; rsch. scientist Express Foods USA, Louisville, 1976-80; dir. R&D Dairyland Products, Savage, Minn., 1980-83; tech. sales mgr. Leprino Foods Co., Denver, 1983-86, dir. whey products mktg., 1986—. Youth coach Arapahoe Youth Baseball League, Highlands Ranch, Colo., 1986-90, Littleton, Colo., 1987—, Douglas County Youth Soccer Coach, Highlands Ranch, 1989—. Mem. Am. Dairy Products

Inst. (tech. com. Chgo. chpt. 1983-86, whey mktg. com. 1986-93, bd. dirs. 1993—), Am. Assn. Cereal Chemists, Nat. Ice Cream Mix Assn., N.C. Dairy Tech. Soc., Inst. Food Technologists (profl.). Office: Leprino Foods Co 1830 W 38th Ave Denver CO 80217-3400

SMITH, RALPH EARL, virologist; b. Yuma, Colo., May 10, 1940; s. Robert C. and Esther C. (Schwarz) S.; m. Sheila L. Kondy, Aug. 29, 1961 (div. 1986); 1 child, Andrea Denise; m. Janet M. Keller, 1988. BS, Colo. State U., 1961; PhD, U. Colo., 1968. Registered microbiologist Am. Soc. Clin. Pathologists. Postdoctoral fellow Duke U. Med. Ctr., Durham, N.C., 1968-70, asst. prof., 1970-74, assoc. prof., 1974-80, prof. virology, 1980-82; prof., head dept. microbiology Colo. State U., Ft. Collins, 1983-88, prof. microbiology, assoc. v.p. rsch., 1989—, interim v.p. rsch., 1990-91, prof. microbiology, assoc. v.p. rsch., 1991—; cons. Bellco Glass Co., Vineland, N.J., 1976-80, Proctor & Gamble Co., Cin., 1985-86, Schering Plough Corp., Bloomfield, N.J., 1987-89. Contbr. articles to profl. jours.; patentee in field. Bd. dirs. Colo. Ctr. for Environ. Mgmt., v.p. for rsch.; mem. pollution prevention adv. bd. Colo. Dept. Health; mem. Rocky Mountain U. Consortium on Environ. Restoration; asst. scoutmaster Boy Scouts Am., Durham, 1972-82, com. mem., Ft. Collins, 1986—; mem. adminstrv. bd. 1st United Meth. Ch., Ft. Collins. Eleanor Roosevelt fellow Internat. Union Against Cancer 1978-79. Mem. AAAS, Am. Soc. Microbiology, N.Y. Acad. Scis., Am. Soc. Virology, Am. Assn. Immunologists, Am. Assn. Avian Pathologists, Am. Assn. Cancer Rsch., Gamma Sigma Delta. Democrat. Methodist. Home: 2406 Creekwood Dr Fort Collins CO 80525-2034 Office: Colo State U VP Rsch Fort Collins CO 80523

SMITH, RAYMOND EDWARD, health care administrator; b. Freeport, N.Y., June 17, 1932; s. Jerry Edward and Madelyn Holman (Jones) S.; B.S. in Edn., Temple U., 1953; M.H.A., Baylor U., 1966; m. Lena Kathryn Jernigan Hughes, Oct. 28, 1983; children: Douglas, Ronald, Kevin, Doris Jean, Raymond. Commd. 2d lt. U.S. Army, 1953, advanced through grades to lt. col., 1973; helicopter ambulance pilot, 1953-63; comdr. helicopter ambulance units, Korea, 1955, Fed. Republic of Germany, 1961; various hosp. adminstrv. assignments, 1963-73; personnel dir. Valley Forge (Pa.) Gen. Hosp., 1966; adminstr. evacuation hosp., Vietnam, 1967; dep. insp. Walter Reed Gen. Hosp., Washington, 1970; dir. personnel div. Office of Army Surgeon Gen., Washington, 1971-73, ret., 1973; adminstr. Health Care Centers, Phila. Coll. Osteo. Medicine, 1974-76; dir. bur. hosps. Pa. Dept. Health, Harrisburg, 1976-79; contract mgr. Blue Cross of Calif., San Diego, 1979-88, Community Care Network, San Diego, 1989—. Decorated Bronze Star, Legion of Merit. Mem. Am. Hosp. Assn., Am. Legion, Ret. Officers Assn., Kappa Alpha Psi. Episcopalian. Club: Masons. Home: 7630 Lake Adlon Dr San Diego CA 92119-2518 Office: Community Care Network 8911 Balboa Ave San Diego CA 92123-1584

SMITH, RAYMOND VICTOR, paper products manufacturing executive; b. Vancouver, B.C., Can., Apr. 28, 1926; s. Stanley Victor and Kathryn Stewart (Hunter) S.; m. Marilyn Joyce Meldrum, Oct. 17, 1947; children—Vicki, Kathi, Stan. Student, U. B.C., Banff Sch. Advanced Mgmt.; student Advanced Mgmt. Program, Harvard U. Trumpeter Dal Richards Band, 1942; ptnr. Warren McCuish Mens' Clothiers, 1947; sales rep. Vancouver Paper Box, 1949-54; with Home Oil Distbrs., 1954-57; domestic rep. kraft paper and board sales MacMillan Bloedel Ltd., 1957-67; asst. mgr. Kraft Paper & Board Sales, 1961-65; newsprint rep. Powell River-Alberni Sales Corp., Pasadena, Calif., 1965-67; mgr. Powell River-Alberni Sales Corp., Pasadena, 1967-68; mgr. supply control and sales adminstrn. MacMillan Bloedel Ltd., Vancouver, 1968-70, gen. mgr., 1970-71, v.p. mktg. paper and pulp, 1971-73, v.p., gen. mgr. newsprint, 1973-77, group v.p. pulp and paper, 1977-79, sr. v.p. pulp and paper, 1979-80, chief oper. officer, 1980-83, pres., 1980-90, chief exec. officer, 1983-90, chmn. bd., 1991—; bd. dirs. Can. Imperial Bank of Commerce. Served with Can. Army, 1944. Clubs: Capilano Golf and Country, Vancouver. Office: MacMillan Bloedel Ltd, 925 W Georgia St, Vancouver, BC Canada V6C 3L2

SMITH, RICHARD FOSTER, education specialist; b. Livingston, Mont., Feb. 7, 1934; s. Alfred Foster and Ruth (Eltzholtz) S.; m. Norma Sachie Yamashita, Oct. 17, 1964; children: Kendall T.F., Melissa M.S. BS in Wildlife Mgmt., Utah State U., 1959; MEd in Secondary Edn., U. Hawaii, 1965. Cert. tchr., Mont. Math/sci. tchr. Bozeman (Mont.) City Sch. System, 1960-61; sci. tchr. Kamehameha Schs., Honolulu, 1961-89; botany collections tech. Bishop Mus., Honolulu, 1989-90; zoo ednl. specialist Honolulu Zoo, 1990—; bd. dirs., sec. Kamehameha Fed. Credit Union, Honolulu, 1965-68, 85; chmn. Kamehameha Faculty Assn., Honolulu, 1976; biology tchr. Am. Sch. of The Hague, Holland, 1978-79; sci., math tchr. Am. Sch. London, 1985-86; agrl. insp. U.S. Dept. Agriculture, Honolulu, 1986-88. Editor, compiler numerous booklets. Pres., vol. Maunawili Estates Community Assn., Kailua, Hawaii, 1971-92; vol. Hawaii Audubon Soc., Honolulu, 1981-86; rec. sec. Save Mt. Olomana Assn., Kailua, 1990-91; mem. Windward Community Arts Coun. NSF grantee, 1962, 63-64, 70. Mem. Lyon Arboretum Assn., Bishop Mus. Assn., Hawaii Mus. Assn., Hawaii Outdoor Edn. Assn., Wilderness Soc., Nature Conservancy, Sandwich Islands Genealogical Soc., New England Historical & Genealogical Soc. Methodist. Home: 1278 Maleko St Kailua HI 96734 Office: Honolulu Zoo 151 Kapahulu Ave Honolulu HI 96815

SMITH, RICHARD I., information systems executive, consultant; b. Columbia, Mo., Oct. 28, 1947; s. William Walter and Nelletha (Lavendar) S.; m. Barbara A. Leuin, June 23, 1985; 1 child, Stormy. BS in Mgmt., U. Fla., 1970; MS in Mgmt., U. So. Fla., 1975. Dir. instl. rsch. Coll. of St. Benedict, St. Joseph, Minn., 1975-77, dir. instl. rsch. and info., 1977-83, assoc. v.p. planning, 1983-86, dir. mgmt. info. systems, 1986-88; dir. mgmt. info. systems Fayetteville (N.C.) State U., 1988-91; chief exec. officer Concept Dynamics-Relational Systems, Prescott, Ariz., 1991—; dir. mgmt. info. systems St. John's U., Collegeville, Minn., 1986-88; cons. colls., univs., med. groups and chs., 1977—. Mem. Med. Planning Coun., St. Joseph, Cen. Minn. Pub. Svc. Consortium, St. Cloud, Minn. 1st lt. U.S. Army, 1971-73. Mem. Acad. Mgmt., Coll. and Univ. Systems Exch., Assn. for Instl. Rsch., Data Processing Mgmt. Assn., So. Assn. Instl. Rsch. Episcopalian. Office: Concept Dynamics-Relational Systems 917 E Gurley St Ste D Prescott AZ 86301

SMITH, RICHARD LAWRENCE, industrial engineering educator; b. St. Louis, Apr. 5, 1933; s. Alfred William and Nannie Irene (Roberson) S.; m. Dixie Lou Koenig, Sept. 6, 1953; children—Robert, William, Dianne. A.A., Southwest Baptist Coll., Bolivar, Mo.; B.S.Indsl. Engring., Washington U., St. Louis; M.S. Indsl. Engring., Ohio State U., Columbus; Ph.D., Ariz. State U., Tempe. Engring. asst. McDonnell Aircraft Co., St. Louis, 1955-56; prin. engr. Battelle Meml. Rsch. Inst., Columbus, Ohio, 1956-60; mem. mgmt. staff GE, Phoenix, 1960-67; prof. engring. Ariz. State U., Tempe, 1967—, chmn. dept. indsl. and mgmt. systems engring., 1981-87, acting v.p. Info. Resource Mgmt., 1987-88; cons. GE, Phoenix, 1967-70, Samaritan Health Services, Phoenix, 1970-85, Flori Corp., Phoenix, 1974-82, McDonnell Douglas Helicopter, Mesa, Ariz., 1985. Author research papers on indsl. engring., ops. research, systems engring. Bd. dirs. Northwest Phoenix YMCA, 1964-67; commr. Phoenix Babe Ruth Baseball, 1968-69; mem. bd. edn. Tempe Union High Sch. Dist., 1976-84; bd. trustees. Ariz. Sch. Bd. Assn. Ins., Phoenix, 1984-86, scholarship fund Am. Inds. Indsl. Engring., Atlanta, 1983-90. Fellow Am. Inst. Indsl. Engring. (sr. mem., pres. local chpt. 1972); mem. Tech. Inst. Mgmt. Sci., Am. Soc. Engring. Educators. Republican. Home: 2116 E Geneva Dr Tempe AZ 85282-4040 Office: Ariz State U Dept Indsl Engring Tempe AZ 85287

SMITH, ROBERT BRUCE, former security consultant, retired army officer; b. De Quincy, La., Apr. 22, 1920; s. Malcolm Monard and Jewell (Perkins) S.; m. Gladys Opal Borel, Feb. 22, 1941; children: Susan, Richard, Bruce. B.J., La. State U., 1941; grad., Command and Gen. Staff Coll., 1951-52, Army War Coll., 1958-59. Commd. 2d lt. U.S. Army, 1941, advanced through grades to maj. gen., 1969; plans and ops. officer 83d Div. Arty., Europe, 1943-45; personnel officer Philippine-Ryukyus Command, Manila, 1947-49; prof. mil. sci. and tactics ROTC, Lanier High Sch., Macon, Ga., 1949-51; chief res. officers sect., procurement br. Dept. Army, 1952-55; chief troop info. Office Chief Info., Dept. Army, 1962-63, dep. chief info., 1968-69; comdg. officer 8th F.A. Bn., 25th Inf. Div., Hawaii, 1955-56; G-1 25th Inf. Div. and U.S. Army Hawaii, Hawaii, 1956-58; mem. staff, faculty Command and Gen. Staff Coll., Fort Leavenworth, Kans., 1959-62; chief Alt. Nat. Mil. Command Center, Fort Ritchie, Md., 1963-64; dep. dir. ops. Office Joint Chiefs of Staff, 1964-65; asst. div. comdr. 7th Inf. Div., Korea, 1965-66; dep. comdt. Army War Coll., Carlisle, Pa., 1966-68; dep. comdg. gen. Ryukyus Islands, 1969-72, 6th U.S. Army, Presidio of San Francisco, 1972-73; ret. active duty, 1973; reporter, news editor Lake Charles (La.), 1946-47; region adminstrv. mgr. Burns Security Service, Oakland, Calif., 1974-76; ptnr. constrn. co. Napa, Calif., 1976-77, Burns Security Service, 1978-81; now ret.; dir. 1st Am. Title Co., Napa, Calif., 1988-92. Trustee Queen of Valley Hosp. Found., 1987-89; mem. Nat. coun. Boy Scouts Am., 1969-70; pres. Silverado Property Owners Assn., Inc., 1990-92. Decorated D.S.M. with oak leaf cluster, Legion of Merit with 2 oak leaf clusters, Bronze Star with oak leaf cluster. Club: Silverado Country (Napa, Calif.). Home: 350 St Andrews Dr Napa CA 94558-1544

SMITH, ROBERT FREEMAN, congressman; b. Portland, Oreg., June 16, 1931; m. Kaye Tomlinson, 1966; children: Christopher, Matthew, Tiffany. B.A., Willamette U., 1953. Mem. Oreg. Ho. of Reps., 1960-72, majority leader and speaker pro tem, 1964-66, speaker, 1968-72; mem. Oreg. Senate, 1972-82, Republican leader, 1978-82; mem. 98th-103rd Congresses from 2d Oreg. dist., Washington, D.C., 1982—; mem. agrl. com., subcom. gen. farm commodities, livestock, dept. ops. and nutrition, natural resource com., subcoms. nat. parks, forests, pub. lands, mem. oversight and investigations. Trustee Willamette U. Mem. Harney County C. of C. Lodges: Masons; Elks. Office: House of Reps 108 Cannon House Office Bldg Washington DC 20515-3702

SMITH, ROBERT HAMIL, fund raiser, author; b. Oak Park, Ill., Nov. 8, 1927; s. Henry Garfield and Mary Ellen (Hamil) S.; student U. Denver, 1946-48, LLB, 1953, JD, 1960; m. Mary Helen Kingsley, Dec. 29, 1948; children: David H., Mark K., Steven H., Rebecca Anne Smith Quintana. Dep. clk. County Ct., City and County of Denver, 1948-53; with Colo. Ins. Group, 1953-59; mgr. claims dept. R.H. Smith & Assocs., 1959-64; cons. Am. Bapt. Home Mission Soc., 1964-68; assoc. dir. devel. Ill. Wesleyan U., 1968-69; asst. to chancellor U. Calif., San Diego, 1969-77; exec. dir. devel. Scripps Clinic and Research Found., La Jolla, Calif., 1977-82, v.p. devel., 1982-88; pres. Cartographic Enterprises, 1981—; bd. dirs. Nat. Com. on Planned Giving, 1990—; fund raising cons. deferred giving. Served with USNR, 1945. Mem. Nat. Soc. Fund Raising Execs., Internat. Yachting Fellowship of Rotarians (San Diego fleet comdr. 1979-81). Baptist. Club: Oceanside Yacht. Author: Guide to Harbors, Anchorages and Marinas So. and No. California edits., 1983; The Physician as a Fundraiser, 1984, Naval Inst. Guide to Maritime Museums in U.S./Canada, 1991, Smith's Guide to Maritime Museums, 1993. Home: PO Box 2785 Del Mar CA 92014-5785 Office: R H Smith & Assocs PO Box 176 Del Mar CA 92014-0176

SMITH, ROBERT HENRY, economist; b. Detroit, Dec. 16, 1941; s. Henry A. and Patricia (Frolich) S.; m. Martha Eshelman, June 1970 (div. 1978); 1 child, Richard G. BA, Occidental Coll., 1963; PhD, U. Hawaii, 1986. Owner, mgr. RHS & Co., Honolulu, 1976—; mem. faculty U. Hawaii, Honolulu, 1984-86. Author: Balance of Payments in Developing Countries, 1986. 1st lt. U.S. Army, 1966-68. Mem. AAAS, Honolulu Club, Waikiki Yacht Club, Hawaii Yacht Club. Home: 3079 Pacific Heights Rd Honolulu HI 96813 Office: RHS & Co PO Box 22490 Honolulu HI 96823

SMITH, ROBERT LONDON, retired air force officer, political scientist, educator; b. Alexandria, La., Oct. 13, 1919; s. Daniel Charleston and Lillie (Roberts) S.; m. Jewel Busch, Feb. 5, 1949; children: Jewel Diane, Robert London, Karl Busch. B.A., Coll. St. Joseph, 1954; M.A., U. Okla., 1955; Ph.D., Am. U., 1964. Commd. 2d lt. USAAF, 1941; advanced through grades to lt. col. USAF, 1961; various assignments in aircraft engring., command and logistics, 1941-60; research logistics Hdqrs. Office Aerospace Research, 1960-63; project scientist, adminstr. postdoctoral research program Nat. Acad. Scis., Hdqrs. Office Sci. Research, 1963-65; ret., 1965; asso. prof. polit. sci., head dept. eve. classes and corr. study U. Alaska, College, 1966-68, dean Coll. Bus., Econs. and Govt., 1968-70, prof., head dept. polit. sci., 1966-84, prof. emeritus, 1984—; commr. Alaska Dept. Health and Social Services, 1983—; mem. govt. panels and planning groups; dir. Arctic 1st Fed. Savs. & Loan Assn.; corporator Mt. McKinley Mut. Savs. Bank. Author: (with others) Squadron Administration, 1951; also publs. on nat. security and nat. def.; Contbr. to: (with others) The United Nations Peace University, 1965. Committeeman Western region Boy Scouts Am., 1968-73; mem. exec. bd. Midnight Sun council, 1973-74, committeeman-at-large nat. council, 1968—; mem. Alaska Gov.'s Employment Commn.; pres. United Service Orgn. Council, Fairbanks, Alaska; mem. active corps execs. SBA. Recipient Silver Beaver award Boy Scouts Am.; named Outstanding Prof. U. Alaska, 1975. Mem. Nat. Acad. Econs. and Polit. Sci., AAAS, Air Force Hist. Found., Nat. Inst. Social and Behavioral Scis., Nat. Inst. U.S. in World Affairs, Am. Polit. Sci. Assn., Assn. U.S. Army (bd. dirs. Polar Bear chpt.), Alaska C. of C. (edn. com.), Pi Gamma Mu, Pi Sigma Alpha. Roman Catholic. Club: Rotary. Home: Smithhaven 100 Goldizen Ave Fairbanks AK 99709-3634 also: Smithport 9994 Salcha Dr North Pole AK 99705 also: Smithawaii Nani Kai Hale Apt 607 73 N Kihei Rd Kihei Maui HI 96753

SMITH, ROBERT MCKAIN, international studies educator; b. Detroit, Sept. 12, 1922; s. Robert McKee and Mary (McKain) S.; m. Margaret Jean Bennett, June 14, 1946; children: Susan, Barbara, Ann, Eric. BS in Bus., Babson Coll., Wellesley, Mass., 1956; MA in Asian History, Am. U., 1963, PhD in Internat. Studies, 1971. Commd. 2d lt. U.S. Army, 1943, advanced through grades to col., 1967, served in U.S., Europe, Asia, 1943-71; asst. internat. policy Joint Chiefs of Staff, 1966-69; asst. project mgr. Dept. of Army, Washington, 1969-70; Asia tng. and supply Comdr.-in Chief of Pacific Forces, Honolulu, 1971; ret. U.S. Army, 1971; prof. internat. studies Chaminade U., Honolulu, 1971—; spl. scholar London Sch. Econs. and Polit. Sci., 1981; prof. Fgn. Affairs Coll., Beijing, China, 1989; cons. U.S. Dept. State, 1990—, USIA, 1989—; lectr. in field. Contbr. articles to profl. jours. Decorated Legion of Merit; recipient grants to study and do rsch. in Taiwan, 1975, 80. Fellow Ctr. of Asian Studies in Hong Kong; mem. Law of Sea Inst., UN Assn. (Hawaii bd. dirs.), Pacific and Asian Affairs Coun. Hawaii (bd. dirs.), Hawaii Geog. Soc. (bd. dirs.), Pacific Sci. Assn., Internat. Geog. Union (commn. on environ. problems), Honolulu Rotary Club (scholarship com. 1977—).

SMITH, ROBERT MICHAEL, lawyer; b. Boston, Nov. 4, 1940; s. Sydney and Minnie (Appel) S.; m. Catherine Kersey, Apr. 14, 1981 (dec. 1983). AB cum laude, Harvard U., 1962; MA in Pub. Law and Govt., Columbia U., 1964, MS in Journalism with High Honors, 1965; JD, Yale U., 1975. Bar: Calif., N.Y., D.C., U.S. Supreme Ct. Intern in econ. devel. UN, Geneva, 1964; corres. Time Mag., N.Y.C., 1965-66, The N.Y. Times, Washington, 1968-72, 75-76; spl. asst. Atty. Gen. of U.S., Washington, 1979-80; dir. Office Pub. Affairs U.S. Dept. Justice, Washington, 1979-80; em. U.S. Delegation Internat. Ct. of Justice, The Hague, 1980; asst. U.S. atty. No. Dist. Calif., San Francisco, 1981-82; counsel, sr. counsel to sr. litigation counsel Bank of Am. NT & SA, San Francisco, 1982-86; assoc. Brobeck, Phleger & Harrison, San Francisco, 1988; pvt. practice law San Francisco, 1988—; lectr. FBI Acad., Quantico, Va., 1980; judge Golden Medallion Broadcast Media awards, State Bar of Calif., 1985; judge pro tem Mcpl. Ct. City and County of San Francisco, 1989—. Bd. editors Yale Law Jour., 1974-75; mem. editorial adv. bd. Bancroft-Whitney Am. Jurisprudence, 1991—; contbr. articles to profl. jours. Bd. dirs. Neighborhood Legal Assistance Found., San Francisco, 1985-87; bd. dirs. Nob Hill Assn., San Francisco, 1985—. 1st lt. USAR, 1965-71. Recipient UPI Award for Newswriting, 1958; Harvard Coll. scholar, 1958-62, Fulbright scholar, 1962-63; Columbia U. Internat. fellow, 1964-65. Mem. ABA (corp. counsel com. 1986—), State Bar of Calif. (pub. affairs com. 1982-85), Bar Assn. of San Francisco (bench-bar-media com. 1985—), Assn. Bus. Trial Lawyers No. Calif., Assn. of Former Asst. U.S. Attys. No. Dist. Calif., Am. Arbitration Assn. (mem. comml. arbitration panel, No. Calif. adv. coun., mediator Am. Arbitration Ctr. for Mediation), French-Am. C. of C., Harvard Club of San Francisco (bd. dirs. 1986—, pres. 1992—), Yale Club of San Francisco (bd. dirs. 1989—), Columbia U. Alumni Club of No. Calif. (exec. com. 1978-92). Democrat.

SMITH, ROBERT VICTOR, university administrator; b. Glendale, N.Y., Feb. 16, 1942; s. Robert Arthur and Marie Marlene (Florence) S.; children: Kevin Christopher, Erin Kathleen. BS in Pharm. Sci., St. John's U., Jamaica, N.Y., 1963; MS in Pharm. Chemistry, U. Mich., 1964, PhD in Pharm. Chemistry, 1968, postgrad., 1988. Asst. prof., then assoc. prof. U. Iowa, Iowa City, 1968-74; assoc. prof., asst. dir. U. Tex., Austin, 1974-77, area coordinator basic pharmaceutics, 1975-76, assoc. dir. Drug Dynamics Inst., 1977-78, dir. Drug Dynamics Inst., Coll. Pharmacy, 1979-85, James E. Bauerle Centennial prof. Coll. Pharmacy, 1983-85; prof., dean Coll. Pharmacy Wash. State U., Pullman, 1985-86, vice provost for research, dean Grad. Sch., 1987—; cons. E. R. Squibb, New Brunswick, N.J., 1979-82, Upjohn Co., Kalamazoo, Mich., 1982-85; external examiner U. Malaysia, Penang, 1981-82; mem. sci. adv. bd. Biodecision Labs., Pitts., 1985-86; Wash. Biotech. Found., 1989-90. Author: Textbook of Biopharmaceutic Analysis, 1981, Graduate Research: A Guide for Students in the Sciences, 1990, Development and Management of University Research Groups, 1986. Bd. dirs. Wash. Tech. Ctr., 1990-92. Recipient award NIH, Bethesda, Md., 1974-83; Acad. Pharm. Scis. fellow, 1981. Mem. Am. Assn. Colls. Pharmacy (chmn. research and grad. affairs com. 1983-84), U.S. Pharmacopeia (revision com. 1985-90), Acad. Pharm. Scis. (chmn., vice chmn. 1983-85, 90, Presdl. citation 1985), Wash. Rsch. Found. (bd. dirs. 1989—). Unitarian. Home: PO Box 2486 CS Pullman WA 99165-2486 Office: Wash State U Grad Sch Pullman WA 99164-1030

SMITH, ROBERT WESLEY, environmental company executive; b. Parrish, Ala., Nov. 27, 1937; s. Wesley Hobson and Nora (Daniel) S.; m. Gwen Marie Hanson, Dec. 30, 1959; children: Kevin Robert, Stacey Rene. BA in Psychology, Willamette U., 1960. Commd. 2d lt. USAF, 1960-86, advanced through grades to Col., 1980, ret., 1986; cons. Sci. Applications Internat. Corp., Las Vegas, 1986—, office mgr., 1987-91, dv. mgr., 1991-93. Mem. Kiwanis Internat. (bd. dirs. 1989-90). Republican. Methodist. Office: Sci Applications Internat 3351 S Highland Dr Ste 101 Las Vegas NV 89109

SMITH, ROBERT WILLIAM, medical director, family physician; b. L.A., Dec. 28, 1951; s. William Davidson and Jane Elizabeth (Young) S.; m. Deborah Ann Hoddick, June 14, 1980; children: Michelle Marie, Stephanie Christine, Christopher Stephen. AB in Psychology, U. So. Calif., L.A., 1973; MD, U. Calif., Irvine, 1976. Diplomate Am. Bd. Family Practice. Commd. ensign USN, 1977; advanced through grades to capt., 1991; intern Naval Regional Med. Ctr., Camp Pendleton, Calif., 1977-78; sr. med. officer Naval Communications Sta., The Philippines, 1978-79; resident Naval Regional Med. Ctr., Camp Pendleton, 1979-81; faculty physician, family practice residency Naval Regional Med. Ctr., 1981-84, Naval Hosp., Pensacola, Fla., 1984-87; med. dir. Amphibious Squadron Two, N.Y.C., 1986; ambulatory svcs. dir. Cen. Ga. Ctr. for Family Health, Macon, 1987-91; med. dir. Family Health Ctr., Macon, 1989-91; chmn. dept. family practice FHP, Inc., Fountain Valley, Calif., 1991—; residency dir. FHP So. Calif., 1991—; asst. prof. Uniformed Svcs. U. Health Scis., Bethesda, Md., 1985-87, Mercer U. Sch. Medicine, Macon, 1987-91; cons. Bibb County Med. Soc., Macon, 1989; assoc. prof. U. Calif. Coll. Medicine, Irvine. Editor GAFP Jour., 1988-91; contbr. articles to profl. jours. Pres. Ashford Park Homeowners' Assn., Macon, 1988. Decorated Navy Commendation medals. Fellow Am. Acad. Family Physicians; mem. AMA, Soc. Tchrs. Family Medicine, Am. Coll. Physicians Execs., Assn. Mil. Surgeons. Republican. Presbyterian. Office: FHP Inc 18129 Brookhurst St Fountain Valley CA 92708-6728

SMITH, RONALD WAYNE, sociology educator, university administrator; b. St. Louis, Sept. 11, 1944; s. Herman Roger and Alice Fay (Kirby) S.; m. Susan Thompson, June 23, 1988; 1 dau., Kelleen Elizabeth. B.S. in Edn., S.E. Mo. U., 1966; M.A. in Sociology, No. Ill. U., 1967; Ph.D. in Sociology, Wash. State U., 1972. Teaching asst. in sociology No. Ill. U., DeKalb, 1966-67; asst. prof. sociology No. Ariz. U., Flagstaff, 1967-70; teaching asst. Wash. State U., Pullman, 1970-72; grad. program coordinator in sociology U. Nev.-Las Vegas, 1975-77, 80-81, asst. dean arts and letters, 1978-79, asst. prof., 1972-76, assoc. prof., 1976-84, prof., 1984—, chmn. dept. sociology, 1973-75, 81-85, co-dir. Ctr. for Survey Research, 1982-86, grad. dean, 1985—; cons. Nev. Humanities Grants, U. Nev.-Las Vegas, 1972—; guest lectr. U. Stirling, Scotland, 1974; speaker in field. Author: Sociology: An Introduction, 1977, 2d rev. edit., 1982; Instructor's Manual for Sociology: An Introduction, 1977, 2d rev. edit., 1982; Social Problems, 1981. Contbr. articles to profl. publs. Group dir. Citizen's Govtl. Forum, Las Vegas, 1974; discussant Clark County Juvenile Ct., Las Vegas, 1975; panelist Nev. Humanities Com., Las Vegas, 1978; adviser Neighborhood Watch Program, Las Vegas, 1982. Named Outstanding Sociology Prof., U. Nev.-Las Vegas Alumni Assn., 1984; grantee Bur. Indian Affairs, 1968, No. Ariz. U., 1969, City of Las Vegas, 1977, U. Nev.-Las Vegas, 1982; recipient William Morris Teaching award, 1985. Mem. Am. Sociol. Assn., Soc. Study Symbolic Interaction, Pacific Sociol. Assn., AAUP, Phi Kappa Phi, Alpha Kappa Delta. Democrat. Home: 258 Sierra Mesa Cir Henderson NV 89014-5935 Office: U Nev-Las Vegas Graduate Coll 4505 S Maryland Pky Las Vegas NV 89154-0002

SMITH, ROSS QUENTIN, computer and communications systems specialist; b. Nacogdoches, Tex., June 22, 1959; s. Roger Qumil and Mary Hilda (Taylor) S. BS in Computer Engring., U. Tex., 1982. Control systems engr. E.I. DuPont de Nemours, Victoria, Tex., 1981-82; research and devel. engr. Geotronics Corp., Austin, Tex., 1982-83; sr. rsch. and devel. engr. Ford Aerospace and Communications Corp., Palo Alto, Calif., 1983-86; def. systems cons., advanced programs, C3I product mktg. mgr. ORI/Intercon Systems Corp., Sunnyvale, Calif., 1986-89; OEM bus. devel. mgr. MIPS Computer Systems, Sunnyvale, 1989—;, 1989-92; dir. sales and bus. devel. Pellucid Inc. (a Media Vision Co.), Santa Clara, Calif., 1992—; dir. ACCC, Inc., Honolulu, 1991—. Patentee in field. Recipient Ethics in Engring. award Hutchinson Found., 1983; Kmiecik fellow Brookview Inst., 1985. Mem. IEEE, Optical Soc. Am., Assn. Computing Machinery, Soc. Photographic and Imaging Engrs., Order of Leon, Hedonism Internat. Home: 169 Waverley St # C Palo Alto CA 94301-1142

SMITH, ROULETTE WILLIAM, educational administrator, researcher; b. N.Y.C., Jan. 19, 1942; s. Timothy and Artisse Eulala (Macomson) S.; m. Norma Abe, Dec. 20, 1964 (div. 1990); children: Nicole Michelle Smith Dinwiddie, Todd Roulette. BS in Math. and Chemistry, Morehouse Coll., 1961; postgrad., N.Mex. Highlands U., 1961; MS in Math., Stanford U., 1964, MS in Computer Sci., 1965, PhD in Math. Models of Edn., 1973; postgrad., U. Calif., San Francisco, 1976-80. Asst. prof. in psychology and edn. U. Calif., Santa Barbara, 1970-75, acting asst. dir. bur. ednl. R&D Sch. Edn., 1973-75; sr. staff mem. Far West Labs., San Francisco, 1975-76; pres., chief exec. officer Humanized Technologies, Inc., Palo Alto, Calif., 1973—; dir. Inst. for Postgrad. Interdisciplinary Studies, Palo Alto, 1984—; mgr. math. lab. Cherry Chase Sch., Sunnyvale, Calif., 1986-87; substitute tchr. Pavenswood City Sch Dist., East Palo Alto, Calif., 1987-89; sr. staff advisor computer ctr. U. Calif., Santa Barbara, 1970-73; rsch. scientist U.S. Naval Missile Ctr., Point Mugu, Calif., 1973; vis. asst. prof. Carnegie-Mellon U., Pitts., 1974-75; vis. scholar inst. math. studies Stanford (Calif.) U., 1981-82, sch. edn., sch. medicine, 1982-83, dept. anthropology, 1987-89; cons. in field. exec. editor Instructional Sci., 1970-83; assoc. editor Health Policy and Edn., 1977-82; patentee in field. Advisor Mental Health Adv. Com. San Francisco Head Start, 1978-90; pres. Concerned Black Parents, Palo Alto, Calif., 1980-83. NASA-Ames Summer Faculty Fellow, 1974. Mem. AAAS, APA, Am. Ednl. Rsch. Assn., Am. Pub. Health Assn., N.Y. Acad. Scis., AIDS and Anthropology Rsch. Group, Bay Area Black Coalition Against AIDS. Democrat. Episcopalian. Office: Inst Postgrad Interdisciplinary Studies PO Box 60846 Palo Alto CA 94306-0846

SMITH, RUSSELL LYNN, JR., engineer, consultant; b. Petaluma, Calif., Dec. 25, 1919; s. Russell Lynn and Marikka (Mikkelson) S.; m. Jean Margaret Austin, July 21, 1942; children: Lynn Suzanne, Dale Austin. Student, Stanford U., 1938-41; BA, U. Hawaii, 1949. Registered profl. engr., Hawaii, Guam. Pilot, photogrammetric engr., surveyor R.M. Towill Corp., Honolulu, 1947-49; jr. engr. Austin & Towill, Honolulu, 1949-53; assoc. engr. H.A.R. Austin, Honolulu, 1953-56; v.p., sec. H.A.R. Austin & Assocs. Ltd., Honolulu, 1956-64; sec. Austin & Towill Ltd., Honolulu, 1957-59; v.p., treas. Austin, Smith & Assocs., Inc., Honolulu, 1959-75; pres. The Russ Smith Corp., Honolulu, 1975-84; chief engr., dir. pub. works City and County of Honolulu, 1985-86; pres. Smith, Young & Assocs. Inc., 1987—; mem. Honolulu Bd. Water Supply, 1985, 86; cons. on water supplies Pub. Utility Agy, Guam, 1966-74; chmn. Interprofl. Council on Environ. Design, U.S., 1982. Founder Hawaii Air N.G., 1946; mem. Gov.'s Com. on Yr. 2000, Hawaii; mem. budget rev. panel Aloha United Way, 1977-81. Served to 1st lt. A.C. U.S. Army, 1942-46, to lt. col. Air N.G. Decorated Air medal with oak leaf cluster; recipient Hawaii Engr. of Yr. award Hawaii Soc. Profl. Engrs., 1976, cert. of Merit Gov. Samuel W. King, Hawaii, 1956. Fellow ASCE (pres. Hawaii sect. 1961), Am. Cons. Engrs. Council (nat. pres. 1982-83, pres. Hawaii council 1970-71); mem. Water Pollution Control Fedn. (pres. Hawaii assn. 1967), Nat. Soc. Profl. Engrs., Engring. Assn. Hawaii (life), Hawaii Pub. Works Assn. (pres. 1985), Am. Water Works Assn., Am. Legion (vice commdr. Hawaii 1956). Republican. Clubs: Stanford (Hawaii) (pres. 1950-52); Pacific, Plaza. Lodge: Rotary. Home: 999 Wilder Ave Apt 1102 Honolulu HI 96822-2635 Office: Smith Young & Assocs Inc 501 Sumner St Ste 502 Honolulu HI 96817-5304

SMITH, SAM CORRY, foundation executive; b. Enid, Okla., July 3, 1922; s. Chester Hubbert and Nelle Kate (Corry) S.; m. Dorothy Jean Bank, Sept. 21, 1945; children: Linda Jean, Nancy Kay, Susan Diane. Student, Phillips U., 1940-43; BS in Chemistry, U. Okla., 1947, MS in Chemistry, 1948; PhD in Biochemistry, U. Wis., 1951. Asst. and assoc. prof. U. Okla., Oklahoma City, 1951-55; assoc. dir. grants Research Corp., N.Y.C., 1957-65, dir., 1965-68, v.p. grants, 1968-75; exec. dir. M.J. Murdock Charitable Trust, Vancouver, Wash., 1975-88; foundation cons., 1988—; pres. Pacific Northwest Grantmakers Forum, 1983-84. Contbr. sci. articles to profl. jours. Trustee Nutrition Found., Washington, 1976-84, Internat. Life Scis. Inst., Washington, 1984-86; bd. councilors U. So. Calif. Med. Sch., L.A., 1977-82; mem. adv. com. Coll. Natural Scis. Colo. State U., 1977-80; pres. Cardiopulmonary Rehab. Programs Oreg., 1990-91; bd dirs. Clark Coll. Found. Named Boss of Yr., Am. Bus. Women's Assn., 1982, Bus. Assoc. of Yr., 1983. Fellow AAAS; mem. Am. Chem. Soc. Home: 5204 DuBois Dr Vancouver WA 98661-6617

SMITH, SAMUEL DAVID, artist, educator; b. Thorndale, Tex., Feb. 11, 1918; s. Otto Frank and Jeanette (Joyce) S.; m. Elizabeth Marie Smith; children: Cezanne, Rembrandt, Michelangelo. Ed. pub. schs. Prof. art U. N.Mex., 1956-84, prof. art emeritus, 1984—. Illustrator: Roots in Adobe, 1967, Cowboy's Christmas Tree, 1956; also: Coronet mag; one man exhbns. include, Corcoran Gallery Art, Washington, 1949, Santa Fe Mus. Art, 1947, Roswell (N.Mex.) Mus. Fine Art, 1953, 64, Goodwell (Okla.) Hist. Mus., 1964, Panhandle Plains Mus., Canyon City, Tex., 1964, Biltomore Galleries, Los Angeles, 1946, First Nat. Bank, Los Alamos, 1968, group exhbns. include, Baker Galleries, Lubbock, Tex., 1964-73, Met. Mus., N.Y.C., 1944, Blue Door Gallery, Taos, N.Mex., 1946-53, Galeria del Sol, Albuquerque, 1968-73, Brandywine Galleries, 1972-73, Watercolor Workshop, Telluride, Colo., 1964; one-man show includes Retrospective Exhbn. U. of N.Mex., Albuquerque, 1986. Served as combat artist AUS, 1942-45. Hon. life mem. N.Mex. Art League. Mem. Artist Equity Assn. (pres. N.Mex. chpt. 1957-58, 66-67, 70-71). Club: Elk. Home and Office: PO Box 2006 Telluride CO 81435-2006

SMITH, SAMUEL HOWARD, university president, plant pathologist; b. Salinas, Calif., Feb. 4, 1940; s. Adrian Reed and Elsa (Jacop) S.; m. Patricia Ann Walter, July 8, 1960; children: Samuel Howard, Linda Marie. BS in Plant Pathology, U. Calif., Berkeley, 1961, PhD, 1964; D (hon.), Nihon U., Tokyo, 1989. NATO fellow Glasshouse Crops Research Inst., Sussex, Eng., 1964-65; asst. prof. plant pathology U. Calif., Berkeley, 1965-69; assoc. prof. Pa. State U., Arendtsville, 1969-71; assoc. prof. Pa. State U., University Park, 1971-74, prof., 1974-85, head dept. plant pathology, 1976-81, dean Coll. Agr., dir. Pa. Agrl. Expt. Sta. and Coop. Extension Service, 1981-85; pres. Wash. State U., 1985—; bd. dirs. Assoc. Western Univs., 1993—; adv. com. Wash. Sch. Employees Credit Union, 1993—; exec. adv. com. Tri-Cities Commercializaton Partnership, 1993—. Bd. dirs. Econ. Devel. Ptnrship. for Wash., 1986—, Wash. Internat. Ag-Trade Ctr., Washington, China Rels. Coun.; nat. adv. com. Air Force ROTC; mem. army adv. panel ROTC affairs; mem. Wash. State Internat. Trade Assistance adv. com.; mem. Wash. Coun. Internat. Trade, Western Interstate Commn. Higher Edn., Am. Coun. on Edn.; bd. dirs. Assn. Western Univs., 1993—; adv. com. Wash. Sch. Employees Credit Union, 1993—; exec. adv. com. Tri-Cities Commercialization Ptnrship, 1993—. Mem. AAAS, Am. Phytopath. Soc., Nat. Assn. State Univs. and Land-Grant Colls., Gamma Sigma Delta, Alpha Zeta, Epsilon Sigma Phi, Sigma Xi, Omicron Delta Kappa, Golden Key. Home: 755 NE Campus Ave Pullman WA 99163-4223 Office: Wash State U French Adminstrn Bldg Pullman WA 99164-1048

SMITH, SELMA MOIDEL, lawyer, composer; b. Warren, Ohio, Apr. 3, 1919; d. Louis and Mary (Oyer) Moidel; 1 child, Mark Lee. Student L.A. City Coll., 1936-37, U. Calif., 1937-39, U. So. Calif., 1939-41; JD, Pacific Coast U., 1942. Bar: Calif. 1943, U.S. Dist. Ct. 1943, U.S. Supreme Ct. 1958. Gen. practice law; mem. firm Moidel, Moidel, Moidel & Smith. Field dir. civilian adv. com. WAC, 1943; mem. nat. bd. Med. Coll. Pa. (formerly Woman's Med. Coll. Pa.), 1953—, exec. bd., 1976-80, pres., 1980-82, chmn. past pres. com., 1990-92. Decorated La Order del Merito Juan Pablo Duarte (Dominican Republic). Mem. ABA, Assn. Learning in Retirement Orgns. in West (pres. 1993—), Calif. Bar Assn. (servicemen's legal com.), L.A. Bar Assn. (psychopathic ct. com.), L.A. Lawyers Club (pub. defenders com.), Nat. Assn. Women Lawyers (chmn. com. unauthorized practice of law, social commn. UN, regional dir. western states, Hawaii 1949-57, mem. jud. adminstrn. com. 1960, nat. chmn. world peace through law com. 1966-67), League of Ams. (dir.), Inter-Am. Bar Assn., So. Calif. Women Lawyers Assn. (pres. 1947, 48, chmn. Law Day com. 1966, subject of oral hist. project, 1986), State Bar Conf. Com., Coun. Bar Assns. L.A. County (charter sec. 1950), Calif. Bus. Women's Coun. (dir. 1951), L.A. Bus. Women's Coun. (pres. 1952), Calif. Pres.'s Coun. (1st v.p.), Nat. Assn. Composers U.S.A. (dir. 1974-79, ann. luncheon chmn. 1975), Nat. Fedn. Music Clubs (nat. vice chmn. for Western region, 1973-78), Calif. Fedn. Music Clubs (state chmn. Am. Music 1971-75, state conv. chmn. 1972), Assn. Learning in Retirement Orgns. in West (pres. 1993—), Docents of L.A. Philharm. (v.p. 1973-83, chmn. Latin Am. community rels. 1972-75, press and pub. rels. 1972-75, cons. coord. 1973-75), Euterpe Opera Club (v.p. 1974-75, chmn. auditions 1972, chmn. awards 1973-75), ASCAP, Iota Tau Tau (dean L.A., supreme treas.), Plato Soc. of UCLA (Toga editor, 1990—, sec. 1991-92, chmn. colloquium com. 1992—, discussion leader UCLA Constitution Bicentennial Project, 1985-87, moderator UCLA extension lecture series 1990). Composer: Espressivo-Four Piano Pieces (orchestral premiere 1987, performance Nat. Mus. Women in the Arts 1989). Home: 5272 Lindley Ave Encino CA 91316-3518

SMITH, SHANE DALE, cultural organization administrator, consultant; b. Denver, Mar. 2, 1954; d. Dale Donovan and Ann (Mee) S.; m. Paige W. Waldvogel, Aug. 23, 1986; 1 child, Rio. BS in Horticulture, Colo. State U., 1977; postgrad., Harvard U., 1989-90. Dir. Cheyenne (Wyo.) Community Solar Greenhouse, 1977-86, Cheyenne Botanic Garden, 1986—; cons. in field, 1979—; cons. Servicio Desarollo E. Paz, Mex., 1986—; radio host weekly program, 1977—. Author: Bountiful Solar Greenhouse, 1987, Greenhouse Gardener's Companion, 1993; columnist Sunday Tribune-Eagle, Cheyenne, Wyo. Bd. dirs. Needs Inc., Cheyenne, 1986-89, Wildflowers for Wyo., Cheyenne, 1988—, Wyo. Outdoor Coun., Lander, 1990—, pres. Recipient Presdl. Citation, Pres. Ronald Reagan, 1986, Point of Light award, Pres. George Bush, 1990. Mem. Am. Community Gardening Assn. (bd. dirs. 1982-86), Am. Horticultural Therapy Assn., Garden Writers Assn. of Am. Office: Cheyenne Botanic Garden 710 S Lions Park Dr Cheyenne WY 82001-7503

SMITH, SIDNEY SHARP, clinical therapist, author; b. Coalville, Utah, July 6, 1928; s. Sidney Sharp and Eliza Catherine (Thomas) S.; m. Shirley Jean McCunne, Mar. 16, 1951; children: Susan Kay, Sandra Lynn, Sharon Eliza, Shelly Ann. BS, Weber State Coll., 1968; MSW, U. Utah, 1970. Brakeman OUR & D Railroad Co., Ogden, Utah, 1948-51; indsl. loan ofcl. Interlake Fin., Salt Lake City, 1953-70; clin. therapist Family Counseling Ctr., Salt Lake City, 1974—. Author, compilor: In Love With Eloquence, 1989, Eloquent Women, 1991. Bd. dirs. Roy (Utah) Kiwanis, 1957-59, Bountiful (Utah) Exchange, 1980-83. With U.S. Army, 1946-48. Mem. Nat. Assn. Social Workers, Acad. Cert. Social Workers. Mormon. Office: Family Counseling Ctr PO Box 25 Midvale UT 84047-0025

SMITH, STANFORD SIDNEY, state treasurer; b. Denver, Oct. 20, 1923; s. Frank Jay and Lelah (Beamer) S.; m. Harriet Holdrege, Feb. 7, 1947; children: Monta Smith Ramirez, Franklin Stanley. Student, Calif. Inst. Tech., 1941-42, Stanford U., 1942-43; BS, U.S. Naval Acad., 1946. Pres. Vebar Livestock Co., Thermopolis, Wyo., 1961-89; mem. Wyo. Senate, 1974-76; pres. Wyo. Wool GrowersAssn., 1976-78; mem. Wyo. Ho. of Reps., Cheyenne, 1978-82; treas. State Wyo., Cheyenne, 1983—; dir. Coun. of State Govts., 1990-92; v.p. Wyo. Wool Growers, dir., 1976-82. County commr. Hot Springs County, Wyo, 1966-74. Lt. USN, 1943-54. Decorated Bronze Star. Mem. Nat. Assn. State Treas. (pres. 1990-91). Republican. Presbyterian. Office: State of Wyoming State Capital Cheyenne WY 82002

SMITH, STANLEY DEAN, biology educator; b. Lihue, Hawaii, Aug. 10, 1951; s. Walter Edward Smith II and Veda Pearl (Edwards) Parsons; m. Gayle Ellen Marrs, Oct. 9, 1982; 1 child, Galen Edward. BS with honors, N.Mex. State U., 1973, MS, 1975; PhD, Ariz. State U., 1981. Postdoctoral fellow U. Calif., L.A., 1981-83; asst. rsch. prof. Biology Desert Rsch. Inst., Reno, 1983-85; asst. prof. Biology U. Nev., Las Vegas, 1985-89, assoc. prof. Biology, 1989—; assoc. editor Am. Midland Naturalist, Notre Dame, Ind., 1989—. Contbr. chpts. to books, articles to profl. jours. Mem. AAAS, Am. Soc. of Plant Physiologists, Ecolog. Soc. of Am., Sigma Xi. Democrat. Home: 4387 E Hacienda Ave Las Vegas NV 89120-1556 Office: U Nev Dept of Biolog Scis Las Vegas NV 89154

SMITH, STEPHANIE MARIE, lawyer; b. Manhattan, Kans., May 15, 1955; d. William C. and Joyce A. (Davis) S. BS in Fgn. Studies, Georgetown U., 1977; JD, U. Mich., 1980. Bar: Colo. 1980, U.S. Dist. Ct. Colo. 1980, U.S. Ct. Appeals (10th cir.) 1980, Ariz. 1985, Nev. 1985, U.S. Dist. Ct. Nev. 1985. Assoc. Fishman & Geman, Denver, 1980-81, Hart & Trinen, Denver, 1982-85; ptnr. Jolley, Urga, Wirth & Woodbury, Las Vegas, Nev., 1985—. Mem. ABA, Nev. Bar Assn., Assn. Trial Lawyers Am., So. Nev. Bankruptcy Lawyers' Assn. Office: Jolley Urga Wirth & Woodbury 300 S 4th St Ste 800 Las Vegas NV 89101-6018

SMITH, STEPHEN ARNOLD, hydrogeologist, geology educator; b. Elmhurst, Ill., Aug. 26, 1946; s. Paul Arnold and Dorothy Ann (Davies) S.; m. Carolyn Ann Lewis, Aug. 31, 1968; children: Sally Jean, Nancy Lynn, Lincoln Andrew, Lucas Paul. BS in Geology, U. Ill., 1970; MS in Water Resources Mgmt., U. Wis., 1972, MS in Hydrogeology, 1973. Registered profl. geologist, Ariz., Calif., Alaska. Staff geologist Moody and Assocs., Inc., Meadville, Pa., 1974-77; pvt. practice cons. Tempe, Ariz., 1977-81; sr. geohydrologist Salt River Project, Tempe, 1981-84; assoc., sr. hydrogeologist Dames and Moore Cons., Phoenix, 1984-89; v.p., prin. hydrogeologist The GeoWest Group, Inc., Scottsdale, Ariz., 1989-91; faculty assoc. Ariz. State U., Tempe, 1990-91; hydrogeologist Wis. Dept. Nat. Resources and U. Wis. Extension, Madison, 1972-74; mgr. hydrogeology EMCON Assocs., Phoenix, 1991—; presenter Ariz. Water Law Conf., 1993, Ariz. Hydrological Soc. Well Rehab. Symposium, 1989, ASTM Symposium, 1988, FOCUS Conf., 1986, Deep Percolation Symposium, 1984. Co-author: Contemporary Hydrogeology, 1979, Practical Handbook of Ground-Water Monitoring, 1990, Ground-Water and Vadose Zone Monitoring, 1990; contbr. articles to profl. jours. Grad. fellow NSF, 1970. Mem. Am. Inst. Profl. Geologists, Nat. Water Well Assn. (mem. editorial rev. bd. 1985—), Mensa, Sigma Xi. Home: 1423 S College Ave Tempe AZ 85281-6616 Office: EMCON Assocs 3922 E Univ Dr Phoenix AZ 85034

SMITH, STEPHEN WAYNE, human resources executive; b. Lewiston, Utah, Dec. 26, 1941; s. Stephen Bybee and Emma LaRue (Robinson) S.; m. Beverly Jean Currell, Oct. 11, 1963; children: Stephen Leslie, Jeffrey Wayne, Nicole Chantel, Gregory Jason. BS, Utah State U., 1967. Cert. compensation profl. Loan officer U.S. Bancorp, Portland, Oreg., 1967-69, mgr. compensation, 1970-76; mgr. compensation and benefits John Fluke Mfg. Co., Seattle, 1976-80; mgr. internat. human resources Solar Turbines, Inc., San Diego, 1980-81; mgr. human resources for Europe and Africa Solar Turbines, Inc., London, 1982-83; dir. human resources Sundstrand Corp., San Diego, 1984-88; mgr. compensation and benefits Morton-Thiokol, Ogden, Utah, 1988-89; mgr. corp. compensation Thiokol Corp., Ogden, 1989—; Speaker in field. Developer, writer medical cost containment legislation State Legis. Com., Salt Lake City, 1990. Mem. Am. Compensation Assn. (faculty 1984-93), Intermountain Compensation and Benefits Assn. (pres. 1986-87, bd. dirs. 1990-92), Soc. Human Resource Mgmt. (dir. pub. affairs 1989-90). Republican. Office: Thiokol Corp 2475 Washington Blvd Ogden UT 84401

SMITH, STEVEN SIDNEY, molecular biologist; b. Idaho Falls, Idaho, Feb. 11, 1946; s. Sidney Ervin and Hermie Phyllis (Robertson) S.; m. Nancy Louise Turner, Dec. 20, 1974. BS, U. Idaho, 1968; PhD, UCLA, 1974. Asst. research scientist Beckman Research Inst. City of Hope Nat. Med. Ctr., Duarte, Calif., 1982-84, staff Cancer Ctr., 1983—, asst. research scientist depts. Thoracic Surgery and Molecular Biology, 1985-87, assoc. research scientist, 1987—, dir. dept. cell and tumor biology, 1990—; cons. Molecular Biosystems Inc., San Diego, 1981-84. Contbr. articles to profl. jours. Grantee NIH, 1983—, Coun. for Tobacco Rsch., 1983-92, March of Dimes, 1988-91, Smokeless Tobacco Rsch. Coun., 1992—; Swiss Nat. Sci. Found. fellow U. Bern, 1974-77, Scripps Clinic and Rsch. Found., La Jolla, Calif., 1978-82, NIH fellow Scripps Clinic, 1979-81. Mem. Am. Soc. Cell Biology, Am. Assn. Cancer Rsch., Am. Crystallographic Assn., Am. Chem. Soc., Am. Weightlifting Assn., Phi Beta Kappa. Office: City of Hope Nat Med Ctr 1500 Duarte Rd Duarte CA 91010-3012

SMITH, STUART ROBERT, foundation executive; b. South Amboy, N.J., Aug. 14, 1942; s. Stuart Conroy and Elizabeth Beatrice (Keenan) S.; m. Nancy Jo Roberts, Apr. 24, 1965; children: Mark Christopher, Melissa Jo. BA in Psychology, St. Vincent Coll., Latrobe, Pa., 1964; postgrad., Stanford U., 1986. Dist. exec. Raritan coun. Boy Scouts Am., Perth Amboy, N.J., 1965-68, Greater Niagara Frontier Coun., Buffalo, 1968-69; assoc. dir. devel. Canisius Coll., Buffalo, 1969-70; dir. devel. Kenmore (N.Y.) Mercy Hosp., 1971-74; dir. community rels. and devel. United Hosp., Port Chester, N.Y., 1974-77; exec. dir. Shadyside Hosp. Found., Pitts., 1977-79; exec. v.p. Samaritan Med. Found., Phoenix, 1979-87, pres., chief exec. officer, 1988—; cons. fundraising and golf tournaments. Contbr. articles to profl. jours., newsletters. Pres., bd. dirs. Crisis Nursery, Phoenix, 1990—, v.p., 1987, 88; chmn. Fiesta Bowl Golf Classic, Phoenix, 1988, 89; mem. com. Fiesta Bowl, Phoenix, 1986—; bd. dirs. Palms Clinic & Hosp. Found., Phoenix, Crisis Nursery, 1993, exec. com., v.p. Fellow Assn. for Healthcare Philanthropy (nat. v.p. 1977-80, bd. examiners 1986—); mem. Ariz. Assn. Hosp. Devel. (pres. 1990, exec. com. 1989—), Nat. Soc. Fund Raising Execs. (cert. various offices local chpts., Outstanding Fundraising Exec. award Ariz. chpt. 1989), LPGA (sponsors bd., treas. 1988-92), Moon Valley Country Club. Republican. Roman Catholic. Office: The Samaritan Found 1441 N 12th St Phoenix AZ 85006-2887

SMITH, SUSAN BITTER, trade association exeuctive, consultant; b. Phoenix, Aug. 23, 1955; d. Charles R. and Judith (Anderson) Bitter; m. Paul H. Smith, Mar. 10, 1979; 1 child, Prescott R. BS, Ariz. State U., 1977, MBA, 1982. Supr. Inmate Legal Svcs., Phoenix, 1978-80; exec. dir. Ariz. Cable TV Assn., Phoenix, 1980—; cons. Bell Atlantic CTS, Phoenix, 1986—, Sears Sch. Driving, Phoenix, 1987-92. Mem. Rep. Party of Ariz., Phoenix, 1976—; mem. Scottsdale (Ariz.) City Coun., 1988-92; bd. dirs. Morrison Inst. Pub. Policy, Tempe, Ariz., 1986-90, Family Emergency Shelter, Mesa, Ariz., 1990—. Mem. Am. Soc. Assn. Execs. (pres. 1989-90, Exec. of Yr. 1987, bd. dirs.), Am. Fedn. Bus. and Profl. Women, Valley Leadership Alumni (bd. dirs. 1987-88), Ariz. State U. Coll. Bus. Alumni Assn. (pres. 1976-77), Ariz. State U. Alumni Assn. (bd. dirs. 1985—). Congregationalist. Home: 5806 E Lewis Ave Scottsdale AZ 85257-1926

SMITH, TERRY LEE, business owner; b. Eugene, Oreg., July 19, 1954; s. Robert Eugene and Rebecca Anne (Atkinson) S.; m. Kellie Lurline Henry, May 3, 1975. Cert. journeyman, Oreg. Cleanup/delivery man Chase Co., Eugene, Oreg., 1976; apprentice Durbin Heating and Sheet Metal, Eugene, Oreg., 1976-78, Harvey & Price, Eugene, Oreg., 1978-80, Brainard Sheet Metal, Springfield, Oreg., 1980-82; owner Smith Sheet Metal, Inc., Springfield, Oreg., 1983—; chmn. Area III Apprenticeship Com., 1987—. Mem. Am. Soc. Heating, Refrigeration, and Air Conditioning Engrs., Am. Subcontractors Assn., Nat. Roofing Assn., Associated Bldg. Contractors, Construction Specialists Inst. Republican. Office: Smith Sheet Metal Inc PO Box 639 Springfield OR 97477

SMITH, TERUKO, physician's assistant; b. Stockton, Calif., Jan. 10, 1936; d. Masaru and Shizuyo (Hara) Kuwada; m. James Nobuhiko Ono (div. 1970); children: Michele M., Marla M., Mireya M.; m. George Irving Smith, Aug. 2, 1974. BS, Coll. Notre Dame, 1982; Physician's Asst., Stanford U., 1974. RN, Calif; cert. physician's asst. Staff neonatal nurse O'Connor Hosp., San Jose, 1957-60; team leader med. floor nurse Peninsula Hosp., Millbrae, Calif., 1960-62; pediatric supr., office nurse Sunnyvale (Calif.) Med. Clinic, 1962-70; pediatric office nurse Donald Allari, M.D., San Jose, 1970-73; physician asst. Stanford Coronary Prevention Trial, 1974-83, Dept. Psychiatry, Stanford, 1983-84; physician asst., laser specialist Palo Alto (Calif.) Med. Found., 1984—; rsch. investigator Collagen Corp., Palo Alto, 1989—; cons. Coherent Inc., Palo Alto, 1991—. Contbr. articles to profl. jours. Fellow Am. Soc. for Laser Medicine and Surgery (awards com. 1993-94), Calif. Acad. Physician Assts., Am. Acad. Physician Assts. Home: 15 Siesta Ct Portola Valley CA 94028

SMITH, THOMAS WINSTON, cotton marketing executive; b. Crosbyton, Tex., Mar. 16, 1935; s. Lance L. and Willie Mae (Little) S.; m. Patricia Mae Zachary, Dec. 13, 1958; children—Janna Olean, Thomas Mark. B.S., Tex. A&M U., 1957; P.M.D., Harvard U., 1964. Various positions Calcot Ltd., Bakersfield, Calif., 1957-77, exec. v.p., pres., 1977—; v.p. Amcot, Inc., Amcot Internat., Inc., Bakersfield, 1977—, also bd. dirs.; v.p. Nat. Cotton Coun., Memphis; bd. mgrs. N.Y. Cotton Exchange, N.Y.C. Bd. dir. Greater Bakersfield Meml. Hosp.; mem. pres.'s adv. commn. Calif. State Coll., Bakersfield. Mem. Rotary.

SMITH, VERNON LOMAX, economist, researcher; b. Wichita, Kans., Jan. 1, 1927; s. Vernon Chessman and Lula Belle (Lomax) S.; m. Joyce Harkleroad, June 6, 1950 (div. Aug. 1975); m. Carol Breckner, Jan. 1, 1980. BSEE, Calif. Inst. Tech., 1949; MA in Econs., U. Kans., 1952; PhD in Econs., Harvard U., 1955; D of Mgmt. (hon.), Purdue U., 1990. Asst. prof. econs. Purdue U., West Lafayette, Ind., 1955-58, assoc. prof., 1958-61, prof., 1961-65, Krannert prof., 1965-67; prof. Brown U., Providence, 1967-68, U. Mass., Amherst, 1968-75; prof. U. Ariz., Tucson, 1975—, Regents' prof.; Contbr. articles to profl. jours. Fellow Ctr. for Advanced Study in Behavioral Scis., Stanford, Calif., 1972-73; Sherman Fairchild Disting. Scholar Calif. Inst. Tech., Pasadena, 1973-74; adj. scholar CATO Inst., Washington, 1983—. Fellow AAAS, Am. Acad. Arts and Scis., Econometric Soc. Home: 2122 E Camino El Ganado Tucson AZ 85718-4108 Office: Univ Ariz Dept Economics Tucson AZ 85718

SMITH, VICTORIA TAYLOR, museum special events-public relations consultant; b. Salt Lake City, July 6, 1956; d. John Ralph and Sue (Taylor) Smith; m. Lawrence Joel Smith, Nov. 29, 1975; children: Ariel Alexandria, Andrea Lauren. BA in Anthropology magna cum laude, U. Utah, 1983. Asst. curator edn. Utah Mus. Natural History, Salt Lake City, 1984-87, assoc. curator edn., 1987-88, programmer lecture series, 1988-91, mem. pub. rels. dept., 1988-92; cons. to mus. on spl. events and pub. rels., Salt Lake City, 1992—; coord. spl. event Sta. KRCL, community radio, Salt Lake City, 1990; pub. rels. and film event coord., Salt Lake City, 1991. Co-chmn. Citizens for Preservation Hotel Utah, Salt Lake City, 1987; vol. Sta. KRCL, 1989—. Grantee Utah Endowment for Humanities, 1990. Mem. Utah Mus. Natural History, Wilderness Soc. Democrat. Home and Office: 1431 Beacon Dr Salt Lake City UT 84108

SMITH, VIN, sports editor, business owner, novelist; b. Whittier, Calif., May 19, 1944; s. M. Clifford and Anna Eugenia (Hill) S.; m. Marthea Karen Callaham, May 15, 1969 (div. 1979); children: Jayare Smith, Eric Smith; m. Ginger Hammon, Oct. 20, 1984; children: Amy Michelle, Stacey Erin, Kellie Rae. Student, Columbia Sch. Broadcasting, San Francisco, 1967; AA, Cuesta Coll., 1974; grad., Am. Sch. of Piano Tuning, 1978. Sales mgr. Sta. KTAT, Frederick, Okla., 1967-69; owner Melmart Markets, San Luis Obispo, Calif., 1971-73, Am. Direct Sales, Grover City, Calif., 1973-79; instr. piano Valley View Acad., Arroyo Grande, Calif., 1977-78; instr. piano Long Piano Co., San Luis Obispo, 1977-79, piano technician, 1978-79; owner Chocolate Piano, Yreka, Calif., 1979—; instr. piano Makah Indian Tribe, Neah Bay, Wash., 1981-82; sports editor New Words Digest, Bakersfield, Calif., 1988—; cons., stress evaluator seminar Yreka Stress Therapy Clinic, 1986-87. Sports columnist New Words Digest, 1987-91; guest columnist Siskiyou Daily News, 1991—; contbr. articles to profl. jours. Chmn. heart fund Tillman County, Okla., 1968; campaign worker Ken Jourdan for sheriff, Yreka, 1986. Recipient Cert. of Appreciation, Siskiyou County, 1988, Achievement award, 1988; winner Golden Poet award World of Poetry, 1989. Mem. Nat. Writers Club (chmn. student com. Yreka chpt. 1988), Author's Guild, Inc., Author's League of Am., Mystery Writers Am., Soc. Children's Book Writers, Jr. C. of C. (sgt.-at-arms Frederick chpt. 1967-69), Kiwanis, Moose. Home: 710 Knapp St Yreka CA 96097-2343 Office: Chocolate Piano Svcs PO Box 447 Yreka CA 96097-0447

SMITH, WALDO GREGORIUS, former government official; b. Bklyn., July 29, 1911; s. John Henry and Margaret (Gregorius) S.; m. Mildred Pearl Prescott, July 30, 1935 (dec. Jan. 1992); 1 dau., Carole Elizabeth Smith Levin. Student CCNY, N.Y., 1928-29; B.S. in Forestry, Cornell U., 1933. Registered prof. engr., Colo. Forester Forest Service, U.S. Dept. Agr., Atlanta, 1933-41, Ala. Div. Forestry, Brewton, 1941-42; engr., civil engring. technician Geol. Survey, U.S. Dept. Interior, 1942-71, cartographic technician, 1972-75; chmn. Public Transp. Council, 1975-89; legislator aide to individuals Colo. State Legis. Internship Program, 1987—. Recipient 40 Yr. Civil Service award pin and scroll; 42 Yr. Govt. Service award plaque. Fellow Am. Congress Surveying and Mapping (life, sec.-treas. Colo. chpt. 1961, program chmn. 1962, reporter 1969, mem. nat. membership devel. com. 1973-74, rep. to Colo. Engring. Council 1976-77); mem. AAAS (emeritus), Denver Fed. Center Profl. Engrs. Group (U.S. Geol. Survey rep. 1973-76, Engr. of Yr. award 1975), Nat. Soc. Profl. Engrs. (pre-coll. guidance com. 1986-91, life 92—), Profl. Engrs. Colo. (chpt. scholarship chmn. 1979—, advt. corr., service award 1983), Cornell U. Alumni Assn. (alumni secondary schs. com. Quadrangle Club), Common Cause, Colo. Engring. Council (chmn. library com. 1970—, spl. rep. Regional Transp. Dist., 1974-75; mem. sci. fair com. 1970-71; rep. ex officio Denver Pub. Library Found. Bd. Trustees 1975-80, Pres.'s Outstanding Service award 1987), Environ. Concerns (chmn. com. 1988—, treas. 1989-91), Fedn. Am. Scientists, Am. Soc. Engring. Edn., People for Am. Way. Contbr. articles to profl. jours. Home: 3821 W 25th Ave Denver CO 80211-4417

SMITH, WALLACE A., radio company executive; b. Nov. 29, 1934. BA, Waynesburg Coll., 1957; ThM., Pitts. Theol. Sem., 1960; MA, U. So. Calif., L.A., 1969, PhD, 1972. Gen. mgr. Sta. KUSC-FM, L.A., 1972-87; v.p., gen. mgr. Sta. WNYC-AM/FM, N.Y.C., 1987-88; pres. USC Radio, U. So. Calif., L.A., 1988—; gen. mgr. Sta. KUSC-FM, U. So. Calif., L.A., 1988—; chair interim internat. working group Corp. for Pub. Broadcasting, 1988—; founding mem., bd. dirs. Am. Pub. Radio, 1983—; mem. radio adv. com. Calif. Pub. Broadcasting Commns.; participant CPB Radio Task Force, Profile of a Pub. Radio Sta., 1980. Mem. Assn. Calif. Pub. Radio Stations (sec. 1975-76, pres. 1976-77). Office: Sta KUSC 3716 S Hope St Los Angeles CA 90007-4344

SMITH, WALTER J., engineering consultant; b. Climax, Kans., Feb. 8, 1921; s. Jacob Walter and Thelma Christina (Stark) S.; m. Wanda Jean Sandys, Apr. 20, 1944 (div. 1965); children: Walter Brooke, Judith Jean; m. Evadean Louise Smith, Sept. 21, 1965; stepchildren: Stephen Henslee, Kimberly Ann; 1 adopted child, Nancy Louise. BEE, Cleve. State U., 1948; postgrad., UCLA, 1955-58, Western State U. Law, Anaheim, Calif., 1970-71. Lic. profl. engr., Ohio, Calif. Field tech. rep. to Air Force Jack & Heintz, Inc., Maple Hts., Ohio, 1942-44; rsch. engr. Jack & Heintz, Inc., 1948-50, N. Am. Aviation Inc., Downey, Calif., 1950-54; asst. chief engr. Ala. Engring. & Tool Co., Huntsville, Ala., 1954-55; rsch. specialist to dir. prodn. ops. N. Am. Aviation Inc./Rockwell Internat., Anaheim, 1955-86; engring. mgmt. cons. Anaheim, 1986-93; engring. mgmt. cons., Bermuda Dunes, Calif., 1993—. Contbr. articles to profl. jours. Mem. Anaheim Indsl. Devel. Bd., 1982-86, Anaheim Pub. Utilities Bd., 1987-92; bd. dirs. Rep. Cen. Com. of Orange County, 1976-78; pres., bd. dirs. Galerie Homeowners Assn., 1987-93; bd. dirs. Coun. on Environ. Edn. and Econ. Through Devel., Inc., 1974-86, Action Com. to Inform Orage Now, Inc. Mem. Anaheim C. of C. (bd. dirs. 1983-90, pres. 1983-84), Gladhanders Acad. Hospitality Internat. (bd. dirs. 1989—, Man of Yr. 1989). Republican. Religious Science. Home and Office: 78615 Purple Sagebrush Ave Bermuda Dunes CA 92201-9051

SMITH, WALTER ROGERS, protective services administrator; b. Burlington, Vt., Jan. 20, 1945; s. LeRoy F. and Gertrude (Spurbeck) S.; m. Carolyn S. Snidow, July 11, 1978; 1 child, Nancy C. BA, U. Tex., 1970;

MPA, U. Colo., Denver, 1978. Dep. sheriff Denver Sheriff Dept., 1971-77, sgt., 1977-78, lt., 1978-80, capt., 1980-85, major, 1985-90, div. chief, 1990—; mem. curriculum devel. com. detentions Colo. Law Enforcement Tng. Acad., Golden, Colo., 1989-92. Mem. Am. Correctional Assn., NAt. Sheriff Assn., Western Correctional Assn. (pres. 1991), Colo. Correctional Assn. (pres. 1989, Merit Award 1986), Am. Jail Assn. (bd. dirs. 1992—), Colo. Jail Assn. (pres. 1987-88). Office: Denver Sheriff Dept PO Box 1108 Denver CO 80201-1108

SMITH, WILLARD GRANT, psychologist; b. Sidney, N.Y., June 29, 1934; s. Frank Charles and Myrtle Belle (Empet) S.; m. Ruth Ann Dissly, Sept. 14, 1957; children—Deborah Sue Henri, Cynthia Lynn Koster, Andrea Kay Richards, John Charles. BS, U. Md., 1976; MS, U. Utah, 1978, PhD, 1981. Lic. psychologist, Utah; cert. sch. psychologist, sch. adminstr., tchr., Utah, nat. cert. sch. psychologist. Rsch. asst. Med. Ctr., U. Utah, 1977, teaching asst. dept. ednl. psychology, 1976-78, rsch. cons. dept. edn., 1977; program evaluator Salt Lake City Sch. Dist.; program evaluator and auditor Utah State Bd. Edn., 1978; sch. psychologist Jordan Sch. Dist., Sandy, Utah, 1978-82, tchr., 1979-80; exec. dir. Utah Ind. Living Ctr., Salt Lake City, 1982-83; spl. edn. cons. Southeastern Edn. Svc. Ctr., 1983-85; sch. psychologist Jordan Sch. Dist., Sandy, 1985—; assoc. psychologist Don W. McBride & Assocs., Bountiful, Utah, 1989-91; pvt. practice Salt Lake City, 1991—. Master sgt. USAF, 1953-76. Decorated Air Force Commendation medal with 2 clusters; recipient U. Md. scholastic achievement award, 1975. Mem. Am. Psychol. Assn., Nat. Assn. Sch. Psychologists, Am. Ednl. Rsch. Assn., Air Force Sgts. Assn., Ret. Enlisted Assn., Phi Kappa Phi, Alpha Sigma Lambda. Home: 6879 Maverick Cir Salt Lake City UT 84121-3301 Office: Jordan Sch Dist 7500 S 1000 E Midvale UT 84047-2910

SMITH, WILLIAM CASON, III, broadcaster; b. Canyon, Tex., Aug. 26, 1961; s. William Cason Jr. and Bonnie (Reeves) S. AA in Radio and TV Broadcasting, Mt. San Antonio Coll., Walnut, Calif., 1982, cert. in electronic components assembly, 1982, AS in Electronic Communications, 1985; BA in Psychology with high honors, Calif. State U., Fullerton, 1988. Lic. real estate salesman, Calif. Broadcast engr. Sta. KWOW, Pomona, Calif., 1981-82, Stas. KLOS and KABC, L.A., 1982, 84, Global Satellite Network, Sherman Oaks, Calif., 1984; announcer, engr. Money Radio Network, Sta. KMNY, Pomona, Anaheim, Calif., 1988-89; anchorman Metro Traffic Control, Inc., L.A., 1989; radio personality Sta. KCAL-FM, Redlands, Calif., 1988—; voice over artist A.E.I. Music Network, Orange, Calif., 1990—; guest lectr. Sta. KSAK, Mt. San Antonio Coll., 1985—. Mem. Nat. Assn. Broadcast Employees and Technicians, Golden Key, Phi Kappa Phi, Psi Chi.

SMITH, WILLIAM FRANCIS, educator, author, poet; b. La Crescenta, Calif., Dec. 18, 1922; s. George Joseph and Hazel Delight (Newcomb) S.; m. Rosemary Gladys Boose, Sept. 12, 1948; children: Rosemary K. West, Lawrence Bradford, Philip Steven, Rebecca Sue. AA, Santa Ana Jr. Coll., 1947; BA, U. Redlands, 1949, MA, 1952. Cert. tchr., secondary sch. adminstr., Calif. Tchr. Perris (Calif.) Union High Sch., 1950-53, Garden Grove (Calif.) High Sch., 1953-91. Sgt. U.S. Army, 1943-46, ETO. Fulbright teaching grantee U.S. Ednl. Commn., Fed. Republic of Germany, 1960-61; fgn. lang. grantee U.S. office Edn., U. Colo., 1964. Mem. Mystery Writers Am., Am. Legion. Home: 11401 Reva Dr Garden Grove CA 92640-2301

SMITH, WILLIAM MORLEY, electric power research institute official; b. Bklyn., Mar. 6, 1948; s. William R. and Catherine (Morley) S.; m. Anita Weber, Nov. 30, 1968; 1 child, William C. AA, Manhattan C.C., N.Y.C., 1969; BS, SUNY, Stony Brook, 1971, MS, 1972, PhD, 1977. Load mgmt. analyst Pacific Gas & Electric Co., San Francisco, 1977-80, supr. load mgmt., 1980-85; mgr. demand-side planning and info. Electric Power Rsch. Inst., Palo Alto, Calif., 1985-89, program mgr. power electronics and controls, 1989-91, mgr. office delivery systems, 1991-93, exec. program mgr. partnership for industrial competitiveness, 1993—. Contbr. numerous articles on demand-side mgmt., power quality, power electronics, and technology transfers to profl. jours. Vice pres. Homeowners Assn., Oakland, Calif., 1987-88. Mem. IEEE (sr., demand-side mgmt. subcom. 1982-89, vice chmn. power quality standards coordinating com. 1990-91), Sigma Pi Sigma. Office: Electric Power Rsch Inst Customer Systems Div 3412 Hillview Ave Palo Alto CA 94304

SMITH, WILLIAM RAY, biophysicist, engineer; b. Lyman, Okla., June 26, 1925; s. Harry Wait and Daisy Belle (Hull) S. BA, Bethany Nazarene Coll., 1948; MA, Wichita State U., 1950; postgrad. U. Kans., 1950-51; PhD, UCLA, 1967. Engr., Beech Aircraft Corp., Wichita, Kans., 1951-53; sr. group engr. McDonnell Aircraft Corp., St. Louis, 1953-60; sr. engr. Lockheed Aircraft Corp., Burbank, Calif., 1961-63; sr. engr. scientist McDonnell Douglas Corp., Long Beach, Calif., 1966-71; mem. tech. staff Rockwell Internat., L.A., 1973-86, CDI Corp.-West, Costa Mesa, Calif., 1986-88, McDonnell Douglas Aircraft Corp., Long Beach, 1988—; tchr. math. Pasadena Coll. (now Point Loma Coll., San Diego), 1960-62, Glendale Coll., Calif., 1972; asst. prof. math. Mt. St. Mary's Coll., L.A., 1972-73. Contbr. articles to sci. jours. L.A. World Affairs Coun.; docent Nature Mus. Will Rogers State Pk. Recipient citation McDonnell Douglas Corp., 1968; Tech. Utilization award Rockwell Internat., 1981; cert. of recognition NASA, 1982. Mem. UCLA Chancellor's Assocs., Internat. Visitors Coun. L.A., Town Hall Calif., Yosemite Assocs., Sigma Xi, Pi Mu Epsilon. Republican. Presbyterian (deacon). Office: McDonnell Douglas Corp 3855 N Lakewood Blvd # 4159 Long Beach CA 90846-0001

SMITH, ZACHARY ALDEN, political science and public administration educator; b. Stanford, Calif., Aug. 8, 1953; s. Alden Wallace and Lelia (Anderson) S.; m. Lisa Friel, May 20, 1983. BA, Calif. State U., Fullerton, 1975; MA, U. Calif., Santa Barbara, 1979, PhD, 1984. Adj. lectr. polit. sci. U. Calif., Santa Barbara, 1981-82; asst. prof., dir. Ctr. for Island and Ocean Resources Mgmt. U. Hawaii, Hilo, 1982-87, assoc. prof., 1987-89; assoc. prof. No. Ariz. U., Flagstaff, 1989-93, prof., 1993—. Author: Groundwater and the Future of the Southwest, 1984, Groundwater Policy in the Southwest, 1985, Groundwater in the West, 1989, The Environmental Policy Paradox, 1992, Politics and Public Policy in Arizona, 1993, Environmental Politics and Policy in the West, 1993; co-author: Politics and Public Policy in Hawaii, 1992; contbr. articles to profl. jours. Active campaign Jimmy Carter for Pres., 1976, campaign for various state propositions, 1970, 74, 76; elected to Orange County (Calif.) Dem. Cen. Com., 1976—. Research grantee U. Calif., Los Alamos (N.Mex.) Sci. Lab., Water Resources Ctr., Davis., Calif. Mem. Am. water Resources Assn., Am. Polit. Sci. Assn., Western Polit. Sci. Assn., Am. Soc. Pub. Adminstrn. Office: No Ariz U Dept Polit Sci Flagstaff AZ 86011

SMITH, ZDENKA KOPAL, physicist; b. Boston, Apr. 3, 1943; d. Zdeněk and Alena (Müldner) Kopal; m. Dean Francis Smith; children: Helena, Lara. BA, Bryn Mawr Coll., 1965; MS, Stanford U., 1967. Scientist NASA/AMES, Moffett Field, Calif., 1967-70; physicist NOAA/SEL, Boulder, Colo., 1970—. Contbr. articles to profl. jours. Mem. Am. Geophys. Union, Sigma Xi. Home: 290 Green Rock Dr Boulder CO 80302-4705 Office: NOAA/SEL R/E/SE 325 S Broadway St Boulder CO 80303-3464

SMITHRUD, RICKY LEE, academic development director; b. Hillsboro, Oreg., Oct. 8, 1958; s. Arne Magnus and Clara Belle (Pierce) S.; m. Jordanna Chiara Christensen, Apr. 20, 1991; 1 child, Christian Quinn. BS, U. Oreg., 1981. Asst. dir. community svc. U. Oreg., Eugene, 1981-83, asst. dir. ann. giving, 1984-88; dir. ann. giving Willamette U., Salem, Oreg., 1988-92, U. Conn., 1992—. Bd. dirs. Willamette chpt. ARC, Salem, Oreg., 1989-92; mem. Coun. for Advancement and Support Edn. Mem. Elks. Lutheran.

SMITH-THOMPSON, PATRICIA ANN, public relations consultant, educator; b. Chgo., June 7, 1933; d. Clarence Richard and Ruth Margaret (Jacobson) Nowack; m. Tyler Thompson, Aug. 1, 1992. Student Cornell U., 1951-52; B.A., Centenary Coll., Hackettstown, N.J., 1983. Prodn. asst. Your Hit Parade Batten, Barton, Durstine & Osborne, 1953-54; pvt. practice polit. cons., 1954-66; legal sec., asst. Atty. John C. Cushman, 1966-68; field dep. L.A. County Assessor, 1968-69, pub. info. officer L.A. County Probation Dept., 1969-73; dir. consumer rels. Fireman's Fund, San Francisco, 1973-76; pvt. practice pub. rels. cons., 1976-77; spl. projects officer L.A. County Transp. Commn., 1977-78; tchr. Calif. State U.-Dominguez Hills, 1979-86; editor, writer Jet Propulsion Lab., 1979-80; pub. info. dir. L.A. Bd. Pub. Works, 1980-82; pub. info. cons. City of Pasadena, (Calif.), 1982-84; pub. rels. cons., 1983-90, community rels./Worldport L.A., 1990-92. Mem. First United Methodist Ch. Commn. on Missions and Social Concerns, 1983-89; bd. dirs. Depot, 1983-87; mem. devel. com. Pasadena Guidance Clinics, 1984-85. Recipient Pro award L.A. Publicity Club, 1978, Outstanding Achievement award Soc. Consumer Affairs Profls. in Bus., 1976, Disting. Alumni award Centenary Coll., 1992. Mem. Pub. Relations Soc. Am. (accredited mem.; award for consumer program 1977, 2 awards 1984, Joseph Roos Community Service award 1985), Nat. Press Women (pub. relations award 1986), Calif. Press Women (awards 1974, 78, 83, 84, 85, community relations 1stplace winner 1986, 87, 88, 89), Nat. Assn. Mental Health Info. Offices (3 regional awards 1986). Republican. Clubs: Pasadena Women's City. Contbr. articles to profl. jours.

SMOLARSKI, DENNIS CHESTER, mathematics educator; b. Harvey, Ill., Sept. 2, 1947; s. Chester Francis and Genevieve Josephine (Pasek) S. BS, Santa Clara U., 1969; MA, U. Calif., Santa Barbara, 1975; MDiv, STM, Jesuit Sch. of Theology, Berkeley, Calif., 1979; PhD, U. Ill., 1982. Instr. math. Santa Clara (Calif.) U., 1975-76, asst. prof., 1982-88, assoc. prof., 1988—; Ordained priest Roman Cath. Ch., 1979; mem. Jesuit Order, 1969—. Author: Eucharistia, 1982, How Not To Say Mass, 1986 (Hon. Mention 1986), Liturgical Literacy, 1990; contbr. articles to profl. jours.; author booklets. Mem. Math. Assn. Am. (sect. chmn. 1991-92), Am. Math. Soc., Assn. Computing Machinery, Sigma Xi (club pres. 1987-89). Democrat. Home: Jesuit Community Santa Clara Univ Santa Clara CA 95053 Office: Santa Clara Univ Math Dept Santa Clara CA 95053

SMOLENSKY, EUGENE, economics educator; b. Bklyn., Mar. 4, 1932; s. Abraham and Jennie (Miller) S.; m. Natalie Joan Rabinowitz, Aug. 16, 1952; children: Paul, Beth. B.A., Bklyn. Coll., 1952; M.A., Am. U., 1956; Ph.D., U. Pa., 1961. Prof. econs. U. Wis., Madison, 1968-88, chmn. dept., 1978-80, 86-88; dir. Inst. for Research on Poverty, U. Wis., 1980-83; dean Grad. Sch. Pub. Policy U. Calif., Berkeley, 1988—. Author: Public Expenditures, Taxation and the Distribution of Income: The U.S., 1950, 61, 70, 77. Mem. com. on child devel. research and pub. policy NAS, Washington, 1982-87, mem. com. on status of women in labor market, 1985-87. Served with USN, 1952-56. Mem. Am. Econs. Assn. Democrat. Jewish. Home: 669 Woodmont Ave Berkeley CA 94708-1233 Office: U Calif Dept Pub Policy 2607 Hearst Ave Berkeley CA 94720-0001

SMOLKA, JAMES WILLIAM, aerospace research pilot; b. Mt. Clemens, Mich., July 31, 1950; s. Joseph William and Patricia Joan (Righetti) S.; m. Diane Sue McCoin. BS in Astronautics, USAF Acad., 1972; MS in Aero., Astronautics, MIT, 1980; postgrad., Stanford U., 1988—. Commd. 2d lt. USAF, 1972, advanced through grades to lt. col., 1992; resigned, 1983; served as pilot 3d Tactical Fighter Squadron, Korat RT AFB, Thailand, 1974, 21 Tactical Air Support Squadron, Shaw AFBSC, 1975-77; test pilot 6510 Test Wing, Edwards AFB CA, 1981-83; exptl. test pilot Ft. Worth div. Gen. Dynamics, Edwards AFB, 1984-85; aerospace rsch. pilot N.A.S.A. Ames-Dryden FRF, Edwards AFB, 1985—; lt. col. USAFR, 1992—; adj. prof. Calif. State U., Fresno, 1984—. Author: Analysis and Testing of Aircraft Flight Control Systems, 1982. Mem. Soc. Exptl. Test Pilots. Home: PO Box 2123 Lancaster CA 93539-2123 Office: NASA Ames-Dryden FRF PO Box 273 Edwards CA 93523-0273

SMOLKER, GARY STEVEN, lawyer; b. L.A., Nov. 5, 1945; s. Paul and Shayndy Charolette (Sirott) S.; m. Alice Graham; children: Terra, Judy, Leah. BS, U. Calif.-Berkeley, 1967; MS, Cornell U., 1968; JD cum laude, Loyola U., L.A., 1973. Bar: Calif. 1973, U.S. Dist. Ct. (cen. dist.) Calif. 1973, U.S. Tax Ct. 1973, U.S. Ct. Appeals (9th cir.) 1973, U.S. Supreme Ct. 1978, U.S. Dist. Ct. (so., ea. and no. dists.) Calif. 1981. Guest researcher Lawrence Radiation Lab., U. Calif., 1967; teaching fellow Sch. Chem. Engring., Cornell U.; mem. tech. staff Hughes Aircraft Co., Culver City, Calif., 1968-70; in advanced mktg. and tech. TRW, Redondo Beach, Calif., 1970-72; sole practice, Beverly Hills, Calif., 1973-89, L.A., 1989—; guest lectr. UCLA Extension, 1973-74, Loyola U. Law Sch., 1979; speaker, panelist in field; adv. Loyola U. Law Sch., 1973—. Contbr. articles to profl. jours.; inventor self-destruct aluminum tungstic oxide films, electrolytic anticompromise process. Mem. Nat. Assn. Real Estate Editors, Calif. State Bar Assn., L.A. County Bar Assn., Beverly Hills Bar Assn. (sr. editor jour. 1978-79, contbg. editor jour. 1980-82, 86-90, editor-in-chief 1984-86, pub. Smolker Letter 1985—). Jewish. Lodge: B'nai B'rith (anti-defamation league). Office: 5456 McConnell Ave Ste 245 Los Angeles CA 90066

SMOLLAN, DAVID LESLIE, tax practitioner; b. Middlesbrough, Eng., June 22, 1928; came to U.S., 1948, naturalized, 1954; s. Philip and Sarah (Freedman) S.; B.B.A., Woodbury Coll., 1950; m. Sheila Joy Glassman, Aug. 5, 1956 (dec.); children: Jeffrey, Debbie. Chief acct. Lucky Plastic Co., Inc., Los Angeles, 1951-64; self-employed tax practitioner, Encino, Northridge, Calif, 1965—. Named Kiwanian of Yr., Pacoima Kiwanis Club, 1968; enrolled to practice before the IRS, 1967. Mem. Nat. Assn. Enrolled Agts. (pres. 1973-74), Calif. Soc. Enrolled Agts., Kiwanis (pres. Encino 1985-86, treas. 1989-91), IRS Practitioners' Forum (L.A. dist. 1991—). Office: 8448 Reseda Blvd Ste 104 Northridge CA 91324-4627

SMOOT, LEON DOUGLAS, university dean, chemical engineering educator; b. Provo, Utah, July 26, 1934; s. Douglas Parley and Jennie (Hallam) S.; m. Marian Bird, Sept. 7, 1953; children: Analee, LaCinda, Michelle, Melinda Lee. BS, Brigham Young U., 1956, B in Engring. Sci., 1957; MS, U. Wash., 1958, PhD, 1960. Registered profl. engr., Utah. Engr. Boeing Corp., Seattle, 1956; teaching and research asst. Brigham Young U., 1954-57; engr. Phillips Petroleum Co., Arco, Idaho, 1957; engr., cons. Hercules Powder Co., Bacchus, Utah, 1961-63; asst. prof. Brigham Young U., 1960-63; engr. Lockheed Propulsion, Redlands, Calif., 1963-67; vis. asst. prof. Calif. Inst. Tech., 1966-67; asso. prof. to prof. Brigham Young U., 1967—, chmn. dept. chem. engring., 1970-77, dean Coll. Engring. and Tech., 1977—; dir. Advanced Combustion Engring. Rsch. Ctr., 1986—; expert witness on combustion and explosions; dir. Advanced Combustion Engring. Research Ctr. (NSF), 1986—; cons. Hercules, Thiokol, Lockheed, Teledyne, Atlantic Research Corp., Raytheon, Redd and Redd, Billings Energy, Ford, Bacon & Davis, Jaycor, Intel Com Radiation Tech., Phys. Dynamics, Nat. Soc. Propellants and Explosives, France, DFVLR, West Germany, Martin Marietta, Honeywell, Phillips Petroleum Co., Exxon, Nat. Bur. Standards, Eyring Research Inst., Systems, Sci. and Software., Los Alamos Nat. Lab., others. Contbr. over 200 articles to tech. jours.; Author 5 books on coal combustion. Mem. Am. Inst. Chem. Engrs., Am. Inst. Aeros. and Astronautics, Am. Soc. Engring. Edn., Combustion Inst., Research Soc. Am., Tau Beta Pi, Phi Lambda Epsilon, Sigma Xi. Republican. Mem. LDS Ch. Home: 1811 N 1550 Provo UT 84604-5709 Office: Brigham Young U-Advance Combuston Engring Rsch Ctr 45 Crabtree Tech Bldg Provo UT 84602

SMOOT, WENDELL MCMEANS, JR., investment counselor; b. Salt Lake City, Jan. 15, 1921; s. Wendell M. and Rebecca (Clawson) S.; m. Barbara Davis, June 24, 1942; children—Wendell M. III, Margaret, David, John, Mary. B.A., U. Utah, 1942. Gen. ptnr. J.A. Hogle & Co., Salt Lake City, 1945-63, Goodbody & Co., N.Y.C., 1963-70; chmn. Smoot, Miller, Cheney & Co., Salt Lake City, 1971—. Pres. Great Salt Lake council Boy Scouts Am., 1968-70; chmn. Utah State Pioneer Meml. Theatre, 1978-79; pres. Mormon Tabernacle Choir. Served to capt., U.S. Army, 1942-45; ETO. Mem. Fin. Analysts Soc. Republican. Mem. Ch. of Jesus Christ of Latter Day Saints. Club: The Country. Lodge: Rotary.

SMUDIN, RICHARD STANLEY, computer company executive; b. Brockton, Mass., Apr. 21, 1966; s. Stanley Frank and Patricia Ellen (Reardon) S. Student, U.S. Mil. Acad., 1984-86; BSBA, Boston U., 1988. Commd. 2d lt. U.S. Army, 1988; project control asst. Raytheon Co., Waltham, Mass., 1989-90; customer svc. rep. Orion Systems, Inc., Santa Clara, Calif., 1990-92; software prodns. mgr., system adminstr. Advanced Micro Devices, Sunnyvale, Calif., 1992—. Mem. Am. Prodn. Inventory Control Soc. (cert.), World Affairs Coun. No. Calif., Res. Officers Assn. Republican. Home: 2758 Mabury Sq San Jose CA 95133

SMULDERS, ANTHONY PETER, biology educator; b. Oss, North Brabant, The Netherlands, July 6, 1942; came to U.S., 1963; s. Arnoldus A.P. and Maria A.A. (Horsten) S. T.C. in Edn. and Psychology, St. Stanislaus T.T.C., Tilburg, The Netherlands, 1962; BS in Biology summa cum laude, Loyola U., Los Angeles, 1966; PhD in Physiology with distinction, UCLA, 1970. Joined Bros. of Our Lady Mother of Mercy, Roman Cath. Ch., 1959. Tchr. Loon op Zand (The Netherlands) elem. schs., 1962-63, Santa Clara High Sch., Oxnard, Calif., 1965-67; research physiologist UCLA, 1970—; prof. biology Loyola Marymount U., Los Angeles, 1970—, assoc. dean sci., 1972—; mem. Los Angeles County Narcotics and Dangerous Drugs Commn., 1973—, Calif. State Adv. Bd. on Drug Programs, 1982—. Contbr. articles to profl. jours. Mem. AAUP, AAAS, The Biophys. Soc., Nat. Assn. Advisors for Health Professions (pres. 1978-84), Western Assn. Advisors for Health Professions, Sigma Xi, Sigma Pi Sigma. Democrat. Lodge: KC. Office: Loyola Marymount U 7101 W 80th St Los Angeles CA 90045-2659

SMULLIN, DONALD EVAN, communications company executive; b. Eureka, Calif., July 15, 1947; m. Cecilia Mattana. BS in Fin., U. Calif., Berkeley; student, Harvard U. Engr. KIEM-TV, 1966, Pacific Teletronics, 1968; mgr. So. Cable TV, 1970-73, KOTI-TV, 1973-76; pres. Oreg. Broadcasting Co., 1976-82; ptnr. TV 58, Sacramento, 1984-86; mgr. KSMS-TV, Monterey, Calif., 1987-89; prin. TRC Communications, Corvallis, Oreg., 1982—, Pacific Broadcasting Co, Oreg., 1993—; prin. Cam Internat., Italy, TRC Leasing, Oreg., Cividale, Italy, Internat. Teletronics, Princeton, N.J.; mem. Univision Spanish TV affiliate bd., 1987-89; bd. dirs. affiliates bd. CBS TV Network, 1977; del. to World Conf. Broadcasting Unions, Algiers, 1983, Prague, 1986, Washington, 1989, Internat. Assn. Broadcasters Gen. Assembly, Rio de Janeiro,1 983, Madrid, 1984, Venice, 1986, Montevideo, 1987. Mem. Nat. Assn. Broadcasters (chmn. internat. com. 1987—), Internat. Assn. Broadcasters (pres. bus. com. Madrid 1986-90, bd. dirs. Montevideo, Uruguay 1986-90), Oreg. Assn. Broadcasters (pres. 1979), Broadcast Pioneers Assn. Office: TRC Communications Inc PO Box 731 Corvallis OR 97339-0731

SMYER, MYRNA RUTH, drama educator; b. Albuquerque, June 10, 1946; d. Paul Anthony and Ruth Kelly (Klein) S.; m. Carlton Weaver Canaday, July 5, 1980. BFA, U. N.Mex., 1969; MA, Northwestern U., 1971. Pvt. practice drama instr. Albuquerque, 1974-78; dir. drama Sandia Preparatory Sch., Albuquerque, 1977—, chmn. dept. fine arts, 1980—; dialect coach, dir. Chgo. Acting Ensemble, 1969-71; lectr., performer Albuquerque Pub. Schs. and various civic orgns., Albuquerque, 1974—; writer, dir., performer Arts in the Pks., Albuquerque, 1977-80; performer, crew various indsl. videos, 1981-86; instr. workshops and continuing edn. U. N.Mex. 1977-80. Writer, dir., designer children's plays including May The Best Mammal (Or Whatever) Win, 1977, A Holiday Celebration, 1977, Puppets on Parade, 1978, A Witch's Historical Switches, 1979, Once Upon a Rhyme, 1987—, Little Red Riding Hood, 1987, Goldilocks and The Three Bears, 1988, Cinderella, 1989, Hansel and Gretel, 1990, Rumpelstiltskin, 1991, The Dancing Princesses, 1992; dir. numerous other children and adult plays. Instr., writer, dir. various community theatres including Albuquerque Little Theatre, Corrales Adobe Theatre, Kimo Theatre, Albuquerque Civic Light Opera, Now We Are Theatre; mem. Albuquerque Cable TV Adv. Bd.; mem. task force on the arts for children Albuquerque Little Theatre. Recipient 1st Pl. award for quality in edn. N.Mex. Rsch. and Study Coun., U. N.Mex., 1989-90. Mem. Am. Alliance for Theatre and Edn., Women in Communications. Office: Sandia Preparatory Sch 532 Osuna Rd NE Albuquerque NM 87113-1099

SMYSER, ADAM ALBERT, newspaper editor; b. York, Pa., Dec. 18, 1920; s. Adam Milton and Miriam (Stein) S.; m. Elizabeth Harrison Avery, Dec. 25, 1943 (dec. 1983); children: Heidi, Avery; m. Doris H. Prather, Apr. 24, 1984. B.A., Pa. State U., 1941. Rewrite man Pitts. Press, 1941-42; with Honolulu Star-Bull., 1946—, city editor, 1953-60, mng. editor, 1960-65, editor, 1966-75, editor editorial page, 1975-83, contbg. editor, 1983—; mem. Pulitzer Journalism Awards Jury, 1970. Author: Hawaii's Future in the Pacific: Disaster, Backwater or Future State?, 1988, Hawaii as an East-West Bridge, 1990; past freelance writer McGraw-Hill mags. Chmn. temp. commn. on statewide environ. planning, 1973; bd. dirs. Corp. for Community TV; chmn. steering com. Gov.'s Congress on Hawaii's Internat. Role, 1988; mem. community adv. bd. Tokai U. Pacific Ctr.; Lt. USNR, 1942-46, PTO. Recipient Distinguished Alumnus award Pa. State U., 1976. Mem. Hawaii C. of C., Coun. on Fgn. Rels., Hawaii Econ. Assn., Honolulu Social Sci. Assn., Honolulu Acad. Arts, Am. Soc. Newspaper Editors, Japan-Am. Soc. Hawaii, Honolulu Community-Media Coun. Clubs: Honolulu Press (named to Hall of Fame 1987), Honolulu Rotary. Home: 1052 Iiwi St Honolulu HI 96816-5111 Office: Honolulu Star-Bull 605 Kapiolani Blvd Honolulu HI 96813-5195

SMYSER, CHARLES ARVIL (SKIP SMYSER), senator, lawyer; b. Caldwell, Idaho, Nov. 14, 1949; s. Samuel H. and Mildred (Skelton) S.; m. Melinda Sloviaczek, Aug. 22, 1981; children: Lincoln, Logan, Landon. BA, Ea. Wash. U., 1972; JD, Gonzaga U., 1977. Bar: Idaho 1977. Dep. pros. atty. Ada County, Boise, Idaho, 1977-79; dep. atty. gen. State of Idaho, Boise, 1979-80; ptnr. Connolly & Smyser, Boise and Parma, Idaho, 1980—; senator State of Idaho, 1982-90. Mem. Idaho Ho. of Reps., Canyon County, 1980-82; bd. dirs. Idaho State Sch. and Hosp., Nampa, Idaho, 1982-88. Capt. Q.M.C., U.S. Army, 1972-74. Named Legis. of Yr. Idaho Prosecuting Atty.'s Assn., one of Outstanding Young Men of Am. U.S. Jaycees, 1977-86. Mem. Idaho State Bar Assn., Lions, Masons, Scottish Rite, Shriners. Republican. Presbyterian. Office: Connolly & Smyser 134 S 5th St Boise ID 83702-5949

SMYTH, BERNARD JOHN, retired newspaper editor; b. Renovo, Pa., Nov. 16, 1915; s. John Bernard and Alice C. (Russell) S.; m. Eva Mae Stone, Dec. 31, 1936; children: Constance, Joe, Pamela, Lisa. Grad., Dickinson Jr. Coll., 1935. Machinist helper Pa. R.R. Renovo Shops, 1936-39; mgr. Smyth Bros., Renovo, 1939-45; editor, pub., owner Renovo Daily Record, 1946-53; owner, editor, pub. Del. State News, Dover, 1953-70; chmn. bd. Independent Newspapers Inc., 1970-85; pres. Valley Newspapers Inc., Tempe, Ariz., 1971-85. Served with AUS, 1944-45. Mem. Soc. Profl. Journalists, Ariz. Newspaper Assn., Sigma Delta Chi. Home: 4200 N Miller Rd Apt 422 Scottsdale AZ 85251-3631

SMYTH, DAVID SHANNON, real estate investor, commercial and retail builder and developer; b. Denver, May 13, 1943; s. William James and Constance Ruth (Sherman) S.; student Regis Coll., 1967-69, USAF Acad., 1961-65, U. No. Colo., 1965-67; m. Sharon Kaye Swiderski, Jan. 3, 1980; children—Julia Caitlin, Alexander Jeremiah, Matthew Davis; 1 son by previous marriage, Shannon David. Accountant, Colo. Nat. Bank, 1966-69; bus. analyst Dun & Bradstreet, 1969-70; pres., dir. Georgetown Valley Water & Sanitation Dist., 1973-74, Realists, Inc., 1973-74, Silver Queen Constrn. Co., 1973-74; v.p., sec., dir. Georgetown Assocs., Inc. (Colo.), 1970-74; pres., chief ops. officer Lincoln Cos., Denver, 1975-76; project mgr., sales mgr., prin. Brooks-Morris Homes, Fox Ridge, Colo., 1976-77; project mgr. U.S. West Homes, Denver, 1977-78; pres., dir. Denver Venture Capital, 1978-81; prin., dir., exec. v.p. Shelter Equities, Inc., 1982-87; prin., dir., exec. v.p. Comml. Constrn. Mgmt. Services, Inc., 1987-88, Shelter Equities, Inc., 1984-87; owner, dir., exec. v.p. Maple Leaf Realty Corp.; v.p., dir. Gibraltar Devel. Corp., Dominion Properties Ltd., 1978-82; investment dir. Van Schaack & Co., 1987-91; prin. investor, head devel. The Farkas Group, 1991-92; sr. residential loan officer, Freedom Mortgage Co., 1992—. Served with USAF, 1961-65. Lic. real estate broker. Home: 8052 S Rosemary Ct Englewood CO 80112-1020 Office: Freedom Mortgage Co 6432 S Quebec St # 108 Englewood CO 80111-2931

SMYTH, JOHN R., state official, lawyer; b. Rawlins, Wyo., Oct. 5, 1932; s. Ed A. and Sarah (Murphy) S.; m. Ruth L. Long; children: Suzanne, Diane, Carolyn, Teresa. BA, U. Santa Clara, 1954; JD, U. Wyo., 1959. Bar: Wyo. 1959. Asst. atty. gen. State of Wyo., 1959-60; pvt. practice, Wyo., 1960-77; mem. Wyo. Pub. Svc. Commn., Cheyenne, 1977—, chmn.; former judge Cheyenne Mcpl. Juvenile Ct. Mem. Wyo. Ho. of Reps., 1967-77. With F.A., U.S. Army, 1954-56. Office: Wyo Pub Svc Commn 700 W 21st St Cheyenne WY 82002

SNAPE, WILLIAM JOHN, JR., physician; b. Camden, N.J., Aug. 24, 1943; s. William John and Barbara (Fleischman) S.; m. Margaret Fry, Mar. 7, 1982; children: William John III, Rebecca Jane. BA, Princeton U., 1965; MD, Jefferson Med. Coll., 1969. Intern Bronx (N.Y.) Municipal Hosp., 1969-70, resident, 1970-71; fellow in gerontology U. Pa., 1973-75; asst. to assoc. prof. U. Pa., Phila., 1975-82; prof. UCLA, 1982—. Lt. comdr.

USNR, 1971-73. Fellow ACP, Am. Coll. Gastroenterology. Office: Harbor UCLA 1124 W Carson St A-4 Annex Torrance CA 90502

SNARE, CARL LAWRENCE, JR., business executive; b. Chgo., Oct. 25, 1936; s. Carl Lawrence and Lillian Marie (Luoma) S.; B.B.A., Northwestern U., 1968; postgrad. Roosevelt U.; postgrad. in econs. San Francisco State U., 1976-77, Calif. Coast U. Cert. fin. planner. Asst. sec., controller Bache Halsey Stuart & Shields Inc. (now Prudential Bache), Chgo., 1968-73; controller Innisfree Corp. div. Hyatt Corp., Burlingame, Calif., 1973-76; cash mgr. Portland (Oreg.) Gen. Electric Co., 1976-79; chief fin. officer, controller Vistar Fin. Inc., Marina del Rey, Calif., 1979-82; v.p., treas. Carson Estate Co., Rancho Dominguez, Calif., 1988—; pres. Snare Properties Co., Long Beach, Calif., 1984—, Snare Fin. Services Corp., Rialto, Calif., 1985-89, Carl Snare & Assocs., Long Beach. CPA, cert. fin. planner, Calif. Mem. AICPA, Calif. Soc. CPAs. Founder Cash Mgmt. Assn., Portland, Oreg. Home: 3746 Palo Verde Ave Long Beach CA 90808-2221 Office: 18710 S Wilmington Ave Ste 200 Compton CA 90220-5912

SNASDELL, SUSAN KATHLEEN, computer company executive; b. St. Louis, July 17, 1948; d. Russell John and Gertrude Burnett (Gassman) S. BA, So. Nazarene U., 1972. Office adminstr. Lake, Van Dyke & Browne Med. Group, Pasadena, Calif., 1972-83; founder, ptnr., adminstr. ComputerEase, Oxnard, Calif., 1984—. Contbr. articles to profl. jours. Mem. Better Bus. Bur., Oxnard C. of C. Office: ComputerEase 1201 S Escalon Dr Oxnard CA 93035-2731

SNEDKER, CLIVE JOHN, advertising executive; b. London, Dec. 5, 1947; came to U.S., 1979; s. Henry Morris and Iris May (Clapham) S.; m. Judith Ann Stevens, Dec. 5, 1970; children; Sarah Louise, Clare Jane, Karen Ann. Grad., Tollington Grammar Sch., London. Shipping clk. Thomas Meadow & Co., Ltd., London, 1965-67; comml. dir. F.W. Stephens & Co. Ltd., Cuffley, Eng., 1967-77; owner CJs Design, Hoddesdon, Eng., 1977-79; account exec. Process Displays, Hayward, Calif., 1979-87; owner The Freelance Consortium, Tracy, Calif., 1987—. Chmn. fund raising Tracy (Calif.) Tritons Swim Club, 1987-89, M.C. swim meets, 1986-89; artist Tracy High Sch. Water Polo, 1990; mktg. rep. Tracy Arts Commn., 1991; artist, photographer Tracy Drama Club, 1990-92; artist Trouble Inc. Dance Group, 1990. Mem. Internat. Freelance Photographers Orgn. Office: The Freelance Consortium Ste B 950 E Grant Line Rd Tracy CA 95376

SNEED, JOSEPH TYREE, III, federal judge; b. Calvert, Tex., July 21, 1920; s. Harold Marvin and Cara (Weber) S.; m. Madelon Juergens, Mar. 15, 1944; children—Clara Hall, Cara Carleton, Joseph Tyree IV. B.B.A., Southwestern U., 1941; LL.B., U. Tex., Austin, 1947; S.J.D., Harvard, 1958. Bar: Tex. bar 1948. Instr. bus. law U. Tex., Austin, 1947; asst. prof. law U. Tex., 1947-51, asso. prof., 1951-54, prof., 1954-57, asst. dean, 1949-50; counsel Graves, Dougherty & Greenhill, Austin, 1954-56; prof. law Cornell U., 1957-62, Stanford Law Sch., 1962-71; dean Duke Law Sch., 1971-73; dep. atty. gen. U.S. justice dept., 1973; judge U.S. Ct. Appeals (9th cir.), San Francisco, 1973—; Cons. estate and gift tax project Am. Law Inst., 1960-69. Author: The Configurations of Gross Income, 1967; Contbr. articles to profl. jours. Served with USAAF, 1942-46. Mem. ABA (chairperson appellate judges conf. jud. adminstrn. div.), State Bar Tex., Am. Law Inst., Order of Coif. Office: US Ct Appeals PO Box 547 San Francisco CA 94101-0547

SNELL, NED COLWELL, financial planner; b. Cowley, Wyo., May 16, 1944; s. Jay Hatton and Freda Hope (Colwell) S.; m. Barbara Anne Frandsen, Apr. 24, 1969; children: Taylor Anthony, Trevor Cameron. BA, U. Utah, 1969; CLU, Am. Coll., 1983, ChFC, 1985. English tchr. Granite Sch. Dist., Salt Lake City, 1969-71; ins. agt. Prudential Ins. Co., Salt Lake City, 1971-76; pres. Snell Fin. Corp., Salt Lake City, 1976—. Bd. dirs. Utah chpt. Arthritis Found., Salt Lake City, 1980-82, pres., 1982-83; missionary Mormon Ch., 1963-66. Mem. NALU (Nat. Sales Achievement award 1971-89, Nat. Quality award), Am. Soc. CLU and ChFC (bd. dirs. Utah chpt. 1990-93, treas. 1993—, Golden Key Soc. Devel. award 1990), Million Dollar Round Table (knight 1988-91), Salt Lake Assn. Life Underwriters (bd. dirs. 1974-76, 80-82). Republican. Home: 1101 S 2000 E Salt Lake City UT 84108-1971 Office: 1800 SW Temple Ste 416 Salt Lake City UT 84115

SNELL, RICHARD, holding company executive; b. Phoenix, Nov. 26, 1930; s. Frank L. and Elizabeth (Berlin) S.; m. Alice Cosette Wiley, Aug. 1, 1954. BA, Stanford U., 1952, JD, 1954. Bar: Ariz. Ptnr. firm Snell & Wilmer, Phoenix, 1956-81; pres., chmn., chief exec. officer Ramada Inc., Phoenix, 1981-89; chmn., chief exec. officer Aztar Corp., 1989-90, chmn., bd. dirs., 1990-92; chmn., chief exec. officer, pres. Pinnacle West Capital Corp., Phoenix, 1990—, bd. dirs.; bd. dirs. Bank One Ariz. Corp., Bank One Ariz. NA, Aztar Corp.; bd. dirs., chmn. Ariz. Pub. Svc. Co. Chmn. bd. trustees Am. Grad. Sch. Internat. Mgmt., Phoenix; past pres. YMCA Met. Phoenix and Valley of Sun. With U.S. Army, 1954-56. Mem. ABA, Ariz. Bar Assn., Paradise Valley Country Club, Phoenix Country Club, John Gardiner's Tennis Ranch. Republican. Lutheran. Office: Pinnacle West Capital Corp PO Box 52132 Phoenix AZ 85072-2132 also: Arizona Public Service Co PO Box 53999 Sta 9960 Phoenix AZ 85072

SNEVA, THOMAS EDSOL, race car driver; b. Spokane, Wash., June 1, 1948; s. Edsol Hilmer and Joan (Giles) S.; m. Sharon Setchell, Aug. 17, 1968; children: Joey, Amanda. B.A. in Edn, Eastern Wash. State Coll., 1970. Tchr., coach, prin. Sprague (Wash.) Sch. Dist., 1970-73; race car driver for Grant King, 1974, for Roger Penske Racing Team, 1975-78, for Jerry Oconell, 1979. Recipient U.S. Auto Club Rookie of the Year award, 1973, Jimmy Clark award, 1976, Eddie Sachs Scholarship award, 1977, U.S. Auto Club Nat. Champion, 1977, 78, Triple Crown, 1977, Jim Malloy Meml. award, 1977; U.S. Auto Club Champion, 1977, 78. Mem. U.S. Auto Club, Fedn. Internationale de L'Automobile. Lutheran. Home: 3301 E Valley Vista Ln Paradise Valley AZ 85253-3739

SNIEZEK, PATRICK WILLIAM, real estate loan officer; b. Zainesville, Ohio, Apr. 25, 1964; s. Richard Anton and Wanda Lee (Sir) S. BSBA in Mktg., U. Ariz., 1987. Customer svc. rep. Great Am. Bank, Tucson, 1983-85, customer svc. rep. II, 1985-87, real estate loan officer, 1987-91; real estate loan officer Waterfield Fin. Corp., Tucson, 1991—. Bd. mem. So. Ariz. Kidney Found., Tucson, 1987-88; bus. cons. Jr. Achievement, Tucson, 1987—; treas. Active 20/30 Club, Tucson, 1987-88, sec. 1988-89, bd. dirs., 1989-90. Named Outstanding Young Man of Yr., Outstanding Young Men of Am., Montgomery, Ala., 1988, Future Bus. Leader of Yr., Future Bus. Leaders of Am., Phoenix, 1988. Republican. Roman Catholic. Home: Apt # 1007 3690 N Country Club Rd Tucson AZ 85716-1293 Office: Waterfield Fin Corp 333 N Wilmot Rd # 205 Tucson AZ 85711

SNOOK, QUINTON, construction company executive; b. Atlanta, July 15, 1925; s. John Wilson and Charlotte Louise (Clayson) S.; student U. Idaho, 1949-51; m. Lois Mullen, Jan. 19, 1947; children: Lois Ann Snook Matteson, Quinton A., Edward M., Clayson S., Charlotte T. Rancher, Lemhi Valley, Idaho, 1942—; owner, mgr. Snook Constrn., Salmon, Idaho, 1952—; owner Snook Trucking, 1967—, Lemhi Posts and Poles, 1980—. Mem. Lemhi County Comm., Dist. 2, 1980-93. Mem. Am. Quarter Horse Assn., Farm Bur., Nat. Rifleman's Assn., Idaho Assn. Commrs. and Clerks (sec. 1986, v.p. 1987, pres. 1988), Am. Hereford Assn., Idaho Cattlemen's Assn., Elks. Republican. Episcopalian. Home: RR 1 Box 49 Salmon ID 83467-9712

SNOW, ALAN ALBERT, publisher; b. Van Nuys, Calif., July 20, 1946; s. Perry William and Virginia (Show) S. BA, Pepperdine U., L.A., 1969; MA, Sch. of Theology, Claremont, Calif., 1974; Magister Operae Onerosae (hon.), Inst. Antiquity-Christianity, Claremont, 1972. bd. dirs. Inst. for Study of Judeo-Christian Origins Calif. State U., Long Beach. Contbg. author to anthologies: The Book Your Church Does Not Want You to Read, 1993; contbr. articles to profl. jours. and newspapers. Mem. Nat. Notary Assn. (ethics com., Cert. Accomplishment), Am. Soc. Notaries, Dead Sea Scroll Rsch. Coun., Bibl. Archaeology Soc. Democrat. Home: 518 S Bay Front Newport Beach CA 92662-1040

SNOW, CHET BONINE, clinical hypnotherapist, researcher, lecturer; b. Paterson, N.J., July 6, 1945; s. Walter A. and Ann Whiteman (Bonine) S.; m. Benedicte Kallista Abelé, Dec. 12, 1992. BA, Johns Hopkins U., 1967; MA, Columbia U., 1970, PhM, 1976; PhD, Internat. Inst. for Advanced Studies (Greenwich U.), Clayton, Mo., 1985. Cert. Am. Coun. Hypnotherapist Examiners. Instr. Columbia U., N.Y.C., 1973-75; command historian USAF, Travis AFB, Calif., 1978-85; ind. rschr., Paris, 1985-89; asst. dir. Mountain Psychol. Clinic, Lake Arrowhead, Calif., 1989-91; pvt. practice, Scottsdale, Ariz., 1991—; assoc. Dr. Helen Wambach, Berkeley, Calif., 1984-85. Author: Mass Dreams of the Future, 1989 (German, Brit., French, Japanese and Dutch edits.) (Book of Yr. award Mag. 2000, 1991); co-author: Regression Therapy: A Handbook for Professionals, 1992; asst. editor Jour. Regression Therapy, 1986-89; also articles. Herbert H. Lehman fellow Columbia U., 1969-71. Mem. Assn. for Rsch. and Enlightenment, Assn. for Past Life Rsch. and Therapies (bd. dirs. 1986—, pres. 1991—), Phi Beta Kappa, Sigma Phi Epsilon. Democrat. Office: PO Box 9732 Scottsdale AZ 85252

SNOW, DEXTER CLINTON, accountant; b. St. George, Utah, Aug. 12, 1932; s. Jeter Clinton and Wanda (Esplin) S.; m. Deneice Truman, Aug. 12, 1954; children: Devery Clinton, Diane Snow Hoefelmann. BS in Econs., U. Utah, 1954. CPA, Nev. Staff acct. Lincoln G. Kelly & Co. (now Coopers), Salt Lake City, 1956-59; pvt. practice St. George, 1960-69; ptnr. Bradshaw, Snow and Mathis, Las Vegas, 1960-69, Fox & Co., Salt Lake City, 1969-76; real estate broker Snow, Truman Realty Inc., St. George, 1977-83, Grubb & Ellis, Salt Lake City, 1983, ERA West Realtors, St. George, 1983-86; acct. Bradshaw Smith & Co., Las Vegas, 1986-88; pvt. practice Las Vegas, 1988—. Rep. Utah State Sch. Bd., Salt Lake City, 1969-70. Capt. USAF, 1954-62. Mem. AICPA, Nev. Soc. CPAs. Republican. Mem. Ch. LDS. Office: 1055 E Tropicana #590 Las Vegas NV 89119

SNOW, LEE ERLIN, artist, educator; b. Buffalo, Jan. 2, 1924; d. Edward and MRY (Gaffe) Erlin; m. Herbert Snow, Apr. 2, 1952; 1 child, Dana Alan. BA in Psychology and Sociology, U. Buffalo, 1947; course in art, Otis Art Inst., L.A., 1964-65; ESL accreditation, UCLA, 1980. Instr. multimedia fibre Barnsdall Arts and Crafts Ctr., L.A., 1972-76, L.A. County Mus. Art, 1975; instr. adult edn. Santa Barbara (Calif.) City Coll., 1984—, Santa Barbara Art Mus., 1987; workshop leader non-loom weaving World Crafts Conf., Toronto, Ont., Can., 1974. One-man shows include S.W. Craft Ctr. Gallery, San Antonio, 1975, Front Rm., Dallas, 1976; group shows include Galeria de Sol, Santa Barbara, 1976. Art Rental Gallery, L.A.County Mus. Art., 1976-80, Jewish Fedn. Craft Show, L.A., 1983, L.A. Art Assn. Exibit Craft and Folk Art Mus., Santa Barbara Art Assn., 1984—, Juried Weavers Guild, 1984, 85, Adult Edn. Fac Shows, 1985—, Gallery 113, Santa Barbara, Santa Barbara Art Walk, 1990—, De Vere Gallery, Mendecino, 1992—, Philip Campbell Assoc. Gallery, Los Olivos, 1993, Cubrillo Gallery, Santa Barbara, 1993; rep. in pub. collections Skirball Mus., L.A., Halls Crown Ctr., Kansas City, Craft and Folk Art Mus., L.A.; co-author: Weaving Off-Loom, 1973, Creative Stitchery with Dona Meilach. Bd. dirs. Adult Edn. Tchrs. Senate, Santa Barbara, 1990-91. Scholar, UCLA; recipient 3rd Prize Painting award Westwood Art Assn., 1963. Mem. Soc. Calif. Designer Craftsmen (sr. advisor 1978-80, pres. 1976-78), L.A. Art Assn., Am. Crafts Coun., So. Calif. Weavers Guild, Santa Barbara Art Assn. Gallery 113 (Artist of Month 1990). Home and Office: 333 Old Mill Rd Apt 284 Santa Barbara CA 93110-3420

SNOW, MARCELLUS SCOWCROFT, economics educator; b. Ogden, Utah, Apr. 2, 1942; s. Marcellus Keyting and Charlene (Scowcroft) S.; m. Edwina Jo Burton, Mar. 27, 1967; children: David Burton, Jonathan Marcellus, Matthew Stephen. BA magna cum laude, U. Utah, 1965; MS, MIT, 1967; MA, Johns Hopkins U., 1969; PhD, U. Calif., Berkeley, 1974. Rsch. asst. World Bank, Washington, 1969; fin., polit. analyst Communications Satellite Corp., Washington, 1969-71, summer 1972; instr. econs. Calif. State U., San Francisco, 1972; rsch. asst. dept. econs. U. Calif., Berkeley, 1971-74; asst. prof. econs. U. Hawaii, Honolulu, 1974-79, assoc. prof., 1979-86, prof., 1986—; Fulbright rsch. prof. U. Bonn, 1980-81; vis. scholar Stanford U., summer 1983; cons. ITT, 1978, Dept. Commerce, 1979, Max Planck Inst., 1986-87. Author: International Commercial Satellite Communications, 1976, The International Telecommunications Satellite Orgn. (INTELSAT), 1987, INTELSAT: An Economic Assessment, 1988; co-editor: Economic and Policy Problems in Satellite Communications, 1977; editor: Marketplace for Telecommunications: Regulation and Deregulation in Industrialized Democracies, 1986; co-author: Telecommunication Economics and Internat Regulatory Policy, 1986; book review editor Information Economics and Policy, 1993—; contbr. articles to profl. jours. Scoutmaster, Boy Scouts Am., Honolulu, 1984-90, scouting unit commnr., 1990-93. NSF fellow, 1965-68, NSF grantee, 1984; Harvard U. fellow, 1988-89. Mem. Am. Econ. Assn., Pacific Telecommunications Council, Internat. Inst. Communications, Econometric Soc. , Hawaii Coun. Econ. Edn. Home: 4774 Aukai Ave Honolulu HI 96816-5242 Office: U Hawaii Dept Econs 2424 Maile Way Honolulu HI 96822-2281

SNOW, W. STERLING, biology and chemistry educator; b. Devils Lake, N.D., Feb. 14, 1947; s. Morgan Williams and Josephine Elizabeth Ann (Erickstad) S.; m. Barbara Kay Jolley, Aug. 29, 1976; 1 child, Michelle Rene. AB, U. Calif., Santa Cruz, 1970; tchr. credential, U. Calif., Santa Barbara, 1971; MA, Chapman Coll., 1976. Cert. secondary sch. tchr., Calif., Alaska; cert. adminstrn., Calif. Tchr., coach Monterey (Calif.) Peninsula Unified Sch. Dist., 1972-76; tchr., coach Anchorage (Alaska) Sch. Dist., 1976—, athletic dir., 1987-92, tchr., 1992—; conf. asst. U. Calif., Santa Cruz, 1971-78. Bd. dirs. Dimond Alumni Found., Anchorage, 1987-92 (award of excellence 1992). Mem. AAAS, ASCD, Nat. Assn. Biology Tchrs., Nat. Interscholastic Athletic Adminstrs. Assn. (life), Nat. Assn. Basketball Coaches, Alaska Sci. Tchrs. Assn., N.Y. Acad. Scis. Lutheran.

SNYDER, ALLEGRA FULLER, dance educator; b. Chgo., Aug. 28, 1927; d. R. Buckminster and Anne (Hewlett) Fuller; m. Robert Snyder, June 30, 1951 (div. Apr. 1975, remarried Sept. 1980); children: Alexandra, Jaime. BA in Dance, Bennington Coll., 1951; MA in Dance, UCLA, 1967. Asst. to curator, dance archives Mus. Modern Art, N.Y.C., 1945-47; dancer Ballet Soc. of N.Y.C. Ballet Co., 1945-47; mem. office and prodn. staff Internat. Film Found., N.Y.C., 1950-52; editor, dance films Film News mag., N.Y.C., 1966-72; lectr. dance and film adv., dept. dance UCLA, 1967-73, chmn. dept. dance, 1974-80, 90-91, acting chair, spring 1985, chair of faculty Sch. of the Arts, 1989-91, prof. dance and dance ethnology, 1973-91, prof. emeritus, 1991—; vis. lectr. Calif. Inst. of Arts, Valencia, 1972; co-dir. dance and TV workshop Am. Dance Fest., Conn. Coll., New London, 1973; dir. NEH summer seminar for coll. tchrs. Asian Performing Arts, 1978, 81; coord. Ethnic Arts Intercoll. Interdisciplinary program, 1974-83, acting chmn., 1986; vis. prof. performance studies NYU, 1982-83; hon. vis. prof. U. Surrey, Guildford, Eng., 1983-84; bd. dirs. Buckminster Fuller Inst.; cons. Thyodia Found., Salt Lake City, 1973-74; mem. dance adv. panel Nat. Endowment Arts, 1968-72, Calif. Arts Commn., 1974-91; mem. adv. screening com. Council Internat. Exchange of Scholars, 1979-82; mem. various panels NEH, 1979-85; mem. adv. bd. Los Angeles Dance Alliance, 1978-84; core cons. for Dancing Sta. WNET-TV, 1988—. Dir. film Baroque Dance 1625-1725, in 1977; co-dir. film Gods of Bali, 1952; dir. and wrote film Bayanihan, 1962 (named Best Folkloric Documentary at Bilboa Film Festival, winner Golden Eagle award); asst. dir. and asst. editor film The Bennington Story, 1952; created films Gestures of Sand, 1968, Reflections on Choreography, 1973, When the Fire Dances Between Two Poles, 1982; created film, video loop and text Celebration: A World of Art and Ritual, 1982-83; supr. post-prodn. film Erick Hawkins, 1964, in 1973. Also contbr. articles to profl. jours. and mags. Adv. com. Pacific Asia Mus., 1980-84, Festival of the Mask, Craft and Folk Art Mus., 1979-84; adv. panel Los Angeles Dance Currents II, Mus. Ctr. Dance Assn., 1974-75; bd. dirs. Council Grove Sch. III, Compton, Calif., 1976-81; apptd. mem. Adv. Dance Com., Pasadena (Calif.) Art Mus., 1970-71, Los Angeles Festival of Performing Arts com., Studio Watts, 1970; mem. Technology and Cultural Transformation com., UNESCO, 1977. Fulbright research fellow, 1983-84; grantee Nat. Endowment Arts, 1981, Nat. Endowment Humanities, 1977, 79, 81, UCLA, 1968, 77, 80, 82, 85. Mem. Am. Dance Therapy Assn., Congress on Research in Dance (bd. dirs. 1970-76, chairperson 1975-77, nat. conf. chair 1972), Council Dance Adminstrs., Am. Dance Guild (chairperson com. awards 1972, Honoree of Yr. 1992), Soc. for Ethnomusicology, Am. Anthropol. Assn., Am. Folklore Soc., Soc. Anthropology of Visual Communication, Soc. Humanistic Anthropology, Calif. Dance Educators Assn. (conf. chair 1972), Los Angeles Area Dance Alliance (adv. bd. 1978-84, selection com. Dance Kaleidoscope project 1979-81), Fulbright Alumni Assn. Home: 15313 Whitfield Ave Pacific Palisades CA 90272-2548 Office: UCLA Dept Dance 124 Dance Bldg Los Angeles CA 90024

SNYDER, GEORGE LEONARD, geologist; b. Kingston, N.Y., Sept. 17, 1927; s. Raymond Tracy and Orpha Hesley (Bishop) S.; m. Margaret Mary Sloan, Sept. 27, 1952; children: Marilee Bishop, Jane M., Sandra Pauline, Daniel George. Student, MIT, 1945; AB, Dartmouth Coll., 1950; MS, U. Chgo., 1952; postgrad., Colo. Sch. Mines, 1977. Geologist U.S. Geol. Survey, Denver, 1949—, chief area pubs. unit, 1962-63; dep. asst. chief geologist U.S. Geol. Survey, Washington, 1967-69; mem. oil shale environ. adv. panel U.S. Geol. Survey, Denver, 1974-75. Author: (with others) Early Precambrian Basic Magmatism, 1990; contbd. articles to profl. jours. With USN, 1945-47. Mem. Colo. Sci. Soc. (hon. life, pres. 1977). Home: 2121 S Allison Ct Denver CO 80227-2407 Office: US Geol Survey Federal Ctr Mail Stop 913 Denver CO 80225

SNYDER, HOWARD ARTHUR, aerospace engineering sciences educator, industrial consultant; b. Palmerton, Pa., Mar. 7, 1930; s. Howard Franklin and Mary Rachel (Landis) S.; m. Nancy Jane Simon, Sept. 14, 1961 (div. Feb. 1975); m. Kaye Elizabeth Bache, Mar. 21, 1975. BS in Physics, Rensselaer Poly. Inst., 1952; MS in Physics, U. Chgo., 1957, PhD in Physics, 1961. From asst. prof. to assoc. prof. Brown U., Providence, 1961-68; prof. aerospace engring. U. Colo., Boulder, 1968—; cons. Storage Tech. Corp., Louisville, Colo., 1980-84, 89-91, Ball Aerospace Systems, Boulder, 1984—, Superconducting Super Collider, 1992—. Contbr. articles to profl. jours. Served to lt. (j.g.) USN, 1948-55. Mem. Am. Phys. Soc. Club: Colo. Mountain (Denver). Home: 251 Gay St Longmont CO 80501-5336 Office: U Colo Dept Aerospace Engring Sci Campus Box 429 Boulder CO 80309

SNYDER, JOHN HENRY, computer science teacher, consultant; b. Wichita, Kans., Mar. 16, 1947; s. Melvin Henry and Cathleen Ann (Collins) S.; m. Patricia Reilly, Mar. 11, 1984; children: Matthew Melvin George, Mark John Joseph. BA, U. Kans., 1970; MS, Nova U., Ft. Lauderdale, Fla., 1984. Cert. tchr. Nev., N.D. Computer sci. tchr. Hyde Park Jr. High Sch., Las Vegas, Nev., 1981-86, Chapparal High sch., Las Vegas, 1986-91, Cimarron Meml. High Sch., Las Vegas, 1991—; copywriter pub. info. office CCSD, Las Vegas, 1982-84; chmn. gifted children spl. interest group, Am. Mensa, 1984; cons. Office Supt. Clark County Sch. Dist., Las Vegas, 1984, 85, IBM Corp., Atlanta, 1991—; systems analyst Holmes & Narver, 1988 (summer); adminstrv. aide EG&G Energy Measurements, Las Vegas, 1989 (summer); adj. instr. computer sci. Nova U., 1984-93, U. Nev. Las Vegas, 1990—, The Meadows Sch., 1991—; bd. dirs. Ctr. for Teaching Resources, The Mazer Corp., N.Y., Akron, Ohio, 1990—. Contbr. articles to profl. jours. Co-chmn. Ednl. Exposition, Las Vegas, 1984; tech. cons. Henry Reid for U.S. Senate, 1986, '92. Named Tchr. of Yr., State of Nev., 1989-90, U. Nev., Las Vegas, Southland Tchr. of Yr., 1990, Tandy Tech. Scholar, 1991, Nev. Educator of Yr., Milken Family Found., 1992; recipient Innovative Teaching award Bus. Week Mag., 1990. Mem. NEA (Instrn. and Profl. Devel. chmn. 1979-80), ASCD, KC (sec., v.p., pres., past pres., local lodge newsletter editor), Am. Legion, Phi Delta Kappa (newsletter editor Overall Excellence award 1990). Democrat. Roman Catholic. Office: Cimmaron Meml High Sch 2301 N Tenaya Way Las Vegas NV 89128

SNYDER, JOHN JOSEPH, optometrist; b. Wonewoc, Wis., June 30, 1908; s. Burt Frederick and Alta Lavinia (Hearn) S.; A.B., UCLA, 1931, postgrad., 1931-32; postgrad. U. Colo., 1936, 38, 40, 41, U. So. Calif., 1945-46; B.S. in Optometry, Los Angeles Coll. Optometry, 1948, O.D., 1949. Tchr., La Plata County (Colo.) Pub. Schs., 1927-28; supt. Marvel (Colo.) Pub. Schs., 1932-33; tchr. Durango (Colo.) High Sch., 1933-41; pvt. practice optometry, Los Angeles, 1952-72, Torrance, Calif., 1972-78; now retired. Former bd. dirs. Francis Boys' Club, Los Angeles; former pres. Exchange Club South Los Angeles, also sec. Mem. AAAS, Am. Inst. Biol. Scis., Am., Calif., Los Angeles County Optometric Assn., Internat. Biog. Assn. Republican. Home: 25937 Reynolds St Loma Linda CA 92354-3962

SNYDER, JUDITH ARMSTRONG, dean; b. Washington, Nov. 11, 1946; d. John Bertram and Agnes (Winning) Armstrong; m. Ralph A. Snyder, Oct. 28, 1972 (div. Nov. 1981). AB, U. Calif., Berkeley, 1968, PhD, 1972. Teaching assoc. U. Calif., Berkeley, 1969-72; post-doctoral U. Colo., Boulder, 1973-78; asst. prof. Denver U., 1978-83, assoc. prof., 1983-89, prof., 1989—, dean of the coll., 1989-93; bd. dirs. Phycotech, Inc., Boulder, 1983-89. Contbr. articles profl. jours. Bd. dirs. Am. Cancer Soc., Denver, 1988—. Mem. Am. Assn. Cell Biology (mem. edn. com. 1987-89), Phi Beta Kappa. Office: U Denver Dept Biological Scis Denver CO 80210

SNYDER, KAREN LEE, graphics executive; b. Rockford, Ill., May 8, 1946; d. William F. and Leatrice Joyce (Atz) Highbarger; m. James Lewis Snyder, July 11, 1964; children: Brent, Shelley. Grad. high sch., Rockford. Sec. Rockford (Ill.) Med. Clinic, 1963-69; sch. bus driver Jelco, Rockford, 1974-80; office mgr. Rockford Access Mobilization Project for Disabled, 1980-81; advocate For Disabled Ill., Rockford, 1980-82; office mgr. Sun Tribune/Rancho News, Lake Elsinore, Calif., 1984-87; adminstrv. asst. Realty World Lake Elsinore Valley, 1987-88; owner Just Your Type, Lake Elsinore, 1988—; pub. relations dir. Rockford Deaf Awareness, 1981-82; exec. dir. Mt. San Jacinto (Calif.) Coll. Found., 1989—. Active Rights for the Handicapped Coalition, Ill., 1981, Planning Commn. for the Developmentally Disabled, Ill., 1981; commr. Riverside County Commn. on the Status of Women, Riverside, 1984-85, various local campaigns; bd. dirs. United Cerebral Palsy Inland Empire. Grantee State of Ill. Disabled Program, Springfield, 1981. Office: Just Your Type 150 N Pennsylvania St Lake Elsinore CA 92530-1823

SNYDER, MARTIN BRADFORD, mechanical engineering educator; b. Evergreen Park, Ill., Dec. 19, 1942; s. Bernard A. and Helena M. (Piro) S. BS in Physics, MIT, 1964; PhD in Nuclear Engring., Northwestern U., 1972; PhD in Bioengring., U. Mich., 1985. Presdl. intern Argonne Nat. Lab., Chgo., 1972-73; staff engr. Sargent and Lundy Co., Chgo., 1973-74; Parker B. Francis fellow U. Fla., Gainesville, 1979-81; vis. scholar U. Mich., Ann Arbor, 1981-82, asst. rsch. scientist Sch. Medicine, 1984-85; biomed. engr. VA Hosp., Ann Arbor, 1982-84; assoc. prof. dept. mech. engring. U. Nev., Reno, 1985—. Contbr. articles on nuclear engring., physiology and mech. engring. to profl. publs. Sci. tchr. U.S. Peace Corps, India, 1965-67. NSF fellow, 1971; recipient Mark Mills award Am. Nuclear Soc., 1973; NIH trainee, 1975; rsch. fellow Whitaker Found., 1985. Mem. Am. Phys. Soc. Office: Dept Mech Engring Univ Nev Reno Reno NV 89557

SNYDER, RICHARD GERALD, research scientist, administrator, educator, consultant; b. Northampton, Mass., Feb. 14, 1928; s. Grant B. and Ruth (Putnam) S.; m. Phoebe Jones, Mar. 2, 1949; children: Dorinda, Sherrill, Paul, Jeff, Jon, David. Student Amherst Coll., 1946-48; BA, U. Ariz., 1956, MA, 1957, PhD, 1959. Diplomate Am. Bd. Forensic Anthropology. Teaching asst. dept. anthropology U. Ariz., Tucson, 1957-58, assoc. rsch. engr. Applied Rsch. Lab., Coll. Engring., 1958-60, mem. staff Ariz. Transp. and Traffic Inst., 1959-60, assoc. prof. systems engring., 1960; chief phys. anthropology Civil Aeromed. Rsch. Inst., FAA, Oklahoma City, 1960-66, rsch. pilot, 1962-66, acting chief Protection and Survival Labs., 1963-66; mgr. biomechanics dept. Office of Automotive Safety Rsch., Ford Motor Co., Dearborn, Mich., 1966-68, prin. rsch. scientist, 1968; assoc. prof. anthropology U. Mich., Ann Arbor, 1968-73, prof., 1973-85 , rsch. scientist Hwy. Safety Rsch. Inst., 1968-85, head biomed. dept., 1969-84, dir. NASA Ctr. of Excellence in Man-Vehicle Systems, 1984-85, prof. emeritus, 1985—, rsch. scientist emeritus, 1989—; pres. Biodynamics Internat., Tucson, Ariz., 1986—; pres. George Snively Rsch. Found., 1992—; adj. assoc. prof. U. Okla., 1963; rsch. assoc. Zoller Lab. U. Chgo., 1964-65, rsch. assoc. dept. anthropology, 1965-67; assoc. prof. Mich. State U., East Lansing, 1967-68; cons. USAF Aerospace Med. Rsch. Labs., Nat. Acad. Scis., U.S. Dept. Transp., adv. com. Office Naval Rsch. Dept. Navy, numerous others. Assoc. editor: Jour. of Communication, 1961-63; cons. editor: Jour. of Biomechanics, 1967-81; editorial bd. Product Safety News, 1973—; adv. bd. Aviation Space and Environ. Medicine, 1980-91; contbr. chpts. to books and numerous articles to profl. jours. Judge, Internat. Sci. Fair, Detroit. 1968; mem. coun. Explorer Scouts, Ann Arbor, 1968-70; dir. Am. Bd. Forensic Anthropology, 1978-84, 85-91; dir. Snell Meml. Found., 1990—; dir. George Snively Rsch. Found., 1992—. 1st lt. USAF, 1949-54, Korea. Recipient Met. Life award, Nat. Safety Coun., 1970; Arch T. Colwell Merit award, Soc. Automotive Engrs., 1973; Award for Profl. Excellence Aerospace Med.

Assn., 1978; Admiral Luis de Flores Flight Safety award, Flight Safety Found., 1981; named to Safety and Health Hall of Fame Internat., 1993. Fellow Aerospace Med. Assn., Royal Anthrop. Inst., AAAS, Am. Anthropl. Assn., Am. Acad. Forensic Scis. (T. Dale Stewart award 1992), AIAA (assoc.); mem. Am. Assn. Phys. Anthropologists, Ariz.-Nev. Acad. Sci., Survival and Equipment Assn., Assn. Aviation Psychologists, Soc. Automotive Engrs. (Aerospace Congress award 1982, Tech. contributions to Air Transport Safety), Internat. Soc. Aircraft Safety Investigators, Am. Assn. Automotive Medicine, Aerospace Physiologists Soc., Sigma Xi, Beta Beta Beta. Republican. Congregationalist. Avocations: aviation, aerospace medicine, forensic anthropology. Home: 3720 N Silver Dr Tucson AZ 85749-9709 Office: Biodynamics Internat Tucson AZ 85749

SNYDER, ROBERT MICHAEL, chess trainer; b. L.A., May 4, 1954; s. Alan Charles and Cecilia Ruth (Perea) S. AA in Bus., Santa Ana Coll., 1975; BA in Geography, Calif. State U., Long Beach, 1977. Cert. coll. tchr., Calif. Chess instr. Santa Ana (Calif.) Coll., 1972-80, Calif. U., Long Beach, 1977-78; chess dir. Boys Clubs Am., Placentia, Calif., 1984—; chess columnist Register Newspaper, Santa Ana, 1979-81; writer, columnist U.S. Chess Fedn., New Windsor, N.Y., 1981-84; dir., trainer Chess for Jrs., Garden Grove, Calif., 1983—; bd. dirs. Orange County Chess Assn., Buena Park, Calif., 1974—; chess instr. Long Beach (Calif.) Recreation Dept., 1984—, Gardena (Calif.) Recreation Dept., 1988—; mem. U.S. Olympic Chess Team Internat. Corr. Chess Fedn. 1977. Author: Snyder Sicilian, 1984, Chess for Juniors, 1991; producer, host Chess with Robert Snyder, 1982, Chess for Juniors, 1989. Named Nat. Chess Master, 1973, chess co-champion We. U.S., 1973, Orange County Chess Champion, 1974, So. Calif. High Sch. Chess Champion, 1972. Mem. U.S. Chess Fedn., Anaheim Chess Club, Orange County Chess Assn. Home: 14282 Jessica St Garden Grove CA 92643-5037 Office: Chess for Juniors 10090 Westminster Ave Garden Grove CA 92643-4721

SNYDER, WILLIAM HARRY, financial advisor; b. Newport, Pa., May 11, 1934; s. William Harry and Mary (Barner) S.; m. Irvil Kear, June, 1956 (div. 1961); 1 child, Geoffrey W.; m. Sandra Elizabeth Wolff, June 25, 1966; 1 child, Tara Elizabeth. BS in Indsl. Engring., Lehigh U., 1956; MS in Applied Stats., Rutgers U., 1961. Cert. fin. planner. Research engr. Johns-Manville Corp., Manville, N.J., 1956-61; indsl. engr., mgr. services and quality control Johns-Manville Corp., Nashua, N.H., 1961-69; mgr. phys. distbn. Johns-Manville Corp., N.Y.C., 1969-72; mgr. div. and corp. planning. Johns-Manville Corp., Denver, 1972-82; dir. corp. devel. Manville Corp. (formerly Johns-Manville Corp.), Denver, 1982-85; prin. Snyder Fin. Services, Littleton, Colo., 1985—; bd. dirs. Manville Employees Fed. Credit Union, Denver, 1985-88; sec., founding mem. Manville Retirees Assn., 1992—. Patentee process for making chalkboard; author: (with others) Standard Handbook of Plant Engineering, 1983. Vol. AARP Tax Coun. Program for the Elderly, 1987—. Served as 2d lt. U.S. Army, 1957-58. Mem. Colo. Soc. of Cert. Fin. Planners, Inst. of Cert. Fin. Planners, Pi Kappa Alpha (pres. 1954-55). Republican. Methodist. Lodge: Mason. Home and Office: Snyder Fin Svcs 1952 W Ridge Rd Littleton CO 80120-3139

SNYDER, WILLIAM REGIS, JR., construction company executive; b. Pitts., Mar. 14, 1954; s. William R. Sr. and Laverne V. (Krebs) S.; m. Nancy Mary Meglio, May 31, 1980; children: Sarah Elizabeth, William Joseph, Kathryn Lee. Student, U. Pitts., Pa. State U., McKeesport, Mesa Community Coll. Checker Three Rivers Drafting Co., Pitts., 1973-75; estimator, project mgr. Plasteel Products, Washington, Pa., 1975-77; draftsman Siciliano Interiors, Pitts., 1977-78; engineered inside salesman Steelite, Inc., Pitts., 1978-80; assoc. Ariz. Joist & Deck Co., Scottsdale, 1980-82; sales mgr. George D. Widman, Inc., Gardena, Calif., 1982-83, mgr. Ariz. ops., 1983-84; pres. WRS & Assocs., Inc., Tempe, Ariz., 1984—. Mem. Constrn. News West. Office: WRS & Assocs Inc PO Box 24664 Tempe AZ 85285-4664

SOBEK, IRVIN GENE, consulting engineer, sales engineer, farmer; b. Cheney, Wash., Apr. 24, 1934; s. Louie and Lena (Schmitt) S.; m. Mary Elizabeth Cottles, Dec. 28, 1958; children: Craig Allen, Julie Ann. BS in Agr., Washington State Coll., 1957; BS in Agrl. Engring., Wash. State U., 1962. Exptl. aide agrl. engring. dept. Wash. State U., Pullman, 1959-61; agrl. engr. Gen. Food Corp., Walla Walla, Wash., 1962-66; plant engr. Gen. Food Corp., Nampa, Wash., 1966-70; plant engr. Gen. Food Corp., Walla Walla, Wash., 1970-73, prodn. supr., 1973-74, corp. project constrn. engr., 1974-75; farmer Edwall, Wash., 1975—; cons. engr. Edwall, 1977—, sales engr., 1988. Mem. alumni bd. Agrl. Coll. Wash. State U., Pullman, 1980-90; bd. dirs., pres. Edwall Grain Growers Inc., 1978-87; bd. dirs. United Grain Grower Inc., Harrington, Wash., 1987-89. With U.S. Army, 1957-59. Mem. Am. Soc. Agrl. Engrs., Washington State Grange, Lions, Alpha Zeta. Methodist. Home: RR 1 Box 7 Edwall WA 99008-9703

SOBON, LEON EDWARD, vintner, consultant; b. Lackawanna, N.Y., Aug. 11, 1934; s. Edward Stanley and Alexandra Marie (Woyshner) S.; m. Shirley Elaine Shangeniuk, June 20, 1959; children: David, Caroline, Paul, Elaine, Robert, Kenneth,. BS in Ceramic Engring., Alfred U., 1958. Ceramic engr. Stanford Rsch. Inst., Menlo Park, Calif., 1958-61; sr. scientist Gen. Telephone, Mountain View, Calif., 1961-63; rsch. chemist Hewlett-Packard, Palo Alto, Calif., 1963-65; sr. scientist Lockheed Missles & Space Co., Palo Alto, 1965-77; owner, winemaker Shenandoah Vineyards, Plymouth, Calif., 1977—, Sobon Estate, Plymouth, Calif., 1990—; dir. Wine Inst., San Francisco, 1991—. Contbr. articles to profl. jours.; patentee in scientific field. Mem. Am. Soc. Viticulture and Enology, Amador Vintners Assn. (pres. 1986-88, v.p. 1991-93), Sierra Foothill Winery Assn. (pres. 1982-86), Amador County C. of C. (dir. 1987-89). Home and Office: 12300 Steiner Rd Plymouth CA 95669

SOCHA, DOUGLAS DAVID, computer systems analyst; b. San Bernardino, Calif., Jan. 27, 1960; s. Daniel John and Patricia Marguerite (Jankowski) S.; m. Shan Suzanne Ames, Mar. 12, 1988. AS, San Bernardino Valley Coll., 1982; BS in Computer Sci. cum laude, Calif. State Polytech. U., 1985; postgrad., Torrey Bible Inst., 1991—. Cook McDonald's Rest. Corp., Redlands, Calif., 1978-80; tutor, pvt. practice Redlands, Pomona, Calif.; counselor Camp Yollijwa, Oak Glenn, Calif.; firefighter, stonemason Calif. Conservation Corps, Del Norte County, Calif., 1980-81; asst. lab. technician Calif. State Polytech. U., Pomona, Calif., 1984; subst. tchr. Ontario-Montclair Sch. Dist., Ontario, Calif., 1985; instr. English lang. ASA Community Salon, TOEIC Tng. Ctr., Tokyo, 1985-87; computer programmer Alta-Dena Dairy, Industry, Calif., 1987-89; computer systems analyst Mission Foods Corp., L.A., 1989—; computer cons. Scholarship Resource Ctr. Mentone, Calif., 1991. Teens backpack leader Ch. of the Nazarene, Redlans, 1981-83; mem. Olympic Choir 23d Olympiad, L.A., 1984; Sunday sch. tchr. Kurume Bible Fellowship, Higashi-Kurume, Japan, 1986; counselor, tchr. Camp Wynolla, Julian, Calif., 1990-92. Lions Club scholar, 1977; recipient Writing award Photojournalism Club, Morongo Unified Sch. Dist., 1977. Mem. Ch. of the Open Door (class treas., 1992), Calif. Scholarship Fedn. (life), Inter-Varsity Christian Fellowship (chpt. pres. 1984-85), Olympic Alumni Orgn., Golden Key. Evangelical Christian. Office: Mission Foods Corp 5750 Grace Pl Los Angeles CA 90022

SOCHACKI, ANDRZEJ, mechanical engineer, researcher; b. Warsaw, Poland, July 26, 1948; came to U.S., 1973; s. Jerzy and Halina (Błażejczyk) S. MS, Tech. Acad., Warsaw, 1969; AAS, Maricopa Tech. Coll., Phoenix, 1983. Sr. mech. engr. Roger Bus. Products div. Rogers Corp., Mesa, Ariz., 1986-87; sr. mech. design engr. Parker Aerospace Co., Phoenix, 1987-88; sr. project engr. Micro-Rel Inc., Tempe, Ariz., 1988-90; cons., project engr., pres., owner Design & Fabricating Co., Phoenix, 1985—; founder, pres., chmn. The Vagabond Ctr., Phoenix. Pres. Vagabond Ctr. Found., 1992. Recipient award Medtronic Corp., Phoenix, 1989. Mem. Soc. Mfg. Engrs. (sr.). Roman Catholic. Home and Office: The Vagabond Ctr 3715 E Taylor St Phoenix AZ 85008

SODEN, DALE EDWARD, historian, educator; b. Spokane, Wash., May 4, 1951; s. Dale Arthur and Margaret (Priestley) S.; m. Margaret Ann Kringen, Dec. 29, 1974; children: Joel, Marta. BA in History, Pacific Luth. U., 1973; MA, U. Wash., 1976, PhD, 1980. Instr. Pacific Luth. U., Tacoma, Wash., 1978-80; asst. prof. Okla. Bapt. U., Shawnee, 1980-85; assoc. prof. Whitworth Coll., Spokane, 1985—, dir. continuing studies, 1988—. Author: History of Whitworth College, 1990; contbr. articles to profl. jours. Bd. dirs. YMCA, Spokane, 1990—, Spokane Christian Coalition, 1986—, Project Self Sufficiency, Spokane, 1989-91; active St. Mark's Luth. Ch. Mem. Ea. Wash. Hist. Soc. (com. mem.). Home: W 1012 28th Ave Spokane WA 99203 Office: Whitworth Coll Dept History Spokane WA 99251

SODEN, RUTH M., geriatrics nurse, educator; b. Tipton, Iowa, Nov. 29, 1940; d. Tony and Clarissa Arlene (Beall) Koreman; m. James D. Soden; children: Shannon, Scott, Suzan, Staci. AA, Highline Community Coll., Midway, Wash. Cert. in intravenous therapy. Charge nurse Wildwood Health Care Ctr., Puyallup, Wash.; admissions coord. Forestglen Nursing Ctr., Seattle, staff devel. dir.; charge nurse Green River Terrace Nursing Ctr., Auburn, Wash.; unit coord. Tacoma Luth. Home; mem. Clover Park Tech. Coll., Tacoma. Mem. Nat. Gerontol. Nursing Assn. (practical nurse program adv. com.), Wash. State Nurses Assn., Assn. for Practitioners in Infection Control, Nat. Coun. on Family Rels., Phi Theta Kappa. Home: 25650 29th Ave S Kent WA 98032-5532

SOELBERG, BARBARA JOYCE, accountant; b. Tucson, Oct. 16, 1963; d. William Ray and Ellen Bernice (Mills) Parslow; m. Mark Budge Soelberg, Sept. 6, 1985; children: Andrew Mark, Matthew William. AAS, Ricks Coll., 1984; BS in Acctg., Utah State U., 1986. CPA. Sr. acct. Deloitte & Touche, Salt Lake City, 1986-91; pvt. practice Farmington, Utah, 1991—. Mem. AICPA, Utah Assn. CPA. Republican. Mem. LDS Ch. Home and Office: 172 N 100 E Farmington UT 84025-3524

SOELDNER, JOHN STUART, physician, educator; b. Boston, Sept. 22, 1932; s. Frank and Mary Amelia (Stuart) S.; m. Elsie Irene Harnish, Aug. 25, 1962; children: Judith Marie, Elizabeth Anne, Stephen J.D. BS magna cum laude, Tufts U., 1954; Dr.med., Dalhousie U., Halifax, N.S., 1959. Diplomate Am. Bd. Med. Examiners; lic. Med. Coun. Can. Intern then resident Victoria Gen. Hosp., Halifax, 1958-61; from instr. medicine to assoc. prof. medicine Harvard U., Boston, 1964-87; prof. medicine Davis Med. Ctr. U. Calif., Sacramento, 1987—. Contbr. 300 articles to sci. publs.; patentee in field. Founding mem. med. bd. Juvenile Diabetes Found., N.Y.C. Recipient Sci. award Juvenile Diabetes Found., 1973, U.S. Sr. Scientist award Von Humboldt Found., 1975; fellow Dalhousie U., 1959-60, Harvard Med. Sch., 1961-63, Pfizer traveling fellow, 1973. Mem. Am. Physol. Soc., Am. Soc. Clin. Investigation, Am. Diabetes Assn. (profl. edn. com. 1975-81, 83-85, bd. dirs. 1982-85, Calif. affiliate bd. dirs. 1989—), Columbian Assn. Internal Medicine (corr.), New Eng. Diabetes Assn., Am. Fedn. Clin. Rsch., European Assn. Study of Diabetes, Endocrine Soc., Soc. Exptl. Biology and Medicine, Assn. Advancement Med. Instrumentation, Am. Soc. Artificial Internal Organs, Internat. Soc. Artificial Organs, Dalhousie Med. Alumni Assn. (bd. dirs. Can. 1977). Democrat. Roman Catholic. Office: Diabetes Clin Rsch Unit 1625 Alhambra Blvd Ste 2901 Sacramento CA 95816-7051

SOFFER, PHILIP J., technical writer; b. N.Y.C., Feb. 19, 1954; s. Paul and Florence (Hoffman) S.; m. Asuncion Ramos, Nov. 16, 1986; 1 child, Jessica Shannon. BS, Southwest U., New Orleans; MS, NRI Inst., Washington. Pres. Barrets Schs. Inc., N.Y.C., 1980-85; ind. tech. writer Chatsworth, Calif., 1985—; lectr. in field. Author: Robotics, 1988; contbr. articles to profl. jours. Mem. San Fernando Bd. Realtors, Calif. Assn. Realtors, Nat. Assn. Realtors. Home: 21735 Wahoo Trl Chatsworth CA 91311-1425

SOFIN, H. JONARDEN S. (JON SOFIAN), analyst, environmental engineer, consultant; b. Northern Sumatra, Indonesia, Jan. 23, 1958; came to U.S., 1968; s. Kosen Sofin and Lusia Tanilla. BS in Math., Calif. State U., Long Beach, 1976; BS in EE, West Coast U., Orange, Calif., 1981; MS in Fin. Mgmt., So. State U., Huntington Beach, Calif., 1992. Registered environ. assessor. Mem. tech. staff Rockwell Internat., Anaheim, Calif., 1984-91; rsch. scientist/engr. Teledyne Systems Co., Northridge, Calif., 1991—; bd. dirs. G-Investments Internat., Inc., Corona, Calif. Office: G Investments Internat 1099 Salinas Ave # 1A Costa Mesa CA 92626

SOFOS, STEPHANY LOUISE, real estate executive; b. Honolulu, Sept. 16, 1954; d. Thomas A. and Catherine B. (Seros) S. BA in History, U. Hawaii, 1976. Assoc. Chaney Brooks Realty, Inc., Honolulu, 1976-77; supr. property/mgr. shopping ctr. Hawaii Mgmt. Corp., Honolulu, 1977-79; mgr. mktg. and customer relations Kaiser Devel. Co., Honolulu, 1979-82; gen. mgr. Kuhio Mall, Honolulu, 1982-86; pres. SL Sofos and Co., Ltd., Honolulu, 1986—. Mem. Nat. Assn. Realtors, Inst. Real Estate Mgmt. (cert. property mgr., bd. dirs. Hawaii chpt. 1987), Internat. Coun. Shopping Ctrs. (cert. shopping ctr. mgr.), Bldg. Owners and Mgrs. Assn. (real property adminstr.). Greek Orthodox. Clubs: Honolulu, Outrigger Canoe, Oahu Country (Honolulu). Office: 770 Kapiolani Blvd Ste 605 Honolulu HI 96813-5240

SOHMER, STEVE, writer, producer. Grad., Yale U., 1963. Doubleday Fellow in creative writing Columbia U.; v.p. advt., promotion CBS, 1987-82; v.p. advt., creative svcs. NBC, 1982-84, exec. v.p., 1984-85; pres., COO COLUMBIA Pictures, 1985-87; pres. Steve Sohmer Inc., 1987-89; pres. CEO Nelson TV, 1989—. Author: (short story) The Way It Was, 1966, (novels) Favorite Son, 1987, Patriots, 1991; co-exec. producer (film) Leonard Part 6, 1987; producer (TV series) Mancuso FBI. Office: care NBC Productions 3000 W Alameda Ave Burbank CA 91523-0001*

SOHNEN-MOE, CHERIE MARILYN, business consultant; b. Tucson, Jan. 2, 1956; d. D. Ralph and Angelina Helen (Spiro) Sohnen; m. James Madison Moe, Jr., May 23, 1981. BA, UCLA, 1977. Rsch. asst. UCLA, 1975-77; ind. cons. L.A., 1978-83; cons. Sohnen-Moe Assocs., Tucson, 1984—. Author: Business Mastery, 1988, 2d edit., 1991; contbr. Compendium mag., 1987-90, Massage Mag., 1992—, (jour.) Am. Massage Therapy Assn., 1989—. Vol. Am. Cancer Soc., Tucson, 1984—; mem. Ariz. Sonora Desert Mus., Tucson; pres. Women in Tucson, 1989. Recipient Outstanding Instr. award Desert Inst. of Healing Arts, 1992. Mem. NOW, NAFE, ASTD (dir. mem. svcs. 1988, Achievement award 1987, Disting. Svc. award 1988), Pub.s Mktg. Assn., New Age Pub. and Retailing Alliance, Sierra Club, COSMEP, Women in Tucson. Office: Sohnen-Moe Assocs 3906 W Ina Rd # 200-348 Tucson AZ 85741-2295

SOKKAPPA, PRABHU MARCOS, lawyer; b. Seattle, Nov. 13, 1958; s. Balraj Ghana and Betty Lorraine S.; m. Kitty Fan, Nov. 13, 1989; 1 child, Cody Fan. BA in Polit. Sci., Grinnell Coll., 1980; JD, U. Mont., 1983. Bar: Mont., Alaska. Staff atty. Mont. Legal Svcs., Warm Springs, 1983-85; clk. Hotel Weisses Kreuz, Grindelwald, Switzerland, 1987-88; prof. Taiwan Army Acad., Fungsan, 1989-90; staff atty. Alaska Legal Svcs., Kotzebue, 1990-91, Juneau, 1991—. Contbr. articles to profl. jours. Bd. dirs. AWARE Group Home, Anaconda, Mont., 1984-85, Big Bros./Sisters, Anaconda, 1985; vol. Poverello Ctr., Missoula, Mont., 1980; organizer Mont. Pub. Interest Rsch. Group, Missoula, 1980-85. Reginald Heber Smith fellow Howard U., Washington, 1983-85. Mem. Alaska Bar Assn., Mont. Bar Assn., Juneau Bar Assn., Juneau Human Rights Commn. Democrat. Home: PO Box 22819 Juneau AK 99802 Office: Alaska Legal Svcs 419 6th St Ste 322 Juneau AK 99801

SOKOL, LARRY NIDES, lawyer, educator; b. Dayton, Ohio, Sept. 28, 1946; s. Boris Franklin and Kathryn (Konowitch) S.; m. Beverly Butler, Aug. 3, 1975; children: Addie Teller, Maxwell Philip. BA, U. Pa., 1968; JD, Case Western Res. U., 1971. Bar: Oreg. 1972, U.S. Dist Ct. Oreg. 1972, U.S. Ct. Appeals (9th cir.) 1973, U.S. Supreme Ct. 1980. Law clk. chief judge Oreg. Ct. Appeals, Salem, 1971-72; pvt. practice Portland, Oreg., 1972—; prof. law Lewis and Clark Law Sch., Portland; adj. prof. law sch. environ. litigation Lewis & Clark U., 1984—. Commr. planning City of Lake Oswego, Oreg., 1981-84. Sgt. USAR, 1968-74. Mem. Oreg. State Bar Assn. (chmn. litigation sect. 1983, disciplinary rev. bd. 1982-85), Oreg. Trial Lawyers Assn. Democrat. Jewish. Office: 721 SW Oak St Portland OR 97205-3712

SOKOLOFF, ALEXANDER DIMITROVITCH, biology educator; b. Tokyo, Japan, May 16, 1920; came to U.S., 1938; s. Dimitri Fyodorovitch and Sofia Alexandrovna (Solovieff) S.; m. Barbara B. Bryant, June 24, 1956; children: Alexandra, Elaine A., Michael A. AA, UCLA, 1942, AB, 1948; PhD, U. Chgo., 1954. Instr. Hofstra U., L.I., N.Y., 1955-56, asst. prof., 1956-58; geneticist W.H. Miner Agrl. Research Inst., Chazy, N.Y., 1958-60; assoc. research botanist UCLA, 1960; assoc. research geneticist U. Calif., Berkeley, 1961-66, research geneticist, 1966-68; assoc. prof. Calif. State U., San Bernardino, 1965-66, prof. biology, 1966—, prof. emeritus, 1990—. Author: Genetics of Tribolium, 1966, The Biology of Tribolium, vol. 1., 1972, vo. 2, 1975, vol. 3, 1977; mem. editorial bd.: Jour. Stored Product Research, 1965—; assoc. editor: Evolution, 1972-74, Jour. Advanced Zoology, 1980—; editor Tribolium Info. Bull., 1960—. Served to sgt. USAAF, 1942-46. Research grantee USPHS, 1961, NSF, 1957-59, 67-69, 69-71, 71-73, Army Research Office 1973-76, 79. Fellow Royal Entomol. Soc. of London; mem. Soc. Study of Evolution, Genetics Soc. Am., Am. Genetic Assn., Am. Soc. Naturalists, Am. Soc. Zoologists, Genetics Soc. Can., Japanese Soc. Population Ecology, Entomol. Soc. Am., Sigma Xi. Democrat. Lodge: Elks. Home: 3324 Sepulveda Ave San Bernardino CA 92404-2218 Office: Calif State U 5500 University Pky San Bernardino CA 92407-2318

SOKOLOV, JACQUE JENNING, health care executive, nuclear cardiologist; b. L.A., Sept. 13, 1954; s. Albert I. and Frances (Burgess) S. BA in Medicine magna cum laude, U. So. Calif., 1974, MD with hons., 1978; postgrad., Mayo Clinic, Rochester, Minn., 1978-81, U. Tex., Dallas, 1981-83. Med. diplomate. Cardiologist, nuclear cardiologist Health Sci. Ctr. U. Tex., 1981-84; chief med. officer Baylor Ctr. for Health Promotion Wellness & Lifestyle Corp., Dallas, 1985-87; v.p., dir. health care dept., corp. med. dir. So. Calif. Edison Co., Rosemead, Calif., 1987-92; pres. Sokolov Strategic Alliance, L.A., 1992—; cons. Health Care Strategic Planning Southwestern Bell, AT&T, Wang, Rosewood Corp., Dallas, 1985-87; bd. dirs. Calif. Health Decisions. Contbr. to articles in profl. jours. Tech. advisor Coun. Social Security; bd. dirs. Washington Bus. Group Health. Grantee NIH, Bethesda, Md., 1983. Office: Ste 1300 10100 Santa Monica Blvd Los Angeles CA 90067

SOLANO, NANCY VOGT, chemist; b. Buffalo, Jan. 16, 1958; d. Arthur Charles and Carol (Ford) Vogt; m. Romeo I. Solano, Aug. 7, 1982; children: Dawn M., Ryan R. BS in Chemistry, Baldwin-Wallace Coll., 1980. Toxicologist Cuyahoga County Coroner's Office, Cleve., 1980-84; med. tech. Roche Biomed. Lab., Inc., Highland Heights, Ohio, 1984-86, Cleve. Clinic Found., 1986-89, South Bend Med. Found., 1989-90; devel. scientist Miles, Inc., Elkhart, Ind., 1990-91; mgr. R&D Utak Labs., Inc., Canyon Country, Calif., 1992—. Mem. AAAS, Am. Chem. Soc., Am. Assc. Clin. Chemistry. Home: 27350 Blueridge Dr Valencia CA 91354-1906 Office: Utak Labs Inc Ste J 26752 Oak Ave Canyon Country CA 91351

SOLDNER, PAUL EDMUND, ceramist, educator; b. Summerfield, Ill.; s. Grover and Beulah (Geiger) S.; m. Virginia I. Geiger, June 15, 1947; 1 child, Stephanie. BA, Bluffton Coll., 1946; MA, U. Colo., 1954; MFA, L.A. County Art Inst., 1956; DFA (hon.), Westminster Coll., 1992. Tchr. art Medina (Ohio) County Schs., 1946-47; supr. art, asst. county supr. Wayne County Schs., Wooster, Ohio, 1951-54; tchr. adult edn. Wooster Coll., 1952-54; vis. asst. prof. ceramics Scripps Coll., 1957-66, prof., 1970-91, prof. emeritus, 1991—; prof. Claremont (Calif.) Grad. Sch., 1957-66, prof., 1970-92; prof. U. Colo., Boulder, 1966-67, U. Iowa, Iowa City, 1967-68; pres. Soldner Pottery Equipment, Inc., Aspen, Colo., 1956-77; mem. steering com. Internat. Sch. Ceramics, Rome, 1965-77; advisor Vols. for Internat. Assistance, Balt., 1966-75; craftsman, trustee Am. Craft Coun., N.Y.C., 1970-74, trustee emeritus, 1976-77; dir. U.S. sect. World Craft Coun., 1970-74; dir. Anderson Ranch Ctr. for Hand Art Sch., 1974-76; speaker 6th Internat. Ceramics Symposium Syracuse, 1989; participant Internat. Russian Artists Exchange Program, Riga, Latvia, 1989; cons. in field. Author: Kilns and Their Construction, 1965, Raku, 1964, Paul Soldner, A Retrospective View, 1991; contbr. articles to profl. jours.; subject of 5 films; 156 one-man shows including Cantini Mus. Modern Art, Marseille, France, 1981, Thomas Segal Gallery, Boston, 1982, Elements Gallery, N.Y., 1983, Louis Newman Gallery, L.A., 1985, Susan Cummins Gallery, Mill Valley, Calif., 1989, Great Am. Gallery, Atlanta, 1986, Patricia Moore Gallery, Aspen Colo., 1987, Coleg Prifysgol Cymru, Aberystwyth, Wales, 1987, Joan Hodgell Gallery, Sarasota, Fla., 1988, Esther Saks Gallery, Chgo., 1986, 88, El Camino Gallery Art, Toraance, Calif., 1987, San Antonio Art Ctr., San Angelo, Tex., 1988, traveling exhibit, 12 U.S. mus., 1992—; 335 group shows including Nelson-Atkins Mus., Kansas City, Mo., 1983, Los Angeles Mcpl. Art Gallery, 1984, 27th Ceramic Nat. Exhibition, Everson Mus. Art, Syracuse, N.Y., 1986, Victoria & Albert Mus., London, 1986, Chicago Internat. New Art Forms Exposition, 1986, Hanover Gallery, Syracuse, N.Y., 1987, L.A. County Mus. of Art, 1987, Crain/Wolov Gallery, Tulsa, 1987, Contem Crafts Gallery, Portland, Oreg., 1988, Oakland (Calif.) Art Mus., 1988, Munson Gallery, Santa Fe, 1988, Japanese Influence on Am. Ceramics, Everson Mus., Syracuse, N.Y., 1989; works in permanent collections, Nat. Mus. Modern Art, Kyoto, Japan, Victoria and Albert Mus., London, Smithsonian Instn., Washington, Los Angeles County Mus. Art, Oakland Art Mus., Everson Mus. Art, Syracuse Australian Nat. Gallery, Taipei Fine Arts Mus.; curator Mirror Images Exhibit, Craft Alliance Gallery, St. Louis, 1989. Served with U.S. Army, 1941-46. Decorated Purple Heart; grantee NEA, 1991, Louis Comfort Tiffany Found., 1966, 72, Nat. Endowment for Arts, 1976, Colo. Gov.'s award for the Arts & Humanities, 1975; voted one of Top Twelve Potters World-Wide, Ceramics Monthly mag., 1981; Scripps Coll. Faculty Recognition award, 1985; named Hon. Mem. Coun., Nat. Coun. on Edn. for Ceramic Arts, 1989. Fellow Collequim of Craftsmen of the U.S.; mem. Internat. Acad. Ceramics, Nat. Coun. on Edn. for Ceramic Arts. Home: PO Box 90 Aspen CO 81612-0090

SOLERI, PAOLO, architect, urban planner; b. Turin, Italy, June 21, 1919; came to U.S., 1947; m. Corolyn Woods, 1949 (dec. 1982); children: Kristine, Daniela. D.Arch., Turin Poly., 1946; hon. doctorates, Dickinson Coll., Moore Coll. Art, Ariz. State U. Fellowship with Frank Lloyd Wright, Taliesin West, Ariz., 1947-49; pvt. practice Turin and So., Italy, 1950-55; founder Cosanti Found., Scottsdale, Ariz. Major works include Dome House, Cave Creek, Ariz., 1949, Earth House, Scottsdale, Ariz., 1956, Mesa City project, 1958-61, Outdoor Theatre, Inst. Am. Indian Arts, Santa Fe, 1966, Arcosanti (community for 5,000 people), nr. Cordes Junction, Ariz., 1970—, Minds for History Inst., 1986, Via Deliziosa (NEA grantee), 1987; exhbns., Mus. Modern Art, N.Y.C., 1961, Brandeis U., Waltham, Mass., 1964, Corcoran Gallery, Washington, 1970, Space for Peace, 1985, also on tour, Xerox Center, Rochester, N.Y., 1976, Space for Peace Exhbn. at NAD and Pacific Design Ctr., San Diego, 1989; collection Howe Architecture Library, Ariz. State U., Tempe; author 7 books. Recipient Craftsmanship medal AIA, 1963, Silver medal Academie d'Architecture in Paris, 1984, Gold medal World Biennale of Architecture, Sofia, Bulgaria, 1981, Gugenheim Found. grantee, 1964-67. Address: Cosanti Found 6433 Doubletree Rd Scottsdale AZ 85253

SOLIDAY, WILLIAM THOMPSON, journalist; b. Balt., Sept. 8, 1943; s. William Thompson Soliday and Martha Nethers Hodges; m. Martha Ann Munday, July 25, 1981; children: Heather Ann, Kent Charles. BA in Journalism, San Jose State U., 1965. Writer, editor San Carlos (Calif.) Enquirer, 1965; writer/columnist Fremont (Calif.) News Register, 1966; writer, sports columnist The Daily Rev., Hayward, Calif., 1968—. Contbg. author: Oakland Raiders Compendium, 1977. Pres. Monte Vista Homeowners Assn., Hayward, 1984-87. With U.S. Army, 1966-68. Recipient 1st pl. best feature San Francisco Press Club, 1970, 1st pl. best sports story Calif./Nev. APNEC, 1970, 4th pl. best sports story APSE Nat. Contest, 1989, 6th pl., 1988. Mem. Profl. Football Writers Assn., Nat. Sportswriters and Sportcasters Assn., Sigma Delta Chi (pres. San Jose State chpt. 1964). Democrat. Office: The Daily Rev 116 W Winton Ave Hayward CA 94544

SOLIS, HILDA LUCIA, educational administrator, state legislator; b. Los Angeles, Oct. 20, 1957; d. Raul and Juana (Sequiera) S.; m. Sam H. Sayyad, June 26, 1982. BA in Polit. Sci., Calif. State Poly U., 179; MA in Pub. Adminstrn., U. So. Calif., 1981. Interpreter Immigration and Naturalization Service, Los Angeles, 1977-79; editor in chief Office Hispanic Affairs, The White House, Washington, 1980-81; mgmt. analyst Office Mgmt. and Budget, Washington, 1981-82; field rep. Office Assemblyman Art Torres, L.A., 1982; dir. Calif. Student Opportunity and Access, Whittier, 1982—; rep. 57th assembly dist. Calif. State Assembly, Sacramento, 1992—; cons. South Coast Consortium, L.A., 1986—; mem. South Coast Ednl. Opportunity Pers. Consortium. Bd. dirs. Calif. Commn. on Status of Women, 1993—; corr. pres. Friendly El Monte (Calif.) Dem. Club, 1986—; mem.

credentials com. Calif. Dem. Com., 1987-88; trustee Rio Hondo C.C., 1985—. Recipient Meritorious Svc. award Dept. Def., 1981, Young Careerist award El Monte Bus. and Profl. Women, 1987; fellow Nat. Edn. Inst., Kellogg Found., 1984-85. Mem. Western Assn. Ednl. Opportunity Pers. (sec. bd. dirs. 1986—), Comision Feminil de Los Angeles (bd. dirs. 1983-84, edn. chmn.), Women of Moose. Roman Catholic. Home: 11724 E Roseglen St El Monte CA 91732-1446 Office: Calif Student Opportunity and Access 9401 Painter Ave Whittier CA 90605-2729

SOLL, LAUREN SABIN, accountant; b. Chgo., Oct. 3, 1942; s. Roy and Dorothy (Sabin) S.; m. Susie Elizabeth Dean, May 6,1 982; children: Natasha Jacqueline, Bradley Dean. BBA, U. Wis., 1964. CPA, Calif. Revenue agt. IRS, Chgo., 1964-69; options mgr. Loeb Rhoades & Co., Beverly Hills, Calif., 1969-74; gen. ptnr. Chgo. Pizza Works, L.A., 1974-77; pres., mng. dir. Grunts Investments Ltd., London, 1977-88. Jewish. Home: 18707 Lunada Point San Diego CA 92128

SOLOMON, ARTHUR CHARLES, pharmacist; b. Gary, Ind., May 30, 1947; s. Laurence A. and Dorothy B. (Klippel) S.; m. Janet Evelyn Irak, Aug. 23, 1969; children: Thomas, Michael, Mark, Jill. BS in Pharmacy, Purdue U., 1970, MS in Clin. Pharmacy, 1972; PharmD. Registered pharmacist; cert. nuclear pharmacist. Clin. prof. pharmacy U. Tex., Austin, 1972-75; v.p. Nuclear Pharmacy, Inc., Atlanta, 1975-83; exec. v.p., chief oper. officer Diagnostek, Inc., Albuquerque, 1983—; pres. Health Care Svcs., Inc., 1990—; adj. prof. U. N.Mex., 1992—. Contbr. articles to profl. jours. Mem. Am. Pharm. Assn., Am. Soc. Hosp. Pharmacy, Nat. Assn. Retail Druggists, Nat. Coun. Prescription Drug Programs, Am. Managed Care Pharmacy Assn., Kiwanis, Elks, Rho Chi, Pi Kappa Phi. Republican. Roman Catholic. Home: 1504 Catron Ave SE Albuquerque NM 87123-4218 Office: Diagnostek Inc 4500 Alexander Blvd NE Albuquerque NM 87107-6805

SOLOMON, GEORGE FREEMAN, academic psychiatrist; b. Freeport, N.Y., Nov. 25, 1931; s. Joseph C. and Ruth (Freeman) S.; children: Joshua Ben, Jared Freeman. A.B., Stanford U., 1952, M.D., 1955. Intern, Barnes Hosp., St. Louis, 1955-56; resident in psychiatry Langley Porter Neuropsychiat. Inst., U. Calif. Med. Sch., San Francisco, 1956-59; asst. to asso. prof. psychiatry Stanford U. Med. Sch., 1962-73; dir. med. edn. Fresno County (Calif.) Dept. Health, 1973-83; clin. prof. UCLA Med. Sch., 1974-78; clin. prof. psychiatry U. Calif. Med. Sch., San Francisco, 1976-79, prof., 1980-84, vice-chmn. dept., 1978-83; adj. prof. U. Calif., San Francisco, 1984-90; prof. psychiatry UCLA, 1984—; chief chem. dependency treatment ctr. VA Med. Ctr., Sepulveda, Calif., 1984-89; chief psychoneuroimmunology, 1989—; chief psychiatry Valley Med. Center, Fresno, 1974-83. Co-author: The Psychology of Strength, 1975; contbr. over 150 papers and articles on psychoneuroimmunology, violence, Vietnam and other topics to profl. jours. and various publs. Served to capt. USAR, 1959-61. Fellow Internat. Coll. Psychosomatic Medicine, Am. Psychiat. Assn., Acad. of Behavioral Med. Research., Royal Coll. Psychiatrists. Home: 19054 Pacific Coast Hwy Malibu CA 90265-5406 Office: VA Med Ctr 16111 Plummer St Sepulveda CA 91343-2036

SOLOMON, JULIUS OSCAR LEE, pharmacist, hypnotherapist; b. N.Y.C., Aug. 14, 1917; s. John and Jeannette (Krieger) S.; student Bklyn. Coll., 1935-36, CCNY, 1936-37; BS in Pharmacy, U. So. Calif., 1949; postgrad. Long Beach State U., 1971-72, Southwestern Colls., 1979, 81-82; PhD, Am. Inst. Hypnotherapy, 1988; m. Sylvia Smith, June 26, 1941 (div. Jan. 1975); children: Marc Irwin, Evan Scott, Jeri Lee. Cert. hypnotherapist; cert. hypnoanaesthesia therapist. Dye maker Fred Fear & Co., Bklyn., 1935; apprentice interior decorator Dorothy Draper, 1936; various jobs, N.Y. State Police, 1940-45; rsch. asst. Union Oil Co., 1945; lighting cons. Joe Rosenberg & Co., 1946-49; owner Banner Drug, Lomita, 1949-53, Redondo Beach, Calif., 1953-72, El Prado Pharmacy, Redondo Beach, 1961-65; pres. Banner Drug, Inc., Redondo Beach, 1953-72, Thrifty Drugs, 1972-74, also Guild Drug, Longs Drug, Drug King, 1976-83; pres. Socoma, Inc. doing bus. as Lee & Ana Pharmacy, 1983-86, now Two Hearts Help Clinic, 1986-91. Charter commr., founder Redondo Beach Youth Baseball Council; sponsor Little League Baseball, basketball, football, bowling; pres. Redondo Beach Boys Club; v.p. South Bay Children's Health Ctr., 1974, Redondo Beach Coordinating Coun., 1975; founder Redondo Beach Community Theater, 1975; active maj. gift drive YMCA, 1975; mem. SCAG Com. on Criminal Justice, 1974, League Calif. Environ. Quality Com., 1975; mem. Dem. State Cen. Com., Los Angeles County Dem. Cen. Com.; del. Dem. Nat. Conv., 1972; chmn. Redondo Beach Recreation and Parks Commn.; mem. San Diego County Parks Adv. Commn., 1982; mem. San Diego Juvenile Justice Commn., 1986—; mem. San Diego County Adv. Com. Adult Detention, 1987—; mem. human resource devel. com., pub. improvement com. Nat. League of Cities; v.p. Redondo Beach Coordinating Coun.; councilman, Redondo Beach, 1961-69, 73-77; treas. 46th Assembly Dist. Coun.; candidate 46 Assembly dist. 1966; nat. chmn. Pharmacists for Humphrey, 1968, 72; pres. bd. dirs. South Bay Exceptional Childrens Soc., Chapel Theatre; bd. dirs. so. div. League Calif. Cities, U.S.-Mex. Sister Cities Assn., Boy's Club Found. San Diego County, Autumn Hills Condominium Assn. (pres.), Calif. Employee Pharmacists Assn. (pres. 1985), Our House, Chula Vista, Calif., 1984—; mem. South Bay Inter-City Hwy. Com., Redondo Beach Round Table, 1973-77; mem. State Calif. Commn. of Californias (U.S.-Mexico), 1975-78; mem. Chula Vista Safety Commn., 1978, chmn., 1980-81; chmn. San Diego County Juvenile Camp Contract Com., 1982-83; mem. San Diego County Juvenile Delinquency Prevention Commn., 1983-85, 89—, San Diego County Juvenile Justice Commn., 1986—, San Diego County Adv. Com. for Adult Detention, 1987—; spl. participant Calif. Crime and Violence Workshop; mem. Montgomery Planning Commn., 1983-86; mem. Constnl. Observance Com., 1990—, Troubled Teenagers Hypnosis Treatment Program, 1989—. With USCGR, 1942-45. Recipient Pop Warner Youth award, 1960, 1962, award of merit Calif. Pharm. Assn., 1962, award Am. Assn. Blood Banks, 1982. Diplomate Am. Bd. Diplomates Pharmacy Internat., 1977-81; Fellow Am. Coll. Pharmacists (pres. 1949-57); mem. South Bay Pharm. Assn. (pres.), South Bay Councilman Assn. (founder, pres.), Palos Verdes Peninsula Navy League (charter), Am. Legion, U. So. Calif. Alumni Assn. (life), Assn. Former N.Y. State Troopers (life), AFTRA, Am. Pharm. Assn., Nat. Assn. Retail Druggists, Calif. Pharmacists Assn., Calif. Employee Pharmacist Assn. (bd. dirs. 1980-81), Hon. Dep. Sheriff's Assn., San Ysidro C. of C. (bd. dirs. 1985-87), Fraternal Order of Police, San Diego County Fish and Game Assn., Rho Pi Phi (pres. alumni). Club: Trojan (life). Lodges: Elks (life), Masons (32 deg.; life), Lions (charter mem. North Redondo). Established Lee and Ana Solomon award for varsity athlete with highest scholastic average at 10 L.A. South Bay High Schs. in Los Angeles County and 3 San Diego area South Bay High Schs.

SOLOMON, MARK ALAN, human resources executive; b. N.Y.C., June 4, 1943; s. Charles Solomon and Anne (Waxberg) Solomon Baietti; m. Cora Lee Watson, Oct. 20, 1973; 1 child, Elizabeth Joann. BA, Adelphi U., 1965. Dir. pers. Biltmore Hotel, L.A., 1969-73; chief acct. Ask Mr. Foster Travel Svc., Encino, Calif., 1973; adminstrv. svcs. mgr. Great S.W. Corp., L.A., 1974; dir. pers. Lady Luck Casino, Las Vegas, Nev., 1974-77; dir. human resources Las Vegas Hilton/Falmingo, 1977-87, Bally's Casino Resort, Las Vegas, 1987—; ptnr. Adia Pers. Svcs., Las Vegas, 1987—; instr. U. Nev., Las Vegas, 1992—. Trustee Civil Svc. Bd., Las Vegas, 1987-89; mem. Bd. of Zoning Adjustment, Las Vegas, 1989—; commr. Planning Commn., Las Vegas, 1990—; mediator Neighborhood Justice Ctr., Las Vegas, 1992—; mem. Nev. Com. for Employer Support of Guard and Res. Mem. Am. Soc. Human Resource Mgmt., Nev. Self-Insurers Assn., So. Nev. Human Resource Assn., Indsl. Rels. Rsch. Assn., Toastmasters Internat., Lions Internat. Democrat. Office: Bally's Casino Resort 3645 Las Vegas Blvd S Las Vegas NV 89109

SOLOMON, PAUL MARSHALL See MARSHALL, PAUL

SOLOMON, RHONDA HOPE, school and educational psychologist; b. L.A., Dec. 1, 1962; d. Jerry and Lynn (Cabin) S. BA in Psychology and Child Devel., Calif. State U., Northridge, 1985, MA in Psychology, 1987; postgrad., Calif. Grad. Inst., 1987—. Lic. ednl. psychologist, Calif. Play therapist, children's counselor family stress program San Fernando Valley Child Guidance Clinic, Van Nuys, Calif., 1981-84; sch. psychologist, cons., presenter L.A. Unified Sch. Dist., 1987—; pvt. practice ednl. psychology, 1987—. Crisis counselor, helpline worker Haven Hills Shelter for Battered Women, 1983-84. Mem. APA (assoc.), Nat. Assn. Sch. Psychologists, Calif. Assn. Sch. Psychologists, Western Assn. Psychologists, L.A. Assn. Sch. Psychologists, Psi Chi. Home: 5620 Yolanda Ave #104 Tarzana CA 91356 Office: LA Unified Sch Dist Psychol Svcs Cen Ednl Support Ctr 15530 Hesby St Encino CA 91436-1519

SOLONE, RAYMOND JOSEPH, advertising executive; b. Chgo., Feb. 6, 1960; s. Arthur Romeo and Florence Marie (Kilgallon) S.; m. Lindsay Fetterman, Jan. 8, 1983 (div. 1988); 1 child, Caitlin Jean. BS in Mktg., So. Ill. U., 1982, MS in Orgn. Communications, 1984. Account mgr. Hill & Knowlton, Santa Clara, Calif., 1984-85, Carlson Assocs., Sacramento, Calif., 1985-87; mktg. communications mgr. Intel Corp., Folsom, Calif., 1987-90; v.p., ptnr. Anderson Solone Inc., Sacramento, 1990—. Bd. dirs. NorCal Ctr. on Deafness, Sacramento, 1986-87; pub. rels. cons. United Way Sacramento, 1985-87. Recipient Award of Excellence-Trademark Communication Arts Mag., 1986. Mem. Am. Mktg. Assn., Sacramento Valley Mktg. Assn., Sacramento Ad Club (Gold award direct mail 1986, Silver award newsletter 1986, Silver award advt. 1986, Delta award direct mail 1988). Republican. Roman Catholic. Office: Anderson Solone Inc Mktg Comm 3100 Fite Circle Ste 101 Sacramento CA 95827-1805

SOLOW, HERBERT FRANKLIN, film producer, writer; b. N.Y.C., Dec. 14, 1930; s. Morris David and Frances Louise (Birnbaum) S.; m. Maxine Debra Turner, Aug. 6, 1954 (div. 1974); children: Jody, Bonnie, Jamie. AB, Dartmouth Coll., 1953. Agt. William Morris Agy., N.Y.C., 1954-58; dir., exec. NBC, N.Y.C., 1958-59, Los Angeles, 1958-60, CBS, Los Angeles, 1961-63; v.p. Desilu Studios, Los Angeles, 1964-69; v.p. prodn. Paramount TV, Los Angeles, 1969; v.p. worldwide prodn. Metro-Goldwyn-Mayer, Los Angeles, 1969-73; pres. Solow Prodn. Co., Los Angeles, 1976-79; v.p. Sherwood Prodns., Los Angeles, 1980-83; ind. producer, writer Los Angeles, 1984—. Mem. Writers Guild Am., Dirs. Guild Am., Acad. Motion Picture Arts and Scis., Acad. TV Arts and Scis.

SOLOW, LEE HOWARD, psychologist, consultant; b. Fairfield, Calif., Jan. 16, 1953; s. Robert Avrom and Marilyn Cynthia (Anes) S.; m. Toni Elleen Gingold, Apr. 5, 1987; children: Max (dec.), Hannah, Sophie. BA, U. Calif., Irvine, 1974; MA, Calif. Sch. Profl. Psychology, 1976, PhD, 1978. Lic. psychologist, Calif. Psychology dir. U. Athletic Club, Newport Beach, Calif., 1980—; dir. Wellness Resources, Newport Beach, Calif., 1980—; pvt. practice psychologist Newport Beach, 1980—; mem. adj. faculty Coestine Community Coll., Fountain Valley, Calif., 1980—, Pepperdine U., Irvine, 1984-86. Mem. APA, Calif. Psychol. Assn. Democrat. Jewish. Office: 1101 Dove St Ste 260 Newport Beach CA 92660-2803

SOLOW, ROBERT A., physician; b. Newark, Sept. 11, 1925; m. Marilyn Anes, Dec. 25, 1949; children: Lawrence Jay, Lee Howard, Bruce Alan, Brian Keith, Margaret Ann. AA, Princeton U., 1944; MD, N.Y. Med. Coll., 1948. Diplomate Am. Bd. Psychiatry and Neurology. Intern Jersey City Med. Ctr., 1948-49; resident in psychiatry Winter VA Hosp., Topeka, Kans., 1949-52; fellow Menninger Found. Sch. Psychiatry, Topeka, Kans., 1949-52; staff psychiatrist Topeka State Hosp., 1952; attending staff psychiatrist Mt. Sinai Hosp., Los Angeles, 1956-59; child psychiatrist Reiss Davis Child Study Ctr., 1955-70; vis. staff psychiatrist U. Calif. Hosp. and Clinics, Los Angeles, 1958-86, UCLA Neuropsychiat. Inst., 1958—; mem. courtesy staff Westwood Hosp., L.A., 1960-77; mem. teaching staff Menninger Found. Sch. Psychiatry, 1958-62; asst. clin. prof. psychiatry, UCLA Sch. Medicine, 1962-69, assoc. clin. prof. 1969-78, clin. prof., 1978—; med. examiner State of Calif.; ind. med. examiner State of Calif. Dept. Indsl. Med.; med. adv. com. Muscular Dystrophy Assn. Am., 1955-80. Co-author: The Joys and Sorrows of Parenthood, 1973, Speaking Out for Psychiatry, 1987; mem. editorial bd. Adolescent Psychiatry, 1969-76; mem. editorial rev. bd. Am. Jour. Psychiatry, Am. Jour. Hosp. and Community Psychiatry. Chmn. exec. com. Boy Scouts Am., L.A. chpt., 1968-74. Capt. M.C., USAF, 1952-54. Recipient Silver Bruin award Boy Scouts Am., 1969, Hon. Svc. award Calif. Congress Parents and Tchrs., 1970, Resolution, City of L.A., 1977. Fellow Am. Psychiat. Assn. (life), Am. Soc. for Adolescent Psychiatry (life), So. Calif. Psychiat. Soc. (life, past. pres.), So. Calif. Soc. for Adolescent Psychiatry (life), Am. Coll. Psychiatrists, Am. Assn. Social Psychiatry, World Assn. for Social Psychiatry; mem. Internat. Assn. for Adolescent Psychiatry (exec. bd.), Group for Advancement of Psychiatry (editorial bd.), Calif. Med. Assn. (past chmn. sect. on psychiatry), So. Calif. Soc. Child Psychiatry (past pres.), Physicians for Social Responsibility, Calif. Soc. Indsl. Medicine and Surgery. Club: Mountaingate Country. Office: 152 S Lasky Dr Beverly Hills CA 90212-1720

SOLOWAY, BARRY H., engineering executive; b. Jersey City, July 30, 1942; m. Elaine Soloway; children: Brett, Abby, Marc. BSEE, Fairleigh Dickinson U., 1964; MSEE, NYU, 1966. Group supr. Bell Labs., Allentown, Pa., 1966-74; ops. mgr. Bowmar Instruments, Phoenix, 1974-75; product line mgr. Fairchild Semiconductor, Mountain View, Calif., 1975-76; dir. ITT Advanced Tech. Ctr., Shelton, Conn., 1976-85; pres. Grove Hill Industries, Inc., Woodbridge, Conn., 1985-91; v.p. engring. Verilink Corp., San Jose, Calif., 1991—. Author: Demystifying Computer, 1987; author, editor newsletter Streams of Change, 1986—; contbr. articles to profl. publs.; patentee in field. Mem. IEEE (sr.). Office: Verilink Corp 145 Baytech Dr San Jose CA 95134-2303

SOLTISIAK, CHRISTINA ANN, management consultant; b. Bridgeport, Conn., Sept. 22, 1945; d. Frank Edward and Ann Georgiana (Pjura) Tomek; m. Aug. 31, 1967 (dec. 1986); 1 child, Scott William Soltisiak; m. Steven Earl Howell, Apr. 25, 1987. AA, Bryant Coll., 1965. Exec. sec. Glass Tite Mfg., Providence, 1965-67; legal sec. Robert D. Moilanen, Atty., Vancouver, Wash., 1974-77; exec. asst., sales and mktg. Devel. Svcs. Corp., Portland, Oreg., 1978-83; mgmt. cons. Exec. Forum, Vancouver and Denver, 1983—; bd. dirs. Columbia Credit Union. Bd. edn. Grace Luth. Ch., Vancouver, 1988-89; mem. Clark County YWCA, Columbia River Econ. Devel. Coun. Recipient Customer Care award U.S. Army C.E., 1989. Mem. Am. Soc. Tng. and Devel., C. of C., Nat. Speaker Assn. Democrat. Lutheran. Office: Exec Forum 404 E 15th St Ste 7 Vancouver WA 98663-3451

SOLTOW, PAUL CARL, JR., civil engineer; b. Reno, Nev., Dec. 15, 1930; s. Paul Carl and Louisa (Arriola) S.; m. Lilian Parker, Jan. 17, 1958. BS, U. Calif., Berkeley, 1952; MPA, Golden Gate U., 1968. Registered profl. engr., Calif., Nev. Engr. officer Aviation Engrs., various locations, 1953-54; hwy. engr. Calif. Div. Hwys., San Francisco, 1954-58; engr.-mgr. San Pablo (Calif.) Sanitary Dist., 1958-71; gen. mgr. Bay Area Sewage Svc. Agy., Berkeley, Calif., 1971-74; v.p. Koretsky-King Assocs., San Francisco, 1975-78; pres. Paul Soltow/Cen. Engrs., Inc., Richmond and El Sobrante, Calif., 1979—. Contbr. articles to profl. jours. Sec. North Bay Water Adv. Coun., Richmond, Calif., 1961-71, East Bay Conf. on Sewer Practice, San Pablo, 1959-71. Capt. C.E., U.S. Army, 1951-52. Recipient Cert. Calif. State Assy., Contra Costa Bd. Suprs., City of Richmond, City of San Pablo. Mem. ASCE, Am. Pub. Wks. Assn. (chmn. infiltration com. 1968-70), Calif. Assn. Sanitation Agys. (editor newsletter 1965-71), El Sobrante C. of C. (pres. 1970), Navy League (Richmond chpt. pres. 1971), West Contra Costa Bus. and Profl. Assn. (pres.. 1982), Rotary (chpt. pres. 1971-73), Berkeley Camera Club. Republican. Office: Paul Soltow/Cen Engring Ste 629 3817 San Pablo Dam Rd El Sobrante CA 94803

SOLYMOSSY, EMERIC, management consultant, engineer; b. Wolfratshausen, Germany, Dec. 1, 1948; came to U.S., 1952; s. Martin Akos V. and Maria Rosalia (Mailath) S.; m. Sharon Dale Fults, Aug. 3, 1974; children: Christine Maria, Martin Emeric. Cert. in Energy Mgmt., NYU, Chgo., 1979; BS in Engring., Century U., 1991; postgrad., Colo. State U., Denver, 1992—. Registered master electrician, Wyo. Chief estimator Carlton Electric, Denver, 1974-76; coord. Amco Electric, Denver, 1976-77; chief estimator Modern Electric Inc., Casper, Wyo., 1977-83; pres., CEO A & E Electric/A & E Petroleum, Casper, Wyo., 1983-90, Custom Electronics, Casper, Wyo., 1986-92; prin. Emeric Solymossy, Cons., Grand Junction, Colo., 1989—; cons. Moores-Eikenhorst, Denver, 1989-92; turnaround cons. Redlands Video and Tan, Grand Junction, Colo., 1991. Author: Project Management, 1988. Dir. Panorama Improvement Dist., Mesa County, Colo., 1990-92; bd. dirs. Casper, Natrona County Licensing Bd., 1985-89; co-chmn. Tourism Com. Wyo. Centennial, 1985-86; scoutmaster Boy Scouts of Am., Grand Junction, 1989-92. Named Outstanding Young Man of Am., 1978; recipient Paul Harris fellowship Rotary, 1988. Mem. Associated Bulders and Contractors (pres. 1987-88), Redlands Rotary. Office: Emeric Solymossy Cons 2390 Crabtree Dr Littleton CO 80121

SOMA, MANI, electrical engineering educator; b. Cantho, Vietnam, Mar. 23, 1953; came to U.S. 1972; s. Sundram and Manh Thi (Duong) S.; m. Karen N. Bloomer, Dec. 21, 1985. BSEE, Calif. State U., Fresno, 1975, BA in Math., 1975; MSEE, Stanford U., 1977, PhD in Elec. Engring., 1980. Tech. staff GE Rsch. and Devel. Ctr., Schenectady, 1980-82; asst. prof. elec. engring. U. Wash., Seattle, 1982-87, assoc. prof. elec. engring., 1987-90, prof. elec. engring., 1990—; assoc. dir. Nat. Sci. Found. Ctr. for Design of Analog/Digital IC, Seattle, 1989—; acting dir. Computer Systems/Software Ctr., Wash. Tech. Ctrs., Seattle, 1990—. Contbr. articles to profl. jours.; editor: Kluwers Rsch. Jour., 1991—, IEEE Design/Test mag., 1991—. Mem. IEEE (Tchr. of the Yr. 1983, 89, significant contbn. 1990, 91), Tau Beta Pi, Phi Kappa Phi, Eta Kappa Nu. Office: Univ Wash FT 10 Dept Elec Engring Seattle WA 98195

SOMANI, ARUN KUMAR, electrical engineer, educator; b. Beawar, India, July 16, 1951; came to the U.S., 1985; s. Kanwar Lal and Dulari Devi (Mundra) S.; m. Deepa-Toshniwal, Jan. 21, 1976 (dec. 1985); children: Ashutosh, Paritosh; m. Manju-Kankani, July 6, 1987; 1 child, Anju. BS with honors, B.I.T.S., Pilani, India, 1973; MTech, IIT, Delhi, 1979; MSEE, McGill U., 1983, PhD, 1985. Tech. officer Electronics Corp. India, Hyderabad, 1973-74; scientist Dept. Electronics, Delhi, 1974-82; asst. prof. dept. elec. engring. U. Wash., Seattle, 1985-90, assoc. prof. dept. computer sci. and engring., 1990—. Patentee in field; contbr. articles to profl. jours. and chpts. to books. Mem. IEEE (sr.), Assn. for Computing Machinery, Eta Kappa Nu. Hindu. Home: 16609 126th Ave NE Woodinville WA 98072-7979 Office: U Wash Dept Elec Engring Ft-10 Seattle WA 98195

SOMERSET, HAROLD RICHARD, sugar company executive; b. Woodbury, Conn., Sept. 25, 1935; s. Harold Kitchener and Margaret Mary (Roche) S.; m. Marjory Deborah Ghiselin, June 22, 1957 (dec. Jan. 1984); children: Timothy Craig, Paul Alexander; m. Jean MacAlpine DesMarais, Jan. 2, 1985; stepchildren: Cheryl Lyn DesMarais, James Fenelon DesMarais. B.S., U.S. Naval Acad., 1957; B.C.E., Rensselaer Poly. Inst., Troy, N.Y., 1959; LL.B., Harvard U., 1967. Bar: Mass. 1967, Hawaii 1973. Commd. ensign U.S. Navy, 1957, advanced through grades to lt., 1961; service in U.S. and Hawaii; resigned, 1964; with firm Goodwin, Procter & Hoar, Boston, 1967-72; corp. counsel Alexander & Baldwin, Inc., Honolulu, 1972-74, v.p., gen. counsel, 1974-78, group v.p.-sugar, 1978-79, exec. v.p.-agr., 1979-84; with Calif. & Hawaiian Sugar Co., San Francisco, 1984—, exec. v.p., chief operating officer, 1984-88, pres., chief exec. officer, 1988—, mem. exec. com., also bd. dirs.; bd. dirs. World Sugar Rsch. Orgn., Longs Drug Stores Corp. Mem. exec. bd. Bay Area Coun., San Francisco; bd. dirs., mem. exec. bd. Mt. Diablo coun. Boy Scouts Am.; trustee San Francisco Nat. Maritime Mus. Mem. Sugar Assn. (bd. dirs., fin. com.). Home: 19 Donald Dr Orinda CA 94563-3646 Office: Calif & Hawaiian Sugar Co 830 Loring Ave Crockett CA 94525-1199

SOMOGYI, LASZLO PETER, food technologist; b. Budapest, Hungary, June 1, 1931; came to U.S., 1957, naturalized, 1962; s. Istvan and Szerena (Wiesel) S.; m. Marika Harmat, June 1, 1951; children—Peter, George. B.S., U. Agrl. Scis., Budapest, 1956; M.S., Rutgers U., 1960, Ph.D., 1962; postdoctoral fellow U. Calif.-David, 1962-64. Jr. research pomologist U. Calif.-Davis, 1962-64; project leader Hunt-Wesson Foods, Fullerton, Calif., 1964-70; tech. dir. VacuDry Co., Emeryville, Calif., 1970-74, Biophys. Research Corp., Hayward, Calif., 1974-75; sr. food scientist Stanford Research Inst., Menlo Park, Calif., 1975-78; v.p. research and devel. Finn-Cal, Inc., San Rafael, Calif., 1978-83; pres. ETEL, Inc., Berkeley, 1983-89; sr. cons. SRI Internat., Menlo Park, 1989—. Fellow Inst. Food Technologists (named No. Calif. sect. Mem. of Yr. 1984); mem. Am. Assn. Cereal Chemists, Am. Oil Chemists Soc. Home: 12 Highgate Ct Kensington CA 94707-1115

SOMORJAI, GABOR ARPAD, chemist, educator; b. Budapest, Hungary, May 4, 1935; came to U.S., 1957, naturalized, 1962; s. Charles and Livia (Ormos) S.; m. Judith Kaldor, Sept. 2, 1957; children: Nicole, John. B-SChemE, U. Tech. Scis., Budapest, 1956; PhD, U. Calif., Berkeley, 1960; D (hon.), Tech. U. Budapest, 1989, U. Paris, 1990, Free Univ Brussels, Belgium, 1992. Mem. research staff IBM, Yorktown Heights, N.Y., 1960-64; dir. Surface Sci. and Catalysis Program Lawrence Berkeley Lab., Calif., 1964—; mem. faculty dept. chemistry U. Calif.-Berkeley, 1964—, assoc. prof., 1967-72, prof., 1972—, Miller prof., 1978; Unilever prof. dept. chemistry U. Bristol, Eng., 1972; vis. fellow Emmanuel Coll., Cambridge, Eng., 1989; Baker lectr., Cornell U., Ithaca, N.Y., 1977; mem. editorial bds. Progress in Solid State Chemistry, 1973—, Jour Solid State Chemistry, 1976—, Nouveau Jour de Chemie, 1977-80, Colloid and Interface Sci., 1979—, Catalysis Revs., 1981, Jour. Phys. Chm. 1981—, Langmuir, 1985, Jour. Applied Catalysis, Molecular Physics, 1992—. Author: Principles of Surface Chemistry, 1972, Chemistry in Two Dimensions, 1981, Introduction to Surface Chemistry and Catalysis, 1993; editor in chief Catalysis Letters, 1988—; contbr. articles to profl. jours. Recipient Emmett award Am. Catalysis Soc., 1977, Kokes award Johns Hopkins U., 1976, Albert award Precious Metal Inst., 1986, Sr. Disting. Scientist award Alexander von Humboldt Found., 1989, E.W. Mueller award U. Wis.; Guggenheim fellow, 1969. Fellow AAAS, Am. Phys. Soc.; mem. NAS, Am. Acad. Arts and Scis., Am. Chem. Soc. (chmn. colloid and surface chemistry 1981, Surface and Colloid Chemistry award 1981, Peter Debye award 1989), Am. Phys. Soc., Catalysis Soc. N.Am., Hungarian Acad. Scis. (hon. 1990). Office: U Calif Dept Chemistry D 58 Hildebrand Hall Berkeley CA 94720 Home: 665 San Luis Rd Berkeley CA 94707-1725

SONDAK, BRADLEY WAYNE, sports editor; b. Far Rockaway, N.Y., Apr. 7, 1962; s. Norman Edward and Eileen Lorraine (Miller) S. BS, San Diego State U., 1984. Sports editor San Diego Weekly News, 1984--, Inn Rm. Mag., 1985-87, Coast Dispatch, Encinitas, Calif., 1987--; on-the-spot reporter The Sports Network, Phila., 1986--; sportswriter Coast Dispatch, Encinitas, Calif., 1986-87; cons. KGTV Channel 10 Sports Dept., San Diego, 1986--; sports commentator Sta. KVSD, Carlsbad, Calif., 1988-91; freelance sportswriter UPI, 1991—; sports commentator Xtra-AM Sta., 1991—. Contbr. articles to profl. jours. Home: 6344 Lake Lomond Dr San Diego CA 92119-3032 Office: Coast Dispatch 687 Forrest St Encinitas CA 92024-5829

SONETT, CHARLES PHILIP, physicist; b. Pitts., Jan. 15, 1924; s. Erwin and Helen (Dorner) S.; m. Virginia Hooten, June 20, 1948; children: Eric Erwin, Maria Lisa. BA in Physics, U. Calif., Berkeley, 1949; MS, U. Calif., 1951; PhD in Nuclear Physics, UCLA, 1954. Assoc. physics UCLA, 1953-54; head range devel. group Ramo Wooldridge Corp., 1954-57; mem. sr. staff, head space physics sect., project scientist Pioneer 1, 2, 5, Explorer 6 Space Tech. Labs., 1957-60; chief scis. lunar and planetary programs NASA Hdqrs., 1960-62, chief space sci. div., 1962-70; dep. dir. astronautics Ames Rsch. Ctr., 1970-73; prin. investigator Pioneer 1, 2, 5, 9; Explorer 6, 33, 35; Apollo 12, 15; prof. planetary scis., head dept., dir. lunar and planetary lab. U. Ariz., Tucson, 1973-77, prof. planetary scis., 1977-92, regents prof. planetary scis., 1990—, prof. emeritus, 1992—; lectr. engring. UCLA, 1955-58; cons. NASA Hdqrs., Jet Propulsion Lab., Rockwell Internat. Editor Cosmic Electrodynamics, 1970-72; co-editor Astrophysics and Space Sci., 1973-80, mem. editorial bd., 1980—; co-editor The Moon and the Planets, 1973—; mem. editorial com. Ann. Rev. Earth and Planet Scis., 1973-76. With U.S. Army, 1943-46. Decorated Purple Heart; recipient Exceptional Sci. Achievement medal NASA, 1969, 72, Space Sci. award AIAA, 1969; Guggenheim fellow, 1968-69, Carnegie fellow U. Edinburgh, 1985; grantee NASA, 1959—, NSF, 1978, 83-86. Fellow Am. Geophys. Union; mem. AAAS, Internat. Astron. Union, Univ. Space Rsch. Assn. (trustee 1977-83). Home: 5745 N Camino Real Tucson AZ 85718-4213 Office: Univ Ariz Dept Planetary Scis Lunar and Planetary Lab Tucson AZ 85721

SONG, TAE-SUNG, real estate appraiser, consultant; b. Seoul, June 11, 1941; came to U.S., 1967; s. Won Do Song and Un Hae Lim; m. Chae-Ryong Moon, Dec. 27, 1969; children: Edward, Sumie. BBA in Acctg. and Mgmt., Yonsei U., Seoul, 1964; MBA in Real Estate and Urban Land Econs., U. Wis., 1971. Appraiser, analyst Am. Appraisal Co., Milw., 1971-74, Real Estate Research Corp., St. Louis, 1974-78; v.p. Marshall and Stevens, Inc., St. Louis, 1978-87, Los Angeles, 1987—; cons. in field. Mem.

Appraisal Inst. (nat. grader/reviewer demonstration report 1983-89, co-vice chmn. subcom. non-residential reports, bd. dirs. examiners), Am. Real Estate and Urban Econs. Assn. (membership chmn.), Mo. Real Estate and Urban Econs. Assn. Office: Marshall & Stevens Inc 600 S Commonwealth Ave Los Angeles CA 90005-4001

SONNEMANN, DOUGLAS WILLIAM, appraiser; b. Ft. Collins, Colo., Nov. 12, 1956; s. William K. and Doris Jane (Hill) S.; m. Valerie R. Purvis, Aug. 17, 1991. BS, U. Nev., 1979, MS, 1982. Cert. appraiser. Grad. rsch. fellow U. Nev., Reno, 1979-81; economist U.S. Forest Svc., Reno, 1981-82; asst. county supr. USDA Farmers Home Adminstrn., Minden, Nev., 1982-83, county supr., 1983-87; appraiser Douglas County Assessor's Office, Minden, 1988—. Mem. Douglas County Engine Co. Vol. Fire Dept., 1984—, pres., 1987-93, named Ambulance Attendant of Yr., 1985; bd. dirs. Douglas County Paramedic Dist., Minden, 1990-91, Gardnerville (Nev.) Town Bd., 1991—, chmn., 1993; bd. dirs. Western Nev. Devel. Dist., Carson City, 1992—. Mem. Nev. State Fireman's Assn., Western Agrl. Econs. Assn. Republican. Methodist. Home: 1169 Mill St Gardnerville NV 89410 Office: Douglas County Assessor's Office PO Box 218 Minden NV 89423

SONNENFELD, ALBERT, French language and comparative literature educator, food critic; b. Berlin, July 22, 1934; came to U.S. 1938; s. Arthur and Anni (Lichtenstein) S.; m. Portia B. Leys, June 15, 1955 (div.); children: Mark David, Carole Marie Geithner; m. Noel Riley Fitch, Aug. 23, 1987. AB, Oberlin (Ohio) Coll., 1955; AM, Princeton U., 1957, PhD, 1958. Prof. French and comparative lit. Princeton U., 1958-86; M.F. Chevalier prof. French and dept. chmn. U. So. Calif., L.A., 1986—; vis. prof. Dartmouth Coll., UCLA, U. Wis., NYU, CUNY, also others; cons. Linguaphone Inst., London, 1974—; food critic; restaurant cons. Author: L'Oeuvre poetique de Tristan Corbiere, 1961, Crossroads, 1982, Thirty-Six French Poems, 1961; co-author: Temoins de l'Homme, 1965. Fulbright fellow, 1966-67; NEH fellow, 1978-79, 80, 83; recipient Raubenheimer Outstanding Faculty award, U. So. Calif., 1990. Mem. Am. Inst. Wine and Food (bd. dirs.), The Athenaeum (London), Phi Beta Kappa. Home: 11829 Mayfield Ave # 303 Los Angeles CA 90049 Office: U of So Calif THH 126 University Pk Los Angeles CA 90089-0359

SONTAG, FREDERICK EARL, philosophy educator; b. Long Beach, Calif., Oct. 2, 1924; s. M. Burnett and Cornelia (Nicholson) S.; m. Carol Furth, June 10, 1950; children: Grant Furth, Anne Burnett Karch. BA with great distinction, Stanford U., 1949; MA, Yale U., 1951, PhD, 1952; LLD (hon.), Coll. Idaho, 1971. Instr. Yale U., 1951-52; asst. prof. philosophy Pomona Coll., Claremont, Calif., 1952-55, assoc. prof., 1955-60, prof., 1970—, Robert C. Denison prof. philosophy, 1972—, chmn. dept. philosophy, 1960-67, 76-77, 80-84; chmn. coordinating com. in philosophy Claremont Grad. Sch. and Univ. Ctr., 1962-65; vis. prof. Union Theol. Sem., N.Y.C., 1959-60, Collegio di Sant' Anselmo, Rome, 1966-67, U. Copenhagen, fall 1972; theologian-in-residence Am. Ch. in Paris, fall 1973; Fulbright regional vis. prof., India, East Asia, Pacific areas, 1977-78; mem. nat. adv. council Kent Fellowship Program of Danforth Found., 1963-66. Author numerous books, the most recent being: Love Beyond Pain: Mysticism Within Christianity, 1977; Sun Myung Moon and the Unification Church, 1977, also German, Japanese and Korean transl.; (with John K. Roth) God and America's Future, 1977; What Can God Do?, 1979; A Kierkegaard Handbook, 1979; The Elements of Philosophy, 1984, (with John K. Roth) The Questions of Philosophy, 1988, Emotion, 1989, The Return of the Gods, 1989. Pres. bd. dirs. Claremont Family Service, 1960-64; trustee The Coro Found., Los Angeles and San Francisco, 1967-71; bd. dirs., chmn. ways and means com. Pilgrim Place, Claremont, 1970-77. Served with AUS, 1943-46. Vis. scholar Ctr. for Study Japanese Religions, Kyoto, Japan, spring 1974; vis. fellow East-West Ctr., Honolulu, summer 1974. Wig Disting. Prof. award, 1970, 76; Fulbright regional vis. prof. India, East Asia, Pacific Areas, 1977-78. Mem. Am. Philos. Assn., Metaphys. Soc. Am., Soc. on Religion in Higher Edn. (Kent fellow 1950-52), Am. Acad. Religion, Phi Beta Kappa. Congregationalist. Office: Pomona Coll 333 N College Ave Claremont CA 91711-6337

SORBY, DONALD LLOYD, university dean; b. Fremont, Nebr., Aug. 12, 1933; s. Lloyd A. and Orpha M. (Simmons) S.; m. Jacquelyn J. Burchard, Nov. 7, 1959; children: Thomas, Sharon. B.S. in Pharmacy, U. Nebr., 1955; M.S., U. Wash., 1958, Ph.D., 1960. Dir. pharm. services U. Calif., San Francisco, 1970-72; chmn. dept. pharmacy practice Sch. Pharmacy, U. Wash., Seattle, 1972-74; dean Sch. of Pharmacy, U. Mo., Kansas City, 1974-84, Sch. of Pharmacy, U. Pacific, Stockton, Calif., 1984—. Contbr. articles in field to profl. jours. Assoc. fellow Am. Coll. Apothecaries; mem. Am. Pharm. Assn., Am. Assn. Colls. of Pharmacy (pres. 1980-81), Fedn. Internat. Pharmaceutique, Calif. Pharm. Assn., Acad. Pharm. Rsch. and Scis., Calif. Soc. Hosp. Pharmacists, Assn. Pharm. Scis., Sigma Xi, Phi Kappa Phi, Rho Chi. Home: 4362 Yacht Harbor Dr Stockton CA 95204-1126 Office: U Pacific Sch Pharmacy Stockton CA 95211

SORCSEK, JEROME PAUL, composer, conductor; b. Lebanon, Pa., Sept. 22, 1949; s. Martin Raymond and Agnes Geraldine (Ondrusek) S.; m. Joan Marie Kissinger, Nov. 20, 1976. BMus, Temple U., 1974; MMus, U. Miami, Coral Gables, Fla., 1975. Staff Pa. Dept. Edn., Harrisburg, 1976-77; composer-in-residence Nat. Endowment for Arts/Pa. Coun. of the Arts, Lebanon, 1977-78; prof. music Modesto (Calif.) Jr. Coll., 1979-80, Calif. State U., Northridge, 1980-81; guest conductor Harrisburg Symphony Orch., 1977, Westmar Coll. Wind Orch., Le Mars, Iowa, 1984, Marshall U. Wind Orch., Dunn, N.C., 1987; guest composer Internat. Gesellschaft zur Erforschung und Foerderung der Blasmusik, Uster, Switzerland, 1981, 85. Composer: Symphony No. 1, 1980, Symphony No. 2, 1981, Music of the Pearl, 1985, Orchestral Variations, 1989. With U.S. Army, 1967-70. Recipient Nat. Band Assn. De Moulin Composition award, 1978, New Music for Young Ensembles composition award, 1987. Mem. Am. Soc. Composers, Authors and Pubs. Home: 11018 Swinton Ave Granada Hills CA 91344-5336

SOREM, RONALD KEITH, geologist, mineral resources consultant; b. Northfield, Minn., June 18, 1924; s. Melvin L. Sorem; m. Judith Bacon LaFollette, Feb. 21, 1953; children: Kaia, Keith, Sam, Tom. BA, U. Minn., 1946, MS, 1948; PhD, U. Wis., 1958. Strategic minerals advisor U.S. Fgn. Ops. Adminstrn., Philippines, 1953-55; geologist U.S. Geol. Survey, Washington, Maine, Philippines and Cuba, 1948-55; postdoctoral rsch. assoc. U. Wis., Madison, 1957-58; prof. geology Wash. State U., Pullman, 1959-83; cons. geologist Rks Geol. Rsch., Pullman, 1973—; co-chief scientist NOAA-U.S. Geol. Survey Expeditions, Deep Ocean Mining Environ. Studies Project, Pacific Ocean, 1975, 76, 77, observer rsch. vessel Deepsea Miner II, 1978; pres. Rks Geol. Rsch. Svcs., Pullman, 1972; pres. Commn. on Manganese, Internat. Assn. of the Genesis of Ore Deposits, 1986-90; vis. lectr. Japan Soc. for Promotion of Sci. Hokkaido, 1981; fgn. invited scientist USSR Pacific Vinogradov Expdn., 1986. Sr. author: Manganese Nodules, 1979; donor of first extensive deep-sea manganese nodule collection to be archived in the Smithsonian Institution, Washington, 1991; contbr. over 50 articles to profl. jours. and govt. publs. Informal cons. City Coun., NOAA, Wash. State Govt., 1980-90; volcanic ash cons. Mt. St. Helens eruption 1980, Wash. State U. Vis. rsch. fellow in geology Manchester (England) U., 1969, U. Geneva, Switzerland, 1969-70; recipient numerous rsch. grants NSF, U.S. Bur. Mines, others, 1960—. Fellow Mineralogical Soc. of Am., Geol. Soc. of Am., Soc. Econ. Geologists; mem. Sigma Xi. Home: 925 SE Spring St Pullman WA 99163-2245 Office: Rks Geol Rsch Svcs 1345 NE Terre View Dr Ste 4W Pullman WA 99163-5101

SOREN, DAVID, archaeology educator, administrator; b. Phila., Oct. 7, 1946; s. Harry Friedman and Erma Elizabeth (Salamon) Soren; m. Noelle Louise Schattyn, Dec. 22, 1967. B.A., Dartmouth Coll., 1968; M.A., Harvard U., 1972, Ph.D., 1973. Cert. Rome Classics Ctr. Curator of coins Fogg Art Mus., Cambridge, Mass., 1972; asst. prof. U. Mo., Columbia, 1972-76, assoc. prof., dept. head, 1976-81; prof. archaeology U. Ariz., Tucson, 1982-83, dept. head, 1984-89; guest curator Am. Mus. Natural History, N.Y.C., 1983-90, lectr., 1993—; creator dir. Kourion excavations, Cyprus, 1982-89, Portugal, 1983-84, pot cons., field dir. Tunisia Excavations Chgo. Oriental Inst./Smithsonian Instn., 1973-78; creator/dir. Am. Excavations at Lugnano, Italy, 1988—; dir. U. Ariz. humanities program, 1992. Author: (books) Unreal Reality, 1978, Rise and Fall of Fantasy Film, 1980, Carthage, 1990; co-author: Kourion: Search for a Lost Roman City, 1988, Corpus des Mosaiques de Tunisie, 1972, 3rd rev. edit., 1986, Carthage: A Mosaic of Ancient Tunisia, 1987; editor: Excavations at Kourion I, 1987; producer: (film) Carthage: A Mirage of Antiquity, 1987; creator and guest curator: (internat. traveling exhbn.) Carthage: A Mosaic of Ancient Tunisia, 1987-92; editor, founder Roscius, 1993—; contbr. articles to profl. jours. Subject of National Geographic spl. Archeological Detectives, 1985; work subject of feature articles in Newsweek, Conoisseur, National Geographic and others; recipient Cine Golden Eagle, 1980, Angenieux Film award Industrial Photography mag., 1980, Outstanding American Under 40 award C. Johns Hopkins-Britain's Royal Inst. Internat. Affairs, 1985; named Outstanding American Under 40 Esquire mag., 1985, hon. Italian citizen Lugnano, Italy, 1989; grantee NEH, 1979, 87, Fulbright, Lisbon, 1983. Mem. Nat. Geog. Soc. (project dir. 1983-84), Am. Sch. Oriental Rsch. (dept. rep. 1981-85), Archaeol. Inst. Tucson (pres. 1983-86), Luso-Am. Commn. (citation 1983-84), Explorer's Club. Office: U Ariz Dept Classics 371 MLB Tucson AZ 85721

SORENSEN, CARL DAVID, mechanical engineering educator; b. Washington, Mar. 2, 1958; s. Neil R. and Lu Ann (Merrill) S.; m. Cynthia Louise Cobabe, Apr. 28, 1981; children: Neil William, Michael Paul, Daniel Carl. BS in Physics, Brigham Young U., 1981; PhD in Materials Sci., MIT, 1988. Engr.-in-tng., Utah. Rsch. asst. MIT, Cambridge, 1981-85, postdoctoral assoc., 1985-87; asst. prof. mech. & mfg. engring. Brigham Young U., Provo, Utah, 1987—; mem. adj. faculty U. Lowell, Mass., 1981-86; cons. Chrysler Motors Co., Detroit, 1986-87, Wilson Products, Salt Lake City, 1988. Contbr. articles to profl. jours. Mem. ASME, Am. Soc. Engring. Edn., ASM Internat., Sigma Xi. Republican. Mem. LDS Ch. Home: 286 E 4840 N Provo UT 84604-5438 Office: Brigham Young U 435 CTB Provo UT 84602

SORENSEN, CRAIG BURG, county official; b. Salt Lake City, Oct. 17, 1946; s. William Homer and Winona (Burg) S.; m. Aug. 3, 1977; children: Craig Jr., Cameron, Clinton, Crystal, Candice, Carlyn. BS, U. Utah, 1970; postgrad., UCLA, 1970-71. Auditor Peat Marwick Main, Salt Lake City, 1972-74; county auditor Salt Lake County Auditors Office, Salt Lake City, 1978—. Bd. dirs. Salt Lake County Planning Commn., 1986-91, Foothill Western Boys Baseball Assn.; pres. bd. dirs. Work Activity Ctr. for Handicapped Adults, Salt Lake City, 1972-91. Recipient Cert. Achievement for Excellence in Fin. Reporting Govt. Fin. Officers Assn. U.S. and Can., 1988-92. Republican. Mem. Church Latter Day Saints. Home: 1642 Maple Ave Salt Lake City UT 84106 Office: Salt Lake County Auditor 2001 S State St N 2200 Salt Lake City UT 84190-1100

SORENSEN, DOROTHY ALLAN, allergy nurse; b. Butte, Mont., July 25, 1932; d. Charles Harwood and Margaret P. (Shea) Allan; m. Oscar John Sorensen, Feb. 4, 1956; children: Erick Andrew, Erin Anne, Craig Michael. Diploma in nursing, Mt. Zion Hosp., San Francisco, 1957; student, City Coll., San Francisco, 1954, U. San Francisco, 1956. RN, Calif. Office mgr. Yvonne Knighten, M.D., Berkeley, Calif., Ralph G. Bennett, M.D., Hayward, Calif.; nurse San Francisco Airport Clinic; immunotherapy coord. The Allergy Clinic, San Mateo, Calif., 1991—. Mem. Dermatol. Nurses Assn. (cert.), Office Nursing Assn. Home: 453 Beech Ave San Bruno CA 94066-4153 Office: The Allergy Clinic 50 S San Mateo Dr San Mateo CA 94401

SORENSEN, ELAINE SHAW, nurse, educator, researcher; b. Ogden, Utah, Mar. 3, 1949; d. Rulon C. and Jean (Blodgett) Shaw; children: Brian, Chad, Todd and Johanna Sorensen. AA, Weber State Coll., Ogden, 1970; BS, U. Utah, 1972, MS, 1979, PhD, 1988. RN. Community worker Operation Outreach, Pippa Passes, Ky., 1969; staff nurse LDS Hosp., Salt Lake City, 1970-71, St. Benedict's Hosp., Ogden, Utah, 1971-72; health missionary LDS Ch., Colombia, 1972-74; sch. nurse Ogden City Schs., 1974; instr. nursing U. Utah, Salt Lake City, 1978-80; staff nurse Primary Children's Med. Ctr., Salt Lake City, 1981-82; asst. prof. nursing Brigham Young U., Provo, Utah, 1987-92, assoc. prof., 1992—; com. mem. Brigham Young U./LDS Women's Conf., Provo, 1990—; health missionary LDS Ch., Colombia, 1972-74; mem. adv. com. Ohlsten Health Care, Provo, 1990—. Author: Children's Stress and Coping, 1993. Recipient New Profl. Book award Nat. Coun. on Family Rels., 1991, Excellence in Writing award Utah Nurses Assn., 1991; Faculty fellow Charles Redd Ctr., 1992. Mem. ANA, We. Inst. of Nursing (sec. 1989-91), We. Soc. for Rsch. in Nursing (exec. com. 1989-91), Phi Kappa Phi. Mormon.

SORENSEN, SHEILA, state legislator; b. Chgo., Sept. 20, 1947; d. Martin Thomas Moloney and Elizabeth (Koehr) Paulus; m. Wayne B. Slaughter, May 1969 (div. 1976); 1 child, Wayne Benjamin III; m. Dean E. Sorensen, Feb. 14, 1977; (stepchildren) Michael, Debbie, Kevin, Dean C. BS, Loretto Heights Coll., Denver, 1965; postgrad. pediatric nurse practicioner, U. Colo., Denver, 1969-70. Pediatric nurse practicioner Pub. Health Dept., Denver, 1970-71, Boise, Idaho, 1971-72; pediatric nurse practicioner Boise (Idaho) Pediatric Group, 1972-74, Pediatric Assocs., Boise, 1974-77; mem. Idaho State Ho. Reps., 1987-92, Idaho State Senate, 1992—. Pct. committeeman Ada County Rep. Cen. Com., Boise, 1982-86, dist. vice-chairperson, 1985—; polit. chmn. Idaho Med. Assn. Aux., 1984-87, Ada County Med. Assocs., 1986-87; bd. dirs. Family Practice Residency Program, 1992—, Univ./Community Health Sci. Assn. Mem. Nat. Conf. State Legislators, Nat. Orgn. Women Legislators, Am. Legis. Exch. Coun. Roman Catholic.

SORENSON, CRAIG ALLEN, business executive; b. Belle Fourche, S.D., Mar. 11, 1954; s. LaMoine Charles and Verla Leulla (Twombley) S.; m. Vicki Ann Fitzgerald, Nov. 28, 1981; children: Joshua, Amanda, Carin, Casey. AS, NW Community Coll., Powell, Wyo., 1974; BS in Agrl. Engring., U. Wyo., 1978. Reclamation engr. Decker (Mont.) Coal Co., 1978-81; contract adminstr. Am. Line Builders Inc., Dayton, Wash., 1981-83; exec. owner SE Inc., Deaver, Wyo., 1983—; bd. dirs. SE Inc., 1983—, Calif.-Wyo. Ventures West, Inc., Blythe, Calif. Council mem. Town of Deaver, 1984-88, mayor elect, 1988, mayor 1989—; vol. fireman Frannie, Wyo., 1984—; bd. dirs. joint powers bd. Shoshone Mcpl. Water System. Mem. Wyo. Assn. Municipalities (voting del. 1988, 92). Republican. Lutheran. Home: 727 Rd 1 Deaver WY 82421

SORENSON, MARC BRUCE, health resort owner, writer; b. Ely, Nev., June 20, 1943; s. Marcus C. and Mildred (Wheat) S.; m. Nancy Arnett, June 2, 1966 (dec. Dec. 1982); m. Vicki Lynn Cummings, Sept. 16, 1983; children: Marc A., Kathleen, Suzanne, Samantha. BS, Brigham Young U., 1966, MS, 1968, PhD, 1973. Owner, CEO Nat. Inst. of Fitness, St. George, Utah, 1973-92. Author: (books) Slim Nutrition, 1982, Eat More, Move More, Lose More, 1987, Essays in Happiness, 1991, Megahealth, 1992 (Nutrition award Money Sch. Boston 1992); contbr. articles to fitness and popular fin. mags. Named Ky. Col., State of Ky., 1992, Arkansas Traveler, State of Ark.; Megahealth(his book) resulted in State of Utah declaring Fitness Week. LDS ch. Home: 2501 S Tonaquint Lot 5 Saint George UT 84770 Office: Nat Inst of Fitness 202 N Snow Canyon Rd Ivins UT 84738

SORENSON, RALPH ZELLAR, II, management educator; b. Evanston, Ill., Sept. 20, 1933; s. Ralph Zellar and Verna Mary (Koenig) S.; m. Charlotte Bacon Ripley, June 25, 1960; children: Kristin Elizabeth, Katrina Anne, Eric Ripley. AB magna cum laude, Amherst Coll., 1955; MBA with distinction, Harvard U., 1959, DBA, 1967; LLD (hon.), Babson Coll., 1985. Rsch. asst. IMEDE Mgmt. Devel. Inst., Lausanne, Switzerland, 1959-61; exec. Nestle Alimentana (SA), Vevey, Switzerland, 1961-63; prof. Bus. Sch. Harvard U., 1964-74, adj. prof. mgmt., 1989—; pres. Babson Coll., Wellesley, Mass., 1974-81; pres., chief exec. officer Barry-Wright Corp., 1981-89, chmn. bd., bd. dir.; bd. dir. Houghton-Mifflin Co., Springs Industries Inc., Affiliated Publs. Inc., Polaroid Corp., Eaton Vance Corp.; past. bd. dirs. Fed. Res. Bank Boston. Vice chmn., trustee Boston Mus. Sci.; mem. corp. Babson Coll., Mass. Gen. Hosp.; bd. overseers Boston Symphony Orch., Mus. Fine Arts, Boston. Lt. USAF, 1955-57. Ford Found. fellow; recipient spl. award appreciation Asian Inst. Mgmt., Manila, Disting. Citizen award Boy Scouts Am., 1985. Mem. Amherst Coll. Alumni Soc. (past pres.), Phi Beta Kappa. Clubs: The Country (Brookline); Comml., Univ. Home: 603 Spruce St Boulder CO 80302-5017 Office: Univ Colo Dean of Bus Sch University Of Colorado CO 80309

SORIA, HUMBERTO ARREOLA, accountant; b. Durango, Mexico, Aug. 24, 1949; came to U.S., 1973; s. Luis and Dolores (Arreola) S.; m. Maria C. Soria, Oct. 17, 1973; children: Cinthya Marie, Crystal Marie, Stephanie Marie. BS in Acctg., Instituto Thecnologico, Durango; postgrad., Instituto Comercial, Durango. Jr. acct. Amex Systems, El Segundo, Calif., 1974-77; bus. mgr. Djalma Constrn., Redondo Beach, Calif., 1977-79; fin. analyst Rockwell Internat., Cypres, Calif., 1980-87; pvt. practice tax cons. and fin. planning Harbor City, Calif., 1988—; cons. Nat. Inst. Adult Edn., L.A., 1985—. Recipient Certs. of Appreciation L.A. Unified Sch. Dist., 1986, Lomita (Calif.) Fundamental CIMI, 1987. Office: Tax Cons PO Box 452 Harbor City CA 90710-0452

SOROM, TERRY ALLEN, ophthalmic surgeon; b. Lanesboro, Minn., Jan. 9, 1940; s. Martin John and Elvira (Lodahl) S.; m. Suzanne A. Johnson, children: Martin, Jeb, Abraham, Theodore. BS, Luther Coll., 1962; MD, U. Minn.-Mpls., 1966. Diplomate Am. Bd. Ophthalmology. Intern. U. Oreg., Portland, 1967, resident in ophthalmology, 1969-73; ophthalmic surgeon Eye and Ear Clinic, Inc., Wenatchee, Wash., 1973—. Charter trustee Wenatchee Visitor and Conv. Bur., 1980; bd. dirs. Blue Cross Wash., and Alaska; pres. Wenatchee Valley Coll. Found., 1986-88. Capt. M.C., USAF, 1967-69. Mem. AMA, Am. Acad. Ophthalmology, Contact Lens Assn. Ophthalmology, Am. Intraocular Implant Soc., Wash. State Acad. Ophthalmology (trustee 1978-80), Oregon Ophthalmologic Alumni Assn. (pres. 1988—), Greater Wenatchee Found. (bd. dirs.), Chelan-Douglas County Med. Assn., Rotary (pres. 1983-84). Republican. Lutheran. Office: Eye & Ear Clinic Wenatchee Inc PS 600 Orondo Ave PO Box 3027 Wenatchee WA 98801

SORRENTINO, GILBERT, English language educator, novelist, poet; b. Bklyn., Apr. 27, 1929; s. August E. and Ann Marie (Davis) S.; m. Victoria Ortiz; children: Jesse, Delia, Christopher. Student, Bklyn. Coll., 1949-51, 54-56. In various positions, 1947-70; including reins. clk. Fidelity and Casualty Co., N.Y.C., 1947-48; freight checker Ace Assembly Agy., N.Y.C., 1954-56; packer Bennett Bros. Inc., N.Y.C., 1956-57; messenger Am. Houses, Inc., N.Y.C., 1948-49; shipping-room supr. Thermo-fax Sales, Inc., Queens, N.Y., 1957-60; editor Grove Press, N.Y., 1965-70; tchr. Columbia U., 1966, Aspen Writers Workshop, 1967, Sarah Lawrence Coll., 1972, The New Sch. for Social Rsch., 1976—; NEH chairperson in lit. U. Scranton, 1979; prof. English Stanford (Calif.) U., 1982—; editorial cons. Contemporary Lit., 1989—. Author: The Darkness Surrounds Us, 1960, Black and White, 1964, The Sky Changes, 1966, The Perfect Fiction, 1968, Steelwork, 1970, Imaginative Qualities of Actual Things, 1971, Corrosive Sublimate, 1971, Splendide-Hotel, 1973, Flawless Play Restored, 1974, A Dozen Oranges, 1976, White Sail, 1977, Sulpiciae Elegidia/Elegiacs of Sulpicia, 1977, The Orangery, 1978, Mulligan Stew, 1979, Aberration of Starlight, 1980, Selected Poems, 1958-80, 1981, Crystal Vision, 1981, Blue Pastoral, 1983, Something Said: Essays, 1984, Odd Number, 1985, Rose Theatre, 1987, Misterioso, 1989, Under the Shadow, 1991. With U.S. Army, 1951-53. Recipient Samuel Fels award in fiction Coord. Coun. Lit. Mags., 1974, John Dos Passos prize, 1981, Am. Acad. and Inst. Arts and Letters award in lit., 1985, Lannan Lit. award for fiction, 1992; John Simon Guggenheim Meml. fellow, 1973-74, 87-88; grantee Creative Artists Pub. Svc. Program, 1974-75, Nat. Endowment for Arts, 1974-75, 78-79, 83-84. Mem. PEN Am. Ctr. Office: Stanford U Dept English Stanford CA 94305

SORSTOKKE, SUSAN EILEEN, systems engineer; b. Seattle, May 2, 1955; d. Harold William and Carrol Jean (Russ) S. BS in Systems Engring., U. Ariz., 1976; MBA, U. Wash., Richland, 1983. Warehouse team mgr. Procter and Gamble Paper Products, Modesto, Calif., 1976-78; quality assurance engr. Westinghouse Hanford Co., Richland, Wash., 1978-80; supr. engring. document ctr. Westinghouse Hanford Co., Richland, 1980-81; mgr. data control and adminstrn. Westinghouse Electric Corp., Madison, Pa., 1981-82, mgr. data control and records mgmt., 1982-84; prin. engr. Westinghouse Elevator Co., Morristown, N.J., 1984-87; region adminstrn. mgr. Westinghouse Elevator Co., Arleta, Calif., 1987-90; ops. rsch. analyst Am. Honda Motor Co. Inc., Torrance, Calif., 1990—; adj. prof. U. LaVerne, Calif., 1991-92. Advisor Jr. Achievement, 1982-83; literacy tutor Westmoreland Literacy Coun., 1983-84, host parent EF Found., Saugus, Calif., 1987-88, Am. Edn. Connection, Saugus, 1988-89, 91, 93; instr. Excell, L.A., 1991-92. Mem. Soc. Women Engrs., Am. Inst. Indsl. Engrs., Optimists Charities, Inc. (bd. dirs. Acton, Calif. 1991—). Republican. Methodist. Home: 21647 Spice Ct Santa Clarita CA 91350-1656 Office: Am Honda Motor Co Inc Dept Parts Rsch and Planning 1919 Torrance Blvd Torrance CA 90501-2746

SORTLAND, TRUDITH ANN, educator, speech and language therapist; b. Butte, Mont., Dec. 3, 1940; d. Kenneth Hjalmer Sortland and Sigrid V. (Kotka) Strand. BS, Minot (N.D.) State U., 1965. Tchr. Westby (Mont.) Sch., 1960-61, Glasgow (Mont.) Southside Sch., 1962-65, Glasgow AFB, Mont., 1965-80; tchr., speech and lang. pathologist Mineral County Sch. Dist., Hawthorne, Nev., 1965-68, 78—; kindergarten tchr. Mineral County Sch. Dist., Mina, Nev., 1968-72; elem. tchr. Mineral County Sch. Dist., Mina, 1978-80; speech, language pathologist Mineral County Sch. Dist., Mina, Republic of Korea, 1980—; tchr. Dept. Def., Pusan, Republic of Kores, 1972-73, Illesheim, Fed. Republic Germany, 1973-78; tchr. Mohall (N.D.) Pub. Sch., 1964-65; cons. Mary Kay Cosmetics, tchr. Glasgow Air Force Base, 1965-68. Supt. Sunday sch. Bethany Luth. Ch., Hawthorne, 1987—, sec. Ladies Aid, 1987—. Mem. NEA, Nev. Edn. Assn., AAUW (past sec., pres.), Pair O Dice Square Dance Club (sec. 1989—), Delta Kappa Gamma. Home: PO Box 816 Hawthorne NV 89415-0816 Office: Mineral County Sch Dist A St Hawthorne NV 89415

SOSKIN, STEVE, computer software consultant; b. N.Y.C., Feb. 20, 1947; s. Al and Beatrice (Gordon) Mandel; m. Tobi Eisentein, 1972 (div. 1982); children: Deena Lyn, Sheela Beth; m. Diane Kathie Behling, Mar. 21, 1992. BA, L.I. U., 1969; MA in Psychology, New Sch. for Social Rsch., 1972. Tchr. N.Y.C. Bd. Edn., Bklyn., 1969-76; computer programmer Con Edison, N.Y.C., 1975-79; computer analyst Colgate Palmolive, N.Y.C., 1979-80, Paine Webber, N.Y.C., 1980-81; system analyst Merrill Lynch, N.Y.C., 1981-84; sales engr. Tarkenton Software/Knowledgeware, Atlanta, 1984-87; cons. Interactive Info. Systems, San Francisco, 1987-88; sales engr., mech. mktg. mgr. Micro Focus, Palo Alto, Calif., 1988-91; cons. Interactive Info. Systems, Los Gatos, Calif., 1991—; lectr. U. Calif. at Berkeley Ext., San Francisco, 1990-91. Mem. Psi Chi Nat. Honor Soc.

SOSS, ALEXANDER LESTER, business and management executive, consultant; b. Cleve., Nov. 2, 1938; s. Lester A. and Elizabeth (Osiecki) S.; m. July 10, 1971; div. Aug. 1984. Student, Calif. State U., Northridge; diploma, Stanford U., 1969, U. So. Calif., 1975; student, San Fernando Valley State Coll. Asst. to chancellor Calif. State Univs. and Colls., 1966-68; regional mgr. South Bay U.S. Census, L.A., 1969-70; treas. United Rep. Fin. Com. L.A. County, L.A., 1970-73; v.p. St. Johns & Talmadge, L.A., 1973-79; dir. mktg. Showcase U.S.A., L.A., 1979-80; pvt. practice cons. L.A., 1980—, Leif & Soss, 1987—; with KLS Assocs., 1987—; bd. dirs. Hall Enterprises, Inc., Granada Contractors, Inc., Terran Group, Inc., hearts and Lands, inc. Contbr. poetry to mags., articles to profl. jours. Chmn. bd. SCAG/DWP SFV Groundwater Contamination Commn., 1981-83; mem. Roosvelt Ctr. Am. Policy Studies (San Fernando Valley Citizens Assembly 1988-90), Ctr. Entreprenurial Mgmt., 1987—, Tierra del Sol Found., Sunland (bd. dirs. 1981-83). With U.S. Army, 1961-69. Recipient honorary resolutions by Calif. legislature, L.A. County Bd., L.A. City Coun., L.A. Dept. Water and Power and others. Mem. Order of APEHA (pres. Beverly Hills chpt., nat. del.), Nat. Football Found. Hall of Fame (bd. dirs.), San Fernando Valley Pub. Rel. Round Table (pres. 1978-79), L.A. Pub. Affairs Officers Assn., Am. Soc. Pub. Adminstrn., Pub. Rels. Soc. Am., Splty. Equipment Mfrs. Assn., Calif. C. of C. (small bus. task force), United C. of C. (bd. dirs.), San Fernando Valley Regional C. of C. (v.p., bd. dirs. 1975-81), Mid San Fernando C. of C. (Pres.'s Excellence award 1991, v.p. govt. affairs, bd. dirs. 1990-93), United C. of C. San Fernando Valley (v.p. govt., chair, govt. affairs, bd. dirs. 1989—), Valley Transp. Summit, Greater Van Nuys Area C. of C. (v.p. state and fed. gov. 1989—), San Francisco Valley UNITY Coalition, MIT Enterprise Forum, Inc., Burbank Elks, Blue Key, Phi Mu Alpha, Pi Sigma Alpha, Sigma Chi. Lutheran. Office: 11257 Calvert St North Hollywood CA 91606-4243

SOSSAMAN, JAMES J., state legislator; b. Phoenix, July 17, 1932; s. Jasper H. and Faith Carolyn (Mather) S.; m. Carolyn Sue Peters, Dec. 12, 1953; children—Kimberlee, Stephen, Scott. Student, Ariz. State U., 1950-52. Mem. Ariz. Ho. of Reps., 1969-93, majority whip, 1976-84, speaker, 1985-

87, senator, 1987-93. Precinct committeeman, 1958—; mem. Queen Creek Sch. Bd., 1965-80. Lt. USN, 1952-56, Korea. Recipient Outstanding Young Farmer award Flying Farmers, 1966, Legislator of Yr. award Ariz. Students' Assn., 1977, 78, Disting. Citizen award U. Ariz., 1979, hon. state farmer degree Future Farmers Am., 1980. Mem. Am. Legis. Exchange Council, Western Conf. Council State Govts., Maricopa County Farm Bur. (pres.), Ariz. Cotton Growers Bd. (agriculturalist for 1986). Republican. Methodist. Home: 19105 E Ocotillo Rd Queen Creek AZ 85242

SOTER, NICHOLAS GREGORY, advertising agency executive; b. Great Falls, Mont., Apr. 26, 1947; s. Sam Nick and Bernice (Bennett) S.; m. Kathleen Lyman, Feb. 20, 1970; children: Nichole, Erin, Samuel Scott, Kara, Stephen Andrew, Riley Kyle. BS, Brigham Young U., 1971. With McLean Assocs., Provo, Utah, 1970-75; chmn. bd., chief exec. officer Soter Assocs. Inc., Provo, 1975—; founder, pres. RS Corp., 1986-88, Plum C Corp., 1988; instr. advt. Utah Valley Community Coll., Orem, 1971-75, Brigham Young U., Provo, 1980-84. Publisher: Journal of Joseph, 1979, Journal of Brigham, 1980, LaVell Edwards, 1980, Amos Wright, 1981, Moments in Motherhood, 1981, What It Means to Know Christ, 1981, Mormon Fortune Builders, 1982, Utah History, 1982; contbr. articles to profl. jours. Active Utah Valley Pub. Communications Coun. for LSD Ch., 1982-87; mem. adv. coun. Monte L. Bean Life Sci. Mus., 1987-89; Rep. dist. chmn.; v.p. exec. com. Am.'s Freedom Festival at Provo, 1990-91; jury chmn. Coun. for Advancement and Support of Edn., 1989; vocalist Ralph Woodward Chorale, 1991—, pres., 1992—. Recipient N.Y. Art Dir.'s The One Show award, Salt Lake Art Dirs. Communications Assn. of Utah Valley awards. Mem. Utah Advt. Fedn., Pub. Rels. Soc. Am., Communications Assn. Utah Valley (past pres.), Provo C. of C. (bd. dirs.), Innisbrook Network of Advt. Agys. (pres. 1986-87). Home: 1728 S 290 E Orem UT 84058-7928 Office: Soter Assocs Inc 209 N 400 W Provo UT 84601-2799

SOTH, CAROLYN MARIE, academic program director; b. Long Beach, Calif., Oct. 11, 1964; d. Robert Charles and Mary Beth (House) S. AA, Long Beach City Coll., 1986, cert. mktg., 1986, cert. mgmt., 1986; BSBA, Calif. State Polytechnic U., 1989. Nat. chpt. devel. cons. Kappa Delta Nat. Sorority, Denver, 1989-90; asst. activities advisor U. Calif., Santa Barbara, 1990-92; coord. Greek Life San Jose (Calif.) State U., 1992—; adminstrv. asst. Western Regional Greek Conf., Santa Barbara, 1990-92, dir. pubs. 1992—. Donor Long Beach Day Nursery, 1989—. Named Outstanding Alumni Interfrat. and Panhellenic Couns., 1992. Mem. Assn. Frat. Advisors (area coord. 1992—, Outstanding Area Coord., 1992), Kappa Delta.

SOULÉ, MICHAEL HOWARD, educational administrator; b. Portland, Oreg., Oct. 5, 1952; s. James Frederick and Dorothy Helen (Boentje) S.; m. Holly Ann Bushbaum, Apr. 19, 1987; stepchildren: Japhet Koteen, Azur Koteen. BS, Northwestern U., 1974; MS, U. Calif., Berkeley, 1975. Rsch. asst. Clearlake (Calif.) Algal Rsch. Unit, 1975; exec. dir. Oreg. Environ. Found., Portland, 1976-81; dir. Environ. Edn. Project Portland State U., 1977-83; dir. Children of the Green Earth, Seattle, 1980—; adminstr. Seattle Waldorf Sch., 1986-91; regional coord. Columbia River Watch, Portland, 1980; regional coord. Project Learning Tree Am. Forest Inst., Portland, 1979-82; cons. Can. Trees for Life, Toronto, Ont., 1982. Author booklet: Treesong, 1981; founder, editor Clearing Magazine, Jour. for Environ. Edn., 1977-83, Children of Green Earth News, 1980—; Green Book Curriculum Guide, 1981. NSF grad. fellow, 1975; recipient One Earth award Bahai Internat. Community, 1982. Mem. Anthroposophical Soc. Democrat. Home and Office: 3055 NE 98th Seattle WA 98115

SOULES, CHARLES WEBSTER, engineering executive; b. Mpls., Sept. 27, 1936; s. Webster Fladlin and Helen Virginia (Wildes) S.; m. Beatrice Karain Farmer, Apr. 12, 1963; children: Lynnae Michelle, Heather Marie Soules Dillon. BSEE, Ill. Inst. of Tech., 1958; MSEE, U.S. Naval Postgrad. Sch., 1965. Commd. ensign USN, 1958, advanced through grades to capt.; various duties, 1958-72; project mgr. Puget Sound Naval Shipyard, Bremerton, Wash., 1972-75; chief engr. USS Midway, Yokosuka, Japan, 1975-77; asst. maintenance ofcer to aircraft carrier maintenance officer Naval Air Force Pacific, San Diego, 1977-82; prodn. officer to comdg. officer Ship Repair Facility, Yokosuka, Japan, 1982-87; comdg. officer Supr. of Shipbuilding Conversion and Repair, San Francisco, 1987-89, ret., 1989; engrng. mgr. CALEX Mfg. Co. Inc., Concord, Calif., 1989—. Mem. IEEE, Am. Soc. of Naval Engrs. (chpt. pres. 1986-87), Treasure Island Yacht Club (rear commodore 1990), Yokosuka Sailing Assn. (commodore 1982-83), Al Bahr Temple, Disabled Am. Vets. (life), Sigma Chi. Republican. Presbyterian. Office: CALEX Mfg Co Inc 2401 Stanwell Dr Concord CA 94520

SOUTHARD, MARY ELLEN, pianist, organist, language educator; b. Detroit, July 4, 1941; d. Thomas Hollister and Dorothy Elisabeth Southard; 1 child, Ari Bustin. Student, U. Calif., Santa Barbara, 1959-61, Staatliche Hochschule Musik, Munich, 1961-62; BA, Calif. State U., San Francisco, 1964, MA, 1966. Organist, choir dir. Plymouth Ch., Oakland, Calif., 1968-72; music instr. Yamaha Music Sch., Berkeley, Calif., 1968-72; dance accompanist Oakland (Calif.) Recreation Dept., 1969-72; music dir., mgr. Epic West Theatre, Berkeley, 1975-76; music specialist Centro Vida Bilingual Ctr., Berkeley, 1977-81; composer, vocal coach San Francisco Bay Area Theatres, 1978-83; music instr. Akademi Musik Indonesia, Yogyakarta, Java, 1984-85; music accompanist Shasta Coll., Redding, Calif., 1990—, ESL instr., 1987—; pianist, performer Shasta Symphony Orch., Redding, 1987—; program dir. Performing Arts Soc., Redding, 1988—. Composer: (theatre music) Schweyk, 1978, Orfee, 1979, Simone Machard, 1982, (radio music) Psychobabble, 1977. Mem. Am. Guild of Organists, Calif. Assn. Tchrs. ESL. Office: Shasta Coll 11555 Old Oregon Trail Redding CA 96003

SOUTHARD, PEGGY-DEE ANN, sociologist, anthropologist; b. San Francisco, Jan. 27, 1956; d. Layfette Fate and Wilma May (Trobridge) S. AA in Social Sci., Cen. Oreg. C.C., 1989; BA in Sociology, Anthropology, So. Oreg. State Coll., 1991; postgrad., U. Colo., 1991-92, U. Oreg., Eugene, 1992—. Adminstrv. analyst Proteus Adult Tng. Non-Profit Employment and Tng., Visalia, Calif., 1975-83; co-dir. Low Income Families Together, Bend, Oreg., 1984-86; owner, mgr. book store Yesterday's Gone, Bend, 1983-86; spl. collections manuscript processor U. Oreg., Eugene, 1987-88; prof.'s asst. Cen. Oreg. C.C., Bend, 1988-89; tutor sociology, anthropology So. Oreg. State Coll., Ashland, 1989-91; asst. editor, adminstrv. asst. U. Colo., Boulder, 1991-92, teaching asst. sociology, 1991-92; NSF rsch. fellow in sociology U. Oreg., Eugene, 1992-93, teaching asst. sociology, 1993—; bus. cons. Pageantry Book Co., Ashland, 1989-91, Eugene, 1992—. Author: Shelters Are for Scum; and I Ain't No Bum, 1992; contbr. to various publs. Bd. dirs. Cen. Oreg. Community Action Agy., Bend, 1984-86. Mem. NOW, Am. Sociol. Assn., Sociologists for Women in Soc., So. Oreg. Sociol. Assn. (chair 1989-91), Pacific Sociological Assn., Phi Kappa Phi, Omicron Delta Kappa. Home: PO Box 1784 Eugene OR 97440

SOUTHERN, RONALD DONALD, diversified corporation executive; b. Calgary, Alta., Can., July 25, 1930; s. Samuel Donald and Alexandra (Cuthill) S.; m. Margaret Visser, July 30, 1954; children: Nancy, Linda. BSc, U. Alta., Edmonton, 1953; LLD (hon.), U. Calgary, 1976, U. Alberta, 1991. Pres., CEO ATCO Ltd., Calgary, 1954-85, dep. chmn., CEO, 1985-91, chmn., pres., CEO, 1985—; chmn. Can. Utilities Ltd., Edmonton; hon. assoc. mem. Calgary Exhbn. and Stampede Bd.; bd. dirs. ATCO Ltd., Fletcher Challenge Can Ltd., Can. Airlines Ltd., Chrysler Can. Ltd., IMASCO Ltd., LaFarge Corp., Royal Inst. Ltd., Xerox of Can. Inc., Fletcher Challenge Ltd. Recipient Holland Trade award Govt. of The Netherlands, 1985, (with wife) Sportsmen of Yr. award Calgary Booster Club; named Businessman of Yr. U. Alta., 1986, to Order of Can., 1986; mem. Brit. Empire. Mem. United Church of Can. Clubs: Calgary Petroleum, Earl Grey Golf, U. Calgary Chancellors, Ranchmen's Club. Home: 67 Massey Pl SW, Calgary, AB Canada T2V 2G7 Office: ATCO Ltd, 909 11th Ave SW # 1600, Calgary, AB Canada T2R 1N6 also: Canadian Utilities, 10035 105th St, Edmonton, AB Canada T5J 2V6

SOUTHWARD, WALTER WILLIAM, public relations company executive; b. Pitts., July 16, 1936; s. Walter William and Hilda (Geider) S.; m. Leilani Akoni, Mar. 30, 1963. Student, Marshall U., 1957-59. Reporter Herald-Dispatch, Huntington, W.Va., 1957-59; reporter, asst. Sunday editor Hilo (Hawaii) Tribune-Herald, 1959-62; asst. Sunday editor Honolulu Advertiser, 1962-63; Big Island bur. chief Honolulu Advertiser, Hilo, 1963-70; mgr. pub. affairs Waikoloa, Hilo, 1970-77; pvt. practice pub. relations Hilo, 1977—; various sportscasting and freelance writing assignments, 1957—. Pres. Hilo Nat. Little League, 1966-68, Big Island Women's Softball League, 1968-73, Waikoloa Village Assn., 1971-74; head coach Hilo Comets Women's Softball Team, 1970-88, U. Hawaii at Hilo Athletic Boosters, 1976-77. With U.S. Army, 1954-57. Named Booster of Yr. U. Hawaii at Hilo, 1974. Mem. Am. Numismatic Assn. (life), Pub. Relations Soc. Am., Geothermal Resources Council, Hawaii Island C. of C. (pres. 1982-83), Big Island Coin Club (pres. 1964), Big Island Press, Lions, Hilo Yacht Club. Home: 94 Pakalana St Hilo HI 96720-1734 Office: PO Box 251 Hilo HI 96721-0251

SOUTHWICK, CHARLES HENRY, zoologist, educator; b. Wooster, Ohio, Aug. 28, 1928; s. Arthur F. and Faye (Motz) S.; m. Heather Milne Beck, July 12, 1952; children: Steven, Karen. B.A., Coll. Wooster, 1949; M.S., U. Wis., 1951, Ph.D., 1953. NIH fellow, 1951-53; asst. prof. biology Hamilton Coll., 1953-54; NSF fellow Oxford (Eng.) U., 1954-55; faculty Ohio U., 1955-61; assoc. prof. pathobiology Johns Hopkins Sch. Hygiene and Pub. Health, Balt., 1961-68; prof. Johns Hopkins Sch. Hygiene and Pub. Health, 1968-79; assoc. dir. Johns Hopkins Internat. Ctr. for Med. Rsch. and Tng., Calcutta, India, 1964-65; chmn. dept. environ., population and organismic biology U. Colo., Boulder, 1979-82, prof. biology, 1979—; researcher and author publs. on animal social behavior and population dynamics, influences animal social behavior on demographic characteristic mammal populations, primate ecology and behavior, estuarine ecology and environmental quality; mem. primate adv. com. Nat. Acad. Sci.-NRC, 1963-75, com. primate conservation, 1974-75; mem. Gov.'s Sci. Adv. Com. State of Md., 1975-78; mem. com. on rsch. and exploration Nat. Geog. Soc., 1979—; mem. adv. bd. Caribbean Primate Rsch. Ctr., 1987—, Wis. Primate Rsch. Ctr., 1990—; mem. Integrated Conservation Rsch., 1989—. Editor: Primate Social Behavior, 1963, Animal Aggression, 1970, Nonhuman Primates in Biomedical Research, 1975, Ecology and the Quality of Our Environment, 1976, Global Ecology, 1985; Ecology and Behavior of Food-Enhanced Primate Groups, 1988. Recipient Fulbright Rsch. award India, 1959-60. Fellow AAAS, Acad. Zoology, Animal Behavior Soc.; mem. Am. Soc. Zoologists, Ecol. Soc. Am., Am. Soc. Mammalogists, Am. Soc. Primatology, Internat. Primatology Soc., Am. Inst. Biol. Scis., Primatology Soc. Great Britain, Internat. Soc. Study Aggression.

SOUTHWICK, STEPHEN MARK, agricultural scientist; b. Woodland, Calif., May 14, 1956; s. Franklin Walburg and Rita (Anderson) s.; m. Perpetua Mary Santa Ana, July 8, 1989. BS, Cornell U., 1978; MS, U. Fla., 1980, PhD, 1986. Asst. rsch. specialist E.I. duPont de Nemours, Phila., 1977; owner Irrigation Sci. Svcs., Vero Beach, Fla., 1983-85; mng. ptnr. Agricultural Resource Mgmt., Vero Beach, 1982-84; extension specialist U. Calif., Davis, 1986—; owner, ptnr. Calyx Fruit, Winters, Calif., 1990—. Contbr. chpts. in ency.; contbr. articles to profl. jours. Grantee in field. Mem. Am. Soc. for Horticultural Sci. Republican. Home: 108 Almond Dr Winters CA 95694-2104 Office: U Calif Pomology Dept Davis CA 95616

SOUTHWORTH, ROD BRAND, computer science educator; b. Binghampton, N.Y., Aug. 24, 1941; s. William Tanner Southworth and Ruth Evelyn (Brabham) Woods; m. Patrice Marie Gapen, Jan. 10, 1978; children: Suzi Lynn, Judi Leigh, Megan Marie, Robin Ashley. BS in Bus., U. Ariz., 1965; MS in Mgmt. Sci. and Info Systems, Colo. State U., 1978. Mktg. rep. IBM, Denver, 1966-69; system analyst Colo. State U., Fort Collins, 1969-73, grad. teaching asst., 1978-79; project mgr. Systems and Computer Tech., Portland, Oreg., 1973-75; asst. dir. Systems and Computer Tech., Fairbanks, Alaska, 1975-77; instr. in computer info. systems Laramie County C.C., Cheyenne, Wyo., 1979—. Author: (software) PC-DOS/MS-DOS Simplified, 1st edit. 1988, 3rd edit. 1992, DOS Complete and Simplified, 1990, DOS Essentials, 1991, DOS 5 Simplified, 1992. Mem. Civil Air Patrol, Cheyenne, 1991. Mem. Data Processing Mgmt. Assn. (mem. assoc. level model curriculum 1984-85), Assn. Computing Machinery (mem. assoc. level computer info. processing model curriculum 1991-92). Home: PO Box 5457 Cheyenne WY 82003 Office: Laramie County Comm Coll 1400 East College Dr Cheyenne WY 82007

SOUVIRON, ALVARO, mining executive; b. Valparaiso, Chile, Feb. 15, 1933; came to U.S., 1973; s. Jose Maria and Olivia Margaret (Rose-Price) S.; m. Ximena Grebe, Sept. 14, 1958 (div. 1991); children: Pilar S. Bracero, Beatriz D'Amico, Alvaro J.; m. Aida Cordoba-Core, June 15, 1991. BS in Geology, Rensselaer Polytechnic Inst., 1956. Exploration mgr. L.Am. Atlantic Richfield Corp., Denver, 1977-82; pres. Mineracao Anaconda Brasil, Rio de Janeiro, 1982-85; internat. cons. Littleton, Colo., 1985—; Cons. UN, N.Y.C., 1986-91. Fellow So. Econ. Geologists; mem. Inst. Ingenieros de Minas (Chile) (Silver medal 1982). Home and Office: 5236 S Perry Ct Littleton CO 80123

SOUZA, BLASE CAMACHO, media specialist, writer; b. Kohala, Hawaii, Feb. 3, 1918; d. Lawrence Lorenzo Ramos and Mary Maria (Caravalho) Camacho; m. Alfred Patrick Souza, Nov. 26, 1949; children: Michelle Louise, Patricia Ann. EdB, U. Hawaii, Honolulu, 1939; MLS with honors, Pratt Inst., 1947. Cert. tchr., Hawaii. Tchr. Honolulu Dept. Pub. Instruction, 1940-42, Lahaina (Maui, Hawaii) Dept. Pub. Instruction, 1941-42; tchr. Waialua (Oahu, Hawaii) Dept. Pub. Instruction, 1943-46, libr., 1947-66; rsch. libr. dept. of edn. U. Hawaii, Honolulu, 1967-68, adminstr., rsch. libr. dept. of edn., 1968-70; edn. officer, program specialist Hawaii Dept. of Edn., Honolulu, 1970-75; local historian media svcs., writer P.R. Heritage Soc. of Hawaii, Honolulu, 1976—; cons. Hawaii Multi-Cultural Ctr., Honolulu, 1976-80, Hawaii Heritage Ctr., Honolulu, 1981—; lectr., cons. P.R. Heritage Soc. of Hawaii, Honolulu, 1984—. Author: Boricua Hawaiiana: Puerto Ricans of Hawaii, Reflections of the Past and Mirror of the Future, 1983, De Borinquen a Hawaii, 1985, (chpt.) Legacy of Diversity, 1975, MONTAGE-An Ethnic History of Women in Hawaii, 1977; contbr. articles to profl. jours. Dir. Friends of Waipahu Cultural Garden Park, 1983-92; active Hist. Hawaii Found., Honolulu, 1984, Bishop Mus., Honolulu, 1985—. Hawaii Com. for the Humanities grantee, 1980, 91. Mem. Hawaii Assn. Sch. Librs. (pres. 1965), Hawaii Libr. Assn. (pres. 1975), Hawaii Mus. Assn., P.R. Heritage Soc. Hawaii (founder, pres. 1980-84), AAUW. Roman Catholic. Home and office: 5180 Nohu St Honolulu HI 96821-1844

SOUZA, WADE ANTHONY, management professional; b. Honolulu, Feb. 1, 1958; s. Alfred Edward and Evelyn Elvira (Moniz) S.; m. Ellen Durchlaub, May 5, 1990. BA magna cum laude, U. Hawaii, 1980; MBA, U. Mich., 1982. Assoc. cons. Strategic Mgmt. Services, Detroit, 1981-82; mktg. analyst for product devel. then sr. mktg. planner then sr. project cons. CIGNA Conn. Gen. Ins., Hartford, 1982-85; assoc. mktg. mgr. then sr. assoc. mktg. mgr. RJR-Nabisco Inc., Farmington, Conn., 1985-87; brand mgr. for chocolate bars Nestle Foods Corp., Purchase, N.Y., 1987-88; sr. product mgr. Lea and Perrins Corp., Fair Lawn, N.J., 1988-90; gen. mgr. Castle & Cooke Consumer Ops Hawaiian Plantations Inc., Honolulu, 1990—; bd. dirs. Kilohana Mgmt. Group, Honolulu (mktg. cons. 1982-90), Pacific Cons. Inc., N.Y.C., Honolulu. Recipient fellowship Ctr. Japanese Studies, 1981. Mem. Planning Execs. Inst. Democrat. Roman Catholic. Home: 95-255 Waioleka St #77 Mililani HI 96789 Office: Castle & Cooke Hawaiian Plantations Inc 650 Iwilei Rd Honolulu HI 96817-5086

SOVATSKY, STUART CHARLES, psychotherapist; b. Rochester, N.Y., Apr. 14, 1949; s. Jacob J. Sovatsky and Lillian (Kaplan) Sawyer. AB, Princeton U., 1971; MA, Fairleigh Dickinson U., 1975; PhD, Calif. Inst. Integral Studies, San Francisco, 1984. Cert. marriage and family counselor. Probation officer Atlantic County, N.J., 1972-75; dir., asst. dir. Youth Svcs., Atlantic City, N.J., 1975-78; dir. projects Atlantic County Mental Health, Atlantic City, 1978-79; pvt. practice psychotherapy San Francisco, 1980—; asst. prof. Calif. Inst. Integral Studies, 1989—; instr., supr. J.F.K. U., Orinda, Calif., 1988—; clin. dir. Blue Oak and Insight Counseling, Berkeley and San Franciso, 1990—; bd. dirs., Calif. Inst. Integral Studies. Author: Passions of Innocence, 1993, Inner Traditions International, 1992; contbg. author Enlightened Sexuality, 1989; contbr. articles to profl. jours. Scholar Princeton U., 1967-71, Calif. Inst. Integral Studies, 1980-82; N.J. Judiciary Study grantee, 1973-75. Mem. Assn. Transpersonal Psychology, Calif. Marriage-Family Counselor Assn. Home And Office: 3040 Richmond Bl Oakland CA 94611

SOVETKY, JACK, entrepreneur, lawyer; b. Chgo., Aug. 13, 1930; s. Morris M. and Sadie (Kutchinsky) S.; m. Marion Elaine Leon, Aug. 13, 1955 (div. 1983); children: Rose Leon, Ralph Arthur, Susan Ruth, Daniel Louis. AA, L.A. City Coll., 1951; BA, L.A. State Coll., 1953; MA, Calif. State U., Northridge, 1960; JD, U. San Fernando Valley, Sepulveda, Calif., 1975. Bar: Calif. 1975. Tchr. L.A. City Schs., 1954-80; spl. agt. CIC, U.S. Army, L.A., 1954-56; pvt. practice law Reseda, Calif., 1976—. With U.S. Army, 1954-56. Mem. Calif. Bar Assn., Reseda C. of C. (bd. dirs. 1992), Valley Socialites (pres. 1989). Office: 7219 Canby Ave Ste G Reseda CA 91335-3004

SOVINEE, RUDY WILLIAM, chemist, lecturer; b. Elizabeth, N.J., June 28, 1948; s. Rudolph William and Freda Mae (Hixson) S.; m. Vivian Ama Donko Dakua, Sept. 4, 1971 (div. May 1, 1983); m. Ellen Gayle Wiggins, Oct. 10, 1987 (div. Mar. 15, 1990); 1 stepchild, Matthew. BS in Chemistry, Lehigh U., 1970. Cert. holistic health practitioner. Tchr., lexicographer Peace Corps Ghana, Kumasi, Ashanti, 1970-73; product, market analyst mgr. Union Carbide Corp., N.Y.C., Danbury, Conn., 1974-84; tech. sales support Execucom Systems, Inc., L.A., 1984-85; owner, chief cons. RWS Mgmt. Consulting, San Diego, 1986-92; creator, presenter Rudy Sovinee, Photographer for Peace, San Diego, 1990—; CFO San Diego Peace Corps Assn., 1988, 89, 90, 92, 93, pres., 1991; tour photographer World Peace Tours, China, Russia, 1986. Author: English-Twi Dictionary...of Chemistry of Physics, 1973; creator (multimedia show) One World, Our World, 1990. CPR instr. ARC, Danbury, 1978-84, fundraiser, 1981-84; coord. "Formando Puentes" Multiagency Binational Symposium, 1990, 92, 93. Recipient Math. scholarship NSF, 1965. Mem. Coalition for Equality, Difference Makers Internat., Citizen Diplomacy, San Diego-Vladivostok Sister City. Office: Photographer for Peace PO Box 436 Solana Beach CA 92075-0436

SOVISH, RICHARD CHARLES, retired manufacturing executive, consultant; b. Cleve., July 22, 1925; s. Charles and Clara Rita (Spiewak) S.; m. Amelia Martin, Jan. 9, 1954; children: Leslie Jean, Linda Gale, Eric Richard. BS, Ohio U., 1949; MS, Case Western Res. U., 1951, PhD, 1954. Chemist Dow Chem. Co., Midland, Mich., 1954-62; tech. assoc. Lockheed M&S Co., Sunnyvale, Calif., 1962-63; mem. tech. staff Raychem Corp., Menlo Park, Calif., 1963-75; tech. dir. telecom Europe Raychem Corp., Brussels, 1975-78; tech. dir. telecom group Raychem Corp., Menlo Park, 1978-80; tech. dir., U.K., rsch. and devel. Raychem Corp., Swindon, Eng., 1980-83; tech. dir. electronics group Raychem Corp., Menlo Park, 1983-85, dir. corp. rsch. and devel., 1985-89, v.p., corp. tech., 1989-91; ret. Raychem Corp., 1991; cons. R&D mgmt., innovation, 1991—. Patentee in field; contbr. articles to profl. jours. Cpl. U.S. Army, 1943-46, ETO. Mem. Am. Chem. Soc., Soc. Plastic Engrs., Materials Soc., Sigma Xi, Phi Beta Kappa. Home: 1 Ashdown Pl Half Moon Bay CA 94019-2275 Office: Raychem Corp 300 Constitution Dr Menlo Park CA 94025-1111

SOWDEN, WILLIAM CARL, orchardist; b. Marysville, Calif., June 7, 1951; s. Raymond Uren and Florence Ellen (Vander Ploeg) S.; m. Deborah Ann Garrison, Nov. 13, 1976; children: Heather Robin, Brian Jeffery. AA in Adminstrn. Justice, Yuba Coll., 1971; BA in Criminal Justice, Sacramento State U., 1973; MA in Criminal Justice, Calif. State U., Sacramento, 1975. Co-owner Sowden Bros., Live Oak, Calif., 1976—. Developed first organic prune juice, 1985. Coach Little League, Live Oak, 1986—; asst. coach Youth Football, Gridley, Calif., 1990. Mem. Farm Verified Organic (chartered, area coord. 1988-90). Home: 8888 Township Rd Live Oak CA 95953-9718

SOWDER, ROBERT ROBERTSON, architect; b. Kansas City, Kans., Dec. 29, 1928; s. James Robert and Agnes (Robertson) S.; m. Joan Goddard, July 26, 1954; 1 dau., Lisa Robertson Lee. B.A., U. Wash., 1953; B.Arch., U. Va., 1958; grad. diploma in Architecture, Ecole Des Beaux Arts, Fontainebleau, France, 1952. Designer Architects Collaborative, Boston, 1958-59, Peirce & Pierce (architects), Boston, 1959-63; asso. Fred. Bassetti & Co. (architects), Seattle, 1963-67; partner Naramore, Bain, Brady & Johanson (architects), Seattle, 1967-81; pres. NBBJ Internat., 1976-81; architect TRA, Seattle, 1981-83; v.p. Daniel, Mann, Johnson & Mendenhall, San Francisco, 1983—; archtl. design critic Boston Archtl. Ctr., 1961-62. Important works include Ridgeway III Dormitories, Bellingham, Wash. (Dept. Housing and Urban Devel. Honor award), Seattle Rapid Transit (HUD Excellence award), Safeco Ins. Co. Home Office Complex, Seattle, King County Stadium, Balt. Conv. Ctr., Oreg. Conv. Ctr., San Francisco (Moscone) Conv. Ctr. Expansion, Honolulu Conv. Ctr., Wilmington (Del.) Conv. Ctr. Served with CIC U.S. Army, 1954-56. Recipient Premier Prix D'Architecture Ecole Des Beaux Arts, Fontainebleau, 1951, 52, Prix D'Remondet Fontainebleau, 1952. Mem. AIA, Internat. Assn. Auditorium Mgrs., Nat. Assn. Expo. Mgrs., Scarab, Sigma Chi. Episcopalian. Clubs: Seattle Tennis, Rainier. Home: 2390 Hyde St San Francisco CA 94109-1505 Office: Daniel Mann Johnson & Mendenhall 222 Kearny St San Francisco CA 94108-4510

SOWELL, MADISON UPSHAW, language educator, farmer; b. Piggott, Ark., Mar. 8, 1952; s. Madison Upshaw Sowell Sr. and Ora (Hosey) Blair; m. Debra Sue Hickenlooper, June 18, 1977; children: MariLouise, Laura Elizabeth. BA summa cum laude, Brigham Young U., 1975; AM, Harvard U., 1976, PhD, 1979. Asst. prof. Italian and comparative lit. Brigham Young U., Provo, Utah, 1979-83, assoc. prof. Italian and comparative lit., 1983-91; prof. of Italian and comparative lit. Brigham Young U., Provo, 1991—; chair Italian and French depts. Brigham Young U., Provo, Utah, 1989—. Author: (exhbn. catalog) Italian Renaissance Books, 1988; editor: Italian Echoes in the Rocky Mountains, 1990, Dante and Ovid, 1991, The Age of Exploration, 1992. Missionary Ch. Jesus Christ Latter-day Saints, Italy, 1971-73; patron Harold B. Lee Libr., Provo, 1980—. Mem. Am. Assn. for Italian Studies (regional rep. 1988-90), Am. Assn. for Tchrs. of Italian (regional rep. 1982-83), Modern Lang. Assn., Medieval Acad. Am., Dante Soc. Am., Rocky Mountain Medieval and Renaissance Assn. (assoc. editor jour. 1985-86, mng. editor 1987-89, cons. editor 1990-91). Republican.

SOWERS, MIRIAM RUTH, painter; b. Bluffton, Ohio, Oct. 4, 1922; d. Paul S. and Edith E. (Triplehorn) Hochstettler; m. H. Frank Sowers, Apr. 15, 1944; children: Craig V., Keith A. BFA, Miami U., Oxford, Ohio, 1944; postgrad., Chgo. Art Inst., 1946, U. N.Mex., 1957. Draftsman Army Map Service, Chgo., 1945-46; owner studio Findlay, Ohio, 1949-53, Albuquerque, 1953-60; owner Old Town Gallery, Albuquerque, 1961-80; owner pvt. studio Albuquerque, 1980—. One-woman shows include Tex. Agrl. and Indsl. U., Kingville, Houston Bapt. Coll., Winblad Galleries, San Francisco, L'Atelier Gallery, Cedar Falls, Iowa, Southwestern Galleries, Dallas, Albuquerque Unitarian Ch., Am. Bible Soc., N.Y.C., Peacock Gallery, Corrales, N.Mex., 1984, U. N.Mex. Community Ctr. Arts, Las Cruces, 1985, Wharton's Gallery, Santa Fe, 1985, Aliso Gallery, Albuquerque, 1986, Statesman Club, Albuquerque, Arts Internat. Gallery, Findlay, Findlay Coll., Springfield (Ohio) Mus. Art, Provenance Gallery, Maui, Hawaii, 1988, Saint Johns Coll., Santa Fe, 1988, King Kamehameha Hotel, Kailua-Kona, Hawaii, 1989, Marine Gallery, Kona, 1990, Kona Surf Hotel, 1990, Luigi De Rossi Gallery, Kealakaua, Hawaii, Blankley Gallery, Albuquerque; group and gallery exhibits include Dayton (Ohio) Art Inst., Butler (Ohio) Art Inst., Akron (Ohio) Art Inst., Massilon (Ohio) Art Inst., Toledo Mus. Art (prize), Sun Carnival, El Paso, Chelmont Nat., El Paso, Tucson Fiesta Show, Santa Fe Biennial, Corrales All State Show (prize), N.Mex. State Fair (prize), Ohio Tri-State Show, Ohio State Fair, I.P.A. Nat., Washington, Roswell (N.Mex.) Mus., All Albuquerque Show and Jonson Gallery (prize), Galeria de Artesanos, Albuquerque, 1985, Little Studio Gallery, N.Y.C., Ft. Smith (Ark.) Art Ctr., The Gallery, Roswell, Gallery D., Mesilla, N.Mex., Creative Endeavors, Taos, N.Mex., Smith LTD. Galleries, Ruidoso, N.Mex., Alice Moxey Gallery, Midland, Tex., Linda Lundeen Gallery, Las Cruces, Hand Made U.S.A., Albuquerque, Reynolds Gallery, Albuquerque, El Dor Gallery, Albuquerque, Weems Gallery, Albuquerque, My Place, Albuquerque, Casa Manana Gallery, Albuquerque, Preusser Gallery, Albuquerque, Argosy Arts & Artifacts Gallery, Albuquerque, Fuller Lodge, Los Alamos, Kona Arts & Crafts, Volcano House Gallery, Volcano Nat. Pk., Hawaii, Universal Ctr. for the Arts, Las Cruces, N.Mex., Milagro Gallery, Taos, N.Mex., Eloise Contemporary, Taos, Wakefield Gardens Gallery, Honaunau-Kona, Hawaii, 1992, Kona Arts & Crafts Gallery, Kailua-Kona, Hawaii, 1992, Crystal Star Gallery, Kealaka Kua, Hawaii, 1992, others; works pub.: (mags.) Western Rev., 1967, N.Mex. Cultural News, 1968, Albuquerque Clubwoman, 1969, S.W. Art Mag., 1973, Art Voices South, 1980, (books) Parables from Paradise, 1975, The Suns of Man, 1981, (poetry quar.) Encore, 1979, (video) Layerist Artists, 1990; included in books Leap, Limited Edition Art Prints, 1979-80, American Artists, 1985, New York Artists, 1988, Artists of New Mexico vol. 3, 1989, Layerist Artists, 1991, Merto Plus, Albuquerque Jour., 1992. Home and Office: 3020 Glenwood Dr NW Albuquerque NM 87107-2925

SOWERWINE, ELBERT ORLA, JR., chemical engineer; b. Tooele, Utah, Mar. 15, 1915; s. Elbert Orla and Margaret Alice (Evans) S.; B in Chemistry, Cornell U., 1937, MSChemE, 1938; m. Norma Borge; children: Sue-Ann Sowerwine Jacobson, Sandra Sowerwine Montgomery, Elbert Orla 3d, John Frederick, Avril Ruth Taylor, Albaro Francisco, Octavio Evans, Zaida Margaret. Analytical chemist Raritan Copper Works, Perth Amboy, N.J., summers 1936, 37; rsch. chem. engr. Socony-Vacuum Oil Co., Paulsboro, N.J., 1938-43; prodn. supr. Merck & Co., Elkton, Va., 1943-45; asst. plant mgr. U.S. Indsl. Chems. Co., Newark, 1945-48; project engr. and rsch. dir. Wigton-Abbott Corp., Newark, 1948-50, Cody, Wyo., 1950-55; cons. engring., planning, indsl. and community devel., resource evaluation and mgmt. Wapiti, Wyo., also Cent. Am., 1955—. Commr. N.J., Boy Scouts Am., 1938-43; mem. Wapiti and Park County (Wyo.) Sch. Bds., 1954-58; dir. Mont. State Planning Bd., 1959-61; exec. bd. Mo. Basin Rsch. and Devel. Coun., 1959-61. Fellow Am. Inst. Chemists; mem. Am. Inst. Chem. Engrs., Am. Planning Assn., Nicaraguan Assn. Engrs. and Architects. Libertarian. Mem. Christian Ch. Researcher desulfurization of petroleum products, process control, alternate energy projects; patentee in petroleum and chem. processes and equipment. Home: Broken H Ranch Wapiti WY 82450 Office: Sowerwine Cons Wapiti WY 82450

SOWINSKI, STANISLAUS JOSEPH, artist, retired naval officer; b. Milw., May 7, 1927; s. Francis Anthony and Stefania (Zakszewski) S.; m. R. Jackie Giddens, Oct. 2, 1948; children: Stephanie Ann, Lisa Renée. BA, San Diego State U., 1952; postgrad., Def. Intelligence Sch., 1964-65; cert., San Diego Sch. Arts, 1948-49. Ensign USN, 1952, advanced through grades to comdr., jr. officer, 1952-60; comdg. officer USS Abnaki, Oahu, Hawaii, 1960-62, USS Surfbird, Sasebo, Japan, 1962-64, USN, London, 1965-67; comdr. landing ship squadron USN, San Diego, 1967-69; comdg. officer U.S.S. Fresno, San Diego, 1969-71; ret. USN, 1971, enlisted, 1945-48; painting instr. San Diego Art Inst., 1973-75; painting demonstrator Grumbacher Art Supplies, Inc., N.Y., 1980-85, Inveresk Paper Co., Bath, Eng., 1980-85; instr. painting workshops, San Diego, Rapid City, S.D., 1980-85. One-man shows include Laguna Beach (Calif.) Mus. of Art, 1955, USN, 1963, Dept. Def., Washington, 1964, Am. Embassy, London, 1967, San Diego Art Inst. Gallery, 1980, 86, Dahl Fine Art Ctr., Rapid City, S.D., 1982, Wind Gap Gallery of Fine Art, Sacramento, 1983, Art Ctr. Gallery, Rancho Santa Fe, Calif., 1984, Thackeray Gallery of Fine Art, San Diego, 1985, 87, San Diego Mus. of Art, 1985, A. Huney Gallery of Fine Art, San Diego, 1990; artist 21 major Icons including Saint Constantine and Helen Greek Orthodox Ch., 1985-90. Curator major art exhibit Felicita Found. of the Arts, Escondido, Calif., 1985. Mem. Internat. Westerners, The Retired Officers Assn. Republican. Roman Catholic. Home and Office: 13040 Cedilla Pl San Diego CA 92128-1811

SOWLE, JOHN STEVEN, systems analyst, director; b. Havre De Grace, Md., Oct. 13, 1944; s. William Hart and Lois Nadine (Groskinsky) S.; m. Elin Calvin, July 19, 1970 (div.); 1 child, Meadow Lynn; life ptnr. Steven Patterson. SB, MIT, 1966; MA, U. Calif., Berkeley, 1970, PhD, 1982. Artistic dir. Kaliyuga Arts, L.A. and San Francisco, 1984-91; systems mgr. Fireman's Fund Ins., San Rafael, Calif., 1985—. Producer: (play) Soul Survivor, 1988; producer, dir., designer (play) In Circles, 1985, King of the Crystal Palace, 1987, The Public, 1989, The Client, 1993. Fulbright fellow U. Calif., 1973-74. Home: 141 Albion St San Francisco CA 94110-1116

SOZA, MICHAEL WILLIAM, accountant; b. Castro Valley, Calif., Feb. 28, 1964; s. Ernest and Beverly Ann (Brown) S.; m. Chérie Jeanne Hughes, Aug. 23, 1986; 1 child, Jennifer Erin. BS, U. So. Calif., 1986; MBA, St. Mary's Coll. Calif., 1989. CPA. Asst. acct. KPMG Peat Marwick, San Francisco, 1986-87, staff acct., 1987-88, sr. acct., 1988-89, supervising sr., 1989-90, mgr., 1990-92, sr. mgr., 1992—; bd. dirs. U. So. Calif. Acctg. Cir., L.A. Mem. U. So. Calif. Assocs., L.A., 1992, Grad. Bus. Alumni Assn. St. Mary's Coll., Moraga, Calif., 1989, U. So. Calif. Alumni Assn., L.A., 1986. Mem. AICPA, Calif. Soc. CPAs (chmn. San Francisco chpt. depository instns. com. 1992—, mem. state com. on depository instns.), Commonwealth Club Calif. Republican. Roman Catholic. Office: KPMG Peat Marwick 3 Embarcadero Ctr San Francisco CA 94111

SPADE, GEORGE LAWRENCE, scientist; b. Sioux City, Iowa, Dec. 14, 1945; s. Walter Charles and LaVancha May (Green) S.; m. Carol Margaret Deaton, Mar. 14, 1966 (div. June 1985); children: Aaron Michael, Margaret. Mem. earthquake study group for China, U.S. Citizen Amb. Programs, 1989. Contbr. articles to profl. jours. Mem. AAAS, Am. Math. Soc., Math. Assn. Am., N.Y. Acad. Scis., Mensa. Home and Office: PO Box 2260 Columbia Falls MT 59912-2260

SPAETH, JOSEPH LOUIS, lawyer; b. Buffalo, Feb. 20, 1940; s. Joseph L. and Carolyn M. (Deibel) S.; m. Sparkie Weisberger, Feb. 18, 1984. AB, Hamilton Coll., 1961; JD, SUNY, Buffalo, 1969. Bar: N.Y. 1970, Calif. 1972; cert. criminal law specialist, Calif. Staff acct. Arthur Young & Co., San Francisco, 1970-72; atty. San Francisco Office Pub. Defender, 1973-81, head trial atty., supr. misdemeanor and felony attys., 1981-83, mng. atty. juvenile div., 1983—; instr. criminal procedure Lincoln U. Law Sch., San Francisco, 1987, 88; mem. Jud. Coun. Adv. Com. on Juvenile Ct. Law, 1988-93; mem. Jud. Coun. Family and Juvenile Standing Adv. Com., 1993—; lectr. on juvenile law to legal assns., also Nat. Coun. Juvenile and Family Ct. Judges, Calif. Ctr. for Jud. Edn. and Rsch. Mem. tech. adv. com. San Francisco Dept. Social Svcs.; chmn. AB90 Youth Svcs. Task Force, San Francisco, 1989-92; mem. San Francisco Mayor's Task Force on Dependent Children, 1987-89; mem. out-of-home care task force-populations working com. Health and Welfare Agy., San Francisco, 1987-88. Lt. (j.g.) USNR, 1961-66. Mem. State Bar Calif. (com. on juvenile justice 1988—, vice-chair 1990, chair 1991—), Calif. Pub. Defenders Assn. (rep. chief victim witness jud. adv. com. 1987-88, select com. on children and youth task force 1987-88, bd. dirs. 1989—), San Francisco Bar Assn., San Francisco Child Abuse Coun., Olympic Club. Democrat. Office: Office Pub Defender 375 Woodside Ave Rm 118 San Francisco CA 94127

SPAFFORD, MICHAEL CHARLES, artist; b. Palm Springs, Calif., Nov. 6, 1935. BA, Pomona Coll., 1959; MA, Harvard U., 1960. One man shows include Seattle Art Mus., 1982, 86, Reed Coll., 1984, Whtcom county Mus., 1987, U. Puget Sound, Tacoma, Wash., 1973, Tacoma Art Mus., 1975, 86, Utah Mus. Fine Arts, Salt Lake City, 1975, Francine Seders Gallery, Seattle, 1965—, Bellevue Art Mus., 1991; exhibited in group shows at Wilcox Gallery, Swarthmore Coll., Pa., 1977, Seattle Art Mus., 1977, 80, 84, Am. Acad. and Inst. Arts and Letters, N.Y.C., 1980, 83, 89, Kobe, Japan, 1981, Eastern Wash. U., 1982, Henry Art Gallery, 1982, 86, Bellevue Art Mus., 1987, Cheney Cowles Mus., 1988. Recipient Prix de Rome, 1967-69, award Am. Acad. and Inst. Arts and Letters, 1983; Louis Comfort Tiffany Found. grantee, 1965-66. Home: 2418 E Interlaken Blvd Seattle WA 98112-3029

SPAHLE, MICHAEL THOMAS, engineer, volunteer; b. Montclair, N.J., Oct. 20, 1952; s. Thomas Patrick Spahle and Maryanne (Dowd) Cutlip; children: Matthew Peter, Nicholas Adam, Julia Marguerite; m. Sue Anne Shackelford, 1992. AS in Elem. Edn., Essex County Community Coll., 1973; BS in Liberal Arts, Ariz. State U., 1988, postgrad., 1988—. Cert. configuration mgr. Am. Def. Preparedness Assn. Engring. change cord. ITT Courier Terminal Systems, Inc., Tempe, Ariz., 1976-84; configuration and data specialist Motorola, Inc., GED, Scottsdale, Ariz., 1984-87; configuration/standard parts control adminstr. Allied Signal Aerospace Co., GAPD, Phoenix, 1987—; contract data adminstr. Lear Siegler, Santa Monica, Calif., 1985. Tribal chief, mem. fedn. bd. Scottsdale-Paradise Valley YMCA, Scottsdale, 1988-90; chair planning com. Greater East Phoenix Neighborhood Assn., 1986, chmn. exec. search com., 1987; mgr. pub. rels. com. Linda Nadolski for City Coun., Phoenix, 1988; chmn. publs. com. Desert S.W. chpt. MS Soc., 1990; mem. sanctuary choir Shepherd of the Hills Congl. Ch., 1989—, chmn. youth sub-com., 1990-91, co-chmn. ch. camp, 1990, dir. sr. high youth programs, 1991—, capital fund drive chmn., 1992; camp counselor, 1991—; commr. Arcadia Interfaith Softball League, 1992—, SAE tech. com. 1991—. Mem. Soc. Automotive Engrs. (E-25, aerospace fastners tech. adv. com. 1991), Ariz. Alliance Health and Phys. Edn., Greater Ariz. Bike Assn., Golden Key Nat. Honor Soc. (past pres., nat. student rep. 1989-90, dir. corp. funding 1991), Scottsdale Bike Club (bd. dirs. 1990), Perimeter Bicycling Assn. of Am. (bike patrol 1990—). Home: 5437 E Pinchot Phoenix AZ 85018-8141 Office: Allied Signal Aerospace Co PO Box 52180 2739 E Washington St Phoenix AZ 85072-2180

SPAHN, GERARD JOSEPH, biologist, consultant; b. Balt., May 4, 1938; s. James A. and Amalia A. (Schafer) S.; m. Jane J. Skozilas, Aug. 26, 1961; children: Sheila M., Julie A., David G., Anne M. MS, St. John's U., 1962; PhD, U. Md., College Park, 1965. Staff scientist Microbiol. Assocs., Inc., Walkersville, Md., 1965-72; sr. scientist Litton Bionetics, Inc., Frederick, Md., 1972-76; dir. safety Microbiol. Assocs., Inc., La Jolla, Calif., 1976-77; sr. scientist Enviro Control, Inc., Rockville, Md., 1977-79; dir. occupational health and safety The Salk Inst., San Diego, 1979—; cons. Sci. Air Systems, Chico, Calif., 1986-87, Baxter Healthcare, Deerfield, Ill., 1991—, JWP Pacific Internat., Inc., 1991—. Pres. Exchange Club, Frederick, Md., 1975; v.p. Bobby Sox Softball, San Diego, 1989. Mem. APHA, Am. Indsl. Hygiene Assn., Am. Biol. Safety Assn. (pres. 1991-92), Rsch. Soc. Am., Tissue Culture Assn., Am. Assn. Lab. Animal Sci. Roman Catholic. Office: The Salk Inst PO Box 85800 San Diego CA 92186-5800

SPAIN, RUSSELL KEITH, television station executive; b. Twin Falls, Idaho, June 21, 1944; s. Delmar Ernest and Mary Virginia (Somerville) S.; m. Carol Elaine Cantral, Jun. 4, 1966; children: Lara Kathleen, Mark David. BS in Drama, Idaho State U., 1973; postgrad., U. Idaho, Moscow, 1988, 89. Producer, dir. KISU-TV, Pocatello, Idaho, 1975-82; ops. mgr. KISU-TV, Pocatello, 1982-85, acting mgr., 1982, 84; station mgr. KUID-TV, Moscow, 1985—. Mem. State Bd. to choose Idaho Young Woman of Yr., 1988-91, pres. 1989-91. Broadcast Best Agrl. Program, Idaho State Broadcasters Assn., 1980, 2nd Best Sports Program, 1982; recipient Jay Silverheels/Will Simpson Collection L.A. County Libr., 1981. Mem. Moscow C. of C., Couer d' Alene C. of C., Lewiston C. of C., Moscow Cen. Lions Club. Office: KUID-TV Radio-TV Ctr Moscow ID 83843

SPAKES, PATRICIA ANN, academic administrator; b. Canton, Ohio, June 16, 1948; m. Jerry Finn, Jan. 1, 1990; children: Brantlee Spakes, Lauren Finn. BA cum laude, Winthrop Coll., 1969; MSW, U. S.C., 1973; PhD, U. Wis., 1979. Tchr. Spartanburg (S.C.) County Dist. Schs., 1969-70; family counselor Family Svcs. Assn., Jackson, Miss., 1973-74; clin. svcs. dir. Youth Svcs. Bur., Spartanburg, 1974-75; dir. family impact project Wis. Dept. Health and Social Svcs., Madison, 1978-80; asst. prof., then assoc. prof. social work U. N.C., Greensboro, 1980-90; coord. women's studies Ariz. State U., West, Phoenix, 1990-92, assoc. provost, acad. pers. adminstr., 1992—. Author: Family Policy and Family Impact Analysis, 1983; mem. editorial bd. Lifestyles: Family and Economic Issues, 1986-88; contbr. articles to profl. publs. Pres. bd. dirs. Mental Health Assn., Greensboro, 1989-90; rsch. cons. Ariz. Women's Town Hall, 1992—. Grantee NIMH, 1971-73, Nat. Inst. on Aging, 1976-78; recipient Women of Achievment award Commn. on Status of Women, 1989. Mem. Nat. Women's Studies Assn., Nat. Coun. on Family Rels. Office: Ariz State U West 4701 W Thunderbird Rd Phoenix AZ 85069

SPANEL, HARRIET ROSE ALBERTSEN, state senator; b. Audubon, Iowa, Jan. 15, 1939; m. Leslie E. Spanel, June 3, 1961; 3 children. BS in Math., Iowa State U., 1961. Rep. Wash. State, 1987-93, senator, 1993—. Home: 901 Liberty St Bellingham WA 98225-5632 Office: PO Box 40440 Olympia WA 98504-0440

SPANGLER, LORNA CARRIE, pharmacy technician; b. San Jose, Calif., Feb. 4, 1938; d. Earl Albert and Elsie Carol (Lincoln) LaPorte; children: Kirk Earl, Eric Clair, David Paul, Linda Jean Spangler-Whiting. AA, Monterey Peninsula Coll., 1958; AS in Pharmacy Tech., Santa Ana (Calif.) Coll., 1982; BSBA, Calif. State U., Long Beach, 1986, MS in Vocat. Edn., 1992. Cert. pharmacy technician; cert. C.C. instr., Calif. Pharmacy technician Meml. Med. Ctr., Long Beach, Calif., 1974-77, technician coord., 1979-87; pharmacy technician Hoag Meml. Hosp., Newport Beach, Calif., 1987-92, Sharp Health Care, Murrieta, Calif., 1992—; accreditation team Am. Bur. Health Edn. Schs., 1987-91; adv. com. Cerritos (Calif.) Coll., 1982-87; speaker in field. Mem. Assn. of Pharmacy Technicians (founder, treas. 1989-91), Valley Computer Soc. (founder 1991), So. Calif. Assn. Pharmacy Technicians (treas. 1990-92, sec. 1992—), Am. Vocat. Assn., Calif. Soc. of Hosp. Pharmacy (task force mem. 1982, nominating com. technician div., 1988), Omicron Tau Theta (Nu chpt. 1988). Office: Sharp Health Care Murrieta 25500 Medical Center Dr Murrieta CA 92562

SPANIER, JEROME, mathematics educator; b. St. Paul, June 3, 1930; s. David Howard and Anne (Goldman) S.; m. Bernice Hoffman, Aug. 31, 1952; children: Stephen, Ruth, Adrienne. BA, U. Minn., 1951; MS, U. Chgo., 1952, PhD, 1955. Sr. mathematician and fellow mathematician Bettis Atomic Power Lab., 1955-66, adv. mathematician, 1966-67; mem. tech. staff N. Am. Rockwell Sci. Ctr., 1967-70; group leader math. group N. Am. Rockwell Sci. Ctr., Thousand Oaks, Calif., 1970-71; prof. math., co-dir. math. clinic to dir. math. clinic The Claremont Grad. Sch., 1971—, dean of faculty, 1982-87, v.p. acad. affairs and dean of faculty, 1985-87, v.p. acad. affairs, dean grad. sch., 1987-90; vis. prof. Royal Inst. Tech., Stockholm, 1981, Swiss Fed. Inst. Tech., Zurich, 1981; lectr. in field. Contbr. articles to profl. jours.; editorial bd. Internat. Jour. Math. Modeling, 1979—, Jour. Statis. Physics, 1971—; author: An Atlas of Functions, 1987, The Fractional Calculus, 1974, Monte Carlo Principles and Neutron Transport Problems, 1969. Recipient Westinghouse Disting. Svc. awad, 1963, President's medal Claremont Grad. Sch., 1990; fellow NSF, 1952-55, U. Chgo., 1951-52; grantee U.S. Energy R&D Adminstrn., 1976-80, NSF, 1976-80; Fulbright sr. rsch. scholar Massey U., New Zealand, 1990. Mem. AAAS, Am. Math. Assn., AAUP, Internat. Assn. Math. Modeling, Soc. for Indsl. and Applied Math., Am. Math. Soc., Sigma Xi, Phi Beta Kappa. Office: The Claremont Grad Sch 143 E 10th St Claremont CA 91711-3988

SPANN, KATHARINE DOYLE, marketing and communications executive; b. Holton, Kans.; d. Edward James and Josephine (Hurla) Doyle; m. Hugh J. Spann; 1 dau., Susan Katharine. BS, Emporia State Coll. V.p. Bozell & Jacobs Advt. (formerly L.C. Cole Co.), San Francisco, 1951-76; pres. Katharine Doyle Spann Assos., 1977—; propr. Kate's Vineyard, Napa Valley, Calif. Bd. dirs. No. Calif. Am. Inst. Wine and Food, Napa Valley Opera House. Named Advt. Woman of Yr., 1962; recipient El Capitan award Peninsula chpt. Pub. Relations Soc. Am., 1962, 66, Am. Silver Anvil award, Pub. Relations Soc. Am., 1962, 66, Excellence award Publicity Club of Bay Area, 1966. Trustee, bd. dirs., mem. exhbn. com., audience devel. com. Fine Arts Mus. San Francisco. Mem. Am. Soc. Enology, Am. Inst. Wine and Food, Napa Valley Women in Wine, Calif. Vintage Wine Soc. (wine com.), Commandeur, Conferie des Chevaliers du Tastevin (events com.), Delta Sigma Epsilon. Club: Metropolitan (San Francisco). Home: 1447 S Whitehall Ln Saint Helena CA 94574-9787

SPANN, STEPHEN ALLISON, civil engineer, state official; b. Albuquerque, May 22, 1941; s. Ben Allison and Doris Lovern (Carson) S.; m. Annemie Weinelt, July 24, 1970; children: Stefan Oliver, Christopher Andrew. BSCE, Colo. State U., 1969; MPA, U. Denver, 1984. Registered profl. engr., Colo. Project engr. Continental Pipeline Co., Ponca City, Okla., 1969-71; sr. engr. W.W. Wheeler & Assocs., Denver, 1971-73, Batchley & Assocs., Denver, 1973-76; chief design rev. and constrn. inspection unit for dam safety Colo. Divsn. Water Resources, Denver, 1976—; commdg. officer Support Unit Two Naval Constrn. Force, Colo. and Wyo., 1989-91. Exec. sec. Como (Colo.) Civic Assn., 1982—; mem. 208 Water Quality Com., Fairplay, Colo., 1986; chmn. Upper South Platte Water Conservancy Dist., Fairplay, 1986, 92—. Fellow Soc. Am. Mil. Engrs. (bd. dirs. 1985-90); mem. U.S. Com. on Large Dams, Assn. State Dam Safety Ofcls. Home: 4801 S Galapago St Englewood CO 80110-6432 Office: Colo Divsn Water Resources 1313 Sherman St Rm 818 Denver CO 80203

SPANNER, GARY EARL, mechanical engineer, researcher; b. San Diego, Mar. 16, 1954; s. Jack Clyde and E. Nadine (Fischer) S.; m. Cody Christine Burns, July 1, 1977; 1 child, Griffan T. BME, Wash. State U., 1976; MBA, U. Wash., 1986; postgrad., Ariz. State U., 1990—. Registered profl. engr., Wash. Design engr. Tex. Instruments, Dallas, 1976-80; testing engr. Babcock & Wilcox, Lynchburg, Va., 1980-81; sr. rsch. engr. Battelle Meml. Inst., Richland, Wash., 1981—; session chmn. Nat. Energy Program Evaluation Conf., Chgo., 1992—. Contbr. articles to profl. jours. Recipient Excellence in Tech. Transfer award Fed. Lab. Consortium, 1990. Mem. ASME, Inst. Indsl. Engrs., Am. soc for Nondestructive Testing (sect. chmn. 1984-85), Alpha Pi Mu, Phi Kappa Phi. Office: Battelle NW Lab Battelle Blvd K8-18 Richland WA 99352

SPANNER, JACK C., utility company engineer; b. Denver, Aug. 5, 1952; s. Jack C. and E. Nadine (Fischer) S.; m. Kathy T. Spanner, Nov. 9, 1978; children: Jeffrey, Jennifer, Becky, Brian. BS in Phys. Metallurgy, Wash. State U., 1974; MS in Welding Engring., Ohio State U., 1979. Cert. level III, Am. Soc. for Nondestructive Testing. Nondestructive exam. engr. Pacific Gas & Electric, San Ramon, Calif., 1979-83, sr. nondestructive exam. engr., 1983—, corp. level III, 1982—; presenter in field. Asst. coach Ballistics United Soccer Club, Pleasanton, Calif., 1990. 1st lt. U.S. Army, 1974-78. Mem. Electric Power Rsch. Inst. (chmn. codes nondestructive exam. subcom. 1987—). Office: Pacific Gas & Electric 3400 Crow Canyon Rd San Ramon CA 94583

SPANOS, ALEXANDER GUS, professional football team executive; b. Stockton, Calif., Sept. 28, 1923; m. Faye Spanos; children: Dean, Dea, Alexis Spanos Ruhl, Michael. LLD (hon.), U. Pacific, 1984. Chmn. bd. dirs. A.G. Spanos Constrn. Inc., Stockton, Calif., 1960—, A.G. Spanos Properties Inc., Stockton, Calif., 1960—, A.G. Spanos Mgmt. Inc., Stockton, Calif., 1967—, A.G. Spanos Enterprises Inc., Stockton, Calif., 1971—, A.G. Spanos Devel. Inc., Stockton, Calif., 1973—, A.G. Spanos Realty Inc., Stockton, Calif., 1978—, A.G. Spanos Jet Ctr. Inc., Stockton, Calif., 1980—, A.G.S. Fin. Corp., Stockton, Calif., 1980—; pres., chmn. bd. dirs. San Diego Chargers, 1984—. Former trustee Children's Hosp., San Francisco, San Francisco Fine Arts Mus.; trustee Eisenhower Med. Ctr., Rancho Mirage, Calif.; hon. regent U. Pacific, Stockton, 1972-82; gov. USO, , Washington, 1982—. Served with USAF, 1942-46. Recipient Albert Gallatin award Zurich-Am. Ins. Co., 1973, Horatio Alger award Horatio Alger Found., 1982, medal of Honor Statue of Liberty-Ellis Islan Found., 1982. Mem. Am. Hellenic Ednl. Progressive Assn., Calif. C. of C. (bd. dirs. 1980-85). Republican. Greek Orthodox. Office: San Diego Jack Murphy Jack Murphy Stadium PO Box 609609 San Diego CA 92160-0001 also: A G Spanos Constrn Co 1341 W Robinhood Dr Stockton CA 95207*

SPARGER, WILLIAM HARRY, gas transmission company executive; b. Durant, Okla., June 13, 1942; s. Alan Jeff Sparger and Ruth S. Strickland Lytton. BSCE, N.Mex. State U., 1965. Registered profl. engr., Tex., La. With Mountain States Tel. & Tel., Santa Fe, N.Mex., 1965-67, Transcontinental Gas Pipeline Corp., Houston, 1967-92; v.p. engring. Colo. Interstate Gas Co., Colorado Springs, 1992—. Mem. ASCE, NSPE, Tex. Soc. Profl. Engrs., La. Soc. Profl. Engrs., Am. Gas Assn. (pipeline rsch. com.), Interstate Natural Gas Assn. of Am. Republican. Office: Colo Interstate Gas Co PO Box 1087 Colorado Springs CO 80944

SPARKS, IRVING ALAN, biblical scholar, educator; b. Ft. Wayne, Ind., June 15, 1933; s. James Edwin and Isabelle Mildred S.; A.B., Davidson (N.C.) Coll., 1954; B.D., Union Theol. Sem., Richmond, Va., 1959; S.T.M., Lancaster (Pa.) Theol. Sem., 1970; Ph.D., Claremont (Calif.) Grad. Sch., 1970; m. Helen Daniels, Sept. 3, 1954; children—Lydia Isabelle Sparksworthy, Leslie Bishop, Robin Alan. Lectr. philosophy and religion LaVerne (Calif.) Coll., 1965-69; asst. prof. religion Claremont Grad. Sch., 1970-74, assoc. dir. Inst. Antiquity and Christianity, 1970-74; mem. faculty San Diego State U., 1974—, prof. religious studies, 1980—, chmn. dept. religious studies, 1983-90, 92, assoc. dean grad. div. and research, 1974-83; adj. faculty Sch. Theol. Claremont, Calif., 1970-74, 89—; founder/pres. Inst. Bibl. Studies, 1983-85; cons. photog. archival conservation of Dead Sea Scrolls in Jerusalem, 1980; mem adv. bd. Inst. Antiquity and Christianity, 1974—. Trustee, Claremont Collegiate Sch., 1970-75, pres., 1972-74; trustee, mem. exec. com. Ancient Bibl. Manuscript Ctr., 1981—. Fellow Lilly Found., 1964-65, Layne Found., 1965-66; disting. vis. scholar James Madison U., 1982. Mem. Am. Soc. Papyrologists, Soc. Bibl. Lit., Phi Beta Delta. Author: The Pastoral Epistles: Introduction and Commentary, 1981, Exploring World Religions: A Reading and Writing Workbook, 1986, 4th edit., 1991; editor Studies and Documents, 1971-92; contbr. articles on papyrology and bibl. studies to scholarly jours. Office: San Diego State U San Diego CA 92182-0304

SPARKS, JACK NORMAN, college dean; b. Lebanon, Ind., Dec. 3, 1928; s. Oakley and Geraldine Ruth (Edrington) S.; m. Esther Lois Bowen, Apr. 11, 1953; children: Stephen Michael, Robert Norman, Ruth Ann, Jonathan Russell. BS, Purdue U., 1950; MA, U. Iowa, 1951, PhD, 1960. Tchr. math. Leyden Community High Sch., Franklin Park, Ill., 1954-58; rsch. asst. U. Iowa, Iowa City, 1958-60; assoc. prof. applied stats., dir. bur. of rsch. U. No. Colo., Greeley, 1960-65; assoc. prof. ednl. psychology Pa. State U., State Coll., 1965-68; dir. corr. Campus Crusade for Christ, San Bernardino, Calif., 1968-69; dir. Christian World Liberation Front, Berkeley, Calif., 1969-75; pastor, ch. overseer New Covenant Apostolic Order, Berkeley, 1975-77; dean St. Athanasius Acad. Orthodox Theology, Santa Barbara, Calif., 1977-87, St. Athanasius Coll., Santa Barbara, 1987-93, St. Athanasius Acad. of Orthodox Theology, Ben Lomnd, Calif., 1993—; cons. Measurement Rsch. Ctr., Iowa City, 1959-60, Western States Small Schs. Project, Greeley, 1962-65, Colo. Coun. on Edn. Rsch., Denver, 1963-65. Author: Letters to Street Christians, 1971, The Mind Benders, 1977, 79, The Resurrection Letters, 1978, The Preaching of the Apostles, 1987; editor: Apostolic Fathers; gen. editor The Orthodox Study Bible, 1993. Trustee Rock Mont Coll., Denver, 1962-77, Thomas Nelson Co., Nashville, 1977-78. 1st lt. U.S. Army, 1952-54. Mem. Am. Scientific Affiliation, Assn. Orthodox Theologians, Conf. on Faith and History, Phi Delta Kappa (Epsilon chpt. pres. 1959-60). Democrat. Orthodox Christian. Home: 9792 Live Oak Ave Ben Lomond CA 95005 Office: St Athanasium Acad Orthodox Theology 9540-2 Central Ave Ben Lomond CA 95005

SPARKS, JESSICA J., organization executive, lawyer. BA, U. Nev., Las Vegas, 1976; JD, UCLA, 1983. Bar: Calif. 1984. Assoc. field editor Action Pursuit Games mag., Burbank, Calif., 1988—; founder, bd. dirs. Internat. Paintball Players Assn., L.A., 1988—; editor Paintball mag., Burbank, 1991—; freelance writer, 1987—; cons. to various cos. in paintball industry, 1987—; script cons. for numerous video and movie scripts, 1987—. Contbr. numerous articles to mags. and newspapers. Named Industry Leader of Yr., Paintcheck mag., 1990.

SPARKS, ROBERT DEAN, medical administrator, physician; b. Newton, Iowa, May 6, 1932; s. Albert John and Josephine Emma (Kleinendorst) S.; children: Steven, Robert, Ann Louise, John James. BA, U. Iowa, 1955, MD, 1957; D of Humanitarian Service, Creighton U., 1978. Diplomate Am. Bd. Internal Medicine. Intern Charity Hosp. of La., New Orleans, 1957-58, resident in internal medicine, 1958-59; asst. in medicine Charity Hosp. of La., 1958-59; fellow in gen. medicine and gastroenterology Tulane U. Sch. Medicine, 1959-62, instr. medicine, 1959-63, asst. prof., 1963-64, assoc. prof., 1964-68, prof., 1968-72, asst. dean, 1964-67, assoc. dean, acting dean, 1967-68, vice dean, 1968-69, dean, 1969-72, chief sect. gastroenterology, 1968-72; chancellor Med. Ctr. U. Nebr., 1972-76, prof. medicine, 1972-76; v.p. U. Nebr. System, 1972-76; health program dir. W.K. Kellogg Found., Battle Creek, Mich., 1976-81, v.p. programming, 1981-82, sr. v.p., 1982, pres., chief programming officer, 1982-86, pres., 1982-87, trustee, 1986-87, pres. emeritus, cons., 1988-92; cons. U. Tenn. Health Svc. Ctr., 1988-90, Boston U. Health Policy Inst., 1989-90; bd. dirs., mem. sci., compensation and trust rev. coms. Syntex Corp., Palo Alto, Calif., 1987-91; mem. overseers com. to visit Harvard U. Med. and Dental Schs., 1984-90; mem. vis. com. U. Miami Sch. Medicine,. 1982-86; assoc. med. dir. for addiction treatment svcs., dir. for edn. and rsch. Battle Creek Adventist Hosp., 1990-91; v.p. product safety and compliance Syntex Corp., Palo Alto, Calif., 1991—. Contbr. articles to profl. jours. Bd. dirs. Nat. Coun. on Alcoholism and Drug Dependence, N.Y.C., 1982-93, treas., 1986-88, chmn., 1989-90, past chmn., 1991-92; bd. dirs. Battle Creek Symphony Orch., 1981-88, Lakeview Sch. Dist., Battle Creek, 1979-83, 88-91; trustee Monsour Med. Found., Jeannette, Pa., 1976-90, interim pres., 1989, chmn. bd., pres., 1989-90; mem. Pres. Reagan's Adv. Bd. Pvt. Sector Initiatives, Washington, 1986-89; chmn. bd. dirs. Bard Coll. Health Policy and Practice Inst., 1988—, Consumer Health Info. Rsch. Inst., 1990—, Chelsea-Arbor Treatment Ctr., 1990-91, Calhoun County Bd. Health, 1988-91, chmn., 1989-91; mem., bd. dirs. Mental Health and Addictions Found. of Mich., Battle Creek, 1991-93. Recipient Harvard Dental award Harvard U. Sch. Dental Medicien, 1992. Fellow ACP; mem. AMA, Nat. Acad. Scis. Inst. Medicine (com. study of treatment and rehab. svcs. for alcoholism and alcohol abuse, bd. mental health and behavioral medicine), Coun. Mich. Founds. (trustee 1986-88), Assn. Am. Med. Colls. (disting. svc. mem. award 1975), Phi Eta Sigma, Alpha Omega Alpha. Republican. Presbyterian. Home: 7 Robert S Dr Menlo Park CA 94025 Office: Syntex Corp 3401 Hillview Ave PO Box 10850 Palo Alto CA 94303

SPARKS, ROBERT WILLIAM, publishing executive; b. Seattle, Dec. 30, 1925; s. James Donald and Gladys (Simmons) S. Student, U. Wash., 1947-50; B.A., U. Hawaii, 1954, M.A., 1965. Editor, various publs., 1947-64; mng. editor U. Hawaii Press, 1964-66, dir., 1967-87; cons. East-West Ctr., Jour. Hawaiian History, Japanese and Chinese book pubs., 1987-92; mem. adv. bd. to pres. Kamehameha Schs. Served with AUS, 1944-46, PTO. Recipient McInerny editorship, 1953; Pacific House citation Pacific and Asian Affairs Council, 1974. Mem. Assn. Am. Univ. Presses, Assn. Am. Publishers, Internat. Assn. Scholarly Publishers, Soc. for Scholarly Pub., Hawaiian Hist. Soc., Hawaii Found. History and Humanities, Honolulu Acad. Arts, Bishop Mus. Assn. Home: 3634 Nihipali Pl Honolulu HI 96816-3308

SPARKS, WALTER CHAPPEL, horticulturist, educator; b. New Castle, Colo., Aug. 22, 1918; s. Lester Elroy and Jean Ivene (Murray) S.; m. Barbara Ferne Gardner, May 31, 1942; children: Robert, Richard, Eugene. Student, Western State Coll., 1936-37; BS, Colo. State U., 1941, MS, 1943; postgrad., U. Minn., 1945, Wash. State U., 1949, 56-57; DSc (hon.), U. Idaho, 1984. Instr., head dept. agr. Pueblo Jr. Coll., 1941; grad. asst. Colo. State U., 1941-43, instr. horticulture, 1943-44, asst. prof., 1944-47, assoc. prof., 1947; assoc. horticulturist U. Idaho, Aberdeen, 1947-57; acting supt. Aberdeen br. Agrl. Expt. Sta., 1951, 57, 65, horticulturist, 1957—, research prof. horticulture, 1968—, prin. liaison coordinator for potato program, 1976—; exchange prof. Research Inst., Kolding, Denmark, 1972-73; adviser and lectr. on potato problems to various fgn. govts.; cons., adv., Israel, 1980, Philippines, 1981, Jamaica, 1988; dir. Postharvest Inst. Perishables, 1980—. Contbr. articles to profl. jours. Recipient 50th Anniversary medal Fed. Land Banks, 1967; Disting. Svc. in Potato Industry award Gov. of Idaho, 1967; named to Hall of Fame Potato Mus. Brussels, 1977, Alumni Svc. award, 1980, Disting. Faculty award Phi Kappa Phi, 1980, Disting. Svc. award rsch. in potato postharvest storage tech., 1987, Cert. of Appreciation Nat. Potato Rsch. Edn. Found., 1986, Agriculture Svc. award N.W. Food Processor Field Reps., 1987; elected Idaho Agrl. Hall of Fame, 1983; Eldred Jenne Rsch. fellow, 1957; named 1 of 100 "People Make the Difference" in Idaho, 1990. Mem. AAAS, Am. Inst. Biol. Scis., Am. Soc. Hort. Sci. (life), European Assn. Potato Research, N.W. Assn. Horticulturists, Entomologists and Plant Pathologists, Idaho Acad. Sci., Nat. Potato Research and Edn. Found. (cert. appreciation seed potato storage tech. 1986), N.W. Food Processors Assn. (Disting. Service award, 1987), N.W. Fieldman's Assn. (Disting. Agrl. Service award, 1987), Potato Assn. Am. (life mem., past pres., dir.), Western Regional Potato Improvement Group (past pres.), C. of C., Scabbard and Blade, Sigma Xi (Outstanding Research Paper award 1974), Gamma Sigma Delta (Outstanding Research Worker award 1977, award of merit 1978), Alpha Zeta, Beta Beta Beta, Epsilon Rho Epsilon. Club: Rotary. Home: 1100 Burnett Dr # 513 Nampa ID 83651 Office: U Idaho Rsch and Extension Ctr Aberdeen ID 83210

SPARR, DANIEL BEATTIE, federal judge; b. Denver, June 8, 1931; s. Daniel John and Mary Isabel (Beattie) S.; m. Virginia Sue Long Sparr, June 28, 1952; children: Stephen Glenwood, Douglas Lloyd, Michael Christopher. BSBA, U. Denver, 1952, JD, 1966. Bar: Colo. U.S. Dist. Ct. Assoc. White & Steele, Denver, 1966-70; atty. Mountain States Telephone & Telegraph Co., Denver, 1970-71; ptnr. White & Steele, Denver, 1971-74; atty. Wesley H. Doan, Lakewood, Colo., 1974-75; prin. Law Offices of Daniel B. Sparr, Denver, 1975-77; judge 2d dist. Colo. Dist. Ct., Denver, 1977-90; judge U.S. Dist. Ct. Colo., Denver, 1990—. Mem. Denver Bar Assn. (trustee 1975-78), Denver Paralegal Inst. (bd. advs. 1976-88), William E. Doyle's/Am. Inns of Ct., Am. Bd. Trial Advs., ABA, Colo. Bar Assn. Office: US Dist Ct US Courthouse C-540 1929 Stout St Denver CO 80294-2900

SPARREVOHN, FREDERIC REIDTZ, engineering executive; b. L.A., Dec. 2, 1943; s. Frederic D.R. and Dorthy Mae (Utter) S. AA, Mount San Antonio Jr. Coll., 1964; BS, Calif. State U., L.A., 1967. Devel. engr. Communications Mfg. Co., Long Beach, Calif., 1971-77; engr. HTL K West, Santa Ana, Calif., 1975—; owner Sparrevohn Engring., Long Beach, 1975—. Inventor in field. Mem. Heritage Found., Washington, 1987—. Capt. USAF, 1967-71. Republican. Home and Office: 143 Nieto Ave Apt 1 Long Beach CA 90803-3363

SPARROW, DONALD, Canadian provincial government official, municipal and farm land assessor and electrician. Student NAIT, SAIT, U. Alberta. Co-founder Sparrow Electric, Ltd., 1960. Chmn. Leduc Recreation Bd.; mem. Province of Alta. Legis. Assembly, Wetaskiwin-Leduc Legis. Assembly, 1982-89; former assoc. minister pub. lands and wildlife, now minister tourism; apptd. minister forestry lands and wildlife, 1986, minister tourism, parks and recreation, 1992. Mem. Leduc C. of C., LIons (pres. 2 terms), Knights of Columbus. Office: Minister of Tourism Parks & Rec, Legislature Bldg Rm 424, Edmonton, AB Canada T5K 2B6

SPARROW, LARRY J., telecommunications executive. Pres. GTE Inc., Thousand Oaks, Calif. Office: GTE/West Area One GTE Pl CA500AA Thousand Oaks CA 91362

SPATZ, JACOB WILLIAM, criminology educator; b. Beacercreek, Oreg., Jan. 21, 1909; s. Daniel Milton and Henrietta L. (Kalbfleisch) S.; m. Dorothy McConnel, 1930 (div. 1946); children: Ronald W., Anita L.; m. Doris L. Andrew, June 6, 1946. Student, Inst. Applied Sci., 1936-38, Internat. Sch. Criminology, 1940-41. Instr. in civil and criminal investigation Portland, Oreg., 1939-42; asst. chief of identification USCG Intelligence Div., Washington, 1942-45; instr. in criminal investigation L.A., 1948-63. Home: 261 Susan Ln Hemet CA 92543-5932

SPATZ, RONALD MARVIN, English language educator, editor, filmmaker, writer; b. N.Y.C., Apr. 10, 1949; s. Jacob John R. and Estelle (Jacobs) S.; m. Barbara L. Larlin; 1 child, Benjamin. Student, CUNY, 1967-70; BA, U. Iowa, 1971, MFA, 1973. Instr., dir. Writers Workshop Corr. Program in Faction Writing, Iowa City, 1972-73; instr. English U. Mo., Columbia, 1973-74; instr., asst. prof. Western Mich. U., Kalamazoo, 1974-78; asst. prof. Mo. Western State Coll., St. Joseph, 1979-80; asst. prof., assoc. prof. U. Alaska, Anchorage, 1980-88, prof., 1988—, dir. program in creative writing, 1984—, 1st v.p. faculty senate, 1985-87, pres. assembly, chmn. statewide assembly, 1986-87, asst. to assoc. vice chancellor for acad. affairs, 1987-88. Founding, exec. and fiction editor Alaska Quar. Rev., 1982—; contbr. short stories to anthologies and jours.; dir., prodr., editor film and video For the Love of Ben, 1988-89, also 9 others. Creative Writing fellow NEA, 1982, fellow Alaska Coun. for Arts, 1985; grantee Alaska Coun. for Arts, 1982—, Alaska Humanities Forum grantee, Mich. Coun. for Arts grantee, Literary Pub. grantee NEA, 1986; recipient Disting. Tchr. of Yr. award U. Alaska Alumni Assn., 1986, resolution of appreciation U. Alaska Bd. Regents, 1987, cert. of appreciation for outstanding leadership U. Alaska Statewide Assembly, 1987, Chancellor's award for excellence in teaching U. Alaska, 1990. Office: U Alaska 3211 Providence Dr Anchorage AK 99508

SPAULDING, JOHN PIERSON, public relations executive, marine consultant; b. N.Y.C., June 25, 1917; s. Forrest Brisbine and Genevieve Anderson (Pierson) S.; m. Eleanor Rita Bonner, Aug. 18, 1947; children: Anne Spaulding Balzhiser, John F., Mary T. Spaulding Calvert; m. 2d, Donna Alene Abrescia, May 15, 1966. Student Iowa State Coll., 1935-36, Grinnell Coll., 1936-38, U. Chgo., 1938-39. Reporter, Chgo. City News Bur., UPI, 1939-40; editor Cedar Falls (Iowa) Daily Record, 1940-41; picture editor Des Moines Register & Tribune, 1941-42, 47-50; pub. relations dir. Motor Club Iowa, Davenport, 1950-51; commd. 2d. lt. USAF, 1942, advanced through grades to maj., 1947, recalled, 1951, advanced through grades to lt. col.; ret., 1968; v.p. Vacations Hawaii, Honolulu, 1969-70; dir. pub. relations, mgr. pub. relations services Alexander & Balwin, Inc., Honolulu, 1970-76; mgr. community relations Matson Navigation Co., Honolulu, 1976-81. Pres., Econ. Devel. Assn., Skagit County, Wash., 1983-85; mem. Anacortes (Wash.) Sch. Bd., 1982-88; mem. Gov.'s Tourism Devel. Council, 1983-85; mem. adv. com. State Ferry System, 1982—, productivity coun., 1990—; chmn. Everett chpt. S.C.O.R.E., 1984-86, Bellingham chpt., 1991—. Decorated Air medal. Mem. Pub. Relations Soc. Am. (pres. Hawaii chpt. 1974), Hawaii Communicators (pres. 1973), Nat. Def. Transp. Assn. (pres. Aloha chpt. 1980-81, Disting. Service award 1978-79), Air Force Assn., Can. Inst. Internat. Affairs, Anacortes C. of C., Sigma Delta Chi (life). Clubs: Propeller (pres. Port of Honolulu 1979-80), Honolulu Press, Fidelgo Yacht, Hawaii Yacht, Royal Hawaiian 400 Yacht (comdr. 1977-81), Rotary, Elks. Home: 6002 Sands Way Anacortes WA 98221-4015

SPEAKER, GARY DAVID, company president; b. Kenosha, Wis., Mar. 24, 1948; s. David and Betty (Demmer) S.; m. Rosalind (div. 1981); 1 child, Adrienne. BS, Carroll Coll., 1970. Prodn. control supr. Honeywell, Mpls., 1977-79, Cyclotron, Berkley, Calif., 1980-81; prodn. control mgr. Atari, San Jose, Calif., 1981-83; material mgr. Visicorp, San Jose, Calif., 1983-84; ops. mgr. Atlas, Penang, Malaysia, 1984-85; pres. Spinneret Inc., Sunnyvale, Calif., 1985—. Mem. APICS.

SPEAKER, RAY, Canadian government official; b. Enchant, Alta., Can., Dec. 13, 1935; m. Ingrid Marie Schwab, 1966; children: Kari Rae Anne, Michael Ray Mark. BEd, U. Alta. Tchr., coach; mem. Alta. Legis., 1963—, Minister Without Portfolio, 1967, Minister of Health and Social Devel., 1968, chmn. human resources devel. authority, 1969, house leader of ofcl. opposition, 1982-85, leader of rep. party, 1984; Minister Mcpl. Affairs Alta. Cabinet, 1989—; owner, operator family farm, 1975—. Coach various community sports programs. Lutheran. Office: Legis Blvd, Room 127, Edmonton, AB Canada T5K 2B6

SPEAKS, J(ERRY) MARK, marketing professional; b. Visalia, Calif., Oct. 24, 1956; s. Gerald Ray and Margaret Ann (Broyles) S.; m. Marjorie Marie Tolson, July 16, 1981. BSBA, Calif. Poly., 1978. Dist. mgr. Yamaha Motor Corp. USA, Salt Lake City, 1979-81, San Francisco, 1981-87, L.A., 1987-89; regional mgr. Yamaha Motor Corp. USA, Milw., 1989-91; divsn. sales mgr. Yamaha Motor Corp. USA, Calif., 1992—. Inventor speaks reed piston. Mem. Am. Mktg. Assn., Sales and Mktg. Execs. Internat., Mensa. Republican. Home: 11692 Tammany Circle Santa Ana CA 92705-9999 Office: Yamaha Motor Corp USA 6555 Katella Ave Cypress CA 90630

SPEARLY, JAMES LUTHER, academic administrator, educator; b. Bellefonte, Pa., June 15, 1950; s. Grove Alton and Edna (Gales) S.; m. Diane Lynn Hawk, May 12, 1973; 1 child, Stefan Hawk. BA, Pa. State U., 1972; JD, Yale U., 1975; PhD, U. Tex., Austin, 1981. Rsch. asst. Child Abuse Resource Ctr., Austin, Tex., 1980-81; instr. U. Tex., Austin, 1982; legis. counsel Tex. Senate, Austin, 1982-85; v.p. adminstrn. The Naropa Inst., Boulder, Colo., 1985-91, dir. masters program gerontology and long-term care mgmt., 1991—; cons. rsch. and planning Bexar County Hosp., San Antonio, 1985-86; cons. Nuclear Waste Disposal Impact, State of Tex., Austin, 1986; cons. nursing home mental health svcs. Piñon Mgmt. Co., Denver, 1992. Contbr. articles to profl. jours. Recipient Commendation for Meritorious Svc., State of Tex., Austin, 1985, Cert. of Appreciation, Coalition of Mental and Developmental Disabilities, Austin, 1985; rsch. fellow Hogg Found. for Mental Health, Austin, 1978. Mem. APA. Office: The Naropa Inst 2130 Arapahoe Ave Boulder CO 80302-6697

SPEARS, CAROLYN LEE, small business owner; b. Springfield, Ill., June 11, 1944; d. Theodore Leo and Clover Fawn (Notley) Ratterree; m. William Arthur Rowland, May 4, 1963 (div. 1971); 1 child, Kimberly Carol; m. Roger Erwin Spears, Dec. 21, 1979. Grad. high sch., Springfield. Sec. Sangamo Electric Co., Springfield, 1961-63, Nat. Soc. Crippled Children and Adults, Chgo., 1963-65, Regency Life Ins. Co., Springfield, 1965-67; with Prescription Learning Co. (name changed to Jostens Learning Corp. 1989), Phoenix, 1971—; v.p. field ops. Prescription Learning Co., Phoenix, 1986—; owner Picture Perfect Photo Lab, Inc., 1990—; group v.p. edn. svcs. Jostens Learning Corp., Phoenix, 1989-92; rep. Ednl. Svcs. Am., 1993. Home: 5714 N 22d St Phoenix AZ 85016

SPEARS, ROBERT LEE, pediatrics educator, dean; b. Santa Ana, Calif., May 9, 1932; s. Harvey M. and Ruth (Hall) S.; m. Ann Brigham, June 20, 1956 (div. 1979); children: Robert, Elizabeth, Carolyn; m. Fran Sassé, Jan 1, 1982. BA, Dartmouth Coll., 1954; MD, U. So. Calif., 1957. Diplomate Am. Acad. Pediatrics. Resident in pediatrics Children's Hosp., L.A., 1958-60, med. dir., 1981-87; Neonta fellow NATO, NIH, Paris, France, 1960-62; asst. dir. nurseries L.A. County, U. So. Calif. Med. Ctr., 1962-68, assoc. dir. pediatrics, 1973-75, assoc. med. dir., 1975-77; dir. pediatrics John Wesley County Hosp., L.A., 1968-73; assoc. prof. pediatrics U. So. Calif., L.A., 1969—; med. dir. Rancho Los Amigos Hosp., Downey, Calif., 1977-81; assoc. dean U. So. Calif. Sch. of Medicine, L.A., 1987-91; med. adv. bd. March of Dimes, 1969-72. Contbr. numerous articles to med. jours. Fellow Am. Coll. Phys. Execs. (bd. dirs. 1984-87); mem. Am. Acad. Pediatrics (naat fetus/newborn com. 1974-77), Phi Beta Kappa. Office: Univ Southern Calif 1420 San Pablo St PMB C-202 Los Angeles CA 90033

SPEAS, ROBERT DIXON, aeronautical engineer, aviation company executive; b. Davis County, N.C., Apr. 14, 1916; s. William Paul and Nora Estelle (Dixon) S.; m. Manette Lansing Hollingsworth, Mar. 4, 1944; children: Robert Dixon, Jay Hollingsworth. BS, MIT, 1940; grad., Boeing Sch. Aero., 1938. Aviation reporter Winston Salem Jour., 1934; sales rep. Trans World Airlines, 1937-38; engr. Am. Airlines, 1940-44, asst. to v.p., 1944-46, dir. maintenance and engring., cargo div., 1946-47, spl. asst. to pres., 1947-50; U.S. rep. A.V. Roe Can., Ltd., 1950-51; pres., chmn. bd. R. Dixon Speas Assocs., Inc. (aviation cons.), 1951-76; chmn., chief exec. officer Speas-Harris Airport Devel., Inc., 1974-76; chmn. bd., pres. Aviation Consulting, Inc., 1976-84; pres. PRC Aviation, 1984—; Mem. aeros. and space engring. bd. Nat. Research Council, 1980-84. Author: Airplane Performance and Operations, 1945, Pilots' Technical Manual, 1946, Airline Operation, 1949, Technical Aspects of Air Transport Management, 1955, Financial Benefits and Intangible Advantages of Business Aircraft Operations, 1989. Recipient 1st award Ann. Nat. Boeing Thesis Competition, 1937; research award; Am. Air Transport Assn., 1942, William A. Downes Airport Operators Coun. Internat. award, 1992. Fellow AIAA (treas. 1963-64, council 1963-64, chmn. ethics com. 1989—), Royal Aero. Soc., Soc. Automotive Engrs. (v.p. 1955, mem. council 1964-66); mem. ASME, Flight Safety Found. (bd. govs. 1958-71, 79-90, exec. com. 1979-90), Inst. Aero. Scis. (past treas.; council 1959-62, exec. com. 1962), Coll. Aeronautics (trustee 1967—), Soc. Aircraft Investigators, 1964—. Manhasset C. of C. (pres. 1962), Wings Club (sight lectr. 1992), Wings (pres. 1968-69, coun. 1966-71, 73-90, chmn. devel. com. 1989—), Skyline Country. Home: 4771 E Country Villa Dr Tucson AZ 85718-2640 Office: 6262 N Swan Rd Tucson AZ 85718-3600

SPECHT, LINDA GAYLE, budget analyst, computer programmer; b. Gainesville, Fla., July 9, 1953; d. Charles William and Janet Gale (Heironymus) Mullis; m. Charles Herbert Specht, July 10, 1976; children: Charles James, Janet Dorothy. BA, N.Mex. State U., 1985. Clk.-typist Naval Ordnance Missile Test Sta., White Sands Missile Range, N.Mex., 1989; acctg. technician Naval Ordnance Missile Test Sta., WSMR, N.Mex., 1989-90; budget analyst Plans and Programming Divsn. Naval Air Warfare Ctr. Weapons Divsn., White Sands Missile Range, N.Mex., 1990—; auditor Navy Wives Club and 1st Class Assn., White Sands Missile Range, N.Mex., 1990—. Pub. newsletter Rio-Grande chpt. Assn. Computing Machines. Mem. TGIF Mixed Bowling League (sec.-treas. 1989—), Blue Key, Delta Sigma Pi, Beta Alpha Psi, Beta Gamma Sigma, Alpha Chi, Phi Kappa Phi. Mem. Christian Disciples Ch. Office: Naval Air Warfare Ctr Weapons Div White Sands Code W31204 White Sands Missle Range NM 88002

SPECK, ROBERT CHARLES, geological engineer; b. Bklyn., June 15, 1944; s. Charles Ernest and Helen Gertrude (York) S.; m. Pia Rey Polanco, July 4, 1971; 1 child, Stephen Ruben. BA, Franklin and Marshal Coll., 1968; BS, U. Missouri, Rolla, 1974, MS, 1975, PhD, 1979. Geologist Peace Corps, Dominican Republic, 1968-70; resident geologist Geokinetics, Inc., Dominican Republic, 1970-72; project geologist Hanson-Rodriguez, S.A., Dominican Republic, 1972-73; staff engr. GAI Cons., Inc., Pitts., 1979-84; assoc. prof. U. Alaska, Fairbanks, 1984—. Contbr. articles to profl. jours. Mem. Assn. Engring. Geologists (sect. vice chmn. 1985-89), Soc. Mining Engrs., Am. Inst. Profl. Geologists (lic.), Internat. Soc. for Rock Mechanics, Tau Beta Pi, Sigma Gamma Epsilon. Home: 3030 Forrest Dr Fairbanks AK 99709-5741 Office: U Alaska Dept Mining & Geol Engring Fairbanks AK 99775-1190

SPECTER, RICHARD BRUCE, lawyer; b. Phila., Sept. 6, 1952; s. Jacob E. and Marilyn B. (Kron) S.; m. Jill Ossenfort, May 30, 1981; children: Lauren Elizabeth, Lindsey Anne, Allison Lee. BA cum laude, Washington U., St. Louis, 1974; JD, George Washington U., 1977. Bar: Mo. 1977, U.S. Dist. Ct. (ea. and we. dists.) Mo. 1977, U.S. Ct. Appeals (8th cir.) 1977, Ill. 1978, Pa. 1978, U.S. Dist. Ct. (ea. dist.) Ill. 1979, U.S. Ct. Appeals (7th cir.) 1979, Calif. 1984, U.S. Dist. Ct. (cen. dist.) Calif. 1985, U.S. Ct. Appeals (9th cir.) 1986, U.S. Dist. Ct. (so. dist.) Calif. 1987, U.S. Dist. Ct. (no. dist.) Calif. 1988. Assoc. Coburn, Croft, Shepherd, Herzog & Putzell, St. Louis, 1977-79; ptnr. Herzog, Kral, Burroughs & Specter, St. Louis, 1979-82; exec. v.p. Uniqey Internat., Santa Ana, Calif., 1982-84; pvt. practice law L.A. and Irvine, Calif., 1984-87; ptnr. Corbett & Steelman, Irvine, 1987—; instr. Nat. Law Ctr. George Washington U. 1975. Mem. ABA, Ill. Bar Assn., Mo. Bar Assn., Pa. Bar Assn., Calif. Bar Assn. Jewish. Home: 37 Bull Run Irvine CA 92720-2510 Office: Corbett & Steelman 18200 Von Karman Ave Ste 200 Irvine CA 92715

SPECTOR, PHIL, record company executive; b. Bronx, N.Y., Dec. 25, 1940; m. Veronica Bennett, 1968 (div. 1974); children: Gary Phillip and Louis Phillip (twins), Donte Phillip, Nicole and Phillip (twins). Student, UCLA. Producer with Atlantic Records, 1960-61; founder Philles Records, 1962; now pres. Warner-Spector Records, Inc.; also Mother Bertha Music. Mem. mus. group: Teddy Bears, 1958-59; producer records for Gene Pitney, Ike and Tina Turner, Ben E. King, the Beatles, Righteous Bros., Checkmates, Crystals, Ronettes, John Lennon, George Harrison, The Ramones, Yoko Ono, others; producer album A Concert for Bangladesh (Grammy award); composer songs including You've Lost That Lovin' Feelin', others; appeared in films Tami, Easy Rider; prod., TV documentary film A Giant Stands 5 Ft. 7 In.; prod. film That Was Rock. Named to: Rock and Roll Hall of Fame, 1989. Office: Care Warner-Spector Records Inc 686 S Arroyo Pky Pasadena CA 91105-3262

SPEER, PHILLIP BRADFORD, commercial business executive; b. Deering, Mo., Jan. 31, 1927; s. Aiser Jacob and Bertha Mary (Black) S.; m. Sylvia June Petersen, Nov. 5, 1948; children: Mark Stephen, Philip Craig, Kim Gregory, Todd Jeffrey, Dana Paige. Grad., Logistics Devel. Sch., Ft. Lee, Va., 1977; BA, U. Ariz., 1954, Command & Gen. Staff Coll., Ft. Leavenworth, Kans., 1969, Nat. Def. U., 1972; MA, George Washington U., 1982. Cert. logistician. Pres., CEO Lollesgard Splty. Co., Inc., Tucson, 1954-84, TLC Med. Alert, Inc., Tucson, 1984-87, Treasured Family Ties, Inc., Tucson, 1990—; cons. Kwik Change Tables, Inc., Tucson, 1990—. V.p., charter mem. Srs. Achievement and Growth through Edn., Tucson, 1989-90. Col. U.S. Army, 1977-82. Decorated Legion of Merit. Mem. Res. Officers Assn., Ret. Officers Assn. Home: 1316 S Camino Seco Tucson AZ 85710

SPEERS, J. ALVIN, editor, publisher, accountant; b. Orangeville, Ont., Can., June 30, 1930; s. Frank A. and Pauline (Albrecht) S.; m. Esther Roth, May 5, 1962; children: Kelly A., Craig J. Student pub. sch., Caledon, Ont., Can.; grad. (corr.), Am. School, Chgo., 1965. Communications installer No. Electric Co. Ltd., Toronto, Ont., Can., 1956-59; owner Small Land Devel., Caledon, Ont., Can., 1959-60; collection mgr. Laurendide Fin. Co., Calgary, Alta., Can., 1960-62; br. mgr. Niagara Fin. Co. Ltd., Calgary, 1962-65; credit and time sales ins. mgr. Stampede Pontiac Buice Ltd., Calgary, 1965-66; mgr. acctg. sect. Alta. Wheat Pool, 1967-69; mgr. surety dept. Morrison & Tait Ins. Ltd., 1969-73; editor, pub., mgr. Aardvark Enterprises div. Speers Investments Ltd., 1973—; pub. Breakthrough! mag. Author poetry and prose. Candidate Penticton (B.C., Can.) City Coun., 1983; pack leader Boy Scouts Am., Calgary, 1972; treas. ch., Calgary, 1972; pres. Eugene Coste Home & Sch. Assn., Calgary, 1970-71. With RCAF, 1951-56. Mem. Am. Bookdealers Exch., Can. Poetry Assn., Christian Writers League Am. Presbyterian. Home and Office: 204 Millbank Dr SW, Calgary, AB Canada T2Y 2H9

SPEIGHT, JOHN BLAIN, lawyer; b. Cheyenne, Wyo., May 29, 1940; s. Jack B. and Kathryn Elizabeth (Schmidt) S.; m. Sally Karolee Sullivan, Aug. 20, 1960 (div. Apr. 1977); children: Sheryl, Tricia, Jackie; m. Carol Ann McBee, Sept. 16, 1979. BA, U. Wyo., 1962, JD, 1965. Bar: Wyo. 1965. Atty. Standard Oil Calif., 1965-67; asst. atty. gen. State of Wyo., Cheyenne, 1967-69, adminstrv. legal asst. to gov., 1969-71, atty. for reorgn. com., 1969-71; asst. U.S. atty. litigation div. Dist. Wyo., Cheyenne, 1971-72; ptnr. Hanes, Carmichael, Johnson, Gage & Speight, Cheyenne, 1972-75, Hathaway, Speight, Kunz & Trautwein, Cheyenne, 1976—; cons. to sec. interior Dept. Interior, Washington, summer, 1975; mem. Commn. for Uniform State Laws, 1986-90; chmn. Wyo. Jud. Supervisory Commn., 1986-90; bd. dirs. various banks. Chmn. Wyo. Republican. Com., 1973-75; bd. dirs. various civic orgns. Recipient numerous awards for civic activities. Mem. ABA, Wyo. Bar Assn., Laramie County Bar Assn., ATLA, Wyo. Trial Lawyers Assn., Am. Bd. Trial Advs. (diplomate), Young Men's Literary Club. Roman Catholic. Home: 4021 Snyder Ave Cheyenne WY 82001-1165 Office: Hathaway Speight Kunz 2424 Pioneer Ave Ste 402 PO Box 1208 Cheyenne WY 82003

SPEISER, THEODORE WESLEY, astrophysics, planetary and atmospheric sciences educator; b. Del Norte, Colo., Nov. 23, 1934; s. Alfred Theodore and Virginia Melva (Pickens) S.; m. Patricia Jane McCrummen, June 10, 1956; children: Tanya Lee, Kelly Ann, Tertia Ava. BS, Colo. State U., 1956; MS, Calif. Inst. Tech., 1959; PhD, Pa. State U., 1964. Asst. prof. U. Colo., Boulder, 1969-74, assoc. prof., 1974-85, prof. astrophysics, planetary and atmospheric scis., 1985—; cons. NOAA, Boulder, 1970—. Contbr. articles to profl. jours. Served to capt. U.S. Army, 1960-61. Recipient U.S. Sr. Scientist award A.V. Humboldt Found., 1977; Fulbright fellow, 1956. Mem. Am. Geophys. Union (local br. v.p. 1986-87, pres. 1987). Home: 2335 Dartmouth Ave Boulder CO 80303-5209 Office: U Colo Dept of Astrophysics Planetary & Atmospheric Scis C Box 391 Boulder CO 80309

SPELLMAN, DOUGLAS TOBY, advertising executive; b. Bronx, N.Y., May 12, 1942; s. Sydney M. and Leah B. (Rosenberg) S.; BS, Fairleigh Dickinson U., 1964; m. Ronni I. Epstein, Jan. 16, 1966 (div. Mar. 1985); children: Laurel Nicole, Daren Scott; m. Michelle Ward, Dec. 31, 1986, 1 child, Dallas Ward Spellman. Media buyer Doyle, Dane, Bernbach, Inc., N.Y.C., 1964-66, Needham, Harper & Steers, Inc., N.Y.C., 1966; media supr. Ogilvy & Mather, Inc., N.Y.C., 1967-69; media dir. Sinay Advt., L.A., 1969-70; chief ops. officer S.H.H. Creative Mktg., Inc., L.A., 1969—; assoc. media dir. Warren, Mullen, Dolobowsky, Inc., N.Y.C., 1970—; dir. West Coast ops. Ed Libov Assocs., Inc., Los Angeles, 1970-71; media supr. Carson/Roberts Advt. div. Ogilvy & Mather, Inc., L.A., 1971-72; assoc. media dir. Ogilvy & Mather, Inc., L.A., 1972-73; media dir. Vitt Media Internat., Inc., L.A., 1973-74; v.p., dir. West Coast ops. Ind. Media Svcs., Inc., L.A., 1974-75; owner Douglas T. Spellman, Inc., L.A., 1975-77, pres., chmn. bd., 1977-82; pres., chief operating officer Douglas T. Spellman Co. div. Ad Mktg., Inc., L.A., 1982-85; pres., chief exec. officer, chmn. bd. Spellbound Prodns. and Spellman Media divs. Spellbound Communications, Inc., L.A., 1984-86; gen. ptnr. Faso & Spellman, L.A., 1984-86; chief oper. officer, pres. Yacht Mgmt. Internat., Ltd., L.A., 1984-86; v.p. media Snyder, Longino Advt. div. Snyder Advt., L.A., 1985-86; advt./media cons., L.A., 1986-91; gen. mgr. Nucleus Nuance, L.A., 1987-88; gen. ptnr. Convention Photos Unltd, Hawaii, 1988-89; v.p. mktg. Pacific Med. Products, Inc., L.A., 1990-91; media dir., Kennedy-Wilson Inc., L.A., 1991—; guest lectr. sch. bus UCLA, 1975, U. So. Calif., 1976. Served with U.S. Army Res. N.G., 1964-69. Mem. Aircraft Owners and Pilots Assn., Nat. Rifle Assn., Phi Zeta Kappa, Phi Omega Epsilon. Jewish. Clubs: Rolls Royce Owners, Mercedes Benz Am., Aston Martin Owners. Office: Kennedy-Wilson Inc 2950 31st St Santa Monica CA 90405

SPELLMAN, JOHN DAVID, retired electrical engineer; b. Beaver Dam, Wis., July 27, 1935; s. John Joseph and Elsie Marguerite (Schultz) S.; B.S. in Elec. Engring., U. Wis., 1959; m. Kathleen Burns King, May 26, 1972; stepchildren: Kathleen Biegel, Karen Zarling, Kimberly Lyon. Jr. engr., part time, Malleable Iron Range Co., Beaver Dam, 1952-59; mem. tech. staff Rockwell Internat., Anaheim, Calif., 1961-85, lead engr., 1969-78, 81-85; mgr. ground instrumentation ops. unit Rockwell Internat., Vandenberg AFB, 1985-88, mgr. data ops., 1988-91; cons. Data Processing, Santa Maria, Calif., 1965. Served to 1st lt. Signal Corps, AUS, 1959-61. Recipient U.S. Army Accomodation award, 1961, USAF Outstanding Achievement award for Civilian Personnel. Mem. Assn. Computing Machinery, Air Force Assn.,

Res. Officers Assn. Clubs: Birnam Wood Golf (Montecito, Calif.); Santa Maria Country. Contbr. publs. on minutemen data systems, PCM Telemetry systems. Home: 642 Meadowbrook Dr Santa Maria CA 93455-3604 Office: PO Box 2669 Santa Maria CA 93457-2669

SPELTS, RICHARD JOHN, lawyer; b. Yuma, Colo., July 29, 1939; s. Richard Clark and Barbara Eve (Pletcher) S.; children: Melinda, Meghan, Richard John Jr.; m. Gayle Merves, Nov. 14, 1992. BS cum laude, U. Colo., 1961, JD, 1964. Bar: Colo. 1964, U.S. Dist. Ct. Colo. 1964, U.S. Supreme Ct. 1968, U.S. Ct. Appeals (10th cir.) 1970, U.S. Dist. Ct. (ea. dist.) Mich. 1986. With Ford Motor Internat., Cologne, Germany, 1964-65; legis. counsel to U.S. Senator, 89th and 90th Congresses, 1967-68; minority counsel U.S. Senate Subcom., 90th and 91st Congresses, 1968-70; asst. U.S. atty., 1st asst. U.S. atty. Fed. Dist. of Colo., 1970-77; pvt. practice Denver, 1977-89; risk mgr. sheriff's dept. Jefferson County, Golden, Colo., 1990-91; prodr. Video Prodn. for Lawyers, 1991—. Appointed for Leadership Denver, 1977. Selected for Leadership Denver, 1977. Mem. Fed. Bar Assn. (chmn. govt. torts seminar 1980), Colo. Bar Assn. (bd. govs. 1976-78), Denver Bar Assn., Colo. Trial Lawyers Assn., Denver Law Club, Order of Coif. Republican. Methodist. Home and Office: 6697 W Hinsdale Ave Littleton CO 80123-4511

SPENCE, A. MICHAEL, economics educator, university dean; b. Montclair, N.J., 1943; m. Ann. BA, Princeton U., 1966; MA, Oxford U., 1968; PhD, Harvard U., 1972. Instr. Harvard U., 1971-72, prof. econs., 1976-90, prof. bus. adminstrn., 1979-90, dean faculty arts and scis., 1984-90; instr. Stanford U., 1973-75, prof. econs. and bus. adminstrn., 1990—, dean Grad. Sch. Bus., 1990—; bd. dirs. BankAm. Corp., Sun Microsystems, Gen. Mills Inc., VeriFone, Inc., Bay Area Coun.; chmn. Nat. Rsch. Coun. on Sci., Tech. and Econ. Policy; mem. econs. adv. panel, NSF, 1977-79. Author: Market Signaling: Information Transfer in Hiring and Related Screening Processes, 1974; (with R.E. Caves and M.E. Porter) Competition in the Open Economy, 1980; mem. editorial bd. various jours. including Bell Jour. Econs., Jour. Econ. Theory, Pub. Policy. Rhodes scholar, 1966-68; recipient Galbraith Prize for Teaching Excellence, 1978, John Bates Clark Medal, Am. Econ. Assn., 1981. Office: Stanford U Grad Sch Bus Stanford CA 94305-5015

SPENCE, GERALD LEONARD, lawyer, writer; b. Laramie, Wyo., Jan. 8, 1929; s. Gerald M. and Esther Sophie (Pfleeger) S.; m. Anna Wilson, June 20, 1947; children: Kip, Kerry, Kent, Katy; m. LaNelle Hampton Peterson, Nov. 18, 1969. BSL, U. Wyo., 1949, LLB, 1952, LLD (hon.), 1990. Bar: Wyo. 1952, U.S. Ct. Claims 1952, U.S. Supreme Ct. 1982. Sole practice Riverton, Wyo., 1952-54; county and pros. atty. Fremont County, Wyo., 1954-62; ptnr. various law firms, Riverton and Casper, Wyo., 1962-78; sr. ptnr. Spence, Moriarity & Schuster, Jackson, Wyo., 1978—; lectr. legal orgns. and law schs. Author: (with others) Gunning for Justice, 1982, Of Murder and Madness, 1983, Trial By Fire, 1986, With Justice for None, 1989, From Freedom to Slavery, 1993. Mem. ABA, Wyo. Bar Assn., Wyo. Trial Lawyers Assn., Assn. Trial Lawyers Am., Nat. Assn. Criminal Def. Lawyers. Office: Spence Moriarty & Schuster PO Box 548 Jackson WY 83001-0548

SPENCER, CAROLINE, library director. Dir. Honolulu br. Hawaii State Libr. Office: HI State Public Lib 478 S King St Honolulu HI 96813*

SPENCER, DOUGLAS LLOYD, chemist, manufactuing executive; b. Berkeley, Calif., July 19, 1952; s. Alma Glenn and Anna Lea (Lloyd) S.; m. Connie Jeanette Whitesel, Aug. 23, 1974; children: Jeanette Dawn, Jared Douglas, Jilissa Annette, Janine Marie, Janelle Renee, Jeffrey Brian. AA, Diablo Valley Coll., 1971; BS, Brigham Young U., 1974. Lab. instr. chemistry dept. Brigham Young U., 1973-74; rsch. chemist Dow Chem. Western div., Pittsburg, Calif., 1975-80; pres. Sunset Distbg., Inc., Brentwood, Calif., 1980-82; pres. Maier & Assocs., Inc., Brentwood, 1982-83; pres. Doug Spencer & Assocs., Placerville, 1983—. Mem. Brentwood Planning Commn., 1980-81; missionary, dist. zone leader Eastern States Mission, 1971-73; active Boy Scouts of Am.. Rossmoor residents scholar, 1969-71, Brigham Young U. scholar, 1973-74. Mem. Liahona Club. Republican. Mormon. Avocations: camping, fishing, gardening. Office: 6500 Wagon Loop Placerville CA 95667-8795

SPENCER, HERBERT WARD, III, air pollution control manufacturing company executive; b. Louisville, June 12, 1945; s. Herbert W. Jr. and Mary (Armstrong) S.; m. Elizabeth Ryan, Sept. 2, 1967 (div. Feb. 1984); children—Andrew Heath, Jennifer Coates; m. Amy R. Soejoto, Aug. 12, 1984. B.A., Vanderbilt U., 1967; M.S., Auburn U., 1969, Ph.D., 1974. Research physicist So. Research Inst., Birmingham, Ala., 1974-76; research engr. Joy Mfg., Los Anegeles, 1976-79, mgr. advanced tech., 1979-85, chief devel. engr., 1985-86, mgr. new tech., 1986-87, founder, exec. v.p. EC&C Techs., La Canada, Calif., 1988—; owner HWS Engrng. and Rsch. Co., 1989—. Mem. bd. mgrs. Santa Clara Valley YMCA, 1986—. Contbr. articles to profl. publs. NDEA fellow Auburn U., Ala., 1971-73; NSF summer trainee Auburn U., 1969. Mem. Am. Phys. Soc., Air and Waste Mgmt. Assn., Sigma Xi. Republican. Presbyterian. Office: EC&C Techs 4234 Chevy Chase Dr La Canada Flintridge CA 91011-3844

SPENCER, NEAL RAYMOND, entomolgist; b. Honolulu, Hawaii, July 9, 1936; s. Henry Jackson and Florence Lillian (Evans) S.; m. Patricia Louise Wilbur, Feb. 15, 1965; children: Quentin Reynolds, Nathan Patrick, Lisa Louise, Creighton Reynolds. BS, U. Fla., 1961, postgrad., 1970-77; postgrad., U. Mo., 1965-67. Staff entomologist Govt. of Am.Samoa, Pago Pago, 1963-65, Govt of Guam, Agana, 1968-70; entomologist USDA/ARS, Gainesville, Fla., 1970-77, Rome, Italy, 1977-81, Stoneville, MS, 1981-88, Sidney, Mont., 1988—. Contbr. numerous articles to profl. jours. Scoutmaster, cubmaster, chief exec. officer Boy Scouts of Am. Mem. Entomol. Soc. Am., Weed Sci. Soc. Am. Republican. Office: USDA/ARS PO Box 1109 1500 N Central Ave Sidney MT 59270

SPENCER, PAUL ROGER, physicist; b. Madison, Wis., Dec. 24, 1941; s. Guy Roger and Irene Anna (Joy) S.; m. Diane Dee Tullius, Feb. 1, 1969 (dec. May 1990); children: Timothy David, Rebecca Joy; m. Susan Daniels, Feb. 22, 1992. BS in Physics, Wash. State U., 1963; MS in Physics, U. Ill., 1965, PhD in Physics, 1969. Sci. co-worker Stuttgart (Fed. Republic of Germany) Univ., 1969-70; mem. rsch. staff Xerox Corp., Webster, N.Y., 1970-79; mem. tech. staff Hewlett Packard Corp., Boise, Idaho, 1979—. Patentee in electrophotography and ink jet printing; contbr. articles to profl. publs. Scoutmaster Boy Scouts Am., Meridian, Idaho, 1984-88. Exch. scholar to Bonn (Fed. Republic of Germany) Univ., 1961-62. Mem. Am. Phys. Soc., Phi Beta Kappa, Sigma Xi, Phi Kappa Phi. Democrat. Mem. United Ch. of Christ. Home: 6045 Becky Dr Meridian ID 83642-5333 Office: Hewlett Packard Corp Network Printer Divsn 11311 Chinden Blvd Boise ID 83714-1023

SPENCER, ROBERT C., political science educator; b. Chgo., Mar. 28, 1920; m. Edith Maxham McCarthy, Sept. 13, 1941; children: Margaret, Catherine, Anne, Thomas More, David. AB, U. Chgo., 1943, MA, 1952, PhD in Polit. Sci. (Univ. fellow 1952-53), 1955. Instr. polit. sci. and sociology St. Michaels Coll., 1949-51, asst., then assoc. prof. polit. sci., 1953-60, prof. govt., 1960-63, dir. summer sessions, 1960-61, asst. to pres., 1963-65; prof. polit. sci., chmn. dept., dean summer sessions U. R.I., 1965-67; grad. dean U. R.I. (Grad. Sch.), 1967-69; founding pres. Sangamon State U., Springfield, Ill., 1969-78; prof. govt. and public affairs Sangamon State U., 1978-88, prof. emeritus, 1988—; research assoc. Indsl. Relations Center, U. Chgo., 1952-53; extension lectr. N.Y. State Sch. Indsl. and Labor Relations, Cornell U., 1956-57; vice chmn. West Central Ill. Ednl. Telecommunications Consortium, 1975-77, chmn., 1977-78; chmn. task force personnel Vt. Little Hoover Commn., 1957-58; mem. Ill. adv. com. U.S. Commn. on Civil Rights, 1979-87; bd. mgrs. Franklin Life Variable Annuity Funds, 1974—; vis. prof. polit. sci., sr. rsch. assoc. local govt. ctr. Mont. State U., Bozeman, 1985, 89, 90—. Author: (with Robert J. Huckshorn) The Politics of Defeat, 1971. Bd. dirs. City Day Sch., Springfield, 1979-83, Gt. Am. People Show Repertory Co., 1980-90; vice-chmn. Petersburg Library Bd., 1982-88; chmn. Petersburg Zoning Bd. Appeals, 1984-90; mem. Vt. Senate, 1959-63; Nat. Com. faculty fellow, research dir. Democratic Nat. Com., 1962-63; mem. adv. bd. Landmark Preservation Council of Ill., 1986-89. Lt. (j.g.) USCGR, 1943-45. Mem. Mont. Hist. Soc. Roman Catholic. Home: 2303 S 3d Ave Bozeman MT 59715

SPENCER, ROBERT WILFORD, education educator, administrator; b. Logan, Utah, May 19, 1938; s. Farrell J. and Bertha (Farnsworth) S.; m. Alice Marie Anderson; children: Catherine, Douglas, Steven, David, Deborah. BS, Utah State U., 1963, MS, 1965; EdD, Brigham Young U., 1971. Cert. tchr., counselor, Utah. Tchr., counselor Tooele (Utah) Sch. Dist., 1963-64, dir. pupil personnel, 1964-67; admissions counselor, then dir. admissions, asst. dean Brigham Young U., Provo, Utah, 1967-70, assoc. prof. ednl. psychology, chair counselor edn., 1970-71, dean admissions and records, 1971-90, prof. instructional sci., 1990—. With U.S. Army, 1956-57, 61-62, Berlin. Mem. Pacific Assn. of Admissions Officers and Collegiate Registrars (past. officer, pres.). Republican. Mem. LDS Ch. Home: 1665 W 1400 N Provo UT 84604-2223

SPENCER-DAVIDSON, PAUL KEINER, process control specialist; b. Exeter, Calif., July 17, 1957; s. Franklin Dillard and Polly Ann (Mann) Davidson; m. Peggy Spencer, June 26, 1982; children: Serena Melody, Derek. BS in Applied Math., Northern Ariz. U., 1980, BS in Environ. Sci., 1980, MS in Applied Math., 1982. Programmer, analyst Sudor Corp., Tucson, 1983-84; pres. Sun Data Inc., Albuquerque, 1984—, W.I.S. Inc., Albuquerque, 1992—; cons. USS, Pitts., 1990—, Aerojet Ordnance, 1992—, N.I.S.T., 1993—, Conoco Oil, Ponce City, Okla., 1991, Babcock & Wilcox, Barberton, Ohio, 1990—. Speaker of house Ariz. Boys State, Flagstaff, 1974. NAV Environ. Sci. scholar, 1979, 80, 81. Mem. Phi Kappa Phi, Sigma Pi Sigma. Office: Sun Data Inc PO Box 37197 Albuquerque NM 87176

SPENDLOVE, REX S., research laboratory administrator, microbiologist; b. Hoytsville, Utah, Apr. 29, 1926; s. Janus Albern and Hazel Tressie (Stonebreaker) S.; m. Reta Bright Allen, May 9, 1949; children: Cheri Lynn, Rex Alan, Debbi Susan, Lisa Janette, Lori Jeanne. BS, Brigham Young U., 1951, MS, 1952; PhD, Ohio State U., 1955; Doctoral (hon.), Utah State Univ., 1989. Instr. U. Conn., Storrs, 1955-58; research microbiologist Calif. State Dept. Pub. Health, Berkeley, 1958-66; head dept. bacteriology Utah State U., Logan, 1966-73, prof. biology, 1973-81; pres. Sci. Advt. and Mktg., Inc., Logan, 1981—, HyClone Labs. Inc., Logan, 1975—. Mem. editorial bd. excerpta medica Internat. Abstracting Service, Amsterdam, The Netherlands; contbr. chpts. to books; also articles to profl. jours. Named Utah Busman. of Yr., 1982. Mem. AAAS, Nat. Com. Clin. Lab. Standards (serum standardization com. 1989—), Tissue Culture Assn. (serum standardization com. 1981-85), Am. Soc. Microbiology (pres. Intermountain Br. 1970), Am. Acad. Microbiology, Am. Assn. Immunologists, Soc. Exptl. Biology and Medicine, N.Y. Acad. Scis., Internat. Com. Nomenclature Viruses (reovirus study group vertebrate virus subcom. 1978-79), Sigma Xi (pres. Utah State U. chpt. 1973-74). Republican. Mormon. Home: PO Box 229 Millville UT 84326 Office: HyClone Labs Inc 1725 S State Hwy 89-91 Logan UT 84321

SPERO, STANLEY LEONARD, broadcast executive; b. Cleve., Oct. 17, 1919; s. Morris B. and Hermine (Harve) S.; m. Frieda Kessler, June 30, 1946; children—Laurie, Lisa, Leslie. BS cum laude, U. So. Calif., 1942; postgrad., Cleve. Coll., 1943. Account exec. Sta. WHKK, Akron, Ohio, 1946-48, Sta. KFAC, Los Angeles, 1948-52; account exec. Sta. KMPC, Hollywood, 1952-53, v.p., gen. sales mgr., 1953-68, v.p., gen. mgr., 1968-78; v.p. Golden West Broadcasters, 1978—; dir. Major Market Radio, Los Angeles, 1969. Pres. permanent charities com. entertainment industry, 1972; Served with U.S. Maritime Service, 1942-43. Mem. So. Calif. Broadcasters Assn. (chmn. 1972), Am. Advt. Fedn. (gov. 1972), Advt. Assn. West, Hollywood C. of C. (dir. 1972-90, chmn. bd. dirs. 1985-87). Club: Hollywood Advertising (dir. 1972, pres. 1960-61). Home: 5027 Hayvenhurst Ave Encino CA 91436-1114 Office: Sta KMPC 5858 W Sunset Blvd Los Angeles CA 90028-6661

SPERRY, ROGER WOLCOTT, neurobiologist, educator; b. Hartford, Conn., Aug. 20, 1913; s. Francis B. and Florence (Kraemer) S.; m. Norma G. Deupree, Dec. 28, 1949; children: Glenn Tad, Jan Hope. AB, Oberlin Coll., 1935, M.A., 1937, D.Sc. (hon.), 1982; Ph.D., U. Chgo., 1941, D.Sc. (hon.), 1976; D.Sc. (hon.), Cambridge U., 1972, Kenyon Coll., 1979, Rockefeller U., 1980; Oberlin Coll., 1982. Rsch. fellow Harvard and Yerkes Labs., 1941-46; asst. prof. anatomy U. Chgo., 1946-52, sect. chief Nat. Inst. Neurol. Diseases of NIH, also asso. prof. psychology, 1952-53; Hixon prof. psychobiology Calif. Inst. Tech., 1954-84, Bd. Trustees prof. emeritus, 1984—; rsch. brain orgn., neurospecificity, split-brain rsch., hemispheric specialization, consciousness revolution. Author: Science and Moral Priority, 1983, Nobel Prize Conversations, 1985; contbr. articles to profl. jours. Recipient Oberlin Coll. Alumni citation, 1954, Howard Crosby Warren medal Soc. Exptl. Psychologists, 1969, Disting. Sci. Contbn. award Am. Psychol. Assn. 1971, Calif. Scientist of Year award Calif. Mus. Sci. and Industry, 1972, award Passano Found., 1973, Albert Lasker Basic Med. Rsch. award, 1979, co-recipient William Thomas Wakeman Rsch. award Nat. Paraplegia Found., 1972, Claude Bernard sci. journalism award, 1975, Disting. Rsch. award Internat. Visual Literacy Assn., 1979, Wolf Found. prize in medicine, 1979, Nobel prize in physiology or medicine, 1981, Realia award Inst. for Advanced Philos. Rsch., 1986, Mentor Soc. award, 1987, Nat. medal of sci., 1989; William James fellow Am. Psychol. Soc.,1990. Fellow NAS, AAAS, Am. Acad. Arts & Scis., Am. Philos. Soc.(Karl Lashley award), Am. Neurol. Assn., Royal Soc. (fgn. mem.), Pontifical Acad. Scis., USSR Acad. Scis. (fgn. mem.). Office: Calif Inst Tech Div Biology 156-29 1201 E. California St Pasadena CA 91125

SPERRY, VICTORIA B. See COURTNEY, VICTORIA BLACK

SPESER, PHILIP LESTER, social scientist, consultant; b. Buffalo, N.Y., Mar. 17, 1951; s. David and Theodora (Cowen) S.; m. Nancy Jean Parafinczyk, Nov. 27, 1980; children: Arendt, Ariel. BA in Polit. Sci. and Journalism, Case Western Res. U., 1973; JD, SUNY, Buffalo, 1980, PhD in Polit. Sci., 1981. Spl. asst. for sci. and tech. Fedn. Am. Scientists, Washington, 1980-81; pres. Foresight Sci. and Tech., Port Townsend, Wash., 1981—; Wash. rep. Soc. Am. Archeology, 1982-89; exec. dir. Nat. Coalition for Sci. and Tech., Washington, 1985-89; session chair Nat. Biotech. Edn. Sharing Conf., Madison, Wis., 1991; cons. Office of Gov. State of N.Y., 1980; adj. prof. dept. anthropology Am. U., Washington, 1988; adv. panelist on univ. small bus. ctrs., NSF, Washington, 1985. Author: The Defense-Space Market, 1985, The Politics of Science, 1987, Technology Transfer Handbook, 1990, The Federal Laser and Optics Market, 1990, Small Business Guide to Federal Research and Development Funding, 1991, others; author, editor numerous reports, articles. Founding chair Glen Echo (Md.) Park Found., 1987-88; bd. dirs. Jefferson County Edn. Found., Port Townsend, 1991—, v.p., 1993—; bd. dirs., exec. com. Jefferson County Econ. Devel. Coun., Port Townsend, 1991—, v.p., 1992—; lead lobbyist Small Bus. Innovation Devel. Act of 1982; founding pres. Olympic Penninsula Found., 1993. Grantee USDA, Small Bus. Adminstrn., Dept. Energy, NSF, others. Mem. AAAS, Tech. Transfer Soc. (bd. dirs., chair task force on nat. tech. transfer policy 1988-91), Bar Assn. D.C. Democrat. Office: Foresight Sci and Tech 1200 W Simms Way Port Townsend WA 98368

SPICER, JANETH LEE, business educator; b. Sidney, Mont., June 18, 1936; d. Walter William and Alice Lorrene (Lowry) Mende; m. Leonard Oakes Spicer, Apr. 14, 1962; 1 child, Jeffrey. BS, U. Mont., 1958; MS, U. N.D., 1968; EdD, Mont. State U., Bozeman, 1980. Educator Unity Pub. Schs., Petersburg, N.D., 1965-67, Grand Forks (N.D.) Pub. Schs., 1967-68, Denver Pub. Schs., 1969-70, Ea. Mont. Coll., Billings, 1972—. Faculty amb. Ea. Mont. Coll., 1987-90; judge U.S. Swimming, 1978-87; presenter Billings Pub. Schs., 1985-88; adjudicator State AA Forensics Meet, Billings, 1990—. Ea. Mont. Coll. Found. grantee, 1985. Mem. Assn. Bus. Communication, Data Processing Mgmt. Assn., Mont. Bus. Edn. Assn. (sec. 1977-78, officer membership com. 1978-79), Nat. Bus. Edn. Assn., AAUP, Delta Pi Epsilon Nat. Bus. Hon. Soc. (treas. 1968—).

SPIEGEL, JERRY ALLEN, organizational development consultant; b. Chgo., June 22, 1935; s. Maurice and Edith (Goldman) S.; m. Eleanor Heit, Oct. 12, 1958 (div. Jan. 1973); children: Stephanie, Jodi, Susan; m. Linda Savage, May 5, 1977 (div. Aug. 1980); 1 child, Sarah. BS, U. Wis., 1956; MSW, Columbia U., 1959; PhD, U. Chgo., 1972. Social worker Social Group Work, Chgo., N.Y.C., 1959-64; dir. tng. Commn. on Youth Welfare City of Chgo., 1965-70; quality cir. coord. Nat. Steel Shipbuilding Co., San Diego, 1980-85; pres. Leadership-Edn.-Achievement, San Diego, 1975—; mgmt., orgnl. cons. Rohr, Inc., San Diego, 1992—; human resource mgmt. advisor, faculty Chapman U., San Diego, 1990—. Co-author: Self Directed Work Teams-A Primar, 1990, Teamworking The Official Guide, 1993; dir. (video) Carl Rogers "Walk Softly Through Life", 1986. Master sgt. U.S. Army, 1954-56. Mem. ASTD, Orgnl. Devel. Network. Home: 6061 Caminito Del Oeste San Diego CA 92124-6874

SPIEGEL, ROBERT MOORE, publishing executive, writer; b. Pontiac, Mich., Aug. 13, 1950; s. Thomas Burdette and Phyllis (Moore) S.; m. Jean Spiegel (div. Nov. 1976); m. C. Eleanor Bravo (div. Jan. 1991); m. Jill Sullivan, 1991; children: Jesse Bravo, Mara Terese. B, U. N.Mex., 1980. Dir. mktg. Access Innovations, Albuquerque, 1982-85; v.p. S.W. Press, Albuquerque, 1985-86; pres. Out West Pub., Albuquerque, 1986—; CFO Border Books, Inc., 1993—. Author: (book of poems) Stepping in the Field, 1985; pub. (mag.) The Whole Chile Pepper (now Chile Pepper Mag.), 1988—. Dem. Ward chmn., Albuquerque, 1988. Mem. Am. Mktg. Assn. (pres. N.Mex. chpt. 1987-88), Mag. Pubs. Am. (edn. com. 1992—). Home: 10308 Oso Grande NE Albuquerque NM 87111 Office: PO Box 80780 Albuquerque NM 87198-0780

SPIEGEL, RONALD STUART, insurance company executive; b. Chgo., Sept. 12, 1942; s. Arthur I. and Elaine M. (Young); m; Carol J. Lieberthal, July 25, 1964; children: Eric, Elissa. BA, Calif. State U., Los Angeles, 1966. Pres. Newhouse Automotive, Los Angeles, 1966-78; agt. N.Y. Life Ins. Co., Santa Fe Springs, Calif., 1978-82, sales mgr., 1982-86, assoc. gen. mgr., 1986-88, gen. mgr., 1989-91; assoc. gen. mgr. N.Y. Life Ins. Co., Fullerton, Calif., 1991—; v.p. Cerritos Valley Br. Life Underwriters Assn. of Los Angeles, 1984-86, pres., 1987-88. Pres. Temple Shalom, West Covina, Calif., 1975-77, 88-89, 93—, treas., 1978-83; pres. Jewish Fedn. Coun. Ea. Region, L.A., 1986-88, v.p., 1984-85. Mem. Am. Soc. CLUs, Gen. Agts. and Mgrs. Assn., Airline Owners and Pilots Assn., Nat. Assn. Life Underwriters. Democrat. Lodge: Kiwanis. Home: 1720 S Orchard Hill Ln Hacienda Heights CA 91745-3843 Office: NY Life Ins Co 3230 E Imperial Hwy Ste 100 Brea CA 92621

SPIER, LUISE EMMA, film editor, director; b. Laramie, Wyo., Aug. 22, 1928; d. Louis Constantine Cames and Vina Jane Cochran; m. John Spier, Sept., 1957 (div. 1962). Student, U. Wyo., 1947, U. Calif., Berkeley, 1948-53. Head news film editor Sta. KRON-TV, San Francisco, 1960-70, film editor, 1980—; freelance film editor, director San Francisco, 1970-80, 83—. Edited and directed numerous news specials and documentaries, including The Lonely Basque, Whaler, The American Way of Eating. Recipient numerous awards for film editing and directing, including Cine Golden Eagle, Best Med. Res. Film award John Muir Med. Found., Chris Statuette, Bronze and Silver Cindy awards Info. Film Producers Am.

SPIES, HAROLD GLEN, anatomy and physiology educator; b. Mt. View, Okla., Mar. 30, 1934; s. Chester Charles and Tessie Elizabeth (Hawkins) S.; children; Russell Lee, Terry Wayne (dec.); m. Diane Wilp, 1990. BS, Okla State U., 1956; MS, U. Wis., 1957, PhD, 1959. Rsch. asst. animal genetics and physiology U. Wis., Madison, 1956-59; asst. prof. animal physiology Kans. State U., Manhattan, 1959-64, assoc. prof., 1964-66; rsch. assoc. dept. anatomy UCLA, 1967-68, Delta Regional Primate RSch. Ctr., New Orleans, 1968-72; assoc. prof. dept. anatomy Tulane U., New Orleans, 1968-72; chmn. reprodn. physiology Oreg. Regional Primate Rsch. Ctr., Beaverton, 1972-82, assoc. dir. rsch., 1983—; prof. dept. anatomy Oreg. Health Sci. U., Portland, 1973—. Contbr. numerous articles to profl. jours.; mem. editorial bd. Biology of Reprodn., 1974-78, Endocrinology, 1975-79, Jour. Animal Sci., 1983-86, Neuendocinology, 1990-93. NIH spl fellow UCLA, 1966-67. Mem. Am. Physiol. Soc., Endocrine Soc., Soc. Study of Reprodn. (dir. 1978-79, v.p. 1979-80, pres. 1980-81) Neurosci. Soc., Internat. Neuroendocrine Soc. (mem. coun. 1993—), Am. Assn. Anantomy, Soc. Study Exptl. Biol. Medicine, Am. Soc. Animal Sci., Sigma Xi, Phi Kappa Phi, Phi Eta Sigma, Alpha Zeta, Gamma Sigma Delta. Office: Oreg Regional Primate Rsch Ctr 505 NW 185th Ave Beaverton OR 97006-3499

SPIES, KAREN BORNEMANN, writer, education consultant; b. Renton, Wash., Sept. 5, 1949; d. William Edward and Aina Jeanette (Johnson) Bornemann; m. Allan Roy Spies, July 18, 1970; children: Karsten, Astrid. BA, Calif. Luth. U., Thousand Oaks, 1970; MEd, U. Wash., 1974. Vice prin., tchr. Lake Washington Sch. Dist., Kirkland, Wash., 1971-79; tchr. various pub. schs. N.J., 1979-82; kindergarten tchr. Mt. Park Sch., Lake Oswego, Oreg., 1982-84; writer, seminar leader, cons. Wash., 1984-87, Oreg., 1984-87, Littleton, Colo., 1987—; lectr. Arapahoe Community Coll., Littleton, 1988—; ski instr. various locations, 1974-87, Copper Mountain Resort, Colo., 1987—; curriculum writer Augsburg-Fortress Pubs.; lectr. in field. Author: Family Activities for the Christmas Season, 1988, Denver, 1988, Raffi: The Children's Voice, 1989, Visiting in the Global Village, Vol. IV, 1993, Vol. III, 1992, Vol. II, 1991, Vol. I., 1990, Everything You Need to Know About Grieving, 1990, Competitiveness, 1991, Our National Holidays, 1992, Our Money, 1992, The Changing American Family, 1993, Everything You Need to Know About Diet Fads, 1993, George Bush, 1991, Barbara Bush, 1991, Everything You Need to Know About Incest, 1992, others. Organist Wooden Cross Luth. Ch., 1977-79. Title III grantee, 1974. Mem. Soc. of Children's Book Writers, AAUW, Mensa, Profl. Ski Instrs. Am., Pi Lambda Theta. Republican. Lutheran.

SPILLER, GENE ALAN, nutritionist, clinical human nutrition research consultant, research center administrator, writer, editor; b. Milan, Italy, Feb. 19, 1927; came to U.S., 1950, naturalized, 1962; s. Silvio and Beatrice (Galli) S. D.Chemistry, U. Milan, 1949; MS, U. Calif.-Berkeley, 1968, PhD in Nutrition, 1972. Cons. nutrition rsch. and edn., Los Angeles, 1952-65; rsch. chemist U. Calif.-Berkeley, 1966-67, assoc. specialist physiology dept., 1968-72; prin. scientist, head nutritional physiology Syntex Rsch., Palo Alto, Calif., 1972-80; cons. clin. nutrition rsch., Los Altos, Calif., 1981—; head Health Rsch. and Studies Ctr., 1988—; mem. SPHERA Found., 1990—; lectr. Mills Coll., Oakland, Calif., 1971-81, Foothill Coll., Los Altos, 1974—. Co-author: The Last Puff, 1990; editor: Fiber in Human Nutrition, 1976, Topics in Dietary Fiber, 1978, Medical Aspects of Dietary Fiber, 1980, Nutritional Pharmacology, 1981, The Methylxanthine Beverages and Foods, 1984, CRC Handbook of Dietary Fiber in Human Nutrition, 1986, 2d edit., 1992, New Protective Roles for Selected Nutrients, 1989, The Mediterranean Diets in Health And Disease, 1991, The Superpyramid Eating Program, 1993; reviewer papers Am. Jour. Clin. Nutrition, 1976-83. Mem. Am. Inst. Nutrition, Am. Soc. Clin. Nutrition, Brit. Nutrition Soc., Am. Assn. Cereal Chemists, Am. Diabetes Assn., Am. Coll. Nutrition, Alpine Hills Club. Rsch. on human nutrition; prin. investigator in human nutrition studies; dietary fiber, lipids, and carbohydrates effect on human health; role of lesser known food components in nutrition. Office: Health Rsch and Studies Ctr 340 2d St PO Box 338 Los Altos CA 94023

SPILMAN, JAMES BRUCE, biologist, educator; b. Marysville, Calif., July 27, 1947; s. James M. and Mary E. (Stafford) S. BA, Calif. State U., Chico, 1969. Cert. secondary tchr., Calif. Chemistry, advanced placement biology tchr. Lompoc (Calif.) Valley Middle Sch., 1970-85; biology tchr. Lompoc High Sch., 1985—. Mem. Am. Chem. Soc., Lompoc Valley Club, Elks. Republican. Mem. LDS Ch. Office: Lompoc High Sch 515 W College Ave Lompoc CA 93436-4498

SPINDEL, ROBERT CHARLES, electrical engineer; b. N.Y.C., Sept. 5, 1944; s. Morris Tayson and Isabel (Glazer) S.; m. Barbara June Sullivan, June 12, 1966; children—Jennifer Susan, Miranda Ellen. B.S.E.E., Cooper Union, 1965; M.S., Yale U., 1966, M.Phil., 1968, Ph.D., 1971. Postdoctoral fellow Woods Hole Oceanographic Instn, Mass., 1971-72, asst. scientist, 1972-76; assoc. scientist Woods Hole Oceanographic Instn., Mass., 1976-82; sr. scientist Woods Hole Oceanographic Instn, Mass., 1982-87, chmn. dept. ocean engrng., 1982-87; dir. applied physics lab. U. Wash., 1987—. Contbr. articles to profl. jours.; patentee on underwater nav. Recipient A.B. Wood medal Brit. Inst. Acoustics, 1981, Gano Dunn medal The Cooper Union, 1989. Fellow IEEE (assoc. editor jour. 1982—), Acoustical Soc. Am. (exec. coun. 1985-86), Marine Tech. Soc. (pres. elect 1991-93, pres. 1993—). Democrat. Jewish. Home: 14859 SE 51st St Bellevue WA 98006-3515 Office: U Wash Applied Physics Lab 1013 NE 40th St Seattle WA 98105-6698

SPINDLER, GEORGE DEARBORN, anthropologist, educator, author, editor; b. Stevens Point, Wis., Feb. 28, 1920; s. Frank Nicholas and Winifred (Hatch) S.; m. Louise Schaubel, May 29, 1942; 1 dau., Sue Carol Spindler Coleman. B.S., Central State Tchrs. Coll., Wis., 1940; M.A., U. Wis., 1947;

Ph.D., U. Calif. at Los Angeles, 1952. Tchr. sch. in Wis., 1940-42; research asso. Stanford, 1950-51, mem. faculty, 1951—, prof. anthropology and edn., 1960-78, exec. head dept., 1963-67, 84; vis. prof. U. Wis., Madison, 1979, 80, 81, 82, 83, 84, 85; editor Am. Anthropologist, 1962-66; cons. editor Holt, Rinehart & Winston, 1965-91, Harcourt, Brce, 1991—; vis. prof. U. Calif., Santa Barbara, 1986-91. Author: Menomini Acculturation, 1955, (with A. Beals and L. Spindler) Culture in Process, 1967, rev. edit., 1973, Transmission of American Culture, 1959, (with L. Spindler) Dreamers Without Power, 1971, rev. edit., 1984, Burgbach: Urbanization and Identity in a German Village, 1973, (with Louise Spindler) The American Cultural Dialogue and its Transmission, 1990; editor: Education and Anthropology, 1955, (with Louise Spindler) Case Studies in Cultural Anthropology, 1960—, Methods in Cultural Anthropology, 1965—, Case Studies in Education and Culture, 1966—, Basic Units in Anthropology, 1970; editor, contbr.: Education and Culture, 1963, Being An Anthropologist, 1970, Education and Cultural Process, 1974, rev. edit., 1987, The Making of Psychological Anthropology, 1978, 2nd edit., 1993, Doing the Ethnography of Schooling, 1982, Interpretive Ethnography of Schooling at Home and Abroad, 1987. Pres. Peninsula Sch. Bd., Menlo Park, Calif., 1954-56. Served with AUS, 1942-45. Recipient Lloyd W. Dinkelspell award Stanford U., 1978, Disting. Svc. award Soc. Internat. Diplomacy and Third World Anthropologists, 1984, Disting. Career Contbn. award Com. on Role and Status of Minorities, Am. Edn. Rsch. Assn., 1992; fellow Ctr. Advanced Study Behavioral Scis., 1956-57; subject of Vol. 17 Psychoanalytic Study of Soc. essays. Fellow Am. Anthrop. Assn.; mem. Southwestern Anthrop. Assn. (pres. 1962-63), Coun. for Anthropology and Edn. (pres. 1982, George and Louise Spindler award for outstanding contbns. to ednl. anthropology 1987). Home: 489 Kortum Canyon Rd Calistoga CA 94515 Office: Ethnographics PO Box 38 Calistoga CA 94515-0038

SPINDLER, MICHAEL H., computer company executive; b. 1942. MBA, Rheinische Fachochschule. European mktg. mgr. Apple Computer Inc., 1980-88, pres. Apple Europe divsn., 1988-90, exec. v.p., COO, 1990-91, pres., COO, 1991-93, now pres., CEO, 1993—. Office: Apple Computer Inc 20525 Mariani Ave Cupertino CA 95014-6201*

SPINELLA, CHRISTOPHER DAMIAN, health care company executive; b. Fallbrook, Calif., Apr. 20, 1960; s. Anthony and Jeanne B. (Buytaers) S. BS, Ariz. State U., 1983; MBA, Harvard U., 1990. Devel. cons. Cigna Corp., Dallas, 1984-85, devel. mgr., 1985-86; sr. devel. mgr. Cigna Corp., Hartford, Conn., 1986-87, dir. devel., 1987-88; asst. v.p. Salick Health Care, Inc., Beverly Hills, Calif., 1990-91, v.p., 1992—. Bd. dirs. City of Glendale Parks and Recreation, 1978; mem. City of Glendale Juvenile Concerns Task Force, 1978. Mem. Harvard Alumni Assn., Ariz. State U. Alumni Assn., Pi Kappa Alpha. Home: 855 S Wooster St # 300 Los Angeles CA 90035 Office: Salick Health Care Inc 8201 Beverly Blvd Los Angeles CA 90048-4520

SPINN, MARIAN ROSE, artist, retired realtor; b. St. Louis, June 29, 1926; d. Leo J. and Alvina (Luepker) Schneider; m. Robert D Spinn, Oct. 15, 1946; 1 child, Douglas R. Student, Washington U., St. Louis, 1945, U. Hawaii, 1982, 84, 87, Palomar, 1990-91. Prin. Marian Spinn Realty, Honolulu, 1976-88. Exhibited in group shows including Hawaii Watercolor Soc., 1975-88, Assn. Honolulu Artists, 1977-80, Nat. League Am. Pen Women, 1977-88, City & County Honolulu, 1981, Office of Lt. Gov. Hawaii, 1981, Gov.'s Office, Honolulu, 1982, Hawaii Artists League, 1985, Hawaii Women's History Week Show, 1987; represented in permanent collections including, State Hawaii Collection, Castle & Cook Collection (Dole), Hawaii, Senator Salii of Saipan, Sun Gold Investment Co., San Francisco, Russ Tummelson, Martin & MacArthur Co., Honolulu, Knish Collection, Honolulu; represented in numerous private collections; contbr. articles to profl. jours. Mem. Hawaii Watercolor Soc. (pres. 1980-81, Best of Show award 1977, 1st Pl. Ann. Dinner awards 1975, 80, 2d Pl. award 1982), Nat. League Am. Pen Women (v.p. 1985-86), Assn. Honolulu Artists, San Diego Watercolor Soc., Honolulu Acad. Arts. Home: 1476 Sierra Linda Dr Escondido CA 92025

SPINRAD, ROBERT JOSEPH, computer scientist; b. N.Y.C., Mar. 20, 1932; s. Sidney and Isabel (Reiff) S.; m. Verna Winderman, June 27, 1954; children: Susan Irene, Paul Reiff. B.S., Columbia U., 1953, M.S. (Bridgham fellow), 1954; Ph.D. (Whitney fellow), MIT, 1963. Registered profl. engr., N.Y. Project engr. Bulova Research & Devel. Lab., N.Y.C., 1953-55; sr. scientist Brookhaven Nat. Lab., Upton, N.Y., 1955-68; v.p. Sci. Data Systems, Santa Monica, Calif., 1968-69; v.p. programming Xerox Corp., El Segundo, Calif., 1969-71; dir. info. scis. Xerox Corp., 1971-76, v.p. systems devel., 1976-78; v.p. research Xerox Corp., Palo Alto, 1978-83; dir. systems tech. Xerox Corp., 1983-87, dir. corp. tech., 1987-92, v.p. tech. analysis and devel., 1992—; cons. Contbr. articles to profl. jours. Mem. IEEE, Nat. Acad. Engring., Assn. Computing Machinery, Sigma Xi, Tau Beta Pi. Office: Xerox Corp 3333 Coyote Hill Rd Palo Alto CA 94304-1314

SPINWEBER, CHERYL LYNN, research psychologist; b. Jersey City, July 26, 1950; d. Stanley A. And Evelyn M. (Pfleger) S.; m. Michael E. Bruich, June 18, 1977; children: Sean Michael Bruich, Gregory Alan Bruich. AB with distinction, Cornell U., 1972; PhD in Exptl. Psychology, Harvard U., 1977. Lic. psychologist, Calif. Asst. prof. psychiatry Tufts U. Sch. Medicine, Medford, Mass., 1977-79; asst. dir. sleep lab. Boston State Hosp., 1973-79; dep. head dept. behavioral psychopharmacology Naval Health Research Ctr., San Diego, 1978-86, head dept. behavioral psychopharmacology, 1986-89; research asst. prof. dept. psychiatry Uniformed Svcs. U. of the Health Scis., Bethesda, Md., 1985—; lectr. workshop instr. U. Calif. San Diego, La Jolla, 1979-81, vis. lectr. 1979-86; assoc. adj. prof. Dept. Psychology, 1989—; courtesy clin. staff appointee dept. psychiatry Naval Hosp., San Diego, 1984—; clin. dir. Sleep Disorders Ctr. Mercy Hosp., San Diego, 1991—; pediatric sleep specialist Children's Hosp., San Diego, 1992—. Contbr. articles to profl. jours. Scholar Cornell U., Ithaca, N.Y., 1968-72, West Essex Tuition, 1968-72, Cornell U. Fedn. Women, 1917-72, Harvard U., 1972-73, 74-76, NDEA Title IV, 1973-74; postdoctoral associateship Nat. Research Council, 1978-80. Fellow Clin. Sleep Soc.; mem. Am. Men and Women of Sci., Sleep Rsch. Soc. (exec. com. 1986-89), Am. Psychol. Assn., Western Psychol. Assn. (sec., treas. 1986—), Calif. Sleep Soc., Sigma Xi. Office: U Calif San Diego Dept Psychology 0109 La Jolla CA 92093

SPIRA, JULIE MARGO, communications executive; b. Glen Rock, N.J., May 28, 1957; d. Hillard and Myra Regina (Schmertz) S. BS in TV and Radio, Ithaca Coll., 1979. Program dir., on-air personality WAAL-FM Radio, Binghamton, N.Y., 1977-79; N.E. sales mgr. Watermark Prodns., Hollywood, Calif., 1979-80; dir. nat. sales Golden Egg Prodns., Hollywood, Calif., 1980-81; dir. affiliate rels. RKO Radio Networks, N.Y. and L.A., 1981-87; v.p. sales IDB Communications Group, Culver City, Calif., 1987—; media cons. Julie Spira & Assocs., L.A., 1985-87. Mem. Am. Women in TV and Radio, Soc. of Satellite Profls., Internat. TV and Radio Soc. Home: 13219 Fiji Way # F Marina del Rey CA 90292 Office: IDB Communications Group 10525 Washington Blvd Culver City CA 90232-3311

SPIRA, ROBERT SAMUEL, mathematician; b. Detroit, Dec. 12, 1927; s. Adolph and Leta Belle (Hopkins) S.; m. Cyla Siev, Oct. 20, 1946 (div. May 1949); m. Harriett Robena Keeler, Nov. 22, 1953; children: Constance Olivia Simonsen, Bradford Ace Burdick. BA, U. Calif., Berkeley, 1957, PhD, 1962. Asst. prof. Duke U., Durham, N.C., 1962-64, U. Tenn., Knoxville, 1964-67; assoc. prof. Mich. State U., East Lansing, 1967-82; artistic dir. Quartz Theatre, Ashland, Oreg., 1982—; adj. prof. So. Oreg. State Coll., Ashland, Oreg., 1992—; asst. cons. Walter Reed Army Inst., Washington, 1962-64, Armed Forces Inst. of Pathology, Washington, 1962-64. Author: A Course in Playwrighting, 1991; translator: Matthew, 1981; author plays, 1973—; contbr. articles to profl. jours. Ombudsman Linda Vista, Ashland, Oreg., 1992; vol. Crisis Intervention Svcs., Medford, Oreg., 1985-90. Democrat. Jewish. Office: Quartz Theatre 392 Taylor Ashland OR 97520-3058

SPIRA-SOLOMON, DARLENE JOY, industrial chemist, researcher, project manager; b. Walnut Creek, Calif., Feb. 7, 1959; d. Erwin Irving and Beverly Sue (Davis) Spira; m. Edward Ira Solomon, Sept. 15, 1984; children: Mitchell Landau, Paige Elana. BS, Stanford U., 1980; PhD, MIT, 1984. Rsch. asst. Beckman Instruments, Palo Alto, Calif., 1978-79; rsch. assoc. MIT, Cambridge, 1980-84; rsch. assoc. Stanford (Calif.) U., 1982-84, asst. in instrn. FT-IR spectroscopy, 1982-83; rsch. scientist Hewlett-Packard Labs., Palo Alto, 1984—. Contbr. numerous articles to profl. jours. Coll. recruiter Hewlett-Packard, 1985—; co-chmn. Hewlett-Packard Tech. Women's Conf., 1988, chmn. adv. bd., 1989-91; workshop coord. Expanding Your Horizons Conf., Humboldt State U., 1987. Fellow chemistry dept. MIT, 1980-82, Stanford U., 1976-80. Mem. Am. Chem. Soc., Sigma Xi, Phi Beta Kappa. Office: Hewlett Packard Labs PO Box 10350 Palo Alto CA 94303-0867

SPIRTOS, NICHOLAS GEORGE, lawyer, financial company executive; b. Youngstown, Ohio, Mar. 19, 1950; s. George Nicholas Spirtos and Tulla (Palaologos) Waldron; m. Andrea Carel DeFrane, Aug. 19, 1979. BA in Physics, Philosophy, UCLA, 1969, MA in Biochemistry, 1974, JD, 1978. Bar: Calif., 1978. Intelligence analyst, 1969-72; dir. product devel. Adolph's Food Products, Burbank, Calif., 1972-73; asst. to pres. Eckel Research and Devel., San Fernando, Calif., 1973-74; dep. State Public Defender Los Angeles, 1977-82; sole practice Pacific Palisades, Calif., 1982—; co-founder, Tekni-Query Cons., 1990; appellate lawyer Calif. and U.S. Supreme Ct., 1982; exec. v.p. Gen. Counsel Compensation Strategies Group, Santa Ana, Calif., 1988—; pro bono legal counsel Junipero Serra High Sch., Gardena, Calif., 1987-88; cons. to U.S. Govt., 1982—. Patentee solubilization of Sodium CMC at room temperature, 1972. Founder, fund raiser Pacific Multiple Sclerosis Research Found., Beverly Hills, Calif., 1982—, coordinator with Reed Neurology Ctr. at UCLA. Westinghouse Sci. scholar, 1965; recipient Gregor Mendell award in genetics, 1962; named Jr. Engr. of Yr. Am. Assn. Aero. Engrs., 1963, Outstanding Speaker U. So. Calif., 1965. Mem. State Bar Calif., Internat. Platform Assn. Republican. Greek Orthodox. Office: 44489 Town Center Way D-404 Palm Desert CA 92260

SPISAK, JOHN FRANCIS, environmental company executive; b. Cleve., Mar. 27, 1950; s. Ernest Lawrence and Adele Marie (Chipko) S.; m. Barbara Ann Heisman, June 10, 1972; children: John Stefan, Theresa Rose. BS in Chemistry, Purdue U., 1972, BS in Biology with honors, 1972. Rsch. engr. Anaconda Minerals, Tucson, 1972-79; chief metallurgist Fed. Am. Uranium, Riverton, Wyo., 1979-80; v.p. ops. Anschutz Mining Corp., Denver, 1980-87; chmn. bd. dirs. Warrenton Refining (subs. of Anschutz Corp.), Denver, 1987-89; CEO SP Environ./Indsl. Compliance, Denver, 1989—. Contbr. articles to profl. publs.; patentee sequential flotation of sulfide ores. Mem. AIME, Soc. Mining, Metallurgy and Exploration, Nat. Assn. Environ. Mgrs. (co-founder, bd. dirs. Washington chpg., co-chmn. govt. liaison and advocacy com.), Denver Club, Elks. Republican. Roman Catholic. Home: 9570 LaCosta Ln Littleton CO 80124 Office: Indsl Compliance 1746 Cole Blvd Bldg 21 #300 Golden CO 80401

SPITALERI, VERNON ROSARIO, newspaper publisher, manufacturing company executive; b. Pelham, N.Y., Aug. 2, 1922; s. Rosario S. and Martha (Landerer) S.; m. Marjorie A. Ferrar, Oct. 14, 1952; children: Marc, Eric, Kris, Lynn. B.S., Carnegie Inst. Tech., 1942. Mgr. mech. dept. Am. Newspaper Pubs. Assn., N.Y.C., 1946-53; research dir., gen. adminstr. Miami Herald and Knight Newspapers (Fla.), 1953-57; chmn. bd., pres. Sta-Hi Corp., Newport Beach, Calif., 1957-74; chmn. bd. Sta-Hi Color Service, Sta-Hi Europe, Brussels, Concrete Floats-Huntington Engring. Corp., Huntington Beach, Calif.; editor, pub. Laguna Beach (Calif.) News-Post, 1967-81; pres. Laguna Pub. Co., Nat. Newspaper Found.; dir. Suburban Newspapers Am. ; chmn. bd. Victory Profl. Products, Mango Surfware. Pres., Boys Club, Laguna Beach; mem. citizens adv. com. Laguna Beach; pres. Laguna Beach Library Bd., Laguna Playhouse, Laguna Coordinating Council; bd. dirs. Sta-Hi Found.; dir. Opera Pacific. Served to lt. comdr. USNR, 1942-46. Decorated Purple Heart. Mem. Am. Mgmt. Assn., Nat. Newspaper Assn. (dir.), Calif. Newspaper Pubs. Assn. (dir.), Laguna Beach C. of C. (bd. dir.), Alpha Tau Omega. Republican. Roman Catholic. Club: Dana Point Yacht.

SPITZ, LEWIS WILLIAM, historian, educator; b. Bertrand, Nebr., Dec. 14, 1922; s. Lewis William and Pauline Mary (Griebel) S.; m. Edna Marie Huttenmaier, Aug. 14, 1948; children: Stephen Andrew, Philip Mathew. AB, Concordia Coll., 1944; MDiv, Concordia Sem., 1946; MA, U. Mo., 1947; PhD, Harvard U., 1954; DD (hon.), Concordia Theol. Sem., 1977; LLD (hon.), Valparaiso (Ind.) U., 1978; LittD (hon.), Wittenberg U., 1983; DLitt (hon.), Concordia Coll., 1988. With U. Mo., Columbia, 1953-60, assoc. prof. history, 1958-60; Fulbright prof. U. Mainz, Fed. Republic of Germany, 1960-61; prof. history Stanford (Calif.) U., 1960—, William R. Kenan Jr. prof., 1974—, assoc. dean humanities and scis., 1973-77; vis. prof. Harvard U., Cambridge, Mass., 1964-65; dir. rsch. Ctr. for Reformation Rsch., Clayton, Mo., summer 1964, mem. bd. control, 1973—; sr. fellow Southeastern Medieval and Renaissance Inst., Duke U., summer 1968; vis. prof. Barnard Coll., 1980-81; sr. fellow Inst. Advance Study Princeton U., 1979-80; vis. prof. Institut für Europäische Geschichte, Mainz, Ger., 1992. Author: Conrad Celtis: The German Arch-Humanist, 1957, The Religious Renaissance of the German Humanists, 1963, Life in Two Worlds: A Biography of William Sihler, 1968, The Renaissance and Reformation Movements, 2 vols., 1987, Humanismus und Reformation in der Deutschen Geschichte, 1980, The Protestant Reformation, 1517-1559, 1985; contbr. The Harvest of Humanism in Central Europe: Essays in Honor of Lewis W. Spitz, 1993, Johann Sturm on Education, 1993; mem. editorial bd.: Soundings, 1973-79, Ch. History, 1982-86; mng. editor: Archive for Reformation History, 1968-76. Recipient Harbison award for teaching Danforth Found., 1964; Guggenheim fellow, 1956; Nat. Endowment for Humanities sr. fellow, 1965; Am. Council Learned Socs. fellow, 1971; Huntington Library fellow, 1959; Inst. Advanced Study Princeton fellow, 1979-80; Pew Found. fellow, 1983. Fellow Am. Acad. Arts and Scis.; mem. Am. Soc. Reformation Rsch. (pres. 1963-64), Am. Hist. Assn., No. Calif. Renaissance Soc. (pres. 1964-65), Am. Soc. Ch. History (pres. 1976-77). Home: 827 Lathrop Dr Palo Alto CA 94305-1054 Office: Stanford U Dept History Stanford CA 94305

SPITZER, LAURA CLAIRE, concert pianist, educator; b. Syracuse, N.Y., Oct. 10, 1952; d. Charles Frederick and Jannette (Rinehart) S.; m. Kenneth Martin Hanlon, June 14, 1985 (div. Feb. 1989). Klavier Solodiplom, Mozarteum, Salzburg, Austria, 1976; MM, Peabody Inst., Balt., 1979. Concert pianist, 1980—; mem. piano faculty U. Nev., Las Vegas, 1981-86, Nev. Sch. of the Arts, Las Vegas, 1980-86, Idyllwild (Calif.) Sch. Music and the Arts, 1986, summers 1986-91; asst. lectr. U. So. Calif., L.A., 1990-92, lectr., 1992—; artist-in-residence, various western locations, 1985—; piano master classes, tchr. workshops and children's concerts throughout U.S. and Can., 1980—. Author feature article in Nev. mag., 1988. Bd. dirs. Las Vegas Symphony, 1981-86. Named Steinway Artist, Steinway and Sons, 1985; recipient Gov.'s Arts award as outstanding musician State of Nev., 1986; Nev. State Coun. on Arts grantee, 1984-86, Nev. Humanities Com. grantee, 1988. Mem. Music Tchrs. Nat. Assn., SWAP N.W. Democrat. Unitarian. Office: PO Box 72343 Las Vegas NV 89170

SPITZER, MARC LEE, lawyer; b. Pitts., Sept. 12, 1957; s. Richard A. and Edith (Brodie) S. BA in History and Polit. Sci. summa cum laude, Dickinson Coll., 1979; JD cum laude, U. Mich., 1982. Bar: Ariz. 1982, U.S. Dist. Ct. Ariz. 1982, U.S. Tax Ct. 1982, U.S. Ct. Appeals (9th cir.) 1985. Ptnr. Fennemore, Craig, Phoenix, 1982—. Bd. dirs. Ariz. Rep. Caucus, Phoenix, 1982—, Ariz. Acad., 1990; mem. devel. com. Dickinson Coll., 1985-86; mem. Soc. for the Arts; vice-chmn. Ariz. 18th Dist., 1986—; alternate del. 1988 Rep. Nat. Conv. GOP; legal counsel Maricopa County Rps.; apptd. by pres. Ariz. senate and speaker of house Ariz. Commn. Mcpl. Taxation. Mem. ABA (vice-chmn., tax legis. sect.), State Bar Ariz. (cert. specialist taxation), Ariz. Tax Research Found. (bd. dirs. 1984—), Ariz. Tax Research Assn., Maricopa County Bar Assn., Phi Beta Kappa, Sigma Alpha Epsilon. Jewish. Clubs: Arizona, Phoenix City, Captain's (bd. dirs.). Home: 36 E Harmont Dr Phoenix AZ 85020-3612

SPITZER, MATTHEW L., retail store executive; b. Pitts., June 20, 1929; s. Martin and Ruth G. S.; student U. Buffalo, 1948-50; children: Mark, Edward, Eric, Joseph. Lic. airline transport pilot. Product line mgr. Gen. Dynamics, Rochester, N.Y., 1962-67; dir. contracts Friden div. Singer, San Leandro, Calif., 1968-69; asst. v.p. Talcott Computer Leasing, San Francisco, 1970-71; pres. Spitzer Music Mgmt. Co., Hayward, Calif., 1972—, J.M. Sanlein Music Co., Inc., Hayward; chmn. bd. Leo's Audio and Music Techs., Oakland, Calif.; Masons, Mensa. Office: 1859 Sabre St Hayward CA 94545

SPITZER, PETER GEORGE, information systems executive, consultant; b. Oradea, Romania, July 16, 1956; m. Anne Taylor, 1985. BS in Bioelec. Engring., MIT, 1979, MS in Elec. Engring. and Computer Sci., 1980; MD cum laude, Harvard U., 1980; MBA, UCLA, 1986. Sr. systems analyst Nat. Cash Register Co., Los Angeles, 1976-77; dir. pathology diagnosis registry Peter Brigham Hosps., Boston, 1978-80; research analyst Mass. Gen. Hosp., Boston, 1978-80; resident obstetrics and gynecologist UCLA Ctr. for Health Scis., Los Angeles, 1980-81; asst. v.p. Am. Med. Internat., Info. Systems Group, Beverly Hills, Calif., 1981-87; chief info. officer Tex. Children's Hosp., Houston, 1988-90; asst. rsch. prof. pediatrics Baylor Coll. of Medicine, Houston, 1988-90; pres. Spitzer Assocs., 1990—; cons. advanced info. tech., 1990—. Smith-Kline Found. fellow, 1978-80. Fellow Healthcare Info. Mgmt. Systems Soc.; mem. AMA, IEEE, Am. Hosp. Assn., Am. Coll. Physician Execs., Soc. for Info. Mgmt., Am. Soc. Quality Control, Am. Med. Info. Assn., European Community Com. for Standardization (CEN/TC251 - healthcare systems standardization com.), Eta Kappa Nu, Sigma Xi. Office: 612 S Barrington Ave Los Angeles CA 90049

SPIVAK, JACQUE R., bank executive; b. San Francisco, Nov. 5, 1929; d. Robert Morris and Sadonia Clardine Breitstein; m. Herbert Spivak, Aug. 26, 1960; children—Susan, Donald, Joel, Sheri. B.S., U. So. Calif., 1949, M.S., 1950, M.B.A., 1959. Mgr. Internat. Escrow, Inc., Los Angeles, 1960-65, Greater Los Angeles Investment Co., 1965-75; mgr. escrow Transam. Title Ins. Co., Los Angeles, 1975-78; mgr. escrow, asst. v.p. Wells Fargo Bank, Beverly Hills, Calif., 1979-80; adminstr. escrow, v.p. 1st Pacific Bank, Beverly Hills, 1980-85; escrow adminstr. Century City Savs. & Loan Assn., Los Angeles, 1986-87; pres. Producers Escrow Corp., Beverly Hills., 1987—. Recipient awards PTA, Girl Scouts U.S.A., Jewish Fedn. Los Angeles, Hadassah. Mem. Calif. Escrow Assn., Nat. Assn. Bank Women, Inst. Trustees Sales officers. Republican. Jewish. Office: Producers Escrow Corp 9328 Civic Center Dr Beverly Hills CA 90210-3964

SPIVEY, LISA, entrepreneur; b. Spirit Lake, Iowa, July 10, 1958; d. Bruce Eldon and Nancy (Howe) S. BA, U. Calif., Santa Barbara, 1980; postgrad., Beijing Lang. Inst., 1982. Ops. mgr. bookstore U. Calif., Santa Barbara, 1976-80; distbn. mgr. Going Internat., San Francisco, 1982; cruise mgr. Lindblad Travel, Chongqing, China, 1983-84; China mgr. Lindblad Travel, Beijing, 1985-86; dir. Anywhere Travel, San Francisco, 1987; sr. v.p. By Enterprises, Hong Kong, 1987-88; prin. Spivey Internat. Inc., San Francisco, 1989—. Mem. Internat. Trade Coun., Women in Internat. Trade, Am. Found. Traditional Chinese Medicine (adv. bd.), Leadership Am., Asian Bus. League (Pacific Rim com.), U.S. China Ednl. Inst., China Bus. Assn., Malaysian Profl. and Bus. Assn., World Affairs Coun., 1990 Inst., Calif.-SE Asia Bus. Coun., San Francisco-Shanghai Sister City Com. Bus. Mgmt. Program, U.S.-Vietnam Trade Coun. Home: 58 Genebern Way San Francisco CA 94112 Office: 384 Oyster Point Blvd Ste 11 South San Francisco CA 94080

SPIZIZEN, JOHN, microbiologist, b. Winnipeg, Man., Can., Feb. 7, 1917; came to U.S., 1939, naturalized, 1944; s. Nathan and Sarah Spizizen; m. Louise Myers, Apr., 1969; 1 child, Gary. B.A., U. Toronto, 1939; Ph.D., Calif. Inst. Tech., 1942. Assoc. in virus rsch. Merck, Sharp and Dohme, West Point, Pa., 1946-54; assoc. prof. dept. Microbiology Western Res. U., Cleve., 1954-61; prof., head dept. microbiology U. Minn., Mpls., 1961-65; chmn. dept. microbiology Scripps Clinic and Rsch. Found., La Jolla, Calif., 1965-79; prof., head dept. microbiology and immunology U. Ariz., Tucson, 1979-87, prof. emeritus, 1987—; bd. govs. Weizmann Inst. Sci., Israel, 1970-82. bd. sci. advisors La Jolla Cancer Rsch. Found., 1978—; mem. com. for rsch. and tng. NIH, 1962-79, Am. Cancer Soc., 1967—; mem. coms. NASA, 1970-78. Served to capt. U.S. Army, 1943-46. Recipient Career Devel. award NIH, Western Res. U., 1955; rsch. grantee NIH, NSF; fellow NRC; Fullbright scolar U. Lund, Sweden, 1982. Mem. Am. Soc. Microbiology, Am. Soc. Biochem. and Molecular Biology. Home: 2540 E Camino La Zorrela Tucson AZ 85718-3122 Office: U Ariz Sch Medicine Dept Microbiology 1501 N Campbell Ave Tucson AZ 85724-0001

SPIZIZEN, LOUISE MYERS, musician, composer, writer; b. Lynn, Mass.. AB, Vassar Coll., 1949; MA, U. Calif., San Diego, 1972. Cert. instr., Calif. Composer, mus. dir. Interplayers, Inc., N.Y.C., 1949-51, Dorothea Spaeth Dancers, N.Y.C., 1949-51, Invisible Theatre, Tucson, 1980—; freelance and/or staff music writer L.A. Times, La Jolla Light, and Applause mag., 1974-79; music critic Tucson Weekly, 1984—; tchr., lectr. music history and lit., Conn., Calif., Ariz., 1960—; annotator, lectr. Norwalk (Conn.) Symphony, Sta. WNLK-FM, 1962-65, Tucson Symphony, Sta. KUAT-FM, 1981-83; scriptwriter, panelist L.A. Philharm., San Diego Symphony, 1975-79; music panelist, Calif. Arts Coun., 1978, Ariz. Commn. on Arts, 1988, 92; teaching-performance resident Chinese Ministry Arts Edn., 1985. Harpsichordist La Jolla Chamber Orch., 1972—, Soloist de Alcala, Old Globe Theatre, Basically Baroque Ensembles, San Diego, 1972—, Anna Magdalena Bach Quartet, Tucson, 1984—, Tucson Symphony Orch., 1982—, Ariz. Opera, Phoenix and Tucson, 1982—; commd. works include Weary with Toil, 1970, Sacred Service, 1967, Come Let's Away, 1986; contbr. articles and revs. to Mus. Am., Mus. Quarterly, Ovation, and newspapers. Founder, artistic dir. San Diego Mini-Concerts, Inc., 1972, Ariz. Mini-Concerts, Inc., Tucson, 1980—; music program com. Tucson Symphony Orch., 1988—. NARAS grantee, 1988. Mem. Music Critics Assn., Early Music Am. (founding), Am. Fedn. Musicians, Ariz. Composers Forum (composer designee), Ariz. Early Music Soc. (pres. 1989—), Ariz. Music Tchrs. Assn. (pres. 1985-86), Am. Musicological Soc., Sorneck Soc. for Am. Mus., Coll. Mus. Soc. Home and Office: 2540 E Camino La Zorrela Tucson AZ 85718-3122

SPLANE, RICHARD BEVERLEY, social work educator; b. Calgary, Alta., Can., Sept. 25, 1916; s. Alfred William and Clara Jane (Allyn) S.; m. Verna Marie Huffman, Feb. 22, 1971. BA, McMaster U., 1940, LLD (hon.), 1990; cert. social sci. and adminstrn., London Sch. Econs., 1947; MA, U. Toronto, 1948, MSW, 1951, PhD, 1961; LLD (hon.), Wilfrid Laurier U., 1988. Exec. dir. Children's Aid Soc., Cornwall, Ont., Can., 1948-50; with Health and Welfare Can., Ottawa, 1952-72; exec. asst. to dep. minister nat. welfare Health and Welfare Can., 1959-60, dir. unemployment assistance, 1960-62, dir. gen. welfare assistance and services, 1960-70, asst. dep. minister social allowances and services, 1970-72; vis. prof. U. Alta., Edmonton, 1972-73; prof. social policy Sch. Social Work, U. B.C., Vancouver, 1973—; cons. Govt. Can., Govt. Alta., UNICEF. Author: The Development of Social Welfare in Ontario, 1965. Served with RCAF, 1942-45. Recipient Centennial medal Govt. Can., 1967, Charles E. Hendry award U. Toronto, 1981. Mem. Can. Assn. Social Workers (Outstanding Nat. Svc. award 1985), Can. Inst. Public Adminstrn., Can. Hist. Assn., Can. Coun. on Social Devel., Internat. Assn. Schs. Social Work. Mem. United Ch. Can. Club: Vancouver. Office: Sch Social Work U BC, Vancouver, BC Canada V6T 1W5

SPOFFORD, ROBERT HOUSTON, advertising agency executive; b. N.Y.C., Apr. 3, 1941; s. Robert Knowlton and Linda Prieber (Houston) S.; m. Susan Proctor Allerton; children—Margaret, Robert Christopher. B.E.E., Cornell U., 1964. Account exec. Batten, Barton, Durstine & Osborn, Inc., N.Y.C., 1964-71, v.p., 1971-84, sr. v.p., 1984-88, exec. v.p., dir. strategic planning, 1988—. Contbr. articles to advt. and data processing jours. Mem. Westchester County Democratic Com. N.Y. 1974-78; ch. organist. First recipient Founder's medal Batten, Barton, Durstine & Osborn, Inc., 1985. Unitarian. Home: 449 35th St Manhattan Beach CA 90266-3320 Office: BBDO Los Angeles 10960 Wilshire Blvd Los Angeles CA 90024-3702

SPOHN, DANIEL JAY, mechanical engineer; b. Montgomery, Ala., Dec. 18, 1956; s. Harry Ray and Grace Delight (Davison) S.; m. Mary Elizabeth Fielder, Apr. 10, 1987; children: Ian Michael, Stuart Thomas, Christopher James. Grad., Naval Nuclear Power Sch., 1976. Mech. designer Shrader Sci. Inc., Hayward, Calif., 1981-85; mfg. engr. Machine Tech. Inc., San Jose, Calif., 1985-87, Surface Sci. Instruments, Mountain View, Calif., 1987-89; chief mech. engr. CONSARC, Albany, Oreg., 1989-92; prodn. mgr. Tulip Memory Systems Inc., Fremont, Calif., 1992—. With submarine svc. USN, 1975-81. Mem. Am. Vacuum Soc., Am. Soc. Metals. Office: Tulip Memory Systems Inc 3450 W Warren Ave Fremont CA 94538

SPOLTER, PARI DOKHT, writer of scientific books; b. Teheran, Iran, Jan. 30, 1930; came to U.S., 1957; m. Herbert Spolter, Aug. 16, 1958; children: David, Deborah. Licence chimie biologique, U. Geneva, 1952; PhD in Biochemistry, U. Wis., 1961. Rsch. assoc., instr. Temple U., Phila., 1961-65; researcher U.S. Pub. Health Svc. Hosp., San Francisco, 1965-68; writer Orb Pub. Co., Granada Hills, Calif., 1988—. Mem. AAAS, Am. Math. Soc.

Office: Orb Pub Co 11862 Balboa Blvd # 182 Granada Hills CA 91344-2798

SPOOR, JAMES EDWARD, company executive; b. Rockford, Ill., Feb. 19, 1936; s. Frank Kendall and Genevieve Eileen (Johnson) S.; B.S. in Psychology, U. Ill., 1958; m. Nancy E. Carlson, Sept. 8, 1962; children—Sybil K., Kendall P., Andrea K., Marcie K. Personnel mgr. Nat. Sugar Refining Co., N.Y.C., 1960-64, Pepsico, Inc., N.Y.C., Auburn, N.Y., 1964-67; mgr. internat. pers. Control Data Corp., Mpls., 1967-75; v.p. personnel and employee rels. Vetco, Inc., Ventura, Calif., 1975-79; v.p. employee rels. Hamilton Bros. Oil Co., Denver, 1979-84; pres., chief exec. officer Spectrum Human Resource Systems Corp., 1984—; cons., author, speaker on human resources and entrepreneurism. Mem. adv. bd. Salvation Army, 1978-79; chmn. Spl. Commn. for Ventura County Bd. Suprs., 1978; mem. task force on human resources Colo. Sch. Mines, 1983; state chairperson Coun. Growing Cos., 1991-92, nat. pres., 1992-94. With U.S. Army, 1958-60. Mem. Am. Soc. Pers. Adminstrn. (contbg. author handbook), Assn. for Human Resource Systems Profls., Colo. Soc. Pers. Adminstrn. Republican. Episcopalian. Clubs: Denver, Masons, Shriners. Contbg. author: Am. Soc. Personnel Adminstrn. Personnel and Indsl. Relations Handbook.

SPRAGUE, DEWEY DEAN, health physicist, consultant; b. Neoshoe, Mo., June 27, 1954; s. Ralph Norse and Lotta June (Rayburn) S. BA, U. Mo., 1976. Rsch. technician Mo. U. Rsch. Reactor, Columbia, 1977-78; facilities asst. U. Mo., Columbia, 1978-80; health physicist RadPharm, Inc., Burlingame, Calif., 1980-85; sr. health physicist Radiation Safety Svc., Fremont, Calif., 1985-86; health physicist U. Calif., San Francisco, 1986-87; safety officer DNAX Rsch. Inst., Palo Alto, Calif., 1988-89; mgr. environ. health & safety LifeScan, Inc., Milpitas, Calif., 1989; health physicst U. Calif., Berkeley, 1990—; cons. Childen's Hosp. of San Francisco, 1984, Cor Therapeutics, Palo Alto, 1988. Mem. Health Physics Soc. (plenary, com. 1990—). Democrat. Office: U Calif Office of Environ Health & Safety 2223 Fulton St Fl 4 Berkeley CA 94720-0001

SPRAGUE, PETER JULIAN, semiconductor company executive, lecturer; b. Detroit, Apr. 29, 1939; s. Julian K. and Helene (Coughlin) S.; m. Tjasa Krofta, Dec. 19, 1959; children: Carl, Steven, Kevin, Michael. Student, Yale U., 1961, MIT, 1961, Columbia U., 1962-66. Chmn. bd. dirs. Nat. Semiconductor Corp., Santa Clara, Calif.; pres. Wave Systems Inc. Trustee Strang Clinic. Club: Yale. Home: 249 Under Mountain Rd Lenox MA 01240-2035 Office: Wave Systems Corp 885 Third Ave New York NY 10022 also: Nat Semiconductor Corp 2900 Semiconductor Dr PO Box 58090 Santa Clara CA 95051

SPRAGUE, RODERICK, III, anthropologist, educator; b. Albany, Oregon, Feb. 18, 1933; s. Roderick and Mary Curtis (Willis) S.; m. Linda Ferguson, May 28, 1975; children: Roderick IV, Katherine K., Frederick L., Alexander W. BA, Wash. State U., 1955, MA, 1959; PhD, U. Ariz., 1967. Staff archaeologist Wash. State U., Pullman, 1965-67; asst. prof. U. Idaho, Moscow, 1967-69, head dept. anthropology, 1968-81, dir. anthropology lab., 1968—, assoc. prof., 1969-72, prof. anthropolgy, 1972—; fgn. expert Inner Mongolia U., Huhhot, Peoples Republic of China, 1986-87; bd. trustees N.W. Sci. Assn., 1968-71. Co-author: A Bibliography of Glass Trade Beads in North America, 1980; editor N.W. Anthrop. Rsch. Notes jour., 1970—. With U.S. Army, 1956-58. Fellow Am. Anthrop. Assn.; mem. AAAS, Soc. for Hist. Archaeology (sec., treas. 1971-74, pres. 1976, 90, rev. editor 1977—), Soc. for Am. Archaeology, Sigma Xi (pres. local chpt. 1980). Office: U Idaho Lab Anthropology Moscow ID 83844

SPRAINGS, VIOLET EVELYN, psychologist; b. Omaha, Aug. 1, 1930; d. Henry Elbert and Straunella (Hunter) S.; A.B., U. Calif., Berkeley, 1948, M.A., 1951, postgrad., 1960-64; Ph.D., U. San Francisco, 1982. Tchr., Oakland (Calif.) Public Schs., 1951-58; psychologist Med. Edn. Diagnostic Ctr., San Francisco, 1959-62; dir. psychol. edn. and lang. services Calif. Dept. Edn., 1963-71; asst. prof. San Francisco State U., 1964-71; assoc. prof. ednl. psychology Calif. State U., Hayward, 1971-79; dir. Spraings Acad., Orinda, Lafayette and Walnut Creek, 1971—; psychologist in pvt. practice, 1962—; dir. Western Women's Bank, Spraings Acad.; mem. adv. bd. Bay Area Health Systems Agy.; instr. U. Calif., Berkeley extension, 1964—; mem. oral bd. for Ednl. Psychologists, 1972—; mem. Calif. Dept. Task Force on Psychol. Assessment, 1987—. Mem. adv. com. Foothill Jr. Coll. Dist. Recipient Phoebe Apperson Heart award San Francisco Examiner, 1968. Mem. Am. Psychol. Assn., Internat. Neuropsychol. Assn. (charter), Calif. Psychol. Assn., Calif. Assn. Sch. Psychologists and Psychometrists, Western Psychol. Assn., Nat. Council Negro Women, AAUP, Delta Sigma Theta, Psi Chi, Pi Lambda Theta. Contbr. articles to profl. jours. Home: 170 Glorietta Blvd Orinda CA 94563-3543 Office: 89 Moraga Way Orinda CA 94563

SPRIGGS, EVERETT LEE, lawyer; b. Safford, Ariz., July 30, 1930; s. Claude E. and Evelyn (Lee) S.; m. Betty Medley, Aug. 22, 1953; children: Claudia Lynn Reynolds, Scott B. BS, Ariz. State U., 1955; JD, U. Ariz., 1958. Bar: Calif. 1960, U.S. Supreme Ct. 1983. City atty. criminal dept. Los Angeles, 1960-61; mem. firm Kinkle & Rodiger, Riverside, Calif., 1961-64; pres. Kinkle, Rodiger & Spriggs (P.C.), Riverside, 1965—; chmn. bd. dirs. Riverside Nat. Bank. With AUS, 1951-52. Mem. ABA, Calif. Bar Assn., Riverside County Bar Assn., L.A. County Bar Assn., Def. Rsch. Inst., So. Calif. Def. Counsel (editorial staff 1970-71), Assn. Trial Lawyers Am., Riverside Downtown Assn., Am. Bd. Trial Advocates, Supreme Ct. Hist. Soc., Def. Orientation Conf. Assn. Home: 1456 Muirfield Rd Riverside CA 92506-5576 also: 1126 E Balboa Blvd Balboa CA 92661 Office: Kinkle Rodiger & Spriggs 3801 University Ave Ste 700 Riverside CA 92501-3255 also: 621 Sunset Blvd Los Angeles CA 90012-2191 also: 837 N Ross St Santa Ana CA 92701-1558 also: 1620 5th Ave San Diego CA 92101 also: 4195 Thousand Oaks Blvd Thousand Oaks CA 91362

SPRINCZ, KEITH STEVEN, financial services company professional; b. Whitewater, Wis., Mar. 8, 1956; s. Steven B. Sprincz and Mary Lou (Crotte) Zolle; m. Renee Michele Werner, Sept. 11, 1982; children: Nicholas, Cameron. BS in Mktg., Colo. State U., 1978; student, Am. Coll., 1985-86. CLU, ChFC. Agt. Prudential, Denver, 1978-83; ins. broker Nolen/Western, Denver, 1983-88, ptnr., 1988—; tchr. Life Underwriters Tng. Coun., Bethesda, Md., 1991-92. Chmn. bd. elders Bethlehem Luth. Ch., Lakewood, Colo., 1989; campmaster coord. Denver Area coun. Boys Scouts Am., Denver, 1989—; mem. Boys Scouts Am., scoutmaster, 1983—; capt. March of Dimes, Denver, 1981, Big Bros., Denver, 1984; pres. Centennial Assn. Life Underwriters, 1986-87. Recipient Outstanding Family award Boy Scouts Am., 1986. Mem. Colo. Assn. Life Underwriters, Tahosa Alumni Assn. (bd. dirs. 1982—). Lutheran. Office: Nolen Western 5690 DTC Blvd Ste 140 Englewood CO 80111

SPRING, DEE, psychotherapist, educator; b. Clayton, Ga., Sept. 22, 1934; d. James Rusk and Maxie Marie (Thompson) Grant; m. John Bowan Spring Jr., Mar. 15, 1957 (div. 1981); children: Jay, Angela, David. BA, Calif. State U., Fullerton, 1976; MA, Goddard Coll., 1977; Ma, The Fielding Inst., 1985, PhD, 1988. Lic. marriage and family therapist, Calif.; lic. counselor, Ohio. Prof. Calif. State U., Fullerton, 1976-81, Ea. Mont. Coll., Billings, 1982-83; exec. dir., psychotherapist Earthwood Ctr., Ventura, Calif., 1983—; prof. Marylhurst Coll., Oreg., 1988—; nat. pvt. cons., 1976—; exec. dir. Women's Crisis Ctr., Placentia, Calif., 1974-82; psychologist Ea. Mont. Mental Health, Colstrip, 1982083; counselor Ventura County Alcohol Svcs., 1983-88; prof. U. Calif., Santa Barbara, 1989—. Author: Shattered Images: Phenomenological Language of Sexual Trauma, 1992; contbg. author: In Imagery, Vol. I, 1980, Vol. II, 1981, Vol. III, 1983; also articles. Recipient Vol. award Ventura County, 1984, 86. Mem. Am. Art Therapy Assn. (profl., chmn. program com. 1980, treas. 1985-89), Internat. Soc. for Multiple Personality Disorder (profl.), Soc. for Post Traumatic Studies, So. Calif. Soc. for Clin. Hypnosis (clin.), Calif. Soc. for Study Multiple Personality and Disorder (pres. 1993-95). Office: 2021 Sperry Ave Ste 23 Ventura CA 93003-7417

SPRING, GLENN ERNEST, composer; b. Hot Springs, Ark., Apr. 19, 1939; s. Glenn Ernest Sr. and Ellen (Maddox) S.; m. Ingrid Kathryn Olesen, Aug. 5, 1962 (dec. Jan. 1973); 1 child, Brian Glenn; m. Kathleen Marie Klein, Dec. 16, 1973; children; Christopher, Heidi. BA, La Sierra U., 1962; M.Mus., Tex. Christian U., 1964; D. Mus. Arts, U. Wash., 1972. Instr. music Otterbein Coll., Westerville, Ohio, 1964-65; prof. music Walla Walla Coll., College Place, Wash., 1965-75, 87-89; concertmaster Walla Walla (Wash.) Symphony, 1965-75, 87-90; sect. violionist (1st) Columbus (Ohio) Symphony, 1964-65; sect. violinist (1st and 2d) Ft. Worth Symphony, 1962-64. Composer Shapes: a short symphony, 1973 (Indpls. Symphony award 1974), (orchestral composition) Perceptions, 1977, Dona nobis pacem for baritone and orch., 1984, Contrasts for organ, 1986, Hold in your memory the land, 1990, many other works. Recipient commn. Wash. State Arts Commn., 1973, Musiklager Margess, Switzerland, 1988, 89, Alienor Harpsichord Composition award SE Hist. Keyboard Soc., 1990. Mem. ASCAP (ann. awards 1988-92), Coll. Music Soc. (Burlington-No. award 1991). Office: Walla Walla Coll 204 S College Ave College Place WA 99324-1139

SPRING, JEFFREY DAVID, architect; b. Spokane, Wash., Dec. 18, 1955; s. James David and Dorothy Mae (Smith) S.; m. Rebecca Louise Haugen, Aug. 19, 1978; children: Molly Jean, Annie Mae, Jesse Joseph. Student, Mont. State U. Lic. architect, Wash. Designer Indsl. Drafting, Spokane, 1977; constrn. supt. Quantum Constrn., Spokane, 1977-78; pres. DDI-Architecture & Planning Co., Spokane, Kirkland, Wash., 1978—. Recipient 1st and 2d People's choice awards Spokane Home Builders Assn., 1986, 1st place, 1987. Mem. AIA, Nat. Assn. Home Builders (bd. dirs. Spokane chpt. 1985-86, v.p. 1986). Republican. Lutheran.

SPRING, KATHLEEN MARIE, musical program director, educator; b. L.A., Apr. 6, 1951; d. James David and Mabel Katherine (Nobbe) Klein; m. Glenn Ernest Spring, Dec. 16, 1973; children: Christopher, Heidi, Brian. BA in Music, Walla Walla Coll., 1974; student, Hochschule für Musik, Vienna, Austria, 1970-71, 85, 88. Registered tchr. trainer, Suzuki Assn. of Ams. Violin instr. College Place, Wash., 1977—, string techniques instr., 1977—; string and orchs. tchr. Rogers Elem., College Place, 1980—; dir. Walla Walla Suzuki Program, Wash., 1984—; asst. prin. first violin Walla Walla Symphony, 1986-91, prin. second violin, 1991—. Performer: (duo recital) Duo LeClair, Switzerland, Austria, 1983, (solo) Walla Walla, 1985, 88, WWC Centenial Chamber Music Series, 1992. Dir. Rogers String Ensembles, 1985—. Mem. Am. String Tchrs. Assn., Internat. Suzuki Assn., Suzuki Assn. of Ams. (cert.), Suzuki Assn. of Wash. Seventh-day Adventist. Home: 1057 Brickner College Place WA 99324 Office: Rogers Elem Sch 4th and Bade College Place WA 99342

SPRINGER, CAROL, state legislator. Mem. Ariz. State Senate from dist. 1. Home: 973 W Curley Prescott AZ 86301 Office: Arizona State House 620 Lester Dr Prescott AZ 86301

SPRINGER, CHARLES EDWARD, state supreme court justice; b. Reno, Feb. 20, 1928; s. Edwin and Rose Mary Cecelia (Kelly) S.; m. Jacqueline Sirkegian, Mar. 17, 1951; 1 dau., Kelli Ann. BA, U. Nev., Reno, 1950; LLB, Georgetown U., 1953; LLM, U. Va., 1984; student Grad. Program for Am. Judges, Oriel Coll., Oxford (Eng.), 1984. Bar: Nev. 1953, U.S. Dist. Ct. Nev. 1953, D.C. 1954, U.S. Supreme Ct. 1962. Pvt. practice law Reno, 1953-80; atty. gen. State of Nev., 1962, legis. legal adv. to gov., 1958-62; legis. bill drafter Nev. Legislature, 1955-57; mem. faculty Nat. Coll. Juvenile Justice, Reno, 1978—; juvenile master 2d Jud. Dist. Nev., 1973-80; also chmn. Gender Bias Task Force Supreme Ct. Nev., Carson City, 1981—; chmn. Jud. Selection Commn., 1981; trustee Nat. Coun. Juvenile and Family Ct. Judges, 1983; mem. faculty U. Nev., Reno, McGeorge Sch. Law, 1982—; mem. Nev. Commn. for Women, 1991—. With AUS, 1945-47. Recipient Outstanding Contbn. to Juvenile Justice award Nat. Coun. Juvenile and Family Ct. Judges, 1989, Midby-Byron Disting. Leadership award U. Nev., 1988. Mem. ABA, Am. Judicature Soc., Am. Trial Lawyers Assn., Phi Kappa Phi. Office: Nev Supreme Ct Capitol Complex 201 S Carson St Carson City NV 89710-0001

SPRINGER, FLOYD LADEAN, architect; b. Goodrich, N.D., Feb. 1, 1922; s. George Roy Springer and Louise Baumbach; m. Dorothy Mae Shepard; children: Debra Louise, Tami June. Student, U. Denver, 1948-51; BS in Archtl. Engring., U. Colo., 1952; postgrad., U. Wash., 1953-54, U. Utah, Portland, Oreg., 1980. With Seattle Delta Investment Group, 1984—. Cpl. inf. U.S. Army, 1941-44, PTO. Mem. Frank Lloyd Wright Conservancy (N.W. chpt.). Presbyterian. Home and Office: 18548 60th Ave NE Seattle WA 98155

SPRINGER, GEORGE STEPHEN, mechanical engineering educator; b. Budapest, Hungary, Dec. 12, 1933; came to U.S., 1959; s. Joseph and Susan (Grausz) S.; m. Susan Martha Flory, Sept. 15, 1963; children: Elizabeth Anne, Mary Katherine. B in Engring., U. Sydney, Australia, 1959; M in Engring., Yale U., 1960, MSc in Engring., 1961, PhD, 1962. Registered profl. engr., Mass. Asst. prof. mech. engring. MIT, Cambridge, Mass., 1962-67; prof. mech. engring. U. Mich., Ann Arbor, 1967-83; prof. mech. engring., chmn. dept. aeronautics/astronautics Stanford (Calif.) U., 1983—. Author: Erosion by Liquid Impact, 1975; co-author, co-editor 12 books; contbr. over 150 articles to scholarly and profl. jours. Recipient Pub. Svc. Group Achievement award NASA, 1988. Fellow AIAA, ASME; mem. Am. Physical Soc., Soc. Automotive Engrs. (Ralph Teeter award 1978), Soc. for the Advancement of Materials and Process Engring. (Del Monte award 1991). Office: Stanford U Dept Aeronautics and Astronautics Stanford CA 94305

SPRINGER, GERALD WILLIAM, sales executive; b. Amherst, Ohio, Nov. 13, 1943; s. Raymond W. and Ione J. (Myers) S.; m. Marilyn F. Gregg, Aug. 28, 1971. BBA, Kent State U., 1966. Dist. sales mgr. Flintkote Co., Kent, Ohio, 1970-72, US Gypson Co., Denver, 1972-75, Ameron Corp., Denver, 1975-79; nat. sales mgr. Blue Bird Internat. Co., Englewood, Colo., 1979-81; sales mgr. Smith & Wesson, Golden, Colo., 1981-85; pres. The West & Assocs., Inc., Golden, 1985—. Served with Ohio N.G., 1963-67. Jeffco Posse Club. Republican. Congregationalist. Office: The West and Assocs Inc 4895 Easley Rd Golden CO 80403-1600

SPRINGER, PAUL DAVID, lawyer, motion picture company executive; b. N.Y.C., Apr. 27, 1942; s. William W. and Alma (Markowitz) S.; m. Mariann Frankfurt, Aug. 16, 1964; children: Robert, William. BA, U. Bridgeport, 1963; JD, Bklyn. Law Sch., 1967. Bar: N.Y. 1968, U.S. Dist. Ct. (so. and ea. dists.) N.Y. 1968, U.S. Ct. Appeals (2d cir.) 1970, U.S. Supreme Ct. 1973, Calif. 1989. Assoc. Johnson & Tannenbaum, N.Y.C., 1968-70; assoc. counsel Columbia Pictures, N.Y.C., 1970; assoc. counsel Paramount Pictures, N.Y.C., 1970-79, v.p., theatrical distbn. counsel, 1979-85, sr. v.p., chief resident counsel East Coast, 1985-87; sr. v.p., asst. gen. counsel Paramount Pictures, L.A., 1987—; Bar: N.Y. 1968, U.S. Dist. Ct. (so. and ea. dists.) N.Y. 1968, U.S. Ct. Appeals (2d cir.) 1970, U.S. Supreme Ct. 1973, Calif. 1989. Trustee West Cunningham Park Civic Assn., Fresh Meadows, N.Y., 1978—. Mem. ABA, Assn. of Bar of City of N.Y., L.A. Copyright Soc., Acad. Motion Picture Arts and Scis.

SPRINGER, RANDY RAYMOND, handicap sit ski instructor; b. Delta, Colo., Mar. 14, 1959; s. Daniel Patrick and Mary Ann (Knob) S.; m. Tracie Lee Wahl, Dec. 13, 1979 (div. Mar. 1984); 1 child, Kimberly Marie. Grad., Delta High Sch., 1977. Cert. Nat. Handicap Sports, Profl. Ski Instrs. Am. Carpenter Delta, 1980-81; in constrn. Schmidt & Tiego, Rifle, Colo., 1981; ski instr. Colo. Discover Ability/Nat. Handicap Sports, 1985—; handicap cons., vol. Hilltop Rehab. Hosp., Grand Juncion, Colo., 1986-89, St. Mary Hosp., Grand Junction, 1988-90, Vets. Hosp., Grand Junction, 1988—; dir. First Wheelchair Tennis Tournament in We. Colo., 1989; instr. DAV's Winter Sport's Clinic, 1988-93, Disabled Veteran Winter Sports Clinic. With U.S. Army, 1977-80, Germany. Named to Outstanding Young Ams., 1989. Mem. Nat. Handicap Sports, Profl. Ski Instrs. Am., Dyno Wheelers Sports Team (past pres., Presdl. Appreciation award 1991), Colo. Discover Ability, Black Canyon Posse, Paralyzed Vets. Am. (Sportsman of the Yr. 1990). Roman Catholic. Home: 2815 Elm Ave Grand Junction CO 81501

SPRINGER, SALLY PEARL, university administrator; b. Bklyn., Mar. 19, 1947; d. Nathaniel Margulies and Fanny (Schoen) S.; m. Hakon Hope; children: Erik Jacob Hope, Mollie Liv Hope. BS, Bklyn. Coll., 1967; PhD, Stanford U., 1971. Postdoctoral fellow Stanford U. Med. Sch., Calif., 1971-73; asst. prof. SUNY-Stony Brook, 1973-78, assoc. provost, 1981-85, assoc. prof., 1978-87; exec. asst. to chancellor U. Calif., Davis, 1987-92; asst chancellor, 1992—. Author (with others): Left Brain, Right Brain, 1981 (Am. Psychol. Found. Disting. Contbr. award 1981), 4th rev. edit., 1993, How to Succeed in College, 1982; contbr. articles to profl. jours. Mem. Internat. Neuropsychol. Soc., Psychonomic Soc. Office: U Calif Office Chancellor Davis CA 95616

SPROUL, JOHN ALLAN, retired public utility executive; b. Oakland, Calif., Mar. 28, 1924; s. Robert Gordon and Ida Amelia (Wittschen) S.; m. Marjorie Ann Hauck, June 20, 1945; children: John Allan, Malcolm J., Richard O., Catherine E. A.B., U. Calif., Berkeley, 1947, LL.B., 1949. Bar: Calif. 1950. Atty. Pacific Gas & Electric Co., San Francisco, 1949-52, 56-62, sr. atty., 1962-70, asst. gen. counsel, 1970-71, v.p. gas supply, 1971-76, sr. v.p., 1976-77, exec. v.p., 1977-89, cons., 1989—; gen. counsel Pacific Gas Transmission Co., 1970-73, v.p., 1973-79, chmn. bd., 1979-89, also bd. dirs.; atty. Johnson & Stanton, San Francisco, 1952-56; bd. dirs. Oreg. Steel Mills, Inc. Bd. dirs. Hastings Coll. of Law. Served to 1st lt. USAAF, 1943-46. Mem. Calif. Bar Assn., Am. Gas Assn., Pacific Coast Gas Assn., Engrs. Club, World Trade Club (San Francisco), Pacific-Union Club, Orinda Country Club. Home: 8413 Buckingham Dr El Cerrito CA 94530-2531 Office: Mail Code F31 PO Box 770000 1 California St Ste 3125 San Francisco CA 94177

SPROULE, BETTY ANN, computer industry market researcher; b. Evanston, Ill., Dec. 30, 1948; d. Harold Fletcher and Lois (Reno) Mathis; m. J. Michael Sproule, Mar. 3, 1973; children: John Harold, Kevin William. BS, Ohio State U., 1969, MS, 1970, PhD, 1972. Mem. tech. staff Bell Telephone Labs., Columbus, Ohio, 1973-74; asst. prof. U. Tex., Odessa, 1974-77; analyst bus. systems Maj. Appliance Bus. div. GE, Louisville, 1977-78; dir. forecasting and analysis Brown and Williamson Tobacco, Louisville, 1978-86; mgr. market rsch. Hewlett-Packard Co., Cupertino, Calif., 1986—. Contbr. articles to profl. jours.; patentee in field. Sr. mem. IEEE, Soc. Women Engrs. Home: 4135 Briarwood Way Palo Alto CA 94306-4610 Office: Hewlett-Packard Co 19483 Pruneridge Ave Cupertino CA 95014-0781

SPROUSE, ROBERT ALLEN, II, retail chain director; b. Portland, Oreg., Dec. 25, 1935; s. John Alwyn and Mary.Louise (Burpee) S.; m. Frances Carolyn Russell, June 22, 1957. Student, Williams Coll., 1953-57. With Sprouse-Reitz Stores Inc., Portland, 1957—; buyer, sec. Sprouse-Reitz Stores Inc., 1963-69, v.p., 1969-73, pres., 1973—, chief exec. officer, 1986-91, also bd. dirs., chmn., 1991—. Active Good Samaritan Hosp. Found. Mem. Chief Execs. Orgn., Theta Delta Chi. Republican. Episcopalian. Clubs: Multnomah Athletic (Portland); Arlington. Lodge: Rotary. Office: Sprouse-Reitz Stores Inc PO Box 8996 Portland OR 97208-8996

SPUDICH, JAMES A., biology educator; b. Collinsville, Ill., Jan. 7, 1942; married, 1964; 2 children. BS, U. Ill., 1963; PhD in Biochemistry, Stanford U., 1967. USPHS trainee Stanford (Calif.) U., 1968, now prof. biochemistry and devel. biology, dept. biochemistry; asst. prof. biochemistry U. Calif., San Francisco, 1970-74, assoc. prof., from 1974. USAF Sci. Rsch. fellow Cambridge U., 1969, NSF fellow, 1970; Am. Cancer Soc. rsch. grantee U. Calif., San Francisco, 1970. Mem. AAAS, NAS, Am. Soc. Cell Biologists (pres. 1989). Office: Stanford U Dept Biochemistry Stanford Med Ctr Stanford CA 94305-5307

SQUIER, CHARLES LABARGE, English language educator; b. Milw., Apr. 28, 1931; s. Theodore Louis and Nina Amelie (LaBarge) S.; m. Janice Helen Stevenson, July 6, 1957; children: Alison Anne Stevenson, Charles LaBarge Stevenson. AB, Harvard Coll., 1953; AMT, Harvard U., 1957; PhD, U. Mich., 1963. Instr. U. Mich., Ann Arbor, 1961-63; prof. Dept. English U. Colo., Boulder, 1963—, chmn. Dept. English, 1989-91, assoc. chmn., 1992—. Author: Sir John Suckling, 1978, John Fletcher, 1986; editor: The Sonnet, 1965, 87; author of articles, short fiction, poetry. With U.S. Army, 1953-55. Mem. Internat. Shakespeare Assn., Shakespeare Assn. Am., Rocky Mountain Medieval and Renaissance Soc. Democrat. Episcopalian. Office: U Colo Dept English Campus Box 226 Boulder CO 80309

SQUIRE, JUDITH MAUREEN, aviation company executive; b. Hollywood, Calif., Nov. 21, 1942; d. James Francis and Virginia E. (Joham) Power; m. Dennis Davis, May 30, 1969 (div. Dec. 1970); m. Robert George Squire, Feb. 10, 1978. AA, Pierce Coll., 1962; BA, Valley State U., 1964. Cert. paralegal. Mgr. Dow Jones & Co., L.A., 1965-70, Power & Assocs., Colorado Springs, Colo., 1970-71; sec., paralegal, mgr. Sklar, Coben, Stashower, L.A., 1971-78; owner Judy's Secretarial Svcs., Ennis, Mont., 1978-89; paralegal, mgr. Ben Johnson Properties, Ennis, 1979-87; ptnr., mgr. Bob's Aircraft, Ennis, 1979-88; ptnr., mgr. Squire Aircraft, Inc., Buhl, Idaho, 1988—, also bd. dirs.; cons. Madison Valley Land Mgmt., Ennis, 1980—. Mem. Buhl Econ. Coun., 1992. Mem. Twentieth Century Club (pres. 1991—, bd. dirs. 1989—), Idaho Fedn. Women Clubs (scholarship chmn. 1992—, 1st v.p. dist. II 1992—), Buhl C. of C. Office: Squire Aircraft Inc PO Box 428 Buhl ID 83316

SQUIRES-GROHE, LINDA LEE, college administrator; b. San Francisco, Aug. 1, 1944; d. Alan Francis and Edna May (Rafael) Squires; m. William Edward Grohe, Apr. 28, 1984. BA, San Jose State U., 1966, MA, 1969. Instr. Humboldt State U., Arcata, Calif., 1968-69; instr. City Coll. San Francisco, 1969-75, pub. rels. officer, 1975-78, dean of instruction, 1978-92, contract edn. coord., 1992—. Mem. Am. Assn. Community and Jr. Coll. Women (pres. Bay Area chpt. 1988—). Office: City Coll San Francisco 800 Mission St San Francisco CA 94103

SRIVASTAVA, HARI MOHAN, mathematics educator; b. Karon, Ballia, Uttar Pradesh, India, July 5, 1940; came to U.S., 1967, Can., 1969; s. Harihar and Bela (Devi) Prasad; m. Rekha Panda, July 30, 1978; children: Sapna, Gautam Mohan. BSc, Allahabad (India) U., 1957, MSc, 1959; PhD, Jodhpur (India) U., 1965. Chartered mathematician, U.K. Lectr. Manipur Univ., Imphal, India, 1959-60, U. Roorkee, India, 1960-63; lectr. Jodhpur U., 1963-68, reader (on leave), 1968-69; asst. prof. W.Va. U., Morgantown, 1967-69; assoc. prof. U. Victoria, B.C., Can., 1969-74, prof., 1974—; hon. prof. Inst. Basic Rsch., Palm Harbor, Fla., 1992—; mem. editorial bd. numerous math. and sci. publs. including Internat. Jour. Sci. and Engring., Internat. Jour. Math. and Mathematical Scis., Jour. of Nat. Acad. Math., Pan Am. Math. Jour., Soochow Jour. Math., Jour. Bihar Math. Soc., Bulletin Calcutta Math. Soc., Astrophysics and Space Sci., Integral Transforms and Spl. Functions, Indian Jour. Pure and Applied Math., Jour. Indian Acad. Math., Ganita Sandesh, Jour. Inst. Math. and Computer Scis., Ganita, facta Universitatis, Hardonic Jour., Indian Jour. Phys. and Natural Scis., Hadronic Jour. Supplement, Jour. Natural Geometry, Jour. Math. Phys. Scis.; editorial advisor The Math. Edn.; reviewer Applied Mechanics Revs., 1973—, Math. Revs., 1966—, Zentralblatt für Mathematik, 1965—; referee, editorial cons. several Asian, European, Am. jours.; referee for rsch. grant projects NSF, Nat. Scis. and Engring. Rsch. Coun. of Can.; mem. exec. coun. Bharata Ganita Parisad, 1980-81, 1984-85. Co-author: Convolution Integral Equations with Special Function Kernels, 1977, Special Functions in Queuing Theory and Related Stochastic Processes, 1982, The H-Functions of One and Two Variables with Applications, 1982, A Treatise on Generating Functions, 1984, Multiple Gaussian Hypergeometric Series, 1985, Theory and Applications of Convolution Integral Equations, 1992; co-editor Univalent Functions, Fractional Calculus, and Their Applications, 1989, Current Topics in Analytic Function Theory, 1992, Topics in Polynomials of One and Several Variables and Their Applications, 1993; editor Jñānābha; communicating editor Simon Stevin; regional editor in Can. Pure and Applied Mathematika Scis.; contbr. over 300 articles to profl. jours. Fellow Royal Astronomical Soc., Nat. Acad. Scis. of India, Inst. of Math. and Its Applications U.K. (hon. fgn. mem.) Royal Acad. of Scis., Lit. and Fine Arts Belgium. Office: Univ Victoria, Dept Math and Statistics, Victoria, BC Canada V8W 3P4

STAAB, JOSEPH RAYMOND, retired federal agency administrator; b. Hays, Kans., Jan. 2, 1932; s. Joseph Leo and Esther Isea (Eaton) S.; m. Joan Annette Schumacher, Nov. 25, 1961; children: Gregory Joseph, William Eric. BSBA, Fort Hays State U., 1958; MS, Kans. State U., 1959. Various auditing positions, 1959-67; acct. exec. Dean Witter & Co. Inc., San Marino, Pasadena, Calif., 1967-69; fin. advisor, planner Powell, Johnson & Assocs. Inc., Pasadena, 1969-70; sr. fin. analyst Standard and Poor's Corp., L.A., 1970-71; ind. fin. mgmt. cons. L.A., 1971-74; chief mgmt. systems divsn. FAA N.W. Region, Seattle, 1974-76; dir. ctr. for small bus. Urbana (Ohio) Coll., 1976-77; chief mgmt. info. br. FAA, Washington, 1977-80; mgr. tech. and adminstrv. support staff FAA Transport Airplane Directorate, Seattle,

1980-93; retired, 1993; pres. coop. edn. adv. com. & bus. edn. adv. bds. Green River C.C., Auburn, Wash., 1991-93; freelance fin. mgmt. cons., Federal Way, Wash., 1992—. With USN, 1952-56. Mem. Fraternal Order of Eagles, Sigma Tau Gamma (treas. 1957-58). Republican. Roman Catholic. Home: 3703 SW 319th St Federal Way WA 98023-2154

STACK, GEOFFREY LAWRENCE, real estate developer; b. Trinidad, British West Indies, Sept. 16, 1943; s. Gerald Francis and V. Louise (Bell) S.; m. Victoria Hammack, 1970 (div. 1986); 1 child, Kathryn; m. Nancy J. Haarer, Apr. 19, 1987; children: Alexandra, Natalie. BA, Georgetown U., 1965; MBA, U. Pa., 1972. Dir. acquisitions J.H. Snyder Co., L.A., 1972-75; from project mgr. to exec. v.p. Richards West, Newport Beach, Calif., 1975-77; pres. Regis Homes Corp., Newport Beach, 1977—; bd. dirs. WJS, Inc., Newport Beach, 1988—, Arral & Ptnrs., Hong Kong, 1981—, Calif. Housing Coun., Sacramento, 1986—. Mem. adv. bd. Coro So. Calif., Santa Ana, 1991—; bd. regents Franciscan Sch. of Theology, Berkeley, Calif., 1991—; bd. advisors Grad. Sch. Bus., U. Calif., Irvine, 1992. Capt. USMC, 1967-70. Decorated 2 Bronze Stars, 21 Air medals, Navy Commendation medal, Purple Heart. Mem. Young Pres. Orgn., Big Canyon Country Club, Pacific Club, Ctr. Club. Democrat. Roman Catholic. Office: Sares Regis Group 5120 Campus Dr 18802 Bardeen Ave Irvine CA 92715

STACKHOUSE, CHRISTIAN PAUL, computer company executive; b. Lynnwood, Wash., Mar. 24, 1960; s. Paul Sullivan Stackhouse and Trilby Mary (Schultz) Roman; m. MyPhuong Ngoc Le, Sept. 1, 1984; 1 child, Andre Le. BSEE, U. Wash., 1983; MSEE, U. Ariz., 1987. Cert. engr.-in-tng. Elec. engr. IBM, Tucson, 1983-86; software engr. IBM Palo Alto (Calif.) Scientific Ctr., 1986-88, IBM Knowledge Based Systems Lab., Menlo Park, Calif., 1988-90, LaserAccess Corp., Bothell, Wash., 1990-91; mgr. of product devel. LaserAccess Corp., Bothell, 1991—. Mem. IEEE, AAAI, Assn. Computing Machinery, Amnesty Internat., Nature Conservancy. Home: 15510 92nd Pl NE Bothell WA 98011 Office: LaserAccess 22122 20th Ave SE P O Box 3020 Bothell WA 98041-3020

STACKHOUSE, WILL, III, laboratory technologist; b. Washington, Dec. 19, 1942; s. Will Jr. and Frances Louise (Stouffer) S. BS in Engring. Sci., USAF Acad., 1964; MS in Engring. Mechanics, U. Mich., 1972; PhD in Engring. Design and Bioengring., Oxford U., 1978; postgrad, Def. Systems Mgmt. Coll., Ft. Belvoir, Va., 1982. Commd. 2d lt. USAF, 1964, advanced through grades to col, 1985; pilot F4D, chief F4 standardization and evaluation 8th TFW Ubon RTAFB, Thailand; instr. dept. engring. sci., mechanics and materials, pilot USAF Acad., Colo., 1972-74, assoc. prof. engring. mechanics, pilot, dir. rsch., 1978-81; dir. systems integration, requirements and analysis Air Force Satellite Communications Program Office Space Div., L.A., 1981; dir. spacecraft acquisition and space segment integration MILSTAR Joint Program Office, L.A., 1982-86; asst. high leverage tech. Sec. of Air Force for Acquisitions, Washington, 1986-89; asst. high leverage tech. space systems div. L.A. AFB, Calif., 1989-91; asst. high leverage tech. NASA-Jet Propulsion Lab., Pasadena, Calif., 1991—; ret. USAF, 1991; speaker USAF Recruiting Svc., U.S. Competitiveness, Econ. amd Nat. Security and civic groups; adivsor L.A. area youth on Air Force Acad. opportunities, 1981-91. Chmn. Lee's Heights Homeowners Asns., Charlbury, Oxfordshire, Eng., 1975-77. Recipient Mil. Order of Purple Heart, Pres. Commn. for Handicapped, 1979, Laurel, Aviation Week and Space Tech., 1991, Profl. Achievement award IEEE, 1991, Disting. Flying Cross. Mem. IEEE (comm. and info. policy com.), Assn. Grads. USAF Acad. (life), Air Force Assn., Soc. Motion Picture and TV Engrs. (chmn. task forces on future of HDTV in U.S.). Office: Jet Propulson Lab MS 138-307 4800 Oak Grove Dr Pasadena CA 91109-8099

STACY, BILL WAYNE, college president; b. Bristol, Va., July 26, 1938; s. Charles Frank and Louise Nelson (Altwater) S.; m. Sue Stacy; children: Mark, Sara, James. B.S.Ed., S.E. Mo. State U., 1960; M.S., So. Ill. U., 1965, Ph.D., 1968. Tchr. Malden High Sch., Mo., 1960-64; asst. prof. communication Southeast Mo. State U., Cape Girardeau, 1967-71, assoc. prof., 1971-74, prof., from 1974, asst. to pres., 1972-76, dean Grad. Sch., 1976-79, interim pres., 1979, pres., 1980-89; pres. Calif. State U., San Marcos, 1989—; dir. Boatmen's Nat. Bank. Mem. San Diego United Way. Mem. Cape Girardeau C. of C. (chmn.), Am. Assn. State Colls. and Univs., Am. Assn. Higher Edn., Rotary. Presbyterian.

STACY, THOMAS DONNIE, oil company executive; b. Houston, Jan. 13, 1934; s. Thomas Dillard and Bonnie (Batts) S.; m. Wanda Taylor, Aug. 20, 1954; children: Chris A., Kathy Stacy Cameron, David W., Shari Stacy Riley. BS in Engring., La. Tech U., 1957, MS in Engring., 1963; PhD in Engring. Sci., Miss. State U., 1967. Registered profl. engr., La. Engr. Amoco Prodn. Co., Duncan, Okla., 1957-58; sr. engr. Amoco Prodn. Co., Houston, 1967-72, reg. engr. mgr., 1976-77; mgr. product rsch. Amoco Prodn. Co., Tulsa, 1977-80; regional engr. mgr. Amoco Prodn. Co., Chgo., 1980-83; gen. mgr. prodn. svcs. Amoco Prodn. Co., Houston, 1983-85; chief engr. Amoco Can., Calgary, Alta., 1972-75, pres., 1986—, chmn. bd. dirs., 1988—; chmn. Offshore Tech. Conf., 1985-88. Contbr. Articles to tech. jours. Bd. dirs. Jr. Achievement Alta., 1986—. 1st lt. USAF, 1958-62. Recipient 100 Yr. Alumni award Miss. State U., 1985, Alumni of Yr. award La. Tech U., 1989. Mem. Soc. Petroleum Engr. (bd. dirs., treas. 1976-80, Svc. award 1991), Can. Assn. Petroleum Prodrs., Calgary Golf and Country Club. Republican. Home: 419 Lake Placid Green SE, Calgary, AB Canada T2J 5A4 Office: Amoco Can Petroleum Co, 240 4th Ave SW PO Box 200, Calgary, AB Canada T2P 2H8

STADLER, CRAIG ROBERT, professional golfer; b. San Diego, June 2, 1953; s. Donald Edwin and Betty M. (Adams) S.; m. Susan Barrett, Jan. 6, 1979; children: Kevin Craig, Christopher Barrett. Student, U. So. Calif. Profl. golfer Palm Beach Gardens, Fla.; winner Hope Classic, 1980, Greater Greensboro Open, 1980, Kemper Open, 1981-82, Tucson Open, 1982, Masters, 1982, World Series of Golf, 1982, 92. Named U.S. amateur champion, 1973, to U.S. Walker Cup team, 1975, PGA Tour Leading Money Winner, 1982. Mem. Golf Mag. (Player of Yr. 1982). Home: PO Box 3504 Rancho Santa Fe CA 92067-3504 Office: PO Box 2753 Rancho Santa Fe CA 92067-2753

STADLEY, PAT ANNA MAY GOUGH (MRS. JAMES M. STADLEY), author; b. El Paso, Tex., Aug. 31, 1918; d. Thomas and Leona (Plitt) Gough; A.A., Chaffey Jr. Coll., 1936; m. James M. Stadley, Aug. 15, 1936; children—William T., Jerry M. Author books, anthologies, short stories published in over 15 fgn. langs., works include: The Black Leather Barbarians, 1960; Autumn of a Hunter (Edgar Allen Poe spl. award 1970, produced as The Deadly Hunt TV Friday Night Movie Week 1971), 1970; The Deadly Hunt; 1977; The Murder Hunt, 1977; also numerous short stories including The Doe and The Gantlet, 1957, The Waiting Game, 1961, Kurdistan Payload, 1962, Something for the Club, 1963, The Big Measure, 1976, The Tender Trap, 1977, The Stranger, 1980. Democrat. Mem. Christian Ch. Clubs: Calif. Writers (v.p. 1967) (Citrus Heights), Calif. Writers (v.p. 1967—), Mystery Writers Am. Home: 15079 Pinon Rd Magalia CA 95954-9124

STAEHELIN, LUCAS ANDREW, cell biology educator; b. Sydney, Australia, Feb. 10, 1939; came to U.S., 1969; s. Lucas Eduard and Isobel (Malloch) S.; m. Margrit Weibel, Sept. 17, 1965; children: Daniel Thomas, Philip Roland, Marcel Felix. Dipl. Natw., Swiss Fed. Inst. Tech., Zurich, 1963, Ph.D. in Biology, 1966. Research scientist N.Z. Dept. Sci. and Indsl. Research, 1966-69; research fellow in cell biology Harvard U., Cambridge, Mass., 1969-70; asst. prof. cell biology U. Colo., Boulder, 1970-73, assoc. prof., 1973-79, prof., 1979—; vis. prof. U. Freiburg, 1978, Swiss Fed. Inst. Tech., 1984, 92; mem. cellular biology and physiology study sect. NIH, Bethesda, Md., 1980-84; mem. DOE panel on rsch. directions for the energy bioscis., 1988, 92. Editor Jour. Cell Biology, 1977-81, European Jour. Cell Biology, 1981-90, Plant Physiology, 1986-92, Plant Jour., 1991—, (with C.J. Antzen) Ency. Plant Physio., Vol. 19, Photosynthesis III, 1986; contbr. numerous articles to sci. jours. Recipient Humboldt award Humboldt Found., 1978, Sci. Tchr. award U. Colo., 1984, NIH research grants, 1971—. Mem. AAAS, Am. Soc. Cell Biology, Am. Soc. Plant Physiology, Internat. Soc. Plant Molecular Biology. Home: 2855 Dover Dr Boulder CO 80303-5305 Office: U Colo Dept Molecular Cell/Devel Biology Campus Box 347 Boulder CO 80309-0347

STAFF, ROBERT JAMES, JR., international economist; b. 1946; s. Robert J. and Harriet G. (Karber) S.; m. Martha Lee Coleman, 1976; children: Adrian, Marika. Student Wilhelms Universität, W.Ger., 1966; BA, Kalamazoo Coll., 1968; postgrad. Ateneo de Manila Univ., Philippines, 1969; MBA, Am. Mgmt. Assn., 1970; MPA, Harvard U., 1990. Sr. cons. George Odiorne Assocs., Ann Arbor, Mich., 1972-74; assoc. cons. Hutchings Orgn., Palo Alto, Calif., 1974-75; sr. mgmt. cons. E.H. White & Co., Inc., San Francisco, 1975-78; pres. The Wavelink Orgn., Honolulu, 1978—; internat. economist dept. fin. econ. Coll. Bus. Adminstrn U. Hawaii, 1991—; consulting analyst State of Hawaii, Honolulu, 1979—; research mgr. Inst. Philippine Culture, Manila, 1969; sector adviser U.S. Dept. State, Washington, 1978; fiscal project mgr. U. Hawaii, Honolulu, 1980; vis. lectr. Pacific Asian Mgmt. Inst., 1981; coordinator Pacific Devel. Program East-West Ctr., Honolulu, 1981; mem. staff Prime Minister's Disaster Relief Com., Fiji, 1981; mem. adv. staff Kahauale'a Geothermal Energy Project, 1982-83; mem. Gov.'s Adv. Com. on Criminal Justice Info. Systems, 1984; vis. lectr. Inst. Econ. Devel. and Policy, East-West Ctr., Honolulu, 1992; mem. state innovations task force Nat. Govs. Assn, 1992. Author: Political Aspects of Modernization: Buddhist Experiences in Southeast Asia, 1968, Assessment of International Health Manpower Planning, 3 vols., 1978-80; Consolidated Fiscal Procedures in Education, 1981, Trades and Tradeoffs: Strategic Policy Operants in Public-Private Partnerships, 1990, Bioregionalism as a Public Policy Operant, 1992; co-author: MBO Systems Manual, 1974; National Manpower Utilization Study, 1976. Dep. dir. Anchorage Econ. Opportunity Agy., Alaska, 1971-72; diplomatic liaison Coll. Fgn. Study Program, W.Ger., 1966. Served with USAFR, 1970-72. Hughes Meml. scholar Kalamazoo Coll., 1965-68; invited scholar Internat. Negotiations Workshop Harvard Law Sch., 1990. InterPacific fellow, 1989-90; recipient Rewick award, McMannis award Harvard U. Sch. Govt., 1989-90, Internat. Peace award Beyond War Found., 1987. Home: PO Box 1873 Honolulu HI 96805-1873 Office: State Capitol PO Box 150 Honolulu HI 96810-0150

STAFFORD, J. FRANCIS, archbishop; b. Balt., July 26, 1932; s. F. Emmett and Mary Dorothy S. Student, Loyola Coll., Balt., 1950-52; B.A., St. Mary's Sem., Balt., 1954; S.T.B., S.T.L., Gregorian U., Rome, 1958; M.S.W., Catholic U., 1964; postgrad., Rutgers U., 1963, U. Wis.-Madison, 1969, St. Mary's Sem. and Univ., Balt., 1973-75. Spiritual moderator Ladies of Charity Ch., Balt., 1966-76; spiritual moderator Soc. St. Vincent de Paul, Balt., 1965-76; urban vicar Archdiocese of Balt., 1966-76, monsignor, 1970, vicar gen., auxiliary bishop, 1976-83; bishop Diocese of Memphis, 1983-86; archbishop Archdiocese of Denver, 1986—; dir. Assn. Cath. Charities, Balt., 1966-76; archdiocesan liaison to Md. Cath. Conf., Balt, 1975-78; Oriental Orthodox/Roman Cath. consultation Nat. Cath. Conf. Bishops, 1977-85, com. on doctrine, 1978-82, chmn. ecumenical and interreligious affairs com., 1987-90; co-chmn. bilateral dialogue Roman Cath./World Meth. Council, 1977-86; co-chmn. U.S. Roman Cath.-Luth. Dialogue, 1986—; chmn. Bishops' com. marriage and family life U.S. Cath. Conf., 1978-84; mem. gen. Synod Bishops, Vatican City, 1980. Contbr. articles to profl. jours. Trustee Good Samaritan Hosp., Balt., 1973-77, Cath. U. Am., 1990—, Blue Cross of Md., Inc., 1973-76, Balt. Urban Coalition, 1970-75; trustee, chmn., St. Thomas Theol. Sem., 1987—; bd. dirs. Sch. Social Work and Planning, U. Md., 1973-76. Recipient Father Kelly Alumni award Loyola High Sch., 1978; Alumni Laureate, Loyola Coll., 1979. Mem. World Meth. Conf. Roman Cath. Dialogue (co-chmn. 1977-86), Oriental Orthodox Roman Cath. Consultation (co-chmn. 1977-85), Nat. Conf. Cath. Bishops, Luth. Roman Cath. Dialogue, Congregation for Doctrine of Faith. Office: Archdiocese of Denver PO Box 6017A Denver CO 80206-0199*

STAFFORD, JOHN R., consulting firm executive; b. Las Vegas, Nev., Feb. 16, 1968. Diploma, So. Tech. Inst., Las Vegas, 1990. Evangelist Affiliated Inst., Washington, 1974-89; pastor WAI Internat., 1982-85, teens pastor, 1985-87; founder, pres. Home Bus. Adminstrn., Washington, 1987—; CEO United Svcs. Commn., Denver, 1989—; cons. H.B.A., Las Vegas, 1987—; bd. dirs. Desert Star Prodns., Las Vegas, Infinite Images. Republican. Home: 4706 Kay Pl Las Vegas NV 89107-4126

STAFFORD, WILLIAM EDGAR, author, retired educator; b. Hutchinson, Kans., Jan. 17, 1914; s. Earl Ingersoll and Ruby Nina (Mayher) S.; m. Dorothy Hope Frantz, Apr. 8, 1944; children: Bret William (dec.), Kim Robert, Kathryn Lee, Barbara Claire. BA, U. Kans., 1937, MA, 1946; PhD, State U. Iowa, 1954; LittD, Ripon Coll., 1965; LHD, Linfield Coll., 1970. Faculty Lewis and Clark Coll., Portland, Oreg., 1948-80, prof. English, 1960-80; faculty San Jose (Calif.) State Coll., 1956-57, Manchester (Ind.) Coll., 1955-56; cons. poetry Library of Congress, Washington, 1970. Author: West of Your City, 1960, Traveling Through the Dark, 1962 (Nat. Book award 1963), The Rescued Year, 1966, Eleven Untitled Poems, 1968, Weather: Poems, 1969, Temporary Facts, 1970, Allegiances, 1970, Poems for Tennessee, 1971, In the Clock of Reason, 1973, Someday, Maybe, 1973, Going Places: Poems, 1974, North By West, 1975, Braided Apart, 1976, I Would Also Like to Menion Aluminum: Poems and a Conversation, 1976, Late, Passing Prairie Farm: A Poem, 1976, Stories That Could Be True, New and Collected Poems, 1977, The Design on the Oriole, 1977, All About Light, 1978, A Meeting with Disma Tumminello and William Stafford, 1978, Possinga Creche, 1978, Tuft by Puff. 1978, Two About Music, 1978, Around You, Your Horse and A Catechism, 1979, Absolution, 1980, Things That Happen Where There Aren't Any People, 1980, Unmuzzled Ox, 1980, Sometimes Like a Legend, 1981, A Glass Face in the Rain, 1982, Roving Across Fields: A Conversation and Uncollected Poems 1942-82, 1983, Smoke's Way: Poems From Limited Editions, 1968-81, 1983, Segues: A Correspondence in Poetry, 1984, Listening Deep, 1984, Wyoming, 1985, You Must Revise Your Life, 1986, An Oregon Message, 1987, A Scripture of Leaves, 1989, How to Hold Your Arms When It Rains, 1990, Passwords, 1991, History Is Loose Again, 1991, The Long Sigh the Wind Makes, 1991, My Name is William Tell, 1992, Holding Onto the Grass, 1992; non-fiction Down in My Heart, 1947, Friends to this Ground: A Statement for Readers, Teachers, and Writers of Literature, 1967, Leftovers, A Care Package: Two Lectures, 1973, Writing the Australian Crawl: Views on the Writer's Vocation, 1978, You Must Revise Your Life, 1986, The Mozart Myths: A Critical Reassessment, 1991; regular contbr. to periodicals. Edn1. sec. civilian pub. service sect. Ch. of Brethren, 1943-44; mem. Oreg. bd. Fellowship of Reconciliation, 1959—. Yaddo Found. fellow, 1956, Guggenheim grantee for creative writing, 1966-67, NEA grantee, 1966, Danforth Found. grantee; recipient short story and poetry prize Oreg. Centennial 1959, Union Civic League award Poetry Mag., 1959, Shelley Meml. award, 1964, Melville Cane award, 1974, Am. Acad. Inst. Arts and Letters Lit. award, 1981. Mem. AAUP, Modern Lang. Assn., Nat. Council Tchrs. English, War Registers League, Modern Poetry Assn. Home: 1050 Sunningdale Rd Lake Oswego OR 97034-1735

STAGER, DONALD K., construction company executive. Chief exec. officer Dillingham Construction, Calif. Office: Dillingham Constrn Corp 5960 Inglewood Dr Pleasanton CA 94588-8515

STAHL, JACK LELAND, real estate company executive; b. Lincoln, Ill., June 28, 1934; s. Edwin R. and Edna M. (Burns) S.; m. Carol Anne Townsend, June 23, 1956; children: Cheryl, Nancy, Kellea. BS in Edn., U. N.Mex., 1957. Tchr. Albuquerque Public Schs., 1956-59; pres. House Finders, Inc., Albuquerque, 1959-65; v.p. N.Mex. Savs. & Loan Assn., Albuquerque, 1965-67; chmn. bd. Hooten-Stahl, Inc., Albuquerque, 1967-77; mem. N.Mex. Ho. of Reps., 1969-70; pres. The Jack Stahl Co., Albuquerque, 1977—; mem. N.Mex. Senate, 1981-86; lt. gov. State of N.Mex., 1987-90. Mem. N.Mex. Ho. of Reps., 1969-70; mem. exec. bd. Gt. SW coun. Boy Scouts Am., 1982-89; bd. dirs. Better Bus. Bur. N.Mex., 1968-82, pres., 1975-76; trustee Univ. Heights Hosp., 1980-85; vice chmn. N.Mex. Bd. Fin., 1987-90, N.Mex. Community Devel. Coun., 1987-90. Named Realtor of Yr., Albuquerque Bd. Realtors, 1972. Mem. Nat. Assn. Realtors, Nat. Homebuilders Assn., N.Mex. Amigos, 20-30 Club (pres. 1963-64), Rotary. Republican. Methodist. Office: 1911 Wyoming Blvd NE Albuquerque NM 87112-2865

STAHL, MARGO SCHNEEBALG, ecologist, environmental scientist; b. Coral Gables, Fla., June 24, 1947; d. Martin and Rose (Osman) Schneebalg; m. Glenn Stahl, Aug. 17, 1969 (div. June 1988); 1 child, Shaina Flori Georgina. BS in Biology, U. Miami, 1969, MS in Marine Biology, 1973. Fish and wildlife aide Calif. Dept. Fish and Game, Long Beach, 1973; assoc. rsch. engr. So. Calif. Edison Co., Rosemead, 1973-75; rsch. assoc. in urban and regional planning U. Hawaii, Honolulu, 1975-76, Hawaii Inst. Marine Biology, Kaneohe, 1975-77, Anuenue Fisheries Rsch. Ctr., Honolulu, 1977-79; aquatic biology Hawaii Dept. Land and Natural Resources, Honolulu, 1979-83; instr. sci. U. Hawaii Windward C.C., Kaneohe, 1985-88; ecologist U.S. Army C.E., Honolulu, 1988—; pres. Mermaid Aquatic Cons., Honolulu, 1979-81, 84-88; mem. Hawaii Water Quality Tng. Interagy. Com., Honolulu, 1991-93. Contbg. author: Taste of Aloha, 1983 (Jr. League award 1985); contbr. articles to profl. jours. Project mgr. Kokokahi Aquaculture Model, Kaneohe, 1978-80; mem. adv. bd. Windward C.C., 1982-83; hon. coord. RESULTS Hunger Lobby, Honolulu, 1989. Recipient Stoye award in icythyology Am. Soc. Ichtyologists and Herpetologists, 1972, Career Woman award Sierra Mar dist. Calif. Bus. and Profl. Womens Club, 1975, Comdr's award for exceptional performance U.S. Army C.E., Ft. Shafter, Hawaii, 1990. Mem. Nat. Assn. Environ. Profls. (cert. environ. profl., chmn. cert. com. 1992-93, C.E.P. award 1991), Assn. for Women in Sci. (bd. dirs. 1985), Hawaii Assn. Environ. Profls. (bd. dirs. 1991-93), World Mariculture Soc. (bd. dirs. 1981), Am. Fisheries Soc., Western Soc. Naturalists. Home: 46-436 Holopeki St Kaneohe HI 96744 Office: US Army Corps Engrs Fort Shafter Honolulu HI 96858

STAHL, RICHARD G. C., journalist, editor; b. Chgo., Feb. 22, 1934; m. Gladys C. Weisbecker; 1 child, Laura Ann. Student, Northwestern U., U. Ill., Chgo. Editor Railway Purchases and Stores Mag., Chgo., 1960-63; editor pub. rels. dept. Sears Roebuck & Co., Chgo., 1963-68; dir. pub. rels. dept. St. Joseph's Hosp. Med. Ctr., Phoenix, 1968-72; v.p. pub. rels. Consultation Svcs., Inc., Phoenix, 1972-73; creative dir. Don Jackson and Assoc., Phoenix, 1973; editor, pub. rels. mgr. Maricopa County Med. Soc., Phoenix, 1974-76; mng. editor Ariz. Hwys. mag., Phoenix, 1977—. Regional editor: (travel guides) Budget Travel, 1985, USA, 1986, Arizona, 1986; free-lance writer and editor. Mem. Soc. Profl. Journalists. Office: Ariz Hwys Mag 2039 W Lewis Ave Phoenix AZ 85009-2893

STAHLGREN, LEROY HENRY, educator, surgeon, researcher; b. Erie, Pa., June 21, 1924; s. Henry William and Cecilia (Lander) S.; m. Anita Elliot, Aug. 20,1978; children: Leroy Jr., Julia, Clark, William. MD, U. Pa., 1948. Diplomate Am. Bd. Surgery. Surg. residency in Grad. Hosp. U. Pa., Phila., 1948-50, 53-54; surg. svc. USNR, Guam, Marianas, 1950-53; chief surgery Phila. Gen. Hosp., 1959-66, Episcopal Hosp., Phila., 1966-79; prof. surgery Temple U., 1966-79; chief surgery St. Barnabas Med. Ctr., Livingston, N.J., 1979-83, St. Joseph Hosp., Denver, 1983-93; prof. surgery U. Colo., 1983—. Editor: Cost Effective Surgery Management, 1989, Biliary Lithotripsy, 1989, Primary Care Jour., 1976; contbr. articles profl. jours. com. Chmn. Ch. Edn. Program, Denver, 1990, dir. rsch. dept., 1991—; surg. svc. USNR, 1950-53. Lt. (j.g.) USNR, 1950-53. Fellow CIDC, Denver Acad. Surgery (pres. 1990-92), Am. Coll. Surgeons (pres. 1989-90), Am. Gastroenterology Soc., Internat. Soc. Surgery, Soc. Surgery Alimentary Tract. Office: Research Dept 2005 Franklin St Denver CO 80218-1191

STAHLKE, RICHARD DAVID, human services administrator; b. Waconia, Minn., Dec. 16, 1939; s. Ernst Henry and Clara Ida (Schneider) S.; m. Shirley Mae Anderson, Aug. 22, 1962; children: James Andrew, Karen Andrea. AA, Concordia Jr. Coll., St. Paul, 1959; student, Concordia Sr. Coll., Ft. Wayne, Ind., 1959-60; BA, Augsburg Coll., 1962; MSW, Fla. State U., 1965. Case worker Todd County Welfare Dept., Long Prairie, Minn., 1962-63; social worker Luth. Social Svc. Kans., Wichita, 1965-70; exec. dir. Luth. Social Ministry Ariz., Phoenix, 1970-78; pres. Luth. Social Svcs. No. Calif., San Francisco, 1978—; peer reviewer Coun. on Accreditation, N.Y.C., 1980—; social svc. cons. Evang. Luth. Ch. Am., Chgo., 1986—. Contbr. articles to profl. jours. Mem. Gov.'s Earthquake Preparedness Task Force, Calif., 1982-88; chair disaster preparedness No. Calif. Ecumenical Coun., Calif., 1982-84. Mem. NASW (Calif. Social Worker of Yr. 1992, pres. Calif. chpt. 1984-86), Coalition of Exec. Luth. Agys. (dir. com. 1980—). Lutheran. Office: Luth Social Svcs No Calif 1101 O'Farrell St San Francisco CA 94109

STALDER, MARGARET ANN, dance educator; b. Laramie, Wyo., Sept. 1, 1959; d. Howard Lee and Ruth (Saathoff) Wilson; m. Dale Alan Stalder, June 21, 1979; 1 child, Jessica Rae. BA in Theatre and Dance, U. Wyo., 1981, MS in Phys. Edn., 1987. Part-time instr. dept. health and phys. edn. U. Wyo., Laramie, 1982-84, part-time lectr. dept. theatre and dance, 1985—; coord. Wyo. Summer Arts Inst., 1991—; mem. task force, coord. Wyo. Arts Coun., 1990-91. Choreographer and dance performer modern dance and ballet, 1980-92; contbr. articles to profl. jours. Sec. joint powers bd. Laramie Plains Civic Ctr., 1990—; bd. dirs. Creative Arts Inst., Laramie, 1989—. Performing Arts fellow Wyo. Arts Coun., 1991. Mem. Nat. Dance Assn., Wyo. Alliance for Health, Phys. Edn., Recreation and Dance (v.p. elect for dance 1991-93), Wyo. Arts Alliance for Edn. (v.p. 1991-93), Internat. Assn. for Dance Medicine and Sci. Office: U Wyo PO Box 3951 Laramie WY 82071

STALDER, ROBERT DEAN, safety specialist; b. Casper, Wyo., Jan. 11, 1955; s. Carl C. and Imogene Louise (Keeler) S.; m. Debra Ann Foster, May 25, 1974; children: Misty Marie, Shawn Carl, Kiara Lynette. BA in Edn., U. Wyo., 1977; MBA, U. Phoenix, 1991. Tchr./coach St. Anthony's Sch., Casper, Wyo., 1977-78, Rawlins (Wyo.) High Sch., 1978-80, Moffat County High Sch., Craig, Colo., 1980-81; underground miner Cyprus Empire Corp., Craig, 1981-85; safety rep. Cyprus Empire Corp., 1985-87, safety dir., 1987—. Pres. NCSW Dist. Coun. Holmes Safety, Rawlins, 1986—; leader Boy Scouts Am., 1988—, Girl Scouts U.S.A., 1985-91; chmn. Colo. Bd. Mine Examiners, 1985-91; chmn. Colo. Bd. Examiners, 1985-91, Wyo. Bd. of Mine Examiners, 1993—; boys basketball coach Hanna High Sch., 1992—. Mem. Am. Soc. Safety Engrs., Holmes Safety Assn. (dist. pres. 1985—), Colo. Mining Assn. (health/safety com. 1986-90). Republican. Baptist. Home: PO Box 153 Elk Mountain WY 82324-0153 Office: Cyprus Shoshone Coal PO Box 830 Hanna WY 82327

STALEY, CLINTON ANDREW, educator; b. Arlington, Va., Dec. 31, 1958; s. Samuel Sorber Staley and Dorinda Merle Reed-Doerr. BA, Principia Coll., 1980; MS, U. Calif., Santa Barbara, 1982, PhD, 1986. Asst. prof. Principia Coll., Elsah, Ill., 1986-87; assoc. prof. Calif. Poly. State U., San Luis Obispo, Calif., 1988—; mgr. software devel., AROFA, Calif. Poly. State U., 1990—; designer database Pacific Gas and Electric, Atascardero, 1989—. Contbr. articles to profl. confs. Mem. IEEE, Assn. for Computing Machinery, Upsilon Pi Epsilon. Republican. Office: Calif Poly State U San Luis Obispo CA 93407

STALEY, JAMES TROTTER, microbiology educator; b. Brookings, S.D., Mar. 14, 1938; s. Newton Clarence and Isabelle (Trotter) S.; m. Sonja Jeanne Erickson, Dec. 28, 1963; children: Greg, Wendy. BA, U. Minn., 1960; MS, Ohio State U., 1963; PhD, U. Calif., Davis, 1967. From instr. to asst. prof. Mich. State U., East Lansing, 1967-69; asst. prof. U. N.C., Chapel Hill, 1969-71; asst. prof. U. Wash., Seattle, 1971-74, assoc. prof., 1974-82, prof. microbiology, 1982—; cons. Weyerhauser, Federal Way, Wash., Biotechniques Labs., Redmond, Wash., 1983-84, Biocontrol Systems, Kent, Wash., 1985—. Mem. editorial bd. Microbial Ecology, 1977, Applied Environ. Microbiology, 1975; editor: Bergey's Manual, 1981; contbr. articles to jours. Mem. AAAS, Am. Soc. Microbiology (vice chmn., chmn. gen. microbiology sect. 1975-76, div. lectr. 1983), Internat. Assn. Microbiology Soc. (judicial commn. 1983—), Internat. Symposium on Environ. Biogeochemistry. Office: U Wash Dept Microbiology SC 42 Seattle WA 98195

STALEY, PATRICK AUREL, mathematics educator; b. Bethesda, Md., Feb. 20, 1948; s. Joseph Francis and Josephine (Hernandez) S.; m. Seanne Detmer, June, 1980 (div.); children: Michael Aaron, Patrick Andrew. BA in Maths., U. Calif., San Diego, 1969; MS in Maths., San Diego State U., 1971. Rsch. scientist Teledyne Aeronautics, San Diego, 1971-74; sr. engr. Teledyne Systems Co., Northridge, Calif., 1974-77; mgr. software group Data Ware Devel., Sorrento Valley, Calif., 1978-81; pres. Staley Enterprises Inc., San Diego, 1981-84; tchr. Southwestern Coll., Chula Vista, Calif., 1984—. Author video tapes. Bd. dirs. Girls & Boys Club of Chula Vista, 1984-89. Mem. Maths. Assn. Am., Faculty Assn. of Calif. Communtiy Colls., Calif. Maths. Coun. Community Colls. South. Home: PO Box 704 Bonita CA 91908-0704 Office: Southwestern Coll 900 Otay Lakes Rd Chula Vista CA 91910-7223

STALL, WILLIAM READ, writer; b. Phila., Feb. 21, 1937; s. Sidney Joseph and Helen (Read) S.; m. Carolee Ramsey, July, 1961 (div. 1979);

children: Melissa Stall Demeter, Tracy Stall Ko, Erica; m. Anne Elizabeth Baker, Dec. 8, 1979. BS, U. Wyo., 1959. Reporter Laramie (Wyo.) Boomerang, 1956-59, Associated Press, Cheyenne, Wyo., 1960-63; corres. Associated Press, Reno, 1963-66; bur. chief, polit. writer Associated Press, Sacramento, 1966-74; press sec. Edmund G. Brown Jr., Sacramento, 1974-76; staff writer, asst. met. editor, corres. L.A. Times, 1976-81, editorial writer, 1984-90, polit. writer, 1990—; bur. chief Hartford Courant, Washington, 1981-84; sr. lectr. journalism dept. U. So. Calif., 1985—. With USNG, 1960-67. Mem. Am. Alpine Club (dir. 1992—). Episcopalian. Office: L A Times Times Mirror Sq Los Angeles CA 90053

STALLARD, GEORGE THOMAS (DUKE STALLARD), retired retail store owner; b. Lakin, Kans., Oct. 1, 1937; s. George Aubry and Gladys Agnes (Prather) S.; m. Carolyn Diane Flower, Mar. 18, 1967. Student, Colo. State U., 1955-56; cert. of agriculture, Lamar (Colo.) Community Coll., 1958-60; student, Adams State Coll., Alamosa, Colo., 1963, 67. Parts mgr. Irrigation and Power Co., Greeley, Colo., 1965-67; owner, mgr. Shelpers, Inc., Roswell, N.M., 1967-87; bd. dirs. Tabosa Devel. and Tng. Ctr., Roswell; cons. numerous establishments in N.M. including N.M. Rehab. Ctr. and Ea. N.M. Med. Ctr. Vice chmn. Gov.'s Com. Concerns of Handicapped, Sante Fe, 1981-87; past pres. Roswell Area Com. Concerns of Handicapped, 1978-79; rep. Nat. Conf. for Coalition of Handicapped, Houston, 1978; life mem. Disabled Am. Vets., Roswell, Paralized Vets. Am.; mem. Agrl. Council Chaves County, Roswell. Served with U.S. Army, 1961-66. Recipient Outstanding Handicapped New Mexican N.M. Gov.'s Com. Concerns of Handicapped, 1983; agrl. scholarship Lamar Coll., 1958. Republican. Methodist. Clubs: Roswell Sertoma, Paralized Vets. Am., Disabled Am. Vets. Lodges: Elks, York Rite, Scottish Rite, Masons, Shriners. Home: 227 Peaceful Valley Rd Roswell NM 88201-9801

STALLEY, ROBERT DELMER, retired mathematics educator; b. Mpls., Oct. 25, 1924; s. Francis Charles and Florence Camille (Goode) S.; m. Dorothy Ann Jeffery, Aug. 27, 1950; children: Mark, Jeffery, John, Lorena. BS, Oreg. State U., 1946, MA, 1948; PhD, U. Oreg., 1953. Instr. U. Ariz., Tucson, 1949-51, Fresno (Calif.) State U., 1955-56; instr. Iowa State U., Ames, 1953-54, asst. prof., 1954-55; mathematician Sperry Rand, St. Paul, 1955; mathematician U.S. Naval Ordnance Test Sta., China Lake, Calif., 1956, cons., 1956-60; asst. prof., assoc. prof. math. Oreg. State U., Corvallis, 1956-66, prof., 1966-89, prof. emeritus, 1989—; jour. referee, reviewer; speaker, cons. in field, mem. various sci. panels; dir. Summer Insts. in Math., NSF, 1965-67. Contbr. articles to math. jours. Rsch. grantee NSF, 1967-71. Mem. Am. Math. Soc., Sierra Club, Sigma Xi, Pi Kappa Phi. Home: 1405 NW Forest Dr Corvallis OR 97330-1705 Office: Oreg State U Dept Math Corvallis OR 97331

STALLINGS, GENE CLIFTON, professional, university athletic coach; b. Paris, Tex., Mar. 2, 1935; s. Eugene C. and Neil (Moye) S.; m. Ruth Ann Jack, Dec. 1, 1956; children: Anna Lee, Laura Nell, John Mark, Jacklyn Ruth, Martha Kate. B.S., Tex. A&M U., 1958. Asst. football coach U. Ala., 1958-64; head football coach, dir. athletics Tex. A&M U., 1964-72; asst. coach Dallas Cowboys, 1972-85; head football coach St. Louis Cardinals (now known as Phoenix Cardinals), 1986-89, U. Ala. Crimson Tide, 1990—; dir. Bank of A&M, College Station, Tex., Rolling Internat., Inc., Dallas; Spalding sports cons. Mem. Sam Houston council Boy Scouts Am.; trustee Abilene (Tex.) Christian U. Named 1983 Dallas Father of the Yr.; elected to Tex. A&M U. Hall of Fame, 1982. Mem. Nat. Assn. Collegiate Dirs. Athletics, Am. Football Coaches Assn., Fellowship Christian Athletes. Mem. Ch. of Christ. Office: Univ Ala Box 870323 Tuscaloosa AL 35487-0323

STALLKNECHT-ROBERTS, CLOIS FREDA, publisher, publicist; b. Birmingham, Ala., Dec. 31, 1934; d. August and Sadie Bell (Wisener) Anton; m. Randall Scott Roberts; children: Yvonne Denise, April O'dell, Kurt William. Publicist Ms. Clois Presents, L.A., 1968—; advt. Engineered Magic, Advt., Santa Ana, Calif., 1976, 77, 81; pub. Internat. Printing, L.A., 1981—. Editor: Nostradamus, William Bartram, Apuleious, 1990-92. Home: PO Box 165 Inyokern CA 93527 Office: Engineered Magic 510 De La Estrella San Clemente CA 92672

STALLONE, THOMAS MICHAEL, mental health services professional; b. N.Y.C., Dec. 5, 1952; s. Vito Joseph and Mary Ellen (Kearney) S.; m. Bonnie Elizabeth Wenk, May 30, 1982. B of Profl. Studies, N.Y. Inst. Tech., 1987; MA, Spalding U., 1991. Cert. psychol. assoc. in clin. psychology, rational emotive therapy. Internat. banker Sumitomo Bank, Ltd., N.Y.C., 1980-82; pvt. practice hypnosis cons. LaGrange, Ky. and N.Y.C., 1982—; internat. banker Bank of N.Y., N.Y.C., 1982-87; rehab. specialist Goodwill Industries Ky., Louisville, 1989; psychol. assoc. div. mental health Ky. Corrections Cabinet, La Grange, 1989-91; teaching and rsch. asst. Pacific U., Forest Grove, Oreg., 1991—; psychotherapist Portland, Oreg., 1991—. Author: The Boke of Taliesyne, 1979, The Effects of Psychodrama on Inmates Within a Structured Residential Behavior Modification Program, 1993. Cons. Hist. Arms, Ltd., N.Y.C., 1983-87, N.Y. Medieval Festival, 1984-86; dir., cons. Whitestone (N.Y.) Creative Arts Workshop, 1977, Ky. Shakespeare Festival, Louisville, 1987-88; treas., advisor 4H Exec. Coun., La Grange, 1988-91. Decorated Grant of Arms Chief Herald of Ireland, Ky. Col. Mem. Am. Psychol. Assn., Am. Soc. Group Psychotherapy and Psychodrama, Internat. Soc. for Profl. Hypnosis, Ky. Psychol. Assn., Western Psychol. Assn., Ancient Order Hibernians, Mensa, Hon. Order Ky. Cols. Internat. Platform Assn.

STALLWORTH, DAISY MARIE, county official; b. Ardmore, Okla., Oct. 18, 1939; d. Alfred and Mazola (Holman) McKerson; m. Luke A. Stevenson Sr., 1957 (div.); children: Luke A. Jr., Stephanie, Sonja; m. Leroy Stallworth, June 24, 1967. BBA in Bus., Pacific Luth. U., 1976; cert. economic development inst., U. Okla., 1988; cert. economic developer, Am. Econ. Devel. Coun., 1990. Planning aide City of Tacoma, 1972-74, program devel. specialist, 1974-78, sr. program devel. specialist, 1978-83; mgr. County of Pierce, Tacoma, 1983-86, dir., 1986—; thesis cons. Econ. Devel. Inst., U. Okla., Norman, 1991—; dir. World Trade Ctr. Bd., Tacoma. Member adv. com. U. Wash., Tacoma, 1991—; mem. bd. visitors U. Puget Sound Sch. of Bus., Tacoma, 1990—; chair community adv. com. St. Joseph Hosp. Capital Campaign, Tacoma, 1991. Named News Maker of Tomorrow, Morning News Tribune & Time Mag., 1983; recipient Centennial Alumni award Pacific Luth. U., 1991. Mem. Am. Econ. Devel. Coun., Am. Leadership Forum, Nat. Coun. Urban Econ. Devel., Alpha Kappa Alpha, Zeta Omega Omega (chpt. pres. 1990-94). Methodist. Office: County of Pierce Dept Community Econ Devel 4916 S Center St Tacoma WA 98409-3121

STALNAKER, JOHN HULBERT, physician; b. Portland, Oreg., Aug. 29, 1918; s. William Park II and Helen Caryl (Hulbert) S.; m. Louise Isabel Lucas, Sept. 8, 1946; children: Carol Ann, Janet Lee, Mary Louise, John Park, Laurie Jean, James Mark. Student, Reed Coll., Portland, 1936-38; AB, Willamette U., Salem, Oreg., 1941; MD, Oreg. Health Scis. U., 1945. Diplomate Am. Bd. Internal Medicine. Intern Emanuel Hosp., Portland, 1945-46; resident in internal medicine St. Vincent Hosp., Portland, 1948-51; clin. instr. U. Oreg. Med. Sch., 1951-54, 60-62; staff physician VA Hosp., Vancouver, Wash., 1970-79; cons. in internal medicine, 1951-79. Contbr. articles to profl. jours. Pianist various civic and club meetings, Portland; leader Johnny Stalnaker's Dance Orch., 1936-39. Lt. (j.g.) USNR, 1946-48. Fellow ACP; mem. AMA, Multnomah County Med. Soc., Oreg. State Med. Assn., N.Am. Lily Soc., Am. Rose Soc. Republican. Home: 2204 SW Sunset Dr Portland OR 97201-2068

STAMBAUGH, HARRIETT MCCARDELL (HARRIETT WYNN MCCARDELL), social worker; b. Philipsburg, Pa., May 10, 1922; d. Horace Andrew and Vivian Annabel (Wynn) McCardell; m. James Arthur Stambaugh Sr., May 1, 1954; children: James Arthur Jr., David Monroe, Richard Thomas. BA, Juniata Coll., 1942; MS in Social Svc., Boston U., 1947. Instr. in pediatrics Southwestern Med. Sch. U. Tex. Health Sci. Ctr., Dallas, 1966-67, asst. prof. pediatrics, 1968-80; dir. dept. clinical social work Children's Med. Ctr. of Dallas, 1967-80; dir. clin. social work dept. U. N.Mex. Hosp., Albuquerque, 1981-84; contract therapist Family Counseling Svcs., Inc., Albuquerque, 1984-85; supr. Chaparral Maternity and Adoption Svcs., Albuquerque, 1985-87; interim exec. dir. Family & Children Svcs., Inc., Albuquerque, 1987-88; part-time clin. social worker Chaparral Maternity Adoptions div. Chaparral Maternity and Adoption Svcs., Albuquerque, 1988-92; exec. dir. Family and Children's Svc's., Inc., 1992; cons. Terrell (Tex.) State Hosp., 1966-67, Tex. Child Welfare Dept., Dallas, 1966-67, Dallas Assn. for Retarded Citizens, 1966-67, Community Mental Health Program, Corsicana, Tex., 1968, Britain Nursing Home, Irving, Tex., 1968-70, Turtle Creek Nursing Home, Dallas, 1969, North Tex. Hemophilia Found., Dallas, 1969, Four Seasons Nursing Home, Dallas, 1970-71, YWCA Park North Br., Dallas, 1972, Children's Hosp. of Phila., 1972, Dialysis Ctr., Inc., Albuquerque, 1982-84, Carrie Tingley Hosp., Albuquerque, 1982-84; adj. prof. Dept. of Sociology adn Social Work Tex. Women's U., Denton, 1977-80. Contbr. articles to profl. jours. Mem. Child Care Coun. of Dallas County, 1971-74; mem. Human Devel. Fund Rev. Com. City of Dallas, 1975-77, mem. Children and Youth Adv. Com., 1975-80; mem. Profl. Adv. Com. Parents Without Ptnrs., 1967-74, Creative Learning Ctr., 1968-74, Mental Health Assn. Greater Dallas 1966-72, 1976-79, bd. dirs. 1972-80, Dallas County Community Action Com., 1967-68, Routh St. Ctr., 1972-80; profl. adv. com. Epilepsy Assn., 1971-80, Vis. Nurse Assn., 1977-80; mem. med. adv. com. March of Dimes, and others. Mem. NASW (Chmn. subcom. to est. responsibilities for summer employment 1964-65, chmn. profl. standards div. 1967-68, chmn. battered child com. 1968-73, v.p. Dallas chpt. 1974-75), Am. Assn. Marriage and Family Therapists (bd. dirs. N.Mex. chpt. 1969-92), Nat. Registry Clin. Soc. Workers, Acad. Cert. Social Workers. Methodist. Home: 5023 Calle De Luna NE Albuquerque NM 87111-2918

STAMES, WILLIAM ALEXANDER, realtor, cost management executive; b. Douglas, Ariz., Mar. 26, 1917; s. Alex Basil and Teresa (Ruis) S.; AA, Long Beach Coll., 1941; postgrad. U. Calif., Berkeley, 1962-64; cert. mgmt. practices Naval Officers CIC Sch., Glenview, Ill., 1955; grad. Real Estate Inst., Calif.; m. Marguerite Winifred Nelson, June 11, 1943; 1 child, Wynn Lorain. Owner, Stames Beverage Co., Brawley, Calif., 1945-50; liaison engr. Lockheed Missiles & Space Co., Sunnyvale, Calif., 1958-60, liaison engr. sr., 1960, adminstr., 1960-62, staff adminstr., 1962-63, liaison engr., sr., design engr. sr., 1965-76; owner, mgr. Cost Reduction Equipment Sales & Tech., Sunnyvale, 1967-76; realtor Cornish & Carey, 1988—. Comdr. USNR, 1941-69, ret., World War II, Korea, Vietnam. Decorated D.F.C., Air medal with two gold stars, Presdl. citation. Mem. Am. Mgmt. Assn., Mountain View Real Estate Bd. (pres.), Calif. Assn. Realtors (bd. dirs.), Tailhook Assn. Clubs: Commonwealth San Francisco, Ret. Officers (past pres. Peninsula chpt.), Lions. Author: Polaris Electrical Subsystems Design History, 1964; Poseidon Subsystem Invention, 1971. Home: 1060 Coronado Ave Coronado CA 92118-2439 also: Cornish and Carey Real Estate 2754 Middlefield Rd Palo Alto CA 94306

STAMM, RICHARD WILLIAM, podiatrist; b. Meadville, Pa., July 9, 1944; s. William Henry and Norma Marie (Bertocci) S.; divorced; chilren: Aileen Johnine, William Tarkington. AA, Hershey Jr. Coll., 1965; BA, Washington and Jefferson Coll., 1967; D Podiatric Medicine, Ohio Coll. Podiatric Medicine, 1978. Diplomate Am. Bd. Podiatric Surgeons. Resident in podiatric surgery Cleve. Foot Clinic, 1978-79; practice medicine specializing in podiatry Albuquerque, 1979—, Clovis, 1993—;, 1979-93; chief podiatric surgery St. Joseph's N.E. Heights Hosp., Albuquerque, 1990-92. Contbr. articles to profl. jours. Bd. dirs. Albuquerque Wild Turkey Fedn., 1984-88, SVC, 1984-88, Bernalillo chpt. Vis. Nurses Found., 1983-88, pres. bd. dirs., 1985-86, Hospice and Home Care Found., 1989-91; mem. citizens adv. coun. Albuquerque Pub. Schs., 1985-86. Served with U.S. Army, 1967-71, Vietnam. Fellow Am. Coll. Foot and Enkle Surgeons, Am. Coll. Foot Orthopedists; mem. Am. Podiatric Podopediatrics (sec. 1988—), Am. Podiatric Med. Assn. (ho. of del. 1982-90), N.Mex. Podiatric Med. Assn. (pres. 1984-88, appreciation awards 1981, 85, 86), Am. Diabetes Assn. (bd. dirs. Albuquerque chpt. 1986-88), Rotary. Republican. Greek Orthodox. Lodge: Rotary. Home: 208 Lakeview Terr Clovis NM 88101 Office: 120 W 21st St Clovis NM 88101

STAMM, ROBERT FRANZ, research physicist; b. Mt. Vernon, Ohio, Mar. 28, 1915; s. John Frederick William and Alice Maude (Swartout) S.; m. Elizabeth Ona Ladd, June 1, 1947 (div. Oct. 1958); m. Isabel Golinski, Jan. 28, 1964. AB with 1st honors, Kenyon Coll., 1937; PhD, Iowa State U., 1942. Rsch. physicist Am. Cyanamid Co. Cen. Rsch. Lab., Stamford, Conn., 1942-72, Clairol Rsch. Lab., Stamford, 1973-82. Contbr. 35 tech. articles to profl. jours. Prin. flutist Norwalk (Conn.) Community Symphony Orch., 1948-79, Greenwich (Conn.) Philharm. Orch., 1954-65, Stamford Symphony Orch. Recipient cert. for work essential to prodn. of atomic bomb U.S. Army, War Dept., Armed Forces, Corps of Engrs., Manhattan Dist., 1945. Mem. Phi Beta Kappa, Sigma Xi. Republican. Episcopalian. Home: 158 Rufous Ln Sedona AZ 86336-7116

STAMNES, KNUT HENRIK, physics educator; b. Rost, Norway, June 30, 1943; s. Alfred Johannes and Petra (Antonsen) S.; m. Anja Elisabeth Moen, Feb. 17, 1984; children: Snorre, Kaja. BS in Physics, U. Oslo, 1969, MS in Physics, 1972; PHD in Astro-Geophysics, U. Colo., 1978. Rsch. assoc. geophysical inst. U. Alaska, Fairbanks, 1978-83; assoc. prof. U. Tromso (Norway), 1983-88; prof. U. Alaska, Fairbanks, 1988—; adj. assoc. prof. U. Alaska, Fairbanks, 1983-88. Contbr. more than 50 articles to profl. jours. Rsch. grantee NSF, NASA, U.S. Dept. Energy, Norwegian Funding Agys. Mem. Am. Geophys. Union, Am. Meteorol. Soc., Norwegian Phys. Soc., European Geophys. Soc., Oceanograph Soc. Office: U Alaska Geophysical Inst Fairbanks AK 99775

STAMOS, JAMES WILLIAM, computer science researcher; b. Salem, Mass., Aug. 17, 1959; s. William James and Jenny James (Pappas) S.; m. Mary Ellen Muldoon, Oct. 27, 1990. BS and MS, MIT, 1982, PhD, 1986. Rsch. staff mem. IBM Almaden Rsch. Ctr., San Jose, Calif., 1986—. Contbr. articles to profl. jours. Recipient grad. fellowship IBM, 1983-85. Mem. Assn. Computing Machinery, Sigma Xi, Tau Beta Pi, Eta Kappa Nu. Home: 1515 Constanso Ct San Jose CA 95129-4905 Office: IBM Almaden Rsch Ctr 650 Harry Rd San Jose CA 95120-6099

STAMPER, MALCOLM THEODORE, aerospace company executive; b. Detroit, Apr. 4, 1925; s. Fred Theodore and Lucille (Cayce) S.; m. Marion Philbin Guinan, Feb. 25, 1946; children: Geoffrey, Kevin, Jamie, David, Mary, Anne. Student, U. Richmond, Va., 1943-44; BEE, Ga. Inst. Tech., 1946; postgrad., U. Mich., 1946-49. With Gen. Motors Corp., 1949-62; with Boeing Co., Seattle, 1962-90; mgr. electronics ops., v.p., gen. mgr. turbine div. Boeing Co., 1964-66; v.p., gen. mgr. Boeing Co. (747 Airplane program), 1966-69, v.p., gen. mgr. comml. airplane group, 1969-71, corp. sr. v.p. ops., 1971-72; pres. Boeing Co., 1972-85, vice chmn., 1985-90; chief exec. officer Storytellers Ink Pub., Seattle, 1990—, also chmn. bd. dirs.; bd. dirs. Travelers Ins. Cos., Nordstrom Co., Esterline Co., Chrysler Co., Whittaker Corp.; trustee The Conf. Bd., 1988—. Candidate for U.S. Ho. of Reps., Detroit, 1952; trustee, chmn. Seattle Art Mus.; nat. bd. dirs. Smithsonian Assocs. With USNR, 1943-46. Named Industrialist of Year, 1967; recipient Educator's Golden Key award, 1970, Elmer A. Sperry award, 1982, AIEE award, Ga. Inst. Tech. award, Sec. Dept. Health and Human Services award, Silver Beaver award Boy Scouts Am., 1989. Mem. Nat. Alliance Businessmen, Phi Gamma Delta.

STAMPS, PETER DAVID, production supervisor; b. Dearborn, Mich., June 4, 1963; s. David William and Alice Janette (Travis) S.; m. Pamela Krishelle Orkis, Sept. 26, 1986 (div. 1990); m. Sherry Lee Shelton, Mar. 25, 1992. BSME, USN Acad., 1985. Registered engr.-in-tng. Comd. ensign USN, 1985, advanced through grades to lt., 1992; comms. officer USN, Norfolk, Va., 1988-90; current ops. and tng. officer USN, San Diego, 1990-92; with USNR, 1992—; prodn. supr., quality steering com., quality edn. trainer Cargill Incorp., Lynwood, Calif., 1992—. Vol. County Registrar of Voters, San Diego, 1992, store front ops. dir. H. Ross Perot Petition Com., San Diego, 1992. Mem. Am. Soc. for Quality Control, ASME (assoc., pres. student chpt. 1984-85), USN Inst. (command liaison 1990—), Am. Assn. Individual Investors, Surface Navy Assn., Naval Res. Assn., USN Acad. Alumni Assn., Sigma Xi (assoc.). Office: Cargill Incorp Resin Products Div Lynwood CA 90262

STANDLEE, KEVIN ALLEN, systems analyst, technical writer; b. Oroville, Calif., Aug. 27, 1965; s. William Thomas and Della Louise (Reynolds) S. BS in Computer Sci., Calif. State U., Chico, 1988. Asst. mgr. Affiliated Discount Comics, Marysville, Calif., 1984-88; agt., mgr. Edward A. Luena, profl. artist, Marysville, 1985-87; systems analyst, tech. writer Blue Shield Calif., Chico, 1988-90, Folsom, 1990-93; mem. exec. com. ConFrancisco, 1993 World Sci. Fiction Conv., sec., 1989—, div. chief, 1991—; mem., exec. com. Conadian, 1994 World Sci. Fiction Conv., Winnipeg, Manitoba, divsn. chief, 1992—; bd. dirs., sec. San Francisco Sci. Fiction Convs., Inc., Pleasant Hill and Walnut Creek, 1991—. Democrat. Home: PO Box 95 Sutter CA 95982-0095

STANDRING, JAMES DOUGLAS, real estate developer; b. Fresno, Calif., Dec. 2, 1951; s. James Robert Pusey and Jacquelin (Moore); m. Paula Jean Monson, Oct. 27, 1972; children: Craig Douglas, Ryan Scott, Melinda Jean, Kevin Paul. BS, Calif. State U., Fresno, 1975. Pres. Westland Industries, Inc., Portland, Oreg., 1976—; ptnr. Aloha Land and Cattle, Inc., Portland, 1982—; bd. dirs. Homebuilders Assn., Metro Portland, Oreg. State Homebuilders Assn., Nat. Assn. Homebuilders, Washington; v.p. Homebuilders Assn. Metro Portland, 1988-90, pres., 1990-91. Bd. dirs. Tualitin Valley Econ. Devel. Corp., Portland, 1988—; co-founder, dir. People for Washington County Charities, Beaverton, Oreg., 1985-88. Named Portland Metro. Builder of Yr., 1992, Oregon Builder of Yr., 1992. Mem. Tualitin Valley Econ. Devel. Commn., Multnomah Athletic Club, Portland City Club, Portland Golf Club, 1000 Friends of Oreg., Sierra Club, Elks. Republican. Episcopalian. Home: 5 Nansen Smt Lake Oswego OR 97035-1029 Office: Aloha Land/Cattle Co 17980 SW Kemmer Rd Beaverton OR 97007-6078

STANEK, ALAN EDWARD, music educator; b. Longmont, Colo., July 3, 1939; s. Edward Thomas Stanek and Mary Rose (Hicks) Stanek MacDougall; m. Janette Elizabeth Swanson, Aug. 23, 1963; children—Michael Alan, Karen Leigh. Mus. Ed. B., U. Colo., 1961; Mus.M., Eastman Sch. Music, 1965; Mus.D., U. Mich., 1974. Dir. instrumental music Ainsworth Pub. Sch., Nebr., 1961-64, Cozad Pub. Sch., Nebr., 1965-67; asst. prof. music Hastings Coll., Nebr., 1967-76; prof., chmn. Idaho State U., Pocatello, 1976—. . Contbr., editor, reviewer for profl. jours. including Clarinet, Idaho Music Notes, Nebr. Music Educator. Mem. Music Educators Nat. Conf., Idaho Music Educators Assn. (chmn. higher edn. 1978-86, pres. 1988-90, chair state solo contest 1990-92), Internat. Clarinet Soc. (sec. 1978-84, v.p. 1986-88), Coll. Music Soc., Nat. Assn. Coll. Wind and Percussion Instruments (chmn. Idaho 1978-88), Nat. Assn. Schs. Music (sec. N.W. region 1979-82, vis. evaluator 1990—, chair N.W. region 1991-94). Office: Idaho State U Dept Music PO Box 8099 Pocatello ID 83209-8099

STANFILL, DENNIS CAROTHERS, business executive; b. Centerville, Tenn., Apr. 1, 1927; s. Sam Broome and Hattie (Carothers) S.; m. Therese Olivieri, June 29, 1951; children: Francesca (Mrs. Peter Tufo), Sara, Dennis Carothers. B.S., U.S. Naval Acad., 1949; M.A. (Rhodes scholar), Oxford U., 1953; L.H.D. (hon.), U. S.C. Corporate finance specialist Lehman Bros., N.Y.C., 1959-65; v.p. finance Times Mirror Co., Los Angeles, 1965-69; exec. v.p. 20th Century-Fox Film Corp., 1969-71, pres., 1971, chmn. bd., chief exec. officer, 1971-81; pres. Stanfill, Bowen & Co., 1981-90; chmn. bd. dirs., chief exec. officer AME, Inc., 1990-91; co-chmn., co-CEO Metro-Goldwyn-Mayer, Inc., 1992-93; bd. dirs. Dial Corp. (formerly Greyhound Corp.), Carter Hawley Hale, Weingart Found. Trustee John F. Kennedy Ctr. Performing Arts, Calif. Inst. Tech. Served to lt. USN, 1949-59; politico-mil. policy div. Office Chief Naval Ops. 1956-59.

STANFORD, JACK ARTHUR, biological station administrator; b. Delta, Colo., Feb. 18, 1947; s. LeRoy and Wilma (Tucker) S.; children: Jake, Chriss. BS in Fisheries Sci., Colo. State U., 1969, MS in Limnology, 1971; PhD in Limnology, U. Utah, 1975. Fisheries biologist Alaska-Fish and Game, Dillingham, 1968-69; rsch. biologist and limnologist instr. U. Mont., Missoula, 1973-74; dir. Flathead Lake Biol. Sta. U. Mont., Polson, 1980—; research prof. zoology U. Mont., Missoula, 1983-86; prof. N. Tex. State U., Denton, 1974-81; panelist div. biotic system NSF, Washington, 1985-89. Editor: Ecology of Regulated Streams, 1979; mem. bd. editors: Regulated Rivers: Research and Management, 1985—; contbr. over 75 articles to profl. jours. Advisor Nature Conservancy, Boulder, Colo., 1982—. Named Bierman Prof. Ecology U. Mont., 1986—; grantee N. Tex. State U., EPA, U.S. Army, U.S. Bur. Reclamation, NSF, U.S. Nat. Park Svc. Mem. Mont. Acad. Sci., Am. Soc. Limnology and Oceanography, Ecol. Soc. Am., N.Am. Benthological Soc. (exec. com. 1979, 1988-89), AAAS. Home and Office: U Mont Flathead Lake Biol Sta 311 Bio Station Ln Polson MT 59860-9659

STANFORD, JAMES M., oil company executive. B.S. in Mining Engring., Loyola Coll., Montreal; B.S. in Petroleum Engring., U. Alta., Can. With Mobil Oil Can. Ltd., 1959-78; gen. mgr. conventional prodn. Petro-Can. Inc., Calgary, Alta., from 1978-80; v.p., sr. v.p. Prodn. Petro-Can. Inc., 1980-82; pres. Petro-Can. Resources, 1982-90; pres., chief oper. officer Petro-Can., 1990—; bd. dirs. Westcoast Energy Inc., Hibernia Mgmt. and Devel. Co. Ltd., Can. Petroleum Assn., the Oil Industry Internat. Exploration & Prodn. Forum, Panarctic Oils Ltd., Syncrude Can. Ltd., Westcoast Petroleum Ltd., Can. Roxy Petroleum Ltd. Bd. dirs. Calgary Philharm. Soc., Alta. Theatre Projects. Mem. Assn. Profl. Engrs., Geologists and Geophysicists of Alta., Can. Inst. Mining and Metallurgy, Can. Petroleum Assn. (bd. dirs.), Chancellor's Club & Pres'. Circle U. Calgary (bd. dirs), Can. Petroleum Products Inst., Can. Com. World Energy Coun. (bd. dirs.). Office: Petro-Can, 150-6th Ave SW PO Box 2844, Calgary, AB Canada T2P 3E3

STANFORD, RAY EDMUND, pathologist; b. San Diego, Dec. 4, 1939; s. Dwight Edmund and Ida Maxine (Harris) S.; m. Katharine Ann Doyle, June 20, 1964; children: Linda Jean, Scott Edmund. BS in Math. with highest honors, Stanford U., 1961; MD, UCLA, 1966; PhD, U. Colo., 1970. Diplomate Am. Bd. Anatomic Pathology. Intern, then resident, lectr. in pathology Med. Sch. U. Colo., Denver, 1967-70, from asst. prof. to clin. prof. pathology, 1972—; chief pathologist Walson Army Hosp., Ft. Dix, N.J., 1971-72; rsch. assoc. Denver Mus. Natural History, 1966—; intermittent tchr. Garland Dist. Pub. Sch., Colo., 1966—; curatorial asst. Denver Mus. Natural History; mem. various coms. U. Colo. Med. Ctr., 1972—. Co-author: Butterflies RM States, 1981, Pulmonary Pathology, 1989. Pres. Stanford Young Reps., 1959-60; asst. organist Palo Alto (Calif.) Meth. Ch.; cubmaster coun. Boy Scouts Am., Denver, 1980-82. Maj. U.S. Army, 1970-72. Rsch. grantee U. Colo. Med. Ctr., 1972-87. Mem. AAAS, Internat. Acad. Pathology, Lepidopterists' Soc., Audubon Soc., Xerces Soc., Sierra Club (field trip leader DMNH 1966—). Republican. Home: 720 Fairfax St Denver CO 80220-5151

STANG, ERIC BRADFORD, corporate executive; b. Henderson, Nev., Sept. 1, 1959; s. Fred William and Adrienne Thalia (Kost) S.; m. Helen Marguerite Robinson, Apr. 5, 1987; 1 child, Anna Laurel Robison. BA with honors and distinction, Stanford U., 1981; MBA, Harvard U., 1983. Software engr. Ford Aerospace, Palo Alto, Calif., 1980-81; cons. McKinsey & Co., San Francisco, 1983-85; dir. Monitor Co. Europe, London, 1985-90; cons. Monitor Co., Boston, 1988-90; mgr. strategic planning Raychem, Menlo Park, Calif., 1990-91, dir. corp. strategy, 1991—; bd. dirs. Buttner Properties, Oakland, Calif. Mem. Phi Beta Kappa. Office: Raychem 300 Constitution Dr Menlo Park CA 94303

STANG, PETER JOHN, organic chemist; b. Nûrnberg, Germany, Nov. 17, 1941; came to U.S., 1956; s. John Stang and Margaret Stang Pollman; m. Christine Schirmer, 1969; children: Antonia, Alexandra. BS, DePaul U., Chicago, 1963; Ph. D., U. California, Berkeley, 1966; hon. degr., Moscow State Lomonossov U., 1992, Russian Academy of Sciences, 1992. Instr. Princeton (N.J.) U., 1967-68; from asst. to assoc. prof. U. Utah, Salt Lake City, 1969-79, prof., 1979-92, Disting. prof. chemistry, 1992—. Co-author: Organic Spectroscopy, 1971; author: (with others) Vinyl Cations, 1979; contbr. 250 articles to sci. publs. Humboldt-Forschungspreis, 1977; JSPS Fellowship, 1985; Fulbright-Hays Sr. Scholarship, 1988. Fellow AAAS; mem. Am. Chem. Soc. (assoc. editor jour. 1982—). Office: Univ Utah Dept Chemistry Salt Lake City UT 84112

STANG, ROBERT GEORGE, engineering educator; b. L.A., June 20, 1938; s. Edward Richard and Mildred Marie (Stohler) S.; m. Kathleen Desmond, Aug. 8, 1964. BS in Engring., Calif. State U., Long Beach, 1961; MS in Materials, UCLA, 1965; PhD in Materials Sci. and Engring., Stanford U., 1972. Teaching asst. UCLA, 1963-65; instr. mech. engring. Calif. State U., Long Beach, 1965-66; Inco fellow/rsch. asst. Stanford U., 1966-71; asst. prof. Inst. Mil. Engring., Rio de Janerio, 1971-72; rsch. assoc. dept. materials sci. and engring. Stanford U., 1972-73; asst. prof. metall. engring. U. Wash.,

Seattle, 1973-79, assoc. prof. matl. sci. engring., 1979—; sr. Fulbright-Hayes lectr./researcher Montanuniversitat, Leoben, Austria, 1980-81; assoc. program dir. metallurgy materials rsch. div. NSF, Washington, 1984-85, program dir. metallurgy, 1985-86. Bd. review Metall. Transactions, 1987—. Mem. The Metall. Soc. of AIME, ASM, Am. Soc. Engring. Edn., Sigma Xi. Home: 4573 Purdue Ave NE Seattle WA 98105-2141 Office: U Washington Matl Sci Engring FB10 Seattle WA 98195

STANGELAND, ROGER EARL, retail chain store executive; b. Chgo., Oct. 4, 1929; s. Earl and Mae E. (Shaw) S.; m. Lilah Fisher, Dec. 27, 1951; children: Brett, Cyndi Stangeland Meili, Brad. Student, St. Johns Mil. Acad., 1943-47, Carleton Coll., 1947-48; B.S., U. Ill., 1949-51. With Coast to Coast Stores, Mpls., 1960-78, pres., 1972-77; sr. v.p., exec. v.p. Household Merchandising, Chgo., 1978-84; chief exec. officer, chmn. bd. Vons Grocery Co., Los Angeles, 1984-85; chmn., chief exec. officer The Vons Cos., Inc., Arcadia, Calif., 1986—. Chmn. Wauconda (Ill.) Bd. Edn., 1957-60, Hopkins (Minn.) Bd. Edn., 1968-74; bd. fellows Claremont (Calif.) U. Ctr. and Grad. Sch., 1986; bd. dirs. L.A. area Boy Scouts Am.; trustee Hugh O'Brian Youth Found.; mem. CEO bd. advisors U. So. Calif. Sch. Bus. Adminstrn.; trustee St. John's Mil. Acad; bd. visitors Peter F. Drucker Grad. Mgmt. Ctr. Mem. Am. Inst. Wine and Food (bd. dirs.), Food Mktg. Inst. (chmn. bd. dirs.), Food Employers Coun. (exec. com., bd. dirs.), Mchts. & Mfrs. Assn. (bd. dirs.), L.A. Area C. of C. (bd. dirs.), Jonathan Club (L.A.), Calif. Club. Home: 842 Oxford Rd San Marino CA 91108-1214 Office: Vons Cos Inc PO Box 3338 618 Michillinda Ave Arcadia CA 91007-6300

STANLEY, FORREST EDWIN, fundraiser, university program director; b. Bakersfield, Calif., Sept. 6, 1942; s. James Edwin and Lucile Haworth (Sloan) S.; student U. Calif., Los Angeles, 1960-63, M.S., 1970; B.S., Calif. State U., Northridge, 1969; m. Suzanne Roberts, June 15, 1968 (div. 1984); children—John Forrest, Cheryl Suzanne; m. Virginia Louise Sorenson, Jan. 18, 1987. Sr. clk. So. Calif. Gas Co., 1963-65, programmer analyst, 1965-70; fin. analyst Continental Bldgs. Co., Burbank, Calif., 1970-72; fin. analyst McKinsey & Co., Inc., Los Angeles, 1972-74; analyst Unionamerica Advisors, Beverly Hills, Calif., asst. v.p., asst. treas., 1974-75; dir. alumni and devel. Grad. Sch. Mgmt., UCLA, 1976-80; dir. spl. campaigns U. Calif., Berkeley, 1980-84; dir. devel. U. Colo., Colorado Springs, 1984-86; dir. devel. pub. affairs, Calif. State U., Bakersfield, 1987—, asst. sec., 1989—; v.p. U. Colo. Found., Inc., 1984-86. Mem. Am. Inst. Cert. Computer Profls., Assn. for Computing Machinery, Council for Advancement and Support of Edn., UCLA Mgmt. Alumni Assn. (v.p. 1974, pres. 1975-77), Sons Am. Colonists, Mensa, Lambda Chi Alpha (UCLA alumni chpt. pres. 1974-77, treas. 1977-80). Clubs: North Kern. Office: PO Box 10705 Bakersfield CA 93389-0705

STANLEY, GEORGE DABNEY, JR., geology educator; b. Chattanooga, Jan. 25, 1948; s. George Dabney and Lucille (Proctor) S. B.A., U. Tenn.-Chattanooga, 1970; M.S., Memphis State U., 1972; Ph.D., U. Kans., 1977. Lectr. in geology U. Calif., Davis, 1977-78; geologist, research assoc. Smithsonian Instn., Washington, 1978-81; sr. prof. Fulbright-Hayes, Erlangen, West Germany, 1981-82; assoc. prof. U. Mont., Missoula, 1982-91, prof., 1991—; mem. organizing com. 4th Internat. Com. on Fossil Corals, Washington, 1981-84. Author monograph; editor books; contbr. numerous articles in field to profl. jours. Served to capt. U.S. Army, 1970-72. Grantee NSF, 1976-77, 83—; hon. research assoc. Smithsonian Instn., 1980—; Orgn. for Tropical Studies fellow, 1974, Fulbright-Hayes fellow, 1981-82. Mem. Geol. Soc. Am., Soc. Econ. Paleontologists and Mineralogists (metal com. 1990-93), Paleontol. Soc. Washington (pres. 1980-81), Internat. Paleontol. Soc., Paleontol. Assn. Gr. Britain, Com. on Coral Reefs (founding mem.). Home: 1900 Alvina Dr Missoula MT 59802-3659

STANLEY, JOHN LANGLEY, political science educator; b. Boston, Nov. 16, 1937; s. John Willis and Marion (Langley) S.; m. Charlotte Whitcomb Colony, Nov. 28, 1964; children: John Colony, Andrea Page, Marjorie Page. BA, Kenyon Coll., 1960; postgrad., Cambridge (Eng.) U., 1960-61; PhD, Cornell U., 1966. Asst. prof. polit. sci. U. Calif., Riverside, 1965-71, assoc. prof., 1971-79, prof., 1979—; vis. lectr. Hertford Coll., Oxford (Eng.) U., 1986; adv. editor Transaction Books, New Brunswick, N.J., 1976—. Author: The Sociology of Virtue, 1981; editor, translator: From Georges Sorel, 1976, From Georges Sorel II, 1990, The Illusions of Progress By Georges Sorel, 1969; mem. editorial bd. Cahiers Georges Sorel, Paris, 1983—, The Polit. Sci. Reviewer, 1990—; contbr. articles to profl. jours. Woodrow Wilson Found. fellow, 1961, NEH fellow, 1970. Mem. Am. Polit. Sci. Assn., Am. soc. for Polit. and Legal Philosophy, Polit. Studies Assn., United Oxford and Cambridge U. Club, Am. Hist. Assn., Assn. Francaise des Historiens des Idees Politiques. Democrat. Episcopalian. Office: U Calif Dept Polit Sci Riverside CA 92521

STANLEY, PETER WILLIAM, college president; b. Bronxville, N.Y., Feb. 17, 1940; s. Arnold and Mildred Jeanette (Pattison) S.; m. Joan Olivia Hersey, Sept. 14, 1963 (div. 1978); m. Mary-Jane Cullen Cosgrove, Sept. 2, 1978; 1 dau., Laura. B.A. magna cum laude, Harvard U., 1962, M.A., 1964, Ph.D., 1970. Asst. prof. history U. Ill., Chgo., 1970-72; asst. prof. history Harvard U., 1972-78, lectr. history, 1978-79; dean of coll. Carleton Coll., Northfield, Minn., 1979-84; program officer in charge edn. and culture program Ford Found., 1984-87, dir. edn. and culture program, 1987-91; pres. Pomona Coll., Claremont, Calif., 1991—; lectr. Fgn. Service Inst., Arlington, Va., 1977-89. Author: A Nation in the Making: The Philippines and the United States, 1974; co-author: Sentimental Imperialists: The American Experience in East Asia, 1981; editor, contbr.: Reappraising an Empire: New Perspectives on Philippine-American History, 1984; contbr. numerous articles to scholastic jours., 1966—. Trustee The Coll. Bd., 1991—; dir. The Hitachi Found., 1993—; active humanities and scis. coun. Stanford U., 1986—; nat. adv. bd. Ctr. for Rsch. on Effective Schooling for Disadvantaged Students, John Hopkins U., 1989-92; nat. adv. coun. Nat. Fgn. Language Ctr., 1992—; mem. exec. com. Consortium Financing Higher Edn., 1992—; bd. dirs. Nat. Assn. Latino Elected Officials Ednl. Fund, 1992—, Commn. on Internat. Edn., Am. Coun. Edn., 1992—. Fellow Charles Warren Ctr. for Studies in Am. History-Harvard U., 1975-76; Frank Knox Meml. fellow Harvard U., 1962-63. Mem. AAUP, Am. Hist. Assn., Assn. Asian Studies, Coun. on Fgn. Rels., Phi Beta Kappa. Home: 345 N College Ave Claremont CA 91711-4408 Office: Pomona Coll Pres Office Claremont CA 91711-6301

STANNARD, RALPH ELY, aeronautical, electrical engineer; b. Chgo.; s. Ely Martin and Ina Maude (Perego) S. AB in Psychology, San Jose State U., postgrad.; postgrad. in elec. engring., Colo. Coll; postgrad. in aero. engring., St. Louis U. Sr. staff reliability engr. Canadair, Ltd., Montreal, Quebec, Can., 1977-78; mem. tech. staff United Techs., Farmington, Conn., 1978-79; sr. reliability engr. specialist Boeing Airplane Co., Wichita, Kans., 1980-82; sr. reliability engr. Hughes Aircraft Co., Fullerton, Calif., 1983-84, Magnavox Advanced Products Co., Torrance, Calif., 1984-85, Mainstream Engring. Co., Costa Mesa, Calif., 1985; reliability cons. R. Stannard & Assocs., Irvine, Calif., 1985-86; staff reliability engr. Airspace Tech. Corp., Irvine, 1987-88; founder, pres. ODASER Techs., Newport Beach, Calif., 1988—. Avia cadet Navy Air Corps. Mem. IEEE, Soc. Automotive Engrs., Optical Soc. So. Calif., Navy League, Mil. & Hospitaler Order of St. Lazarus of Jerusalem, Opera Pacific, Beverly Hills Pop Orch. Episcopalian. Home: PO Box 7458 Newport Beach CA 92658 Office: ODASER Technologies 1133 Camelback Newport Beach CA 92658

STANTON, CAMPBELL EDGAR, energy technician; b. Chgo., Nov. 25, 1947; s. Francis Rew and Louise (Parsons) S.; m. Susan Pesses, Mar. 9, 1980; children: Aleta Rose, Corey Elizabeth. BA in Geography, U. Denver, 1970; cert. in Solar Retrofit Tech., Colo. Mt. Coll., 1983; cert. in Energy Auditing, Western Area Power Adminstrn., Glenwood Springs, Colo., 1990. Manual laborer Denver and Boulder, 1970-74; owner and mgr. Saw-Whet Orchards., Paonia, Colo., 1974—; founder, mgr. KVNF-FM pub. radio, Paonia, 1976-83; station mgr. KVNF-FM pub. radio, Paonia, Colo, 1986-89; sales rep. and installer Sunrise Energy Co., Delta, Colo., 1983-85; ptnr., sales rep., installer Sun Dragon Svcs., Hotchkiss, Colo., 1985-86; energy technician The Energy Office, Inc., Grand Junction, Colo., 1989—. Home: 503 Reed Mesa Dr Grand Junction CO 81503

STANTON, LEWIS HARRIS, publishing company executive; b. London, Apr. 2, 1954; came to U.S., 1980; s. Gerald and Carole (Harris) S.; m. Victoria Frances Patterson, Sept. 17, 1977; children: Graham, Joshua. BS, U. Birmingham, Eng., 1976. CPA, Calif.; chartered acct., Eng. Sr. mgr. Arthur Andersen & Co., L.A., London, 1976-88; chief fin. officer Data Analysis Inc., L.A., 1988—. Fellow Inst. Chartered Accts.; mem. AICPA, Calif. Soc. CPA's, Assn. Western Securities Mgmt. (pres. 1989). Office: Data Analysis Inc 12655 Beatrice St Los Angeles CA 90066

STANTON, WILLIAM JOHN, JR., marketing educator, author; b. Chgo., Dec. 15, 1919; s. William John and Winifred (McGann) S.; m. Imma Mair, Sept. 14, 1978; children by previous marriage: Kathleen Louise, William John III. BS, Ill. Inst. Tech., 1940; MBA, Northwestern U., 1941, PhD, 1948. Mgmt. trainee Sears Roebuck & Co., 1940-41; instr. U. Ala., 1941-44; auditor Olan Mills Portrait Studios, Chattanooga, 1944-46; asst. prof., asso. prof. U. Wash., 1948-55; prof. U. Colo., Boulder, 1955-90; prof. emeritus, 1990—; head mktg. dept. U. Colo., 1955-71, acting dean, 1963-64; assoc. dean U. Colo. (Sch. Bus.), 1964-67; vis. prof. summers U. Utah, 1946, 49, U. Calif., Berkeley, 1950, UCLA, 1957; mktg. cons. to various bus. firms and govt. agys., 1950—; lectr. univs. Austria, India, Mex., New Zealand; mem. faculty exec. devel. programs sponsored by Sales and Mktg. Execs. and by Internat. Advanced Mgmt. Rsch., 1963-71. Author: Economic Aspects of Recreation in Alaska, 1953; (with Richard H. Buskirk and Rosann Spiro) Management of a Sales Force, 8th edit., 1991 (also Spanish transl.); (with others) Challenge of Business, 1975; (with M. Etzel and B. Walker) Fundamentals of Marketing, 10th edit., 1994 (also Spanish, Portuguese and Indonesian transls.); (with M.S. Sommers and J. G. Barnes) Can. edit. Fundamentals of Marketing, 5th edit., 1989, (with K. Miller and R. Layton) Australian edit., 2d edit. 1991, (with R. Varaldo) Italian edit., 2d edit., 1990, (with others) South African edit., 1992; (with R. Abratt, L. Pitt, G. Staude) South African edit., 1992; monographs on Alaska Tourist Industry, 1953-54; contbr. articles to profl. jours. Mem. Am., So., Southwestern, Western mktg. assns., Beta Gamma Sigma. Roman Catholic. Home: 1445 Sierra Dr Boulder CO 80302-7846

STAPLES, LORENA JO, transition home director; b. Whittier, Calif., Aug. 4, 1962; d. James Edmund Thornton; d. William Paul and Sally Ann (McKinney) Sullivan; m. Timothy Darrell Mantlo, June 2, 1984 (div. Sept. 1988); children: Tanesha Mantlo, Milea Mantlo; m. John Raymond Staples, Nov. 15, 1991; 1 child, Jeffrey Staples. BS in Home Econs., AA in Mktg., So. Utah State Coll., 1985, BS in Edn., 1990. Mgr., dir. State Home for Mentally Ill Women, St. George, Utah, 1985-86; asst. mgr. County Seat, Goodlettsville, Tenn., 1986-87; mgr. Brooks Fashions, Goodlettsville, 1987-88; owner, dir. Transition Home for Girls, St. George, 1988—. Vol. LDS Ch.; judge beauty pagents. Royden C. Braithwaite scholar So. Utah U., 1981-83. Republican. Mem. LDS Ch.

STAPLES, ROBERT EUGENE, nursing educator; b. Roanoke, Va., June 28, 1942; s. John Ambrose and Anna Theresa (Anthony) S. AA, L.A. Valley Coll., Van Nuys, Calif., 1960; AB, Calif. State U., 1963; MA, San Jose State U., 1965; PhD, U. Minn., 1970. Assoc. prof. sociology Howard U., Washington, 1971-73; prof. sociology U. Calif., San Francisco, 1973—. Editor: The Black Family, 1971; author: The Black Woman In America, 1973, Introduction to Black Sociology, 1976, World of Black Singles, 1981, Black Masculinity, 1982, The Urban Plantation, 1987, Black Families Essays, 1991, Black Families at the Crossroads, 1993. Mem. Nat. Coun. on Family Rels., Assn. Black Sociologists, Am. Sociol. Assn. Office: U Calif 3rd & Parnassus St Box 0612 San Francisco CA 94143

STAPLETON, KATHARINE HALL (KATIE STAPLETON), food broadcaster, author; b. Kansas City, Mo., Oct. 29, 1919; d. William Mabin and Katharine (Hall) Foster; B.A., Vassar Coll., 1941; m. Benjamin Franklin Stapleton, June 20, 1942; children: Benjamin Franklin, III, Craig Roberts, Katharine Hall. Cookbook reviewer Denver Post, 1974-84; producer, writer, host On the Front Burner, daily radio program Sta. KOA-CBS, Denver, 1976-79, Sta. WGN, Portland, Maine, 1979-81, Cooking with Katie, live one-hour weekly, Sta. KOA, 1979-88; guest broadcaster Geneva Radio, 1974, London Broadcasting Corp., 1981, 82; tour leader culinaries to Britain, France and Switzerland, 1978-85. Eng., 1978. Chmm. women's div. United Fund, 1955-56; founder, chmn. Denver Debutante Ball, 1956, 57; hon. chmn. Nat. Travelers Aid Assn., 1952-56; commr. Denver Centennial Authority, 1958-60; trustee Washington Cathedral, regional v.p., 1967-73; mem. world service council YWCA, 1961-87; trustee, Colo. Women's Coll., 1975-80; sole trustee Harmes C. Fishback Found. Decorated Chevalier de L'Etoile Noire (France); recipient People-to-People citation, 1960, 66, Beautiful Activist award Altrusa Club, 1972, Gran Skillet award Colo./Wyo. Restaurant Assn., 1981; named Chevalier du Tastevin, 1989. Republican. Episcopalian. Clubs: Denver Country, Denver. Author: Denver Delicious: 150 Past and Present Recipes from the Queen City, 1980, 3d. edit., 1983; High Notes: Favorite Recipes of KOA, 1984. Home: 8 Village Rd Englewood CO 80110-4908

STAPLETON, SHIRLEY ANN, retired real estate executive; b. Boise, Idaho, June 17, 1936; d. Charles Edward and Eleanor Lucille (Swiggart) Lee; m. Larry J. Stapleton, July 10, 1954 (div. 1976); children: Terry Michael, William Carroll, Tamara Lee; m. Bruce Frederick Wauters, May 23, 1986. AA, DeAnza Community Coll., Cupertino, Calif., 1976; BS in Bus. Mgmt., Ariz. State U., 1979. Lic. in real estate, Ariz. Exec. sec. Sys. Devel. Corp., Wash., 1961-63; with Cupertino Sch. Dist., Calif., 1968-71; coordinator Women's Opportunity Ctr., DeAnza Coll., Cupertino, 1972-74; owner, mgr. Ariz. Women's Yellow Pages, Inc., 1975-78; realtor assoc. Coldwell Banker Resdl. Real Estate, Scottsdale, Ariz., 1979-82; assoc., ptnr. The Weigelt Corp., Scottsdale, 1982-86; br. mgr., assoc. Carol Vernon & Assocs., Inc., Scottsdale, 1986-88; v.p. real estate sales TransWestern Consolidated Realty, Inc., Scottsdale, 1988-89; assoc., cons. comml. real estate Internat. Ariz. Investments Inc., Scottsdale, 1989—; sec. Ctr. for Environ. Studies, Ariz. State U., 1992—. Bd. dirs. Cupertino Sch. Vol. Bd. Mem. bus. and Profl. Women's Club, Cupertino Fine Arts Assn., NAFE, Women in Comml. Real Estate, Ariz. State U. Alumni Assn., Ariz. State U. Bus. Coll. Alumni Assn. Democrat. Home: 7701 E Palm Ln Scottsdale AZ 85257-2230

STARING, GRAYDON SHAW, lawyer; b. Deansboro, N.Y., Apr. 9, 1923; s. William Luther and Eleanor Mary (Shaw) S.; m. Joyce Lydia Allum-Poon, Sept. 1, 1949; children: Diana Hilary Agnes, Christopher Paul Norman. Student, Colgate U., 1943-44; A.B., Hamilton Coll., 1947; J.D., U. Calif.-Berkeley, 1951. Bar: Calif. 1952, U.S. Supreme Ct. 1958. Atty. Office Gen. Counsel, Navy Dept., San Francisco, 1952-53; atty. admiralty and shipping sect. U.S. Dept. Justice, San Francisco, 1953-60; assoc. Lillick & Charles, San Francisco, 1960-64, ptnr., 1965—; titulary mem. Internat. Maritime Com.; bd. dirs. Marine Exchange at San Francisco, 1984-88, pres. 1986-88; instr. pub. speaking Hamilton Coll., 1947-48. Author: Law of Reinsurance, 1993; assoc. editor Am. Maritime Cases, 1966-92, editor, 1992—; contbr. articles to leval jours. Mem. San Francisco Lawyers Com. for Urban Affairs, 1972-90; bd. dirs. Legal Aid Soc., San Francisco, 1974-90, v.p., 1975-80, pres., 1980-82. With USN, 1943-46, comdr. USNR. Fellow Am. Bar Found., Am. Coll. Trial Lawyers; mem. ABA (chmn. maritime ins. com. 1975-76, mem. standing com. admiralty law 1976-82, 86-90, chmn. 1990, ho. dels. 1986-90), Fed. Bar Assn. (pres. San Francisco chpt. 1968), Bar Assn. San Francisco (sec. 1972, treas. 1973), Calif. Acad. Appellate Lawyers, Maritime Law Assn. U.S. (exec. com. 1977-88, v.p. 1980-84, pres. 1984-86), Brit. Ins. Law Assn., Brit.-Am. C. of C. (bd. dirs. 1987—), World Trade Club San Francisco, Tulane Admiralty Inst. (permanent adv. bd.), Assocs. Maritime Mus. Libr. (dir. 1990-92, pres. 1992—). Republican. Episcopalian. Home: 195 San Anselmo Ave San Francisco CA 94127-1513 Office: 2 Embarcadero Ctr Ste 2600 San Francisco CA 94111-3911

STARK, BETTY ANDREWS, corporate executive; b. Holyoke, Mass., July 3, 1920; d. George Francis and Elizabeth (Casey) Purser; m. Virgil Ray Andrews (dec. 1981); m. Wilbur H. Stark, Apr. 4, 1982; 1 child, Sara Ann Andrews Clayton. Student, Stetson U., 1938-39; AA, San Antonio Jr. Coll., Walnut, Calif., 1964; BS, Calif. State Poly., 1971, postgrad., 1972. Comml. artist Stafford Lowdon Litho, Ft. Worth, 1942-43; artist Walt Disney, Burbank, Calif., 1943-44; co-owner Sabo Co., L.A., 1944-46; advt. display Andrews Co., So. Calif., 1953-71, Andrella Kennels, Templeton & West Covina, Calif., 1988—; co-owner Ridgecrest Heights (Calif.) Water Co., 1988—, No. Mojave Lands Inc., Ridgecrest, 1988—, Miss. Valley Investment corp., 1982—; educator Sierra Sands Unified Sch. Dist., Ridgecrest, 1973-86. Illustrator, writer ethnic booklets for sch. dist., 1984-86; also advt. ednl. posters; art exhibited in galleries in San Luis Obispo, San Simeon, Cambria, Puerta Jallarta, Mexico. Supporter, charter mem. Reagan Task Force, Washington, 1982; supporter Battered Women Hot Line, Ridgecrest, 1982-84; mem. Homeless Animal Rescue Team Cambria. Mem. AAUW, Allied Arts Assn. Cambria (bd. dirs. 1987—), San Luis Obispo Art League, Ridgecrest Women's Club (charter, bd. dirs., parliamentarian), Pewter Plough Players, Cayucos Art Assn., Morro Bay Art Assn., Sweet Adeliners. Episcopalian. Home: 5752 Moonstone Beach Dr Cambria CA 93428

STARK, FORTNEY HILLMAN (PETE STARK), congressman; b. Milw., Nov. 11, 1931; s. Fortney Hillman Sr. and Dorothy M. (Mueller) S.; children: Jeffrey Peter, Beatrice Ann, Thekla Brumder, Sarah Gallup; m. Deborah Roderick. BS, MIT; MBA, U. Calif. Teaching asst. MIT, Cambridge, 1953-54; prin. Skaife & Co., Berkeley, Calif., 1957-61; founder Beacon Savs. & Loan Assn., Antioch, Calif., 1961; pres., founder Security Nat. Bank, Walnut Creek, Calif., 1963-72; mem. 93d-102nd Congresses from 9th Calif. dist., 1973—; chmn. ways and means subcom. on health 93d-103d Congresses from 13th dist. Calif., 1973—; mem. D.C. com., Ways and Means com., subcom. Health, Select Revenue Measures, joint econ. com. Bd. dirs. ACLU, 1971, Common Cause, 1971, Starr King Sch.; del. Dem. State Cen. Com.; trustee Calif. Dem. Coun. Capt. USAF, 1955-57. Mem. Delta Kappa Epsilon. Office: House of Representatives 239 Cannon Bldg Washington DC 20515-0513

STARK, JACK LEE, college president; b. Urbana, Ind., Sept. 26, 1934; s. Lynn C. and Helen (Haley) S.; m. Jil Carolyn Harris, June 14, 1958; children: Janet, Jeffrey, Jennifer, Jonathan. BA, Claremont McKenna Coll., 1957; hon. degree, Redlands U., LDH, 1973. Asst. to pres. Claremont (Calif.) McKenna Coll., 1961-70, pres., 1970—; bd. dirs. Angeles Corp., Los Angeles. Chmn. Pomona Valley Community Hosp., Region II United Way, El Monte, Calif.; bd. dirs. Foothill Country Day Sch., Claremont. Served to capt. USMCR, 1957-60. Mem. Assn. Ind. Calif. Colls. and Univs. (chmn.), Ind. Colls. So. Calif. (bd. dirs.), Western Coll. Assn. (bd. dirs.). Club: California (Los Angeles). Office: Claremont McKenna Coll Office of Pres Bauer Ctr Claremont CA 91711

STARK, MARTIN J., management consultant; b. N.Y.C., May 29, 1941; s. Nathan and Lola (Belmont) S.; m. Shigemi Matsumoto, Apr. 27, 1967; AA Glendale Coll., 1960; BA, Calif. State U., 1966; postgrad. San Fernando Valley Coll. Law, 1967-70. Systems analyst Industrial Electronic Engrs., Van Nuys, Calif., 1969-71; sales mgr., 1971-73; sales rep. Columbia Artists Mgmt., Inc., N.Y.C., 1973-78, sales mgr., 1978-79, v.p. bus. affairs, mgr. data processing, 1979-82; dir. corp. affairs Kolmar-Luth Entertainment, Inc., N.Y.C., 1982-84; pres. Oryx Corp., N.Y.C., 1984-85; exec. v.p. Asco Aerospace Products, Inc., El Segundo, Calif., 1985-87; exec. v.p. Internat. Engine Parts, Inc., Chatsworth, Calif., 1987—; pres. Stark & Assocs., Northridge, Calif., 1985—; lectr. Calif. State U., Long Beach; cons. City of N.Y., Memory Data Software, IEPO, Inc., and others. Mem. Opera Guild of So. Calif., Am. Symphony Orch. League, Assn. Coll., Univ. and Community Arts Adminstrs., Internat. Soc. Performing Arts Adminstrs., Am. Mgmt. Assn., Northridge C. of C., Chatsworth C. of C., Delta Upsilon. Avocations: sports cars, antiques, travel. Home: 18342 Chatham Ln Northridge CA 91326-3603

STARK, MILTON DALE, sports association executive; b. Fellows, Calif., Apr. 28, 1932; s. Ernest Esco and Ruth Hazel (Keeney) S.; m. Katherine Margaret Boyd, Dec. 17, 1955 (div. June 1978); children: Mark Boyd, Kimberly Kay, Matthew Scott, Martin Dean; m. Diana Lynn Mead, July 26, 1980; 1 child, Ryan. AA, Taft Coll., 1956; BA, Whittier Coll., 1958, MEd, 1963. Cert. ednl. adminstr., Calif. Sec. Western Softball Congress, Hollywood, Calif., 1962-70; commr. Internat. Softball Congress, Anaheim Hills, Calif., 1966-75, sec., 1975-83, exec. dir., 1983—; sports cons. Whittier (Calif.) News, 1959-70. Editor in chief Softball Illus. mag., 1966-69; contbr. articles to softball mags. Served with USAF, 1951-55. Named to Internat. Softball Congress Hall of Fame, 1981, recipient Alumni Achievement award Whittier Coll. Lancer Soc., 1989. Mem. U.S. Fastpitch Assn. (v.p. 1992—), Whittier Coll. Alumni (bd. dirs. 1989). Republican. Home and Office: Internat Softball Congress 6007 E Hillcrest Cir Anaheim CA 92807-3921

STARK, RAY, motion picture producer. Student, Rutgers U. Publicity agt., lit. agt.; talent agt. Famous Artist Agy., to 1957; co-founder Seven Arts Prodn. Co., 1957; ind. film producer, 1966—. Producer: (films) The World of Suzie Wong, 1960, The Night of the Iguana, 1964, Reflections in a Golden Eye, 1967, Funny Girl, 1968, The Owl and the Pussycat, 1970, Fat City, 1972, The Way We Were, 1973, Funny Lady, 1975, The Sunshine Boys, 1975, Murder By Death, 1976, Smokey and the Bandit, 1977, The Goodbye Girl, 1977, The Cheap Detective, 1978, California Suite, 1978, Chapter Two, 1979, The Electric Horseman, 1979, Seems Like Old Times, 1980, Annie, 1982, Blue Thunder, 1983, Nothing in Common, 1986, Peggy Sue Got Married, 1986, The Secret of My Success, 1987, Biloxi Blues, 1988, Steel Magnolias, 1989, Revenge, 1990, Lost in Yonkers, 1993, Barbarians at the Gate, 1993, Mr. Jones, 1993. Recipient Thalberg award Acad. Motion Picture Arts and Scis., 1980. Office: Rastar Prodns 335 N Maple Dr Ste 356 Beverly Hills CA 90210-3857

STARK, S. DANIEL, JR., convention and visitors bureau executive; b. Port Hueneme, Calif., Mar. 26, 1953; s. S. Daniel and Eloise Marie (Fisher) S.; m. Renee Elizabeth Perry, Apr. 21, 1981 (div. Apr. 1990); 1 child, Kaitlyn Elizabeth. BS, Calif. Poly. U., Pomona, 1981; cert. in exec. mgmt., Claremont Grad. Sch., 1989, MA in Mgmt., 1992. Driver-guide San Diego Wild Animal Pk., Escondido, Calif., 1974-76; attractions host Disneyland div. The Walt Disney Co., Anaheim, Calif., 1976-80; mgmt. intern Disneyland div. The Walt Disney Co., Anaheim, 1981; supr. ops. Disneyland div. The Walt Disney Co., Anaheim, Calif., 1981-82; area supr. ops., 1982-87; mgmt. cons. S.D. Stark, Jr., Riverside, Calif., 1987-88; dir. mktg. Ramada Express Hotel & Casino, Laughlin, Nev., 1988-89; exec. dir. San Bernardino (Calif.) Conv. and Visitors Bur., 1989—; cons. Hemmeter Devel. Corp., Honolulu, 1985, Calif. Authority Racing Fairs, Sacramento, 1987-88, USIA for Latvian Ministry Transp., tourism div., 1992; adj. prof. Sch. Bus.and Pub. Adminstrn., Calif. State U., San Bernardino, 1992—. Guest columnist San Bernardino Bus., 1989-93. Recipient resolution Calif. Assembly, 1989, San Bernardino County Bd. Suprs., 1989, City of San Bernardino Mayor and Coun., 1989, Calif. Senate, 1989; selected as one of 1991 Up and Coming Young Bus. Leaders in San Bernardino County; named one of Inland Empire Bus. All Stars, 1991. Mem. Assn. Travel Mktg. Execs., Internat. Assn. Conv. and Visitors Burs. (cert. comm., conv. mktg., tourism mktg.), Pub. Rels. Soc. Am. (bd. dirs. Calif. Inland Empire chpt. 1990—), Meeting Planners Internat., Travel Industry Assn. Am., Hospitality Sales and Mktg. Assn. Internat., Calif. Travel Industry Assn., Am. Mktg. Assn., Tourism Assn. So. Calif. (bd. dirs. 1990—, vice chair 1992—), Western Assn. Convs. and Vis. Bur. (chmn. Calif. coun. 1992—), Rotary (bd. dirs., program chair 1992-93), FarmHouse Fraternity (internat. bd. dirs. 1986—, v.p. 1990-92, Snyder Alumni award 1984). Office: San Barnardino Conv and Visitors Bur 201 N E St Ste 101 San Bernardino CA 92401-1530

STARK-ADAMEC, CANNIE, psychology educator, researcher; b. Fredericton, N.B., Can., June 2, 1945; d. Bazil Millan and Inez Muriel (Pearce) S. BA with honors, McGill U., Montreal, Que., Can., 1966, MSc in Applied Psychology, 1968, PhD, 1975; cert., Regina Citizens' Police Acad., Sask., Can., 1990. Sr. experimenter Le Dain Commission, Can., 1971; asst. prof. Dalhousie U., Halifax, N.S., Can., 1975-77; co-dir. Scott Lab., Wellesley Hosp., Toronto, Ont., Can., 1977-84; contbg. editor Resources for Feminist Rsch., Toronto, 1979—; sci. editor Eden Press, Montreal, 1980-86; asst. prof. Faculty of Medicine, Toronto, 1981-84; rsch. assoc. Dept Psychiatry, Toronto, 1983-84; assoc. prof. U. Regina, Sask., 1984-87; head Dept. Psychology U. Regina, 1984-92; prof. U. Regina, Sask., 1987—; dir. organizational and social psychology rsch unit U. Regina, 1992—; cons. Sask. Internat. Rescue Team, Saskatoon, 1989—, mem. Sask Health Rsch. Bd., Saskatoon, 1989-92. Author: Sex Roles, 1980; contbr. articles to profl. jours. Nat. Health Rsch. scholar, Health & Welfare Can., 1981-84; Women & Work Strategic grantee Social Scis. & Humanities Rsch. Coun. of Can., 1988—, Sask grantee Health Rsch. Bd., 1990-93, grantee Health Svcs. Utilization and Rsch. Commn., 1993—. Fellow Can. Psychol. Assn. (pres. 1991-92, Outstanding Contbns. award 1989); mem. Can. Police Canine Assn. (assoc.), Social Sci. Fedn. Can. (bd. dirs. 1991-92, 93—). Office: Univ of Regina, OSPRU, Regina, SK Canada S4S 0A2

STARKEY, HARRY CHARLES, geologist; b. Wheeling, W.Va., Dec. 10, 1925; s. Burtice Johannes and Mary Irene (Hilton) S.; BS, W.Va. U., 1950; m. Ruth Woods, May 16, 1964. With U.S. Geol. Survey, 1955-84, geologist specializing in clay mineralogy, Denver, 1958-84. With inf. U.S. Army, 1944-46. Mem. Mensa. Methodist. Research in clay mineralogy, ion-exchange in clay and zeolites, chem. reactions involving clays; contbr. articles to profl. jours. Home: 1636 S Yarrow Ct Denver CO 80232-6754

STARKEY, JOE WARREN, farmer; b. Chico, Calif., Jan. 14, 1948; s. Carl E. and Henretta Jean (Brattan) S.; m. Judi W. Smith, June 26, 1971; children: Emily, Alyssa. B of Geography, Chico State U., 1971. Cert. secondary edn. tchr. Tchr. Montebello (Calif.) Unified Sch. Dist., 1972-74; ptnr. J.G. Brattan Co., Chico, 1974—. Mem. Calif. Grain and Feed, Rotary. Roman Catholic. Home: 1030 Dias Dr Chico CA 95926 Office: JC Brattan Co 2604 Hwy 32 Chico CA 95926

STARKWEATHER, FREDERICK THOMAS, data processing executive; b. Sioux City, Iowa, Feb. 24, 1933; s. Fred Ervin and Gertrude Faye (Madden) S.; m. Margot Glassen, Nov. 19, 1959; children: Thomas Frederick, Jerry Russell, Michael Glassen. BA in Math. and Physics, U. Nebr., Omaha, 1955. Mathematician Flight Determination Lab., White Sands Missile Range, N.Mex., 1955-56; supervisory mathematician Analysis & Computation, White Sands Missile Range, 1956-81; chief data scis. div. Nat. Range Ops., White Sands Missile Range, 1981—; Nat. council rep. Am. Def. Preparedness Assn., Washington, 1980—; pres. White Sands Pioneer Group, White Sands Missile Range, 1983-86; bd. dirs. Assn. U.S. Army, Washington. Author hist. and genealog. books; contbr. book reviews and articles to newspapers and mags. Chmn. El Paso (Tex.) City Planning Commn., 1980-84; bd. dirs. El Paso County Hist. Soc., 1983-87; mem. El Paso County Hist. Commn., 1983—. With USAR, 1955-63. Recipient Profl. Secs. Internat. Exec. of Yr. award, 1987, Conquistador award City of El Paso, 1980; named Disting. Alumnus U. Nebr., Omaha, 1985; named to Hon. Order of St. Barbara U.S. Field Arty. Assn., 1988; cited for svcs. to mankind El Paso chpt. Sertoma, 1985. Mem. Fed. Mgrs. Assn. (bd. dirs.), Freedom Found. at Valley Forge (pres. El Paso chpt., George Washington Hon. medal 1982), El Paso C. of C. (assoc. dir. 1984—, bd. dirs.), Toastmasters (dist. gov. 1970-71), Masons, Tau Kappa Epsilon (Hall of Fame 1986). Office: Nat Range Ops Chief Data Scis Div White Sands Missile Range NM 88002

STARKWEATHER, WILLIAM HENRY, bank officer, educator, consultant; b. Topeka, Nov. 2, 1944; s. William Otto and Marjory (Bales) S.; m. Leslie Ann Birch, Dec. 30, 1970; children: Laurel Ann., Jonathan James. BS, Brigham Young U., 1966; JD, U. Mich., 1971. Ptnr. Bean, Bean, Smedley & Starkweather, Layton, Utah, 1971-74; mortgage loan officer, mortgage coord., v.p., mgr. incom property fin. dept. 1st Security Bank Utah, N.A., Salt Lake City, 1974—; lectr. Sch. Mortgage Banking-Mortgage Bankers, 1984—; instr. U. Utah, 1979-88. Bd. dirs., officer Salt Lake Neighborhood Housing Svcs., 1985-89; adminstr. LDS Ch., Bountiful, Utah, 1988—, Boy Scouts of Am., 1980—. Willis Bryant scholar Mortgage Bankers Assn., 1983. Mem. Mortgage Bankers Assn. Am. (cert. mortgage banker, faculty fellow award, comml. real estate com., constrn. lending subcom., vice chmn. edn. com.), Utah State Bar, Salt Lake Area C. of C. (com. 1989—). Republican. Office: 1st Security Bank Utah NA 405 S Main St Fl 12 Salt Lake City UT 84111-3417

STARR, CHARLES LEONARD, air force historian; b. Sacramento, Sept. 3, 1951; s. Lawrence Allen and Mary Alice (Julien) S.; m. Melodie Joy Keller, June 23, 1984. BA in History, Calif. Bapt. Coll., 1981; MA in Nat. Security, Calif. State U., 1986; AA in Aerospace History, C.C. of Air Force, 1992. Enlisted USAF, 1974-79, 83—, advanced through grades to tech. sgt., 1991; munitions specialist USAF, Hill AFB, Utah, 1975-77, RAF Lakenheath, U.K., 1977-79; munitions specialist USAF, George AFB, Calif., 1983-85, historian, 1985-87, 88-90; historian USAF, Kunsan AB, Korea, 1987-88, Shaikh Isa AB, Bahrain, 1990-91, George AFB, 1991-92, Norton AFB, Calif., 1992—. Author: USAF History--History of the 8th Tactical Fighter Wing, 1987 (Best in USAF, Best in Tactical Air Force, 1988, USAF History--History of the 831st Air Division, 1990-91 (Best in 12th Air Force), USAF Historical Spl. Study--History of the 35th Tactical Fighter Wing--Operations Desert Shield and Desert Storm, 1990-91.

STARR, GRIER FORSYTHE, retired pathologist; b. Jamestown, N.D., Oct. 6, 1926; s. Earl Grier and Grace (Forsythe) S.; m. Virginia Lucille Heidinger, June 25, 1948; children: William Grier, Joan Elizabeth Starr Ferguson. BS cum laude, Jamestown (N.D.) Coll., 1947; MD, Northwestern U., 1951; MS in Pathology, U. Minn., 1956. Diplomate Nat. Bd. Med. Examiners, 1952, Minn., Mich., Oreg. and Wash. state bds., Am. Bd. Pathology in Clin. Pathology, 1956, and in Pathol. Anatomy, 1957. Intern Evanston (Ill.) Hosp., 1951-52; sr. resident in pathology Henry Ford Hosp., Detroit, 1955-56; fellow in pathology Mayo Clinic, Rochester, Minn., 1952-55, cons. surgical pathology, 1956-59; cons., pathologist Lab. Pathology and Pathology Cons., Eugene, Oreg., 1959-91, pres., 1973-85; mem. staff McKenzie-Willamette Hosp., Springfield, Oreg., 1959-91—; mem. staff Sacred Heart Gen. Hosp., Eugene, Oreg., 1959-91, chief of staff, 1969-71, dir. labs., 1973-86, emeritus staff, 1992—; chmn. bd., chief ops. officer Oreg. Consol. Labs., Eugene, Oreg., 1986-89; bd. dirs. Oreg. Blue Cross-Blue Shield, Portland, 1985—, Sisters of St. Joseph of Peace Health & Hosp. Svcs., Bellevue, Wash., 1990—; affiliate in pathology Oreg. Health Scis. Ctr., Portland, 1972-88; assoc. prof. U. Oreg., Eugene, 1986. Contbr. articles to profl. jours. Served with USN, 1944-46. Fellow Am. Coll. Pathologists, Am. Soc. Clin. Pathologists; mem. AMA, Lane County Med. Soc. (pres. 1984-85), Am. Soc. Cytology, Internat. Acad. Pathologists, Pacific NW Soc. Pathologists (pres. 1979-80), Oreg. State Soc. Pathologists, Am. Soc. Dermatopathology (chmn. 1984, peer review com. 1976—). Republican. Presbyterian. Home: 2455 S Louis Ln Eugene OR 97405-1026 Office: Pathology Cons PO Box 369 Eugene OR 97440-0369

STARR, JAMES EDWARD, logistics management officer; b. Iowa City, Iowa, June 12, 1944; s. Donald Edward and Lucille (Waggoner) S. BBA, U. Iowa, 1967. Supr. internat. bank ops. Continental Ill. Bank, Chgo., 1973-77; mgr. office svcs. McMaster Carr Supply Co., Chgo., 1977-78; mktg., contracts rep. Astronautics Corp. of Am., Milw., 1979-82; logistics prog. analyst 442 Fighter Wing, Richards-Gebaur AFB, Mo., 1983-87, 302 Airlift Wing, Peterson AFB, Colo., 1987—. Capt. USAF, 1967-73, lt. col. res., 1975—. Recipient Finkbine Leadership award, Pres./U. Iowa, Iowa City, 1966, 67; named Resource Officer of Yr. USAF Res., Robins AFB, Ga., 1985, Unit of Yr., 1989. Mem. Air Force Assn., Res. Officers Assn. of U.S. (pres. Colo. State 1990-91, nat. officer 1981-82, various state offices 1978—, chmn. nat. AF com. 1992-93), U.S. Space Found., Soc. Logistics Engrs., U. Iowa Alumni Assn., Colorado Springs Club (chmn.), Am. Legion, I Club, Alpha Kappa Psi, others. Lutheran. Home: 9025 Aragon Dr Colorado Springs CO 80920-7543

STARR, MELVIN LEE, counselor; b. N.Y.C., Mar. 17, 1922; s. Herman and Martha (Aberman) S.; m. Eileen Ferne Kagan, Sept. 7, 1947; children: Marianne, Lisa Caren. BBA, U. Miami, 1947; postgrad. Columbia U., 1949-53, U. Denver, 1955-56, Ariz. State U., 1956-57; MA, U. Ariz., 1950; EdD, Western Colo. U., 1974. Faculty, adminstrn. Tucson Pub. Schs., 1950—; tchr. Doolen Jr. High Sch., 1951-53, cochran high sch., 1953-62, asst. prin. Alice Vail Jr. High Sch., 1962-64, Catalina High Sch., 1964-68; prin. Rincon High Sch., 1968-71, Tucson High Sch., 1971-74; asst. supt. Tucson Pub. Schs., 1974-78, assoc. supt., 1978-82; pvt. practice family counseling. Mem. Tucson Mayor's Com. on Human Relations, 1969—; mem. Ariz. state com. Anti Defamation League, 1971; Ariz. state adv. bd. Good Shepherd Sch. for Girls, 1971; mem. Dem. Cen. Com., Pima City, Ariz., 1968—; bd. dirs., Mobile Meals of Tucson, Pima County Bd. Health, So. Arix. Girl Scouts U.S. Council; chmn. Tucson Community Ctr. Commn.; bd. dirs. Amigos dos los Americanos, AnyTown, Ariz., Lighthouse YMCA, Beacon Found., Big Bros., NCCJ, Jr. Achievement, Tucson Community Center, Pacific Western region Anti-Defamation League, Handmaker Nursing Home Pima County, United Way, CODAC, Planned Parenthood, Girl Scouts Am., Ariz. Mobile Meals, Epilepsy Soc. So. Ariz., Drug Abuse and Alcohol Consortium; adv. bd. Tucson Free Med. Clinic; bd. dirs. Los Ninos Crisis Center. Mem. Ariz. Assn. Student Teaching (state treas.), NEA, Ariz. Interscholastic Assn. (pres. conf. 1971, legis. council), Ariz. Personnel and Guidance Assn., Nat. Assn. Secondary Sch. Prins., Am. Assn. Sch. Adminstrs., Assn. Supervision and Curriculum Devel., Ariz. Sch. Adminstrs., Phi Epsilon Pi, Phi Delta Kappa. Home: 7101 E River Canyon Rd Tucson AZ 85715-2111 Office: PO Box 30163 Tucson AZ 85751-0163

STARR, ROBERT IRVING, plant physiologist, chemist; b. Laramie, Wyo., Dec. 11, 1932; s. George Herman and Meriel Louise (Spooner) S.; m. Lavon Fabricius, June 10, 1956; children: Deborah Ann, Kenneth Irving. BS in Chemistry, U. Wyo., 1956, MS in Soil and Biochemistry, 1959, PhD in Plant Physiology and Chemistry, 1972. Ordained deacon, Presbyn. Ch. Chemist Shell Chem. Corp., Dominguez, Calif., 1956-57; biochemist Bur. Sport Fisheries and Wildlife, Denver, 1960-63; plant physiologist U.S. Bur. Sport Fisheries and Wildlife, Denver, 1968-74; plant physiologist Colo. State U., Ft. Collins, 1963-64, chemist, 1965-68, mem. environ. faculty dept. botany and plant pathology, 1973—; analytical chemist FDA, Denver, 1964-65; environ. scientist coal mining U.S. Geol. Survey, Denver, 1974-77, chief environ. tech. unit, 1977-78; chief biol. and ecol. scis. br. Office of Surface Mining U.S. Dept. Interior, Denver, 1979-81, sr. tech. coord., cons. environ. chemistry, 1984-89; sr. scientist pesticide rsch. Wildlife Rsch. Ctr. USDA, Denver, 1989—; cons. in environ. chemistry and fin. planning/real estate, 1982-84. Reviewer Jour. Agrl. Food Chemistry, 1970; editor, Reclamation Rev., 1981; contbr. articles to profl. jours. Served to 1st lt., AUS, 1957-64. Fellow Am. Inst. Chemists; mem. AAAS, Am. Chem. Soc., Nat. Water Well Assn., Sigma Xi. Club: Ft. Collins Swimming.

STARRATT, PATRICIA ELIZABETH, writer, actress, composer; b. Boston, Nov. 7, 1943; d. Alfred Byron and Anna (Mazur) S.; AB, Smith Coll., 1965; grad. prep. dept. Peabody Conservatory Music, 1961. Teaching asst. Harvard U. Grad. Sch. Bus. Aminstrn., 1965-67; mng. dir. INS Assocs., Washington, 1967-68; adminstrv. asst. George Washington U. Hosp., 1970-71; legal asst. Morgan, Lewis & Bockius, Washington, 1971-72; profl. staff energy analyst Nat. Fuels and Energy Policy Study, U.S. Senate Interior Com., 1972-74; cons., exec. asst. energy resource devel. Fed. Energy Adminstrn., Washington, 1974-75; sr. cons. energy policy Atlantic Richfield Co., 1975-76; energy cons., Alaska, 1977-78; govt. affairs assoc. Sohio Alaska Petroleum Co., Anchorage, 1978-85; legal asst. Hughes, Thorsness, Gantz, Powell and Brudin, Anchorage, 1989—; writer, media specialist corp. affairs Alyeska Pipeline Svc., Co., 1990—; pres. Starratt Monarch Prodns., 1986—; Econ. Devel. Commn., Municipality of Anchorage, 1981; actress/asst. dir. Brattle St. Players, Boston, 1966-67, Washington Theater Club 1967-68, Gene Frankel, Broadway 1968-69; actress Aspen Resident Theater, Colo. 1985-86; writer and assoc. producer Then One Night I Hit Her, 1983; appeared Off-Broadway in To Be Young, Gifted and Black; performed as Mary in Tennessee, Blanche in A Streetcar Named Desire, Stephanie Dickinson in Cactus Flower, Angela in Papa's Wine, Elizabeth Procter in The Crucible, Candida in Candida, Zeuss in J.B., Martha in Who's Afraid of Virginia Woolf, Amy in Dinny and The Witches, as Columbina in Servant of Two Masters, as Singer in Death of Morris Biederman, as Joan in Joan of Lorraine, as Mado in Amadee, as Mrs. Rowlands in Before Breakfast, as the girl in Hello Out There, as Angela in Bedtime Story, as Hannah in Night of the Iguana, as Lavinia in Androcles and the Lion, as Catherine in Great Catherine, as Julie in Lilliom, as First Nurse in Death of Bessie Smith, as Laura in Tea and Sympathy, as Amelia Earheart in Chamber Music; appeared at Detroit Summer Theatre in Oklahoma, Guys and Dolls, Carousel, Brigadoon, Kiss Me Kate, Finnian's Rainbow; asst. to dir. Broadway plays A Cry Of Players, A Way Of Life, Off-Broadway play To Be Young, Gifted, and Black; screenwriter Challenge in Alaska, 1986, Martin Poll Films; asst. dir. Dustin Hoffman, 1974; contbr. articles on natural gas and Alaskan econ. and environ. to profl. jours. Bd. dirs. Anchorage Community Theatre; industry rep. Alaska Eskimo Whaling Commn.; mem. Alaska New Music Forum. Mem. Actors' Equity. Episcopalian. Avocations: skiing, horseback riding, biking, hiking. Home: 1054 W 20th Ave Apt 4 Anchorage AK 99503-1749

STARRATT, RICHARD COURTNEY, banker; b. Boston, Dec. 4, 1936; s. Clarence Winfield and Marie (Hevey) S.; m. Ellen Van Alstyne, Jan. 3, 1959; children: Richard W., Michael G., Courtney. BA, Yale U., 1958. From trainee to v.p. Morgan Guarnaty Trust Co., N.Y.C., 1962-81; exec. v.p. First Nat. Bank, Palm Beach, Fla., 1981-84, Resources Planning Corp., Palm Beach, 1984-87; v.p. Meritor Savings Bank, Phila., 1987-90; v.p. pvt. banking Wells Fargo Bank, San Francisco, 1990—. Treas. Enterprise for High Sch. Students, San Francisco, 1991—; bd. dirs. Internat. Visitors Ctr. Mem. The Club at Point o' Woods, Belvedere Tennis Club. Republican. Roman Catholic. Home: 2001 Sacramento Apt. 5 San Francisco CA 94109

STARRFIELD, SUMNER GROSBY, astrophysics educator, researcher; b. L.A., Dec. 29, 1940; s. Harold Ernest and Eve (Grosby) S.; m. Susan Lee Hutt, Aug. 7, 1966; children: Barry, Brian, Sara. BA, U. Calif., Berkeley, 1962; MA, UCLA, 1965, PhD, 1969. From lectr. to asst. prof. Yale U., New Haven, 1967-71; rsch. scientist IBM, Yorktown Heights, N.Y., 1971-72; asst. prof. Ariz. State U., Tempe, 1972-75, assoc. prof., 1975-80, prof., 1980—; vis. assoc. prof. Steward Observatory, Tucson, 1978-79; vis. staff mem. Los Alamos (N.Mex.) Nat. Lab., 1974—. Author numerous scientific papers. Grantee Ariz. State U., 1973, NSF, 1974—, NASA, 1981—; Los Alamos Summer fellow, 1974, 86; Joint Inst. of Lab. Astrophysics fellow 1985-86. Fellow Royal Astron. Soc.; mem. Internat. Astron. Union, Am. Astron. Soc. (high energy astrophyics div., mem. publs. bd. 1978-81), Am. Physical Soc. (astrophysics div.). Office: Ariz State U Dept Physics/Astronomy Po Box 871504 Tempe AZ 85287-1504

STARRFIELD, SUSAN LEE, research and development coordinator; b. N.Y.C., Aug. 30, 1945; d. Benjamin and Grace (Rothman) Hutt; m. Sumner Grosby Starrfield, Aug. 7, 1966; children: Barry Adam, Brian Jay, Sara Beth. BA, UCLA, 1965; PhD, Ariz. State U., 1981. Cert. community coll. English, communications, social scis. Asst. dir. adolescent rsch. lab. Ariz. State U., Tempe, 1979-81; instr. Rio Salado Community Coll., Phoenix, 1982—, supr., 1988-89; coord. rsch. South Mountain Community Coll., Phoenix, 1989—. Mem. editorial bd. MCCD Vision Jour., 1990—; contbr. articles to profl. jours. Mem. Ariz. State U. Alumni Assn. (treas. 1984-86, 89-90, pres.-elect 1986-87, pres. 1987-88, past pres. 1988-89), Azair, Aero, Phi Delta Kappa. Democrat. Home: 1833 E Auburn Dr Tempe AZ 85283-2219 Office: South Mountain Community Coll 7050 S 24th St Phoenix AZ 85040-5898

STASENKO, RICHARD EDWARD, educator, educational administrator; b. Cleve., Oct. 14, 1941; s. John and Elizabeth Katherine (Roth) S.; m. Laree Ronda Harman, June 1, 1968 (div. Apr. 1976); 1 child, Rhett; m. Rachel Sinnok, Dec. 22, 1976; children: Mary, Katheirne, Stacey, Tommy. BS in Edn., Ohio State U., 1966; MEd, U. Mont., 1973. Cert. type A secondary lang. arts tchr., Alaska. Tchr. Alaska State Operated Schs., Delta Junction, 1966-68, Santa Rosa (Calif.) City Schs., 1968-74, Unorganized Burrough Sch. Dist., Deering, Alaska, 1976; tchr. Bering Strait Sch. Dist., Shishmaref, Alaska, 1976—, asst. prin., 1991—; cons. N.W. Region Ednl. Lab., Portland, Oreg., 1991-93. Contbr. articles to newsletters. At-large mem. Shishmaref Health Coun., 1985—; mem. adv. coun. N.W. C.C., Nome, Alaska, 1991—. Recipient Gold Pan award Bering Strait Sch. Dist., 1979, Eagle award, 1981; fellow Alaska Math. Consortium, 1987, Alaska Writing Consortium, 1989, Sci. and Math. Acads. for Rural Tchrs., 1991-93. Mem. NEA (legis. contact team Alaska 1985—). Lutheran. Home: City Hall Rd Shishmaref AK 99772 Office: Shishmaref Sch Icy View Ln Shishmaref AK 99772

STASHOWER, ARTHUR L., lawyer; b. Cleve., Apr. 12, 1930; s. Joseph G. and Tillie (Merlin) S.; m. Joy Schary, Sept. 1, 1957 (div. 1982); children: Keren, Saul, David; m. Barbara Hayden, Jan. 17, 1985. AB, U. Mich., 1951, JD with distinction, 1953. Bar: Ohio 1953, Mich. 1953, Calif. 1957, U.S. Dist. Ct. (mid. dist.) Calif. 1957, U.S. Ct. Appeals (9th cir.) 1962. Assoc. Kaplan Livingston Goodwin & Berkowitz, Beverly Hills, Calif., 1957-64; exec. United Artists Corp., L.A., 1964-65, Artists Agy. Corp., L.A., 1965-67; assoc. Greenberg & Glusker, Beverly Hills, 1967-68; ptnr. Swerdlow Glikbarg & Shimer, Beverly Hills, 1968-71, Sklar Cohen & Stashower, L.A., 1971-84; of counsel Shea & Gould, L.A., 1985-88; ptnr. Chrystie & Berle, L.A., 1988-92, of counsel, 1993—; arbitrator Hughes Aircraft, E.A.S.T. Mem. Anti-Defamation League, 1961-79, exec. com. 1967-73; mem. Assn. Alternative Pub. Schs., L.A., 1973-79. Lt. USCGR, 1953-57. Mem. ABA, Am. Arbitration Assn., L.A. Bar Assn., State Bar Assn. Calif., Beverly Hills Bar Assn., L.A. Copyright Soc. (trustee 1986-90), Fed. Mediation and Conciliation Svc. Democrat. Jewish. Office: Chrystie & Berle 1925 Century Park E # 2200 Los Angeles CA 90067-2736

STATLER, IRVING CARL, aerospace engineer; b. Buffalo, N.Y., Nov. 23, 1923; s. Samuel William and Sarah (Strauss) S.; m. Renee Roll, Aug. 23, 1953; children—William Scott, Thomas Stuart. B.S. in Aero. Engring., U. Mich., 1945, B.S. in Engring. Math., 1945; Ph.D., Calif. Inst. Tech., 1956. Research engr. flight research dept. Cornell Aero. Lab., Inc., Buffalo, 1946-53; prin. engr. flight research dept. Cornell Aero. Lab., Inc., 1956-57, asst. head aero-mechanics dept., 1957-63, head applied mechanics dept., 1963-70, sr. staff scientist aeroscis. div., 1970-71; research scientist U.S. Army Air Mobility Research and Devel. Lab., Moffett Field, Calif., 1971-73; dir. Aeromechanics Lab. U.S. Army Air Mobility Research and Devel. Lab., 1973-85, dir. AGARD, 1985-88; sr. staff scientist NASA Ames Rsch. Ctr., 1988-92, chief Human Factors Rsch. Divsn., 1992—; research scientist research analysis group Jet Propulsion Lab., Pasadena, Calif., 1953-55; chmn. flight mechanics panel adv. group aerospace research and devel. NATO, 1974-76; lectr. U. Buffalo, Millard-Fillmore Coll., Buffalo, 1957-58. Served with USAAF, 1945-46. Fellow AIAA, AAAS, Royal Aero. Soc.; mem. Am. Helicopter Soc., Sigma Xi. Home: 1362 Cuernavaca Circulo Mountain View CA 94040-3571 Office: NASA Ames Rsch Ctr MS262-1 Moffett Field CA 94035

STAUTER, SUSAN ELLEN, conservatory director; b. East Hartford, Conn., Aug. 29, 1949; d. Thomas Alfred Charest and Margery Lucille (Leroy) Scanlon; 1 child, Jeanine A. Payer. BA, MA, Calif. State U., Fullerton. Tchr. English and drama Esperanza High Sch., Placentia, Calif., 1975-84; dir. summer drama program Placentia Unified Sch. Dist., 1976; mentor, tchr. oral communications Placentia Unitied Sch. Dist., 1984; dir., coord. young co. summer drama program Lincoln High Sch., Stockton, Calif., 1978; founding chair dept. theater L.A. County High Sch. for the Arts, 1985-87; young conservatory dir. Am. Conservatory Theater, San Francisco, 1987-88, conservatory dir., 1988—; also bd. dirs.; creative cons. Holocaust Oral History Project, San Francisco, 1987—; bd. dirs. Bay Area Theatre Sports, San Francisco; creative cons., dir., writer Disneyland, Anaheim, Calif., 1983-84. Playwright: Miss Fairchild Sings, To Whom It May Concern, Who Are These People, The Wildest Storm of All, Find Me A Hero, Song for Granada, Metamorphosis Project, Shattered Rainbows, Amy and Friends; Women of Courage; actress: (repertory theater) Hedda Gabler, Hay Fever, Blithe Spirit, A Thousand Clowns, You're a Good Man Charlie Brown, Chapter Two; dir. numerous profl., coll. and high sch. prodns. Mem. Suprintendent's Task Force for the High Sch. for the Arts, San Francisco, 1987—; sponsor Teens Kick Off, San Francisco, 1991—. Office: Am Conservatory Theater 450 Geary St San Francisco CA 94102-1243

STEAD LEE, POLLY JAE See LEE, PALI JAE

STEADMAN, ROBERT KEMPTON, oral and maxillofacial surgeon; b. Mpls., July 8, 1943; s. Henry Kempton and Helen Vivian (Berg) S.; m. Susan E. Hoffman; children: Andrea Helene, Darcy Joanne, Richard Kempton, Micheal D. Wendlandt. BS, U. Wash., Seattle, 1969, DDS, 1974. Diplomate Am. Bd. Oral and Maxillofacial Surgery. Residency USAF, Elgin AFB, Fla., 1974-75; resident oral and maxillofacial surgery U. Okla., 1977-80, La. State U., Shreveport, 1980-81; pvt. practice Spokane, Wash., 1981—; cons. Group Health Coop., 1989—; mem. adv. bd. Osteoporosis Awareness Resource, 1988—. Select recruiting ptnr. U. Wash. Sch. Dentistry, 1990. Lt. col. USAFR, 1974—. Fellow Am. Coll. Oral & Maxillofacial Surgery, Am. Soc. Oral & Maxillofacial Surgery, Acad. Gen. Dentistry; mem. Internat. Soc. Plastic, Aesthetic and Reconstructive Surgery, Delta Sigma Delta (pres. 1987-88). Office: 801W E 5th Ave # 212 Spokane WA 99204-2823

STEARS, PAULA DENINE, retail owner; b. Pensicola, Fla., Mar. 31, 1965; d. Thomas Michael and Barbara (Kidwiler) S. BS in Textiles, Clothing, Ariz. State U., 1987. Sr. mdse. mgr. J.C. Penney Co., San Diego, 1987-91; owner Check It Out Apparel, Prescott, Ariz., 1992—. Advisor Alpha Chi Omega Sorority, San Diego, 1988-90. Named Dist. Merchandiser, J.C. Penney, 1989, 90. Mem. Yavapai Big Brother/Big Sister. Republican. Roman Catholic. Office: Check It Out 1316 Iron Springs Rd Prescott AZ 86303

STEBBINS, DENNIS ROBERT, business and environmental management consultant; b. Evergreen Park, Ill., Mar. 4, 1948; s. Daniel Mathew and Alberta Irene (Schmidt) S.; m. Ida Gattinger, Feb. 14, 1989. AA in Bus. Mgmt./Sci., Mohegan C. C., Norwich, Conn., 1983; BS in Environ. Studies, Chadwick U., 1993, MBA, 1993. Enlisted USN, 1966, advanced through grades to chief warrant officer, ret., 1989; pres., CEO Fanciful Notions, Inc., Honolulu, 1989-91; Hawaii state mgr. of field ops. Census '90 U.S. Dept. Commerce/U.S. Bur. of Census, Honolulu, 1990; pres., CEO Stebbins Internat. Ltd., Honolulu, 1990—; bd. dirs. I-Power, Reno, Nev., Water Caye Resort Devel. LTD, Belize, Ctrl. Am., 1993—; instr. Can. Fed. Staff Coll., B.C., 1992; spl. advisor UN Environ. Program, 1992—, internat. corp. adv. coun., 1992—. Contbr. articles to internat. profl. jours. Advisor, trustee The Tanager Found., Reno, Nev., 1992—; bd. dirs. Neighborhood Bd., Honolulu, 1992—, Mayor's Complete Count Com., Honolulu, 1990. Mem. UN Assn. of U.S. (bd. dirs. 1992—), Am. Meteorol. Soc., Am. Soc. for Tng. and Devel. (Hawaii chpt. bd. dirs., pres.-elect 1991), C. of C. of Hawaii (bd. dirs. sml. bus. coun. 1990-91), Ret. Officers Assn. (chpt. bd. dirs., pub. rels. dir. 1992—), N. Am. Environ. Edn. Assn., Am. Assn. of Corp. Environ. Officers, Nat. Assn. Environ. Profls. Democrat. Home: 1520 Ward Ave #1302 Honolulu HI 96822-3556 Office: Stebbins Internat Ltd 1750 Kalakaua Ave #3-775 Honolulu HI 96826-3709

STEBBINS, MICHAEL WILLIAM, business educator; b. Modesto, Calif., Sept. 19, 1943; s. William L. and Wanda (Ord) S.; m. Margaret Jane Hughes, May 22, 1964; children: Eric Todd, Anne Elizabeth. BS, U. Calif., Berkeley, 1966, MBA, 1967, PhD, 1972. Cert. orgn. devel. cons. Staff analyst Kaiser Industries, Oakland, Calif., 1968-72; coord. orgn. devel. Kaiser Permanente, L.A., 1972-78; owner Cambria Consultants, Cambria, Calif., 1978—; assoc. prof. Calif. Poly. Sch. Bus., San Luis Obispo, 1981-87, prof., 1988—; cons. U. So. Calif. Andrus Gerontology Ctr., L.A., 1977-84, Kaiser Permanente, So. Calif. region, 1978-93, USN, Port Hueneme, Calif., 1981-93, USN, Point Mugu, (Calif.) NAS, 1988-92. Contbr. articles to profl. jours. Mem. Acad. of Mgmt. Home: 1110 Suffolk Cambria CA 93428 Office: Calif Poly Coll Bus San Luis Obispo CA 93407

STEBLAY, CRAIG DOUGLAS, real estate executive, entrepreneur; b. San Bernardino, Calif., Mar. 1, 1948; s. Ralph Edward and Grace J. (Rhody) S.; m. Amina Marie Nickell, Sept. 28, 1968; children: Lavee, Kari Ann, Jennifer. V.p. Phototron Corp., San Bernardino, Calif., 1982—, also dir.; sec., treas. Sunmass Corp., Phoenix, Ariz., 1986—; pres. Sunmass Corp., Phoenix, 1987—. Served with USMC, 1969-71. Lodge: Knights of Malta (named Knight of Honor 1984), Cedam Internat.

STECKEL, RICHARD J., radiologist, academic administrator; b. Scranton, Pa., Apr. 17, 1936; s. Morris Leo and Lucille (Yellin) S.; m. Julie Raskin, June 16, 1960; children: Jan Marie, David Matthew. BS magna cum laude, Harvard U., 1957, MD cum laude, 1961. Diplomate: Am. Bd. Radiology. Intern UCLA Hosp., 1961-62; resident in radiology Mass. Gen. Hosp., Boston, 1962-65; clin./rsch. assoc. Nat. Cancer Inst., 1965-67; mem. faculty UCLA Med. Sch., 1967—, prof. radiol. scis. and radiation oncology, dir. Jonsson Comprehensive Cancer Ctr., 1974—; pres. Assn. Am. Cancer Insts., 1981. Author two books; contbr. over 130 articles on radiology and cancer diagnosis to profl. publs. Fellow Am. Coll. Radiology; mem. Radiol. Soc. N. Am., Am. Roentgen Ray Soc., Assn. Univ. Radiologists. Office: UCLA Med Ctr Jonsson Comp Cancer Ctr 10833 Le Conte Ave Los Angeles CA 90024-1602

STECKER, CARL ROBERT, lawyer; b. Syracuse, N.Y., Apr. 24, 1951; s. Leroy Henry and Laura Mary (Harter) S.; m. Anne Veronica Yurecko, Sept. 21, 1974; children: Bryan Stephen, Christine Anne. BA, U. Conn., 1973; JD, Willamette U., 1979. Bar: Oreg. 1979, U.S. Dist. Ct. Oreg. 1992. Engring. aide Port of N.Y. Authority, N.Y.C., 1972-73; fleet supt. Kramer Bros Corp., Pine Brook, N.J., 1974-76; title officer Key Title & Escrow, Salem, Oreg., 1977-78; law clk. Marion County Cir. Ct. Bench, Salem, 1979-80; dep. dist. atty. Marion County Dist. Atty., Salem, 1980-85, chief dep. dist. atty.,

1985—; instr. Chemeketa C.C., Salem, 1979—; mem. Oreg. Atty. Gen.'s Task Force on Guidelines, 1989-90. Contbr. articles to profl. jours. Founder Exch. Club Child Abuse Prevention Ctr., Salem, 1984; exec. fin. com. Morningside Meth. Ch., Salem, 1989-91; cubmaster Salem area Boy Scouts Am., 1990-91; mem. Marion County Labor-Mgmt. Task Force, Salem, 1991—. Named Exchangite of Yr. Exch. Club Salem, 1986. Mem. Oreg. State Bar (exec. com. family and juvenile law sect. 1988-92), Oreg. Dist. Attys. Assn. (legis. liaison 1981—, cert. of appreciation 1987), Family Support Enforcement Assn. (exec. 1992). Office: Marion County Dist Atty Ste 345 388 State St Salem OR 97301

STECKLER, LARRY, publisher, editor; b. Bklyn., Nov. 3, 1933; s. Morris and Ida (Beekman) S.; m. Catherine Coccozza, June 6, 1959; children: Gail Denise, Glenn Eric, Kerri Lynn, Adria Lauren. Student, CCNY, 1951. Assoc. editor Radio-Electronics mag., N.Y.C., 1957-62, editor, 1967-85; pub., editor in chief Radio Electronics mag., 1985-92; electronics editor Popular Mechanics mag., N.Y.C., 1962-65; assoc. editor Electronic Products mag., Garden City, N.Y., 1965-67; editorial dir. Merchandising 2-Way Radio mag., N.Y.C., 1975-77; v.p., dir. Gernsback Publs., N.Y.C., 1975-84, pres., dir., 1984—; pub., editorial dir. Spl. Projects mag., 1980-84, Radio-Electronics Ann., 1982-84; pub., editor in chief Hands-On Electronics, 1984-88; Popular Electronics mag., 1988—, Hobbyists Handbook, 1989—; pub., editor in chief Experimenters Handbook, 1986-92; Radio Craft, 1993—, High-Voltage Electronics, 1993—; pub., editor in chief Computer Digest, 1985-90; pres. Claggk, Inc., 1986—; Silicon Chip, 1993—; pub., editor in chief The Magic Course, Eating In/Dining Out on Long Island, Faxsimile Newsletter, 1987—, Modern Short Stories, 1987-90, GIZMO, 1988—, Video/Stereo Digest, 1989-91, Experimenters' Handbook, 1992—; pres. Sci. Probe Inc., 1989-93; pub., editor in chief Sci. Probe! mag., 1989-93, StoryMasters, 1989—, Electronics Shopper, 1990—, Electronics Market Ctr., 1991—, Radio Craft, High Voltage Electronics, 1993—; mem. electronics adv. bd. Bd. Coop. Ednl. Services, Nassau County, N.Y., 1975-77; pres. Electronics Industry Hall of Fame, 1985—; bd. dirs. Pub. Hall of Fame, 1987-89. Author books, handbooks; pub.; contbr. articles to profl. jours. Bd. dirs. Nassau County council Camp Fire Girls, 1971-72. Served with U.S. Army, 1953-56. Recipient Coop. award Nat. Alliance TV and Electronic Services Assns., 1974, 75; inducted into Electronics Industry Hall of Fame, 1985. Mem. IEEE, Internat. Soc. Cert. Electronic Technicians (chmn. 1974-76, 79-81, Pres.'s award 1985, dir. at large 1991—, rep. to NESDA bd. 1991—), Nat. Electronics Sales and Service Dealers Assn. (rec. sec. N.Y. State 1976-78, Man of Yr. award 1975, 85, treas. 1991—), Am. Mgmt. Assn., Radio Club Am., Internat. Underwater Explorers Soc., Am. Soc. Bus. Press Editors (sr.), Internat. Performing Magicians (exec. dir.), Soc. Profl. Journalists, L.I. Press Club, Sierra Club. Home: 2601 Springridge Dr Las Vegas NV 89134-8848 Office: Gernsback Pub Inc 500B Bi County Blvd Farmingdale NY 11735-3931 also: Claggk Inc 4820 Alpine Pl # A101 Las Vegas NV 89107

STECKLER, PHYLLIS BETTY, publishing company executive; b. N.Y.C.; d. Irwin H. and Bertha (Fellner) Schwartzbard; m. Stuart J. Steckler; children: Randall, Sharon Steckler-Slotky. BA, Hunter Coll.; MA, NYU. Editorial dir. R.R. Bowker Co., N.Y.C., 1954-69, Crowell Collier Macmillan Info. Pub. Co., N.Y.C., 1969-71, Holt Rinehart & Winston Info. Systems, N.Y.C., 1971-73; pres., CEO Oryx Press, Scottsdale, Ariz., 1973-76, Phoenix, 1976—; adj. prof. history Ariz. St. U., Tempe. Past chmn. Info. Industry Assn.; pres. Ariz. Ctr. for the Book; past pres. Friends Librs., U.S.A.; mem. exec. com. Ednl. Resources Info. Ctr., U.S. Dept. Edn.; mem. Senator John McCains Edn. Adv. Com. Elected to Hunter Coll. Hall of Fame, 1985. Mem. ALA, Spl. Librs. Assn., Am. Soc. Info. Sci., Ariz. Libr. Assn., Phoenix Pub. Libr. Friends (bd. dirs.), Univ. Club of Phoenix (bd. dirs.). Home: 6711 E Camelback Rd #32 Scottsdale AZ 85251 Office: Oryx Press 4041 N Central at Indian School Rd Phoenix AZ 85012

STEDMAN, JOHN ADDIS, financial planner; b. L.A., June 30, 1958; s. Saul Addis Fonseca and Marie Edith (Pereyra) Duggan; m. Kelly Jean Francis, Mar. 29, 1989; 1 child, Abrielle Francis. AS, U. State N.Y., 1981, BS, 1991; postgrad., San Diego State U., 1992—. Enlisted USN, 1977, advanced through grades to chief petty officer, ret., 1987; coach sailing, rsch. assoc. Bus. Sch. Harvard U., Cambridge, Mass., 1987-88; dir. mktg. U.S. Mktg., San Diego, 1988-89; securities prin. Brokers Investment Corp., La Jolla, Calif., 1990-91; fin. planning exec. Prin. Fin. Group, San Diego, 1991-92, CIGNA Individual Fin. Svcs. Co., San Diego, 1992—; cons. Nat. Bus. Cons., Inc., San Diego, 1992. Coach Murphy Canyon Little League, San Diego, 1985; organizer Pete Navarro Mayoral Campaign, San Diego, 1991-92; writer Planned Legis. Action Network, Des Moines, Iowa, 1991-92. Recipient Civic Leadership award The Philippines, Olongapo City, 1983. Fellow Life Underwriting Tng. Coun.; mem. Nat. Assn. Securities Dealers (registered prin.), U.S. Naval Inst. (Essay award 1986), Nat. Assn. Life Underwriters, Nat. Mgmt. Assn., Navy League U.S. (bd. dirs. 1992—, Leadership award 1981), Mission Bay Yacht Club (bd. dirs. 1992), Kiwanis (chair 1991-92). Republican. Roman Catholic. Home: 11577 Madera Rosa San Diego CA 92124 Office: CIGNA Individual Fin Svc Co Ste 410 4510 Executive Dr Ste 215 San Diego CA 92121-3098

STEECE, BERT MAURICE, university dean; b. Maywood, Calif., Sept. 9, 1945; s. Guy and Agnes (Sisco) S.; m. Joyce Elaine McCulley, Aug. 12, 1967; 1 child, Troy Devon. AB, U. So. Calif., 1967, PhD, 1974. Applied statistician Rand Corp., Santa Monica, Calif.; mem. tech. staff Jet Propulsion Lab., Pasadena; chmn./assoc. prof. U. Oreg., Eugene; prof. statistics and dean of faculty Sch. Bus. Adminstrn., U. So. Calif., L.A. Contbr. articles to profl. jours. Mem. Decision Sci. Inst. (pres. 1985-86), Am. Statis. Assn. (prog. chmn. 1989-90), City Club, Phi Kappa Phi. Republican. Methodist. Home: 1455 Mirasol Dr San Marino CA 91108-2736 Office: Office of the Dean Univ Southern California Los Angeles CA 90089

STEED, EMMETT DALE, hotel executive; b. Logan, Utah, July 14, 1950; s. Dale R. and Elizabeth (Emmett) S.; m. Jana Carol Jones, July 31, 1976; children: Carolyn, Mark, Elisa. BA in Journalism, Utah State U., 1974; M in Internat. Mgmt., Am. Grad. Sch., 1975. Asst. contr. Marriott Hotels Camelback Inn, Scottsdale, Ariz., 1975-76, Marriott Hotels Essex Ho., N.Y.C., 1976-78; contr. Marriott Mexicana Paraiso, Acapulco, Mex., 1978-80, Marriott Hotel, L.A., 1980-82; regional contr. Marriott Hotels, Plantation, Fla., 1982-85; resident mgr. Marriott Hotels, Panama City, Panama, 1985-89, Scottsdale, Ariz., 1985-89; v.p. Red Lion Hotels and Inns, Vancouver, Wash., 1989—. Mem. PTO, Vancouver, 1991-92; mem. Utah State U. Support Coun., 1992-93; dir. LDS Ch. Employment, Ft. Lauderdale, 1984-85. Mem. Am. Mgmt. Assn., Am. Grad. Sch. of Internat. Mgmt. Alumni Assn., Sigma Chi (life). Republican. Office: Red Lion Hotels and Inns 4001 Main St Vancouver WA 98663

STEEL, DAWN, motion picture studio executive; b. N.Y.C., Aug. 19; m. Charles Roven; 1 child, Rebecca. Student in mktg., Boston U., 1964-65, NYU, 1966-67. Sportswriter Major League Baseball Digest and NFL, N.Y.C., 1968-69; editor Penthouse Mag., N.Y.C., 1969-75; pres. Oh Dawn!, Inc., N.Y.C., 1975-78; v.p. merchandising, cons. Playboy mag., N.Y.C., 1978-79; v.p. merchandising Paramount Pictures, N.Y.C., 1979-80; v.p. prodn. Paramount Pictures, L.A., 1980-83, sr. v.p. prodn., 1983-85, 1983-85, pres. prodn., 1985-87; pres. Columbia Pictures, 1987-90; formed Steel Pictures (with Touchstone Pictures and Walt Disney Film & TV), 1990—; mem. dean's adv. bd. UCLA Sch. Theater, Film, TV, 1993. First women studio pres.; prodns. for Paramount include Flashdance, Footloose, Top Gun, Star Trek III, Beverly Hills Cop II, The Untouchables, The Accused, Fatal Attraction, 1985-87; prodns. for Columbia include Ghostbusters II, Karate Kid III, When Harry Met Sally, Look Who's Talking, Casualties of War, Postcards from the Edge, Flatliners, and Awakenings; prodr. Steel Pictures for Disney: Honey, I Blew Up the Kid, 1992, Cool Runnings, 1993, Sister Act 2, 1993; prodr. (benefit concert) For Our Children, 1992; author: They Can Kill You, But They Can't Eat You, 1993. Appointee Presdl. Commn. Scholars, 1993; mem. L.A. Mayor Richard Riordan's Transition Team, 1993; bd. dirs. Hollywood Supports, 1993. Recipient Women Film Crystal award, 1989. Mem. Acad. Motion Picture Arts and Scis. Office: Steel Pictures 345 N Maple Dr # 275 Beverly Hills CA 90210

STEELE, GERDA GOVINE, company president; b. St. Thomas, V.I., Apr. 25, 1942; d. Conrad Govine and Irene (Chinnery) Vanterpool; m. Richard Steele, June 16, 1962 (div. Nov. 19, 1971); children: Lisa (dec.), Dorie. BS, NYU, 1967, MA, 1970; MA, Tchrs. Coll., Columbia U., 1976, EdD, 1982. Community coll. teaching credential, Calif. Asst. dean sch. of continuing edn. Pace U., N.Y.C., 1975-77; urban sch. supr. State of N.Y. Edn. Dept., N.Y.C., 1977-78; nat. dir. of edn. NAACP, N.Y.C., 1978-80; exec. dir. Commn. on Status of Women, Pasadena, Calif., 1983-90; pres. G.G. Steele Consulting, Pasadena, Calif., 1990—; cons. Walt Disney, Burbank, Calif., 1992—, Hughes Aircraft, L.A., 1988—, City of Pasadena, 1992, Calif. State U., L.A., 1988—, Women & Minority Bus. Enterprise Ctr., L.A., 1991—, Fannie Mae Mortgage Co., 1992—. Co-producer: (video) Women For A Change, 1990; host/producer: Ebony '93 Radio Show, 1986—, As We Speak Cable TV Show, 1986—. Bd. pres. Women At Work, Pasadena, 1991; founding bd. mem. Pasadena AIDS Resource Ctr., 1991, African-Am. Cultural Ctr., Pasadena, 1990; bd.d irs. Foothill Family Svcs., Pasadena, 1992; mem. Friends of the Pasadena Commn. on Women, 1991. Named Outstanding Women of Pasadena, 1989, Woman of Yr., Magna Carta Bus. & Profl. Women, 1988, Outstanding Work in Civil and Human Rights, 1978. Mem. NAACP, LWV, Black Journalist Assn., Black Women's Network. Office: G G Steele Consulting 260 N Mar Vista Ste #2 Pasadena CA 91106

STEELE, JOELLE, writer, artist, photographer; b. San Francisco, Apr. 19, 1951; d. LeRoy Basilio and Norma Elisabeth (Steele) Martelli. Ind. mgmt. cons. San Francisco, 1973-78; gen. mgr. Richard L. Segal & Assocs., Santa Monica, Calif., 1980-84; ind. mgmt. cons. L.A., 1985-89; ind. pub., editor The New Leaf Press Newsletter, L.A., 1985-90; ind. writer, artist, photographer L.A., 1989—. Author 8 books; contbr. over 400 articles to jours. and publs. Mem. Mensa.

STEELE, JOHN PATRICK HENRY, engineering educator; b. Portland, Oreg., Oct. 19, 1948; s. Orvie Allen and Eleanor Steele; m. Kathleen Higdon, June 4, 1969 (div. June 1974); 1 child, Eleanor. BS in Physics cum laude, N.Mex. State U., 1970; MSME, U. N.Mex., 1986; PhD in Engring., U. N.M., 1988. Coop. rsch. asst. phys. sci. lab. Satellite Tracking Program N.Mex. State U., Las Cruces, 1967-70; engr., shop foreman Ampex Corp., Albuquerque, 1970-72; cartographer Alaska Task Force Nat. Park Svc., Anchorage, 1972-73; apprentice/journeyman steamfitter and welder United Assn. Plumbers and Steamfitters Local #367, Anchorage, 1973-81; rsch. asst. Tribology Program U. N.Mex. Dept. Mech. Engring., Albuquerque, 1982-84, instr., 1983-84; rsch. asst. Robotics Rsch. Lab. U. N.Mex. and Sandia Nat. Labs., Albuquerque, 1984-87; project engr. Advantage Prodn. Tech., Albuquerque, 1987-88; asst. prof. Engring. Dept. Colo. Sch. Mines, Golden, 1988—. Contbr. numerous articles to profl. jours. Dir. credit union Colo. Sch. Mines, 1990. Named Outstanding Faculty Mem. graduating srs. Colo. Sch. Mines, 1990. Mem. ASME (vice chmn. Colo. chpt. 1992-93, chmn. 1993—), IEEE, Am. Assn. Artifical Intelligence, Soc. Mfg. Engrs.-Robotics Internat. Office: Colo Sch Mines Divsn Engring Brown Hall Golden CO 80401

STEELE, KEVIN D., business owner; b. Greenfield, Ind., Dec. 5, 1958; s. Kerry D. and Marilyn S. Steele; m. Mary Steele, Oct. 14, 1987. AA, Sacramento City Coll., 1979; BS, Pepperdine U., 1981; PhD, Columbia U., 1988. Adj. prof. phys. edn. Pepperdine U., Malibu, Calif., 1983-88, cross country coach, 1986-89; fitness dir. Mgmt. Health, Malibu, Calif., 1981-89; dir. edn. Health and Tennis Corp., L.A., 1988-93; chmn. Steele Assocs., Malibu, 1989—. Pres. Team Malibu, 1992—; del. U.S. Olympic Com., Colorado Springs, Colo., 1983, People to People Amb., Spokane, Wash. Mem. AAPHERD, Am. Med. Athletic Assn., Am. Heart Assn., Am. Running and Fitness Assn., U.S. Olympics Acad. Home and Office: Box 594 Malibu CA 90265

STEELE, THOMAS JOSEPH, English language educator, writer; b. St. Louis, Nov. 6, 1933; s. Harry L. and Genevieve E. (Harder) S. BA, St. Louis U., 1957, licentiate in Philosophy, 1958, MA, 1959, licentiate in Theology, 1965; PhD, U. N.Mex., 1968. Tchr. Chaplain Kapaun High Sch., Wichita, Kans., 1959-61, Regis Coll., Denver, 1968—; vis. prof. U. N.Mex., Albuquerque, 1982—, Colo. Coll., Colorado Springs, 1987—. Author: Santos and Saints, 1974, (with others) Penitente Self-Government, 1985, Fraser Haps and Mishaps, 1990, Guidebook to Zen & The Art of Motorcycle Maintenance, 1990. Regis Centenary scholar, 1977. Mem. Soc. of Jesus. Roman Catholic. Office: Regis Jesuit Community 3333 Regis Blvd Denver CO 80221

STEELE, WILLIAM ARTHUR, financial analyst, public utilities executive; b. Albuquerque, Dec. 21, 1953; s. William Robert and Lois Ellen (Garvett) S. BSBA, U. No. Colo., 1976; MBA, U. Phoenix, Denver, 1987. Buyer Joslins Dept. Stores, Denver, 1978-79; transp. specialist Colo. Pub. Utilities Commn., Denver, 1979-80, fin. analyst, 1980-83, sr. fin. analyst, 1983-87, prin. fin. analyst, 1987—. Mem. Colo. State Mgr. Assn., Nat. Assn. Regulatory Commn. (staff subcom. on mgmt. analysis). Office: Pub Utilities Commn 1580 Logan St Denver CO 80203-1914

STEEN, DAVID SAMUEL, pastor; b. Williston, N.D., Oct. 30, 1935; s. Ernest B. and Inez V. (Ingebrigtson) S.; m. Lorilie J. Hefty, Aug. 11, 1957; children: Susan, Mark, Sari, Michael, Timothy. BA, Pacific Lutheran U., 1957; MDiv, Luther Theol. Sem., 1961. Pastor Comstock (Minn.) Luth. Ch., 1961-64, Faith Luth. Ch., Hoyt Lakes, Minn., 1964-68, Ascension Luth. Ch., Seattle, 1968-72, Good Shepherd Luth. Ch., Olympia, Wash., 1972—. Regent Pacific Luth. U., Tacoma, 1979—, chmn. acad. affairs com., 1990-92; dean South Sound Conf., Olympia, 1988-92; chaplain Wash. State Patrol, Olympia, 1978—; pres. South Sound Athletic Ofcls., Olympia, 1972-88. Named Outstanding Alumnus Pacific Luth. U., 1991; recipient Ofcls. award Wash. Interscholastic Athletics Assn., 1988. Lutheran. Home: 2717 Raintree Ct SE Olympia WA 98501-3818 Office: Good Shepherd Luth Ch 1601 North St SE Olympia WA 98501

STEEN, PAUL JOSEPH, retired broadcasting executive; b. Williston, N.D., July 4, 1932; s. Ernest B. and Inez (Ingebrigtson) S.; m. Judith Smith; children—Michael M., Melanie. BA, Pacific Luth. U., 1954; MS, Syracuse U., 1957. Producer, dir. Sta. KNTV, San Jose, Calif., 1957-58, Sta. KVIE, Sacramento, 1958-60; asst. prof. telecommunications Pacific Luth. U., Tacoma, 1960-67; dir. ops. Sta. KPBS San Diego State U., 1967-74; gen. mgr., 1974-93, prof. telecommunications and film, 1974-93, dir. univ. telecommunications; co-chmn. Office of New Tech. Initiatives. Dir. (tel. program) Troubled Waters (winner Nat. Ednl. TV award of excellence 1970). With AUS. Named Danforth Assoc. Mem. Pacific Mountain Network (bd. dirs., chmn., bd. of govs. award 1993), NATAS, Assn. Calif. Pub. TV Stas. (pres.), Pi Kappa Delta. Home: 4930 Campanile Dr San Diego CA 92115-2331

STEENSGAARD, ANTHONY HARVEY, federal agent; b. Rapid City, S.D., Mar. 21, 1963; s. Harvey Hans and Dorothy Lorraine (Hansen) S. Student, U. Alaska, 1981-83, Anchorage C.C., 1983-84; AAS in Indsl. Security, C.C. Air Force, 1989; BS in Criminal Justice, Wayland U., 1989. Lic. pilot, radio operator. Bookseller B. Dalton Bookseller, Rapid City, S.D., 1978-81, Anchorage, Alaska, 1981-83; warehouseman Sears, Roebuck & Co., Anchorage, 1983-85; security specialist Alaska Air N.G., Anchorage, 1985-88; agt., draftsman, engring. cons. U.S. Border Patrol, El Centro, Calif., 1988—. Author: Unit Security Manager's Guide Book, 1988. Vol. U.S. Senator George McGovern's Campaign, Rapid City, 1980, Congressman Tom Daschle's Campaign, Rapid City, 1980, Spl. Olympics, Rapid City, 1981; observer CAP, Anchorage, 1981. Tech. sgt. USAFR, 1985—, Ops. Desert Shield, Desert Storm, 1990-91. Mem. Am. Legion, Air Force Assn., Fraternal Order of Eagles. Democrat. Lutheran. Office: US Border Patrol 1111 N Imperial Ave El Centro CA 92243

STEFANKI, JOHN X., airline pilot; b. Chgo., July 14, 1920; s. Stephen and Anastasia (Stopak) S.; m. Dorothy Lancaster, Apr. 4, 1945; children: Cathy Ann, Steve, John, Mike, Judy, Larry, Mary, Megan, Dorothy. Student, Western Ill. U., 1940-41, Northwestern U., 1942, U. Iowa, Elmhurst Coll. Capt. United Air Lines, 1946-85, ret.; aviation safety cons. Lt. USN, 1942-46. Recipient Gen. Spruance award SAFE, 1973, Pfizer award of Merit U.S. Civil Def. Coun., 1974, Outstanding Alumni Achievement award Western Ill. U., 1975, Cert. Appreciation NFPA, 1976, Silver Plate award Internat. Assn. Airport and Seaport Police, London UK, 1977,cert. Commendation State of Calif., 1981, Laura Taber Barbour Air Safety award Flight Safety Found., 1990, others. Mem. NFPA (former chmn. 424 airport/community emergency planning, mem. planning com.), Ret. Airline Pilots Assn. (legis. chmn., v.p. legis. com., Am. Safety award 1978), others. Democrat. Roman Catholic. Home: 26901 Beatrice Ln Los Altos Hills CA 94022

STEFANOV, WILLIAM LOUIS, geologist; b. Webster, Mass., July 19, 1965; s. Edward Cyril and Jeannette Arzelea (Scheffler) S. BS, U. Lowell, 1988; MS, Ariz. State U., 1992. Geologist-in-tng., Ariz. Geographic asst. U.S. Dept. Commerce, Boston, 1987; optical mineralogist HYGEIA, Inc., Waltham, Mass., 1988-89; rsch./teaching asst. dept. geology Ariz. State U., Tempe, 1989-91; staff geologist Foree & Vann, Inc., Phoenix, Ariz., 1992—. Vol. Tempe (Ariz.) Fire Dept., 1991, Mus. Geology Ariz. State U., Tempe, 1989-90; vol., trail worker Recreational Equipment, Inc., Tempe, 1991-92. Mem. Geol. Soc. Am., Am. Geophys. Union, Ariz. Geol. Soc., Preserve Ams. Wolves, Ariz. Hydrological Soc., Sigma Gamma Epsilon, Sigma Xi (Undergrad. Rsch. award 1988). Office: Foree & Vann Inc 9013 N 24th Ave # 7 Phoenix AZ 85021

STEFFAN, WALLACE ALLAN, entomologist, educator, museum director; b. St. Paul, Aug. 10, 1934; m. Sylvia Behler, July 16, 1966; 1 child, Sharon. B.S., U. Calif.-Berkeley, 1961, Ph.D., 1965. Entomologist dept. entomology Bishop Mus., Honolulu, 1964-85, head diptera sect., 1966-85, asst. chmn., 1979-85; dir. Idaho Mus. Natural History, Idaho State U., Pocatello, 1985-89, U. Alaska Mus., 1989-92; prof. biology U. Alaska Fairbanks, 1989-92; exec. dir. Great Valley Mus. Natural History, 1992—; mem. grad. affiliate faculty dept. entomology U. Hawaii, 1969-85; liaison officer Bishop Mus., Mus. Computer Network, 1980-85; reviewer NSF, 1976—; mem. internat. editorial adv. com. World Diptera Catalog, Systematic Entomology Lab., U.S. Dept. Agr., 1983-85; mem. affiliate faculty biology, Idaho State U., 1986-89; bd. dirs. Idaho State U. Fed. Credit Union, 1986-89; mem. adv. coun. Modesto Conv. & Visitors Bureau, 1992—; mem. Ft. Hall Replica Commn., 1986-89. Acting editor Jour. Med. Entomology, 1966; assoc. editor Pacific Insects, 1980-85. Judge Hawaii State Sci. and Engring. Fair, 1966-85, chief judge sr. display div., 1982, 83, 84; advisor to bd. Fairbanks Conv. and Visitors Bur., 1989-91; mem. vestry St. Christophers Episcopal Ch., 1974-76, St. Matthew's Episcopal Ch., Fairbanks, 1990-91; pres. Alaska Visitors Assn., Fairbanks, 1991; advisor Fairbanks Conv. Visitors Bur. Bd., 1989-91; bd. dirs. Kamehameha Fed. Credit Union, 1975-77, chmn., mem. supervisory com., 1980-84. Served with USAF, 1954-57. Grantee NIH, 1962, 63, 67-74, 76-81, 83-85. U.S. Army Med. Research and Devel. Command, 1964-67, 73-74, NSF, 1968-76, 83-89, City and County of Honolulu, 1977, U.S. Dept. Interior, 1980, 81. Mem. Entomol. Soc. Am. (mem. standing com. on systematics resources 1983-87), Am. Mosquito Control Assn., Pacific Coast Entomol. Soc., Soc. Systematic Zoology, Hawaiian Entomol. Soc. (pres. 1974, chmn. coms. 1966-85, editor procs. 1966), Hawaiian Acad. (councillor 1976-78), Entomol. Soc. Wash., Fairbanks C. of C. (adv. bd. Conv. Visitors Bur. 1989), Alaska Visitors Assn. (pres. Fairbanks chpt. 1991), Modesto Convention and Visitors Bur. (adv. coun. 1992—) Sigma Xi (pres.-elect San Joaquin chpt. 1993). Office: Great Valley Museum of Natural Hist 1100 Stoddard Ave Modesto CA 95350

STEFFEN, THOMAS LEE, state supreme court justice; b. Tremonton, Utah, July 9, 1930; s. Conrad Richard and Jewel (McGuire) S.; m. LaVona Ericksen, Mar. 20, 1953; children—Elizabeth, Catherine, Conrad, John, Jennifer. Student, U. So. Calif., 1955-56; BS, U. Utah, 1957; JD with honors, George Washington U., 1964; LLM, U. Va., 1988. Bar: Nev. 1965, U.S. Dist. Ct. Nev. 1965, U.S. Tax Ct. 1966, U.S. Ct. Appeals 1967, U.S. Supreme Ct. 1977. Contracts negotiator U.S. Bur. Naval Weapons, Washington, 1961-64; private practice Las Vegas, 1965-82; justice Supreme Ct. Nev., Carson City, 1982—, chmn. code of jud. conduct study com., 1991; vice chmn. Nev. State Jud. Edn. Coun., 1983-84; chmn. Nev. State-Fed. Jud. Coun., 1986-91, mem., 1986—. Mem. editorial staff George Washington U. Law Rev., 1963-64; contbr. articles to legal jours. Bd. dirs. So. Nev. chpt. NCCJ, 1974-75; mem. exec. bd. Boulder Dam Area coun. Boy Scouts Am., 1979-83; bd. visitors Brigham Young U., 1985-89. Recipient merit citation Utah State U., 1983. Mem. Nev. Bar Assn. (former chmn. So. Nev. med.-legal screening panel), Nev. Trial Lawyers Assn. (former dir.). Republican. Mem. LDS Ch. Office: Nev Supreme Ct 100 N Carson St Carson City NV 89710-0001

STEFFENSEN, DWIGHT A., medical products and data processing services executive; b. Fresno, Calif., 1943. BA, Stanford U., 1965. Corp. contr. Synergex Corp. (merged with Bergen Brunswig Corp. 1985), Orange, Calif., 1969-72, chief fin. officer, v.p., 1972-80, chief oper. officer, chief fin. officer, exec. v.p., treas., 1980-83, pres., chief exec. officer, 1983-85, exec. v.p., 1985—; pres. Drug Service Inc., 1975-80. Office: Bergen Brunswig Corp 4000 W Metropolitan Dr Orange CA 92668-3502

STEFFEY, EUGENE PAUL, veterinary medicine educator; b. Reading, Pa., Oct. 27, 1942; s. Paul E. and Mary M. (Balthaser) S.; children: Michele A., Bret E., Michael R., Brian T. Student, Muhlenberg Coll., 1960-63; D in Vet. Medicine, U. Pa., 1967; PhD, U. Calif., Davis, 1973. Diplomate Am. Coll. Vet. Anesthesiologists (pres. 1980). NIH spl. research fellow U. Calif., San Francisco, 1973; asst. prof. U. Calif., Davis, 1974-77, assoc. prof., 1977-80, prof. vet. medicine, 1980—, also chmn. dept. vet. surgery; mem. scientific reviewers Am. Jour. Vet. Research, Schaumburg, Ill., 1984-87. Contbr. numerous articles to profl. jours. Mem. AVMA, Am. Coll. Vet. Anesthesiologists, Am. Physiol. Soc., Am. Soc. Pharmacology Exptl. Therapeutics, Am. Soc. Anesthesiologists, Assn. Vet. Anaesthetists, Calif. Soc. Anesthesiologists, Comparative Respiratory Soc., Internat. Anesthesia Research Soc., Pa. Vet. Med. Assn., Sigma Xi, Phi Zeta. Office: U Calif Dept Surgery Sch Vet Medicine Davis CA 95616

STEFFEY, LELA, state legislator, banker; b. Idaho Falls, Idaho, Aug. 8, 1928; d. Orawell and Mary Ethel (Owen) Gardner; m. Carl A. Hendershott, Jr., Apr. 16, 1949 (div. 1961); children: Barry G., Bradley Carl, Barton P.; m. 2d Warren D. Steffey, July 13, 1973; children: Dean, Wayne, Luann, Scott, Susan. Grad. Am. Inst. Banking, 1972. With Pacific Tel. & Tel., San Diego, 1948-49, Bank of Am., San Diego, 1949-52, Gen. Dynamics/Astro, San Diego, 1960-61; escrow officer, mgr. consumer loans Bank of Am., San Diego, 1961-73; real estate agt. Steffey Realty, Mesa, Ariz., 1978—; mem. Ariz. Ho. of Reps, Phoenix, 1982-86, vice chmn. banking and ins. com., 1982-86, mem. house appropriations, judiciary, counties and municipalities coms., 1986-90, chmn. transp. 1991—, chmn. counties and municpalities com., 1987-90. Founder, Citizens Com. Against Domestic Abuse; precinct com. Legis. Dist. 29, 1978—, dep. registrar, 1978—; pres. Mesa Rep. Women, 1980; chmn. Mesa Mus. Adv. bd., 1981-83; del. to Rep. Nat. Conv., Dallas, 1984. Bd. dirs. Mesa Community Coun., 1985—, Ariz. Hist. Soc., Ariz. Life Found., Aide to Women Ctr. Mem. Nat. Order Women Legislators (v.p. 1987-88, pres. 1989-90), Am. Mothers Assn., Nat. Fedn. Rep. Women, Ariz. Fedn. Rep. Women (dir.), Ariz. Assn. of Women (dir.), Am. Legis. Exchange Coun., Pi Beta Phi. Mem. Ch. of Jesus Christ of Latter-Day Saints. Office: Ariz Ho Reps 1439 E Ivglen St Mesa AZ 85203

STEFFEY, RICHARD DUDLEY, former land use consultant; b. Plymouth, Ind., Apr. 13, 1929; s. Albert Otto and Ethel (Williams) S.; m. Evelyn Jean Brunn, Apr. 5, 1952 (div. Nov. 4, 1985); children: Janet, Diane, Steffey-Smith, Kay; m. Barbara Mae Clark, Nov. 28, 1985. Student, Northwestern U., 1949-51. Mgmt. trainee, mgr. Lockheed Aircraft Corp., Burbank, Calif., 1953-59; asst. mgr., registered rep. Schwabacher & Co., Palo Alto, Calif., 1959-63; v.p. Colby's, Northbrook, Ill., 1963-67; pres. Steffey Fruit Ranch, Temecula, Calif., 1967-85. Dir., pres. Rancho Calif. Water Dist., Temecula, 1974-79, 85— (Distinguished Svc. award 1979); dir. Elsinore Murrieta Anza Resource Conservation Dist., Temecula, 1977-81, 86-90; commr., chmn. Riverside (Calif.) County Planning Commn., 1980-85 (Distinguished Svc. award 1985); commr. Local Agy. Formation Commn., Riverside, 1986—, chmn., 1992. With USAF, 1951-53.

STEGEMEIER, RICHARD JOSEPH, oil company executive; b. Alton, Ill., Apr. 1, 1928; s. George Henry and Rose Ann (Smola) S.; m. Marjorie Ann Spess, Feb. 9, 1952; children: Richard Michael, David Scott, Laura Ann, Martha Louise. BS in Petroleum Engring., U. Mo., Rolla, 1950, cert. petroleum engr. (hon.), 1981; MS in Petroleum Engring., Tex. A&M U., 1951; D of Engring. (hon.), U. Mo., Rolla, 1990. Registered profl. engr., Calif. Various nat. and internat. mgmt. positions with Unocal Corp. (formerly Union Oil Co.), L.A., 1951—, pres. sci. and tech. div., 1979-80, sr. v.p. corp. devel., 1980-85, pres., chief operating officer, 1985—, chief exec. officer, 1988—, chmn. bd. dirs., 1989—; bd. dirs. First Interstate Bancorp,

Northrop Corp., Outboard Marine Corp. Patentee in field. Bd. dirs. Calif. Econ. Devel. Corp., Nat. Coun. Bus. Advisors; bd. govs. Town Hall of Calif., The Music Ctr. of L.A. County; bd. overseers Exec. Coun. on Fgn. Diplomats, Huntington Libr.; chmn. L.A. World Affairs Coun.; pres. World Affairs Coun. of Orange County, 1980-82; chmn. Brea (Calif.) Blue Ribbon Com., 1979-80 ; trustee Com. for Econ. Devel., U. So. Calif., Harvey Mudd Coll., Loyola Marymount U.; mem. adv. bds. Northwestern U. Kellogg Grad. Sch. of Mgmt.; bd. vis. UCLA Anderson Grad. Sch. of Mgmt., U. Mo., Rolla; mem. adv. bd. Calif. State U., Fullerton, adv. coun., Long Beach; bd. dirs. YMCA of L.A., L.A. Philharm. Assn., Orange County Performing Arts Ctr., John Tracy Clinic; bd. dirs. French Found. for Alzheimer Rsch.; chmn. L.A. area coun. Boy Scouts of Am., Calif. C. of C. (elect.); gen. campaign chmn. United Way of Greater L.A., 1990-91; trustee Hugh O'Brian Youth Found., L.A. Archidiocese Found. Recipient Merit award Orange County Engring. Coun., 1980, Outstanding Engr. Merit award Inst. Advancement Engring., 1981, Disting. Achievement medal Tex. A&M U., Hugh O'Brian Youth Found. Albert Schweitzer Leadership award, 1990, Human Rels. award Am. Jewish Com., 1990. Mem. NAM (bd. dirs.), Nat. Acad. Engring., Am. Petroleum Inst. (bd. dirs.), Soc. Petroleum Engrs. (lectr. 1978), Nat. Petroleum Coun., Am. Inst. Chem. Engrs. (Disting. Career award So. Calif. sect. 1989), 25 Yr. Club of Petroleum Industry (past pres.), Calif. Bus. Roundtable, Calif. Coun. on Sci. and Tech., The Conf. Bd., Coun. on Fgn. Rels., Calif. C. of C. (chmn.-elect), Calif. Club. Republican. Roman Catholic. Office: Unocal Corp PO Box 7600 1201 W Fifth Los Angeles CA 90051-0600

STEGENGA, DAVID A., mathematics educator; b. Chgo., Aug. 20, 1946; s. Louis A. and Dorothy (Hamater) S.; m. Bridgit Kristen Folstad, Nov. 29, 1972. BS, Purdue U., 1968; MS, U Wis., 1970, PhD, 1973. Teaching asst. U. Wis., Madison, 1968-73; mem. Inst. Adv. Study, Princeton, N.J., 1973-74; asst. prof. math. Ind. U., Bloomington, 1973-80, U. Hawaii, Honolulu, 1980-82; assoc. prof. math. U. Hawaii, 1982-88, prof. math., 1988—; vis. prof. U. N.C., Chapel Hill, 1987, U. Tenn., Knoxville, 1988. Contbr. articles to profl. jours. NSF grantee, 1975-86; Sloan Found. fellow, 1987-88. Mem. Am. Math. Soc., Math. Assn. Am. Office: Dept Mathematics Univ Hawaii Honolulu HI 96822

STEIN, ARTHUR OSCAR, pediatrician; b. Bklyn., Apr. 3, 1932; s. Irving I. and Sadie (Brander) S.; A.B., Harvard U., 1953; M.D., Tufts U., 1957; postgrad. U. Chgo., 1963-66; m. Judith Lenore Hurwitz, Aug. 27, 1955; children: Susan, Jeffrey, Benjamin. Intern U. Chgo. Hosps., 1957-58, resident, 1958-59; resident N.Y. Hosp.-Cornell U. Med. Center, 1959-61; practice medicine specializing in pediatrics, 1963—; instr. pediatrics U. Chgo., 1963-66, asst. prof. pediatrics, 1966-70; mem. Healthguard Med. Group, San Jose, Calif., 1970-72; mem. Permanente Med. Group, San Jose, 1972—; asst. chief pediatrics Santa Teresa Med. Center, 1979-87; clin. instr. Santa Clara Valley Med. Center, Stanford U., 1970-72. Served to capt., M.C., AUS, 1961-63. USPHS Postdoctoral fellow, 1963-66. Fellow Am. Acad. Pediatrics. Jewish (v.p. congregation 1969-70, pres. 1972-73). Clubs: Light and Shadow Camera (pres. 1978-80) (San Jose); Central Coast Counties Camera (v.p. 1980-81, pres. 1981-82), Santa Clara Camera. (pres. 1991). Co-discoverer (with Glyn Dawson) genetic disease Lactosylceramidosis, 1969. Home: 956 Redmond Ave San Jose CA 95120-1831 Office: Kaiser/ Permanente Med Group 260 Internat Circle San Jose CA 95119

STEIN, ELIZABETH ANN, research immunologist; b. Burlington, Kans., May 27, 1931; d. Alfred Brunner Koch and Alice Medworth (Miller) Rhoads; m. Joseph Stein, Sept. 1, 1956 (div. 1986); children: Beth, David. BA, BS in Edn., Kans. State Tchrs. Coll., 1952; MA, UCLA, 1954, PhD, 1960. Teaching asst. Kans. State Tchrs. Coll., Emporia, 1950-52, tchr. Lab. High Sch., 1952-53; grad. teaching asst. dept. zoology UCLA, 1953-56, NSF rsch. fellow, 1956-58, postgrad. rsch. anatomist, 1975-79, asst. rsch. anatomist, 1979-86, asst. rsch. immunologist, 1986-90, assoc. rsch. immunologist, 1990—. Contbr. articles on immunology and diabetes rsch. to sci. jours. Mem. Internat. Soc. for Devel. and Comparative Immunology, Western Soc. Naturalists, Sigma Xi. Home: 3647 Keystone Ave Apt 4 Los Angeles CA 90034-5611 Office: UCLA Dept Medicine Div Endocrinology Los Angeles CA 90024

STEIN, HOLLY JAYNE, geochemist, geologist; b. Memphis, Oct. 4, 1954. BS in Geology, Western Ill. U., 1976; MS in Geology, U. N.C., 1978, PhD in Geology, 1985. Geologist Climax Molybdenum Co., Golden, Colo., 1978-80; postdoctoral appointee U.S. Geol. Survey, Denver, 1985, geologist, 1986—; adj. faculty U. Vt., Burlington, 1990—; invited speaker various geol. orgns., 1978—; mem. sci. adv. com. U.S. Geol. Survey, 1991—. Editor: Granite-Related Ore Deposits, 1990; mem. editorial bd. Econ. Geology Jour., 1991—; contbr. articles to profl. jours. Councilor Colo. Scientific Soc., Golden, 1989-90. Mem. Geochem. and Meteoritical Soc., Geol. Soc. of Am., Soc. of Econ. Geologists, Am. Geophys. Union, Soc. Geology Applied to Mineral Deposits, Colo. Scientific Soc., Sigma Xi, Phi Kappa Phi. Office: US Geol Survey MS 905 Fed Ctr Denver CO 80225

STEIN, JEFFREY HOWARD, dentist; b. N.Y.C., Nov. 16, 1960; s. Arthur Oscar and Judith Lenore (Hurwitz) S.; m. Beth Ann Brown, Aug. 12, 1984; children: Michelle Ilana, Stephanie Elise. BA, U. of the Pacific, 1983; DDS, U. So. Calif., 1987. Pvt. practice dentistry Lancaster, Calif., 1987—. Mem. ADA, Calif. Dental Assn., L.A. Dental Soc., Alpha Omega. Democrat. Home: 27131 Rexford Pl Valencia CA 91354-2107

STEIN, RICHARD ALLEN, theatre director; b. Sacramento, Mar. 16, 1953; s. Bernard George and Iris (Trueheart) S.; m. Alison Archer Bly, Sept. 6, 1981. BA, Columbia U., 1976; MA, Syracuse U., 1978. Assoc. producer Contemporary Theatre, Syracuse, N.Y., 1978-81; faculty mem. Syracuse (N.Y.) U., 1976-81; exec. dir. Oswego County Coun. on Arts, Fulton, N.Y., 1978-80; sales promotion mgr. Syracuse Symphony Orch., 1980-81; dir. mktg. and pub. rels. The Fla. Orch., Tampa Bay, 1981-82; dir. Lincoln Theater, U. Hartford (Conn.), 1982-87; mng. dir. Grove Shakespeare Festival, Garden Grove, Calif., 1987-90; exec. dir. The Laguna Playhouse, Laguna Beach, Calif., 1990—; panel mem. New Eng. Found. for Arts, Cambridge, Mass., 1983-87, Western States Arts Found., Santa Fe, N.Mex., 1987; panel mem., cons. Conn. Commn. on the Arts, Hartford, Conn., 1983-87; emissary Internat. Theatre Inst., Seoul, South Korea, 1988; cons. Calif. Arts Coun., 1992—; participant Leadership Greater Hartford, 1985-86. Stage dir.: Teibele and Her Demon, 1986, Seascape, 1987; producer: Albertine, In Five Times, 1986 (Conn State Arts award 1987); contbr. articles to profl. jours. Pres. adv. bd. WRVO-FM Pub. Radio, Oswego, N.Y., 1981-82; mem. adv. bd. Oswego County CETA, Oswego, 1981-82; mem. John Wayne Airport Arts Commn., Orange County 1990—, chmn., 1991—; co-chmn. Nat. Philanthropy Day Orange County, 1990. NEH fellow, Columbia U., N.Y.C., 1984. Mem. Nat. Soc. Fund Raising Execs. (sec. Orange county chpt. 1993—, cert.), Sierra Club, Garden Grove C. of C. (v.p. 1989-90), Garden Grove Sister City Assn. (v.p. 1988-90). Democrat. Jewish. Office: Laguna Playhouse 606 Laguna Canyon Rd Laguna Beach CA 92651-1898

STEIN, ROBERT GEORGE, mathematics educator, author; b. N.Y.C., Apr. 16, 1939; s. Ernest and Doris (Blumenthal) S.; m. Veronika Kirschner, Nov. 13, 1970; children: Joseph, Lucy. B.A., Harvard U., 1961; M.A.T., Conn. Wesleyan U., 1962; M.A., Dartmouth Coll., 1967; Ph.D., U. Tex.-Austin, 1975. Math. tchr. Ethical Culture Schs., N.Y.C., 1962-64, Acad. la Castellana, Caracas, Venezuela, 1964-65; mem. faculty Calif. State U., San Bernardino, 1967—, prof., 1982—, chmn. math. dept., 1976-89; mem. coms. Entry Level Math. Test Devel. Com. Author: Mathematics, An Exploratory Approach, 1975; Fundamentals of College Algebra and Trigonometry, 1986, Fundamentals of College Algebra, 1986; also articles; reviewer; reader Advanced Placement Calculus Test. Bd. dirs. Crestline Community Ambulance Assn., Calif., 1979-91; mem. Rim of the World Bd. Edn., 1989—. Fellow Danforth Assn.; mem. San Bernardino County Math. Tchrs. Assn. (founding pres. 1984—), Math. Assn. Am., Nat. Coun. Tchrs. of Math. Republican. Home: PO Box 494 Crestline CA 92325-0494 Office: Calif State Coll 5500 State College Pky San Bernardino CA 92407-2318

STEIN, ROBERT GESTRICH, dean, educator; b. Bedford, Ohio, Nov. 5, 1934; s. Karl Wise and Florence (Gestrich) S.; m. Arlene Paterson Stein, July 30, 1959; children: Robert G. II, Robyn Raye, Gifford P. BSBA, Ohio State U., 1956; MBA, U. Detroit, 1966; BS in Logistics, Weber State U., 1977; PhD in Ednl. Adminstrn., U. Utah, 1975. Commd. 2d lt. U.S. Air Force, 1957; advanced through grades, 1987; logistics officer U.S. Air Force, 1957-70, advanced through grades, resigned, 1970; prof. logistics Weber State U., Ogden, Utah, 1970-84; sr. logistics engr. Rsch. Analysis Corp., San Diego, 1984-86; dir. logistics programs Nat. U., San Diego, 1986-88; dean sch. arts, mgmt. and logistics Colo. Tech., Colorado Springs, 1989—. Brigadier gen. U.S. Air Force Res., 1970-91. Fellow Soc. Logistics Engrs. (dist. dir. 1978-83, editor jour. 1984—, Eccles medal 1986); mem. Logistics Edn. Found. Home: 5965 Wilson Rd Colorado Springs CO 80919 Office: Colo Tech 4435 Chestnut St Colorado Springs CO 80907

STEIN, RONALD BLEY, physician; b. L.A., Jan. 30, 1935; s. I. Bley and Adele (Gitelson) S.; divorced; m. Katherine Garcia, Sept. 16, 1966; 1 child, Jane; 1 child by previious marriage, Timothy. BA in Chemistry and Econs. summa cum laude, U. Calif., Berkeley, 1957; MD, U. Calif., San Francisco, 1961. Cert. Am. Bd. Internatl Medicine, 1969. Intern L.A. County Gen. Hosp., 1961-62; resident, fellow in internal medicine Mayo Clinic, 1962-64; resident Wadsworth V.A. Hosp., UCLA Hosp., 1964-67, fellow in endocrinology, 1965-67; clin. instr. medicine UCLA, 1967-70; clin. instr. medicine U. So. Calif., 1970-71, clin. asst. prof. medicine, 1971-74, asst. prof. medicine, 1975—; med. dir., founder Endo Labs., Burbank. Trustee The Bley Stein Found. Fellow ACP; mem. The Endocrine Soc., Am. Thyroid Assn., Am. Diabetes Assn. (pres. 1975, bd. dirs. 1982-85), Cross Town Endocrine Soc., L.A. Soc. Internal Medicine, Los Angeles County Med. Assn. (pres. dist. 17 1990-91), Calif. Med. Assn., U. Calif. Alumni Asns., Phi Beta Kappa, Sigma Alpha Mu. Office: 1624 W Olive Ave Burbank CA 91506-2459

STEIN, SHERMAN KOPALD, mathematics educator; b. Mpls., Aug. 11, 1926; s. Harry and Fannie (Kopald) S.; m. Hannah Dunitz, June 11, 1950; children: Joshua, Rebecca, Susanna. BS, Calif. Inst. Tech., 1946; PhD, Columbia U., 1952; LittD (hon.), Marietta Coll., 1975. Prof. U. Calif., Davis, 1953—. Author: Calculus and Analytic Geometry, 1968, 5th edit. 1992, Mathematics: The Manmade Universe, 1963, 3d edit. 1976, Geometry, A Guided Inquiry, 1986. Mem. Math. Assn. Am. (Lester R. Ford Expository award 1975), Am. Math. Soc. Office: Univ Calif Math Dept Davis CA 95616

STEIN, STEPHEN, electronics executive; b. N.Y.C., May 5, 1943; s. Solomon and Freda (Nyman) S.; m. Karen M. Rothstein, June 23, 1968; children: Alan, Gabrielle. BA in Physics, Columbia U., 1964, MA in Physics, 1965, PhD in Physics, 1969. Rsch. assoc. SLAC, Stanford, Calif., 1970-74; vis. researcher CERN, Geneva, 1974-77; vis. researcher Coll. De France, Paris, 1976-77, staff physicist, 1977-78; physicist TCI, Mountain View, Calif., 1978-82, mgr. data processing, 1982-84, dir. data processing, 1984-85, dir. advanced systems, 1985-87, v.p. advanced programs, 1987-92, v.p. advanced tech., 1992—. Office: TCI 222 Caspian Dr Sunnyvale CA 94089-1014

STEINBACH, LYNNE SUSAN, radiologist, educator; b. San Francisco, Dec. 28, 1953; d. Howard Lynne and Ilse (Rosengarten) S.; m. Eric Franklin Tepper, Aug. 14, 1977; 1 child, Mark Evan. Student, Vassar Coll.; BA, Stanford U., 1975; MD, Med. Coll. Pa., 1979. Intern Coll. Medicine and Dentistry N.J., Newark, 1979-80; resident radiology N.Y. Hosp.-Cornell Med. Ctr., N.Y.C., 1980-83; fellow musculoskeletal radiology Hosp. Spl. Surgery Cornell Med. Ctr., N.Y.C., 1983-84; asst. prof. radiology U. Calif., San Francisco, 1984-92, assoc. prof., 1992—. Contbr. articles on radiology, chpts. on musculoskeletal radiology to profl. publs. Mem. Internat. Skeletal Soc., Radiol. Soc. N.Am., Am. Assn. Women Radiologists (mem.-at-large 1987-88, pres. San Francisco chpt. 1987-88, sec. 1989-91, v.p. 1991-92, pres. elect 1992—), Am. Roentgen Ray Soc., Soc. Magnetic Resonance Imaging, Assn. Univ. Radiologists, Soc. Magnetic Resonance Imaging in Medicine, Am. Coll. Radiology, Soc. Skeletal Radiology. Democrat. Jewish.

STEINBERG, DANIEL, preventive medicine physician, educator; b. Windsor, Ont., Can., July 21, 1922; came to U.S., 1922; s. Maxwell Robert and Bess (Krupp) S.; m. Sara Murdock, Nov. 30, 1946 (dec. July 1986); children—Jonathan Henry, Ann Ballard, David Ethan; m. Mary Ellen Stratthaus, Aug. 11, 1991. B.S. with highest distinction, Wayne State U., 1941, M.D. with highest distinction, 1944; Ph.D. with distinction (fellow Am. Cancer Soc. 1950-51), Harvard U., 1951; M.D. (hon.), U. Gothenburg, 1991. Intern Boston City Hosp., 1944-45; physician Detroit Receiving Hosp., 1945-46; instr. physiology Boston U. Sch. Medicine, 1947-48; joined USPHS, 1951, med. dir., 1959; research staff lab. cellular physiology and metabolism Nat. Heart Inst., 1951-53, chief sect. metabolism, 1956-61, chief of lab. metabolism, 1962-68; lectr. grad. program NIH, 1955, mem. sci. adv. com. ednl. activities, 1955-61, com. chmn., 1955-60; mem. metabolism study sect. USPHS, 1959-61; chmn. heart and lung research rev. com. B Nat. Heart, Lung and Blood Inst., 1977-79; vis. scientist Carlsberg Labs., Copenhagen, 1952-53, Nat. Inst. Med. Research, London, 1960-61, Rockefeller U., 1981; pres. Lipid Research Inc., 1961-64, adv. bd., 1964-73; prof. medicine, head div. metabolic disease Sch. Medicine, U. Calif., San Diego and La Jolla; also program dir. basic scis. medicine Sch. Medicine, U. Calif., 1968—. Former editor Jour. Lipid Research; mem. editorial bd. Jour Clin. Investigation, 1969-74, Jour. Biol. Chemistry, 1980-84, Arteriosclerosis, 1980—; exec. editor Analytical Biochemistry, 1978-80; contbr. articles to profl. jours. Bd. dirs. Found. Advanced Edn. in Scis., 1959-68, pres., 1956-62, 65-67. Served to capt. M.C. AUS, World War II. Mem. Nat. Acad. Scis., AAAS, Am. Acad. Arts and Scis., Am. Heart Assn. (mem. exec. com. council on arteriosclerosis 1960-63, 65-73, chmn. council arteriosclerosis 1967-69), Fedn. Am. Scientists (exec. com. 1957-58), Am. Soc. Biol. Chemists, Am. Soc. Clin. Investigation, Assn. Am. Physicians, Am. Fedn. Clin. Research, AMA, European Atherosclerosis Discussion Group, Am. Physiol. Soc., Alpha Omega Alpha. Home: 7742 Whitefield Pl La Jolla CA 92037-3810 Office: U Calif San Diego Dept Medicine 0682 9500 Gilman Dr La Jolla CA 92093-0682

STEINBERG, JACK, lawyer; b. Seattle, Jan. 6, 1915; s. Solomon Reuben and Mary (Rashall) S.; widower; children: Roosevelt, Mary Ann Steinberg Shulman, Quentin. BA, U. Wash., 1936, JD, 1938. Bar: Wash. 1938, U.S. Dist. Ct. (we. dist.) Wash. 1938, U.S. Ct. Appeals (9th cir.) 1938. Ptnr. Steinberg & Steinberg, Seattle, 1938—. Former editor and pub. The Washington Examiner; contbr. numerous articles to legal jours. Judge pro tem Seattle Mcpl. Ct., Seattle, 1952; past pres. Emanuel Congregation, Seattle, Seattle chpt. Zionist Orgn. Am. Recipient Scrolls of Honor award (3) The State of Israel. Mem. Assn. Trial Lawyers Am., Am. Judicature Soc., Wash. Bar Assn., Wash. Assn. Trial Lawyers, Seattle-King County Bar Assn. Jewish Orthodox. Office: Steinberg & Steinberg 1210 Vance Bldg Seattle WA 98101

STEINBERG, JOAN EMILY, educator; b. San Francisco, Dec. 9, 1932; d. John Emil and Kathleen Helen (Montgomery) S. BA, U. Calif.-Berkeley, 1954; EdD, U. San Francisco, 1981. Tchr., Vallejo (Calif.) Unified Sch. Dist., 1959-61, San Francisco Unified Sch. Dist., 1961—, tchr. life and phys. sci. jr. high sch., 1978-85, 87—, sci. cons., 1985-87. Contbr. articles to profl. jours. Fulbright scholar U. Sydney (Australia), 1955-56; recipient Calif. Educator award, 1988, Outstanding Educator in Teaching award U. San Francisco Alumni Soc., 1989. Mem. Audubon Soc., Nat. Wildlife Fedn., Nature Conservancy, Astron. Soc. Pacific, Am. Fedn. Tchrs., Calif. Acad. Scis., Calif. Malacozool. Soc., Nat. Sci. Tchrs. Assn., Elem. Sch. Sci. Assn. (sec. 1984-85, pres. 1986-87), Calif. Sci. Tchrs. Assn., Internat. Reading Assn., Sigma Xi. Democrat. Office: Presidio Middle Sch 450 30th Ave San Francisco CA 94121-1797

STEINBERG, LESLIE R., director of public information; b. N.Y.C., Apr. 11, 1954; d. J. Leonard and Carol S.; m. John B. Ward, June 19, 1987; 1 child, Erin Taylor Ward. BA, UCLA, 1976. Tchr. L.A. Unified Sch. Dist., 1977-80, Beverly Hills (Calif.) Unified Sch. Dist., 1980-81; asst. to dean Southwestern U. Sch. of Law, L.A., 1981-84, dir. publs./special projects, 1984-86, dir. pub. info., 1986—. Contbr. articles to profl. jour. Active edn. com. Constl. Rights Found., 1981. Mem. Internat. Assn. Bus. Communicators (L.A. chpt. v.p. comm. 1988), Coun. for Advancement and Support of Edn. (advancement of women and minorities com.), U. Club L.A. Office: Southwestern U Sch of Law 675 S Westmoreland Ave Los Angeles CA 90005

STEINBERG, WARREN LINNINGTON, school principal; b. N.Y.C., Jan. 20, 1924; s. John M. and Gertrude (Vogel) S.; student U. So. Calif., 1943-44, UCLA, 1942-43, 46-47, BA, 1949, MEd, 1951, EdD, 1962; m. Beatrice Ruth Blass, June 29, 1947; children: Leigh William, James Robert, Donald Kenneth. Tchr., counselor, coach Jordan High Sch., Watts, Los Angeles, 1951-57; tchr. athletic coordinator Hamilton High Sch., Los Angeles, 1957-62; boys' vice prin. Univ. High Sch., Los Angeles, 1962-67, Crenshaw Hig Sch., Los Angeles, 1967-68; cons. Ctr. for Planned Change, Los Angeles City Sch., 1968-69; instr. edn. UCLA, 1965-71; boys' vice prin. LeConte Jr. High Sch., Los Angeles, 1969-71, sch. prin., 1971-77; adminstrv. cons. integration, 1977-81, adminstr. student to student interaction program, 1981-82; prin. Gage Jr. High Sch., 1982-83, Fairfax High Sch., 1983-90. Pres. Athletic Coordinators Assn., Los Angeles City Schs., 1959-60; v.p. P-3 Enterprises, Inc., Port Washington, N.Y., 1967-77, Century City (Calif.) Enterprises, 1966-88. V.p. B'nai B'rith Anti-Defamation League, 1968-70; mem. adv. com. Los Angeles City Commn. on Human Relations, 1966-71, 72-76, commr., 1976—, also chmn. edn. com.; pres. Los Angeles City Human Relations Commn., 1978-87; mem. del. assembly Community Relations Conf. of So. Calif., 1975-91; mem. citizens adv. com. for student integration Los Angeles Unified Sch. Dist., 1976-79; chmn. So. Calif. Drug Abuse Edn. Month com., 1970. Bd. dirs. DAWN, an anti-narcotics youth group. Served with USMCR, 1943-46. Recipient Beverly Hills B'nai B'rith Presdl. award, 1965, Pres.'s awardCommunity Rels. Conf. So. Calif., 1990; commended Los Angeles City Council, 1968, 88. Mem. West Los Angeles Coordinating Council (chmn. case conf., human relations), Beverly-Fairfax C. of C. (bd. dirs. 1986-88). Lodges: Lions (dir. 1960-62), Kiwanis. Contbr. articles on race relations, youth behavior to profl. jours. and newspapers. Home: 2737 Dunleer Pl Los Angeles CA 90064-4303

STEINBERG-PODGORNY, JUDY ELLEN, company travel executive; b. Gilroy, Calif.; d. Joseph M. and Eleanor (Gagliardi) Frusetta; m. Victor Serge Podgorny, June 14, 1980. BS, San Francisco State U., 1974. Cert. corp. travel exec. Mgr. transp. E.F. MacDonald Incentive Travel Co., San Francisco, 1974-80; mgr. corp. travel Del Monte Foods, San Francisco, 1980—; bd. dirs. Pan Am. Corp. Adv. Bd., 1990, Holiday Inn Corp. Adv. Bd., 1990. Mem. Nat. Bus. Travel Assn. (dir. 1986-89, treas. 1989-91, bd. dirs. 1991—), Bay Area Bus. Travel Assn. (sec. 1982-84, pres. 1984-86, chmn. bd. 1986-88), Meeting Planners Internat., Italian Cath. Fedn., Diabled Am. Vets. Aux.

STEINBOCK, JOHN T., bishop; b. L.A., July 16, 1937. Student, Los Angeles Diocesan sems. Ordained priest Roman Cath. Ch., 1963. Aux. bishop Diocese of Orange, Calif., 1984-87; bishop Diocese of Santa Rosa, Calif., 1987-91; titular bishop of Midila, 1984; bishop Diocese of Fresno, Calif., 1991—. Office: Diocese of Fresno PO Box 1668 1550N Fresno St Fresno CA 93717

STEINER, FREDERICK RAY, educator; b. Dayton, Ohio; s. John Frederick Jr. and Martha Jewell (Potts) S.; m. Anna Ostrowska, Feb. 5, 1981; children: Halina Jewell, Andrew John. BS, U. Cin., 1972, MCP, 1975; M in Regional Planning, U. Pa., 1977, MA, PhD, 1986. Adminstrv. asst. Newfields New Community, Dayton, 1970-72; environ. designer H.L. Malt Assocs., Washington, 1973; asst. design mgr. C.K.R. Investments, Columbia, Ill., 1974; community planner, organizer Downtown Community Ctr., Covington, Ky., 1975; outdoor recreation planner U.S. Nat. Park Svc., Phila., 1984; asst. to assoc. prof. Wash. State U., Pullman, 1977-87; from assoc. dir. to dir. Ctr. for Built Environ. Studies U. Colo., Denver, 1987-89, from assoc. prof. to prof. Sch. of Architecture and Planning, 1987-89; prof., chair Dept. Planning, Ariz. State U., Tempe, 1989—; ecol. planning cons. New Denver Internat. Airport, 1988-89; expert witness Yakima County, Wash., 1984; regional planning cons. Whitman County, Wash., Colfax, 1978-83. Author: The Living Landscape, 1991, Soil Conservation in the U.S., 1990; co-editor: Planning for Agroforestry, 1990, Land Conservation and Development, 1984; editorial bd. Jour. Planning Edn. and Rsch., Landscape Jour. Conservation colleague Nat. Pk. Svc., Washington, 1989—; coun. mem. Pullman Main St. Program, 1986-87; co-founder, bd. dirs. Pullman Civic Trust, 1983—; mem. planning commn. City of Pullman, 1978-79; bd. trustees Desert Bot. Garden, 1993—. Recipient Fulbright-Hays fellowship Netherlands Am. Commn. for Ednl. Exch., 1980. Mem. Am. Planning Assn., Coun. of Educators in Landscape Architecture (2d v.p. 1987-91), Soil and Water Conservation Soc. (bd. dirs. 1993—, program chair 1991, Pres. Citation 1991), Am. Soc. Landscape Architects (Nat. awards jury 1991), Lambda Alpha, Sigma Lambda Alpha. Home: 1830 E LaJolla Tempe AZ 85282 Office: Dept Planning Ariz State U Tempe AZ 85287-2005

STEINER, HERBERT MAX, physics educator; b. Goeppingen, Germany, Dec. 8, 1927; came to U.S., 1939, naturalized, 1944; s. Albert and Martha (Epstein) S. B.S., U. Calif., Berkeley, 1951, Ph.D., 1956. Physicist Lawrence Berkeley Lab., Berkeley, Calif., 1956—; mem. faculty U. Calif., Berkeley, 1958—, prof. physics, 1966—, William H. McAdams prof. physics, chmn. dept., 1992—; vis. scientist European Center Nuclear Research, 1960-61, 64, 68-69, 82-83, Max Planck Inst. Physics and Astrophysics, Munich, 1976-77; vis. prof. Japanese Soc. Promotion Sci., 1978; vis. prof. physics U. Paris, 1989-90. Author articles in field. Served with AUS, 1946-47. Recipient Sr. Am. Scientist award Alexander von Humboldt Found., 1976-77; Guggenheim fellow, 1960-61. Fellow Am. Phys. Soc. Office: U Calif Berkeley Dept Physics Berkeley CA 94720

STEINER, KENNETH DONALD, bishop; b. David City, Nebr., Nov. 25, 1936; s. Lawrence Nicholas and Florine Marie (Pieters) S. B.A., Mt. Angel Sem., 1958; M.Div., St. Thomas Sem., 1962. Ordained priest Roman Catholic Ch., 1962, bishop, 1978; asso. pastor various parishes Portland and Coos Bay, Oreg., 1962-72; pastor Coquille Ch., Myrtle Point, Powers, Oreg., 1972-76, St. Francis Ch., Roy, Oreg., 1976-77; aux. bishop Diocese of Portland, Oreg., 1977—; vicar of worship and ministries and personnel dir. clergy personnel Portland Archdiocese. Democrat. Office: 2838 E Burnside St Portland OR 97214-1895

STEINER, RICHARD RUSSELL, conglomerate executive; b. Chgo., Feb. 26, 1923; s. Frank Gardner and Ruth (Cowie) S.; m. Colleen M. Kearns, Dec. 6, 1949; children—Robert C., Kevin K., Sheila M. B.A., Dartmouth Coll., 1948. With Steiner Corp., Salt Lake City, 1948—; divisonal dir., v.p. Steiner Corp., 1951-59, pres., 1959—; dir. Am. Uniform Co. Served with USAAF, 1942-46. Decorated D.F.C. Mem. Phi Beta Kappa. Clubs: Alta, Salt Lake Country. Office: 505 E South Temple Salt Lake City UT 84102-1061

STEINHARDT, HENRY, photographer; b. N.Y.C., Nov. 15, 1920; s. Maxwell and Ruth (Davis) S.; m. Elizabeth Smith, 1946 (dec. 1955); children: Elizabeth, Maxwell; m. Helene Fleck, Feb. 1, 1958; 1 child, Henry III. AB, Harvard U., 1942, MArch, 1949. Registered architect. Office mgr. R.H. Cutting, Architect, N.Y.C., 1951-53; ptnr., architect Steinhardt & Thompson, Architects, N.Y.C., 1953-61; architect The Cerny Assocs., St. Paul, 1961-63, John Graham & Co., Seattle, 1963-67, Morse/Kirk, Seattle, 1967-68, N.G. Jacobson & Assocs., Seattle, 1968-69; pvt. practice Mercer Island, Wash., 1969-75; architect USN, Bremerton, Wash., 1975-78; photographer Mercer Island, 1979—. Prin. works exhibited at Washington, Seattle and Andover, Mass.; contbr. articles to fgn. archtl. jours. 1st lt. U.S. Army, 1943-46; capt. USAF, 1950-52. Recipient Design award Progressive Architecture, 1959, Archtl. award Fifth Ave. Assn., 1960. Fellow AIA. Democrat. Episcopalian. Home and Office: 7825 SE 63rd Pl Mercer Island WA 98040-4813

STEINHARDT, RICHARD ANTHONY, molecular and cell biology educator; b. Washington, Sept. 23, 1939; s. Jacinto and Hazel Steinhardt. AB in Zoology, Columbia U., 1961, PhD in Biol. Scis., 1966. Asst. prof. dept. zoology U. Calif., Berkeley, 1967-74, assoc. prof., 1974-79, prof., 1979-88, prof. molecular and cell biology, 1988—, Miller prof. basic sci., 1979-80; co-founder, minority ptnr. Ambion, Inc., Austin, Tex. Chmn. bd. dirs. The Crowden Sch., Berkeley, 1990—. NSF fellow Cambridge (Eng.) U., 1966-67, overseas fellow Churchill Coll., 1981. Fellow AAAS; mem. Soc. for Devel. Biology, Am. Soc. for Cell Biology. Home: 1508 Spruce St Berkeley CA 94709 Office: U Calif Dept Molecular and Cell Biology 391 LSA Berkeley CA 94720

STEINHART, DAWN ZUCKERMAN, artist; b. Stockton, Calif., Sept. 6, 1920; d. Roscoe Conkling and Florence Erna (Schwartz) Zuckerman; m. Carl Steinhar Jr., May 11, 1941; children: Sally, Carlsteinhart III. Student, Stockton Jr. Coll., 1938-39, Principia Coll., 1939-40, Coll. of the Pacific, Stockton, 1940-41. Mgr., owner art gallery Kahana Ki'i Gallery, Lihue, Hawaii, 1979-88, Koloa, Hawaii, 1989-92; head scenery dir. Stockton Ballet Guild, 1955-59. Recipient numerous art awards. Mem. Mokihana Club, Soc. of Artists, Kauai Hist. Soc., Kauai Concert Assn., Nat. Botanical Tropical Gardens, Nat. Pen Women's Assn. Home: 4321 Palama Rd Kalaheo HI 96741

STEINHAUSER, JOHN STUART (JACK STEINHAUSER), oil company executive; b. Grosse Pointe, Mich., Mar. 28, 1958; s. John William and Patricia Elizabeth (Mooney) S.; m. Barbara Jeanne Shirley, Aug. 23, 1985; children: Cassandra Lorraine, Robert William, Alexandra Elizabeth. BA in Econs., Claremont McKenna Coll., Claremont, Calif., 1979; M.Internat.Mgmt., U. Denver, 1982; postgrad., Inst. Superieur des Affairs, Jouyen-Josas, France, 1981. Fin. analyst Martin Marietta, Denver, 1980; intern analyst UN, Vienna, Austria, summer 1981; land mgr. Sharon Resources Inc., Englewood, Colo., 1982-84; exec. dir. Sharon Resources Inc., 1984-87, exec. v.p., 1987-88, pres., 1988—, CEO, 1992—; exec. v.p. Sharon Energy Ltd., Vancouver, B.C., 1987—; dir. Sharon Resources, Inc. Advisor Jr. Achievement, Parker, Colo., 1985-86; dir. Student Entrepreneurs, Parker, 1987-88; pres. Claremont McKenna Coll. Colo. Alumni Assn., Denver, 1988—. Mem. Racquet World. Republican. Lutheran. Office: Sharon Resources Inc 5995 Greenwood Plz Blvd Greenwood Village CO 80111

STEINHAUSER, JOHN WILLIAM, lawyer; b. Akron, Ohio, June 25, 1924; s. John Hugo and Francis Lillian (Pearson) S.; BSc in Bus. Adminstrn., Ohio State U., 1949; JD, U. Mich., 1950; m. Patricia E. Mooney, Dec. 1, 1956; children: John, Christian, Mark, Sharon. Bar: Colo. 1972, Mich. 1950. With Chrysler Corp., 1950-71, beginning as atty., successively dir. Latin Am., dir. export sales, gen. mgr. Africa-Far East, dir. Chrysler Internat., Geneva, dir. Africa-Far East, 1950-71; corp. atty., Denver, 1971—; founder, pres. Pearson Energy Corp., 1977, Sharon Energy, Ltd., Denver, 1980, also dir., 1971—. Sponsor Platte Valley Pony Club, Denver Symphony; active Colo. Rep. Party. With USNR, 1943-46. Mem. Colo. Bar Assn., Mich. Bar Assn., ABA, Soc. Internat. Law, Rocky Mountain Mineral Law Found., Cherry Hills Country Club, Naples Sailing & Yacht Club, Rotary (Denver). Home: 46 Charlou Cir Englewood CO 80111 Office: Sharon Resources Inc Ste 220 5995 Greenwood Plaza Blvd Englewood CO 80111-4714

STEINHAUSER, SHELDON ELI, communal executive, educator, consultant; b. N.Y.C., Aug. 11, 1930; s. Charles W. and Helen (Rosenstein) S.; m. Frances Goldfarb, June 28, 1953 (div. 1963); children: Karen, Lisa Steinhauser Hackel; m. Janice M. Glass, May 2, 1965; children: Shayle, David, Susan Hirschman. BS, L.I. U., 1963. Community cons. Anti-Defamation League, Columbus, Ohio, 1951-57; regional dir. Anti-Defamation League, Denver, 1957-85, dir. nat. field svcs., 1977-85, dir. nat. community svcs. divsn., 1979-81, western area dir., 1975-85; exec. v.p. Allied Jewish Fedn. of Denver, 1985-91; pres. Sheldon Steinhauser & Assocs., Denver, 1991—; asst. prof. sociology Met. State Coll., Denver, 1971—; arbitrator Am. Arbitration Assn., Denver, 1988—; pres. Anti-Defamation League Profl. Staff Assn., N.Y.C., Denver, 1967-70; chmn. Intergroup Agy. Orgn., Denver, 1963; past cons. EEOC. Leader Congl. Missions to Egypt and Israel, 1982, 83; staff dir. Mission to Israel, 1986, 87, 90; former mem. Denver Anti-Crime Coun.; chmn. Mountain States Inst. of Judaism, Denver, 1958-59; pres. Adult Edn. Coun. Met. Denver; past mem. community adv. bd. Jr. League Denver; mem. Colo. Martin Luther King Holiday Planning Com., Latin Am. Rsch. and Svc. Agy. Recipient M.L. King Jr. Humanitarian award Colo. M.L. King Commn., Denver, 1986, 1st Ann. Human Rels. award Colo. Civil Rights Commn., Denver, 1965, Humanitarian award NAACP, Denver, 1980, ADL Civil Rights Achievement award, 1989; named to Gallery of Fame, Denver Post, 1979, 80. Mem. Western Social Sci. Assn., Am. Sociol. Assn., Colo. Jewish Reconstructionist Fedn., Am. Soc. on Aging, Sociol. Practice Assn. (mem. Gov.'s Holocaust Com.), B'nai Brith (Columbus v.p., Denver).

STEINHOFF, MONIKA ANNELIESE, artist, educator; b. Swienemünde, East Germany, Oct. 19, 1941; came to U.S., 1947; d. Ernst August and Hildegard (Madee) S.; m. Daniel J. O'Friel, May 20, 1977; 1 child, Sean; adopted children: Paolo, Melissa, Heather. BA, UCLA, 1962, MA, 1964; postgrad., U. Calif., Berkeley, 1965-69; student, U. Saarbrucken of Munich, 1964-65. Tchr. Holy Name High Sch., Oakland, Calif., 1969-72; part-time tchr. Coll. of Santa Fe, 1973-80; freelance artist Santa Fe, 1979—. Bronze sculpture bust Werner von Braun, Smithsonian Inst., 1982; exhibited in group shows, including Southwest '90, Mus. of N.Mex., 1990, Fla. Mus. Latin Am. Art, 1993; 2-person show Edith Lambert Gallery, Santa Fe, 1990, Goethe Inst. Houston, 1991; 1-person show Peyton Wright Gallery, Santa Fe, 1991, Galarie Jakob Kohnert, Berlin, 1992, Dezember Salon, 1992, Taube Galarie; Gallery Representation: Turner Carrol, Santa Fe, Sherry French, Boca Raton, Fla.; Permanent Collection: Fine Arts Mus., N.Mex., Mus. of N.Mex. Mem. Environ. Task Force, Santa Fe, 1990—; participant All Species/Earth Day Painted Mural, Santa Fe, 1989, 90. Mem. Santa Fe Coun. for the Arts (artist's advocacy com.), One of a Kind Artists Coop. (pres. 1975-78). Home and Studio: 1298 Lejano Ln Santa Fe NM 87501

STEINMAN, BETTY ANN, human resources executive; b. Waterbury, Conn., Nov. 16, 1939; d. Harry I. and Rose (Levin) S.; m. M. Warner, Oct. 15, 1959 (dec. Oct. 18, 1965); m. Roger W. Gerhardt, Nov. 18, 1968 (div. Feb. 14, 1980). BFA, Julliard Sch. Music, 1962; MBA, Harvard U., 1983; postgrad., Cornell U., 1983-84. Sr. human resources profl. Music tchr. High Sch. System, Hartford, Conn., 1963-68; personnel adminstr. EDI/Windsor Gardens, Denver, 1968-72; personnel mgr. Opt, Dyne, Inc., Denver, 1972-78; mgr. employee rels. H.D. Heinz/ORE-Ida/FNI Div., Wethersfield, Conn., 1978-85; mgr. human resources UNIPAC, Denver, 1985-89; human resources cons. self-employed, Denver, 1985-86; dir. N.R.-Unipac, Denver, 1986-89; dir. human resources Mile High Equipment, Denver, 1989-90, CBMS, Inc., Denver, 1990—; founder, past pres., v.p., Conn. Personnel Assn., Hartford, 1980s. Contbr. articles, short stories and poems to profl. jours. and mags. Bd. dirs. Gen. Rose Meml. Hosp., Denver, 1970-75, Spl. Olympics, Hartford, 1978-85. Mem. ASTD, Soc. Human Resource Mgmt. (v.p. 1975-76), Colo. Human Resource Mgmt. Assn., Conn. Human Resource Mgmt. Assn. Office: CBMS Inc 208 S Kalamath St Denver CO 80223

STEINMAN, CLAYTON MARSHALL, communications educator, writer; b. N.Y.C., Aug. 11, 1950; s. Allan and Florence (Liebman) S.; m. Patricia Lynn Garrett, Aug. 21, 1976; 1 child, Daniel P. Garrett-Steinman. BA, Duke U., 1971; MS, Columbia U., 1972; MA, NYU, 1976, PhD, 1979. Reporter, film reviewer Vancouver (Wash.) Columbian newspaper, 1972-73; reporter Capitol Hill News Svc., Washington, 1973-74; editorial writer The Nation, N.Y.C., 1975-76; asst. prof. communications Fla. Atlantic U., Boca Raton, 1977-82, assoc. prof., 1982-89; prof. communications Calif. State U., Bakersfield, 1989—; editorial advisor New China News Agy., Beijing, 1985-86. Contbr. numerous articles to profl. mags. Mem. NEA, Assn. for Edn. in Journalism and Mass Communication, Calif. Faculty Assn., Soc. for Cinema Studies, Speech Communication Assn., Union for Democratic Communications, Univ. Film & Video Assn., United Faculty of Fla. (pres. Fla. Atlantic U. chpt. 1988-89). Mem. Green Party. Jewish. Office: Calif State U Bakersfield Dept English & Communications 9001 Stockdale Hwy Bakersfield CA 93311-1022

STEINMAN, JOHN FRANCIS, psychiatrist; b. N.Y.C., May 5, 1916; s. David Barnard and Irene Stella (Hoffman) S.; m. Helen G. Meyer (div. 1963); children: James, Judith, Jill; m. Roxane Bear (div. 1972); m. Ellen M. Sears, Nov. 16, 1985. AB with hons., Columbia U., 1936, MD, 1940. Diplomate Am. Bd. Psychiatry and Neurology. Intern Strong Meml. Hosp., Rochester, N.Y. and Cin. Gen. Hosp., 1940-43; resident psychiatry Nebr. Psychiat. Inst., 1948, 58, R.I. Med. Ctr., 1961; psychiatrist, dir. Lincoln (Nebr.) and Lancaster County Child Guidance Ctr., 1948-61; instr. pediatrics, psychiatry and neurology U. Nebr., Lincoln, 1951-52; postdoctoral fellow in psychiatry Yale U., New Haven, Conn., 1962-64; psychiatrist U. Conn., Storrs, 1964-69, Community Mental Health Services, San Francisco, 1971-79; pvt. practice psychiatry San Francisco, 1979—. Delgate, chmn. Nebr. health com. White House Conf. Children and Youth, Washington, 1960. Served to capt. M.C., AUS, 1943-46, PTO. Mem. Am. Psychiat. Assn. (life), Am. Orthopsychiat. Assn., N.Y. Acad. Scis., Phi Beta Kappa. Home and Office: 164 Otsego Ave San Francisco CA 94112-2590

STEINMAN, LISA MALINOWSKI, English literature educator, writer; b. Willimantic, Conn., Apr. 8, 1950; d. Zenon Stanislaus and Shirley Belle (Nathanson) Malinowski; m. James A. Steinman, Apr. 1968 (div. 1980); m. James L. Shugrue, July 23, 1984. BA, Cornell U., 1971, MFA, 1973, PhD, 1976. Asst. prof. English Reed Coll., Portland, Oreg., 1976-82, assoc. prof., 1982-90, prof., 1990—, Kenan prof. English lit. and humanities, 1993—; cons. NEH, Washington, 1984-85. Author: Lost Poems, 1976, Made in America, 1987, All That Comes To Light, 1989, A Book of Other Days, 1992; editor Hubbub Mag., 1983—; editorial bd. Williams Rev., 1991—; contbr. articles to profl. jours. Fellow Nat. Endowment for Arts, 1984, Oreg. Arts Commn., 1983-84, NEH, 1983, Danforth Found., 1971-75; recipient Pablo Neruda award, 1987; Rockefeller Found. scholar, 1987-88. Mem. MLA, Poets and Writers, PEN (N.W. chpt., co-founder, officer 1989—). Home: 5344 SE 38th Ave Portland OR 97202-4208 Office: Reed Coll Dept English 3203 SE Woodstock Blvd Portland OR 97202-8199

STEINMANN, JOHN COLBURN, architect; b. Monroe, Wis., Oct. 24, 1941; s. John Wilbur and Irene Marie (Steil) S.; m. Susan Koslosky, Aug. 12, 1978 (div. July 1989). BArch., U. Ill., 1964; postgrad. Ill. Inst. Tech., 1970-71; Project designer C.F. Murphy Assocs., Chgo., 1968-71, Steinmann Architects, Monticello, Wis., 1971-73; design chief, chief project architect State of Alaska, Juneau, 1973-78; project designer Mithun Assos., architects, Bellevue, Wash., 1978-80; owner, prin. John C. Steinmann Assos., Architect, Kirkland, Wash., 1980—; bd. dirs. Storytell Internat.; lectr. Ill. Inst. Tech., 1971-72; prin. works include: Grant Park Music Bowl, Chgo., 1971, Menomonee Falls (Wis.) Med. Clinic, 1972, Hidden Valley Office Bldg., Bellevue, 1978, Kezner Office Bldg., Bellevue, 1979, The Pines at Sunriver, Oreg., 1980, also Phase II, 1984, Phase III, 1986, The Pines at Sunriver Lodge Bldg., 1986, 2d and Lenora highrise, Seattle, 1981, Bob Hope Cardiovascular Research Inst. lab. animal facility, Seattle, 1982, Wash. Ct., Bellevue, 1982, Anchorage Bus. Park, 1982, Garden Townhouses, Anchorage, 1983, Vacation Internationale, Ltd. corp. hdqrs., Bellevue, 1983, Vallarta Torres III, Puerto Vallarta, Mex., 1987, Torres Mazatlan (Mex.) II, 1988, Canterwood Townhouses, Gig Harbor Wash., 1988, Inn at Ceres (Calif.), 1989, Woodard Creek Inn, Olympia, Wash., 1989, Northgate Corp. Ctr., Seattle, 1990, Icicle Creek Hotel and Restaurant, Leavenworth, Wash., 1990, Bellingham (Wash.) Market Pl., 1990, Boeing Hot Gas Test Facility, Renton, Wash., 1991, Boeing Longacres Customer Svc. Tng. Ctr. Support Facilities, Renton, 1992, also pvt. residences. Served to 1st lt. C.E., USAR, 1964-66; Vietnam. Decorated Bronze Star. Registered architect, Wash., Oreg., Calif., N.Mex., Ariz., Utah, Alaska, Wis., Ill. Mem. AIA, Am. Mgmt. Assn., Nat. Council Archtl. Registration Bds., Alpha Rho Chi. Republican. Roman Catholic. Clubs: U. Wash. Yacht, Columbia Athletic. Address: 4316 106th Pl NE Kirkland WA 98033

STEINMETZ, JOHN CHARLES, paleontologist, geologist; b. St. Paul, Sept. 26, 1947; s. Charles Leonard and Ruth Naomi (Osteraas) S.; m. Sarah Cook Tristán, May 29, 1982; children: Katherine Ruth, Elizabeth Margaret. BS, U. Ill., 1969, MS, 1975; PhD, U. Miami, 1977. Asst. prof. U. South Fla., St. Petersburg, 1977-82; advanced rsch. geologist Marathon Oil Co., Littleton, Colo., 1982-86, sr. geologist, 1986-90, advanced sr. geologist, 1990—; bd. dirs. Scanning Electron Microscope Facility U. South Fla., 1980-82; chief fin. officer Palynodata, Inc., Reno, Nev., 1989—. Mem. bd. advisors Micropaleontology Press, N.Y.C., 1986—. Trustee Paleontol. Rsch. Instn., Ithaca, N.Y., 1990—, v.p., 1992—; trustee Arapahoe Libr. Dist., 1993—. Mem. Am. Assn. Petroleum Geologists, Am. Assn. Stratiographic Palynologists, Internat. Nannoplankton Assn. (U.S. treas. 1982-92), Brit. Micropaleontol. Soc., Paleontol. Soc., Soc. Econ. Paleontologists and Mineralogists (mem. publs. com. 1987-92). Home: 6043 S Cherrywood Cir Littleton CO 80121-2407 Office: Marathon Oil Co Denver Rsch Ctr 7400 S Broadway Littleton CO 80122-2609

STEINMETZ, WAYNE EDWARD, chemistry educator; b. Huron, Ohio, Feb. 16, 1945; s. Ralph Freeman and Helen Louise (Rossman) S. AB, Oberlin Coll., 1967; AM, Harvard U., 1968, PhD, 1973. Asst. prof. chemistry Pomona Coll., Claremont, Calif., 1973-79, assoc. prof., 1979-88; prof. Pomona Coll., Claremont, 1988-91, Carnegie prof., 1991—; akademischer Gast (vis. prof.) Eidgenössiche Technische Hochschule, Zurich, Switzerland, 1979-80, 86-87. Contbr. articles on spectroscopy and molecular structure to profl. jours. Scoutmaster, adult leader trainer Old Baldy council Boy Scouts Am., 1973—. Fellow NSF, Woodrow Wilson Found.; recipient Dist. Merit award Boy Scouts Am., 1978, Silver Beaver award, Boy Scouts Am., 1993. Mem. AAUP, Am. Chem. Soc., Phi Beta Kappa (local sec.-treas. 1980-89). Democrat. Roman Catholic. Home: 1081 W Cascade Pl Claremont CA 91711-2525 Office: Pomona Coll Dept Chemistry 645 N College Ave Claremont CA 91711-6338

STEKOLL, MICHAEL STEVEN, biochemist, marine biologist, educator; b. Tulsa, May 7, 1947; s. Marion H. and Virginia (Bell) S.; m. Deborah Hansen, Apr. 20, 1976; children: Justin, Skye, Spencer, Kokii. BS in Chemistry, Stanford U., 1971; PhD in Biochemistry, UCLA, 1976. Postdoctoral fellow U. Alaska, Fairbanks, 1976-78; rsch. biochemist Nat. Marine Fisheries Service, Auke Bay, Alaska, 1979; asst. prof. chemistry U. Alaska, Juneau, 1978-83, from assoc. prof. to prof. chemistry and biochemistry, 1983-91; from assoc. prof. to prof. chemistry and biochemistry U. Alaska, Southeast, Fairbanks, 1991—. Contbr. articles to profl. jours. Mem. AAAS, Phycol. Soc. Am., Western Soc. Naturalists. Office: U Alaska Juneau Fisheries and Ocean Scis 11120 Glacier Hwy Juneau AK 99801-8625

STELL, JOE M., JR., state legislator; b. Wilson, Tex., June 15, 1928; s. Joe M. Sr. and Mary Louise (Stiles) S.; m. Verna Jeanne Renfro, Aug. 30, 1948; children: James William, Cathy Jeanne Stell Kinzer, Jo Beth Stell Hawk, Linda Lee. BS, U. N.Mex., 1950; MS, Western N.Mex. U., 1956; postgrad., N.Mex. State U., Ea. N.Mex. U., 1960-80. Tchr., coach Deming (N.Mex.) Pub. Schs., 1950-53, Carlsbad (N.Mex.) Mcpl. Schs., 1953-86; rancher, farmer Eddy County, Carlsbad, 1955—; mem. dist. 54 N.Mex. Ho. Reps., Carlsbad and Artesia, 1986—. Bd. dirs. Eddy County Soil and Water Conservation, Carlsbad, 1986; active Mountain States Legal Found., Denver, 1980, Eddy County Sheriff's Posse, Carlsbad, 1986. Named Outstanding Legislator, N.Mex. Farm and Livestock Bur., 1992. Mem. NEA, N.Mex. Cattle Growers, S.E. N.Mex. Grazing Assn., Elks, Carlsbad Sportsman Club. Democrat. Methodist. Home: 22 Colwell Ranch Rd Carlsbad NM 88220 Office: Hat Bar Ranch 1705 Quay Carlsbad NM 88220

STELLWAGEN, ROBERT HARWOOD, biochemistry educator; b. Joliet, Ill., Jan. 6, 1941; s. Harwood John and Alma Dorothy (Handorf) S.; m. Joanne Kovacs, June 15, 1963; children: Robert Harwood, Alise Anne. AB, Harvard U., 1963; PhD, U. Calif.-Berkeley, 1968. Staff fellow NIH, Bethesda, Md., 1968-69; postdoctoral scholar U. Calif.-San Francisco, 1969-70; asst. prof. biochemistry U. So. Calif., L.A., 1970-74, assoc. prof., 1974-80, prof., 1980—, chmn. dept., 1981-86; vis. scientist Nat. Inst. for Med. Research, Mill Hill, Eng., 1979. Contbr. articles to profl. jours. Recipient Henderson prize Harvard U., 1963; NSF fellow, 1963-67; NIH grantee, 1971-84. Mem. AAAS, Am. Soc. Biochemistry and Molecular Biology, Sierra Club, Phi Beta Kappa. Democrat. Office: U So Calif 2011 Zonal Ave Los Angeles CA 90033-1054

STEMMER, JAY JOHN, safety engineer, consultant; b. Wilkes-Barre, Pa., Apr. 29, 1939. BSCE, N.J. Inst. Tech., 1962; MBA, Calif. State U., Long Beach, 1969. Registered profl. engr., Calif.; cert. safety profl.; cert. hazard control mgmt. Engr. Factory Mut., N.J., 1973-77; cons. McKay & Assoc., Calif., 1977-81, Index Research, Calif., 1981-83, Fireman's Fund, Calif., 1983-85, AIG Cons., Calif., 1985-87; sr. cons. Argonaut, Calif., 1987—; assoc. prof. Sierra Coll., Los Angeles, 1979-80. Author: Medical Manual of Industrial Toxicology, 1965, Latin America, A Study of Air Transport Development and Potential in the Decade Ahead, 1970. Served to lt. USAF, 1962-65. Mem. NSPE, Calif. Soc. Profl. Engrs., Am. Soc. Safety Engrs., Am. Bd. Motion Pictures and TV Engrs., Screen Actors Guild, Actors Equity Assn., AFTRA. Home: 1935 Alpha Rd Ste 225 Glendale CA 91208

STEMPER, MARILYN MILLER, manufacturing management consultant; b. Cleve., Sept. 22, 1962; d. Daniel D. and Jocyce Beverly Miller; m. Jack Stemper, Sept 3, 1989. BSBA, Ohio State U., 1984. Shop scheduler Martin Marietta Missile Systems, Orlando, Fla., 1984-86; sr. fin. adminstr. Martin Marietta Missile Systems, Orlando, 1986-89; mfg. cons. Price, Waterhouse, Costa Mesa, Calif., 1989—. Author: (methodology) Conf. Room Pilot, 1992. Mem. Assn. for Mfg. Excellence, Am. Prodn. and Inventory Control Soc. (cert. prodn. and inventory mgr., bd. dirs. 1984—, tchr. 1991—). Home: 17 Amistad Irvine CA 92720

STEMPLE, ALAN DOUGLAS, aerospace engineer; b. Elkins, W.Va., July 19, 1963; s. Stephen Warren and C. Phyllis (Cavalier) S. BS cum laude, Davis and Elkins Coll., 1984; BS in Aero. Engring. cum laude, W.Va. U., 1985; MS, U. Md., 1986, PhD, 1989. Rotorcraft fellow Ctr. for Rotorcraft Edn. and Rsch., U. Md., College Park, 1985-89; structures rsch. engr. McDonnell Douglas Helicopter Co., Mesa, Ariz., 1989—; reviewer tech. papers, 1990—. Contbr. articles to profl. publs. Army Rotorcraft fellow U. Md., 1985-89. Mem. AIAA, Am. Helicopter Soc. (Vertical Flight Found. scholar 1988). Home: 1233 N Mesa Dr #2084 Mesa AZ 85201-2763 Office: McDonnell Douglas Mail Stop 530/B337 5000 E McDowell Rd Mesa AZ 85205-9797

STENDER, CHARLES FREDERICK, aeronautical operations manager; b. East Orange, N.J., Nov. 17, 1940; s. Robert Conrad and Ruth Warne (Cobb) S. BSCE, Pa. State U., 1962; MS in Systems Mgmt., U. So. Calif., University Park, Calif., 1982. Commd. ensign USN, 1962; advanced through grades to capt. USNR, 1983, ret., 1991; naval aviator USN, various, 1962-72; test pilot Grumman Aerospace, Point Mugu, Calif., 1972-77; airline pilot TWA, L.A., 1977-80; mgr., test pilot Hughes Aircraft Co., L.A., 1980—. Decorated Disting. Flying Cross (3), Vietnam, Air medal (13), Vietnam, Navy Commendation medal. Mem. Soc. Exptl. Test Pilots (assoc. fellow), Tailhook Assn., Air Line Pilots Assn. Office: Hughes Aircraft Co 16101 Saticoy St Van Nuys CA 91406-2915

STENDER, LAURA LYN, scientific researcher; b. Reno, May 24, 1960; d. Ernest Leo and Carol Suzanne (Kettering) Whitaker; m. Lee Stender, May 21, 1983; children: Jackie, Justin, Jason. AA, Scottsdale Community Coll., 1982. Habilitation technician Gomper's Rehab. Ctr. and Ariz. Tng. Program, Phoenix, 1979-82; sec., bookkeeper CEW Sound Recordings, Phoenix, 1979-82; sec. Electronic Test Ctr., Groton, Mass., 1984; exec. v.p., dir. sci. rsch., devel. and investment Children United to Save the Planet, Phoenix, 1991—. Mem. Mentally Ill Kids In Distress, Phoenix, 1990, Lithium Alliance, Phoenix, 1992, Nat. Alliance for Mentally Ill, Phoenix, 1992, Smithsonian Inst., 1992. Named Internat. Woman of Yr., Internat. Biog. Ctr., England, 1991-92, Woman of Yr., Am. Biog. Inst., 1992; recipient Silver Shield of Honor, 1992. Mem. NAFE (assoc.), World Found. Successful Women (assoc.), Women's Inner Circle of Achievement, Lifetime Achievement Acad., Am. Biog. Inst. Rsch. Assn. (assoc. and advisor). Office: Children United Save Planet PO Box 54964 Phoenix AZ 85078-4964

STENGELE, HARRY EVEREST, manager, technical company administrator; b. San Antonio, July 29, 1945; s. Harry E. and Hazel Dean (Maverick) S.; m. Nancy Burkett, Aug. 28, 1947; children: William, John. BBA in Fin., Tex. A&M U., 1967; MBA, Sam Houston State U., 1968. Dir. adminstrn. Acurex Corp., Mountain View, Calif., 1972-87; v.p. fin. and adminstrn. Aptech Engring. Svcs., Inc., Sunnyvale, Calif., 1987—; bd. dirs. CMT Communications, Santa Clara, Calif. Capt. USAF, 1968-72. Mem. Nat. Contracts Mgmt. Assn., Am. Electronics Assn. (govt.-bus. com. 1980—). Republican. Episcopalian. Home: 104 Ann Arbor Ct Los Gatos CA 95032 Office: Aptech Engring Svcs Inc 1282 Reamwood St Sunnyvale CA 94089

STENGER, MARTIN LANE, financial planner; b. Dallas, Jan. 13, 1949; s. Tressie Marie (Merritt) S.; m. Miriam Rose Yant, Mar. 5, 1972; children: Jason Alexander, Michael Lawrence, Amanda Marie. AA, Riverside Community Coll., 1969; BA, Calif. State U., 1972. V.p. United Calif. Bus. & Estate, Riverside, 1975-80; prin. Perkins, Stenger, Baird & Staffieri, San Bernardino, Calif., 1980-83; pres. Consol. Westchester Fin., Riverside, 1983—. Contbr. articles to profl. jours. Bd. dirs. Estate Planning Coun., Riverside, 1983—. Mem. Am. Soc. Pension Actuaries, Internat. Assn. Registered Fin. Planners, Internat. Assn. Fin. Planners, Life Underwriters Assn. (pres. 1981). Republican. Mem. LDS Ch. Office: Consol Westchester Fin 3741 Merced Dr Ste F2 Riverside CA 92503

STENGER, VICTOR JOHN, physics educator; b. Bayonne, N.J., Jan. 29, 1935; s. Victor and Mary (Wagner) S.; m. Phyllis Marcia Black, Oct. 6, 1962; children: Noelle, Victor Andrew. BS, Newark Coll. Engring., 1956; MS, UCLA, 1958, PhD, 1963. Engr. Hughes Aircraft Co., Culver City, Calif., 1956-59; grad. asst. UCLA, 1959-63; prof. physics U. Hawaii, Honolulu, 1963—; vis. prof. U. Heidelberg, Germany, 1967-68, Oxford (England) U., 1977-78, INFN, Frascati, Italy, 1987; co-prin. investigator DUMAND Project, Honolulu, 1980—. Author: Not By Design, 1988, Physics and Psychics, 1990. Mem. Humanists Hawaii (pres. 1990—), Hawaii Secular Humanists (chair 1990—). Office: U Hawaii Dept Physics 2505 Correa Rd Honolulu HI 96822

STENNETT, WILLIAM CLINTON (CLINT STENNETT), television station executive, state legislator; b. Winona, Minn., Oct. 1, 1956; s. William Jessie and Carole Lee (Halsey) S. BA in Journalism, Idaho State U., 1979. Gen. mgr. Wood River Jour., Hailey, Idaho, pres., pub.; pres. Sta. KWRV-TV, Ketchum, Idaho; mem. Idaho Ho. of Reps., Boise, 1990—. Recipient Gen. Excellence award Idaho Newspaper Assn., 1985, 86, 87. Mem. Rotary Internat., Ketchum Sun Valley C. of C. (bd. dirs. 1990—). Democrat.

STENSTROM, MICHAEL KNUDSON, civil engineering educator; b. Anderson, S.C., Nov. 28, 1948; s. Edward Farnum and Virginia Frances (Garrett) S.; m. Linda Ann Moxley, Aug. 15, 1974 (div. Nov. 1976); m. Margaret Merle Allen, Jan. 13, 1977. BSEE, Clemson U., 1971, MS in Environ. Engring., 1972, PhD in Environ. Engring., 1976. Registered profl. engr., Calif. Project mgr. Amoco Oil Co., Naperville, Ill., 1975-77; asst. prof. civil engring. UCLA, 1977-81, assoc. prof., 1981-84, prof., 1984—, dir. Engring. Computer Ctr., 1985-89, asst. dean, 1989—, chair dept. Civil Engring, 1991—; cons. on pollution control to numerous cos. and state and city govts. Contbr. articles to profl. jours. Chmn. sci. adv. bd. Heal-the-Bay, L.A., 1987-88. With USAF, 1969-70. Recipient numerous grants. Mem. ASCE (Walter L. Huber award 1989), Am. Acad. Environ. Engrs., Assn. Environ. Engring. Profs., Water Environ. Fedn. (Harrison Prescott Eddy medal 1992), Internat. Assn. on Water Quality, Am. Chem. Soc., Blue Key, Sigma Xi, Tau Beta Pi. Democrat. Home: 1829 S Crescent Heights Los Angeles CA 90035 Office: 4173 Engring I 4173 Boelter Hall Los Angeles CA 90024-1600

STENTZ, STEVEN THOMAS, researcher, systems analyst; b. Sidney, Nebr., May 4, 1951; s. Howard William and Orletha Maxine (Gardner) S.; m. Patricia Marie Thompson, Oct. 9, 1971 (div. 1979); 1 child, Carrie Lee; m. Barbara Ann Willie, Dec. 29, 1990. BA magna cum laude, We. Wash. U., 1979; MS, U. Wash., 1982, doctoral postgrad., 1982-85. Counselor Auburn (Wash.) Youth Svcs., 1977-79, Renton (Wash.) Area Youth Svcs., 1980; research analyst Dept. Social & Health Svcs., Olympia, Wash., 1981-82; computer, rsch. cons. U. Wash., Seattle, 1982-85, instr., 1986; instr. We. Wash. U., Bellingham, 1986-88; systems analyst S. Stentz & Assocs., Olympia, 1981—; researcher Wash. Supreme Ct., Olympia, 1986—; Mem. Human Subjecs Rev. Com. U. Wash., Seattle, 1982-85; cons. King County Dept. of Youth Svcs., Seattle, 1984-88, Wash. Assn. Rehab. Psychologists, Seattle, 1983-88, King County Health Planning Coun., Seattle, 1983-84, Children's Home Soc. Wash., Seattle, 1985-86. Contbr. articles to profl. jours.; author software reference manuals. Speaker Assn. Hosp. Adminstrs., 1983-86, Coun. Social Work Edn., Detroit, 1983, Alliance for Children, Youth and Families, Seattle, 1986, Pacific Northwest Assn. Hosp. Adminstrs., 1983-86, Ann. Wash. Jud. Conf., 1987-91, Dist. and Mcpl. Judges Spring Conf., 1988-89, Wash. State Assn. County Clks., 1988-92. With U.S. Army, 1971-72.

STEPANEK, JOSEPH EDWARD, industrial development consultant; b. Ellinwood, Kans., Oct. 29, 1917; s. Joseph August and Leona Mae (Wilson) S.; m. Antoinette Farnham, June 10, 1942; children: Joseph F., James B., Antoinette L., Debra L. BSChemE, U. Colo., 1939; DEng in Chem. Engring., Yale U., 1942. Registered profl. engr., Colo. Engr. Stearns-Roger

Mfg., Denver, 1939-45; from asst. to assoc. prof. U. Colo., Boulder, 1945-47; from cons. to dir. UN, various countries, 1947-73; cons. internat. indsl devel., U.S.-China bus. relations Boulder, 1973—; bd. dirs. 12 corps., 1973—. Author 3 books on indsl. devel.; contbr. 50 articles to profl. jours. Exec. dir. Boulder Tomorrow, 1965-67. Recipient Yale Engring. award Yale Engring. Assn., 1957, Norlin award U. Colo. 1978, Annual award India League of Am., 1982. Mem. AAAS. Democrat. Unitarian. Club: Yale (N.Y.C.). Home: 1622 High St Boulder CO 80304-4224

STEPHAN, JOHN DAVID, ophthalmologist; b. Columbus, Ohio, July 25, 1926; s. Lewis B. and Dorothy Fair (Fuller) S.; m. Phyllis Jean Proctor, July 8, 1950 (div. June 1990); children: Peggy Jean, John William, Sarah Louise; m. Y'vonne Marie Kime, July 27, 1990. AB, Oberlin Coll., 1950; MSc, Ohio State U., 1955, MD, 1956. Diplomate Am. Bd. Ophthalmology. Intern Mercy Hosp., Toledo, Ohio, 1956-57; resident Univ. Hosp., Columbus, 1957-60; clin. instr. dept. ophthalmology Ohio State U., Columbus, 1960-69, clin. asst. prof. dept. indsl. and aviation medicine, 1960-69; ophthalmologist Western Mont. Clinic, Missoula, 1969-71; ophthalmologist in pvt. practice Kalispell, Mont., 1971—; lectr. ophthalmology FAA med. seminars, 1962—. Mem. Coun. on Aging, Kalispell, 1992, Am. 2000 Com., Kalispell, 1992. Pvt. USAAC, 1945-46. Mem. AMA (Physicians award 1992), Am. Acad. Ophthalmology, Mont. Acad. Ophthalmology, Mont. Med. Assn., Glacier Eagles Soaring Club (sec.), Mont. Pilots Assn. (pres. 1979), Kalispell Unitarian Fellowship (vice chmn. 1992), Kiwanis. Office: Family Eye Clinic 1286 Burns Way Kalispell MT 59901

STEPHEN, WILLIAM PROCURONOFF, entomologist, educator; b. St. Boniface, Manitoba, Canada, June 6, 1927; s. Steven and Amalia (Hoppe) S.; m. Dorris Jo Williams, June 8, 1952; children: Dana Ann, Jan Marie, Mary Beth, William Thaddeus. BS, U. Manitoba, 1948; postgrad., Iowa State U., 1949-50; PhD, U. Kans., 1952. Asst. assoc. entomologist Canada-Agriculture, Brandon, Ottawa, 1946-53; from asst. prof. to assoc. prof. Oreg. State U., Corvallis, 1953—, prof., 1963—; cons. OAS, Santiago, Chile, 1971-72; program dir. FAO, Buenos Aires, 1973-76; dir. Junto Inc., Corvallis. Contbr. articles to profl. jours. Mem. Entomol. Soc. Am., Kans. Entomol. Soc., Internat. Bee Rsch. Assn., Soc. Study Evolution. Democrat. Office: Oreg State U Corvallis OR 97331

STEPHENS, ALBERT LEE, JR., federal judge. Judge U.S. Dist. Ct. (cen. dist.) Calif., Los Angeles. Office: US Dist Ct 312 N Spring St Los Angeles CA 90012-4701

STEPHENS, DANIEL AMOS, biology educator; b. Twin Falls, Idaho, Dec. 30, 1955; s. Edward and Maria Luisa (Ferbal) S.; m. Pamela ann McHargue, Sept. 25, 1978; children: Zachary Amos, William Rush. AS, Treasure Valley C.C., 1976; BS, Boise State U., 1981; MS, Cen. Wash. U., 1985; ArtsD, Idaho State U., 1990. Smokejumper U.S. Forest Svc., McCall, Idaho, 1978-83; naturalist Cispus Environ. Ctr., Radle, Wash., 1985-87; biology instr. Treasure Valley C.C., Ontario, Oreg., 1990, Idaho State U., Pocatello, 1989; biology prof. Wenatchee (Wash.) Valley Coll., 1990—; master bird bander U.S. Fish and Wildlife Svc., Laurel, Md., 1986—; rschr., cons. BLM, Wenatchee. Author: Idaho Bird Distribution, 1991; contbr. articles to profl. jours. Mem. Nat. Assn. of Biology Tchrs., Soc. of N.W. Vertebrate Biology, Am. Ornthologists Union, NC Wash. Audubon Soc. (pres. 1991-92), Western Bird Banding Assn., We Field Ornithologists, Phi Kappa Phi, Sigma Xi. Office: Wenatchee Valley Coll Biology Dept 1300 5th St Wenatchee WA 98801

STEPHENS, DAVID BISEL, college administrator; b. Tooele, Utah, Apr. 23, 1944; s. Francis John and Gwendolyn (Bisel) S.; m. Susan Williams, Dec. 22, 1965; children: Robert David, Audrey, Wendy, Sally. BA, Brigham Young U., 1968; MBA, U. Pitts., 1969; PhD, U. Tex., Austin, 1975. Asst. prof. Fla. State U., Tallahassee, 1974-76, Tex. Tech. U., Lubbock, 1976-78; prof., chair dept. bus. U. Tex., El Paso, 1978-85; prof., dean Coll. Bus. Utah State U., Logan, 1985—. Co-author: Strategic Management and Policy, 1985; contbr. articles to profl. publs. Mem. Indsl. Rels. Rsch. Assn., Am. Arbitration Assn. (panel of arbitrators). Republican. Mormon. Home: 1725 E 1220 N Logan UT 84321-3041 Office: Coll Bus Utah State Univ Logan UT 84322-3500

STEPHENS, FREDRIC MILO, airline pilot; b. Laredo, Tex., Sept. 24, 1955; s. Albert Milo and Wanda Joann (White) S.; m. Marcia Lynn MacSwain, Sept. 30, 1989; 1 child, Taylor Lane. BA in Polit. Sci., U. N.Mex., 1977; MBA, U. Fla., 1987. Commd. ensign USN, 1977, pilot trainee, 1977-79, maintenance officer, patrol plane comdr., 1979-82, instr. pilot, 1982-85; resigned, 1985; pilot Northwest Airlines, Inc., Mpls., 1985—. Comdr. USNR, 1985—. Mem. Airline Pilots Assn., Naval Inst., Experimental Aircraft Assn. Democrat. Presbyterian. Address: 3611 350th Ave W Oak Harbor WA 98277

STEPHENS, JEFFREY DANIEL, pharmacist, owner; b. El Paso, Tex., May 4, 1954; s. Otis Daniel and Emma Katharine (Scruggs) S.; m. Carrie Ruth Jordan, May 21, 1982; children: Scott Daniel, Mark Jeffrey. BS in Biology, Memphis (Tenn.) State U., 1977; Bs in Pharmacy, U. N.Mex., 1986. Pharmacy intern U. N.Mex. Hosp., Albuquerque, 1983-87; staff pharmacist Smiths Food and Drug, Albuquerque, 1987-90; owner, pharmacist Jeff's Valley Pharmacy, Colorado City, Colo., 1990—. Vol. EMT Rye (Colo.) Fire Dept., 1992—. Mem. Pueblo County Pharm. Assn. Republican. Hme: P O Box 543 Colorado City CO 81019 Office: 4491 Bent Brothers Blvd Colorado City CO 81019

STEPHENS, LARRY DEAN, engineer; b. Sterling, Colo., Sept. 1, 1937; s. John Robert and Shirley Berniece (Rudel) S.; m. Carol Ann Wertz, Sept. 1, 1957 (div. May 1975); children: Deborah Lynn, Janell Diane, Dana Larry, Hilary Elizabeth Melton. BS in Engring., Colo. State U., 1960; MBA, U. Colo., 1967. Registered profl. engr., Colo. Engr. Bur. Reclamation, Denver, 1960-90, cons., 1991—; exec. v.p. U.S. Com. on Irrigation and Drainage, Denver, 1971—; exec. dir. U.S. Com. on Large Dams, Denver, 1986—. V.p. Internat. Commn. on Irrigation and Drainage, 1989-92. With USNG, 1961-62. Mem. Am. Soc. Agrl. Engrs., Assn. State Dam Safety Officials, Colo. River Water Users Assn., Coun. on Engring. and Sci. Soc. Execs. Republican. Methodist. Home: 1625 Larimer St Apt 1505 Denver CO 80202-1532 Office: USCID 1616 17th St Ste 483 Denver CO 80202-1277

STEPHENS, LEE AMIEL, business development executive; b. Indpls., Dec. 9, 1962; s. Philip David and Verlee Ester (Foertsch) S.; m. Linda Anne Montrois, Mar. 14, 1986; 1 child, Philip Sterling. Student, Phoenix Coll., 1982, Scottsdale (Ariz.) Community Coll., 1982-83. Supr. automotive testing Lighting Scis., Inc., Scottsdale, Ariz., 1982-88; product design engr. Sylvania div. GTE, Seymour, Ind., 1988-90; bus. development mgr. Lighting Scis., Inc., Scottsdale, Ariz., 1990-91; sales engr. Hoffman Engring. Corp., Phoenix, Ariz., 1992—. Pres. Pepper Ridge Townhomes Homeowner's Assn., Phoenix, 1986-88. Named Explorer of the Yr. Boy Scouts Am., Phoenix, 1981. Mem. Soc. Automotive Engrs., Illuminating Engring. Soc. (edn. chmn. Ariz. sect. 1986-87), Nat. Eagle Scout Assn., Nat. Assn. Outstanding Jr. & Community Coll. Students, Elks. Republican. Methodist. Office: Hoffman Engring 3432 E Utopia St Phoenix AZ 85024

STEPHENS, MARIA CARMELA, environmental planner, aviation planner; b. Altoona, Pa., Nov. 5, 1963; m. H. Jackson Stephens, Sept. 29, 1990. BS in Environ. Resource Mgmt., Pa. State U., 1985. Planning intern Blair County Planning Commn., Hollidaysburg, Pa., 1984-85; airport planner L. Robert Kimball & Assocs., Ebensburg, Pa., 1985-86, Howard Needles Tammen & Bergendoff, Alexandria, Va., 1986-90; environ. specialist Washington Met. Airports Authority, 1990; airport, environ. planner Belt Collins & Assocs., Honolulu, 1990—. Mem. Nat. Assn. Environ. Profls., Am Assn. Airport Execs., Sierra Club, Nature Conservancy, Audubon Soc. Roman Catholic. Office: Belt Collins & Assocs 680 Ala Moana Blvd Honolulu HI 96813

STEPHENS, PHILLIP, screenwriter, producer; b. Council Bluffs, Iowa, June 25, 1940; s. Ronald Donald and Alice Margrete (Skelton) S.; m. Elaine Jensen, July 1, 1961 (div. June 1983); children: Christopher Roland, Denise Andrea. BA in Theatre/Film, U. Denver, 1973, MA in Mass Communications, 1979. Screenwriter Mary Muphy Agy., Hollywood, Calif., 1975-78, Concept Continuum, Denver, 1978-79; prof. TV and Film Studies U. Denver, 1979—; writer, producer C-Star Internat. Entertainment, 1988-89; writer, dir., exec. producer Ravenshead Communications, Denver, 1990-92. Vol. moutain search and rescue team. Recipient Bronze medal Internat. Film and TV Festival, N.Y., 1973, 79; Phillip Stephens' Libr. Collection named in his honor U. Wyo. Mem. Author's League of Am., Dramatist's Guild, U. Film and Video Assn., Broadcast Edn. Assn., Internat. Freelance Photographers Assn., Internat. Film and Video Assn. Office: U Denver University Blvd Denver CO 80208-0001

STEPHENS, RICHARD MERRITT, lawyer; b. Arcadia, Calif., Oct. 2, 1960; s. Ray Manning and Rita Lee (Merritt) S. BA cum laude, Bob Jones U., 1982; JD cum laude, Pepperdine U., 1985. Bar: Calif. 1985, Oreg. 1986, Wash. 1992. Atty. Pacific Legal Found., Sacramento, 1985—; faculty mem. Am/ Law Inst.-ABA Conf. on Inverse Condemnation, Seattle, 1992. Contbr. articles to profl. publs.

STEPHENS, RONALD CARLYLE, retired military officer, academic director; b. L.A., Feb. 25, 1941; s. Ronald Francis Stephens and Martha Virginia (Wright) Hubbard. BA in History, UCLA, 1963; grad., Purdue U., 1964. World wide tour mgr. Laughlin Tours, L.A., 1960-64; commd. ensign USN, 1964, advanced through grades to capt., intelligence officer, 1964-74; sci. and tech. intelligence liaison officer Naval Sea Systems Command, Naval Ship, Port Hueneme, Calif., 1975-85; mil. dir. tech. transfer data base program, reserve liaison officer Office Sec. Def. Def. Tech. Security Adminstrn., Pentagon, Washington, 1985-91; ret. USN, 1991; dir. Coachella Valley Acad. Ctr. Chapman U., Palm Desert, Calif., 1991—; ops. security cons. Chief of Naval Material, Washington, 1981-85; ops. security officer Naval Sea Systems Command, Washington and Port Hueneme, 1981-85; dir. res. programs trade security policy Office Dep. Undersecretary Def., Pentagon, 1986-91; cons. Def. Dept. Author: course curr. Fleet Operational Intelligence, 1982; author: Shipboard: Over-the-Horizon Targeting Capabilities and Limitations, 1982, 84. Player, coach community sports, L.A., 1975-85; tutor, counselor Oxnard (Calif.) Sch. Systems, 1978-85. Recipient Defense Meritorious Svc. medal, 1987, Defense Superior Svc. medal, 1989. Mem. Naval Res. Assn., Ret. Officers Assn. (life), U.S. Naval Inst., UCLA Alumni Assn. (scholarship com. 1970-82), Blue and Gold Circle, Coachella Valley Industry and Edn. Coun., Palm Desert C. of C. (edn. com.), Assn. Old Crows, Phi Kappa Sigma. Republican. Episcopalian. Home: PO Box 457 Palm Desert CA 92261-0457 Office: Chapman U 41-555 Cook St Ste 100 Palm Desert CA 92260

STEPHENS, SHAND SCOTT, lawyer; b. Pasadena, Calif., Mar. 25, 1949; s. Elmer Shand and Gladys Joy (Baker) S.; m. Marcia Pizzo, July 25, 1982 (div. Dec. 1985). BA, Yale U., 1971; JD, U. Calif., San Francisco, 1975. Bar: Calif. 1975, U.S. Dist. Ct. (no., so., ea. and cen. dists.) Calif. 1975, U.S. Ct. Appeals (9th cir.) 1975. Assoc. Bronson, Bronson & McKinnon, San Francisco, 1978-82, ptnr., 1982—; gen. counsel San Francisco State U. Found., 1986—; gen. counsel Westamerica Bank, San Rafael, Calif., 1987—, Uapa Valley Bank, 1993—. Mem. ABA, Calif. Bar Assn., Order of Coif. Office: Bronson Bronson & McKinnon 505 Montgomery St San Francisco CA 94111-2552

STEPHENS, WILLIAM LEONARD, university provost; b. Covington, Ky., Apr. 19, 1929; s. Leonard Edwin and Mary Blanche S.; m. Claire Neall, Apr. 12, 1957. B.A. with honors, Calif. State U., Sacramento; Ph.D. in Microbiology, U. Calif., Davis, 1963. Research asst. U. Calif., Davis, 1957-63; mem. faculty Calif. State U., Chico, 1963—; prof. biol. scis. Calif. State U., 1970—, chmn. dept., 1968-74; dean Calif. State U. (Coll. Natural Scis.), Chico, 1977-91, provost, v.p. for acad. affairs, 1991—; researcher in bacterial pigments, microbial metabolism. Served with USN, 1950-54. Mem. Am. Soc. Microbiology. Home: 1661 Oak Vista Ave Chico CA 95926-1724 Office: Calif State U Office of Vice Pres Chico CA 95929

STEPHENS, WILLIAM THOMAS, forest products manufacturing company executive; married. BS, U. Ark., 1965, MS, 1966. Various mgmt. positions Manville Forest Products Corp., from 1963; asst. to pres., then sr. v.p., pres. forest products group Manville Corp., Denver, exec. v.p. fin. and adminstrn., from 1984, now pres., chief exec. officer, chmn. Office: Manville Corp PO Box 5108 Manville Plz Denver CO 80202*

STEPHENSON, BARBERA WERTZ, lawyer; b. Bryan, Ohio, Dec. 10, 1938; d. Emerson D. and Beryl B. (Barber) Wertz; m. Gerard J. Stephenson Jr., June 22, 1960; 1 child, Thomas. Student, Smith Coll., 1956-57; BSEE, MIT, 1961; JD, U. N.Mex., 1981. Bar: N.Mex. 1981. Electronic engr. Digital Equipment Corp., Maynard, Mass., 1960-66; logic analyst Librascope, Glendale, Calif., 1966; electronic engr. Md. Dept. of Def., Ft. Meade, 1966-68; mem. tech. staff Xerox Data Systems, Rockville, Md., 1968; pvt. practice cons., Silver Spring, Md., 1969-78; pvt. practice law, Albuquerque, 1981—. Author: Financing Your Home Purchase in New Mexico, 1992; patentee analog to digital converter, kitchen calculator. Mem. ABA, N.Mex. Bar Assn. Office: 4221 Silver Ave SE Albuquerque NM 87108-2720

STEPHENSON, GARY VAN, electro-optics systems engineer; b. Huron, S.D., Mar. 25, 1958; s. Phillip Carlyle Stephenson and Barbara Jean (O'Leary) Young; m. Sandra Lynn Deault, June 4, 1977 (div. Feb. 1989); m. Nancy Watkins Gossett, July 19, 1991. BS in Physics, BA in Philosophy, Mont. State U., 1983. Mem. tech. staff Hughes Aircraft Co., El Segundo, Calif., 1983-86; sr. engr. ITT-Aerospace Optical Div., Ft. Wayne, Ind., 1986-88; electro-optics engr. Weyerhaeuser Co., Federal Way, Wash., 1988-89; systems engr. Hughes Aircraft Co., Seattle, 1989—; pres. Seculine Consulting, Seattle, 1989—. With U.S. Army, 1976-79. Mem. Soc. Photo-Optical and Instrumentation Engrs., Sigma Pi Sigma. Home: 6802 142d Ct NE Redmond CA 98052 Office: Hughes Aircraft Co Kent Space Ctr Mailstop 8Y50 PO Box 3700 Seattle WA 98124

STEPHENSON, HERMAN HOWARD, banker; b. Wichita, Kans., July 15, 1929; s. Herman Horace and Edith May (Wayland) S.; m. Virginia Anne Ross, Dec. 24, 1950; children: Ross Wayland, Neal Bevan, Jann Edith. BA, U. Mich., 1950; JD with distinction, U. Mo., Kansas City, 1958. Bar: Kans. 1958. With City Nat. Bank, Kansas City, Mo., 1952-54, City Bond & Mortgage Co., Kansas City, 1954-59, Bank of Hawaii, Honolulu, 1959—; now chmn. bd., ceo Bancorp Hawaii Inc. and subs. Bank Hawaii, First Fed. Am. Inc., 1st Nat. Bank Ariz., Honolulu; bd. dirs. Banque de Nouvelle-Caledonie, Banque Tahiti. Bd. dirs. Honolulu Symphony, Maunalani Found., Aloha United Way, Pacific Fleet Submarine Meml. Assn.; co-chmn. Ellison Onizuka Meml. Scholarship Fund Com.; chmn. bd. regents U. Hawaii; commr. Kaho'olawe Island Conveyance Commn. With U.S. Army, 1950-52. Mem. ABA, Am. Bankers Assn. (past chmn. exec. com. housing and real estate fin. div., dir. 1976-77, mem. governing coun. 1976-77, mem. govt. rels. coun. 1986-89), Kans. Bar Assn., Hawaii Bankers Assn. (pres. 1991-92), U.S.-Japan Bus. Coun., Pacific Asia Travel Assn. (Hawaii chpt., assoc.), Navy League of U.S., Hawaii Bus. Roundtable (chmn.), Pacific Forum/CSIS (bd. govs.), Japan-Hawaii Econ. Coun., Assn. Res. City Bankers, U.S.-Korea Bus. Coun., Kappa Sigma, Pi Eta Sigma, Oahu Country Club, Pacific Club, Waialae Country Club, Rotary. Office: Bank of Hawaii PO Box 2900 Honolulu HI 96846-0001

STEPHENSON, IRENE HAMLEN, biorhythm analyst, consultant, editor, educator; b. Chgo., Oct. 7, 1923; d. Charles Martin and Carolyn Hilda (Hilgers) Hamlin; m. Edgar B. Stephenson, Sr., Aug. 16, 1941 (div. 1946); 1 child, Edgar B. Author biorhythm compatibilities column Nat. Singles Register, Norwalk, Calif., 1979-81; instr. biorhythm Learning Tree Open U., Canoga Park, Calif., 1982-83; instr. biorhythm character analysis 1980—; instr. biorhythm compatibility, 1982—; owner, pres. matchmaking svc. Pen Pals Using Biorhythm, Chatsworth, Calif., 1979—; editor newsletter The Truth, 1979-85, Mini Examiner, Chatsworth, 1985—; researcher biorhythm character and compatibility, 1974—, biorhythm columnist Psychic Astrology Horoscope, 1989—, True Astrology Forecast, 1989—, Psychic Astrology Predictions, 1990—; author: Learn Biorhythm Character Analysis, 1980; Do-It-Yourself Biorhythm Compatibilities, 1982; contbr. numerous articles to mags.; frequent guests clubs, radio, TV. Office: PO Box 3893-WW Chatsworth CA 91313-3893

STEPHENSON, LARRY KIRK, strategic planner, management and geography educator; b. Seattle, Sept. 22, 1944; s. Norman Eugene and Virginia Dare (Frost) S.; m. Tamara Leah Ladin, June 24, 1967; children: Mathew Alan, Leah Anela. BS, Ariz. State U., 1966, MA, 1971; PhD, U. Cin., 1973; Manpower research analyst Employment Security Commn. of Ariz., 1969-70; asst. prof. dept. geography U. Hawaii, Hilo, 1973-76, assoc. prof., 1976-78, chmn. dept., 1975-77; vis. lectr. dept. geography Ariz. State U., 1978, adj. assoc. prof., 1979—; planner Ariz. Dept. Health Services, Phoenix, 1978-84; vis. assoc. prof. dept. geography, area devel. and urban planning U. Ariz., 1978; strategic plannner City of Glendale, Ariz., 1984-92; pub. health analyst Gila River Indian Community, 1992—; mem. faculty U. Phoenix, 1979—; adj. prof. Golden Gate U., 1981—; ptnr. Urban Research Assocs., Phoenix, 1981—; adj. prof. Coll. St. Francis, 1982—; mem. faculty Troy State U., 1990—. Mem. Hawaii Island Health Planning Council, 1974-78; mem. Glendale Community Colls. Pres.'s Council, 1986—. Served with U.S. Army, 1966-68. NDEA fellow, 1971-72. Mem. Am. Inst. Cert. Planners, Am. Planning Assn., Assn. Am. Geographers, Ariz. Planning Assn. (pres. 1987—), Southwest Profl. Geog. Assn., Lambda Alpha. Unitarian. Author books in field; contbr. chpts. to textbooks, articles to profl. jours. Home: RR 1 Box 453-F Laveen AZ 85339 Office: PO Box 7 Sacaton AZ 85247

STEPHENSON, LEE JOSEPH, tax accountant, consultant; b. Ogden, Utah, Aug. 15, 1953; s. Melvin Joseph and Nedra (Haskell) S.; m. Sandra Lee Lewis, Sept. 18, 1981; children: Kelly Lyn, Robert Joseph, Blake Taylor, Jennifer Anne. BS, U. Utah, 1977. CPA, Colo. Tax acct. Richard Francis & Co., Salt Lake City, 1977-81; sr. tax acct. KPMG Peat Marwick Main & Co., Denver, 1981-83; tax mgr. Duncan Energy Co., Denver, 1983—; cons. Plz. Motor Co., Denver, 1981-86, Gt. Divide Weather Instruments, Inc., Denver, 1981—, Abcoil Prodn., Inc., Denver, 1989-92, Mut. of N.Y., Denver, 1989—. Mem. AICPA, Colo. Soc. CPAs, Ind. Petrol Assn. of Mountain States, N. Am. Falconers Assn. Republican. Mem. LDS Ch. Home: 8557 E Kettle Pl Englewood CO 80112 Office: Duncan Energy Co 1777 S Harrison St PH1 Denver CO 80210

STEPHENSON, MICHAEL MURRAY, lawyer; b. San Pedro, Calif., July 31, 1943; s. George Murray and Josephine Ann (Wathen) S. Student, U. Okla., 1961, 62, 65, 66; student Harbor Coll., 1962-63, Universidad Ibero-Americana, Mexico City, summer 1964; A.B., U. So. Calif., 1965; J.D., Southwestern U., 1970. Bar: Calif. 1971. Dep. dist. atty. Los Angeles County, 1971-74; ptnr. Stephenson & Stephenson, San Pedro, Calif., 1974—; legal advisor Los Angeles County Underwater Instrs. Assn.; dir. Los Angeles County Underwater Instrs. Assn.; staff instr. Los Angeles Underwater Instrs. Certification Progrm and Advanced Diving progrm. Bd. dirs. ARC, San Pedro, 1975-76; alt. mem. Los Angeles County Dem. Central Com. Recipient Outstanding Teaching award, 28th Underwater Instrs. Cert. Course, Los Angeles, 1980, LA. County Outstanding Underwater Instr., 1990. Mem. State Bar Calif., Los Angeles Trial Lawyers Assn., Am. Trial Lawyers Assn., ABA, Calif. Trial Lawyers Assn. (lectr. underwater instr. liability), Harbor Bar Assn. (pres.), S. Bay Bar Assn., Nat. Assn. Underwater Instrs., Elks, YMCA Underwater Instrs. Assn. Democrat. Roman Catholic. Contbr. articles to profl. jours. Office: 150 W 7th St Ste 120 San Pedro CA 90731-3341

STEPNEY, PHILIP HAROLD ROBERT, museum director; b. Edmonton, Alta., Can., Nov. 19, 1947; s. Harold Albert and Elenor Blanche (Landals) S.; m. Donna Maureen Kelly, Sept. 4, 1967; children: Sean Philip Stuart, Erin Maureen, Lindsay Dawn. B.Sc. with honors, U. Alta., Edmonton, Can., 1969; M.Sc., U. Toronto, Ont., Can., 1971, Ph.D., 1979. Wildlife biologist Renewable Resources Cons. Svc., Edmonton, 1975, project mgr., 1976, dir. bus. devel., 1977; curator ornithology Provincial Mus. Alta., Edmonton, 1978-81, asst. dir. natural history, 1981-87, asst. dir., curatorial, 1987-89, dir., 1989—; mem. collections com. U. Alta., Edmonton, 1982-89, adj. rsch. assoc. dept. forest sci., 1987—; chmn. Lakeland Coll Curriculum Adv. Com., Vermillion, Alta., 1984—. Editor: (exhbn. catalog) The Scriver Blackfoot Collection, 1990; mem. editorial bd. Alta. Studies Jour., 1986-90; contbr. artices to jours. in field. Recipient Can. Nat. Sportsman Show award U. Toronto, 1973; collections registration grantee Mus. Assistance Program, 1972, 79, 80, 83, Alta. Hist. Resources Found. grantee, 1988, Alta. Recreation, Pks., Wildlife Found. grantee, 1989; Can. Cultural Property Export Rev. Bd. grantee, 1989, 90, 91, Can. Museums Assn. grantee, 1990; U. Toronto scholar, 1972, 73, 74. Mem. Am. Ornithologists Union (co-chair collections com. 1984—), Soc. Can. Ornithologists (treas. membership sect. 1985—), Cooper Ornithol. Soc., Wilson Ornithol. Soc. Office: Provincial Mus of Alberta, 12845 102nd Ave, Edmonton, AB Canada T5N 0M6

STEPOVICH, MICHAEL LEO, orthodontist; b. Fairbanks, Alaska, Nov. 17, 1929; s. Mike and Vuka (Radovich) S.; A.B., San Jose State U., 1956; D.D.S., Marquette U., 1961; M.S., St. Louis U., 1964; m. Arline Audry Gentry, June 10, 1956; children—Michael John, Matthew James, Dean Alexander, Lynn Diane. Intern, USPHS Hosp., Fort Worth, 1961-62; pvt. practice orthodontics, San Jose, Calif., 1964—; mem. staff Good Samaritan Hosp., San Jose. Pres., Orthodontic Edn. and Research Found., St. Louis, 1969; bd. dirs. Tweed Found. for Orthodontic Research, 1978-84, pres. Western sect., 1985-87. Served with AUS, 1953-54; PTO. Diplomate Am. Bd. Orthodontists. Mem. Am., Calif., Santa Clara County dental assns., Am. Assn. Orthodontists, Pacific Coast Soc. Orthodontists (pres. Central sect. 1975), Angle Soc., DeMolay, Interfrat. Council San Jose State U. Alumni (chmn. 1966), Omicron Kappa Upsilon, Delta Upsilon. Contbr. articles to profl. jours. Home: 19557 Arden Ct Saratoga CA 95070-3301 Office: 4110 Moorpark Ave San Jose CA 95117

STEPP, GEORGE ALLAN, JR., state official; b. Inglewood, Calif., Apr. 26, 1922; s. George Allan and Ida Johanna (Wehselau) S.; m. Margit Lindblad, Oct. 15, 1966; 1 dau., Elizabeth. B.A., U. Hawaii, 1948, M.A. in Govt., 1950. Personnel technician and adminstr. Hawaii Dept. Civil Service, Honolulu, 1950-59; asst. dir. research Hawaii Employers Council, Honolulu, 1959-61; mgmt. services adminstr. Hawaii State Dept. Budget and Fin., Honolulu, 1961-88; mgmt. cons. DHB Inc., Honolulu, 1988—. Served with USCG, 1942-45, to comdr. Res. (ret.), 1952-82. Mem. Western Govtl. Research Assn. (pres. 1971-72), Am. Soc. Pub. Adminstrn., Am. Mgmt. Assn., Am. Cons. League. Res. Officers Assn. of U.S. Democrat. Home: 2999 Kalakaua Ave Honolulu HI 96815-4654 Office: DHB Inc 1173 Lunalilo Home Rd Honolulu HI 96825-3204

STEPP, WILLIAM EDWARD, retired military operations analyst; b. Turtle Creek, Pa., Feb. 23, 1930; s. William George and Emma Jean (McLean) S.; m. Barbara Johanna Barth, Oct. 23, 1965; children: Randal R., Roger W. BS in Physics, Carnegie-Mellon U., 1951; MS in Engring., U. So. Calif., 1977. Physicist Bell Aircraft Co., Buffalo, 1951-53, Convair Aircraft Co., San Diego, 1953-56, Bendix Co., North Hollywood, Calif., 1956-59; ops. analyst ORI, Santa Monica, Calif., 1959-61, Douglas Aircraft Co., Santa Monica, 1961-63; sr. mil. ops. analyst Lockheed Calif. Co., Burbank, 1963-91, ret., 1991.

STERBICK, PETER LAWRENCE, lawyer; b. Tacoma, Nov. 12, 1917; s. Anton John and Pearl (Medak) S.; m. Rita J. Morrell, Dec. 26, 1946; children: Marilyn, Lawrence, Thomas, David, Colleen. BBA, U. Wash., 1941, LLB, 1948. Bar: Wash. 1949. Adjuster Gen. Accidenty Ins. Co., Seattle, 1948-49, Farmers Ins. Group, Tacoma, 1949-50; dep. pros. atty. Pierce County, Tacoma, 1950-51; ptnr. Sterbick and Sterbick, Tacoma, 1951-57, Sterbick, Manza, Moceri and Sterbick, Tacoma, 1958-72, Sterbick, Abel and Sterbick, Tacoma, 1972—. 2d lt. USAAF, 1943-45. Mem. Wash. Bar Assn., Tacoma-Pierce County Bar Assn., Kiwanis, KC, Elks. Roman Catholic. Home: 3143 Olympic Blvd W Tacoma WA 98466-1605 Office: Sterbick Abel & Sterbick 15 Oregon Ave Ste 303 Tacoma WA 98409

STERLING, DONALD JUSTUS, JR., retired newspaper editor; b. Portland, Oreg., Sept. 27, 1927; s. Donald Justus and Adelaide (Armstrong) S.; m. Julie Ann Courteol, June 7, 1963; children: Sarah, William, John. A.B., Princeton U., 1948; postgrad. (Nieman fellow), Harvard U., 1955-56. Reporter Denver Post, 1948-52; news staff mem. Oreg. Jour., Portland, 1952-82; editor Oreg. Jour., 1972-82; asst. to pub. The Oregonian, 1982-92, ret., 1992. Pres. Tri-County Community Coun., 1972-73. Recipient Izaak Walton League Golden Beaver award, 1969, Edith Knight Hill award, 1978, Jessie Laird Brodie award Planned Parenthood Assn., 1983, McCall award Women in Communications, 1987, Roger W. Williams Freedom of Info. award Oreg. Newspaper Pubs. Assn., 1989; English-Speaking Union traveling fellow,

1959. Mem. Soc. Nieman Fellows, Soc. Profl. Journalists, Oreg. Hist. Soc. (pres. 1977-79). Clubs: City (Portland) (pres. 1973-74), Multnomah Athletic (Portland); Dial, Elm, Cannon (Princeton). Home: 1718 SW Myrtle St Portland OR 97201-2300

STERLING, DONALD T., professional basketball team executive; b. Chgo.. Lawyer Los Angeles (formerly San Diego) Clippers, Nat. Basketball Assn., owner. Office: care Los Angeles Clippers Los Angeles Meml Sports Arena 3939 S Figueroa St Los Angeles CA 90037-1207*

STERMAN, LORRAINE TAYLOR, psychologist; b. L.A., Mar. 8, 1944; d. Thomas M. and Helen (Christiansen) Taylor; m. Maurice B. Sterman, Aug. 16, 1964; children: Felicia, Paul Bradley. AA, Pasadena City Coll., 1964; BSN, Mt. St. Marys Coll., 1973; MSN, UCLA, 1975; PhD, Wright Inst., L.A., 1985. RN UCLA Med. Ctr., 1969-70; rsch. nurse County/Women's Hosp., U. So. Calif., L.A., 1971-73; lectr. UCLA Sch. Nursing, 1974, asst. prof., 1975-79; assoc. dir. B. Rush, Crisis Ctr., L.A., 1975; clinician UCLA Neuropsychiat. Inst., 1978-86, psychologist, 1986-90, assoc. dir. speciality clinic, psychologist, 1990—; pvt. practice in clin. psychology Beverly Hills, Calif., 1984—; lectr., cons. pub. and pvt. schs. and univs. Contbr. articles to profl. jours. Grantee NIMH, 1973-75. Mem. Am. Psychol. Assn. (bd. of div. 39, 1981—), Calif. Psychol. Assn., Calif. Nurses Assn. Democrat. Office: UCLA Neuropsychiat Inst & Hosp 300 Medical Pla Los Angeles CA 90024

STERMER, DUGALD ROBERT, designer, illustrator, writer, consultant; b. Los Angeles, Dec. 17, 1936; s. Robert Newton and Mary (Blue) S.; m. Jeanie Kortum; children: Dugald, Megan, Chris, Colin, Crystal. B.A., UCLA, 1960. Art dir., v.p. Ramparts mag., 1965-70; freelance designer, illustrator, writer, cons. San Francisco, 1970—; founder Pub. Interest Communications, San Francisco, 1974; pres. Frisco Pub Group Ltd.; bd. dirs Am. Inst. Graphic Arts. Cons. editor Communication Arts mag., Palo Alto, Calif., 1974—; designer Oceans mag., 1976-82; editor: The Environment, 1972, Vanishing Creatures, 1980; author: The Art of Revolution, 1970, Vanishing Creatures, 1980; designer 1984 Olympic medals; illustration exhbn. Calif. Acad. Scis., 1986. Mem. Grand Jury City and County San Francisco, 1989; bd. dirs. Delancey St. Found., 1990—. Recipient various medals, awards for design and illustration nat. and internat. competitions. Office: #204 600 The Embarcadero San Francisco CA 94107

STERN, ARTHUR PAUL, electronics company executive, electrical engineer; b. Budapest, Hungary, July 20, 1925; came to U.S., 1951, naturalized, 1956; s. Leon and Bertha (Frankfurter) S.; m. Edith M. Samuel; children: Daniel, Claude, Jacqueline. Diploma in Elec. Engring., Swiss Fed. Inst. Tech., Zurich, 1948; MSEE, Syracuse U., 1955. Mgr. electronic devices and applications lab. Gen. Electric Co., Syracuse, N.Y., 1957-61; dir. engring. Martin Marietta Corp., Balt., 1961-64; dir. ops. Bunker Ramo Corp., Canoga Park, Calif., 1964-66; v.p., gen. mgr. advanced products div. Magnavox, Torrance, Calif., 1966-79, pres. Magnavox Advanced Products and Systems Co., Torrance, 1980-90; vice chmn., bd. dirs. Magnavox Govt. and Indsl. Electronics Co., Ft. Wayne, Ind., 1987-90; pres. Ea. Beverly Hills Corp., 1991—; non-resident staff mem. MIT, 1956-59; instr. Gen. Elec. Bus. Mgmt., 1955-57. Chmn. engring. div. United Jewish Appeal, Syracuse, 1955-57; mem. adv. bd. dept. elec. engring. U. Calif., Santa Barbara, 1980-92; mem. Sch. Engring. Adv. and Devel. Council Calif. State U., Long Beach, 1985-90. Co-author: Transistor Circuit Engineering, 1957, Handbook of Automation, Computation and Control, 1961; also articles; U.S., fgn. patentee in field. Fellow AAAS, IEEE (pres. 1975, bd. dirs., officer 1970-77, guest editor spl. issue IEEE Trans. on Circuit Theory 1956, invited guest editor spl. issue Procs. IEEE on Integrated Electronics 1964, Centennial medal 1984). Jewish.

STERN, LOUIS, gallery executive; b. Casablanca, Morocco, Jan. 7, 1945; s. Frederic and Sultana (Ifergan) S.; m. Karen Anne Honeman, Oct. 12, 1969; children: Deborah Beth, Daniel William. BA, Calif. State U., Northridge, 1968. Dir. Wally Findlay Galleries, Inc., Beverly Hills, Calif., 1975-78; pres. Wally Findlay Galleries, Inc., 1978-80, Louis Stern Galleries, Inc., 1980—. Expert witness L.A. Police Dept., 1984—, L.A. Superior Ct., 1984—. With U.S. Army, 1968-71. U.S. Dept. Def. Joint Commendation medal, 1971. Mem. Art Dealers Assn. Calif. (v.p. 1988—), Am. Arts Coun., Am. Friends of Blerancourt (Paris), Pres. Cir. of L.A. County Mus., L.A. Art Galleries. Office: 9528 Brighton Way Beverly Hills CA 90210-4506

STERN, MARC IRWIN, financial services executive; b. Vineland, N.J., Apr. 17, 1944; s. Albert B. and Sylvia (Goodman) S.; m. Eva Suzanne Kuhn, Aug. 14, 1966; children: Adam Bryan, Suzanne Rona. BA cum laude in Polit. Sci., Dickinson Coll., Carlisle, Pa., 1965; MA, Columbia U., 1966; JD magna cum laude, 1969. Bar: N.Y. 1969, N.H. 1975. Law clk. U.S. Ct. Appeals 2d Circuit, 1969-70; assoc. Debevoise & Plimpton, 1970-74; v.p., gen. counsel Wheelabrator-Frye Inc., Hampton, N.H., 1974-80; sr. v.p. Wheelabrator-Frye Inc., 1980-83; sr. v.p. adminstrn. The Signal Cos., Inc., La Jolla, Calif., 1983-85, Allied-Signal Inc., Morristown, N.J., 1985-86; mng. dir., chief adminstrv. officer The Henley Group, Inc., N.Y.C. and La Jolla, 1986-88; pres. Broad, Inc., L.A., 1988-90, The TCW Group, Inc., L.A., 1992—; chmn. bd. TCW Ams. Devel., Inc., 1990—, TCW Funds, Inc., 1990—. Trustee Salk Inst. for Biol. Studies, La Jolla, Dickinson Coll., Carlisle, Pa., UCLA Med. Ctr.; bd. dirs. L.A. Music Ctr. Opera. Home: 10247 Century Woods Dr Los Angeles CA 90067-6312 Office: Trust Co of the West 865 S Figueroa St # 1800 Los Angeles CA 90017 also: 200 Park Ave Ste 2200 New York NY 10166

STERN, MILTON REID, educator, university administrator; b. N.Y.C., Feb. 1, 1918; s. Charles and Sadie (Reid) S.; m. Margaret Halsey, Mar. 22, 1944; 1 child, Deborah; m. Virginia Harriman, Sept. 15, 1970; m. Isabel Singer, May 23, 1987; children: Amee, Andrea, Amanda. BS, MA, Columbia U., 1939; LHD (hon.), Johns Hopkins U., 1989, SUNY, 1992; LittD (hon.), Tulane U., 1993. Asst. d'Anglais Lycee De Bayonne, Basses Pyrennes, France, 1936-37; asst. to dean NYU, N.Y.C., 1946-66, from asst. prof. to assoc. prof., 1951-66; assoc. prof., dir. Ctr. for Adult Edn. U. Mich., Ann Arbor, 1966-71; dean Univ. Extension U. Calif., Berkeley, 1971-91, dean emeritus, 1991—; cons. Ford Found., N.Y.C., 1965-66; lectr. British Univs., Edinburgh, Scotland, 1967, 71, Sheffield, England, 1967, Keele and Liverpool, 1964-65; vis. com. Harvard U., Cambridge, Mass., 1977-83; vis. fellow Oxford U., England, 1989, Inst. Govt. Studies U. Calif., Berkeley, 1991—. Author: People, Programs and Persuasion, 1960; co-editor: The First Years in College, 1965; editor, contbg. author: Power and Conflict in Continuing Professional Education, 1983. Mem. scholarship com. Richard III Soc., 1958—, English Speaking Union, 1984—; treas. Western Consortium for Pub. Health, 1975-91; trustee Royal Oak Found., 1975—, French Am. Internat. Sch., San Francisco Calif., 1989—, Athenian Sch., Danville, Calif., 1993—. Sgt. U.S. Signals Corps, 1941-45, ETO. Recipient Silver medal, Order of Oak Crown Grand Duchy of Luxembourg, 1945, Julius Nolte award Nat. Continuing Edn. Assn., 1984, Paul A. McGhee medal NYU, 1986, Chevalier, Palmes Academiques, Govt. of France, 1988, Wilbur Cohen award U. Mich., 1990. Mem. Nat. Assn. State Univs. and Landgrant Colls. (exec. com. 1985-88). Democrat. Home: 44 Southridge W Belvedere Tiburon CA 94920 Office: U Calif Berkeley Inst Govtl Studies 109 Moses Hall Berkeley CA 94720-0001

STERN, STANLEY, psychiatrist; b. N.Y.C., Apr. 5, 1933; s. Frank and Gussie S.; children: Marcus F., David S. BA cum laude, N.Y. U., 1953; MD, SUNY, 1957. Intern Ohio State U. Hosp., Columbus, 1957-58; resident in psychiatry Inst. Living, Hartford, Conn., 1958-60, Austen Riggs Ctr., Stockbridge, Mass., 1960-61; psychoanalytic tng. We. New Eng. Inst. for Psychoanalysis, New Haven, Conn., 1965-73; asst. clin. prof. psychiatry Yale U., New Haven, Conn., 1975-81; assoc. clin. prof. psychiatry U. Calif., San Diego, 1982-84; pvt. practice New Haven, 1965-82, La Jolla, Calif., 1982-84, Phoenix, 1984—; mem. faculty San Diego Psychoanalytic Inst., 1980-84; pres. Ariz. Psychoanalytic Study Group, Phoenix, 1986-88, Phoenix Psychoanalytic Study Group, 1986-88; tng. and supervising analyst So. Calif. Psychoanalytic Inst., 1989; chmn. edn. com. Ariz. Psychoanalytic New Tng. Facility, 1990-91; lectr., presenter, participant seminars and confs. in field. Contbr. article to profl. jours. Trustee, Gesell Inst., New Haven, 1986-88, Ctr. for the Exceptional Patient, New Haven; bd. dirs. ACLU. Capt. USAF, 1961-63. Mem. Am. Coll. Psychoanalysts, Am. Psychoanalytic Assn. (cert.), Am. Psychiatric Assn., Am. Acad. Psychoanalysts, Irene Josselyn Group Advancement of Psychoanalysis, So. Calif. Psychoanalytic Inst. and Soc. (faculty), San Diego Psychoanalytic Inst., Council for the Advancement of Psychoanalysis (treas. 1972-73, pres.-elect 1973-74, pres. 1974-75, councillor 1975-80), Phi Beta Kappa, Beta Lambda Sigma, Psi Chi. Home and Office: 3352 E Camelback Rd Ste D Phoenix AZ 85018-2397

STERNBERG, BEN KOLLOCK, geophysicist; b. Wausau, Wis., Sept. 11, 1947; s. Lawrence Walter and Jane (Kollock) S.; m. Christine Marie Streiff, Oct. 24, 1970; children: Petra Jane Streiff, Andrew Dennis Kollock, William Lawrence Fredrickson. B.S. in Physics, U. Wis., 1970, M.S. in Geophysics, 1974, Ph.D. in Geophysics, 1977. Rsch. scientist Conoco Inc., Ponca City, Okla., 1977-79, sr. rsch. scientist, 1980, group leader, 1980-83, supr. elec. methods group, 1979-83; chief geophysicist Barringer Resources, Golden, Colo., 1983-84, mgr. geophysics and computer services dept., 1983-84; mgr. controlled source elec. methods Phoenix Geophysics Inc., Denver, 1984-86; assoc. prof., dir. lab. advanced subsurface imaging, dept. head, mining and geol. engr. U. Ariz., Tucson, 1986—. Contbr. articles to profl. jours. Patentee in field. Mem. Soc. Exploration Geophysicists, European Assn. Exploration Geophysicists, Sigma Xi, Phi Eta Sigma. Presbyterian. Office: U Ariz Dept Mining & Geol Engring Bldg 12 Tucson AZ 85721

STERNFELS, LEWIS BERNARD, patent lawyer; b. Waterbury, Conn., Oct. 31, 1933; s. Martin M. and Jeanette C. (Wolff) S.; m. Diane B. Olefsky, Dec. 14, 1969; children: Jessica M., Sarah E. AB, Columbia Coll., 1955, BS, 1956; LLB, George Washington U., 1963. Bar: Calif. 1966, U.S. Patent and Trademark Office 1963. Patent examiner U.S. Patent and Trademark Office, Washington, 1956-63; pvt. practice L.A., 1963-66, 88—; sr. patent atty. Hughes Aircraft Co., L.A., 1966-88. With U.S. Army, 1956-58. Mem. L.A. Intellectual Property Law Assn., Am. Intellectual Property Law Assn., State Bar of Calif., Patent and Trademark Office Soc. Home and Office: 3100 Inglewood Blvd Los Angeles CA 90066-1062

STERNS, PATRICIA MARGARET, lawyer, consultant; b. Phoenix, Jan. 30, 1952; d. Lawrence Page and Mildred Dorothy (Barbaras) S. BA, Ariz. State U., 1974; JD, U. Ariz., 1977. Bar: Ariz. bar, 1978, U.S. Dist. Ct. Ariz., 1978, U.S. Supreme Ct. 1986. With Sterns and Tennen, Phoenix, 1978—; judge pro tempore Superior Ct. Ariz., County of Maricopa, 1983—; mem. Domestic Rels. Study Com., 1984-86, judge Jessup Internat. Moot Ct. Competition and semi-finals rounds, 1984—, regional rounds, 1981—; cons. internat. law; lectr. Am. Grad. Sch. Internat. Mgmt., 1982, Princeton U. Space Mfg. Facilities Conf., 1979, Internat. Astronautical Fedn., 1978—. Fellow Ariz. Bar Found.; mem. AIAA, ABA (family law, internat. law sects., aerospace law com.), Am. Quarterhorse Assn., Am. Soc. Internat. Law (space law sect.), Maricopa County Bar Assn. (family law sect.), Internat. Inst. Space Law (bd. dirs., sec., bd. dirs. U.S. membership IISL), Internat. Bar Assn., Aviation/Space Writers Assn., Ariz. Bar Assn., Profl. Rodeo Cowboys Assn. (assoc.), Am. Quarter Horse Assn. Contbr. articles to profl. publs.; mem. Ariz. Law Rev. Office: 849 N 3d Ave Phoenix AZ 85003-1439

STERRETT, JAMES MELVILLE, accountant; b. Chicago, Dec. 25, 1949; s. James McAnlis and Antoinette (Galligan) S.; m. Joyce Mieko Motoda, Sept. 1, 1989; 1 child, Victoria Hanako. BS in Acctg., Chaminade U., Honolulu, 1988; MBA, Chaminade U., 1991. CPA, Hawaii. Cons. Profitability Cons., Honolulu, 1985-87; pres. Sterrett Cons. Group, Honolulu, 1987-88; auditor Deloitte & Touche, Honolulu, 1988-90; pvt. practice acctg. Honolulu, 1990—. Mem. Delta Epsilon Sigma.

STETLER, CHARLES EDWARD, English language educator; b. Pitts., Sept. 12, 1927; s. Charles Edward and Catherine (Seidel) S.; m. Ellen Donovan, June 25, 1956 (div. Jan. 1981); children: Peter, Paul, Casey; m. Kristin Jill Brown, July 17, 1984 (div. 1993). BA, Duquesne U., 1950, MA, 1962; PhD, Tulane U., 1966. Reporter Pitts. Sun Telegraph, 1957-62; instr. in English Rollins Coll., Winter Park, Fla., 1962-63; asst. prof. English Loyola U., New Orleans, 1963-67; prof. English Calif. State U., Long Beach, 1967—; exch. prof. English U. Hull, Eng., fall 1984. Author poetry; contbr. articles to profl. jours. With USN, 1945-46, 50-52. Mem. Honor Soc. for Internat. Scholars, Phi Beta Kappa. Democrat. Home: 5905 E Pacific Coast Hwy #4 Long Beach CA 90803-3449 Office: Calif State U 1250 N Bellflower Blvd Long Beach CA 90840-0001

STETLER, LARRY D., geologist; b. Rapid City, S.D., Dec. 2, 1956; s. Harold Lawrence and Alice Elaine (Kellum) S.; m. Jeanette Marie Gross, Aug. 6, 1988. BS in Geol. Engring., S.D. Sch. Mines and Tech., 1979, MS in Geol. Engring., 1989; PhD in Geology, Wash. State U., 1993. Field engr. Schlumberger, Williston, N.D., 1979-81, Casper, Wyo., 1983-86; fluids engr. Newpark Drilling Fluids, Casper, 1981-82; rsch. asst., teaching asst. S.D. Sch. Mines and Tech., Rapid City, 1987-89, Wash. State U., Pullman, 1989-92; rsch. scientist Northwest Coll. and Univ. Assn. for Sci., Pullman and Richland, Wash., 1992—. Author lab. manuals on fluids engring.; contbr. articles to profl. publs. Grantee Battelle Meml. Inst., 1990, 92, Wash. State U., 1991. Mem. Am. Assn. Petroleum Geologists, Geol. Assn. Am., Soc. Sedimentary Geologists. Republican. Home: NW 435 Irving Pullman WA 99163 Office: Phys Sci Bldg Wash State Univ Pullman WA 99164-1228

STEVENS, AMY DIRKS, public relations professional; b. Bethesda, Md., Nov. 11, 1965; d. LeRoy John Dirks and Sharon Ann (Powers) Clarke; m. John Gerald Stevens. Student, Brigham Young U., 1983-84; BA, Purdue U., 1990; postgrad., Calif. State U., Sacramento, 1991—. Senate page Md. Gen. Assembly, Annapolis, 1983; exec. sec. Foulger-Pratt Constn. Co., Rockville, Md., 1983-85, SMA Fin. Svcs., Pitts., 1985-86; clk. II Tarkington Residence Hall, West Lafayette, Ind., 1986-87; continuing edn. coord. Sch. of Vet. Medicine, West Lafayette, 1987-91; teaching assoc. Calif. State U., Sacramento, 1991-92; resident assoc. Argonne Nat. Lab.-West, Idaho Falls, Idaho, 1991, 92; pub. participation specialist Sci. Applications Internat. Corp., Idaho Falls, Idaho, 1993—. Author: Use of NIMBY Strategies, 1992, Issue Lifecycle Analysis, 1992; author conf. papers. Speaker, host INEL Women's Career Day, Idaho Falls, 1991, 92; Purdue U. liaison Ind. Acad. Vet. Medicine, West Lafayette, 1988-91; Purdue vet. medicine coord. Ind. State Fair, West Lafayette, 1989-91; mem. Idaho Falls Hist. Preservation Commn., 1993—. Mem. Internat. Assn. Bus. Communicators, Internat. Communication Assn., Am. Nuclear Soc., Speech Communicaton Assn., Motar Bd. (life, pres. Purdue U. 1990-91), Golden Key Nat. Honor Soc. (pres. 1989-90, regional rep. Purdue U. 1989-90), Phi Kappa Phi, Phi Beta Kappa. Office: SAIC 545 Shoup Ave Idaho Falls ID 83402

STEVENS, ARTHUR WILBER, JR., English language educator, writer, editor; b. Bklyn., Aug. 16, 1921; s. Arthur Wilber and Isabella Ellen (MacGibbon) S.; m. Marjorie Athene Rogers, Feb. 15, 1955 (dec. Feb. 1979); children: Arthur Wilber III, Christopher Rivers; m. Joan Cutuly, Mar. 6, 1992. AB, Brown U., 1942; MA, U. Wash., 1956, PhD, 1957. Teaching fellow, assoc., then instr. U. Wash., Seattle, 1944-54; vis. lectr., then asst. prof. Idaho State U., Pocatello, 1954-60; assoc. prof., chmn. dept. English, 1961-64; Fulbright prof. Am. and English lit. U. Mandalay (Burma) and U. Chulalongkorn, Thailand, 1956-57; Fulbright prof. Am. lit. U. Brazil, Rio de Janeiro, 1959; prof., chmn. dept. lit. Park Coll., Parkville, Mo., 1964-66; prof. English, chmn. Center Lang. and Lit. Studies; Prescott (Ariz.) Coll., 1966-69, provost, 1968-71, dir. Prescott Coll. Press,, 1968-73, prof. English and comparative lit., 1972-73; prof. English and humanities U. Nev., Las Vegas, 1973—; dean Coll. Arts and Letters U. Nev., 1973-75, chmn. Asian Studies program, 1980-88; vis. prof. Ariz. State U., Tempe, summer 1968, SUNY, Buffalo, summer 1971, Utah Shakespeare Festival, 1972, Baylor U., summer 1976; vis. prof. U. Pa., 1983, 84; dramatic and music critic Billboard, 1947-54, Intermountain, 1954-64, Seattle Home News, 1947-53, Prescott Courier and The Paper, 1966-73, Las Vegas Rev.-Jour., 1973-77, Las Vegas Sun, 1977-84, Sta. KLAV-Radio, The Las Vegan. Author, editor: Poems Southwest, 1967, Stories Southwest, 1973; author: Pocatello; The World is Going to End Up in Burma; co-editor: Indian Poetry in English, 1988, Seven Nevada Poets, Desert Wind: Anthology of Nevada Poets, 1991; contbr. poems and articles to profl. jours. and anthologies; editor, founder lit. mag. Interim, 1944-55, 85—; theatre critic Las Vegas Rev. Jour., 1984—. Del. Theatre Libr. Assn. UNESCO Conf., San Francisco, 1957; mem. Nev. Humanities Com., 1982-88, Internat. James Joyce Found. Recipient Spanos Disting. Teaching award U. Nev., Las Vegas, 1986, Exemplary Svc. award Nev. Humanities Com., 1992; Frances Wayland scholar, 1940-42; inductee Nev. Writers Hall of Fame, Friends of Libr., U. Nev., Reno, 1992. Mem. MLA, Rocky Mountain MLA (pres. 1971), Conf. Christianity and Lit., Music Critics Assn. Am., Philol. Assn. Pacific Coast (exec. bd. 1978-80), Burma Studies Group, Modern Humanities Rsch. Assn., Am. Theatre Critics Assn., Renaissance Soc. Am., F. Scott Fitzgerald Soc., Theatre Libr. Assn., Brown Club (N.Y.C.), Princeton Club (N.Y.C.), Phi Kappa Phi, Beta Theta Pi. Home: 3770 Forestcrest Dr Las Vegas NV 89121-4909

STEVENS, CLYDE BENJAMIN, JR., property manager, retired naval offier; b. Denver, Oct. 10, 1908; s. Clyde Benjamin and Maybelle Olive (Boot) S.; m. Lucile Lillian-Louise Kip, May 5, 1933; children: Jane Stevens White, Donald Kip, Patricia Louise Stevens Schley. BS, U.S. Naval Acad., 1930; postgrad., U.S. Naval Postgrad. Sch., Annapolis, Md., 1939, U.S. Naval War Coll., Newport, R.I., 1947. Registered profl. engr. Commd. ensign USN, advanced through grades to rear adm., 1959; comdg. officer USS R-20, S-33 and Plaice, 1939-45; with torpedo prodn. and undersea weapons div. Bur. Ordnance, Washington, 1947-59, program dir., 1952-55, 56-59; ret., 1959; product mgr. TRW, Inc., Cleve., 1959-65; rsch. engr. Boeing Co., Seattle, 1965-74, torpedo cons., 1985; apt. owner and mgr., Seattle, 1967—; torpedo cons. Goodyear Aerospace Co., Akron, Ohio, 1965. Patentee automobile generator. Decorated Navy Cross, Silver Star with oak leaf cluster. Mem. Seattle Apt. Assn. (bd. dirs. 1967-91), Army and Navy Club, Rainier Club. Republican. Episcopalian. Home and Office: 2339 Franklin Ave E Seattle WA 98102-3342

STEVENS, DALE JOHN, geography educator; b. Ogden, Utah, June 27, 1936; s. Lawrence C. and M. Elma (Aldous) S.; m. Mary Lasson, June 1, 1962; children: J. Clarke, Alan, Jill, Sue Ann, Kaylene, Cherie. A.A., Weber State Coll., 1956; B.A., Brigham Young U., 1961; M.A., Ind. U., 1963; Ph.D., UCLA, 1969. Instr., U. Wyo., Laramie, 1963-64; asst. prof. geography Brigham Young U., Provo, Utah, 1966-72; assoc. prof. geography, 1972-82; prof. geography, 1982—; dept. chmn., 1988—; assoc. dir. Study Abroad, Vienna, 1985, dir., 1991—; observer U.S. Weather Service, Provo, 1980—. Author: Utah Weather, 1979; Field Projects in Physical Geography, 1981; Utah Weather Guide, 1983; Arches of Arches National Park, 1988, 91. Author: (with R. Clayton Brough) Climatography of Salt Lake City Snowfall, Precipitation and Temperatures, 1874-1988, 1988, (with others) Utah's High Winds, Intensities, Frequencies and Distribution, 1989, (with J. Edward McCarrick) Arches of Arches National Park, 1989, Using Physical Geography, 1990, (with others) Outline Map Blackline Masters: Set A, 1991, (with J. Edward McCarrick) Arches of Arches National Park, Supplement, 1991, Physical Geography Applications, 1992; contbr. entries to encyclopedias, articles to profl. jours. Mem. Orem Bd. Adjustments, Utah, 1984-85. Brigham Young U. grantee Arches Nat. Park, 1984. Mem. Assn. Am. Geographers, Soc. Applied Climatology (pres. 1983-86), Natural Arch and Bridge Soc. (exec. com. 1991—). Republican. Mormon. Office: Brigham Young U 690 SWKT Provo UT 84602

STEVENS, DAVID KING, civil engineer, educator; b. Kans. City, Kans., Dec. 17, 1954; s. Arthur David and Patricia (Williams) S.; m. Margaret Marie Cashell, May 18, 1985; children: Michael James, Abby Elizabeth. BSCE, Tufts U., 1976; PhD, U. Wis., 1983. Registered profl. engr., Ohio. Engr. irrigation U.S. Peace Corps, Malacca, Malaysia, 1976-78; rsch. assoc. U. Cin., 1984-86; asst. prof. Utah State U., Logan, 1986-90, assoc. prof., 1990—; cons. Soap and Detergent Assn., N.Y.C., 1982, Peer Cons., Washington, 1987-88, Dynamac Corp., Rockville, Md., 1989—, Am. Petroleum Inst. Contbr. articles to profl. jours. Recipient Cen. States Water Pollution Control Assn. Acad. Excellence award, 1981, Lewis H. Kessler award U. Wis., 1982; grantee EPA, U.S. Geol. Survey, Battelle Meml. Inst., 1984—, Nat. Inst. Environ. Health Scis., Electric Power Rsch. Inst. Mem. ASCE, Am. Water Works Assn., Internat. Assn. for Environment Rsch. and Control, Water Pollution Control Fedn., Sigma Xi, Phi Kappa Phi, Tau Beta Pi. Office: Utah State U UMC 4110 Logan UT 84322

STEVENS, DOUGLAS WILLIAM, inventor, entrepreneur; b. Jefferson, Iowa, Nov. 26, 1960; s. Richard Henry and Pat Van (McCurdy) S. Grad. high sch., Stewartville, Minn. Casino dealer Harrahs, Stateline, Nev., 1981-92; prin., inventor DWS Enterprises, South Lake Tahoe, Calif., 1986-92, Stateline, 1992. Patentee rangefinder. Mem. Nev. Inventors Assn. Home: 2605 Fountain Ave South Lake Tahoe CA 96150 Office: DWS Enterprises PO Box 6575 Stateline NV 89449

STEVENS, EDWARD FRANKLIN, college president; b. Newcastle, Wyo., Sept. 7, 1940; s. Edward Downey and Esther Elizabeth (Watt) S.; m. Linda Elaine Loewenstein, June 3, 1962; children: Carla Sue, Cathy Lynne. Student, U. Denver, 1959-60; BA in Edn., Physics, Chemistry cum laude, Nebr. Wesleyan U., 1963; MA in Ednl. Psychology, Stats. and Measurement, U. Nebr., 1967; PhD in Higher Edn., Mktg., Mgmt., U. Minn., 1983; postdoctoral, Harvard U., 1991. Tchr., head basketball coach Alvo-Eagle (Nebr.) High Sch., 1963-64, Madison (Nebr.) High Sch., 1964-65; asst. basketball coach U. Nebr., Lincoln, 1965-67; head basketball coach, asst. prof. edn. Augustana Coll., Sioux Falls, S.D., 1967-71; v.p., gen. mgr. tng. Iseman divsn. U.S. Inds., Sioux Falls, 1971-74; chief devel. and instl. advancement officer Sioux Falls Coll., 1974-79, asst. prof. then prof., 1980-83; exec. v.p. Kearny (Nebr.) State Coll. Found., 1979-80; pres. George Fox Coll., Newberg, Oreg., 1983—. Chmn. campaign Yamhill County United Way, Newberg, 1988; bd. commrs. Newberg Community Hosp., 1988-91. NDEA fellow, 1965; recipient Young Alumni Achievement award, Nebr. Wesleyan U., 1973, Leadership Fellows award, Bush Found., St. Paul, 1976. Mem. Am. Assn. Pres. Indep. Colls. and Univs., Nat. Christian Coll. Consortium (chmn. 1987-88), Nat. Assn. Intercollegiate Athletics (council pres., exec. com. 1988-92, chmn. 1992), Nat. Assn. Evangelists (Christian higher edn. com.), Nat. Assn. Indep. Colls. and Univs., Oreg. Ind. Colls. Assn. (bd. dirs. 1983-92, chmn. 1986-87), Oreg. Ind. Colls. Found. (bd. dirs. 1983-92, vice chmn. 1993), Coun. of Ind. Colls. (bd. dirs. 1990), N.W. Assn. Schs. and Colls. (commn. on colls.), Internat. Assn. Univs. Pres., New Life 200 (internat. com. reference), Rotary. Republican. Mem. Soc. Friends. Office: George Fox Coll Office of Pres 414 N Meridian St Newberg OR 97132-2625

STEVENS, ELEANOR SANDRA, professional services executive; b. Oklahoma City, Nov. 1, 1932; d. Benjamin Franklin and Mary Lou (Smith) Williams; children: Fred W., Nathandra, Benjiman, Ola Enaid. AS in medicine, Fresno State U., 1954; student Fresno Adult Edn., Los Angeles Trade Tech., 1972-73. Radio disc jockey, Fresno, Calif., 1954-55; bookkeeper Los Angeles County Assessor, 1961-69; supervisor Holzman-Begue Real Estate Co., Los Angeles, 1969-73; dist. mgr. United Systems, Inc., Los Angeles, 1973-77; pub. relations cons. Harold G. Simon & Assoc., Vernon, Calif., 1977-81; pres. Stevens Personalized Services, Los Angeles, 1982—. Recipient cert. profl. devel. State of Calif., 1983. Mem. Van Nuys Women's Referral Service, D.B. & O. Charity and Social Club, Los Angeles Good Neighbor Council, Nat. Assn. Female Execs., Order Ea. Star. Methodist. Office: 4614 S Western Ave Ste B Los Angeles CA 90062-2319

STEVENS, ELIZABETH ELLEN (BETTY STEVENS), academic dean; b. Manhattan, Kans., May 28, 1943; d. Nelson Lorenzo Dow and Crescentia C. (Gufler) Cary; m. Verl G. Stevens, Dec. 29, 1971; children: Cary Teresa, Emily Susan. BA, Kans. State U., 1965, MA, 1966; PhD, U. Kans., 1990. Diplomate Coun. of North Ctrl. Community and Jr. Coll., Dean's Acad., 1988-92. Instr. Crowder Coll., Neosho, Mo., 1966-67; asst. instr. U. Kans., Lawrence, 1967-70; instr. Pratt (Kans.) Community Coll., 1970-73, div. dir., 1976-85, acting dean continuing dean, 1985-87, coord. curriculum and instr., 1987-88, dean of instl. svcs., 1988-91; dean of instr. Northern Wyo. Community Coll., Sheridan, 1991—; dir. Western Kans. Community Svcs. Consortium, Pratt, 1979-91, S.W. Kans. Area Agy. on Aging, 1985-87; cons. Kans. State U. Gerontology Project, St. Joseph, Mo., 1988; dir., charter mem., bd. dirs. Wyo. Vols. of Am., 1992; cons., evaluator No. Ctrl. Assn. Colls. Schs., 1993—. Adv., editor coll. yearbook, 1976-79; editor, photographer coll. viewbook, 1979; editor coll. catalogue, 1977-81, 87-89.. Producer Feast & Follies Summer Theatre, Pratt, 1978-82; logo designer Pratt Kans. centennial com., 1984; hon. mem. Gov.'s task force on Alzheimer's Disease, Kans., 1986; bd. dirs. Assoc. Community Arts. Coun., Kans., 1987-88. Mem. P.E.O., Nat. Assn. Humanities Edn., Rotary. Home: PO Box 7277 Sheridan WY 82801-7028 Office: Northern Wyo Community Coll PO Box 1500 Sheridan WY 82801-1500

STEVENS, GEORGE ALEXANDER, farmer, realtor; b. Loma, Mont., Nov. 10, 1923; s. Otto Oliver and Josephine (Dale) S.; m. Martha Evie Fultz,

Sept. 16, 1944 (div. 1978); children: Gary, Kathleen, Arlene, Tina; m. Arleen Dorothea Largent, Nov. 14, 1978. A in Bus Admisntrn., SUNY, 1992. Prin. George Stevens Farm, Loma, Mont., 1946—, George Stevens, Realtor, Loma, Mont., 1957—; pres. George A. Stevens Corp., Loma, 1976—. Trustee Sch. Dist. # 32, Loma, 1947-50; election judge Precinct # 7, Loma, 1953-88. With USN, 1944-46, PTO. Mem. Nat. Assn. Realtors, VFW (life), Am. Legion, Elks (life), Eagles Lodge. Democrat. Lutheran. Home: HCR67 Box 19 Loma MT 59460-9702

STEVENS, HENRY AUGUST, insurance agent, educator; b. Frankfurt, Main, Germany, July 21, 1921; came to U.S., 1940; m. Rosemary O'Neil, Mar. 23, 1963; children: Michael, Patrick; 1 child from previous marriage, H. Jack Fay. Student, U. Wis., 1943-44; grad., Dale Carnegie Sch., Richland, Wash., 1974. Theatre mgr. Sterling Theatres, Seattle, 1946-54, Alliance Amusement Co., Chgo., 1955-68; ins. agt. N.Y. Life Ins. Co., Richland, 1968—; regional v.p. Washington Assn. Life Underwriters, Richland, 1980; mem. adv. com. Wash. State Ins., Olympia, 1983-89. Chmn. bd. Richland YMCA, 1968; commr. Benton County Dyking Dist., Richland, 1970; chmn. Benton-Franklin Counties Bi-Centennial Commn., Tri-Cities, Wash., 1976; precinct capt. Rep. Party, Benton County, 1980—. Staff sgt. U.S. Army 1943-46. Recipient Nat. Quality award, Nat. Sales Achievement award. Mem. Tri-Cities Life Underwriters Assn. (pres. 1975, bd. dirs.), Tri-Cities Estate Planning Coun. (pres. 1984), Kiwanis (pres. Chgo. club 1963, Richland club 1986-87, lt. gov. Pacific N.W. dist. club 1983, chmn. dit. conv. 1971, 81, 91, v.p. Pacific N.W. Found. 1975—). Home: 712 Riverside Dr Richland WA 99352-5216 Office: NY Life Ins Co 8203 W Quinault Ave Kennewick WA 99336

STEVENS, LELAND ROBERT, minister; b. Mpls., July 1, 1929; s. Leland J. and Mathilda Marie (Cloeter) S.; m. Meta Adele Asendorf, June 15, 1952; children: Kathryn, David, Elizabeth, Jonathan. BA, Concordia Seminary, St. Louis, 1950; MA, Syracuse U., 1968; MDiv, Concordia Seminary, St. Louis, 1983; PhD, St. Louis U., 1987. Ordained to ministry Lutheran Ch., 1953. Mil. chaplain USAF, 1953-73, commd., 1953, advanced through grades to col., retired, 1973; pastor First Luth. Ch., Bowie, Md., 1970-76, Trinity Luth., Alamogordo, N.Mex., 1976-79; editor Luth. Witness, St. Louis, 1979-84; pastor Shepherd of the Hills, Ruidoso, N.Mex., 1984-90; freelance religious editor Alamogordo, 1990—; instr. Park Coll., Ctrl. Tex. Coll., Holloman AFB, N.Mex., 1988—; commd. armed forces Luth. Ch./Mo. Synod, St. Louis, 1974-81; dir. of communications Rocky Mountain dist., Luth. Ch./Mo. Synod, Denver, 1989—. Republican. Home: 403 Sunglow Ave Alamogordo NM 88310-4126

STEVENS, NEIL GEORGE, school system administrator; b. Burley, Idaho, Aug. 6, 1951; s. Geroge Nettie and Louise Minerva (Powers) S.; m. Denise Diane Tracy, July 31, 1983; children: Faustin, Hannah. MA, U. Nev., 1991, EdS, 1992. Tchr., coach Minico High Sch., Rupert, Idaho, 1979-81, Kootenai High Sch., Harrison, Idaho, 1981-83; tchr., coach, vice-prin. McDermitt (Nev.) High Sch., 1983-91; prin. Eureka (Nev.) High Sch., 1991—.

STEVENS, ROBERT BOCKING, lawyer, educator; b. U.K., June 8, 1933; naturalized, 1971; s. John Skevington and Enid Dororthy (Bocking) S.; m. Katherine Booth, Dec. 23, 1985; 1 child, Robin; children by previous marriage: Carey, Richard. BA, Oxford U., 1955, BCL, 1956, MA, 1959, DCL, 1984; LLM, Yale U., 1958; LLD (hon.), N.Y. Law Sch., 1984, Villanova U., 1985, U. Pa., 1987; D.Litt. (hon.), Haverford Coll., 1991. Barrister-at-law London, 1956; tutor in law Keble Coll. Oxford U., 1958-59; asst. prof. law Yale U., 1959-61, assoc. prof., 1961-65, prof., 1965-76; provost, prof. law and history Tulane U., 1976-78; pres. Haverford Coll., 1978-87; chancellor U. Calif., Santa Cruz, 1987-91; of counsel Covington and Burling, Washington and London, 1992—; master Pembroke Coll., Oxford, 1993—; vis. prof. U. Tex., 1961, U. East Africa, 1962, Stanford U., 1966, U. Coll. London, 1991—; cons. UN, HEW, U.S. Dept. State. Author: The Restrictive Practices Court, 1965, Lawyers and the Courts, 1967, In Search of Justice, 1968, Income Security, 1970, Welfare Medicine in America, 1974, Law and Politics, 1978, The Law School, 1983, The Independence of the Judiciary, 1993. Rockefeller Found. grantee, 1962-64, Ford Found. grantee, 1962-64, 73-74, NEH grantee, 1973-74, Nuffield Found. grantee, 1975, Russell Sage Found. grantee, 1967-68; Hon. fellow Keble Coll. Oxford U., 1985, Socio-Legal Ctr. Mem. Nat. Coun. Humanities, United Oxford and Cambridge Univs. (London) Club. Home: The Lodging, Masters Lodgings, Pembroke Coll, Oxford OX1 1DW, England Office: Pembroke Coll, Eng and Leconfield House, Curzon St, W1Y 7FT London W1Y 7TF, England

STEVENS, ROGER SEYMOUR, retired music educator, musician; b. N.Y.C., Jan. 25, 1921; s. Roger Babington Stevens and Thelma Mae (Seymour) S.; m. Margaret Maureen Elsner, May 28, 1944; children: Roger Elsner, David Seymour, Ann Hunter. MusB, Eastman Sch. Music, 1942. Flutist L.A. Philharmonic, 1946-77; lectr. music U. So. Calif., L.A., 1948-78, prof. music, 1978-91; lectr. music Claremont (Calif.) Associated Colls., 1950-67, Occidental Coll., Eagle Rock, Calif., 1954-67; lectr. music Calif. State U., Northridge, 1955-88, Long Beach, 1955-60; freelance music, 1947-80. Author: (text) Artistic Flute, 1967; contbr. articles to profl. jours. With USAF, 1942-46. Recipient 13 Coaching awards Coleman Chamber Music Assn., 8 Coaching awards Monterey Peninsula Chamber Music, Coaching award Colmar (France) Competition, 1985. Mem. Chamber Music Am., Nat. Flute Assn.

STEVENS, STEPHEN EDWARD, psychiatrist; b. Phila.; s. Edward and Antonia S.; BA cum laude, LaSalle Coll., 1950; MD, Temple U., Phila., 1954; LLB, Blackstone Sch. Law, 1973; m. Isabelle Helen Gallacher, Dec. 27, 1953. Intern, Frankford Hosp., Phila., 1954-55; resident in psychiatry Phila. State Hosp., 1955-58; practice medicine specializing in psychiatry Woodland Hills, Calif., 1958-63, Santa Barbara, Calif., 1970-77; asst. supt. Camarillo (Calif.) State Hosp., 1963-70; cons. ct. psychiatrist Santa Barbara County, 1974-77; clin. dir. Kailua Mental Health Ctr., Oahu, Hawaii, 1977—. Author: Treating Mental Illness, 1961. Served with M.C., USAAF. Diplomate Am. Bd. Psychiatry and Neurology. Decorated Purple Heart. Fellow Am. Geriatrics Soc. (founding); mem. Am. Acad. Psychiatry and Law, AMA, Am. Psychiat. Assn., Am. Legion, DAV (Oahu chpt. 1), Caledonia Soc., Am. Hypnosis Soc., Am. Soc. Adolescent Psychiatry, Hawaiian Canoe Club, Honolulu Club, Elks, Aloha String Band (founder and pres.). Home: PO Box 26413 Honolulu HI 96825-6413 Office: 2333 Kapiolani Blvd Honolulu HI 96826

STEVENS, SUSAN FLUHR, preschool administrator; b. N.Y.C., June 26, 1954; d. Arthur Joseph and Helen E. (Ball) Fluhr; m. Martin E. Stevens, Jan. 6, 1979; children: Shane Michael, Rachel Alyssa. BA in Liberal Arts, Ariz. State U., 1976; postgrad., U. Alaska, Juneau, 1985, 86. Tchr. Sunrise Presch., Inc., Scottsdale, Ariz., 1986-88; asst. dir. Sunrise Presch., Inc., Chandler, Ariz., 1988-89; dir. 1 sch. Sunrise Presch., Inc., Tempe, Ariz., 1989-91; exec. dir. 2 schs. Sunrise Presch., Inc., Phoenix and Tempe, 1991-92; dir. 1 sch. Sunrise Presch., Inc., Phoenix, 1992—; kindergarten coord. Sunrise Presch., Scottsdale, 1989—. Roman Catholic. Office: Sunrise Presch 4111 E Ray Rd Phoenix AZ 85044

STEVENS, THEODORE FULTON, senator; b. Indpls., Nov. 18, 1923; s. George A. and Gertrude (Chancellor) S.; m. Ann Mary Cherrington, Mar. 29, 1952 (dec. 1978); children—Susan B., Elizabeth H., Walter C., Theodore Fulton, Ben A.; m. Catherine Chandler, 1980; 1 dau.; Lily Irene. B.A., U. Calif. at Los Angeles, 1947; LL.B., Harvard U., 1950. Bar: Calif., Alaska, D.C., U.S. Supreme Ct. bars. Pvt. practice Washington, 1950-52, Fairbanks, Alaska, 1953; U.S. atty. Dist. Alaska, 1953-56; legis. counsel, asst. to sec., solicitor Dept. Interior, 1956-60; pvt. practice law Anchorage, 1961-68; mem. Alaska Ho. of Reps., 1965-68, majority leader, speaker pro tem, 1967-68; U.S. senator for Alaska, 1968—, asst. Rep. leader, 1977-85. Served as 1st lt. USAAF, World War II. Mem. ABA, Alaska Bar Assn., Calif. Bar Assn., D.C. Bar Assn., Am. Legion, VFW. Lodges: Rotary, Pioneers of Alaska, Igloo #4. Home: PO Box 100879 Anchorage AK 99510-0879 Office: US Senate 522 Hart Senate Bldg Washington DC 20510

STEVENS, WALTER SCOTT, insurance company executive; b. Houston, July 21, 1962; s. William David and Barbara Ann (Duncan) S.; m. Kathleen Ann Martin, Feb. 2, 1985. BA in Fin., Bethany (W.Va.) Coll., 1984; MBA, Carnegie Mellon U., 1990. Ins. underwriter Hartford Ins., East Hartford/Bridgeport, Conn., 1984-87; ins. supr. Hartford Ins., East Hartford, 1987-88; fin. analyst Tex. Commerce Bank, Houston, 1989; project mgr. Fireman's Fund Ins., Novato, Calif., 1990-91; comml. ins. mgr. Fireman's Fund Ins., Sacramento, 1991—. Tutor Lit. Vols. Am., Middleton, Conn., 1987. Republican. Lutheran. Office: Firemans Fund Ins White Rock Rd Rancho Cordova CA 94949

STEVENS, WENDELL CLAIRE, anesthesiology educator; b. Mason City, Iowa, June 28, 1931; s. Lloyd Leroy and Amy Luella (Hodson) S.; m. Lola C. Claycomb, July 27, 1958; children: Amy P., Eric C., Mitchell L. AA, Mason City Jr. Coll., 1951; MD, U. Iowa, 1956. Diplomate Am. Bd. Anesthesiology. Intern City Hosp., Cleve., 1956-57; resident in gen. surgery U. Iowa Hosp., Iowa City, 1957-58, 60-61, resident in anesthesia, 1961-63; assoc. in anesthesia U. Iowa Coll. Medicine, Iowa City, 1963, asst. prof. anesthesia dept., 1963-67; asst. prof. U. Calif. Sch. Medicine, San Francisco, 1967-72, assoc. prof., 1972-77, prof., 1977; prof., chmn. anesthesia dept. U. Iowa Coll. Medicine, Iowa City, 1978-82, Oregon Health Scis. U., Portland, 1982—. Contbr. papers and book chpts. to profl. publs. Lt. USNR, 1958-60. Recipient anesthesiology rsch. grant U. Calif., San Francisco NIH, 1969-78. Mem. Oreg. Soc. Anesthesiologists, Am. Soc. Anesthesiologists, Oreg. Med. Assn., AMA, Christian Med. Soc. Republican. Baptist. Office: Oreg Health Scis Ctr Dept of Anesthesiology 3181 SW Sam Jackson Park Rd Portland OR 97201-3011

STEVENS, WILBUR HUNT, accountant; b. Spencer, Ind., June 20, 1918; s. John Vosburgh and Isabelle Jane (Strawser) S.; m. Maxine Dodge Stevens, Sept. 28, 1941; children: Linda Maxine Piffero, Deborah Anne Augello. BS, U. Calif., Berkeley, 1949, MBA, 1949. CPA, Calif. Staff acct. McLaren, Goode, West & Co., San Francisco, 1949-52; mng. ptnr. Wilbur H. Stevens & Co., Salinas, Calif., 1952-70; regional ptnr. Fox & Co., CPAs, Salinas, 1970-73; nat. dir. banking practice Fox & Co., CPAs, Denver, 1973-80; pres., chmn. Wilbur H. Stevens, CPA, PC, Salinas, 1980—; adj. prof. acctg. U. Denver, 1975-78; faculty mem. Nat. Banking Sch., U. Va., Charlottesville, 1976-86; chmn., dir. Valley Nat. Bank, 1963-71. Editor Issues in CPA Practice, 1975; contbr. articles to profl. jours. Capt. AUS, 1942-53. Decorated Bronze Star, China War medal, China Victory medal; Frank G. Drum fellow U. Calif., Berkeley, 1949; Paul Harris fellow Rotary Internat., Evanston, Ill., 1978. Mem. Nat. Assn. State Bds. Accountancy (pres. 1976-77), Acctg. Rsch. Assn. (pres. 1973-75), Calif. Soc. CPAs (pres. 1968-69, Disting. Svc. award 1988), AICPAs (v.p. 1971), Burma Star Assn., CBI Vets. Assn., Commonwealth Club Calif., Masons (master 1992), Rotary (dist. gov. 1983), Phi Beta Kappa. Republican. Methodist. Home and Office: 38 Santa Ana Dr Salinas CA 93901-4136

STEVENS-ALLEN, DAVID JOSEPH (MARQUESS OF ALN, VISCOUNT OF ST. ETIENNE BARON OF ST. JOHN AND OF ZELLAN), construction executive; b. Portland, Oreg., Apr. 12, 1925; s. John Raymond and Merle Cleone (Stevens) A. BA, San Diego State U., 1960, MA, 1971; PhD, U. Sarsota, 1972. V.p. Auto Mechanics Inst., L.A., 1965-67; labor rels. specialist Pacific Architects and Engrs., Saigon, Vietnam, 1967-70; edn. cons. Pacific States U., L.A., Paris, 1972-74; labor rels. mgr. Constructeurs Inga/Shaba, Kinshasa, Zaire, 1974-76. Author: The Lexarchy, 1983. Cand. for County Commr., Josephine County, Oreg., 1984, 1992. Ensign U.S. Merchant Marine, 1945, U.S. Army. Decorated Labor medal Republic of South Vietnam, 1969; decorated knight comdr. Merit Order St. John Jerusalem, knight comdr. Order Aztec Crown. Mem. Am. Merchant Marine Vets. (bd. dirs. Rogue Valley chpt.), Am. Legion, Josephine County Taxpayers Assn. Home: 442 Honeylynn Ln Grants Pass OR 97527-9013

STEVENSON, FRANCES GRACE, small business owner; b. Colorado Springs, Colo., Aug. 4, 1921; d. Albert Earl and Grace Margaret (Cahill) Storey; m. Robert Louis Stevenson, Oct. 23, 1943; children: Donald Maurice, Nancy Jean, Richard Dean (dec.), James Kirk. Grad. high sch., Las Vegas, Nev. Owner, mgr. Francie's Fancies, Napa, Calif., 1973-78, Cheyenne, Wyo., 1979-92. Organizer Citizens Com. for Sylvan Dist. Schs., Citrus Heights, Calif., 1954; mem. Napa (Calif.) County Dem. Cen. Com., 1966-78, chmn., 1975-78; hdqrs. chmn. McGovern for Pres., Napa, 1972; mem. Calif. State Dem. Cen. Com., 1975-78; chmn. Klee for U.S. Congress, Napa County, 1976, Brown for Gov., Napa County, 1976; candidate 2d Congl. Dist. Calif. Assembly, 1976; elector Carter for U.S. Pres., Napa County, 1976. Mem. Am. Cut Glass Assn., Am. Carnival Glass Assn., Am. Bell Assn., Cheyenne C. of C. Episcopalian. Home: PO Box 2263 Carson City NV 89701

STEVENSON, JAMES RALPH, school psychologist, author; b. Kemmerer, Wyo., June 29, 1949; s. Harold Ralph and Dora (Borino) S.; m. Alice M. Paolucci, June 17, 1972; children: Tiffany Jo, Brian Jeffrey. BA, U. No. Colo., 1971, MA, 1974, EdS, 1975. cert. elem. sch. counselor, Colo., nationally cert. sch. psychologist. Sch. psychologist Jefferson County Pub. Schs., Golden, Colo., 1975-87, 89-91, Weld County Sch. Dist. 6, Greeley, Colo., 1987-89, Weld Bd. Coop. Edn. Svcs., LaSalle, Colo., 1991—, Greeley, 1992—. Asst. coach Young Am. Baseball, Greeley, 1989, 90, head coach, 1992, 93; asst. basketball coach Recreation League for 6th-7th Grades, 1992, 93. U. No. Colo. scholar, 1974. Mem. NEA, NASP (alt. del. Colo. chpt. 1975-77, dir. Apple II users group Washington chpt. 1989—), Colo. Soc. Sch. Psychologists (chmn. task force on presch. assessment 1991—), Colo. Edn. Assn., Ft. Lupton Edn. Assn., Jefferson County Psychologists Assn. (sec. 1986-87). Democrat. Roman Catholic. Home: 1937 24th Ave Greeley CO 80631-5027 Office: Weld County BOCES PO Box 578 204 Main St LaSalle CO 80645

STEVENSON, JAMES RICHARD, radiologist, lawyer; b. Ft. Dodge, Iowa, May 30, 1937; s. Lester Lawrence and Esther Irene (Johnson) S.; m. Sara Jean Hayman, Sept. 4, 1958; children: Bradford Allen, Tiffany Ann, Jill Renee, Trevor Ashley. BS, U. N.Mex., 1959; MD, U. Colo., 1963; JD, U. N.Mex. 1987. Diplomate Am. Bd. Radiology, Am. Bd. Nuclear Medicine, Am. Bd. Legal Medicine, 1989; Bar: N.Mex. 1987, U.S. Dist. Ct. N.Mex. 1988. Intern U.S. Gen. Hosp., Tripler, Honolulu, 1963-64; resident in radiology U.S. Gen. Hosp., Brook and San Antonio, Tex., 1964-67; radiologist, ptnr. Van Atta Labs., Albuquerque, 1970-88, Radiology Assocs. of Albuquerque, 1988—, Civerolo, Hansen & Wolf, Albuquerque, 1988-89; adj. asst. prof. radiology U. N.Mex., 1970-71; pres. med. staff AT & SF Meml. Hosp., 1979-80, chief of staff, 1980-81, trustee, 1981-83. Author: District Attorney manual, 1987. Participant breast screening, Am. Cancer Soc., Albuquerque, 1987-88; dir. profl. div. United Way, Albuquerque, 1975. Maj. U.S. Army 1963-70, Vietnam; col. M.C. USAR, 1988—. Decorated Bronze Star. Allergy fellow, 1960. Med.-Legal Tort Scholar award, 1987. Fellow Am. Coll. Radiology (councilor 1980-86, mem. med. legal com. 1990—), Am. Coll. Legal Medicine, Am. Coll. Nuclear Medicine, Radiology Assn. of Albuquerque; mem. AMA (Physicians' Recognition award 1969—), Albuquerque Bar Assn., Am. Coll. Nuclear Physicians (charter), Soc. Nuclear Medicine (v.p. Rocky Mountain chpt. 1975-76), Am. Inst. Ultrasound in Medicine, N.Am. Radiol. Soc. (chmn. med. legal com. 1992—), N.Mex. Radiol. Soc. (pres. 1978-79), N.Mex. Med. Soc. (chmn. grievance com.), Albuquerque-Bernalillo County Med. Soc. (scholar 1959), Nat. Assn. Health Lawyers, ABA (antitrust sect. 1986—), N. Mex. State Bar, Albuquerque Bar Assn., Sigma Chi. Republican. Methodist. Club: Albuquerque Country. Lodges: Elks, Masons, Shriners. Home: 3333 Santa Clara Ave SE Albuquerque NM 87106-1530 Office: Van Atta Imaging Ctr A-6 Med Arts Sq 801 Encino Pl NE Albuquerque NM 87102-2612

STEVENSON, RICHARD GRAY, III, dentist; b. Long Beach, Calif., July 9, 1958; s. Richard Gray and Carla (Wood) S.; m. Victoria Puthumana, Sept. 15, 1985; 1 child, Richard Gray IV. BS, UCLA, 1982, DDS, 1986. Lic. dentist, Calif. Paramed. vol. Project Nepal, Palo Alto, Calif., 1979-80; dental rschr. Va. Med. Ctr., Sepulveda, Calif., 1980-83; pvt. practice Laguna Niguel, Calif., 1986—, Santa Ana, Calif., 1987-90; vis. lectr. Dental Sch. Faculty Operative Dept. UCLA. Active Youth Evolving Solutions, Palo Alto, 1980, Creative Initiative Found., Palo Alto, 1976-82, Students for Global Awareness, UCLA, 1980-82, Beyond War, Palo Alto, 1985—. Mem. ADA, Acad. Operative Dentistry, Acad. Gen. Dentistry, Calif. Dental Assn., Orange County Dental Soc., Crown Pacific Dental Study Club (co-pres. 1986—), Orange County Richard V. Tucker Cast Gold Study Club (co-founder, sec. 1991—), Lions (bd. dirs. 1987-88), Delta Sigma Delta (v.p. 1984-86). Office: 32241 Crown Valley Pky Laguna Beach CA 92677-6800

STEWARD, LESTER HOWARD, psychiatrist, academic administrator; b. Burt, Iowa, Nov. 6, 1930; m. Patricia Byrness Roach, June 17, 1953; children: Donald Howard, Thomas Eugene, Susan Elaine, Joan Marsha. BS, Ariz. State U., 1958, MA in Sci. Edn., 1969; PhD in Psychology, Calif. Coast U., 1974; postgrad., Escuela Nat. U., Mex., 1971-80; MD, Western U. Hahnemann Coll., 1980. Rscher. drug abuse and alcoholism Western Australia U., Perth, Australia, 1970-71; intern in psychiatry Helix Hosp., San Diego, Calif., 1971-72; rscher. drug addiction North Mountain Behavioral Inst., Phoenix, 1975-77; exec. v.p., chief exec. officer James Tyler Kent Coll., 1977-80; pres., chief exec. officer Western U. Sch. Medicine, 1980-86; instr. psychology USN Westpac, Subic Bay, Philippines, 1988-91; pvt. practice preventive medicine Tecate, Baja California, Mexico, 1971-88; instr. Modern Hypnosis Instrn. Ctr., 1974—, Maricopa Tech. Community Coll., Phoenix, 1975-77; mem. Nt. Ctr. Homeopathy, Washington, Menninger Found., Wichita, Kans. Contbr. numerous papers to profl. confs. Leader Creighton Sch. dist. Boy Scouts Am., Phoenix, 1954-58. With USN, 1949-54, 60, Korea. Fellow Am. Acad. Med. Adminstrs., Am. Assn. Clinic Physicians and Surgeons, Internat. Coll. Physicians and Surgeons, Am. Coll. Homeopathic Physicians, Am. Counc. Sex Therapy; mem. numerous orgns. including Nat. Psychol. Assn., Am. Psychotherapy Assn., Royal Soc. Physicians, World Med. Assn., Am. Acad. Preventive Medicine, Am. Bd. Examiners in Psychotherapy, Am. Bd. Examiners in Homeopathy, Western Homeopathic Med. Soc. (exec. dir.), Ariz. Profl. Soc. Hypnosis (founder 1974). Home: 515 W Townley Ave Phoenix AZ 85021-4566

STEWART, ANGUS BYNON, ophthalmologist; b. Klamath Falls, Oreg., Mar. 22, 1934; s. Ivor Neal and Lois Virginia (Bynon) S.; m. Joan Havland, Dec. 24, 1956; children: Sara E., Ian H., Avery H., Malcolm A.H., Thea L. BS, U. Oreg., 1956, MD, 1958. Diplomate Am. Bd. Ophthalmology. Pvt. practice Eureka, Calif., 1965—. Lt. USN, 1959-61. Office: 2840 O'Neil Ln Eureka CA 95503

STEWART, CHARLES F(RANKLIN), JR., clergyman, consultant; b. Evanston, Ill., Apr. 6, 1942; s. Charles Franklin and Constance (Brocker) S.; m. Nancy Jean Autio, Jan. 1, 1983. BA, Ariz. State U., 1967; MDiv, San Francisco Theol. Sem., 1970, DMin, 1973. Ordained to ministry, Presbyn. Ch., 1971. Pastor Fruitvale Presbyn. Ch., Oakland, Calif., 1973—, Immanuel Presbyn. Ch., San Jose, Calif., 1985, Christ Presbyn. Ch., San Leandro, Calif., 1987; stated clk. Presbytery of San Francisco, 1990-92; cons. gerontolgoy, Alameda, Calif., 1986—; pension cons. Older Adult Svc. Agys. Contbr. articles on ch. mgmt., aging, to various publs. Chmn. bd. dirs. MM Fed. Credit Union, Berkeley, Calif., 1988-90, Fred Finch Youth Ctr., Berkeley, 1988-90; vice-chmn. Mental Health Svc. Dist.; hon. chmn. campaign com. County supr. election, Alameda County. Mem. Am. Assn. Aging. Republican. Office: Presbytery San Francisco 890 Fargo Ave San Leandro CA 94579

STEWART, DALE LYNN, management consultant; b. Indpls., May 13, 1954; s. Paul John and Delores Loretta S.; m. Joy Ann Jenness, June 14, 1986; 1 child, Nicholas Allen. AS, St. Leo Coll., Fla., 1975, BBA, 1981; M. Bus., WEstern Internat., Phoenix, 1983. Lic. project mgmt. profl. Ptnr. S & C Constrn., Virginia Beach, Va., 1973-79; sr. engr. Bechtel Power, Gaithersburg, Md., 1979-80; supr. Ariz. Pub. Svc., Phoenix, 1980-83; owner DLS & Assocs., Loveland, Colo., 1983—; v.p. edn. Project Mgmt. Inst., Denver, 1988-92, chpt. pres., 1992—; assoc. prof. Metro. Coll., Denver, 1988-89. Commr. Planning/Zoning Bd., Loveland, 1991-92; mem. Young Reps., Phoenix, 1981. With USN, 1972—. Mem. Am. Nuclear Soc., Am. Mgmt. Assn. Roman Catholic. Home: 6006 Jordan Dr Loveland CO 80537 Office: DLS & Assocs PO Box 3 Loveland CO 80538

STEWART, DAVID WAYNE, psychologist, marketing educator, consultant; b. Baton Rouge, La., Oct. 23, 1951; s. Wesley A. Stewart and Edith L. (Richhart) Moore; m. Lenora Francois, June 6, 1975; children: Sarah Elizabeth, Rachel Dawn. BA, N.E. La. U., 1972; MA, Baylor U., 1973, PhD, 1974. Research psychologist Dept. Health & Human Svcs., La., 1974-76; reseach mgr. Needham, Harper & Steers Advt., Chgo., 1976-78; assoc. prof. Jacksonville (Ala.) State U., 1978-80; assoc. prof. Vanderbilt U., Nashville, 1980-86, sr. assoc. dean, 1984-86; prof. U. So. Calif., 1986-90, Ernest W. Hahn prof. mktg., 1990-91, Robert Brooker rsch. prof. of mktg., 1991—; mgmt. cons., 1978—. Author and co-author: Secondary Research: Sources and Methods, Effective Television Advertising: A Study of 1000 Commercials, Consumer Behavior and the Practice of Marketing, Focus Groups: Theory and Practice, Advertising and Consumer Psychology, Nonverbal Communication and Advertising; contbr. articles to profl. jours.; mem. editorial bd. Jour. of Mktg. Rsch., Jour. of Consumer Mktg., Jour. Mktg., Jour. Adv., Jour of Promotion Mgmt., Current Issues and Rsch. in Advertising, Jour. of Internat. Consumer Mktg., Jour. Managerial Issues, Jour. Promotion Mgmt.; past pres. policy bd. Jour. of Consumer Rsch. Fellow APA (coun. rep.), Am. Psychol. Soc. (charter); mem. Soc. for Consumer Psychol. (past pres.), Inst. Mgmt. Scis., Decision Sci. Inst., Am. Mktg. Assn., Assoc. for Consumer Rsch., Acad. of Mgmt. Republican. Baptist. Office: U So Calif Sch Bus Adminstrn Dept Mktg Los Angeles CA 90089

STEWART, DONALD EDWIN, association director; b. Modale, Iowa, Aug. 7, 1926; s. Cecil Davis and Ruby Jeanne (Baxter) S.; m. Barbara Joan Swaggerty, Jan. 1, 1977; children: Michael, Kathleen. Student, U. No. Idaho, 1946-47, Coll. of Idaho, 1955-59, Boise State U., 1958-59, Ariz. State U., 1968-70. Ind. bldg. contractor Caldwell, Idaho, 1946-65; owner lumber yard Caldwell, 1958-65; dist./city mgr. ABC Theatres of Ariz., Phoenix, 1966-71; owner DeNovo Stamp & Coin Co., Phoenix, 1972-82, Classic Signs/Western Printer, Phoenix, 1982-90; exec. dir. Key Collectors Internat., Phoenix, 1978—; Author 34 books including Standard Guide to Key Collecting; contbr. articles to profl. jours. Pres. Jaycees, Caldwell, 1955. With USN, 1943-54, World War II, Korea. Named Man of Yr. Caldwell Jaycees, 1955. Home and Office: 902 E Country Gables Phoenix AZ 85022

STEWART, FRED RAY, journalism educator; b. Ranger, Tex., Dec. 28, 1950; s. Montie R. Stewart and Irene (Norris) Burge; m. Vaunie L. Von Storch, June 23, 1987; children: Brent, Dheren, Ian. BA, U. Tex., Tyler, 1976; MA, Morehead (Ky.) State U., 1980. Editor Mt. Pleasant (Tex.) Daily Times, 1971-72, Tex. East Times Newspaper, Troup, 1974-75; sports editor Mid-Cities Daily News, Hurst, Tex., 1972-74; dir. pub. info. East Tex. State U., Texarkana, 1976-78; dir pub. info. Santa Maria (Calif.) High Sch. Dist., 1990-91; dir. news svcs. Morehead State U., 1978-81; head dept. jouranlism Yavapai Coll., Prescott, Ariz., 1981-85; asst. prof. No. Ariz. U., Flagstaff, 1985-90; head dept. journalism, instr. journalism, newspaper advisor Ohlone Coll., Fremont, Calif., 1991—; exec. dir. Rocky Mountain Collegiate Press Assn., Flagstaff, 1990. Editor sports mag., 1984-85; contbr. articles to mags. Coach Pop Warner Youth Football, Prescott, 1982-85, No. Ariz. Youth Football, Flagstaff, 1988-90; den leader Boy Scouts Am., Pleasanton, Calif., 1991. Recipient Outstanding Svc. award Kappa Tau Alpha, 1989. Mem. Journalism Assn. Calif. C.C.'s, Coll. Media Advisers, Phi Kappa Phi. Office: Ohlone Coll 43600 Mission Blvd Fremont CA 94539

STEWART, ISAAC DANIEL, JR., state supreme court justice; b. Salt Lake City, Nov. 21, 1932; s. Isaac Daniel and Orabelle (Iverson) S.; m. Elizabeth Bryan, Sept. 10, 1959; children: Elizabeth Ann, Shannon. B.A., U. Utah, 1959, J.D., 1962. Bar: Utah 1962, U.S. Ct. Appeals (4th, 8th, 9th and 10th cirs.) 1965, U.S. Supreme Ct. 1965. Atty. Dept. Justice, 1962-65; asst. prof., then assoc. prof. with tenure U. Utah Coll. Law, 1965-70, chmn. curriculum com., rsch. com., 1967-69; ptnr. firm Jones, Waldo, Holbrook & McDonough, Salt Lake City, 1970-79; justice Utah Supreme Ct., 1979—, assoc. chief justice, 1986-88; lectr. in field; mem. Utah Bd. Oil, Gas and Mining, 1976-78, chmn., 1977-78; Utah rep. Interstate Oil Compact Commn., 1977-78, exec. com. 1978-79; mem. adv. com. rules of procedure Utah Supreme Ct., 1983-87; chmn. com. on bar-press guidelines Utah Bar. Contbr. articles to legal jours. Chmn. subcom. on legal rights and responsibilities of youth Utah Gov's Com. on Youth, 1972; pres. Salt Lake chpt. Coun. Fgn. Rels., 1982; mem. Salt Lake City C. of C., 1974-79, mem. govtl. modernization com., 1976-78; missionary for Mormon Ch. in Fed. Republic Germany, 1953-56; bd. dirs. U. Utah Alumni Assn., 1986-89. Recipient Alumnus of Yr. award U. Utah Coll. Law, 1989. Mem. ABA, Utah Bar Assn. (com. on law and poverty 1967-69, com. on specialization 1977-78, pub. rels. com. 1968-69, chmn. com. on antitrust law 1977-78, com. on civil procedure reform 1968, mem. exec. com. bd. of appellate judges 1990—, Appellate Judge of Yr. 1986), Salt Lake County Bar Assn., Am. Judicature Soc., Order of Coif, Phi Beta Kappa, Phi Kappa Phi, Sigma Chi (Significant Sig award 1987). Office: Utah Supreme Ct 332 State Capitol Salt Lake City UT 84114-1181

STEWART, JAMES, lawyer; b. Salt Lake City, Oct. 23, 1951; s. James William and Francine (Robbins) S.; m. Peneé Wood, Apr. 21, 1979; children: James, Jason, Sherstin, Matthew. BA in Polit. Sci., Brigham Young U., 1975, MBA, 1981, JD, 1981. Bar: Utah 1983, U.S. Dist. Ct. Utah 1983, U.S. Ct. Appeals (10th cir.) 1983, Colo. 1985. Senate aide U.S. Senate Jud. Com., Washington, 1979; law clk. U.S. Ct. Appeals (10th cir.), Tulsa and Denver, 1981-82; assoc. VanCott, Bagley, Cornwall & McCarthy, Salt Lake City, 1982-85; assoc. Jones, Waldo, Holbrook & McDonough, Salt Lake City, 1985-87, ptnr., 1987—. Mem. Utah Bar Assn. (exec. com. young lawyers sect. 1987-88, program chmn. labor sect. 1988-89, continuing legal edn. dir. 1990—), Inns of Ct. I. Office: Jones Waldo Holbrook & McDonough 170 S Main St Ste 1500 Salt Lake City UT 84101-1644

STEWART, JAMES M., insurance and securities broker; b. L.A., July 9, 1946; s. Robert Lawrence and Maxine Madeline (Lininger) Stewart; m. Christina Jean Caruso; 4 children. BA, UCLA, 1971, MPH, MBA, 1975. Lic. series 7 securities, probate referee appointment. Dept. head UCLA Med. Ctr., L.A., 1971-77; dir. Children's Hosp., L.A., 1977-80; pres. J.M. Stewart Inc., Beverly Hills, Calif., 1980—; founder First Profl. Bank, Santa Monica, Calif., 1988—. Mem. Calif. Probate Referee Assn. (standards/ethics com., bd. dirs.), Provident Mutual Leaders Assn., St. James's Club. Republican. Office: 9595 Wilshire Blvd Ste 711 Beverly Hills CA 90212-2507

STEWART, JOHN MORROW, biochemistry educator; b. Greensboro, N.C., Oct. 31, 1924; s. David Henry and Mary Ellen (Morrow) S.; m. Joyce Loraine Clark, Sept. 3, 1949 (dec. 1989); children: Ellen Elizabeth, Susan Elaine, David Clark. BS, Davidson (N.C.) Coll., 1948; MS, U. Ill., 1950, PhD, 1952. Instr. Davidson Coll., 1948-49; rsch. assoc. Rockefeller Inst. Med. Rsch., N.Y.C., 1952-57; asst. prof. Rockefeller U., N.Y.C., 1957-64; assoc. prof. Rockefeller U., 1964-68; prof. biochemistry U. Colo. Med. Sch., Denver, 1968—; cons. in field; vis. prof. U. Sao Paulo, Brazil, 1987, Escola Paulista de Medicine, Sao Paulo, 1971, 73, 84, 88. Contbr. 280 scientific articles to profl. jours.; author: Solid Phase Peptide Synthesis, 1969, 2nd edit. 1984; inventor in field; patentee in field. With U.S. Army, 1943-46. NIH grantee, 1967—; Japan Found. for Promotion of Cancer Rsch. fellow, 1987; recipient Merit award U.S. NIH, 1986, Disting. Alumnus award Davidson Coll., 1993; Gold medal for discovery of bradykinin antagonists Frey-Werle Found., Germany, 1991. Fellow N.Y. Acad. Sci.; mem. Am. chem. Soc., Am. Soc. Biochemistry and Molecular Biology, Am. Soc. Pharmacology and Exptl. Therapeutics, Endocrine Soc., Soc. for Neurosci., The Protein Soc., Am. Peptide Soc., Am. Orchid Soc. (trustee 1987—). Office: Univ of Colo Med Sch 4200 E 9th Ave Denver CO 80262-0001

STEWART, JOHN WRAY BLACK, college dean; b. Coleraine, Northern Ireland, Jan. 16, 1936; s. John Wray and Margaret Reid (Black) S.; m. Felicity Ann Patricia Poole, Aug. 7, 1965; children: J.W. Matthew, Hannah Louise. BSc with honors, Queen's U., Belfast, Northern Ireland, 1958, B.Agr. with honors, 1959, PhD, 1963, DSc, 1988. Registered profl. agrologist. Sci. officer chem. rsch. div. Ministry of Agr., Belfast, 1959-64; asst. prof. soil sci. dept. U. Sask., Saskatoon, Can., 1966-71, assoc. prof., 1971-76, prof., 1976-81; dir. Sask. Inst. Pedology U. Sask., 1981-89; dean Coll. Agr. U. Sask., Saskatoon, 1989—; tech. expert, cons. FAO/IAEA, U.N.D.P., Vienna, Austria, 1971, 1974-75; sec.-gen. Sci. Com. on Problems of Environment, Paris, 1988-92; cons. UNESCO, Paris, 1990, pres. Sci. Com on problems of the Environment, 1992. Contbr. articles to profl. publs., chpts. to books. Fellow Can. Soc. Soil Sci., Berlin Inst. Advanced Study, Am. Soc. Agronomy, Soil Sci. Soc. Am.; mem. Brit. Soc. Soil Sci., Brazilian Soc. Soil Sci., Internat. Soc. Soil Sci., Agrl. Inst. Can. Office: U Sask, Coll Agr, Saskatoon, SK Canada S7N 0W0

STEWART, LARRY R., engineer, financial director, quality consultant; b. Rock Springs, Wyo., Mar. 26, 1948; s. Raymond Melvin and Mary Jane (Fillin) S.; m. Della Jean Warren, Aug. 25, 1967; children: Stephanie M., Kara K., Gina R., Laura J. BS in Engring., U. Wyo., 1970, MS in Engring., 1972. Registered profl. engr., Ariz., Colo., Idaho, Mont., N.Mex., Oreg., Tex., Utah, Wyo. Mgr. apt. Willey Enterprises, Laramie, Wyo., 1966-70; grad. asst. U. Wyo., Laramie, 1970-72; systems analyst Dept. Def., Corona, Calif., 1972-73; engr. Mountain Bell, Cheyenne, Wyo., 1973-77; adminstr. Mountain Bell, Denver, 1977-79; mgr. Mountain Bell, Englewood, Colo., 1979-84; dist. mgr. Mountain Bell, Denver, 1985-87; dir. Bell TRICO Services, Englewood, 1984-85, U.S. West CGI, Denver, 1987-92; divsn. mgr. Hamlin Electric Services, Inc., Ft. Morgan, Colo., 1993—; mem. adv. bd. U. Wyoming Grad. Sch., Laramie, 1970-72; IOF co-chair AT&T/Bell System, Basking Ridge, N.J., 1980-83; curriculum advisor Network Tng., Englewood, 1980-83; fin. advisor Employee Suggestion Plan, Denver, 1984-86. Editor (coll. mag.) Enginews, 1970. Pres. Maplewood Homeowners, Arvada, Colo., 1986; key chair United Way, Denver, 1988. Served with USAF, 1970-76. Mem. IEEE, Nat. Soc. Profl. Engrs. Republican. Lodge: Optimist (lt. gov. of Colo./Wyo. Dist.). Office: Hamlin Electric Svcs 138 West St Fort Morgan CO 80701

STEWART, LELAND PERRY, minister, educator, administrator; b. Detroit, Mar. 4, 1928; s. Hoyt Clifford and Gladys (Woodward) S.; m. Elizabeth Elliot, June 13, 1953; children: Deanna Jennings, Dana, Lynn Murphy. BS in Math. and Mech. Engring., U. Mich., 1949; STB, Harvard Divinity Sch., 1953. Cert. secondary edn. tchr., Calif. Minister Universalist Ch. of Hollywood, Calif., 1959-60; tchr. Glendale (Calif.) Unified Sch. Dist., 1960-62, L.A. Unified Sch. Dist., 1962-72; cen. coord. Unity-and-Diversity World Coun., L.A., 1965—; founding minister Unity-and-Diversity Fellowship, L.A., 1974—; substitute tchr. L.A. Unified Sch. Dist., 1972—; mem. faculty World U. in L.A., 1987—; bd. dirs. Interfaith Coun. for UN, L.A. Author: From Industrial Power to Lasting Peace, 1953; compiler World Scripture, 1954, Central Scriptures, 1954. Recipient Community Svc. award UNICEF, 1986. Democrat. Office: Unity-and-Diversity World Coun 1010 S Flower St Ste 401 Los Angeles CA 90015-1428

STEWART, MARLENE METZGER, financial planner, insurance agent; b. Portland, Oreg., Nov. 1, 1937; d. Eddie Charles and Helen M. (Grant) Metzger; m. Robert W. Stewart, Aug. 1, 1964 (dec. Jan. 1967); m. Melvin N. McBurney, Feb. 14, 1985. BA, U. Oreg., 1959; MA, U. Tex., El Paso, 1971. Exec. dir. Summer 72 Youth Com. Office of Mayor, Portland, 1972; registered rep. Mut. Life Ins. Co. N.Y., Portland, 1973-76, Prudential Life Ins. Co., Portland, 1976-77; ptnr. N.W. Fin. Planning, Portland, 1977-79; pres. Horizons Unltd. Fin. Planning, Portland, 1979-86; prin. EMR Fin. Adv. Svcs., Inc., Portland, 1986-89; registered rep. KMS Fin. Svcs., Inc., Portland, 1979—; owner Stewart Fin. Group, 1991—. Mem.-at-large Nat. Bd. YMCAs, 1971-73; bd. dirs. Met. YMCA Portland, 1972-75, YWCA Portland, 1989-92, treas. 1990-92; chmn. planned giving com. Arthritis Found., 1984-86. Bill Bottler scholar Portland chpt. CLU and Chartered Fin. Cons., 1981. Mem. Inst. Cert. Fin. Planners, Oreg. Soc. Inst. Cert. Fin. Planners (treas. 1985-86), Internat. Assn. Fin. Planners (pres. Oreg. chpt. 1987-88), Nat. Assn. Life Underwriters, CLU and Chartered Fin. Cons. (treas. Portland chpt. 1985-86), Assocs. Good Samaritan (steering com., chmn. 1991-92), Portland Downtown Rotary Internat., YWCA (bd. dirs. 1989-92, tres. 1990-92, fin. investment coms. 1989—). Republican. Presbyterian. Office: 4380 SW Macadam Ave Ste 525 Portland OR 97201-6408

STEWART, NANCY LEE, artist, art consultant; b. Pharr, Tex., Dec. 30, 1935; d. Elmer Lee and Willie Delilah (Epley) Shortes; m. James Edgar Davis, Aug. 24, 1956 (dec. Dec. 1961); children: James N., Glenn B., Garth A.; m. Charles Andrew Stewart, Nov. 24, 1982. BS in Art Edn., Tex. Tech U., 1965, M Art Edn., 1973, PhD in Fine Arts, 1982. Secondary tchr. art, dept. chmn. Lubbock Pub. Schs., 1967-78, 79-81; elem. art cons., program designer art magnet schs. Ector County Pub. Schs., Odessa, Tex., 1983-84; artist, art cons., Taos, N.Mex., 1985—; instr. drawing Tex. Tech U., Lubbock, 1979-80; dir. Stewart Studios, Taos, 1985—; condr. workshops for educators and adminstrs., Tex., 1972-85. Exhibited works in N.Mex. Traveling Exhbn., 1989, Highlands U., Las Vegas, 1988, Ea. N.Mex. U., Portales, 1990. Midland (Tex.) Coll., 1991, Milagro Gallery, Taos, N.Mex., 1991, Taos Fine Arts Gallery, 1993; represented in permanent collections at Town Hall, Red River, N.Mex., Tandy Corp., Ft. Worth, Meth. Hosp., Lubbock, Tex., also pvt. collections. Campaign chmn. Save the Trees, Carson Nat. Forest, 1983-85; sec. bd. dirs. Midland (Tex.) Arts Assembly, 1984-85, organizer Arts Everywhere, 1985; set designer Midland Opera Theater Centennial, 1985. Rsch. grantee Tandy Corp., 1972. Presbyterian. Home and Studio: PO Box 1872 Taos NM 87571

STEWART, NORMA LEE, communications executive; b. Odon, Ind., June 7, 1925; d. Wallace Cecil and Nova Arena (O'Donald) Hunter; m. Loren Dean Adams, May 10, 1945 (div. 1956); children: Loren Dean Jr., Dana Neill, Terrance Drake; m. Floyd Cecil Stewart, June 6, 1956; children: Rebecca Lynn, Brenda Alice. Student, Mesa Coll., 1984-85. Apt. mgr. Stanton, Calif., 1968-69; ins. salesperson Am. Nat. Ins. Co. Felix and Assocs., Escondido, Calif., 1973-74; mgr. Call Co., San Marcos, Calif., 1989—; regional dir. Fin. Planning Assocs., NYC; disk jockey, radio announcer ATS Radio Network, San Diego, 1984-85. Active Penasquitas City Coun., San Diego, 1977-82, Friends in Service to Humanity, 1982—. Home: 1750 W Citracado Pky Space 96 Escondido CA 92029-4129

STEWART, PAUL ANTHONY, II, author, association executive; b. Oakland, Calif., Apr. 14, 1952; s. Paul Anthony Sr. and Hilda Hensley (Monger) S.; m. Stephanie Anne Pitts, July 8, 1972; children: Jana Lorraine, Robyn Lynne. BA, San Jose (Calif.) State U., 1974, MS, 1975. News editor various pubs., 1974-77; v.p. legis. svcs. Bldg. Industry Assn. of Superior Calif., Sacramento, 1977-82; exec. v.p. So. div. Bldg. Industry Assn. of No. Calif., San Jose, 1982-86; exec. v.p. Bldg. Industry Assn. of San Joaquin Valley, Fresno, Calif., 1986-90; CEO Bldg. Industry Assn. of Cen. Calif., Modesto, 1990-91; chmn. Sacramento Regional Legis. Advs. Group, 1977-82. Host (TV show) Stewarts Sports Challenge, 1974 (Emmy nomination 1975); contbr. articles to profl. jours. Chmn. housing element update com. City of Sacramento, 1980, Transp. 2000 Steering LCom., San Jose, 1985-87; transp. commr. County of Santa Clara, Calif., 1986-87; pres. San Joaquin Valley Community Housing Leadership Bd., Fresno, 1988-90. Recipient Community Involvement award Calif. Hwy. Patrol, 1977; named one of Outstanding Young Men of Am., U.S. Jaycees, 1984. Mem. Nat. Assn. Home Bldrs., Calif. Bldg. Industry Assn. (exec. officers coun., pres. 1990-91), Internat. Soc. Poets, Poetry Soc. Am., Calif. Writer's Club, Sigma Delta Chi. Baptist.

STEWART, RENICE ANN, public relations consultant, writer; b. Milw., Jan. 2, 1947; d. Fredrick and Lucia (Stewart) Fregin; m. Thomas George Muehlbauer, July 5, 1968; children: Jennifer Jean, Whitney Susan. BA, U. San Diego, 1988, MA, 1990. Pres. Chubby Bumpkins, Inc., Houston, 1980-82; contracts adminstr. Gulf States Computer Svcs., Houston, 1980-82; pres. RAM Prodns., Houston, 1981-82, Pizza Internat., Inc., Houston, 1982-84; contracts adminstr. First Alliance Corp., Houston, 1982-85; freelance pub. rels. cons. San Diego, 1985—. Tutor U. San Diego Writing Ctr., 1987-89; founder, dir. pub. rels.-tng. Montgomery County (Tex.) Crisis Action Line, Houston, 1979-84; founder, v.p., bd. dirs. Montgomery County Rape Crisis Coalition, 1982-84, speaker, 1982-84; speaker Rape Trauma Coalition, 1982-84; mem. prodn. com. Community Women Together, Montgomery County, 1980-82; pres. Living Arts Coun., Houston, 1980-81. Named Woman of Yr. YWCA, 1981, 82. Mem. Am. Assn. Bus. Women (dir. activities Houston chpt. 1983-84), Bus. Women's Forum (bd. dir. community awareness Houston chpt. 1982-83), Assn. Women Bus. Owners, Lions (hon.), Phi Alpha Delta.

STEWART, RICHARD ALFRED, business executive; b. Hartford, Conn., Nov. 2, 1945; s. Charles Alfred and Theresa (Procopio) S. BS, Valley Coll., 1967. Account exec. Bank Printing Inc., Los Angeles, 1967-70; pres. Carpet Closet Inc., Los Angeles, 1970-73; western sales mgr. Josten's, Los Angeles, 1973-84; pres. Western Internat. Premiums, Los Angeles, 1984-87; dir. corp. sales Tiffany and Co., Beverly Hills, Calif., 1987-90, dir. major program sales, 1990-92; dir. regional sales Tiffany and Co., N.Y.C., 1992-93, dir. major programs, 1992-93; v.p. sales and recognition div. Jostens, Memphis, 1993—; recognition cons. Los Angeles Olympic Com., 1983-84. Contbr. articles to profl. mags.; developer medals for 1984 summer Olympics. Chmn. bd. dirs. Athletes and Entertainers for Kids.

STEWART, ROBERT LEE, retired army officer, astronaut; b. Washington, Aug. 13, 1942; s. Lee Olin and Mildred Kathleen (Wann) S.; m. Mary Jane Murphy; children: Ragon Annette, Jennifer Lee. BS in Math., U. So. Miss., 1964; MS in Aerospace Engring., U. Tex., 1972; grad., U.S. Army Air Def. Sch., 1964, grad. advanced course, guided missile systems officers course, 1970. Commd. 2d lt. U.S. Army, 1964, advanced through grades to brig. gen., 1986, fire team leader armed helicopter platoon 101st Aviation Bn., instr. pilot Primary Helicopter Sch., 1967-69; bn. ops. officer, bn. exec. officer 309th Aviation Bn., U.S. Army, Seoul, Korea, 1972-73; exptl. test pilot Aviation Engring. Flight Activity U.S. Army, Edwards AFB, Calif., 1974-78; astronaut candidate NASA, 1978, mission specialist Space Shuttle Mission 41-B, 1984; mission specialist STS-51J, 1985; dep. comdr. U.S. Army Strategic Def. Command, Huntsville, Ala., 1987-89; dir. of plans U.S. Space Command, 1989-92. Decorated D.S.M., (2) Legion of Merit, (4) DFC, (2) Purple Hearts, Bronze star, others; recipient NASA Space Flight medal, 1984, 85; named Army Aviator of Yr., 1984. Mem. Soc. Exptl. Test Pilots, Assn. U.S. Army, Army Aviation Assn. Am., Assn. Space Explorers. Home: 815 Sun Valley Dr Woodland Park CO 80863 Office: Nichols Rsch Corp 5575 Tech Ctr Dr Colorado Springs CO 80909

STEWART, SUSAN KAY, school administrator; b. Yuba City, Calif., June 3, 1951; d. Leo Max and Velma Claire (Dunlap) Luse; m. Robert Marion Stewart, Dec. 17, 1971; children: Karen, Robert Leo, Bryon. BA in Liberal Studies, Calif. State U., 1976. Substitute tchr. Tehachapi (Calif.) Unified Sch. Dist., 1975-80; tchr./ISP coord. Tehachapi Christian Sch., 1982-85; adminstr. Highland Christian Schs., Tehachapi, 1988—. Field dir. REACT Internat., Chgo., 1980-82; sec., bd. dirs. Tehachapi Crisis Pregnancy Ctr., 1991-93. Recipient Competent Toastmaster Toastmaster Internat., 1980. Mem. Christian Home Educators Assn. Calif. (area contact 1982-84, 90—, mem. svcs. dir. 1993—), Tehachapi Home Educators Group (newsletter editor 1990-93). Republican. Office: Highland Christian Schs PO Box 262 Tehachapi CA 93581

STEWART, TRENT ANTHONY, pharmacist; b. Cin., Dec. 10, 1954; s. Philip Howard and Essie Mae (Kilgore) S. B.S., U. Cin., 1978. Registered Pharmacist. Staff pharmacist Kettering Med. Ctr., 1978-81; staff pharmacist St. Elizabeth Med. Ctr., Dayton, Ohio, 1981-83; sales rep. Eli Lilly & Co., Portland, Oreg., 1983-84; mgr. pharmacy Dunbar Pharmacy and Med. Supply, Inc., Dayton, 1984-85; intravenous admixture pharmacist Dayton VA Med Ctr., 1985-88; staff pharmacist Portland (Oreg.) VA Med. Ctr., 1988—. Sponsor, Big Bros. and Big Sisters of Dayton, 1981. Mem. Dayton Area Soc. Hosp. Pharmacists (sec. 1985), Ohio Soc. Hosp. Pharmacists, Cin. Pharm. Soc., Internat. Platform Assn. Home: 5609 NW 179th Ave Portland OR 97229-1776 Office: Portland VA Med Ctr 3710 SW Us Veterans Hospital Rd Portland OR 97201-2964

STEZOSKI, LORISE ANN, critical care nurse, educator; b. Pitts., July 11, 1963; d. Walter and Pauline (Kurutz) S. ASN, Mt. San Antonio Coll., 1985; BSN, Calif. State U., L.A., 1987, postgrad., 1987—. RN, Calif. Part-time mem. faculty Calif. State U., L.A.; staff nurse Huntington Meml. Hosp., Pasadena, Calif.; clin. edn. specialist Hosp. of the Good Samaritan, L.A.; mgr. staff devel. Healthcare Ptnrs. Mem. AACN, Sigma Theta Tau.

STICH, SALLY SIMON, educator, newspaper columnist, writer; b. Omaha, Apr. 18, 1950; d. Stuart E. and Esther (Fox) Simon; m. Thomas M. Stich, Aug. 9, 1975; children: Max, Sarah. BA in French, U. Denver, 1972; MA in English, U. Colo., 1983. Cert. tchr., Colo. Tchr. St. Mary's Acad., Englewood, Colo., 1973-79; instr. writing U. Colo., Denver, 1980—; columnist Family Fun, Denver Post, 1986-92, edn. cons., 1987—; freelance writer, 1986—; adj. faculty U. Denver. Author: Writing with Today's Text, 1987; former contbg. editor New Choices Mag. Mem. women's com. Brandeis U., Denver, 1983—; bd. dirs. Herzl Jewish Day Sch., Denver, 1988—. Named Tchr. of Yr., St. Mary's Acad., 1976-78. Mem. Denver Women's Press Club (bd. dirs. 1992—), Colo. Authors League (pres., bd. dirs. 1993), Am. Soc. Journalists and Authors. Democrat. Home: 3227 S Niagara St Denver CO 80224-2825

STICKEL, FREDERICK A., publisher; b. Weehawken, N.J., Nov. 18, 1921; s. Fred and Eva (Madigan) S.; m. Margaret A. Dunne, Dec. 4, 1943; children—Fred A., Patrick F., Daisy E., Geoffrey M., James E., Bridget A. Student, Georgetown U., 1939-42; BS, St. Peter's Coll., 1943. Advt. salesperson Jersey Observer daily, Hoboken, N.J., 1945-51; retail advt. salesperson Jersey Jour., Jersey City, 1951-55; advt. dir. Jersey Jour., 1955-66, publisher, 1966-67; gen. mgr. Oregonian Pub. Co., Portland, Oreg., 1967-72, pres., 1972—, publisher, 1975—. Bd. regents U. Portland; mem. adv. bd. Portland State U.; bd. dirs. Portland Rose Festival Assn., United Way Oreg.; chmn. Portland Citizens Crime Commn.; mem. adv. bd. St. Vincent's Hosp. Capt. USMC, 1942-45. Mem. Assn. for Portland Progress (dir.), Portland C. of C. (dir.), Oreg. Newspaper Pubs. Assn. (past pres.), Pacific N.W. Newspaper Assn. (pres.), Am. Newspaper Pubs. Assn., University Club, Multnomah Athletic Waverley Country Club, Arlington Club, Rotary. Office: Oregonian Pub Co 1320 SW Broadway Portland OR 97201-3469

STICKEL, PATRICK FRANCIS, publishing executive, newspaper; b. Hoboken, N.J., Apr. 17, 1950; s. Fred A. and Margaret (Dunne) S.; m. Debra Isaak, May 10, 1986. Degree in bus. mgmt., U. Portland, 1975. With advt. dept. Jersey Jour., Jersey City, 1966-67; with Oregonian Pub. Co., Portland, 1967-68, 70-75, pressman, with retail advt. dept., 1975-77, with retail & circulation depts., 1980-86, adminstrv. asst., 1987-89, gen. mgr., 1990—; project mgr. Times Picayune, New Orleans, 1986-87. Bd. dirs. Oreg. Ind. Coll. Found., Portland, Oreg. Symphony Assn., Associated Oreg. Industries; exec. com. Oregon Forum, Portland; coun. advisors Youth Today, Inc., Portland. 1st lt. USMC, 1977-80. Oreg. Newspaper Pubs. Assn. (bd. dirs.), Rotary, Waverley Country Club, Univ. Club, Multnomah Athletic Club. Office: Oregonian Pub Co 1320 SW Broadway Portland OR 97201-3469

STICKNEY, ROBERT ROY, fisheries educator; b. Mpls., July 2, 1941; s. Roy E. and Helen Doris (Nelson) S.; m. LuVerne C. Whiteley, Dec. 29, 1961; children: Robert Roy, Marolan Margaret. BS, U. Nebr., 1967; MA, U. Mo., 1968; PhD, Fla. State U., 1971. Cert. fisheries scientist. Research assoc. Skidaway Inst. Oceanography, Savannah, Ga., 1971-73, asst. prof., 1973-75; asst. prof. Texas A&M U., College Station, 1975-78, assoc. prof., 1978-83, prof., 1983-84; prof. zoology, dir. Fisheries Research Lab., So. Ill. U., Carbondale, 1984-85; dir. Sch. of Fisheries U. Wash., Seattle, 1985-91, prof., 1985—; chmn. S-168 com. So. Regional Coop. Research Project, 1981-84. Author: Principles of Warmwater Aquaculture, 1979, Estuarine Ecology of the Southeastern United States and Gulf of Mexico., 1984; editor: Culture of Non-Salmonid Freshwater Fisheries, 1986, 92, Flagship: A History of Fisheries at the University of Washington, 1989; co-editor: Fisheries: Harvesting Life from Water, 1989, Culture of Salmonid Fishes, 1992, revs. in Aquatic, Fisheries Scis.; contbr. articles to profl. jours. Served with USAF, 1959-63. Fellow Am. Inst. Fisheries Rsch. Biologists (past bd. dirs. Tex. div.); mem. Am. Fisheries Soc. (pres. fish culture sect. 1983-84, pres. fish edn. sect. 1990-91, Tex. Aquaculturist of Yr. 1979), Am. Inst. Nutrition, World Aquaculture Soc. (bd. dirs., pres. 1991-92), Western Region Aquaculture Consortium (chmn. bd. dirs. 1987). Office: U Wash Sch Fisheries WH-10 Seattle WA 98195

STIEFEL, SHERYL KAY, museum curator; b. Tucson, June 12, 1958; d. Gilbert Roy and Rita Doris (Zimmerman) Cooperman; m. Mark Jonathan Stiefel, May 30, 1982; children: Elana Ruth, Miriam Rose. BA in Anthropology, Pitzer Coll., Claremont, Calif., 1980; MA in Anthropology, U. B.C., 1985. Mus. guide Griffith Obs., L.A., 1977-80; rsch. asst. Joint Sci. Ctr., Claremont Coll., 1977-80; teaching asst./lectr. U. B.C., Vancouver, 1980-82; curatorial asst. Mus. Anthropology, U. B.C., 1981; preparator Mus. of History and Industry, Seattle, 1983-84; asst. curator Mus. of History and Industry, 1984-86, chief curator, 1986—. Chmn. Leadership Devel. Grp., Seattle, 1984-85. Mem. Am. Assn. for State and Local History, Am. Assn. Mus., Sigma Xi. Home: 10026 NE 140th St Bothell WA 98011-5214 Office: Museum of History & Ind 24th Ave E Seattle WA 98112

STIFEL, FREDERICK BENTON, pastor, biochemist, nutritionist; b. St. Louis, Jan. 30, 1940; s. Carl Gottfried and Alma J. (Clark) S.; m. Gail Joane Stewart, Aug. 10, 1963; children: Tim, Faith, Seth, Elizabeth. BS, Iowa State U., 1962, PhD, 1967; MDiv., Melodyland Sch. Theol., Anaheim, Calif., 1979. Ordained to ministry Evang. Presbyn. Ch., 1981. Lab. supr., research chemist U.S. Army Med. Research and Nutrition Lab., Denver, 1968-74, Letterman Army Inst. Research, San Francisco, 1974-76; intern pastor Melodyland Christian Ctr., Anaheim, 1979-80; assoc. pastor Faith Presbyn. Ch., Aurora, Colo., 1980—; chmn. care of candidates com. Presbytery of West, Denver, 1985-88, 91—; bd. dirs., v.p. Love Inc. of Metro Denver, 1987-90; regional coord. Nat. Assn. Single Adult Leaders, 1987-90, coord. Denver area, 1990—, Colo. Pregnancy Ctrs., Inc., 1992—. Contbr. clin. med. and nutritional articles to profl. jours. Del. Iowa State Rep. Conv., Denver, 1984; mem. parent adv. coun. IMPACT drug intervention team Rangeview High Sch., Aurora, 1985-89, accountability com., 1989—; mem. Friends of the Arts, 1992—; young life leader Hinkley High Sch., Aurora, 1968-74; vice chmn. Young Life Com., Marin County, Calif., 1974-76. Capt. U.S. Army Med. Svc. Corps, 1967-70. Recipient Sci. Achievement award U.S. Army Sci. Conf., West Point, N.Y., 1968, 70, Parents of the Yr. award Rangeview High Sch., 1992-93. Mem. Am. Inst. Nutrition, Am. Soc. Clin. Nutrition, Am. Sci. Affiliation, Evang. Theol. Soc., Phi Eta Sigma, Phi Kappa Phi, Alpha Zeta, Gamma Sigma Delta, Kappa Sigma, Sigma Xi. Home: 3492 S Blackhawk Way Aurora CO 80014-3909 Office: Faith Presbyn Ch 11373 E Alameda Ave Aurora CO 80012-1023

STIGLICH, JACOB JOHN, JR., engineering consultant; b. Milw., Dec. 21, 1938; s. Jacob John Sr. and Augusta (Prezel) S. BSME, Marquette U., 1961; PhD, Northwestern U., 1970. Chief engr. Boride Products, Traverse City, Mich., 1971-74; mgr. ceramic materials Valeron Corp., Madison Heights, Mich., 1974-76; group leader, asst. dir. tech. Eagle Picher, Miami, Okla., 1976-78; program mgr. San Fernando Lab., Pacoima, Calif., 1978-84; tech. specialist Aerojet Ordnance Co., Tustin, Calif., 1984-85; cons. Sierra Madre, Calif., 1985—. Contbr. articles to profl. jours.; patentee in field. Col. USAR, 1961-92. Mem. AIME, Am. Soc. Metals, Am. Ceramic Soc., Mensa, Sigma Xi.

STIGLITZ, JOSEPH EUGENE, economics educator; b. Gary, Ind., Feb. 9, 1943; s. Nathaniel David and Charlotte (Fishman) S.; m. Jane Hannaway, Dec. 23, 1978; children: Siobhan, Michael, Edward, Julia. B.A., Amherst Coll., Mass, 1964; D.H.L., Amherst Coll., 1974; Ph.D. in Econs., MIT, 1966; M.A. (hon.), Yale U., 1970. Prof. econs. Cowles Found., Yale U., New Haven, 1970-74; vis. fellow St. Catherine's Coll., Oxford, Eng., 1973-74; Joan Kenney prof. econs. Stanford U., 1974-76, 88—; Oskar Morgenstern dist. fellow Inst. Advanced Studies Math., Princeton, N.J., 1978-79; Drummond prof. polit. economy Oxford U., Eng., 1976-79; prof. econs. Princeton U., 1979-88; with Pres. Clinton's Coun. Econ. Advisers, Washington, 1993—; mem. Pres.'s Coun. Econ. Advisers, 1993—; cons. World Bank, State of Alaska, Seneca Indian Nation, Bell Communications Rsch. Editor: Jour. Econ. Perspectives, 1986—; Am. editor Rev. of Econ. Studies, 1968-76; assoc. editor Am. Econ. Rev., 1968-76, Energy Econs., Managerial and Decision Econs.; mem. editorial bd. World Bank Econ. Rev. Recipient John Bates Clark award Am. Econ. Assn., 1979, Internat. prize Accademia Lincei, 1988, Union des Assurances de Paris prize, 1989; Guggenheim fellow, 1969-70; Hoover Instn. sr. fellow, 1988—. Fellow NAS (inst. policy reform), Econometric Soc. (coun.); mem. Am. Econ. Assn. (exec. com. 1982-84, v.p. 1985), Am. Acad. Arts and Scis.

STILES, KATHLEEN O'SHEA, wearable art designer, educator; b. Bangor, Maine, Dec. 25, 1956; d. David Lloyd and Lis B. (Sorensen) Peat; m. Gary E. Stiles, Apr. 13, 1986; children: Amber, Christopher, Robin, Steven. AA in Liberal Arts, Merced (Calif.) C.C., 1980; student, Calif. State U., Fresno, 1981-82. Freelance photographer Ctrl. San Joaquin Valley, Calif., 1979-84; broadcaster McClatchy Broadcasting, Fresno, 1984-86; owner Styles by Stiles, Fresno, 1986—, Kathi Stiles Sewing and Crafts Sch., 1993—; master licensee Simplicity Kids Can Sew, 1993—; instr. sewing, design and crafts Clovis (Calif.) Adult Sch., 1991—, Fresno Adult Sch., 1992—; cons. Knittin' Kitten, Clovis, 1990—; contbr., cons. Designer Kids, Lebanon, Oreg., 1990-92. Author: Sewing Machine Art, 1991, Jewelry-Making Techniques, 1992; designer, author Designer Kids Appliqués, 1990; contbg. designer Wearable Wonders mag., Berne, Ind., 1992—. Vol., Girl Scouts Am., Fresno, 1990—; mem., vol. KVPT-Channel 18, Fresno, 1989—.

Mem. Soc. Craft Designers, Coun. Am. Embroiderers, Fresno Arts Coun., Calif. Coun. for Adult Edn. Democrat. Christian. Office: Styles by Stiles 6751 N Blackstone Ste 254 Fresno CA 93710 also: Sewing and Crafts Sch 5265 N Blackstone Ave Fresno CA 93710

STILL, HAROLD HENRY, JR., engineering company executive; b. Beggs, Okla., Sept. 17, 1925; s. Harold Henry and Hannah Jane (Blackburn) S.; student U. Calif., Santa Barbara, 1946-49, USC, 1949-50, UCLA, 1975-76. Sr. specification writer Welton Becket and Assocs., L.A., 1968-71; dept. head Maxwell Starkman and Assocs., Beverly Hills Architect, 1971-72; project mgr. May Dept. Stores Co., L.A., 1972-74; sr. coordinator C.F. Braun and Co., Alhambra, Calif., 1975—, on leave, constrn. mgr. spl. project Runhau Evans Runhau Assocs., Riverside, Calif., 1978-79; architect, project adminstr. developing May Co. Dept. Store Complex for firm Leach Cleveland, Hyakawa, Barry & Assocs.; project mgr. constrn. Lyon Assocs., Inc.; pvt. cons. in constrn. practices, 1983—. With U.S. Army, 1943-45. Decorated Purple Heart. Mem. CSI, ICBO, ASTM, VFW (comdr. post 10965), Constrn. Inspection Assn. Republican. Congregationalist. Home: 503 Beverly Ave Paso Robles CA 93446-1227

STILLWELL, KATHLEEN ANN, healthcare consultant; b. Glendale, Calif., Aug. 12, 1950; d. Robert Dowayne and Irene Margaret (Sawatzky) Swanger; m. Joseph Wayne Stillwell, Nov. 11, 1971; children: Shannon Kristine, Nathan Joseph. AA, Cypress Coll., 1971; AS & diploma, Golden West Coll., 1981; BA in English Lit., Long Beach State U., 1982; MPA, Health Svcs. Adminstrn., U. San Francisco, 1989. RN Calif. Staff nurse Long Beach (Calif.) Meml. Hosp., 1981-84; sr. claims analyst Caronia Corp., Tustin, Calif., 1984-87; dir. quality assurance & risk mgmt. St. Mary Med. Ctr., Long Beach, 1987-89; cons. quality assurance, risk mgmt. Am. Med. Internat., Costa Mesa, Calif., 1989-91; cons. healthcare O'Mara & Assocs., L.A., 1991—; adj. faculty U. San Francisco; v.p. Patient Care Assessment Coun., L.A., 1988-89, pres., 1989-90, bd. dirs.; pres. State Bd. Patient Care Coun., 1990-92, past pres., 1992-94; speaker in field. Vol. Calif. Health Decisions, Orange County, 1989—, PTA, Am. Cancer Soc. Mem. Nat. League Nursing, Am. Soc. Healthcare Risk Mgmt., Nat. Assn. Healthcare Quality, Am. Soc. Quality Control Profls., So. Calif. Assn. Healthcare Risk Mgrs. (sec. 1989-90, membership chmn. 1989-90), Calif. League for Nurses (bd. dirs. 1993-95), Patient Care Assessment Coun. (v.p. So. Calif. 1988, pres. So. Calif. 1989-90, state bd. pres. 1990-92, state bd. dirs. 1992-94). Democrat. Lutheran. Home: 825 Coastline Dr Seal Beach CA 90740 Office: O'Mara & Assocs 3731 Wilshire Blvd Ste 770 Los Angeles CA 90010

STILSON, WALTER LESLIE, radiologist, educator; b. Sioux Falls, S.D., Dec. 13, 1908; s. George Warren and Elizabeth Margaret (Zager) S.; m. Grace Beall Bramble, Aug. 15, 1933 (dec. June 1984); children: Carolyn G. Palmieri, Walter E., Judith A. Stirling; m. Lula Ann Birchel, June 30, 1985. BA, Columbia Union Coll., 1929; MD, Loma Linda U., 1934. Diplomate Am. Bd. Radiology, Nat. Bd. Med. Examiners. Intern White Meml. Hosp., Los Angeles, 1933-34; resident radiology Los Angeles County Gen. Hosp., 1934-36; instr. radiology Loma Linda (Calif.) U. Sch. Medicine, 1935-41, asst. prof., 1941-49, exec. sec. radiology, 1945-50, assoc. prof., 1949-55, head dept. radiology, 1950-55, prof. radiology, 1955-83, chmn. dept. radiology, 1955-69, emeritus prof., 1983—; chief radiology service White Meml. Hosp., Los Angeles, 1941-65, Loma Linda U. Med. Ctr., 1966-69; chmn. dept. radiologic tech. Sch. Allied Health Professions, 1966-75, med. dir. dept. radiologic tech., 1975-83. Contbr. articles to health jours. Fellow Am. Coll. Radiology; mem. AAAS, Los Angeles Radiol. Soc. (sec. 1960-61, treas. 1961-62, pres. 1963-64), Radiol. Soc. N.Am., Am. Roentgen Ray Soc., N.Y. Acad. Sci., Inland Radiol. Soc. (pres. 1971), Alpha Omega Alpha. Republican. Adventist. Home: 25045 Crestview Dr Loma Linda CA 92354-3414 Office: Loma Linda Radiol Med Group 11234 Anderson St Loma Linda CA 92354-2870

STILWILL, BELLE JEAN, record company executive; b. Mackay, Idaho, Oct. 27, 1955; d. Allen LeRoy Stilwill and Galia Vee (Larter) Stilwill Dodd. Student, Ricks Coll., 1974-79, Def. Language Inst., 1980. Quality control Best Foods, Hermiston, Oreg., 1972-73; leader dance band Ricks Coll., Rexburg, Idaho, 1975-77; reporter Standard Jour., Rexburg, Idaho, 1976-77; news editor Chronicle-News, St. Anthony, Idaho, 1978; editor-in-chief The Scroll Ricks Coll., 1979-80; exec. asst. Rapid Printers, Monterey, Calif., 1981-82; corp. acct. Color-Ad Printers, Monterey, Calif., 1983—. Author (record albums) 1st Step, 1988 (Sam Segal award 1988), Mixed Signals, 1989 (Sam Segal award 1990, Album of Month Sta. KOFE Radio Idaho), Lovin' Arms, 1990. Faculty scholar Ricks Coll., 1979-80. Mem. NAFE, NARAS, Nat. Assn. Ind. Record Distributors, Broadcast Music Industry. Home: 1199 Luxton St Seaside CA 93955-6008 Office: Color Ad Printers 1187 Del Monte Ave Monterey CA 93940-2493

STIMMEL, DARREN CLARK, futures broker; b. Spokane, Wash., Sept. 12, 1962; s. Monty Clark and Linda Kay (Schultz) S.; m. Cristy Jeanne Bergevin, Dec. 3, 1989. BA in Fin., Ea. Wash. U., 1986. Salesman Western Auto, Davenport, Wash., 1977-80, NAPA, Cheney, Wash., 1982-86; broker Stotler & Co., Spokane, 1986-88, Walla Walla, Wash., 1988-90; owner Cycle Logical Trading Co., Walla Walla, 1990—. Mem. Libertarian Party of Wash. State, Seattle, 1987—; student ambassador People to People Internat., Davenport, 1978-81. Recipient nat. award Math. Assn. Am., Davenport, 1979, Dale Wilson Edn. Trust scholarship, Cheney, Wash., 1981-86, Century award Am. Bowling Congress, Walla Walla, 1992. Mem. Walla Walla Valley Amateur Radio Club, Nat. Futures Assn., Am. Bowling Congress, Elks. United Methodist. Office: Cycle Logical Trading Co 510 Menlo Walla Walla WA 99362

STIMMEL, JAMES RUSSELL, chemist; b. Columbus, Ohio, Apr. 9, 1950; s. James Eugene and Evelyn (Rose) S.; m. Cynthia Gay Freckleton, Aug. 6, 1977; children: Sandra Rose, Ilona Michelle, Jessica Leigh, James Russell II. BA in Chemistry, U. Calif. San Diego, LaJolla, 1973. Scientist Allied Chem. Corp., Idaho Falls, Idaho, 1974-80; sr. scientist Exxon Nuclear Idaho, Idaho Falls, 1980-83; from scientist to sr. scientist West Valley (N.Y.) Nuclear Svcs. Co., 1983-90; sci. supr. Lockheed Environ. Systems and Techs. Co., Las Vegas, Nev., 1990—. Bd. dirs. League for Handicapped, Springville, N.Y., 1985-90, sec. 1988-90. Recipient Quality Achievement award Westinghouse Electric, 1988, George Westinghouse award, 1989. Mem. ASTM (D19 com.), Am. Chem. Soc. Mem. LDS Ch. Office: Lockheed Analytical Lab 975 Kelly Dr Las Vegas NV 89119-2501

STINE, GEORGE HARRY, consulting engineer, author; b. Phila., Mar. 26, 1928; s. George Haeberle and Rhea (Matilda) (O'Neill) S.; m. Barbara Ann Kauth, June 10, 1952; children: Constance Rhea Stine Molde, Eleanor Anne Stine Trepas, George Willard. B.A. in Physics, Colo. Coll., 1952. Chief controls and instruments sect., propulsion br. White Sands (N.Mex.) Proving Grounds, 1952-55; chief range ops. div. U.S. Naval Ordnance Missile Test Facility at proving grounds, 1955-57; design specialist Martin Co., Denver, 1957; chief engr., pres. Model Missiles, Inc., Denver, 1957-59; design engr. Stanley Aviation Corp., Denver, 1959-60; asst. dir. research Huyck Corp., Stamford, Conn., 1960-65; sci. cons. CBS-TV, 1969, CBC, Toronto, 1969; sci. reporter Metromedia Radio News, N.Y.C., 1968; cons. Young & Rubicam Inc., N.Y.C., also Gen. Electric Co., Valley Forge, Pa., 1966-69; lectr. Franklin Inst., Phila., 1966-72; mktg. mgr. Flow Technology, Inc., Phoenix, 1973-76; cons. curator Internat. Space Hall of Fame, 1976; cons. astronautical history Nat. Air and Space Museum, Smithsonian Instn., 1965—; cons. mktg. research and surveys Talley Industries, Inc., Mesa, Ariz., 1977; cons. mktg. and communications Flow Tech., Inc., 1976-79; cons. Sci. Applications, Inc., 1976-81, Visions of the Future, 1982-86, McDonnell Douglas Corp., 1988-90, Sci. Applications Internat. Corp., 1990, Quest Aerospace Edn., Inc., 1992—, Aero Tech, Inc., 1991—; expert witness, fireworks injury cases, 1984—; pres. The Enterprise Inst., Inc., 1987—; cons., writer Discover Space Computer Program, Broderbond Software, Ind., 1992-93; moderator aviation conf., Bix on-line computer network, 1986—. Freelance writer, 1951—; author more than 50 books on astronautics and sci., including The Model Rocketry Manual, 1975, The Third Industrial Revolution, 2d edit, 1979, The New Model Rocketry Manual, 1977, Shuttle Into Space, 1978, The Space Enterprise, 1980, Space Power, 1981, Confrontation in Space, 1981, The Hopeful Future, 1983, The Untold Story of the Computer Revolution, 1984, The Silicon Gods, 1984, Handbook for Space Colonists, 1985, The Corporate Survivors, 1986, Thirty Years of Model Rocketry, A Safety Report, 1988, Mind Machines You Can Build, 1991, ICBM, The Making of the Weapon That Changed the World, 1991, The Handbook of Model Rocketry sixth edit., 1994; author: (as Lee Correy) sci. fiction novels and stories, including, Starship Through Space, 1954, Rocket Man, 1955, Contraband Rocket, 1956, Star Driver, 1980, Shuttle Down, 1981, Space Doctor, 1981, The Abode of Life, 1982, Manna, 1984, A Matter of Metalaw, 1986; (under own name) Warbots, Operation Steel Band, The Bastaard Rebellion, Sierra Madre, Operation High Dragon, The Lost Battalion, Operation Iron Fist, Force of Arms, Blood Siege, Guts and Glory, Warrior Shield, Judgement Day, Star-sea Invaders #1, First Action, Star-sea Invaders #2, Second Contact; contbr. numerous articles to jours. Charter mem. citizen's adv. coun. Nat. Space Policy, 1981—; Ariz. Space Commn., 1992—. Recipient Silver medal Assn. U.S. Army, 1967, Spl. award Hobby Industry Assn., 1969; Paul Tissandier diploma Fedn. Aeronautique Internationale, 1985. Fellow Explorers Club, Brit. Interplanetary Soc., AIAA (assoc.), Am. Rocket Soc.; mem. N.Y. Acad. Scis., Nat. Assn. Rocketry (hon. trustee 1967-82, founder 1957, pres. 1957-67, trustee 1978-81, Spl. Founder's award 1967, Howard Galloway Service award 1978, 83, 85, 87), Nat. Fire Protection Assn. (chmn. com. pyrotechnics 1974—), Aircraft Owners and Pilots Assn., Ariz. Pilots Assn. (dir. 1980-93, v.p. 1981-84), L-5 Soc (v.p. 1984). Home: 2419 W Saint Moritz Ln Phoenix AZ 85023

STINI, WILLIAM ARTHUR, anthropologist, educator; b. Oshkosh, Wis., Oct. 9, 1930; s. Louis Alois and Clara (Larsen) S.; m. Mary Ruth Kalous, Feb. 11, 1950; children—Patricia Laraine, Paulette Ann, Suzanne Kay. B.B.A., U. Wis., 1960, M.S., 1967, Ph.D., 1969. Planner cost acct. Kimberly-Clark Corp., Niagara Falls, N.Y., 1960-62; asst. prof. Cornell U., Ithaca, N.Y., 1968-71, assoc. prof., 1971-73; assoc. prof. U. Kans., Lawrence, 1973-76; prof. anthropology U. Ariz., Tucson, 1976—; head dept. anthropology U. Ariz., 1980-89; panelist anthropology program NSF, 1976-78; cons. NIH, 1974—; panelist NRC/NSF Graduate Fellowship Program, 1991—. Author: Ecology and Human Adaptation, 1975, Nature, Culture and Human History - A Biocultural Introduction to Anthropology, (with Davydd J. Greenwood), 1977, Physiological and Morphological Adaptation and Evolution, 1979 (with Frank E. Poirier and Kathy B. Wreden) In Search of Ourselves: An Introduction to Physical Anthropology, 1990; field editor for phys. anthropology The Am. Anthropologist, 1980-83; editor in chief Am. Jour. Phys. Anthropology, 1983-89; assoc. editor Nutrition and Cancer, 1981—; cons. editor Collegium Antropologicum, 1985—; contbr. articles. Mem. Gov.'s Adv. Council on Aging, State of Ariz., 1980-83. Nat. Inst. Dental Rsch. tng. grantee, 1964-68; Clark Found. grantee, Cornell U., 1973; Nat. Dairy Coun. grantee, 1985-88; Wenner-Gren Found. grantee, 1991—; fellow Linacre Coll., Oxford, 1985; vis. fellow U. London, 1991. Fellow AAAS (steering group sect. H 1987-91), Am. Anthrop. Assn., N.Y. Acad. Scis.; mem. Am. Assn. Phys. Anthropologists (exec. com. 1978-81, pres. 1989-91), Soc. for Study Human Biology, Human Biology Coun. (exec. com. 1978-81), Soc. for Study Social Biology, Am. Inst. Nutrition, Am. Soc. on Aging, Sigma Xi. Home: 6240 N Camino Miraval Tucson AZ 85718-3025 Office: U Ariz Dept Anthropology Tucson AZ 85721

STINSON, DAVID DONNEL, commuter programs and services administrator; b. Dilla, Sidamo, Ethiopia, June 16, 1957; arrived in Can., 1960; s. David Lloyd and Muriel Ruth (Bouck) S.; m. Rebecca Ann Buhler, Apr. 2, 1988; children: David Michael, Timothy Ryan, Matthew Douglas. BA, U. Calgary, Alta., Can., 1981; M of Missiology, Can. Theol. Sem., Regina, Sask., 1984; MEd, Western Wash. U., 1992. Resident dir. Trinity Western U., Langley, B.C., Can., 1984-87, dir. student svcs., 1987-91, dir. commuter programs and svcs., 1992—. Mem. Assn. Christians in Student Devel. Office: Trinity Western Univ, 7600 Glover Rd, Langley, BC Canada V3A 6H4

STIRLING, DALE ALEXANDER, environmental historian, consultant; b. Corona, Calif., Oct. 5, 1956; s. Alexander James and Marilyn Ann (Garrett) S.; m. Stephanie Kay Fox, Jan. 17, 1981. BA in History, U. Alaska, Anchorage, 1980; MA in History, Alaska Pacific U., 1984. Environ. historian Alaska Dept. Natural Resources, Anchorage, 1980-86; records mgr. Seattle Dept. Constrn. and Land Use, 1987; environ. historian Hart Crowser, Inc., Seattle, 1987-89, Landau Assocs., Inc., Edmonds, Wash., 1989—. Author: The Alaska Records Survey, 1986, Bibliography of Aviation History, 1985; contbr. articles to profl. jours. Mem. adv. bd. MA program Alaska Pacific U., Anchorage, 1984-86; bd. dirs. Friends of the Anchorage Libr., 1984-85, Friends of the U. Wash. Librs., 1990-92. Literary Artists Guild of Alaska grantee, 1982, Alaska Hist. Commn. grantee, 1983-85. Mem. Assn. Groundwater Scis. and Engrs., Environ. Assessment Assn., Assn. for the Bibliography of History, Nat. Coun. on Pub. History, N.W. Archivists, Soc. Am. Archivists, Pacific N.W. Historians Guild, Am. Assn. for State and Local History (Alaska state chair 1985-86), N.W. Oral History Assn. (Alaska del. 1984-86), Assn. N.W. Environ. Profls., Phi Alpha Theta. Home: 11502 Phinney Ave N Seattle WA 98133-8623 Office: Landau Assocs Inc PO Box 1029 Edmonds WA 98020-9129

STIRLING, THOMAS FLUCKIGER, programmer, analyst; b. Henderson, Nev., Sept. 23, 1955; s. Thomas Eldon and Louise (Fluckiger) S. AA, Dixie Jr. Coll., St. George, Uta, 1981. Ops. officer Sun Capital Bank, St. George, Utah, 1982-86; programmer, annalyst Murdock Travel, Salt Lake City, 1986—. Republican. Mem. LDS Ch. Home: PO Box 510933 Salt Lake City UT 84151-0933 Office: Murdock Travel 36 S State Ste 900 Salt Lake City UT 84111

STIRM, EUGENE ROBERT, artist, graphic arts company executive; b. Portland, Oreg., Jan. 6, 1945; s. Robert Adolf and Matilda Herminia (Niehaus) S.; m. Patricia Dale Button; Feb. 25, 1972; children: Malinda, Daniel, Mark. AA in Fine Arts, West Valley Coll., Campbell, Calif., 1965; postgrad., San Jose State Coll., 1965-66; BA in Comml. Art, N. Am. Coll., 1969; cert., Word of Faith Bible Coll., Dallas, 1983. Ordained minister of the Gospel. Art dir. Joston's Pub. Co., Visalia, Calif., 1972-76; owner, prin. Word Print Shop, Ivanhoe, Calif., 1976-79; freelance artist Orange County, Calif., 1979-85; pastor Christ's Love Fellowship Ch., Corina, Calif., 1980-85; gen. mgr. Menu Printers Inc., Orange, Calif., 1985-87; v.p., ptnr. Stirm/Collins & Assocs., Inc., Anaheim, Calif., 1987-91; lectr. in field. Author: Israel, Is Your Fig Tree Budding?, 1978; designer menus Plaza Hotel; executed mural of history of Yorba Linda, Calif., Yorba Linda C. of C., 1991; contbr. art work to profl. jours. Founder, Coarsegold (Calif.) Artist Assn., 1972-74; advisor Yorba Linda (Calif.) Light Opera, 1988-90. Recipient Fine Arts award Bank of Am., 1963, Strathmore Graphics Gallery Gold award, 1989. Mem. Printing Industry Am., Am. Orchid Soc. (editor newsletter 1984). Republican. Presbyterian. Home: 4665 School St Yorba Linda CA 92686-2441 Office: Artco Printers & Lithographers 1015 E Vermont Ave Anaheim CA 92805

STITES, FRANCIS NOEL, historian; b. Indpls., Dec. 25, 1938; s. Francis Charles and Grace Travis (Cooper) S.; m. Joan Carol, Aug. 27, 1966; children: Madelaine Marie, Audrey Elizabeth. BA, Marian Coll., 1960; MA in History, Ind. U., 1965, PhD in History, 1968. Prof. history San Diego State U., 1968—. Author: Private Interest and Public Gain: The Dartmouth College Case, 1819, 1972, John Marshall, 1981. Bd. dirs. San Diego Hist. Site Bd., 1988-91. Recipient Outstanding Faculty Contbn. to Univ. award San Diego State U., 1992. Mem. Orgn. Am. Historians, Am. Soc. for Legal History, Soc. for Historians of Early Am. Republic, Inst. of Early Am. History and Culture, Ind. Hist. Soc. Democrat. Office: San Diego State U Dept History San Diego CA 92182

STITNIZKY, JOHN LOUIS, health facilities and hospital services professional; b. Chgo., Oct. 10, 1939; s. John and Laura Lucille (Elzroth) S.; m. Yasuko Terada, June 2, 1961; children: Janet Laura, Diane Lynn, Sherry Jean. BA in Bus., Chaminade U. of Honolulu, 1977, postgrad., 1980-81. Enlisted USN, 1956, advanced through grades to sr. chief, ret., 1977; ins. underwriter Conn. Mut., Honolulu, 1977-80; gen. mgr. Waikiki Grand Hotel, Honolulu, 1980-81; auditor, night mgr. Outrigger Hotel, Honolulu, 1981-86; asst. dir. environ. svcs. St. Mary Med. Ctr. United Health Services, Inc., Long Beach, Calif., 1987-88; dir. environ. svcs. Fairview Devel. Ctr., Costa Mesa, Calif., 1988-89, Marriott Facilities Mgmt., Camarillo State Hosp., 1989-91; mgr., dir. environ. svcs. L.A. Dodgers Stadium, 1991-92; mgr. Gene Autry Western Heritage Mus., 1993—. Big borther Big Bros. of Hawaii, Honolulu, 1975-76; del. Rep. Conv., Honolulu, 1980. Mem. Navy League U.S. (life, sec., v.p. 1978-79, Sailor of Yr. award 1977), Am. Legion (comdr., dist. vice comdr. Post 56 1979), Fleet Res. (bd. dirs. bd. 46 1978), VFW, NRA (Cert. saftey instructor), Nat. Exec. Housekeepers Assn. (reg. mem.), Elks. Lutheran. Office: Marriott Corp Svcs 4700 Western Heritage Way Los Angeles CA 90027

STITT, GUY AMES, management consultant; b. San Fernando, Calif., June 24, 1957; s. Ronald Hannah and Jeanne Ann (Binckley) S.; m. Mary Ann Grangroth, May 28, 1982; children: Michael Andrew, Jeremy Ryan. Submarine weapons specialist USN, 1974-79; test asst. Todd Shipyards Corp., Seattle, 1979-81; project adminstr. Todd Shipyards Corp., 1981-82, dep. prog. mgr., 1982-83; dir. comml. ops. Applied Tech. Sys., Bremerton, Wash., 1983; cons. Am. Maritime Internat., Bremerton, 1983-84; pres., chief exec. officer AMI Internat., Bremerton, 1984—; naval advisor various cos. Editor: Worldwide Naval Projections Report, 1992. Mem. Bremerton Visitor & Conv. Bur., 1988—; strategist Mentor for Mayor campaign, 1989; mem. Bremerton Main St. Assn., 1987-89. With USN, 1974-79. Mem. Am. Soc. Naval Engrs., Am. Def. Preparedness Assn., U.S. Naval Inst., U.S. Naval League, Naval Submarine League, U.S. Navy Meml., The Mountaineers, The Sierra Club. Office: AMI Internat PO Box 30 Bremerton WA 98310-0087

STITT, ROBERT R., electrical engineer; b. Mpls., Dec. 5, 1941; s. Rhea Emerson and Katherine May (Knoop) S.; m. Kay Frances Reinartz, Sept. 4, 1965 (div. July 1980); m. Marcia Elston, Dec. 28, 1985; stepchildren: Marisa, Lisa, Rachel. BSEE, Mont. State U., 1965. Equipment engr. Boeing Comml. Airplane, Seattle, 1965-69; maintenance engr. Sparton S.W., Albuquerque, 1969-70; facilities elec. engr. Molybdenum Corp. Am., Questa, N.Mex., 1970-71; design engr. Gen. Mills, Mpls., 1972-73; sr. facilities engr. Boeing Aerospace, Seattle, 1975-80; sr. facilities engr. fabrication div. Boeing Comml. Airplane, Auburn, Wash., 1980-88; prin. engr. Boeing Comml. Airplane, Auburn, 1988—. Editor, co-author: Cave Gating, 1975; editor: SpeleoDigest, 1983, People Underground, 1992—; publisher, Cave Conservationist, 1990—; contbr. articles to profl. jours. Bd. dirs. Nat. Speleological Soc., Huntsville, Ala., 1973-85, exec. v.p., 1977-78, pres., 1981-83; bd. dirs., pres., treas. Seattle Folklore Soc., 1978-85; bd. dirs., pres. N.W. Folklife Festival, Seattle, 1980-85; joint venture Cave Rsch. Found., Columbus, Ohio, 1975-81, hon. mem., 1985; pres. N.W. Cave Rsch. Inst., 1987-89. Mem. Instrument Soc. Am., Nat. Speleological Soc. (dir. 1973-85, exec. v.p. 1977-78, pres. 1981-83, Cert. of Merit 1975, Outstanding Svc. award 1986), Seattle Folklore Soc. (dir., pres. 1978-85), N.W. Cave Rsch. Inst. (pres. 1987-89), NSS Cave Conservation and Mgmt. (chmn., sect. 1987—, treas. NSS Human Sci. sect. 1992—), Wash. State Folklife Coun. (treas. 1991—). Democrat. Office: Boeing Comml Airplane PO Box 3707 Mail Stop 51-AA Seattle WA 98124-2207

STITT, WILLIAM D., small business owner, marketing professional, consultant; b. Clarinda, Iowa, Oct. 15, 1913; s. William Porter and Mary C. (Standage) S.; m. Marjorie Brenneman, Sept. 5, 1937; children: Jolana, Orlo, John, Jeanne, Margaret. BSA, Iowa State U., 1936; BS in Bus., U. Chgo., 1943. Salesman various cos., Iowa, Wash. and Ill., 1936-43; br. mgr. Thompson-Hayward Chem., Memphis, 1944-45; sales mgr. Buckman Labs., Inc., Memphis, 1946-47, v.p. mktg., 1947-73; owner, mgr. Stittwood Properties, Anacortes, Wash., 1974—. Councilman City of Anacortes, 1987-88. Mem. Rotary (Paul Harris fellow 1985), Elks, Moose. Presbyterian. Office: Stittwood Properties PO Box 726 Anacortes WA 98221-0726

STITTICH, ELEANOR MARYANN, nursing educator; b. Blawnox, Pa.; d. Joseph John and Mary T. Stittich. BS in Nursing Ed., U. Pitts., 1951, M.Litt., 1954; postgrad., Johns Hopkins U., 1958-60, Humphrey's Sch. Law, Fresno, Calif., 1973-74. Staff nurse Sinai Hosp., Balt., 1947, Univ. Hosps., Cleve., 1947-48; staff nurse, clin. instr. St. Francis Med. Ctr., Pitts., 1948-51, med.-surg. instr., 1951-56; lectr. fundamentals, asst. in charge fundamentals U. Mich. Sch. Nursing, Ann Arbor, 1956-57; assoc. dir. nursing edn. Sinai Hosp. Sch. Nursing, Balt., 1957-64; prof. dept. nursing Calif. State U., Fresno, 1964-93, prof. emeritus, 1993—; western region cons. Neuman Systems Model, 1986—, trustee, exec. com., 1988—; researcher program for RN, Calif. State U., Fresno, 1982, programs for BSN degree students, 1988. Author: (with others) Neuman Systems Model, 1989. Educator program planning Alpha Tau Delta, 1975; mem. Cen. Valley chpt. Am. Heart Assn., Fresno, 1978-87, chairperson, 1982-85; mem., chairperson Cen. Valley Cancer Soc., Fresno, 1980-86; chairperson, vol. hospice com. St. Agnes Med. Ctr., Fresno, 1978-80, task force for pastoral care, hospice com., 1978-79; mem. exec. com. regional med. program UCLA, 1977-82. Recipient Cert. of Merit, Am. Heart Assn., 1986, Meritorious Performance & Profl. Promise awards, 1987, 90, Nurse of Yr. award Calif. Nurses Assn., 1991; scholar Sinai Hosp. Sch. Nursing, Balt., 1947. Mem. Am. Assn. Critical Care Nurses (bd. dirs. 1979—, pres. 1982-83, corr. sec. 1984—), Sigma Theta Tau (faculty advisor, bd. dirs., pres.-elect Mu Nu chpt. 1991-92, pres. 1992—), Delta Kappa Gamma (Eta Tau chpt., Chi state 1991—, chair legis. com., 1992—). Roman Catholic. Office: Calif State U Shaw & Maple Aves Fresno CA 93740

STIVISON, THOMAS HOMER, federal credit union executive; b. Boise, July 5, 1948; s. Homer M. and Del (Sanford) S.; m. Ernestine Mary Bell, May 20, 1970; children: Matthew, Kali. BA in Fin., Boise State U., 1972. Mktg. officer Bank of Idaho, Boise, 1972-76; pres. Grange Co-op Fed. Credit Union, Meridian, Idaho, 1976-84, Albertsons Employees' Fed. Credit Union, Boise, 1984—; mem. credit union adv. com. Dept. Fin. State of Idaho, Boise, 1980—. 1st lt. U.S. Army, 1968-75. Mem. Credit Union Nat. Assn. (nat. dir. 1987—), Idaho Credit Union League (1st vice-chmn. 1979-84, chmn. 1984-85, 2d vice-chmn. 1992-93, Outstanding Credit Union Profl. of Yr. 1990), Elks. Home: 1748 Gekeler Ln Boise ID 83706-4004 Office: Albersons Employees' Fed Credit Union 501 E Highland St Boise ID 83706-6598

STOCK, RONALD WILFRED, lawyer; b. Appleton, Minn., July 30, 1950; s. Wilfred F. and Leonora S. (Maynard) S.; m. Sharon Kay Fossen, Sept. 12, 1970; children: Krystal Meehee, Stephen Seungwhan. BA, S.W. Minn. State U., 1972; JD, U. Denver, 1974. Bar: Colo. 1975, Minn. 1975, Hawaii 1993, U.S. Dist. Ct. Colo. 1975, U.S. Ct. Appeals (10th cir.) Colo., 1983, U.S. Supreme Ct. 1984, U.S. Dist. Ct. Minn. 1975, U.S. Dist. Ct. Hawaii, 1993. Ptnr. Bennett & Stock, P.C., Appleton, 1975-76; city atty. City of Sterling, Colo., 1976-77, City of Aspen, Colo., 1977-81, City of Steamboat Springs, Colo., 1989—; spl. counsel Dept. of Interior, Washington, 1981-82; county atty. Adams County, Brighton, Colo., 1984; gen. counsel Front Range Airport, Watkins, Colo., 1982-89. Mem. sch. bd. RE-2 Sch. Dist., Steamboat Springs, 1991-93; advisory council appointment by Gov. of Colo., Colo. Legal Svc. 1990—. Mem. ABA, Colo. Bar Assn., Assn. Trial Lawyers Am., Nat. Dist. Atty. Assn., N.W. Colo. Bar Assn., Colo. Trial Lawyers Assn., Colo. Mcpl. League (pres. city atty.'s sect. 1990-91), Hawaii Bar Assn., Nat. Inst. Mcpl. Law Officers (state chair 1990—), Rotary. Democrat. Lutheran. Home: PO Box 772892 1735 Highland Way Steamboat Springs CO 80477 Office: City of Steamboat 137 10th St PO Box 775088 Steamboat Springs CO 80477

STOCKING, SHERL DEE, retail executive; b. Boise, Idaho, Aug. 20, 1945; s. Parley Dean and Iola Merrill (Linford) S.; m. Debra Lynn Hunt, Sept. 5, 1982. BS, Brigham Young U., 1968. Automotive specialist Bradshaw Auto Parts, Provo, Utah, 1964-68, J.C. Penney Co., Salt Lake City, 1969-70; store mgr. Uniroyal Tire Co., Salt Lake City, 1970-71; corp. tng. coordinator Uniroyal Tire Co., Houston, 1971, corp. advt. coordinator, 1972; store supr. Uniroyal Tire Co., Norfolk, Va., 1973-76; mgr. automotive dept. K-Mart Corp., Rapid City, S.D., 1976-79; dist. mgr. automotive dept. K-Mart Corp., N.Mex., 1979-80; mgr. Service Mdse. subs. K-Mart Corp., Denver, 1980-88; pres., owner S. & H. Svcs. Inc., Denver, 1988—. Pres. Quail Crossing Homeowner Assn., Denver, 1986—. Mem. Samuel Hall Soc. Mormon. Home: 115 146th St SE Lynnwood WA 98037-6711 Office: 4779 Lincoln St Denver CO 80216-2725

STOCKLAND, ALAN E., microbiology educator; b. Huron, S.D., July 18, 1938; s. C.O. and B.L. (Dawes) S.; m. Pak Moi Lim, Sept. 14, 1968; children: Brian, Tanya. BA/BS, U. Nebr., 1961; MSc, Mich. State U., 1967, PhD, 1970. Tchr. U.S. Peace Corps., Kuantan, Malaysia, 1962-63; prof. Weber State U., Ogden, Utah, 1970—. Office: Weber State U Dept Microbiology Ogden UT 84408

STOCKTON, ANDERSON BERRIAN, electronics company executive, consultant, genealogist; b. Lithonia, Ga., Oct. 7, 1943; s. Berrian Henry and Mary Grace (Warbington) S.; m. Linda Arlene Milligan, June 9, 1963; 1

child, Christopher Lee. Cert. in cryptographic engring., USAF Acad., Wichita Falls, Tex., 1963. Supr. Western Union Telegraph Co., East Point, Ga., 1965-67; mgr. RCA Corp., Cherry Hill, N.J., 1967-72; v.p. Universal Tech., Inc., Verona, N.J., 1972-76, Siemens Am., Anaheim, Calif., 1976-84, Concorde, El Toro, Calif., 1984-85, Data Card Troy, Inc., Santa Ana, Calif., 1985-86; dir. laser engring. div. ITT, San Jose, Calif., 1986-87; v.p. S.T.A.R. Ricoh Corp., San Jose, 1988-92; exec. dir. mktg. QUS, Inc., Mobile, Ala., 1992—; cons. Hutchinson (Minn.) Tech. Corp., 1984-87. Author: Polled Network Communications, 1976, A Quest for the Past, 1991; patentee in field. With USAF, 1961-65. Mem. IEEE, Am. Electronics Assn. Home: 2086 Silence Dr San Jose CA 95148

STOCKTON, DAVID KNAPP, professional golfer; b. San Bernardino, Calif., Nov. 2, 1941; s. Gail Rufus and Audrey (Knapp) S.; m. Catherine Fay Hales, Feb. 27, 1965; children—David Bradley, Ronald Edwin. B.S. in Gen. Mgmt., U. So. Calif., 1964. Mem. Golf's All Am. Team, 1974-76. Republican. Roman Catholic. Club: Elk. Office: 32373 Tres Lagos St Mentone CA 92359-9611

STOCKTON, RODERICK ALAN, chemist; b. Lafayette, La., Jan. 18, 1951; s. Herbert Raymond and Olivet (Smith) S.; m. Pamela Sue Jones, Aug. 1, 1981 (div. 1992). BS, Stephen F. Austin State U., Nacogdoches, Tex., 1974; PhD, Tex. A&M U., College Station, 1985. Rsch. assoc. Tex. A&M U., College Station, 1975-85; sr. chemist Midwest Rsch. Inst., Kansas City, Mo., 1985-87, EG&G Idaho, Idaho Falls, 1987-89; prin. chemist Westinghouse Hanford Co., Richland, Wash., 1989-92; owner SLR Systems, Richland, 1992—; owner Stockton Consulting Svc., Richland, 1990-92. Contbr. articles to profl. jours. Welch Found. fellow. Mem. Am. Chem. Soc. Home: PO Box 1265 Richland WA 99352-1265 Office: SLR Systems 2950 George Washington Way Richland WA 99352

STODDARD, ARTHUR GRANT, pilot; b. Twin Falls, Idaho, Jan. 8, 1947; s. Donald and Merle (Nelson) S.; m. Elfriede Anna Elizabeth Laburda, Apr. 22, 1978; 1 child, Ryan Erich. BS, U. Utah, 1969. Field worker Cornelli Seed Co., Twin Falls, 1963-69; stream guard Dept. Fish and Game, State of Alaska, Anchorage, 1967-69; mill cutter Jackalot Logging Camp, Homer, Alaska, 1969; counselor YWCA Kokokani, Kailua, Hawaii, 1968; waiter Rustler Lodge, Alta, Utah, 1966-69; pilot Sky Valley Aviation, Minden, Nev., 1970-71, Fairbanks (Alaska) Air Svc., 1972-74, Wien Air Alaska, Anchorage, 1974-84, Hawaiian Air, Honolulu, 1986—. Mem. Airline Pilots Assn. Home: 2825 S King St Apt 601 Honolulu HI 96826-3533

STODDARD, STEPHEN DAVIDSON, ceramic engineer, former state senator; b. Everett, Wash., Feb. 8, 1925; s. Albert and Mary Louise (Billings) S.; m. Joann Elizabeth Burt, June 18, 1949; children: Dorcas Ann, Stephanie Kay. Student, Tacoma Coll., 1944, Conn. Coll., 1946; B.S., U. Ill., 1950. Asst. prodn. supr., asst. ceramic engr. Coors Porcelain Co., Golden, Colo., 1950-52; ceramics-powder metallurgy sect. leader Los Alamos (N.Mex.) Sci. Lab., U. Calif., 1952-80; pres., treas. Materials Tech. Assocs., Inc., 1978—; cons. Ceramic Age Mag., 1958-60; Cons. Nuclear Applications for Ceramic Materials, 1958-60; Jury commr. Los Alamos County, 1969; justice of peace, 1956-62; mem. Los Alamos Sch. Adv. Council, 1966; mcpl. judge, 1976-77; chmn. Los Alamos Ordinance Rev. Com., 1958; Mem. Republican County and State Central Com., 1955—; county commr. Los Alamos, N.Mex., 1966-68; mem. Los Alamos County Planning Commn., 1962-63, N.Mex. Senate, 1981-92; bd. dirs. Bank of Los Alamos, 1982—; bd. dirs., exec. officer Los Alamos Econ. Devel. Corp. Patentee in field. Bd. dirs. Sangre de Cristo coun. Girl Scouts U.S.A., 1965-71, N.Mex. chpt. Nature Conservancy, 1987—, Southwestern Assn. on Indian Affairs, Inc., 1987-91. With AUS, 1943-46. Decorated Bronze Star, Purple Heart; recipient Disting. Alumni award U. Ill. Coll. Engring., 1986, Leopold Conservation award N.Mex. Nature Conservancy, 1988. Fellow Am. Inst. Chemists, Am. Ceramic Soc. (treas. 1972-74, pres. 1976-77, disting. life mem. 1984); mem. Nat. Inst. Ceramic Engrs. (PACE award 1965, Greaves Walker award 1984), Am. Soc. Metals, Los Alamos C. of C. (Citizen of Yr. award 1992), Sigma Xi, Alpha Tau Omega. Episcopalian. Clubs: Masons, Shriners, Elks, Kiwanis (pres. 1963-64, dist. dep. grand exalted ruler 1968-69, lt. gov. 1968-69), Los Alamos Golf Assn. (dir. 1964-66). Home: 326 Kimberly Ln Los Alamos NM 87544-3528 Office: PO Box 11 Los Alamos NM 87544-0011

STOEBE, THOMAS GAINES, materials science educator, department administrator; b. Upland, Calif., Apr. 26, 1939; s. Wallace Theodore and Martha Thomas (Gaines) S.; m. Jessica Rae Trout, June 20, 1959 (div. Jan. 1981); children: Brian, Paul, Diane; m. Janet Eleanor Dumm, Aug. 7, 1982. BS, Stanford U., 1961, MS, 1963, PhD, 1965. Instr. Imperial Coll., London, Eng., 1965-66; from asst. to assoc. prof. U. Wash., Seattle, 1966-75, prof., 1975—, assoc. dean, 1982-87, chmn. dept. materials sci. and engring., 1987—; vis. prof. U. Sao Paulo, Brazil, 1972-73; fellow USAF Materials Lab., Wright-Patterson AFB, Ohio, 1975; dir. materials and mfg. Wash. Tech. Ctr., 1992—. Patentee direct response dosimeter system; contbr. numerous tech. articles to profl. jours. Bd. dirs. Wash. Math., Engring., Sci. Achievement Program, Seattle, 1984—. Spl. fellow Atomic Energy Commn. Fellow Am. Soc. for Metals Internat.; mem. Am. Soc. Engring. Edn. (young faculty award 1972, Western Electric award 1977), Am. Phys. Soc., Materials Rsch. Soc., Metall. Soc. (chmn. No. Pacific sect. 1973), Am. Ceramic Soc., PRO Sports Club (Redmond, Wash.). Spl. fellow AEC. Home: 11106 NE 38th Pl Bellevue WA 98004-7653 Office: U Wash Roberts Hall FB-10 Seattle WA 98195

STOEN, J. THOMAS, energy company executive, land developer, investor; b. Milw., June 20, 1939; s. Joel A. and Lucile V. (Oliver) S.; m. Sara Peterson (div. 1980); children: Eric Thomas, Erin Kristen. BA, Wheaton (Ill.) Coll., 1961. V.p. Columbia Savs., Denver, 1964-72; pres. Crown Properties, Denver, 1972-74, Columbia Corp., Denver, 1972-74, Cimmaron Corp., Colorado Springs, Colo., 1974-79; chmn. Pacific Energy and Minerals Ltd., Colorado Springs, 1979-87; pres. Remington Oil and Gas Co., 1986—. Served to lt. U.S. Army, 1961-64. Clubs: Garden of the Gods, Broadmoor Golf (Colorado Springs); Castle Pines Golf Club (Castle Rock, Colo.). Home: 1911 Mesa Ave Colorado Springs CO 80906-2922

STOERMER, THOMAS GREGORY, title insurance company executive; b. Berkeley, Calif., June 12, 1954; s. Roy Robert and Elinore Frances (Cowles) S.; m. Betty Ann Cunningham, July 3, 1981; children: Andrew Robert, Jennifer Marie. AA, Diablo Valley Coll., Pleasant Hill, Calif., 1975; student, Humphries Sch. of Law, Stockton, Calif., 1992—. Title officer First Am. Title Co., Walnut Creek, Calif., 1972-77; adv. title officer Chgo. Title Ins., Hayward, Calif., 1977-80; chief title officer Yosemite Title Co., San Andreas, Calif., 1980-88; v.p. Yosemite Title Co., Sonora, Calif., 1988—; cons. speaker Calif. Land Surveyors Assn., Sonora, 1991-92, Bldg. Industry Assn., Tuolumne County, 1990-91. Cubmaster Boy Scouts Am., 1989-91; founding mem. Ebbetts Pass Recreation Dist., 1990—. Mem. Lions (zone chmn. Dist. 4A-1 1984-85, pres. 1991-92). Republican. Home: 1922 Deer Run Way Arnold CA 95223 Office: Yosemite Title Co 208 S Washington St Sonora CA 95370

STOHL, ESTHER A., senior citizen advocate; b. Olympia, Wash., Apr. 13, 1919; d. James Vernon and Anna Marie (Rixe) Snodgrass; m. Edwin F. Crowell, Sept. 4, 1938 (div. Apr. 1958); children: John Steven Crowell, Charles Edwin Crowell; m. Donald L. Stohl, Oct. 16, 1960 (dec. 1983). Grad. high sch., Olympia. Asst. to sales mgr. Ga.-Pacific Plywood, Olympia, 1937-41, 46-54; adminstrv. asst. Wash. Fedn. State Employees, Olympia, 1954-79; senate healthcare com. aide Wash. State Legislature, Olympia, 1980; office mgr. Sr. Citizens Lobby, Olympia, 1980-83, 84-89; office asst. Wash. State Ret. Tchrs. Assn., Olympia, 1989—; pres. Srs. Educating Srs., Olympia, 1984—; chmn. Area Agy. on Aging Adv. Coun., 1991-92. Author, editor Srs. Educating Srs. jour., 1984—. Consumer advocate Wash. State Long Term Care Commn., Olympia, 1989-90. Mem. AFSCME (life), Wash. Fedn. State Employees (life), Am. Assn. Ret. Persons (lobbyist 1988—), Sr. Citizens Lobby Wash., Ret. Pub. Employees Wash. Democrat. Lutheran. Home: 1347 NE Pear St Olympia WA 98506-3945 Office: Wash State Ret Tchrs Assn 910-B Lakeridge Way SW Olympia WA 98502-6036

STOKES, GERALD MADISON, research and development executive; b. Burlington, Vt., Aug. 19, 1947; s. Konrad Howard and Lois Batchelder (Brown) S.; m. Brooke Lee Buchanan, Sept. 11, 1971; children: Samantha, Garrett. BA in Physics, U. Calif., Santa Cruz, 1969; MS in Astronomy and Astrophysics, U. Chgo., 1971, PhD, 1977. Rsch. scientist Battelle Pacific NW Lab., Richland, Wash., 1978-84, sect. mgr., 1984-85, project mgr., 1985-86, mgr. computational scis., 1986-88, mgr. applied physics, 1988-90, dir. global studies, 1989—; tech. dir. DOE Atmospheric Radiation Measurement Program, Washington, 1989—; bd. dirs. Am. Coun. for Energy Efficient Economy, Washington, 1988-92. Contbr. articles to profl. jours. Mem. AAAS, Am. Geophys. Soc., Nat. Commn. on Sci. Edn. Standards and Assessment of Nat. Rsch. Coun. Home: 124 Orchard Way Richland WA 99352-9658 Office: Battelle Pacific NW Lab Battelle Blvd Richland WA 99352

STOKES, WANDA BERNICE, mortgage loan consultant; b. Cleve., Apr. 12, 1962; d. William Stokes and Irene Carter. Student, Banking Inst. Dir. fin. aid various career colls.; admission rep. Nat. Edn. Ctr., L.A., 1987-89; membership devel. dir. Better Bus. Bur., L.A., 1989—; mortgage cons. Gt. Western Bank, L.A., 1992—. Home: 5719 1/2 Condon Los Angeles CA 90056

STOKES, WILLIAM LEE, writer, geologist; b. Hiawatha, Utah, Mar. 27, 1915; s. William Peace and Grace Elizabeth (Cox) S.; m. Betty Asenath Curtis, Sept. 7, 1939; children—Betty Lee Stokes Huff, Mary Susan Stokes Griffith, William Michael, Patricia Jane, Jennifer Joy. B.S., Brigham Young U., 1937, M.S., 1938; Ph.D., Princeton U., 1941. Geologist, U.S. Geol. Survey, western states, 1942-47; prof. geology U. Utah, Salt Lake City, 1947-82, dept. head, 1954-68; cons. U.S. AEC, Colo., Utah, 1952-55, Standard Oil of Calif., Utah, Nev., 1950-51. Author: Essentials of Earth History, 1960, 66, 73, 82; co-author: Introduction to Geology 1968, 78; The Genesis Answer, 1984; The Great Salt Lake, 1985; Scenes of the Plateau Lands, 1969—; co-author: Messages on Stone, 1981, Geology of Utah, 1986; Glossary of Selected Geologic Terms, 1955; articles profl. and tech. papers, ann. rev. articles. Fellow Geol. Soc. Am.; mem. Am. Assn. Petroleum Geologists, Soc. Econ. Paleontologists and Mineralogists, Am. Geophys. Union, AAAS, Soc. Vertebrate Paleontology, Utah Geol. Assn. (pres.). Mormon. Club: Explorers (N.Y.C.). Home: 1283 E South Temple Apt 504 Salt Lake City UT 84102-1735

STOLL, CLIFFORD, astronomer, author; b. Buffalo, June 4, 1950. BA, SUNY, Buffalo; PhD, U. Ariz. Astronomer Purple Mountain Obs., Nanjing, China, 1980-81, U. Ariz., Tucson, 1981-82, Space Telescope Inst., Balt., 1982-85; rsch. assoc. Lawrence Berkeley (Calif.) Labs., 1985-89, Harvard-Smithsonian Astrophys. Obs., Cambridge, Mass., 1989-91. Author: The Cuckoo's Egg, 1989 (Best Book award Fgn. Intelligence Lit. Orgn. 1989). Recipient cert. of appreciation CIA, 1987, Giraffe award Giraffe Assn., 1988. Mem. Am. Astron. Assn., Assn. for Computing Machinery, Nat. Speleological Soc. (life), Am. Radio Relay League (life). Home: 6270 Colby St Oakland CA 94618

STOLL, PETER ALAN, electrical engineer; b. Cleve., Oct. 7, 1948; s. Donald Christian and Katherine Grace (Sharp) S.; m. Elizabeth Christine Luebbert, June 22, 1974; children: Virginia Lynn, Rebecca Anne. BS, MIT, 1972, MS, 1972, EE, 1974. Design engr. Intel Corp., Santa Clara, Calif., 1974-77, design engr., mgr., 1978-83, design mgr., 1987-88; reliability mgr. Intel Corp., Rio Rancho, N.Mex., 1988-92, mgr. yield engr., 1992—; design engr. Hewlett Packard, Palo Alto, 1977-78; hardware devel. engr. fellow Daisy Sys., Mountain View, Calif., 1983-87; cons. Brooktree Corp., San Diego, 1981-84. Patentee infield. Chmn. fin. com. Santa Clara United Meth. Ch., 1980, lay leader, 1979; Sun. sch. supt. Covenant United Meth. Ch., Albuquerque, 1990. Hertz fellow, 1972. Mem. IEEE, AAAS, Sigma Xi. Republican. Methodist.

STOLOV, WALTER CHARLES, educator, physician; b. N.Y.C., Jan. 6, 1928; s. Arthur and Rose F. (Gordon) S.; m. Anita Carvel Noodelman, Aug. 9, 1953; children: Nancy, Amy, Lynne. BS in Physics, CCNY, 1948; MA in Physics, U. Minn., 1951, MD, 1956. Diplomate Am. Bd. Phys. Med. and Rehab., Am. Bd. Electrodiagnostic Medicine. Physicist U.S. Naval Gun Factory, Nat. Bur. Stds., Washington, 1948-49; teaching and rsch. asst. U. Minn., Mpls., 1950-54; from instr. to assoc. prof. U. Washington, Seattle, 1960-70, prof., 1970—, also chmn., 1987—; editorial bd. Archives Phys. Medicine and Rehab., 1967-78, Muscle & Nerve, 1983-89; cons. Social Security Adminstrn., Seattle, 1970. Co-editor: Handbook of Severe Disability, 1981; contbr. articles to profl. jours. Surgeon USPHS, 1956-57. Recipient Townsend Harris medal CCNY, 1990. Fellow AAAS, Am. Heart Assn.; mem. Am. Acad. Phys. Medicine & Rehab. (Disting. Clinician award 1987), Am. Congress Rehab. Medicine (Essay award 1959), Assn. Acad. Physiatrists, Am. Assn. Electrodiagnostic Medicine (pres. 1987-88), Am. Spinal Cord Injury Assn. Office: Univ Washington Dept Rehab Medicine Seattle WA 98195

STOLPMAN, THOMAS GERARD, lawyer; b. Cleve., June 2, 1949; s. Joseph Eugene and Katherine Ann (Berry) S.; m. Marilyn Heise, Aug. 17, 1974; children: Jennifer, Peter. BA, UCLA, 1972; JD, Los Angeles, 1976. Bar: Calif. 1976, U.S. Dist. Ct. (cen. dist.) Calif. 1976, U.S. Dist. Ct. (ea. dist.) Calif. 1985. Ptnr. Carriage Trade Parking Service, Los Angeles, 1970-75, Silver, McWilliams, Stolpman, Mandel & Katzman, Wilmington and Los Angeles, Calif., 1976—. Editor The Forum, 1978-84; editor-in-chief The Advocate, 1984-87; contbr. articles to profl. jours. Bd. dirs. Miraleste Recreation and Park Dist., Rancho Palos Verdes, Calif., 1982—, Citizens Against Forced Annexation, Rancho Palos Verdes, 1978-83; del. Rancho Palos Verdes Council of Homeowners Assns., 1979-86, v.p. 1986; v.p., gov. Miraleste Assn., Rancho Palos Verdes, 1976-82. Named Trial Lawyer of Yr. So. Calif., Verdictum Juris, 1984. Mem. L.A. Trial Lawyers Assn. (bd. govs. 1979-83, pres. 1989), Calif. Trial Lawyers Assn. (bd. govs. 1987-90, exec. com. 1989-90), Assn. Trial Lawyers Am., Am. Bd. Trial Advocates, Nat. Bd. Trial Advocacy (cert.), L.A. Bar Assn., South Bay Bar Assn., Long Beach Bar Assn. Democrat. Roman Catholic. Office: Silver McWilliams Stolpman Mandel & Katzman 1121 N Avalon Blvd PO Box 1118 Wilmington CA 90744-3598

STOLTENBERG, CARL HENRY, university dean emeritus; b. Monterey, Calif., May 17, 1924; s. George L. and Eloise (Hyatt) S.; m. Rosemary Johnson, Apr. 20, 1973; children by previous marriage—Bruce C., Gail L., Susan I., Paul L., Shirley J.; stepchildren—Michael Johnson, Jillean Johnson. B.S., U. Calif.-Berkeley, 1948, M.F., 1949; Ph.D., U. Minn., 1952. Instr. U. Minn., 1949-51; asst. prof. Duke U., 1951-56; forest economist U.S. Forest Service, Washington, 1956; chief div. forest econs. research N.E. Forest Expt. Sta., Forest Service, USDA, Upper Darby, Pa., 1956-60; head dept. forestry Iowa State U., 1960-67; dean, prof. Oreg. State U. Coll. Forestry, Corvallis, 1967-90, dean emeritus, 1990; mem. adv. bd. Coop. Forestry Research, USDA, 1963-67, 86—, mem. adv. com. for state and pvt. forestry, 1970-74; mem. Oreg. Bd. Forestry, 1967-87, chmn., 1974-83; bd. dirs. Resources for Future, 1980-89. Author: Research Planning for Resource Decisions, 1970. Served with AUS, 1943-45, ETO. Mem. AAAS, Soc. Am. Foresters (pres. 1988, past mem. council, com. chmn.), Forest Products Research Soc., Am. Econ. Assn., Sigma Xi, Xi Sigma Pi. Methodist. Home: 14720 N Summerstar Blvd Tucson AZ 85737

STOLTZFUS, BEN FRANK, language educator, novelist, literary critic; b. Sofia, Bulgaria, Sept. 15, 1927; s. B. Frank and Esther (Johnson) S.; m. Elizabeth Burton, Aug. 20, 1955 ; div. 1975; children: Jan, Celia, Andrew; m. Judith Palmer, Nov. 8, 1975. BA, Amherst (Mass.) Coll., 1949, LittD (hon.), 1974; MA, Middlebury (Vt.) Coll., 1954; postgrad., U. Paris, 1955-56; PhD, U. Wis., 1959. Teaching asst. U. Wis., Madison, 1956-58; instr. in French Smith Coll., Northampton, Mass., 1958-60; prof. French, comparative lit. and creative writing U. Calif., Riverside, 1960-93, emeritus, 1993—. Author: (novels) The Eye of the Needle, 1967, Black Lazarus, 1972, Red White and Blue, 1989, (literary criticism) Alain Robbe-Grillet and the New French Novel, 1964, Georges Chenneviere et l'unanimisme, 1965, Gide's Eagles, 1969, Gide and Hemingway: Rebels Against God, 1978, Alain Robbe-Grillet: The Body of the Text, 1985, Alain Robbe-Grillet: Life, Work, and Criticism, 1987, Postmodern Poetics: Noveau Roman and Innovative Fiction, 1987; contbr. articles to profl. jours. Recipient Creative Arts Inst. awards U. Calif., 1967-75, Humanities Inst. awards, 1969-72; Fulbright-Hays rsch. grantee Paris, 1955-56, 63-64, Camargo Found. grantee, 1983, 85; U. Calif. fellow, 1991—. Mem. ALA, MLA, Am. Comparative Lit. Assn., Hemingway Soc., New Novel Assn., Camus Soc., PEN, Associated Writing Programs, Poets and Writers. Democrat. Home: 2040 Arroyo Dr Riverside CA 92506-1609 Office: U Calif Dept Literatures and Langs Riverside CA 92521

STONE, ALEXANDER PAUL, mathematics educator; b. West New York, N.J., June 28, 1928; s. Samuel Bradford and Violet Elizabeth (Schuessler) S.; m. Mary Ann Majeski, July 23, 1960; 1 child, Christopher Bradford. BSEE, Columbia U., 1952; MSEE, Newark Coll. Engring., 1956; PhD, U. Ill., 1965. Field engr. Western Elec./Bell Telephone Labs., Whippany, N.J., 1952-56; instr. in elec. engring. Manhattan Coll., Riverdale, N.Y., 1956-58; asst. prof. physics Dickinson Coll., Carlisle, Pa., 1958-60; asst. prof. math. U. Ill., Chgo., 1965-69; assoc. prof. math. U. Ill., 1969-70, U. N.Mex., Albuquerque, 1970-76; prof. math. U. N.Mex., 1976—, chmn. dept. math. and stats., 1991—; cons. Air Force Weapons Lab., 1984—. Editor: Improperly Posed Boundary Value Problems, 1976; author: Transient Lens Synthesis, 1990; contbr. articles to profl. jours. With USN, 1946-48, 2d lt. U.S. Army, 1951-52. NSF grantee, 1966-70, AFOSR grantee, 1984-85. Mem. Am. Math. Soc., Internat. Union of Radio Sci. (commn. E on electro-magnetic noise and interference). Office: Univ NMex Dept Math and Statistics Albuquerque NM 87131

STONE, BRINTON HARVEY, retired university official; b. Balt., Mar. 30, 1907; s. Harvey Brinton and Ethel (Hoffman) S.; m. Margaret Keeler, Aug. 19, 1933 (dec. Dec. 1975); children: Gregory B., David M., Melinda, Nancy E. AB, Johns Hopkins U., 1927, postgrad., 1928-32; MA, Columbia U., 1937. Asst. to pres. Haverford (Pa.) Coll., 1942-45; asst. to pres., dean men Alfred (N.Y.) U., 1946-48; asst. to v.p. U. Chgo., 1948-51; asst. to pres. Beloit (Wis.) Coll., 1951-52; exec. dir. Assoc. Colls. Ill., Chgo., 1952-53; v.p. Coll. of Idaho, Caldwell, 1953-54, Boise (Idaho) Jr. Coll., 1955-56; mem. staff higher edn. survey U. Calif., Berkeley, 1956-58, coll. and univ. placement adviser, 1958-74; ret., 1974. Author advice and info. commentaries.

STONE, DAVID GUY, public relations executive; b. Tualatin, Oreg., June 26, 1957; s. Dale Eugene Stone and Donna Mae (Phelps) Rowles; m. Brenda Lee Pugh, Sept. 3, 1977 (div. Feb. 1990); children: Carlin, Brandon; m. Melanie Anne Anderson, May 25, 1991; 1 stepchild, Ashley Elena. Student, Alaska Meth. U., 1975-76; BS in Geology, U. Alaska, 1979. V.p., dir. consumer affairs Alaska Electric Light & Power Co., Juneau, Alaska, 1980-89; mgr. pub. rels. Echo Bay Mines, Juneau, 1990—. Author: Hard Rock Gold, 1980. Bd. dirs. Alaska Coun. on Econ. Edn., 1991—; mem. Gov.'s coun. on vocat. edn., 1992—; mem. Gov.'s statewide private industry coun., 1992—. Mem. Alaska Miners Assn. (Juneau br., chmn.-bd. dirs. 1989—), Alaska Producers Coun. (vice chair-bd. dirs. 1990—, pres. 1992—), Alaska Mineral Energy Resource Edn. Found. (bd. dirs. 1990—), Juneau C. of C. (bd. dirs. 1989—), Rotary. Republican. Presbyterian. Home: 9348 Center Ct Juneau AK 99801-9633 Office: Echo Bay Mines 3100 Channel Dr Ste 2 Juneau AK 99801-7814

STONE, DAVID ULRIC, management executive; author; b. Santa Cruz, Calif., Feb. 4, 1927; s. Ernest Marshall and Grace (Stone) S.; student Theol. Ministry Sch., San Jose, Calif., 1945-48; grad. Real Estate Inst., Nat. Inst. Real Estate, 1964; m. Iva Dell Frazier, July 20, 1947; children—Katherine LaVerne, Russell Keith, Susan Marie. With E.M. Stone Realty, San Jose, 1945-48; mgr. Broadway-Hale Co., San Jose, 1948-52; sales mgr. William Perry Co., San Francisco, 1952-56; gen. mgr., ptnr. Stone & Schulte, Inc., San Jose, 1956-66; pres., chmn. bd. dirs. Stone Inst., Los Gatos, Calif., 1966; chmn. bd. Sunchoke Internat., Inc. 1983—, Custom One Internat. Inc., 1986—; pres. The Mktg. Forum, Inc., Mpls., 1986—; dir. Realty Programming Corp. St. Louis; chmn. bd. dirs. Custom One Internat., Inc., Mpls.; pres. Sunchoke Internat. San Juan Bautista, Calif, 1984. Named Realtor of Yr. Homes for Living Network, 1982. Mem. Nat. Inst. Real Estate Brokers (faculty mem. 1965—), Nat. Assn. Real Estate Bds. (chmn. joint task force 1966-68), Builder's Mktg. Soc. (founder, chmn. 1985), Calif. Real Estate Assn. (dir.), Nat. Assn. Home Builders (award 1960, Sales Mgr. of Year 1960, chmn. joint task force 1966-68, faculty mem. Inst. Residential Mktg. 1982—), The Builder Marketing Soc. (founder, chmn. bd.). Author: How to Operate a Real Estate Trade-In Program, 1962; Training Manual for Real Estate Salesmen, 1966; Guaranteed Sales Plan for Realtors and Builders, 1968 New Home Sales Training Course; The Professional Approach To Selling Real Estate; How To Communicate with Persuasive Power; How to Sell New Homes and Environmental Communities; How to Market and Sell Condominiums; How to Hire, Train and Motivate Real Estate Salespeople, How to Profitably Manage a Real Estate Office, 1977; The Road to Success in Real Estate, 1978; New Horizons in Real Estate, 1980; New Home Sales, 1982, Sales Power: American Sales Masters, 1986, The Gold Series, 1986, New Home Marketing, 1988. Home: 236 Camino Del Cerro Los Gatos CA 95032-4829

STONE, DONALD D., investment and sales executive; b. Chgo., June 25, 1924; s. Frank J. and Mary N. (Miller) Diamondstone; student U. Ill., 1942-43; B.S., DePaul U., 1949; m. Catherine Mauro, Dec. 20, 1970; 1 child, Jeffrey. Pres., Poster Bros., Inc., Chgo., 1950-71, Revere Leather Goods, Inc., Chgo., 1953-71; owner Don Stone Enterprises, Chgo., 1954—; v.p. Horton & Hubbard Mfg. Co., Inc. div. Brown Group, Nashua, N.H., 1969-71, Neevel Mfg. Co., Kansas City, Mo., 1969-71. Mem. adv. bd. San Diego Opera; founder Don Diego Meml. Scholarship Fund; mem. bd. overseers U. Calif., San Diego, chancellor's assoc.; mem. exec. bd. Chgo. Area council Boy Scouts of Am. Served with U.S. Army, 1943-46. Clubs: Bryn Mawr Country (Lincolnwood, Ill.) (dir.), Carlton, La Jolla Beach and Tennis, La Jolla Country, Del Mar Thoroughbred. Home: 8240 Caminito Maritimo La Jolla CA 92037-2204

STONE, EDWARD CARROLL, physicist, educator; b. Knoxville, Iowa, Jan. 23, 1936; s. Edward Carroll and Ferne Elizabeth (Baber) S.; m. Alice Trabue Wickliffe, Aug. 4, 1962; children—Susan, Janet. AA, Burlington Jr. Coll., 1956; MS, U. Chgo., 1959, PhD, 1964; DSc (hon.), Washington U., Saint Louis, 1992, Harvard U., 1992, U. Chgo., 1992. Rsch. fellow in physics Calif. Inst. Tech., Pasadena, 1964-66, sr. rsch. fellow, 1967, mem. faculty, 1967—, prof. physics, 1976—, chmn. div. physics, math. and astronomy, 1983-88, v.p. for astron. facilities, 1988-90, v.p., dir. Jet Propulsion Lab., 1991—; Voyager project scientist, 1972—; cons. Office of Space Scis., NASA, 1969-85, mem. adv. com. outer planets, 1972-73; mem. NASA Solar System Exploration Com., 1983; mem. com. on space astronomy and astrophysics Space Sci. Bd., 1979-82; mem. NASA high energy astrophysics mgmt. operating working group, 1976-84, NASA Cosmic Ray Program Working Group, 1980-82, Outer Planets Working Group, NASA Solar System Exploration Com., 1981-82, Space Sci. Bd., NRC, 1982-85, NASA Univ. Relations Study Group, 1983, steering group Space Sci. Bd. Study on Major Directions for Space Sci., 1995-2015, 1984-85; mem. exec. com. Com. on Space Research Interdisciplinary Sci. Commn., 1982-86; mem. commn. on phys. scis., math. and resources NRC, 1986-89; mem. adv. com. NASA/Jet Propulsion Labs. vis. sr. scientist program, 1986-90; mem. com. on space policy NRC, 1988-89; chmn. adv. panel for The Astronomers, KCET, 1989—. Mem. editorial bd. Space Sci. Instrumentation, 1975-81, Space Sci. Rev., 1982-85, Astrophysics and Space Sci., 1982—. Recipient medal for exceptional sci. achievement NASA, 1980, Disting. Service medal, 1981; Am. Edn. award, 1981; Dryden award, 1983; Space Sci. award AIAA, 1984; Sloan Found. fellow, 1971-73; NASA Disting. Pub. Service medal, 1985, NASA Outstanding Leadership Medal, 1986; Aviation Week and Space Tech. Aerospace Laureate, 1989, Science award Nat. Space Club, 1990, Sci. Man of Yr. award ARCS Found., 1991, Pres.'s Nat. medal of Sci., 1991, Am. Philos. Soc. Magellanic award, 1992, Am. Acad. Achievement Golden Plate award, 1992, COSPAR award for outstanding contribution to space sci., 1992, LeRoy Randle Grumman medal, 1992, Disting. Pub. Svc. award Aviation/Space Writers Assn., 1993. Fellow AIAA (assoc.), Am. Phys. Soc. (chmn. cosmic physics divsn. 1979-80, exec. com. 1974-76), Am. Geophys. Union; mem. NAS, AAAS, Internat. Astron. Union, Internat. Acad. Astronautics, Am. Astron. Soc. (com. mem. divsn. planetary scis. 1981-84), Am. Assn. Physics Tchrs., Am. Philos. Soc., Calif. Assn. Rsch. in Astronomy (bd. dirs. 1985—, vice chmn. 1987-88, 90—), Astron. Soc. Pacific (hon.), Am. Philos. Soc. Office: Jet Propulsion Lab 4800 Oak Grove Dr M/S 180-904 Pasadena CA 91109

STONE, HARRY, English language educator, writer, consultant, researcher; b. N.Y.C., Feb. 1, 1926; s. Bernard and Annie (Rappaport) S.; m. Esther M. Brucker, July 01, 1951 (dec. June 1970); children: Jonathan Bernard, Ann Melanie. BA, UCLA, 1946, MA, 1950, PhD, 1955. Teaching asst. UCLA,

1948-51, assoc. English, 1952-54, instr., summer 1956; instr. English Northwestern U., Evanston, Ill., 1955-57, asst. prof., 1957-60; asst. prof. English Calif. State U., Northridge, 1960-63, assoc. prof., 1963-66, prof., 1966—. Author: Dickens' Uncollected Writings, 2 vols., 1968 (Best Books of 1969 Am. Assn. Univ. Presses), Dickens' and the Invisible World, 1979 (Pres.'s prize Calif. State Univ./Northridge), Dickens' Working Notes for His Novels, 1987 (Honor book Chgo. Book Show); editor: George Silverman's Explanation, 1984 (Outstanding Western Book, Western Book Dealers Assn. 1984); mem. editorial bd. Dickens Studies Annual, 1972—, Nineteenth Century Lit., 1976-84; contbr. articles and revs. to profl. publs. Lt. (j.g.) USN, 1943-45. Univ. fellow UCLA, 1950, Guggenheim fellow, 1968-69, NEH Sr. fellow, 1975-76; Am. Coun. Learned Socs. travel grantee, 1970, rsch. grantee, 1974, 80, numerous others. Mem. AAUP, MLA, Philological Assn. Pacific Coast, Dickens Soc. Am. (v.p. 1976-77, pres. 1977-78), Nat. Coun. Tchrs. English, NEA, Internat. Assn. Univ. Profs. English. Office: Calif State U Dept English Northridge CA 91330

STONE, JAMES ROBERT, surgeon; b. Greeley, Colo., Jan. 8, 1948; s. Anthony Joseph and Dolores Concetta (Pietrafeso) S.; m. Kaye Janet Friedman, May 16, 1970; children: Jeffrey, Marisa. BA, U. Colo., 1970; MD, U. Guadalajara, Mex., 1976. Diplomate Am. Bd. Surgery, Am. Bd. Surg. Critical Care. Intern Md. Gen. Hosp., Balt., 1978-79; resident in surgery St. Joseph Hosp., Denver, 1979-83; practice medicine specializing in surgery Grand Junction, Colo., 1983-87; staff surgeon, dir. critical care Va. Med. Ctr., Grand Junction, 1987-88; dir. trauma surgery and critical care, chief surgery St. Francis Hosp., Colorado Springs, Colo., 1988-91; pvt. practice Kodiak, Alaska, 1991-92; with Surgical & Trauma Assocs., Englewood, Colo., 1992—; asst. clin. prof. surgery U. Colo. Health Sci. Ctr., Denver, 1984—; pres. Stone Aire Cons., Grand Junction, 1988—; owner, operator Jjnka Ranch, Flourissant, Colo.; spl. advisor CAP; med. advisor med. com. unit, 1990-92; recipient Bronze medal of Valor. Contbr. articles to profl. jours.; inventor in field. Bd. dirs. Mesa County Cancer Soc., 1988-89, Colo. Trauma Inst., 1988-91. Colo. Speaks out on Health grantee, 1988; recipient Bronze medal of Valor Civil Air Patrol. Fellow Denver Acad. Surgery, Southwestern Surg. Congress, Am. Coll. Chest Physicians, Am. Coll. Surgeons (trauma com. Colo. chpt.), Am. Coll. Critical Care; mem. Am. Coll. Physician Execs., Soc. Critical Care (task force 1988—). Roman Catholic.

STONE, JOE ALLAN, economics educator; b. Seminole, Tex., Mar. 17, 1948; s. Richard Elick and Ivy Lillian (Childs) S.; m. Crystal Lee Barnes, Aug. 30, 1969; children: Christopher Dylan, Elizabeth Ivy. BA, U. Tex., El Paso, 1970; MA, Mich. State U., 1974, PhD, 1977. Research economist U.S. Bur. Labor Stats., Washington, 1977-79; asst. prof. U. Oreg., Eugene, 1979-82, assoc. prof., 1982-84, W.E. Miner prof. econs., 1985—, head dept., 1988-92, assoc. dean Coll. Arts and Scis., 1992—; sr. economist Pres.' Council Econ. Advisors, Washington, 1984-85; vis. scholar Fed. Res. Bank Cleve., 1986. Author: (with others) Unions and Public Schools, 1984, Wage and Employment Adjustment in Local Labor Markets, 1992; contbr. articles to profl. jours. Served with U.S. Army, 1970-72. Mem. AAUP (pres. U. Oreg. chpt. 1986-87), Am. Econ. Assn., Western Econ. Assn., So. Econ. Assn., Indsl. Rels. Rsch. Inst. Episcopalian. Home: 3820 Onyx St Eugene OR 97405-4515 Office: U Oreg Dept Econs Eugene OR 97403

STONE, JOHN HELMS, JR., admiralty advisor; b. Andalusia, Ala., Dec. 3, 1927; s. John Helms and Ruth May (Barker) S.;m. Mary Ham, July 24, 1950; children: Malcolm, Mary Ruth, Ronald, John T. Student Ga. Mil. Coll., U.S. Merchant Marine Sch., 1945; student, Tulane U., 1975. Master mariner, USCG. Master capt. Sea-Land Steamship, Port Newark, N.J., 1947-60; sr. pilot Panama Canal Co., Balboa Canal Zone, 1960-73; chief of transit op. Panama Canal Commn., Balboa Canal Zone, 1973-76; chmn. bd. local inspection Panama Canal Commn., Balboa, Republic of Panama, 1976-85; admiralty cons. John H. Stone & Assocs., Boulder, Colo., 1985—; admiralty advisor Phelps-Dunbar, New Orleans, 1958-79, Fowler White, Tampa, Fla., 1984, Terriberry & Assocs., New Orleans, 1992. County treas. Dem. Party, Boulder, 1989. Mem. NRA (v.p. 1970, master pistol and rifle shot), Master, Mates and Pilots Union (v.p. 1970-72). Presbyterian. Home: 3795 Wild Plum Ct Boulder CO 80304 Office: John H Stone & Assoc PO Box 17471 Boulder CO 80308

STONE, MARTHA BARNES, food science educator; b. Paris, Tenn., Nov. 20, 1952; d. George Carroll and Minnie (Hudson) Barnes; m. James Moore Stone, Sept. 8, 1973; children: Steven Stone, Christopher Stone. BS, U. Tenn., Martin, 1973; MS, U. Tenn., Knoxville, 1974, PhD, 1977. Grad. rsch. asst. U. Tenn., Knoxville, 1973-77; asst. prof. Food Sci. Kans. State U., Manhattan, 1978-84, assoc. prof. Food Sci., 1984-89; prof. Food Sci. Colo. State U., Ft. Collins, 1989—. Methodist. Office: dept Food Sci/Humanities Colo State U Fort Collins CO 80523

STONE, MICHAEL DAVID, landscape architect; b. Moscow, Idaho, Apr. 11, 1953; s. Frank Seymour Stone and Barbara Lu (Wahl) Stone/Schonthaller; m. Luann Dobaran, Aug. 12, 1978; children: Stephanie Nicole, David Michael. B in Landscape Architecture, U. Idaho, 1976; postgrad., Oreg. State U., 1986, Harvard U., 1990; MA in Orgnl. Leadership, Gonzaga U., 1990. Registered landscape architect, Wash., cert. leisure profl. Landscape designer Robert L. Woerner, ASLA, Spokane, Wash., 1976-77; park planner Spokane County Pks. and Recreation, 1977-82; landscape architect City of Spokane Pks. and Recreation, 1982-84, asst. parks mgr., 1984-86; golf and community devel. mgr. City of Spokane Parks and Recreation, 1986—; cons. Lake Chelan (Wash.) Golf Course, 1988. Pres. Sacred Heart Parish Coun., Spokane, 1987-89; v.p. Cataldo Sch. Bd. Dirs., Spokane, 1987-89; pres. South Spokane Jaycees, 1977-86; active Leadership Spokane, 1989. Named Outstanding Young Man Am., 1980, 85, Outstanding Knight, Intercollegiate Knights, 1972-73, Jaycee of the Yr., South Spokane Jaycees, 1981, Vet. of the Yr., South Spokane Jaycees, 1984-85; recipient Holy Grail award Intercollegiate Knights, 1972-73. Mem. Nat. Recreation and Park Assn., Am. Soc. Landscape Architects, Wash. Recreation and Park Assn., N.W. Turfgrass Assn., Beta Chi, Delta Tau Delta. Roman Catholic. Home: S 5428 Arthur Spokane WA 99223 Office: City of Spokane 808 W Spokane Falls Blvd Spokane WA 99201-3333

STONE, NORMAN MICHAEL, psychologist; b. Balt., Mar. 23, 1949; s. Forrest Leon and Beverly Iola (Gendason) S.; m. Susan Foster Hoitt, May 18, 1981; children: Shannon, Caroline, Brittany Rain, Forrest. BA, UCLA, 1971; PhD, U. Iowa, 1976. Lic. psychologist, Tex., Calif. Chief youth and family svcs. Abilene (Tex.) Mental Health-Mental Retardation Regional Ctr., 1976-79; coord. family crisis team San Fernando Valley Guidance Clinic, Northridge, Calif., 1980-88, sr. clin. supr., 1989—; mem. psychiat. panel of experts on dependency and family law Calif. Superior Ct., 1987—; mem. adj. faculty Hardin-Simmons U., Abilene, 1977-79; vis. prof. UCLA, 1980-81; clin. prof. Fuller Theol. Sem., L.A., 1982—. Contbr. numerous articles on psychology, psychiatry, law and social welfare to internat. profl. jours., books and film. USPHS fellow, 1972-76; Simon Found. rsch. grantee, 1982, 89. Mem. APA, Assn. Family and Conciliation Cts., Am. Profl. Soc. on Abuse of Children, Sojourners. Office: San Fernando Valley Child Guidance Clinic 9650 Zelzah Ave Northridge CA 91325-2098

STONE, RALPH B. (BARRY), real estate executive; b. Jamestown, N.Y., Apr. 14, 1943; s. Theodore Roosevelt and Helen Marie (Bailey) S.; m. Kathleen Jane Poston, Apr. 2, 1967; children: Darci Elizabeth, Melony Lynn, Margaret Kathleen, Monique Corrine. AA, Palo Verde Coll., Blythe, Calif., 1963; BS, Colo. State U., 1970; MBA, Golden Gate U., 1976. Staff announcer Sta. KYOR Radio, Blythe, 1963-64; inventory mgr. Braden Machinery Co., Blythe, 1961-64; commd. 2d lt. USAF, 1964, advanced through grades to major, 1983, ret., 1985; real estate cons. Century 21 Realty Cons., Inc., Albuquerque, 1985-88, Wheeler Realty Better Homes & Gardens, Estes Park, Colo., 1989-90, Century 21, AAA and Colucci Realtors, 1992—; assoc. prof. aerospace studies N.Mex. State U., Las Cruces, 1980-82. Com. chmn. Saguenay Valley Schs., Arvida, Quebec, Can., 1979-80, bd. mem., 1979-80; parents' com. elem. sch., Las Cruces, 1980-82; kitchen cabinet com. Mayor of Albuquerque, 1985-87; sch. accountability com. Park Sch. Dist., Estes Park, 1988-89; cadet comdr. Civil Air Patrol, Albuquerque, 1985-87. Mem. Comml. Investment Real Estate Coun., Buick Club Am. Republican. Lutheran. Home: PO Box 1024 Cedar Crest NM 87008-1024 Office: 35 Sandia Haven Dr Cedar Crest NM 87008-9425

STONE, RICHARD LEHMAN, chemical engineer, consultant; b. Cleve., Dec. 5, 1916; s. Lawrence Edward and Nina (Lehman) S.; m. Isabelle Stewart, Oct. 24, 1943; children: Richard, Rosalind, Elizabeth, Susan. B-SChemE, U. Mich., 1938, MSChemE, 1940; postgrad., Case Western Res. U., 1949-50. Lic. profl. engr. Sr. rsch. engr. Am. Gas Assn. Labs., Cleve., 1946-53; dir. rsch. and engring. Metalbestos Systems, Selkirk Metlabestos div. Household Internat., Belmont, Calif., 1953-85; cons. Selkirk Metalbestos, Los Altos Hills, Calif., 1985-88; pvt. practice cons. Bodega Bay, Calif., 1988—. Contbr. numerous articles to profl. jours. Capt. USAF, 1943-46. Recipient Pioneer Award Fireplace Inst., 1978. Mem. ASME, ASHRAE (fuels and combustion com.), Am. Chem. Soc., Am. Soc. Gas Engrs., Nat. Fire Protection Assn. (sectional com. chimneys, fireplaces venting systems). Home: 20205 Osprey Dr Box 940 Bodega Bay CA 94923-0940

STONE, RUBY R., state legislator; b. Portal, Ga., Feb. 6, 1924; d. Eddie Lee and Della (Taylor) Rocker; widowed; children: Dianne Carolyn Stone Milhollin, Raymond Edward Stone. Office mgr., dental asst. to Dr. Richard W. Collins; asst. to mgr. Am. Machine & Foundry Spl. Missile project Vandenberg AFB; aide to Gov. Don Samuelson; mem. Idaho Ho. Reps., chmn. local govt. com., 1991—. Active Am. Red Cross. Recipient Sportsmanship award Idaho State Women's Amateur Golf Tournament, 1980, Plantation Ladies Gold Assn. Outstanding Woman award, 1992; inducted into Idaho Sports Hall of Fame, 1993, Idaho New Agenda Hall of Fame, 1993. Mem. Nat. Orgn. Women Legislators, U.S. Golf Assn. (mem. jr. girls championship com. 1981), Idaho Golf Assn. (bd. dirs. 1975-87), Plantation Golf Club, Gowen Field Officers Club, Gowen Field Officers Wives Club, Daus. of Nile, El Korah Shrine Club, Elks. Republican. Protestant. Home: 6604 Holiday Dr Boise ID 83709-2022

STONE, SALLY ANNE, enrolled tax agent, tax consultant; b. Seattle, Sept. 25, 1957; d. Ian Laing-Malcolmson and Frances Rutherford (Arold) Cook; m. daniel John Quandt, Apr. 19, 1980 (div. Oct. 1983); 1 child, Rhiannon Ethel Quandt; m. Charles Richard Stone, May 25, 1985; children: Peter Eugene, Benjamin Elliott. AS in Bus., SUNY, 1989. Cert. individual tax profl. With accounts payable dept. King County Airport, Seattle, 1984-86; bookkeeper Driftmeir Architects, P.S., Kirkland, Wash., 1986; pvt. practice tax cons. Bellevue, Wash., 1987—; tax specialist Puget Sound Nat. Bank, Tacoma, 1990-92; bookkeeper Papillon, Inc.; sec. Washington State Tax Cons., Bellevue, 1991—, Am. Bus. Women's Assn., Bellevue, 1992—. Active Word of His Grace Fellowship, PTA, newsletter editor, 1991—. Mem. Pentecostal Ch. Home and Office: 16227 SE 8th Bellevue WA 98008

STONE, SAMUEL DWIGHT, mechanical engineer, engineering executive; b. Driggs, Idaho, Nov. 22, 1955; s. Dwight Clifton and Zelda (Richards) S.; m. Shari Stone, Dec. 27, 1979; children: Melissa, Paul, Robert, Annaliese. BS, Brigham Young U., 1980; MBA, U. Utah, 1990. Registered profl. engr., Utah, Idaho, Wyo. Field engr. Bucyrus-Erie Co., Milw., 1978-79; project engr. Heath Engring. Co., Salt Lake City, 1980-85, dir., v.p., 1985-87, adminstrv. v.p., dir., 1987—. Mem. ASHRAE (chmn. tech. com. 1989), Cons. Engrs. Coun. (profl. devel. com. 1990), Salt Lake City C. of C. Office: Heath Engring Co 377 W 800 N Salt Lake City UT 84103

STONE, WILLIAM EDWARD, association executive; b. Peoria, Ill., Aug. 13, 1945; s. Dean Proctor and Katherine (Jamison) S.; m. Deborah Ann Duncan; children: Jennifer, Allison, Molly. A.B., Stanford U., 1967, M.B.A., 1969. Asst. dean Stanford U., 1969-71, asst. to pres., 1971-77; exec. dir. Stanford Alumni Assn., 1977-90, pres., chief exec. officer, 1990—; pres., dir. Alpine Chalet, Inc., Alpine Meadows, Calif., 1987—; dir. Coun. Alumni Assn. Execs., 1989—, v.p., 1990-91, pres., 1991-92; trustee Coun. for Advancement and Support of Edn., 1988-91; bd. dirs. Univ. ProNet, Inc., chmn., 1990-92. Bd. dirs. North County YMCA, 1975-76; bd. dirs., chmn. nominating com. faculty club Stanford U., 1979-81; trustee Watkins Discretionary Fund, 1979-82; mem. community adv. bd. Resource Ctr. for Women. Recipient K.M. Cuthbertson award Stanford U., 1987, Tribute award Coun. for Advancement and Support of Edn., 1991. Mem. Stanford Hist. Soc., Stanford Assocs., Bay Area Profl. Women's Club. Democrat. Club: Stanford Faculty. Home: 1061 Cathcart Way Stanford CA 94305-1048 Office: Stanford Alumni Assn Inc 416 Santa Teresa St Stanford CA 94305-4005

STONEHILL, BRIAN ALLAN, English language educator; b. Bklyn., Dec. 20, 1953; s. Elliott H. and Harriett Renée (Mayblum) S.; m. Brenda Jane Lunger, June 22, 1986. BA, Haverford (Pa.) Coll., 1973; MA with honors, U. Chgo., 1974, PhD with honors, 1978. Fiction editor Chgo. Rev., 1976-78; asst. prof. Pomona Coll., Claremont, Calif., 1979-85, assoc. prof., 1985—; book reviewer L.A. Times, 1981—, Washington Post, 1981—; op-ed essayist Christian Sci. Monitor, 1985—, Internat. Herald Tribune, 1985—; film critic, historian Voyager Co., Santa Monica, Calif., 1987—. Author: The Self-Conscious Novel, 1988; script cons. PBS French in Action, 1987—; prodr. (laserdisc) Children of Paradise, 1991, The 400 Blows, 1993. Bd. dirs. Claremont Pub. Access TV, 1987—; chair cable TV adv. com. Claremont Coll., 1988—. Mem. Modern Lang. Assn., Internat. Visual Literacy Assn., Phi Beta Kappa. Office: Pomona Coll Dept of English Claremont CA 91711

STONEHOUSE, JAMES ADAM, lawyer; b. Alameda, Calif., Nov. 10, 1937; s. Maurice Adam and Edna Sigrid (Thuesen) S.; m. Marilyn Jean Kotkas, Aug. 6, 1966; children: Julie Aileen, Stephen Adam. AB, U. Calif., Berkeley, 1961; JD, Hastings Coll. Law, U. Calif., San Francisco, 1965. Bar: Calif. 1966; cert. specialist probate, estate planning & trust law.. Assoc. Hall, Henry, Oliver & McReavy, San Francisco, 1966-71; ptnr. firm Whitney, Hanson & Stonehouse, Alameda, 1971-77; pvt. practice, Alameda, 1977-79; ptnr. firm Stonehouse & Silva, Alameda, 1979—; judge advc. Alameda council Navy League, 1978—. Founding dir. Alameda Clara Barton Found., 1977-80; mem. Oakland (Calif.) Marathon-Exec. Com., 1979; mem. exec. bd. Alameda council Boy Scouts Am., 1979—, pres., 1986-88; mem. Nat. council Boy Scouts Am., 1986—; trustee Golden Gate Scouting, 1986—, treas. 1989-91, v.p. 1991-92, pres. 1993, v.p. area III western region, 1990—, bd. dirs. western region, 1991—; bd. dirs. Lincoln Child Ctr. Found., 1981-87, pres., 1983-85. Recipient Lord Baden-Powell Merit award Boy Scouts Am., 1988, Silver Beaver award, 1991; named Boss of Yr. Alameda Jaycees, 1977; Coro Found. fellow in pub. affairs, 1961-62. Mem. ABA, State Bar Calif., Alameda County Bar (vice chmn. com. office econs., 1977-78). Republican. Roman Catholic. Club: Commonwealth. Lodges: Rotary (dir. club 1976-78), Elks (past exalted ruler, all state officer 1975-76, all dist. officer 1975-77, 78-79) (Alameda). Home: 2990 Northwood Dr Alameda CA 94501-1606 Office: Stonehouse & Silva 512 Westline Dr Ste 300 Alameda CA 94501-5870

STONE-MANNING, TRACY, freelance environment media relations professional; b. Springfield, Va., Sept. 18, 1965; d. James Mullen and Audrey Marie (Hammel) Stone; m. Richard Dale Manning, Sept. 8, 1990. Student, U. Exeter (Eng.), 1985-86; BA, U. Md., 1988; MS, U. Mont., 1992. Naturalist Wintergreen (Va.) Resort, 1985-87; freelance writer High Country News, Paonia, Colo., 1990—; video prodr. Craighead Wildlife-Wildlands Inst., Missoula, Mont., 1992; traveling wolf booth mgr. Defenders of Wildlife, Missoula, 1992; freelance pub. rels. profl. Missoula, 1990—; dir. Five Valleys Land Trust, 1992—. Contbr. articles to profl. jours. Vice-chair bd. dirs. Rock Creek Adv. Coun., Missoula, 1989—; judging chair Internat. Wildlife Film Festival, Missoula, 1988-90; activist Coalition for Social Responsibility, Missoula, 1991, Environ. Studies Advocates, Missoula, 1988-90. Democrat. Home and office: 11000 Sleeman Gulch Lolo MT 59847

STONER, MADELEINE RUSKIN, social work educator; b. N.Y.C., Sept. 13, 1937; d. Morris and Mae (Stetsky) Ruskin; m. Bartine A. Stoner Jr., Dec. 21, 1977 (div. 1990); children: Alan Harrison, Katherine Anne Stoner Cushman. BA, Sarah Lawrence Coll., N.Y.C., 1960; M of Social Svc., Bryn Mawr (Pa.) Coll., 1969, PhD, 1979. Dir. Urban League of Phila., 1969-71; chmn. admissions Bryn Mawr Coll. Sch. Social Wk. and Social Rsch., 1971-74; ass.t dep. dir. Nat. Coun. Social Svc., London, 1977-80; asst. dean sch. social work U. So. Calif., L.A., 1980-85; assoc. prof. sch. social work U. So. Calif., 1980—. Author: Inventing a Non-Homeless Future, 1989; contbr. articles to profl. jours. Bd. dirs. Women's Polit. Com., L.A., 1989—, L.A. Free Clinic, 1980-87; trustee Hood Coll., 1972-76; commr. Santa Monica Commn. on Status of Women. Mem. Coun. on Social Work Edn., Nat. Assn. Social Workers. Democrat. Office: Univ of Southern Calif University Park MC0411 Los Angeles CA 90089-0411

STONEY, GORDON ADAIR, physician; b. Detroit, Oct. 10, 1930; s. Ernest Gordon and Mary (Dodwell) S.; m. Joanne Eleanor Toepfer, June 18, 1955; children: Kurt, Shawna Lee. Student, U. British Columbia, 1948-50; BS, U. Cin., 1951, MD, 1955. Intern Stanford U., San Francisco, 1955-56; resident U. Mich., Ann Arbor, 1961-64; flight surgeon USAF, various, 1956-59; pvt. practice gen. physician Cin., 1960-61; chmn. radiology Mt. Hood Med. Ctr., Gresham, Oreg., 1964—; chief of staff Mt. Hood Med. Ctr., Gresham, 1978-79; pres. Oreg. Radiology Soc., 1978-88, Pacific N.W. Radiology Soc., 1985-86. Chmn. Boy Scouts of Am., Gresham, 1972-73; bd. mem. Mt. Hood Festival Jazz, Gresham, 1985—. Capt. USAF, 1956-59. Fellow Am. Coll. Radiology; mem. AMA, Radiol. Soc. N.Am. Libertarian. Unitarian. Home: 20121 NE Broadway Ct Troutdale OR 97060-9736 Office: Mt Hood Med Ctr 24800 SE Stark St Gresham OR 97030-3399

STONG, JOHN ELLIOTT, retail electronics company executive; b. Elkater, Iowa, Sept. 20, 1921; s. Elliott Sheldon and Nora Elizabeth (Daly) S.; m. Olive Miriam Foley, Dec. 11, 1943; children: Mary Myers, Jon, Miriam. Grad. U. Colo., 1943. Salesman, Purucker Music, Medford, Oreg., 1946-48, dept. mgr., 1949-56, store mgr., 1957, partner, 1958-61, owner, 1962-64; pres. Purucker Music Houses, Medford, 1965-67, Music West, Inc., Eugene, Oreg., 1968-70, Magnavox Centers, Medford, 1971—, exec. asst., Consultants Internat., 1972—. Served with USAF, 1943-45. Decorated Air medal. Mem. Nat. Assn. Music Mchts. (dir. 1969-72), Scull Mchts. Rsch. Group (dir., chmn.). Republican. Roman Catholic. Home: 2120 Woodlawn Dr Medford OR 97504-7678 Office: Cons Internat 117 N Central Ave Medford OR 97501-5925

STOOKEY, RICHARD, writer, lawyer; b. Rockford, Ill., Mar. 2, 1938; s. Dale Jeffries and Dorotha Amy (Phelps) S.; m. Martha Marie Milton, Mar. 24, 1962; children: Margaret Amy, Nathaniel Milton. AB, U. Calif., Davis, 1960; LLB, Stanford U., 1963. Bar: Calif. 1963. Rsch. atty. Supreme Ct. Calif., San Francisco, 1964-88; pvt. practice as writer San Francisco, 1988—. Author: A Still and Woven Blue, 1974 (Friends of Am. Writers award 1975); translator: The Affirmation: Late Entries From the Journals of Andre Gide, 1979; contbr. articles to various publs. Mem. Authors Guild, Phi Beta Kappa. Home: 361 Laidley St San Francisco CA 94131

STOREY, BRIT ALLAN, historian; b. Boulder, Colo., Dec. 10, 1941; s. Harold Albert and Gladys Roberta (Althouse) S.; m. Carol DeArman, Dec. 19, 1970; 1 child, Christine Roberta. AB, Adams State Coll., Alamosa, Colo., 1963; MA, U. Ky., 1965, PhD, 1968. Instr. history Auburn (Ala.) U., 1967-68, asst. prof., 1968-70; dep. state historian State Hist. Soc. Colo., Denver, 1970-71, acting state historian, 1971-72, rsch. historian, 1972-74; hist. preservation specialist Adv. Coun. on Hist. Preservation, Lakewood, Colo., 1974-88; sr. historian Bur. Reclamation, Lakewood, 1988—. Contbr. articles to profl. publs. Mem. Fed. Preservation Forum (pres. 1990-91), Nat. Coun. Pub. History (sec. 1987, pres.-elect 1990-91, pres. 1991-92), Orgn. Am. Historians (com. 1983-86, chmn. 1985-86), Victorian Soc. Am. (bd. dirs. 1977-79), Western History Assn. (chmn. com. 1982-86), Colo.-Wyo. Assn. Mus. (sec. 1974-76, pres. 1976-77). Home: 7264 W Otero Ave Littleton CO 80123-5639 Office: Bur Reclamation D-5650 Bldg 67 Denver Fed Ctr PO Box 25007 Denver CO 80225-0007

STOREY, FRANCIS HAROLD, business owner, retired bank executive; b. Calgary, Alberta, Can., June 20, 1933; s. Bertwyn Morrell and Hilda Josephine (Masters) S.; m. Willomae Saiter, Apr. 25, 1954; children: Daryl, Elizabeth, Brian, Shelley. Student, Gonzaga U., 1953, Pacific Coast Bankers Sch., 1974-76. Designated Certified Profl. Cons. Bank trainee Wash. Trust Bank, Spokane, 1950-56; owner Storey & Storey, Spokane, 1956-64; agt. Bankers Life Nebr., Spokane, 1964-67; sr. v.p. Old Nat. Bank, Spokane, 1967-87, U.S. Bank of Wash., Spokane, 1987-90; pvt. practice cons. Spokane, 1990—; bd. dirs. Alloy Trailers Inc., Output Tech. Corp. Bd. dirs. United Way of Spokane, 1990—; bd. dirs., treas., fin. chair Episcopal Diocese Spokane Conf. Dep., 1969—; trustee Spokane Symphony Soc., 1986-93, Spokane Area Devel. Coun., 1982-89; mem. adv. bd. Intercollegiate Ctr. Nursing Edn.; bd. dirs. Spokane Bus. Incubator, Spokane Marketplace. Mem. Acad. Profl. Cons. and Advisors, Spokane Rotary, Spokane Country Club, Spokane Club. Episcopalian. Home: E 214-13th Spokane WA 99202

STOREY, LEE HEROLD, lawyer; b. Ypsilanti, Mich., Nov. 28, 1959; d. Henry Perry Herold and Elsie Lorraine (Long) Wolf; m. William Storey; children: Jason Michael, Jenifer Lorraine. Student, U. Mich., 1977-79; BA, UCLA, 1982, MA, 1984; JD, U. Calif., Berkeley, 1987. Bar: Ariz. 1988, U.S. Dist. Ct. 1990. Circulations mgr. Inst. Archaeology UCLA, 1980-84; rsch. asst. John Muir Inst., Napa, Calif., 1985, Am. Indian Resources Inst., Oakland, Calif., 1985; assoc. editor Ecology Law Quarterly U. Calif., Berkeley, 1985-86; assoc. Evans, Kitchel & Jenckes, Phoenix, 1987-89, Gallagher & Kennedy, Phoenix, 1989-90, Meyer, Hendricks, Victor, Osborn & Maledon, Phoenix, 1991—; guest lectr. water transfers Hydrological Soc. Symposium, Phoenix, 1989, environ. studies Ariz. State U., Tempe, Ariz., 1990, water quality Soc. Mining Engrs., Denver, 1991, water transfers Wind River Assocs., Denver, 1991-92, Phoenix, 1992, Central Ariz. Project Utilization, Am. Water Resources Assn. Symposium, Tucson, 1992, Colo. RIver Basin Tribes, Coun. Energy Resource Tribes, Tucson, 1993, Indian Sovereignty, U.S. Dept. Interior, Bureau Reclamation, Phoenix, 1993; adj. prof. Indian water rights Sch. Law Ariz. State U., 1992. Co-author: Leasing Indian Water: Choices in Colorado River Basin, 1988; asst. editor Ariz. State Bar Environ. and Natural Resources Newsletter, 1990—; contbr. articles to profl. jours.; mem. Calif. Law Rev. U. Calif. Berkeley, 1985-87. Landlord tenant clinics Vols. Lawyers Program, Phoenix, 1988-89; mem. Ariz. Ctr. for Law-Related Edn., Ariz. Bar Found., Drug Awareness Program for Schs., 1990—. Scholar UCLA, 1980-84; recipient Am. Jurisprudence award Lawyers Coop., 1986. Mem. ABA, Ariz. Bar Assn., Maricopa County Bar Assn., Ariz. Women Lawyers Assn. Office: Meyer Hendricks Victor Osborn & Maledon 2929 N Central Ave Phoenix AZ 85012-2703

STORM, DONALD JOHN, archaeologist, historian; b. Bradford, Pa., Nov. 20, 1947; s. John Ross and Jean Lamar (Frederick) S. AA, Yuba Coll., 1967; BA, Sacramento State U., 1972; postgrad., Calif. State U., Sacramento, 1972-74, Calif. State U., Chico, 1980, U. Nev., Reno, 1988-89. Instr. Marysville (Calif.) Joint Unified Sch. Dist., 1977-78; state archaeologist Calif. Dept. Parks and Recreation, Sacramento, 1981-84; owner North Yuba Contracting, Oregon House, Calif., 1984-87; archaeologist Elko dist. Nev. Bur. Land Mgmt., Elko, 1988; asst. forest archaeologist Sierra Nat. Forest, Clovis, Calif., 1990-91; archaeol. tech. Tahoe Nat. Forest, Camptonville, Calif., summer 1980; archaeol. cons. Oregon House, 1976-81, 88—; instr. Yuba Coll., Marysville, Calif., 1976-78, 88—. Activist various conservation/environ. groups; candidate for Yuba County Supr., 1992. With U.S. Army, 1967-70. Mem. Soc. Am. Archaeology, Soc. Hist. Archaeology, Soc. for Calif. Archaeology, Calif. Hist. Soc., Nat. Trust for Historic Preservation, So. Pacific Hist. and Tech. Soc. Home and Office: PO Box 552 Oregon House CA 95962-0552

STORMONT, CLYDE JUNIOR, laboratory company executive; b. Viola, Wis., June 25, 1916; s. Clyde James and Lulu Elizabeth (Mathews) S.; m. Marguerite Butzen, Aug. 31, 1940; children: Bonnie Lu, Michael Clyde, Robert Thomas, Charles James, Janet Jean. BA in Zoology, U. Wis., 1938, PhD in Genetics, 1947. Instr., lectr. then asst. prof. U. Wis.-Madison, 1946-50; asst. prof. dept. vet. microbiology U. Calif.-Davis, 1950-54, assoc. prof., 1954-59, prof., 1959-73, prof. dept. reprodn., 1973-82, prof. emeritus, 1982—; chmn. Stormont Labs., Inc., Woodland, Calif., 1981—. Contbr. articles to profl. jours. Lt. (j.g.) USNR, 1944-46, PTO. Fulbright fellow, 1949-50, Ellen B. Scripps fellow, 1957-58, 64-65. Mem. AAAS, Am. Genetic Assn., Genetics Soc. Am., Nat. Buffalo Assn., N.Y. Acad. Sci., Am. Soc. Human Genetics, Soc. Exptl. Biology and Medicine, Internat. Soc. for Animal Genetics, Sigma Xi. Office: Stormont Labs Inc 1237 E Beamer St Ste D Woodland CA 95776-6000

STORMS, LESTER (C STORMS), retired veterinarian; b. Camas, Wash., Oct. 13, 1920; s. Roy Lester and Helen Violet (Belshe) S.; m. Marjorie Louise Hudson, Apr. 10, 1943 (div.); children: Marjorie Maureen, Terry Jo, Sandra Diane. BS in Animal Husbandry, Wash. State U., 1951, DVM, 1952. Intern Portland, 1952; gen. practice vet. medicine Camas, 1952-54; dr.'s asst. pvt. practice vet. office, Hollywood, Calif., 1954, L.A., 1954, Whittier, Calif., 1954; vet. in charge pvt. practice vet. office, Artesia, Calif., 1955-56; owner, pvt. practice vet. medicine Buena Park, Calif., 1956-86; ret.,

1986; mem. adv. bd. Guide Dogs for Blind, San Rafael, Calif., 1957-58; mem. steering com. Children's Hosp., Fullerton, Calif., 1960-61. With USN, 1940-51, PTO. Decorated Air medal with 3 gold stars, DFC. Mem. NRA, So. Calif. Vet. Medicine Assn. (life), Am. Vet. Medicine Assn., Orange County Vet. Medicine Assn. (pres. 1958), Olde '78 Fraser's Highlanders (chief-of-staff), Explorer's Club, Adventurer's Club L.A. (sec. 1984, bd. dirs., 1980-82), Long Beach Yacht Club, Rotary (Paul Harris fellow, pres. Buena Park chpt. 1963). Home: 17367 Modoc Apt # 13 Fountain Valley CA 92708

STOROZUM, STEVEN LEE, marketing professional; b. St. Louis, Jan. 14, 1954. AB, Washington U., St. Louis, 1975; MS, Carnegie Mellon U., 1976; postgrad., Va. Poly. U., 1979. Assoc. engr. IITRI-ECAC, Annapolis, Md., 1977; applications engr. ITT, Roanoke, Va., 1977-79; sr. engr. McDonnell Douglas Corp., St. Louis, 1979-82; mgr. LAN systems Am. Photonics, Inc., Brookfield, Conn., 1982-88; product mgr. PCO, Inc., Chatsworth, Calif., 1988-90, Fibermux Corp., Chatsworth, 1990—; cons. Wilton Industries, Ridgefield, Conn., 1988. Lighting designer theatrical prodns., 1978-79, 86-88; contbr. articles to profl. jours. Mem. Am. Phys. Soc., Optical Soc. of Am., Mensa.

STORVICK, CLARA AMANDA, nutrition educator emerita; b. Emmons, Minn., Oct. 31, 1906; d. Ole A. and Elise A. (Opdahl) S. AB, St. Olaf Coll., 1929; MS, Iowa State U., 1933; PhD, Cornell U., 1941. Instr. chemistry Augustanta Acad., Canton, S.D., 1930-32; rsch. asst. Iowa State U., Ames, 1932-34; nutiritionist Fed. Emergency Relief Adminstrn., Brainerd, Minn., 1934-36; asst. prof. nutrition Okla. State U., Stillwater, 1936-38; rsch. asst. Cornell U., Ithaca, N.Y., 1938-41; asst. prof. nutrition U. Wash., Seattle, 1941-45; assoc. prof. nutrition to prof. Oreg. State U., Corvallis, 1945-72, prof. nutrition and head home econ. rsch., 1955-72, dir. nutrition rsch. inst., 1965-72; ret., 1972. Contbr. over 70 articles to profl. jours. Recipient Borden award Am. Home Econs. Assn., 1952, Disting. Alumni award St. Olaf Coll., 1955, Alumni Achievement award Iowa State U., Ames, 1966. Fellow AAAS, Am. Pub. Health Assn., Am. Inst. Nutrition; mem. N.Y. Acad. Scis., Am. Chem. Soc., Phi Kappa Phi, Sigma Xi., Iota Sigma Pi (nat. pres.), Omicron Nu. Republican. Lutheran. Home: 124 NW 29th St Corvallis OR 97330-5343

STOSIC, MICHAEL RICHARD, insurance company executive; b. Reno, May 28, 1953; s. John Michael and Nancy (Velma) S.; m. Joan Elizabeth Cavilia, July 10, 1976; children: Kristofer Michael, Kelsey Joan, Katie Marie. BA, U. Nev., 1975. Owner Farmers Ins. Agy., Reno, 1974-83, Total Fitness Ctr., Reno, 1982-83; dist. mgr. Farmers Ins. Group, Seattle, 1983—; pres., owner The Love Light Co. Rec. Studio, 1989; owner Misto Music Pub. Co., 1990; voice tchr., 1991, record producer, arranger, 1991. Author: The Singers Bible, 1988; albums include Brand New Love, 1986 (Peoples Choice award 1986), Symphony of Praise, 1989, Psalms From the Heart, 1992; performer TV Show Symphony of Praise, 1990. Home: 23629 NE 7th Ct Redmond WA 98053-3616

STOSICH, DAVIDJOHN, company executive; b. Idaho Falls, Idaho, May 24, 1938; s. Vaughn T. and Esther (Smith) S.; m. Adeana Marshall, Aug. 28, 1962; children: Jennifer Lynne, Jacquelyn, Bryan, Jill, Jon, Anthony, Vaughndavid, Jelair, Hartman, Jeanne. BS, Brigham Young U., 1964; BPA in Profl. Illustrator, Art Ctr. Coll. Design, L.A., 1967. Graphic support Computer Scis. Corp., El Segundo, Calif., 1967-68; corp. communications staff Geotech, Salt Lake City, 1968-69; asst. to pres. Computer Update, Salt Lake City, 1969-70; corp. communications staff Omnico, Salt Lake City & Tacoma, 1970-71; support staff Big Sky of Mont., Big Sky, Mont., 1972-73; art dir. Artcraft, Bozeman, Mont., 1973-75; owner Stosich Advt., Idaho Falls, 1975-78; pres. Worldwide Achievements, Idaho Falls, 1980-81, Hive Systems, Idaho Falls, 1982-92; pres. Stosich Woodlock, Idaho Falls, 1986-92. Graphic designer Crapo for U.S. Congress, Boise, 1992; active Idaho Falls Arts Coun., Exch. Club Am. Mem. Art Guild (Pocatello, Idaho), Cowboy Artists of Am. Republican. Church of Jesus Christ of Latter-Day Saints. Home: 2300 Charlotte Idaho Falls ID 83402

STOTLER, ALICEMARIE H., federal judge; b. Alhambra, Calif., May 29, 1942; d. James R. and Loretta M. Huber; m. James Allen Stotler, Sept. 11, 1971. BA, U. So. Calif., 1964, JD, 1967. Bar: Calif. 1967, U.S. Dist. Ct. (no. dist.) Calif. 1967, U.S. Dist. Ct. (cen. dist.) Calif. 1973, U.S. Supreme Ct., 1976; cert. criminal law specialist. Dep. Orange County Dist. Atty.'s Office, 1967-73; mem. Stotler & Stotler, Santa Ana, Calif., 1973-76, 83-84; judge Orange County Mcpl. Ct., 1976-78, Orange County Superior Ct., 1978-83, U.S. Dist. Ct. (cen. dist.) Calif., L.A., 1984—; assoc. dean Calif. Trial Judges Coll., 1982; lectr., panelist, numerous orgns.; mem. standing com. on rules of practice and procedure U.S. Jud. Conf., 1991—; mem. judicial working group U.S. Sentencing Commn., 1992-93; mem. exec. com. 9th Cir. Jud. Conf., 1989—, Fed. State Jud. Coun., 1989—, jury com., 1990-92, planning com. for Nat. Conf. on Fed.-State Judicial Relsationships, Orlando, 1991-92, planning com for We. Regional Conf. on State-Fed. Judicial Relationships, Stevens, Wash., 1992-93; chair dist. ct. symposium and jury utilization Ctrl. Dist. Calif., 1985, chair atty. liason, 1989-90, chair U.S. Constitution Bicentennial com., 1986-91, chair magistrate judge com.; mem. State Adv. Group. on Juvenile Justice and Delinquency Prevention, 1983-84, Bd. Legal Speciliazations Criminal Law Adv. Commn., 1983-84, victim/witness adv. com. Office Criminal Justice Planning, 1980-83, women's law inst. adv. bd. coll. law We. State U., 1979-82; instr. Orange County Sherrif's Acad., 1982. Mem. planned giving com. Orange County br. Arthritis Found., 1976-81; bd. trustees George A. Parker Law Found., 1979-82; bd. dirs. Legion Lex U. So. Calif. Sch. Law Support Group, 1981-83; active team in tng. Leukemia Soc. Am., 1993. Winner Hale Moot Ct. Competition, State of Calif., 1967; named Judge of Yr., Orange County Trial Lawyers Assn., 1978, Most Outstanding Judge, Orange County Bus. Litigation Sect., 1990; recipient Franklin G. West award Orange County Bar Assn., 1985. Mem. ABA (jud. adminstrn. divsn.and litigation sect. 1984—, nat. conf. fed. trial judges com. on legis. affairs 1990-91), Am. Law Inst., Am. Judicature Soc., Fed. Judges Assn. (bd. dirs. 1989-92), Nat. Assn. Women Judges, U.S. Supreme Ct. Hist. Soc., Ninth Cir. Dist. Judges Assn., Calif. Supreme Ct. Hist. Soc., Orange County Bar Assn. (mem. numerous coms., Franklin G. West award 1984), Calif. Judges Assn. (mem. com. on judicial coll. 1978-80, com. on civil law and procedure 1980-82, Dean's coll. cirriculum commn. 1981), Calif. Judges Found. Office: US Dist Ct PO Box 12339 751 W Santa Ana Blvd Santa Ana CA 92701

STOTT, BRIAN, software company executive; b. Eccles, Eng., Aug. 5, 1941; came to U.S., 1983; s. Harold and Mary (Stephens) S.; m. Patricia Ann Farrar, Dec. 3, 1983. BSc, Manchester U., 1962, MSc, 1963, PhD, 1971. Asst. prof. Middle East Tech. U., Ankara, Turkey, 1965-68; lectr. Inst. Sci. and Tech., U. Manchester (Eng.), 1968-74; assoc. prof. U. Waterloo (Ont., Can.), 1974-76; cons. Electric Energy Rsch. Ctr. Brazil, Rio de Janeiro, 1976-83; prof. Ariz. State U., Tempe, 1983-84; pres. Power Computer Applications Corp., Mesa, Ariz., 1984—; cons. in field. Contbr. numerous articles to rsch. publs. Fellow IEEE. Office: Power Computer Applications 1921 S Alma School Rd # 207 Mesa AZ 85210

STOTT, JAMES CHARLES, chemical company executive; b. Portland, Oreg., Sept. 5, 1945; s. Walter Joseph and Rellalee (Gray) S.; m. Caroline Loveriane Barnes, Dec. 7, 1973; children: William Joseph, Maryann Lee. BBA, Portland State U., 1969. Ops. mgr. Pacific States Express, Inc., Portland, 1970-73; bus. mgr. Mogul Corp., Portland, 1974-80; v.p. Market Transport, Ltd., Portland, 1980-85; pres., founder, chmn. bd. dirs. Chem. Corp. Am., Portland, 1985—, also bd. dirs.; chmn. bd. dirs. Carolina Industries, Portland. Mem. TAPPI. Republican. Roman Catholic. Club: University (Portland). Home: 3842 Wellington Ct West Linn OR 97068-3651 Office: Chem Corp Am 2525 SE 9th Ave Portland OR 97202-1048

STOTT, PETER WALTER, timber company executive; b. Spokane, Wash., May 26, 1944; s. Walter Joseph and Rellalee (Gray) S. Student Portland State U., 1962-63, 65-68, U. Americas, Mexico City, 1964-65. Founder, chmn. bd. dirs. Market Transport Ltd., Portland, Oreg., 1969—; bd. dirs., pres., CEO, prin. Crown Pacific, Ltd. Bd. dirs. Sunshine div. Portland Police Bur.; assoc. mem. adv. bd. Pacific Crest Outward Bound Sch.; mem. pres.'s adv. bd. for athletics Portland State U. With USAR, 1966-72. Mem. Nat. Football Found. and Hall of Fame, Oreg. Sports Hall Fame (lifetime), Oreg. Trucking Assn., Arlington Club, Astoria Golf and Country, Mazamas Club, Multnomah Athletic Club, Portland Golf Club, Univ. Club. Republican. Roman Catholic. Office: Crown Pacific Ltd 121 SW Morrison St Ste 900 Portland OR 97204-3139

STOTTER, JAMES, II, lawyer, legal consultant; b. Cleve., Oct. 12, 1929; s. Raymond H. and Janet H. (Stern) S.; m. Hollie McGlohn, Oct. 31, 1954; children: Raymond Judd, Hillary Margaret, James Robin, Cameron Elizabeth. BA, Yale Coll., 1951; LLB, Yale U., 1954; M in Law Studies, U. So. Calif., 1961. Bar: Calif., U.S. Supreme Ct., U.S. Ct. Mil. Appeals. Asst. U.S. atty. U.S. Dept. Justice, L.A., 1957-59, 73-89, asst. chief civil div., chief drug forfeiture unit, 1980-89; pvt. practice L.A., Beverly Hills, Calif., 1960-67; instr., adj. prof. law U.S. Atty. Gen.'s Advocacy Inst. Calif. Coll. Law, U. West L.A., 1970-87; judge pro tem Mcpl. and Small Claims Ct., L.A., 1970-88; atty. at law Cambria, Calif., 1989—. Guide trainee hist. monument Hearst Castle, San Simeon, Calif., 1991; active civic and vol. orgns., Cambria and San Luis Obispo, Calif. Capt. USAF, 1954-57. Mem. Am. Arbitration Assn. (mediator/arbitrator 1970—). Home and Office: 1595 Cardiff Dr Cambria CA 93428-5703

STOUFFER, DANIEL HENRY, JR., artist; b. Paulding, Ohio, Sept. 26, 1937; s. Daniel H. and Alverda C. (Hanenkratt) S.; m. Jean D. Diederich, June 8, 1968; children: Daniel III, Laura. BFA, Ohio State U., 1959. Prodn. dir. Charles E. Merrill Pub., Columbus, 1965-70, mng. editor, 1970-72; dir. art and prodn. U. N.Mex. Press, Albuquerque, 1972-79. Exhibited in group shows at Nat. Sml. Painting Show, Albuquerque, 1983 (first pl. 1983, 89), Watercolor U.S.A., Springfield (Mo.) Art Mus., 1987, 93, Rocky Mountain Nat., Golden, Colo., 1987, 88, 93, Albuquerque Mus., 1984, Carlsbad (N.Mex.) Mus., 1985, Nature Conservancy Show, Gingrass Gallery, Milw., 1990, Gov.'s Show, Alberquerque, 1992, Arts for the Parks, 1992, Magnifico, 1993; spl. commns. include commemerative poster, Sandia Fed. Savs. and Loan, 1986, N.Mex. Arts and Crafts Fair, 1988, Annual Fine Art Print, Pub. Svc. Co. of N.Mex., 1976. Fundraiser Bright Horizons, Albuquerque, 1988, Rio Grande Nature Ctr., 1992. Named Artist of Yr., Bright Horizons, 1988; recipient eight nat. awards in book design, 10 awards of merit and purchase, N.Mex. Arts and Crafts Fair, Albuquerque, 1980-90. Mem. Nature Conservancy, Wilderness Soc., Sierra Club. Home: 3817 Chelwood Dr NE Albuquerque NM 87111-4109

STOUFFER, DEBORAH MARIE, public relations practitioner; b. Upland, Calif., June 27, 1968; d. Gary Allen and Avalla Ann (Kilgo) S. AA, Fla. Coll., 1988; B. in Communication, Calif. State U., Fullerton, 1991. Memory book rep. Lifetouch Pub., San Dimas, Calif., 1989-91; publicity specialist City of San Dimas, 1991-92; pub. rels. asst. Citrus Coll., Glendora, Calif., 1991-92, coll. promotions specialist, 1992-93; cons. Citrus Coll. Found., Glendora, 1992-93, San Dimas Pub. Access Channel, 1992-93. Pres. Fla. Coll. Booster Club of So. Calif., 1992; chmn. corp. relay Orange County Performing Arts Ctr. Triathlon, Costa Mesa, Calif., 1991. Republican. Home: 998 Church St # 20 Ventura CA 93001

STOUGH, STEPHEN ALAN, aerospace and railroad company executive; b. Wichita, Kans., Sept. 13, 1950; s. David Allen and Ramona June (York) S.; m. Lydia Kow, Nov. 20, 1981. B. in Physics, U. Calif., Berkeley, 1972. Aerospace engr. Lockheed Missiles & Space, Sunnyvale, Calif., 1972-77; aerospace engr. internat. Lockheed Missiles & Space, 1977-82; group engr. Lockheed Missiles & Space, Sunnyvale, 1982—; dir. Expressway Corp., Cupertino, Calif., 1985-86; CFO Ascesis Corp., Sunnyvale, 1988—; new bus. mgr. Lockheed Missiles & Space, Sunnyvale, 1984-86, systems engring. mgr., 1986-89, dir. anti-submarine warfare systems, 1989-90, systems engring. mgr. Space Systems div., 1990—; exec. v.p., sec. Nev. Copper Belt RR, Stagecoach, 1992—. Mem. Nat. Rep. Congl. Com., Washington, 1989—. Mem. Armed Forces Communications and Electronics Assn., Nat. Security Indsl. Assn., Security Affairs Support Assn., Commonwealth Club Calif., Alpha Gamma Sigma. Office: Lockheed Space Systems Div 68-61 1111 Lockheed Way Sunnyvale CA 94089-1212

STOUT, DENNIS LEE, lawyer, mayor; b. Upland, Calif., Feb. 25, 1948; s. Daniel L. and Vena C. (Bryan) S.; m. Linda M. Flaaten, Aug. 2, 1969; 1 child, Todd C. BA, U. Calif., Riverside, 1970; JD, U. LaVerne, 1977. Bar: Calif. 1977, U.S. Supreme Ct. 1988. Adminstrv. asst. Dept. Mental Health, San Bernardino (Calif.) County, San Bernardino, 1973-77; dep. dist. atty. San Bernardino County Dist. Atty., Rancho Cucamonga, Calif., 1977—. Commr. Citizen's Adv. Commn., City of Rancho Cucamonga, 1978-82, chmn. planning commn., 1982-86, mayor, 1986—, bd. dirs. Rancho Cucamonga Redevelopment Agy. (chmn. 1986—), pres. Rancho Cucamonga Fire Protection Dist., 1990—. Sgt. U.S. Army, 1971-72, Vietnam. Named Mayor of the Year, Nat. WeTip, 1990, Alumnus of Yr., U. LaVerne, 1986, Vet. of the Year, San Bernardino County, 1988. Mem. Western San Bernardino County Bar Assn. (bd. dirs. 1985-88), Kiwanis. Republican. Office: City of Rancho Cucamonga 10500 Civic Center Dr Rancho Cucamonga CA 91730-3801

STOUT, JAMES TILMAN, minister; b. Pitts., Feb. 20, 1942; s. Randall Stuart and Alice Margaret (Stevenson) S.; m. Leah Ann Hayden, June 24, 1967; children: James T. Jr., John Davis. Student, U. Pitts., 1960-63; BA, Miami U. of Ohio, 1965; MDiv, Gorden Conwell Sem., 1969; DMin, Fuller Sem., 1980. Ordained to ministry Presbyn. Ch., 1969. Assoc. pastor Key Biscayne (Fla.) Presbyn. Ch., 1969-74; pastor First Presbyn. Ch., North Palm Beach, Fla., 1974-81, St. Andrews Presbyn. Ch., Beaumont, Tex., 1981-83, Covenant Presbyn. Ch., Sharon, Pa., 1983-87; assoc. pastor St. Andrews Presbyn. Ch., Newport Beach, Calif., 1987-91; area dir. Gathering of Men, Costa Mesa, Calif., 1992—. Author: Winning Over Depression, 1992. Named Golden Glove Heavyweight Champion, Pitts., 1961. Mem. Exch. Club, Rotary. Office: Gathering of Men 2093 Santa Ana Costa Mesa CA 92627

STOUT, LOWELL, lawyer; b. Tamaha, Okla., July 23, 1928; s. Charles W. and Rosetta (Easley) S.; m. Liliane Josue, Nov. 29, 1952; children: Georgianna, Mark Lowell. Student, Northeastern State Coll., Tahlequah, Okla., 1946-49, U. Okla., 1949-51; LLB, U. N.Mex., 1952. Bar: N.Mex. 1952. Ptnr. Easley, Quinn & Stout, Hobbs, N.Mex., 1954-58, Girand & Stout, Hobbs, 1958-60; pvt. practice Hobbs, 1960-80; ptnr. Stout & Stout, Hobbs, 1980—. Cpl. U.S. Army, 1952-54. Fellow Am. Coll. Trial Lawyers; mem. ABA, Assn. Trial Lawyers Am., State Bar N.Mex., N.Mex. Trial Lawyers Assn., Lea County Bar Assn. Home: 218 W Lea St Hobbs NM 88240-5199 Office: Stout & Stout PO Box 716 Hobbs NM 88241-0716

STOUT, ROGER PAUL, mechanical engineer; b. Phoenix, July 10, 1956; s. Arthur Paul and Marilyn Sue (Munsil) S.; m. Carol Louise Gordon, Mar. 24, 1979; children: Julia Renee, Matthew Paul, Joshua Michael. BSE, Ariz. State U., 1977; MSME, Calif. Inst. Tech., 1979. Registered profl. engr., Ariz. Mem. tech. staff Hughes Aircraft Co., Culver City, Calif., 1977-79; sr. engr. Motorola, Phoenix, 1979-80, staff engr., 1980-82; sr. staff engr. Motorola, Chandler, Ariz., 1982-84, prin. staff engr., 1984-86, mem. tech. staff, 1986-92, sr. mem. tech. staff, 1992—; guest lectr. Coll. Engring. Ariz. State U., Tempe, 1991. Contbr. articles to profl. jours. Inventor die pick mechanism, voice coil motor with integral capacitor. Lay leader St. Andrews United Meth. Ch., Mesa, Ariz., 1992—, fin. chairperson, 1986-91. Mem. ASME, Soc. Mfg. Engrs. (robotics internat. divsn. 1984), Ariz. Assn. for the Gifted and Talented (treas. exec. bd. dirs. 1992), Tau Beta Pi, Phi Kappa Phi, Pi Tau Sigma, Phi Eta Sigma. Methodist.

STOVALL, DENNIS MICHAEL, publishing executive, writer; b. Portland, Oreg., June 22, 1946; s. Frank Riley and Ruth Reeva (Freeman) S.; m. Linny Singer, May 22, 1978. BA in Polit. Sci., U. Oreg., 1968. Freelance writer, 1968-78; owner Proseworthy & Wordsmith, Pitts., 1978-83; pres., prin. Dennis Stovall & Assocs., Hillsboro, Oreg., 1983-85; pres. Blue Heron Pub., Inc., Hillsboro, 1985—. Editor: Writer's Northwest Handbook, 1990 (grantee 1990-91); editor, pub.: (series) Left Bank Anthologies, 1991-92; co-author: Classroom Publishing, 1992; contbr. articles to profl. jours. Vol. career speaker to local and regional schs., Oreg., Wash., 1987—; cons. Skyline Ridge Assn., Oreg., 1989-90. Mem. Pacific N.W. Writers (dir. 1987-89), N.W. Writers, Inc. (dir. 1989), Oreg. Writers Colony (dir. 1987-89), N.W. Assn. Book Pubs. (dir. 1989-90), Pacific N.W. Booksellers Assn., Willamette Writers. Office: Blue Heron Pub Inc 24450 NW Hansen Rd Hillsboro OR 97124

STOVER-MCBRIDE, TAMA SUE, quality assurance manager; b. Dayton, Ohio, Mar. 20, 1957; d. Robert E. and Florence Alberta (Wilson) Stover; m. David James McBride, Jan. 2, 1988; 1 child, Ian David. BS in Math./Computer Sci. and Chemistry, Prin. Coll., 1979. Cert. quality analyst. Adminstrv. asst. chemistry dept. Prin. Coll., Elsah, Ill., 1976-79; sci. programmer Goodyear (Ariz.) Aerospace, 1979-82; MTS III Hughes Helicopter, Mesa, Ariz., 1982-83; mgr. product line Texscan, Phoenix, 1983-84; mgr. customer support/quality assurance Internat. Anasazi, Phoenix, 1984-86; mgr. quality assurance Anasazi, Inc., Phoenix, 1986—. Mem. IEEE (assoc.), NAFE, Mensa. Republican. Office: Anasazi Inc 7500 N Dreamy Draw Dr # 120 Phoenix AZ 85020-4691

STOWE, NOEL JAMES, historian, educator; b. Sacramento, Jan. 16, 1942; s. Harold James and R. Elaine (Hildreth) S.; m. Gwendolyn Joyce Lee, Nov. 1965; 1 son, James. A.A., Sacramento City Coll., 1961; B.A., U. So. Calif., 1963, Ph.D., 1970. Lectr. U. Nev., Las Vegas, 1967; prof. history Ariz. State U., Tempe, 1967—, assoc. dean grad. coll. acad. programs, 1987—, co-dir. pub. history, 1980—, dir. grad. studies in history, 1979-87. Author: California Government: The Challenge of Change, 1975, 2d edit. 1980; co-editor: Arizona at 75: The Next Twenty-five Years, 1987, Accountancy in Arizona: A History of the Profession, 1990; contbr. articles to profl. jours. Bd. dirs. Coordinating Com. for History in Ariz., 1988—. Mem. Nat. Council Pub. History (chmn. 1985-86, mem. bd. dirs.), Conf. on Latin Am. History, Am. Hist. Assn., Southwest Oral History Assn. (exec. com. 1988—, pres. 1992-93), Western Hist. Assn., Orgn. Am. Historians, Phi Beta Kappa, Phi Kappa Phi. Christian Scientist. Office: Ariz State U Grad Coll Tempe AZ 85287-1003

STOWELL, GERALDINE CASE, treasurer, secretary; b. Chgo., Apr. 6, 1942; d. Joseph Anthony and Catherine Geraldine (Pierce) Case; m. John Fowler Schaefer, June 13, 1964 (div. Jan. 1979); children: Richard, Lauren; m. Christopher Eldon Stowell, June 20, 1981; stepchildren: Therese, Alex, Julia. BS in Home Econs. and Sci., U. Md., 1964; MA in Home Econs. and English, Calif. State U., Long Beach, 1968; MBA in Fin., George Washington U., 1982. Asst. dept. mgr. Bullock's Dept. Store, Torrance, Calif., 1974; with Zellerbach Paper Co., 1974-80; inventory mgr. So. region Zellerbach Paper Co., L.A., 1978-79, asst. merchandising mgr. So. region, 1979-80; with inside and outside sales VIP Travel, McLean, Va., 1983-86; pres., owner Firstworld Travel of McLean, 1986-89; corp. sec., treas. WJS, Inc., Newport Beach, Calif., 1989—; v.p Zellerbach Employees Assn., L.A., 1978-79; chmn. mgmt. adv. coun. Zellerbach Paper Co., San Francisco, 1979-80; bd. dirs. Zelpaco Credit Union. Loaned corp. chmn. campaign, United Way, San Francisco, 1977. Mem. Nat. Acctg. Assn. (chmn. meeting arrangements com. San Francisco chpt. 1977-78). Home: 2815 Setting Sun Dr Corona Del Mar CA 92625-1520

STOYER, MARK ALAN, chemist; b. Cin., May 17, 1963; s. Lyn Paul and Dorothy Louise (Warner) S. BS in Chemistry, Purdue U., 1984; PhD in Nuclear Chemistry, U. Calif., Berkeley, 1990. Postdoctoral fellow in nuclear chemistry U. Calif., Berkeley, 1990-91, Lawrence Livermore (Calif.) Nat. Lab., 1991—. Mem. Am. Phys. Soc., Am. Chem. Soc. Office: Lawrence Livermore Nat Lab Mail Stop L-231 Livermore CA 94550

STRAATMEYER, JEAN ELLEN, economist; b. Chancellor, S.D., Nov. 25, 1938; d. M.E.J. and Dena (Thaden) Plucker; m. H. Gene Straatmeyer, June ll, 1957; children: Cynthia Jean, Sandra Jean, Michael Gene. Student, U. Dubuque, 1958, U. No. Iowa, 1965, 66; BA in Sociology, U. Alaska, 1977. Dir. Literacy Coun. Alaska, Fairbanks, 1977-78; project mgr., program supr., mgmt. advisor East Ctrl. Intergovtl. Assn., Dubuque, Iowa, 1978-86; contracts mgr. Ariz. Dept. Health, Phoenix, 1986-87; energy econ. devel. specialist Ariz. Dept. Commerce, Phoenix, 1987—. Editor: Profile Fact Book, 1985, (directory) Arizona Built, 1988, 89, 91. Democrat. Presbyterian. Home: 1249 W 12th Pl Tempe AZ 85281 Office: Ariz Energy Office 3800 N Central Ste 1200 Phoenix AZ 85012

STRACK, STEPHEN NAYLOR, psychologist; b. Rome, N.Y., Nov. 13, 1955; s. Ralph and Grace (Naylor) S.; m. Leni Ferrero. BA, U. Calif., Berkeley, 1978; PhD, U. Miami, Fla., 1983. Psychologist L.A. County Dept. Mental Health, 1984-85; staff psychologist VA Outpatient Clinic, L.A., 1985-92, dir. tng., 1992—; clin. assoc. U. So. Calif., L.A., 1986—; adj. assoc. prof. Calif. Sch. Profl. Psychology, L.A., 1989—; clin. assoc. prof. Fuller Grad. Sch. Psychology, Pasadena, 1986—; cons. editor Jour. of Personality Disorders, N.Y.C., 1992—. Author test: Personality Adjective Check List, 1987; contbr. articles to profl. jours. U.S. Dept. Vets. Affairs grantee, 1986—. Fellow Soc. for Personality Assessment; mem. APA, Calif. Psychol. Assn., European Assn. of Psychol. Assessment, Soc. for Rsch. in Psychopathology, Western Psychol. Assn., Sigma Xi. Office: VA Outpatient Clinic 351 E Temple St Los Angeles CA 90012-3328

STRACZYNSKI, JOSEPH MICHAEL, writer; b. Paterson, N.J., July 17, 1954; s. Charles and Evelyn (Pate) S.; m. Kathryn May Drennan, Sept. 30, 1983. AA in Interdisciplinary Studies, Southwestern Coll., 1975; BA in Clin. Psychology, San Diego State U., 1976, BA in Sociology, 1978. Acad. counselor San Diego State U., 1974-75, orientation counselor, 1974-76; editor Racquetball News, El Cajon, Calif., 1975-77; spl. corr. Daily Californian, El Cajon, 1977-78; entertainment editor KSDO-AM Newsradio, San Diego, 1978-80; freelance writer Calif.; host Hour 25 Sta. KPFK-FM, Los Angeles, 1987—; artistic dir. Airstage Radiodrama Prodns., San Diego, 1979-80; spl. corr. Los Angeles Times, San Diego Bur., 1977-79, TV Cable Week, Time Inc., Los Angeles, 1981-82, Anthology Tales from the New Twilight Zone, 1989; creative writing instr. San Diego State U., 1977-78; staff writer Filmation Studios, Reseda, Calif., 1984-85; story editor DIC Enterprises, Encino, Calif., 1985-86, Landmark Entertainment, Hollywood, Calif., 1986-87, London Films, Hollywood, 1987-88; devel. writer TMS Enterprises, 1985-87, Nelvana Entertainment, 1988, Warner Bros., 1988—. Author: (novel) Othersyde, 1991, Demon Night, 1988, shortstories appearing in Amazing Stories and Pulphouse mag., numerous articles, plays, radio dramas, TV shows including He-Man and the Masters of the Universe, She-Ra, Princess of Power, Jayce and the Wheeled Warriors, CBS Storybreak, Nightmare Classics, V: The Next Chapter; story editor: The Real Ghostbusters, Captain Power and the Soldiers of the Future, The Twilight Zone; producer Jake and the Fatman, Murder She Wrote, Walker Texas Ranger; contbg. editor Writer's Digest, 1981—, Twilight Zone mag., 1983—; creator: Aragon and the Wuff, ABC-TV; exec. producer/creator: Bablyon 5, Prime Time Entertainment Network, 1992—. Mem. citizen's com. People for the Am. Way, Washington, 1985—. Mem. Writers Guild of Am. West, Horror Writers of Am., Psi Chi. Democrat.

STRAHAN, JULIA CELESTINE, electronics company executive; b. Indpls., Feb. 10, 1938; d. Edgar Paul Pauley and Pauline Barbara (Myers) Shawver; m. Norman Strahan, Oct. 2, 1962 (div. 1982); children: Daniel Keven, Natalie Kay. Grad. high sch., Indpls. With EG&G/Energy Measurements, Inc., Las Vegas, Nev., 1967—; sect. head EG&G Co., 1979-83, mgr. electronics dept., 1984—. Recipient award Am. Legion, 1952, Excellence award, 1986. Mem. NAFE, Am. Nuclear Soc. (models and mentors), Internat. Platform Assn. Home: 5222 Stacey Ave Las Vegas NV 89108-3078 Office: EG&G PO Box 1912 Las Vegas NV 89125-1912

STRAHLER, ARTHUR NEWELL, former geology educator, author; b. Kolhapur, India, Feb. 20, 1918; s. Milton W. and Harriet (Brittan) S.; m. Margaret E. Wanless, Aug. 10, 1940; children: Alan H., Marjorie E. A.B., Coll. Wooster, 1938; A.M., Columbia U., 1940, Ph.D. (Univ. fellow), 1944. Faculty Columbia U., 1941-71, prof. geomorphology, 1958-68, adj. prof. geology, 1968-71, chmn. dept. geology, 1959-62. Author: Physical Geography, rev. edit., 1975, The Earth Sciences, rev. edit., 1971, Introduction to Physical Geography, rev. edit., 1973, Planet Earth, 1971, Environmental Geoscience, 1973, Introduction to Environmental Science, 1974, Elements of Physical Geography, 2d edit., 1979, 3d edit., 1984, 4th edit., 1989, Principles of Earth Science, 1976, Principles of Physical Geology, 1977, Geography and Man's Environment, 1977, Modern Physical Geography, 1978, 4th edit., 1992, Physical Geology, 1981, Science and Earth History—The Evolution/Creation Controversy, 1987, Investigating Physical Geography, 1989, Understanding Science: An Introduction to Concepts and Issues, 1992. Fellow Geol. Soc. Am., Am. Geog. Soc.; mem. Am. Geophys. Union, Phi Beta Kappa, Sigma Xi. Home: 1039 Cima Linda Ln Santa Barbara CA 93108-1818

STRAIN, JOHN THOMAS, electronics engineer; b. Raymondville, Mo., Oct. 25, 1939; s. Thomas and Lillie (Merckling) S.; m. Bonnie J. Cline, 1967 (div. 1980); children: Robert Vidmar, Anthony Vidmar. BSEE, U. Mo., Rolla, 1964. Electronics technician Exec. Aircraft Co., Kansas City, Mo., 1960-61; electronic engring. technician Wilcox Electric Co., Kansas City, 1963, sr. electronics technician, 1964-67; sr. electronics technician Exec. Aircraft Co., 1964; electronic engring. tech. Gianni Voltex Co., San Diego, 1967-68; electronic fabricator Bendix Atomic Energy Commn., Kansas City, 1968; electronics engr. Electronic Research Corp., Overland Park, Kans., 1968-69, Monitor Products Co., South Pasadena, Calif., 1969-73, NBC, Burbank, Calif., 1973--. Designed and developed original TV stereo encoder; responsible (with Ron Estes) for first recorded stereo TV program (nominated for Emmy 1983); developer first DIP style crystal controled oscillator for use in computer and areospace industries. With USAF, 1964-65. Home: 6450 Clybourn Ave North Hollywood CA 91606-2728 Office: NBC 3000 W Alameda Ave Burbank CA 91523-0001

STRAIT, LINDSY EDWARD, systems engineering and computer science executive; b. Delta, Colo., Nov. 4, 1955; s. Lindsy Dean and Diana Pearl (Wright) S. BA, MWC U. Va., 1980; grad., Computer Sci. Sch., Quantico, Va., 1981; MS, U. So. Calif., 1984. Commd. 2d lt. USMC, 1980, advanced through grades to maj., 1982—; tech. dir. Software AG of N. Am., L.A., 1984-86; asst. v.p. Profl. Hosp. Svcs., L.A., 1986-89; v.p. Interpractice Systems, San Francisco, 1989-91; dir. Teradata Profl. Svcs., Greenbrae, Calif., 1991-93; v.p. Knowledge Data, Ameritech Health Connections, Greenbrae, Calif., 1993—; pres., founder Sytem Builder Assoc., Irvine, Calif., 1986—, Cognizance Tech. Systems, Marin, Calif., 1989—. Author and Presentor: Strategic Technology Initiatives, 1988. Recipient Outstanding Presentor, Data Gen. Worldwide Systems Supplier, USMCR. Mem. Nat. Riffle Assn., Marine Corps Meml. Assn., Assn. Computer Machinery, IEEE, Digital Cons. Assoc. (advisory bd. mem. 1984—), Homeowners Assn. (pres. 1982-84), Nat. Honor Soc., Elks. Home: 329 Via La Cumbre San Rafael CA 94904-1336 Office: Knowledge Data Ameritech 32A Via La Cumbre Greenbrae CA 94904

STRAIT, RAYMOND EARL (RUSTY), biographer; b. Akron, Ohio, May 17, 1924; s. Charles Earl and Geraldine Oma (Shirkey) S.; m. Nanette E. Logan, Aug. 19, 1965 (div. 1975); children: Mark, Russell; stepchildren: Dane Block, Shaunna Citrowski. Student, U. Charleston, 1946-47; Degree in Bus., Capitol City Bus. Coll., Charleston, 1952; grad., Stenotype Inst., Tampa, Fla., 1951; student, U. Calif., Riverside, 1988. Cert. ct. reporter, paralegal. tchr. U. Calif., Riverside, Mt. San Jacinto (Calif.) Coll., Menefee Campus, Coll. of the Desert, Palm Desert, Calif., Capitol City Bus. Coll., St. Louis, Baker Bus. Coll., St. Louis, San Jacinto Valley Sch. of the Arts. Author: Mrs. Howard Hughes, 1970, High Rider, 1971, A State of Disgrace, 1971, Star Babies, 1980, Hollywood's Children, 1982, Alan Alda, 1985, James Garner, 1985, The Tragic Secret Life of Jayne Mansfield, 1976, This for Remembrance (The Rosemary Clooney Story), 1976; (with Chris Costello) Lou's On First, 1980;(with Patte Barham, Maria Rasputin) Rasputin: The Man and The Myth, 1976; (with Fred-Otash) Investigation Hollywood, 1976, (with Terry Robinson) Lanza, His Tragic Life, 1980, (with Leif Henie) Queen of Ice, Queen of Shadows-The Unsuspected Life of Sonja Henie, 1985, Harry Langdon, a biography, 1986, Get Me Otash, 1991, Hollywood's Star Children, 1992, Here They Are, Jayne Mansfield, 1992, The Godlings, 1993, The Corpse Below the Credits, 1993; motion picture credits include S.L.I.P., 1969; TV credits include The Musical World of Rudolf Friml, 1971, The Rosemary Clooney Story, 1982. Mem. state exec. bd. Calif. Dem. Party, 1990—; vice chair Calif. 73d Assembly Dist. Com., 1990-93, Riverside County Dem. Ctrl. Com., 1990—; Dem. candidate Calif. State Assembly 73d Dist., 1990, 65th Dist., 1992. With USN, 1941, USAAC, 1944-47, USAF, 1947-50, World War II PTO, Berlin Airlift. Mem. Writers Guild Am., Authors Guild, Author's League, Nat. Writers Union, Hemet C. of C., San Jacinto Valley Sch. of Arts (sec.). Democrat. Home and Office: PO Box 5307 Hemet CA 92544-0307

STRAKA, WILLIAM CHARLES, II, astronomer; b. Phoenix, Oct. 21, 1940; s. William Charles and Martha Nadine (Marshall) S.; m. Barbara Ellen Thayer, Jan. 29, 1966; 1 child, William Charles III. BS, Calif. Inst. Tech., 1962; MA, UCLA, 1965, PhD, 1969. Tchr. Long Beach (Calif.) City Coll., 1966-70; asst. prof. Boston U., 1970-74; prof., dept. head Jackson (Miss.) State U., 1974-84; sr. staff scientist Lockheed Palo Alto (Calif.) Rsch. Lab., 1984—. Contbr. articles to profl. jours. Mem. Am. Astron. Soc., Sigma Xi. Office: Lockheed Palo Alto Rsch Lab 3251 Hanover St Palo Alto CA 94304-1187

STRALING, PHILLIP FRANCIS, bishop; b. San Bernardino, Calif., Apr. 25, 1933; s. Sylvester J. and Florence E. (Robinson) S. B.A., U. San Diego, 1963; M.S. in Child and Family Counseling, San Diego State U., 1971. Ordained priest Roman Catholic Ch., 1959, consecrated bishop, 1978. Mem. faculty St. John Acad., El Cajon, Calif., 1959-60, St. Therese Acad., San Diego, 1960-63; chaplain Newman Club, San Diego State U., 1960-72; mem. faculty St. Francis Sem., San Diego, 1972-76; pastor Holy Rosary Parish, San Bernardino, 1976-78; bishop Diocese of San Bernardino, 1978—; pub. Inland Catholic newspaper, 1979—; bd. dirs. Calif. Assn. Cath. Campus Ministers, 1960s; exec. sec. Diocesan Synod II, 1972-76; Episcopal vicar San Bernardino Deanery, 1976-78. Office: Diocesan Pastoral Ctr 1450 N D St San Bernardino CA 92405-4790

STRAND, MARK, poet; b. Summerside, P.E.I., Can., Apr. 11, 1934; came to U.S., 1938; s. Robert Joseph and Sonia (Apter) S.; m. Antonia Ratensky, Sept. 14, 1961 (div. June 1973); 1 dau., Jessica; m. Julia Rumsey Garretson, Mar. 15, 1976; 1 child, Thomas Summerfield. BA, Antioch, 1957; BFA, Yale, 1959; MA, U. Iowa, 1962. Instr. English U. Iowa, 1962-65; asst. prof. Mt. Holyoke Coll., 1967; adj. assoc. prof. Columbia U., 1969-72; assoc. prof. Bklyn. Coll., 1971-72; vis. prof. U. Wash., 1968; vis. lectr. Yale, 1969-70, U. Va., 1976, Calif. State U., Fresno, 1977, U. Calif., Irvine, 1979; Bain-Swiggett lectr. Princeton, 1973; Hurst prof. poetry Brandeis U., 1974-75; vis. prof. U. Va., 1978, Wesleyan U., 1979, Harvard U., 1980; prof. U. Utah, 1981—; poet laureate of U.S. Library of Congress, Washington, 1990-91. Author: Sleeping with One Eye Open, 1964, Reasons for Moving, 1968, Darker, 1970, New Poetry of Mexico, 1970, The Contemporary American Poets, 1969, 18 Poems from the Quechua, 1971, The Story of Our Lives, 1973, The Owl's Insomnia, 1973, The Sargentville Notebook, 1973, Another Republic, 1976, The Monument, 1978, The Late Hour, 1978, Selected Poems, 1980, The Planet of Lost Things, 1982, The Art of the Real: Nine American Figurative Painters, 1983, The Night Book, 1985, Rembrandt Takes a Walk, 1986, William Bailey, 1987, New Poems, 1990; co-editor: Travelling in the Family, 1986; (short stories) Mr. and Mrs. Baby and Other Stories, 1985; Recipient award Am. Acad. and Inst. Arts and Letters 1975, Edgar Allen Poe prize 1974. Recipient award Am. Acad. and Inst. Arts and Letters, 1975, Edgar Allen Poe prize, 1974, Utah Gov.'s award in Arts, 1992, The Bobbitt Nat. prize for Poetry, 1992, The Bollingen award, 1993; named U.S. Poet Laureate, 1990, Fulbright scholar to Italy, 1960-61, Fulbright lectr. U. Brazil, 1965-66, Ingram Merrill fellow, 1966, Nat. Endowment for Arts fellow, 1967-68, 78-79, 86-87, Rockefeller fellow, 1968-69, Guggenheim fellow, 1975, Disting. Prof., 1987, MacArthur fellow, 1987—. Fellow Acad. Am. Poets; mem. Am. Acad. and Inst. Arts and Letters. Office: Univ of Utah Eng 332 Orson Spencer Hall Salt Lake City UT 84112 Home: 716 4th Ave Salt Lake City UT 84103

STRAND, RAY WALTER, general contractor; b. Seattle, July 23, 1924; s. Arvid O. and Antonia (Sjogren) S.; m. Luella Oak, Oct. 1948 (div. 1959); m. Ruby Good, Jan. 8, 1960; children: Timothy Ray, Donald Brent. Student, U. Wash., 1945-48. Ptnr. Strand & Sons, Seattle, 1939-54; CEO, pres. Strand Inc., Seattle and Bellevue, Wash., 1954-92; chmn., CEO Strand Hunt Constrn., Kirkland, Wash., 1992—. Staff sgt. U.S. Army Air Corps, 1943-45. Mem. Assn. Gen. Contractors, Wash. Athletic Club, Bellevue Athletic Club, Lakes Club, Broadmoor Golf Club. Republican. Congregational. Home: 5800 Princeton Ave NE Seattle WA 98105-2134

STRAND, ROGER GORDON, federal judge; b. Peekskill, N.Y., Apr. 28, 1934; s. Ernest Gordon Strand and Lisabeth Laurine (Phin) Steinmetz; m. Joan Williams, Nov. 25, 1961. AB, Hamilton Coll., 1955; LLB, Cornell U., 1961; grad., Nat. Coll. State Trial Judges, 1968. Bar: Ariz. 1961, U.S. Dist. Ct. Ariz. 1961, U.S. Supreme Ct. 1980. Assoc. Fennemore, Craig, Allen & McClennen, Phoenix, 1961-67; judge Ariz. Superior Ct., Phoenix, 1967-85, U.S. Dist. Ct. Ariz., Phoenix, 1985—; assoc. presiding judge Ariz. Superior Ct., 1971-85; lectr. Nat. Jud. Coll., Reno, 1978-87. Past pres. cen. Ariz. chpt. Arthritis Found. Lt. USN, 1955-61. Mem. ABA, Ariz. Bar Assn., Maricopa County Bar Assn., Nat. Conf. Fed. Trial Judges, Phi Delta Phi, Aircraft Owners and Pilots Assn. Lodge: Rotary. Home: 5825 N 3d Ave Phoenix AZ 85013 Office: US Dist Ct Courthouse and Fed Bldg 230 N 1st Ave Ste 3013 Phoenix AZ 85025-0002

STRANDBERG, LEE R., pharmacist; b. Valley City, N.D., Oct. 12, 1945; s. Merrill H. and Myrtle A. (Olson) S.; m. Rebecca L. Sandal, Aug. 9, 1969; children: Jennifer, Jon. BS in Pharmacy, N.D. State U., 1968, MS in Social Scis., 1970; PhD, U. Colo., 1975. Asst. prof. pharmacy N.D. State U., Fargo, 1968-72; instr. Oreg. State U., Boulder, 1972-75; assoc. prof. Oreg. State U., Coll. Pharmacy, Corvallis, 1975—; cons. State Oreg. Medicaid, Salem, 1976-86, Colo. Bus. Coalition on Health, Denver, 1990—, Oreg. Dept. Corrections, Salem, 1989—, Adolph Coors Co., Golden, Colo., 1990—, Teamsters, 1991—; dir. rsch. and devel. Pharmacists Svc. Group, Salem, Oreg., 1984—. Contbr. articles and videos in field. Mem. Am. Pharm. Assn. (chmn. ESAS sect., 1989), Am. Soc. Pharmacy Law, Assn. Health Svcs. Rsch., Oreg. State Pharmacists Assn. Democrat. Lutheran. Office: Oreg State U Coll Pharmacy Corvallis OR 97331-3507

STRANG, CHARLES WARD, business educator; b. Mineola, N.Y., May 8, 1932; s. Charles Ward and Martha Elsie (Lenzner) S.; m. Loretta Elennor Pruss, Oct. 3, 1959 (div. 1980); children: Jane Patricia, Lori Leilani, Ruth Marta; m. Carrol Eva Sauer, Nov. 27, 1981. BS, Va. Poly. Inst., 1954; MBA, U. Hawaii, 1967; DED, U. So. Calif., 1985. CPA, Hawaii. Commd. 2d lt. U.S. Army, 1954, advanced through grades to lt. col., ret., 1974; rsch. dir. Hawaii Trucking Assn., Honolulu, 1974-75; mgr. Yellow Freight System, Honolulu, 1975-79; asst. prof. Embry Riddle Aeornautical U., Prescott, Ariz., 1980-81; asst. prof. Chaminade U., Honolulu, 1982-83, dean bus. sch., 1983-86; prof. Western N.Mex. U., Silver City, 1986—; bd. dirs. S.W. N.Mex. Econ. Devel. Corp., Silver City; cons., instr. S.W. N.Mex. Bus. Assistance Ctr., Silver City, 1989—; dir. N.Mex. Community Econ. Devel. Leadership Inst. Decorated Bronze star, Legion of Merit, Soldier's medal. Mem. AICPA, Am. Mktg. Assn., Am. Acctg. Assn., Nat. Assn. Accts., Am. Assn. U. Profs., Hawaii Soc. CPAs, N.Mex. Soc. CPAs. Home: 4257 N Swan St Silver City NM 88061-6050 Office: Western NMex U Bus Dept Silver City NM 88062

STRANGE, RICHARD EUGENE, conductor, music educator; b. Hutchinson, Kans., Sept. 14, 1928; s. Virgil and Dorothy (Lusk) S.; m. Marian Lucille Box; children: Steven Lynn, Phillip Michael. MusB in Edn., Wichita U., 1950; MusM in Edn., U. Colo., 1957; D Mus. Arts, Boston U., 1962. Tchr. music Clifton (Kans.) High Sch., 1951-57; grad. asst. band dir. Boston U., 1957-59; asst. prof. music Tex. State Coll. A&I, Kingsville, 1959-60; dir. bands W.Va. U., Morgantown, 1960-61, Carnegie-Mellon U., Pitts., 1961-74, Ariz. State U., Tempe, 1974—; condr. Carnegie (Pa.) Civic Symphony, 1961-74, Butler (Pa.) County Symphony, 1965-74, Tempe Symphony Orch., 1975—; adjudicator, condr. mus. groups worldwide. Music reviewer: (mags.) Sch. Musician, Bandworld, 1987—. With U.S. Army, 1950-51. Recipient Outstanding Contbn. to the Arts award Tempe City Con., 1984, Excellence in Teaching award Ariz. Music Educators Assn., 1989; Faculty Rsch. grantee Ariz. State U., 1986, 88, 89, Citation of Excellence Nat. Band Assn., 1991. Mem. Am. Bandmasters Assn. (various offices including pres. 1989—), Coll. Band Dirs. Nat. Assn. (various offices including pres. 1990—), Music Educators Assn., Ariz. Band & Orch. Dirs. Assn., Kappa Kappa Psi (Disting. Svc. to Music award 1991, Tau Beta Sigma, Phi Mu Alpha Sinfonia. Office: Ariz State U Sch Music Tempe AZ 85287-0405

STRANGWAY, DAVID WILLIAM, university president; b. Can., June 7, 1934. BA in Physics and Geology, U. Toronto, 1956, MA in Physics, 1958, PhD, 1960; DLittS (hon.), Victoria U., U. Toronto, 1986; DSc (hon.), Meml. U. Nfld., 1986, McGill U., Montreal, Que., Can., 1989, Ritsumeikan U., Japan, 1990; D.Ag.Sc. (hon.), Tokyo U. Agr., 1991. Sr. geophysicist Dominion Gulf Co. Ltd., Toronto, 1956; chief geophysicist Ventures Ltd., 1956-57, sr. geophysicist, summer 1958; research geophysicist Kennecott Copper Corp., Denver, 1960-61; asst. prof. U. Colo., Boulder, 1961-64, M.I.T., 1965-68; mem. faculty U. Toronto, 1968-85, prof. physics, 1971-85, chmn. dept. geology, 1972-80, v.p., provost, 1980-83, pres., 1983-84; pres. U. B.C., 1985—; chief geophysics br. Johnson Space Ctr., NASA, Houston, 1970-72, chief physics br., 1972-73, acting chief planetary and earth sci. div., 1973; vis. prof. geology U. Houston, 1971-73; interim dir. Lunar Sci. Inst., Houston, 1973; vis. com. geol. scis. Brown U., 1974-76, Meml. U., St. John's Nfld., 1974-79, Princeton U.; v.p. Can. Geosci. Coun., 1977; chmn. proposal evaluating program Univs. Space Rsch. Assocs., 1977-78, Ont. Geosci. Rsch. Fund; Pahlavi lectr. Govt. Iran, 1978; cons. to govt. and industry, mem. numerous govt. and sci. adv. and investigative panels; hon. prof. Changchun Coll. Geology, People's Republic China, 1985, Guilin Coll. Geology, People's Republic China, 1987; bd. dirs. MacMillan Bloedel Ltd., Echo Bay Mines, Ltd., BC Gas, Corp.-Higher Edn. Forum, Internat. Inst. for Sustainable Devel. Author numerous papers, reports in field. Active Royal Trust Adv. Coun. Recipient Exceptional Sci. Achievement medal NASA, 1972. Fellow Royal Astron. Soc., Royal Soc. Can.; mem. AAAS, Soc. Exploration Geophysicists (Virgil Kauffman Gold medal 1974), Geol. Assn. Can. (pres. 1978-79, Logan Gold medal), Can. Geophys. Union (chmn. 1977-79, J. Tuzo Wilson medal 1987), Am. Geophys. Union (sect. planetology sect. 1978-81), European Assn. Exploration Geophysicists, Soc. Geomagnetism and Geoelectricity Japan, Can. Geosci. Council (pres. 1980), Can. Exploration Geophysicists, Soc. Exptl. Geophysics (hon.), Canada-Japan Soc., Japan Soc. Can. (founding bd. dirs.), Internat. House Japan, Inc.

STRANSKE, TIMOTHY W., superintendent; b. Khartown, Sudan, Oct. 26, 1949; s. Harvey Raymond and Evadene Charlotte (Johnson) S.; m. Mary Gaye Murphy, Aug. 25, 1973; children: Tim R., Gail L., Sarah E. BA in Social Scis., Biola Coll., 1972; MA in Sch. Adminstrn., Biola U., 1979; PhD in Edn., Claremont Grad. Sch., 1990. Cert. social studies tchr., Calif.; cert. adminstr. Christian Schs. Tchr. L.A. Unified Sch. Dist., 1973, Whittier (Calif.) Christian Schs., 1973-74; dept. mgr. Inst. in Basic Youth Conflicts, Oakbrook, Ill., 1974-77; curriculum dir., prin. Whittier Christian Sch. of Yorba Linda, Calif., 1977-83; supt. Brethren Elem. and Jr. High Schs., Whittier, 1983—; asst. prof. Biola U., La Mirada, Calif., 1982-87, 91—; chmn. accreditation com. Assn. Christian Schs. Internat., La Habra, Calif., 1983, 85, 89. Co-author: (brochure) A Biblical Perspective for Early Childhood Education, 1988; contbr. articles to profl. jours. Office: Brethren Elem/Jr High Sch 11000 E Washington Blvd Whittier CA 90606

STRASBURGER, VICTOR C., pediatrician; b. Balt., Oct. 7, 1949; s. Arthur Charles and Marjorie (Cohen) S.; m. Alison Reeve, Aug. 18, 1984; children: Max, Katya. BA summa cum laude, Yale U., 1971; MD, Harvard U., 1975. Intern Children's Hosp.- U. Wash., Seattle, 1975-76, residency, 1976-77; residency Boston Children's Hosp., 1977-78; dir. adolescent medicine Bridgeport (Conn.) Hosp., 1979-86; vis. lectr. St. Mary's Hosp. Med. Sch., London, 1986-87; chief div. adolescent medicine sch. medicine U. N.Mex., Albuquerque, 1987—; cons. Nat. PTA, Washington and Chgo., 1978-86. Author: Rounding Third and Heading Home, 1974, Adolescent Medicine: A Practical Guide, 1991; editor: Basic Adolescent Gynecology, 1990; editor-in-chief Adolescent Medicine: State of the Art Revs., 1989—. Fellow Am. Acad. Pediatrics, Soc. for Adolescent Medicine; mem. Phi Beta Kappa. Office: U NM Sch Medicine Dept Pediatrics Albuquerque NM 87131

STRATFORD, JOHN HENRY, cattle farmer; b. Billings, Mont., Feb. 29, 1920; s. Harry Haines and Katherine Louise (Denton) S.; m. Mary Katherine Maxon, Aug. 26, 1947 (div. Aug. 1979); children: Michael, Scott, Steven; m. Rita Arrasmith Kennedy, Feb. 26, 1990. Grad., high sch., 1938. V.p., owner Stratford Farms Inc., Billings, 1946—; ptnr. Indsl. Land-Realty, Billings, Stratford Bros. Farm, Billings; v.p. R.L. Stratford & Co., Billings. Chmn. City-County Planning Bd., Billings, 1985-86; mem. Nat. Orgn. Police, 1992—; chmn. Yellowstone County Weed Bd., Billings, 1984-91; del. Rep. Platform Com., Billings, 1992. Sgt. U.S. Army, 1943-45, PTO, Japan. Decorated Bronze Star medal (2). Mem. Mont. Grain Growers Assn. (founder, 1st treas. 1972), Am. Legion, Masons, Elks. Presbyterian. Home and Office: 9543 Stratford Hill Rd Billings MT 59101

STRATTON, A(LLAN) DONALD, computer industry executive, writer; b. South Amboy, N.J., Mar. 23, 1934; s. Rupell M. and Francis (Kososky) S.; m. Leah R. Fillhower, May 7, 1955; children: Todd Donald, Mark Allan. Bachelors, Rutgers U., 1957; MBA, Fairleigh Dickinson U., 1963. Mgr. in engring. and installation quality AT&T, Atlanta, 1957-88; v.p. in corp. quality and edn. StorageTek, Louisville, Colo., 1988—. Author: An Approach to Quality Improvement That Works, 1991 (Golden Quill award 1991). With U.S. Army, 1953-56.

STRATTON, DAVID HODGES, history educator; b. Tucumcari, N.Mex., Jan. 6, 1927; s. Samuel Houston and Lottie (Hodges) S.; m. Wanda Lee Cummings, Nov. 23, 1949; children: John Michael, Nancy Ellen, Scott David. BA in History, Ea. N.Mex. U., Portales, 1951; MA in History, U. Colo., 1953, PhD in History, 1955. Asst. prof. Baylor U., Waco, Tex., 1955-58, assoc. prof., 1958-62; assoc. prof. Wash. State U., Pullman, 1962-66, prof., 1966-93, prof. emeritus, 1993—, dir. Am. studies program, 1968-71, chair dept. history, 1979-85; mem. State Adv. Coun. on Hist. Preservation, 1969-80, Wash. Centennial Commn., 1982-90. Author: First Century of Baptists in New Mexico, 1954; editor: Memoirs of Albert B. Fall, 1966, Spokane and the Inland Empire, 1991, Washington Comes of Age, 1992; co-editor: The Changing Pacific Northwest, 1988; bd. editors: Pacific N.W. Quarterly, 1968-93, mem. editorial bd. Wash. State Univ. Press, 1989—. Mem. adv. com. on history Supt. of Pub. Instruction, Wash., 1963-67; bd. dirs. adv. coun. Nat. Archives & Records Svc., Seattle, 1969-73; bd. dirs. Wash. State Hist. Soc., Tacoma, 1973-79, 92—. With USNR, 1945, Sgt. U.S. Army, 1946-47. Huntington Libr. grantee, 1961, NEH grantee, 1980, 81; recipient Spl. Recognition award Gov. of Wash.'s Writers Awards, 1990, Capt. Robert Gray award Wash. State Hist. Soc., 1993. Mem. Am. Historical Assn. (coun. Pacific Coast br. 1980-83), Orgn. Am. Historians (hist. preservation com. 1979-81), Western History Assn. Home: SW 635 Fountain Pullman WA 99163 Office: Wash State U Dept of History Pullman WA 99164

STRATTON, GREGORY ALEXANDER, computer specialist, administrator, mayor; b. Glendale, Calif., July 31, 1946; s. William Jaspar and Rita Phyllis (Smith) S.; m. Yolanda Margot Soler, 1967 (div. 1974); 1 child, Tiffany; m. Edith Carter, Sept. 27, 1975; stepchildren: John Henkell, Paul Henkell, D'Lorah Henkell. Student, Harvey Mudd Coll., 1964-65; BS in Physics, UCLA, 1968; MBA, Calif. Luth. U., 1977. Elec. engr. Naval Ship Weapon System Engring. Sta., Port Hueneme, Calif., 1968-73; sr. staff mem. Univac, Valencia, Calif., 1973-74; v.p. Digital Applications, Camarillo, Calif., 1974-75; cons. Grumman Aerospace, Point Mugu, Calif., 1975-76; F-14 software mgr. Pacific Missle Test Ctr., Pt. Mugu, 1976-84; software mgr. Teledyne Systems, Northridge, Calif., 1984-92, dir. engring. software dept., 1992—. Mem. City Coun., City of Simi Valley, Calif., 1979-86, mayor, 1986—; alt. Rep. County Cen. Com., Ventura County, 1986-88; mem. Rep. State Cen. Com., Calif., 1990—; bd. dirs. Simi Valley Hosp., 1987—. Mem. Assn. Ventura County Cities (chair 1990-91), Rotary (Paul Harris award Simi Sunrise chpt. 1989), Jaycees (pres. Simi Valley chpt. 1974-75, nat. bd. dirs. 1975-76, v.p. Calif. state 1976-77). Republican. Lutheran. Home: 254 Goldenwood Cir Simi Valley CA 93065-6771 Office: Office of Mayor 2929 Tapo Canyon Rd Simi Valley CA 93063-2199

STRAUB, KENNETH RICHARD, educator; b. Denver, Dec. 1, 1945; s. Eugene Curtis Sr. and Helen Margaret (Russ) S.; m. Norine Ann Forde, Dec. 18, 1971; 1 child, Nicole Kristina. BA, Adam's State Coll., Alamosa, Colo., 1970; postgrad., Metro State Coll., Denver, 1981-83, Denver U., 1989. Cert. secondary tchr. English and social studies. Team leader, tchr. Adam's County Dist. 27J, Brighton, Colo., 1971-72; asst. mgr. Gano-Downs Men's Store, Cherry Creek, Colo., 1972-75; adminstr. Adam's County Dist 12 Alternative High Sch., Northglenn, Colo., 1975-80; educator, tchr. Adam's County Five Star Sch. System, Northglenn, 1980—; mem. alternative edn. task force Adam's County Dist. 12, Northglenn, 1990-91; pres. Colo. Options in Edn. Assn., Denver, 1976-77; cons. Adam's County Dist. 14 schs., Commerce City, Colo., 1977-78; team leader curriculum devel. Adam's County Dist. 27J, Brighton, Colo., 1971-72. Co-chmn. author: Comprehensive District Wide Alternative Program, 1991. Recipient awards of appreciation Jr. Achievement, 1989, 90. Mem. NEA, Colo. Edn. Assn., Polit. Action Com. in Edn., Dist. 12 Tchrs. Assn. (rep. Alternative Sch. 1975-80). Roman Catholic. Home: 11767 Keough Dr Northglenn CO 80233 Office: Adams County 5 Star Schs 11285 Highline Dr Northglenn CO 80233

STRAUBEL, JOHN FREDERICK, public relations executive; b. Green Bay, Wis., May 19, 1928; s. Clarence Weise and Ethel (Puchner) S. B.S. in English, Northwestern U., 1950. Dir. pub. relations Hiller Aircraft Corp., Palo Alto, Calif., 1956-64; dir. communications Fairchild Hiller Corp., Washington, 1964-66; owner, pres. Straubel Communications, Portola Valley, Calif., 1966—. Author, editor: Pacific Diary I, 1952; Pacific Diary II, 1953; One Way Up, 1963. Mgr. pub. relations Volunteers for Nixon-Lodge, Washington, 1960. Served to lt. USN, 1950-53; Korea. Mem. Pub. Relations Soc. Am. Presbyterian. Office: Straubel Communications 4370 Alpine Rd Ste 206 Menlo Park CA 94028-7927

STRAUS, LEONARD H., retail company executive; b. 1914; married. LL.B., Harvard U., 1938. With Thrifty Corp., Los Angeles, 1945—, officer legal dept., from 1948, chmn., 1979—, now chief exec. officer, also dir. Served with USCG, 1943-45. Office: Thrifty Corp Worldway Postal Ctr PO Box 92333 Los Angeles CA 90009-2333

STRAWA, ANTHONY WALTER, researcher; b. Chgo., Apr. 22, 1950. BS, USAF Acad., Colorado Springs, Colo., 1973; PhD, MS, Stanford (Calif.) U., 1986. Rsch. asst. Stanford U., 1982-86; lead researcher ballistic range NASA-Ames Rsch. Ctr., Moffett Field, Calif., 1986-89, prin. investigator Aerosissit flight expt., 1990-91, rsch. scientist, 1991—; mem. NASA Aerodynamic Sensors Working Group, 1989—. Mem. AIAA (sec. aerodynamic measurement tech. com. 1989—), AAAS, Aeroballistic Range Assn. Office: NASA-Ames Rsch Ctr Mail Stop 245-4 Moffett Field CA 94035

STRAWBERRY, DARRYL, professional baseball player; b. L.A., Mar. 12, 1962; s. Henry and Ruby S.; 1 child, Darryl Jr. Baseball player New York Mets, 1983-90, L.A. Dodgers, 1990—; mem. Nat. League All-Star Team, 1984-91, World Series Champions, 1986. Named Nat. League Rookie of Yr., 1983; Sporting News All-Star Team, 1988, 90; recipient Silver Slugger award, 1988, 90; Nat. League Home Run Leader, 1988. Office: Los Angeles Dodgers Dodger Stadium Los Angeles CA 90012

STRAWN, JOHN, musical instrument company executive, consultant; b. Lima, Ohio, Jan. 22, 1950. BMus, Oberlin Coll., 1973; PhD, Stanford U., 1985. Programmer Droid Works/Lucasfilm, San Rafael, Calif., 1985-87; cons. S Systems, San Rafael, 1987-88; pres. Yamaha Music Tech. U.S.A., Larkspur, Calif., 1988-92; ind. cons., 1992—. Editor: Digital Audio Signal Process, 1985, Digital Audio Engineering, 1985, Foundations of Computer Music, 1985. Fulbright fellow, 1973-75, Watson fellow IBM, 1975-76. Mem. Audio Engring. Soc., IEEE, Assn. Computer Machinery, Computer Music Assn.

STREALY, JERRY LEE, educational administrator, consultant; b. San Diego, Oct. 3, 1941; s. Cecil Charles and Blanche (Peters) S.; m. Jean Sue Ryal, Aug. 26, 1966; children: Dorothy, Christina. BA, Pepperdine U., 1973, MA, 1977; PhD, Columbia Pacific U., 1980. Ordained to ministry Ch. of Christ, 1973. Min. Chs. of Christ, Calif., 1973-82; materiel mgr. Aerospace Industries, L.A., 1982-85; ch. devel. cons. to nonprofit orgns. Calif., 1985—; founder Hughson (Calif.) Christian Sch., 1978. Mem. Green Valley (Calif.) Town Coun., 1990-94. Republican. Home: 39136 Calle Escondido Green Valley CA 91350

STREET, ROBERT LYNNWOOD, civil and mechanical engineer; b. Honolulu, Dec. 18, 1934; s. Evelyn Mansel and Dorothy Heather (Brook) S.; m. Norma Jeanette Ensminger, Feb. 6, 1959; children: Brian Clarke (dec.), Deborah Lynne, Kimberley Anne. Student, USN ROTC Program, 1952-57; M.S., Stanford U., 1957, Ph.D. (NSF grad. fellow 1960-62), 1963. Mem. faculty sch. engring. Stanford U., 1962—, prof. civil engring., assoc. chmn. dept., 1970-72, chmn. dept., 1972-80, prof. fluid mechanics and applied math., 1972—, dir. environ. fluid mechanics lab., 1985-91, assoc. dean research, 1971-83, vice provost for acad. computing and info. systems, 1983-

85, vice provost and dean of research and acad. info. systems, 1985-87, v.p. for info. resources, 1987-90, acting provost, 1987, v.p. librs. and info. resources, 1990-92; vice provost, dean of librs. and info. resources Stanford U., 1992—; vis. prof. U. Liverpool, Eng., 1970-71; trustee Univ. Corp. Atmospheric Rsch., 1983-94, chmn. sci. programs evaluation com., 1981, treas. corp., 1985, vice chmn. bd., 1986, chmn. bd., 1987-91; bd. dirs., sec.-treas. UCAR Found., 1987-91; bd. govs. Rsch. Libr. Group, 1990-91; chair Com. Preservation Rsch. Libr. Materials, Assn. Rsch. Librs., 1993; mem. higher edn. adv. bds. of computer corps. Author: The Analysis and Solution of Partial Differential Equations, 1973; co-author: Elementary Fluid Mechanics, 6th edit, 1982; asso. editor: Jour. Fluids Engring, 1978-81; author articles in field; mem. editorial bds. profl. jours. Trustee Pacific Graduate Sch. Psychology, 1993—. Served with C.E.C., USN, 1957-60. Sr. postdoctoral fellow Nat. Center Atmospheric Research, 1978-79; sr. Queen's fellow in marine sci., Australia, 1985; fellow N.E. Asia-U.S. Forum on Internat. Policy at Stanford U., 1985-89. Mem. Am. Soc. Engring. Edn., ASCE (chmn. publs. com. hydraulics div. 1978-80, Walter Huber prize 1972), ASME (R.T. Knapp award 1986), Am. Geophys. Union, The Oceanographic Soc., Phi Beta Kappa, Sigma Xi, Tau Beta Pi. Office: Stanford U Librs & Info Resources Green Libr Stanford CA 94305-6004

STREGE, TIM MELVIN, economic consultant; b. Tacoma, Wash., Sept. 6, 1952; m. Dawn Bernstein; children: Rachel, Nathan. BA, Pacific Luth. U.; MPA, Harvard U., 1986. Dist. adminstrv. asst. U.S. Congressman Norm Dicks, 1976-79; dir. Wash. state Kennedy for Pres. campaign, 1979-80; dep. campaign mgr. U.S. Senator Warren G. Magnuson, 1980; rsch. analyst, legis. asst. Ho. of Reps., Olympia, 1980-83; chmn. Pierce (Wash.) Transit Authority, 1978-83; dir. dist. rels. office Ho. of Reps., Olympia, 1983-84, sr. policy analyst, 1984-85; dep. mayor City of Tacoma, 1984-85; chief fin. analyst Puget Sound Water Quality Authority, Seattle, 1986-87; fin. advisor, then. exec. dir. Coun. Vocat. Tech. Insts., Renton, 1987-91; exec. v.p. Job Training Execs. of Wash., 1991—; chmn. TAPCO Credit Union, 1991—; labor & natural resources economist, 1986—. Author: Employment & Job Training Impacts of Increased U.S.-Canadian Trade, 1991. Bd. dirs. western Wash. chpt. Am. Health Edn. Consortium, 1990-92; mem. Gov.'s Adv. Coun. on Investment in Human Capital, 1990-91, Wash. State Com. on Health Occupations, 1992, Govs. Econ. Devel. Task Force, 1992—; chmn. Pierce County Law & Justice Commn., 1978-79, Community Health Care Delivery System, Pierce County, 1988-89; numerous others. Recipient Disting. Svc. award Clover Park chpt. Wash. Vocat. Assn., 1988; named one of Outstanding Young Men in Am., U.S. Jaycees, 1984. Mem. Rotary. Democrat. Roman Catholic. Home: 8340 6th Ave Tacoma WA 98465-1044

STREITWIESER, ANDREW, JR., chemistry educator; b. Buffalo, June 23, 1927; s. Andrew and Sophie (Morlock) S.; m. Mary Ann Good, Aug. 19, 1950 (dec. May 1965); children—David Roy, Susan Ann; m. Suzanne Cope Beier, July 29, 1967. A.B., Columbia U., 1949, M.A., 1950, Ph.D., 1952; postgrad. (AEC fellow), MIT, 1951-52. Faculty U. Calif., Berkeley, 1952-92, prof. chemistry, 1963-92, prof. emeritus, 1993—; researcher on organic reaction mechanisms, application molecular orbital theory to organic chemistry, effect chem. structure on carbon acidities, f-element organometallic chemistry; cons. to industry, 1957—. Author: Molecular Orbital Theory for Organic Chemists, 1961, Solvolytic Displacement Reactions, 1962, (with J.I. Brauman) Supplemental Tables of Molecular Orbital Calculations, 1965, (with C.A. Coulson) Dictionary of Pi Electron Calculations, 1965, (with P.H. Owens) Orbital and Electron Density Diagrams, 1973, (with C.H. Heathcock and E.M. Kosower) Introduction to Organic Chemistry, 4th edit., 1992; also numerous articles; co-editor: Progress in Physical Organic Chemistry, 11 vols., 1963-74. Recipient Humboldt Found. Sr. Scientist award, 1976, Humboldt medal, 1979. Fellow AAAS; mem. NAS, Am. Chem. Soc. (Calif. sect. award 1964, award in Petroleum Chemistry 1967, Norris award in phys. organic chemistry 1982, Cope scholar award 1989), Am. Acad. Arts and Scis., German Chem. Soc., Bavarian Acad. Scis. (corr.), Phi Beta Kappa, Sigma Xi. Office: U Calif Dept Chemistry Berkeley CA 94720

STREMBITSKY, MICHAEL ALEXANDER, school administrator; b. Smoky Lake, Alta., Can., Mar. 5, 1935; s. Alec and Rose (Fedoretz) S.; m. Victoria Semeniuk, Aug. 12, 1954; children: Michael, William-John. BA, U. Alta., 1955, BEd, 1958; MA, Columbia U., 1968, MEd, 1972, LLD, 1989. With Edmonton (Alta.) pub. schs., now supt. of schs. Mem. Am. Assn. Sch. Adminstrs., Am. Mgmt. Assn., Am. Sch. Bus. Ofls., Assn. for Supr. and Curriculum Devel., Can. Assn. Sch. Adminstrs., Can. Coll. Tchrs., Can. Edn. Assn., Conf. Alta. Sch. Suptds., Alberta Tchr's Assn., Pub. Sch. Admstrs. Assn., Council Ednl. Facility Planners Internat., Edmonton C. of C., Edmonton-Harbin (China) Friendship Soc., Edmonton Edn. Soc., U. Alta. Faculty Edn. Alumni Assn., Large City Sch. Supts., Nat. Assn. Ednl. Negotiators, Nat. Assn. Elementary Sch. Prins., Nat. Ukrainian Profl. Bus. Club, World Coun. for Curriculum and Instruction, Phi Delta Kappa. Office: Edmonton Pub Schs, Ctr for Edn, 1 Kingsway, Edmonton, AB Canada T5H 4G9

STRENA, ROBERT VICTOR, research laboratory manager; b. Seattle, June 28, 1929; s. Robert Lafayette Peel and Mary Oliva (Holmes) S.; m. Rita Mae Brodovsky, Aug. 1957; children: Robert Victor, Adrienne Amelia. AB, Stanford U., 1952. Survey mathematician Hazen Engring., San Jose, Calif., 1952-53; field engr. Menlo Sanitary Dist., Menlo Park, Calif., 1954-55; ind. fin. reporter Los Altos, Calif., 1956-59; asst. dir. Hansen Labs. Stanford U., 1959-90, asst. dir. Ginzton Lab., 1990—; ind. fin. cons., Los Altos, 1965—. Active Edn. System Politics, Los Altos, 1965-80, local Boy Scouts Am., 1968-80. Maj. USAR, 1948-70. Mem. AAAS, Soc. Rsch. Adminstrs., Mus. Soc. Republican. Home: 735 Raymundo Los Altos CA 94024 Office: Ginzton Lab Stanford Univ Stanford CA 94305

STRENGER, GEORGE, surgeon; b. N.Y., Sept. 5, 1906; s. Philip and Tillie (Strassman) S.; m. Florence Serxner, June 9, 1931; children: Philip J., Laurence N. BA, Columbia U., 1928, MD, 1931. Diplomate Am. Bd. Surg., 1942. surgeon Bklyn. Jew. Hosp., N.Y., 1934-72, Goldwater Meml. Hosp., N.Y., 1939-53; chief surg. svc. N.Y. regional office VA, 1948-72; surgeon Coney Island Hosp., N.Y., 1953-72; instr. Long Island Med. Coll., N.Y., 1934-36. Mem. Ditmas Pk. Assn. (pres. 1953-54). Comdr. field hosp. U.S. Army, 1942-46, ETO. Recipient commendation Gen. Eisenhower, 1945. Fellow Am. Coll. Surgeons. Home: 31397 E Nine Dr Laguna Niguel CA 92677-2909

STRENK, YASMINE SYLVIA, environmental planner; b. Fresno, Calif., Oct. 17, 1966; d. Don Tomas Lopez and Olivia (Cardenas) Guerra; m. Jeffrey Paul Strenk, July 8, 1989. BS Environ. Policy Analysis and Planning, U. Calif., Davis, 1990. Grievance counselor Assoc. Students of U. Calif. Davis Acad. Affairs, 1987-89; staff asst. Assemblyman Sam Farr, Monterey, Calif., 1989; environ. planner EMCON Assocs., San Jose, Calif., 1989—. Co-author: (manual) Permanent Household Hazardous Waste Programs, 1992. Publicity task leader Community Outreach; bd. dirs. Silicon Valley Rainforest Action Coalition, San Jose, 1991—; big sister Big Bros./Big Sisters of Santa Clara County, San Jose, 1991-92. Mem. Women in Waste Mgmt. Professions, Rose Villa Home Owner Assn. (bd. dirs. 1992—), Toastmasters (ednl. v.p. San Jose). Office: EMCON Assocs 1921 Ringwood Ave San Jose CA 95131

STRETZ, LAWRENCE ALBERT, chemical engineer; b. Santa Rita, N.Mex., Oct. 5, 1946; s. Charles and Myrtle Belle (Gray) S.; 1 child, Curtis Charles. BS, N.Mex. State U., 1969; MS, Iowa State U., 1971, PhD, 1973. Registered profl. engr., N.Mex. Engr. Consumer's Power, Jackson, Mich., 1973-74; engr. El Paso Products Co., Odessa, Tex., 1974-78; staff mem. Los Alamos Nat. Lab., 1978-85, sect. leader, 1985-89, dep. group leader, 1989-91, group leader, 1991—. Contbr. articles to profl. jours. Mem. Los Alamos Sch. Bd., 1989-93. Mem. Am. Inst. Chem. Engrs., Sigma Xi. Republican. Baptist. Office: Los Alamos Nat Lab 1663 MS C930 MS C920 Los Alamos NM 87545

STRICHARTZ, JAMES LEONARD, lawyer; b. N.Y.C., Feb. 5, 1951; s. Morris Harvey and Estelle (Flatow) S.; m. Cheryl Rene Johnson, July 10, 1982. BA in Urban Studies, U. Mich., 1973, M in Pub. Policy, 1976, JD, 1977. Bar: Mich. 1977, D.C. 1978, Wash. 1980. Law clk. Mich. Ct. Appeals, Detroit, 1977-78; assoc. atty. Weinrich, Gilmore & Adolph, Seattle, 1978-79; gen. counsel The 13th Regional Corp., Seattle, 1979-81; pvt. practice Seattle, 1981—; mem. Senate Jud. Com. Condominium Law Task Force, Seattle, 1986-87, Condominium Act Statutory Revision Com., 1987-91; speaker 22d and 23d nat. confs. Community Assn. Inst., Alexandria, Va. Pres., bd. dirs. Fremont Community Health Clinic, 1982-83, 45th St. Community Health Clinic, 1984-89; gen. counsel, trustee Wash. Trust for Hist. Preservation, 1982-87; mem. Corp. Coun. For The Arts, 1987-88, Coun. for Corp. Responsibility, 1984—; founding mem., founding dir. Shoreline Arts Coun., 1989-92. Mem. CAI, Nat. Conf. of Chpts. (vice chmn. N.W. region 1988-89, chmn. 1990-91), Community Assns. Inst. Wash. (bd. dirs. 1986-92, v.p. 1987, pres. 1988-90, faculty mem. ops. and mgmt. community assns. leadership tng. program 1987, 89, 90, 91, chmn. 1992, 93), Community Assns. Inst. Rsch. Found. (chmn. symposium on community 1990, bd. dirs. 1991—, speaker symposium on uniform multiple ownership acts 1991). Democrat. Unitarian. Office: 200 W Mercer St # 511 Seattle WA 98119-3958

STRICKER, ANDREW GERALD, air force officer, psychologist, educator; b. San Diego, May 5, 1957; s. Larry Wayne and Jesse (Wilson) S.; m. Kathy Ann Duncan, June 4, 1977; children: Jaime, Shannon. BS, U. Evansville, 1979; MA, Ea. N.Mex. U., 1982; PhD, Tex. A&M U., 1988. Commd. 2d lt. USAF, 1980, advanced through grades to maj., 1992; command contr. 27th tactical fighter wing USAF, Clovis, N.Mex., 1980-83; test psychologist Occupational Measurement Ctr. USAF, San Antonio, 1983-85; sponsor Air Force Inst. Tech. USAF, College Station, Tex., 1985-88; assoc. prof. behavioral scis. USAF Acad. USAF, Colorado Springs, Colo., 1988—; dir. learning ctr. USAF Acad.,1 990—, dir. of curriculum, 1992—; chief consulting team Delta Rocket project NASA, Cape Canaveral, Fla., 1992—; cons. U. Denver, 1989—, Martin Marietta Corp., Denver, 1990—, Colorado Springs Sch. Dist., 1991—; diagnostician Right to Read program, Colorado Springs, 1990—. Author: Cognitive Behavioral Psychology, 1988; author book, software: Social-Cognitive Skills, 1992; author software: Language Skills, 1988, Assessment, 1991. Mem. Am. Psychol. Assn. (chpt. pres. 1982), Am. Ednl. Rsch. Assn., Human Factors Soc. (symposium chair 1988), Psi Chi. Republican. Methodist. Home: 4211 E Douglas St USAF Academy CO 80840 Office: USAF Acad Behavioral Scis Fairchild Hall USAF Academy CO 80840

STRICKER, FRANK ALOYSIUS, history educator; b. Evanston, Ill., May 10, 1943; s. Aloys and Ann (Grotz) S.; m. Sharon Genelly, July 1965 (div. June 1981); m. Deborah A. Schopp, Dec. 27, 1984; children: Vonn, Alexis. BS in History, Loyola U., Chgo., 1965; MA in History, Princeton U., 1970, PhD in History, 1974. Vis. lectr. UCLA, 1970-71; asst. prof. Calif. State U., Dominguez Hills, 1972-75, assoc. prof., 1975-80, prof. history, 1980—, chair history dept., 1982-84, 1992—, coord. labor studies, 1985—, coord. interdisciplinary studies, 1990-92. Contbr. articles to profl. jours. Mem. New Am. Movement, L.A., 1972-74; mem., organizer Westcoast Assn. of Marxist Historians, L.A., 1980-83. Woodrow Wilson fellow, 1965-66, Shelby Cullom Davis fellow, 1965-67, Woodrow Wilson Dissertation fellow, 1967-68. Mem. Soc. Sci. History Assn., S.W. Labor Studies Assn. (various offices). Home: 14509 Dublin Ave Gardena CA 90249-3207 Office: Calif State U History Dept Dominguez Hills Carson CA 90747

STRICKER, RAPHAEL BECHER, hematologist; b. N.Y.C., Jan. 7, 1950; s. William and Jenny (Becher) S. BA, Columbia U., 1971, MD, 1978. Resident St. Lukes-Roosevelt Hosp., N.Y.C., 1978-81; fellow U. Calif., San Francisco, 1981-84, rsch. scholar, 1984-85, instr., 1985-86, asst. prof., 1986-89; assoc. dir. immunotherapy div. Calif. Pacific Med. Ctr., San Francisco, 1989—; assoc. dir. Bay Area Mobile Apheresis Program, San Francisco, 1990—. Contbr. articles to profl. jours. and chpts. to books. NIH grantee, 1982-84, 87-89, Am. Heart Assn. grantee, 1985-87, AIDS Task Force grantee, 1987-89, Taylor Found. grantee, 1989—. Mem. So. Med. Assn., AAAS, WWF, Am. Soc. Hematology, Am. Fedn. for Clin. Rsch., Am. Soc. for Apheresis, World Affairs Coun., Smithsonian Assocs., Nat. Geographic Soc. Democrat. Jewish. Office: Calif Pacific Med Ctr 3801 Sacramento St # 623 San Francisco CA 94118-1625

STRICKLAND, SYLVIA RAYE, social worker; b. Grand Prarie, Tex., Feb. 21, 1945; d. Nathaniel and Flora Evelyn (Miller) S.; m. Julian B. Angel, Oct. 6, 1973 (div. Apr. 1983); 1 child, Sarah Renee. BSW, U. So. Colo., Pueblo, 1986; MSW, N.Mex. Highlands U., Las Vegas, Nev., 1987. Social worker Highland Park Nursing Home, Pueblo, 1988; social worker III El Paso County Social Svcs., Colorado Springs, Colo., 1988-89; resident svcs. coord. Villa Santa Maria, Colorado Springs, Colo., 1990-92, ballot initative circulator, 1992; activities dir. social svcs. Medalion Health Ctr. and Personal Care Unit, Colorado Springs, Colo., 1993—. Sec. Social Work Action Team, U. So. Colo., 1984-85. Mem. Nat. Assn. Social Workers. Home: PO Box 3067 Colorado Springs CO 80934-3067

STRID, GAIL KEYS, occupational therapist; b. Calif., Aug. 4, 1953; d. Walter Scott and Shirley Mae (MacDonald) Keys; m. Gene R. Strid, July 22, 1978; children: Kyla Joann, Carl Everett. BS in Occupational Therapy, Colo. State U., 1975; postgrad., U. of Alaska, 1976-78, U. Wash., 1992. Registered occupational therapist. Staff occupational therapist Nakoyia Skilled Nursing Facility, Anchorage, 1976-78; supr. occupational therapy Alaska Treatment Ctr., Anchorage, 1978-81; occupational therapist Humana Hosp. Alaska, Anchorage, 1982-84; staff occupational therapist Providence Hosp., Anchorage, 1987-90; pvt. practice occupational therapy Anchorage, 1992—; mem. med. adv. bd. Alaska chpt. Muscular Dystrophy Assn., 1980-90. Vol. Parent Tchr. Assn., Anchorage, 1985—; vol. clinic staff Muscular Dystrophy Assn., Anchorage, 1976-90; troop leader, organizer, adult trainer Susitna coun. Girl Scouts, Anchorage, 1987—. Recipient Maddak award for phys. disabilities, Maddak, Inc., 1981. Mem. Am. Occupational Therapy Assn., Alaska Occupational Therapy Assn. (pres. 1980-82, v.p. 1978-80, various coms. 1982—), Nat. Head Injury Found., MADD. Home: 15001 Curvell Dr Anchorage AK 99516

STRINGER, WILLIAM JEREMY, university official; b. Oakland, Calif., Nov. 8, 1944; s. William Duane and Mildred May (Andrus) S.; BA in English, So. Meth. U., 1966; MA in English, U. Wis., 1968, PhD in Ednl. Adminstrn., 1973; m. Susan Lee Hildebrand; children: Shannon Lee, Kelly Erin, Courtney Elizabeth. Dir. men's housing Southwestern U., Georgetown, Tex., 1968-69; asst. dir. housing U. Wis., Madison, 1969-73; dir. residential life, asso. dean student life, adj. prof. Pacific Luth., Tacoma, 1973-78; dir. residential life U. So. Calif., 1978-79, asst. v.p., 1979-84, asst. prof. higher and post-secondary edn., 1980-84; v.p. student life Seattle U., 1984-89, v.p. student devel., assoc. provost, 1989, assoc. prof. edn., 1990—. Author: How to Survive as a Single Student, 1972, The Role of the Assistant in Higher Education, 1973. Bd. dirs. N.W. area Luth. Social Services of Wash. and Idaho, pres.-elect, 1989, pres., 1990—. Danforth Found. grantee, 1976-77. Mem. Am. Assn. Higher Edn., Nat. Assn. Student Pers. Adminstrs. (bd. dirs. region V), Phi Eta Sigma, Sigma Tau Delta, Phi Alpha Theta. Lutheran. Home: 4553 169th Ave SE Issaquah WA 98027-7813 Office: Seattle U Seattle WA 98122

STRITTMATTER, PETER ALBERT, astronomer, educator; b. London, Eng., Sept. 12, 1939; came to U.S., 1970.; s. Albert and Rosa S.; m. Janet Hubbard Parkhurst, Mar. 18, 1967; children—Catherine D., Robert P. B.A., Cambridge U., Eng., 1961, M.A., 1963, Ph.D., 1967. Staff scientist Inst. for Astronomy, Cambridge, Eng., 1967-70; staff scientist dept. physics U. Calif.-San Diego, La Jolla, Calif., 1970-71; assoc. prof. dept. astronomy U. Ariz., Tucson, 1971-74, prof. dept. astronomy, 1974—; dir. Steward Observatory, Tucson, 1975—; mem. staff Max Planck Inst. Radio-astronomy, Bonn, W. Germany, 1981—. Contbr. articles to profl. jours. Recipient Sr. award Humboldt Found., 1979-80. Fellow Royal Astron. Soc.; mem. Am. Astron. Soc., Astronomische Gesellschaft. Office: U Ariz Steward Observatory Tucson AZ 85721

STROBEL, DAVID ALLEN, psychology educator; b. Madison, Wis., Jan. 17, 1942; s. Carl Herbert and Anita (Wells) S.; m. Harriet Hartshorne, June 12, 1964 (div.); 1 child, Laura Wells; m. Linda Zimmermann, Mar. 31, 1982. B.A., Lake Forest Coll., 1964; M.A., U. Wis., 1971; Ph.D., U. Mont., 1972. Asst. prof. Northwestern U., Evanston, Ill., 1972-73; asst. prof., assoc. prof. then prof. psychology, U. Mont., Missoula, 1973—, chmn. dept., 1981, 83-90, assoc. dean Grad. Sch., 1990—; dir. Ft. Missoula Primate Lab., 1973-92. Contbr. chpts. to books. Cons. Missoula Drug Treatment Program, 1978, Missoula Spl. Edn. Coop., 1983. Grantee NIH, 1973-77, Dept. Agr./Agrl. Research Service, 1977-84. Mem. Mont. Psychol. Assn., Rocky Mountain Psychol. Assn., Western Psychol. Assn., Am. Assn. Primatologists, Internat. Soc. Primatologists, Missoula Humane Soc., Mont. Wilderness Assn., N. Rocky Mountain Assn. Lab. Animal Sci., Psychologists for Ethical Treatment Animals, Phi Beta Kappa, Sigma Xi. Home: 11284 Grant Creek Rd Missoula MT 59802-9345 Office: U of Montana Dept Psychology Missoula MT 59812

STROBER, SAMUEL, immunologist, educator; b. N.Y.C., May 8, 1940; s. Julius and Lee (Lander) S.; m. Linda Carol Higgins, July 6, 1991; children from previous marriage: Jason, Elizabeth. AB in Liberal Arts, Columbia U., 1961; MD magna cum laude, Harvard U., 1966. Intern Mass. Gen. Hosp., Boston, 1966-67; resident in internal medicine Stanford U. Hosp., Calif., 1970-71; research fellow Peter Bent Brigham Hosp., Boston, 1962-63, 65-66, Oxford U., Eng., 1963-64; research assoc. Lab. Cell Biology, Nat. Cancer Inst., NIH, Bethesda, Md., 1967-70; instr. medicine Stanford U., 1971-72, asst. prof., 1972-78, assoc. prof. medicine, 1978-82, prof. medicine, 1982—, Diane Goldstone Meml. lectr., John Putnam Merrill Meml. lectr., chief div. immunology and rheumatology, 1978—; investigator Howard Hughes Med. Inst., Miami, Fla., 1976-81. Assoc. editor Jour. Immunology, 1981-84, Transplantation, 1981-85, Internat. Jour. Immunotherapy, 1985—, Transplant Immunology, 1992—; contbr. articles to profl. jours. Bd. dirs. La Jolla Inst. for Allergy and Immunology, Activated Cell Therapy, Inc. Served with USPHS, 1967-70. Recipient Leon Reznick Meml. Research prize Harvard U., 1966, Career Devel. award Nat. Insts. Allergy and Infectious Diseases, 1971-76. Mem. Am. Assn. Immunology, Am. Soc. Clin. Investigation, Am. Rheumatism Assn., Transplantation Soc. (councilor 1986-89), Am. Soc. Transplantation Physicians, Western Soc. Medicine, Am. Assn. Physicians, Clin. Immunology Soc. (councilor), Alpha Omega. Home: 435 Golden Oak Dr Menlo Park CA 94028-7734 Office: Stanford U Sch Medicine 300 Pasteur Dr Palo Alto CA 94305

STROCK, DAVID RANDOLPH, brokerage house executive; b. Salt Lake City, Jan. 31, 1944; s. Clarence Randolph and Francis (Hornibrook) S.; m. Phyllis A. Tingley, Dec. 13, 1945 (div. June 15, 1982); children: Sarah, Heidi. AA, San Mateo Coll., 1967; BS, San Jose State U., 1970. Investment exec. Paine Webber, San Jose, Calif., 1970-78; corp. trainer Paine Webber, N.Y.C., 1978-79, rsch. coord., 1979-82; br. mgr. Paine Webber, Northbrook, Ill., 1982-84, Palos Verdes, Calif., 1984-89, Napa, Calif., 1989-90; investment exec. Paine Webber, Napa, 1990—. Contbr. articles to profl. jours. Mem. San Jose Jr. C. of C. (chmn. 1977, v.p. 1978), North Napa Rotary, Moose. Republican. Home: 3324 Homestead Ct Napa CA 94558 Office: Paine Webber 703 Trancas St Napa CA 94558

STROHMEYER, JOHN, former editor, writer; b. Cascade, Wis., June 26, 1924; s. Louis A. and Anna Rose (Saladunas) S.; m. Nancy Jordan, Aug. 20, 1949; children: Mark, John, Sarah. Student, Moravian Coll., 1941-43; A.B., Muhlenberg Coll., 1947; M.A. in Journalism, Columbia, 1948; L.H.D. (hon.), Lehigh U., 1983. With Nazareth Item, 1940-41; night reporter Bethlehem (Pa.) Globe-Times, 1941-43, 45-47; investigative reporter Providence Jour.-Bull., 1949-56; editor Bethlehem Globe-Times, 1956-84, v.p., 1961-84, dir., 1963-84; African-Am. journalism tchr. in Nairobi, Freetown, 1964; Atwood prof. journalism U. Alaska Anchorage, 1987-88, writer-in-residence, 1989—. Author: Crisis in Bethlehem: Big Steel's Struggle to Survive, 1986, Extreme Conditions: big Oil and The Transformation of Alaska, 1993. Lt. (j.g.) USNR, 1943-45. Pulitzer Traveling fellow, 1948; Nieman fellow, 1952-53; recipient Comenius award Moravian Coll., 1971; Pulitzer prize for editorial writing, 1972; Alicia Patterson Found. fellow, 1984, 85. Mem. Am. Soc. Newspaper Editors, Pa. Soc. Newspaper Editors (pres. 1965-66). Club: Hiawatha Hunting and Fishing (E. Stroudsburg, Pa.). Home: 6633 Lunar Dr Anchorage AK 99504-4550

STROLLE, JON MARTIN, academic dean, language studies educator; b. Gaylord, Mich., Apr. 21, 1940; s. Edward Gustave and Nellie Dorothy (Yuill) S.; children: Carl, Thomas. BA, Oberlin Coll., 1962; MA, U. Wis., 1964, PhD, 1968. Asst. prof. Spanish Ind. U., Bloomington, 1967-74, SUNY Brockport, 1974-76; dean of the Spanish Sch. Middlebury (Vt.) Coll., 1976-80; edn. policy fellow U.S. Dept. Edn., Washington, 1980-81; dean of the coll. Jr. Coll. of Albany, N.Y., 1981-85; dean of lang. studies Monterey (Calif.) Inst. Internat. Studies, 1985—; cons. NEH, Washington, 1980-85; bd. dirs. Coun. on Internat. Edn. Exch., N.Y.C., 1990—. Contbr. articles to profl. jours. Pres. bd. Monterey Bay Pub. Broadcasting, Monterey, 1989-92. Woodrow Wilson fellow U. Wis., Madison, 1962. Mem. Rotary, Phi Beta Kappa. Office: Monterey Inst Internat Studies 425 Van Buren St Monterey CA 93940-2623

STROM, ARTHUR VAN WATERS, design and manufacturing company executive; b. Seattle, Sept. 25, 1946; s. Arthur Albin and Barbara Jean (Van Waters) S.; m. Nancy Jane Stocker, Aug. 10, 1985. Cert., Nat. Fabric Care Inst. Pres. Liberty Group Inc., Bellevue, Wash., 1972-80, Liberty Devel. Corp., Carnation, Wash., 1981-87, Am. Design and Mfg. Inc., Seattle, 1987—; pres. bd. dirs. Liberty Group, Carnation. Co-founder arbitration system Better Bus. Bur., Seattle, 1973, mem. arbitration bd., 1988-91; vol. Fall City (Wash. Fire Dept., 1980-90, capt., tng. officer, 1988-90; mem. Grass Roots Gubernatorial Campaign, Seattle, 1992; pres. Profl. Cleaners Assn., Bellevue, 1975-78. Mem. Exec. Club, Washington Athletic Club, Columbia Tower Club, Rainier Club. Home: 1202 W Snoqualmie River Rd NE Carnation WA 98014 Office: Am Design and Mfg 1407 S Dearborn Seattle WA 98144

STROM, MARK ALAN, manufacturing executive; b. Kalamazoo, Mich., Feb. 9, 1962; s. John Rutledge and Marjorie Josephine (Griffin) S.; m. Andrea Logan Thompson, Aug. 2, 1986. BS summa cum laude, Biola U., 1984; MBA, Stanford U., 1990. Material coord. McDonnell Douglas Corp., Long Beach, Calif., 1984-86, sect. mgr., 1986-87, br. mgr., 1987-88, prin. staff specialist, 1990; assoc. Pittiglio, Rabin, Todd & McGrath, Mountain View, Calif., 1990-91, mgr., 1992-93, prin., 1993—. Arjay Miller scholar Stanford U., 1990. Mem. Am. Prodn. & Inventory Soc. Republican. Evangelical Free Christian. Home: Apt A 219 Backs Ln Placentia CA 92670

STROMBOM, MARI DIANE, college administrator; b. Ogema, Wis., Feb. 21, 1964; d. Frederick Arthur and Inez May (Trebil) S. BS, U. Wis., Stevens Point, 1987; MEd, Colo. State U., 1989. Asst. hall dir. U. Wis., Stevens Point, 1984-85, spl. events coord., 1986-87; program coord. Colo. State U., Ft. Collins, 1987-89, program advisor, 1990-93, asst. dir. student devel. for staff tng. leadership devel., 1993—; asst. dir. activities Bucknell U., Lewisburg, Pa., 1989-90; cons. Multicultural Edn. Team, Ft. Collins, 1990—; advisor Nat. Assn. Coll. and Univ. Residence Halls, Nat. Conf. Program, Greeley, Colo., 1988-89; instr. Colo. State U., Ft. Collins, 1988-89, 90—. Trainer ARC, Ft. Collins, instr. HIV/AIDS 1990—, instr.-trainer HIV/AIDS, 1992— ; activity dir. Big Bros./Big Sisters, Phillips, Wis., 1985. Mem. Assn. Coll. Unions Internat., Am. Coll. Pers. Assn., Nat. Assn. Campus Activities (regional conf. com. 1992-93, regional steering com. 1993—). Office: Colo State U Palmer Ctr Fort Collins CO 80523

STROMER, PETER ROBERT, lawyer; b. Norwich, Conn., July 16, 1929; s. Benjamin and Sadie (Rabin) S.; m. Martha Best, Feb. 28, 1959 (div. 1981); children: Philip, Daniel. BA, Syracuse U., 1952; JD, Lincoln U., 1968. Bar: Calif. 1969. Pvt. practice Los Gatos, Calif., 1969—. With U.S. Army, 1946-47, Japan. Unitarian. Office: 15951 Los Gatos Blvd # 11A Los Gatos CA 95032-3488

STROMME, GARY L., law librarian; b. Willmar, Minn., July 8, 1939; s. William A. and Edla A. (Soderberg) S.; m. Suzanne Readman, July 21, 1990. B.A., Pacific Lutheran U., 1965; B.L.S., U. B.C. (Can.), Vancouver, 1967; J.D., Hastings Coll. of Law; 1973. Bar: Calif. 1973, U.S. Sup. Ct. 1977. Serials librarian U. Minn. St. Paul Campus Library, 1967-69; asst. librarian McCutchen, Doyle, Brown and Enersen, San Francisco, 1970-71, Graham & James, San Francisco, 1971-73; ind. contracting atty., 1973-74; law librarian Pacific Gas and Electric Co., San Francisco, 1974—; lectr. in field. Served with USAF, 1959-63. Mem. Am. Assn. Law Libraries (chmn. com. on indexing of legal periodicals, 1986-88)., Western Pacific Assn. Law Libraries, No. Calif. Assn. Law Libraries, Pvt. Law Libraries, Corp. Law Libraries, ABA (chmn. library com. of sect. econs. of law practice 1978-82). Author: An Introduction to the use of the Law Library, 1974, 76; Basic Legal Research Techniques, 1979. Home: 6106 Ocean View Dr Oakland CA 94618-1841 Office: PO Box 7442 San Francisco CA 94120-7442

STRONG, DEBRA KAY, sales executive; b. Chambersburg, Pa., Feb. 18, 1954; d. Samuel Wilson and Delores Jean (Varner) Holch; m. Wayne C. Strong, Oct. 28, 1978 (div. Sept. 1991); 1 child, Jennifer Austine Roe. Sales mgr. Sears, Iowa City, 1974-86; data entry clk. U. Iowa Dental Coll., Iowa City, 1986-88; sales mgr. This End Up Furniture Co., Torrance, Calif., 1988—. Home: 1200 Esplanade #318 Redondo Beach CA 90277 Office: This End Up Furniture Co 310 D Del Amo Fashion Ctr Torrance CA 90503

STRONG, GARY EUGENE, librarian; b. Moscow, Idaho, June 26, 1944; s. Authur Dwight and Cleora Anna (Nirk) S.; m. Carolyn Jean Roetker, Mar. 14, 1970; children: Christopher Eric, Jennifer Rebecca. BS in Edn., U. Idaho, 1966; AMLS, U. Mich., 1967. Adminstrv. and reference asst. U. Idaho, 1963-66; extension librarian Latah County Free Library, Moscow, 1966; head librarian Markeley Residence Library, U. Mich., 1966-67; library dir. Lake Oswego (Oreg.) Public Library, 1967-73, Everett (Wash.) Public Library, 1973-76; asso. dir. services Wash. State Library, Olympia, 1976-79; dep. state librarian Wash. State Library, 1979-80; state librarian Calif. State Library, Sacramento, 1980—; chief exec. Calif. Library Services Bd., 1980—; founder, bd. dirs. Calif. State Library Found., 1982—, Calif. Literary Campaign, 1984—, Calif. Rsch. Bureau, 1992; bd. dirs. No. Regional Library Bd., 1983—; mem. adv. bd. Ctr. for Book in Libr. of Congress, 1983-86; mem. nat. adv. com. Libr. of Congress, 1987-89; chmn. adv. bd. Calif. Libr. Constrn. and Rennovation Bond Act Bd., 1989—; vis. lectr. Marylhurst Coll., Oreg., 1968, Oreg. Div. Continuing Edn., 1972, San Jose State U. Sch. Libr. Svc., 1990; lectr. and cons. in field. Host, producer: cable TV Signatures Program, 1974-76, nationwide videoconfs. on illiteracy, censorship, 1985; author: On Reading-in the Year of the Reader, 1987; editor Calif. State Library Found. Bull., 1982— (H.W. Wilson Periodical award 1988), Western Americana in the Calif. State Library, 1986, On Reading-In the Year of the Reader, 1987, Chinatown Photographer: Louis J. Stellman, 1989, Local History Genealogical Resources, 1990, Literate America Emerging, 1991; contbr. articles to profl. jours.; editor, designer and pub. of various books. Bd. dirs., v.p. Pacific N.W. Bibliog. Ctr., 1977-80; bd. dirs. Thurston Mason County Mental Health Ctr., 1977-80, pres., 1979-80; bd. dirs. Coop. Library Agy. for Systems and Services, 1980—, vice chmn., 1981-84; bd. dirs. Sr. Services Snohomish County, 1973-76, HISPANEX (Calif. Spanish lang. database), 1983-86; bd. govs. Snohomish County Hist. Assn., 1974-76; mem. Oreg. Coun. Pub. Broadcasting, 1969-73; mem. psychiat. task force St. Peters Hosp., Olympia, 1979-80; co-founder Calif. Ctr. for the Book, bd. dirs., 1987—; mem. adv. bd. Calif. State PTA, 1981-86; mem. adv. com. Sch. Libr. Sci., UCLA, 1991—, Sch. Libr. and Info. Studies, U. Calif., Berkeley, 1991—; mem. Calif. Adult Edn. Steering Com., 1988—; chmn. collaborative coun. Calif. State Literacy Resource Ctr., 1993—. Recipient Disting. Alumnus award U. Mich., 1984, Disting. Service award Calif. Literacy Inc., 1985, Spl. Achievement award Literacy Action, 1988, Assn. Specialized and Cooperative Library Agencies Exceptional Achievement award, 1992; Oreg. Library scholar, 1966. Mem. ALA (legis. com. 1980-82, Commn. on Freedom and Equality of Access to Info. 1983-86), Libr. Adminstrn. and Mgmt. Assn. (dir. 1980-88, pres. 1984-85), Oreg. Libr. Assn. (hon. life mem., pres. 1970-71), Pacific N.W. Libr. Assn. (hon. life mem., pres. 1978-79), Calif. Libr. Assn. (govt. rels. com. 1980—), Chief Officers of State Libr. Agys. (pres. 1984-86), Western Coun. State Librs. (pres. 1989-91, Assn. Specialized and Coop. Libr. Agys., Everett Area C. of C. (bd. dirs. 1974-76). Clubs: Book of Calif., Sacramento Book Collectors, Roxburghe, The Book Collectors (L.A.). Office: Calif State Libr PO Box 942837 Sacramento CA 94237-0001

STRONG, JOHN OLIVER, plastic surgeon, educator; b. Montclair, N.J., Feb. 1, 1930; s. George Joseph and Olivia (LeBrun) S.; m. Helen Louise Vrooman, July 19, 1958 (dec. Mar. 1973); m. Deborah Sperberg, May 20, 1978; children: John Jr., Jean LeB., Andrew D. BS, Yale U., 1952; MD, U. Pa., 1957. Practice medicine specializing in plastic and reconstructive surgery Santa Ana, Calif., 1964—; asst. clin. prof. plastic and reconstructive surgery U. Calif., Irvine, 1970—. Fellow ACS; mem. Calif. Med. Assn. (chmn. sci. adv. panel 1983-89), Calif. Soc. Plastic Surgeons (pres. 1991-92). Republican. Office: 2200 E Fruit St Ste 103 Santa Ana CA 92701-4479

STRONG, MAYDA NEL, psychologist, educator; b. Albuquerque, May 6, 1942; d. Floyd Samuel and Wanda Christmas (Martin) Strong; 1 child, Robert Allen Willingham. BA in Speech-Theatre cum laude, Tex. Western Coll., 1963; EdM, U. Tex., Austin, 1972, PhD in Counseling Psychology, 1978; lic. clin. psychologist, Colo., 1984; cert. alcohol counselor III, Colo., 1987, nat. addiction counselor II, 1991. Asst. instr. in ednl. psychology U. Tex., Austin, 1974-78; instr. psychology Austin Community Coll., 1974-78, Otero Jr. Coll., La Junta, Colo., 1979—; dir. outpatient and emergency svcs. S.E. Colo. Family Guidance and Mental Health Ctr., Inc., La Junta, 1978-81; pvt. practice psychol. therapy, La Junta, 1981—; exec. dir. Pathfinders Chem. Dependency program, 1985—; clin. psychologist Inst. for Forensic Psychiatry, Colo. Mental Health Inst., Pueblo, 1989—; adj. faculty Adams State Coll., 1992. Del. to County Dem. Conv., 1988. Co-star The Good Doctor, 1980, On Golden Pond, 1981, Plaza Suite, 1987, Otero Jr. Coll. Players, 1987, Chase Me Comrade, 1989. AAUW fellow, 1974-76. Mem. Bus. and Profl. People (legis. chairperson 1982-83, chmn. news election svc. 1982-88), Colo. Psychol. Assn. (legis. chmn. for dist.), Am. Contract Bridge League. Contbr. articles in field to profl. publs. Author poems in Chinook: Paths through the Puzzle, Decisions, Passion. Home: 500 Holly Ave PO Box 177 Swink CO 81077 Office: 2071 2 Colorado Ave La Junta CO 81050-1517

STRONG, PAMELA KAY, material and process engineer, chemical engineer; b. Mesa, Ariz., Oct. 17, 1950; d. Wayland Thorton and Adele (Gaumer) S. BS in Organic Chemistry, Phila. Coll. Pharmacy and Sci., 1972; MS in Organic Chemistry, Bryn Mawr Coll., 1974. Cons. formulation, rsch. chemist Western Indsl. Enterprises, Phoenix, 1974-75; analytical chemist Henkel Corp., Hawthorne, Calif., 1975-80; mem. tech. staff, process engr. Radar div. Hughes Aircraft, El Segundo, Calif., 1980-83; sr. process engr. Irvine Sensors Corp., Costa Mesa, Calif., 1983; sr. advanced composite and composite quality engr. Aircraft Engine Bus. Group, GE, Albuquerque, 1983-85; mantech engring. specialist sr., sr. quality assurance engr. Advanced Systems div. Northrop Corp., Pico Rivera, Calif., 1985-87; material and process engring. tech. specialist, lead engr. McDonnell Douglas Missile and Space Systems Co., Huntington Beach, Calif., 1987—. Recipient GE Mfg. Tech. Excellence award, 1984; Bryn Mawr Coll. scholar; NSF rsch. fellow, 1971. Mem. Am. Chem. Soc. (Petroleum Rsch. fellow 1971, Scholastic award 1972), Am. Inst. Chemists, AAAS, Soc. Applied Spectroscopy (chairperson 1977-79, sec. 1979-81), Soc. Women Chemists, Soc. Women Engrs., Soc. Advancement Materials and Process Engrs. (treas. 1984-85), NAFE, Iota Sigma Pi. Home: 4912 Hilo Cir Huntington Beach CA 92649-2306 Office: McDonnell Douglas Space 207/T-50 5301 Bolsa Ave # A-3 Huntington Beach CA 92647

STRONG, THOMAS FREMONT, agricultural products supplier; b. Pasadena, Calif., Mar. 30, 1946; s. Thomas Foster and Oakalla (Bellis) S.; m. Marilyn Myers, Aug. 1, 1988 (div. 1992); 1 child, Kassandra Constance. BA, Calif. State U., L.A., 1974, MA, 1975. Design engr. SWECO, Inc., L.A., 1968-72; mktg. mgr. James Hardie Irrigation, El Cajon, Calif., 1972-75; owner, mgr. TFS Injector Systems, Monrovia, Calif., 1975—. Recipient Outstanding Product Design award Am. Soc. Agrl. Engrs., 1985, 87, 89, Contbn. award San Diego Xeriscape Conf. Mem. Irrigation Assn., Calif. Assn. Nurserymen. Republican. Office: TFS Injector Systems 211 W Maple Ave Monrovia CA 91016

STRONGIN, DANIEL OTTO, food service executive; b. Huntington, N.Y., Apr. 8, 1951; s. Theodore Monroe; m. Rovena de Araujo Mahfuz, Oct. 30, 1992; children: Thiago, Daniel. Student, Bard Coll., 1970-71. Cert. applied food svc. sanitation. First cook, apprentice chef Ferdinands Restaurant, Cambridge, Mass., 1972-75; sous-chef Lily's Restaurant, Boston, 1976, The Sonesta Hotel, Cambridge, 1976-78; chef garde-mgr., night chef, Cafe de Partie The Ritz Carlton Hotel, Boston, 1975, 76; exec. sous chef Ritz Carlton Corp., Boston, 1978-81; working chef Augusta's Restaurant, Berkeley, Calif., 1981-83, La Petit Cafe, San Francisco, 1983-84; exec. chef The Claremont Resort Hotel and Spa, Oakland, Calif., 1984-85, The Lakeview Club, Oakland, 1985-86; corp. chef, dir. deli ops. Vasilio's Kitchen at Andronico's Markets, Berkeley, 1986—; cons. on technique Ortho Books, Cooking A to Z; cons., writer, performer videos Fabricating Venison, Preparing Venison for food svc. ednl. programs nationwide New Zealand Venison Coun.; owner, chief instr. The Cooking Workshop, Cambridge, 1973-81. Recipient Silver medal The San Francisco Chefs de Cuisine Culinary Salon, 1986. Mem. Am. Culinary Fedn. (founding pres., chmn. bd. Greater East Bay chpt. 1987, Chef of Yr. 1988), San Francisco Profl. Food Soc., Am. Cheese Soc. (bd. mem. 1992—), Am. Inst. Wine and Food, Inst. on Studies in Ontological Nuclei. Democrat. Office: Andronico's Park and Shop 1109 Washington Ave Albany CA 94530

STROOCK, THOMAS FRANK, diplomat; b. N.Y.C., Oct. 10, 1925; s. Samuel and Dorothy (Frank) S.; B.A. in Econs., Yale U., 1948; m. Marta Freyre de Andrade, June 19, 1949; children—Margaret, Sandra, Elizabeth, Anne. Landman Stanolind Oil & Gas Co., Tulsa, 1948-52; pres. Stroock Leasing Corp., Casper, Wyo., 1952-89, Alpha Exploration, Inc., 1980-89; ptnr. Stroock, Rogers & Dymond, Casper, 1960-82; dir. Wyo. Bancorp., Cheyenne, First Wyo. Bank, Casper; mem. Wyo. Senate, 1967-69, 71-75, 79-89, chmn. appropriations com. 1983, co-chmn. joint appropriations com., 1983-89, mem. mgmt. and audit com. P; mem. steering com. Edn. Commn. of States; ambassador to Guatemala, 1989-92; pres. Alpha Devel. Corp., 1992—. Rep. precinct committeeman, 1950-68; pres. Natrona County Sch. Bd., 1960-69; pres. Wyo. State Sch. Bds. Assn., 1965-66; chmn. Casper Community Recreation, 1955-60; chmn. Natrona County United Fund, 1963-64; chmn. Wyo. State Republican Com., 1975-78, exec. com. 1954-60; delegate Rep. Nat. Convetion, 1956, 76; regional coord. campaign George Bush for pres., 1979-80, 87-88; chmn. Western States Rep. Chmn. Assn., 1977-78; chmn. Wyo. Higher Edn. Commn., 1969-71; mem. Nat. Petroleum Council, 1972-77; chmn. trustees Sierra Madre Found. for Geol. Research, New Haven; chmn. Wyo. Nat. Gas Pipeline Authority 1987-88; bd. dirs. Ucross Found., Denver; mem. Nat. Pub. Lands Adv. Council, 1981-85. Served with USMC, 1943-46. Mem. Rocky Mountain Oil and Gas Assn., Petroleum Assn. Wyo. Republican. Unitarian. Lodge: Kiwanis. Clubs: Casper Country; Casper Petroleum; Denver. Home and Office: PO Box 2875 Casper WY 82602

STROTHER, LYNN BREHM, professional association executive; b. Hazleton, Pa., Oct. 30, 1951; d. George W. III and Gloria (Staber) Brehm; 1 child, Sarah Elizabeth. BA cum laude, U. Pa., 1972. Editorial asst. Biosys, Inc., Phila., 1971-73; broadcast prodn. asst. APCL & K Advt., Phila., 1973-74; grant adminstr. dept. psychology U. Pa., Phila., 1974-75; asst. coordinating editor Brentwood Pub. Corp., L.A., 1975-77; freelance writer and editor, L.A., 1977-81; mgr. publs. Human Factors and Ergonomics Soc., Santa Monica, Calif., 1981-86, exec. adminstr., 1990—; sr. mgr. publs. UCLA Med. Ctr., 1987; mng. editor Med. Device & Diagnostic Industry, Santa Monica,, 1988-89. Editor: Graduate Programs in Human Factors, 1982; contbr. articles to profl. jours. Paraprofl. counselor Nat. Coun. Jewish Women, L.A., 1985-87; sec., treas. St. Paul's Luth. Ch., Santa Monica, 1991-92. Mem. Am. Soc. Assn. Execs., Coun. Engring. and Sci. Soc. Execs., Metro L.A. Assn. Execs., NOW. Office: Human Factors Ergonomics Sc PO Box 1369 Santa Monica CA 90406

STROUD, ROBERT LEE, JR., retail store manager; b. Monticello, Iowa, Feb. 11, 1962; s. Robert Lee Stroud Sr. and Dorothy Mae (McGuirk) Ehlts; m. Tamara Kay Deibert, Oct. 9, 1992. Student, Blair Coll., 1987-88, Pikes Peak C.C., 1988-89, Nazarene Bible Coll., 1990, Nat. Coll., 1991—. Cert. notary pub., Colo. Asst. store mgr. Cavey's Hardware, Olin, Iowa, 1983-85; store clk. Ace Hardware, Colorado Springs, Co., 1985-86; apt. maintenance person Hitch-n-Post Apts., Fountain, Colo., 1986; store clk. Southland Corp., Colorado Springs, 1986-87, Phillip's 66, Colorado Springs, 1987-88; cashier Walgreen's, Colorado Springs, 1990-92; store mgr. Gen. Nutrition Inc., Colorado Springs, 1988—; tax preparer, fin. cons. Lee's Tax Acctg. Svc., Colorado Springs, 1988—. With USAF, 1980-82. Republican. Home: 4725 Scenic Circle Colorado Springs CO 80917 Office: Gen Nutrition Inc 1710 Briargate Blvd #195 Colorado Springs CO 80920

STROUP, ELIZABETH FAYE, librarian; b. Tulsa, Mar. 25, 1939; d. Milton Earl and Lois (Buhl) S. BA in Philosophy, U. Wash., 1962, MLS, 1964. Intern Libr. of Congress, Washington, 1964-65; asst. dir. North Cen. Regional Libr., Wenatchee, Wash., 1966-69; reference specialist Congl. Reference div. Libr. of Congress, Washington, 1970-71, head nat. collections Div. for the Blind and Physically Handicapped, 1971-73, chief Congl. Reference div., 1973-78, dir. gen. reference, 1978-88; city libr., chief exec. officer Seattle Pub. Libr., 1988—; cons. U.S. Info. Svc., Indonesia, Feb. 1987. Mem. adv. bd. KCTS 9 Pub. TV, Seattle, 1988—; bd. visitors Sch. Librarianship, U. Wash., 1988—; bd. dirs. Wash. Literacy, 1988—. Mem. ALA (pres. reference and adult svcs. div. 1986-87, div. bd. 1985-88), Wash. Libr. Assn., D.C. Libr. Assn. (bd. dirs. 1975-76), City Club, Ranier Club. Office: Seattle Pub Libr 1000 4th Ave Seattle WA 98104-1193

STROUP, RICHARD LYNDELL, economics educator, writer; b. Sunnyside, Wash., Jan. 3, 1943; s. Edgar Ivan and Inez Louise (Kellet) S.; m. Sandra Lee Price, Sept. 13, 1962 (div. Sept. 1981); children—Michael, Craig; m. Jane Bartlett Steidemann Shaw, Jan. 1, 1985; 1 child, David. Student, MIT, 1961-62; B.A., M.A., U. Wash., 1966, Ph.D. in Econs., 1970. Asst. prof. econs. Mont. State U., Bozeman, 1969-74; assoc. prof. econs. Mont. State U., 1974-78, prof. econs., 1978—; dir. Office Policy Analysis, Dept. Interior, Washington, 1982-84; vis. assoc. prof. Fla. State U., Tallahassee, 1977-78; sr. assoc. Polit. Economy Research Ctr., Bozeman, 1980—/lectr. summer univ., U. Aix (France), 1985—. Co-author: Natural Resources, 1983, Economics: Private and Public Choice, 6th edit., 1992, Basic Economics, 1993, What Everyone Should Know About Economics and Prosperity, 1993; also articles, 1972—. Mem. Am. Econs. Assn., Western Econs. Assn. (exec. com. mem. 1985-88), Mont Pelerin Soc., Phila. Soc., Pub. Choice Soc., Agrl. Econs. Assn. , So. Econs. Assn. Episcopalian. Home: 9 W Arnold St Bozeman MT 59715-6127 Office: Polit Economy Rsch Ctr 502 S 19th Ave Bozeman MT 59715-6827

STRUDWICK, LINDSEY HOWARD, consultant company executive; b. Durham, N.C., Aug. 8, 1946; s. London Lincoln and Mable Christine (Alston) S.; children: Lindsey Howard Jr., Casandra, James Christopher. AAS in Bus. Adminstrn., Durham (N.C.) Bus. Coll., 1975; BA in Econs., Shaw U., Raleigh, N.C., 1976; MBA in Bus. Adminstrn., Southeastern U., Greenville, S.C., 1977. Cert. purchasing mgr. Mgr. purchasing and facilities Northrop Corp., Research Triangle Park, N.C., 1976-78; personnel asst. Gen. Telephone Co., Durham, 1978-79; group leader purchasing No. Telecom, Inc., Research Triangle Park, 1979-81; mgr. purchasing and contracts Sci. Atlanta, 1982-86; dir. purchasing and materials mgmt. Coors Brewing Co., Golden, Colo., 1986-88, dir. project materials/contracts, 1988-89, bus. unit dir. purchasing/materials mgmt., 1989-90; v.p. purchasing and contracts SDS Petroleum Products, Inc., Denver, 1990-92; pres. LNC Group Ltd., Denver, 1992—; vis. prof. Nat. Urban League, Inc., Black Exec. Exchange Program, 1983—; instr. Jr. Achievement Met. Denver, Inc., 1986-87. Bd. dirs. Denver City Ptnrs., 1986-87; active Operation Push, INc., 1985—, Colo. PTA, 1986—. Capt. U.S. Army, 1966-70, Vietnam. Named Hon. Citizen, State of Tenn., 1986, Corp. Supplier of Yr., Rocky Mountain Purchasing Coun., 1986, 1986, Interracial Coun. Bus. Opportunity, 1986, U.S. SBA, 1987, Corp. of Yr., U.S. Dept. Commerce, 1988, Advocate of Yr., Rocky Mountain Regional Purchasing Coun., 1988, Disting. Alumnus Shaw U., 1990; recipient Corp. Citizenship award United Indian Devel. Assn., 1988, Disting. Alumni Citation, Nat. Assn. Equal Opportunity in Higher Edn., 1990. Mem. NAACP (life and golden mem.), Nat. Minority Bus. Directories (bd. dirs. 1988-90), Nat. Assn. Purchasing Mgmt., Nat. Minority Supplier Devel. Coun. (bd. dirs.), Nat. Optometric Assn. (bd. dirs.), Rocky Mountain Minority Supplier Purchasing Coun. (past pres., bd. dirs.), Rocky Mountain Regional Minority Supplier Devel. Coun. (bd. dirs. 1986-89), Purchasing Mgmt. Assn. Denver, Masons, Shriners. Home: PO Box 18528 Denver CO 80218-0528 Office: LNC Group Ltd Ste 625 6825 E Tennessee Ave Bldg 1 Denver CO 80224-5012

STRUHL, STANLEY FREDERICK, real estate developer; b. Bklyn., Oct. 10, 1939; s. Isidore and Yvette (Miller) S.; BS with honors in Engring., UCLA, 1961, MBA in Data Processing, 1963; m. Patricia Joyce Wald, Feb. 26, 1966; children: Marc Howard, Lisa Lynn. Mem. tech. staff Hughes Aircraft Co., Fullerton, Calif., 1963-65; sr. asso. Planning Research Corp., Los Angeles, 1965-70; mgr. corporate info. systems Logicon, Inc., Torrance, Calif., 1970-73; mgr. operations analysis System Devel. Corp., Santa Monica, Calif., 1973-77; gen. partner TST Developers, Canyon Country, Calif., 1977-81; pres. Struhl Enterprises, Inc., Northridge, Calif., 1977-85; owner Struhl Properties, Northridge, 1979—. Mem. planning sub. com. 12th council dist., Los Angeles, 1986—. Lic. real estate broker, Calif. Mem. Assn. For Computing Machinery, San Fernando Valley Bd. Realtors, Tau Beta Pi, Beta Gamma Sigma, Alpha Phi Omega. Home: 17074 Knapp St Northridge CA 91325-2637

STRUIK, RUTH REBEKKA, mathematics educator; b. Worcester, Mass., Dec. 15, 1928; d. Dirk Jan and Ruth (Ramler) S.; div. 1969; children: Marion, Margo, Louise. BA, Swarthmore Coll., 1949; MA, U. Ill., 1951; PhD in Math., NYU, 1955. Lectr. math. Columbia U., N.Y.C., 1955; asst. prof. Drexel Inst. Tech., Phila., 1956-57; lectr. U. British Columbia, 1957-61; from asst. prof. to prof. math. U. Colo., Boulder, 1961—. Mem. Am. Math. Soc., Math. Assn. Am., Assn. Women Math., Sigma Xi. Office: Univ Colo Math Dept Box 395 Boulder CO 80309

STRUTHERS, RALPH CHARLES, inventor, energy company executive; b. Vona, Colo., Feb. 28, 1933; s. Alex H. and Maude M. (Williams) S.; m. Erma L. Barnett, July 20, 1951 (div. June 1966); children: Cheryl, Belinda, Carol, Kay, Ronda, Diana, April; m. Darlene L. Struthers, Sept. 11, 1968. Pres., dir. Electro Sonic Industries, Inc., San Fernando, Calif., 1960-62; data engr. Jet Propulsion Lab., Pasadena, Calif., 1962-68; systems analyst System Devel. Corp., Santa Monica, Calif., 1968-74; pres., dir. Universal Fuel Systems, Saugus, Calif., 1974-88, Clean Energy & Air Am., Saugus, 1988—; chmn. bd. dirs. Patentee in field. Home: 31347 Woodridge Dr Shingletown CA 96088-9791 Office: Clean Energy & Air For Am 39503 Calle El Fuente Santa Clarita CA 91350-1009

STRUTTON, LARRY D., newspaper executive; b. Colorado Springs, Colo., Sept. 12, 1940; s. Merril and Gladys (Sheldon) S.; m. Carolyn Ann Croak, Dec. 3, 1960; children—Gregory L., Kristen. A.A. in Electronics Engring., Emily Griffith Electronics Sch., 1968; B.S. in Bus. Mgmt. and Systems Mgmt., Met. State Coll., 1971; diploma in Advanced Mgmt. Program, Harvard U., 1988. Printer Gazette Telegraph, Colorado Springs, Colo., 1961-64; prodn. dir. Rocky Mountain News, Denver, 1964-80; exec. v.p. ops. and advt. Detroit Free Press, 1981-83; v.p. ops. Los Angeles Times, 1983-85, exec. v.p. ops., 1986—. Mem. adv. com. Rochester Inst. Tech., 1984—. Mem. Am. Newspaper Pubs. Assn. (chmn. 1987, chmn. TEC com. 1985-86), R&E Council (research and engring. council of the Graphic Arts Industry Inc.). Club: Lakeside Golf (Los Angeles). Home: 50 Glenmoor Cir Englewood CO 80110-7121 also: Rocky Mountain News 400 W. Colfax Ave Denver CO 80204

STRUTZEL, J(OD) C(HRISTOPHER), escrow company executive; b. L.A., Sept. 20, 1947; s. James Rudolph and Charlotte Elizabeth (Weiss) S.; m. Christine Melba Kemp, Dec. 28, 1969; children: Jason James, Jess Warren. BS in Bus. Mgmt., Calif. State U., Long Beach, 1970. Bellman Edgewater Hyatt House Hotel, Long Beach, 1970, night auditor, 1970-71; asst. mgr. Sands Resort Hotel, Palm Springs, Calif., 1971-72; gen. mgr. Sands Resort Hotel, Palm Springs, 1972-73; sales coordinator Bendix Home Systems, Santa Fe Springs, Calif., 1973-74; loan rep. J.E. Wells Fin. Co., L.A., 1974-75; v.p. Express Escrow Co., Huntington Beach, Calif., 1976-78; pres., chmn. bd., bd. dirs. Express Escrow Co., Westminster, Calif., 1978—; pres., chmn. bd., bd. dirs. Elsinore (Calif.) Escrow, Inc., 1977-79; bd. dirs. Sorrel Devel., Redondo Beach, Calif.; expert witness on escrow, litigation and cons., 1982—; chmn. liability reduction com. Fidelity Corp., 1983-84, legis. chmn., 1985-86, 87-90, vice-chmn. bd. 1989-90, treas. 1992—; bd. dirs., sec. Discovery Escrow Co., 1989—; drafted sections of Calif. Fin. Code, Health and Safety Code, Calif. Adminstrv. Code. Contbr. articles to trade publs. Campaign treas. Californians to Elect Ted Cook, 1982; bd. dirs. publicitiy chmn. Fountain Valley (Calif.) Youth Baseball, 1986-87; AD HOC com. on Escrow Regulations Dept. Housing and Community Devel., 1980; escrow adv. com. Dept. Corps., 1990. Recipient J.E. Wells Meml. award, 1988. Mem. Escrow Agts. Fidelity Corp. (bd. dirs. 1983-90), Escrow Inst. of Calif. (bd. dirs. 1991), Calif. Manufactured Housing Assn. (treas., bd. dirs. 1984-86), Calif. Manufactured Housing Inst. (bd. dirs. 1986—, treas. 1986-87, Polit. Action Com. Man of Yr. award 1988, Orange County chpt. Man of Yr. award 1988). Republican. Office: Express Escrow Co 14441 Beach Blvd Ste 100 Westminster CA 92683-5309

STRYGLER, BERNARDO, physician, researcher; b. Mexico, Jan. 31, 1959; came to U.S., 1988; s. Marcos and Lily (Zagursky) S.; m. Sandra Sommer. BS in Biol. Chemistry Sci., Israelite Coll. of Mex., 1979; MD, Nat. Autonomous U. Mex., 1985. Intern in internal medicine Am. Brit. Cowdray Hosp., Mexico, 1983-84, asst. resident in internal medicine, 1984-87; instr. in internal medicine Donald McKenzie Clinic, Mexico, 1986-88; fellow in internal medicine and gastroenterology Baylor U. Med. Ctr., Dallas, 1988-89; fellow in geriatric medicine U. Calif., Sacramento, 1989-92; prin. investigator memory disorders clinic for the Spanish speaking population U. Calif. at Davis Med. Ctr., Sacramento, 1989—. Mem. Nat. Hispanic Coun. on Aging, Washington, 1989, Alzheimer's Disease Internat., Chgo., 1989. Fellow InterAm. Coll. of Physicians and Surgeons; mem. ACPE, Am. Med. Dirs. Assn., Am. Geriatric Soc., N.Y. Acad. Scis., So. Med. Assn., Calif. Med. Assn., Gerontol. Soc. Am. Office: #650-503, Ave Ejercito Nacional, Districto Federale 11520, Mexico

STUART, BRIAN MICHAEL, employee benefits and insurance sales consultant; b. Marin, Calif., Nov. 23, 1961; s. Martin T. and Inez S. S. BA in Econs., Princeton U., 1984; cert. in internat. bus., U. Copenhagen, 1982. Sr. marketer Link-Allen and Assocs., Inc., Foster City, Calif., 1986-92; prin. Stuart Planning Group, San Mateo, Calif., 1992—. Author: Airline Regulation and Deregulation, 1984. Mem. Am. Soc. CLUs, Princeton Club No. Calif. (exec. bd. 1988—), San Francisco Estate Planning Coun., Estate Planning Coun. Peninsula, Ivy League Club San Francisco (v.p. 1986-88, pres. 1988-91, exec. bd. 1992—), Zeta Psi. Office: Stuart Planning Group Ste 304 1670 S Amphlett Blvd San Mateo CA 94402

STUART, DAVID EDWARD, anthropologist, columnist; b. Calhoun County, Ala., Jan. 9, 1945; s. Edward George and Avis Elsie (Densmore) S.; B.A. (Wesleyan Merit scholar 1965-66), W.V.A. Wesleyan Coll., 1967; M.A. in Anthropology, U. N.Mex., 1970, Ph.D., 1972, postdoctoral student, 1975-76; m. Cynthia K. Morgan, June 14, 1971. Research assoc. Andean Center, Quito, Ecuador, 1970; continuing edn. instr. anthropology U. N.Mex., 1971, research archeologist Office Contract Archeology, 1974, research coordinator, 1974-77, asst. prof. anthropology, 1975-77, assoc. prof. anthropology, 1984—, asst. v.p. acad. affairs, 1987—; asst. prof. Eckerd Coll., St. Petersburg, Fla., 1972-74; cons. archeologist right-of-way div. Pub. Service Co. N.Mex., Albuquerque, 1977-78; cons. anthropologist Bur. Indian Affairs, Albuquerque, 1978, Historic Preservation Bur. N.Mex., Santa Fe, 1978-81, Nat. Park Service, 1980, Albuquerque Mus., 1981; sr. research assoc. Human Systems Research, Inc., 1981-83, Quivira Research Center, Albuquerque, 1984-86; bd. dirs. Table Ind. Scholars, 1979-83, pres., bd. dirs. Rio Grande Heritage Found., Albuquerque and Las Cruces, 1985-87; advisor Human Systems Research, Inc., Tularosa, N.Mex., 1978-80, Albuquerque Commn. on Hist. Preservation, 1984-86. Grantee Eckerd Coll., 1973, Historic Preservation Bur., 1978-80. Essayist award N.Mex. Humanities Council, 1986. Mem. Am. Anthrop. Assn., Royal Anthrop. Inst. Gt. Britain, N.Mex. Archeol. Council, Albuquerque Archeol. Soc. (pres. 1986-88), Descs. Signers Declaration Independence, Sigma Xi, Phi Kappa Phi. Presbyterian. Co-author: Archeological Survey: 4 Corners to Ambrosia, N.Mex., 1976, A Proposed Project Design for the Timber Management Archeological Surveys, 1978, Ethnoarcheological Investigations of Shepherding in the Pueblo of Laguna, 1983; Author: Prehistoric New Mexico, 1981, 2d edit., 1984, 3d edit., 1988, Glimpses of the Ancient Southwest, 1985, The Magic of Bandelier National Monument, 1989, others; columnist New Mexico's Heritage, 1983-87, others. Editor: Archeological Reports, No. 1, 1975, No. 2, 1981. Address: U NMex Rm 262 Student Svcs Ctr Albuquerque NM 87131

STUART, DOROTHY MAE, artist; b. Fresno, Calif., Jan. 8, 1933; d. Robert Wesley Williams and Maria Theresa (Gad) Tressler; m. Reginald Ross Stuart, May 18, 1952; children: Doris Lynne Stuart Willis, Darlene Mae Stuart Cavalletto, Sue Anne Stuart Peters. Student, Calif. State U., Fresno, 1951-52, Fresno City Coll., 1962-64. Artist, art judge, presenter demonstrations at schs., fairs and art orgns. Calif., 1962—. Editor, art dir. Fresno High School Centennial 1889-1989, 1989; art advisor Portrait of Fresno, 1885-1985; contbg. artist Heritage Fresno, 1975; exhibited in group shows, including M.H. De Young Mus., San Francisco, 1971, Charles and Emma Frye Mus., Seattle, 1971, Calif. State U.-Fresno tour of China, 1974.

Mem. adv. com. Calif. State Ken Maddy Cen. Calif. Conf. on Women, 1989-93, Patrons for Cultural Arts, Fresno, 1987-92, bd. dirs. 1991-92. Recipient 53 art awards, 1966-84. Mem. Soc. Western Artists (bd. dirs. 1968-74, v.p. 1968-70), Fresno Womens Trade Club (bd. dirs. 1986-93, pres. 1988-90), Fresno Art Mus., Fresno Met. Mus., Native Daus. Golden West Fresno. Republican. Home and Office: 326 S Linda Ln Fresno CA 93727-5737

STUART, GARY LESTER, lawyer; b. Gallup, N.Mex., Oct. 8, 1939; s. Arthur Lester and DeAva (Cato) S.; m. Kathleen Ann Stuart, Aug. 31, 1962; children: Gregory Lester, Kara Stuart Lewis, Tosh Forrest. Student, St. Michael's Coll., Santa Fe, N.Mex., 1961-62; BS, U. Ariz., 1965, JD, 1967. Bar: Ariz. 1967, U.S. Dist. Ct. Ariz. 1967, U.S. Ct. Appeals (9th cir.) 1968, U.S. Supreme Ct. 1973, U.S. Tax Ct. 1976. Assoc. Jennings, Strouss & Salmon, Phoenix, 1967-71, ptnr., 1971—; chmn. ethics com. Ariz. Bar, Phoenix, 1976-86; mem. faculty Ariz. Coll. Trial Advocacy, 1987—; chmn. Ariz. Adv. Commn. on Litigation, Phoenix, 1989—. Fellow Ariz. Bar Found.; mem. Am. Bd. Trial Advocates (faculty mem. 1976—, pres. 1986), Ariz. Inn. of Ct. Roman Catholic. Home: 618 W Moon Valley Dr Phoenix AZ 85023-6233 Office: Jennings Strouss & Salmon 2 N Central Ave Phoenix AZ 85004-2322

STUART, GEORGE MICHEL, accountant; b. Columbus, Ohio, Feb. 21, 1963; s. George Frederick and Marcena Paulene (Michel) S. B. magna cum laude, San Diego State U., 1986. CPA, Calif. Asst. Deloitte & Touche, San Diego, 1986-88, sr. acct., 1987-91, mgr., 1991—. Vol. Holiday Bowl Com., San Diego, 1991—. Mem. Calif. Soc. CPA's, San Diego State U. Young Alumni (bd. dirs. 1991—). Republican. Office: Deloitte & Touche Ste 1900 701 B St San Diego CA 92101

STUART, GERARD WILLIAM, JR., corporate executive, councilman; b. Yuba City, Calif., July 28, 1939; s. Gerard William and Geneva Bernice (Stuke) S.; student Yuba Jr. Coll., 1957-59, Chico State Coll., 1959-60; A.B., U. Calif., Davis, 1962; M.L.S., U. Calif., Berkeley, 1963; m. Lenore Frances Loroña, 1981. Rare book librarian Cornell U., 1964-68; bibliographer of scholarly collections Huntington Library, San Marino, Calif., 1968-73, head acquisitions librarian, 1973-75; sec.-treas., dir. Ravenstree Corp., 1969-80, pres., chmn. bd., 1980—; pres., chmn. bd. William Penn Ltd., 1981—. Councilman City of Yuma, 1992—; bd. dirs. Ariz. Humanities Coun., 1993—. Lilly fellow Ind. U., 1963-64. Mem. Bibliog. Soc. Am., Phi Beta Kappa, Alpha Gamma Sigma, Phi Kappa Phi. Clubs: Rolls-Royce Owners; Grolier (N.Y.C.); Zamorano (Los Angeles). Office: 204 S Madison Ave Yuma AZ 85364

STUART, WILLIAM ROY, information services executive; b. Redwood City, Calif., June 7, 1972; s. Larry Howard and Happy Helen Francis (Hockabout) S. Mgr. info. svcs. Am. Data Mgmt., Inc., Mountain View, Calif., 1991-93. Vol. Tom Nolan for Supr., Redwood City, 1984, Kevin Kelly for Assembly, Belmont, Calif., 1986, Ted Lempert for Assembly, San Mateo, Calif., 1988, PC specialist, 1990. Democrat.

STUBBLEFIELD, JAMES IRVIN, physician, surgeon, army officer; b. Phila., Aug. 17, 1953; s. James Irvin Sr. and Geri (Harvey) S.; m. Linda Marie Simms, Aug. 12, 1978; children: Lindsay, Shannon. BSEE, MS in Bioengring., U. Pa., 1977; MD, Hahnemann U., Phila., 1982. Diplomate Am. Bd. Emergency Medicine, 1991. Mgr. energy engring. Norcross, Inc., Bryn Mawr, Pa., 1977-78; commd. 2d lt. U.S. Army, 1977, advanced through grades to maj., 1988; intern in gen. surgery Letterman Army Med. Ctr., San Francisco, 1982-83; flight surgeon, brigade surgeon 101st Airborne Div., Ft. Campbell, Ky., 1983-87; resident in emergency medicine Madigan Army Med. Ctr., Ft. Lewis, Wash., 1987-90; chief emergency. med. svcs. Silas B. Hays Army Hosp., Ft. Ord, Calif., 1990-92, chief Dept. Emergency Medicine and Primary Care, 1992—; flight surgeon attack helicopter battalion Operation Desert Storm, Persian Gulf, 1991. Mem. AMA, Am. Coll. Emergency Physicians, U.S. Army Flight Surgeon Soc., Assn. Mil. Surgeons U.S., Tau Beta Pi, Eta Kappa Nu, Alpha Epsilon Delta. Roman Catholic. Home: 22586 Oak Canyon Rd Salinas CA 93908-9606

STUBBLEFIELD, THOMAS MASON, agricultural economist, educator; b. Taxhoma, Okla., Apr. 16, 1922; s. Temple Roscoe and Martha Lacy (Acree) S.; BS, N.Mex. State U., 1948; MS, A. and M. Coll. Tex., 1951, PhD, 1956; postgrad. U. Ariz., 1954; m. Martha Lee Miller, Mar. 7, 1943; children: Ellen (Mrs. Richard Damron), Paula (Mrs. James T. Culbertson), Thommye (Mrs. Gary D. Zingsheim). Specialist cotton mktg. N.Mex. State U., 1948; extension economist, then asst. agrl. economist U. Ariz., Tucson, 1951-58, from assoc. prof. to prof., 1958-64, prof. and agrl. economist, 1964-83, emeritus prof., 1983—, acting asst. dir. agrl. expt. sta., 1966-68, asst. to dir. sta., 1973-74, chief party Brazil contract, 1968-70. Mem. Pima Council Aging, 1974-77, 80-90; chmn. adv. com. Ret. Sr. Vol. Program, Pima County, 1980-90, mem. 1974-93. Chmn. bd. Saguaro Home Found., 1980-85. With AUS, 1942-45. Author bulls. Home: 810 W Calle Milu Tucson AZ 85706-3925

STUBBS, DANIEL GAIE, labor relations consultant; b. Charleston, S.C., Nov. 13, 1940; s. Daniel Hamer and Esther Virginia (Garlow) S.; m. Sherrill Ann Sloan, July 8, 1984; children: Kimberly, Allison, Don; student U. Fla., 1959-60; BA, W.Va. U., 1965; postgrad. Temple U., 1965-67. Tchr., Sch. Dist. of Phila., 1965-67; rep. Am. Fedn. Tchrs., Washington, 1967; exec. sec. Calif. State Coll. Coun., Am. Fedn. Tchrs., AFL-CIO, L.A., 1967-68; rep. Am. Fedn. Tchrs., AFL-CIO, L.A., 1968-69, dir. orgn. Balt. Tchrs. Union, 1969-70; employee relations specialist Calif. Nurses Assn., L.A., 1971-72; exec. dir. United Nurses Assn. Calif., L.A., 1972-74; labor rels. cons. Social Svcs. Union, Svc. Employees Internat. Union, Local 535, AFL-CIO, L.A., 1974-76; exec. dir. Met. Riverside UniServ Unit, Calif. Tchrs. Assn., 1976-79, exec. dir. San Bernardino/Colton Uniserv Unit, 1979-80; gen. svcs. adminstr. Housing Authority, City of L.A., 1980-82; cons. Blanning & Baker Assocs., Tujunga, Calif., 1983-84; asst. exec. dir. adminstrv. svcs. L.A. Housing Authority, 1984-86; labor rels. con., L.A., 1986—; lectr. in field. With U.S. Army, 1961-62. Recipient W.Va. U. Waitman Barbe Prize for creative writing, 1965. Mem. So. Calif. Indsl. Rels. Rsch. Assn., Orange County Indsl. Relations Research Assn., Indsl. Rels. Rsch. Assn., UCLA Inst. Indsl. Rels. Assn., Soc. of Profls. in Dispute Resolution, Town Hall Club of Calif. Presbyterian. Home: 3200 Fairesta St Apt 11 La Crescenta CA 91214-2681

STUBBS, MARK DARWIN, lawyer; b. Spanish Fork, Utah, Oct. 4, 1950; s. R. Eugene and Joan (Loveless) S.; m. Jan Green, Aug. 28, 1973; children: Julie, Jared, Michael, Melissa, Richard. BA, Brigham Young U., 1974, JD, 1977. Bar: Ariz. 1977, U.S. Dist. Ct. Ariz. 1977, Idaho 1980, U.S. Dist. Ct. Idaho 1980. Assoc. Ryley, Carlock & Ralson, Phoenix, 1976-79; ptnr. May & May Law Offices, Twin Falls, Idaho, 1979—; mem. Idaho Ho. of Reps., Boise, 1990—. Bd. dirs. Lawyers Involved for Idaho, 1986-90; Rep. dist. chmn., Twin Falls, 1982, 83. Named Outstanding Precinct Committeeman, Twin Falls, 1983. Mem. ABA, Ariz. Bar Assn., Idaho Bar Assn., Idaho Trial Lawyers Assn. (bd. govs., bd. dirs. 1984-87), Idaho World Trade Assn., Twin Falls C. of C., Am. Arbitration Assn. (panel of arbitrators 1990—). Republican. Home: 1025 Sawtooth Blvd Twin Falls ID 83301-3583 Office: May & May Law Offices 516 2nd St E PO Box 1846 Twin Falls ID 83303

STUBBS, RANDALL ARTHUR, fund raising executive; b. Billings, Mont., June 10, 1952; s. William Arthur and Betty Lou (Roberts) S.; m. Loraine Lynn Hatton, Oct. 18, 1980; children: Amanda, Mitchell. BA, U. Colo., 1975; postgrad., U. Tulsa, 1977-78, Regis. U., 1993—. Owner, operator Petroleum Land Cons., Denver, 1978-86; v.p. AMC Cancer Rsch. Ctr., Denver, 1986-90; devel. dir. Denver Zool. Found., Denver, 1990—. Mem. Nat. Com. on Planned Giving. Mem. Nat. Soc. Fund Raising Execs., Am. Assn. of Zool. Parks and Aquariums. Office: Denver Zool Found 825 E Speer Blvd # 10 Denver CO 80218-3719

STUCKEY, WAYNE KEITH, chemist, materials scientist; b. Pittsburg, Kans., Apr. 12, 1940; s. Russell S. and Lavon Edith (Sellers) S.; m. Nancy Dee Johns (div. 1974); chldren: Debbie, Dana, Kenny; m. Miyoko Nakashimo, Apr. 17, 1975. BA, Pittsburg State U., 1962, MS, 1964; PhD, Kans. State U., 1966. Mem. tech. staff Aerospace Corp., El Segundo, Calif., 1966-76, mgr. analytical techniques sect., 1976-82, dept. head materials analysis dept., 1982-89; dept. head analytical and polymer scis. Aerospace Corp., 1989-91, rsch. scientist, 1991—. Home: 2049 W 235th St Torrance CA 90501-5811 Office: The Aerospace Corp PO Box 92957 MS: M2/250 Los Angeles CA 90009-2957

STUDEBAKER, IRVING GLEN, engineering educator, researcher; b. Ellensburg, Wash., July 22, 1931; s. Clement Glen and Ruth (Krause) S.; (widowed); children: Ruth, Betty, Raymond, Karl, Donna. BS in Geol. Engring., U. Ariz., 1957, MS in Geology, 1959, PhD in Geol. Engring., 1977. Registered profl. engr., Wash., Nev., Ariz., Colo., Mont. Geophys. engr. Mobil, 1959-61; civil engr. City of Yakima, Wash., 1964-66; instr. Yakima Valley Coll., 1962-67; sr. rsch. geologist Roan Selection Trust, Kalulushi, Zambia, 1967-72; sr. mining engr. Occidental Oil Shale, Grand Junction, Colo., 1974-81; prof. Mont. Coll. Mining Sch., Butte, 1982—; cons. in field. Sgt. U.S. Army, 1951-54, Korea. Mem. N.W. Mining Assn., Geol. Soc. Am., Soc. for Mining and Metall. Engring., Mont. Mining Assn., Sigma Xi (pres. Mont. tech. chpt. 1990-91). Home: 5 Cedar Lake Dr Butte MT 59701-4337 Office: Mont Tech Mining Dept West Park Butte MT 59701

STUDEMEISTER, PAUL ALEXANDER, geologist; b. Caracas, Venezuela, Mar. 20, 1954; came to U.S., 1966; s. Alexander E. and Marguerite (Preobrajensky) S. BA, U. Calif., Berkeley, 1977; PhD, U. Western Ont., London, Can., 1982. Lic. engring. geologist, Calif.; lic. geologist, Ariz. Geology instr. U. Ottawa, Can., 1982-83; project geologist Dunraine Mines Ltd., Toronto, Can., 1983-84; geology instr. Laurentian U., Sudbury, Can., 1984-85; project geologist Agassiz Resources, Ltd., Toronto, 1985; rsch. petrographer Constrn. Tech. Labs., Skokie, Ill., 1985-90; project geologist Applied GeoSystems, Fremont, Calif., 1990; sr. geologist EVAX Techs., Inc., Scotts Valley, Calif., 1990-93, AGS Inc., San Francisco, 1993—. Contbr. articles to profl. jours. Mem. Assn. Engring. Geologists, Groundwater Resources Assn. Calif. Lutheran. Home: 2140 Santa Cruz Ave # 105D Menlo Park CA 94025 Office: AGS Inc 120 Howard St Ste 600 San Francisco CA 94105

STUDLEY, HELEN ORMSON, artist, poet, writer, designer; b. Elroy, Wis., Sept. 8, 1937; d. Clarence Ormson and Hilda (Johnson) O.; m. William Frank Studley, Aug. 1965 (div.); 1 son, William Harrison. Owner RJK Original Art, Sherman Oaks, Calif., 1979—; designer Aspen Series custom greeting cards and stationery notes, lithographs Love is All Colors, 1982, Flowers for Ruth (Best of Art Show award). One woman show includes Sherman Oaks, Calif., 1991, Toluca Lake Art Festival, 1991, Art Show for Srs., 1992, Art Show for Youth, 1991; represented in numerous pub. and pvt. collections throughout U.S., Can., Norway, Sweden, Austria, Germany, Eng., France; group exhibits include Art Show for Homeless, L.A., 1990; author poetry Love is Care, Changes, 1988; contbr. poems to publs. Active Luth. Brotherhood, Emmanuel Luth. Ch. Honors include display of lithograph Snow Dreams, Snow Queens at 1980 Winter Olympics, Lake Placid, N.Y., lithograph Summer Dreams, Summer Queens at 1984 Summer Olympics, Los Angeles; named finalist in competition for John Simon Guggenheim fellowship; recipient Golden Poet award World Poetry, 1987-92, Art Show for Youth, 1991, Art Show for Srs., 1992, Art Show at the Park, 1992, Diamond Pin award Carter Hawley Hale, 1991, 92, Outstanding Achievements in Poetry award, 1993, . Mem. Internat. Soc. Poets (publ. in Disting. Poets Am. 1993), Soc. Illustrators, Am. Watercolor Soc., Internat. Soc. Artists, Internat. Platform Assn., Calif. Woman's Art Guild, Sons of Norway Club. Office: RJK Original Art 5020 Hazeltine Ave Sherman Oaks CA 91423-1174

STUHLMILLER, JOHN CHRISTOPHER, legislature staff member; b. Reardan, Wash., Apr. 22, 1963; s. E. Robert and Willamae Josephine (Anderson) S.; m. Allyson Elizabeth Smith, June 1, 1985; children: David Michael, Rachael Bethany. BA in Polit. Sci., Pacific Luth. U., 1985; MPA, Evergreen State Coll., 1990. Claims processor Wash. State Atty. Gen., Tacoma, 1984; senate intern Wash. State Senate, Olympia, 1985, senate aide, 1985, rsch. analyst Rep. caucus, 1985-87, rsch. analyst Agri. com., 1987—. Sun. sch. tchr. Luth. Ch. Good Shepherd, 1990—; ch. coun. Luth. Ch. Good Shepherd, 1989—; chmn. worship com. Luth Ch. Good Shepherd, 1986—; youth minstry team Luth. Ch. Good Shepherd, 1987-88; Sunday Sch. superintendent, teacher Summit Lake Community Ch.; founding mem., sec.-treas. Project Little Lamb, 1992. Bd. dirs. Lake Lucinda Community Club (pres. 1987-90). Office: Wash State Senate PO Box 40461 Jac Bldg Olympia WA 98504

STULBERG, NEAL HOWARD, conductor, pianist; b. Detroit, Apr. 12, 1954; s. Samuel and Judith (Victor) S.; m. Leah Shahmoon, July 12, 1987. B.A. magna cum laude, Harvard Coll., 1976; M.Mus., U. Mich., 1978; postgrad., Juilliard Sch. Music, 1979-80. Condr. MIT Symphony Orch., Cambridge, 1980-82, Young Musicians Found. Debut Orch., Los Angeles, 1981-84; Exxon Arts Endowment asst. condr. Los Angeles Philharm. Orch., 1983-85; music dir., condr. N.Mex. Symphony Orch., 1985—. Recipient 2d prize Balt. Symphony Orch. Young Condrs. Competition, 1980, Seaver/Nat. Endowment Arts Conductor award, 1988; Henry Russell Shaw fellow, 1976-77. Office: NMex Symphony Orch PO Box 769 Albuquerque NM 87103-0769

STULL, ERICA HEATH, public relations executive; b. N.Y.C., Sept. 29, 1951; d. Norton Jay and Pearl (Stark) Bramesco; m. Dennis M. Stull, June 30, 1974; children: Gabriel Bramesco, Cameron Paul. BA, U. Colo., 1973. Traffic mgr. KVOD Radio, Denver, 1974-76; traffic mgr., producer KCFR Radio, Denver, 1976-78; bus. mgr., columnist Straight Creek Jour., Denver, 1978-80; tech. writer Petro-Lewis Corp., Denver, 1980-84; writer Jones Intercable, Inc., Englewood, Colo., 1985-88, mgr. corp. communications, 1988-91, dir. corp. communications, 1991—; publicity and mktg. chair Women in Cable 1992 Mgmt. Conf., Denver. Mem. Pub. Rels. Soc. Am. (accredited in pub. rels.), Cable TV Pub. Affairs Assn. Office: Jones Intercable Inc 9697 E Mineral Ave Englewood CO 80112

STULTS, JOHN EDWIN, administrative law judge; b. Evanston, Ill., Mar. 1, 1950; s. Allen Parker and Elizabeth (Van Horne) S.; m. Daphne Ann Crosbie, Nov. 19, 1977. BA, Carroll Coll., 1979; postgrad., Nat. Judicial Coll., 1990-91. Resource technician U.S Bur. Land Mgmt., Fairbanks, Alaska, 1977-80; land surveyor U.S. Forest Svc., Helena, Mont., 1980-84; water rights specialist Mont. Dept. Nat. Resources and Conservation, Helena, 1984-87, adminstrv. officer, 1987-89, adminstrv. law judge, 1990—. Chmn Helena Citizens Coun., 1991-92, treas., 1989-90; chmn. bd. dirs. Water Quality Protection Dist., Lewis & Clark County, Mont., 1992-93; mem. bd. zoning adjustment, Helena, 1989—. Mem. Nat. Judges Assn., Nat. Assn. Adminstrv. Law Judges, Western Conf. Adminstrv. Law Judges (chmn. bd. trustees 1990-92). Home: 714 Red Letter St Helena MT 59601-5808 Office: Dept Natural Resources & Conservation 1520 W 6th Ave Helena MT 89620-2301

STULTS, LAURENCE ALLEN, airline pilot; b. Evanston, Ill., Nov. 2, 1940; s. Allen Parker and Elizabeth Van Horne; m. Karen Frashure, Feb. 13, 1965 (div. 1986); m. Takako Yajima, Mar. 25, 1986; children: Rex Allen, Mark Edwin. AB in Econs., Colgate U., 1962; MS, George Washington U., 1978; postgrad., Cath. U., 1977; cert. in Japanese Lang., U. Guam, Maniglao, 1991. Commd. 2d lt. U.S. Marine Corps, 1962, fighter pilot, 1962-83; test pilot, mgr. fighter Naval Air Test Ctr., 1972-76; advanced through grades to lt. col. commdg. officer USMC, 1980; capt. Continental Air Micronesia, 1984-91; chief pilot World Fish and Agriculture, 1991; capt. B-727 Continental Airlines, Denver, 1991—; cons. real estate sales, Honolulu, 1983-86. Pres. Mariners Ridge Homeowners, Honolulu, 1980-86, Tumon View (Guam) Homeowners, 1987-91. Decorated Disting. Flying Cross, Bronze Star, Cross of Gallantry. Mem. Soc. Exptl. Test Pilots (life), Ind. Assn. Continental Pilots, Continental Ops. Group, Marine Corps Assn. Republican. Congregationalist. Home: 28602 16th Ave S Redondo Apt 204 Federal Way WA 98003-3613 Office: Continental Airlines PO Box 38371 Denver CO 80238-0371

STUMBLES, JAMES RUBIDGE WASHINGTON, multinational company executive; b. Harare, Zimbabwe, Aug. 13, 1939; came to U.S., 1980; s. Albert R.W. and Mary Dallas (Atherstone) S.; m. Vyvienne Clare Shaw, Dec. 19, 1964; children: Christopher, Timothy, Jonathan. BA, U. Cape Town, Republic of South Africa, 1960, LLB, 1962. Adv. Supreme Ct. of S. Africa. Mng. dir. Pritchard Services Group of South Africa, Johannesburg, 1972-80; dir. security, pres. subs. Pritchard Svcs. Group Am., Columbus, Ohio, 1980-83; exec. v.p., pres. subs. Mayne Nickless/ Loomis Corp., Seattle, 1984-87; v.p. N.W. Protective Svc. Inc., Seattle, 1987-91, pres., CEO, 1991—; pres., CEO Western Security Svc. Inc., Spokane, 1991—, Northwest Protective Svc. Inc.-Oreg., Portland, 1992—. Sec. Boy Scouts, Johannesburg, 1978-80. Mem. Rand Club, Columbia Tower Club, Rotary, Kiwanis, Round Table (officer 1969-80). Office: NW Protective Svc Inc 2700 Elliott Ave Seattle WA 98121-1189

STUMP, BOB, congressman; b. Phoenix, Apr. 4, 1927; s. Jesse Patrick and Floy Bethany (Fields) S.; children: Karen, Bob, Bruce. B.S. in Agronomy, Ariz. State U., 1951. Mem. Ariz. Ho. of Reps., 1957-67; mem. Ariz. Senate, 1967-76, pres., 1975-76; mem. 95th-103rd Congresses from 3rd Dist.Ariz., 1976—; mem. Armed Svcs. com., subcoms. rsch., tech., mil. installations, facilities, veteran affairs com., Hosps., Health care, Edn., Tng. Employment. With USN, 1943-46. Mem. Am. Legion, Ariz. Farm Bur. Republican. Seventh-day Adventist. Office: 211 Canon House of Representatives Washington DC 20515-0303 also: 230 N 1st Ave Rm 5001 Phoenix AZ 85025*

STUMP, D. MICHAEL, librarian; b. Santa Monica, Calif., Dec. 22, 1947; s. H. Walter and Margaret June (Stetler) S. B.A. in History, Pasadena Coll., 1971; M.L.S., U. So. Calif., 1977. Library asst. Calif. Inst. Tech., Pasadena, Calif., 1970-74; librarian First Baptist Ch. of Van Nuys, Calif., 1974-81, 1982-87, Laurence/2000, Van Nuys, 1981-82; Van Nuys Christian Coll., 1975-76, Hillcrest Christian Sch., Granada Hills, Calif., 1987—. Asst. scoutmaster San Fernando council Boy Scouts Am., 1970-73. Named to Outstanding Young Men Am. U.S. Jaycees, 1976. Mem. ALA, Am. Assn. Sch. Librs., Evang. Ch. Libr. Assn. (So. Calif. chpt.). Republican. Baptist. Office: Hillcrest Christian Sch 17531 Rinaldi St Granada Hills CA 91344-3319

STUMPF, BERNHARD JOSEF, physicist; b. Neustadt der Weinstrasse, Rhineland, Germany, Sept. 21, 1948; came to U.S., 1981; s. Josef and Katharina (Cervinka) S. Diploma physics, Saarland U., Saarbrucken, West Germany, 1975, Dr.rer.nat., 1981. Rsch. asst. physics dept. Saarland U., Saarbrucken, 1976-81; rsch. assoc. Joint Inst. Lab. Astrophysics, U. Colo., Boulder, 1981-84; instr. physics, physics dept. NYU, N.Y.C., 1984-86, asst. rsch. scientist Atomic Beams Lab., 1984-85, assoc. rsch. scientist Atomic Beams Lab., 1985-86; vis. assoc. prof. physics dept. U. Windsor (Ont., Can.), 1986-88; assoc. prof. physics dept. U. Idaho, Moscow, 1988—; chmn. Conf. on Atomic and Molecular Collisions in Excited States, Moscow, 1990. Contbr. articles to profl. jours. German Sci. Found. postdoctoral fellow U. Colo., Boulder, 1981-83; recipient Rsch. Opportunity award NSF, U. Idaho, 1990-91. Mem. AAAS, AAUP, German Phys. Soc., Am. Phys. Soc., N.Y. Acad. Scis. Office: U Idaho Dept Physics Moscow ID 83843

STUMPF, MICHAEL HOWARD, psychiatrist; b. Indpls., Aug. 7, 1952; s. Joseph A. and Nettie (Weinberg) S.; m. Sandra Kay Beams, Sept. 2, 1974; 1 child, Amanda Laura. BA in Biology, Ind. U., Bloomington, 1978; MD, Ind. U., Indpls, 1982. Diplomat Am. Bd. Psychiatry and Neurology. Intern, then resident Psych. Residency Trng. Program, Maricopa Med. Ctr., Phoenix, 1982-86; Psychiatrist homeless shelter program Phoenix South Community Mental Health Ctr., 1983-84; psychiatrist Tri-City Behavioral Health Ctr., Mesa, Ariz., 1984; attending psychiatrist County Homeless Alternative Psychiat. Svcs., Phoenix, 1984-86; teaching psychiatrist Maricopa Med. Ctr., Phoenix, 1986-90, chief psychiatrist psychiat. inpatient unit III, 1986-87, attending and chief psychiatrist psychiat. crisis ctr., 1987-88; attending psychiatrist Maricopa County Correctional Health Svcs., Phoenix, 1987-89, 90-92; dir. psychiat. and med. svcs. Community Orgn. for Drug Abuse, Mental Health and Alcoholism, Phoenix, 1989-92; attending psychiatrist Psychiat. Outreach Project, Phoenix, 1988-89; instr. SMI program Rio Salado Community Coll.; med. dirs. Superstition Mountain Mental Health Ctr., Apache Junction, Ariz., 1992—, Rainbows Way Inn, Mesa, Ariz., 1992—; attending psychiatrist Pinal-Gila Behavioral Health Assn., Apache Junction, 1992—. Chmn. com. to rev. other states Ariz. Gov.'s Task Force on Homelesss Chronically Mentally Ill., Phoenix, 1989. Named Psychiat. Attending of Yr. psychiat. nursing svc. Maricopa Med. Ctr., 1987. Mem. Am. Psychiat. Assn., Am. Assn. Community Psychiatrists, Ariz. Psychiat. Soc. (co-chmn. pub. affairs com. 1987—, sec. 1991, v.p. 1992), Phoenix Psychiat. Coun. (sec.-treas. 1990-91, v.p. 1992), Mental Health Assn. Maricopa County (bd. dirs. 1992—). Jewish. Office: Superstition Mountain Mental Health Ctr PO Box 3160 150 N Ocotillo Dr Apache Junction AZ 85217-3160

STUMPF, PAUL KARL, former biochemistry educator; b. N.Y.C., N.Y., Feb. 23, 1919; s. Karl and Annette (Schreyer) S.; married, June 1947; children: Ann Carol, Kathryn Lee, Margaret Ruth, David Karl, Richard Frederic. AB, Harvard U., 1941; PhD, Columbia U., 1945. Instr. biochemistry U. Mich., Ann Arbor, 1946-48; from asst. prof. to prof. U. Calif., Berkeley, 1948-58; prof. U. Calif., Davis, 1958-84, prof. emeritus, 1984—; chief scientist Competitive Rsch. Grants Office USDA, Washington, 1988-91; cons. Palm Oil Rsch. Inst., Kuala Lumpur, Malaysia, 1982-92; sci. adv. bd. Calgene, Inc., Davis, Calif., 1990—; sci. adv. panel Md. Biotech. Inst., 1990-92. Co-Author: Outlines of Enzyme Chemistry, 1955, Outlines of Biochemistry, 5th ed. 1987; co-editor-in-chief Biochemistry of Plants, 1980; exec. editor Archives of Biochemistry/Biophysics, 1965-88; contbr. over 250 articles to profl. jours. Mem. planning commn. City of Davis, 1966-68. Guggenheim fellow, 1962, 69; recipient Lipid Chemistry award Am. Oil Chemists Soc., 1974, Sr. Scientist award Alexander von Humboldt Found., 1976, Superior Svc. Group award USDA, 1992. Fellow Linnean Soc. London; mem. NAS, Royal Danish Acad. Scis., Am. Soc. Plant Physiologists (pres. 1979-80, chmn. bd. trustees 1986-90, Stephen Hales award 1974, Charles Reid Barnes Life Membership award 1992), Yolo Fliers Country Club (Woodland, Calif.). Home: 764 Elmwood Dr Davis CA 95616-3517 Office: Univ of Calif Biochemistry & Biophysics Dept Davis CA 95616

STUPSKI, LAWRENCE J., investment company executive; b. 1945. JD, Yale U., 1970. V.p. Bradford Nat. Corp., N.Y.C., 1971-78; with Western Bradford Tr. Inc., San Francisco, 1978-80; pres., COO, CEO Charles Schwab & Co. Inc. (formerly Charles Schwab Corp.), 1980—, also bd. dirs. Office: Charles Schwab & Co Inc 101 Montgomery St San Francisco CA 94104-4122*

STURE, STEIN, civil engineering educator; b. Oslo, Norway, Nov. 12, 1947; came to U.S., 1970; s. Alf and Gunnvor (Een) S.; m. Karen J. Marley, June 3, 1989. Student, Schous Inst. Tech., Oslo, 1970; BSCE, U. Colo., 1971, MSCE, 1973, PhD, 1976. Asst. prof. Va. Polytechnic Inst., Blacksburg, 1976-80; rsch. scientist Marshall Space Flight Ctr. NASA, Huntsville, Ala., 1979; from asst. prof. to prof. civil engring. U. Colo., Boulder, 1980—, acting chmn. dept. civil engring., 1990-91; sr. vis. dept. engring. sci. U. Oxford, Eng., 1985; vis. prof. Norway Inst. Tech., Trondheim, 1985-86. Jenkin fellow, 1986. Mem. Am. Soc. Civil Engrs. (pres. Colo. sect. 1990-91, Walter Huber Civil Engring. Rsch. prize 1990), Am. Assn. Advancement Sci., Am. Geophys. Union, Am. Soc. Engring. Edn., NASA Ctr. Space Construction, Internat. Soc. Soil Mech. Found. Engrs., ASTM (affiliate). Home: 1077 Diamond Ct Boulder CO 80303-3244 Office: Univ Colo Dept Civil Engring Boulder CO 80309-0428

STURGEN, WINSTON, photographer, printmaker, artist; b. Harrisburg, Pa., Aug. 27, 1938; s. George Winston and Gladys Erma (Lenker) S.; m. Nancy Kathryn Otto, Jan. 23, 1959 (div. 1981); 1 child, Bruce Eugene Sturgen; m. Jessica Sheldon, Mar. 15, 1988. BS in Forestry, Pa. State U., 1960; postgrad., U. N.H., 1961-62; M of Forestry, Pa. State U., 1964; postgrad., U. Oreg., 1966-68. Cert. profl. photographer. Devel. engr. Weyerhaeuser Co., Longview, Wash., 1964-66; mgr. Wickes Lumber Co., Elkhorn, Wis., 1968-70; owner, mgr. Wickes Wanderland, Delavan, Wis., 1970-72, Sturgen's Cleaners, Delavan, 1972-80, Images by Sturgen, Delavan, 1980-84; instr. photography continuing edn. dept. Western N.Mex. U., 1988-90; juror numerous orgns., 1982—. One-man shows include Artesia (N.Mex.) Mus. and Art Ctr., 1992, Delavan Art Mus., 1984, Donnell Libr., N.Y.C., 1992; exhibited in group shows at Carlsbad (N.Mex.) Mus., 1992, Sister Kenny Inst., 1992, (3rd Pl.), Deming Ctr. for the Arts, N.Mex., 1991, Tex Fine Arts Assn., 1991-93, Shellfish Collection, Silver City, N.Mex., 1989, 90, Thompson Gallery, U. N.Mex., 1989, Profl. Photographers Assn. of N.Mex., 1985, 86, 88 (awards), Union Gallery, U. N.Mex., 1987, Gallery Sigala, Taos, N.Mex., 1986, World Trade Ctr., N.Y.C., 1992, Internat. Exposition of Photography, 1983, 84, 85, 87, and many others; pub. poetry, numerous articles in field. Founder, chmn. Winter Arts Festival, Silver City,

N.Mex., 1988-90; com. mem. Taos Fall Arts Festival, 1985; com. chair Oktoberfest, Delavan, 1976-80. Residency grant Wurlitzer Found., 1987, 89. Mem. Resources for Artists with Disabilities, Enabled Artists United, Disabled Artists Network, Fuller Lodge Art Ctr. Home: PO Box 370 Silver City NM 88062

STURGIS, G. KENT, book publisher, writer, editor; b. Fairbanks, Alaska, Dec. 4, 1947; s. George and Mary (Hayes) S.; m. Patricia E. Lesko, Aug. 16, 1967 (div. Oct. 1978); children: Victoria, Christine; m. Patricia Mary Tanner, May 4, 1981. Student, U. Alaska, 1966-67, U. Wash., 1967-70. Corr. The Assoc. Press, Anchorage, Juneau, Alaska, 1970-73; chief of bureau The Assoc. Press, Seattle, 1973-75; mng. editor Fairbanks Daily News-Miner, 1975-86; pres. Epicenter Press Inc., Seattle, Fairbanks, 1988—. Author: Four Generations on the Yukon, 1988 (Best Travel Writing Benjamin Franklin award 1989).

STURGULEWSKI, ARLISS, state senator; b. Blaine, Wash., Sept. 27, 1927; B.A., U. Wash.; LLD (hon.) U. Alaska, Anchorage, 1993. Mem. Assembly Municipality of Anchorage; vice chmn. New Capital Site Planning Commn., mem. Capital Site Selection Com.; chmn. Greater Anchorage Area Planning and Zoning Commn.; mem. Alaska State Senate, 1978-93. Rep. nominee Office Gov. Alaska, 1986, 90. Home: 2957 Sheldon Jackson St Anchorage AK 99508-4469 Office: 3301 C St Ste 520 Anchorage AK 99503

STUTMAN, HARRIS RONALD, pediatrician; b. Phila., May 7, 1947; s. Sydney and Sally (Press) S.; m. Eileen Elizabeth Letson, Apr. 18, 1971; children: Jessica, Timothy. BA, U. Pa., 1968; MD, Pa. State U., 1972. Diplomate Am. Bd. Pediatrics. Pediatric resident Univ. Hosp., Pitts., 1972-75; chief pediatric resident Univ. Hosp., 1975-76; rsch. fellow U. and Children's Hosp. of Okla., Oklahoma City, 1982-84; asst. prof. pediatrics U. Okla. Health Sci. Ctr., Oklahoma City, 1984-86, U. Calif., Irvine, 1986—; dir. pediatric infectious disease Meml. Miller Children's Hosp., Long Beach, Calif., 1986—; assoc. dir. cystic fibrosis ctr. Meml. Miller Children's Hosp., 1987—; pvt. practice pediatrics Lakewood, N.J., 1976-82; cons. computer implementation medicine Long Beach Meml. Med. Ctr., 1989—; chmn. data rev. com. Bur. Maternal-Child Health, 1988-89. Contbr. articles to profl. jours., chpts. to books; editor: Handbook for Pediatric Infectious Disease, 1990. NIH grantee, 1986—, Cystic Fibrosis Found. grantee, 1986—, So. Med. Assn. grantee, 1984-85; recipient Mosby award, Pa. State U., 1972, Pediatric Dept. award, U. Okla. Health Sci. Ctr., 1984. Fellow Am. Acad. Pediatrics (co-chmn. com. computer tech. 1986-88); mem. Western Soc. Pediatric Rsch., Am. Soc. Microbiology, Infectious Disease Soc. Am., Pediatric Infectious Disease Soc., Mensa (prog. v.p. 1985-86). Democrat. Office: Memorial Miller Childrens 2801 Atlantic Ave Long Beach CA 90806-1799

STYLES, BEVERLY, entertainer; b. Richmond, Va., June 6, 1923; d. John Harry Kenealy and Juanita Russell (Robins) Carpenter; m. Wilbur Cox, Mar. 14, 1942 (div.); m. Robert Marascia, Oct. 5, 1951 (div. Apr. 1964). Studies with Ike Carpenter, Hollywood, Calif., 1965—; student, Am. Nat. Theatre Acad., 1968-69; studies with Paula Raymond, Hollywood, 1969-70. Freelance performer, musician, 1947-81; owner Beverly Styles Music, Joshua Tree, Calif., 1971—; v.p. spl. programs Lawrence Program of Calif., Yucca Valley, Calif. Composer (songs) Joshua Tree, 1975, I'm Thankful, 1978, Wow, Wow, Wow, 1986, Colour Chords (and Moods), Piano Arrangement, 1990; records include The Perpetual Styles of Beverly, 1978; albums include The Primitive Styles of Beverly, 1977; author: A Special Plan to Think Upon, The Truth as Seen by A Composer, 1978. Mem. ASCAP (Gold Pin award), Am. Fedn. Musicians, Internat. Platform Assn. Republican. Office: PO Box 615 Joshua Tree CA 92252-0615

SUBACH, JAMES ALAN, infosystems company executive, consultant; b. Lawrence, Mass., Mar. 24, 1948; s. Anthony John and Bernice Ruth (Pekarski) S. m. Marilyn Butler, Feb. 16, 1980. BS with distinction, U. Maine, 1970; MS, U. Ariz., 1975, PhD, 1979. Vis. scientist NASA Johnson Space Ctr., Houston, 1977-79; rsch. assoc. Baylor Coll. Medicine, Houston, 1977-79; pres. Subach Ventures, Inc., San Antonio, 1980-84, JAS & Assocs., Inc., Phoenix, 1984—, C.I.O. Inc., 1987-90; v.p. PTIMS, Inc., Phoenix, 1992—; faculty assoc. Ariz. State U., Tempe, 1992—. Assoc. editor Jour. Applied Photog. Engring., 1973-78; author software Gen. Acctg. System, 1987; bus. computing columnist, 1987. Pres. Forest Trails Homeowners Assn., Phoenix, 1987-88. Mem. SPIE, Phoenix C. of C. (Pres.'s Roundtable), Toastmasters (treas. Phoenix chpt. 1984), Tau Beta pi, Sigma Pi Sigma. Republican. Office: JAS & Assoc Inc 3625 N 16th St Ste 100 Phoenix AZ 85016-6446

SUBADYA, KORNELIUS TJANDRA, chiropractor; b. Jakarta, Java, Indonesia, Oct. 20, 1958; came to U.S., 1977; s. Peter Tjandra Subadya and Suzana (Hosiuna) Nugroho; m. Ester Tiana Noegroho, Dec. 10, 1983; children: Jeremy, Natasha. BS magna cum laude, Cleve. Chiropractic Coll., 1983, D. Chiropody, 1983. Diplomate chiropractic. Chmn. Indonesian Christian Ch., Pasadena, Calif., 1991—. Recipient cert. Found. for Athletic Rsch. and Edn., L.A., 1983, Motion Palpation Inst., L.A., 1981, award Parker Chiropractic Rsch. Found., L.A., 1983. Mem. Am. Chiropractic Assn., Christian Chiropractic Assn., Bus. Indsl. Chiropractic Svcs., Christian Bus. Men's Com. Republican. Office: 1234 S Garfield Ave Alhambra CA 91801

SUBER, ROBIN HALL, former medical/surgical nurse; b. Bethlehem, Pa., Mar. 14, 1952; d. Arthur Albert and Sarah Virginia (Smith) Hall; m. David A. Suber, July 28, 1979; 1 child, Benjamin A. BSN, Ohio State U., 1974. RN, Ariz., Ohio. Formerly staff nurse Desert Samaritan Hosp., Mesa, Ariz. Lt. USN, 1974-80. Mem. ANA, Sigma Theta Tau.

SUBRAMANIAN, RAVANASAMUDRAM VENKATACHALAM, materials science educator, consultant; b. Kalakad, Tamilnadu, India, Jan. 16, 1933; s. Ravanasamudram V. Venkatachalam and Sankari (hariharan) V.; m. Chellam, June 29, 1953; children: Venkatachalam, Balaji. BS (with honors), U. Madras, Madras, India, 1953, MS, 1954, PhD, 1957. Sci. officer Nat. Chem. Lab., Poona, India, 1957-63; rsch. assoc. Case Western Res. U., Cleve., 1963-66; asst. prof. H.B. Technol. Inst., Kanpur, India, 1967-69; asst. chem. Wash. State U., Pullman, Wash., 1969-71, assoc. prof., 1971-78, prof., 1978—. Patentee: Basalt Fibers, 1979, Fiber Fragment Release, 1981. Mem. Kiwanis Club of Pullman, Wash. Recipient Best Paper Award Soc. of the Plastics Industry, 1978, rsch. excellence, Wash. State U. Coll. of Engring., Pullman, Wash., 1987. Mem. Am. Chem. Soc., Soc. of Mfg. Engrs., Sigma Xi, Materials Rsch. Soc. Democrat. Hindu. Office: Wash State Univ Pullman WA 99164-2920

SUBRAMANIAN, SUNDARAM, electronics engineer; b. Emaneswaram, Madras, India, July 9, 1934; came to U.S., 1968; s. Sundaram and Velammal (Subbiah) S.; m. Hemavathy Vadivelu, Feb. 18, 1968; children: Anand Kumar, Malathy. BE, Madras (India) U., 1959; PhD, Glasgow (Scotland) U., 1967; MBA, Roosevelt U., Chgo., 1977. Research engr. Zenith, Inc., Chgo., 1968-75; project engr. Motorola, Inc., Chgo., 1975-77; prof. Chapman Coll., Orange, Calif., 1977-78; cons. MCS, Orange, 1978-80; project engr. Endevco, San Juan Capistrano, Calif., 1980-84; project mgr. Unisys Corp., Mission Viejo, Calif., 1984—; bd. dirs. P.S.B. Inc., Torrance, Calif., 1984—. Patentee in field. Bd. dirs. Tamil Nadu Found. Inc., Balt. and Washington, 1976-79; pres. S. India Cultural Assn., Villa Park, Calif., 1977-78. Mem. IEEE, Inst. Environ. Sci. (sr.). Office: Unisys Corp 25725 Jeronimo Rd Mission Viejo CA 92691

SUBRAMANYA, SHIVA, aerospace systems engineer; b. Hole-Narasipur, India, Apr. 8, 1933; s. S.T. Srikantaiah and S. Gundamma; m. Lee. S. Silva, Mar. 3, 1967; children: Paul Kailas, Kevin Shankar. BSc, Mysore U., Bangalore, India, 1956; MSc, Karnatak U., Dharwar, India, 1962; postgrad., Clark U., 1963; MBA, Calif. State U., Dominguez Hills, 1973; D in Bus. Adminstrn., PhD in Bus. Adminstrn., Nova U., 1986. Sr. scientific officer AEC, Bombay, India, 1961-63; chief engr. TEI, Newport, R.I., 1964-67; prin. engr. Gen. Dynamics Corp., San Diego, 1967-73; asst. project mgr. def. and systems group TRW, Colorado Springs, Colo., 1973-87; asst. project mgr. space and def. group TRW, Redondo Beach, Calif., 1987—. Contbr. over 150 articles to profl. jours. V.p. VHP of Am., Berlin, Conn., 1984-88; pres. IPF of Am., Redondo Beach, 1981-88; appointed by Pres. of India to Atomic Energy Commn., India. Winner of dozens of awards and commendations from U.S. Dept. of Defense and the Aerospace Industry. Mem. Armed Forces Communications and Electronics Assn. (v.p.-elect Rocky Mountain chpt. 1986—, Meritorious svc. award 1985, medal of merit 1990), Am. Acad. Mgmt. Hindu. Home: 2115 Shelburne Way Torrance CA 90503-9344 Office: TRW Def and Space Group 1 Space Park Blvd Redondo Beach CA 90278-1071

SUCHENEK, MAREK ANDRZEJ, computer science educator; b. Warsaw, Poland, May 2, 1949; came to U.S., 1986; s. Tadeusz Aleksander and Barbara Krystyna (Zych) S.; m. Ewa Aleksandra Czerny, July 30, 1974 (div. 1991). MSc in Math. Engring., Warsaw Tech. U., 1973, PhD in Tech. Scis. with distinction, 1979. Instr. Warsaw (Poland) Tech. U., 1973-79, asst. prof., 1979-88; assoc. Nat. Inst. for Aviation Rsch., Wichita, 1987-90; assoc. prof. Wichita (Kans.) State U., 1988-89, assoc. prof., chair, 1989-90; prof. Calif. State U.-Dominguez Hills, Carson, 1990—; vis. asst. prof. Wichita (Kans.) State U., 1986-88; organizing com. Internat. Symposium on Methodologies for Intelligent Systems, 1989-90; program com. Annual Ulam Math. Conf., 1990-91, Internat. Conf. on Computing and Info., 1992—; referee NSF, 1990—, Annals of Math. and Artificial Intelligence, 1992—, Jour. Logic Programming, 1992—; presenter in field. Author: (with Jan Bielecki) ANS FORTRAN, 1980, (with Jan Bielecki) FORTRAN for Advanced Programmers, 1981, 2d edit., 83, 3d edit., 88 (Minister of Sci. Higher Edn. and Techs. prize 1982); reviewer Zentralblatt fur Mathematik, 1980-89, Math. Reviews, 1989-91; mem. editorial bd.: Ulam Quarterly, 1990—; contbr. articles to profl. jours. Recipient rsch. grants Polish Govt., 1974-76, 85-86, FAA, 1988-90. Mem. AAUP, The Assn. for Logic Programming, Computer Soc. IEEE, Assn. for Computing Machinery, Sigma Xi. Home: 830 N Juanita Ave Redondo Beach CA 90277 Office: Calif State Univ Dominguez Hills 1000 E Victoria St Carson CA 90747

SUCKIEL, ELLEN KAPPY, philosophy educator; b. Bklyn., June 15, 1943; d. Jack and Lilyan (Banchefsky) Kappy; m. Joseph Suckiel, June 22, 1973. A.B., Douglass Coll., 1965; M.A. in Philosophy, U. Wis., 1969, Ph.D. in Philosophy, 1972. Lectr. philosophy U. Wis., Madison, 1969-71; asst. prof. philosophy Fla. State U., Tallahassee, 1972-73; asst. prof. philosophy U. Calif., Santa Cruz, 1973-80, assoc. prof., 1980—, provost Kresge Coll., 1983-89. Author: The Pragmatic Philosophy of William James, 1982, also articles. Mem. Am. Philos. Assn., Soc. for Advancement Am. Philosophy. Office: U Calif Stevenson Coll Santa Cruz CA 95064

SUCZEK, CHRISTOPHER A., geologist, educator, department chair; b. Detroit, Sept. 6, 1942; parents: Robert F. and Barbara (Haining) S.; divorced 1974; 1 child, Patrick Muir. BA, U. Calif., Berkeley, 1972; PhD, Stanford U., 1977. Asst. prof. geology Western Wash. U., Bellingham, 1977-82, assoc. prof., 1982—, chair geology dept., 1990—; pres. faculty senate Western Wash. U., 1989-90. Assoc. editor Jour. of Sedimentary Petrology, 1986-88. Fellow Geol. Assn. Can.; mem. Soc. Sedimentary Geology, Internat. Assn. Sedimentologists, Geol. Soc. Am., Am. Geophys. Union, Am. Geol. Inst. Office: Western Wash U Dept Geology Bellingham WA 98225-9080

SUDBECK, RICHARD JAMES, medical systems engineer; b. Sioux Falls, S.D., Apr. 20, 1957; s. Gorman Francis and Lois Mae (Lawless) S.; m. Margaret Loretta Lochray, Oct. 11, 1986. AAS in Tech. Communication, U. S.D., 1980, AAS in Indsl. Electronics, 1980, BSEET, 1980. With Taylor Oil Co., Worthing, S.D., 1973-76; civil technician S.D. Dept. Transp., Beresford, S.D., 1976; hwy. maint. worker S.D. Dept. Transp., Sioux Falls, 1977; temp. supt. Springfield (S.D.) Water Treatment, 1978, plant operator, 1978-79; tech. writer Sundstrand Aviation Ops., Rockford, Ill., 1980-82; field svc. engr. Gen. Elec. Med. Sys., Des Moines, 1982-86; sr. field svc. engr. R Squared Scan Sys., Fresno, Calif., 1986—. Mem. Fresno PC User's Group. Democrat. Roman Catholic. Home: 772 E Vartikian Ave Fresno CA 93710-5435 Office: R Squared Scan Systems Inc 1611B Pomona Rd Corona CA 91720-1704

SUDDOCK, FRANCES SUTER THORSON, gerontology educator; b. Estelline, S.D., Oct. 23, 1914; d. William Henry and Anna Mary (Oakland) Suter; m. Carl Edwin Thorson, July 6, 1941 (dec. Apr. 1976); children: Sarah Thorson Little, Mary Frances; m. Edwin Matthew Suddock, Aug. 7, 1982 (dec. Sept. 1986). BA, Iowa State Tchrs. Coll., 1936; postgrad., Syracuse U., 1940-41, U. Iowa, 1946; MA, Antioch U., San Francisco, 1981. Cert. tchr. Tchr. various high schs., Correctionville and Eagle Grove, Iowa, 1936-38, 38-40, 41-43, 45-47; chief clk. War Price and Rationing Bd., Eagle Grove, 1943-45; instr. (part time) Eagle Grove Jr. Coll., 1953-61; adminstr. Eagle Grove Pub. Library, 1961-77; facilitator Will Schutz Assocs., Muir Beach, Calif., 1987-88; facilitator indep. grief workshops, Anchorage, 1989—. Keynote speaker Nat. Widowed Persons Conf. of Am. Assn. Retired Persons, 1988. Vol. Nat. Trainer Widowed Persons Svc. Am. Assn. Retired Persons, 1989—, ret. sr. vol. program, Anchorage, 1988—; pres., bd. dirs. Anchorage Widowed Persons Svc., 1992—; bd. dirs. North Iowa Mental Health Ctr., Mason City, 1959-76, Eagle Grove Community Chest, 1960, Help Line, Inc., Ft. Dodge, Iowa, 1976-77; chmn. Community Mental Health Fund, Eagle Grove, 1966-73; charter pres. Eagle Grove Concerned, Inc., 1973-77; charter pres. Eagle Grove br. AAUW, 1973-75; active various civic orgns. Mem. Am. Soc. on Aging, Alaska Assn. Gerontology (treas. 1992—), P.E.O., Kappa Delta Pi. Home: 333 M St Apt 404 Anchorage AK 99501-1902

SUE, ALAN KWAI KEONG, dentist; b. Honolulu, Apr. 26, 1946; s. Henry Tin Yee and Chiyoko (Ohata) S.; m. Ginger Kazue Fukushima, Mar. 19, 1972; 1 child, Dawn Marie. BS in Chemistry with honors, U. Hawaii, 1968; BS, U. Calif., San Francisco, 1972, DDS, 1972. Film editor, photographer Sta. KHVH-TV ABC, Honolulu, 1964-71; staff dentist Strong-Carter Dental Clinic, Honolulu, 1972-73; dentist Waianae Dental Clinic, Honolulu, 1972-73; pvt. practice Pearl City, Hawaii, 1973—; chief exec. officer Dental Image Specialists, Pearl City, 1975—; dental dir. Hawaii Dental Health Plan, Honolulu, 1987—; dental cons. Calif. Dental Health Plan, Tustin, 1987—; bd. dirs. Kula Bay Tropical Clothing Co.; mem. exec. bd. St. Francis Hosp., Honolulu, 1976-78, chief dept. dentistry, 1976-78. Mem adv. bd. Health Svcs. for Sr. Citizens, 1976—; mem. West Honolulu Sub-Area Health Planning Coun., 1981-84; mem. dental task force Hawaii Statewide Health Coordinating Coun., 1980, mem. plan devel. com., 1981-84; vol. oral cancer screening program Am. Cancer Soc.; v.p. Pearl City Shopping Ctr. Mchts. Assn., 1975-84, 92—. Regents' scholar U. Calif., San Francisco, 1968-72. Fellow Pierre Fauchard Acad., Acad. Gen. Dentistry; mem. ADA, Acad. Implants and Transplants, Am. Acad. Implant Dentistry, Hawaii Dental Assn. (trustee 1978-80), Honolulu County Dental Soc. (pres. 1982), Am. Acad. and Bd. Head, Facial, Neck Pain and TMJ Orthopedics, Intertel, Internat. Platform Assn., Mensa, Porsche Club, Pantera Owners Club, Mercedes Benz Club. Democrat. Office: Dental Image Specialists 850 Kam Hwy Ste 116 Pearl City HI 96782

SUE, LAWRENCE GENE, statistician; b. Portland, Oreg., Sept. 22, 1939; s. Henry Lock Sue and Dorothy Helen (Wong) Chung. BS in Math., Brigham Young U., 1967, MS in Statistics, 1973. Assoc. engr. Boeing Co., Seattle, 1967-69; math. statistician Ultrasystems Inc., Hill AFB, Utah, 1974-77; mem. tech. staff TRW Systems, Hill AFB, 1977-81; sr. staff engr. Motorola Inc., Phoenix, 1981-84, mgr. engring., 1984-85, statis. engr., 1985—; statis. cons. Motorola Semiconductor Research and Devel. Lab., Phoenix, 1985—; instr. Rio Salado Community Coll., Phoenix, 1984—, Brigham Young U. Extension, Salt Lake City, 1975-81, Highline Coll., Midway, Wash., 1967-69. Voting del. Salt Lake County Rep. Conv., 1973. Mem. Am. Statis. Assn. (2d v.p. Utah chpt., pres. Ariz. chpt. 1988—), Am. Soc. Quality Control (vice chair Phoenix sect. 1989-90, chair Phoenix sect. 1990-91), Sigma Xi. Home: 2308 W Sagebrush Dr Chandler AZ 85224-2155

SUFFIELD, FREDERICK GLANVILLE, consulting engineer; b. Chgo., Oct. 22, 1920; s. Frederick and Harriett (Schaeffer) S.; m. Patricia Dolores, July 4, 1981. Student pvt. tutors, equivalent to B.S. in Physics and M.B.A. Registered profl. engr., Calif. Engr. Westinghouse, Balt., 1940-46; cons. engr. Los Angeles, 1946-49; chief engr. The Houston Corp. and RCA, W. Coast div., Los Angeles, 1949-52; dept. head The RAND Corp., Santa Monica, Calif., 1952-57; project mgr. Hughes Aircraft, Culver City, Calif., 1957-63; mgr. dept. TRW Inc., Redondo Beach, Calif., 1963-68; tech. and mgmt. cons., Los Angeles, 1969-70; cons. FGS & Assocs., Los Angeles/San Diego, 1970-85, Sequim, Washington, 1986—. Contbr. articles to profl. jours.; patentee in field. Mem. planning commn. City of Sequim, 1988-89. Fellow AIAA (assoc.), IEEE (sr., bd. dirs. 1981-82, Nominations and Appointments Com., 1983-84, Centennial medal 1984), Radio Club of Am., Inc., Air Force Assn.; mem. Assn. Old Crows, Fund Coms (life), Masons. Republican. Avocations: photography, flying. Home: 227 Fairway Dr Sequim WA 98382-9371

SUGANUMA, ERIC KAZUTO, music educator, missionary; b. Honolulu, Dec. 28, 1958; s. Henry Yozo and Barbara Kazue (Miyoshi) S. BEd, U. Hawaii, 1989. Piano tuner, technician, 1980—; music tchr. Hokulani Elem. Sch., Honolulu, 1990; trumpet, trombone and euphonium player 25th Inf. Div. Band, Honolulu, 1977-80; euphonium player 111th Army NG Band, Honolulu, 1982-92; trombonist Celebrant Singers, Visalia, Calif., 1990—; mem. 40th inf. divsn. (mechanized) band Army N.G., 1992—. Chmn. properties com. Olivet Bapt. Ch., Hawaii, 1985; minister of music and youth, Honolulu Bapt. Ch., 1989-90. Mem. Internat. Trombone Assn., Tubist Universal Brotherhood Assn., Piano Technician Guild, Golden Key, Phi Kappa Phi (one of Oustanding Young Men of Am.). Home: 17803 McNab Ave Bellflower CA 90706-7014

SUGERMAN, RICHARD ALAN, anatomy educator, administrator, researcher; b. San Diego, Oct. 10, 1944; s. David and Betty (Starr) S.; m. Beverly Elaine Katz, Mar. 25, 1972; children: Benjamin Eli, Rachel Estelle. B.A., Calif. State U.-San Diego, 1967; M.S., U. N.Mex., 1971, Ph.D., 1975. Asst. prof. Wichita State U. (Kans.), 1975-80; asst. prof. Coll. Osteo. Medicine of the Pacific, Pomona, Calif., 1980-84, assoc. prof., 1984-92, prof., 1992—, chmn. research com., 1982-84, dir. continuing edn., 1983-87, dir. continuing med. edn., 1984-87, chmn. facility planning com., 1986-87, coord. neurosensory system, 1981-90, coord. renal system, 1990—, head anatomy group, 1984, 1987-88, mem. long range planning com., 1986, chmn. grievance com., 1987-88, mem. faculty coun., 1990, chmn., 1992-93. Author lab. manual Human Anatomy, 1979, also articles. With Army N.G., 1968-74; capt. USAR, 1982—; maj. USAR, 1991. Grantee Wichita State U., 1975-79, Coll. Osteo. Medicine of Pacific, 1983—. Mem. Soc. for Neurosci., Sigma Xi (pres. Wichita State U. 1979), Phi Sigma. Democrat. Jewish. Office: Coll Osteo Medicine of Pacific College Plz Pomona CA 91766-1853

SUGIKI, SHIGEMI, ophthalmologist, educator; b. Wailuku, Hawaii, May 12, 1936; s. Sentaro and Kameno (Matoba) S.; AB, Washington U., St. Louis, 1957, M.D., 1961; m. Bernice T. Murakami, Dec. 28, 1958; children: Kevin S., Boyd R. Intern St. Luke's Hosp., St. Louis, 1961-62, resident ophthalmology, Washington U., St. Louis, 1962-65; chmn. dept. ophthalmology Straub Clinic, Honolulu, 1965-70, Queen's Med. Ctr., Honolulu, 1970-73, 80-83, 88-90, 93—; assoc. clin. prof. ophthalmology Sch. Medicine, U. Hawaii, 1973—. Served to maj. M.C., AUS, 1968-70. Decorated Hawaiian NG Commendation medal, 1968. Fellow ACS; mem. Am., Hawaii med. assns., Honolulu County Med. Soc., Am. Acad. Ophthalmology, Contact Lens Assn. Opthalmologists, Pacific Coast Oto-Ophthal. Soc., Pan-Pacific Surg. Assn., Am. Soc. Cataract and Refractive Surgery, Am. Glaucoma Soc., Internat. Assn. Ocular Surgeons, Am. Soc. Contemporary Ophthalmology, Washington U. Eye Alumni Assn., Hawaii Ophthal. Soc., Rsch. To Prevent Blindness. Home: 2398 Aina Lani Pl Honolulu HI 96822-2024 Office: 1380 Lusitana St Ste 714 Honolulu HI 96813-2449

SUHL, HARRY, physics educator; b. Leipzig, Fed. Republic Germany, Oct. 18, 1922; s. Bernhard and Klara (Bergwerk) S.; widowed. BSc, U. Wales, 1943; PhD, U. Oxford, 1948, DSc (hon.), 1970. Temp. exptl. officer British Admiralty, England, 1943-46; mem. tech. staff Bell Labs., Murray Hill, N.J., 1948-60; prof. physics U. Calif.-San Diego, La Jolla, 1961—; cons. Aerospace Corp., El Segundo, Calif., 1961—, Exxon Research & Engring., Clinton Twp., N.J., 1977—. Editor (with others) book series: Magnetism, 1961-74; editor (mag.): Solid State Communication, 1961—. Guggenheim fellow, 1968-69, NSF fellow, 1971. Fellow Am. Phys. Soc.; mem. Nat. Acad. Scis., Calif. Catalysis Soc. Office: U Calif Dept Physics 9500 Gilman Dr La Jolla CA 92093

SUINN, RICHARD MICHAEL, psychologist; b. Honolulu, May 8, 1933; s. Maurice and Edith (Wong) S.; m. Grace D. Toy, July 26, 1958; children: Susan, Randall, Staci, Bradley. Student, U. Hawaii, 1951-53; B.A. summa cum laude, Ohio State U., 1955; MA in Clin. Psychology, Stanford U., 1957, PhD in Clin. Psychology, 1959. Lic. psychologist, Colo. Counselor Stanford (Calif.) U., 1958-59, rsch. assoc. Med. Sch., 1964-66; asst. prof. psychology Whitman Coll., Walla Walla, Wash., 1959-64; assoc. prof. U. Hawaii, Honolulu, 1966-68; prof. Colo. State U., Ft. Collins, 1968—, head dept. psychology, 1972-93; cons. in field; psychologist U.S. Ski Teams, 1976 Olympic Games, U.S. Women's Track and Field, 1980 Olympic games, U.S. Ski Jumping Team, 1988; mem. sports psychology adv. com. U.S. Olympic Com., 1983-89; reviewer NIMH, 1977-80. Author: The Predictive Validity of Projective Measures, 1969, Fundamentals of Behavior Pathology, 1970, The Innovative Psychological Therapies, 1975, The Innovative Medical-Psychiatric Therapies, 1976, Psychology in Sport: Methods and Applications, 1980, Fundamentals of Abnormal Psychology, 1984, 88, Seven Steps to Peak Performance, 1986, Anxiety Management Training, 1991; editorial bd.: Jour. Cons. and Clin. Psychology, 1973-86, Jour. Counseling Psychology, 1974-91, Behavior Therapy, 1977-80, Behavior Modification, 1977-78, Jour. Behavioral Medicine, 1978—, Behavior Counseling Quar., 1979-83, Jour. Sports Psychology, 1980—; author: tests Math. Anxiety Rating Scale, Suinn Test Anxiety Behavior Scale, Suinn-Lew Asian Self-identity Acculturation Scale. Mem. City Council, Ft. Collins, 1975-79, mayor, 1978-79; mem. Gov.'s Mental Health Adv. Council, 1983, Colo. Bd. Psychologist Examiners, 1983-86. Recipient cert. merit U.S. Ski Team, 1976; NIMH grantee, 1963-64; Office Edn. grantee, 1970-71. Fellow APA (chmn. bd. ethnic minority affairs 1982-83, chmn. edn. and tng. bd. 1986-87, policy and planning bd. 1987-89, bd. dirs. 1990-93), Behavior Therapy and Rsch. Soc. (charter); mem. Assn. for Advancement Psychology (trustee 1983-86), Assn. for Advancement Behavior Therapy (sec.-treas. 1986-89, pres.-elect 1991, pres. 1992-93), Asian Am. Psychol. Assn. (bd. dirs. 1983-88), Am. Bd. Behavior Therapy (bd. dirs. 1987—), Phi Beta Kappa, Sigma Xi. Home: 808 Cheyenne Dr Fort Collins CO 80525-1560 Office: Colo State U Dept Psychology Fort Collins CO 80523

SUKO, LONNY RAY, lawyer; b. Spokane, Wash., Oct. 12, 1943; s. Ray R. and Leila B. (Snyder) S.; m. Marcia A. Michaelsen, Aug. 26, 1967; children—Jolynn R., David M. B.A., Wash. State U., 1965; J.D., U. Idaho, 1968. Bar: Wash. 1968, U.S. Dist. Ct. (ea. dist.) Wash. 1969, U.S. Dist. Ct. (we. dist.) Wash. 1978, U.S. Ct. Appeals (9th cir.) 1978. Law clk. U.S. Dist. Ct. Ea. Dist. Wash., 1968-69; assoc. Lyon, Beaulaurier & Aaron, Yakima, Wash., 1969-72; ptnr. Lyon, Beaulaurier, Weigand, Suko & Gustafson, Yakima, 1972-91, Lyon, Weigand, Suko & Gustafson, P.S., 1991—; U.S. magistrate, Yakima, 1971-91. Mem. Wash. State Trial Lawyers Assn., Wash. Council Sch. Attys., Phi Beta Kappa, Phi Kappa Phi, Phi Eta Sigma. Office: PO Box 1689 Yakima WA 98907-1689

SUKOV, RICHARD JOEL, radiologist; b. Mpls., Nov. 13, 1944; s. Marvin and Annette (Ivry) S.; m. Susan Judith Grossman, Aug. 11, 1968; children: Stacy Faye, Jessica Erin. BA, BS, U. Minn., 1967, MD, 1970; student, U. Calif.-Berkeley, 1962-64. Lic. physician, Minn., D.C., Calif.; diplomate Am. Bd. Radiology. Intern pediatrics U. Minn., Mpls., 1970-71; resident radiology UCLA Ctr. for Health Sci., 1973-76; fellow in ultrasound and computed tomography UCLA, 1976-77; staff radiologist Centinela Hosp. Med. Ctr., Inglewood, Calif., 1977-85, Daniel Freeman Marina Hosp. Med. Ctr., Marina del Rey, Calif., 1980—; dir. radiology Daniel Freeman Marina Hosp. Med. Ctr., Inglewood, Calif., 1988-90; asst. clin. prof. radiology UCLA Ctr. for Health Scis., 1977-83; adv. bd. Aerobics and Fitness Assn. Am., 1983—. Contbr. articles to profl. jours. Vol. Venice Family Clinic, 1985—. Lt. comdr. USPHS, 1970-72. U. Minn. fellow, 1964-65, 66, 70. Mem. AMA, Royal Soc. Medicine, Soc. Radiologists in Ultrasound (charter), Minn. Med. Alumni Assn., Los Angeles County Med. Assn., Calif. Med. Assn., Radiol. Soc. N.Am., L.A. Radiol. Soc. (continuing edn. com. 1990—, treas.), L.A. Ultrasound Soc., Am. Coll. Radiology. Office: Inglewood Radiology 323 N Prairie Ave Ste 160 Inglewood CA 90301-4597

SULENTIC, DANIEL MCINTYRE, contractor; b. Waterloo, Iowa, Apr. 20, 1964; s. Anton Roger Sulentic and Cathie (Davidson) Waugh. Grad., high sch. Ptnr. BCR Constrn., Denison, Tex., 1985-86; foreman LARCO Constrn., Anaheim, Calif., 1991-92; owner Suncastle Constrn., Garden Grove, Calif., 1992—. With USMC, 1987-91, Saudi Arabia. Decorated

D.S.M. with 2 bronze stars. Office: Suncastle Constrn 10425 Dozier Dr Garden Grove CA 92643

SULLIVAN, CLAIRE FERGUSON, marketing educator; b. Pittsburg, Tex., Sept. 28, 1937; d. Almon Lafayette and Mabel Clara (Williams) Potter; m. Richard Wayne Ferguson, Jan. 31, 1959 (div. Jan. 1980); 1 child, Mark Jeffrey Ferguson; m. David Edward Sullivan, Nov. 2, 1984. BBA, U. Tex., 1958, MBA, 1961; PhD, U. North Tex., 1973; grad., Harvard Inst. Ednl. Mgmt., 1991. Instr. So. Meth. U., Dallas, 1965-70; asst. prof. U. Utah, Salt Lake City, 1972-74; assoc. prof. U. Ark., Little Rock, 1974-77, U. Tex., Arlington, 1977-80, Ill. State U., Normal, 1980-84; prof., chmn. mktg. Bentley Coll., Waltham, Mass., 1984-89; dean sch. bus. Met. State Coll. Denver, 1989-92, prof. mktg., 1992—; cons. Denver Partnership, 1989-90, Gen. Tel. Co., Irving, Tex., 1983, McKnight Pub. Co., Bloomington, Ill., 1983, dental practitioner, Bloomington, 1982-83, Olympic Fed., Berwyn, Ill., 1982, Denver Partnership Econ. Devel. Adv. Coun., 1989-91; mem. African-Am. Leadership Inst. Gov. Bd. Contbr. mktg. articles to profl. jours. Direct Mktg. Inst. fellow, 1981; Ill. State U. rsch. grantee, 1981-83. Mem. Am. Mktg. Assn. (faculty fellow 1984-85), So. Mktg. Assn., Southwestern Mktg. Assn., Denver World Trade Ctr., Denver Partnership (econ. devel. adv. bd.), Rotary, Beta Gamma Sigma. Republican. Methodist. Home: 4715 W 11th St Greeley CO 80634 Office: Met State Coll Dept Mktg MSCD Box 79 PO Box 173362 Denver CO 80217-3362

SULLIVAN, CORNELIUS WAYNE, marine biology researcher, educator; b. Pitts., June 11, 1943; s. John Wayne and Hilda Sullivan; m. Jill Hajjar, Oct. 28, 1966; children: Shane, Preston, Chelsea. BS in Biochemistry, Pa. State U., 1965, MS in Microbiology, 1967; PhD in Marine Biology, Scripps Inst. Oceanography, 1971. Postdoctoral fellow Scripps Inst. Oceanography, La Jolla, Calif., 1971-74; asst. prof. marine biology U. So. Calif., L.A., 1974-80, assoc. prof., 1980-85, prof., 1985—, dir. marine biology sect., 1982-91; dir. Hancock Inst. Marine Studies, L.A., 1991-93; dir. Office of Polar Programs Nat. Sci. Found., Washington, 1993—; vis. prof. U. Colo., Boulder, 1981-82, MIT, Cambridge, 1981-82; field team leader Sea Ice Microbial Communities Studies, McMurdo Sound, Antarctica, 1980-86; chief scientist/cruise coord. Antartic Marine Ecosystem Rsch. at the Ice Edge Zone Project, Weddell Sea, 1983, 86, 88; mem. BIOMASS Working Party on Pack-Ice Zone Studies, 1983-86, ecol. rsch. rev. bd. Dept. Navy, 1982-85; So. Ocean Ecology Group Specialist Sci. Com. on Antarctic Rsch.; chmn. SCOR working group 86 "Sea Ice Ecology" sci. com. on oceanic rsch.; mem. polar rsch. bd. NAS, 1983-86; chmn. com. to evaluate polar rsch. platforms Nat. Rsch. Coun., 1985—. Editorial bd. Jour. Microbiol. Methods, 1982-85, Polar Biology, 1987—; contbr. articles to profl. jours. USPHS fellow; recipient Antarctic Service Medal of U.S., NSF, 1981. Office: U So Calif Dept Biol Scis University Pk Los Angeles CA 90089-0371

SULLIVAN, DENNIS JOHN, consulting company owner; b. Bklyn., July 5, 1940; s. John Francis and Helen M. Sullivan; m. Barbara Lynn Short, Apr. 29, 1968; 1 child, Patrick John. BA, Fairleigh Dickinson U., 1965; MS, U. So. Calif., 1972. Lead engr. Matrix Corp., Arlington, Va., 1965-66; mem. tech. staff Bunker Ramo Corp., Westlake Village, Calif., 1966-71; rsch. psychologist Hughes Aircraft Co., L.A., 1971-76; sr. scientist Canyon Rsch.Group, Westlake Village, 1976-79; sr. v.p. Am. Productivity & Quality Ctr., Houston, 1979-80; exec. scientist Vreuls Rsch. Corp., Thousand Oaks, Calif., 1980-86; sr. analyst United Airlines Svc. Corp., Denver, 1986-88; pres. Sunavia, Inc., 1988—; mgr. program Hernandez Engring., Inc., Denver, 1989-91; asst. prof. Calif. State U., L.A., 1977; cons. in field. Contbr. articles to profl. jours. With U.S. Army, 1963-65, Vietnam. Mem. Nat. Soc. Performance and Instruction, Soc. Applied Learning Tech., Am. Assn. Artificial Intelligence. Office: Sunavia Inc Hangar 9 Box B-5 7375 S Peoria St Englewood CO 80112

SULLIVAN, G. CRAIG, chemical executive; b. 1940. BS, Boston Coll., 1964. With Proctor & Gamble Co., 1964-69, Am. Express Co., 1969-70; regional sales mgr. Clorox Co., Oakland, Calif., 1971-76, v.p. mktg., 1976-78, mgr. food svc. sales devel., mgr. bus. devel., 1978-79, gen. mgr. food svc. products divsn., 1979-81, v.p. food svc. products divsn., 1981, v.p. household products, 1981-89, group v.p. household products, 1989-92, chmn. bd., CEO, 1992—. Office: The Clorox Co 1221 Broadway Oakland CA 94623-1837*

SULLIVAN, GEORGE ANERSON, orthodontist; b. Bon Aqua, Tenn.; s. Joe Marble and Ruby Christine (Luther) S.; m. Edith Melvina Timmons, May 11, 1957; children: Scott Patrick, Shawn Michael. AS, Henry Ford Community Coll., Dearborn, Mich., 1957; student, Eastern Mich. U., 1958-59; DDS, U. Mich., 1963, MS, 1966. Diplomate Am. Bd. Orthodontics. Pvt. practice specializing in orthodontics Phoenix, 1966—; pres. Ammons Meml. Dental Clinic, Phoenix, 1979-80. Chmn. Phoenix Meml. Hosp., 1977-80. Served with USNR, 1955-63. Mem. Am. Assn. Orthodontics, Cen. Ariz. Dental Soc., Ariz. State Dental Assn., ADA, Ariz. Orthodontic Soc., Pacific Coast Soc. Orthodontics, Optimist Club (pres. Phoenix chpt. 1967-68), Lions (pres. 1972-73), Elks. Republican. Office: 4909 N 44th St Ste E Phoenix AZ 85018-2767 also: 4805 W Thomas Rd Ste D Phoenix AZ 85031 also: 10752 N 69th Pl Ste 111 Scottsdale AZ 85260

SULLIVAN, GERALD JAMES, insurance company executive; b. Olympia, Wash., Sept. 30, 1937; s. John F. and Elizabeth J. (Yater) S.; B.B.A., U. Wash., 1959; M.B.A., Wharton Sch. U. Pa., 1966; m. Wendy D. Edmunds, Sept. 2, 1987; children—Gerald James, Thomas, Katheleen, Shannon. Security analyst Hartford Ins. Group (Conn.), 1966-67; chief dep. ins. commr. State of Wash., Olympia, 1967-68; sec. John F. Sullivan Co., Seattle, 1968-71; pres. Walker Sullivan Co., Los Angeles, 1971-80, chmn., 1979; chmn. bd., pres. Gerald J. Sullivan & Assocs., Inc., ins. brokers, 1980—; mem. exec. com., chmn. security com. Calif. Surplus Lines Assns., San Francisco, 1974; mem. NAIC Industry Adv. Com. on Surplus Lines Laws and Reins. Served to capt. USAF, 1959-64. C.P.C.U., C.L.U. Roman Catholic. Clubs: Wilshire Country, Jonathan, Calif., Stock Exchange, K.C. Author: Trends in International Reinsurance Affecting American Reinsurers, 1966. Office: 800 W 6th St Los Angeles CA 90017-2704

SULLIVAN, JAMES AUSTIN, landscape contractor, writer; b. Santa Rosa, Calif., Sept. 18, 1936; s. Harvey and Elizabeth (Staats) S.; m. Rewa Gilmoure, 1970 (div. 1976); 1 child, Maya-Li; m. Linda E. Parker. Cert., Inst. European Studies, Vienna, Austria, 1957; BS, U. Notre Dame, 1958. Lic. contractor, Calif. Free lance writer Santa Barbara, Calif., 1962—; gen. mgr. New Age Natural Foods, San Francisco, 1967-71, cons., 1968-74; owner Jim Sullivan Landscaping, Bodega, Calif., 1971-91; free lance writer Bodega, 1991—; ptnr. Inch Worm Press, Bodega, 1992. Writer (column) Bodega Bay Naviagtor, 1986-92; contbr. articles to mags., newspaper and quars. Bd. dirs. Land Trust C.O.A.A.S.T. Sonoma County Tomorrow Inst. for Better Health, 1979-85; founding pres. Western Sonoma County Rural Alliance, 1979, Sonoma County Farm Lands Group, 1980; bd. dirs. Sonoma County Conservation Action, 1992. 1st lt. U.S. Army, 1958-62. Recipient cert. of appreciation Sonoma County Farm Land Group, 1984; grantee Sonoma County Land Trust, 1983. Mem. Calif. Landscape Contractors Assn. Democrat. Home and Office: Inch Worm Press PO Box 92 Bodega CA 94922

SULLIVAN, JAMES JEROME, lawyer, consultant; b. Fargo, N.D., Feb. 23, 1943; m. Roberta Jean Ranes, Nov. 8, 1980; children: Kristen, Jason, Eric, Amy. PhB, U. N.D., 1966, JD, 1970. Bar: N.D. 1970, Wash. 1982. Atty. Northwestern Nat. Life Ins. Co., Mpls., 1970-73; regional counsel Econ. Devel. Admin. of U.S. Dept. Commerce, Seattle, 1973-90; pvt. practice Bellevue and Issaquah, Wash., 1986—. Editor, contbr. articles to numerous periodicals. Recipient numerous legal awards. Mem. Wash. State Bar Assn. Home: 11110 NE 38th Pl Bellevue WA 98004-7653 Office: 800 Bellevue Way NE 300 MGM Bldg Bellevue WA 98004 Office: 385 Front St N Issaquah WA 98027-2929

SULLIVAN, JAMES KIRK, forest products company executive; b. Greenwood, S.C., Aug. 25, 1935; s. Daniel Jones and Addie (Brown) S.; m. Elizabeth Miller, June 18, 1960; children: Hal N., Kim J. BS in Chemistry, Clemson U., 1957, MS, 1964, PhD, 1966; postgrad. program for sr. execs., MIT, 1975; DSc (hon.), U. Idaho, 1990. Prodn. supr. FMC Corp., South Charleston, W.Va., 1957-62; tech. supt. FMC Corp., Pocatello, Idaho, 1966-69; mktg. mgr. FMC Corp., N.Y.C., 1969-70; v.p. govtl. and environ. affairs Boise (Idaho) Cascade Corp., 1971—; bd. dirs. Key Bank Idaho, chmn. trust and investment com., 1983-90, exec. com., 1983—; chmn. adv. bd. U. Idaho Coll. Engring., 1966-70, 80-87, centennial campaign, 1987-89, rsch. found., 1980-82. Contbr. articles to profl. jours.; patentee in field. Mem. Coll. of Forest and Recreation Resources com. Clemson U., Idaho Found. for Pvt. Enterprise and Econ. Edn., Idaho Rsch. Found., Inc., Idaho Task Force on Higher Edn.; bd. dirs. Idaho Found. for Excellence in Higher Edn., Exptl. Program to Stimulate Competitive Rsch. NSF, N.W. Nazarene Coll., 1988-90, active Len. B. Jordan Pub. Affairs Symposium; trustee Idaho Children's Emergency Fund, 1984—, Bishop Kelly High Sch., chmn. 1987-89; chmn. Bishop Kelly Found., 1972-79, 85-89; chmn. adv. bd. U. Idaho Coll. Engring., Am. Forest and Paper Assn., Govtl. Affairs Com., Environ. Com., Future options Group; pub. affairs com. NAM; active Idaho Found. Pvt. Enterprise and Econ. Edn., 1988—; chmn. centennial campaign U. Idaho, U, Idaho Found., others; mem. environ. com. Future Options Group. 1st lt. U.S. Army, 1958-59. Recipient Presdl. Citation U. Idaho, 1990. Mem. Am. Chem. Soc., Am. Inst. Chem. Engrs., Bus. Week Found. (chmn. Bus. Week 1980), Am. Paper Isnt. (environ. steering com.), Bus. Roundtable (environ. com.), Idaho Assn. Commerce and Industry (chmn. bd. dirs.), C. of C. of U.S. (pub. affairs com.). Republican. Home: 5206 Sorrento Cir Boise ID 83704-2347 Office: Boise Cascade Corp One Jefferson Sq Boise ID 83728

SULLIVAN, JAMES N., fuel company executive; b. San Francisco, 1937. Student, U. Notre Dame, 1959. Formerly v.p. Chevron Corp., until 1988, now vice chmn., dir., 1988—. Office: Chevron Corp 225 Bush St San Francisco CA 94104-4207

SULLIVAN, KRISPIN NISSA, small business owner, nutritionist; b. Boston, July 17, 1946; d. Norman Sigvold and Viola Mae (Brown) Brugger; m. Alfred Joseph Bishop, Nov. 23, 1970 (div. 1976); 1 child, Elden Gregory; m. Eugene Michael Sullivan, Oct. 25, 1976 (div. 1979); 1 child, Bridgett Alexis. Student, U. Vt., 1964-67; Cert. Nutritionist, Nat. Inst. Nutrition Edn., Aurora, Colo., 1988. Nutritionist in pvt. practice Marin County, Calif., 1970-74; co-tchr. John F. Kennedy U., Orinda, Calif., 1975-76; nutritionist Peter Mutke, M.D., San Anselmo, Calif., 1974-76; tchr. nutritional physiology Alive & Well Sch. of C. Bodywork, San Anselmo, Calif., 1988—; nutritionist Recovery Systems, Mill Valley, Calif., 1988-90; clin. nutritionist in pvt. practice San Anselmo, 1990—; owner, formulator Middle Marin Lab., Woodacre, Calif., 1986—; cons. Super Natural Foods, Corte Madera, Calif., 1985—, Marine Minerals, Roy, Utah, 1989—, various corps.; lectr. in field. Formulator:" Metabasic (enhances healing time), 1988, Aminogold (athletic recovery), others; author: Imagine This, 1992. Expert witness Calif. Child Abuse Commn., Sacramento, 1984—;vol. counselor for abuse victims in ct. Marin County, 1985—. Mem. Soc. of Cert. Nutritionists, Woodacre Improvement Club. Republican. Home: 230 Redwood Woodacre CA 94973 Office: Middle Marin Lab PO Box 961 Woodacre CA 94973

SULLIVAN, MICHAEL EVAN, investment and management company executive; b. Phila., Dec. 30, 1940; s. Albert and Ruth (Liebert) S.; BS, N.Mex. State U., 1966, MA (Ednl. Research Tng. Program fellow), 1967; BS, U. Tex., 1969; MBA, U. Houston, 1974; MS, U. So. Calif., 1976, MPA, 1977, PhD in Adminstrn., 1983; BS in Acctg., U. La Verne, 1981. Sr. adminstrv. and tech. analyst Houston Lighting & Power Co., 1969-74; electronics engr. U.S. Govt., Point Mugu, Calif., 1974-77; mem. tech. staff Hughes Aircraft Co., El Segundo, Calif., 1977-78; staff program adminstr. Ventura div. Northrop Corp., Newbury Park, Calif., 1978-79; div. head engring. div. Navastrogru, Point Mugu, 1979-82; br. head, div. head spl. programs head operational systems integraton office Pacific Missile Test Ctr., Calif., 1983-90; CNO, Dir. Rsch., Devel., and Acquisition in the Pentagon, Washington, 1987-88, dir. rsch. devel. test and evaluation and tech. in the Pentagon, 1990—; pres., chmn. bd. Diversified Mgmt. Systems, Inc., Camarillo, Calif., 1978—. Author: The Management of Research, Development, Test and Evaluation Organizations; Organizational Behavior Characteristics of Supervisors-Public versus Private Sectors, Organizational Behavior Characteristics of Supervisors, Public versus Private Sectors; Self-Actualization in RDT & E Organizations; Self-Actualization in a Health Care Agency; others. V.p., bd. dirs. Ventura County Master Chorale and Opera Assn; bd. dirs. Southern Calif. Assn. of Pub. Adminstrn. (also mem. fin. com., programs com., student aid com.). Served with U.S. Army, 1958-62. Ednl. Research Info. Clearing House fellow, 1965-67. Mem. IEEE, Am. Math. Soc., Math. Assn. Am., Am. Statis. Assn., IEEE Engring. Mgmt. Soc., Am. Soc. Pub. Adminstrn., So. Calif. Assn. Pub. Adminstrn. (bd. dirs., various coms.), Am. Personnel and Guidance Assn., Fed. Mgrs. Assn., Am. Assn. Individual Investors, Mcpl. Mgmt. Assts. So. Calif., Acad. Polit. Sci., Internat. Soc. for the Systems Scis., Assn. MBA Execs., Internat. Fedn. for Systems Rsch., Phi Kappa Phi, Pi Gamma Mu. Home: PO Box 273 Port Hueneme CA 93044-0273 Office: PO Box 447 Camarillo CA 93010

SULLIVAN, MICHAEL JOHN, governor, lawyer; b. Omaha, Sept. 23, 1939; s. Joseph Byrne and Margaret (Hamilton) S.; m. Jane Metzler, Sept. 2, 1961; children: Michelle, Patrick, Theresa. BS in Petroleum Engring., U. Wyo., 1961, JD, 1964. Bar: Wyo. 1964. Assoc. Brown, Drew, Apostolos, Barton & Massey, Casper, Wyo., 1964-67; ptnr. Brown, Drew, Apostolos, Massey & Sullivan, Casper, 1967—; gov. State of Wyo., Casper, 1987—. Trustee St. Joseph's Children's Home, Torrington, Wyo., 1986-87; bd. dirs. Natrona County Meml. Hosp., Casper, 1976-86. Mem. ABA, Wyo. Bar Assn., Assn. Trial Lawyers Am., Wyo. Trial Lawyers Assn., Rotary (pres. Casper club). Democrat. Roman Catholic. Home: 5001 Central Ave Cheyenne WY 82002-0001 Office: Office of Gov State Capitol Cheyenne WY 82002*

SULLIVAN, MICHAEL JOHN, finance educator; b. Rochester, N.Y., May 13, 1957; s. Paul Anthony and Louise (Folker) S. BS, St. John Fisher Coll., 1979; MBA, U. Fla., 1982; PhD, Fla. State U., 1989. Account exec. Merrill Lynch, Gainesville, Fla., 1982-83; v.p. First Realty Group, Inc., Bethesda, Md., 1983-85; instr. Fla. State U., Tallahassee, 1985-88; asst. prof. Auburn (Ala.) U., 1989-91, U. Nev., Las Vegas, 1991—; Presenter in field, 1987—. Contbr. articles to profl. jours.; author proceedings; reviewer various profl. jours. Homer Hoyt Rsch. grantee Homer Hoyt Ctr., Tallahassee, 1986. Mem. Fin. Mgmt. Assn. Republican. Home: PO Box 71751 Las Vegas NV 89170-1751 Office: U Nev Las Vegas 4505 Maryland Pkwy Las Vegas NV 89154-6008

SULLIVAN, PATRICK ALLEN, strategic management educator; b. Peoria, Ill., Oct. 31, 1932; s. Francis Richard and Carmela Marie (Smith) S.; m. Gwendolyn Jo Herndon, Aug. 25, 1958; children: Richard John, Sharon Louise Little, Patrick Michael, Cecelia Anne, Catherine Marie Markee. BCE, Marquette U., 1955; MBA, San Diego State U., 1975; DBA, U.S. Internat. U., San Diego, 1988. Engr. USMC, 29 Palms, Calif., 1958-63; engr. USN, San Diego, 1963-67, mgmt. analyst, 1967-88; asst. prof. strategic mgmt. U.S. Internat. U., San Diego, 1988-89, assoc. prof. strategic mgmt., 1989—; ptnr. Sullivan and Assocs. Mgmt. Cons., San Diego, 1988-89. Pres. St. Pius Ch. Parish Coun., Chula Vista, Calif., 1984. 1st lt. USMC, 1955-58. Mem. ASCE, Acad. Mgmt., Strategic Mgmt. Soc. Planning Forum, K.C., Chi Epsilon, Tau Beta Pi, Sigma Iota Epsilon, Beta Gamma Sigma. Democrat. Roman Catholic. Home: 98 E Emerson St Chula Vista CA 91911-3545

SULLIVAN, ROBERT SCOTT, architect; b. Alexandria, La., Sept. 8, 1955; s. Robert Wallace and Harriette Henri (Fedric) S. BA cum laude, Tulane U., 1979, BArch, 1979. Registered architect, N.Y., Calif.; cert. Nat. Coun. of Archtl. Registrations Bds. Staff architect Cavitt, McKnight, Weymouth, Inc., Houston, 1979-81, Hardy, Holzman, Pfeiffer Assocs., N.Y.C., 1981-83; ptnr. Sullivan, Briggs Assocs., N.Y.C., 1983-86; project architect Butler, Rogers, Baskett, N.Y.C., 1985-86; prin. R. Scott Sullivan AIA, Berkeley, Calif., 1986-89; ptnr. Talbott Sullivan Architects, Albany, Calif., 1989—; cons. Neometry Graphics, N.Y.C., 1983-86, dir, 1986—; dir. Middleton/Sullivan Inc., Alexandria, 1981—. Works include specific design projects at N.Y. Hist. Soc. exhibit Grand Cen. Terminal, N.Y.C., 1982, The Houston Sch. of Performing Visual Arts, 1980, The Pingry Sch., Bernards Twp., N.J., 1982, Arts Ctr. at Oak Knoll Sch., Summit, N.J., 1986. Vestry member St. Mark's Episc. Ch., Berkeley, 1988-89; bd. dirs. The Parsonage, Episcopal Diocese Calif., 1992—; cons. Commn. Accessibility, Episcopal Diocese Calif., 1991—. Mem. AIA, Calif. Council Architects, Archtl. League N.Y.C., Nat. Trust for Hist. Preservation, Victorian Soc. in Am., Tau Sigma Delta. Democrat. Episcopalian. Home: 1060 Sterling Ave Berkeley CA 94708 Office: 1323 Solano Ave Albany CA 94706

SULLIVAN, STUART FRANCIS, anesthesiologist, educator; b. Buffalo, July 15, 1928; s. Charles S. and Kathryn (Duggan) S.; m. Dorothy Elizabeth Faytol, Apr. 18, 1959; children: John, Irene, Paul, Kathryn. BS, Canisius Coll., 1950; MD, SUNY, Syracuse, 1955. Diplomate Am. Bd. Anesthesiology. Intern Ohio State Univ. Hosp., Columbus, 1955-56; resident Columbia Presbyn. Med. Ctr., 1958-60; instr. Coll. of Physicians and Surgeons Columbia U., N.Y.C., 1961-62; assoc., 1962-64; assoc. prof. Columbia Presbyn. Med. Ctr., Columbus, 1967-73; prof., vice-chmn. dept. anesthesiology Sch. Medicine UCLA, 1973-91, acting chmn., 1983-84, 87-88, 90-91, prof. emeritus, 1991—. Served to capt. M.C., USAR, 1956-58. Fellow NIH, 1960-61; recipient research career devel. award NIH, 1966-69. Mem. Assn. Univ. Anesthetists, Am. Physiol. Soc., Am. Soc. Anesthesiologists. Home: 101 Foxtail Dr Santa Monica CA 90402-2047 Office: UCLA Sch Medicine Dept Anesthesiology Los Angeles CA 90024-1778

SULLIVAN, WHITNEY BRAYTON, municipal court judge; b. Pueblo, Colo., Jan. 6, 1922; s. Clyde A. Sullivan and Lucy Estelle (Patch) Johnson; m. Virginia Ruth Lower, July 27, 1946; children: Kerry Jay, Carol Anne, Brian Gordon. BBA, U. N.Mex., 1948; grad., Air War Coll., 1968; post-grad., Nat. Jud. Coll., Reno, Nev., 1976-87, Am. Acad. Jud. Edn., Boulder, Colo., 1981. Appointed county ct. judge Gov. Lamm Colo. State Jud. Dept., 1976,. Commd. 2d lt. USAAF, 1943; advanced through grades to lt. col. USAF, 1965, served in CBI, ETO, 1943-46, officer, pilot various locations including Korea, 1946-53, officer, sr. pilot U. Utah ROTC, 1953-56, command pilot SAC, 1956-72, ret., 1972; county ct. judge Colo. State Jud. Dept., Westcliffe, 1977-92; mcpl. ct. judge Towns of Westcliffe and Silver Cliff, Colo., 1984-87, 89—; jud. planning com. Colo. State Jud. Dept., Denver, 1985-87; faculty adviser Nat. Jud. Coll., 1987-89; 1st pres. Custer County Airport Authority; founder Custer County Credit Union. Editor: The Gavel, 1982-83; contbr. to profl. publs. Pres. Wet Mountain Valley Rotary Club, Westcliffe, 1974-75; chmn. County Centennial/Bicentennial Com., Westcliffe, 1975-76. Recipient 7 decorations, 17 medals USAF, pilot wings RAF, 1943. Mem. Nat. Judges Assn. (exec. dir., pres. 1982-83, McEachern Meml. award for Outstanding Non-Atty. Judge in U.S. 1987), Colo. Assn. County Judges (pres. 1984-85), Westcliffe Ctr. for Arts (pres. 1990-91), Post Master Masonic Lodge. Republican. Methodist. Home: 42 Little Horn Rd Westcliffe CO 81252-9693

SULLIVAN, WILLIAM JAMES, university president; b. Freeport, Ill., Dec. 20, 1930; s. Arlend Eugene and Bessie (Burton) S. B.A. in Philosophy, St. Louis U., 1954, M.A. in Philosophy, 1956, Ph.L., 1956; S.T.L., Faculté de Theologie, Lyons, France, 1962; M.A., Yale U., 1966, M.Phil. in Religious Studies, 1967, Ph.D. in Religious Studies, 1971; D.D. (hon.), Concordia Sem. in Exile, 1977. Joined S.J., Roman Cath. Ch. Tchr. classical lang. Creighton Prep. Sch., 1955-58; asst. prof. theology Marquette U., 1967-71; dean Sch. Div., St. Louis U., 1971-75; provost Seattle U., 1975-76, pres., 1976—; bd. dirs. Internat. Fedn. Catholic Univs., 1978-88, Maryville Coll., 1972-75, Am. Council Edn., 1978-81, U. San Francisco, 1976-84; founder, bd. dirs. Wash. Student Loan Guaranty Assn.; trustee Carnegie Found. Advancement of Teaching, 1985—; mem. Wash. State Higher Edn. Facilities Authority, 1984—, Wash. State Math. Coalition, co-chair with Gov. Gardner, 1990—, Wash. State Coalition for Student Svc., 1990—; bd. dirs. U.S. Bank of Wash. Contbr. articles on theology, edn. and cultural topics to profl. jours., popular publs. Bd. dirs. World Without War Council, Seattle, 1978-81; bd. dirs. Seattle United Way, 1979-81, Creighton U., 1982-86, Loyola U. Chgo., 1983-87; chmn. host com. 1990 Goodwill Games, 1986-90. Recipient Edmund Campion award Campion High Sch., 1970; Pope John XXIII award Viterbo Coll., 1979; Brotherhood award NCCJ, 1981; Torch of Liberty award Anti-Defamation League, B'nai Brith; named Seattle First Citizen, 1990. Mem. Assn. Cath. Colls. and Univs. (bd. dirs. 1986—), Nat. Assn. Ind. Colls. and Univs. (bd. dirs. 1983-86), Assn. Jesuit Colls. and Univs. (bd. dirs. 1986—), Wash. Friends Higher Edn., Ind. Colls. Wash., Seattle C. of C. (dir. 1979-82, 88—). Catholic. Clubs: Rainier, Seattle Yacht, Columbia Tower (bd. dirs.), University (Seattle). Lodge: Rotary (Seattle). Home and Office: Seattle U Broadway and Madison Seattle WA 98122

SULLIVAN-BOYLE, KATHLEEN MARIE, association administrator; b. Tulsa, Feb. 9, 1958; d. Thomas Anthony and Jeanne Lee (Agnew) Sullivan; m. Thomas C. Boyle. BS in Polit. Sci., Ariz. State U., 1980; MA in Govt., Coll. William and Mary, 1982. Sec. Ariz. Rep. Party, Phoenix, 1980-81; rsch. asst. Pete Dunn for U.S. Senate Campaign, Phoenix, 1982; adminstr. sec Ariz. Corp. Commn., Phoenix, 1983-84; pub. relations dir. Epoch Univs. Publ., Phoenix, 1984-86; membership dir. Tempe (Ariz.) C. of C., 1986—. Sec., chmn. publicity Cactus Wren Rep. Women, Phoenix, 1983-80, Fiesta Bowl. Mem. Soroptimist (past pres.), Pub. Rels. Soc. Am., Alpha Phi. (chmn. conv.). Republican. Office: Tempe C of C 60 E 5th St # 3 Tempe AZ 85281-3633

SUMIDA, GERALD AQUINAS, lawyer; b. Hilo, Hawaii, June 19, 1944; s. Sadamu and Kimiyo (Miyahara) S.; m. Sylvia Whitehead, June 23, 1970. AB summa cum laude, Princeton U., 1966, cert. in pub. and internat. affairs, 1966; JD, Yale U., 1969. Bar: Hawaii 1970, U.S. Dist. Ct. Hawaii 1970, U.S. Ct. Appeals (9th cir.) 1970, U.S. Supreme Ct. 1981. Rsch. assoc. Ctr. Internat. Studies, Princeton U., 1969; assoc. Carlsmith, Ball, Wichman, Murray, Case, Mukai & Ichiki, Honolulu, 1970-76, ptnr., 1976—; mem. cameras in courtroom evaluation com. Hawaii Supreme Ct., 1984—. Mem. sci. and statis. com. Western Pacific Fishery Mgmt. Council, 1979—; mem. study group on law of armed conflict and the law of the sea Comdr. in Chief Pacific, U.S. Navy, 1979-82; chmn. Pacific and Asian Affairs Council Hawaii, 1991, pres., 1982-91, bd. govs., 1976—, Paul S. Bachman award, 1978; chmn. internat. com. Hawaii chpt. ARC, 1983—, bd. dirs., 1983—, vice chmn. 1990—, recipient chmn.'s cup award, 1990; vice chmn. Honolulu Com. on Fgn. Relations, 1983—; pres., dir., founding mem. Hawaii Ocean Law Assn., 1978—; mem. Hawaii Adv. Group for Law of Sea Inst., 1977—; pres. Hawaii Inst. Continuing Legal Edn., 1979-83, dir., 1976-87; pres., founding mem. Hawaii Council Legal Edn. for Youth, 1980-83, dir., 1983-88; chmn. Hawaii Commn. on Yr. 2000, 1976-79; mem. Honolulu Community Media Council, exec. com., 1976-84, legal counsel, 1979-83; bd. dirs. Hawaii Imin Centennial Corp., 1983—, Hawaii Pub. Radio, 1983-88, Legal Aid Soc. Hawaii, 1984. Mem. Pacific Alliance Trade and Devel., 1984-88; founding gov., exec. v.p., chmn. rules and procedures Ctr. Internat. Comml. Dispute Resolution, 1987—; mem. Pacific Rim Found., 1987—; exec. com. Pacific Islands Assn., 1988—; bd. dir. Pacific Aerospace Mus., 1991—; exec. com. Asia-Pacific Ctr. for Res. Internat. Bus. Disputes, 1991—; mem. Coun. Asia-Pacific Dispute Res. Ctrs., 1991—. Recipient cert. of appreciation Gov. of Hawaii, 1979, resolutions of appreciation Hawaii Senate and Ho. of Reps., 1979; grantee Japan Found., 1979. Mem. ABA, Hawaii Bar Assn. (pres. young lawyers sect. 1974, v.p. 1984), Japan-Hawaii Lawyers Assn., Am. Soc. Internat. Law, Japan-Hawaii Lawyers Assn., Internat. Bar Assn., Hawaii C. of C. (energy com. 1981-87, chmn. 1985-87, bd. dir. 1990—), Am. Judicature Soc., Asia Pacific Lawyers Assn., Internat. Bar Assn., Phi Beta Kappa. Democrat. Clubs: Yale (N.Y.C.); Plaza (Honolulu); Colonial (Princeton). Author: (with others) Legal, Institutional and Financial Aspects of An Inter-Island Electrical Transmission Cable, 1984, Alternative Approaches to the Legal, Institutional and Financial Aspects of Developing an Inter-Island, Electrical Transmission Cable System, 1986; editor Hawaii Bar News, 1972-73; contbr. chpts. to books. Home: 1130 Wilder Ave Apt 1401 Honolulu HI 96822-2755 Office: Carlsmith Ball et al Pacific Tower 1001 Bishop St Honolulu HI 96813-3429 also: Carlsmith Ball Wichman Murray Case Mukai Ichiki 1001 Bishop Pacific Tower #2200 Honolulu HI 96813

SUMIDA, KEVIN P.H., lawyer; b. Honolulu, Feb. 14, 1954; s. William H. and Dorothy A. (Iwamoto) S. BA in Philosphy, Case Western Res. U., 1976; JD, U. Pa., 1979. Bar: Hawaii 1979, U.S. Ct. Appeals (9th cir.) 1981. Assoc. Fong & Miho, Honolulu, 1979-81; law clk. to hon. judge Harold M. Fung U.S. Dist. Ct., Honolulu, 1981-82; assoc. Matsui & Chung, Honolulu, 1982-89; ptnr., 1989—. Bd. dirs., officer Farrington Alumni and Community Found., Honolulu, 1980—. Mem. ABA (litigation sect., tort and ins. practice sect.), Hawaii Bar Assn. Office: Matsui Chung & Sumida 737 Bishop St Ste 1490 Honolulu HI 96813-3293

SUMMERILL, JOHN FREDERICK, retired mortuary science college dean and educator; b. Long Beach, Calif., Aug. 25, 1917; s. Theo Samuel and Nellie May (Goodall) S.; m. Edna Bull (div. 1962); 1 child, Adrianne Summerill Burton; m. Betty Ohlstrom, June 1988 (div.). BS, Calif. Maritime Acad., 1938, San Francisco Coll. Mortuary Sci., 1945; D Mortuary Sci.

(hon.), San Francisco Coll. Mortuary Sci., 1962. 3d, 2d and chief mate U.S. Mcht. Marines, 1938-40; chief dep. coroner Marin County, San Rafael, Calif., 1947-48; locum tenens mng. and funeral dir. Calif., 1948-49; owner, funeral dir. Chapel of Lake Mortuary, Lakeport, Calif., 1949-62; dean students, prof. pathology, adminstrn. and pub. rels. San Francisco Coll. Mortuary Sci., 1962-82. Author: West Coast Piloting, 1940, Training Tanker Manual, 1947, Ancient Funeral Customs, 1960. Post leader, dist. chmn. Boy Scouts Am., Lakeport and Lake County, 1958-61; county gen. chmn., state dist. chmn. Am. Cancer Soc., 1959-60; dist. chmn. Calif. Tb Assn., Lake County. Lt. comdr. USN, 1941-45, mem. Res. ret. Recipient hon. award Boy Scouts Am., 1960, Am. Cancer Soc., Calif. Tb Assn. Mem. Funeral Dirs. and Doctors Soc., Redwood Empire Funeral Dirs. Assn. (past pres.), Lake County Officers Assn., Am. Mensa Soc. (dist. and nat. judge scholarship awards), Internat. Mark Twain Soc., Masons, Lions, Rotary, KP (past sec., chancellor comdr.), Clearlake Grange (past master), Elks (chmn. events com.). Home: 1350 S Main St Apt 13 Lakeport CA 95453

SUMMERS, MARIE JEAN, artist, fabric designer, researcher; b. Lompoc, Calif., Mar. 15, 1956; d. Charles Franklin and Jane Ming-Hwa (Hsu) S.; m. Scott Thomas Edmondson, June 4, 1978; 1 child, Chloe Ming-Hwa. BA, U. Calif., Berkeley, 1978; MST, Rochester (N.Y.) Inst. Tech., 1981. Free-lance translator Van Nostrand Reinhold Pub. Co., N.Y.C., 1978; grad. asst. The Met. Mus., N.Y.C., 1981; curatorial intern The Textile Mus., Washington, 1982; textile artist Mitchell Designs, L.A., 1983; self employed textile artist Paris, 1983-84, L.A., 1984-85, San Francisco, 1985—. Mem. Internat. Ctr. for Study of Ancient Textiles, The Textile Arts Coun. Democrat.

SUMNER, GORDON, JR., retired military officer; b. Albuquerque, July 23, 1924; s. Gordon and Esstella (Berry) S.; m. Frances Fernandes, May, 1991; children: Ward T., Holly Rose. AS, N.Mex. Mil. Inst., 1943; BA, La. State U., 1955; MA, U. Md., 1963. Commd. 2d. lt. U.S. Army, 1944, advanced through grades to lt. gen., 1975, ret., 1978; founder, chmn. Cypress Internat., 1978-81; chmn. La Mancha Co., Inc., 1981—; cons. U.S. Depts. State and Def; amabassador at large for Latin Am.; spl. ambassador U.S. Dept. State; nat. security advisor Pres.' Bi-Partisan Commn. Cen. Am.; vis. staff mem. Los Alamos Nat. Lab. Contbr. articles to profl. jours. Decorated D.S.M., Silver Star, Legion of Merit with three oak leaf clusters, Disting. Flying Cross with 13 oak leaf clusters, Bronze Star, Army Commendation medal with oak leaf cluster, Purple Heart. Mem. Phi Kappa Phi, Pi Sigma Alpha. Office: La Mancha Co 100 Cienega St Ste D Santa Fe NM 87501-2003

SUMNER, NORMAN LESLIE, JR., air traffic controller; b. San Fernando, Calif., Aug. 4, 1943; s. Norman Leslie Sumner and Edna Mae (Occleston) Wall; m. Susan Engle Fairchild, Aug. 21, 1966; children: Kenneth Warren, Keith Norman. AA, Antelope Valley Coll., 1984. USAF, Norton AFB, Calif., 1964-66, Dnang AFB, Vietnam, 1966-67, McChord AFB, Wash., 1967-68; Lapidary self-employed, Canoga Park, Calif., 1968-69, Palmdale, Calif., 1985—; air traffic controller L.A. Air Route Traffic Control Ctr., Palmdale, Calif., 1969—; instr. FAA, Palmdale, 1974—, evaluator, 1983—; sec. L.A. Ctr. Nat. Air Traffic Controllers Assn., 1991-92, rep., 1989-91. Contbr. articles to local newspapers. Mem. Rep. Nat. Com., 1981—. Recipient Air Force Accomodation medal USAF, 1967, Dist. Award of Merit, Boy Scouts of Am., 1978. Mem. So. Calif. Paleontol. Soc. Fluorescent Mineral Soc., Antelope Valley Gem and Mineral Club, DAV Commanders Club. Republican. Presbyterian. Home: 37633 Dalzell St Palmdale CA 93550 Office: FAA 2555 E Ave P Palmdale CA 93550

SUMNER, RODNEY WILLIAM, political consultant; b. Chgo., May 28, 1950; s. Ronald Eugene and MaryLou (Fehr) S.; m. Jean G. Rogge, Apr. 2, 1977 (dec.); m. Carey Ruth Rogers, Dec. 3, 1988. BS in Psychology, Bradley U., 1973. Cons. Jack Orr Co., Cardiff, Calif., 1984-88; sole prop. Rod Sumner & Assocs., Santa Barbara, Calif., 1988—. Republican. Methodist. Home: 37-A N San Marcos Rd Santa Barbara CA 93111 Office: Rod Sumner & Assocs 32 W Anapamu # 291 Santa Barbara CA 93101

SUMNER, THOMAS BARRY, international petroleum executive; b. Happy, Tex., May 24, 1931; s. Charles Lynn and Emmie (Harris) S.; m. Marguerite Anne Watson, Mar. 5, 1989; children: Merry Anne, Catherine Gail. BS in Petroleum Engring., Tex. A&M U., 1954. Registered petroleum engr., N.Mex. Gen. mgr. drilling Gulf Oil Corp., New Orleans, La., 1982-86; mgr. drilling tech. ctr. Chevron USA, Houston, 1986-89; div. mgr. Chevron USA, Midland, Tex., 1989-91; v.p., gen. mgr. Chevron USA, Denver, 1991—; pres. Chevron Shale Oil Co., Denver, 1991—. With U.S. Army, 1954-56. Home: 11 Red Tail Dr Highlands Ranch CO 80126

SUN, HUGO SUI-HWAN, mathematics educator, researcher; b. Hong Kong, Oct. 19, 1940; came to U.S., 1956; s. Jun Tao and Sarah Hung Kwan (Hu) S.; m. Ixin Wen, June 6, 1989. BA, U. Calif., Berkeley, 1963; MA, U. Md., 1966; PhD, U. N.B., Can., 1969. Asst. prof. U. N.B., Fredericton, Can., 1969-70; asst. prof. Calif. State U., Fresno, 1970-74, assoc. prof., 1974-78, prof., 1978—; hon. prof. math. and Chinese lit. Fu Yang (Peoples Rep. China) Normal U., 1987—; vis. prof. math. Peking (Peoples Rep. China) U., 1987; vis. rsch. prof. Academia Sinica, Nan Kang, Taiwan, 1980. Recipient First Award 5th Cong. World Poets, 1981. Mem. Am. Math. Soc., Math. Assn. Am., Soc. Indsl. and Applied Maths., Chinese Combinatorial Math. Soc. (hon. dir. 1989—). Republican. Office: Calif State U Shaw & Cedar Ave Fresno CA 93740

SUNDARESH, SUBRAMANIAN, marketing executive; b. Madras, India, May 24, 1956; s. Kuppuswami and Lakshmi (Ananta Krishnan) Subramanian; m. Sudha Venkataraman, Sept. 13, 1983; children: Suman, Sushant. B Tech.EE, Indian Inst. Tech., 1978; MEE, Cornell U., 1979; MBA, U. Pa., 1983. Test engr. Nat. Semiconductor, Santa Clara, Calif., 1979-80, systems engr., 1980-81; product mgr. Hewlett-Packard, Roseville, Calif., 1983-85, Cupertino, Calif., 1987-88; mktg. mgr. Hewlett-Packard, Aquadilla, P.R., 1985-87; product mktg. mgr. Hewlett-Packard, Sunnyvale, Calif., 1988-89, market devel. mgr., 1989-91; dir. mktg. Hyundai Electronics Am., San Jose, 1991-93, Adaptec, Inc., Milpitas, Calif., 1993—. IEEE scholar, 1978. Mem. Bay Area Wharton Club, Beta Gamma Sigma. Office: Adaptec Inc 691 S Milpitas Blvd Milpitas CA 95035

SUNDBERG, NORMAN DALE, psychology educator; b. Aurora, Nebr., Sept. 15, 1922; s. Cedric William and Nellie Mae (Akerson) S.; m. Donna Varner, Sept. 25, 1948; children: Kent Alan, Gregory Paul, Scott Donald, Mark William. BA, U. Nebr., 1947; MA, U. Minn., 1949, PhD, 1952. Lic. psychologist, Oreg. Teaching asst, instr. U. Minn., Mpls., 1947-52; from asst. to prof. U. Oreg., Eugene, 1952-88, prof. emeritus, 1988—; vis. prof. U. Calif., Berkeley, 1959-61, LaTrobe U., Melbourne, Australia, 1976, 80, Macquarie U., Sydney, Australia, 1980, U. Hong Kong, 1984; dean Wallace Sch. Community Svc. and Pub. Affairs, U. Oreg., Eugene, 1967-72; cons. VA, 1953—; dir. clin. and community psychology program U. Oreg., 1977-80, 84-88; lectr., cons. U.S. Ednl. Found., New Delhi, 1965-66, 73. Author: Assessment of Persons, 1977; (with Leona Tyler) Clinical Psychology, 1962; (with Leona Tyler, Julian Taplin) Clinical Psychology, 1973, 83; contbr. articles to profl. jours.; editorial com. Annual Rev. Psychology, 1976-80. Field assessment officer Peace Corps, Oreg., 1963. 1st lt. arty. U.S. Army, 1943-46. Grantee Fulbright-Hays, 1965-66, 73. Fellow Am. Psychol. Assn. (ethics com. 1970-73), Soc. Personality Assessment (Walter Klopfer award 1987); mem. Oreg. Psychol. Assn. (pres. 1962-63), Internat. Coun. Psychologists, Internat. Assn. Cross-Cultural Psychology. Democrat. Office: Univ Oreg Dept Psychology Eugene OR 97403

SUNDEL, HARVEY H., marketing research analyst and consultant; b. Bronx, NY, July 24, 1944; s. Louis and Pauline (Brotman) S. BBA, St. Mary's U., San Antonio, 1969, MBA, 1970; PhD, St. Louis U., 1974. Asst. dir. research Lone Star Brewery, San Antonio, 1970-71; cons. Tri-Mark, Inc., San Antonio, 1972-73; asst. prof. mktg. Lewis and Clark Coll., Godfrey, Ill., 1973-74; asst. prof. mktg. Met. State Coll., Denver, 1974-77, chmn., prof. mktg., 1977-86; pres. Sundel Rsch., Inc., Denver, 1976—; cons. Frederick Ross Co., Denver, 1979-84, U.S. West Direct, Denver, 1986—, Monsanto Chems. Co., St. Louis, 1985—, Mountain Bell, Denver, 1979-88, U.S. West Communications, Denver, 1988—, AT&T, 1986—, Melco Industries, 1987—, Norwest Banks, 1990—, PACE Membership Warehouse, 1992—; expert witness in legal cases. Contbr. papers and proceedings to profl. jours.; expert witness. Com. mem. Mile High United Way, Denver, 1975-80. Jewish. Home: 1616 Glen Bar Dr Lakewood CO 80215-3014 Office: Sundel Rsch Inc 1150 Delaware St Denver CO 80204-3608

SUNDELL, KENT ALLAN, geologist; b. Olathe, Kans., July 5, 1955; s. Allan R. S. and Joyce H. (Jensen) Bonebright; m. Margaret B. Bertolino, Aug. 31, 1980; children: Jessica Ann, Andrew Kent, Emily Grace. BS in Geology, U. Wyo., 1977, MS, 1980; PhD, U. Calif., Santa Barbara, 1985. Profl. geologist, Wyo. Geologist WGM Inc., Anchorage, 1977; teaching asst. U. Wyo., Laramie, 1978-80, U. Calif., Santa Barbara, 1980-82; pres., owner Ram Oil Co. Inc., Casper, Wyo., 1980—; pres. Absaroka Exploration Co. Inc., Casper, 1986—. Author: Geology of North Fork of Owl Creek, 1982; co-editor: Wyoming Geology Association 1990 Guidebook, 1990; contbr. articles to profl. jours. Mem. Wyo. Geol. Assn. (treas. 1989, chmn. field conf. 1990, Best Paper award 1984, 88, Frank Morgan award 1991), Geol. Soc. Am., Rocky Mountain Assn. Geologists (Best Paper award 1989), Sigma Xi. Office: Absaroka Exploration Co Inc PO Box 1543 Casper WY 82602

SUNDET, EDWIN ODELL STUART, art educator; b. Wells County, N.D., Aug. 26, 1929; s. James Edvin and Petra Ovedja (Flaskerud) S.; m. Kay Eileen Haline Ames, Jan. 7, 1937; children: Laura, Robin, Rochelle. BA, U. Wash., 1960, MFA, 1963. Cert. tchr., Wash. Art tchr. Tyee Jr. High Sch., Bellevue, Wash., 1960-61; teaching fellow in art U. Wash., Seattle, 1961-63; asst. prof. Mills Coll., Oakland, Calif., 1963-68; prof. Humboldt State U., Arcata, Calif., 1968-93; prof. emeritus, 1992—; dir., founder Centering Elem. Sch., Arcata, 1974-81; chair elem. tchr. preparation program Humboldt State U., Arcata, Calif., 1990-92. Exhibited drawings and paintings in group shows throughout U.S., 1960—. Founder, dir. Ctr. Children's Creative Arts, Arcata, 1972-76; Cpl. U.S. Army Corps Engrs., 1951-53. J. Paul Getty Art Edn. grantee, 1989. Mem. Gideons Internat. (chaplain 1989—), VFW (chaplain 1987-92), Am. Legion (chaplain 1990—, 1st vice comdr. 1986-90), Foursquare Internat. (coun. mem.). Office: Humboldt State U Art Dept Arcata CA 95521

SUNDIN, THEODORE ALAN, military officer, engineer; b. Mpls., Nov. 30, 1932; s. August Theodore Sundin and Evelyn Mable (Emerson) Sheaff; m. Judith Adell, Apr. 28, 1962 (div. Aug. 1977); children: Brian, Charles; m. Michelle Madonna, Mar. 31, 1983; children: Kristie Scofield, Tracie Scofield. B in Mech. Engring., U. Minn., 1955. Registered mech. engr. Enlisted USAF, 1955; advanced through grades to col. USAF, USAFR, 1962; engr. USAF, Carswell AFB, Tex., 1955-58; test engr. Convair, Ft. Worth, Tex., 1958-59; sr. engr. Delco Electronics, GMC, Santa Barbara, Calif., 1959-71; freelance cons. Ashland, Oreg., 1971-77; mgr. Comptech Research Inc., Santa Barbara, 1977-81; sr. staff engr. Martin Marietta, Vandenberg AFB, Calif., 1981-83; system program dir. USAF, Tyndell AFB, Fla., 1983-87; engr. Martin Marietta, Denver, 1987—; v.p. Aviation Hall of Fame, Dayton, Ohio, 1974-77. appointed to bldg. commn. Ashland (Oreg.) City Govt., 1976-77. Decorated Legion of Merit, USAF. Mem. Am. Inst. Aeronautics and Astronautics (sr.) (sect. chmn. 1979-83, cert. 1983, mem. tech. com. 1986—), La. Engring. Soc., Air Force Assn. (life), Res. Officers Assn. (life), Rotary. Avocations: boating, classic autos, home restoration.

SUNDT, HARRY WILSON, construction company executive; b. Woodbury, N.J., July 5, 1932; s. Thoralf Mauritz and Elinor (Stout) S.; m. Dorothy Van Gilder, June 26, 1954; children: Thomas D., Perri Lee Sundt Touche, Gerald W. BS in Bus. Adminstrn., U. Ariz., 1954, postgrad., 1957-59. Salesman ins. VanGilder Agys., Denver, 1956-57; apprentice carpenter M.M. Sundt Constrn. Co., Tucson, 1957-58, estimator, 1958-59; adminstrv. asst. M.M. Sundt Constrn. Co., Vandenberg AFB, 1959-62; sr. estimator M.M. Sundt Constrn. Co., Tucson, 1962-64, div. mgr., 1964-65, exec. v.p., gen. mgr., 1965-75, pres., chmn., 1975-79; pres., chmn. Sundt Corp., Tucson, 1980-83, chmn., chief exec. officer, 1983—; bd. dirs. Tucson Electric Power Co., Magma Copper Co., 1987—. Pres. Tucson Airport Authority, 1982; bd. dirs. U. Ariz. Found. 1981. 1st lt. U.S. Army, 1954-56. Recipient Disting. Citizen award U. Ariz., 1982, Centennial Medallion award, 1989. Mem. Tucson Country Club, Old Pueblo Club. Republican. Episcopalian. Home: 6002 E San Leandro Tucson AZ 85715-3014 Office: Sundt Corp PO Box 26685 4101 E Irvington Rd Tucson AZ 85726

SUNG, ANDREW HSI-LIN, computer science educator; b. Taipei, Taiwan, Nov. 29, 1953; came to U.S., 1978; s. Chen H. and Ching Y. (Wang) S.; m. Cindy S. Lin, Oct. 22, 1983; 1 child, David L. BSEE, Nat. Taiwan U., Taipei, 1976; MS in Math. Scis., U. Tex., Dallas, 1980; PhD in Computer Sci., SUNY, Stony Brook, 1984. Asst. prof. computer sci. dept. U. Tex., Dallas, 1984-87; asst. prof. computer sci. dept. N.Mex. Inst. Mining and Tech., Socorro, 1987-88, dept. chmn., 1988—, assoc. prof., 1989—; prin. investigator rsch. grants Cray Rsch. Inc., Minn., 1986-87, Sandia Nat. Labs., N.Mex., 1988-89, TRW, Calif., 1989. Contbr. numerous articles to profl. jours. 2d lt. Air Force, Taiwan, 1976-78. Mem. IEEE, Assn. Computing Machinery. Home: 115 Stallion Cir Socorro NM 87801-4453 Office: N Mex Inst Mining and Tech Computer Sci Dept Socorro NM 87801

SUNG, CHIN KYUNG, research scientist; b. Seoul, Calif., Jan. 26, 1957; came to U.S., 1979; m. Kalvin Won Lee, Nov. 23, 1984; children: Janice, Michelle. BS, Yonsei U., Seoul, 1979; PhD, Baylor U., 1984. Postdoctoral fellow U. Calif., San Francisco, 1984-88; rsch. scientist Mt. Zion Hosp. of U. Calif., San Francisco, 1988—. Mem. AAAS, Am. Diabetes Assn., Endocrine Soc. Mem. Christian Ch. Office: Mt Zion Hosp 1600 Divisadero St San Francisco CA 94115-3066

SUNG, SUSAN CHU, social work educator, associate dean; b. Shanghai, People's Republic China, Jan. 28, 1947; d. Philip Kia-Siang and Dorothy Shu-Fan (Tsai) Chu; m. Oscar Anthony Sung, Sept. 7, 1947; children: Kenzo, Karl. AB, U. Calif., Berkeley, 1969, MSW, 1972, PhD, 1977. Rsch. assoc. Inst. of Race Rels., U. Calif., Berkeley, 1969-70; program evaluator, social worker Chinatown Child Devel. Ctr., San Francisco, 1972-75; lectr. Sch. Social Work San Diego State U., 1975-76; prof. dept. social work edn. and ctr. cross-cultural rsch. San Francisco State U., 1977—; dir. Ctr. for Cross Cultural Rsch., San Francisco State U., 1985-86; pres. Chinese Am. Faculty Assn., San Francisco State U., 1989-90, senator acad. senate, 1989-90. Editor: The Americans Amongs Us, 1990, Jour. of Social Devel., Jour. of Social Svc. Rsch.; author: The Infusion Model, 1983. Bd. dirs. United Way of the Bay Area, San Francisco, 1984-87; chair affirmative action com. San Francisco State U., 1985-88; mem., chair com. Coun. on Asian Mental Health, San Francisco, 1978-83. NIMH grantee, 1986-89; grad. fellow U. Calif., Berkeley, 1970-72, Child Welfare fellow (Calif.) State Child Welfare Grant, 1969-72. Mem. Coun. on Social Work Edn. (Asian educator, symposium coord. accreditation team 1984-89), Nat. Assn. Social Workers, Asian Pacific Am. Coalition U.S.A., Asian Social Work Educators (symposium coord.), Nat. Assn. Women Social Work Educators, U. Calif. Berkeley Alumni Assn. Home: 635 Spruce St Berkeley CA 94707-1729 Office: San Francisco State U 1600 Holloway Ave San Francisco CA 94132-1722

SUPAN, RICHARD MATTHEW, controller; b. Palo Alto, Calif., June 22, 1953; s. James Arthur and Nancy Ann (Rhein) S.; m. Bernadette Joan Bayer, Sept. 8, 1979; children: Raymond, Valerie, Joanna. AA, Foothill Coll., 1973; BSC, Santa Clara U., 1975, MBA, 1979. Cost acctg. supr. Electron Devices div. Litton Industries, San Carlos, Calif., 1975-78; cost acctg. mgr. Microwave Tube div. Varian Assocs., Palo Alto, Calif., 1978-81, ops. controller, 1981-84; dir. acctg. Varian Assocs., Palo Alto, Calif., 1984-85; controller Electron Device & Systems Group, Varian Assocs., Palo Alto, Calif., 1985-89, Oncology Systems, Varian Assocs., Palo Alto, Calif., 1989—. Mem. Beta Gamma Sigma (hon.). Home: 5915 Amapola Dr San Jose CA 95129 Office: Varian Assocs Inc 911 Hansen Way Palo Alto CA 94303

SURFACE, STEPHEN WALTER, water treatment chemist, environmental protection specialist; b. Dayton, Ohio, Feb. 25, 1943; s. Lorin Wilfred and Virginia (Marsh) S.; m. Suzanne MacDonald, Aug. 29, 1964 (div.); 1 child, Jennifer Nalani; m. Sinfrosa Garay, Sept. 16, 1978; children: Maria Lourdes, Stephanie Alcantara. BS, Otterbein Coll., 1965; MA, U. So. Calif., 1970; postgrad., U. Hawaii, 1971. Tchr. Hawaii State Dept. Edn., Honolulu, 1970-71; staff chemist Del Monte Corp., Honolulu, 1971; head chemist USNPearl Harbor, Honolulu, 1971-76; staff chemist USN Pearl Harbor, Honolulu, 1976-90; chief office installation svcs., environ. protection Def. Logistics Agy., Camp Smith, Hawaii, 1990—. Contbr. articles to profl. jours. Recipient DuPont Teaching award, U. So. Calif., 1966. Fellow Internat. Biog. Assn., Am. Inst. Chemists; mem. Am. Chem. Soc., Am. Water Works Assn., Am. Def. Preparedness Assn., N.Y. Acad. Scis., Sigma Zeta, Phi Lambda Upsilon. Democrat. Methodist. Home: 94-1139 Noheaiki St Waipahu HI 96797 Office: Def Logistics Agy DPAC-W Camp Smith HI 96861-4110

SURLA, EDWARD DAVID, artist, writer; b. Houston, Aug. 16, 1937; s. Leandro Tizon and Pearle Naomi (De Monbrun) S. Artist Boeing, New Orleans, 1963-68; graphic designer Bechtel, L.A., 1969-86; ind. artist, writer San Diego, 1986—. One-man shows include San Diego Art Inst, 1992, 93, Indigo Nights Fine Art and Antique Gallery, New Orleans, 1993; exhibited at Art Site Inc., San Diego, 1990, San Diego Art Inst., 1990, 91, 92, 93, Signature Art Gallery, San Diego, 1992. Mem. COVA, Nat. Trust for Historic Preservation (assoc.).

SURWILL, BENEDICT JOSEPH, JR., college dean, educator; b. Chgo., Oct. 8, 1925; s. Benedict Joseph and Emily (Zemgolis) S.; m. Frances May Welling, Oct. 16, 1948; children: Thomas, Benedict, Robert, Patricia; m. Charlene R. McClintock, Feb. 17, 1991; 1 child, Michael McClintock. BS in Edn., Ariz. State Coll., 1951, MS in Edn., 1954; EdD, U. Colo., 1962. Elem. tchr. Winnetka (Ill.) Pub. Schs., 1958-61; jr. high sch. prin. Champaign (Ill.) Pub. Schs., 1961-63; dir. Campus Sch. SUNY, Buffalo, 1963-68; dean. Sch. Edn. Ea. Mont. Coll., Billings, 1968-88, asst. to pres., 1988-91, dean Sch. Edn., prof. edn. emeritus, 1991—; chmn. dean's coun. Mont. Univ. System, 1974; mem. Mont. Supts. Adv. Com. on Tchr. Edn. and Cert., 1969-76, chmn., 1972-73; mem. ednl. forum State Supt. Pub. Instrn., 1977-83, Mont. Rural Youth Adv. Coun., Billings, 1979-81; lectr. in field. Editor: A Critical Examination of American Education, 1985; mem. editorial bd., contbg. editor Jour. Creative Behavior, 1966-93. Co-chmn. cancer drive Billings chpt. Am. Cancer Soc., 1988-89, Mont. State Cancer Crusade, 1989. With inf. U.S. Army. Recipient Am. Assn. of Coll. for Tchr. Edn. award, 1972, Presdl. citation Ill. Assn. Sch. Adminstrs., 1973. Mem. Nat. Coun. Accreditation Tchr. Edn. (mem. standards com., mem. multicultural edn. com. 1977, bd. appeals 1980-83, bd. examiners 1988-90), Elks, Yellowstone Country Club, Phi Delta Kappa, Kappa Delta Pi. Home: 5864 Sam Snead Trl Billings MT 59106-1021

SURYADHARMA, HANDAJANY DEVI, information systems/systems integration consultant; b. Jakarta, Indonesia, Oct. 16, 1968; came to U.S., 1987; d. Juliany (Setiawan) S. BS magna cum laude, U. Calif., Irvine, 1991. Cons. Andersen Cons., L.A., 1991—. Mem. Assn. Computing Machinery, Ind. Profl. Assn., U. Calif. Irvine Alumni Orgn., Golden Key (v.p. chpt. 1990-91), Phi Beta Kappa. Office: 633 W 5th St Los Angeles CA 90071

SUSAN, ANNE-LOUISE, foundation consultant; b. Schurz, Nev., Apr. 24, 1958; d. Raymond and Lucille (Harvey) Willie; m. Lloyd W. Susan, Apr. 30, 1988; children: Ashley Na'ilihn, Taylor Tailbi' Denzhoone'. BA, U. Nev., 1981; MPH, U. Calif., Berkeley, 1992, MSW, 1993. Congl. intern U.S. Senate, Washington, 1981; exec. dir. Community Action Program, Schurz, 1981-82; educator community health Nev. Urban Indian Health, Reno, 1982-83; exec. dir. juvenile div. White Mountain Apache Tribe, Whiteview, Ariz., 1986, exec. asst. tribal chmn., 1986-87, exec. dir. div. social svcs., 1987-90; adminstv. resident Dept. Vets. Affairs, Martinez, Calif., 1991-92; cons. Calif. Urban-Rural Indian Health Bd., Sacramento, 1992—; with VA Western Region, San Francisco, 1992-93; clin. fellow Minority Health Professions, Washington, 1992. Vol. Howard Cannon U.S. Senate Campaign, Reno, 1982, Bill Sperazza Mayor Campaign, Reno, 1982, Bill Clinton for Pres. Campaign, Oakland, Calif., 1992; participant nat. think tank Ctrs. for Disease Control, Atlanta, 1992; regional adminstv. resident Dept. Vets. Affairs, San Francisco, 1992—. NIMH scholar, 1992-93; named Miss Indian Nev., Nev. Indian Rodeo Assn., 1979-80, Miss Indian Am., Am. Indian Found., 1984-85; recipient Outstanding Youth award U.S. Indian Pub. Health Svc., 1988. Mem. Am. Indian Heritage Found. (pageant asst. 1987—), U. Nev. Alumni Assn., U. Calif. Berkeley Alumni Assn., Gamma Phi Beta. Democrat. Methodist. Home: 143 Wilson St # 67 Albany CA 94710

SUSMAN, BENJAMIN MAYER, retail sales company executive; b. Denver, Apr. 4, 1937; s. Israel Burnett and Ethel (Zalben) S.; m. Brenda Norma Litrow, Jan. 6, 1943 (div. Feb. 1980); children: Barry Samuel, Lauren Michelle; m. Michele Bledstein, Dec. 19, 1989. BS, UCLA, 1959. Staff acct. Gold, Eisenberg and Co., CPAs, Beverly Hills, Calif., 1959-60, Bernard Bloch and Co., CPAs, Beverly Hills, Calif., 1960-62, Kahn, Seltzer and Eckstein, CPAs, Beverly Hills, Calif., 1961-62; mgr. Van Nuys (Calif.) Army and Navy Stores, Inc., 1962-64; dept. mgr. Sears Roebuck and Co., Santa Monica, Calif., 1964-70; pres. Van Nuys Army and Navy Stores, Inc., 1970—; pres. Unified Wholesale Distbrs., L.A., 1973-74. Co-chmn. San Fernando Valley Jewish Fedn., Canogo Park, Calif., 1983-84; bd. dirs. Adat Ari El Synagogue, North Hollywood, Calif., 1988-90. Mem. Associated Surplus Dealers (Buyers award 1993), Western Shoe Retailers, N.Am. Conf. Ethiopian Jewery (bd. dirs. 1979—), Valley Beth Shalom Synagogue. Home: 13909 Hesby St Sherman Oaks CA 91423 Office: Van Nuys Army Navy Stores Inc 6179 Van Nuys Blvd Van Nuys CA 91401

SUSSKIND, TERESA GABRIEL, publisher; b. Watford, Eng., came to U.S., 1945, naturalized, 1948; d. Aaron and Betty (Fox) Gabriel; m. Charles Susskind, May 1, 1945; children: Pamela Pettler, Peter Gabriel, Amanda. Ed. U. London, 1938-40. Profl. libr. Calif. Inst. Tech., Pasadena, 1946-48, Yale U., New Haven, Conn., 1948-51, Stanford U., Calif., 1951-52, SRI Internat., Menlo Park, Calif., 1953; founder, pres. San Francisco Press, Inc., 1959—. With Women's Royal Naval Svc., 1943-45. Author: A Room of One's Own Revisited, 1977. Active in cultural affairs; bd. govs. San Francisco Symphony, 1986-89. Mem. Town and Gown Club (Berkeley, Calif., pres. 1984-85). Office: PO Box 426800 San Francisco CA 94142-6800

SUSSMAN, BRIAN JAY, meteorologist, weather broadcaster; b. L.A., Apr. 3, 1956; s. Alan E. and Beverly A. (Carlson) S.; m. Sue Ann Rittenhouse, June 18, 1978; chilren: Elisa, Samuel, Benjamin. BS, U. Mo., 1978. Reporter, anchor Sta. KCBJ-TV, Columbia, Mo., 1977-80; weather anchor Sta. KOLO-TV, Reno, 1980-83; on-air meteorologist Sta. KNTV-TV, San Jose, Calif., 1983-87, Sta. KDKA-TV, Pitts., 1987-89; substitute weatherman CBS This Morning, N.Y.C., 1988—; on-air meteorologist Sta. KPIX-TV, San Francisco, 1989—. Co-author: (textbook) For Spacious Skies, 1987, rev. edit., 1989. Recipient Best Weathercast award Radio-TV News Dirs. Assn., 1987, 90, 91, 92, Associated Press, 1989, 92, Advancement of Learning Through Broadcasting award NEA, 1989. Mem. Am. Meteorol. Soc. (Seal of Approval cert.). Office: Sta KPIX-TV 855 Battery St San Francisco CA 94111

SUSSMAN, HAROLD LOUIS, marketing professional; b. Ann Arbor, Mich., Mar. 24, 1955; s. Alfred Shepard and Selma (Feinman) S.; m. Shekoofeh Manzoor, July 24, 1983; children: Sabrina Sanam, Cyrus Samuel. BA in Math. and Computer Sci., U. Mass., 1983; MS, U. So. Calif., L.A., 1985; student, Stanford U., 1973-76. Teaching asst. U. Mass., Boston, 1981-83; assoc. mem. program staff Xerox Corp., El Segundo, Calif., 1983-84, sr. mem. program staff, 1984-85, mgr. data mgmt. svcs., tech. program mgr., 1986-88; systems integration mktg. mgr. Xerox Corp., Santa Ana, Calif., 1988—. Mem. DECUS, Xerox Pres. Club. Jewish. Home: 1 Estrade Ln El Toro CA 92610-2202

SUSSMAN, KAREN ANN, professional society administrator; b. Clearfield, Pa., Jan. 11, 1947; d. Leonard Wilhelm and Theresa Emma (Schmidt) Kuntz; divorced; children: Jennifer Lynne, Amy Nicole. Diploma in nursing, Temple U., 1967. Critical care nurse Scottsdale (Ariz.) Meml. Hosp., 1974-89; pres. Internat. Soc. for the Protection of Mustangs & Burros, 1989—; pvt. practice piano instr., Scottsdale, 1976-89. Author short stories. Exec. dir. Wild Horses of Am. Registry, mem. nat. adv. bd. Wild Horse & Burro Mgmt., 1990-92, Adv. Bd. U.S. Depts. Interior & Agr., 1990-92. Home and Office: 6212 E Sweetwater Ave Scottsdale AZ 85254-4461

SUSSMAN, PETER YEGER, journalist; b. Phila., May 29, 1941; s. Sidney and Ann (Rosenberg) S.; m. Patricia Carson, Apr. 10, 1971; children: Deborah, Katherine, Stephanie. Student, St. Andrews Univ., Scotland, 1961-62; BA summa cum laude, Union Coll., 1963; postgrad, Stanford U., 1978-79. Copy editor San Francisco Chronicle, 1964-67, asst. news editor,

1967-81, editor Sunday mag., 1981-83, editor Sunday supplement, 1983—; freelance writer and lectr. Co-author: Committing Journalism, 1993. Recipient Nat. Journalism award Scripps Howard, 1989, Bill Farr Freedom of Info. award Calif. Soc. Newspaper Editors, 1990, hon. mention Freedom of Info. award Brechner Ctr., U. Fla., 1990 and James Aronson award for pub. conscience journalism CUNY, 1992, journalism award Prison Law Office-San Francisco Bar Assn., 1991, Hugh M. Hefner First Amendment award Playboy Found., 1992, PEN/Newman's Own First Amendment spl. citation, 1993; NEH-Knight fellow Stanford U., 1978-79. Mem. Media Alliance (Elsa Knight Thompson award 1988), Soc. Profl. Journalists (James Madison Freedom Info. award No. Calif. chpt. 1989; Nat. Freedom Info. award 1990). Home: 2636 Woolsey St Berkeley CA 94705 Office: San Francisco Chronicle 901 Mission St San Francisco CA 94103

SUSSMAN, STEVEN YALE, preventive medicine educator; b. Chgo., Mar. 16, 1955; s. Max and Rosamond (Vishny) S.; m. Sun Cha Lim, Sept. 20, 1992. BS, U. Ill., Champaign-Urbana, 1976; PhD, U. Ill., Chgo., 1984. Rsch. assoc. U. So. Calif., L.A., 1984-86; asst. prof. rsch. U. So. Calif., Pasadena, 1986-88, asst. prof., 1988-92; assoc. prof. Inst. Health Promotion-Disease Prevention Rsch. U. So. Calif., Alhambra, 1992—; mem. expert adv. group on spitting tobacco prevention and cessation Nat. Cancer Inst., Rockville, Md., 1992; reviewer 1992 Surgeon Gen.'s Report on Tobacco Use in Young People. Contbr. articles on health behavior research to profl. pubis. Grantee Nat. Cancer Inst., 1987-92, Nat. Inst. Drug Abuse, 1992—, Tobacco Related Disease Rsch. Program, 1992—. Mem. Assn. Advancement Behavior Therapy, Am. Psychol. Assn. Office: Inst Health Promotion and Disease Prevention Rsch 1000 S Fremont Ave Ste 641 Alhambra CA 91803-1358

SUTARDJI, JOHNY SASTRA, software engineer; b. Jakarta, Indonesia, Dec. 28, 1960; came to U.S., 1979; s. Hendra and Anggraini S.; m. Fanti Tandean, Sept. 28, 1985; 1 child, Kevin Sastra. BS in Computer Sci., San Francisco State U., 1983. Softwre engr. Personal CAD Systems, Inc., Los Gatos, Calif., 1983-85, CalComp, Inc., Campbell, Calif., 1985-86; sr. software engr. Innovative Data Design, Concord, Calif., 1987-88, Claris Corp., Santa Clara, Calif., 1988—. Mem. Indonesian Profl. Assn. (founder, mgr. comm. group 1991—, bd. dirs. 1991—, chief editor NEWSantara newsletter 1991—).

SUTCLIFFE, ERIC, lawyer; b. Calif., Jan. 10, 1909; s. Thomas and Annie (Beare) S.; m. Joan Basché, Aug. 7, 1937; children: Victoria, Marcia, Thomas; m. Marie C. Paige, Nov. 1, 1975. AB, U. Calif. at Berkeley, 1929, LLB, 1932. Bar: Calif. 1932. Mem. firm Orrick, Herrington & Sutcliffe, San Francisco, 1943-85, mng. ptnr., 1947-78. Trustee, treas., v.p. San Francisco Law Libr., 1974-88; bd. dirs. Merritt Peralta Found., 1988. Fellow Am. Bar Found (life); mem. ABA (chmn state regulation securities com. 1960-65), San Francisco Bar Assn. (chmn. corp. law com., 1964-65), San Francisco C. of C. (past treas., dir.), State Bar Calif., Pacific Union Club, Bohemian Club, Phi Gamma Delta, Phi Delta Phi, Order of Coif. Home: 260 King Ave Oakland CA 94610-1231 Office: Old Fed Reserve Bank Bldg 400 Sansome St San Francisco CA 94111-3308

SUTCLIFFE, RICHARD JOSEPH (RICK SUTCLIFFE), computer science educator; b. Calgary, Alta., Can., July 3, 1947; s. Thomas Joseph and Mary Elizabeth (Tobin) S.; m. Joyce Arlene Madland; children: Nathan, Joel. BSc, Simon Fraser U., Burnaby, B.C., Can., 1969, MSc, 1973. Math. tchr., dept. head Sch. Dist. # 35, Langley, B.C., 1971-83; assoc. prof. computer sci. Trinity Western U., Langley, 1983—; Can. chair, del. Internat. Stds. Orgn. Modula 2 working group, 1987—. Author: Introduction to Programming Using Modula 2, 1987; contbr. columns, articles and revs. to trade publs. Deacon, treas. Aldergrove (B.C.) Bapt. Ch., 1985-91; bd. mem. N.W. Bapt. Theol. Coll. and Sem., Vancouver, B.C., 1987. Mem. IEEE, Assn. Computing Machinery, Nat. Coun. Tchrs. Math., Math. Assn. Am. Baptist. Home: 28964 64th Ave Starr Rd, Mount Lehman, BC Canada V0X 1V0 Office: Trinity Western U, 7600 Glover Rd, Langley, BC Canada V3A 6H4

SUTER, DAVID WINSTON, religion educator, minister; b. Staunton, Va., Mar. 1, 1942; s. Beverly Wills and Sarah Frances (Anderson) S.; m. Kristine Ann Pearson, July 8, 1978; 1 child, Jessica Eden. BA, Davidson Coll., 1964; BD, U. Chgo., 1967, MA, 1970, PhD, 1977. Ordained to ministry Presbyn. Ch. (U.S.A.), 1967. Pastor Longbranch (Wash.) Community Ch., 1986-90; prof. St. Martin's Coll., Lacey, Wash., 1983—, dean of humanities, 1991—. Author: Tradition and Composition in the Parables of Enoch, 1979; contbr. articles to profl. publs. Mem. Soc. Biblical Lit. Democrat. Office: St Martin's Coll 5300 Pacific Ave SE Lacey WA 98503

SUTHERLAND, BRUCE, composer, pianist; b. Daytona Beach, Fla.; s. Kenneth Francis and Norma (Williams) S.; Mus.B., U. So. Calif., 1957, Mus.M., 1959; studies with Halsey Stevens, Ellis Kohs, Ethel Leginska, Amparo Iturbi. Harpsichord soloist with Telemann Trio in concert tour, 1969-70; tchr. master class for pianists U. Tex., Austin, 1971; dir. Bach festivals Music Tchrs. Assn. Calif., 1972-73, dir. Artists of Tomorrow Music Festivals Music Tchrs. Assn. Calif., 1984—, competitions performed in numerous contemporary music festivals in U.S., 1957—; piano faculty Calif. State U. at Northridge, 1977—; adjudicator music competitions and auditions Nat. Guild Piano Tchrs., others; dir. Brentwood-Westwood Symphony ann. competition for young artists, 1981—; composer: Allegro Fanfara for Orch., world premiere conducted by José Iturbi with Bridgeport Symphony Orch., 1970; Saxophone Quartet, 1971; Quintet for Flute, Strings, Piano, 1972; Notturno for Flute and Guitar, 1973; also string trio, piano and vocal works. Recipient grand prize Internat. Competition Louis Moreau Gottschalk, 1970; Stairway of Stars award Music Arts Soc., Santa Monica, 1973; named one of Los Angeles' Finest Piano Tchrs., New West Mag., 1977; honored as Dist. Tchr. of Anders Martinson, presdl. scholar in arts, 1991; honored by Nat. Found. Advancement Arts. Mem. Nat. Assn. Am. Composers and Condrs., Music Tchrs. Nat. Assn., Music Tchrs. Assn., Calif. Assn. Profl. Music Tchrs., Pi Kappa Lambda.

SUTHERLAND, EARL CHRISTIAN, engineering executive; b. Detroit, July 23, 1923; s. Earl Jefferson and Mildred Fredricka (Schroeder) S.; m. Faith B. Maier, Aug. 12, 1946 (dec.); m. Marion Elizabeth Schultz; 1 child, Earl Maier. BS, Mich. Coll. Mining Tech., 1950, MS, 1950; MBA, Portland State U., 1974. Engr. IBM Corp., Endicott, N.Y., 1941-52; metallurgist Fansteel Metall., N. Chgo., 1956; v.p. tech. Eriez S.A. Produtos Metall., Sao Paulo, Brazil, 1956-60; research scientist NASA Lewis Ctr., Cleve., 1960-62; mfg. mgr. Precision Castparts Corp., Portland, 1962-64; engrng. mgr. Omark Industries, Milw., 1964-68; cons. engr. MEI Charlton, Inc., Portland, 1968-75; pres. Cellufibres Internat., Inc., Seattle, 1977—; cons. engr. Earl C. Sutherland & Assocs., 1975. Author: numerous books and articles. Served to col. U.S. Army, 1946-75, ret. Decorated Legion of Merit. Mem. Am. Cons. Engrs. Council, Cons. Engrs. Wash., Nat. Soc. Profl. Engrs., Am. Soc. Metals, AIME, Nat. Assn. Corrosion Engrs., Soc. Automotive Engrs. Baptist. Home: 2655 Dexter Ave N Seattle WA 98109-1913 Office: Earl C Sutherland & Assocs 10307 Stewart Dr Eagle River AK 99577-9514

SUTHERLAND, JOHN CAMPBELL, pathologist, educator; b. Tamingfu, Hopei, People's Republic of China, Oct. 28, 1921; came to U.S., 1926; s. Francis Campbell and Ann Findlay (Bowman) S.; m. Eunice Lucille Kindschi, June 16, 1950; 1 child, John Mark. AB, N.W. Nazarene Coll., 1941; MD, Med. Coll. Wis., 1946. Intern Milw. Hosp., 1946-47; resident in pathology St. Francis Hosp., Wichita, Kans., 1950-52, Barnes Hosp., St. Louis, 1952-54, Stanford (Calif.) Med. Ctr., 1967-68; gen. practitioner Mangum Clinic, Nampa, Idaho, 1949-50; gen. med. officer Raleigh Fitkin Meml. Hosp., Manzini, Swaziland, 1955-56, Ethel Lucas Meml. Hosp., Acornhoek, South Africa, 1956-61, 62-67; acting head biology dept. N.W. Nazarene Coll., Nampa, 1961-62; head rsch. pathology dept. Balt. Cancer Rsch. Ctr., 1968-74; asst. prof. dept. pathology U. Md., Balt., 1974-76, assoc. prof., 1976-84, mem. grad. faculty, 1982-84; vis. assoc. prof. dept. surgery U. Ariz., Tucson, 1984—. Co-author: Guinea Pig Doctors, 1984; contbr. articles to sci. jours. Capt. USAF, 1947-49. Mem. Alumni Assn. of N.W. Nazarene Coll. (Profl. Achievement award 1984), Toastmasters, Gideons. Republican. Mem. Nazarene Ch. Home: 3411 S Camino Seco Unit 337 Tucson AZ 85730-2829 Office: Univ Ariz Dept Surgery 1501 N Campbell Ave Tucson AZ 85724-0001

SUTHERLAND, LOWELL FRANCIS, lawyer; b. Lincoln, Nebr., Dec. 17, 1939; s. Lowell Williams and Doris Genevieve (Peterson) S.; m. Virginia Kay Edwards, Aug. 29, 1992. AB, San Diego State Coll., 1962; LLB, Hastings Coll. Law, 1965; children: Scott Thorpe, Mark James, Sandra Doris. With Cooper, White & Cooper, attys., San Francisco, 1963-66; admitted to Calif. bar, 1966; with Wien & Thorpe, attys., El Centro, 1966-67; ptnr. Wien, Thorpe & Sutherland, El Centro, 1967-74, Wien, Thorpe, Sutherland & Stamper, 1973-74, Sutherland, Stamper & Feingold, 1974-77, Sutherland & Gerber, 1977—, Sutherland & Sutherland. Mem. ABA, Calif. Bar Assn., Imperial County Bar Assn. (Recognition of Experience awards), San Diego (named Outstanding Trial Lawyer April 1981, Oct. 1983, Trial Lawyer of Yr. 1982), Trial Lawyers Assns., Thurston Soc., Nat. Bd. Trial Advs. (diplomate), Am. Bd. Trial Advocates (assoc.), Theta Chi. Mem. editorial staff Hastings Law Jour., 1964-65. Home: 1853 Sunset Rd El Centro CA 92243-3518 Office: 300 S Imperial Ave # 7 El Centro CA 92243-3192

SUTJIPTO, SUGANTO, virologist, researcher; b. Medan, Sumatra, Indonesia, Mar. 20, 1946; came to U.S., 1967; s. Sutjipto and Surjani Tandela; m. Lucia Ching-Hwa Wang, May 6, 1984. BS, Nebr. Wesleyan U., 1972; MS, N.W. Mo. State U., 1974; PhD, N.C. State U., 1979. Rsch. asst. sch. vet. medicine N.C. State U., Raleigh, 1975-79; postdoctoral rsch. assoc. dept. microbiology and immunology Duke U. Med. Ctr., Durham, N.C., 1980-82, postdoctoral rsch. assoc. dept. surgery, 1983-85; postdoctoral fellow Calif. Primate Rsch. Ctr. U. Calif., Davis, 1985-88, rsch. virologist Calif. Primate Rsch. Ctr., 1989—; rsch. cons. Bio-Trends, Sacramento, 1989. Contbr. articles to profl. jours. NIH grantee 1986-91, 1990—. Mem. AAAS, Am. Soc. for Microbiology, N.Y. Acad. Scis. Home: 2913 Erin Dr Sacramento CA 95833-2859

SUTTER, HARVEY MACK, consultant, engineer; b. Jennings, La., Oct. 5, 1906; s. Josiah Harvey and Effie Relief (Murray) S.; AB, U. Wichita, 1932; m. Julia Genevieve Wright, Sept. 19, 1936; children: James Houston, Robert Mack, Julia Ann Boyd, John Norman. Design and prodn. engr. Boeing Aircraft, Wichita, Kans., 1936-38; supr. arts, crafts and coop. activities Bur. Indian Affairs, U.S. Dept. of Interior, 1938-42, chief procurement br. Bur. of Reclamation, Washington, 1946-54, chief div. procurement and property mgmt., 1954-58; asst. to adminstr. Bonneville Power Adminstrn., 1958-61, asst. to chief engr., 1962-66; cons. engr., 1967—; analyst, chief prodn. service WPB, Denver, 1942-44; chief div. supply C.E., Denver, 1944-46. Mem. exec. bd. Portland area Boy Scouts Am. Recipient Silver Beaver award. Presbyterian. Mem. Nat., Western woodcarvers assns., Internat. Wood Collectors Soc., Electric of Oreg. Author or co-author books and articles on woodcarving. Home: 3803 SE Carlton St Portland OR 97202-7635

SUTTER, JOSEPH F., aeronautical engineer, consultant, retired airline company executive; b. Seattle, Wash., Mar. 21, 1921; m. Nancy Ann French, June 14, 1943. B.A., U. Wash., 1943. Various engrng. positions Boeing Comml. Airplane Co., Seattle, 1946-65, dir. engrng. for Boeing 747, 1965-71, v.p., gen. mgr. 747 div., 1971-74, v.p. program ops., 1974-76, v.p. ops. and product devel., 1976-81, exec. v.p., 1981-86, cons., 1986-87; cons. Boeing Comml. Airplane Co., 1987—; chmn. aerospace safety adv. panel NASA, 1986; mem. Challenger Accident Commn., 1986. Served to lt. j.g. USN, 1943-45. Recipient Master Design award Product Engring. mag., 1965, Franklin W. Kolk Air Transp. Progress award Soc. Aero. Aerospace Coun., 1980, Elmer A. Sperry award, 1980, Nuts & Bolts award Transport Assn., 1983, Nat. Medal Tech., U.S. Pres. Reagan, 1985, Sir Kingsford Smith award Royal Aero. Soc. in Sydney, 1980, Wright Bros. Meml. Trophy, 1986; Joseph F. Sutter professorship established in his honor at U. Wash., Boeing Co., 1992. Hon. fellow AIAA, Royal Aero. Soc. Gt. Brit.; mem. Internat. Fedn. Airworthiness (pres. 1989, Danial Guggenheim award 1991). Office: Boeing Comml Airplane Co PO Box 3707 Mail Stop 13-43 Seattle WA 98124

SUTTERBY, LARRY QUENTIN, internist; b. North Kansas City, Mo., Sept. 11, 1950; s. John Albert and Wilma Elizabeth (Henry) S.; m. Luciana Rises Magpuri, July 5, 1980; children: Leah Lourdes, Liza Bernadette. BA in Chemistry, William Jewell Coll., 1972; MD, U. Mo., Kans. City, 1976. Diplomate Am. Bd. Internal Medicine. Resident in internal medicine Mt. Sinai Hosp., Chgo., 1976-79; physician Mojave Desert Health Svc., Barstow, Calif., 1979-86; pvt. practice Barstow, 1986—; med. dir. Rimrock Villa Convalescent Hosp., Barstow, 1986-89, Mojave Valley Hospice, 1983—. Recipient Long Care award Vis. Nurse Assn. Inland Counties, 1988. Mem. AMA, Calif. Med. Assn., San Bernardino County Med. Soc., Am. Soc. Internal Medicine, Am. Geriatric Soc., Acad. Hospice Physicians, Soc. Gen. Internal Medicine, Physicians Who Care, Am. Numismatic Assn., Combined Orgns. Numismatic Error Collectors Am. Democrat. Roman Catholic. Office: 209 N 2d Ave Barstow CA 92311

SUTTLES, VIRGINIA GRANT, advertising executive; b. Urbana, Ill., June 13, 1931; d. William Henry and Lenora (Fitzsimmons) Grant; m. John Henry Suttles, Sept. 24, 1977; step-children: Linda Suttles Daniels, Peg Suttles La Croix, Pamela Suttles Diaz, Randall. Grad. pub. schs., Mahomet, Ill. Media estimator and Procter & Gamble budget control Tatham-Laird, Inc., Chgo., 1955-60; media planner, supr. Tracy-Locke Co., Inc., Dallas and Denver, 1961-68; media dir., account exec. Lorie-Lotito, Inc., 1968-72; v.p., media dir. Sam Lusky Assos., Inc., Denver, 1972-86; ind. media buyer, 1984-89; mktg. asst. media dept. Del E. Webb Communities, Inc., Sun City West, Ariz., 1985-88, with telemarketing dept., 1989-90; mktg. coord. asst./media buyer, Del Webb Corp., Phoenix, 1990—; lectr. sr. journalism class U. Colo., Boulder, 1975-80; condr. class in media seminars Denver Advt. Fedn., 1974, 77; Colo. State U. panelist Broadcast Day, 1978, High Sch. Inst., 1979, 80, 81, 82, 83. Founder, Del E. Webb Meml. Hosp. Found.; patron founder Tree of Life Nat. Kidney Found. of Colo.- Rockies Snow Mountain YMCA Ranch, Winter Park, Colo. Mem. Denver Advt. Fedn. (bd. dir. 1973-75, program chmn. 1974-76, 80-82, exec. bd., v.p. ops. 1980-81, chmn. Alfie awards com. 1980-81, advt. profl. of Yr. 1981-82), Denver Advt. Golf Assn. (v.p. 1976-77, pres. 1977-78), Colo. Broadcasters Assn., Sun City West Bowling Assn. (bd. dirs. 1987-88), Sun City West Women's Social Club. Republican. Congregationalist. Club: Denver Broncos Quarterback. Home: 20002 Greenview Dr Sun City West AZ 85375-4710 Office: Del Webb Corp Inc PO Box 29040 Phoenix AZ 85038-9040

SUTTON, BARBARA POWDERLY, marketing executive; b. Scranton, Pa., Oct. 29, 1940; d. Eugene Thomas and Kathryn Dorothy (Loftus) Powderly. Student, Miami (Fla.)-Dade Jr. Coll., 1960. Ordained minister, 1992. Asst. controller Oak Ridge, Inc., Hialeah, Fla., 1959-63; v.p., media dir. Harold Gardner Assocs., Inc., Miami Beach, Fla., 1963-67; media dir., adminstrv. asst. Stern, Hays & Lang Advt., Inc., Miami, 1967-69; exec. asst. Los Angeles Times, 1969-71; media dir., adminstrv. asst. Greenman Advt., Inc., Hollywood, Fla., 1971-73; asst. to gen. mgr. Sta. WGMA-FM, Hollywood, 1974; with acctg. and settlement dept. Fed. Res. Bank, Miami, 1974-75; bus. mgr. Impart Pub. Corp., Reno, 1975-76; adminstrv. asst., office mgr. Edn. Advancement Inst., Reno, 1976-78; ind. contractor Du-Bar Internat., Reno, 1979-80; pres. Capital Advt., Reno, 1980-81; dir. media Mktg. Systems Internat., Reno, 1981-82; owner Dolphin Secretarial Service, Reno, 1982-88, Dolphin Services, Reno, 1983-88, Powderly Assocs., Reno, 1982—; pres. Bus.-Promotional Services, Inc., Reno, 1986-89; ptnr. Investigative Rsch. Report Svcs., Sedona, Ariz., 1993—, B & B Graphics, Sedona, 1991—, Beyond Belief Metaphysical & Spiritual Resources, Sedona, 1991—, Megatrends Mktg. Assocs., Sedona, 1991—, Atkinson Fine Artist's Reps., Sedona, 1992—; speaker Mktg. Fedn., Inc., N.Y.C., 1986; seminar developer and presenter Advt. and Mktg. for Small Bus., U. Nev. Small Bus. Devel. Ctr., 1987-88; editor non-fiction books Atkinson World Publishing, Sedona, 1992—; writer, rschr. non-fiction studies Expecting Publication, 1993. Bd. dirs. March of Dimes, Reno, 1982; mem. Presdl. Task Force, Washington, 1983-85, Reno Women's Network, 1982-84, Reno Commn. on Status of Women, 1987-88. Named one of 2,000 Women of Achievement, London, 1971. Mem. Entrepreneurial Women of Reno (rec. sec., bd. dirs. 1987-88). Metaphysician.

SUTTON, LEONARD VON BIBRA, lawyer; b. Colorado Springs, Colo., Dec. 21, 1914; s. Benjamin Edmund and Anne (von Bibra) S.; B.A., Colo. Coll., 1937; fellow Nat. Inst. Pub. Affairs, 1937-38; J.D., U. Denver, 1941; grad. Inf. Officers Sch., Ft. Benning, Ga., 1942; LLD (hon.) Colo. Coll., 1987, U. Denver, 1989, U. Colo., 1990. Bar: Colo. 1941, U.S. Supreme Ct., U.S. Tax Ct., U.S. Ct. Claims, U.S. Ct. Internat. Trade (former Customs Ct.), U.S. Ct. Mil. Appeals. Practiced law, Colorado Springs, 1941-42, 46-56; justice Colo. Supreme Ct., 1956-68, chief justice, 1960, 66; chmn. Fgn. Claims Settlement Commn. U.S., 1968-69; pvt. practice law, Denver and Washington, 1969—. Chmn. Colo. Statute Revision Com., 1964-67; participant Fgn. Trade Seminar, 1935, Germany; del. various nat. and internat. bar assn. confs.; lectr.; past vice chmn. com. internat. cts. World Peace Through Law Commn.; past chmn. Colo. World Peace through Law Com., World Habeas Corpus Com., Colo.; hon. mem. N.J. World Trade Com., 1976—; mem. Colo. Democratic Cen. Com., 1948-56, mem. exec. com., 1948-58, chmn. rules com., 1955-56; del. Dem. Nat. Conv., 1952; past pres. Garden of the Gods Rotary Club. Former trustee Inst. Internat. Edn., N.Y.C.; regent Dana Coll., Blair, Nebr., 1976-78; chmn. bd. govs. U. Denver, 1985-90, mwm., 1991—; chmn. Pioneer Soc. U. Denver, 1989—. Capt., AUS, World War II. Recipient Grand Order of Merit Fed. Republic Germany, 1987. Mem. Colo. (Jr. Bar past chmn.), Internat., Inter-Am. (council), Am. (past chmn. com. on internat. cts., former mem. council sect. internat. law), Denver, D.C. bar assns., Mexican Acad. Internat. Law, Bremos Aires Bar Assn. (U.S. mem.), Am. Arbitration Assn., Can. Arbitration, Conciliation and Amicable Composition Cen., Inc. (internat. assoc.), Washington Fgn. Law Soc. (pres. 1970-71, now hon. mem.), Royal Danish Guards Assn. Calif., Consular Law Soc. N.Y. (hon.), Phi Delta Phi. Episcopalian. Clubs: Wyoming One Shot Antelope Past Shooter's (pres. 1985-86); Colo. Harvard Bus. Sch. (assoc.); Mason (33 degree), Shriners; Garden of Gods, Kissing Camels (Colorado Springs); Cosmos (Washington). Author: Constitution of Mexico, 1973. Contbr. articles on law, jud. adminstrn. and internat. relations to jours. Home: Unit 1908 3131 E Alameda Ave Denver CO 80209

SUTTON, MARCELLA FRENCH, interior designer; b. Prague, Czechoslovakia, Sept. 4, 1946; came to U.S., 1952, naturalized, 1956; d. Eugen E. and Frances V. (Pruchovia) French; BS in Profl. Arts, Woodbury U., 1971; m. Michael D. Sutton, Feb. 11, 1978; 1 child, Kevin Christopher. Mgr. design dept. W. & J. Sloane, Beverly Hills, Calif., 1972-76; project dir. Milton I. Swimmer, Beverly Hills, 1977-78; owner, interior designer Marcella French Designs, Woodland Hills and La Crescenta, Calif., 1969—; v.p. Shepherd of the Valley Sch.; property mgmt. coord., interior designer Home Savs. and Loan., State of Calif., L.A., 1979-82; regional premises officer, asst. v.p. regional hdqrs. Bank of Am., L.A., 1981-86; v.p. M.D. Sutton Ins. Agy.; prin. designer Marcella French Designs, Woodland Hills; cons. pvt. residences, comml. bldgs., office and banks. Project mgr., 1st v.p. fundraising Shephard of the Valley Sch., 1989-90, enrichment chmn., 1990-91, mem. enrichment program pub. sch. calendar, 1991; active Young Reps., Vinyard Ch.; treas. West Hills Baseball Aux., 1989-91; coord. Taffy Festival, Agoura; arcades coord., chmn. ways and means RTRWF, 1993—. Recipient various scholarships.

SUTTON, ROBERT EDWARD, investment company executive; b. Burlington, Vt., July 3, 1943; s. Rollin Robert and Blanche Margaret (Deforge) S.; m. Julie Robin Levine, Feb. 1, 1975; children: Katherine Vanessa, David Robert. BA in Econs., St. Michaels Coll., 1962-66. V.p. Compretic, Inc., Beverly Hills, Calif., 1967-70; brokerage cons. Conn. Gen. Life Ins. Co., Denver, 1970-74; pres. The Core Corp., Denver, 1975-80; mng. dir. Willshire Investments & Holding Co., Denver, 1981-91; pres., chmn. Gen. Capital, Inc., Denver, 1991—; dir. NAt. Assn. Indep. Contr., Denver. 1991—, Nat. Endowment Trust, Denver, 1990—, Tri Corp, Denver, 1980-89, Nat. Acceptance Corp., L.A., 1991—, Nat. Investment Holdings, L.A., 1990—. Mem. Nat. Rep. Eagles, Washington, 1986-90, Inner Circle, Washington, 1985-90, Denver Ctr. Performing Arts, 1976-86. Mem. Am. Cancer League, Glenmoor Country Club. Home: 57 Glenmoor Circle Cherry Hills Village CO 80110 Office: Gen Capital Inc 4155 E Jewell Ave Ste 800 Denver CO 80222

SUTTON, SAMUEL J., lawyer, educator; b. Chgo., July 21, 1941; s. Samuel J. and Elaine (Blossom) S.; m. Anne V. Sutton, Aug. 28, 1965; children: Paige, Jean, Leah, Jepson. BA in History and Philosophy, U. Ariz., 1964, BSEE, 1967; JD, George Washington U., 1969. Bar: Ariz. 1969, D.C. 1970, U.S. Ct. Appeals (fed. cir.) 1983. Patent atty. Gen. Electric Co., Washington, Phoenix, 1967-70; ptnr. Cahill, Sutton & Thomas, Phoenix, 1970—; prof. law Ariz. State U., Tempe, 1975—; expert witness Fed. Dist. Cts., 1983—; trial cons. to numerous lawyers, 1972—; arbitrator Am. Arbitration Assn., Phoenix, 1971—. Author: Patent Preparation, 1976, Intellectual Property, 1978, Commercial Torts, 1980, Art Law, 1988, Law, Science and Technology, 1991. Chmn. air pollution hearing bd. City of Phoenix, 1970-85. Recipient Patent prize Patent Resources Group, 1979, Publ. award IEEE, 1967, Genematus award U. Ariz., 1964, Disting. Achievement award Ariz. State U., 1980. Office: Cahill Sutton & Thomas 2141 E Highland Ave Ste 155 Phoenix AZ 85016-4737

SUTTON, THOMAS C., insurance company executive; b. Atlanta, June 2, 1942; m. Marilyn Sutton; children: Stephen, Paul, Matthew, Meagan. BS in Math. and Physics, U. Toronto, 1965; postgrad., Harvard U., 1982. With Pacific Mut. Life Ins. Co., Newport Beach, Calif., 1963—, actuarial asst., 1966-69, successively asst. actuary, assoc. actuary, asst. v.p., 2d v.p., v.p. individual ins., 1969-80, successively v.p. individual fin., sr. v.p. corp. devel., exec. v.p. individual ins., 1980-87, pres., from 1987, now chmn. bd., chief exec. officer, also bd. dirs.; mem. affiliates adv. bd. U. Calif. Irvine Grad. Sch. Mgmt. Trustee South Coast Repertory; bd. dirs. Ind. Colls. So. Calif. Fellow Soc. of Actuaries (mem. numerous coms.); mem. Am. Acad. Actuaries (com. on dividend prins. and practices, 1978), Pacific States Actuarial Club, L.A. Actuarial Club (sec. 1974-75, pres. 1978-79). Office: Pacific Mut Life Ins Co 700 Newport Center Dr Newport Beach CA 92660-6397

SUTTON, TIMOTHY WAYNE, engineering executive; b. Phoenix, Aug. 13, 1960; s. Everett Harmon and Anna Minnie (Paetzold) S.; m. Rebecca Sue Pflueger, Dec. 27, 1986; 1 child, Lindsey Hope. BSEE, Ariz. State U., 1982. Integrated circuit design engrng. aide semiconductor sector Motorola, Mesa, Ariz., 1981-82, integrated circuit design engr. semiconductor sector, 1982-85, integrated circuit design engrng. sect. leader semiconductor sector, 1985-88, integrated circuit design engrng. dept. mgr. semiconductor sector, 1988—. Co-inventor improved power-on-reset circuit. Bd. dirs. Child Improvement Through Therapy, Mesa, 1986-89, pres., 1988. Mem. IEEE, Alta Mesa Country Club, Eta Kappa Nu, Tau Beta Pi. Republican. Presbyterian. Home: 1565 N Sinova St Mesa AZ 85205-4373 Office: Motorola M235 2200 W Broadway Rd Mesa AZ 85202

SUTTON, VALERIE JEAN, educational administrator, inventor, consultant; b. N.Y.C., Feb. 22, 1951; d. Paul McCullough and Doris (Nichols) S.; m. Kim Darling, Sept. 1984 (div. 1986). Student dance with Lila Zali, Laguna Beach, Calif., 1961-70; with Edite Frandsen and Edel Pederson, Copenhagen, 1970-72. Tchr. dance notation Royal Danish Ballet, Copenhagen, 1974, Boston Conservatory Music, 1976-80, Walnut Hill Sch., Natick, Mass., 1976-80; tchr. sign notation U. Copenhagen, 1974-75; founder, editor The Sign Writer newspaper, Newport Beach, Calif., 1981-84; founder Movement Shorthand Soc., Ctr. for Sutton Movement Writing, Newport Beach, 1973, pres., 1976—, exec. dir., 1978—; tchr., cons. Nat. Tech. Inst. for Deaf, Rochester, N.Y., 1979. Author: Book I, The Classical Ballet Key, 1973, Bournonville Barres, 1975, Monday School, 1976, Sign Writing for Everyday Use, 1981; also numerous works on dance notation and sign writing. Office: PO Box 517 La Jolla CA 92038-0517

SUYETSUGU, GRACE TAMIKO, nurse; b. San Mateo, Calif., Feb. 16, 1957; d. Frank Takiji and Mitsuka (Shimizu) S. BS magna cum laude in Nursing, San Francisco State U., 1979. RN, Calif. Charge nurse med./surg. unit Peninsula Hosp. and Med. Ctr., Burlingame, Calif., 1979-84, staff nurse ICU, 1984-88, charge nurse ICU, 1988-91, staff nurse endoscopy and ICU, 1991-92, recovery room same day surgery and endoscopy, ICU, 1992—. Mem. Nat. Nurses Assn., Calif. Nurses Assn., Am. Assn. Critical Care Nurses. Democrat. Buddhist. Avocations: travel, photography, cooking, needlework, sports. Home: 3682 Bobwhite Ter Fremont CA 94555-1524 Office: Peninsula Hosp and Med Ctr 1783 El Camino Real Burlingame CA 94010-3282

SUZUKI, BOB H., university president. Formerly v.p. acad. affairs Calif. State Univ., Northridge; pres. Calif. State Poly. Univ., Pomona, 1991—. Office: Calif State Poly Univ Office of Pres 3801 W Temple Ave Pomona CA 91768-2557*

SVEC, RICHARD STANLEY, insurance executive; b. L.A., Oct. 16, 1942; s. Stanley F. and Dorothy E. (Whaley) S.; m. Barbara A. Gerzin, Sept. 24, 1966; 1 child, David M. BA, St. Mary's Coll., 1964. Jr. underwriter Fireman's Fund Ins. Co., San Francisco, 1965-67; sales rep. Fireman's Fund Ins. Co., L.A., 1967-69; surety mgr. Fireman's Fund Ins. Co., San Jose, Calif., 1969-77; surety mgr. Alexander & Alexander, San Jose, 1977-81, v.p., 1981-88, sr. v.p., 1988—. Contbr. articles to profl. jours. Bd. dirs. Almaden Valley Youth Athletic Assn., San Jose, 1971-80. Mem. Assoc. Gen. Contractors (chmn. mktg. com. 1989—), Nat. Assn. Surety Bond Producers, Bldg. Industry Assn., Almaden Valley Athletic Club. Home: 7007 Quail Cliff Way San Jose CA 95120-4138 Office: Alexander & Alexander 1530 Meridian Ave Ste 300 San Jose CA 95125-5318

SVEE, GARY DUANE, newspaper editor, author, journalist; b. Billings, Mont., Nov. 11, 1943; s. Sigvart Oluf and Beatrice Evelyn (Lund) S.; m. C. Diane Schmidt, June 26, 1966; children—Darren Kirk, Nathan Jared. B.A., U. Mont., 1967. Unit mgr. Midland Bank, Billings, Mont., 1967-69; reporter Billings Gazette, 1969-76, opinion editor, 1982—; pub. Bridger (Mont.) Bonanza, 1976-77; feature editor Missoulian, Missoula, Mont., 1977-81. Author: Spirit Wolf, 1987, Incident at Pishkin Creek, 1989, Sanctuary, 1990 (Best Western novel Western Writers Am. 1990). vestryman St. Luke's Meml. Bd., Billings, 1989, Salvation Army, Missoula, 1980-82; vestryman Holy Spirit Parish, Missoula, 1980-82. Served to lt. USAR, 1966-72. Recipient Business Writing award U. Mo., 1974, Minority Affairs Reporting award N.W. region Sigma Delta Chi, 1980. Mem. Kiwanis (bd. dirs. Billings club 1988-89, 2d v.p. 1989, pres. 1990, 91-92), Theta Chi. Episcopalian. Home: 474 Indian Trl Billings MT 59105-2706 Office: Billings Gazette PO Box 36300 Billings MT 59107-6300

SVIKHART, EDWIN GLADDIN, equipment manufacturing executive; b. Chgo., July 12, 1930; s. Edwin Gabriel and Mildred Charlotte (Slapnicka) S.; m. Joann Barbara Frisk, Aug. 22, 1954; children: David E., Robert E. BA, Beloit (Wis.) Coll., 1952; postgrad., Bradley U., 1957-59. With Caterpillar Tractor Co., Peoria, Ill., 1956-66; chief fin. officer Berglund Inc., Napa, Calif., 1966-71; chief fin. officer, treas. Galion (Ohio) Mfg. Co., Galion, 1971-77; chief operating officer constrn. equip. internat. div. Dresser Industries, Columbus, Ohio, 1977-81; chief operating officer Rocky Mountain Machinery Co., Salt Lake City, 1981-87; chief oper. officer Custom Equipment Corp., Salt Lake City, 1989-92; ptnr. Travis Capital Mkts., Salt Lake City, 1992—. Served to lt. (j.g.) USN, 1952-56. Named an Outstanding Young Man of Am., U.S. C. of C., 1966. Republican.

SVINOS, JOHN GEORGIOS, software consulting firm executive; b. Kos, Greece, Aug. 3, 1957; came to U.S., 1975; s. Georgios I. and Maria (Kouyoumzoglou) S.; m. Allyson Mary Mazzarulli, Dec. 16, 1981; children: Geo, Alexandra. BSME, West Va. U., 1981, M in Mech. Engring., 1982. Engr. Gulf Oil Corp., Harmarville, Pa., 1981-83; rsch. engr. Gulf Oil Corp., Houston, 1983-85; sr. rsch. engr. Chevron Oil Field Rsch., La Habra, Calif., 1985-89; pres., owner Theta Enterprises, Fullerton, Calif., 1989—; cons. Theta Enterprises, Fullerton, 1989-92, software devel., 1989-02. Author: (software) Rodstar, Roddiag, CBalance, 1991; contbr. tech. papers to publs. Mem. Soc. Petroleum Engrs. (chmn. 1991). Home: 3906 San Marcos Fullerton CA 92635-1231 Office: Theta Enterprises 3906 San Marcos Fullerton CA 92635-1231

SWAGEL, DENNIS JAY, lawyer; b. N.Y.C., May 25, 1946; s. Harry R. and Sah Belle (Fisher) S.; student Harvard U., 1966; certificat de langue pratique U. Paris, 1967; AB (Dana scholar), Hamilton Coll., 1968; JD, Fordham U., 1971; postgrad. U. So. Calif. Sch. Law, Los Angeles, 1976, 79. Bar: N.Y. 1972, Calif. 1974. Law clk. firm Lord, Day & Lord, N.Y.C., 1969; legal asst. Legal Aid Soc., N.Y.C., 1969-70; law clk. Greenbaum, Wolff & Ernst, N.Y.C., 1970-71; ptnr. Casa de Cynjaden Co., Cypress, Calif., 1972-73; assoc. firm William J. Bluestein, Beverly Hills, Calif., 1974; ptnr. firm Bluestein, Heimbach & Swagel, Beverly Hills, 1975; sole practice, Los Angeles, 1975-84, Beverly Hills, Calif., 1984—. Active Environ. Def. Fund; benefactor Da Camera Soc.; friend Joffrey Ballet,Statue of Liberty Found., World Wildlife Fund, Natural Resources Def. Coun., Cousteau Soc., People for the Ethical Treatment of Animals, Gene Autry Western Heritage Mus. Mem. ABA, Los Angeles County Bar Assn., Beverly Hills Bar Assn., Assn. Trial Lawyers Am., L.A. County Bar (profl. responsibility and ethics com.), Los Angeles Trial Lawyers Assn., Fordham Law Alumni Assn., Am. Film Inst., U.S. Olympic Soc., ACLU, Los Angeles County Mus. Art, Mus. Contemporary Art Los Angeles, Town Hall, Internat. Platform Assn., Tree People, Sierra Club. Democrat. Jewish. Club: B'nai B'rith. Home: 4329 Latona Ave Los Angeles CA 90031-1425

SWAIN, HOWARD LYLE, electronics engineer, educator; b. Des Moines, May 10, 1946; s. Lyle and Harriet Swain. BSEE, Iowa State U., 1969; MSEE, Stanford U., 1972. Design engr. Hewlett-Packard Corp., Palo Alto, Calif., 1969-78, project mgr., 1979-91; sr. engr. Hewlett-Packard Corp., Santa Clara, Calif., 1991—; lectr. Stanford U., 1980—. Inventor method and structure. Mem. IEEE, Phi Kappa Phi, Eta Kappa Nu, Tau Beta Pi. Office: Hewlett Packard 5301 Stevens Creek Blvd Santa Clara CA 95052

SWAIN, ROBERT EDSON, architect; b. Wareham, Mass., Apr. 19, 1946; s. Albert Hampton and Ellen Nora (Spillane) S. Urban Design Cert., Istituto Univ. di Architettura, Venice, Italy, 1970; BArch, U. Ariz., 1972. Field engr., estimator Eastern Erection Co., Woburn, Mass., 1972-73; project mgr., designer The Architects Collaborative Inc., Cambridge, Mass., 1973-76; architect in pvt. practice Cambridge, 1977-90; real estate prin. various trust properties, Cambridge, 1977—; pilot, prin. SWAIR, Cambridge, 1984-90; pres., prin., architect Swain Assocs. Inc., Cambridge, 1983-90; architect in pvt. practice Seattle, 1990—; trustee Conway (Mass.) Sch. Landscape Design, 1990—; dir. McKinnon's Neck Conservancy, Argyle, Nova Scotia, Can., 1991—; tchr., guest critic Harvard, MIT, Boston Archtl. Ctr., Boston U., Conway Sch., U. Calif. at Berkeley, 1977—; critic-in-residence U. Nebr. Coll. Architecture, 1986. Architect more than 300 projects including bldgs., landscapes and interiors, 1977—. Recipient Merit award Am. Sch. and Univ., Rindge, N.H., 1987, Best Office Interior award New Eng. Real Estate Dirs., Boston, 1984, others. Mem. AIA. Home and Office: 5002 Greenwood Ave N Seattle WA 98103-6015

SWALLING, JOHN CHRISTIAN, accountant, president; b. Anchorage, Sept. 13, 1949; s. Albert Christian and Minnie H. (Dooley) S.; m. Mary Ann Campbell, May 29, 1972; children: Kate, Matthew, Paul, Ryann. BBA, Notre Dame U., 1971. CPA, Alaska. Various staff and mgmt. positions Arthur Young & Co., Anchorage, San Francisco, 1971-83; ptnr. Arthur Young & Co., Anchorage, 1983-87, Ernst & Whitney & Co., Anchorage, 1987-89, Ernst & Young & Co., Anchorage, 1989-91; pres. John C. Swalling, CPA, Anchorage, 1991—. Active Providence Hosp., Anchorage, 1986—, Anchorage Conv. and Visitors Bur., 1986—, Cath. Social Svcs., 1991—, Multiple Sclerosis Soc., 1982-92; mem. Anchorage organizing com. Winter Olympic Games, chmn., 1990-93, bd. dirs., 1984-93, treas., 1984-89. Mem. AICPA (pub. svc. award 1990), Alaska State Bd. Pub. Accountancy (bd. mem. 1991—), Alaska Soc. CPAs (bd. dirs. 1979-85, sec. 1981, pres. 1983, pub. svc. award 1990), Anchorage Rotary (bd. dirs. 1992-93). Office: John C Swalling CPA 3301 C St Ste 520 Anchorage AK 99503

SWAMINATHAN, VENKATES VADAKANCHERY, electrical engineer, software company executive; b. Bombay, Maharashtra, India, Dec. 31, 1963; came to U.S., 1985; s. Venkateswaran and Radha V. Iyer; m. Debra Kay Ragan, Dec. 20, 1991. B Tech. in Elec. Engring., Indian Inst. Tech., Delhi, India, 1985; MS in Elec. Engring., U. Ill., 1988. Software engr. Teknekron Comm. Systems, Inc., Berkeley, Calif., 1988-91; sr. software engr. Teknekron Comm. Systems, Inc., Berkeley, 1991-92, project mgr., 1992—. Designer (computer software) schematic generator, 1985 (Best Project award 1985), chief architect NMS/Core, 1992. Bd. dirs. Beacon High Sch., Oakland, Calif., 1992. Recipient fellowship U. Ill., 1985. Mem. Assn. for Computing Machinery. Home: 6901 Fairmont Ave El Cerrito CA 94530 Office: Teknekron Comm Systems Inc 2121 Allston Way Berkeley CA 94704

SWAN, ALLAN HOLLISTER, minister; b. Ridgewood, N.J., Oct. 29, 1929; s. Merriam Hollister and Irene Louise (Ferres) S.; m. Janet Louise Peterson, June 6, 1958; children: Jennifer, David, Kimberly, Rebecca. BA, Lafayette Coll., 1951; MDiv, Princeton Sem., 1954; D of Min., San Francisco Theol. Sem., 1975. Ordained to ministry Presbyn. Ch., 1954. Pastor Valmont and Nederland Presbyn. Chs., Boulder, Colo., 1954-57; assoc. pastor 1st Presbyn. Ch., Boulder, 1958-62; pastor Westminster Presbyn. Ch., Ft. Collins, Colo., 1963-70, Lincoln Presbyn. Ch., Stockton, Calif., 1970-80, Covenant Presbyn Ch., Boise, 1981-90; interim pastor Whitworth Presbyn Ch., Spokane, 1990-91, First Presbyn. Ch., Coeur d'Alene, Idaho, 1992—; bd. dirs. Coun. Evangelism, N.Y.C., 1967-69; bd. dirs., exec. com. Vocation Agy., N.Y.C., 1979-86. Mem. orgn. bd. Larimer County Youth Home, Ft. Collins, 1966-70; bd. dirs. Rotary, Stockton, Calif. and Boise, 1970-90. Mem. Psi Chi, Pi Gamma Mu. Home: 15520 N Meadowglen Ct Spokane WA 99208-9527

SWAN, JOSEPH BISHOP, JR., lawyer; b. Evanston, Ill., Aug. 19, 1942; s. Joseph B. Sr. and Virginia (Weber) S.; m. Karyn A. Geislin, Apr. 13, 1989; children: Joseph B. III, Brian M. BA, U. Ariz., 1964, JD, 1967. Bar: Ariz. 1967, U.S. Dist. Ct. Ariz. 1967, U.S. Ct. Appeals (9th cir.) 1971. Law clk. to presiding judge Ariz. U.S. Ct. Appeals, Phoenix, 1967-78; dep. county atty. Maricopa County Atty.'s Office, Phoenix, 1968-70; ptnr. Swan & Woodford, Phoenix, 1970-71, Tempe, Ariz., 1975-77; asst. fed. pub. defender Fed. Pub. Defender's Office, Phoenix, 1971-75; assoc. Renaud, Cook & Videan, Phoenix, 1977-83; ptnr. Oake, Hathaway & Swan, Phoenix, 1983-88, Shelley, Turley, Swan & Bethea, Phoenix, 1988-91, Turley & Swan P.C., Phoenix, 1991—; arbitrator Am. Arbitration Assn., Phoenix, 1984—; judge pro tem Maricopa County Superior Ct., Phoenix, 1986—. Mem. State Bar Ariz. (personal injury and wrongful death specialist 1990), Am. Bd. Trial Advocates (mem. exec. bd. state bar trial sect. 1989—), Phoenix Assn. Def. Coun. (bd. dirs. 1983-84), Ariz. Country Club. Republican. Lutheran. Office: Turley & SwanPC 2025 N 3rd St Ste 350 Phoenix AZ 85004-4531

SWAN, KENNETH CARL, physician, surgeon; b. Kansas City, Mo., Jan. 1, 1912; s. Carl E. and Blanche (Peters) S.; m. Virginia Grone, Feb. 5, 1938; children: Steven Carl, Kenneth, Susan. A.B., U. Oreg., 1933, M.D., 1936. Diplomate: Am. Bd. Ophthalmology (chmn. 1960-61). Intern U. Wis., 1936-37; resident in ophthalmology State U. Iowa, 1937-40; practice medicine specializing in ophthalmology Portland, Oreg., 1945—; staff Good Samaritan Hosp.; asst. prof. ophthalmology State U. Iowa, Iowa City, 1941-44; asso. prof. U. Oreg. Med. Sch., Portland, 1944-45, prof. and head dept. ophthalmology, 1945-78; Chmn. sensory diseases study sect. NIH; mem. adv. council Nat. Eye Inst.; also adv. council Nat. Inst. Neurol. Diseases and Blindness. Contbr. articles on ophthalmic subjects to med. publs. Recipient Proctor Rsch. medal, 1953; Disting. Svc. award U. Oreg., 1963; Meritorious Achievement award U. Oreg. Med. Sch., 1968; Howe Ophthalmology medal, 1977; Aubrey Watzek Pioneer award Lewis and Clark Coll., 1979, Disting. Alumnus award Oreg. Health Scis. U. Alumni Assn., 1988, Disting. Svc. award, 1988; named Oreg. Scientist of Yr. Oreg. Mus. Sci. and Industry, 1959. Mem. Assn. Research in Ophthalmology, Am. Acad. Ophthalmology (v.p. 1978, historian), Soc. Exptl. Biology and Medicine, AAAS, AMA, Am. Ophthal. Soc. (Howe medal for distinguished service 1977), Oreg. Med. Soc., Sigma Xi, Sigma Chi (Significant Sig award 1977). Home: 4645 SW Fairview Blvd Portland OR 97221-2624 Office: Oreg Health Scis U Portland OR 97201

SWAN, RICHARD ALAN, executive recruiter; b. Hollywood, Calif., May 5, 1944; s. Morris George and Mary Theresa (Fenusz) S.; m. Carol Ann Jacobs, Apr. 15, 1967; children: David Michael, Jennifer Marie, Matthew Richard. BS in Indsl. Mgmt., U. So. Calif., 1966; MS in Health Care Adminstrn., Trinity U., 1970. Adminstrv. resident Tucson (Ariz.) Med. Ctr., 1971; assoc. cons. A.T. Kearney and Co. Inc., Chgo., 1971-72; v.p. Tribrook Group Inc., Oakbrook, Ill., 1972-82; dir. program and spl. studies div. James A. Hamilton Assocs. Inc., Dallas, 1982-83; v.p. corp. devel. Vincentian Health Services, L.A., 1983-88; v.p., dir. healthcare group Boyden Internat., L.A., 1988-89; regional v.p. Kieffer Ford & Assocs., Ltd., Orange, Calif., 1989-92; ptnr. Witt/Kieffer, Ford, Hadelman & Lloyd, Irvine, Calif., 1992—. Contbr. articles to profl. jours. Served to capt. Med. Service Corps, U.S. Army, 1967-69. Fellow Am. Assn. Hosp. Cons., Am. Coll. Healthcare Execs.; mem. Soc. Hosp. Planning and Mktg., So. Calif. Soc. Hosp. Planners (charter), Health Care Execs. of So. Calif., Am. Hosp. Assn. Republican. Roman Catholic. Office: Witt Kieffer Ford Hadelman & Lloyd Ste 620 2030 Main St Irvine CA 92714

SWAN, RICHARD HENRY, educator; b. Toledo, Aug. 6, 1956; s. Howard Dean and Elizabeth Kathleen (Carpenter) S. B Instrumental Music Edn., Ea. Mich. U., 1979. Tchr. music, dir. Gila River Indian Reservation, Sacaton, Ariz., 1982—; contbr. to essential skills in edn. State of Ariz., 1988. Office: Sacaton Schs PO Box 98 Sacaton AZ 85247

SWANER, PAULA MARGETTS, clinical psychologist; b. Salt Lake City, Nov. 23, 1927; d. Sumner Gray and Pauline (Moyle) M.; m. Leland Scowcroft, May 22, 1951; children: Leland S., Jr., Sumner Margetts, Paula June Swaner-Sargetakis. BA in Eng. Lit., U. Utah, 1949, MA in Eng. Lit., 1972, MS in Ednl. Psychol., 1978, PhD in Clin. Psychology, 1986; postgrad. in Brit. object rels. theory, Washington Sch. Psychiatry, 1991; postgrad., Mill Valley Calif. Acad., 1990. Lic. clin. psychologist, Utah. Psychotherapist Granite Mental Health Ctr., Salt Lake City, 1978-80; postdoctoral intern Mental Health Unit, Juvenile Ct., Salt Lake City, 1984-87; pvt. practice Salt Lake City, 1986—; courtesy mem. profl. staff Western Inst. Neuropsychiatry, Psychiat. Insts. Am., Salt Lake City; mem. Washington Sch. Psychiatry; cons. Olympus View Hosp., Salt Lake City. Lector, All Saints Episcopal Ch., Salt Lake City. Mem. Am. Psychol. Assn., Utah Psychol. Assn., Wasatch Mountain Club. Democrat. Episcopalian. Office: Paula M Swaner 1775 E 4500 S Salt Lake City UT 84117-4298

SWANK, BRADD A, lawyer; b. Normal, Ill., July 8, 1949; s. George Dearborn and Ruth Eileen (Ruggles) S.; m. Nancy McKay (div. 1976); m. Claudia Lynn Howells Williams, Oct. 3, 1987; 1 child, Devon Atticus. BA, Ind. U., Ft. Wayne, 1973; JD, Willamette U., 1976. Bar: Oreg. 1976. Dep. legis. counsel Oreg. Legis. Assembly, Salem, 1976-84; sr. counsel Oreg. Legis. Judiciary Com., Salem, 1984-86; legal/mgmt. analyst Oreg. State Ct. Adminstr., Salem, 1986—; recorder Uniform Trial Ct. Rules Com., Salem, 1987—; mem. staff Oreg. Jud. Conf. Case Disposition Benchmarks Com., Salem, 1991—, Ju. Dept. Uniform Citations Com., Salem, 1991—. Author: Oregon Judicial Department Manual on Garnishments, 1987; author: (with others) Oregon Bar Civil Litigation Manual, 1990; drafter (legis./law) Oreg. Vehicle Code, 1983. Office: Oreg Jud Dept 1163 State St Salem OR 97310

SWANK, ROY LAVER, physician, educator, inventor; b. Camas, Wash., Mar. 5, 1909; s. Wilmer and Hannah Jane (Laver) S.; m. Eulalia F. Shively, Sept. 14, 1936 (dec.); children: Robert L., Susan Jane (Mrs. Joel Keizer) Stephen (dec.); m. Betty Harris, May 23, 1987. Student, U. Wash., 1926-30; M.D., Northwestern U., 1935; Ph.D., 1935. House officer, resident Peter Bent Brigham Hosp., Boston, 1936-39; fellow pathology Harvard Med. Sch., 1938-39; prof. neurology Oreg. Med. Sch., 1954-74, prof. emeritus, 1974—, also former head div. neurology; pres. Pioneer Filters. Served to maj. M.C. AUS, 1942-46. Recipient Oreg. Gov.'s award for research in multiple sclerosis, 1966. Mem. Am. Physiol. Soc., Am. Neurol. Assn., European Microcirculation Soc., Sigma Xi. Home: 789 SW Summit View Dr Portland OR 97225-6185

SWANN, STEVEN CHARLES, television company executive; b. Bradford, Yorkshire, Eng., Sept. 20, 1951; s. Charles Percival and Olive (Jackson) S.; m. Susan Lynne Nielson, Nov. 26, 1974; children: Alicia Lynne, Alexander Freeman. BS in Bus. Mgmt., U. Utah, 1977. Asst. sec. Am. Savs., Salt Lake City, 1977-84; mgr. comm. LDS Ch., Salt Lake City, 1985-87; mgr. Apple TV Apple Computer Inc., Cupertino, Calif., 1987-90; dir. tech. Orange County Newschannel, Santa Ana, Calif., 1990—. Mem. Data Processing Mgmt. Assn. (cert., chpt. pres. 1985-86), Intecom Users Group (pres. 1987-88), Soc. Motion Picture and TV Engrs. LDS Ch. Home: 16 Mykonos Laguna Niguel CA 92677 Office: Orange County Newschannel 625 N Grand Ave Santa Ana CA 92701-4347

SWANSON, DEBORAH CLAIRE, social scientist, researcher; b. Alhambra, Calif., May 22, 1952; d. Warren Dean and Esther June (Fisher) Collins; m. Tadashi Nitasaka, July 15, 1989. BA, Calif. State U., L.A., 1983, MA, 1986; postgrad., Claremont Grad. Sch., 1988—. Instrl. support asst. Calif. State U., L.A., 1983-87; instr. adult edn. Temple City (Calif.) Adult Sch., 1987-90; social worker L.A. County Dept. Children's Svcs., 1987-90, rschr. social sci., 1990-92; cons. Sonoma Valley Migrant Farm Worker Housing Task Force, 1992—; commr. Sonoma County Human Rights, 1993—; cons. Gt. Western Bank-Ctr. for Applied Social Rsch., Claremont, Calif. 1989, Kaiser Permanente, L.A., 1989. Author conf. presentations. Mem. Com. for Nuclear Responsibility, San Francisco, 1984; charter mem. Japanese Am. Nat. Mus., L.A., 1990. Recipient Alumni Cert. of Honor, Dept. Psychology, Calif. State U., 1985. Mem. Soc. Psychol. Study Social Issues. Home: PO Box 1054 Glen Ellen CA 95442-1054

SWANSON, DONALD ALAN, geologist; b. Tacoma, July 25, 1938; s. Leonard Walter and Edith Christine (Bowers) S.; m. Barbara Joan White, May 25, 1974. BS in Geology, Wash. State U., 1960; PhD in Geology, Johns Hopkins U., 1964. Geologist U.S. Geol. Survey, Menlo Park, Calif., 1965-68, 71-80, Hawaii National Park, 1968-71; sr. geologist Cascades Volcano Obs. U.S. Geol. Survey, Vancouver, Wash., 1980-90, rsch. scientist-in-charge, 1986-89; sr. geologist U.S. Geol. Survey, Seattle, 1990—; affiliate prof. U. Wash., 1992—; cons. U.S. Dept. Energy, Richland, Wash., 1979-83; volcanologist New Zealand Geol. Survey, Taupo, 1984; advisor Colombian Volcano Obs., Manizales, 1986. Assoc. editor Jour. Volcanolgy and Geothermal Rsch., 1976—, Jour. Geophys. Rsch., 1992—; editor Bull. of Volcanology, 1985-90; contbr. numerous articles to profl. jours. Recipient Superior Service award U.S. Geol. Survey, 1980, Meritorious Service award U.S. Dept. Interior, 1985; postdoctoral fellow NATO, 1964-65. Fellow Geol. Soc. Am.; mem. AAAS, Am. Geophys. Union, Sigma Xi. Home: 7537 34th Ave NE Seattle WA 98115-4802 Office: U Washington US Geol Survey Dept Geol Sci AJ-20 Seattle WA 98195

SWANSON, EDWIN ARCHIE, business educator; b. Boone County, Nebr., July 5, 1908; s. Andrew E. and Alma (Nordgren) S.; student George Washington U., 1933-34; B.S., Nebr. State Tchrs. Coll., Kearney, 1932; M.S., U. So. Calif., 1936, Ed.D., 1949; m. Fern E. Anderson, Aug. 25, 1933; children—Edwin Burton, John LeRoy. Elementary, high sch. tchr., Nebr., 1925-35; instr. Fullerton Jr. Coll., 1936-37, 38-39; teaching and research fellow in edn. U. So. Calif., 1935-36, instr. edn. and commerce, 1937-38; asso. prof., dept. head Ariz. State Coll., 1939-46; prof. bus. San Jose (Calif.) State U., 1946-79, emeritus prof. bus., 1979—, chmn. dept., 1957-68. Vis. faculty mem., summer sessions U. Tenn., Woman's Coll. U. N.C., Armstrong Coll., Colo. State Coll., U. So. Calif., U. Fla. Editor: New Media in Teaching the Business Subjects, 1965; editorial bd. Nat. Bus. Edn. Quar., 1939-48, editor, 1939-41. Mem. AAUP, AAAS, Am. Mgmt. Assn., Nat. (pres. 1950-51, mem. and chmn. publs. com. and editorial bd. 1959-62, editor Yearbook 1965), Western (pres. 1954-55, gen. program chmn. conv. 1965), Cal. bus. edn. assns., NEA, Calif. Tchrs. Assn., Phi Delta Kappa (chpt. pres. 1945-46, 54-55, area coordinator 1955-66), Kappa Delta Pi, Pi Omega Pi, Delta Pi Epsilon (mem. nat. commn. bus. and econ. edn. 1964-65, mem. bd. govs. for research and devel. in bus. edn. 1968-74), Gamma Rho Tau, Xi Phi, Phi Kappa Phi (chpt. pres. 1956-57). Presbyn. Club: Commonwealth (San Francisco). Contbr. publs. in field. Home: 2390 Mazzaglia Ave San Jose CA 95125-3626

SWANSON, LEE RICHARD, computer security executive; b. Mpls., Apr. 21, 1957; s. Donald Jerome and Wildie (Greenwood) S.; m. Amy Jane Shutkin, Jan. 1, 1980 (div. Apr. 1991). BS, U. Minn., 1983. Owner, prin. Environ. Landforms, Inc., Minnetonka, Minn., 1974-80; v.p. Blomfield-Swanson, Inc., Mpls., 1981-85; contractor Citicorp Card Acceptance Svcs., Seattle, 1986-88; pres., mktg. dir., cons. Room Svcs. Computers, Bellevue, Wash., 1988-91; exec. v.p. First Step Computer Consultants, Inc., Novato, Calif., 1991—. Libertarian. Office: First Step Computer Consultants Inc 60 Galli Dr Ste T Novato CA 94949

SWANSON, MARK TODD, archaeologist; b. Raleigh, N.C., Dec. 5, 1951; s. Haywood Lee and Rachel (Britt) S. BA, U. N.C., 1974; MA, U. de las Americas, Cholulu, Mex., 1981. Assoc. archaeologist New World Rsch., Inc., Polloc, La., 1978-86, Fort Walton Beach, Fla., 1978-86; ptnr. Rsch. Assocs., Yucaipa, Calif., 1987-89, proprietor, 1989—. Mem. Soc. of Profl. Archaeologists. Home: 35240 Ave D Yucaipa CA 92399 Office: Rsch Assocs 35240 Ave D Yucaipa CA 92399

SWANSON, PAUL RUBERT, minister; b. Bakersfield, Calif., May 13, 1943; s. Roland Hilding and Myrtle Isabelle (Magnuson) S.; m. Mary Elizabeth Greene, June 18, 1967; children: Kristen Ann, Karlynn Marie, Jonathan Paul. BA, Pacific Luth. U., 1966; MDiv, Luth. Sch. Theology, 1970. Ordained minister, Luth. Ch. Pastor 1st Luth. Ch., Anaconda, Mont., 1970-76, King of Kings Luth. Ch., Milwaukie, Oreg., 1976-84; asst. to bishop Pacific N.W. Synod-Luth. Ch. in Am., Portland, Oreg., 1984-87; bishop Oreg. Synod-Evang. Luth. Ch. Am., Portland, 1987—; bd. dirs. Legacy Health System, Portland. Regent Pacific Luth. U., Tacoma, 1987—; bd. dirs. Emanuel Hosp., Portland, 1987; chmn. bd. dirs. Hearthstone, Inc., Anaconda, 1973-76; bd. dirs. Ecumenical Ministries Oreg., Portland, 1984—. Recipient Disting. Svc. award Pacific Luth. U., 1993.

SWANSON, RICHARD MARVIN, criminal psychology educator; b. El Paso, Tex., May 4, 1943; s. Joseph Paul and Dorothy Elizabeth (Bryce) S. BA, U. Tex., 1965; MA, U. Colo., 1968, PhD, 1970; JD, U. Denver, 1985. Bar: Fla., 1985; lic. psychologist, Fla., Colo. Research assoc. Ft. Logan Mental Health Ctr., Denver, 1969-71; research dir. Ctr. Study of Crime, Delinquency and Corrections Southern Ill. U., Carbondale, 1971-72; asst. prof. psychology U. Fla., Gainesville, 1972-75, assoc. prof. psychology, 1975-87; asst. dir. County of Alachua (Fla.) Dept. Corrections, Gainesville, 1975-76; dir. criminal justice program U. Fla., Gainesville, 1976-79; chmn., prof. Dept. Law and Mental Health, Fla. Mental Health Ctr. U. South Fla., Tampa, 1987-91; dir. PsyLaw Inst., Tampa, 1988-91; chief mental health diagnostics Colo. Dept. Corrections, Denver, 1991—; clin. prof. dept. psychiatry U. Colo., 1992—; pres. Nat. Research Found., Gainesville, 1976-81; cons. Nat. Inst. Corrections Jail Ctr., Boulder, 1977-86, Belize, Cen. Am., 1988-91; rsch. prof. Fla. Mental Health Inst., 1991—. Contbr. articles to profl. jours. Active Gov.'s Task Force on Criminal Justice Research State of Fla., Tallahassee, 1977-80; chmn. Corrections Adv. Bd. Alachua County, Gainesville, 1972-84. Named Tchr. of Yr. Coll. Liberal Arts and Scis. U. Fla., 1986-87. Mem. ABA, APA (Psychology Tchr. of Yr. 1987), Am. Correctional Assn. (prof. edn. com. 1978-80), Fla. Bar Assn. (corrections com. 1987-90). Democrat. Methodist. Office: CO Dept Corrections 10900 Old Smith Rd Denver CO 80239

SWANSON, RICHARD WILLIAM, statistician; b. Rockford, Ill., July 26, 1934; s. Richard and Erma Marie (Herman) S.; m. Laura Yoko Arai, Dec. 30, 1970. BS, Iowa State U., 1958, MS, 1964. Ops. analyst Stanford Rsch. Inst., Monterey, Calif., 1958-62; statistician ARINC Rsch. Corp., Washington, 1964-65; sr. scientist Booz-Allen Applied Rsch., Vietnam, 1965-67, L.A., 1967-68; sr. ops. analyst Control Data Corp., Honolulu, 1968-70; mgmt. cons., Honolulu, 1970-73; exec. v.p. SEQUEL Corp., Honolulu, 1973-75; bus. cons. Hawaii Dept. Planning and Econ. Devel., Honolulu, 1975-77, tax rsch. and planning officer Dept. Taxation, 1977-82; ops. rsch. analyst U.S. Govt., 1982-89; shipyard statistician U.S. Govt., 1989—. Served with AUS, 1954-56. Mem. Hawaiian Acad. Sci., Sigma Xi. Home: 583 Kamoku St Apt 3505 Honolulu HI 96826-5240 Office: Pearl Harbor Naval Shipyard PO Box 400 Honolulu HI 96860-5350

SWANSON, ROBERT KILLEN, management consultant; b. Deadwood, S.D., Aug. 11, 1932; s. Robert Claude and Marie Elizabeth (Kersten) S.; m. Nancy Anne Oyaas, July 19, 1958; children: Cathryn Lynn, Robert Stuart, Bart Killen. B.A., U. S.D., 1954; postgrad., U. Melbourne, Australia, 1955. With Gen. Mills, Inc., Mpls., 1955-58, 71-79, v.p., 1971-73, group v.p., 1973-77, exec. v.p., 1977-79; with Marathon Oil Co., Findlay, Ohio, 1958-60; sr. v.p., dir. Needham, Harper & Steers, Inc., Chgo., 1961-69; joint mng. dir. S. H. Benson (Holdings) Ltd., Eng., 1969-71; pres., chief operating officer Greyhound Corp., Phoenix, 1980; chmn., chief exec. officer Del E. Webb Corp., Phoenix, 1981-87; chmn. RKS Inc., Phoenix, 1987—; bd. dirs. Grossman's Inc., Conzept Internat., ST Internat. Ltd., Am. S.W. Concepts Inc., Internat. Imports Inc. Bd. dirs. Univ. S.D. Found. 2d lt. U.S. Army, 1955. Fulbright scholar, 1954-55; Woodrow Wilson scholar. Mem. U.S. Coun. Fgn. Rels., U.K. Dirs. Inst., U.S. Internat. Scholars Assn., English Speaking Union. Episcopalian. Home and Office: RKS Inc 5600 N Palo Cristi Rd Paradise Valley AZ 85253-7543

SWARD, ROBERT STUART, author; b. Chgo., June 23, 1933; s. Irving Michael and Gertrude (Huebsch) S.; children: Cheryl, Barbara, Michael,

Hannah, Nicholas. BA with hons., U. Ill., 1956; MA, U. Iowa, 1958; post-grad., U. Bristol (Eng.), 1960-61, Middlebury (Vt.) Coll., 1956-60. Instr. English Conn. Coll., New London, 1958-59; writer-in-residence Cornell U., Ithaca, N.Y., 1962-64, U. Iowa, 1967-68; asst. prof. English/writer-in-residence U. Victoria (B.C.), 1969-73; editor/pubr. Soft Press, Victoria, 1970-79; radio broadcaster Can. Broadcasting Corp., Toronto, Ont., 1979-84; tech. writer Santa Cruz Op. (SCO), Santa Cruz, Calif., 1987-89; writer-in-residence extension program U. Calif., Santa Cruz, 1988—; writer-in-residence Cabrillo Coll., Aptos, Calif., 1988—; vis. poet creative writing program U. Calif., Santa Cruz, 1992—; writer in the schs. Ont. Arts Coun., Toronto, 1979-84, Cultural Coun., Santa Cruz, 1984—; cons. to pubs.; book reviewer Toronto Star, others. Author: Uncle Dog and Other Poems, 1962, Autobiography, CAAS, 1991, Poems: New and Selected, 1983, Four Incarnations: New & Selected Poems, 1957-91. Tchr. Oak Bay Sr. Citizens, Victoria, 1973-74; editor, advisor Jazz Press, Poet Santa Cruz Pubs., 1985-87. With USN, 1951-54. Fulbright grantee, 1961, Guggenheim fellow, 1964-65, D.H. Lawrence fellow, U. N.Mex., 1966-67, Yaddo MacDowell Colony grantee, 1959-82; Djerassi Found. grantee, 1990—; recipient Villa Montalvo Lit. Arts award, 1989-90. Mem. League of Can. Poets, Writers Union of Can. (newsletter editor 1983-84), Nat. Writers Union. Democrat. Home: PO Box 7062 Santa Cruz CA 95061-7062 Office: 435 Meder St Santa Cruz CA 95060-2307

SWART, VERNON DAVID, JR., technology company executive; b. Redwood City, Calif., Oct. 12, 1955; s. Vernon David Sr. and Elizabeth Marie (Eberhard) S.; m. Robin Jean Hubert, Aug. 10, 1980; 3 children: Alexandra Nicole, Hunter Colton, Spencer Hamilton. BSBA, San Jose State U., 1981. Lic. real estate broker, Calif. Regional mgr. Augat Inc., Arlington Heights, Ill., 1983-86; exec. v.p., bd. dirs. McKenzie Tech., Fremont, Calif., 1987-90; ceo Precision Plastics and Swart Interconnect Divsns. of Swart Industries Corp., South San Francisco, Calif., 1991—. Active Planning Commn., Deer Park, Ill., 1985. Mem. Internat. Inst. Connector Interconnection Tech. (no. Calif. chpt.). Republican. Office: Swart Industries Inc Precision Plastics Swart Intercon Divsns 340 Roebling Rd South San Francisco CA 94080-4813

SWARTOUT, EDWIN LESTER, engineering executive, mechanical engineer; b. Boonville, N.Y., Aug. 31, 1949; s. Lester Leroy and Vera Edna (Watson) S.; m. Greta Louise Young, June 4, 1971 (div. Aug. 1972); m. Carolyn Joyce Seelye, Sept. 5, 1973; 1 child, Ryan Eastman. BA in Philosophy, Wadhams Hall Sem., 1971; AAS in Mech. Design, Canton Agrl. and Tech. Coll., 1980. Outpatient therapist Mental Health Ctr. Mercy Hosp., Watertown, N.Y., 1972-76; family therapist Family Counseling Svc., Watertown, 1977-78; design trainee N.Y. Airbrake, Watertown, 1980-81, devel. lab. technician, 1981-82; mech. designer Maxlight (div. of Raychem), Phoenix, 1982-84; coord. program, supr. engring svcs. Kroy Inc., Scottsdale, Ariz., 1984-86, mgr. engring., 1986-90, dir. engring., 1990-92, v.p. engring., 1992—. Patentee in field. Bd. dirs. Transitional Living Svcs., Watertown, 1974, 77. Named Mental Health Worker of Yr., Jefferson County Mental Health Assn., 1975. Office: Kroy Inc 14555 N Hayden Rd Scottsdale AZ 85260

SWARTOUT, GLEN MARTIN, optometrist; b. Troy, N.Y., Mar. 25, 1956; s. J. Baxter and Dorothy (Porter) S.; m. Karen Aubrey Niles, Mar. 14, 1987. AB, Dartmouth Coll., 1978; OD, SUNY, N.Y.C., 1982; D of Naturopathy, Clayton Sch., 1989; BD (hon.), Universal Brotherhood, Duluth, Ga., 1990. Vision therapist Swartwout & Lazarus, Latham, N.Y., 1972; dir. Optometric Ctr. Tokyo, 1982-84; clin. dir. Learning Disabilities Assocs., Latham, 1984-89; mem. clinic staff Nat. Coll. Naturopathic Medicine, Portland, Oreg., 1989-90; co-founder Hawaii Ctr. Natural Medicine, Hilo, 1990—; dir. Vision Fitness, Hilo, 1991—; pres. Achievement of Excellence Rsch. Acad. Internat., Hilo, 1990—; cons. Am. Optometric Assn., St. Louis, 1982-84; mem. adv. bd. Pediatric Optometry and Vision Therapy. Author: Electromagnetic Pollution Solutions, 1990, Electromagnetic Health Research Manual, 1990; contbg. editor Jour. N.Y. State Optemetric Assn., 1985—; patentee VDT stress reduction lens, 1990. Cons. Easter Seals Soc., Hilo, 1991—; minister Universal Brotherhood Movement, Hilo, 1991—; bd. dirs. Hawaii Island Environ. Coun., 1991; pres. Holistic Health Network, N.Y., 1985-89, Blackwood Inst. Holistic Studies, N.Y., 1985; pres. Starfire Internat., 1992; co-founder Parents Active for Vision Edn., Hawaii chpt., 1992. Recipient Cert. Appreciation NCAA, 1978. Fellow Coll. Syntonic Optometry (sec., trustee 1987—), Internat. Coll. Applied Nutrition; mem. Coll. Optometrists in Vision Devel., Optometric Extension Program Found., Internat. Soc. Holistic Optometry (state dir. 1984-89, Optometrist of Yr. 1985), Japanese C. of C., Beta Sigma Kappa (chpt. pres. 1981-82). Office: Achievement of Excellence 311 Kalanianaole Ave Hilo HI 96720

SWARTZ, RAY, data processing executive; b. Glendale, Calif., May 3, 1952; s. Albert and Ethel S. BA, U. Calif., Irvine, 1974; MBA, U. Calif., Berkeley, 1981. Mng. dir. Berkeley Decision Systems, Santa Cruz, Calif., 1981—; adj. lectr. U. Santa Clara, 1982-84; vis. lectr. U. Calif., Santa Cruz, 1984-87, India-sponsored by NIIT, 1988. Author: Doing Business with C, 1989, UNIX Application Development, 1990; editor conf. proc. Modeling and Simulation, 1984; columnist Answers on UNIX, 1989—; creator tng. on video line of C Programming and UNIX system video tng. courses. Coach Community Basketball League, Santa Cruz, 1987. Mem. Soc. Computer Simulation (bd. dirs. 1985-89, sec. 1988), USENIX, Uniforum, Nat. Speakers Assn. Office: Berkeley Decision/Systems 803 Pine St Santa Cruz CA 95062-2444

SWARTZ, RICHARD JOEL, restaurant executive; b. Beverly Hills, Calif., Dec. 3, 1942; s. Louis A. and Charlotte (Litwin) S.; children: Todd L., Dee Ann; m. Marlene B. Among, Nov. 30, 1987. BS in Fin. Mgmt., U. So. Calif., 1964; JD, U. Calif., Berkeley, 1968. Hotel internal auditor Haskins & Sells, CPAs, San Francisco, 1968-69; contr. Tropicana Hotel and Country Club, Las Vegas, Nev., 1969-71; v.p. food and beverage Harrah's Hotels, Reno and Lake Tahoe, 1971-75; mgr. legal affairs AMFAC Restaurants, Resorts and Retail Mgmt., Nev., 1976-78; pres. CECO Resort Pers. Tng. Programs, Honolulu, 1979-83; resident gen. mgr. Kaua'i (Hawaii) Surf Resort, 1986-87; CFO, ptnr. Hale'iwa (Hawaii) Restaurants Ltd., 1989-91; pres. PRL Restaurants, Honolulu, 1986—. Co-author: The Hotel Employee Mutual Trust Network, 1986. Mem. Soc. Resort Accts. (audit com.), Nat. Restaurant Assn. (polit. action com.), Hawaii Hotel Assn., U.S. Tennis Assn., Nat. Eagle Scout Assn., Friends of 'Iolani, Prince Kuhiō Hawaiian Civic Club. Republican. Home: 2746 Ferdinand Ave Honolulu HI 96822-1741 Office: PRL Restaurants 1200 Ala Moana Blvd 4A Honolulu HI 96814

SWARTZ, ROSLYN HOLT, real estate investment executive; b. Los Angeles, Dec. 9, 1940; d. Abe Jack and Helen (Canter) Holt; m. Allan Joel Swartz, June 2, 1963. AA, Santa Monica (Calif.) Coll., 1970; BA summa cum laude, UCLA, 1975; MA, Pepperdine U., 1976. Cert. community coll. instr., student-personnel worker, Calif. Mgr. pub. relations Leader Holdings, Inc., L.A., 1968-75, pres., 1991—; sec., treas. Leader Holdings, Inc., North Hollywood, Calif., 1975-81, pres., 1981-91; chief exec. officer Beverly Stanley Investments, L.A., 1979—. Condr. An Oral History of the Elderly Jewish Community of Venice, Calif. at Los Angeles County Planning Dept. Library, 1974. Trainer VITA, L.A., 1975; mem. Friends of the Hollywood Bowl; bd. dirs. Am. Friends of Haifa Med. Ctr.; founder Music Ctr. L.A., L.A. County Mus. Art; capital patron Simon Wiesenthal Ctr. Fellow Phi Beta Kappa (bicentennial); mem. NAFE, AAUW, Am. Soc. Profl. and Exec. Women, Am. Pub. Health Assn., Am. Pharm. Assn., Women in Comml. Real Estate, L.A. World Affairs Coun., Town Hall (life), Century City C. of C., UCLA Alumni Assn. (life), UCLA Founders Circle, Women's Coun. Women's Guild Cedars-Sinai Med. Ctr., UCLA Alumni Assn. (life), Santa Monica Coll. Alumni Assn. (life), Order of Eastern Star, Phi Alpha Theta, Alpha Gamma Sigma, Alpha Kappa Delta, Phi Delta Kappa, Pi Gamma Mu.

SWARTZ, TERESA ANNE, marketing educator, researcher, consultant; b. Port Alleghany, Pa., May 3, 1953; d. Robert Wilson and Geraldine Elizabeth (Hess) S. B.S. in Edn., Clarion U., Pa., 1974, M.B.A., 1977; Ph.D. in Bus. Adminstrn., Ohio State U., 1981. Cert. secondary tchr., Pa. High sch. tchr. Bradford Area Schs., Bradford, Pa., 1975-76; grad. asst. Clarion U., Pa., 1976-77; researcher, teaching assoc., Ohio State U., Columbus, 1977-80; lectr. Ariz. State U., Tempe, 1980-81, asst. prof., 1981-86, assoc. prof., 1986-91; prof. mktg. Calif. Poly. U., San Luis Obispo, 1991—; mktg. cons., Tempe, 1981—; vis. prof. Dailey and Assocs., L.A., 1983. Mem. Am. Mktg. Assn. (Phoenix bd. dirs. 1982-85, nat. bd. dirs. 1991—, v.p. elect western region 1985-86, v.p. 1986-87, v.p. elect svcs. mktg. div. 1991-92, v.p. svcs. mktg. divsn. 1992-93), Assn. Consumer Research, Am. Acad. Advt., Acad. Mktg. Sci., Assn. Women in Psychology, Beta Gamma Sigma. Democrat. Avocations: golf, tennis, travel, softball. Office: Calif Poly U Dept Bus Adminstrn San Luis Obispo CA 93407

SWARTZENDRUBER, DOUGLAS EDWARD, biology educator; b. Goshen, Ind., May 3, 1946; s. Edward Glen and Mary Adeline (Aschliman) S.; m. Rhonda Lou Willems, June 15, 1969; children: Douglas A., Nick A., Rachel L. BA, Goshen Coll., 1968; PhD, U. Colo. Health Sci. Ctr., 1974. Staff mem. Los Alamos (N.Mex.) Nat. Lab., 1974-80; assoc. prof. U. Tex. M.D. Anderson Hosp. and Tumor Inst., Houston, 1980-82; prof., chmn. biology U. Colo., Colorado Springs, 1982—; dir. OncoMetrics, Colorado Springs. Contbr. 50 rsch. papers. Mem. Citizens Goals, Colorado Springs, 1992—. Grantee in field, 1974—. Mem. AAAS, Am. Assn. Cancer Rsch., Internat. Soc. Analytical Cytology, Sigma Xi. Office: U Colo 1420 Austin BLuffs Pkwy Colorado Springs CO 80918-3733

SWARTZLANDER, EARL EUGENE, JR., engineering educator, former electronics company executive; b. San Antonio, Feb. 1, 1945; s. Earl Eugene and Jane (Nicholas) S.; m. Joan Vickery, June 9, 1968. BSEE, Purdue U., 1967; MSEE, U. Colo., 1969; PhD, U. So. Calif., 1972. Registered profl. engr., Ala., Calif., Colo., Tex. Devel. engr. Ball Bros. Rsch. Corp., Boulder, Colo., 1967-69; Hughes fellow, mem. tech. staff Hughes Aircraft Co., Culver City, Calif., 1969-73; mem. rsch. staff Tech. Svc. Co., Santa Monica, Calif., 1973-74; chief engr. Geophys. Systems Corp., Pasadena, Calif., 1974-75, staff engr. to sr. staff engr., 1975-79, project mgr., 1979-84, lab. mgr., 1985-87; dir. ind. R&D TRW Inc., Redondo Beach, Calif., 1987-90; Schlumberger Centennial prof. engring. dept. elec. and computer engring. U. Tex., Austin, 1990—; hon. conf. chair 3rd Internat Conf. Parallel and Distributed Systems, Taiwan, 1993; hon. chair 3d Internat. Conf. on Parallel and Distributed Systems, Taiwan, 1992; gen. chair 11th Internat. Symposium Computer Arithmetic, 1992, Internat. Conf. Application Specific Array Processors, 1990, Internat. Conf. Wafer Scale Integration, 1989, Internat. Conf. Distbg. Computing Systems, 1985. Author: VLSI Signal Processing Systems, 1986; editor: Computer Design Development, 1976, Systolic Signal Processing Systems, 1987, Wafer Scale Integration, 1989, Computer Arithmetic Vol. 1 and 2, 1990; editor-in-chief Jour. of VLSI Signal Processing, 1989—, IEEE Transactions on Computers, 1991—, editor 1982-86, IEEE Transactions on Parallel and Distributed Systems, 1989-90; Hardware Area Editor ACM Computing Reviews, 1985—; assoc. editor: IEEE Jour. Solid-State Circuits, 1984-88; contbr. over 75 articles to profl. jours. and tech. conf. proc. Bd. dirs. Casiano Estates Homeowners Assn., Bel Air, Calif., 1976-78, pres. 1978-80; bd. dirs. Benedict Hills Estates Homeowners Assn., Beverly Hills, Calif., 1984—, pres. 1990—. Recipient Disting. Engring. Alumnus award Purdue U., West Lafayette, Ind., 1989, named Outstanding Elec. Engr. Purdue U., 1992. Fellow IEEE; mem. Computer Soc. IEEE (bd. govs. 1987-91), Signal Proc. Soc. IEEE(Adcom 1992—), IEEE Solid-State Circuits Coun. (sec. 1992—), Knights of Malta (knight Imperial Russian Order St. John of Jerusalem, 1993), Eta Kappa Nu, Sigma Tau, Omicron Delta Kappa.

SWARTZWELDER, JOHN JOSEPH, writer, producer television show; b. Seattle, Feb. 8, 1949; s. John Joseph Sr. and Gloria Mae (Matthews) S. Student, U. Wash., 1967. Writer various advt. agys., Chgo., Los Angeles, Houston, 1970-85; comedy writer TV shows Saturday Night Live, N.Y.C., 1985-86, David Brenner Show, N.Y.C., 1987; freelance writer TV episodes for shows Women in Prison, Mr. President, The Dictator, L.A., 1987-89; freelance writer TV episodes for shows The Simpsons, L.A., 1989, story editor, 1989-91, producer, 1991—. Recipient Emmy award for The Simpsons, 1990, numerous advt. awards. Mem. Writers Guild Am. East, AFTRA. Home: 14311 Addison St Apt 209 Sherman Oaks CA 91423-1846 Office: care Fox Broadcasting Co PO Box 900 Beverly Hills CA 90213-0900

SWATT, STEPHEN BENTON, communications executive, consultant; b. L.A., June 26, 1944; s. Maurice I. and Lucille E. (Sternberger) S.; m. Susan Ruth Edelstein, Sept. 7, 1968; 1 child, Jeffrey Michael. BSBA, U. Calif., 1966, M in Journalism, 1967. Writer San Francisco Examiner, 1967; reporter United Press Internat., L.A., 1968-69; producer news Sta. KCRA-TV, Sacramento, Calif., 1969-70, reporter news, 1970-79, chief polit. and capitol corres., 1979-92; exec. v.p. Nelson-Lucas Communications, Sacramento, 1992—; guest lectr. Calif. State U., Sacramento. Contbr. articles to profl. jours. With USCG, 1966. Recipient No. Calif. Emmy NATAS, 1976-77, Pub. Svc. award Calif. State Bar, 1977, Exceptional Achievement Coun. advancement and Support of Edn., 1976, Nat. Health Journalism award Am. Chiropractic Assn., 1978. Mem. Soc. Profl. Journalists (8 awards), Capitol Corres. Assn., U. Calif. Alumni Assn., Sacramento Press Club. Office: Nelson-Lucas Communications 1029 J St Sacramento CA 95814

SWEANEY, JAMES LEO, gemologist, jewelry designer; b. Ft. Stockton, Tex., Mar. 4, 1944; s. James William and Wanda Jo (Burcham) S.; m. Kaye Lynn Swanson, Aug. 14, 1971; 1 child, Jennifer Lynn. BA, Calif. State U., Fullerton, 1971. Jewelry designer Guerneville, Calif., 1971-76; lab. supr. Gemol. Inst. Am., Santa Monica, Calif., 1976-81; exec. v.p. Am. Pearl Co., Camden, Tenn., 1981-84; gemologist, designer Mardon Jewelers, Inc., Riverside, Calif., 1984—. Contbr. articles to industry publs. Fellow Gemol. Assn. Gt. Britain (with distinction); mem. Gemol. Inst. Am. (grad. gemologist). Office: Mardon Jewelers Inc 3630 Riverside Plz Riverside CA 92506

SWEARENGEN, JACK CLAYTON, II, research and development manager, systems engineer; b. Zanesville, Ohio, Feb. 11, 1940; s. Jack Clayton and Margaret Ann (Bowman) S.; m. Nancy Lee Hubbard, Sept. 5, 1962; 1 child, Alan Peter. BS, U. Idaho, 1961; MS, U. Ariz., 1963; PhD, U. Wash., 1970. Rsch. engr. FMC Corp. Cen. Engring. Labs., Santa Clara, Calif., 1963-66; teaching assoc. U. Wash., Seattle, 1966-70; mem. tech. staff Sandia Nat. Labs., Albuquerque, 1970-78; supr. matls. sci. div. Sandia Nat. Labs., Livermore, Calif., 1978-84, supr. solar components div., 1984-86; supr. adv. sys. div. Sandia Nat. Labs., 1986-88; arms control sci. advisor Office of Sec. of Def., The Pentagon, Washington, 1988-90; mgr. tech. applications Sandia Nat. Labs., Livermore, 1990—; mem. awards panel NSF, 1988; reviewer various tech. jours., 1980-88. Contbr. fifty-five articles to profl. jours.; editor: Mechanical Testing for Deformation Model Development, 1980. Founder, chmn. Good Samaritan Ministries, Dublin, Calif., 1984—; mem. Bread for the World, Washington, 1980—. Fellow Am. Sci. Affiliation; mem. AIAA, ASME. Democrat. Home: 1151 Vienna St Livermore CA 94550-5618

SWEDBERG, GERTRUDE LALIAH, director women's programs, biology educator; b. Shanghai, China, Oct. 24, 1933; came to U.S., 1940; d. Robert Joseph and Frances Willard (King) Salmon; m. Kenneth Charles Swedberg, June 7, 1958; children: Jeffrey Eugene, Claire Ellen. BA, Radcliffe Coll., 1955; postgrad., U. Minn., 1957-58; MS, Oreg. State U., 1960. Tchr. Mary C. Wheeler Sch., Providence, 1955-57; rsch. assoc. Oreg. State U., Corvallis, 1959-60; coord. women's studies Ea. Wash. U., Cheney, 1979-83, dir. women's programs, 1983—, asst. prof., 1975—. Contbr. articles to profl. jours. Pres. Spokane (Wash.) Regional Women's Commn., 1988-90. Danforth assoc.; recipient Outstanding Achievement award YWCA, 1989. Mem. AAAS, N.Y. Acad. Scis., Nat. Women's Studies Assn., N.W. Women's Studies Assn. (co-coord. 1987-91), LWV, Phi Kappa Phi. Home: 19607 S Cheney Spangle Rd Cheney WA 99004-9606 Office: Ea Wash U MS 166 Cheney WA 99004

SWEDBERG, STEVEN HAROLD, research scientist; b. Bellingham, Wash., Aug. 1, 1964; s. Byron Lincoln and Shirley Aileen (Hague) S.; m. Nicole Annette Montague, June 25, 1988. BS, Harvey Mudd Coll., Claremont, Calif., 1987; MD, U. Wash., 1992. Rsch. technologist U. Wash., Seattle, 1987-88, rsch. scientist, 1992—. Contbr. articles to profl. jours. Mem. Sigma Xi, Phi Lambda Upsilon. Home: 5844 NE 75th St A109 Seattle WA 98115-6303 Office: U Wash RC-09 Seattle WA 98195

SWEENEY, CHRISTOPHER LEE, applied mathematics engineer; b. Denver, Oct. 14, 1959; s. Roger Lee Sweeney and Beverly Ann (Wagoner) Good; m. Susan Ann Merrell, May 24, 1986. Student, Community Coll. Denver; grad., U. Colo., 1988. Technican Ball Computer Products, Boulder, Colo., 1978-82, devel. engr., 1982-83; devel. engr. Ball Electronic Systems, Westminster, Colo., 1983-88; reliability engr. StorageTek, Louisville, Colo., 1989—. Inventor in field. Mem. Eta Kappa Nu, Tau Beta Pi. Home: 9836 Jellison St Broomfield CO 80021-4272 Office: StorageTek 2270 S 88th St Louisville CO 80028-0002

SWEENEY, DANIEL BRYAN, JR., financial adviser, pension fund administrator; b. Providence, Oct. 23, 1946; s. Daniel Bryan Sr. and Clara Perene (Hodgdon) S.; m. Carol Jane Weir, June 18, 1966; children: Heather, Holly. AS in Electronic Engring., San Mateo Community Coll., 1969. CLU. Tax specialist Northwestern Nat. Life, Minn., 1974-81; pres. Dan Sweeney & Assocs., Inc., Bellevue, Wash., 1981—; pres., trustee Davis-Bacon Pension Adminstrn., Inc., Kirkland, Wash., 1987—. Author: Investment Planning Ideas, 1983. With USN, 1964-70. Mem. Internat. Assn. Fin. Planners, Eastside Estate Planning Coun., Masons. Office: Davis-Bacon Pension Adminstrn 10532 NE 68th Ste 130 Kirkland WA 98033

SWEENEY, JAMES AUGUSTUS, retired marine engineer; b. Chelsea, Mass., Oct. 5, 1912; s. Michael James and Jane Ann (Goggin) S.; m. Leonora Bixby, Nov. 11, 1939; children: Janet Sweeney Armstrong, Cari Sweeney Damoose, Michelle Sweeney Mellen. BS in Naval Architecture and Marine Engring., MIT, 1934, MS in Naval Architecture and Marine Engring., 1936. Registered profl. engr., N.Y., N.J. Trainee United Shipyards, N.Y.C., 1936-38; structural designer George G. Sharp, Inc., Naval Architect, N.Y.C., 1938-40, freelance rep., 1947-52, constrn. rep., 1972-74; gen. outfitting supt. Ingalls Shipbuilding Corp., Pascagoula, Miss., 1940-47, 52-53; various managerial positions N.Y. Shipbuilding Corp., Camden, N.J., 1953-62; tech. advisor to gen. mgr. L.A. Div. Todd Shipyards Corp., N.Y.C., 1962-63; ind. cons. shipbuilding, 1963-65, 70-72; project engr./mgr. Nat. Steel & Shipbuilding Co., San Diego, 1965-68; mgr. prodn./design support Advanced Marine Tech. div. Litton Systems, El Segundo, Calif., 1968-70; sr. engr. John J. McMullen Assocs., Inc., N.Y.C., 1974-75; naval architect tanker analysis dept.marine and rail equipment div. FMC Corp., Portland, Oreg., 1975-77; cons. James M. Montgomery Internat., Inc., Pasadena, Calif., 1977-78; ret., 1978; instr. warship design MIT, 1934-36. Active various civic and community orgns. Scholarship recipient MIT, 1932-35. Mem. Soc. Naval Architects and Marine Engrs., Am. Soc. Naval Engrs., KC. Republican. Roman Catholic. Home: 16387 Gabarda Rd San Diego CA 92128-3048

SWEENEY, MICHAEL, mayor; b. Oakland, Calif., 1950. BA, Calif. State U., MA in Polit. Sci. Elected to Hayward City Coun., 1982, re-elected, 1986; mayor pro tem City of Hayward, 1983-84, 88-89, mayor, 1990—; guest speaker planning action conf. ABAG, 1988, Oceanic Soc., 1988. Chmn. Citizen/Industry Task Force, 1984; established Household Toxics Removal Day with League of Women Voters, 1984; chmn. Hayward Area Shoreline Planning Agy.; pres., ciry rep. Alameda County Waste Mgmt. Authority, 1992. Recipient Outstanding Svc. award to community Hayward Neighborhood Alert for Crime Prevention, 1985, 86. Office: City of Hayward 25151 Clawiter Rd Hayward CA 94545*

SWEENEY, PAMELA ALISON, lawyer; b. Norwalk, Conn., Sept. 18, 1958; d. Joseph M. and Barbara C. Sweeney. BA, Newcomb Coll., New Orleans, 1979; JD, Tulane U., 1986. Bar: La. 1986. Asst. dist. atty. New Orleans Dist. Atty.'s Office, 1986-88; assoc. McGlinchey, Stafford et al, New Orleans, 1988-91; jud. law clk. Magistrate Judge Patricia Trumbull, No. Dist. of Calif., San Jose, 1991—. Mem. Assn. for Women Attys. (legis. com. chair 1990, v.p. 1991). Democrat. Episcopalian. Home: 2752 Byron St Palo Alto CA 94306

SWEENEY, WILLIAM ALAN, chemist, researcher; b. Ocean Falls, B.C., Can., Sept. 12, 1926; came to U.S., 1950; s. William Patrick and Florence Harriet (Lewthwaite) S.; m. Sally Lou Grant, Apr. 11, 1953; children: Michael Alan, Peter Grant, Alison Elizabeth. BSChemE, U. B.C., Vancouver, 1949; PhD, U. Wash., 1954; postgrad., U. Calif., Berkeley, 1967-71. Devel. chemist Can. Industries, Ltd., Toronto, Ont., Can., 1949-50; from rsch. chemist to rsch. scientist Chevron Rsch. & Tech. Co., Richmond, Calif., 1954-90; cons. Chevron Rsch., Richmond, Calif., 1976-90, Teltech, Inc., Mpls., 1990—, U.S. Dept. of Energy, Idaho Falls, Idaho, 1990. Contbr. articles to profl. jours.; patentee in field. Pres., bd. dirs. Homeowners Assn., Larkspur, Calif., 1979-82; chmn., dept. lt. comdr. United Way campaign, 1972; mem. PTA. U. B.C. scholar, 1944, 45; U. Wash. fellow, 1952. Mem. Am. Chem. Soc., N.Y. Acad. Scis., Chevron Retirees Club, Sigma Xi. Republican. Home and Office: 27 Corte Del Bayo Larkspur CA 94939-1501

SWEET, ANDREW ARNOLD, psychologist; b. Mt. Kisco, N.Y., Aug. 26, 1956; s. John Stevens and Deana (Baron) S.; m. Nancy Rainwater, May 19, 1984; 1 child, Adrienne Elizabeth Sweetwater. BS, SUNY, Oneonta, 1978; Psychology D., Denver U., 1982. Lic. psychologist. Asst. prof. U. Colo., Greeley, 1982-83; pvt. practice Assocs. for Change, Denver, Colo., 1982—; clin. supr. Wallace Village for Children, Broomfield, Colo., 1983-84; clin. affiliate sch. profl. psychology U. Denver, 1983—; clin. psychologist Human Performance Inst., Lakewood, Colo., 1985-87. Co-author: Behavior Therapy Outcome, 1986, Anxiety & Stress Disorders, 1987; contbr. articles to profl. jours. Mem. Assn. for Advancement Behavior Therapy, Am. Psychol. Soc. Democrat. Home: 1900 Leyden St Denver CO 80220-1626 Office: 1720 S Bellaire St # 808 Denver CO 80220

SWEET, CHARLES W., retired firefighter; b. Providence, R.I., Nov. 5, 1934; s. Ronald H. and Glayds (Fairbroter) S.; m. Joann Collantonio, Sept. 23, 1966; children: Monica Ann, Charles W. Jr. Grad., Internat. Corr. Sch., Scranton, Pa.; grad. in fire sci., R.I. Coll., 1982. Fire capt. Warwick (R.I.) Fire Dept., 1958-85; technician Bugs Burger "ext", Miami, 1988-91; greenskeeper Bernardo Heights Country Club, San Diego, 1991—; life mem. Apponacug Fire Co., pres., 1972-74; mem. Oakland Beach Vol. Fire Co., 1960—, sec.-treas., 1955; life mem. Warwick Fire Dept. Sgt. U.S. Army, 1954-59, Korea. Recipient Fire Sci. award, Fire proclamation, Fire Retirement award, Fire Life award, Warwick, R.I., 1985. Mem. Warwick Police and Fire Assn., Warwick Firemans Lodge, Elks. Mem. Christian Ch. Home: 10897 Buckhurst Ave San Diego CA 92126

SWEETMAN, LORETTA VINETTE, social worker; b. Niagara Falls, N.Y., Sept. 27, 1941; d. Vincent and Loretta Viola (Williams) Leone; m. George W. Sweetman, Sept. 14, 1967 (div. July 1972); children: Loretta, Mary, GiGi. AS, Claremore (Okla.) Jr. Coll., 1975; BS in Sociology, East Cen. State Coll., 1978; MSW, U. Okla., 1980. With Tulsa Dist. Office Corp Engrs., 1975; with practicum placement dept. VA Hosp., Muskogee, Okla., 1979-80; clin. social worker VA Hosp., Sheridan, Wyo., 1980—, St. Joseph Hosp., Ponca City, Okla., 1980; tchr. Sheridan Community Coll., 1983—; presenter seminars. Bd. dirs. Wyo. Health Care, Sheridan, 1982-85, Sr. Citizens Coord. Council, Sheridan, 1982-84, exec. bd. pres., 1984-87; Sheridan County Hospice rep. Nat. Hospice Mgrs., 1984-87; bd. pres., owner exec. ste. Edn., Conseling Svc., Sheridan. Named one of Women of the Yr. Sheridan chpt. Bus. and Profl. Women, 1982, one of Women of the Day Sheridan chpt. Bus. and Profl. Women, 1982. Mem. NAFE, Nat. Assn. Social Workers. Democrat. Roman Catholic. Home: 150 W 11th St Lot 15 Sheridan WY 82801-2650

SWEETOW, ELIZABETH SWOOPE, bank executive; b. Philipsburg, Pa., Aug. 7, 1947; d. Walter Moore and Mary Louise (Fryberger) Swoope; m. Walter Allen McDougall, Aug. 8, 1970 (div. Dec. 1978); m. Michael Richard Sweetow, Dec. 22, 1984. BA, Smith Coll., 1969; MA, U. Mich., 1970. Fin. analyst Harris Trust, Chgo., 1970-75, Fed. Home Loan Bank, San Francisco, 1975-76; dir. planning World Savs., Oakland, Calif., 1976-82; v.p. Bank of Am., San Francisco, 1982-90, sr. v.p., 1990—. Mem. Bay Area Profl. Women's Network (pres. 1989-90), San Francisco C. of C. (bus. vol. for the arts 1990—), Phi Beta Kappa. Office: Bank of America PO Box 37000 San Francisco CA 94137-0001

SWELGIN, JAMES HERMAN, logistics, materials management executive; b. Wilkes-Barre, Pa., May 3, 1942; s. Herman Gustof and Jennie (Malkoski) S.; ; children from previous marriage: Kim, Jim; m. Carol L. Bailey; Cameron, Cord. BA in Math., King's Coll., Willes-Barre, 1965; BSEE, U. Detroit, 1965; postgrad., San Diego State U. With mfg. mgmt. program GE, 1963-72; investment control mgr. Honeywell, Phoenix, 1972-78; materials mgr. Loral Corp., San Diego, 1978-81, Digital Devices Corp., San Diego,

1981-83, Transport Designs and Tech., San Diego, 1983-85, Allied-Signal, San Diego, 1985—; cons., San Diego, 1982-85; prof. San Diego State U., 1981—; v.p. edn. A.P.I.C.S., San Diego, 1981-83. Mem. adv. bd. San Diego State U., 1981—; pres. Home Owners Assn., Carlsbad, Calif., 1988-91. Mem. Am. Prodn. and Inventory Control Soc.

SWENKA, ARTHUR JOHN, food products executive; b. Lone Tree, Iowa, Oct. 21, 1937; s. Samuel Joseph and Verdis Mary (Weed) S.; m. Elizabeth Simms, July 1956 (div. 1976); children: Lee Arthur, Timothy John; m. Dixie Jo Meade, Feb. 1982. Gen. equivalency diploma, U.S. Army, 1957. Truck driver U.S. Mail, Oelwein, Iowa, 1958-59, Stiles Supermarket, Oelwein, 1959-60; salesman Hoxie Inst. Wholesale Co., Waterloo, Iowa, 1960-68, slaes mgr., 1968-69, br. mgr., 1969-70; br. mgr. Hoxie Inst. Wholesale Co., Waterloo and Mason City, Iowa, 1970-72, Nobel Inc., Albuquerque, 1972-81; pres. Nobel/Sysco Food Svcs. Co., Albuquerque, 1981-84; pres., chief exec. officer Nobel/Sysco Food Svcs. Co., Denver, 1984—; chmn. bd. dirs. Nobel/Sysco Food Svcs, Albuquerque, Sysco Food Svcs., Billings, Mont; mem. Dirs. Coun., Houston, 1985—; bd. dirs Mountain States Employee Coun. Treas., bd. dirs. Albuqerque Conv. and Visitors Bus., 1975-80; v.p., bd. dirs. Albuquerque Internat. Balloon Festival, 1975-82; bd. dirs. New Day Home for Runaway Children, Albuquerque, 1980-89; bd. dirs. St. Joseph's Hosp. Found., 1990—. Democrat. Roman Catholic. Clubs: Colo. Balloon, Quad A. Balloon. Lodge: Moose. Home: 2870 W 116th Pl # 204 Westminster CO 80234 Office: Nobel/Sysco Food Svcs Co 1101 W 48th Ave Denver CO 80217

SWENSEN, LAIRD S., orthopedic surgeon; b. Provo, Utah, Oct. 5, 1944; s. Russel Brown and Beulah (Strickler) S.; m. Gloria Elaine Matoza, Sept. 23, 1973; children: Lara Ann, Christine, Russel, Tracy, Laird. BA in Chemistry, Brigham Young U., 1968; MD, George Washington U., 1972. Diplomate Am. Bd. Orthopedic Surgery; cert. added qualifications in surgery of hand, 1992. Fellow in hand and microvascular surgery Jack Tupper, 1970-78; intern San Francisco Gen. Hosp., 1972-73; resident in orthopedics U. Calif., San Francisco, 1973-77; pvt. practice orthopedic surgery Salt Lake City, 1978—; vice chmn. dept. surgery LDS Hosp.; chmn. div. orthopedics LDS Hosp., 1991, 192; assoc. clin. prof. dept. orthopedic surgery U. Utah, 1979, asst. clin. prof., 1990—; vol. surgeon Orthopedics Overseas, Nepal, 1988, 90, Bhutan, 1992; med. project advisor Tibetan Resettlement Project, Salt Lake City. Fellow Am. Acad. Orthopedic Surgery; mem. Western Orthopedic Assn. (pres. Utah chpt. 1991), Utah State Med. Assn. Office: 324 10th Ave Salt Lake City UT 84103

SWENSEN, MARY JEAN HAMILTON, graphic artist; b. Laurens, S.C., June 25, 1910; d. Elvin A. and Della (Brown) Hamilton; m. Oliver Severn Swensen, Mar. 3, 1943 (dec.). BS, Columbia U., 1956, MA, 1960; Cert. Notable, U. Madrid, Spain; postgrad., Ariz. State U., 1974-80. One person shows at Colo. Fed. Savs. and Loan Assn., Denver, 1978, Panoras Gallery, N.Y.C., 1963; exhibited in group shows at Soc. Western Artist, M.H. de Young Mus., San Francisco, 1964, Nat. Art Roundup, Las Vegas, 1965, Fine Arts Bldg., Colo. State Fair, Pueblo, 1965, Duncan Gallery, Paris, 1974, Colo. Fed. Savs. & Loan Assn., Denver, 1978; graphics arts in pub. collections at Met. Mus. Art, N.Y.C., Nat. Graphic Arts Collection, Smithsonian Inst., Laurens (S.C.) Pub. Libr., N.Y.C. Pub. Libr. Pres. Hamilton Found. Recipient Duncan Gallery Prix de Paris, 1974, others. Mem. Am. Mensa, Delta Phi Delta.

SWENSEN, PHILIP ROMNEY, business administration educator; b. Washington, Oct. 24, 1943; s. Albert Donald and Jennie (Romney) W.; m. MarKay Bruggeman, May 25, 1967 (dec. 1979); children: Jennifer Ann, Stephen Romney, Heather, Mark Philip, Matthew Joseph. BS, Brigham Young U., 1968; MBA, Ind. U., 1971, D of Bus. Adminstr., 1972. Asst. prof. U. Wis., Oshkosh, Wis., 1972-75; assoc. prof. Utah State U., Logan, 1975-83; pres. Integrated Systems Engring., Logan, Utah, 1983-85; prof., dept. head Utah State U., Logan, 1985—; bd. dirs. Integrated Systems Engring., Logan. Author: (with others) Financial Planning for the Executive, 1981, Managing Your Money, 1979. Home: PO Box 819 Hyde Park UT 84318-0819 Office: Utah State U UMC-3510 Logan UT 84322

SWENSON, KATHLEEN SUSAN, music and art teacher; b. Reno, Nev., Oct. 23, 1938; d. Harold Ruthaford McNeil and Hollyce Margaret (Scruggs) McNeil Biggs; m. James Michael Phalan, 1956 (div. 1974); children: David Michael, Jeanine Louise Phalan Lawrence, Gregory Shaun; m. Gerald Allen Swensen, Nov. 1976 (div. 1987); stepchildren: Craig Allen, Sarah Ann, Eric Sander. Student, U. Nev., Reno, 1956-58, Foothill Coll., 1966-68; AA, West Valley Coll.; BA, U. Calif., Santa Cruz, 1983. Concert pianist Nev.,Calif, 1950-64; pvt. piano instr. various locations, 1963—, pvt. art instr., 1970—, pvt. astrology instr., 1973—; founder, pres. AAM Triple Arts, Aptos, Calif., 1974—. Producer, instr. art instrn. videos. Mem. Soc Western Artists, Calif. Piano Tchrs. Assn., Los Gatos Art Assn. (pres. 1985-86), Saratoga Contemporary Artists (v.p. 1984-85), Nat. League Am. Pen Women (honorarian 1985), Soroptomists. Republican. Episcopalian. Home and Office: AAM Triple Arts 3000 Wisteria Way Aptos CA 95003-3318

SWENSON, MARY ANN, bishop. Bishop Rocky Mountain Diocese, Denver. Office: Rocky Mountain Diocese 2200 S University Blvd Denver CO 80210*

SWERDA, PATRICIA FINE, artist, author, educator; b. Ft. Worth, Aug. 10, 1916; d. William Emerson and Margaret Ellen (Cull) Fine; B.S. cum laude, Tex. Woman's U., 1941; grad. Ikenobo U., Tokyo, 1965-66, Ikenobo Dojo, Kyoto, Japan, 1976, 77, 83, 85, 87, 91; m. John Swerda, July 7, 1941; children: John Patrick James, Susan Ann Mary Swerda Foss, Margaret Rose Swerda Kownover. Exhibited ikebana in one-woman shows including: Bon Marche, Tacoma, 1966, Seattle, 1967, 85, Gallery Kokoro, Seattle, 1972-78; exhibited in group shows including: Takashimaya Dept. Store, 1965, 77, 83, 85, Matsuzakaya Dept. Store, Tokyo, 1966, Ikenobo Center, Kyoto, 1966, 77, Seattle Art Mus., 1974-80, Sangyo Kaikan, Kyoto, 1976, Burke Mus., U. Wash., ann. Cherry Blossom Festival, Seattle, Bellevue Art Mus., 1984, 85, 87, 89, 90, 91, 92; demonstrations in field for various groups, including Greater Northwest Flower and Garden Show. Master of Ikebana of Ikenobo Ikebana Soc., Kyoto. Pres. Bellevue Sister Cities Assn. 1985; mem. Sister Cities for State of Wash. Named Disting. Alumna class of 1941 Tex. Woman's U., 1991. Mem. N.W. Sakura Chpt. of the Ikenobo Ikebana Soc. (pres. 1960-91), Bonsai Clubs Internat., Puget Sound Bonsai Assn. Democrat. Greek Orthodox. Author: Japanese Flower Arranging: Practical and Aesthetic Bases of Ikebana, 1969; Creating Japanese Shoka, 1979, Art Deco-Free Style Art Cards, 1990; contbr. articles to mags. in field; creator Ikenobo Gardens, Redmond; numerous radio and TV appearances. Home and Office: 23025 NE 8th St Redmond WA 98053-7230

SWETT, DALE EVERETT, physical therapist; b. Eagle River, Wis., June 12, 1937; s. Jess Floyd Swett and Velma O. (Vreeland) Swett-Rozich; children: Jess Scott (dec.), Deanna Marie. BS, Cen. State U., Stevens Point, Wis., 1960; Cert. Phys. Therapy, Northwestern U., Chgo., 1962. Cert. phys. therapist. Commd. USPHS, 1962, advanced through grades to capt., 1983, ret., 1992; staff therapist USPHS, Seattle, 1962-65; chief phys. therapy USPHS/Indian Health Svc., Sitka, Alaska, 1965-70; dep. chief phys. therapy Div. Hosp. and Clinics USPHS, Norfolk, Va., 1970-72; chief phys. therapy USPHS/Indian Health Svc., Gallup, N.Mex., 1972-75; clin. coord. field ops. USPHS/Indian Health Svc., 1975-85; chief, rehab. br. USPHS/Indian Health Svc., Window Rock, Ariz., 1975—; acting sr. clinician USPHS/Indian Health Svc., 1985-88; therapy program dir. Indian Health Svc., Gallup, N.Mex., 1989-92; Indian Health Svc. rep. to Navajo Nation Coun. on Handicapped, Window Rock; cons. in sports medicine Gallup H.S. wrestling team, Gallup Gymnastics Club. Mem. Commd. Officer's Assn., Assn. USPHS (sec. Mt. Edgecumbe chpt. 1968-70, pres. Gallup chpt. 1980-83), Am. Phys. Therapy Assn. (named Therapist of Yr. N.Mex. chpt. 1988, Surgeon Gen.'s Profl. Adv. Com. 1988-92, Meritorious Svcs. medal 1991), Res. Officers Assn. of Uniformed Svcs. of U.S., Gallup Country Club, N.Am. Hunting Club, NRA, others. Presbyterian. Home: 500 Calle Pinon Gallup NM 87301-6761

SWETTE, ROBERT FRANCIS, business executive; b. Plainfield, N.J., Oct. 26, 1956; s. Glen John and Muriel (Murtagh) S.; m. Dana Swette, Oct. 26, 1985. BS in Engring., Ariz. State U., 1979; M in Bus., Ashland U., 1982; postgrad., Claremont U., 1987, U. So. Calif., 1992. Indsl. engr. Reynolds Metals, Phoenix, 1977-79; bus. planning assoc. Westinghouse Electric, Concordville, Pa., 1979-81; mgr. mktg. Morgan Engring./AMCA Internat., Alliance, Ohio, 1981-83; from computer aided engine specialist to ops. mgr. Northrop, Hawthorne, Calif., 1983-87; mgr. bus. devel. MagneTex, Anaheim, Calif., 1987-90; dir. bus. devel. MagneTex, Anaheim, 1990—; assoc. faculty mem. Antioch U., L.A., 1987-91. Mem. Claremont Grad. Sch. Alumni Assn. (pres. 1988-91).

SWIFT, AL, congressman; b. Tacoma, Wash., Sept. 12, 1935; m. Paula Jean Jackson, 1956; children—Amy, Lauri. Student, Whitman Coll., 1953-55, Central Wash. U., 1956; 57. Broadcaster; public affairs dir. Sta. KVOS-TV; adminstrv. asst. to U.S. rep. Lloyd Meeds, 1965-69, 77; mem. 96th-103rd Congresses from 2d Wash. dist., Washington, D.C., 1979—; mem. Energy and Commerce com., subcoms. Energy and Power, transp. and hazardous materials, house adminstrn. com., subcom. elections, accts., joint com. orgn. congress; mem. Bellingham (Wash.) City Charter Revision Com.; chmn., mem. Bellingham Citizens Adv. Com.; mem. Bellingham Housing Authority. Democrat. Office: House of Representatives 1502 Longworth House Bldg Washington DC 20515-4702

SWIFT, WILLIAM CHARLES, professional baseball player, olympic athlete; b. Portland, Maine, Oct. 27, 1961. Student, Maine. Mem. U.S. Olympic Team, 1984; with Seattle Mariners, 1985-91; pitcher San Francisco Giants, 1992—. Office: San Francisco Giants Candlestick Park San Francisco CA 94124

SWIHART, H. GREGG, real estate company executive; b. San Francisco, Sept. 25, 1938; s. Lawson Benjamin and Violet Mary (Watters) S.; B.A., U. Ariz., 1958; postgrad. U. Heidelberg (W.Ger.), 1958-59, Harvard U., 1959-60; M.A., Boston U., 1961; postgrad. U. Freiburg (West Germany), 1961-65; m. Ilse Paula Rambacher, Dec. 24, 1958; children—Tatjana Etta, Brett Marc, Natascha Theda. Stock broker Walston & Co., Tucson, 1966-71; with Solot Co., Tucson, 1971-74; pres. Cienega Properties, Inc., property mgmt. and investment, Tucson, 1975-77; pres. GT Realty Assocs., Ltd., Tucson, 1977—. Mem. Tucson Com. Fgn. Relations, 1973—; pres. Forum for Greater Outdoors, 1977-79; bd. dirs. Tucson Mus. Art, 1968-74, pres. 1969-70; pres. and trustee Canelo Hills Sch., 1977-79. Cert. property mgr. Mem. Tucson Bd. Realtors, Inst. Real Estate Mgmt. (pres. Tucson-So. Ariz. chpt. 1982, mem. nat. governing council 1985-87), Inst. Real Estate Mgmt. (governing council 1985-87, Property Mgr. of Yr. award So. Ariz. chpt. 1988), Realtors Nat. Mktg. Inst. Clubs: Harvard (pres. 1973-74), Active 20-30 (pres. 1969), Downtown Tucson. Home: PO Box 555 Tunnel Springs Ranch Sonoita AZ 85637 Office: 4003 E Speedway Blvd Ste 110 Tucson AZ 85712-4555

SWIHART, JOHN MARION, retired aircraft manufacturing company executive; b. New Winchester, Ohio, Dec. 27, 1923; s. Harry Miron and Fay I. (Cress) S.; m. Gail G. Carter, Nov. 8, 1986; children from previous marriages: Vicki Ann, John Richard, Thomas Marion, Mark Andrew, Karen Lee, Laurie Christine, Stacey Anne. BS in Physics, Bowling Green State U., 1947; BS in Aero. Engring., Ga. Inst. Tech., 1949, postgrad., 1951-53; postgrad., U. Va., 1951-53. Asst. group leader propulsion group NASA, 1956-58, group leader spl. projects, 1958-59, head advanced configurations group aircraft, 1959-62, chief large supersonic tunnels br., 1962; with Boeing Co., 1962-89; dep. dir. internat. sales Boeing Co., Renton, Wash., 1974-75; v.p. Japan Boeing Internat. Corp. Boeing Co., Tokyo, 1973-74; program mgr. 7X7 Boeing Co., Kent, Wash., 1975-76; dir. new airplane product devel., sales, mktg. Boeing Co., Seattle, 1976-78; dir. product devel., sales mktg. Boeing Co., 1978-79, v.p. U.S., Can. sales, 1979-83, v.p. govt. tech. liaison, 1983-85, corp. v.p. airplane market analysis, 1985; corp. v.p. internat. affairs Boeing Co., Seattle, 1985-89; ret., 1989. Contbr. over 100 articles to profl. jours. 1st lt. USAAF, 1943-45. Decorated D.F.C., Air medal with 3 oak leaf clusters; recipient Wright Bros. Meml. Lectureship award, 1987. Fellow AIAA (chmn. aircraft design com., chmn. Pacific N.W. sect. 1969-70, gen. chmn. aircraft systems and design meeting 1977, pres.-elect, pres. 1990-91), Royal Aero. Soc.; mem. Internat. Soc. for Air-Breathing Engines (pres. 1993—), Japan-Am. Soc. (pres. 1978-79), Wash. State China Rels. Coun. (past pres.), Nat. Ctr. Advanced Techs. (vice chmn. 1993—).

SWIM, HELEN WILSON, school psychologist, counselor, retired; b. Lava Hot Springs, Idaho, Feb. 14, 1928; d. Charles E. aand Delania (Potter) Wilson; m. H. Hugh Swim, Apr. 10, 1949; children: David, Linda, Laura, Zane, Kathy, Bill, Sherri. Student, U. Wyo., 1948-50; BA in English and Edn. with high honors, Idaho State U., 1967, MEd in Counseling and Guidance, 1971; EdS in Sch. Psychology, U. Idaho, 1980. Cert. tchr., sch. psychologist, Idaho; lic. counselor, Idaho. Sec. Cypress View Mausoleum, San Diego, 1948; tchr. Lava Hot Springs Elem. Sch., 1948-49, McCammon (Idaho) Elem. Sch., 1959-60, Marsh Valley High Sch., Arimo, Idaho, 1960-72; sch. counselor, tchr. Melba (Idaho) Sch. Dist., 1972-80, psychologist, counselor, tchr., 1980-83, psychologist, tchr., 1983-88; sch. psychologist Emmett (Idaho) Sch. Dist., 1989-93, coord. spl. svcs., 1989-93, ret., 1993. Author book of poetry, 1962, biographies, 1984, 90. Mem. Idaho Sch. Psychologists Assn., Idaho Sch. Counselors Assn. (state pres. 1977-78), Am. Legion Aux. (unit sec. 1950-54, pres. 1955, 60-Yr. Mem. award), Delta Kappa Gamma. Mem. LDS Ch. Home: 222 Southside Rd Melba ID 83641-5142

SWINDELLS, WILLIAM, JR., lumber and paper company executive; b. Oakland, CA, 1930; married. B.S., Stanford U., 1953. With Willamette Industries, Inc., Portland, Oreg., 1953—; sr. v.p. prodn., mktg. bldg. materials Willamette Industries, Inc., until 1978, exec. v.p., 1978-80, pres. forest products div., 1980-82, pres., chief exec. officer, 1982—, also dir., chmn., 1984—; dir. Oreg. Bank, Portland. Office: Willamette Industries Inc 1300 S W 5th Ave Portland OR 97201*

SWINDLER, DARIS RAY, physical anthropologist, forensic anthropologist; b. Morgantown, W.Va., Aug. 13, 1925; s. George Raymond and Minnie Mildred (McElroy) S.; m. Kathryn Pardo, Nov. 10, 1977; children: Gary, Darece, Linda, Dana, Bruce, Geoffry, Jason. AB, W.Va. U., 1950; MA, U. Pa., 1952, PhD, 1959. Instr. Cornell Med. Sch., N.Y.C., 1956-57, W.Va. Med. Sch., Morgantown, 1957-59; asst. prof. Med. Coll. S.C., Charleston, 1959-64; assoc. prof. Mich. State U., East Lansing, 1964-68; prof. phys. anthropology, comparative primate anatomy, dental anthropology U. Wash., Seattle, 1968-91, prof. emeritus anthropology, 1991—; emeritus curator comparative primate anatomy Burke Mus., Seattle, 1991—; cons. King County Med. Examiner, Seattle, 1968—; vis. sr. scientist Com. on Scholarly Comms. with People's Republic China, 1987-88; vis. prof. U. Zurich, Switzerland, 1992; field participant Valley of the Kings expdn., Egypt, 1990-93. Author: A Racial Study of the West Nakani of New Britain, 1962, Dentition of Living Primates, 1976, Systematics, Evolution and Anatomy, Comparative Primate Biology; (with C.D. Wood) Atlas of Primate Gross Anatomy, 1973 (Gov's. award 1973), (with J. Sirianni) Growth and Development of Pigtailed Macaque, 1985. Served with USN, 1943-46. Recipient Alexander von Homboldt Sr. U.S. Scientist award, Frankfurt, Fed. Republic Germany, 1981. Fellow AAAS, Explorer's Club; mem. Am. Assn. Phys. Anthropologists (v.p. 1976-78), Dental Anthropology Assn. (pres. 1990-92), Internat. Primatology Soc., N.Y. Acad. Sci., Italian Primatol. Assn., Sigma Xi.

SWING, WILLIAM EDWIN, bishop; b. Huntington, W.Va., Aug. 26, 1936; s. William Lee and Elsie Bell (Holliday) S.; M. Mary Willis Taylor, Oct. 7, 1961; children—Alice Marshall, William Edwin. B.A., Kenyon Coll., Ohio, 1954-58; D.Div. (hon.), Kenyon Coll., 1980; M.A., Va. Theol. Sem., 1958-61, D.Div., 1980. Ordained priest Episcopal Ch. Asst. St. Matthews Ch., Wheeling, W.Va., 1961-63; vicar St. Matthews Ch., Chester, W.Va., 1963-69, St. Thomas Ch., Weirton, W.Va., 1963-69; rector St. Columba's Episcopal Ch., Washington, 1969-79; bishop Episcopal Ch. Calif., San Francisco, 1980—; chmn. bd. Ch. Div. Sch. of the Pacific, 1983-84; founder, chmn. Episcopal Found. for Drama, 1976—. Republican. Home: 2006 Lyon St San Francisco CA 94115-1610 Office: Episcopal Ch Diocesan Office 1055 Taylor St San Francisco CA 94108-2209*

SWINGLE, DONALD MORGAN, physicist, engineer, meteorologist, consultant; b. Washington, Sept. 1, 1922; s. Louis Morgan and Anna Pearl (Fenby) S.; m. Hazel Elizabeth O'Hara, Mar. 5, 1943; children: Donna Beth, Donald Morgan, Jonathan Warne. BS, Wilson Tchrs. Coll., Washington, 1943; MS, NYU, 1947; MA, Harvard U., 1948, M of Engring. Sci., 1949, PhD, 1950; MBA, George Washington U., 1962; cert., Indsl. Coll. Armed Forces, 1962. Registered profl. engr. N.Y., N.J. Commd. 2nd lt. U.S. Army, 1944, advanced through grades to lt. col., 1964, research and devel. project officer, 1944-46; radio engr. Signal Corps Lab. U.S. Army, Ft. Monmouth, N.J., 1946-47; research asst. Harvard U., Cambridge, Mass., 1949-50; physicist Signal Corps Lab., Ft. Monmouth, N.J., 1950-66; sr. scientist Atmospheric Sci. Lab. U.S. Army Electronics Command, Ft. Monmouth, N.J., 1966-71, sr. scientist Exploratory and Engring. Devel. Tech Area, 1971-74, Spl. Sensors Tech. Area, Combat Surveillance, 1974-78; research physicist, cons. U.S. Army, White Sands Missile Range, N.M., 1978-80; pvt. practice, 1980—; U.S. mem. Commn. for Instruments and Methods of Observation, World Meteorol. Orgn., UN, 1952-72; cons. Nat. Security Mgmt. Radar Design and Military Meteorology, Forensic Meteorology, 1980—. Mem. Army Research Council, 1964-65. Fellow AIAA (assoc., mem. com. on unidentified flying objects 1965-75), N.Y. Acad. Scis.; mem. IEEE (sr.), AAAS, NSPE, Am. Meteorol. Soc., Am. Geophys. Union, N.Mex. Rsch. Inst., Mensa. Methodist. Home: 1765 Pomona Dr Las Cruces NM 88001-4919 Office: PO Box 160 Las Cruces NM 88004-0160

SWINGLE, ROY SPENCER, nutritionist, educator; b. Harvey, Ill., Oct. 15, 1944; s. Roy C. and Marjory (Ames) S.; m. Carmen Roberts, Aug. 6, 1966; children: Brian, Gary. BS in Agr., U. Ariz., 1966; MS in Nutrition, Wash. State U., 1969, Phd in Nutrition, 1972. Asst. prof. to assoc. prof. dept. animal sci. U. Ariz., Tucson, 1972—. Mem. Am. Soc. Animal Sci., Am. Inst. Nutrition, Am. Dairy Sci. Assn., Coun. Agrl. Sci. and Tech. Office: Univ Ariz Dept Animal Sci Tucson AZ 85721

SWINSON, DEREK BERTRAM, physics educator, consultant; b. Belfast, No. Ireland, Nov. 5, 1938; came to U.S., 1965; m. Shelagh Nagira Pike, Aug. 25, 1965 (div. Apr. 1976); children: Brian Edward, Kevin Henry; m. Jo Ann Harrison, May 5, 1979. BSc in Math., Queen's U., Belfast, 1959, BSc in Physics with honors, 1960; MSc in Physics, U. Alta, Calgary, Can., 1961, PhD in Physics, 1965. Grad. teaching asst. U. Alta, Calgary, 1960-65; asst. prof. physics U. N.Mex., Albuquerque, 1965-71, assoc. prof., 1971-76, prof., 1976—; cons. accident reconstruction, Albuquerque, 1968—. Contbr. numerous articles, mostly on cosmic radiation, to profl. jours., 1963—. Home: 3417 Mackland Ave NE Albuquerque NM 87106-1216 Office: Univ N Mex Dept Physics 800 Yale Blvd NE Albuquerque NM 87131-0001

SWISHER, JOSEPH PERRY, utilities executive; b. Bruneau, Idaho, Sept. 21, 1923; s. James Joyce and Mary Louise (Blakeslee) S.; m. Nicky Nichols, May 7, 1948; children: Lawrence A., Eric N. BA in Govt., Idaho State U., 1968. News bur. mgr. Salt Lake Tribune, Pocatello, Idaho, 1943-52; editor, pub. The Intermountain, Pocatello, Idaho, 1953-67; spl. asst. to pres. Idaho State U., Pocatello, 1969-76; night mng. editor Lewiston (Idaho) Morning Tribune, 1977-79; commr., pres. Idaho Pub. Utilities Commn., Boise, 1979—. Contbr. articles to profl. jours. and books. Mem. Idaho Ho. of Reps., 1951-57, 75-76; mem. Idaho Senate, 1963-67; city councilman City of Pocatello, 1969-73. Named Statesman of Yr. Idaho State U. Polysci. Fraternity, 1985. Mem. Nat. Assn. Regulatory Utilities Commrs. (mem. exec. com. 1983—). Democrat. Home: 8660 Oakmont Dr Boise ID 83704-3345 Office: Idaho Pub Utilities Commn Statehouse Boise ID 83720-0001

SWISZCZ, PAUL GERARD, textile chemist; b. New Bedford, Mass., Nov. 25, 1958; s. Tadeusz and Jeanne (Weaver) S. BS in Textile Chemistry, S.E. Mass. U., 1981. Mgr. technican svc. Julius Koch USA Inc., New Bedford, Mass., 1979-86; mgr. product devel. Hunter Douglas Inc., Broomfield, Colo., 1986-89; sr. product devel. mgr. Hunter Douglas Inc., 1989-92, dir. fabric devel., 1992—. Recipient Rosco award, Ductte Fresco, 1989, 91. Mem. Am. Assn. Textile Chemists and Colorists. Home: 2210 Howard Pl Boulder CO 80303-5628

SWITLIK, JOHN ANDREW, electronic engineer; b. Parsons, Kans., Nov. 22, 1943; s. John Andrew and Marie Jeanette (Every) S. BSEE, San Diego State U., 1990. Joined USN, 1965, advanced through grades, ret., 1987; electronic maintenance officer USN Communications Schs., San Diego, 1978-82, USS Tripoli, 1982-87; electronic engr. Naval Command Control and Ocean Surveilance Ctr., San Diego, 1991—; adj. faculty San Diego State U., 1992—. Author: Electronic Engineering Lab Manual Part 1, 1990; co-author: Electronic Engineering Lab Manual Part 2, 1989. Republican. Roman Catholic. Office: NCCOSC RDTE Div Code 823 271 Catalina Blvd San Diego CA 92152-5000

SWORD, CHARLES HEGE, JR., geophysicist; b. Fullerton, Calif., Dec. 30, 1957; s. Charles Hege and Lois Maxine (Beebe) S. BS in Physics, Stanford U., 1980, MS in Geophysics, 1983, PhD in Geophysics, 1988. Exhibit guide U.S. Info. Agy., Washington, 1987-88; sr. rsch. geophysicist Chevron Petroleum Tech. Co., La Habra, Calif., 1988—. Author: (computer program) Limbr/Alrt, 1990. Mem. Am. Geophysical Union, European Assn. Exploration Geophysicists, Soc. Exploration Geophysicists (assoc.).

SWORD, ROBERT RANDOLPH, inventory planning specialist, consultant; b. Grundy, Va., Oct. 17, 1954; s. Robert Edward and Esther Lea (Vasuary) S.; m. Joy Geraldine Hodges, Oct. 15, 1976; 1 child, Robyn Joy. AS in Bus., West L.A. Coll., 1984. With Time Electronics West, Inglewood, Calif., 1973-74; jr. planner Ampex, L.A., 1974-75; fabrication planner Ampex, El Segundo, Calif., 1975-78; mgr. Pic N Save, Lancaster, Calif., 1978-79; field repairer Citicorp TTI, L.A., 1979-80, inventory planning specialist, 1980—; cons. Robynhood Svcs., Culver City, Calif., 1982—. Mem. SANE, L.A., 1987-90; scoutmaster Boy Scouts Am. Troop 193, L.A., 1974-80; youth dir. Bapt. Temple, L.A., 1977-81; chmn. activities com. 1st Luth. Sch., L.A., 1989-90, treas. 1990-91, chmn. activities com. 1990-91, sec. annual fund assn. 1990-93; treas. 1st Luth. Christian Parents Tchrs. Forum, 1991-93; mgr. Culver City Little League softball team, 1992-93. With U.S. Army, 1973-74. Republican. Office: Citicorp/TTI 12959 Coral Tree Pl Los Angeles CA 90066-7020

SYDNOR, ROBERT HADLEY, state government geologist; b. Whittier, Calif., July 1, 1947; s. Thurston Edward and Mary Edith (Thompson) S.; divorced; 1 child, Christopher. BA, Whittier Coll., 1969; MS, U. Calif.-Riverside, 1975. Registered geologist, Calif., Alaska, Ariz.; cert. engring. geologist, Calif. Asst. petroleum geologist Mobil Oil Corp., Anchorage, 1970-71; staff engring. geologist Leighton & Assocs., Irvine, Calif., 1973-77; assoc. engring. geologist Orange County, Laguna Niguel, Calif., 1977-79; sr. engring. geologist VTN Corp., Irvine, 1979; chief engring. geologist R&M Cons., Inc., Irvine, 1979-82; supervising geologist Calif. Div. Mines and Geology, San Francisco, 1982-90, sr. engr. geologist, Sacramento, 1990—; mem. exam. com. Calif. State Bd. of Registration for Geologists and Geophysicists, Sacramento, 1977—, chmn., 1978. Co-editor CDMG spl. publ. on the 1989 Loma Prieta earthquake, 1992 Cape Mendocino earthquake, 1992 Landers earthquake; contbr. many cons. reports on landslides and seismicity. Mem. alumni scholarship com. U. Calif.-Riverside, 1978-86; mem. City of Los Angeles Grading Appeals Bd., 1979-84; alt. mem. County of Orange Grading Appeals Bd., 1980-84. Donnel Foster Hewett fellow U. Calif., 1972. Mem. Calif. Acad. Sci. (life), Assn. Engring. Geologists (assoc. editor Bull. 1979-86, chmn. So. Calif. sect. 1979-80), Geol. Soc. Am., Seismol. Soc. Am. (life), Am. Assn. Petroleum Geologists, Am. Inst. Profl. Geologists, Nat. Assn. Geology Tchrs., Arctic Inst. N.Am. (life), ASTM, Am. Geophys. Union (life), Sigma Gamma Epsilon (life). Republican. Home: 4930 Huntridge Ln Fair Oaks CA 95628-4823 Office: Calif Div Mines and Geology 801 K St MS13-35 Sacramento CA 95814-3531

SYGALL, SUSAN E., international educational exchange director; b. N.Y.C., June 4, 1953; d. Michael and Lisa S. BS, U. Calif., Berkeley, 1975; MS, U. Oreg., 1981. Co-founder, dir. Berkeley Outreach Recreation Program, 1975-78, Mobility Internat. USA, Eugene, Oreg., 1981—; mem. exec. bd. Mobility Internat., London, 1989-92. Co-author: A World of Options, 1991, Global Perspectives on Disability, 1992; co-prodr. (videos) Look Back-Looking Forward, 1990, Emerging Leaders, 1992. Kellogg Nat. Leadership fellow Kellogg Found., 1988; Rotary grad. fellow Rotary Found., 1978. Jewish. Office: Mobility Internat USA PO Box 3551 Eugene OR 97403

SYKE, CAMERON JOHN, lawyer; b. Oak Park, Ill., Jan. 29, 1957; s. A. John and Rosemarie (Grasso) S.; m. Susan Royer, Jan. 2, 1982; children: Caroline, Jared. BSBA cum laude, U. Denver, 1977, LLM in Taxation, 1986; JD with honors, DePaul U., 1982. Bar: CPA, Colo. 1983, U.S. Tax Ct. 1985. Acct. Touche, Ross, Chgo., 1978-79, Denver, 1980-83; investment broker Boettcher & Co., Denver, 1983-84; CPA Laventhol & Horwath, Denver, 1984-85; assoc. Roath & Brega, Denver, 1985-87; dir. Hopper and Kanouff, P.C., Denver, 1987—; adj. prof. U. Denver, 1985; instr. Colo. Soc. CPA's, 1986-87; lectr. Nat. Bus. Inst., 1986-87. Candidate councilman City of Denver, 1987. Mem. Colo. Bar Assn., Colo. Soc. CPA's. Republican. Presbyterian. Home: 6942 E Costilla Pl Englewood CO 80112 Office: Hopper & Kanouff 1610 Wynkoop St Ste 200 Denver CO 80202-1100

SYKES, ROY ARNOLD, JR., computer consultant business executive; b. N.J., Sept. 30, 1948; s. Roy Arnold and Grace (Brickman) S.; m. Kathy Grazulis, Mar. 1980 (div. 1982); m. Kyle Parr, Aug. 31, 1985; children: Roy Mackenzie; stepchildren: Andy Lutz, Zack Lutz. BA in Mgmt. Data Systems, Syracuse U. Mktg. rep. to v.p. STSC, Inc., Bethesda, Md. and L.A., 1971-85; pres. Sykes Systems, Inc., L.A., 1985—; guest lectr. UCLA Grad. Sch. Mgmt., 1978-87. Contbr. articles to profl. jours. Candidate for Calif. state assembly Libertarian Party, 41st Dist., 1992. Mem. Assn. ofr Computing Machinery (pres. So. Calif. spl. interest group APL 1979—). Episcopalian. Home: 4649 Willens Ave Woodland Hills CA 91364 Office: Sykes Systems Inc 4649 Willens Ave Woodland Hills CA 91364-3812

SYLLA, JOHN RICHARD, telecommunications executive; b. Salt Lake City, Feb. 8, 1959; s. James Robert and Virginia Joy (Elder) S.; m. Jessica Herbold, May 20, 1989. AB, Harvard U., 1981; JD, MBA, U. Chgo., 1985. Bar: Calif. Atty. Cooley Godward Law Firm, 1985-88; corp. counsel Network Equipment Tech., 1988-90, european mktg. dir., 1990-91, european sales dir., 1991-92, european dir. and asst. to v.p., 1992; pres. Foton Microsystems, Inc., Santa Clara, Calif., 1992—, Paris, 1992—. Office: Foton Microsystems Inc 350 Page St San Francisco CA 94102

SYLTE, JUDITH ANN OSTERBERG, educator, historian, consultant; b. Santa Monica, Calif., Oct. 22, 1943; d. Arthur Dean and Gretha (Press) Ostergerg; m. Gordon D. Sylte, Aug. 1, 1965 (div. 1978); children: Anne Elisebeth, John Christian; m. James R. McLeod, June 11, 1982; stepchildren: Brock, Rory. BA with honors, Whitworth Coll., 1965; MA in English, UCLA, 1968; postgrad., U. Idaho, Ea. Wash. U., Sonoma State U., Lewis-Clark State Coll., Seattle Pacific U., St. Andrews U., 1968—. Tchr. Glendale (Calif.) Pub. Schs., 1965-68, Glendale Community Coll., 1967-68; prof., adminstr. North Idaho Coll., Coeur D'Alene, 1975—; humanities chair North Idaho Coll., 1989—, studies abroad leader, 1982—; vis. instr. Lewis-Clark State Coll., Lewiston, Idaho, 1990, U. Idaho, Moscow, 1990; presenter, lectr. in field. Editor: Hangar Flying: Float Country Bush Pilot Stories, 1985, Mysterious Lake Pend Oreille and Its "Monster": Fact and Folklore, 1987; contbr. articles to profl. jours. Dir. Centennial Living History Project, Idaho, 1988-90, North Idaho Oral History Project, 1987—; project dir. NEH, 1990—; cons. Idaho Humanities Coun., 1977-85; active Dem. Party, 1965—; various community arts projects, hist. preservation projects. Named Outstanding Humanities Educator NEH/Am. Assn. Comm. and Jr. Colls., 1989-90, grantee, 1990—. Mem. Am. Assn. for Higher Edn., Am. Assn. for State and Local History, Community Coll. Humanities Assn., The Washington Ctr. for Improvement Undergrad. Edn., Ctr. for Critical Thinking and Moral Critique, Assn. for Gen. and Liberal Studies, Pacific N.W. Historians Guild, N.W. Oral History Assn., Pacific N.W. Conf. English in Two-Yr. Colls. Presbyterian. Home: 701 S 12th St Coeur D Alene ID 83814-3815 Office: North Idaho Coll 1000 W Garden Ave Coeur D Alene ID 83814-2161

SYLVANUS, JOANNE MARGARET, accountant, business consultant; b. Cleve., Aug. 21, 1931; d. Norman D. Raymer and Florence F. (Kuntz) Tupper; widowed; children: Leslie L., Judith M. BBA, Cleve. State U., 1970. CPA, Ariz. Staff acct. Walthall & Drake CPA's, Cleve., 1965-70, Schulman & Trobman CPA's, Phoenix, 1970-73; office mgr. Wolftang & Robertson CPA's, Phoenix, 1973-74; pvt. practice acctg. Phoenix, 1974—; tchr. Phoenix Community Coll., 1972-84. Named Adv. of Yr. Small Bus. Adminstrn., 1987. Mem. AICPA's, Ariz. Soc. CPA's, Am. Women's Soc. CPA's, Am. Soc. Women Accts. (cons. 1980—, pres. 1988-89, numerous chairmanships, treas., bd. dirs. 1972—). Office: # 110H 4628 N 17th St Phoenix AZ 85016-4646

SYLVESTER, EDWARD JOSEPH, science writer, journalism educator; b. Hackensack, N.J., Oct. 10, 1942; s. Edward Joseph Jr. and Ellen Marian (Hopkins) S.; m. Ginny Ross Gowanloch, Sept. 6, 1969; children: Daniel, Kathleen. AB, Princeton U., 1965; MA, CCNY, 1974. Reporter The Jersey Jour., Jersey City, 1962-63, The Morning Call, Paterson, N.J., 1968-69, The Ariz. Star, Tucson, 1973-76, L.A. Times, 1978-80; rewriteman The Star Ledger, Newark, 1970-72; reporter, editor The Tucson Citizen, 1976-78; prof. Ariz. State U. Walter Cronkite Sch. Journalism, Tempe, 1980—; corr. Wall Street Jour., N.Y.C., 1975-78. Prin. author: The Gene Age, 1983, rev. edit., 1987; author: Target: Cancer, 1986, The Healing Blade: A Tale of Neurosurgery, 1993. With U.S. Army, 1965-67. Recipient teaching award Burlington Resources Found., 1991. Mem. AAAS, Nat. Assn. Sci. Writers, Soc. Profl. Journalists, Investigative Reports and Editors. Office: Walter Cronkite Sch Journ Ariz State U Tempe AZ 85287

SYMCOX, GEOFFREY WALTER, history educator; b. Swindon, Wiltshire, England, Nov. 8, 1938; came to U.S., 1962; s. Sydney Walter and Gladys (Thewlis) S.; m. Linda Sharon Silvers, Sept. 4, 1971; children: Alexander, Adrian. BA, Oxford U., England, 1960; MA, U. Stockholm, 1962; PhD, UCLA, 1967. Asst. prof. dept. history UCLA, 1969-74, assoc. prof. dept. history, 1974-82, prof. dept. history, 1982—. Author: The Crisis of French Sea Power 1688-1697, 1974, Victor Amadeus II, 1983; gen. editor Repertorium Columbianum, UCLA, 1989—. Guggenheim fellow, 1977-78. Mem. Am. Hist. Assn., Deputazione Subalpina di Storia Patria (Turin, Italy). Office: UCLA Dept History Los Angeles CA 90024-1473

SYMINGTON, FIFE, governor; b. N.Y.C., Aug. 12, 1945; s. John Fife Jr. and Martha (Frick) S.; m. Leslie Marion Barker, June 1, 1968 (div. Jan. 1973); childen: Fife IV, Scott; m. Ann Pritzlaff, Feb. 7, 1976; children: Whitney, Richard, Tom. Student, Harvard U., 1968. Ptnr. Lincoln Property Co., Phoenix, 1972-76; chmn. of the bd. The Symington Co., Phoenix, 1976-89; gov. State of Ariz., 1991—. Precinct committeeman Ariz.'s Legis. Dist. 24, Paradise Valley; fin. chmn. State Republican Party, Phoenix, 1982-84; campaign advisor Rep. John Rhodes, Sen. John McCain, Ariz.; chmn. Phoenix Citizens Police Protection Bond Com., 1988; v.p. bd. trustees Heard Mus.; mem. Men's Art Coun., Environ. Quality Commn., 1971-73, Ariz. Children's Found.; dep. sheriff Maricopa County Air Posse; exec. bd. Phoenix Community Alliance. Capt. USAF, 1968-71. Mem. Western Govs.' Assn. (chmn. 1992—). Episcopalian. Office: Govs Office 1700 W Washington Phoenix AZ 85007

SYMMES, DANIEL LESLIE, three-dimensional technology executive, producer, director; b. Los Angeles, June 26, 1949; s. Louis Leslie and Mary (Warkentine) S.; m. Joanne Iriye Symmes, June 4, 1988. Student, Columbia Coll., Hollywood, Calif., 1970-71. Co-founder Stereovision Internat., Inc., North Hollywood, Calif., 1971; cons. Dimension 3e, Beverly Hills, Calif., 1975-87; pres., chmn. Spatial Techs. Inc., 3D Video Corp., Hollywood, Calif., 1987—; responsible for comml. 3D TV in U.S. and abroad; known worldwide as Mr. 3D. Author: Amazing 3-D; contbr. numerous articles to profl. jours.; dir. photography local 659 IATSE; patentee 3-D TV; inventor 1st reflex widescreen 3D filming system. Mem. SMPTE. Office: Spatial Techs Inc 801 N La Brea Ave Ste 104 Los Angeles CA 90038-3340

SYMONDS, NORMAN LESLIE, computer programming specialist; b. Hawthorne, Calif., July 10, 1953; s. Malcolm F. and Nancy J. (Raab) S. BA in Math., U. Calif., Berkeley, 1978; MBA in Mgmt. Sci., U. So. Calif., 1981. Programmer Burroughs Corp. (Unisys), Pasadena, Calif., 1978-81; sr. systems analyst Sungard Fin. Systems, Canoga Park, Calif., 1981-89; programming project leader Dames & Moore, L.A., 1989—. Home: 19211 Haynes St Apt 4 Reseda CA 91335 Office: Dames & Moore Ste 700 911 Wilshire Blvd Los Angeles CA 90017

SYMONIK, DANIEL MICHAEL, toxicologist; b. Milw., July 10, 1960; s. Emil F. and Trudy C. (Sternig) S. BS, U. Wis., Stevens Point, 1982; MS, Iowa State U., 1987. Scientist USEPA Environ. Rsch. Lab., Duluth, Minn., 1982-84; analytical chemist dept. entomology Iowa State U., Ames, 1984-88; staff toxicologist Utah Div. Environ. Response and Remediation, Salt Lake City, 1988-91; Superfund sect. mgr. Utah Dept. Environ. Quality, Salt Lake City, 1991—. Contbr. articles to profl. jours. Vol. Habitat for Humanity, Salt Lake City, 1991—, Salvation Army Kitchen, Salt Lake City, 1991—. Mem. AAAS, Soc. Environ. Toxicology and Chemistry, Nat. Wildlife Fedn., Sigma Xi. Office: Div Environ Response Remed 1960 W North Temple Salt Lake City UT 84116

SYMONS, JAMES MARTIN, theater and dance educator; b. Jacksonville, Ill., May 7, 1937; s. James and Pauline (Barton) S.; m. Judith White, Nov. 14, 1959; children: Tracy, Kelly, Carrie. BA, Ill. Coll., 1959; MA, So. Ill. U., 1964; PhD, Cornell U., 1970. Asst. prof. Yankton (S.D.) Coll., 1964-67; assoc. prof. Coll. St. Catherine, St. Paul, 1970-74, SUNY, Albany, 1974-77; prof., chair Trinity U., San Antonio, 1977-84; prof., chair theatre and dance dept. U. Colo., Boulder, 1984—; actor Off-Broadway, N.Y.C., 1959, Mo. Repertory Theatre, Kansas City, 1984; dir., actor Colo. Shakespeare Festival, Boulder, 1985—; leader People-to-People Del. of Theater Educators, USSR and Czechoslovakia, 1991. Author: Meyerhold's Theatre of the Grotesque, 1971 (Freedley Meml. award Theatre Libr. Assn. 1971); contbr. articles to scholarly jours. Lt. (j.g.) USN, 1960-63. Mem. Assn. for Theatre in Higher Edn. (pres. 1989-91), Assn. for Communication Adminstrn. (pres. 1990). Democrat. Methodist. Office: U of Colorado Dept Theatre and Dance Boulder CO 80309-0261

SYMONS, ROBERT SPENCER, electronic engineer; b. San Francisco, July 3, 1925; s. Spencer W. and Avesia (Atkins) S.; m. Alice Faye Smith, Dec. 21, 1960; children: Julia Ann, Robert Spencer Jr. BS, Stanford U., 1946, MS, 1948. Engr. Eitel-McCullough, Inc., San Bruno, Calif., 1947, Heinz & Kaufman, South San Francisco, 1948, Pacific Electronics Co., Los Gatos, Calif., 1949; sr. engring. mgr. Varian Assocs., Palo Alto, Calif., 1950-83; tech. dir. Litton Industries, San Carlos, Calif., 1983—. Recipient Charles B. Thornton award for Advanced Technology Achievement, 1991. Patentee in field. Served to 1st lt. AUS, 1950-53. Fellow IEEE (assoc. editor Transactions on Electron Devices jour. 1980-83); mem. Phi Beta Kappa, Tau Beta Pi. Club: Commonwealth of Calif. Home: 290 Surrey Pl Los Altos CA 94022-2146 Office: Litton Industries 960 Industrial Rd San Carlos CA 94070-4194

SYRETT, (JOHN) BARRY, airline pilot; b. Barkingside, Essex, Eng., June 15, 1934; came to U.S., 1966; s. John Victor and Molly Mackrell (Skelcher) S.; m. Cecile F. Boucher, June 15, 1957; children: Louise, Denise, Claire. Air traffic control asst. RAF, Uxbridge, Middlesex, Eng., 1952-54; pilot Aer Lingus, Dublin, Ireland, 1961-66; pilot, capt. Am. Airlines Inc., Los Angeles, 1966—. Flying Officer RCAF, 1955-60. Mem. Guild of Air Pilots and Air Navigators, London, Allied Pilots Assn. (bd. dirs. 1968-77, editor 1980-87, 89-90). Republican. Home: 3615 11th Ave NW Gig Harbor WA 78335

SYRING, JAMES JOHN, television news editor; b. N.Y.C., Oct. 4, 1942; s. John Joseph and Genevieve (Reynolds) S.; m. Virginia Catherine Zemaitis, July 20, 1968. BA in Mass Communications, SUNY, N.Y.C., 1975. Chief editor Sta. KUSA-TV, Denver, 1976-80; news editor Sta. KCNC-TV, Denver, 1980-89; media cons., 1989-93; tech. coord. ABC News, Denver, 1993—. Cpl. USMC, 1961-64. Recipient, Kodak award, Nat. Press Photographers Assn., 1976, Colo. Broadcasters award, Colo. Broadcasters Assn., 1988. Mem. NATAS (Emmy award 1973, regional Emmy, Denver, 1988), Colo. Film and Video Assn. Democrat. Home: 3229 S Forest St Denver CO 80222-7553 Office: 2460 W 26 Ave Ste C-130 Denver CO 80211

SYVERTSON, CLARENCE ALFRED, aerospace engineering consultant; b. Mpls., Jan. 12, 1926; s. Alfred and Esther Louise (Goertemiller) S.; m. Helen Hammond Gonnella, May 4, 1953 (dec. May 1981); 1 child, Marguerite Louise.; m. JoAnn Mary Caruso, May 8, 1982. B. Aero. Engring., U. Minn., 1946, M.S., 1948; postgrad., Stanford U., 1950-57; grad., Advanced Mgmt. Program, Harvard U., 1977. Research scientist Ames Aero. Lab., NACA, Moffett Field, Calif., 1948-58; exec. dir. Joint Dept. Transp./NASA Civil Aviation Research and Devel. Policy Study, 1970-71; with Ames Research Center, NASA, Moffett Field, 1958-84; dep. dir. Ames Research Center, NASA, 1969-78, dir., 1978-84; mem. adv. bd. Coll. Engring., U. Calif., Berkeley, 1980-85; cons. prof. Stanford U., 1985-88. Served with U.S. Army, 1946-47. Recipient invention and contbn. award NASA, 1964, Exceptional Service medal, 1971, Disting. Service medal, 1984, Outstanding Achievement award U. Minn., 1982, Commanders award for civilian service U.S. Army, 1984. Fellow AIAA (Lawrence Sperry award 1957), Am. Astronautical Soc.; mem. Nat. Acad. Engring. Home: 15725 Apollo Heights Ct Saratoga CA 95070-6302

SZABLYA, HELEN MARY, author, language professional, lecturer; b. Budapest, Pest, Hungary, Sept. 6, 1934; came to U.S., 1963; d. Louis and Helen (Bartha) Kovacs; m. John Francis Szablya, June 12, 1951; children: Helen, Janos, Louis, Stephen, Alexandra, Rita, Dominique-Mary. Diploma in Sales, Mktg., U.B.C., 1962; BA in Fgn. Lang., Lit., Wash. State U., 1976. Freelance writer, translator, 1967—; columnist Cath. News, Trinidad, W.I., 1980-91; adult educator TELOS Bellevue (Wash.) Community Coll., 1987-89; adult educator Pullman-Spokane (Wash.) Community Coll., 1976-80; faculty Christian Writers' Conf., Seattle, 1983-88, Pacific Northwest Writers' Conf., Seattle, Tacoma, 1987—; consul Republic of Hungary, 1993—; lectr. Washington Commn. for Humanities, 1987-89. Author: (with others) Hungary Remembered, 1986 (Guardian of Liberty award 1986, George Washington Honor medal, Freedoms Found. award 1988), 56-os Cserkészcsapat, 1986, numerous articles; pub., editor Hungary Internat. newsletter; translator: Emlékezünk, 1986, Mind Twisters, 1987. Recipient Nat. 1st place editorial Nat. Fedn. Press Women, 1987, Senator Tom Martin Meml. award Pacific N.W. Writers Conf., 1979; grantee Hungarian Am. Assn. Wash., 1986, Wash. Com. for Humanities, 1986; named Community Woman of Yr., Am. Bus. Women Assn., 1990. Mem. AAUW, Wash. Press Assn. (pres. 1987-88, 1st and 2d place awards, several editorial and profile awards 1983, 87, 89, 90, 91, 92, Communicator of Achievement award 1987), Nat. Fedn. Press Women (Affiliate Pres.' award 1988, bd. dirs. edn. fund northwest quadrant, mem. 21st century planning com.), Authors Guild, Am. Translators Assn., Arpad Acad. (Gold medal 1987), Nat. Writers Club, Internat. P.E.N. Club, Sigma Delta Chi (editorial award 1989). Home and Office: 4416 134th Pl SE Bellevue WA 98006-2104

SZABO, NICHOLAS, mayor, manufacturing executive; b. Budapest, Hungary, Feb. 2, 1930; came to the U.S., 1949; s. Nicholas and Charlotte (Nagy) S.; m. Marcia Purcifull, Dec. 4, 1955; children: Alex, Andrew. BS in Physics, Calif. Inst. Tech., 1953; MEE, Stanford U., 1959; D in Engring., U. Calif., Berkeley, 1976. Engr. Tracerlab, Inc., Richmond, Calif., 1956-57; scientist Lockheed, Palo Alto, Calif., 1959-66; dir. R&D Link div. Singer, Sunnyvale, Calif., 1966-84; dir. govt. programs KLA Instruments Corp., San Jose, Calif., 1984—; mayor City of Cupertino, Calif., 1992—; tech. adv. com. U.S. Dept. Commerce, 1990—. Author: Residue Arithmetic, 1967; patentee in field. Planning commr. City of Cupertino, Calif., 1983-89, councilman, 1989-90, vice mayor, 1990-92. With U.S. Army, 1953-55. Democrat. Home: 10235 Creston Dr Cupertino CA 95014-1013 Office: KLA Instruments Corp 160 Rio Robles Dr San Jose CA 95161-9055

SZABO, ROBERT JOSEPH, family entertainment company executive; b. San Jose, Calif., July 29, 1962; s. Joseph John and Katalin Rozalia Szabo. BS in Fgn. Svc., Georgetown U., 1983. Pres. Futuretainment, Inc., San Jose, 1983—. Adviser Jr. Achievement, Santa Clara County, Calif., 1980-90; mem. alumni admissions com. Georgetown U.; mem. Better Bus. Bur., Santa Clara. Mem. Nat. Fedn. Ind. Bus., Calif. Mchts. Safety Assn., Santa Clara C. of C., Union City C. of C., San Jose C. of C., Mountain View C. of C., Amusement and Music Operators Assn., Calif. Coin Machine Assn. (bd. dirs. 1990—), Jr. Achievement Nat. Alumni Assn., Los Altos Rotaract., San Jose Jaycees.

SZABO, ZOLTAN, medical science educator, medical institute administrator; b. Szeged, Hungary, Oct. 5, 1943; came to U.S., 1967; s. Imre and Maria (Szikora) S.; m. Wanda Toy, Dec. 5, 1976; children: Eva, Maria. Student, U. Med. Sch., Szeged, 1962-65; PhD, Columbia Pacific U., 1983. Tech. dir. microsurgery lab. R.K. Davies Med. Ctr., San Francisco, 1972-80; dir. Microsurg. Research Inst., San Francisco, 1980—; assoc. dir. advanced laparoscopic surgery tng. ctr. Dept. Surgery, U. Calif. Sch. Medicine, San Francisco, 1992—; research assoc. oral and maxillofacial surgery U. of the Pacific, San Francisco, 1980-83, adj. asst. prof., 1983—. Author: Microsurgery Techniques, vol. 1 1974, vol. 2 1984 (1st Place award for excellence in med. writing, 1982); contbr. chpt. books, articles to profl. jours. Served with U.S. Army, 1969-71, Vietnam. Recipient 1st prize sci. exhibit Am. Soc. Plastic and Reconstructive Surgeons, 1977, Cert. of Merit, AMA, 1978, Commendation, Accreditation Council for Continuing Med. Edn., 1984, 1990, Spl. Recognition award Cen. U. Venezuela Sch. Medicine, 1988, Residents and Fellows Rsch. and Scientific Presentation 1st Prize award Soc. Am. Gastrointestinal Endoscopic Surgeons, 1992, Techniques For In-Utero Endoscopic Surgery award Soc. Am. Gastrointestinal Endoscopic Surgeons, 1992, Scientific Poste Sessions Hon. Mention award Am. Urological Assn., 1992, Roundtable for New Techs. and Innovations 1st Prize award, we. sect. 1992, James Barrett Brown award Am. Assn. Plastic Surgeons, 1993. Fellow Internat. Coll. Surgeons; mem. Hungarian Gynecol. Soc. (hon.), Medico-Dental Study Guild of Calif., Internat. Microsurg. Soc., Am. Fertility Soc., Am. Soc. Reconstructive Microsurgery (assoc.), Soc. for Study of Impotence. Office: Microsurgery Operative Endoscopy Tng Inst 153 States St San Francisco CA 94114-1403

SZCZERBA, VICTOR BOGDAN, electrical engineer, sales executive, consultant; b. Chgo., Oct. 21, 1966; s. Bogdan and Zosia (Mika) S. BSEE, Marquette U., 1989. Sales engr. New Vision Computers, Milw., 1988-89; mktg. engr. Cypress Semicondr., San Jose, Calif., 1989-91; sales engr. Trinity Tech., Mountainview, Calif., 1991-92, AMD, Santa Clara, Calif., 1992—; cons. S3, Santa Clara, 1992. Mem. Knights of St. Patrick (pres. 1988-89), Sigma Phi Delta (v.p. 1987-88). Republican. Roman Catholic. Home: 687 Belden Ct Los Altos CA 94022

SZEGO, CLARA MARIAN, cell biologist, educator; b. Budapest, Hungary, Mar. 23, 1916; came to U.S., 1921, naturalized, 1927; d. Paul S. and Helen (Elek) S.; m. Sidney Roberts, Sept. 14, 1943. A.B., Hunter Coll., 1937; M.S. (Garvan fellow), U. Minn., 1939, Ph.D., 1942. Instr. physiology U. Minn., 1942-43; Minn. Cancer Research Inst. fellow, 1943-44; rsch. assoc. OSRD, Nat. Bur. Standards, 1944-45, Worcester Found. Exptl. Biology, 1945-47; rsch. instr. physiol. chemistry Yale U. Sch. Medicine, 1947-48; mem. faculty UCLA, 1948—, prof. biology, 1960—. Named Woman of Year in Sci. Los Angeles Times, 1957-58; Guggenheim fellow, 1956; named to Hunter Coll. Hall of Fame, 1987. Fellow AAAS; mem. Am. Physiol. Soc., Am. Soc. Cell Biology, Endocrine Soc. (CIBA award 1953), Soc. for Endocrinology (Gt. Britain), Biochem. Soc. (Gt. Britain), Internat. Soc. Rsch. Reprodn., Phi Beta Kappa (pres. UCLA chpt. 1973-74), Sigma Xi (pres. UCLA chpt. 1976-77). Home: 1371 Marinette Rd Pacific Palisades CA 90272-2627 Office: U Calif Dept Biology Los Angeles CA 90024-1606

SZEGO, PETER A., government staff consultant, mechanical engineer; b. Berlin, July 18, 1925; came to U.S., 1934; s. Gabor and Anne E. Szegö. P-rin. cons. Calif. State Senate, Sacramento. Contbr. articles to profl. jours. Served as sgt. U.S. Army, 1944-46, ETO. Mem. ASME, IEEE, SIAM, Am. Math. Soc., ACM. Democrat. Home: 75 Glen Eyrie Ave Apt 19 San Jose CA 95125-3131 Office: Office Senator Dan McCorquodale State Capitol Room 4032 Sacramento CA 95814

SZETO, HUNG, publisher; b. Hoyping, Canton, People's Republic of China, Sept. 8, 1936; s. Cheong Yee and Sau King(Kwan) S.; m. Sau Hing Chow, Jan. 27, 1962; children: Roland, Lisa, Nancy. B in adminstrn., Tsing Hua Coll., Hong Kong, 1969. Mgr. Far East Trade Ctr., Seattle, 1975-81; editor Seattle Chinese Post, 1982; pub. Asia Pub. Co., Seattle, 1986—, Chinese Bus. Jour., 1989—; Investment Letter, Investment Plans, 1992—. Mem. Asian Am. Journalists Assn., Chinese-Lang. Press. Inst., Northwest Minority Pubs. Assn. Office: Chinese Bus Jour 659 S Weller St Seattle WA 98104-2944

SZETO, PAUL (CHEUK-CHING), religious mission executive; b. Canton, China, July 28, 1940; came to U.S., 1962; s. Fai and Oi-wan (Wong) S.; m. Dorcas Chow, July 8, 1967; children: Tedd, Christine, Melissa. BA, Seattle Pacific U., 1966, MA, 1968; MDiv, Yale U., 1970; D of Missiology, Fuller Theol. Sem., Pasadena, Calif., 1980. Sr. minister Chinese Bapt. Ch., Seattle, 1971-78; dir. ch. planting ABC Pacific N.W., Seattle, 1978-80; gen. dir. Evangelize China Fellowship, Inc., Monterey Park, Calif., 1980—; founding dir. N.Am. of Chinese Evangelicals, 1972; participant Internat. Conf. for Itinerant Evangelists, 1983-86; bd. dirs. Chnese Coordination Centre of West, Hong Kong, 1976-80. Author: Seven Directions of Modern Theology, 1978, Suffering and Hope, 1982; translator: Evangelical Awakening in Eastern Asia, 1981; compiler: The Abundant Life, 1987. Mem. Greater Seattle Asian Am. Coun., 1972; mem. Royal Brougham Found., Seattle, 1974; mem. Campaign for Yale, L.A., 1977. Resident scholar Oxford U., 1991. Mem. Greater L.A. Chinese Ministers Assn. Home: 437 S Garfield Ave Monterey Park CA 91754 Office: Evangelize China Fellowship 437 S Garfield Ave Monterey Park CA 91754

SZYNAKA, EDWARD M., library director, consultant; b. N.Y.C., Sept. 26, 1948; s. Edward J. and Catherine A. (Regan) S.; m. Diane Pickering; children—Edward, Andrew, Emily. B.A. in Polit. Sci., SUNY-Fredonia, 1972; M.L.A., Syracuse U., 1973. Dir. libraries, Massena, N.Y., 1972-75, Midland, Mich., 1975-80; dir. Pasadena (Calif.) Pub. Library, 1980—; mgmt. cons. Bd. dirs. ARC; active Big Bros. Served to lt. U.S. Army, 1966-68. Mem. ALA, Calif. Library Assn., Mich. Library Assn. Democrat. Roman Catholic. Club: Kiwanis.

TABACHNICK, WALTER JAY, geneticist, researcher; b. Bklyn., June 14, 1947; s. Jack and Sylvia (Breidbart) T.; m. Darlene K. Virchow. BS, CUNY Bklyn. Coll., 1968; MS, Rutgers U., 1971, PhD, 1974. Asst. prof. life scis. U. Wis., Parkside, 1973-75; postdoctoral fellow Yale U., New Haven, 1975-78, rsch. assoc., 1979-82; lectr. UCLA, 1978-79; asst. prof. biology Loyola U., Chgo., 1982-87; rsch. entomologist Anthropod-borne Animal Diseases Rsch. Lab., Agrl. Rsch. Svc., Laramie, Wyo., 1987—; rsch. leader USDA-ARS, Laramie, Wyo., 1992—; cons. Anthrpod and Infectious Diseases Lab., Ft. Collins, Colo., 1988—; mem. exec. com. MacArthur Found. vector biology program Colo. State U., Ft. Collins, 1988—. Co-editor: Recent Developments in the Genetics of Insect Disease Vectors, 1982; contbr. numerous articles to profl. jours. NDEA fellow Rutgers U., 1970-73; NIH grantee Yale U., 1975-78, 80-82, Loyola U., 1982-85, USDA grantee ARS, 1992-94. Mem. Am. Genetics Assn., Am. Soc. Tropical Medicine and Hygiene, Am. Mosquito Control Assn., Genetics Soc. Am., Entomological Soc. Am., Soc. for the Study Evolution, Sigma Xi. Office: USDA Agrl Rsch Svc Arthrop-Bn Animal Dis Rsch PO Box 3965 Laramie WY 82071-3965

TABASCIO, STEFANO ANTONINO, chemical lubricant company executive; b. Toronto, Ont. Can., Sept. 26, 1965; s. Josef Antonino and Helena Ana (Neuhort) T.; m. Linda Ann Wade. Degree in Engring., Karlova U., Prague, Czechoslovakia, 1984; degree in Bus. Adminstrn., Calif. State U., L.A., 1989; degree in Chemistry, U. Nev., Las Vegas, 1991. Automotive engr. Zavodi Crevena Zastava, Knagujevac, Yugoslavia, 1984-85, Yugo Cars, Sun Valley, Calif., 1985; cons. Yugo Am., N.J., 1985-86; automobile dealer Mik Auto Inc./Bertone, North Hollywood, Calif., 1986-89; automotive designer Moretti, Torino, Italy, 1989-90; v.p. engring. Skocar, Markham, Ont., 1990-91; CEO Pentagram Products/Synlube, Las Vegas, 1991—. Author: All About Oil, 1989. Mem. Soc. Automotive Engrs., Soc. Tribologists and Lubrication Engrs., Sports Car Club Am. Office: Pentagram Products Synlube 2961 Industrial Rd # 300 Las Vegas NV 89109

TABB, WILLIAM HOWARD, podiatrist; b. Bklyn., Oct. 27, 1951; s. Irving and Miriam (Feldman) T.; m. Patty Bernice Sokolecki, Aug. 19, 1973 (div. Jan. 1978); m. Carolyn Jean Stallard, Nov. 20, 1983. BSEE, Poly. Inst. Bklyn., 1972; postgrad., UCLA, 1974-76; BS in Basic Med. Sci., Calif. Coll. Podiatric Medicine, 1978, D Podiatric Medicine, 1979. Diplomate Nat. Bd. Podiatric Examiners. Staff engr. PRD Electronics, Syosset, N.Y., 1972-73; mem. tech. staff Hughes Aircraft Co., Culver City, Calif., 1973-76; preceptor Harbor Podiatric Group, Torrance, Calif., 1979-80; pvt. practice Torrance, 1980-81, Anaheim, Calif., 1982—; attending staff Riviera Hosp., Torrance, 1979-81, Bay Harbor Hosp., Harbor City, Calif., 1980-81, H. Claude

Hudson County Clinic, L.A., 1980-81; podiatric med. dir. Gericare Podiatry Group, Anaheim, Calif., 1989—. Republican. Jewish. Home: 6930 E Avenida De Santiago Anaheim CA 92807-5104 Office: Gericare Podiatry Group 6312 E Santa Ana Canyon Rd # 292 Anaheim CA 92807-2300

TABLER, RONALD DWIGHT, snow and wind engineering consultant; b. Denver, May 18, 1937; s. Dwight Glen and Carol Arline (Turman) T.; m. Alicia Virginia Revollo, May 11, 1964; children: Edward Ronald, Alice Arlene. BS, Colo. State U., 1959, PhD, 1965. Rsch. forester USDA Forest Svc., Laramie, Wyo., 1959-65; rsch. hydrologist, project leader USDA Forest Svc., Laramie, 1965-85; snow and wind engrng. cons. Tabler & Assocs., Laramie, 1985-89, Niwot, Colo., 1989—; adj. prof. Dept. Mech. Engring., Univ. Wyo., Laramie, 1986—; rsch. affiliate Geophysical Inst., Univ. Alaska, Fairbanks, 1988—. Author: Snow Fence Handbook, 1988; contbr. articles to profl. jours. Recipient USDA Superior Svc. Honor award USDA, Washington, 1976, D. Grant Mickle award Nat. Acad. Scis., Washington, 1979, Rsch. award for fgn. specialists Japan Sci. & Tech. Agy., Tokyo, 1980-81. Fellow AAAS; mem. Am. Geophysical Union, Internat. Glaciological Soc., Am. Railway Engring. Assn., Am. Water Resources Assn., Western Snow Conf. (life, chmn. N. Cont. area 1980-84). Home: 7505 Estate Cir Longmont CO 80503-7260 Office: Tabler & Assocs PO Box 483 Niwot CO 80544-0483

TABRISKY, JOSEPH, radiologist, educator; b. Boston, June 23, 1931; s. Henry and Gertrude Tabrisky; BA cum laude, Harvard U., 1952; MD cum laude, Tufts U., 1956; m. Phyllis Eleanor Page, Apr. 23, 1955; children: Joseph Page, Elizabeth Ann, William Page. Flexible intern U. Ill. Hosp., 1956-57; resident in radiology Fitzsimons Army Hosp., 1958-60; instr. radiology Tufts U. Med. Sch., 1964-65; cons. radiologist Swedish Med. Center, Denver, 1966-68; chief radiologist Kaiser Found. Hosp., Harbor City, Calif., 1968-72; mem. faculty UCLA Med. Sch., 1972—, prof. radiol. scis., 1975-92, prof emeritus, 1993—, vice chmn. dept., 1976-92 , exec. policy com. radiol. scis.; chmn. radiology dept. Harbor-UCLA Med. Ctr., 1975-92 , pres. faculty soc., 1979-80, exec. dir. MR/CT Imaging Ctr., bd. dirs. Rsch. Ednl. Inst., Harbor Collegium/UCLA Found.; chief exec. officer Vascular Biometrics Inc.; steering com. Harvard U., 1952; cons. L.A. County Dept. Pub. Health; chmn. L.A. County Radiol. Standards Com., 1979. Mem. Harvard-Radcliffe Schs. Com.; chmn., bd. dirs., treas., Harbor-UCLA Med. Found.; chmn. UCLA Coun. for Ednl. Devel. Maj. M.C., U.S. Army, 1957-63. Recipient Silver Knight award Nat, Mgmt, Assn., 1992. Diplomate Am. Bd. Radiology. Fellow Am. Coll. Radiology, Univ. Radcom Assn. (chief exec. officer 1987—); mem. Radiol. Soc. N. Am., Calif. Med. Assn., Calif. Radiol. Soc., L.A. Med. Assn., L.A. Radiol. Soc., Alpha Omega Alpha. Contbr. articles to med. jours. Office: 1000 W Carson St Torrance CA 90509

TACHA, DEANELL REECE, federal judge; b. Jan. 26, 1946. BA, U. Kans., 1968; JD, U. Mich., 1971. Spl. asst. to U.S. Sec. of Labor, Washington, 1971-72; assoc. Hogan & Hartson, Washington, 1973, Thomas J. Pitner, Concordia, Kans., 1973-74; dir. Douglas County Legal Aid Clinic, Lawrence, Kans., 1974-77; assoc. prof. law U. Kans., Lawrence, 1974-77, prof., 1977-85, assoc. dean, 1977-79, assoc. vice chancellor, 1979-81, vice chancellor, 1981-85; judge U.S. Ct. Appeals (10th cir.), Denver, 1985—. Office: US Ct Appeals10th Circuit 4830 W 15th St Ste 100 Lawrence KS 66049-3846

TACHOUET, JOHN JAMES, real estate executive; b. San Rafael, Calif., Feb. 11, 1943; s. John Jacques and Mary K. (Bailey) T.; m. Mary Elizabeth Bergevin, Aug. 21, 1971; children: Matthew John, Stephen James, Marie Elizabeth. BS, U. Oreg., 1964. Pres. The Equity Group, Inc., Beaverton, Oreg., 1984—, also bd. dirs.; bd. dirs. E.G. Devel., Inc., Beaverton, Mountain Devel., Inc., Portland, Oreg. Mem. Nat. Assn. Realtors (residential specialist cert. 1985, residential brokerage mgr. 1988), Oreg. Assn. Realtors (bd. dirs., grad. realtors inst. 1975), Washington County Assn. Realtors (pres. 1990, Broker of Yr. 1988, Realtor of Yr. 1991), Multnomah Athletic Club. Office: The Equity Group Inc 1905 NW 169th Pl Beaverton OR 97006-7303

TACK, THERESA ROSE, women's health nurse; b. Lunenburg, Vt., Nov. 10, 1940; d. Gustave L. and Blanche Rose Fournier; m. Dennis M. Tack, Sept. 2, 1961; children: Lynelle Dannecker, Karyn Terry, LeAnn. Diploma, Cen. Maine Gen. Hosp., 1961. Cert. ACLS, neonatal resuscitation Am. Heart Assn. Staff nurse neurosurgery unit Hillcrest Med. Ctr., Tulsa, 1961-62; staff nurse cardiovascular unit Meth. Hosp., Houston, 1962-65; staff nurse St. John's Hosp., Red Wing, Minn., 1979-85, Wasatch County Hosp., Heber City, Utah, 1985—. columnist, Nurses Notes in Wasatch Wave, Heber City, Utah, 1990—.

TACKMAN, ARTHUR LESTER, newspaper publisher, management consultant; b. Chgo., July 28, 1916; s. Arthur Lester and Lucy Louise (Gutekunst) T.; m. Mary Lillian Connor, Mar. 31, 1939; children: Arthur Lester III, Laurence Connor, Alan Rhead. BA, Ohio State U., 1938, MPA, 1939. With various depts. U.S. Govt., Washington, 1938-49; staff asst., mem. pers. policy bd. Dept. Def., Washington, 1949; asst. mgr. Savannah river plant AEC, Aiken, S.C., 1950-55; asst. dir. inspection AEC, Washington, 1955-59, dir. pers., 1959-65; dir. pers. HUD, Washington, 1965-70; mgmt. cons. Glenwood, N.Mex., 1970-78; owner, operator Deep Creek Ranch, Inc., Glenwood, 1972—; publisher Catron Co. Pub. Co., Inc., Reserve, N.Mex., 1987—. Pres. Gila Nat. Forest Permittees, Reserve, 1978-86; mem., treas. N.Mex. Pub. Lands Coun., Albuquerque, 1967-87; coun. mem. Boy Scouts Am., S.C., Washington, 1950-65. Lt. USN, 1943-46. Recipient Man Yr. Award Aiken County C. of C., 1953, Citation for Meritorious Svc. United Def. Fund, 1957. Mem. N.Mex. Press Assn. Democrat. Unitarian. Home: Deep Creek Ranch Glenwood NM 88039 Office: Catron County Courier PO Box 644 Reserve NM 87830-0644

TACY, ROBERT E., JR., professional speaker, seminar presenter; b. Boston, June 11, 1943; s. Robert Edson and Rita Lorain (Gaudreagh) T.; children: Julia C. Goble, Cari S., Alan E., Michelle M. Sales rep. Arrowhead Water Co., Long Beach, Calif., 1964-68; dist. sales mgr. GTE Directory Co., Long Beach, Calif., 1968-74; area sales mgr. Gen. Tire and Rubber Co., Orange, Calif., 1975-78; founder, pres. Modern Creative Seminars, Kent, Wash., 1978—. Author of 6 tng. programs and monthly columns. Mem. Pacific NW Speakers Assn. (v.p. 1986-87, treas. 1987-88), Internat. Platform Assn. Office: Modern Creative Seminars PO Box 1125 Kent WA 98035-1125

TADDEI, MIRIAN H., corporate secretary; b. Cedar City, Utah, Apr. 18, 1930; d. William R. and Nola (Smith) Hunter; m. Armando Taddei, June 20, 1954; children: Max William, Amy Breda. BA in Lit., U. Wash., 1952; MA in Lit., Ariz. State U., 1959, PhD in Lit., 1989. Corp. sec. Hunter Contracting Co., Gilbert, Ariz., 1961—. Republican. Mem. Christian Ch. Office: Hunter Contracting Co 701 N Cooper Rd Gilbert AZ 85234-4301

TAFF, JEFFERY LYNN, computer programmer; b. Reno, Apr. 6, 1963; s. Dee C. and Freda May (Christy) T.; m. Tracy Heather Rogers, Sept. 28, 1987. BS in computing info. systems, Loma Linda U., La Sierra, Calif., 1985. Software engr. Electronic Data Systems, L.A., 1986-87; asst. mgr. Thermal (Calif.) Pallet Mfg., 1987-88; computer programmer Coachella (Calif.) Valley Water Dist., 1988—; computer cons. U.S. Lining, Palm Desert, Calif., 1984; computer programmer cons. Pavlof Electric, Palm Springs, Calif., 1985; owner small mail order bus. Grantee State of Calif., 1981-85; scholar Masonic Found., 1982-83. Home: 45-560 Holly Ct Indio CA 92201 Office: Coachella Valley Water Dist Ave 52 and Hwy 111 Coachella CA 92236

TAFF, WARREN RUSSELL, psychiatrist; b. Newark, Apr. 6, 1947; s. Harry and Edith Joyce (Tobias) T.; m. Barbara Ann Zordan, Apr. 13, 1986. BA, Rutgers U., 1968; MD, Birmingham (Eng.) U., 1974; MPH, UCLA, 1977. Diplomate Am. Bd. Psychiatry and Neurology. Intern VA Hosp., Sepulveda, Calif., 1974-75; resident in psychiatry U. So. Calif. Med. Ctr., L.A., 1975-78; resident Auckland Hosp., New Zealand, 1978, Royal Prince Alfred Hosp., Sydney, Australia, 1987-89; med. dir. Charter Hosp., Long Beach, Calif., 1990—; ptnr. Brea (Calif.) Mental Health Assocs., 1983—; chief of staff Coll. Hosp., Cerritos, 1984-86, assoc. med. dir., 1987-89, med. dir., 1989-90; asst. clin. prof. U. So. Calif. Med. Sch., L.A., 1984-92. Mem. Am. Psychiat. Assn., Royal Coll. Psychiatrists (Eng.) (treas. 1986-89, pres. 1989-93). Office: 6060 N Paramount Blvd Long Beach CA 90805-3798 also: 1203 W Imperial Hwy 102 Brea CA 92621

TAFOYA, ARTHUR N., bishop; b. Alameda, N.Mex., Mar. 2, 1933; s. Nicholas and Rosita Tafoya. Ed., St. Thomas Sem., Denver, Conception (Mo.) Sem. Ordained priest Roman Cath. Ch., 1962. Asst. pastor Holy Rosary Parish, Albuquerque, 1962-65; pastor Northern N.Mex., from 1965, San Jose Parish, Albuquerque; rector Immaculate Heart of Mary Sem., Santa Fe; ordained bishop of Pueblo Colo., 1980—. Office: 1001 N Grand Ave Pueblo CO 81003-2915

TAFT, PETER R., lawyer; b. Cin., Mar. 3, 1936; s. Charles P. and Eleanor (Chase) T.; m. Diana F. Todd, Nov. 17, 1979; children: Travis Todd, Tyler Frost, Julia Chase. B.A., Yale U., 1958, LL.B., 1961. Bar: D.C. 1963, Calif. 1969. Law clk. U.S. Ct. Appeals (5th cir.), 1961-62; law clk. to Chief Justice Earl Warren, U.S. Supreme Ct., 1962-63; assoc. Williams & Connolly, Washington, 1963-67, ptnr., 1967-69; asst. atty. gen. Land and Natural Resources div. Dept. Justice, Washington, 1975-77; ptnr. Munger Tolles & Olson, Los Angeles, 1969-75, 77—. Mem. D.C. Bar Assn., Calif. Bar Assn., Los Angeles Bar Assn., ABA. Republican. Episcopalian. Home: 17058 Avenida De Santa Ynez Pacific Palisades CA 90272 Office: 35th Fl 355 S Grand St Los Angeles CA 90071-1560

TAGGART, DENNIS DEVERE, physician; b. Logan, Utah, Sept. 19, 1938; s. DeVere Jerome and Faye (Hodges) T.; m. Karen Miller, June 29, 1966; children: Dennis, Pamela. BS, Utah State U., 1960; MD, George Washington U., 1963. Diplomate Am. Bd. Internal Medicine. Intership Wash. U., St. Louis, 1963-64, resident, 1964-65, fellow in nephrology, 1968-70, instr., 1970-71; resident U. N.Mex., Albequerque, 1965-66; pvt. practice Salt Lake City, 1971—; asst. prof. U. Utah, Salt Lake City, 1971-74; chief of medicine Holy Cross Hosp., Salt Lake City, 1974-75, pres. med. staff, 1988-90; pres. Premier Med. Physicians Group, 1991—, Chairman Premier Med. Network Bd. Capt. U.S. Army, 1966-68, Vietnam. Mem. Salt Lake City Med. Soc., Utah State Med. Assn., Am. Coll. Physician, Am. Soc. Nephrology, Ft. Douglas Club. Office: 24 S 1100 E Ste 306 Salt Lake City UT 84102-1500

TAGGART, SONDRA, financial planner, investment advisor; b. N.Y.C., July 22, 1934; d. Louis and Rose (Birnbaum) Hamov; children: Eric, Karen. BA, Hunter Coll., 1955. Cert. fin. planner, registered investment advisor; registered prin. Nat. Assn. Securities Dealers. Founder, dir., officer Copyright Svc. Bur., Ltd., N.Y.C., 1957-69; dir., officer Maclen Music, Inc., N.Y.C., 1964-69, The Beatles Ltd., 1964-69; pres. Westshore, Inc., Mill Valley, Calif., 1969-82; investment advisor, securities broker, chief exec. officer The Taggart Co. Ltd., 1982—. Editor: The Red Tapes: Commentaries on Doing Business With The Russians and East Europeans, 1978. Mem. Internat. Assn. Fin. Planners, Registry Fin. Planning Practitioners. Republican. Club: Bankers. Office: 9720 Wilshire Blvd # 205 Beverly Hills CA 90212

TAGGART, WILLIAM AREND, government educator; b. Lakehurst, N.J., July 29, 1955; s. Robert and Martha B. (Kraan) T.; m. Vicki A. Mills, Mar. 14, 1989; children: Germaine S., Robert E. AA, Pensacola (Fla.) Jr. Coll., 1975; BA, Fla. Atlantic U., 1978, MPA, 1979; PhD, Fla. State U., 1982. Records clk. City of Melbourne, Fla., 1978-79; rsch./teaching asst. Fla. State U., Tallahassee, 1979-82; asst. prof. N.Mex. State U., Las Cruces, 1982-86, assoc. prof., head dept. govt., 1986-92, prof., head dept. govt., 1992—. Contbr. chpts. to books and articles to profl. jours. Mem. ASPA (v.p. local chpt., pub. budgeting sect., criminal justice adminstrn. sect.), Acad. of Criminal Justice Scis., Am. Polit. Sci. Assn., Law and Soc. Assn., Midwest Polit. Sci. Assn., Policy Studies Orgn., So. Polit. Sci. Assn., Southwestern Social Sci. Assn., Western Polit. Sci. Assn. Office: Dept Govt NMex State U Dept 3BN Box 30001 Las Cruces NM 88003

TAI, FRANK, aerospace engineer; b. Omaha, Apr. 10, 1955; s. Shou Nan and May (Chuang) T.; m. Lorraine Mae Fesq, May 14, 1988. BSME, U. Calif., Berkeley, 1977; MS in Automatic Controls Engring., MIT, 1979. Design engr. satellite attitude control systems Ball Aerospace, Boulder, Colo., 1979-84; mgr. satellite attitude control systems TRW, Redondo Beach, Calif., 1984-88; mgr. engring. Microcosm, Inc., Torrance, Calif., 1988-89; pres., engring. cons., founder Tech. Advancements, Inc., Playa del Rey, Calif., 1989—. Contbr. articles to profl. jours. Mem. AIAA, Am. Astronautical Soc., Sigma Xi, Tau Beta Pi, Pi Tau Sigma. Home: 6738 Esplanade Playa Del Rey CA 90293-7525 Office: Tech Advancements Inc 6738 Esplanade # 300 Playa Del Rey CA 90293-7525

TAIMUTY, SAMUEL ISAAC, physicist; b. West Newton, Pa., Dec. 20, 1917; s. Elias and Samia (Hawatt) T.; BS, Carnegie Inst. Tech., 1940; PhD, U. So. Calif., 1951; m. Betty Jo Travis, Sept. 12, 1953 (dec.); children: Matthew, Martha; m. Rosalie Richards, Apr. 3, 1976. Physicist, U.S. Naval Shipyard, Phila. and Long Beach, Calif., 1942-46; rsch. asst. U. So. Calif., 1947-51; sr. physicist U.S. Naval Radiol. Def. Lab., 1950-52, SRI Internat., Menlo Park, Calif., 1952-72; sr. staff engr. Lockheed Missiles & Space Co., Sunnyvale, Calif., 1972-89; cons. physicist, 1971—. Mem. Am. Phys. Soc., Sigma Xi. Episcopalian. Contbr. articles to sci. publs. Patentee in field. Home: 3346 Kenneth Dr Palo Alto CA 94303-4217

TAIRA, MASA MORIOKA, gallery director, volunteer; b. Kagoshima City, Japan, Nov. 25, 1923; d. Masakiyo Morioka and Kin (Masuda) Morioka Uyeno; m. Tom Keizo Taira, Aug. 8, 1954; 1 child, Mikilani. BS in Food Nutrition, Madison (Tenn.) Coll., 1947; postgrad., George Peabody Tchrs. Coll., 1949-50; MS in Food Nutrition, U. Calif., L.A., 1953. Various positions statewide, 1947-63; dir. Queen Emma Gallery, Honolulu, 1977—. Office: Queen Emma Gallery 1301 Punchbowl St Honolulu HI 96813-2419

TAIT, JOHN REID, lawyer; b. Toledo, Ohio, Apr. 7, 1946; s. Paul Reid and Lucy Richardson (Rudderow) T.; m. Christina Ruth Bjornstad, Mar. 12, 1972; children: Gretchen, Mary. BA, Columbia Coll., 1968; JD, Vanderbilt U., 1974. Bar: Idaho 1974, U.S. Dist. Ct. Idaho 1974. Assoc. Keeton & Tait, Lewiston, Idaho, 1974-76, ptnr., 1976-86, 89—, Keeton, Tait & Petrie, 1986-88, Keeton & Tait, 1989—. Chmn. bd. No. Rockies Action Group, Helena, Mont., 1985-86, bd. dirs. 1981-88, Lewiston Hist. Preservation Commn., Idaho, 1975—, chmn., 1988—; bd. dirs. Idaho Legal Aid Services, Boise, 1975—, Idaho Housing Agy., Boise, 1984-91, St. Joseph Regional Med. Ctr. Found., Inc., 1989—; Dem. precinct committeeman, 1976-86, state committeeman, 1977—; co-chmn. Idaho state re-election com. John V. Evans, 1978; Idaho del. Nat. Dem. Conv., N.Y., 1980, standing com. on credentials, N.Y., 1980, San Francisco, 1984; treas. Larry LaRocco for Congress, 1990, 92. Served with U.S. Army, 1968-71. Recipient Pro Bono Svc. award Idaho State Bar 1988. Mem. ABA, Assn. Trial Lawyers Am., Idaho Trial Lawyers Assn. (regional dir. 1976-77, 86-88), Clearwater Bar Assn. (sec. 1974-76, pres. 1984-86). Democrat. Office: Keeton & Tait 312 Miller St # E Lewiston ID 83501-1944

TAIT, JOSEPH EDWARD, public water utility executive; b. L.A., Oct. 31, 1957; s. William Richard and Corrine Fay (Harris) T.; m. Denise Patricia Boutelle, Aug. 23, 1980; children: Jeffrey William, Gregory Charles, Jason Andrew. Student, Brigham Young U., 1977, Utah Valley Community Coll., 1978-80; BA in Mgmt., U. Phoenix, 1988. Field supt. Met. Water Dist. of Salt Lake City, Pleasant Grove, Utah, 1984-88; asst. mgr. Met. Water Dist. of Salt Lake City, Salt Lake City, 1989-91; adminstrv. mgr., 1992—; pres. Utah Network for Profl. Devel., Salt Lake City, 1987-90. Corp. campaign mgr. United Way, 1986—; scout troop com. chmn. Boy Scouts Am., Pleasant Grove, Utah, 1991—; chmn. Salt Lake County Drinking Water Week Com., 1992. Recipient Excellence in Mgmt. award Utah Network for Profl. Devel., 1986, Diamond Pin award Am. Water Works Assn., 1990; named Most Valuable Player, Utah Valley C.C., 1978-79, 79-80. Mem. Am. Water Works Assn., Utah Network for Profl. Devel. (pres. 1987-89), Nat. Safety Coun. Democrat. Mem. LDS Ch. Home: 3846 W 8800 N Pleasant Grove UT 84062-9412 Office: First Interstate Pla 170 S Main St Ste # 650 Salt Lake City UT 84101

TAJON, ENCARNACION FONTECHA (CONNIE TAJON), retired educator, association executive; b. San Narciso, Zambales, Philippines, Mar. 25, 1920; came to U.S., 1948; d. Espiridion Maggay and Gregoria (Labrador) Fontecha; m. Felix B. Tajon, Nov. 17, 1948; children: Ruth F., Edward F. Teacher's cert., Philippine Normal Coll., 1941; BEd, Far Eastern U., Manila, 1947; MEd, Seattle Pacific U., 1976. Cert. tchr., Philippines. Tchr. pub. schs. San Narciso and Manila, 1941-47; coll. educator Union Coll. Manila, 1947-48; tchr. Auburn (Wash.) Sch. Dist., 1956-58, Renton (Wash.) Sch. Dist., 1958-78; owner, operator Manila-Zambales Internat. Grill, Seattle, 1980-81, Connie's Lumpia House Internat. Restaurant, Seattle, 1981-84; founder, pres. Tajon-Fontecha, Inc., Renton, 1980—, United Friends of Filipinos in Am. Found., Renton, 1985—; founder Labrador Fontecha and Baldovi-Tajon Permanent Scholarship Fund of The Philippine Normal Coll., 1990; bd. mem. World Div. of the Gen. Bd. of Global Ministries of the United Meth. Ch., 1982-84, Ch. Women United Seattle Chapt.; mem. advisory bd Univ. Wash. Burke Mus., 1991—. Bd. dirs. women's div. Gen. Bd. Global Ministries United Meth. Ch., 1982-84, Renton Area Youth Svcs., 1980-85, Girls' Club of Puget Sound, Ethnic Heritage Coun. of Pacific N.W., 1989—; mem. Mcpl. Arts Commn. Renton, 1980—; chair fundraising steering com. Washington State Women's Polit. Caucus, 1985-89; governing mem. nat. steering com. Nat. Women's Polit. Caucus Wash. State Coun., 1990—, mem. vol. action, 1990 Goodwill Games, Seattle, vol. worker Native Am. Urban Ministries, 1990—; adv. bd. Renton Community Housing Devel.; community adv. bd. U. Wash. Thomas Burke Meml. Mus., 1990—. Recipient spl. cert. of award Project Hope, 1976, U.S. Bicentennial Commn., 1976, UNICEF, 1977, Spirit of Liberty award Ethnic Heritage Coun. Pacific Northwest, 1991; named Parent of Yr. Filipino Community of Seattle, Inc., 1984, One of 500 Seattle Pacific U. Centennial "Alumni of a Growing Vision", 1991. Mem. NEA, U. Wash. Alumni Assn. (life), U. Wash. Filipino Alumni Assn. (pres. Wash. State chpt. 1985-87), Renton Retired Tchrs. Assn., Wash. State Edn. Assn. (bd. dirs. 1990—), Am. Assn. Ret. Persons, Nat. Ret. Tchrs. Assn., Renton Hist. Mus. (life), Internat. Platform Assn., United Meth. Women, Pres.'s Forum, Am. Biog. Inst. Rsch., Assn. (dep. gov.), Alpha Sigma, Delta Kappa Gamma. Democrat. Home and Office: 2033 Harrington Pl NE Renton WA 98056-2303

TAKACS, JAMES ERIC, accountant; b. Prince Albert, Canada, May 1, 1935; came to the U.S., 1957; s. Joseph and Flora (Tarcy) T.; m. Hilda Ethel Lendvoy, June 16, 1954 (div. 1982); children: David, Gerald, Phillip, Donald; m. Shirley Ann Bracewell, July 19, 1982; children: Walter, Crawford, Patricia. BS in Acctg., Tri-State U., Angola, Ind., 1961. Regional mgr. Studebaker Corp., Atlanta, 1961-64; pres. Cobb Electric Co., Marietta, Ga., 1965-82; mgr. Rimrock Lighting, Billings, Mont., 1982-85; owner, tax acct. Interstate Svcs. Co., Tacoma, Wash., 1986—; instr. IRS, Tacoma, 1991. Mem. Nat. Assn. Pub. Accts. (del. 1991), Wash. Assn. Pub. Accts. (pres. 1991—, v.p. 1990-91, treas. 1989-90). Republican. Baptist. Office: Interstate Svcs Co 10510 Gravelly Lake Dr SW Tacoma WA 98499-5036

TAKAHASHI, BRIAN TOSHIO, architectural firm executive; b. Honolulu, Jan. 13, 1954; s. Robert Kazuo and Martha (Saito) T.; m. Faye Nakamoto, Aug. 16, 1981; children: Nicholas, Tracy. BA in Fine Arts, U. Hawaii, 1977, MArch, 1983. Registered architect, Hawaii. Designer, drafter Johnson and Reese Architects, Honolulu, 1979; designer Zephyr Architects, Honolulu, 1980; designer, drafter Environ. Design Works, Honolulu, 1981; designer, drafter Group 70 Architects, Honolulu, 1981-83, assoc., 1984-87; assoc. AM Ptnrs., Inc., Honolulu, 1987, prin., v.p., 1987—. Principal in Charge: Dole Cannery Sq. Archtl. Design BIA Renaissance, 1989 (Merit award 1989), Dole Kids Shop Designing to Sell, 1989; Prin. works include King Kamuaii Elementary Sch., Kauei, Hi. (award of excellence Am. Sch. and Univ. Archtl. Portifolio 1992). Named Architect in Residence, State Found. Culture & Arts, Honolulu, 1987. Mem. Am. Planning Assn. (treas. 1989—, newsletter chmn. 1988-89, spl. publicity co-chmn. 1987-88, Hawaii chpt.), AIA (public ed. chmn., Hawaii chpt., 1987—), Nat. Historic Pres. Found., Hawaii Soc. of Corp. Planners, Japan Am. Soc., Constrn. Specifications Inst.. Office: AM Partners Inc Ste 1000 1164 Bishop St Honolulu HI 96813-2810

TAKAHASHI, HIROYASU, computer scientist; b. Morioka, Iwate, Japan, Nov. 23, 1945; came to U.S., 1990; s. Ryozo and Eiko T.; m. Akiko Karino; Apr. 23, 1983; children: Yuta, Kazuma, Yoko. BA, U. Tokyo, Japan, 1969; MA, U. Tokyo, 1971, PhD, 1974. Systems engr. IBM Japan, Tokyo, 1974-78; researcher in Tokyo sci. ctr. IBM Japan, 1978-82, rsch. mgr. in Tokyo rsch. lab., 1982-89; rsch. staff mem. in Almaden rsch. ctr. IBM, San Jose, Calif., 1990—. Mem. IEEE, Assn. Computing Machinery, Inst. Electronics, Info. and Comm. Engrs., Info. Processing Soc. Japan. Home: 1498 Montalban Dr San Jose CA 95120 Office: IBM Almaden Rsch Ctr 605 Harry Rd San Jose CA 95120

TAKAMURA, JEANETTE CHIYOKO, state agency administrator; b. Honolulu, Aug. 1, 1947; d. Jiro and Jane Chiseko (Ishida) Chikamoto; m. Carl Takeshi Takamura, May 17, 1974; 1 child, Mari Leigh. BA, U. Hawaii, 1969, MSW, 1972; PhD, Brandeis U., 1985. Program dir. Moiliili Community Ctr., Honolulu, 1972-74; instr. sch. medicine and social work U. Hawaii, Honolulu, 1975-78, asst. prof., 1982-86; dir. exec. office on aging Office of Gov., Honolulu, 1987—; ptnr. Browne/Takamura, Honolulu, 1985-86. Contbr. articles to profl. jours. and chpts. to books; editorial bd.: Aging Today, 1991—. V.p. Moiliili Community Ctr., 1977. Grantee NIMH, 1982-84, U.S. Dept. HHS, 1985, 86, 89-90, 91. Mem. Nat. Assn. Statute Units on Aging (2d v.p. 1991-92), Am. Soc. on Aging (program planning com. 1992—), Gerontology Soc. Am., Futurist Soc. Congregationalist. Office: Exec Office on Aging 335 Merchant St Ste 241 Honolulu HI 96813

TAKANO, MARK A, congressman, educator; b. Riverside, Calif., 1961; s. William and Nancy T. BA in Govt., Harvard U., 1983. Cert. tchr., Calif. English/History tchr. Rialto Jr. High Sch., Riverside, Calif.; mem. 103d Congress from 43d Calif. Dist., 1993—; pres., bd. trustees Riverside C.C., 1991-93. Chmn. Greater Riverside Urban League, 1989-93; mem. Rialto Edn. Assn., Chancellors Commn. on Innovation in Calif. Community Colls.; mem. bd. Japanese-Am. Citizens League, State Democratic Ctrl. Com.; so. sec. Calif. Dem. Party's Asian Pacific Islander Caucus; mem. exec. bd. Calif. Dem. Party, 1988-90. Office: US Ho Reps Office House Members Washington DC 20515

TAKASUGI, NAO, business developer; b. Oxnard, Calif., Apr. 5, 1922; s. Shingoro and Yasuye (Hayashi) T.; m. Judith Shigeko Mayeda, Mar. 23, 1952; children—Scott, Russell, Ronald, Tricia, Lea. B.S., Temple U., 1945; M.B.A., U. Pa. Wharton Sch., 1946. Mem. city council City of Oxnard, Calif., 1976-82, mayor, 1982-92; mem. Calif. State Assembly, 1992—; bus. developer, cons. Mem. Oxnard Planning Commn., 1974-76; pres. World Trade Ctr. Assn., Oxnard; apptd. (by Calif. gov.) chmn. UN Anniversary; assemblyman Calif. State Assembly 37th Dist. Mem. Ventura County Japanese Am. Citizens League, World Trade Ctr. Assn. (pres. Oxnard chpt.), U.S. Conf. Mayors (mem. nat. adv. bd.), Nat. League of Cities (nat. bd. dirs.), Ventura County Transp. Com., League Calif. Cities (bd. dirs.), South Coast Area Bd. Dirs. (chmn. transp. com.), Assn. Ventura County Cities, Oxnard Housing Authoritry (chmn.), Oxnard Redevel. Agy. (chmn.), Optimists Club (Oxnard). Republican. Methodist. Home: 1221 El Portal Way Oxnard CA 93035-2511 Office: State Capital Room 2016 Sacramento CA 95814 also: 221 Daily Dr Ste 7 Camarillo CA 93010

TAKASUGI, ROBERT MITSUHIRO, federal judge; b. Tacoma, Sept. 12, 1930; s. Hidesaburo and Kayo (Otsuki) T.; m. Dorothy O. Takasugi; children: Jon Robert, Lesli Mari. BS, UCLA, Los Angeles, 1953; LLB, JD, U. So. Calif., 1959. Bar: Calif. bar 1960. Practiced law Los Angeles, 1960-73; judge East Los Angeles Municipal Ct., 1973-75, adminstrv. judge, 1974, presiding judge, 1975; judge Superior Ct., County of Los Angeles, 1975-76; U.S. dist. judge U.S. Dist. Ct. (cen. dist.) Calif., 1976—; nat. legal counsel Japanese Am. Citizens League; guest lectr. law seminars Harvard U. Law Sch. Careers Symposium; commencement speaker; mem. Legion Lex U. So. Calif. Law Center; chmn. Pub. Defs. Indigent Def. & Psychiat. Panel Com.; mem. Affirmative Action Com., Habeas Corpus-Death Penalty Com., Exec. Com., Jury Com., Settlement Rule Com., Adv. Com. on Codes of Conduct of the Jud. Conf. of the U.S., 1988—, Code of Conduct of Judges. Mem. editorial bd. U. So. Calif. Law Rev., 1959; contbr. articles to profl. jours. Mem. Calif. adv. com. Western Regional Office, U.S. Commn. on Civil Rights. Served with U.S. Army, 1953-55. Recipient U.S. Mil. Man of Yr. award for Far East Theater U.S. Army, 1954, Jud. Excellence award Criminal Cts. Bar Assn.; certificate of merit Japanese-Am. Bar Assn.; other awards; Harry J. Bauer scholar, 1959. Mem. U. So. Calif. Law Alumni (dir.). Office: US Dist Ct 312 N Spring St Los Angeles CA 90012-4701

TAKATA, KEVIN KENJI, lawyer; b. Lanai City, Hawaii, Feb. 9, 1956; s. Kengo and Evelyn S. (Ishida) T. BA, U. Hawaii, 1978; JD, Case Western Res. U., 1984. Bar: Hawaii 1984, U.S. Dist. Ct. Hawaii 1984. Assoc. Oliver, Lee, Cuskaden & Ogawa, Honolulu, 1984-87; dep. prosecutor specializing in homicides Dept. of Prosecuting Atty., Honolulu, 1987—. Mem. ABA, Hawaii Bar Assn., Nat. Dist. Attys. Assn., Honolulu C. of C. Office: Dept of Prosecuting Atty 10th fl 1060 Richards St Honolulu HI 96813

TAKATA, NOBU, electrical engineer; b. Pepeekeo, Hawaii, July 23, 1938; s. Ichibei and Hanayo (Okano) T.; m. Mae Sadako Morita, Aug. 21, 1965; children: Michelle, Cheryl, Kevin. BSEE, West Coast U., 1964. Engr. Gilfillan div. ITT, L.A., 1963-70, Actron, Monrovia, Calif., 1970-77, Dept. Def., USN, Corona, Calif., 1977—. With U.S. Army, 1961-63. Office: Naval Warfare Assessment Ct SE 13 Corona CA 91720

TAKATA, SAYOKO, retired educator; b. L.A., July 12, 1937; d. Henry Takuji and Fujie (Udo) Nishi; m. Isao Jon Takata, Nov. 24, 1961; 1 child, Stephen Isamu. BA in Bus., U. No. Colo., 1959; M.Ed. in Vocat. Edn., Colo. State U., 1980. Life teaching cert., Colo. Tchr. home econs. Erie (Colo.) Jr. and Sr. High Sch., 1959-60; tchr. bus. and office edn. Manual High Sch., Denver, 1960-63, 68-78, chmn. dept., 1977-78; asst. bookkeeper Century Fixtures, Inc., Los Angeles, 1963-64; tchr. bus. and office edn. East High Sch., Denver, 1978-79; tchr. bus. and office edn. Met. Youth Edn. Ctr., Zuni Ctr., 1978-79; tchr. bus. and office edn. East extension, Denver, 1979-92, chmn. dept., 1980-92; mem. Colo. Spl. Needs Ad Hoc Com., 1980. Mem. Am. Vocat. Assn., Nat. Bus. Edn. Assn. (chmn. decorations NBEA conv. 1988), NEA, Colo. Educators For/About Bus. (treas. 1981-83, Profl. Merit award 1987), Internat. Soc. bus. Educators, Colo. Vocat. Assn., Mountain Plains Bus. Edn. Assn. (Colo. rep. 1986-92, chmn. conv. pres. reception 1992), Denver Classroom Tchrs. Assn., Colo. Edn. Assn., Delta Pi Epsilon, Delta Kappa Gamma (asst. treas. 1986-88, treas. 1988—). Buddhist. Home: 561 W 87th Pl Denver CO 80221-4314 Office: 3800 York St Bldg 1 Unit A Denver CO 80205

TAKAYAMA, LINDA CHU, state agency administrator; b. Honolulu, Feb. 12, 1948; d. Charles Chung and Beatrice (Chang) Chu; m. Gregg T. Takayama, Nov. 1, 1975; children: Kelly, Teal, Sage. BA, U. Hawaii, 1974; JD, George Mason U., 1986. Bar: Pa. 1990, Hawaii 1991. Dir. advt. Gibson's Dept. Store, Honolulu, 1975-76; asst. dir. advt. Parkview Gem Dept. Store, Honolulu, 1976-77; dir. staff State Rep. Benjamin Cayetano, Honolulu, 1977-78; dir. state legis. Grocery Mfrs. Am. Inc., Washington, 1979-87; adminstv. asst., gen. counsel U.S. Senate Sgt. at Arms, Washington, 1987-91; ins. commr. State of Hawaii, Honolulu, 1991—. Bd. dirs. Hawaii Foodbank Inc., Honolulu, 1991—. Mem. Hawaii Bar Assn. Democrat. Home: 1639 Hoolana St Pearl City HI 96782

TAKEDA, TIMOTHY SCOTT, accountant; b. San Jose, Calif., Oct. 22, 1956; s. Herbert Kingo and Chiye (Kogura) T. BS in Bus. Adminstrn., San Jose State U., 1979; MBA, Santa Clara U., 1989. CPA, cert. internal auditor. Sr. tax analyst Acuson Corp., Mountain View, Calif. Active The Kenna Club, Santa Clara, 1989, Univ. of Santa Clara (Calif.) MBA Assn., 1989, San Jose (Calif.) State Univ. Spartan Found., 1989. Mem. AICPA, Calif. Soc. CPA's, Inst. Internal Auditors. Office: Acuson Corp 1220 Charleston Rd Mountain View CA 94039-7393

TAKEI, TOSHIHISA, otolaryngologist; b. L.A., Apr. 19, 1931; s. Taketomi and Mitsue (Hagihara) T.; m. Emiko Kubota, Jan. 25, 1955; children: H. Thomas, T. Robert. BA, UCLA, 1954; MD, Boston U., 1962. Diplomate, Am. Bd. Otolaryngology. Intern L.A. County Harbor Gen. Hosp., 1962-63; resident in otolaryngology L.A. County/U. So. Calif. Med. Ctr., 1963-67; staff physician Covina (Calif.) Ear, Nose & Throat Med. Group, 1968—; asst. prof. Sch. Medicine, U. So. Calif., L.A., 1968—. 1st lt. U.S. Army, 1955-56, Korea. Fellow Am. Acad. Otolaryngology, Royal Soc. Medicine. Republican. Buddhist. Office: Covina ENT Med Group Inc 236 W College St Covina CA 91723-1902

TAKEUCHI, HAJIME JIM, airline executive, electrical engineer; b. Ishikawa, Japan, Nov. 4, 1941; came to U.S., 1961; s. Kazuo and Modori (Genmei) T.; m. Elaine Tsuha, Mar. 20, 1975; children: Mitsuko, Erica, Rodger. BSEE, U. Ill., 1966. Mgr. space shuttle United Svcs. Co., Cape Kennedy, Fla., 1982-83; contract mgr. Air Crew Tng. Co., Denver, 1983-84; engr. United Air Lines, San Francisco, 1967-76, staff engr., 1976-79; mgr. aircraft sales United Air Lines, Chgo., 1979-82; mgr. tech. svcs. United Air Lines, San Francisco, 1984-89, mgr. engring., 1989-91, dir. engring., 1991—. Home: 2436 Wright Ct South San Francisco CA 94080 Office: United Airlines San Francisco Internat Airport San Francisco CA 94128

TAKEUCHI, SYLVIA FUJIE, marketing executive; b. Portland, Oreg., Jan. 15, 1939; d. Thomas K. and Tomie (Miyake) T.; m. Donald D. Owens, Aug. 30, 1985. Student, Willamette U.; BABA, Portland State U., 1975. Cert. in internat. bus. Adminstrv. asst. Gov. Mark O. Hatfield, Salem, Oreg., 1960-63, Nelson Rockefeller and John D. Rockefeller III, N.Y.C., 1963-66, Senator Mark O. Hatfield, Washington, 1966-67; personnel dir. Donaldson, Lufkin & Jenrette, N.Y.C., 1967-70; sales rep. Boise Casdade, Portland, 1976-81; owner, gen. mgr. Far West Office Systems, Phoenix, 1981-86; cons. NBI"s The Office Pl., Seattle, 1987-88; gen. sales mgr. Eastman, Inc., Phoenix; mem. Phoenix IDA Bd. Chmn. Gov.'s Energy Policy, Salem, Oreg., 1983-85. Republican.

TAKIURA, MITSURU, pharmaceutical company executive; b. Tokyo, Japan, Dec. 28, 1939; s. Kiyoshi and Sada (Orihara) T.; m. Masako Tanigaki, July 26, 1976. BBA, Hitotsubashi U., Tokyo, 1965. Acctg. staff Takeda Chem. Industries, Osaka, Japan, 1965-67; acctg. mgr. Nippondo Co., Tokyo, 1967-70; import mgr. Narisako & Co., Osaka, 1971-72; import staff Nissin Transp. Co., Osaka, 1972-74; acctg. mgr. Wakunaga Pharm. Co., Osaka, 1974-77, dir. acctg., 1981-85, dir. sales, 1985-90; contr. Wakunaga of Am. Co., Torrance, Calif., 1977-81; exec. v.p. Wakunaga of Am. Co., Mission Viejo, Calif., 1990-91, pres., 1992—. Presbyterian. Office: Wakunaga of Am Co Ltd 23501 Madero Mission Viejo CA 92691

TAKO, GABRIELLA, art historian; b. N.Y.C., Dec 1; d. Norma Susan (Schmetterer) Reiner. BA, Ariz. State U., 1988, Certificate in Women's Studies, 1992. Jeweler Michael Bondanza, Inc., N.Y.C., 1983-86, Takashi Wada Jewelers, N.Y.C., 1986-87; peer counselor, women's studies Ariz. State U., Tempe, 1987-88, teaching asst., 1990; freelance curator Tempe, 1989-91; grad. asst. art slide collection Ariz. State U., Tempe, 1990-91, grad. asst., archivist, 1992—. Recipient Best of Show (painting) Masako I, 1991, Aware scholarship, Ariz. StateU., Tempe, 1990, Women's Studies scholarship, Ariz. State U., Tempe, 1990, 91, 92. Mem. Woman Image Now, Coll. Art Assn., Women's Caucus of Art, Assn. Grad. Art Students (art history rep. 1990-91). Jewish. Office: Ariz State U Tempe AZ 85287-1505

TAKUMI, ROY MITSUO, state representative; b. Honolulu, Oct. 13, 1952; m. Wanda A. Kutaka; children: Aisha, Jaron. BA, Friends World Coll., 1991; MPA, U. Hawaii, 1993. Program dir. Am. Friends Svc. Com., Honolulu, 1984-90; polit. coord. Hawaii State AFL-CIO, Honolulu, 1990-92; rep. Ho. of Reps., Honolulu, 1992—. Office: State Ho of Reps State Capitol Honolulu HI 96813

TALBERT, MELVIN GEORGE, bishop; b. Clinton, La., June 14, 1934; s. Nettles and Florence (George) T.; m. Ethlelou Douglas, June 3, 1961; 1 child, Evangeline. BA, So. U., 1959; MDiv, Interdenominational Theol. Ctr., Gammon Theol. Sem., Atlanta, 1962; DD hon., Huston Tillotson Coll., Austin, 1972; LLD (hon.), U. Puget Sound, Tacoma, 1987. Ordained deacon, Meth. Ch., 1960 , elder, 1962, elected to episcopacy, United Meth. Ch., 1980. Pastor Boyd Chapel, Jefferson City, Tenn., 1960-61, Rising Sun, Sunrise, Tenn., 1960-61, St. John's Ch., L.A., 1961-62, Wesley Ch., L.A., 1962-64, Hamilton Ch., L.A., 1964-67; mem. staff So. Calif.-Ariz. Conf. United Meth. Ch., L.A., 1967-68; dist. supr. Long Beach dist. So. Calif.-Ariz. Conf. United Meth. Ch., 1968-73; gen. sec. Gen. Bd. Discipleship, Nashville, 1973-80; resident bishop Seattle area Pacific N.W. conf. United Meth. Ch., 1980-88, resident bishop San Francisco area Calif.-Nev. Conf., 1988—, sec. coun. bishops, 1988—; mem. exec. com. World Meth. Coun., 1976-81, 84—; mem. governing bd. Nat. Coun. Chs., 1980—; v.p., chmn. funding com. Gen. Commn. on Religion and Race, 1980-84, pres., 1984-88; chmn. Missional Priority Coordinating com. Gen. Coun. Ministries, 1980-84; mem. Gen. Commn. on Christian Unity and Interreligious Concerns, 1984—, African Ch. Growth and Devel. Com., 1981-84. Mem. steering com. Student Non-Violent Coordinating com. Atlanta U. Ctr., 1960-61; trustee Gammon Theol. Sem., Atlanta, 1976—, U. Puget Sound, Tacoma, 1980-88 , Sch. Theology at Claremont, Calif., 1981-88, Pacific Sch. Religion, 1988—; bd. dirs. Glide Found., 1988—. Recipient award of merit for outstanding svc. in Christian edn. Gen. Bd. Edn., 1971; recipient Spl. achievement award Nat. Assn. Black Bus. Women, 1971; Nat. Meth. scholar, 1960; Crusade scholar, 1961. Mem. Theta Phi. Democrat. Home: 13816 Campus Dr Oakland CA 94605-3830*

TALBERT, WILLARD LINDLEY, JR., physicist; b. Casper, Wyo., Mar. 8, 1932; s. Willard L. Sr. and Ellen Lunette (Goodlander) T.; m. Mary Alice Williams, Aug. 29, 1952; children: Marc Alan, Kenneth Earl, Linda Sue, Cynthia Lunette. BA cum laude, U. Colo., 1954; PhD, Iowa State U., 1960. Rsch. physicist Ohio Oil Co., Littleton, Colo., 1959-62; prof. physics Iowa State U., Ames, 1962-76; staff mem. Los Alamos Nat. Lab., 1976—; vis. fellow Nobel Inst., Stockholm, 1970-71; mem. various adv. panels. Editor Procs. of 11th Internat. Conf. on Isotope Separators, 1977; jour. and proposal referee, 1964—; contbr. numerous articles to profl. jours. NSF fellow, 1956-59. Fellow Am. Phys. Soc.; mem. AAAS, Phi Beta Kappa, Phi Kappa Phi. Home: 1 E Sunrise Dr Santa Fe NM 87501 Office: Los Alamos Nat Lab PO Box 1663 Los Alamos NM 87545

TALBOT, JAMES EDWARD, food service executive; b. San Jose, Calif., Nov. 12, 1947; s. Joseph Parker and Barbara (Holbrook) T.; m. Marisa Isobel Talbot, Dec. 30, 1973; children: Stephen, Kathrine, Erin, Colleen. BBA, U. Portland, 1970; MBA in Fin. and Acctg., Regis U., 1992. Food svc. mgr. Saga Corp., Spokane, Wash., 1970-72; food svc. dir. Saga Corp., Canon City, Colo., 1972-74, Newberg, Oreg., 1974-80; food svc. mgr. Saga Corp., Salem, Oreg., 1980-82, food svc. dir., 1982-84, sr. food svc. dir., 1984-86; dist. mgr. Marriott Corp., Rocklin, Calif., 1986-89; food svc. dir. Marriott Corp., Colorado Springs, Colo., 1989—. Active Liberty Boone Neighborhood Assn., Salem, 1983-85; chmn. Sumpter Park Selfg Help Park, Salem, 1983-85. With N.G., 1970-78. Home: 2670 Himalaya Ct Colorado Springs CO 80919 Office: Marriott Corp 7408 Duryea Rd Bldg B Colorado Springs CO 80920

TALBOT, PATRICK JAMES, aerospace engineer, researcher; b. Bethlehem, Pa., Oct. 5, 1948; s. John Joseph and Geraldine (Benner) T.; m. Evelyn May Strickland, Oct. 10, 1966 (div.); 1 child, Stephanie; m. Sheila Lynn Scheetz, Aug. 25, 1979; children: Zachary, Joshua, Cody, Brittany. BS in Math., Pa. State U., 1972, BS in Physics, 1972, MS in Physics, 1974. Tech. staff TRW Space and Def. Sector, Washington, 1972-74; profl. staff TRW Space and Def. Sector, Redondo Beach, Calif., 1974-77, prin. investigator, space object identification, 1977-79; lead engr. TRW Space and Def. Sector, Colorado Springs, Colo., 1980-85; project mgr. TRW Space and Def. Sector, Albuquerque, N.Mex., 1985-89; sr. project engr. TRW Space and Def. Sector, Colorado Springs, Colo., 1989—; pres., founder TRW Colo. Springs Employees Assn., 1984-85; program mgr. TRW Software Devel. Project, Albuquerque, N.Mex., 1988-89; project mgr. TRW Internal rsch. & devel., Redondo Beach, Calif., 1977-80. Author: Space Defense Algorithms, 1991, Aircraft Survivability, 1989, Battle management, 1977; inventor: Satellite Attitude Control Kit., 1979. Leader Boy Scouts, 1990-91; lectr. Falcon Elem. Sch., 1990-91. Recipient Profl. Achievement, NASA, 1978, Tech. Achievement award, TRW, 1979, Disting. Paper award, U.S.A.F., 1989. Mem. Am. Inst. Aeronautics and Astronautics. Office: TRW 1555 Newport Rd N Colorado Springs CO 80916-2790

TALBOTT, DOROTHY ADAMS, artist; b. Grosse Pointe, Mich., Nov. 23, 1928; d. Merrill Cooper and Vanche Elizabeth (Shesler) Adams; m. John Leroy Talbott, Oct. 14, 1950; children: Carol Jane Turpin, Elizabeth Hunt Melzer, Martha Adams Barta. BA, U. Colo., 1950. Pvt. practice artist Englewood, Golden, Colo., 1957—; workshop tchr., Englewood, Golden, 1970—, UKpper Edge Gallery, Snowmass, Colo., 1991, 93, Dillman's Creative Arts Found., Lac du Flambeau, Wis., 1993. Artist over 600 paintings. Leader Girl Scouts U.S., Englewood, 1964-66; artist Wellshire Presbyn. Ch., Denver, 1954-93; dir. Genesee Found., Golden, 1985-86; vol. Women's Bean Project, Denver, 1991-93, Republican Party, Englewood, 1960-78. Named 1st for painting Nat. Soc. for Painters in Casein and Acrylic, N.Y.C., 1982. Mem. North Coast Collage Soc. (signature mem.). Home and office: 1615 Foothills Dr S Golden CO 80401

TALBOTT, GEORGE ROBERT, physicist, mathematician, educator; b. San Diego, Oct. 1, 1925; s. George Fletcher and Mary (Lanz) T.; BA with honors, UCLA, 1960; DSc, Ind. No. U., 1973. Physicist, mem. tech. staff Rockwell Internat. Co., Anaheim, Calif., 1960-85; mem. faculty thermodynamics Pacific States U., 1971-77, prof., 1972-80, chmn. dept. math. studies, 1973-80; lectr. computer sci. Calif. State U., Fullerton, 1979—; cons. physics, computer sci.; disting. guest lectr. Brunel U., London, 1974, 76; spl. guest Forschungsbibliothek, Hannover, W. Ger., 1979; assoc. editor KRONOS jour., Glassboro (N.J.) U., 1978—; chief computer scientist and ednl. videotape dir. Specialized Software, Wilmot, Wis., 1982—. With M.C., U.S. Army, 1956. Recipient Vis. Scholar's award Western Mich. U., 1979. Mem. Am. Soc. Med. Technologists, Am. Math. Soc., Math. Assn. Am., Am. Soc. Clin. Pathologists (lic. med. lab. technologist). Buddhist. Author: Electronic Thermodynamics, 1973; Philosophy and Unified Science, 1977, Computer Applications, 1989, Sir Arthur and Gravity, 1990, Fermat's Last Theorem, 1991; co-inventor burner. Home: 4031 E Charter Oak Dr Orange CA 92669-2611

TALBOTT, JONATHAN L., electrical engineer; b. Denver, May 30, 1952; s. Richard L. and Mary Margaret (Junger) T.; m. Debra K. Gahagen, Jan. 5, 1975 (div. Dec. 18, 1981); m. Donna M. Rodriguez, Apr. 11, 1987; 1 child, Brigette M. BSEE, U. Colo., 1974; MBA, Regis U., 1987. Registered profl. engr. Summer intern Pub. Svc. of Colo., Boulder, 1973; engr. Stone and Webster, various cities, 1974-76, Ernst/Comstock Elec. Constrn., various cities, 1976-78, Stearns-Roger, Denver, 1978-80, Behrent Engring., Denver, 1980-83; owner, prin., cons. Talbott Co., Denver, 1983-90; project mgr. The RMH Group, Lakewood, Colo., 1990—. Bd. dirs. City of Thornton (Colo.) Archtl. Rev., 1981-83, City of Westminster (Colo.) Code Bd. of Appeals, 1989—. Mem. IEEE, Soc. Profl. Engrs., Bldg. Owners Mgmt. Assn., Metro North C. of C. Home: 10383 Irving Ct Westminster CO 80030

TALEBI, NAHID, psychotherapist; b. Tehran, Iran, May 9, 1954; came to U.S., 1976; s. Esmaiel and Liaghat (Tavakol) Rezazadeh; divorced. BA in Psychology, Pars Coll., Tehran, 1976; MEd, Loyola U., L.A., 1978; MA in Psychology, Loyola Marymount U., 1981; postgrad., U.S. Internat. U., 1992. Cert. marriage, family and child therapist, sch. psychologist. Counselor View Height Hosp., L.A., 1979-81; program coord. Regional Ctr. for Devel. Disabled, Torrance, Calif., 1981-84; prof. Yuin U., El Monte, Calif., 1983-85; asst. prof. Loyola U., L.A., 1985; program dir. Tierra Del Sol for Devel. Disabled, Sun Valley, Calif., 1985-86; sch. psychologist L.A. Unified Sch. Dist., 1986-90; pvt. practice Westwood, Calif., 1989—; Bd. dirs. Youth Support and Counseling Ctr., L.A., 1986—; host Persian radio program, L.A., 1983-85; host Persian and Am. TV program, L.A., 1983—. Contbr. articles to profl. jours. Mem. Calif. Mariage and Family Therapists, Group Psychotherapy Assn., Western Psychol. Svcs., Music Ctr. Office: 1100 Glendon Ave Penthouse Los Angeles CA 90024

TALIAFERRO, ROBERT See BROOKE, TAL

TALIAFERRO, YVON ROCHELLE, accountant, consultant; b. Washington, May 1, 1957; d. Kenneth Wayne and Shirley Yvonne (Dixon) Smith. BS in Acctg., Loma Linda U., 1981. Mgr., personnel cons., acct. K&W Security Patrol, Valiejo, Calif., 1981-85; account exec. Alamo Assocs., Concord, Calif., 1986-88; credit mgr. BTS Group, Oakland, Calif., 1988-91; owner, pres. AAA Notary Svc., Danville, Calif., 1990—; adminstrv. asst. Strategic Fin. Svcs., Walnut Creek, Calif., 1992—; contracting cons. VIP Bus. Svcs., Danville, Calif., 1990-91; entreprenuer, investor, Walnut Creek, 1991—. Mem. NAFE, Nat. Notary Assn. (notary pub.).

TALLEY, MARTHA ANN, sales and marketing administrator; b. Hobart, Okla., May 22, 1941; d. William W. and Jacquita E. Talley. BS in Adult Bus. Edn., U. Okla., 1972; MEd in Bus. summa cum laude, Ctrl. State U., Edmond, Okla., 1978. Tchr. bus., coord. Putnam City Schs., Oklahoma City, 1972-78; tng. mgr. Howard Johnsons Sales Res. Ctr., Oklahoma City, 1978-80; mgr. computer ctr. Radio Shack, Oklahoma City, 1980-82; adj. prof. U. Okla., Okla. State U., South Western State U., VoTech., Army, Okla., 1982-85; dist. mgr. sales and mktg. computer and edn. divsns. Radio Shack, Scottsdale, Ariz., 1985-90; nat. mgr. sales and mktg. Intechnica Internat., Inc., Oklahoma City, 1990-92; dir. sales and mktg. Mindplay Methods and Solutions, Inc., Tucson, 1992—; cons. Okla. Dept. Vocat. Tech., Stillwater, 1981-85, IBM, Okla., 1982-84. Speaker Am. Cancer Soc., Nev., Ariz.; mem. Make a Wish Found., Nev., Jr. Hospitality, Okla., Rep. Party, Okla., Nev., Ariz. Mem. Tucson Bus. Alliance, Tucson Literacy Coalition. Office: Mindplay 3130 N Dodge Blvd Tucson AZ 85716

TALLEY, WARREN DENNIS RICK, journalist, broadcaster; b. Pinckneyville, Ill., Aug. 12, 1934; s. Virgil and Hannah (Maxwell) T.; m. Frances Jane Herr, Aug. 9, 1958; children: Wendy Warren, Scott Ryan, Jennifer Jane. B.S. in Journalism, So. Ill. U., 1958. Sports writer Decatur (Ill.) Herald, 1958; sports editor Menlo Park (Calif.) Recorder, 1958-59; reporter UPI, San Francisco, 1959-60; sports editor Rockford (Ill.) Morning Star, also Register Republic, 1960-69; sports editor, columnist Chgo. Today, 1969-74; daily columnist Chgo. Tribune, 1974-79; TV host, interviewer WLS-TV, Chgo.; commentator WLS Radio, Chgo., FNN Sports, L.A.; sports columnist Daily News, Los Angeles, 1979-88; sportstalk host Sta. KABC, Los Angeles, 1980-82; sports host Sta. KVE6 Am. Sports, Las Vegas. Author: (with Jay Johnstone) Temporary Insanity, 1985, Some of My Best Friends Are Crazy, 1990; Over the Edge, 1987, The Cubs of '69, 1989, (with Art Manteris) Super Bookie, 1991; contbr. articles to sports mags. Served with AUS, 1953-55, Korea. Recipient Outstanding Journalism Alumni award So. Ill. U., 1967; Bronze medal Olympic Journalism Assn., 1970; named Ill. Sportswriter of Yr., 1974. Mem. Football Writers Assn., Baseball Writers Assn. Home: 7628 Rolling View Dr # 101 Las Vegas NV 89129-6465

TALLMADGE, DIANE JOYCE, bookstore manager; b. Racine, Wis., May 10, 1934; d. Robert William and LuLu A (Steinike) Sperberg; m. Guy Kasten Tallmadge Jr. Sept. 12, 1957. BA, U. Wis., 1956; MA, 1957; MLS, UCLA, 1962. Ballet instr., choreographer Madison, Wis., 1952-57; tchr. pub. schs. Melbourne, Australia, 1957-58; ballet instr., choreographer Los Angeles, 1959-62; libr./physical sci. cataloger UCLA, 1962-64, Slavic lang. cataloger, 1964-66; docent libr. Stanford U. Mus., 1974--; mgr. Stanford U. Art Gallery Bookshop, 1985-89. Bd. govs. Com. for Art, Stanford, 1985--; mem. Santa Monica and Westside Jr. Philharmonic, 1964-66. Mem. AAUW (pres. 1970-71), Phi Beta Kappa, Phi Kappa Phi, Beta Phi MU, Chi Omega. Republican. Congregationalist. Home: 446 Guadalupe Dr Los Altos CA 94022-2108

TALLMADGE, GUY KASTEN, research psychologist; b. Milw., Mar. 2, 1932; s. Guy Kasten and Alice (LaBoule) T.; m. Diane Joyce Sperberg, Sept. 12, 1957. AB, Princeton U., 1954; MS, Purdue U., 1956, PhD, 1959. Rsch. scientist Douglas Aircraft Co., Santa Monica, Calif., 1959-61; mgr. behavioral psychology Humetrics div. Thiokol Chem. Corp., L.A., 1961-63; sr. assoc. Planning Rsch. Corp., L.A., 1963-65; dir. instrnl. methods Am. Insts. for Rsch., Palo Alto, Calif., 1965-73; v.p., pres. RMC Rsch. Corp., Mountain View, Calif., 1973-83, sr. v.p., 1987-90; sr. v.p. SRA Techs., Mountain View, 1983-86. Contbr. articles to profl. jours. Fulbright scholar U. Melbourne (Australia), 1957-58; sr. rsch. fellow Am. Insts. for Rsch., Palo Alto, Calif., 1990-92. Mem. Am. Ednl. Rsch. Assn., Nat. Coun. on Measurement in Edn., Am. Evaluation Assn., Los Altos Golf and Country Club, Princeton Club No. Calif. Office: Am Inst for Rsch PO Box 1113 Palo Alto CA 94302-1113

TALLMAN, JOHANNA ELEONORE, former library administrator; b. Luebeck, Germany, Aug. 18, 1914; came to U.S., 1923, naturalized, 1930; d. Friedrich Franz and Johanna Cornelia (Voget) Allerding; m. Lloyd Anthony Tallman, May 8, 1954 (dec.). AA, Los Angeles Jr. Coll., 1934; BA, U. Calif., Berkeley, 1936; Cert. in Librarianship, 1937. Asst. librarian San Marino (Calif.) Pub. Library, 1937-38; various positions Los Angeles County Pub. Library, 1938-40, tech. reference librarian, 1940-42; asst. librarian Pacific Aero. Library, Hollywood, Calif., 1942-43; head librarian Pacific Aero. Library, 1943-44; librarian Engring. and Math. Scis. Library, U. Calif., Los Angeles, 1945-73; coordinator phys. scis. libraries U. Calif., Los Angeles, 1962-73; faculty Sch. Library Service, 1961-73; dir. libraries Calif. Inst. Tech., Pasadena, 1973-82; Dir. re-cataloging project U.S. Naval Ordnance Test Sta. Library., China Lake, Calif., 1951; cons. to indsl., research, ednl. instns., 1950-73; mem. trade adv. com. for library assts. Los Angeles Trade Tech. Coll., 1958-73. Author: Check Out a Librarian, 1985. Contbr. articles to profl. jours. Pres. Zonta Club Pasadena, 1976-78, United Svc. Clubs Officers Assn., 1978-79, 88-89, 90-91, Fine Arts Club Pasadena, 1982-84; trustee Pasadena Hist. Soc., 1980-90. Fulbright lectr. Brazil, 1966-67. Mem. ALA (chmn. engring. sch. libraries sect. 1949-50), Calif. Library Assn. (chmn. coll., univ. and research libraries sect. So. dist. 1954), Spl. Libraries Assn. (pres. So. Calif. chpt. 1965-66, chmn. sci.-tech. div. 1969-70), Librarians Assn. U. Calif. (pres. 1971). Home: 4731 Daleridge Rd La Canada Flintridge CA 91011-3724

TALLON, JOSEPH CHARLES, research and development director, researcher; b. Lewistown, Mont., Aug. 10, 1949; s. Joseph F. and Opal L. (Norlee) T.; m. Linda M. Hoogland, 1979 (div. 1988); children: Timothy Joseph, Casie Opal Marie. AA, El Camino Coll., 1970. Rt. operator Tallon Termite & Pest Control, Long Beach, Calif.; field operator Tallon Termite & Pest Control, Long Beach; rsch. and devel. dir. Tallon Termite & Pest Control, Bakersfield, Calif., 1989—; laborer, driver Golden Bear Forest Products, Calif., 1976-78; owner Cal Pacific Termite Co., Redondo Beach, Calif., 1978-82; owner, inventor Blizzard Systems, Bakerfield, 1982-89; panelist U.S. EPA Methyl Bromide Workship, Washington, 1992. Patentee pest control systems The Blizzard and The HeatWave Method; developer nonchem. urban pest control. Coach littl league, Kern Valley, Calif., 1975; mem. 65 Roses/Cystic Fibrosis Found., L.A., 1990—. Mem. AAAS, N.Y. Acad. Scis., Smithsonian Assocs., Audobon Soc. Lutheran. Home and Office: Tallon Termite & Pest Control 5702 Pioneer Dr Bakersfield CA 93306

TALLY, BRETT RICHARD, systems analyst; b. Big Spring, Tex., Apr. 8, 1963; s. James Carrey and Louise Marie (Stewart) T. BS in Physics, U. Calif., Santa Barbara, 1986. Rsch. engr. Lumonics, Camarillo, Calif., 1986-88; systems analyst engring. div. Ball Systems, San Diego, 1989—; cons. Transglobal Environ., Encinitas, Calif., 1992—. Mem. Planetary Soc., Wilson Ctr. Assn., San Diego Flight Mus. Home: 1161 Hermes Ave Leucadia CA 92024

TALMADGE, WOODDALL WELLS, lawyer; b. Portland, Oreg., May 14, 1958; s. Marion Lyman and Frances Louise (Wooddall) T.; m. Sarah E. Banks; 1 child, Clair. BA, Colgate U., 1980; JD, Cornell U., 1983. Bar: Oreg. 1983. Assoc. Miller, Nash, Wiener, Hager & Carlsen, Portland, Oreg., 1983-85; assoc. Weiss, Jensen, Ellis & Botteri, Portland, 1985-91, shareholder, 1991—. Trustee, pres. N.W. Svc. Ctr., Portland, 1986-92; trustee Boys and Girls Aid Soc. Oreg., 1987—. Mem. ABA, Oreg. Bar Assn., Multnomah County Bar Assn., Univ. Club, Multnomah Athletic Club, City Club of Portland. Episcopalian. Office: Weiss Jensen Ellis & Botteri 111 SW 5th Ave Ste 2300 Portland OR 97204-3689

TALMAGE, KENNETH KELLOGG, business executive; b. Morristown, N.J., Jan. 16, 1946; s. Edward Taylor Hunt Talmage Jr. and Dorothy (Rogers) Kaye. BA, Claremont Men's Coll., 1968; MBA, Boston U., Brussels, 1976. Assoc., Hon. Leonard K. Firestone, L.A., 1973-74; attaché Am. Embassy, Brussels, 1974-77; mgmt. cons. strategic planning and fin. Arthur D. Little, Inc., Cambridge, Mass., 1977-80; sr. v.p. Boston Safe Deposit & Trust Co., 1980-87; pres. Lloyd's Furs, Inc., Denver, Colo., 1987-92; prin. Monterey Water Co., 1992—. Trustee Colo. Outward Bound Sch., 1990—, Vols. for Outdoor Colo., 1988—, Breckenridge Outdoor Edn. Ctr., 1989-92; advisor Hurricane Island Outward Bound Sch., Maine, 1987—, trustee, 1979-87, chmn. bd. trustees, 1980-83; mem. exec. com. Outward Bound, U.S.A., 1980-85; asst. to chmn. fin. com. to Re-elect the President, 1972-73.

With USNR, 1968-69. Mem. The Country Club (Mass.), Denver Country Club. Home: 1510 E 10th Ave Denver CO 80218-3104

TALMI, YOAV, conductor, composer; b. Kibbutz Merhavia, Israel, Apr. 28, 1943; diploma Rubin Acad. Music, Tel Aviv; postgrad. diploma Juilliard Sch. Music; m. Erella Gottesmann; 2 children. Assoc. condr. Louisville Orch., 1968-70; co-condr. Israel Chamber Orch., 1970-72; artistic dir., condr. Gelders Symphony Orch., Arnhem, 1974-80; prin. guest condr. Munich Philharm. Orch., 1979-80; artistic dir., condr. Israel Chamber Orch., 1984-88; music dir. New Israeli Opera, 1985-89, San Diego Symphony Orch., 1990—; guest condr. Berlin Philharm., Munich Philharm., London Philharm., Philharmonia, Concertgebouw, Rotterdam Philharm., Israel Philharm., Tokyo Symphony, New Japan Philarm., Vienna Symphony, St. Petersburg Philharm., Detroit Symphony, St. Louis Symphony, Houston Symphony, Dallas Symphony, N.Y. Chamber Symphony, L.A. Chamber Orch., Oslo Philharm., Tonhalle Orch. Zurich, others. Composer: Dreams for choir a capella, Music for Flute and Strings; Overture on Mexican Themes (recorded), 3 Monologues for Flute Solo (pub.); recs. include: Bruckner 9th Symphony (Oslo Philharm.), Glière 3rd Symphony (San Diego Symphony), Brahms Sextet/4 Serious Songs (San Diego Symphony), Tchaikowsky/Scoenberg, Bloch/Barber/Grieg/Puccini (Israel Chamber Orch.); (with Erella Talmi) works for flute and piano. Recipient Boskovitch prize for composition, Israel, 1965; Koussevitzky Meml. Conducting prize, Tanglewood, 1969; award Ruppert Found. Condr. competition, London, 1973. Home: PO Box 1384, Kfar Saba 44113, Israel Office: Shaw Concerts Inc 1900 Broadway New York NY 10023-7004 also: San Diego Symphony Orch 1245 7th Ave San Diego CA 92101

TALTON, CHESTER LOVELLE, bishop; b. El Dorado, Ark., Sept. 22, 1941; s. Chester Talton and Mae Ola (Shells) Henry; m. Karen Louise Warren, Aug. 25, 1963; children: Kathy Louise, Linda Karen, Frederick Douglass, Benjamin Albert. BS, Calif. State U., Hayward, 1967; MDiv, Ch. Divinity Sch. of Pacific, 1970. Ordained to ministry Episcopal Ch., as deacon, 1970, as priest, 1971, as bishop, 1991. Vicar Good Shepherd Episc. Ch., Berkeley, Calif., 1970-71, St. Mathias Mission, Seaside, Calif., 1971-73, Ch. of the Holy Cross, Chgo., 1973-76; curate All Sts. Episc. Ch., Carmel, Calif., 1971-73; rector St. Philips Episc. Ch., St. Paul, 1976-81, St. Philips Ch., N.Y.C., 1985-90; mission officer Parish of Trinity Ch., N.Y.C., 1981-85; suffragan bishop Diocese of L.A., Episc. Ch., 1990—. Pres. Community Svc. Coun. Greater Harlem, N.Y.C., 1985-90, Upper Manhattan Child Devel. Ctr., N.Y.C., 1985-90, Peter Williams Jr. Housing Corp., N.Y.C., 1988-90. Mem. Union of Black Episcopalians. Office: Episc Diocese LA PO Box 2164 1220 W 4th St Los Angeles CA 90051

TAM, ROD, state legislator; b. Honolulu, Oct. 3, 1953; s. Robert H.C. and Patsy Y.T. (Young) T.; m. Lynnette Tam. BBA, U. Hawaii, 1977. Mem. Hawaii Ho. of Reps., Honolulu, 1982—. Chmn. Neighborhood Bd., Honolulu, 1979-82. Named to Three Outstanding Young Persons ol 1983, Hawaii Jaycees, 1983; recipient Freedom award Sertoma Club, 1984, Librs. award for Leadership and Support, Librs. Assn. Hawaii, 1987. Democrat. Roman Catholic. Home: 2751 C-2 Booth Rd Honolulu HI 96813

TAM, ROLAND FOOK SENG, physician; b. Honolulu, Feb. 19, 1946. BA, U. Hawaii, 1968; MD, U. Wash., 1972. Intern surgery Orange County Med. Ctr., Orange, Calif.; resident otolaryngology U. Calif., San Francisco. Fellow Am. Bd. Otolarngology; mem. AMA, Hi Soc. Otolaryngology, Hawaii Med. Assn., Honolulu County Med. Soc. Episcopalian.

TAMBURINI, JOSEPH URBAN, civil engineer; b. New Brunswick, N.J., May 23, 1951; s. John Eugene and Barbara Elizabeth (Gunther) T.; m. Connie Lynn Murray, July 3, 1976; children: Steven, Joe. BSCE, Bucknell U., 1973; MSCE, U. Colo., 1977. Registered profl. engr., Colo., N.J., N.Mex., Ohio. Project engr. Van Cleef Engring. Assocs., Clinton, N.J., 1972-76; rsch. asst. U. Colo., Boulder, 1976-78; project mgr. Wright-McLaughlin Engrs., Denver, 1978-80; sr. engr. Culp-Wesner-Culp, Denver, 1980-84; v.p. Rothberg, Tamburini & Winsor, Inc., Denver, 1984—. Contbg. author: (textbook) Handbook of Public Water Systems, 1986; contbr. articles to profl. jours. Recipient Arthur Sidney Bidell award Water Environ. Fedn., 1990. Mem. Rocky Mountain Water Pollution Control Assn. (pres. 1988-89), Am. Water Works Assn. (mem. standards com. on fluorides), The Denver Club. Office: Rothberg Tamburini & Winsor 1600 Stout St Ste 1800 Denver CO 80202

TAMKIN, CURTIS SLOANE, real estate development company executive; b. Boston, Sept. 21, 1936; s. Hayward and Etta (Goldfarb) T.; BA in Econs., Stanford U., 1958; m. Priscilla Martin, Oct. 18, 1975; 1 child, Curtis Sloane. V.p., treas., dir. Hayward Tamkin & Co., Inc., mortgage bankers, L.A., 1963-70; mng. ptnr. Property Devel. Co., L.A., 1970-82; pres. The Tamkin Co., 1982—. Bd. govs. Music Ctr. L.A., 1974—; pres. Los Angeles Master Chorale Assn., 1974-78; mem. vis. com. Stanford U. Libraries, 1982-86; bd. dirs. L.A. Philharm. Assn., 1985—. Served to lt. (j.g.) USNR, 1960-63. Mem. Founders League of L.A. Music Ctr. (pres. 1988—), L.A. Jr. C. of C. (dir. 1968-69). Republican. Clubs: Burlingame Country, L.A., University. Office: 9460 Wilshire Blvd Beverly Hills CA 90212

TAMMANY, ALBERT SQUIRE, III, trust and bank executive; b. Paget, Bermuda, Aug. 21, 1946; s. Albert Squire Jr. and Marion Genevieve (Galloway) T.; m. Teresa Reznor, Sept. 8, 1973. BA, Stanford U., 1968; MBA, U. Pa., 1973. Budget and planning officer Tuskegee Univ., Ala., 1973-74; budget analyst contrs. dept. Chase Manhattan Bank, N.Y.C., 1974-75; v.p., div. contr. Wells Fargo Bank, San Francisco, 1975-78, v.p., retail group contr., 1978-79; v.p., contr. Imperial Bank, L.A., 1979-81, sr. v.p. fin., 1981-83; exec. v.p., First Network Savs. Bank, L.A., 1983-87, chief oper. officer, 1987-89, North Am. Trust Co., San Diego, 1990-93, Trustguard, San Diego, 1993—; cons., Torrance, Calif., 1990—; cons. Inst. for Svcs. to Edn., Inc., 1973-74. Woodrow Wilson fellow U. Pa. Served with USMC, 1968-71. Wharton Pub. Policy fellow, 1972. Mem. Am. Bankers Assn. (trust ops. com.), Wharton Club, Stanford Club. Baptist.

TAMURA, CARY KAORU, developer, fundraiser; b. Honolulu, Jan. 9, 1944; s. Akira and Harue (Otake) T.; m. Sharon Irene Gray, Aug. 1968 (div. Oct. 1982); children: Jennifer Joy, Matthew D.; m. Denise Jeane Mitts, Oct. 17, 1987. Student, U. Hawaii, 1961-63; BA in Philosophy, Nyack Coll., 1966; MA in Theology, Fuller Sem., 1986. Cert. fund-raising exec. Dir. svc. tng. ops. Fin. Adv. Clinic of Hawaii, Honolulu, 1972-76; dir. planned giving The Salvation Army, Honolulu, 1976-78; planned giving cons. InterVarsity Christian Fellowship, Portland, Oreg., 1978-80; account exec. Am. Income Life, Portland, Oreg., 1980-81; dir. planned giving The Salvation Army, Portland, Oreg., 1981-84, L.A., 1984-85; dir. devel., planned giving U. So. Calif., L.A., 1985-90; dir. gift planning UniHealth America, Burbank, Calif., 1990—; bd. dirs. Nat. Com. on Planned Giving, Indpls., 1991—, sec. exec. com., 1993; mem. adv. com., instr. cert. program in fund raising UCLA Extension; lectr. in field. Bd. dirs. Japanese Evang. Missionary Soc., 1990—, v.p. 1993—; bd. deacons Evang. Free Ch., 1992—. With U.S. Army, 1969-72. Named Outstanding Nominee in profl. category Nat. Philanthropy Day, 1992. Mem. Planned Giving Round Table So. Calif. (pres. 1989-91, Pres.'s award 1992), Nat. Soc. Fund Raising Execs. (Greater L.A. chpt. bd. dirs. 1990—, v.p. 1993), So. Calif. Assn. Hosp. Developers, Assn. for Healthcare Philanthropy. Republican. Office: UniHealth America 4100 W Alameda Ave #205 Burbank CA 91505

TAMURA, NEAL NOBORU, dentist, consultant; b. Honolulu, May 3, 1953; s. Tony T. and Doris (Fujiki) T.; m. Liana N.N. Pang, May 31, 1980 (div.); 1 child, Randi M.A. BS in Biology with distinction, U. Mo., Kansas City, 1975; DDS, Northwestern U., 1985. Resident asst. in counselling U. Mo., Kansas City, 1974-75; emergency med. technician Pacific Ambulance, Honolulu, 1975-77, mgr. ops., mobile intensive care technician, 1977-79; gen. practice dentistry Honolulu, 1985—; cons. Nuuanu Hale Hosp., Honolulu, 1985—, Hale Nani Hosp., Honolulu, 1990—, Dept. Corrections, State of Hawaii, 1987-89, Job Corps Hawaii, 1989-91, Lilina Healthcare Ctr., 1992—, PACE program Maluhia Hosp., 1993—. Vice chair mgmt. area hosps. State of Hawaii Bd. Commrs., Honolulu, 1987, chair, 1989, exec. com., 1989; mem. YMCA, Honolulu, 1987— (svc. award 1972, 73). Mem. ADA, Hawaii Dental Assn., Hawaii Implant Soc., Honolulu County Dental Soc., Papaniho Study Club (founder, sec. 1987-89), Phi Kappa Phi. Democrat. Home: 2016 Metcalf St Honolulu HI 96822-3333 Office: 1600 Kapiolani Blvd Ste 508 Honolulu HI 96814

TAN, TERESA, lawyer; b. Hartford, Conn., Sept. 7, 1948; d. Chi-Ming and Hsing (Chow) t. AB magna cum laude, Smith Coll., 1969; MA, U. Calif., Berkeley, 1971; JD, U Calif., Berkeley, 1973. Bar: Calif. 1973; U.S. Dist. Ct. (no. dist.) Calif. 1973, U.S. Dist. Ct. (no. dist.) Tex. 1990; U.S. Ct. Appeals (9th cir.) 1986. Lawyer Nat. Ctr. for State Cts., San Francisco, 1976-80; dep. atty. gen. Office of the Atty.-Gen., San Francisco, 1980-88; sr. litigation counsel Motorola, Inc., San Jose, Calif., 1988—. Fellowship Smith Coll. Mem. Legal Aid Soc. of San Francisco (bd. dirs. 1991—, exec. com. state bar litigation sect. 1991—). Office: Motorola Inc Law Dept Ste 1740 2 Embarcadero Ctr San Francisco CA 94111

TAN, WILLIAM LEW, lawyer; b. West Hollywood, Calif., July 25, 1949; s. James Tan Lew and Choon Guey Louie. BA, U. Pa., 1971; JD, U. Calif. Hastings Coll. Law, San Francisco, 1974. Bar: Calif. 1975, U.S. Dist. Ct. (cen. dist.) Calif. 1975, U.S. Ct. Appeals (9th cir.) 1975, U.S. Supreme Ct. 1979. Assoc. Hiram W. Kwan, Los Angeles, 1974-79; ptnr. Mock & Tan, Los Angeles, 1979-80; sole practice Los Angeles, 1980-81; ptnr. Tan & Sakiyama, P.C., Los Angeles, 1981-87, Tan & Sakiyama, Los Angeles, 1987—; bd. dirs. Pacific Career Opportunities, Los Angeles, Am. Bus. Network, Los Angeles; pres., bd. dirs. Asian Research Cons., Los Angeles; mem. adv. bd. Cathay Bank. Co-founder Asian Pacific Am. Roundtable, Los Angeles, 1981; chmn. bd. dirs. Leaderhip Edn. for Asian-Pacifics, Los Angeles, 1984-87; alt. del. Dem. Nat. Conv., San Francisco, 1984; mem. Calif. State Bd. Pharmacy, Sacramento, 1984-92, v.p., 1988-91, pres., 1991-92; mem. Los Angeles City and County Crime Crisis Task Force, Los Angeles, 1981, Los Angeles Asian Pacific Heritage Week Com., 1980-85, Asian Pacific Women's Network, Los Angeles, 1981, Los Angeles City Atty.'s Blue Ribbon Con. of Advisors, 1981, community adv. bd. to Mayor of Los Angeles, 1984, allocations vol. liaison team health and therapy div. United Way, Los Angeles, 1986; bd. dirs. Chinatown Service Ctr., Los Angeles, 1983; conf. advisor U.S.-Asia, Los Angeles, 1981-83; atty. Los Angeles City Housing Adv. Com.; mem. Pacific Bell Consumer Product Adv. Panel; mem. community adv. bd. Sta. KCET-TV, PBS; mem. adv. commn. State of Calif. Com. on State Procurement Practices, 1989—; mem. L.A. City Attys. Citizens' Task Force on Pvt. Club Discrimination, 1989-90; mem. Calif. Med. Summit, 1993. Named one of Outstanding Young Men of Am., 1979. Mem. ABA (mem. numerous coms.), Calif. State Bar Assn. (vice chmn. com. ethnic minority relations 1983-85, chmn. pub. affairs com. 1981-82, mem. others), Los Angeles County Bar Assn. (vice chmn. 1980-82, mem. numerous coms.), So. Calif. Chinese Lawyers Assn. (pres. 1980-81, chmn., 1987-88, mem. various coms.), Minority Bar Assn. (chmn. 1981-82, sec. 1980-81, chmn. adv. bd. 1982-83), Asian Pacific Bar of Calif., Nat. Asian Pacific Am. Bar, Japanese Am. Bar Assn., Assn. Trial Lawyers Am., Bench and Bar Media Council, Calif. Trial Lawyers Assn., Soc. Intercultural Edn. (conf. coordinator, advisor panelist tng. and research com. 1983),. Office: 300 S Grand Ave Ste 2750 Los Angeles CA 90071-5918

TANAKA, JEANNIE E., lawyer; b. Los Angeles, Jan. 21, 1942; d. Togo William and Jean M. Tanaka. BA, Internat. Christian U., Tokyo, 1966; MSW, UCLA, 1968; JD, Washington Coll. Law, 1984. Bar: Calif. 1984, U.S. Dist. Ct. (cen., no. dists.) Calif. 1985, U.S. Ct. Appeals (9th cir.) 1985, D.C. 1987. Instr. Aoyama Gakuin, Meiji Gakuin, Sophia U., Tokyo, 1968-75; with program devel. Encyclopedia Britannica Inst., Tokyo, 1976-78; instr. Honda, Mitsubishi, Ricoh Corps., Tokyo, 1975-80; with editorial dept. Simul Internat., Tokyo; assoc. Seki and Jarvis, L.A., 1984-86, Jones, Day, Reavis & Pogue, L.A., 1986-87, Fulbright, Jaworsky and Reavis, McGrath, L.A., 1987-89; asst. counsel Unocal, L.A., 1989-91; pvt. practice, L.A., 1991—. Active Japan-Am. Soc., L.A., 1984—, Asia Soc., L.A., 1984—, Japanese-Am. Citizens League, L.A., 1981, 92—, Japanese Am. Cultural and Community Ctr., 1986-89; vol. Asian Pacific Am. Legal Ctr. So. Calif., 1985-86. Mem. ABA, Los Angeles County Bar Assn., Japanese-Am. Bar Assn., Women Lawyers Assn. L.A., Mensa. Democrat. Methodist. Office: 100 S Doheny Dr Ste 322 Los Angeles CA 90048

TANAKA, JOHN AUGUSTUS, natural resource economist, educator, researcher; b. N.Y.C., Oct. 8, 1955; s. Augustus Masashi and Teruko (Wada) T.; m. Ann Therese Fuller, Aug. 10, 1985; children: Alison Michelle, Megan Elizabeth, Briana Nicole. BS, Oreg. State U., 1978, MS, 1982; PhD, Utah State U., 1986. Rsch. assoc. U. Ariz., Tucson, 1980-82; asst. prof. Oreg. State U., Corvallis, 1985-91, assoc. prof., 1991—; rsch. coord. Blue Mountains. Nat. Resources Inst., 1991-93; cons. U.S. Forest Svc.-Sawtooth Nat. Forest, Twin Falls, Idaho, 1990-91, U.S. Dept. Justice, 1992—. Mem Farmer Svc. Group South 40 Club, Island City, Oreg., 1987—. U.S. Dept. Agrl. Competitive grant, 1986-88. Mem. Nat. Assn. Colls. and Tchrs. Agriculture, Am. Agrl. Econs. Assn., Western Agrl. Econs. Assn., Soc. for Range Mgmt. (Pacific northwest sect. 2nd v.p. 1990-91, 1st v.p. 1991-92, pres. 1992-93). Home: 10808 S E St La Grande OR 97850-8436 Office: Oreg State U Agr Program Ea Oreg State Coll 204 Zabel Hall La Grande OR 97850

TANAKA, RICHARD KOICHI, JR., architect, planner; b. San Jose, Calif., Oct. 16, 1931; s. Richard Inoru and Mae Yoshiko (Koga) T.; m. Barbara Hisako Kumagai, Oct. 7, 1961; children: Craig, Todd, Sandra, Trent. BArch, U. Mich., 1954; M in Urban Planning, Calif. State U., San Jose, 1978. Exec. v.p. Steinberg Group, San Jose, 1954—. Author: American on Trial, 1988. Dir. Human Rels. Com., San Jose, 1969-73; dir., pres. Bicentennial Com., San Jose, 1974-77; bd. dirs. Santa Clara County Sch. Bd. Assn., 1980—; pres. Internment of Local Japanese Ams., San Jose, 1984—; past pres., trustee East Side High Sch. Dist., San Jose, 1971-92, Japanese Am. Citizens League, San Jose; bd. govs. Boy Scouts Am., San Jose, 1978—, NCCJ, San Jose, 1978—; past pres. Tapestry and Talent, 1976-80; trustee San Jose/Evergreen Community Coll., 1992, v.p.. Mem. AIA, Am. Planning Inst., Constrn. Specification Inst., Rotary. Home: 14811 Whipple Ct San Jose CA 95127 Office: Steinberg Group 60 Pierce Ave San Jose CA 95110

TANEJA, ARUN K., computer company executive; b. D'Doon, India, June 24, 1947; came to U.S., 1969; m. Linda M. Mercadante, Sept. 28, 1973; children: Nathan, Tara, Nevin. BSEE, Indian Inst. Tech., New Delhi, 1968; MSEE, U. N.H., 1972, MBA, 1973. Sr. bus. analyst IBM Corp., Don Mills, Ont., Can., 1973-78; div. mktg. mgr. Data Gen. Corp., Westboro, Mass., 1978-85; dir. mktg. Sun Microsystems, Inc., Mountain View, Calif., 1985-88; v.p. mktg. Convergent Techs., San Jose, Calif., 1988-91, Univel subs. Novell, San Jose, Calif., 1992—.

TANENBAUM, BASIL SAMUEL, college dean, engineering educator; b. Providence, R.I., Dec. 1, 1934; s. Harry Milton and Rena Ada (Herr) T.; m. Carol Binder, Aug. 26, 1956; children: Laurie, Stephen, David. B.S. summa cum laude, Brown U., 1956; M.S. (NSF fellow, 1956-60), Yale U., 1957, Ph.D. in Physics, 1960. Staff physicist Raytheon Co., Waltham, Mass., 1960-63; prof. engring. Case Western Res. U., Cleve., 1963-75; dean of faculty Harvey Mudd Coll., Claremont, Calif., 1975—; vis. scientist Cornell U., Arecibo (P.R.) Obs., 1968-69; vis. asso. prof. Northwestern U., Evanston, Ill., 1970; sci. adv. com. Nat. Astronomy and Ionosphere Center, 1972-77, Calif. Poly. Inst., Pomona, 1976-87; engring. and sci. adv. com. Calif. State U., Fullerton, 1976-87; bd. dirs. University Circle, Inc., 1973-75; dir. Minority Engrs. Indsl. Opportunity Program, 1973-75; dir. summer sci. program Thacher Sch., Ojai, Calif., 1977-82; cons. various corps., univ. labs., govt. agencies. Author: Plasma Physics, 1967. Woods Hole Oceanog. Inst. fellow, 1959; sr. Sterling fellow, 1959; recipient Wittke teaching award, 1974. Mem. AAAS, Am. Phys. Soc., Am. Soc. for Engring. Edn., IEEE, AAUP, Sigma Xi (research award 1969). Home: 611 W Delaware Dr Claremont CA 91711-3458 Office: Harvey Mudd Coll 301 East 12th St Claremont CA 91711

TANENBAUM, MARC HARRIS, physician; b. Phila., Aug. 17, 1943; s. Sam and Esther (Fishman) T.; m. Deborah Tanenbaum, Sept. 20, 1965; children: Dean, Adam, Alison; m. Patricia Stutz, Aug. 20, 1983; 1 child, Griffin. BS, St. Joseph Coll., Phila., 1965; postgrad., Georgetown U., 1966; MD, U. Louisville, 1970. Intern San Bernardino (Calif.) County Hosp., 1970-71; pvt. practice in obstetrics, internal medicine, pediatrics Longmont, Colo., 1973—, head family practice dept., 1985-86. Lt. USN, 1971-73. Recipient grant Georgetown U., 1965. Mem. AMA, Colo. Med. Soc., Boulder Med. Soc., C. of C. Jewish. Home: 8069 Neva Rd Niwot CO 80503 Office: 1350 Stuart St Longmont CO 80501

TANENBAUM, ROBERT EARL, artist; b. Chillicothe, Mo., July 31, 1936; s. David and Henrietta (Drumbelvitz) T.; m. Patricia Rea Olian, Sept. 7, 1958; children: David James, Jill Lauren. BFA, Washington U., St. Louis, 1959. Freelance artist Watkins & Assocs., St. Louis, 1960-64, Studio Artist Inc., L.A., 1964-73; pres. Robert Tanenbaum Inc., Tarzana, Calif., 1973—; tchr. Brandes Art Sch., L.A., 1982-84. Represented in permanent collections. Capt. U.S. Army, 1959-65. Mem. Soc. Illustrators, Nat. Watercolor Soc., Am. Portrait Soc. (cert. mem.). Jewish. Home and Office: 5505 Corbin Ave Tarzana CA 91356-2986

TANG, JOHN C., design engineer, researcher; b. Indpls., Nov. 9, 1960; s. Yu-Sun and Lillian Y. D. (Mao) T.; m. Jean M. Hsia, July 1, 1989; 1 child, Julia Jiazhen. BSME, Stanford U., 1982, MSME, 1983, PhD in Mech. Engring., 1989. Engr. R & D Ctr. Westinghouse, Pitts., summer 1981-82; biomed. engr. Rehab. R & D Ctr. VA, Palo Alto, Calif., 1983-84; rsch. assoc. Palo Alto Rsch. Ctr. Xerox, 1986-90; staff engr. Sun Microsystems Labs., Inc., Mountain View, Calif., 1990—; vis. lectr. U. Sci. and Tech., Beijing, summer 1990. Contbr. articles to profl. jours.; patentee in field. Mem. Foothill Covenant Ch., Los Altos, Calif., 1990—. Timothy Francis Kennedy meml. fellow, 1982. Mem. Assn. for Computing Machinery (spl. interest group on computer and human interaction), Phi Beta Kappa, Tau Beta Pi. Mem. Christian Ch. Office: Sun Microsystems Inc 2550 Garcia Ave Mountain View CA 94043

TANG, KUNIKYO, educator; b. Kowloon, Hong Kong, Feb. 5, 1966; s. Hok-Gie and Ume (Shimizu) T. BS, U. Victoria, B.C., Can., 1988, MS, 1990. Rsch. asst. dept. math U. Victoria, 1988—. Pres. scholar, 1986, Stephen A. Jennings Meml. scholar, 1987, Mark E. Hooney Meml. scholar, 1987; U. Victoria fellow, 1988-91. Mem. Am. Math. Soc., Can. Math. Soc. Office: U Victoria Dept Math, PO Box 3045, Victoria, BC Canada V8W 3P4

TANG, THOMAS, federal judge; b. Phoenix, Jan. 11, 1922. B.S., U. Santa Clara, 1947, law student, 1948-50; LL.B. with distinction, U. Ariz., 1950. Bar: Ariz. 1950, Calif. 1951. Dep. county atty. Maricopa County, Ariz., 1953-57; asst. atty. gen. State of Ariz., 1957-58; judge Ariz. Superior Ct., 1963-70; mem. firm Sullivan, Mahoney & Tang, Phoenix, 1971-77; councilman City of Phoenix, 1960-62, vice mayor, 1962; judge U.S. Ct. of Appeals 9th Circuit, Phoenix, 1977—. Mem. State Bar Ariz. (bd. govs. 1971-77, pres. 1977), State Bar Calif. Office: US Ct Appeals 9th Cir 6412 Courthouse & Fed Bldg 230 N 1st Ave Phoenix AZ 85025-0230

TANG, TOM, banking executive; b. Tiensuei, Peoples Republic of China, Nov. 24, 1946; came to the U.S., 1974; s. Hsun Hei and Hui Hsing (Fan) T.; m. Gloria Tang, Aug. 13, 1974; children: Jonathan, Kevin. BA, Nat. Chung Hsing U., Taipei, Taiwan, 1974; MBA, Okla. State U., 1977; postgrad., UCLA Ext., 1978-79, Inst. Fin. Edn., L.A., 1979-82. Loan officer Topa T&L, Lakewood, Calif., 1977-78; acct. Gibraltar Savs., Beverly Hills, Calif., 1978-80; asst. v.p., br. mgr. 1st Pub. Savs. Bank, L.A., 1980-84; v.p. Gateway Savs. Bank, L.A., 1984-85; v.p., regional mgr. East-West Fed. Bank, San Marino, Calif., 1985-90; sr. v.p. Far-East Nat. Bank, L.A., 1990—. Fellow Optimists (Outstanding Svc. award 1984); mem. Chinese Coll. Alumni Basketball Assn. So. Calif. (chairperson 1990-91), Nat. Chung-Hsing U. Alumni Assn. So. Calif. (bd. dirs. 1987-93, pres. 1989-90, v.p. 1988-89, 90-91), Joint Chinese Coll. Alumni Assn. So. Calif. (bd. dirs. 1988-93), Monterey Park C. of C. (bd. dirs. 1983-84, chairperson Chinese-Am. com. 1984). Home: 2135 Urmston Pl San Marino CA 91108-2342 Office: Far East Nat Bank 200 S Garfield Ave # 103 Alhambra CA 91801-3890

TANG, WING TSANG, chemical researcher; b. Kowloon, Hong Kong, July 16, 1958; came to U.S., 1977; s. Pak Chiu and Pui Tsang (Chan) T.; m. Wai-Chun Wong, Aug. 11, 1984; children: Ming-Yun, Tin-Yun. AA, Vincennes (Ind.) U., 1978; BA, Hamilton Coll., 1981; MS, Stanford U., 1985, PhD, 1987. Vis. scientist IBM, San Jose, Calif., 1987-88, staff scientist, 1988-92; R&D project engr. Komag Inc., Milipitas, Calif., 1992-93; process engr. mgr. Corner Peripherals, San Jose, Calif., 1993—; rsch. asst. Stanford (Calif.) U., 1981-86. Patentee ferroelectric liquid crystal, a novel thin film disk lubricant. Recipient Root fellowship in sci., 1981. Mem. Material Rsch. Soc. Home: #C206 1775 Milmont Dr Milpitas CA 95035 Office: Corner Peripherals 3081 Zanker Rd San Jose CA 95134

TANIGUCHI, IZUMI, economics educator; b. Stockton, Calif., Feb. 3, 1926; s. Isamu and Sadayo (Miyagi) T.; m. Barbara Kazuko Nishi, June 11, 1960; children: Neal Izumi, Ian Kei. BBA, U. Houston, 1952, MBA, 1954; PhD, U. Tex., 1970. Statis. analyst Anderson Clayton and Co., Houston, 1953-54; instr., research assoc. U. Houston, 1956; teaching asst., research assoc. U. Tex., Austin, 1956-59, lectr. in econs., 1959-60; asst. prof. Econs. U. Mo., Columbia, 1960-63; asst. prof. Econs. Calif. State U., Fresno, 1963-70, dept. chmn., assoc. prof. Econs., 1971-74, prof. Econs., 1974-92, dept. chmn., 1979-90; ret., 1992. Nat. v.p. Japanese-Am. Citizens League, San Francisco, 1974-76, gov. Cen. Calif. Dist. Council in Fresno, 1973-74, pres. Fresno chpt., 1971; active Beyond War, Fresno, 1985-89; mem. Ednl. Innovation and Planning Commn., Sacramento, 1979-82, State Supr. of Instruction Council on Asian, Pacific Islander Affairs, Sacramento, 1984-85; mem. Adv. Bd. Sch. Edn. Calif. State U., Fresno, 1976-90; mem. Legal Compliance Panel State Dept. Edn., Sacramento, 1974-79; mem. exec. bd. Jesse Marvin Unruh Assembly Fellowship Program, Sacramento, 1989—; mem. scholarly adv. coun. Japanese Am. Nat. Mus., L.A., 1989—. Recipient Wall Street Jour. Achievement award U. Houston, 1952. Mem. Am. Econs. Assn., Southwestern Social Sci. Assn., Assn. Evolutionary Econs., Assn. Asian Studies, Western Social Sci. Assn., Phi Kappa Phi. Democrat. Clubs: U.S. Judo Fedn. (Fresno) (advisor), Japanese Lang. Sch. (pres. 1971). Home: 738 E Tenaya Way Fresno CA 93710-5439 Office: Calif State U Fresno Dept of Econs Fresno CA 93740

TANIGUCHI, RAYMOND MASAYUKI, neurosurgeon; b. Waipahu, Hawaii, May 14, 1934; s. James Takeo and Yoshiko (Yamaguchi) T.; m. Helen Akiki Fujiyoshi, Oct. 6, 1971; 1 child, Stacy. Student, U. Hawaii, 1952-54; BA, Washington U., St. Louis, 1956; MD, Tulane U., 1960. Diplomate Am. Bd. Neurological Surgery, 1973. Rotating internship McLeod Infirmary, Florence, S.C., 1960-61; resident, gen. pathology and neuropath Duke Med. Ctr., 1961-62; resident in gen. surgery N.C. Baptist Hosp., 1962-63; resident in neurology Duke Med. Ctr., 1963-64; resident in clin. neurosurgery N.C. Baptist Hosp., 1964-65, Duke Med. Ctr., 1965-66, 68-70; clin. assoc. prof. U. Hawaii Sch. of Med., Honolulu, 1980—; pvt. practice, neurosurgeon Honolulu, to date; cons. in neurosurgery, Tripler Army Med. Ctr., Kaiser Found. Hosp., spl. physician cons. on spinal cord injury and trauma, Hawaii Med. Assn., Emergency Med. Svcs. Program, ADHOC com. on trauma, State of Hawaii, 1981-82. Contbr. articles to profl. jours. Capt. U.S. Army Med. Corps, 1966-68, Vietnam, Japan. Fellow ACS (chmn. credential com.); mem. Am. Assn. Neurol. Surgeons, Pan Pacific Surg. Assn. (past chmn. bd. trustees), Congress of Neurol. Surgeons. Office: 1380 Lusitana St # 415 Honolulu HI 96813-2449

TANIGUCHI, TOKUSO, surgeon; b. Eleele, Kauai, Hawaii, June 26, 1915; s. Tokuichi and Sana (Omaye) T.; BA, U. Hawaii, 1941; MD, Tulane U., 1946; 1 son, Jan Tokuichi. Intern Knoxville (Tenn.) Gen. Hosp., 1946-47; resident in surgery St. Joseph Hosp., also Marquette Med. Sch., Milw., 1947-52; practice medicine, specializing in surgery, Hilo, Hawaii, 1955—; chief surgery Hilo Hosp.; teaching fellow Marquette Med. Sch., 1947-49; v.p., dir. Hawaii Hardware Co., Ltd. Capt. M.C., AUS, 1952-55. Diplomate Am. Bd. Surgery. Fellow Internat., Am. colls. surgeons; mem. Am., Hawaii med. assns., Hawaii County Med. Soc., Pan-Pacific Surg. Assn., Phi Kappa Phi. Contbr. articles in field to profl. jours. Patentee automated catheter. Home: 277 Kaiulani St Hilo HI 96720-2530

TANIMOTO, GEORGE, agricultural executive, farmer; b. Gridley, Calif., Feb. 10, 1926; s. Hikoichi and Rewa Tanimoto; m. Hanami Yamasaki, Dec. 19, 1946; 1 child, Patricia. Grad., Coyne Electric Sch., Chgo., 1950. Elec. technician, 1951, owner peach and prune orchards, 1952; founder Kiwifruit Nursery, Calif., 1965; pres. Tanimoto Bros., Gridley, Calif., 1977—, Tanimoto Enterprises, Inc., Gridley, 1979—; bd. dirs. Blue Anchor, Inc., Sacramento; chmn. Calif. Fruit Exchange, Inc.; U.S. rep. Internat. Kiwifruit

Orgn., Lake Tahoe, Calif., 1985, Rome, 1986, Biarritz, France, 1987, Hong Kong, 1988, chmn. Orgn.,Rome, 1986; dir. Butte County Agrl. Adv. Commn., Oroville, Calif.; founder, chmn. Calif. Kiwifruit Commn., 1980-84, vice chmn., 1985-87, chmn., 1988-89. Pres. South Shore Assn., Bucks Lake, Calif., 1989. Mem. Kiwifruit Growers Calif. (founder, bd. dirs., pres. 1973-80), Kiwifruit Mktg. Assn. Calif. (founder, chmn. 1989), Gridley Sportsman Club (founder, pres. 1975-78). Republican. Buddhist. Home: 948 River Ave Gridley CA 95948-9774

TANIMOTO, STEVEN LARRY, computer science educator; b. Chgo., May 18, 1949; s. Taffee Tadashi and Mary-Mae Muriel (Whistler) T.; m. Gunnel Birgitta Neander, Sept. 19, 1981; children: Elise Marie, Anna Sofia. AB, Harvard U., 1971; PhD, Princeton U., 1975. Asst. prof. U. Conn., Storrs, 1975-77; asst. prof. U. Wash., Seattle, 1977-81, assoc. prof., 1981-87, prof., 1987—. Author: Elements of Artificial Intelligence, 1987 (Book of Month award 1987); area editor CVGIP: Image Understanding, 1989—; adv. editor J. Visual Langs. and Computing, 1990—; patentee in field. Mem. IEEE (sr. computer soc., editor-in-chief transactions on pattern analysis and machine intelligence 1986-90, Outstanding Contbn. award 1991). Office: U Wash Dept Computer Sci and Eng FR-35 Seattle WA 98195

TANK, HIMAT G., pediatrician; b. Kalana, India, Aug. 1, 1951; came to U.S., 1976; s. Gangdas V. and Maniben G. (Chotala) T.; m. Mina H.; children: Sumi, Pinki, Niki, Rikin. MD, Meghji Pethraj Shah Med. Coll., Jamnagar, India, 1975; FAAP (hon.), Am. Acad. Pediatrics, 1985. Resident in pediatrics N.Y.C., 1976-79, pvt. practice in pediatrics, 1979-81; pvt. practice in pediatrics Santa Maria, 1981—. Fellow Am. Acad. Pediatrics; chmn. Child Health and Disability Prevention Program adv. bd., Santa Barbara County, 1992-93. Office: 1414 S Miller St Ste 10 Santa Maria CA 93454

TANKE, THOMAS JOHN, engineer; b. Chgo., Mar. 17, 1944; s. Raymond and Catherine (Dybas) T.; m. Virginia Rae Coyne, July 3, 1965; children: Kimberly, Michael, Kelly, Carrie. BSME, U. Ill., Urbana, 1966; MSME, U. Wis., 1969; PhD in Bus. Adminstrn., U. Colo., Boulder, 1987. Registered profl. engr.; Calif., Ill., Tex., Colo. Loss prevention engr. Royal-Globe, Inc. Co., Chgo., 1966-69; corp. safety dir. Wright, Corp., Des Moines, 1969-72; loss prevention mgr. Green Construction Co., Pueblo, Colo., 1972-75; mgr. safety and emergency svcs. Kentron Internat., Pueblo, 1975-76; mgr., safety, quality and emergency svcs. U.S. Dept. Transp., Pueblo, 1976-81; mgr. project integration Kaiser, Engrs., Houston, 1981-83; project mgr. Kaiser, Engrs., L.A., 1983-90; exec. v.p. Rail Construction Corp./L.A. County Transp. Commn., 1990-91; sr. engring. mgr. Parsons, Brinkerhoss, Quade & Douglas, Oakland, Calif., 1991—. Contbr. articles profl. publs.; speaker profl. confs. Scoutmaster, Boys Scouts Am., Houston, 1981-83; mem. Assn. Retarded Citizens, Houston, 1982, Spl. Olympics, Ventura, Calif., 1987. Recipient Outstanding Achievement award, Am. Pub. Transit Assn., Washington, 1987, Award of Merit, U.S. Dept. Trans., Washington, 1980, Sr. Exec. Service designation, Office of Personnel Mgmt., Washington, 1980. Mem. Am. Soc. Safety Engrs. (pres. 1973-75), Nat. Safety Mgmt. Soc. (pres. 1974-78), Nat. Fire Protection Assn., Am. Mgmt. Assn., NSPE, Calif. Assn. Profl. Engrs. (sec. 1987), Am. Soc. for Quality Control (cert. quality examiner). Home: 2757 Las Posas Cir Camarillo CA 93012-8255 Office: Parsons Brinkerhoff Ste 400 1000 Broadway Oakland CA 94607

TANKELEVICH, ROMAN LVOVICH, computer scientist; b. Odessa, USSR, Apr. 25, 1941; came to U.S., 1990; s. Lev Faivel and Irina Rudolph (Novak) T.; m. Raye Ja. Sapiro, Jan. 28, 1961; children: Alex, Kate. BS in Physics, Moscow Phys. Engring. Inst., 1963, MS in Physics, 1965; PhD in Computer Sci., Moscow State U., 1968. Rscher., head rsch. lab. Moscow Rsch. Inst. for Computing Tech., 1965-74; prof. Moscow Tech. Inst., 1974-81; dir. rsch. lab. Moscow Comml. Inst., 1981-89; dir. R & D Micrel, Inc., Denver, 1990; v.p. R & D System 6, Inc., Denver, 1989—. Author: Simulation of Physical Fields, 1968, Analog Systems for Simulation, 1974, Microprocessor Systems, 1979; tech. writer, translator All-Union Inst. for Sci. and Tech. Info., Moscow, 1963-85; patentee in field. Mem. Scientists for Polit. Freedoms Com., Moscow, 1981-86. Recipient Gold Medal Int. Exhbn., Moscow, 1987. Mem. N.Y. Acad. Scis. Jewish. Office: System 6 Inc Ste 130 602 Park Point Dr Golden CO 80401

TANNER, DAVID EARL, education educator; b. Lethbridge, Alberta, Canada, July 31, 1948; s. Earl Pingree and Betty (Bridge) T.; m. Susan Elizabeth Bodell, Aug. 21, 1972; children: Dylan, David, Gillian, John, Suzanna. BA, Brigham Young U., 1973, MA, 1977; PhD, Tex. A&M U., 1984. Tchr. Jordan Sch. Dist., Sandy, Utah, 1977-81; lectr. Tex. A&M U., College Station, 1981-84; asst. prof. U. Tex., Tyler, 1984-85; asst. prof. Calif. State U., Fresno, 1985-87, assoc. prof., 1987-90, prof., 1990—, chmn. dept. ednl. rsch., adminstrn. and founds., 1990—; cons. Calif. Dept. Edn., 1985-86; coord. spl. projects div. grad. studies Calif. State U., Fresno, 1989-90. Editor: The Network Journal, 1986-89; contbr. articles to profl. jours. Mem. Am. Ednl. Rsch. Assn. Mem. Latter-day Saints. Office: Calif State U Fresno MS #2 Fresno CA 93740-0002

TANNER, DEE BOSHARD, lawyer; b. Provo, Utah, Jan. 16, 1913; s. Myron Clark and Marie (Boshard) T.; m. Jane Barwick, Dec. 26, 1936 (div. Aug. 1962); children: Barry, Diane McDowell; m. Reeta Walker, Dec. 6, 1981. BA, U. Utah, 1935; LLB, Pacific Coast U., 1940; postgrad., Harvard U., 1936, Loyola U., L.A., 1937. Bar: Calif. 1943, U.S. Dist. Ct. (so. dist.) Calif. 1944, U.S. Ct. Appeals (9th cir.) 1947, ICC 1964, U.S. Dist. Ct. (ea. dist.) Calif. 1969, U.S. Supreme Ct. 1971. Assoc. Spray, Davis & Gould, L.A., 1943-44; pvt. practice L.A., 1944; assoc. Tanner and Sievers, L.A., 1944-47, Tanner and Thornton, L.A., 1947-54, Tanner, Hanson, Meyers, L.A., 1954-64; ptnr. Tanner and Van Dyke, L.A., 1964-65, Gallagher and Tanner, L.A., 1965-70; pvt. practice Pasadena, Calif., 1970—. Mem. L.A. Bar Assn., World Affairs Assn., Harvard Law Sch. Assn., Lawyers' Club L.A. Home and Office: 1720 Lombardy Rd Pasadena CA 91106-4127

TANNER, JACK EDWARD, federal judge; b. 1919; m. Glenda M. Martin; children: Maryetta J. Greaves, Donnetta M. Gillum. Sole practice Tacoma, 1955-78; judge U.S. Dist. Ct. (we. dist.) Wash., Tacoma, 1978—, now sr. judge. Mem. Nat. Bar Assn. Office: US Dist Ct PO Box 2015 Tacoma WA 98401-2015

TANNER, JOHN DOUGLAS, JR., history educator, author; b. Quantico, Va., Oct. 2, 1943; s. John Douglas and Dorothy Lucille (Walker) T.; m. Jo Ann Boyd, Jan. 1964 (div. Aug. 1966); 1 child, Lorena Desiree; m. Laurel Jean Selfridge, Dec. 19, 1967 (div. Oct. 1987); children: John DouglasIII, Stephen Douglas, Elizabeth Jane; m. Karen M. Olson, Apr. 16, 1988. BA, Pomona Coll., 1966; MA, Claremont Calif. Grad. Sch., 1968; postgrad., U. Calif., Riverside, 1976, 84-86, U. Calif., San Diego, 1984-87. Cert. tchr., Calif. Asst. swimming, water polo coach Pomona Coll., 1966-69; rsch. asst. history dept. Claremont Grad. Sch., 1967-69; assoc. prof. history Palomar Coll., San Marcos, Calif., 1969—, pres. faculty, 1970-71, v.p. faculty senate, 1971-72. Author: Olaf Swenson and his Siberian Imports jour., 1978 (Dog Writers Assn. Am. Best Series award 1979), Campaign for Los Angeles, 1846-47, 69; co-editor: Don Juan Forster, 1970; contbr. articles to profl. jours. Mem. citizens com. Fallbrook (Calif.) San. Dist., 1980; merit badge counselor Boy Scouts Am., 1975-85; Martin County Hist. Soc., Morgan County Hist. Soc., Fallbrook Hist. Soc., San Diego Opera Guild, San Diego Classical Music Soc., Opera Pacific Guild. Chautauqua fellow NSF, 1979. Mem. Custer Battlefield Hist. & Mus. Assn. (life), The Westerners, Siberian Husky Am. (bd. dirs. 1974-78, 1st v.p. 1978-79), So. Calif. Siberian Husky (pres. 1972-79). Republican. Episcopalian. Home: 2308 Willow Glen Rd Fallbrook CA 92028-9752 Office: Palomar Coll 1140 W Mission Rd San Marcos CA 92069-1415

TANNER, LYNN, actress; b. N.Y.C., Mar. 22, 1953; d. Harry J. and Barbara Sylvia (Hirschman) Maurer; m. Allen Barry Witz, Aug. 31, 1975. BS, NYU, 1975; JD, DePaul U., 1980. Bar: Ill. 1980. Actress various, 1980—. Appeared in (film) Human Error, 1987, Another Time, Another Place, 1988, (theatre) Pack of Lies, Back at the Blue Dolphin Saloon. Mem. SAG, AFTRA, Actors Equity Assn., Women in Film, Women in Theater, Friends and Artists Theatre Ensemble. Office: Ste 1094 505 S Beverly Dr Beverly Hills CA 90212

TANNER, RICHARD DEAN, physician; b. Palo Alto, Calif., June 9, 1952; s. O. Ralph and June (Phillips) T. BA cum laude, Amherst Coll., 1974; MD, Boston U., 1978. Bd. cert. internal medicine. Intern, then resident in internal medicine Tucson Hopitals Med. Ed. Program, Tucson, 1978-81; Attending in medicine Kino Community Hosp., Tucson, 1981-83; group practice Group Health Med. Assocs., Tucson, 1983—. Mem. P.M.A. County Med. Soc., AMA. Office: Group Health Med Assocs 6565 E Carondelet Dr Tucson AZ 85710-2157

TANNER, WILLIAM COATS, JR., business owner; b. Magna, Utah, Oct. 22, 1920; s. William Coats and Clara (Sutton) T.; m. Athelia Sears, Feb. 14, 1942; children: Roberta Graham, Athelia Woolley, Terri Mitchell, William Coats Tanner III, John Sears Tanner, Richard Sears Tanner, Mark Sears Tanner, Claralyn Palfreyman, Kaye Whitworth, Daken Sears Tanner, Scott Sears Tanner, Janet Perry, Bryan Sears Tanner. BS, U. Utah, 1943; MA, U. Minn., 1948; PhD, U. Utah, 1952. Lic. psychologist, Calif. Instr. Ea. Montana Coll. Edn., Billings, 1952; rsch./statis. assoc. Ednl. Testing Svc., L.A., 1952-54; prin. Tanner Thought Dynamics, L.A., 1954—; instr. U. So. Calif., L.A., 1972-76; therapist, therapists trainer; lecturer. Author in field. Pres. Mormons Ill. Chgo. Mission, Oakbrook, 1986-89. 1st lt. arty. U.S. Army, 1943-46. Mem. Rotary Club, Phi Kappa Phi. Republican. Home: 5055 Holladay Blvd Salt Lake City UT 84117-6307

TANNO, RONALD LOUIS, dentist; b. San Jose, Calif., Dec. 17, 1937; s. George Anthony and Rose Marie (Manghisi) T. BS, Santa Clara U., 1959; DDS magna cum laude, U. of Pacific, 1963. Lic. DDS. Dentist Santa Clara County Health Dept., San Martin, Calif., 1965-67, Alameda County Health Dept., Oakland, Calif., 1965-67; pvt. practice San Jose, 1966—; dental cons. Found. Med. Care, San. Jose, 1977-81, Dental Ins. Cons., Saratoga, Calif., 1980-88, Santa Clara County Sch. Dists. Dental Plan, San Jose, 1983-93; cons. quality rev. Delta Dental Plan Calif., San Francisco, 1983-93; mem. dental staff Los Gatos (Calif.) Community Hosp., 1978—, chief dental dept., 1983, 84. Capt. USAF, 1963-65. Mem. Santa Clara County Dental Soc., Calif. Dental Assn., Am. Dental Assn., Elks, Lions, Xi Psi Phi, Omicron Kappa Upsilon. Office: 1610 Westwood Dr Ste 3 San Jose CA 95125

TANOUS, MICHAEL ALLAN, consulting company executive; b. Hettinger, N.D., Dec. 11, 1939; s. Alfred George and Wilma Verna (Potter) T.; m. Jean Marie Maercklein, Aug. 22, 1960; (div. Dec. 1974); children: Stephen, David, Carl, Jennifer, Elizabeth; m. Valerie Ann Pokoyski, June 6, 1986. B in Philosophy, U. N.D., 1961; postgrad., U. Calif., L.A., 1970-72. Mathematician System Devel. Corp., Grand Forks, N.D., 1961-63; systems analyst System Devel. Corp., Santa Monica, Calif., 1963-68; group mgr. System Devel. Corp., Santa Monica, 1968-75; program mgr. Gen. Electric Co., Valley Forge, Pa., 1976-77; v.p. Sci. Applications Internat. Corp., Colorado Springs, Colo., 1978-86; v.p., ptnr. Booz, Allen & Hamilton, Inc., Colorado Springs, 1986-89; pres. The Matrix Group, Colorado Springs, 1990-92; v.p. Nat. Systems & Rsch. Co., Colorado Springs, 1992—; Contbr. articles to profl. jours. Mem. engring. adv. com. U. Colo., 1987—; mem. Multiple sclerosis Soc., Colorado Springs, 1986—. Mem. IEEE, AIAA. Republican. Office: Nat Systems & Rsch Co 5475 Mark Dabling Blvd Colorado Springs CO 80918

TANOUYE, MARIAN NATSUKO, accountant; b. Honolulu, July 30, 1965; d. Masao and Hanayo T. BS in Math., U. Hawaii, 1987; AS in acctg., Leeward C.C., Pearl City, Hawaii, 1988. Bookkeeper Enterprise Realty, Honolulu, 1985-87; acctg. clk. Wayne Choo, CPA, Honolulu, 1988-89; secondary mktg. clk. Am. Savs. Bank, Honolulu, 1989-90, acct., 1990-91, sr. acct., 1991—. Office: Am Savs Bank 915 Fort St Honolulu HI 96813

TANZMANN, VIRGINIA WARD, architect; b. Tuxedo, N.Y., July 6, 1945; d. John A. Ward and Helen Pfund. BA in Architecture, Syracuse U., 1968, BArch, 1969. Registered architect, Calif., Nev. Intern architect Burke Kober Nicolais Archuleta, Los Angeles, 1969-72; project architect Daniel L. Dworsky & Assocs., Los Angeles, 1972-74, SUA, Inc., Los Angeles, 1974-75; staff architect So. Calif. Rapid Transit Dist., L.A., 1975-78; prin. The Tanzmann Assocs., L.A., 1978—. Prin. works, clients, include transp. facilities, retail stores, comml. and office facilities 6 railroad stations, Los Angeles to Long Beach Light Rail Transit, Conv. Ctr. Expansion Team, Renovation of Hollywood Bowl, Petroleum Lab. Chevron USA, Inc., El Segundo, Calif., Hyperion Treatment Plant UCLA Med. Ctr., L.A. Unified Sch. Dist., L.A. Mission, So. Calif. Gas Co. Valencia, Gas Co. Computer Ctr., L.A. Dept. Water and Power, Oxnard Housing Authority, L.A. Housing Authority. Work exhibited: Monterey Design Conf., Calif., 1981, 87. Pres. YWCA of L.A., 1984-87. founder, Kay Bixby Libr. on Volunteerism, 1992; mem. exec. com. United Way of L.A., 1992-93, bd. dirs. 1992-93; vol. Ctr. L.A., 1984-86, pres.; bd. dirs. Dorland Mountain Arts Colony, 1990-91; mem. Mus. Contemporary Art, L.A. Conservancy. Recipient Vesta award, 1991. Fellow AIA (CCAIA bd., 1989-91, v.p., pres.-elect, 1993); mem. Assn. Women in Architecture (pres. 1977-78, 87-88), Archtl. Guild (treas. 1987-88, v.p. 1988-89, pres. 1990), Calif. Women in Environ. Design (founder), Architects Designers and Planners for Social Responsibility, L'Union International des Femmes Architectes. Office: The Tanzmann Assocs 820 E 3rd St Los Angeles CA 90013-1820

TAPIA, ARTHUR ALBERT, lawyer; b. San Jose, Calif., July 26, 1959; s. Amador E. and Martha (Gonzalez) T. BS, U. Santa Clara, 1981; JD, U. Pa., 1984. Assoc. Caputo, Liccardo, Rossi, Sturges & McNeil, San Jose. Bd. dirs. Mexican-Am. Community Svcs. Agy., San Jose; commr. Consumer Affairs Adv. Commn. County of Santa Clara, San Jose. Mem. United Way (budget allocations rev. com.), Phi Alpha Theta. Democrat. Roman Catholic.

TAPIA, JOHN REYNA, foreign language educator; b. Ajo, Ariz., Jan. 29, 1922; s. Genaro Villa-Gomez and Gillerma (Reyna) T.; m. Bertha Velasco Cervantes, Sept. 21, 1942. BA, W.Va. State Coll., 1960; LLB, U. Chgo., 1960, JD, 1961; MA, U. Utah, 1966, PhD, 1969. Asst. prof. Western Mich. U., Kalamazoo, 1969-70, So. Ill. U., Edwardsville, 1970-71; prof., chmn. Ft. Lewis Coll., Durango, Colo., 1971-84, prof. emeritus, 1984—; part-time prof. Yavapai Coll., Prescott, Ariz., 1981—. Author: Alecia En Flowerland, 1970, Tierra Comprometida, 1980, Indian in Spanish-American Novel, 1981; author poetry. Mem. exec. com. Ariz. Rep. Party, Phoenix, 1989—; commr. Prescott Preservation Commn., 1986-89; chmn. Yavapai County Rep. Party, 1989-91. Decorated 3 Bronze Stars, 7 Purple Hearts; named to Hon. Order of Ky. Cols. Mem. Nat. Assn. Civilian Conservation Corp Alumni, Internat. Acad. Poets (vice chancellor 1982—), Ret. Officers Assn. (life), Mil. Order of the Purple Heart Hall of Honor, Rocky Mountain Modern Langs. Assn., Vets. of the Battle of the Bulge/70th Tank Btn. Assn., Order Don Quijote, Phi Kappa Phi. Home: 326 S Mt Vernon Ave Prescott AZ 86303-4349

TAPIA, STEVEN PAUL, lawyer; b. Torrance, Calif., Mar. 15, 1955; s. Amado Bernal and Magdalena (Angulo) T.; m. Stephani Siudmak, Oct. 11, 1986. BA, Yale U., 1980; JD, U. So. Calif., 1983. Bar: Calif. 1983, U.S. Dist. Ct. (cen. dist.) Calif. 1983, U.S. Ct. Appeals (9th cir.) 1983, U.S. Dist. Ct. (ea., no. and so. dists.) Calif. 1986. Assoc. Loeb & Loeb, Los Angeles, 1983-90; dir. legal affairs Community TV of So. Calif. KCET, L.A., 1990—. Mem. ABA, Mex. Am. Bar Assn., L.A. County Bar Assn., ACLU, Calif. State Bar (com. on adminstrn. of justice 1989-92), Yale Club (bd. dirs. So. Calif. chpt. 1988—). Democrat. Lutheran. Office: KCET 4401 W Sunset Blvd Los Angeles CA 90027-6090

TAPP, CHARLES MILLARD, quality management professional, consultant; b. Memphis, Nov. 9, 1936; s. Millard Brown and Lillian (Bodyston) T.; m. Frances Elouise Billings, Jan. 3, 1978; children: Barbara Frances, David Charles. BA in Philosophy, Union U., 1958; BS in Physics, Memphis State U., 1960; MS in Physics, U. Va., 1962, PhD in Physics, 1964. Mem. tech. staff div. radiation effects Sandia Nat. Labs., 1964-66; supr. div. neutron tube devel. Sandia Nat. Labs., Livermore, Calif., 1966-69, mgr. dept. component devel., 1969-78, mgr. dept. instrumentation devel., 1978-82; mgr. dept. instrumentation devel. Sandia Nat. Labs., Albuquerque, 1982-89, dir. devel. test, 1989-91, acting v.p. devel. support, 1991, dir. quality improvement and primary stds., 1991—; tech. chmn. Electronic Components Conf., 1975, vice chmn., 1976, gen. chmn., 1977; nat. examiner AT&T Malcolm Baldridge Award, 1991, sr. nat. examiner, 1992; sr. judge N.Mex. State Quality Award, 1992; disting. vis. lectr. N.Mex. State U., 1992-93. Editor IEEE Trans. on Mfg. Tech. and Components, 1972-77; contbr. articles to profl. jours. Pres. Osuna PTA, 1971; parental advisor East Area Albuquerque PTA, 1972. Home: 9201 Lona Ln Albuquerque NM 87111 Office: Sandia Nat Labs 4300 Box 5800 Albuquerque NM 87111

TAPP, JESSE WASHINGTON, JR., physician, educator; b. N.Y.C., July 10, 1930; s. Jesse Washington Sr. and Isabel Converse (Dickey) T.; m. Marie Jean Glasse, July 10, 1952; children: Elizabeth, Jane, Cathleen, Jessie, Mary. BA, Stanford U., 1952; MD, U. Chgo., 1955; MPH, Harvard U., 1962. Diplomate Am. Bd. Preventive Medicine, Am. Bd. Family Practice. Rotating intern Alameda County Hosp., Oakland, Calif., 1955-56; family physician Presbyn. Nat. Missions, San Sebastian, P.R., 1956-61; asst. prof. U. Ky. Sch. Medicine, Lexington, 1962-68, assoc. prof., 1968-70; assoc. prof. U. Ariz. Sch. Medicine, Tucson, 1970-73, prof., 1973-79; chief physician svcs. Seattle-King County Dept. Pub. Health, 1979-80, dir., 1980-85, communicable disease control officer, 1985-89; clin. prof. dept. health svcs. U. Wash., Seattle, 1982—; vis. prof., hon. cons. St. Thomas Hosp. Med. Sch., London, 1968-69. Contbr. articles to med. jours. Milbank Meml. Fund faculty fellow. Mme. Am. Coll. Preventive Medicine (v.p. 1977, regent 1980-83), Internat. Epidemiol. Assn., Am. Pub. Health Assn., King County Med. Soc. Home: 4234 51st Ave NE Seattle WA 98105-4931 Office: Univ Wash NW Ctr Pub Health Practice SC-37 1959 NE Pacific St Seattle WA 98195

TAPPAN, JANICE RUTH VOGEL, animal behavior researcher; b. Pasadena, Mar. 13, 1948; d. Robert Samuel and Etta (Berry) Vogel; m. David Stanton Tappan IV, Dec. 20, 1970; children: Stacey, Christina, Danny. BA in Anthropology, U. Calif., Berkeley, 1970. Rsch. asst. L.A. Zoo, 1982—; owner Fiddlers Crossing, Pasadena, 1989—. Calif. Arts Coun. folklore grantee, 1989-90. Mem. Scottish Fiddling Revival (v.p. 1986—, judge fiddling 1989—), Scottish Fiddlers of Calif. (v.p. 1986—), Calif. Traditional Music Soc. (devel. dir. 1990—), Scottish Fiddlers of L.A. (music dir. 1990—), Phi Beta Kappa. Democrat. Soc. of Friends. Home: 1938 Rose Villa St Pasadena CA 91107-5046

TAPPAN, WILLIAM MANNING, physician, surgeon; b. Holland, Mich., Apr. 23, 1920; s. William Manning and Mary Christine (Lokker) T.; m. Sally L. Ross, Mar. 31, 1949; children: William Ross, John Manning. AB, Hope Coll., Holland, 1942; MD, U. Mich., 1945. Diplomate Am. Bd. Surgery. Resident in gen. surgery Univ. Hosp., Ann Arbor, Mich., 1945-52; pvt. practice surgery Reno, 1952—. Capt. U.S. Army, 1946-48, Italy. Fellow ACS; mem. AMA, Nev. State Med. Assn. (pres.), Washoe County Med. Soc. (pres.), Reno Surg. Soc. (pres.), F.A. Colle Surg. Soc. (coun.), Pan Pacific Surg. Soc., Southwestern Surg. Congress. Republican. Presbyterian. Home: 4857 Lakeridge Terr W Reno NV 89509 Office: Ste 302 236 W 6th St Reno NV 89503

TAPPER, CHARLES E., mechanical engineer; b. Portland, Oreg., June 15, 1930; s. Charles Ejidious and Darcevus Dorothy (Murphy) T.; m. Elizabeth Ann Nelson, Dec. 28, 1955 (div. 1979); children: Lisa Hardy, Perry M.; m. Karen Yvonne Foss, July 3, 1987; children: Larry Lightner Jr., Lisa Holloway. BSME, Oreg. State U., 1951; postgrad., LaSalle U., Chgo., 1958, U. Wash., 1961, Seattle U., 1971. Registered profl. engr., Wash. Aero. engr. Boeing Co., Seattle, 1951-58; profl. mech. engr. Boeing Co., Seattle, Everett, 1958—; mech. design engr. Boeing Co., Seattle, 1960-80; design/test engr. Boeing Co., Kent, Wash., 1980—; cons. engr. Wash. Civil Svc., Olympia, 1960—. Comdr. USNR, 1955-58. Mem. ASME, U.S. Naval Inst., Inst. Aero. Scis., Mus. of Flight, Grange, Eagles, Western Wash. Dance Club, Tau Kappa Epsilon. Republican. Presbyterian. Home: PO Box 976 Maple Valley WA 98038 Office: Boeing Def & Space Group PO Box 3999 Seattle WA 98124

TAPPER, JOAN JUDITH, magazine editor; b. Chgo., June 12, 1947; d. Samuel Jack and Anna (Swoiskin) T.; m. Steven Richard Siegel, Oct. 15, 1971. BA, U. Chgo., 1968; MA, Harvard U., 1969. Editor manuscripts Chelsea House, N.Y.C., 1969-71, Scribners, N.Y.C., 1971; editor books Nat. Acad. Scis., Washington, 1972-73; assoc. editor Praeger Pubs., Washington, 1973-74; editor New Rep. Books, Washington, 1974-79; mng. editor spl. pubs. Nat. Geog. Soc., Washington, 1979-83; editor Nat. Geog. Traveler, Washington, 1984-88; editor-in-chief Islands (internat. mag.), Santa Barbara, Calif., 1989—. Mem. Am. Soc. Mag. Editors, Soc. Am. Travel Writers (editors' council). Democrat. Jewish. Home: 603 Island View Dr Santa Barbara CA 93109-1508 Office: Islands Mag 3886 State St Santa Barbara CA 93105-3112

TARA (TARA SINGH), research chemist; b. Kotdata, Punjab, India, June 11, 1921; came to U.S., 1966; naturalized, 1972; s. Nand and Isar (Kaur) Singh; m. Rani Surinder, Dec. 29, 1954; children: Nina, Roopinder, Sylvia, Sonya. BS with honors, Punjab U., 1944, MS with 1st class honors, 1946; AM, Harvard U., 1949, PhD, 1950. Post doctorate fellow with Prof. R.B. Woodward Harvard U., 1950-51; Post doctorate fellow NRC, Can., 1953-54; prof. chemistry govt. colls., Punjab, India, 1954-58; prin. govt. colls., India, 1958-64; rsch. and devel. chemist PEBOC Ltd., Northolt, Eng., 1964-65, Unilever Rsch. Lab., Isleworth, Eng., 1965-66, Aldrich Chem.Co., Milw., 1966-76, Polyscis., Inc., Warrington, Pa., 1976-88, Calbiochem, La Jolla, Calif., 1989—. Author many books; contbr. numerous articles to profl. jours. Mem. Am. Chem. Soc. Home: 4202 Appleton St San Diego CA 92117-1901 Office: Calbiochem Corp 10933 N Torrey Pines Rd La Jolla CA 92037-1080

TARANIK, JAMES VLADIMIR, geologist, educator; b. Los Angeles, Apr. 23, 1940; s. Vladimir James and Jeanette Downing (Smith) T.; m. Colleen Sue Glessner, Dec. 4, 1971; children: Debra Lynn, Danny Lee. B.Sc. in Geology, Stanford U., 1964; Ph.D., Colo. Sch. Mines, 1974. Chief remote sensing Iowa Geol. Survey, Iowa City, 1971-74; prin. remote sensing scientist Earth Resources Observation Systems Data Ctr., U.S. Geol. Survey, Sioux Falls, S.D., 1975-79; chief non-renewable resources br., resource observation div. Office of Space and Terrestrial Applications, NASA Hdqrs., Washington, 1979-82; dean mines Mackay Sch. Mines U. Nev., Reno, 1982-87, prof. of geology and geophysics, 1982—; pres. Desert Research Inst., Univ. and Community Coll. System Nev., 1987—; adj. prof. geology U. Iowa, 1971-79; vis. prof. civil engring. Iowa State U., 1972-74; adj. prof. earth sci. U. S.D., 1976-79; program scientist for space shuttle large format camera expt. for heat capacity mapping mission, liaison Geol. Scis. Bd., Nat. Acad. Scis., 1981-82; dir. NOAA Coop. Inst. Aerospace Sci. & Terrestrial Applications, 1986—; program dir. NASA Space Grant consortium Univ. and Community Coll. System Nev., Reno, 1991—; team mem. Shuttle Imaging Radar-B Sci. Team NASA, 1983-88, mem. space applications adv. com. 1986-88; chmn. remote sensing subcom. SAAC, 1986-88; chmn. working group on civil space commercialization U.S. Dept. Commerce, 1982-84, mem. civil operational remote sensing satellite com., 1983-84; bd. dirs. Newmont Gold Co.; mem. NASA Space Sci. and Applications adv. com., 1988—, Nat. Def. Exec. Res., 1986—, AF Studies Bd., Com. on Strategic Relocatable Targets, 1989-91; developer remote sensing program and remote sensing lab. for State of Iowa, ednl. program in remote sensing for Iowa univs. and U. Nev., Reno; Office Space and Terrestrial Applications program scientist for 2d space shuttle flight; terrestrial geol. applications program NASA, 1986—. Contbr. to profl. jours. Served with C.E. U.S. Army, 1965-67; mil. intelligence officer Res. Decorated Bronze Star medal; recipient Spl. Achievement award U.S. Geol. Survey, 1978, Exceptional Sci. Achievement medal NASA, 1982, NASA Group Achievement award Shuttle imaging radar, 1990, NASA Johnson Space Ctr. Group Achievement award for large format camera, 1985; NASA prin. investigator, 1973, 83-88; NDEA fellow, 1968-71. Fellow AAAS, Explorers Club, Geol. Soc. Am.; mem. Am. Assn. Petroleum Geologists (charter, mem. energy minerals divsn., divsn. environ. geoscis.), Soc. Mining Engrs., Am. Inst. Profl. Geologists (certified, pres. Nev. sect. 1985-87), AIAA (sr. mem.), Am. Astronautical Soc. (sr. mem.), Soc. Exploration Geophysicists, Geosci. and Remote Sensing Soc. of IEEE (bd. dirs., geosat com. 1983—), Am. Soc. Photogrammetry (certified), Am. Soc. Photogrammetry and Remote Sensing (dep. dir. for remote sensing cert.), Internat. Soc. Photogrammetry and Remote Sensing (pres. working group II/4 1976-80, working group VII-5 non-renewable resources 1980-88, working group VII-4 geology and mineral resources applications 1992—), Nev. Quality and Productivity Inst. (chmn. bd.), Nev. Industry Sci., Engring., and Tech. Task Force, Grand Canyon Visibility Commn. (pub. adv. com. 1992—), Sigma Xi, Phi Kappa Phi (life). Home: 3075 Susileen Dr Reno NV 89509-3855 also: 2108 calle De Espana Las Vegas NV 89120

Office: Univ and Community Coll Sys Nev Desert Rsch Inst Pres' Office Reno NV 89512

TARBETT, DOUGLAS GENE, air force officer; b. Fayetteville, Tenn., Oct. 21, 1959; s. Gene Porter and Marilyn Gail (Wilkes) T.; m. June Kristine Cromer, July 19, 1987; children: Brendan Douglas, Joshua Ryan. BSCE, U. Tenn., 1982; MBA, So. Ill. U., 1985. Commd. 2nd lt. USAF, 1982, advanced through grades to capt., 1986; project mgr. USAF, Norton AFB, Calif., 1982-86; dep. site comdr. USAF, Yma, Ariz., 1986-87; comprehensive planner USAF, Hahn AB, Germany, 1987-88; chief ops. USAF, Wueschheim AS, Germany, 1988-90; project mgr. USAF, Elmendorf AFB, Alaska, 1990-91, chief environ. compliance, 1991—. Mem. ASCE, Soc. Am. Mil. Engrs. Home: 18829 Mills Bay Dr Eagle River AK 99577 Office: 3 SPTG/DEVC 22040 Maple St Elmendorf AFB AK 99506-3240

TARBI, WILLIAM RHEINLANDER, educator, curriculum consultant, educational technology researcher; b. San Bernardino, Calif., Feb. 23, 1949; s. William Metro and Sue (Rheinlander) T.; m. Jenny Workman, Apr. 10, 1980 (div. 1985); m. Michele Hastings, July 4, 1990; children: Amy, Melissa. AA, Santa Barbara City Coll., 1969; BA in History, U. Calif., Santa Barbara, 1976; MA, U. Redlands, 1992. Cert. secondary edn. social studies tchr., Calif. Reporter Associated Press, Santa Barbara, Calif., 1976-80, United Press Internat., Seattle, 1980-85, Golden West Radio Network, Seattle, 1980-85; tchr. Redlands (Calif.) Unified Sch. Dist., 1988—; cons. IMCOM, Redlands, 1985—. Mrm. E Clampus Vitus, Phi Delta Kappa.

TARDIF, GILMAN NORMAND, transplant immunologist, educator; b. Van Buren, Maine, Feb. 25, 1947; s. Alderic Hector and Celenie Martha (Cyr) T.; m. Cathy Ellen Bernthal, Oct. 25, 1980; children: Timothy Christopher, Kristina Catherine. BS in Biology magna cum laude, Mass. State Coll., Fitchburg, 1970; MS in Genetics, Western Ill. U., 1974; postgrad., Mich. State U., East Lansing, 1975-80. Tchr. biology Grafton (Mass.) High Sch., 1970-71; tech. dir. Life Link Found., Tampa, Fla., 1980-89; asst. dir. Immunological Assoc. Denver, 1989—; tech. advisor Southeastern Organ Procurement Found., Richmond, Va., 1983—; cons. Biotest Corp., Denville, N.J., 1987-92, Astroscan Ltd., W.I., 1988. Editor: Immunology Reference Manual, 1987, 93; author: (chpts.) Immunology Technical Manual, 1987, 90, 93; inventor single color fluorescent class II typing. Elder Messiah Luth. Congregation, Tampa, 1988, Sunday sch. tchr., 1989; pres. All Sts. Luth. Congregation, Tampa, 1986; stewardship com. The Shepherd on the Hill Luth. Ch., Denver, 1992—; chmn. ROP tray and tech. workshop coms. South-Eastern Procurement Found. Recipient Achievement award Life Link Found., 1989. Mem. Am. Assn. Blood Banks, United Network of Organ Sharing, Am. Soc. for Histocompatibility and Immunogenetics (councilor 1988-91, councilor at large 1989-90), Am. Bd. for Histocompatibility and Immunogenetics (treas. 1990—, chmn. examination and self-assessment program coms. mem. continuing cert. com.), Lone Tree Golfers Club, Lambda Phi Sigma. Republican. Home: 9831 S Venneford Ranch Rd Highlands Ranch CO 80126 Office: Immunological Assocs Denver 101 University Blvd Ste 330 Denver CO 80206-4632

TARIN, WILLIAM MICHAEL, senior publications engineer; b. San Antonio, July 15, 1942; s. Joseph Walter and Dorothy Mae (Perry) T.; m. Elizabeth Ann Scout, Feb. 1, 1969; children: Dorothy Elizabeth, William Michael, Joseph Clement. BS in Info. Systems, Nat. Coll., 1988. Communications analyst USAF, Ft. Meade, Md., 1961-81; tech. writer Docu-Data Corp., Millersville, Md., 1981-83; document control mgr. Ford Aerospace & Communications Corp., Hanover, Md., 1983; data processing mgr. Dept. Defense, Ft. Meade, 1983-84; tech. writer Intercon Systems Corp., Aurora, Colo., 1984-87; sr. publ. engr. Lockheed Missiles & Space Co., Aurora, 1987—; cons. in field. Recipient Air Force Commendation Medal Air Force, 1967, 1979, 1981, Commendation Cert. Nat. Security Agy., 1977. Mem. Am. Legion (Elizabeth, Colo.). Democrat. Methodist. Home: 5064 Pine Ridge Dr Elizabeth CO 80107-7820 Office: Lockheed Missiles & Space 16000 E Lockheed Dr Aurora CO 80011

TARIO, TERRY C(HARLES), broadcasting executive; b. Los Angeles, Aug. 28, 1950; s. Clifford Alexander and Marion Charlene (Olive) T.; m. Bonnie L. Eisen; children: Brian Paul, Caycee Nicole. Grad. high sch., Hermosa Beach, Calif., 1968. Gen. mgr. South Bay Power Tools, Hermosa Beach, 1973-76; broadcaster Sta. KEZJ FM, Twin Falls, Idaho, 1976—; dir. mktg. Pet Complex, Boise and Salt Lake City, 1985-90. Creator comms. John Lennon Meml. (Best of Yr. award 1982), Pets Unltd., 1983 (Best of Yr. award 1983), Depot Grill, 1984 (Best of Yr. award 1984), Eyecenter (Best of Yr. award 1986). Served with USN, 1968-72. Recipient Best of Yr. Pub. Svc. award, 1990. Mem. Idaho State Broadcasters Assn. (Best Pub. Svc. award 1990), Advt. and Mktg.Cons. (pres.), Broadcast Music Inc.; v.p. Admagination. Office: Stas KEZJ FM, KLIX AM/FM 415 Park Ave Twin Falls ID 83301-7752

TARN, NATHANIEL, poet, translator, educator; b. Paris, June 30, 1928; s. Marcel and Yvonne (Suchar) T.; children : Andrea, Marc. BA with honors, Cambridge (Eng.) U., 1948, MA, 1952; postgrad., U. Sorbonne, U. Paris, 1949-51; MA, U. Chgo., 1952, PhD, 1957; postgrad., London Sch. Econs., 1953-58. Anthropologist Guatemala, Burma, Alaska, and other locations, 1952—; prof. comparative lit. Rutgers U., 1970-85; vis. prof. SUNY, Buffalo and Princeton, 1969-70. Author: Old Savage/Young City, 1964, Where Babylon Ends, 1968, The Beautiful Contradictions, 1969, October, 1969, A Nowhere for Vallejo, 1971, Lyrics for the Bride of God: Section: The Artemision, 1972, The Persephones, 1974, Lyrics for the Bride of God, 1975, The House of Leaves, 1976, Birdscapes, with Seaside, 1978, The Desert Mothers, 1985, At the Western Gates, 1985, Palenque, 1986, Seeing America First, 1989, Flying the Body, 1993, Views from the Weaving Mountain: Selected Essays in Poetics and Anthropology, 1991; co-author: (with Janet Rodney) The Forest, 1978, Atitlan/Alashka, 1979, The Ground of Our Great Admiration of Nature, 1978; contbg. author: Penguin Modern Poets No. Seven: Richard Murphy, Jon Silkin, Nathaniel Tarn, 1965, A.P.E.N. Anthology of Contemporary Poetry, 1966, The Penguin Book of Modern Verse Translation, 1966, Poems Addressed to Hugh MacDiarmid, 1967, Music and Sweet Poetry: A Verse Anthology, 1968, Frontier of Going: Anthology of Space Poetry, 1969, Shaking the Pumpkin, 1972, America: A Prophecy, 1973, Open Poetry, 1973, Active Anthology, 1974, Symposium of the Whole, 1983, Random House Book of Twentieth Century French Poetry, 1983, Beneath a Single Moon: Buddhism in American Poetry, 1991, American Poetry since 1950, 1993; translator: The Heights of Macchu Picchu (Pablo Neruda), 1966, Stelae (Victor Segalen), 1969; editor, co-translator: Con Cuba: An Anthology of Cuban Poetry of the Last Sixty Years, 1969, Selected Poems (Pablo Neruda), 1970; editor Cape Edits. and founder-dir. Cape Goliard Press, J. Cape Ltd., 1967-69. Recipient Guinness prize for poetry, 1963. Office: PO Box 8187 Santa Fe NM 87504-8187

TARR, DAVID EUGENE, college administrator; b. Washington, Pa., Jan. 11, 1932; s. Charles E. and Zoe (Donel) T.; m. Dorothy Irene Gray, Sept. 2, 1950; children: Diane, David, Dale, Darren. B in Sacred Music, Nyack Coll., 1956; MM, U. Hartford, 1960; postgrad., W.Va. U., 1960-64; PhD, Pacific State U., 1977. Music dept. chmn. Can. Alliance Coll., Regina, Sask., Can., 1955-63; music chmn. Fairmont (W.Va.) High Sch., 1963-65; music dept. chmn. Rowland High Sch., Rowland Heights, Calif., 1965-69; music chmn., prof. Alderson-Broaddus Coll., Philippi, W.Va., 1969-75; acad. dean Simpson Coll., San Francisco, 1975-77; founder, dir. The West Virginians, Philippi, 1977-82; dean of external edn. Alderson-Broaddus Coll., Philippi, 1982-85; acad. dean Simpson Coll., San Francisco, 1985-88, exec. dir., 1988—; assoc. dir. The Young Americans, Hollywood, Calif., 1971; dir. The A-B Singers, W.Va., 1972-74. Author: Appalachian Chains, 1980; composer various choral works, 1975-85. Recipient Nat. Teaching fellowship U.S. Govt., Washington, 1969-70; named Outstanding Educator in Am., 1974. Office: Simpson Coll 2211 College View Dr Redding CA 96003-8606

TARRAN, MATTHEW JAY, psychologist; b. Bklyn., Mar. 15, 1961; s. Alvin K. and Adele (Smith) T. BA, SUNY, Buffalo, 1983; MA, NYU, 1985; PhD, U. Vt., 1990. Lic. psychologist, Calif. Rsch. asst. N.Y. State Psychiat. Inst., 1983-84, Columbia U., N.Y.C., 1984-85, U. Vt., Burlington, 1985-88; psychology intern VA Med. Ctr., Palo Alto, Calif., 1988-89; staff psychologist Atascadero (Calif.) State Hosp., 1990-91; psychologist Community Counseling Ctr., Fremont, Calif., 1991—; pvt. practice Mountain View, Calif., 1992—; cons. Daytop Village, Redwood City, Calif., 1992—. Commr. parks and recreation dept. City of Menlo Park, Calif. Grantee Vt. Dept. of Correction, 1987. Mem. Am. Psychol. Assn. Office: Bldg 2 2500 Hospital Dr Mountain View CA 94040

TARSON, HERBERT HARVEY, university administrator emeritus; b. N.Y.C., Aug. 28, 1910; s. Harry and Elizabeth (Miller) T.; m. Lynne Barnett, June 27, 1941; 1 son, Stephen. Grad., Army Command Gen. Staff Coll., 1942, Armed Forces Staff Coll., 1951, Adavnced Mgmt. Sch. Sr. Air Force Comdrs., George Washington U., 1954; B.A., U. Calif., Los Angeles, 1949; Ph.D., U.S. Internat. U., 1972. Entered U.S. Army as pvt., 1933, advanced through grades to maj., 1942; transfered to U.S. Air Force, 1947, advanced through grades to lt. col., 1949; adj. exec. officer Ft. Snelling, Minn., 1940-42; asst. adj. gen. 91st Inf. Div., 1942-43; chief of personnel, advance sec. Comd. Zone, ETO, 1944-45; dir. personnel services 8th Air Force, 1946-47; dep. dir. dept. info. and edn. Armed Forces Info. Sch., 1949-51; dir. personnel services Japan Air Def. Force, 1951-53, Continental Air Command, 1953-62; dir. adminstrv. services, spl. asst. to Comdr. 6th Air Force Res. Region, 1962-64; ret., 1964; asst. to chancellor L.I. U., Brookville, 1964-69; dean admissions Tex. State Tech. Inst., San Diego Indsl. Center, 1970-72; v.p. acad. affairs Nat. U., San Diego, 1972-75, sr. v.p., 1975-88, founding sr. v.p. emeritus, 1988—. Decorated Bronze Star medal with oak leaf cluster, Air Force Commendation medal with 2 oak leaf clusters. Fellow Bio-Med Research Inst.; mem. Doctoral Soc. U.S. Internat. U., Am. Soc. Tng., Devel., World Affairs Council, Air Force Assn., Navy League U.S., Pres.'s Assos. of Nat. U. (presidential life). Home: 4611 Denwood Rd La Mesa CA 91941-4803

TARTER, BLODWEN, marketing executive; b. Sacramento, Dec. 2, 1954; d. Bill and Blodwen Edwards (Coburn) Tarter; m. Alan May, Aug. 6, 1983. BA, MA, Stanford U., 1976; MBA, U. Chgo., 1978; PhD, Golden Gate U., 1991. Mgr. mkt. rsch. Mead Products, Dayton, Ohio, 1978-79; assoc. mktg. mgr. Mead Products, 1979-80; mgr. mktg. svcs. Mead Paperboard Products, 1980-81; mgr. mktg. planning Mead Data Cen., N.Y.C., 1981-82; v.p. mktg. Info. Access Co., Belmont, Calif., 1982-86; dir. mktg. Channelmark Corp., San Mateo, Calif., 1986-87; v.p. mktg. Ins. Equities Corp., Palo Alto, Calif., 1987-89; dir. product mgmt. Charles Schwab & Co., Inc., San Francisco, 1989-91, v.p. info. systems divsn., 1991-93, v.p. telecom., 1993—. Fundraiser Stanford Keystone campaign, 1988-91. Mem. Stanford Profl. Women. Office: Charles Schwab & Co Inc 101 Montgomery St San Francisco CA 94104-4122

TARTIKOFF, BRANDON, motion picture company executive, retired; b. L.I., N.Y., Jan. 13, 1949; m. Lilly Samuels, 1982; 1 child, Calla Lianne. B.A. with honors, Yale U., 1970. With promotion dept. ABC TV, New Haven, Conn., 1971-73; program exec. dramatic programming Sta. WLS-TV (ABC), Chgo., 1973-76; mgr. dramatic devel. ABC TV, N.Y.C., 1976-77; writer, producer Graffiti; dir. comedy programs NBC Entertainment, Burbank, Calif., 1977-78, v.p. programs, 1978-80, pres., 1980-90; chmn. NBC Entertainment Group, until 1991, Paramount Pictures, 1991-92. Co-author: The Last Great Ride,1992. Named 1 of 10 Outstanding Young Men Am. U.S. Jaycees, 1981; recipient Tree of Life award Jewish Nat. Found., 1986.

TARVER, PETER LYNN, electrical engineer; b. Fresno, Calif., Sept. 29, 1958; s. Eddie P. and Juanita Faye (Dorrough) T.; m. Tammy Marie Cappelli, June 5, 1987; children: Kathryyn Elizabeth Plambeck, Chelsea Victoria T. BSEE, Calif. State U., Fresno, 1984. Registered profl. engr., Calif. Sr. project engr. Underwriters Labs., Santa Clara, Calif., 1984—. Mem. Industry Adv. Conf. on Tel. Appliances and Equipment. Office: Underwriters Labs 1655 Scott Blvd Santa Clara CA 95050

TARZANIN, FRANK JULIUS, computer systems engineer; b. Media, Pa., Oct. 9, 1964; s. Frank Julius and Eloise Carmen (NuNez) T. BSME, Rensselaer Poly. Inst., 1986. Application engr. Applicon/Slumberger, Ann Arbor, Mich., 1987, Computervision/Prime, Natick, Mass., 1987-90; systems engr. Ingres-Ask, Alameda, Calif., 1990-92; support cons. Uniface, Alameda, 1992—. Earthwatch scholar Keck Found., 1982, Storch scholar Soc. Am. Mil. Engrs., 1984, scholar ROTC, 1985-86. Mem. Sierra Club, Police Activities League. Mem. Green Party. Home: 1430 St Charles Alameda CA 94501 Office: Uniface Alameda CA 94501

TASAKA, MASAICHI, hospital executive; b. Hilo, Hawaii, Feb. 3, 1925; s. Sunao and Shizue (Katayama) T.; m. Toshiko Kohatsu, Aug. 30, 1952; children: Sharon Lei, Russell Ken. M.S. in Hosp. Adminstrn., Northwestern U., 1955. Bookkeeper, Francis Hiu & Co., 1948-50; bus. mgr. South Shore Hosp., 1950-53; asst. adminstr. Highland Park Hosp., 1955-64; asst. adminstr. Kuakini Med. Ctr., Honolulu, 1964-69, pres., 1969-90, healthcare cons., 1990—; asst. prof. Sch. Pub. Health; chmn. United Laundry Svcs. Inc. Mem. Am. Hosp. Assn. (life), Am. Coll. Hosp. Adminstrs., Japanese Cultural Cntr. of Hawaii, Honolulu Japanese C. of C., Lions.

TASHIMA, ATSUSHI WALLACE, federal judge; b. Santa Maria, Calif., June 24, 1934; s. Yasutaro and Aya (Sasaki) T.; m. Nora Kiyo Inadomi, Jan. 27, 1957; children: Catherine Y., Christopher I., Jonathan I. A.B. in Polit. Sci., UCLA, 1958; LL.B., Harvard U., 1961. Bar: Calif. 1962. Dep. atty. gen. State of Calif., 1962-67; atty. Spreckels Sugar div. Amstar Corp., 1968-72, v.p., gen. atty., 1972-77; partner Morrison & Foerster, Los Angeles, 1977-80; judge U.S. Dist. Ct. Central Dist. Calif., Los Angeles, 1980—; mem. Calif. Com. Bar Examiners, 1978-80. Served with USMC, 1953-55. Mem. ABA, State Bar Calif., Los Angeles County Bar Assn. Democrat. Office: US Dist Ct 312 N Spring St Los Angeles CA 90012-4701

TATA, GIOVANNI, publishing executive; b. Taranto, Italy, Apr. 26, 1954; came to U.S., 1974, naturalized, 1982; s. Vito and Angela (Colucci) T.; m. Brenda Susan Smith, Feb. 14, 1978; children: Elizabeth Ariana, Katherine Allison, Margaret Anne. BS cum laude (scholar), Brigham Young U., 1977, MA, 1980; grad. cert. area studies U. Utah, 1980; PhD, 1986; postgrad. U. Turin (Italy), 1980-81. Archaeologist, Utah State Hist. Soc., Salt Lake City, 1979; instr. dept. langs. U. Utah, Salt Lake City, 1983-85; Mediterranean specialist Soc. Early Hist. Archaeology, Provo, Utah, 1978-91; mus. curator Pioneer Trail State Park, Salt Lake City, 1982-83; instr. dept. art Brigham Young U., Provo, 1982-84; research fellow Direzione Generale per la Cooperazione Scientifica Culturale e Technica, Rome, 1980-81; research curator Utah Mus. Fine Arts, Salt Lake City, 1985-87; chmn. 35th Ann. Symposium on the Archaeology of the Scriptures, 1986; pres. Transoft Internat., Inc., 1988—, Mus. Info. Systems, 1987—. Republican. Mem. Ch. Jesus Christ of Latter-day Saints. Mem. Am. Assn. Museums, Internat. Coun. Museums, Utah State Hist. Soc. Home: 510 East 3950 No Provo UT 84604 Office: 3707 N Canyon Rd Ste 8H Provo UT 84604-4575

TATARSKII, VALERIAN IL'ICH, physics researcher; b. Kharkov, USSR, Oct. 13, 1929; s. Il'ya A. and Elizabeth A. (Lapis) T.; m. Maia S. Granovskaia, Dec. 22, 1955; 1 child, Viatcheslav V. MS, Moscow State U., 1952; PhD, Acoustical Inst. Acad. Scis., 1957; DSc, Gorky State U., 1962. Scientific rschr. Geophys. Inst. Acad. Sci. USSR, Moscow, 1953-56; scientific rschr. Inst. Atmospheric Physics, Acad. Sci. USSR, Moscow, 1956-59, sr. scientific rschr., 1959-78, head lab., 1978-90; head dept. Lebedev. Phys. Inst. Acad. Sci., Moscow, 1990-91; sr. rsch. assoc. U. Colo. Coop. Inst. for Rsch. in Environ. Sci., Boulder, 1991—. Nat. Oceanic and Atmospheric Adminstrn., Boulder, 1991—, ERL/Wave Propagation Lab., Boulder, 1991—. Author: Wave Propagation in a Turbulent Medium, 1961, 67, The Effect of the Turbulent Atmosphere on Wave Propagation, 1971, Principles of Statistical Radiophysics, 1989; contbr. articles to profl. jours. Fellow Optical Soc. of Am; mem. Russian Acad. Sci. Office: NOAA/ERL/WPL 325 Broadway Boulder CO 80303

TATE, JERRY ALLEN, mechanical engineer; b. De Kalb, Ill., Mar. 10, 1956; s. Kenneth Jean and Doris Jean (Parks) T. BSME, Ariz. State U., 1983. Devel engr. assoc. Allied-Signal Garrett Fluid Systems, Tempe, Ariz., 1983-84; devel. engr. Allied-Signal Aerospace Co., Garrett Fluid Systems Div., Tempe, 1984-86, sr. devel. engr., 1986-89; devel. specialist Allied-Signal Aerospace Co., Garrett Fluid Systems Div., 1989—. Co-inventor flow straightener for fluidic devices, 1984. Mem. Soc. Automotive Engrs., Am. Soc. Mech. Engrs., Phi Theta Kappa, Tau Beta Pi, Pi Tau Sigma. Republican. Club: Cen. Ariz. Trials, Inc. (Tempe) (pres. 1987-88).

TATEISHI, YOSHIHARU, aviation company executive; b. Japan, Mar. 21, 1946; came to U.S., 1991; s. Shinkichi and Yoshiko Tateishi. BA in Econs., Keio U., Tokyo, 1969. Mgr. Toyota Motor Corp., Tokyo, 1969-91; sr. exec. coord. Toyota Aviation, U.S.A., Long Beach, Calif., 1991—; v.p. Airflite, Long Beach, 1991—. Home: 727 Esplanade #107 Redondo Beach CA 90277 Office: Airflite 3250 Airflite Way Long Beach CA 90807

TATHAM, GREGORY ARTHUR, university administrator; b. Macomb, Ill., Mar. 13, 1953; s. Victor Otis and Patricia Ann (Mulica) T.; m. Mary Teresa O'Dell, Apr. 5, 1986; children: Kelli Ann, Nicole Joyce. BS in Recreation, Park Adminstrn., Western Ill. U., 1978; MS in Phys. Edn., Recreation, Mont. State U., 1987; postgrad., U. Wyo. Lab. technician Amax Coal Co., Astoria, Ill., 1980-83; grad. teaching asst. Mont. State U., Bozeman, 1983-87; asst. dir. Wyo. Union U. Wyo., Laramie, 1987-90, dir. Wyo. Union, 1990—; bd. dirs. Wyo. Acad. Decathalon, 1989-91; regional rep. Assn. Coll. Unions Internat., Bloomington, Ind., 1991-94 (top position in Wyo., Ariz, Utah., Colo., N.Mex. Mem. Leadership Laramie Area C. of C., 1991. Named one of Outstanding Young Men in Am., 1988. Mem. Jacoby Park Men's Golf Assn. (pres. 1990-91), Rotary, Elks. Republican. Presbyterian. Office: U Wyo Wyo Union 101 13th St Box 3105 Laramie WY 82071

TATMAN, ROBIN REICH, pilot; b. Walnut Creek, Calif., July 21, 1959. AA with honors, Coll. San Mateo (Calif.), 1983; BS, Calif. State U., Hayward, 1985. Sr. patient service rep. Mills Meml. Hosp., San Mateo, 1981-87; sr. flight instr. West Valley Flying Club, Palo Alto, Calif., 1986-89; chief pilot Flight Simulation, San Carlos, Calif., 1989-92; pilot Ameriflight, Oakland, Calif., 1992-93, Atlantic Coast Airlines, Washington, 1993. Vol. San Mateo Hist. Assn., 1975-82, Planned Parenthood, San Mateo, 1975-85. Mem. Aircraft Owners and Pilots Assn., Air and Space Smithsonian, Calif. Scholarship Fedn. (life), Sierra Club. Democrat.

TATUM, RONALD WINSTON, physician, endocrinologist; b. Joplin, Mo., Apr. 29, 1935; s. Dorothy Elizabeth (Messick) T.; m. Phyllis Wainman, June 25 (div. May 1974); children: Jeffrey, Stacey; m. Ruby Germaine Trujillo, Aug. 21, 1983; children: Tracea, Susan. AB, Harvard U., 1957; MD, U. Rochester, 1961. Intern Strong Meml. Hosp., Rochester, N.Y., 1961-62; resident U. Rochester, 1962-64, fellow, 1964-66; clin. endocrinologist in pvt. practice Albuquerque, 1966—; active staff Presbyn. Hosp. and St. Joseph Hosp., Albuquerque, 1966—; med. dir. Cottonwood Treatment Ctr., Albuquerque, 1985-90, N.Mex. Monitored Treatment Program, Albuquerque, 1990—; clin. endocrine cons. Chareter Hosp. and Heights Psychiat. Hosp., Albuquerque, 1985—. Contbr. articles to profl. jours. Mem. med. adv. com. Hospice Home Health Care, Albuquerque, 1991—. Mem. Am. Assn. Clin. Endocrinologists (charter), Am. Assn. Internal Medicine, Am. Diabetes Assn. (pres. N.Mex. chpt. 1970, 74), Am. Soc. Addiction Medicine, Assn. for Med. Rsch. in Substance Abuse. Home: 538 Chamiso Ln NW Albuquerque NM 87107 Office: 8008 Constitution Pl NE Albuquerque NM 87110

TATUM, THOMAS DESKINS, film and television producer, director; b. Pineville, Ky., Feb. 16, 1946; s. Clinton Turner and Gaynelle (Deskins) T.; m. Laura Ann Smith, Aug. 15, 1968 (div. 1974); m. Suzanne Pettit, Sept. 29, 1983; children: Rhett Cowden, Walker Edwin. BA, Vanderbilt U., 1968; JD, Emory U., 1974. Bar: Ga. 1974, D.C. 1980. Spl. asst. City of Atlanta, 1974-76; dep. dir. fed. relations Fed. Relations Nat. League of Cities, Washington, 1977-78; dir. communications Office of Conservation and Solar Energy, Washington, 1979-80; chmn. exec. producer Tatum Communications., Inc., Telluride, and Burbank, Calif., 1981—; chmn., pres. Western Film & Video, Inc., Telluride, 1987—; mem. adv. bd. Electric Light Fund, Washington, 1990—. Producer: (feature film) Winners Take All, 1987; producer dir.: (documentary) Double High, 1982 (award), Maui Windsurf, 1983, (home video) Greenpeace in Action, Girls of Winter/Skiing mag., Am. Ultra Sports with Prime Network, 1989-93, various TV, cable, home video sprots programs, 1982—. Dep. campaign mgr. Maynard Jackson, 1973, Jimmy Carter campaign, 1976, staff conf. Dem. Mayors, 1974-75, media cons. Greepeace, 1988; bd. dirs. Atlanta Ballet, v.p., 1975; nat. urban affairs coord. Carter Mondale campaign 1976, mem. Carter Mondale transition team 1976-77; mem. adv. bd. Solar Electric Light Fund, Washington, 1990-93. Mem. Ga. Bar Assn., Washington Bar Assn., Hollywood Film and TV Soc., L.A. Tennis Club. Presbyterian. Home: 103 Davis St Telluride CO 81435-9999 Office: Tatum Communications Inc 2920 W Olive Ave Ste 102 Burbank CA 91505-4546

TATUS, RONALD PETER, account executive; b. Detroit, Sept. 9, 1944; s. Peter Stanley and Irene Delphine (Gburzynski) T.; m. Kathryn Elizabeth Stutsman, Dec. 17, 1970; children: Elizabeth, Matthew, Jonathan. BA in Psychology, U. Detroit, 1966, MA in Indsl. Psychology, 1968. Chief of protocol 32d Tactical Fighter Squadron, Camp New Amsterdam, The Netherlands, 1978-81; from chief staff comm. and applications to sr. instr. Air Command and Staff Coll., Maxwell AFB, Ala., 1982-85; comdr. 302d Tactical Missile Squadron, Comiso AS, Italy, 1986-87; dep. comdr. resource mgmt. 341st Strategic Missile Wing, Malmstrom AFB, Mont., 1987-89, 40th Air Div., Malmstrom AFB, 1989-90; dep. chief of staff pers. Strategic Missile Ctr., Vandenberg AFB, Calif., 1990-91; community liaison Western Space and Missile Ctr., Vandenberg AFB, 1991-92; account executive Heritage Corp., Sherwood, Ark., 1992—. Composer numerous poems and songs. Mem. Air Force Assn (coun. mem. Goddard chpt. 1991-93), Industry Edn. Coun. Calif. (bd. dirs. 1991-92), Santa Maria C. of C. (bd. dirs. 1990-92), Solvang C. of C. (bd. dirs. 1990-92). Roman Catholic.

TAUB, ABRAHAM HASKEL, mathematician; b. Chgo., Feb. 1, 1911; s. Joseph Haskell and Mary (Sherman) T.; m. Cecilia Vaslow, Dec. 26, 1933; children: Mara, Nadine, Haskell Joseph. B.S., U. Chgo., 1931; Ph.D., Princeton U., 1935. Asst. Inst. Advanced Study, Princeton, 1935-36; from instr. to prof. U. Wash., 1936-48; research prof. applied math. U. Ill. at Urbana, 1948-64, head digital computer lab., 1961-64; prof. math. U. Calif., Berkeley, 1964-78, prof. emeritus, 1978—; dir. computer center, 1964-68; mem. Inst. Advanced Study, 1940-41, 47-48, 62-63; vis. prof. Coll. de France, Paris, 1967, 75, 76; mem. theoretical physicist div. 2 Nat. Def. Research Com., 1942-45; mem. adv. panel applied math. Nat. Bur. Standards, 1951-60. Editor: Collected Works of John von Neumann, 1961-63, (with S. Fernbach) Computers and Their Role in the Physical Sciences, 1971, Studies in Applied Mathematics, 1972; editorial bd.: Communications in Mathematical Physics, 1965-74. Recipient Pres.'s Cert. of Merit, 1946, medal City of Lille, France, 1969, Berkeley citation, 1978; Guggenheim fellow 1947-48, 58. Fellow Am. Acad. Arts and Scis., AAAS (v.p. sect. A 1968-69), Am. Phys. Soc.; mem. Soc. Indsl. and Applied Math. (past trustee), Am. Math. Soc. (past trustee), Math. Assn. Am. Home: 1526 Arch St Berkeley CA 94708-1850

TAUBE, HENRY, chemistry educator; b. Sask., Can., Nov. 30, 1915; came to U.S., 1937, naturalized, 1942; s. Samuel and Albertina (Tiledetski) T.; m. Mary Alice Wesche, Nov. 27, 1952; children: Linda, Marianna, Heinrich, Karl. B.S., U. Sask., 1935, M.S., 1937, LL.D., 1973; Ph.D., U. Calif., 1940; Ph.D. (hon.), Hebrew U. of Jerusalem, 1979; D.Sc. (hon.), U. Chgo., 1983, Poly. Inst., N.Y., 1984, SUNY, 1985, U. Guelph, 1987; D.Sc. honoris causa, Seton Hall U., 1988; Lajos Kossuth U. of Debrecen, Hungary, 1988; DSc, Northwestern U., 1990, Northwestern U., 1991. Instr. U. Calif., 1940-41; instr., asst. prof. Cornell U., 1941-46; faculty U. Chgo., 1946-62, prof., 1952-62, chmn. dept. chemistry, 1955-59; prof. chemistry Stanford U., 1962—, Marguerite Blake Wilbur prof., 1976, chmn. dept., 1971-74; Baker lectr. Cornell U., 1965. Hon. mem. Hungarian Acad., Scis., 1988. Recipient Harrison Howe award, 1961; Chandler medal Columbia U., 1964; F.P. Dwyer medal U. N.S.W., Australia, 1973; Nat. medal of Sci., 1976, 77; Allied Chem. award for Excellence in Grad. Teaching and Innovative Sci., 1979; Nobel Prize in Chemistry, 1983; Bailar medal U. Ill., 1983; Robert A. Welch Found. Award in chemistry, 1983; Disting. Achievement award Internat. Precious Metals Inst., 1986; Guggenheim fellow, 1949, 55. Fellow Royal Soc. Chemistry (hon.), Indian Chem. Soc. (hon.); mem. NAS (award in chem. scis. 1983), Am. Acad. Arts and Scis., Am. Chem. Soc. (Kirkwood award New Haven sect. 1965, award for nuclear applications in chemistry 1955, Nichols medal N.Y. sect. 1971, Willard Gibbs medal Chgo. sect. 1971, Disting. Svc. in Advancement Inorganic Chemistry award 1967, T.W. Richards medal NE sect. 1980, Monsanto Co. award in inorganic chemistry 1981, Linus Pauling award Puget Sound sect. 1981, Priestley medal 1985, Oesper award Cin. sect. 1986, G.M. Kosolapoff award Auburn sect. 1990),

Royal Physiographical Soc. of Lund (fgn. mem.), Am. Philos. Soc., Finnish Acad. Sci. and Letters, Royal Danish Acad. Scis. and Letters, Coll. Chemists of Catalonia and Beleares (hon.), Can. Soc. Chemistry (hon.), Hungarian Acad. Scis. (hon. mem.), Royal Soc. (fgn. mem.), Brazilian Acad. Scis. (corr.), Engring. Acad. Japan (fgn. assoc.), Australian Acad. Scis. (corr.), Chem. Soc. Japan (hon. mem. 1993), Phi Beta Kappa, Sigma Xi, Phi Lambda Upsilon (hon.). Office: Stanford U Dept Chemistry Stanford CA 94305

TAUCK, DAVID LAWRENCE, biology educator; b. Dearborn, Mich., June 7, 1956; s. William Howard and Helen Jean (Ballard) T. AB, Middlebury (Vt.) Coll., 1977; PhD, Duke U., 1983. Postdoctoral fellow Stanford (Calif.) U., 1983-85, Harvard U.-Children's Hosp., Boston, 1985-87; asst., then assoc. prof. Santa Clara (Calif.) U., 1987—; ad hoc reviewer Benjamin Cummings Pub. Co., Redwood City, Calif., 1991—; reviewer NSF Aviation, Space and Environmental Medicine. Contbr. articles to profl. jours. Recipient Nat. Rsch. Svc. award Pub. Health Svc., 1978, 85; Pilot Rsch. grantee Alzheimer's Assn., 1990. Mem. AAAS, Soc. of Neurosci., N.Y. Acad. Sci., Internat. Brain Rsch. Orgn., Phi Beta Kappa. (pres. Pi of Calif.). Office: Santa Clara U Biology Dept Santa Clara CA 95053

TAUER, PAUL E., mayor, educator; b. 1935; m. Kate Tauer, 1956; 8 children. BA in Historyand Edn., Regis Coll.; MA in Edn. Adminstrn., U. No. Colo. Tchr. Denver Pub. Schs., 1961-92; ret., 1992. Mayor City of Aurora, Colo., 1987—, mem. Aurora City Coun., 1979-1987; mem. Adams County Coordinating Com., Gov.'s Met. Transp. Roundtable; active Aurora airport coms. Mem. Noise. Office: Office of Mayor 1470 S Havana St Aurora CO 80012-4015

TAUFEN, PAUL MICHAEL, geochemist; b. West Chester, Pa., Nov. 3, 1952; s. Harvey James and Helen Ann (Krznofski) T.; m. Glenda Sue Gabbert, Oct. 8, 1977; children: Amber Simone, Arthur Benhamin, Justin James. BS in Chemistry, Georgetown U., 1974; MSc in Geochemistry, Colo. Sch. Mines, 1976. From geochemist to mgr. geochemistry Texasgulf Inc., Golden, Colo., 1977-83; chief geochemist British Petroleum Minerals, Rio de Janeiro, Brazil, 1983-87; sr. geochemist Western Mining Corp., Rio de Janeiro, 1987-89; chief geochemist Western Mining Corp.-Am. Bus. Group, Lakewood, Colo., 1991—; chmn. gen. program 13th Internat. Geochem. Exploration Symposium. Editor symposium procs.; patentee in field; contbr. articles to profl. jours. Bd. dirs. Escola Americana, Rio de Janeiro, 1987-89, pres. bd. dirs., 1989. Fellow Assn. Exploration Geochemists (coun. mem. 1987—); mem. Am. Inst. Mining Engrs., Soc. Econ. Geologists, Computer Oriented Geologists Soc. Office: Western Mining Corp 141 Union Blvd Ste 475 Lakewood CO 80228

TAUNTON, HAROLD DEAN, naval officer; b. Bennetsville, S.C., Sept. 29, 1953; s. Harold Dean Sr. and Delma Dolores (Clark) T.; m. Katherine Ann Hesse, Dec. 3, 1983; 1 child, Sandra Nicole. BSEE, N.C. State U., 1975; MSEE, Kans. U., 1981. Registered profl. engr., Nev.; lic. 1st class comml. radio telephone. Commd. ensign USN, 1975, advanced through grades to comdr., 1992; activity civil engr. Navy Pub. Works Ctr., Norfolk, Va., 1975-76; asst. resident officer in charge of constrn. Naval Air Sta. Oceana, Virginia Beach, Va., 1978-80; co. comdr. Amphibious Constrn. Bat. II, Little Creek, Va., 1981-84; pub. works officer Marine Corps Air Sta., Iwakuni, Japan, 1984-87; test group engr. Def. Nuclear Agy, Mercury, Nev., 1987-89; dir. pub. works mgmt. div. Naval Sch., Civil Engr. Corps Officer, Port Hueneme, Calif., 1989-92; fin. mgmt. officer, base ops. support Office of the Navy Contr., Washington, 1992—; mem. Child Devel. Coun., Port Hueneme, 1991-92. Author/editor: Guide to Public Works Management, 1991. Mem. IEEE, Am. Radio Relay League, Soc. of Am. Mil. Engrs., Am. Modelers Assn., Eta Kappa Nu. Republican. Office: Naval Sch Civil Engring Corps Officer Port Hueneme CA 93043

TAUSCHEK, TERRENCE ALAN, dentist, consultant; b. Cleve., June 29, 1948; s. Max Joseph and Marilyn (Kuhl) T.; m. Debora Jon Farr, June 10, 1972; children: Heather, Megan, Heidi. DDS, Marquette U., 1972. Staff dentist, resident USPHS Hosp., Seattle, 1972-73; staff dentist Alaska Native Med. Ctr., Anchorage, 1973-75; pvt. practice Anchorage, 1975—; mem. staff Surgery Ctr., Inc., 1979—; mem. staff Providence Hosp., 1975—, chmn. dental staff, 1985-86; contract dentist Indian Health Svc., Kokhanok and Pedro Bay, Alaska, 1973-89; cons., expert witness U.S. Govt., State of Alaska, 1979—; mem. Alaska Bd. Dental Examiners, 1987-81, pres., 1990-91, examiner for Western region examining bd., 1988—. Recipient svc. award Alaska Native Med. Ctr., 1975, commendation USPHS, 1986, Alaska State Legis., 1987. Mem. ADA, Am. Assn. Dental Examiners, Alaska Dental Soc. (chmn. peer rev. com. 1979-84), South Dental Dist. Dental Soc. Office: Alaska Dental Assocs 1600 E Tudor Rd Ste 201 Anchorage AK 99507-1090

TAUSIG, MICHAEL ROBERT, college administrator, higher education planning consultant; b. L.A., May 3, 1948; s. Maurice James and Georgia Ann (Bullgreen) T.; m. Cheryl Irvin, Jan. 30, 1972; children: Michael Robert Jr., Matthew Paul. BA in Music, Whittier Coll., 1971; MA, Calif. State U., Sacramento, 1973; postgrad., Nova U., 1987—. Dir. summer music programs Anaheim (Calif.) Arts Dept., 1968-73; tchr. music Borrego Springs (Calif.) High Sch., 1973-75; div. chmn., asst. to v.p. instrn. Napa (Calif.) Valley Coll., 1975-88; v.p. planning and devel. Mt. San Jacinto (Calif.) Coll., 1988-92, 1992—. Author: Fundamentals of Music, 1985. Chmn., pres. Napa County Arts Coun., 1985; chmn. spl. issues San Jacinto Planning Commn., 1990-91; elder Presbyn. Ch., Napa, 1985-87. Mem. Nat. Coun. Rsch. and Planning, Rsch. and Planning Group for Calif., C.C., Kiwanis (bd. dirs. Hemet, Calif. 1990—, pres.-elect 1993—). Republican. Office: Mt San Jacinto Coll 1499 N State St San Jacinto CA 92583-2399

TAUSSIG, ROBERT TRIMBLE, engineering executive; b. St. Louis, Apr. 26, 1938; s. Joseph Bondi and Frances Shackleford (McConnell) T.; m. Judith Ann Pryor, July 13, 1963; 1 child, Emily Barr. BA, Harvard Coll., 1960; MA, Columbia U., 1963, PhD, 1965. Rsch. assoc. Columbia U., N.Y.C., 1965-66, Inst. for Plasma Physics, Nagoya, Japan, 1966-67; lectr. Harvard U., Cambridge, Mass., 1968-69; assoc. prof. Sch. of Engring. Columbia U., 1969-75; v.p. Spectra Tech., Inc., Bellevue, Wash., 1975-90; bus. devel. mgr. Bechtel Rsch. and Devel., San Francisco, 1990-92, mgr. applied physics, 1992—; cons. Allerton Press, N.Y.C., 1974-76, Edison Electric Inst., N.Y.C., 1974-75; bd. dirs. Spectra Tech., Inc., Bellevue. Contbg. author: Efficient Electricity Use, 1976; referee and assoc. editor: Energy jour., 1978. Intern sponsor Seattle (Wash.) Sch. System, 1980-88. Recipient award for Acad. Excellence, Harvard Coll., 1957-58. Mem. AAAS, ASME, AIAA. Democrat. Presbyterian. Office: The Bechtel Corp 50 Beale St San Francisco CA 94105-1813

TAVARES, DENNIS JOSEPH, professional driver; b. Providence, Apr. 12, 1951; s. Daniel Joseph and Mary Constance (Faria) T. BA, Monmouth Coll., 1974; postgrad., U. Denver, 1988. Spl. agt. Met. Life Ins. Co., Cranston, R.I., 1974-79; stock tr. agt. United Bank of Denver, N.A., 1979-81; lift-operator Vail Assocs., Inc., Vail, Colo., 1981-84; account exec. Jones Boys of Colo./Aurora, Aurora, Colo., 1985-86, USA Today, Denver, 1986-87; sr. account exec. TeleMarketing Communications of Denver, 1983-88; driver Edson Express, Inc., Commerce City, Colo., 1987-88; sales cons. ATEO Copier Systems, Inc., Denver, 1989; sr. account exec. DialAmerica Mktg. Inc., Denver, 1989—; sales asst.-cons. DialAmerica Mktg. Inc., Denver, 1989—. Mem. Pro Denver, 1980—. Mem. NRA (charter mem. Golden Eagles), Racquet World Athletic Club, Sigma Phi Epsilon (life mem., alumni rels. bd. 1990—, senate 1971-73, Scholar awards 1970-74, Buchanan award 1973-74). Republican. Office: USTDS 8150 W 48th Ave Wheat Ridge CO 80033

TAVEGGIA, THOMAS CHARLES, educator; b. Oak Lawn, Ill., June 15, 1943; s. Thomas Angelo and Eunice Louise (Harriss) T.; m. Brigitte I. Adams, Jan. 23, 1965; children—Michaela, Francesca. BS, Ill. Inst. Tech., 1965; MA, U. Oreg., 1968, PhD, 1971. Prof., U. Oreg., Eugene, 1970, U. B.C. (Can.), Vancouver, 1970-73, U. Calif.-Irvine, 1973-74, Ill. Inst. Tech., Chgo., 1974-77; mgmt. cons. Towers, Perrin, Forster & Crosby, Chgo., 1977-80; ptnr. Manplan Cons., Chgo., 1980-81; ptnr. Coopers & Lybrand, San Francisco, 1981-86; ptnr. Touche Ross, San Francisco, 1986-88; prof. Calif. Sch. Profl. Psychology, Berkeley, 1989—. NDEA Title IV fellow, 1967-71; U. B.C. faculty research grantee, 1970, 71, 73. Mem. Acad. Mgmt. Soc., Am. Sociol. Assn., Human Resource Mgmt. Soc., Inst. Mgmt. Cons. Presbyterian. Author: (with R. Dubin and R. Arends) From Family and School To Work, 1967; (with Dubin) The Teaching-Learning Paradox: A Comparative Analysis of College Teaching Methods, 1968; (with Dubin and R.A. Hedley) The Medium May Be Related to the Message: College Instruction by TV, 1969; contbr. numerous articles to profl. jours. Home: 2188 Lariat Ln Walnut Creek CA 94596-6515 Office: Calif Sch Profl Psychology 1005 Atlantic Ave Alameda CA 94501-1148

TAVENNER, FRANK LEE, hydropower company executive, consultant; b. Deer Lodge, Mont., Aug. 12, 1948; s. Don Williams and Mary Ellen (Bielenberg) T.; m. Adele Patricia Furby, July 8, 1978. Student, Harvard U., 1966-68; BA in Comm., Antioch Coll., 1971. Co-dir. Granite County Alliance, Maxville, Mont., 1982; pres. Mont. Small Hydro Assn., Hall, 1982-83; gen. ptnr. Boulder Hydro Ltd. Partnership, Hall, 1983—; cons., Missoula, 1989—; PSC rep. Mont. Small Hydro Assn., Missoula, 1989—. Home and Office: 413 Eddy Apt 2 Missoula MT 59801

TAVERNA, RODNEY ELWARD, retired marine corps officer, marketing company executive; b. Springfield, Ill., Aug. 8, 1947; s. Jerome Thomas and Virginia (Holcomb) T.; m. Cheryl Ann Walters, Sept. 4, 1968 (div. 1983); children: Lara Lyn, Melinda Marie, Ryan Thomas; m. Caroline Whiffen, Apr. 1985. BA, U. Mo., 1969; MBA in Fin., Nat. U., 1988. Commd. 2d lt., supply officer USMC, 1969, advanced through grades to maj., 1979; supply officer Central Svcs. Agy., Danang, Vietnam, 1970-71, Marine Air Control Squadron, Futenma, Okinawa, 1977-78; logistics officer Hdqrs. Marine Corps Recruit Depot, Paris Island, S.C., 1972-75; support officer Marine Barracks, Treasure Island, San Francisco, 1975-77; regimental supply officer 1st Marine Div., Camp Pendleton, Calif., 1978-79; brigade supply officer 1st Marine Brigade, Kaneohe Bay, Hawaii, 1980-82; exec. officer 1st Maintenance Bn., Camp Pendleton, 1982-85; asst div. supply officer 1st Marine Div., 1985-88; pres., fin. svcs. specialist R.E. Taverna, Inc., 1991—; owner, mgr. Opportunities Unltd., Oceanside, Calif., 1985—; cons. Incentive Leasing Corp., San Diego, 1985-86, The Profit Ctr., Santa Ana, Calif., 1991; founding mgr. Meditrend Internat., San Diego, 1987-88; founding dir. Am. 3-D Corp., Henderson, Nev., 1989-90; cons. CYI Corp., Cathedral City, Calif., 1990-91. Republican. Home and Office: 1632 Avenida Andante Oceanside CA 92057

TAXER, ERIC JOHN, civil engineer; b. Portland, Oreg., June 7, 1963; s. Milton and Mildred Ida (Fahlen) T. BS, Oreg. State U., 1986. Registered profl. engr., Calif. Assoc. water resource control engr. Calif. Regional Water Quality Control Bd., South Lake Tahoe, Calif., 1987—. Treas. Lake Tahoe Community Orch., South Lake Tahoe, 1990-91; mem. Lake Tahoe AIDS Task Force, South Lake Tahoe, 1992, pres., 1993. Mem. ASCE, Am. Soc. Surface Mining and Reclamation (ecological restoration del. to Russia and Estonia 1992). Republican. Unitarian. Office: Calif Regional Water Qual Control Bd 2092 Lake Tahoe Blvd South Lake Tahoe CA 96150

TAYLOR, B. ELDON, human potential researcher; b. Anchorage, Utah, Jan. 27, 1945; s. Blaine Eldon and Helen Gertrude (George) T.; m. Ravinder Kaur Sadana, June 17, 1990; children: Angela, Eric, Cassandra, Hillarie, Preston. Student, Weber State Coll., Ogden, Utah, 1971-74; BS, MS, DD, U. Metaphysics, L.A., PhD in Pastoral Psychology, 1986; PhD in Clin. Psychology, St. John's U., Springfield, La., 1990; HHD (hon.), Sem. Coll., 1987; PhD in Pastoral Psychology (hon.), World U. Roundtable, Benson, Ariz., 1988. Sales mgr. Sears, Roebuck & Co., Salt Lake City, 1964-76; v.p. mktg. Dictograph Security, Salt Lake City, 1976-77; dir. Bulwark, Salt Lake City, 1977-84; pres., dir. Progressive Awareness Rsch., Big Bear City, Calif., 1984—; bd. dirs. World U. Roundtable, Benson, Ariz.; co-dir. Creative Living Inst., 1993; mem. adj. faculty St. John's U., 1989—. Author: Subliminal Communication, 1986, Subliminal Learning, 1988, Simple Things and Simple Thoughts, 1989, Wellness: Just a State of Mind, 1993, also others; contbr. numerous articles and poetry to various publs.; author over 300 audio cassettes on self-improvement; patentee whole brain info. audio processor. Spiritual advisor Intermountain Hospice Ctr., Salt Lake City, 1987-88; counselor Utah State Prison, Draper, 1986-88; sports motivation trainer U.S. Judo Team, Colorado Springs, Colo., 1989—. Named Ky. Col., State of Ky., 1984; recipient Golden Poet award Am. Poetry Soc., 1985-87. Fellow Nat. Assn. Clergy Hypnotherapists; mem. Am. Psychol. Practitioners Assn., Am. Law Enforcement Officers Assn., Internat. Assn. for Forensic Hypnosis, Am. Counselors Soc., Internat. Soc. Stress Analysts, Am. Assn. Religious Counselors. Home: PO Box 691 Big Bear City CA 92314 Office: Progressive Awarenesss Rsch 816 W Big Bear Blvd Big Bear City CA 92314

TAYLOR, BARRY LLEWELLYN, microbiologist, educator; b. Sydney, Australia, May 7, 1937; came to U.S., 1967; s. Fredrick Llewelyn and Vera Lavina (Clarke) T.; m. Desmyrna Ruth Tolhurst, Jan. 4, 1961; children: Lyndon, Nerida, Darrin. BA, Avondale Coll., Cooranbong, New South Wales, 1959; BSc with honors, U. New South Wales, Sydney, 1966; PhD, Case Western Res. U., 1973; postgrad., U. Calif., Berkeley, 1973-75. Vis. postdoctoral fellow Australian Nat. U., Canberra, 1975-76; asst. prof. biochemistry Loma Linda (Calif.) U., 1976-78, assoc. prof. biochemistry, 1978-83, prof. biochemistry, 1983—, prof., chmn. dept. microbiology, 1988—, interim dir. Ctr. for Molecular Biology, 1989—. Contbr. articles to profl. publs. Rsch. grantee Am. Heart Assn., 1978-85, NIH, 1981—. Mem. Am. Soc. Microbiology, Am. Soc. Biochemistry and Molecular Biology. Office: Loma Linda U Dept Microbiology Loma Linda CA 92350

TAYLOR, BRIAN DAVID, art and photography educator, artist; b. Tucson, June 14, 1954; s. Porter C. and Irene Francis (Munaretto) T.; m. Patrice Katherine Garrett, July 28, 1984. BA cum laude, U. Calif., San Diego, 1975; MA, Stanford U., 1976; MFA, U. N.Mex., 1979. Hon. teaching fellow Stanford U., 1976; lectr. various univs., workshops; coord. photography program San Jose State U. One-man exhibits include San Jose Mus. Art, 1982, Susan Spiritus Gallery, Newport Beach, Calif., 1983, Ithaca (N.Y.) Coll., 1983, Houston Ctr. Photography, 1984, Nagase Photo Salon, Tokyo, Japan, 1985, Etherton Gallery, Tucson, U. Oreg. Art Mus., Eugene, 1986, James Madison U., Harrisonburg, Va., 1987, Monterey (Calif.) Peninsula Mus. Art, Northlight Gallery, Ariz. State U., Tempe, 1989; represented in permanent collections Bibliotheque Nationale, Paris, Victoria and Albert Mus., London, San Francisco Mus. Modern Art, Australian Photographic Soc., Victoria. Recipient Fellowship award Western Regional Nat. Endowment for the Arts, 1991; resident artist's grantee Polaroid Corp., 1989. Mem. AAUP, Soc. for Photog. Edn., Coll. Art Assn., Phi Kappa Phi, Phi Delta Kappa. Republican. Roman Catholic.

TAYLOR, DOUGLAS STERLING, civil engineer; b. Victoria, Tex., June 9, 1956; s. Fred Sturdevant III and Mary Elizabeth (Short) T.; m. Patricia Ann Betts, May 10, 1980; children: Jennifer, Stephanie, Kelly, Ryan. BSCE, Syracuse U., 1978. Registered profl. engr., Calif., Alaska. Project mgr. Alaska Dist. C.E., Anchorage, 1982-89; v.p. Twining Labs., Inc., Fresno, Calif., 1989—. Elder Abbott Loop Christian Ctr., Anchorage, 1982-89, Clovis Christian Ctr., Fresno, 1992—. 1st lt. USAF, 1978-82. Mem. ASCE, NSPE, Calif. Soc. Profl. Engrs., Constrn. Specifications Inst., Internat. Conf. Bldg. Ofcls. Republican. Office: Twining Labs Inc 2527 Fresno St Fresno CA 93721

TAYLOR, EDDIE MILTON, operations manager, country music historian; b. Rutherford, N.C., Jan. 2, 1945; s. Thurman and Mary (Russell) T. Textiles purchasing mgmt. Deering-Milliken, Columbus, N.C., 1963-74; purchasing svc. Gan-ED, Inc., Columbus, N.C., 1975-80; mgr. Kangaroo Nev. Co., Carson City, Nev., 1980-90, v.p., 1990—. Democrat. Baptist. Home: 170 Koontz Ln Trlr 136 Carson City NV 89701-5511 Office: Kangaroo Nevada Co 1012 Mallory Way Carson City NV 89701-5309

TAYLOR, EDNA JANE, employment program counselor; b. Flint, Mich., May 16, 1934; d. Leonard Lee and Wynona Ruth (Davis) Harvey; children: Wynona Jane MacDonald, Cynthia Lee Zellmer. BS, No. Ariz. U., 1963; MEd, U. Ariz., 1967. Tchr. high sch. Sunnyside Sch. Dist., Tucson, 1963-68; employment program counselor employment devel. dept. State of Calif., Canoga Park, 1968—. Mem. adv. coun. Van Nuys Community Adult Sch., Calif., 1983-93, steering com., 1989-91, leadership coun., 1991-92; mem. adv. coun. Pierce Community Coll., Woodland Hills, Calif., 1979-81; first aid instr., recreational leader ARC. Mem. NAFE, Internat. Assn. of Pers. in Employment Security, Calif. Employment Counselors Assn. (state treas. 1978-79, state sec. 1980), Delta Psi Kappa (life). Office: State of Calif Employment Devel Dept 21010 Vanowen St Canoga Park CA 91303-2803

TAYLOR, GARY L., federal judge; b. 1938. AB, UCLA, 1960, JD, 1963. Assoc. Wenke, Taylor, Evans & Ikola, 1986-90; judge Orange County Superior Ct., 1986-90, U.S. Dist. Ct. (ctrl. dist.) Calif., Santa Ana, 1990—. With U.S. Army, 1964-66. Mem. Am. Coll. Trial Lawyers, State Bar Calif., Orange County Bar Assn. (bd. dirs. 1980-82, founder, chmn. bus. litigation com., Disting. Svc. award 1983), Calif. Judges Assn. Office: US District Courts Rm 801 715 W SA Blvd Los Angeles CA 90012*

TAYLOR, GEORGE ALLEN, advertising agency executive; b. Lake City, Iowa, Oct. 26, 1906; s. Bertrand Franklin and Mabel (Minard) T.; m. Regina Helen Wickland, July 3, 1938 (div. 1956). PhB in Fine Arts, Northwestern U., 1947, MEd, 1951, postgrad., 1951-54; art edn. diploma, U. No. Iowa, 1926. Art supr. pub. schs. Indianola, Iowa, 1926-29; instr. art Simpson Coll., Indianola, 1926-29; designer Modern Art Studios, Chgo., 1929-30; display designer W.J. Rankin Corp., Chgo., 1930-35; creative dir. Arthur Meyerhoff Assocs., Inc., Milw., 1935-38; br. mgr. Arthur Meyerhoff Assocs., Inc., L.A., 1938-42; account exec. Arthur Meyerhoff Assocs., Inc., Chgo., 1942-59, account supr., 1959-61, v.p. adminstrn., 1961-65, vice chmn., 1965-80; pres. GATA Ltd.; lectr. semantics Ill. Inst. Tech., Chgo., 1947-50, Northwestern U. Sch. Commerce, 1948. Lyricist popular songs. Reader Recs. for Blind, Inc., 1956—, CRIS Radio, 1981-85; mem. Chgo. Architecture Found., Landmarks Preservation Coun. Ill. Recipient 1st place awards in copy and layout L.A. Advt. Club, 1940. Mem. AAAS, Friends of Downtown, Art Inst. Chgo. Home (summer): 1212 N Lake Shore Dr Apt 29A-S Chicago IL 60610 Home (winter): 4767 Ocean Bldv Apt 201 San Diego CA 92109

TAYLOR, GEORGE FREDERICK, newspaper publisher, editor; b. Portland, Oreg., Feb. 28, 1928; s. George Noble and Ida Louise (Dixon) T.; m. Georgia Bray, Oct. 6, 1951; children—Amelia Ruth, Ross Noble. B.S., U. Oreg., 1950. Reporter Astoria (Oreg.) Budget, 1950-52, Portland Oregonian, 1952-54; copy reader Wall St. Jour., 1955-57, reporter, 1957-59, Detroit Bur. chief, 1959-64, Washington corr., 1964-68; asst. mng. editor Wall St. Jour., San Francisco, 1968-69; mng. editor Wall St. Jour., N.Y.C., 1970-77, exec. editor, 1977-86; pub. North Bend (Oreg.) News, 1986—, Prime Time, 1987—, Coquille Valley Sentinel, 1989—. Served to lt. USAF, 1955-57. Office: 1 Barton's Alley Coquille OR 97423

TAYLOR, IRVING, mechanical engineer, consultant; b. Schenectady, N.Y., Oct. 25, 1912; s. John Bellamy and Marcia Estabrook (Jones) T.; m. Shirley Ann Milker, Dec. 22, 1943; children: Bronwen D., Marcia L., John I., Jerome E. BME, Cornell U., 1934. Registered profl. engr., N.Y., Mass., Calif. Test engr. Gen. Electric Co., Lynn, Mass., 1934-37; asst. mech. engr. M.W. Kellogg Co., N.Y.C., 1937-39; sect. head engring. dept. The Lummus Co., N.Y.C., 1939-57; research engr. Gilbert and Barker, West Springfield, Mass., 1957-58, Marquardt Corp., Ogden, Utah, 1958-60, Bechtel, Inc., San Francisco, 1960-77; cons. engr. Berkeley, Calif., 1977-91; adj. prof. Columbia U., 1950-60, NYU, 1950-60. Contbr. articles to profl. jours. Fellow ASME (life, Henry R. worthington medal 1990); mem. Pacific Energy Assn., Soaring Soc. Am. (life), Sigma Xi (assoc.). Unitarian. Home: 300 Deer Valley Rd Apt 2P San Rafael CA 94903-5514

TAYLOR, J. THOMAS, III, financial executive; b. Flagstaff, Ariz., Dec. 12, 1947; s. John Thomas and Helen Corene (Nieman) T.; m. Janet Elaine Clough, Aug. 8, 1970; children—Mary Caroline, John Thomas, Jesse Charles. B.S., Miss. Valley Coll., 1970. C.L.U.; cert. fin. planner. Sales rep. Bus. Men's Assurance Co., Kansas City, Mo., 1970-73; owner, planner Taylor Fin. Planners, Camp Verde, Ariz., 1973—; instr. Yavapai Community Coll., Prescott, Ariz., 1984—; cons. Ariz. Edn. Assn., 1981-82, Okla. Edn. Assn., N.Mex. Edn. Assn., 1982; founding dir. Bank of Verde Valley; pres. Verde Valley Bancorp. Author Money Talk weekly newspaper column, fin. planning workbook. Pres. Yavapai Assn. Retarded Citizens, Cottonwood, Ariz., 1983-85; bd. dirs. Marcus J. Lawrence Meml. Hosp. Paul Harris fellow, Rotary Internat., 1984. Mem. Internat. Assn. Fin. Planning (cert.), Nat. Assn. Securities Dealers, Integrated Resources Equity Corp., Verde Valley C. of C., Camp Verde C. of C. (pres. 1983—). Republican. Baptist. Lodge: Rotary. Home: 137 Silver Bugle Dr Camp Verde AZ 86322 Office: PO Box 1350 31 Lane St Camp Verde AZ 86322

TAYLOR, JAMES BARTON, petroleum company executive; b. Harrisburg, Pa., Apr. 12, 1938; s. James B. and Jean Taylor; m. Sarah Williams Taylor; children: Dale, Karen. BSc in Geology, U. Redlands, 1961; MSc in Geology, UCLA, 1963. Geologist in Alaska, Calif. and S.Am., Texaco, 1963-68; various positions Occidental Petroleum Corp., 1968-90, v.p. Colombian ops., v.p. L.Am. ops.; exec. v.p. Ea. Hemisphere ops.; COO, exec. v.p. Can. Occidental Petroleum Ltd., Calgary, Alta., 1990—. Chmn. Alta. regional coun. Nature Conservancy Can., Calgary, 1992-93. Mem. Am. Assn. Petroleum Geologists, Nature Conservancy U.S.A. Office: Can Occidental Petroleum Ltd, 635 8th Ave SW Ste 1500, Calgary, AB Canada T2P 3Z1

TAYLOR, JAMES GAVIN, mechanical engineer; b. Chgo., Nov. 19, 1932; s. William James Taylor and Ethel (Adele) Robb; m. Helen Lucille Rowe, Feb. 11, 1955; children: Julianne Marie, Gavin Lee. Student, U. Wash., 1954-59. Registered profl. engr., Wash. Design engr. Black Clawson, Everett, Wash., 1960-63, asst. chief engr., 1970-73; asst. plant engr. Weyerhaeuser Co., Everett, 1963-67; project mgr. Weyerhaeuser Co., Tacoma, 1968-70; engring. mgr. Stetson-Ross, Seattle, 1973-76; project engr. Western Gear, Everett, 1976-79; project mgr. Scott Paper Co., Everett, 1979—. Patentee in field. Mem. Planning Commn., Snohomish County, Wash., 1982-92. With USN, 1950-53. Republican. Lutheran. Home: 15020 123d Ave SE Snohomish WA 98290-6810 Office: Scott Paper Co 2600 Federal Ave Everett WA 98201-3490

TAYLOR, JAMES WALTER, marketing educator; b. St. Cloud, Minn., Feb. 15, 1933; s. James T. and Nina C. Taylor; m. Joanne Syktte, Feb. 3, 1956; children: Theodore James, Samuel Bennett, Christopher John. BBA, U. Minn., 1957; MBA, NYU, 1960; DBA, U. So. Calif., 1975. Mgr. research div. Atlantic Refining, Phila., 1960-65; dir. new product devel. Hunt-Wesson Foods, Fullerton, Calif., 1965-72; prof. mktg. Calif. State U., Fullerton, 1972—; cons. Smithkline Beecham Corp., Tokyo, Govt. of Portugal, Lisbon, Sealand Svcs., Seattle, KF Fackhandel, Stockholm. Author: Profitable New Product Strategies, 1984, How To Create A Winning Business Plan, 1986, Competitive Marketing Strategies, 1986, The 101 Best Performing Companies In America, 1987, How to Write A Successful Advertising Plan, 1988, The Complete Manual for Developing Winning Strategic Plans, 1988, Every Manager's Survival Guide, 1989, Developing Winning Strategic Plans, 1990, How to Develop Successful Advertising Plans, 1993. Fulbright scholar Ministry of Industry, Lisbon, Portugal, 1986-87, U. We. Sydney, Australia, 1989-90; recipient Merit award Calif. State U., 1986-90. Mem. The Planning Forum, Am. Mktg. Assn., Strategic Mgmt. Assn., Assn. for Consumer Rsch., Acad. Mktg. Sci. Home: 3190 Mountain View Dr Laguna Beach CA 92651-2056 Office: Calif State U Dept of Mktg Nutwood at State College Fullerton CA 92634

TAYLOR, JOHN FELTON, II (JACK TAYLOR), insurance company executive; b. San Francisco, Feb. 10, 1925; s. John Felton Sr. and Mary Madeline (Sicocan) T.; m. Wilburta Estelle Prather, Oct. 23, 1948; children: Stephanie, Sharon, Suzanne, Stacie, John III, Saundra, Shelby. BA, San Jose State U., 1950. Dist. mgr. Farmers Ins. Group Cos., San Jose, Calif., 1952—. Mem. bd. fellows U.Santa Clara. 1st lt. USAAF, 1943-46, PTO. Mem. Saratoga Men's Club (Calif.), Desert Island Country Club, Spyglass Hill Country Club, Monterey Peninsula Country Club (Pebble Beach, Calif.), PGA West Country Club (LaQuinta, Calif.). Republican. Roman Catholic. Home: 13177 Ten Oak Ct Saratoga CA 95070-4420 Office: Farmers Ins Group Cos 1471 Saratoga Ave San Jose CA 95129

TAYLOR, JOHN FREDERICK, clinical psychologist; b. Akron, Ohio, Dec. 13, 1944; s. John Idris and Winnifred Jane (Fletcher) T.; m. Linda Jean Bolinger, Mar. 20, 1965; children: Tamara, Brian, Dana, Beth, Sharon, John, Amy, Michael. BS in Psychology, Ohio State U., 1966; MA in Psychology, Kent State U., 1969, PhD in Clin. Psychology, 1970. Psychologist Chattanooga Psychiat. Clinic, 1970-71; instr. U. Tenn., Chattanooga, 1971;

psychologist Marion County Mental Health Program, Salem, Oreg., 1971-76; instr. Chemeketa Community Coll., Salem, 1974-76, Linn-Benton Community Coll., Lebanon, Oreg., 1976-77; pvt. practice psychology Salem, 1976—; dir. Seminars Unltd. Northwest (SUN) seminars, Salem, 1985—. Author: Hyperactive Child and the Family, 1980, Person to Person: Awareness Techniques, 1984, Special Diets and Kids (with others), 1987, Diagnostic Interviewing of MIsbehaving Child, 1988, Motivating the Uncooperative Student, 1990, The Attention Deficit Hyperactive Student at School, 1990, Helping Your Hyperactive Child, 1990, Anger Control Training for Children and Teens, 1991; contbr. articles to various jours. Chair family life steering com. Northwest YMCA, Salem, 1974-75. Capt. U.S. Army, 1970. Recipient vol. award YMCA, Salem, 1974, 75, 76. Mem. APA, Assn. for Childhood Edn. Internat., Mental Health Assn. Oreg. (Communications award 1974). Republican. Office: 1095 25th St SE Ste 107 Salem OR 97301-5050

TAYLOR, JOHN LOCKHART, city official; b. N.Y.C., Nov. 4, 1927; s. Floyd and Marian (Lockhart) T.; m. Barbara Becker, July 19, 1952; children: Catherine, Robert, William, Susan. A.B., Middlebury Coll., 1952; M.Govtl. Adminstrn., U. Pa., 1956. Reporter Providence Jour.-Bull., 1952-54; adminstrv. intern City of Xenia, Ohio, 1955-56; mcpl. mgr. Borough of Narberth, Pa., 1956-60, Twp. of Lakewood, N.J., 1960-64; asst. city mgr. Fresno, Calif., 1964-65; city mgr., 1965-68, Kansas City, Mo., 1968-74, Berkeley, Calif., 1974-76; lectr. U. Pa., 1957-58, Golden Gate U., 1977; sr. urban mgmt. specialist Stanford Research Inst., 1977-80; dir. Internat. Devel. Center, 1980-82; clk. of bd. suprs. City of San Francisco, 1982—; pres. Calif. Clks. Bd. Suprs. Assn., 1988-89. Served with USN, 1945-48. Mem. Internat. City Mgrs. Assn., Am. Soc. Pub. Adminstrn., Mcpl. Execs. Assn. (pres. 1991-93). Home: 2133 Stockton St San Francisco CA 94133-2067 Office: 235 City Hall San Francisco CA 94102

TAYLOR, JOHN O'MARA, engineer; b. Birmingham, U.K., Aug. 11, 1953; came to U.S., 1990; s. Dennis O. and Renee (Franklin) T. BSc, U. Aston, Birmingham, 1975; PhD, U. Birmingham, Birmingham, 1983. Registered profl. engr., England. Core metallurgist Rolls Royce & Assocs., Derby, U.K., 1979-80; section mgr. GKN Tech. Ltd., Wolverhampton, U.K., 1980-90; engring. specialist Rohr Inc., Chula Vista, Calif., 1990—. Author (patent application) Crack Detecting Apparatus, 1989. Mem. British Inst. of NDT, Acoustic Emission Working Group. Home: 5290 Vickie Dr San Diego CA 92109-1332

TAYLOR, JOLYNN, art director; b. Milw., Jan. 24, 1948; d. Bernard William and Clarice June (Yakel) Goecks; m. Dennis Michael Holtz, Apr. 23, 1967 (div. Sept. 1972); m. David William Taylor, Feb. 21, 1992. Student, Sch. Art Inst., Chgo., 1972-76, Northwestern U., 1972-76; AA, City Coll. San Francisco, 1978. Prodn. mgr. Folkwear, Inc., San Rafael, Calif., 1979-84; art dir. Craftways, Corp., Richmond, Calif., 1984—. Office: Craftways 4118 Lakeside Dr Richmond CA 94806

TAYLOR, JUDITH ANN, sales executive; b. Sheridan, Wyo., July 9, 1944; d. Milo G. and Eleanor M. (Wood) Rinker; m. George I. Taylor, Sept. 15, 1962; children: Monte G., Bret A. Fashion dept. mgr. Montgomery Ward, Sheridan, 1968-73; pers. mgr., asst. mgr. Dan's Ranchwear, Sheridan, 1973-80; sales/prodn. coord. KWYO Radio, Sheridan, 1981-83; sales mgr., promotions coord. KROE Radio, Sheridan, 1984—; notary pub. State of Wyo., 1985—. Sec.-treas. Sheridan County Centennial Com., 1986-89; local sec.-treas. Wyo. Centennial Com., Sheridan, 1986-90; exec. dir. Sheridan-Wyo. Rodeo Bd., 1983—; bd. dirs. Sheridan County Fair Bd., 1991—, "Christmas in April" Sheridan County, 1992—; mem. WJTP Coun., Cheyenne, 1990-92; active Tutor-Literacy Vols. of Am.; Mrs. Santa Claus for local groups. Mem. Wyo. Assn. Broadcasters, S.C. C. of C. (dir. 1988—, pres. 1989-91), UMWA Aux. (pres. 1982-89), Kiwanis (v.p. 1992—). Democrat. Christian Ch. Home: 98 Decker Rd Sheridan WY 82801 Office: KROE AM PO Box 5086 Sheridan WY 82801-1386

TAYLOR, KENDRICK JAY, microbiologist; b. Manhattan, Mont., Mar. 17, 1914; s. William Henry and Rose (Carney) T.; BS, Mont. State U., 1938; postgrad. (fellow) U. Wash., 1938-41, U. Calif. at Berkeley, 1952, Drama Studio of London, 1985; m. Hazel Marguerite Griffith, July 28, 1945; children: Stanley, Paul, Richard. Rsch. microbiologist Cutter Labs., Berkeley, Calif., 1945-74; microbiologist Berkeley Biologicals, 1975-86. Committeeman Mount Diablo coun. Boy Scouts Am., 1955, dist. vice-chmn., 1960-61, dist. chmn., 1962-65, cubmaster, 1957, scoutmaster, 1966; active Contact Ministries, 1977-80; bd. dirs. Santa Clara Community Players, 1980-84; vol. instr. English as a Second Lang., 1979-80; vol. ARC Blood Ctr., VA Hosp., San Jose; life mem. PTA; census taker, 1980; mem. Berkely Jr. C. of C., 1946-49. Served with AUS, 1941-46, lt. col. Res., ret. Recipient Scout's Wood badge Boy Scouts Am., 1962; recipient Golden Diploma Mont. State U., 1988. Mem. Am. Soc. Microbiology (chmn. local com. 1953, v.p. No. Calif. br. 1963-65, pres. 1965-67), Sons and Daus. Mont. Pioneers, Mont. State Univ. Alumni Assn., Mont. Hist. Soc., Gallatin County Hist. Soc., Ret. Officers' Assn., Headwaters-Heritage Hist. Soc., Am. Legion Post 89, Commonwealth Club Calif., Parent-Tchrs. Assn. Calif. (life). Presbyterian (trustee 1951-53, elder 1954—). Home: 550 S 13th St San Jose CA 95112-2361

TAYLOR, LARRY ARTHUR, computer scientist, programmer analyst; b. Phoenix, Dec. 31, 1951; s. Melvin Robert and Lucille Mary (Cole) T.; m. Mary Alice Slider, Dec. 28, 1976 (div. Apr. 1981); m. Beverly Victoria Serbell, Nov. 17, 1984; children: Margaret Rose, David Wakeman. BA, Ambassador Coll., 1973; MA in History, Calif. State U., 1982; MS in Computer Sci., Calif. State Poly. U., 1988; postgrad., UCLA, 1988—. Sr. computer programmer Ambassador Coll., Worldwide Ch. of God, Pasadena, Calif., 1970-78; sr. programmer/analyst Security Pacific Nat. Bank, Glendale, Calif., 1978-82; sr. programmer/analyst, dir. programmer edn. City Nat. Bank, L.A., 1982-91; instr. Calif. State Poly. U., Pomona, 1988; cons., sr. programmer UCLA Office of Acad. Computing, 1991-92; teaching fellow, rsch. asst. UCLA Computer Sci. Dept., 1993—. Coord., editor Humanist Spl. Interest Group, Calif., 1983-89; dir. humanist ext. Am. Humanist Assn., So. Calif., 1983-92; dir. Humanist Assn. L.A., 1984-88, 90—. Recipient HUMCON Pioneer award Humanist Conf., Highland Springs, Calif., 1992. Mem. IEEE, Assn. for Computing Machinery, Am. Assn. Artificial Intelligence, Mensa (dir. human spl. interest group 1983-89), Phi Alpha Theta. Democrat. Humanist.

TAYLOR, LEE ROGER, JR., English language educator; b. Long Beach, Calif., Apr. 15, 1944; s. Lee Roger and Penny (Woody) T.; m. Gaye Diane Elliott, Aug. 20, 1968; children: Patrick Andrew, Jacqueline Yvonne. AB in English, East Carolina U., 1970, MA in English, 1972. English and reading specialist Beaufort C.C., Washington, N.C., 1973-76; asst. prof. Brevard (N.C.) Coll., 1976-78; assoc. prof. English, Western Wyo. Coll., Rock Springs, 1978—; columnist, film reviewer Casper (Wyo.) Star-Tribune, 1991—. Author: English Grammar Made Difficult, 1975; also articles. Mem. Wyo. Coun. for Humanities, Laramie, 1980-84, Rock Springs Downtown Adv. Com., 1991—. With USAF, 1962-65. Grantee NEH, 1986, NSF, 1991; Fulbright scholar, 1987. Office: Western Wyo Coll 2500 College Dr Rock Springs WY 82901

TAYLOR, LESLIE GEORGE, mining and financial company executive; b. London, Oct. 8, 1922; came to U.S., 1925; s. Charles Henry and Florence Louisa (Renouf) T.; m. Monique S. Schuster, May, 1964 (div. 1974); children: Leslie G. Anthony II, Sandra J. Mira, Linda S. Marshall; m. Wendy Ann Ward, July 4, 1979. BBA, U. Buffalo, 1952. Asst. to pres. Kelsey Co., 1952-60; pres. Aluminum Industries and Glen Alden Co., Cin. and N.Y.C., 1960-63; pres., chmn. bd. dirs. DC Internat. (and European subs.), Denver, 1963-68; prin. Taylor Energy Enterprises, Denver, 1968—, Taylor Mining Enterprises, Denver, 1968—, Leslie G. Taylor and Co., Denver, 1968—; pres. Lucky Break Gold, Inc., Vancouver, B.C., Can., 1992—; cons. Lucky Break Gold Inc., Vancouver, B.C.; bd. dirs., pres. Aberdeen Minerals, Ltd., Vancouver, B.C.; bd. dirs. Amiron Inc., Boulder, Colo.; del. Internat. Astronautical Soc., Stockholm, 1968, London, 1969, Speditur Conv., 1976. Mem. USCG Aux. Mem. Internat. Bus. Brokers Assn., Soc. Automotive Engrs., Denver Country Club, Shriners, Masons, Scottish Rites. Republican. Episcopalian. Office: 5031 S Ulster St Ste 200 Denver CO 80237-2810

TAYLOR, LINDAJEAN THORTON, information systems executive; b. Cambridge, Mass., Apr. 16, 1942; d. Ferdinand and Hazel Irene (Towne) Karamanoukian; m. John Robert Thornton, Jan. 21, 1961; 1 child, John Robert; m. F. Jason Gaskell, Nov. 30, 1978. AA in Bus. Adminstrn., West L.A. Coll., 1976; BS, West Coast U., 1978, MS in Bus. and Info. Scis., 1980. Cert. quality analyst, systems profl. Asst. to chief indsl. engr. Pitts. Plate Glass Co., Boston, 1960-64; corp. sec., gen. mgr. Seaboard Planning Corp., Boston, 1967-67, L.A., 1969-72; prin. Tay-Kara Mgmt., L.A., 1972-73; chief systems adminstrn. Comp-La, L.A., 1973-74; mgr. systems analysis Trans Tech Inc., L.A., 1974-77; mgr. software engring. and tech. audit depts. System Devel. Corp., L.A., 1977-81; v.p. Gaskell and Taylor Engring., Inc., L.A., 1981-86; pres. Taylor and Zeno Systems, Inc., 1986—; mem. faculty, sr. lectr. West Coast U., L.A., 1980—; vis. lectr. sr. seminar Calif. Poly. U., Pomona, 1978, 87-89, 90; del. 11th World Computing Congress, San Francisco, 1989, Internat. Fedn. Info. Processing, del. 12th, Madrid, 1992, speaker security conf. '90, Helsinki, Finland, del., Dublin, Ireland, 1986; leader ednl. exch. del to People's Republic China, 1987; del. to 10th World Computing Congress; keynote speaker Hong Kong Computer Soc., Hong Kong Assn. for Advancement Sci. and Tech., 1987, NEC Inc. Software Engring. Lab., Tokyo, 1987, Tarleton State U., 1992. Appeared in 8 episodes of The New Literacy: An Introduction to Computers, Pub. Broadcasting System; mem. editorial bd.: Data Processing Quality jour. Chmn. bus. and profl. women's com. Calif. Rep. Cen. Com., 1974; mem. White House Com. on Workers Compensation, 1976; mem. fiscal adv. com. Santa Monica Unified Sch. Bd. Edn., 1979-81. Recipient Pub. Svc. award West L.A. C. of C., 1974. Mem. Assn. Women in Computing (pres. 1980-84, v.p. L.A. chpt. 1979-80), Nat. Computer Conf. (vice chmn., program com. 1980, mem. adv. com. 1983), Data Processing Mgmt. Assn. (v.p. South Bay chpt. 1979-80, bd. dirs. L.A. chpt. 1984, chmn. program com., media rels. com. 1984 internat. conf., pres. L.A. chpt. 1992, chmn. internat. conf. 1990, Individual Performance awards), IEEE (software engring. terminology task force 1980), Am. Def. Preparedness Assn. (congl. legis. adv. com. 1991-92), Assn. Systems Mgmt. (sec. local chpt. 1974-75), EDP Auditors Assn., Assn. for Computing Machinery, Women in Mgmt., Nat. Assn. Women Bus. Owners, Internat. Fedn. for Information Processing (delegate security conf. Toronto 1993), Ind. Computer Cons. Assn., Inst. for Cert. of Computer Profls. (cert., bd. dirs., v.p. 1992, 93).

TAYLOR, LOUIS HENRY, laboratory geologist; b. Albion, Pa., Feb. 2, 1944; s. Stanley Mearl and Doris Aleen (Redfoot) T.; m. Mary Jean Soine, Dec. 21, 1971; 1 child, Taito Clayton. BS, Edinboro State Coll., 1965; MA, No. Ariz. U., 1971; MS, U. Ariz., 1977, PhD, 1984. Tchr. NW High Sch., Albion, 1965-71; instr. Cen. Ariz. Coll., Coolidge, Ariz., 1971-74; lab. geologist Texaco Inc., Midland, Tex., 1981-84, Denver, 1984-92; pres. Standard Geol. Svcs., Inc., Englewood, Colo., 1992—. Contbr. articles to profl. jours. Mem. Soc. Econ. Paleontologists and Mineralogists (sec. Permian Basin Sect. 1983), Western Interior Paleontological Soc. (pres. 1988), Am. Assn. Petroleum Geologists, Paleontology Soc., Soc. Vertebrate Paleontology, Rocky Mountain Assn. Geologists. Democrat. Home: 4931 Rowland Ave Littleton CO 80123-6419 Office: Standard Geol Svcs 6920 Jordan Rd Englewood CO 80112

TAYLOR, MARY ELIZABETH, retired dietitian; b. Medina, N.Y., Dec. 10, 1933; d. Glenn Aaron and Viola Hazel (Lansill) Grimes; m. Wilbur Alvin Fredlund, Apr. 12, 1952 (div. Jan. 1980); 1 child, Wilbur Jr.; m. Frederick Herbert Taylor, Mar. 15, 1981; children: Martha Dayton, Jean Grout, Beth Stern, Cindy Hey, Carol McLellan, Cheryl, Robert. BS in Food and Nutrition, SUCB, Buffalo, 1973; MEd in Health Sci. Edn. and Evaluation, SUNY, 1978. Registered dietitian, 1977. Diet cook Niagara Sanitorium, Lockport, N.Y., 1953-56; cook Mount View Hosp., Lockport, N.Y., 1956-60, asst. dietitian, 1960-73, dietitian, food svc. dir., 1973-79, cons. dietitian, 1979-81; instr. Erie Community Coll., Williamsville, N.Y., 1979-81; sch. lunch coord. Nye County Sch. Dist., Tonopah, Nev., 1970-93; cons. dietitian Nye Gen. Hosp., Tonopah, 1983-88; adj. instr. Erie Community Coll., Williamsville, 1978-79; nutrition instr. for coop. extension Clark County Community Coll., 1990—; cons. Group Purchasing Western N.Y. Hosp. Adminstrs., Buffalo, 1975-79, vice-chmn. adv. com., 1976-78; cons. BOCES, Lockport, 1979-81. Nutrition counselor Migrant Workers Clinic, Lockports, 1974-80; mem. Western N.Y. Soc. for Hosp. Food Svc. Adminstrs., 1974-81; nutritionist Niagara County Nutrition Adv. Com., 1977-81. Recipient Outstanding Woman of the Yr., YWCA-UAW Lockport, 1981, Disting. Health Care Food Adminstrn. Recognition award Am. Soc. for Hosp. Food Svc. Adminstrs., 1979, USDA award Outstanding Lunch Program in Nev. and Western Region, 1986, 91. Mem. Am. Assn. Ret. Persons, Am. Sch. Food Svc. Assn. (bd. dirs. 1987, 92-93, cert. dir. II 1987, 5-yr. planning com. 1990, mem. ann. confs. 1988-92), Am. Dietetic Assn. (nat. referral system for registered dietitians 1992-93), So. Nev. Dietetic Assn. (pres. 1985-86), Nev. Food Svc. Assn. (participant ann. meetings 1990-92), Nutrition Today Soc., Nev. Sch. Food Svcs. Assn. (dietary guidelines com. 1991-93). Republican. Baptist. Home: 481 N Murphy PO Box 656 Pahrump NV 89041-0656

TAYLOR, MICHAEL JAMES, engineering and construction company executive; b. Des Moines, June 20, 1941; s. Robert Phillip and Evelyn (Brown) T.; m. Judith Brissette, Dec. 27, 1966; children: Jason Edmond, Bryan Michael, Jennifer Marie. BSCE, Carnegie Mellon, 1963; MSCE, Carnegie Mellon U., 1965. Registered profl. engr., Colo., Ill., Md., Mich., Minn., Mont., Nev., N.Mex., N.D., Ohio, Pa., Va., W.Va., Wyo. Engr. E. D'Appolonia, Pitts., 1964-65, from asst. project engr. to asst. project mgr., 1967-76; project mgr., v.p. tech. E. D'Appolonia, Denver, 1976-83; from v.p. to exec. v.p. Canonie Environ. Service Corp., Denver, 1983—. Contbr. articles to profl. jours.; chpts. to books; patentee in field. Served to lt. C.E., U.S. Army, 1965-67. Mem. ASCE, Am. Inst. Mining Engrs. Home: 9807 Bayou Ridge Trl Parker CO 80134-5142 Office: Canonie Environ Svc Corp 94 Inverness Ter E # 100 Englewood CO 80112-5303

TAYLOR, MINNA, lawyer; b. Washington, Jan. 25, 1947; d. Morris P. and Anne (Williams) Glushien; m. Charles Ellett Taylor, June 22, 1969; 1 child, Amy Caroline. BA, SUNY, Stony Brook, 1969; MA, SUNY, 1973; JD, U. So. Calif., 1977. Bar: Calif. 1977, U.S. Dist. Ct. (cen. dist.) Calif. 1978. Extern to presiding justice Calif. Supreme Ct., 1977; field atty. NLRB, L.A., 1977-82; dir. employee rels., legal svcs. Paramount Pictures Corp., L.A., 1982-85, v.p. employee rels. legal svcs., 1985-89; dir. bus. and legal affairs Wilshire Ct. Prodns., L.A., 1989-91; sr. counsel Fox Broadcasting Co., L.A., 1991-92, v.p. legal affairs, 1992—. Editor notes and articles: U. So. Calif. Law Rev., 1976-77. Mentor MOSTE, L.A., 1986-87, 88-89; pres. Beverly Hills chpt. ACLU, L.A., 1985. Fellow ABA, L.A. County Bar Assn.; mem. Beverly Hills Bar Assn., L.A. Bead Soc. (membership sec. 1992—), Order of Coif. Office: Fox Broadcasting Co 10201 W Pico Blvd Los Angeles CA 90035

TAYLOR, NEVIN J., air force officer, investment company executive; b. Bakersfield, Calif., May 28, 1966; s. Martin Van and Joan Lorraine (Kunkle) T. Student, Acad. Mil. Sci., 1987. Exec. trainee Dynasonic Corp., Bakersfield, 1980-82; ptnr. Bitron Investment Co., Bakersfield, 1982-85, owner, 1985-90; property mgr. Chelsea Investment Co., Bakersfield, 1982-84; commd. 1st lt. U.S. Air Force, 1984, airman communications, computers, adminstrn., 1984-87; honor guard comdr. 146th Tactical Airlift Wing, Channel Islands, Calif., 1987-91, mgr. communications and computer systems, 1989—; comdr. 146th Mission Support Flight, Channel Islands, 1990—; owner Triad Investments, Ventura, Calif., 1990—. Mem. Nat. Guard Assn. Episcopalian. Office: 146th MSF/CC PO Box 4001 4146 Navalair Rd Port Hueneme CA 93041-4001

TAYLOR, PETER VAN VOORHEES, advertising and public relations consultant; b. Montclair, N.J., Aug. 25, 1934; s. John Coard and Mildred (McLaughlin) T.; m. Janet Kristine Kirkebo, Nov. 4, 1978; 1 son, John Coard III. BA in English, Duke U., 1956. Announcer Sta. WQAM, Miami, 1956; announcer, program dir. Sta. KHVH, Honolulu, 1959-61; promotion mgr. Sta. KPEN, San Francisco, 1962; with Kaiser Broadcasting, 1962-74, GE Broadcasting Co., 1974-78; program/ops. mgr. Sta. KFOG, San Francisco, 1962-66; mgr. Sta. WXHR AM/FM, Cambridge, Mass., 1966-67; gen. mgr. Sta. WJIB, Boston, 1967-70; v.p., mgr. FM div. Kaiser Broadcasting, 1969-72; v.p., gen. mgr. Sta. KFOG, San Francisco, 1970-78; pres. Taylor Communications, 1978-90, Baggott & Taylor, Inc., 1990-91, Taylor Advt. & Pub. Rels., 1991—, No. Calif. Broadcasters Assn., 1975-77, Broadcast Skills Bank, 1975-76. Trustee, WDBS, Inc., Duke U., 1974-80; bd. dirs. San Francisco Better Bus. Bur., 1976-78, 89—, San Francisco Boys & Girls Club, 1991—, Coast Guard Found., 1991—, Leukemia Soc., San Francisco, 1992—; mem. Better Bus. Bur. Mem. Nat., Internat. Radio Clubs, Mus. Assn., San Francisco Symphony, Bay Area Publicity Club, San Francisco Advt. Club, Pub. Rels. Soc. Am., Worldwide TV/FM Dx Assn., Advt. Tennis Assn. (pres. 1975-77), Olympic Club, Bacchus Club, The Family Club, Rotary (bd. dirs. 1988-93, 1st v.p. 1990-91, pres. 1991-92, dist. pub. rels. chmn. 1986-89, conf. chmn. 1990, area rep. 1992-93). Lt. USCGR, 1957-63. Home: 2614 Jackson St San Francisco CA 94115-1123 Office: Ste 801 442 Post St San Francisco CA 94102-1522

TAYLOR, PHILIP HARLEY, JR., software engineer; b. Pensacola, Fla., Mar. 27, 1959; s. Philip Harley Sr. and Sheila Ann (McNamee) T. BS, U. Md., 1984. Programmer Gee & Jenson, West Palm Beach, Fla., 1982; programmer Goddard Space Flight Ctr. NASA, Greenbelt, Md., 1983-84; programmer Intran, Rosslyn, Va., 1984-85, SAIC, Tysons Corner, Va., 1985; sr. programmer TRW, Alexandria, Va., 1985-87, Claritas, Alexandria, 1987-88; cons. Boeing, IBM, Microsoft, Chase Manhattan, A.C. Neilson, Vienna, Va., 1988-90; mgr. spl projects Softview, Oxnard, Calif., 1990-91; sr. software engr. Borland, Scotts Valley, Calif., 1991-92. Author: 3D Graphics Programming in Windows; contbr. book revs., instrnl. courseware. Mem. North Monterey County (Calif.) High Sch. Restructin Bus. Com., 1991-92. Mem. IEEE, Assn. Computer Machinery. Home: 320 Miraflores Rd Scotts Valley CA 95066 Office: Borland Langs Devel Unit C2 1700 Green Hills Rd Scotts Valley CA 95066

TAYLOR, RICHARD EDWARD, physicist, educator; b. Medicine Hat, Alta., Can., Nov. 2, 1929; came to U.S., 1952; s. Clarence Richard and Delia Alena (Brunsdale) T.; m. Rita Jean Bonneau, Aug. 25, 1951; 1 child, Norman Edward. B.S., U. Alta., 1950, M.S., 1952; Ph.D., Stanford U., 1962; Docteur honoris causa, U. Paris-Sud, 1980; DSc, U. Alta., 1991; LLD (hon.), U. Calgary, Alta., 1993. Boursier Lab. de l'Accelerateur Lineaire, Orsay, France, 1958-61; physicist Lawrence Berkeley Lab., Berkeley, Calif., 1961-62; staff mem. Stanford (Calif.) Linear Accelerator Ctr., 1962-68, assoc. dir., 1982-86, prof., 1968—. Fellow Guggenheim Found., 1971-72, von Humboldt Found., 1982; recipient Nobel prize in physics, 1990. Fellow AAAS, Am. Phys. Soc. (W.K.H. Panofsky prize div. particles and fields 1989), Royal Soc. Can.; mem. Am. Acad. Arts and Scis., Can. Assn. Physicists, Nat. Acad. Scis. (foreign assoc.). Office: Stanford Linear Accelerator Ctr PO Box 4349 Palo Alto CA 94309-4349

TAYLOR, RICHARD KEITH, scriptwriter, security director; b. Lomita, Calif., Feb. 22, 1949; s. Marion Luther and Vesta Irene (Tiller) T.; m. Karen Sponaugle, 1978 (div. 1984). Dir. security, fire and safety Warner Bros., West Hollywood, Calif., 1975—. Author screenplays: Psyche, 1985, Deceptions, 1990 (Ace nomination); author short stories. With U.S. Army, 1967-70, Vietnam. Recipient Screenwriting award Writer's Digest, 1986.

TAYLOR, ROBERT BROWN, medical educator; b. Elmira, N.Y., May 31, 1936; s. Olaf C. Taylor and Elizabeth (Place) Brown; m. Anita Dopico; children: Diana Marie, Sharon Jean. Student, Bucknell U., 1954-57; MD, Temple U., 1961. Diplomate Am. Bd. Family Practice. Gen. practice medicine New Paltz, N.Y., 1964-78; faculty physician Bowman Gray Sch. Medicine Wake Forest U., Winston-Salem, N.C., 1978-84; prof., chmn. dept. family medicine Oreg. Health Scis. U. Sch. Medicine, Portland, 1984—; mem. comprehensive part II com. Nat. Bd. Med. Examiners, Phila., 1986-91. Author: Common Problems in Office Practice, 1972, The Practical Art of Medicine, 1974; editor: Family Medicine: Principles and Practice, 1978, 4th edit., 1993, Health Promotion: Principles and Clinical Applications, 1982, Difficult Diagnosis, 1985, Difficult Medical Management, 1991, Difficult Diagnosis II, 1992; contbg. editor Physicians Mgmt. Mag., 1972—; editorial bd. The Family Practice Rsch. Jour., 1980-90, The Female Patient, 1984—, Frontiers of Primary Medicine, 1983—, Am. Family Physician, 1990—, Jour. of Family Practice, 1990—. Served as surgeon USPHS, 1961-64. Fellow Am. Acad. Family Physicians, Am. Coll. Preventive Medicine; mem. Soc. Tchrs. Family Medicine (bd. dirs. cert. of excellence), Assn. Am. Med. Colls., Am. Assn. for the Study of Headache, Phi Beta Kappa, Alpha Omega Alpha. Clubs: City, Multnomah Athletic (Portland). Home: 680 SW Regency Ter Portland OR 97225-6070 Office: Oreg Health Scis U Sch Medicine Mail Code FP 3181 Sam Jackson Pk Rd Portland OR 97201

TAYLOR, RONALD E., real estate manager; b. Longview, Tex., Dec. 8, 1962; s. Charles A. and Mary E. (Nolan) T. BA in Journalism, U. Tex., 1986; M. Real Estate Devel., U. So. Calif., 1991. State senator Tex. Legislature, Austin, 1981-83; broker CAP Oil Co., Austin, 1983-84; account exec. MCI, Austin, 1984-86, Hill & Knowlton PR, Austin, 1985-86; rep. City Coun. of San Diego, 1986-88, deputy mayor, 1986-88; gen. mgr. The Hahn Devel. Co., San Diego, 1988-90; pres., CEO Taylor Com./Re Consulting, L.A., 1989-91; asst. to dir. U. So. Calif. Develop., 1990-91; real estate mgr. Pepsico, L.A., Chgo., 1991—; pres., CEO TNT Real Estate Devel., 1991—; bd. dirs. Univ. Real Estate Tng. Svc. (chmn. 1990-91), L.A., Univ. So. Calif. Inclusivness Commn., 1991-92. Active NAACP, L.A., 1990-92; coord. entertainment United Negro Coll. Fund Nat. Telethon, 1992; founder Alana Soc., U. So. Calif., L.A., 1990, Taylor Tri-Star Scholarship, Longview, 1991; mem. Trust Leaders, 1989; co-founder Project I Believe, San Diego, 1988; metro bd. Urban League, Chgo., 1989—; bd. UNCF, Chgo., 1992. Recipient Thirty Leaders of the Future award Ebony Mag., Chgo., 1984, Most Disting. Alumni award Longview High Sch., 1991. Mem. Nat. Assn. of Corp. Real Estate Exec's., Nat. MBA Assn., Internat. Coun. of Shopping Ctr's., L.A. Foreign Affairs Coun., Univ. So. Calif. Rotary Com. Home: 4 Elm Creek Dr # 219 Elmhurst IL 60126

TAYLOR, ROSE PERRIN, social worker; b. Lander, Wyo., Feb. 11, 1916; d. Wilbur Rexford Perrin and Agatha Catherine (Hartman) Perrin DeMars; m. Louis Kempf Kugland, Sept. 1942 (div. 1951); children: Mary Louise, Carolyn Kugland McElhany; m. Wilfred Taylor, Oct. 13, 1962 (dec. 1991). AB, U. Mich., 1937; MSW, U. Denver, 1956; student, Columbia U., 1936, Santa Rosa Jr. Coll., 1974-92. Group worker Dodge Community House, Detroit, 1937-38; case worker Detroit Welfare Dept., Detroit, 1938-40; child welfare worker Fremont County Welfare Dept., Lander, Wyo., 1940-42; worker children's svcs. Laramie County Welfare Dept., Cheyenne, Wyo., 1951-57, dir., 1957-58; supr. San Mateo (Calif.) County Health & Welfare, 1958-74; dir. Fed. Day Care Project, San Mateo, 1964—; tchr. Sch. Pub. Health Nursing, U. Wyo., 1951-55; tchr. Sch. Social Work, U. Calif., San Jose, 1962-63; workshop leader NIMH, Prescott, Ariz., 1961, Ariz. State U., Phoenix, 1962, Oreg. State Welfare Dept., Otter Crest, 1973; cons. day care workshops. Contbr. articles to profl. jours. Bd. dirs. YMCA, Sonoma County, Calif., 1980-84. Recipient Resolution of Commendation, Calif. State Senate, 1974; Annual Rose Taylor award San Mateo Child Care Coordinating Coun., 1982. Mem. NASW. Democrat. Methodist. Home: 137 Wild Moor Reach Box 15 The Sea Ranch CA 95497

TAYLOR, ROSLYN DONNY, family practice physician; b. Columbia, S.C., Feb. 14, 1941; d. Otto Gary and Roslyn (Alfriend) Donny; children: Cynthia Gambill, Kevin Emory. BA, Emory U., 1963, MD, 1967. Diplomate Am. Bd. Family Practice. Intern USN, Jacksonville, Fla., 1967-68; resident in family practice Spartanburg (S.C.) Gen. Hosp., 1974-76; pvt. practice Green Cove Springs, Fla., 1968-70, Inman, S.C., 1976-78; student health physician U.S.C., Columbia, 1978-81; with faculty sch. med. U.S.C. Richland Meml. Hosp., 1979-87; vis. prof. family practice U. Utah, Salt Lake City, 1987-88, residency dir. family practice, 1988—; med. dir. Woodrow Dormitory for Disabled U. S.C., 1984-86; attending physician pain therapy ctr. Richland Meml. Hosp., 1986-87. Rural physician fin. assistance com. State of Utah, 1990—. Lt. comdr. USNR, 1967-68, 72-73. Named Physician of Yr. Mayor's Com. Employment of Handicapped, Columbia, 1984. Fellow Am. Acad. Family Physicians (Mead-Johnson awards com. 1985-87, commn. on continuing med. edn. 1988—), Utah Acad. Family Physicians (alternate del. 1990—, pres.-elect, pres. 1989-90), Salt Lake County Med. Soc., AMA, Utah Med. Assn. Presbyterian. Office: U Utah Sch Medicine Dept Family Practice 50 N Medical Dr Salt Lake City UT 84132-0002

TAYLOR, RUTH ANNE, lawyer; b. Honolulu, Feb. 18, 1961; d. Gerald Lou and Charlotte Anne (Nelson) Allison; m. Thomas Scott Taylor, Dec. 28, 1985; children: Kyle Thomas, Kelly Gerald. BA in Journalism, U. So. Calif., 1984; JD, N.Y. Law Sch., 1987. Bar: Calif. 1987, U.S. Dist. Ct. (so. dist.) Calif., U.S. Ct. Appeals (9th cir.). Assoc. Carlsmith, Wichman, Case Mukai & Ichiki, L.A., L.A., 1987-89, Christensen, White, Miller, Fink & Jacobs, L.A., 1989—. Mem. Los Angeles County Bar Assn., Beverly Hills

Bar Assn. Republican. Office: Christensen White Miller Fink & Jacobs 2121 Avenue Of The Stars Fl 18 Los Angeles CA 90067-5010

TAYLOR, SCOTT DOUGLAS, publishing company official, infosystems specialist; b. Salt Lake City, Apr. 12, 1954. BS in Mktg., U. Utah, 1975; MBA in Fin., U. Colo., 1978. Corp. fin. analyst Manville Corp., Denver, 1978-80; sr. product design analyst Standard & Poor's Compustat, Englewood, Colo., 1980-82, corp. planning systems analyst, 1982-84, mgr. product tech., 1984--; developer CD-ROM technology McGraw-Hill Corp., Englewood, 1987-89, editor newsletter update, 1987-92. H.G.B. Gould Meml. scholar U. Colo., 1977-78. Mem. Planning Forum (bd. dirs. Denver chpt. 1987-92). Avocations: golf, squash, computer programming. Office: SPCS/McGraw Hill 7400 S Alton Ct Englewood CO 80112-2310

TAYLOR, STEVEN BRUCE, agriculture company executive; b. Salinas, Calif., Dec. 29, 1954; s. Edward Horton and Joanne (Church) T.; m. Kathryn Hagler, Dec. 17, 1978; children: Meghan Jean, Kyle Hagler, Christian Steven. BA, U. Calif., Berkeley, 1978; MBA, Harvard U., 1985. Pres. Fresh Concepts, San Marino, Calif., 1985-87; mktg. staff Bruce Church, Inc., Salinas, Calif., 1987-91; pres. Fresh Express Retail Mktg., Salinas, 1991—, Fresh Internat., Salinas, 1991—; v.p. Salinas Valley Lettuce Co-op, Salinas, 1990—; bd. dirs. Produce for Better Health, Del., 1991—. Bd. Elders First Presbyn. Ch., Salinas, 1989-92, personnel com. 1989-94, bldg. com. 1990—; founding mem. Lincoln Club of Monterey County, Salinas, 1990. Home: 515 Santa Paula Dr Salinas CA 93901 Office: Fresh Internat 1020 Merrill St Salinas CA 93912

TAYLOR, T. RABER, lawyer; b. Colorado Springs, Colo., Dec. 31, 1910; s. Ralph Franklin and Mary Catherine (Burns) T.; m. Josephine Loretto Reddin, Sept. 20, 1938; children: Mary Therese, Carol Anne, Margaret Claire, Josephine R., Rae Marie, Kathleen Mae, Anne Marie. BA magna cum laude, Regis Coll., 1933; JD, Harvard U., 1937. Bar: Colo. 1937, U.S. Dist. Ct. Colo. 1937, U.S. Tax Ct. 1938, U.S. Ct. Appeals (10th cir.) 1940, U.S. Supreme Ct. 1950. Pvt. practice law Denver, 1937—. Bd. dirs. Denver Cath. Charities, 1946-71; v.p. Nat. Conf. Cath. Charities, 1956-57, 69-75; mem. gov.'s com., White House Conf. on Children and Youth, 1971. Lt. comdr. USNR, 1943-45, NATOUSA, ETO. Knight Order St. Gregory, 1971, Equestrian Order of Holy Sepulchre of Jerusalem, 1973; recipient St. Vincent de Paul medal St. John's U., Jamaica, N.Y., 1971, St. Thomas More award Cath. Lawyers Guild Denver, 1981. Fellow Am. Coll. Probate Counsel; mem. ABA, Colo. Bar Assn., Denver Bar Assn., Denver Estate Planning Coun. (pres. 1962-63), Greater Denver Tax Counsel Assn., Serra Club Denver, Denver Athletic Club. Home: 790 Fillmore St Denver CO 80206-3848 Office: 250 Century Bank Pla 3300 E 1st Ave Denver CO 80206-5810

TAYLOR, THOMAS DANIEL, military officer; b. Derby, Conn., July 2, 1957; s. Malcolm Leigh and Susan Yates (Hawley) T.; m. Scarlett Maria Fiveash, Aug. 29, 1987. BA in History, The Citadel, 1981. Cert. cannon battery officer U.S. Army Field Artillery Sch. Commd. officer U.S. Army, 1981, advanced through grades to capt., 1984; fire direction officer A Battery, 6th Battalion, 10th Artillery, Bamberg, Germany, 1981-82; exec. officer A Battery, 6th Battalion, 10th Artillery, Bamberg, 1982-83; spl. nuclear ops. officer 6th Battalion, 10th Artillery, Bamberg, 1983-85, battalion motor officer, 1985; range control officer U.S. Field Artillery Ctr., Fort Sill, Okla., 1986-87; battery commdr. C Battery, 4th Battalion, 4th Artillery, Fort Sill, 1987-89; emergency actions officers Ops. J3, U.S. Pacific Command, Camp H. M. Smith, 1989-92; targeting officer G3 Ops. Hdqrs. III Corps Arty., Ft. Sill, Okla., 1992—; tng. NCO 5th Signal Command Co. SCNG, North Charleston, 1979-81; pres. Protestant adv. coun. Aliamanu Mil. Chapel, Honolulu, 1991-92. Asst. scoutmaster Boy Scout Troop 1, Huntington, Conn., 1975-76; deacon First Presbyn. Ch., Lawton, Okla., 1988-89; scout master Boy Scout Troop 180, Honolulu, 1989-91; orgnl. rep. Boy Scout and Cub Scout Troop Park 1980, Honolulu, 1990-92. Decorated Two-Army Achievement medals Commdr. 6th/10th Artillery, Bamberg, Germany, 1984-85, Army Commendation medal Commdr. 72d Artillery Brigade, Wertheim, Germany, 1985, Army Meritorious Svc. medal Commanding Gen., Fort Sill, Okla., 1989, Joint Svc. Commendation medal Comdr. in Chief, U.S. Pacific Command, 1993. Mem. Am. Numismatic Assn., Am. Philatelic Soc., Nat. Eagle Scout Assn. (Eagle Scout 1975), Sons of Union Vets. of the Civil War. Home: 4707 NW Cheryl Blvd Lawton OK 73505 Office: Hdqs III Corps Artillery Fort Sill OK 73503

TAYLOR, TIMOTHY DAVIES, psychologist; b. Tacoma, Jan. 25, 1945; s. Thomas Gibson and Eleanor Jane (Davies) T.; B.A., Central Wash. U., 1968; M.A., U. Puget Sound, Tacoma, 1975; Ph.D., U.S. Internat. U., 1980. Tchr. schs. in Wash., 1968-72; v.p. Tom Taylor Ins. Brokers, Tacoma, 1972-81; pvt. practice psychology, Tacoma, 1981—. Vice chmn. Pierce County March of Dimes, 1977-78, chmn., 1980; active Tacoma-Pierce County YMCA; assoc. chmn. United Way Pierce County, 1981-82. Mem. Ind. Ins. Agts. and Brokers Am., Family Service Assn. Am., Profl. Ins. Agts. Wash., Am. Psychol. Assn., Am. Assn. Marriage and Family Therapy. Democrat. Clubs: W. Tacoma Optimist (pres. 1977, Optimist of Yr. award 1977), Elks. Home: 4412 N 27th St Tacoma WA 98407-4608 Office: Trust Office Bldg 808 N 2d St Tacoma WA 98403

TAYLOR, TIMOTHY KIVEN, business owner; b. Raymond, Wash., May 22, 1944; s. John Hunt Taylor and Helen Lenor (Howdeshell) Johnson; 1 child, Derrick Kiven Taylor. Student, Sitka (Alaska) C.C., 1973. Comml. fisherman S.E. Alaska, 1959-69; superintendent mainenance Sitka Sch Dist., 1970-76; owner M.H.P., Sitka, 1972-79, South Bend, Wash., 1977-86; owner Mini Mall, South Bend, 1979-81, Peppertree West Motor Inn, Centralia, Wash., 1985—; owner restaurant Peppermill Inc. Ltd., Centralia, 1987—. Mem. City Coun., South Bend, 1979; mem. Planning and Zoning Com., Sitka, 1975. Mem. Masons, Shriners. Home: 1208 Alder St Centralia WA 98531 Office: Peppermill Inc Ltd 1208 Alder St Centralia WA 98531

TAYLOR, WALTER WALLACE, lawyer; b. Newton, Iowa, Sept. 18, 1925; s. Carrol W. and Eva (Greenly) T.; A.A., Yuba Coll., 1948, A.B., 1950; M.A., U. Calif., 1955, J.D., McGeorge Coll. Law, 1962; m. Mavis A. Harvey, Oct. 9, 1948; children—Joshua Michael (dec. 1980), Kevin Eileen, Kristin Lisa, Jeremy Walter, Margaret Jane, Melissa E., Amy M. Adminstrv. analyst USAF, Sacramento, 1951-53; personnel, research analyst Calif. Personnel Bd., Sacramento, 1954-56; civil service, personnel analyst, chief counsel, gen. mgr. Calif. Employees Assn., Sacramento, 1956-75; staff counsel, chief profl. standards Calif. Commn. Tchr. Credentialing, 1975-88, ret. 1988; staff counsel State Office Real Estate appraiser Licensing and Certification, 1992—; tchr. discipline civil service, personnel cons. Served USCGR, 1943-46. Mem. Calif. State Bar, Am., Sacramento County bar assns. Democrat. Author: Know Your Rights, 1963-64. Home: 4572 Fair Oaks Blvd Sacramento CA 95864-5336

TAYLOR, WAYNE MICHAEL, controller; b. Newark, Aug. 15, 1945; s. Lester George and Genevieve Julia (Jaros) T.; 1 child, Kimberly Darlene. BS, Am. Internat. Coll., Springfield, Mass., 1968; MBA, Ea. N.Mex. U., 1971. Group acctg. mgr. Frito-Lay, Inc., Dallas, 1972-89; group contr. Borden Inc., Salt Lake City, Utah, 1989—. Sgt. USAF, 1968-72. Republican. Roman Catholic. Office: Borden Inc PO Box 620 Salt Lake City UT 84110-0620

TAYLOR, WILLIAM AL, judge; b. Lusk, Wyo., Nov. 2, 1928. BA, U. Wyo., 1951, LLB, 1959. Bar: Wyo. 1959. Pvt. practice Lusk, 1959-80; city atty. Town of Lusk, 1962-74; atty. Niobrara County, Wyo., 1964-78; judge Wyo. Dist. Ct. (8th dist.), Cheyenne, 1980—. Staff sgt. U.S. Army, 1951-53. Mem. Wyo. State Bar, Wyo. Judicial Conf. (chmn. 1984-85), Sigma Alpha Epsilon. Office: Wyo Dist Ct 8th Judicial Dist PO Box 189 Douglas WY 82633*

TAYLOR, WILLIAM MALCOLM, executive recruiter; b. South Hiram, Maine, June 18, 1933; s. William Myers and Gladys Marie (Weldy) T.; m. Carrie Mae Fiedler, Aug. 31, 1957 (div. Sept. 1980); children: William Stephan, Alyson Marie, Eric Fiedler; m. Elizabeth Van Horn, June 18, 1983. Student, George Sch., 1948-50; BA in Liberal Arts, Pa. State U., 1956; MEd in Sci., U. N.C., 1961. Cert. secondary sch. tchr. Chemistry and biology tchr. Coral Shores High Sch., Tavernier, Fla., 1961-62; pk. naturalist Everglades Nat. Pk., Fla., 1962-65; tech. editor Nat. Pk. Svc., Washington, 1965-67; chief naturalist Canyonlands Nat. Pk., Utah, 1967-71; environ. edn. specialist western regional office Nat. Pk. Svc., Calif., 1971-77; programs devel. dir. Living History Ctr., Novato, Calif., 1981-83; ptnr. Van Horn, Taylor & Assocs., Santa Cruz, Calif., 1983—. Originator: (ednl. program) Environ. Living Program, 1973 (Calif. Bicentennial Commn. award 1974, Don Perryman award Calif. Social Studies Coun., 1975, Calif. Conservation Coun. award 1975, Nat. Bicentennial Adminstrn. sponsorship 1976). Bd. dirs. Novato Environ. Quality Commn., 1973-76; mem. Calif. Conservation Coun., 1973-76. Men. AAAS, Am. Assn. Clin. Chemistry, Lighthawk/Environ. Air Force, Air Life Line, Flying Samaritans, Mensa. Home: 30714 Ty Valley Rd Lebanon OR 97355

TAYLOR, ZACK, broadcast executive; b. L.A., Mar. 30, 1964; s. Horatio Cornelius and Agness (Dombrowski) T.; m. Marianne Appleby, Oct. 7, 1989; 1 child, Gomer. BA in Broadcasting, U. Miss., 1984. Air personality WOOR-FM, Oxford, Miss., 1982-84, WNUE, Ft. Walton Beach, Fla., 1984-86, WSUH, Oxford, 1988-90; meteorologist WJM-TV, Mpls., 1986-88; program dir. WKRP, Cin., 1988-89, Antelope Broadcasting Co., Inc., Lancaster, Calif., 1990—. Author: Programming Primer, 1991; patented sponge cleaner. Office: KAVL/KAVS-FM 2501 W Ave I Lancaster CA 93536

TAYLOR-GRIGSBY, QUEENIE DELORES, consultant; b. Oklahoma City, Aug. 21, 1948; d. Barnett C., Sr. and Bedell (Boles) Taylor; m. Walter Thomas White II, Nov. 26, 1966 (div. June 1976); children: Walter Thomas III, Robin Orlando; m. James O. Grigsby, Oct. 19, 1976 (dec. Dec. 1976); 1 child, James Tumaané. BS, Howard U., 1970. Ordained to ministry Ray Deliverance Found., 1989. Assoc. cons. Trust Inc., Richmond, Va., 1974-80, Orgnl. Devel. Consultants, Richmond, 1980-82; cons., pres. Taylor & Co., Phoenix, 1974—; minister Man Child Ministries, Phoenix, 1988—; cons. Met. Atlanta, 1980-82, Fredrick County, Md., 1974, Richond Pub. Sch. System, 1977, Black Police Officers, Tulsa, 1986. Author poetry. Advocate child welfare Dept. of Corrections, Phoenix, 1990, advocate tchr. rights, 1991; active tchr. rights Phoenix Pub. Sch. System, 1992; supr. elections County Election Bd., Maricopa County, Ariz., 1987. Recipient Lucille McMahn scholarship, 1965, Nellie Green scholarsip, 1965, Golden Feet award, 1991. Mem. Soc. Tng. and Devel. (cert. housing specialist), Housing Specialist Inst., YWCA. Republican. Office: Taylor & Co PO Box 9605 Phoenix AZ 85068

TAYLOR-HUNT, MARY BERNIS BUCHANAN, educator, artist; b. Marion, Ind., Aug. 16, 1904; d. Walter Scott and Nora Elizabeth (Kinslear) B.; m. Robert Rush Taylor, Jan. 26, 1929 (dec. Mar. 1975); m. Ralph Van Nice Hunt, May 20, 1978; stepchildren: Penelope Clark, Diane Stockmar. AB in English, UCLA, 1926; MA in Drama, U. So. Calif., 1931. Tchr. speech and dramatics Los Angeles City Schs., 1929-44; vol. instr. Ikebana (Japanese Flower Arranging) Huntington Library, San Marino, Calif., 1957—,; produced Japanese Festival at Huntington Library, for Olympic Fine Arts Festival in L.A., 1984. represented in permanent collection at Japanese House in Japanese Garden at Huntington Library, 1957—. Mem. bd. overseers Huntington Libr. Art Collections and Bot. Gardens, 1993—. Recipient Gold Crown award Pasadena Arts Coun. Mem. L.A. Soc. Ikenobo (bd. dirs. 1987—), San Marino League (fine arts projects), Valley Hunt Club, Calif. Club, Arabella and Henry Huntington Heritage Soc. of the Huntington Libr. Republican. Mem. Christian Ch. Club: San Marino League (founding pres. 1954-55). Home: 1300 S Sierra Madre Blvd San Marino CA 91108-2140

TEACHOUT, WALTER FLOYD, psychologist; b. Zeeland, Mich., Feb. 10, 1957; s. Floyd W. Teachout and Sieglinde (Gottschalk) Tausend. BA, Grand Rapids Bapt. Coll., 1979; MA, We. Mich. U., 1982; PhD, Calif. Sch. Profl. Psychology, 1988. Assoc. regional dir. Pacific We. region VA, San Francisco, 1992—; lectr. in field. Contbr. articles to profl. jours. Capt. U.S. Army, 1987-92. Mem. APA. Home: 92 Sanchez San Francisco CA 94114

TEAGUE, LAVETTE COX, JR., educator, systems consultant; b. Birmingham, Ala., Oct. 8, 1934; s. Lavette Cox and Caroline Green (Stokes) T.; student Auburn U., 1951-54; B.Arch., MIT, 1957, M.S.C.E., 1965, Ph.D., 1968; MDiv with distinction Ch. Div. Sch. Pacific, 1979. Cert. system profl. Inst. Cert. of Computer Profls. Archtl. designer Carroll C. Harmon, Birmingham, 1957, Fred Renneker, Jr., Birmingham, 1958-59; architect Rust Engring. Co., Birmingham, 1959-62, Synergetics, Inc., Raleigh, N.C., 1962-64, Rust Engring. Co., Birmingham, 1964-68; research asst., inst., research assoc. MIT, Cambridge, 1964-68; dir. computer services Skidmore, Owings & Merrill, San Francisco, Chgo., 1968-74; postdoctoral fellow UCLA, 1972; adj. assoc. prof. architecture and civil engring. Carnegie-Mellon U., Pitts., 1973-74; archtl. systems cons., Chgo., 1974-75, Berkeley, Calif., 1975-80, Pasadena, Calif., 1980-82, Altadena, Calif., 1982—; lectr. info. systems Calif. State Poly. U., Pomona, 1980-81, prof., 1981—, asst. chair, 1990-91, chair, 1991—. Fulbright lectr., Uruguay, 1985. Co-author: Structured Analysis Methods for Computer Information Systems, 1985. Recipient Tucker-Voss award M.I.T., 1967; Fulbright scholar, 1985. Mem. AIA (Arnold W. Brunner scholar 1966), Assn. Computing Machinery, Sigma Xi, Phi Eta Sigma, Scarab, Scabbard and Blade, Tau Beta Pi, Chi Epsilon. Episcopalian. Home: 1696 N Altadena Dr Altadena CA 91001-3623 Office: 3801 W Temple Ave Pomona CA 91768

TEAMAN, RICHARD ALAN, accountant; b. Fairfield, Calif., Aug. 19, 1960; s. Glenn Richard and Dorothy Teaman; m. Lisa A. Turner, June 22, 1985 (div. Nov. 1990); 1 child, Grace Ann; Sally Thomas, July 5, 1991. AA, Riverside (Calif.) City Coll., 1981; BS, Calif. State U., San Bernardino, 1983. CPA, Calif. Staff acct. Thomas, Byrne & Smith, Riverside, 1983-85, sr. acct., 1985-88, mgr., 1988-92, ptnr., 1992-93; ptnr. Thomas, Bigbie & Smith, Riverside, 1993—. Mem. AICPA, Calif. Soc. CPA's, Assn. Govt. Accts., Govt. Fin. Officers Assn., Calif. Soc. Mcpl. Fin. Officers. Home: 11503 Chaucer St Moreno Valley CA 92557 Office: Thomas Bigbie & Smith 4201 Brockton Ave Ste 100 Riverside CA 92501-3829

TEBEDO, MARYANNE, state legislator; b. Oct. 30, 1936; m. Don Tebedo; children: Kevin, Ronald, Linda, Thomas, Christine. Former mem. Colo. Ho. of Reps.; now mem. Colo. Senate; profl. parliamentarian. Republican. Office: Colorado State Senate State Capitol Bldg Denver CO 80203

TEDFORD, CHARLES FRANKLIN, biophysicist; b. Lawton, Okla., June 26, 1928; s. Charles E. and Loula B. (Waters) T.; m. Julie Reme Sauret, Sept. 15, 1951; children: Gary Franklin, Mark Charles, Philip John. BS with distinction in Chemistry, S.W. Tex. State U., 1950, MS, 1954; postgrad. in radiobiology Reed Coll., 1957, in biophysics U. Calif., Berkeley, 1961-63. Enlisted USN, 1945-47, commd. ensign, 1950, advanced through grades to capt., 1968; biochemist U.S. Naval Hosp., San Diego, 1953-54, U.S. Naval Biol. Lab., Oakland, Calif., 1954-56; sr. instr., radiation safety officer Nuclear, Biol. and Chem. Warfare Def. Sch., Treasure Island, Calif., 1956-61; asst. chief nuclear medicine div. Navy Med. Sch., Bethesda, Md., 1963-66; adminstrv. program mgr. radiation safety br. Bur. Medicine and Surgery, Washington, 1966-72; dir. radiation safety and health physics program Navy Regional Med. Center, San Diego, 1972-74; mgr. Navy Regional Med. Clinic, Seattle, 1974-78, ret., 1978; dir. radiation health unit Ga. Dept. Human Resources, Atlanta, 1978-79; dir. Ariz. Radiation Regulatory Agy., Tempe, 1979-91; chief, Radiological Health Prog., Juneau, Alaska, 1991— ; elected chmn. Conf. Radiation Program Dirs., 1987; named Ariz. Southwestern Low Level Radioactive Waste Compact Commr., 1990. Recipient Ariz. Adminstr. of Yr. award Ariz. Adminstrs. Assn., 1988; decorated Legion of Merit, Meritorious Service medal. Mem. Health Physics Soc., Am. Nuclear Soc. Contbr. articles on radiation safety to profl. publs.

TEDFORD, JACK NOWLAN, III, construction executive, small business owner; b. Reno, Jan. 1, 1943; s. Jack Nowlan Jr. and Elizabeth (Kolhoss) T.; m. Nancy Joanne Stiles, Feb. 27, 1971; children: Jack Nowlan IV, James Nathan. BS, U. Nev., 1966, MBA, 1969. Bus. mgr. Los Angeles Bapt. Coll., Newhall, Calif., 1969-71; v.p. Jack N. Tedford, Inc., Fallon, Nev., 1971—; owner/broker Tedford Realty, Fallon, 1974—; owner/mgr. Tedford Bus. Systems, Fallon, 1978—; bd. dirs. Masters Coll., Newhall, Calif., 1972—. Author numerous computer programs. Mem. Selective Svc. Local Bd., Fallon, 1971-76; chmn. City of Fallon Bd. Adjustment, 1975—, Churchill Co. Reps., Fallon, 1976-80; mem. ctrl. com. Nev. Reps., 1976—; del. Nat. Conv., Detroit, 1980, Dallas, 1984; coun. officials Western Nev. Devel. Dist. Mem. Assn. Gen. Contractors (bd. dirs.), Nat., State and Fallon Bd. Realtors, CEDA Bus. Coun. (bd. dirs.), Nev. Motor Transport Assn., NAt. Asphalt Pavement Assn., Am. Trucking Assn., Rotary (bd. dirs. 1969-71). Republican. Baptist. Home: 115 N Bailey St Fallon NV 89406-2720 Office: 235 E Williams Ave PO Box 1505 Fallon NV 89407-1505

TEERLINK, J(OSEPH) LELAND, real estate developer; b. Salt Lake City, July 16, 1935; s. Nicholas John and Mary Luella (Love) T.; student U. Utah, 1953-55; m. Leslie Dowdle, Nov. 5, 1975; children: Steven, David, Andrew, Suzanne, Benjamin. Sales rep. Eastman Kodak Co., Salt Lake City, 1960-69; founder Graphic Systems, Inc., Salt Lake City, 1969-82, pres., 1969-79, chmn. bd., 1979-82; founder Graphic Ink Co., Salt Lake City, 1973, pres., 1975-79, chmn. bd., 1979-82; founder G.S.I. Leasing Co., Salt Lake City, 1975, pres., 1975-82; chmn. bd. Graphic Systems Holding Co., Inc., Salt Lake City, 1978-82; dir. leasing and acquisitions Terra Industries, Inc., real estate developers, 1982-86, ptnr., 1986—; bd. dirs. ARC, Salt Lake City, 1979-82, Hope Living Ctr. Found., 1993-; vice consulate of the Netherlands for Utah, 1977-92; mem. active corps of execs., SBA, 1979-83; mem. adv. bd. House of Hope Mothers and Children Utah Alcoholism Found., 1992—. Named Small Businessman of the Yr. for Utah, SBA, 1978. Mem. Graphic Arts Equipment and Supply Dealers of Am. (dir. 1978-82), Printing Industry of Am., Nat. Assn. Indsl. and Office Parks (pres. Utah chpt., 1986-87), Nat. Fedn. Ind. Businessmen, Million Dollar Club (life). Republican. Mormon. Home: 2984 Thackeray Pl Salt Lake City UT 84108-2517 Office: 6925 Union Park Ctr Midvale UT 84047

TEETER, LORNA MADSEN, art educator; b. Salt Lake City, Dec. 10, 1948; d. Orrin Andersen and Marie Eliza (Hunter) Madsen; m. Steven Church Teeter, June 9, 1971; children: Heather, Michael Patrick, Michelle, Russell Scott, Kurt Andrew, Ryan Anthony, Sean Douglas. BS, U. Utah, 1971; MOE, Keene (N.H.) State Coll., 1978; postgrad., Novosibirsk (Russia) State U. Cert. tchr. secondary edn. and mid. sch. in art, home econs., geography and bus., Utah. Instr. Keene State Coll., 1975-77; ptnr. The Tack and Hammer/Mobile Decorator Showroom, Nelson, N.H., 1976-84; tchr. Provo (Utah) Sch. Dist., 1984—; presenter Getty Ctr. for Arts Conf., L.A., 1989; dist. art curriculum leader Provo Sch. Dist., 1989-91; gifted and talented specialist Farrer Mid. Sch., Provo, 1991-93. Leader 4-H, Nelson, 1973-76; den mother Cub Scouts, Provo, 1984-86. Mem. NEA, Nat. Art Edn. Assn., Utah Edn. Assn., Utah Art Edn. Assn., Provo Edn. Assn. (instrnl. and profl. devel. 1989-91). Mem. Ch. of Jesus Christ of Latter-day Saints. Home: 1152 W 400 N Provo UT 84601 Office: 100 N 600 E Provo UT 84606

TEETER, ROB R., technical operations specialist; b. Rexburg, Idaho, Oct. 4, 1957; s. LaVerl Edward and Kita Dawn (Burns) T. Grad., DeVry Inst. of Tech., 1979. Quality control technician I Sundstrand Data Control, Redmond, Wash., 1979-81; quality control technician I Physio Control Corp., Redmond, 1981-82, quality control technician II, 1982-83, quality control technician II lead, 1983-85, quality control coord., 1985-86, quality control technician III, 1986-90, tech. ops. specialist surface mount tech., 1990-92, calibration supr., 1992—. Home: PO Box 367 Clinton WA 98236 Office: Physio Control Co 11811 Willows Rd NE Redmond WA 98073

TEETERS, CLARENCE, salt company manager; b. Mt. Pleasant, Pa., Dec. 22, 1933; s. Clarence and Edna Marie (Grimm) T.; student U. Toledo, 1952-55, U. So. Calif., 1978; m. Sandra Jean Ulery, Aug. 2, 1958; children: Deanna Marie, Douglas James. Buyer, mgr. Tiedtkes, Toledo, 1955-60; sales rep. Morton Salt Co., 1960-69, dist. sales mgr., No. Calif., Nev., Hawaii, 1969-78; mgr. consumer products .Cargill Salt Co., Newark, Calif., 1978—. Mem. The Illuminators, San Francisco Sales Mgrs. Club, Masons. Republican. Presbyterian. Address: 7200 Central Ave Newark CA 94560

TEETS, JOHN WILLIAM, diversifed company executive; b. Elgin, Ill., Sept. 15, 1933; s. John William and Maudie T.; m. Nancy Kerchenfaut, June 25, 1965; children: Jerri, Valerie Sue, Heide Jane, Suzanne. Student, U. Ill. Pres., ptnr. Winter Garden Restaurant, Inc., Carpenterville, Ill., 1957-63; v.p. Greyhound Food Mgmt. Co.; pres. Post Houses, Inc., and Horne's Enterprises, Chgo., 1964-68; pres., chief operating officer John R. Thompson Co., Chgo., 1968-71; pres., chief operating officer Restaurant div., also corp. v.p Canteen Corp., Chgo., 1971-74; exec. v.p., chief operating officer Bonanza Internat. Co., Dallas, 1974-76; chmn., chief exec. officer Greyhound Food Mgmt., Inc., Phoenix, 1976; group v.p. food service Greyhound Corp., Phoenix, 1976-81, group v.p. services group, 1980-81, vice chmn., 1980-82; chmn., chief exec. officer Greyhound Corp. (now The Dial Corp.), Phoenix, 1981—, now also pres. and dir.; chmn., pres. Armour & Co., from 1981; chmn., chief exec. officer Greyhound Food Mgmt. Inc. (now Restaura Inc.), Phoenix, 1982—; vice chmn. President's Conf. on Foodservice Industry; mem. adv. bd. Phoenix and Valley of Sun Conv. and Visitors Bur., 1979-82. Recipient Silver Plate award, Golden Plate award Internat. Foodservice Mfrs. Assn., 1980. Mem. Nat. Automatic Mdsg. Assn., Nat. Restaurant Assn., Nat. Inst. Foodservice Industry (trustee), Am. Mgmt. Assn., Christian Businessmen's Assn. (chmn. steering com. 1977), Nat. Speakers Assn. Club: Arizona. Office: The Dial Corp 111 W Clarendon Ave Phoenix AZ 85077-0001*

TEGELER, DOROTHY, writer; b. Effingham, Ill., Oct. 12, 1950; d. Albert Bernard and Mildred Elizabeth (Haarmann) T.; children: Paul Anthony, Laura Ann. BS cum laude, Ill. State U., 1971. Cert. elem. tchr., Ill., Ariz. Tchr. Camp Point Sch. Dist., Golden, Ill., 1971-72; elem. career devel. specialist McKnight Pub. Co., Bloomington, Ill., 1972-74; sales rep. Bobbs Merrill Pub. Co., Indpls., 1981-82; tchr. Lincoln Coll., Lincoln, Ill., 1980-82; employee communications adminstr. Ill. Farm Bur., Bloomington, Ill., 1982-84; freelance writer Phoenix, 1972—; pres. Fiesta Books Inc., Phoenix, 1987—. Author: Retiring Arizona, 1987, 2d edit., 1990, Hello Arizona, 1987, Moving to Arizona, 1988, 2d edit., 1992, Destination: Phoenix, 1990, Arizona Favorites, 1992; contbr. articles to popular mags. Mem. Nat. Assn. Realtors, Ariz. Authors Assn. (pres. 1987-88). Office: PO Box 51234 Phoenix AZ 85076-1234

TEGTMEIER, RONALD EUGENE, physician, surgeon; b. Omaha, Jan. 16, 1943; s. Harvey and Edna T.; children: Anne, Amy; m. Victoria Susan, June 28, 1985; children: Justina Becerra, Gregory Galvan, Mark Tegtmeier. AB, Dartmouth Coll., 1965; BMS, Dartmouth Med. Sch., 1966; MD, Harvard Med. Sch., 1968. Diplomate Am. Bd. Plastic Surgery. Internship in surgery U. Colo. Med. Ctr., Denver, 1968-69, residency in gen. surgery, 1969-70; plastic surgery preceptorship Kingston-upon-Hull, England, 1973; residency in plastic surgery U. Mexico, Albuquerque, 1974-76, fellowship, 1976; plastic surgeon pvt. practice Arvada, Colo., 1977—, Artistic Ctr. for Cosmetic Surgery, Golden, Colo., 1988—; pres. Clear Creek Valley Med. Soc., Lakewood, Colo., 1983-84; speaker of ho. Colo. Med. Soc., denver, 1985-87. Author: Aesthetica Tapes, 1988—; patentee in field; contbr. numerous papers and publs. to profl. jours. Named Outstanding Bus. Person, Arvada Jaycees, 1978; recipient Arvada Image award, 1981, Denver Post Gallery of Fame award, 1979. Mem. Am. Soc. Plastic and Reconstructive Surgeons, Am. Soc. for Aesthetic Plastic Surgery. Office: Artistic Ctr Cosmetic Surgery 14062 Denver West Pky Bldg 52 Golden CO 80401-3121

TEICHROB, CAROL, Canadian provincial official; b. Sask., Can., Aug. 27, 1939; d. J. Delbert and Elizabeth (Spenst) Sproxton; m. Donald P. Teichrib, Mar. 1, 1958; children: Lori, Sharon, James. Sr. matriculation, Notre Dame Convent, Morinville, Alta., Can. Cert. profl. ct. reporter, exec. mem. Can. and Saskatchewan Fedns. Agriculture, 1976-81; chmn. Can. Turkey Mktg. Agy., 1980-81, Plains Poultry Wynyard, Sask., 1981-88; founding ptnr. Primrose Books, Saskatoon, Sask., 1988—; now also min. edn., min. responsible for Sask. Property Mgmt. Corp., min responsible for Sask. Comm. Network Province of Sask., Regina. Reeve, Rural Municipality of Corman Park, Saskatoon, Sask., 1981-91; active U. Sask. Senate, 1981-86; mem. legis. assembly N.D.P. Caucus. Recipient Golden WHeel award Sask. Rotary, 1990; named Woman of Yr. in Bus., Saskatoon YWCA, 1981. Mem. Saskatton C. of C. Office: Minister of Education, Room 361 Legislative Bldg, Regina, SK Canada S4S OB3

TELFER, RICHARD GREENWELL, educational consultant; b. Ann Arbor, Mich., Dec. 28, 1922; s. William and Minnie T.; m. Norinne Elizabeth Gale, Dec. 23, 1949; children: Janet, Brian, Gary. BA, Ea. Mich. U., 1948; MA, U. Mich., 1953; EdS, Wayne State U., 1964. Dir. instrn.

Cheyenne Mountain Schs., Colorado Springs, Colo., 1959-62; curriculum cons. The Jam Handy Orgn., Detroit, 1962-63; dir. instrn. Shorewood (Wis.) Schs., 1964-68; cons. Colo. Dept. Edn., Denver, 1968-71; dir. instrn. Boulder (Colo.) Valley Schs., 1971-73; sales cons. A.N. Palmer Co., Schaumburg, Ill., 1976-78; owner/cons. Ednl. Directions, Las Vegas, Nev., 1973—; vis. prof. edn. Ea. Mich. U., U. No. Colo., Colo. Coll., Adams State Coll.; cons. (DECAT) Reynolds Elec. and Engring.; guest cons. Ford Motor Co., GM, Army Air Def. Command.; cons. in field; conductor workshops in field. Author: Up to Date With Nuclear Energy, Don't Be Afraid of the Atom, Bringing About Instructional Improvement; mem. editorial bd. Franklin Pubs., Milw., 1965-68; contbr. numerous articles to profl. jours. Chmn. edn. com. Las Vegas 2000 and Beyond Task Force, 1991; mem. steering com. nev. Nuclear Waste Study Com.; mem., cons. Colo. Safety Coun.; evaluator N.Y. State Regents Exams; resource leader Colo. PTA Coun.; advisor budget com. Colo. State Legis.; evaluator N.Mex. Rural Edn. project, U. N.Mex.; advisor testing Constrn. Industries div. State of N.Mex.; chmn. So. Nev. of U. Mich. Ann. Giving Scholarship program, other activities in past. With U.S. Army, 1943-45; ETO. Mem. ASCD (bd. dirs.). Home: 5357 Spencer Las Vegas NV 89119 Office: Ednl Directions 1222 S Rainbow Blvd Las Vegas NV 89102

TELGÁRSKY, RASTISLAV JOZEF, mathematician, computer scientist; b. Martin, Slovakia, July 24, 1943; came to U.S., 1983; s. Jozef and Olga (Steliarova) T.; m. Anna Maria Romanowska, Jan. 5, 1974; children: Marek, Olga, Matus. MS in Math., Wroclaw U., Poland, 1967; PhD in Math., Polish Acad. Scis., Warsaw, 1970. Rsch. fellow Slovak Acad. Scis., Bratislava, Slovakia, 1970-74; asst. prof. Wroclaw Tech. U., 1974-77, assoc. prof., 1977-85, prof., 1985-86, vice chmn. Math. Inst., 1981-83; sr. mathematician Tech. Solutions, Inc., Mesilla Park, N.Mex., 1988—; cons. DJH Engring. Ctr., Salt Lake City, 1987-88; vis. prof. So. Ill. U., Carbondale, 1979-80, Va. Tech., Blacksburg, 1983-85, Ohio U., Athens, 1985-86, U. Tex. El Paso, 1986-88. Introduced topological games and contbd. to their theory and application; contbr. 50 articles to profl. jours. Referee Math. Revs. and Zentralblatt Für Mathematik, 1968-89. Recipient awards for rsch. papers Pres. Wroclaw Tech. U., 1976, 78, 80, 81, 82, Ministry Edn. of Polish Republic, 1977, 81. Mem. IEEE, Am. Math. Soc., Assn. for Computing Machinery. Roman Catholic. Home: 1801 Pomona Dr Las Cruces NM 88001-4921 Office: Tech Solutions Inc PO Box 1148 Mesilla Park NM 88047-1148

TELLEEN, STEVEN LOUIS, marketing professional; b. Ft. Dodge, Iowa, Mar. 21, 1947; s. Carl Laurel and Opal Eleanor (Johnson) T.; m. Clare Elizabeth Adams, Aug. 7, 1971; children: Adam Carl, Ashley Clare, Jacob Charles. BA in English, U. Colo., 1973, MA in Biology, 1976, PhD in Biology, 1978. Lic. psychiat. technician Ft. Logan Mental Health Ctr., Denver, 1969-71; teaching asst. U. Colo., Boulder, 1973-78; sr. rsch. assoc. Info. Sci./Genetic Resources Program, Boulder, 1978; project mgr. Lab. for Info. Sci. in Agrl., Ft. Collins, Colo., 1978-84; mgr. Applications Mktg. ETA Systems, Inc., St. Paul, 1984-89; mgr. open systems mktg. programs Amdahl Corp., Sunnyvale, Calif., 1989-91, mgr. open systems tech. mktg., 1991—; cons., field ecologist Lab. of Mountain Ecology for Man, Boulder, 1973-75. Mem. Sci. Rsch. Soc., Sigma Xi. Home: 3458 Windsor Ct Pleasanton CA 94588-3546 Office: Amdahl Corp 1250 E Arques Ave M/S 213 Sunnyvale CA 94088

TELLEM, SUSAN MARY, public relations executive; b. N.Y.C, May 23, 1945; d. John F. and Rita C. (Lietz) Cain; divorced; children: Tori, John, Daniel. BS, Mt. St. Mary's Coll., L.A., 1967. Cert. pub. health nurse; RN. Pres. Tellem Pub. Rels. Agy., Marina del Rey, Calif., 1977-80, Rowland Grody Tellem, L.A., 1980-89, Tellem, Inc., Beverly Hills, Calif., 1990—; chmn. The Rowland Co., L.A., 1989-90; sr. v.p., mng. dir. Burson-Marsteller, L.A., 1992—; instr. UCLA Extension, 1983—; speaker numerous seminars and confs. on pub. rels. Editor: Sports Medicine for the '80's, Sports Medicine Digest, 1982-84. Bd. dirs. Marymount High Sch., 1984-87, pres., 1984-86; bd. dirs. L.A. Police Dept. Booster Assn., 1984-87; mem. Cath. Press Coun.; mem. pres.'s coun. Mus. Sci. and Industry. Mem. Am. Soc. Hosp. Mktg. and Pub. Rels., Healthcare Mktg. and Pub. Rels. Assn., Pub. Rels. Soc. Am., L.A. Counselors, Nat. Investor Rels. Inst. Roman Catholic. Club: Sports (L.A.).

TELLEP, DANIEL MICHAEL, aerospace executive, mechanical engineer; b. Forest City, Pa., Nov. 20, 1931. B.S. in Mech. Engring. with highest honors, U. Calif., Berkeley, 1954, M.S., 1955; grad. Advanced Mgmt. Program, Harvard U., 1971. With Lockheed Missiles & Space Co., 1955—, chief engr. missile systems div., 1969-75, v.p., asst. gen. mgr. advanced systems div., 1975-83, exec. v.p., 1983-84, pres., 1984—, 1986—; chmn., chief exec. officer Lockheed Corp., 1989—; cons. in field; bd. dirs. 1st Interstate Bancorp., SCECorp. Contbr. article to profl. jours. Bd. govs. Music Ctr. L.A. County, 1991—; mem. adv. bd. U. Clalif. Berkeley Sch. Engring.; mem. Calif. Bus. Roundtable, 1992—; nat. chmn. vol. com. U.S. Savs. Bond Campaign, 1993. Recipient Tower award San Jose State U., 1985, Aerospace Laurels award Aviation Week and Space Tech., 1993. Fellow AIAA (Lawrence Sperry award 1964, Missile Systems award 1986); Am. Astronautical Soc.; mem. NAE, Nat. Aero. Assn., Soc. Mfg. Engrs., Sigma Xi, Pi Tau Sigma, Tau Beta Pi. Office: Lockheed Corp 4500 Park Granada Calabasas CA 91399

TELSON, STANLEY ALAN, engineer; b. Tucson, Sept. 6, 1957; s. Samuel Aaron and Beverly (Broder) T.; m. Lynn Hope Zaminsky, Aug. 14, 1982; children: Sarah Elizabeth, Aaron Samuel, Joshua Solomon. BSEE, U. Ariz., 1979; MSEE, Stanford U., 1982. Mem. tech. staff Hewlett-Packard Co., Palo Alto, Calif., 1979-83; devel. engring. mgr. ROLM Systems, Santa Clara, Calif., 1983-91; systems engring. mgr. E-mu Systems, Inc., Scotts Valley, Calif., 1991-92; engring. mgr. Acuson Corp., Mountain View, Calif., 1992—; instr. Coll. of San Mateo, Calif., 1982, U. Calif. Extension, Berkeley, 1991—. Mem. IEEE, Am. Soc. Quality Control, Tau Beta Pi. Home: 100 Cherry Ln Campbell CA 95008 Office: Acuson Corp PO Box 7393 1220 Charleston Rd Mountain View CA 94039

TEMES, GABOR CHARLES, electrical engineering educator; b. Budapest, Hungary, Oct. 14, 1929; s. Erno and Rozsa (Angyal) Wohl-Temes; m. Ibi Kutasi-Temes, Feb. 6, 1954; children: Roy Thomas, Carla Andrea. Dipl.Ing., Tech. U. Budapest, 1952, DSc (hon.), 1991; Dipl. Phys., Eotvos U., Budapest, 1954; Ph.D., U. Ottawa, Ont., Can., 1961. Asst. prof. Tech. U. Budapest, 1952-56; project engr. Measurement Engring. Ltd., 1956-59; dept. head No. Electric Co. Ltd., 1959-64; group leader Stanford Linear Accelerator Center, 1964-66; corp. cons. Ampex Corp., 1966-69; prof. elec. engring. UCLA, 1969-90, chmn. dept., 1975-80; dept. head Oreg. State U., Corvallis, 1990—; cons. Xerox Corp., ANT GmbH. Author: (with others) Introduction to Circuit Synthesis and Design, 1977, Analog MOS Integrated Circuits for Signal Processing, 1986; assoc. editor: (with others) Jour. Franklin Inst, 1971-82; co-editor, contbg. author: (with others) Modern Filter Theory and Design, 1973, Oversampling Delta-Sigma Data Converters, 1991. Recipient Western Electric Fund award Am. Soc. Engring. Edn., 1982, Humboldt Sr. Rsch. award, 1991; NSF grantee, 1970—. Fellow IEEE (editor Transactions on Circuit Theory 1969-71 Best Paper award 1969, 81, 85, Centennial medal 1984, Edn. award 1987, Tech. Achievement award 1989). Home: 7100 NW Grandview Dr Corvallis OR 97330-2708 Office: Oreg State U Corvallis OR 97330

TEMKO, ALLAN BERNARD, writer; b. N.Y.C., Feb. 4, 1924; s. Emanuel and Betty (Alderman) T.; m. Elizabeth Ostroff, July 1, 1950; children: Susannah, Alexander. A.B., Columbia U., 1947; postgrad, U. Calif., Berkeley, 1949-51, Sorbonne, 1948-49, 51-52. Lectr. Sorbonne, 1953-54, Ecole des Arts et Metiers, Paris, 1954-55; asst. prof. journalism U. Calif., Berkeley, 1956-62; lectr. in city planning and social scis. U. Calif., 1966-70; prof. art Calif. State U., Hayward, 1971-80; lectr. art Stanford U., 1981, 82; architecture critic San Francisco Chronicle, 1961—, art editor, 1979-82; lectr. Grad. Sch. Journalism, U. Calif., Berkeley, 1991; archtl. planning cons.; chmn. Yosemite Falls Design Workshop, 1992; Pulitzer Prize juror, 1991-92; chmn. Yosemite Falls Design Workshop, Nat. Park, 1992. Author: Notre Dame of Paris, 1955, Eero Saarinen, 1962, No Way To Build a Ballpark and Other Irreverent Essays on Architecture, 1993; contbr. articles to U.S. and fgn. mags. and newspapers; West Coast editor, Archtl. Forum, 1959-62. Served with USNR, 1943-46. Recipient Gold medal Commonwealth Club Calif., 1956, Journalism award AIA, 1961, Silver Spur award San Francisco Planning & Urban Renewal Assn., 1985, Inst. Honor award, 1991, 1st prize in archtl. criticism Mfrs. Hanover/Art World, 1986, Critic's award Mfrs. Hanover/Art World, 1967, Profl. Achievement award Soc. Profl. Journalists, 1988, Pulitzer Prize for criticism, 1990; grantee Rockefeller Found., 1962-63, 20th Century Fund, 1963-66, NEA, 1988, Graham Found., 1990; Guggenheim fellow, 1956-57. Office: Chronicle Pub Co 901 Mission St San Francisco CA 94103-2988

TEMPELMAN, STEVEN CARLOS, transportation company executive; b. Caracas, Venezuela, Mar. 22, 1967; came to U.S., 1967; s. Russell Neil and Hannelore (Keck) T. B of Individualized Studies, U. Minn., 1990. Air ops. mgr. UPS, Mpls., 1985-87; self-employed, 1987-90; human resources exec. Northwest Transp. Svc., Denver, 1990—. Recipient Pres'. Student Leadership and Svc. award, 1988. Mem. Sigma Alpha Epsilon (pres. 1988-89, Merill Cragun award 1989). Home: 7777 E Yale Ave D201 Denver CO 80231

TEMPEST, PETER ROB, surgeon; b. Phila., Dec. 23, 1962; s. Bruce Dean and Phyllis Jackson (Rems) T.; m. Janet Mayfan Li, Oct. 6, 1990. BS, N.Mex. Inst. Mining and Tech., 1983; MD, UCLA, 1989. Lab. technologist Advanced Mineral Techs., Socorro, N.Mex., 1984; resident in gen. surgery Valley Med. Ctr., Fresno, Calif., 1989—. Med. vol. Luke Soc., Catacamas, Honduras, 1984-85. Mem. Nat. Off Road Bicycle Assn., Ultimate Players Assn. Home: 4828 E Florence Ave Fresno CA 93725 Office: Valley Med Ctr 445 S Cedar Ave Fresno CA 93702

TEMPLE, JAMES FREDERICK, II, auditor; b. Norman, Okla., June 4, 1944; s. James Frederick and Jane (Adams) T.; m. Geri Kazue Irinaka, Jan. 28, 1984; children: Jay, Jana. BA, Reed Coll., 1966; MBA with distinction, Hawaii Pacific U., 1991. Acct. Arthur Andersen & Co., Portland, 1967-70; sr. auditor Deloitte Haskins & Sells, Honolulu, 1970-73, audit mgr., 1973-79; asst. contr. Pacific Resources, Inc., Honolulu, 1979-80, contr., 1980-83, dir. of internal audit, 1983-89; regional auditor The Broken Hill Pty Co. Ltd. (aquired Pacific Resources), Honolulu, 1989—. Past pres., dir. The Samaritan Counseling Ctr. of Hawaii; past pres., bd. dirs., Hale Kipa, Inc.; trustee Waiokeola Congreg. Ch., Honolulu. Mem. AICPA (Disting. Pub. Svc. 1985), Hawaii Soc. of CPAs (bd. dirs. 1987-89, Disting. Pub. Svc. 1985), Inst. of Internal Auditors (pres. 1985-86, gov. 1986-92, Hawaii chpt. gov., past pres. 1985-92), Inst. of Mgmt. Accts. (nat. dir. 1982-84, pres. Hawaii chpt. 1979-80), Assn. of Cert. Fraud Examiners (Hawaii chpt. bd. dirs. 1992—).

TEMPLEMAN, JOHN ALDEN, lawyer; b. Urbana, Ill., Jan. 26, 1945; s. William Darby and Marion Helen (Gillespie) T. AB, U. Calif., Berkeley, 1966, JD, 1969. Bar: Calif., N.Mex. Atty. Edn. Dept. State of N.Mex., Santa Fe, 1973-76, atty. Fin. Dept., 1978-83, atty. Risk Mgmt. Div., 1983-86, atty. Pub. Safety Dept., 1988—. Home: 2720 Paseo de Tularosa Santa Fe NM 87505 Office: NMex Dept Pub Safety PO Box 1628 Santa Fe NM 87504

TEMPLIN, JOHN ALTON, historical theology educator, minister; b. Hoehne, Colo., Sept. 27, 1927; s. John Wesley and Stella Mable (Canterbury) T.; m. Dorothy Jean Lear, Dec. 31, 1952; children: Kayla Jean, Ann Revae, Bryce Alton. BA, U. Denver, 1950; ThM, The Iliff Sch. Theology, 1953, ThD, 1956; PhD, Harvard U., 1966. Ordained United Meth. Ch., 1951. Asst. prof. Southwestern Coll., Winfield, Kans., 1954-57; min. Meth. Ch., Mass., 1957-66; asst. prof. U. S.D., Vermillion, 1966-67; asst. to full prof. The Iliff Sch. Theology, Denver, 1967—. Editor: The United Methodist, Evangelical and United Brethren Churches in the Rockies, 1977; author: Ideology on a Frontier: The Theological Foundation of Afrikaner Nationalism, 1652-1910, 1984; author, editor: An Intellectual History of the Iliff School of Theology: A Centennial Tribute, 1892-1992, 1992. Cpl. USAF, 1945-47. Named Alumnus of Yr., The Iliff Sch. Theology, Denver, 1989. Mem. Am. Soc. Ch. History, Am. Soc. Reformation History, Am. Hist. Assn., Sixteenth Century Study Conf. Democrat. Office: The Iliff Sch Theology 2201 S University Blvd Denver CO 80210

TEMPLIN, KATHLEEN ANN, nursing educator; b. Santa Monica, Calif., June 13, 1947; d. Charles Richard and Marion Elizabeth (Taylor) Allen; children: Christine, Joanna. BSN, Georgetown U., 1969; MSN, U. Calif., L.A., 1981. RN, Calif., CCRN. Critical care nurse St. Vincent Charity Hosp., Cleve., 1969-77, UCLA Med. Ctr., 1977-79; intensive care nurse Meml. Med. Ctr., Long Beach, Calif., 1982; asst. prof. nursing Calif. State U., Long Beach, 1982-89; clin. nurse specialist MICU VA Med. Ctr., San Diego, 1989—; cons. and educator in field. Author/editor critical care texts; contbg. author Nursing Care Planning Guides; editor profl. jours.; pub. rsch. in critical care nursing. Mem. Am. Assn. Critical Care Nurses, Honor Soc. of Nursng, Sigma Theta Tau Internat. (Iota Eta chpt. pres. 1986-87). Roman Catholic.

TENER, WILLIAM TERRENCE, information services executive; b. San Francisco, Jan. 25, 1941; s. William Morris and Josephine Marie (Brehm) T.; m. Dianne Mae Neuwirth, 1964 (div. 1978); children: Ward, David; m. Susan Ann Berry, June 9, 1979. AA in Natural Sci., Diablo Valley Coll., 1965; BS in Bus. Sci., San Francisco State U., 1967; MBA in Fin. and Strategy, Claremont (Calif.) Grad. Sch., 1986, postgrad. Rsch. assoc. Dow Chem. Co., Walnut Creek, Calif., 1965-67; asst. dir. ops. Sunset House, Culver City, Calif., 1967-69; asst. regional data collection mgr. TRW Credit Data Div., Orange, Calif., 1969-71, mgr. nat. data ops. analysis, 1971-73, mgr. data acquisition policies and procedures, 1973-75, mgr. security and internal auditing, 1975-81, dir. operational and regulatory compliance, 1981-90, dir. legis. and regulatory affairs, 1990-93; mem. adv. bd. Inst. Internal Auditors Rsch. Found., Orlando, Fla., 1986—; chmn. disting. panel experts advanced techs. in info. systems program U. So. Calif., L.A., 1990-91. Author: (chpt.) Expert Systems in Business & Finance, 1993, (monograph) Adapting the Integrated Audit Approach, 1992; contbg. editor EDP Auditors Assn. Computer Crime Rsch. Project, 1991-93; contbr. articles to profl. jours. Del. Chinese Computer Soc./People to People China, Hong Kong, 1986; bd. dirs. Calif. Assn. Credit Burs., 1991-93, v.p. 1992; lectr. Internat. Fedn. for Info. Processing, Ireland, 1985, Monte Carlo, 1986, Brisbane, Australia, 1988, Brighton, Eng., 1991. With USNR, 1963-67. Mem. Inst. Internal Auditors (v.p. Orange County chpt. 1985-86, bd. dirs. 1988—, Grantee 1989), Computer Soc. IEEE (security and privacy tech. com. 1988—), Assn. for Computing Machinery (contbr. blue ribbon panel on hacking), Computer Security Inst. (lectr.), EDP Auditors Assn. (founding dir. 1985, pres. Orange County chpt. 1990-91, lectr.), Info. Systems Security Assn. (lectr., pres. Orange County chpt. 1993-94), Internat. Assn. Knowledge Engrs. (lectr.). Republican.

TENNANT, HOWARD EDWARD, academic administrator; b. Lethbridge, Alberta, Can., May 13, 1941; s. Rex. Joseph and Jean Sylvia (Engle) T.; m. Sharon Lea Buckley, Sept. 7, 1963; children: Carmen, Patricia, Daniel. BBA cum laude, Gonzaga U., 1963; MBA, U. Oreg., 1964, PhD, 1970. Asst. prof. U. Saskatchewan, Saskatoon, Can., 1966-70, assoc. prof., 1970-74, prof. mgmt., head dept. mgmt. and mktg., 1972-77, assoc. dean grad. studies, prof. mgmt., 1977-84, dean grad. studies, assoc. v.p. rsch., 1984-87; pres., vice-chancellor U. Lethbridge, 1987—; chmn. bd. dirs. SED Systems Inc., Saskatoon, 1980-90; bd. dirs. Assn. Univ. & Colls. Can., Ottawa, Ontario, 1987—; chmn. Univs. Coordinating Coun., Edmonton, Alberta, 1989-91; bd. dirs. Alberta Rsch. Coun., Edmonton, 1990—; instr. Banff Sch. Advanced Mgmt., 1970-87; labor mediator U. Saskatchewan, 1989; vis. scholar U. Wash. Grad. Sch. Bus., Seattle, 1974-75. Dir. Saskatchewan Rsch. Coun., Saskatoon, 1984-87; bd. dirs. Can. Plains Rsch. Ctr., Regina, Saskatchewan, 1984—, Saskatchewan Expo 86 Corp., Regina., 1985-86. Named adopted son and chief Bull Horn Soc., 1987, 90, Kainai Chief by Blood Indians, 1991; decorated 125th Can. medal Gov. Gen., 1992. Mem. Rotary, Beta Gamma Sigma. Roman Catholic. Home: 61 Ridgewood Cres W, Lethbridge, AB Canada T1K 6C3 Office: Univ Lethbridge, Pres Office, Lethbridge, AB Canada T1K 3M4

TENNEN, KEN, property management executive, commercial arbitrator; b. Belmont Shore, Calif., June 30, 1949; s. Morris and Clair (Rose) T.; m. Diane Janet Sussman, Dec. 25, 1982; children: Sterling M, Skyler Alexander. Cert. counseling, UCLA, 1973; lic., U. Los Ams., Cholula Puebla, Mex., 1975; MA, Georgetown U., 1977. Cons. Booz Allen & Hamilton, Washington, 1974-77; with Multinat. Corp., L.A., 1977-86; owner, mgr. Share-Tel Internat. Hostel, Venice Beach, Calif., 1986-92; bd. dirs., chief exec. officer Suntree Townhomes, Tarzana, Calif. Pres. Happy Valley Sch. Bd., Ojai, Calif., 1991—; mem. Happy Valley Found., 1990—; bd. dirs., chief exec. officer Calvin Homeowners Assn., 1989-92. Home and Office: 20 Brooks Ave Venice Beach CA 90291-1961 also: PO Box 570 970 Tarzana CA 91357-0970

TENNENT, VALENTINE LESLIE, accountant; b. Apia, Western Samoa, Apr. 5, 1919; came to U.S., 1922; s. Hugh Cowper and Madge Grace (Cook) T.; m. Jeanne Marie Elder, Dec. 10, 1941; children: Madeline Jeanne Walls, Hugh Cowper II, Michael Waller, Val Leslie, Paul Anthony. Student, U. Calif., Berkeley, 1938-40. CPA, Hawaii, La. Mgr. Tennent & Greaney, CPA's, Hilo, Hawaii, 1945-50; ptnr. Cameron, Tennent & Dunn, CPA's, Honolulu, 1950-56; ptnr. Peat, Marwick, Mitchell & Co. CPAs, Honolulu, 1956-79, cons., 1979-84; ind. researcher pub. fin. and banking San Diego, 1984—. Pres., treas. Tennent Art Found., Honolulu, 1955-77; trustee, treas. Watumull Found., Honolulu, 1963-90 (G.J. Watumull award for disting. achievement 1982); bd. dirs. Iolani Sch., Lyman Mus., Inst. for Human Svcs., Honolulu. Capt. USAF, 1941-45, MTO. Recipient Bishop's Cross for Disting. Svc. Protestant Episcopal Ch., Dist. of Hawaii, 1965. Mem. AICPA (governing coun. 1961-64), Hawaii Soc. CPAs (pres. 1960), Univ. Club (San Diego). Episcopalian. Home and Office: 700 Front St No 2005 San Diego CA 92101

TENNEY, ROBERT NELSON, finance company executive; b. Detroit, Jan. 14, 1942; s. Elmer L. and Marguerite E. (Proper) T. BS, Ferris State Coll., 1965. Asst. v.p. Congress Fin. Corp., N.Y.C., 1970-76; sr. v.p. Congress Fin. Corp., L.A., 1984-88; v.p. A.J. Armstrong Corp., L.A., 1976-81, Chase Comml. Corp., L.A., 1981-84; pres. Commonwealth Fin. Corp., Santa Monica, Calif., 1989—. Pres. Park Kenwood Homeowners Assn., Glendale, Calif., 1983-84. Mem. Comml. Fin. Conf. of Calif. (bd. dirs. 1981—, pres. 1983-85, chmn. bd. 1985-87—), Nat. Comml. Fin. Assn. (Far Western edn. com. 1983—, program com. 1985, dir. 1989—), Tau Kappa Epsilon (chmn. bd. trustees Calif. Poly. State U. Pomona chpt., 1984—), L.A. Club, L.A. Athletic Club. Office: Fremont Fin Corp 1633 26th St Santa Monica CA 90404-4023

TENNEY, WILLIAM FRANK, pediatrician; b. Shreveport, La., June 5, 1946; s. William Bonds and Pat (Patton) T.; m. Elizabeth Carter Steadman, Oct. 4, 1973; children: Amy Karen, William Allen. BA, Vanderbilt U., 1968; MD, La. State U., New Orleans, 1972. Diplomate Am. Bd. Pediatrics, sub-Bd. Pediatric Nephrology. Intern Grady Meml. Hosp., Atlanta, 1972-73; resident in pediatrics Emory U. Affiliated Hosps., Atlanta, 1973-74, fellow in pediatric nephrology and inorganic metabolism, 1974-76; practice medicine specializing in pediatric nephrology St. Helens, Oreg., 1976-79, Shreveport, 1979-85, Seattle, 1985—; mem. staff Children's Orthopedic Hosp. and Med. Ctr., Seattle; chief dept. pediatrics Swedish Hosp. Med. Ctr., Seattle, 1987-90; clin. asst. prof. pediatrics La. State U. Sch. Medicine, 1979-85, U. Wash. Sch. Medicine, Seattle, 1985—; chmn. Renal com. Schumpert Med. Ctr., Shreveport, 1982, co-chmn. 1979-81, mem. 1983-84, co-dir. Renal Dialysis Unit, 1979-84, mem. renal transplantation com., 1984; cons. pediatric nephrology Shriner's Hosp. Crippled Children, Shreveport, 1979-84, Shreveport Regional Dialysis Ctr., 1979-84, Bossier Dialysis Ctr., Bossier City, La., 1983-84, Natchitoches (La.) Dialysis Facility, 1984. Author: (with others) Pediatric Case Studies, 1985; contbr. articles to profl. jours. Mem. Union Concerned Scientists, Cambridge, Mass., 1986—, Internat. Physicians for Prevention of Nuclear War, Boston, 1986—. Fellow Am. Acad. Pediatrics; mem. Am. Soc. Pediatric Nephrology, North Pacific Pediatric Soc., AMA, Wash. State Med. Assn., Internat. Soc. Peritoneal Dialysis, Empirical Soc. Emory U., King County Med. Soc., AAAS, Northwest Renal Soc., Southwest Pediatric Nephrology (mem. study group 1981-84). Home: 1133 16th Ave E Seattle WA 98112-3310 Office: 1221 Madison St Seattle WA 98104-1360

TENNISON, DON, entertainer; b. Dallas, Aug. 4, 1950; s. Ross R. Tennison and June Marie (Hibbard) Underwood; m. Mary Alice Ledeen, Nov. 30, 1968; children: Kenneth Donald, Ronald Brian. Grad., Palomar Coll., 1978. Newsman Tex. State Network, Ft. Worth, 1974-75; news dir. Sta. KCLE, Cleaburne, Tex., 1976-77; keyboardist Marty Robbins Enterprises, Nashville, 1980-82; producer von Allman Advt. Agy., Nacogdotches, Tex., 1983-84; rec. artist Dean Records, Escondido, Calif., 1985; songwriter Don Tennison Music, Escondido, 1985. Writer numerous songs. Served as cpl. USMC, 1969-72. Mem. Broadcast Music, Inc. Republican.

TENNISON, WILLIAM RAY, JR., financial planner, stock broker, recreational facility executive; b. Deming, N.Mex., July 22, 1941; s. William Ray and Mildred Rose (Frei) T.; m. Mary Kay Reid, Jan. 27, 1963; children: William Ervin, Bradley Joseph, Stephanie Kay (dec.). BS in Indsl. Mgmt., Ariz. State U., 1963; MBA in Econs., U. Ariz., 1966. Indsl. engr. USAF, 1963-71; from account exec. to br. office mgr., stockbroker E. F. Hutton & Co., Mesa, Ariz., 1971-88, first v.p., also mem. Dirs. Adv. Coun.; sr. v.p., stockbroker Kemper Security Group, Mesa, Ariz., 1988-92, sr. v.p. Boettcher divsn., also Kemper Exec. Coun.; exec. v.p D.E. Frey, Mesa, Ariz., 1992—; pres. Tennison and Assocs., Inc., Mesa, Ariz., 1992—; owner Crystal Meadows Ranch, Inc., Somerset, Colo.; speaker in field at sales confs. and conventions. Author: (book/tng. program) Bill Tennison Master Class, 1990.; featured in Registered Representative Mag., 1989, Rsch. Mag., 1992, 93, Arizona Business Mag., 1993; contbr. articles to profl. jours; presenter weekly radio show. Chmn. East Valley Sr. Found., 1986-91. Mem. Mesa Rotary Club. Republican. Mem. Christian Ch. Home: 1735 N Val Vista Mesa AZ 85213 Office: DE Frey & Co 40 N Center Ste 100 Mesa AZ 85213

TENNO, JEANNE HIROKO, credit union executive; b. Honolulu, June 14, 1960; d. Ronald Wayne and Cynthia Yasuko (Chinen) Naylor. Grad., Western CUNA Mgmt. Sch., 1991. Clk. Kwikset Credit Union, Anaheim, Calif., 1978-80; head teller Orange County Postal Credit Union, Santa Ana, Calif., 1980-81, EAC Fed. Credit Union, Garden Grove, Calif., 1981-82; ops. mgr. Orange County Postal/ Fed. Employee Credit Union, Garden Grove, 1982-88; regional membership mgr. Calif. Credit Union League, Pomona, Calif., 1988-92; pres., CEO Cal West Credit Union, Newport Beach, Calif., 1992—. Office: Cal West Credit Union 4311 Jamboree Rd Newport Beach CA 92660

TENNY, EDWARD MILLARD, utility executive; b. Kansas City, Mo., Oct. 1, 1941; s. Kenneth E. and Ila (Millard) T.; m. Laura Jean Pakiser, May 30, 1963; children: Nathan E., Alison R. BA, San Francisco State U., 1968; MA, U. Calif., Berkeley, 1970; MPA, Lewis and Clark Coll., 1990. Reporting mgr. Dun & Bradstreet, Inc., San Francisco, 1963-72; regional credit mgr. Nikon, USA, San Francisco, 1973-74, product developer, 1974-77; v.p., gen. mgr. St. Johns Camera Ctrs., inc., Portland, Oreg., 1977-80; mgr. bus. lics. City of Portland, 1980-85; adminstr. Portland Water Bur., 1985—. Chmn. Citizens for Sch. Support, Beaverton, Oreg., 1984-86. Mem. ASPA (bd. dirs. 1986-87, Career Achievement award), Nat. Water Resources Assn., Am. Water Works Assn., Assn. Met. Water Agys. (v.p. 1990-91, President's award). Office: Portland Water Bur 1120 SW 5th Ave Portland OR 97204

TENNYSON, GEORG BERNHARD, English educator; b. Washington, July 13, 1930; s. Georg B. and Emily (Zimmerli) T.; m. Elizabeth Caroline Johnstone, July 13, 1953; children: Cameron, Holly. BA, George Wash. U., 1953, MA, 1959; MA, Princeton U., 1959, PhD, 1963. Instr. English U. N.C., Chapel Hill, 1962-64; asst. prof. to prof. English UCLA, 1964—. Author: Sartor Called Resartus, 1965, An Introduction to Drama, 1969, Victorian Devotional Poetry, 1981, Owen Barfield on C.S. Lewis, 1990, A Carlyle Reader, 1984, Nature and the Victorian Imagination, 1977, An Index to Nineteenth-Century Fiction, 1977, Religion and Modern Literature, 1975, Victorian Literature: Prose and Poetry (2 vols.), 1976; contbr. articles to profl. jours.; editor: Nineteenth Century Fiction, 1971-73, Nineteenth Century Literature, 1983—. With U.S. Army, 1954-56. Fullbright fellow, Freiburg, Germany, 1953-54, Guggenheim fellow, Guggenheim Found., London, 1970-71. Mem. MLA (chmn. Victorian sect. 1973), Philological Assn. of Pacific Coast (chmn. English 2 1969), Carlyle Soc. (Edinburgh). Republican. Anglican. Office: Univ of California Press Journals Division 2120 Berkeley Way Berkeley CA 94720

TENORIO, VICTOR, community college official, researcher; b. Trinidad, Colo., Dec. 30, 1937; s. Felix and Porfiria (Montoya) T.; divorced; children: Victor Jr., Yvonne Rene, Mark Anthony. BS in History, Psychology and

Edn., So. Colo. State Coll. (now U. So. Colo.), 1971. Neighborhood aide So. Colo. State Coll. (name now U. So. Colo.), Pueblo, 1971-72, admissions and records counselor, 1972-74; asst. dir. fin. aide Adams State Coll., Alamosa, Colo., 1974-75; asst. dir. admissions So. Colo. State U. (now U. So. Colo.), Pueblo, 1975-78, asst. dir. fin. aid, 1975-79; dir. student svcs. Pueblo Community Coll., 1979—, dir. admissions, fin. aid and vet. affairs, 1979-83, coord. instrnl. support, 1983-85, coord. student employment, 1985—; owner Joe's Miffler & Brake Ctr., Pueblo, Colo.; organizer, mem. Community Referral System, Canon City, Colo., 1985, Employer Svc. System (for Disabled), Pueblo, 1985—. With USMC, 1956-59. Recipient Outstanding Staff Svc. award U. So. Colo., 1979. Mem. Latin Am. Rsch. and Svcs. Agy, Colo. Ednl. Svcs. and Devel. Assn. Democrat. Roman Catholic. Office: Joes Muffler & Brake Ctr 2114 S Prairie Ave Bldg C Pueblo CO 81004

TEPPER, ROBERT JOSEPH, writer; b. N.Y.C., June 15, 1920; s. Abram Samuel and Esther Rose (Nebenzahl) T.; m. Anne Hathaway, June 24, 1946 (div. 1966); 1 child, Robert; m. Sheila Ann Finch, Nov. 20, 1976. Student, Coll. William and Mary, 1938-40; BA of Fgn. Affairs, George Washington U., 1949. Fgn. svc. officer U.S. State Dept., 1950-70; city mgr. City of Opa-Locka (Fla.), 1971; staff mem. Dade County Community Rels. Bd., Miami, Fla., 1972; dir. City Housing Authority, Clearwater, Fla., 1972-73; mktg. analysis Montgomery Capital Co., Portland, Oreg., 1973-74; dir. Washington County Area Agy. Aging, Hillsboro, Oreg., 1978-87; freelance writer, 1988—; dir. Down Town Community Assn., Portland, 1990-92, Unitarian UN Office, N.Y., 1990-92; advisor Ctr. Defense Info., Washington, 1987-92; bd. dirs. World Affairs Coun. Oreg., 1975-; chmn. Police Budget Adv. Com., Portland, 1991. Contbr. articles to profl. jours. Mem. City Club Portland, 1975-92, Defense Orientation Conf. Assn., Washington, 1989-92, Patrol Sailors Assn., 1986-92. With USN, 1940-47, comdr. USNR. Named Eagle Scout, 1934. Mem. Oreg. Hist. Soc., West Bay Yacht Club. Home: The Ambassador 1209 SW 6 Apt 301 Portland OR 97204

TERESI, JOSEPH, publishing executive; b. Mpls., Mar. 13, 1941; s. Cliff I.A. and Helen Ione (Leslie) T.; divorced; 1 child, Nicholas. Chief exec. officer Jammer Cycle Products Inc., Burbank, Calif., 1968-80, Paisano Pubs. Inc., Agoura Hills, Calif., 1970—. Pub. (mags.) Easyriders, 1971—, In the Wind, 1974—, Biker Lifestyle, 1986—, Tattoo, 1986—, Am. Rodder, 1987—, Womens Enterprise, 1987-89, Eagles Eye, 1989—. Office: Paisano Pubs Inc PO Box 3000 Agoura Hills CA 91376-3000

TERNES, DONAVON PETER, savings and loan association executive; b. Aberdeen, Dec. 20, 1959; s. Vernor and Stella (Friesz) T. AS in Agr., N.D. State U., 1982. Loan officer trainee Farmers Home Adminstrn., Denver, 1981-82; acctg. supr. Encino (Calif.) Savs. and Loan, 1982-83; asst. v.p. fin. svcs. Signal Savs. and Loan, Signal Hill, Calif., 1983-85; v.p., chief fin. officer Calif. Profl. Savs. & Loan, Beverly Hills, 1985-89; pres., chief exec. officer, chief fin. officer Mission Savs. and Loan, F.A., Riverside, Calif., 1989—, also bd. dirs. Mem. Fin. Mgrs. Soc., Tri-County chpt., Calif. League of Savs. Instns. (bd. dirs. 1991—, funds mgmt. com. 1985-89, smaller assns. com. 1989—). Office: Mission Savs and Loan FA 4860 La Sierra Ave Riverside CA 92505

TERPIN, MICHAEL JAMES, public relations executive; b. Buffalo, Feb. 3, 1957; s. Walter M. and Jeanne E. (Jackson) T. BA, Syracuse U., 1978; MFA, SUNY, Buffalo, 1982. Pub. rels. mgr. U. Redlands, Calif., 1982-84; pres., gen. mgr. Avatar Communications, Del Rosa, Calif., 1984-86; v.p. pub. rels. Canyon Studios, Agoura Hills, Calif., 1986-89; pres. The Terpin Group, Manhattan Beach, Calif., 1989—. Office: The Terpin Group Ste 301 228 Manhattan Beach Blvd Manhattan Beach CA 90266

TERRA, DALE EDWARD, personnel executive; b. Berkeley, Calif., July 16, 1948; s. Albert Lewis Terra and Norma (Angeles) Bernardi; m. Robin Davison, Aug. 24, 1976 (div. 1978); m. Diane Mae Sankari, July 3, 1983; 1 child, Dana Miglietto. Student, Coll. of Redwoods, 1968-70, Solano State Coll., Fairfield, CAlif., 1980-82; BA, Calif. State U., Sacramento, 1974, postgrad., 1977. Mgr. security Burns Internat. Security Svcs., Inc., Concord, Calif., 1974-76; rsch. asst. Calif. State U., Sacramento, 1976-77; grad. student asst. Calif. State Pers. Bd., Sacramento, 1976-77, staff svcs. analyst, 1977-80, test validation and devel. specialist, 1980-84, pers. selection cons., 1984-89; mgr. Dept. Corrections, Sacramento, 1989—; pers. cons. Orange County Corrections Dept., Orlando, Fla., 1988-92. Contbr. reports to profl. publs. Sgt. USAF, 1966-70, Vietnam. Mem. Internat. Pers. Mgmt. Assn., Pers. Testing Coun., NOW, Phi Kappa Phi, Psi Chi. Home: 336 Chisum Ave Rio Linda CA 95673-4004

TERRAIL, PATRICK ANDRÉ, restaurant and hotel consultant; b. Paris, Sept. 19, 1942; came to U.S., 1959; s. Jean Claude and Gabrielle (Sirigo) T. Student, Cornell U., 1960-63. Assoc. dir. Brasserie Restaurant, N.Y.C., 1964-65; asst. to owner El Morocco, N.Y.C., 1965-66; mng. dir. Brody Corp. Celebrity Room, Palm Beach, Fla., 1966-68, The Pier Restaurant, Palm Beach, 1968; pres., co-founder Four Elements, Inc. and Info. Clearing House, N.Y.C., 1968-72; propr. Ma Maison Restaurant, L.A., 1973-85; founder, ptnr. Ma Cuisine Cooking Sch., L.A. and Newport Beach, Calif., 1979-85; dir. food and beverage Ma Maison Sofitel Hotel, 1985-90; pres. Dining Prodns. Inc., 1990-92; spl. asst. to pres. Hiram Walker & Sons Inc., 1992—; lectr. Palm Beach Jr. Coll., 1968; asst. prof. N.Y. C.C., Bklyn., 1968-70; assoc. prof. Calif. Poly. U. Pomona, 1985-90; spokesman for Simi Winery, 1985-90; asst. to pres. Hiram Walker & Sons, Inc., 1991—, RJM Enterprises, L.A.; cons. to vice chmn. Omni Hotels; pres. Riva Richemond Hotel, St. Tropez, France. Co-author: The L.A. Wedding Organizer; appeared on TV and radio, including David Letterman Show, Regis Philbin, AM L.A., AM N.Y. Decorated chevalier Ordre Merite Agricole (France); named to Restaurant Hall of Fame, Nat. Restaurant News, 1980; recipient Ivy award Restaurants and Instns., 1982. Home and Office: 7963 Willow Glen Rd Los Angeles CA 90046

TERRANOVA, PATRICIA HELEN, treasurer; b. Tacoma, Mar. 25, 1952; d. Donald John and Alicia Katherine (Rose) Marcan; m. Richard James McDonald, Aug. 28, 1971 (div. 1974); 1 child, Christopher Ryan; m. Anthony James Terranova, July 3, 1986. A.Acctg., Ft. Steilacoom Coll., Tacoma, 1974. Contract adminstr. Titan Pacific Corp., Ft. Lewis, Wash., 1974-77; office mgr. Sequoia Supply, Tacoma, 1977-78; treas., chief fin. officer Woodworth & Co., Inc., Tacoma, 1978—. Active PTA, Tacoma, 1978—; sec.-treas. Adelaine Acres Homeowners' Assn. Mem. Nat. Assn. Credit Mgrs., Credit Execs. of Puget Sound, Women in Constrn. Republican. Roman Catholic. Office: Woodworth & Co Inc 1200 E D St Tacoma WA 98421-1795

TERRAZAS, PAUL EDWARD, facility administrator; b. L.A., June 5, 1947; s. Raul Juan and Lucy Maria (Montoya) T.; m. Cynthia Maria Mussenden, Oct. 19, 1968; children: Christpher Allen, Jennifer Joy. AA, El Camino Coll., Torrance, Calif., 1972; BS in Indsl. Tech., Calif. State U., Long Beach, 1978. Engring. aide Bendix Nav. and Control Div., Lakewood, Calif., 1971-74; product svc. technician Bendix Flight Systems Div., Lakewood, 1974-75, supr. computer shop, 1975-76, svc. shop mgr., 1976-92; facility mgr. Bendix Guidance and Control Systems, Lakewood, 1992—. Advisor, L.A. Archdiocese Office of Family Life, 1988—; leader, presenter Worldwide Marriage Encounter, L.A., 1979—. Sgt. USAF, 1966-70. Democrat. Roman Catholic. Office: Alied Signal Aerospace Co 3625 Industry Ave Lakewood CA 90712-4111

TERRELL, A. JOHN, university telecommunications director; b. Pasadena, Calif., Dec. 27, 1927; s. Harry Evans and Elizabeth (Eaton) T.; m. Elizabeth Schalk, June 6, 1949; children—Patricia Elyse, Marilee Diane, John Scott. Student, Chaffey Coll., 1947-48; B.B.A., U. N. Mex., 1952. Communications cons. Mountain States Tel. & Tel., Albuquerque, 1951-56; mgr. office and communications services A.C.F. Industries, Inc., Albuquerque, 1956-62; mgr. communications and services Norton Simon Industries, Inc., Fullerton, Ca., 1962-68; v.p. gen. mgr. Wells Fargo Security Guard Service Div. Baker Industries, Fullerton, Ca., 1968-71; adminstrv. mgr., budget adminstr. Hyland div. Baxter-Trevenol Labs. Inc., Costa Mesa, CA, 1971-77; exec. v.p. Am. Tel. Mgmt. Inst Inc., Newport Beach, Calif., 1977-78; telecommunications dir. UCLA, 1978-89, retired, 1989. Contbr. articles to profl. jours. Republican. candidate for state rep., Albuquerque, 1960; precinct chmn. and mem. Bernalillo County Rep. Central Com., 1961-62; Rep. candidate for N. Mex. State Bd. Edn., 2nd Jud. Dist., 1962; colonial aide-de-camp Gov. N. Mex., Santa Fe, 1968. Served with U.S. Mcht. Marine, 1944-45, U.S. Army, 1946-47, USAR, 1947-50. Mem. Nat. Assn. Accts. (dir. 1967-77) (Most Valuable mem. 1974-75), Telecommunications Assn., Am. Legion, Am. Legion Yacht Club , VFW. Episcopalian. Lodges: Greater Irvine Lions (charter pres. 1975-76), Albuquerque Jaycees (v.p., treas. 1956-62). Home: 1725 Port Charles Pl Newport Beach CA 92660-5319

TERRELL, HOWARD BRUCE, psychiatrist; b. Cleveland, Calif., Feb. 19, 1952. BS magna cum laude, Calif. State U., Hayward, 1974; MD, U. Calif., San Diego, 1980. Intern. Kaiser Found. Hosp., Oakland, Calif., 1980-81; resident in psychiatry U. Calif., San Francisco/Fresno, 1982-85; staff psychiatrist Kings View Corp., Reedley, Calif., 1985-87, sr. staff psychiatrist, 1987-88, dir. outpatient psychiatry, 1988-89; dir. dual diagnosis and affective disorders programs Sierra Gateway Hosp., Clovis, Calif., 1989-91. Contbr. articles to profl. jours. Fellow Am. Coll. Forensic Psychiatry; mem. Am. Acad. Psychiatry and the Law, Am. Psychiat. Assn., U. Calif.-San Francisco-Fresno Psychiat. Residency Program (alumni pres. 1985—). Office: 3100 Willow Ave Ste 102 Clovis CA 93612-4741

TERRELL, LAWRENCE P., lawyer; b. Phila., Sept. 21, 1948; s. Allen MacKay and Josephine (Peters) T.; m. Ingrid Eckmann, June 20, 1972. AB cum laude, Harvard U., 1970; JD, Georgetown U., 1975. Atty. Fed. Energy Adminstrn., Washington, 1976-77; assoc. Gorsuch, Kirgis, Campbell, Walker and Grover, Denver, 1977-81, ptnr., 1981-85; ptnr. Mayer, Brown and Pratt, Denver, 1985-88; dir., officer Ireland, Stapleton, Pryor and Pascoe, Denver, 1988—. Co-author: Law of Federal Oil and Gas Leases, 1985, 35 Rocky Mountain Mineral Law Institute, 1989. Mem. ABA, Rocky Mountain Mineral Law Found., Colo. Bar Assn., Denver Bar Assn., Ind. Petroleum Assn. Mountain States, Rocky Mountain Harvard Club. Office: Ireland Stapleton Pryor & Pascoe 1675 Broadway Ste 2600 Denver CO 80202-4685

TERRELL, W(ILLIAM) GLENN, university president emeritus; b. Tallahassee, May 24, 1920; s. William Glenn and Esther (Collins) T.; m. Gail Strandberg Terrell; children by previous marriage: Francine Elizabeth, William Glenn III. BA, Davidson Coll., 1942, LLD (hon.), 1969; MS, Fla. State U., 1948; PhD, State U. Iowa, 1952; LLD (hon.), Gonzaga U., 1984, Seattle U., 1985. Instr., then asst. prof. Fla. State U., Tallahassee, 1948-55; asst. prof., then assoc. prof., chmn. dept. psychology U. Colo., Boulder, 1955-59, assoc., acting dean Coll Arts and Scis., 1959-63; prof. psychology, dean Coll. Liberal Arts and Scis., U. Ill. at Chgo. Circle, 1963-65, dean faculties, 1965-67; pres. Wash. State U., Pullman, 1967-85, pres. emeritus, 1985—; Pres. Nat. Assn. State Univs. and Land-Grant Colls., 1977-78; cons. The Pacific Inst., Seattle, 1987—. Contbr. articles to profl. jours. Served to capt. inf. U.S. Army, 1942-46, ETO. Recipient Disting. Alumnus award U. Iowa, 1985. Fellow APA, Soc. Rsch. in Child Devel.; mem. AAAS, Sigma Xi, Phi Kappa Phi. Home: 2438 36th Ave W Seattle WA 98199 Office: The Pacific Inst 1011 Western Ave Seattle WA 98104-1040

TERRILL, KAREN STAPLETON, medical planning consultant; b. Milw., Mar. 21, 1939; d. Thomas John and Olive Patrea (Thorbjornsen) Stapleton; m. Max Kurt Winkler, Dec. 18, 1965 (dec. June 1976); m. Richard Terrill, Jan. 23, 1991 (dec. May 1991). BS in Nursing, U. Mich., 1961; MBA, U. Nev., 1974. RN, Calif. Project nurse Langley Porter N.P.I., San Francisco, 1962-64; asst. dir. nursing Milw. County Mental Health Ctr., 1964-66; instr. Fond du Lac (Wis.) Sch. Dist., 1966-67; sch. nurse Inglewood (Calif.) Sch. Dist., 1968-69; instr. nursing U. Nev., Reno, 1969-74; health planner manpower State of Nev. Comp B. Agy., Carson City, 1974-75; planning analyst St. Mary's Hosp., Reno, 1974-76; sr. system analyst U. Calif., San Francisco, 1976-79; med. planning cons. Stone Marraccini & Patterson, San Francisco, 1979—. Mem. citizen's adv. group for Shoreline Plan, City of Richmond, Calif., 1987-88, found. dir. Bay Organization for Aquatic Travel, 1979—. Mountain State Regional Planning Commn. grantee, 1973-74. Home: 1308 Mallard Dr Richmond CA 94801-4113 Office: Stone Marraccini et al One Markert Pla San Francisco CA 94105

TERRY, DALE RANDOLPH, controller; b. Phila., Jan. 15, 1947; s. Richard Arthur Terry and Anne (Schwab) Williams; m. (Polly) Elides Isabel Ramos, June 16, 1974; children: David, Joseph, Tamera, Kurt. BS in Hotel Adminstrn., Cornell U., 1970; MBA, Golden Gate U., 1978. Food svc. mgr. Svc. Systems, Davis, Calif., 1976-80; food svc. dir. Svc. Systems, Davis, 1980-81; fin. analyst Del Monte, San Francisco, 1981-85; system adminstr. Chaminade, Santa Cruz, Calif., 1985-87; contr. Charter at Beaver Creek (Colo.), 1987-88, Manor Vail (Colo.) Condominium Assn., 1988—. Scoutmaster Eagle, Colo. Boy Scouts Am., 1988. With U.S. Army, 1972-75. Recipient On My Honor award Mormon Ch., 1988. Mem. Internat. Assn. Hospitality Accts., Cornell Soc. Hotelmen. Republican. Home: PO Box 329 Edwards CO 81632-0329

TERRY, DARRELL MERLE, sociology educator, consultant; b. Council Bluffs, Iowa, Nov. 11, 1933; s. Riley Merle and Sara Blanche (Grove) T.; m. Alice Rebecca Beams, Dec. 27, 1957 (div. 1975); children: Crescent Lynn, Angela Anne. BA, Lincoln (Ill.) Christian Coll., 1956; MDiv, Lincon Christian Sem., 1963; BA in Sociology, Whittier (Calif.) Coll., 1968, MA in Sociology, 1969; PhD in Human Behavior, U.S. Internat. U., San Diego, 1975. Founding minister First Christian Ch., La Mirada, Calif., 1961-64; founder, dir. Project Challenge, Inc., Avalon, Calif., 1963-71; prof. Cypress (Calif.) Coll., 1971-80, chmn. dept. human svcs., 1981-88, prof. human svcs., 1988—; dir. DM Terry Cons., Long Beach, Calif., 1980—; bd. dirs. U.S. Div. of Toc-H, London, City of Refuge, Tijuana, Mex., Resource Inst., Long Beach. Bd. dirs. LAOS, Inc., El Toro, Calif., 1975—; creator Eagles Nest Self Esteem program. Mem. Calif. Assn. Drug and Alcohol Educators (v.p. bd. dirs. Mission Viejo, Calif. chpt. 1984—), Lincoln Christian Coll. Alumni Assn. (Restoration award 1968, Alumni of Yr.), Alpha Kappa Delta. Mem. Christian Ch. Home: 5796 Campo Walk Long Beach CA 90803-5035 Office: Cypress Coll 9200 Valley View St Cypress CA 90630-5897

TERRY, FRANK JEFFREY, bishop. Bishop Diocese of Spokane, Wash., 1991—. Office: Diocese of Spokane 245 E 13th Ave Spokane WA 99202*

TERRY, RICHARD FRANK, data transcriber; b. Ogden, Utah, July 19, 1949; s. Frank Nebeker and Gertrude Angeline (Berghout) T. BA, Weber State Coll., 1979. Data transcriber IRS, Marriott, Utah, 1976—. Mem. Ch. of Jesus Christ of Latter Day Saints.

TERRY, ROBERT DAVIS, neuropathologist, educator; b. Hartford, Conn., Jan. 13, 1924; m. Patricia Ann Blech, June 27, 1952; 1 son, Nicolas Saul. AB, Williams Coll., 1946, DSc (hon.), 1991; M.D., Albany (N.Y.) Med. Coll., 1950. Diplomate: Am. Bd. Pathology, Am. Bd. Neuropathology. Postdoctoral tng. St. Francis Hosp., Hartford, 1950, Bellevue Hosp., N.Y.C., 1951, Montefiore Hosp., N.Y.C., 1952-53, 54-55, Inst. Recherches sur le Cancer, Paris, France, 1953-54; sr. postdoctoral fellow Inst. Recherches sur le Cancer, 1965-66; asst. pathologist Montefiore Hosp., 1955-59; assoc. prof. dept. pathology Einstein Coll. Medicine, Bronx, N.Y., 1959-64; prof. Einstein Coll. Medicine, 1964-84, acting chmn. dept. pathology, 1969-70, chmn., 1970-84; prof. depts. neuroscis. and pathology U. Calif.-San Diego, 1984—; mem. study sect. pathology NIH, 1964-68; study sects. Nat. Multiple Sclerosis Soc., 1964-72, 74-78; mem. bd. sci. counselors Nat. Inst. Neurol. and Communicative Disorders and Stroke, NIH, 1976-80, chmn., 1977-80; mem. nat. sci. council Huntington's Disease Assn., 1978-81; mem. med. and sci. adv. bd. Alzheimer Assn., 1978-88; mem. sci. adv. bd. Max Planck Inst., Munich, 1990—. Mem. editorial adv. bd. Jour. Neuropathology and Exptl. Neurology, 1963-83, 85-88, Lab. Investigation, 1967-77, Revue Neurologique, 1977-87, Annals of Neurology, 1978-82, Ultrastructural Pathology, 1978-86, Am. Jour. Pathology, 1985-89. Served with AUS, 1943-46. Recipient Potamkin prize for Alzheimer Rsch., 1988, Met. Life Found. award, 1991. Fellow AAAS; mem. Am. Assn. Neuropathologists (pres. 1969-70, Meritorious Contbn. award 1989), N.Y. Path. Soc. (v.p. 1969-70, pres. 1971-73), Am. Assn. Pathologists, Am. Neurol. Assn., Am. Acad. Neurologists. Office: U Calif San Diego Dept Neuroscis La Jolla CA 92093

TERRY, STEVEN SPENCER, mathematics educator, consultant; b. Hoodriver, Oreg., July 9, 1942; s. Steven Bliss and Kathryn (Spencer) T.; m. Vivian Hickman, Aug. 20, 1964; children: Yvette, Kathryn, S. Matthew, Spencer, Stuart, Heather. BS, Utah State U., 1964, MS, 1967. Tchr. math Clayton Jr. High, Salt Lake City, 1964-67, 29 Palms (Calif.) High Sch., 1967-68; tchr. math, coach Yucca Valley (Calif.) High Sch., 1968-76; prof. math. Ricks Coll., Rexburg, Idaho, 1976—. Author: (textbook) Elementary Teachers' Math, 1985. Pres. Yucca Valley City Coun., 1972-76, mem. water bd., fire and streets bd., lighting bd., recreation bd.; judge Young Woman of Yr. contests, Idaho; officer Madison County (Idaho) Baseball Assn. Recipient Outstanding Tchrs. award San Bernardino and Riverside Counties, Calif., 1976, Outstanding Secondary Educator, 1974, 75. Mem. Am. Math. Assn. Two Yr. Colls. (v.p. 1980-86), Outstanding Contribution award 1982, 84, 86, co-chair Summer Inst. at Ricks Coll. co-chair 1988 Conv.), Nat. Coun. Tchrs. of Math., NEA (life), Phi Delta Kappa (life, sec. 1974-76, Outstanding Contribution award 1984). Republican. Mormon. Home: 221 S 2D E Rexburg ID 83440 Office: Ricks Coll Rexburg ID 83460-0515

TERWILLIGER, CYNTHIA LOU, software designer; b. Cherry Pt., N.C., May 28, 1955; d. James Alexander and Shirley Mae (Zent) Marks; m. Paul Wayne Terwilliger Jr., Sept. 23, 1978; children: Bryce Ashley, Natalie Cadence. BA, U. Redlands, Redlands, 1977; MA, U. Calif., Riverside, 1980; EdD, U.S. Internat. U., 1987. Classroom tchr. Yucaipa (Calif.) Joint Unified Sch. Dist., 1977-83; edn. therapist Learning Devel. Svcs., San Diego, 1983-88; instrnl. designer Perspective Instrnl. Communication, San Diego, 1984, ISSCO, San Diego, 1985, Jostens Learning Corp., San Diego, 1986—; dir. Corp. Partnerships, 1992—. Designer of software including Elementary Math Curricula, 1987, Take Home Computer, 1990, Home Learning System, 1990, TEAMS & TAAS Inventory, 1988-90, Tapestry, 1991-92. Swim instr. ARC, Redlands, 1973-84; fundraiser Am. Heart Assn., Yucaipa, 1982. Mem. Learning Disabilities Assn., Phi Delta Kappa. Republican. Home: 4636 Serenata Pl San Diego CA 92130-2462 Office: Jostens Learning Corp 6170 Cornerstone Ct E San Diego CA 92121-3766

TERWILLIGER, ROBERT BARDEN, computer science researcher; b. Ithaca, N.Y., Aug. 23, 1956; s. Ernest William and Elizabeth (Barden) T. BA in Chemistry magna cum laude, Ithaca Coll., 1980; MS in Computer Sci., U. Ill., 1982, PhD in Computer Sci., 1987. Computer operator, computer programmer Ithaco, Inc., Ithaca, 1975-80; asst. prof. U. Colo., Boulder, 1987-92, rsch. assoc., 1992—. Contbr. articles to profl. jours. Fellowship U. Ill., 1980; Regents scholarshp, 1974-80. Mem. IEEE Computer Soc., Assn. for Computing Machinery, Assn. for Artificial Intelligence, Phi Kappa Phi, Sigma Xi. Office: Dept Computer Sci CB430 U Colo Boulder CO 80309

TERZIAN, JAMES RICHARD, marketing executive; b. L.A., Mar. 9, 1961; s. Carl Richard and Lynne (Morgan) T. Student, Oxford U., 1981; BA, U. Calif., Berkeley, 1984. Polit. cons. Gov. George Deukmajian and Sen. Becky Morgan, Calif., 1984; senate cons. Calif. State Senate Select Com. Bus. Devel., Sacramento, 1985-86; cons. to bus. devel. and fundraising firms Sacramento and Santa Rosa, Calif., 1986-88; exec. officer Terzian Internat. Group (TIGR), San Mateo, L.A., 1987—. Mem. Royal Oak Found., Boy Scouts Am.; assoc. mem. Calif. Rep. Cen. Com. Named to Order of St. Dunstan Episc. Ch., 1979. Mem. Soc. Creative Anachronism, Order of De Molay, Am. Gem. Soc., Pi Kappa Alpha. Office: 1543 Shoal Dr San Mateo CA 94404-1521

TERZICH, MICHAEL IRVING, planner, landscape architect; b. Sonora, Calif., Feb. 13, 1951; s. Irving M. and June (Dixon) T.; m. Geneen Granger, Aug. 18, 1988. BS, U. Calif., Davis, 1974; student, Humboldt State U., 1976; M of Landscape Architecture, U. Calif., Berkeley, 1988. Ednl. cons. Sch. Dists. in San Francisco Bay Area, 1974-79; program mgr. Marine Biology Lab., Alameda County Schs., Point Richmond, Calif., 1982-84; outdoor recreation planner Bur. of Reclamation, U.S. Dept. Interior, Lake Berryessa, Calif., 1984-88; landscape architect, project mgr. U.S. Forest Svc.-Tongass Nat. Forest, Ketchikan, Alaska, 1988-91; project mgr. U.S. Forest Svc.-Tongass Nat. Forest, Juneau, Alaska, 1991—; Presdl. mgmt. intern U.S. Forest Svc., Ketchikan, 1988-90. Mgr. design project Visitor Ctr. Bldg., S.E. Alsaka Visitor Info. Ctr., 1988-91, Mendenhall Glacier Visitor Ctr., 1991—. Office: US Forest Svc Juneau Ranger Dist 8465 Old Dairy Rd Juneau AK 99801

TESLER, LAWRENCE GORDON, computer company executive; b. N.Y.C., Apr. 24, 1945; s. Isidore and Muriel (Krechmer) T.; m. Shelagh Elisabeth Leuterio, Oct 4, 1964 (div. 1970); 1 child, Lisa Traci; m. Colleen Ann Barton, Feb. 17, 1987. BS in Math., Stanford U., 1965. Pres. Info. Processing Corp., Palo Alto, Calif., 1963-68; rsch. asst. Stanford U. Artificial Intelligence Lab., 1968-73; mem. rsch. staff Xerox Corp., Palo Alto, 1973-80; sect. mgr. Lisa div. Apple Computer, Inc., Cupertino, Calif., 1980-82, cons. engr., 1983-86, v.p. advanced tech., 1986-90, v.p. advanced products, 1990-92, v.p. engring., 1992-93, chief scientist, 1993—; bd. dirs. Advanced RISC Machines Ltd.; mem. Computer Sci. and Telecom. Bd. Contbr. articles to profl. jours., various computer software. Bd. dirs. Peninsula Sch., Menlo Park, Calif., 1974-78, C.S. and Telecom., 1991—. Mem. Assn. Computing Machinery (conf. co-chmn. 1987-88). Office: Apple Computer Inc 20525 Mariani Ave Cupertino CA 95014-6201

TESLUK, NICHOLAS GEORGE, field engineer; b. Chgo., Oct. 27, 1948; s. Walter Leonard and Alyce Grace (Manos) T.; m. Barbara Jean Frettem, July 17, 1980; children: Erik, Kristen. B. Electronic Engring., Devry Inst. Tech., Chgo., 1969. Lab. tech. Midwest Am. Dental, Waukegan, Ill., 1970-73; customer engr. IBM Corp., Greeley, Colo., 1973-88; field engr. Eastman Kodak Co., Englewood, Colo., 1988—. Mem. ASCAP. Republican. Lutheran. Home: 2303 Mountair Ln Greeley CO 80631

TESS, ROY WILLIAM HENRY, chemist; b. Chgo., Apr. 25, 1915; s. Reinhold W. and Augusta (Detl) T.; m. Marjorie Kohler, Feb. 19, 1944; children: Roxanne, Steven. BS in Chemistry, U. Ill., 1939; PhD, U. Minn., 1944. Rsch. chemist, group leader Shell Devel. Co., Emeryville, Calif., 1944—, rsch. supr., 1959-61, 63-66; rsch. supr. Royal Dutch/Shell Plastics Lab., Delft, The Netherlands, 1962-63; tech. planning supr. Shell Chem. Co., N.Y.C., 1967-70; tech. mgr. solvents Shell Chem. Co., Houston, 1970-77, cons., 1977-79; ind. cons. Fallbrook, Calif., 1979—; pres. Paint Rsch. Inst., Phila., 1973-76. Editor, organizer: Solvents Theory and Practice, 1973; (with others) Applied Polymer Science, 1975, Applied Polymer Science, 2d edit., 1985. Pres. Assn. Indsl. Scientists, Berkeley, Calif., 1948-50, Minerinda Property Owners Assn., Orinda, Calif., 1965-67, Houston Camellia Soc., 1973-74. Fellow Am. Inst. Chemists; mem. Nat. Paint and Coatings Assn. (air quality com. 1967-79), Fedn. Socs. Coatings Tech. (bd. dirs. 1973-76, Roon award 1957, Heckel award 1978), Am. Chem. Soc. (divsn. polymeric materials chmn. 1978, exec. com. 1977, Disting. Svc. award 1993). Home: 1615 Chandelle Ln Fallbrook CA 92028-1707 Office: 1615 Chandelle Ln Fallbrook CA 92028-1707

TESSIER-LAVIGNE, MARC TREVOR, neurobiologist, researcher; b. Trenton, Ont., Can., Dec. 18, 1959; came to U.S., 1987; s. Yves Jacques and Sheila Christine (Midgley) Tessier-L.; m. Mary Alanna Hynes, Feb. 4, 1989; children: Christian, Kyle. BSc, McGill U., 1980; BA, Oxford U., 1982; PhD, U. London, 1986. Exec. dir. Can. Student Pugwash Orgn., Ottawa, Ont., 1982-83; rsch. fellow devel. neurobiology unit Med. Rsch. Coun., London, 1986-87; rsch. fellow Ctr. for Neurobiology, Columbia U., N.Y.C., 1987-91; asst. prof. dept. anatomy U. Calif., San Francisco, 1991—. Contbr. articles on neurobiology to profl. jours. Rhodes scholar, 1980, Commonwealth scholar, 1983, Markey scholar, 1989, Searle scholar, 1991, McKnight scholar, 1991; Klingenstein fellow, 1992. Home: 1000 Chenery St San Francisco CA 94131 Office: U Calif Dept Anatomy San Francisco CA 94143-0452

TESTA-SMITH, MARY, recovery center administrator; b. N.Y.C., Sept. 25, 1949; d. William V. and Kathleen T. (Fitzpatrick) Nickas; m. Ronald P. Testa, Sept. 28, 1969 (div. 1990); children: Richard Italo, Sean Douglas, Brianne Kathleen; m. Barry Ray Smith, June 9, 1990; children: Charles Clinton, Grace Kiernan. AA, Mohegan C.C., 1978; BA, U. Cen. Fla., 1981; MS, Chapman Coll., 1986. Cert. chem. dependency specialist; cert. drug abuse counselor. Program coord. Navy Alcohol and Drug Safety Action, Bremerton, Wash., 1984-90; lead counselor Cabrini Hosp. Addiction Treatment, Seattle, 1990; treatment dir. Kitsap Recovery Ctr., Bremerton, 1990-91; family therapist New Beginnings of NW, Seattle, 1991; pvt. practice Family Svcs. Clinic, Port Orchard, Wash., 1990—; faculty Olympia Coll., Bremerton, 1988—; treatment dir. Lakeside Recovery Ctr., Silverdale, Wash.,

1992—; educator Dept. of Alcohol and Substance Abuse, 1988—. Editor Red Fox Rev., 1979. Bd. dirs. Olympic Coll. Human Svcs. Adv. Bd., Bremerton, 1988—. Mem. Chem. Dependency Profls. of Wash. State, Nat. Assn. of Alcohol and Drug Abuse Counselors, Assn. of Substance Abuse Providers. Office: Family Svcs Clinic 2501 Mile Hill Dr Port Orchard WA 98366

TETER, ROBERT DEAN, avionics engineer, commercial pilot; b. Alton, Ill., Feb. 22, 1946; s. Kenneth L. and Mary E. Teter; m. Karen Marie Wheeler, Jan. 20, 1968; 1 child, Kenneth. BSEE, U. Mo., Rolla, 1969; postgrad., N.C. State U., 1974, U. Mo., Kansas City, 1975, Ariz. State U., 1985-88. Engr. Western Electric/Gen. Electric HMED, Syracuse, N.Y., 1971-72; devel. engr. Western Electric/Bell Labs, Greensboro, N.C., 1972-74; design engr. King Radio, Olathe, Kans., 1974-76; sr. project engr. Sperry Comml. Flight Systems, Phoenix, 1976-79; from prin. engr. to engring. dept. head Sperry Avionics Div., Phoenix, 1979-87; from engring. mgr. to dir. radio frequency ops. Honeywell Bus. Aviation Div., Phoenix, 1987-92, dir. radio frequency ops., 1992—; mem. AIAA Tech. Com. on Gen. Aviation Systems, 1991. Patentee vibrating cylinder pressure transducer. Mem. elec. engring. indsl. adv. coun. S.D. Sch. Mines, 1989—. Home: 9678 E Adobe Dr Scottsdale AZ 85255-4402 Office: Honeywell Bus Aviation Div PO Box 29000 Phoenix AZ 85038-9000

TETHER, ANTHONY JOHN, aerospace executive; b. Middletown, N.Y., Nov. 28, 1941; s. John Arthur and Antoinette Rose (Gesualdo) T.; m. Nancy Engel Pierson, Dec. 26, 1963 (div. July 1971); 1 child, Jennifer; m. Carol Susan Dunbar, Mar. 3, 1973; 1 child, Michael. AAS, Orange County Community Coll., N.Y., 1961; BS, Rensselaer Poly Inst., 1963; MSEE, Stanford (Calif.) U., 1965, PhD, 1969. V.p., gen. mgr. Systems Control Inc., Palo Alto, Calif., 1968-78; dir. nat. intelligence Office Sec. of Def., Washington, 1978-82; dir. strategic tech. DARPA, Washington, 1982-86; corp. v.p. Ford Aerospace, Newport Beach, Calif., 1986-90, LORAL, Newport Beach, 1990-92; corp. v.p., sector mgr. Sci. Application Internat., Inc., San Diego, Calif., 1992—; chmn., bd. dirs. Condyne Tech., Inc., Orlando, Fla., 1990-92; dir. Orincon, La Jolla, Calif. Contbr. articles to profl. jours. Recipient Nat. Intelligence medal DCI, 1986, Civilian Meritorious medal U.S. Sec. Def., 1986. Mem. IEEE, Cosmos Club, Sigma Xi, Eta Kappa Nu, Tau Beta Pi. Home: 4518 Roxbury Rd Corona Del Mar CA 92625-3125

TETLOW, WILLIAM LLOYD, computer consultant; b. Phila., July 2, 1938; s. William Lloyd and Mary Eleanor (Ferris) T.; m. Amber Jane Riederer, June 13, 1964; children: Jennifer Kay, Rebecca Dawn, Derek William. Student, Cornell U., 1956-60; B in Gen. Edn., U. Omaha, 1961; MA, Cornell U., 1965, PhD, 1973. Dir. instl. research Cornell U., Ithaca, N.Y., 1965-70; dir. planning U. B.C., Vancouver, Can., 1970-82; dir. NCHEMS Mgmt. Products, Boulder, Colo., 1982-85; pres., dir. Vantage Info. Products, Inc., Boulder, 1985-87; pres., propr. Vantage Computer Svcs., Boulder, 1986—; cons. various univs. U.S., Can. and Australia, 1970—. Editor/author: Using Microcomputers for Planning and Decision Support, 1984; contbr. numerous articles to profl. jours. Mem. Mt. Calvary Luth. Ch. Coun., 1985-86, 89—, pres., 1991-92. Served to 1st lt. AUS, 1961-63. Recipient U. Colo. medal, 1987. Mem. Assn. Inst. Research (sec. 1973-75, v.p. 1980-81, pres. 1981-82). Republican. Lodges: Concordia, Tsawwassen, Kiwanis. Home: 3650 Smuggler Way Boulder CO 80303-7224

TETTEGAH, SHARON YVONNE, educator; b. Wichita Falls, Tex., Jan. 14, 1956; d. Lawrence Guice and Doris Jean (Leak) Oliver; m. Joseph Miller Zangai, Dec. 22, 1978 (div. 1983); 1 child, Tonia Manjay Zangai; m. George Tettegah, Apr. 28, 1989; 1 child, Nicole Jennifer Tettegah. AA, Coll. Alameda, 1985; BA, U. Calif., Davis, 1988, teaching cert., 1989, MA, 1991. Cert. elem. tchr., Calif. Clk. II Alameda County Mcpl. Ct., Oakland, Calif., 1976-77; acct. clk. Alameda County Social Svcs., Oakland, 1977-78, eligibility technician, 1978-82; supervising clk. Alameda County Health Care Svcs., Oakland, 1982-84; tchr. Davis (Calif.) Joint Unified Sch. Dist., 1988-89, L.A. Unified Schs., L.A., 1990-92; tchr. Oakland Unified Sch. Dist., Oakland, 1992—, tchr. sci. mentor, 1993—; cons. U. Calif., Davis, 1988-89; multicultural cons. Davis Unified Sch. Dist., 1988-89. Pres. African-Am. Grad. and Profl. Student's Orgn., Davis, 1988-89. Recipient Charlene Richardson Acad. Honors award Coll. Alameda, 1985; Calif. State Acad. fellow, 1989-91. Mem. Calif. Sci. Tchrs. Assn., Calif. Advocacy for Math and Sci., PTA, Multicultural Curriculum Assn., Supervision and Curriculum Leadership Assn., Bay ARa Sci.and Tech. Educators Consortium, Pan-African Students Assn., Calif. Tchrs. Assn., Calif. Media Libr. Educators Assn. Office: Oakland Unified Sch Dist PO Box 6433 Oakland CA 94603-0433

TEUGH, THOMAS WILLIAM, chemist, market researcher; b. Lansing, Mich., Nov. 13, 1953; s. William Clarence and Laura May (Hively) T.; children: Joseph Jackow, Janet Marie Wilson. Diploma in chemistry, Mich. State U., 1979; diploma in computers, Ariz. Tech. U., 1982; diploma in chemistry, U. Mich., 1991; ChD (hon.), MIT, 1991. Spray painter Ford Motor Co., Wixom, Mich., 1977-79; plant mgr. ThermoFil Inc., Brighton, Mich., 1979-80; rsch. interviewer Rsch. Info. Ctr. Inc./Winona, Phoenix, 1981-84; cons., songwriter, mgr. Magic Enterprises, Phoenix, 1982-92; rschr., interviewer Audience Studies Inc. Market Rschr. L.A., 1984-85; stock clk. Allied Signal Aviation Aerospace Co., Inc., Phoenix, 1985-86; with Castle Studios, Hollywood, Calif. Inventor in field (award 1979). Rschr. Behavior Rsch. Ctr., Inc., Phoenix, 1988-90. Recipient highest award Plastic's Assn., 1979, Grammy award, 1984. Republican. Office: Castle Studios Hollywood Ave Hollywood CA 90069

TEVIS, BARRY LEE, television producer, marketing executive; b. Pasadena, Calif., Feb. 5, 1956; s. John Larry Tevis and Renee Lydia Clement; m. Julie Marie Knauss, Mar. 31, 1990; children: Ben, Ann Marie, Hilary, Andrew. Student, Bates Vocat. Tech. Inst., Tacoma, 1973-75. Master control operator KTBN-TV, Santa Ana, Calif., 1975-76; producer, dir. KOTI-TV, Klamath Falls, Oreg., 1976-77, KPAZ-TV, Phoenix, Ariz., 1977-78; prodn. mgr., dir. advt. and promotion KTVL-TV, Medford, Oreg., 1978—. Recipient various broadcast awards. Mem. Broadcast Promotion and Mktg. Execs. (award of merit 1990). Christian. Office: KTVL-TV 1440 Rossanley Dr Medford OR 97501

TEVRIZIAN, DICKRAN M., JR., federal judge; b. Los Angeles, Aug. 4, 1940; s. Dickran and Rose Tevrizian; m. Geraldine Tevrizian, Aug. 22, 1964; children: Allyson Tracy, Leslie Sara. BS, U. So. Calif., 1962, JD, 1965. Tax acct. Arthur Andersen and Co., Los Angeles, 1965-66; atty., ptnr. Kirtland and Packard, Los Angeles, 1966-72; judge Los Angeles Mcpl. Ct., Los Angeles, 1972-78, State of Calif. Superior Ct., Los Angeles, 1978-82; ptnr. Manatt, Phelps, Rothenberg & Tunney, Los Angeles, 1982-85, Lewis, D'Amato, Brisbois & Bisgaard, Los Angeles, 1985-86; judge U.S. Dist. Ct., Los Angeles, 1986—. Office: US Dist Ct Royal Federal Bldg 255 E Temple St Los Angeles CA 90012-4701

THACHER, CARTER POMEROY, diversified manufacturing company executive; b. 1926. With Wilbur-Ellis Co., San Francisco, 1960—, v.p., 1963-67, pres., from 1967, chmn. bd., 1989—, also bd. dirs. Office: Wilbur-Ellis Co 320 California St San Francisco CA 94104-1403

THACHER, HENRY CLARKE, JR., computer science educator; b. N.Y.C., Aug. 8, 1918; s. Henry Clarke and Ethel (Anderson) T.; m. Ann Babcock Peters, Aug. 29, 1942; children: Mary B. Thacher Kelly, Ann K. Thacher-Renshaw, Harriet Thacher Holbrook, Alida, Henry C. III. BA, Yale U., 1940; MS, Harvard U., 1942; PhD, Yale U., 1949. Instr. chemistry Yale U., New Haven, Conn., 1947-48; asst. prof. chemistry Ind. U., Bloomington, 1949-54; task scientist Aero. Rsch. Lab., Wright Paterson AFB, 1954-58; assoc. chemist Argonne (Ill.) Nat. Lab., 1958-66, cons., 1966-76; prof. computing sci. U. Notre Dame, Ind., 1966-71; prof. computer sci. U. Ky., Lexington, 1971-85, prof. emeritus, 1985—; cons. Holloman AFB, Alamagordo, N.Mex., 1960, Jet Propulsion Lab., Pasadena, Calif., 1967. Contbr. over 70 articles to profl. jours. Fellow AAAS; mem. N.Y. Acad. Scis., Soc. Indsl. and Applied Maths. (vis. lectr. 1959-61). Democrat. Home: 924 W Cliff Dr Santa Cruz CA 95060

THACKER, DANIEL DEAN, electrical engineer, consultant; b. Sandpoint, Idaho, May 12, 1955; s. William Rufus and Teresa (Driggs) T.; m. Susan Amante, Sept. 5, 1992. BSEE, U. Idaho, 1978; MSEE, U. Mo., 1987. Elec. engr. Boeing MAC, Wichita, Kans., 1978-79; SW design engr. IFR, Inc., Wichita, 1979-80; design engr. Sundstrand, Rockford, Ill., 1980-83; project, systems engr. Emerson Electric, St. Louis, 1983-88; sr. systems engr. Eldec, Bothell, Wash., 1988-91; proprietor, chief engr. Foresight Techs., Sultan, Wash., 1989—; prin. engr. Boeing Commerical Aircraft Co., 1991—. Mem. IEEE. Office: Foresight Techs 35110 Mann Rd Sultan WA 98294-9734

THAGARD, SHIRLEY STAFFORD, sales and marketing executive; b. Detroit, Nov. 29, 1940; d. Walter Jay Stafford and Marjorie Gertrude (LaRa) Stafford Goode; children: Grayson Jay, Devon Charles. Assoc. Bus., Webber Coll., 1961; cert. Pierce Coll., 1973, UCLA, 1989. Dir. pub. relations Miami Herald, Fla., 1963-67; pres. Thagard Enterprises, Woodland Hills, Calif., 1980—; v.p. mktg. R.T. Durable Med. Products, Inc., Miami, also Woodland Hills, 1983-85; investment cons., lectr. investments Palisades Fin. Services, Sherman Oaks, Calif., 1985-86; v.p. real estate investments, M.W. Palmer and Assocs., 1986-87, with real estate sales dept. Country Club West Realtors, 1987-89; comml./investment mgr. Century 21 Town & Country Realty, Coeur d'Alene, Idaho, 1990-92; owner Property Mgmt. North Idaho, 1991—; ind. lectr. women's issues and children's health care, 1980—. Editor, pub. Pediatric Network, 1980-85. Contbr. articles to various jours. Creator Med. Moppets healthcare teaching tools, 1983. Chairperson Los Angeles County Mental Health (Expressing Feelings), 1985-87; ind. lobbyist for child abuse lAvocations: travel, water and snow skiing, writing..

THAI, PHILIP PHI, financial information company executive; b. People's Republic of China, Mar. 15, 1947; s. Thi Thai and Hgoc Ma; m. Kin San, Mar. 10, 1980; children: Susie, Nancy, Lily. Student, De Anzlo Coll., 1983. V.p. fin. officer P&T Info. Svc., San Jose, Calif., 1985—; money svcs. cons. P&T Info. Svc., San Jose, 1985—. Author: Where and How to Expense Control Save Money For Any Purpose, 1990. Mem. Highlander Club. Office: P&T Info Svc 467 Saratoga Ave Ste 275 San Jose CA 95129

THAL, MICHAEL LEWIS, educator; b. Oceanside, N.Y., Feb. 28, 1949; s. Herman Leon and Vivian (Friedman) T.; m. Daphna Oded, Dec. 23, 1980 (div. 1991); children: Channie Anne, Koren Ellen. BA in History, U. Buffalo, 1971; MA in Elem. Edn., Wash. U., 1973; MA in Reading, Calif. State U., Northridge, 1978, sch. adminstrv. credential, 1991. Cert. elem. and secondary tchr., reading specialist, Calif. Tchr. L.A. Unified Sch. Dist., L.A., 1973-78; dir. edn. Readwrite Ednl. Program, Newport Beach, Calif., 1978-80; tchr. Montobello (Calif.) Unified Sch. Dist., 1980-85; tchr., dept. chmn. Glendale (Calif.) Unified Sch. Dist., 1985-91, elem. tchr. specialist, 1991—; instr. The Learning Annex, L.A., 1986-89; sales rep. World Book, Inc., Chgo. 1986-91; chmn. Parent-Tchr.'s Adv. Coun., Roosevelt Jr. High Sch., Glendale, 1986—, reading dept.; reader Glendale Unified Sch. Dist., 1986-90, mentor tchr., 1989-91. Contbr. articles to profl. jours. Treas. Orgn. for Advancement of Space Industrialization and Settlements, L.A., 1978-80; bd. dirs. Glendale Beautification Project, 1987. Mem. Glendale Tchrs. Assn., Calif. Tchrs. Assn., NEA, Sports Connection. Republican. Jewish. Home: 5811 Woodman Ave # 18 Van Nuys CA 91401 Office: John Marshall Elem Sch 1201 E Broadway Glendale CA 91205

THALER, MANNING MICHAEL, pediatrics educator; b. Poland, Sept. 29, 1934; came to U.S., 1965; s. Morris and Fanny Thaler; m. Libby L. Fuss, Jan. 24, 1966; children: Eva, Joshua. MD, U. Toronto, Can., 1958. Prof. pediatrics U. Calif., San Francisco, 1967—, also dir. pediatric gastroenterology and nutrition; bd. dirs. U. Calif., San Francisco, 1967—. Contbr. articles to profl. jours. and chpts. to books. Pres. Holocaust Ctr. of No. Calif., San Francisco, 1982. Josiah Macy Jr. Found. scholar, 1974. Mem. Am. Soc. Biol. Chemists, Am. Pediatric Soc., Am. Soc. Clin. Investigation, Assn. for Study Liver Disease, Soc. Pediatric Research, Am. Gastroenterol. Assn. Office: U Calif M680 San Francisco CA 94143-0136

THALL, RICHARD VINCENT, school program coordinator; b. San Francisco, Sept. 12, 1940; s. Albert Vincent and Alice Stella (O'Brien) T.; m. Ellyn Marie Wisherop, June 15, 1963; children: Kristen Ellyn, Richard Vincent Jr. AA, City Coll. San Francisco, 1961; BA, San Francisco State Coll., 1964; MA, San Francisco State U., 1971. Cert. elem. tchr., Calif.; cert. secondary tchr., Calif.; cert. community coll. tchr., Calif. Tchr. biology San Francisco Unified Sch. Dist., 1965-66; tchr. biology Mt. Diablo Unified Sch. Dist., Concord, Calif., 1966-79, coord. water environ. studies program, 1979—; ranger/naturalist State of Calif., Brannan Island, 1973-78; naturalist Adventure Internat., Oakland, Calif., 1979-81; lectr. Princess Cruise Lines, 1982-84, Sea Goddess, 1986—, Sun Lines, 1987, Sitmar Lines, 1989, RCCL, 1991-93; speaker commencements U. Calif., Berkeley, 1989. Author: Ecological Sampling of the Sacramento-San Joaquin Delta, 1976; Water Environment Studies Program, 1986; co-author: Project MER Laboratory Manual, 1982. Mem. Contra Costa County (Calif.) Natural Resources Commn., 1975-78, vice-chmn., 1977-78; active Save Mt. Diablo, Concord, 1969-76, v.p., 1974-75; mem. citizens com. Assn. Bay Area Govt. Water Quality, 1979-82, vice-chmn., 1980-82; active John Marsh Home Restoration Com., Martinez, Calif., 1977-78; mem. edn. adv. com. Marine World/Africa USAd, Vallejo, Calif., 1988—; troop com. chmn. Boy Scouts Am., Concord, 1984-86, asst. scoutmaster, 1985-87. Recipient Recognition and Excellence cert. Assn. Calif. Sch. Adminstrs., 1984, Wood Badge award Boy Scouts Am., 1986; grantee State Calif., 1982, 84, San Francisco Estuary Project, 1992, EPA, 1992. Mem. AAAS, Nat. Assn. Biology Tchrs., Nat., Audubon Soc., Am. Mus. Natural Hist., Nat. Geog. Soc., Smithsonian Instn. (assoc.). Republican. Roman Catholic. Home: 1712 Lindenwood Dr Concord CA 94521-1109 Office: Mt Diablo Unified Sch Dist 1936 Carlotta Dr Concord CA 94519-1397

THAMES, CARROLL THOMAS, financial consultant; b. Webbers Falls, Okla., Sept. 26, 1938; s. Carroll Hilton and Opal (Gillespie) T.; m. Ramona Pepin, Dec. 16, 1961 (div. July 1980); children: Kimberly Ann, Gavin Thomas. BA, Coll. of Notre Dame, Belmont, Calif., 1972; MBA, U. Santa Clara, 1974. CLU, chartered fin. cons.; cert. fin. planner. Chief industr. engr. Kaiser Aluminum Chem. Corp., Oakland, Calif., 1966-83; registered prin. Anchor Nat. Fin. Svcs. Inc., Phoenix, 1980—; pres. Capital Mgmt. Network, Inc., Woodbridge, Calif., 1985—; lectr. U. Calif., Santa Cruz, 1986, Golden Gate U., Monterey, Calif., 1984-85, Hartnell Coll., Salinas, Calif., 1986-87. Contbr. fin. planning articles to profl. jours. Bd. dirs. YMCA, Salinas, 1986-87. Mem. Internat. Assn. for Fin. Planning Inc. (pres.-chmn. Monterey Bay chpt. 1985-88), Am. Soc. CLU & Chartered Fin. Consultants (pres. Monterey Bay chpt. 1984-85), Calif. Assn. for Fin. Planning (sec. 1986-87), Inst. Cert. Fin. Planners, Internat. Bd. Cert. Fin. Planners, Alpha Gamma Sigma. Republican. Office: PO Box 1024 Woodbridge CA 95258-1024

THATCHER, REGINALD, retired real estate broker; b. Los Angeles, June 18, 1927; s. Howard Russell and Regina (Cremer) T.; m. Nancy Dale Hemmings, Nov. 27, 1954 (div. 1991); 1 child, Kimberly Dale. Student, Chouinard, Los Angeles, 1939-44, UCLA Extension, West Los Angeles, 1951-66, Glendale Community Coll., 1980. Cert. real estate appraiser. Regional sales mgr. Stewart-Warner Microcircuits, Los Angeles, 1968-70; ptnr. and mfgs. rep. Compar L.A., Gardena, Calif., 1970-72; sales engr. De Angelo-Rothman & Co., Culver City, Calif., 1972-73; dist. sales mgr. Teledyne Semiconductor, Hawthorne, Calif., 1973-74; v.p. V & L Assocs., Encino, Calif., 1974-76; regional sales mgr. Triridge Corp., Goleta, Calif., 1976; realtor assoc. Pro Realty Inc., Glendale, Calif., 1976-78, O.E. Higgs Realtor, Glendale, 1978; sole proprietor Thatcher Enterprises, Newport Beach, 1978—; founder, past pres. Glendale (Calif.) Exchangors, 1979-85; dir., treas. Inst. for Cryobiol. Ext., Newport Beach, 1979—; dir. Glendale Bd. Realtors, 1981-83. Contbr. numerous articles to profl. mags.; inventor wrist worn cardiotachometer, catamaran airboat. Bd. dirs. Glendale Regional Arts Coun., 1981. Mem. Realty Investment Assn. Calif.

THAYER, JAMES NORRIS, financial corporation executive; b. Janesville, Wis., July 9, 1926; s. James Norris and Hazel (VanWormer) T.; m. Sylvia Lucille Kittell, June 26, 1948; children: Scott Norris, Diane Marie, Bradley Raymond. B.S., UCLA, 1948. With Prudential Ins. Co. Am., 1948-55; with William R. Staats & Co., 1955-65, partner, 1960-65; sr. v.p. Glore Forgan-Wm. R. Staats Inc., 1965-67; treas. Lear Siegler, Inc., 1967—, v.p., 1969—, sec., 1972—, sr. v.p. fin., 1977-87; chmn., chief exec. officer Gibraltar Fin. Corp., Beverly Hills, Calif., 1988-91; bd. dirs. Bunker Hill Income Securities. Bd. dirs., treas. Hathaway Home Children, Highland Park, Calif., 1956-62. Served with USAAF, 1944-47. Mem. UCLA Alumni Assn. (pres. 1982-84), Delta Sigma Phi, Beta Gamma Sigma. Clubs: Bel Air Country, Regency (Los Angeles). Home: 305 S Camden Dr Beverly Hills CA 90212-4202

THAYER, WILLIAM WENTWORTH, hematologist, medical oncologist; b. L.A., Mar. 17, 1926. AB with distinction, Stanfor (Calif.) U., 1949, MD, 1954. Diplomate Am. Bd. Internal Medicine. Intern in straight medicine Stanford U. Hosp., San Francisco, 1953-54, asst. resident clinic svc. medicine, 1954-55; resident in medicine VA Hosp., Boston, 1955-56; sr. resident in hematology Boston City Hosp., 1956-57; pvt. practice Stockton, Calif., 1958-72; chief div. hematology and oncology, asst. chief of medicine Harkness Community Hosp. (So. Pacific Hosp.), San Francisco, 1973-75; pvt. practice San Francisco, 1975-81; dir. dept. gen. and consultive medicine City of Hope Nat. Med. Ctr., Duarte, Calif., 1981-85; pvt. practice Monterey Park, Calif., 1986; physician dept. hematology and med. oncology CIGNA Healthplans of So. Calif., L.A., 1986—; mem. teaching staff San Joaquin Gen. Hosp., Stockton, 1958-72, reader all bone marrow exams, 1962-72; asst. clin. prof. medicine U. Calif., San Francisco, 1973-81, assoc. prof. medicine, 1981; instr., mem. resident staff teaching program Presbyn. Hosp. of Pacific Med. Ctr., San Francisco, 1981; staff physician-specialist Laguna Honda Hosp., San Francisco, 1971-81; mem. dept. gen. and consultive medicine City of Hope Nat. Med. Ctr., 1981-86. Contbr. articles to profl. jours. Chmn. cancer com., dir. tumor bd. and tumor registry French Hosp., San Francisco, 1978-81; chmn. library support com. City of Hope Nat. Med. Ctr., Duarte, 1982-86, chmn. med. records com., 1983-85; chmn. nutritional support subcom. CIGNA Hosp., L.A., 1987—, mem. tissue and transfusion com., 1989, dir. tumor registry, 1989—. Mem. Am. Fedn. for Clin. Rsch., Am. Soc. Clin. Oncology, Am. Soc. Hematology, No. Calif. Acad. Clin. Oncology (charter), ACP (life fellow), Calif. Acad. Medicine, Calif. Tissue Culture Assn., So. Calif. Bone and Mineral Rsch., So. Calif. Acad. Clin. Oncology, Phi Beta Kappa, Phi Rho Sigma. Home: 3634 Yorkshire Rd Pasadena CA 91107-5433

THEILEN, GORDON HENRY, veterinary surgery educator; b. Montevideo, Minn., May 29, 1928; s. Lou Ernst and Ema Kathryn (Schaller) T.; m. Carolyn June Simon, Mar. 6, 1953; children—Kyle, John, Ann. B.S., U. Calif.-Davis, 1953, D.V.M., 1955. Pvt. practice, Tillamook, Oreg., 1955-56; specialist, lectr. U. Calif.-Davis, 1956-57, instr., 1957-58, asst. prof., 1958-64, assoc. prof., 1964-70, prof., chief clin. oncology, 1970—. Co-author: Veterinary Cancer Medicine, 1979; co-discoverer Feline sarcoma virus and simian sarcoma virus, 1968, 70; patentee Bovine leukemia virus, 1980; feline leukemia virus vaccine, 1977; contbr. articles to profl. jours. Served with U.S. Army, 1946-48. NIH fellow, 1964-66; N.Y. Cancer Immunology fellow, 1972-73; Alexander von Humboldt Sr. Scientist award, 1979-80; Fleishmann Found. award, 1980—; Ralston Purina award in Small Animal Medicine, 1982. Mem. AVMA, Assn. Vet. Clinicians, Am. Assn. Cancer Research, Vet. Cancer Soc., Phi Zeta, Sigma Xi. Democrat. Lutheran. Club: N. Calif. Brittany Spaniel. Office: U Calif Dept Veterinary Surgery Davis CA 95616

THEIS, JOAN C., accountant; b. Flushing, N.Y., Feb. 22, 1948; d. Phillip Martin and Juanita Elizabeth (Weigelt) Brown; m. John H. Theis, Jr., Mar. 24, 1979; children: Mathew, Jacqueline. BA, U. Denver, 1970; MA, U. Colo., 1978; BS summa cum laude, Met. State Coll., Denver, 1984. CPA, Colo.; cert. master tchr., Colo. Tchr. Englewood (Colo.) Pub. Schs., 1976-82; acct. Diane D. Blackman, CPA, Denver, 1984-88, Peters & Co., CPAs, P.C., Denver, 1989-91; ptnr. Grubb, Theis & Assocs. PC CPAs, 1991—. Pres. Englewood Educators, 1981-82. Mem. AICPA, Colo. Soc. CPAs, Phi Beta Kappa, Toastmasters (v.p. 1992—), Colo. Women's C. of C. (chair 1992—). Office: Grubb Theis & Assocs PC CPAs 1660 S Albion # 403 Denver CO 80222

THEISEN, MARISSA ROCHE, organizational consultant; b. Boston, Mar. 31, 1952; d. John Francis and Elizabeth Barbara (Brooks) Roche; m. J. Charles Theisen, Feb. 6, 1982 (div. Nov. 1986); children: Victoria, Nicholas. BA, U. N.H., 1974; M in Regional Planning, Harvard U., 1976; MBA, Ariz. State U., 1987. Rsch. assoc. The Conservation Found., Washington, 1976-81; pub. involvement specialist Wirth Assocs., Phoenix, 1981-82; ind. cons. Phoenix, 1982-89; ptnr., cons. Win-Win Creations Inc., Phoenix, 1989—. Co-author: (monograph) National Forest Management, 1977. Bd. dirs. Jr. League of Phoenix, 1988, 92, Literacy Vol. of Maricopa County, Phoenix, 1987-90. Recipient FPA fellowship EPA, 1975. Mem. YWCA of Maricopa County (bd. dirs. 1991—). Democrat. Home: 5244 E Calle Redonda Phoenix AZ 85018 Office: Win-Win Creations Inc 5244 E Calle Redonda Phoenix AZ 85018

THEOBALD, MICHAEL PAUL, training executive; b. Delta, Utah, Apr. 18, 1949; s. Paul Homer and Dorothy Carol (Henderson) T.; m. Shauna Don Leavitt, Sept. 1, 1971; children: Jonathan, Jae, Jenna, Richard Tyler. BS in Social Psychology, Brigham Young U., 1974, MA in Orgn. Behavior, 1976; Cert. Orgn. Devel., Columbia U., 1979-80. Cert. sr. profl. human resources. Orgn. devel. specialist Diamond Shamrock Corp., Cleve., 1976-78; sr. specialist orgn. devel. Marathon Oil Co., Findlay, Ohio, 1978-80; cons. self-employed San Jose, Calif., 1980-81; v.p. J. Fielding Nelson & Assocs., Salt Lake City, 1981-85; tng. mgr. LDS Ch., Salt Lake City, 1985-90, dir. orgn. devel. tng., 1990—; faculty U. Phoenix, Salt Lake City, 1990—. Adv. coun. Marriott Sch Mgmt., dept. org. behavior, Brigham Young U., 1991—. Recipient Scholarship, J. Winter Smith Meml., 1975-76. Mem. Am. Soc. for Tng. & Devel. (Utah chpt. pres. 1991, Region 8 leadership coun. 1990-91), Phi Kappa Phi. Republican. Mormon. Office: LDS Ch 50 E North Temple Salt Lake City UT 84150-0001

THEROUX, PETER CHRISTOPHER SEBASTIAN, writer, translator; b. Boston, Nov. 29, 1956; s. Albert Eugene and Anne Frances (Dittami) T. AB, Harvard U., 1974; postgrad., Am. U. in Cairo, 1978-79. Author: The Strange Disappearance of Imam Moussa Sadr, 1987, Sandstorms, 1990; translator (books by Abdelrahman Munif): Cities of Salt, 1988, The Trench, 1991, Variations on Night and Day, 1993. Mem. L.A. schs. com. Harvard U. Recipient Arab League award Columbia U. Transl. Ctr., 1991. Mem. Am. Translators Assn., Am. Lit. Translators Assn., Laubach Literacy Action, Ams. for Peace Now/Shalom Achshav. Address: PO Box 14931 Long Beach CA 90803

THEURER, BYRON W., business owner, aerospace engineer; b. Glendale, Calif., July 1, 1939; s. William Louis and Roberta Cecelia (Sturgis) T.; m. Sue Ann McKay, Sept. 15, 1962 (div. 1980); children: Karen Marie, William Thomas, Alison Lee. BS in Engring. Sci., USAF Acad., 1961; MS in Aero. Sci., U. Calif., Berkeley, 1965; MBA, U. Redlands, 1991. Commd. USAF, 1961, advanced through grades to lt. col., ret. 1978; project officer Space Shuttle Devel. Prog., Houston, 1971-76; chief of test F-15 Systems Prog. Office Wright Patterson AFB, Ohio, 1976-78; sr. engr. Veda, Inc., Dayton, 1979-81, Logicon Inc., Dayton, 1981-83; project mgr. Support Systems Assocs., Inc., Dayton, 1983-84, CTA Inc., Ridgecrest, Calif., 1985-89; owner, operator The Princeton Rev. of Cen. Calif., Ridgecrest, 1989—; cons. in field. Decorated Silver Star, D.F.C., Air Medals (16); named Officer of the Yr., Air Force Flight Test Ctr., Edwards AFB, 1970. Mem. Air Force Assn., Assn. Old Crows, USAF Acad. Assn. Grads. (nat. bd. dirs. 1972-75, chpt. pres. 1981-83). Republican. Episcopalian. Home: PO Box 697 Cayucos CA 93430

THIBAUT, RICHARD L., controller; b. Vientiane, Laos, Aug. 15, 1968; came to U.S., 1983; s. William L. Thibaut and Lan T. Le. BSBA in Fin., U. Fla., 1988. CPA. Contr. Advanced Systems Installers, San Diego, 1989—; cons. Integrated Bus. Svcs., San Diego, 1989—, Calwest Mortgage Co., San Diego, 1991—. Republican. Home: 778 Mosaic Cir Oceanside CA 92057

THIELEN, CYNTHIA, state legislator. Student, Stanford U., 1951-52, UCLA, 1952-53; BA with high honors, U. Hawaii, 1975, JD, 1978. Staff atty. Legal Aid Soc. Hawaii, 1979-84; staff atty. planning and zoning com. Honolulu City Coun., 1984-85; sr. litigation assoc. Brown, Johnston & Day, 1985-88; pvt. practice Honolulu, 1988—. Editor Windward Community Newspaper, 1969-71. Mem. State Hwy. Safety Coun., 1977-81, State Environ. Coun., 1984-87, State Ho. of Reps., 1990—, Nature Conservancy, Hist. Hawai'i; bd. dirs. Hanahauoli Sch., 1976-86, Hawaii Women's Polit. Action League, 1987; candidate for lt. gov., Hawaii, 1986; v.p. State Helicopter and Tour Aircraft Adv. Bd., 1986-88, Kailua Neighborhood Bd., 1987-89; pres. Hawaii Children's Mus. Arts, Sci. and Tech., 1987-88, mem.,

1987-90; chair Mayor's Adv. Task Force on the Environ., 1989-90. Mem. LWV, ABA, Hawaii Bar Assn., Hawaii Women Lawyers (chartered), Orgn. Women Leaders, Stanford Club. Office: House of Reps Rm 1308 235 S Beretania St Honolulu HI 96813

THIERIOT, RICHARD TOBIN, publisher; b. San Francisco, Jan. 18, 1942; s. Charles de Young and Barbara Mary (Tobin) T.; m. Angelica Maria Reynal, Sept. 30, 1972; children: Charles de Young, II, Richard Reynal; stepchildren—Juan P. Withers, Simon Withers. B.A., Yale U., 1963; M.B.A., Stanford U., 1969. Reporter, Camden (N.J.) Courier-Post, 1963-64; asso. editor San Francisco Chronicle, 1969-77, editor, pub., 1977—; treas. Chronicle Pub. Co., 1969-77, pres., 1977—. Served with USMCR, 1964-67. Mem. Am. Newspaper Pubs. Assn., AP, Am. Soc. Newspaper Editors, Am. Press Inst., Calif. Press Assn., Calif. Newspaper Pubs. Assn., Sigma Delta Chi. Office: Chronicle Pub Co 901 Mission St San Francisco CA 94103-2988

THIEROLF, RICHARD BURTON, JR., lawyer; b. Medford, Oreg., Oct. 27, 1948; s. Richard Burton Sr. and Helen Dorothy (Rivolta) T. BA, Columbia U., N.Y.C., 1970. Bar: Oreg. 1976, U.S. Dist. Ct. Oreg. 1976, U.S. Ct. Appeals (9th cir.) 1977, U.S. Dist. Ct. (no. dist.) Calif. 1980, U.S. Supreme Ct., 1993. Staff atty. Orgn. of the Forgotten Am., Inc., Klamath Falls, Oreg., 1976-77, exec. dir., 1977-79; ptnr. Jacobson, Jewett & Thierolf, P.C., Medford, 1980—. Mem. City of Medford Planning Commn., 1990-92; mem. Medford Sch. Dist. 549-C Budget Com., 1991-92, chmn., 1991. Mem. ABA, Fed. Bar Assn., Oreg. Bar Assn. (local profl. responsibility com. Lake Oswego, Oreg., 1987-89), Jackson County Bar Assn. (sec. Medford chpt. 1988). Episcopalian. Home: 234 Ridge Rd Ashland OR 97520 Office: Jacobson Jewett & Thierolf PC 426 W Main St Medford OR 97501-2731

THIERS, EUGENE ANDRES, mineral economist, educator; b. Santiago, Chile, Aug. 25, 1941; came to U.S., 1962, naturalized, 1976; s. Eugenio A. and Elena (Lillo) T.; m. Marie H. Stuart, Dec. 23, 1965 (div. 1979); children: Ximena, Eugene, Alexander; m. Patricia Van Metre, Jan. 29, 1983. B.S., U. Chile, 1962; M.S., Columbia U., 1965, D.Eng.Sc., 1970. Mgr.-tech. Minbanco Corp., N.Y.C., 1966-70; dir. iron info. Battelle Inst., Columbus, Ohio, 1970-75; minerals economist SRI Internat., Menlo Park, Calif., 1975-79, dir.-minerals and metals, 1979-83, sr. cons., 1983-86; bus. mgr. inorganics, 1986—; vis. prof. mineral econs. Stanford U., Calif., 1983—; bd. dirs Small Mines Internat. Contbr. articles, chpts. to profl. publs. Campbell and Krumb fellow Columbia U., 1965-67. Fellow AAAS; mem. AIME (chmn. Columbus sect. of Ohio chpt. 1973-75, chmn. Bay Area chpt. of metall. sect. 1979-80), AIME (San Francisco sect.). Home: 426 27th Ave San Mateo CA 94403-2402 Office: SRI Internat 333 Ravenswood Ave Menlo Park CA 94025-3493

THIESEN, GREGORY ALAN, accountant; b. Denver, Apr. 24, 1958; s. Gene Duane and Virginia Ruth (Haas) T.; m. Karen Elise McGrew, Aug. 17, 1984; children: Jeffrey Richard, Jeremy Eugene. BS in Bus., U. Colo., 1980. CPA, Colo. Sr. mgr. Ernst & Whinney, Denver, 1980-89; v.p., contr. Monfort, Inc., Greeley, 1989—, now pres. Mem. student adv. coun. U. No. Colo.; mem. exec. com. Pvt. Industry Coun. Weld County; active Weld County Retirement Bd. Mem. MIT Enterprise Forum Colo. (mem. exec. com. 1987-89), Greeley Country Club, No. Colo. Acctg. Club. Office: MonFort Inc PO Box G Greeley CO 80632-0350

THIGPEN, RICH, engineer; b. Florence, Ala., Dec. 7, 1966; s. Junior Edward and Mary (Moore) T. B of Indsl. Engring., Auburn U., 1990. Trainee indsl. engr. Marshall Space Flight Ctr. NASA, Huntsville, Ala., 1986-89; indsl. engr. EER Systems, El Segundo, Calif., 1990-91; quality assurance engr. PRC Inc./Jet Propulsion Lab., Pasadena, Calif., 1991—. Author (tng. manual) District Officer Resource Manual, 1990, (tng. brochures) Direct Currents, 1990. Vol. Children of the Night, Van Nuys, Calif., 1992, AIDS Project L.A., 1991—, Heal the Bay, Santa Monica, Calif., 1991—, San Diego Comic Con, San Diego, 1991-92, Starlight Foundn. Wish Granter, 1992—. Named Disting. Lt. Gov. Circle K Internat., 1989; recipient Leader of Leaders award Tex.-Okla. Kiwanis Dist., 1990. Mem. Inst. Indsl. Engrs., Soc. Disting. Collegians, Culver City Toastmasters (pres. 1992), Cal-Nev-Ha CKI Alumni Assn. (sec.-treas. 1991-93), Tau Beta Pi, Alpha Pi Mu, Phi Kappa Phi. Home: 630 Venice Way #202 Inglewood CA 90302-2869

THISSELL, CHARLES WILLIAM, lawyer; b. Sioux Falls, S.D., Nov. 23, 1931; s. Oscar H. and Bernice Grace Janet (Olbertson) T.; m. Leila Amoret Rossner; Jan. 24, 1959; children—Amoret Gates, William Richards. B.A., Augustana Coll., Sioux Falls, 1953; J.D., U. Calif.-Berkeley, 1959. Bar: Calif. 1960, U.S. Dist. Ct. (no. and ea. dists.) Calif. 1960, Ct. Appeals (9th cir.) 1966, U.S. Claims Ct. 1974, U.S. Ct. Appeals (D.C., 5th cirs.) 1985, U.S. Supreme Ct. 1985. Cert.in trial advocacy Nat. Bd. Trial Advocacy. Trial counsel Calif. Dept. Transp. San Francisco, 1959-66; asst. gen. counsel law dept. Pacific Gas and Electric Co., San Francisco, 1966-91; ptnr. Morris, Taylor & Hill (formerly Morris, Taylor, Hays & Higaki), San Francisco, 1991-93; pvt. practice law, 1993—; instr. San Francisco Law Sch., 1962-63; arbitrator Superior Cts. San Francisco and Marin County, 1979—. Vice chmn. Marin County Rep. Cen. Com., 1983-84; pres. Marin County Rep. Coun., 1981-82; chancellor, vestry mem. St. Luke's Episcopal Ch., San Francisco, 1979-82. Served to lt. (j.g.) USNR, 1953-56; comdr. Ret. Mem. ABA, San Francisco Bar Assn. (chmn. trial lawyers sect. 1974), Am. Arbitration Assn., Am. Judicature Soc. Clubs: Commonwealth of Calif. (chmn. environ. energy sect. 1981-83), Engineers (San Francisco), Marines Meml. Home: 2 Garden Rd Ross CA 94957-9999 Office: Morris Taylor & Hill 1 Bush St Ste 200 San Francisco CA 94104-4408

THISSELL, JAMES DENNIS, physicist; b. Lincoln County, S.D., June 1, 1935; s. Oscar H. and Bernice G.J. (Olbertson) T. BA cum laude, Augustana Coll., 1957; MS, U. Iowa, 1963. Rsch. physicist U. Iowa, Iowa City, 1958-64; engr. McDonnell Douglas, St. Louis, 1965-66; scientist E.G. & G., Inc., Las Vegas, Nev., 1967-68; engr. Bendix Field Engring. Corp. Ames Rsch. Ctr., Moffett Field, Calif., 1970-77, Lockheed Missiles & Space Co., Sunnyvale, Calif., 1978—. Mem. AIAA, IEEE, Am. Phys. Soc., Am. Geophys. Soc., Sigma Xi. Republican. Lutheran. Home: 38475 Jacaranda Dr Newark CA 94560-4727 Office: Lockheed Corp 0/23-20 B-100 FAC 1 PO Box 61687 Sunnyvale CA 94088-1687

THISTEL, CYNTHIA GRELLE, nursing educator, infection control clinician; b. Pitts., June 2, 1955; d. Albert Charles and Mary Jane (Hol) Grelle; m. James N. Thistel, Sept. 22, 1985. BSN, U. Fla., 1978; MSN, U. Md., 1985. Nurse epidemiologist Washington Adventist Hosp., Takoma Park, Md., 1986-89, Malcolm Grow Med. Ctr., Andrews AFB, Md., 1989; infection control clinician Porter Meml. Hosp., Denver, 1989—. Mem. Assn. for Practitioners in Infection Control, Sigma Theta Tau.

THOENNES, KARL E(VALD), III, district court supervisor; b. New Haven, Conn., Mar. 31, 1962; s. Karl E. and Phyllis J. (Petz) T. BA in English Lit., U. Alaska, 1987. Lead diver Nuclear Utility Constrn., Essex, Conn., 1980-82; deputy ct. clk. Alaska Ct. System, Palmer, 1987-90; ct. calendar supr. Alaska Ct. System, Anchorage, 1990—; membership adv. com. Local Elec. Utility, Palmer, 1988-89. Pres., bd. dirs. Ballet Alaska Inc., Anchorage, 1989—; mem. Rep. Nat. Com.; com. chmn. U. Statewide Assembly, Fairbanks, 1986-87; student body pres. U. Alaska, 1983-84, 85-86. Recipient Alaska State Legislature Commendation, 1984, Writing award U. Alaska and Anchorage Daily News Writing Competition, 1989. Mem. Nat. Assn. for Ct. Mgmt. Baptist. Office: Alaska Ct System 941 W 4th Ave Anchorage AK 99501

THOLBORN, BRETT LEWIS, accountant; b. Stockton, Calif., Dec. 10, 1957; s. George F. and Betty A. (Lewis) T.; m. Lauren D. Brungardt, June 23, 1979 (div. Sept. 1988); children: Casey L., Brooke A.; m. Laura L. Rathhaus, Nov. 30, 1990. AA, San Joaquin Delta Coll., 1978; BA, Calif. State U., Turlock, 1980. CPA Libhart, Cook & Rosek, Stockton, 1980-82, Dowden & Barker, Stockton, 1982-83, Scott, Wardell & Sands, Stockton, 1983-88; prin., CPA Tholborn Cert. Pub. Acctg., Stockton, 1988—; owner BLT Software, Stockton, 1988—. Pres. Chamber Bus. Exchange, Stockton, 1990; treas. St. Andrew's Luth. Ch., Stockton, 1984-88. Mem. AICPA, Calif. Soc. CPA, Greater Stockton C. of C. Republican. Home: 6851 Atlanta Cir Stockton CA 95219 Office: Tholborn CPA 1743 Grand Canal Blvd Ste 17 Stockton CA 95207-8108

THOMAN, JOHN EVERETT, architect, mediator; b. Dixon, Ill., Aug. 6, 1925; s. George Dewey and Agnes Katherine (Fane) T.; m. Paula Ann Finnegan, Oct. 31, 1953; children: Shawn Michael, Brian Gerard, Kevin Charles, Trace Marie, Patricia Ann, Ronan Patrick, Caron Lynn. AA, UCLA, 1948; BArch cum laude, U. So. Calif., 1955. Registered architect and gen. contractor, Calif. Project dir. A. Quincy Jones & Frederick E. Emmons, L.A., 1956-57, assoc., 1958, dir. constrn., 1958-73; dir. specifications A. Quincy Jones, FAIA & Assocs., L.A., 1973-77; dir. specifications Albert C. Martin and Assocs., L.A., 1977-79, dir. constrn. and industry rels., 1979—, assoc., 1979-90, sr. assoc., 1990—, prin., 1991—; gen. contractor Martin of Calif., L.A., 1984—, v.p., 1985—; guest lectr. U. So. Calif. Lusk Sch. Real Estate, UCLA Grad. Sch., also various student, trade and tech. groups. Mem., vice chmn. Culver City (Calif.) Planning Commn., 1959; mem. Calif. Gov.'s Housing Commn., L.A., 1960, Community Redevel. Agy., Culver City, 1992—. With U.S. Army, 1943-45, USAF, 1950-51. Mem. AIA (chmn. design awards com. L.A. 1960), Constrn. Specifications Inst. (bd. dirs. 1977-80, guest lectr.), Phi Eta Sigma, Tau Sigma Delta. Office: Albert C Martin and Assocs 811 W 7th St Los Angeles CA 90017

THOMAS, BRIAN CHESTER, state legislator, engineer; b. Tacoma, Wash., May 19, 1939; s. Ralph R. and Katheryne (Chester) T.; m. Judith Lynn Adams, Feb. 20, 1965; children: Jeffrey, Kyle, Cheryl. BS in Indsl. Engring., Oreg. State U., 1961; postgrad., U. Wash., 1968-70; MBA, Pacific Luth. U., 1979. Civil engr. U.S. Coast Guard, Seattle, 1962-63; ops. officer U.S. Coast Guard, Astoria, Oreg., 1964-65; sr. sales engr. Puget Sound Power & Light Co., Bellevue, Wash., 1965-70, mgr. market rsch., 1971-80, rsch. adminstr., 1981-89, prin. engr., 1989-93; mem. Wash. Ho. Reps., Olympia, 1993—; chair EEI Rsch. Mgmt. Com., Washington, 1988-89, EPRI Renewable Com., Palo Alto, Calif., 1989-90; adv. bd. Nat. Renewable Energy Lab., Golden, Colo., 1990-92; mem. adv. bd. sch. elec. engring. Oreg. State U., Corvallis, 1991-93; dep. dir. region 10 U.S. Dept. Transp. Emergency Orgn., Seattle, 1989-93. Bd. dirs. Issaquah (Wash.), Sch. Dist., 1989-93. Capt. USCGR, 1961-84. Mem. Issaquah Rotary (pres. 1982-83). Republican. Home: 14715 182nd Pl SE Renton WA 98059 Office: Wash Ho Reps PO Box 40610 Olympia WA 98504-0610

THOMAS, CHARLES CARLISLE, JR., nuclear technologist; b. Rochester, N.Y., Aug. 18, 1925; s. Charles Carlisle and Pleasantine Virginia (Doan) T.; m. Marilyn Bee Smith, Dec. 1, 1945; children: Charles C. III, Frank C., Jeffrey C., Jonathan C. BS in Chemistry, U. Iowa, 1947; MS, U. Rochester, 1950. Prin. chemist Battelle Meml. Inst., Columbus, Ohio, 1953-55; fellow engr. Westinghouse Electric, Pitts., 1955-60; nuclear chemist Quantum, Inc., Wallingford, Conn., 1960-62; research mgr. Western N.Y. Nuclear Research Ctr., Buffalo, 1962-72; dir. Nuclear Sci. and Tech. Facility Nuclear Sci. and Tech. Facility, Buffalo, 1972-78; staff mem. Los Alamos (N.Mex.) Nat. Lab., 1978-90; ret., 1990; vis. prof. Tsing Hua U., Hsin Chu, Taiwan, 1964-65; prin. cons. Nuclear Tech. Cons., Santa Fe, N.Mex., 1986-91; instr. No. N.Mex. C.C., Espanola, 1987-91, program advisor, 1991—. Author: (with others) Handbook of Nuclear Safeguards and Measurement Methods, 1983; contbr. articles to profl. jours. Active Repub. County Com., Santa Fe, 1985-92. Fellow Am. Nuclear Soc. (chmn. biology and medicine div. 1988-89, 91-92); mem. Am. Chem. Soc., Health Physics Soc. (plenary). Home: 3373 La Avenida de San Marcos Santa Fe NM 87505

THOMAS, CLAUDEWELL SIDNEY, psychiatry educator; b. N.Y.C., Oct. 5, 1932; s. Humphrey Sidney and Frances Elizabeth (Collins) T.; m. Carolyn Pauline Rozansky, Sept. 6, 1958; children: Jeffrey Evan, Julie-Anne Elizabeth, Jessica Edith. BA, Columbia U., 1952; MD, SUNY, Downstate Med. Ctr., 1956; MPH, Yale U., 1964. Diplomate Nat. Bd. Med. Examiners, Am. Bd. Psychiatry. From instr. to assoc. prof. Yale U., New Haven, 1963-68, dir. Yale tng. program in social community psychiatry, 1967-70; dir. div. mental health service programs NIMH, Washington, 1970-73; chmn. dept. psychiatry U.M.D.N.J., Newark, 1973-83; prof., chmn. dept. psychiatry Drew Med. Sch., 1983—; prof., vice chmn. dept. psychiatry UCLA, 1983—; cons. A.K. Rice Inst., Washington, 1978-80. Author: (with B. Bergen) Issues and Problems in Contemporary Society, 1966; editor (with R. Bryce LaPorte) Alienation in Contemporary Society, 1976, (with J. Lindenthal) Psychiatry and Mental Health Science Handbook; mem. editorial bd. Internat. Jour. Mental Health, Adminstrn. In Mental Health. Served to capt. USAF, 1959-61. Fellow: Am. Psychoanalytic Assn. (hon.), Am. Psychiat. Assn., Am. Pub. Health Assn., Royal Soc. Health, N.Y. Acad. Sci., N.Y. Acad. Medicine; mem. Am. Sociol. Assn. Home: 30676 Palos Verdes Dr E Palos Verdes Peninsula CA 90274-6354 Office: Charles R Drew Med Sch Dept Psychiatry 1720 E 120th St Los Angeles CA 90059-3097

THOMAS, CRAIG, congressman; b. Cody, Wyo., Feb. 17, 1933; s. Craig E. and Marge Oweta (Lynn) T.; m. Susan Roberts; children: Peter, Paul, Patrick, Alexis. BS, U. Wyo., 1955. Exec. v.p. Wyo. Farm Bur., Laramie, 1960-69; asst. legis. dir. Am. Farm Bur., Wash., 1969-71; dir. nat. resource Am. Farm Bur., Chgo., 1971-75; gen. mgr. Wyo. Rural Elec. Assn., 1975-89; mem. Wyo. Ho. of Reps., 1985-1989, 101st-103rd Congresses from Wyo., Washington, D.C., 1989—. Former chmn. Natrona County (Wyo.) Rep. Com.; state rep. Natrona County Dist.; del. Rep. Nat. Conv., 1980. Capt. USMC. Mem. Am. Soc. Trade Execs., Masons. Methodist. Office: US Ho of Reps 1019 Longworth Ho Office Bldg Washington DC 20515

THOMAS, DARRELL DENMAN, lawyer; b. Lake Cormorant, Miss., Sept. 10, 1931; s. Darrell Dane and Maggie Adele (McKay) T.; m. Dora Ann Bailey, Feb. 12, 1957 (div. 1988). BS, Memphis State U., 1957; JD, U. Denver, 1960. Bar: Colo. 1960, U.S. Dist. Ct. Colo. 1960, U.S. Supreme Ct. 1967, U.S. Ct. Appeals (10th cir.) 1971. Law clk. to presiding justice U.S. Dist. Ct., Colo., 1960-61; ptnr. Mills & Thomas, Colorado Springs, Colo., 1961-65; pvt. practice Colorado Springs, 1965—; U.S. commr. U.S. Dist. Ct., 1961-71, U.S. magistrate, 1971-91. Pres. Colorado Springs Symphony, 1979-82; v.p. Colorado Springs Symphony Orch. Found. With U.S. Army, 1952-54. Mem. ABA, Colo. Bar Assn., El Paso County Bar Assn., El Paso Club (dir. 1985-88), Broadmoor Golf Club, Garden of the Gods Club, Masons, Shriner. Republican. Office: 115 E Vermijo Ave Colorado Springs CO 80903-2004

THOMAS, DAVID STANLEY, sales executive; b. Malad, Idaho, July 4, 1946; s. Stanley and Erma (Peterson) T.; m. Rochelle Skinner, Sept. 27, 1974; children: Aaron, Adam, Amanda. BS in Acctg., Brigham Young U., 1969. Ptnr. Emporium Gift Shop and Union Block Inc., Provo, Utah, 1971-73; prin. Keith Warshaw & Co., Salt Lake City, 1973-79; regional sales mgr. Eddie Parker Sales, Dallas, 1979-84; v.p. mktg. Country Cozy's Inc., Buena Park, Calif., 1984—. Bd. dirs. AYSO Soccer. Mem. Am. Legion. Republican. Mem. LDS Ch. Home: 13126 San Felipe St La Mirada CA 90638-3450 Office: Country Cozy's Inc 8011 Orangethorpe Ave Buena Park CA 90621

THOMAS, E(DWARD) DONNALL, physician, researcher; b. Mart, Tex., Mar. 15, 1920; married; 3 children. BA, U. Tex., 1941, MA, 1943; MD, Harvard U., 1946; MD (hon.), U. Cagliari, Sardinia, 1981, U. Verona, 1991, U. Parma, 1992. Lic. physician Mass., N.Y., Wash.; diplomate Am. Bd. Internal Medicine. Intern in medicine Peter Bent Brigham Hosp., Boston, 1946-47, rsch. fellow hematology, 1947-48; NRC postdoctoral fellow in medicine dept. biology MIT, Cambridge, 1950-51; chief med. resident, sr. asst. resident Peter Bent Brigham Hosp., 1951-53, hematologist, 1953-55; instr. medicine Harvard Med. Sch., Boston, 1953-55; rsch. assoc. Cancer Rsch. Found. Children's Med. Ctr., Boston, 1953-55; physician-in-chief Mary Imogene Bassett Hosp., Cooperstown, N.Y., 1955-63; assoc. clin. prof. medicine Coll. Physicians and Surgeons Columbia U., N.Y.C., 1955-63; attending physician U. Wash. Hosp., Seattle, 1963—; prof. medicine Sch. Medicine U. Wash., Seattle, 1963-90, head divsn. oncology Sch. Medicine, 1963-85, prof. emeritus medicine Sch. Medicine, 1990—; dir. med. oncology Fred Hutchinson Cancer Rsch. Ctr., Seattle, 1974-89, assoc. dir. clin. rsch. programs, 1982-89, mem., 1974—; attending physician Harborview Med. Ctr., Seattle, 1963—, VA Hosp., Seattle, 1963—, Providence Med. Ctr., Seattle, 1973—, Swedish Hosp., Seattle, 1975—; consulting physician Children's Orthopedic Hosp. and Med. Ctr., Seattle, 1963—; mem. hematology study sect. NIH, 1965-69; mem. bd. trustees and med. sci. adv. com. Leukemia Soc. Am., Inc., 1969-73; mem. clin. cancer investigation review com. Nat. Cancer Inst., 1970-74; 1st ann. Eugene C. Eppinger lectr. Peter Bent Brigham Hosp. and Harvard Med. Sch., 1974; Lilly lectr. Royal Coll. Physicians, London, 1977; Stratton lectr. Internation Soc. Hematology, 1982; Paul Aggeler lectr. U. Calif., San Francisco, 1982; 65th Mellon lectr. U. Pitts. Sch. Medicine, 1984; Stanley Wright Meml. lectr. Western Soc. Pediatric Rsch., 1985; Adolfo Ferrata lectr. Italian Soc. Hematology, Verona, Italy, 1991. Mem. editorial bd. Blood, 1962-75, 77-82, Transplantation, 1970-76, Proceedings of Soc. for Exptl. Biology and Medicine, 1974-81, Leukemia Rsch., 1977—, Hematological Oncology, 1982—, Jour. Clin. Immunology, 1982—, Am. Jour. Hematology, 1985—, Bone Marrow Transplantation, 1986—. With U.S. Army, 1948-50. Recipient A. Ross McIntyre award U. Nebr. Med. Ctr., 1975, Philip Levine award Am. Soc. Clin. Pathologists, 1979, Disting. Svc. in Basic Rsch. award Am. Cancer Soc., 1980, Kettering prize Gen. Motors Cancer Rsch. Found., 1981, Spl. Keynote Address award Am. Soc. Therapeutic Radiologists, 1981, Robert Roesler de Villiers award Leukemia Soc. Am., 1983, Karl Landsteiner Meml. award Am. Assn. Blood Banks, 1987, Terry Fox award Can., 1990, Internat. award Gairdner Found., 1990, N.Am. Med. Assn. Hong Kong prize, 1990, Nobel prize in medicine, 1990, Presdl. medal of sci., 1990,. Mem. NAS, Am. Assn. Cancer Rsch., Am. Assn. Physicians (Kober medal 1992), Am. Fedn. Clin. Rsch., Am. Soc. Clin. Oncology (David A. Karnoksky Meml. lectr. 1983), Am. Soc. Clin. Investigation, Am. Soc. Hematology (pres. 1987-88, Henry M. Stratton lectr. 1975), Internat. Soc. Exptl. Hematology, Internat. Soc. Hematology, Academie Royale de Medicine de Belgique (corresponding mem.), Swedish Soc. Hematology (hon.), Swiss Soc. Hematology, Royal Coll. Physicians and Surgeons Can. (hon.), Western Assn. Physicians, Soc. Exptl. Biology and Medicine, Transplantation Soc. Office: Fred Hutchinson Cancer Ct 1124 Columbia St Seattle WA 98104

THOMAS, ESTHER MERLENE, educator; b. San Diego, Oct. 16, 1945; d. Merton Alfred and Nellie Lida (Von Pilz) T. AA with honors, Grossmont Coll., 1966; BA with honors, San Diego State U., 1969; MA, U. Redlands, 1977. Cert. elem. and adult edn. tchr. Tchr. Cajon Valley Union Sch. Dist., El Cajon, 1969—; sci. fair coord. Flying Hills Sch.; tchr. Hopi and Navajo Native Americans, Ariz, Calif., Utah, 1964-74, Goose and Gander Nursery School, Lakeside, Calif., 1964-66; dir., supt. Bible and Sunday schs. various chs., Lakeside, 1961-87; mem. sci. com., math coun. Cajon Valley Union Sch. Dist., 1990-91. Author: (with others) Campbell County, The Treasured Years, 1990, Legends of Lakeside; contbr. articles to profl. jours. and newspapers. Mem. U.S. Senatorial Club, Washington, 1984—, Conservative Caucus, Inc., Washington, 1988—, Ronald Reagan Presdl. Found., Ronald Reagan Rep. Ctr., 1988, Rep. Presdl. Citizen's Adv. Commn., 1989—, Rep. Platform Planning Com., Calif., 1992, at-large del. representing dist. #45, Lakeside, Calif., 1992; mem. health articulation com. project AIDS, Cajon Valley Union Sch. Dist., 1988—, Concerned Women Am., Washington, Recruit Depot Hist. Mus., San Diego, 1989—, Citizen's Drug Free Am., Calif., 1989—, The Heritage Found., 1988—; charter mem. Marine Corps; mem. Lakeside Centennial Com., 1985-86; hon. mem. Rep. Presl. Task Force, Washington, 1986; mus. curator Lakeside Hist. Soc., 1992-93. Recipient Outstanding Svc. award PTA, 1972-74; recognized for various contbns. Commdg. Post Gen., San Diego Bd. Edn., 1989. Mem. Nat. Tchrs. Assn., Calif. Tchrs. Assn., Cajon Valley Educators Assn. (faculty advisor, rep. 1980-82, 84-86, 87-88), Christian Bus. & Profl. Women, Lakeside Hist. Soc., Lakeside Hist. Soc. (mus. curator 1992), Capitol Hill Women's Club, Internat. Christian Women's Club (Christian amb. to Taiwan, Korea, 1974). Republican. Home: 13594 Hwy 8 Apt 3 Lakeside CA 92040 Office: Flying Hills Elem Sch 1251 Finch St El Cajon CA 92020-1499

THOMAS, ETHEL COLVIN NICHOLS (MRS. LEWIS VICTOR THOMAS), educator; b. Cranston, R.I., Mar. 31, 1913; d. Charles Russell and Mabel Maria (Colvin) Nichols; Ph.B., Pembroke Coll. in Brown U., 1934; M.A., Brown U., 1938; Ed.D., Rutgers U., 1979; m. Lewis Victor Thomas, July 26, 1945 (dec. Oct. 1965); 1 child, Glenn Nichols. Tchr. English, Cranston High Sch., 1934-39; social dir. and adviser to freshmen, Fox Hall, Boston U., 1939-40; instr. to asst. prof. English Am. Coll. for Girls, Istanbul, Turkey, 1940-44; dean freshman, dir. admission Women's Coll. of Middlebury, Vt., 1944-45; tchr. English, Robert Coll., Istanbul, 1945-46; instr. English, Rider Coll., Trenton, N.J., 1950-51; tchr. English, Princeton (N.J.) High Sch., 1951-61, counselor, 1960-62, 72-83, coll. counselor, 1962-72, sr. peer counselor, 1986—. Mem. NEA, AAUW, Nat. Assn. Women Deans Adminstrs. and Counselors, Am. Assn. Counseling and Devel., Bus. and Profl. Women's Club (named Woman of Yr., Princeton chpt. 1977), Met. Mus. Art, Phi Delta Kappa, Kappa Delta Pi. Presbyn. Clubs: Brown University (N.Y.C.); Nassau.

THOMAS, FRANK JOSEPH, nuclear engineer; b. Pocatello, Idaho, Apr. 15, 1930; s. Emil C. and Jean (Jones) T.; m. Carol Jones, Feb. 4, 1949; children: Dale, Wayne, Keith. BSEE, U. Idaho, 1952; MS, U. Calif., Berkeley, 1957. Registered profl. mech. engr., Calif. Engr. Sandia Corp., Albuquerque, 1952-56; mgr. engring. div. Aerojet Gen., San Ramon, Calif., 1957-64; dir. nuclear program Office Sec. Defense, Washington, 1964-67; sr. scientist Rand Corp., Santa Monica, Calif., 1967-71; pres. Pacific-Sierra Rsch. Corp., L.A., 1971—; lectr. U. Calif., Berkeley, 1956-58; chmn. treaty evaluation panel Def. Advanced Rsch. Projects Agy., Washington, 1969-71; clear sky panel USAF, Washington, 1967-73. Author: Evasive Foreign Nuclear Testing, 1971, Blackjack Strategy, 1961; contbr. articles to profl. jours. including Nature, Physics Letters. Recipient Master Design award Product Engring. Mag., 1963. Mem. AAAS, Am. Inst. Aeronautics and Astro. Office: Pacific Sierra Rsch Corp 2901 28th St Santa Monica CA 90405

THOMAS, GARETH, metallurgy educator; b. Maesteg, U.K., Aug. 9, 1932; came to U.S., 1960, naturalized, 1977; s. David Bassett and Edith May (Gregory) T.; m. Elizabeth Virginia Cawdry, Jan. 5, 1960; 1 son, Julian Guy David. B.Sc., U. Wales, 1952; Ph.D., Cambridge U., 1955, Sc.D., 1969. I.C.I. fellow Cambridge U., 1956-59; asst. prof. U. Calif., Berkeley, 1960-63; asso. prof. U. Calif., 1963-67, prof. metallurgy, 1967—, assoc. dean grad. div., 1968-69, asst. chancellor, acting vice chancellor for acad. affairs, 1969-72; sci. dir. Nat. Ctr. Electron Microscopy, 1982—; cons. to industry. Author: Transmission Electron Microscopy of Metals, 1962, Electron Micoscopy and Strength of Crystals, 1963, (with O. Johari) Stereographic Projection and Applications, 1969, Transmission Electron Microscopy of Materials, 1980; contbr. articles to profl. jours. Recipient Curtis McGraw Research award Am. Soc. Engring. Edn., 1966, E.O. Lawrence award Dept. Energy, 1978, I-R 100 award R & D mag., 1987, Henry Clifton Sorby award, Internat. Metallographic Soc., 1987; Guggenheim fellow, 1972. Fellow Am. Soc. Metals (Bradley Stoughton Young Tchrs. award 1965, Grossman Publ. award 1966), Am. Inst. Mining, Metall. and Petroleum Engrs.; mem. Electron Microscopy Soc. Am. (prize 1965, pres. 1976), Am. Phys. Soc., Nat. Acad. Scis., Nat. Acad. Engring., Brit. Inst. Metals (Rosenheim medal 1977), Internat. Fedn. Electron Microscopy Socs. (pres. 1986-90), Brit. Iron and Steel Inst. Club: Marylebone Cricket (Eng.). Office: U Calif Dept Math Sci and Engring 284 Heanot Mining Bldg Berkeley CA 94720

THOMAS, GWENDOLYN JEANNE (PRAVRAJIKA BHAKTIPRANA), member of religious order; b. San Jose, Calif., Sept. 21, 1922; d. Elmer Willis and Beatrice Genevieve (Johnson) T. BA in Music Edn., Calif. State U., San Jose, 1945; BSc in Violin, Juilliard Sch., N.Y.C., 1947, MSc in Violin, 1949. Ordained to ministry, Vedanta Soc. of So. Calif., Ramakrishna Order of India. Violin tchr. Turtle Bay Music Sch., N.Y.C., 1949-54; novice nun Sarada Convent, Vedanta Soc., Hollywood, Calif., 1954-59, brahmacharini, 1959-65; sannyasini or Pravrajika (Woman Swami), Vedanta Soc., Hollywood, 1965—; lectr., performer of other ministerial duties, 1977—; dir. women's choir Temple of Vedanta Soc., Hollywood, 1965-77; mem. Hindu-Roman Cath. Dialog Com., L.A., 1990—. Mem. Interreligious Coun. of So. Calif. (del. 1988—). Home and office: 2027 N Vine St Hollywood CA 90068

THOMAS, HAYWARD, manufacturing company executive; b. Los Angeles, Aug. 9, 1921; s. Charles Sparks and Julia (Hayward) T.; m. Phyllis Mary Wilson, July 1, 1943; children: H. David, Steven T. BS, U. Calif., Berkeley, 1943. Registered profl. engr. Staff engr. Joshua Hendy Corp., Los Angeles, 1946-50; prodn. mgr. Byron Jackson Co., Los Angeles, 1950-55; mgr. mfg. Frigidaire div. Gen. Motors Corp., Dayton, Ohio, 1955-70; group v.p. White Motor Corp., Cleve., 1971-73; sr. v.p. Broan Mfg. Co., Hartford, Wis., 1973-85; pres. Jensen Industries, Los Angeles, 1985-87; retired, 1987. Served to lt.

USNR, 1943-46. Mem. Soc. Mfg. Engrs. (chmn. mfg. mgmt. council 1984-86). Republican. Episcopalian. Home: 1320 Granvia Altamira Palos Verdes Peninsula CA 90274-2006

THOMAS, HOWARD PAUL, civil engineer, consultant; b. Cambridge, Mass., Aug. 20, 1942; s. Charles Calvin and Helen Elizabeth (Hook) T.; m. Ingrid Nybo, Jan. 4, 1969; children: Kent Michael, Lisa Karen, Karina Michelle. BS in Engring., U. Mich., 1965, MS in Engring., 1966. Registered profl. engr., Alaska, Calif. Engr. Ove Arup & Ptnrs., London, 1966-67; project engr. Woodward-Clyde Cons., San Francisco, 1967-73; assoc. Woodward-Clyde Cons., Anchorage, 1975-89; spl. cons. Cowiconsult Cons., Copenhagen, 1973-75; prin. engr. Harding-Lawson Assocs., Anchorage, 1989-90; dir. engring. Am. North/EMCON, Inc., Anchorage, 1991—; chmn. Nat. Tech. Coun. Cold Regions Engring., 1988-89, chmn. com. program and publs., 1982-84; chmn. 4th Internat. Conf. cold Regions Engring., Anchorage, 1986; liaison Nat. Acad. Sci./Nat. Rsch. Coun. Polar Rsch. Bd., 1991—; advisor U.S. Arctic Rsch. Commn., 1989-93. Contbr. articles to profl. jours. Named Alaskan Engr. Yr., 1986. Fellow ASCE (pres. Anchorage chpt. 1985-86); mem. Internat. Soc. Soil Mechs. and Found. Engring., Soc. Am.'s Mil. Engrs., Cons. Engrs. Coun. of Alaska (pres. 1989-90), Am. Cons. Engrs. Coun. (nat. dir. 1990-91), Project Mgmt. Inst. (v.p. Alaska chpt. 1991—), Toastmasters (pres. Anchorage club 1984), Sons of Norway. Lutheran. Home: 2611 Brittany Dr Anchorage AK 99504-3332 Office: Am North/EMCON Inc 201 E 56th Ave #300 Anchorage AK 99518-1241

THOMAS, JACK WARD, wildlife biologist; b. Fort Worth, Sept. 7, 1934; s. Scranton Boulware and Lillian Louise (List) T.; m. Farrar Margaret Schindler, June 29, 1957; children: Britt Ward, Scranton Gregory. BS, Tex. A&M U., 1957; MS, W.Va. U., 1969; PhD, U. Mass., 1972. Wildlife biologist Tex. Game & Fish Commn., Sonora, 1957-60, Tex. Parks & Wildlife Dept., Llano, 1961-66; research biologist U.S. Forest Svc., Morgantown, W.Va., 1966-69, Amherst, Mass., 1970-73, LaGrande, Oreg., 1974—. Author, editor: Wildlife Habitats in Managed Forests, 1979 (award The Wildlife Soc. 1980), Elk of North America, 1984 (award The Wildlife Soc. 1985); contbr. numerous articles to profl. jours. Served to lt. USAF, 1957. Recipient Conservation award Gulf Oil Corp., 1983, Earle A. Childs award Childs Found., 1984, Disting. Svc. award USDA, Disting. Citizen's award, E. Oreg. State Coll., Nat Wildlife Fedn. award for Sci., 1990, Disting. Achievement award Soc. for Cons. Biology, 1990, Giraffe award The Giraffe Project, 1990, Scientist of Yr. award Oreg. Acad. Sci., 1990. Fellow Soc. Am. Foresters; mem. The Wildlife Soc. (cert., hon., pres. 1977-78, Oreg. chpt. award 1980, Arthur Einarsen award 1981, Spl. Svcs. award 1984, Also Leopold medal 1990, Group Achievement award 1990), Am. Ornithol. Union, Am. Soc. Mammalogists, Lions, Elks. Office: US Forest Svc 1401 Gekeler Ln La Grande OR 97850-9802

THOMAS, JAMES GORDON, sales and marketing consultant; b. Kansas City, Mo., Sept. 19, 1946; s. Jack Nelson and Rosemary Dorothy (Bose) T. BA, U. Calif., Santa Barbara, 1968. Field sales rep. Sues, Young & Brown, L.A., 1968-70; tele-sales rep. Eurasian Automotive, Sunnyvale, Calif., 1971-76, sales mgr., 1976-79, dir. sales, 1979-80; dir. sales World Wide Trading Corp., Mountain View, Calif., 1980-84; CEO Autohaus Mgmt., Saratoga, Calif., 1984-89, Acquired EXCELLENCE Defined, Saratoga, 1989—. Mem. Churchill Club. Democrat. Roman Catholic. Office: Acquired Excellence Defined PO Box 2873 Saratoga CA 95070

THOMAS, JAMES HENRY, III, federal agency administrator, statesman; b. Lewiston, Maine, May 14, 1960; s. James H. II and Arleen (Dube) T.; m. Kathryn England, Nov. 9, 1979; children: Brian, Matthew, Steven. BGS, Weber State Coll., 1982; MPA, Brigham Young U., 1990. Security specialist Corp. of the Pres., Salt Lake City, 1982-85; contract negotiator USAF Dept. of Def., Ogden, Utah, 1985-88; mgr. purchasing and customer svc. Fountain Fresh Inc., Salt Lake City, 1988-89; contract specialist U.S. Army Dept. of Def., Tooele, Utah, 1989—. City councilman Roy (Utah) City Corp., 1986-90, 1991—; pres. Police Sci. Assn., Rexburg, Idaho, 1978-79; pres. elect Lakeview Elem. PTA, Roy, 1990—; chmn. Roy Days Ann. Celebration, 1986, 87. Mem. Internat. City Mgmt. Assn., Utah League of Cities and Towns Assn. Republican. Home: 2055 W 5025 S Roy UT 84067-2553

THOMAS, JEANETTE MAE, accountant; b. Winona, Minn., Dec. 19, 1946; d. Herbert and Arline (Shank) Harmon; m. Gerald F. Thomas, Aug. 9, 1969; children: Bradley, Christopher. BS, Winona State U., 1968; postgrad., Colo. State U.; CFP, Coll. for Fin. Planning, Denver, 1985. Enrolled agt.; cert. fin. planner; registered rep. NASD; registered investment advisor; accredited tax advisor. Tchr. pub. schs. systems Colo., N.Mex., Mich., 1968-72; adminstrv. asst. Bus. Men's Svcs., Ft. Collins, Colo., 1974-75; tax cons. Tax Corp. Am., Ft. Collins, Colo., 1972-80; chief acct. Jayland Electric, La Porte, Colo., 1981-90; chief exec. officer Thomas Fin. Svcs. Inc., Ft. Collins, 1980—; mem. Colo. State U. Extension Adv. Bd. Contbr. articles to newspapers and profl. newsletters. Bd. dirs. local PTO, 1984-85; treas. Boy Scouts Am., 1985-88; master food preserver coop. extension Colo. State U., 1988—; speaker, mem. steering com. AARP Women's Fin. Info. Program, 1988—; mem. adv. bd. Larimer County Coop. Extension. Mem. Internat. Assn. Fin. Planning (past officer), Am. Soc. Women Accts. (bd. dirs. 1984-86), Pvt. Industry Coun. (fin. com. 1987—), Nat. Soc. Pub. Accts., Am. Notary Assn., Ft. Collins C. of C. (red carpet com. bus. assistance coun. 1989—), Inst. Cert. Fin. Planners. Home: PO Box 370 Laporte CO 80535-0370

THOMAS, JIM, professional sports team executive. Mng. gen. ptnr. Sacramento Kings. Office: Sacramento Kings 1 Sports Pkwy Sacramento CA 95834

THOMAS, KEITH VERN, bank executive; b. Provo, Utah, Oct. 21, 1946; s. Vern R. and Lois (Doran) T.; m. Sherrie Hunter, Oct. 7, 1969; children: Genevieve, Joshua, Rachel, William, Rebecca. AA, Dixie Coll., 1969; BS, Brigham Young U., 1971; MBA, St. Mary's Coll., 1980. Examiner Fed. Home Loan Bank Bd., San Francisco, 1971-79, field mgr., 1979-84, asst. dir., 1984-85; sr. v.p., dir. exams. and supervision Fed. Home Loan Bank, Seattle, 1985-88; exec. v.p. and COO Frontier Savings Assn., Las Vegas, Nev., 1988-89, pres., CEO, dir., 1989-90; 1st v.p. Am. Fed. Savs. Bank, Las Vegas, 1991—; bd. dirs. Nev. Community Found.; mem. bd. inquiry Las Vegas Met. Police Dept.; active Leadership Las Vegas; v.p., bd. dirs. Nev. Clearing House Assn.; trustee Nev. Community Reinvestment Corp. Editor: Real Estate Textbook, 1983-84. Trustee Nev. Sch. of Arts; mem. adv. bd. Clark County Community Devel.; co-chmn. fin. com. North Las Vegas Neighborhood Housing Svcs. Named Outstanding Instr., Inst. Fin. Edn. 1984. Mem. Nat. Assn. Rev. Appraisers and Mortgage Underwriters, U.S. League Gov. Affairs Coun., Brigham Young U. Mgmt. Soc. (bd. dirs.), So. Nev. Exec. Coun., Rotary. Republican. Mormon. Office: Am FSB 2887 S Maryland Pky Las Vegas NV 89109

THOMAS, KENT SWENSON, sales executive; b. Logan, Ut., Jan. 8, 1955; s. Don Wylie and Merla (Swenson) T.; m. Laurie Belle Jackson, Dec. 17, 1976; children: Joel, Jared, Katie, Jacob, Hollie. BS in Mktg. and Distribut, Utah State U., Logan, 1982. Mktg. Mgr. Metroshare Inc., Salt Lake City, Utah, 1982-83; nat. sales mgr. Wescor Inc., Logan, Utah, 1983--. Mem. Planning and Zoning Commn., Hyde Park, 1988. Republican. Mormon. Office: Wescor Inc 459 S Main St Logan UT 84321-5294

THOMAS, LAURA MARLENE, artist, private antique dealer; b. Chico, Calif., Apr. 29, 1936; d. Boyd Stanley Beck and Lois Velma (Behrke) Lyons; m. Charles Rex Thomas; children: Tracy Loraine, Jeffory Norris. AA in Fine Arts, Sacramento City Coll., 1978; BA in Fine Arts, Calif. State U., 1981. Tchrs. asst. Hanford Elem. Sch., Hanford, Calif., 1963-68; asst. dir. RSVP: Retired Sr. Vol. Program, Hanford, 1971-74; dir. of Art Bank Sacramento City Coll., Sacramento, 1976-78; pub. asst. Student Activities Calif. State Univ., Sacramento, 1978-81; antique dealer pvt. practice, Sacramento, 1981--, arts and crafts bus., 1976--; social worker Cath. Social Svcs., Sacramento, 1985--. Artist: weaving, Double Image, 1977, 2nd Place 1977; ceramic sculptor, Bird. Charter mem. YWCA, Sacramento, 1972, Folsum Hist. Soc., 1988. Cert. of appreciation, Carmellia City Ctr. Adv. Council, Sacramento, 1986. Mem. Statue of Liberty-Ellis Island Found., 1985, North Shore Animal League (Benefactors award 1985), Calif. State U. Alumni Assn., Hanford Sportsman Club (v.p. 1963-68). Republican. Protestant. Home: 2721 I St # 8 Sacramento CA 95816-4355

THOMAS, LOWELL, JR., former lieutenant governor Alaska, former state senator, author, lecturer; b. London, Oct. 6, 1923; s. Lowell Jackson and Frances (Ryan) T.; m. Mary Taylor Pryor, May 20, 1950; children: Anne Frazier, David Lowell. Student, Taft Sch., 1942; B.A., Dartmouth Coll., 1948; postgrad., Princeton Sch. Pub. and Internat. Affairs, 1952. Asst. cameraman Fox Movietone News, S.Am., 1939, Bradford Washburn Alaskan mountaineering expdn., 1940; illustrated lecturer, 1946—; asst. economist, photographer with Max Weston Thornburg, Turkey, 1947, Iran, 1948; film prodn. Iran, 1949; Tibet expdn. with Lowell Thomas, Sr., 1949; field work Cinerama, S.Am., Africa, Asia, 1951-52; travels by small airplane with wife, writing and filming Europe, Africa, Middle East, 1954-55; mem. Rockwell Polar Flight, first flight around the world over both poles, Nov., 1965; mem. Alaska State Senate, 1967-74; lt. gov. State of Alaska, 1974-79; owner Talkeetna Air Taxi, Inc., air contract carrier, Anchorage, Alaska, 1980—. Producer series of films Flight to Adventure, NBC-TV, 1956; producer, writer TV series High Adventure, 1957-59; producer documentary film Adaq, King of Alaskan Seas, 1960; producer two films on Alaska, 1962, 63, film on U. Alaska, 1964, South Pacific travel documentary, 1965, film on Arctic oil exploration, Atlantic-Richfield Co., 1969. Author: Out of this World, A Journey to Tibet, 1950, (with Mrs. Lowell Thomas, Jr.) Our Flight to Adventure, 1956, The Silent War in Tibet, 1959, The Dalai Lama, 1961, The Trail of Ninety-Eight, 1962, (with Lowell Thomas Sr.) More Great True Adventures, 1963, Famous First Flights that Changed History, 1968. Past pres. Western Alaska council Boy Scouts Am.; bd. dirs. Anchorage unit Salvation Army, Alaska Conservation Fund. Served 1st lt. USAAF, 1943-45. Mem. Nat. Parks and Conservation Assn., Alaska C. of C., Aircraft Owners and Pilots Assn. Clubs: Explorers, Marco Polo, Dutch Treat (N.Y.C.); Rotary, (Anchorage), Press (Anchorage); Dartmouth Outing; American Alpine. Address: 10800 Hideaway Lake Dr Anchorage AK 99516

THOMAS, MERRILL PATRICK, automotive sales and service executive; b. Madras, Oreg., July 15, 1932; s. William John and Loma Lenore (Laughlin) T.; m. Joan Frances Heartt, Aug. 30, 1952; children: Mark Patrick, William Bryan, Matthew John. BS, U. Oreg., 1954. Owner Thomas Sales and Svc., Inc., Madras, Redmond and Bend, Oreg., 1957—; Mem. Dealer Truck Com., 1965-70, Dealer Adv. Coun., 1962-78. Pres. Jaycees, Madrass, 1957-67, Madras C. of C., 1967-80; v.p. Madras Sch. Bd., 1962-82. Recipient Pentastar award, Quality Dealer award, award of excellence Chrysler Corp. Mem. Wheels LIfe (v.p. 1980—), Dodge One Group, Elks, Masons, Shriners. Republican. Methodist. Home: PO Box 5519 Bend OR 97708 Office: Thomas Sales & Svc Inc 2060 NE Hwy 20 Bend OR 97701

THOMAS, PAUL DENIS, aerospace scientist; b. Pueblo, Colo., Oct. 9, 1935; s. Paul Albert and Mary Louise (Klintz) T.; m. Anne Geraldine Girimonte, June 5, 1965 (div. Oct. 1991); children: Paul Denis, Christian Joseph, Elizabeth Anne. BS in Engring. with honors, UCLA, 1957, MS in Engring., 1958; postgrad., Stanford U., 1959-60. Teaching asst. UCLA, West Los Angeles, 1956-57; thermodynamics engr. Gen. Dynamics/Convair, Pomona, Calif., 1957; sr. thermodynamicist Lockheed Rsch. Lab., Palo Alto, Calif., 1958-61, sr. scientist, 1962-63, rsch. scientist, 1964-67, staff scientist, 1968-82; sr. staff scientist Lockheed R&D Div., Palo Alto, 1983—; cons. Battelle Meml. Inst., Columbus, Ohio, 1989, Corvus Rsch., Vienna, Va., 1988-89, McGraw-Hill, Dayton, Ohio, 1976-80. Contbr. numerous articles to profl. jours. Active Am. Youth Soccer Orgn., Los Altos, Calif., 1974-89. Recipient cert. of recognition NASA, 1982, 83, Sci. commendation Air Force Astronautics Lab., 1987. Fellow AIAA (assoc.; mem. fluid dynamics tech. com. 1989-92), Phi Beta Kappa, Tau Beta Pi, Phi Eta Sigma. Home: 2080 Marich Way # 11 Mountain View CA 94040 Office: Lockheed R&D O/97-10 B/256 3251 Hanover St Palo Alto CA 94304

THOMAS, PAUL MASSENNA, JR., retail executive, investment holding company executive; b. Darby, Pa., Sept. 7, 1935; s. Paul Massenna Sr. and Leota L. (Errett) T.; m. Eloise Whitney Fletcher, Aug. 28, 1957; children: Carolyn, Peter, James. Student, San Diego State U., 1953-55, U. Calif., various locations, 1955-56, 78-70. Licensed realtor Calif. Ptnr., founder Thomas Fletcher Nicol Co., San Diego, 1968-80; pres., founder Sierra S.W. Cos., San Diego, 1980—; chmn., co-owner Nat. Theme Prodn., San Diego, 1982—; owner, mng. ptnr. Thomas Jaeger Winery, San Diego, 1988—; bd. dirs., founder Rancho Santa Fe Nat. Bank. Owner, curator Mus. Show of posters since 1896 of Olympic athletes in Art. Bd. dirs. Rancho Santa Fe Assn., 1988—, pres., 1990; trustee, founding mem. Rancho Santa Fe Youth, Rancho Santa Fe Community Found.; trustee Rancho Santa Fe Little League, La Jolla Theater Arts Found., La Jolla Country Day Sch., Fountain Valley Sch., Colorado Springs; ruling elder Rancho Santa Fe Presbyn. Ch. Mem. Confrerie des Chevaliers de Tastevin (La Jolla chpt.). Republican. Clubs: Rancho Santa Fe Garden, Rancho Santa Fe Golf, Rancho Santa Fe Supper. Lodge: Rotary (Paul Harris fellow), Internat. Order St. Hubert (knight officer), Los Ancianos. Office: Thomas Jaeger Winery 13455 San Pasqual Rd Escondido CA 92025-7898

THOMAS, RICHARD VAN, state supreme court justice; b. Superior, Wyo., Oct. 11, 1932; s. John W. and Gertrude (McCloskey) T.; m. Lesley Arlene Ekman, June 23, 1956; children: Tara Lynn, Richard Ross, Laura Lee, Sidney Marie. B.S. in Bus. Adminstrn. with honors, U. Wyo., 1954, LL.B. with honors, 1956; LL.M., NYU, 1961. Bar: Wyo. 1956, U.S. Ct. Appeals (10th cir.) 1960, U.S. Ct. Mil. Appeals 1960, U.S. Supreme Ct. 1960. Law clk. to judge U.S. Ct. Appeals (10th Circuit), Cheyenne, 1960-63; assoc. firm Hirst & Applegate, Cheyenne, 1963-64; partner firm Hirst, Applegate & Thomas, Cheyenne, 1964-69; U.S. atty. Dist. Wyo., Cheyenne, 1969-74; justice Wyo. Supreme Ct., Cheyenne, 1974—, chief justice, 1985-86. Pres. Laramie County United Way, 1972, trustee, 1973-74, chmn. admissions and allocations com., 1968-69, chmn. exec. com., 1973, chmn. combined fed. campaign, 1974; bd. dirs. Goodwill Industries Wyo., Inc., 1974-77; exec. com. Cheyenne Crusade for Christ, 1974; v.p., exec. com. Wyo. Billy Graham Crusade, 1987; bd. dirs. Cheyenne Youth for Christ, 1978-81; chancellor Episcopal Diocese of Wyo., 1972—, lay dep. gen. conv., 1973—, chmn. search evaluation nomination com., 1976-77, lay reader, 1969—; bd. dirs. Community Action of Laramie County, 1977-82; chmn. Cheyenne dist. Boy Scouts Am., 1977-78, mem. nat. council, 1982-84, mem. Longs Peak council, 1977—, v.p. dist. ops., v.p. membership relationships, 1979-81, pres., 1981-83; mem. North Cen. Region Exec. Bd., 1986—, pres. Old West Trails Area, 1988—; chmn. Laramie County Health Planning Com., 1980-84. Served with JAGC USAF, 1957-60. Named Boss of Year, Indian Paintbrush chpt. Nat. Secs. Assn., 1974; Civil Servant of Year, Cheyenne Assn. Govt. Employees, 1973; Vol. of Yr., Cheyenne Office, Youth Alternatives, 1979; recipient St. George Episcopal award, 1982, Silver Beaver award Boy Scouts Am., 1985. Mem. Am., Laramie County bar assns., Wyo. State Bar, Phi Kappa Phi, Phi Alpha Delta, Omicron Delta Kappa, Sigma Nu. Clubs: Kiwanis (Cheyenne) (program com. 1969-70, dir. 1970-72, chmn. key club com. 1973-76, disting. pres. 1980-81), Masons (Cheyenne) (33 deg., past master); Shriners; Nat. Sojourners (Cheyenne). Office: Wyo Supreme Ct Supreme Ct Bldg Cheyenne WY 82002*

THOMAS, ROBERT JOSEPH, columnist, author; b. San Diego, Jan. 26, 1922; s. George H. and Marguerite (Creelman) T.; m. Patricia Thompson, Sept. 6, 1947; children: Nancy Katherine, Janet Elizabeth, Caroline Brooke. Student, UCLA, 1943. With AP, 1943—, Hollywood columnist, 1944—; radio, TV, lecture appearances; editor Action Mag., 1968-74. Author: The Art of Animation, 1958; (novel) Flesh Merchants, 1959; The Massie Case, 1966, King Cohn, 1967, Walt Disney: Magician of the Movies, 1967, Will Penny, Star, 1968, Thalberg, 1969, Selznick, 1970, The Heart of Hollywood, The Secret Boss of California, Winchell, 1971; (novel) Weekend '33, 1972; Marlon, 1974, Walt Disney, An American Original, 1976, Bud and Lou, The Abbott and Costello Story, 1977, The Road to Hollywood (with Bob Hope), 1977, The One and Only Bing, 1977, Joan Crawford, 1978, Golden Boy, the Untold Story of William Holden, 1983, Astaire, 1984, I Got Rhythm, The Ethel Merman Story, 1985; also numerous mag. articles. Mem. Beta Theta Pi. Office: Associated Press 1111 S Hill St Los Angeles CA 90015-2245

THOMAS, ROBERT LANCEFIELD, psychiatrist, surgeon; b. Forest Grove, Oreg., Feb. 23, 1909; s. Horace Estes and Georgia (Lancefield) T.; student Reed Coll., 1926-27; AB with distinction, Stanford U., 1930; MD cum laude, Harvard, 1933; children: Randolph Woodson, Suzanne Chilton, Robert W., Barbara Jelen, Gwen Thomas. Diplomate Am. Bd. Surgery. Intern, Mass. Gen. Hosp., Boston, 1933-36; fellow Lahey Clinic, Boston, 1936-37; practice medicine, specializing in surgery, Portland, Oreg., 1937-42, Oakland, Calif., 1946-64, Whitefield, N.H., 1964, Nev. Test Site, AEC, 1964-66; med. dir. Yolo Gen. Hosp., Woodland, Calif., 1966-67, Yerington, Nev., 1967-68; asst. med. dir. Multnomah Med. Svc. Bur., Portland, 1938-42; med. dir. Hosp. Svc. of Calif., Oakland, 1948-58; resident psychiatry Napa-Sonoma State Hosps., 1969-72; staff psychiatrist Napa State Hosp., 1972-80, 84-88; practice medicine, specializing in psychiatry, 1969-88; with Rehab. Mental Health Svcs., San Jose, 1980-84. With USNR, 1938—, Capt. M.C. 1942-46. Decorated Asiatic Pacific medal with 4 bronze stars. Fellow ACS; mem. Huguenot Soc., Order First Families VA 1607-1624/5, Soc. Mayflower Descs. (mem.-at-large exec. com. gen. soc. 1972-75, surgeon gen. 1969-72, gov. Calif. soc. 1970-73, gov. gen. 1975-78), Soc. of Cincinnati in State of R.I., Hereditary Order Descs. Colonial Govs., Jamestowne Soc., Soc. Calif. Pioneers, SAR, Sons and Daus. Oreg. Pioneers, Naval Order U.S., Sovereign Colonial Soc., Ams. of Royal Descent, Barons of Magna Charta, Soc. Descs. Colonial Clergy, Alden Kindred Am., Order of Crown in Am., Sons of Colonial New England, Phi Beta Kappa, Alpha Omega Alpha, Phi Gamma Delta, Nu Sigma Nu, Order Am. Armorial Ancestry, Order of Crown of Charlemagne USA. Home: 41359 Whitecrest Ct Fremont CA 94539-4529

THOMAS, ROGER PARRY, interior designer, art consultant; b. Salt Lake City, Nov. 4, 1951; s. E. Parry and Peggy Chatterton T.; m. Marilyn Harris Hite, Nov. 21, 1976 (div. Apr. 1979); m. H. Andrea Wahn, Nov. 20, 1982; 1 child, Andrew Chatterton. Student, Interlochen Arts Acad., 1969; BFA, Tufts U., 1973. Pres. Miller-Thomas, Inc., Las Vegas, Nev., 1973-76; v.p. Yates-Silverman, Inc., Las Vegas, 1976-81; v.p. design Atlandia Design a Mirage Resorts Inc. Co., Las Vegas, 1981—. Mem. Nev. State Coun. on the Arts, McCarren Arts Adv. Bd.; vice chmn. McCarren Arts. Mem. Country Club (Las Vegas). Republican. Mem. LDS Ch. Office: Atlandia Design 3260 Industrial Rd Las Vegas NV 89109-1141

THOMAS, STEPHANIE GRACE, nurse; b. Hannibal, Mo., June 2, 1964; d. Dewayne Eugene and Penny Kay (Armour) Larenson; m. Gary Ray Thomas, June 30, 1984; children: Kari Ann, Joshua Seth. ADN, Hannibal-Lagrange Coll., 1984. RN, Mo., Alaska. Charge nurse Levering Hosp., Hannibal, 1984-86, Audrain Med. Ctr., Mexico, Mo., 1986-89; staff devel. coord., infection control nurse St. Ann's Nursing Home, Juneau, Alaska, 1989-92; surgical office nurse Med. Arts Surg. Group, Fairbanks, Alaska, 1992—; instr. Lamaze childbirth, breast-feeding, Hannibal and Mexico, 1984-89; tchr. cert. nurse assts., Juneau, 1989-92; crisis pregnancy counselor, Juneau, 1989-92. Baptist.

THOMAS, STEPHEN DOUGLAS, forest development officer; b. Kyoto, Japan, May 2, 1954; came to U.S., 1955; s. Jesse Reamer and Louise (Gay) T.; m. Holly Virginia King, Aug. 12, 1978. BS in Forestry and Wildlife, Va. Poly. Inst. and State U., 1976. Cert. silviculturist Dept. Interior. Agrl. rsch. technician Agrl. Rsch. Svc. USDA, Suffolk, Va., 1977-81; forester BIA Navajo Area Office Bur. Indian Affairs Navajo Area Office, Dept. Interior, Ft. Defiance, Ariz., 1981-86; forest devel. officer, silviculturist BIA Albuquerque area Bur. Indian Affairs Albuquerque Area, Dept. Interior, Dulce, N.Mex., 1986—. Photographer (book) A Forest In Trust, 1987. Mem. Soc. Am. Foresters, Am. Peanut Rsch. and Edn. Soc. Home: Gen Delivery Dulce NM 87528 Office: Dept Interior BIA Jicarilla Agy PO Box 167 Dulce NM 87528

THOMAS, STEVE D., infosystem specialist; b. Butte, Mont., Aug. 8, 1951; s. William James and Catherine (Murphy) T.; m. Kathy Ann McCarthy, Aug. 22, 1971; children: Shawn, Heather. Programmer analyst Anaconda Co., Butte, 1973-81, systems analyst, 1981-82; systems programmer ARCO Metals, Columbia Falls, Mont., 1982-83, supr. ops. and tech. support, 1983-85; supr. of mgmt. info. systems Columbia Falls Aluminum Co., Columbia Falls, 1985—. Office: CFAC 2000 Aluminum Dr Columbia Falls MT 59912-9424

THOMAS, SYLVIA ANN, educator; b. Hanford, Calif., Jan. 16, 1947; d. Antonio R. and Esperanza R. (Gonzales) Vallejo; m. Francis Thomas, June 24, 1970; 1 child, Aric Vincent. BA, UCLA, 1968; teaching degree, Fresno State U., 1970; MA, Pepperdine U., 1973, postgrad., 1992. Cert. tchr., elem. K-9, jr. coll. and adminstrn. Tchr. Colton (Ill.) Sch. Dist., 1970-83; dean instrnl. support svcs., faculty and programs, 1993—; dean instrnl. support svcs. Moreno Valley Campus of Riverside Community Coll., 1993—. Mem. Jr. League of Riverside, 1985—. Mem. Akita Club Am. (sec., nat. liaison), Kin Ken Akita Club (newsletter editor), Inland Empire Akita Club (newsletter editor), Lake Mathews Kennel Club (treas.), Channel Islands Akita Club, Orange Empire Dog Club, Lake Mathews Kennel Club, Samoyed Club Am. Democrat. Roman Catholic. Home: 2155 Hackamore Pl Riverside CA 92506-4616

THOMAS, TERESA ANN, microbiologist, educator; b. Wilkes-Barre, Pa., Oct. 17, 1939; d. Sam Charles and Edna Grace T. BS cum laude, Coll. Misericordia, 1961; MS in Biology, Am. U. Beirut, 1965; MS in Microbiology, U. So. Calif., 1973. Tchr., sci. supr., curriculum coord. Meyers High Sch., Wilkes-Barre, 1962-64, Wilkes-Barre Area Public Schs., 1961-66; rsch. assoc. Proctor Found. for Rsch. in Ophthalmology U. Calif. Med. Ctr., San Francisco, 1966-68; instr. Robert Coll. of Istanbul (Turkey), 1968-71, Am. Edn. in Luxembourg, 1971-72, Bosco Tech. Inst., Rosemead, Calif., 1973-74, San Diego Community Coll. Dist., 1974-80; prof. math.-sci. div. Southwestern Coll., Chula Vista, Calif., 1980—, pres. acad. senate, 1984-85, del., 1986-89; chmn., coord., steering com. project Cultural Rsch. Educational and Trade Exchange, Southwestern Coll.-Shanghai Inst. Fgn. Trade; coord. Southwestern Coll. Great Teaching Seminar, 1987, 88, 89, coord. scholars program, 1988-90, Best Alliance, CREATE, 1991—; mem. exec. com. Acad. Senate for Calif. Community Colls., 1985-86, Chancellor of Calif. Community Colls. Adv. and Rev. Council Fund for Instrnl. Improvement, 1984-86; adj. asst. prof. Chapman Coll., San Diego, 1974-83; asst. prof. San Diego State U., 1977-79; chmn. Am. Colls. Istanbul Sci. Week, 1969-71; mem. adv. bd. Chapman Coll. Community Center, 1979-80; cons. sci. curriculum Calif. Dept. Edn., 1986—; pres. Internat. Relations Club 1959-61; mem. San Francisco World Affairs Coun., 1966-68, San Diego World Affairs Coun., 1992—; v.p. Palomar Palace Estates Home Owners Assn., 1983-85, pres. 1987—. mem. editorial rev. bd. Jour. of Coll. Sci. Teaching, NSTA, 1988-92; bd. dirs. San Diego-Leon Sister Cities Soc., 1991-94. Mem. Chula Vista Nature Interpretive Ctr. (life), Internat. Friendship Commn., Chula Vista, 1985—, vice chmn. 1989-90, chmn. 1990-92, Chula Vista, Calif., 1987—; mem. U.S.-Mex. Sister Cities Assn., nat. bd. dirs., 1992—, gen. chair 30th nat. conv., 1993. NSF fellow, 1965 ; USPHS fellow, 1972-73; recipient Nat. Teaching Excellence award Nat. Inst. Staff and Orgnl. Devel., 1989; recognized at Internat. Conf. Teaching Excellence, Austin, 1989; Pa. Heart Assn. research grantee, 1962; named Southwestern Coll. Woman of Distinction, 1987. Mem. Am. Soc. Microbiology, Nat. Sci. Tchrs. Assn. (life, internat. com., coord. internat. honors exchange lectr. competition sponsored with Assn. Sci Educators Great Britain, 1986), Nat. Assn. Biology Tchrs. (life), Soc. Coll. Sci. Tchrs., S.D. Zool. Soc., Calif. Tchrs. Assn., NEA, Am. Assn. Community and Jr. Colls., MENSA, Arab Am. Med. Assn., Am.-Lebanese Assn. San Diego (chmn. scholarship com., pres. 1988-93), Am. U. of Beirut Alumni and Friends of San Diego (1st v.p. 1984-91), Lions Intern. (S.W. chpt. 1990—, bull. editor 1991-93, best bull. award 1992, 93, 2nd v.p. 1992-93, 1st v.p. 1993-94, editor Roaring Times Newsletter 1993—), Kappa Gamma Pi (pres. Wilkes-Barre chpt. 1963-64, San Francisco chpt. 1967-68), Sigma Phi Sigma, Phi Theta Kappa, Alpha Pi Epsilon (advisor Southwestern Coll. chpt. 1989-90). Club: Am. Lebanese Syrian Ladies (pres. 1982-83). Office: Southwestern Coll 900 Otay Lakes Rd Chula Vista CA 91910-7223

THOMAS, VERNEDA ESTELLA, perfusionist; b. Chgo., June 21, 1936; d. Russel Huston and Verneda (Williams) T. BS, Graceland Coll., Lamoni, Iowa, 1973. Cardiovascualr technician Michael Reese Hosp., Chgo., 1962; cardiopulmonary technician Chgo. State Tuberculosis Sanitorium, Chgo., 1962-66, Loyola U. Sch. Medicine, Maywood, Ill., 1966-68; physiology technician Loyola U. Sch. Medicine, 1968-69; med. technologist Cook County Hosp., Chgo., 1969-71; rsch. assoc. Queen's Med. Ctr., Honolulu, 1973-78; intra aortic balloon pump technician Queen's Med. Ctr., 1973—; perfusionist for pvt. med. practice Honolulu, 1978-82; perfusionist Mid

Pacific Perfusion, Honolulu, 1982-88, Psicor, Inc., Honolulu, 1988—; referee, U.S. Volleyball Assn., 1978. Contbr. articles to med. publs. Mem. U.S. Pan-Am. high jump team, Mex., 1955; mem. U.S. Olympic volleyball team, Tokyo, 1964. Mem. Am. Soc. Cardiopulmonary Technology, Am. Bd. Cardiovascular Perfusion. Baptist. Home: 217 Prospect St Apt D7 Honolulu HI 96813-1724 Office: Psicor Inc 16818 Via Del Campo Ct San Diego CA 92127-1799

THOMAS, VIOLETA DE LOS ANGELES, real estate broker; b. Buenos Aires, Dec. 21, 1949; came to U.S., 1968; d. Angel and Lola (Andino) de Rios; m. Jess Thomas, Dec. 23, 1974; 1 child, Victor Justin. BA, Pine Manor Coll., 1970; BBA, U. Bus. Adminstrn., Buenos Aires, 1971. Mgr. book div. Time-Life, N.Y.C., 1970-74; real estate broker First Marin Realty, Inc., Mill Valley, Calif., 1985—. Bd. dirs. City of Tiburon, Calif., 1987—, Art and Heritage Commn., Tiburon. Named Woman of Yr. City of Buenos Aires, 1977, Agy. of Yr. Marin County and San Francisco, 1987-92. Home: PO Box 662 Belvedere Tiburon CA 94920-0662

THOMAS, WILLIAM ELWOOD (WILL THOMAS), newspaper editor; b. Willows, Calif., Feb. 5, 1932; s. Ralph E. and Bertha A. (Adam) T.; B.S. in Agrl. Journalism, Calif. State Poly. U., 1956; m. Nancy Rae Eisenbeiss, Aug. 27, 1955; children—William Scott, Brian Edward, Bradley Westlund, Karen Jessica. Reporter, Merced (Calif.) Sun-Star, 1956-57; patrolman-clk. Willows (Calif.) Police Dept., 1957-58; staff announcer, news dir. KHSL-TV and Radio Sta., Chico, Calif., 1958-60; editor Lakeport (Calif.) Record-Bee, 1960-66; weekly pubs. editor, columnist San Mateo Times Newspaper Group, 1966—. Active San Mateo coun. Boy Scouts Am., 1970-71; pres. Benjamin Franklin Jr. High Sch. PTA, 1971-72, del. state conv., 1971, 76; pres. Broadmoor Property Owners Assn., 1976-77. With U.S. Army, 1953-55. Recipient Hon. Svc. award Jefferson Coun. of PTA, 1976. Mem. Peninsula Press Club, South San Francisco C. of C. (past mem. bd. dirs.). Republican. Home: 723 87th St Colma CA 94015 Office: 1080 S Amphlett Blvd San Mateo CA 94402-1802

THOMAS, WILLIAM ESMANT, JR., air force officer; b. Euclid, Ohio, July 3, 1958; s. William Esmant and Frances Alice (Buttolph) T. BS, Miami U., 1980; MS, Air Force Inst. Tech., 1985. Commd. USAF, 1980, advanced through grades to maj., 1992; lauch and integration mgr. Space Div. Los Angeles, 1980-84; project officer Weapons Lab. Albuquerque, 1986-88; chief optical components br. Weapons Lab., Albuquerque, 1988-89, dep. program mgr. additional sci. Relay Mirror Expt., 1989-90; space systems analyst Air Force Operational Test and Evaluation Ctr., Albuquerque, 1990-93, test mgr., 1993—. Mem. Air Force Assn., Jr. Officers Group (chmn. 1987). Mem. Ch. of Christ. Home: 10616 Pennyback Park Dr NE Albuquerque NM 87123-4845 Office: USAF Operational Test and Evaliation Ctr Kirtland A F B NM 87117

THOMAS, WILLIAM GERAINT, museum administrator; b. Columbo, Sri Lanka, June 27, 1931; came to U.S., 1941; s. Cecil James and Iris Katharine (Evans) T.; m. Maria Alcalde, Jan. 2, 1976; 1 child, Laura. BA, U. Calif., Berkeley, 1952. Reporter, editor San Francisco Chronicle, 1952-64; asst. to mayor City of San Francisco, 1964-66; chief cons. majority caucus Calif. State Assembly, Sacramento, 1966-68; adminstrv. asst. U.S. Congressman Phillip Burson, Washington, 1968-70; cons. interior com. U.S. Ho. of Reps., Washington, 1972-78; ptnr. Thomas & Iovino, San Francisco, 1972-78; asst. regional dir. Nat. Park Svc., San Francisco, 1978-89; supt. San Francisco Maritime NHP, 1989—. Mem. Nat. Dem. Club; bd. dirs. Nat. Libery Ship Meml., 1978-80. Sgt. U.S. Army, 1952-54, Korea. Mem. Nat. Maritime Mus. Assn., Nat. Maritime Hist. Soc., Press Club of San Francisco (pres. 1973-74, Best News Story 1963). Episcopalian. Office: San Francisco Maritime Bldg 201 Ft Mason Bldg 204 San Francisco CA 94123

THOMAS, WILLIAM MARSHALL, congressman; b. Wallace, Idaho, Dec. 6, 1941; s. Virgil and Gertrude T.; m. Sharon Lynn Hamilton, Jan., 1967; children: Christopher, Amelia. B.A., San Francisco State U., 1963, M.A., 1965. Mem. faculty dept. Am. govt. Bakersfield (Calif.) Coll., 1965-74, prof., 1965-74; mem. Calif. State Assembly, 1974-78, 96th-102nd Congresses from 18th, now 21st Calif. Dist., 1979—; vice chmn. of House Task Force on Campaign Fin. Reform; mem. Ho. of Reps. Ways and Means Com.; ranking Rep. House Adminstrn. Com., Ways & Means subcom on Health; mem. Ways & Means subcom on Trade; mem. del. to Soviet Union, by Am. Council Young Polit. Leaders, 1977; chmn. Kern County Republican Central Com., 1972-74; mem. Calif. Rep. Com., 1972-80; del. Republican Party Nat. Conv., 1980, 84, 88; mem. Rep. Leader's Task Force on Health Care Reform. Office: House of Representative 2209 Rayburn House Office Bldg Washington DC 20515

THOMAS, WILLIAM SCOTT, lawyer; b. Joliet, Ill., Aug. 16, 1949; s. William Edward and Audrey Ann (Johnson) T.; m. Carolyn Smith Cotter, Aug. 10, 1974; children: Derek Cotter, Kimberley Cotter. AB, Stanford U., 1971; JD, U. Calif., Hastings, 1974; LLM in Taxation, Golden Gate U., 1981. Bar: Calif. 1975, U.S. Dist. Ct. (no. dist.) Calif. 1975, U.S. Tax Ct. 1982. Tax editor Internat. Bur. Fiscal Documentation, Amsterdam, Holland, 1974-75; tax atty. Chevron Corp., San Francisco, 1975-77; from assoc. to ptnr. Brobeck, Phleger & Harrison, San Francisco, 1978—; bd. dirs. Value Line Inc., N.Y.C. Mem. ABA (taxation sect.), Calif. Bar Assn. (exec. com. taxation sect. 1984-89, chmn. 1987-88). Office: Brobeck Phleger & Harrison 1 Market Plz San Francisco CA 94105-1019

THOMASON, C. JO, special education association administrator; b. Chgo., Mar. 7, 1937; d. Clarence Walker-Failor and Mary (Springer) Dotts; m. Duncan MacDonald, June 4, 1956 (div. 1959); m. Tom William Thomason, June 6, 1960. Student, U. Colo., 1954-56; BS, U. Minn., 1958; MS, U. N.Mex., 1968, Ed.D., 1977. Cert. spl. edn. tchr., elem. edn., adminstrn., N.Mex. Tchr. spl. edn. Taos (N.Mex.) Pub. Schs., 1958-59; tchr. elem edn. Albuquerque Pub. Schs., 1959-66, tchr. spl. edn., 1966-69, coordinator spl. edn., 1969-76, area coordinator spl. edn., 1976-78, asst. dir. spl. edn., 1978-86; ednl. cons. Albuquerque, 1986—; exec. dir. Coun. Adminstrs. of Spl. Edn., Albuquerque, 1988—; lectr., presenter numerous state depts. edn., local dists., pvt. bus. in U.S., Can., Gt. Britain, 1967—; cons. Malagasy Republic, 1967, White House Conf. on Handicapped, 1978, IBM, Albuquerque, 1986-88; adj. prof. U. N.Mex., Albuquerque, 1969-80; vis. faculty U. B.C., Vancouver, Can., 1987; program chmn. Internat. Conf. on Spl. Edn., Beijing, 1988; delegation leader Adminstrn. of Spl. Edn. to USSR, 1991, delegation leader Adminstrs. of Spl. Edn. to People's Republic of China, 1993. Author: (chpt.) Managerial Models of Mainstreaming, 1986; contbr. articles to profl. jours. Bd. dirs. Foster Grandparents Program, Albuquerque, pres. 1988-89; pres. YWCA, Albuquerque, 1986-87. Mem. Internat. Council for Exceptional Children (pres. 1981-82, chmn. N.Mex. Polit. Action Network 1982-88, Leadership awards, Service award), N.Mex. Council Adminstrn. Spl. Edn. (pres. 1985-86), Found. for Exceptional Children (bd. dirs.), N.Mex. Sch. Adminstrs. (bd. dirs.). Democrat. Mem. Unitarian Ch. Home: 615 16th St NW Albuquerque NM 87104-1303 Office: CASE 615 16th St NW Albuquerque NM 87104-1303

THOMASON, DOUGLAS NAAMAN, lawyer; b. San Bernardino, Calif., Oct. 29, 1949; s. Ryland M. and Evelyn A. (McCutcheon) T. BA, U. Calif., Berkeley, 1979; JD, Santa Clara U., 1985. Bar: Calif. Assoc. Erickson, Arbuthnot, Brown, Kilduff & Day, Oakland, Calif., 1989-90, Law Offices of John C. Shaffer, Jr., Menlo Park, Calif., 1991—. Chmn. fundraising com. No. Alameda County Dem. Party, Oakland, 1988. Presdl. Rsch. grantee Santa Clara Coll., 1986. Mem. San Mateo County Bar Assn. Democrat. Home: 3653 20th St San Francisco CA 94110 Office: Law Offices John C Shaffer Jr 750 Menlo Ave Ste 250 Menlo Park CA 94025-4735

THOMASON, PHILLIP BRIAN, Spanish language educator; b. Shawmut, Ala., Dec. 12, 1949; s. Earl Marchel and Margaret Evelyn (Wall) T.; m. Cathy Lea Ray, Aug. 19, 1972; 1 child, Brian Michael. AB, U. Montevallo, 1972; M of Hispanic Studies, Auburn U., 1975; PhD, U. Ky., 1987. Cert. tchr. Spanish tchr. Kendrick High Sch. Muscogee County Schs., Columbus, Ga., 1972-74; grad. teaching asst., instr. Auburn (Ala.) U., 1974-75, 82; instr. econs. and Spanish Marion (Ala.) Mil. Inst., 1975-81; grad. teaching asst., dir. Spanish House U. Ala., Tuscaloosa, 1981; grad. teaching asst. U. Ky., Lexington, 1982-86; instr. Spanish Asbury Coll., Wilmore, Ky., 1986; assoc. prof. Spanish Pepperdine U., Malibu, Calif., 1986—, lang. divsn. coord., 1992-94; adv. coun. Cen. States Conf. on Lang. Teaching, 1991, Fgn. Lang. Alliance of So. Calif.; dir. lang. program Madrid; fellow Ministry of Culture of Spain; presenter in field. Author and translator articles to profl. jours. Deacon Ch. of Christ, Thousand Oaks, Calif., 1988-92. Fellow Ministry of Spain, 1985. Mem. Am. Assn. Tchrs. Spanish and Portuguese, Modern Lang. Assn. (grant for profl. devel.), Southwest Conf. on Lang. Teaching (adv. coun. 1989-91), Calif. Fgn. Lang. Tchrs. Assn., Soc. of Seven Sages, Adult Children of Alcoholics, Sigma Delta Pi. Home: 76 W Avenida De Las Flores Thousand Oaks CA 91360-3109 Office: Pepperdine U 24255 Pacific Coast Hwy Malibu CA 90263-4212

THOMAS-ORR, BETTY JO, retired public relations specialist; b. Chgo., Sept. 28, 1937; d. William H. and Elizabeth (Brown) Shannon; m. Wilbur E. Thomas, June 28, 1958 (div. 1979); m. Vernon A. Orr, June 2, 1980 (dec. 1985); children: Pamela F., Kenneth E., Neil A. BBA, Nat. U., 1988, MBA, 1989. Campaign and project dir. Chgo. 17th Ward, 1970-75, communmity project dir., 1978-79; customer svc. rep. Mainliner Reservations United Airlines, Chgo., 1967-83; customer svc. rep. United Airlines, Las Vegas, Nev., 1983-92; ret., 1992; asst. dir. pub. rels. Am. Lung Assn., Las Vegas, 1989, 92; mem. Bd. Vet. Med. Examiners, Reno, Nev., 1990-93. Named 4-H Leader of Yr., State of Ill., 1978. Mem. Am. Bus. Women Assn., Nat. Univ. Student Alumni Assn. (treas. 1990), Las Vegas Drifters (past pres., sec., treas.), The Links, Alpha Kappa Alpha. Democrat. Roman Catholic. Home: 5155 Myrtlewood St Las Vegas NV 89122

THOMASSON, GEORGE ORIN, physician, insurance company executive; b. Davenport, Iowa, Apr. 22, 1937; s. Loris and Elsie Mae (Parker) T.; m. Dorothy Jane Adams, Nov. 25, 1962 (div. 1978); m. Jacqueline Jean Soter, July 6, 1984; children: Laura, William, Patrick, David, Elizabeth, Elaine Kristen, Jill, Paul. BA, North Tex. State U., 1959; MD, U. Tex., Dallas, 1962; postgrad., U. Ga., 1976. Cert. pub. mgr. Intern. U. Ark. Med. Ctr, 1962-63; residence USPHS, 1963-65; pvt. practice Russellville, Ark., 1965-66; instr. U. Fla. Med. Sch., Gainesville, 1966-71; univ. physician U. Ga., Athens, 1971-73; dist. health officer Ga. Dept. Human Resources, Athens, 1973-78; asst. prof. U. Colo. Health Scis. Ctr., Denver, 1978-83, clin. asst. prof. dept. family practice, 1983-92, grad. faculty, 1990—, clin. assoc. prof. dept. family medicine, 1992—; risk mgr. Med. Liability Cons. Program, Denver, 1983-88; v.p. risk mgmt. COPIC Ins. Co., Denver, 1988—; med. dir. Alachua County Head Start project, Gainesville, 1968-71; med. cons. Robert Wood Johnson Sch. Health Project, Denver, 1978-80, Clin. Reference Systems Inc., Englewood, Colo., Colo. Lt. Gov.'s Rural Coun., 1983-86; bd. dirs. Pricare, Inc., Englewood; mem. mammography advocacy project Colo. Dept. Health, 1988—, future of pub. health task force, 1989; breast cancer task force Colo. chpt. Am. Cancer Soc., 1987—; Colo. Vascular Disease Prevention Coalition, 1989—. Contbr. articles to med. publs. Cons. Gilpin County Health Ctr., Black Hawk, Colo., 1983-85, Clinica Compasina, Lafayette, Colo., 1984-87, Colo. Health Dept., 1984—. Recipient outstanding contbn. award Colo. Hosp. Assn., 1985. Mem. Am. Assn. Med. Systems and Informatics, Am. Acad. Med. Dirs., AMA, Colo. Med. Assn. (chmn. community health issues coun. 1984-91, chmn. med. informatics com. 1989—), Denver Med. Soc. Pres. (Gold Star award 1986), Colo. Med. Soc. (Commendation award 1989), Denver Med. Soc. (pub. health com. 1985—), Am. Coll. Physician Execs. Democrat. Office: COPIC Ins Co 5575 Dtc Pky Englewood CO 80111-3008

THOMLISON, RAY J., university dean, educator; b. Edmonton, Alta., Can., Jan. 22, 1943; s. Herbert MacLeod and Margaret Patricia (Hagen) T.; m. Barbara Buckler, Aug. 22, 1964; children: Lynn, Breanne. BSc, U. Alta., 1963; B in Social Work, U. B.C., 1964, MSW, 1965; PhD, U. Toronto, 1972. Social worker Dept. Pub. Welfare, Edmonton, 1964-65; psychiat. social worker Mental Health Ctr., Burnaby, B.C., Can., 1965-67; mental health cons. Lower Mainland & North B.C., 1967-68; assoc. prof. Wilfrid Laurier U., Waterloo, Ont., Can., 1971-73; prof. U. Toronto, Ont., 1973-83; prof., dean U. Calgary, Alta., 1983—; vis. prof. U. B.C., Vancouver, 1980-81, U. Regina, Saskatchewan, Can., 1977; sessional faculty York U., Downsview, Ont., 1978-83, Wilfrid Laurier U., 1974-83; chairperson Com. Native Social Work Edn., Alta., 1986—, Profl. Exam. Bd. Social Work, Alta., 1983-87; bd. accreditation Can. Assn. Schs. Social Work, 1978-81; mem. Univs. Coordinating Coun., Alta., 1984-86, Atkinson Coll. York U., Nat. Film Bd., Esso Can., Bank of Montreal, Que. Editor: Perspectives on Industrial Social Work Practice, 1983; (with J.S. Ismael) Perspectives on Social Services and Social Issues, 1987, (with C.R. Bagley) Child Sexual Abuse: Critical Perspectives on Prevention, Intervention, and Treatment, 1991, (with J. Hudson and J. Mayne) Action-Oriented Evaluation in Organizations: Canadian Practices, 1992; contbr. articles to profl. jours., book chpts., reports, and papers to confs. U. Toronto Faculty teaching fellow, 1974. Mem. Coun. Social Work. Edn., Assn. Advancement Behaviour Therapy, Assn. Behavioral Social Work, Rsch. Inst. Social Work (People's Rep. of China), Assn. Social Workers of Russia, Alberta Assn. Social Workers, Met. Toronto Children's Aid (bd. dirs. 1979-83), Family Service Assn. Met. Toronto Employee Assistance Program (adv. bd. 1977-83). Home: 1139 Varsity Estates Dr NW, Calgary, AB Canada T3B 3B5 Office: U of Calgary, Faculty of Social Work, 2500 Univ Dr NW, Calgary, AB Canada T2N 1N4

THOM OXFORD, JULIA RAE, biochemist, researcher, consultant, educator; b. Seattle, Dec. 31, 1958; d. Donaldson Ellery and Jean Ruth (Holt) Thom; m. Rex Oxford, May 18, 1991. BA, Linfield Coll., 1981; MS, Wash. State U., 1985, PhD, 1986. Postdoctoral fellow Swiss Inst. Cancer Rsch., Lausanne, Switzerland, 1986-88; postdoctoral fellow biochemistry dept. Wash. State U., Pullman, 1988; postdoctoral fellow Oreg. Health Scis. U., Portland, 1988-92; rsch. assoc. Shriners Hosp. Crippled Children, Portland, 1992—; test item writer Am. Coll. Testing Program, Iowa City, Iowa, 1989—; cons. Nature's Mist, Portland, 1991-92; instr. Portland State U., 1991; asst. prof. Lewis and Clark Coll., Portland, 1992. Contbr. articles to profl. jours. Vol. Shriners Hosp. Crippled Children, Mt. Hood, 1991, Shared Outdoor Activities Recreation, 1991, Mt. Hood. Grantee Wash. State U., 1985, C. Glenn King fellow, 1981; fellow Swiss Inst. Experimental Cancer Rsch., 1987, 88. Mem. AAAS, N.Y. Acad. Sci., Swiss Biochemistry Soc., Protein Soc. Home: 14115 NW Mason Hill Rd Hillsboro OR 97124 Office: Shriners Hosp Crippled Children 3101 SW Sam Jackson Rd Portland OR 97201

THOMPSON, ANNA BLANCHE, educator; b. Ft. Worth, Oct. 8, 1914; d. George Lewis and Gula Gertrude (Cook) Turnbow; m. Jess Lee, May 27, 1939; children: Jess Lee II, Mary Ann Thompson Archbold. BA in Edn., Ariz. State U., Tempe, 1935; postgrad., U. Ariz., 1940, U. Hawaii, 1964, Pepperdine U., 1967. Tchr. Parke (Ariz.) Elem. Sch., 1935-40; tchr. music Parker High Sch., 1940-42; tchr. Scottsdale (Ariz.) Elem. Sch., 1948-71; tchr. U. Hawaii, Laie, 1971-72; tchr. U. Hawaii, 1972-79, ret., 1979. Mem. edn. bd. Phoenix Women's Club, 1983-84; pres. Ariz. Res. Officers Ladies, Phoenix, 1982-84, state pres., 1986-87; pres. Ladies of the Ribbon, Phoenix, 1987-90, Tempe Garden Club, 1987-88. Recipient Mus. plaque Phoenix Symphony Symphonette, 1982-83, Cert. of Appreciation, St. Luke's Hosp. Aux., 1985, Cert. of Appreciation, Mil. Order of World Wars, 1989. Mem. Ariz. Res. Officers Ladies (state sec. 1990—), Tri-City Angels of Ariz. (pres. 1984—), Collectors Club Am. (nat. pres. 1987—), Ikebana Internat., AAUW (historian Tempe chpt. 1987-90), Delta Kappa Gamma (pres. Phoenix chpt. 1974-76, 88-90, parliamentarian 1990—). Home: 533 E Fairmont Dr Tempe AZ 85282-3722

THOMPSON, ANNE MARIE, newspaper publisher; b. Des Moines, Feb. 7, 1920; d. George Horace and Esther Mayer Sheely; m. J. Ross Thompson, July 31, 1949; children: Annette McCracken, James Ross. BA, U Iowa, 1940; postgrad. U. Colo., 1971. Co-pub. Baca County Banner, Springfield, Colo., 1951-54, Rocky Ford (Colo.) Daily Gazette, 1954-82, pub., 1982—. Editor Colo. Bus. Prof. Women Mag. Colo. Bus. Women, Rocky Ford, 1981-92, The Sage Quar. Publ. Toastmasters dist. 26, 1983—. Mem. Otero Jr. Coll. Coun., 1987-93, Colo. Ho. of Reps., 1957-61; Colo. presdl. elector, 1972; chmn. Colo. adv. com. SBA, 1979-81. Recipient Community Service award Rocky Ford C. of C., 1975; named Colo. Woman of Achievement in Journalism, 1959, Colo. Bus. Person of Yr., Future Bus. Leaders of Am., 1981; elected to Colo. Community Journalism Hall of Fame, 1981. Mem. Nat. Fedn. Press Women (dir. 1971-81), Nat. Newspaper Assn. (Emma C. McKinney award 1984), Colo. Press Assn. (dir. 1981-83, Golden Make-Up award 1991) , Colo. Press Women, PEO, Bus. and Profl. Women's Club. Republican. Methodist.

THOMPSON, ARLENE RITA, nursing educator; b. Yakima, Wash., May 17, 1933; d. Paul James and Esther Margaret (Danroth) T. BS in Nursing, U. Wash., 1966, Masters in Nursing, 1970, postgrad., 1982—. Staff nurse Univ. Teaching Hosp., Seattle, 1966-69; mem. nursing faculty U. Wash. Sch. Nurses, Seattle, 1971-73; critical care nurse Virginia Mason Hosp., Seattle, 1973—; educator Seattle Pacific U. Sch. Nursing, 1981—; nurse legal cons. nursing edn., critical care nurse. Contbr. articles to profl. jours. USPHS grantee, 1969; nursing scholar Virginia Mason Hosp., 1965. Mem. Am. Assn. Critical Care Nurses (cert.), Am. Nurses Assn., Am. Heart Assn., Nat. League Nursing, Sigma Theta Tau, Alpha Tau Omega. Republican. Presbyterian. Home: 2320 W Newton St Seattle WA 98199-4115 Office: Seattle Pacific U 3307 3d Ave West Seattle WA 98199

THOMPSON, AYLMER HENRY, meteorologist, educator, consultant; b. Lake Bluff, Ill., Sept. 11, 1922; s. Aylmer and Katharine (Pitt) T.; m. Ann Dillon, Dec. 26, 1941; children: Bruce H., Kenneth A., Patricia A. AA, L.A. City Coll., 1942; BA, UCLA, 1947, MA, 1948, PhD, 1960. Instr. UCLA, 1943-44, lectr., 1949-52; asst. prof. meteorology U. Utah, Salt Lake City, 1952-60; prof. meteorology Tex. A&M U., College Station, 1960-88, emeritus prof., 1988—; cons. Port Angeles, Wash., 1990—; vis. prof. U. Alaska, Fairbanks, 1967-68, 71-72; resource scientist Found. for Glacier and Environ. Rsch., Juneau, Alaska, 1968-92; cons. Dow Chem. Co., Freeport, Tex., 1981-86. Contbr. chpts. to books, numerous articles to profl. jours. Capt. USAAC, 1942-46. J.P. Parks fellow U. Utah, 1959. Fellow Royal Meteorol. Soc.; mem. Am. Meteorol. Soc., Internat. Glaciological Soc., Nat. Weather Assn., Res. Officers Assn. Home and Office: PO Box 1948 Port Angeles WA 98362-0406

THOMPSON, BETTY JANE, small business owner; b. Ladysmith, Wis., Nov. 18, 1923; d. Edward Thomas and Mayme Selma (Kratwell) Potter; m. Frederick Sturdee Thompson, Apr. 19, 1945 (div. Apr. 1973); children: Denise Alana, Kent Marshall; m. J.R. Critchfield, Feb. 14, 1977 (div. 1989). Student, Jamestown (N.D.) Coll., 1946-47, U. Calif., Long Beach, 1964-69; AA, Orange Coast Coll., 1976; postgrad., Monterey Peninsula Coll., 1979-80; SBA Cert., Hartnell Coll., 1982. Cert. fashion cons. Owner, mgr., buyer Goodview (Minn.) Food Mart, 1947-50; dist. mgr. Beauty Counselor of Minn., Winona County, 1951-61; Boy Scout liaison J.C. Penney Co., Newport Beach, Calif., 1969-72; dept. mgr. and buyer boyswear At Ease, Newport Beach, 1972-77; mgr. Top Notch Boys Wear, Carmel, Calif., 1977-83, propr., 1984-88; owner, mgr. Top Notch Watch, Sun City, Ariz., 1989—; v.p., chmn. Don Loper Fashion Show, 1967, pres., 1968, bd. dirs., 1969. Co-editor Aux. Antics mag., 1965. Vol. fundraising leadership Family Svc. Assn., Orange County, Calif., 1962-68, other orgns.; chmn. publicity, study group, Sunday sch. tchr., Congl. Ch., Winona, Minn., 1956-58, fellowship pres., Santa Ana, Calif., 1963-65; pres. Goodview Civic Club, 1948. Recipient Athena award Panhellenic Assn. Orange City, Calif., 1968, El Camino Real Dist. Svc. award Orange Empire coun. Boy Scouts Am., Baden-Powell award, Outstanding Leadership award, El Camino Real Dist., Calif., 1972J. Ringling North award, 1949; named Outstanding Svc. Vol. Family Svc. Assn., 1969. Mem. Carmel Bus. Assn. Home and Office: 10048 W Hawthorn Dr Sun City AZ 85351-2829

THOMPSON, BONNIE RANSA, secondary educator, chemistry educator; b. Charleroi, Pa., Oct. 12, 1940; d. William Edward and Edith Lorraine Ransa; m. Joel E. Thompson, June 15, 1963 (div. Dec. 1980). BA, Seton Hill Coll., Greensburg, Pa., 1963; MEd, Ariz. State U., 1979, postgrad. Cert. in secondary chemistry, anthropology, and gifted edn., Ariz. Tchr. chemistry Scotch Plains (N.J.)-Fanwood High Sch., 1963-74; tchr. chemistry and anthropology Tolleson (Ariz.) Union High Sch., 1974-93; tchr. chemistry Westview High Sch., Phoenix, 1992—; instr. anthropology and archaeology Rio Salado C.C., Sun City, Ariz., 1981-88; instr. chemistry Glendale (Ariz.) C.C., 1988—; pres. Brite Ednl. Programs, Ltd., Phoenix, 1988-91; mem. Ariz. Reagent and Task Force on Lab. Sci., Tempe, 1987; tchr., cons. Pitts. SuperComputer Project, Tolleson, 1992—; amb. People to People Sci. Exchange, Russia, Australia, New Zealand, summer 1989-92; rsch partnership High Sch./Coll. Flinn Found. Rsch. Corp., 1988-91. Editor: Starting at Ground Zero, 1988, others; editor: Energy Education Kits, 1985; contbr. articles to mags. V.p. Villa Casitas Townhouse Assn., Phoenix, 1991-92, pres., 1993—; vol. Perot Orgn. for Pres., Phoenix, 1992. Woodrow Wilson fellow, 1983; recipient Golden Bell award Ariz. Sch. Bd. Assn., 1985, 88; recipient Growth Incentives for Tchrs. award GTE Corp., 1987, Tech. Scholar award Tandy Corp., 1990; named Outstanding High Sch. Sci. Tchr. Ariz. Coun. for Engring. and Scientific Assocs., 1993. Mem. NEA, Ariz. Edn. Assn., Tolleson Edn. Assn. (pres. 1981-83), Nat. Sci. Tchrs. Assn., Ariz. Sci. Tchrs. Assn., Ariz. Alliance for Math., Sci. and Tech., S.W. Archeol. Team. Office: Tolleson Union HS Dist 9419 W Van Buren St Tolleson AZ 85353

THOMPSON, (IRVING) BOYD, association executive; b. Stockton, Calif., Dec. 6, 1921; s. Irving Boyd and Winnifred Lucille (Taylor) T.; m. Virginia Woodall Graham, July 8, 1948; children: Boyd Taylor, Susan, Scott. B.A., Coll. of Pacific, Stockton, Calif., 1943, M.A., 1948, secondary adminstrn. cert., 1949. Mem. faculty Coll. of Pacific, 1946-52; exec. dir. San Joaquin Med. Soc., 1952-74, San Joaquin Found. Med. Care, 1952-74; exec. v.p. Am. Med. Care and Rev. Assn., Potomac, Md., 1974—; pres. Med. Dental Hosp. Burs. Am., 1965, Nat. Council Community Blood Banks, 1965; Med. Execs. Assn. Calif., 1962-63; past exec. dir. Delta Blood Bank Calif., San Joaquin Bur. Med. Econs. Pres. Stockton Family Service Agy., 1959-61; adv. bd. Salvation Army, Stockton, 1961-62. Served with USN, 1943-46. Mem. Profl. Conv. Mgmt. Assn., Am. Assn. Med. Soc. Execs. (pres. 1972-73), Am. Soc. Assn. Execs., Am. Public Health Assn., U. Pacific Alumni Assn. (past pres.). Republican. Presbyterian. Office: Ste 2 2087 Grand Canal Blvd Stockton CA 95207

THOMPSON, CHARLES CURTIS, management consultant; b. Decatur, Ill., Feb. 10, 1953; s. Wayne Jewell and Jacquelyn Mercedes (Phipps) T.; m. Debbie Ann Sanford, Nov. 16, 1976 (div. 1987); 1 child, Jason Thomas; m. Linda Carol Lundgren, Dec. 31; children: Ryan Scott Winter, Jaime Dawn Winter. BS, U. Ariz., 1987. Internal cons. Magma Copper Co., San Manuel, Ariz., 1976-90; mgmt. cons., owner Progressive Mgmt. Svcs., Tucson, 1990—. Mem. Am. Inst. Mining Engrs. (com. chair 1990), Assn. for Quality & Productivity, Ariz. Coun. for Excellence. Home and Office: 10351 N Shannon Rd Tucson AZ 85741

THOMPSON, CHRISTOPHER JOHN, computer company executive, marketing analyst; b. Oshawa, Ontario, Can., July 9, 1964; s. Maurice James and Karen Ann (King) T. BA in Econs.-Macro, McMaster U., 1990, MBA in Mktg., 1992. Strategic analyst No. Telecom. Can., Toronto, 1990; sr. analyst No. Bus. Info., Toronto, 1990-91; dir. product mktg. Forté Advanced Mgmt. Software, Carlsbad, Calif., 1991-92; strategic analyst VMX, Inc., San José, Calif., 1992—; cons. No. Bus. Info., Toronto, 1991, Forté Advanced Mgmt. Software, Carlsbad, 1991. Author: Canadian 9-1-1 Market Report, 1990, Canadian PBX Market Report, 1991. Vol. Arthritis Soc. San Diego, 1992, United Way Can., Toronto, 1984-91. Recipient Chief Scout award Boy Scouts Can., 1982. Mem. Phi Delta Theta (alumni). Mem. Progressive Conservative Party. Mem. United Ch. Can. Home: 1632 Willow Lake Ln San Jose CA 95131-3553 Office: VMX Inc. 2115 O'Nel Dr San Jose CA 95131-2032

THOMPSON, CLAYTON HOWARD, computer engineer; b. Albert Lea, Minn., Aug. 29, 1939; s. Howard Truman and Bernice Nelsena (Munson) T.; m. George Ann Devault, Mar. 5, 1961 (div. Aug. 1979); children: Clayton, David; m. Karen Joan Dahlinger Baughman, Apr. 6, 1985; stepchildren: Kit, Juliana. BS in Computer Sci., Colo. State U., 1973, MBA, 1974. Aviation cadet USAF, 1959, commd. lt. col., 1976, ret., 1980; chief computer resources div. USAF, Wright Patterson, Ohio, 1976-80; sr. software engr. Hughes Aircraft Co., El Segundo, Calif., 1980-81; software mgr. Contel Info. Systems, Dayton, Ohio, 1981-82, Ford Aerospace Corp., Colorado Springs, Colo., 1982-86; program dir. Northrop Corp., L.A., 1986—. Mem. Soc. of Concurrent Engring., Assn. Computing Machinery, Phi Kappa Phi, Beta Gamma Sigma. Home: 300 Pebble Beach Dr Thousand Oaks CA 91320-4124 Office: Northrop Corp One Northrop Ave Hawthorne CA 90250-3277

THOMPSON, CRAIG SNOVER, corporate communications executive; b. Bklyn., May 24, 1932; s. Craig F. and Edith (Williams) T.; m. Masae Sugizaki, Feb. 21, 1957; children: Lee Anne, Jane Laura. Grad., Valley

Forge Mil. Acad., 1951; B.A., Johns Hopkins U., 1954. Newspaper and radio reporter Easton (Pa.) Express, 1954-55, 57-59, Wall St. Jour., 1959-60; account exec. Moore, Meldrum & Assocs., 1960; mgr. pub. relations Cen. Nat. Bank of Cleve., 1961-62; account exec. Edward Howard & Co., Cleve., 1962-67; v.p. Edward Howard & Co., 1967-69, sr. v.p., 1969-71; dir. pub. relations White Motor Corp., Cleve., 1971-76; v.p. pub. relations No. Telecom Inc., Nashville, 1976-77, White Motor Corp., Farmington Hills, Mich., 1977-80; v.p. corp. communications White Motor Corp., 1980-81; dir. exec. communications Rockwell Internat. Corp., Pitts., 1981-86, El Segundo, Calif., 1986-91, Seal Beach, Calif., 1992—. Bd. dirs. Shaker Lakes Regional Nature Center, 1970-73. Served to 1st lt., inf. U.S. Army, 1955-57. Mem. Pub. Relations Soc. Am. (accredited), Alumni Assn. Valley Forge Mil. Acad. (bd. dirs. 1988—). Office: Rockwell Internat Corp 2201 Seal Beach Blvd Seal Beach CA 90740-8250

THOMPSON, DANIEL EMERSON, vending machine service company; b. Fairbanks, Alaska, Jan. 24, 1947; s. George Edmond and Emma Jean (Burns) T.; m. Yvette Clarice Brazeau, Aug. 16, 1980. Student, U. Notre Dame, 1965-67. Vice-pres. Music Inc., Fairbanks, 1965-67; pres. Music Inc. (doing bus. as Alaska Music Co.), Fairbanks, 1967-81; sec.-treas. Music Inc. (doing bus. as Alaska Music Co. and TLC Vend), Anchorage, 1981-84; sec. Music Inc. (doing bus. as Vend Alaska-Fairbanks), Fairbanks, 1984-87, pres., 1987—; pres. Vend Inc. (doing bus. as Vend Alaska-Anchorage), Anchorage, 1984—; bd. dirs. Music Inc., Fairbanks, Vend Inc., Anchorage, Denali State Bank, Fairbanks; ptnr. Thompson Investment Co., Fairbanks, 1976—. Trustee Hi Pow, Fairbanks, 1972—; pres. Fairbanks Downtown Assn., 1987-88, bd. dirs., 1984—; bd. dirs. Alaska State Devel. Corp., Juneau, 1971-82, Monroe Found., Fairbanks, 1991—. Mem. Amusement Music Operators Am., Nat. Automatic Merchandising Assn., Northwest Automatic Vending Assn. (bd. govs. 1983—), Rotary, Fairbanks C. of C. (co-chmn. local govt. com. 1988-90). Roman Catholic. Office: Vend Alaska 1890 Marika Rd Fairbanks AK 99709-5540

THOMPSON, DAVID CHARLES, SR., management executive; b. Oneonta, N.Y., Jan. 27, 1942; s. Gordon George and Evelyn Beatrice (Michaels) T.; m. Carol Anne Peele, Dec. 24, 1976; children: David Charles Jr., Robert Edward. BS in Mgmt., U. La Verne, 1989, MS in Mgmt., 1991. Mgr. Hughes, West Covina, Calif., 1968-93, CH2M Hill, Santa Ana, Calif., 1993—; bd. dirs. Honeywell West Coast Fed. Credit Union, Azusa, Calif. Officer Glendora (Calif.) Police Aux., 1972-74; agt. South Pasadena Police Res., 1978-82; active Foothill Apt. Owners Assn., Pasadena, Calif., 1979—. Served with USN, 1960-68. Mem. Soc. Logistics Engrs., Soc. Tech. Communication, Assn. Proposal Mgmt. Profls., NRA, Rogues Club (chief Arcadia, Calif. chpt. 1987-88), Elks. Republican. Home: 6792 N Country Club Dr La Verne CA 91750-1347 Office: CH2M Hill 2510 Red Hill Ave Santa Ana CA 92705

THOMPSON, DAVID RALPH, food products executive; b. Boston, Sept. 14, 1959; s. Peter Hunter and Alice (Kreps) T.; m. Bernadette O'Brien, Mar. 28, 1987; children: Caroline Sinnott, Andrew Hunter. BA, Bates Coll., 1981; M of Mgmt., Northwestern U., 1988. With Gen. Foods Corp., Dedham, Mass., 1981-86; retail sales rep. Food Enterprises, Canton, Mass., 1986; mktg. strategic planning intern Jam Lane, Inc., Meriden, Conn., 1987; asst. product mgr. Kraft Gen. Foods Frozen Products, White Plains, N.Y., 1988-89; mktg. mgr. The All Am. Gourmet Co. Birds Eye Frozen Vegetable Div., Orange, Calif., 1989—. Mem. Alumni Admissions Orgn. Northwestern U. Home: 1141 Via Viento Ln Corona CA 91720-3636

THOMPSON, DAVID RENWICK, federal judge. BS in Bus., U. So. Calif., 1952, LLB, 1955. Pvt. practice law with Thompson & Thompson (and predecessor firms), 1957-85; judge U.S. Ct. Appeals (9th cir.), 1985—. Served with USN, 1955-57. Mem. ABA, San Diego County Bar Assn., Am. Bd. Trial Lawyers (sec. San Diego chpt. 1983, v.p. 1984, pres. 1985). Office: US Ct Appeals 940 Front St San Diego CA 92189-0010

THOMPSON, DENNIS PETERS, plastic surgeon; b. Chgo., Mar. 18, 1937; s. David John and Ruth Dorothy (Peters) T.; m. Virginia Louise Williams, June 17, 1961; children: Laura Faye, Victoria Ruth, Elizabeth Jan. BS, U. Ill., 1957, BS in Medicine, 1959, MS in Physiology, MD, 1961. Diplomate Am. Bd. Surgery, Am. Bd. Plastic Surgery. Intern Presbyn.-St. Lukes Hosp., Chgo., 1961-62; resident in gen. surgery Mayo Clinic, Rochester, Minn., 1964-66, fellow in gen. surgery, 1964-66; resident in gen. surgery Harbor Gen. Hosp., Los Angeles, 1968-70; resident in plastic surgery UCLA, 1971-73, clin. instr. plastic surgery, 1975-82, asst. clin. prof. surgery, 1982—; practice medicine specializing in plastic and reconstructive surgery, Los Angeles, 1974-78, Santa Monica, Calif., 1978—; chmn. plastic surgery sect. St. John's Hosp., 1986-91; mem. staff Santa Monica Hosp., UCLA Ctr. Health Scis., Brotman Med. Ctr.; chmn. dept. surgery Beverly Glen Hosp., 1978-79; pres. Coop. of Am. Physicians Credit Union, 1978-80, bd. dirs., 1980—, chmn. promotion com., 1983—, treas., 1985—. Contbr. articles to med. jours. Moderator Congl. Ch. of Northridge (Calif.), 1975-76, chmn. bd. trustees, 1973-74, 80-82; bd. dirs. L.A. Bus. Coun., 1987-90. Am. Tobacco Inst. research grantee, 1959-60. Fellow ACS; mem. AMA (Physicians Recognition award 1971, 74, 77, 81, 84, 87), Calif. Med. Assn., Los Angeles County Med. Assn. (chmn. bylaws com. 1979-80, chmn. ethics com. 1980-81, sec.-treas. dist. 5 1982-83, program chmn. 1983-84, pres. 1985-86, councilor 1988—), Pan-Pacific Surgical Assn., Am. Soc. Plastic and Reconstructive Surgeons, Calif. Soc. Plastic Surgeons (chmn. bylaws com. 1982-83, chmn. liability com. 1983-85, councilor 1988-91, sec. 1993—), Los Angeles Soc. Plastic Surgeons (sec. 1980-82, pres. 1982—), Lipoplasty Soc. N.Am., UCLA Plastic Surgery Soc. (treas. 1983-84), Am. Soc. Aesthetic Plastic Surgery, Western Los Angeles Regional C. of C. (bd. dirs. 1981-84, 86-89, chmn. legis. action com. 1978-80), Phi Beta Kappa, Alpha Omega Alpha, Nu Sigma Nu, Phi Kappa Phi, Delta Sigma Delta, Omega Beta Pi, Phi Eta Sigma. Republican. Office: 2001 Santa Monica Blvd Santa Monica CA 90404-2102

THOMPSON, DOUGLAS EVAN, association executive; b. Brigham, Utah, June 7, 1947; s. Evan C. Thompson and Ruby Willardsen Westergard; m. Martha McClellan, Aug. 3, 1973; children: Joshua Evan, Marshall McClellan, Katey. BS in Econs., Utah State U., 1971; MBA, U. Utah, 1974. With Sears Roebuck & Co., Salt Lake City, 1972-73; account rep. Burroughs (Unisys) Corp., Salt Lake City, 1973-76; chief exec. officer Thompson, Cook and Assocs., Bountiful, Utah, 1976-78; dep. dir. Utah Energy Office, Salt Lake City, 1978-80; dir. coll. rels. So. Utah State Coll., Cedar City, Utah, 1980-82; alumni dir. Utah State U., Logan, 1982-88; pres., CEO Cache C. of C., Logan, 1988—; lectr. in field. Pub. Cache Chamber Newsletter, 1988—; author numerous brochures on energy conservation. Exec. dir. Bridgerland Travel Bd., Logan, 1988, Cache Econ. Devel., 1986; exec. com. Utah State U., 1988; treas., dir. Heart of the Rockies, Provo, 1988; active Boy Scouts Am., 1978-88; bd. dirs. Cache Performances, 1990; chmn. Abrams for Congress Com., Logan, 1986; mem. Gov.'s Coun. on Volunteerism, 1991—. Recipient Gold medal, Coun. for Advancement and Support of Edn., 1987. Mem. U.S. C. of C., Utah C. of C. Assn. (pres.-elect, bd. dirs. 1988-89). Mem. Ch. of Jesus Christ of Latter Day Saints. Home: 1567 Lynnwood Ave Logan UT 84321-3031 Office: Cache C of C 160 N Main St Logan UT 84321-4541

THOMPSON, DWIGHT ALAN, vocational rehabilitation expert; b. Monterey Park, Calif., Mar. 2, 1955; s. Irvin Edward and Lydia (Busch) T.; m. Irene Anita Arden, June 18, 1977; children: Dwight Christopher, Meredith Irene, Hilda Arden. BA in Social Welfare, U. Wash., 1978, MSW, 1980. Registered vocat. rehab. counselor, Wash., Oreg.; cert. social worker, Wash.; diplomate Am. Bd. Clin. Examiners in Social Work; cert. Ins. Rehab. Specialist Commn. Houseparent Parkview Home for Exceptional Children, Seattle, 1976-77; rsch. analyst Wash. State Ho. Reps., Olympia, 1979-81; v.p. The James L. Groves Co., Everett, Wash., 1982-86; exec. dir. Evaluation & Tng. Assocs., Seattle, 1984-86; pres., owner Rehab. & Evaluation Svcs., Seattle, 1986—; social work officer 50th Gen. Army Res. Hosp., Seattle, 1982-87, 91—; med. adminstrv. officer Operation Desert Storm, Riyadh, Saudi Arabia, 1990-91; aide-de-camp 2d Hosp. Ctr., San Francisco, 1987-88, pub. affairs officer, 1988-90. Co-author Correction Study Report, 1981. Registered lobbyist Wash. State, 1983-87; conf. pres. St. Vincent de Paul Soc., 1975-78; lt. Thurston County Fire Dist #6, East Olympia, Wash., 1980-83; alumni rep. COS Track Com. U. Wash., 1984-87; primary candidate Dem. Primary for State Rep., Renton, Wash., 1984; mem. Wash. Vocat. Rehab. adv. com. Dept. Labor Industires, 1992—. Capt. USAR, 1982—, Persian Gulf. Mem. NASW (cert.), Nat. Assn. Rehab. Profls. (pvt. sector), Acad. Cert. Social Workers, Wash. Self-Insurers Assn. (mem. legis. com.), Assn. Mil. Surgeons U.S., Res. Officers Assn., Theta Xi (pres. 1975-77). Roman Catholic. Home: 16136 41st Ave NE Seattle WA 98155-6726 Office: Rehab and Evaluation Svcs 226 Summit Ave E Seattle WA 98102-5619

THOMPSON, EDGAR JOSEPH, musician, educator. BS, MS in Physics and Math., Brigham Young U.; MA in Music, Calif. State U., Long Beach; PhD in Choral Music Edn., U. Utah; studies with Frank Pooler, Newell B. Weight. Asst. dir. Choral Activities Calif. State U., Long Beach; mem. faculty U. Utah, Salt Lake City, 1978, chmn. Music dept., conductor Univ. A Cappella Choir, 1979—; mus. dir. Utah Symphony Chorus, 1982—; conductor clinics, guest conductor in field. Producer film on new choral literature and techniques, 1972; developer computer program to teach fundamental music skills. Mem. Music Educators Nat. Conf., Utah Music Educators Assn., Am. Choral Dirs. Assn. (past state pres.). Office: U Utah Music Dept 204 Gardner Hall Salt Lake City UT 84112

THOMPSON, ELBERT ORSON, retired dentist, consultant; b. Salt Lake City, Aug. 31, 1910; s. Orson David and Lillian (Greenwood) T.; m. Gayle Larsen, Sept. 12, 1935; children: Ronald Elbert, Karen Thompson Toone, Edward David, Gay Lynne. Student, U. Utah, 1928-30, 33-35; DDS, Northwestern U., 1939; hon. degree, Am. Coll. Dentistry, Miami, Fla., 1958, Internat. Coll. Dentistry, San Francisco, 1962. Pvt. practice dentistry Salt Lake City, 1939-78; ret., 1978; inventor, developer and internat. lectr. post-grad./undergrad. courses various dental schs. and study groups, 1953-83; developer, tchr. Euthenics Dentistry Concept; cons. in field. Contbr. numerous dental articles to profl. jours. Life mem. Rep. Presdl. Task Force, Washington, 1985—. Recipient Merit Honor award U. Utah, 1985; named Dentist of the Yr. Utah Acad. Gen. Dentistry, 1991, Father of Modern Dentistry, 1991. Mem. ADA (life), Utah Dental Assn. (life, sec. 1948-49, Disting. Svc. award 1980), Salt Lake City Dental Soc. (life, pres. 1945-46), Utah Dental Hygiene Soc. (hon.), Am. Acad. Dental Practice Adminstrn. (life, pres. 1965-66), Internat. Coll. Dentists, Am. Coll. Dentists, Sons of Utah Pioneers (life), Dinorators Club (charter), Northwestern U. Alumni Assn. (Merit award 1961), Omicron Kappa Upsilon. Mormons. Home: 3535 Hillside Ln Salt Lake City UT 84109-4099

THOMPSON, FLOYD HENRY, cytogenetic oncologist; b. Blue Earth, Minn., Aug. 18, 1951; s. Ansel Clinton and Dorothy June Thompson. BA, So. Ill. U., 1972; MS, U. Ill., Chgo., 1981. Cytogenetic technician Cook County Hosp., Chgo., 1972-73; cytogenetics lab. mgr. U. Ill. Med. Ctr., Chgo., 1973-81; cytogenetic oncology lab. mgr. Ariz. Cancer Ctr., Tucson, 1981-90, dir. cytogenetic oncology lab., 1990—; cons. U.S. Congress, Washington, 1974-76; lectr. So. Ill. U. Sch. Medicine, Carbondale, 1973-77; organizer, coord. workshops on chromosomes in solid tumors, 1985-93. Author: (with others) Association of Cytogenetic Techonogists Lab Manual, 2d edit., 1991; mem. editorial staff Applied Cytogenetics, 1986—; contbr. articles to profl. jours. Mem. AAAS, Am. Soc. Human Genetics, Found. for Sci. and the Handicapped, Assn. Cytogenetic Technologists. Office: Ariz Cancer Ctr 1515 N Campbell Ave Tucson AZ 85724

THOMPSON, GEORGE ALBERT, geophysics educator; b. Swissvale, Pa., June 5, 1919; s. George Albert Sr. and Maude Alice (Harkness) T.; m. Anita Kimmell, July 20, 1944; children: Albert J., Dan A., David C. BS, Pa. State U., 1941; MS, MIT, 1942; PhD, Stanford U., 1949. Geologist, geophysicist U.S. Geol. Survey, Menlo Park, Calif., 1942-76; asst. prof. Stanford (Calif.) U., 1949-55, assoc. prof., 1955-60, prof. geophysics, 1960—, chmn. geophysics dept., 1967-86, chmn. geology dept., 1979-82, Otto N. Miller prof. earth scis., 1980-89, dean sch. earth scis., 1987-89; cons. adv. com. reactor safeguards Nuclear Regulation Commn., Washington, 1974—; mem. bd. earth sci. NRC, 1986-88, vice chmn. Yucca Mountain Hydrology-tectonics panel NRC, 1990-92; bd. dirs. Inc. Rsch. Inst. for Seismology, Washington, 1984-92, exec. com., 1990-92; mem. sr. external events rev. com. Lawrence Livermore Nat. Lab., 1989-93; mem. Coun. on Continental Sci. Drilling, 1990-93. Author over 100 research papers. With USNR, 1944-46. Recipient G.K. Gilbert award in seismic geology, 1964; NSF postdoctoral fellow, 1956-57; Guggenheim Found. fellow, 1963-64. Fellow AAAS, Geol. Soc. Am. (coun. mem. 1983-86, George P. Woollard award 1983), Am. Geophys. Union; mem. NAS, Seismol. Soc. Am., Soc. Exploration Geophysicists. Home: 421 Adobe Pl Palo Alto CA 94306-4501 Office: Stanford U Geophysics Dept Stanford CA 94305-2215

THOMPSON, GLENN MICHAEL, environmental consulting firm executive; b. Providence, Sept. 21, 1946; s. Jack Edward Thompson and Adelaide (Spurdutti) Reeves; m. Lawana Jacqueline Robertson, June 1973 (div. Jan. 1982); m. Shannan Kaye Marty. BS, U. R.I., 1970; MS, Memphis State U., 1973; PhD, Ind. U., 1976. Asst. prof. dept. hydrology U. Ariz., Tucson, 1977-83; founder, pres. Tracer Rsch. Corp., Tucson, 1984—. Contbr. articles to profl. jours.; inventor, patentee various facets of tracer leak detection technology. 2d lt. U.S. Army, 1973. Mem. Nat. Water Well Assn., Am. Chem. Soc., Am. Geophysical Union. Office: Tracer Rsch Corp 3855 N Business Center Dr Tucson AZ 85705-2944

THOMPSON, GORDON, JR., federal judge; b. San Diego, Dec. 28, 1929; s. Gordon and Garnet (Meese) T.; m. Jean Peters, Mar. 17, 1951; children—John M., Peter Renwick, Gordon III. Grad., U. So. Calif., 1951, Southwestern U. Sch. Law, Los Angeles, 1956. Bar: Calif. 1956. With Dist. Atty.'s Office, County of San Diego, 1957-60; partner firm Thompson & Thompson, San Diego, 1960-70; U.S. dist. judge So. Dist. Calif., San Diego, 1970—, chief judge, 1984-91. Bd. dirs. Sharp Meml. Hosp. Mem. Am. Bd. Trial Advocates, ABA, San Diego County Bar Assn. (v.p. 1970), Delta Chi. Club: San Diego Yacht. Office: US Dist Ct 940 Front St San Diego CA 92189-0010

THOMPSON, GREG ALAN, computer sciences consulting executive; b. Palo Alto, Calif., Sept. 15, 1955; s. Jack Edward and Elaine Irene (Palmer) T.; m. Michelle Marie Barnes, Dec. 26, 1987; children: Amy, Beth, Julie, Kimberly. BSEE and Computer Sci., MIT, 1977. Cons. engr. Informatics-PMI Ames Rsch. Ctr. NASA, Moffett Field, Calif., 1975-78; prin. software specialist Digital Equipment Corp., Santa Clara, Calif., 1978-83; lead engr. computer aided design-CAM ctr. Digital Equipment Corp., 1982; lead cons. engr., mgr. Interlink computer Scis., Inc., Fremont, Calif., 1983-93; sr. scientist nCUBE, Foster City, Calif., 1993—. Bank of Am. and Hertz Found. scholar, 1973. Mem. IEEE Computer Soc., Bay Area MIT Alumni. Office: nCUBE 919 E Hillsdale Blvd Foster City CA 94404-2112

THOMPSON, HERBERT ERNEST, tool and die company executive; b. Jamaica, N.Y., Sept. 8, 1923; s. Walter and Louise (Joly) T.; student Stevens Inst. Tech., 1949-51; m. Patricia Elaine Osborn, Aug. 2, 1968; children: Robert Steven, Debra Lynn. Foreman, Conner Tool Co., 1961-62, Eason & Waller Grinding Corp., 1962-63; owner Endco Machined Products, 1966-67, Thompson Enterprises, 1974—; pres. Method Machined Products, Phoenix, 1967; pres., owner Quality Tool, Inc., 1967—. Served to capt. USAAF, 1942-46. Decorated D.F.C., Air medal with cluster. Home: 14009 N 42d Ave Phoenix AZ 85023 Office: 4223 W Clarendon Ave Phoenix AZ 85019

THOMPSON, JAMES HAROLD, judge; b. Chgo., Aug. 15, 1927; s. Robert Bruce and Jimmie Lee (Walls) T.; m. Jean Fay Ruttenbur, Sept. 21, 1953; 1 child, Irene Lee. BS in Pub. Adminstrn., The Am. Univ., 1958, LLB, 1961. Bar: D.C. 1962, Nev. 1963. Chief counsel Nev. Dept. Hwys., 1965-70; atty. gen. State of Nev., 1971-78, spl. dep. atty. gen., 1979-81, judge 2d jud. dist., 1981-83, judge Reno Justice Ct., 1983—; rep. State of Nev. to U.S. Supreme Ct. in Calif. vs. Nev. boundary litigation, 1979-81. Past mem. editorial bd. Better Roads mag., 1968-69; contbr. articles to profl. jours. With U.S. Army, 1946-47, 51-53. Recipient Am. Jurisprudence prize for Excellence in Trusts. Mem. Washoe County Bar Assn., First Jud. Dist. Bar Assn. (v.p. 1967-68), Am. Arbitration Assn. (nat. constrn. panel), Delta Theta Phi. Democrat. Methodist. Home: 136 Greenridge Dr Reno NV 89509-3927

THOMPSON, JAMES KIRK, transportation executive; b. Little Rock, 1953. Grad., U. Ark., 1978. Pres., CEO, dir. J.B. Hunt Transport Svcs., Inc., Lowell, Ark. Office: J B Hunt Transport Svcs Inc PO Box 130 Lowell AR 72745

THOMPSON, JAMES WILLIAM, lawyer; b. Dallas, Oct. 22, 1936; s. John Charles and Frances (Van Slyke) T.; BS, U. Mont., 1958, JD, 1962; m. Marie Hertz, June 26, 1965; children: Elizabeth, Margaret, John. Acct., Arthur Young & Co., N.Y.C., summer 1959; instr. bus. adminstrn. Eastern Mont. Coll., Billings, 1959-60, U. Mont., Missoula, 1960-61; admitted to Mont. bar, 1962; assoc. Cooke, Moulton, Bellingham & Longo, Billings, 1962-64, James R. Felt, Billings, 1964-65; asst. atty. City of Billings, 1963-64, atty., 1964-66; ptnr. Felt, Speare & Thompson, Billings, 1966-72, McNamer, Thompson & Cashmore, 1973-86, McNamer & Thompson PC, 1986-89, McNamer, Thompson, Werner & Stanley, P.C., 1990—; bd. dirs. Associated Industries of Mont., Inc. Mem. Billings Zoning Commn., 1966-69; v.p. Billings Community Action Program (now Dist. 7 Human Resources Devel. Council), 1968-70, pres., 1970-75, trustee, 1975—; mem. Yellowstone County Legal Services Bd., 1969-70; City-County Air Pollution Control Bd., 1969-70; pres. Billings Symphony Soc., 1970-71; bd. dirs. Billings Studio Theatre, 1967-73, Mont. Inst. of Arts Found., 1986-89, Downtown Billings Assn., 1986-90, Billings Area Bus. Incubator, Inc., 1991—, Ea. Mont. Coll. Found., 1992—; mem. Diocesan exec. council, 1972-75; mem. Billings Transit Commn., 1971-73; mem. City Devel. Agy., 1972-73; bd. dirs. United Way, Billings, 1973-81. C.P.A., Mont. Mem. ABA, State Bar Mont., Yellowstone County Bar Assn. (bd. dirs. 1983-87, pres. 1985-86), Mont. Soc. CPAs, C. of C., Elks, Kiwanis, Sigma Chi (pres. Billings alumni assn. 1963-65). Episcopalian. Home: 123 Lewis Ave Billings MT 59101-6034 Office: Transwestern 1 Bldg Billings MT 59101

THOMPSON, JESSE JACKSON, former university educator, clinical psychologist, consultant; b. Sanger, Calif., July 26, 1919; s. Lewis Elmer and Lucy Jane (Hamilton) T.; m. Clara Lucile Roy, Feb. 4, 1945; children: Lyle Blair, Carolrae, Jon Royal, Mark Alan. BA, Santa Barbara State Coll., 1941; MS in Edn., U. So. Calif., 1947, PhD, 1957. Lic. psychologist, speech pathologist, Calif. Speech therapist Pasadena (Calif.) City Schs., 1947-51; coord. spl. svcs Riverside (Calif.) County Schs., 1951-53, asst. supt. schs., 1953-56; prof. communicative disorders Calif. State U., Long Beach, 1956-79, dir. ctr. for health manpower edn., 1970-74; pvt. practice in clin. psychology Westminster and Santa Ana, Calif., 1979-87; coord. mental health svcs. AIDS Response Program of Orange County, Garden Grove, Calif., 1988-89, 90; adv. bd. Speech and Lang. Devel. Ctr., Buena Park, Calif., 1966—, Nat. Coun. YMCA, 1970-75, Orange County County YMCA's, 1968-72, pres., 1970-72; pres. West Orange County YMCA, 1960-72; cons. Orange County Schs., Santa Ana, Calif., 1969-71, Child Devel. Clinic, Long Beach, 1961-64, Head Start Program, Compton, Calif., 1967-72. Co-author: Talking Time, 2d edit., 1966, Speech Ways, 1955, Phonics, 1962, Rhymes for Fingers and Flannel Boards, 1962, 87. Pres. Orange County Community Action Coun., Santa Ana, 1970-71; chmn. bd. dirs. Orange County-Long Beach Health Consortium, Santa Ana, 1974; vol. AIDS Response Program, Garden Grove, Calif., 1987— (Disting. Svc. award 1992), coord. mental health svcs., 1988-89, 90; facilitator AIDS Ministry Ecumenical Network, 1989—; mem. constitution com. Southeastern conf. Seventh-Day Adventist Ch., 1966-92, vice chmn., 1989-92, chmn., 1992; mem. constitution com. PAcific Union conf., 1992—. Fellow Am. Speech, Lang. and Hearing Assn.; mem. Calif. Speech, Lang. and HEaring Assn. (pres. 1959-60, honors 1979), Christian Assn. Psychol. Studies, Assn. Emeritii Profs., ACLU, Common Cause, People for the Am. Way. Democrat. Office: AIDS Response Program 12832 Garden Grove Blvd Ste B Garden Grove CA 92643-2014

THOMPSON, JOHN LESTER, III, bishop; b. Youngstown, Ohio, May 11, 1926; s. John Lester and Irene (Brown) T.; m. Shirley Amanda Scott, Aug. 1, 1951; children: Amanda, Ian. B.A., Youngstown Coll., 1948; S.T.B., Episcopal Theol. Sch., Cambridge, Mass., 1951. Ordained priest Episcopal Ch., 1951; curate, then rector chs. Ohio, Oreg. and Calif., 1951-78; bishop Episcopal Diocese No. Calif., Sacramento, 1978-92, Diocese No. Calif., Sacramento, 1992—; trustee Ch. Divinity Sch. Pacific, Berkeley, Calif. Pres., Oreg. Shakespeare Festival, 1955-56, chmn. bldg. com. for outdoor theatre, 1957-58. Served with USNR, 1943-46. Office: PO Box 131268 Sacramento CA 95816-1268*

THOMPSON, JOHN WILLIAM, international management consultant; b. Hurricane, Utah, Oct. 14, 1945; s. Thomas Thurman and Lula (Brinkerhoff) T.; m. Pamela Ruth Williams, Sept. 14, 1991. BSEE, Utah State U., 1969, MBA, 1972; PhD, U. Oreg., 1978. Rsch. asst. Utah State U., Logan, Utah, 1967-69, tching. asst., 1971-72; elec. engr. Collins Radio, Newport Beach, Calif., 1969-72; tching. fellow U. Oreg., Eugene, 1972-78; tng. dir. Lifespring Inc., San Rafael, Calif., 1978-80; pres., CEO Human Factors Inc., San Rafael, Calif., 1980—; chmn. bd. Acumen Internat., San Rafael, Calif., 1985—. Author: The Human Factor: An Inquiry into Communication and Consciousness, 1983, Leadership in the 21st Century in New Dimensions of Business, 1992, The Renaissance of Business, 1993; author of software based management assessment programs, system theory based management development courses, 1980-92. Rockefeller Found. grantee, 1971. Avocations: raising koi, gardening, bicycling. Office: Human Factors Inc 4000 Civic Ctr Dr Ste 302 San Rafael CA 94903

THOMPSON, JOSIE, nursing administrator; b. Ark., Apr. 16, 1949; d. James Andrew and Oneda Fay (Watson) Rhoads; m. Mark O. Thompson, Feb. 14, 1980. Diploma, Lake View Sch. Nursing, 1970; student, Danville Community Coll., 1974-75, St. Petersburg Jr. Coll., 1979. RN, Ill., Wyo. Staff nurse St. Elizabeth Hosp., Danville, Ill., 1970-78, Osteopathetic Hosp., St. Petersburg, Fla., 1980-81, Wyo. State Hosp., Evanston, 1981-83; staff nurse Wyo. Home Health Care, Rock Springs, 1984—, adminstr., 1986—; pres. Home Health Care Alliance Wyo., 1991-92. Mem. nursing program adv. bd. Western Wyo. Community Coll.; mem. Coalition for the Elderly, Spl. Needs Com. Sweetwater County, 1992-93. Home: PO Box 1154 1207 McCabe Rock Springs WY 82902

THOMPSON, JUDITH KASTRUP, nursing researcher; b. Marstal, Denmark, Oct. 1, 1933; came to the U.S., 1951; d. Edward Kastrup and Anna Hansa (Knudsen) Pedersen; m. Richard Frederick Thompson, May 22, 1960; children: Kathryn Marr, Elizabeth Kastrup, Virginia St. Claire. BS, RN, U. Oreg., 1958, MSN, 1963. RN, Calif., Oreg. Staff nurse U. Oreg. Med. Sch., Eugene, 1957-58; staff nurse U. Oreg. Med. Sch., Portland, 1958-61, head staff nurse, 1960-61; instr. psychiat. nursing U. Oreg. Sch. Nursing, Portland, 1963-64; rsch. asst. U. Oreg. Med. Sch., Portland, 1964-65, U. Calif., Irvine, 1971-72; rsch. assoc. Stanford (Calif.) U., 1982-87; rsch. asst. Harvard U., Cambridge, Mass., 1973-74; rsch. assoc. U. So. Calif., L.A., 1987—. Contbg. author: Behavioral Control and Role of Sensory Biofeedback, 1976; contbr. articles to profl. jours. Treas. LWV, Newport Beach, Calif., 1970-74; scout leader Girl Scouts Am., Newport Beach, 1970-78. Named Citizen of Yr. State of Oreg., 1966. Mem. Soc. for Neurosci., Am. Psychol. Soc. (charter), ANA, Oreg. Nurses Assn. Republican. Lutheran. Home: 28 Sky Sail Dr Corona Del Mar CA 92625-1436 Office: U So Calif University Park Los Angeles CA 90089-2520

THOMPSON, LINDSAY TAYLOR, lawyer; b. Fayetteville, N.C., Dec. 13, 1955; s. Tommy J. and Margaret Ruth (Comer) T. BA, St. Andrews Presbyn. Coll., 1978; MA, Oxford (Eng.) U., 1980; JD, Lewis & Clark Coll., 1983. Bar: Wash. 1985, U.S. Dist. Ct. (we. dist.) Wash. 1986. Assoc. Green & Thompson, P.C., Portland, Oreg., 1985-86, Weber, Gunn, Nicholson, Nordeen & Marshack, P.S., Vancouver, Wash., 1986-91; dep. prosecuting atty. Prosecutor's Office, Cowlitz County, Wash., 1991—. Editor The Advocate, 1983—, Wash. State Bar News, 1988—. Bd. dirs. The Old Ch. Soc., Portland, 1984-89, pres., 1986-88, life mem., 1989; bd. dirs. Heritage Trust of Clark County, Vancouver, 1987-89, West Coast Chamber Orch., Portland, 1988-91, pres. 1989-91. Mem. Clark County Bar Assn. (trustee 1988-91), Wash. State Bar Assn., U.S. Rowing Assn. (masters com. 1987-89, safety adv. com. 1988—), Cowlitz-Wahkiakum County Bar Assn., Rotary Internat. (pres. North Portland 1990-91). Republican. Presbyterian. Office: Prosecutors Office Hall of Justice 312 SW 1st Ave Kelso WA 98626-1724

THOMPSON, LOHREN MATTHEW, oil company executive; b. Sutherland, Nebr., Jan. 21, 1926; s. John M. and Anna (Ecklund) T.; children—Terence M., Sheila M., Clark M. Ed., U. Denver. Spl. rep. Standard Oil Co., Omaha, 1948-56; sales mgr. Frontier REF. Co., 1956-67, v.p. mktg., 1967-68; mgr. mktg. U.S. region Husky Oil Co., Denver, 1968-72; v.p.

Westar Stas., Inc., Denver, 1967-70; pres., chmn. bd. Colo. Petroleum, Denver, 1971—. Served with USAAF, 1944-46. Mem. Colo. Petroleum Council, Am. Petroleum Inst., Am. Legion. Democrat. Lutheran. Clubs: Denver Petroleum, Denver Oilman's Lodge: Lions. Home: 2410 Spruce Ave Estes Park CO 80517-7146 Office: Colo Petroleum 4080 Globeville Rd Denver CO 80216-4906

THOMPSON, LOIS JEAN HEIDKE ORE, industrial psychologist; b. Chgo., Feb. 22, 1933; d. Harold William and Ethel Rose (Neumann) Heidke; m. Henry Thomas Ore, Aug. 28, 1954 (div. May 1972); children: Christopher, Douglas; m. Joseph Lippard Thompson, Aug. 3, 1972; children: Scott, Les, Melanie. BA, Cornell Coll., Mt. Vernon, Iowa, 1955; MA, Idaho State U., 1964, EdD, 1981. Lic. psychologist, N.Mex. Tchr. pub. schs. various locations, 1956-67; tchr., instr. Idaho State U., Pocatello, 1967-72; employee/orgn. devel. specialist Los Alamos (N.Mex.) Nat. Lab., 1981-84, tng. specialist, 1984-89, sect. leader, 1989—; pvt. practice Los Alamos, 1988—; sec. Cornell Coll. Alumni Office, 1954-55, also other orgns.; bd. dirs. Parent Edn. Ctr., Idaho State U., 1980; counselor, Los Alamos, 1981-88. Editor newsletter LWV, Laramie, Wyo., 1957; contbr. articles to profl. jours. Pres. Newcomers Club, Pocatello, 1967, Faculty Womens Club, Pocatello, 1968; chmn. edn. com. AAUW, Pocatello, 1969. Mem. APA, AACD, N.Mex. Psychol. Assn. (bd. dirs. div. II, 1990, sec. 1988-90, chmn. 1990), N.Am. Soc. Adlerian Psychology, N.Mex. Soc. Adlerian Psychology (pres. 1990, treas. 1991-93), Soc. Indsl. and Orgnl. Psychology, Nat. Career Counseling Assn. Mem. LDS Ch. Home: 340 Aragon Ave Los Alamos NM 87544-3505 Office: Los Alamos Nat Lab MS M589 HRD-3 Los Alamos NM 87545

THOMPSON, LYLE EUGENE, electrical engineer; b. Pocatello, Idaho, May 16, 1956; s. Clyde Eugene and Doris (Pratt) T.; m. Barbara Mae Dickerson, Dec. 31, 1986. Grad. high sch. Sr. diagnostic engr. Calma/GE, Santa Clara, Calif., 1978-83; mem. tech. staff Telecommunications Tech., Inc., Milpitas, Calif., 1983-84; proprietor/cons. Lyle Thompson Cons., Fremont, Calif., 1984-87; sys. analyst Raynet Corp., Menlo Park, Calif., 1987-88; proprietor/cons. Lyle Thompson Cons., Hayward, Calif., 1988-89; mgr. sys. design Raylan Corp., Menlo Park, Calif., 1989-90; dir. system design Raylan Corp., Menlo Park, 1990-91; pvt. practice cons. San Lorenzo, Calif., 1991—; cons. in field. Patentee in field. Mem. ACM, IEEE. Home: 664 Paseo Grande San Lorenzo CA 94580-2364

THOMPSON, MALCOLM FRANCIS, electrical engineer; b. Charleston, S.C., Sept. 2, 1921; s. Allen R. and Lydia (Brunson) T.; m. Ada Rose O'Quinn, Jan. 20, 1943 (dec. 1987); children: Rose Mary, Nancy Belle, Susan Elizabeth, Frances Josephine; m. Milena N. Winckler, June 22, 1989. BS, Ga. Inst. Tech., 1943, MS, 1947; postgrad., MIT, 1947-49. Instr. dept. elec. engring. MIT, 1947-49; rsch. engr. Autonetics Co., Anaheim, Calif., 1949-70; tech. dir. SRC div. Moxon, Inc., Irvine, Calif., 1970-73; engring. mgr., mgr. computers and armament controls. Northrop Aircraft Div., Hawthorne, Calif., 1973-87; ind. cons., 1987—. Patentee in field. Capt. AUS, 1943-46. Mem. IEEE, NRA, Nat. Geog. Soc., Am. Ordnance Assn., Eta Kappa Nu. Home and Office: 1602 Indus St Santa Ana CA 92707-5308

THOMPSON, MARK DUAINE, electrical engineer; b. Blue Island, Ill., July 4, 1956; s. James Alvin and Nella (Frances) T.; m. Cynthia Lee Zelasko, Sept. 24, 1977; children: James Irwin, Rebecca Louise. BSEET, DeVry Inst. Tech., Chgo., 1977; MSEE, U. N.Mex., 1983. Mem. tech. staff Sandia Nat. Labs., Albuquerque, 1977-83; field application engr. Intel Corp., Albuquerque, 1983-89; application engring. mgr. Alliance Electronics, Albuquerque, 1989—; cons. systems div. BFANM, Albuquerque, 1982-83. Contbr. articles to tech. pubs. Bell & Howell scholar, 1974-77. Mem. Armed Forces Communications and Electronics Assn., Am. Def. Preparedness Assn., Assn. Old Crows, Surface Mount Tech. Assn. Republican. Baptist. Office: Alliance Electronics 10510 Research Ct SE Albuquerque NM 87123-3424

THOMPSON, MARTHA ELLEN, physiology educator; b. St. Charles, Mo., May 18, 1947; d. James Edgar and Florence Charlotte (Gutermuth) T.; m. Robert Andrew Goetz, June 25, 1975; 1 child, Evan Andrew. B Med. Sci., U. Mo., 1970, MS, 1971; PhD, U. Ariz., 1976. Cert. med. technologist Am. Soc. Clin. Pathologists. Med. technologist U. Mo. Med. Ctr., Columbia, 1970-72, sr. med. technologist, 1972; grad. teaching asst. U. Ariz., Tucson, 1972-75, rsch. assoc., 1975-76; fellow Oreg. Health Scis. U., Portland, 1976-78, asst. prof. physiology, 1978-83, assoc. prof., 1983—, pres. faculty senate, 1990-91. Contbr. articles to profl. jours. Unit Chmn. United Way, Portland, 1988; com. chmn. Boy Scouts Am., Portland, 1991—. USPHS traineeship, 1970. Mem. Endocrine Soc., Internat. Soc. for Endorcinology, Soc. for Neurosci., Am. Assn. Dental Schs., Internat. Assn. for Dental Rsch., City Club Portland (sci. and high tech. com. 1986), Sigma Xi (chpt. del. 1991), Iota Sigma Pi (nat. bd. dirs. 1987—). Office: Oreg Health Scis U 611 SW Campus Dr Portland OR 97201

THOMPSON, (GERRY) MAXINE LEAK, supply technician, inventory consultant; b. Brigham, Utah, Nov. 25, 1938; d. Gerald L. and Luetta Grace (Peterson) Leak; m. Gordon Wise Thompson, Sept. 27, 1957; children: Kellee, Kris, Kasey. A in Bus. Adminstrn., GTE, 1992, A in Mktg., 1992; BS in Bus. Adminstrn. and Mgmt., U. Phoenix, 1992. Plant clk. Contel, Tremonton, Utah, 1977-78, warehouse person, 1978-82, storekeeper, 1982-89, Utah state purchasing/supply agt., 1989-91; Utah state purchasing/supply agt. GTE, Tremonton, 1992—. Editor: T-P Times, 1970-74. Active LDS Primary Orgn., LDS Mutual Improvement Assn. Orgn., Thatcher-Penrose, Utah, 1960-80; exhibit chmn. Box Elder County Fair, 1969, 74. Recipient award LDS Ch., 1981. Home: 9073 N 11600 W Tremonton UT 84337

THOMPSON, MICHAEL JOHN, elementary educator; b. Green Bay, Wis., Apr. 28, 1944; s. Guy Franklin and Delilah Martha (Westphal) T.; m. Olivia Harris Reischling, Oct. 29, 1989; 1 child, Kirsten. Student, U. Wis., Green Bay, 1962-63; BA in Econs. & Sociology, Beloit Coll., 1966; postgrad., U. Tex., El Paso, 1966-67; MA in Elem. Edn., San Francisco State U., 1972. Instr. U.S. Army, El Paso, 1967-68, U.S. Army/U. Wis., Korea, 1968-69; classroom tchr. San Francisco Unified Sch. Dist., 1970-72; classroom tchr. Old Adobe Union Sch. Dist., Petaluma, Calif., 1972—, vice-prin., tchr., 1991—; coord. Year Round Sch. Program, Old Adobe Union Sch. Dist., 1974-87; speaker staff devel. Old Adobe Union Sch. Dist., 1982—; mem., rep. Sch./Community Site Coun., Petaluma, 1987—; adminstr. Spl. Edn. Program Rev.-La Tercera Elem. Sch., Petaluma, 1990—. Co-founder, tchr. Clown Coll., 1979-84; creator reading program for slow learners, 1975, lit.-based reading program for classroom, 1986. Co-founder Dist. Outdoor Edn. Program, 1974; coord. Sch.-Bus. Rels., Petaluma, 1985; judge essay contest Elks Club, Petaluma, 1987. 1st lt. U.S. Army, 1966-69, Korea. Recipient Recognition award Petaluma Area C. of C., 1985, Lit.-based reading grant Petaluma Ednl. Found., 1989, Jack London award ednl. excellence Calif. Faculty Assn.-Sonoma State U., 1990, Program Excellence award Sonoma County Office Edn., 1991. Mem. NEA, Internat. Reading Assn., Calif. Tchrs. Assn., Old Adobe Tchrs. Assn. (dir. community rels. 1988-92, v.p. 1974-77, pres. 1984-86, chmn. 1986—). Home: 706 B St Petaluma CA 94952 Office: Old Adobe Union Sch Dist 1600 Albin Way Petaluma CA 94954

THOMPSON, NEIL BRUCE, foundation executive; b. Tuscaloosa, Ala., Oct. 14, 1941; s. Donald Eugene and Jean (Beecher) T.; m. Diane Sorrita Ramsey, Aug. 13, 1966; children: Marnie, Karina. BA, Rutgers U., 1963; MS, San Diego State U., 1974. Enlisted USN, 1965, advanced through grades to lt. comdr., 1965-86, pub. affairs officer, 1965-70; dep. dir. USN Pub. Affairs Office Midwest, Chgo., 1970-72; pub. affairs officer Carrier Div. 5/CTF-77 USN, 1972-73; pub. affairs officer Taiwan Def. Command USN, Taipei, 1975-78; pub. affairs officer USN, Bklyn., 1978-81, exec. officer, 1980-81; pub. affairs officer Naval Postgrad. Sch. USN, Monterey, Calif., 1981-86; ret. USN, 1986; exec. dir. Monterey County Spl. Olympics, 1986-88, Food Bank for Monterey County, 1988—. Co-chmn. Fleet Week, Monterey, 1987; active Leadership Monterey Peninsula, 1987-88; commr. City of Marina Planning Commn., 1988-90; bd. dirs. Monterey County Homeless Coalition, 1989-90; commr. Monterey County Social Svcs. Commn., 1989—; mem. Monterey County Homeless Task Force, 1989-90. Mem. Navy League U.S. (bd. dirs. Monterey Peninsula council 1987-89), Devel. Execs. Network. Republican. Home: 270 Reindollar Ave Marina CA 93933 Office: Food Bank for Monterey Cty 815 W Market St Salinas CA 93901

THOMPSON, PAUL HAROLD, university president; b. Ogden, Utah, Nov. 28, 1938; s. Harold Merwin and Elda (Skeen) T.; m. Carolyn Lee Nelson, Mar. 9, 1961; children: Loralyn, Kristyn, Shannyn, Robbyn, Daylyn, Nathan. BS, U. Utah, 1964; MBA, Harvard U., 1966, D Bus. Adminstrn., 1969. Rsch. assoc. Harvard U., Cambridge, Mass., 1966-69; asst. prof. Harvard U., Cambridge, 1969-73; assoc. prof. bus. Brigham Young U., Provo, Utah, 1973-78, prof., 1978-84, asst. dean, 1978-81, dean, 1984-89, v.p., 1989-90; pres. Weber State U., Ogden, Utah, 1990—; cons. Goodyear, Hughes Aircraft, Portland GE, Esso Resources Ltd., GE. Co-author: Organization and People: Readings, Cases, and Exercises in Organizational Behavior, 1976, Novations: Strategies for Career Management, 1986; also articles. Vice chmn. Utah Gov.'s Econ. Devel. Bd., Salt Lake City, 1986—; mem. Utah Gov.'s Task Force on Entrepreneurship, 1989-90; mem. exec. com. Weber Econ. Devel. Corp., Ogden, 1990—. Named Outstanding Prof. of Yr., Brigham Young U., 1981; Baker scholar Harvard U., 1966. Mem. Am. Assn. State Colls. and Univs. (com. 1991—), Ogden C. of C. (exec. com. 1990—), Rotary (prograam com. Ogden 1991—, Harris fellow 1992—), Phi Beta Kappa. Office: Weber State U 3750 Harrison Blvd Ogden UT 84408-1001

THOMPSON, PHILIP MASON, museum director; b. N.Y.C., June 9, 1942; s. William R. and Marie J. (Buckovecky) T.; m. Vilja Maria Horner, Sept. 4, 1966; children: Philip Jr., Tyra. BA, Ariz. State U., 1969, MA, 1986. Asst. dir. Phoenix Art Mus., 1971-73, Phila. Mus. Art, 1973-78; dir. devels. and community affairs Phoenix Meml. Hosp., 1978-81; dir. devels. St. Joseph's Hosp., Phoenix, 1981-83; dir. Mus. No. Ariz., Flagstaff, 1983—; nat. adv. bd. practitioners No. Ariz. U., Flagstaff, 1986; bd. dirs. Western Mus. Conf., Ariz. Mus. Assn. Mem., vice chmn. Ariz. Hist. Gov.'s Adv. Commn., Phoenix, 1984—; mem. steering com. BLOC Grant Program, 1980-83. Served with U.S. Army, 1963-66. Mem. Am. Assn. Mus., Am. Anthropol. Assn., Sigma Xi. Republican. Presbyterian. Club: Continental Country (Flagstaff). Home: RR 4 Box 718 Flagstaff AZ 86001-9301 Office: Mus No Ariz RR 4 Box 720 Flagstaff AZ 86001-9302

THOMPSON, RICHARD DICKSON, lawyer; b. Lexington, Ky., Aug. 14, 1955; s. Lawrence Sidney and Algernon Smith (Dickson) T.; m. Bobbi Dale Magidoff, Aug. 3, 1980; 1 child, Anne Katherine. AB, Harvard U., 1977; JD, Stanford U., 1980. Bar: Calif. 1980, U.S. Dist. Ct. (so. dist.) Calif. 1980. Assoc. Rosenfield Meyer & Susman, Beverly Hills, Calif., 1980-83, Silverberg Rosen Leon & Behr, L.A., 1983-86; ptnr. Silverberg Rosen Leon & Behr, 1986-89; assoc., then ptnr. Silverberg Katz Thompson & Braun, L.A., 1989—. Mem. L.A. Copyright Soc., Order of Coif, Phi Beta Kappa. Office: Silverberg Katz Thompson Braun & Klein 11766 Wilshire Blvd Ste 700 Los Angeles CA 90025-6538

THOMPSON, RITA MARIE, retired counselor, writer; b. Rochester, N.Y., July 12, 1930; d. Horace Kenneth and Doris Marie (Brown) Lawrence; m. James Frederick Thompson (div. Apr. 1964); children: Mary Thompson Shank, Margaret. BS, Cortland State U., 1952; MS, Syracuse U., 1965. Cert. counselor, social worker. Tchr. phys. edn. Pittsford (N.Y.) Pub. High Sch., 1952-55, West Palm Beach (Fla.) Schs., 1955-59, 63-64; counselor Fulton (N.Y.) High Sch., 1965-67, Orange (Calif.) Unified Sch. Dist., 1967-92; pres. JoyCo, Newport Beach, Calif., 1973—. Author: Bed & Breakfast Travel Guide and Cookbook, 1986, Lunch, Brunch, and Happy Hour in Orange County, 1985, 86. Eucharistic min. to sick Our Lady Queen Angels Cath. Ch., Newport Beach, 1988—.

THOMPSON, ROBERT CHARLES, lawyer; b. Council, Idaho, Apr. 20, 1942; s. Ernest Lavelle and Evangeline Montgomery (Carlson) T.; m. Marilyn Anne Wilcox, Jan. 17, 1960 (dec. Mar. 1962); m. Patricia Joan Price, June 1, 1963 (div. 1969); m. Jan Nesbitt, June 29, 1973; children: Christopher Andrew, Eric Robert, Tanya. AB, Harvard U., 1963, LLB, 1967. Bar: Mass. 1967, Calif. 1983, U.S. Dist. Ct. (ea. dist.) Mass. 1975, U.S. Ct. Appeals (1st cir.) 1976, U.S. Ct. Appeals (9th cir.) 1984, U.S. Dist. Ct. (no. dist.) Calif. 1983. Assoc. Choate, Hall & Stewart, Boston, 1967-73; asst. regional counsel EPA, Boston, 1973-75, regional counsel, 1975-82, assoc. gen. counsel, 1979-82; regional counsel EPA, San Francisco, 1982-84; ptnr. Graham & James, San Francisco, 1984-91, LeBoeuf, Lamb, Leiby & MacRae, San Francisco, 1992—. Contbr. articles to profl. jours. Bd. dirs. Peninsula Indsl. and Bus. Assn., Palo Alto, Calif., 1986—; chmn. Cambridge (Mass.) Conservation Commn., 1972-74; co-chmn. The Clift Confs. on Environ. Law, 1983-93. John Russell Shaw traveling fellow Harvard Coll., 1963-64; recipient Regional Adminstrs. Bronze medal EPA, 1976, 84. Mem. ABA (natural resources sect., com. on native Am. natural resources law, spl. com. on mktg.), Natural Resources Def. Coun., Sierra Club, Commonwealth Club. Democrat. Episcopalian. Office: LeBoeuf Lamb Leiby & MacRae One Embarcadero Ctr San Francisco CA 94111

THOMPSON, ROBERT RANDALL (ROBBY THOMPSON), professional baseball player; b. West Palm Beach, Fla., May 10, 1962. Student, Palm Beach Jr. Coll., Fla. State U. With San Francisco Giants, 1986—; mem. Nat. League All-Star Team, 1988, 93. Named Sporting News Rookie Player of Yr., 1986, Nat. League Leader in Triples, 1989. Office: San Francisco Giants Candlestick Park San Francisco CA 94124

THOMPSON, ROGER CRAIG, manufacturing company executive; b. Detroit, July 22, 1941; s. Wilford George and Lucille (Watson) T.; m. Victoria Renee Baughn, July 3, 1964; children: Laura, David, Douglas, Jeanette, Sharon. Student bus. adminstrn., Colo. State U., 1959-60, Brigham Young U., Liae, Hawaii, 1961; student fin. and mktg., Ariz. State U., 1963-64. Mgmt. trainee Theo. H. Davies & Co., Ltd., Honolulu, 1961-62; div. mgr. Sears, Roebuck & Co., Phoenix, 1964-67; program mgr. Talley Def. Systems, Mesa, Ariz., 1968-69; area mgr. Fotomat Corp., Phoenix, 1970-71; mktg. mgr. Fotomat Corp., La Jolla, Calif., 1972-73; regional dir. Fotomat Corp., Stamford, Conn., 1974-79; v.p., co-owner Biesemeyer Mfg. Corp., Mesa, 1980—; mem. adv. bd. Powermatic div. Houdaille Industries, McMinnville, Tenn., 1985-86; lectr. Brigham Young U., Provo, Utah, 1988—. Exec. com., chmn. mktg. com., bd. dirs. YMCA, Mesa, 1987—, Mesa Symphony Orch. Assn., 1988-90; bd. dirs. El Tour de Tucson, 1988—; chmn. Project Eagle, Boy Scouts Am., Mesa, 1988-89; vice chair, bd. dirs. Mesa Crime Prevention Adv. Bd., 1989—; grad. Valley Leadership, 1991; bicyclist from L.A. to Boston to raise funds for Heart, Cancer and Multiple Sclerosis charities, 1992. Mem. Wood Machinery Mfg. Assn. Am. (bd. dirs. 1987—). Republican. Mormon. Home: 1717 E Ivy Glen Mesa AZ 85203 Office: Biesemeyer Mfg Corp 216 S Alma School Rd Mesa AZ 85210-1006

THOMPSON, RONALD EDWARD, lawyer; b. Bremerton, Wash., May 24, 1931; s. Melville Herbert and Clara Mildred (Griggs) T.; m. Marilyn Christine Woods, Dec. 15, 1956; children—Donald Jeffery, Karen, Susan, Nancy, Sally, Claire. B.A., U. Wash., 1953, J.D., 1958. Bar: Wash. 1959. Asst. city atty. City of Tacoma, 1960-61; pres. firm Thompson, Krilich, LaPorte, Tucci, Prather & West, P.S., Tacoma, 1961—; judge pro tem Mcpl. Ct., City of Tacoma, Pierce County Dist., 1972—, Pierce County Superior Ct., 1972—. Chmn. housing and social welfare com. City of Tacoma, 1965-69; mem. Tacoma Bd. Adjustment, 1967-71, chmn., 1968; mem. Tacoma Com. Future Devel., 1961-64, Tacoma Planning Commn., 1971-72; bd. dirs., pres. Mcpl. League Tacoma; bd. dirs. Pres. Tacoma Rescue Mission, Tacoma Pierce County Cancer Soc., Tacoma-Pierce County Heart Assn., Tacoma-Pierce County Council for Arts, Econ. Devel. Council Puget Sound, Tacoma Youth Symphony, Kleiner Group Home, Tacoma Community Coll. Found., Pierce County Econ. Devel. Corp., Wash. Transp. Policy Inst.; Coalition to Keep Wash. Moving, precinct committeeman Republican party, 1969-73. Served with AUS, 1953-55; col. Res. Recipient Internat. Community Service award Optimist Club, 1970, Patriotism award Am. Fedn. Police, 1974, citation for community service HUD, 1974, Disting. Citizen award Mcpl. League Tacoma-Pierce County, 1985; named Lawyer of the Yr. Pierce County Legal Secs. Assn., 1992. Mem. Am. Arbitration Assn. (panel of arbitrators), ABA, Wash. State Bar Assn., Tacoma-Pierce County Bar Assn. (sec. 1964, pres. 1979, mem. cts. and judiciary com. 1981-82), Assn. Trial Lawyers Am., Wash. State Trial Lawyers Assn., Tacoma-Pierce County C. of C. (bd. dirs., exec. com., v.p., chmn.), Downtown Tacoma Assn. (com. chmn., bd. dirs. exec. com., chmn.), Phi Delta Phi, Sigma Nu. Roman Catholic. Clubs: Variety (Seattle); Lawn Tennis, Tacoma, Optimist (Tacoma, Internat. Pres. 1973-74). Home: 3101 East Bay Dr NW Gig Harbor WA 98335 Office: 524 Tacoma Ave S Tacoma WA 98402-5416

THOMPSON, RONALD MACKINNON, family physician, artist; b. N.Y.C., Oct. 19, 1916; s. George Harold and Pearl Anita (Hatfield) T.; m. Ethel Joyce Chastant, June 30, 1950; children: Phyllis Anita, Walter MacKinnon, Charles Chastant, Richard Douglas. BS, U. Chgo., 1947, MS, 1948, MD, 1949. Diplomate Am. Bd. Family Practice. Intern U. Mich., Ann Arbor, 1950-51; resident in psychiatry U. Tex., Galveston, 1951-52; pvt. practice, family South Dixie Med. Ctr., West Palm Beach, Fla., 1952-85; instr. Anatomy, U. Chgo., 1946-47, Pharmacology, 1948-49. Contbr. articles to profl. jours. Artist: Paintings in permanent collections of 5 mus. Mem. Civitan Club W. Palm Beach, Fla., 1951. Cadet Army Air Force, 1943-44. Over thirty awards for painting in regional and nat. shows. Mem. AMA, Fla. Med. Assn., Nat. Watercolor Soc., Ariz. Watercolor Soc. Republican. Episcopalian. Home: 308 Leisure World Mesa AZ 85206

THOMPSON, SHERMAN LEE, producer; b. Perris, Calif., Jan. 13, 1934; s. Leo and Anna Margaret (Schwarz) T. Student, Chouinard Art Inst., 1957-60. Staff artist Churchill Films, Inc., Hollywood, Calif., 1960-64; prod. mgr. Murakami-Wolf Swenson Films, Hollywood, 1964-72; prod. supr. Focus Films Inc., N.Y.C., 1972-74; producer Film Fair, Inc., Studio City, Calif., 1974-78; exec. producer Murakami-Wolf Swenson Films, Hollywood, 1978-80; bd. dirs. Camera Services Inc., Burbank, Calif., 1980-81; sr. producer Ogilvy & Mather Advt., Los Angeles, 1981—; animation instr. Art Ctr. Sch. Design, Los Angeles, 1968-70. Mem. Acad. TV Arts and Sci. (animation peer group exec. com. 1991-93). Office: Ogilvy & Mather 11766 Wilshire Blvd Los Angeles CA 90025

THOMPSON, STEPHEN MARK, artist, educator; b. Denver, June 21, 1947; s. Chester Collom and Maxine (Elson) T.; m. Angela Cunningham; children: Jesse Cameron, Spencer Collom. BFA, Colo. State U., 1972. Illustrator Feldkamp-Malloy Studios, Chgo., 1969-70; tchr. Jefferson County Pub. Schs., Arvada, Colo., 1972-81; ind. artist Golden, Colo., 1972—; tchr. Art Students' League, Denver, 1987—. Recipient Philip Isenberg award Knickerbocker Artists, N.Y.C., 1985, Cert. of Merit Salmagundi Club, N.Y.C., 1986. Mem. Am. Artists Profl. League (John Grabach Meml. award 1985), Allied Artists Am. (R. Brackman Meml. award 1989). Home and Office: 452 Rudi Ln Golden CO 80403

THOMPSON, TERENCE WILLIAM, lawyer; b. Moberly, Mo., July 3, 1952; s. Donald Gene and Carolyn (Stringer) T.; m. Caryn Elizabeth Hildebrand, Aug. 30, 1975; children: Cory Elizabeth, Christopher William. BA in Govt. with honors and high distinction, U. Ariz., 1974; JD, Harvard U., 1977. Bar: Ariz. 1977, U.S. Dist. Ct. Ariz. 1977, U.S. Tax Ct. 1979. Assoc. Brown & Bain P.A., Phoenix, 1977-83, ptnr., 1983-92; ptnr. Gallagher and Kennedy, P.A., Phoenix, 1992—; legis. aide Rep. Richard Burgess, Ariz. Ho. of Reps., 1974; mem. bus. adv. bd. Citibank Ariz. (formerly Great Western Bank & Trust, Phoenix), 1985-86. Mem. staff Harvard Law Record, 1974-75; rsch. editor Harvard Internat. Law Jour. , 1976; contbr. articles to profl. jours. Mem. Phoenix Mayor's Youth Adv. Bd. 1968-70, Phoenix Internat.; active 20-30 Club, 1978-81, sec. 1978-80, Valley Leadership, Phoenix, 1983-84, citizens task force future financing needs City of Phoenix, 1985-86; exec. coun. Boys and Girls Clubs of Met. Phoenix, 1990—; bd. dirs. Phoenix Bach Choir, 1992—; deacon Shepherd of Hills Congl. Ch., Phoenix, 1984-85; pres. Maricopa County Young Dems., 1982-83, Ariz. Young Dems., 1983-84, sec. 1981-82, v.p. 1982-83; exec. dir. Young Dems. Am., 1985, exec. com. 1983-85; others. Fellow Ariz. Bar Found.; mem. ABA, State Bar Ariz. (vice chmn. internat. law sect. 1978, sec. securities law sect. 1990-91, vice chmn. sect. 1991-92, chmn.-elect 1992—, sec. bus. law sect. 1992—), Maricopa County Bar Assn., Nat. Assn. Bond Lawyers, Am. Acad. Hosp. Attys., Blue Key, Phi Beta Kappa, Phi Kappa Phi, Phi Eta Sigma. Home: 202 W Lawrence Rd Phoenix AZ 85013-1226 Office: Gallagher & Kennedy PA 2600 N Central Ave Phoenix AZ 85004

THOMPSON, THOMAS MICHAEL, logistics management executive; b. Eureka, Calif., Dec. 3, 1943; s. Henry Clay Harman and Marion Margaret (Lee) Thompson. BA in Polit. Sci., Seattle U., 1965; MA in Counseling Psychology, U. San Francisco, 1989. Supply specialist Weapons Command U.S. Army, Rock Island, Ill., 1966-67; supply specialist Sharpe Army Depot, Lathrop, Calif., 1967-68, supply systems analyst, 1968-69; inventory mgmt. specialist PHD, NSWC, Port Hueneme, Calif., 1969-72, logistics mgmt. specialist, 1972-83, asst. for logistics tech. ops., 1983-86, divsn. mgr., 1986-90, dept. mgr., 1990—. Roman Catholic. Home: 2507 Grapevine Dr Oxnard CA 93030

THOMPSON, TIMOTHY HOWARD, computers and data communications consultant; b. Seattle, Feb. 16, 1955; s. Terry and Lucile (Mildred) T. BA, U. Pa., 1976; MBA, U. Wash., 1987. Fgn. exch. trader Rainier Nat. Bank, Seattle, 1975; underwriter Terry Thompson & Co., Seattle, 1975-85; ptnr. Ulterior Design R&D Partnership, Seattle, 1985-88; investments mgr. Paul G. Allen & Asymetrix Corp., Bellevue, Wash., 1988; pres. Silicon Forest Co., Seattle, 1988—. Benjamin Franklin scholar U. Pa., Phila., 1972. Mem. Athenaeum of Phila., Seattle Yacht Club, Sigma Chi. Home: 3803 42d Ave NE Seattle WA 98105-5444 Office: Silicon Forest Co 717 N 45th St No 301 Seattle WA 98103-6500

THOMPSON, TINA LEWIS CHRYAR, publisher; b. Houston, Dec. 31, 1929; d. Joshua and Mary Christine (Brown) Thompson; m. Joseph Chryar, May 25, 1943; 1 child, Joseph Jr. Cosmetologist, Franklin Coll., Houston, 1950; student, Crenshaw Coll., L.A., 1961. Pubr., composer, author B.M.I., N.Y.C., 1964-74; pubr. ASCAP, N.Y.C., 1974-86, The Fox Agy., N.Y.C., 1986—, Tech. World, L.A., 1990—; v.p. music Asset Records, L.A., 1978—; music dir., v.p. Roach Records, L.A., 1968; music dir. Rendezvous Records, Hollywood, 1950; v.p. Assoc. Internat., L.A., 1973; pres. Cling Music Pub., ASCAP, 1974. Author: Soprano Poems, 1985; creator/designer Baby Napkin brand form-fitting, no-leak, no pins baby diaper, 1967; patentee/publisher Letter's Tech. in Word, used by TV stas. to advertise, 1972. Recipient recognition award IBC, Cambridge, Eng., 1991, cert. of proclamation Internat. Woman of Yr., 1991-92; named Most Admired Woman of Decade, ABI, 1993. Mem. NARAS, Am. Soc. Authors and Composers, Nat. Music Pubs. Assn., Songwriters Build Am., Am. Fedn. Label Company Unions, Am. Theatre Assn., Broadcast Music Inc. (pres. Soprano Music Publ. 1968), Rec. Acad. Country Music Acad. Home: PO Box 7731 Beverly Hills CA 90212-7731

THOMPSON, VIRGINIA LOU, agricultural products supplier and importer; b. Malcolm, Iowa, July 15, 1928; d. Isaac Cleveland and Viola (Montgomery) Griffin; m. Alfred Thompson, Mar. 1, 1946 (dec. March 1992); children: Michael Duane, Cathryn Lynn, Steven Curtis, Laura Lue. Student Phoenix Coll., 1962, Phoenix-Scottsdale Jr. Coll., 1973-74. With sales dept. Trend House, Phoenix, 1962-67; importer World Wide Imports, Ft. Collins, Colo., 1974-79; owner, mgr. Windsor Elevator Inc. (Colo.), 1979-89; participant in trade shows, seminars. Pres. Am. Luth. Ch. Women, 1973-74. Mem. Nat. Grain and Feed Assn., Colo. Grain and Feed Assn., Rocky Mountain Bean Dealers, Colo. Cattle Feeders Assn., Western U.S. Agrl. Assn., Rice Millers Assn. Democrat. Lutheran. Clubs: Christian Women (Greeley, Colo.); Order of Eastern Star (Iowa). Home: 3331 Riva Ridge Dr Fort Collins CO 80526-2887

THOMPSON, WADE MARSHALL, electrical engineering exective; b. Livermore, Calif., Aug. 4, 1959; s. James Allan and Shirley Ann (Whalen) T.; div.; children: Ali Albright, Aaron Albright; m. Athene Marie Perakis, June 24, 1987; 1 child, Tyler Nathan. AA in Machine Tech., Chabot Coll., 1980; BSEE, Fresno State U., 1985. Gas sta. attendent East Ave Texaco, Livermore, Calif., 1973-76; welder Calif. Steel Works, Livermore, 1976-77; mechanic, sales rep. Halyak Cylce, Livermore, 1973-77; waiter, mgr. Hungry Hunter, Pleasanton, Calif., 1978-86; engr. assoc. Bendix Field Engring., Livermore, 1978-80; engr. Lawrence Livermore Lab., 1980—; pilot, cons., Livermore, 1980—. Home: 3124 Chateau Way Livermore CA 94550 Office: Lawrence Livermore Nat Lab PO Box 808 L-352 Livermore CA 94550

THOMPSON, WILLIAM BENBOW, JR., obstetrician/gynecologist, educator; b. Detroit, July 26, 1923; s. William Benbow and Ruth Wood (Locke) T.; m. Constance Carter, July 30, 1947 (div. Feb. 1958); 1 child, William Benbow IV; m. Jane Gilliland, Mar. 12, 1958; children: Reese Ellison, Belinda Day. AB, U. So. Calif., 1947, MD, 1951. Diplomate Am. Bd. Ob-Gyn. Resident Gallinger Mun. Hosp., Washington, 1952-53; resident George Washington U. Hosp., Washington, 1953-55; asst. ob-gyn. La. State U.,

1955-56; asst. clinical prof. UCLA, 1957-64; assoc. prof. U. Calif.-Irvine Sch. Med., Orange, Calif., 1964-92; dir. gynecology U. Calif.-Irvine Sch. Med., 1977-92; prof. emeritus U. Calif.-Irvine Sch. Med., Orange, 1993—; vice chmn. ob-gyn. U. Calif.-Irvine Sch. Med., 1978-89; assoc. dean U. Calif.-Irvine Coll. Med., Irvine, 1969-73. Inventor: Thompson Retractor, 1976; Thompson Manipulator, 1977. Bd. dirs. Monarch Bay Assn. Laguna Niguel, Calif. 1969-77, Monarch Summitt II A ssn. 1981-83. With U.S. Army, 1942-44, PTO. Fellow ACS, Am. Coll. Ob-Gyn., L.A. Ob-Gyn. Soc. (life); mem. Orange County Gynecology and Obstetrics Soc. (hon.), Am. Soc. Law and Medicine, Capistrano Bay Yacht Club (commodore 1975), Internat. Order Blue Gavel. Office: UCI Med Ctr OB/GYN 101 City Blvd W Orange CA 92668-2901

THOMPSON, WILLIAM CHARLES, law educator; b. San Diego, Mar. 16, 1954; s. Lewayne and Helen Bernice (Lean) T.; m. Claudia Laverne Cowan, June 21, 1980; children: Jessica, Graham, Elliot. BA, U. So. Calif., 1976; JD, U. Calif., Berkeley, 1982; PhD, Stanford U., 1984. Bar: Calif. 1982. Lawyer Clark Deichler, Oakland, Calif., 1982-83; asst. prof. U. Calif., Irvine, 1983-89, assoc. prof., 1990—. Contbr. articles to profl. jours. NSF rsch. grantee, Washington, 1987-90. Mem. Am. Psychology-Law Soc. (program chmn. 1990). Office: U Calif Dept Criminology Law & Soc Irvine CA 92717

THOMPSON, WILLIAM DENNISON, JR., aeronautical consultant; b. Chgo., Jan. 26, 1920; s. William Dennison and Bertha Helen (Lachnit) T.; m. Jeanne Ann Burkholder, Dec. 26, 1942; children: William III, Burk Blair, Constance Gail. BA in Aero. Engring., Purdue U., 1947. Draftsman/engr. Curtis-Wright Airplane Co., St. Louis, 1940-41; army air corps flight instr. Hawthorne Flying Svc., Orangeburg, S.C., 1942-45; flight instr. Purdue Aeronautics Corp., West Lafayette, Ind., 1946-47; engring. test pilot Cessna Aircraft Co., Wichita, Kans., 1947-53, mgr. flight test and aerodynamics, 1953-74; tech. cons. SIAI Marchetti, Sesto Calende, Italy, 1975-77; owner Thompson Aeronautical Cons., Sunriver, Oreg., 1978—; pres. Precise Flight, Inc., Bend, Oreg., 1980-83; owner Thompson Aero Products, Sunriver, 1984—; cons. for aerodynamics and aeronautics coms. NASA, 1969-73. Author: Cessna Wings for the World-The Single-Engine Development Story, 1991; editor (booklets) Cessna Owners Manuals, 1953-74; co-inventor, patentee integrated spoiler/throttle assembly, 1984. Loaned exec. United Fund, Wichita, 1965; designated engring. rep., flight test pilot, flight analyst FAA, Seattle, Washington, 1980—. Fellow Soc. Exptl. Test Pilots (1st chmn. Wichita sect. 1962-63); mem. Soc. Automotive Engrs. (chmn. Wichita sect. 1970-71), Exptl. Aircraft Assn. Internat., Internat. 195 Club, Cardinal Club. Republican. Presbyterian. Home and Office: 4 Jackpine Ln Bend OR 97707-2706

THOMPSON, WILLIAM PAUL, JR., aerospace company executive; b. Elmira, N.Y., June 3, 1934; s. W. Paul and Helen Katharine (Bruce) T.; m. Sally W. Lessig, Aug. 1955 (div. Apr. 1977); children: Helen W., Bruce A., Leila E., Judith A.; m. Anne Stevenson, Dec. 11, 1977. BS in physics, Yale U., 1955; MS in Physics, Lehigh U., 1957, PhD in Physics, 1963. Research and teaching asst. Lehigh U., Bethlehem, Pa., 1955-61; instr. Moravian Coll., Bethlehem, 1957-58, Los Angeles Trade-Tech., 1967; mem. tech. staff labs Aerospace Corp, Los Angeles, 1961-68; head dept. reentry systems Aerospace Corp., San Bernardino, Calif., 1968-72; assoc. group dir. Aerospace Corp., Los Angeles, 1972-79, dir. space tech., 1979-81, dir. aerophysics lab, 1981-89; prin. scientist devel. group Aerospace Corp., L.A., 1989—; vis. com. Sch. Aerospace Engring. U. Okla., 1987—; adv. bd. minority engring. program UCLA, 1987—. Contbr. articles to profl. publs., chpt. to books. Fellow AIAA (assoc., mem. laser tech. com. 1986-89, chmn. 1989-91); mem. Am. Phys. Soc., Sigma Xi. Republican. Episcopalian. Home: 361 Glensummer Rd Pasadena CA 91105-1422

THOMS, BONNIE ANNE, elementary school educator; b. Vancouver, B.C., Can., Dec. 6, 1952; d. Arthur and Irna T. AA, Flathead Valley Community Coll, Kalispell, Mont., 1973; BS, Dickinson State U., 1975; MA, Lesley Coll., 1986. Cert. phys. fitness specialist, helath promotion dir. Coach, instr. Bozeman (Mont.) Sch. Dist.; instr. health, phys. edn., driver's edn. Campbell County Sch. Dist., Gillette, Wyo.; tchr. gifted & talented Campbell County Sch. Dist., Gillette; active in TESA, Wellness, & Curriculum programs. State and regional volleyball ofcl., 1986-93. Named Young Educator of Yr., Jaycees, 1990. Mem. AAHPERD, NEA, AHA, ASA, Wyo. Edn. Assn., Nat. Coaches Assn., Campbell County Edn. Assn., Epsilon Sigma Alpha, Alpha Sigma Alpha. Home: 916 Fairway Dr Gillette WY 82718-7608

THOMSEN, MICHAEL BERNARD, geologist; b. Milw., Jan. 18, 1952; s. Myron Ernst and Marcella Barbara (Hodan) T.; m. Diane Marie Lynch, Aug. 29, 1988; 1 child, William Michael. BS in Geology cum laude, U. Wis., 1974, MS, 1976. Teaching asst. U. Wis., Madison, 1974-76; geologist Freeport Exploration Co., Tucson, Ariz., 1977-80; chief geologist Freeport Indonesia Inc., Irian Jaya, 1980-83; sr. geologist Freeport McMoRan Inc., Denver, 1983-85; chief geologist Freeport Sulphur Co., New Orleans, 1985-87; sr. mgr. Sulphur Rsch. Group, Lakewood, Colo., 1987-88; sr. geologist Gold Fields Mining Co., Golden, Colo., 1988-93; consulting geologist Lakewood, Colo., 1993—; bd. dirs. Sulphur Rsch. Group, 1987-92. Author: Native Sulphur, 1990. Active Rep. Cen. Com., Denver, 1992. Mem. Am. Inst. Mining Engrs., Colo. Mining Assn., Denver Mining Club, N.Mex. Geologic Soc., Soc. Econ. Geologists. Roman Catholic. Office: Kohls Exploration Ltd 12567 W Cedar Dr Ste 105 Denver CO 80228

THOMSEN, NANCY LEE, advertising consultant; b. Memphis, May 8; d. Julius A. and Selma L. T. AA, Wright Coll., 1957. Advt. mgr. Wham-O Toys, San Gabriel, Calif., 1970; media dir. Carl Falkenhainer Advt., L.A., 1971-72; account mgr. Metromedia/Metro TV Sales, L.A., 1972; media dir. Jack Wodell Assocs., L.A., 1972-76; v.p., ptnr. Charles Martin & Assocs., L.A., 1976-79; media dir. Filmways Pictures, Beverly Hills, Calif., 1979-82, Media Buying Svcs./West, Santa Monica, Calif., 1983-85; v.p. L'Ermitage Hotels, L.A., 1985-91; owner Thomsen & Assocs., L.A., 1991-93; assoc. dir. of co-op advertising Orion Pictures, L.A., 1993—. Editor arts and entertainment The Jewish News, 1985—. Writer, producer Gore Vidal for U.S. Senate, Calif., 1982. Mem. NAFE, Am. Bus. Womens Assn., Am. Bd. Hypnotherapy. Office: 1888 Century Park E 7th Fl Los Angeles CA 90067

THOMSON, CHARLES LEROY, district water conservation administrator; b. Leadville, Colo., Apr. 4, 1924; s. Laurence William and Viola Joyce (Foster) T.; m. Helen J. Nowocin, Sept. 12, 1945; children: Kathrine Ann, Karen Lee, Laurence William. Student, Colo. State U.; postgrad., U. Colo. Mgr. Salida C. of C., 1952-57; gen. mgr. Pueblo (Colo.) C. of C., 1957-66, Southeastern Colo. Water Conservancy Dist., 1966—; former tchr. adult edn. Pueblo Jr. Coll., So. Colo. State Coll.; lectr. in field. With USMC, PTO, Korea. Mem. Am. Legion, Masons (grand master of masons Colo. 1964, master Salida lodge 1954, high priest Royal Arch chpt. Salida), Knights Templar, Elks, Rotary. Republican. Methodist. Home: 1754 Mackenzie Rd Pueblo CO 81001-1735 Office: SE Colo Water Conservancy Dist 905 W Us Hwy 50 Pueblo CO 81008-1606

THOMSON, GRACE MARIE, nurse, minister; b. Pecos, Tex., Mar. 30, 1932; d. William McKinley and Elzora (Wilson) Olliff; m. Radford Chaplin, Nov. 3, 1952; children: Deborah C., William Earnest. Assoc. Applied Sci., Odessa Coll., 1965; extension student U. Pa. Sch. Nursing, U. Calif., Irvine, Golden West Coll. RN, Calif., Okla., Ariz., Md., Tex. Dir. nursing Grays Nursing Home, Odessa, Tex., 1965; supr. nursing Med. Hill, Oakland, Calif.; charge nurse pediatrics Med. Ctr., Odessa; dir. nursing Elmwood Extended Care, Berkeley, Calif.; surg. nurse Childrens Hosp., Berkeley; med./surg. charge nurse Merritt Hosp., Oakland, Calif.; adminstr. Grace and Assocs.; advocate for emotionally abused children; active Watchtower and Bible Tract Soc.; evangelist for Jehovah's Witnesses, 1954—.

THOMSON, JAMES ALAN, research company executive; b. Boston, Jan. 21, 1945; s. James Alan and Mary Elizabeth (Pluff) T.; m. Darlene Thomson; children: Kristen Ann, David Alan. BS, U. N.H., 1967; MS, Purdue U., 1970, PhD, 1972. Research fellow U. Wis., Madison, 1972-74; systems analyst Office Sec. Def., U.S. Dept. Def., Washington, 1974-77; staff mem. Nat. Security Council, White House, Washington, 1977-81; v.p. RAND, Santa Monica, Calif., 1981-89, pres., chief exec. officer, 1989—. Contbr. articles to profl. jours. and chpts. to books. Mem. Internat. Inst. for Strategic Studies (council 1985—), Coun. Fgn. Rels. Office: Rand PO Box 2138 1700 Main St Santa Monica CA 90407-2138

THOMSON, JOHN ANSEL ARMSTRONG, biochemist; b. Detroit, Nov. 23, 1911; s. John Russell and Florence (Antisdel) T.; m. June Anna Mae Hummel, June 24, 1938; children: Sheryll Linn, Patrisha Diane, Robert Royce. AA, Pasadena (Calif.) City Coll., 1935; AB cum laude, U. So. Calif., 1957; BGS (hon.), Calif. Poly. State U., 1961; MA, PhD, Columbia Pacific U., 1978, 79; DA, Internat. Inst. Advanced Studies, Clayton, Mo., 1979. Cert. secondary tchr., Calif. Chemist J.A. Thomson Bio-Organic Chemist, L.A., 1938, Vitamin Inst. (formerly J.A. Thomson Bio-Organic Chemist), L.A. and North Hollywood, Calif., 1939—; vocat. edn. instr. U.S. War Manpower Commn., 1943-44; chmn. activities coun. World Coun. of Youth, L.A., 1932; pres. Coun. of Young Men's Divs. Athletic Commns., YMCA Pasadena area, 1931, chmn. exec. coun., 1932; dist. officer Boy Scouts Am., San Fernando Valley coun., 1954-64, del. to nat. conf., 1959, and others. Author: (booklets) Whose Are the Myths?, 1949, Open Eyes, Illegaliza Agency Abuses, 1968, Non-toxic Vitamins-hormones Answers to Environmental, Public Problems, 1972, Lobby Interest Goals to Sequester Nutrients Among Those Rarely Educated in Them, 1973, Support of Pressures to Homeostasis, Normality, 1990, Minimization of Toxics in Agriculture, 1991; contbr. articles to jours. Prog. leader United Meth. Men Quadrennial Conf., Lafayette, Ind., 1982, instr. United Methodist Ch. nat. seminar for profls., Nashville, Tenn., 1983, pres. United Meth. Men, 1979-80, mem. adminstv. bd., 1952—, chmn. commn. ch. and soc., 1986—, First United Meth. Ch., North Hollywood; mem. Rep. county ctrl. Com. L.A. County, 1941-50, chmn. 63d assembly dist., 1948-50, Rep. state ctrl. com., Calif. 1948-50. Recipient Sci. and Industry award San Francisco Internat. Expn., 1940, various scouting leadership awards Boy Scouts Am., Civic Svc. award State of Calif., 1949, others. Mem. AAAS (life), Am. Inst. Biol. Scis., Soc. Nutrition Edn., N.Y. Acad. Scis., Am. Horticultural Soc., Am. Chem. Soc. (So. Calif. sect.), Internat. Acad. Nutrition and Preventive Medicine, Western Gerontol. Assn., Am. Forestry Assn., Am. Assn. Nurserymen, Soc. Am. Florists and Ornamental Horticulturists, Internat. Soc. Hort. Sci., Nat. Coun. Improved Health, Nat. Recreation and Parks Assn., Nat. Landscape Assn., Nat. Nutritional Foods Assn. (Pioneer Svc. award 1970), Nat. Health Fedn., Sierra Club, Soc. Colonial Wars (life), Kiwanis (projects panelist internat. confs. 1987, 91), numerous others. Republican. Office: Vitamin Inst PO Box 230 5411 Satsuma Ave North Hollywood CA 91603-0230

THOMSON, JOHN RANKIN, city manager; b. Oakland, Calif., Nov. 1, 1935; s. John Stalker and Mary Josephine (Estes) T.; m. Loretta Earlene Edwards, Aug. 13, 1960 (div. June 1982); children: John Christopher, Deborah Ann. AB, San Diego State U., 1960, MPA, 1973. Budget analyst City of San Diego, 1960-62, adminstrv. analyst, 1962-64, asst. sanitation supt., 1964-67, asst. utilities supt., 1967-68; asst. city mgr. City of Chula Vista, Calif., 1968-70; city mgr. City of Chula Vista, 1970-75, City of Lawton, Okla., 1975-76, City of Medford, Oreg., 1976-87, City of Covina, Calif., 1987—; bd. dirs. Covina Irrigating Co., 1990-92; Covina city clk., 1990-92. Author: manual Municipal Budgeting for Smaller Cities, 1973. With USMC, 1954-56. Recipient ASPA Community Svc. award, 1976. Mem. Internat. City Mgmt. Assn., Rotary, MENSA. Democrat. Roman Catholic. Home: 561 W Puente Ave # 2 Covina CA 91722-3779 Office: City of Covina 125 E College St Covina CA 91723-2197

THOMSON, ROBERT GEORGE, lawyer; b. Weehawken, N.J., Aug. 10, 1949; s. Robert and Teresa Margaret (Turley) T.; m. Teresa Joycelyn Huestis, June 22, 1980. BA in Polit. Sci., Calif. State U., Northridge, 1972; JD, U. San Diego, 1976. Dep. dist. atty. Imperial County, El Centro, Calif., 1977, San Diego County, 1977-80, Lane County, Eugene, Oreg., 1980-81; dep. dist. atty. Josephine County, Grants Pass, Oreg., 1981-87, chief dep. dist. atty., 1987-90; asst. U.S. atty. U.S. Atty. Office, Dist. Oreg., Portland, 1990—; part-time instr. Rogue Community Coll., Grants Pass, 1985-89; lectr. Oreg. Dist. Attys. Assn., Portland, 1989. Recipient scholarship State of Calif., 1968. Mem. Oreg. Bar Assn., Calif. Bar Assn., Aberdeen and N.E. Scotland Family History Soc., Nat. Audobon Soc. Republican. Roman Catholic. Office: US Atty Dist Oreg 888 SW Fifth Ave # 1000 Portland OR 97204

THOMSON, THYRA GODFREY, former state official; b. Florence, Colo., July 30, 1916; d. John and Rosalie (Altman) Godfrey; m. Keith Thomson, Aug. 6, 1939 (dec. Dec. 1960); children—William John, Bruce Godfrey, Keith Coffey. B.A. cum laude, U. Wyo., 1939. With dept. agronomy and agrl. econs. U. Wyo., 1938-39; writer weekly column Watching Washington pub. in 14 papers, Wyo., 1955-60; planning chmn. Nat. Fedn. Republican Women, Washington, 1961; sec. state Wyo. Cheyenne, 1962-86; mem. Marshall Scholarships Com. for Pacific region, 1964-68; del. 72d Wilton Park Conf., Eng., 1965; mem. youth commn. UNESCO, 1970-71, Allied Health Professions Council HEW, 1971-72; del. U.S.-Republic of China Trade Conf., Taipei, Taiwan, 1983; mem. lt. gov.'s trade and fact-finding mission to Saudi Arabia, Jordan, and Egypt, 1985. Bd. dirs. Buffalo Bill Mus., Cody, Wyo., 1987—; adv. bd. Coll. Arts and Scis., U. Wyo., 1989, Cheyenne Symphony Orch. Found., 1990—. Recipient Disting. Alumni award U. Wyo., 1969, Disting. U. Wyo. Arts and Scis. Alumna award, 1987; named Internat. Woman of Distinction, Alpha Delta Kappa; recipient citation Omicron Delta Epsilon, 1965, citation Beta Gamma Sigma, 1968, citation Delta Kappa Gamma, 1973, citation Wyo. Commn. Women, 1986. Mem. N.Am. Securities Adminstrs. (pres. 1973-74), Nat. Assn. Secs. of State, Council State Govts. (chmn. natural resources com. Western states 1966-68), Nat. Conf. Lt. Govs. (exec. com. 1976-79). Home: 3102 Sunrise Rd Cheyenne WY 82001-6136

THONG, TRAN, scientist, engineer, researcher; b. Saigon, Vietnam, Dec. 8, 1951; came to U.S., 1969, naturalized, 1980; s. Vy and Vinh-Thi (Nguyen) T.; m. Thuy Thi-Bich Nguyen, Jan. 12, 1978. BSEE, Ill. Inst. Tech., 1972; MS in Engring., Princeton U., 1974, MA, 1974, PhD, 1975. Research scientist Western Geophys. Houston, 1975-76; computer devel. engr. Gen. Electric Co., Syracuse, N.Y., 1976-79; dir. electronic system lab. Tektronix, Inc., Beaverton, Oreg., 1980-90, v.p. engring., and digital signal processing gen. mgr., Tektronix Fed. Systems Inc., Beaverton, Oreg., 1990—; adj. asst. prof. Syracuse U., 1979-81, Oreg. State U., Corvallis, 1980-83, U. Portland, Oreg., 1981-83; adj. assoc. prof. Oreg. Grad. Ctr., Beaverton, 1984. Author numerous sci. papers and U.S. patents. Princeton U. fellow, 1974. Fellow IEEE (com. chmn. 1982-88), assoc. editor transaction 1979-81, gen. chmn. internat. symposium on circuits and systems, exec. v.p., 1989; mem. Soc. Motion Picture and TV Engrs., Eta Kappa Nu, Tau Beta Pi, Sigma Xi. Republican. Office: Tektronix Inc PO Box 4495 MS 38-386 Beaverton OR 97076

THOR, LINDA M., college president; b. Los Angeles, Feb. 21, 1950; d. Karl Gustav and Mildred Dorrine (Hofius) T.; m. Robert Paul Huntsinger, Nov. 22, 1974; children: Erik, Marie. BA, Pepperdine U., 1971, EdD, 1986; MPA, Calif. State U., Los Angeles, 1980. Dir. pub. info. Pepperdine U., Los Angeles, 1971-73; pub. info. officer Los Angeles Community Coll. Dist., 1974-75, dir. communications, 1975-81, dir. edn. services, 1981-82, dir. high tech., 1982-83, sr. dir. occupational and tech. edn., 1983-86; pres. West Los Angeles Coll., Culver City, Calif., 1986-90, Rio Salado Community Coll., Phoenix, 1990—; bd. dirs. Coun. for Adult and Experiential Learning, Nat. Inst. Leadership Devel. Adv. Com., AAWCJC Leaders Found., Tech. Exch. Ctr., CASE Commn. on Two-Yr. Instns. Editor: Curriculum Design and Development for Effective Learning, 1973; author: (with others) Effective Media Relations, 1982, Performance Contracting, 1987. Active AACJC Commn. Urban Community Coll., Continuous Quality Improvement Network for Community Colls; mem. Ariz. Gov.'s Adv. Coun. on Quality. Recipient Delores award Pepperdine U., 1986, Alumni Medal of Honor, 1987, Outstanding Achievement award Women's Bus. Network, 1989; named Woman of the Yr., Culver City Bus. and Profl. Women, 1988. Office: Rio Salado C C Phoenix AZ 85003

THORDARSON, WILLIAM, hydrogeologist; b. N.Y.C., Mar. 14, 1929; s. William and Lillian (Hirsch) T. BA, Columbia U., 1950; postgrad., U. Kans., Lawrence, 1953-55; MA, U. Colo., 1987. Hydrogeologist U.S. Geol. Survey, Denver, 1955—. Author: Perched Groundwater, Nevada, 1965, Hydrogeology of Test Wells, 1975, Hydrogeology of South-Central Great Basin, 1983, Hydrogeologic Monitoring, Nevada, 1985, Hydrogeology of Anhydrite, 1989. Served with U.S. Army, 1950-52. Mem. AAAS, Geol. Soc. Am., Am. Assn. Petroleum Geologists, Am. Geophys. Union, Assn. Groundwater Scientists and Engrs., Am. Water Resources Assn., Am. Inst. Profl. Geologists (cert.), Am. Inst. Hydrology (cert.), Assn. Engring. Geologists, Geol. Soc. Wash., Precision Measurements Assn., Internat. Assn. Mat. Geologists, Rocky Mountain Assn. Geologists, Soc. Econ. Paleontologists and Minerologists, Am. Geol. Inst., Nat. Geographic Soc., Am. Mus. Nat. History, Denver Mus. Nat. History, others.

THOREN-PEDEN, DEBORAH SUZANNE, lawyer; b. Rockford, Ill., Mar. 28, 1958; d. Robert Roy and Marguerite Natalie (Geoghegan) Thoren; m. Steven E. Peden, Aug. 10, 1985. BA in Philosophy, Polit. Sci./Psychology, U. Mich., 1978; JD, U. So. Calif., 1982. Bar: Calif. 1982. Assoc. Bushkin, Gaines & Gaims, L.A., 1982-84, Rutan & Tucker, Costa Mesa, Calif., 1984-86; sr. counsel First Interstate Bank Calif., L.A., 1986—; lectr. on Bank Secrecy Act; chair CBA Regulatory Compliance Com. Supervising editor U. So. Calif. Entertainment Law Jour., 1982-83, Entertainment Publishing and the Arts Handbook, 1983-84. Mem. ABA, State Bar Calif. Office: First Interstate Bank Calif 707 Wilshire Blvd 20th Fl Los Angeles CA 90017

THORNBURY, WILLIAM MITCHELL, lawyer, educator; b. Kansas City, Mo., Feb. 11, 1944; s. Paul Cobb and Marguerite Madellaine (Schulz) T.; m. Joy Frances Barrett, Feb. 2, 1973; children: Barrett Mitchell, Adele Frances. BA, UCLA, 1964; JD, U. So. Calif., 1967, postgrad. 1967-69. Bar: Calif. 1968, U.S. Dist. Ct. (cen. dist.) Calif. 1968, U.S. Dist. Ct. (no. dist.) Calif. 1973, U.S. Dist. Ct. (so. dist.) Calif. 1980, U.S. Dist. Ct. (ea. dist.) Calif. 1980, U.S. Ct. Appeals (9th cir.) 1973, U.S. Ct. Claims 1980, U.S. Ct. Internat. Trade, 1981, U.S. Ct. Customs and Patent Appeals 1980, U.S. Ct. Mil. Appeals 1980, U.S. Supreme Ct. 1973, U.S. Ct. Appeals (Fed. cir.) 1984. Dep. L.A. County Pub. Defender, 1969—, dep.-in-charge traffic ct., 1982-84, supervising atty. Juvenile Svcs. div., 1984, dep. in charge, Inglewood, Calif., 1984-85; legal asst. prof. Calif. State U., L.A., 1983—; mem. adv. com. on alcohol determination State Dept. Health, 1984—; appointed to apprenticeship council by Gov. Deukmejian State of Calif., 1986—, chmn. equal opportunity com. 1987-90, chmn. forums com., 1991-92; chmn., vice chmn. Santa Monica Fair Election Practices Commn., Calif., 1981-85; advisor on drunk driving Calif. Pub. Defenders Assn., 1984—; alt. mem. L.A. County Commn. on Drunk Driving, 1983-84; mem. steering com. Santa Monica Coalition, nominations com., 1984; bd. dirs. Westside Legal Svcs., 1984-86, v.p., 1986-87, pres., 1987-88. Columnist Calif. Defender; editor Drunk Driving Manual, 1984; contbr. article to Forum. Exec. bd. dirs. Santa Monica Young Rep., 1967-72, pres. 1972-73, treas. 1973-75, bd. dirs. 1968-72; del., precinct chmn., registration chmn. L. A. County Young Rep., 1968-70; chmn. legal com. L.A. County Rep. Cen. Com., 1977-81, 83-85; chmn. jud. evaluation com., 1978-80; pres. Santa Monica Rep. Club 1986-88, bd. dirs., 1966-90; bd. dirs. West L.A. Rep. Club, 1986—; mem. Beverly Hills Rep. Club, Rep. State Cen. com., 1983-85, 89-91, assoc. mem., 1980-83, 86-89, platform com. 1990 State Rep. Party, Non-Partisan Candidate Evaluating Coun., Inc. (bd. dirs. 1980-86, v.p. 1986-89, pres. 1989—); mem. Pasadena Rep. Club, 1984—; bd. dirs. Santa Monicans Against Crime, 1979—; chmn. 44th Assembly Dist. Rep. Cen. Com. 1974-87; chmn. Western part of L.A. County for George Murphy for U.S. Senate, 1970, John T. LaFollette for Congress, 1970; campaign chmn. Donna A. Little for City Council, 1984; adv. Pat Geffner for City Council, 1979, 81; campaign mgr. Experienced Coll. Team, 1983; mem. adv. com. Fred Beteta for Assembly, 1989-90; mem. platform com. Rep. State Party, 1990. Recipient Outstanding Chmn. award Los Angeles County Rep. Party, 1974, sec.-treas. 1968-75, chmn. legal com. 1977-82, 83-85; named Outstanding Service to Rep. Party Legal Counsel, 1978; recipient award Am. Assn. UN, 1961. Mem. ABA, L.A. County Bar Assn. (vice chmn. indigent and criminal def. com., jud. evaluation com. 1986-88, 2d vice chmn. 1989-90, 1st vice chmn., 1990-91, chair, 1991-92, criminal justice com. 1986—, criminal law and law enforcement com., 1986—), Santa Monica Bar Assn. (trustee 1976-77, 79-87, chmn. legis. and publicity com., chmn. jud. evaluation com. 1982-84, pres.-elect 1984-85, pres. 1985-86, del. to state bar conv. 1974-88, liaison to L.A. County Bar Assn. 1986-87, chmn. legis. com. 1983-84, 88), L.A. County Pub. Defenders Assn. (advisor, bd. dirs. 1980-88), Calif. Pub. Defenders Assn. (advisor), Santa Monica Hist. Soc., San Fernando Valley Criminal Bar Assn. (membership chmn. 1986-88, bd. trustees 1986—, treas. 1987-88, v.p. 1988, pres.-elect 1988, pres. 1989-90, chmn. judicial evaluations com. 1988), Assn. Trial Lawyers Am., Supreme Ct. Hist. Soc., Nat. Legal Aid and Defenders Assn., Nat. Assn. Criminal Def. Attys., Acad. Criminal Justice Scis., U. So. Calif. Law Alumni Assn., UCLA Alumni Assn., N.Y. Acad. Scis., Am. Assn. Polit. Sci., Criminal Law sect. of State Bar of Calif., Am. Soc. Criminology (life), Criminal Cts. Bar Assn., Western Region Criminal Law Educatorsca C. of C. (inebriate task force 1980), Calif. Hist. Soc., Santa Monica Coll. Patron's Assn., Nat. Assn. Criminal Def. Counsel, Navy League (life, bd. dirs. 1979—, legis. chmn. 1982, judge adv. 1983-89, 2d vice pres. 1989-90, 1st v.p. 1991-92, pres. navy league coun. 1992—), Nat. Rifle Assn. (life), Calif. Rifle and Pistol Assn. (life).

THORNDAL, JOHN LAFLEUR, lawyer; b. Ironwood, Mich., June 13, 1936; s. Herbert Ladegard and Lucille (LaFleur) T.; m. Loretta Ann Vendramin, June 8, 1968; children: Daniel Leyton, Debra Louise, Jason Andrew. BS, U. N.D., 1958; JD, U. Denver, 1965. Bar: Colo. 1965, U.S. Dist. Ct. Colo. 1966, Nev. 1967, U.S. Dist. Ct. Nev. 1967, U.S. Supreme Ct. 1971, U.S. Ct. Appeals (9th cir.) 1972. Law clerk Law Office Morton Galane, Las Vegas, 1965-67; asst. legal counsel Reynolds Elec. and Engring. Co., Inc., Las Vegas, 1967-69; asst. U.S. atty. U.S. Dept. Justice, Las Vegas, 1969-70; asst. pub. defender Clark County Pub. Defender, Las Vegas, 1970; ptnr. Austin & Thorndal, Las Vegas, 1970-72, Austin, Thorndal & Liles, Ltd., Las Vegas, 1972-75, Thorndal & Liles, Las Vegas, 1975-78, Thorndal, Backus, Maupin & Armstrong, Las Vegas, 1978—; spl. asst. U.S. atty. U.S. Dept. Justice, Las Vegas, 1978-79, contract atty., 1981-83; lawyer del. 9th Cir. Judicial Conf., Las Vegas, 1984-87, chmn., lawyer del., 1986-87; treas. Clark County Bar Assn., Las Vegas, 1972-74, v.p., 1974-75, pres., 1976. Note editor: Denver Law jour., 1964-65. Bd. trustees Cath. Community Svc. Nev., 1980-92, pres., 1985-87 (Community Individual Svc. award 1991). Lt. Col. USAF Res., 1958-62. Mem. Am. Bd. Trial Advocates (assoc.), Nev. Am. Inns of Ct. (master). Roman Catholic. Office: Thorndal Backus Maupin Armstrong 1100 E Bridger Ave Las Vegas NV 89101

THORNE, KIP STEPHEN, physicist, educator; b. Logan, Utah, June 1, 1940; s. David Wynne and Alison (Comish) T.; m. Linda Jeanne Peterson, Sept. 12, 1960 (div. 1977); children: Kares Anne, Bret Carter; m. Carolee Joyce Winstein, July 7, 1984. B.S. in Physics, Calif. Inst. Tech., 1962; A.M. in Physics (Woodrow Wilson fellow, Danforth Found. fellow), Princeton U., 1963, Ph.D. in Physics (Danforth Found. fellow, NSF fellow), 1965, postgrad. (NSF postdoctoral fellow), 1965-66; D.Sc. (hon.), Ill. Coll., 1979; Dr.h.c., Moscow U., 1981. Research fellow Calif. Inst. Tech., 1966-67, assoc. prof. theoretical physics, 1967-70, prof., 1970—, William R. Kenan, Jr. prof., 1981-91, Feynman prof. theoretical physics, 1991—; Fulbright lectr., France, 1966; vis. assoc. prof. U. Chgo., 1968; vis. prof. Moscow U., 1969, 75, 78, 82, 83, 86, 88, 90; vis. sr. rsch. assoc. Cornell U., 1977, A.D. White prof.-at-large, 1968-92; adj. prof. U. Utah, 1971-92; mem. Internat. Com. on Gen. Relativity and Gravitation, 1971-80, Com. on U.S.-USSR Coop. in Physics, 1978-79, Space Sci. Bd., NASA, 1980-83. Co-author: Gravitation Theory and Gravitational Collapse, 1965, Gravitation, 1973, Black Holes: The Membrane Paradigm, 1986. Alfred P. Sloan Found. Research fellow, 1966-68; John Simon Guggenheim fellow, 1967; recipient Sci. Writing award in physics and astronomy Am. Inst. Physics-U.S. Steel Found., 1969. Mem. Nat. Acad. Scis., Am. Acad. Arts and Scis., Am. Astron. Soc., Am. Phys. Soc., Internat. Astron. Union, AAAS, Sigma Xi, Tau Beta Pi. Office: Calif Inst Tech 130-33 Pasadena CA 91125

THORNGATE, JOHN HILL, physicist; b. Eau Claire, Wis., Dec. 23, 1935; s. John Harold and Dorothy Geraldine (Maxon) T.; m. Carole Joan Rye, Aug. 5, 1956; children: FayAnne, John, Sharon. BA, Ripon Coll., 1957; MS, Vanderbilt U., 1961, PhD, 1976. Insp. U.S. Atomic Energy Commn., Oak Ridge, Tenn., 1959; physicist Oak Ridge Nat. Lab., 1960-78, Lawrence Livermore (Calif.) Nat. Lab., 1978--. Inventor determining Radon in air, stable pulsed light source, fast neutron solid state dosimeter, method of improving BEO as a thermoluminescent dosimeter. Mem. Am. Phys. Soc., Health Physics Soc., IEEE, Sigma Xi. Office: Lawrence Livermore Nat Lab L-383 PO Box 5505 Livermore CA 94550

THORNSJO, DOUGLAS FREDRIC, insurance company executive, lawyer, consultant; b. Mpls., July 10, 1927; s. Adolph Fredric and Agnes Emily (Grynikewski) T.; m. Barbara Jean Bachmann, Aug. 10, 1950 (div. June 1990); children: Claudia, Douglas Fredric Jr.; m. My Turner, August 18, 1990. BS in Law, U. Minn., 1948, JD, 1951. Bar: Minn. 1950, N.Y. 1951, Maine 1966, Calif. 1990, U.S. Dist. Ct. Maine 1966, U.S. Dist. Ct. Minn. 1955, U.S. Dist Ct. (so. dist.), N.Y. 1954, U.S. Ct. Appeals (2d and 8th cirs.) 1954 and 1956, U.S. Supreme Ct. 1955. Assoc. Dewey, Ballentine, et al, N.Y.C., 1951-52, 54-55; spl. counsel Investors Diversified Svcs., Mpls., 1955-61; chief exec. officer Thornsjo, Smith & Johnson, Mpls., 1961-66, Midwest Tech. Devel. Corp. and Investment Policies Inc., Mpls., 1961-66; sr. v.p., counsel Union Mut. Life Ins. Co., Portland, Maine, 1966-76, Bradford Nat. Corp., N.Y.C., 1976-83; 1st sr. v.p. Dime Savs. Bank N.Y., N.Y.C., 1984-88; vice chmn., chief operating officer Gen. Svcs. Life Ins. Co., Petaluma, Calif., 1987-93; also bd. dirs. Gen. Svcs. Life Ins. Co., Novato, Calif. Author: The Mutual Company-Use of a Downstream Holding Company in Process of Self-Analysis, 1973; contbr. numerous articles to mags. Bd. dirs. Nat. Multiple Sclerosis Soc., N.Y.C., 1980-90. Officer U.S. Mcht. Marines, 1945-46; lt. USNR, 1952-54. Mem. ABA, Am. Corp. Counsel Assn. (pres. N.Y. chpt. 1987-88), Nat. Assn. Bus. Economists, Lotos Club (N.Y.C.). Home: 1085 Bel Marin Keys Blvd Novato CA 94949-5348

THORNTON, DEAN DICKSON, airplane company executive; b. Yakima, Wash., Jan. 5, 1929; s. Dean Stoker and Elva Maud (Dickson) T.; m. Joan Madison, Aug. 25, 1956 (div. Apr. 1978); children—Steven, Jane Thornton; m. Mary Shultz, Nov. 25, 1981; children—Volney, Scott, Peter, Todd Richmond. B.S. in Bus., U. Idaho, 1952. C.P.A., Wash. Acct. Touche, Ross & Co., Seattle, 1954-63; treas., controller Boeing Co., Seattle, 1963-70; various exec. positions Boeing Co., 1974-85; pres. Boeing Comml. Airplane Co., 1985—; sr. v.p. Wyly Co., Dallas, 1970-74; bd. dirs. Seafirst Corp, Prin. Fin. Group. Bd. dirs. YMCA, Seattle, 1966-68, Jr. Achievement, Seattle, 1966-68; chmn. Wash. Council on Internat. Trade, Seattle, 1984-87. Served to 1st lt. USAF, 1952-54. Named to U. Idaho Alumni Hall of Fame. Mem. Phi Gamma Delta. Republican. Presbyterian. Clubs: Rainier, Seattle Tennis, Seattle Yacht, Conquistadores de Cielo. Home: 1602-34 Ct W Seattle WA 98199 Office: Boeing Co 7755 E Marginal Way PO Box 3707 Seattle WA 98124-2207

THORNTON, J. DUKE, lawyer; b. Murray, Ky., July 11, 1944; s. Arthur Lee and Ruth Maxine (Billings) T.; m. Carol Caceres, Dec. 26, 1966 (dec.); children: Jennifer, Carey. BBA, U. N.Mex., Albuquerque, 1966, JD, 1969. Bar: N.Mex. 1969, U.S. Ct. Appeals (10th cir.) 1969, N.Y. 1985. With Butt, Thornton & Baehr, P.C., Albuquerque, 1971—; legal counsel N.Mex. Jaycees, 1972; clk. N.Mex. Supreme Ct., Santa Fe, 1969; mem. com. N.Mex. Uniform Jury Instructions, 1987-88. Author: Trial Handbook for New Mexico Lawyers, 1992. Bd. dirs. N.Mex. Bd. of Dentistry, Santa Fe, 1987-88; commr. N.Mex. Racing Commn., Albuquerque, 1988—. Mem. ABA, Assn. Coll. and Univ. Counsel, Internat. Assn. Ins. Counsel, Am. Bd. Trial Advs., Albuquerque Bar Assn. (bd. dirs. 1978-79), Nat. Collegiate Athletic Assn. (agt.). Office: Butt Thornton & Baehr PC 2500 Louisiana Blvd NE Albuquerque NM 87110-4319

THORNTON, JACK NELSON, publishing company executive; b. Columbia, Mo., Nov. 9, 1932; s. Samuel Calvin and Mary Elizabeth (Nelson) T.; m. Patricia Helmke, Sept. 15, 1973; children: Gray Nelson, Elizabeth Susan. BA, U. Mo., 1985. Also bd. dirs. Wadsworth Inc., Belmont, Calif.; pres. Brooks/Cole Pub. Co., Monterey, Calif., 1966-80; Pres., chief exec. officer Wadsworth Inc., Belmont, Calif., 1985—; bd. dirs. Nelson-Can., Southwestern Pub. Co. Served with USAF, 1954-57. Mem. Am. Math. Assn., Am. Soc. Engring. Edn., Am. Rocket Soc., Nat. Council Tchrs. Math., Greater El Paso Area Council Tchrs. Math., Kappa Alpha Order. Lodge: Knights of the Vine. Office: Wadsworth Inc 10 Davis Dr Belmont CA 94002-3098

THORNTON, JAMES SCOTT, consultant, trainer; b. Detroit, Aug. 23, 1941; s. Thomas George and Iris Irene (Malcolm) T.; m. Diana Louise Barker, Nov. 18, 1961; children: James Scott Jr., Christian Stuart. BA, U. Olso, 1972, Eastern Wash. U., 1976; MS, Eastern Wash. U., 1977. With USAF, 1961, advance through grades to master sgt., 1972; flight comdr. USAF, S.E. Asia, 1964-66; med. adminstr. USAF, Fairchild AFB, Wash., 1966-68, 72-73, Oslo, 1968-72; resigned USAF, 1973; pres. N.W. Tng. Cons., Spokane, Wash., 1973-78; exec. dir. Am. Heart Assn., Spokane, 1978-83; exec. v.p. Am. Heart Assn., San Jose, Calif., 1983-89; v.p. field svcs. Calif. Affiliate Am. Heart Assn., 1987-98; adj. instr. Ea. Wash. U., C. Cheney, 1977-80; cons., speaker Thornton Leadership Group Internat., San Jose, 1983—. Mem. SEITAR, Assn. United Way Agys. (pres. San Jose chpt. 1987-88), Am. Soc. Assn. Execs., No. Calif. Soc. Assn. Execs. (bd. dirs., chmn. South Bay chpt. 1987-89), Internat. Platform Assn., Am. Motorcyclist Assn., Rotary. Office: Thornton Leadership Group PO Box 32730 San Jose CA 95152-2730

THORNTON, JOHN S., IV, bishop. Bishop Diocese of Idaho, Boise, 1990—. Office: Diocese of Idaho Box 936 510 W Washington Boise ID 83701*

THORNTON, LAURIE ANNE, veterinarian; b. Kansas City, Mo., Sept. 20, 1962; d. William Clements and Marianne (MacMain) T.; m. Ernest Daniel Stefely, Oct. 28, 1989. BS, Coll. of William and Mary, 1984; DVM, Colo. State U., 1989. Assoc. veterinarian Hermosa Vet. Clinic, Denver, 1989-91, Deer Creek Animal Hosp., Littleton, Colo., 1991—. Mem. Am. Vet. Med. Assn., Colo. Vet. Med. Assn., Denver Area Vet. Med. Soc., Am. Animal Hosp. Assn. Home: 8010 A Garrison Ct Arvada CO 80005 Office: Deer Creek Animal Hosp 10148 W Chatfield Ave Littleton CO 80127

THORNTON, LEO MAZE, clergyman, educator, political consultant; b. Dayton, Oreg., Apr. 13, 1922; s. Ladrue Leslie and Radda (Antrin) T.; m. Patricia Pearl Remster, June 27, 1943; children: Virginia Wildermuth, Elizabeth Seward. BA, Cascade Coll., Portland, Oreg., 1946; MDiv., U. Oreg., 1952; LLD, Azusa Pacific U., 1969; DD (hon.), Western Evang. Sem., Portland, 1987. Ordained to ministry Evang. United Brethren Ch., 1947. Pastor Evang. Ch., Portland, 1942-48, 50-52, Meth. Ch., Portland, 1948-50; missionary rep. Oriental Ministry Soc., L.A., 1952-54; pastor Evang. Ch., Eugene, Oreg., 1954-58; pres. Western Evang. Sem., Portland, 1958-87; in pub. rels. OMS Internat. (formerly Oriental Missionary Soc.), Portland, 1987-92, Oreg. Republican Party, Portland, 1992—. Mem. Oreg. State Legislature, Salem, 1967-72; mem. exec. com. Columbia Dist. coun. Boy Scouts Am., 1967-72. Mem. Billy Graham Assocs. (vice chair 1991-92), Rotary (mem. exec. com. 1968-92), Saltshakers. Home: 5452 SE Sierra Vista Dr Milwaukie OR 97267

THORNTON, LESLIE EILEEN, educator; b. San Francisco, Feb. 15, 1953; d. Gerald Herman and Ruth (Coffman) Cohl; m. Gregory Alan Thornton, June 20, 1975; children: Sarah Eileen, James Gregory. BA, Seattle Pacific U., 1975. Cert. elem. tchr., Calif. 1st grade tchr. Mill Valley Sch. Dist., Van Nuys, Calif., 1976-77, kindergarten tchr., 1977-78; substitute tchr., tutor Mill Valley Sch. Dist., Marin County, Calif., 1991—. Mem. Calif. Lit. Project. Home: 45 Molino Ave Mill Valley CA 94941

THORNTON, WAYNE ALLEN, naval officer, engineer; b. Manchester, Conn., Dec. 17, 1952; s. Warren George and Dorothy Marie (Brooks) T. BS in Ocean Engring. with honors, U.S. Naval Acad., 1974; MS in Mech. Engring., Stanford U., 1980; MA in Nat. Security Studies, Georgetown U., 1991. Commd. ensign USN, 1974, advanced through grades to comdr., 1989; naval liaison officer to U.S. Senate Office of Legis. Affairs, Washington, 1974; elec. and reactor controls officer, main propulsion asst. USS Barb, San Diego, 1976-78, combat systems officer, 1978-79; rsch. asst. Stanford U., 1980-81; engring. officer USS Gurnard, San Diego, 1981-84; engring. officer submarine group five staff San Diego, 1984-86; engring. officer submarine squadron 11 staff USN, San Diego, 1986; exec. officer USS Pollack, San Diego, 1987-88; br. head undersea manpower, staff ACNO for undersea warfare Washington, 1988-91; commanding officer USS Drum, San Diego, 1991—. Mem. ASME, AIAA, Soc. Naval Architects and Marine Engrs., Stanford Alumni Assn., Georgetown Alumni Assn., Porsche Club of Am., Sigma Xi.

THORP, EDWARD OAKLEY, investment management company executive; b. Chgo., Aug. 14, 1932; s. Oakley Glenn and Josephine (Gebert) T.; B.A. in Physics, UCLA, 1953, M.A., 1955, Ph.D. in Math., 1958; m. Vivian Sinetar, Jan. 28, 1956; children: Raun, Karen, Jeffrey. Instr., UCLA, 1956-59, C.L.E. Moore instr. MIT, Cambridge, Mass., 1959-61; asst. prof. N.Mex. State U., 1961-63, assoc. prof. math., 1963-65, U. Calif., Irvine, 1965-67, prof. math., 1967-82, adj. prof. fin., 1982—; regents lectr. U. Calif., Irvine, 1992-93; vis. prof. UCLA, 1991; chmn. Oakley Sutton Mgmt. Corp., Newport Beach, Calif., 1972-91; mng. gen. ptnr. Princeton/Newport Ptnrs., Newport Beach, 1969-91, OSM Ptnrs., MIDAS Advisors, Newport Beach, 1986-89; gen. ptnr. Edward O. Thorp & Assocs., L.P., Newport Beach, 1989—; portfolio mgr., cons. Glenwood Investment Corp., Chgo., 1992—; prin., cons. Grosvenor Capital Mgmt., Chgo., 1992—. Grantee NSF, 1954-55, 62-64, Air Force Office Sci. Research, 1964-73. Fellow NSF, Inst. Math. Stats.; mem. Phi Beta Kappa, Sigma Xi. Author: Beat The Dealer: A Winning Strategy for the Game of Twenty-One, 1962, rev. edit., 1966, Elementary Probability, 1966, The Mathematics of Gambling 1984; co-author: Beat The Market, 1967; The Gambling Times Guide to Blackjack, 1984; columnist Gambling Times, 1979-84. Avocations: astronomy, distance running. Office: Edward O Thorpe & Assocs LP 620 Newport Ctr Dr # 1075 Newport Beach CA 92660

THORP, RODERICK MAYNE, JR., writer; b. N.Y.C., Sept. 1, 1936; s. Roderick Mayne and Irene Elizabeth (Rehill) T.; m. Noel Margaret Kennel, Apr. 22, 1957 (div. 1981); children: Roderick M. III, Stephen Philip; m. Claudia Lucille Yancey, Mar. 17, 1988. BA, Ramapo Coll. of N.J., 1957. Assoc. prof. literature Ramado Coll. of N.J., Mahwah, 1971-76; cons. Bank of Am., L.A., 1981. Author: Into the Forest, 1961, The Detective, 1966, Dionysus, 1969, Slaves, 1972, The Cirle of Love, 1974, Westfield, 1977, Die Hard, 1979, Jennie and Barnum, 1981, Rainbow Drive, 1986, Devlin, 1992; author: (nonfiction) The Music of Their Laughter, 1970, Wives, 1971. Recipient Theodore Goodman Meml. Short Story award CCNY, 1957. Mem. Authors League of Am., Authors Guild of Am., Mystery Writers of Am., Am. Crime Writers League, Nat. Writers Union, Writers Guild of Am. Home: 494 Royalview St Duarte CA 91010

THORPE, CALVIN E., lawyer, legal educator, legal journalist; b. Springville, Utah, May 22, 1938; s. Ronald Eaton and Lillian (Thorn) T.; m. Patricia Warren, Feb. 2, 1961; children—Amber, Jill, Marc, Linda, Michael. B.S. in Physics, Brigham Young U., 1962; M.S. in Engring., U. Pa., 1963; J.D., Seton Hall U., 1969. Bar: N.J. 1969, Tex. 1971, Utah, 1974, U.S. Dist. Ct. Utah 1974, U.S. Ct. Customs and Patent Appeals 1975, U.S. Ct. Appeals (10th cir.) 1980. Assoc. Law Offices Giles C. Clegg, Dallas, 1971-73; ptnr. Thorpe, North & Western, Sandy, Utah, 1973—; adj. assoc. prof. U. Utah, Salt Lake City, 1975—; lectr. Brigham Young U., Provo, 1983-88; dir. I.E. Sensors, Inc., Salt Lake City, Quartstronics, Inc., Salt Lake City. Chmn., mem. Sandy City Planning Commn., 1975-84; mem. Sandy City Bd. Adjustment, 1980-81, Utah Citizen's Coun. on Alcoholic Beverage Control; chmn. Sandy Econ. Devel. Council, 1984-88; bd. dirs. Salt Lake City Metro Water Dist. Editor-in-chief, Utah Bar Journal, 1987—. Mem. Am. Planning Assn. (Utah chpt., Citizen Planner award 1985), Utah C. of C. (Total Citizen award 1986), Sandy Area C. of C. (chmn. 1985), Am. intellectual Property Law Assn., Sigma Pi Sigma. Mormon. Office: Thorpe North & Western 9035 S 700 E Sandy UT 84070-2418

THORPE, GARY STEPHEN, chemistry educator; b. Los Angeles, Mar. 9, 1951; s. David Winston and Jeanette M. (Harris) T.; m. Patricia Marion Eison, Apr. 13, 1949; children: Kristin Anne, Erin Michelle. BS, U. Redlands, 1973; MS, Calif. State U., Northridge, 1975. Tchr. L.A. Schs., 1975-80, L.A. Community Colls., 1976-81, Beverly Hills (Calif.) High Sch., 1980—. Author: AP Chemistry Study Guide, 1993. Res. police officer L.A. Police Dept., 1991. Recipient Commendation, L.A. County Bd. Supers., 1983, 84, Commendation Beverly Hills City Council, 1983, 84, Resolution of Commendation, State of Calif. Senate and Assembly, 1983, 84, Cert. Appreciation, L.A. County Bd. Edn., 1984-85, Cert. Appreciation, Gov. George Deukmejian, Sacramento, 1984-85. Mem. Am. Chem. Soc. (Selected as Outstanding Chemistry Tchr. of So. Calif. 1989, 92), NEA, Calif. Tchrs. Assn., Phi Delta Kappa. Republican. Lutheran. Lodge: Masons. Home: 6127 Balcom Ave Reseda CA 91335-7207

THORPE, JAMES, humanities scholar; b. Aiken, S.C., Aug. 17, 1915; s. J. Ernest and Ruby (Holloway) T.; m. Elizabeth McLean Daniells, July 19, 1941; children: James III, John D., Sally Jans-Thorpe. A.B., The Citadel, 1936, LL.D., 1971; M.A., U. N.C., 1937; Ph.D., Harvard U., 1941; Litt.D., Occidental Coll., 1968; L.H.D., Claremont Grad. Sch., 1968; H.H.D., U. Toledo, 1977. Instr. to prof. English Princeton, 1946-66; dir. Huntington Libr., Art Gallery and Bot. Gardens, San Marino, Calif., 1966-83; sr. research assoc. Huntington Libr., San Marino, Calif., 1966—. Author: Bibliography of the Writings of George Lyman Kittredge, 1948, Milton Criticism, 1950, Rochester's Poems on Several Occasions, 1950, Poems of Sir George Etherege, 1963, Aims and Methods of Scholarship, 1963, 70, Literary Scholarship, 1964, Relations of Literary Study, 1967, Bunyan's Grace Abounding and Pilgrim's Progress, 1969, Principles of Textual Criticism, 1972, 2d edit., 1979, Use of Manuscripts in Literary Research, 1974, 2d edit., 1979, Gifts of Genius, 1980, A Word to the Wise, 1982, John Milton: The Inner Life, 1983, The Sense of Style: Reading English Prose, 1987, Henry Edwards Huntington: A Biography, 1993. Served to col. USAAF, 1941-46. Decorated Bronze Star medal.; Guggenheim fellow, 1949-50, 65-66. Fellow Am. Acad. Arts and Scis., Am. Philos. Soc.; mem. MLA, Am. Antiquarian Soc., Soc. for Textual Scholarship (pres.). Democrat. Episcopalian. Clubs: Zamorano, Twilight. Home: 1199 Arden Rd Pasadena CA 91106-4143 Office: Huntington Libr San Marino CA 91108

THORPE, JAMES ALFRED, utilities executive; b. Fall River, Mass., Apr. 19, 1929; s. James and Charlotte Ann (Brearley) T.; m. Maxine Elva Thompson, Mar. 4, 1950; children: James Alfred, Peter R., David T., Carol L., Mark W. B.S., Northeastern U., 1951. Asst. supt. prodn. Fall River Gas Co., 1951-55; chief engr. Lake Shore Gas Co., Ashtabula, Ohio, 1955-57; cons. Stone & Webster Mgmt. Corp., 1958-67; pres. Wash. Natural Gas Co., Seattle, 1972; chmn., chief exec. officer Wash. Natural Gas Co., 1980—; dir. Sea First Corp., Unigard Ins. Group. Bd. dirs. Salvation Army; trustee U. Puget Sound. Mem. Am. Gas Assn., Pacific Coast Gas Assn. (pres. 1977-78). Methodist. Clubs: Rainier (Seattle), Wash. Athletic (Seattle), Rotary (Seattle). Home: 11160 SE 59th St Bellevue WA 98006-2606 Office: Wash Energy Co PO Box 1869 815 Mercer St Seattle WA 98111

THORPE, JUDITH KATHLEEN, cultural organization administrator and artist, educator; b. Denver, July 26, 1951; d. Austin Thomas and Veronica Agnes (Dwyer) T.; m. J. Pritchard; children: Sean Austin Pritchard-Thorpe, James Whitney Pritchard-Thorpe. BS, Regis Coll., 1973; MFA, U. Colo., 1983. Gallery dir. Fine Arts Ctr. U. Colo., Boulder, 1980-83; asst. exhbn. coord. Visual Studies Workshop, Rochester, N.Y., 1983-84; exec. dir. waterworks Contemporary Arts Ctr., Salisbury, N.C., 1984-85; dir. exhbns. Ctr. for Contemporary Arts, Santa Fe, 1985-86, exec. dir. Soc. for Photographic Edn., 1986-91; chair dept. art U. Colo., Denver, 1991—; site reviewer Nat. Endowment for the Arts, Washington, 1987-89; grant reviewer Inst. for Mus. Svcs., Washington, 1985-87. Exhibited at Atlanta Gallery of Photography, 1992, Emmanuel Gallery, Denver, 1992, Ark. State U. Art Gallery, 1992. Mem. Coll. Arts Assn., Pi Delta Phi, Alpha Sigma Nu. Office: U Colo Campus Box 177 PO Box 173364 Denver CO 80217

THORSEN, JAMES HUGH, aviation director, airport manager; b. Evanston, Ill., Feb. 5, 1943; s. Chester A. and Mary Jane (Currie) T.; m. Nancy Dain, May 30, 1980. BA, Ripon Coll., 1965. Asst. dean of admissions Ripon (Wis.) Coll., 1965-69; adminstrv. asst. Greater Rockford (Ill.) Airport Authority, 1969-70; airport mgr. Bowman Field, Louisville, 1970-71; asst. dir. St. Louis Met. Airport Authority, 1971-80; dir. aviation, airport mgr. City of Idaho Falls (Idaho), 1980—. Named hon. citizen State of Ill. Legislature, 1976, Ky. Col., Flying Col. Delta Airlines; FAA cert. comml. pilot, flight instr. airplanes and instruments. Mem. Am. Assn. Airport Execs. (accredited airport exec.), Idaho Airport Mgmt. Assn. (pres. 1991—), Internat. NW Aviation Council, Greater Idaho Falls C. of C. (bd. dir. 1986-89), Mensa, Quiet Birdmen Club, Sigma Alpha Epsilon. Home: 1270 1st St Idaho Falls ID 83401-4175 Office: Mcpl Airport Idaho Falls ID 83401

THORSEN, NANCY DAIN, real estate broker; b. Edwardsville, Ill., June 23, 1944; d. Clifford Earl and Suzanne Eleanor (Kribs) Dain; m. David Massie, 1968 (div. 1975); 1 child, Suzanne Dain Massie; m. James Hugh Thorsen, May 30, 1980. BSc in Mktg., So. Ill. U., 1968, MSc in Bus. Edn., 1975; grad. Realtor Inst., Idaho, 1983. Cert. resdl. and investment specialist. Personnel officer J.H. Little & Co. Ltd., London, 1969-72; instr. in bus. edn. Spl. Sch. Dist. St. Louis, 1974-77; mgr. mktg./ops. Isis Foods, Inc., St. Louis, 1978-80; asst. mgr. store Stix, Baer & Fuller, St. Louis, 1980; assoc. broker Century 21 Sayer Realty, Inc., Idaho Falls, Idaho, 1981-88, RE/MAX Homestead Realty, 1989—; speaker RE/MAX Internat. Conv., 1990. Bd. dirs. Idaho Vol., Boise, 1981-84, Idaho Falls Symphony, 1982; pres. Friends of Idaho Falls Library, 1981-83; chmn. Idaho Falls Mayor's Com. for Vol. Coordination, 1981-84. Recipient Idaho Gov.'s award, 1982, cert. appreciation City of Idaho Falls/Mayor Campbell, 1982, 87, Civitan Disting. Pres. award, 1990; named to Two Million Dollar Club, Three Million Dollar Club, 1987, 88, Four Million Dollar Club, 1989, 90, Top Investment Sales Person for Eastern Idaho, 1985, Realtor of Yr. Idaho Falls Bd. Realtors, 1990, Outstanding Realtors Active in Politics, Mem. of Yr. Idaho Assn. Realtors, 1991, Women of Yr. Am. Biog. Inst., 1991. Mem. Idaho Falls Bd. Realtors (chmn. orientation 1982-83, chmn. edn. 1983, chmn. legis. com. 1989, chmn. program com. 1990, 91), Idaho Assn. Realtors (pres. Million Dollar Club 1988—, edn. com. 1990-93), So. Ill. U. Alumni Assn., Idaho Falls C. of C., Newcomers Club, Civitan (pres. Idaho Falls chpt. 1988-89, Civitan of Yr. 1986, 87, outstanding pres. award 1990). Office: RE/MAX Homestead Inc 1301 E 17th St Ste 1 Idaho Falls ID 83404-6273

THORSON, JAMES LLEWELLYN, English language educator; b. Yankton, S.D., Jan. 7, 1934; s. James Albert and Doris Reece (Burgi) T.; m. Barbara Gay Jelgerhuis, Sept. 6, 1957 (div. 1970); m. Connie Capers, June 6, 1970. BS in Edn., Nebr. U., 1956, MA, 1961; PhD, Cornell U., 1966; MA (hon.), Oxford U., Oxford, England, 1976. Instr. English U. Nebr., Lincoln, 1961-62; asst. prof. U. N.Mex., Albuquerque, 1965-70; assoc. prof. U. N.Mex., 1970-84; vis. prof. U. Kiril i Metodij, Skopje, Yugoslavia, 1971-72, U. Wurzburg, Wurzburg, Fed. Republic of Germany, 1983; prof. English U. N.Mex., Albuquerque, 1984—; vis. prof. U. Munster, Munster, Fed. Republic of Germany, 1985-86, 92-93; lectr. USIA, Yugoslavia, Denmark, Czechoslovakia, Fed. Republic of Germany, England, 1971. Editor: Yugoslav Perspectives on American Literature, 1980, Humphry Clinker, 1983, (with Connie Thorson) A Pocket Companion for Oxford, 1988. Lt. USN, 1956-59. Fulbright professorship Skopje, 1971-72, Munster, 1985-86. Mem. Modern Lang. Assn., AAUP (pres. U. N.Mex. chpt. 1968-70), Old Mems. Jesus College Oxford, Am. Soc. for Eighteenth-Century Studies (patron), Wig and Pen Club (London). Democrat. Home: Apt 412 1331 Park Ave SW Albuquerque NM 87102 Office: U New Mexico Dept English Univ Of New Mexico NM 87131

THRAEN-FISHER, ANNETTE CHRISTINE, financial executive; b. Omaha, July 11, 1959; d. LaVerne Nicholas and Iona Maria (Wellendorf) Thraen; m. James Michael Fisher, June 22, 1991. BSBA, U. Nebr., Omaha, 1981; MBA, Calif. State U., Long Beach, 1993. CPA. Auditor Arthur Anderson and Co., Omaha, 1981-83, Farm Credit Banks, Omaha, 1983-84; contr. York (Nebr.) Gen. Hosp., 1984-86; dir. acctg. Pioneer Hosp., Mulliken Med. Ctr., Cerritos, Calif., 1986-87, FHP, Inc., Long Beach, Calif., 1987-91; dir. fin. FHP, Inc., Las Vegas, Nev., 1992-93, assoc. v.p., 1993—. Youth dir. First United Meth. Ch., York, 1984-86; nursery worker Seabreeze Community Ch., Huntington Beach, Calif., 1988-91. Mem. Nebr. CPAs, Calif. CPAs, Healthcare Fin. Mgmt. Assn., Las Vegas C. of C. Office: FHP Inc 2300 W Sahara Ste 700 Las Vegas NV 89102

THREAT, N.E., military officer; b. Forrest City, Ariz., Nov. 18, 1944; s. John Ervan and Nancy Bell (Pieler) T.; m. Tokiko Toma, Apr. 13, 1970; children: Junichi, Nicky Eugene. Commd. sgt. U.S. Army, 1964, advanced through grades to major, 1981; detailed to U.S. Army Info. Systems Command Signal Bn., Ft. Buckner, Okinawa, 1981-86, U.S. Army Info. Systems, White Sands, N.Mex., 1986-87; stationed at 1109th Signal Brigade, Ft. Clayton, Panama, 1987-90, U.S. Army Info. Systems Engring. Command, Ft. Huachuca, Ariz., 1990—. Contbr. articles to mags. and newspaper. Decorated Legion of Merit, 1990. Mem. NRA, Noncommd. Officers Assn., Armed Forces Communications, Signal Corp Regimental Assn., Tucson Rod and Gun Club, Cochise Gun Club. Republican. Baptist. Home: 8218 S Placita Del Barquero Tucson AZ 85747 Office: US Army Info System Engring Command Fort Huachuca AZ 85613

THRELKELD, STEVEN WAYNE, civil engineer; b. La Jolla, Calif., Feb. 22, 1956; s. Willard Wayne and Sylvia Eileen (Daugherety) T.; m. Sheree Leslie Chabot, Nov. 17, 1984; children: Tristan David, Kayla Lee. BS in Geol. Scis., San Diego State U., 1985. Geophys. trainee Western Geophys., Bakersfield, Calif., 1985; civil engr. Dee Jaspar & Assocs., Bakersfield, 1986, Bement, Dainwood & Sturgeon, Lemon Grove, Calif., 1987, Calif. Dept. Transp., San Diego, 1988—; comml. scuba diver, San Diego, 1987-88. Photo editor Montezuma Life Mag., San Diego, 1981; portrait photographer Coast Prodns., San Diego, 1975. Mem. ASCE Transportation Study Group, San Diego sect., Profl. Engrs. in Calif. Govt., Smithsonian Assocs., Soc. Young Am. Profls., Common Cause, Nat. Parks and Conservation Assn. Home: 4262 Bancroft Dr La Mesa CA 91941-6744

THRELKELD-WESAW, SALLIE EASLEY, art educator; b. Blacksburg, Va., Dec. 19, 1934; d. William Logan and Louise (Vaden) Threlkeld; m. Joseph L. Thompson, July 15, 1955 (div. 1969); children: Scott Thompson, Les Thompson, Melanie T. Rozewski; m. George E. Wesaw, July 11, 1972 (div. 1975); 1 chil, Sallie Isabelle Wesaw. BA, Shorter Coll., 1955; MFA, Idaho State U., 1972. Artist Wind River Reservation, Ft. Washakie, Wyo.; prof. art Cen. Wyoming Coll., Riverton, Wyo., 1975—. Exhibited in group works at Casper, Wyo., 1988, Laramie, Wyo., 1989, LCCC, Cheyenne, Wyo., 1989, Nova Eocles Mus., Logan, Utah, 1990, Wind River Valley Art Assn. Exhibit, Dubois, Wyo., 1986, 1990, Pottsdam, N.Y., 1984, American Traveling Basket Show, Brainard Gallery, Alaska State Mus., Juneau, 1975. Demonstrator Sch. Dist. 25, Riverton; children's basket workshop, middle sch., Riverton, 1988; mus. and county fairs spinning demonstrator, Riverton, 1986-87; fiber affair/workshop guest, Douglas, Wyo., 1985-91; swimming instr. ARC, 1985-90; mem. Am. Crafts Coun. Slide Libr., N.Y.C., slide registry Wyo. Coun. on the Arts, Cheyenne. Recipient 1st place pastel Audubon Art Show, Lander, Wyo., 1989, 2d place watercolor Audubon Art Show, Lander, 1987, 2d place pottery Wyo. State Art Assn. Exhibit, Worland, Wyo., 1986, purchase award Cen. Wyo. Coll., 1985. Mem. Wyo. Art Assn., Wind River Valley Artist Guild, Fremont Fiber Artists, Arts in Action, Riverton Art Guild, NCECA, Great Artist Guild Cen. Wyo. Coll. (sponsor). Home: 3060 Cooper Rd Rte 1 Box 23G Riverton WY 82501 Office: Cen Wyo Coll Peck Ave Riverton WY 82501-2222

THROCKMORTON, REX DENTON, lawyer; b. Lima, Ohio, June 4, 1941; s. Francis and Jane (Corwin) T.; m. Barbara Catherine Poore, July 21, 1962; children: Scott, John. BS, Denison U., 1963; JD, Ohio State U., 1965. Bar: Ohio 1966, N. Mex. 1971, U.S. Dist. Ct. N. Mex. 1971, U.S. Ct. Appeals (10th cir.) 1973. Assoc. Squire, Sanders & Dempsey, Cleve., 1965-66; shareholder, bd. dirs. Rodey, Dickason, Sloan, Akin & Robb, P.A., Albuquerque, 1971—, chmn. comml. litigation dept., 1985--. Editor Ohio State Law Jour., 1965. Pres. Albuquerque Civic Light Opera Assn., 1985. Capt. JAGC, USAF, 1966-71. Mem. ABA, N.Mex. Bar Assn. (bd. of bar commrs. 1990—), Albuquerque Bar Assn. (bd. dirs. 1980-83, pres. 1982), N.Mex. Bar Found., Tanoan Country Club. Republican. Home: 9109 Luna De Oro Rd NE Albuquerque NM 87111-1640 Office: Rodey Dickson Sloan Akin & Robb PO Box 1888 Albuquerque NM 87103-1888

THROPAY, JOHN PAUL, radiation oncologist; b. L.A., Aug. 1, 1949; s. Adam Joseph and Marianita (Lopez) T.; m. Maricela Oropeza Rojas, Sept. 2, 1972; children: John Adams, Natalie Sarah, Jacquelyn Grace. BS in Chemistry, UCLA, 1971, MD, 1975. Diplomate Am. Bd. Radiology. Intern L.A. County/U. So. Calif. Med.Ctr., 1975-76, resident in radiation oncology, 1976-79, instr. radiation therapy, 1983, 85; spl. tng. in endocurietherapy Calif. Med. Group, Inc., L.A., 1979-80; practice medicine specializing in radiation oncology Montebello, Calif., 1980—; dir. Queen of Angels Presbyn. Hosp.; chmn. cancer com. Monterey Park Hosp.; mem. staff, trustee Beverly Hosp., Montebello Midway Hosp.; staff Community Hosp., Huntington Park, Greater El Monte Hosp., Temple Hosp., L.A.; staff Hollywood Community Hosp.; chmn. cancer com. Santa Marta Hosp. Mem. AMA,

Calif. Med. Assn., L.A., County Med. Assn., Am. Coll. Radiology, Am. Cancer Soc., Am. Endocurietherapy Soc., Am. Soc. Therapeutic Radiologists and Oncologists, L.A. Radiol. Soc., So. Calif. Radiation Therapy Assn., Assn. Medicos Hispanos Calif. Office: Beverly Oncology & Imagin 120 W Beverly Blvd Montebello CA 90640-4373

THUESON, DAVID OREL, pharmaceutical executive, researcher, educator, writer; b. Twin Falls, Idaho, May 9, 1947; s. Orel Grover and Shirley Jean (Archer) T.; m. Sherrie Linn Lowe, June 14, 1969; children: Sean, Kirsten, Eric, Ryan, Todd. BS, Brigham Young U., 1971; PhD, U. Utah, 1976. Postdoctoral fellow U. Tex. Med. Br., Galveston, 1976-77, asst. prof., 1977-82; sr. rsch. assoc. Parke-Davis Pharms., Ann Arbor, Mich., 1982-88; dir. pharmacology Immunetech Pharms., San Diego, 1988-90; dir. immunopharmacology Tanabe Rsch. Labs., San Diego, 1990-92; v.p. discovery Cosmederm Techs., San Diego, 1992—. Contbr. articles to profl. jours. Scout leader Boy Scouts Am., Mich., Tex. and Calif., 1979—. NIH grantee, 1978-81. Mem. Am. Acad. Allergy and Clin. Immunology, Am. Assn. Immunologists, Am. Thoracic Soc. Republican. Mormon. Home: 12740 Boxwood Ct Poway CA 92064-2643 Office: Cosmederm Techs PO Box 1300 Cardiff By The Sea CA 92007

THUMS, CHARLES WILLIAM, designer, consultant; b. Manitowoc, Wis., Sept. 5, 1945; s. Earl Oscar and Helen Margaret (Rusch) T. B. in Arch., Ariz. State U., 1972. Ptnr., Grafic, Tempe, Ariz., 1967-70; founder, prin. I-Squared Environ. Cons., Tempe, Ariz., 1970-78; designer and cons. design morphology, procedural programming and algorithms, 1978—. Author: (with Jonathan Craig Thums) Tempe's Grand Hotel, 1973, The Rossen House, 1975; (with Daniel Peter Aiello) Shelter and Culture, 1976; contbg. author: Tombstone Planning Guide, 5 vols., 1974. Office: PO Box 3126 Tempe AZ 85280-3126

THUNDER, SPENCER K, elementary school principal; b. Longview, Wash., Dec. 5, 1939; s. Maynard King and Aarah Avona (Hearn) T.; m. Joyce Marie Sjogren, June 22, 1959 (div. June 1972); children: Scott, Mark, Karen; m. Jeanine Louise Pratt. BA, Cen. Wash. U., 1962; MEd, U. Wash., 1975. Cert. elem. educator, prin., reality therapist. Tchr. jr. and sr. high Yakima (Wash.) Sch. Dist., 1962-66; tchr. elem. Olympia (Wash.) Sch. Dist., 1966-67; tchr. high sch. Edmonds (Wash.) Sch. Dist., 1967-71, program mgr., high sch. spl. edn., 1971-76; prin. Maplewood Handicapped Children's Ctr., Edmonds, 1976-87, Mountlake Terrace (Wash.) Elem. Sch., 1987—; adj. prof. Seattle Pacific U., 1991—; instr. Edmonds Community Coll., 1978-79; vis. faculty Cen. Wash. U., Ellensberg, 1976; instr. Olympia Vocat. Tech, 1966-67, Yakima Valley Coll., 1964-66. Author: (pamphlet) Work Evil in Schools, 1975; contbr. articles to profl. jours. Bd. dirs. Smithwright Estates Group Home, Edmonds, Wash., 1980-91. Sgt. Wash. Nat. Guard, 1955-63. Home: 708 Hoyt Ave Everett WA 98201-1320 Office: Mountlake Terrace Elem Sch 22001 52nd Ave W Mountlake Terrace WA 98043-3311

THURMAN, ALLEN GEORGE, engineer; b. Gt. Falls, Mont., Feb. 12, 1933; s. John Louis and Ruth (Gallihur) T.; m. Martha Jane Meinhardt, Feb. 5, 1956; children: Harold Lawrence, Lura Jane, John Allen. BSCE, Wash. State U., 1955; MS, Mont. State U., 1961; PhD, Carnegie Mellon U., 1964. Registered profl. engr., Colo., Mont., Oreg., Wyo., Utah. Various engring. positions Mont., Calif., Oreg., 1955-60; assoc. prof. Engring., dept. chmn. U. Denver, Denver, 1964-71; dir. rsch. and devel. Stanley Structures, Denver, 1971-73; freelance cons. engr. Denver, 1973-74, 83-91; dir. corp. devel. D'Appolonia Cons. Engrs. Inc., Denver, 1974-81; mgr. mining svcs. Kellogg Corp., Denver, 1981-83; pres. Denver Moscow Assocs., Denver, 1991—, also bd. dirs.; bd. dirs. Siberia West Ltd., Denver, Avia West Inc., Denver. Contbg. author (book) Principles and Practice of Explosive Metal Working, 1973; contbg. editor (book) Engineering and Design Manual, Coal Refuse Disposal Facilities, 1973; contbr. articles to profl. jours. Founder Pushkin Goncharov Hist. Found., Denver, 1992. Mem. World Trade Ctr., Soc. for Mining Metallurgy & Exploration (bd. dirs. Rocky Mountain chpt. 1984), Tau Beta Pi. Republican. Home and Office: 5455 S Clarkson St Greenwood Village CO 80121

THURMAN, SAM WESLEY, aerospace engineer; b. Tulsa, Nov. 22, 1961; s. Stephen Phelps and Katherine Noreen (Kribbs) T.; m. Lisa Gail Nolan, Oct. 4, 1987. BS, Purdue U., 1983; MS, MIT, 1985; postgrad., U. So. Calif. Staff engr. Draper Lab., Cambridge, Mass., 1985-87; mem. tech. staff Jet Propulsion Lab., Pasadena, Calif., 1987-91, tech. mgr., 1991—. Contbr. articles to profl. jours. 2d lt. USAR, 1987—. Mem. AIAA (sr.), Am. Astron. Soc., Tau Beta Pi, Sigma Gamma Tau. Episcopalian. Home: 25947 Sandalia Dr Santa Clarita CA 91355 Office: Jet Propulsion Lab 4800 Oak Grove Dr Pasadena CA 91109

THURSTON, RALPH LLOYD, small business owner; b. Des Moines, Apr. 3, 1952; s. Ray Lealand and Leatrice Ione (Babcock) T.; m. Joyce Lynn Weinberg, Aug. 28, 1982; children: Randall Lloyd, Rebecca Lynn. AA, Long Beach City Coll., 1973; BS, Calif. Polytech. U., Pomona, 1976. Cert. tax preparer, notary. Cons. SBA, L.A., 1976; internal auditor Van Ordt Inc., Ontario, Calif., 1976-77; branch acct. Comtronn Corp., Santa Ana, Calif., 1978; office mgr. Barovich Konecky Braun Schwartz & Kay, Beverly Hills, Calif., 1979; controller Sheppard Mullin Richler & Hampton, L.A., 1980-85, Biles & Cook Adminstrs., No. Hollywood, Calif., 1986; bus. mgr. Psychol. Svcs., Inc., Glendale, Calif., 1987-90; tax preparer Robert Hall & Assocs., Glendale, Calif., 1990-91; gen. mgr. Image Transfer Systems, Thousand Oaks, Calif., 1988-91; mgr. retail sales CV Custom T-Shirts, La Crescenta, Calif., 1991—; cons. David Blake Films, W. Hollywood, Calif., 1986-87, Sessions Payroll Mgmt., Burbank, Calif., 1987-88, Dadco Inc., Long Beach, Calif., 1987-88. Pres. Kings Villas Home Owners Assn., W. Hollywood, Calif., 1986-87; treas., bd. deacons Covenant Presbyn. Ch., 1970-72. Mem. Assn. Legal Adminstrs., Am. Mgmt. Assn., Crescenta Valley C. of C. (pres. 1989-90, dir. 1988), Nat. Notary Assn. Republican. Mem. Christian Ch. Home: 6922 Day St Tujunga CA 91042-2045 Office: Thurston & Assoc 3115 Foothill Blvd # M La Crescenta CA 91214-2691

THURSTON, WILLIAM RICHARDSON, oil and gas industry executive, geologist; b. New Haven, Sept. 20, 1920; s. Edward S. and Florence (Holbrooke) T.; m. Ruth A. Nelson, Apr. 30, 1944 (div. 1966); children: Karin R., Amy R., Ruth A.; m. Beatrice Furnas, Sept. 11, 1971; children: Mark P., Stephen P., Douglas P., Jennifer P. AB in Geol. Sci. with honors, Harvard U., 1942. Registered profl. engr., Colo. Field geologist Sun Oil Co., Corpus Christi, Tex., 1946-47; asst. to div. geologist Sun Oil Co., Dallas, 1947-50; chief geologist The Kimbark Co., Denver, 1952-59; head exploration dept. Kimbark Exploration Co., Denver, 1959-66; co-owner Kimbark Exploration Ltd., Denver, 1966-67, Kimbark Assocs., Denver, 1967-76, Hardscrabble Assocs., Denver, 1976-80; pres. Weaselskin Corp., Durango, Colo., 1980—. Bd. dirs. Denver Bot. Gardens, 1972—, Crow Canyon Ctr. for Archaeology, Cortez, Colo., 1980-92. Comdr. USNR, World War II, Korea. Decorated D.F.C. (with 3 stars). Mem. Am. Assn. Petroleum Geologists, Denver Assn. Petroleum Landmen, Rocky Mountain Assn. Petroleum Geologists, Four Corners Geol. Soc. Republican. Office: Weaselskin Corp 12995 US Hwy 550 Durango CO 81301

THYDEN, JAMES ESKEL, diplomat, researcher, educator; b. L.A., Apr. 10, 1939; s. Eskel A. and Mildred Aileene (Rock) T.; m. Patricia Irene Kelsey, Dec. 15, 1959; children: Teresa Lynn, Janice Kay, James Blaine. BA in Biology, Pepperdine U., 1961; MA in Scandinavian Area Studies, U. Wash., 1992. Cert. secondary tchr., Calif., Wash. Tchr. Gompers Jr. High Sch., L.A., 1962-64; fgn. svc. officer U.S. Dept. State, Washington, 1964-90; rschr. U. Wash., Seattle, 1991—. Editor govt. report, ann. human rights report, 1983-86; author in-house govt. reports, documents. Dir. Office Human Rights, 1983-86; counselor Embassy for Polit. Affairs, Am. Embassy, Oslo, Norway, 1986-90. Named Outstanding Young Man Am., 1969, Alumnus of Yr., Pepperdine U., 1984. Mem. Am. Fgn. Svc. Assn., Internat. Inst. for Strategic Studies, Soc. for Advancement of Scandinavian Studies. Home: 5631 153 Place SW Edmonds WA 98026-4239

TIBBETS, ROBIN FRANK, writer; b. Alanreed, Tex., Nov. 7, 1924; s. Marvin Frank and Hazel Kenneth (Porter) T.; m. Dorothy Louise McMahan, Sept. 15, 1952; children: Marlin D., Judith L. BS, McMurry Coll., 1950. Various reporter, photographer positions Daily News and Daily Spokesman, Pampa, Tex., 1946-52; publ. dir. McMurry Coll. and Abilene (Tex.) High Sch., 1953-57; editor Sunday feature Abilene Tex. Reporter-News, 1957; mng. editor Artesia (N.Mex.) Daily Press, 1957-58; city editor Carlsbad (N. Mex.) Current-Argus, 1958-59; mng. editor, asst. to pub. Free Press, Colorado Springs, Colo., 1959-64; city editor Gazette-Telegraph, Colorado Springs, 1964-65, Standard-Examiner, Ogden, Utah, 1968-69; reporter, feature writer, 1970-77, sports columnist, photographer, 1977-87, freelance writer, 1987—. Contbr. various articles to mags. Bd. dirs. Colo. Schs. for Deaf/Blind, Colorado Springs, 1963-67; mem. Colo. Manpower Adv. Com., Colorado Springs, 1963-65, Pikes peak or Bust Rodeo Com., Colorado Springs, 1964, Ogden (Utah) Pioneer Days Exec. Com., 1967-77. Recipient 3d Pl. Typography award N.Mex. Press Assn., 1959, Appreciation award Pikes Peak Scout Coun., 1960, McKay-Dee Found., 1969, Outstanding Citizenship award Am. Heritage Found., 1961, Golden Spike Centennial Appreciation award, 1970, Award of Excellence Ogden City Coun., 1973, 1st Pl. award Utah-Idaho Assoc. Press Assn., 1979, Friends of 4-H award, 1983, Community Svc. award South Ogden City Coun., 1986. Mem. Sigma Delta Chi. Republican. Baptist. Home and Office: 1444 N 250 W Clearfield UT 84015-2850

TIBBITTS, SAMUEL JOHN, hospital administrator; b. Chgo., Oct. 7, 1924; s. Samuel and Marion (Swanson) T.; m. Audrey Slottelid, Aug. 28, 1949; children: Scott, Brett. B.S., UCLA, 1949; M.S., U. Calif.-Berkeley, 1950. Adminstrv. resident Calif. Hosp., Los Angeles, 1950-51; adminstrv. asst. Calif. Hosp., 1951-52, asst. supt., 1954-59, admistr., 1959-66; chmn. mgmt. com., asst. sec. Luth. Hosp. Soc. So. Calif., 1962-66, pres., 1966-88; chmn. Pacificare Health Systems, 1979—; chmn. bd. Health Network Am., 1982—, Am. Healthcare Systems, 1983-88; now chmn. bd. UniHealth America; asst. supt. Santa Monica (Calif.) Hosp., 1952-54; pres. Commn. for Adminstrv. Services in Hosps., 1963, 64, 67, Calif. Health Data Corp., 1968-71; mem. Calif. Health Planning Council and Steering Com., 1968—, Los Angeles City Adv. Med. Council, 1971, 73, Pres.'s Com. Health Services Industry, Adv. Health Council, Calif., 1973; mem. adv. panel Pres.'s Cost of Living Council, Price Commn. and Pay Bd., Phase II; mem. Calif. Hosp. Commn., 1974—; mem. adv. bd. programs health service adminstrn. U. So. Calif. Bd. dirs. Calif. Hosp. Med. Center, Martin Luther Hosp., Henry Mayo Newhall Meml. Hosp.; trustee, exec. com. Blue Cross So. Calif., 1966-75. Served with M.C., U.S. Army, 1946-47. Recipient Service to Humanity award Luth. Mut. Life Ins. Co., Outstanding Achievement award Hosp. Council So. Calif., 1972, ACHE Gold Medal award, 1987, CAHHS Award of Merit, 1987; Lester Breslow Disting. lectr., 1983; named asso. officer most Venerable Order of St. John, 1972. Fellow Am. Coll. Hosp. Adminstrs.; mem. Am. Hosp. Assn. (chmn. council research and planning 1964-67, trustee 1968-70, chmn. bd. trustees 1978, Meritorious Service citation 1973, Trustees' award 1979), San Diego Hosp. Assn. (dir.), Calif. Hosp. Assn. (pres. 1968-69, trustee 1966-70, Ritz E. Heerman award 1960, Award of Merit, 1987), Hosp. Council So. Calif. (pres. 1961-62), U. Minn. Alumni Assn. Hosp. and Health Care Adminstrn. (hon.), Delta Omega. Home: 1224 Adair St San Marino CA 91108-1805 Office: Pacificare Health Systems 5995 Plaza Drive Cypress CA 90630

TICE, CLIFFORD RAY, state legislator, oil company executive; b. Dexter, N.Mex., Aug. 18, 1927; s. Nina Sherod (Williams) Tice; m. Mary Smith, June 15, 1946 (dec. 1970); children: Karen, Thomas (dec.), Kenneth (dec.), Ronald. Student in pstroleum, I.C.S., 1946-51. With Malco Refineries, Inc., Artesia, N.Mex., 1949-53; yard foreman Malco Asphalt & Refining Co., Artesia, 1953-59; craft foreman Continental Oil Co., Artesia, 1959—; mem. N.Mex. State Sen., Santa Fe. Mem. City/County Planning and Zoning Commn., Artesia, 1986-87; pres. Parents and Boosters Club, Artesia, 1967-71. With USN, 1945-46, PTO. Decorated Victory Medal. Mem. Sertoma (membership chmn. 1989-90), Elks. Democrat. Home: 537 El Rey Dr Corrales NM 87048-7121

TICE, ROBERT GALEN, consultant; b. Lincoln, Nebr., June 8, 1956; s. Wayne Kilmer and Jean Louise (Bell) T. Student, Tex. Christian U., 1976; BS in Fin., Samford U., 1978; MBA in Fin., Rockhurst Coll., 1984. Asst. debate coach Samford U., Birmingham, Ala., 1978-79; asst. mgr. Barclay's Am. Credit, Birmingham, 1978-82; credit analyst Home State Bank, Kansas City, Kans., 1982-83; asst. cashier, loan officer Landmark K.C.I. Bank, Kansas City, Mo., 1983-85; dir. bus. devel. Centerre Bank Northland, North Kansas City, Mo., 1985-87; loan brokerage and investment cons. The Provo Group, Kansas City, Mo., 1987-88; bus. banking officer Nev. Nat. BAnk, Las Vegas, 1987-88; pres. Fin. Services Co., Las Vegas, 1988—; v.p. sales Prime Merchant Svcs., Inc., Las Vegas, 1988—; sales mgr. Sta. KJUL, Las Vegas, 1990—; bd. dirs. Indsl. Devel. Com., Platte County, Mo., Clay County Indsl. Deve. Com., Ambassadors Com.; v.p. sales Prime Mcht. Svcs., Inc., with Genre mag. and the Chritopher St. West Parade and Prode program; adminstr. Job Tng. Placement Act Word Processing and Computer Sci., instr. Century Bus. Coll., 1992—. Mem. race rels. com., issue selection & edn. com. Kansas City (Mo.) Consensus, 1986, pub. improvements adv. com. City of Kansas City, 1986, issue selection com. and mail-in ballot task force, reelection campaign Bonnie Sue Cooper for State Rep.; key gifts chmn. Boy Scouts of Am., Kansas City, 1985; Platte County chmn. Friends of Margaret Kelley CPA for State Auditor, 1986; media coord. Nat. Coming Out Day; bd. dirs. Citizens for Equal Justice & Gay Pride; Las Vegas coord. Human Rights Campaign Fund; active Shanti Found., L.A., Lesbian & Gay Acad. Union, Aid for AIDS of L.A., Las Vegas (Nev.) Met. Community Ch., The Experience. Mem. Suburban Bankers Assn. (bd. dirs. 1985-86), United Ostomy Assn. (bd. dirs, treas. 1984-86), Bus. and Profl. Assn. of Platte County (legis. action com., pub. rels. com. 1985-86), Gay and Lesbian Community Svcs. Ctr., Citizens Assn. of Kansas City, Greater Kansas City C. of C. (co-host Bus. After Hours 1985-86), Northland C. of C. (legis. com., Look North com. 1985-86), Rotary (Las Vegas chpt.). Presbyterian. Lodges: Rotary (local bd. dirs. 1986), Lions (bd. dirs. 1984-85). Home: 10456 Riverside Dr Toluca Lake CA 91602

TIDWELL, JOSEPH PAUL, JR., technical specialist research and engineering; b. Tuscaloosa, Ala., Oct. 29, 1943; s. Joseph Paul and Jeanette (Steinwinder) T.; m. Susan Kay White, Oct. 3, 1970; children: Joseph Paul III, James Boland, Heather Loran, Shawn Damon. A.S., NYU, 1978, BS, 1984; postgrad. Murray (Ky.) State U., 1984-85; MBA Embry Riddle Aero. U., 1991. Lic. pilot rotorcraft, cert. safety mgr., safety exec. Commd. aviation ops. officer U.S. Army, 1976, advanced through grades to maj., 1985; aviation safety officer Ft. Campbell, Ky., 1982-85, Chun Chon, Korea, 1981-82; chief aviation and product safety/flight safety parts programs McDonnell Douglas Helicopter, Co., Mesa, Ariz., 1985-89, dept. mgr., supplier evaluation and requirements Quality Control div., 1989-91, sr. systems safety engr. Advanced Devel. and Tech. div., 1991-93; rsch., engring. tech. specialist (aviation and product safety) advanced devel. and engring. divsn. McDonnell Douglas Corp., 1993—. Adj. instr. Embry Riddle Aero. Univ.; developer safety engring., safety cons., safety instr. Webelos den leader Clarksville council Cub Scouts Am., Tenn., 1983-85; asst. scout master Clarksville council Boy Scouts Am., 1983-85, scoutmaster Mesa council, 1985—; bd. dirs., vice-chairperson External Affairs S.W. Health and Safety Congress, 1985-86. Decorated Purple Heart, Meritorious Service medal, recipient Den Leaders Tng. Key Middle Tenn. council Boy Scouts Am., 1985, Woodbadge Beads Middle Tenn. Council Boy Scouts Am., 1985. Named Scoutmaster of Yr., Mesa Dist., Theodore Roosevelt Council Boy Scouts Am., 1986, award of merit Mesa Dist. 1988.. Mem. Am. Soc. Safety Engrs. (profl.; Safety Officer of Month award 1985, chmn. awards and elections Ariz. chpt. 1985-87), System Safety Soc. (leader Ariz. chpt.), Army Aviation Assn. Am. (air assault chpt. exec. treas. 1983-85, Aviation Safety Officer of Yr. award 1984), U.S. Army Warrant Officer's Assn. (Ky.-Tenn. chpt. pres. 1984-85, Disting. Service plaque 1984, Cert. of Merit for Disting. Achievement in Youth Leadership Devel. Men of Achievement, Cambridge, Eng., 1987. World Safety Orgn. (affiliate), Internat. Soc. Air Safety Investigators, S.W. Safety Congress and Exposition (bd. govs., conv. and advt. dir.), Aviation Edn. Coun. of Ariz. (bd. govs.), System Safety Soc. (organizer Ariz. chpt. 1993). Republican. Roman Catholic. Lodge: WIPALA WIKI, Order of Arrow. Avocations: golfing, camping, cycling. Home: 2338 W Lindner # 10 Mesa AZ 85202 Office: McDonnell Douglas Helicopter Co 5000 E McDowell Rd Mesa AZ 85205

TIEDEMAN, JOHN DENBY, computer consultant; b. Greensboro, N.C., Mar. 6, 1937; s. John Albert and Kathryn Wright (Price) T.; m. Dorothy McShane, Sept. 1, 1962 (div. June 1982); children: James P., William G. BSBA, La. State U., Baton Rouge, 1970. Data processing coord. Combellick, O'Connor & Reynolds, Englewood, Colo., 1977-81; asst. controller Signal Oilfield Svc. Co., Denver, 1982; computer systems/info. systems liaison World Savs. & Loan Assn., Denver, 1983; pvt. practice Fresno, Calif., 1983-87, San Francisco, 1987—. Active Golden Gate Mens Chorus. With USN, 1957-58. Mem. Bay Area Modula 2 Users Group, Integrity/San Francisco Bay Area. Episcopalian. Home: 1800 Market St # 39 San Francisco CA 94102-6227

TIEDEMANN, ARTHUR RALPH, ecologist, researcher; b. Grand Junction, Colo., Mar. 21, 1938; s. Henry Frederick and Elizabeth Mildred (Montgomery) T.; m. Sharon Estelle Bjorsness, Aug. 19, 1962. MS, U. Ariz., 1966, PhD, 1970. Rsch. range scientist Pacific N.W. Rsch. Sta., Wenatchee, Wash., 1969-72, rsch. project leader, 1972-79; rsch. project leader Intermountain Rsch. Sta., Provo, Utah, 1979-83; chief rsch. ecologist Pacific N.W. Rsch. Sta., La Grande, Oreg., 1983—; chmn. Shrub Rsch. Consortium, Provo, Utah, 1983, sustainable forest and range mgt. com. Blue Mountains Natural Resources Inst., La Grande, 1992-93. Author, editor: Research and Management of Bitterbrush, 1983; editor: Biology of Atriplex and Related Chenopods, 1984. Recipient Superior Services award U.S. Dept. Agr., 1974, 90; named Outstanding Alumnus, U. Ariz. Sch. Renewable Natural Resources, 1992. Mem. Soc. Range Mgmt., N.W. Scientific (assoc. editor 1977-83), Soc. Am. Foresters (assoc. editor forest sci. 1980-92), Sigma Xi (pres. ea. Oreg. state coll. chpt. 1992-93). Republican. Lutheran. Office: Pacific N W Rsch Sta 1401 Gekeler La Grande OR 97850

TIEDEMANN, DALE MERRIT, infosystems specialist; b. Milw., Dec. 4, 1944; s. Edward H.J. and Dorothy F. (Vedner) T.; m. Dixie L. White, May 2, 1970. AA in Data Processing, Milw. Inst. Tech., 1973; BA in Mgmt., U. Phoenix, 1984. Cert. systems profl., cert. quality analyst; cert. info. systems security profl. Assoc. systems analyst Globe Union, Milw., 1969-70; programmer/analyst Clark Oil & Refining, Milw., 1970-73; systems analyst Am. Petrofina, Dallas, 1973-77, electronic data processing auditor, 1977-78; cons. Arthur D. Little, Phoenix, 1978-80; mgr. electronic data processing auditing Am. Express, Phoenix, 1980-84; dir. mgmt. info. systems auditing Greyhound Dial Corp., Phoenix, 1984-90; dir. info. systems standards The Dial Corp., Phoenix, 1990-92; dir. Andersen Cons., 1992-93; ind. cons. Enterprising Assocs., Ltd., 1993—. Mem. Assn. for Systems Mgmt.

TIEKOTTER, KENNETH LOUIS, electron microscopist; b. Montgomery, Ala., Jan. 23, 1955; s. Kenneth Heil and Elaine June (Krause) T.; m. Kathryn Parks, July 29, 1978. BS, Portland State U., 1983. Cert. electron microscopy technologist. Histology technician U. Nebr. Sch. Dentistry, Lincoln, 1978-80; rsch. assoc. neurology rsch. VA Med. Ctr., Portland, Oreg., 1980-84; electron microscopy coord., dir. dept. ophthalmology Good Samaritan Hosp. and Med. Ctr., Portland, 1984—; adj. prof. U. Portland; electron microscopy cons. neurology rsch. VA Med. Ctr., Portland, 1984—, Portland State U., Pacific U., Forest Grove, 1992—. Contbr. articles to profl. jours. Recipient awards Polaroid Corp., 1984, 89, Nikon Corp., 1989, 90. Mem. Am. Soc. Parasitologists, Am. Microscopical Soc., Electron Microscopical Soc. Am., Helminthological Soc. Wash., B.C. Parasitologists, N.Y. Acad. Scis., Sigma Xi. Home: 2920 NE 25th Ave Portland OR 97212-3459 Office: Good Samaritan Hosp N320 1015 NW 22d Ave Portland OR 97210

TIEMAN, MICHAEL LAVERNE, graphic design executive; b. Keokuk, Iowa, Aug. 20, 1950; s. Malcolm LaVerne and Doris Earline (Morrill) T.; m. Nancy Lee Marshall, June 16, 1972; children: Heather Anne, Katherine Jane. BFA, Columbus Coll. Art and Design, 1972. Art dir. Kersker Advt., Columbus, Ohio, 1969-72; graphic designer The Studio, Inc., Columbus, 1972-74; sr. art dir. Cocfield & Brown Advt., Vancouver, B.C., Can., 1974-75; ptnr., graphic designer Designers West, Ltd., Vancouver, 1975-78; owner, graphic designer Tieman & Friends, North Vancouver, 1978-86; ptnr., art dir. Printpac Mktg., Ltd., Richmond, B.C., 1978-81; sr. art dir. McKim Advt., Ltd., Vancouver, 1981-84; sr. graphic designer EXPO 86, Vancouver, 1984-86; exec. graphic designer Gilchrist & Assocs., Inc., Portland, Oreg., 1986—. Recipient First Pl. Presentation Folders award Lithographers & Printing House Craftsmen, 1990, Cert. of Merit award Printing Industries Am., 1988, First Pl. Ann. Report award Internat. Fedn. Advt. Agys. 1985, PRSA, 1987; named World's Best 30 Second Comedy Spot, Hollywood Radio & TV Soc., 1981. Mem. Nat. Geog. Soc., Am. Inst. Graphic Artists, The Smithsonian Assocs. (Nat.), New England Hist. Geneal. Soc., Trout Unlimited, Friends of the Zoo. Office: Gilchrist & Assoc 319 SW Washington Portland OR 97214

TIEN, CHANG LIN, chancellor; b. Wuhan, China, July 24, 1935; came to U.S., 1956, naturalized, 1969; s. Yun Chien and Yun Di (Lee) T.; m. Di Hwa Liu, July 25, 1959; children: Norman Chihnan, Phyllis Chihping, Christine Chihyih. BS, Nat. Taiwan U., 1955; MME, U. Louisville, 1957; MA, PhD, Princeton U., 1959. Acting asst. prof. dept. mech. engring. U. Calif., Berkeley, 1959-60, asst. prof., 1960-64, assoc. prof., 1964-68, prof., 1968-89, 90—, A. Martin Berlin prof., 1987-89, 90—, dept. chmn., 1974-81, also vice chancellor for research, 1983-85; exec. vice chancellor U. Calif., Irvine, 1988-90; chancellor U. Calif., Berkeley, 1990—; tech. cons. Lockheed Missiles and Space Co., GE; trustee Princeton (N.J.) U., 1991—; bd. dirs. Wells Fargo Bank. Contbr. articles to profl jours. Guggenheim fellow, 1965; recipient Heat Transfer Meml. award, 1974, Larson Meml. award Am. Inst. Chem. Engrs, 1975. Fellow AAAS, ASME (Max Jakob Meml. award), AIAA (Thermophysics award 1977); mem. NAE. Office: U Calif Chancellor's Office Berkeley CA 94720

TIERNAN, PETER JAY, union representative, painter; b. Santa Monica, Calif., Sept. 18, 1955; s. Paul Joseph and Katherine (Letts) T.; m. Mary Theresa Shanahan, Aug. 20, 1977. Bachelor degree, U. San Francisco, 1990; postgrad., Golden State U., 1990-92. Cert. journeyman painter. Trustee Bay Area Painter Trust Fund, San Francisco, 1991—; bus. rep. Painter Local 83, San Rafael, Calif., 1984—; pres. Painters Dist. Coun. 8, San Francisco, 1982-86. Commr. Adult Criminal Justice Commn., San Rafael, 1992; mem. Planning Commn., Novato, Calif., 1989-91; del. Dem. Cen. Com., Marin County, Calif., 1992; bd. dirs. Pvt. Industry Coun., Marin County, 1987—. Recipient Ray Castel-Blake award 9th Assembly Dist., 1992, Cert. of Honor, Novato C. of C., 1991. Mem. Rotary. Roman Catholic. Home: Box 184 Novato CA 94947 Office: Painters Local 83 4174 Redwood Hwy San Rafael CA 94903

TIETZ, WILLIAM JOHN, JR., research institute executive, university president emeritus; b. Chgo., Mar. 6, 1927; s. William John and Irma (Neuman) T.; children: Karyn Elizabeth, William John, Julia Wells. BA, Swarthmore Coll., 1950; MS, U. Wis., 1952; DVM, Colo. State U., 1957; PhD, Purdue U., 1961, DSc, 1982; fellow, Va. Poly. and State U., 1991. Rsch. assoc. Baxter Labs., Morton Grove, Ill., 1952-53; instr., then assoc. prof. Purdue U., 1957-64; faculty Colo. State U., 1964-77, prof., chmn. physiology and biophysics, 1967-70, v.p. student and univ. relations, 1970-71, dean Coll. Vet. Medicine and Biomed. Scis/, 1971-77, assoc. dir. Agrl. Expt. Sta., 1975-77; pres. Mont. State U., Bozeman, 1977-90, Deaconess Rsch. Inst., Bozeman, 1992—; pres., COO Deaconess Rsch. Inst., Billings, Mont., 1992—; mem. Gov.'s Com. on Econ. Devel., 1984-87; mem. Mont. Sci. and Tech. Alliance, 1985-87; chmn. bd. Intermountain Community Learning and Info. Svc., 1987-89, N.W. Commn. of Schs. and Colls., Commn. on Colls., 1982-89. Bd. dirs. Children's House, Montessori Sch., 1966-70, chmn., 1968-70; bd. dirs. Colo. State U. Found., 1970-71, Colo. chpt. Am. Cancer Soc., 1976-79; mem. rsch. bd. Denver Zool. Soc., 1975-77; treas. Mont. Energy Rsch. and Devel. Inst., 1977-78, v.p. 1978-80, pres., 1981-83; bd. dirs. Greater Mont. Foun., 1979-91, 93—; mem. Mont. Com. for Humanities, 1980-83; mem. div. rsch. resources adv. coun. NIH, 1979-82; trustee Yellowstone Pk. Found., 1981-93, chmn., 1989-92; adv. com. Yellowstone Ctr. for. Recipient Svc. award Colo. Vet. Med. Assn., 1976; named Honor Alumnus Colo. State U., 1977, Coll. Vet. Medicine, 1979; recipient Blue and Gold award Mont. State U., 1993. Mem. Larimer County Vet. Med. Assn. (pres. 1968-69), Am. Assn. Vet. Physiologists and Pharmacologists (pres. 1971-72), Am. Physiol. Soc., Sigma Xi, Phi Zeta (sec.-treas. 1970-71), Assn. Am. Colls. Vet. Medicine (chmn. council of deans 1975-76), Phi Kappa Phi, Phi Sigma Kappa, Omicron Delta Kappa, Beta Beta Beta. Home and Office: 10030 Cottonwood Rd Bozeman MT 59715

TIFFANY, MARIAN CATHERINE, social worker; b. Seattle, Dec. 22, 1919; d. Evald Martiness and Amy Myrtle (Wampler) Petersen; m. William Robert Tiffany, Nov. 5, 1943; children: Susan Margaret, Ruston William (dec.), Lisa Ann Amy, William W. BA in Social Work, U. Wash., 1974.

Dir. social svcs. Wash. Villa Care, Inc., Seattle, 1973-74; instr. home and family edn., coord. sr. adult edn. North Seattle Community Coll., 1974-84; real estate saleswoman William Bruce Co., Seattle, 1984-86, Richard James Realtors, Seattle, 1986-88, Relo Resources, Kirkland, Wash., 1988—; cons. to families of aging parents, Seattle, 1989—. V.p. U. Wash. Faculty Wives, 1966; mem. dept. health Seattle-King County North Multi-Svc. Ctr., 1982-83, chairwoman, 1983-84. Democrat. Methodist. Home: 8005 Sand Point Way NE A-34 Seattle WA 98115

TIFFANY, WILLIAM BENJAMIN, physicist; b. Shawnee, Okla., Mar. 28, 1937; s. William Edwin and Alberta Rebecca (Guzzardo) T.; m. Lise Tiffany Dearborn, Mar. 15, 1974; children: Sherryl, Elise, Nicole Teresa. BS in Physics with highest honors, U. Okla., 1959; MS in Physics, Stanford (Calif.) U., 1963, PhD in Physics, 1967. Engring. specialist GTE Sylvania Electro-Optics, Mountain View, Calif., 1959-70; v.p. Molectron Corp., Sunnyvale, Calif., 1970-77; mgr. R&D R.R. Donnelley & Sons Co., Chgo., 1978-84; program mgr. Coherent Inc., Palo Alto, Calif., 1984-89; pres. Micro-Habitat Systems, Inc., Palo Alto, 1989—; cons. Advanced Cardiovascular Systems, Santa Clara, Calif., 1989-91, Biomedica Inc., Neenah, Wis., 1992—. Contbr. articles to profl. jours; inventor gas-transport laser, isopic laser for surgery. Fulbright fellowship U. Heidelberg, 1959-60. Fellow Laser Inst. of Am. (pres. 1976); mem. IEEE, Am. Phys. Soc., Optical Soc. of No. Calif., Sigma Xi. Home and Office: 1110 Harker Ave Palo Alto CA 94301

TILLERY, BILL W., physics educator; b. Muskogee, Okla., Sept. 15, 1938; s. William Earnest and Bessie C. (Smith) Freeman; m. Patricia Weeks Northrop, Aug. 1, 1981; 1 child, Elizabeth Fielding; children by previous marriage: Tonya Lynn, Lisa Gail. BS, Northeastern U., 1960; MA, U. No. Colo., 1965, EdD, 1967. Tchr. Guthrie Pub. Schs., Okla., 1960-62; tchr. Jefferson County schs., Colo., 1962-64; teaching asst. U. No. Colo., 1965-67; asst. prof. Fla. State U., 1967-69; assoc. prof. U. Wyo., 1969-73, dir. sci. and math. teaching ctr., 1969-73; assoc. prof. dept. physics Ariz. State U., Tempe, 1973-75, prof., 1976—; cons. in field. Author: (with Ploutz) Basic Physical Science, 1964; (with Sund and Trowbridge) Elementary Science Activities, 1967, Elementary Biological Science, 1970, Elementary Physical Science, 1970, Elementary Earth Science, 1970, Investigate and Discover, 1975; Space, Time, Energy and Matter: Activity Books, 1976; (with Bartholomew) Heath Earth Science, 1984; (with Bartholomew and Gary) Heath Earth Science Activities, 1984, 2d edit. 1987, Heath Earth Science Teacher Resource Book, 1987, Heath Earth Science Laboratory Activity, 1987, Physical Science, 1991, 2d edit. 1993, Physical Science Laboratory Manual, 1991, 2d edit. 1993, Physical Science Instructor's Manual, 1991, 2d edit. 1993, Physical Science Laboratory Manual Instructor's Manual, 1991, 2d edit. 1993, (with Grant) Physical Science Student Study Guide, 1991, 2d edit. (with Claassen) 1993, Introduction to Physics and Chemistry: Foundations of Physical Science, 1992, Laboratory Manual in Conceptual Physics, 1992, Physics, 1993, Chemistry, 1993, Astronomy, 1993, Earth Science, 1993; editor: Ariz. Sci. Tchrs. Jour., 1975-85, Ariz. Energy Edn., 1978-84. Fellow AAAS; mem. Nat. Sci. Tchrs. Assn., Ariz. Sci. Tchrs. Assn., Assn. Edn. of Tchrs. in Sci., Nat. Assn. Research in Sci. Teaching. Republican. Episcopalian. Home: 8986 S Forest Ave Tempe AZ 85284-3142 Office: Ariz State U Dept Physics Tempe AZ 85287-1504

TILLERY, CAROLYN DENISE, lawyer, deputy district attorney; b. Asheville, N.C., July 6, 1957; d. John Gordon and Delores Gweindolyn (Adams) Quick; m. Jackie R. Tillery, May 15m 1978; 1 child, Ashley. BA in English, Tuskegee Inst., 1979; JD, U. Denver, 1989. Jud. fellow Colo. Supreme Ct., Denver, 1988-89, law clk., 1990-91; law clk. El Paso Dist. Ct., Colorado Springs, Colo., 1989-90; dep. dist. atty. Fourth Jud. Dist., Colorado Springs, 1991—. Bd. dirs. Battered Women's Shelter Bldg. Fund, 1992—; del. Fifth Rep. Dist., 1991, 92; founder Save Our Children, Colorado Springs, 1992; chair Joint Coun. Minority Law Students, Denver, 1989. Capt. USAF, 1980-85. Recipient Philip E. Lowry award, 1989, Irving P. Andrew award Sam Carey Bar Assn., 1989; named to Outstanding Young Women of Am., 1984. Mem. Colo. Bar Assn., Nat. Inst. Trial Advocacy. Home: 5137 Windgate Ct Colorado Springs CO 80917 Office: 326 S Tejon Colorado Springs CO 80903

TILLMAN, HENRY BARRETT, author; b. Pendleton, Oreg., Dec. 24, 1948; s. John Henry and Beverly Jean (Barrett) T. BS in Journalism, U. Oreg., 1971. Freelance author Athena, Oreg., 1972-82, 1989—; pub. Champlin Mus. Press, Mesa, Ariz., 1982-86; mng. editor The Hook Mag., Bonita, Calif., 1986-89. Author: (nonfiction) Wildcat: F4F in WW II, 1983, reprint 1990, MiG Master, 1980, reprint 1990, (novel) Warriors, 1990, The Sixth Battle, 1992, Dauntless, 1992; co-author: (nonfiction) On Yankee Station, 1987. Pres. C. of C., Athena, 1976-77, Caledonian Games, Athena, 1978-79; commr. County Planning Commn., Umatilla County, Oreg., 1976-79; councilor City Coun., Athena, 1990, commr. police, parks, libr. Recipient Contbrs. award Am. Aviation Hist. Soc., L.A., 1978, Writing award USAF Hist. Found., Washington, 1981, Writing award N.Am. Oceanographic Soc., 1987. Mem. U.S. Naval Inst., NRA, Tailhook Assn. (all life). Republican. Baptist. Home: 3536 E Camino Cir Mesa AZ 85213-7033

TILLMAN, JOSEPH NATHANIEL, engineer; b. Augusta, Ga., Aug. 1, 1926; s. Leroy and Canarie (Kelly) T.; m. Alice Lavonia Walton, Sept. 5, 1950 (dec. 1983); children: Alice Lavonia, Robert Bertram; m. Areerat Usahaviriyakit, Nov. 24, 1986. BA magna cum laude, Paine Coll., 1948; MS, Northrop U., 1975, MBA, 1976; DBA, Nova U., 1989. Dir. Rockwell Internat., Anaheim, Calif., 1958-84; pres. Tillman Enterprises, Corona, Calif., 1985—; guest lectr. UCLA, 1980-85. Contbr. articles to profl. jours. Capt. USAF, 1948-57, Korea. Recipient Presdl. Citation Nat. Assn. for Equal Opportunity in Higher Edn., 1986. Mem. Acad. Mgmt. (chmn. 1985-86), Soc. Logistics Engrs. (pres. 1985-86), Paine Coll. Alumni Assn. (v.p. 1976—), NAACP (pres. 1984-88). Office: Tillman Enterprises 1550 S Rimpau Ave # 45 Corona CA 91719-3206

TILSON, DONALD HEATH, JR., orthopedist; b. Tarrytown, N.Y., Mar. 23, 1930; s. Donald Heath and Anne (Coe) T.; m. Kirtley Gunn, July 26, 1952; children: Donald H. III, John G., Charles E., William W. AB, Harvard Coll., 1951; MD, Washington U., St. Louis, 1955; MHA, Baylor U., 1968. Diplomate Am. Bd. Orthopaedic Surgery, Am. Bd. Prevention Medicine; lic. physician, Oreg., Wash., Calif., N.Mex., Mo., Va., N.C., N.Y. Commd. 1st lt. U.S. Army, 1955, advanced through grades to col., 1971; commd. USAR, 1957, advanced through grades to col., 1971, intern surgery, 1955-56; resident orthopedics Buffalo Gen. Hosp., 1956; preceptee anesthesiology Madigan Gen. Hosp., Tacoma, Wash., 1956-58, resident surgery, 1958-59; resident orthopedics Tripler Gen. Hosp., Honolulu, 1959-62, Shriners Hosp., Honolulu, 1962; various assigments U.S. Army, 1962-72; chief orthopaedics Gorgas Hosp., Canal Zone, 1972-75, Womack Hosp., Ft. Bragg, N.C., 1975-77; ret. USAR, 1977; orthopaedist Kaiser West Interstate Offices, Portland, Oreg., 1977—; resident in occupational medicine Duke U. Med. Ctr., Durham, N.C., 1984; cons. indsl. medicine svc. Kaiser HCW, 1980-89, Riverfront Med. Svcs., N.Y., 1986-89, Occupational Health Svc. Kaiser, 1980—. Decorated Bronze Star, Legion of Merit. Mem. APHA, Am. Acad. Orthopaedic Surgeons, Am. Coll. Occupational Medicine, Alpha Omega Alpha, Phi Beta Kappa. Republican. Episcopalian. Office: Kaiser W Interstate Offices 3325 N Interstate Ave Portland OR 97227-1099

TILSWORTH, TIMOTHY, environmental and civil engineering educator; b. Norfolk, Nebr., Apr. 6, 1939; s. Brooke and Mildred (Palmer) T.; m. Joanne Novak, Apr. 19, 1966 (div. Jan. 1984); children: Craig Scott, Patrick Joseph; m. Debbie J. May, July 20, 1984. BSCE, U. Nebr., Lincoln, 1967; PhD, U. Kans, 1970. Registered profl. engr., Alaska. Instr. U. Nebr., Lincoln, 1967; prof. environ. quality and civil engring. U. Alaska, Fairbanks, 1970—, dir. program environ. quality engring. and sci., 1972-76, 78—, asst. to pres. for acad. affairs, 1976-78, head dept. civil engring, 1990-91, chmn. grad. coun., chmn. chancellor search com., 1990-91; owner Raven Press Pub. Co., Fairbanks, 1990—; pres. faculty senate U. Alaska, Fairbanks, 1992-93; owner Alaska Arctic Environ. Services, Fairbanks, 1972—, DJT's Shelties Delight, Fairbanks, 1985—; project mgr. superconducting super collider proposal State of Alaska, Fairbanks, 1987-88. Chmn. exec. com. Cowper for Gov. Alaska, Fairbanks, 1986. Recipient commendation State of Alaska, 1988. Mem. Assn. for Environ. Engring. Profs., ASCE (Outstanding Service award 1975), Am. Water Works Assn. Water Pollution Control Fedn., Chi Epsilon. Roman Catholic. Home: 1900 Raven Dr Fairbanks AK 99709-6661 Office: U Alaska Civil Engring Dept 306 Tanana Dr Fairbanks AK 99775

TILTON, GEORGE ROBERT, geochemistry educator; b. Danville, Ill., June 3, 1923; s. Edgar Josiah and Caroline Lenore (Burkmeyer) T.; m. Elizabeth Jane Foster, Feb. 7, 1948; children—Linda Ruth, Helen Elizabeth, Elaine Lee, David Foster, John Robert. Student, Blackburn Coll., 1940-42; B.S., U. Ill., 1947; Ph.D., U. Chgo., 1951; D.Sc. (hon.), Swiss Fed. Inst. Tech., Zurich, 1984. Phys. chemist Carnegie Instn., Washington, 1951-65; prof. geochemistry U. Calif.-Santa Barbara, 1965-91, emeritus, 1991—, chmn. dept. geol. scis., 1973-77; guest prof. Swiss Fed. Inst., Zurich, 1971-72; prin. investigator NSF research grant, 1965—; mem. earth scis. panel NSF, 1966-69, 82-85. Assoc. editor Jour. Geophys. Research, 1962-65, Geochimica et Cosmochimica Acta, 1973—; contbr. articles to profl. jours. Served with AUS, 1942-45. Decorated Purple Heart; recipient Sr. Scientist award Alexander von Humboldt Found., 1989. Fellow AAAS, Am. Geophys. Union, Geol. Soc. Am.; mem. Nat. Acad. Scis., Geochem. Soc. (pres. 1981), Sigma Xi. Episcopalian. Home: 3425 Madrona Dr Santa Barbara CA 93105-2652 Office: U Calif Dept Geol Scis Santa Barbara CA 93106

TILTON, RONALD WILLIAM, naval officer; b. Brookline, Mass., Dec. 28, 1944; s. John Walter and Audrey Muriel (Rice) T.; m. Thuy-Nhi Tran, Jan. 2, 1993. BA in Mgmt., Jacksonville U., 1967; cert., Naval War Coll., 1979, Air U., 1985; MS in Systems Mgmt., U. Southern Calif., 1985. Commd. ens. USN, 1967, advanced through grades to comdr., 1982; sr. pilot evaluator of Atlantic fleet patrol squadrons Patrol Squadron Thirty, Jacksonville, Fla., 1975-78; patrol plane comdr., maintenance officer Patrol Squadron 17, Barbers Point, Hawaii, 1980-82; ops. and plans officer Commander in Chief Pacific, Camp H.M. Smith, Hawaii, 1982-84; comptroller Naval Air Sta., Barbers Point, 1984-86; exec. officer, chief test pilot NAVPRO, Lockheed Aero. Systems Co., Burbank, Calif., 1986-90; pilot UPS, Louisville, 1990—. Loaned exec. United Way, Jacksonville, 1975. Mem. Naval Air Exec. Inst., Order of Daedalians, Phi Delta Theta. Home: 24660A Brighton Dr Santa Clarita CA 91355-3539

TIMBLIN, LLOYD O., JR., water resources scientist; b. Denver, June 25, 1927; s. Lloyd Oswald and Winona Mary (Crosby) T.; m. Barbara Helen McNiel, Sept. 16, 1950; 1 child, Carol Lynn. BS in Engring. Physics, U. Colo., 1950; MS in Physics, U. Denver, 1967. Registered profl. engr., Colo.; cert. corrosion specialist. Physicist U.S. Bur. Reclamation, Denver, 1950-58; head spl. investigations lab. sect. U.S. Bur. Reclamation, 1958-63, chief chem. engring. br., 1963-70, chief applied scis. br., 1970-91, ind. water resources cons., 1992—; chair tech. program Internat. Symposium Geomembranes, Denver, 1984; chair U.S. team U.S./USSR Joint study plastics in hydotechnical constrn., 1975-85; mem. com. on envrion. Internat. Commn. Large Dams, 1987—; gen. reporter Question 60-Reservoirs and the Environ., Internat. Commn. on Large Dams 16th Congress, San Francisco, 1988; mem. U.S. com. on Large Dams; chmn. com. Materials for Embankment Dams, 1981-86, Environ. Effects, 1990—; mem. bur. reclamation nat. sanitation found. joint com. for flexible membrane liners, 1978-83, mem. Am. Water Works Assn. standards com. on thermosetting fiberglass reinforced plastic pipe, 1971-89; mem. Colo. Adv. Coun. for Seminar on Environ. Arts and Scis., 1971-74; bd. dirs. Timless Tales Inc., 1992—. Contbr. articles to profl. jours. With USN, 1944-45. Recipient Merit Svc., 1977, Disting. Svc. award, 1991, U.S. Dept. Interior. Presbyterian. Home and Office: 355 Martin Dr Boulder CO 80303

TIMM, JERRY ROGER, fiberglass manufacturing company executive; b. Nampa, Idaho, Apr. 16, 1942; s. Sheldon A. and Beulah M. (Bell) T.; children: Bryan Lee, Michelle Ann; m. Marcy Marrs, Oct. 18, 1991. B.S. in Acctg, U. Idaho, 1965; student, Stanford Fin. Mgmt. Program, 1986. C.P.A., Idaho. With Touche Ross & Co. (C.P.A.), 1965-73; mgr. Touche Ross & Co. (C.P.A.), Boise, Idaho, 1973; asst. controller to controller corp. div. Albertson's, Inc., Boise, 1973-76; controller Albertson's, Inc., 1976-81, v.p. and controller, 1981-89; v.p., chief fin., adminstrv. officer Fiberglass Systems, Inc., Boise, 1990—; pres., dir. Albertson's Fed. Credit Union, 1976-84; past chmn. Idaho Bd. Accountancy. Bd. dirs. Boise Family YMCA, 1978-81; chmn., dir. Boise chpt. ARC, 1986-90; campaign chmn. United Way of ADA Countk Inc., 1985, pres. elect 1986, pres. 1987; bd. dirs. Associated Taxpayers of Idaho, Inc., 1983-89. Mem. AICPA, Nat. Assn. Accts. (past pres. Boise chpt.), Idaho Soc. CPAs, Boise Capital Lions (pres. 1970-83), Boise Sunrise Rotary (pres. 1984—). Office: Fiberglass Systems Inc 4545 Enterprise St Boise ID 83705-5425

TIMM, ROBERT MERLE, wildlife specialist; b. Pomona, Calif., Oct. 7, 1949; s. Herbert Merle and Mary Elsie (Beasley) T.; m. Janice Howard Hawthorne, May 31, 1986; children: Anna Elizabeth Howard, Sarah Beatrice Howard. BS, U. of Redlands, 1971; MS, U. Calif., Davis, 1973, PhD, 1977. Extension wildlife specialist, assoc. prof. U. Nebr., Lincoln, 1978-87; supt., extension wildlife specialist Hopland Rsch. and Ext. Ctr., U. Calif., Hopland, 1987—; cons. rodent control USAID/Denver Wildlife Rsch. Ctr.-USDA, Bangladesh, 1989. Editor: Prevention and Control of Wildlife Damage, 1983; contbr. articles to profl. jours. Chmn. coun. 1st Evang. Covenant Ch., Lincoln, 1983-85; group study exch. mem. Rotary Internat. to Natal province, Republic South Africa, 1982. Named Outstanding New Specialist, NE Coop. Extension Assn., Lincoln, 1982. Mem. Soc. for Range Mgmt., Am. Soc. Mammalogists, Nat. Animal Damage Control Assn. (co-editor newsletter 1990—), The Wildlife Soc. (animal damage com., cert. wildlife biologist), Sigma Xi, Gamma Sigma Delta. Mem. United Ch. Christ-Congl. Home: 968 Riverside Dr Ukiah CA 95482-9606 Office: U Calif Hopland Rsch and Ext Ctr 4070 University Rd Hopland CA 95449-9718

TIMMERHAUS, KLAUS DIETER, chemical engineering educator; b. Mpls., Sept. 10, 1924; s. Paul P. and Elsa L. (Bever) T.; m. Jean L. Mevis, Aug. 3, 1952; 1 dau., Carol Jane. BS in Chem. Engring, U. Ill., 1948, MS, 1949, PhD, 1951. Registered profl. engr., Colo. Process design engr. Calif. Rsch. Corp., Richmond, 1952-53; extension lectr. U. Calif., Berkeley, 1952; mem. faculty U. Colo., Boulder, 1953—, prof. chem. engring., 1961—, asso. dean engring., 1963-86, dir. engring. rsch. ctr. coll. engring., 1963-86, chmn. aerospace dept., 1979-80, chmn. chem. engring. dept., 1986-89, Patten Chair Disting. prof., 1986—, presdl. teaching scholar, 1989—; chem. engr. cryogenics lab. Nat. Bur. Standards, Boulder, summers 1955,57,59,61; lectr. U. Calif. at L.A., 1961-62; sect. head engring. div. NSF, 1972-73; cons. in field. Bd. dirs. Colo. Engring. Expt. Sta., Inc., Engring. Measurements Co., both Boulder. Editor: Advances in Cryogenic Engineering, vols. 1-25, 1954-80; co-editor: Internat. Cryogenic Monograph Series, 1965—. Served with USNR, 1944-46. Recipient Disting. Svc. award Dept. Commerce, 1957; Samuel C. Collins award outstnding contbns. to cyrogenic tech., 1967; George Westinghouse award, 1968; Alpha Chi Sigma award for chem. engring. rsch., 1968; Meritorious Svc. award Cryogenic Engring. Conf., 1987; R.L. Stearns Profl. Chievement award U. Colo., 1981, Hazel E. Barnes Rsch. and Teaching Excellence award U. Colo., 1992; Disting. Pub. Svc. award NSF, 1984. Fellow AAAS (Southwestern and Rocky Mountain div. Pres.'s award 1989); mem. NAE, Am. Astron. Soc., Am. Inst. Chem. Engrs. (v.p. 1975, pres. 1976, Founders award 1978, Eminent Chem. Engr. award 1983, W. K. Lewis award 1987, F.J. Van Antwerpen award 1991), Am. Soc. for Engring. Edn. (bd. dirs. 1986-88, 3M Chem Engring. div. award 1980, Engring. Rsch. Coun. award 1990, Delos Svc. award 1991, F. Merryfield Design award 1992), Internat. Inst. Refrigeration (v.p. 1979-87, pres. 1987—, U.S. nat. commn. 1983—, pres. 1983-86, W.T. Pentzer award 1989), Austrian Acad. Sci., Cryogenic Engring. Conf. (chmn. 1956-67, bd. dirs. 1956—), Soc. Automotive Engrs. (Ralph Teetor award 1991), Sigma Xi (v.p. 1986-87, pres. 1987-88, bd. dirs. 1981-89), Sigma Tau, Tau Beta Pi, Phi Lambda Upsilon. Home: 905 Brooklawn Dr Boulder CO 80303-2708

TIMMINS, JAMES DONALD, venture capitalist; b. Hamilton, Ont., Can., Oct. 3, 1955; came to U.S., 1979; s. Donald G. and Myrna L. (Seymour) T. BA, U. Toronto, 1977; LLB, Queen's U., 1979; MBA, Stanford U., 1981. Investment banker Wood Gundy, Toronto, 1980, Salomon Bros., San Francisco, 1981-84; mng. dir. and chief exec. officer McKewon & Timmins, San Diego, 1984-87; ptnr. Hambrecht & Quist, San Francisco, 1987-90, Glenwood Capital, Menlo Park, 1991—; bd. dirs. Iwerks Entertainment, Inc., Burbank, Magllan Systems, West Covina, Visualization Techs., Inc., Fremont, Calif.; chmn. Paradigm Tech., San Jose, Calif., Inc. Mem. Olympic Club of San Francisco. Home: 735 Laurelwood Dr San Mateo CA 94403-4058 Office: Glenwood Capital 3000 Sandhill Rd Ste 230 Menlo Park CA 94025-7116

TIMMONS, ROBERT G., physician, educator; b. Erie, Pa., May 1, 1938; s. James D. and Beatrice M. (Kelly) T.; m. Barbara Jo Ann Wengert, June 30, 1962; children: Patrick, Ann, Bobby, John, Victor, Dan. BA in Biology, Gannon U., 1960; MD, Thomas Jefferson U., 1966. Diplomate Am. Bd. Internal Medicine, Am. Bd. Internal Medicine. Rotating intern St. Vincent Health Ctr., Erie, 1966-67; resident in medicine Lankenau Hosp., Phila., 1970-72, sr. resident in medicine, fellow in infectious diseases, 1972-73; staff resident Hamot Med. Ctr., Erie, 1973-82, chmn., dir. med. edn. com., 1974-82; instr. in family medicine Gannon U., Erie, 1975-82; pvt. practice Portales, N.Mex., 1982—; clin. assoc. prof., preceptor dept. family medicine and emergency medicine U. N.Mex., Albuquerque, 1983—; chief exec. officer Roosevelt Gen. Hosp., Portales, 1989-93; adj. prof. dept. psychology Ea. N.Mex. U., Portales, 1982—, adj. prof. dept. natural sci., 1988; cons. staff mem. Shriners Hosp. for Crippled Children, Erie, VA Hosp., Erie; clin. asst. prof. family and community medicine Pa. State U., Hershey, 1979-80; clin. asst. prof. dept. medicine Hahnemann Med. Coll. and Hosp., Phila., 1981; chief of staff Roosevelt Gen. Hosp., Portales, 1983, 86, 87-88; pvt. practice internal medicine and infectious diseases Bayview Internist, Inc., Erie, 1973-82; med. dir. Plains Regional Med. Ctr., Clovis/Portales. Contbr. numerous articles to profl. jours. Mem. Rotary, Portales, 1982-86. Capt. USAF, 1967-70. Fellow ACP; mem. AMA, Assn. for Hosp. Med. Edn., Assn. for Practitioners in Infection Control, Erie County Med. Soc., Pa. Med. Soc., Pa. Assn. for Med. Edn., Tri-County Med. Soc., N.Mex. Med. Soc. Office: Roosevelt Gen Hosp 1700 S Ave O PO Drawer 60 Portales NM 88130

TIMMONS, WILLIAM MILTON, retired cinema arts educator, publisher, free-lance writer, film maker; b. Houston, Apr. 21, 1933; s. Carter Charles and Gertrude Monte (Lee) T.; m. Pamela Cadorette, Dec. 24, 1975 (div. 1977). BS, U. Houston, 1958; MA, UCLA, 1961; PhD, U. So. Calif., 1975. Child actor Houston Jr. Theater, 1945-46; staff announcer Sta. KMCO, Conroe, Tex., 1951-52; prodn. asst. Sta. KUHT-TV, Houston, 1953-54, 56-57; teaching fellow UCLA, 1960-61; ops. asst. CBS-TV, Hollywood, Calif., 1961-62; prof. speech and drama Sam Houston State U., Huntsville, Tex., 1963-67; chmn. dept. cinema Los Angeles Valley Coll., Van Nuys, Calif., 1970-91, ret., 1992; producer Sta. KPFK, Los Angeles, 1959-60, 1983—; pub. Acad. Assocs., L.A., 1976—; proofreader, cons. Focal Press Pub. Co., N.Y.C., 1983—. Author: Orientation to Cinema, 1986; contbr. articles to mags.; producer, dir.: (radio program) Campus Comments, 1963-67, numerous ednl. films, 1963—. With USNR, 1954-56. Named Hon. Tex. Ranger, State of Tex., Austin, 1946; U. Houston scholar, 1957. Mem. Soc. for Scholary Pub., Mensa, U. So. Calif. Cinema-TV Alumni Assn., Red Masque Players, Secular Humanists L.A., Alpha Epsilon Rho, Delta Kappa Alpha. Democrat.

TIMMRECK, THOMAS C., health sciences and health administration educator; b. Montpelier, Idaho, June 15, 1946; s. Archie Carl and Janone (Jensen) T.; m. Ellen Prusse, Jan. 27, 1971; children: Chad Thomas, Benjamin Brian, Julie Anne. AA, Ricks Coll., 1968; BS, Brigham Young U., 1971; MEd, Oreg. State U., 1972; MA, No. Ariz. U., 1981; PhD, U. Utah, 1976. Program dir. Cache County Aging Program, Logan, Utah, 1972-73; asst. prof. div. health edn. Tex. Tech U., Lubbock, 1976-77; asst. prof. dept. health care adminstrn. Idaho State U., Pocatello, 1977-78; program dir., asst. prof. health services program No. Ariz. U., Flagstaff, 1978-84; cons., dir. grants Beth Israel Hosp., Denver, 1985; assoc. prof. dept. health scis. and human ecology, coordinator grad. studies, coordinator health adminstrn. and planning Calif. State U., San Bernardino, 1985—; pres. Health Care Mgmt. Assocs., 1985—; presenter at nat. confs.; mem. faculty Loretto Heights Coll., Denver, Dept. Mgmt. U. Denver, Dept. Mgmt. and Health Adminstrn. U. Colo., Denver. Author: Dictionary of Health Services Management, rev. 2d edit., 1987, An Introduction to Epidemiology, Handbook of Planning and Program Development for Health and Social Services; editorial bd. Jour. Health Values, 1986—, Introduction to Epidemiology; contbr. numerous articles on health care adminstrn., behavioral health, gerontology and health edn. to profl. jours. Chmn., bd. dirs. Inland Counties Health System Agy.; bd. dirs. health svc. orgns. Served with U.S. Army, 1966-72, Vietnam. Mem. Assn. Advancement of Health Edn., Am. Acad. Mgmt., Assn. Univ. Programs in Health Care Adminstrn., Healthcare Forum. Republican. Mormon. Office: Calif State U Dept Health Scis and Human Ecology San Bernardino CA 92407

TIMMS, EUGENE DALE, wholesale business owner, state senator; b. Burns, Oreg., May 15, 1932; s. Morgan Oscar and Dorothy Vera (Payne) T.; m. Edna May Evans, Aug. 24, 1953; children: Tobi Eugene, Trina Maria. BA, Willamette U., 1954. Sen. State of Oreg., 1982, 84, 88, 92; pres. Harney City C. of C.; bd. trustees Assoc. Oreg. Industries; chmn. Parks & Recreation Dist. Bd.; mem. Harney City Hosp. Bd. Mem. SBA, Jaycees (state v.p.), Elk Lodge, Masonic Lodge, Al Kader Harney City Shrine Club. Presbyterian. Home: 1049 N Court Burns OR 97720

TINDAL, RALPH LAWRENCE, career officer; b. Columbus, Ohio, Jan. 10, 1940; s. Charles Howard and Dorthy (Limpert) T.; m. Sally Joan Tankalavage, June 17, 1961; children: Ralph Lawrence III, William Charles, John Patrick. BSEE, Pa. State U., 1961; MS, Naval Postgrad. Sch., Monterey, Calif., 1971. Commd. ensign USN, 1961, advanced through grades to rear adm., 1988; navigator, ops. officer USS Skipjack USN, Norfolk, Va., 1971-73, exec. officer USS Shark, 1973-76; mgr. enlisted nuclear programs Dept. Navy, Washington, 1976-78, mgr. nuclear power pers., 1986-88, dir. strategic and theater nuclear warfare, 1990-92; dir. ops./logistics U.S. Strategic Command, 1992—; comdg. officer USS Dace USN, New London, Conn., 1978-82; comdg. officer USS Henry M. Jackson USN, Bangor, Wash., 1982-86; asst. chief of staff, logistics Allied Forces So. Europe USN, Naples, Italy, 1988-90; mem. sci. adv. group Joint Strategic Targeting Planning Staff, Omaha, 1990-92. Mem. exec. com. No. Va. Cursillio Movement. Decorated Navy Commendation medal (2), Meritorious Svc. medal (3), Legion of Merit with two gold stars, Def. Superior Svc. medal. Mem. U.S. Naval Inst. Roman Catholic. Home: Quarters 3 Custer Dr Offutt A F B NE 68113 Office: Dir Ops/Logistics US Strategic Command Offutt A F B NE 68113

TINDALL, ROBERT EMMETT, lawyer, educator; b. N.Y.C., Jan. 2, 1934; s. Robert E. and Alice (McGonigle) T.; B.S. in Marine Engring., SUNY, 1955; postgrad. Georgetown U. Law Sch., 1960-61; LL.B., U. Ariz., 1963; LL.M., N.Y.U., 1967; Ph.D., City U., London, 1975; children: Robert Emmett IV, Elizabeth Mary. Mgmt. trainee Gen. Electric Co., Schenectady, N.Y., Lynn, Mass., Glen Falls, N.Y., 1955-56, 58-60; law clk. firm Haight, Gardner, Poor and Havens, N.Y.C., 1961; admitted to Ariz. bar, 1963; prin., mem. firm Robert Emmett Tindall & Assocs., Tucson, 1963—; asso. prof. mgmt. U. Ariz., Tucson, 1969—; vis. prof. Grad. Sch. of Law, Soochow U., Republic of China, 1972, Grad. Bus. Centre, London, 1974, NYU, 1991-92; dir. MBA program U. Ariz., Tucson, 1975-81; investment cons. Kingdom of Saudi Arabia, 1981—; dir. entrepreneurship program, U. Ariz., Tucson, 1984-86; lectr. USIA in Eng., India, Middle East, 1974; lectr. bus. orgn. and regulatory laws Southwestern Legal Found., Acad. Am. and Internat. Law, 1976-80. Actor community theatres of Schenectady, 1955-56, Harrisburgh, Pa., 1957-58, Tucson, 1961-71; appeared in films Rage, 1971, Showdown at OK Corral, 1971, Lost Horizon, 1972; appeared in TV programs Gunsmoke, 1972, Petrocelli, 1974. Served to lt. USN, 1956-58. Ford Found. fellow, 1965-67; Asia Found. grantee, 1972-73. Mem. Strategic Mgmt. Soc., State Bar of Ariz., Acad. Internat. Bus., Screen Actors Guild, Honourable Soc. of Middle Temple (London), Phi Delta Phi, Beta Gamma Sigma, Assoc. for Corp. Growth. Clubs: Royal Overseas League (London). Author: Multinational Enterprises, 1975; contbr. articles on legal aspects of domestic and internat. bus. to profl. jours. Home: PO Box 43153 Tucson AZ 85733-3153 Office: Coll Bus and Public Adminstrn U Ariz Dept Mgmt and Policy Tucson AZ 85721

TING, BENJAMIN SHIU-MING, engineer, consultant; b. Hong Kong, Mar. 4, 1950; came to U.S., 1968; s. Sing Wu and Grace (Fu) T.; m. Dora Choi, Dec. 25, 1972; 1 child, Douglas. BS, U. Md., 1972; MS, U. Calif., Berkeley, 1973, PhD, 1976. Mem. tech. staff Bell Labs., Holmdel, N.J., 1976-77; staff engr. IBM, East Fishkill, N.Y., 1977-78; mgr. Hughes Aircraft Co., Newport Beach, Calif., 1978-84; dir. Synertek, Inc., Santa Clara, Calif., 1984; v.p. Gould AMI, Santa Clara, 1985-87, Concurrent Logic, Inc., Sunnyvale, Calif., 1991—; chmn. Orcas Systems, Inc., Cupertino, Calif., 1987—; cons. Gould, Cupertino, 1984, 85, Burroughs, Rancho Bernardo, Calif., 1987, Cadence Design Systems, Inc., San Jose, 1989; presenter papers at profl. confs. Contbr. articles to tech. jours. Bd. dirs. Seventh-day Adventist Ch., various cities, Calif., 1982-91; mem. sch. bd. Seventh-day Adventist Ch., Los Altos, 1990-92. Mem. IEEE (CAS adminstrv. bd. 1988-90). Office: Concurrent Logic Inc 1092 E Arques Ave Sunnyvale CA 94086

TINGLEY, WALTER WATSON, computer programmer, analyst; b. Portland, Maine, July 24, 1946; s. Edward Allen Tingley and Ruth Annie (Howard) Tuttle; m. Elizabeth A. Fletcher, May 1970 (div. 1975). BS, U. Md., 1974. Programmer analyst U.S. Ry. Assn., Washington, 1974-80, Digital Equipment Corp., Maynard, Mass., 1980-81, Interactive Mgmt. Systems, Belmont, Mass., 1981; systems designer Martin Marietta Data Systems, Greenbelt, Md., 1982-84; mgr. computer ops. Genex, Rockville, Md., 1984; system mgr. Applied Rsch. Corp., Landover, Md., 1985; programmer analyst Input/Output Computer Svcs., Washington, 1986-87, Lockheed Engring. and Scis., Las Vegas, Nev., 1987-91, Computer Profls., Inc., Los Alamos, N.Mex., 1992—. Author tech. book revs., software revs. With USAF, 1964-68. Mem. IEEE Computer Soc., Assn. Computing Machinery. Home: PO Box 429 Los Alamos NM 87544

TINKER, MARK CHRISTIAN, producer, director; b. Stamford, Conn., Jan. 16, 1951; s. Grant Almerin Tinker and Ruth Prince Eyerly Fricke; m. Kristin Harmon, Apr. 16, 1988; 1 child, James. BS, Syracuse U., 1973. Producer, dir., writer TV series: The White Shadow, 1978-81, St. Elsewhere, 1981-88 (Emmy, Peabody award, Peoples Choice award); dir. TV Movie: Babe Ruth, 1991; producer, dir. TV series: Civil Wars, 1991—. Mem. Nat. Acad. TV Arts and Scis.

TINKER, PETER ALLMOND, computer science researcher; b. Richmond, Va., Nov. 8, 1956; s. Bertram Hanna and Dorris Elizabeth (Shankroff) Tinker; m. M. Kathy Igo, Sept. 9, 1989. BA in Physics, Oberlin Coll., 1978; PhD in Computer Sci., U. Utah, 1987. Sr. programmer Sci. Applications Inc., La Jolla, Calif., 1978-81; programmer Evans & Sutherland, Salt Lake City, 1983-85; mem. tech. staff Rockwell Internat. Sci. Ctr., Thousand Oaks, Calif., 1987—. Contbr. articles to profl. jours. Mem. Assn. for Computing Machinery. Office: Rockwell Internat Sci Ctr PO Box 1085 Thousand Oaks CA 91358

TINKLER, NANCY EMILY, credit union executive; b. Canal Zone, Panama, Aug. 5, 1948; came to U.S., 1967; d. Melvin F. and Judith (Vega) T. BA, Whittier Coll., 1971, postgrad. in theater arts, 1971-72; postgrad. in theater arts, Am. Ctr. for Music Theater, 1977; MBA, Whittier Coll., 1987. V.p., asst. mgr., ops. lending officer United Fin. Credit Union, Whittier, Calif., 1968-89, pres., CEO, 1989—; sec. Calif. Credit Union League Palm Tree Conf., Pomona, Calif., 1988; treas. VISTA USERS-Electronic Data Systems, Phoenix, 1988—; mem. Sec. Pacific Nat. Bank Adv. Coun., L.A., 1990—. Mem. Tri-cities Regional Occupational Banking Advisory Com., Whittier, 1991-92; v.p., bd. dirs. Rio Hondo Symphony, Whittier, Calif., 1987-92; active Rep. Ctrl. com., Whittier. Mem. Credit Union Execs. Soc., Whittier Republican Women Federated Club. Home: 12208 E Orange Dr Whittier CA 90601 Office: United Fin Credit Union 9925 Painter Ave Ste D Whittier CA 90605

TINNIN, THOMAS PECK, real estate professional; b. Albuquerque, May 15, 1948; s. Robert Priest and Frances (Ferree) T.; m. Jamie Tinnin Garrett, Dec. 12, 1986; children: Megan Ashley, Courtney Nicole, Robert Garrett. Student, U. Md., 1969-72; BA, U. N.Mex., 1973. Ins. agt. Occidental Life of Calif., Albuquerque, 1972—; gen. agt. Transamerica-Occidental Life, Albuquerque, 1978—; pres. Tinnin Investments, Albuquerque, 1978—, Tinnin Enterprises, Albuquerque, 1978—, Tinnin Real Estate & Devel., Albuquerque, 1989—; mem. N.Mex. State Bd. Fin., Santa Fe., 1985-87, 90—, sec. 1990-92; del. White House Conf. on Small Bus., Washington, 1986; bd. dirs. Albuquerque Econ. Devel., 1987-88. Bd. dirs. Albuquerque Conv. and Visitor's Bureau, 1982-84, St. Joseph's Hosp, Better Bus. Bur., 1983, Albuquerque, 1984-86, N.Mex. Jr. Livestock Found., pres. 1988, Presbyn. Heart Inst., 1989—, N.Mex. First Confs., 1992; chmn. Manzano Dist. Boy Scouts Am., 1981-82; chmn. Manzano Dist. Finance, 1983; del. White House Conf. Small Bus., 1986; pres. N.Mex. Jr. Livestock Investment Found., Albuquerque, 1988—; trustee N.Mex. Performing Arts Coun., 1989-90. Mem. NALU, N.Mex. Life Leaders Assn., Nat. Assn. Real Estate Appraisers, Albuquerqye Armed Forces Adv. Assn., Albuquerque C. of C. (bd. dirs. 1978-84, chmn. ambassador's com. 1983), N.Mex. Life Underwriters Assn., Albuquerque Country Club. Republican. Presbyterian. Home: 2312 Calle de Estavan Albuquerque NM 87104 Office: Tinnin Enterprises 20 First Plaza Ctr NW Ste 518 Albuquerque NM 87102-3352

TINTAREV, KYRIL, mathematician, educator; b. St. Petersburg, USSR, Aug. 9, 1956; came to U.S., 1985; MSc, Leningrad U., 1978; PhD, Weizman Inst., Rehovot, Israel, 1986. Asst. prof. math. U. Calif., Irvine, 1987—; sr. lecturer Uppsala Univ., Sweden, 1993—. Contbr. articles to profl. publs. Home: 23 Virgil Ct Irvine CA 92715-4054 Office: Dept Math Univ Calif Irvine Irvine CA 92717

TIPPNER, NORMAN ALBERT, writer; b. Silverton, Oreg., Nov. 15, 1943; s. Albert and Gladys Virginia (Anderson) T.; divorced; children: Derek Norman, Bryce Matthews, Rebecca Elizabeth Tippner-Hedges. BS with honors, Ariz. State U., 1966; MS in Edn., Oreg. Coll. Edn., 1972. Counselor Oreg. State Penitentiary, Salem, 1969-74; supr. Oreg. State Correctional Inst., Salem, 1974-79; parole and probation officer Marion County Community Corrections, Salem, 1979-92; facility mgr. Marion County Community Corrections Restitution Ctr., Salem, 1982-84, parole and probation officer, 1984-88; ptnr. PLAS-TECH-FAB, Salem, 1988-89; crew leader U.S. Bur. Census, Salem, 1990; instrnl. asst. Mary Eyre Elem. Sch., Salem, 1990-91; founder, chmn. bd. Emanation, Salem, 1985—; owner No Broken Hearts Co., Salem, 1991—. Author: The Development of Public Policy and the Next Step of Democracy for the 21st Century, 1992, Developing a Personal, Loving-God Theology, 1992; inventor sewing machine aid Pin-Catcher, 1978, sweet corn meal, 1975. 1st lt. U.S. Army, 1967-69, Vietnam. Mem. Alpha Kappa Delta. Home: 4937 Saddle Horn Ct SE Salem OR 97301-5764 Office: Emanation PO Box 12883 Salem OR 97309-0883

TIPPY, ALAN CLAY, banker; b. Albuquerque, Nov. 6, 1953; s. Marshall Wayne and Dorothy Nell (Matthews) T. BA with distinction, U. N.Mex., 1976; M. Internat. Mgmt., Am. Grad. Sch. Internat. Mgmt., Glendale, Ariz., 1979. Asst. mgr., diamond gemologist Feathers Jewelers, Albuquerque, 1977-78; diamond gemologist Grunewald and Adams, Scottsdale, Ariz., 1980; front office supr. Sheraton Palace Hotel, San Francisco, 1980-84; adminstrn. mgr. Bank of Am., San Francisco, 1985—. Mem. The Experiment in Internat. Living, Fed. Republic Germany, 1971. Mem. Gemological Inst. Am. (cert.), San Francisco Ballet Assn., San Francisco Opera Guild, Phi Alpha Theta. Libertarian. Presbyterian. Home: 26 Carl St San Francisco CA 94117-3918 Office: Bank of Am BASE Div 2000 Clayton Rd Concord CA 94520-2402

TIPTON, GARY LEE, services company executive; b. Salem, Oreg., July 3, 1941; s. James Rains and Dorothy Velma (Dierks) T. BS, Oreg. Coll. Edn., 1964. Credit rep. Standard Oil Co. Calif., Portland, Oreg., 1964-67; credit mgr. Uniroyal Inc., Dallas, 1967-68; ptnr., mgr. bus. Tipton Barbers, Portland, 1968—. Mem. Rep. Nat. Com., 1980—, Sen. Howard Baker's Presdl. Steering Com., 1980; apptd. dep. dir. gen. Internat. Biog. Ctr., Cambridge, Eng., 1987—; mem. U.S. Congl. adv. bd. Am. Security Coun., 1984—; mem. steering com. Coun. on Fgn. Rels. Portland Com., 1983-84, chmn. 1984-86, mem. exec. com., 1988-90, bd. dirs., 1990-91. Recipient World Culture prize Accademia Italia, 1984, Presdl. Achievement award, 1982, cert. disting. Contbn. Sunset High Sch. Dad's Club, 1972, 73. Fellow Internat. Biog. Assn. (life, Key award 1983, U.K.); mem. Sunset Mchts. Assn. (co-founder, treas. 1974-79, pres. 1982-83), Internat. Platform Assn., Smithsonian Assocs., UN Assn. (steering com. UN day 1985), World Affairs Coun. of Oreg., City Club of Portland. Office: Tipton Barbers 1085 NW Murray Rd Portland OR 97229-5501

TIPTON, HARRY BASIL, JR., state legislator, physician; b. Salida, Colo., Mar. 14, 1927; s. Harry Basil Sr. and Nina Belle (Hailey) T.; m. Dorothy Joan Alexander, Sept. 16, 1950; children: Leslie Louise, Harry Basil III, Robert Alexander. BA, U. Colo., 1950, MD, 1953. Diplomate Am. Bd. Family Practice. Postgrad. med. tng. Good Samaritan Hosp., Phoenix., Ariz., Maricoma County Hosp., Phoenix; ptnr., dir. Lander (Wyo.) Med. Clinic, 1954—; mem. Wyo. Ho. Reps., Cheyenne, 1981—, chmn. judiciary com., 1986—; cons. Indian Health Svc., Ft. Washakie, Wyo., 1968—; dir NOWCAP Family Planning, Worland, Wyo., 1975-90. Mem., pres. Fremont County Sch. Dist. # 1, Lander, 1958-78. With USMC, 1945-46, capt. USNR Med. Corps, 1950-87. Named Capt. Med. Corps. USNR, 1974. Fellow Am. Coll. Ob.-Gyn., Am. Assn. Family Practice (charter); mem. Wyo. Med. Soc. (Physician of Yr. 1989), Rotary (pres. 1960-61), Elks. Republican. Office: Lander Med Clin PC 745 Buena Vista Lander WY 82520

TIPTON, JAMES CEAMON, resort executive; b. Ardmore, Okla., Jan. 8, 1938; s. James Marcus Tipton and Georgia Muriel (Terrell) Freiberger; m. Ruth Eve Green, May 1, 1971; children by previous marriage: Martha, Marcus. BA in Bus., East Cen. U., 1961. Contr. Aetna Life & Casualty Co., various locations, 1962-72; pension regional mgr. Aetna Life & Casualty Co., Oakland, Calif., 1972-74; pension mgr. Aetna Life & Casualty Co., Salt Lake City, 1974-77, San Jose, Calif., 1977-81; owner, mgr. Valhalla Resort, Inc., Estes Park, Colo., 1981—. With U.S. Army, 1961. Mem. Estes Park Accommodations Assn. (pres., bd. dirs. 1986-87). Republican. Methodist. Home: PO Box 5103 Estes Park CO 80517-5103 Office: PO Box 1439 Estes Park CO 80517-1439

TISCHENDORF, JOHN ALLEN, applied statistician; b. Lincoln City, Ind., July 22, 1929; s. Oswald Edgar and Violet Sophia (Katterjohn) T.; m. Norma Joan Sies, Apr. 11, 1959; children: Lisa Kay, Diana Joan, John Eric. AB in Sec. Edn. cum laude, U. Evansville, 1950; MS in Math., Purdue U., 1952, PhD in Math. Statistics, 1955. Sr. asst. scientist USPHS, Boston, 1955-57; mem. tech. staff Bell Telephone Labs., Allentown, Pa., 1957-59, supr. reliability & statistics, 1959-64; supr. applied statistics Bell Telephone Labs., Holmdel, N.J., 1964-68, supr. statistical applications, 1969-78, supr. engring. data analysis, 1978-83; supr. product quality & reliability AT&T Gen. Bus. Systems Lab., Middletown, N.J., 1983-89; mgr. product & performance assurance AT&T Gen. Bus. Systems Svcs., Englewood, Colo., 1989-92; ret., 1992; adj. assoc. prof. statistics Stanford U., 1968-69, Rutgers U., 1966-67; adj. instr. Pa. State U., Wyomissing, 1961; mem. short course faculty Cornell U., George Washington U., others; mem., chmn. Elec. Device Engring. Com., N.Y.C., 1959-64. Author (with others): Semiconductor Reliability, vol. II, 1962; contbr. articles to profl. jours. Mem. planning bd. Colts Neck, N.J., 1976; mem. bd. adjustment Colts Neck, 1977-86, chmn., 1983-84. Cited among Purdue Engrs. & Mathematicians in the Space Age Purdue U., 1963. Mem. Am. Statis. Assn., Sigma Xi, Sigma Pi Sigma. Home: 7798 Oakview Pl Castle Rock CO 80104

TISCHLER, DAVID WILLIAM, music educator; b. Sacramento, Dec. 16, 1935; s. William and Myrta Holland (Smith) T. Diploma, U. Paris, 1956; BA, U. Calif., Berkeley, 1958. Tchr. Loomis (Calif.) High Sch., 1960-61, John F. Kennedy Sch., Berlin, Fed. Republic of Germany, 1962-64; pvt. studio, piano tchr. Cypress, Calif. Performer: (piano concerts) Bridges Hall of Music, Pomona Coll., 1978, UCLA, 1978. With U.S. Army, 1958-60, 61-62. Mem. Music Tchrs. Assn. of Calif., Mensa. Home: 8801 Walker St Apt 57 Cypress CA 90630-5920

TISCHLER, GARY LOWELL, psychiatrist, educator; b. N.Y.C., Oct. 30, 1935; s. Louis and Dorothy (Green) T.; m. Judith Post, Aug. 18, 1957; children: Laurie Dee, Marc David, Rachel Mara. AB, Hamilton Coll., 1957; MD, U. Pa., 1961; MS, Yale U., 1975. Intern Kings County Hosp., Bklyn., 1961-62; resident in psychiatry Yale U. Sch. Medicine, New Haven, 1962-65, asst. prof., 1967-70, assoc. prof., 1970-75, prof. psychiatry, 1975-90; prof., chmn. dept. psychiatry and biobehavioral scis., dir. neuropsychiatric inst. UCLA Sch. Medicine, 1990—; chmn. dept. psychiatry Yale U. Sch. Medicine, New Haven, 1986-87; dir. Yale Psychiatric Inst., New Haven, 1978-87; chief psychiatry Yale-New Haven Hosp., 1986-87; clin. dir. Hill-West Haven div. Conn. Mental Health Ctr., New Haven, 1968-70, dir., 1970-77; study dir. Pres.'s Commn. on Mental Health, Washington, 1977-78; cons. Arthur D. Little Inc., Boston, 1973-75, IBM Corp., Armonk, N.Y., 1986-87; mem. profl. adv. com. Am. Med. Internat., Los Angeles, 1984-86; mem. bd. mental health and behavioral medicine Inst. Medicine, Washington, 1986—, com. on clin. evaluation Inst. Medicine, 1990—. Author: Quality Assurance Thru Utilization and Peer Review, 1982; editor: Patient Care Evaluation in Mental Health, 1985, Diagnosis and Classification in Psychiatry, 1987; contbr. articles to profl. jours. Mem. Gov.'s transition staff on mental health, Conn., 1975; vice chmn. Bd. Mental Health State of Conn., 1986. Served to capt. U.S. Army, 1965-67, Vietnam. Fellow Am. Psychiat. Assn., Am. Coll. Mental Health Adminstrn., Am. Assn. for Social Psychiatry, Am. Coll. Psychiatry. Democrat. Jewish. Home: 16314 Meadowridge Rd Encino CA 91436-3607 Office: UCLA Dept Psychiatry 760 Westwood Pla Los Angeles CA 90024

TISDALE, DOUGLAS MICHAEL, lawyer; b. Detroit, May 3, 1949; s. Charles Walker and Violet Lucille (Battani) T.; m. Patricia Claire Brennan, Dec. 29, 1972; children: Douglas Michael, Jr., Sara Elizabeth, Margaret Patricia, Victoria Claire. BA in Psychology with honors, U. Mich., 1971, JD, 1975. Bar: Colo. 1975, U.S. Dist. Ct. Colo. 1975, U.S. Ct. Appeals (10th cir.) 1976, U.S. Supreme Ct. 1979. Law clk. to chief judge U.S. Dist. Ct. Colo., Denver, 1975-76; assoc. Brownstein Hyatt Farber & Madden, P.C. ; ptnr., dir. Brownstein Hyatt Farber & Strickland, P.C., 1976-92; shareholder Popham, Haik, Schnobrich & Kaufman, Ltd., 1992—. lectr. Law Seminars, Inc., 1984—, Continuing Legal Edn. in Colo., Inc., 1984—, Nat. Bus. Insts., 1985—, ABA Nat. Insts. 1988-92; Colo. Law-Related Edn. Coord., 1982-88; bd. dirs. Vail Valley Med. Ctr., 1992—. Mem. ABA (mem. litigation sect. trial evidence com. 1981—, vice chmn. real property sect. com. on enforcement of creditors rights and bankruptcy 1984-90, vice chmn. real property sect. com. on pub. edn. concerning the lawyers role 1984-87, chmn. 1987-90, chmn. real property sect. sub-com. on foreclosures in bankruptcy 1982-90), Colo. Bar Assn. (conv. com. 1979-88), Denver Bar Assn. (jud. adminstrn. com. 1978-89), Am. Judicature Soc., Assn. Trial Lawyers Am., Colo. Trial Lawyers Assn., Law Club of Denver (sec. 1984-85, v.p. 1990-91), Phi Alpha Delta, Phi Beta Kappa. Democrat. Roman Catholic. Home: 4662 S Elizabeth Ct Cherry Hills Village CO 80110-7106 Office: Popham Haik Schnobrich & Kauffman Ltd 1200-17th St # 2400 Denver CO 80202

TISE, GEORGE FRANCIS, II, air pollution inspector, retired air force officer; b. Polk County, Mo., Dec. 4, 1937; s. George Francis and Eunice Etta (Gilden) T.; m. Ofelia Ostos, Mar. 21, 1959; children: Victor, Georgetta. AA, Alan Hancock Coll., Santa Maria, Calif., 1974, AS, 1980, AAS, 1991; cert., U. Calif., Davis, 1988, U. Calif., Berkeley, 1990; BS in Bus. Mgmt., U. La Verne, 1988. Commd. 2d lt. USAF, 1956, advanced through grades to 1st sgt., 1979, positions include airman, weather observer, Rawinsonde operator, rocketeer, chief observer, ret., 1982; game warden State of Calif.; vets. rep. VA; insp. Santa Barbara Air Pollution Control Dist., Buellton, Calif., 1985—; spl. game warden, Calif. 1970-82.; vet. rep. VA, 1982-85. Author: (booklet) Asbestos, 1990. VA scholar 1983-88; County of Santa Barbara grantee, 1988, 90. Mem. Non-Commissioned Officers Assn. (chmn., life), Air Force Assn. (mem.-at-large, life), Air Force Sergeants Assn. (life), NRA (life), Air and Waste (West Coast sect.), Arroyo Grande Rifle and Pistol (pres. 1973-79), Space Shooter Rifle Club (v.p. 1972-76), VAFB Rod and Gun Club, Elks, Am. Legion. Republican. Home: 1901 Elmwood Dr Santa Maria CA 93455-2820 Office: Santa Barbara Air Pollution Control Dist 240 E Hwy Ste 207 Buellton CA 93427

TISOPULOS, LAKI T., chemical engineer; b. Istanbul, Turkey, May 26, 1959; came to U.S., 1982; s. Peter and Angela (Zahariadou) Tsitsopoulos; m. Theresa Ann Patzakis, July 18, 1987. BS, Tech. U. Istanbul, 1982; MS, U. So. Calif., 1984, PhD, 1988. Asst. air quality engr. South Coast Air Quality Mgmt. Dist., El Monte, Calif., 1988, air quality engr. I, 1988, air quality engr. II, 1988-90, program supr., 1990—. Contbr. articles to sci. jours. Mem. AICE, AWMA. Home: 2644 San Pasqual St Pasadena CA 91107

TISS, GEORGE JOHN, pediatrician, educator; b. Weiser, Idaho, Aug. 24, 1925; s. George Joseph and Mildred Gwendolyn (Barham) T.; m. Catherine Cassady, June 6, 1968; children: Randy, Carolyn, Danny, Mary, Andy. BS, U. Oreg., 1950, MD, 1954. Diplomate Am. Bd. Pediatrics. Intern U. Oreg. Hosps. and Clinics, Portland, 1954-55, resident in pediatrics, 1955-57; practice medicine specializing in pediatrics Visalia (Calif.) Med. Clinic, 1957—, chmn. bd., 1959-70; specialist Care Medico, Malaysia, 1969, Indonesia, 1976; specialist Managua, Nicaragua, 1979; med. dir. Free Good News Clinic, 1991—; cons. Keweah Delta Dist. Hosp., Visalia, Tulare (Calif.) Dist. Hosp., Tulare County Hosp.; chmn. 1st Rubella mass immunization program in U.S., Tulare, 1960; chmn. Visalia Comprehensive Health Planning Bd., 1973-74; mem. bd. consortium San Joaquin Valley, 1975—; co-chmn. Calif. Immunization adv. com., 1973-76, chmn., 1976-77, chmn. Toddler Immunization adv. com., Calif., 1983—; assoc. clin. prof. pediatrics U. Calif., San Francisco. Mem. sch. bd. Liberty Sch., 1980—. Served with USAAF, 1945-46. Fellow Am. Bd. Allergy and Immunology, 1987; recipient Lyda M. Smiley award, Calif. Assn. Sch. Nurses, 1981; named Man of Yr. Kaweah Delta Hosp., 1992. Mem. AMA, Calif. Med. Assn. Tulare County Med. Soc. (pres. 1969-70), Am. Acad. Pediatrics (bd. dirs. 1992—), West Coast Allergy Soc., L.A. Pediatric Soc., Calif. Thoracic Soc., Am. Legion, Am. Coll. Allergy, Christian Med. Soc. (missions to Mex. 1987, 90, Dominican Republic 1988, Ecuador, 1992). Office: 5400 W Hillsdale Ave Visalia CA 93291-5140

TISSER, DORON MOSHE, lawyer, educator; b. Tel Aviv, Israel, Mar. 3, 1955; came to U.S., 1958; s. Leon Tisser and Livia H. (Lorber) S.; m. Laurie J. Satnick, Nov. 18, 1978; children: Benjamin A., Jeremy N. BA in Polit. Sci., UCLA, 1978; JD cum laude, Southwestern U., 1981; LLM in Taxation, NYU, 1982. Bar: Calif. 1981, U.S. Dist. Ct. (cen. dist.) Calif. 1982, U.S. Tax Ct. 1982, U.S. Ct. Appeals (9th cir.) 1982. Pvt. practice Woodland Hills, Calif., 1987—; instr. Coll. Continuing Edn., U. So. Calif., Los Angeles, 1984-85, dept. bus. and mgmt. UCLA, 1985-88, Calif. Luth. U., Thousand Oaks, 1985-87; panel mem. pro se program U.S. Tax Ct., 1984—; lectr. to profl. orgns., 1985—. Contbg. editor (taxation) Calif. Bus. Law Reporter, 1986—; contbr. articles to legal publs. Mem. steering com. Warner Ctr. bus. and profl. div. San Fernando Valley region Jewish Fedn. Coun. Greater Los Angeles, 1987—. Mem. ABA, Calif. State Bar (cert. taxation specialist), Phi Alpha Delta. Democrat. Jewish. Office: 21031 Ventura Blvd Fl 12 Woodland Hills CA 91364-2203

TITUS, EDWARD DEPUE, psychiatrist, administrator; b. N.Y.C., May 24, 1931; s. Edward Kleinhans and Mary (Brown) Chadbourne; m. Virginia Van Den Steenhoven, Mar. 24, 1963 (div.); m. Catherine Brown, Apr. 22, 1990. BA, Occidental Coll., 1953; MS, U. Wis., 1955; MD, Stanford U., 1962; PhD, So. Calif. Psychoanalytic Inst., 1977. Mng. ptnr. Hacker Clinic Assn., Lynwood, Calif., 1968-90; chief psychiatrist parole outpatient clinic region III Calif. Dept. Corrections, L.A., 1991—; chmn. dept. psychiatry St. Francis Hosp., Lynwood, 1979-80. Fellow Am. Psychiat. Assn.; mem. Calif. Med. Assn. (del. Ho. of Dels. 1982-92), So. Calif. Psychiat. Soc. (sec. 1984-85), L.A. County Med. Assn. (dist. pres. 1980-81), L.A. County Med. Assn. Sect. on Psychiatry (pres. 1990-92). Office: Parole Outpatient Clinic 307 W 4th St Los Angeles CA 90013

TITUS, JON ALAN, lawyer; b. Milw., Oct. 6, 1955; s. Mary (Irwin) Stephenson; m. Laura Jean Newman, Sept. 5, 1982; children: Katherine, Derek. BA, U. Ariz., 1977; JD, Ariz. State U., 1980. Bar: Ariz. 1980, U.S. Dist. Ct. Ariz. 1980; cert. real estate specialist. Ptnr. Titus, Brueckner & Berry, P.C., Scottsdale, Ariz., 1980—. Mem. Ariz. Kidney Found., 1984—, pres., 1991-92. Mem. ABA, Ariz. Bar Assn. (chmn. securities regulation sect. 1986-87), Maricopa County Bar Assn., Scottsdale Bar Assn. (dir. 1993—). Office: Titus Brueckner & Berry PC 7373 N Scottsdale Rd Ste 252B Scottsdale AZ 85253-3527

TJOELKER, MICHAEL LYLE, dermatologist; b. Bellingham, Wash., Dec. 9, 1954; s. Lawrence Earl and Lyla Louise (McIvor) T.; m. Christina Jean Reagan, May 16, 1981; children: Danielle Jean, Kimberly Louise, Kelsey Christina. BS in Biology, Wash. State U., 1977; MD, St. Louis U., 1981. Diplomate Am. Bd. Dermatology. Intern SUNY Buffalo Affiliated Hosps., 1981-82, resident in dermatology, 1982-84; resident in dermatology U. Calif., San Diego, 1984-85; pvt. practice dermatology Everett, Wash., 1985—. Mem. AMA, Am. Acad. Dermatology, Assn. Am. Physicians & Surgeons Inc., Snohomish County Med. Assn., Physicians Who Care, Rotary, Alpha Omega Alpha. Office: 3327 Colby Ave Everett WA 98201

TOADVINE, JOANNE ELIZABETH, physical therapy foundation executive; b. Covington, Ky., Nov. 29, 1933; d. Ralph and Myrtle (Wasson) Bailer; children: Daniel, Michael, Patrick, Michell, Joseph. Student, St. Benedict Coll. Bus. Sch., 1948; PhD, U. for Humanistic Studies, Las Vegas, Nev., 1986. Cert. rehab. technician in functional elec. stimulation, Nev. Founder, pres. Help Them Walk Again Found., Inc., Las Vegas, 1976—. Contbr. articles to profl. jours. Mem. State of Nev. Dem. Cen. Com., Clark Clunty (Nev.) Dem. Cen. Com. Recipient Humanitarian award Chiropractic Assn. of Ariz., Channel 3 Spirit award, Humanitarian award Dr. Otto Kestler; named to Honorable Order Ky. Colonels, Mother of Yr. Clark County, 1988. Mem. Am. Acad. of Neurol. Orthopedic Surgeons (nat. coordinating council on spinal cord injury), Nat. Coordinating Coun. on Spinal Cord Injury, Las Vegas C. of C. (Women's Achievement award in health care), VFW, NAFE, The Pilot Club Internat. Office: Help Them Walk Again Found 5300 W Charleston Blvd Las Vegas NV 89102-1307

TOAL, CHRISTOPHER ANTHONY, legislative aide; b. Wichita Falls, Tex., Jan. 16, 1953; s. Robert A. and Joan L. (Preising) T. BA, U. Alaska, Anchorage, 1987; cert. in welding tech., Mesa Coll., 1975. Exec. dir. SANE/Alaska, Anchorage, 1987-92; legis. aide Alaska State Legislature, Anchorage, 1992—. Contbr. articles to local newspapers. campaign coord. Alaska Freeze '86, Anchorage, 1986; mem. steering com. Spohnholz for State House, Anchorage, 1990, Clinton for Pres., Anchorage, 1992; organizer Alaskans for Harkin, Anchorage, 1992. Recipient Community Svc. award Ecumenical Peach With Justice Coun., 1990. Democrat.

TOBIAS, CHRISTOPHER ORD, software company executive; b. Phila., Aug. 17, 1962; s. Joel Allen Tobias and Lucy Cresap (Beebe) T. Student, Reed Coll., 1980-82. Mgr. DaVinci Personal Tech., Portland, Oreg., 1982-84, Computer One, Portland, 1984-85; ptnr. PC Profls., Portland, 1985-87; devel. mgr. Somex, Lake Oswego, Oreg., 1987-91; owner Tobias Cons., 1992—; bd. dirs. Oreg. Computer Cons., Portland, 1986-87. Contbr. articles to profl. jours. Mem. Am. Seed Trade Assn. Office: Somex 2829 NW 68th Seattle WA 98117

TOBIAS, CYNTHIA LEE, data processing executive; b. Dayton, Ohio, July 6, 1945; d. Raymond Wilbur and Dorothy Virginia Tobias; divorced. BS in Lang., Georgetown U., 1967; MA in Sociology, U. Chgo., 1969, PhD, 1977; MS in Indsl. Engring., U. Ariz., 1986. Lectr. Bayero U., Kano, Nigeria, 1977-78; cons., 1979—; research assoc. U. Ariz., Tucson, 1984-87, dir. Office Med. Computing, Coll. Medicine, 1987—. Contbr. articles to profl. jours. Participant 1989 Ariz. Women's Town Hall. NIMH fellow, 1969-72, OAS fellow, 1975-76. Mem. APHA, Am. Sociol. Assn., Human Factors Soc. (treas. 1988-89). Democrat. Home: PO Box 42064 Tucson AZ 85733-2064

TOBIN, JAMES MICHAEL, lawyer; b. Santa Monica, Calif., Sept. 27, 1948; s. James Joseph and Glada Marie (Meisner) T.; m. Kathleen Marie Espy, Sept. 14, 1985. BA with honors, U. Calif., Riverside, 1970; JD, Georgetown U., 1974. Bar: Calif. 1974, Mich. 1987. From atty. to gen. atty. So. Pacific Co., San Francisco, 1975-82; v.p. regulatory affairs So. Pacific Communications Co., Washington, 1982-83; v.p., gen. counsel Lexitel Corp., Washington, 1983-85; v.p., gen. counsel, sec. ALC Communications Corp., Birmingham, Mich., 1985-87, sr. v.p., gen. counsel, sec., 1987-88; of counsel Morrison & Foerster, San Francisco, 1988-90, ptnr., 1990—. Mem. ABA, Calif. Bar Assn., Mich. Bar Assn., Fed. Communications Bar Assn. Republican. Unitarian. Home: 2739 Octavia St San Francisco CA 94123-4303 Office: Morrison & Foerster 345 California St San Francisco CA 94104-2606

TOBIN, KATHERINE COLLEEN, quality management educator; b. Norfolk, Va., Oct. 27, 1950; d. Richard Gilmore and Helen (Collins) T. BA, Skidmore Coll., 1972; MAT, U. Mass., 1974; MA, Stanford U., 1980, PhD, 1984. Instr. English dept. Holyoke (Mass.) Community Coll., 1974-75; instr. sch. humanities and arts Hampshire Coll., Amherst, Mass., 1975; dir. career planning and field experience programs Skidmore Coll., Saratoga Springs, N.Y., 1976-79; teaching, rsch. asst. Stanford U., Stanford, Calif., 1979-84;

mgr. market rsch., quality Hewlett-Packard Co., Cupertino, 1984-92; instr. U. Nev. Coll. Hotel Administrn., Las Vegas, 1993—; dancer, writer Summer Sch. Dance, Harvard U., Cambridge, Mass., 1974; adminstrv. intern Carnegie Corp. Elmira (N.Y.) Coll., 1974-75; cons. Stanford U. Devel. Office, 1981-84; bd. dirs. Isadora Duncan Internat. Inst., Euphrat Gallery, De Anza Coll., v.p., 1989-91, pres., 1991-92. Editor: Education and Urban Society-The Finance of Adult Education, 1981; contbr. articles to profl. jours. Bd. dirs. Clark County chpt. ARC, Inst. Nev. Quality and Productivity, sec., treas. Home: 9001 Robinson Ridge Las Vegas NV 89117 Office: U Nev PO Box 456021 Las Vegas NV 89154

TOBIN, KIEFER A., acoustical engineer, consultant; b. Honolulu, Oct. 24, 1937; s. Albert and Mary Helen (Jordan) T.; m. Sharlene Tobin, June 23, 1960; children: Mari, Kerri, Sean. BS, Oreg. State U., 1960; MS, Naval Postgrad. Sch., 1977. Ensign U.S. Navy, 1960, mgr. submarine silencing program, 1977-80, ret., 1980; sr. engr., scientist Tracr Inc., Austin, Tex., 1980-84; pres. W. Sound Assocs., Bremerton, Wash., 1984—; instr. Chapman Coll., Silverdale, Wash., 1982—. Mem. Acoustical Soc. Am. (pres. NW chpt. 1982-83). Lodge: Rotary. Office: West Sound Assocs 202 Pacific Ave Bremerton WA 98310-1979

TOBIN, ROBERT MANFORD, JR., karate instructor; b. Idaho Falls, Idaho, Feb. 17, 1958; s. Robert Manford and Marilyn Hilma (Harju) T. BS in Fin. and Acctg., U. Colo., 1979. Asst. instr. taekwon-do U. Colo., Boulder, 1977-85, instr. basketball team, 1985-88, head instr., 1985—; fin. mgr. Tobin Engrs. & Constructors, Longmont, Colo., 1979-80, gen. mgr., 1981-82; gen. mgr. Roofguard of Colo., Longmont, 1981-83; oximetry rschr. Biox-B.T.I.-Ohmeda Boulder, Boulder and Louisville, Colo., 1984—; instr. Sereff Taekwon-Do, Broomfield, Colo., 1984-85. Contbr. articles to various publs. Del. Colo. Dem. Com., 1980, Boulder County Dem. Com., 1984. Mem. U.S. Taekwon-Do Fedn. (test bd. 1985—, bd. dirs. 1986—), Internat. Taekwon-Do Fedn. (1st thru 5th degree black belts). Democrat. Presbyterian. Home: 1365 Brown Cir Boulder CO 80303-6724 Office: Ohmeda Boulder 1315 W Century Dr Louisville CO 80027

TOBIN, SAUL, real estate developer; b. Boston, May 25, 1928; s. David and Bertha (Tanfield) T.; m. Susan Rae Cohen, July 11, 1954; children: Eric Alan, Sarah Ann. BBA cum laude, CCNY, 1953; postgrad., U. Ariz., 1961-63. Asst. to pres. Chester Barrie Ltd., N.Y.C., 1948-59; salesman Batavia Realty and Krones Realty, Tucson, 1959-62; gen. ptnr. KTZ Builders & Developers, Tucson, 1963-68; exec. v.p. Marved Constrn., Inc., Tucson, 1968-71; exec. v.p. Tucson div. U.S. Home Corp., 1971-75, pres. Tucson div., 1975-80; sr. v.p. parent co. U.S. Home Corp., Clearwater, Fla., 1976-77; pres. The Tobin Co., Tucson, 1980-90, Tucson Land and Devel. Corp., 1990—. Life bd. dirs. Jewish Fedn. So. Ariz., Tucson, 1970—, pres. 1982-84; pres. Congrgation Anshei Israel, Tucson, 1969-70; gen. chmn. Tucson Combined Jewish Appeals, 1975; pres. Tucson Jewish Community Found., 1991—. Named Man of Yr., Jewish Fedn. So. Ariz., 1976, 84, Congregation Anshei Israel, 1983. Mem. Nat. Assn. Home Builders (nat. rep. 1975), Nat. Assn. Realtors, So. Ariz. Home Builders Assn. (life bd. dirs. 1966—, pres. 1973-74, Builder of Yr. 1973, '74, '83). Home: 6901 N Gleneagles Dr Tucson AZ 85718-1844 Office: 635 N Craycroft Rd Ste 103 Tucson AZ 85711-1451

TOBIN, TIMOTHY BRUCE, aerospace engineering company executive; b. El Paso, Tex., May 23, 1956; s. Lawrence Tobin and Mary Ann (Keesee) Tobin; m. Sandra Eileen Major, Aug. 12, 1979; children: Nicholas, Justin, Jonathan, Brittany. BS in Aerospace Engring., Ill. Inst. Tech., 1979; MSEE, U. So. Calif., 1988. Navigator, trainee 452d TFS USAF, Mather AFB, Calif., 1979-80; navigator 524th TFTS USAF, Cannon AFB, N.Mex., 1980-81; spacecraft project officer Space div. USAF, L.A. AFS, 1981-83, br. chief spacecraft engring., 1983-85; project mgr. Northrop Electronic Systems Div., Hawthorne, Calif., 1985-89; engring. mgr.. Aerojet Electronic Systems Div., Azusa, Calif., 1989—; cons. T T Cons., Carson, Calif., 1988—; asst. systems operator Genie Info. Svcs., Rockville, Md., 1991—; founder Apple II Lost Classics Project 1992—. Author, editor (manual) F-111D Systems Training Manual, 1981. Newsletter editor YMCA Indian Guides Program, Torrance, Calif., 1990-91. Capt. USAF, 1979-85. Mem. Am. Inst. Aero. & Astronautics (sr.). Office: Aerojet Electronic Systems Div 1100 W Hollyvale PO Box 296 Azusa CA 91702

TOBIN, WILLIAM JOSEPH, newspaper editor; b. Joplin, Mo., July 28, 1927; s. John J. and Lucy T. (Shoppach) T.; m. Marjorie Stuhldreher, Apr. 26, 1952; children—Michael Gerard, David Joseph, James Patrick. BJ, Butler U., 1948. Staff writer AP, Indpls., 1947-52, news feature writer, N.Y.C., 1952-54, regional membership exec., Louisville, 1954-56, corr., Juneau, Alaska, 1956-60, asst. chief of bur., Balt., 1960-61, chief of bur., Helena, Mont., 1961-63; mng. editor Anchorage Times, 1963-73, assoc. editor, 1973-85, gen. mgr., 1974-85, v.p., editor-in-chief, 1985-89, editor editorial page, 1990, asst. pub., 1991, senior editor Voice of the Times, 1991—; bd. dirs. Enstar Corp., 1982-84. Mem. devel. com. Anchorage Winter Olympics, 1984-91, bd. dirs. Anchorage organizing com., 1985-91; bd. dirs. Alaska Coun. on Econ. Edn., 1978-84, Boys Clubs Alaska, 1979-83, Anchorage Symphony Orch., 1986-87, Blue Cross Wash. and Alaska, 1987—, chmn. 1990-91; mem. adv. bd. Providence Hosp., Anchorage, 1974-91, chmn., 1980-85. Served to sgt. AUS, 1950-52. Mem. Alaska AP Mems. Assn. (pres. 1964), Anchorage C. of C. (bd. dirs. 1969-74, pres. 1972-73), Alaska World Affairs Council (pres. 1967-68), Phi Delta Theta. Clubs: Alaska Press (pres. 1968-69), Commonwealth North (Anchorage). Home: 2130 Lord Baranof Dr Anchorage AK 99517-1257 Office: Anchorage Times PO Box 100040 Anchorage AK 99510-0040

TOBKIN, VINCENT HENRY, management consultant; b. Pelican Rapids, Minn., July 4, 1951; s. Henry Edward and Kathryn Mary (Johnson) T.; m. Christine Marie Anderson, Aug. 28, 1976; children: Gregory, Carolyn, Alexander. SB, SM, MIT, 1973; MBA with high distinction, JD, Harvard U., 1977. Bar: N.Y. Elec. engr. Fairchild Semicondr. Co., Calif., 1969-70, 72, Hewlett-Packard Co., 1971, 73; fin. analyst Memorex, 1974; founder Kodon, Inc., Wellesley, Mass., 1971-72; prin. MC Kinsey & Co., N.Y.C., 1976-84; mgmt. cons. MC Kinsey & Co., San Francisco, 1979-84, ptnr., 1983-84; v.p. Wood River Capital, Calif. and N.Y., 1984—, Prospect Group, N.Y.C., 1985-88; gen. ptnr. Sierra Ventures I & II Mgmt. Co., Menlo Park, Calif. and N.Y.C., 1984-92, Sierra Ventures III & IV, Menlo Park, 1988-92; ptnr., dir. Bain & Co., San Francisco, 1992—; bd. dirs. Advanced Tech. Materials, New Milford, Conn., Bain & Co., San Francisco; mem. com. on indsl. econs. NRC, 1991; mem. Bus. Sch. adv. bd. San Francisco State U. Editor: (mag.) Tech. Engring. News, 1969-73. Hughes fellow, 1973. Mem. IEEE, Assn. Computing Machinery, Oceanic Soc., Assn. Old Crows, Lincoln's Inn (Cambridge), Hasty Pudding (Cambridge), Commonwealth Club of San Francisco, Olympic Club of San Francisco, Tau Beta Pi, Eta Kappa Nu. Republican. Roman Catholic. Home: 2644 Webster St San Francisco CA 94123-4719 Office: Bain & Co One Embarcadero Ctr Ste 3400 San Francisco CA 94111

TOBUREN, LARRY HOWARD, research physicist; b. Clay Center, Kans., July 9, 1940; s. Howard H. and Beulah (Boyd) T.; m. Lana L. Henry, June 16, 1962; children: Debra L., Tina L. BA, Emporia State U., 1962; PhD, Vanderbilt U., 1968. Research scientist Battelle Northwest Lab., Richland, Wash., 1967-80, mgr. radiol. research, radiation physics and chemistry, 1980-93; sr. program officer NRC/NAS, Washington, 1993—; affiliate asst. prof. radiological physics U. Wash., 1982-91, affiliate assoc. prof. environ. health U. Wash., 1991—; adj. lectr. environ. scis. Wash. State U., 1991—. Contbr. articles to profl. jours. Fellow Am. Phys. Soc.; mem. AAAS, Radiation Research Soc., Internat. Radiation Physics Soc. Home: 631 N Tazewell St Arlington VA 22203 Office: NAS 2101 Constitution NW Washington DC 20418

TODD, DAVID FRANZA, career military officer; b. Houston, Apr. 12, 1952; s. David William and Alice Juanita (Franza) T.; m. Janet Marie Walsh, Nov. 20, 1976; children: Mary Elizabeth, Margaret Anne. BA in Govt., U. Ariz., 1974; MA in Mgmt., Webster U., 1983; MS in Systems Mgmt., U. So. Calif., 1986. Commd. 2d lt. USAF, 1974, advanced through grades to lt. col., 1990; C-141A aircraft comdr. 53rd Mil. Airlift Squadron, Norton AFB, Calif., 1976-80; chief pilot officer to spl. airlift dir. Hdqr. Mil. Airlift Command, Scott AFB, 1980-84; asst. chief pilot and C-141B aircraft comdr. 53rd Mil. Airlift Squadron, Norton AFB, Calif., 1984-86; faculty instr. Air Command and Staff Coll., Maxwell AFB, 1987-89; chief pilot 52d Airlift Squadron, Norton AFB, 1989-90, ops. officer and C-141B instr. pilot, 1991-92; sr. rsch. fellow RAND Corp., Santa Monica, Calif., 1992—. Mem. Order of Daedalians (life), Air Force Assn. (life).

TODD, HAROLD WADE, retired air force officer, consultant; b. Chgo., Jan. 17, 1938; s. Harold Wade and Jeanne (Fayal) T.; m. Wendy Yvonne Kendrick, July 12, 1981; children by previous marriage: Hellen J. Wilson, Kenneth J., Stephen D., Joseph M., Michelle M. Adams, Mark A.; stepchildren: Jamie Y. White, James K. Mills, Timothy S. Emerson. B.S., U.S. Air Force Acad., 1959; grad., Nat. War Coll., 1975. Commd. 2d lt. U.S. Air Force, 1959, advanced through grades to maj. gen., 1982; aide to comdr. (2d Air Force (SAC)), Barksdale AFB, La., 1970-71; exec. aide to comdr.-in-chief U.S. Air Forces Europe, Germany, 1971-74; spl. asst. chief of staff USAF, 1975-76; chief Concept Devel. Div., 1976-77, chief Readiness and NATO Staff Group, Hdqrs. USAF, 1977-78; exec. asst. to chmn. Joint Chiefs Staff Washington, 1978-80; comdr. 25th region N. Am. Aerospace Def. Command McChord AFB, Wash., 1980-82; chief staff 4th Allied Tactical Air Force Heidelberg, 1982-85; commandant Air War Coll., 1985-89; vice comdr. Air U., 1985-89, ret., 1989; ind. cons. Colorado Springs, Colo., 1989—. Founder, pres. Bossier City (La.) chpt. Nat. Assn. for Children with Learning Disabilities, 1970-71. Decorated Def. D.S.M., Air Force D.S.M. (2), Legion of Merit (2), D.F.C., Air medal (8), Air Force Commendation medal. Mem. Air Force Assn., USAF Acad. Assn. Grads., Nat. War Coll. Alumni Assn. Home: 1250 Big Valley Dr Colorado Springs CO 80919-1015

TODD, JAMES GILBERT, art and humanities educator, artist; b. Mpls., Oct. 12, 1937; s. James Gilbert and Doris Elizabeth (Linn) T., Sr.; m. Julia Katarina Brozio, Aug. 3, 1963; children: Seamus, Riel, Baird. BA, Coll. Great Falls, 1964; MA, U. Mont., 1965, MFA, 1969. Art instr. Oberndorf Gymnasium, Fed. Republic Germany, 1966-68; art and humanities instr. Okaloosa-Walton Jr. Coll., Niceville, Fla., 1969-70; prof. humanities U. Mont., Missoula, 1970-80, chmn. art dept., 1980-88; instr. English, Kepler Gymnasium, Freiburg, Fed. Republic Germany, 1965-66; instr. humanities Mont. State Prison, Deer Lodge, 1973-78; coord. internat. traveling exhibit selected German and Am. artists, 1991-92. Executed murals Liberal Arts Bldg., U. Mont., 1973, Mont. Fedn. Tchrs., Helena, 1976; illustrator: Fire in the Bushes, 1978; A Radiant Map of the World, 1981; one man shows include: Univ. Ctr. Gallery, U. Mont., 1978, Keller Gallery, Salem, Oreg., 1978, Western Ga. Coll., Carrollton, 1979, Black Orchid Gallery, Butte, Mont., 1981, Amerika-Haus, Hamburg, Germany, 1984, Armstron-Prior Gallery, Phoenix, 1985, Blufton (Ohio) Coll., 1986, Image Gallery, Portland, Oreg., 1990; exhibited in group shows: Yellowstone Art Ctr., Billings, Mont., 1980, Gabrova, Bulgaria, 1981, Missoula (Mont.) Mus. Arts, 1981, LaGrange (Ga.) Coll., 1981, U. Calif., 1981, Boston Printmakers, Lincoln, Mass., 1982, San Diego Print Club, 1989, Nat. Print Invitational, Anchorage, 1990, Intergrafik 90, Berlin, 1990, VII Premio de Gravado-Maximo Ramos, Ferrol, Spain, 1990, 4th Internat. Print Exhibit, Taiwan, 1990. Contbr. cover designs, articles, reviews to profl. publs. Served with U.S. Army, 1961-63. Rsch. grantee German Acad. Exchange, Leipzig, Germany, 1991. Mem. AAUP, Am./Popular Culture Assn., Am. Soc. Wood Engravers, English Soc. Wood Engravers, Northwest Print Coun. Office: U Mont Dept Art Missoula MT 59812

TODD, JUDITH, nursing educator; b. Bangor, Maine, Nov. 30, 1936; d. Roger Eastman and Christine (Bates) Blackmer; m. Paul W. Todd, June 16, 1957; children: Kevin, Dana, Trevor, Andrea. BA, Radcliffe Coll., 1958; diploma, Mass. Gen. Hosp. Sch. Nursing, 1960; MS, Pa. State U., 1984; PhD, Temple U., 1991. RN, cert. sch. nurse, Pa. Staff nurse Children's Hosp., Oakland, Calif., 1960-62; pub. health nurse Alameda County Health Dept., Oakland, 1962-63; sch. nurse substitute State College Area Sch. Dist., 1979-86; dir. Christian edn. Presbyn. Ch., State College, Pa., 1977-84; instr. nursing Pa. State U., University Park, 1985-88; asst. prof. U. Colo. Sch. Nursing, Denver, 1988—. Officer AAUW, State College, 1980-84, PTA, State College, 1970-79; mem. LWV, State College. Scholar AAUW, 1979; recipient nursing traineeship U.S. Govt., Pa. State U., 1980-82, Outstanding Woman award AAUW, 1978. Mem. ANA, Colo. Nurses Assn., Western Soc. for Rsch. in Nursing, Western Inst. Nursing, Phi Kappa Phi, Sigma Theta Tau (membership chair 1990—). Republican. Presbyterian. Home: 2595 Vassar Dr Boulder CO 80303-5730 Office: U Colo Sch of Nursing 4200 E 9th Ave Denver CO 80262-0001

TODD, MATTHEW DEAN, design engineer; b. Bozeman, Mont., Aug. 29, 1958; s. Ernest Glen and Margaret Ellen (Hough) T.; m. Martha Jean Freese, June 13, 1981; children: Megan, Matthew Benjamin, Maura. BS in Agrl. Engring., Wash. State U., 1981. Registered profl. engr., Wash., Oreg. Sales engr. Carrier Corp., L.A., 1981-82, Syracuse, N.Y., 1981, Dallas, 1982-84; sales engr. Airefco, Inc., Tualatin, Oreg., 1984-90; engr., mgr. Entek Corp., Vancouver, Wash., 1991—. Basketball ofcl. Evergreen Ofcls., Clark County, Wash., 1984—. Recipient Group Study Exch. award Rotary Internat., 1992. Mem. ASHRAE (rsch. chair 1992), Am. Soc. Agrl. Engring. (local v.p. 1979-80), Lewis River Rotary. Republican. Presbyterian. Home: 20902 NE Lucia Falls Rd Yacolt WA 98675

TODD, PAUL WILSON, biophysicist, educator; b. Bangor, Maine, June 15, 1936; s. Albert Clayton and Sylvia May (Preble) T.; m. Judith Stow Blackmer, June 16, 1957; children: Kevin, Dana, Trevor, Andrea. BA, Bowdoin Coll., Brunswick, Maine, 1959; BS, Mass. Inst. Tech., 1959; MS, U. Rochester, 1960; PhD, U. Calif., Berkeley, 1964. Lectr. U. Calif., Berkeley, 1964-66; asst. prof. Pa. State U., University Park, 1966-72; assoc. prof. Pa. State U., 1972-77, chmn. genetics program, 1974-79, prof., 1977-86; dir. Bioprocessing & Pharm. Rsch. Ctr., Phila., 1984-87; physicist Nat. Inst. Stds. and Tech., Boulder, Colo., 1988-91; adj. prof. U. Colo., Boulder, 1990-91, rsch. prof., 1991—. Co-editor: Space Radiation Biology, 1973, Frontiers in Bioprocessing, 1989, Gravity and the Cell, 1991, Frontiers in Bioprocessing II, 1991, Cell Separation Science and Technology, 1990; inventor in field; contbr. articles to profl. jours. Radiol. Physics fellow AEC, 1959, Eleanor Roosevelt fellow Am. Cancer Soc., 1967, Fogarty Internat. fellow NIH, Moscow, 1979, Yamagiwa-Yoshida fellow Internat. Union Against Cancer, Sweden, 1979, R & D 100 award, 1990. Mem. AAAS, AIAA, AICE, Am. Chem. Soc., Electrophoresis Soc. (assoc. editor 1986-92), Cell Kinetics Soc., Radiation Rsch. Soc. (assoc. editor 1975-79), Soc. for Analytical Cytology (assoc. editor 1979-88), Am. Soc. for Gravational and Space Biology (coun. 1988-91), Tissue Culture Assn., Am. Soc. Engring. Edn., Com. on Space Rsch. Home: 2595 Vassar Dr Boulder CO 80303-5730 Office: U Colo Dept Chem Engring Campus Box 424 Boulder CO 80309-0424

TODEA, ROCKLING, organizational development consultant; b. Naschitti, N.Mex., Aug. 9, 1942; s. John Jr. and Norma (Bell) T.; m. Nancy Dine Yazzie, Nov. 13, 1962; children: Rwanda, Rachelle, Nathaniel. BA, Ft. Lewis Coll., Durango, Colo., 1986; MBA, U. Denver, 1990. Acct. Navajo Agrl. Products Industry, Farmington, N.Mex., 1975-76; plant mgr. The Navajo Tribe, Window Rock, Ariz., 1976-77; bus. mgr. acctg. The Coll. of Ganado, Ariz., 1978-79; dir. fin./adminstrn. Alamo Navajo Sch. Bd., Inc., Magdalena, N.Mex., 1979-84; policy analyst The Navajo Nation, Window Rock, 1986-87; exec. dir. Denver Indian Health & Family Svc., 1989-91; systems analyst Regional Bus. Devel., Crownpoint, N.Mex., 1991-92; bus. cons. Fundamental Mgmt. Group, Denver, 1985-87; mgmt. cons. Mgmt. Exponent, Denver, 1988—; mem. Johnson-O'Malley Adv., Ignacio, Colo., 1985-86, Denver Indian Health Bd., 1987-89. Author: Managing Volunteers, 1991. Pollster MacDonald for Chairman, Window Rock, 1986; activist Govt. for Navajos, Window Rock, 1991; founder Spring Intertribal Thanksgiving: Celebration to Advance Indian Art, Crownpoint, 1992.

TODESCHI, JOSEPH L., sales executive; b. Murray, Utah, June 17, 1935; s. Andrew and Ottilia (Valentine) T.; m. Carol Mary DeYoung, Nov. 7, 1957; children: Kevin, Kurt, Heidi, Kellie. AS, Weber Coll., 1957; BS, U. Utah, 1959. With territory sales dept. McKesson & Robbins, Salt Lake City, 1957-58; with chem. sales dept. Wasatch Chems., Salt Lake City, 1959-60; with territory sales dept. Wyeth Labs, 1960-64; with territory sales dept. Wallace Pharms., Cranbury, N.J., 1964-72, dist. mgr., 1972-73, regional mgr., 1973-86; dist. mgr. Boehringer Ingelheim, Ridgefield, Conn., 1986-87, dir. cardiovascular spltys., 1986-87, regional dir., 1987—. With U.S. Army, 1954-56. Roman Catholic. Office: 25909 Pala # 290 Mission Viejo CA 92691

TODSEN, THOMAS KAMP, botanist; b. Pittsfield, Mass., Oct. 21, 1918; s. Lorenz and Ellen Paula (Christensen) T.; m. Margaret Cumming Dorsey, Aug. 4, 1939 (dec. 1988); children: Thomas A., William L. BS, U. Fla., 1939, MS, 1942, PhD, 1950. Instr. N.Mex. Coll. of A & MA, State College, 1950-51; chief chemist White Sands Proving Ground, N.Mex., 1951-53; chief warheads and spl. projects White Sands Proving Ground, 1953-57; chief sci. adv. office White Sands Missile Range, 1957-59, chief surf-to-surf project, 1959-65, dir. test ops., 1965-68, chief land combat project, 1968-72, tech. dir. Army test and evaluation, 1972-78; asst. prof. botany N.Mex. State U., Las Cruces, 1978—; chmn. Joint AEC-DOD subcom., Washington, 1953-62; cons. in field. Contbr. articles to profl. jours., chpts. to books; co-editor: Rare and Endemic Plants of New Mexico; asst. editor the Heliograph Jour.; author: New Mexico Territorial Postmarks; editor La Posta jour., 1974-76. Elder First Presbyn. Ch., Las Cruces, 1960—; dir. Rio Grande Hist. Collections, Inc., Las Cruces, 1975-85; wildflower chmn. N.Mex. Garden Clubs, Inc., Albuquerque, 1987-91. Tenn. Corp. rsch. fellow, Atlanta, 1949. Fellow Ariz.-Nev. Acad. Scis.; mem. Am. Chem. Soc. (emeritus), Am. Soc. Mag. Photographers (emeritus), AAAS, Am. Soc. Plant Taxonomists, Assn. for Tropical Biology, Sigma Xi.

TOEDT, ELIZABETH MARY, naval officer; b. Duluth, Minn., Oct. 2, 1957; d. Dell Charles and Gloria Barbara (Miletich) T.; m. Robert Howard Rudolph Jr., Dec. 31, 1986; 1 child, Jordan Robert Toedt Rudolph. BA in Biology, St. Mary's U., 1977. Commd. ensign USN, 1978, advanced through grades to comdr., naval aviator, 1980—, carrier pilot, 1981—; AME/PR divsn. officer to asst. adminstrn. officer Fleet Logistics Support Squadron 30, 1980-83; officer in charge NAF Misawa, Seoul, Republic of Korea, 1983-85; tng. schedules officer to maintenance tng. officer Tng. Squadron 4, NAS, Pensacola, Fla., 1985-87; asst. ops. officer, asst. adminstrn. officer, pers. officer Attack Squadron 128, Whidbey Island, Wash., 1987-91; VR-61 adminstrn. officer, ops. officer USN, 1991—, ops. officer, RSTARS officer, legal officer, 1991—; guest speaker Profl. Businesswomen's Assn., Oak Harbor, Wash., 1991, Soroptimists, Oak Harbor, 1990-91. Contbr. articles to newspapers. Decorated Navy Commendation medal, Navy Achievement medal. Mem. Tailhook Assn. (life, nat. com. chmn.), Naval Res. Assn., Order of Daedalians (life).

TOELLE, RICHARD ALAN, operations management educator; b. Tokyo, Nov. 3, 1949; s. George A. and Margaret A. (Young) T.; m. Lois Mae Ihle, Sept. 30, 1978 (div.); children: Erica Marie, Lisa Ann. BA in Psychology, U. Ariz., 1971; MBA, U. Okla., 1981, PhD, 1988; postgrad., U. Hawaii, 1980-81. Br. mgr. Household Fin. Corp., Tucson, San Fernando, 1975-78; grad. asst. U. Okla., Norman, 1981-83, instr., 1984-86; asst. prof. ops. mgmt. U. Idaho, Moscow, 1986—. Book reviewer Irwin Pub., West Pub., Dellen Pub.; contbr. articles to profl. jours. Pres. Concerned Citizens for Edn., Moscow, 1989; campaign chmn. Moscow Sch. Dist. Bldg. Bond Levy, 1989. 1st lt. U.S. Army, 1971-75. Recipient fellowships Richard D. Irwin Found., Homewood, Ill., 1985, Robert Schumann Found., U. Okla., 1982. Mem. Am. Prodn. and Inventory Control Soc., Decision Scis. Inst. Home: 214 N Home St Moscow ID 83843-2139 Office: U Idaho Coll Bus and Econs Moscow ID 83843

TOEPPE, WILLIAM JOSEPH, JR, retired aerospace engineer; b. Buffton, Ohio, Feb. 27, 1931; s. William Joseph Sr. and Ruth May (Hipple) T. BSEE, Rose-Hulman Inst. Tech., Terre Haute, Ind., 1953. Engr. Electronics divsn. Ralph M. Parsons Co., Pasadena, Calif., 1953-55; pvt. practice cons. Orange, Calif., 1961-62; engring. supr. Lockheed Electronics Co., City of Commerce, Calif., 1962-64; staff engr. Interstate Electronics Corp., Anaheim, Calif., 1957-61; engring. supr. Interstate Electronics Corp., Anaheim, 1964-89, ret., 1989. Author: Finding Your German Village, 1990, Gazetteers and Maps of France for Genealogical Research, 1990. Pres. Golden Circle Home Owners' Assn., Orange, 1989-93. With U.S. Army, 1953-57. Mem. Ohio Geneal. Soc. (life), Geneal. Soc. Pa., So. Calif. Geneal. Soc. Home: 700 E Taft Ave Unit 19 Orange CA 92665-4400

TOFTNESS, CECIL GILLMAN, lawyer, consultant; b. Glasgow, Mont., Sept. 13, 1920; s. Anton Bernt and Nettie (Pedersen) T.; m. Chloe Catherine Vincent, Sept. 8, 1951. AA, San Diego Jr. Coll., 1943; student Purdue U., Northwestern U.; BS, UCLA, 1947; JD, Southwestern U., 1953. Bar: Calif. 1954, U.S. Dist. Ct. (so. dist.) Calif. 1954, U.S. Tax Ct. 1974, U.S. Supreme Ct. 1979. Sole practice, Palos Verdes Estates, Calif., 1954—; dir., pres., chmn. bd. Fisherman & Mchts. Bank, San Pedro, Calif., 1963-67; dir., v.p. Palos Verdes Estates Bd. Realtors, 1964-65. Chmn. Capital Campaign Fund, Richstone Charity, Hawthorne, Calif., 1983. Served to lt. (j.g.) USN, 1938-46, ETO, PTO. Decorated Silver Star; named Man of Yr., Glasgow, 1984. Mem. South Bay Bar Assn., Southwestern Law Sch. Alumni Assn. (class rep. 1980—), Internat. Physicians for the Prevention of Nuclear War (del. 7th World Congress, 1987), Themis Soc.-Southwestern Law Sch., Schumacher Founder's Circle-Southwestern Law Sch. (charter). Democrat. Lutheran. Lodges: Kiwanis (sec.-treas. 1955-83, v.p., pres., bd. dirs.), Masons, K.T. Participant Soc. Expedition thur the N.W. Passage. Home: 2229 Via Acalones Palos Verdes Peninsula CA 90274-1646 Office: 2516 Via Tejon Palos Verdes Peninsula CA 90274-6802

TOGERSON, JOHN DENNIS, computer software company executive; b. Newcastle, England, July 2, 1939; arrived in Can., 1949; s. John Marius and Margaret (McLaughlin) T.; m. Donna Elizabeth Jones, Oct. 3, 1964 (div. 1972); children: Denise, Brenda, Judson; m. Patricia Willis, May 5, 1984. BME, GM Inst., Flint, Mich., 1961; MBA, York U., Toronto, Ont., 1971. Sr. prodn. engr. GM of Can., Oshawa, Ont., 1961-69; with sales, investment banking Cochran Murray, Toronto, 1969-72; pres. Unitec, Inc., Denver, 1972-79, All Seasons Properties, Denver, 1979-81, Resort Computer Corp., Denver, 1981—; mng. dir. VCC London (subs. of Resort Computer Corp.), 1992; bd. dirs. VCC London (sub. of 1st Nat. Bank U.K.), London, 1989—, mng. dir., 1992; pres., bd. dirs. Resort Mgmt. Corp., Dillon, Colo., 1980-81. Office: Resort Computer Corp 2801 Youngfield St Ste 300 Golden CO 80401-2266

TOGLIA, THOMAS VINCENT, automotive technology educator; b. Tucson, July 29, 1954; s. Gabriel Anthony and June Isabel (Rahm) T. AS in Automotive Tech., Pima C.C., Tucson, 1974; BS in Vocat. Indsl. Edn. magna cum laude, No. Ariz. U., 1976; MEdin Ednl. Adminstrn., Ea. N.Mex. U., 1993. Cert. master automobile technician. Automotive technician Ramsowers Garage, Tucson, 1973-75; automotive instr. Amphitheater High Sch., Tucson, 1977-84; prof. automotive tech. N.Mex. Jr. Coll., Hobbs, 1984—; instr. Pima C.C., 1976-84. Named one of Outstanding Young Men Am., U.S. Jaycees, 1982, Instr. of Yr. Gen. Motors Corp., 1990. Mem. Am. Vocat. Assn., Vocat. Indsl. Clubs Am., N.Am. Coun. Automotive Tchrs., N.Mex. Vocat. Assn., N.Mex. Vocat. Indsl. Clubs Am. (bd. dirs. 1988—), Epsilon Pi Tau.

TOGO, YUKIYASU, automotive executive; b. Yokohama, Kanagawa, Japan, Nov. 13, 1924; came to U.S., 1983; s. Kinji Togo and Nobuko Watanabe; m. Misako Mineta, Apr. 2, 1948; children: Yukinori, Yumi. Gen. mgr. Toyota Motor Sales, Tokyo, Japan, 1976-78, assoc. dir., 78-79, dir., 1979-80; pres. Toyota Can. Inc., Ontario, Can., 1980-82; dir. Toyota Motor Corp., Aichi, Japan, 1982, mng. dir., 1982-83; pres. Can. Auto Parts Toyota Inc., B.C., Can., 1983—; pres., chief exec. officer Toyota Motor Sales U.S.A. Inc., Torrance, Calif., 1983—; pres. Toyota Motor Credit Corp., Torrance, Calif., 1989—, Toyota Motor Ins. Svcs., Torrance, Calif., 1989—, Toyota Aviation USA Inc., Torrance, Calif., 1989—. Bd. dirs. Los Angeles World Affairs Coun., 1989. Office: Toyota Motor Sales USA Inc Ste 2991 19001 S Western AVe Torrance CA 90501-1106*

TOGUCHI, CHARLES TERUO, state agency superintendent; b. Kahaluu, Oahu, Hawaii, Nov. 13, 1941; m. Elaine A. Toguchi; children: Jodi, Ryan. BE, Brigham Young U., 1964; postgrad., UCLA, 1967; M in Ednl. Adminstrn., Calif. State U., Long Beach, 1969. Cert. profl. tchr.; licensed real estate broker. Math. tchr. Ewa Sch., 1965, Kailua Intermediate, 1965-66, Muir Jr. High Sch., L.A., 1966-68, adult edn. Farrington High Sch., 1968, Kailua High Sch., 1968-69; adminstrv. asst., staff engr. Pacific Concrete and Rock Co. Ltd., 1969-72; political action and legis. dir. Hawaii State Tchrs. Assn., 1972-76; mem. Hawaii Ho. Reps., 1977-82, Hawaii Senate, 1983-87; supt. Hawaii State Dept. Edn., 1987—; chair edn. com. Ho. Reps., Hawaii, 1981, 82, ocean and marine resources com., 1977-80; vice-chair edn. com. Hawaii State Senate, 1984, transp. com., 1985, 86, chair edn. com.,

1985, 86, agriculture com., 1983; prodn. supr. Jacqueline's of Hawaii, 1972; safety officer Pan-Pacific Corp., 1982; commr. Edn. Commn. States; bd. dirs. Northern Koolau Health Edn. Ctr.; guest lectr., workshop leader, forum participant numerous ednl. orgns. Active Hawaii Edn. Roundtable, Kahaluu Meth. Ch., Ahuimanu Homeowners Assn. With US Army Nat. Guard Res. Mem. Lions Club. Home: 47-640 Hui Ulili St Kaneohe HI 96744 Office: Hawaii Dept Edn PO Box 2360 Honolulu HI 96804-2360

TOKAR, DANIEL, mining company executive; b. Detroit, Nov. 27, 1937; s. Alex and Olga (Leme) T.; m. Marian Carol Wilson, Dec. 10, 1970 (div. 1981); 1 child, Jonathan Wilson; m. Taffy Jill Stubbs, Sept. 19, 1986. BS in Engring., Boston U., 1962, MBA, 1964. With Ford Motor Co., Dearborn, Mich., 1964-67; fin. analyst Sperry Corp., N.Y.C., 1967-68; mgr. acctg. Am. Motors Corp., Southfield, Mich., 1969-74; controller Gen. Vehicle, Inc., Livonia, Mich., 1974-75; pres. Motor City Container, Romulus, Mich., 1975-80; dir. fin. planning Mountain States Mineral Enterprises, Inc., Tucson, 1981-89, corp. sec., 1990-92; CFO Western States Engring. and Constrn. Inc., Tucson, 1992—; chmn. Addax Corp., Livonia, 1976-79; freelance cons., 1979—; bd. dirs. Zytex Corp., Tucson, 1980-91; teaching fellow Boston U., 1962-64; assoc. faculty Henry Ford Coll., Dearborn, 1969-79; adj. prof. U. Phoenix, 1980-82, Pima Coll., Tucson, 1988-91. Trustee local ch., Detroit, 1971-79; chmn. fin. com. local ch., Tucson, 1985-87. Mem. Engring. Soc. Detroit, Phi Mu Delta (nat. sec. 1971-74), Delta Phi (nat. treas. 1974). Democrat. Unitarian. Home: 1830 N Norton Ave Tucson AZ 85719-3827 Office: Western States Engring and Constrn Inc 3480 E Britannia Dr Tucson AZ 85706

TOKAR, LOUIS JOHN, company executive; b. Sioux City, Iowa, July 21, 1923; s. John N. and Mary (Homa) T.; m. Mary Jo Trafton, Aug. 30, 1947; children: Robert Louis, Mary Lou. BS, Morningside Coll., 1952. Mgr. Tower Constrn., Inc., Sioux City, 1948-56; asst. to pres. Tower Communications, Inc., Sioux City, 1957-63; pres. Advance Industries, Inc., Sioux City, 1964-84, dir., 1985-88; cons. in field Scottsdale, Ariz., 1988—. With USN, 1942-46. Home: 9160 N 81 St Scottsdale AZ 85258

TOKHEIM, ROBERT EDWARD, physicist; b. Eastport, Maine, Apr. 25, 1936; s. Edward George and Ruth Lillian (Koenig) T.; m. Diane Alice Green, July 1, 1962; children: Shirley Diane, William Robert, David Eric, Heidi Jean. BS, Calif. Inst. Tech., 1958, MS, 1959; Degree of Engr., Stanford U., 1962, PhD, 1965. Rsch. asst. Hansen Labs Physics Stanford (Calif.) U., 1960-65; microwave engr. Watkins-Johnson Co., Palo Alto, Calif., 1965-73, staff scientist, head ferrimagnetic R&D dept., 1966-69; physicist SRI Internat., Menlo Park, Calif., 1973—. Co-author: Tutorial Handbook on X-ray Effects on Materials and Structures, 1992; contbr. articles to Jour. Applied Physics, IEEE Transactions on Magnetics, conf. proceedings on shock compressions. Mem. IEEE (sr. mem.), Am. Phys. Soc., Toastmasters Internat., Tau Beta Pi, Sigma Xi. Home: 5 Trinity Ct Menlo Park CA 94025 Office: SRI International 333 Ravenswood Ave Menlo Park CA 94025

TOKMAKOFF, GEORGE, history educator; b. Tientsin, Hopei, China, July 9, 1928; s. Vasili and Claudia (Kalinin) T.; m. Erika Berzewski, Aug. 30, 1959 (dec. 1988); children: Andrei, Larisa. BA, U. Wash., 1952, MA, 1957; PhD, U. London, 1963. Instr. U. Md., London, 1959-61; asst. prof. history U. Wis., Milw., 1962-63; prof. history Calif. State U., Sacramento, 1963-93, prof. emeritus of History, 1993—. Author: Stolypin and the Third Duma, 1981; contbr. articles to profl. jours. With USAF, 1951-54. Named Faculty of the Yr., Calif. State U., Sacramento, 1964; NEH grantee, 1971; recipient Outstanding Faculty award, Phi Kappa Phi, 1975. Mem. Am. Assn. for Advancement of Slavic Studies. Democrat. Orthodox Ch. Home: 4837 Foster Way Carmichael CA 95608-2912

TOKOFSKY, JERRY HERBERT, film producer; b. N.Y.C., Apr. 14, 1936; s. Julius H. and Rose (Trager) T.; m. Myrna Weinstein, Feb. 21, 1956 (div.); children: David, Peter; m. Fiammetta Bettuzzi, 1970 (div.); 1 child, Tatianna; m. Karen Oliver, Oct. 4, 1981. BS in Journalism, NYU, 1957, LLD, 1959. Talent agt. William Morris Agy., N.Y.C., 1953-59; v.p. William Morris Agy., L.A., 1959-64; exec. v.p. Columbia Pictures, L.A., 1964-69; v.p. Paramount Pictures, London, 1970, MGM, London, 1971; pres. Jerry Tokofsky Prodns., L.A., 1972-82; exec. v.p. Zupnik Enterprises, L.A., 1982-92; pres. Jerry Tokofsky Entertainment, Encino, Calif., 1992—. Prodr. films Where's Poppa, 1971, Born To Win, 1972, Dreamscape, 1985, Fear City, 1986, Wildfire, 1988, Glengarry Glen Ross, 1992, Indubious Battle, 1992. With U.S. Army, 1959, res. 1959-63. Named Man of Yr. B'nai Brith, 1981; recipient L.A. Resolution City of L.A., 1981. Mem. Variety Club Internat.

TOLENTINO, CASIMIRO URBANO, lawyer; b. Manila, May 18, 1949; came to U.S., 1959; s. Lucio Rubio and Florence (Jose) T.; m. Jennifer Masculino, June 5, 1982; 2 children: Casimiro Masculino, Cristina Cecelia Masculino. BA in Zoology, UCLA, 1972, JD, 1975. Bar: Calif. 1976. Gen. counsel civil rights div. HEW, Washington, 1975-76; regional atty. Agrl. Labor Relations Bd., Fresno, Calif., 1976-78; regional dir. Sacramento and San Diego, 1978-81; regional atty. Pub. Employment Relations Bd., Los Angeles, 1981; counsel, west div. Writers Guild Am., Los Angeles, 1982-84; dir. legal affairs Embassy TV, Los Angeles, 1984-86; sole practice Los Angeles, 1986—; mediator Ctr. Dispute Resolution, Santa Monica, Calif., 1986—; asst. chief counsel Dept. of Fair Employment and Housing, State of Calif., 1986-92, adminstrv. law judge dept. social svcs., 1992—. Editor: Letters in Exile, 1976; contbr. articles and revs. to Amerasia Jour. Chmn., adv. bd. UCLA Asian Am. Studies Ctr., 1983—; chmn. bd. Asian Pacific Legal Ctr., L.A., 1983—; pres. bd. civil svc. commrs., City of L.A., 1984-85, 1990—; mem. United Way (bd. dirs. met. region); bd. dirs. Rebuild L.A., 1992—. Mem. State Bar Calif. (exec. com. labor law sect. 1985—), Los Angeles County Bar Assn., Minority Bar Assn. (sec. 1984-85), Philippine Lawyers of So. Calif. (pres. 1984—, Award of Merit 1982). Democrat. Roman Catholic.

TOLIVER, HAROLD EARL, language professional, English; b. McMinnville, Oreg., Feb. 16, 1932; s. Marion E. and Mable A. (Mallery) T.; m. Mary Bennette, June 20, 1954; children: Tricia, Brooks. BA, U. Oreg., 1954; MA, Johns Hopkins U., 1958; PhD, U. Wash., 1961. Asst. prof. Ohio State U., Columbus, 1961-64, UCLA, 1965-66; asst. prof., prof. U. Calif., Irvine, 1966—. Author: Marvell's Ironic Vision, 1965, Pastoral Forms and Attitudes, 1971, Animate Illusions, 1974, Lyric Provinces, 1985, The Past That Poets Make, 1981, Transported Styles, 1989, Herbert's Christian Narrative, 1993. Pvt. first class, U.S. Army, 1954-56. Recipient Guggenheim fellowship, 1964, 76. Home: 1405 Skyline Dr Laguna Beach CA 92651 Office: U of Calif Dept of English Irvine CA 92717

TOLIVER, LEE, mechanical engineer; b. Wildhorse, Okla., Oct. 3, 1921; s. Clinton Leslie and Mary (O'Neall) T.; m. Barbara Anne O'Reilly, Jan. 24, 1942; children: Margaret Anne, Michael Edward. BSME, U. Okla., 1942. Registered profl. engr., Ohio. Engr. Douglas Aircraft Co., Santa Monica, Calif., 1942, Oklahoma City, 1942-44; engr. Los Alamos (N.Mex.) Sci. Lab., 1946; instr. mech. engring. Ohio State U., Columbus, 1946-47; engr. Sandia Nat. Labs., Albuquerque, 1947-82; instr. computer sci. and math. U. N.Mex., Valencia County, 1982-84; number theory researcher Belen, N.Mex., 1982—. Co-author: (computer manuals with G. Carli, A.F. Schkade, L. Toliver) Experiences with an Intelligent Remote Batch Terminal, 1972, (with C.R. Borgman, T.I. Ristine) Transmitting Data from the PDP-10 to Precision Graphics, 1973, (with C.R. Borgman, T.I. Ristine) Data Transmission-PDP-10/Sykes/Precision Graphics, 1975. With Manhattan Project (Atomic Bomb) U.S. Army, 1944-46. Mem. Math. Assn. Am., Am. Math. Soc. Home: 206 Howell St Belen NM 87002-6225

TOLL, CHARLES HULBERT, construction executive; b. Los Angeles, June 30, 1931; s. Charles Hulbert Sr. and Kathryn (Burrows) T.; m. Barbara Jean Tressler, Mar. 5, 1955; 1 child, Wendy Warren Toll Greene. Grad. high sch., North Hollywood, Calif. Various positions The Flinkote Co., Blue Diamond, Nev., 1955-67, works mgr., 1967-75; v.p. The Grail Co., Santa Ana, Calif., 1975-78, H.G. Toll Co., El Segundo, Calif., 1978-80; pres. H.G. Toll Co., Scottsdale, Ariz., 1980-89, Toll Constrn., Scottsdale, Ariz., 1989—. Republican. Episcopalian. Office: Toll Constrn Co 7762 E Gray Rd Scottsdale AZ 85260-6957

TOLL, ERIC JAY, corporate executive; b. Phila., Apr. 15, 1951; s. Jay H. and Celia-Ann (Teitelman) T.; m. Linda Joan Holland, Jan. 13, 1973; children: Erica Lynne, Michael Edward. BA, So. Ill. U., 1971, Sonoma State U., 1980. Registered environ. assessor, Calif. Local sales mgr. WQLR-FM, Kalamazoo, Mich., 1972-74; gen. sales mgr. KBDF-AM, Eugene, Oreg., 1974-76; account exec. Advt. Svcs., Santa Rosa, Calif., 1976-79; sr. policy planner County of Calaveras, San Andreas, Calif., 1980-87; dep. dir. community devel. Consol. Municipality and State Capital of Carson City, Nev., 1987-89; prin. Eric Jay Toll AICP, Inc., Carson City, Nev., 1989—; mem. Nev. State Population Steering Com., 1988-90; alternate governing bd.Tahoe Regional Planning Agy. 1989-93. Sec., Ebbetts Pass Fire Fighters Assn., Arnold, Calif., 1984-86; pres. Meadowmont Property Owners Assn., Arnold, 1985-87. Mem. Am. Planning Assn. (exec. bd. Nev. chpt. 1988—), Am. Inst. Cert. Planners (cert.), Santa Rosa Jaycees (bd. dirs. 1976-80). Democrat. Home: 2401 Michael Dr Carson City NV 89703-1512

TOLLENAERE, LAWRENCE ROBERT, industrial products company executive; b. Berwyn, Ill., Nov. 19, 1922; s. Cyrille and Modesta (Van Damme) T.; m. Mary Elizabeth Hansen, Aug. 14, 1948; children: Elizabeth, Homer, Stephanie, Caswell, Mary Jennifer. BS in Engring., Iowa State U., 1944, MS in Engring., 1949; MBA, U. So. Calif., 1969; LLD (hon.), Claremont Grad. Sch., 1977. Specification engr. Aluminum Co. Am., Vernon, Calif., 1946-47; asst. prof. indsl. engring. Iowa State U., Ames, 1947-50; sales rep. Am. Pipe and Constrn. Co. (name changed to AMERON 1970), South Gate, Calif., 1950-53; spl. rep. Am. Pipe and Constrn. Co. (name changed to AMERON 1970), S.Am., 1952-54; 2d v.p., div. mgr. Colombian div. Am. Pipe and Constrn. Co. (name changed to AMERON 1970), Bogota, S.Am., 1955-57; div. v.p., mgr. Am. Pipe and Constrn. Co. (name changed to AMERON 1970), Calif., 1957-63; v.p. concrete pipe ops. Am. Pipe and Constrn. Co. (name changed to AMERON 1970), Monterey Park, Calif., 1963-65, pres. corp. hdqrs., 1965-67; pres., chief exec. officer Ameron Inc., Monterrey Park, Calif., 1967-89; chmn. bd., CEO, pres. Ameron Inc., Pasadena, 1989-93, chmn. bd., 1993—; bd. dirs. Avery Dennison, Pasadena, Calif., Newhall Land and Farming Co., Valencia, Calif., Pacific Mut. Life Ins. Co., Newport Beach, Calif., The Parsons Corp., Pasadena, Gifford-Hill-American, Dallas, Tamco, Etiwanda. Trustee The Huntington Library, Art Gallery and Bot. Gardens; emeritus mem. bd. fellows Claremont U. Ctr.; bd. gov.'s Iowa State U. Found. Mem. Merchants and Mfrs. Assn. (past chmn. bd. dirs.), Nat. Assn. Mfrs., Soc. Advancement Mgmt., AMA Pres. Assn., Newcomen Soc. N.Am., Calif. C. of C. (bd. dirs. 1977-92), Alpha Tau Omega. Republican. Clubs: California (bd. dirs.), Jonathan, Pauma Valley Country, San Gabriel Country, Bohemian, San Francisco, Commanderie de Bordeaux, Los Angeles, Los Angeles Confrerie des Chevaliers du Tastevin, Twilight, Lincoln, Beavers (past. pres., hon. dir.), Valley of Montecito (Santa Barbara, Calif.). Home: 1400 Milan Ave South Pasadena CA 91030-3930 Office: Ameron Inc 245 S Los Robles Ave Pasadena CA 91101-2894

TOLLEY, JOHN STEWART, state transportation administrator, urban planner; b. Greenville, Miss., Feb. 3, 1953; s. Frank Edward and Rachel Lee (Roberts) T. BA, U. Alaska, 1977; M in Urban Planning, Princeton U., 1979. Research asst. Princeton (N.J.) U., 1978-79; planner transp. Alaska Dept. Transp., Anchorage, 1979-81, mgr. statewide planning, 1982-84, chief of planning, 1985—. Mem. AIA, Am. Planning Assn., Transp. Research Bd. of Nat. Acad. Scis. (mem. various coms.). Home: 1200 I St Apt 416 Anchorage AK 99501-4372

TOLLIVER, JAMES DAVID, JR., aerospace engineer; b. Long Branch, N.J., Dec. 27, 1938; s. James David and Daisy E. (Brabham) T.; m. Evelyn C. Davis, Jan. 16, 1965 (div. 1982); children: Yvette, James D. III; m. Rachel Evelyn Thornton, June 14, 1986. BS in Law, Glendale U., 1974; postgrad., UCLA, 1965-72, cert. numerical analysis, 1968. Mem. staff Cambridge (Mass.) electron accelerator div. Harvard U. and MIT, 1963-64; mem. staff Cyclotron lab. UCLA, 1964-73; elec. engr., 1973-77; system engr. Honeywell Systems Co., West Covina, Calif., 1977-80, Magnavox Systems Co., Torrance, Calif., 1980-86, Teledyne Systems Co., Northridge, Calif., 1986—; speaker at profl. seminars. With USMC, 1958-62. Mem. Am. Math. Soc., Bioelectromagnets Soc., Elec. Discharge and Elec. Over Stress Soc., Toastmasters Internat. (pres. Magnavox Toastmasters, Torrance, 1985-86). Home: PO Box 67426 Los Angeles CA 90067

TOLLIVER-PALMA, CALVIN EUGENE, violist, instructor, performer; b. Corpus Christi, Tex., Sept. 24, 1950; s. Jack Terrell Tolliver and Sara Lee (Palma) Denmon. MusB, Baylor U., 1973; MusD, U. Colo., 1981; studied with Mary Ellen Proudfit, Waco, Tex., 1969-71; studied with Wayne Crouse, Houston, 1971-72. Violist Corpus Christi (Tex.) Symphony, 1967-69, Waco (Tex.) Symphony, 1970-73, Tucson Symphony, 1971; union musician Denver and Boulder (Colo.) Locals, 1973-88; violist, violinist Boulder Philharmonic, 1974-88; pvt. music instr., performer Boulder, 1973—. Home: 664 Manhattan Dr # 3A Boulder CO 80303

TOLMAN, RICHARD ROBINS, zoology educator; b. Ogden, Utah, Dec. 1, 1937; s. Dale Richards and Dorothy (Robins) T.; m. Bonnie Bjornn, Aug. 18, 1964; children: David, Alicia, Brett, Matthew. BS, U. Utah, 1963, MSEd, 1964; PhD, Oreg. State U., 1969. Tchr. sci. Davis County Sch. Dist., Bountiful, Utah, 1964-66; instr. Mt. Hood C.C., Gresham, Oreg., 1968-69; staff assoc., project dir. Biol. Scis. Curriculum Study, Boulder, Colo., 1969-82; prof. Zoology Brigham Young U., Provo, Utah, 1982—. Contbr. articles to profl. jours. Scoutmaster Boy Scouts Am., Orem, Utah, 1992. With USAR, 1956-63. Alcuin fellow Brigham Young U., 1991. Mem. Nat. Sci. Tchrs. Assn., Utah Sci. Tchrs. Assn. (exec. sec. 1991—), Nat. Assn. for Rsch. in Sci. Teaching, Nat. Assn. of Biology Tchrs. Mem. Ch. of LDS. Home: 174 East 1825 South Orem UT 84058 Office: Dept Zoology Brigham Young U Provo UT 84602

TOLPO, CAROLYN LEE MARY, artist; b. Detroit, Feb. 1, 1940; d. James J.E. and Ethel Lucy Lee (Greener) Robiscoe; m. Vincent Tolpo;, June 24, 1976; 1 child, Michael Coleman Inglesh. BA, Wayne State U., 1962. Cert. tchr., Mich., Ill. Art tchr. Detroit Pub. Schs., 1962-64; art tchr., coord. Freeport (Ill.) Cath. Sch. System, 1972-78; artist Tolpo Studios, Rock Island, Ill., 1979-81, Shawnee Mountain Studios, Shawnee, Colo., 1981—; co-owner Shawnee Mountain Gallery, 1981—; art advisor Mountain Cable Channel, Bailey, Ill., 1990—. Principal works include (wrapped fiber sculpture) Rampart Range, 1988, Spirit Case, 1990, Anasazi, 1991, Opposition, 1992, (watercolor) Ruffled Lily, 1983 (Amoco collection: Works on paper by living Am. artists, 1983), Bye Bye Broadway, 1981 (silver award 1981). Founding pres. Womens Caucus for Art-Midwest Region, Rock Island, 1979-81; mem. Park County Hist. Soc., Shawnee, 1985—, Denver Art Mus., 1988—, Park County Friends of the Libr., 1985—; activist Save Shawnee environ. orgn., 1985—; founding v.p. Rock Island Preservation Assn., 1980-81; founder Cultural Coun. of Park County, 1992. Named Guild V, Kraus/Sikes, 1990, Guild VI, 1991, Guild VII, 1992. Mem. Am. Crafts Coun., Nat. Hist. Trust. Home and Office: Shawnee Mountain Gallery & Studios 55918 US Hwy 285 Shawnee CO 80475

TOLPO, VINCENT CARL, artist; b. Chgo., Apr. 26, 1950; s. Carl A.E. and Lily Rose (Mark) T.; m. Carolyn L. Tolpo, June 24, 1976. Student, U. Wyo., 1968-69; BFA, Ariz. State U., 1974; AA, Chgo. City Coll., 1971. Exec. dir. Freeport (Ill.) Art Mus., 1975-78, Quad City Arts Coun., Rock Island, Ill., 1978-81; artist, co-owner Shawnee (Colo.) Mt. Gallery, 1981—; arts advisor Mt. Cable Channel, Bailey, Colo., 1990—. Commd. work includes oil painting, Pima Point, 1985, sculpture, Spires, 1990, Books & Pages, 1992, Learning, 1992; wall sculpture, Accelleration, 1988, fiber-wrapped sculpture, Iridies, 1986; represented in permanent collections Kraft Corp., Englewood, Colo., Beaumont Properties, Denver, Colo. Bankshares, Denver, Blue Cross/Blue Shield, Denver, Digital Corp., Denver, others. Pres. Shawnee Water Commrs., 1983—; com. chmn. Park County Hist. Soc., Bailey, 1985—; organizer Save Shawnee Com., 1988—; founder Cultural Coun. Parks County; active Park County Historical Soc. Recipient Colo. Arts Coun. grant for Parks County Libr. sculpture, 1992. Mem. Am. Crafts Coun., Denver Art Mus., Park County Friends of Libr. Home: 55918 Us Hwy 285 Shawnee CO 80475-9999 Office: Shawnee Mountain Gallery 55918 Us Hwy 285 Shawnee CO 80475-9999

TOLSON, JON HART, investment advisor; b. San Francisco, Aug. 10, 1939; s. Herschel and Loe (Swart) T.; m. Linda Ann Lew, Jan. 20, 1967; children: Andrew, Leigh. BS, U. Calif., Berkeley, 1961, LLB, 1964. Bar: Calif. 1965. Acct. Arthur Young & Co., San Francisco, 1965-68; 1st v.p. Sutro Co. Inc., San Francisco, 1968-80; v.p. Barclay and Co., Inc., San Francisco, 1980-90; owner Tolson Capital Mgmt., San Francisco, 1991—. Bd. dirs. Lowell High Sch. Alumni Assn., San Francisco, 1990. With USAR. Mem. Calif. Bar Assn., Pacific Rowing Club (bd. dirs.). Home: 165 29th Ave San Francisco CA 94121-1037

TOM, CLARENCE YUNG CHEN, retired city and county official; b. Honolulu, Jan. 25, 1927; s. John Chong and Dorothy Oi Fook (Ing) T.; m. Vivian Kam Oi Lum, July 19, 1969; children: Claire-Anne, Karen-Anne, Patricia-Anne. BS in Chem. Engring., Purdue U., 1947, MS in Chem. Engring., 1957; M City Planning, Harvard U., 1959. Chem. engr. Libby, McNeill & Libby, Honolulu, 1947-50, 52-54; planner City and County Honolulu, 1958-89, chief environ. and plans assessment br. dept. gen. planning, 1960-88; mem. Hawaii Census Tract Com., 1960-89. Jr. warden St. Mary's Ch., Honolulu, 1970-82; vestryman Ch. Holy Nativity, Honolulu, 1984-86. Served with U.S. Army, 1950-52, Korea. Mem. Hawaii Govt. Employees Assn. (steward 1971-72, 81-82, alt. steward 1988). Democrat. Home: 2911A Koali Rd Honolulu HI 96826-1805

TOM, CREIGHTON HARVEY, aerospace engineer, consultant; b. Oakland, Calif., Mar. 29, 1944; s. Harvey and Katherine (Lew) T. BS in Forestry, U. Calif., Berkeley, 1966; MS in Stats., Colo. State U., 1972, PhD in Computer Sci., 1978. Sr. environ. analyst HRB-Singer, Inc., Ft. Collins, Colo., 1977-78; staff scientist Sci. Applications, Golden, Colo., 1979-80; cons. Golden, 1981; scientist, specialist ConTel Info. Systems, Littleton, Colo., 1981-84; sr. staff engr. Hughes Aircraft Co., Aurora, Colo., 1984-91; shuttle astronaut cand. NASA, Houston, 1980; cons. to companies and schs. Contbr. articles to profl. jours. Adviser CAP, Golden, 1981—; mem. YMCA. Served to maj. U.S. Army, 1966-67, with Res. 1967—. Decorated Bronze Star and Air medals, U.S. Army, 1967. Mem. Am. Soc. Photogrammetry, AAAS, NRA, Mensa, Intertel, Sigma Xi, Xi Sigma Pi, Phi Kappa Phi. Republican. Methodist. Home: 7951 S Cedar St Littleton CO 80120-4432 Office: C&H Enterprises 7951 S Cedar St Littleton CO 80120-4432

TOM, LAWRENCE, engineering executive; b. L.A., Jan. 21, 1950; BS Harvey Mudd Coll., 1972; JD Western State U., San Diego, 1978; spl. diploma U. Calif., San Diego, 1991. Design engr. Rockwell Internat., L.A., 1972-73; design engr. Rohr Industries, Inc., Chula Vista, Calif., 1973-76, sr. design engr., 1980, computer graphics engring. specialist, 1980-83, chief engring. svs., 1989-91, chief engring. quality, 1991-93, project engr. 1993—; pvt. practice design engring. cons., L.A., 1975-77; sr. engr. Rohr Marine, Inc., Chula Vista, 1977-79; chief exec. officer Computer Aided Tech. Svcs., San Diego, 1983-87; software cons. Small Systems Software, San Diego, 1984-85; computer graphics engring. specialist TOM & ROMAN, San Diego, 1986-88; dir. Computervision Users Group, 1986-88, vice chmn. 1988-91, pres., 1991—, exec. chmn., 1992—; bd. dirs. Exec. Program for Scientists and Engrs.-Alumni Assn. U. Calif., San Diego, 1991—; cons. in field. George H. Mayr Found. scholar, 1971, Bates Found. Aero. Edn. scholar, 1970-72. Mem. Aircraft Owners and Pilots Assn., Infiniti Club. Office: 7770 Regents Rd Ste 113-190 San Diego CA 92122-1937

TOMA, KYLE TAKEYOSHI, recreational therapist; b. Honokaa, Hawaii, Aug. 30, 1953; s. Takeo and Kikue (Ishiki) T. BA in Sociology, U. Hawaii, 1976, BS in Recreation, 1978, student, 1992—. Recreation dir., dormitory coun. Mid-Pacific Inst., Honolulu, 1985—; display specialist Shirokiya Dept. Store, Honolulu, 1986-88; fitness specialist Hickam (Hawaii) AFB, 1988-90; aerobics instr. Manoa Recreation Ctr., Honolulu, 1990—, Kaiser Permanente, 1990—; recreation therapist III State Dept. of Health, Honolulu, 1990—; aerobics instr. U. Hawaii, 1991—. Mem. YMCA, Am. Alliance Health, Physical Edn., Recreation, and Dance, Hawaii Assn. for Health, Physical Edn., Recreation, and Dance, Internat. Dance Exercise Assn., Reebpk Profl. Instr. Alliance. Democrat. Home: 2445 Kaala St Honolulu HI 96822

TOMASCHKE, JOHN EDWARD, chemist; b. San Diego, Sept. 23, 1949; s. Frederick Louis and Mary Ellen (Reinhart) T.; m. Christine Lorenzen, Apr. 19, 1973; children: James, Jennifer. BS, San Diego State U., 1972. Chemistry technician Salk Inst. for Biol. Studies, San Diego, 1972-78; dir. R&D Hydranautics, San Diego, 1978—. Inventor 5 patents in field. Mem. Am. Chem. Soc. (div. polymer chemistry, div. polymeric materials: sci. & engring.). Office: Hydranautics 8444 Miralani Dr San Diego CA 92126

TOMASELLI, KEVIN JAMES, neuroscientist, researcher; b. Providence, July 9, 1957; s. Rosario Vito and Mary Frances (Carlstrom) T. BS, Tufts U., 1979; PhD, U. Calif., San Francisco, 1987. Rsch. asst. Tufts U. Med. Sch., Boston, 1978-79, Harvard Med. Sch., Boston, 1979-81; postdoctoral scientist Howard Hughes Med. Inst., San Francisco, 1987-89; scientist Athena Neuroscis. Inc., South San Francisco, Calif., 1989—; cons. Calif. Biotech. Inc., Mountain View, 1987, Huntington's Disease Found., L.A., 1989, Early Stage Biotech. Startup Co., San Francisco, 1992. Contbr. articles to profl. jours.; patentee in field. Active AIDS Found., San Francisco, 1990. Mem. AAAS, Am. Soc. Cell Biologists, Soc. for Neurosci. Home: 485 Vallejo St San Francisco CA 94133

TOMASSON, HELGI, dancer, choreographer, dance company executive; b. Reykjavik, Iceland, 1942; m. Marlene Rizzo, 1965; children: Kristinn, Erik. Student, Sigridur Arman, Erik Bidsted, Vera Volkova, Sch. Am. Ballet, Tivoli Pantomime Theatre, Copenhagen. With Joffrey Ballet, 1961-64; prin. dancer Harkness Ballet, 1964-70, N.Y.C. Ballet, 1970-85; artistic dir. San Francisco Ballet, 1985—. Debut with Tivoli Pantomime Theatre, 1958; created roles in A Season of Hell, 1967, Stages and Reflections, 1968, La Favorita, 1969, The Goldberg Variations, 1971, Symphony in Three Movements, 1972, Coppélia, 1974, Dybbuk Variations, 1974, Chansons Madecasses, 1975, Introduction and Allegro, 1975, Union Jack, 1976, Vienna Waltzes, 1977; choreographer Menuetto (for N.Y.C. Ballet) 1984, Swan Lake, 1988, Handel-a Celebration, 1989, Sleeping Beauty, 1990, others. Decorated Knight Order of Falcon (Iceland), 1974, Comdr. Order of Falcon, 1990; recipient Silver medal Internat. Moscow Ballet Competition, 1969, Dance Mag. award, 1992. Office: care San Francisco Ballet 455 Franklin St San Francisco CA 94102-4471

TOMBACH, IVAR HARALD, environmental scientist; b. Tallinn, Estonia, Sept. 20, 1941; came to U.S., 1947; s. Harald and Milli Tombach; m. Evelyn Maria Renson, Sept. 11, 1966; children: Christina Michelle, Joanna Moon. BS honors, Calif. Inst. Tech., 1963, PhD, 1969; M in Aerospace Engring., Cornell U., 1966; MusM, Azusa Pacific U., 1991. Dir. advanced devel. Meteorology Rsch., Inc., Altadena, Calif., 1969-71; v.p. and co-founder AeroVironment Inc., Monrovia, Calif., 1971-91; environ. cons. Altadena, 1991-92; v.p. ENSR Consulting & Engring., Camarillo, Calif., 1992—; instr. U. Calif. Irvine, 1985-87, Kuwait Inst. Sci. Rsch., 1983. Inventor: Particulate Sampler Shield, 1979, patent 1981; contbr. articles to profl. jours. Mem. ASME, AIAA, Air and Waste Mgmt. Assn. (chmn. visibility com. 1982-83), Am. Meteorol. Soc., Am. Assn. for Aerosol Rsch., Sierra Club, Nature Conservancy, Wilderness Soc., Common Cause, Sigma Xi. Democrat. Mem. Nazarene Ch. Office: 1220 Avenida Acaso Camarillo CA 93012

TOMBES, AVERETT SNEAD, academic administrator; b. Easton, Md., Sept. 13, 1932; s. Thomas N. and Susie (Broaddus) T.; m. Jane R. Gill, June 15, 1957; children: Thomas, Robert, Jonathan, Susan. BA, U. Richmond, 1954; MS, Va. Poly. Inst., 1956; PhD, Rutgers U., 1961. Asst. prof., assoc. prof., then prof. Clemson (S.C.) U., 1961-77; chmn. dept. biology George Mason U., Fairfax, Va., 1977-81, dean Grad. Sch., 1981-86; v.p. grad. studies and rsch. Wichita (Kans.) State U., 1986-88; v.p. rsch., econ. devel. N.Mex. State U., Las Cruces, 1988—; cons. NSF, Washington, 1968-69, Oconee (S.C.) Hosp., 1972-73, Fairfax Hosp., 1978-80. Author textbook; contbr. chpts. to books, articles to profl. jours. Capt. U.S. Army, 1956-58. A.I. DuPont fellow U. Richmond, 1953-54; Thomas Headlee fellow Rutgers U., 1958-61; Am. Coun. Edn. fellow U. Del., U. Md., 1980-81. Fellow AAAS (counselor 1971-74); mem. Am. Soc. Cell Biology, Soc. Rsch. Adminstrs., Am. Physiol. Soc., Am. Soc. Zoologists, Soc. Gen. Physiologists, Sigma Xi, Phi Kappa Phi. Presbyterian. Home: 6621 Vista Hermosa Las Cruces NM 88005-4958 Office: NMex State U Las Cruces NM 88003

TOMBRELLO, THOMAS ANTHONY, JR., physics educator, consultant; b. Austin, Tex., Sept. 20, 1936; s. Thomas Anthony and Jeanette Lilian (Marcuse) T.; m. Esther Ann Hall, May 30, 1957 (div. Jan. 1976); children: Christopher Thomas, Susan Elaine, Karen Elizabeth; m. Stephanie Carhart Merton, Jan. 15, 1977; 1 stepchild, Kerstin Arusha. B.A. in Physics, Rice U., 1958, M.A., 1960, Ph.D., 1961. Research fellow in physics Calif. Inst. Tech., Pasadena, 1961-62, 64-65, asst. prof. physics, 1965-67, assoc. prof., 1967-71, prof., 1971—; asst. prof. Yale U., New Haven, 1963; cons. in field; disting. vis. prof. U. Calif.-Davis, 1984; v.p., dir. rsch. Schlumberger-Doll Rsch., Ridgefield, Conn., 1987-89; mem. U.S. V.P.'s Space Policy Adv. Bd., 1992. Assoc. editor Nuclear Physics, 1971-91, Applications of Nuclear Physics, 1980—, Radiation Effects, 1985-88, Nuclear Instruments and Methods B, 1993—. Recipient Alexander von Humboldt award von Humboldt Stiftung, U. Frankfurt, Federal Republic of Germany, 1984-85; NSF fellow Calif. Inst. Tech. 1961-62; A.P. Sloan fellow, 1971-73. Fellow Am. Phys. Soc.; mem. AAAS, Materials Rsch. Soc., Phi Beta Kappa, Sigma Xi, Delta Phi Alpha. Avocations: reading, jogging. Democrat. Office: Calif Inst Tech Dept Physics Mail Code 91125 Pasadena CA 91125

TOMICH, LILLIAN, lawyer; b. L.A., Mar. 28, 1935; d. Peter S. and Yovanka P. (Ivanovic) T. AA, Pasadena City Coll., 1954; BA in Polit. Sci., UCLA, 1956, cert. secondary teaching, 1957, MA, 1958; JD, U. So. Calif., 1961. Bar: Calif. Sole practice, 1961-66; house counsel Mfrs. Bank, Los Angeles, 1966; ptnr. Hurley, Shaw & Tomich, San Marino, Calif., 1968-76; assoc. Driscoll & Tomich, San Marino, 1976—; dir. Continental Culture Specialists Inc., Glendale, Calif. Trustee, St. Sava Serbian Orthodox Ch., San Gabriel, Calif. Charles Fletcher Scott fellow, 1957; U. So. Calif. Law Sch. scholar, 1958. Mem. ABA, Calif. Bar Assn., Los Angeles County Bar Assn., Women Lawyers Assn., San Marino C. of C., UCLA Alumni Assn., Town Hall and World Affairs Council, Order Mast and Dagger, Iota Tau Tau, Alpha Gamma Sigma. Office: 2460 Huntington Dr San Marino CA 91108-2460

TOMINAGA, BRENDA ELAINE, tutor coordinator; b. Kellogg, Idaho, May 14, 1958; d. Emil A. and Beulah F. (Bohannon) Hirte; m. Lynn S. Tominaga, Aug. 1, 1981; children: Andrew, Anna. BA, U. Idaho, 1980, postgrad., 1988. Substitute tchr. grades K-12 Minidoka County Schs., Rupert, Idaho, 1982-84, 85-86; instr. GED Coll. So. Idaho, Twin Falls, 1986-90; tutor coord. student support program Boise (Idaho) State U., 1991—. Tutor ESL Vista Vol. Program, 1985-86; mem. planning com., bd. dirs. Family Community Leadership Program, 1987-91; mem. adv. bd. minicassia breastfeeding project South Ctrl. Health Dist., 1988-89; mem. planning and adv. bd. Women and Econ. Devel., Coll. So. Idaho, 1989-91, cosponsor Ctr. for New Directions, 1989-91; vol. Librs. 2000, 1990; 4-H judge Western Idaho State Fair, 1991; facilitator Gov.'s Conf. on Tourism and Recreation, 1992; co-pres. Franklin Elem. PTO, Boise, 1992; and others. Mem. Idaho Assn. Adult Educators, Phi Beta Kappa, Phi Kappa Phi, Pi Gamma Mu.

TOMITA, VINCENT SADAO, electrical engineer; b. Torrence, Calif., Oct. 3, 1957; s. James Sadao and Arleen Yuriko T. BS, Calif. State U., Pomona, 1986. Elec. engr. CalComp, Inc., Anaheim, Calif., 1987-90. Recipient Eagle Scout, Boy Scouts Am. Mem. Tau Alpha Pi. Home: 311 Cascade Ave Oxnard CA 93033

TOMIZUKA, MASAYOSHI, mechanical engineering educator, researcher; b. Tokyo, Mar. 31, 1946; came to U.S., 1970; s. Makoto and Shizuko (Nagatome) T.; m. Miwako Tomizawa, Sept. 5, 1971; children: Lica, Yumi. MS, Keio U., Japan, 1970; PhD, MIT, 1974. Rsch. assoc. Keio U., 1974; asst. prof. U. Calif., Berkeley, 1974-80, assoc. prof., 1980-86, prof., 1986—. Tech. editor ASME Jour. Dynamic Systems Measurement and Control, 1988—; assoc. editor IEEE Control Systems Mag., 1986-88; contbr. more than 100 articles to profl. jours. NSF grantee, 1976-78, 81-83, 86-89, State of Calif. grantee, 1984-86, 88—. Fellow ASME (chmn. dynamic systems and control div. 1986-87); mem. IEEE, Soc. Mfg. Engrs. (sr.). Office: U Calif Dept Mech Engring Berkeley CA 94720

TOMKIEL, JUDITH IRENE, small business owner; b. St. Louis, Nov. 4, 1949; d. Melvin Charles William and Mildred Neva (Kayhart) Linders; m. William George Tomkiel, Dec. 15, 1972; children: Soteara, William, Kimberli, Jennifer, Christopher. Order filler Baker & Taylor Co., Sommerville, N.J., 1972-74; owner, founder The Idea Shoppe, Garden Grove, 1983-90; seamstress, crafts person Cloth World, Anaheim, Calif., 1987-89; mgr. S.M.T. Dental Lab., San Clemente, Calif., 1990—; Vol. Reading Is Fundamental Program, Garden Grove, 1988-89; freedom writer Amnesty Internat., Garden Grove, 1988-91. Author numerous poems; pub., editor (newsletter) Shoppe Talk, 1987-90; pub. Fakatale, 1988. Fellow World Literary Acad.; mem. Nat. Writer's Club, NAFE, Soc. Scholarly Pub., Dental Lab Owners Assn.

TOMKINS, ALLYSON JONES, psychotherapist, author; b. New Orleans, July 14, 1954; d. Nelson Buckner and Martha (Mitchel) Jones; m. James Patrick Tomkins, Jan. 6, 1989; children: Kelsey Alexandra. BA in Edn., St. Mary's Dominican Coll., New Orleans, 1976; MA in Psychology, Pepperdine U., Malibu, Calif., 1981. Lic. elem. sch. tchr., La.; marriage/family/child counselor, Calif.; lic. profl. counselor, La. Tchr. Trinity Episcopal Sch., New Orleans, 1977-79; teaching asst. Pepperdine U., 1979-81, adj. prof., 1989; product mgr. Interactive Health Systems, Santa Monica, Calif., 1981-86; psychotherapist, dir. Counseling Ctr. of Malibu, 1987-92, Connections Counseling Ctr., Covington, La., 1992. Author, editor: (workbook) The Intervention Workbook, 1984; author: The Joy Connection, 1993, Joy to the World, 1993. Bd. dirs. Mallinson Sch. of Malibu, 1983-85; pres. Episcopal Ch. Women, Malibu, 1985-87; bishop's warden St. Aidan's Episcopal Ch., Malibu, 1986-88.

TOMLINSON, JERRY LANNING, entrepreneur; b. Hermosa Beach, Calif., May 14, 1944; s. Walter Negus and Sharra (Sale) Toml.inson; m. Linda Ann Brown, May 1, 1969 (div. 1975); 1 child, Shadlock Ryan; m. Caroleigh Joan Williamson, Dec. 31, 1986. Grad., Aviation High Sch., Redondo Beach, Calif., 1962. Claims adjuster Blue Shield Ins., Fairfax, Calif., 1971-72; feature editor Collectors Voice Mag., Mill Valley, Calif., 1972-75; staff writer/sales mgr. Sausalito (Calif.) Revue, 1975-84; owner, dir. Pacific Crystal Guild, Sausalito, 1986—; promoter Great San Francisco Crystal Fair, 1987—; dir. Homestead Valley Land Trust, Mill Valley. Contbr. articles to profl. jours. Mem. Pacific Crystal Guild (dir. 1986-92), San Francisco Gem and Mineral Soc., San Francisco Tesla Soc. (v.p. 1991-92). Democrat. Buddhist. Office: Pacific Crystal Guild PO Box 1371 Sausalito CA 94966

TOMLINSON, ROBERT EUGENE, purchasing manager; b. Phoenix, Aug. 29, 1931; s. Charles Edward and Maud Margaret (Savage) T.; m. Nedra Kay Moore, Feb. 5, 1956; children: Robert, Todd, Cynthia, David, Shauna, Krista, Thomas, Tiana. Student, Danville (Ill.) Jr. Coll., 1964-67; grad. in materials mgmt., U. Utah, 1974; grad. in prodn./inventory control, U. Ill., Danville, 1975, 78. Cert. material mgmt. profl. Purchasing agt. Mallco Distbrs., Phoenix, 1950-62; ptnr. Moore's Disposal Svc., Danville, 1962-66; purchasing mgr. FMC Corp., Hoopeston, Ill., 1966-69; export purchasing coord. Hyster Co., Danville, 1969-73; materials mgr. Caravelle Industries, Jacksonville, Ark., 1973-75; dir. materials Wyman-Gordon Co., Danville, 1975-79; purchasing mgr. projects Cyprus-Miami Mining Corp., Miami, Ariz., 1979—. Mem. Purchasing Mgmt. Assn. Ariz., Internat. Lumber Assn. Republican. Mem. LDS Ch. Home: 821 S Santa Barbara St Mesa AZ 85202-2818

TOMLINSON-KEASEY, CAROL ANN, university administrator; b. Washington, Oct. 15, 1942; d. Robert Bruce and Geraldine (Howe) Tomlinson; m. Charles Blake Keasey, June 13, 1964; children: Kai Linson, Amber Lynn. BS, Pa. State U., 1964; MS, Iowa State U., 1966; PhD, U. Calif., Berkeley, 1970. Lic. psychologist, Calif. Asst. prof. psychology Trenton (N.J.) State Coll., 1969-70, Rutgers U., New Brunswick, N.J., 1970-72; prof. U. Nebr., Lincoln, 1972-77; prof. U. Calif., Riverside, 1977-92, acting dean coll. humanities and social scis., 1986-88, chmn. dept. psychology, 1989-92; vice provost for faculty rels. U. Calif., Davis, 1992—. Author: Child's Eye View, 1980, Child Development, 1985; also numerous chpts. to books; articles to profl. jours. Recipient Disting. Tchr. award U. Calif., 1986. Mem. Am. Psychol. Assn., Soc. Rsch. in Child Devel., Riverside Aquatics Assn. (pres. 1985). Office: Office of Provost U Calif Davis Davis CA 95616

TOMOEDA, CHERYL KUNIKO, academic researcher; b. Honolulu, Sept. 24, 1958; d. Charles Kunio and Doris Masue (Takehara) T. BS, U. Hawaii, 1980; MS, U. Ariz., 1982. Cert. speech-lang. pathology. Speech pathologist Amphitheater Pub. Schs., Tucson, 1983-84; rsch. asst. U. Ariz., Tucson, 1982-83, rsch. asst. II, 1984-86, rsch. coord., 1985-91, sr. rsch. specialist, 1991—. Author: (test) Ariz. Battery for Communication Disorders of Dementia, 1991. Mem. Acad. Neurologic Communication Disorders and Scis. (acting sec. 1991, sec. 1992—), Internat. Neuropsychol. Soc., Am. Speech-Lang.-Hearing Assn., Ariz. Speech-Lang.-Hearing Assn. Office: U Ariz Dept Speech & Hearing Scis Tucson AZ 85721

TOMPKINS, DANIEL NELSON, university lecturer, consultant; b. Phila., May 19, 1928; s. Daniel Nelson Tompkins and Helen Sculthorp Downs; m. Virginia Ann Morris, Dec. 23, 1950 (div. 1970); children: Lois Diane Maggette, Barbara Ann Brown, Claudia Brooks. BS in Physics, West Chester (Pa.) U., 1950; BS in Elec. Engring., Purdue U., 1955, MS in Elec. Engring., 1956, PhD in Elec. Engring., 1960. Lic. real estate broker, Calif. Space sci. engr. Hughes Aircraft Co., Culver City, Calif., 1957-60; mgr. space sci. Ford Aeroneutronic, Newport Beach, Calif., 1960-70; ptnr. Info-Data Systems, Gardena, Calif., 1984-86, Danvic Mfg., Van Nuys, Calif., 1977-87; v.p. Nelson Pers. & Media Svcs., Pasadena, Calif., 1972—; pres. Univ. and Coll. Lectures, Pasadena, 1972—; chmn. MacKenzie-Wells Co., Pasadena, 1971—; chmn., CEO Bus. Devel. Assocs., Pasadena, 1969—; dir. The Pasadena Inst., 1993—. Author: Easy Ways to Easy Days, 1971, Six Paydays a Week, 1978, Make Money with Computers, 1982; discoverer mathematical concept Tompkins Codes; contbr. articles to space sci. and instrumentation to profl. jours. Lt. (j.g.) USN, 1950-54. Gen. Electric Co. fellow, 1955, 56; Howard Hughes fellow, 1957. Home and Office: 920 E Colorado Blvd # 262 Pasadena CA 91106

TOMS, MICHAEL ANTHONY, electronic journalist; b. Washington, June 7, 1940; s. Austin Herman Toms and Margart Dorothy (Pitcher) Slavinsky; m. Justine Willis, Dec. 16, 1972; children: Michael Anthony, Robert Welch. Postgrad., Calif. Inst. Integral Studies, San Francisco, 1973-75; DrTheology, Sem. St. Basil the Great, Sydney, Australia, 1981; DHL (hon.), U. Humanistic Studies, San Diego, 1983. Field govt. rep. VariTyper Corp., Washington, 1960-64; sales mgr. VariTyper Corp., San Francisco, 1964-67; regional sales mgr. VariTyper Corp., San Bernardino, 1967-68; pres. Creative Mktg. Assocs., San Francisco, 1968-73; chmn. bd. The Response Mktg. Group, San Francisco, 1971-73; CEO Michael A. Toms & Assocs., San Francisco, 1973-76; pres. New Dimensions Found., San Francisco, 1973—; sr. acquisitions editor Harper Collins, San Francisco, 1989—; exec. prodr., host nat. pub. radio interview series New Dimensions, 1980—; chmn. bd. emeritus Calif. Inst. Integral Studies, San Francisco, 1979-83; exec. dir. Audio Inds., Inc., San Francisco, 1981-83. Author: Worlds Beyond, 1978, The New Healers, 1980, An Open Life, 1988, At The Leading Edge, 1991. Mem. Task Force to Promote Self Esteem and Personal and Social Responsibility, Mendocino County, Calif., 1988-89; mem. internat. adv. bd. Radio Peace Internat. Mem. Internat. Assn. for Socially Responsible Radio (founding dir. 1991—). Home: PO Box 569 Ukiah CA 95482 Office: New Dimensions Found PO Box 410510 San Francisco CA 94141

TOMSKY, JUDY, fundraiser and event planner; b. Oklahoma City, Nov. 28, 1959; d. Mervin and Helen (Broude) T. Student, Hebrew U. of Jerusalem, 1979-80; BA in Liberal Studies, Sonoma State U., 1981. Internat. tour group dir. Kibbutz Yahel, Israel, 1981-83; telemktg. supr., mktg. and advt. coord. The Sharper Image, San Francisco, 1983-85; br. mgr., acct. exec. advt. Marin Express Ltd., Corte Madera, Calif., 1986; spl. events coord., fundraiser Sausalito, Calif., 1987; Pacific N.W. regional dir. Jewish Nat. Fund, San Francisco, 1987-90; event mgmt., mktg. and promotion specialist, 1990-93; devel. dir. Insight Meditation West, Woodacre, Calif., 1993—. Office: Insight Meditation West PO Box 909 Woodacre CA 94973

TONAY, VERONICA KATHERINE, psychology educator; b. LaJolla, Calif., Mar. 28, 1960. BA with honors, U. Calif., Santa Cruz, 1985; MA, U. Calif., Berkeley, 1988, PhD, 1993. Teaching asst. U. Calif.-Berkeley, U. Calif.-Santa Cruz, 1985-88; psychology intern Family Svcs. Assn., Santa Cruz, 1989-90; lectr. psychology U. Calif., Santa Cruz, 1989—, Berkeley, 1992—; dream educator, researcher, Santa Cruz. Contbr. articles to profl. jours. Fellow State of Calif., 1985-89. Mem. APA (assoc., program chmn. div. 32, 1989-90), Assn. for Study Dreams (conf. organizer 1987-88, 91-92). Office: U Calif Psychology Dept Santa Cruz CA 95064

TONELLO-STUART, ENRICA MARIA, political economist; b. Monza, Italy; d. Alessandro P. and Maddalena M. (Marangoni) Tonello; m. Albert E. Smith; m. Charles L. Stuart. BA in Internat. Affairs, Econs., U. Colo., 1961; MA, Claremont Grad. Sch., 1966, PhD, 1971. Sales mgr. Met. Life Ins. Co., 1974-79; pres. E.T.S. Rsch. and Devel., Inc., 1977—; dean internat. studies program Union U., L.A.-Tokyo; lectr. internat. affairs and mktg. UCLA Extention, Union U.; chief exec. officer E.T.S. R & D, Inc., 1986—. Pub., editor Tomorrow Outline Journal, 1963—, The Monitor, 1988; pub. World Regionalism--An Ecological Analysis, 1971, A Proposal for the Reorganization of the United Nations, 1966, The Persuasion Technocracy, Its Forms, Techniques, and Potentials, 1966, The Role of the Multinationals in the Emerging Globalism, 1978, The Monitor, 1988; developed the theory of social ecology and econsociometry. Bd. dirs. Caesarea World Monument; mem. L.A. World Affairs Coun.; organized first family assistance program Langley AFB Tactical Air Command Commandation, 1956-58; editorial bd. C. of C. Bus. Jours., Nat. Italian Am. Found.; mem. transit adv. com. City of Rancho Palos Verdes, Calif. Recipient vol. svc. award VA, 1956-58, ARC svc. award, 1950-58. Mem. Corp. Planners Assn. (treas. 1974-79), Investigative Reporters and Editors, World Future Soc. (pres. 1974—), US-China Journalists Fellowship Assn. (founder, pres. 1984—), L.A. Venture Assn., Fgn. Trade Assn., Palos Verdes C. of C., Pi Sigma Alpha, Sigma Delta Chi. Clubs: Los Angeles Press (bd. dirs.). Lodge: Zonta (chmn. internat. com. South Bay).

TONG, LARRY WINGLOON, information systems consultant; b. Hong Kong, Apr. 26, 1962; came to the U.S., 1976; s. Young Kwain and Chow Hung (Tam) T.; m. Rita Yewling Chan, July 28, 1990; 1 child, Melody April Wei-Ming. BS with distinction, Harvey Mudd Coll., 1984; MS in Engring., Claremont Grad. Sch., 1985. Cert. data processing profl., engr. Mgr. Pacific Bell, Santee, Calif., 1985, Pasadena, Calif., 1985; system engr. Rockwell Internat., Anaheim, Calif., 1985-86; sr. mfg. cons. Ernst & Young, Irvine, Calif., 1987-88; project mgr. MIS Sugar Foods Corp., Panorama City, Calif., 1989-92; owner, cons. RT Lawrence Cons., La Mirada, Calif., 1992—; bus. advisor Miracle Info. Svcs., Ontario, Calif., 1990-92. Active planning com. Pomona (Calif.) Chinese United Meth. Ch., 1981-91. Mem. Am. Prodn. Inventory Control Soc., Mfg. Engr. Soc., Computer Profl. Inst., Am. Mgmt. Assn., Mech. Engring. Soc. (student chmn. 1983-84). Office: RT Lawrence Cons 14700 Firestone Blvd # 123 La Mirada CA 90638

TONG, RICHARD DARE, anesthesiologist; b. Chgo., Oct. 20, 1930; s. George Dare and June (Jung) T.; student U. Calif., Berkeley, 1949-52; MD, U. Calif., Irvine, 1956; postgrad. UCLA, 1965-67; m. Diane Helene Davies, Apr. 12, 1970; children: Erin, Jason, Jeffery, Ryan; m. Deanna Johnson, Jan. 5, 1993. Intern, Phoenix Gen. Hosp., 1956-57; resident in anesthesiology UCLA, 1965-67; pvt. practice, Lakewood, Calif., 1967—; clin. instr. UCLA Sch. Medicine, 1968—. Dep. sheriff reserve med. emergency team, L.A. County. With USNR, 1947-53. Diplomate Am. Bd. Anesthesiology. Fellow Am. Coll. Anesthesiology; mem. Am. Soc. Anesthesiologists, AMA, Calif. Med. Assn., L.A. County Med. Assns. Democrat. Office: PO Box 1131 Lakewood CA 90714

TONG, SIU WING, computer programmer; b. Hong Kong, Hong Kong, May 20, 1950; came to U.S., 1968; BA, U. Calif., Berkeley, 1972; PhD, Harvard U., 1979; MS, U. Lowell, 1984. Research assoc. Brookhaven Nat. Lab., Upton, N.Y., 1979-83; software engr. Honeywell Info. Systems, Billerica, Mass., 1984-85; sr. programmer, analyst Hui Computer Cons., Berkeley, Calif., 1985-88; sr. v.p. devel., chief fin. officer Surgicenter Info. Systems, Inc., Orinda, Calif., 1989—. Vol. tchr. Boston Chinatown Saturday Adult Edn. Program of Tufts Med. Sch., 1977-79. Muscular Dystrophy Assn. fellow, 1980-82. Mem. AAAS, IEEE, Assn. Computing Machinery, N.Y. Acad. Scis. Home: 1076 Carol Ln Apt 25 Lafayette CA 94549-4737 Office: Surgicenter Info Systems Inc 4 Orinda Way Ste 110B Orinda CA 94563-2518

TONICK, ILLENE, clinical psychologist; b. Bronx, N.Y.; d. Benjamin and Mollie (Airov) T.; m. Michael S. Levine, May 30, 1984. BA, SUNY-Stony Brook, 1973; MS, U. Utah, 1979, PhD, 1981. Staff psychologist Neuropsychiat. Inst., UCLA, 1980-82, asst. clin. prof. dept. psychiatry, 1984—; clin. supr. Ctr. Legal Psychiatry, L.A., 1982-83; pvt. practice psychology, L.A., 1982—. Dir. Acad. Rev. Psychol. Lic. Workshops., L.A., 1983—. Contbr. articles to profl. jours. NIMH fellow, 1973-76, Solomon Baker fellow 1979-80. Mem. Am. Psychol. Assn., Nat. Register Health Providers in Psychology, So. Calif. Psychotherapy Affiliation, Phi Kappa Phi. Office: 941 Westwood Blvd Ste 221 Los Angeles CA 90024-2904

TONINI, LEON RICHARD, sales professional; b. Pittsfield, Mass., May 16, 1931; s. John Richard and Mabel Grayce (Rushbrook) T.; B.A. in Mgmt., U. Md., 1951; m. Helen Jo, Aug. 15, 1966; 1 son, John Richard, II. Enlisted in U.S. Army, 1947, advanced through grades to master sgt., 1968; service in W.Ger., Vietnam; ret., 1974; dir. vets. employment and assistance Non-Commd. Officers Assn., San Antonio, 1974-75; supr. security Pinkerton's Inc., Dallas, 1975-78; gen. mgr. civic center Travelodge Motor Hotel and Restaurant, San Francisco, 1978-85; sales representative Vernon Co., 1985—. Chmn. San Francisco Vets. Employment Com., 1981. Served as sgt. maj. Calif. N.G., res. Decorated Bronze Star; Republic Vietnam Honor medal 2d class. Mem. San Francisco Hotel Assn. (dir.), Non-Commd. Officers Assn. (dir. Calif. chpt.), Am. Legion, Regular Vets. Assn. (nat. sr. vice comdr.), Amvets, Patrons of Husbandry. Republican. Baptist. Club: Masons. Home and Office: 205 Collins St Apt 9 San Francisco CA 94118-3429

TONJES, MARIAN JEANNETTE BENTON, reading educator; b. Rockville Center, N.Y., Feb. 16, 1929; d. Millard Warren and Felicia E. (Tyler) Benton; m. Charles F. Tonjes (div. 1965); children: Jeffrey Charles, Kenneth Warren. BA, U. N.Mex., 1951, cert., 1966, MA, 1969; EdD, U. Miami, 1975. Dir. recreation Stuyvesant Town Housing Project, N.Y.C., 1951-53; tchr. music., phys. edn. Sunset Mesa Day Sch., Albuquerque, 1953-54; tchr. remedial reading Zia Elem. Sch., Albuquerque, 1965-67; tchr. secondary devel. reading Rio Grande High Sch., Albuquerque, 1967-69; research asst. reading Southwestern Coop. Ednl. Lab., Albuquerque, 1969-71; assoc. dir., vis. instr. Fla. Ctr. Tchr. Tng. Materials U. Miami, 1971-72; asst. prof. U.S. Internat. U., San Diego, 1972-75; prof. edn. Western Wash. U., Bellingham, 1975—, dir. summer study at Oxford (Eng.) U., 1975-93; vis. prof. adult edn. Palomar (Calif.) Jr. Coll., 1974; reading supr. Manzanita Ctr. U. N.Mex., Albuquerque, 1968; vis. prof. U. Guam, Mangilao, 1989-90; speaker, cons. in field; invited guest Russian Reading Assn., Moscow, 1992. Author: (with Miles V. Zintz) Teaching Reading/Thinking Study Skills in Content Classrooms, 3d edit., 1991; author: Secondary Reading, Writing and Learning, 1991; contbr. articles to profl. jours. Mem. English Speaking Union/Dartmouth House, London. Recipient Disting. Tchr. award Western Wash. U., 1981; TTT grantee; NDEA fellow Okla. State U. Mem. Am. Reading Forum (chmn. bd. dirs. 1983-85), Internat. Reading Assn. (travel, interchange and study tours com. 1984-86, non-print media and reading com. 1980-83, workshop dir. S.W. regional conf. 1982, com. internat. devel. N.Am. 1991—, outstanding tchr. educator 1988-90), U.K. Reading Assn. (speaker), European Conf. Reading Berlin, Edinburgh and Malmo (speaker), PEO (past chpt. pres.), Phi Delta Kappa (chpt. nominating com. 1984, alt. del. 1982), Delta Delta Delta. Office: Western Wash U Coll Edn Bellingham WA 98225

TONN, ELVERNE MERYL, pediatric dentist, dental insurance consultant; b. Stockton, Calif., Dec. 10, 1929; s. Emanuel M. and Lorna Darlene (Bryant) T.; m. Ann G. Richardson, Oct. 28, 1951; children: James Edward, Susan Elaine Tonn Yee. AA, La Sierra U., Riverside, Calif., 1949; DDS, U. So. Calif., 1955; BS, SUNY, Albany, 1984. Lic. dentist; cert. tchr., Calif., dental ins. cons. Pediatric dentist, assoc. Walker Dental Group, Long Beach, Calif., 1957-59, Children's Dental Clinic, Sunnyvale, Calif., 1959-61; pediatric dentist in pvt. practice Mountain View, Calif., 1961-72; pediatric dentist, ptnr. Pediatric Dentistry Assocs., Los Altos, Calif., 1972-83; assoc. prof. U. Calif., San Francisco, 1984-86; pediatric dentist, ptnr. Valley Oak Dental Group, Manteca, Calif., 1987—; from asst. prof. to assoc. prof. U. of the Pacific, San Francisco, 1964-84; pediatric dental cons. Delta Dental Plan, San Francisco, 1985—; chief dental staff El Camino Hosp., Mountain View, 1964-65, 84-85; lectr. in field. Weekly columnist Manteca Bull., 1987-92; producer 2 teaching videos, 1986; contbr. articles to profl. jours. Lectr. to elem. students on dental health Manteca Unified Sch. Dist., 1982-92; dental health screener Elem. Schs., San Joaquin County Pub. Health, 1989-92; dental cons. Interplast program Stanford U. Sch. Medicine. Capt. U.S. Army, 1955-57. Fellow Am. Acad. Pediatric Dentistry, Am. Coll. Dentists, Royal Soc. Health (Eng.), Acad. of Dentistry for Handicapped, Pierre Fauchard Acad., Acad. Dental Mateirals; mem. ADA, Am. Assn. Dental Cons., Calif. Dental Assn., Internat. Coll. Dentists, Internat. Assn. Pediatric Dentistry, Internat. Assn. Dental Rsch., Fedn. Dentaire Internationale, Calif. Soc. Dentistry for Children (pres. 1968), Calif. Soc. Pediatric Dentists, N.Y. Acad. Scis., Rotary Internat. Republican. Seventh-day Adventist. Home: 374 Laurelwood Cir Manteca CA 95336 Office: Valley Oak Dental Group Inc 1507 W Yosemite Ave Manteca CA 95336

TONTZ, JAY LOGAN, university dean, educator; b. Balt., July 20, 1938; s. E. Logan and Charlotte (Mullikin) T.; m. Frances Anne Deems, June 26, 1982; children: Michelle Anne, Brandon Logan. B.A., Denison U., 1960; M.S., Cornell U., 1962; Ph.D., U. N.C., 1966. Asst. prof. econs. U.S. Air Force Acad., 1966-69; prof. econs. Calif. State U., Hayward, 1969—, acting assoc. dean, 1970-72, chmn. dept. econs., 1972-73, acting dean, 1973-74, dean Sch. Bus. and Econs., 1974—. Trustee St. Rose Hosp., Hayward, Calif., 1979-85, chmn. bd. trustees, 1981-85. Mem. Nat. Assn. Drs. in U.S., Am. Econ. Assn., Western Econ. Assn., Rotary (pres. Hayward chpt. 1986-87), Omicron Delta Epsilon, Delta Sigma Pi. Home: 602 Lomond Cir San Ramon CA 94583-2557 Office: Calif State U Sch Bus and Econs Hayward CA 94542

TOO, DANNY, educator; b. Montreal, Oct. 14, 1958; s. Nie Suey and Sook King (Moy) T. DCS, Vanier Coll., Montreal, 1977; BEd, McGill U., Montreal, 1980, MA, 1984; PhD, U. Ill., 1989. Grad. rsch./teaching asst. McGill U., Montreal, 1980-83, U. Ill., Urbana, 1983-88; asst. prof. sports biomechanics Calif. State U., Fullerton, 1988-92, U. Nev., Las Vegas, 1992—. Contbr. articles to profl.. jours. McGill U. scholar, 1977-79, James McGill awardee, 1977-79, Gold medal, 1980. Mem. AAHPERD, Internat. Soc. for Biomechanics of Sports (bd. dirs. 1990-92), Am. Coll. Sports Medicine, Can. Assn. Sport Scis., Nat. Strength and Conditioning Assn., Sigma Xi. Office: Univ of Nev 4505 Maryland Pkwy Las Vegas NV 89154-3034

TOOKEY, ROBERT CLARENCE, consulting actuary; b. Santa Monica, Calif., Mar. 21, 1925; s. Clarence Hall and Minerva Maconachie (Anderson) T.; BS, Calif. Inst. Tech., 1945; MS, U. Mich., 1947; m. Marcia Louise Hickman, Sept. 15, 1956; children: John Hall, Jennifer Louise, Thomas Anderson. Actuarial clk. Occidental Life Ins. Co., Los Angeles, 1945-46; with Prudential Ins. Co. Am., Newark, 1947-49; assoc. actuary in group Pacific Mut. Life Ins. Co., Los Angeles, 1949-55; asst. v.p. in charge reins. sales and service for 17 western states Lincoln Nat. Life Ins. Co., Ft. Wayne, Ind., 1955-61; dir. actuarial services Peat, Marwick, Mitchell & Co., Chgo., 1961-63; mng. partner So. Calif. office Milliman & Robertson, cons. actuaries, Pasadena, 1963-76; pres. Robert Tookey Assos., Inc., 1977—. Committeeman troop 501 Boy Scouts Am., 1969-72. Served to lt. (j.g.) USNR, 1943-45, 51-52. Fellow Soc. Actuaries, Conf. Consulting Actuaries; mem. Am. Acad. Actuaries, Pacific States Actuarial Club, Pacific Ins. Conf. Clubs: San Gabriel Country; Rotary (Pasadena); Union League (Chgo.). Home and Office: 3950 San Augustine Dr Glendale CA 91206 also: PO Box 646 La Canada Flintridge CA 91012

TOOLE, CLYDE ROWLAND, JR., physicist; b. Seattle, July 24, 1933; s. Clyde Rowland and Esther Stanun (Magnuson) T.; m. Hazel Ruth Coppess, June 15, 1957; children: Kelli, Shauna Toole Pawlowski, Erin Toole Albertson, Megan Toole Teckmeyer. BS in Physics, U. Wash., 1955; postgrad., U. Idaho, 1956-60. Research physicist Phillips Petroleum, Idaho Falls, Idaho, 1955-59; spl. power excursion reactor test facility, ops. mgr. Phillips Petroleum, Idaho Falls, 1959-68, Aerojet Nuclear, Idaho Falls, 1968-71;

power burst facility, ops. mgr. EG&G, Inc., Idaho Falls, 1971-75, power burst facility mgr., 1975-77, tech. asst. to loft facility mgr., 1977-81; rep. to fed. lab. consortium Idaho Nat. Engring. Lab., Idaho Falls, 1981-85; mgr., exploratory rsch. and devel. EG&G, Inc., Idaho Falls, 1985-93; loaned exec., endowed chair Idaho State Dept. Edn., 1993—; gen. chmn. 8th Topical Mtg. on Tech. of Fusion Energy, Salt Lake City, 1988; cons. Dept. of Energy, Buffalo, N.Y., 1969; lectr. U. Wash., Seattle, 1968, Naval Officer's Tng., Idaho Falls, 1966. Contbr. articles to profl. jours. Vice-chmn. Idaho Sch. Bd., Dist. #91, Idaho Falls, 1979-92; bd. dirs. Idaho Falls Aquatic Ctr., 1987—; chmn. Idaho Falls Youth/Adult Assn., 1978; precinct com. Republican Party, Idaho Falls, 1968-72; active Idaho Assn. Commerce and Industry Edn. Com., 1992—. Mem. Am. Nuclear Soc. (program com. 1978, chmn. Idaho sect. 1985-86, Exceptional Service award 1980, sect. liason for Spectrum Internat. Waste Mgmt. MTG 1992), Idaho Acad. Sci., Pinecrest Golf Assn., Sigma Alpha Epsilon. Republican. Episcopalian. Home: 356 Redwood Dr Idaho Falls ID 83401-2948 Office: EG&G Inc PO Box 1625 Idaho Falls ID 83415-0001

TOOLE, FLOYD EDWARD, manufacturing company executive; b. Moncton, N.B., Can., June 19, 1938; s. Harold Osman and Arilla Adeltha (Allen) T.; m. Noreen Beckie, June 31, 1961. BSc in EE, U. N.B., Fredericton, 1961; PhD in EE, U. London, 1965. Sr. rsch. officer NRC Can., Ottawa, Ont., 1965-91; v.p. engring. Harman Internat. Industries Inc., Northridge, Calif., 1991—. Contbr. articles to profl. jours. Fellow Audio Engring. Soc. (pres. 1992-93, Publs. award 1988, 90); mem. Acoustical Soc. Am. Office: Harman Internat Industries 8500 Balboa Blvd Northridge CA 91329

TOOLE, HOWARD, lawyer; b. Missoula, Mont., Aug. 2, 1949; s. John H. and Barbara T. BA, Lawrence U., 1972; JD, U. Mont., 1978. Bar: Mont. 1978. Deputy prosecutor Missoula County Attys. Office, 1978-82; pvt. practice Missoula, 1982—; rep. Mont. House Reps., Helena, Mont., 1990—; owner No. Rockies Arbitration & Mediation, Missoula, 1985—. Office: Howard Toole Law Offices 126 E Broadway #25 Missoula MT 59802 Home: 1625 McDonald Missoula MT 59801

TOOLE, JOAN TRIMBLE, financial consultant; b. Ipswich, Mass., Apr. 3, 1923; d. Dana Newcomb and Barbara (Campbell) T.; m. John R. Marchi, Dec. 28, 1943 (div. Aug. 1959); children: Jon, Jael, Charis, Peter; m. Kenneth Ross Toole, Apr. 22, 1960 (dec. Aug. 1981); children: Dana O'Keefe, David Campbell. BA, Antioch Coll., Yellow Springs, Ohio, 1946; MS in Fin., U. Mont., 1976; MPA, Harvard U., 1985. Rancher J/J and KJ Ranches, 1955-82; Mont. legis. asst., researcher, 1981-83; cons. Mont. Dept. Revenue, 1985-87, U. Mont. Biol. Sta., 1987-89; pvt. practice, 1987—. State coord. Cranston for Pres., 1983-84; lobbyist Office Pub. Instrn., 1989-90; mem. tax appeals bd., Ravalli County, 1981-84; mem. Mont. Bd. Natural Resources and Conservation, 1986-90; bd. dirs. Forever Wild Endowment; active League Women Voters, Mont. Environ. Info. Ctr., No. Plains Resource Coun.; bd. dirs., treas. Mont. Conservation Voters, 1992—. Mem. Harvard Club (bd. dirs. ch. schs. and scholarships). Democrat. Episcopalian. Home: 269 Westside Dr N Polson MT 59860-9618 Office: 1220 8th Ave Helena MT 59601-3901

TOOLEY, WILLIAM LANDER, real estate company executive; b. El Paso, Tex., Apr. 23, 1934; s. William Lander and Virginia Mary (Ryan) T.; m. Reva Berger, Mar. 5, 1966; children: William Ryan, Patrick Boyer, James Eugene. BA, Stanford U., 1956; MBA, Harvard U., 1960. Treas., mgr. Pickwick Hotel Co., San Diego, 1960-63, David H. Murdock Devel. Co., Phoenix, 1963-66; ptnr. Ketchum, Peck & Tooley, L.A., 1967-74; chmn. Tooley & Co., L.A., 1974—; bd. dirs. Fed. Res. Bank San Francisco, 1988—; dir. Nat. Realty Com., Washington, 1975—. Trustee Loyola Marymount U., L.A., 1975-82, bd. regents, 1982—, mem. task force, 1988—. Lt. (j.g.) USNR, 1956-58. Recipient Lifetime Achievement award L.A. Area C. of C., 1992, Civic Achievement award Am. Jewish Com., 1989. Mem. Urban Land Inst. (award 1988), Calif. Club, Calif. Yacht Club, Lambda Alpha. Office: 3303 Wilshire Blvd Los Angeles CA 90010-1704

TOOMIN, LOUIS ALLEN, small business owner, state legislator; b. Newark, Aug. 20, 1935; s. Maurice Aaron and Lydia (Simkins) T,; m. Loretta Faber, Apr. 29, 1956 (div. 1961); children: Lawrence Scott, Lance Steven; m. Mary Ellen Toomin, Apr. 13, 1993; stepchildren: Charles Troy Sitter, Jennifer Jean Sitter. Student, L.A. City Coll., 1954-55, UCLA, 1955. V.P., sales mgr. Faber Enterprises, Inc., Santa Monica, Calif., 1955-62; owner Aircraft Surplus, LA, 1963-73, T-Shirt Printing Business, LA, 1973-83; mgr. Las Vegas Sporting House, 1983-86; owner Monterey Pools, Las Vegas, 1986—; mem. Nev. State Assembly, Las Vegas, 1992—. Charter treas. Temple Beth Am, 1984, treas., 1992; mem. Dem. Ctrl. Com., 1990-91, 92, 93; del. State of Nev. Dem. Conv., 1990-92, Clark County Dem. Conv., 1990-92; active Better Bus. Bureau, 1987—, Citizens Com. for Mass Transit, 1990—; dir. exec. bd. Goodwill Industries, 1991, 92. With USAF, 1954-59. Mem. Fed. Bus. Assn., Nat. Pool and Spa Inst., B'Nai B'Rith (Ted Mack chpt.), Latin C. of C., Las Vegas C. of C., Kiwanis (Uptown Las Vegas chpt., bd. dirs.), Women's Dem. Club, Paradise Dem. Club. Office: 3852 Topaz St Las Vegas NV 89121 also: 401 S Carson St Carson City NV 89710

TOON, LEONARD EUGENE, chiropractor; b. San Fernando, Calif., Dec. 19, 1932; s. Lester F. and Bessie M. (Rucker) T.; m. Jillian D. Gibbs, May 14, 1975, (div. Mar. 1979); children: Donna J., Susan J. D Chiropractic, L.A. Chiropractic, 1956. Diplomate Am. Bd. Chiropractic Orthopedists. Pvt. practice, chiropractic Chatsworth, Calif., to date; treas. Am. Bd. Chiropractic Orthopedists, 1981-91. Mem. Am. Coll. Chiropractic Orthopedists (pres. 1980), Coun. on Chiropractic Orthopedics (pres. 1985-86); fellow Acad. Chiropractic Orthopedists (sec. 1980-90). Office: 20529 Devonshire St Chatsworth CA 91311-3296

TOPAZ, DAVID ETHAN, congressional staff assistant; b. Salem, Oreg., Nov. 19, 1967; s. Lionel Victor and Rachael Jo (Spinning) T.; m. Lisa Dawn Robnett, June 17, 1990. BA in Polit. Sci., Oreg. State U., 1990; postgrad., U. San Francisco, Sacramento, 1991—. Campaign mgr. Kevin Mannix and Jeff Gilmour for Oreg. Ho. of Reps., Salem, 1990; staff asst. to Rep. Robert T. Matsui U.S. Ho. of Reps., Sacramento, 1991—. Mem. adv. coun. Nat. Youth Sports Program, Sacramento, 1991—; mem. McClellan AFB Installation Restoration Task Force, Sacramento, 1991—, co-chmn.; vol. Bill Clinton for Pres. Del. Caucus, Sacramento, 1992; mem. vol. rev. team United Way Sacramento, 1993. Mem. U.S. Jaycees. Democrat. Jewish. Office: Office Rep Robert T Matsui 8058 Federal Bldg 650 Capitol Mall Sacramento CA 95814

TOPE, DWIGHT HAROLD, retired management consultant; b. Grand Junction, Colo., Aug. 29, 1918; s. Richard E. and Elizabeth (Jones) T.; m. Carolyn Stagg, Apr. 29, 1949; children: Stephen R., Chris L. AS, Mesa Coll., 1940; student, George Washington U. With Fgn. Funds Control, a Div. of U.S. Treasury Dept.; staff adjuster Fire Cos. Adjustment Bur., Denver, Albuquerque, 1946-48; br. mgr. Gen. Adjustment Bur., Deming, N.Mex., 1948-50; spl. agt. Cliff Kealey State Agy., Albuquerque, 1950-56; pres. Dwight Tope State Agy., Inc., Albuquerque, 1956-84, also chmn. bd., sr. cons., 1985-87. Mem. adv. bd. Salvation Army, Albuquerque, 1974—, Meals on Wheels, 1987—; past chmn. bd., pres. Presbyn. Heart Inst., Albuquerque, 1977—. Maj. Coast Arty. Anti-Aircraft, 1941-45. Mem. N.Mex. Ins. Assn. (past chmn.), Ins. Info. Inst. (past chmn.), N.Mex. Surplus Lines Assn. (past pres.), Air Force Assn., Assn. of U.S. Army, Am. Legion, Albuquerque C. of C. (mil. rels. com.), Rotary, Masons, Shriners, Albuquerque Country Club, Petroleum Club. Republican. Home: 1812 Stanford Dr NE Albuquerque NM 87106-2538 Office: 8100 Mountain Rd NE Ste 204E Albuquerque NM 87110-7818

TOPHAM, DOUGLAS WILLIAM, writer, consultant; b. Hollywood, Calif.; s. Ollie Austin and Harriet Winifred (Scott) T. BS, Stanford U., 1964, AM, 1965. Cert. secondary tchr., Calif. Tchr. The Principia, St. Louis, 1969-72; instr. Can. Coll., Redwood City, Calif., 1973-74; writer Varian Assocs., Palo Alto, Calif., 1977, Four-Phase Systems Inc., Cupertino, Calif., 1977-80, MicroPro Internat., San Rafael, Calif., 1980-81, Zentec Corp., Santa Clara, Calif., 1981-85; contract writer various cos., 1985—, TeleVideo Systems Inc., Sunnyvale, Calif., 1988-89; freelance writer, cons. Santa Clara, 1989—; cons. ABC-TV, Burbank, Calif., 1974. Author: WordStar Training Guide, 1981, UNIX and XENIX, 1985 (Small Computer Club Book of Month 1985), Using WordStar, 1988, WordPerfect 5.0 with 5.1 Extensions, 1990, A DOS User's Guide to UNIX, 1990, First Book of UNIX, 1990 (Small Computer Club Book of Month 1992), A System V Guide to UNIX and XENIX, 1990, Up and Running with Q & A, 1991, Portable UNIX, 1992 (Small Computer Club Book of Month 1993). Bd. dirs. Las Brisas Condominium Assn., 1988-89, Christian Sci. Ch., 1988-89. Capt. USAF, 1965-69. Acad. scholar Stanford U., 1960-64. Mem. Authors Guild, Writers Connection, Nat. Writers Union.

TOPIK, STEVEN CURTIS, history educator; b. Montebello, Calif., Aug. 6, 1949; s. Kurt and Gertrude Irene (Kriszanich) T.; m. Martha Jane Marcy, Feb. 3, 1979; children: Julia, Natalia. BA, U. Calif., San Diego, 1971; MA, U. Tex., 1973, PhD, 1978. Asst. prof. Universidade Fed. Fluminense, Rio de Janeiro, 1978-81, vis. prof., 1984; asst. prof. Colgate U., Hamilton, N.Y., 1981-84; vis. prof. Univ. Ibero Americana, Mexico City, 1982; assoc. prof. U. Calif., Irvine, 1984—; vis. prof. Ecols des Hautes Etudes en Sci. Social, Paris, 1990; cons. in field; mem. editorial com. U. Calif. Press, Berkeley, 1987-89. Author: The Political Economy of the Brazilian State, 1987; contbr. articles, revs. to profl. publs. Mem. Mayor's Adv. Bd. on Sister Cities, Irvine, 1989-90; mem. adv. bd. Orange County (Calif.) Com. on Latin Am., 1989-90. Fellow NEH, 1987, 89-90, Rockefeller Found., 1977, Social Sci. Rsch. Coun. Mexico City, 1982-83, Fulbright-Hayes Found., 1978-79, 84, U. Calif., 1988-89. Mem. Latin Am. Studies Assn., Am. Hist. Assn., Conf. Latin Am. History (com. on hist. statistics, com. on projects and publs., chair Brazilian studies com. 1988-90), Pacific Coast Coun. on Latin Am. Studies (bd. govs. 1987-90).

TOPJON, ANN JOHNSON, librarian; b. Los Angeles, Dec. 2, 1940; d. Carl Burdett and Margaret Elizabeth (Tildesley) Johnson; m. Gary M. Topjon, 1963; children: Gregory Eric and Cynthia Elizabeth (twins); m. Philip M. O'Brien, 1990. BA, Occidental Coll., 1962; MLS, UCLA, 1963. Reference asst. Whittier (Calif.) Pub. Library, 1973-78; pub. services and reference librarian Whittier Coll., 1981—. Author, bibliography: Carl Larsson. Faculty rsch. grantee Whittier Coll., 1987-88, 91-92, grantee The Am.-Scandinavian Found., N.Y., 1991. Mem. Calif. Acad. and Rsch. Librs. (liaison at Whittier Coll. 1990—), AAUW (Whittier br. 1968-77, Brea-La Habra br., Calif. 1977—, chmn. lit. group, 1977—, chmn. scholarship fund raising 1988-89). Office: Whittier Coll Wardman Libr 7031 Founders Rd Whittier CA 90608

TOPP, ALPHONSO AXEL, JR., environmental scientist, consultant; b. Indpls., Oct. 15, 1920; s. Alphonso Axel and Emilia (Karlsson) T.; m. Mary Catherine Virtue, July 7, 1942; children: Karen, Susan, Linda, Sylvia, Peter, Astrid, Heidi, Eric, Megan, Katrina. BS in Chem. Engring., Purdue U., 1942; MS, UCLA, 1948. Commd. 2d lt. U.S. Army, 1942, advanced through grades to col., 1966, ret., 1970; environ. scientist Radiation Protection Sect., State of N.Mex., Santa Fe, 1970, program mgr., licensing and registration sect., 1978, chief radiation protection bur., 1981-83; cons., 1984—. Decorated Legion of Merit, Bronze Star with 2 oak leaf clusters. Mem. Health Physics Soc., Sigma Xi, Rotary. Republican. Presbyterian. Home and Office: 872 Highland Dr Los Osos CA 93402-3902

TORBERT, MEG BIRCH, artist, design and color consultant; b. Faribault, Minn., Sept. 30, 1912; d. William Alfred and Lucille Birch; m. Arnnold Clair, Aug. 30, 1937 (dec.); m. Donald Torbert, Aug. 12, 1940 (dec. 1985); 1 child, Stephanie B. BA, U. Minn., 1934; MA, U. Iowa, 1938. Prof. Kans. Wesleyan U., Salina, 1934-35, U. Mont., Dillon, 1937-38; assoc. prof. U. Minn., Mpls., 1939-49; curator, editor Walker Art Ctr., Mpls., 1950-63; film dir. NSF, Mpls., 1963-68; freelance color cons., Mpls., 1968-78. Editor Design Quar., 1950-63; dir. (films): Vectors, 1967, Equidecomposable Polygons, 1968; one-woman shows: Hutchins Gallery, Cambria, Calif., 1986, 88, 90, Elizabeth Fortner, Santa Barbara, Calif., 1987, 88, 90, 91, Santa Barbara Art Co., 1992. Carnegie fellow U. Iowa, 1935-37. Home and Studio: 2643 State St Apt 1 Santa Barbara CA 93105

TORBET, WALTER, mechanical engineer; b. Oakland, Calif., May 20, 1933; s. John Allen and Helen (Calver) T.; m. Geraldine Roldanus, Mar. 28, 1960; children: Hugo, Elizabeth, Jessica, Eric. BS in Mech. Engring., U. Calif., Berkeley, 1958. Engr. FMC Corp., San Jose, Calif., 1959-63, SCM Corp., Oakland, 1963-68, Siltec Corp., Menlo Park, Calif., 1976-87; chief engr. Wolff Mfg. Co., Haywark, Calif., 1989. Editor: The Naming of Parts With 30 Characters or Less, 1989; patentee in field. With U.S. Army, 1955-57. Recipient Cert. of Recognition NASA, 1982, 83. Libertarian.

TOREN, ROBERT, photojournalist; b. Grand Rapids, Mich., Oct. 9, 1915; s. Clarence J. and Helen (Holcomb) T.; student Winona Sch. Profl. Photography, 1957, West Coast Sch. Photography, 1959-62; m. Miriam Jeanette Smith, July 17, 1940. Photographer, Harris and Ewing, Washington, 1938-39, Versluis Studios, Grand Rapids, Mich., 1939-43, prodn. mgr., 1940-43; owner, photographer Toren Galleries, San Francisco, 1946-70; photographer Combat Tribes of World, Rich Lee Orgn., 1978-84, Darien jungle expdn. Am. Motors, 1979; feature writer Auburn (Calif.) Jour., El Dorado Gazette, 1983-87, Georgetown Gazette, 1983-93. One man shows various univs.; prints in permanent collections: Photog. Hall of Fame, Coyote Point Mus., San Mateo County Hist. Mus.; photog. column San Mateo Times, Georgetown Gazette; lectr. Am. Pres. Lines, Coll. San Mateo, Peninsula Art Assn., Mendicino Art Ctr. Historian City of Foster City; vice chmn. Art Commn. Foster City. Trustee, West Coast Sch.; bd. dirs. Foster City Art League, Hillbarn Theatre, San Mateo County Arts Council; mem. art com. San Mateo County Fair, 1979-87; coord., dir. Georgetown (Calif.) Mountain Mus., 1982-88; founding pres. Music on The Divide, 1989; pres. El Dorado County Arts Coun. Served from pvt. to staff sgt. AUS, 1943-46. Mem. Calif. Writers (br. pres.), Profl. Photographers Am. Presbyn. Author: Peninsula Wilderness. Illustrator: The Tainted Tree, 1963. Editor: The Evolution of Portraiture, 1965; The Western Way of Portraiture, 1965, Conquest of the Darien, 1984. Home: 3140 Cascade Trl Cool CA 95614-2615

TORGET, ARNE O., electrical engineer; b. Cathlamet, Wash., Oct. 10, 1916; s. John B. and Anna J. (Olson) T.; m. Dorothy M. Lackie, Aug. 30, 1941; children: Kathleen, James, Thomas. BSEE, U. Wash., 1940. Registered prof. elec. engr., Calif. Design engr. Boeing, Seattle, 1940-41, asst. group engr., 1941-46; design specialist N.Am. Aviation, L.A., 1946-50, 60-64, elec. supr., 1950-55; design specialist Rocketdyne N.Am. Aviation, Canoga Park, Calif., 1955-60; design specialist Space Div. Rockwell Internat., Downey, Calif., 1964-79; commr. Wahkiakum Count Pub. Utility, Cathlamet, 1985—; Bd. dirs. Wash. Pub. Utility Dist. Utility Systems, Seattle, 1985—, Wash. Pub. Power Supply System, Richland, 1987—, Wash. Pub. Utility Dist. Assn., Seattle, 1985—. Mem. AAAS, IEEE, Elks. Republican. Roman Catholic. Home: 166 E Sunny Sands Rd Cathlamet WA 98612-9708 Office: Wahkiakum County Pub Utilities Dist 45 Riv St Cathlamet WA 98612

TORKLEP, LYNLEE (LINDA LEE TORKLEP), education educator; b. Rochester, N.Y., Mar. 15, 1942; d. Donald Webster and Marjorie Elizabeth (Loeffler) Crombie; m. Hans Arthur Torklep, Nov. 28, 1964; children: Tracianne Nicole, Tamara Kirsten. BS, Cornell U., 1964; MS, Nova U., 1983. Cert. tchr., vocat. tchr., Wash. Tchr. Auburn (Wash.) Sch. Dist., 1965-67; dir. Children's Ctr. Kent (Wash.), 1979-87, Daybridge Learning Ctrs., Renton, Wash., 1987-88; group ctr. mgr. Children's World Learning Ctrs., Renton, 1988—; on-site trainer Renton Vocat. Tech. Inst., 1981-87, mem. child care specialist adv. bd., 1982-84; validator Nat. Acad. Early Childhood Programs, Washington, 1986—. Mem. occupational adv. com. Highline Community Coll., Midway, Wash., 1979-81; adv. bd. Resource and Referral Ctr., 1990—; del. Seattle-Managua Sister Cities, 1986. Recipient cert. of appreciation Renton Vocat. Inst. Tech., 1982, 83, 84, Highline Community Coll., 1986. Mem. Nat. Assn. for Edn. Young Children, Assn. Childhood Edn. Internat. Republican. Lutheran. Home: 11440 SE 290th Pl Auburn WA 98002

TORRES, ART, state senator; b. L.A.; children: Joaquin, Danielle. AA, East L.A. C.C.; BA, U. Calif., Santa Cruz; JD, U. Calif. John F. Kennedy teaching fellow Harvard U.; senator State of Calif., L.A.; chmn. Senate Com. Ins., Claims and Corps., Assembly Health Com., Senate Toxics and Pub. Safety Mgmt. Com., Select Com. Pacific Rim, Senate Spl. Rask Force on New L.A.; founder Calif. EPA; sr. mem. Senate Edn. Com.; author 1992 Immigrant Workforce Preparation Act; mem. Nat. Conf. State Legislatures Coalition on Immigration, Senate Appropriations Com., Senate Energy and Pub. Utilities Com., Senate Govtl. Orgn. Com., Senate Judiciary Com., Senate Natural Resources Com., Senate Transp. Com. Mem. Coun. Fgn. Rels., N.Y., Nat. Commn. Internat. Migration and Econ. Devel.; participant IVth Nobel Prizewinners Meeting Nova Spes Internat. Found., Vatican, Rome, 1989—. Recipient Legislator of Yr. award Calif. Orgn. Policy and Sheriffs, 1990, Outstanding Legislator of Yr. award Calif. Sch. Bd. Assn., 1990, Outstanding Alumnus award U. Calif. Santa Cruz, Dreamer award Boys and Girls Club Am., 1990, Achievement award Latin Am. Law Enforcement Assn., 1992. Office: Office of State Senate 101 S Broadway #2105 Los Angeles CA 90012

TORRES, CARLOS ALBERTO, education educator; b. Buenos Aires, Oct. 1, 1950; came to U.S., 1980; s. Domingo Roberto and Maria Laura (Novoa) T.; m. Maria Cristina Pons, Mar. 10, 1973; children: Carlos Alberto, Pablo Sebastian, Laura Silvina. BA in Sociology, U. del Salvador, 1974; M. Polit. Sci., Flacso, Mexico City, 1978; MEd, Stanford U., 1982, PhD in Edn., 1984. Cert. sociology tchr., Argentina. Gen. sec. Inst. for Study Sci. Latin Am., Buenos Aires, 1973-75; asst. prof. U. del Salvador, Buenos Aires, 1974-75; assoc. prof. U. Pedagógica Nacional, Mexico City, 1979; prof., researcher Flacso, Mexico City, 1984-86; scholar-in-residence World Coll. W., Petaluma, Calif., 1986; Killam fellow U. Alta., Edmonton, Can., 1986-88, asst. prof., 1988-90; asst. prof. UCLA, 1990-92, assoc. prof., asst. dean for student affairs, 1992—, coord. comparative & topical programs Latin Am. Ctr., 1992—; vis. prof. U. Toronto (Ont., Can.)-Oise, 1989; ind. cons. UNESCO, Paris, 1990-91. Author: The Politics of Nonformal Education, 1990; co-author: The State, Corporatist Politics and Educational Policy Making in Mexico, 1990; author, editor 17 books, over 60 rsch. articles. Fulbright fellow, 1986, Spencer fellow Nat. Acad. Edn., 1990-92; fellow OAS, 1982-84, Stanford U., 1980-83. Fellow Latin Am. Studies Assn.; mem. Internat. Polit. Sci. Assn. (bd. dirs., mem. rsch. com. polit. edn. 1985—), Internat. Sociol. Assn. (bd. dirs. rsch. com. sociology of edn. 1990—), Comparative Internat. Edn. Soc. bd. dirs. 1991—). Office: UCLA Grad Sch Edn Moore Hall 405 Hilgard Ave Los Angeles CA 90024

TORRES, ESTEBAN EDWARD, congressman, business executive; b. Miami, Ariz., Jan. 27, 1930; s. Esteban Torres and Rena Baron (Gomez) T.; m. Arcy Sanchez, Jan. 22, 1955; children: Carmen D'Arcy, Rena Denise, Camille Bianca, Selina Andre, Esteban Adrian. Student, East Los Angeles Coll., 1960, Calif. State U., Los Angeles, 1963, U. Md., 1965, Am. U., 1966; PhD (hon.), Nat. U., 1987. Chief steward United Auto Workers, local 230, 1954-63, dir. polit. com., 1963; organizer, internat. rep. United Auto Workers (local 230), Washington, 1964; asst. dir. Internat. Affairs Dept., 1975-77; dir. Inter-Am. Bureau for Latin Am., Caribbean, 1965-67; exec. dir. E. Los Angeles Community Union (TELACU), 1967-74; U.S. ambassador to UNESCO, Paris, 1977-79; chmn. Geneva Grp., 1977-78; chmn. U.S. del. Gen. Conf., 1978; spl. asst. to pres. U.S., dir. White House Office Hispanic Affairs, 1979-81; mem. 98th-103rd Congresses from 34th Dist. Calif., 1983—, mem. appropriations com., subcom. fgn. opinions, veteran HUD and indep. agys.; campaign coordinator Jerry Brown for Gov., 1974; Hispanic coordinator Los Angeles County campaign Jimmy Carter for Pres., 1976; mem. Sec. of State Adv. Group, 1979-81; v.p. Nat. Congress Community Econ. Devel., 1973-74; pres. Congress Mex.-Am. Unity, 1970-71, Los Angeles Plaza de la Raza Cultural Center, 1974; dir. Nat. Com. on Citizens Broadcasting, 1977; cons. U.S. Congress office of tech. assessment, 1976-77; del to U.S. Congress European Parliament meetings, 1984—; ofcl. congl. observer Geneva Arms Control Talks; chmn. Congl. Hispanic Caucus, 1987; speaker Wrights Del. to USSR, 1987; Dem. dep. Whip, 1990. Contbr. numerous articles to profl. jours. Co-chmn. Nat. Hispanic Dems., 1988—; chmn. Japan-Hispanic Inst. Inc.; bd. visitors Sch. Architecture U. Calif. at Los Angeles, 1971-73; bd. dirs. Los Angeles County Econ. Devel. Com., 1972-75, Internat. Devel. Conf., 1976-78. Served in AUS, 1949-53, ETO. Recipient various awards for public service. Mem. Americans for Dem. Action (exec. bd. 1975-77). Office: House of Representatives Rm 1740 Longworth Office Bldg Washington DC 20515-0534*

TORRES, MICHAEL ALFONSO, insurance underwriter; b. San Diego, Dec. 10, 1956; s. Alfonso and Adele Marie (Mazzeo) T.; m. Teresa Ortiz, June 20, 1975 (div. 1977); 1 child, Elaine M.; m. Virginia Shirley Teas, July 6, 1985; children: Michael A., John M. BA, San Diego State U., 1988; postgrad., Western State U. Sch. Law, 1992—. Fund auditor State Compensation Ins., San Diego, 1988-92, dist. underwriter, 1992—. Res. officer San Diego Police Dept.; mem. Redevel. Project Area Com., San Diego, 1991. With U.S. Army, 1975-78. Mem. Calif. Res. Peace Officers Assn., San Diego State Alumni Assn., Phi Mu Alpha. Office: State Compensation Ins 9444 Waples St San Diego CA 92121

TORREY, JAMES D., communications executive, consultant; b. Drayton, N.D., July 16, 1940; s. Howard J. Torrey and Gertrude (Carpenter) Steenson; m. Katherine Joann Kowal, Sept. 2, 1958; children: Tamara, Timonthy (dec.), Teresa, Todd. Student, U. Oreg. Mgr. Waldport (Oreg.) Food Market, 1959-67; dist. mgr. Obie Outdoor Advt., Aberdeen, Wash., 1967-68; dir. sales Obie Media Corp., Eugene, Oreg., 1968-71, exec. v.p., 1971-78, pres., CEO, 1980-88; pres., CEO Total Comm., Inc., Eugene, Oreg., 1989—; N.W. area market mgr. 3M Nat. Advt., Eugene, Oreg., 1978-80; dir. mktg. State Accident Ins. Fund, Salem, Oreg., 1988-89; mem. exec. com. affiliate bd. Mut. Broadcasting, 1981-87. Pres. Waldport City Coun., 1962-67; coach Eugene Kidsports, 1968-92, ASA Girls Softball Team, 1988; mem. adv. com. 4 J Sch. Dist., 1988-90; bd. dirs. Lane County United Way, 1983-86, dir., 1992, Lane County Goodwill Industries, 1989-90. Named JCI senator, Oreg. State Jaycees, 1966, Citizen of Yr., City of Waldport, 1967, Outstanding Vol., City of Eugene, 1991. Mem. Oreg. Outdoor Advt. Assn. (pres. 1971-80), Oreg. Assn. Broadcasters (dir. 1984-87), Eugene C. of C. (bd. dirs., pres. 1991-92), Eugene Rotary (dir., pres. 1984, Paul Harris fellow 1985). Republican. Roman Catholic. Home: 2545 Chuckanut St Eugene OR 97401 Office: Station KUGN-AM & FM 2545 Chestnut St Eugene OR 97401

TORREZ, NAOMI E., copyright review editor, librarian; b. Scranton, Pa., July 3, 1939; d. Sterling E. and Naomi (Reynolds) Hess; m. Lupe F. Torrez, Dec. 23, 1961; children: Sterling Edward, Stanley Marshall. BA, U. Ariz., 1961; MA, U. Calif., Berkeley, 1964, MLS, 1970; DRE, Golden State Sch. Theology, Oakland, Calif., 1988. Libr. asst. Oakland Pub. Libr., 1966-67, U. Calif. Libr., Berkeley, 1967-70; tutor, couns. Sonoma State Hosp., Eldridge, Calif., 1973-77, libr. tech. asst., 1977-79; health scis. libr. Kaiser Hosp., Vallejo, Calif., 1979-87; copyright review editor Kaiser Dept. Med. Editing, Oakland, 1987—. Author: Not in My Pew, 1990, GSST Research Manual, 1990. Mem. Albany 75th Anniversary Com., 1983. Nat. Merit scholar, 1957, Woodrow Wilson fellow, 1961. Mem. Kaiser Permanente Latino Assn., Kaiser Affirmative Action Com., Kaiser Health Edn. Com., K.P. Regional Libr's. Group (chair 1988), Phi Beta Kappa, Phi Kappa Phi. Baptist. Home: 829 Jackson St Albany CA 94706 Office: Kaiser Dept Med Editing 1800 Harrison 16th Fl Oakland CA 94612

TORRU, JOHN EGON, sales executive; b. San Francisco, Aug. 9, 1963; s. Egon and Marina (Skoblin) T.; m. Katharine Anne Lucas, Aug. 27, 1989. BA in Internat. Econs. and Russian, UCLA, 1986. Sales rep. Procter & Gamble, San Jose, Calif., 1986-87; dist. field rep. Procter & Gamble, San Francisco, 1987-88, sales mgr., 1988—. Mem. Commonwealth Club. Calif. Republican. Russian Orthodox. Home: 109 Arlene Dr Walnut Creek CA 94595

TORRU, KATHARINE LUCAS, bank officer; b. Los Altos, Calif., Apr. 10, 1964; d. John Townsend and Elizabeth (Bergamini) Lucas; m. John Egon Torru, Aug. 27, 1988. BA magna cum laude, UCLA, 1986. CPA, Calif. Sr. auditor Arthur Anderson & Co., San Francisco, 1986-89; bank acctg. dept. mgr. Fremont (Calif.) Bank, 1989—. Mem. Phi Beta Kappa, Chi Omega. Republican. Episcopalian. Office: Fremont Bank 39150 Fremont Blvd Fremont CA 94538-1397

TORTEN, MICHAEL, microbiologist, educator; b. Haifa, Israel, Sept. 25, 1935; came to U.S. 1956; s. Joseph and Fella (Vierny) T.; m. Judith Ann Keller, Aug. 25, 1959; children: Dina, Dan, Ron. BSc, U. Calif., Davis, 1959, DVM, 1963; PhD, Hebrew U., Jerusalem, 1968. Prof. microbiology Israel U. Bio Rsch., Ness Ziona, 1965-90, Tel-Aviv U. Sch. Medicine, 1970—; prof. immunology and surg. oncology UCLA, 1981-83; vis. prof. vet. medicine U. Calif., Davis, 1988-90, rsch. virologist, 1991—; dir. WHO/FAD

Leptospirosis Lab., Ness Ziona, 1965-90. Contbr. over 100 articles to sci. publs.; editor-in-chief Israel Jour. Vet. Medicine, 1985-88; co-editor 2 handbooks on diseases common to man and animal, 1980, 93. Recipient Zur award Israel Ministry of Agr., 1975; Hon. Diplomate Am. Vet. Epidemiology Soc., 1985. Mem. Internat. Immunology Soc., Internat. Microbiology Soc., Internat. Vet. Soc., Rotary (chpt. pres. 1975-76). Office: Univ of Calif Sch Vet Medicine Davis CA 95616

TOSCAN, RICHARD ERIC, college dean, theatre educator; b. N.Y.C., July 1, 1941; s. Vincent E. and Stella (Werner) T.; m. Sharon Walker, Dec. 22, 1979. BA, Purdue U., 1963; MA, U. Ill., 1965, PhD, 1970. Postdoctoral teaching resident NEH, 1967-69; dir. Exptl. Coll. Calif. State U., Fresno, 1968-70; asst. chair div. drama U. So. Calif., L.A., 1970-76, assoc. dean sch. performing arts, 1976-79, assoc. prof. div. of drama, 1979-86, assoc. dean sch. of cinema, 1986-90, dean sch. of theatre, 1990-92; dean sch. fine and performing arts Portland (Oreg.) State U., 1992—; adv. bd. Internat. Contemporary Art Fair, L.A., 1989-91, Tygres Heart Shakespeare Co., Portland, 1992—, Portland Ctr. Performing Arts, 1992—; mem. theatre panel Cultural Affairs Dept., L.A., 1990-92; mem. selection com. Javits fellows U.S. Dept. Edn., Washington, 1990—. Author numerous stage plays, articles to profl. jours.; producer Radio Drama Series, 1981 (recipient Armstrong award 1982). Woodrow Wilson Found. fellow, 1963-64, U. Ill. fellow, 1964. Fellow (assoc.) East Asian Study Ctr., Am. Soc. Theatre Rsch., Assn. Theatre in Higher Edn., Internat. Coun. Fine Arts Deans. Office: Portland State U Sch Fine and Performing Arts Portland OR 97207-0751

TOTH, ELIZABETH LEVAY, retired educational organization executive, lawyer; b. Woodbridge Twp., N.J.; d. Nicholas and Elizabeth (Nagy) Levay; m. Frederick Louis Toth; children: Frederick Albert, Thomas Franklin. BA, Rutgers U., 1970; JD, Seton Hall U., 1973; LLM, NYU, 1980. Bar: N.J. 1973. Mgr., dispatcher, prin. Tri-R-Bus Svc., Inc., Metuchen, N.J., 1959-71; arbitration atty. Robert J. Casulli, East Orange, N.J., 1973; mediator, hearing officer N.J. Pub. Employment Relations Commn., Trenton, 1974-75; assoc. dir. employee relations Woodbridge (N.J.) Twp. Pub. Schs., 1975-81; dir. govt. and community relations Ariz. Sch. Bd. Assn., Phoenix, 1981-85; exec. dir. Greater Phoenix Ednl. Mgmt. Coun., 1985-92; ret., 1992; completed Insts. for Orgnl. Mgmt., San Jose (Calif.) State U. and Stanford U., Calif., 1985-90. Mem. community adv. bd. Sta. KAET-TV, Ariz. State U., Tempe, 1985-91; bd. dirs. North Community Behavioral Health Ctr. (merged into Terros Community Mental Health Orgn. 1988), Phoenix, 1984-88, Ariz. Partnership, 1988-92, Ariz. Alliance Sci., Math. & Tech., 1989-92; sr. arbitrator Better Bus. Bur., Phoenix, 1987—; judge Acad. Decathlon, 1988-92. Recipient plaque and pub. recognition North Community Behavioral Health Ctr., 1987. Mem. Am. Arbitration Assn. (arbitrator), Nat. Panel Mediators, Am. Soc. Assn. Execs., Ariz. Soc. Assn. Execs. (life, bd. dirs. 1987-88, Exec. of Yr. 1987), Soc. Profls. in Dispute Resolution), Pub. Affairs Profls. Ariz., Rutgers U. Alumni Club (pres. 1992-93), Ariz. State U. West Alumni Assn. (sec. 1990-92), Phi Alpha Delta, Alpha Sigma Lambda. Home: 1731 E Alameda Dr Tempe AZ 85282

TOTH, JOSEPH MICHAEL, JR., structural engineer; b. Somerville, N.J., Mar. 8, 1935; s. Joseph Michael and Anna Theresa (Horvath) T.; m. Ann Todd Carlton, Aug. 22, 1959; children: Joseph Michael III, Sarah Ann, Deborah Lynn. Student, Lafayette Coll., 1951-53; BS, MIT, 1956; MS, U. Ariz., 1965, postgrad., 1965-68. Registered profl. engr., Colo. Design engr. U.S. Steel Corp., Fairless Hills, Pa., 1956-58; rsch. assoc. U. Ariz., Tucson, 1958-61; design engr. McDonnell Douglas Corp., Huntington Beach, Calif., 1961-72; program mgr. Martin Marietta Astronautics Group, Denver, 1972—. Contbr. articles to profl. jours.; patentee in field. Mem. ASTM (com. D-30, composites), Soc. for Advancement of Material and Process Engring., AIAA (mem. materials and structures standards panel), MIL-HDBK-17 Coordination Group. Home: 4551 N Lariat Dr Castle Rock CO 80104-9304 Office: PO Box 179 Denver CO 80201-0179

TOTTEN, GEORGE OAKLEY, III, political science educator; b. Washington, July 21, 1922; s. George Oakley Totten Jr. and Vicken (von Post) Totten Barrois; m. Astrid Maria Anderson, June, 1948 (dec. Apr. 26, 1975); children: Vicken Yuriko, Linnea Catherine; m. Lilia Huiying Li, July 1, 1976; 1 child, Blanche Maluk Lemes. Cert., U. Mich., 1943; A.B., Columbia U., 1946, A.M., 1949; M.A., Yale U., 1950, Ph.D., 1954; docenturi Japanologi, U. Stockholm, 1977; docentur i japanologi. Lectr. Columbia U., N.Y.C., 1954-55; asst. prof. MIT, Cambridge, 1958-59, Boston U., 1959-61; assoc. prof. U. R.I., Kingston, 1961-64; assoc. prof. polit. sci. U. So. Calif., L.A., 1965-68, prof., 1968-92, dir. East Asian Studies Ctr., 1974-77, chmn. dept., 1980-86, prof. emeritus, 1992—, affiliated scholar Ctr. for Multiethnic and Transnat. Studies, 1993—; dir., founder Calif. Pvt. Univs. and Colls. (CALPUC) yr.-in-Japan program Weseda U., 1967-73, So. Calif.-UCLA Joint East Asia Ctr., 1976-77; affiliated scholar Ctr. for Multicultural Transnat. Studies, 1993—; vis. prof. U. Stockholm, 1977-79; 1st dir. Ctr. Pacific Asia Studies, 1985-89, sr. counselor bd. dirs., 1989—. Author: Social Democratic Movement in Prewar Japan, 1966, Chinese edit., 1987; co-author: Socialist Parties in Postwar Japan, 1966, Japan and the New Ocean Regime, 1984; co-editor, author: Developing Nations: Quest for a Model, 1970, Japanese edit., 1975, China's Economic Reform: Administering the Introduction of the Market Mechanism, 1992; co-translator; Chien Mu's Traditional Government in Imperial China, 1982; contbr. The Politics of Divided Nations, 1991. Mem. U.S.-China People's Friendship Assn., Washington, 1974—; mem. Com. on U.S.-China Relations, N.Y.C., 1975—; chmn. Los Angeles-Pusan Sister City Assn., Los Angeles, 1976-77; bd. dirs. Los Angeles-Guangzhou Sister City Assn., 1982—, Japan-Am. Soc. Los Angeles, 1981—; mem. nat. adv. com. Japan Am. Student Conf., 1984—, Assn. of Korean Pol. Studies in No. Am., 1992—. 1st lt. AUS, 1942-46, PTO. Recipient Plaque for program on Korean studies Consulate Gen. of Republic of Korea, 1975; Social Sci. Rsch. Coun. fellow, 1952-53; Ford Found. grantee, 1955-58, NSF grantee, 1979-81, Korea Found. grantee, 1993, Rebuild L.A. grantee, 1993. Mem. Assn. for Asian Studies, Am. Polit. Sci. Assn., Asia Soc., Internat. Polit. Sci. Assn., Asia Soc., Internat. Polit. Sci. Assn., Internat. Studies Assn., Japanese Polit. Sci. Assn., European Assn. Japanese Studies, U. So. Calif. Faculty Club, Phi Beta Delta (founding mem. Beta Kappa chpt. 1993—). Episcopalian. Home: 5129 Village Green Los Angeles CA 90016 Office: U So Calif Kerckhoff Hall 734 W Adams Blvd Los Angeles CA 90089

TOUCHBERRY, ROBERT WALTON, animal genetics eduator; b. Manning, S.C., Oct. 27, 1921; s. Samuel Lee and Linwood Miller (Gibson) T.; m. Caroline Fuhrmeister, Sept. 1, 1948; children: Robert Walton Jr., Pamela, Forrest Lee, Alan Bruce. BS, Clemson U., 1945; MS, Iowa State U., 1947, PhD, 1948. Asst. prof., assoc. prof., then prof. genetics U. Ill., Urbana, 1948-70; prof., head dept. animal sci. U. Minn., St. Paul, 1970-82; Senson prof. U. Calif., Davis, 1982-90, chair dept. animal sci., 1982-87, prof. animal sci., 1990—; cons. in animal genetics FAO, USAID, Worldbank, various locations, 1965-89; tech. rep. genetics div. biology and medicine AEC, Germantown, Md., 1967-68; adv. com. Ctr. Vet. Medicine, FDA, Rockville, Md., 1987—. Contbr. sci. papers to profl. publs. Elder Presbyn. Ch., Ill., Minn., Calif., 1960-90; pres. Ill. Congress PTA, Champaign, 1961; coun. com. Champaign area Boy Scouts Am., 1965-70. 2d lt. inf. U.S. Army, 1943-45. Fellow AAAS, Am. Soc. Animal Sci. (program com., Animal Breeding and Genetics award 1971); mem. Am. Dairy Sci. Assn. (bd. dirs. 1977-80), Am. Genetics Assn. Republican. Home: 35 Ely Rd Ely IA 52227 Office: Univ Calif Davis Meyer Hall Davis CA 95616-3521

TOUR, ROBERT LOUIS, ophthalmologist; b. Sheffield, Ala., Dec. 30, 1918; s. R.S. and Marguerite (Meyer) T. Chem.E., U. Cin., 1942, M.D., 1950. Intern, U. Chgo. Clinics, 1950-51; resident U. Calif. Med. Center-San Francisco, 1951-54; practice medicine, specializing in ophthalmology, occupational medicine and plasmapheresis, San Francisco, 1954-76, Fairbanks, Alaska, 1976-79, Phoenix, 1979—; clin. prof. ophthalmology U. Calif.-San Francisco, 1974-76. Maj. AUS, 1942-45. Diplomate Am. Bd. Ophthalmology. Fellow ACS, Am. Acad. Ophthalmology; mem. AMA, MENSA, Ariz. Ophthal. Soc., Phoenix Ophthal. Soc., Calif. Assn. Ophthalmology, Contact Lens Assn. Ophthalmologists, Pacific Coast Oto-Ophthal. Soc., Ariz. Med. Assn., Maricopa County Med. Soc., F.C. Cordes Eye Soc., Sigma Xi, Nu Sigma Nu, Alpha Tau Omega, Tau Beta Pi, Alpha Omega Alpha, Phi Lambda Upsilon, Omicron Delta Kappa, Kappa Kappa Psi. Clubs: Masons, K.T., Lions. Shriners. Home: 2201 E Palmaire Ave Phoenix AZ 85020-5633

TOUSLEY, RUSSELL FREDERICK, lawyer; b. New Haven, Nov. 19, 1938; s. Russell F. and Della (Ermer) T.; m. Sarah Morford, July 23, 1963; children: Ellen Elizabeth, Kenneth Morford. BA cum laude, Yale Coll., 1960; JD, U. Wash., 1967. Bar: Wash. 1967. Assoc. Davis Wright, Seattle, 1967-69; v.p. Safecare Co., Inc., Seattle, 1969-78, Winmar Co., Inc., Seattle, 1977-78; ptnr. Tousley Brain, Seattle, 1978—. Trustee Seattle Opera Assn., 1980—, pres., chmn. bd., 1985-87; trustee Seattle Chamber Music Festival, 1990-93; moderator Plymouth Congl. Ch., Seattle, 1975-77, 83-85, trustee, 1969=93. Lt. (j.g.) USN, 1960-64. Mem. ABA, Wash. State Bar Assn., Seattle King County State Bar Assn., Internat. Coun. Shopping Ctrs. (assoc.), Rainier Club, Seattle Tennis Club. Office: Tousley Brain 700 Fifth Ave AT&T Gateway Tower 56th Fl Seattle WA 98104-5056

TOVAR, CAROLE L., real estate manager; b. Toppenish, Wash., May 19, 1940; d. Harold Max and Gertrude Louisa (Spicer) Smith; m. Duane E. Clark, Aug. 1959 (div. 1963); 1 child, David Allen; m. Vance William Gribble, May 19, 1966 (div. 1989), m. Conrad T. Tovar, June 25, 1992. Student Seattle Pacific Coll. With B.F. Shearer, Seattle, 1959-60, Standard Oil, Seattle, 1960-62, Seattle Platen Co., 1962-70; ptnr. West Coast Platen, Los Angeles, 1970-87, Waldorf Towers Apts., Seattle, 1970—, Cascade Golf Course, North Bend, Wash., 1970-88; co-owner Pacific Wholesale Office Equipment, Seattle and L.A., 1972-87; owner Pacific Wholesale Office Equip., Seattle, L.A. and San Pablo, Calif., 1988-92, Pac Electronic Service Ctr., Commerce and San Pablo, Calif., 1988-90, Waldorf Mgmt. Co., 1988—. Republican. Methodist. Office: 706 Pike St Seattle WA 98101

TOVAR, NICHOLAS MARIO, mechanical engineer; b. Ogden, Utah, Jan. 18, 1960; s. Gerdo and Alice (Martinez) T.; m. Suzanne Oxborrow, Sept. 17, 1982; children: Ashley, Nicholas Brock, Clinton Gregory, Lance Edward. BSME in Logistics Engring., Weber State U., 1986; BSME in Mech. Engring. and Mfg., Nat. U., 1990. Warehouseman R.C. Willey & Son Co., Syracuse, Utah, 1982-85; logistics contr. Utah-Idaho Supply Co., Salt Lake City, 1985-86; assoc. engr. Aerojet TechSystems Co., Sacramento, 1986-87, engr., 1988-89; mech. engr. Aerojet Solid Propulsion, Sacramento, 1990; sr. mech. engr. Aerojet Propulsion div. GenCorp, Sacramento, 1991—. Republican. Mormon. Home: 2360 Cobbleoak Ct Rancho Cordova CA 95670-4230 Office: Aeroject Propulsion Div GenCorp PO Box 13222 Dept 5329 Bldg 49015 Sacramento CA 95813-6000

TOVEY, WELDON REYNOLDS, college dean, engineering educator; b. Malad City, Idaho, Oct. 19, 1938; s. Lester Malcolm and Edith (Reynolds) T.; m. Vicki Rae Bowman, July 15, 1964; children: Kristina, Bradley, Kimberli, Daniel, Camille, Laura Lee. BSME, U. Idaho, 1961, MEd, 1964; EdD, Brigham Young U., 1971. Instr. engring. U. Idaho, Moscow, 1962-64, asst. prof., 1965-71, assoc. prof., asst. dean, 1971-76, prof., asst. dean, 1976-80, prof., assoc. dean, 1980—. Author: Engineering Analysis and Design, 1974, Engineering Graphics Problems, 1975. Bishop LDS Ch., Moscow, 1968-74; counselor LDS Ch. Stake Presidency, Pullman, Wash., 1974-80; pres. LDS Ch. Stake, Pullman, 1980-89; regional rep. LDS Ch. 1991—. Mem. Am. Soc. for Engring. Edn. (Western Electric Fund award 1971), Tau Beta Pi, Sigma Tau, Phi Delta Kappa. Republican. Home: 1130 E 7th St Moscow ID 83843-3713 Office: U Idaho Coll Engring Moscow ID 83843

TOW, BRUCE LINCOLN, computer software architect, consultant; b. Pasadena, Calif., Jan. 6, 1952; s. Philip Samuel and Lois Mary (Rogers) T.; m. Lois Mary Gadway, June 22, 1974; 1 child, Emily Winona. BA in Math., Dartmouth Coll., 1973. Systems programmer Dartmouth Coll., Hanover, N.H., 1971-73; systems rep. Honeywell Info. Systems, Manchester, N.H., 1973-77; sr. systems rep. Honeywell Info. Systems, Evansville, Ind., 1977-78; sr. systems cons. Honeywell Info. Systems, Phoenix, 1979-82; product mgr. Walker Intractive Products, San Francisco, 1982-85; software cons., San Francisco, 1985; dir. application architecture Oracle Corp., Redwood Shores, Calif., 1985—; prin. Synovation, San Francisco, 1990—; presenter Software Monterey Conf., 1992; multi-disciplinary cons. Mem. Synthesis Inst. (founder), N.Y. Acad. Scis. Home: 455 Hazelwood Ave San Francisco CA 94127 Office: Oracle Corp 500 Oracle Park Dr M/S 5659511 Redwood Shores CA 94065

TOWE, THOMAS EDWARD, lawyer; b. Cherokee, Iowa, June 25, 1937; s. Edward and Florence (Tow) T.; m. Ruth James, Aug. 21, 1960; children: James Thomas, Kristofer Edward. Student, U. Paris, 1956; BA, Earlham Coll., 1959; LLB, U. Mont., 1962; LLM, Georgetown U., 1965. Ptnr. Towe, Ball, Enright, Mackey & Sommerfeld, Billings, Mont., 1967—; legislator Mont. House of Rep., Billings, 1971-75, Mont. State Senate, Billings, 1975-87, 91—; served on various coms. Mont. Senate, 1975-87, 91—. Contbr. articles to law revs. Pres. Alternatives, Inc. Halfway House, Billings, 1985-86, mem. 1977—; mem. adv. com. Mont. Crime Control Bd. 1973-78, Youth Justice council, 1981-83; mem. State Dem. Exec. com., 1969-71, Yellowstone County Dem. Exec. Com., 1969-73; clk. Billings Friends Meeting; bd. dirs. Mont. Consumer Affairs Council, Regional Community Services for the Devel. Disabled, 1975-77, Rimrock Guidance Found., 1975-80, Vols. of Am., Billings, 1984-89, Youth Dynamics Inc., 1989—. Capt. U.S. Army, 1962-65. Mem. Mont. Bar Assn., Yellowstone County Bar Assn., Am. Hereford Assn., Billings C. of C., Optimists. Mem. Soc. of Friends. Home: 2739 Gregory Dr S Billings MT 59102 Office: 2525 6th Ave N Billings MT 59101

TOWERS, T. GORDON, Canadian lieutenant governor; b. Red Deer, Alta., Can., July 5, 1919; s. Thomas Henry and Janet (Morrison) T.; m. Doris Roberta Nicholson, Dec. 22, 1940; children: Thomas Robert, Gary Lee, Lynda Marie, Ross Gordon, Leona. Farmer Red Deer; mem. Can. Ho. of Commons, 1972—; lt. gov. Edmonton, Alta., 1991—; del. UN Gen. Assembly, 1978, Can. br. Commonwealth Parliamentary Assn. to the 29th Parliamentary Seminar; chmn. Standing Com. on Privileges and Elections; vice chmn. Standing Com. on Agr.; official Opposition Critic for the Ministry of Supply and Svcs.; dep. official Opposition Critic for the Min. of Vets. Affairs; parliamentary sec. to the Solicitor Gen.; parliamentary sec. to the Min. of State for Sci. and Tech. Pres. River Glen Home and Sch. Assn., Red Deer Exhib. Assn., Prairie Fairs Assn., Red Deer 4-H Coun. Named Paul Harris fellow Rotary Internat., 1989, Citizen of Yr. Red Deer C. of C., 1990. Presbyterian. Office: Office of Lt Gov, 3d Flr Legislature Bldg, Edmonton, AB Canada T5K 2B6

TOWNER, GEORGE RUTHERFORD, writer; b. N.Y.C., Sept. 15, 1933; s. Rutherford Hamilton and Marion (Washburn) T.; m. Danielle Lemoine, Apr. 30, 1985; children: Stephane, Diane, Philip, Claire. BA, U. Calif., 1955, MA, 1956. Asst. dir. Kaiser Found., Richmond, Calif., 1958-60; rsch. engr. Advanced Instrument Corp., Richmond, Calif., 1960-61; pres. Berkeley Instruments, Oakland, Calif., 1962-67; chmn. bd. Towner Systems Corp., San Leandro, Calif., 1968-78; cons. Towner Systems Corp., San Leandro, 1968-78; editor The Ecphorizer, 1981-86; sr. writer Apple Computer, Cupertino, Calif., 1987—. Inventor: Teladvisor Data System, 1962 (awarded 3 Patents 1966-76),. Recipient award of Merit Soc. Technical Communication 1985, 1988. Mem. Soc. Technical Communication, Assn. Computing Machinery, Mensa. Home: 814 Gail Ave Sunnyvale CA 94086-8564 Office: Apple Computer 20525 Mariani Ave Cupertino CA 95014-6201

TOWNER, HOWARD FROST, biologist, educator; b. Los Angeles, Aug. 10, 1943; s. Leonard Wimberley and Caroline Warren (Frost) T.; m. Linda Lorraine Pardee, Aug. 25, 1978; children: Mary, Elizabeth. AB, U. Calif., Riverside, 1965; PhD, Stanford U., 1970. Prof. biology Loyola Marymount U., Los Angeles, 1972—. Bd. dirs. Friends of Ballona Wetlands, Los Angeles, 1977—. Mem. Ecol. Soc. Am., Calif. Bot. Soc., Phi Beta Kappa, Sigma Xi. Home: 8114 Westlawn Ave Los Angeles CA 90045-2753 Office: Loyola Marymount U Dept Biology 7101 W 80th St Los Angeles CA 90045-2699

TOWNER, LARRY EDWIN, consulting company executive; b. Gallup, N.Mex., Sept. 27, 1937; s. Edwin Robert and Esther Kathryn (Kern) T.; m. D. Yvonne Turner, Mar. 12, 1966; children: Kristina Kay, Jennifer Kate. BS in Tech. Mgmt., Am. U., Washington, 1976. Project mgr. Wolf Research, Houston, 1965-66, Gulton SRG, Arlington, Va., 1966-67; dep. for database devel. USN, Washington, 1967-79; mgr., BTP teleprocessing RCA, Cherry Hill, N.J., 1979-80; mgr., data base adminstrn., solid state div. RCA, Somerville, N.J., 1980-82; mgr., systems devel. Hughes Aircraft, El Segundo, Calif., 1982-89; pres. TCSI, Richland, Wash., 1989—. Author: Ads/Online Cookbook, 1986, A Professionals Guide, 1989, Case: Concepts and Implementation, 1989, Oracle: The Professionals Reference, 1991; contbr. articles to profl. jours. Treas. Va. Hills Recreation Assn., Alexandria, 1970-72, pres. 1975-77; active Civil Air Patrol, Alexandria, 1968-79; bd. dirs. Northwest Citizens Radio Emergency Service, Spokane, Wash., 1960-63. Recipient Meritorious Service award Civil Air Patrol, 1976. Mem. IDMS User Assn. (bd. dirs.) (Outstanding Service award, 1984), Hughes Mgmt. Club, Amateur Radio Relay League. Methodist. Home and Office: TCSI 266 Adair Dr Richland WA 99352-9453

TOWNES, CHARLES HARD, physics educator; b. Greenville, S.C., July 28, 1915; s. Henry Keith and Ellen Sumter (Hard) T.; m. Frances H. Brown, May 4, 1941; children: Linda Lewis, Ellen Screven, Carla Keith, Holly Robinson. B.A., B.S., Furman U., 1935; M.A., Duke U., 1937; Ph.D., Calif. Inst. Tech., 1939. Mem. tech. staff Bell Telephone Lab., 1939-47; assoc. prof. physics Columbia U., 1948-50, prof. physics, 1950-61; exec. dir. Columbia Radiation Lab., 1950-52, chmn. physics dept., 1952-55; provost and prof. physics MIT, 1961-66, Inst. prof., 1966-67; v.p., dir. research Inst. Def. Analyses, Washington, 1959-61; prof. physics U. Calif., Berkeley, 1967-86, prof. physics emeritus, 1986—; Guggenheim fellow, 1955-56; Fulbright lectr. U. Paris, 1955-56, U. Tokyo, 1956; lectr., 1955, 60; dir. Enrico Fermi Internat. Sch. Physics, 1963; Richtmeyer lectr. Am. Phys. Soc., 1959; Scott lectr. U. Cambridge, 1963; Centennial lectr. U. Toronto, 1967; Lincoln lectr., 1972-73, Halley lectr., 1976, Krishman lectr., 1992, Nishina lectr., 1992; dir. Gen. Motors Corp., 1973-86; mem. Pres.'s Sci. Adv. Com., 1966-69, vice chmn., 1967-69; chmn. sci. and tech. adv. com. for manned space flight NASA, 1964-69; mem. Pres.'s Com. on Sci. and Tech., 1976; researcher on nuclear and molecular structure, quantum electronics, interstellar molecules, radio and infrared astrophysics. Author: (with A.L. Schawlow) Microwave Spectroscopy, 1955; author, co-editor: Quantum Electronics, 1960, Quantum Electronics and Coherent Light, 1964; editorial bd.; Rev. Sci. Instruments, 1950-52, Phys. Rev., 1951-53, Jour. Molecular Spectroscopy, 1957-60, Procs. Nat. Acad. Scis., 1978-84; contbr. articles to sci. publs.; patentee masers and lasers. Trustee Calif. Inst. Tech., Carnegie Instn. of Washington, Grad. Theol. Union, Calif. Acad. Scis.; mem. corp. Woods Hole Oceanographic Instn. Decorated officier Légion d'Honneur (France); recipient numerous hon. degrees and awards including Nobel prize for physics, 1964; Stuart Ballantine medal Franklin Inst., 1959, 62; Thomas Young medal and prize Inst. Physics and Phys. Soc., Eng., 1963; Disting. Public Service medal NASA, 1969; Wilhelm Exner award Austria, 1970; Niels Bohr Internat. Gold medal, 1979; Nat. Sci. medal, 1983, Berkeley citation U. Calif., 1986; named to Nat. Inventors Hall of Fame, 1976, Engring. and Sci. Hall of Fame, 1983; recipient Common Wealth award, 1993. Fellow IEEE (life medal of honor 1967), Am. Phys. Soc. (pres. 1967, Plyler prize 1977), Optical Soc. Am. (hon., Mees medal 1968), Indian Nat. Sci. Acad., Calif. Acad. Scis.; mem. NAS (coun. 1969-72, 78-81, chmn. space sci. bd. 1970-73, Comstock award 1959), Am. Philos. Soc., Am. Astron. Soc., Am. Acad. Arts and Scis., Royal Soc. (fgn.), Pontifical Acad. Scis., Max-Planck Inst. for Physics and Astrophysics (fgn.). Office: U Calif Dept Physics Berkeley CA 94720

TOWNSEND, GREG, professional football player; b. Los Angeles, Nov. 3, 1961. Student, Long Beach City Coll., Tex. Christian U. Defensive end L.A. Raiders, 1983—. Office: L A Raiders 332 Center St El Segundo CA 90245

TOWNSEND, NEAL, educator, ceramic artist; b. Rock Island, Tex., Oct. 26, 1934; s. Archie Lee and Synthia Ellen (Westbrook) T.; m. Phyllis Virginia Keyes, Mar. 15, 1955 (div. Apr. 1959); 1 dau., Phyllis Lynn; m. Betsy Brown, June 23, 1959; children—Brita, Lissi, Shana, Kristinn. B.F.A., U. N.Mex., 1961, M.A. in Fine Arts, 1962. Grad. asst. U. N.Mex., Albuquerque, 1961-62, asst. prof. art edn., 1970-73, assoc. prof., 1973-81, prof., 1981-91, prof. recreation, 1985-89, prof. emeritus, 1991, lectr. ceramics and jewelry, continuing edn., 1962-72, dir. art edn. gallery, 1982-86; instr. art N.E. La. State U., Monroe, 1962; base crafts dir. GS-9, U.S. Army, Sandia Base, N.Mex., 1962-69, post crafts dir., Ft. Belvoir, Va., 1969-70; owner, operator, exhibitor 10 Craftsmen Gallery, Albuquerque, 1967-69; vis. instr. ceramics Vancouver Sch. Art (B.C., Can.), summer 1972; vis. prof. art No. Ariz. U., Flagstaff, summer 1984; juror art shows, 1986 N.Mex. Arts and Crafts Fair; pres. Albuquerque Designer-Craftsmen, 1966-67, N.Mex. Designer Craftsmen, 1967. One-man shows Fine Arts Gallery N.Mex., Albuquerque, 1961, Johnson Gallery, Albuquerque, 1979, No. Ariz. U., 1980, Fletcher-Brownbuilt Ceramics, Auckland, New Zealand, 1982; numerous group shows include Salzbrand '83, '86, 89, 93, Koblenz, Germany, 1983, IX Biennale de Ceramique d'Art, France, 1984; represented in permanent collections No. Ariz. U., Mus. Albuquerque, Jonson Gallery, U. N.Mex. Art Mus. Bd. dirs. S.W. Arts and Crafts Festival, Albuquerque, 1979-80; panel mem. N.Mex. Bd. Edn., Albuquerque, 1984. Served with USN, 1953-57. Recipient First Pl. award for ceramics Craftsmen N.Mex., 1966, Mus. Internat. Folk Art, Santa Fe, 1967. Democrat. Home: 2583 Ramirez Rd SW Albuquerque NM 87105-4149 Office: U N Mex Dept Art Edn Albuquerque NM 87131

TOWNSEND, RUSSELL HENRY, lawyer; b. Ft. Lewis, Wash., Dec. 27, 1949; s. Peter Lee and Irma Matilda (Greisberger) T.; m. Patricia Susan Parks, Feb. 9, 1985; children: Alexander Peter, Jennifer Sabrina. BS, Calif. Maritime Acad., 1971; JD, Lincoln U., San Francisco, 1979. Bar: Calif., U.S. Dist. Ct. (no. and ea. dists.) Calif. Title examiner Western Title Ins. Co., Oakland, Calif., 1971-74; clk. Garrison, Townsend, Hall and predecessor, San Francisco, 1974-79; ptnr. Amberg & Townsend, San Francisco, 1980-83, Townsend and Bardellini, San Francisco, 1983-87, Townsend, Bardellini, Townsend and Wechsler, San Francisco, 1988-92. Lt.j.g. USNR, 1971-75. Mem. State Bar Calif. Republican. Home: 5 Mae Ct Novato CA 94947-1961 Office: Townsend Law Offices Ste D 2169 E Francisco Blvd San Rafael CA 94901

TOWSE, SALLY JOAN, software engineer, consultant; b. Grand Forks, N.D., Aug. 12, 1952; d. Donald Frederick and Marjorie Janice (Riley) T.; m. Frederic Scott Adams, Nov. 1974 (div. 1978); m. Burton Nathaniel Kendall, Feb. 1979; children: James, Samuel. BA in Biol. Sci., San Jose State U., 1974. Applications engr. Systems Control Inc., Palo Alto, Calif., 1977-83; sr. software engr. Measurex Inc., Cupertino, Calif., 1987-91, cons., 1992—; cons. San Jose City (Calif.) Pub. Libr., 1981-83. Treas. pack 549 Cub Scouts Am., Saratoga, Calif., 1990—; mem. Saratoga Libr. Commn., 1991—, dep. chair, 1992—; table capt. YWCA Santa Clara Valley; ptnrs. in edn. com. Saratoga Edn. Found., 1992—; mem. Friends of Saratoga Pub. Libr. Mem. Writers Connection, Friends of Filoli, Planned Parenthood, MADD. Home: 15211 Bellecourt Saratoga CA 95070

TOYER, RICHARD HENRY, accountant; b. Snohomish, Wash., Aug. 6, 1944; s. Henry James Toyer and Bertha Maud (Darrow) Gilmore; m. Jean Ann Moore, July 1, 1966; 1 child, David K. BS in Acctg., Cen. Wash. U., 1973. CPA. Staff acct. Moss, Adams and Co., Everett, Wash., 1973-74, sr. staff acct., 1975-77; prin. CPA's Inc. PS Toyer and Assocs., CPAs Inc., PS, Everett, Wash., 1977—. Mayor City of Lake Stevens, Wash., 1983-91, city councilman, 1977-83; state treas. Wash. Jaycees, 1975-76; pres. Snohomish Jaycees, 1974-75; mem. Snohomish County Estate Planning Coun.; chmn. Snohomish County Subregional Coun., 1981-82; exec. bd. Puget Sound regional coun., 1981-83; chmn. City of Everett Navy Review Task Force, 1987-88, Snohomish County HUD policy adv. bd., 1982-91; chmn. Snohomish County Cities and Towns, 1983-84, Snohomish County Transp. Authority, 1987-89, Snohomish County Dept. Emergency Mgmt., 1981-91, Snohomish County Tomorrow Steering Com., 1989-91; treas. Lake Stevens Aquafest, 1983-84; sponsor Miss Lake Stevens Pageant, 1983-84; bd. dirs. Josephine Sunset Home, 1993—. Served as Seargent U.S. Army, 1965-67, Vietnam. Mem. AICPA, Wash. Soc. CPAs, Everett C. of C. (treas. 1990—). Lutheran. Home: 15128 76th St SE Snohomish WA 98290 Office: 3201 Broadway Ste C Everett WA 98201-4470

TOYOMURA, DENNIS TAKESHI, architect; b. Honolulu, July 6, 1926; s. Sansuke Fujimoto and Take (Sata) T.; m. Akiko Charlotte Nakamura, May 27, 1949; children—Wayne J., Gerald F., Amy J., Lyle D. BS in Archtl. Engring., Chgo. Tech. Coll., 1949; cert., U. Ill., Chgo., 1950, 53, 54; student, Ill. Inst. Tech., Chgo., 1953-54; cert., U. Hawaii-Dept. Def., Honolulu, 1966-67, 73. Lic. architect, Ill. 1954, Hawaii 1963; lic. real estate broker Ill., 1957. Designer, draftsman James M. Turner, Architect, Hammond, Ind., 1950-51, Wimberly and Cook, Architects, Honolulu, 1952, Gregg, Briggs & Foley, Architects, Chgo., 1952-54; architect Holabird, Root & Burgee,

Architects, Chgo., 1954-55, Loebl, Schlossman & Bennett, Architects, Chgo., 1955-62; prin. Dennis T. Toyomura, AIA, Architect, Honolulu, 1963-83, Dennis T. Toyomura, FAIA, Architect, Honolulu, 1983—; fallout shelter analyst Dept. Def., 1967—; cert. analyst multi-distaster design, Dept. Def., 1973; cert. value engr. NavFacEngCom., Gen. Svc. Adminstrn., Environ. Protection Agy., Fed. Housing Agy., U.S. Corps. of Engrs., 1988; cons. Aloha Tower Devel. Corp., State of Hawaii Project Devel. Evaluation Team, 1989, archl. cons. 1991—; mem. Provost Selection Interview Com., Leeward Community Coll., U. Hawaii, 1987; design profl. conciliation panelist Dept. of Commerce and Consumer Affairs, State of Hawaii, 1983, 84; archtl. design examiner Nat. Council of Archtl. Registration Bd., State of Hawaii, 1974-78; cons. Honolulu Redevel. Agy., City and County of Honolulu, 1967-71; sec., dir. Maiko of Hawaii, Honolulu, 1972-74, Pacific Canal of Hawaii, 1972; mem. steering com. IX world conf. World Futures Studies Fedn., U. Hawaii, 1986; conf. organizer pub. forum 10th Hawaii Conf. in High Energy Physics, U. Hawaii, 1985, 60th Ann. Nat. Council of Archtl. Registration Bd. Conv., Maui, Hawaii, 1981, Hawaii State Bd. Conv. steering com.; del. Nat. Credential Com., NCARB, 1981, 125th Nat. AIA Com., Honolulu, 1982, HS/AIA Conv. Com., steering com., budget and fin. chmn., treas., 1981-82, appointments State of Hawaii; mem. legis. adv. com. Hawaii State Legis.; vice chmn. Rsch. Corp. U. Hawaii, 1991-93, bd. dirs. 1986—; commr. Hawaii State Found. on Culture and the Arts, 1982-86, Gov.'s Com. on Hawaii Econ. Future, 1984; archtl. mem. Bd. Registration for Profl. Engrs., Architects, Land Surveyors and Landscape Architects, State of Hawaii, 1974-82, sec. 1980, vice chmn. 1981, chmn., 1982; mem. Nat. Coun. Engring. Examiners, 1974-82; mem. Nat. Coun. Archtl. Registration Bds., Western region del. 1974-82, nat. del. 1974-82. Editor, pub.: (directory) Japanese Companies Registered to do Business in Hawaii, 1991. Del. commr. state assembly Synod of Ill., United Presbyn. Ch. U.S.A., 1958, alt. del. commr. nat. gen. assembly, 1958, del. commr. L.A. Presbytery, 1965; mem. bd. session 2d Presbyn. Ch., Chgo., 1956-62, trustee, 1958-62; trustee 1st Presbyn. Ch., Honolulu, 1964-66, 69-72, sec., 1965, bd. sessions, 1964-72, 74-79; founding assoc. Hawaii Loa Coll., Kaneohe, 1964; mem. adv. commn. drafting tech. Leeward Community Coll., U. Hawaii, 1965—; bd. dirs. Lyon Arboretum Assn., U. Hawaii, 1976-77, treas.,1976. With AUS, 1945-46. Recipient Human Resources of U.S.A. award Am. Bicentennial Rsch. Inst., 1973, Outstanding Citizen Recognition award Cons. Engrs. Coun. Hawaii, 1975, cert. appreciation Gov. Hawaii, 1982, 86, 89, commendation Hawaii Ho. of Reps. and Senate, 1983, 90, 91, cert. appreciation Leeward Community Coll., U. Hawaii Adv. Com., 1971-86, 87—, medal for peace Albert Einstein Internat. Acad. Found., 1990, commendation resolution Honolulu, Japanese C. of C., 1991. Fellow AIA (Coll. Fellows 1983, bd. dirs. Hawaii Soc. 1973-74, treas. 1975, pres. Hawaii coun. 1990, Pres.'s Mahalo award 1981, Fellows medal 1983); mem. AAAS (life), ASTM, Am. Arbitration Assn. (mem. panel of arbitrators, 1983—), Acad. Polit. Sci. (life), Am. Acad. Polit. and Social Scis., N.Y. Acad. Scis., Chgo. Art Inst., Chgo. Natural History Mus., HonoAcad. Arts, Nat. Geog. Soc., Coun. Ednl. Facility Planners Internat. (bd. govs. N.W. region 1980-86, 89—), Bldg. Rsch. Inst. (adv. bd. of Nat. Acad. Sci.), Ill. Assn. Professions, Constrn. Specifications Inst. (charter mem. Hawaii), Constrn. Industry Legis. Orgn. (bd. dirs. 1973-81, 83—, treas. 1976-77, v.p. 1990-91, pres. 1991—), Japan-Am. Soc., Hawaii State C. of C. (bd. dirs. 1984-87), U. Hawaii Kokua O'Hui, O'Nahe Popo (bd. dirs. 1984—), Hawaii-Pacific Rim Soc. (bd. trustees 1988—, sec. 1991—), Malolo Mariners Club (purser 1964, skipper 19865, Hawaii), Alpha Lambda Rho, Kappa Sigma Kappa. Home: 2602 Manoa Rd Honolulu HI 96822-1703 Office: Dennis T Toyomura FAIA Architect 1370 Kapiolani Blvd Honolulu HI 96814-3605

TRABANT, DENNIS CARLYLE, glaciologist; b. Lawrence, Kans., Oct. 2, 1943; s. Carlyle Earl and Lauretta Louise (Gerstenberger) T.; m. Evelyn Irene Johnson, Jan. 28, 1966; children: Tonya Denise, Chad Michael. BS, Kans. State U., 1966; MS, U. Alaska, 1970. Sr. rsch. asst. Geophys. Inst., U. Alaska, Fairbanks, 1970-73; hydrologist, glaciologist U.S. Geol. Survey-Nat. Rsch. Program, Fairbanks, 1973-87, U.S. Geol. Survey-Alaska Dist. Office Staff, Fairbanks, 1987—; reviewer Internat. Glaciol. Soc., Cambridge, Eng., 1988; speaker in field. Contbr. numerous articles to profl. jours. Recipient Spl. Achievement award U.S. Geol. Survey, 1990. Mem. Internat. Glaciol. Soc., Arctic Inst. North Am., Interagy. Hydrology Com. for Alaska, Am. Inst. Hydrology (local chpt. sec. 1988—, cert. profl. hydrologist), Am. Geophys. Union. Office: US Geol Survey 800 Yukon Dr Fairbanks AK 99775-5170

TRABITZ, EUGENE LEONARD, aerospace company executive; b. Cleve., Aug. 13, 1937; s. Emanuel and Anna (Berman) T.; m. Caryl Lee Rine, Dec. 22, 1963 (div. Aug. 1981); children: Claire Marie, Honey Caryl; m. Kathryn Lynn Bates, Sept. 24, 1983. BA, Ohio State U., 1965. Enlisted USAF, 1954, advanced through grades to maj.; served as crew commdr. 91st Stragetic Missile Div., Minot, S.D., 1968-70; intelligence officer Fgn. Tech. Div., Dayton, Ohio, 1970-73; dir. external affairs Aero Systems Div., Dayton, 1973-75; program mgr. Air Force Armament Div., Valparaiso, Fla., 1975-80; dir. ship ops. Air Force Ea. Test Range, Satellite Beach, Fla., 1980-83; dep. program mgr. Air Force Satellite Text Ctr., Sunnyvale, Calif., 1983-84; ret., 1984; sr. staff engr. Ultrasystems Inc., 1984-86; pres. TAWD Systems Inc., Palo Alto, Calif., 1986-92, Am. Telenetics Co., San Mateo, Calif., 1992—; cons. Space Applications Corp., Sunnyvale, 1986-87, Litton Computer Svcs., Mountain View, Calif., 1987-91. Pres. bd. County Mental Health Clinic, Ft. Walton Beach, Fla., 1973-75. Decorated Bronze Star. Mem. DAV (life), World Affairs Coun., U.S. Space Found. (charter), Air Force Assn. (life), Assn. Old Crows, Nat. Sojourners, Masons. Home: 425 Anchor Rd Ste 317 San Mateo CA 94404

TRACHTENBERG, ALAN ISRAEL, public health physician; b. Phila., Oct. 27, 1956; s. Jesse Myron and Myra Rose (Glogover) T. BS cum laude, Rensselaer Poly. Inst., 1978; MD, Tuft U. Sch. Medicine, 1980; intern's cert., Oreg. Health Scis. U., 1981; MPH, U. Calif., Berkeley, 1986. Diplomate Am. Bd. Preventive Medicine, Nat. Bd. Med. Examiners. Resident in family practice Oreg. Health Sci. U., Portland, 1980-81; resident in preventive medicine U. Calif., Sch. Pub. Health, Berkeley, 1984-86; clinic physician West Berkeley Community Health Ctr., 1985; med. advisor Social Security Adminstrn., Office Hearing and Appeals, 1987-91; physician City of Berkeley Health Dept., 1987-88; pub. health med. officer III Calif. Dept. Health Svcs., 1988-89; med. dir. Bay Area Addiction Rsch. and Treatment, San Francisco, 1989-90; med. officer NIH/Nat. Inst. on Drug Abuse/Office of Sci. Policy, Rockville, Md., 1991—; cons. Calif. Med. Assn. Task force on AIDS and Sexually Transmitted Diseases, 1988—, U. Calif., San Francisco AIDS Profl. Edn. Project, 1988—, Calif. Dept. Health Svcs., Office of Family Planning, 1986-88; cons., vol. physician Oakland Feminist Women's Health Ctr.; clin. instr. Claemore Comprehensive Indian Health Fac ility, 1983-84; instr. Am. Coll. Traditional Chinese Medicine, San Francisco, 1985-90; mem. task force against MDR-TB USPHS, 1992—; mem. interdepartmental working group Presdl. Task Force Health Care Reform, 1993—. Ad hoc referee Jour. of AMA, 1988—; contbr. articles to profl. jours. Lt. USPHS, 1982-84. Recipient Physician Recognition awards AMA, 1983, 87, Med. Svc. award Rogers County Cherokee Assn., 1984. Fellow Am. Coll. Preventive Medicine, Am. Acad. Family Physicians; mem. AAAS, N.Y. Acad. Scis., Am. Acad. Family Physicians, Am. Pub. Health Assn., Physicians for Social Responsibility, Assn. Tchr. of Preventive Medicine, Physicians for a Nat. Health Program, Physicians for Reproductive Health, Am. Coll. Preventive Medicine. Jewish.

TRACY, (DEBORAH) ANN, director, actress, freelance writer; b. Waltham, Mass., Aug. 9, 1951; d. David McElroy and Mary Elizabeth (Maher) Sinclaire; m. Patrick Tracy, 1974 (div. 1977); m. John A. Kreutzberger, July 13, 1979. BA in Liberal Arts, Western Ill. U., 1992. News anchor Sta. KTLK radio, Denver, 1977, Stas. WXJY and WOKY radio, Milw., 1978-80; news/pub. affairs dir. Sta. WQFM radio, Milw., 1980-81; asst. news dir., anchor Sta. WBCS AM-FM radio, Milw., 1981-83; news/pub. affairs dir. Sta. KWSS radio, San Jose, Calif., 1983-84; morning news anchor Sta. KGNR radio, Sacramento, 1985-87; comml. voice-overs various prodn. cos. and agys. Milw., Sacramento, 1981—; freelance writer Sacramento, 1986—. Asst. dir. "The Curious Savage," Theatre El Dorado, Placerville, Calif., 1992; dir. "The Play" by Beckett-Bilhenny Studios, Milw., 1982, "Chamber Music" by A. Kopit, Highland Exptl. Theatre, Boulder, 1975; author (play) Liver Lips/Carrot Hips, 1991; dir. premier The Atelier, 1993; artistic dir. Foothill Actors Theatre, Placerville, 1992—; installation artist: Gotta Go; dir. 1959 Pink Thunderbird, 1993. Mem. El Dorado Arts Coun. (treas. 1986, pres. 1987-88), Soc. Stage Dirs. and Choreographers. Home and Office: 4781 Gold Creek Ln Diamond Springs CA 95619

TRACY, EMILY ANNE MILLER, social services administrator; b. N.Y.C., June 5, 1947; d. James Edward and Margaret Howard (Kinsey) Miller; m. Jack Herbert Tracy, June 7, 1969 (div. 1986); children: Christopher Ryan, Neil Brendan. BA, U. Colo., 1969, MPA, 1983. Writer, reporter Fremont County SUN Newspapers, Canon City, Colo., 1981-83; quality control compliance reviewer Colo. Dept. Social Svcs., Colo. Springs, 1983-85; child protection caseworker Fremont County Dept. Social Svcs., 1985-90; foster care reviewer, team leader Colo. Dept. Social Svcs., Denver, 1990—. Mem. Canon City City Coun., 1983-92; mem. Jud. Performance Commn. 11th Jud. Dist. Colo., Gt. Outdoors Colo.; bd. dirs. Fremont County Econ. Devel. Corp., 1985-91, Main Street U.S.A., Canon City, 1987-89. Mem. Zonta, Phi Beta Kappa, Pi Alpha Alpha. Democrat. Home: 612 N 11th St Canon City CO 81212-3049

TRACY, JAMES JARED, JR., law firm administrator; b. Cleve., Jan. 17, 1929; s. James Jared and Florence (Comey) T.; m. Elizabeth Jane Bourne, June 30, 1953 (div. 1988); children: Jane Mackintosh, Elizabeth Boyd, James Jared IV, Margaret Gardiner; m. Judith Anne Cooper, Feb. 18, 1989. AB, Harvard U., 1950, MBA, 1953. CPA, Ohio. Acct., mgr. Price Waterhouse & Co., Cleve., 1953-65; treas., CFO Clevite Corp., Cleve., 1965-69; asst. treas. Republic Steel Corp., Cleve., 1969-70, treas., 1970-75; v.p., treas. Johns-Manville Corp., Denver, 1976-81; v.p., treas., CFO I. T. Corp., L.A., 1981-82; exec. dir. Hufstedler, Miller, Carlson & Beardsley, L.A., 1983-84, Shank, Irwin & Conant, Dallas, 1984-85, Pachter, Gold & Schaffer, L.A., 1985-86; v.p., sr. cons. Right Assocs., L.A., 1987-91; dir. adminstrn. Larson & Burnham, Oakland, Calif., 1991—; trustee and v.p. Miss Hall's Sch., Pittsfield, Mass., 1970-78; dir. Union Commerce Bank, Cleve., 1971-76; adv. bd. mem. Arkwright-Boston Ins. Co., Boston, 1976-81. Trustee and v.p. Cleve. Soc. for Blind, 1965-76; trustee Western Res. Hist. Soc., Cleve., 1972-76; treas. St. Peters by the Sea Presbyn. Ch., Palos Verdes, Calif., 1981-91. Recipient Alumni award Harvard U., Denver, 1981. Mem. AICPA, Ohio Soc. CPAs, Assn. Legal Adminstrs., Nat. Assn. Realtors, Piedmont Montclair Rotary Club, Harvard Club of San Francisco. Home: 180 Lombardy Ln Orinda CA 94563 Office: Larson & Burnham 1901 Harrison St 11th Fl Oakland CA 94612

TRAEGER, RICHARD K., engineer; b. Madison, Wis., Aug. 27, 1932; s. Edgar A. and Hildegard A. (Hessert) T.; m. Carol R. Sonnenburg, Sept. 15, 1954; children: Richard K., Mark S.,Scott R., Kim L. BS, U. Wis., 1954; MS, Case Western Res. U., 1958; PhD, U. N.Mex., Albuquerque, 1965. Process devel. engr. B.F. Goodrich Chem. Co., Avon Lake, Ohio, 1954-57; process design engr. B.F. Goodrich Chem. Co., Cleve., 1957-58; fellow Inst. Paper Chemistry, Appleton, Wis., 1958-59; instr. U. N.Mex., Albuquerque, 1959-63, adj. prof., 1963-80; supr., staff mem. Sandia Nat. Labs., Albuquerque, 1963-79, dept. mgr., 1979—; mem. continental drilling com. NRC, Washington, 1979-82; mem. ocean drilling-downhole measurements panel NSF, College Station, Tex., 1986-88. Contbr. articles to profl. jours. Asst. scoutmaster, scoutmaster Boy Scouts Am., Albuquerque, 1954-76; chmn., mem. Luth. Student Ctr., Albuquerque, 1954-58. Mem. IEEE, Am. Soc. Engring. Edn., Am. Inst. Chem. Engrs. (nat. bd. dirs. 1986-89, sec.). Republican. Home: 11721 Tivoli Ave NE Albuquerque NM 87111-5240 Office: Sandia Nat Labs Dept 7022 PO Box 5800 Albuquerque NM 87185-5800

TRAFTON, STEPHEN J., banking executive; b. Mt. Vernon, Wash., Sept. 17, 1946; m. Diane Trafton; children: John, Roland. BS in Zoology, Wash. State U., 1968. V.p., mgr. dept. money market Seattle-First Nat. Bank, 1968-79; v.p., mgr. bank consulting group Donaldson Lufkin Jennrette, N.Y.C., 1980; exec. v.p., treas. Gibraltar Savings Bank, L.A., 1980-84; banking cons., 1984-86; v.p., treas. Hibernia Bank, San Francisco, 1986-88; sr. v.p., treas. Goldome Bank, Buffalo, N.Y., 1988-90; sr. exec. v.p., CFO Glenfed Inc., 1990-91, vice chmn., CFO, 1991—, pres., 1992—; sr. exec. v.p., CFO Glendale Fed. Bank, 1990-91, vice chmn., CFO, 1991, pres., COO, 1991-92, chmn. bd., pres., CEO, 1992—. Mem. Phi Eta Sigma. Office: Glenfed Inc 700 N Brand Blvd Glendale CA 91203-1238*

TRAGER, RUSSELL HARLAN, publishing company executive; b. Cambridge, Mass., Sept. 26, 1945; s. Nathan Allan and Shirley (Gibbs) T.; m. V. Jan Adams, Aug. 19, 1968 (div. July 1975); 1 child, Eric Todd; m. Edna Marie Sanchez, Feb. 16, 1980; children: Felice Rosanne, Justin Tomas. AA, Newton Jr. Coll., 1965; BS, U. Miami, 1968; postgrad., Harvard U., 1968-69. Account rep. Hervic Corp., Sherman Oaks, Calif., 1972-75, Canon USA, Lake Success, N.Y., 1975-78; key account sales rep. Yashica Inc., Glendale, Calif., 1978-79; sales rep. Region I United Pubs. Corp., Beverly Hills, Calif., 1979-81, sales mgr., 1981-83; regional pres. United Pubs. Corp., Carson, Calif., 1983-86, region v.p., 1986-88; v.p. sales United Pubs. Corp. divsn. of Nynex Co., El Segundo, Calif., 1988-91; dir. sales Yelex Corp., L.A., 1991-92; sales mgr. Trader Publishing Co., L.A., 1992—. Home: 1201 11th St Manhattan Beach CA 90266-6025 Office: Trader Publishing Co 16114 Sherman Way Van Nuys CA 91406

TRAHERN, GEORGE EUGENE, real estate appraiser and owner; b. Grants Pass, Oreg., June 29, 1936; s. Eugene Goodyear and Lela Marie (Feldmaier) T.; m. Darlene Irma Taylor, Dec. 22, 1956; children: Karen Marie Bodeving, Eugene Lyle, Keith Charles. BS, U. Oreg., 1960. Owner, dealer, gen. mgr. Trahern Motors, Inc., Grants Pass, Oreg., 1960-68, John Day, Oreg., 1969-71; asst. mgr. Keith Roberts Ford, Cottage Grove, Oreg., 1959-60; dep. assessor Josephine County, Grants Pass, 1971-73, county assessor, 1973-81; owner, appraiser Trahern Real Estate Appraiser, Grants Pass, 1981—; owner, dealer, gen. mgr. N.Valley Auto Ctr., Inc., Grants Pass, 1985-87. Capt., sec. Josephine County Sheriff's Mounted Posse, Grants Pass, 1971-88; Rep. Oreg. Legis. Assembly, Salem, Oreg., 1981-88, Oreg. State Senate, 1988-89; bd. dirs. shooting sports com. Oreg. 4-H Club, Corvallis, Oreg., 1986-87. With USN, 1954-56, USNR, 1956-62. Recipient 3 Quality Dealer awards Chrysler Corp., 1961, 62, 64, Merit award Internat. Harvester, Inc., 1964, Pentastar Club award Chrysler Corp., 1986. Mem. Nat. Assn. Real Estate Appraisers (cert. comml. real estate appraiser), Josephine County Hist. Soc. (bd. dirs. Grants Pass chpt. 1975-88), Grants Pass Knife & Fork Club (pres. 1978-79), Rotary, Order of Ea. Star (worthy patron 1966-67). Republican. Methodist (past pastor parish rels., bd. dirs.). Home: 4011 Williams Hwy Grants Pass OR 97527-8751 Office: 514 NE 7th St Grants Pass OR 97526

TRAILL, DAVID ANGUS, classics educator; b. Helensburgh, Scotland, Jan. 28, 1942; came to U.S., 1965; s. Angus Nicolson and Elizabeth Blyth (Wilson) Trail. MA, U. St. Andrews, Scotland, 1964; PhD, U. Calif.-Berkeley, 1971. Lectr. classics McGill U., Montreal, Que., Can., 1964-65; teaching asst. U. Calif.-Berkeley, 1965-68; asst. prof. U. Calif.-Davis, 1970-78, assoc. prof., 1978-85; prof., 1985—; cons. prodn. documentaries on Schliemann and Troy, Brit. Broadcasting Corp., London, 1980-81, 84. Author: Walahfrid Strabo's Visio Wettini: Text, Translation and Commentary, 1974; co-editor: Myth, Scandal, and History: The Heinrich Schliemann Controversy, 1986; contbr. articles to profl. jours. Mem. Am. Philol. Assn., Archaeol. Inst. Am. Home: 1351 Monarch Ln Davis CA 95616-1636 Office: Classics Dept U Calif Davis CA 95616

TRAMMELL, MARTIN GIL, humanities educator; b. Seattle, Apr. 13, 1959; s. Charles and Joyce (Reeves) T.; m. Linda Elaine Markwood, Aug. 28, 1982; children: Justin, Christopher, Joshua. BS, We. Oreg. State U., 1982, MA, 1986; BEd, We. Bapt. Coll., 1983, ThB, 1985. Rte. coord. Stovers, Seattle, 1982; dir. of field edn. We. Bapt. Coll., Salem, Oreg., 1983, instr., 1982-84; asst. prof. We. Bapt. Coll., Salem, 1985-86, assoc. prof., 1986—; pastor of youth and family Valley Bapt. Ch., Perrydale, Oreg., 1982-91; seminar speaker We. Bapt. Coll., 1982—. Asst. dir. Salem-Willamette Area Teens, Salem, 1987—. Mem. Internat. Soc. for Gen. Semantics. Office: Western Bapt Coll 5000 Deer Park Dr SE Salem OR 97301

TRAN, NGHIA T., mechanical engineer; b. Saigon, Vietnam, Nov. 10, 1963; came to U.S., 1975; s. Nhan Van Tran and Oanh Thu Nguyen; m. Carolyn Michelle Marlett, June 10, 1989. BS in Mech. Engring., Seattle U., 1985; MSCE, U. Colo., 1987. Admnstrv. asst. City of Seattle, 1984-85; structural engr. Boeing Co., Seattle, 1985; rsch. asst. U. Colo., Boulder, 1985-86; co-op engr. Rockwell Internat., Golden, Colo., 1986-87, sr. process engr., 1988-90; project engr. Merrick & Co., Denver, 1987-88; sr. process engr. E G & G Rocky Flats, Inc., Golden, 1990-91; project mgr. Merrick & Co., Denver, 1991—; pres. Tran Engring. Corp., Westminster, Colo., 1986. Author: Field Measurement of Chilled Water Storage System Thermal Performance, 1987. Grantee ASHRAE, 1987-89. Mem. Tau Beta Pi, Sigma Nu. Republican. Roman Catholic. Home: 14533 W 69th Pl Arvada CO 80004-5916

TRANG, KIEN, pharmacist; b. Quang Ngai, Vietnam, Dec. 17, 1933; came to U.S., 1975; s. Cha Van and Chat Thi Trang; m. Duythanh Tonnu, Mar. 21, 1961; children: Thien-Tam, Thien-Chau, Duc, Nhan. Degree pharmacy, U. Saigon, Vietnam, 1959; postgrad., U. Paris, 1965-66; BS in Pharmacy, U. Tex., 1977. Owner Duythanh Pharmacy, Saigon, 1960-65; chief pharmacist Conghoa Gen. Hosp., Saigon, 1966-71; dep. dir. med. logistics Dept. Health, Saigon, 1971-75; staff pharmacist Bay Gen. Hosp., San Diego, 1978-80; owner Kien's Pharmacy, San Diego, 1980—; bd. dirs. Linda Vista Health Care Ctr., San Diego, 1982-84, 91—. Pub. and editor: San Diego Tin Tuc Mag., 1982-86; pub. Bantin Datlanh, San Diego, 1989—. Maj. Vietnam Med. Corps, 1959-75. Mem. Vietnamese Pharmacist Assn. in U.S.A. (v.p. 1980-82), Indochinese C. of C. (founder and pres. 1982-85), Vietnamese Fedn. San Diego (founder and pres. 1989-91). Office: Kien's Pharmacy 2354 Ulric St San Diego CA 92111

TRANQUADA, ROBERT ERNEST, medical educator, physician; b. Los Angeles, Aug. 27, 1930; s. Ernest Alvro and Katharine (Jacobus) T.; m. Janet Martin, Aug. 31, 1951; children: John Martin, James Robert, Katherine Anne. B.A., Pomona Coll., 1951; M.D., Stanford U., 1955; D.Sc. (hon.), Worcester Poly. Inst., 1985. Diplomate Am. Bd. Internal Medicine. Intern in medicine UCLA Med. Center, 1955-56, resident in medicine, 1956-57; resident Los Angeles VA Hosp., 1957-58; fellow in diabetes and metabolic diseases UCLA, 1958-59; fellow in diabetes U. So. Calif., 1959-60, asst. prof. medicine, 1960-63, assoc. prof., 1964-68, chmn. dept. community medicine, 1967-75, prof. medicine, 1986—; med. dir. Los Angeles County/U. So. Calif. Med. Center, 1969-74; regional dir. Central Region, Los Angeles County Dept. Health Services, 1974-76; assoc. dean UCLA, 1976-79; chancellor and dean U. Mass. Med. Sch., 1979-86; dean sch. medicine U. So. Calif. Sch. Medicine, 1986-91; prof. medicine U. So. Calif., 1986—; mem., chair L.A. County Task Force on Health Care Access, 1992—. Contbr. numerous articles to profl. publs. Trustee Pomona Coll., 1969—; vice chmn., 1987-91, chmn., 1991—; mem. bd. fellows Claremont U. Ctr., 1971-79, 91—; corporator Worcester Art Mus., 1980-86; bd. dirs. Nat. Med. Fellowships, Inc., 1973—, chmn., 1980-85; trustee Charles Drew U. Medicine and Sch., 1968-79, 86—, Orthopaedic Hosp., 1986-91, Barlow Hosp., 1987-89; bd. dirs. Worcester Acad., 1984-86, Worcester County Inst. for Savs., 1982-86, U. So. Calif. Univ. Hosp., 1988-91; mem. Ind. Commn. on L.A. Police Dept., 1991—. Milbank faculty fellow, 1967-72. Fellow AAAS, Am. Antiquarian Soc.; mem. AMA, Am. Diabetes Assn., Western Soc. Clin. Investigation, Los Angeles County Med. Assn., Los Angeles Acad. Medicine, Calif. Med. Assn., Inst. Medicine of Nat. Acad. Scis., Phi Beta Kappa, Sigma Xi, Alpha Omega Alpha. Office: U So Calif VKC 368A Los Angeles CA 90089-0041

TRANSUE, PAMELA JEAN, dean; b. Caldwell, Idaho, Apr. 5, 1950; d. Howard L. and Melba I. (Kimmell) T.; m. Ben Drake, June, 1972 (div. June 1981). BA summa cum laude, U. Wash., 1972; MA, Ohio State U., 1976, PhD, 1981. Asst. dir. continuing edn. Ohio State U., Columbus, 1980-82; spl. asst. to pres. U. Wash., Seattle, 1982-88; exec. dean Portland (Oreg.) Community Coll., 1989—. Author: Virginia Woolf & the Politics of Style, 1986; co-editor: Rebirth, Reform, Resilience: Universities in Transition, 1300-1700, 1984; contbr. articles to profl. jours. Mem. Mayor's Task Force on Pub. Works, 1990, Portland Fire Bur. Adv. Com., 1990—; bd. dirs. Portland Devel. Commn./Jobnet, 1990—, No. Region Welfare Reform Adv. Com., 1990—. Presdl. fellow Ohio State U., 1980-81; White House regional fin. fellow, 1985. Mem. Nat. Inst. for Leadership Devel. of Community Coll. CEOs, Am. Assn. Women in Community and Jr. Colls., Oreg. Assn. Minority Entrepreneurs, Am. Assn. Community Colls., N.W. Adult Edn. Assn., Community Based Edn. (inst. rep.), Japan-Am. Soc., Oreg. Community Coll. Pres.'s Coun., Oreg. Coun. Instrnl. Adminstrs., Portland C. of C., City Club, Rotary, Phi Beta Kappa. Office: Portland CC PO Box 19000 RI-B4 Portland OR 97280-0990

TRAPANI, RALPH JAMES, transportation engineer; b. Buffalo, May 21, 1952; s. Ralph James and Estelle (Silvaroli) T. BS in Archtl. Engring., U. Colo., 1974. Registered profl. engr., Colo. Hwy. engr. Colo. Dept. Hwys., Glenwood Springs, 1975-80, Glenwood Canyon I-70 project mgr., 1980-92; pres. Colo. Transp. Inst., 1992—. Contbr. articles to profl. jours. Mem. ASCE, Nat. Soc. Profl. Engrs. Home: 714 Cowdin Ave Glenwood Springs CO 81601-9710 Office: Colo Dept Hwys PO Box 1430 Glenwood Springs CO 81602-1430

TRAPP, GERALD BERNARD, journalist; b. St. Paul, May 7, 1932; s. Bernard Edward and Lauretta (Mueller) T.; m. Bente Joan Moe, Jan. 29, 1954; children—Eric Gerald, Lise Joan, Alex Harold. B.A., Macalester Coll., St. Paul, 1954. Editor Mankato (Minn.) Free Press, 1954-57; with AP, 1957-80; nat. broadcast exec. charge sales AP, East of Miss., 1966-68; gen. broadcast news editor AP, N.Y.C., 1968-79; dep. dir. broadcast services AP, 1979-80, liaison broadcast networks, 1968-80; v.p., gen. mgr. Intermountain Network, Salt Lake City, 1980-87; v.p., dir. mktg. Travel Motivation, Inc., Salt Lake City, 1987-88; ops./program mgr. Mountain Cable Network, Inc., Salt Lake City, 1988-89; sr. v.p. Travel Motivation, Inc., Salt Lake City, 1990—; mktg. specialist Morris Travel, 1992—. Bd. dirs. Westminster Coll. Found. Mem. Radio TV News Dirs. Assn., Oratorio Soc. Utah (bd. dirs.), Pro Musica, Sigma Delta Chi. Mem. United Ch. Christ. Home: 1615 Millcreek Way Salt Lake City UT 84106-3231 Office: 3487 W 2100 S Ste 105 Salt Lake City UT 84119-1162

TRASK, LINDA ANN, sales executive; b. Cambria Heights, N.Y., Oct. 13, 1956; d. Lewis Volkert and Ethel May (Sheid) T. Cert. Transp., Delta Coll., 1985. Office mgr. Roofers Supply, Modesto, Calif., 1978-80; terminal mgr. Prouty Trucking, Modesto, 1980-82; mgr. Cert. Transpn., Modesto, 1982-86; mgr. regional sales Provisioners Express, Modesto, 1987-91; mktg. mgr. Willis Shaw Express, Modesto, Calif., 1991—; Mem. Cen. Valley Transpn., Modesto, 1987—.

TRASK, ROBERT CHAUNCEY RILEY, author, lecturer, foundation executive; b. Albuquerque, Jan. 2, 1939; s. Edward Almon Trask and Florence Jane (White) Jones; m. Katie Lucille Bitters (div. 1981); m. Mary Jo Chiarottino, Dec. 1, 1984; 1 child, Chauncey Anne. Student pub. schs., San Diego. Lic. master sea capt. Entertainer, singer, comedian, 1964--; founder, pres. Nat. Health & Safety Svcs., San Francisco, 1968-71, ARAS Found., Issaquah, Wash., 1978—; capt., dive master San Diego Dive Charters, 1972-75; sr. capt., dive master Pacific Sport Diving Corp., Long Beach, Calif., 1975-77; lectr., bus. cons., 1978—; cons., tng. developer Nissan, Gen. Dynamics, AT&T, religious orgns., also other corps., 1978--. Author: (manual) Tulip, 1971, Living Free, 1982, God's Phone Number, 1987, (video program for adolescents) Breaking Free, also seminar manuals. Mem. SAG. Office: ARAS Found # 93 3020 Issaquah Pine Lk Rd SE Issaquah WA 98027

TRASK, TALLMAN HARLOW, III, university administrator; b. L.A., Dec. 1, 1947; s. Tallman Harlow Jr. and Nancy Lou (Hargrave) T.; m. Marcy Muchmore, Mar. 15, 1986; children: Tallman IV, Merrill Kathryn. AB in History, Occidental Coll., 1969; MBA, Northwestern U., 1971; PhD, UCLA, 1974. Spl. cons. Calif. State Dept. Fin., Sacramento, 1973; asst. to pres. Occidental Coll., L.A., 1973-76; asst. to exec. vice chancellor UCLA, 1976-78, asst. exec. vice chancellor, asst. to chancellor, 1978-84, vice chancellor for acad. adminstrn., 1984-86; v.p. for fin. and adminstrn. U. Wash., Seattle, 1986-87, exec. v.p., 1987—; affiliate assoc. prof. coll. of edn. U. Wash., 1987—. Office: U Wash Office of Pres Seattle WA 98195

TRATNER, ALAN ARTHUR, foundation administrator, designer, inventor; b. Detroit, Jan. 21, 1947; s. Max and Shirley Cyril (Tribuck) T.; m. Stephanie Dawn Medvin. Student, Woodbury U., Art Ctr. Coll. Design, Detroit Inst. Arts and Scis., Student Art Ctr. Coll. Design. Indsl., graphic, transport designer, 1966—; v.p. Design Vectors, Inc., Mission Hills, Calif., 1969-73; exec. dir. Environ. Edn. Group, Canoga Park, Calif., 1970-90; prof. environment and energy Pepperdine U. Sch. Continuing Edn., L.A., 1973; bd.

dirs. Nat. Found. Creative, Gifted and Talented Children, Hungton Beach, Calif. Tech. editor Environ. Quality mag., 1970s; editor-in-chief Energies mag., 1975, Solar Energy Soc. of Am.; pub. Geothermal World Corp., 1975-85; mem. editorial adv. bd. Invent! mag., 1989—; contbr. articles to profl. jours. including Time Mag., Wall Street Jour., Entrepreneur, Inc.; co-host radio show Inventors Workshop of Air; 8 U.S. patents in fields of environment, alternative energy and transp. So. Calif. coord. "Sun Day" Internat. Solar Energy Celebration, Calif., 1978; served in numerous environ., energy, transp. coms., agys., and groups; conf. dir. Green Bus. Conf. ECO Expo; dir. New Environ. Techs. Project. Recipient Great Idea Contest award Am. Initiative for Creativity, Invention & Entrepreneurship, 1979. Mem. Inventors Workshop Internat.

TRATT, DAVID MICHAEL, physicist; b. Southampton, Hampshire, U.K., July 3, 1955; came to U.S. 1986; s. Alfred Oliver and Margaret Aline (Harding) T. BSc in Physics, U. Wales, 1976; MSc in Physics, Heriot-Watt U., Edinburgh, 1981; PhD in Physics, Heriot-Watt U., 1984. Chartered physicist, U.K. Exptl. officer Heriot-Watt U., Edinburgh, 1976-86; rsch. assoc. Jet Propulsion Lab., Pasadena, 1986-88; exptl. officer Heriot-Watt U., 1988-89; mem. tech. staff Jet Propulsion Lab., Pasadena, 1989—. Contbr. articles to profl. jours. Fellow Brit. Interplanetary Soc.; mem. IEEE, IEEE Lasers and Electro-Optics Soc., Optics Soc. Am., Inst. Physics (U.K.), Am. Geophys. Union. Home: 355 S Los Robles Ave Apt 107 Pasadena CA 91101-3283 Office: Jet Propulsion Lab 4800 Oak Grove Dr Pasadena CA 91109-8099

TRAUTENBERG, DAVID HERBERT, investment advisor; b. Atlantic City, July 23, 1958; s. Edward Samuel and Beatrice Trautenberg; m. Nancy Leigh Fritts, Feb. 25, 1989; children: Zeke, Edward, Nathan, Lee. BA, MS, U. Pa., 1980; MA, Leeds (Eng.) U., 1981; MBA, Stanford (Calif.) U., 1990. Account mgr. GE Info. Systems, N.Y.C., 1986-88; founding ptnr. The Suit Boys, Stanford, 1989-90; assoc. Morgan Stanley & Co., L.A., 1990—. Author, editor: (newspaper) The Reporter, 1988-90. Thouron scholar U. Pa., 1980. Mem. Phi Beta Kappa. Jewish. Office: Morgan Stanley & Co Ste 2400 199 Avenue of the Stars Los Angeles CA 90067

TRAUTMAN, LEO C., JR., bank executive; b. Perryville, Mo., Feb. 11, 1954; s. Leo C. and Janet R. (Siebert) T.; m. Debra M. Mohr, Aug. 22, 1975; children: Scott E., Jody L., Gregory L. BSBA, U. Nebr., Omaha, 1976. CPA, CMA. Staff acct./asst. treas. Nebr. Fed. Savs. and Loan Assn., Omaha, 1975-81; acctg. mgr. Am. Charter Fed. Savs. and Loan, Lincoln, Nebr., 1981-82; chief fin. officer, sr. v.p. Platte Valley Fed. Savs. and Loan, Gering, Nebr., 1982-87; pres., chief operating officer Platte Valley Mortgage Corp., Denver, 1987-88; pres., chief exec. officer Colorado Springs (Colo.) Savs. and Loan, 1989-92; pres. Trautman & Assocs., Colorado Springs, 1992-93; pres., CEO Skyline Fin. Corp., Skyline Mortgage Corp., Colorado Springs, 1993—. Fin. com. chmn. Christ the King Cath. Ch., Gering, 1985-88; audit com. chmn. St. Patrick's Cath. Ch., Colorado Springs, 1991—. Mem. Nat. Assn. Accts., U.S. League of Fin. Insts., Mortgage Bankers Am., Colo. Mortgage Bankers Assn., Colo. League of Savs. and Loans (chmn. bd. 1990-92). Republican. Roman Catholic. Office: Skyline Fin Corp 5376 Tomah Dr Ste 201 Colorado Springs CO 80918-6968

TRAVELLER, BRUCE FRANK, engineer; b. Richmond, Utah, July 31, 1955; s. Wayne Peart and Melba (Christensen) T.; m. Leanne Erekson, Mar. 17, 1978; children: Amber, Justin Bruce, Heather, Bryce Wayne, Chelsea. BSCE, Utah State U., 1979, MBA, 1988. Registered profl. engr., Utah. Surveyor, inspector Forsgren, Perkins & Assocs., Logan, Utah, 1977-78; facilities engr. Thiokol Corp., Brigham City, Utah, 1979, Presto Products, Inc., Lewiston, Utah, 1979-84; sr. engr. United Design Internat., Logan, 1985-86; structural design engr. Thiokol Corp., Brigham City, Utah, 1984-89, reliability engring. supr., 1989-91, quality engring. supr., 1991-92, quality engring. mgr., 1992—; cons. in field, 1984—. Leader Boy Scouts Am., Cache Valley, Utah, 1978—; coach Utah Youth Soccer Assn., Richmond, 1991-93. Recipient Silver Beaver award Boy Scouts Am., 1990. Mem. LDS Ch. Home: 272 N 300 E Richmond UT 84333

TRAVERS, JUDITH LYNNETTE, human resource executive; b. Buffalo, Feb. 25, 1950; d. Harold Elwin and Dorothy (Helsel) Howes; m. David Jon Travers, Oct. 21, 1972; 1 child, Heather Lynne. BA in Psychology, Barrington Coll., 1972; cert. in paralegal course, St. Mary's Coll., Moraga, Calif., 1983; postgrad., Southland U., 1982-84. Exec. sec. Sherman C. Weeks, P.A., Derry, N.H., 1973-75; legal asst. Mason-McDuffie Co., Berkeley, Calif., 1975-82; paralegal asst. Blum, Kay, Merkle & Kauftheil, Oakland, Calif., 1982-83; exec. v.p. Dela Pers. Svcs. Inc., Concord, Calif., 1983—; pres. All Ages Sitters Agy., Concord, 1986—. Vocalist record album The Loved Ones, 1978. Vol. local Congl. campaign, 1980, Circle of Friends, Children's Hosp. No. Calif., Oakland, 1987—; mem. Alameda County Sheriff's Mounted Posse, 1989, Contra Costa Child Abuse Prevention Coun., 1989. Mem. NAFE, Am. Assn. Respiratory Therapy, Calif. Soc. Respiratory Care, Am. Mgmt. Assn., Gospel Music Assn., Palomino Horse Breeders Am., DAR, Barrington Oratorio Soc., Commonwealth Club Calif., Nat. Trust Hist. Preservation, Alpha Theta Sigma. Republican. Baptist. Home: 3900 Brown Rd Oakley CA 94561-2532 Office: Delta Pers Svcs Inc 1820 Galindo St Ste 225 Concord CA 94520-2447

TRAVERSO, PEGGY BOSWORTH, speech pathologist; b. Stockton, Calif., Nov. 1, 1938; d. James Everett Bosworth and Jeanne (Owens) Sturla; divorced; children: Gregory, Douglas. BA, Stanford U., 1960; MA in Early Childhood Edn., Calif. State U., Sacramento, 1989. Cert. tchr., Calif. Speech therapist Stockton Unified Sch. Dist., 1960-65, 77—; mem. early childhood adv. com. San Joaquin Delta Coll., 1985-92; tchr. Lincoln Presbyn. Nursery Sch., Stockton, 1968-70; owner, mgr. restaurants, Stockton, 1969-77. Speaker Child Abuse Prevention Coun., Stockton, 1981—, pres. bd. dirs., 1982-84. Recipient Sammy Davis Jr. award Child Abuse Prevention Coun., 1987. Mem. Calif. Speech-Lang. Hearing Assn., Nat. Assn. for Edn. of Young Children (mem. Coun. for Exceptional Children), Calif. Children's Lobby. Avocation: travel. Office: McKinley Sch 30 W 9th St Stockton CA 95206-2599

TRAVIS, JOHN RICHARD, nuclear and mechanical engineer; b. Billings, Mont., Sept. 3, 1942; s. Lynn E. and Dorothy (Howard) T.; m. Carole M. Lahti, Aug. 1, 1963 (div. 1980); children: Kristi Ann, Patti Sue; m. Linda M. Hasenbank, May 24, 1985; 1 child, Jason Allan. BSME with hons., U. Wyo., 1965; MS, Purdue U., 1969, PhD, 1971. Registered profl. engr., N.Mex. Instr. engring. sci. U. Wyo., Laramie, 1965-66; instr. fluid mechanics Purdue U., Lafayette, Ind., 1970-71; staff Argonne (Ill.) Nat. Lab., 1971-73, Los Alamos (N.Mex.) Nat. Lab., 1973-90; sr. scientist Sci. Applications Internat. Corp., Albuquerque, 1990—; summer staff Argonne Nat. Lab., Idaho Falls, Idaho, 1965, Battelle Meml. Inst., Columbus, Ohio, 1966; cons. in field; official U.S. Cons. to Internat. Atomic Energy Agy. on nuclear reactor safety issues, Vienna, 1984—; official U.S. Del. to Fed. Republic of Germany on nuclear reactor safety issues, 1989—. Contbr. articles to profl. jours. Nat. Ctr. Atmospheric Rsch. fellow, 1970. Mem. ASME, Am. Nuclear Soc., Los Alamos Ski Club, Sigma Xi, Sigma Pi Sigma, Sigma Tau, Elks. Home: 5422 Avenida Cuesta NE Albuquerque NM 87111 Office: Sci Applications Internat 2109 Airpark Rd SE Albuquerque NM 87106-3258

TRAVIS, PAUL NICHOLAS, international banker; b. N.Y.C., Jan. 11, 1949; s. Nicholas and Mary (Bondar) T.; m. Carol Ann Rush; children: Tanya Ann, Paul John. BA, Rutgers U., New Brunswick, N.J., 1971; M, Sch. Advanced Internat. Studies, Washington, 1973. Mgmt. trainee Marine Midland Bank, N.Y.C., 1973-74; asst. agt., credit Bank of Montreal, N.Y.C., 1974-76; rep. Bank of Montreal, Tokyo, 1976; dep. v.p. Algemene Bank-The Netherlands, N.Y.C., 1976-79; mgr. Banco Real S.A., N.Y.C., 1979-80; gen. mgr. Banco Real S.A., Houston, 1980-88; v.p. corp. fin., merger & acquisitions The Sumimoto Trust & Banking Co., Ltd. L.A. Agy., L.A., 1989-93; mktg. officer Riyad Bank, Houston, 1993—. Mem. Boys Club of N.Y., Alumni, 1974—. Mem. Western Coun. Internat. Banking, Houston Inter-Am. C. of C. (bd. dirs. 1987—), Boys Club N.Y. Alumni Assn., Assn. Energy Engrs. Republican.

TRAVIS, ROY, composer; b. N.Y.C., June 24, 1922; s. Marion M. and Diane (Aaronson) T.; m. Victoria Elizabeth Khodadad, July 24, 1946; children: Gabriel, Naomi Stoller, Adam. BA, Columbia U., 1947, MA, 1951; BS, Julliard Sch. Music, 1949, MS, 1950. Tchr. Columbia U., 1952-53, Mannes Coll., 1952-57; mem. faculty UCLA, 1957-68, prof. dept. music, 1968-91. Composer: (operas) The Passion of Oedipus, 1965, The Black Bacchants, 1982; composer Symphonic Allegro, 1951 (1st prize 7th annual Gershwin Contest), Collage, 1968, Piano Concerto, 1969, Songs and Epilogues for bass and orch., 1975, Dorian Air for piano, 1954, Capriccio "The Minotaur" for piano, 1954, Sonata no. 1 for piano, 1954, String Quartet, 1958, African Sonata, 1966, Duo Concertante, 1967, Septet: Barma, 1968, Switched-on Ashanti, 1973, Dover Beach for bass and piano, 1983, Concerto for Violin, Tabla, and Orchestra, 1988, other vocal and instrumental works; author: Tonal Coherence in the First Movement of Bartok's Fourth String Quartet, 1970, The Recurrent Figure in the Britten/Piper Opera Death in Venice, 1987. Guggenheim fellow, 1972-73, Nat. Endowment for the Arts fellow, 1976, 78; Martha Baird Rockefeller grantee, 1986, Ford Found. Recording/Publ. grantee, 1975, grantee UCLA Rsch. Com.; recipient ASCAP Standard awards, 1969-91. Office: UCLA Dept Music Los Angeles CA 90024-1616

TRAVSKY, AMBER LONG, wildlife biologist, environmental consultant; b. Gillette, Wyo., Sept. 22, 1955; d. John Raymond and Amber Francis (McLeod) Long; m. Richard William Travsky, Aug. 7, 1982. AD in Biology, Casper (Wyo.) Coll., 1976; BS in Wildlife Mgmt., U. Wyo., 1978, MS in Zoology, 1981, MS in Exercise Physiology, 1988. Rsch. biologist U. Wyo., Laramie, 1978-81, fitness instr., 1985-88; wildlife biologist Laramie, 1981-85; dir. residential life Wyo. Tech. Inst., Laramie, 1985-91; owner, dir. Laramie Kempo Karate Sch., 1986—; sr. wildlife ecologist Hayden-Wing Assocs., Environ. Cons., Laramie, 1991-93; environ. cons., edn. specialist Real West Wildlife Inst., 1993—; bd. dirs. Laramie Tri's Corp. Contbr. articles to profl. jours. Mem. City Coun., City of Laramie, 1988—, mayor, 1991—; coun. liaison Environ. Commn., 1988-90, Laramie Parks and Recreation Bd., 1988-90, Laramie Planning Commn., 1990—; mem., chmn. Jail/Communications Joint Powers Bd., 1989—; bd. dirs. Laramie Econ. Devel. Corp., 1990—, Laramie Jubilee Days, 1988-92, Women in Mcpl. Govt. Bd. Nat. League Cities, 1992—. Named to Outstanding Young Women of Am., 1991; Honor Student scholar U. Wyo., 1978. Mem. Wyo. Assn. of Municipalities (econ. devel. com. 1988-90, legis. steering com. 1990—, Exec. Mgmt. scholar 1992). Home: 1116 Albin Laramie WY 82070

TRAYLOR, CLAIRE GUTHRIE, state senator; b. Kansas City, Mo., Jan. 18, 1931; d. Frank and Janet Guthrie; m. Frank A. Traylor, 1954; children: Nancy, Frank, Susan, David. BS, Northwestern U., 1952; MA, Washington U., St. Louis, 1955. Primary sch. tchr., 1955-57; mem. Colo. Ho. of Reps., 1978-82, majority caucus chmn., 1980-82; mem. Colo. State Senate, 1987—, chair bus. affairs and labor, 1985—, capital devel. com., 1988; mem. health, environ. and insts., audit coms., 1987—; mem. Colo. Commn. on Aging, Colo. Commn. on Children and Families, Colo. Housing Fin. Authority Bd., Colo. Guaranteed Student Loan Bd., Colo. Indsl. Commn. Adv. Com., Colo. Internat. Trade Adv. Commn., Colo. Capital Complex Commn., Wheat Ridge, Golden, Arvada, Lakewood, Jefferson County, Rep. Cen. Coms., del. rules com. Rep. Nat. Com., 1988; Jr. League, Clear Creek (Colo.) Valley Med. Aux., pres. bd. Highland West-Highland So. (Colo.). Presbyterian. Mem. Lakewood C. of C., Nat. Conf. State Legislators (dir. western region), Women's Network (chair Human Svcs. com. 1988-89), vice chair internat. trade com.). Office: Colo State Senate State Capitol Bldg Rm 259 Denver CO 80203

TRAYLOR, WILLIAM ROBERT, publisher; b. Texarkana, Ark., May 21, 1921; s. Clarence Edington and Seba Ann (Talley) T.; m. Elvirez Traylor, Oct. 9, 1945; children: Kenneth Warren, Gary Robert, Mark Daniel, Timothy Ryan. Student, U. Houston, 1945-46, U. Omaha, 1947-48. Div. mgr. Lily-Tulip Cup Corp., N.Y.C., 1948-61; asst. to pres. Johnson & Johnson, New Brunswick, N.J., 1961-63; mgr. western region Rexall Drug & Chem. subs. Dart Industries, L.A., 1963-67; pres. Prudential Pub. Co., Diamonds Springs, Calif., 1967—; cons. to printing industry, 1976—; syndicated writer (under pseudonym)s. Bill Friday's Bus. Bull., 1989—. Author: Instant Printing, 1976 (transl. into Japanese), Successful Management, 979, Quick Printing Ency., 1982, 7th edit., 1988, How to Sell Your Product Through (Not to) Wholesalers, 1980; pubr. Profl. Estimator and Mgmt. Software for Printing Industry, 1992. With USCG, 1942-45. Named Man of Yr. Quick Printing Mag., 1987. Mem. Nat. Assn. Quick Printers (hon. lifetime), C. of C., Kiwanis, Toastmasters. Democrat. Office: Prudential Pub Co 7089 Crystal Blvd Diamond Springs CA 95619-9634

TREADWAY, FRANK DEWITT, sociologist; b. Mount Shasta, Calif., Dec. 13, 1941; s. Jesse De Witt and Helen Ann (Talmadge) T. AA, Shasta Coll., 1992; postgrad., Chico State U., 1992—. Owner, designer DeWitt of Calif. Custom Apparel, Redding, Calif., 1967-71; owner Golden Rose Coffee-Tea-Spices, Redding, 1971-75; sr. care provider Shasta Co. Homemakers, Redding, 1975-85; asst. dir. March of Dimes, Redding, 1985-87; AIDS educator Calif. Nurses Assn., San Francisco, 1987—; tutor Shasta Coll., Redding, 1989—; phone counselor HELP Line, Inc., Redding, 1982—. Campaign activist Shasta County Dems., Redding, 1965—; initiator North State AIDS Project, Redding, 1980, ACLU No. Chpt. Guard; escort coord. Feminist Women's Health Ctr., Redding, 1989-91. With USNG, 1964-70. Recipient Grotefend scholarship Shasta Coll., Redding, 1992, John Mack award for Outstanding Grass Roots Vol., Dem. Com., 1993. Home: PO Box 422 Anderson CA 96007

TREANOR, WALTER JOHN, physician; b. County Tyrone, No. Ireland, May 14, 1922; came to U.S., 1949, naturalized, 1954; s. Hugh and Marion (deVine) T.; M.D., Nat. U. Ireland, 1947; Diplomate Am. Bd. Phys. Medicine & Rehab.; m. Mary Stewart, Dec. 29, 1971; children: James P., Wanden, Dona, June. Intern, St. Mary's Hosp., San Francisco, 1949-52; resident Mayo Found., Rochester, Minn.; practice medicine specializing in rehab. medicine, Santa Rosa, Calif.; emeritus prof. medicine U. Nev., Reno, 1979—. Served to capt., M.C., U.S. Army, 1953-55. Fellow ACP, Royal Soc. Medicine; mem. Am. Acad. Neurology, Internat. Med. Soc. Paraplegia, Am. Acad. Phys. & Rehab. Medicine. Republican. Contbr. articles to profl. jours. Home: 1370 Spring St Santa Rosa CA 95404-3656

TREAT, JOHN ELTING, management consultant; b. Evanston, Ill., June 20, 1946; s. Carlin Alexander and Majorie Ann (Mayland) T.; m. Barbara Laflin, May 27, 1984; children: Charles, Luli, Tyler. B.A., Princeton U., 1967; M.A., Johns Hopkins U., 1969. Legis. asst. U.S. Senate, 1966; assoc. ops. officer Office of Sec., U.S. Dept. State, 1971-73; research coordinator Presdl.-Congressional Commn. on Orgn. of Govt. for Conduct of Fgn. Policy, Washington, 1973-74; dir. research trade U.S. Fed. Energy Adminstrn., Washington, 1974-78; dep. asst. sec. U.S. Dept. Energy, Washington, 1979-80; staff mem. Nat. Security Council, 1980-81; sr. v.p. N.Y. Merc. Exchange, N.Y.C., 1981-82, pres., 1982-84; ptnr. Bear Stearns & Co., Los Angeles, 1984-85; exec. pub. Petroleum Intelligence Weekly, N.Y.C., 1985-87; pres. Regent Internat., Washington and The Hague, 1987-89; v.p., ptnr. Booz, Allen & Hamilton, Inc., San Francisco, 1989—. Chmn. spl. gifts Am. Cancer Soc., 1983; chmn. bd. dirs. Mirror Repertory Co., 1987—; trustee No. Calif. World Affairs Coun.; mem. San Francisco Fgn. Rels. Com. With USNR, 1969-71. Decorated AF Commendation medal; Ford Found. European Area Travel grantee, 1972; Woodrow Wilson fellow, 1967; McConnell fellow, 1966. Mem. Coun. Fgn. Rels., Internat. Assn. for Energy Econs. Democrat. Unitarian. Clubs: Colonial (Princeton, N.J.), St. Francis Yacht Club, Bankers (San Francisco). Home: 39 Cooper Ln Sausalito CA 94965-2010

TREECE, JAMES LYLE, lawyer; b. Colorado Springs, Colo., Feb. 6, 1925; s. Lee Oren and Ruth Ida (Smith) T.; m. Ruth Julie Treece, Aug. 7, 1949 (div. 1984); children—James (dec.), Karen Peterson, Teryl Wait, Jamilyn Smyser, Carol Crowder. Student Colo. State U., 1943, Colo. U., 1943, U.S. Naval Acad., 1944-46; B.S., Mesa Coll., 1946; J.D., U. Colo., 1950; postgrad. U. N.C., 1976-77. Bar: Colo. 1952, U.S. Dist. Ct. Colo. 1952, U.S. Ct. Appeals (10th cir.) 1952, U.S. Supreme Ct. 1967. Assoc., Yegge, Hall, Treece & Evans and predecessors, 1951-59, ptnr., 1959-69; U.S. atty., Colo., 1969-77; pres. Treece & Bahr and predecessor firms, Littleton, Colo., 1977-91; mcpl. judge, 1967-68; mem. faculty Nat. Trial Advocacy Inst., 1973-76, Law-Sci. Acad., 1964. Chmn. Colo. Dept. Pub. Welfare, 1963-68; chmn. Colo. Dept. Social Services, 1968-69; mem. Littleton Bd. Edn., 1977-81. Served with USNR, 1944-46. Recipient awards Colo. Assn. Sch. Bds., 1981, IRS, 1977, FBI, 1977, DEA, 1977, Fed. Exec. Bd., 1977. Mem. Fed. Bar Assn. (pres. Colo. 1975), Colo. Bar Assn. (bd. govs.), Denver Bar Assn. (v.p., trustee). Republican. Episcopalian. Home: 12651 N Pebble Beach Dr Sun City AZ 85351

TREECE, JOSEPH CHARLES, insurance broker; b. Loma Linda, Calif., Sept. 1, 1934; s. Roy G. and Jeane L. (Reade) T.; m. Diane D. Shuck, Sept. 10, 1960; children: Debbie, Mike, David. BA, Chapman Coll., 1956. Cert. Ins. Counselor, Assoc. in Risk Mgmt. Comml. banker Security Pacific Nat. Bank, Hemet, Calif., 1959-72; ins. broker H.I.S./Kent & Hamilton, Hemet, 1972-89, Russell & Kaufmann, Hemet, 1989—. Dir. YMCA, Hemet. Lt. USN, 1956-59. Recipient Associate Achievement award Am. Assn. Mng. Gen. Agts., 1991. Mem. Ramona Pageant Assn. (life, chmn.-supr. 1962-92), Profl. Ins. Assn. (state dir. 1988-91), Profl. Ins. Agts., (pres. Riverside and San Bernardino, Calif. 1989-90), Joint Ins. Assn. (pres. Riverside and san Bernardino 1991), Ind. Ins. Agents (pres.), Cert. Profl. Ins. Agts. (nat. pres. 1992), Hemet C. of C. (pres. 1970), Kiwanis Club (life, Hemet chpt., pres. 1971, lt. gov. div. 6 Cal-Na-HA 1972). Home: 40370 Melrose Ave Hemet CA 92544 Office: Russell & Kaufmann Ins Agts 400 S State St Hemet CA 92543

TREFNY, JOHN ULRIC, physics educator; b. Greenwich, Conn., Jan. 28, 1942; s. Ulric John and Mary Elizabeth (Leech) T.; m. Sharon Livingston, 1992; 1 child from previous marriage, Benjamin Robin. BS, Fordham U., 1963; PhD, Rutgers U., 1968. Rsch. assoc. Cornell U., Ithaca, N.Y., 1967-69; asst. prof. physics Wesleyan U., Middletown, Conn., 1969-77; asst. prof. physics Colo. Sch. Mines, Golden, 1977-79, assoc. prof., 1979-85, prof. 1985—, dir. Amorphous Materials Ctr., 1986—, assoc. dean rsch., 1988-90, head physics dept., 1990—; cons. Solar Energy Rsch. Inst., Golden, Energy Conversion Devices, Troy, Mich., various other cos. Contbr. articles to profl. jours. Recipient Teaching award AMOCO Found., 1984, Friend of Sci. Edn. award, 1990. Mem. Am. Ceramic Soc., Am. Phys. Soc., Am. Assn. Physics Tchrs., Colo. Assn. Sci. Tchrs. (bd. dirs. 1986-88), Sigma Xi, Sigma Pi Sigma. Avocations: golfing, traveling, whiskey. Home: 14268 W 1st Ave Golden CO 80401-5336

TREGER, MARK ALAN, physician, surgeon; b. Buffalo, Mar. 21, 1938; s. Joseph and Lena (Goldman) T.; m. Marilyn Treger, June 21, 1959; children: Lisa, Julie, Stephen, Matthew. Student, Syracuse (N.Y.) U., 1955-56, U. Buffalo, 1956-58; MD, SUNY, Syracuse, 1962. Intern L.A. County Hosp., 1962-63; resident ob-gyn. SUNY, Buffalo, 1965-69; pvt. practice San Diego, 1969—; cons. U. Calif., San Diego, 1969—, asst. clin. prof. dept. ob-gyn. Capt. U.S. Army, 1963-65. Fellow ACS, Am. Coll. Ob-gyn.; mem. AMA, Am. Fertility Soc., Soc. Reproductive Surgeons, Calif. Med. Assn. Office: Ctr Infertility & Reproductive Medicine 6719 Alvarado Rd Ste 109 San Diego CA 92120-5009

TREGLIO, JAMES RONALD, business executive, physicist; b. Orange, N.J., May 18, 1946; s. James and Rose (Trovato) T.; m. Carol Elaine Klotz, Aug. 28, 1971; children: James Michael, Richard Thomas, Dante Andrew. BS, Brown U., 1968; MS, Rutgers U., 1975; PhD, Stevens Inst. of Tech., 1977. Staff physicist Fusion Engergy Corp., Princeton, N.J., 1973-77; sr. engr. Gen. Dynamics/Convair, San Diego, 1977-80; sr. scientist Gen. Atomic Co., San Diego, 1980-83, sr. bus. planner, 1984-85; founder, chief exec. officer ISM Techs., Inc., San Diego, 1985—. Contbr. articles to profl. jours. Legis. asst. U.S. Senate, Washington, 1982-83. Mem. Am. Phys. Soc. (Congl. Sci. fellow 1982), Am. Vacuum Soc., ASM Internat., Materials Rsch. Soc. Home: 12202 Spruce Grove Pl San Diego CA 92131-2215 Office: ISM Techs Inc 9965 Carroll Canyon Rd San Diego CA 92131-1105

TREIGER, IRWIN LOUIS, lawyer; b. Seattle, Sept. 10, 1934; s. Sam S. and Rose (Steinberg) T.; m. Betty Lou Friedlander, Aug. 18, 1957; children: Louis H., Karen I., Kenneth B. BA, U. Wash., 1955, JD, 1957; LLM in Taxation, NYU, 1958. Bar: Wash. 1958, D.C. 1982, U.S. Dist. Ct. (we. dist.) Wash., U.S. Ct. Appeals (9th cir.), U.S. Supreme Ct. Assoc. Bogle & Gates, Seattle, 1958-63, ptnr., 1964—. Pres. Jewish Fedn. Greater Seattle, 1993; chmn. Mayor's Symphony Panel, 1986, Corp. Coun. for the Arts, 1987-88; pres. Seattle Symphony Found., 1986—; trustee, co-chmn. Cornish Coll. of the Arts, 1990—; trustee The Seattle Found., 1992—. Fellow Am. Coll. Tax Counsel; mem. ABA (chmn. taxation sect. 1988-89, sect. del. 1990—), Wash. State Bar Assn. (chmn. taxation sect. 1975), Greater Seattle C. of C. (pres. 1993—). Jewish. Office: Bogle & Gates 601 Union St Seattle WA 98101-2327

TREINEN, SYLVESTER WILLIAM, bishop; b. Donnelly, Minn., Nov. 19, 1917; s. William John and Kathryn (Krausert) T. Student, Crosier Sem., Onamia, Minn., 1935-41; B.A., St. Paul's Sem., 1943. Ordained priest Roman Cath. Ch., 1946; asst. pastor Dickinson, N.D., 1946-50; sec. to bishops Ryan and Hoch, 1950-53; asst. pastor Cathedral Holy Spirit, Bismarck, N.D., 1950-57; chancellor Diocese Bismarck, 1953-59; asst. pastor St. Anne's Ch., Bismarck, 1957-59; pastor St. Joseph's Ch., Mandan, N.D., 1959-62; bishop Boise, Idaho, 1962-88; retired bishop Diocese of Boise, Idaho, 1988—. Office: 303 Federal Way Box 769 Boise ID 83701 also: 4450 N Five Mile Rd Boise ID 83704

TREMBLAY, LAURIER JOSEPH, JR., surgeon; b. Jacksonville, N.C., Oct. 10, 1955; s. Laurier Joseph and Magdeline Marie (Fortin) T.; m. Janet Lynn Mason, May 9, 1981. BS in Biology, U. Cen. Fla., 1977; MD, U. South Fla., 1980. Lic. physician., Calif. Intern, 1980-81, resident, 1981-86; gen. surgeon Four County Surg. Assocs., Henderson, N.C., 1988-90, Inland East Med. Clinics, La Mesa, Calif., 1990-92; pvt. practice San Diego, 1992—. Comdr. USN, 1977-88. Fellow ACS, Southea. Surg. Congress; mem. AMA, Calif. Med. Assn., San Diego County Med. Soc., Soc. Am. Gastrointestinal Endoscopic Surgeons. Roman Catholic. Office: 6719 Alvarado Rd # 307 San Diego CA 92120

TREMBLY, CRISTY, television executive; b. Oakland, Md., July 11, 1958; d. Charles Dee and Mary Louise (Cassidy) T. BA in Russian, German and Linguistics cum laude, W.Va. U., 1978, BS in Journalism, 1978, MS in Broadcast Journalism, 1979; advanced cert. travel, West L.A. Coll., 1982; advanced cert. recording engring., Soundmaster Schs., North Hollywood, Calif., 1985. Videotape engr. Sta. WWVU-TV, Morgantown, W.Va., 1976-80; announcer, engr. Sta. WVVW Radio, Grafton, W.Va., 1979; tech. dir., videotape supr. Sta. KMEX-TV, L.A., 1980-85; broadcast supr. Sta. KADY-TV, Oxnard, Calif., 1988-89; news tech. dir. Sta. KVEA-TV, Glendale, Calif., 1985-89; asst. editor, videotape technician CBS TV Network, Hollywood, Calif., 1989-90; videotape supr. Sta. KCBS-TV, Hollywood, 1990-91, mgr. electronic news gathering ops., 1991-92; studio mgr., engr.-in-charge CBS TV Network, Hollywood, 1992—; radio operator KJ6BX Malibu Disaster Comm., 1987—. Producer (TV show) The Mountain Scene, 1976-78. Sr. org. pres. Children of the Am. Revolution, Malibu, Calif., 1992—; sec., adv. com. Tamassee (S.C.) Sch., 1992—; vol. Ch. Coun., LA Riot Rebuilding, Homeless shelter work, VA Hosps., Mus. docent; sponsor 3 overseas foster children. Recipient Outstanding Young Woman of Am., 1988, Asst. editor Emmy award Young and the Restless, 1989-90, Golden Mike award Radio/TV News assn., 1991, 92. Mem. DAR (state chmn. jr. membership 1987-88 state chmn. scholarships, 1992-94, others, organizing regent Malibu chpt. 1992, state chmn. motion pictures radio and TV, Calif., 1988-90, Mex. 1990—, Nat. Outstanding Jr. 1993), Soc. of Profl. Journalists, Women in Comm., Travelers Century Club (program chmn. 1987—), Mensa (life), Beta Sigma Phi. Democrat. Methodist. Home: 11837 Ellice St Malibu CA 90265 Office: CBS TV City 7800 Beverly Blvd Los Angeles CA 90036

TREMBLY, DENNIS MICHAEL, musician; b. Long Beach, Calif., Apr. 16, 1947; s. Fred Lel and Jewel Fern (Bouldin) T. Student, Juilliard Sch. Music, 1965-68. Asst. adj. prof. U. So. Calif., 1981—. Bass player, 1959—, with Los Angeles Philharmonic Orch., 1970-73, co-prin. bass, 1973—. Recipient 2d pl. Internat. Solo Bass competition, Isle of Man, 1978. Mem. Internat. Soc. Bassists. Office: L A Philharm Orch 135 N Grand Ave Los Angeles CA 90012-3013

TRENBERTH, KEVIN EDWARD, atmospheric scientist; b. Christchurch, New Zealand, Nov. 8, 1944; came to U.S., 1977; s. Edward Maurice and Ngaira Ivy (Eyre) T.; m. Gail Neville Thompson, Mar. 21, 1970; children: Annika Gail, Angela Dawn. BSc with honors, U. Canterbury, Christchurch,

1966; ScD, MIT, 1972. Meteorologist New Zealand Meteorol. Service, Wellington, 1966-76, supt. dynamic meteorology, 1976-77; assoc. prof. meteorology U. Ill., Urbana, 1977-82, prof., 1982-84; scientist Nat. Ctr. Atmospheric Research, Boulder, Colo., 1984-86, sr. scientist, 1986—, leader empirical studies group, 1987, head sect. climate analysis, 1987—; dep. dir. climate and global dynamics divsn. Nat. Ctr. Atmospheric Rsch., Boulder, Colo., 1991—; adj. prof. U. Ill., 1984-89; cons. NOAA, 1980—, NASA, 1981—; mem. joint sci. com. for world climate programme, com. climate changes and the ocean Tropical Oceans Global Atmosphere Program Sci. Steering Group, 1990—. Editor: Climate System Modeling, 1992; contbr. articles to profl. jours. Fellow Am. Meteorol. Soc. (editor sci. jour. 1981-86, com. chmn. 1985-87, editor's award 1989); mem. NAS (earth scis. com. 1982-85, tropical oceans global atmosphere adv. panel 1984-87, polar rsch. bd. 1986-90, climate rsch. com. 1987-90), AAAS (coun. del. sect. on atmospheric and hydrospheric scis. 1993—), Royal Soc. of New Zealand, Meteorol. Soc. of New Zealand. Grantee NSF, NOAA, NASA. Fellow Am. Meteorol. Soc. (editor sci. jour. 1981-86, com. chmn. 1985-87, editors's award 1989); mem. NAS (earth scis. com. 1982-85, tropical oceans global atmosphere adv. panel 1984-87, polar research bd. 1986-90, climate research com. 1987-90), AAAS (coun. del. sect. atmosphere and hydrospheric sci. 1993—), Royal Soc. of New Zealand, Meteorol. Soc. of New Zealand. Home: 1445 Landis Ct Boulder CO 80303-1122 Office: Nat Ctr Atmospheric Research PO Box 3000 Boulder CO 80307-3000

TRENCHARD, WARREN CHARLES, academic administrator, religion educator; b. St. John's, Nfld., Can., July 16, 1944; s. Charles Edward and Violet Frances (Noseworthy) T.; m. Marilyn Joyce Beaumont, Aug. 20, 1967; children: Mark Edward, David Wayne, Kevin Scott. BA, Andrews U., 1966, MA, BD, 1968; PhD, U. Chgo., 1981. Ordained to ministry Seventh-day Adventists, 1982. Instr. religion Andrews U., Berrien Springs, Mich., 1968; pastor Seventh-day Adventist Ch., Lancaster, Mass., 1968-69, Atleboro, Mass., 1969-70; prof. religious studies Can. Union Coll., College Heights, Alta., 1975—, v.p. acad. adminstrn., 1989—; mem. Pvt. Colls. Accreditation Bd., Edmonton, Alta., 1987-93. Author: Ben Sira's View of Women, 1982, The Student's Complete Vocabulary Guide to the Greek New Testament, 1992; contbr. articles to religious publs. Fellow Inst. Bibl. Rsch.; mem. Andrews Soc. Religious Studies (pres. 1992-93), Cath. Bibl. Assn. Am., Internat. Orgn. Septuagint and Cognate Studies, Soc. Bibl. Lit., Am. Assn. Higher Edn. Home: Box 458, College Heights, AB Canada T0C 0Z0 Office: Can Union Coll, Box 430, College Heights, AB Canada T0C 0Z0

TRENNERT, ROBERT ANTHONY, JR., historian, educator; b. South Gate, Calif., Dec. 15, 1937; s. Robert Anthony Sr. and Mabel Valentine (Chesnut) T.; m. Linda Lee Griffith, July 31, 1965; children: Robert Anthony III, Kristina M. BA, Occidental Coll., 1961; MA, L.A. State Coll., 1963; Phd, U. Calif., Santa Barbara, 1969. Asst. prof. Temple U., Phila., 1967-74; Asst. prof. Ariz. State U., Tempe, 1974-76, assoc. prof., 1976-81, prof. history, 1981--, chmn. dept. history, 1986-91; chmn. Ariz. Hist. Sites Rev. Com., 1989-91. Author: Alternative to Extinction, 1975, Indian Traders on Middle Border, 1981, Phoenix Indian Sch., 1988. Bd. dirs. Ariz. Hist. Found. Mem. Orgn. of Am. Historians. Home: 3581 W Golden Ln Chandler AZ 85226-1347 Office: Ariz State U Dept of History Tempe AZ 85287

TRENOWETH, ROY WILBUR, state forester; b. Athol, Mass., Oct. 18, 1942; s. Roy Wilbur and Emma Mary (Moschini) T.; m. Candy Rae Julius, Sept. 27, 1967; children: Tricia Rae, Traci Jann. AAS, Paul Smiths (N.Y.) Coll., 1962; BS in Forest Mgmt., U. Mont., 1965. Sr. forester Idaho Dept. of Lands, Orofino, 1968-73; asst. state forester Nev. Div. of Forestry, Carson City, 1973-80, dep. state forester, 1980-92, state forester, 1992—. Lt. col. USAR. Mem. Sierra Sertoma (pes. 1990-91). Home: 1512 Palo Verde Carson City NV 89701-4423

TRETBAR, HAROLD CARL, internist; b. Stafford, Kans., Mar. 13, 1931; s. J. J. and Gladys (Reid) T.; m. Dorothy Ann Lott, June 5, 1955; children: Bruce, Brian, David, Nancy. AB in Chemistry, Southwestern Coll., Winfield, Kans., 1952; MD, Kans. U., Kansas City, 1956. Diplomate Am. Bd. Internal Medicine, Am. Bd. Rheumatology. Intern St. Vincents Hosp., Portland, 1957; resident, fellow Cleve. Clinic, 1961-65; pvt. practice internal medicine Tucson, 1965—; staff Fairview Home for Mentally Retarded, Salem, Oreg., 1957, Tucson VA Hosp., 1965; chmn. dept. medicine Tucson Med. Assocs., Ltd.; sr. clin. lectr. Dept. Medicine, U. Ariz.; cons. in arthritis Tucson VA Med. Ctr., Kino Community Hosp.; past chmn. bd. Intergroup Prepaid Health Plans of Ariz.; pres. Tucson Med. Assocs., Ltd.; past pres. med. staff El Dorado Hosp. Contbr. articles to profl. jours. Capt. U.S. Army, 1958-61. Arthritis Found. Disting. Pub. Svc. awardee, 1972, Nat. Vol. Svc. Citation, 1973, others. Fellow ACP, Am. Coll. Rheumatology; mem. Ariz. Med. Assn., AMA, Pima County Med. Soc., Arthritis Found. Republican. Methodist. Home: 401 S Brighton Ln Tucson AZ 85711-4509 Office: Tucson Med Assocs 116 N Tucson Blvd Tucson AZ 85716-4794

TREVITHICK, RONALD JAMES, underwriter; b. Portland, Oreg., Sept. 13, 1944; s. Clifford Vincent and Amy Lois (Turner) T.; m. Delberta Russell, Sept. 11, 1965; children: Pamela, Carmen, Marla, Sheryl. BBA U. Wash., 1966. CLU, CPA, ChFC. Mem. audit staff Ernst & Ernst, Anchorage, 1966, 68-70; pvt. practice acctg., Fairbanks, Alaska, 1970-73; with Touche Ross & Co., Anchorage, 1973-78, audit ptnr., 1976-78; exec. v.p., treas., bd. dirs. Veco Internat., Inc., 1978-82; pres., bd. dirs. Petroleum Contractors Ltd., 1980-82; bd. dirs. P.S. Contractors A/S, Norcon, Inc., OFC of Alaska, Inc., V.E. Systems Svcs., Inc., Veco Turbo Services, Inc., Veco Drilling, Inc., Vemar, Inc., 1978-82; with Coopers & Lybrand, Anchorage, 1982-85; field underwriter, registered rep. New York Life Ins., 1985—; instr. acctg. U. Alaska, 1971-72; lectr. acctg. and taxation The Am. Coll., 1972, instr. adv. sales Life Underwriters Tng. Coun., 1988-89; bd. dirs. Ahtna Devel. Corp., 1985-86. Div. chmn. United Way, 1975-76, YMCA, 1979; bd. dirs., fin. chmn. Anchorage Arts Coun., 1975-78, Am. Diabetes Assn., Alaska affiliate, 1985-91, chmn. bd. 1988-89, chmn. hon. bd. 1992—, Am. Heart Assn., Alaska affiliate, 1986-87. With U.S. Army, 1967-68. Fellow Life Underwriting Tng. Coun.; mem. AICPA, Petroleum Accts. Soc. (bd. dirs. Alaska 1976; nat. tax com. 1978-80), Fin. Execs. Inst. (pres. Alaska chpt. 1981-83), Am. Soc. CLUs & ChFCs (v.p. Alaska chpt. 1993—), Nat. Assn. Life Underwriters, So. Alaska Assn. Life Underwriters, Alaska Assn. Life Underwriters (sec., treas. 1987-90), Million Dollar Roundtable, Rotary, Beta Alpha Psi. Clubs: Alaska Goldstrikers Soccer (pres. 1992—); Petroleum. Home: 4421 Huffman Rd Anchorage AK 99516-2211 Office: 1400 W Benson Blvd Anchorage AK 99503-3660

TREXLER, VERNON LEE, portfolio manager; b. Enid, Okla., July 13, 1948; s. Vernon Lee and Mary Joe (Brown) T.; m. Pamela Sue Brown, 1971 (div. 1973); m. Jane B. Carver, 1982 (div. 1985); m. Leslie Marie Roberts, 1988. BBA, U. N.Mex., 1971. Sales rep. foods divsn. Coca Cola, Colorado Springs, Colo., 1972-74; territory mgr. Gen. Foods Corp., Grand Junction, Colo., 1975-76; account exec. E.F. Hutton Co. Inc., Denver, 1976-88; v.p., portfolio mgr. Prudential Securities, Denver, 1988—. Bd. dirs. Friends of Family Crisis Ctr., Denver, 1991-92. Staff sgt. USAF N.G., 1969-75. Mem. Sertoma Club (v.p. 1992).

TREYBIG, JAMES G., computer company executive; b. Clarendon, TX, 1940. BS, Rice U., 1963; MBA, Stanford, 1968. Mkgt. mgr. Hewlett-Packard Co., 1968-72; with Kleiner and Perkins, 1972-74; with Tandem Computer Inc., Cupertino, Calif., 1974—, now pres., chief exec. officer, dir. Office: Tandem Computers Inc 19333 Vallco Pky Cupertino CA 95014-2506*

TRIANT, THANOS MICHAEL, information services executive; b. Athens, Greece, Feb. 6, 1946; came to U.S., 1965; s. Michael and Georgia (Siorvane) T.; m. Deborah Howard Diller, June 2, 1973; children: Mark, Theodore. BA in Math., Hamilton Coll., 1968; BS in Elec. Engring. and Computer Sci., Columbia U., 1970, MS in Elec. Engring. and Computer Sci., 1972. Cons. various cos., N.Y. and N.J., 1971-73; programmer analyst Fed. Res. Bank N.Y., N.Y.C., 1973-76, mgr., 1976-79; v.p. teleprocessing ops. Data Resources Inc., Lexington, Mass., 1979-83, v.p. planning, 1983-84, v.p. electronic delivery svcs., 1984-85; v.p. systems and tech. McGraw-Hill Inc., N.Y.C., 1985-88; sr. v.p. product devel. McGraw-Hill Fin. Svcs., N.Y.C., 1988-90; dir. bus. systems Sun Microsystems Inc., Palo Alto, Calif., 1990—. Mem. IEEE, Assn. Computing Machinery. Christian Orthodox. Home: 165 Canyon Dr Portola Valley CA 94028 Office: Sun Microsystems Inc 901 San Antonio Ave Palo Alto CA

TRIBBLE, RICHARD WALTER, brokerage executive; b. San Diego, Oct. 19, 1948; s. Walter Perrin and Catherine Janet (Miller) T.; m. Joan Catherine Sliter, June 26, 1980. BS, U. Ala., Tuscaloosa, 1968; student, Gulf Coast Sch. Drilling Practices, U. Southwestern La., 1977. Stockbroker Shearson, Am. Express, Washington, 1971-76; ind. oil and gas investment sales, Falls Church, Va., 1976-77; pres. Monroe & Keusink, Inc., Falls Church and Columbus, Ohio, 1977-87; institutional investment officer FCA Asset Mgmt., 1983-85; fin. cons. Merrill Lynch Pierce, Fenner & Smith, Inc., Phoenix, 1987—, cert. fin. mgr., 1989-92, sr. fin. cons., 1992—. Served with USMC, 1969-70. Republican. Methodist. Office: 2525 E Camelback Rd Phoenix AZ 85016-4219

TRICK, ROGER LEE, national park ranger; b. Port Clinton, Ohio, Aug. 28, 1950; s. Carl Franklin and Marilyn Mae (Kemp) T.; m. Terri Ann Jacob, Aug. 8, 1977; children: Randy, Hillary, Brian. BA, U. Pa., 1972; MA, U. Ariz., 1975. Park technician Grand Canyon (Ariz.) Nat. Park, 1975-77; park ranger Mesa Verde (Colo.) Nat. Park, 1977-79; area mgr. Hovenweep Nat. Monument, Cortez, Colo., 1979-83; chief ranger Whitman Mission Nat. Historic Site, Walla Walla, Wash., 1983—; instr. in vegetation mgmt. Nat. Park Svc., Washington, 1990—; instr. Oreg. Trail seminar Whitman Mission Nat. Historic Site, 1991—. Editor: Hovenweep Trail Guide, 1981; contbr. chpts. to books. Bd. dirs. Little Theatre Walla Walla, 1985-89; cubmaster Walla Walla area Boy Scouts Am., 1989—. Mem. Nat. Assn. Interpreters, Assn. Nat. Park Rangers, Kiwanis Club Walla Walla (bd. dirs. 1985-87). Home: 2141 Leonard Dr Walla Walla WA 99362-4427 Office: Whitman Mission Nat Historic Site RR 2 Box 247 Walla Walla WA 99362-9699

TRICOLES, GUS PETER, electromagnetics engineer, physicist, consultant; b. San Francisco, Oct. 18, 1931; s. Constantine Peter and Eugenia (Elias) T.; m. Beverly Mildred Ralsky, Dec. 20, 1953 (dec. Dec. 1974); children: Rosanne, Robin; m. Aileen Irma Aronson, Apr. 1, 1980 (div. June 1980). BA in Physics, UCLA, 1955; MS in Applied Math., San Diego State U., 1958; MS in Applied Physics, U. Calif., San Diego, 1962, PhD in Applied Physics, 1971. Engr. Convair div. Gen. Dynamics, San Diego, 1955-59, engr. Electronics div., 1962-75, engring. mgr. Electronics div., 1975-89, sr. engring. staff specialist, 1989-92; sr. engring. staff specialist GDE Systems Inc., 1992—; engr. Smyth Rsch. Assn., San Diego, 1959-61; rsch. asst. Scripps Instn. Oceanography, La Jolla, Calif., 1961-62; sr. engring. staff specialist G.D.E. Systems, Inc., San Diego, 1992—; cons. Ga. Inst. Tech., Atlanta, 1972, 79-80, Transco Industries, L.A., 1973, Aero Geo Industries, San Antonio, 1980-82, Vantage Assocs., San Diego, 1988; rsch. reviewer NRC, NAS, Boulder, Colo., 1986-88. Author: (with others) Radome Engineering Handbook, 1970, Antenna Handbook, 1988; contbr. articles to profl. jours.; holder 18 patents. With USN, 1952-53. Fellow IEEE (antenna standards com. 1980—, advancement com. 1988), Optical Soc. Am. (local sect. v.p. 1966); mem. N.Y. Acad. Scis., Am. Geophys. Union. Home: 4633 Euclid Ave San Diego CA 92115-3226 Office: GDE Systems Inc PO Box 85310 San Diego CA 92186-5310

TRIER, WILLIAM CRONIN, medical educator, plastic surgeon; b. N.Y.C., Feb. 11, 1922; s. John and Anne (Cronin) T.; m. Kathleen Emily Renz, June 14, 1947; children: William Cronin, Peter L. AB, Dartmouth Coll., 1943; MD, N.Y. Med. Coll., 1947. Diplomate Am. Bd. Surgery, Am. Bd. Plastic Surgery (dir. 1976-82, vice-chmn. 1981-82). Intern St. Agnes Hosp., White Plains, N.Y., 1947-48; intern Grasslands Hosp., Valhalla, N.Y., 1948-49, resident in surgery, 1949-50; commd. lt. (j.g.) USN, 1948, advanced through grades to capt., 1964; asst. med. officer USS Midway and USS Wasp, 1950-52; residen in surgery St. Albans Hosp., L.I., N.Y., 1952-55; fellow plastic surgery Washington U. Barnes Hosp., St. Louis, 1956-58; mem. plastic surgery staff Naval Hosp., St. Albans, 1958-60; chief plastic surgery Naval Hosp., Phila., 1960-63; chief plastice surgery Nat. Naval Med. Ctr., Bethesda, Md., 1963-67; asst. prof. surgery, plastic surgery U. N.C., Chapel Hill, 1967-69, prof. surgery, plastic surgery, 1976-85, prof. dental ecology Sch. Dentistry, 1976-85; assoc. prof., chief plastic surgery U. Ariz. Coll. Medicine, Tucson, 1969-76; prof. surgery U. Wash. Sch. Medicine, Seattle, 1985-90; retired, 1990; mem. com. on study evaluation procedures Am. Bd. Med. Specialties, 1981-85, sci. adv. com. Contbr. articles to profl. jours. Bd. dirs., pres. Pima County unit and Ariz. divs. Am. Cancer Soc., 1970-76, bd. dirs. N.C. Div., pres. Orange County (N.C.) unit, 1976-82. Mem. ACS, Am. Assn. Plastic Surgeons (historian 1973-76, v.p. 1984-85, pres.-elect 1985-86, pres. 1986-87), Am. Soc. Plastic and Reconstructive Surgeons, Am. Soc. Aesthetic Plastic Surgery (at large bd. dirs. 1979-81, treas. 1984-87), Am. Soc. Maxillofacial Surgeons, Am. Acad. Pediatrics, Am. Cleft Palate Assn. (pres. 1980-81), Am. Cleft Palate Found. (pres., 1984-90), Gamma Delta Chi, Alpha Kappa Kappa. Episcopalian. Home: 6321 Seaview Ave NW Apt 20 Seattle WA 98107-2671

TRIEWEILER, TERRY NICHOLAS, lawyer; b. Dubuque, Iowa, Mar. 21, 1948; s. George Nicholas and Anne Marie (Oastern) T.; m. Carol M. Jacobson, Aug. 11, 1972; children: Kathryn Anne, Christina Marie, Anna Theresa. BA, Drake U., 1970, JD, 1972. Bar: Iowa 1973, Wash. 1973, U.S. Dist. Ct. (so. dist.) Iowa 1973, U.S. Dist. Ct. (we. dist.) Wash. 1973, Mont. 1975, U.S. Dist. Ct. Mont. 1977. Staff atty. Polk County Legal Services, Des Moines, 1973; assoc. Hullin, Roberts, Mines, Fite & Riveland, Seattle, 1973-75, Morrison & Hedman, Whitefish, Mont., 1975-77; sole practice, Whitefish; now justice Mont. Supreme Ct., Helena; lectr. U. Mont. Law Sch., 1981—; mem. com. to amend civil proc. rules Mont. Supreme Ct., Helena, 1984, commn. to draft pattern jury instrns., 1985; mem. Gov.'s Adv. Com. on Amendment to Work Compensation Act, adv. com. Mont. Work Compensation Ct. Mem. ABA, Mont. Bar Assn. (pres. 1986-87), Wash. Bar Assn., Iowa Bar Assn., Assn. Trial Lawyers Am., Mont. Trial Lawyers Assn. (dir., pres.). Democrat. Roman Catholic. Home: 1615 Virginia Dale St Helena MT 59601-5823 Office: 215 N Sanders St Helena MT 59620 also: Mont Supreme Ct Justice Bldg 215 N Sanders St Rm 323 Helena MT 59620*

TRIFONIDIS, BEVERLY ANN, associate dean, opera company manager, accountant; b. Dallas, Dec. 19, 1947; d. Philo McGill and Mary Elizabeth (Sikes) Burney; m. Paul Douglas Spikes, June, 1968 (div. 1976); m. Chris Trifonidis, August 1979 (div. 1986); 1 child, Alexandra. BBA, U. Tex., 1971, M in Profl. Acctg., 1976. CPA, Tex. Mgmt. trainee J.C. Penney Co., Austin, Tex., 1971-72; acctg. clk. SW Ednl. Devel. Lab., Austin, 1972-73; editorial asst. Jour. of Mktg., Austin, 1974-76; staff auditor Hurdman & Cranstoun, CPA's, San Francisco, 1976; instr. acctg. U. Tex., San Antonio, 1976-77; lectr. U. Tex., Austin, 1991; lectr. acctg. Simon Fraser U., Burnaby, B.C., Can., 1978-79, 81-84; gen. mgr. Vancouver (Can.) Opera, 1984-91; Bd. dirs. B.C. Devel. Corp., Banff Sch. Advanced Mgmt. Bd. dirs. United Way, 1988; mem. spl. coun. Com. on Arts, Vancouver, 1987; exec. bd. Vancouver Cultural Alliance, 1987. Mem. AICPA, Tex. Soc. CPAs. Presbyterian. Office: U BC Profl Programmes, 2053 Main Mall Rm 110, Vancouver, BC Canada V6T 1Z2

TRIGGS, WILLIAM MICHAEL, microelectronics executive; b. South Amboy, N.J., Aug. 15, 1937; s. William E. Triggs and Stella V. (Szatkowski) Kasper; m. Mary Ellen Banfield, Sept. 10, 1960 (div. Dec. 1979); children: William J., Matthew H., Anne; m. Bonnie L. Cascio, Jan. 3, 1981. BS in Metall. Engring., Lafayette U., Easton, Pa., 1960; MS in Metall., Stevens Inst. Tech., Hoboken, N.J., 1965. Rsch. investigator Asarco, South Plainfield, N.J., 1960-61; engr. RCA Solid State div., Somerville, N.J., 1961-66; unit mgr. GE IC div., Syracuse, N.Y., 1966-71; dir. Harris Corp. IC div., Melbourne, Fla., 1971-84; ops. mgr. Mass. Microelectronics Ctr., 1984-89; dri. tech. support MRC, Phoenix, 1989—; tech. program chmn. Univ. Govt. and Industry Micro Symp., Westboro, 1989; session chmn. Semicon East, Boston, 1987. Inventor in field. Pres. Homeowners Assn., Fla., 1972-73; dir. South Beaches Exec. Coun., Fla., 1972-74; treas. Nursery Sch., Liverpool, N.Y., 1967-68. Mem. Electrochem. Soc., Tau Beta Pi, Alpha Sigma Mu. Home: 7793 E Aster Dr Scottsdale AZ 85260-4845

TRIGIANO, LUCIEN LEWIS, physician; b. Easton, Pa., Feb. 9, 1926; s. Nicholas and Angeline (Lewis) T.; children: Lynn Anita, Glenn Larry, Robert Nicholas. Student Tex. Christian U., 1944-45, Ohio U., 1943-44, 46-47, Milligan Coll., 1944, Northwestern U., 1945, Temple U., 1948-52. Intern, Meml. Hosp., Johnstown, Pa., 1952-53; resident Lee Hosp., Johnstown, 1953-54; gen. practice, Johnstown, 1953-59; med. dir. Pa. Rehab. Center, Johnstown, 1959-62, chief phys. medicine and rehab., 1964-70; fellow phys. medicine and rehab. N.Y. Inst. Phys. Medicine and Rehab., 1962-64; dir. rehab. medicine Lee Hosp., 1964-71, Ralph K. Davies Med. Center, San Francisco, 1973-75, St. Joseph's Hosp., San Francisco, 1975-78, St. Francis Meml. Hosp., San Francisco, 1978-83; asst. prof. phys. medicine and rehab. Temple U. Sch. Medicine; founder Disability Alert. Served with USNR, 1944-46. Diplomate Am. Bd. Phys. Medicine and Rehab. Mem. AMA, A.C.P., Pa., San Francisco County Med. socs., Am. Acad. Phys. Medicine and Rehab., Am. Congress Phys. Medicine, Calif. Acad. Phys. Medicine, Nat. Rehab. Assn., Babcock Surg. Soc. Author various med. articles. Home: 1050 North Point St San Francisco CA 94109-8302 Office: 1150 Bush St Ste 4B San Francisco CA 94109

TRIGUEIRO, RONALD DEAN, legal researcher; b. Fresno, Calif., Mar. 11, 1959; s. Stanley Joseph and Lena Dolores (Azevedo) T. Student, Fresno City Coll., 1979-83; BA in Polit. Sci., Calif. State U., Fresno, 1988. Data transcriber IRS, Fresno, 1983-86; rsch. asst. Law Offices of Edward V. Marouk, Fresno, 1992—; mem. staff Trial & Win, Fresno, 1992—. Mem. Future Bus. Leaders Am. (nat. parliamentarian 1976-77), Phi Beta Lambda, Inc. Democrat. Roman Catholic. Home: 11337 S Hughes Ave Caruthers CA 93609

TRIMBLE, RICHARD DOUGLAS, utilities engineer, electrical engineer; b. San Antonio, Sept. 28, 1962; s. Harold Vincent and Frances Lynette (Allen) T.; m. Deborah Susan Treick, June 3, 1987 (div. Feb. 1992); children: Gini Kathleen, Richard Douglas II, Kaitlyn Rebecca; m. Marla Jean Sharp-Peters, Jan. 4, 1993; stepchildren: Travis Justin Sharp, Lindsay Jean Sharp, Braden William Sharp. AS, Olympic Coll., Bremerton, Wash., 1983; BSEE, U. Wash., 1985. Registered profl. engr., Alaska, Wash. Engring. mgr. Ketchikan (Alaska) Pub. Utilities, 1990—. Chmn. nominating com. Ketchikan Campus Adv. Coun., 1992. Lt. USN, 1985-90. Mem. NSPE, Phi Beta Kappa, Tau Beta Pi. Office: Ketchikan Pub Utilities 2930 Tongass Ketchikan AK 99901

TRIMBLE, STANLEY WAYNE, hydrology and geography educator; b. Columbia, Tenn., Dec. 8, 1940; s. Stanley Drake and Clara Faye (Smith) T.; m. Alice Erle Gunn, Aug. 16, 1964; children: Alicia Anne, Jennifer Lusanne. BS, U. North Ala., 1964; MA, U. Ga., 1970, PhD, 1973. Asst. prof. hydrology and geography U. Wis., Milw., 1972-75; from asst. prof. to prof. UCLA, 1975—; vis. asst. prof. U. Chgo., 1978, vis. assoc. prof., 1981, vis. prof. environ. geography, 1990; vis. lectr. U. London, 1985; hydrologist U.S. Geol. Survey, 1974-84. Author: Culturally Accelerated Sedimentation on the Middle Georgia Piedmont, 1971, Man-Induced Erosion on the Southern Piedmont, 1700-1970, 1974, Soil Conservation and the Reduction, 1982, Sediment Characteristics of Tennesee Streams, 1984. Served to 1st lt. U.S. Army, 1963-65. Grantee U.S. Geol. Survey, Washington, 1974-79, Wis. Dept. Nat. Resources, Madison, 1978, 82, NSF, Washington, 1976, Agrl. Research Service of USDA, Washington, 1972. Mem. Assn. Am. Geographers, Am. Geophys. Union, Soil Conservation Soc. Am., Brit. Geomorphol. Rsch. Group, Sigma Xi. Republican. Office: UCLA Dept Geography 405 Hilgard Ave Los Angeles CA 90024-1301

TRIMBLE, THOMAS JAMES, utility company executive; b. Carters Creek, Tenn., Sept. 3, 1931; s. John Elijah and Mittie (Rountree) T.; m. Glenna Kay Jones, Sept. 3, 1957; children: James Jefferson, Julie Kay. BA, David Lipscomb U., 1953; JD, Vanderbilt U., 1956; LLM, NYU, 1959. Bar: Tenn. 1956, Ariz. 1961, U.S. Dist. Ct. Ariz. 1961, U.S. Dist. Ct. D.C. 1963, U.S. Ct. Appeals (10th cir.) 1971, U.S. Supreme Ct. 1972, U.S. Ct. Appeals (9th cir.) 1975. From assoc. to ptnr. Jennings, Strouss & Salmon, Phoenix, 1960-85, mng. ptnr., 1985-87; sr. v.p., gen. counsel, corp. sec. S.W. Gas Corp., Las Vegas, Nev., 1987—, gen. counsel, 1987-92; corp. sec. Primerit Bank, 1990-92; exec. v.p., bd. dirs. Energy Ins. (Bermuda) Ltd., 1992—; bd. dirs. Energy Ins. Mut. Ltd., 1988—, vice chmn., 1992—. Mem. editorial bd. Vanderbilt U. Law Rev., 1954-56. Mem. Pepperdine U. Bd. Regents, Malibu, Calif., 1981—, sec., 1982—, mem. exec. com., 1982-89; bd. visitors Pepperdine Sch. Law, Malibu; pres. Big Sisters Ariz., Phoenix, 1975, bd. dirs., 1970-76; chmn. Sunnydale Children's Home, Phoenix, 1966-69, bd. dirs., 1965-75; pres. Clearwater Hills Improvement Assn., Phoenix, 1977-79, bd. dirs., 1975-80; trustee Nev. Sch. of Arts, 1988-92, chmn., 1989-90. 1st lt. JAGC, USAF, 1957-60. Fellow Ariz. Bar Found. (founding); mem. ABA, Ariz. Bar Assn. (editorial bd. Jour. 1975-80), Am. Gas. Assn. (legal sect. mng. com. 1987—), Order of Coif, Phi Delta Phi. Republican. Mem. Ch. Christ. Club: Spanish Trail Country (Las Vegas). Lodge: Kiwanis (pres. Phoenix 1972-73). Home: 5104 Turnberry Ln Las Vegas NV 89113-1394 Office: SW Gas Corp PO Box 98510 5241 Spring Mountain Rd Las Vegas NV 89193-8510

TRIPLEHORN, DON MURRAY, geology educator; b. Bluffton, Ohio, July 24, 1934; s. Murray and Alice (Lora) T.; m. Julia Evans Hardesty; Sept. 14, 1957; children: Clay, Carl, Joel, Stella. BA, Ohio Wesleyan U., 1956; MA, Ind. u., 1957; PhD, U. Ill., 1961. Instr. Coll. Wooster, Ohio, 1960-61; rsch. geologist Sinclair Rsch., Tulsa, Ohio, 1961-69; geologist U. Alaska, Fairbanks, 1969—. Lt. USAF, 1957-58. Home: PO Box 80826 Fairbanks AK 99708-0826 Office: U Alaska-Fairbanks Dept Geology & Geophysics Fairbanks AK 99775

TRIPLETT, RAYMOND FRANCIS, insurance underwriter; b. Detroit Lakes, Minn., Oct. 14, 1921; s. Raymond LeRoy Triplett and Barbara A. (Wambach) Van Der Wey; m. Shirley J. Koenig, Feb. 14, 1942; children: Kathleen, Barbara, Joan, Therese, Raymond J. CLU. Mgr. western sales Minn. & Ont. Paper Co., Calif., 1950-53; field underwiter N.Y. Life Ins. Co., San Jose, Calif., 1953—; faculty 2nd annual Inst. Estate Planning, Law Ctr. U. Miami, 1968, Inst. Fed. Taxation, Law Ctr. U. So. Calif., 1971. Author: Voyage of Commitment, 1983. Mem. personnel bd. Santa Clara County, 1965-66; mem. Jud. Selection Adv. Bd., San Jose, 1976-74; bd. dirs. O'Connor Hosp. Found., bd. fellows Santa Clara U. Lt. USMS, 1942-44. Recipient Circumnavigators award Cruising Club Am. Mem. Santa Clara County Estate Planning Council (pres. 1958), San Jose Life Underwriters Assn., CLU (pres. Santa Jose chpt. 1964), N.Y. Life Ins. Co. (pres. council 1964), Am. Soc. CLU (nat. pres. 1972-73), Am. Coll. Life Underwriters (trustee), Cath. Layman's Retreat Assn. Home: 16203 Hillvale Ave Monte Sereno CA 95030 Office: 255 Metro Dr Ste 228 San Jose CA 95110-1316

TRIPP, LEONARD LEE, software engineer; b. L.A., Oct. 21, 1941; s. Leonard Henry and Allie Marie (Haws) T.; m. Celia Frank, Nov. 28, 1963; children: Valerie, Monica, Allyson, Justin, Mary Esther, Lee. BS, Brigham Young U., 1965, MS, 1967. Sci. programmer Boeing Co., Seattle, 1967-75, computer scientist, 1975-85, sr. computer scientist, 1985-91, assoc. tech. fellow, 1991—. Contbr. to profl. publs. Commr. King County Water Dist. 124, Federal Way, Wash., 1977-82, Lakehaven Sewer Dist., Federal Way, 1979-82, Federal Way Water and Sewer Bd., 1983-84. Recipient Silver Beaver award Boy Scouts Am., 1984. Mem. IEEE (vice-chair computer soc. std. activity bd. 1989-93, exec. vice-chair IEEE software engring. stds. sub-com. 1985-92, chair IEEE software engring. stds. com. 1993—, chair U.S. tech. adv. group to ISO/IEC JTC1/SC7 software engring), Assn. Computing Machinery, Math. Assn. Am., Boy Scouts Am. Home: 28632 8th Pl S Federal Way WA 98003 Office: Boeing Comml Airplane PO Box 3707 MS 6Y-07 Seattle WA 98124

TRIPP, RAYMOND PLUMMER, JR., English literature educator; b. Acushnet, Mass., Dec. 15, 1932; s. Raymond Plummer and Mildred Evelyn (Willis) T.; m. Susan Jane Scofield, June 6, 1959. BA, U. Mass., 1960; MA, U. Toronto, Ont., 1963; PhD, Union Grad. Sch., 1971. Asst. prof. Clarion (Pa.) State Coll., 1964-67; prof. U. Denver, 1968—; vis. prof. Hirosaki Coll., Japan, 1980-81. Author: Reflections on Walden, 1972, Beyond Canterbury, 1977 (Acad. Book of Yr.), More About the Fight with the Dragon: The Dragon in Beowulf, 1983, The Mysterious Kingdom of Emily Dickinson's Poetry, 1988, Literary Essays on Beowulf, 1992. Pres. Univ. Profs. for Acad. Order, Washington, 1989-90. With U.S. Army, 1954-57. Mem. Soc. for New Lang. Study (founder 1972). Western Rite Orthodox. Home: 885 S Vine St Denver CO 80209-4618 Office: U Denver Dept English Lit Denver CO 80208-0182

TRISKA, BRADLEY FRANK, sales executive; b. Sewickley, Pa., Mar. 13, 1950; s. Frank and Mary Florence (Kopy) T.; m. Linda Carol Freno, Aug. 25, 1973; 1 child, Tawny Lin. BSBA in Mktg., Robert Morris Coll., 1973.

With Kellogg Sales Co., various locations, 1973—; met. dist. mgr. Kellogg Sales Co., L.A., 1979-82, unit mgr., 1982-84; dir. div. sales Kellogg Sales Co., St. Louis, 1984-87, L.A., 1987—. Mem. Food Industry Sales Mgrs. Club. Republican. Mem. Assemblies of God Ch. Office: Kellogg Sales Co Ste 830 7755 Center Ave Huntington Beach CA 92647

TRISKA, JAN FRANCIS, retired political science educator; b. Prague, Czechoslovakia, Jan. 26, 1922; came to U.S., 1948, naturalized, 1955; s. Jan and Bozena (Kubiznak) T.; m. Carmel Lena Burastero, Aug. 26, 1951; children: Mark Lawrence, John William. J.U.D., Charles U., Prague, 1948; LL.M., Yale U., 1950, J.S.D., 1952; Ph.D., Harvard U., 1957. Co-dir. Soviet treaties Hoover Instn., Stanford, Calif., 1956-58; lectr. dept. polit. sci. U. Calif.-Berkeley, 1957-58; asst. prof. Cornell U., Ithaca, N.Y., 1958-60; assoc. prof. Stanford U., Calif., 1960-65, prof. polit. sci., 1965-89, prof. emeritus, 1989—, assoc. chmn. dept., 1965-66, 68-69, 71-72, 74-75, emeritus prof. polit. sci., 1990—. Co-author: (with Slusser) The Theory, Law and Policy of Soviet Treaties, 1962, (with Finley) Soviet Foreign Policy, 1968, (with Cocks) Political Development and Political Change in Eastern Europe, 1977, (with Ike, North) The World of Superpowers, 1981, (with Gati) Blue Collar Workers in Eastern Europe, 1981, Dominant Powers and Subordinate States, 1986; bd. editors: East European Quar. Comparative Politics, Internat. Jour. Sociology, Jour. Comparative Politics, Studies in Comparative Communism, Soviet Statutes and Decisions, Documents in Communist Affairs. Recipient Rsch. award Ford Found., 1963-68, Josef Hlavka Commemorative medal Czechoslovak Acad. Scis., 1992, M.A. Comenius 1592-1992 Meml. medal Czechoslovak Pedagogical Mus., Prague, 1991; fellow NSF, 1971-72, Sen. Fulbright fellow, 1973-74, Woodrow Wilson fellow Internat. Ctr. for Scholars, 1980-81. Mem. Am. Polit. Sci. Assn. (sec. pres. conf. on communist studies 1970-76l), Assn. Advancement Slavic Studies (bd. dirs. 1975-83), Am. Soc. Internat. Law (exec. coun. 1964-67), Czechoslovak Soc. Arts and Scis. (pres. 1978-80, 90-92), Inst. for Human Scis. Vienna (acting for Commn. European Communities, Brussels, com. experts on transformation of nat. higher edn. and rsch. system in Ctrl. Europe, Brussels 1991—). Democrat. Club: Fly Fishers (Palo Alto, Calif.). Home: 720 Vine St Menlo Park CA 94025-6154 Office: Stanford U Dept Polit Sci Stanford CA 94305

TRITTEN, JAMES JOHN, national security educator; b. Yonkers, N.Y., Oct. 3, 1945; s. James Hanley and Jennie (Szucs) T.; m. Kathleen Tritten, (div. 1983); children: Kimberly, James John Jr.; m. Jasmine Clark, Dec. 29, 1990. BA in Internat. Studies, Am. U., 1971; MA in Internat. Affairs, Fla. State U., 1978; AM in Internat. Rels., U. So. Calif., L.A., 1982, PhD in Internat. Rels., 1984. Commd. officer USN, 1967, advanced through grades to commdr., 1981; joint strategic plans officer Office of the Chief of Naval Ops., Washington, 1984-85; asst. dir. net assessment Office of the Sec. of Def., Washington, 1985-86; chmn. dept. nat. security affairs Naval Postgrad. Sch., Monterey, Calif., 1986-89; ret. USN, 1989; assoc. prof. nat. security affairs Naval Postgrad. Sch., Monterey, 1989—; cons. Rand Corp., Santa Monica, Calif., 1982-84; with Nat. Security Rsch., Fairfax, Va., 1992. Author: Soviet Naval Forces and Nuclear Warfare, 1986, Our New National Security Strategy, 1992 (George Washington Honor medal 1991); co-editor: Reconstituting National Defense, 1992; contbr. chpts. to books and articles to profl. jours. Mem. Adv. Bd. on Alcohol Related Problems, Monterey County, Calif., 1987-90; bd., officer Leadership Monterey (Calif.) Peninsula, 1989-92, Carmel Valley (Calif.) Property Owners Assn., 1989-91; commr. Airport Land Use Commn., Monterey County, 1990—, mem. Nat Eagle Scout Assn. Decorated Def. Superior Svc. medal Sec. Def., Washington, 1986, Meritorious Svc. medal Sec. Navy, Monterey, 1989; recipient Alfred Thayer Mahan award for literary achievement Navy League of U.S., Arlington, Va., 1986. Mem. Mil. Ops. Rsch. Soc. (v.p. 1990-91), Internat. Inst. for Strategic Studies, U.S. Naval Inst. (Silver and Bronze medals), Royal United Svcs. Insts. for Def. Studies, Pi Sigma Alpha, Pi Gamma Mu. Republican. Presbyterian. Office: Naval Postgrad Sch Code NS/TR Monterey CA 93943-5100

TRNKA, ZDENEK, engineering company executive, consultant; b. Prague, Czechoslovakia, Feb. 3, 1943; came to U.S., 1968; s. Zdenek and Helena (Ružková) T.; m. Jana Lukešová, Oct. 29, 1965; children: Michael Jan, Hana Helena. MSME, Tech. U. Prague, Czechoslovakia, 1965. Registered profl. engr., Wash. Rsch. asst. Tech. U. Prague, 1966-68; sr. project engr. Kaiser Aluminum & Chem., Tacoma, Wash., 1969-79; plant engr., facilities mgr. Advanced Tech. Labs., Bellevue, Wash., 1983-85; prin. Trnka Engrs. Co., Bellevue, Wash., 1979-83, 85—. Patentee cooling system for continuous casting machines. Home: 5413 126th Pl SE Bellevue WA 98006 Office: 1050 140th NE Bellevue WA 98005

TROAN, GORDON TRYGVE, accountant, financial planner, entrepreneur; b. Mpls., Mar. 1, 1960; s. John Trygve and Janet Lillian (Cook) T.; m. Stefanie Louise Mock, July 15, 1989. BS in Acctg., Ariz. State U., 1982, MBA, 1985. CPA, CFP, Ariz. Pres., chief fin. officer Five Star Enterprises, Inc., Phoenix, 1982-90, chief exec. officer, 1990—, also bd. dirs.; cons. St. Andrew's Found., Phoenix, 1988—. Precinct commiteeman Ariz. Dems., Phoenix, 1982; mem. coun. of deacons St. Andrew Luth. Ch., Phoenix, 1982-84. Mem. Ariz. Soc. CPAs, North Valley C. of C., Son's of Norway (sec. fin. com. 1986—). Office: Five Star Enterprises Inc 5927 W Bell Rd Glendale AZ 85308-3711

TROCHAK, STEPHANIE ELLEN, army officer; b. McAllen, Tex., Sept. 19, 1953; d. Frank Luke and Margaret Jean (Myers) T. BS in Biology, S.W. Tex. State U., 1975; BBA in Fin., U. Tex.-Pan Am., Edinburg, 1986. Mortgage loan processor Valley Fed. Savs. & Loan, McAllen, Tex., 1977-83; commd. U.S. Army, 1986—, advanced through grades to capt.; chief disbursing/cash control 106th Fin. Support Unit, Ludwigsburg, Germany, 1987-89; asst. chief fin. support div. 7th Fin. group, Stuttgart, Germany, 1989-90; joint svc. software depolyment team leader Def. Fin. & Acctg. Svcs., Indpls., 1990-92, fin. officer advanced course, 1992-93; detachment comdr., S1-S4 officer 125th Fin. Support Unit, Schofield Barracks, Hawaii, 1993—. Decorated Army Commendation medal with oak leaf cluster. Mem. Am. Soc. Mil Comptrollers (transp. com. 1991), Fin. Corps Assn., Assn. U.S. Army, AAUW (treas. 1980-84), Alpha Kappa Psi. Methodist. Address: 125th Fin Support Unit Schofield Barracks HI 96857-5200

TROCKI, LINDA KATHERINE, geoscientist, natural resource economist; b. Erie, Pa., Oct. 7, 1952; d. Bernard Joseph and Catherine Frances (Manczka) T. BS in Geology with highest honors, N.Mex. Inst. Mining and Tech., 1976; MS in Geochemistry, Pa. State U., 1983, PhD in Mineral Econs., 1985. Staff mem. Los Alamos (N.Mex.) Nat. Lab., 1976-78, 83-90; geologist Internat. Atomic Energy Agy., Vienna, Austria, 1978-80; grad. rsch. asst. Los Alamos (N.Mex.) Nat. Lab., 1981-83, dep. group leader, 1990-92, dep. program dir., 1992—; com. mem. Global Found., Coral Gables, Fla., 1988—; mem. Strategic Lab. Coun., U.S. Dept. Energy, 1992—; mem. Chief of Naval Ops. Task force on Energy, Alexandria, Va., 1990-91. Contbr. to profl. publs. Pres. Vista Encantada Neighborhood Assn., Santa Fe, 1988-89. Fellow East West Ctr., Honolulu, 1988. Mem. AAAS, Internat. Assn. Energy Economists, Mineral Econs. and Mgmt. Soc. (pres.-elect). Office: Los Alamos Nat Lab MS F641 PO Box 1663 Los Alamos NM 87545-0001

TROISE, JOSEPH LOUIS, writer; b. N.Y.C., Aug. 28, 1942; s. Louis Carlo and Anne (Bivona) T. BA, Bklyn. Coll., 1964. Cert. tchr., N.Y. Tchr. honors English Erasmus Hall, Bklyn., 1964-66; asst. editor Harcourt Brace Javonovich, N.Y.C., 1966-68; asst. dir. of admissions and fin. aide Columbia U., N.Y.C., 1968-69; spl. rep. Mercedes Benz of N.Am., Montvale, N.J., 1969-71; writer, cartoonist Sausalito, Calif., 1972—. Author: Dare to be Dull, 1982, Drive It Til It Drops, 1981, Cherries and Lemons, 1977; contbr. over 200 articles to nat. mags. Acessions and rsch. mem. Sausalito Hist. Soc.; bd. dirs. Galilee Harbor Community Assn., Sausalito, 1990-91, ArtZone, Sausalito, 1984-88. With USAR, 1965-70. Mem. Soc. of Automotive Historians, Internat. Dull Men's Club (pres. and founder). American Buddhist. Home and Office: 300 Napa St Sausalito CA 94965

TROMBLEY, WILLIAM HOLDEN, journalist; b. Buffalo, June 18, 1929; s. William Albert and Eva (Atkinson) T.; m. Audrey Louise Ramsdell, Mar. 21, 1954; children—Suzanne, Patricia. B.A., Johns Hopkins U., 1952; M.S. in Journalism, Columbia U., 1953. Reporter Life Mag., N.Y.C., Chgo. and San Francisco, 1953-61; writer, editor Saturday Evening Post, Phila., 1962-63; staff writer Los Angeles Times, 1965-92; sr. editor Calif. Higher Edn. Policy Ctr., 1993. Recipient numerous awards for pub. affairs and ednl. reporting AAUP, Los Angeles Press Club, Calif. Tchrs. Assn., others, 1969-77. Home: 7070 Flintwood Way Sacramento CA 95831-3004 Office: Calif Higher Edn Policy Ctr 160 W Santa Clara St San Jose CA 95113

TRONE, DONALD BURNELL, investment company executive; b. Gettysburg, Pa., Jan. 22, 1954; s. Donald Burnell and Mary Ann (Moreau) T.; children from previous marriage, Tara C., Donald Timothy. BS in Govt., USCG Acad., 1977; MS in Fin. Svcs., Am. Coll., Bryn Mawr, Pa., 1989. Registered investment adviser; cert. fin. planner. Commd. ensign USCG, 1977, advanced through ranks to lt. comdr., 1988, aviator, 1977-87; resigned, 1987; fin. planner Fla. Fin. Advisers, Tampa, 1987; sr v.p. Investment Adv. Svcs. of Raymond James, St. Petersburg, Fla., 1987-89, USF&G, Cin., 1989; v.p. mktg. SEI Wealth Mgmt., 1989-91; dir. investment mgmt. coun. div dir. Callan Assocs. Inc., San Francisco, 1991—. Pilot (film) Cocoon, 1985; coauthor: Procedural Prudence. Recipient Sikorsky Heroism award United Techs., 1981. Mem. Internat. Bd. Cert. Fin. Planners (dir. 1987—). Republican. Episcopalian. Home: 3 Rose Ct Sausalito CA 94965 Office: Callan Assocs Inc 71 Stevenson St Ste 1300 San Francisco CA 94105

TROPPER, JOSHUA, lawyer; b. Birmingham, Ala., Jan. 30, 1955; s. Sol and Pearl (Kessler) T.; m. Jeanne Lynn Watson, Jan. 5, 1980. BA, Columbia U., 1975; JD, MPP, Harvard U., 1979. Bar: N.Y. 1980, U.S. Dist Ct. (so. and ea. dists.) N.Y. 1980, U.S. Ct. Appeals (9th cir.) 1983, Calif. 1984, U.S. Dist. Ct. (so. dist.) Calif. 1984, U.S. Supreme Ct. 1986, U.S. Dist. Ct. (cen. dist.) Calif. 1987, U.S. Dist. Ct. (ea. dist.) Wis. 1987. Assoc. Seward & Kissel, N.Y.C., 1979-83, Gaston Snow & Ely Bartlett, Palo Alto, Calif., 1983-87; corp. counsel Atari Corp., Sunnyvale, Calif., 1987-90; ptnr. Lee & Tropper, San Mateo, Calif., 1990—. Office: Lee & Tropper 2121 S El Camino Real San Mateo CA 94403-1819

TROST, BARRY MARTIN, chemist, educator; b. Philadelphia, Pa., June 13, 1941; s. Joseph and Esther T.; m. Susan Paula Shapiro, Nov. 25, 1967; children: Aaron David, Carey Daniel. B.A. cum laude, U. Pa., 1962; Ph.D., MIT, 1965. Mem. faculty U. Wis., Madison, 1965—; prof., chemistry U. Wis., 1969—, Evan P. and Marion Helfaer prof. chemistry, from 1976, Vilas research prof. chemistry; prof. chemistry Stanford U., 1987—, Tamaki prof. humanities and scis., 1990; cons. Merck, Sharp & Dohme, E.I. duPont de Nemours.; Chem. Soc. centenary lectr., 1982. Author: Problems in Spectroscopy, 1967, Sulfur Ylides, 1975; editor-in-chief Comprehensive Organic Synthesis, 1991—; editor: Structure and Reactivity Concepts in Organic Chemistry series, 1972—; assoc. editor: Jour. Am. Chem. Soc, 1974-80; editorial bd.: Organic Reactions Series, 1971—; editor-in-chief Comprehensive Organic Synthesis, 1991; contbr. numerous articles to profl. jours. Recipient Dreyfus Found. Tchr.-Scholar award, 1970, 77, Creative work in synthetic organic chemistry award, 1981, Baekeland medal, 1981, Alexander von Humboldt award, 1984, Guenther award, 1990, Janssen prize, 1990; named Chem. Pioneer, Am. Inst. Chemists, 1983; NSF fellow, 1963-65, Sloan Found. fellow, 1967-69, Am. Swiss Found. fellow, 1975—; Cope scholar, 1989. Mem. Am. Chem. Soc. (award in pure chemistry 1977), Nat. Acad. Scis., Am. Acad. Arts and Scis., AAAS, Chem. Soc. London. Office: Stanford U Dept Chemistry Stanford CA 94305

TROST, MARTHA ANN, educator; b. Ft. Monmouth, N.J., Nov. 30, 1951; d. Oscar F. and Anna M. (Connor) T. BS, N.Mex. State U., 1974, MA in Teaching, 1977. Tchr. Gadsden Ind. Schs., Anthony, N.Mex., 1974-82; learning ctr. dir. Ednl. Svcs., White Sands Missile Range, N.Mex., 1983-85; tchr. Santa Fe Community Coll., 1985-90, adminstr. corrections edn. div., 1990-91; instr. Espanola Valley Pub. Schs., Espanola, N.Mex., 1991—; computer cons. M&M Connection, Santa Fe, 1988—; speaker at profl. confs. Mem. N.Mex. Jaycees (mgmt. v.p. 1990-91, mgmt. v.p. Capital City unit 1986-87, pres. 1989-90), Leadership Santa Fe (v.p. 1990-91). Home: 1115 Calle Del Pajarito Santa Fe NM 87505-5030 Office: Espanola Valley Schs PO Box 3039 Espanola NM 87532

TROTT, STEPHEN SPANGLER, lawyer, musician; b. Glen Ridge, N.J., Dec. 12, 1939; s. David Herman and Virginia (Spangler) T.; divorced; children: Christina, Shelley. B.A., Wesleyan U., 1962; LL.B., Harvard U., 1965. Bar: Calif. 1966, U.S. Dist. Ct. (cen. dist.) Calif. 1966, U.S. Ct. Appeals (9th cir.) 1983, U.S. Supreme Ct. 1984. Guitarist, mem. The Highwaymen, 1958—; dep. dist. atty. Los Angeles County Dist. Atty.'s Office, Los Angeles, 1966-75; chief dep. dist. atty. Los Angeles County Dist. Atty.'s Office, 1975-79; U.S. dist. atty. Central Dist. Calif., Los Angeles, 1981-83; asst. atty. gen. criminal div. Dept. Justice, Washington, 1983-86; mem. faculty Nat. Coll. Dist. Attys., Houston, 1973—; chmn. central dist. Calif. Law Enforcement Coordinating Com., Houston, 1981-83; coordinator Los Angeles-Nev. Drug Enforcement Task Force, 1982-83; assoc. atty. gen. Justice Dept., Washington, 1986-88; judge U.S. Ct. of Appeals 9th Cir., Boise, Idaho, 1988—. Recipient Gold record as singer-guitarist for Michael Row the Boat Ashore, 1961, Disting. Faculty award Nat. Coll. Dist. Attys., 1977. Mem. Am. Coll. Trial Lawyers, Wilderness Fly Fishers Club (pres. 1975-77), Brentwood Racing Pigeon Club (pres. 1977-82), Magic Castle. Republican. Office: US Ct Appeals9th Circuit 550 West Fort St Boise ID 83724

TROTTER, F(REDERICK) THOMAS, university president; b. Los Angeles, Apr. 17, 1926; s. Fred B. and Hazel (Thomas) T.; m. Gania Demaree, June 27, 1953; children—Ruth Elizabeth, Paula Anne (dec.), Tania, Mary. AB, Occidental Coll., 1950, DD, 1968; STB, Boston U., 1953, PhD, 1958; LHD, Ill. Wesleyan U., 1974, Cornell Coll., 1985, Westmar Coll., 1987; LLD, U. Pacific, 1978, Wesleyan Coll., 1981; EdD, Columbia Coll., 1984; LittD, Alaska Pacific U., 1987. Exec. sec. Boston U. Student Christian Assn., 1951-54; ordained elder Calif.-Pacific, Methodist Ch., 1953; pastor Montclair (Calif.) Meth. Ch., 1956-59; lectr. So. Calif. Sch. Theology at Claremont, 1957-59, instr., 1959-60, asst. prof., 1960-63, assoc. prof., 1963-66, prof., 1966, dean, 1961; prof. religion and arts, dean Sch. Theology Claremont, 1961-73; mem. Bd. Higher Edn. and Ministry, United Meth. Ch., 1972-73, gen. sec., 1973-87; pres. Alaska Pacific U., Anchorage, 1988—; dir. Inst. for Antiquity and Christianity at Claremont. Author: Jesus and the Historian, 1968, Loving God with One's Mind, 1987, weekly column local newspapers; editor-at-large: Christian Century, 1969-84. Trustee Dillard U. Served with USAAF, 1944-46. Kent fellow Soc. for Values in Higher Edn., 1954; Dempster fellow Meth. Ch., 1954. Mem. Rotary Internat. (Anchorage Downtown), Commonwealth North. Office: Alaska Pacific U Office Pres 4101 University Dr Anchorage AK 99508-4672

TROUP, MALCOLM GRAHAM, retired army officer, real estate developer; b. Olean, N.Y., May 19, 1918; s. Norman Irving Graham Troup and Mildred (Brink) Mahley; m. Alma May Henry, June 12, 1941; children: Malcolm Brian, Stephen Preston. BS, U.S. Mil. Acad., 1941; MBA, Harvard U., 1949. Commd. 2d lt. U.S. Army, 1941, advanced through grades to col., 1956; logistics mgr. U.S. Army, Tokyo, Seoul, Washington, Phila., West Point, N.Y., Ft. Lee, Va., Colorado Springs, Colo., 1941-66; ret., 1966; developer, salesman Colo. Mountain Property, 1966-72. Decorated Legion of Merit. Mem. Ret. Officers Assn., Am. Philatelic Soc. Republican. Home: 202 Pine Ave Colorado Springs CO 80906-3251

TROUT, LINDA COPPLE, judge; b. Tokyo, Sept. 1, 1951. BA, U. Idaho, 1973, JD, 1977. Bar: Idaho 1977. Judge magistrate divsn. Idaho Dist. Ct. (2d jud. divsn.), 1982-88; dist. judge Idaho Dist. Ct. (2d jud. divsn.), Boise, 1991—; acting trial ct. adminstr. Idaho Dist. Ct. (2d jud. divsn.); instr. coll. law U. Idaho, 1983, 88. Mem. Idaho State Bar Assn., Clearwater Bar Assn. (pers. 1980-81). *

TROUT, MONROE EUGENE, hospital systems executive; b. Harrisburg, Pa., Apr. 5, 1931; s. David Michael and Florence Margaret (Kashner) T.; m. Sandra Louise Lemke, June 11, 1960; children: Monroe Eugene, Timothy William. AB, U. Pa., 1953, MD, 1957; LLB, Dickinson Sch. of Law, 1964, JD, 1969. Intern Great Lakes (Ill.) Naval Hosp., 1957-58; resident in internal medicine Portsmouth (Va.) Naval Hosp., 1959-61; chief med. dept. Harrisburg State Hosp., 1961-64; dir. drug regulatory affairs Pfizer, Inc., N.Y.C., 1964-68; v.p., med. dir. Winthrop Labs., N.Y.C., 1968-70; med. dir. Sterling Drug, Inc., N.Y.C., 1970-74, v.p., dir. med. affairs, 1974-78, sr. v.p., dir. med. affairs, bd. dirs., mem. exec. com., 1978-86; pres., chief exec. officer Am. Healthcare Systems, Inc., 1986—, chmn., 1987—, also bd. dirs.; chmn. bd. dirs. Am. Excess Ins. LTd.; adj. assoc. prof. Bklyn. Coll. Pharmacy; spl. lectr. legal medicine, trustee Dickinson Sch. Law; trustee Ariz. State U. Sch. Health Adminstrn.; mem. Sterling Winthrop Rsch. Bd., 1977-86; sec. Commn. on Med. Malpractice, HEW, 1971-73, cons., 1974; mem. Joint Commn. Prescription Drug Use, 1976-80; co-chmn. San Diego County Health Commn. Mem. editorial bd. Hosp. Formulary Mgmt, 1969-79, Forensic Science, 1971—, Jour. Legal Medicine, 1973-79, Reg. Tox. and Pharmac, 1981-87, Medical Malpractice Prevention, 1985—; contbr. articles to profl. jours. Exec. com. White House mini conf. on aging, 1980; Republican dist. leader, New Canaan, Conn., 1966-68; mem. Town Council New Canaan, 1978-86 , vice chmn., 1985-86; bd. dirs. New Canaan Interchurch Svc. com., 1965-69, Athletes Kidney Found., Circle in Sq. Theater Inc., 1984-86, Nat. Com. for Quality Health Care, 1988-90, Friends Nat. Libr. Medicine, Criticare, Inc., West Co., Inc., Cytran, Inc., Cytyc, Inc., Gensia Inc., UCSD Found.; trustee Dickinson Sch. of Law, Cleve. Clin., 1971-87, U. Calif.-San Diego Thornton Hosp. and Med. Ctr., Albany Med. Coll., 1977-86, St. Vincent DePaul. Ctr. for the Homeless, 1987-90; trustee, vice chmn. Morehouse Med. Sch., 1980-89; assoc. trustee U. Pa.; bd. visitors U. Pa. Sch. Nursing; vice-chmn. Med. Commn. for Food and Shelter, Inc.; mem. Nat. Health Advisory Bd. AAA, N.Y. State Commn. Substance Abuse, 1978-80; chmn. bd. ACLM Found., 1983-87; chmn. Internat. B'nai B'rith Dinner, 1989. Served to lt. comdr. USNR, 1956-61. Recipient Alumni award of merit U. Pa., 1953, Disting. Alumni award Dickinson Sch. Law, 1989, Nat. Healthcare award Internat. B'nai B'rith, 1991; named to Hon. Order Ky. Cols., Tenn. Cols. Fellow Am. Coll. Legal Medicine (v.p., pres., bd. govs.); mem. AMA (Physicians Recognition awards 1969, 72, 76, 82, 85, 88, 92), Med. Execs. (pres. 1975-76), Delta Tau Delta. Lutheran. Office: 12730 High Bluff Dr Ste 300 San Diego CA 92130-2099

TROUT, ROSCOE MARSHALL, JR., health care and insurance executive; b. Alexandria, La., July 24, 1944; s. Roscoe Marshall Sr. and Clara (de la Croix) T.; m. Myra Susan Segerson; children: Heather Reneé, Tiffany Linnea. BA, NW State U., Natchitoches, La., 1967; MA, NW State U., 1973; EdD, U. No. Colo., 1976; postdoctoral study, U. Pa., 1986. Cert. med. rehab. counselor; registered health underwriter, registered employee benefits cons. Regional ops. dir. Tex. edn. Agy., Beaumont, Tex., 1976-77; mgmt./ops. cons. Tex. Dept. Mental Health-Mentala Retardation, Austin, 1977-79; chief exec. officer Mytro, Inc., Shreveport, La., 1979-84; COO, CEO, NME Health Plans, New Orleans, 1985-88; v.p. mktg. HSI Health Plans, Ft. Collins, Colo., 1989-92; pres. TSOP Fin. Strategies, Austin, Tex., 1989-93; state dir. Coordinated Health Care, TDHS, 1992—; cons. HEW, Denver, 1975, U.S. Dept. Labor, Denver, 1975; mem. Colo. Task Force on Health Care Reform. Com. mem. Shreveport (La.) C. of C., 1980-83; mem. New Orleans Health Adminstrs., 1986-88, Greater No. La. C. of C., New Orleans, 1985-88; com. mem. Exchange Club, Mandeville, La., 1987-88, Ft. Collins C. of C., 1988-89; bd. dirs. Medicom Internat. (Med. Interface), 1989—. Recipient Leadiing Producers Round Table award, 1989; La. State Legis. scholar, 1962, Colo. State Legis. scholar, 1976. Mem. New Orleans Assn. Health Underwriters (bd. dirs. 1987-88), Employee Benefit Planners New Orleans, New Orleans Assn. Health Care Adminstrs., Colo. Assn. Health Underwriters (bd. dirs. 1990-92), No. Colo. Assn. Health Underwriters (pres. 1992-93). Republican. Mem. Ch. of Christ.

TROVER, ELLEN LLOYD, lawyer; b. Richmond, Va., Nov. 23, 1947; d. Robert Van Buren and Hazel (Urban) Lloyd; m. Denis William Trover, June 12, 1971; 1 dau., Florence Emma. AB, Vassar Coll., 1969; JD, Coll. William and Mary, 1972. Asst. editor Bancroft-Whitney, San Francisco, 1973-74; owner Ellen Lloyd Trover Atty.-at-Law, Thousand Oaks, Calif., 1974-82; ptnr. Trover & Fisher, Thousand Oaks, 1982-89; pvt. practice law, Thousand Oaks, 1989—. Editor: Handbooks of State Chronologies, 1972. Trustee, Conejo Future Found., Thousand Oaks, 1978-91, vice chmn., 1982-84, chmn., 1984-88; pres. Zonta Club Conejo Valley Area, 1978-79; trustee Hydro Help for the Handicapped, 1980-85; trustee emeritus Conejo Future Found., 1992. Mem. State Bar Calif., Va. State Bar, Phi Alpha Delta. Democrat. Presbyterian. Home: 11355 Presilla Rd Camarillo CA 93012-8245 Office: 1107E E Thousand Oaks Blvd Thousand Oaks CA 91362-2816

TROW, JD, theater director; b. Mpls., Apr. 5, 1945; d. James Edward and Lois Ruth (Lambert) T.; m. Peter Lind Shaw, Oct. 10, 1970; children: Nora Lind Trow-Shaw, Emily Bayes Trow-Shaw, Max Sundance Trow-Shaw. BA, U. Calif., Berkeley, 1971. Stage mgr. Berkeley Repertory Theatre, 1968-70; assoc. dir. San Jose (Calif.) Repertory Co., 1980-82; freelance dir. Bay Area theaters, San Francisco, 1971—; faculty, acting tchr. Jean Shelton Acting Sch., Berkeley, San Francisco, 1977-87; assoc. dir. One Act Theatre Co., San Francisco, 1977-83; prodn. mgr. Berkeley Jewish Theater, 1983-86; ops. mgr. Berkeley Shakespeare Festival, 1986-88; artistic dir. New Traditions Theater Co., Berkeley, 1988—; conservatory dir. Calif. Shakespeare Festival, Berkeley, 1990—. Judge English-Speaking Union contest, San Francisco, 1990—; chair, bd. dirs. West Berkeley Performing Arts Ctr., Berkeley, 1991—. Recipient Chronicle Drama awards San Francisco Chronicle newspaper, 1986. Mem. Phi Beta Kappa. Democrat. Home: 1610 Martin Luther King Jr Way Berkeley CA 94709 Office: Calif Shakespeare Festival 2531 9th St Berkeley CA 94710

TROWBRIDGE, THOMAS, JR., mortgage banking company executive; b. Troy, N.Y., June 28, 1938; s. of Thomas and Elberta (Wood) T.; m. Delinda Bryan, July 3, 1965; children: Elisabeth Tacy, Wendy Bryan. BA, Yale U., 1960; MBA, Harvard U., 1965. V.p. James W. Rouse & Co., Balt., 1965-66, Washington, 1966-68, San Francisco, 1968-73, 76-78; pres. Rouse Investing Co., Columbia, Md., 1973-76, Trowbridge, Kieselhorst & Co., San Francisco, 1978—. Bd. dirs. Columbia Assn., 1975-76; trustee, treas. The Head-Royce Sch., Oakland, Calif., 1980-84; trustee, pres. Gen. Alumni Assn. Phillips Exeter Acad., 1984-90. Lt. USNR, 1960-63. Mem. Urban Land Inst., Calif. Mortgage Bankers Assn. (bd. dirs. 1991—), Olympic Club, Pacific Union Club, Lambda Alpha Internat. Republican. Presbyterian. Home: 4 Ridge Ln Orinda CA 94563-1318 Office: Trowbridge Kieselhorst & Co 555 California St Ste 2850 San Francisco CA 94104

TROXEL, JOHN MILTON, physician; b. Missoula, Mont., Jan. 14, 1960; s. George Owen and Christina M. (Long) T.; m. Sarah C. Burrell, Jan. 14, 1989. BS, Stanford (Calif.) U., 1982, MD, 1986. Intern in surgery U. Calif., San Francisco, 1986-87; resident in otolaryngology Stanford Med. Ctr., 1987-90, chief resident in otolaryngology, 1990-91, resident plastic surgery, 1991—. Mem. AMA, N.Y. Acad. Scis., Alaska Med. Assn. Office: 950 E Bogard Rd Ste 203 Wasilla AK 99654

TRUAX, DONALD ROBERT, mathematics educator; b. Mpls., Aug. 29, 1927; s. William Raymond and Hermina Wilhelmina (Sobolick) T.; m. Barbara June Eckton, Sept. 16, 1950; children: Mary, Catherine, Patricia, Gail. BS in Math., U. Wash., 1951, MS in Math., 1953; PhD in Statistics, Stanford U., 1955. Rsch. fellow Calif. Inst. Tech., Pasadena, 1955-56; asst. prof. math. U. Kans., Lawrence, 1956-59, U. Oreg., Eugene, 1959-62; assoc. prof. math. U. Oreg., 1962-69, prof. math., 1969—. Mng. editor Inst. Math. Statistics, 1975-81; contbr. articles to profl. jours. With USN, 1945-47. Fellow Inst. Math. Statistics; mem. Am. Statis. Assn. Home: 2323 University St Eugene OR 97403-1547 Office: University of Oregon Dept of Mathematics Eugene OR 97403

TRUBNER, HENRY, museum curator; b. Munich, Ger., June 10, 1920; s. Jorg and Gertrude T.; m. Ruth Trubner, July 10, 1948; children: Susan, Karen. BA, Harvard U., 1942, MA, 1944; postgrad., Fogg Art Mus., 1942-47. Curator Oriental art L.A. County Mus. Art, 1947-58; curator Far Eastern dept. Royal Ont. Mus., Toronto, 1958-68; curator Asian art Seattle Art Mus., 1968-87, assoc. dir. and curator Asian Art, 1976-87, sr. curator emeritus, 1987—; dir. Son of Heaven Exhbn. Imperial Arts of China, Seattle, 1988; mem. art adv. com. The Asia Soc., Japan Soc. Gallery, China Inst. in Am., Inc.; mem. Am. adv. com. The Japan Found., Tokyo, 1978-80. Contbr. articles to profl. jours. Recipient Fujio Koyama Meml. prize, Idemitsu Mus. Art, Tokyo, 1988. Mem. Am. Assn. Mus., Oriental Ceramic Soc. London, The Asia Soc. N.Y., The Japan Soc. N.Y., China Inst. in Am., Acad. Laquer Rsch. Tokyo, Soc. for Japanese Arts. Home: 9341 Vineyard Crest Bellevue WA 98004-4028

TRUDEAU, DEANNA DALLOLIO, environmental engineer; b. Trenton, N.J., Aug. 10, 1963; d. David August and Marjorie (Bezdziecki) Dallolio; m. Michael Andre Trudeau, Sept. 20, 1986. BSChemE, U. Notre Dame, 1985. Registered engr.-in-tng., Calif. Project engr. Nabisco Brands, Inc., East Hanover, N.J., 1984, 85-86; environ. engr. Marine Corps Recruit Depot, San

Diego, 1987—. Recipient Tribute to Women in Industry award San Diego County YWCA, 1988, comdg. gen.'s commendation Marine Corps Recruit Depot, 1989. Mem. AICE, Soc. Women Engrs. (sect. rep. 1987-88, sec. 1988-90), Mil. Spouse Bus. and Profl. Network (v.p. 1990—). Roman Catholic. Home: 8480 Jane St San Diego CA 92129 Office: Facilities Div Marine Corps Recruit Depot San Diego CA 92140-5012

TRUDEAU, PATRICIA MARGARET, education educator, writer; b. Ottawa, Ont., Can., Feb. 19, 1931; d. Donald James and Sarah Cecelia (Sheridan) T. BA, U. Ottawa, 1966; postgrad., U. Calgary, Alta., Can., 1968, 69, 70; BTh, Newman Theol. Coll., Edmonton, Alta., Can., 1977; diploma in edn., U. Alta., 1977. Cert. tchr., Can. Tchr. Peterborough (Ont., Can.) Separate Schs., 1953-54, 56-58, Ottawa Separate Schs., 1954-55, 66-71, St. Joseph's Acad., Lindsay, Ont., Can., 1958-66; tchr. Edmonton Separate Schs., 1972-86, ret., 1986. Author poetry; contbr. puzzles to profl. jours. Vol. Laubental Soc. in Support of Arts, St. Albert, Alta., Can., 1988-93, Heritage Agrl. Soc., Stony Plain, Alta., 1989—; sec. Newman Coll. Alumni Assn., Edmonton, 1982-84; sec. publicity com. St. Alta. Nordic Ski Club, St. Albert, 1970's. Recipient 5 Golden Poet awards World of Poetry, 1985-91, 2 Silver Poet awards, 1989-90. Mem. Contour Artisan Assn. (sec. mgmt. bd. 1984-89, stds. com. 1991-93), Alta. Community Arts Clubs Assn., Edmonton Art Gallery, St. Albert Painters Guild (v.p. Alta. chpt. 1987-88, sec. 1987, pres. 1988-89), St. Albert Writers Circle, Fedn. Can. Artists. Roman Catholic. Home: 7 Grandin Village, Saint Albert, AB Canada T8N 1R9

TRUDEL, JOHN DAVIS, management consultant; b. Trenton, N.J., Aug. 1, 1942; s. Leroy and Elizabeth (Reading) T. BEE cum laude, Ga. Inst. Tech., 1964; MSEE, Kans. State U., 1966. Cert. profl. cons. Engr. Collins Radio, Richardson, Tex., 1966-67, sr. engr., 1969-70; sr. engr. Sanders Assoc., Nashua, N.H., 1967-68, LTV E-Systems, Inc., Greenville, Tex., 1968-69, F&M Systems, Inc., Dallas, 1970; pres. Sci. System Tech., Inc., Dallas, 1970-74; mgr. mktg. Tektronix, Inc., Beaverton, Oreg., 1974-83, mgr. bus. devel., 1983-89; v.p. mktg. Cable Bus. Systems Corp., Beaverton, 1981-83; owner, mng. dir. The Trudel Group, Scappoose, Oreg., 1989—; v.p. TCI, Portland, Oreg., 1992. Author: (software) MAGIC CAE, (book) High Tech with Low Risk, 1990; inventor: Waveform Storage, 1984. Aviation com. mem., OMSI, Portland, 1986-87. Mem. Am. Mgmt. Assn., Inst. Mgmt. Cons., Acad. Profl. Cons. and Advisors, Am. Electronics Assn., Nat. Avionics Soc., IEEE, Product Devel. and Mgmt. Assn., Assn. Old Crows, Aircraft Owners and Pilots Assn. Office: The Trudel Group 52001 Columbia River Hwy Scappoose OR 97056-3724

TRUE, DIEMER D., trucking company executive; b. Cody, Wyo., Feb. 12, 1946; s. Henry Alfonso and Jean (Durland) T.; m. Susie Lynn Niethammer, Aug. 28, 1967; children: Diemer Durland, Kyle Shawn, Tara Jeanine, Tracy Lynn. BS, Northwestern U., 1968. With Black Hills Trucking, Inc., Casper, Wyo., 1970—, v.p., 1974—; v.p. Toolpushers Supply Co., Casper, 1981—; dir. Hilltop Nat. Bank, Mountain Plaza Nat. Bank; mem. Wyo. Ho. of Reps., 1972-76; mem. Wyo. State Senate, 1976-92, pres., 1991-92; adv. bd. U. Wyo. Enhanced Oil Recovery Inst. Pres. Natrona County United Way, 1976; vice chmn. Wyo. Rep. Party, 1991-92, chmn. 1993—; mem. bus. adv. coun. Coll. Commerce and Industry U. Wyo. With AUS, 1968. Mem. Wyo. Trucking Assn. (dir. 1972-80, pres. 1983-85), Ind. Petroleum Assn. Am. (regional adv. bd. 1991-93), Rocky Mountain Oil and Gas Assn. (bd. dirs. 1991-93), Western Hwy. Inst. (bd. dirs.) Methodist. Home: PO Box 2360 Casper WY 82602-2360

TRUE, HENRY ALFONSO, JR., entrepreneur; b. Cheyenne, Wyo., June 12, 1915; s. Henry A. and Anna Barbara (Diemer) T.; m. Jean Durland, Mar. 20, 1938; children: Tamma Jean (Mrs. Donald Hatten), Henry Alfonso, III, Diemer D., David L. BS in Indsl. Engring., Mont. State Coll., 1937; PhD in Engring. (hon.), Mont. State U., 1983; LLD (hon.), U. Wyo., 1988. Roustabout, pumper, foreman The Tex. Co., 1937-45, supt. drilling and prodn. for Wyo., 1945-48; mgr. Res. Drilling Co., 1948-51, pres., 1951-59; ptnr. True Drilling Co. and True Oil Co., Casper, Wyo., 1951—; v.p., sec. Toolpushers Supply Co., 1952-53, pres., 1954—; v.p., sec. True Svc. Co., 1953, pres., 1954-70; pres. True Bldg. Corp., 1956-67, Smokey Oil Co., 1975—, Belle Fourche Pipeline Co., 1957—, Black Hills Trucking, Inc., 1977—; owner True Ranches, Inc., 1957-76, pres., 1977-86; pres. True Oil Purchasing Co., 1977-81, True Geothermal Drilling Co., 1981—, True Wyo. Beef, 1987—; ptnr. Eighty-Eight Oil Co., 1955—, True Geothermal Energy Co., 1981—, True Ranches, 1983—; chmn. Powder River Oil Shippers Svc., Inc., 1963-67; pres. Camp Creek Gas Co., 1964-77; v.p. George Mancini Feed Lots, Brighton, Colo., 1964-72; v.p. Black Hills Marketers, Inc., 1966-72, pres., 1973-80; v.p. White Stallion Ranch, Inc., Tucson, 1965—; pres. Res. Oil Purchasing Co., 1972-73; bd. dirs. Midland Fin. Corp.; former bd. dirs. U. Wyo. Rsch. Corp.; chmn. Hilltop Nat. Bank, 1977—, Mountain Plaza Nat. Bank, 1980—; mem. exec. com. Wyo. Oil Industry Com., 1958-74, treas., 1958-59, pres. 1960-62; dir. Rocky Mountain Oil Show, 1955; mem. adv. bd. Internat. Oil and Gas Edn. Ctr., 1964—, vice chmn., 1969-73; mem. natural gas adv. coun. Fed. Power Commn., 1964-65, mem. exec. adv. com., 1971-74; mem. exec. co. com. Gas Supply Com., 1965-69, vice chmn., 1967-69; mem. adv. coun. Pub. Land Rev. Commn., 1965-70; dir. U.S. Bus. and Indsl. Coun., 1971—, exec. com., 1974—; mem. Nat. Petroleum Council, 1962— , nat. oil policy com., 1965, vice chmn., 1970-71, chmn., 1972-73; mem. Rocky Mountain Petroleum Industry Adv. Com., Fed. Energy Office, 1973-77; hon. dir. Mountain Bell, bd. advisors, 1965-84; mem. Wyo. Com. Newcomen Soc. U.S., 1974—. Chmn. advance gifts com. United Fund, 1962; nat. assoc. Boys Clubs Am., 1964-69, hon. chmn. local chpt. 1971; trustee Casper Air Terminal, 1960-71, pres. 1964-65, 67-68; mem. research fellows Southwestern Legal Found., 1968—; trustee U. Wyo., 1965-77, pres. bd., 1971-73, mem. adult edn. and community svc. coun., 1961-64, trustee emeritus, 1991—; bd. govs. Western Ind. Colls. Found., 1963-65; nat. trustee Voice of Youth, 1968; bd. dirs., trustee Nat. Cowboy Hall of Fame and Western Heritage Ctr., 1975—, pres. bd., 1978-80, chmn., 1980-82; dir. Mountain States Legal Found., 1977—, exec. com. 1984—, chmn. bd. 1988-90; dir. Nat. Legal Ctr. for the Pub. Interest, 1988-90; steering com. Wyo. Heritage Soc., 1979—, sec.-treas. 1988— (Heritage award 1991); trustee Buffalo Bill Meml. Assn., 1983-92, emeritus, 1992—; Wyo. state fin. chmn. Reagan-Bush campaign '84. Named Oil Man of Yr., 1959, Disting. Businessman for Small Bus. Mgmt., 1966-67; named to Wisdom Hall Fame, 1970; named Exec. of Yr. Teton chpt. Profl. Secs. Internat., 1985, Hon. Rotarian, Casper Rotary Club, 1990-91; recipient Honored Citizen award, 1964, Casper C. of C., Chief Roughneck of Yr. award, Lone Star Steel award 1965, ann. Indsl. award Wyo. Assn. Realtors, 1965, Pierre F. Goodrich Conservation award Polit. Econ. and Rsch. Ctr., 1982, Oil Man of Century award Casper Centennial Corp., 1989, Soc. centennial alumni Mont. State U., 1992, Century award, 1989. Mem. Internat. Assn. Drilling Contractors (dir. 1950—), Am. Petroleum Inst. (dir. 1960—, exec. com. 1970—, Gold Medal for Disting. Svc. award 1985), Rocky Mountain Oil and Gas Assn. (treas. 1954-55, v.p. Wyo. 1956-58, dir. 1950—, pres. 1962-63, exec. com. 1954—, hon. mem., 1978), Ind. Petroleum Assn. Am. (v.p. Wyo. 1960-61, exec. com. 1962—, pres. 1964-65, Russell B, Karney R. Cochran Gt. Am. Producer award 1991), Rocky Mountain Petroleum Pioneers, Wyo. Stockgrowers Assn., Casper Petroleum (dir. 1954), U.S. C. of C. (dir. 1975-81), Casper C. of C., All-Am Wildcatters, 25 Year Club Petroleum Industry (pres. 1979-80), Ind. Petroleum Assn. Mountain States (Rocky Mountain Wildcatter of Yr. award 1982), Petroleum Assn. Wyo. (dir. 1974—), Am. Judicature Soc. (mem. com. justice 1976), Mont. State U. Soc. Centennial Alumni, Masons, Shriners, Elks, Sigma Chi (Significant Sig award, 1981), Beta Gamma Sigma (hon. mem., 1971 Alpha chpt. Wyo.). Republican. Episcopalian (vestry 1960-62). Office: Belle Fourche Pipeline Co PO Drawer 2360 895 W Rivercross Rd Casper WY 82602

TRUE, LELAND BEYER, civil engineer, consultant; b. Cheyenne, Wyo., Aug. 20, 1921; s. James Beaman and Mary Laura (Beyer) T.; m. Janet R. Hill (dec. Aug. 1976); 1 child, Patricia Ann; m. Alef Collins, May 8, 1977. BSCE, U. Wyo., 1943. Hydrographic field asst. U.S. Geol. Survey, Cheyenne and Laramie, Wyo., 1942-43; engr. P.1 Boysen Dam U.S. Bur. Reclamation, Thermopolis, Wyo., 1946-52; with Morrison-Knudsen Co., Inc., 1952-70, 77-86; project mgr. Greer's Ferry Dam Morrison-Knudsen Co., Inc., Heber Springs, Ark., 1961-63; project mgr. Blue Ridge Dam Morrison-Knudsen Co., Inc., Payson, Ariz., 1963-65; project mgr., estimator home office Morrison-Knudsen Co., Inc., Boise, Idaho, 1965-69; project mgr. Toa Vaca Dam Morrison-Knudsen Co., Inc., Villalba, P.R., 1969-70; resident engr. asst. metro subway A.A. Mathews, Inc., Washington, 1970-77; asst. chief engr. Morrison-Knudsen Co., Inc., Boise, 1977-86; pvt. practice constrn. cons. Boise, 1986—. Staff sgt. U.S. Army Corps Engrs., 1943-46. Mem. ASCE (life). Home and Office: 1143 Santa Maria Dr Boise ID 83712

TRUE, RICHARD BROWNELL, scientist; b. Framingham, Mass., Apr. 4, 1943; s. Charles Richard and Marjorie Brownell (Clapp) T.; m. Sarah Jellison, Feb. 5, 1966; children: Christopher Edmund, Jonathan Richard. BSEE, Brown U., 1966; MS in Microwave Engring., U. Conn., 1968, PhD in Electrophysics, 1972. Elec. engr. Raytheon Co., Inc., Portsmouth, R.I., 1966; lectr., rschr. U. Conn., Storrs, 1966-72; tech. cons., elec. engr. Microwave Assocs., Inc., Burlington, Mass., 1972-73; sr. engr., dept. analyst Litton Systems, Inc., San Carlos, Calif., 1973-78, sr. scientist, 1978-90, chief scientist, 1990—; cons. True Sci., Sunnyvale, 1985—; bd. dirs. AFTER Program U. Utah, 1980-85, chmn. recruiting brochure, 1981, organizer spl. topics course, 1982, 83, lectr. spl. topics course, 1982-86, indsl. thesis advisor, 1982-87; bd. dirs. AFTER Program Stanford U., 1979-81, organizer spl. topics course, 1980, 81, lectr. spl. topics course, 1978-81, indsl. thesis advisor, 1978-81. Patentee in field; contbr. articles to profl. jours. and papers to meetings. NDEA fellow, 1967-70, NSF fellow, 1970-71. Fellow IEEE (sr., mem. adminstrv. com. electron devices soc. 1988—, assoc. editor IEEE Transactions on Electron Devices 1986-90); mem. Sigma Xi. Republican. Home: 1760 Karameos Dr Sunnyvale CA 94087 Office: Litton Systems Inc 960 Industrial Rd San Carlos CA 94070

TRUE, VIRGIL, retired government official, consultant; b. Richview, Ill., July 21, 1925; s.Robert Thurman and Beulah Hazel (Wilson) T.; m. Ruth Louise Hotle, Oct. 7, 1949; children: Kenneth Allen, Virgil David. BSEE, Washington U., St. Louis, 1950. Electronic scientist Naval Rsch. Lab., Washington, 1950-54; supervisory electronic scientist Naval Rsch. Lab., Port Huenene, Calif., 1954-58; br. head Navy Missile Test Ctr., Port Mugu, Calif., 1958-61; sta. dir. Navy Missile Range, Kauai, Hawaii, 1961-65; sta. dir. NASA Network, Kauai, 1965-78, White Sands, N.Mex., 1978-89; cons. NASA, Las Cruces, N.Mex., 1990—. Chmn. Kauai Econ. Devel. Com., 1974-76. With USMCR, 1943-46, PTO. Recipient Exceptional Svc. medal NASA, 1984, 89. Home: 701 Frank Maes Ave Las Cruces NM 88005-1230 Office: NASA Sta Facility PO Drawer GSC Las Cruces NM 88004

TRUE, WILLIAM WADSWORTH, physics educator; b. Rockland, Maine, Dec. 27, 1925; s. Elmer LaForest and Alice Annette (Wadsworth) T.; m. Sarah Elizabeth Goodwin, June 12, 1954; children: William G., Kenneth W., Anne E., Katherine M. BS, U. Maine, 1950; MS, U. R.I., 1952; PhD, Ind. U., 1957. Instr. Princeton (N.J.) U., 1957-60; asst. prof. physics U. Calif., Davis, 1960-64, assoc. prof. phsyics, 1964-69, prof. physics, 1969—. With USAAF, 1944-45. Fellow Am. Phys. Soc.; mem. Phi Kappa Phi, Sigma Xi. Office: Univ of Calif Dept Physics Davis CA 95616

TRUEBLOOD, HARRY ALBERT, JR., oil company executive; b. Wichita Falls, Tex., Aug. 28, 1925; s. Harry A. and Marguerite (Barnhart) T.; m. Lucile Bernard, Jan. 22, 1953; children: Katherine A., John B. Student, Tex. A&M Coll., 1942-43; BS in Petroleum Engring., U. Tex., 1948. Petroleum engr. Cal. Co., 1948-51; chief engr. McDermott & Barnhart Co., Colo., Tex., 1951-52; cons. petroleum and geol. engr. Denver, 1952-55; pres. Colo. Western Exploration Inc., Denver, 1955-58; pres. Consol. Oil and Gas., Inc., 1958-88, chmn. bd., chief exec. officer, 1969-88; chmn. bd., chief exec. officer Princeville Devel. Corp., 1979-87, pres., 1984-86; chmn. bd., chief exec. officer Columbus Energy Corp., 1983—; chmn. bd., chief exec. officer Princeville Airways, Inc., 1979-87. With USNR, 1944-46, ensign, 1949-52. Mem. Soc. Petroleum Engrs., Am. Petroleum Inst., World Bus. Council and Chief Execs. Orgn. (bd. dirs.), Ind. Petroleum Assn. Am. (exec. com.), Natural Gas Supply Assn. (exec. com.), Denver Petroleum Club, Cherry Hills Country Club, Univ. Club, One Hundred Club. Roman Catholic. Home: 2800 S University Blvd Apt 82 Denver CO 80210-6056 Office: Columbus Energy Corp 1660 Lincoln St Ste 2400 Denver CO 80264-2401

TRUEBLOOD, PAUL GRAHAM, emeritus educator, author, editor; b. Macksburg, Iowa, Oct. 21, 1905; s. Charles E. and Adele (Graham) T.; m. Helen Churchill, Aug. 19, 1931; children—Anne Williams, Susan Stuart. BA, Willamette U., 1928; MA, Duke U., 1930, Ph.D., 1935; Litt.D. (hon.), Willamette U., 1984. Instr. Friends U., 1931-34; English master Mohonk Sch. Boys, Lake Mohonk, N.Y., 1935-37; instr. U. Idaho, 1937-40; asso. prof. Stockton Coll., 1940-46; asst. prof. U. Wash., 1947-52; vis. prof. U. Oreg., 1954-55; prof. English, head dept. Willamette U., 1955-70, prof. emeritus, 1971—; vis. lectr. U. B.C., summer 1963. Author: The Flowering of Byron's Genius, 2d edit, 1962, Lord Byron, 2d edit, 1977; Editor: Byron's Political and Cultural Influence in Nineteenth-Century Europe: A Symposium, 1981; Contbr. to charter issues Keats-Shelley Jour, 1952, Byron Jour, 1973. Pendle Hill fellow, 1934-35; fellow Am. Council Learned Socs., 1952-53; recipient Disting. Alumni citation Willamette U., 1975. Mem. MLA, Keats-Shelley Assn. Am., Philol. Assn. Pacific Coast (exec. com. 1964-65), Byron Soc. (founding mem. Am. com. 1973, bd. dirs. 1975, delivered lecture to Byron Soc. in Ho. of Lords 1975), Am. PEN. Home: Capitol Manor 1955 Dallas Rd NW # 903 Salem OR 97304

TRUETT, HAROLD JOSEPH, III (TIM TRUETT), lawyer; b. Alameda, Calif., Feb. 13, 1946; s. Harold Joseph and Lois Lucille (Mellin) T.; 1 child, Harold Joseph IV; m. Anna V. Billante, Oct. 1, 1983; 1 child, James S. Carstensen. BA, U. San Francisco, 1968, JD, 1975. Bar: Calif. 1975, Hawaii 1987, U.S. Dist. Ct. (ea., so., no., and cen. dists.) Calif. 1976, Hawaii 1987, U.S. Ct. Appeals (9th cir.) 1980, U.S. Supreme Ct. 1988. Assoc. Hoberg, Finger et al, San Francisco, 1975-78, Bledsoe, Smith et al, San Francisco, 1979-80, Abramson & Bianco, San Francisco, 1980-83; mem. Ingram & Truett, San Rafael, 1983-90; prin. Law Office of H.J. Tim Truett, San Francisco, 1991—; lectr. trial practice Am. Coll. Legal Medicine, 1989, 90, Calif. Continuing Edn. of the Bar. Bd. dirs. Shining Star Found. 1991—, Marin County, Calif.; mem. Marin Dem. Coun., San Rafael, 1983-90. Lt., aviator USN, 1967-74. Mem. ABA, Hawaii Bar Assn., Assn. Trial Lawyers Am., Calif. Bar Assn. (com. for adminstrn. of justice, conf. of dels.), San Francisco Bar Assn., Calif. Trial Lawyers Assn., Lawyers Pilots Assn. Roman Catholic. Home: 1347 Vallejo St San Francisco CA 94109-2601

TRUFFAUT, MICHELLE, film director; b. San Francisco, Nov. 17, 1942; d. Louis and Eve (Schefski) Mardecich. Student, U. Calif., Berkeley, 1964-65; MFA, Am. Film Inst., 1990. Freelance performer U.S., Eng. and France, 1965-72; pub. rels. asst. Am. Conservatory Theatre, San Francisco, 1972-74; producing and artistic dir. San Francisco Repertory Theatre, San Francisco, 1974-87; artistic dir. San Francisco Shakespeare Festival, 1986-87; freelance filmmaker, dir. L.A., 1987—; mem. adv. bd. Theatre Communications Bay Area, San Francisco, 1983-86. Dir. in field; dir., adapter play Animal Farm Orwell, 1984, Lulu-Wiedkino 1985; writer, dir. screenplay Ralph's Arm, 1988, Willie Won't Dance, 1992. Recipient Best Directing and Best Prodn. Achievement award Bay Area Critics Circle, 1984, 86, Outstanding Best Directing and Best Prodn. Achievement award Bay Area Critics, 1986, Best Directing award Dramalogue, 1984. Democrat. Jewish.

TRUITT, WESLEY BYRON, marketing professional; b. Washington, July 27, 1939; s. Joseph and Esther Truitt; m. Marianne Minarovic, June 22, 1968. BA, U. Pa., 1961; MA, Columbia U., 1963, PhD, 1968; diploma, U. Florence, 1965. Mgr. bus. devel. aircraft div. Northrop Corp., Hawthorne, Calif., 1989—, mgr. advanced planning aircraft div., 1988-89; corp. dir. policy analyst Northrop Corp., L.A., 1983-88, exec. asst. to chief exec. officer, 1980-83; with UCLA Grad. Sch. Mgmt., L.A., 1972-88; adj. prof. Claremont (Calif.) Grad. Sch. Bus., 1976—. Internat. fellow Columbia U., 1962-63, Pres. fellow, 1963, NASA fellow 1964; NSF fellow, 1967. Mem. Calif. Aerospace Alliance (chmn. 1982). Presbyterian.

TRUJILLO, JOSEPH BEN, insurance company executive; b. Santa Fe, Sept. 26, 1947; s. Jose Benito and Annette (Jaramillo) T.; m. Marcelle K. Johnson, Dec. 11, 1976. BA, Wichita State U., 1969; MA, N.Mex. Highlands U., 1972; MBA, U. Phoenix, Denver, 1986. Sales mgmt. trainee Conn. Gen. Co., Bloomfield, 1973-76; sales agt. Conn. Mut. Ins. Co., Hartford, 1976-78; owner, mgr. Larimer Ins. Group, Denver, 1978-84, JBT Fin. Group, Denver, 1984-91; pres. Ins. Resources Inc., Englewood, Colo., 1991—; CLU, ChFC; fin. cons.; dir. Colo. State Bank Bd., 1989. Pres. Rep. Nat. Hispanic Assembly Colo., 1992—, Heritage Village Homeowners Assn., Littleton, Colo., 1984-85; co-chmn. Colo. Gov.'s Latin Am. Task Force, 1988-90, Econ. Devel. com., Hispanic Agenda, 1989—; mem. Colo. Airport Task Force, 1988-90, Colo. Econ. Devel. Task Force, Denver, 1988-90. Mem. Nat. Assn. Life Underwriters, Denver Assn. Life Underwriters, Am. Soc. CLU's, Million Dollar Round Table (life), Colo. Hispanic C. of C. (pres. 1985-87, chmn. U. Phoenix scholar com., Man of Yr. award 1987). Roman Catholic. Office: Ins Resources Inc 12835 E Arapahoe Rd Tower 2 Ste 110 Englewood CO 80112

TRUJILLO, LORENZO A., education consultant; b. Denver, Aug. 10, 1951; s. Filbert G. and Marie O. (Duran) T.; children: Javier Antonio, Lorenzo Feliciano. BA, U. Colo., 1972, MA, 1974, postgrad.; EdD, U. San Francisco, 1979; JD, U. Colo., 1993. Cert. edn. tchr., prin., supt., Colo., Calif. Exec. assoc. Inter-Am. Rsch. Assocs., Rosslyn, Va., 1980-82; exec. dir. humanities Jefferson County Pub. Schs., Golden, Colo., 1982-90; pvt. practice edn. cons. Lakewood, Colo., 1990—; co-chair Mellon fellowships The Coll. Bd., N.Y.C., 1987-93; cons. U.S.I.A. Fulbright Tchr. Exch. Program, Washington, 1987-93; editorial advisor Harcourt, Brace, Jovanovich Pub., Orlando, Fla., 1988-93. Contbr. numerous articles to profl. jours. Pres. bd. Rocky Mountain Symphony, Lakewood, 1987-90; v.p. bd. Festival Summer Symphony, Denver, 1989-90; bd. dirs. S.W. Conf. on Lang. Teaching, 1988-90. Mem. Colo. chpt. Am. Assn. Tchrs. of Spanish and Portuguese (pres. 1985-88), U. San Francisco Alumni Assn. (founder, pres. 1987-90), Phi Delta Kappa (chair internat. edn. com. 1988-89), Phi Alpha Delta. Home: 1556 S Van Dyke Way Lakewood CO 80228-3917

TRUJILLO, LORI SUE, fashion designer; b. Albuquerque, Oct. 3, 1958; d. Donald Daniel and Carol Louise (Anderson) T.; m. Walter Roy Mophett, Aug. 22, 1987. AA, Fashion Inst., Los Angeles, 1980; BA in Art, Calif. State U., Long Beach, 1988. Designer So. Calif. Pleating Co., Los Angeles, 1981-83; owner, designer Fashion by Design, Rancho Palos Verdes, Calif., 1983—, Gentleman's Choice, San Pedro, Calif., 1985—; designer Anvil Cases, Rosemead, Calif., 1989-91, Trujillo Couture, San Pedro, Calif., 1989—; judge sr. fashion show Los Angeles Trade Tech. Sch., 1982; artist. Mem. Mus. Contemporary Art. Recipient 2d place award Nat. Home Sewing contest, 1984, 2d place painting award Harbor Art Show, Los Angeles Harbor Coll., 1984. Mem. Fashion Inst. Alumni Assn.

TRUJILLO, STEPHEN MICHAEL, physicist; b. Culver City, Calif., Mar. 5, 1932; s. Richard Martin and Lena Rue (Kirby) T.; m. Josefina Caravaca, Aug. 22, 1959. BSEE, U. Kans., 1958; PhD in Physics, U. London, 1975. Staff scientist Convair div. Gen. Dynamics, San Diego, 1958-69, Gulf Gen. Atomic Corp., San Diego, 1969-70; vis. rsch. fellow U. London, 1970-75; prin. physicist IRT Corp., San Diego, 1975-80; cons., tech. advisor Gen. Atomic Co., San Diego, 1980; sr. physicist Internat. Nuclear Energy Co., San Diego, 1981-83; staff scientist S-cubed div. Maxwell Labs. Inc., San Diego, 1983-88, sr. staff scientist, 1988-89; prin. physicist IRT Corp., San Diego, 1989-91; sr. scientist ISM Techs., Inc., 1991—; cons., tech. advisor various clients, San Diego, 1984—. Mem. IEEE, Am. Phys. Soc., Inst. Physics (Eng.), N.Y. Acad. Scis., Old Crows Club. Republican. Home: 5931 Bellevue Ave La Jolla CA 92037-7315

TRUMBLE, ROBERT JASPER, fishery biologist; b. Whitmire, S.C., Apr. 21, 1943; s. Robert E. and Jessie (Abrams) T.; m. Cynthia Wright, Sept. 6, 1969. BS, U. Wash., 1965, MS, 1973, PhD, 1979. Oceanographer Naval Oceanographic Office, Washington, 1966-71; fishery biologist Wash. Dept. Fisheries, Seattle, 1975-86, Internat. Pacific Halibut Commn., Seattle, 1986—; mem. Herring plan team Pacific Fishery Mgmt. Coun., Portland, Oreg., 1980-82, Sci. and stats. commn., 1984-86; mem. groundfish plan team North Pacific Fishery Mgmt. Coun., Anchorage, 1986-90. Contbr. 9 articles to profl. jours. Mem. Am. Fisheries Soc., Sigma Xi. Office: Internat Pacific Halibut Commn PO Box 95009 Seattle WA 98145

TRUMBULL, WALTER HENRY, JR., marketing specialist; b. Santa Monica, Calif., Mar. 24, 1959; s. Walter Henry and Elizabeth Lea (Stone) T.; m. Valerie Morgan, July 9, 1988; 1 child, Virginia Armistead. BA, Harvard Coll., 1981; MBA, UCLA, 1984. Fin. analyst Advanced Micro Devices, Sunnyvale, Calif., 1984-85; sales mgr. Electro-Mech Components, Inc., South El Monte, Calif., 1985-89; v.p. mktg. Electro-Mech Components, Inc., South El Monte, 1989—. Republican. Episcopalian. Home: 1401 Pine Ave Manhattan Beach CA 90266-5041 Office: Electro Mech Components Inc 1826 N Floradale Ave South El Monte CA 91733-3689

TRUNK, GARY, physician, consultant; b. Detroit, July 12, 1941. BA, UCLA, 1963; MD, U. Calif., Irvine, 1967; MBA, Century U., 1991. Diplomate Am. Bd. Quality Assurance and Utilization Review Physicians. Intern St. Joseph's Hosp., Phoenix, 1967-68; resident USAF Med. Ctr., Keesler AFB, Miss., 1968-70; fellow USAF Med. Ctr., Scott AFB, Ill., 1970-72; commd. 2d lt. USAF, 1967, advance through grades to Maj., 1970, resigned, 1974; with Dept. Social Svcs. Disability Evaluation, San Diego, 1974—. Am. Coll. Med. Quality fellow, 1987. Fellow Am. Coll. Chest Physicians; mem. Am. Coll. Physicians. Home: 7533 Clear Sky Rd San Diego CA 92120

TRUSSELL, R(OBERT) RHODES, environmental engineer; b. National City, Calif; s. Robert L. and Margaret (Kessing) T.; m. Elizabeth Shane, Nov. 26, 1969; children: Robert Shane, Charles Bryan. BSCE, U. Calif.-Berkeley, 1966, MS, 1967, PhD, 1972. With Montgomery Watson, Inc. (formerly J.M. Montgomery Cons. Engrs.), Pasadena, Calif., 1972—, v.p., 1977, sr. v.p., 1986, dir. applied tech., 1988-92, sr. v.p., dir. of corp. devel., 1992— Mem. com. on water treatment chems. Nat. Acad. Sci., 1980-82, mem. com. 3d part cert., 1982-83, com. on irrigation-induced water quality problems, 1985-88, Am. Water Work Commn. on mixing of water treatment chems., 1988-90; mem. U.S./German research com. on corrosion of water systems, 1984-85; mem. U.S./Dutch research com. on organics in water, 1982-83; mem. U.S./USSR rsch. com. on water treatment, 1985-88, U.S./E.C. Com. Corrosion in Water, 1992—. Mem. joint editorial bd. Standards Methods for Examination of Water and Wastewater, 1980-89; mem. editorial adv. bd. Environ. and Sci. and Tech., 1977-83; contbr. articles to profl. publs. Mem. Am. Water Works Assn. (mem. editorial adv. bd. jour. 1987—, EPA sci. adv. bd. com. on drinking water 1988-91, 93—), Water Pollution Control Fedn., Internat. Water Pollution Rsch. Assn., Am. Chem. Soc., Am. Inst. Chem. Engrs., Nat. Assn. Corrosion Engrs., Sigma Xi. Office: 300 North Lake Ave Ste 1200 Pasadena CA 91101

TRUTA, MARIANNE PATRICIA, oral and maxillofacial surgeon, educator, author; b. N.Y.C., Apr. 28, 1951; d. John J. and Helen Patricia (Donnelly) T.; m. William Christopher Donlon, May 28, 1983; 1 child Sean Liam Riobard Donnelly. BS, St. John's U., 1974; DMD, SUNY, Stonybrook, 1977. Intern The Mt. Sinai Med. Ctr., N.Y.C., 1977-78, resident, 1978-80, chief resident, 1980-81; asst. prof. U. of the Pacific, San Francisco, 1983-85, clin. asst. prof., 1985—; asst. dir. Facial Pain Rsch. Ctr., San Francisco, 1986-92; pvt. practice oral and maxillofacial surgery Peninsula Maxillofacial Surgery, South San Francisco, Calif., 1985—, Burlingame, Calif., 1988—, Menlo Park & Redwood City, Calif., 1990—. Contbr. articles to profl. jours., chpts. to textbooks. Mem. Am. Assn. Oral Maxillofacial Surgeons, Am. Dental Soc. Anesthesiology, Am. Soc. Cosmetic Surgery, Am. Assn. Women Dentists, Western Soc. Oral Maxillofacial Surgeons. No. Calif. Soc. Oral Maxillofacial Surgeons. Office: Peninsula Maxillofacial Surgery 1860 El Camino Real Ste 300 Burlingame CA 94010-3114

TRYBUS, RAYMOND J., academic administrator, psychologist; b. Chgo., Jan. 9, 1944; s. Fred and Cecilia (Liszka) T.; m. Sandra A. Noone, Aug. 19, 1967; children: David, Nicole. BS, St. Louis U., 1965, MS, 1970, PhD, 1971. Lic. psychologist, Md., D.C., Calif. Clin. psychologist Jewish Vocat. Svc., St. Louis, 1968-71; clin. psychologist Gallaudet U., Washington, 1971-72, rsch. psychologist, 1972-74, dir. demographic studies, 1974-78, dean grad. studies and rsch., 1978-88; provost, prof. psychology Calif. Sch. of Profl. Psychology, 1988—, chancellor, 1992—; mem. Sci. Review Bd. Dept. Vets. Affairs Rehab. Rsch. and Devel. Program, 1991—; cons. Mental Health Ctr. for Deaf, Lanham, Md., 1982-88, Congl. Rsch. Svc., 1982-84 , McGill U. Nat. Study Hearing Impairment in Can., 1984-88. Contbg. author: The Future of Mental Health Services for the Deaf, 1978, Hearing-impaired Children and Youth with Devel. Disabilities, 1985; editor Jour. Am. Deafness and Rehab. Assn., 1988-91. Grantee NIMH, Spencer Found., Tex. Edn. Agy., W.K. Kellogg Found. Mem. Am. Assn. Univ. Adminstrs., Am. Psychol. Assn., Calif. Psychol. Assn. (pres. div. edn. and tng. 1990-92), San Diego Psychol. Assn., Am. Coun. Edn., Am. Deafness and Rehab. Assn., Am. Assn. Higher Edn., Am. Psychol. Soc. Roman Catholic. Home: 6342

Cibola Rd San Diego CA 92120-2124 Office: 6212 Ferris Sq San Diego CA 92121-3250

TRZYNA, THOMAS NICHOLAS, college dean; b. Evanston, Ill., Nov. 30, 1946; s. Thaddeus and Irene (Giese) T.; m. Martha Hannah Deutsch, Sept. 13, 1969; children: Alexander, Margaret. BA, U. Calif., Berkeley, 1968; PhD, U. Wash., 1977. Asst. prof. Ohio State U., Columbus, 1978-80; from asst. prof. to prof. Seattle Pacific U., 1980—, dean Sch. Humanities, 1987—; editor Aquaseed Press, Seattle, 1989—, Calif. Inst. Pub. Affairs, Claremont, 1979. Author: (Writing for Technical Professionals, 1987, also poems and textbooks in field; contbr. articles to profl. publs. Episcopalian. Office: Seattle Pacific U 3307 3rd Ave W Seattle WA 98119-1997

TSAI, MICHAEL MING-PING, psychiatrist; b. Chiayi, Taiwan, Mar. 28, 1939; came to U.S., 1966; s. Yang-Ming and Hsien (Wang) T.; m. Pi-Zu Tsai, Apr. 27, 1968; 1 child, Patricia. MD, Kaohsiung Med. Coll., Taiwan, 1965. Diplomate Am. Bd. Psychiatry and Neurology. Intern Meth. Hosp., Bklyn., 1966-67; resident in psychiatry Phila. State Hosp., Phila., 1968-69, VA Hosp., N.Y.C., 1969-71; fellow in child & adolescent psychiatry Hillside Hosp., Glen Oaks, N.Y., 1971-72; clin. psychiatrist N.J. Neuro-psychiatric Inst., Princeton, 1972-75; staff psychiatrist Met. State Hosp., Norwalk, Calif., 1978—. Home and Office: 1878 Calle La Paz Rowland Hills CA 91748

TSAI, WILMAN, chemical engineer; b. Hong Kong, Nov. 2, 1960; came to U.S., 1978; s. John and Cathy (Kwei) T.; m. Wen Lee Wen-Hsing, July 1984; children: Jonathan, Betsy. BSc in Chem. Engring., Environ. Engring., Syracuse U., 1982; MS in Chem. Engring., Calif. Tech. Inst., 1984, PhD in Chem. Engring., 1987. Registered profl. engr., Calif. Sr. chem. engr. Air Products and Chems., Allentown, Pa., 1987-89; sr. engr., rsch. scientist Varian Assocs., Palo Alto, Calif., 1989—. Contbr. numerous articles to tech. publs. Mem. Am. Chemistry Soc., Am. Inst. Chem. Engrs., Tau Beta Pi. Office: Varian Assocs K 224 611 Hansen Way Palo Alto CA 94303

TSALAKY, TERESA, writer; b. Spokane, Wash., July 17, 1959; d. Theophilus John and Magdaline (Barbas) T. BA in Journalism, We. Wash. U., Bellingham, 1981. Reporter Spokane Chronicle, 1982-83; pres. EmployEase, Inc., 1983-86; pub. Whidbey Press, Inc., Whidbey Island, Wash., 1988-91; freelance writer Estes Park, Colo., 1991—. Contbr. articles to Omni mag., Dental Econs. mag.; contbr. poetry to poetry anthology Soundings, 1983. Recipient Best Nonfiction Article award Soc. Profl. Journalists, 1982, 1st place for Page Design, 1988; Spl. citation Edn. Writers Assn., 1983, Gen. Excellence award Wash. Newspaper Pubs. Assn., 1990. Greek Orthodox. Home and Office: 270 Bighorn Dr Estes Park CO 80517

TSANG, CHIT-SANG, engineering educator; b. Hong Kong, Mar. 24, 1952; came to U.S., 1971; s. Chu-Peng and Siu-Han (Ho) T.; m. Jiuan-Min Chang, June 16, 1979; children: Anita Huey-En, Serena Huey-Ning. BS, La. State U., 1974; MS, Ohio State U., 1976; PhD, U. So. Calif., 1982. Network control engr. RCA Am. Communications Corp., Piscataway, N.J., 1976-77; software engr. Digital Equipment Corp., Maynard, Mass., 1977-79; sr. system engr. Lincom Corp., L.A., 1980-88; assoc. prof. Calif. State U., Long Beach, 1988—; cons. Aerospace Corp., El Segundo, Calif., 1991—. Deacon 1st Evang. Ch., Glendale, Calif., 1984-88, steward, 1989—. Mem. IEEE (sr.), Armed Forces Communications and Electronics Assn., Internat. Neural Networks Soc., Chinese Christians for Justice (chmn. bd. dirs. 1990—), Tau Beta Pi, Eta Kappa Nu. Home: 6413 N Lemon Ave San Gabriel CA 91775-1806 Office: Calif State U Dept Elec Engring Long Beach CA 90840

TSANG, SAI KI, aerospace engineer; b. Hong Kong; came to U.S., 1985; s. Chun Wah and Shui Ngor (Chan) T.; m. Ying Hing Li, Aug. 26, 1988; 1 child, Ke Zeng. BS with honors, Queens U., Northern Ireland, 1980; MS, London U., 1981, PhD, 1985. Registered profl. engr., Eng. Rsch. asst. London U., 1981-85; prin. engr. Impell Corp., Walnut Creek, Calif., 1985-87; sr. structural engr. HR Textron, Valencia, Calif., 1987-90; sr. stress engr. Dowty Aerospace L.A., Duarte, Calif., 1990—. Author 14 tech. papers on shell buckling, plasticity, finite element analysis, structural reliability and random vibration.

TSAO, CHICH-HSING ALEX, electrical engineer; b. Taipei, Taiwan, Republic of China, Feb. 8, 1953; arrived in U.S., 1976; m. Hsiao-Jen Ni, May 20, 1978: children: Bohr-Young, Bihn-Young, Ray-Young. BEE, Nat. Taiwan U., 1974; MEE, Duke U., 1978; PhD, U. Ill., 1981. Prin. engr. Space Systems/Loral, Palo Alto, Calif., 1981—. Contbr. articles to profl. jours.; inventor microstrip antennas, 1987. Mem. IEEE. Home: 20567 Brookwood Ln Saratoga CA 95070-5831 Office: Space Systems/Loral 3825 Fabian Way Palo Alto CA 94303-4604

TSIROS, JOHN ANDREAS, accountant; b. Boston, Oct. 2, 1963; s. Constantine Louis and Martha Sophia (Pappas) T. BA, Boston U., 1985; MBA, U. So. Calif., 1990. Acct. Golden/Goldberg Acctg. Corp., L.A., 1990—. Greek Orthodox. Office: Golden/Goldberg Acctg 5757 Wilshire Blvd #240 Los Angeles CA 90036

TSOSIE, WILLIAM BEN-BEGAY, JR., computer services director; b. Tsaile, Ariz., Oct. 12, 1961; s. William B. Sr. and Della Mae (Ben) T. BS in Computer Sci., U. N.Mex., 1983. Adminstrv. asst. Ctrl. Consol. Schs., Shiprock, N.Mex., 1982-84; dir. computer svcs. and communications Chinle (Ariz.) Unified Schs., 1984—; owner Coyote-Pass Hospitality; Navajo nation tourism counsel del., Window Rock, Ariz., 1991-92; speaker in field. Bd. dirs. Native Am. Youth Leadership Coun. Navajo Tribal Pub. Sch. System. Mem. Lions Internat. Home: Lukachukai NHA #40 Tsaile AZ 86503 Office: Chinle Unified Schs Box 587 Chinle AZ 86503

TSUKIJI, RICHARD ISAO, international marketing and financial services consultant; b. Salt Lake City, Jan. 31, 1946; s. Isamu and Mitsuie (Hayashi) T.; children: Angela Jo, Richard Michael. Grad. Sacramento City Coll., 1966; AA, U. Pacific, McGeorge Sch. Law, 1970-72. Grocery mgr. Food Mart, Inc., Sacramento, 1963-65; agy. supr. Takehara Ins. Agy., Sacramento, 1965-68; sales rep. Kraft Foods Co., Sacramento, 1969-71; sales mgr. Olivetti Corp., Sacramento, 1972-73; co-founder Mktg. Devel. and Mgmt. Coll., Sacramento, 1973, pres., 1973-74; pres. Richard Tsukiji Corp., Sacramento, 1974-77; chief exec. officer, chmn. bd. Assocs. Investment Group, Sacramento, 1978-82 ; chmn. bd. RichColor Corp. Sacramento, 1978-83, E.J. Sub Factories, Inc., Elk Grove, Calif., 1978-81; gen. agt. Comml. Bankers Life Ins. Co., 1974-82; chmn. bd. Phoenix Industries, Inc., Carson City, Nev., 1981-84, Databank, Inc., Roseburg, Oreg., 1982-83; pres. Computers, Etc. Corp., Carson City, 1982-84; regional v.p. U.S. BankCard Group, Salem, Oreg., 1993; pres. Richard Tsukiji Cellular Systems, Sacramento, 1993; bd. dirs. Michton, Inc., Pontiac, Mich., Hunt & Johnson, Inc., Phoenix Group, Melbourne, Entertainment Plus, Roseburg, Oreg., A.N.D. Corp., New Orleans, ET World Travel, Salt Lake City, Utah, Bonaventure Group, Inc., Wilmington, Del., Royal Am. Bank, Cayman Islands; exec. v.p. Edco Corp., Glide, Oreg., 1982—; chmn. bd. Computer Edn. Resource Ctr., 1983—, Bonaventure, Inc., Roseburg, 1984—; editor ST World, Melrose, Oreg., 1985-88, publisher, 1988—; editor ST World Reseller, 1988—. Mem. Yolo County Oral Rev. Bd., 1975-76; bd. dirs. Valley Area Constrn. Opportunity Program, 1972-76, chmn., 1976-77; bd. dirs. Douglas County Citizens Community Involvement, 1980-82; bd. dirs. Computer Edn. Found., Sacramento, 1983—, Access Sacramento Cable Television, 1993, Heart to Heart Found., 1993; democratic precinct committeeman, Melrose, Oreg., 1982-86. Served with U.S. Army, 1962-63. Recipient Commendation, Calif. Senate, 1978. Mem. Internat. Assn. Fin. Planners, Associated Gen. Contractors, VIC-20 Users Group (pres. Roseburg 1983-84), Atari Computer Enthusiasts (pres. Sacramento 1983-85), U.S. Commodore Council (pres. Natl. 1984-85), Sacramento Jaycees (dir. 1977-78), Asian Alliance, Japanese Am. Citizens League, Sacramento Urban League. Democrat. Roman Catholic. Office: 9 Heathfield Rd Unit #1, Coolum Beach 4573, Queensland Australia also: 9112 Falcon Creek Circle Elk Grove CA 95624-2757

TSUTAKAWA, EDWARD MASAO, management consultant; b. Seattle, May 15, 1921; s. Jin and Michiko (Oka) T.; student U. Wash., 1941, Wash. State U., 1949; m. Hide Kunugi, Aug. 11, 1949; children: Nancy Joyce Tsutakawa Seigel, Margaret Ann Langston, Mark Edward. Free-lance comml. artist, Spokane, 1943-47; artist Maag & Porter Comml. Printers, Spokane, 1947-54; organizer Litho Art Printers, Inc., Spokane, 1954—, gen. mgr., pres., 1965-80; charter organizer, dir. Am. Comml. Bank, 1965-80; prin. E. M. Tsutakawa Co., bus. cons. and dir., 1980—; v.p., operation officer, dir. Mukogawa Ft. Wright Inst. Pres. emeritus Spokane-Nishinomiya Sister City Soc.; pres. emeritus Sister Cities Assn. of Spokane; mem Eastern Wash. State Hist. Soc.; bd. dirs. Fairmount Cemetery. Recipient Disting. Svc. medal Boy Scouts of Japan, 1967, Cultural medal in Edn., Japan, 1985, Disting. Svc. award City of Nishinomiya, 1971, Disting. Svc. to Expo '74 State of Wash., 1974, Book of Golden Deeds award Exchange Club, 1978, Disting. Community Scv. award UN Assn., 1979, Whitworth Coll., 1987, Svc. to Youth award Spokane YMCA, 1988; decorated Order of Sacred Treasure medal Govt. of Japan, 1984. Mem. Japanese Am. Citizens League. Methodist. Clubs: Kiwanis (Spokane). Home: 4116 S Madelia St Spokane WA 99203-4229

TSUTAKAWA, MAYUMI, writer, editor; b. Seattle, Dec. 13, 1949; d. George and Ayame (Iwasa) T.; children: Kenzan, Yayoi. Student, Scripps Coll., 1968-70; BA, U. Wash., 1972, M Communications, 1977. Program planner Seattle Dept. Human Resources, 1972-74; asst. dir. Asian Multi-Media Ctr., Seattle, 1974; reporter, editor Seattle Times, 1976-82; instr. Seattle Cen. C.C., 1983-84; community arts coord. King County Arts Commn., Seattle, 1984-86, asst. dir., 1986-90; mgr. King County Cultural Resources Div., Seattle, 1990-93; freelance writer, editor, Seattle, 1992—; juror Seattle Arts Commn., 1985, Nat. Endowment for Arts, Washington, 1988, 91, 92, Oreg. State Arts Commn., Salem, 1989, Coun. of Lit. Mags. and Presses, N.Y.C., 1991. Editor anthologies: Turning Shadows into Light, 1982, Gathering Ground, 1984, The Forbidden Stitch, 1988. Charter mem. Wash. state Commn. on Asian Am. Affairs, Olympia, 1972-74; bd. dirs. pub. radio sta. KRAB-FM, Seattle, 1979-81; pres. bd. dirs. Internat. Examiner, Seattle, 1983-90.

TUBBESING, DEBBIE BRLETIC, radio announcer; b. Cleve., Dec. 15, 1954; d. Richard and Ruth (Vuks) Brletic. Student, U. Nev., Las Vegas. With KMJJ/KLUC Radio, 1984-86; copywriter, prodn. asst. KUTP-Channel 45, 1986-87; announcer KCLS Radio, Flagstaff, 1987-88, KMZQ Radio, Las Vegas, 1989-91; studio engr. KVEG Sports Talk Radio, Las Vegas, 1991-92; announcer KEYV Radio, 1992—. Contbr. articles to jours., mags. and newspapers. Active Las Vegas Rescue Mission, Sunshine Rescue Mission, St. Vincent's Ctr., Ctr. Against Domestic Violence, Multiple Sclerosis Soc., Am. Cancer Soc., Easter Seals, Muscular Dystrophy Telethon, Hands Across Am., Marion Residence, others. Named to Outstanding Young Women of Am.; recipient cert. of appreciation Toys for Tots, Aid for AIDS of Nev. Mem. Women in Communications, Toastmasters Internat. (adminstrv. v.p.). Mem. Unity Ch. Home: 787 E Harmon # 27 Las Vegas NV 89119 Office: KEYV Radio 101 Convention Center Dr Las Vegas NV 89109

TUBBS, WILLIAM REID, JR., public service administrator; b. Johnson Air Base, Japan, June 1, 1950; s. William Reid and Roberta Daisy (Krenkel) T.; m. Ellen Lee Duccini, May 19, 1984; 1 child, Catlin Alyse. BA, Calif. State U., Sacramento, 1973, MPA, 1981. Assoc. analyst adminstrn. and fin. agy. County of Sacramento, 1975-84, program coordinator emergency ops., 1984-85; adminstrv. dir. Sacramento County Mental Health Treatment Ctr., 1985—. Chmn. Cable TV Adv. Commn., West Sacramento, Calif., 1987-90. Lt. USCGR. Mem. Am. Soc. Pub. Adminstrn., Res. Officers Assn., U.S. Naval Inst., Am. Radio Relay League. Republican. Home: 1012 Rogers St Broderick CA 95605-2002 Office: Sacramento Co Mental Health 2150 Stockton Blvd Sacramento CA 95817-1337

TUBMAN, WILLIAM CHARLES, lawyer; b. N.Y.C., Mar. 16, 1932; s. William Thomas and Ellen Veronica (Griffin) T.; m. Dorothy Rita Krug, Aug. 15, 1964; children: William Charles Jr., Thomas Davison, Matthew Griffin. BS, Fordham U., 1953, JD, 1960; postdoctoral, NYU Sch. Law, 1960-61. Bar: N.Y. 1960, U.S. Ct. Appeals (2d cir.) 1966, U.S. Supreme Ct. 1967, U.S. Ct. Customs and Patent Appeals 1971. Auditor Peat, Marwick Mitchell & Co., N.Y.C., 1956-60; sr. counsel Kennecott Corp., N.Y.C., 1960-82; sr. counsel Phelps Dodge Corp., N.Y.C., 1982-85, sec., 1985-87, v.p., 1987—; pres. Phelps Dodge Found., Phoenix, 1988—. Author: Legal Status of Minerals Beyond the Continental Shelf, 1966. Mem. scholarship adv. coun. U. Ariz.; active Big Bros. Inc., N.Y.C., 1963-73; trustee Phoenix Art Mus.; bd. dirs. St. Joseph Hosp. Found. Recipient Cert. Disting. Service, Big Brothers Inc., 1968. Mem. ABA, N.Y. State Bar Assn., Maricopa County Bar Assn. Democrat. Roman Catholic. Home: 8008 N 66th St Paradise Valley AZ 85253-2612 Office: Phelps Dodge Corp 2600 N Central Ave Phoenix AZ 85004-3050

TUCCIO, SAM ANTHONY, aerospace executive, physicist; b. Rochester, N.Y., Jan. 15, 1939; s. Manuel Joseph and Phillis (Cannizzo) T.; m. Jenney Laprell Elvington, May 1, 1982; children: David Samuel, Karen Ann, Rebecca Jean, Ashley Lauren. BS, U. Rochester, 1965. Research physicist Eastman Kodak Co., Rochester, 1965-72; program mgr. Lawrence Livermore (Calif.) Labs., 1972-75; sr. physicist Allied Corp., Morristown, N.J., 1975-81; gen. mgr. Allied Laser Products Div., Westlake Village, Calif., 1981-84; sr. bus. mgr. Northrop Corp., Hawthorne, Calif., 1984-89; dir. space bus. Loral Corp., Pasadena, Calif., 1989-92; dir. bus. devel. ThermoTrex Corp., San Diego, 1992—. Patentee in field; contbr. numerous articles to profl. jours. Recipient IR 100 award Indsl. Rsch. Assn., 1971. Republican. Methodist. Home: 18035 Polvera Way San Diego CA 92128-1123 Office: ThermoTrex Corp 9550 Distribution Ave San Diego CA 92121-2306

TUCK, MICHAEL RAY, technical services executive; b. Pocatello, Idaho, Aug. 9, 1941; s. Amos R. and Phyllis (Day) T.; m. Heather K. Fowler, Oct. 22, 1962; children: Lisa M., Jennifer A., M. Mark. BS in Math., Idaho State U., 1964; MS in Math., U. Idaho, 1971. Programmer analyst Argonne Nat. Labs., Idaho Falls, Idaho, 1964-69; computer scientist Argonne Nat. Labs., Idaho Falls, 1969-76; engr., mgr. computer div. Montana Energy Inst., Butte, Mont., 1976-81; v.p. MultiTech Inc. div. MSE Inc., Butte, 1981-82, pres., 1982-83, v.p., CEO, 1983—, also bd. dirs.; cons. TMA Assocs., Butte, 1982-83. Bd. dirs. Jr. Achievement, Mont. Internat. Trade & Devel. Ctr., Tax Increment Fin. Dist. Mem. Am. Soc. Data Processing Profls., Butte C. of C. (bd. dirs.), Mont. Data Processing Soc., Exch. Club, Continental Club. Methodist. Office: MSE Inc PO Box 4078 Butte MT 59702-4078

TUCK, RUSSELL R., JR., college president; b. June 9, 1934; m. Marjorie Gay Tuck; children: Russell R. III, Catherine Elizabeth. BS in Chemistry, Union U., 1956; MS in Biology, Vanderbilt U., 1957, PhD in Curriculum and Instrn., 1971; study, Wash. U., 1960-61. Instr. biology, asst. coordinator Korean Tchr. Edn. Program George Peabody Coll. Vanderbilt U., Nashville, 1957-59; tchr. biology, chmn. sci. dept. University City (Mo.) Sr. High Sch., 1960-63, from asst. prin. to prin., 1963-70; prin. Parkway North Sr. High Sch., St. Louis County, Mo., 1971-78; asst. supt. Parkway Sch. Dist., St. Louis County, 1979-81, assoc. supt., 1981-84; pres. Calif. Bapt. Coll., Riverside, 1984—. Contbr. articles to profl. jours. Bd. dirs. Opera Assn.; pres. Riverside County chpt. ARC, 1989-90; active Bapt. Ch., local hosp. assn. bd., local edn. com.; World Affairs Coun. Mem. Calif. Bapt. Hist. Soc. (bd. dirs.), Calif. Bapt. Devel. Found. (bd. dirs.), Am. Assn. Sch. Adminstrs., Inland Empire Higher Edn. Coun. (pres. 1987-88), Kappa Delta Pi, Phi Delta Kappa. Lodge: Rotary. Office: Calif Bapt Coll 8432 Magnolia Ave Riverside CA 92504-3297

TUCKER, BIL, state official, consultant; b. Wichita, Kans., Mar. 23, 1943; s. Richard Lee and Phoebe Cleo (Grigsby) T.; children: Bill, Shawn. BA, Wichita State U., 1967, MS, 1969; PhD, U. Wyo., 1973. Quality ctrl. and process contr. Boeing Aircraft Co., Wichita, 1961-68; rsch. assoc. Coll. Agr., U. Wyo., Laramie, 1973-75, sr. rsch. assoc. Coll. Engring., 1977-79; process contr., chief chemist Resource Refining, Inc., Laramie, 1975-77; chief chemist, prodn. mgr. Monolith Portland Cement, Laramie, 1979-82; tech. adminstr. EG&G, Laramie, 1983-87; regulatory com. Wyo. Pub. Svc. Commn., Cheyenne, 1987—, chmn., 1991—; instr. Ea. Wyo. Coll., Torrington, 1976; pres. Tucker & Assocs., Laramie, 1978-83; presenter in field; chmn. Com. on Regional Electric Power Cooperation, Denver, 1990—. Contbr. articles to profl. jours. Trustee Albany County Sch. Dist., Laramie, 1975-78; chmn. Albany County Dem. Com., 1985-86; sec. Wyo. Dem. Com., Casper, 1985-87; treas. Safe House/Sexual Assault Svcs., Cheyenne, 1989-93; bd. dirs. Wyo. Territorial Park, Laramie, 1990—. Mem. Nat. Assn. Regulatory Utility Commrs. (chmn. com. on fin. and tech. 1991—, exec. com., internat. relations com.), Western Conf. Pub. Svc. Commrs., Masons. Home: PO Box 3183 Laramie WY 82071 Office: Wyo Pub Svc Commn 700 W 21st St Cheyenne WY 82002

TUCKER, CHARLES CYRIL, information systems consultant; b. N.Y.C., Mar. 7, 1942; s. Bernard Anthony and Charlotte Yvonne (Carron) T.; m. Sue Ann Rasmuson, Apr. 11, 1970; children: Michele, Christine. BS in Mech. Engring., U. Santa Clara, 1964, MBA, 1968. Mktg. rep. IBM, L.A., 1968-72; sr. assoc. McKinsey & Co., L.A., 1972-76; v.p. planning and info. services 20th Century-Fox, L.A., 1977-81; v.p. planning and corp. devel. MSI Data Corp., Costa Mesa, Calif., 1981-83; sr. v.p. planning and control 1st Interstate Services Co., Torrance, Calif., 1983-88; sr. mgr. Nolan, Norton & Co., L.A., 1988-90; pres. Tucker & Assocs., Rancho Palos Verdes, Calif., 1990—; mem. product adv. bd. Teradata Corp., L.A., 1980-83; chmn. computers and info. systems adv. bd. Grad. Sch. Mgmt. UCLA, 1984-85. Served to 1st lt., U.S. Army, 1964-66, Korea. Mem. Soc. for Info. Mgmt. Roman Catholic. Home: 30201 Cartier Dr Palos Verdes Peninsula CA 90274-5721 Office: Tucker & Assocs 3200 La Rotunda Dr Ste 610 Palos Verdes Peninsula CA 90274-6145

TUCKER, CONNIE, legal assistant, insurance consultant; b. Richmond, Calif., Mar. 20, 1956; d. Ray Field Braxton and Maudrie (Harding) Wimbley; m. Keith Dwayne Tucker, Dec. 29, 1974 (div. Nov. 1989); 1 child, Dwayne B. Student, Merritt Coll., 1982. Lic. life and disability, variable annuity, lic. securities. Claims specialist Aetna Life & Casualty, San Francisco, 1973-78; claims rep. Calif. Casualty, San Mateo, 1978-90; legal asst./owner Tucker Claims Assistance, Suisun City, Calif., 1990—. Mem. Life Assn. of Life Underwriters. Office: Tucker Claims Assistance PO Box 144 Suisun City CA 94585

TUCKER, GORDON LOCKE, environmental engineer, air quality consultant; b. Peekskill, N.Y., Dec. 19, 1932; s. Edwin Locke and Eleanor Wardwell (Ramsdell) T.; m. Marlene Rae Culli, Nov. 22, 1959; children: Lisa M., Glenn L., Lori S. BSEE, U. Mass., 1955; postgrad., St. Louis U., 1955-56; MS in Meteorology, U. Wis., 1962; MS in Systems Mgmt., U. So. Calif., 1976. Cert. project mgmt. profl. Commd. 2d lt. USAF, 1955, advanced through grades to maj., 1966, weather officer, staff meteorologist, 1964-75; ret., 1975; sr. scientist, meteorologist, mgr. phys. scis. HDR, Santa Barbara, Calif., 1975-82; engr. Delco Systems Ops., Santa Barbara, 1982-84; environ. scientist Tetra Tech, Inc., San Bernardino, Calif., 1985-86; engring. mgr. Santa Barbara Rsch. Ctr., 1986-88; air quality cons., Santa Barbara, 1988-90; environ. specialist Field Scis. Inst., Albuquerque, 1990—; mem. faculty U. Phoenix, Albuquerque, 1991—. Decorated D.S.M. Mem. AAAS, Am. Meteorol. Soc., Project Mgmt. Inst., Air and Waste Mgmt. Assn., N.Mex.. Hazardous Waste Mgmt. Soc., Kiwanis (pres. Santa Barbara 1981, bd. dirs. Albuquerque 1992). Home: 4608 Glenwood Hills Dr Albuquerque NM 87111

TUCKER, JOEL LAWRENCE, aviation company executive; b. Berkeley, Calif., Feb. 23, 1932; s. Lawrence Otis Tucker and Edythe Lauretta (Pye) Connolly; m. Constance Nadine Finnick, Oct. 19, 1951 (div. Sept. 1975); 1 child, John Lawrence. BS, U. Wash., 1953. Statistician Bell Telephone System, Seattle, 1953-61, AID, Washington, 1961-64; dir. sales Boeing Comml. Airplanes, Seattle, 1965-87; pres. J.E.T. Cons. Ltd., Kirkland, Wash., 1987—; mng. dir. Lorad Boeing Ltd., Hamilton, Bermuda, 1988-89. Chmn. Citizens Sch. Adv. Coun., Bellevue, Wash., 1969-71. With U.S. Army, 1954-56. Republican. Presbyterian.

TUCKER, MARCUS OTHELLO, judge; b. Santa Monica, Calif., Nov. 12, 1934; s. Marcus Othello Sr. and Essie Louvonia (McLendon) T.; m. Indira Hale, May 29, 1965; 1 child, Angelique. BA, U. So. Calif., 1956; JD, Howard U., 1960. Bar: Calif. 1962, U.S. Dist. Ct. (cen. dist.) Calif. 1962, U.S. Ct. Appeals (9th cir.) 1965, U.S. Ct. Internat. Trade 1970, U.S. Supreme Ct. 1971. Pvt. practice, Santa Monica, 1962-63, 67-74; dep. atty. City of Santa Monica, 1963-65; asst. atty. U.S. Dist. Ct. (Cen. Dist.) Calif., 1965-67; commr. L.A. Superior Ct., 1974-76; judge mcpl. ct. Long Beach (Calif.) Jud. Dist., 1976-85; judge superior ct. L.A. Jud. Dist., 1985—; supervising judge L.A. County Dependency Ct. L.A. Superior Ct., 1991-92, presiding judge Juvenile divsn., 1993—; asst. prof. law Pacific U., Long Beach, 1984, 86; justice pro tem U.S. Ct. Appeals (2d cir.), 1981. Mem. editorial staff Howard U. Law Sch. Jour., 1959-60. Pres. Community Rehab. Industries Found., Long Beach, 1983-86, Legal Aid Found., L.A., 1976-77; bd. dirs. Long Beach coun. Boy Scouts Am., 1978-92. With U.S. Army, 1960-66. Named Judge of Yr. Juvenile Ctsd. Bar Assn., 1986, Disting. Jurist Long Beach Trial Trauma Coun., 1987, Honoree in Law Handy Community Ctr., L.A., 1987, Bernard S. Jefferson Jurist of Yr. John M. Langston Bar Assn. of Black Lawyers, 1990, Award for Law-Related Edn. Constl. Rights Found./L.A. County Bar Assn., 1992. Mem. ABA, Calif. Judges Assn. (chmn. juvenile law com. 1986-87), Langston Bar Assn. (pres. bd. dirs. 1972, 73), Calif. Assn. Black Lawyers, Santa Monica Bay Dist. Bar Assn. (treas. 1969-71), Am. Inns of Ct., Selden Soc. Office: 201 Centre Plaza Dr Ste 3 Monterey Park CA 91754-2156

TUCKER, MELVILLE, film company executive; b. N.Y.C., Mar. 4, 1916. Student, Princeton U. Purchasing agt. Consol. Labs., N.Y.C., 1934-36; sound effects and picture editor Republic Prodns., Inc., 1936-38, asst. prodn. mgr., 1st asst. dir., 1938-42, asst. producer, 1946, assoc. producer, 1947-52; producer Universal, 1952-54, exec. v.p., 1955-70; producer Verdon Prodns., 1971—. Producer: (feature films) The Missourians, Thunder in God's Country, Rodeo King and the Senorita, Utah Wagon Train, Drums Across the River, Black Shield of Falworth, A Warm December, Uptown Saturday Night, 1972, Let's Do It Again, 1975, A Piece of the Action, 1977; exec. producer: (feature films) Stir Crazy, 1980, Hanky Panky, 1982, Fast Forward, 1985. Served with U.S. Army, 1942-46. Office: Verdon Cedric Prodns Inc 9350 Wilshire Blvd Ste 310 Beverly Hills CA 90212-3246

TUCKER, ROBIN FLORENCE, non-commissioned officer; b. Wilmington, Ohio, Mar. 7, 1955; s. Edwin Markest Tucker and Thelma Irene (Winterhalter) Wagner. Student, Xavier U., 1973-74; AA, San Antonio Coll., 1980. Enlisted USAF, 1974; real estate cost mgmt. analytical specialist USAF, Ellsworth AFB, S.D., 1974-75; base real estate cost mgmt. analytical specialist USAF, Lackland AFB, Tex., 1975-78; adminstrv. specialist USAF, Pease AFB, N.H., 1981-83; intermediate command adminstrv. specialist USAF, Seoul, Korea, 1983-84, NCOIC investigative adminstr., 1984-86, NCOIC unit adminstr., 1986-88; NCOIC detachment 055 UCLA USAF, 1988—. Mem. Air Force Sgts. Assn. Roman Catholic. Office: AFROTC Det 055 UCLA 405 Hilgard Mens Gym Rm 210 Los Angeles CA 90024-1611

TUCKER, ROY ANTHONY, electro-optical instrumentation engineer, consultant; b. Jackson, Miss., Dec. 11, 1951; s. Roy Anthony and Marjorie Faye (Human) T. BS in Physics, Memphis State U., 1978; MS in Sci. Instrumentation, U. Calif., Santa Barbara, 1981. Planetarium tech. Memphis (Tenn.) Mus. Planetarium, 1976-78; engring. tech. Kitt Peak Nat. Obs., Tucson, 1979; electro-optical engr. Multiple Mirror Telescope Obs., Tucson, 1981-83; rsch. engr., dept. physiology Univ. Ariz., Tucson, 1988-92; electro-optical engr. Applied Tech. Assocs., Inc., Albuquerque, N.Mex., 1992—; cons. Roy Tucker and Assocs., Vancouver, Wash., 1983-84, Tucson, 1984—. Sgt. USAF, 1972-76. Mem. AAAS, Am. Astron. Soc. Home: 5600 Gibson Blvd SE Apt 233 Albuquerque NM 87108

TUCKER, STEVEN BARRY, physician; b. Jersey City, Dec. 13, 1946; s. Harold G. and Lois Nan (Singer) T.; m. Lindsay Ann Hansen, Mar. 10, 1984; 1 child, Jacob Ian. BS, Rutgers U., 1968; MD, SUNY, Buffalo, 1972. Diplomate Am. Bd. Internal Medicine, Am. Bd. Nephrology. Intern in internal medicine SUNY, Buffalo, resident in internal medicine, 1972-74; resident in internal medicine Mercy Hosp. Med. Ctr., San Diego, 1974-75; fellow in nephrology Georgetown U., Washington, 1977-79; pvt. practice nephrology, Internal Med. Assocs., Anchorage, 1979—. Maj. U.S. Army, 1975-77. Fellow ACP. Home: 7146 Candace Cir Anchorage AK 99516-6550

TUCKER, SUSAN MARTIN, nursing administrator; b. Sacramento, Calif.; m. T. Lawrence Tucker, Apr. 24, 1971; children: Karrie, Jill. Diploma, Kaiser Sch. Nursing, 1964; BSN, U. Pa., 1970; MSN, Calif. State U., Dominguez Hills, 1992. RN, Calif. Staff nurse Oakland (Calif.) Hosp., 1964-65; vol. nurse U.S. Peace Corps, Medellin, Colombia, 1965-68; staff nurse VA Hosp., Phila., 1968-70; pub. health nurse Alameda County Health Dept., Oakland, Calif., 1970-71; nurse tchr. practitioner Kaiser Permanente, L.A., 1971-78; DON Kaiser Permanente, Panorama City, Calif., 1978-93; cons. Joint Commn., Chgo., 1989-91; mem. Nat. Adv. Coun. on Nurse Tng., Washington, 1983-86; bd. dirs. NAACOG Cert. Corp., Chgo., 1982-85. Author: Clinical Nursing, 1989, Fetal Monitoring, 1992, Patient Care Standards, 1992. Vol. March of Dimes, L.A., 1992, Am. Heart Assn., L.A., 1992. Mem. ANA, NAACOG, Am. Orgn. Nurse Execs., Orgn. of Nurse Execs. of Calif. (practice com. 1991-93), Calif. Nurses Assn. (resolutions com. 1992-93), Phi Kappa Phi, Sigma Theta Tau. Home: 3116 Canyon Village Circle San Ramon CA 94583 Office: 200 Muir Rd Martinez CA 94553

TUCKER, WALTER RAYFORD, III, congressman, lawyer, mayor; b. Compton, Calif., 1957; s. Walter Rayford Jr. and Martha H. Tucker; m. Robin Tucker; children: Walter Rayford IV, Autumn Monet. BA in Polit. Sci. cum laude, U. So. Calif., 1978; JD, Georgetown U., 1981. Ordained Christian minister. Staff Segrue, Rothwell, McPeak, Washington; dep. dist. atty. County of Los Angeles, 1984-86; pvt. practice Compton, 1986—; mayor City of Compton, Calif., 1991-92; mem. 103rd Congress from 37th Calif. dist., 1993—; mem. pub. works and transp. com., mem. small bus. com. Active Compton Juvenile Delinquency Panel; Sunday Sch. teacher. Mem. NAACP (life), Calif. Bar Assn., South Ctrl. Bar Assn., L.A. Bar Assn., Langston Bar Assn., Kiwanis Club of Compton. Democrat. Office: US Ho of Reps Office of Ho Mems Washington DC 20515

TUDDENHAM, W(ILLIAM) MARVIN, chemist, metallurgist, consultant; b. Salt Lake City, July 8, 1924; s. William Calder and Laura (Pack) T.; m. Dorothy Evelyn Snelgrove, May 1, 1945; children: William Marvin Jr. (dec.), Mary Alice, Evelyn, Laurie. BA in Chemistry, U. Utah, 1947, MS in Chemistry, 1948, PhD in Fuels, 1954, teaching cert., 1984. Rsch. chemist Eastman Kodak Co., Rochester, N.Y., 1948-50; dept. mgr. Kennecott Rsch., Salt Lake City, 1953-83; v.p., gen. mgr. Master Travel, Salt Lake City, 1984-91; pres. Mining & Metall. Assocs., Salt Lake City, 1991—. Editor: Sampling and Analysis Copper, 1983; contbr. articles to tech. jours. and encys., chpts. to books; patentee in electrowinning and refining field. Chmn. Salt Lake City Adv. Com. on Waste Disposal, 1981, Salt Lake City Pub. Utilities Adv. Bd., 1983-90; mem. Salt Lake City Mayor's Budget Adv. Com., 1985-90. Ensign USNR, 1944-46, PTO. Recipient Silver Beaver award Gt. Salt lake coun. Boy Scouts Am., 1978. Mem. AIME (sr.), Metall. Soc. of AIME (past chmn. nat. electrolytic process com.), Am. Chem. Soc. (emeritus, chmn. nat. membership affairs com. 1980-82, various offices 1953—, Utah award Salt Lake-Cen. Utah sects. 1973), Sigma Xi, Alpha Chi Sigma. Republican. Mem. LDS Ch. Office: 1828 Lincoln St Salt Lake City UT 84105

TUDMAN, CATHI GRAVES, educator; b. Fresno, Calif., June 24, 1953; d. Robert Eugene and Bettyelou (Seagraves) Graves; divorced; children: Colleen Melissa, Andrew James. BA in Music cum laude, Calif. State U., Fresno, 1978, MA in Communication, 1991. Gen. elem., English, music and gen. sci. teaching credentials, Calif. Founder, coord. Lake Sequoia Symphonic Music Camp, Miramonte, Calif., 1985—; asst. lectr. communications speech dept. Calif. State U., 1988-91, instr. reading ednl. opportunity program summer bridge, 1990, instr. writing ednl. opportunity program summer bridge, 1991, coach, judge Peach Blossom Festival, 1988-91; band dir. Yosemite Mid. Sch., Mayfair Elem., Hidalgo Elem., 1991-93, Balderas Elem., 1992-93, Turner Elem., 1993; instr. communications dynamics Phillips Coll., Fresno, 1989-90; rsch. assoc. Renshaw Assocs., Fresno, 1989-91; flutist, piccolist Fresno Philharm. Orch., 1981—, libr., 1985, pers. mgr., 1984-85; flute clinician Selmer Corp., Ind., 1988—; festivals chmn. cen. sect. Calif. Music Educators, 1972-82, publicity chmn. 1992-93; pvt. tutor in math., music and social studies. Flute clinician Fresno County Schs., 1980—; founder San Joaquin Valley Instrument Fund, 1984; bd. dirs. Community Concert Series, Fresno County, 1986-88; liaison com. bd. dirs. Fresno Philharm. Orch., 1992-94; asst. chair. FMCMEA Hon. Band, 1992-93. Rsch. grantee Calif. State U., 1991; recipient Outstanding Teaching award Internat. Communication Assn., 1991. Mem. Western States Communication Assn., Fresno-Madera Music Educators Assn., Fresno Tchrs. Assn., Calif. Tchrs. Assn., Fresno Mus. Club (social chmn. 1982-84), Calif. Music Educators (festival chmn. cen. sect. 1972-82), Calif. State U.-Fresno Alumnae Assn. (sec. 1982-83, nat. friendship chmn. 1979-81), Blue Key, Phi Kappa Phi, Mu Phi Epsilon (pres., v.p. Phi Chi chpt.). Home: 5467 E Saginaw Way Fresno CA 93727-7536 Office: Yosemite Mid Sch 1292 N 9th Fresno CA 93703

TUDOR, MARY LOUISE DRUMMOND, educator; b. Long Beach, Calif., Nov. 9, 1937; d. Wesley Carlton and Dora Elizabeth (Blankenbeckler) Drummond; m. Gary Albert Tudor, June 18, 1960 (div. May 1980); children: Tamara Lynn Tudor Craigwell, Michelle Denise. BS in Edn., U. So. Calif., 1959, MS in Edn., 1964; MS in Counseling, Calif. State U., Long Beach, 1984. Cert. elem. adminstr., pupil personnel in counseling. Tchr. Los Angeles Unified Sch. Dist., 1959-68, Long Beach Unified Sch. Dist., 1968—. Past pres. Lake Forest (Calif.) Beach and Tennis Singles Assn., 1980-82; patroness Orange County Performing Arts Ctr., Beverly Sills Guild, Costa Mesa, Calif., 1985-87. Boyd Found. scholar, Long Beach, 1955, Nat. Meth. Bd. scholar, 1955. Mem. DAR, Delta Delta Delta (pres. Saddleback Valley Alumni Assn. 1973-75), U. So. Calif. Alumni Assn., Internat. Soc. of Poets, Phi Delta Kappa, Kappa Delta Pi, Phi Delta Gamma, Psi Chi. Republican. Methodist. Lodge: Internat. Order Job's Daus. (bd. dirs. Mission Viejo, Calif. chpt. 1985-86).

TUELL, JACK MARVIN, retired bishop; b. Tacoma, Nov. 14, 1923; s. Frank Harry and Anne Helen (Bertelson) T.; m. Marjorie Ida Beadles, June 17, 1946; children—Jacqueline, Cynthia, James. B.S., U. Wash., 1947, LL.B., 1948; S.T.B., Boston U., 1955; M.A., U. Puget Sound, 1961, DHS, 1990; D.D., Pacific Sch. Religion, 1966; LLD, Alaska Pacific U., 1980. Bar: Wash. 1948; ordained to ministry Meth. Ch., 1955. Practice law with firm Holte & Tuell, Edmonds, Wash., 1948-50; pastor Grace Meth. Ch., Everett, Wash., 1950-52, South Tewksbury Meth. Ch., Tewksbury, Mass., 1952-55, Lakewood Meth. Ch., Tacoma, 1955-61; dist. supt. Puget Sound dist. Meth. Ch., Everett, 1961-67; pastor 1st United Meth. Ch., Vancouver, Wash., 1967-72; bishop United Meth. Ch., Portland, Oreg., 1972-80, Calif.-Pacific Conf., United Meth. Ch., L.A., 1980-92; Mem. gen. conf. United Meth. Ch., 1964, 66, 68, 70, 72; pres. coun. of Bishops United Meth. Ch., 1989-90. Author: The Organization of the United Methodist Church, 1970. Pres. Tacoma U.S.O., 1959-61, Vancouver YMCA, 1968; v.p. Ft. Vancouver Seamens Cnt., 1969-72; vice chmn. Vancouver Human Rels. Commn., 1970-72; pres. Oreg. Coun. Alcohol Problems, 1972-76; trustee U. Puget Sound, 1961-73, Vancouver Meml. Hosp., 1967-72, Alaska Meth. U., Anchorage, 1972-80, Willamette U., Salem, Oreg., 1972-80, Willamette View Manor, Portland, 1972-80, Rogue Valley Manor, Medford, Oreg., 1972-76, Sch. Theology at Claremont, Calif., 1980-92, Methodist Hosp., Arcadia, Calif., 1983-92; pres. nat. div. bd. global ministries United Meth. Ch., 1972-76, pres. ecumenical and interreligious concerns div., 1976-80, Commn. on Christian Unity and interreligious concerns, 1980-84, Gen. Bd. of Pensions,1984-92, Calif. Coun. Alcohol Problems, 1985-88. Jacob Sleeper fellow, 1955. Mem. Lions. Home and Office: 2697 S North Bluff Rd Greenbank WA 98253

TUKEY, HAROLD BRADFORD, JR., horticulture educator; b. Geneva, N.Y., May 29, 1934; s. Harold Bradford and Ruth (Schweigert) T.; m. Helen Dunbar Parker, June 25, 1955; children: Ruth Thurbon, Carol Tukey Schwartz, Harold Bradford. B.S., Mich. State U., 1955, M.S., 1956, Ph.D., 1958. Research asst. South Haven Expt. Sta., Mich., 1955; AEC grad. research asst. Mich. State U., 1955-58; NSF fellow Calif. Inst. Tech, 1958-59; asst. prof. dept. floriculture and ornamental horticulture Cornell U., Ithaca, N.Y., 1959-64, assoc. prof., 1964-70, prof., 1970-80; prof. urban horticulture U. Wash., Seattle, 1980—, dir. Arboreta, 1980-92, dir. Ctr. Urban Horticulture, 1980-92; cons. Internat. Bonsai mag., Electric Power Rsch. Inst., P.R. Nuclear Ctr., 1965-66; lectr. in field; mem. adv. com. Seattle-U. Wash. Arboretum and Bot. Garden, 1980-92, vice chmn., 1982, chmn., 1986-87; vis. scholar U. Nebr., 1982; vis. prof. U. Calif.-Davis, 1973; mem. various coms. Nat. Acad. Scis.-NRC; bd. dirs. Arbor Fund Bloedel Res., 1980-92, pres., 1983-84. Mem. editorial bd. Jour. Environ. Horticulture, Arboretum Bull. Mem. nat. adv. com. USDA, 1990—; pres. Ithaca PTA; troop advisor Boy Scouts Am., Ithaca. Lt. U.S. Army, 1958. Recipient B.Y. Morrison award USDA, 1987; NSF fellow, 1958-59; named to Lansing (Mich.) Sports Hall of Fame, 1987; grantee NSF, 1962, 75, Bot. Soc. Am., 1964; hon. dr. Portuguese Soc. Hort., 1985. Fellow Am. Soc. Hort. Sci. (dir. 1970-71); mem. Internat. Soc. Hort. Sci. (U.S. del. to council 1971-90, chmn. commn. for amateur horticulture 1974-83, exec. com. 1974-90, v.p. 1978-82, pres. 1982-86, past pres. 1986-90, chmn. commn. Urban Horticulture 1990—), Internat. Plant Propagators Soc. (eastern region dir. 1969-71, v.p. 1972, pres. 1973, internat. pres. 1976), Am. Hort. Soc. (dir. 1972-81, exec. com. 1974-81, v.p. 1978-80, citation of merit 1981), Royal Hort. Soc. (London) (v.p. hon. 1993—), Bot. Soc. Am., N.W. Horticulture Soc. (dir. 1980-92), Arboretum Found. (dir. 1980-92), Rotary, Sigma Xi, Alpha Zeta, Phi Kappa Phi, Pi Alpha Xi, Xi Sigma Pi. Presbyterian. Home: 3300 E St Andrews Way Seattle WA 98112-3750 Office: U Wash Ctr for Urban Horticulture GF-15 Seattle WA 98195

TUKUFU, DARRYL SEKOU, social issues advocate, educator; b. Cleve., July 27, 1949; s. Estus Barham and Bernice Starks; m. Myra C. Duncan, July 8, 1988; children: Ricky and Khari. AB in Social Studies, Youngstown U., 1976; MA in Urban Studies, U. Akron, 1977, PhD in Sociology, 1984. Dep. dir Youngstown (Ohio) Urban League, 1971-75; acting dir., EEO officer Youngstown Hometown Plan, 1975-76; EEO officer City of Akron, Ohio, 1977-79; mgr. Akron-Summit Community Action, 1979-80; exec. dir. Fair Housing Contract Svc., Akron, 1980-82; project dir. Vol. & Employment Project, Akron, 1985; asst. prof. African Am. studies Northeastern U., Boston, 1985-86; asst. prof. sociology and social work Memphis State U., 1986-90; asst. prof. social and behavioral scis. LeMonyne-Owen Coll., Memphis, 1990; pres., CEO Urban League Portland, Oreg., 1990—; vis. asst. prof. Kent (Ohio) State U., 1984-85; adj. assoc. prof. Portland State U., mem. pres.'s coun.; commr. Port of Portland, 1991—; cert. cons. Performax Systems Internat., Personal Dynamics Inst.; mem. minority affairs rev. bd. NIKE, Inc., 1991—, Am.-African Trade Rels. Adv. Bd., adv. bd. Oreg. Peace Inst., 1991—, North/N.E. Econ. Devel. Alliance Bd., 1991—; presenter various regional and nat. sociol. confs.; rschr. in field. Co-founder, pres. Youngstown Sickle Cell Anemia Found., Inc., 1972-73, Akron Black Leadership Forum, 1980-81; convenor Ohio Coun. Urban Leagues Community Svc. staff, 1973-74; Dem. Precinct Committeeman, 1984-85; local dir. Univ. Area Jaycees, 1987-88; advisor Memphis Urban League Male Connection Program, 1988-90; mem. Mayor's Pub. Works Task Force, 1990-91, exec. com. Leaders Roundtable, 1991—; commr. Port of Portland, 1991—; bd. dirs. Memphis Urban League, 1989-90, Emanuel Med. Ctr. Found., 1991—. Recipient Dedicated Svc. Striving for Social Justice award NAACP, 1980, Emerging Leadership award Frontiers Club, 1980, Appreciation award Memphis Edn. Assn., 1991, Gov. Roberts Transition Team, 1991, Youngstown Martin Luther King, Jr. Holiday Com., 1992; named Outstanding Young Man of Am., U.S. Jaycees, 1981. Fellow Am. Leadership Forum (Oreg. chpt.); mem. Am. Sociol. Assn., So. Sociol. Soc., City Club Portland, Kappa Alpha Psi (life, mem. Portland Alumni Chpt. Bd.). Office: Urban League Portland 10 N Russell St Portland OR 97227

TULLIS, GENE EDWARD, cardiovascular surgeon; b. Salem, Ohio, July 17, 1950; s. Gene Elton and Agnes Marie (Kamasky) T.; m. Julie Ella Kandl, Mar. 23, 1973; children: Michael Andrew, Laura Catherine, Matthew Thomas, Sarah Elizabeth. BS in Zoology cum laude, Kent State U., 1976; DMS, Ohio State U. Coll. Med., Columbus, 1979. Bd. Cert. Gen. Surgery, Thoracic Surgery and Surgical Critical Care. Gen. surg. residency St. Joseph Hosp., Denver, 1979-84; thoracic surg. residency Alleghany Gen. Hosp., Pitts., 1984-86; pvt. practice cardiac surgery Jonesboro, Ark., 1986-89; pvt. practice cardiothoracic surgery Denver, Colo., 1990—; asst. clin. prof. surgery, U. Ark. Health Scis. Ctr., Jonesboro, Ark., 1987-89. Contbr. articles to profl. jours., 1986, 87. Staff Sgt. USAF, 1970-73, Vietnam. Major, USAR, 1991, Desert Storm. Recipient Outstanding Surgical Resident, St. Joseph Hosp., Denver, Colo., 1982, 84. Mem. AMA, Denver Med. Soc., Am. Coll. Surgeons, Am. Coll. Chest Physicians, Colo. Med. Soc., Rocky Mountain Cardiac Surgical Soc., Soc. for Thoracic Surgery, Cardiovascular Surgery Coun. of Am. Heart Assn. Office: 1601 E 19th Ave Ste 4450 Denver CO 80218-1250

TULLOCK, GORDON, economics educator; b. Rockford, Ill., Feb. 13, 1922; s. George and Helen T. J.D., U. Chgo., 1947. Fgn. svc. officer China, 1947-56; postdoctoral fellow U. Va., 1958-59; asst. prof. U. S.C., 1959-60, assoc. prof., 1960-62; assoc. prof. U. Va., Charlottesville, 1962-67; prof. econs. and polit. sci. Rice U., Houston, 1967-68; prof. econs. and pub. choice Va. Poly. Inst. and State U., Blacksburg, 1968-72; Univ. disting. prof. econs. and pub. choice Va. Poly. Inst. and State U., 1972-83, George Mason U., Fairfax, Va., 1983-87; prof. U. Ariz., Tucson, 1987—; editorial dir. Center for Study of Pub. Choice, 1968-90; vis. disting. scholar Baruch U., N.Y.C., spring 1987; dir. DHC, Eldora, Iowa. Author: (with J.M. Buchanan) The Calculus of Consent, 1962, The Politics of Bureaucracy, 1965, The Organization of Inquiry, 1966, Toward a Mathematics of Politics, 1967, Private Wants, Public Means, 1970, The Logic of the Law, 1971, The Social Dilemma, 1974, (with Richard B. McKenzie) The New World of Economics, 1975, (with Richard B. McKenzie), Modern Political Economy, 1978, Trials on Trial, 1979, Toward a Theory of the Rent-Seeking Society, 1980, Economics of Income Redistribution, 1983, The Economics of Wealth and Poverty, 1986, Autocracy, 1987, Wealth, Poverty & Politics, 1988, The Economics of Special Privilege and Rent Seeking, 1989. Mem. Am. Econ. Assn., So. Econ. Assn. (past pres.), Western Econ. Assn., Am. Polit. Sci. Assn., Pub. Choice Soc. (sec. 1965—), Assn. for Asian Studies. Home: 6840 E Via Colorada Tucson AZ 85715-6301 Office: U Ariz Dept Econs Tucson AZ 85721-0001

TULMAN, KIMBERLE RUSCHÉ, nonprofit organization administrator; b. Reno, Jan. 15, 1966; d. Robert Charles Rusche' Sr. and Patricia Arlene (Tolotti) Rusche' Jeffers; (stepfather) Jim Jeffers Jr. BA in Journalism, U. Nev., 1989. Pub. rels. asst. Walther/Berkley Agy., Reno, 1988; intern St. Mary's Regional Med. Ctr., Reno, 1988, coord., 1990-91, sr. coord., 1991—; coord. Truckee Meadows Hosp., Reno, 1988-90. Contbr. articles to profl. jours. Pub. rels. task force Biggest Little City Com., Reno, 1988; mem. com. Am. Heart Assn., Reno, 1989, bd. dirs., 1991-93; bd. dirs. Community Child Care Svcs., Reno, 1989-91, v.p., 1990-91. Mem. Internat. Assn. Bus. Communicators (treas. 1991-92), Pub. Rels. Soc. Am. (new profls. com. 1990-91, community svc. com. 1989-90, profl. ptnr. 1990-91, student liaison com. 1990-91), Toastmasters. Home: 5150 Driftstone Ave Reno NV 89523-2600 Office: 1055 S Wells Ave #100 Reno NV 89509

TUMAN, WALTER VLADIMIR, Russian language educator, researcher; b. Heidelberg, Germany, Jan. 21, 1946; came to U.S., 1949; s. Val Alexander Tuman and Valida (Zedins) Grasis; m. Helena Eugenia Makarowsky, June 6, 1970; children: Gregory Vladimir, Larissa Alexandra. BA, Fordham U., 1967; MS in Russian, Linguistics, Georgetown U., 1970, PhD in Russian, 1975. Supr. Russian dept. Def. Lang. Inst., Washington, 1972-75; developer course-curriculum Def. Lang. Inst., Monterey, Calif., 1975-78; asst. prof. Russian Hollins (Va.) Coll., 1978-84; dir. fgn. lang. lab. La. State U., Baton Rouge, 1984-90; assoc. prof., coord. Russian program Thunderbird Campus Am. Grad. Sch. Internat. Mgmt., Glendale, Ariz., 1990—; cons. various univs. Editor: A Bibliography of Computer-Aided Language Learning, 1986; contbg. editor Jour. Ednl. Techniques and Techs., 1987—; author book revs., computer programs, conf. presentations; contbr. articles to profl. jours. Georgetown U. fellow, 1969; recipient Prof.'s Exch. award Internat. Rsch. and Exchs. Bd. (USSR), 1979; Mednick Meml. Fund grantee Va. Found. for Ind. Colls. (Australia), 1983, Apple Computer grantee, 1989. Mem. Am. Assn. Tchrs. Slavic and East European Langs. (v.p. 1981-84, founder Monterey, Calif. chpt.), Am. Coun. on the Teaching Fgn. Langs., Internat. Assn. Learning Lab. Dirs., Assn. Internat. Linguistique Appliquée. Russian Orthodox. Office: Am Grad Sch Internat Mgmt 59th and Greenway Glendale AZ 85306

TUMELSON, RONALD ADRIAN, organization development consultant; b. Grants Pass, Oreg., May 1, 1939; s. Floyd Orville and Alice Evelyn (Adriansen) T.; m. Betsy Destine Martin, Dec. 14, 1963; children: Arlene Dawn, Gretchen Loraine, Ronald Adrian II, Karen Destine. BS, U.S. Mil. Acad., 1962; MS in orgn. devel., Pepperdine U., 1984. Asst. prof. Auburn (Ala.) U., 1970-72; briefing officer U.S. Support Activities Group, Thailand, 1973-74; adjutant 3rd brigade 82nd Airborne Div., Ft. Bragg, N.C., 1974-76; exec. officer 1st batallion, 505th INF 82nd Airborne Div., Ft. Bragg, 1976-77; chief organizational efectivenes USAR, Heidelberg, West Germany, 1977-80; dep. commandant Organizational Effectiveness Sch. Ft. Ord, Calif., 1980-83; dep. dir. Pers. and Community Activities, Ft. Ord, Calif., 1983-86; sr. cons. Systems Excellence, Monterey, Calif., 1986—; cons. Calif. Dept. Motor Vehicles, 1987, Calif. Hwy. Patrol, 1988, Calif. Prison Industry Authority, 1989, Calif. Dept. Transp., 1991, Partnering, 1992. Decorated Purple Heart, 2 Bronze Star medals, 3 Meritorious Svc. medals U.S. Govt., Vietnam, 1968. Mem. Orgn. Devel. Network, Disabled Am. Vets. Methodist. Office: Systems Exellence 177 Webster St Ste 3784A Monterey CA 93940-3182

TUNBERG, KARL ALEXANDER, home building company executive; b. Santa Barbara, Calif., June 4, 1960; s. Karl Alexander and Susan Margaret (Anderson) T.; m. Mary Lynn Huffman, Jan. 2, 1987; 1 child, Karl Alexander III. Student, Ariz. State U., 1984. Editor-in-chief Sunbelt Pub. Group, Phoenix, 1984-86; v.p. Eye Co., Phoenix, 1986-87; sales mgr. Gen. Homes, Phoenix, 1987-89; v.p. sales Colonial Homes, Phoenix, 1989-92; sales rep. Ryland Homes, Scottsdale, Ariz., 1992-93; sales mgr. Forecast Homes, 1993—; bd. dirs. Huffman Trust, Phoenix, 1984—; cons. Rossey Pub., Phoenix, 1986-87.

TUNGPALAN, ELOISE YAMASHITA, state legislator; b. Maui, Hawaii, July 22, 1945; married; 3 children. BA, U. Hawaii. Former instr. U. Hawaii; legis. aide to coms., former mem. Hawaii Ho. of Reps.; now state senator Hawaii Senate; legis. aide and researcher for govt. coms. and depts. State of Hawaii. Mem. Phi Beta Kappa, Phi Kappa Phi. Democrat. Office: Hawaii State Senate Leiopapa A Kamehameha Bldg 235 Beretania St Honolulu HI 96813

TUNISON, ELIZABETH LAMB, education educator; b. Belfast, Northern Ireland, Jan. 7, 1922; came to U.S., 1923; d. Richard Ernest and Ruby (Hill) Lamb; m. Ralph W. Tunison, Jan. 24, 1947 (dec. Apr. 1984); children: Eric Arthur, Christine Wait, Dana Paul. BA, Whittier Coll., 1943, MEd, 1963. Tchr. Whittier (Calif.) Schs., 1943-59; tchr. T.V. Stas. TV Channels 13 and 28, So. Calif. Counties, 1960-75; dir. curriculum Bassett (Calif.) Schs., 1962-65; elem. sch. prin. Rowland Unified Schs., Rowland Heights, Calif., 1965-68; assoc. prof. edn. Calif. State Poly. U., Pomona, 1968-71; prof. Whittier Coll., 1971-88, prof. emerita, 1988—. Bd. dirs. Presbyn. Intercommunity Hosp. Found. Recipient Whittier Coll. Alumni Achievement award 1975; Helen Hefernan scholar 1963. Mem. AAUP, Assn. Calif. Sch. Adminstrs. (state bd., chmn. higher edn. com. 1983-86, region pres. 1981-83, Wilson Grace awrd 1983), PEO (pres. 1990-92), Assistance League of Whittier, Delta Kappa Gamma. Home: 5636 Ben Alder Ave Whittier CA 90601-2111

TUPIN, JOE PAUL, psychiatry educator; b. Comanche, Tex., Feb. 17, 1934; m. Betty Thompson, June 19, 1955; children: Paul, Rebecca, John. BS in Pharmacy, U. Tex., 1955, postgrad., 1955; MD, U. Tex., Galveston, 1959, Wash. Sch. Psychiatry, 1962, NIH Grad. Sch., 1962-64. Lic. psychiatrist, Tex., Calif. Intern U. Calif. Hosps., San Francisco, 1959-60; resident U. Tex. Med. br., Galveston, 1960-62, asst. prof. psychiatry, 1964-68, mem. staff John Sealy Hosp., 1964-69, dir. psychiatric consultation service, 1965-66, dir. psychiatric research, 1965-69, asst. dean medicine, 1967-68, assoc. prof., 1968-69, assoc. dean, 1968-69; resident NIMH div NIH, 1963-64; assoc. prof. psychiatry U. Calif., Davis, 1969-71, mem. staff Davis Med. Ctr., 1969—, vice-chmn. dept. psychiatry, 1970-76, prof., 1971-93, prof. emeritus, 1993, acting chmn. dept. psychiatry, 1977, acting dir. admissions sch. medicine, 1977-78, chmn. dept. psychiatry, 1977-84; med. dir. U. Calif. Davis Med. Ctr., 1984-93; cons. staff St. Mary's Infirmary, Galveston, 1967-69, Moody House Retirement Home for the Aged, Galveston, 1967-69, VA Hosp., Martinez, 1977-82, Yolo Gen. Hosp., 1980-81; dir. psychiatric consultation service U. Calif., Davis, 1969-74, co-director 1974-77; vis. prof. King's Coll. Med. Sch., London, 1974; acting dir. admissions sch. medicine, U. Calif., Davis, 1977-78; chief div. mental health U. Calif. Davis Med. Ctr., 1977-84, also mem. quality care com., 1979-85, chmn. com., 1981-85; med. dir. and assoc. dir. Hosp. and Clinics U. Calif., Davis, 1984-93; cons. U. Calif., Davis, 1993. Referee and book reviewer numerous publs.; mem. sci. editorial bd. Am. Jour. Forensic Psychiatry, 1985-88, Jour. Clin. Psychopharmacology, 1981—, Psychiatry, 1985, Tex. Reports on Biology and Medicine, 1965-67, 68-69; Western Jour. Medicine, 1979-89; contbr. numerous articles to profl. jours. Mem. Academically Talented Child com. Galveston City Sch. Bd., 1966-67; chmn. bd. dirs. William Temple Found., Galveston, 1967-68; bd. dirs. Citizens for Advancement of Pub. Edn., Galveston, 1967-69, pres., 1968-69, Moody House Retirement Home for the Aged, 1968, Cal Aggie Athletic Assn., 1978-82; mem. Davis Master Plan com., 1971. Served to lt. commdr. USPHS, 1962-64, with Res. 1964-80. Recipient Career Teaching award NIMH, 1964-66; named to Friars Soc. U. Tex., 1954; Mosby scholar U. Tex., Ginsberg fellow Group for Advancement of Psychiatry, 1960-62, Nat. Found. Infantile Paralysis fellow, 1957; grantee U. Tex. Med. br., 1964-69, NIMH, 1965-68. Fellow Am. Psychiat. Assn., Am. Coll. Psychiatrists (mem. com., editorial com.); mem. AMA, Yolo County Med. Assn. (chmn. credentials com. 1974-75, nominating com. 1980-84), Calif. Med. Assn. (sec. psychiatry sect. 1977-78, 78-79, sci. adv. panel on psychiatry 1975-80, psychiatry adv. sect. 1977-80, sci. adv. bd. 1978-80), Titus Harris Soc., Cen. Calif. Psychiat. Soc. (chmn. mem. com. 1970-73, pres. 1976), AAAS, Soc. Health and Human Values (exec. council 1970-73), Am. Acad. Psychiatry and the Law, AAUP, West Coast Coll. Biol. Psychiatries Com., Sigma Xi, Rho Chi, Alpha Omega Alpha. Home: 108 Kent Dr Davis CA 95616 Office: U Calif Davis Med Ctr Office of Med Scis 2300 Stockton Blvd Sacramento CA 95817

TURCHAN, OTTO CHARLES, nuclear engineering scientist, consultant; b. Ostrava, Czechoslovakia, Dec. 30, 1925; came to U.S., 1946; s. Karel and Felicia (Szymanski) T.; m. Irene Nairi Arzoumanian, June 7, 1952; children: Carl Michael, Gary Stephan. Diploma, Tech. U., Brünn, Czechoslovakia, 1945; DSc, Charles U., Prague, Czechoslovakia, 1948; MS, U. Detroit, 1953; PhD, UCLA, 1958. Registered profl. engr., Calif. Mem. tech. staff Hughes Rsch. and Devel. Labs., Culver City, Calif., 1955-62; sr. staff mem. Space Tech. Labs., Inc., El Segundo, Calif., 1962-64, Aerospace Corp., El Segundo, 1964-67; sr. tech. specialist N. Am. Aviation/Rockwell, L.A., 1967-72; sr. project engr. Bechtel Power Corp., Norwalk, Calif., 1972-84; pres. Energy Systems Engrng. Co., Beverly Hills, Calif., 1984—. Patentee in field. Fellow AIAA; mem. Am. Geophys. Union, Am. Phys. Soc. (pres. U. Detroit chpt. 1950), Am. Nuclear Soc., N.Y. Acad. Scis., AAAS, Czechoslovak Soc. Arts and Scis. (pres. L.A. chpt. 1970). Office: Energy Systems Devel PO Box 3093 Beverly Hills CA 90212-0093

TURCHI, PATRICE ERNEST ANTOINE, physicist; b. Lorient, Morbihan, France, June 23, 1952; came to U.S., 1985; s. Pietrino and Solange B.A. (Dubois) T.; m. Michele Elise Boyle, Mar. 20, 1986; 1 child, Elodie S.G. Diplome d' Ingenieur, Ecole Nationale Superieure de Chimie de Paris, 1975; These de Docteur Ingenieur, U. Paris VI, 1982, These d'Etat es Scis. Physiques, 1984. Asst. prof. U. Paris VI, Paris, France, 1975-85; vis. rsch. asst. U. Calif., Berkeley, 1985-86; from sr. vis. scientist to sr. scientist Lawrence Livermore (Calif.) Nat. Lab., 1986—. Contbr. articles to profl. jours. Mem. Amnesty Internat. Recipient Materials Scis. Rsch. Competition in the Category of Metallurgy and Ceramics awd., Dept. Energy, 1987. Mem. Am. Phys. Soc., Materials Rsch. Soc., Transaction Metal Soc. (alloy com.), Societe des Ingenieurs et Scientifiques de France, Minerals, Metals and Materials Soc., Am. Orchid Soc. Office: Lawrence Livermore Nat Lab Condensed Matter Div L268 PO Box 808 Livermore CA 94551-0808

TURCO, RONALD NICHOLAS, psychiatrist, educator; b. Phila., Apr. 11, 1940; s. Luigi A. and Antonetta Luci (Tucci) T.; m. Joanne L. Labezius, June 8, 1966; children: Annyce, Diana. BS, Pa. State U., 1962; MD, Jefferson Med. Coll., Phila., 1966. Diplomate Am. Bd. Psychiatry and Neurology, Am. Bd. Med. Examiners. Surg. intern Bryn Mawr (Pa.) Hosp., 1966-67; resident in psychiatry U. N.C., Chapel Hill, 1967-68, U. Oreg. Health Sci. Ctr., Portland, 1968-70; staff psychiatrist Brooklane Psychiat. Ctr., Hagerstown, Md., 1973-74; dir. psychiatry Cedar Hills Psychiat. Hosp., Portland, 1974-75; pvt. practice psychiatry Portland, 1974—; assoc. clin. prof. Oreg. Health Scis. U., Portland, 1974—; cons. Newberg and Portland Police Depts., 1974—, Circuit, Dist. and Fed. Cts., Portland, 1974—, Reed Coll., Portland, 1974—. Contbr. articles to profl. jours. Tchr. First Presbyn. Ch., Portland, 1981—, Portland Film Study Ctr., 1985—; campaign chmn. Jim Davis for Mayor Com., Portland, 1990; sponsor Futures for

Childre, Albuquerque, 1990—. Maj. USAF, 1970-73. Recipient Milton Erickson award Am. Soc. Clin. Hypnosis, 1990, commendation for community svc. Newberg Police Dept., 1991. Mem. Am. Acad. Psychoanalysis (transcultural com.), Portland Psychiatrists in Pvt. Practice (pres. 1985), Am. Acad. Psychoanalytic Physicians, Am. Acad. Psychoanalysis (transcultural com.), Def. for Children Interant., Oreg. Med. Assn., Internat. Assn. Chiefs of Police. Home and Office: 1220 SW Morrison # 805 Portland OR 97205-2227

TURIEL, ISAAC, energy analyst; b. N.Y.C., July 17, 1941; s. Jack and Rachel (Israel) T.; m. Ellen Williams; 1 child, Rachel. BS in Physics, Bklyn. Poly. Inst., 1962; PhD in Physics, NYU, 1968; MPH, U. Calif., Berkeley, 1972. Rsch. physicist Lawrence Livermore (Calif.) Lab., 1967-70; instr. Calif. State U. and San Francisco State U., Hayward, 1970-76; staff scientist Lawrence Berkeley Lab., 1978—. Author: Physics, The Environment and Man, 1975, Indoor Air Quality and Human Health, 1985; also numerous articles. Office: Lawrence Berkeley Lab Bldg 90-4000 1 Cyclotron Rd Berkeley CA 94720

TURK, PENELOPE BRYANT, educator; b. Washington, July 2, 1941; d. David Logan and Marjorie Lenore (Hull) B.; m. Robert Louis Turk, Mar. 25, 1964; children: Marjorie Carol, Susan Elizabeth. BA, UCLA, 1963, MA, 1964. Secondary teaching credential, Calif. Tchr. English Venice High Sch., L.A., 1964-66, Iowa City High Sch., 1966-67, Montgomery Middle Sch., El Cajon, Calif., 1983-84; tchr. for gifted students Murray Manor Elem. Sch., La Mesa, Calif., 1977-79; tchr. English, chmn. dept. Greenfield Jr. High Sch., El Cajon, 1984-91; tchr. English El Capitan High Sch., Lakeside, Calif., 1991—. Elder, deacon Fletcher Hills Presbyn. Ch., El Cajon, 1973—; pres. Friends El Cajon Library, 1974-76, now life mem.; trainer Girl Scouts U.S.A., San Diego, 1975—. Recipient Hon. Svc. award Soroptimist Internat., El Cajon, 1979, Thanks Badge, San Diego coun. Girl Scouts U.S.A., 1984; named San Diego County Tchr. of Yr., 1990; fellow San Diego Area Writers Project, 1987, Calif. Lit. Project, 1988. Mem. Nat. Council Tchrs. English, Calif. Assn. Tchrs. English, NEA, Calif. Tchrs. Assn., Greater San Diego Council Tchrs. English, San Diego Reading Assn., Toastmasters (El Cajon) (past pres., Able Toastmaster award 1983), Phi Delta kappa. Home: 1760 Key Ln El Cajon CA 92021-1507 Office: El Capitan High Sch 10410 Ashwood Ave Lakeside CA 92040

TURK, RUDY HENRY, artist, retired museum director; b. Sheboygan, Wis., June 24, 1927; s. Rudolph Anton and Mary Gertrude (Stanisha) T.; m. Wanda Lee Borders, Aug. 4, 1956; children: Tracy Lynn, Maria Teresa, Andrew Borders, Jennifer Wells. BS in Edn., U. Wis., 1949; MA in History, U. Tenn., 1951; postgrad., Ind. U., 1952-56. Instr. art history, gallery dir. U. Mont., Missoula, 1957-60; dir. Richmond (Calif.) Art Ctr., 1960-65; asst. dir. San Diego Mus. Art, 1965-67; dir. Ariz. State U. Art Mus., 1967-92; from assoc. prof. to prof. art Ariz. State U., 1967-77. Painter, paintings exhibited in solo and group exhbns.; mus. cons., juror, art cons., art lectr; author: (with Cross and Lamm) The Search for Personal Freedom, 2 vols., 1972, 76, 80, 85, Merrill Mahaffey: Monumental Landscapes, 1979, (with others) Scholder, 1983, also commentaries and critiques. Bd. dirs. Chandler Arts Com., 1983-86, Friends of Mex. Art, Ariz., 1986—, pres. 1988-90; mem. Tempe Arts Com., 1987-89, Ariz. Living Treasures Com., 1988-93; bd. dirs. Ariz. Mus. for Youth, 1993—. Recipient merit award Calif. Coll. Arts and Crafts, 1965, Senator's Cultural award State of Ariz., 1987, Golden Crate award Western Assn. Art Mus., 1974, Ariz. Gov.'s Art award, 1992; named Hon. Ariz. Designer Craftsman, 1975; named dir. emeritus Ariz. State U. Art Mus., 1992, Rudy Turk Gallery at Ariz. State U. Art Mus. named in his honor, 1992; Fulbright scholar U. Paris, 1956-57; hon. fellow Am. Craft Coun., 1988. Mem. Nat. Coun. Edn. Ceramic Arts (hon. mem. coun. 1991), Phi Alpha Theta, Phi Kappa Phi. Democrat. Home: 760 E Courtney Ln Tempe AZ 85284-4003 Office: Ariz State U Art Museum Tempe AZ 85287-2911

TURKIN, MARSHALL WILLIAM, symphony orchestra, festival and opera administrator, arranger, composer; b. Chgo., Apr. 1, 1926; 4 children. Student, U. Kans., 1946-48; Mus. B. in Music Composition, Northwestern U., 1950, Mus. M., 1951; postgrad., Juilliard Sch. Music, Columbia U., U. Ind. Record rev. columnist, classical music commentator, gen. mgr., Honolulu Symphony and Opera Co., 1959-66; orch. festival mgr.: Ravinia Festival for Chgo. Symphony, 1966-68; founding mgr.: Blossom Festival for Cleve. Orch., 1968-70; gen. mgr., Detroit Symphony, 1970-73, exec. dir., 1973-79, mng. dir., Pitts. Symphony Orch., 1979-88; gen. dir., Hawaii Opera Theatre, Honolulu, 1988-91; retired, 1991. Served with USN, World War II.

TURLEY, ROBERT STEVEN, physicist, researcher; b. Monterey Park, Calif., May 8, 1954; s. Robert Starling Jr. and Maurine (Johnson) T.; m. Deon Staffanson, Apr. 22, 1978; children: Robert Staffan, Marin, Carole, Allison, Patrick Ansel, Neil Peter. BS summa cum laude, Brigham Young U., 1978; PhD, MIT, 1984. Sr. staff physicist rsch. labs Hughes Aircraft Co., Malibu, Calif., 1975—; mem. computer com. Bates Nat. Lab., Middleton, Mass., 1980-84. Contbr. articles to profl. jours. Chmn. Conejo dist. com. Ventura County coun. Boy Scouts Am., 1992—, site coun. Manzanita Elem. Sch., Newbury Park, Calif., 1989-90. Fellow Hughes Aircraft Co., 1979. Mem. IEEE (sr.), Am. Phys. Soc., Sigma Pi Sigma, Brigham Young U. Alumni Assn. (chmn. Ventura County regional coun. 1990-92). Republican. Mem. LDS Ch. Office: Hughes Aircraft Co Rsch Labs 3011 Malibu Canyon Rd Malibu CA 90265-4797

TURMAN, GEORGE, former lieutenant governor; b. Missoula, Mont., June 25, 1928; s. George Fugett and Corinne (McDonald) T.; m. Kathleen Hager, Mar. 1951; children—Marcia, Linda, George Douglas, John, Laura. B.A., U. Mont., 1951. Various positions Fed. Res. Bank of San Francisco, 1954-64; mayor City of Missoula, 1970-72; mem. Mont. Ho. of Reps. from (Dist. 18), 1973-74; Mont. Pub. Service commr. (Dist. 5), 1975-80; lt. gov. State of Mont., 1981-88, resigned; apptd. Pacific NW Electric Power & Conservation Council, 1988; pres. Nat. Ctr. for Appropriate Tech., Butte, Mont., 1989—. Served with U.S. Army, 1951-53. Decorated Combat Inf. badge. Home: 1525 Gerald Ave Missoula MT 59801

TURMAN, ROBERT LLOYD, lawyer; b. Wiesbaden, Fed. Republic Germany, July 31, 1956; came to U.S., 1956; s. Robert Lee and Maggie Lee (Dossie) T. BA, Howard U., 1978; JD, Georgetown U., 1981. Bar: Colo. 1981, U.S. Dist. Ct. Colo. 1981. Assoc. Sherman & Howard, Denver, 1981-82; prin. Turman & Assocs., Denver and Colorado Springs, Colo., 1982—. Chmn. bd. Urban League of Pikes Peak Region, Colorado Springs, 1986-87; bd. dis. ARC Pikes Peak chpt., Colorado Springs, 1988-90. Mem. ABA, Nat. Bar Assn., Sam Cary Bar Assn., Colo. Bar Assn., El Paso County Bar Assn. Home: 4003 S Rifle Ct Aurora CO 80013-3274 Office: Turman & Assocs 717 17th St Ste 1470 Manville Pla at City Center Denver CO 80202 also: 1401 Potter Dr Ste 104 Colorado Springs CO 80909

TURNAGE, JEAN A., state supreme court chief justice; b. St. Ignatius, Mont., Mar. 10, 1926. JD, Mont. State U., 1951. Bar: Mont. 1951, U.S. Supreme Ct. 1963. Formerly ptnr. Turnage, McNeil & Mercer, Polson, Mont.; formerly Mont. State senator from 13th Dist.; pres. Mont. State Senate, 1981-83; chief justice Supreme Ct. Mont., 1985—. Mem. Mont. State Bar Assn., Nat. Conf. Chief Justices (pres.-elect), Nat. Ctr. State Courts (chair-elect). Office: Mont Supreme Ct 215 N Sanders St Helena MT 59601-4522

TURNAGE, JOE CLAYTON, consulting company executive; b. Tucson, Nov. 19, 1945; s. Clayton Franklin and Ollion Lenore (Sutton) T.; m. Ruth Ellen Ezelle, June 10, 1967; children: Clayton Jonathon, Jason Charles. BS, Miss. State U., 1967; MS, MIT, 1970, PhD, 1972. Dir. nuclear engring. Yankee Atomic Electric, Bolten, Mass., 1974-77; v.p. Mgmt. Analysis Co., San Diego, 1981-82; prin., founder Summit Nuclear Resources, San Diego, 1982-83, Delian Corp., San Diego, 1983-87; v.p., dir. ops. Internat. Tech., San Diego, 1987-88; sr. v.p. Tenera Operating Co., San Diego, 1988—. Capt. U.S. Army, 1970-76. Oak Ridge Associated Univs. spl. fellow in nuclear sci. and engring. U.S. AEC, 1967; named Disting. Engring. fellow Miss. State U., 1992. Mem. Am. Nuclear Soc. (bd. dirs. nuclear reactor safety divsn. 1980-83, chmn. bd. dirs. 1982-83). Office: Tenera L P # 215 9171 Towne Centre Dr San Diego CA 92122-1236

TURNBULL, MILES WATSON, publishing executive; b. Diagonal, Iowa, Oct. 15, 1929; s. Harold Watson and Mildred Anne (Wiley) T.; m. Jane Eloise Howard, June 19, 1960; children: Matthew Watson, Jennifer Jane Turnbull McDonald. BA in English, Simpson Coll., 1951; MA in Journalism, U. Iowa, 1957. Mgr. sales promotion Successful Farming mag. Meredith corp., Des Moines, 1966-67; mktg. mgr. Meredith corp., Chgo., 1967-68, Chgo. mgr., 1968-71; pub., owner San Juan Record, Monticello, Utah, 1971-76, Dove Creek (Colo.) Press, 1973-76, Leavenworth (Wash.) Echo, 1976-88; asst. prof. journalism Central Wash. U., Ellensburg, 1984-87, 93; exec. dir. Wash. Newspaper Pub.'s Assn., Seattle, 1988-92; adv. com. Sch. Journalism, Western Wash. U., 1989, 93; bench bar press com. Wash. Adminstrn. for the Cts., Olympia, 1988-92. Author: column Nobody's Perfect, 1976-88 (1st in State award 1982). Staff sgt. USAF, 1951-55. Mem. Wash. Newspaper Pubs. Assn. (pres. 1982-83, life mem.). Home: 248 Benton St Leavenworth WA 98826-1257 Office: 248 Benton St Box 898 Leavenworth WA 98826

TURNER, ALAN TODD, neuro-radiologist; b. Charleston, W.Va., Sept. 6, 1959; s. Joseph Ellis and Norma Jean (Sims) T.; m. Michele M. Gillenwater, Feb. 18, 1983; children: Greyson Reese, Colin Taylor, Christopher Chase. BA, U. So. Calif., 1981; MD, Morehouse Sch. Medicine, 1986. Resident in internal medicine Martin Luther King Jr. Hosp., L.A., 1986-88, resident in radiology, 1988-92, chief resident in radiology, 1991; fellow in neuroradiology U. So. Calif., L.A., 1992—; pres. Turner Med. Enterprises, L.A., 1992—; presenter at profl. confs. Mem. Rep. Senatorial Inner Circle, Washington, 1991—. Fellow Armed Forces Inst. of Pathology, Washington, 1991; recipient AMA/Burroughs Welcome Leadership award, 1992. Mem. AMA, Nat. Med. Assn., Calif. Radiol. Soc., L.A. Radiol. Soc., Young Black Profls. (exec. com. 1988—). Home: 3714 Floresta Way Los Angeles CA 90043

TURNER, BONESE COLLINS, artist, educator; b. Abilene, Kans.; d. Paul Edwin and Ruby (Seybold) Collins; m. Glenn E. Turner; 1 child, Craig Collins. BS in Edn., U. Idaho, MEd; MA, Calif. State U., Northridge, 1974. Instr. art L.A. Pierce Coll., Woodland Hills, Calif., 1964—; prof. art Calif. State U., Northridge, 1986-87; art instr. L.A. Valley Coll., Van Nuys, 1987-89, Moorpark (Calif.) Coll., 1988—; advisor Coll. Art and Architecture U. Idaho, 1988—; juror for numerous art exhibitions including Nat. Watercolor Soc., 1980, 91, San Diego Art Inst., Brand Nat. Watermedia Exhibition prin. gallery Orlando Gallery, Sherman Oaks, Calif. Prin. works exhibited in The White House, 1984, 85, Smithsonian Inst., 1984, 85, Olympic Arts Festival, L.A., 1984; one woman shows include Angel's Gate Gallery, San Pedro, Calif., 1989, Art Store Gallery, Studio City, Calif., 1988, L.A. Pierce Coll. Gallery, 1988, Brand Art Gallery, Glendale, Calif., 1988, 93, Coos (Oreg.) Art Mus., 1988, U. Nev., 1987, Orlando Gallery, Sherman Oaks, Calif., 1993, others; prin. works represented in pub. collections including Smithsonian Inst., Home Savs. and Loan, San Bernardino Sun Telegram Newspapers, Oreg. Coun. for the Arts, Newport, Nebr. Pub. Librs., Lincoln (Nebr.) Indsl. Tile Corp. Recipient awards Springfield (Mo.) Art Mus., 1989, Butler Art Inst. Mem. Nat. Mortar Bd. Soc., Nat. Watercolor Soc. (life, past pres., Purchase prize 1979), Watercolor U.S.A. Honor Soc. (award), Watercolor West, So. Calif. Women's Caucus for Art.

TURNER, DANIEL STOUGHTON, geologist, engineer; b. Madison, Wis., Feb. 8, 1917; s. Paul Boynton and Ethel (McLaughlin) T.; m. Ruth Lillie Laatsch, Oct. 28, 1944; children: Diane, Sharon, Darlene, Paul. PhD, U. Wis., 1948. Cert. profl. geologist; registered engr., Colo.; registered geologist, Ariz. U. Wyo., 1950-52; Geologist Carter Oil Co., Tulsa, 1952-53; cons. geologist, 1953-65; prof. geology Eastern Mich. U., 1965-85; profl. cons. geologist Englewood, Colo., 1988—; vol. field guide author, Colo. Geol. Survey; vol. to chief Fire Dept., 1958-65. Lt. comdr. USN, 1941-46. Decorated Bronze Star Medal. Mem. Am. Assn. Petroleum Geologists, Geol. Soc. Am., Rocky Mountain Assn. Geologists, Masons (Laramie, Wyo.), Consistory (Denver 32d degree). Home: 7175 S Poplar Way Englewood CO 80112-1632

TURNER, DEAN EDSON, educator, minister; b. Tyrone, Okla., May 24, 1927; s. Jesse Lee and Cora May (Luman) T.; m. Nancy Margaret Roche, Aug. 12, 1964; children: Taos Lee, Summer Marie. BA, Centro de Estudios Universitarios, Mexico City, 1953-55; MEd, Adams State Coll., 1959; PhD in Philosophy and History of Edn., U. Tex., 1966. Cert. tchr., Colo.; ordained to ministry Disciples of Christ Ch., 1967. English tchr. Instituto Taylor Comercial, Mexico City, 1953-55; Spanish tchr. Anchorage High Sch., 1956-58, Carmichael (Calif.) High Sch., 1958, Farmingdale (L.I.) High Sch., 1961, Rye (N.Y.) High Sch., 1963-64; prof. Spanish Sullins Women's Coll., Bristol, Va., 1962-63; prof. sociology, Spanish U. Md., 1959-61; prof. founds. of edn. U. No. Colo., Greeley, 1966—. author: The Autonomous Man, 1970, Commitment to Care, 1978, The Einstein Myth, 1979 (Alt. Book of Month award 1979), Escape from God, 1991; co-author: Classrooms in Crisis, 1986, Benevolent Living, 1988. Served to sgt. U.S. Army, 1950-52. Recipient Colo. Tchr. Who Makes a Difference award Channel 4, Denver, 1986. Mem. Soc. Christian Philosophers, Soc. Christian Ethics, Christian Educators Assn. Internat. Home: 1708 37th Ave Greeley CO 80634-2804 Office: U No Colo Greeley CO 80639

TURNER, DOUGLAS CLARK, analytical chemist; b. Payson, Utah, Jan. 10, 1961; s. Douglas Glen and Marie (Wentz) T.; m. Pamela Peterson, June 23, 1984; children: Douglas Jay, Robert Blake, Sean Michael. BS, Brigham Young U., 1985, PhD, 1991. Lab. technician Signetics Corp., Orem, Utah, 1984-85, lab. supr., 1986-88, sr. engr., 1988-91, lab. mgr., 1991-92; product mgr. Moxtek Corp., Orem, Utah, 1992—. contbr. articles to profl. jours. Bishop Ch. LDS, Orem, 1992—; bd. dirs. Westbridge Homeowners Assn., Provo, 1988-92. Trustee scholarship Brigham Young U., 1979. Mem. AAAS, Am. Chem. Soc., Sigma Xi. Home: 1491 S 135th West Orem UT 84058 Office: Moxtek Corp 452 W 1260 N Orem UT 84057

TURNER, FLORENCE FRANCES, ceramist; b. Detroit, Mar. 9, 1926; d. Paul Pokrywka and Catherine Gagal; m. Dwight Robert Turner, Oct. 23, 1948; children: Thomas Michael, Nancy Louise, Richard Scott, Garry Robert. Student, Oakland C.C., Royal Oak, Mich., 1975-85, U. Ariz., Yuma, 1985, U. Las Vegas, 1989—. Pres., founder Nev. Clay Guild, Henderson, 1990—; workshop leader Greenfield Village, Dearborn, Mich., 1977-78, Plymouth (Mich.) Hist. Soc., 1979, Las Vegas Sch. System, 1989-90, Detroit Met. area, 1977-85. Bd. dir. Las Vegas Art Mus., 1987-91; So. Nev. Creative Art Ctr., Las Vegas, 1990—, rec. sec. Mem. Las Vegas Gem Club, Nev. Camera Club, Golden Key, Phi Kappa Phi. Office: Nev Clay Guild PO Box 50004 Henderson NV 89016

TURNER, GEOFFREY WHITNEY, information security consultant; b. Highland Park, Ill., Sept. 4, 1948; s. Patricia (Busby) Turner; m. Roberta Marie Tidball, Sept. 28, 1969; children: Scott Whitney, Grant Stansfield, Katherine Cass. BA, Oreg. State U., 1973; MA, Naval Postgrad Sch., 1979. Commd. ensign USN, 1973, advanced through grades to comdr., 1982; communications officer USS La Moore County (LST 1194) USN, Norfolk, Va., 1974-76; Soviet navy analyst Naval Ops. Intelligence Ctr. USN, Washington, 1976-77; spl. asst. to nat. intelligence officer CIA, Washington, 1977; intelligence officer Task Force 61 Mediterranean Sea, 1979-80; intelligence officer USS Carl Vinson (CVN-70) USN, Alameda, Calif., 1983-85; chief target systems br. Joint Strategic Target Planning Staff USN, Omaha, 1980-83; ret. USN, 1985; comdr. USNR, 1988—; v.p. Bank Am., San Francisco, 1985-88; sr. mgmt. cons. SRI Internat., Menlo Park, Calif., 1988-92; tech. dir. Mantech Strategic Assn. Ltd.; chmn. data encryption com. Am. Nat. Standards Inst., Washington, 1986-87, mem. fin. svcs. security com., 1986—; mem. Internat. bd. editors Computers and Security, Netherlands, 1987—; mem. steering com. Nat. Computer and Telecommunications Security Coun., Washington, 1987—. Decorated Def. Meritorious Svc. medal. Mem. Info. Systems Security Assn., Armed Forces Communications and Electronics Assn.

TURNER, HAL WESLEY, state agency administrator; b. Winchester, Mass., Nov. 18, 1932; s. Wesley Francis and Anna Louise (Hodgkins) T.; m. Patricia Frances Heastan, Mar. 31, 1984; children: Julie, Karen. BA, Sioux Falls (S.D.) Coll., 1955. Mem. tech. and mgmt. staff Boeing Computer Svcs., Seattle, 1958-69; mgr. prodn. systems Kennecott Copper Corp., Salt Lake City, 1970-71; dir. MIS State of Idaho, Boise, 1971-74, adminstr. of budget, 1974-77; sales assoc. White Riedel Realtors, Boise, 1978-81; chief dep. state auditor Idaho State Auditor's Office, Boise, 1981—; pres., Student Loan Fund Idaho, Inc., Fruitland, 1978—. Idaho Com. for Employer Support of Guard and Reserve. With U.S. Army, 1955-57. Mem. Nat. Assn. State Auditors, Nat. Assn. Govt'l Accts., Comptrollers, Treasurers, Elks, Broadmore Country Club. Democrat. Methodist. Home: 3512 S Brookshore Pl Boise ID 83706-5582 Office: State Auditors Office 700 W State St Boise ID 83720-0001

TURNER, HERBERT BRANCH, designer, builder, artist; b. Mt. Vernon, N.Y., Mar. 20, 1926; s. Oscar Oliver and Irene (Branch) T.; m. Marysa Senn, Oct. 5, 1956 (div.) children: Brent Stockton, Rachel. BS, U.S. Military Acad., 1949. Designer, artist Herbert Turner Designs, Del Mar, Calif., 1952—; prin. Turner Construction, Del Mar, 1954-80, Turner & Assoc., Del Mar, 1968—. Featured in Am. Artist Mag., 1962; exhibited in group shows at Laguna Beach Art Mus., La Jolla Mus., Tex. Fine Arts Assn., Audibon Artist, N.Y.C., Allied Artist, N.Y.C., Purdue U. Chmn. Pub. Access TV Channel 37, Del Mar, Calif., 1984—, Flood Control Com., San Diego County, 1986—; dir. Artists' Space at South Fair, Del Mar, 1987—; mem. Escondido Devel. Adv. Com., 1988—. With U.S. Army, 1945-49. Recipient Citation A.I.A., Sunset Mag., San Francisco, 1974; award of Excellence Builder Industry Assn., 1982, Historic Preservation award, Save Our Heritage Orgn., San Diego, 1984. Mem. Assn. Bldg. Contractors (bd. dirs., legis. chmn. 1976-77), San Diego Mus. Artists' Guild. Republican. Methodist. Home: 606 Zuni Dr Del Mar CA 92014-2449

TURNER, JAMES EDWARD, JR., lawyer; b. Phoenix, Aug. 8, 1942; s. James Edward Turner and Helen Blanche (Whitaker) Greene; m. Lana Sue Rollans, Nov. 3, 1974. BA, U. Va., 1964, JD, 1972; MBA, U. Tex., Arlington, 1983. Bar: Tex. 1972, U.S. Supreme Ct. 1976, N.Y. 1983, Calif. 1988. Legal adminstr. Alcon Labs. Inc., Ft. Worth, 1972-77; trademark atty. Fitch, Even, Tabin & Flannery, Chgo., 1977-78; sr. counsel Alcon Labs. Inc., 1978-84; legal counsel The Salk Inst., La Jolla, Calif., 1984-85; gen. counsel The Salk Inst. Biotech., La Jolla, Calif., 1985—. With USN, 1964-69, USNR, 1969-91. Mem. ABA, Am. Corp. Counsel Assn., Tex. Bar Assn., N.Y. State Bar Assn., Calif. State Bar Assn., Navy Reserve Assn., Reserve Officers Assn., VFW, Am. Legion, Navy League, Masons, Scottish Rite, Shriners, E Clampus Vitus. Republican. Methodist. Home: 1445 Ventana Dr Escondido CA 92029 Office: SIBIA Inc 505 Coast Blvd S Ste 300 La Jolla CA 92037

TURNER, JOHN FREELAND, foundation administrator, former federal agency administrator, former state senator; b. Jackson, Wyo., Mar. 3, 1942; s. John Charles and Mary Louise (Mapes) T.; m. Mary Kay Brady, 1969; children: John Francis, Kathy Mapes, Mark Freeland. BS in Biology, U. Notre Dame, 1964; postgrad., U. Innsbruck, 1964-65, U. Utah, 1965-66; MS in Ecology, U. Mich., 1968. Rancher, outfitter Triangle X Ranch, Moose, Wyo.; chmn. bd. dirs. Bank of Jackson Hole; photo-journalist; state senator from Sublette State of Wyo., Teton County, 1974-89; mem. Wyo. Ho. of Reps. Teton County, 1970-74; pres. Wyo. Senate, 1987-89; chmn. legis., minerals bus. and econ. devel. com. Teton County, Wyo., 1987-89; dir. Fish and Wildlife Svc. Dept. Interior, Washington, 1989-93; v.p. sustained devel. Conservation Fund, Arlington, Va., 1993—; vice chmn. Sec. of Interior's Nat. Parks Adv. Bd.; statewide coordinating Task Force U. Wyo.; exec. commn. State Reps., adv. council Coll. Agriculture U. Wyo.; mem. Teton Sci. Sch. Bd., Nat. Wetland Forum, 1983, 87; mem. exec. com. Council of State Govt.; chmn. Pride in Jackson Hole Campaign, 1986; bd. dirs. Wyo. Waterfowl Trust; chmn. steering com. of UN Convention on Wetlands of Internat. Importance, 1990—; head U.S. delegation to Convention. on Internat. Trade Endangered Species. Author: The Magnificent Bald Eagle: Our National Bird, 1971. Mem. Western River Guides Assn., Jackson Hole Guides and Outfitters. Named Citizen of Yr. County of Teton, 1984; recipient Nat. Conservation Achievement award Nat. Wildlife Fedn., 1984, Sheldon Coleman Great Outdoors award, 1990, Pres.'s Pub. Svc. award The Nature Conservatory, 1990, Stewardship award Audobon Soc., 1992, Nat. Wetland Achievement award Ducks Unlimited, 1993. Republican. Roman Catholic.

TURNER, LILLIAN ERNA, nurse; b. Coalmont, Colo., Apr. 22, 1918; d. Harvey Oliver and Erna Lena (Wackwitz) T. BS, Colo. State U., 1940, Columbia U., 1945; cert. physician asst., U. Utah, 1978. Commd. 2d lt. Nurse Corps, U.S. Army, 1945; advanced through grades to lt. comdr. USPHS, 1964; dean of women U. Alaska, Fairbanks, 1948-50; head nurse Group Health Hosp., Seattle, 1950-53; adviser to chief nurse Hosp. Am. Samoa, Pago Pago, 1954-60; head nurse Meml. Hosp., Twin Falls, Idaho, 1960-61; shift supr. Hosp. Lago Oil and Transport, Siero Colorado, Aruba, 1961-63; nurse adv. Province Hosp., Danang, South Vietnam, 1964-69, Cho Quan Hosp., South Vietnam, 1970-72; chief nurse, advisor Truk Hosp., Moen, Ea. Caroline Islands, 1972-74; nurse advisor Children's Med. Relief Internat., South Vietnam, 1975; physician's asst. U. Utah, 1976-78, Wagon Circle Med. Clinic, Rawlins, Wyo., 1978-89, Energy Basin Clinic Carbon County Meml. Hosp., Hanna, Wyo., 1989—. Named Nat. Humanitarian Pa. of the Yr., 1992, 93. Mem. Wyo. Acad. Physician Assts. (bd. dirs. 1982-83), Am. Acad. Physician Assts., Nat. Assn. Physician Assts. Home: PO Box 337 Hanna WY 82327-0337

TURNER, MARSHALL CHITTENDEN, JR., venture capitalist; b. Santa Monica, Calif., Oct. 10, 1941; s. Marshall C. and Winifred K. (Hudson) T.; m. Ann Curran, Feb. 6, 1965; children: Erin, Benjamin, Brian. BSME, Stanford U., 1964, MS in Product Design, 1965; MBA, Harvard U., 1970. Indsl. designer Mattel Toy Co., Hawthorne, Calif., 1965; rsch. engr. GM Defense Rsch. Lab., Santa Barbara, Calif., 1965-66; med. engr. NIH, Bethesda, Md., 1966-68; White House fellow Washington, 1970-71; dir., ops. coord. EPA, Washington, 1971-73; assoc. Crocker Assocs., L.P., San Francisco, 1973-75; v.p. fin., chief oper. officer Sierra R.R., 1973-75; pres. Liquid Crystal Tech., Inc., San Leandro, Calif., 1975-80; gen. ptnr. Taylor & Turner, San Francisco, 1981—; bd. dirs. Image Data Corp., San Antonio, CongniSeis Devel. Corp., Houston, Alliance Tech. Fund, Corp. Pub. Broadcasting, Washington, chmn., 1990-92, Ramanco Internat., Inc., Wilmington, Mass., Pub. Broadcasting Svc., Arlington, Va. Contbr. articles to profl. jours. Bd. dirs. Sta. KQED, Inc., San Francisco, 1977-87, chmn., 1985-86; trustee Reed Union Sch. Dist., Tiburon, Calif., 1977-81, chmn., 1979-81; bd. dirs. George Lucas Ednl. Found., San Rafael, Calif., 1992—, Pub. Broadcasting Avc., Alexandria, Va., 1993—; trustee Mus. TV and Radio, N.Y.C., 1991-92. Lt. USPHS, 1966-68. Recipient Creative design award Machinery Inst., 1965. Office: Penthouse 10 220 Montgomery St San Francisco CA 94104

TURNER, MAUREEN BARBARA, mathematics educator, researcher; b. Washington, July 20, 1936; d. Max and Florence Estelle (Tanenbaum) T. AB, Cornell U., 1956; postgrad., Johns Hopkin's U., 1960; MA, Columbia U., 1961; postgrad., U. Calif., Berkeley, 1965. Teaching asst. in maths. Columbia U., N.Y.C., 1960-61, U. Calif., Berkely, 1962, 63; instr. in maths. Reed Coll., Portland, Oreg., 1965-66; prof. maths. Calif. State U., Long Beach, 1966—. Bd. reviewers Col. Maths. Jour.; contbr. articles to profl. jours. Mem. Phi Beta Kappa, Phi Kappa Phi, Alpha Epsilon Delta. Office: Calif State U Math Dept 1250 N Bellflower Blvd Long Beach CA 90840-0001

TURNER, MICHAEL SETH, public relations and marketing executive; b. San Diego, July 28, 1948; s. Charles Irwin and Lee (Yomin) T., m. Marlene Carol Meyer, Sept. 7, 1981. BS, San Diego State U., 1970; MS, Iowa State U., 1971. Instr. U. Nebr., Omaha, 1971-72; news dir. Sta. KFJM-AM-FM, Grand Forks, N.D., 1972-78; sta. mgr. Sta. KUOP-FM, Stockton, Calif., 1978-79; dir. pub. relations Sta. KCSN-FM, Northridge, Calif., 1980-92; prin. Turner-Meyer Communications, Chatsworth, Calif., 1989—; dir. pub. rels. Jewish Home for Aging, Reseda, Calif., 1992—; cons. Calif. State U., Northridge, 1987. Host, producer radio shows Morning Jour., 1972-78, L.A. Connection, 1980-87; freelance restaurant critic, 1989—. Bd. dirs. Pine-to-Prairie coun. Girl Scouts U.S., 1972-78; bd. dirs. N. Hills Jaycees, 1980-84, Northridge Recreation and Parks Festival, 1982-84; mem. communication coms. Greater L.A. affiliate Am. Heart Assn., 1989—, N. Angeles region United Way, 1989—. Participant Rotary Internat. Group Study Exchange, Philippines, 1978; named one of Outstanding Young Men of Am., U.S. Jaycees, 1982-84. Mem. So. Calif. Broadcasters, Pub. Interest Radio and TV Ednl. Soc. (pres. 1984-87), Publicity Club L.A. (pres. 1988-89). Home: 10341 Canoga Ave Apt 29 Chatsworth CA 91311-2213

TURNER, MICHAEL WALLACE, lawyer; b. Cheltenham, Gloucester, Eng., Oct. 28, 1960; came to U.S., 1989; s. George Hamilton Turner and Julia Mae Patricia (Wallace) Wales; m. Linda Turner, Aug. 25, 1984; children: Gregory James, Alice Mary. Law, U. Reading, Berkshire, Eng., 1981; Solicitors Exam, Coll. Law, Chester, Eng., 1982. Solicitor Supreme Ct. Eng. and Wales 1984, Fgn. Legal Cons. Calif. 1989. Articled clk. Wilde Sapte, London and N.Y.C., 1982-84; asst. solicitor Wilde Sapte, London, 1984-85, Wiggin and Co., Cheltenham, Eng., 1985-89; ptnr. Wiggin and Co., L.A., 1989—. 1st English atty. admitted as Fgn. Legal Cons. in Calif., State Bar Calif., 1989. Mem. Law Soc. Eng. Church of Eng. Home: 376 Aderno Way Pacific Palisades CA 90272-3344 Office: Wiggin and Co 2121 Ave of the Stars 6th Fl Los Angeles CA 90067

TURNER, MORTIMER DARLING, research geologist; b. Greeley, Colo., Oct. 24, 1920; s. Clarence Earnest and Satia May (Darling) T.; m. Laura Mercedes Perez-Mendez, Jan. 25, 1945 (dec. Mar. 1965); children: Satia Elisa, Ylla Sofia, Robert Stuart; m. Joanne Kay Church, Dec. 5, 1965; 1 stepchild, Christopher Scott Dort. BS, U. Calif., Berkeley, 1943; student, Va. Polytechnic Inst., 1943-44; MS, U. Calif., Berkeley, 1954; PhD, U. Kans., 1972. Registered geologist and engring. geologist, Calif. Asst. mining geologist Calif. Div. Mines and Geology, San Francisco, 1949-54; state geologist P.R. Econ. Devel. Adminstrn., Santurce, 1954-59; phys. sci. adminstr. NSF, Washington, 1959-61, program mgr. polar earth scis., 1965-85; rsch. assoc. U. Kans., Lawrence, 1962-65, Tex. Tech U., Lubbock, 1985; rsch. assoc. Inst. Arctic and Alpine Rsch., U. Colo., Boulder, 1988—; assoc. professorial lectr. George Washington U., Washington, 1972-88, U. Colo., Denver, 1990—; adj. prof. Quaternary studies U. Maine, Orono, 1985—; lectr. Antarctica Expdn. Cruises, Seattle, 1990; cons., ptnr. JCT Enterprises, Boulder, 1977—; chmn. sci. coun. Ctr. for Study of First Ams., Orono, 1989—. Editor: Clays and Clay Technology, 1957, Geology of Central Transantarctic Mountains, 1987; contbr. articles to profl. jours. With U.S. Army, 1943-46. Recipient Presdl. award for mgmt. improvement, White House, 1975; Fellow Shell Oil, 1964. Fellow Geol. Soc. Am.; mem. Internat. Geol. Congress (v.p. 1956), Antarctican Soc. (dir., pres. 1959-68), numerous other sci. and engring. socs. Democrat. Home: 701 Crescent Dr Boulder CO 80303-2712 Office: Univ Colo INSTARR Campus Box 450 Boulder CO 80309-0450

TURNER, NANCY KAY, art educator, artist, art critic; b. Bronx, N.Y., Feb. 26, 1947; d. Murray Aaron and Florence (Drimer) Turner; m. Hoyt Roger Hilsman, July 9, 1982; 1 child, Michael Garrett. Student, Skowhegan Sch. Painting, Sculp, 1966; BA, CUNY, 1967; MA, U. Calif., Berkeley, 1969. Cert. secondary tchr., jr. coll. tchr., Calif. Art instr. Thomas Knowlton Jr. High Sch., South Bronx, N.Y., 1970-72, San Dieguito High Sch., Encinitas, Calif., 1975-77, San Diego City Coll., 1973-79, Mira Costa Coll., Oceanside, Calif., 1978-79, Loyola High Sch., L.A., 1979—, RISD, 1985; adj. prof. U. So. Calif., L.A., 1985, UCLA extension, 1987; asst. prof. Glendale (Calif.) Community Coll., 1979—, gallery dir., 1990-91; art critic Art Week mag., San Jose, Calif., 1984-91, Art Scene, 1989—. Exhibited in numerous one woman shows and group exhbns.; contbr. revs. to profl. publs.; contbg. editor Artweek, Artscene. Bd. dirs. Woman's Bldg., L.A., 1987-88, mem. gallery com., 1988—; bd. dirs. San Diego Mus. Art, 1975. Recipient 1st award San Diego City/County Art Educators Exhibit, 1975, Escondido (Calif.) Regional Arts Gallery, 1976. Mem. Calif. Art Educator's Assn. (Douc Langur award 1987), Women's Caucus for Arts, So. Calif. Women's Caucus for Arts (equity in arts com.), Art Educators L.A. (exec. bd. 1984-87). Office: Loyola High Sch 1901 Venice Blvd Los Angeles CA 90006-4496

TURNER, NORRIS, marketing professional; b. Angelina, Tex., May 3, 1934; s. Ezra and Frankie Turner; m. Katherine Fields, Aug. 16, 1962; 1 child, Tammie Diatrice. BS, Fisk U., 1968. Cert. real estate appraiser; lic. notary pub., ins. agt. Admission officer West Point N.Y., L.A., 1971; dir. vets. programs, profl. recorder, in-sch. coord. L.A. Urban League, 1983; loan officer Empire of Am., Inglewood, Calif., 1983-86; account exec. Imperial Thrift & Loan, Burbank, Calif., 1986-88; v.p., dir. The Mortgage Acad., Ventura, Calif., 1988—; instr. Compton (Calif.) Coll., 1977-78. Author: A Balance Approach to Career Training, 1992. HAC mem. Century Freeway, State of Calif., 1982; chairperson L.A. City Vets. Svcs., 1980-81; treas. reelection svc. L.A. Calif. Reps., 1983; pres. Luth. Day-Care Sch., 1988-89; mem., vol. L.A. Urban League, 1990-92; v.p. local dist. Rep. party, 1987-88. With U.S. Army, 1956-58. Recipient awards L.A. City Coun., 1980, Pres. U.S.A., 1978-79, Cert. of Appreciation U.S. Mil. Acad., 1980, Hon. Admissions Officer award U.S. Mil. Acad., 1980, award L.A. Urban League, 1981-82. Mem. Am. Banking Assn. (treas. 1980-81). Lutheran. Home: 8813 4th Ave Inglewood CA 90305

TURNER, PAUL JESSE, environmental services administrator; b. Culver City, Calif., Jan. 15, 1948; s. Jesse Harold and Mildred Aileen (Roney) T.; m. Georgia Christine Baker, Feb. 25, 1969 (div. Oct. 1983); children: Patrick, Molly; m. Sharon Edythe Scranton, Dec. 26, 1983; two adopted children: Barry, Troy. BS in Biochemistry, U. Calif., Riverside, 1965, MS in Plant Physiology, 1973; PhD in Phys. Chemistry, U. Calif., Santa Barbara, 1979. Post doctoral fellow U. Conn. Dept. Chemistry, 1979-81; asst. prof. chemistry Bucknell U. Dept. Chemistry, Lewisburg, Pa., 1981-85; mgr. hazardous waste facilities Battelle-Pacific N.W. Labs., Richland, Wash., 1985—; tech. expert Internat. Standards Orgn., 1988—. Contbr. articles to profl. jours. Commr. Richard Housing Authority, 1988-91; patrolman Richland Police Dept., 1989—. Fellow N.Y. Acad. Scis. Home: 2102 Davison Ave Richland WA 99352-2017 Office: Battelle Pacific NW Lab PO Box 999 Richland WA 99352-0999

TURNER, PETER HELMER, engineering company executive; b. Macon, Mo., July 17, 1934; s. Clarence Helmer and Sarah Amelia (Cartmell) H.; m. Sally Ann Hawekotte, 1956 (div. 1960); children: Jennifer Lynn, Kimberly Sue; m. Carolyn Lee Behymer, Oct. 21, 1967. BSEE, U. Mo., 1958. Acoustis lab. dir. Gen. Dynamics Corp., Pomona, Calif., 1956-57; mfg. engr. Gen. Dynamics Corp., 1957-58, mgmt. trainee, 1958-59, staff engr., purch, 1959-65; chief engr. Sargent Industries Kahr Div., San Fernando, Calif., 1966-81; v.p., gen. mgr. Networks Elect U.S. Bearing, Chatsworth, Calif., 1981-84; pvt. practice Burbank, Calif., 1984—; v.p. engring. S.W. Products Co., Irwindale, Calif., 1985-91; v.p., gen. mgr. Networks Elect U.S. Bearing, Chatsworth, Calif., 1991—; v.p. L.A. Area Coun. Nat. Mgmt. Assn., 1962-65; mem., group leader Airframe Control Bearing Group, Warminster, Pa., 1966—. Patentee in field. Mem. Navy League (dir. Bel Aire coun.), Masons (master lodge 1979, 81, 82, 83, Hiram award La Canada Oakwood lodge 1985), Shriners (pres. Glendale Shrine Club 1983), Phi Mu Alpha. Republican. Presbyterian. Home: 2850 Delk Rd Apt 14J Marietta GA 30067 Office: US Bearing 9750 De Soto Ave Chatsworth CA 91311-4485

TURNER, RALPH HERBERT, sociologist, educator; b. Effingham, Ill., Dec. 15, 1919; s. Herbert Turner and Hilda Pearl (Bohn) T.; m. Christine Elizabeth Hanks, Nov. 2, 1943; children: Lowell Ralph, Cheryl Christine. B.A., U So. Calif., 1941, M.A., 1942; postgrad., U. Wis., 1942-43; Ph.D., U. Chgo., 1948. Rsch. assoc. Am. Coun. Race Relations, 1947-48; faculty UCLA, 1948—, prof. sociology and anthropology, 1959-90, prof. emeritus, 1990—, chmn. dept. sociology, 1963-68; chmn. Acad. Senate U. Calif. System, 1983-84; bd. dirs. Founds. Fund for Rsch. in Psychiatry; vis. summer prof. U. Wash., 1960, U. Hawaii, 1962; vis. scholar Australian Nat. U., 1972; vis. prof. U. Ga., 1975, Ben Gurion U., Israel, 1983; vis. fellow Nuffield Coll. Oxford U., 1980; disting. vis. prof. Am. U., Cairo, Egypt, 1983; adj. prof. China Acad. Social Scis., Beijing, People's Republic China, 1986; faculty rsch. lectr. UCLA, 1986-87. Author: (with L. Killian) Collective Behavior, 1957, 2d edit., 1972, 3d edit., 1987, The Social Context of Ambition, 1964, Robert Park on Social Control and Collective Behavior, 1967, Family Interaction, 1970, Earthquake Prediction and Public Policy, 1975, (with J. Nigg, D. Paz, B. Young) Community Response to Earthquake Threat in Southern California., 1980, (with J. Nigg and D. Paz) Waiting for Disaster, 1986; editorial cons., 1959-62; editor: Sociometry, 1962-64; acting editor: Ann. Rev. of Sociology, 1977-78; assoc. editor, 1978-79, editor, 1980-86; adv. editor: Am. Jour. Sociology, 1954-56, Sociology and Social Research, 1961-74; editorial staff: Am. Sociol. Rev., 1955-56; assoc. editor: Social Problems, 1959-62, 67-69; cons. editor: Sociol. Inquiry, 1968-73, Western Sociol. Rev., 1975-79; mem. editorial bd. Mass Emergencies, 1975-79, Internat. Jour. Critical Sociology, 1974-76, Symbolic Interaction, 1977-90. Mem. behavioral scis. study sect. NIH, 1961-66, chmn., 1963-64; dir.-at-large Social Sci. Rsch. Coun., 1965-66; chmn. panel on pub. policy implications of earthquake predictions Nat. Acad. Scis., 1974-75, also mem. earthquake study del. to Peoples Republic of China, 1976; mem. policy adv. bd. So. Calif. Earthquake Preparedness program, 1987-92, mem. com. social edn. and action L.A. Presbytery, 1954-56. Served to lt. (j.g.) USNR, 1943-46. Recipient Faculty prize Coll. Letters and Scis. UCLA, 1985; Faculty Rsch. fellow Social Sci. Rsch. Coun., 1953-56; Sr. Fulbright scholar U.K., 1956-57; Guggenheim fellow, U.K., 1964-65. Mem. AAAS (exch. del. to China 1988), AAUP, Am. Sociol. Assn. (coun. 1959-64, chmn. social psychology sect. 1960-61, pres. 1968-69, chmn. sect. theoretical sociology 1973-74, chmn. collective behavior and social movements sect. 1983-84, Cooley-Mead award 1987), Pacific Sociol. Assn. (pres. 1957), Internat. Sociol. Assn. (coun. 1974-82, v.p. 1978-82), Soc. Study Social Problems (exec. com. 1962-63), Soc. for Study Symbolic Interaction (pres. 1982-83, Charles Horton Cooley award 1978, George Herbert Mead award 1990), Sociol. Rsch. Assn. (pres. 1989-90), Am. Coun. of Learned Soc. (exec. com. of coun. 1990-93), UCLA Emeriti Assn. (pres. 1992-93). Home: 1126 Chautauqua Blvd Pacific Palisades CA 90272-3808 Office: UCLA 405 Hilgard Ave Los Angeles CA 90024-1301

TURNER, RALPH JAMES, artist; b. Ashland, Oreg., Oct. 24, 1935; s. Ralph Edwin and Ruth Marie (DeLap) T.; m. Phyllis Irene Wilson, Feb. 25, 1956; children: Sage Russell, Theresa Dawn, Rosalind Ruth, Alys Renee. Diploma, Pacific N.W. Coll. of Art, 1958; BA, Reed Coll., 1958; MFA, U. Oreg., 1962. Tchr. Seward (Alaska) Pub. Schs., 1959-60; teaching asst. Univ. Oreg., Eugene, 1961-62; instr. Univ. Ariz., Tucson, 1962-65, rsch. assoc. Lunar & Planetary Lab., 1964-75; asst. prof. Syracuse (N.Y.) Univ., 1966-70; instr. Pima Community Coll., Tucson, 1970-72, Linfield Coll., McMinnville, Oreg., 1975-80, Chemeketa Community Coll., Salem, Oreg., 1976-80; dir. Rock Creek Experimental Sta., Sheridan, Oreg., 1973—; coord. Art Program, Pima Coll., Tucson, 1970-71. Group shows include 150 Years of Martian Cartography, Staatsbibliothek, Berlin, 1993; permanent exhbns. of planetary models include Smithsonian Inst., NASA hdqs., U. Ariz, Griffith Observatory, 1972-83; murals include Greenly, Colo., Wilsonville, Oreg., Corvallis, Oreg., Portland, Oreg., 1982-92. Pres. Willamina (Oreg.) Sheridan Grand Ronde Kiwanis, 1984-85. Recipient fellowship Nat. Endowment for Humanities, Washington, 1972-73. Mem. Oreg. Art Inst., Internat. Soc. for the Arts, Sci. and Tech., Internat. Sculpture Ctr. Democrat. Unitarian. Home and Office: Rock Creek Experimental Sta 14320 Rock Creek Rd Sheridan OR 97378-9735

TURNER, ROBERT LEE, college administrator; b. Chapel Hill, Tex., Mar. 23, 1939; s. Leon and Lillian Turner; m. Ella M. Brooks, Apr. 4, 1960; children: Karen, Linda. BS, Coll. of S.W., Hobbs, N.Mex., 1972; MBA, Ea. N.Mex. U., 1979; postgrad., No. Colo. Coll., 1981. Truck driver City of Hobbs, N.Mex., 1958-67; miner S.W. Potash Co., Carlsbad, N.Mex., 1967; roustabout Amoco, Eunice, N.Mex., 1967-70, pumper, 1970-73; dir. student ctr. N.Mex. Jr. Coll., Hobbs, N.Mex., 1973-89, fin. aid officer, 1989—. Mem. United Blood Svc. Com., Lubbock, Tex., 1987-90, N.Mex. Health Svc., Santa Fe, N.Mex., 1986-90; treas. Scharbauer St. Ch.; co-chair Commn. on Higher Edn. Com., 1991-92. Mem. NAACP (Outstanding Educator 1991), N.Mex. Jr. Coll. Alumni Assn. (sec. 1991—), Hobbs C. of C. Democrat. Mem. Ch. of Christ. Home: 1117 W Taos Hobbs NM 88240 Office: N Mex Jr Coll 5317 Lovington Hwy Hobbs NM 88240

TURNER, ROGER ORLANDO, quality assurance director, microbiologist; b. Warren, Ohio, May 15, 1938; s. Clarence Ward and Rena Marie (Scot) T.; m. Elizabeth Yanda, Dec. 7, 1965; children: David Alan, Michael Scot, Taylor Sue. BA, Trinity U., 1968; postgrad., Calif. State U., L.A., 1975-76, Marshall U., 1985-87. Microbiologist Becton-Dickinson Inc., Raleigh, N.C., 1968-70; lab. supr. Abbott Labs., Rocky Mount, N.C., 1970-74; lab. mgr. Abbott Sci. Products Divsn., L.A., 1974-75; prodn. supr. Rachelle Labs. Inc., Long Beach, Calif., 1976-78; quality assurance mgr. Inspiron divsn. C.R. Bard Inc., Rancho Cucamonga, Calif., 1978-82; dir. quality assurance Cilco Inc./Intra Optics Inc., Huntington West, Va., 1982-88; ops. mgr. ARC, L.A., 1988-89; dir. product quality Kabi Pharmacia Ophthalmics Inc., Monrovia, Calif., 1989—. Mem. curriculum bd. Chaffey Coll., Rancho Cucamonga, 1979-80. With USAF, 1962-66. Mem. Am. Soc. Quality Control, Am. Mgmt. Assn. Republican. Episcopalian. Office: Kabi Pharmacia Ophthalmics 605 E Huntington Dr Monrovia CA 91017

TURNER, RONALD LEE, accountant; b. Denver, Nov. 4, 1947; s . Howard Lee and Gail Francis (Crane) T.; m. Donna Arlene Turk, Sept. 1976. BSBA, U. Denver, 1969. Sr. acct. Coopers & Lybrand, L.A., 1969-72; sr. auditor City Investing Co., Beverly Hills, Calif., 1972-74; internal audit mgr. Warner Communications Inc., N.Y.C., 1974-76; internat. audit mgr. Warner Communications Inc., London, 1976-78; dir. fin. systems Elektra Asylum Records, L.A., 1978-79; dir. internal audit Gen. Automation Inc., Anaheim, Calif., 1979-81; v.p. internal audit Browning-Ferris Industries, Houston, 1981-88; mgr. internal audit Teledyne Inc., L.A., 1988, asst. to corp. treas., 1988-89, mgr. spl. projects, 1989, fin. advisor to segment pres., 1990-92, fin. mgr. restructured and divested ops., 1993—. Mem. AICPA, Calif. Soc. CPAs, Inst. Internal Auditors. Home: PO Box 34310 Los Angeles CA 90034-0310 Office: Teledyne Inc 1901 Ave of Stars Ste 1800 Los Angeles CA 90069

TURNER, ROSS JAMES, investment corporation executive; b. Winnipeg, Man., Can., May 1, 1930; permanent U.S. resident, 1980; s. James Valentine and Gretta H. (Ross) T.; children: Ralph, Rick, Tracy. U. Man. Extension, 1951, Banff Sch. Advanced Mgmt., 1956. Various sr. operating and mgmt. positions Genstar Corp., San Francisco, 1961-76, chmn./pres., CEO, 1976-86, also bd. dirs.; chmn. Genstar Investment Corp., San Francisco, 1987—; bd. dirs. Rio Algom Ltd., Gt. West Life Assurance Co., Western Corp. Enterprises, Blue Shield of Calif., Guy F. Atkinson Co. of Calif. Bd. dirs. YMCA, San Francisco. Fellow Soc. Mgmt. Accts. Can.; mem. Toronto Club, Pacific Union Club, Rancho Santa Fe Golf Club, Peninsula Golf and Country Club, Loxahatchee Club. Office: Genstar Investment Corp Metro Tower Ste 1170 950 Tower Ln Foster City CA 94404-2121 also: Rio Algom Ltd, 120 Adelaide St W Ste 2600, Toronto, ON Canada M5H 1W5

TURNER, WALLACE L., journalist; b. Titusville, Fla., Mar. 15, 1921; s. Clyde H. and Ina B. (Wallace) T.; m. Pearl Burk, June 12, 1943; children: Kathleen Turner, Elizabeth Turner Everett. B.J., U. Mo., 1943; postgrad. (Nieman fellow), Harvard U., 1958-59. Reporter Springfield (Mo.) Daily News, 1943, Portland Oregonian, 1943-59; news dir. Sta. KPTV, Portland, 1959-61; asst. sec. HEW, Washington, 1961-62; reporter N.Y. Times, San Francisco, 1962—; bur. chief N.Y. Times, 1970-85, Seattle bur. chief, 1985-88. Author: Gamblers Money, 1965, The Morman Establishment, 1967. Recipient Heywood Broun award for reporting, 1952, 56; Pulitzer Prize for reporting, 1957. Office: Box 99269 Magnolia Sta Seattle WA 98199-4260

TURNER, WARREN AUSTIN, state senator; b. Berkeley, Calif., Dec. 21, 1926; s. Warren Mortimer and Rebecca Oline (Noer) T.; m. Daune Mackay, Mar. 29, 1952; children: Daune Scott Marable, Warren Adair, Alan Corey. BA, U. Calif., Berkeley, 1950, BS, 1952, MPH, 1958. Pub. acct. Price Waterhouse, San Francisco, 1951-52, A.W. Blackman, CPA, Las Vegas, 1952-56; asst. adminstr. Marin Gen. Hosp., San Rafael, Calif., 1958-60; assoc. dir. UCLA Hosp., 1960-68; founding adminstr. Walter O. Boswell Meml. Hosp., Sun City, Ariz., 1968-81; pres. Sun Health Corp., Sun City, 1981-90; Arizona state senator Phoenix, 1983-84; bd. dirs. Multi-Hosp. Mutual Ins. Co., Bannackburn, Ill.; active various senate coms., including appropriations, health/welfare and aging, vice-chmn. edn., natural resources, agrl. and environment. Served with USN, 1944-46. Mem. Ariz. Hosp. Assn. (pres., chmn., 1977-78), AHA Governing Coun. for Aging and Long-Term Care Ariz., Coop. Purchasing Assn. (pres. 1981-82, 87), Phoenix Regional Coun. (past pres.), Ariz. Acad., Ariz. State Health Planning Coun., Assn. High Medicare Hosps. (chmn. 1988-90), Lakes Club, Rotary. Republican.

TURNER, WILLIAM COCHRANE, international management consultant; b. Red Oak, Iowa, May 27, 1929; s. James Lyman and Josephine (Cochrane) T.; m. Cynthia Dunbar, July 16, 1955; children: Scott Christopher, Craig Dunbar, Douglas Gordon. BS, Northwestern U., 1952. Pres., chmn. bd. dirs. Western Mgmt. Cons., Inc., Phoenix, 1955-74, Western Mgmt. Cons. Europe, S.A., Brussels, 1968-74; U.S. amb., permanent rep. OECD, Paris, 1974-77, vice chmn. exec. com., 1976-77, U.S. rep. Energy Policy Com., 1976-77, mem. U.S. dels. internat. meetings, 1974-77; mem. western internat. trade group U.S. Dept. Commerce, 1972-74; chmn., chief exec. officer Argyle Atlantic Corp., Phoenix, 1977—; chmn. European adv. coun., 1981-88, Asia Pacific adv. coun.AT&T Internat., 1981-88; mem. European adv. coun. IBM World Trade Europe/Mid. East/Africa Corp., 1977-80; mem. Asia Pacific adv. coun. Am. Can Co., Greenwich, Conn., 1981-85, Gen. Electric of Brazil adv. coun. Gen. Electric Co., Coral Gables, Fla., 1979-81, Caterpillar of Brazil adv. council Caterpillar Tractor Co., Peoria, Ill., 1979-84, Caterpillar Asia Pacific Adv. Council, 1984-90, U.S. adv. com. Trade Negotiations, 1982-84; bd. dirs. Goodyear Tire & Rubber Co., Akron, Ohio, 1978—, Salomon Inc., N.Y.C., 1980-93, Nabisco Brands Inc., Parsippany, N.J., 1977-85, AT&T Internat., Inc., Basking Ridge, N.J., 1980-84, Pullman Inc., Chgo., 1977-80; mem. internat. adv. council Avon Products, Inc., N.Y.C., 1985—; mem. Spencer Stuart adv. council Spencer Stuart and Assocs., N.Y.C., 1984-90; chmn., mem. internat. adv. council Advanced Semiconductor Materials Internat. NV., Bilthoven, The Netherlands, 1985-88; bd. dirs. The Atlantic Council of the U.S., Washington, 1977—; co-chmn. internat. adv. bd. Univ. of Nations, Kona, Hawaii, 1985—; bd. dirs. World Wildlife Fund/U.S., 1983-85, World Wildlife Fund/The Conservation Found., 1985-89, Nat. Coun., 1989—; bd. govs. Joseph H. Lauder Inst. Mgmt. and Internat. Studies, U. Pa., 1983—; trustee Heard Mus., Phoenix, 1983-86, mem. nat. adv. bd., 1986—; trustee Am. Grad. Sch. Internat. Mgmt., 1972—, chmn. bd. trustees, 1987-89; bd. govs. Atlantic Inst. Internat. Affairs, Paris, 1977-88; adv. bd. Ctr. Strategic and Internat. Studies, Georgetown U., 1977-81; dir. Atlantic Inst. Found., Inc., N.Y.C., 1984-90; mem. European Community-U.S. Businessmen's Council, 1978-79; bd. govs. Am. Hosp. of Paris, 1974-77; trustee Nat. Symphony Orch. Assn., Washington, 1973-83, Am. Sch., Paris, 1976-77, Orme Sch., Mayer, Ariz., 1970-74, Phoenix Country Day Sch., 1971-74; mem. nat. coun. Salk Inst., 1978-82; mem. U.S. Adv. Com. Internat. Edn. and Cultural Affairs, 1969-74; nat. rev. bd. Ctr. Cultural and Tech. Interchange between East and West, 1970-74; mem. vestry Am. Cathedral, Paris, 1976-77; pres., bd. dirs. Phoenix Symphony Assn., 1969-70; chmn. Ariz. Joint Econ. Devel. Com., 1967-68; exec. com., bd. dirs. Ariz. Dept. Econ. Planning and Devel., 1968-70; chmn. bd. Ariz. Crippled Children's Services, 1964-65; treas. Ariz. Rep. Com., 1956-57; chmn. Ariz. Young Rep. League, 1955-56; chmn. bd. Mercy Internat., Inc., A Ministry of Youth With A Mission, Lindale, Tex., 1985—; mem. trade and environment com. Nat. Adv. Coun. for Environ. Policy and Tech.-U.S. EPA, Washington, 1991—; dir. exec. com., chmn. internat. com. Ariz. Econ. Coun., Phoenix, 1989-93; dir. exec. com. Orgn. for Free Trade and Devel., Phoenix, 1991—. Recipient East-West Ctr. Disting. Svc. award, 1977. Mem. U.S. Council Internat. Bus. (trustee, exec. com.), U.S.-Japan Bus. Council, Council Fgn. Relations, Council of Am. Ambs. (vice chmn. bd.), Nat. Adv. Council on Bus. Edn., Council Internat. Edn. Exchange, Greater Phoenix Leadership, Met. Club, Links Club (N.Y.C.), Plaza Club (Phoenix), Paradise Valley (Ariz.) Country Club. Episcopalian. Office: 4350 E Camelback Rd Ste 240B Phoenix AZ 85018-2701

TURNER, WILLIAM WEYAND, author; b. Buffalo, N.Y., Apr. 14, 1927; s. William Peter and Magdalen (Weyand) T.; m. Margaret Peiffer, Sept. 12, 1964; children: Mark Peter, Lori Ann. BS, Canisius Coll., 1949. Spl. agt. in various field offices FBI, 1951-61; free-lance writer Calif., 1963—; sr. editor Ramparts Mag., San Francisco, 1967—; investigator and cons. Nat. Wiretap Commn., 1975. Author: The Police Establishment, 1968, Invisible Witness: The Use and Abuse of the New Technology of Crime Investigation, 1968, Hoover's F.B.I.: The Men and the Myth, 1970, (with Warren Hinckle and Eliot Asinof) The Ten Second Jailbreak, 1973, (with John Christian) The Assassination of Robert F. Kennedy, 1978, (with Warren Hinckle) The Fish is Red: The Story of the Secret War Against Castro, 1981, updated, expanded, retitled as Deadly Secrets: The CIA-Mafia War Against Castro and the Assassination of JFK, 1992; contbg. author: Investigating the FBI, 1973; contbr. articles to popular mags. Dem. candidate for U.S. Congress, 1968. Served with USN, 1945-46. Mem. Authors Guild, Internat. Platform Assn., Press Club of San Francisco. Roman Catholic. Home and Office: 163 Mark Twain Ave San Rafael CA 94903-2820

TURNICK, MICHAEL, fire chief, consultant; b. Scalp Level, Pa., Oct. 25, 1925; s. Charles and Anna (Shenigo) T.; m. Alice Elezibeth Kennemer, June 28, 1944 (div. 1965); children: Carol Ann, Michael, Ronald; m. Mary Louise Udey, Aug. 15, 1969; stepchildren: Cynthia Ann, Steven, Neil. Student, Santa Rosa Jr. Coll., U. Calif., Berkeley, U. Calif., L.A., U. Calif., Davis. Logger Union Lumber Co., Ft. Bragg, Calif., 1946-51; lumberer Miranda, Calif., 1951-54; fireman Santa Rosa (Calif.) Fire Dept., 1954-57, capt., 1957-59, fire marshal, 1959-70, asst. fire chief, 1970-72, fire chief, 1972-89; interim fire chief Vallejo (Calif.) Fire Dept., 1992—. Bd. dirs. League Calif. Cities, 1982. With USN, 1943-46. Mem. Calif. Fire Chiefs Assn. (pres. 1984), Kiwanis (lt. gov. 1965, pres. 1966). Democrat. Roman Catholic. Home: 956 Wright St Santa Rosa CA 95404 Office: Fire Dept 1220 Marin St Vallejo CA 94590

TURNIPSEED, RICHARD RUSSELL, sales and leasing company executive; b. Miami, Fla., Dec. 30, 1953; s. Richard Davis and Joyce (Russell) T.; m. Margaret Ann Stroupe, 1982; children: Megan Bailey. BArch in Bldg. Constrn., U. Fla., 1976. Mgmt. trainee Hertz Equipment Rental, Tampa, Fla., 1976-77; br. mgr. Hertz Equipment Rental, Jackson, Miss., 1977-78; br. sales mgr. Gelco Space, Tampa, 1978-79, regional sales mgr., 1979-81, major projects mgr., 1981-84; div. sales mgr. Gelco Space, Chgo., 1984-86; div. gen. mgr. Gelco Space, Dallas, 1986-87, div. v.p., 1987-92; div. v.p. GE Capital Modular Space, 1992—; gen. contractor Gelco Space, Fla., 1973—, S.C., 1982—, La., 1982—, N.C., 1983—. Mem. Assoc. Gen. Contractors, Nat. Home Builders Assn., Modular Bldg. Inst. Home: 5570 Malachite Ave Alta Loma CA 91737 Office: GE Capital Modular Space 701 North Haven #250 Ontario CA 91764

TURNIPSEED, VICTORIA LEE, foundation administrator, public relations executive; b. Yakima, Wash., Jan. 13, 1951; d. Kenneth Ray and Shirley Ann (Dexter) T. BA, Okla. State U., 1973; MSW, U. Okla., 1975. Dir. med. social svcs. Espanola (N.Mex.) Hosp./S.W. Community Health Svcs., 1975-82; assoc. dir. devel. S.W. Community Health Svcs., Albuquerque, 1982-83; exec. dir. found. and pub. rels. Swedish Health Systems, Englewood, Colo., 1983-86; assoc. dir. resource devel. Scripps Meml. Hosp. Found., La Jolla, Calif., 1986-90; v.p. major gifts/found. rels. Sharp Hosps. Found., San Diego, 1990—; devel. cons. Child Abuse Prevention Found., San Diego, 1990, Internat. Aerospace Hall of Fame, San Diego, 1990, Assn. Western Hosps., San Francisco, 1983; program devel. cons. El Centro de Vida Nueva, Espanola, N.Mex. Contbr. articles to profl. jours. Mem. mktg. and spl. events com. LEAD San Diego, Inc., 1990—; vol. Planned Parenthood. Recipient Golden Leaflet award Colo. Hosp. Assn., 1985; named one of Outstanding Young Women of Am., 1983. Mem. Assn. for Healthcare Philanthropy (cert., nat. nominating com. 1990, sec. Region 9/regional conf. 1982-83, pub. rels. com. 1983, pub. rels. chmn. Regions 10 and 11/regional confs. 1988), Women's Inst. for Fin. Edn. (pub. rels. coord. 1988-90), Jr. League of San Diego (nominating com. 1991-92, project and com. chmn. 1987-90, endowment com. 1991-93), City Club of San Diego. Home: 1075 Klish Way Del Mar CA 92014 Office: Sharp Hosp Found 3131 Berger Ave Ste 200 San Diego CA 92123

TUROFF, MARSHALL ARNOLD, consulting company executive; b. Chgo., July 9, 1927; s. Nat and Bertha (Leavitt) T.; m. Gloria Auerbach, May 6, 1951 (div. Apr. 1983); children: Sara Ann, Barbara, Charles; m. Barbara Phillips, Apr. 18, 1983. BSc, Roosevelt Coll., 1950; MBA, U. Chgo., 1954. Asst. mgr. mktg. research Signode Steel Strapping Co., Chgo., 1951-55; mgr., mktg. research Precision Scientific Co., Chgo., 1955-56; dir., mktg. research Ohmite Corp., Skokie, Ill., 1956-57; cons. Booz, Allen & Hamilton, Chgo., 1957-60; pres., chief executive officer Turoff Industries, Ltd., Chgo., 1960-78, Jomar Warehousing Co., Chgo., 1966-78; pres. Photonic Environmental Corp., Chgo., 1972-78, Turoff Consulting Svcs., Chgo., 1978—. Treas. Jewish Vocational Service, Chgo., 1978-79, sec. 1979-80, v.p. 1980-81); pres. North Cen. Home Owners Assn., Skokie, Ill., 1963-65; mem. Bd. Zoning, Skokie, 1961-63. With U.S. Army Air Corps, 1945-46. Mem. Am. Soc. Profl. Cons. (pres. Midwest div. 1980-83), Am. Statistical Assn., Am. Mktg. Assn., Packaging Inst., USA (Chmn. and Excellence awards 1982). Republican. Jewish. Office: Turoff Consulting Svcs Inc PO Box 5740 Scottsdale AZ 85261-5740

TUROFF, RICHARD JOHN, insurance executive; b. Jersey City, Oct. 26, 1945; s. John Joseph and Claire (Sutowski) T.; m. Sandra Jean Battinelli, Aug. 26, 1967 (div. Apr. 1981); 1 child, Cheryll; m. Roma Bhojwani, May

24, 1981; 1 child, Nina Bhojwani. BA, Seton Hall U., 1967; MBA, U. Pa., 1971. CPCU. Mgr. Royal Ins. Co., N.Y., L.A., 1971-83; product mgr. Balboa Ins. Co., Newport Beach, Calif., 1983-84; asst. v.p. Transamerica Premier Ins. Co., Orange, Calif., 1984—. With USN, 1968-70. Mem. Orange County Chpt. of CPCU. Republican. Home: 2336 Wood Ct Claremont CA 91711

TURPIN, RICHARD HAROLD, electrical engineering educator; b. Manning, Iowa, July 30, 1939; s. Harold Bell and Esther (Christian) T.; m. Sylvia Sue Strong, Aug. 21, 1960; children: Timothy Richard, Mark Allan, Rebecca Sue. BSEE, BS in Math., Iowa State U., 1962; MSEE, U. So. Calif., 1964; PhD, Ohio State U., 1969. Technician Hercules Powder Co., Salt Lake City, 1961; elec. engr. Hughes Aircraft Co., Fullerton, Calif., 1962-64; rsch. assoc. electro-sci. lab. Ohio State U., Columbus, 1964-69; from asst. prof. to prof. sch. engring. and tech. Purdue U., Indpls., 1969-84; prof. U. Pacific, Stockton, Calif., 1984-90, chair elec. engring. dept., 1990—; cons. Internat. Energy Mgmt., Indpls., 1976-79, Processor Interface, Inc., Indpls., 1976-77, 84, Bell Telephone Lab., Indpls., 1980-81, Union Carbide, Indpls., 1980-81. Patentee in field. Mem. IEEE, Am. Soc. Engr. Edn., Phi Eta Sigma, Eta Kappa Nu, Tau Beta Pi, Sigma Xi. Office: U Pacific 3601 Pacific Ave Stockton CA 95211-0197

TURRELL, EUGENE SNOW, psychiatrist; b. Hyattsville, Md., Feb. 27, 1919; m. Denise Deuprey, Dec. 26, 1942 (div. Jan. 1976); children: David Hillyer, Gregory Sherman (dec.); m. Zenobia A. Hopper, Apr. 16, 1988; stepchildren: Elizabeth Ann Crofoot, Mary Jane Cooper. BS, Ind. U., 1939, MD, 1947. Diplomate Am. Bd. Psychiatry and Neurology. Intern Peter Bent Brigham Hosp., Boston, 1947-48; resident physician Kandakee (Ill.) State Hosp., 1948-49; clin. asst. psychiatry U. Calif., San Francisco, 1949-51; asst. prof. Ind. U. Sch. Medicine, 1952-53, assoc. prof., 1953-58; prof., chmn. dept. psychiatry Marquette U. Sch. Medicine, 1958-63, clin. prof. psychiatry, 1963-69; lectr. U. Calif., San Francisco, 1969-75; assoc. prof. Ind. U., 1975-80, prof., 1980-89, prof. emeritus, 1989—; staff psychiatrist San Diego County Psychiat. Hosp., 1990—; assoc. clin. prof. U. Calif., San Diego, 1991—; mem., bd. dirs. Community Addictions Svcs. Agy, Indpls., 1975-79, pres. bd., 1976-77. Contr. articles to profl. jours. Lt. USNR, 1950-52. Recipient Certs. of Appreciation Office Sci. Rsch. and Devel., 1945, VA, 1964, Ind. U. Found., 1966. Fellow Am. Psychiat. Assn. (life, Physician's Recognition award 1978); mem. AMA (Physician's Recognition award 1978-89), AAAS, Calif. State Med. Assn., Calif. State Psychiatric Assn., San Diego County Med. Soc., San Diego County Soc. Psychiat. Physicians, Sigma Xi, Alpha Omega Alpha. Democrat. Episcopalian. Office: San Diego County Psychiat Hosp 3851 Rosecrans St San Diego CA 92110-3190

TURRENTINE, HOWARD BOYD, federal judge; b. Escondido, Calif., Jan. 22, 1914; s. Howard and Veda Lillian (Maxfield) T.; m. Virginia Jacobsen, May 13, 1965 (dec.); children: Howard Robert, Terry Beverly; m. Marlene Lipsey, Nov. 1, 1992. A.B., San Diego State Coll., 1936; LL.B., U. So. Calif., 1939. Bar: Calif. 1939. Practiced in San Diego, 1939-68; judge Superior Ct. County of San Diego, 1968-70, U.S. Dist. Ct. (so. dist.) Calif., Calif.; sr. judge U.S. Dist. Ct. (so. dist.) Calif., San Diego, 1970—. Served with USNR, 1941-45. Mem. ABA, Fed. Bar Assn., Am. Judicature Soc. Office: US Dist Ct 940 Front St San Diego CA 92189-0010

TURRENTINE, LYNDA GAYLE, interior designer; b. Carrizozo, N.Mex., Apr. 12, 1941; d. Edward Franklyn and Lora Olive (Allen) Adams; m. Frank George Turrentine, Sept. 5, 1961 (div. 1974); 1 child, Teri Lynn. BA, U. North Tex., 1964. Interior Designer Marsh and Assoc., Denton, Tex., 1964-65, Stewart Office Supply, Dallas, 1965-66, The Paper Mill, Las Cruces, N.Mex., 1966-74; gen. mgr. and interior designer Design Plaza, Las Cruces, 1974-79; acct. rep. Cholla Bus. Interiors, Tucson, 1979-80; owner Interior Concepts, Tucson, 1980—; affiliated with Friedman, Keim, McFerror Architects, Tucson, 1987-92; speaker at several univs.; judge portfolios U. Ariz., 1983, 85; com. chmn. Designer Showhouse, Tucson, 1983, 84, 86, 88, 90, 93, co-chair design com., 1988, 90. Mem. Arts Coun. Las Cruces, 1977-79, PTA, Las Cruces, 1977-84; cookie chmn. Girl Scouts, Las Cruces, 1978; mem. ch. choir; donor Tucson Mus. Art.; com. Casa de los Ninos Angel Nursery Interiors; donor Brewster House for Abused Women; supporter Desert S.W. Soroptimist. Mem. Am. Soc. Interior Designers (pres. 1981-83, nat. bd. dirs. 1981-83, 87-89, Presdl. citation, treas. Ariz. state chpt. 1983-85, bd. dirs. 1981-88, Medalist award 1985), Las Cruces C. of C., Tucson C. of C., Sahuraro Bus. (bd. dirs. Tucson, 1981-88), Chi Omega Sorority Assn., U. North Tex. Alumni Assn. Republican. Methodist. Office: Interior Concepts 812 N Crescent Lane Tucson AZ 85710

TUSHER, THOMAS WILLIAM, apparel company executive; b. Oakland, Calif., Apr. 5, 1941; s. William C. and Betty J. (Brown) T.; m. Pauline B. Kensett, Jan. 1, 1967; children: Gregory Malcolm, Michael Scott. B.A., U. Calif., Berkeley, 1963; M.B.A., Stanford U., 1965. Asst. to v.p. internat. Colgate Palmolive Co., N.Y.C., 1965-67; product mgr. Colgate-Palmolive P.R., 1967-68; supt. corp. planning Levi Strauss & Co., San Francisco, 1969; pres. Levi Strauss Internat., 1977-84; sr. v.p. Levi Straus & Co., before 1984, exec. v.p., chief operating officer, dir., from 1984, now pres., chief oper. officer; regional gen. mgr., Australia/N.Z., Levi Strauss Australia, 1970-74; area gen. mgr. Levi Strauss No. Europe, London, 1974-75; pres. European div. Levi Strauss Internat., San Francisco, 1976; dir. various subs's. Levi Strauss Internat.; dir. Gt. Western Garment Co., Can. Bd. dirs. Calif. Council Internat. Trade, 1977—, U. Calif. Grad. Bus. Sch. Served with Intelligence Corps. USAR, 1966-67. Mem. San Francisco C. of C. (dir.). Republican. Presbyterian. Clubs: World Trade, Bay. Office: Levi Strauss & Co PO Box 7215 San Francisco CA 94120-7215

TUSHINGHAM, GARY, school superintendent. Chief supt. schs. Calgary (Alta.) Sch. Dist. 19, Can. Office: Edn Centre Bldg, 515 MacLeod Trail SE, Calgary, AB Canada T2G 2L9*

TUSHLA, RICHARD J., physician; b. Auburn, Nebr., Jan. 24, 1941; s. Francis Michael and Ruth Jeanette (Shelly) T.; m. Connie Rose Bernard, Aug. 6, 1966; children: Todd, Jennifer. BS, U. Notre Dame, 1963; MD, U. Nebr., 1967. Diplomate Am. Bd. Family Practice. Intern Santa Clara County Hosp., San Jose, Calif., 1968; resident Ventura (Calif.) County Hosp., 1970; pvt. practice, 1973—; clin. prof. medicine U. Calif., Davis, 1976-77; asst. clin. prof. medicine UCLA, 1977—; physician Santa Paula (Calif.) Meml. Hosp., Ventura Gen. Hosp., Community Meml. Hosp., Ventura, St. John's Regional Med. Ctr., Oxnard, Calif. Mem. editorial bd. Patient Care mag. Maj. U.S. Army, 1970-73. Fellow Am. Acad. Family Practice; mem. AMA (Physician Recognition award 1977, 82, 87, 92), Calif. Med. Assn. (alt. del. 1978, 79, 80, del. 1911—), Ventura County Med. Soc. (bd. govs. 1980-86, sec. 1981-83, pres. 1985). Roman Catholic. Home: 615 Teague Dr Santa Paula CA 93060-2511

TUSKA, AGNES, educator; b. Budapest, Hungary, Feb. 29, 1960; came to U.S., 1986; d. Andras Tuska and Vera (Brhlik) Toth; m. Tigest Fesseha Lemlem, Mar. 16, 1990. MA in Math. and Physics Edn., Eötvös L Univ. Sci., Budapest, 1983; MS in Math., Ohio State U., 1988, PhD in Math. Edn., 1992. Cert. math. and physics tchr., Ohio, Hungary. Tchr. math. and physics Arany Janos, Budapest, 1982, Berzsenyi Daniel High Sch., Budapest, 1983-86; tutor math. stats. and physics coll. engring. Ohio State U., Columbus, 1989-90; student asst. Ctr. For Teaching Excellence Ohio State U., 1989, teaching asst. young scholars program, 1990, teaching asst. dept. math., 1986-92; instrnl. faculty Calif. State U., Fresno, 1992—; workshop leader coll. engring. profl. devel. program Ohio State U., 1989-91, course coord. asst. dept. math., 1990-91; sec. conf. NATO/ASI Internat. Orthogonal Polynomials Com., Columbus, 1989. Contbr. articles to publs. Vol. Salvation Army, Columbus, 1990. Mem. Math. Assn. Am., Am. Math. Soc., Libr. of Sci., Nat. Coun. Tchr. Maths. Office: Calif State U Dept Math Fresno CA 93740-0108

TUSO, JOSEPH FREDERICK, English language educator, academic dean emeritus; b. Oak Park, Ill., Nov. 2, 1933; s. Joseph Salvator and Agnes Louise (Berge) T.; m. Mildred Jean Werthmuller, Aug. 30, 1958; children: Ann, Mary, Lisa, Kathleen, Jody. BA, Don Bosco Coll., 1955; MA, U. Ariz., 1964; MSA, Ga. Coll., 1981; PhD, U. Ariz., 1966. Commd. 2d lt. USAF, 1957, advanced through grades to lt. col., 1973, ret., 1976; from asst. prof. to prof. of English U.S. Air Force Acad., Colorado Springs, 1964-76; chmn. English dept. Ga. Coll., Milledgeville, 1976-79; head, English dept. N.Mex. State U., Las Cruces, 1979-82; chmn. English dept. U. of Sci. and Arts of Okla., Chickasha, 1982-84, chmn. Div. Arts & Humanities, 1984-87; acad. dean N.Mex. Mil. Inst., Roswell, 1987-93, prof. English, dean emeritus, 1993—. Editor: Beowulf, A Critical Edition, 1975; author: Singing the Vietnam Blues, 1990. Decorated Meritorious Svc. medal USAF, Disting. Flying Cross, USAF, Bronze Star, USAF, Air medal with 12 oak leaf clusters, USAF, Vietnamese Cross of Gallantry, Republic of Vietnam. Mem. Air Force Assn., Mod. Lang. Assn. of Am., Phi Beta Kappa. Roman Catholic. Home: 200 W College Roswell NM 88201 Office: New Mexico Mil Inst 101 W College Blvd Roswell NM 88201-5174

TUTASHINDA, KWELI (BRIAN P. ALTHEIMER), chiropractic physician, educator; b. Wynne, Ark., May 14, 1956; s. Joe Porché and Lura Ella (Darden) Altheimer; divorced; 1 child, Chinyere R.; m. Leonor Quiñonez, June 13, 1987; children Xihuanel, Rukiya, Jomoké. BA cum laude, U. Ark., 1978; D of Chiropractic cum laude, Life Chiropractic Coll. West, San Lorenzo, Calif., 1989. Tchr. English Oakland (Calif.) Pub. Schs., 1984-86; tchr. spl. programs U. Calif., Berkeley, 1984-92; instr. phys. diagnosis, phys. therapy Life Chiropractic Coll. West, San Lorenzo, Calif., 1989—; pvt. practice chiropractic physician Oakland, Berkeley, 1990—. Editor, pub. Foresight Mag., 1982-84; author, pub. Toward a Holistic Worldview, 1985. Mem. Calif. Chiropractors Assn., Assn. Chiropractic History. Mem. Sufi Order of the West. Office: 3358 Adeline St Berkeley CA 94703

TUTT, WILLIAM BULLARD, hotel management executive; b. Princeton, N.J., Apr. 24, 1941; s. Charles Leeming and Barbara (Shaffer) T.; m. Frankie Campbell, July 13, 1963; 1 child, William Benjamin. BS, Cornell U., 1963. Mgr. Grand Imperial Hotel, Silverton, Colo., 1963-64; food and beverage dir. Continental Plaza Hotel, Chgo., 1966-69; exec. asst. mgr. Georgia Hotel, Vancouver, BC, Can., 1969-71; mgr. Crown Ctr. Hotel, Kansas City, Mo., 1971-74; gen. mgr. Hotel Toronto, Ont., Can., 1974-75; sr. exec. v.p. Broadmoor Hotel, Inc., Colorado Springs, Colo., 1975-92; also pres. Broadmoor Mgmt. Co., Colorado Springs, Colo., 1975-92; bd. dirs. Norwest Banks Colo., Denver, U.S. West Colo., Denver, Colo. Interstate Gas Co., Colorado Springs, Broadmoor Mgmt. Co., exec. com. V.p. Air Force Acad. Found., Colorado Springs, 1977—, U.S. Olympic Com., Colorado Springs, 1979-92; chmn. Colo. Amateur Sports Corp., Colorado Springs, 1979—; vice chmn. U.S. Space Found., Colorado Springs, 1985—; dir. Colo. Wildlife Heritage Found., Colo. Sports Coun., U.S. Ice Hockey Mktg. Com., USA Boxing Found. (trustee); chmn. Olympic Festival Com., 1992—. 1st lt. U.S. Army Spl. Troops, 1964-66, West Germany. Recipient Citizen of Yr. award SAR, 1984, , Pioneer award Colo. Sports Hall of Fame, 1984, Chief of Mission World Taekwondo Championship, Barcelona, Spain, 1987, Chef de Mission U.S. Olympic Com., Calgary XV Winter Olympic Games, 1988, Spl. award Colo. Sports Hall of Fame, 1989. Mem. Internat. Wine and Food Soc. (dir.), Pikes Peak Range Riders Assn., Pikes Peak or Bust Rodeo Assn. (dir.), Cornell Soc. of Hotelmen, Confrerie des Chevaliers de Tastevin, World Sr. Golf Fedn. (exec. coun.), The Thirty Group (co-chmn.), Broadmoor Golf Club, Wigwam Club, Cheyenne Mountain Country Club, El Paso Club, Sanborn Ranch Duck Club, The Cooking Club (pres.), Country Club of Colo. Office: Colo Amateur Sports Corp 12E Boulder St Colorado Springs CO 80903

TUTTLE, DAVID TERRENCE, manufacturing executive; b. Glendale, Calif., Apr. 23, 1937; s. Cecil Madison and Olive Virginia (Gross) T.; m. Jacquelie Marie Lucas, Sept. 16, 1959 (dec. Nov. 1975); children: Deanna, Jeffrey; m. Phyllis Sandra Braunstein, Nov. 7, 1976; 1 child, Lisa. BSBA, U. Redlands, 1987. Sr. buyer Studio Girl Hollywood Inc., Glendale, 1960-64; purchasing agt. Helene Curtis Industries, Chgo., 1964-65; adminstrv. asst. to dir. mktg. Am. Continental Labs., Buena Park, Calif., 1965; mgr. purchasing Nutrilite Products Inc., Buena Park, 1966-80, dir. materials mgmt., 1980-91; dir. strategic ops. Nutrilite Products Inc., Buena Park and Mex., 1992—; v.p. Nutrilite S de R.L. de C.V. With USNR, 1956-58. Mem. Am. Prodn. and Inventory Control Soc., Diamond Bar Jaycees (v.p. charter mem. 1966—). Office: Nutrilite Products Inc PO Box 5940 Buena Park CA 90622-5940

TUTTLE, LEON EIPHRAM, controller; b. Chgo., July 24, 1934; s. Leon E. and Matilda T. (Perona) T.; m. Roberta M. Norton, July 20, 1957; children: Katherine Tuttle Thomas, Karen Tuttle Haenke, John N., Joe L. BSBA, U. Wyo., 1956; MBA, Mich. State U., 1966; M in Bus. Taxation, U. So. Calif., 1976. CPA, Calif. Commd. officer USAF, advanced through grades to col., 1978; ops. staff officer 15th Air Force Strategic Air Command USAF, Riverside, Calif., 1970-74; staff auditor Audit Agy. USAF, San Bernardino, Calif., 1974-76, 1974-76; auditor, gen. rep. Audit Agy. USAF, Denver, 1976-78, auditor gen. rep. Audit Agy., 1976-78, dir. plans and systems Acctg. & Fin. Ctr., 1978-80, ret., 1980; exec. v.p. Resource Systems, Inc., Englewood, Colo., 1980-82; mgr. investor rels. Tri-Ex Oil & Gas, Inc., Denver, 1982-83; assoc. dir. Colo. Lottery, Denver, 1983-85; sr. cons. Sci. Games, Inc., Sacramento, 1985-88; plant contr. Sci. Games, Inc., Gilroy, Calif., 1988—; instr. acctg. U. Md., 1962-70, Chapman Coll., Orange, Calif., 1972-76, Metro U., Denver, 1978-79. Mem. Calif. CPA Soc., Air Force Assn., Ret. Officers Assn., Rotary, Beta Gama Sigma, Alpha Beta Psi. Home: 3825 Clover Valley Rd Rocklin CA 95677 Office: Sci Games 8100 Camino Arroyo Gilroy CA 95020-7308

TUUL, JOHANNES, physics educator, researcher; b. Tarvastu, Viljandi, Estonia, May 23, 1922; came to U.S., 1956, naturalized, 1962; s. Johan and Emilie (Tulf) T.; m. Marjatta Murtoniemi, July 14, 1957 (div. Aug. 1971); children—Melinda, Melissa; m. Sonia Esmeralda Manosalva, Sept. 15, 1976; 1 son, Johannes. B.S., U. Stockholm, 1955, M.A., 1956; Sc.M., Brown U., 1957, Ph.D., 1960. Research physicist Am. Cyanamid Co., Stamford, Conn., 1960-62; sr. research physicist Bell & Howell Research Center, Pasadena, Calif., 1962-65; asst. prof., assoc. prof. Calif. State Poly. U., Pomona, 1965-68; vis. prof. Pahlavi U., Shiraz, Iran, 1968-70; chmn. phys. earth sci. Calif. State Poly. U., Pomona, 1971-75, prof. physics, 1975—; cons. Bell & Howell Research Center, Pasadena, Calif., 1965, Teledyne Co., Pasadena, 1968; guest researcher Naval Weapons Center, China Lake, Calif., 1967, 72; resident dir., Calif. State U. Internat. Programs in Sweden and Denmark, 1977-78. Author: Physics Made Easy, 1974; contbr. articles in field to profl. jours. Pres. Group Against Smoking Pollution, Pomona Valley, Calif., 1976; foster parent Foster Parents Plan, Inc., Warwick, R.I., 1964—; block capt. Neighborhood Watch, West Covina, Calif., 1982-84. Brown U. fellow, 1957-58; U. Namur (Belgium) research grantee, 1978; Centre Nat. de la Recherche Scientifique research grantee, France, 1979; recipient Humanitarian Fellowship award Save the Children Fedn., 1968. Mem. Am. Phys. Soc., AAAS (life), Am. Assn. Physics Tchrs., N.Y. Acad. Scis. Republican. Roman Catholic. Research in energy conservation and new energy technologies. Office: Calif State Poly U 3801 W Temple Ave Pomona CA 91768-2557

TWEEDIE, RICHARD LEWIS, statistics educator, consultant; b. Leeton, NSW, Australia, Aug. 22, 1947; came to U.S., 1991; s. Lewis Chabaud and Nel (Dahlenburg) T.; m. Catherine Robertson, Sept. 13, 1971; 1 child, Marianne Louise Robertson. BA, Australian Nat. U., Canberra, 1968, MA, 1969, DSc, 1986; PhD, Cambridge (Eng.) U., 1972. Sr. rsch. scientist Commonwealth Sci. and Indsl. Rsch. Orgn., Canberra, 1974-77; prin. rsch. scientist Commonwealth Sci. and Indsl. Rsch. Orgn., Melbourne, Australia, 1979-81; assoc. prof. U. Western Australia, Perth, 1978; gen. mgr. Siromath Pty. Ltd., Sydney, Australia, 1981-83, mng. dir., 1983-87; prof., dean Bond U., Gold Coast, Australia, 1987-91; prof. stats. Colo. State U., Ft. Collins, 1991—, chair dept. stats., 1992—. Author: Markov Chains and Stochastic Stability, 1993; also over 80 articles. Fellow Inst. Math. Stats., Internat. Statis. Inst.; mem. Statis. Soc. Australia (pres. 1984-85). Office: Colo State U Dept Stats Fort Collins CO 80523

TWIGG-SMITH, THURSTON, newspaper publisher; b. Honolulu, Aug. 17, 1921; s. William and Margaret Carter (Thurston) Twigg-S.; m. Bessie Bell, June 9, 1942 (div. Feb. 1983); children: Elizabeth, Thurston, William, Margaret, Evelyn.; m. Laila Roster, Feb. 22, 1983. B.Engring., Yale U., 1942. With Honolulu Advertiser, 1946—, mng. editor, 1954-60, asst. bus. mgr., 1960-61, pub., 1961-86; pres., dir., chief exec. officer Honolulu Advertiser, Inc., 1962-93, chmn., 1993—; pres., dir., CEO Persis Corp.; bd. dirs. Am. Savs. Bank, Hawaiian Electric Co. Trustee Punahou Sch., Old Sturbridge Inc., Honolulu Acad. Arts, The Contemporary Mus., Hawaii, Mus. Contemporary Art, L.A., The Skowhegan Sch., Maine, Yale Art Gallery, New Haven, Philatelic Found., N.Y. Maj. AUS, 1942-46. Mem. Honolulu C. of C., Waialae Club, Pacific Club, Oahu Country Club, Outrigger Canoe Club. Office: Persis Corp Po Box 3110 605 Kapiolani Blvd Honolulu HI 96802

TWIST, ROBERT LANPHIER, farmer, rancher, cattle feeder; b. Memphis, Dec. 27, 1926; s. Clarence C. and Edith G. Twist; student Springfield (Ill.) Jr. Coll., 1943; B.S. in Agr., U. Ill., 1950; postgrad. U. Edinburgh (Scotland); 1 dau., Marilyn Edith. Owner, operator farm lands, Twist, Ark., 1949—, Bow Fiddle Ranch, Laramie, Wyo., 1961—, Lost Creek Ranch, Masters, Colo., 1963, Rolling T Ranch, Ft. Morgan, Colo., 1965—, R.L. Twist Ranches Cattle Feeding Enterprises, Greeley, Colo. and Ft. Morgan, 1974—; prin. R.L. Twist Land & Investments, Paradise Valley, Ariz., 1974—; Rocker M Ranch, Douglas, Ariz., 1981—, Circle J Ranch, Gunnison, Colo., 1993; cons. agrl. mgmt. Justice of Peace, Twist, Ark., 1954. Served with USAAF, 1944-46. Mem. Colo. Farm Bur., Wyo. Farm Bur., Nat. Cattlemen's Assn. (charter). Republican. Presbyterian. Home: 4612 E Sparkling Ln Paradise Valley AZ 85253-2924

TWITCHELL, KENT, mural artist; b. Lansing, Mich., Aug. 17, 1942; s. Robert Edward and Wilma Doris (Berry) T.; m. Susan Catherine Fessler, Dec. 27, 1975 (div. 1986); m. Pandora Seaton, Feb. 23, 1990; children: Rory, Artie. AA, East L.A. Coll., 1969; BA, Calif. State U., 1972; MFA, Otis Art Inst., 1977; DA (hon.), Biola U., 1989. Display artist J.C. Penney Co., Atlanta, 1965-66; abstract artist, painter L.A., 1968=70, mural artist, 1971—; instr. L.A. County High Sch. for the Arts, L.A., 1987-90, Otis/Parsons Art Inst., L.A., 1980-83; cons. Olympic Murals Program, L.A., 1983-84. Executed murals at Union at 12th St., L.A., 1971, Hollywood Fwy., L.A., 1974, Hill St. at Olympic, 1987, 405 Fwy., Inglewood, Calif., 1987, 1420 Locust St., Phila., 1989, Hollywood (Calif.) Blvd., 1991-93, Harbor Fwy., L.A., 1991-93; one-man shows include: L.A. Mcpl. Art Gallery, 1980, Thinking Eye Gallery, L.A., 1986, Valparaiso (Ind.) U. Art Mus., 1987, Westmont Coll. Art Gallery, Santa Barbara, Calif., 1987, Biola U. Art Gallery, La Mirada, Calif., 1987, Vincent Price Gallery-East L.A. Coll., 1990, Lizardi-Harp Gallery, Pasadena, Calif., 1991; exibited in group shows at L.A. Mcpl. Art Gallery, 1977, 81, Calif. Polytech. U., Pomona, Calif., 1978, Santa Monica Coll., 1978, L.A.C.E. Gallery, L.A., 1981, Otis/Parsons Art Inst., L.A., 1987, Mayer Schwarz Gallery, Beverly Hills, 1988, 90, Principia Coll., Elsah, Ill., 1989, Koplin Gallery, Santa Monica, 1992, L.A. County Mus. of Art, 1992. Mem. adv. bd. Artists Equity Assn., 1980-93, Mural Conservancy of L.A., 1988-93. Grantee Calif. Arts Coun., 1978, Nat. Endowment for Arts, 1986. Office: 2160 Sunset Blvd Los Angeles CA 90026-3148

TWOGOOD, RICHARD EDWARD, electrical engineer; b. National City, Calif., May 29, 1951; s. Frederick John and Gladys Ruth (Belttary) T.; m. Beth Ellen Norman, June 11, 1972; children: Kate, Sara, Richard. BS, U. Calif., Davis, 1972, MS, 1973, PhD, 1977. Engr. Lawrence Livermore (Calif.) Nat. Lab., 1972-79, group leader, 1979-83, div. leader, 1983-88, prog. leader, 1988—. Contbr. articles to profl. jours. Mem. IEEE. Office: Lawrence Livermore Labs PO Box 808 Livermore CA 94551-0808

TWOMEY, JANINE LOUISE, social psychologist, educator; b. Honolulu, Jan. 12, 1944; d. Lawrence Arver and Celine (Cochran) T.; m. Joseph Norton Roth, Aug. 31, 1965 (div. Dec. 1979); children: Elizabeth Lynn, Emily Michelle, Joseph Norton Jr.; m. John Joseph Hedderson, Sept. 20, 1991. BA, Tex. Christian U., 1965; MA, U. Tex., El Paso, 1978; PhD, N.Mex. State U., Las Cruces, 1991. Lectr. U. Tex., 1978-80; instr. social psychology N.Mex. State U., Alamogordo, 1980-83, asst. prof., 1983-89, assoc. prof., head divsn., 1989-91; instr. social psychology Citrus Coll., Glendora, Calif., 1991—; adj. faculty Grad. Sch. Psychology, Pepperdine U., Culver City, Calif., 1992—; cons. United Way, Alamogordo, 1988, Community Edn., Alamogordo, 1983, 85, 86-87, C. of C. Sr. Program, Alamogordo, 1988. Contbr. articles to profl. jours. Mem. adv. bd. COPE, Alamogordo, 1981-91; bd. dirs. Otero County Mental Health Assn., Alamogordo, 1986-89, Otero County Red Cross, Alamogordo, 1987-89; mem. allocation and budget com. United Way, Alamogordo, 1987-88. NIMH rsch. asst. U. Tex., 1978; N.Mex. Assn. Community, Jr. and Tech. Colls. grantee, 1990. Mem. Population Reference Bur., Western Psychol. Assn., S.W. Sociol. Assn., PEO (v.p., sec. 1986—). Republican. Presbyterian. Home: 4455 Rockland Pl # 12 LaCanada-Flintridge CA 91011-1947 Office: Citrus Coll 1000 W Foothill Blvd Glendora CA 91740

TWOMLEY, BRUCE CLARKE, lawyer, state official; b. Selma, Ala., Jan. 23, 1945; s. Robert Clarke and Eleanor Jane (Wood) Anderson T.; m. Sara Jane Minton, June 13, 1979; children: Christopher Mario, Jonathan Marion. BA in Philosophy, Northwestern U., 1967; LLM, U. Calif., San Francisco, 1970; postgrad. Nat. Jud. Coll., Reno, Nev., 1983, 88. Bar: Calif. 1972, Alaska 1973, U.S. Dist. Ct. Alaska, 1973, U.S. Ct. Appeals (9th cir.) 1982. VISTA vol., Anchorage, 1972-73; lawyer Alaska Legal Services Corp., Anchorage, 1973-82; commr. Alaska Comml. Fisheries Entry Commn., Juneau, 1982-83, chmn., 1983—; mem. Gov.'s Fisheries Cabinet, 1983—; cons. IRS, Sta. WNED-TV, Buffalo, 1988; presenter in field. Co-author: Limited Access Management: A Guidebook to Conservation, 1993. Recipient Alaska Legal Services Disting. Service award, 1983, 92. Mem. Juneau Racquet Club (adv. bd. 1989—), Kappa Sigma (pres. interfraternity council 1966-67). Home: PO Box 20972 Juneau AK 99802-0972 Office: Alaska Comml Fisheries Entry Commn 8800 Glacier Hwy Ste 109 Juneau AK 99801-8106

TYKESON, DONALD ERWIN, broadcasting executive; b. Portland, Oreg., Apr. 11, 1927; s. O. Ansel and Hillie Martha (Haveman) T.; m. Rilda Margaret Steigleder, July 1, 1950; children: Ellen, Amy, Eric. BS, U. Oreg., 1951. V.p., dir. Liberty Communications, Inc., Eugene, Oreg., 1963-67, pres., chief exec. officer, dir., 1967-83; pres. Bend Cable Communications, Inc., 1983—; chmn. bd. Telecomm Systems, Inc., 1983—, Telecomm Svcs. Inc., 1988—; Ctrl. Oreg. Cable Advt., Inc., 1992—; pres. Northwest TV Inc., 1985—. Bd. dirs. Nat. Coalition Rsch. in Neurol. and Communicative Disorders, 1984-89; chmn. Nat. Coalition in Rsch. pub. and govt. info. com., 1986-89, C-SPAn, 1980-89; mem. bus. U. Oreg. Coll. Bus. Adminstrn., 1973—; vice-chmn. we. area Nat. Multiple Sclerosis Soc., 1983—, dir., mem. rsch. and med. programs com., 1986—; trustee Eugene Art Found., 1980-85, Oreg. Health Scis. U. Found., 1988-91, mem. investment com., 1992—; mem. Oreg. Investment Coun. State of Oreg., vice chmn., 1988-92. Mem. Nat. Assn. Broadcasters, Nat. Cable TV Assn. (dir. 1976-83), Chief Execs. Orgn., Vintage Club (dir. Custom Lot Assn. 1992—), Country Club Eugene (dir. 1975-77, sec. 1976—, v.p. 1977), Multnomah Athletic Club, Arlington Club, Rotary, Elks. Home: 447 Spyglass Dr Eugene OR 97401-0101 Office: PO Box 70006 Eugene OR 97401-0101

TYLER, DARLENE JASMER, dietitian; b. Watford City, N.D., Jan. 26, 1939; d. Edwin Arthur and Leola Irene (Walker) Jasmer; BS, Oreg. State U., 1961; m. Richard G. Tyler, Aug. 26, 1977; children: Ronald, Eric, Scott. Clin. dietitian Salem (Oreg.) Hosp., 1965-73; sales supr. Sysco Northwest, Tigard, Oreg., 1975-77; clin. dietitian Physicians & Surgeons Hosp., Portland, Oreg., 1977-79; food svc. dir. Meridian Park Hosp., Tualatin, Oreg., 1979—. Registered dietitian. Mem. Am. Dietetic Assn., Oreg. Dietetic Assn., Portland Dietetic Assn., Am. Soc. Hosp. Food Svc. Adminstrs. Episcopalian. Home: 9472 SW Hume Ct Tualatin OR 97062-9039 Office: 19300 SW 65th St Tualatin OR 97062

TYLER, GAIL MADELEINE, nurse; b. Dhahran, Saudi Arabia, Nov. 21, 1953 (parents Am. citizens); d. Louis Rogers and Nona Jean (Henderson) Tyler; m. Alan J. Moore, Sept. 29, 1990; 1 child, Sean James. AS, Front Range Community Coll., Westminster, Colo., 1979; BS in Nursing, U. Wyo., 1989. RN. Ward sec. Valley View Hosp., Thornton, Colo., 1975-79; nurse Scott and White Hosp., Temple, Tex., 1979-83, Meml. Hosp. Laramie County, Cheyenne, Wyo., 1983-89; dir. DePaul Home Health, 1989-91; field staff nurse Poudre Valley Hosp. Home Care, 1991—. Avocations: collecting internat. dolls, sewing, reading, travel.

TYLER, KENNETH LAURENCE, neurologist, researcher; b. Boston, May 6, 1953; s. H. Richard and Joyce (Colby) T.; m. Lisa Johnson, Oct. 27, 1979; children: Maxwell Johnson, Eric Johnson. AB magna cum laude, Harvard U., 1974; MD, Johns Hopkin's U., 1978. Diplomate Am. Bd. Internal Medicine, Am. Bd. Psychiatry and Neurology. Resident in medicine Brigham S. Women's Hosp., Boston, 1978-80; resident in neurology Mass.

Gen. Hosp., Boston, 1980-83; rsch. fellow Med. Sch. Harvard U., Boston, 1983-84, instr. Med. Sch., 1984-86, asst. prof. Med. Sch., 1986-91; assoc. prof. med. sch. U. Colo., Denver, 1991—. Mem. editorial bd. Microbial Pathogenesis, 1990—, Jour. Neurol. Scis., 1990—, Jour. Virology, 1991—, Jour. Hist. Neurosci., 1993—; editor: Infections in the Central Nervous Systems; contbr. articles to profl. jours. Alfred P. Sloan Found. fellow, 1988-90. Fellow ACP, Am. Acad. Neurology (past pres. history sect. program com., S. Weir Mitchell award); mem. Am. Soc. Neurol. Investigation (past pres., sec., treas.), Am. Soc. Virology, Soc. for Exptl. Neuropathology, Am. Neurol. Assn., Soc. Neurosci. Home: 788 Milwaukee St Denver CO 80206-3902 Office: Denver VA Med Ctr Neurology Svc # 127 1055 Clermont St Denver CO 80220-0001

TYLER, STEVEN ANTHONY, aerospace engineer; b. Chgo., July 8, 1964; s. Edwin Chester and Lillian Josephine (Mierzwinski) Drzymkowski; m. Debra Jean Gaetke, June 15, 1991. BSME, U. Ill., 1986; MSME, Stanford U., 1992. Registered profl. engr., Calif. Design engr. Argonne (Ill.) Nat. Lab., 1986-87; flight test engr. Lockheed - Missiles div., Sunnyvale, Calif., 1987-88; optical phenomenologist Lockheed - Rsch. & Devel., Palo Alto, Calif., 1988—. Mem. NSPE, ASME, AIAA. Democrat.

TYLER BROWNE, MARY ANN, social worker, clergywoman; b. Mitchell, S.D., Apr. 21, 1939; d. William Reaves and Matilda Emma (Boeke) Ball; m. Stanley H. Tyler, Aug. 6,1960 (dec. 1977); children: William R., Michael Greg, Kathy Lynn; m. James Charles Browne, Jan. 23, 1988. BA, Macalester Coll., 1960; MSW, U. Nebr., 1975-78; MDiv, Pacific Sch. Religion, 1988. Ordained to ministry United Ch. of Christ, 1989. Dir. Big Bros./Big Sisters, Norfolk, Nebr., 1973-75; alcohol and drug social worker Mental Health Inst., Clarinda, Iowa, 1977-79; pediatric social worker St. Joseph Hosp., Omaha, 1979-80; dir. career programs YWCA, Omaha, 1980-85; treatment dir. WINDO project North Coast Opportunities, Ukiah, Calif., 1988-93; assoc. pastor United Meth. Ch., Omaha, 1993—; nat. bd. dirs. Displaced Homemakers Network, Washington, 1981-83, Calif. bd. dirs., Sacramento, 1990—; adv. com. Mendocino County Dept. Social Svcs., Ukiah, 1990—. Mem. AAUW (regional dir. 1983-85, women's chair 1978-80, dir. AAUW Found. 1983-85), Acad. Cert. Social Workers, Nat. Assn. Social Workers, Older Women's League. Democrat. Home: 78 Hillside Dr Willits CA 95490-3013 Office: North Coast Opportunities 413A N State St Ukiah CA 95482-4421

TYLER-PARKER, SYDNEY BILLIG, publishing executive, author, consultant; b. L.A., May 11, 1938; d. Harvey Ellsworth Jr. and Sidney Roberta (Woolslair) Billig; m. Thomas True Tyler, July 11, 1969 (div. 1986); 1 child, Lee Harris Tyler Argabrite; m. Minot Harold Parker, Dec. 30, 1988. BA in English Lit., Coll. William and Mary, 1960; MSC in Sci. Edn., U. So. Calif., 1968; post masters, Tavistock Inst. Human Rels., London, 1975. cert. elem. and secondary tchr., U.S., U.K., West Germany, Canada. Tchr. math., social studies Torrance (Calif.) Unified Sch. Dist., 1966-68; math rsch. assoc. southwest Reg. Fed. Lab., Inglewood, Calif., 1967-68; tchr. Am. lit., Latin, great issues of man Palos Verdes USD, Rolling Hills, Calif., 1968-69; tchr. math. Mayfield Comprehensive Sch., London, 1970; tchr. AFCENT NATO Internat. Sch., Brunssum, The Netherlands, 1970-75; internat. primary coord., rsch. head, 1972-74; tchr., program dir. RAF Alcombury (U.K.) U.S. Air Force Schs., 1975-81; pres. Thomas Geale Pubs., Inc., Montara, Calif., 1982—; gifted and talented cons., tchr. Cabrillo Unified Sch. Dist., Half Moon Bay, Calif., 1991—; cons., counselor U.S. Air Force Offices of Social Actions, Alconbury, 1976-79; project dir. The Think Bridge, Inc. Author: Young Think, 1980—, Just Think, 1980—, Stretch Think, 1982—, Think Quest, 1990—; editorial adv., article contbr. THINK Magazine, San Antonio, Tex., 1990—. Recipient 200 Women of Achievement in England award United Kingdom Soc., 1970, Outstanding World-wide Social Actions Cons. Counselor award U.S. Air Force, Alconbury, 1978. Mem. NEA, Overseas Edn. Assn., Phi Delta Kappa (U.K. chpt. treas. 1978-81). Home and Office: P O Box 370540 Montara CA 94037

TYNER, DONNA KING, risk management consultant; b. Cleve., Oct. 16, 1957; d. Jerry and Era (Higgins) King; m. John J Tyner III, Aug. 18, 1984. BA in Polit. Sci., Willamette U., 1979. Mgmt. trainee 1st Interstate Bank, Portland, Oreg., 1980-82; sr. claims adjuster Allstate Ins. Co., Tualatin, Oreg., 1983-88; compliance officer State of Oreg. Ins. Div., Salem, 1988-90; program analyst State of Oreg. Workers' Compensation Div., Salem, 1990-91; risk mgmt. cons. State of Oreg. Risk Mgmt. Div., Salem, 1991—; speaker in field. Layreader St. Bartholomew's Epsicopal Ch., Beaverton, Oreg., 1989—; commr. State of Oreg. Commn. for Women, Salem, 1987-90. Mem. Oreg. Women's Polit. Caucus (chmn. Washington county 1983-85, v.p. Portland area 1986-87, 3d v.p. 1987-89), Jr. League Portland, Willamette U. Alumnae Vols. (recruitment counselor 1985—), Alpha Phi (v.p. 1986-87, pres. 1987-89). Democrat. Home: 15119 W Barcelona Way Beaverton OR 97007

TYRELL-SMITH, PATRICK CREAGH, information systems director; b. Oakland, Calif., Dec. 26, 1933; s. Herbert Creagh and Patricia (McHugh) T.-S.; divorced; children: Lisa Suzanne, Timothy Creagh, Terrence Patrick. BS in Polit. Sci., U. San Francisco, 1955. Systems analyst Am. Fore Ins. Group, San Francisco, 1958-59; data processing mgr. Lockheed Missiles and Space Co., Sunnyvale, Calif., 1959-69; sr. systems mgr., asst. v.p. Fireman's Fund Ins., San Rafael, Calif., 1969-84; bus. cons. Pat Tyrell-Smith & Assocs., San Rafael, 1984-87; dir. info. systems Coll. of Marin, Kentfield, Calif., 1987—. Bus. editor Classified Gazette, San Rafael, 1985—. 1st lt. U.S. Army. Pres. San Rafael C. of C., 1979-80, Marin Arts Coun., 1986-87; chair citizens adv. com. Dominican Coll., San Rafael, 1983-84; chair Mother Lode Musical Theatre, Kentfield, Calif., 1985—. Mem. Nat. Assn. Profl. Saleswomen (bd. dirs. 1989—), Marin Forum, Marvelous Marin Breakfast Club (pres. 1986-87). Home: 53 Beach Dr San Rafael CA 94901 Office: Coll of Marin 835 College Ave Kentfield CA 94904

TYSON, SEAN MICHAEL, research analyst; b. San Pablo, Calif., Sept. 14, 1961; s. John Anthony and Sharon Louise (Marsh) T. BA, U. Wyo., 1987; MA, Monterey Inst. Internat. Study, 1992. Rsch. asst., analyst Emerging Nuclear Suppliers Project, Monterey, Calif., 1991—. Vol. Peace Corps, Kitale, Kenya, 1987-89. Cpl. USMC, 1979-83. Office: Emerging Nuclear Suppliers Project 425 Van Buren St Monterey CA 93940

TYSSELAND, TERRY LAWRENCE, service executive; b. Fargo, N.D., Oct. 28, 1941; s. Milford Selner and Lucile Margaret (Oehlke) T.; m. Shirley Ann Thompson, May 4, 1968. BS, U.S. Merchant Marine Acad., 1964. Plant mgr. Gulf Atlantic Distbn. Services, Arlington, Tex., 1965-80; v.p. and western regional mgr. Trammell Crow, Commerce, Calif., 1980-86; div. mgr. Southland Distbn. Ctr., San Bernardino, Calif., 1986-92; pres. McLane Southern Calif., San Bernardino, 1992—. Republican. Lutheran. Clubs: Newport (Calif.) Sailing; Redlands (Calif.) Country. Office: McLane Southern Calif 4472 Georgia Blvd San Bernardino CA 92407-1857

TYSZKIEWICZ, ROBERT EDWARD, marketing professional; b. Detroit, Oct. 3, 1948; s. Edward Stanley and Geraldine Marie (Drope) T.; m. Susan Eleanor Caine, May 10, 1975; children: Kathryn, Elizabeth. BBA, Ea. Mich. U., 1971. Mgmt. trainee Chrysler Motor Co., Highland Park, Mich., 1971-74; mktg. asst. Lucas Automotive, Inc., Troy, Mich., 1974-76, mktg. svcs. mgr., 1976-79, product mgr., 1979-83, product gen. mgr., 1983-89; v.p. product mktg. ITM Automotive, Inc., Cerritos, Calif., 1989—. Mem. Automotive Svc. Industry Assn., Auto Internat. Assn., Automotive Parts Rebuilders Assn., KC, Alhambra. Republican. Roman Catholic. Home: 3603 E Shallow Brook Ln Orange CA 92667-2054

TYTLER, LINDA JEAN, communications and public affairs executive, state legislator; b. Rochester, N.Y., Aug. 31, 1947; d. Frederick Easton and Marian Elizabeth (Allen) T.; m. George Stephen Dragnich, May 2, 1970 (div. July 1976). AS, So. Sem., Buena Vista, Va., 1967; student U. Va., 1973; student in pub. adminstrn. U. N. Mex., 1981-82. Spl. asst. to Congressman John Buchanan, Washington, 1971-75; legis. analyst U.S. Senator Robert Griffin, Washington, 1975-77; ops. supr. Pres. Ford Com., Washington, 1976; office mgr. U.S. Senator Pete Domenici Re-election, Albuquerque, 1977; pub. info. officer S.W. Community Health Service, Albuquerque, 1978-83; cons. pub. relations and mktg., Albuquerque, 1983-84; account exec. Rick Johnson & Co., Inc., Albuquerque, 1983-84; dir. mktg. and communications St. Joseph Healthcare Corp., 1984-88; mktg. and bus. devel. cons., 1987-90; mgr. communications and pub. affairs Def. Avionics Systems div., Honeywell Inc., 1990—; officer N.Mex. Mounted Patrol, 1993—; mem. N.Mex. Ho. of Reps., Santa Fe, 1983—, vice chmn. appropriations and fin. com., 1985-86, interim com. on children and youth, 1985-86, mem. consumer and pub. affairs com., transp. com., 1992—; chmn. Rep. Caucus, 1985-88; chmn. legis. campaign com. Rep. Com.; del. to Republic of China, Am. Council of Young Polit. Leaders, 1988. Bd. dirs. N. Mex. chpt. ARC, Albuquerque, 1984. Recipient award N.Mex. Advt. Fedn., Albuquerque, 1981, 82, 85, 86, 87. Mem. Am. Soc. Hosp. Pub. Relations (cert.), Nat. Advt. Fedn., Soc. Hosp. Planning and Mktg., Am. Mktg. Assn. Republican. Baptist.

TZAVELLA-EVJEN, HARA, classics educator; b. Pireus, Greece, June 27, 1936; came to U.S., 1966; d. Adam and Markella (Polymeri) Tzavellas; m. Harold D. Evjen, Jan. 30, 1967; 1 child, Harald. BA, U. Athens, Greece, 1959, PhD, 1970. Tchr. classics Pearce Coll., Athens, 1960-66; lectr. U. Colo., Denver, 1968-69; asst. prof. classics U. Colo., Boulder, 1966-67, 70-73, assoc. prof., 1973-91; prof. U. Colo., 1991—; dir. excavation at Lithares Greek Archaeol. Service, Thebes, 1970-77. Author: The Winged Creatures in Aegaean Art, 1970, Lithares, 1984, Lithares An Early Helladic Settlement, 1985; contbr. articles to profl. jours. Mem. Archaeol. Inst. Am., Am. Philol. Assn., Archaeol. Soc. Athens, Classical Assn. Middle West and South, Assn. Greek Writers, Greek Archaeol. Soc. (dir. excavation at Chaeroneia 1983—). Home: 6873 Frying Pan Rd Boulder CO 80301-3604 Office: U Colo Dept of Classics Boulder CO 80309

UBER, RALPH LEROY, rancher, retired physician; b. Grove City, Pa., Aug. 29, 1920; s. Herman Earl and Mary Jeanette (Rainey) U.; m. Edna May Ealy, Apr. 29, 1944; children: Charles H., Rebecca Uber Blair, Julieanne Uber Georgiades. Student, Grove City Coll., 1940-43; MD, Temple U., 1945, MS in Internal Medicine, 1949. Intern, 1945-46, resident, 1946-49; pvt. practice, Yakima, Wash., 1949-91; alpaca and llama rancher, Yakima, 1978—. Bd. dirs. Am. Heart Assn., Wash., 1970-82; bd. dirs. Am. Cancer Soc., Wash., 1968-84, state pres., 1982-83. Mem. Wash. State Med. Soc., Airplane Owners and Pilots Assn., Am. Alpine Club. Home and Office: 521 N Cottonwood Yakima WA 98908

UBEROI, MAHINDER SINGH, aerospace engineering educator; b. Delhi, India, Mar. 13, 1924; came to U.S., 1945, naturalized, 1960; s. Kirpal Singh and Sulaksha (Kosher) U. B.S., Punjab U., Lahore, India, 1944; M.S., Calif. Inst. Tech., 1946; D.Eng., Johns Hopkins U., 1952. Registered profl. engr. Mem. faculty U. Mich., Ann Arbor, 1953-63, prof. aeros., 1959-63, vis. prof., 1963-64; prof. aerospace engring. U. Colo., Boulder, 1963—, chmn. dept. aerospace engring., 1963-75; fellow F. Joint Inst. for Lab. Astrophysics, Boulder, 1963-74; hon. research fellow Harvard U., 1975-76; invited prof. U. Que., Can., 1972-74. Council mem. Ednl. TV Channel 6, Inc., Denver, 1963-66. Guggenheim fellow Royal Inst. Tech., Stockholm, Sweden, 1958; exchange scientist U.S. Nat. Acad. Scis.; exchange scientist Soviet Acad. Scis., 1966. Mem. Am. Phys. Soc., Tau Beta Pi. Home: 819 6th St Boulder CO 80302-7418

UBERSTINE, MITCHELL NEIL, bank executive; b. N.Y.C., Apr. 27, 1956; s. Elliott and Barbara Marilyn (Wernick) U.; m. Janice Diane Wemple, Dec. 26, 1987; children: Jeffrey Aaron, Andrew Louis. AA, Pierce Coll., Woodland Hills, Calif., 1975. Purchasing agt. Workshop West, Inc., Beverly Hills, Calif., 1975-78, Allianz Ins., L.A., 1978-79, Allstate Savs., Glendale, Calif., 1979-80; gen. svc. supr. First Fed. Bank Calif., Santa Monica, 1980-83, asst. v.p., 1983-86, v.p., 1986—. Contbr. articles to profl. jours. Bd. dirs., treas. Jewish Family Svc., Santa Monica, 1991—. Mem. Purchasing Mgmt. Assn. L.A. Republican. Jewish. Office: First Fed Bank Calif 401 Wilshire Blvd # 220 Santa Monica CA 90401

UCHIDA, DEBORAH KNOWLTON, utility company researcher; b. Mpls.. BA, San Francisco State U., 1972; PhD, U. Garcilaso, Lima, Peru, 1992; MLS, U. Hawaii, 1979. Libr. City and County of Honolulu, 1978-79; corp. rschr. Hawaiian Elec. Co., Honolulu, 1979—. Rschr. book: Hawaii: The Electric Century, 1991; contbr. articles/photographs to corp. mags. Mem. Am. Soc. Indexers, Spl. Librs. Assn. (chpt. pres. 1991), Internat. Fedn. of Libr. Assns. and Instns. (del. Belgium 1991—). Home: 1815 Bertram St Honolulu HI 96816 Office: Hawaiian Elec Co PO Box 2750 Honolulu HI 96840

UCHIMOTO, EIJIRO, physicist, educator; b. Tokyo, Oct. 28, 1955; came to the U.S., 1974; s. Heihachiro and Kiyo (Ichikawa) U.; m. Yoshiko Kawasato, Sept. 20, 1983; children: Mari Lisa, Kentaro Jim. BS in Physics and Astrophysics, U. Minn., 1978; MS in Physics, U. Wis., 1981, PhD, 1988. Teaching asst. U. Wis., Madison, 1979-80, rsch. asst., 1980-88; assoc. rsch. scientist Courant Inst. NYU, N.Y.C., 1988-90; asst. prof. dept. physics and astronomy U. Mont., Missoula, 1990—, acting chair, 1991. Contbr. articles and abstracts to profl. jours. Hon. fellow U. Wis., 1992-93. Mem. Am. Astron. Soc., Am. Phys. Soc. (STEP travel grantee 1984), Am. Assn. Physics Tchrs., Sigma Xi, Phi Beta Kappa, Tau Beta Pi, Phi Kappa Phi. Home: 3380 Jack Dr Missoula MT 59803 Office: U Mont Dept Physics Astron Missoula MT 59812

UDALL, MORRIS KING, former congressman; b. St. Johns, Ariz., June 15, 1922; s. Levi S. and Louise (Lee) U.; m. Norma Gilbert, 1989; children by previous marriage: Mark, Judith, Randolph, Anne, Bradley, Katherine. LL.B. with distinction, U. Ariz., 1949. Bar: Ariz. 1949. Player Denver Nuggets, 1948-49; ptnr. firm Udall & Udall, Tucson, 1949-61; chief dep. county atty. Pima County, 1950-52, county atty., 1953-54; lectr. labor law U. Ariz., 1955-56; mem. 87th-101st Congresses, 2d Dist. Ariz., 1961-91; chmn. House Com. on Interior and Insular Affairs; mem. Com. on Post Office and Civil Service; vice chmn. Office Tech. Assessment; mem. Com. on Fgn. Affairs; a founder Bank of Tucson, 1959, former dir.; former chmn. bd. Catalina Savs. and Loan Assn.; chmn. Ariz. Com. for Modern Cts., 1960. Author: Arizona Law of Evidence, 1960, Education of a Congressman, 1972, Too Funny to Be President, 1988; co-author: The Job of the Congressman, 1966. Del. Democratic Nat. Conv., 1956; chmn. Ariz. delegation, 1972, Ariz. Volunteers for Stevenson, 1956; candidate for Dem. nomination for Pres., 1976; keynote speaker Dem. Nat. Conv., 1980. Served to capt. USAAF, 1942-46, PTO. Mem. ABA, Ariz. Bar Assn. (bd. govs.), Pima County Bar Assn. (exec. com.), Am. Judicature Soc., Am. Legion, Phi Kappa Phi, Phi Delta Phi. *

UDALL, TOM, state attorney general; b. Tucson, May 18, 1948; s. Stewart and Lee Udall; m. Jill Z. Cooper; 1 child, Amanda Cooper. BA, Prescott Coll., 1970; LLB, Cambridge U., Eng., 1975; JD, U. N.Mex., 1977. Law clk. to Hon. Oliver Seth U.S. Ct. Appeals (10th cir.), Santa Fe, 1977-78; asst. U.S. atty. U.S. Atty.'s Office, 1978-81; pvt. practice Santa Fe, 1981-83; chief counsel N.Mex. Health & Environ. Dept., 1983-84; ptnr. Miller, Stratvert, Togerson & Schlenker, P.A., Albuquerque, 1985-88; atty. gen. State of N.Mex., 1990—. Dem. candidate U.S. Ho. Reps., 1988; past pres. Rio Chama Preservation Trust; mem. N.Mex. Environ. Improvement Bd., 1986-87; bd. dirs. La Compania de Teatro de Albuquerque, Santa Fe Chamber Music Festival, Law Fund. Mem. Kiwanis. Office: Office of Atty Gen PO Box 1508 Galisteo St Santa Fe NM 87504-1508*

UDWADIA, FIRDAUS ERACH, engineering educator, consultant; b. Bombay, Aug. 28, 1947; came to U.S., 1968.; s. Erach Rustam and Perin P. (Lentin) U.; m. Farida Gagrat, Jan. 6, 1977; children: Shanaira, Zubin. BS, Indian Inst. Tech., Bombay, 1968; MS, Calif. Inst. Tech., 1969, PhD, 1972; MBA, U. So. Calif., 1985. Mem. faculty Calif. Inst. Tech., Pasadena, 1972-74; asst. prof. engring. U. So. Calif., Los Angeles, 1974-77, assoc. prof., 1977-83, prof. mech. engring., civil engring. and bus. adminstrn., 1983-86; prof. engring, bus. adminstrn. U. So. Calif., 1986—; also bd. dirs. Structural Identification Computing Facility U. So. Calif.; cons. Jet Propulsion Lab., Pasadena, Calif., 1978—, Argonne Nat. Lab., Chgo., 1982-83, Air Force Rocket Lab., Edwards AFB, Calif., 1984—. Assoc. editor: Applied Mathematics and Computation, Jour. Optimization Theory and Applications, Jour. Franklin Inst.; mem. adv. bd. Internat. Jour. Tech. Forecasting and Social Change; contbr. articles to profl. jours. Bd. dirs. Crisis Mgmt. Ctr., U. So. Calif. NSF grantee, 1976—; recipient Golden Poet award, 1990. Mem. AIAA, ASCE, Am. Acad. Mechanics, Soc. Indsl. and Applied Math., Seismological Soc. Am., Sigma Xi (Earthquake Engring. Research Inst., 1971, 74, 84). Home: 2100 S Santa Anita Ave Arcadia CA 91006-4611 Office: U So Calif 430K Olin Hall University Park Los Angeles CA 90089-1453

UEBERROTH, JOHN A., air transportation executive; b. Phila., 1944. Student, U. Calif., Berkeley, U. So. Calif. Formerly pres. Ask Mr. Foster Travel, Encino, Calif.; formerly v.p. TCU Travel Corp.; formerly pres., COO 1st Travel Corp., Van Nuys, Calif.; with Carlson Travel Group, Mpls., 1983-89, Contrarian Group Inc., Newport Beach, Calif., 1989—, HAL Inc., 1990—; chmn., CEO Hawaiian Airlines Inc., 1990—. Office: Hawaiian Airlines Inc 1164 Bishop St Honolulu HI 96813-2810 also: First Travel Corp 7833 Haskell Ave Van Nuys CA 91406-1908 also: Carlson Cos Inc 12755 State Hwy 55 Minneapolis MN 55441

UEDA, ISSAKU, medical educator, researcher; b. Tokyo, Mar. 24, 1924; came to U.S., 1968; s. Ichiro and Yoshiko (Uchiyama) U.; m. Setsuko Hirama, Dec. 8, 1955; children—Shunsaku, Marie A. M.D., Keio U., Tokyo, 1948, Ph.D. in Biochemistry, 1960. Diplomate Am. Bd. Anesthesiology. Intern, Keio Univ. Hosp., Tokyo, 1948-49; resident U. Utah Coll. Medicine affiliated hosps., 1957-60; chief Nat. Cancer Ctr., Tokyo, 1962-66; assoc. prof. Osaka U. Med. Sch. (Japan), 1966-68; assoc. prof. U. Utah, Salt Lake City, 1972-74, prof. dept. anesthesia, 1978—; prof. U. Kans., Kansas City, 1974-78. Contbr. research articles on anesthesia to med. jours. Mem. Am. Soc. Anesthesiologists, AMA, Am. Chem. Soc. Home: 1447 Ambassador Way E Salt Lake City UT 84108-2858 Office: U Utah Sch Medicine Dept Anesthesia Salt Lake City UT 84132

UEHLING, BARBARA STANER, educational administrator; b. Wichita, Kans., June 12, 1932; d. Roy W. and Mary Elizabeth (Hilt) Staner; children: Jeffrey Steven, David Edward. B.A., U. Wichita, 1954; M.A., Northwestern U., 1956, Ph.D., 1958; hon. degree, Drury Coll., 1978; LLD (hon.), Ohio State U., 1980. Mem. psychology faculty Oglethorpe U., Atlanta, 1959-64, Emory U., Atlanta, 1966-69; adj. prof. U. R.I., Kingston, 1970-72; dean Roger Williams Coll., Bristol, R.I., 1972-74; dean arts scis. Ill. State U., Normal, 1974-76; provost U. Okla., Norman, 1976-78; chancellor U. Mo.-Columbia, 1978-86, U. Calif., Santa Barbara, 1987—; sr. vis. fellow Am. Council Edn., 1987; mem. Pacific Rim Pub. U. Pres. Conf., 1990—; cons. North Ctrl. Accreditation Assn., 1974-86; mem. nat. educator adv. com. to compt. gen. of U.S., 1978-79; mem. Commn. on Mil.-Higher Edn. Rels., Am. Coun. on Edn., 1978-86, bd. dirs., 1979-83, treas., 1982-83, mem. bus.-higher edn. forum, 1980—, mem. exec. com., 1991—; mem. Commn. on Internat. Edn., 1992—, vice-chair, 1993; bd. dirs. Coun. on Postsecondary Edn., 1986-87, 90—, Meredith Corp., 1980—; mem. Transatlantic Dialogue, PEW Found., 1991-93. Author: Women in Academe: Steps to Greater Equality, 1979; editorial bd. Jour. Higher Edn. Mgmt., 1986—; contbr. articles to profl. jours. Bd. dirs., chmn. Nat. Ctr. Higher Edn. Mgmt. Systems, 1977-80; trustee Carnegie Found. for Advancement of Teaching, 1980-86, Santa Barbara Med. Found. Clinic, 1989—; bd. dirs. Resources for the Future, 1985—; mem. select com. on athletics NCAA, 1983-84, also mem. presdl. commn.; mem. Nat. Coun. on Edn. Rsch., 1980-82. Social Sci. Research Council fellow, 1954-55; NSF fellow, 1956-57; NIMH postdoctoral research fellow, 1964-67; named one of 100 Young Leaders of Acad. Change Mag. and ACE, 1978; recipient Alumni Achievement award Wichita State U., 1978, Alumnae award Northwestern U., 1985, Excellence in Edn. award Pi Lambda Theta, 1989. Mem. Am. Assn. Higher Edn. (bd. dirs. 1974-77, pres. 1977-78), Western Coll. Assn. (pres.-elect 1988-89, pres. 1990-92), Internat. Com. for Study Ednl. Exch. (chmn. 1988—), Nat. Assn. State Univs. and Land Grant Colls. (commn. on human resources and social change 1992—), Golden Key, Sigma Xi. Office: U Calif Office of the Chancellor Santa Barbara CA 93106-2030

UERLINGS, JAMES ROBERT, lawyer; b. Klamath Falls, Oreg., Apr. 25, 1950; s. George Robert and Mary Matilda (Bishop) U.; m. Pamela Kay Norgart, Aug. 19, 1972; children: Matthew Blaine, Amanda Christine, Erin Michelle. BS in Polit. Sci., So. Oreg. State, 1972; JD, U. Puget Sound, 1975. Bar: Oreg. 1976, U.S. Dist Ct. Oreg. 1979, U.S. Ct. Appeals (9th cir.) 1987. Dep. dist. atty. Klamath County, Klamath Falls, Oreg., 1976-79; ptnr. Hoots & Uerlings, Klamath Falls, 1979; pvt. practice law Klamath Falls, 1979-84; ptnr. Boivin, McCobb & Uerlings, P.C., Klamath Falls, 1984-86, Boivin & Uerlings, P.C., Klamath Falls, 1986-89, Boivin, Jones, Uerlings & DiIaconi, Klamath Falls, 1989—; judge mcpl. ct. City of Klamath Falls, 1984—. Bd. dirs., sec. Klamath County Econ. Devel. Assn., Klamath Falls, 1985-91; bd. dirs. Oreg. Mcpl. Judges Assn., 1984-87. Mem. Klamath County Bar Assn. (pres. 1980), Oreg. State Bar (chmn. disciplinary bd. 1988-89, bd. dirs. Future of Legal Profession 1990-92), Klamath County C. of C. (pres. 1986, bd. dirs. 1981-87). Democrat. Roman Catholic. Office: Boivin Jones et al 110 N 6th St Klamath Falls OR 97601

UEZONO, YASUHITO, neuroscientist, researcher; b. Hyuga, Miyazaki, Japan, Apr. 4, 1959; came to U.S., 1990; s. Hiroaki and Michiko (Matsuda) U.; m. Tomoko Ida Uezono, Apr. 30, 1988; 1 child, Eiko. MD, U. Occupational and Environ. Health, Kitakyushu, Japan, 1985; PhD, U. Occupational and Environ. Health, Fukuoka, Japan, 1989. Rsch. asst. U. Occupational and Environ. Health Sch. Medicine, 1989-90; rsch. fellow div. biology Calif. Inst. Tech., Pasadena, 1990—. Japan Rsch. Found. for Clin. Pharmacology fellow Calif. Inst. Tech., 1991, Joseph Drown fellow, 1991-92. Mem. Soc. Neurosci., N.Y. Acad. Scis. Office: Div Biology 156-29 Calif Inst Tech Pasadena CA 91125

UHDE, LARRY JACKSON, joint apprentice administrator; b. Marshalltown, Iowa, June 2, 1939; s. Harold Clarence and Rexine Elizabeth (Clemens) U.; m. Linda-Lee Betty Best, Nov. 19, 1960; children: Mark Harold, Brian Raymon. Student, Sacramento City Coll., 1966, Am. River Coll., Sacramento, 1975. Equipment supr. Granite Constrn., Sacramento, 1962-69; truck driver Iowa Wholesale, Marshalltown, Iowa, 1969-70; mgr. Reedy & Essex, Inc., Sacramento, 1970-71; dispatcher Operating Engrs. Local Union 3, Sacramento, 1971-73; tng. coord. Operating Engrs. Joint Apprenticeship Com., Sacramento, 1973-83, apprenticeship div. mgr., 1983-87, adminstr., 1987—; chmn. First Women in Apprenticeship Seminar, 1972, Calif. Apprentice Coun., 1992, Blue Ribbon com.; com. mem. Sacramento Gen. Jount Apprenticeship Com., 1973-74; rep. Sacramento Sierra's Bldg. and Constrn. Trades Coun., 1973-75; com. mem. Valley Area Constrn. Opportunity Program, 1974-77; commr. State of Calif. Dept. Indsl. Rels., Calif. Apprenticeship Coun; mem. Apprenticeship Adv. Com. Internat. Union of Oper. Engrs. Contbr. articles to trade papers. Mgr., v.p. Little League, 1971-75; co-chmn. Fall Festival St. Roberts Ch., 1973-75; v.p. Navy League Youth Program, 1978-81; instr. ARC, 1978-87; counselor United Way 1980—; bd. mem. County CETA Bd., 1981-82; coun. mem. Calif. Balance of State Pvt. Industry Coun., 1982-83, Sacramento Pvt. Industry Coun., 1982-83; coord. Acholic Recovery Program, 1984—. With USN, 1956-60. Mem. Western Apprenticeship Coords. Assn. (statewide dir. 1987—), U.S. Aprenticeship Assn., Sacramento Valley Apprenticeship Tng. Coords. Assn. (rep.), Rancho Murieta County, U.S. Golf Assn., Bing Maloney Golf Club. Democrat. Roman Catholic. Office: Operating Engrs Apprentice 7388 Murieta Dr Sloughhouse CA 95683-9725

UHL, PHILIP EDWARD, marine artist; b. Toledo, Aug. 19, 1949; s. Philip Edward and Betty Jean (Mayes) U. Student, Dayton Art Inst., 1967-68, Art Students League, 1974. Creative dir. Ctr. for Civic Initiative, Milw., 1969-71; VISTA vol. Office Econ. Opportunity, 1969-71; art dir. Artco Advt. Agy., Honolulu, 1972-73; artist, photographer Assn. Honolulu Artists, 1974-77; pres. Uhl Enterprises div. Makai Photography, Honolulu, 1977—, Videoscapes div. Channel Sea TV, Honolulu, 1977—; cons. Pan Am. Airways, N.Y.C. and Honolulu, 1979-84, ITTC Travel Ctr., Honolulu, 1982-83, Royal Hawaiian Ocean Racing Club, Honolulu, 1984—, Sail Am.-Am's Cup Challenge, Honolulu, 1985-86, Am. 3 Found., Am.'s Cup Def., San Diego, 1991-92. Co-producer video documentary White on Water, 1984 (Emmy 1984), Racing the Winds of Paradise (Golden Monitor award Internat. TV Assn. 1989); producer: Joy of Life (Golden Monitor award Internat. TV Assn. 1988), Sailors on the Sea, 1990, Teamwork, Talent, Technology (Tele award 1993); pub., art dir. mags., promotional publs. Pan Am. Clipper Cup, 1980, 82, 84, and Kenwood Cup, 1986, 88, 90, 92, ESPN Kenwood Cup, 1990, 92, ESPN Am.'s Cup, 1991-92, Transpac, 1991, 93; photographer: (book) Nautical Quar. (Soc. Publ. Designer award 1984); contbr. numerous articles, photos to yachting publs. Mem. Am. Film Inst., Internat. Platform Assn., Soc. Internat. Nautical Scribes, Honolulu Creative Group, Am. Soc. Media Photographers, U.S. Yacht Racing Union (now U.S. Sailing Assn., Royal

Hawaiian Ocean Racing Club, Tutukaka S. Pacific Yacht Club, Waikiki Yacht Club. Office: UHL Enterprises 1750 Kalakaua Century Ctr Ste 3-757 Honolulu HI 96826

UHLANER, JULIUS EARL, psychologist, educator; b. Vienna, Apr. 22, 1917; came to U.S., 1928; naturalized 1928; s. Benjamin and Ethel Uhlaner; m. Vera Kolar, Sept. 3, 1949; children: Carole Jean, Lorraine Uhlaner-Hendrickson, Robert Theodore. BS, CUNY, 1938; MS, Iowa State U., 1941; PhD, NYU, 1947. Indsl. psychology asst. Ford Motor Co., Dearborn, Mich., 1940-41; rsch. asst. Iowa State U., Ames, 1940-41; rsch. assoc. NYU, 1941-42; asst. dir. tng. N.Y. State div. Vets. Affairs, N.Y.C., 1946-49; with U.S. Army Rsch. Inst., Washington, 1947-78, tech. dir., 1964-78; chief psychologist U.S. Army, Washington, 1964-78; adj. prof. psychology George Washington U., 1971—; v.p. Perceptronics, Inc., Woodland Hills, Calif., 1978-81; pres. Uhlaner Cons., Inc., Encino, Calif., 1981—. Author: Psychological Research in National Defense Today, 1964; cons. editor Jour. Applied Psychology, 1970—; contbr. articles to profl. jours. Served with USAF, 1944-46. Recipient Presdl. Mgmt. Improvement award, 1978. Fellow Am. Psychol. Assn. (pres. div. mil. psychology 1969-70), Human Factors Soc., Washington Acad. Scis., Iowa Acad. Scis., Ops. Rsch. Soc. Am.; mem. Cosmos Club, Psi Chi. Home and Office: 4258 Bonavita Dr Encino CA 91436-3525

UHM, JAY YUN, wholesale distribution executive; b. Seoul, Korea, Mar. 10, 1964; came to the U.S., 1981; s. Juseph and Huja (Shin) U.; m. Jungrae Kim, Nov. 6, 1991; 1 child, Lawrence. BA, Claremont Mckenna Coll., 1987. Acct. Arthur Andersen & Co., L.A., 1987-88; gen. mgr. EBI, Inc., Santa Fe Springs, Calif., 1988—; cons. Nat. Forest Products Assn., Washington, 1989, Korea Trade Ctr., L.A., 1991, Claremont Acctg. Assn., 1988. Contbr. articles to profl. jours. Mem. organizing staff Korean Am. Rep. Coalition, L.A., 1991. Recipient Svc. award Korean Am. Rep. Coalition, 1991. Mem. Santa Fe Springs C. of C. (safety com. 1992), Norwalk C. of C. (safety com. 1992), Arthur Andersen Alumni Assn., Omicron Delta Epsilon. Office: EBI Inc 12411 McCann Dr Santa Fe Springs CA 90670

UHRICH, RICHARD BECKLEY, hospital executive, physician; b. Pitts., June 11, 1932; s. Leroy Earl and Mabel Hoffer (Beckley) U.; m. Susan Kay Manning, May 25, 1985; children by previous marriage—Mark, Karen, Kimberly. B.S., Allegheny Coll., 1954; M.D., U. Pa., 1958; M.P.H., U. Calif.-Berkeley, 1966. Diplomate: Am. Bd. Preventive Medicine. Intern Lancaster Gen. Hosp., (Pa.), 1958-59; commd. asst. surg. USPHS, 1959, advanced through grades to med. dir., 1967; resident U. Calif., 1965-66; various adminstrv. positions regional and service unit levels Indian Health Services, until 1971; dir. div. programs ops. Indian Health Service, Health Services Adminstrn. USPHS, Washington, 1971-73; assoc. dir. div. profl. resources Office Internat. Health, Office Asst. Sec. for Health, HEW, Washington, 1973-74; assoc. dir. for program devel. and coordination Office Internat. Health, 1974-78; dir. Phoenix Indian Med. Ctr. and Phoenix Services Unit, 1978-81, ret., 1982; sr. adminstr. Good Samaritan Med Ctr., Phoenix, 1981-82, chief exec. officer, 1982-89; v.p. for managed care programs Samaritan Health Svcs., Phoenix, 1989-90; cons. health care systems Phoenix, 1990-93; dir. S.E. Asia Med. Ambassadors Internat., Modesto, Calif., 1993—; mem. Phoenix Regional Hosp. Coun., 1981-88, pres., 1982-83; bd. dirs. Med. Ctr. Redevel. Corp., Phoenix; v.p. Samaritan Redevel. Corp., 1983-88. Bd. dirs. Phoenix Symphony Orch., 1984-89, Ariz. Sr. Olympics Bd., 1985-89. Recipient Meritorious Service medal USPHS, 1973; recipient citation USPHS, 1973, Commd. Officers award, 1981. Mem. Ariz. Hosp. Assn. (bd. dirs. 1980-86, chmn. council on planning 1980-81, council on human resources 1982-83, council on patient care 1983-84, fin. com. 1984-86), Am. Coll. Health Care Adminstrs., Am. Pub. Health Assn., Christian Med. Soc.

UKROPINA, JAMES ROBERT, lawyer; b. Fresno, Calif., Sept. 10, 1937; s. Robert J. and Persida (Angelich) U.; m. Priscilla Lois Brandenburg, June 16, 1962; children—Michael Steven, David Robert, Mark Gregory. A.B., Stanford U., 1959, M.B.A., 1961; LL.B., U. So. Calif., 1965. Bar: Calif. 1966, D.C. 1980. Assoc. firm O'Melveny & Myers, Los Angeles, 1965-72, ptnr., 1972-80, 92—; exec. v.p., gen. counsel Santa Fe Internat. Corp., Alhambra, Calif., 1980-84, dir., 1981-86; exec. v.p., gen. counsel Pacific Enterprises, Los Angeles, 1984-86, pres. and dir., 1986-89, chmn. bd. and chief exec. officer, 1989-91; bd. dirs. Lockheed Corp., Pacific Mut. Life Ins. Co. Editor in chief So. Calif. Law Rev, 1964-65. Trustee Stanford U. Served with USAF, 1961-62. Mem. ABA, Calif. Bar Assn., Los Angeles County Bar Assn., Annandale Golf Club, Calif. Club, Beta Theta Pi. Office: O'Melveny & Myers 400 S Hope St Los Angeles CA 90071-2899

ULAM, FRANÇOISE, freelance writer, editor; b. Paris, Mar. 8, 1918; came to U.S., 1938, naturalized, 1945; d. Pierre and Madeleine (Carcassonne) Aron; m. Stanislaw M. Ulam, Aug. 19, 1941 (dec. May 1984); 1 child, Claire Anne. BA, Mills Coll., 1939; MA, Mt. Holyoke Coll., 1941. Data analyst Los Alamos (N.Mex.) Sci. Lab., 1946-67; freelance writer book revs., profiles, feature stories, 1965—. Editor: Adventures of a Mathematician (Stanislaw M. Ulam), Analogies Between Analogies. Bd. dirs. Santa Fe Women's Health Com., 1982—.

ULLIMAN, JOSEPH JAMES, forester, educator; b. Springfield, Ohio, July 19, 1935; s. Joseph James Sr. and Iola Mae (Roth) U.; m. Barbara Blessing Gish, Apr. 29, 1961; children: Kathryn Nicole, Barbara Anne, Mark Joseph. BA in English, U. Dayton, 1958; MF in Forest Mgmt., U. Minn., 1968, PhD in Forest Mgmt., 1971. Research asst. U. Minn., Mpls., 1966-68, from instr. to asst. prof., 1968-74; mem. staff land use planning Willamette Nat. Forest, Eugene, Oreg., 1973; from assoc. prof. to prof. U. Idaho, Moscow, 1974-79; dir. U. Idaho FWR Remote Sensing Ctr.; co-dir. U. Idaho Remote Sensing Rsch. Unit, assoc. dean 1988-89, dept. head of forest resources, 1989—; cons. USAID, 1979—. Contbr. numerous articles on forestry and remote sensing to profl. jours. and books. Chmn. Natural Resources Com., Moscow, 1980-81, Environ. Commn., South St. Paul, Minn., 1972-74; pres. Moscow Swim Team Parents Assn., 1976. Recipient Phi Kappa Phi Disting. Faculty award, 1985, German Acad. Exchange Program award, 1985. Mem. Am. Soc. Photogrammetry and Remote Sensing (pres. Minn. chpt. 1974, dep. dir. 1983-85, Ford Bartlett award 1981), Soc. Am. Foresters (counselor 1981-84, chmn. remote sensing working group 1982-84), Internat. Soc. Photogrammetry (chmn. working group 1981-84). Democrat. Roman Catholic. Home: 2226 Weymouth St Moscow ID 83843-9618 Office: U Idaho Coll of Forestry Moscow ID 83844-1133

ULLMAN, JEFFREY DAVID, computer science educator; b. N.Y.C., Nov. 22, 1942; s. Seymour and Nedra L. (Hart) U.; m. Holly E., Nov. 19, 1967; children: Peter, Scott, Jonathan. B.S., Columbia U., 1963; Ph.D., Princeton U., 1966; Ph.D. hon., U. Brussels, 1975, U. Paris-Dauphine, 1992. Mem. tech. staff Bell Labs., Murray Hill, N.J., 1966-69; prof. elec. engring., computer sci. Princeton U., 1969-79; prof. computer sci. Stanford U., 1979—, chmn., 1990—; cons. Bell Labs., 1969-89; mem. examination com for computer sci. grad. record exam. Ednl. Testing service, 1978-86; cons. editor Computer Sci. Press., 1982—; mem. computer sci. adv. panel NSF, 1974-77, infor., robotics and intelligent systems adv. panel, 1986-88; chmn. doctoral rating com. for computer sci. N.Y. State Regents, 1989—. Author: Principles of Database and Knowledge-Base Systems, 1988, 89, (2 vols.), (with A.V. Aho and J.E. Hopcroft) Data Structures and Algorithms, 1983, (with J.E. Hopcroft) Introduction to Automata Theory, Languages and Computation, 1979, (with A.V. Aho, R. Sethi) Compilers: Principles, Techniques and Tools, 1986, (with A.V. Aho) Foundations of Computer Science , 1992. Guggenheim fellow, 1989. Mem. Assn. Computing Machinery (mem. council 1978-80), Spl. Interest Group on Automata and Computability Theory (sec.-treas. 1973-77), Spl. Interest Group on Mgmt. Data (vice-chmn. 1983-85), Nat. Acad. Engring. Home: 1023 Cathcart Way Palo Alto CA 94305-1048 Office: Stanford U 216 Margaret Jacks Hall Stanford CA 94305

ULLMAN, PATRICIA, educator; b. Norfolk, Va., Nov. 27, 1953; d. Cyril Alfred and Beatrice (Halpert) U.; 1 child, Nicole Ullman-Rose. AB, U. So. Calif., 1975; MS, Purdue U., 1983, PhD, 1986. Teaching and rsch. asst. Purdue U., West Lafayette, Ind., 1980-86; NIMH postdoctoral fellow UCLA, 1986-88; staff rsch. assoc. U. Calif., Riverside, 1989; tchr. sci. Mountain View Jr. High Sch., Beaumont, Calif., 1989—; cons. Found. for Advancement Sci. Edn., L.A., 1986-87. Traveling scholar U. Chgo., 1985-86; David Ross fellow Purdue U., 1985; math. and sci. grantee GTE, 1991-92. Mem. NSTA, Hastings Ctr. Home: 25350 Santiago Dr Apt 56 Moreno Valley CA 92553 Office: Mountain View Jr High Sch PO Box 187 Beaumont CA 92223

ULLRICH, DENNIS L., sales engineer; b. Jackson, Mich., Aug. 9, 1947; s. Leonard E. and Violet C. (Kreogher) U.; m. Jami Marie Fiore, June 18, 1988; children: Kyle Edward, Kevin Michael, Kelsey Marie. BS, Calif. Poly. U., 1970; MBA, Pepperdine U., 1978. V.p. Hydraflow, Cerritos, Calif., 1965—; sec. SAE G-3A Subcom., Fullerton, Calif., 1985-90. Capt. U.S. Army, 1966-72. Mem. Rotary. Republican. Roman Catholic. Office: Hydraflow 13259 E 166th St Cerritos CA 90701

ULRICH, (ADELE) CELESTE, retired university dean; b. Balt., Aug. 24, 1924; s. Frank and Adele (Seidewitz) U. B.S., U. N.C.-Greensboro, 1946; M.A., U. N.C.-Chapel Hill, 1947; Ph.D., U.So.Calif., 1956. Asst. prof., assoc. prof. James Madison U., Harrisonburg, Va., 1947-56; assoc. prof., prof. U. N.C., Greensboro, 1956-79; prof., dean Coll. Human Devel. and Performance, U. Oreg., Eugene, 1979—. Author: Physical Education, 1970, Social Matrix of Physical Education, 1975, To Seek and Find, 1977; Editor: Physical Education in the 80's, 1982. Bd. mem. Eugene council Girl Scouts Am., 1980—. Mem. AAHPERD (past pres.; Luther H. Gulick award 1983). Democrat. Presbyterian. Home and Office: 3355 N Delta Rd # 104 Eugene OR 97401-7194

ULRICH, DELMONT MARION, physician; b. Connell, Wash., Jan. 22, 1919; s. Otto Carl and Hannah M. (Zimmerman) U.; m. Doris Pauline Swanson, Mar. 25, 1946; children: Beverly, James, Dean. Student, U. Wash., 1937-40; BS, U. Minn., 1941, MD, 1944. Diplomate Am. Bd. Internal Medicine. Intern Milw. County Hosp., 1944, resident internal medicine, 1944-46; practice medicine specializing in internal medicine Seattle, 1949—; assoc. clin. prof. medicine U. Wash., Seattle, 1950—; pres. med. staff Providence Hosp., Seattle, 1968-69. Served to capt. AUS, 1946-48. Mem. AMA, Seattle Acad. Medicine, NW Soc. Clin. Research, Wash. State Soc. Internat. Medicine (pres. 1956-57), Theta Chi, Phi Rho Sigma. Republican. Episcopalian. Club: Seattle Yacht. Home: 5017 NE Laurelcrest Ln Seattle WA 98105-5245

ULRICH, PAUL GRAHAM, lawyer, author, publisher, editor; b. Spokane, Wash., Nov. 29, 1938; s. Donald Gunn and Kathryn (Vandercook) U.; m. Kathleen Nelson Smith, July 30, 1982; children—Kathleen Elizabeth, Marilee Rae, Michael Graham. B.A. with high honors, U. Mont., 1961; J.D., Stanford U., 1964. Bar: Calif. 1965, Ariz. 1966, U.S. Supreme Ct. 1969, U.S. Ct. Appeals (9th cir.) 1965. Law clk. judge U.S. Ct. Appeals, 9th Circuit, San Francisco, 1964-65; assoc. firm Lewis and Roca, Phoenix, 1965-70; ptnr. Lewis and Roca, 1970-85; pres. Paul G. Ulrich PC, Phoenix, 1985-92, Ulrich, Thompson & Kessler, P.C., 1992—; owner Pathway Enterprises, 1985-91; judge pro tem Div. 1, Ariz. Ct. Appeals, Phoenix, 1986; instr. Thunderbird Grad. Sch. Internat. Mgmt., 1968-69, Ariz. State U. Coll. Law, 1970-73, 78, Scottsdale Community Coll., 1975-77, also continuing legal edn. seminars. Author and pub.: Applying Management and Motivation Concepts to Law Offices, 1985; editor, contbr.: Arizona Appellate Handbook, 1978—; Working with Legal Assistants, 1980, 81; Future Directions for Law Office Management, 1982; People in the Law Office, 1985-86; co-author and publisher: Arizona Healthcare Professional Liability Handbook, 1992, supplement, 1993, Arizona Healthcare Professional Liability Defense Manual, 1992, Arizona Healthcare Professional Liability Update Newsletter, 1992—; contbg. editor Law Office Economics and Management, 1984—; contbr. articles to profl. jours. Mem. Ariz. Supreme Ct. Task Force on Ct. Orgn. and Adminstrn., 1988-89; mem. com. on appellate cts. Ariz. Supreme Ct., 1990-91; bd. visitors Stanford U. Law Sch., 1974-77; adv. com. legal assisting program Phoenix Coll., 1985—. With U.S. Army, 1956. Recipient continuing legal edn. award State Bar Ariz., 1978, 86, 90, Harrison Tweed spl. merit award Am. Law Inst./ABA, 1987. Fellow Ariz. Bar Found. (founding 1985—); mem. ABA (chmn. selection and utilization of staff personnel com., econs. of law sect. 1979-81, mem. standing com. legal assts. 1982-86, co-chmn. joint project on appellate handbooks 1983-85, co-chmn. fed. appellate handbook project 1985-88, chmn. com. on liaison with non-lawyer orgns. Econs. of Law Practice sect. 1985-86), Am. Acad. Appellate Lawyers, Am. Law Inst., Am. Judicature Soc. (Spl. Merit Citation 1987), Ariz. Bar Assn. (chmn. econs. of law practice com. 1980-81, co-chmn. lower ct. improvement com. 1982-85, co-chmn. Ariz. appellate handbook project 1976—), Maricopa County Bar Assn., Calif. Bar Assn., Phi Kappa Phi, Phi Alpha Delta, Sigma Phi Epsilon. Republican. Presbyterian. Home: 107 E El Caminito Dr Phoenix AZ 85020-3503 Office: 3030 N Central Ave Ste 1000 Phoenix AZ 85012-2717

ULUM, JENNIFER LYNN, public relations executive; b. Cedar Rapids, Iowa, Feb. 11, 1957; d. James Clarence and Ann Marie (Shepherd) U.; m. Timothy Wilson Gleason, June 20, 1987. BA, Linfield Coll., McMinnvile, Oreg., 1977; MA, U. Oreg., 1983. Legis. asst. Oreg. State Senate, Salem, 1979; dir. pub. info. Bur. Labor & Ind., Portland, 1979; flight attendant N.W. Airlines, Mpls., 1979-81; grad. teaching fellow U. Oreg., Eugene, 1981-83; editor Seattle Woman Mag., 1983-84; info. specialist U. Wash., Seattle, 1984-85; pub. info. officer Bellevue (Wash.) pub. schs., 1985-87; dir. community rels. Sacred Heart Gen. Hosp., Eugene, 1987-92; dir. external affairs Sacred Heart Health System, Eugene, 1992—. Bd. dirs. Eugene Family YMCA, 1990—; bd. dirs., sec., Am. Cancer Soc., Eugene, 1988—; pub. rels. chmn. Vol. Connection, Eugene, 1989; vice chmn. Great Am. Smokeout Com., Seattle, 1985-87. Recipient Spotlight award, Pub. Rels. Soc. Am., 1990, Award of Excellence, Nat. Sch. Pub. Rels. Assn., 1987. Democrat. Methodist. Home: 3061 Whitbeck Blvd Eugene OR 97405-1977 Office: Sacred Heart Health Sysytem PO Box 1479 Eugene OR 97440-3700

ULVELING, ROGER ALAN, international business consultant; b. Detroit, Dec. 20, 1943; s. Ralph Adrian and Elizabeth (Baer) U.; m. Margaret Jane Eichelberger, Nov. 27, 1968; children: Jennifer Anne, Katherine Emily, Robert Adam. BA, U. Detroit, 1966; grad. advanced mgmt. program, Harvard U., 1981. Dir. mktg. Wailea Land Corp. (subsidiary of Alexander & Balwin, Inc.), Honolulu, 1970-73; project mgr. Pacific Resources, Inc., Portland, Oreg., 1973-75; asst. to exec. v.p. Pacific Resources, Inc., Honolulu, 1975-76, dir. adminstrn., 1976-77, dir. govt. affairs, 1977-80, v.p., 1980-86; dir. dept. planning and econ. devel., dept. bus., econ. devel. & tourism State of Hawaii, 1986-91; internat. bus. cons. Natural Energy Lab. of Hawaii Authority, 1986-91, High Tech. Devel. Corp., 1986-91, Honolulu, 1991—; dir. Hawaii affiliate Am. Heart Assn., 1991—; long range planning com. La Jardin Acad., 1978—. Div. chmn. Aloha United Way, Honolulu, 1977-79; bd. dirs. Child and Family Svc., Honolulu, 1982-83; trustee Le Jardin Acad., Kailua, Hawaii, 1978-90, Palama Settlement, Honolulu, 1980-82. Lt. USNR, 1967-69. Named Hon. Consul of Belgium, Govt. of Belgium, 1980. Clubs: Pacific (Honolulu) (bd. dirs. and chmn. house com. 1981-85), Kaneohe (Hawaii) Yacht. Home: 1556 Mokulua Dr Kailua HI 96734-3241 Office: 700 Bishop St Ste 400 Honolulu HI 96813-4171

UMBERG, THOMAS JOHN, state legislator, lawyer; b. Cin., Sept. 25, 1955; s. John H. and Joan (Jansen) U.; m. Robin Bailey; children: Erin Nicole, Brett Thomas, Thomas Bailey. BA, UCLA, 1977; JD, U. Calif., Hastings, 1980. Bar: Calif. 1980, U.S. Dist. Ct. (ctrl. dist.) Calif. 1981, U.S. Dist. Ct. (so. dist.) Calif. 1986, U.S. Ct. Appeals (9th cir.) 1988. Asst. U.S. atty. U.S Dept. Justice, Santa Ana, Calif., 1987-90; assembly mem. Calif. Assembly, 1990-92; of counsel Palmieri Tyler et al, Irvine, Calif., 1992—. Capt. U.S. Army, 1981-85, Maj. USAR. Roman Catholic. Office: 12387 Lewis St Ste # 203 Garden Grove CA 92640

UMEZAWA, HIROOMI, physics educator, researcher; b. Saitama-ken, Japan, Sept. 20, 1924; came to Can., 1975; s. Junichi and Takako (Sato) U.; m. Tamae Yamagami, July 30, 1958; children: Rui, Ado. B of Engring., U. Nagoya, Japan, 1947, DSc in Physics, 1952. Research asst. U. Nagoya, 1947-53, assoc. prof., 1953; assoc. prof. U. Tokyo, 1955, prof., 1960-64; prof. U. Napoli Inst. Theoretical Physics, Italy, 1964-66; prof. U. Wis., Milw., 1967-67, disting. prof., 1967-75; dir. Inst. Theoretical Physics, Helsinki, Finland, 1965; group leader on structure of matter Centre of Nat. Research Naples div., Italy, 1964-66; Killam Meml. prof. sci., prof. physics U. Alta., Edmonton, Can., 1975-92, Killam prof. emeritus, 1992—; vis. prof. U. Wash., Seattle, 1956, U. Md., College Park, 1957, U. Iowa, Iowa City, 1957, U. Marseille, France, 1959. Mem. editorial bd. Physics Essays, NRC Can.; contbr. numerous articles to profl. jours. ICI fellow U. Manchester, Eng., 1953-55; Lady Davis Sr. scholar, Israel, 1989; Two books published in honor of his 60th birthday, 1985, 86; several internat. workshops held in his honor. Fellow N.Y. Acad. Scis., Am. Phys. Soc., Royal Soc. Can.; mem. Japan Phys. Soc. (life). Office: U Alta, Dept of Physics, Edmonton, AB Canada T6G 2J1

UMLAND, PAULINE SAWYER, retired realtor associate; b. Salem, Mass., June 14, 1903; d. Arthur Franklin and Nellie Susan (Page) Sawyer; m. E. Eugene Umland, Aug. 26, 1932 (dec. May 1969); children: Gretchen Umland Kingsbury, Peter S., Diana Umland Bos. BBA, Boston U., 1925, MBA, 1928. Fin. sec. Walnut Hill Sch., Natick, Mass., 1927-29; buyer Jordan Marsh Co., Boston, 1929-31, R.H. White Co., Boston, 1931-32; sec.-treas. Umland & Co. Advt., San Francisco, 1949-54, Umland-Eastman-Becker Advt., San Francisco, 1954-58; assoc. Rochex & Rochex Realtors, San Mateo, Calif., 1958-77, Jane Powell, Realtor, San Mateo, Calif., 1977-92; retired, 1992. Vol. Mills Hosp. Aux.; mem. life McKinley Sch. PTA, Peninsula Braille Transcribers Guild. Mem. AAUW, Gamma Phi Beta. Republican. Methodist. Home: 416 Villa Ter Apt 1 San Mateo CA 94401-1652

UNDERHILL, KAREN JEAN, university archivist, historian; b. Cambridge, Mass., Dec. 15, 1960; d. Thomas Warren and Anne Winsett (Carter) U.; m. David John Mangelsdorf, May 22, 1983 (div. Apr. 1990); 1 child, Alyssa Seren Mangelsdorf. BS in History, No. Ariz. U., 1982; MA in History, U. Ariz., 1990. Teaching asst. dept. history U. Ariz., Tucson, 1982-84; spl. projects archivist Ariz. Hist. Soc., Tucson, 1984-85, asst. registrar, 1985-88, mus. registrar, 1988; mus. registrar San Diego Hist. Soc., 1988-90; archivist, manuscripts curator No. Ariz. U., Flagstaff, 1990—; hist. cons. Escondido (Calif.) Hist. Soc., 1988-89, Archival Mgmt. & Cons., Tucson, 1985, Environ. Systems, Inc., Tucson, 1985. Copy editor ConservatioNews, 1990-92; contbr. articles to profl. jours. Sunday sch. tchr. Episcopal Ch. of the Epiphany, Flagstaff, 1991—; bd. dirs. Coordinating Com. for History in Ariz., 1991—; mem. Ariz. State Records Mgmt. Coun., 1991—. Named to Outstanding Young Women of Am., 1986. Mem. Am. Assn. for State and Local History (membership chair 1985—, mem. standards, tenure and ethics com. 1991—, Cert. of Commendation 1986, award 1989), Ariz. Paper and Photograph Conservation Group (membership com. 1990—), Soc. S.W. Archivists. Office: No Ariz U Cline Libr PO Box 6022 Flagstaff AZ 86011-6022

UNDERWOOD, RALPH EDWARD, computer systems engineer; b. Houston, Sept. 26, 1947; s. Harry Anson and Ethel Jackson Underwood; m. Linda Sue Merkel, Apr. 10, 1976. BS in Biology, Baker U., 1969; JD, Washburn U., 1973; MS in Computer Sci., Kans. U., 1984. Bar: Kans, 1973. Free-lance stock and options trader Prairie Village, Kans., 1974-79; mem. staff BDM Corp., Leavenworth, Kans., 1982-84; sr. research and devel. engr. Ford Aerospace and Communications Corp., Colorado Springs, Colo., 1984-87, subcontract adminstr., 1987-89; sr. engr., program mgr. CTA Inc., Colorado Springs, 1989—. Patentee in field. Mem. IEEE, Info. System Security Assn., Armed Forces Communications and Electronics Assn., Kans. Bar Assn., Upsilon Pi Epsilon, Sigma Phi Epsilon (social chmn. 1968, asst. house mgr. 1968, sec./treas. sr. coun. 1969), Phi Alpha Delta. Office: CTA Inc 7150 Campus Dr Ste 100 Colorado Springs CO 80920-6592

UNDERWOOD, STEVEN CLARK, publishing executive; b. Arlington Heights, Ill., Dec. 1, 1960; s. Donald William and Mary Frances (Clark) U. BBA, U. Tex., 1982, MBA, 1987; JD, So. Meth. U., 1985. Bar: Tex. 1985. Sr. fin. analyst CBS, Inc., N.Y.C., 1987-89; assoc. bus. mgr. supplementary edn. group Simon & Schuster, Englewood Cliffs, N.J., 1989-90; bus. mgr. Fearon/Janus/Quercus divsn. Simon & Schuster, Belmont, Calif., 1990-92, pres. Fearon/Janus/Quercus divsn., 1992-93, pres. Globe/Fearon divsn., 1993—. Mem. ABA, Am. Mgmt. Assn. (pres.'s assn.), Nat. Eagle Scout Assn., Coll. Bus. Adminstrn. Found., Tex. Bar Assn., Tex. Alumni Assn., Alpha Phi Omega, Beta Gamma Sigma, Phi Kappa Phi, Phi Eta Sigma, Golden Key. Republican. Methodist. Office: Simon & Schuster Globe Fearon Div 500 Harbor Blvd Belmont CA 94002

UNDERWOOD, THOMAS WOODBROOK, communications company executive; b. Royal Oak, Mich., Nov. 29, 1930; s. Elmer and Della Marie (Zimmer) U.; m. Louise Virginia, May 24, 1953 (dec. Feb. 1979); children: Ann Marie Underwood Shuman, Dan and Dave (twins). BAS in Elec. Engring., Milw. Sch. Engring., 1957. Service analyst, writer ITT Gillfillan, Los Angeles, 1958-60; sr. tech. editor, writer Smithkline Beckman, Fullerton, Calif., 1960-78; tech. com. mgr. Smithkline Beckman, Brea, Calif., 1978-85; pres. Tranwood Communications, Santa Ana, Calif., 1985—. Tech. editor, writer manuals for manned space flights to Mars and the moon. Served to staff sgt. USAF, 1950-54, Korea. Mem. Soc. Tech. Communications (Orange County chpt., sr., pres. 1992, 93, treas. 1966, 88), Am. Med. Writers Assn, U.S. C. of C., Santa Ana C. of C. Democrat. Office: Tranwood Communications PO Box 5578 Buena Park CA 90620

UNGER, ARLENE KLEIN, employee assistance consultant and counselor; b. Bklyn., May 12, 1952; d. Eli and Harriet Barbara (Shapiro) Klein; m. Stefan Howard Unger, Aug. 19, 1979; children: Max Elias, Elana Rose. BS with distinction, Emerson Coll., 1974; MS, So. Conn. State Coll., 1976, Calif. State U., Hayward, 1981; Phd, Western Grad. Sch. Psychology, Palo Alto, Calif., 1991. Site adminstr., teaching specialist Severely Delayed Langs. Program Santa Clara (Calif.) County, 1976-81; language-movement counselor Peninsula Children's Ctr., Palo Alto, 1981-83; marriage, family and child counselor Woodside (Calif.) Psychol. Services, 1983-84; dir. tng. and sales Human Resource Services Employee Assistance Program, Sunnyvale, Calif., 1984-86; pvt. practice psychol. counseling Palo Alto, 1984-86; regional Employee Assistance mgr. Occupational Health Services, Sunnyvale, 1986-91; pvt. practice Counseling and Cons. Resources, Palo Alto, 1991—; prin., v.p. operations Allied Health Svs., 1992—; mental health counselor, instr. Foothill Coll., Los Altos, Calif., 1984-85; exec. dir. Sunnyvale Children's Arts and Movement Program, 1979-81, Cafe Motek, 1976-81; vol. instr. in music and movement Ohlone Sch., Palo Alto, 1986—; founder, pres. Boutique Supply, Palo Alto, 1985; founder Let's Talk Program, Western Athletic Clubs, 1991—; speaker to various groups and orgns. Active Palo Alto Docent. Mem. Assn. for Counseling and Devel., Assn. Labor Mgmt. Adminstrs. and Cons. on Alcoholism (conf. chair Santa Clara chpt. 1987—), Calif. Assn. Marriage and Family Counselors, Assn. Tng. and Devel., Am. Dance Therapy Assn. Clubs: Palo Alto Run, Santa Clara Decathlon. Home: 2250 Webster St Palo Alto CA 94301-4053

UNGER, DONALD CHARLES, JR., software engineer, software company executive; b. Detroit, Apr. 17, 1949; s. Donald Charles and Barbara Unger. BS, Eastern Mich. U., 1971. Tchr. Peace Corps, Queen Victoria Sch., Fiji Islands, 1972-76; head dept. math Queen Victoria Sch., 1976-78; test engr. Automotive Environ. Systems, Inc., Westminster, Calif., 1978-80; pres. Data Acquisition Software, Inc., Redondo Beach, Calif., 1980—; software cons. Am. Honda Emission Labs., Torrance, Calif., 1981—; software engr. Am. Honda Motor Co., Torrance, 1991—. Mem. Soc. Automotive Engrs., Assn. for Computing Machinery. Office: Data Acquisition Software 1527 Carver St Redondo Beach CA 90278

UNGER, LENORE, civic worker; b. N.Y.C., June 12, 1929; d. Benedict S. Rosenfeld and Ora (Copel) Kanner; m. Bernard D. Copeland, May 17, 1953 (dec. March 1968); children: Harry (dec.), Robert (dec.); m. C. Wyatt Unger, Mar. 26, 1969 (dec. Feb. 1992); 1 child, Amy Unger; m. F. Lowry Wyatt, Sept. 12, 1992. Student, Mills Coll., 1946-48; BA, Stanford U., 1950, MA, 1952; postgrad., NYU, 1952-53. Instr. Stanford U., Palo Alto, Calif., 1952, Hunter Coll., N.Y.C., 1052-53, Calif. State U., Sacramento, 1056-60, U. Calif., Davis, 1965-68; property mgr. Unger, Demas & Markakis, Sacramento, 1974-83; former actress and model. Pres. Sacramento Opera Assn., 1972-73; treas. Sacramento Children's Home, 1990-92, v.p., 1992—; former mem. bd. dirs. Sutter Hosp. Aux., Sutter Hosp. Med. Rsch. Found., Sacramento Symphony League, Temple B'nai Israel Sisterhood, Sacramento chpt. Hadassah, Sacramento Children's Home Guild; active Sacramento Opera Assn., Crocker Soc. of Crocker Art Gallery, Sacramento Symphony Assn., Sacramento Reportory Theater Assn. Mem. Am. Contract Bridge League, Sacramento Pioneer Assn., Stanford U. Alumni Assn. (past bd. dirs. Sacramento) Sutter club, Kandahar Ski Club, Sutter Lawn Tennis Club, DelPaso Country CLub (capt. women's golf 1983), Tacoma Country and Gulf Club,

Maui Country Club, Orcas Island Yacht Club, Wash. Athletic Club, Tacoma Club. Republican. Jewish.

UNGER, RICHARD ALLAN, health facility administrator, educator; b. Bklyn., May 8, 1948; s. Edwin A. and Ruth (Dunne) U.; divorced; 1 child, Andrina Jones. BA, SUNY, Binghamton, 1971. Fin. planner I.D.S., Houston, 1977-80; dir., founder Internat. Inst. Hand Analysis, San Rafael, Calif., 1985—; lectr., leader workshops nationwide, 1980—. Editor Hand Analysis Jour., Hand Analysis Newsletter. Office: Internat Inst Hand Analysis Box 151313 San Rafael CA 94915

UNGERMAN, KIMBALL REID, computer company executive; b. Vancouver, Wash., Dec. 30, 1957; s. Reid Grant and Patricia (Graves) U.; m. Michelle Conrad, Mar. 17, 1990. Student, Rick's Coll., Rexburg, Idaho, 1976-77, Weber State Coll., Ogden, Utah, 1980-84. Tchr. English as a Second Lang. Davis Area Vocat. Ctr., Kaysville, Utah, 1980-82; sales mgr., trainer Computer Store, Inc., Ogden, 1982-84; trainer Apple Computer, Inc., Salt Lake City, 1984-85; sr. trainer Apple Computer, Inc., Phoenix, 1985-88; tng. devel. specialist Apple Computer, Inc., Cupertino, Calif., 1988—; tng. cons. Red Cross Emergency Svcs., San Mateo, Calif., 1990. Mem. Internat. Interactive Communications Soc. Mormon. Office: Apple Computer Inc 20525 Mariani Ave # 72TS Cupertino CA 95014-6201

UNIS, RICHARD L., state supreme court justice; b. Portland, Oreg., June 11, 1928. Grad., U. Va., U. Oreg. Bar: Oreg. 1954, U.S. Dist. Ct. Oreg. 1957, U.S. Ct. Appeals (9th cir.) 1960, U.S. Supreme Ct. 1965. Judge Portland Mcpl. Ct., 1968-71; judge Multnomah County Dist. Ct., 1972-76, presiding judge, 1972-74; former judge Oreg. Cir. Ct. 4th Judicial Dist., 1977; former sr. dep. city atty. City of Portland; adj. prof. of local govt. law and evidence Lewis & Clark Coll. Northwestern Sch. Law, 1969-76, 77—; faculty mem. The Nat. Judicial Coll., 1971—; former faculty mem. Am. Acad. Judicial Edn. Author: Procedure and Instructions in Traffic Court Cases, 1970, 101 Questions and Answers on Preliminary Hearings, 1974. Bd. dirs. Oreg. Free from Drug Abuse; mem. Oreg. Adv. Com. on Evidence Law Revision, chmn. subcom., 1974-79. Maj. USAFR, JAGC, ret. Recipient Meritorius Svc.award U. Oregon sch. Law, 1988; named Legal Citizen of Yr. Oreg. Law Related Edn., 1987; inducted into The Nat. Judicial Coll. Hall of Honor, 1988. Mem. Am. Judicature Soc. (bd. dirs. 1975), Am. Judges Assn., Multnomah Bar Found., Oregon Judicial Conf. (chmn. Oreg. Judicial Coll. 1973-80, legis. com. 1976—, exec. com. of judicial edn. com., judicial conduct com.), N.Am. Judges Assn. (tenure, selection and compensation judges com.), Dist. Ct. Judges of Oreg. (v.p., chmn. edn. com.), Nat. Conf. Spl. Ct. Judges (exec. com.), Oreg. State Bar (judicial adminstrn. com., sec. local govt. com., com. on continuing certification, uniform jury instrn. com., exec. com. criminal law sect., trial practice sect. standards and certification com., past chmn., among others), Oreg. Trial Lawyers Assn. (named Judge of Yr. 1984). Office: Oreg Supreme Ct Supreme Ct Bldg Salem OR 97310

UNPINGCO, ANTONIO REYES, senator; b. Chalan Pago, Guam, Apr. 21, 1942; s. Jose Aguon and Eliza (Reyes) U.; m. Emilia Cruz Borja, June 19, 1965; children: Eliza, Christine, Raymund, Nicole, Noel, Meriza, Carlo, Aaron, Jerome, Daniel. BBA, Portland State U., 1969. Dep. dir. Dept. Adminstrn., Agana, Guam, 1971-73; chief planner planning and rsch. com. Guam Legis., Agana, 1975-76; mem. Guam Senate, Agana, 1977-86, 88—, asst. minority leader, 1988-90, 91-93; minority leader, 1993—; gen. agt. Moylan's Ins. Co., Agana, 1986-88; bd. dirs. Citizen Security Bank, Agana; chmn. credit com. Govt. of Guam Credit Union, Agana, 1969-70. Exec. dir. Rep. Party of Guam, 1974-75. Recipient Outstanding Svc. award Boy Scouts Am., 1979, Outstanding Support award Jr. ROTC program George Washington High Sch., 1978-79. Mem. K.C. Roman Catholic. Home: 115 Talisay Dr Agana GU 96915-1517 Office: Guam Legis 155 Hesler Pl Agana GU 96910-5010

UNSER, AL, professional auto racer; b. Albuquerque, May 29, 1939; s. Jerry H. and Mary C. (Craven) U.; m. Wanda Jesperson, Apr. 22, 1958 (div.); children: Mary Linda, Debra Ann, Alfred; m. Karen Barnes, Nov. 22, 1977 (div.). Auto racer U.S. Auto Club, Speedway, Ind., 1964—. Home: 7625 Central NW Albuquerque NM 87121

UNSER, BOBBY (ROBERT WILLIAM UNSER), professional auto racer, television commentator; b. Albuquerque, Feb. 20, 1934; s. Jerry and Mary (Craven) U.; m. Barbara Schumacher, 1953 (div. 1966); m. Norma Davis, 1967 (div. 1970); m. Marsha Sale, Oct. 20, 1976; children: Bobby Jr., Cyndi, Robby, Jeri. Former modified stock car race driver; now driver profl. racing cars; commentator ABC, 1987—; cons. Expert Accident Reconstructionist, U.S., 1985—. Co-author: The Unbelievable Unsers, 1970, The Bobby Unser Story, 1978, Unser: An American Family Portrait, 1988. Served with USAF, 1953-56. Recipient 1st pl. Indy 500 award U.S. Auto Club, 1968, 75, 81, 1st pl. Calif. 500 award U.S. Auto Club, 1974, 76, 79, 80, 1st pl. Pocono 500 award Championship Auto Racing Teams, Pa., 1980; named U.S. Auto Club Nat. Driving Champion, 1969, 75, Martini and Rossi Driver of Yr., 1974. Home and Office: 656 N Macdonald St Mesa AZ 85201-5020

UNSOELD, JOLENE, congresswoman; b. Corvallis, Oreg., Dec. 3, 1931; m. William F. Unsoeld (dec.), 1951; children: Regon, Devi (dec.), Krag, Terres. Student, Oreg. State U., 1950-51. Dir. U.S. Info. Svc. English Lang. Inst., Kathmandu, Nepal, 1965-67; mem. Wash. Ho. of Reps., 1985-88, 101st-103rd Congresses from 3rd Wash. dist., Washington, D.C., 1989—; mem. Merchant Marine and Fisheries com., subcom. fisheries and wildlife conservation, environment, merchant marine, edn. and labor com., subcoms. elementary, secondary and vocational edn., labor mgmt. rels., postsecondary edn., tng. Office: US Ho of Reps Office House Mems 1527 Longworth HOB Washington DC 20515-4703*

UNTERMAN, IRA NATHAN, non-profit administrator; b. L.A., June 7, 1964; s. David H. and Jenny L. (Leydesdorff) U. BA, Calif. State U., Fullerton, 1987; MSW, U. So. Calif., 1990, MPA, 1990. Dir. B'nai B'rith Youth, Garden Grove, Calif., 1986-89; intern Orange County Mental Health Assn., Santa Ana, Calif., 1988-89, United Way Orange County, Garden Grove, 1989-90; bus. mgr. Image Pro, Fullerton, Calif., 1986-90; pvt. practice Huntington Beach, Calif., 1983—; v.p./treas. Pacific Greek Inc., L.A., 1990-91; pres. Pacific Greek, Inc., Berkeley, 1991—; field rep. Devel. Corp. for Israel, L.A., 1990-91; city dir. Devel. Corp. for Israel, San Diego, 1991—. Bd. dirs. Jewish Community Ctr. of Cen. Orange County, Garden Grove, treas., 1990; chpt. advisor Sigma Alpha Mu. Mem. B'nai B'rith (Orange Coast Lodge).

UNZICKER, KATERINA DAWN, affirmative action analyst; b. Farmington Hills, Mich., Dec. 28, 1965; d. Jan Roger and Magdalen Martha (Luptak) U. BS, U. Fla., 1989. Guest rels. trainer Walt Disney Co., Orlando, Fla., 1988-91; spl. svc. coord. ITT Ednl. Svcs., West Covina, Calif., 1991-92; affirmative action analyst City of L.A., 1992—. Author: (mag.) The Valencian, 1987. Mem. C. of C., West Covina, 1991-92, Verdugo Hills Dem. Party, 1992—, Assembly Dist. 43 Ctrl. Com., 1993, Women's Caucus, 1993—; del. state conv. Calif. Dem. Party, 1993; vol. Big Sisters of L.A., 1992. Recipient Innsburck Ambassador award U. New Orleans, 1989. Mem. Equal Opportunity Compliance Officers Assn. Democrat. Home: 800 N Verdugo Rd Glendale CA 91206

UPHAM, STEADMAN, anthropology educator, university dean-official; b. Denver, Apr. 4, 1949; s. Albert Tyler and Jane Catherine (Steadman) U; m. Margaret Anne Cooper, Aug. 21, 1971; children: Erin Cooper, Nathan Steadman. BA, U. Redlands, 1971; MA, Ariz. State U., 1977, PhD, 1980. Dist. sales mgr. Ind. News Co. Inc., Los Angeles, 1971-72; regional sales mgr. Petersen Pub. Co, Los Angeles, 1972-74; archeologist, researcher Bur. Land Mgmt., Phoenix, 1979; research asst. Ariz. State U., Tempe, 1979-80; chief archeologist Soil Sytems Inc., Phoenix, 1980-81; chief archeologist N.Mex. State U., Las Cruces, N.Mex., 1981-85, asst. prof. to assoc. prof., 1982-87, assoc. dean, 1987-90; prof. anthropology, vice provost, grad. dean U. Oreg., Eugene, 1990—; interim dir. Cultural Resources Mgmt. div, N.Mex. State U., Las Cruces, 1988. Author: Polities and Power, 1982, A Hopi Social History, 1992; editor: Computer Graphics in Archaeology, 1979, Mogollon Variability, 1986, The Sociopolitical Structure of Prehistoric Southwest Societies, 1989, The Evolution of Political Systems, 1990; also articles. Advanced seminar grantee Sch. of Am. Research, 1987, research grantee NSF, 1979, 1984-85, Hist. Preservation grantee State of N.Mex., 1982-84, 1991, 92, Ford Found. 1991-92, U.S. Dept. Edn. 1991-93. Mem. Nat. Physical Sci Consortium (pres. 1992-95), Western Assn. Grad. Schs. (pres.-elect). Office: U Oreg Grad Sch 125 Chapman Hall Eugene OR 97403

UPHOFF, JOSEPH, publishing executive, editor; b. Iowa City, Nov. 1, 1955; s. Raymond Daniel and Shirley Anne (Johnson) U. BA, U. San Diego, 1979; postgrad., UCLA, 1979-81, PhD, 1991. Libr. UCLA, 1981; pvt. practice info. specialist San Diego, 1982-86; tutor San Diego Mesa Coll., 1983-85; abstract editor Numismatics Internat. Bull., Dallas, 1984—; with libr. City of San Diego, 1986-91; pres. Gold Dragon Publs., San Diego, 1988—. Contbr. articles to profl. jours. Treas. San Diego MacIntosh User's Group, 1988. Mem. Intertel, Royal Numismatic Soc., Ancient Numismatic Soc. San Diego (pres. 1982—), Numismatic Literary Guild, Mensa (poetry editor San Diego chpt. 1989), Phi Alpha Theta.

UPTON, JAMES NATHAN, small business owner; b. Balt., July 26, 1948; s. James Abram and Hazel Marie (Branham) U.; m. Corrine Renee Boudreaux, Sept. 25, 1969 (div. Nov. 1982); children: Kimberly Ann, Joseph Allen; m. Susan Ellen Emra Conn, Dec. 31, 1982; children: Dennis Walter Conn, David Brion Conn, Jon Ryan. Student, Peabody Conservatory, Balt., 1964-66, Towson State Coll., Balt., 1970-72. Music tchr. Corkran Jr. High, Glen Burnie, Md., 1969-70; salesman Tacoma (Wash.) Window Shade Co., 1972-80, mgr., 1980-84, owner, 1984-86; owner Jim's Installation Svc., Puyallup, Wash., 1986—; seminar speaker, cons. Ind. Interior Decorators, Tacoma, 1986-93. Mus. dir. Gospel Quintet, Sounds of Joy, 1985-89. Child advocate speaker Wash. State Legis. Hearings, Olympia, 1989; foster parent Dept. Social and Health Svcs., Tacoma, 1988-91. With U.S. Army, 1966-69. Mem. Nat. Assn. Self-Employed, Monocan Indian Tribal Assn. Mem. Four-Square Ch. Home and Office: 10018 Taylor St E Puyallup WA 98371

URBANSKI, DOUGLAS JAMES, film and theater producer, talent manager; b. Somerville, N.J., Feb. 17, 1957; s. Roman and Diane (Rustic) U. BFA, NYU, 1979. Sr. v.p. prodn. The IndieProd Co. div. Carolco Pictures, L.A., 1987-88; pres. Douglas Mgmt., Ltd., 1990—, Matisce Pictures, 1992—; co-mng. dir. Boston's Met. Ctr., 1982-84; cons. Miami Opera, 1981-84, Houston Grand Opera, 1981-84. Producer Broadway plays including Whodunnitt, Show Boat, 1981-83 (6 Tony nominations), Beethoven's Tenth, 1983-84, The Woman of Independent Means, 1983-84 (L.A. Critics award), Strange Inerlude, 1984-85 (6 Tony nominations), Benefactors, 1984 (winner Best Play Drama Critics Circle award), Aren't We All, 1985-86 (Spl. Drama Critics Circle award), Wild Honey, 1986, Sweet Bird of Youth, 1986, Blithe Spirit, 1987 (3 Tony nominations); London plays include Strange Interlude, Aren't We All, 1984-85, Benefactors, 1985-86, The Caine Mutiny Court Marshall, 1986, Sweet Bird of Youth, 1986-87, The Way of the World, 1986-87, Wild Honey, 1986-87 (9 Olivier awards, Evening Standard award), Tony N'Tina's Wedding, 1989, 90 (L.A. Drama Critics Circle award). Mem. Players Club. Roman Catholic.

URCIA, INGEBORG, English language educator; b. Nurnberg, Germany, Apr. 6, 1934; came to U.S., 1952; d. Werner Edward and Ilse (Lebermann) O.; m. Jose Urcia, July 25, 1958; children: Benjamin Urcia, Gwendolyn Urcia. BA in English, U. Wash., 1955, MA in English, 1956, PhD in English, 1960. Instr. Yakima Valley Coll., Yakima, Wash., 1962-63; asst. prof. U. Nev., Las Vegas, 1963-65, Calif. Poly. U., Pomona, 1965-68; assoc. prof. Eastern Wash. U., Cheney, 1969-83, prof., 1983—; book reviewer and critical adv. Eastern Wash. Book Review Coun., Spokane Sch. Dists., 1983—. Author: All About Rex Cats, 1983, This is the Russian Blue, 1984, For the Love of Cats, 1985, The American Shorthair Cat, 1992, The Russian Blue Cat, 1992. Bd. dirs. Spokanimal Humane Soc., 1985-88; editor Spokanimal newsletter, 1985-88; adv. and judge Spokane area 4-H clubs. Mem. Nat. Conf. Tchrs. and Educators, Modern Lang. Assn., Phi Beta Kappa. Lutheran. Home: PO Box 36 Cheney WA 99004-0036 Office: Ea Wash U Dept English Cheney WA 99004

URENA-ALEXIADES, JOSE LUIS, electrical engineer; b. Madrid, Spain, Sept. 5, 1949; s. Jose L. and Maria (Alexiades Christodulakis) Urena y Pon. MSEE, U. Madrid, Spain, 1976; MS in Computer Science, UCLA, 1978. Rsch. asst. UCLA, 1978; systems analyst Honeywell Info. Systems, L.A., 1978-80; mem. tech. staff Jet Propulsion Lab., Pasadena, Calif., 1980-91; exec. dir. Empresa Nacional de Innovacion S.A., L.A., 1991—. Contbr. various articles to profl. jours. Two times recipient NASA Group Achievement award. Mem. IEEE, IEEE Computer Soc., IEEE Communications Soc., Assn. for Computer Machinery, World Federalist Assn., Spanish Profl. Am. Inc. Roman Catholic. Home: 904 Dickson St Marina Dl Rey CA 90292-5513 Office: Empresa Nacional Innovacion SA 2049 Century Park E Ste 2770 Los Angeles CA 90067-3202

URI, GEORGE WOLFSOHN, accountant; b. San Francisco, Dec. 8, 1920; s. George Washington and Ruby (Wolfsohn) U.; m. Pamela Dorothy O'Keefe, May 15, 1961. A.B., Stanford U., 1941, I.A., 1943, M.B.A., 1946; postgrad., U. Leeds, Eng., 1945. C.P.A., Calif.; Chartered Fin. Cons.; Cert. Fin. Planner. Mem. acctg., econs. and stats. depts. Shell Oil Co., Inc., San Francisco, 1946-48; ptnr. Irelan, Uri, Mayer & Sheppie, San Francisco; pres. F. Uri & Co., Inc., Irelan Accountancy Corp.; instr. acctg. and econs. Golden Gate Coll., 1949-50. Contbr. articles to profl. jours. Chmn. San Rafael Redevel. Adv. Com., 1977-78, mem., 1978-91, mem. emeritus, 1991—; bd. dirs. San Francisco Planning and Urban Renewal Assn., 1958-60. Served with AUS, 1942-46, to col. Res. (ret.). Recipient Key Man award San Francisco Jr. C. of C.; Meritorious Service medal Sec. of Army, 1978. Mem. AICPA (hon. 1991), Inst. Mgmt. Scis. (treas. No. Calif. chpt. 1961-62), Calif. Soc. CPAs (sec.-treas. San Francisco chpt. 1956-57, dir. 1961-63, state dir. 1964-66, mem. Forbes medal com. 1968-69, chmn. 1969-71, hon. 1991), Am. Econs. Assn., Inst. Mgmt. Accts., San Francisco Estate Planning Council (dir. 1965-68), Am. Statis. Assn., Am. Soc. Mil. Comptrollers, Exec. Assn. San Francisco (pres. 1965-66), Inst. Cert. Mgmt. Accts. (cert. mgmt. acctg., Disting. Performance cert. 1978), Inst. Cert. Fin. Planners, Am. Soc. CLUs and Chartered Fin. Cons. Clubs: Engrs. San Francisco, Commonwealth (quar. chmn. 1971), Stanford (dir. 1990—); Army and Navy (Washington). Home: 11 Mcnear Dr San Rafael CA 94901-1545 Office: 100 Pine St Ste 2000 San Francisco CA 94111-5294

URISTA, JUAN, computer scientist; b. L.A., July 3, 1957; s. Pablo and Teresa (Franco) U.; m. Laura, July 31, 1983; children: Timothy James, Tawny Joy. AS, Don Bosco Tech. Inst., Rosemead, Calif., 1976; BS, Calif. State U., L.A., 1990. Software engr. Deep Space Network Jet Propulsion Labs/NASA, Pasadena, Calif., 1982-90, design engr. advanced info. systems, 1990—; mem. speaker's bur. Jet Propulsion Lab., Pasadena, 1992. Author: (design documents) Software Design of Antenna Pointing, 1985. Mem. Pasadena Speech Club (pres. 1991-92, v.p. 1988-89). Home: 712 Charter Oak South Pasadena CA 91030 Office: Jet Propulsion Lab 4800 Oak Grove Pasadena CA 91109

URQUHART, JOHN, physician, corporation executive; b. Pitts., Apr. 24, 1934; s. John and Wilma Nelda (Martin) U.; m. Joan Cooley, Dec. 28, 1957; children: Elizabeth Urquhart Wynne, John Christopher (dec. 1965), Robert Malcolm, Thomas Jubal. BA with honors, Rice U., 1955; MD with honors, Harvard U., 1959. Lic. physician, Calif. Walter B. Cannon fellow in physiology Harvard Med. Sch., Boston, 1956, Josiah Macy, Jr. fellow, 1956-58, 59-61; intern in surgery Mass. Gen. Hosp., Boston, 1959-60, asst. resident, 1960-61; investigator Nat. Heart Inst., NIH, Bethesda, Md., 1961-63; asst. prof. physiology U. Pitts. Sch. Medicine, 1963-66, assoc. prof., 1966-68, prof., 1968-70; prof. biomed. engring. U. So. Calif., Los Angeles, 1970-71; prin. scientist ALZA Corp., Palo Alto, Calif., 1970-86, dir. biol. scis., 1971-74, pres. research div., 1974-78, dir., 1976-78, chief scientist, 1978-82, sr. v.p., 1978-85; co-founder APREX Corp., Fremont, Calif., pres., 1986-88, chmn., 1988-91, chief scientist, 1988—; vis. prof. pharmacology U. Limburg Sch. Medicine, Maastricht, The Netherlands, 1984-85, vis. prof. pharmacoepidemiology, 1986-91; prof. pharmaco-epidemiology, 1992—; adj. prof. pharmacy U. Calif.-San Francisco, 1984—; mem. dir.'s adv. com. NIH, 1986-88. Co-author: Risk Watch, 1984; contbr. numerous articles to sci. jours.; patentee therapeutic systems for controlled drug delivery and regimen compliance monitoring (43). Trustee GMI Engring. and Mgmt. Inst., Flint, Mich., 1983—; bd. dirs. Am. Social Health Assn., Palo Alto, 1983-89, v.p. 1986-87. Served with USPHS, 1961-63. NIH grantee, 1963-70; Bowditch lectr. Am. Physiol. Soc., 1969. Mem. Biomed. Engring. Soc. (pres. 1976), Boyleston Med. Soc., Internat. Soc. Pharmaco-epidemiology, Am. Soc. Clinical Pharmacology and Therapeutics, Soc. for Clinical Trials, Endocrine Soc., Saturday Morning club Palo Alto., Am. Physiol. Soc., Soc. Risk Analysis. Home: 975 Hamilton Ave Palo Alto CA 94301-2213 Office: APREX Corp 47221 Fremont Blvd Fremont CA 94538-6502

URSIN, BJARNE ELLING, manufacturing company executive; b. Bridgeport, Conn., Aug. 8, 1930; s. Bjarne and Esther (Schiott) U.; student Oberlin Coll., 1949-51; BS in Physics, MIT, 1957; m. Mary Elizabeth Locke, July 26, 1969; children: Stephanie, Lara, Matthew, Jonathan, Teri, Kristian. Project engr. Raytheon, Andover, Mass., 1957-60; prin. investigator Gen. Dynamics, San Diego, 1960-62; sr. scientist Philco-Ford, Newport Beach, Calif., 1962-67; with McDonnell Douglas Corp., Huntington Beach, Calif., 1967-76, sr. ops. project mgr., mgr. mfg., 1967-76; prodn. mgr. Eldec Corp., Lynnwood, Wash., 1976-78; v.p. mfg. TCS Inc., Redmond, Wash., 1978-80; bd. dir. new bus. Data I/O Corp., Redmond, 1980-82; prodn. mgr. Atex Inc., A Kodak Co., 1982-83; quality assurance systems mgr. Boeing Electronics Co., Seattle, 1983—; assoc. Coldwell Banker Co., 1981-83, Wallace and Wheeler Realty, 1984—; owner Westechnology, Bellevue, Wash., 1980—; co-owner Lighthouse Interiors, 1982—; community chmn. City of Huntington Beach, 1975-76. With AUS, 1951-53, Korea. Recipient NASA Team award Saturn/Apollo, 1975, Nasa Design VIP award Skylab, 1976, Cert. Appreciation, McDonnell Douglas, 1976. Mem. Am. Assn. Physics Tchrs., AIAA, AAAS, U.S. Internat. Sailing Assn., Am. Mgmt. Assn. Republican. Roman Catholic. Clubs: Bahia Corinthian Yacht (bd. dir. 1972-76, rear commodore 1974, vice commodore 1975, commodore 1976) (Corona Del Mar); Royal Norwegian Yacht (Oslo); Balboa Bay; Seattle Yacht, U.S. Power Squadron, MIT of Puget Sound (bd. dir. 1979—). Home and Office: PO Box 1218 Mercer Island WA 98040-1218 also: PO Box 6968 Bellevue WA 98008-0968

USHER, HARLAN KING, consulting company executive; b. Superior, Nebr., Apr. 12, 1909; s. Grant and Addra Belle (King) U.; m. Lida Marie Hall, June 17, 1928 (dec. 1961); children: Janet Marie Usher Elliott, Ronald Lee Usher; m. Grace Augusta Brinkman Staton, May 15, 1965. BS in Chemistry, U. Wash., 1930, cert. tchr., 1930. Tchr. scis. Chelan (Wash.) High Sch., 1930-34; chemistry mgr. North Cen. Labs., Inc., Wenatchee, Wash., 1935-39; inspector Boeing Airplane Co., Seattle, 1940-45; tech. sales rep. L.H. Butcher Co., Seattle, 1945-46; sales mgr. Beaver & Bohm Mfg. Co., Mt. Vernon, Wash., 1946-48; sales rep. Balfour, Guthrie & Co., Seattle, 1948-52; supr. engring. and mfg. rsch. The Boeing Co., Seattle, 1953-70; owner, mgr. Acme Pers. Agy., Santa Rosa, Calif., 1970-79; pres., dir. Ell Ell Diversified, Inc., Santa Rosa, 1984—. Author: How To Get A Job-With No Experience or Not Enough, 1981, Grown Ups Mother Goose, 1982. Counselor Svc. Corps. of Retired Execs., Santa Rosa, 1981-83. Recipient Spl. SCORE award U.S. SBA, 1982. Office: Ell Ell Diversified Inc PO Box 1702 Santa Rosa CA 95402

USHER, RONALD LEE, government health care consultant, retired county official; b. Wenatchee, Wash., Sept. 14, 1935; s. Harlan King and Lida Marie (Hall) U.; m. Nancy Jean Mallon, Dec. 30, 1961; children: Bradley, Eric, Craig, Michael. BBA, U. Puget Sound, 1957; M in Govtl. Adminstrn., U. Pa., 1959; PhD in Pub. Adminstrn., Golden Gate U., 1980. Adminstrv. intern City of Vallejo (Calif.), 1958-59, asst. city mgr. and personnel dir., 1962-65; adminstrv. analyst Sonoma County, Santa Rosa, Calif., 1959-62; town mgr. Town of Corte Madera (Calif.), 1965-70; city and borough mgr. City and Borough of Juneau (Alaska), 1970-74; city mgr. City of Mill Valley (Calif.), 1974-75; dir. health and human svcs. Marin County, San Rafael, Calif., 1975-78; dir. health Sacramento County, Sacramento, 1978-92; adj. prof. Golden Gate U., San Francisco and Sacramento, 1977—; asst. prof. Calif. State U., Sacramento, 1978-88; cons. Placer County Grand Jury, Auburn, Calif., 1981, County of Sacramento, 1992—, Health For All, Inc., 1992—; asst. clin. prof. U. So. Calif., Sacramento, 1983-84, 90. Contbr. articles to profl. jours. Bd. dirs. Community Svcs. Planning Coun., Sacramento, 1978-92, Parent Support Program, Sacramento, 1984-87, Golden Empire Hypertension Coun., 1987-90, Cities in Schs., Sacramento, 1989-92; exec. couple Sacramento Marriage Encounter, 1988-90. Recipient Exceptional Svc. in Pub. Health award Taxpayers League Sacramento County, 1988. Mem. ASPA (chpt. pres. 1972-73, 86-87, Outstanding Pub. Adminstr. award Sacramento 1991), Calif. Conf. Local Mental Health Dirs. (exec. bd. 1981-86), County Health Execs. Calif. (exec. bd. 1988-92).

USHIJIMA, JEAN M., city official; b. San Francisco, Feb. 14, 1933; d. Toyoharu George and Frances Fujiko (Misumi) Miwa; m. Tad E. Ushijima; 1 child, Carol M. BS, U. San Francisco, 1981. City clk. City of Beverly Hills, Calif., 1973—. Bd. dirs. West L.A. Japanese Am. Citizens League, 1979—, pres., 1988-81, also chmn. bd.; bd. dirs. Leadership Edn. for Asian Pacifics, 1985-90. Mem. Acad. Advanced Edn., City Clks. Assn. Calif. (pres. 1986, City Clerk of Yr. award 1989), Calif. Women in Govt. (program chmn. 1978-79), Beverly Hills C. of C. (Employee of Yr. award 1990), Leadership Edn. for Asian Pacific (chmn. bd. 1987), League Calif. Cities (adminstrv. svcs. com. 1982-86, 93—), Internat. Inst. Mcpl. Clks. (bd dirs. 1988-91). Avocations: reading, Japanese dancing. Office: City Clk 455 N Rexford Dr # 190 Beverly Hills CA 90210-4817

USHMAN, NEAL LESLIE, accounting educator; b. Cornwall, N.Y., Apr. 30, 1951; s. Milton Allen and Lillian (Dubrow) U.; m. Jill Hazel Klion, June 15, 1975 (div. July 1979); m. Linda Diane Hunt, Aug. 15, 1982 (div. Apr. 1992); children: Evanne Alexandra, Kenneth Matthew, Kayla Catherine. AB, Cornell U., 1973, MBA with distinction, 1975, MA, 1981, PhD, 1983. CPA, Calif., Md. Acct. Price Waterhouse & Co., Washington, D.C., 1975-77; asst. prof. acctg. Santa Clara (Calif.) U., 1982-88; assoc. prof. acctg. Santa Clara U., 1988—. Contbr. articles to profl. jours. Doctoral fellow Am. Acctg. Assn., 1981-82. Mem. Am. Acctg. Assn., Am. Inst. CPA. Jewish. Home: 675 Sharon Park Dr-119 Menlo Park CA 94025 Office: Santa Clara Univ Leavey Sch Bus Santa Clara CA 95053

USINGER, MARTHA PUTNAM, educator; b. Pitts., Dec. 10, 1912; d. Milo Boone and Christiana (Haberstroh) Putnam; m. Robert Leslie Usinger, June 24, 1938 (dec. Oct. 1968); children: Roberta Christine, Richard Putnam. AB cum laude, U. Calif., Berkeley, 1934; postgrad., Oreg. State U., 1935, U. Ghana, 1970, Coll. Nairobi, 1970. Tchr. Oakland (Calif.) Pub. Schs., 1936-38; tchr. Berkeley (Calif.) Pub. Schs., 1954-57, dean West Campus, counselor, 1957-78; lectr., photographer in field. Author: Ration Books and Christmas Crackers, 1989. Mem. adv. coun. Lifespan Alta Bates Hosp. Mem. DAR, Berkeley Ret. Tchrs., U. Calif. Emeriti Assn., U. Calif. Alumnae Assn., Prytanean Alumnae Assn. (pres. 1952-54), Mortar Bd., Delta Kappa Gamma. Congregationalist.

USITALO, IRENE JOANN, vocational school educator, small business owner; b. Seattle, June 6, 1921; d. Edwin A. and Vivien I. (Rice) Walton; m. Richard R. Usitalo, Jan. 15, 1940; children: Richard E., Carol Usitalo Donaldson, Clinton D. Grad., Met. Bus. Coll., Seattle, 1940; student, Western Wash. U., 1958-59, Tacoma Community Coll., 1983; AA in Humanities, Highline Coll., Midway, Wash., 1976. Cert. vocat. tchr., Wash. Tchr. Clover Park Vocat. Coll., Tacoma, 1984—; exec. sec. Puyallup (Wash.) Sch. Dist., 1972-86; adminstrv. sec. Auburn (Wash.) Sch. Dist., 1965-72; exec. sec. U. Wis., Milw., 1964-65; adminstrv. sec. Seattle Sch. Dist., 1961-64; bookkeeper McBeath Glass Co., Bellingham, 1960-62, Bellingham Flying Svc., 1959-60, Silverdale (Wash.) Fuel and Transfer, 1947-49; adminstrv. asst. to dietitian Western Wash. U., Bellingham, 1950-53; adminstrv. sec., office mgr. Bellingham (Wash.) High Sch., 1953-58; instr. Highline Community Coll., 1976-84, South Sound Community Coll., Yelm, Wash., 1987; owner, mgr., presenter profl. workshops IJ Usitalo & Assocs., Federal Way, Wash., 1985—; advisor com. for office occupation Tacoma Community, Pierce Community, Highline Community Colls., Federal Way High Sch., 1975-88. Contbr. articles to newsletters and mags. Mem. Wash. Women United, 1984—, Women for Choice, 1989—. Recipient Spl. Dir.'s award Puyallup Sch. Dist., 1984. Mem. NAFE (networking com. 1986), Nat. Assn. Ednl. Office Pers. (life, cert. ednl. office employee award of distinction 1981, advisor profl. standards program 1985-91, chmn. vocat.-adult edn. coun. 1989-91, editor/pub./contbr. Nat. Ednl. Sec. mag. and Crossroads newsletter), Am. Bus. Womens Assn. (chpt. pres. 1986), NW Adult Edn. Assn., Am. Mgmt. Assn., Wash. Assn. Ednl. Office Pers. (life, past pres., Employee of Yr. award 1982, editor/pub./contbr. newsletter), Wash. Assn. Maintenance and Ops. Adminstrs. (editor/pub./contbr. newsletter), Past Pres. Assn.

(treas, pres.), Federal Way C. of C., Order Ea. Star (life). Home: 3025 SW 300th Pl Federal Way WA 98023-2373

USSERY, HARRY MACRAE, lawyer; b. Rockingham, N.C., Jan. 27, 1920; s. Robert Roy and Maggie Estelle (MacRae) U.; m. Olive Dual Simmons, Mar. 19, 1949. AA, Wake Forest U., 1947; JD, George Washington U., 1950. Bar: D.C. 1950. Assoc. firm Geiger & Harmel, Washington, 1950-52; ptnr. firm McNeill & Ussery, Washington, 1952-53; gen. counsel, dir. Harry R. Byers, Inc., Engring. and Constrn. Power Plants, Washington and Denver, 1953-59; procurement counsel Martin Marieta Corp., Denver, 1959-62; authorized agt. RCA, Camden N.J., 1962-69; staff counsel, mgr. internat. subcontract ops. Burns & Roe Constrn. Corp., Paramus, N.J., 1969-74; staff counsel Burns & Roe Indsl. Svcs. Corp., 1975-78; asst. to pres., Burns & Roe Svcs. Corp., Oradell, N.J., 1978-81; investor, Santa Fe, 1981—; broker Collector Cars, 1990—; founder, chmn. Assn. Mortgage Investors, Inc., 1983-86; chmn. Santa Fe Mortgage Investments, Inc., 1984-86; spl. city atty for annexations-contracts, Santa Fe, 1985-87; founder and pres. The House of USSER, Internat., 1993—.editor Investors Voice, 1983-86; chief moderator, dir., Dist. Roundtable, Sta. WWDC, Washington, 1950-53; cons., estate planning counsel Gloyd S. Lovell Trust, 1986—. Served with USAAF, 1941-45. Recipient Community Chest campaign awards, 1951, 52. Mem. ABA, Am. Judicature Soc., Nat. Contract Mgmt. Assn., D.C. Bar Assn. (exec. coun. Jr. bar sect. 1954-56), George Washington U. Law Assn., Wake Forest U. Alumni Assn., Geneal. Soc. Santa Fe (state commr.), Council Scottish Clans Assns., St. Andrew's Soc., Clan MacRae Soc., Clan Donald and Assoc. Scots N.Mex., Delta Theta Phi. Republican. Presbyterian. Club: Santa Fe Vintage Car (pres., editor newsletter 1985—) (Santa Fe). Author: The Origin of the Surname of Ussery, 1983 (founder-pres. The House of Usser, Internat., a Norman-Celtic family soc. 1993); contbr. articles to various publs. Address: 2953 Plaza Azul Santa Fe NM 87505

USUI, LESLIE RAYMOND, clothing executive; b. Wahiawa, Hawaii, Feb. 2, 1946; s. Raymond Isao and Joyce Mitsuyo (Muramoto) U.; m. Annie On Nor Hom, Oct. 23, 1980; 1 child, Atisha. BA in Zool., U. Hawaii, 1969, MA in Edn., 1972. Cert. tchr., Hawaii. Flight steward United Airlines, Honolulu, 1970; spl. tutor Dept. Edn., 1971-73; v.p. Satyuga, Inc., Honolulu, 1974-80; pres. Satyuga, Inc., 1980—; also bd. dirs.; cons. Hawaii Fashion Guild, 1978-79. Composer: Song to Chenrayzee, Song to Karmapa. Co-founder, bd. dirs. Kagyu Thegchen Ling Meditation Ctr., 1974—, Maitreya Inst., 1983-86; bd. dirs. Palpung Found., 1984—; mem. U.S. Senatorial Bus. Adv. Bd., Washington, 1988; charter mem. Citizens Against Govt. Waste, 1988—, Citizens for Sound Economy, 1987-91, Nat. Tax Limitation Com., 1988-89. Mem. Nat. Fedn. Ind. Bus., Am. Biog. Inst. (life, bd. govs. 1990), Hawaii Bus. League, Internat. Biog. Centre (life), Internat. Platform Assn., World Inst. Achievement (life), Cousteau Soc., Nature Conservancy, Honolulu Zool. Soc., Waikiki Aquarium. Republican. Buddhist. Home: 1417 Laamia Pl Honolulu HI 96821-1403 Office: Satyuga Inc 248 Mokauea St Honolulu HI 96819-3110

UTHOFF, MICHAEL, dancer, choreographer, artistic director; b. Santiago, Chile, Nov. 5, 1943; came to U.S., 1962; s. Ernst and Lola (Botka) U.; m. dau., Michelle. Grad. biology, high sch., Chile; dance tng. with Juilliard Sch., 1962-65, Martha Graham, 1962-63, Joffrey Ballet, 1965-68, Sch. Am. Ballet, 1962-64; Laureate in Humanities, St. Joseph Coll., Hartford, Conn. Leading dancer Jose Limon Dance Co., 1964-65, City Center Joffrey Ballet, 1965-68, N.Y.C. Opera, 1968-69; leading dancer, asst. dir. First Chamber Dance Co. N.Y., from 1969; artistic dir. Hartford Ballet Co., 1972-92, Ballet Ariz., 1992—; mem. faculty Juilliard Sch. Music, N.Y.C., from 1969; guest artist, tchr. Princeton Ballet Soc.; prof. dance SUNY, Purchase, 1972-74; instr. dance and drama movement, Yale U.; works premiered by Compania Nacional de Danzas, Mexico City, 1989; guest choreographer Shanghai Ballet, Republic of China, 1986; led Hartford Ballet on 3-week 11-city tour of Peoples Republic of China by invitation of Shanghai Internat. Culture Assn., 1988, 5-week 9-country tour Latin Am., 1991. Choreographer, dancer-actor film Seafall, 1968; opera prodns. Aida and La Cenerentola, Honolulu, 1972, Conn. Opera Romeo et Juliette, 1989, Pitts. Opera Aida, 1988; choreographer Quartet, City Center Joffrey Ballet, 1968, The Pleasure of Merely Circulating, Juilliard Sch. Music, 1969, Windsong, Reflections, Dusk, Promenade, First Chamber Dance Co., 1969-70, Mozart's Idomeneo for Caramoor Music Festival, 1970, Concerto Grosso for Ballet Clasico 70 of Mexico, also restaged Dusk, 1972, Aves Mirabiles, 1973, Danza a Quattro, 1973, Marosszek Dances, 1973, Duo, 1974, Pastorale, 1974, Brahms Variations, 1974, Autumalal, 1975, Mir Ken Geharget Veren, 1976, Tom Dula, 1976, Unstill Life, 1977, Songs of a Wayfarer, 1977, White Mountains Suite, 1978, Bach Cantata, 1978, The Nutcracker, 1979, Romeo and Juliet, 1981, Cachivaches, 1981, Reflections on the Water, 1981, Weeping Willow, 1982, Carmencita Variations, 1982, Hansel and Gretel, 1983, Coppelia, 1986, Speak Easy, 1986, New England Triptych, 1986, Los Copihues, 1988, Petrouchka, 1988, RFD #1, 1989, Classical Symphoniette, 1990, Alice in Wonderland, 1991, Nocturnes, 1991, Sinfonia Danzante, 1991; Nat. Endowment Arts commns. for choreography: Primavera, Minn. Dance Theatre, 1975, Panvezitos, Greater Houston Civic Ballet, 1976, Sonata, The Prodigal Son, Hartford Ballet, 1977, 79. Recipient award for best choreography for Murmurs of the Stream, Chilean Nat. Press, 1983, Critic's Circle Best of Yr. in Arts award, Chile, 1984. Office: Ballet Arizona 3645 E Indian School Rd Phoenix AZ 85018

UTNE, JOHN RICHARD, retired radiation oncologist; b. Fergus Falls, Minn., Oct. 2, 1924; s. John Arndt and Dagney Louise (Thyse) U.; m. Bernice Gertrude Kiefer, June 19, 1948; children: John Stephen, Susan Elizabeth, Barbara Ellen, Linda Louise. Student, Marquette U., 1943; BS, U. Ill., Chgo., 1946, MD, 1948; MS, U. Minn., 1955. Diplomate Am. Bd. Radiology. Intern Mpls. Gen. Hosp., 1948-49; pvt. practice, Mpls., 1948-50, Northfield, Minn., 1951-52; resident in radiology Mayo Clinic, Rochester, Minn., 1953-55; radiologist, chief staff St. John's Mercy Hosp., Mason City, Iowa, 1956-74; radiologist Scripps Meml. Hosp., La Jolla, Calif., 1974-85; locum tenens radiologist, 1985—. Former mem. Mason City Sch. Bd.; former dist. pres. Boy Scouts Am., Mason City; radiologist Project Hope, Managua, Nicaragua, 1965, Tunis, Tunisia, 1969. Lt. M.C., USN, 1951-53, Korea. Named Man of Yr., Sertoma Club, Mason City, 1968. Fellow Am. Coll. Radiology; mem. Radiol. Soc. N.Am. (emeritus). Republican. Lutheran. Home: 220 Coast Blvd La Jolla CA 92037

UTTAL, WILLIAM R(EICHENSTEIN), psychology educator, research scientist; b. Mineola, N.Y., Mar. 24, 1931; s. Joseph and Claire (Reichenstein) U.; m. Michiye Nishimura, Dec. 20, 1954; children: Taneil, Lynet, Lisa. Student, Miami U. Oxford, Ohio, 1947-48; B.S. in Physics, U. Cin., 1951; Ph.D. in Exptl. Psychology and Biophysics, Ohio State U., 1957. Staff Psychologist, mgr. behavioral sci. group IBM Research Center, Yorktown Heights, N.Y., 1957-63; assoc. prof. U. Mich., Ann Arbor, 1963-68, prof. psychology, 1968-86, research scientist, 1963-86, prof. emeritus, 1986—; grad. affiliate faculty dept. psychology U. Hawaii, 1986—; research scientist Naval Ocean Systems Ctr.-Hawaii Lab., Kailua, 1985-88; prof., chmn. dept. psychology Ariz. State U., Tempe, 1988-92, prof. dept. indsl. and mgmt. systems engring., 1992—, affiliated prof., Dept. of Computer Sci. and Engring., 1993—; vis. prof. Kyoto (Japan) Prefectural Med. U., 1965-66, Sensory Sci. Lab., U. Hawaii, 1968, 73, U. Western Australia, 1970-71, U. Hawaii, 1978-79, 80-81; pres. Nat. Conf. on On-Line Uses Computers in Psychology, 1974. Author: Real Time Computers: Techniques and Applications in the Psychological Sciences, 1968, Generative Computer Assisted Instruction in Analytic Geometry, 1972, The Psychobiology of Sensory Coding, 1973, Cellular Neurophysiology and Integration: An Interpretive Introduction, 1975, An Autocorrelation Theory of Visual Form Detection, 1975, The Psychobiology of Mind, 1978, A Taxonomy of Visual Processes, 1981, Visual Form Detection in Three Dimensional Space, 1983, Principles of Psychobiology, 1983, The Detection of Nonplanar Surfaces in Visual Space, 1985, The Perception of Dotted Forms, 1987, On Seeing Forms, 1988, The Swimmer: A Computational Model of a Perceptual Motor System, 1992; also numerous articles; editor: Readings in Sensory Coding, 1972; assoc. editor Behavioral Research Method and Instrn., 1968-90, Computing: Archives for Electronic Computing, 1963-75, Jour. Exptl. Psychology: Perception and Performance, 1974-79. Served to 2d lt. USAF, 1951-53. USPHS spl. postdoctoral fellow, 1965-66; NIMH research scientist award, 1971-76. Fellow AAAS, Am. Psychol. Soc., Soc. Exptl. Psychologists; mem. Psychonomics Soc. Office: Ariz State U Dept Indsl and Mgmt Systems Engring Tempe AZ 85287-1104

UTTER, ROBERT FRENCH, state supreme court justice; b. Seattle, June 19, 1930; s. John and Besse (French) U.; m. Elizabeth J. Stevenson, Dec. 28, 1953; children: Kimberly, Kirk, John. BS, U. Wash., 1952; LLB, 1954. Bar: Wash. 1954. Pros. atty. King County, Wash., 1955-57; individual practice law Seattle, 1957-59; ct. commr. King County Superior Ct., 1959-64, judge, 1964-69; judge Wash. State Ct. Appeals, 1969-71; judge Wash. State Supreme Ct., 1971—, chief justice, 1979-81; lectr. in field; leader comparative law tour Peoples Rep. of China, 1986, 87, 88, 91, USSR, 1989; adj. prof. constl. law U. Puget Sound, 1987, 88, 89, 90, 91. Editor books on real property and appellate practice. Pres., founder Big Brother Assn., Seattle, 1955-67; pres., founder Job Therapy Inc., 1963-71; mem. exec. com. Conf. of Chief Justices, 1979-80, 81-86; pres. Thurston County Big Bros./Big Sisters, 1984; lectr. Soviet Acad. Moscow, 1991; USIA visitor to comment on jud. system, Latvia, 1992. Named Alumnus of Yr. Linfield Coll., 1973, Disting. Jud. Scholar U. Ind., 1987, Judge of Yr. Washington State Trial Lawyers, 1989, Outstanding Judge Washington State Bar Assn., 1990, Outstanding Judge Seattle-King County Bar Assn., 1992. Mem. ABA (commentator on proposed constns. of Albania, Bulgaria, Romania, Russia, Lithuania, Azerbaijan, Uzbekistan, Byelarus, Kazakhstan & Ukraine), Am. Judicature Soc. (Herbert Harley award 1983, sec. 1987—, chmn. bd. dirs., mem. exec. com.), Order of Coif. Baptist. Office: Wash Supreme Ct Temple of Justice Olympia WA 98504*

UYEHARA, CATHERINE FAY TAKAKO (YAMAUCHI), physiologist, educator, pharmacologist; b. Honolulu, Dec. 20, 1959; d. Thomas Takashi and Eiko (Haraguchi) Uyehara; m. Alan Hisao Yamauchi, Feb. 17, 1990. BS, Yale U., 1981; PhD in Physiology, U. Hawaii, Honolulu, 1987. Postdoctoral fellow SmithKline Beecham Pharms., King of Prussia, Pa., 1987-89; rsch. pharmacologist, asst. prof. in pediatrics U. Hawaii John Burns Sch. Medicine, Honolulu, 1989—; statis. cons. dept. clin. investigation Tripler Army Med. Ctr., Honolulu, 1984-87, 89—, chief rsch. pharmacology sect., 1991—. Co-inventor method for preserving renal function in cases of rhabdomyolysis; contbr. articles to profl. jours. Mem. Am. Fedn. for Clin. Rch., Western Oc. Pediatric Rsch., Am. Physiol. Soc., N.Y. Acad. Scis., Soc. of Uniformed Endocrinologists. Democrat. Mem. Christian Ch. Office: Tripler Army Med Ctr Dept Clin Investigation HSHK-CI Honolulu HI 96859-5000

UYEHARA, OTTO ARTHUR, mechanical engineering educator emeritus, consultant; b. Hanford, Calif., Sept. 9, 1916; s. Rikichi and Umi (Nakayama) U.; m. Chisako Suda, Aug. 12, 1945; children: Otto Kenneth, Susan Joy Uyehara Schultheiss, Emi Ryu Uyehara-Stewart. BS, U. Wis., 1942, MS, 1943, PhD, 1946. Postdoctoral fellow U. Wis., Madison, 1945-46, rsch. assoc., 1946-47, asst. prof., then assoc. prof., 1949-57, prof., 1957-82, prof. emeritus, 1982—; pvt. practice cons. Anaheim, Calif., 1985—; mem. sci. adv. com. Eclin Corp., Branford, Conn., 1980—. Recipient Sci. Achievement awrd Japan Soc. Automotive Engrs. Fellow Soc. Automotive Engrs.; mem. ASME, Japan Soc. Mech. Engrs. (hon.). Home: 544 S Bond St Anaheim CA 92805-4823

UZILEVSKY, MARCUS, artist; b. Bklyn., Apr. 10, 1937; s. Chaim and Sarah (Zucker) U.; divorced; children: Bonni Scott, Daniel. Grad. high sch., N.Y.C. Artist, fine art pub. Oaksprings Impressions, Woodacre, Calif., 1980—. Recipient Purchase award 19th Bradley Nat. Print Exhbn., 1988, Alexandra Mus., 1988, Design Excellence award Print Mag., 1988. Home: PO Box 166 Woodacre CA 94973-0166

VACHON, ROGATIEN ROSAIRE (ROGIE VACHON), professional ice hockey executive; b. Palmarolle, Que., Can., Sept. 8, 1945; m. Nicole Vachon; children: Nicholas, Jade, Mary Joy. Goaltender Montreal (Que.) Canadiens, NHL, 1966-72, Los Angeles Kings, NHL, 1972-78, Detroit Red Wings, NHL, 1978-80, Boston Bruins, 1980-82; asst. coach Los Angeles Kings, 1982-84, gen. mgr., 1984—, former alt. gov., now asst. to chmn. Co-recipient Vezina Trophy, 1968. Office: care Los Angeles Kings PO Box 17013 3900 W Manchester Blvd Inglewood CA 90306

VACTOR, ALMA KANE, service executive; b. Cleve., July 7, 1925; d. Marvin A. and Fan (Morgenstern) Kane; m. David C. Vactor, Oct. 8, 1944 (dec. 1984); children: Drew, Wendy Sekovich, Jill Gunzel. Student, Syracuse U., 1942-44, Western Reserve U., 1945-47. Owner, operator, v.p. Rancho Del Rio, Inc., Tucson, 1945—, food cons., 1950—; owner, operator The Tack Room Restaurant, Tucson, 1965—; tchr. cooking U. Ariz. Health Scis. Ctr., 1970—, Brandeis U., 1970—; owner, v.p., sec. K&V Water Co., 1963—; gen. ptnr. Rancho Del Rio Ltd. Ptnrship., 1984—. Bd. dirs. Fan Kane Research Fund Brain Injured Children, 1955-90, So. Ariz. Jewish Hist. Soc. Recipient Five Star award Mobil Travel Guide, 1977-93, 5 Diamond award AAA, 1993. Mem. Tucson Panhellenic (pres. 1965-76). Office: Rancho Del Rio 2800 N Sabino Canyon Rd Tucson AZ 85715-3241

VAIL, DAVID LYNN, military officer; b. Newport, R.I., June 18, 1953; s. Ronald A. and Lois (Reeves) V.; m. Mary B. Leon, Mar. 30, 1980; children: Sean Kristofer, Ashley Noel. BS in Aerospace Engring., U.S. Naval Acad., 1977; postgrad., U. So. Calif., Pt. Mugu, 1992—. Lic. comml. pilot. Commd. ensign USN, 1977, advanced through grades to lt. comdr., 1987; legal, line, electronic warfare and tng. officer Fleet Composite Squadron One, Barbers Point, Hawaii, 1980-83; aviation safety, student control officer Tng. Squadron 22, Kingsville, Tex., 1983-85; safety, asst. maintenance officer Fleet Composite Squadron Ten, Guantanamo Bay, Cuba, 1985-88; ops. officer, targets directorate Pacific Missile Test Ctr., Pt. Mugu, Calif., 1988-91; ops., safety officer Fleet Composite Squadron One, Barbers Point, Hawaii, 1991-92; aviation tng. officer CINCPACFLT Staff, Pearl Harbor, Hawaii, 1992—; cons. Pacific Aerospace Mus., Honolulu; coord. Thunderbirds Pt. Mugu (Calif.) Air Show, 1989. Co-chmn. Fly Through Time-Pacific Aerospace Mus., Honolulu, 1992. Mem. Hickam Aero Club, Naval Acad. Alumni Assn. Home: 15 Honu St Aiea HI 96701 Office: CINCPACFLT N327 Honolulu HI 96860

VAIL, LUKI STYSKAL, investment consultant, author; b. Los Angeles, June 7, 1937; d. Ladislav Jakup and Lucia Marie (Matulich) Styskal; children by previous marriage—Thomas Lad, Jerome David, Tricia Marie. B.S. in Mktg., Loyola-Marymount U., Los Angeles, 1959. Registered securities prin. Nat. Assn. Securities Dealers. Founder San Clemente Savings Bank; pres. Pendleton Press. Author: While Waiting to Win the Lottery!. Mem. Inst. Cert. Fin. Planners, Western Pension Conf., Internat. Assn. Fin. Planners.

VAIL, MARY BARBARA, museum official; b. Kingsville, Tex., Apr. 24, 1956; d. Fred G. and Nora J. (Smith) Leon; m. David L. Vail, Mar. 30, 1980; children: Sean Kristofer, Ashley Noel. Student, Tex. A&I U.; BS, U. Hawaii, 1982; postgrad., Hawaii Pacific U., 1991—. Display specialist Linda's, Kingsville, 1986-87; membership dir. Malibu (Calif.) Riding and Tennis Club, 1990-91; mktg. dir. Pacific Aerospace Mus., Honolulu, 1991—. Vol. Laguna Vista Elem. Sch., Camarillo, Calif., 1990, Barbers Point (Hawaii) Elem. Sch., 1992—, moral, welfare, recreation USN; vol., mil. liaison 1st Night Honolulu, 1991; vol. fundraiser AOWC, Point Mugu, Calif., 1990-91; co-chmn. Aloha Family Festival, Pearl Harbor, Hawaii, 1991; numerous others. Mem. VC-1, Barbers Point Officers Wifes Club. Home: 15 Honu St Aiea HI 96701 Office: Pacific Aerospace Mus HIA Terminal Box # 7 Honolulu HI 96819

VAILE, ROBERT BRAINARD, JR., consulting electrical engineer; b. Oak Park, Ill., May 5, 1907; s. Robert Brainard and Stella (Price) V.; m. Margaret Wichman, Sept. 30, 1930 (dec. 1984); children: Susan, David; m. Kathleen Bardwell, Dec. 13, 1985. BS, Calif. Inst. Tech., 1927, PhD, 1936. Registered profl. engr., Ill., Calif. Engr. GE, Schenectady and L.A., 1927-32; instr. Iowa State Coll., Ames, 1933-36, U. Mo., Columbia, 1937-41; physicist Naval Ordnance Lab., Washington, 1941-46; rsch. physicist Armour Rsch. Found., Chgo., 1946-48; rsch. physicist Stanford Rsch. Inst., Palo Alto, Calif., 1948-58, dir. physics div., 1958-68; cons. engr. GE, Sunnyvale, Calif., Agbabian Jacobsen Assocs., L.A., United Tech. Corp., Sunnyvale, Electric Power Rsch. Inst., Palo Alto, Calif., 1969-79. Patentee in field. Mem. IEEE, Sigma Xi, Tau Beta Pi. Democrat. Home: 850 Webster St Apt 835 Palo Alto CA 94301

VAKIL, JAYSHREE, advertising executive; b. Bombay, Maharashtr, India, Oct. 3, 1957; came to U.S. 1980.; BS in Econ., U. Bombay, Bombay, India, 1979, BS in Fine Art, 1979; MS in Adv., Northwestern, Evanston, Ill., 1981. Exec. trainee J. Walter Thompson, Bombay, India, 1979-80; asst. acct. exec. Greens Adv., Bombay, India, 1980; asst. media planner Ogilvy and Mather Adv., N.Y., 1981-83; media planner Havas Conseil Marsteller, Chgo., 1984-86; media supr. DDB Needham Inc., Chgo., 1986-88; regional adv. mgr. Montgomery Ward, Chgo., 1988-89; assoc. media dir. Wieden and Kennedy, Portland, Oreg., 1988-89; v.p. and COO Whitman Adv. and PR, Portland, Oreg., 1989-90; pres./owner Vakil Advt., Inc., Portland, Oreg., 1990—. Mem. Am. Mktg. Assn., Portland Adv. Fed., Pub. Rels. Acc. of Am., Am. Adv. Museum. Hindu. Office: 6100 Churchill Downs Dr West Linn OR 97068-2523

VAKILI-MIRZAMANI, JALALEDDIN, civil engineer, researcher; b. Tehran, Iran, Sept. 19, 1943; came to U.S., 1979; s. Moussa and Farkhondeh V.; m. Parvin Mojarrab, Aug. 28, 1971; children: Mojgan, Kamran. BS, Tabriz (Iran) U., 1965; MS, PhD in Engring., Sorbonne U., Paris, 1969. Registered profl. engr., Calif., Alaska, Idaho. Rsch. assoc. U. Utah, Salt Lake City, 1971-72; chmn. CE dept Tabriz U., Iran, 1972-75, Arya-Mehr U., Iran, 1975-79; vis. prof. U. Calif., Berkeley, 1979-80; sr. engr. Morrison-Knudsen Co, Boise, Idaho, 1980-85; prin. engr. Battelle Meml. Inst., Columbus, Ohio, 1985-88, Leighton and Assocs., Inc., Irvine, Calif., 1988-93; chief engr. Ninyo & Moore, Inc., Irvine, Calif., 1993—. Author: Linear Viscoelasticity, 1973, Soil Mechanics, 1973; contbr. articles to Jour. Rsch. Mechanica, Jour. Rheology, Jour. Exptl. Mechanics, Transaction of SME-AIME. Mem. transportation com. Indsl. League Orange County, Calif., 1990—. Recipient Fulbright Hays award, U.S. Govt., 1971, 79; Rsch. grant, French Govt., 1965. Mem. ASCE (constn. com. 1987-88), French Soc. Dr.-Engrs., Internat. Soc. Soil Mechanics and Found. Engring. Office: Ninyo & Moore, Inc 15375 Barranca Pkwy Ste A-101 Irvine CA 92718

VALA, ROBERT (DONALD ROBERT MANN), artist; b. Berkeley, Calif., Apr. 19, 1930; s. Robert H. and Nell (Curry) Mann. Student, Coll. Arts & Crafts, Oakland, Calif., 1947, Art Student League, N.Y.C., 1950; BA, U. Calif.-Berkeley, 1951. Designer Ballet Russe, Europe, 1952, San Francisco Opera, 1953-56, San Francisco Ballet, 1953-56, Spanish Dance Co., Santa Cruz, Calif., 1986—, Patri Nader Co., Santa Cruz, Calif., 1986—; artist-in-residence, tchr. Calif. State U., Sacramento, 1987. Multi-media one-man shows include: Art Dirs. Gallery, N.Y.C., 1963, Galeries Raymond Duncan, Paris, 1963, Madison Gallery, N.Y.C., 1964; group shows include: UN Bldg., N.Y.C., 1970, Bohman Gallery, Stockholm, 1965, Arlene Lind Gallery, San Francisco, 1987, Will Stone Gallery, San Francisco, 1987; represented in comml. installations and numerous pvt. collections. Recipient Prix de Paris, L'Art Modern Mus., 1962, 1st prize Salon 50 States, N.Y.C., 1963. Home: 3109 Vista Sandia Santa Fe NM 87501-9999

VALDEZ, ARNOLD, dentist; b. Mojave, Calif., June 27, 1954; s. Stephen Monarez Jr. and Mary Lou (Esparza) V. BS in Biol. Sci., Calif. State U., Hayward, 1976; BS in Dental Sci. and DDS, U. Calif., San Francisco, 1982; MBA, Calif. State Poly. U., 1985; postgrad., Am. Coll. Law. Pvt. practice specializing in temporomandibular joint and Myofascial Pain Dysfunction Disorders Pomona, Calif., 1982-90, Claremont, Calif., 1982—; mem. adv. com. dental assisting program Chaffey Coll., Rancho Cucamonga, Calif., 1982—; mem. staff Pomona Valley Hosp. Med. Ctr. Vol. dentist San Antonio Hosp. Dental Clinic, Rancho Cucamonga, 1984—, Pomona Valley Assistance League Dental Clinic, 1986—. Fellow Acad. Gen. Dentistry; mem. ADA, Calif. Dental Assn., Tri-County Dental Soc. (co-chmn. mktg. 1986, chmn. sch. screening 1987, Golden Grin award), Acad. Gen. Dentistry, Am. Equilibrium Soc., U. Calif.-San Francisco Alumni Assn., U. So. Calif. Sch. Dentistry Gold Century Club, Psi Omega, Delta Theta Phi. Fellow Acad. Gen. Dentistry; mem. ADA, Calif. Dental Assn., Tri-County Dental Soc. (co-chmn. mktg. 1986, chmn. sch. screening 1987, Golden Grin award), Acad. Gen. Dentistry, U. Calif.-San Francisco Alumni Assn., U. So. Calif. Sch. Dentistry Golden Century Club, Psi Omega, Delta Theta Phi. Democrat. Roman Catholic. Home: 1320 Malaga St Upland CA 91786-8602 Office: 410 W Baseline Rd Claremont CA 91711-1698

VALDEZ, ROBERT OTTO BURCIAGA, health policy analyst; b. San Antonio; s. Santiago E. and Gloria (Burciaga) V. ; m. Mary Elizabeth Winter; children: Ariel, Graciela, Camila, Luke Fredrickson. AB, Harvard U., 1978; Master of Health Svcs. Adminstrn., U. Mich., 1980; PhD, Rand Grad. Sch., 1985. Econ. analyst The RAND Corp., Santa Monica, Calif., 1980-85, health policy analyst, 1985—; assoc. prof. sch. of pub. health UCLA, 1985—; sr. rsch. scholar Tomas Rivera Ctr., 1989—; cons. Western Consortium Pub. Health, Berkeley, 1986—; advisor White House Health Care Reform Task Force, 1993. Contbr. articles to profl. jours. Bd. dirs. Minority AIDS Project, L.A., 1988-89, policy adv. bd. Children NOW, 1988—; advisor L.A. Dept. Pub. Works, 1986-87, L.A. Dept. Health, 1984-85, 87—. Predoctoral fellow Bush Program in Child Devel. and Social Policy, U. Mich., 1979-80; vis. scholar Stanford Ctr. Chicano Rsch., Palo Alto, Calif., 1985-88. Fellow Am. Coll. Healthcare Execs.; mem. Am. Pub. Health Assn. (governing coun. 1982-84), Assn. Pub. Policy Analysis and Mgmt., Assn. Health Svcs. Rsch., Population Assn. Am. Roman Catholic.

VALDEZ, VICTOR EDMUND, lawyer; b. Santa Fe, N.Mex., Mar. 20, 1964; s. Ernest E. and Rita J. (Nowak) V. BA, Stanford U., 1986; JD, U. N.Mex., 1989. Bar: N.Mex. 1989. Partner Valdez and Read, Santa Fe, 1989-91, Valdez Law Firm, Santa Fe, 1991—. Mem. ABA, First. Judicial Dist. Bar Assn. Office: Valdez Law Firm PO Box 2385 Santa Fe NM 87504-2385

VALDEZ, VINCENT EMILIO, artist; b. Mora, N.Mex., Mar. 15, 1940; s. Jose Bartolo Valdez and Maria Natividad (Nolan) Henderson; children: Trevor, Tiffney. Student, U. Wyo., 1967-69. Detective Laramie (Wyo.) Police Dept., 1964-84; free-lance artist Laramie, 1983—. Exhibited Allied Artists of Am., 1985, 87. Active Nat. Sculpture Ctr. With U.S. Army, 1962-64. Recipient Best of Show award Wildlife and Western Art Exhbn., Milw., 1985, 2d Pl. sculpture award George Phippen Meml. Art Show, Prescott, Ariz., 1987, Best of Show award Western Regional, 1987. Mem. Laramie Art Guild. Office: Vince Valdez Studio PO Box 581 Laramie WY 82070-0581

VALENTE, ALBERT JOSEPH, electrical engineer, consultant; b. San Francisco, Dec. 24, 1953; s. Joseph and Gertrude (Brockman) V. BS in Electronics Engring., Cogswell Coll., 1987. Engr. in tng., Wash. Elec. designer Boeing Comml. Airplane Div., Seattle, 1981-87; elec. engr. Boeing Mil. Aircraft Div., Seattle, 1987—; pres. PUP Computing Inc., Seattle, 1991—. With USN, 1972-80. Mem. IEEE. Home: 400 NE 50th Seattle WA 98105

VALENTE, ANGELO MARIO, electrical engineer; b. Chgo., Feb. 18, 1941; s. Angelo Mario and Rosalie Valente; m. Linda L. Lieb, June 13, 1964; children: Anthony Joseph, Dominic Mario, Nadine Marie, Dennis John. BEE, Marquette U., 1965; MBA, Loyola U., 1971. Resource mgmt. AG Communication Systems, Phoenix, 1963—. Patentee in field of hardware computer design. Dist. commr. Four Peaks Dist. Boy Scouts Am., Scottsdale, Ariz., 1993; dist. vice chmn. Northstar Dist. Boy Scouts Am., Scottsdale, 1987-90. Recipient Silver Beaver award Boy Scouts Am., 1991; named to Dist. Hall of Fame, Four Peaks Dist., 1992; named Young Man of Yr., Schaumburg Jaycees, 1977. Mem. IEEE, Order of Arrow Boy Scouts Am. (brotherhood mem.), Men's Club of St. Patrick's Ch. Roman Catholic. Home: 13430 N 82d St Scottsdale AZ 85260 Office: AG Communication Systems 2500 W Utopia Rd Phoenix AZ 85027

VALENTE, MICHAEL F., philosopher, consultant; b. Albany, N.Y., Nov. 4, 1937; s. Abel A. and Anna Elizabeth Valente. BA in Philosophy, Stonehill Coll., 1959; MS in Math., Notre Dame U., 1961, MA in Theology, 1962; PhD in Religion, Columbia U., 1968; MSL in Law, Yale U., 1974. Mem. faculty dept. religious studies Seton Hall U., South Orange, N.J., 1967-81, chmn. dept. religious studies, 1968-71; cons. TCIM Consulting Svcs., Santa Monica, Calif., 1981—. Office: TCIM Consulting Svcs 446 San Vicente Blvd Santa Monica CA 90402-1731

VALENTINE, CAROL ANN, director educational program, consultant; b. Mt. Clemens, Mich., Dec. 5, 1942; d. Joseph Eldon and Erna Fredericka (Brandt) V.; married; children: Christopher, David. BA, U. Mich., 1964,

MA, 1965; PhD, Pa. State U., 1971. Tchr. Oak Park (Ill.)-River Forest High Sch., 1965-67; research assoc. U. Md., College Park, 1967; dir. grants Pa. State U., State College, 1967-78; asst. prof. Oreg. State U., Corvallis, 1970-74; vis. prof. U. Oreg., Eugene, 1974-75; assoc. prof. Ariz. State U., Tempe, 1975-85, assoc. dir. women's studies, 1975—; cons. Tempe, 1975—. Author: First Impressions, 1980, Women and Communicative Power, 1988. Bd. dirs. Tempe Pub. Library, 1984—. Named Outstanding Woman of Phoenix, 1987. Mem. Zeta Phi Eta. Democrat. Presbyterian. Home: 2607 S Forest Ave Tempe AZ 85282-3520 Office: Ariz State U Stauffer Hall 412 Tempe AZ 85287

VALENTINE, CHRISTINE SPICER JONES, counselor; b. Newbury, Berks, Eng., Jan. 20, 1942; came to U.S., 1964; d. Percy W. and Mary E. (Brooks) Spicer; m. Robert H. Jones, Dec. 17, 1965 (dec. Nov. 1972); m. Stephen Valentine III, May 11, 1974; stepchildren: Stephen, Cary, John, Samuel, Sarah. Student, Reading Tech. Coll., 1961-64; Assocs. in Human Svcs., Dull Knife Coll., 1986-89. Cert. chem. dependency counselor, Mont. Med. rsch. technician histology dept. radiobiol. unit Atomic Energy Rsch. Establishment, Harwell, Eng., 1958-62, med. rsch. technician genetics dept., 1962-64; head tchr. Headstart Program No. Cheyenne Headstart, Birney, Mont., 1969-72; counselor No. Cheyenne Recovery Ctr., Lame Deer, Mont., 1979-82, sr. counselor, 1982-89, tng. and devel. coord., 1990-92; tech. asst. Billings (Mont.) Area Office, Indian Health Svcs., 1992—. Recipient Svc. award No. Cheyenne Bd. Health, Lame Der, 1987, N.C. Bd. of Health award, 1991. Mem. No. Cheyenne Interdisciplinary Core Team, IHS Clinic, Lame Deer, 1986-89; coord. St. Judes Bikeathon, Birney, 1987-90, 91-92. Recipient Svc. award No. Cheyenne Bd. Health, Lame Deer, 1987, Community Svc. award No. Cheyenne Tribe Community Com., Lame Deer, 1988. Mem. Range Writers Assn. Sheridan Wyo. Home and Office: No Cheyenne Recovery Ctr PO Box 857 Lame Deer MT 59043-0857

VALENTINE, DE WAIN, artist; b. Fort Collins, Colo., Aug. 27, 1936; s. Glenn and Rouine (Lass) V.; m. Jeanne C. Clayman, Feb. 14, 1985; children by previous marriage: Christopher, Sean, Nelsen. BFA, U. Colo., 1958, MFA, 1960; Yale Norfolk fellow, Yale U., 1958. Instr. U. Colo., 1958-61, 64, UCLA, 1965-67; artist-in-residence Aspen Inst., Colo., 1967, 68. One man. shows include U. Colo., 1958, 60, The Gallery, Denver, 1964, Douglas Gallery, Vancouver, Can., 1968, Ace Gallery, Los Angeles, 1968, Galerie Birschofberger, Zurich, Switzerland, 1969, Pasadena Mus. Modern Art, Calif., 1970, San Jose Mus., Calif., 1974, Long Beach Mus. Art, Calif., 1975, La Jolla Mus. Contemporary Art, Calif., 1975, Santa Barbara Mus. Art, Calif., 1977, Los Angeles County Mus. Art, 1979, U. Calif.-Irvine, 1979, Inst. Art and Urban Resources, N.Y.C., 1981, Thomas Babeor Gallery, La Jolla, 1982, Laumeier Internat. Sculpture Park, St. Louis, 1982, Madison Art Ctr., Wis., 1983, Honolulu Acad. Arts, 1985, Contemporary Arts Ctr., Honolulu, 1985; group exhbns. include Whitney Ann. Exhibit, 1966, 68, 70, Walker Art Ctr., Mpls., 1969, Milw. Art Ctr., 1971, Am. Ann. Exhibit, Chgo. Art Inst., 1973; represented in permanent collections Los Angeles County Mus. Art, Milw. Art Center, Whitney Mus. Am. Art, Chgo. Art Inst., Joslyn Mus. Art, others. John Simon Guggenheim fellow, 1980; Nat. Endowment for Arts awardee, 1981. Address: 4223 Glencoe Ave Ste B-127 Marina Del Rey CA 90292

VALENTINE, GENE C., securities dealer; b. Washington, Pa., June 19, 1950; s. John N. and Jane S. Valentine. BS in Psychology, Bethany Coll., 1972; student, U. Vienna, Austria, 1971-72. Commd. ensign USN, 1972, advanced through grades to lt., 1987, hon. discharged, 1978; owner Horizon Realty, San Francisco, 1978-82; dir. land acquisitions Windfarms Ltd. subs. Chevron, U.S.A., San Francisco, 1980-82; v.p. mktg. Christopher Weil & Co., Sherman Oaks, Calif., 1982-85; pres. Pacific Asset Group Inc. (name now Fin. West Group, Inc.), Pasadena, Calif., 1985—; bd. dirs. Fin. West Group, Inc. Mem. Rep. Party, L.A. Mem. Internat. Assn. Fin. Planning (bd. dirs. L.A. chpt. 1982—). Episcopalian. Office: Fin West Group Inc 2977 Willow Ln Ste 101 Thousand Oaks CA 91361

VALENTINE, JAMES WILLIAM, geology educator, author; b. Los Angeles, Nov. 10, 1926; s. Adelbert Cuthbert and Isabel (Davis) V.; m. Grace Evelyn Whysner, Dec. 21, 1957 (div. 1972); children—Anita, Ian; m. Cathryn Alice Campbell, Sept. 10, 1978 (div. 1986); 1 child, Geoffrey; m. Diane Mondragon, Mar. 16, 1987. B.A., Phillips U., 1951; M.A., UCLA, 1954, Ph.D., 1958. From asst. prof. to assoc. prof. U. Mo., Columbia, 1958-64; from assoc. prof. to prof. U. Calif., Davis, 1964-77; prof. geol. scis. U. Calif., Santa Barbara, 1977-90; prof. integrative biology U. Calif., Berkeley, 1990—. Author: Evolutionary Paleoecology of the Marine Biosphere, 1973; editor: Phanerozoic Diversity, 1985; co-author: Evolution, 1977, Evolving, 1979; also numerous articles, 1954—. Served with USNR, 1944-46; PTO. Fulbright research scholar, Australia, 1962-63; Guggenheim fellow Yale U., Oxford U., Eng., 1968-69; Rockefeller Found. scholar in residence, Bellagio, Italy, summer 1974; grantee NSF, NASA. Fellow Am. Acad. Arts and Scis., AAAS, Geol. Soc. Am.; mem. Nat. Acad. Scis., Paleontol. Soc. (pres. 1974-75). Home: 1351 Glendale Ave Berkeley CA 94708-2025 Office: U Calif Dept Integrative Biology Berkeley CA 94720

VALENTINE, JOHN LESTER, state legislator, lawyer; b. Fullerton, Calif., Apr. 26, 1949; s. Robert Lester and Pauline C. (Glood) V.; m. Karen Marie Thorpe, June 1, 1972; children: John Robert, Jeremy Reid, Staci Marie, Jeffrey Mark., David Emerson, Patricia Ann. BS in Acctg. and Econs., Brigham Young U., 1973, JD, 1976. Bar: Utah, U.S. Dist. Ct. Utah, U.S. Ct. Appeals. (10th cir.), U.S. Tax Ct.; CPA. Atty. Howard, Lewis & Petersen, Provo, Utah, 1976—; mem. Utah Ho. Reps., 1988—; instr. probate and estates Utah Valley C.C.; instr. fin. planning., adj. prof. law Brigham Young U.; mem. exec offices, cts., corrections and legis. appropriations sub-com., 1988-90, capital facilities subcom., 1988-90, retirement com., 1988-90, judiciary com., 1988—, strategic planning steering com., 1988-90, interim appropriations com., 1988—, tax. review commn., 1988—, ethics com., 1990-92, human svcs. and health appropriations subcom., 1990-92, revenue and taxation com., 1988—, vice chmn. 1990-92; vice chmn. exec. appropriations., 1990-92, chmn. 1992—; chmn. exec. appropriations com., 1992—; bd. dirs. Utah Corrections Industries. Mem. adv. bd. Internat. Sr. Games, 1988—; active Blue Ribbon Task Force on Local Govt. Funding, Utah League Cities and Towns, 1990—, Criminal Sentencing Guidelines Task Force, Utah Judicial Coun., 1990-92, Access to Health Care Task Force, 1990-92, Utah County Sheriff Search and Rescue, Orem Met. Water Bd., Alpine Sch. Dist. Boundary Line Com., Boy Scouts Am.; bd. regents Legis. Adv. Com. UVCC.; mem. exec. bd. Utah Nat. Parks Coun.; mem. adv. coun. Orchard Elem. Sch., Mountainlands Com. an Aging; bd. trustees Utah Opera Co.; judge nat. and local competitions Moot Ct.; voting dist. chmn.; state, county del.; lt. ICS. Recipient Silver Beaver award Boy Scouts Am., Taxpayer Advocate award Utah Taxpayer Assn. Mem. ABA (tax sect.), Utah State Bar, CPA Com., Tax Sect. Specialization Com., Bicentennial Com. Republican. Mormon. Office: Howard Lewis & Petersen 120 E 300 N Provo UT 84603-0778

VALENTINO, STEPHEN ERIC, production and entertainment company executive; b. N.Y.C., Apr. 2, 1954; s. Joseph and Ina Mae (Diamond) V. Student, Hofstra U., N.Y.C., 1972-74, San Francisco Conservatory Music, 1974-78, Am. Inst. Mus. Studies, Graz, Austria, 1982. Gen. dir., chmn. bd. Mastic Community Theatre, Mastic Beach, N.Y., 1971-74; dir. advt. Marin Opera Co., San Rafael, Calif., 1979-80, Marin Ctr., San Rafael, 1983-85; pres., chief exec. officer Valentino & Assocs., Novato, Calif., 1978—; pres., CEO, co-founder Celebrity Events Internat., 1992—. Contbg. author: Come Barefoot Eating Sensuous Things, 1979; appeared in Firestorm, 1992. Celebrity coord. Kids Say No To Drugs, 1987, MADD, 1987, ARC, San Jose, Calif., 1989; entertainment coord. Earthquake Relief Fund, San Francisco, 1989, Christmas Tree Program for the Needy, San Francisco, 1986, San Francisco Grand Prix BMW Polo Classic, Marin Suicide Prevention Ctr., 1987, Calif. Health Rsch. Found., 1988, UNICEF San Francisco, 1985, Little Sisters of The Poor, 1985, San Francisco Child Abuse Coun., 1988, 92; fundraiser Easter Seals, Marin County, Calif., 1988, Toys for Tots, Bay Area, Calif., 1987—, Global Youth Resource Orgn., Sunnyvale, Calif., 1989-90; mem. Dem. Nat. Com., 1988-90; commr. Bus. Ins. Adv. Commn., 1989; dir. celebrity basketball game Special Olympics, 1992, celebrity basketball game Easter Seals Soc., 1993. Recipient Cert. of Honor, Bd. Suprs., City and County San Francisco, 1986, Awards of Appreciation Easter Seals Soc., 1988, Spl. Olympics, 1992. Mem. AFTRA, SAG. Home and Office: Valentino and Assocs 428 Bloom Ln Novato CA 94947-4202

VALENZUELA, FERNANDO ANGUAMEA, professional baseball player; b. Navajoa, Sonora, Mexico, Nov. 1, 1960; m. Linda, Dec. 29, 1981; children: Fernando, Ricardo, Linda. Pitcher Mexican Leagues, 1978-79, minor league, 1979-80, Los Angeles Dodgers, Nat. League, 1980-91; mem. Nat. League All-Star Team, 1981-86, World Series championship team, 1981; pitcher California Angels, 1991, Baltimore Orioles, 1993—. Recipient Cy Young Meml. award Nat. League, 1981, Silber Bat Nat. League , 1983, Gold Glove Nat. League, 1986; named Rookie of the Yr. Nat. League, Rookie of Yr. Baseball Writers' Assn. Am., 1981. Office: LA Dodgers 1000 Elysian Park Ave Dodger Stadium Los Angeles CA 90012

VALERIO, DAWN ELIZABETH, artist; b. Waltham, Mass., Dec. 31; d. Francis Hector and Hazel Elizabeth (Aldrich) Forest; m. Jean Baptiste Valerio, Dec. 7, 1957. BA, Mass. Sch. Art, 1951; postgrad., Sch. Practical Art, 1952-53, Art Student's League, 1954-55, Beaux Arts, Paris, 1957-58. Art tchr. San Domenico Sch., San Anselmo, Calif., 1981—; represented by galleries in Paris, 1953-60, L.A., 1961-68, San Francisco, 1968—, Marin County, Calif., 1968—, Sausalito, Calif., 1982—. Exhibited in group shows at Gallery Huit, Paris, France, 1991, Chambre des Depute's, Paris, France, 1991, Allen Augustine Gallery, Tahoe, Calif., 1990-93, Bay Model Gallery, Sausalito, Calif., 1993, Resource for Art Gallery, San Francisco, Calif., 1993. Mem. Marin ARts Coun., North Bay Print Makers. Home: 313 Sheffield Ave Mill Valley CA 94945 Studio: 480 Gate 5 Rd Sausalito CA 94941

VALESCO, FRANCES KAY, artist, educator; b. L.A., Aug. 3, 1941; parents Adolph and Ethel Valesco; 1 child, David. BA, UCLA, 1963; postgrad., Sacramento State U., 1964-65; MA, Calif. State U., Long Beach, 1972. Artist in residence Calif. State Arts Coun., San Francisco, 1980-85; instr. U. Calif. Extension, Santa Barbara, 1968-69, Irvine, Riverside, 1970-72; instr. U. Calif., Berkeley, 1975-76, 79, Somoma State U., Rohnert Park, Calif., 1977-80; owner, dir. Big Ink, L.A. and San Francisco, 1969—; instr. Haystack Mountain Sch. Crafts, Maine, 1992; instr. Acad. Art Coll., San Francisco, 1982—; artist San Francisco Neighborhood Arts Commn., 1975-80; cons. HUD, Hartford, Conn., 1978; mem. San Francisco Mural Adv. Bd., 1981—. One-person shows include Hatley Martin Gallery, 1989; exhibited in group shows at Tokyo Met. Mus., 1986, Bronx Mus., 1987, Computer Mus., Boston, 1989; represented in permanent collections N.Y. City Pub. Libr., Fine Arts Mus., San Francisco, Oakland Museum. Recipient Cert. Honor, City of San Francisco, 1987; Mural grantee Neighborhood Initiated Improvement Program, City of San Francisco, HUD, 1981-82, 86, NEA and N.Y. State Coun. for Arts grantee, Lexington N.Y., 1989, 90, 92. Mem. YLEM, Calif. Soc. Printmakers (v.p. 1993-94, historian 1980-82, organizing com Pratt Print Ctr. exhibit 1979).

VALFER, ERNST SIEGMAR, psychologist; b. Frankfurt-Main, Germany, July 4, 1925; came to U.S., 1941; s. Hermann Heinrich and Frieda (Kahn) V.; m. Lois Brandwynne, July 8, 1961; children: Rachel, Lilah. AA, City Coll., San Francisco, 1948; BS, U. Calif.-Berkeley, 1950, MS, 1952, PhD, 1965. Lic. psychologist, registered profl. engr., Calif. Supr. indsl. planning Naval Air Rework Facility, Alameda, Calif., 1952-57; rsch. scientist Maritime Transp. Rsch. Bd., NAS/NRC, Washington, 1957-60; sci. dir. Maritime Cargo Transp. Conf., NRC, Washington, 1960-62; assoc. rsch. engr. U. Calif.-Berkeley, 1961-64, sr. lectr., 1965-68; dean, prof. J.F. Kennedy U., Martinez, Calif., 1970-73; adj. sr. fellow, cons. Inst. Indsl. Rns, 1973-83, UCLA; dir. mgmt. scis. USDA-Forestry Svc., Berkeley and Washington, 1962-88, chief mgmt scientist, 1988-90; counselor, cons., Berkeley, 1966—; cons. govt., pvt. orgns., individuals. Author: (with P.B. Buck and Harvey C. Paige) San Francisco Port Study, 1964, (with L.E. Davis and Alfred W. Clark) Experimenting with Organizational Life, 1976; contbr. articles to profl. jours. Pres. Agy. for Jewish Edn., Oakland, Calif., 1982-85; v.p. Hillel Found., Berkeley, 1988-93; bd. dirs. various orgns. in Bay area, 1970—. Recipient several awards USDA-Forestry Svc., NAS-NRC, 1960—. Mem. Am. Bd. Profl. Psychology, Am. Psychol. Assn., Inst. Indsl. Engrs. (spl. recognition award 1958), Inst. Mgmt. Scis., Sigma Xi, Alpha Pi Mu. Jewish. Home and Office: 2621 Rose St Berkeley CA 94708-1920

VALINE, FREDERICK CHRIST, JR., systems engineer, applied mathematician; b. Sacramento, July 7, 1944; s. Frederick Christ and Nadine (Duncan) V. BA in Math., St. Anselms Coll., Manchester, N.H., 1973; MS in Systems Mgmt., U. So. Calif., 1977. Electronic technician Philco-Ford Co., Palo Alto, Calif., 1970-74; satellite ops. specialist Lockheed Missile & Space Co., Sunnyvale, Calif., 1974-79; rsch. specialist Lockheed Missile & Space Co., Sunnyvale, 1979-81, 83-84, system test engr., 1981-83, staff engr., 1984-92; system engr. IBM Fed. Sector Svc. Corp., Santa Clara, Calif., 1992—. Sgt. USAF, 1966-70. Republican. Roman Catholic.

VALLE, GEORGETTE WALD, state legislator; b. Blue Earth, Minn., Oct. 31, 1924; d. George Wilhelm Endre and Emily (Tenold) Vikingstad; m. Odd Valle, June 30, 1951; children: Peter Odd, Christine Georgette. AA, Waldorf Jr. Coll., 1945; BS, U. Minn., 1949. Occupational therapist Mpls. Curative Workshop, 1949-50; dir. occupational therapy Swedish Polio Rehab. Ctr., Mpls., 1950-51; mem. Wash. Ho. of Reps., Olympia, 1965-67, 72—, chair, exec. chair appropriations com., vice chair environ. affairs, local govt., sci. and tech. coms., ranking minority mem. edn., natural resources and environ. affairs appropriations, human services com., mem. ways and means, rules coms.; clk. Wash. Senate Senator Mike McCormack, Olympia, 1967; cons. occupational therapy Seattle Queen Anne Nursing Home, 1970; dir. occupational therapy Valley Gen. Hosp., Kent, Wash., 1971-72. Mem. state adv. bd. Fed. Water Pollution Act; mem. Coalition Against Oil Pollution, Air Quality Coalition, Wash. Lung Assn., Highline YMCA, Highline West Seattle Mental Health Ctr., Wash. State Environment Policy Act Commn., Fauntleroy Environ. Assn., Adult Literacy Bd., Mothers Against Drunk Drivers; mem. Gov.'s Task Force on High Level Nuclear Waste; bd. dirs. West Seattle Sr. Ctr., Highline Community Council, S.W. Youth Service Bur. Seattle, Wash. State Seismic Safety Bd.; mem. adult edn. bd. Plymouth Congl. Ch.; v.p. bd. dirs. Shoreline Community Hosp.; chair Green River Murder Reward Com. Recipient Friend of Edn. award Highline Ednl. Assn., 1980, Disting. Service award Wash. Lung Assn., Outstanding Achievement for Edn. award Wash. Edn. Assn., 2,000 award Am. Lung Assn., 1985, placque West Seattle Jaycees, Outstanding Alumni award Waldorf Jr. Coll., 1987; cited for Outstanding Dedication for Clean Air Fresh Air for Non-Smokers, Inc., 1987; named Woman of Yr. Evergreen Dem. Club, West Seattle Bus. and Profl. Women, 1985. Mem. NOW, LWV (chair natural resources com. King county South chpt.), Wash. Environ. Council (Outstanding Elected Official 1980), Sierra Club, World Affairs Council (Seattle chpt.), West Seattle C. of C., Highline Assn. Am. Univ. Women. Clubs: Hurstwood Community, West Seattle Garden. Home: 1434 SW 137th St Seattle WA 98166-1051 Office: Wash State Ho Reps 401 Legislative Bldg Olympia WA 98504

VALLERAND, PHILIPPE GEORGES, sales executive; b. Montreal, Que., Can., June 12, 1954; came to U.S., 1982; s. Louis Philippe and Beatrice (Goupil) V.; m. Laura Jean Frombach, Sept. 25, 1979; children: Harmonie May, Jeremy Thomas, Emilie Rose. Student, U. Montreal, 1974, U. Sherbrooke, 1975, U. Que., 1976, White Mgmt. Sch., London, 1981. Dir. resort Club Mediterranee Inc., Bahamas, Switzerland,, Africa,, Guadelupe, West Indies, 1978-80; v.p. Franglo/Sunsaver Inc., London and Hyeres, France, 1980-82; v.p. sales Source Northwest, Inc., Woodinville, Wash., 1982—; dir. Pacific Tech., Seattle; pres. Prime Source, Inc. Sr. comdr. Royal Rangers Boys Club, Monroe, Wash., 1988—; bd. mem. Christian Faith Ctr., Monroe, 1988—; mem. Rep. Nat. Com. Named to 500 Inc. Mag., 1983, 89, Registry of Global Bus. Leaders; recipient Disting. Sales & Mktg. Exec. award Internat. Orgn. Sales & Mktg. Execs., 1993. Mem. Am. Mktg. Assn. (new mem. adv. bd.).

VALNER, RUDY, lawyer; b. Mexico City, Dec. 23, 1960; came to U.S., 1979; s. Benito and Lia (Sod) V.; m. Marci Lynn Zweben, June 22, 1985; children: Danielle Kasey, Alexander Jason, Gabriela Bryn. BA in Polit. Sci. cum laude, UCLA, 1983; JD, Loyola U., L.A., 1987. Bar: Calif. 1989. Assoc. Smylie & Leven, L.A., 1989-90, Warren & Marks, Calabasas, Calif., 1990-92; pvt. practice L.A., 1992—; cons. Mexico-U.S. bus. and real estate devel., transactions, investments, gen. bus. Mem. ABA (real property, bus. and internat. law sects.), L.A. County Bar Assn. (real property, bus. and internat. law sects.), State Bar Calif. Office: Law Offices of Rudy Valner Ste 945 10100 Santa Monica Blvd Los Angeles CA 90067

VALONE, KEITH EMERSON, clinical psychologist; b. Austin, Tex., Aug. 3, 1953; s. James Floyd and Elizabeth Niles (Emerson) V.; m. Leona Marie Lagace, July 22, 1978; children: Kyle Stephen James, Christienne Marie. BA, U. So. Calif., 1975; MA, U. Ill., 1979, PhD, 1981. Lic. psychologist, Calif. Pvt. practice Pasadena, Calif., 1983—; dir. psychology Ingleside Hosp., Rosemead, Calif., 1990-92; candidate Inst. of Contemporary Psychoanalysis, L.A., 1991—; clin. asst. prof. dept. psychology Fuller Theol. Sem., Pasadena, Calif., 1984-85; asst. clin. prof. dept. psychology UCLA, 1984-87; chief psychology svc. Las Encinas Hosp., Pasadena, 1988. Contbr. articles to profl. jours. Mem. APA, Calif. State Psychol. Assn., Phi Beta Kappa. Episcopalian. Office: 301 S Fair Oaks Ave #401 Pasadena CA 91105

VALOT, DANIEL L., oil industry executive; b. 1944. Student, Ecol Nationale d'Administration, Paris. Mng. dir., head corp. planning divsn. Total Petroleum South East Asia, 1981—; chmn. bd., pres., CEO Total Petroleum, Inc., Denver, 1992—; vice chmn. Total Petroleum N.Am. Ltd. Office: Total Petroleum LTD 999 18th St Ste 2201 Denver CO 80202-2492

VALPREDA, MARK DAVID, computer engineering executive, consultant; b. Upland, Calif., Sept. 19, 1964; s. Eugene Michael and Cynthia Jene (Backer) V. BSBA, U. La Verne, 1986, MBA, 1987. Dir. CAMMCO, Claremont, Calif., 1984—; cons. U. La Verne, Calif., 1989—. Supporter Sandy Hester for State Senate, Claremont, Calif., 1992. Recipient Excellence in Bus. award Bank of Am., 1986. Mem. Local Finesse (sec. 1991-92). Republican. Roman Catholic. Office: CAMMCO 976 Foothill Ste 196 Claremont CA 91711

VALVERDE, LEONARD A., academic administrator; b. L.A., May 15, 1943; s. Leopoldo R. and Carmen (Rodriguez) V.; m. Josephine Guzman, Sept. 3, 1966; children: Leo R., Marisa D. AA, East L.A. Coll., 1963; BA, Calif. State U., Los Angeles, 1967; PhD, Claremont Grad. Sch., 1974. Math tchr., supr. L.A. Unified Sch. Dist., 1967-71; prof., dir. U. Tex., Austin, 1974-89; v.p. acad. affairs U. Tex., San Antonio, 1988—; exec. com. U. Coun. Edn. Adminstrn., 1987-88; cons. Mex. Am. Legas & Edn. Defense, San Antonio. Contbr. articles to profl. jours. Pres. Tex. Assn. Chicanos Higher Edn., 1976-77; sec. div. A Am. Edn. Rsch. Assn., 1987-89. Nat. fellow W.K. Kellogg Found., 1984-87; recipient Tomas Rivera Ctr. scholar, Claremont, Calif., 1985—, Rsch. award Nat. Inst. Edn., 1973, 79. Mem. The Coll. Bd. (Edward S. Noyes Leadership award 1989), Am. Assn. Higher Edn. (chmn. Hisp. caucus 1989—), Tex. Acad. Skills Program (policy coun. 1989—), Western Interstate Commn. Higher Edn., Coun. Grad. Schs. (adv. com. minority affairs 1987—). Office: U Ariz Coll Education Tempe AZ 85287

VAN AMRINGE, JOHN HOWARD, oil industry executive, geologist; b. L.A., Oct. 11, 1932; s. Edwin Verne and Viola (Hail) Van A.; m. Mary Jane Lothras, Jan. 29, 1955; children: Kathryn Jean Van Amringe Ball, Kenneth Edwin. AA, Pasadena City Coll., 1954; BA, UCLA, 1956, MA, 1957. Geologist Unocal Corp., Santa Maria, Calif., 1957-58, Santa Fe Springs, Calif., 1958-64, New Orleans, 1964-66; dist. geologist Unocal Corp., Lafayette, La., 1966-68, dist. exploration mgr., 1968-79; exploration mgr. western region Unocal Corp., Pasadena, Calif., 1979-88; v.p. exploration Unocal Corp., L.A., 1988—. Editor: Typical Offshore Oil and Gas Fields, 1973; author profl. paper. Bd. dirs. Pasadena City Coll. Found., 1986—, sec., 1990-91; pres. Pasadena Community Orch., 1990-92. With U.S. Army, 1949-52, Korea. Named Geologist of Yr., Lafayette chpt. Am. Inst. Profl. Geologists, 1972. Mem. Am. Assn. Petroleum Geologists (del. 1972-73), Pacific Sect. of Am. Assn. Petroleum Geologists (editor 1961-63), Lafayette Geological Soc. (pres. 1971-72), Petroleum Club L.A., Jonathan Club. Republican. Home: 1455 Old House Rd Pasadena CA 91107

VAN ARSDALE, DICK, professional sports team executive; b. Indpls., Feb. 22, 1943; m. Barbara V.; children: Jill, Jason. AB in economics, Indiana U., 1965. Player New York Knicks (Nat. Basketball Assn.), N.Y.C., 1965-68; with Phoenix Suns, Phoenix, Ariz., 1968-77; color commentator, TV broadcasts Phoenix Suns, from 1977, interim mgr., 1987, from v.p. basketball ops.to dir. player personnel. Named "Mr. Basketball" of Indiana during high school, NCAA All-American, Indiana U. Office: care Phoenix Suns 2910 N Central Ave Phoenix AZ 85012-2779

VAN ARSDEL, PAUL PARR, JR., allergist, educator; b. Indpls., Nov. 4, 1926; s. Paul Parr and Ellen (Ewing) Van A.; m. Rosemary Thorstenson, July 7, 1950; children: Mary Margaret, Andrew Paul. BS, Yale U., 1948; MD, Columbia U., 1951. Diplomate Am. Bd. Internal Medicine, Am. Bd. Allergy and Immunology. Intern Presbyn. Hosp., N.Y.C., 1951-52; resident in medicine Presbyn. Hosp., 1952-53; research fellow in medicine U. Wash. Sch. Medicine, Seattle, 1953-55, instr. medicine, 1956-58, from asst. prof. to prof. medicine, 1958--, head allergy sect., 1956--; spl. fellow in allergy, Boston U., Columbia U., N.Y.C., 1955-56; mem. staff Univ. Hosp., Seattle, chief of staff, 1983-85; assoc. staff Harborview Med. Ctr., Seattle; cons. Children's Hosp., Seattle VA Hosp.; vis. prof. medicine U. London, 1986. Contbr. to profl. publs. V.p., bd. dirs. Community Assn., Iron Springs, Wash., 1980-82. Served with USN, 1945-46. Fellow ACP, Am. Acad. Allergy and Immunology (pres. 1971-72), Royal Soc. Medicine (London); mem. AMA (alt. del. 1972—), Assn. Am. Med. Colls., Phi Beta Kappa, Sigma Xi, Alpha Omega Alpha. Home: 4702 NE 39th St Seattle WA 98105-5205 Office: U Wash Med Ctr Dept Medicine Seattle WA 98195

VAN ARSDOL, MAURICE DONALD, JR., sociologist, demographer, educator; b. Seattle, May 4, 1928; s. Maurice Donald and Madge (Belts) V.; m. Marian Clide Gatchell, Aug. 18, 1950; 1 child, Pece Durcinovski. B.A. in Sociology, U. Wash., 1949, M.A., 1952, Ph.D., 1957. Research asst. Office Population Research U. Wash., Seattle, 1950-54, pre-doctoral assoc., 1953-57; asst. prof. dept. sociology U. So. Calif., L.A., 1957-61, research coordinator youth studies ctr., 1959-60, assoc. prof. sociology, 1961-65, prof. sociology, 1965—, dir. population research lab., 1965—; vis. prof. dept. sociology U. Hawaii, Honolulu, 1966, Stockholm U., Sweden, 1978, 82; cons., lectr. in field. Co-author: Mortality Trends in the State of Washington, 1955, The Population of Bahrain, 1978, Changing Roles of Arab Women in Bahrain, 1985; contbr. chpts. to books, articles to profl. jours. Served with U.S. Army, 1952-53. Grantee in field from numerous profl. orgns. Fellow AAAS, Am. Sociol. Assn. (conf. com. 1963); mem. Internat. Union Sci. Study of Population, Population Assn. Am., Pacific Sociol. Assn. (adv. council 1965-68), Alpha Kappa Delta, Lambda Alpha. Office: U So Calif Dept Sociology Population Rsch Lab 3716 S Hope St Rm 385 Los Angeles CA 90007-4344

VAN ASPEREN, MORRIS EARL, banker; b. Wessington, S.D., Oct. 5, 1943; s. Andrew and Alyce May (Flagg) Van A.; m. Anne Virginia Merritt, July 2, 1966; 1 child, David Eric. BS in Math., U. Okla., 1966; MBA, Pepperdine U., 1979. Mgr. western dist. Svc. Rev. Inc., Northbrook, Ill., 1970-77; v.p. Hooper Info. Systems Inc., Tustin, Calif., 1977-78; v.p., chief fin. officer ATE Assocs. Inc., Westlake Village, Calif., 1978-84; mgmt. cons. Thousand Oaks, Calif., 1984-92; sr. v.p. Nat. Bank Calif., L.A., 1986—; bd. dirs. Packaging Corp. Am.; chmn. liaison com. region IX, SBA, 1990—. Nat. advocate fin. svcs. SBA, 1989. Lt. USN, 1966-70. Mem. Nat. Assn. Govt. Guaranteed Lenders (bd. dirs. 1990—), Robert Morris Assocs. Office: Nat Bank Calif 145 S Fairfax Ave Los Angeles CA 90036-2166

VANATTA, MERRY JANICE, accountant; b. Mpls., July 18, 1938; d. Lief Erick and Lucille Evelyn (Tucker) Larson; m. Larry Lee VanAtta, Oct. 12, 1956 (div. Dec. 1981); children: Jan Luell, Lori Lee, Erick Donald. Student, Linn Benton Community Coll., 1973-78. Lic. tax cons., Oreg. With various acctg. firms, Lebanon, Oreg., 1956-64, Sharp, Young et al CPAs, Lebanon, Oreg., 1964-72; sole propr. M.J. VanAtta, Acct., Lebanon, Oreg., 1972—. Treas. Oreg. Fedn. Women's Clubs, 1972-74; sec. Lebanon Rural Fire Protection Dist., Lebanon, 1978-87. Mem. Nat. Soc. Pub. Accts. (state dir. 1988-92), Oreg. Assn. Ind. Accts. (pres. 1988-89, 1st v.p. 1987-88, 2d v.p. 1986-87, sec. 1985-86, Martin Fitzgerald award 1988-89, William Blair award 1986-87).

VAN ATTA, SHELLEY GAY, director college relations; b. Billings, Mont., Aug. 21, 1956; d. Charles Augustus and Carra Edna (Burton) George; m. John R. Pingree, May 10, 1980 (dec. May 1984); m. Lawrence Claire Van Atta, Aug. 1, 1992; children: John Morgan, Nicholas Burton. BA in English/Journalism, U. Mont., 1979. Reporter, weather forecaster, weekend anchor KECI TV, Missoula, Mont., 1977-79; legis. asst. U.S. Congressman Cecil Heftel, Washington, 1980-82; asst. alumni dir. Ea. Mont. Coll., Billings, 1985-86; reporter, weather forecaster KTUQ TV, Billings, 1986; dir. coll. and alumni rels. Rocky Mountain Coll., Billings, 1986—; former pres. Leadership Billings (Mont.) Alumni, 1989; bd. mem. Billings (Mont.) Advt. Club, 1990—. Editor: (mag.) Rocky Today, 1989—; writer, producer: (video) The Rocky Difference, 1990 (Bronze award 1990), Building the Future, 1992 (Gold award 1992). Vol. publicist Yellowstone Art Ctr., Billings, 1989—; bd./cabinet United Way of Billings, 1992—. Named Outstanding Young Careerist, Billings (Mont.) Profl. Women, 1986, Outstanding Young Women of Am., 1987. Mem. Mont. Assn. Female Execs., Jr. League, Billings Rotary Club. Democrat. Methodist. Home: 2754 Palm Dr Billings MT 59102 Office: Rocky Mountain College 1511 Poly Dr Billings MT 59102

VAN BELLE, GERALD, environmental health educator; b. The Netherlands, July 23, 1936; came to Can., 1949; m. Johanna van Belle; children: Loeske, William John, Gerard, Christine, Louis. BA in Math., U. Toronto, 1962, MA in Math., 1964, PhD in Math./Stats., 1967. Asst. prof. Fla. State U., Tallahassee, 1967-72, dir. Statis. Cons. Ctr., 1969-72, assoc. prof., 1972-74; vis. assoc. prof. U. Wash., Seattle, 1974-75, assoc. prof., 1975-76, prof., 1976-90, prof., chmn. dept. environ. health, 1991—; Mem. data monitoring bd. VA Collaborative Study of Status Epilepticus, 1988—. Co-author: Biostatistics: A Methodology for the Health Sciences, 1993; mem. editorial bd. Epilepsia, 1991. Bd. mem. Watson-Groen Christian Sch., Seattle, 1975-89. Named Disting. Tchr. U. Wash., Seattle, 1985. Fellow AAAS, Am. Statis. Assn. Office: U Wash Dept Environ Health HSB F-463 SC 34 Seattle WA 98195

VAN BLARICOM, MARGARET ELENA, English language educator; b. Inglewood, Calif., Aug. 6, 1964; d. Roger Guy and Maria Elena (Gomez) Van B. Student, El Camino Coll., 1982-83, 84-86; BA in English and Am. Lit., U. Calif., San Diego, 1989; secondary teaching cert., San Diego State U., 1991. Flight test planning asst. Northrop Corp., Hawthorne, Calif., 1982; cosmetologist Beau Monde Salon, Torrance, Calif., 1983-85; tchr.'s asst. San Diego City Sch. Dist., 1988-91, English tchr., 1991—; adminstrv. asst. Sanford Devel. Co., San Diego, 1990-91; pvt. English tutor San Diego, 1990-92; rsch. asst. for pvt. biographer, San Diego, 1988-90. Mem. Golden Key Nat. Honor Soc.

VAN BORSSUM, JOHN BERNARD, banker; b. Terre Haute, Aug. 14, 1947; s. Jack Maurice and Rosemary (Bright) VanB.; Lesley Sue Ledgerwood, May 25, 19811 child, Jason Aaron. BS in Bus., Ariz. State U., 1980; MBA, U. Redlands, 1991. Cert. info. systems auditor; cert. fraud examiner. Asst. cashier Valley Nat. Bank Ariz., Phoenix, 1975-80; asst. v.p., EDP auditor Security Pacific Nat. Bank, L.A., 1980-82, v.p., auditor, 1982-85; v.p., dep. gen. auditor Security Pacific Corp., L.A., 1985-89, first v.p., dept. gen. auditor, 1989—; v.p. audit group mgr. Bank of Am., San Francisco, 1992—; instr. Security Pacific Audit Svcs. Inc., L.A., 1987. Pres. Affils. of the Webb Schs., Claremont, Calif., 1987-88. With USN, 1969-73. Mem. EDP Auditors Assn. (pres. 1985-86), Nat. Assn. Cert. Fraud Examiners (chair fin. instns. com. 1989-90), Inst. Internal Auditors, Assn. Computing Machinery. Republican. Lutheran. Office: Bank of Am PO Box 37000 # 3276 San Francisco CA 94103

VAN BRUNT, EDMUND EWING, physician; b. Oakland, Calif., Apr. 28, 1926; s. Adrian W. and Kathryn Anne (Shattuck) Van B.; m. Claire Monod, Feb. 28, 1949; children: Karin, Deryk, Jahn. BA in Biophysics, U. Calif., Berkeley, 1952; MD, U. Calif., San Francisco, 1959; ScD, U. Toulouse, France, 1978. Postdoctoral fellow NIH, 1961-63; rsch. assoc. U. Calif., San Francisco, 1963-67; staff physician Kaiser Permanente Med. Ctr., San Francisco, 1964-91; dir. div. rsch. Kaiser Permanente Med. Program, Oakland, Calif., 1979-91; assoc. dir. Kaiser Found. Rsch. Inst., Oakland, 1985-91, sr. cons., 1991—; adj. prof. U. Calif., San Francisco, 1975-92; bd. dirs. Health Svcs. Advisory Group, Oakland, Calif., 1992—; trustee French Found. Med. Edn. and Rsch., San Francisco, 1992—. Contbr. articles to profl. jours. With U.S. Army, 1944-46. Fellow ACP, Am. Coll. Med. Informatics; mem. AAAS, Calif. Med. Assn., Sigma Xi. Office: Kaiser Found Rsch Inst 1800 Harrison St Oakland CA 94612

VAN BRUWAENE, SUSI MARIE, bank executive; b. Cin., Feb. 24, 1964; d. Raymond T. and Connie Marie (Onderko) V. BA in Communications/Mktg., U. Wash., 1986. Personal banker Seattle 1st Nat. Bank, 1986-88, mgr., 1988-89, v.p., mgr., 1989—. Vol. Seafirst Vols., Seattle, 1989-92. Mem. Kiwanis (maj. emphasis chmn. 1991-92, membership chmn. 1992), Univ. C. of C. (bd. dirs. 1989-91), U. Wash. Alumni Assn. Republican. Roman Catholic. Office: Seattle 1st Nat Bank 4701 Univ Way NE Seattle WA 98105

VAN BUHLER, ROBERT ALLAN, broadcast executive; b. Detroit, Aug. 31, 1944; s. Robert Louis and Rosella Marie (Fischer) Van B.; m. Linda Geslani Reyes, May 14, 1970; children: Amie Reyes, Margaret Reyes, Robert R. IV, Alexander Reyes. Student, Kirtland Coll., Roscommon, Mich., 1975-77. Engr. various radio stas., Mich., 1964-66; chief engr. Sta. WIOS, Tawas City, Mich., 1970-77, Sta. KDKB-FM, Phoenix, 1977-85; dir. engring. Sta. WBAL/WIYY-FM, Balt., 1985-89; mgr. engring. KNIX-FM/KCWW-AM and Real Country Network, Phoenix, 1989—. Contbg. author: NAB Engring. Handbook, 7th edit., 1985, co-author 8th edit., 1991; columnist Broadcasting Engring. mag., 1986-92. Served as sgt. USAF, 1966-70. Recipient Presdl. Humanitarian Service award Republic of the Philippines, 1968. Fellow Soc. Broadcast Engrs. (sr., v.p. 1988-89); mem. Nat. Frequency Coordinating Coun. (vice chmn. 1985—), Ariz. Frequency Coordinating Com. (chmn. 1981-85), Rosicrucians (AMORC), Rotary (treas. Tawas City 1976, pres. 1977). Republican.

VANCAS, MARK FRANCIS, chemical engineer; b. Deadwood, S.D., Sept. 7, 1947; s. Francis Michael and Muriel Lois (Sugden) V.; m. Susan Evelyn Loftis, Mar. 21, 1970; 1 child, David Joseph. BSChE, U. Ariz., 1970. Rsch. metallurgist Anaconda Co., Tucson, 1970-71; process engr. Magma Copper Co., San Manuel, Ariz., 1971-87; mgr. process engring. Engring. & Constrn. Internat., Tucson, 1987—. Patentee in field; asst. editor: Bowhunting in Arizona, 3d edit. Capt. U.S. Army, 1970-78. Mem. AIME, Am. Inst. Chem. Engrs., Nat. Rifle Assn., Nat. Wildlife Fedn., Nat. Archery Assn. (pres. 1981-82, treas. 1980-81, 83-85, ranked #1 in U.S. in field archery, nat. field champion 1983), Ariz. Archery Assn., Ariz. Wildlife Fedn., Pope & Young Club, Rocky Mt. Elk Found. Home: 305 N Main St San Manuel AZ 85631-1308 Office: Bateman Engring E&C Divsn 1860 E River Rd Tucson AZ 85718-5838

VANCE, BLAKE, chemist; b. Honolulu; s. Thomas and Phyllis Vance. BS, U. Hawaii, 1972; MS, U. Wyo., 1978, PhD, 1983. Chemist Honolulu Wood Treating Co., Honolulu, 1972-75; teaching asst., instr. U. Wyo., Laramie, 1976-82; postdoctoral fellow U. Conn., Storrs, Conn., 1983-85; guest scientist The Gmelin Inst., Frankfurt, Germany, 1985-87; assoc. chemist Hawaiian Sugar Planters' Assn., Aiea, 1988—. Editor (ref. book series) Gmelin Handbook, 1985-87; contbr. articles to profl. jours. Docent Moanalua Gardens Found., Honolulu, 1988—. Recipient Bd. Dirs. award Hawaii Credit Union League, Honolulu, 1991. Mem. Soc. of Quality Assurance, Hawaiian Sugar Technologists, Am. Crystallographic Assn., Am. Chem. Soc. (chair Honolulu chpt. 1991), Phi Lambda Upsilon, Sigma Xi. Office: Hawaiian Sugar Planters' Assn 99-193 Aiea Heights Dr Aiea HI 96701

VANCE, CARRIE TEMPLE, neonatal nurse; b. Jackson, Miss., Nov. 20, 1944. AA in Nursing, San Joaquin Delta Coll., Stockton, Calif., 1974; BA in Health Svc. Adminstrn., St. Mary's Coll., Moraga, Calif., 1978; MS in Nursing Adminstrn. and Music, PhD in Music Performance, Columbia Pacific U., 1985. Lic. nurse, Calif. Staff nurse Dameron Hosp., Stockton, Calif., 1976-77, charge nurse, 1977-80, supr. nursery, 1980—, dir. maternal neonatal svcs., 1989—. Mem. San Joaquin Gen. Hosp. Delta Coll. Nurse Alumni Assn., NAFE, Columbia Pacific U. Alumni Assn., Nat. Assn. Neonatal Nurses, St. Mary's Coll. Alumni Assn., Internat. Assn. Infant Massage Instrs., Internat. Childbirth Educator Assn., Acad. Cert. Birth Educators, Calif. Perinatal Assn., Nat. League for Nursing; instr. Neonatal Resuscitation Hosp., CPR Instr. Seventh-day Adventist. Office: Dameron Hosp Assn 525 W Acacia St Stockton CA 95203-2484

VANCE, CHARLES ELIJAH, III, electronics store owner; b. Phila., Apr. 21, 1938; s. Arthur William and Doris (MacNamara) V.; m. Susan Rosalie Keener, Nov. 30, 1965 (div. Mar. 1972); 1 child, Cher Dee Elena. BA, Lafayette Coll., 1958; MA, U. Ariz., 1965. Enlisted USMC, 1957-67, sgt., 1957-67; capt. NSA, 1959-63, resigned, 1967; sales mgr. Cali-West Inc., Santa Fe Springs, Calif., 1967-83; owner operator Vance Electronics, Pomona, Calif., 1982-86; with sales G&M Electronics, Industry, Calif., 1986-88; owner operator Charley Three Electronics, Ontario, Calif., 1988—. Author: The Silent Kill, 1961 (NSA Svc. award 1962). Mem. Counseling Assocs. Adv. Bd. (sec. 1988—, v.p. alumni bd. 1991—). Republican. Baptist. Home and office: Charley Three Electronics 701 S Palmetto # 111 Ontario CA 91761

VAN CITTERS, ROBERT LEE, medical educator, physician; b. Alton, Iowa, Jan. 20, 1926; s. Charles and Wilhemina (Heemstra) Van C.; m. Mary E. Barker, Apr. 9, 1949; children: Robert, Mary, David, Sara. A.B., U. Kans., 1949; M.D., U. Kans. Med. Ctr., Kansas City, 1953; Sc.D. hon., Northwestern Coll., Orange City, Iowa, 1977. Intern U. Kans. Med. Ctr., Kansas City, 1953-54, resident, 1955-57, fellow, 1957-58; research fellow Sch. Medicine, U. Wash., Seattle, 1958-61, asst. prof. physiology and biophysics, 1962-65, assoc. prof, 1965-70, prof., 1970—; prof. medicine Sch. Medicine, U. Wash., 1970—, assoc. dean Sch. Medicine, 1968-70, dean Sch. Medicine, 1970-81; mem. staff Scripps Clinic and Research Found., La Jolla, Calif., 1961-62; exchange scientist joint U.S.-U.S.S.R. Sci. Exchange, 1962; mem. Liason Commn. on Med. Edn., Washington, 1981-85; mem. various coms., nat. adv. research council NIH, Bethesda, Md., 1980-83; mem. Va. Spl. Med. Adv. Commn., 1974-78, chmn., 1976-78; chmn. working group on mech. circulatory support systems Nat. Heart, Lung and Blood Inst. NIH, 1985—, mem. adv. coun. clin. applications and prevention, 1985-89. Contbr. numerous articles to profl. jours. Served to 1st lt. U.S. Army, 1943-46, PTO; to capt. M.C., USAF, 1953-55. Recipient research career devel. USPHS. Fellow AAAS; mem. Assn. Am. Med. Colls. (adminstrv. bd. and exec. council 1972-78, Disting. Service mem.), Am. Coll. Cardiology (Cummings medal 1970), Nat. Acad. Sci. Inst. Medicine, Am. Heart Assn., Wash. State Med. Assn. (hon. life). Office: U Wash Sch Medicine Seattle WA 98195

VAN CLEEF, ROBERT EDWARD, computer specialist; b. Fall River, Mass., May 20, 1946; s. Jacque Edward and Ellen Dorothy (Fagan) Van C.; m. Mary Virginia Bradley, June 5, 1971; children: James Edward, Anna-Marie. AS, Santa Barbara City Coll., 1978; BBA magna cum laude, Nat. U., San Diego, 1982, MBA with distinction, 1984. Enlisted man U.S. Navy, 1964-76; field engr. Honeywell Corp., Santa Barbara, Calif., 1976-79; systems analyst Computer Scis. Corp., San Diego, 1979-84, Gateway Computer Systems, San Diego, 1984-85, GE Corp., San Jose, 1985-89; computer specialist NASA, San Jose, 1989—. Editor newsletter of Charismatic Pastoral Svc. Team Diocese of San Jose, 1993—. Mem. IEEE, USENIX, IEEE Computer Soc., San Diego Computer Soc. (pres. 1984-85, bd. dirs. 1983-86, editor Personal Systems 1984-85), Assn. for Computing Machinery (reviewer Computing Revs. 1984-89). Republican. Roman Catholic. Home: 192 Warwick Dr Campbell CA 95008 Office: NASA Ames Rsch Ctr Moffett Field CA 94035

VAN COTT, JEFFREY MARK, manufacturing company executive; b. Lakewood, Ohio, Dec. 1, 1945; s. John F. and Shirley H. Van C.; BS in engring., Oreg. State U., 1973, BS in Bus., 1973; divorced; children: Dustin Mark, Rachel Jean, Jill Anne. Mfg. trainee Unadilla (N.Y.) Silo Co., 1958-66; owner JM Van Cott Trucking, Unadilla, 1966-70; exec. v.p., treas., Unadilla Silo Co., Inc., 1973-85, Unadilla Laminated Products Co., 1973-85; v.p. Am. Laminators, Eugene Oreg., 1985-91; pres. LDI, Denver, 1992—; panelist Am. Arbitration Assn., 1983—. Chmn. fin. Methodist Ch., Unadilla, 1976-79; dir. Sidney Hosp., 1981-85. Mem. Am. Inst. Timber Constructor (dir. 1980-91, treas. 1983-84, 1988-89, v.p. 1984-85, pres. 1985-86), Am. Mgmt. Assn., Am. Wood Preservers Inst., C. of C., Forest Products Research Soc., Midstate Mgmt. Assn., Rotary, (Paul Harris fellow), Elks. Avocations: competitive running, fishing, boxing, travel, languages. Home: PO Box 10154 Eugene OR 97440-2154 Office: LDI PO Box 390262 Denver CO 80239

VANDAL, STEVEN OFFERDAL, plant manager, military reserve officer; b. Mpls., Apr. 25, 1948; s. William Lawson and Doris Alice (Offerdal) V.; m. Carol Anne Werbela, June 13, 1971; children: Susan Anne, James Benjamin, Christine Anne. Student, U.S. Naval Acad. Prep. Sch., 1967, U.S. Mil. Acad., 1971; M in Human Rels., Def. Dept. Race Rels. Inst., 1974. Commd. 2d lt. U.S. Army, 1971, advanced through grades to comdr.; co. comdr. U.S. Army, Ft. Knox, Ky., 1971-79, ret., 1979; team mgr. Procter & Gamble Co., Green Bay, Wis., 1979-80, area dept. mgr., 1980-81; shift supt. Kimberly Clark Corp., Beech Island, S.C., 1981-82; folded products supt. Kimberly Clark Corp., Neenah, Wis., 1982-84; ops. supt. Kimberly Clark Corp., Ogden, Utah, 1984-86, plant supt., 1986-87; ops. mgr. Kimberly Clark Corp., Neenah, Wis., 1987-89; plant mgr. Pope & Talbot Inc., Porterville, Calif., 1989—; bd. dirs. Tule River Indian Reservation Econ. Devel. Corp., Porterville, Calif., Tulare County Pvt. Industry Coun., Visalia, Calif. Coun. commr. Boy Scouts Am., Porterville, 1989-90, Visalia, 1991—; golf coach Monache High Sch., Porterville, 1991—. Maj. USAR, 1971—. Recipient Scoutmaster key Boy Scouts Am., Merit award Boy Scouts Am. Mem. Nat. Model R.R. Assn., Porterville Plant Mgrs. Assn., U.S. Profl. Golf Assn. (assoc.), U.S. Golf Assn. (assoc.), Porterville C. of C. (chair 1989-92). Republican. Lutheran. Home: 9696 SW Ventura Ct Tigard OR 97223 Office: Consumer Products Divsn. 1500 SW 1st Ave Portland OR 97201

VAN DE KAMP, JOHN KALAR, lawyer; b. Pasadena, Calif., Feb. 7, 1936; s. Harry and Georgie (Kalar) Van de K.; m. Andrea Fisher, Mar. 11, 1978; 1 child, Diana. BA, Dartmouth Coll., 1956; JD, Stanford U., 1959. Bar: Calif. 1960. Asst. U.S. atty. L.A., 1960-66, U.S. atty., 1966-67; dep. dir. Exec. Office for U.S. Attys., Washington, 1967-68, dir., 1968-69; spl. asst. Pres.'s Commn. on Campus Unrest, 1970; fed. pub. defender L.A., 1971-75; dist. atty. Los Angeles County, 1975-83; atty. gen. State of Calif., 1983-91; ptnr., chmn. litigation dept. Dewey Ballantine, L.A., 1991—. Mem. Calif. Dist. Attys. Assn. (pres. 1975-83), Nat. Dist. Attys. Assn. (v.p. 1975-83), Peace Officers Assn. L.A. County (past pres.), Nat. Assn. Attys. Gen. (exec. com. 1983-91), Nat. Coll. Dist. Attys. (bd. regents 1991—), Conf. Western Attys. Gen. (pres. 1986). Office: Dewey Ballantine 333 S Hope St Ste 3000 Los Angeles CA 90071-3003

VANDENBERG, PETER RAY, magazine publisher; b. Geneva, Ill., Sept. 8, 1939; s. Don George and Isabel (Frank) V.; m. Kathryn Stock, June 1973 (div. Apr. 1977). BBA, Miami U., 1962. Creative adminstr. E.F. McDonald Incentive Co., Dayton, Ohio, 1966-73; mfrs.' rep. Denver, 1974-75; mgr. Homestake Condominiums, Vail, Colo., 1975-76; desk clk. Vail Run Resort, 1976-77; sales rep. Colo. West Advt., Vail, 1977-79, pres., 1980-83; pres. Colo. West Publ., Vail, 1983—. With U.S. Army, 1963-66. Mem. Sigma Chi.

VAN DEN BERGH, SIDNEY, astronomer; b. Wassenaar, Netherlands, May 20, 1929; emigrated to U.S., 1948; s. Sidney J. and Mieke (van den Berg) vandenB.; m. Paulette Brown; children by previous marriage: Peter, Mieke, Sabine. Student, Leiden (The Netherlands) U., 1947-48; A.B., Princeton U., 1950; M.Sc., Ohio State U., 1952; Dr. rer. nat., Goettingen U., 1956. Asst. prof. Perkins Obs., Ohio State U., Columbus, 1956-58; research assoc. Mt. Wilson Obs., Palomar Obs., Pasadena, Calif., 1968-69; prof. astronomy David Dunlap Obs., U. Toronto, Ont., Can., 1958-77; dir. Dominion Astrophys. Obs., Victoria, B.C., 1977-86; prin. rsch. officer NRC Can., 1977—. Fellow Royal Soc. London, Royal Soc. Can.; mem. Am., Royal Astron. Soc. (assoc.), Canadian Astronomy Soc. (sr. v.p. 1988-90, pres. 1990-92). Home: 418 Lands End Rd, Sidney, BC Canada V8L 5L9

VANDENBERGHE, RONALD GUSTAVE, accountant, real estate developer; b. Oakland, Calif., July 1, 1937; s. Anselm Henri and Margaret B. (Bygum) V.; B.A. with honors, San Jose State Coll., 1959; postgrad. U. Calif. at Berkeley Extension, 1959-60, Golden Gate Coll., 1961-63; CPA, Calif.; m. Patricia W. Dufour, Aug. 18, 1957; children: Camille, Mark, Matthew. Real estate investor, pres. VandenBerghe Fin. Corp., Pleasanton, Calif., 1964—. Instr. accounting U. Cal., Berkeley, 1963-70; CPA, Pleasanton, 1963—. Served with USAF. Mem. Calif. Soc. CPAs. Republican. Presbyterian. Mason (Shriner). Home: PO Box 803 Danville CA 94526-0803 Office: 20 Happy Valley Rd Pleasanton CA 94566

VAN DE POEL, JEFFREY PAUL, data processing executive; b. San Francisco, Nov. 6, 1957; s. John Frederick and Dorothy Agnes (Kern) Van De P.; m. Karen Jean Wentworth, July 12, 1986; children: Andrew Paul, Amy Jean. BS in Info. Systems, San Diego State U., 1981. Programmer, analyst Ins. Co. the West, San Diego, 1981-83, Security Pacific Fin. Corp., San Diego, 1983-84; programmer, analyst XYCOR, Inc., San Diego, 1984-85, project leader, 1985-86, account mgr., client exec., 1990—; programming mgr. ESC Adminstrs., San Diego, 1986-87; v.p. systems, programming Aztec Computer Svcs., San Diego, 1988-89; systems mgr. AVCO Fin. Svcs., Irvine, Calif., 1989-90. Office: XYCOR Inc 10640 Scripps Ranch Blvd San Diego CA 92131-1027

VANDERBILT, KERMIT, English language educator; b. Decorah, Iowa, Sept. 1, 1925; s. Lester and Ella (Qualley) V.; m. Vivian Osmundson, Nov. 15, 1947; 1 dau., Karen Paige. B.A., Luther Coll., Decorah, 1947, Litt. D. (hon.), 1977; M.A., U. Minn., 1949, Ph.D., 1956. Instr. English U. Minn., 1954-57; instr. U. Wash., 1958-60, asst. prof. English, 1960-62; asst. prof. San Diego State U., 1962-65, assoc. prof., 1965-68, prof., 1968-90, prof. emeritus, 1990—; vis. prof. Am. lit. U. B.C., Can., Vancouver, summer 1963; vis. prof. U. Oreg., summer 1968. Author: Charles Eliot Norton: Apostle of Culture in a Democracy, 1959, The Achievement of William Dean Howells: A Reinterpretation, 1968, American Literature and the Academy: The Roots, Growth and Maturity of a Profession, 1986, Theodore Roethke in A Literary History of the American West, 1987; editor: (with others) American Social Thought, 1972, April Hopes (W.D. Howells), 1975, The Rise of Silas Lapham, 1983, spl. issue Am. Literary Realism, winter 1989, La Litterature Americaine, 1991; mem. edit. bd. U. Wash. Press, 1960-62, Twentieth Century Lit., 1969—; contbr. numerous articles to profl. jours. Served with USNR, 1943-46. Outstanding Prof. San Diego State U., 1976; Guggenheim fellow, 1978-79; Huntington Library fellow, 1980; Am. Philos. Soc. grantee, 1964, Am. Council Learned Socs. grantee, 1972, Nat. Endowment for Humanities grantee, 1986. Mem. Am. Studies Assn. (exec. council 1968-69), So. Calif. Am. Studies Assn. (pres. 1968-69), Philol. Assn. Pacific Coast (chmn. sect. Am. lit. 1968), MLA, Internat. Mark Twain Soc. (hon.), United Profs. of Calif. (Disting. prof. 1978). Home: 6937 Coleshill Dr San Diego CA 92119-1920

VANDERGRIFF, JERRY DODSON, computer store executive; b. Ft. Leonard Wood, Mo., Nov. 6, 1943; s. Oliver Wyatt Vandergriff and Mary Ella (Perkins) Myers; m. Donna Jean Niehof, Aug. 14, 1976 (div. Nov. 1987); children: Robert Lee II, William Oliver. BS in Bus., Emporia State U., 1974. Customer svc. mgr. Pictures, Inc., Anchorage, 1975-83, v.p., gen. mgr., 1983-87; gen. mgr. Pictures-The Computer Store, Anchorage, 1987—. Bd. dirs. Community Schs. Coun., Anchorage, 1986-87; mem. Gov.'s Coun. on Edn., 1989-90; bd. dirs. Romig Jr. High Sch., 1989-90, pres. PTSA, 1990-92; mem. exec. bd. Alaska's Youth Ready for Work, 1989-92. Mem. VFW, Moose. Republican. Home: 3831 Balchen Dr Anchorage AK 99517-2446 Office: The Computer Store 601 W 36th Ave # 19 Anchorage AK 99503-5847

VANDERHEIDEN, RICHARD THOMAS, government official, lawyer; b. Omaha, Nov. 10, 1947; s. Frederick Joseph and Margaret (Burke) V.; m. Mary Margaret Schuster, June 1, 1969; children: Brian, Paul. BS, U. Nebr., 1970, JD, 1973. Bar: Nebr. 1974. Dep. county atty. Merrick County, Central City, Nebr., 1974-75; ptnr. Phares Torpin Vanderheiden & Mesner, Central City, 1976-87; v.p. Founders Bank of Ariz., Scottsdale, 1987-88, Chase Trust Co. of Ariz., Scottsdale, 1988-91; pub. fiduciary Maricopa County, Phoenix, 1991—; jud. nominating commn. 21st Jud. Dist., Nebr., 1984-86; bd. dirs. Merrick County Mental Health Ctr., 1975-82; Maricopa County Justice Com., 1991—, exec. team, 1991. Pres. Bd. Edn., Central City, 1975-82; chpt. chmn. ARC, Central City, 1976-80. Mem. ABA, Nat. Guardianship Assn. (bd. dirs. 1992—), Scottsdale Bar Assn., Valley Estate Planners (pres. 1990-91), Ariz. Bankers Assn. (trust com. 1989-91), Sertoma Internat. (pres. 1979), Central City C. of C. (bd. dirs. 1980-84). Democrat. Roman Catholic. Office: First Am Title Bldg 111 W Monroe 5th fl Phoenix AZ 85003

VANDER HOUWEN, BOYD A., marketing and management executive; b. Yakima, Wash., Jan. 17, 1946; s. John W. and Elsie W. (Lanfear) V.; m. Loma Alene Madsen, June 27, 1970; children: Garth John, Dana Madsen. BA in Journalism, U. Mont., 1968; BA in Econs., U. Wash., 1971, MA in Communications/Bus., 1978; grad., Northwest Intermediate Banking Sch., Portland, Oreg., 1985. Edn., city hall reporter Idaho Falls (Idaho) Post-Register, 1971-72; farm bus. writer Tri-City Herald, Kennewick, Wash., 1973-74; bur. mgr., editor Yakima Valley Tri-City Herald, Sunnyside, Wash., 1974-76; editor Jour. Contemporary Bus., mgr. bus. publs. Grad. Sch. Bus. Adminstrn. U. Wash., Seattle, 1978-81; asst. v.p., mgr. communications Rainier Nat. Bank, Seattle, 1981-88; prin. Hawkins Vander Houwen, Inc., Seattle, 1988-89, Vander Houwen Pub. Rels., Bellevue, Wash., 1989—. Mem. publs. redesign com. Hist. Seattle, 1982, selection com. merit scholarship Rainier Nat. Bank, 1983; publicity chmn. United Way One to One Program, 1983, United Way Cabinet, 1982; chmn. communications com. United Way of King County, mem. mktg. com., 1985—; chmn. fiscal adv. com. Mercer Island Pub. Schs., 1985-89; mem. Mercer Island Sch. Bd., 1991—, pres. 1992-93; chmn. CMU Com. United Way of King County, 1985-88, mem. awards com. Washington Gives, 1988—. With U.S. Army, 1969-71. Named IABC Communicator of Yr., 1982, NEH grantee, 1979; recipient Excellence in Publs. award Soc. Tech. Publs., 1979, 81, Merge-Communicator awards IABC, 1987. Mem. Am. Mktg. Assn. (v.p. mktg. Puget Sound chpt. 1990—, pres. elect 1991, pres. 1992-93), Pub. Rels. Soc. Am., Internat. Assn. Bus. Communicators (Pacesetter awards com. 1981-83, Internal Communicatons award of excellence Pacific N.W. chpt. 1982, Silver 6 and Totem awards employee pubs., Puget Sound chpt. 1983, '84, '88, '90), Soc. Profl. Journalists (bus. writing, editing awards 1971, '73, '74). Home: 8575 SE 76th Pl Mercer Island WA 98040-5706 Office: Vander Houwen Pub Rels 11747 NE 1st St Ste 101 Bellevue WA 98005-3018

VANDERLINDEN, CAMILLA DENICE DUNN, telecommunications industry manager; b. Dayton, July 21, 1950; d. Joseph Stanley and Virginia Danley (Martin) Dunn; m. David Henry VanderLinden; Oct. 10, 1980; 1 child, Michael Christopher. Student, U. de Valencia, Spain, 1969; BA in Spanish and Secondary Edn. cum laude, U. Utah, 1972, MS in Human Resource Econs., 1985. Asst. dir. Davis County Community Action Program, Farmington, Utah, 1973-76; dir. South County Community Action, Midvale, Utah, 1976-79; supr. customer service Ideal Nat. Life Ins. Co., Salt Lake City, 1979-80; mgr. customer service Utah Farm Bur. Mutual Ins., Salt Lake City, 1980-82; quality assurance analyst Am. Express Co., Salt Lake City, 1983-86, quality assurance and human resource specialist, 1986-88; mgr. quality assurance and engring. Am. Express Co., Denver, 1988-91; mgr. customer svc. Tel. Express Co., Colorado Springs, Colo., 1991—; mem. adj. faculty Westminster Coll., Salt Lake City, 1987-88. mem. adj. faculty, mem. quality adv. bd. Red Rocks Community Coll., 1990-91. Vol. translator Latin Am. community; vol. naturalist Roxborough State Park; internat. exch. coord. EF Fgn. Exch. Program. Christian. Home: 10857 W Snow Cloud Trail Littleton CO 80125

VANDERLINDEN, CARL RENE, consulting company executive; b. Pella, Iowa, Sept. 26, 1923; s. Marinus and Julia (Fennema) V.; m. Shirley A. Beatty, Mar. 8, 1945; children: Patricia, David. Student, Central Coll., 1941-43; BS in Chem. Engring., U. Wash., 1944; PhD in Chem. Engring., Iowa State U., 1950. Registered profl. engr., Iowa. Rsch. sect. chief Johns-Manville, Manville, N.J., 1953-61, rsch. dept. mgr., 1961-69, dir. R&D, 1969-73, Denver, 1972-75, v.p. dir., R&D, 1975-81; staff v.p. dir. R&D, Manville Sales Corp., Denver, 1981-86; pres. VanderLinden & Assocs., Littleton, Colo., 1987—; treas. Chem. cons. of Colo., 1988—. Pres. Columbine Valley Homeowners Assn., 1986-88, treas., 1988-91; mem. U.S. Dept. of Energy Advanced Indsl. Materials Guidance and Evaluation Bd., 1986—, chmn., 1989-90. Ensign USN, 1943-46. Recipient Profl. Achievement Citation in Engring. Iowa State U., 1982. Fellow Am. Inst. Chem. Engrs. (dir. 1979-81); mem. Am. Chem. Soc., Nat. Inst. Bldg. Scis., Bldg. Futures Council (operating com. 1979-87), Perlite Inst. (pres. 1974-76, Lewis Lloyd award, 1983), Bldg. Thermal Envelope Coordinating Com. (bd. dirs. 1985-

88). Republican. Presbyterian. Club: Columbine Country. Office: Vander-Linden & Assocs 5 Brassie Way Littleton CO 80123-6608

VAN DER MEULEN, JOSEPH PIERRE, neurologist; b. Boston, Aug. 22, 1929; s. Edward Lawrence and Sarah Jane (Robertson) VanDer M.; m. Ann Irene Yadeno, June 18, 1960; children—Elisabeth, Suzanne, Janet. A.B., Boston Coll., 1950; M.D., Boston U., 1954. Diplomate: Am. Bd. Psychiatry and Neurology. Intern Cornell Med. div. Bellevue Hosp., N.Y.C., 1954-55; resident Cornell Med. div. Bellevue Hosp., 1955-56; resident Harvard U., Boston City Hosp., 1958-60, instr., fellow, 1962-66; assoc. Case Western Res. U., Cleve., 1966-67; asst. prof. Case Western Res. U., 1967-69, assoc. prof. neurology and biomed. engring., 1969-71; prof. neurology U. So. Calif., L.A., 1971—; also dir. dept. neurology Los Angeles County/U. So. Calif. Med. Center; chmn. dept. U. So. Calif., 1971-78, v.p. for health affairs, 1977—, dean Sch. Medicine, 1985-86, dir. Allied Health Scis., 1991—; vis. prof. Autonomous U. Guadalajara, Mex., 1974; pres. Norris Cancer Hosp. and Research Inst., 1983—. Contbr. articles to profl. jours. Mem. med. adv. bd. Calif. chpt. Myasthenia Gravis Found., 1971-75, chmn., 1974-75, 77-78; med. adv. bd. Amyotrophic Lateral Sclerosis Found., Calif., 1973-75, chmn., 1974-75; mem. Com. to Combat Huntington's Disease, 1973—; bd. dirs. Calif. Hosp. Med. Ctr., Good Hope Med. Found., Doheny Eye Hosp., House Ear Inst., L.A. Hosp. Good Samaritan, Children's Hosp. of L.A., Barlow Respiratory Hosp., USC U. Hosp., chmn., 1991—; bd. govs. Thomas Aquinas Coll.; bd. dirs. Assn. Acad. Health Ctrs., chmn., 1991-92; pres. Scott Newman Ctr., 1987-89; pres., bd. dirs. Kenneth Norris Cancer Hosp & Rsch. Inst. Served to lt. M.C. USNR, 1956-58. Nobel Inst. fellow Karolinska Inst., Stockholm, 1960-62; NIH grantee, 1968-71. Mem. AMA, Am. Neurol. Assn., Am. Acad. Neurology, L.A. Soc. Neurology and Psychiatry (pres. 1977-78), L.A. Med. Assn., Mass. Med. Soc., Ohio Med. Soc., Calif. Med. Soc., L.A. Acad. Medicine, Alpha Omega Alpha (councillor 1992—), Phi Kappa Phi. Home: 39 Club View Ln Palos Verdes Peninsula CA 90274-4208 Office: U So Calif 1985 Zonal Ave Los Angeles CA 90033-1058

VAN DER MEYDEN, DIEDERICK O., mechanical engineer; b. Porto Alegre, Brazil, Oct. 6, 1960; s. Theo Johannes and Pauline Wendeline (Paarmann) Van Der M. Mech. Engr., Centro Fed. Educacao Tech., Rio de Janeiro, 1987. Trainee engine shop Varig Airlines, Rio de Janeiro, 1984-86, engr. engine shop, 1987-88; project engr. Chromizing Co., Gardena, Calif., 1988—. Office: Chromalloy Nevada 715 Industrial Park Dr Carson City NV 89701-9999

VANDERSPEK, PETER GEORGE, management consultant, writer; b. The Hague, Netherlands, Dec. 15, 1925; came to U.S., 1945; s. Pieter and Catherine Johanna (Rolf) V.; m. Charlotte Louise Branch, Aug. 18, 1957. Student, Tilburg (Netherlands) U., 1944; MA in Econs., Fordham U., 1950, PhD in Econs., 1954; postgrad., George Washington U., 1967-68. Internat. economist Mobil Oil Corp., N.Y.C., 1956-59; mgr. internat. market rsch. Celanese Corp., N.Y.C., 1959-63; internat. economist Bethlehem (Pa.) Steel Corp., 1964-65; sr. tech. adviser Battelle Meml. Inst., Washington, 1965-66; indsl. adviser Inter-Am. Devel. Bank, Washington, 1967-69; economist Fed. Res. Bank, N.Y.C., 1970-72; mgr. internat. market rsch. Brunswick Corp., Skokie, Ill., 1973-76; mgr. advanced planning Sverdrup Corp., St. Louis, 1979-87; cons. Sverdrup Corp., 1988-90; pres. OBEX, Inc., San Luis Obispo, Calif., 1988—. Author: Planning for Factory Automation, 1993; contbr. to profl. jours. Thomas J. Watson fellow, IBM-Fordham U., 1945-49. Mem. Nat. Assn. Bus. Economists, Mensa. Home and Office: 1314 Vega Way San Luis Obispo CA 93405-4815

VAN DERVEER, TARA, university athletic coach. Coach NCAA women's basketball champions Stanford U. Cardinals, 1990, 92. Office: c/o Stanford Univ Stanford CA 94305

VAN DER WERFF, TERRY JAY, management consultant; b. Hammond, Ind., May 16, 1944; s. Sidney and Johanna (Oostman) van der W.; m. Renee Marie Leet, Mar. 2, 1968; children: Anne Cathleen, Valerie Kay, David Edward, Michele Renée, Julia Leigh. SB and SM, MIT, 1968; DPhil, Oxford (Eng.) U., 1972. Registered profl. engr., Colo., South Africa; profl. biomed. engr., South Africa. Staff engr. ARO, Inc., Tullahoma, Tenn., 1968; asst. prof. mech. engring., physiology and biophysics Colo. State U., Ft. Collins, 1970-73; vis. asst. prof. medicine U. Colo., Denver, 1973-74; head biomed. engring. U. Cape Town/Groote Schuur Hosp., Cape Town, South Africa, 1974-80; dean of sci. and engring. Seattle U., 1981-90; exec. v.p. for acad. affairs St. Joseph's U., Phila., 1990-91; pres. van der Werff Assoc., Inc., Seattle, 1991—. Co-author: Mathematical Models of the Dynamics of the Human Eye; author 70 book reviews, monthly newspaper and magazine columns; contbr. articles to profl. jours. Recipient Ralph R. Teetor award Soc. Automotive Engrs., Detroit, 1972. Fellow Royal Soc. South Africa, Biomed. Engring. Soc. South Africa; mem. AAAS, Am. Phys. Soc., Sigma Xi. Republican. Roman Catholic. Home: 2410 NE 123d St Seattle WA 98125-5241

VANDIVER, ROBERT SANFORD, civic association executive; b. Barksdale Field, La., Apr. 2, 1937; s. William Marion and Mattie Katherine (Tiller) V.; m. Patricia Gail Kelly, Feb. 10, 1956; children: Cynthia Ann, Kathleen. AA, U. Md., 1973; BA, SUNY, Albany, 1975; MS, Golden Gate U., 1985, MPA, 1986. Enlisted U.S. Army, 1955, commd. lt., 1967, advanced through grades to maj., 1978; materiel mgr. Pima County Sheriff Dept., Tucson, 1979-81; task leader Computer Scis. Corp., Sierra Vista, Ariz., 1981-83, Mandex, Inc., Sierra Vista, 1983-86; project mgr. Planning Rsch. Corp., Sierra Vista, 1986-90; Boy Scout exec. Catalina Coun., Tucson, 1990—; adj. faculty Cochise Coll., Sierra Vista, 1987-90, Golden Gate U., San Francisco, 1988-92; instr. Sch. Pub. Adminstrn., Ariz. State U., Tucson, 1988-92. Co-editor, South Vietnam Boy Scout Handbook, 1965. Vol. leader Boy Scouts Am., various locations, 1956-90. Decorated Legion of Merit, Bronze Star medal; recipient Silver Beaver award, Boy Scouts Am., 1977. Mem. Nat. Property Mgmt. Assn., Soc. Logistics Engrs., Armed Forces Communications Electronics Assn., Am. Soc. Pub. adminstrn., Co. Mil. Historians. Lutheran. Home: 8345 E Cypress Point Ln Tucson AZ 85710-7164 Office: Catalina Coun Boy Scouts Am 5049 E Broadway Blvd Ste 200 Tucson AZ 85711-3636

VAN DORN, PETER DOUGLAS, accountant; b. Craig, Colo., June 28, 1941; s. Perry Douglas and Gloria Marjorie (Miller) Van D.; m. Joyce Lucille Swanson, Aug. 9, 1964; children: Douglas, Stephen, Marsha. Student Colo. State U., 1959-60; BS, U. Colo., 1969. CPA, Colo., Wyo., La., N.C. With Touche Ross & Co., Denver, 1969-86, ptnr., 1978-86, nat. dir. banking, 1979-86, founder, mng. ptnr. Van Dorn & Bossi, Boulder, Colo., 1986—, bd. of regents Bethel Coll. and Sem., St. Paul. With Army NG, 1963-69. Mem. Am. Inst. CPAs, Colo. Soc. CPAs, Wyo. Soc. CPAs. Republican. Baptist. Clubs: Bear Creek Golf Club, U. Colo. Alumni Dirs.; U. Colo. Alumni Dirs. Home: 5860 Oxford Rd Longmont CO 80503 Office: Van Dorn & Bossi Ste 202 4909 Pearl East Circle Boulder CO 80301

VAN DUSEN, ANN BRENTON, writer; b. Blackfoot, Idaho, June 15, 1919; d. Henry Kirk and Margaret Mary (Burrell) Williams; divorced; children: Delbert Wayne, Brenton John (dec.). Student art history, Univ. of Ams., Mexico City, 1976-78; cert., Famous Writer's Sch., 1981; BA in English, Coll. Idaho, 1985. Cert. tchr., Idaho, cert. vol. tutor Laubach method. Elem. tchr. rural sch. dist. Meridian, Idaho, 1940-42; tchr. English to students who speak another lang. Author: Who's Depressed?, 1984 (Strata merit award 1984). Coord. Am. Cancer Soc., Boise, 1954-69; com. chmn. Idaho Mental Health Assn., 1962-68; vol. Caldwell (Idaho) Hosp. Aux. Mem. PEO (pres. Meridian 1983-85). Republican. Mem. Ch. Religious Sci. Home: 850 Parkway Dr # 19 Blackfoot ID 83221-1638

VAN DYKE, DAVID, broadcast executive; b. Jersey City, N.J., Mar. 1, 1949; s. Sidney Arthur and Wilma Patricia (Heilbrunn) Hass; m. Denise Lynn Spinney, Feb. 14, 1988. BA in Comm., U. Miami, 1971. Air personality Sta. WMFQ-FM, Miami, Fla., 1971, Sta. WWWW-FM, Detroit, 1971-72, Sta. WDAI-FM, Chgo., 1972-76; program dir. Sta. KFWD-FM, Dallas, 1976-78, Sta. KAZY-FM, Denver, 1978-82, Sta. KLUV-FM, Dallas, 1983-87; program dir. Sta. WODS-FM, Boston, 1987-89, v.p., gen. mgr., 1989-91; v.p., gen. mgr. Sta. KCBS-FM, L.A., 1991—; cons. Sta. WOGL-FM, Phila., Sta. KLOU-FM, St. Louis, 1988, Sta. KOJD-FM, L.A., 1989. Mem. So. Calif. Broadcasters (bd. dirs.), Alpha Epsilon Rho. Office: Station KCBS-FM 6121 Sunset Blvd Los Angeles CA 90028

VANE, SYLVIA BRAKKE, anthropologist, cultural resource management company executive; b. Fillmore County, Minn., Feb. 28, 1918; d. John T. and Hulda Christina (Marburger) Brakke; m. Arthur Bayard Vane, May 17, 1942; children: Ronald Arthur, Linda, Laura Vane Ames. AA, Rochester Jr. Coll., 1937; BS with distinction, U. Minn., 1939; postgrad., Radcliffe U., 1944; MA, Calif. State U., Hayward, 1975. Med. technologist Dr. Frost and Hodapp, Willmar, Minn., 1939-41; head labs. Corvallis Gen. Hosp., Oreg., 1941-42; dir. lab. Cambridge Gen. Hosp., Mass., 1942-43, Peninsula Clinic, Redwood City, Calif., 1947-49; v.p. Cultural Systems Rsch., Inc., Menlo Park, Calif., 1978—; pres. Ballena Press, Menlo Park, 1981—; cons. cultural resource mgmt. So. Calif. Edison Co., Rosemead, 1978-81, San Diego Gas and Elec. Co., 1980-83, Pacific Gas and Elec. Co., San Francisco, 1982-83, Wender, Murase & White, Washington, 1983-87, Yosemite Indians, Mariposa, Calif., 1982-91, San Luis Rey Band of Mission Indians, Escondido, Calif., 1986-89, U.S. Ecology, Newport Beach, Calif., 1986—, Riverside County Flood Control and Water Conservation Dist., 1985—, Infotec, Inc., 1989-91, Alexander & Karshmer, Berkeley, Calif., 1989-92, Desert Water Agy., Palm Springs, Calif., 1989-90, Metropolitan Water Dist., 1992—. Author: (with L.J. Bean), California Indians, Primary Resources, 1977, rev. edit., 1990, The Cahuilla and the Santa Rosa Mountains, 1981, The Cahuilla Landscape, 1991; contbr. chpts. to several books. Bd. dirs. Sequoia Area coun. Girl Scouts U.S., 1954-61; bd. dirs., v.p., pres. LWV, S. San Mateo County, Calif., 1960-65, cons. San Francisco coun. Girl Scouts U.S., 1962-69. Fellow Soc. Applied Anthropology; mem. Southwestern Anthrop. Assn. (program chmn. 1976-78, newsletter editor 1976-79), Am. Anthropology Assn., Soc. for Am. Archaeology. Mem. United Ch. of Christ. Office: Ballena Press 823 Valparaiso Ave Menlo Park CA 94025-4206

VAN EECKHOUT, GERALD DUANE, telecommunications executive; b. Fargo, N.D., Sept. 29, 1940; s. Edward Cornelius and Rose (Tuchscherer) Van E.; m. Carolyn Kirk Rush, Aug. 22, 1964; children: Jill Ann, Pamela Sue, Kimberly Lyn. B in Bus., U. N.D., 1962; cert., Stanford U., 1976. CPA, Minn., Colo. CPA Touche, Ross & Co., Mpls., 1962-70; dir. internat. fin. Pillsbury Co., Mpls., 1970-75; v.p., CFO Medtronic, Inc., Mpls., 1975-82; pres., CEO Confer Tech. Internat., Golden, Colo., 1982-89; chmn., CEO ACT Teleconferencing, Golden, 1989—; bd. dirs. Staodyne, Inc., Longmont, Colo., Medivators, Inc., Cannon Falls, Minn., Am. Electronics Assn., Santa Clara, Calif. Mem. Colo. CPA's Soc. Office: ACT Teleconferencing 1658 Cole Blvd #162 Golden CO 80401

VAN EVEREN, BROOKS, historian, educator; b. Boston, Apr. 15, 1934; s. Frank and Louise (Brooks) Van E.; m. Eleanor Goodridge, Aug. 17, 1957; children: Barry, Douglas, Mark, Heather. BA, Boston U., 1960, MA, 1961; PhD, U. Colo., 1970. Instr. history Mass. Bay C.C., Boston, 1961-63, asst. prof. history, 1963-65; assoc. prof. history Mass. Bay C.C., Watertown, Mass., 1965-67; asst. prof. history Met. State Coll., Denver, 1967-68, prof. history, 1970—. Author (with others) Franklin D. Roosevelt and German Problem, 1982: presenter programs on Soviet Union and Cold War for profl. confs. seminars and pub. lectrs . Mem. Phi Alpha Theta. Home: 8789 Baseline Rd Lafayette CO 80026 Office: Met State Coll PO Box 173362 Denver CO 80217

VAN FLEET, JULIA MAE, public relations executive; b. Sharon, Pa., May 6, 1955; d. William Dennis and Joan Marie (Arace) Shisler; m. Kenneth Frank Van Fleet, Nov. 2, 1991. Student, No. Va. C.C., 1984-85. Staff asst. House Com. on Sci. Space and Tech., Washington, 1980-85; exec. asst. Nat. Commn. on Space, Washington, 1985-86; sr. mktg. rep. space systems divsn. Gen. Dynamics, San Diego, 1986-87; pub. relations mgr. Gen. Atomics/San Diego Supercomputer, La Jolla, Calif., 1987-92; head of external rels. Internat. Thermonuclear Exptl. Reactor, La Jolla, Calif., 1992—. Editor: Pioneering the Space Frontier: the Next 50 Years, 1986 (best non-fiction space book, Aerospace Writers of Am., 1986). Bd. dirs. United Svcs. Orgn., San Diego, 1986-93, Alzheimer's Family Ctrs., San Diego, 1990—, Reps. of La Jolla, San Diego, 1992—. Republican. Office: ITER San Diego Co Ctr 11025 N Torrey Pines La Jolla CA 92037

VAN FLEET, WILLIAM MABRY, architect; b. Point Richmond, Calif., Jan. 22, 1915; s. Harvey Lorenz and Allie O'Dell (Taylor) Van F.; m. Colette Sims, Apr. 26, 1940; children: Christine, Ellen, Peter. AB, U. Calif., Berkeley, 1938. Pvt. practice architecture, Eureka, Calif., 1951—; lectr. design Humboldt (Calif.) State U., 1965-66; ptnr. William & Colette Van Fleet, 1954—. Prin. works include Del Norte County Courthouse and Library, Crescent City, Calif., 1957, Freshwater (Calif.) Elem. Sch., 1954, Lee residence, Sunnybrae, Calif., 1962, Zane Jr. High Sch., Eureka, 1965, offices for Brooks-Scanlon Lumber Co., Bend, Oreg., 1967. Chmn., No. Humboldt Vocat. Coun., 1964-65, Humboldt County Scenic Resources Com., 1965; pres. Humboldt-Del Norte Mental Health Soc., 1970-71; mem. Humboldt County Community Svcs. Ctr. 1970, Humboldt Arts Council, 1970, Humboldt County Energy Adv. Com., 1979; chmn. Eureka Beautification Com., 1969, Humboldt Sr. Retirement Homes Com., 1979—; bd. dirs. Humboldt County Assn. Retarded Children, 1960-68, Humboldt Family Svc. Ctr., 1970, Redwoods United Workshop, 1973, Open Door Clinic, 1973, Coordinating Coun. Human Svcs. Humboldt County, 1976, Calif.-Oreg. Community Devel. Soc., 1980—; mem. Humboldt Energy Adv. Com., 1980—, Eureka City Housing Adv. Bd., 1982. Recipient Merit award HHFA, 1964, 1st Honor award Pub. Housing Adminstrn., 1964, Gov. Calif. Design award, 1966, Outstanding Svc. award Far West Indian Hist. Soc., 1973, Man of Yr. award Redwood region Nat. Audubon Soc., 1976, resolutions of commendation Calif. State Senate and Assembly, 1982, Gold medal for 10k cross-country run, 1989. Mem. AIA, Net Energy Assn. (bd. dir.), Humboldt Native Plant Soc., Redwood Art Assn. (pres. 1970), Sierra Club (bd. dir. 1972), Fifty-Plus Runners Assn. (1st place in age group Nat. Fifty-Plus Runners Meet 1981). Unitarian. Club: Six Rivers Running (bd. dirs., All-Am. awards 1987, Hall of Fame, 1992). Lodge: Kiwanis (pres. Eureka 1976-77, Disting. Svc. award 1968). Participant in various marathons and races, including Internat. Marathon, Sacramento, 1983 (1st in 65-69 age group), World Vet. Championships Marathon, Rome, Italy, 1984 (1st in U.S., 8th in World, 70-74 age group), Fifty-Plus 5 mile run, Stanford, Calif., 1985 (1st in 70-74 age group, 2d all-time nationally), course records (70-74 age group) 300-meters and 5-kilometer runs Masters Hayward Classic Track & Field Meet, Eugene, Oreg., 1988, others, course record and Calif. state record (70-74 age group) in Nike Half-Marathon, San Francisco, 1988, Gold medal for 10K cross-country as a member of the U.S. team (70-74 age group), 1989, World Vets. Championships, Eugene, Oreg. (1st in 70-74 age group), 1990, All-Am. certs. 2nd nationally in 800 and 1500 meter run Pacific Assn./TAC Championship, Los Gatos, Calif., 1st half marathon, Calif., 1990. Home: 71 Old Forest Ln Eureka CA 95501-9554 Office: 818 3d St Eureka CA 95501

VAN GRIT, WILLIAM, language educator; b. Meppel, Drente, The Netherlands, Dec. 23, 1937; came to U.S., 1957; s. Jan and Hillegonda Jettina (Zijlstra) Grit; m. Sara del Pilar Mercado, Dec. 26, 1965; 1 child, William Philip. BA in French and German, Atlantic Union Coll., 1960; MA in French, U. Conn., 1963, PhD in French and Italian, 1969; postgrad., Pushkin Inst., Moscow, 1993. Asst. prof. Atlantic Union Coll., South Lancaster, Mass., 1964-70; assoc. prof. Pacific Union Coll., Angwin, Calif., 1970-73; prof. modern langs. Seminar Marienhoehe, Darmstadt, Fed. Republic of Germany, 1973-81; freelance translator. French Embassy of U.S. scholar Ecole Supérieure de Commerce, Lyon, France, 1984, Centre Internat. d'Etude de Langues, Strasbourg, 1991. Mem. Modern Lang. Assn. Am. Republican. Adventist. Office: Pacific Union Coll Dept of Modern Langs Angwin CA 94508

VAN HASSEL, HENRY JOHN, dentist, educator, university dean; b. Paterson, N.J., May 2, 1933; s. William Cornelius and Ina (Sturr) Van H.; m. Ann Newell Wiley, Dec. 28, 1960. BA, Maryville Coll., Tenn., 1954; DDS, U. Md., 1963; MSD, U. Wash., 1967, PhD, 1969. Diplomate Am.Bd. Endodontics. Dental dir. USPHS, Seattle, 1965-81; prof., chmn. dept. endodontics U. Md., Balt., 1981-84; dean dental sch. Oreg. Health Scis. U., Portland, 1984—, v.p. instl. affairs, 1989-91. Recipient Schlack award Assn. Mil. Surgeons U.S., 1976, Borrish award Acad. Gen. Dentistry, 1989. Mem. Am. Assn. Endodontists (pres. 1981-82, Grossman Gold medal 1984), Oreg. Dental Assn. (pres. 1990). Office: Oreg Health Scis U Dental Sch 611 SW Campus Dr Portland OR 97201-3097

VAN HECKE, GERALD RAYMOND, chemist, educator; b. Evanston, Ill., Nov. 1, 1939; s. Joseph Michael and Sylvia Alina (Brygarri) Van H. BS, Harvey Mudd Coll., Claremont, Calif., 1961; MA, Princeton U., 1963, PhD, 1966. Chemist Shell Devel. Co., Emeryville, Calif., 1966-70; prof. chemistry Harvey Mudd Coll., 1970—; bd. govs. Harvey Mudd Coll., pres., 1986-89, 68, v.p., 1967, sec., 1972. Contbr. articles to Jour. Chem. Edn., Liquid Crystals in a Jour., Jour. Phys. Chemistry, Liquid Crystals and Ordered Fluids, Inorganic Chemistry, Jour. Am. Chem. Soc., and others. ARCS scholar Harvey Mudd Coll.; LeRoy Wiley McKay fellow Princeton U., NSF fellow, NASA Sci. Faculty fellow. Fellow Am. Inst. Chemists; mem. AAAS, Am. Chem. Soc. (chair San Gorgonio chpt. 1987-88), Royal Chem. Soc., N.Y. Acad. Scis., N.Am. Soc. for Thermal Analysis, Sigma Xi. Office: Harvey Mudd Coll 301 E 12th St Claremont CA 91711-5992

VANHILST, LUCAS, retired business analyst; b. Amsterdam, The Netherlands, Aug. 6, 1920; came to U.S., 1954, naturalized, 1959; s. Lucas Johannes Arnoldus and Dina (Overtoom) vanH.; m. Ruth Bauersfeld, July 9, 1947 (div. May 1981); children: Anke, Michael; m. Tina M. VanPiggelen, Aug., 1985. BS in Mechanical Engring., Coll. of Amsterdam, 1950; MBA, U. Minn., 1961. Inventory analyst Honeywell, Mpls., 1954-60; programming analyst Univac, St. Paul, 1960-61; mgr. prodn. control electronics div. Gen. Mills, Mpls., 1962; programming cons. Super Valu Stores, Mpls., 1963-65; prin. cons., analyst Control Data Corp., Mpls., 1966-85; ret., 1985; lectr. on bus. practices German Assn. for Bus. Sci., Stuttgart, 1953, Am. Mgmt. Assn., N.Y.C., 1968-72, U. Wis., Madison, 1968, U. Klagenfurt, Austria, 1987-88, Austrian Mgmt. Acad., Vienna, 1988. Chmn. Restructure Sch. Dist. Legis. and Referendum Campaign, Mpls., 1959-60; bd. dirs. Citizens League Mpls.-St. Paul Met. Area, 1960-61; pres. Minn. Coun. for Gifted, 1963-64; bd. dirs. Verde Valley Concert Assn., 1989—; mem.. profl. adv. coun. Marcus J. Lawrence Med. Ctr. Hospice, 1989—; v.p. pub. rels. Marcus J. Lawrence Med. Ctr. Found., 1990-92, treas., 1992-93. Recipient (with wife) Health award Verde Valley C. of C., 1992. Mem. Soc. of Friends. Home: 1646 Destry Ln Cottonwood AZ 86326

VAN HOOMISSEN, GEORGE ALBERT, judge; b. Portland, Oreg., Mar. 7, 1930; s. Fred J. and Helen F. (Flanagan) Van H.; m. Ruth Madeleine Niedermeyer, June 4, 1960; children: Geroge T., Ruth Anne, Madeleine, Matthew. BBA, U. Portland, 1951; JD, Georgetown U., 1955, LLM in Labor Law, 1957; LLM in Jud. Adminstrn., U. Va., 1986. Bar: D.C. 1955, Oreg. 1956, Tex. 1971, U.S. Dist. Ct. Oreg. 1956, U.S. Ct. Mil. Appeals 1955, U.S. Ct. Customs and Patent Appeals 1955, U.S. Ct. Claims 1955, U.S. Ct. Appeals (9th cir.) 1956, U.S. Ct. Appeals (D.C. cir.) 1955, U.S. Supreme Ct. 1960. Law clk. for Chief Justice Harold J. Warner Oreg. Supreme Ct., 1955-56; Keigwin teaching fellow Georgetown Law Sch., 1956-57; dep. dist. atty. Multnomah County, Portland, 1957-59; pvt. practice Portland, 1959-62; dist. atty. Multnomah County, 1962-71; dean nat. coll. dist. attys. U. Houston, 1971-73; judge Cir. Ct., Portland, 1973-81, Oreg. Ct. Appeals, Salem, 1981-88; assoc. justice Oreg. Supreme Ct., Salem, 1988—. Mem. Oreg. Ho. of Reps., Salem, 1959-62, chmn. house judiciary com. Col. USMCR. Recipient Disting. Alumnus award U. Portland, 1972. Mem. ABA, Oreg. State Bar, Tex. Bar Assn., Multnomah Athletic Club, Univ Club. Roman Catholic. Office: Oreg Supreme Ct Supreme Ct Bldg 1163 State St Salem OR 97310

VAN HORN, PHYLLIS MARCIA, American language and culture educator, intercultural communications consultant; b. Balt., Mar. 19, 1943; d. Irving Henry and Estelle (Hochman) Finkler; m. John MacArthur Van Horn, June 7, 1967; children: Brian David, Maureen Tamara. BA in English & Secondary Edn., Austin Coll., 1965; MS in Secondary Edn./Applied Linguistics, U. Idaho, 1972. Tchr. ESL United Ch. Bd. for World Ministries, Izmir & Tarsus, Turkey, 1965-68; instr. ESL U. Idaho, Moscow, 1972-82, internat. student advisor, 1972-80; fgn. expert ESL Nanjing Forestry U., China, 1982, 86-87; pvt. tutor ESL English Lang. Program, Moscow, 1982—. Contbr. articles to NAFSA Newsletter, 1987—. Vol. Internat. Friendship Assn., 1991—. Mem. NAFSA: Assn. Internat. Educators (NAFSAn of Yr. 1991), Wash. Assn. Educators Speakers of Other Langs., B.C. Tchrs. English as Additional Lang., Palouse Asian Am. Assn. (sec. 1983-84). Home: 1185 Foothill Rd Moscow ID 83843

VAN HORSSEN, ARDEN DARRELL, retired manufacturing executive; b. Cottonwood County, Minn., June 14, 1917; s. Charles and Mabel Rosina (Schaffer) Van H.; m. Margaret Eleanor Ellingsen, Nov. 29, 1941; children: Charles A., Ronald D. Student, U. Minn., 1935-38, DePauw U., 1938-40, Lawson Sch. Engring., Chgo., 1941. Trainer Nunn Mfg., Evanston, Ill., 1941-42; dept. supr. Mpls. Moline Mfg., Mpls., 1942-44; plant mgr. Indsl. Tool & Die, Mpls., 1944-47; part owner Tonka Toys, Minnetonka, Minn., 1947-49; plant supt. Woodmark Industries, St. Louis Park, Minn., 1949-51; owner Nu-Line Industries, Mpls., 1951-65; pres. Cinch Nu-Line divsn. Unitec Carr, Mpls., 1965-67; cons. mgmt. and engring., 1968-73. Patentee in field. Home: 13110 Serenade Cir Sun City West AZ 85375

VAN HORSSEN, CHARLES ARDEN, manufacturing executive; b. Mpls., June 28, 1944; s. Arden Darrel and Margaret E. (Ellingsen) V H.; m. Mary Katherine Van Kempen, Sept. 11, 1967 (div. 1975); children: Lisa, Jackie; m. Mary Ann Pashuta, Aug. 11, 1983; children: Vanessa, Garrett. BSEE, U. Minn., 1966. Design engr. Sperry Univac, Mpls., 1966-68; sr. project engr. Sperry Univac, Salt Lake City, 1975-80; systems engr. EMR Computer, Mpls., 1968-75; pres. A&B Industries Inc., Phoenix, 1980—. Patentee in field. Mem. Ariz. Tooling and Machining Assn. (bd. dirs., v.p. 1987-89, pres. 1989-91). Republican. Episcopalian. Office: A&B Industries Inc 9233 N 12th Ave Phoenix AZ 85021-3094

VAN HOUTEN, ROBERT JAN, food service executive; b. Limburg, Netherlands, Sept. 2, 1953; s. Cornelius Willem and Juliana Maria (Runtuwene) van H.; m. Cynthia Ardell Michener, Aug. 12, 1978; children: Courtney Erin, Lauren Kristen, Gwendolyn Martine. Grad., Calif. Culinary Acad., San Francisco, 1981. Registered chef, Calif. Night sous chef Bistrot Les Halles, San Francisco, 1980-81; sous chef La Tour, Restaurante francaise, Palo Alto, Calif., 1981; grill chef Hayes St. Grill, San Francisco, 1981-82; chef, gen. mgr. La Boulangerie, Mammoth Lakes, Calif., 1982-83; chef Saga Food Corp., Newport Beach, Calif., 1983-84; chef de garde manger, sous chef DDL Foodshow, Beverly Hills, Calif., 1984-85; exec. chef Hamlet Gardens, Westwood, Calif., 1985—; caterer pvt. parties, Calif., 1985—; food stylist film and food Marilyn Lewis Prodns. Evian, L.A. Style mag., 1987-88. Mem. Great Chefs Am., Am. Inst. Food and Wine.

VANICEK, MILAN FRANK, mechanical engineer; b. Prague, Czechoslovakia, Jan. 8, 1944; came to U.S., 1989; s. Frank and Ester (Gillern) V.; m. Bobina Klimes, July 3, 1978 (div. 1992); children: Milan, Martin. Degree in engring., U. Tech., Pilsen, Czechoslovakia, 1967; postgrad., U. Tech., Prague, 1983-86. Mgr. design, tech. rep. Skoda Inc., Pilsen, 1960-61, Sokolovské Strojírny K.P., Cheb, Czechoslovakia, 1967-87; mech. engr. B & K Engring., Mountain View, Calif., 1989-91, Spectra Physics Lasers, Oroville, Calif., 1991—. Home: 1661 Forest Ave Chico CA 95928 Office: Spectra Physics Lasers 2001 Challenger Ave Oroville CA 95965

VAN KIRK, JOHN ELLSWORTH, cardiologist; b. Dayton, Ohio, Jan. 13, 1942; s. Herman Corwin and Dorothy Louise (Shafer) Van K.; m. Patricia L. Davis, June 19, 1966 (div. Dec. 1982); 1 child, Linnea Gray. BA cum laude, DePauw U., Greencastle, Ind., 1963; BS, Northwestern U., Chgo., 1964, MD with distinction, 1967. Diplomate Am. Bd. Internal Medicine, Am. Bd. Internal Medicine subspecialty in cardiovascular disease; cert. Nat. Bd. Med. Examiners. Intern Evanston (Ill.) Hosp., 1967-68; staff assoc. Nat. Inst. of Allergy & Infectious Diseases., Bethesda, Md., 1968-70; resident internal medicine U. Mich. Med. Ctr., Ann Arbor, 1970-72, fellow in cardiology, 1972-74, instr. internal medicine, 1973-74; staff cardiologist Mills Meml. Hosp., San Mateo, Calif., 1974—, vice-chief medicine, 1977-78, dir. critical care, 1978—, critical care utilizaton rev., 1988—, dir. pacemaker clinic, 1976—; mem. active staff Peninsular Hosp. and Med. Ctr.; mem. courtesy staff Sequoia Hosp. Contbr. rsch. articles to profl. jours. Recipient 1st prize in landscaping Residential Estates, State of Calif., 1977, Physician's Recognition award AMA, 1968, 72, 75, 77, 80, 82, 85, 87, 89. Fellow Am. Coll. Cardiology; mem. AMA, Calif. Med. Assn., San Mateo County Med.

Soc., Am. Heart Assn., San Mateo County Heart Assn. (bd. dirs. 1975-78, bay area rsch. com. 1975-76, edn. com. 1975-77, pres. elect 1976-77, pres. 1977-79), Alpha Omega Alpha. Republican. United Brethren. Office: San Mateo Med Assocs 50 S San Mateo Dr # 270 San Mateo CA 94401

VAN KLEEK, PETER ERIC, college dean; b. St. Petersburg, Fla., Mar. 15, 1929; s. John R. and Joan (Hill) Van K.; m. Barbara Jane King, June 4, 1954; children: Laura, Jennifer, Erika. BS, Cornell U., 1955; LHD (hon.), Schiller Internat. U., 1984. Founding dean Sch. Hotel Mgmt. U. Ariz. U., Flagstaff, prof. emeritus; ednl. cons. Govt. of St. Maarten, 1983-84, Schiller Internat. U., London, 1983-84; bd. dirs. Rainbow Tech. Group, Phoenix; cons. Cayuga Hospitality Advisors, Duluth, Ga., 1990. Author: Anthology/ Vegetable Cooking, 1966, Cooking With Pride, 1975, Beverage and Bartending, 1981; co-author: Menu Planning, 1974; assoc. editor mag. Cooking For Profit, 1983-85. Sgt. U.S. Army, 1950-52, Korea. Mem. Am. Hotel and Motel Assn. (cert. hotel adminstr., Outstanding Educator of Yr. 1988, Ambassador, trustee Ednl. Inst.), Internat. Hotel Assn. Office: 7397 E Wandering Rd Tucson AZ 85715

VAN KOTEN, ROBERT JAMES, chiropractor; b. Urbana, Ill., Oct. 9, 1951; s. Robert James and Louise Phyllis (Fisher) van K.; m. Flora Margaret Hellrung, Jan. 31, 1972; children: Allison Zoe, Justin Hugh. D of Chiropractic, Logan Coll., 1976; BS, U. State N.Y., 1988. Diplomate Nat. Bd. Chiropractic Examiners. Pvt. practice Northbrook, Ill., 1976-83, L.A., 1983-86, Alton, Ill., 1986-90, Palm Desert, Calif., 1990—; chiropractic researcher Stressology Internat., Long Beach, Calif., 1983—; cons. CSE Inc., Long Beach, 1986—. Author (books) Manual of Practice Standards, 1991, Statistical Analysis of Intact Spine-meningeal Unit Integral Systems, (jour.) Chiropractic's Paradigm Shift, 1991. Mem. Internat. Coll. of Chiropractic Stressology (bd. dirs.). Home: 75-100 La Sierra Dr Palm Desert CA 92260

VAN KULA, GEORGE, III, lawyer; b. Bainbridge, Md., Aug. 28, 1963; s. George Van Kula and Marion Michele (Gallaudet) Willison; m. Catherine Cimpl. BA, U. Notre Dame, 1985; JD, U. Mich., 1988. Bar: Calif. 1988. Assoc. Latham & Watkins, L.A., London, 1988—. Mem. ABA, Calif. Bar Assn., L.A. County Bar Assn. Office: Latham & Watkins, One Angel Ct, London EC2R 7HJ, England

VAN LEER, BETTY LEE, newspaper publisher; b. Louisville, June 28, 1930; d. Earl and Marene (Marriott) Templeman; m. Robert Roy Van Leer, Feb. 16, 1952; children: Sherry Christina, Amy Melinda, Molly Rebecca, Sally Amanda. AA, Stephens Coll., 1950; B in Journalism, U. Mo., 1952. Country corr., then sch. corr. Elizabethtown (Ky.) News, 1942-44, 45-48; reporter, campus editor Stephens Life, Columbia, Mo., 1949-50; country editor Sterling (Ill.) Gazette, 1952-55; pub. Curry County Reporter, Gold Beach, Oreg., 1956—. Bd. dirs. Curry Pub. Libr., Inc., Gold Beach, 1960-85. Mem. DAR, Gold Beach C. of C., Oreg. State Button Soc., Nat. Button Soc., DuBois Family Assn., Huguenot Hist. Soc., Soc. Maureen Duvall Descendents, Delta Kappa Gamma. Democrat. Office: Curry County Reporter 510 N Ellensburg Ave PO Box 766 Gold Beach OR 97444

VANLEEUWEN, LIZ SUSAN (ELIZABETH VANLEEUWEN), farmer, state legislator; b. Lakeview, Oreg., Nov. 5, 1925; d. Charles Arthur and Mary Delphia (Hartzog) Nelson; B.S., Oreg. State U., 1947; m. George VanLeeuwen, June 15, 1947; children—Charles, Mary, James, Timothy. Secondary sch. and adult tchr., 1947-70; news reporter, feature writer The Times, Brownsville, Oreg., 1949—; co-mgr. VanLeeuwen Farm, Halsey, Oreg.; mem. Oreg. Ho. of Reps., 1981—, Western States Forestry Legis. Task Force, Pacific Northwest Econ. Region; weekly radio commentator, 1973-81. Mem. E.R. Jackman Found., PTA, sch. adv. com.; precinct committeewoman; founder Linn County Ct.-Apptd. Spl. Advs. Recipient Outstanding Service award Oreg. Farm Bur., 1975, Oreg. Farm Family of Yr. award, 1983; Chevron Agrl. Spokesman of Yr. award, 1975. Mem. Oreg. Women for Agr. (pres.), Oreg. Women for Timber, Linn-Benton Women for Agr. (pres.), Linn County Farm Bur., Am. Legion (aux.), Linn County Econ. Devel. Com., Grange, Am. Agri-Women. Republican. Office: H386 Capitol Bldg Salem OR 97310

VAN LINT, VICTOR ANTON JACOBUS, physicist; b. Samarinda, Indonesia, May 10, 1928; came to U.S., 1937; s. Victor J. and Margaret (DeJager) Van L.; m. M. June Woolhouse, June 10, 1950; children: Lawrence, Kenneth, Linda, Karen. BS, Calif. Inst. Tech., Pasadena, 1950, PhD, 1954. Instr. Princeton (N.J.) U., 1954-55; staff mem. Gen. Atomic, San Diego, 1957-74; physics cons. San Diego, 1974-75; staff mem. Mission Research Corp., San Diego, 1975-82, 83-91; cons., 1991—; spl. asst. to dep. dir. sci. and tech. Def. Nuclear Agy., Washington, 1982-83. Author, editor: Radiation Effects in Electronic Materials, 1976; contbr. articles to profl. jours. Served with U.S. Army, 1955-57. Recipient Pub. Service award NASA, 1981. Fellow IEEE. Republican. Mem. United Ch. of Christ. Home and Office: 1032 Skylark Dr La Jolla CA 92037

VAN LOM, JOSEPH MILTON, architect firm executive; b. Portland, Oreg., Mar. 23, 1938; s. Francis J. Van Lom and Adel Heide (Nussbaumer) Knusel; m. Linda E. Chevez, Feb. 13, 1971 (div. mar. 1984); children: Todd William, Jeff Alan Van Lom; m. Cynthia Silfversten, Sept. 9, 1989; 1 child, Hannah Silfversten. BArch, U. Oreg., 1965. Registered professional architect Oreg., Wash., Calif., Wyo., Colo., N.Mex., Nev. Assoc. architect Travers/Johnston Architects, Portland, Oreg., 1968-71; owner, architect Van Lom & Assocs., Portland, 1971-73; ptnr., architect Van Lom-Kraxberger Partnership, Portland, 1973-83; prin. Architects Van Lom, Portland and San Diego, 1983-87; pres. Architects Van Lom/Edwards, Portland, 1987—; pub. speaker in field, 1991—; naval intelligence/photo intelligence tng. schs. instr. Chmn. Architects Polit. Action Com., Oreg., 1991; del. Washington County Block Grant Com., Oreg., 1975. With USN, 1955-59. Mem. AIA (del. bd., speakers bur. chmn. 1992), Chanticleers Toastmasters (pres. 1985-87, 92), Oreg. Coun. of Architects (del. 1991, 92). Office: Architects Van Lom/ Edwards 34 NW 1st Ave Ste 309 Portland OR 97209

VAN LOUCKS, MARK LOUIS, venture capitalist, business advisor; b. Tampa, Fla., June 19, 1944; s. Charles Perry and Lenn (Bragg) Van L.; m. Eva Marianne Forsell, June 10, 1968; children: Brandon, Charlie. BA in Communs. and Pub. Policy, U. Calif., Berkeley, 1967. Sr. v.p. mktg., programming and corp. devel. United Cable TV Corp., Denver, Colo., 1970-81, advisor, 1983-89; sr. v.p., office of chmn. Rockefeller Ctr. TV Corp., N.Y.C., 1981-83; advisor United Artists Commun. Corp., Englewood, 1989-91; investor, business advisor in pvt. practice Englewood, 1983—; founder, prin. owner Glory Hole Saloon & Gaming Hall, Central City, Colo., 1990—; bd. dirs. Wild West Devel. Corp., Denver; sr. v.p., bd. dirs. GSI Cable TV Assocs., Inc., San Francisco, 1984-90; guest lectr. on cable TV bus., 1985-91; cons. Telecommunications, Inc., Denver, 1989-93. Producer HBO spl. Green Chili Showdown, 1985; producer TV spl. 3 Days for Earth, 1987; contbr. articles to profl. jours. Chmn. Cops In Crisis, Denver, 1990—; bd. dirs. The NOAH Found., Denver, 1976—; founding dir. Project for Responsible Advt., Denver, 1991-92. Named hon. capt. Denver Police Dept., 1991. Mem. Casino Owners Assn. (founding dir. 1989—), Colo. Gaming Assn. (dir. 1990—), Glenmoor Country Club, The Village Club. Republican. Jewish. Office: MLVL Inc 333 W Hampden Ave # 1005 Englewood CO 80110

VAN MAERSSEN, OTTO L., aerospace engineer, consulting firm executive; b. Amsterdam, The Netherlands, Mar. 2, 1919; came to U.S., 1946; s. Adolph L. and Maria Wilhelmina (Edelmann) Van M.; m. Hortensia Maria Velasquez, Jan. 7, 1956; children: Maria, Patricia, Veronica, Otto, Robert. BS in Chem. Engring., U. Mo., Rolla, 1949. Registered profl. engr., Tex., Mo. Petroleum engr. Mobil Oil, Caracas, Venezuela, 1949-51; sr. reservoir engr. Gulf Oil, Ft. Worth and San Tome, Venezuela, 1952-59; acting dept. mgr. Sedco of Argentina, Comodoro Rivadavia, 1960-61; export planning engr. LTV Aerospace and Def., Dallas, 1962-69, R & D adminstr. ground transp. div., 1970-74, engr. specialist new bus. programs, 1975-80; mgr. cost and estimating LTV Aerospace and Def., San Franciso and Alaska, 1981-84; owner OLVM Cons. Engrs., Walnut Creek, Calif., 1984—; cons. LTV Aerospace and Def., Dallas, 1984—. Served with Brit. Army. Intelligence, 1945, Germany. Mem. SPE (sr.). Democrat. Roman Catholic. Clubs: Toastmasters (Dallas), (sec./treas. 1963-64), Pennywise (Dallas) (treas. 1964-67). Home and Office: OLVM Cons Engrs 1649 Arbutus Dr Walnut Creek CA 94595-1705

VAN MOLS, BRIAN, publishing executive; b. L.A., July 1, 1931; s. Pierre Matthias and Frieda Caryll (MacArthur) M.; m. Barbara Jane Rose, Oct. 1, 1953 (dec. 1968); children—Cynthia Lee, Matthew Howard, Brian; m. Nancy Joan Martell, June 11, 1977; children—Thomas Bentley, Cynthia Bentley, Kristi. A.B. in English, Miami U., Oxford, Ohio, 1953. Media supr. McCann-Erickson Inc., 1955-58; salesman Kelly Smith Co., 1959; with sales Million Market Newspaper Inc., 1959-63; sales mgr. Autoproducts Mag., 1964; sr. salesman True Mag., 1965-68, Look Mag., 1969-70; regional advt. dir. Petersen Pub. Co., Los Angeles, 1971-74; pub. Motor Trend, 1982-84; nat. automotive mktg. mgr. Playboy Enterprises, Inc., N.Y.C., 1984-85, nat. sales mgr., 1985—; western advt. dir. Playboy mag., 1985-86; assoc. pub., advt. dir. Cycle World CBS, Inc., Newport Beach, Calif., 1974-81, pub., 1981; v.p., advt. dir. Four Wheeler Mag., Canoga Pk., Calif., 1986-88; v.p., dir. advt. western div. Gen. Media, Inc., 1988-91; v.p., dir. new bus. devel. Paisano Pub., Inc., Agoura Hills, Calif., 1991-92; dir. mktg. Crown Publs., 1993—. Served with U.S. Army, 1953-55. Mem. Los Angeles Advt. Club, Adcraft Club Detroit, Advt. Sportsmen of N.Y. Republican. Episcopalian. Home: 3668 Twin Lake Rdg Westlake Village CA 91361 Office: Crown Publs 28720 Canwood Agoura Hills CA 91301

VAN NATTA, CAROL ANN, technical writer; b. Tacoma, Wash., May 8, 1956; d. Thomas Fraley and Ann (Harbour) Van N. BA/English Writing, Performance Acting, St. Edward's U., 1984; MA in Theatre History, Calif. State U., Fullerton, 1987. Asst. staff supr. Mountain Bell, Denver, 1979-84; tech. editor/writer Law/Crandall, Inc., L.A., 1990—. Mem. Soc. for Tech. Communication, Soc. for Creative Anachronism.

VAN NATTA, LESLII ANNE, writer, set and costume designer; b. Chgo., Jan. 21, 1950; d. Julian Forrest and Stephanie Lucretia (Robinson) Zimmerman. BA, Calif. State U., Northridge, 1973; MBA, U. So. Calif., 1986. Bus. based in L.A. L.A., 1968-89; prodr. and writer, L.A., 1979-86. Photographer Living History, 1985 (Excellence award); writer Halley's Return, 1986; set and costume designer Nutcracker on Tap, 1988; editor, writer La Pina, 1989-90. Organizer, media spokesperson Vet.'s Peace Convoy, 1988, Women's Network, Austin, Tex., 1989-90. Recipient Excellence award Living History Centre. Mem. Internat. Assn. Theatrical & Stage Employees. Home: 35970 Niles Blvd Fremont CA 94536

VANNESS, CALVIN HANN, architect; b. Oxford, Ohio, June 19, 1926; s. LeRoy and Susan Christine (Hann) V. BArch, Miami U., Oxford, Ohio, 1950; postgrad., Creative Guidelines, Phoenix, 1975. Registered architect, Ariz. Apprentice builder Le Roy Vanness, Contractor, Oxford, 1926-50; archtl. draftsman Wright Patterson AFB, Dayton, Ohio, 1951, Zeller & Hunter, Architects, Springfield, Ohio, 1952, Max Mercer, Architect, Yellow Springs, Ohio, 1953, Robert Johnson, Architect, Phoenix, 1954, Herb Green, Architect, Phoenix, 1955, Charles Polacek, Architect, Phoenix, 1956; architect, owner Calvin H. Vanness, Architect, Phoenix, 1957—; minister, counselor House of th Dawn Ch., Phoenix, 1971—; founder, dir. House of the Dawn Ch., Phoenix, 1971—; counselor self hypnosis, Phoenix; tchr. Kriya Yoga, Phoenix. Author: Rainbows and Rhapsodies, 1988. Deacon Met. Community Ch., Phoenix, 1967-73; mem. S.W. dist. bldgs. and locations com. Meth. Ch., Ariz., Calif., Nev., 1965. With U.S. Army, 1946-48, ETO. Recipient Bldg. award of distinction City of Tempe (Ariz.), 1977. Mem. Constrn. Specifications Inst., AIA, New Age Alliance Chs., Order of Omega, Creative Guidelines, Phys. Fitness Club, Ande's Club, Sun Bear Medicine Circle, Reevis Mountain Native Am. Gathering. Republican. Office: 122 West Way PO Box 637 Yarnell AZ 85362

VANNIX, C(ECIL) ROBERT, programmer, systems analyst; b. Glendale, Calif., June 14, 1953; s. Cecil H. Jr. and Gloria Jenny (Zappia) V.; married, 1980; 1 child, Robert Jeremy. AS in Plant Mgmt., BS in Indsl. Arts, Loma Linda U., 1977; AS in Info. Systems, Ventura City Coll., 1985. Instr. indsl. arts Duarte (Calif.) High Sch., 1977-79, Oxnard (Calif.) High Sch., 1979-81; computer cons. Litton Data Comand Systems, Agoura, Calif., 1976-81, sr. engr. instr., 1981-85; computer cons. McLaughlin Research Corp., Camarillo, Calif., 1976-77, sr. program analyst, 1985-88; sr. program analyst Computer Software Analysts, Camarillo, Calif., 1988-90; sr. systems analyst, mgr. S/W systems devel. Metters Industries, 1990—. Recipient Spl. Achievement award One Way Singers, Glendale, 1975. Republican. Adventist. Clubs: Apple PI Computer, Litton Computer (pres. 1975-76). Home: 407 Appletree Ave Camarillo CA 93012-5125 Office: 1001 Flynn Rd Camarillo CA 93012-5125

VAN NORDSTRAND, ROBERT ALEXANDER, retired research chemist; b. Schenectady, N.Y., Feb. 17, 1917; s. Robert Daniel and Amelia Gertrude (Pierson) Van N.; m. Wanda Zentera, Feb. 22, 1941 (dec. Dec. 1989); children: Carol Worden, Nancy Cantu, Peggy. Student, Union Coll., 1934-35; BS in Chemistry, U. Mich., 1938, MS in Chemistry, 1940. Rsch. chemist Sherwin-Williams Co., Chgo., 1940-42; rsch. chemist Sinclair Oil Co., Harvey, Ill., 1942-61, Tulsa, 1961-69; chemistry prof. U. Tulsa, Okla., 1969-72; rsch. chemist Filtrol Corp., L.A., 1972-77, Chevron Rsch. Co., Richmond, Calif., 1977-92. Contbr. articles to profl. jours. Mem. Am. Chem. Soc., Royal Soc. Chemistry (life), The Catalysis Soc., British Zeolite Assn. (life). Home: 520 Monticello Rd San Rafael CA 94903-3223

VAN NOY, TERRY WILLARD, insurance company executive; b. Alhambra, Calif., Aug. 31, 1947; s. Barney Willard and Cora Ellen (Simms) V.; m. Betsy Helen Pothen, Dec. 27, 1968; children: Bryan, Mark. BS in Bus. Mgmt., Calif. State Poly. U., 1970; MBA, Pepperdine U., 1991. CLU. Group sales rep. Mutual of Omaha, Atlanta, 1970-74, dist. mgr., 1974-77; regional mgr. Mutual of Omaha, Dallas, 1977-82; nat. sales mgr. Mutual of Omaha, Omaha, Neb., 1982-83; v.p. group mktg. Mutual of Omaha, Omaha, 1983-87; div. dir. Mutual of Omaha, Orange, Calif., 1987—. Presenter: Health Ins. Assn. of Am., Chgo, 1984, Life Insur Mktg. & Rsch. Assn., San Francisco, 1987. Vice chmn. Morning Star Luth. Ch., Omaha, 1987; mem. adv. bd. Chapman U. Sch. Bus. Mem. Am. Soc. CLUS, Orange County Employee Benefit Coun. Republican. Home: 381 S Smokeridge Ter Anaheim CA 92807-3711 Office: Mut of Omaha PO Box 11018 Orange CA 92668-8118

VAN ORDEN, HARRIS OLSON, retired chemistry educator, researcher; b. Smithfield, Utah, Oct. 6, 1917; s. Harris Olonzo Van Orden and Ingra (Pearson) Olson; m. Eleanor Young, Oct. 16, 1948; 1 child, Peter Lee. BS, Utah State U., 1938; MS, Wash. State U., 1942; PhD, MIT, 1951; postgrad., U. Utah, 1953-54, U. Calif., Berkeley, 1962-63. Asst. prof. chemistry Utah State U., Logan, 1946-47, assoc. prof., 1950-59, acting dept. head, 1958-59, prof., 1959-83, emeritus prof., 1983—; dir. Summer Inst. for High Sch. Tchrs. Chemistry, Logan, 1957, 58. Co-author textbooks on gen. chemistry, 1960-73; also articles. Maj. AUS, 1942-46, PTO. Univ. fellow MIT, 1947-49, fellow NIH U. Utah, 1953. Fellow AAAS, Am. Chem. Soc., Sigma Xi, Phi Lambda Upsilon. Republican. Mem. LDS Ch. Home: 281 E 8th N Logan UT 84321-3329

VAN ORDEN, LUCAS SCHUYLER, III, psychiatrist; b. Chgo., Nov. 3, 1928; s. Lucas Schuyler II and Florence (Peterson) Van O.; m. Aug. 22, 1953 (dec. Aug. 5, 1989); children: William Eddy, Christine Lee, Katherine Rouseau, Lucas Schuyler IV; m. Shirley Ann Mason, Dec. 30, 1989. BS in Chemistry, Northwestern U., 1950, MS in Biochemistry, 1952, MD, 1956; PhD in Pharmacology, Yale U., 1966. Diplomate Am. Bd. Psychiatry and Neurology. Prof. pharmacology U. Iowa, Iowa City, 1967-78, prof. pharmacology & psychiatry, 1976-78; dir. chem. dependency unit Mental Health Inst., Mount Pleasant, Iowa, 1978-79; med. dir. substance abuse unit Schoitz Med. Ctr., Waterloo, Iowa, 1980-83; resident in psychiatry Wash. U., St. Louis, 1984-86; med. dir. alcohol & drug unit Mental Health Inst., Independence, Iowa, 1987-89; med. dir. Careunit Hosp., Albuquerque, 1990; staff psychiatrist forensic unit New Mex. State Hosp., Las Vegas, 1991—; psychotherapist pvt. practice, Santa Fe, N.Mex., 1991—. Editor: Jour. Pharmacology & Experimental Therapeutics, 1975-78; contbr. articles to profl. jours. Capt. USNR, 1957-78. Grantee NIH, 1967-78. Mem. Am. Psychiat. Assn., Am. Soc. on Addiction Medicine. Anglican Catholic. Home: 327 Calle Loma N Santa Fe NM 87501

VAN OVERVEEN, JOSEPH PETER, mechanical engineer, consultant; b. Amsterdam, The Netherlands, Dec. 3, 1916; came to U.S., 1939, naturalized.; s. Hartog and Henrietta Berendina (Polak) Van O.; m. Irene Eva Loewenberg, Mar. 6, 1943; children: Joann, David. BSc in Mech. Engring., Higher Tech. Coll., Haarlem, The Netherlands, 1939; MSME in Ry. Mech. Engring., Purdue U., 1940; postgrad., U. Calif., Berkeley. Registered profl. engr., Calif. Jr. engr. Am. Locomotive Co., N.Y.C., 1940-41; sales engr. Estes Co., Inc., export machinery, N.Y.C., 1946-48; design engr. Paragon Gear Works, Taunton, Mass., 1948-49; mgr. design and devel. Shand & Jurs Co., Berkeley, Calif., 1949-60; mech. engr. Systron Donner Co., Concord, Calif., 1960-63; sr. equipment engr. BART project Parsons-Brinckerhoff-Tudor-Bechtel, San Francisco, 1964-66; sr. mech. engr. San Francisco Bay Area Rapid Transit, Oakland, Calif., 1966—; cons., rep. Kennedy & Donkin, Godalming, Eng., 1985—. Co-editor: Hundred Year Railway Mechanical Engineering, 1979; contbr. articles on fluid flow, wheel rail dynamics, shop installation and design rail transit to tech. publs. Bd. dirs. Lafayette (Calif.) Community Ctr., 1958-74, chmn. bd., 1960-74; mem. Lafayette City Recreation Commn., 1975-82. 1st lt. U.S. Army, 1941-46, PTO. Named Man of Yr., City of Lafayette, 1962. Fellow ASME (life, chmn. San Francisco sect. 1972-73, mem. nat. com. on profl. ethics and practice 1974-79, chmn. rail transp. com. 1987, exec. bd. region IX, Dedicated Svc. award 1986); mem. NSPE, Soc. Automotive Engrs. Home: 1057 Dolores Dr Lafayette CA 94549

VAN PELT, MEREDITH ALDEN, general and vascular surgeon; b. Lake Preston, S.D., June 22, 1923; s. Herman Earl and Pearl Glenn (Williams) Van P.; m. Margaret E. Springs, Nov. 9, 1947 (div. Feb. 1969); children: Gregory Alden, Sharman Louise Van Pelt Halloran, Susan Lee Van Pelt Lockett, Stephanie Lane Van Pelt Stemmark; m. Sheila Mae Kimball, July 19, 1969; 1 child, Stephen. BA, U. Iowa, 1943, MD, 1946; postgrad., U. Vienna, 1948. Diplomate Am. Bd. Surgery. Intern Good Samaritan Hosp., Cin., 1946-47; resdent in surgery Swedish Med. Ctr., Seattle, 1949-53; asst. chief surgery VA Hosp., Fresno, Calif., 1953-55; pvt. practice gen. and vascular surgery San Rafael, Calif., 1955-92; surgeon, cons. San Quentin State Prison, San Rafael, 1989—; chief of surgery San Rafael Gen. Hosp., 1962-65, Terra Linda Valley Hosp., San Rafael, 1962-68; chief of gen. surgery Ross (Calif.) Gen. Hosp., 1987-88, Marin Gen. Hosp., San Rafael, 1964-65; commr. Calif. State Bd. Med. Examiners 1992—; instr. vascular surg. clinic U. Calif., San Francisco, 1957-69; civilian cons. in surgery U.S. Air Force, Hamilton Field, Calif., 1960-65. Capt. M.C., U.S. Army, 1947-49. Fellow ACS, Am. Coll. Angiology, Internat. Coll. Angiology; mem. AMA, Calif. Med. Assn., Marin Med. Soc., San Francisco Yacht Club (life). Episcopalian. Home: 14 Eucalyptus Belvedere CA 94920

VAN REMMEN, ROGER, advertising executive; b. Los Angeles, Sept. 30, 1950; s. Thomas J. and Elizabeth (Vincent) V.; B.S. in Bus., U. So. Calif., 1972. Account mgr. BBDO, Los Angeles, 1972-78; account mgr. Dailey & Assocs. Advt., L.A., 1978—, v.p., mgmt. supr., 1980-84, sr. v.p., 1985-90; dir. Aux. Aids Inc., Richstone Family Ctr; dir. mktg. communications, Teradata, 1990-91, ptnr. Brown, Bernardy, Van Remmen Exec. Search, L.A., 1991—. Chmn. adv. bd. El Segundo (Calif.) First Nat. Bank; bd. dirs. Advt. Emergency Relief Fund. Mem. Univ. So. Calif. Alumni Assn., Advt. Club of Los Angeles. Roman Catholic. Home: 220 9th St Manhattan Beach CA 90266-4937 Office: Brown Bernardy Van Remmen 12100 Wilshire Blvd Ste 40M Los Angeles CA 90025-7120

VAN SEVENTER, A., accountant; b. Amsterdam, The Netherlands, Sept. 25, 1913; came to U.S., 1940; s. A. and Maria (van Dijk) van S.; m. Ruth E. Smith, Nov. 5, 1949; children: Antony, Ronald E. AB, U. Amsterdam, 1934; MBA, Stanford U., 1949; PhD, U. Mich., 1966. Acct. C.A. Gall and Co., N.Y.C., 1940-41, Credit Suisse, N.Y.C., 1941, Haskins and Sells, San Francisco, 1949, Philip A. Hershey, San Francisco, 1949, O.M. Beaver CPA, Anchorage, 1950, Beaver and van Seventer CPAs, Anchorage, 1950-62; pvt. practice acctg. Anchorage and Palo Alto, Calif., 1957-62; instr. acctg. Cleary (Mich.) Coll., 1963; instr., lectr. acctg. U. Mich., Ann Arbor, 1963-66; asst. and assoc. prof. acctg. San Jose (Calif.) State U., 1966-76; prof. acctg. San Francisco State U., 1976-84; pres. Bay Books Publishing, Palo Alto, Calif., 1976—; vis. lectr. taxation Ea. Mich. U., Ypsilanti, 1963; instr. acctg. Anchorage Community Coll., 1954-62. Author: The History of Accountancy - translation, 1976, 2nd edit., 1986, Intermediate Accounting Problems, 1973, 3rd edit. 1981; editor: Accounting Bibliography, 1986; contbr. articles to profl. jours., chpt. to book. Sec. Alaska Bd. Pub. Accountancy, 1953-57. With USAAF, 1942-45. Lybrand fellow, 1965; decorated French Medal of Honor in Bronze. Mem. AICPA, Am. Acctg. Assn., Acad. Acctg. Historians (Hourglass award 1977), Calif. Soc. CPAs, Peninsula Symphony, Phi Beta Kappa (pres. No. Calif. chpt. 1980-81), Rotary (Anchorage chpt.).

VAN SICKLE, FREDERICK L., federal judge; b. 1943; m. Jane Bloomquist. BS, U. Wis., 1965; JD, U. Wash., 1968. Ptnr. Clark & Van Sickle, 1970-75; prosecuting atty. Douglas County, Waterville, Wash., 1971-75; judge State of Wash. Superior Ct., Grant and Douglas counties, 1975-79, Chelan and Douglas Counties, 1979-91; judge U.S. Dist. Ct. (ea. dist.) Wash., Spokane, 1991—; co-chair rural ct. com. Nat Conf. State Trial Judges, 1987—. Bd. dirs. YMCA, 1984—. 1st lt. U.S. Army, 1968-70. Mem. ABA (nat. conf. state trial judges judicial adminstrn.), Am. Adjudicature Soc., Superior Ct. Judges Assn. (sec. 1980-82, bd. trustees 1987-90, criminal law and edn. coms.), Washington State Bar Assn., Eagles, Elks, Masons (pres. badger Mountain lodge 1972—), Scottish Rite, Waterville C. of C. (bd. dirs.), Centipiede Dance Club (bd. dirs.), Wenatchee Rotary (bd. dirs. 1988—). Office: US Dist Cts US Courthouse W 920 Riverside Ave Rm 921 Spokane WA 99210*

VAN STEKELENBURG, MARK, food service executive. Pres., CEO G.V.A., The Netherlands; exec. v.p., now CEO Rykoff-Sexton Inc., L.A. Office: Rykoff-Sexton Inc 761 Terminal St Los Angeles CA 90021-1112

VANSTRALEN, ERIC, title company executive; b. Montebello, Calif., Dec. 4, 1952; s. Albert Phillip and Evelyn Ruth (Murray) VanS.; m. Linda K. Hunt, June 30, 1972 (div. Feb. 1976); 1 child, Katrina Meagan; m. Diane Alene Laizure, May 18, 1980; children: Heather Annalisa, Rebecca Lynn, Candice Marie. Student, Long Beach City Coll., 1971, 75, Solano Community Coll., Fairfield, Calif., 1980-83, U. Calif., Davis, 1981-82. L.A. County mgr. Title-Tax, Inc., L.A., 1976-80; title searcher, examiner First Am. Title Co., Fairfield, 1980-82; mgr. title ops. Transam. Title Ins. Co., Walnut Creek, Calif., 1982-87, Stewart Title Calif., Santa Ana, 1987; mgr. Southbay area N.Am. Title Co., Torrance, Calif., 1987-90; title ops. mgr. World Title Co., Burbank, Calif., 1990-92; mgr. Alameda county World Title Co., Pleasanton, Calif., 1992—. Rescue sgt. Long Beach (Calif.) Search and Rescue Team, 1970; chief Tribe of Tahquitz coun. Boy Scouts Am., 1970-71, activities dir. Camp Tahquitz, Barton Flats, Calif., 1971, dir. mountain man program, Long Beach, 1975. With USN, 1972-75. Recipient appreciation award Exchange Club, Concord, Calif., 1986. Mem. Calif. Land Title Assn. (speakers' bur. 1986-87), Calif. Escrow Assn., Calif. Trustees Assn. Republican. Episcopalian. Office: World Title Co 7031 Koll Center Pkwy # 120 Pleasanton CA 94566

VAN TASSELL, JAY LEE, geology educator; b. Mt. Kisco, N.Y., Oct. 19, 1952; s. David Wayne and Ruth Charity (Van Steenburgh) Van T.; m. April Diane Krueger, June 29, 1991. BA, Bowdoin Coll., 1974; MS, U. Wis., 1975; PhD, Duke U., 1979. Vis. asst. prof. Guilford Coll., Greensboro, N.C., 1979-87; assoc. prof. Ea. Oreg. State Coll., LaGrande, 1988—. Contbr. numerous articles to profl. jours. Mem. Geol. Soc. of Am., Internat. Assn. of Sedimentologists, Soc. of Econ. Paleontologists and Mineralogists, Sigma Xi, Phi Beta Kappa. Office: Ea Oreg State Coll 1410 L La Grande OR 97850-2899

VAN VALKENBURG, HOLLI BEADELL, real estate company executive; b. Blue Island, Ill., Dec. 25, 1950; d. Robert Morton and Vivian (Doberstein) Beadell; m. Gerard William Van Valkenburg, May 26, 1984. BS, U. Nebr., 1973; cert. paralegal, Colo. Paralegal Inst., 1978. Child care counselor Father Flanagan's Boys Home, Boys Town, Nebr., 1974-77; service rep. Blue Cross & Blue Shield, Denver, 1977-78; escrow asst. Transamerica Title, Denver, 1978; paralegal Pendleton & Sabian, P.C., Denver, 1978-84, Isaacson, Rosenbaum, Woods & Levy, P.C., Denver, 1984-88; dir. adminstrn. Pan-Terra, Inc., Kirkland, Wash., 1988-92; dir. Rocky Mountain Legal Assistance Assn., Denver, 1979-82. Recipient Betty King Grainger scholarship for Excellence in Journalism, U. Nebr., 1970. Mem. Alpha Chi Omega (newsletter editor 1970-73), Univ. Club. Home: 12419 106th Pl NE Kirkland WA 98034-2861

VAN VEEN, DAVID JOSEPH, customer engineer; b. St. Ignatius, Mont., Apr. 5, 1956; s. Francis Leonard and Patricia (Konrad) van V.; m. Jessica Lynn Devlin, Aug. 29, 1992. Sr. customer engr. Northwest Computer Maintenance, Bellevue, Wash., 1981—. Office: Northwest Computer Maint 1331 118 SE Bellevue WA 98005

VAN VELZER, VERNA JEAN, retired research librarian; b. State College, Pa., Jan. 22, 1929; d. Harry Leland and Golda Lillian (Cline) Van V. BS in Library Sci., U. Ill., 1950; MLS, Syracuse U., 1957. Head librarian Orton Library, Ohio State U., Columbus, 1952-54; serials assoc. Syracuse (N.Y.) U. Library, 1954-57; head cataolger SRI Internat., Menlo Park, Calif., 1957-58; head librarian GE Microwave Lab., Palo Alto, Calif., 1958-64, Fairchild Rsch. and Devel. Lab., Palo Alto, 1964-65, Sylvania Intelligence Library, Mountain View, Calif., 1965-66; rsch. librarian ESL Inc. subs. TRW, Sunnyvale, Calif., 1966-92; cons. in field. Vol. Lantos Re-election Campaign, San Mateo, Calif., 1972—, Wildlife Rescue, Palo Alto, 1980—; mem. Barron Park Assn., Palo Alto, 1975—; mem. Calif. Polit. Action Com. for Animals, San Francisco, 1986—. Recipient Commemorative medal of Honor, Am. Biographical Inst., 1946, Paul Revere Cup, Santa Clara Camellia Soc., 1968, Internat. Cultural Diploma of Honor, Am. Biographical Inst., 1988. Mem. Spl. Librs. Assn., IEEE, AIAA, Calif. Holistic Vet. Assn., Internat. Primate Protection League, People for Ethical Treatment of Animals, Assn. Old Crows, In Def. of Animals, Primarily Primates, Sierra Club, World Wildlife Club, Greenpeace. Home: 4048 Laguna Way Palo Alto CA 94306-3122 Office: ESL Inc subs TRW 495 E Java Dr # 3510 Sunnyvale CA 94089-1150

VAN VLEET, HAROLD ALAN, insurance executive; b. Salt Lake City, Mar. 28, 1947; s. Harold and Vivian (Stone) Van V.; m. Jolene Taylor, Apr. 10, 1974; children: Keri, Jill, Andrew, Erin, Katy. BS in Acctg., U. Utah, 1972, MBA, 1973; M. Fin. Svcs., Am. Coll., Bryn Mawr, Pa., 1988. CLU, ChFC; cert. life underwriter tng. coun. fellow. With property mgmt. dept. Western Mortgage Loan Co., Ogden, Utah, 1973-74; field underwriter N.Y. Life-Salt Lake City Gen. Office, 1974-76, sales mgr., 1976-77; field underwriter N.Y. Life-Salt Lake City Gen. Office, Salt Lake City, 1978, tng. supr., 1978-82; tng. supr. N.Y. Life Provo (Utah) Gen. Office, 1983-84; tng. mgr. N.Y. Life Ogden (Utah) Gen. Office, 1984-86, N.Y. Life N.Mex. Gen. Office, Albuquerque, 1986—. Com. mem. N.Mex. Continuing Edn. Com., Albuquerque, 1991; com. chmn. pack and troop 210 Boy Scouts Am., Albuquerque. Mem. Salt Lake City Assn. Life Underwriters (LUTC chmn. 1980-81, moderator), No. Utah Chpt. of CLUs (bd. dirs., edn. chmn.), Ogden Chpt. Life Underwriters (bd. dirs.), Cen. Assn. Life Underwriters (moderator), N.Mex. Chpt. CLU/ChFC (bd. dirs.), N.Mex. Chpt. CLU/ChFC (v.p., pres. 1988-90). Mem. LDS Church. Office: NY Life NMex GO Ste 500 6565 Americas Pkwy NE Albuquerque NM 87110

VAN VOORHIES, WAYNE ALAN, biologist; b. Plainfield, N.J., Apr. 4, 1956; s. Robert Leon and Dolores E. (Schiffel) Van V.; m. Laurie Abbott, Nov. 1992. BA, Prescott Coll., 1978; MS, U. Ariz., 1988, PhD, 1993. Rsch. specialist U. Ill., Antarctica, 1978-81; instr. Outward Bound, Portland, Oreg., 1981-84; river guide Expeditions, Grand Canyon, Ariz., 1984; grad. teaching asst. U. Ariz., Tucson, 1985—; foreign fishers observer Nat. Marine Fisheries, Alaska, 1989. Contbr. article on sci. discovery to Nature mag. Recipient Teagle scholarship Exxon Found., 1986, grad. fellowship grant U. Ariz., 1991, NSF Tng. grant, 1992. Home: 1125 N Olsen Ave Tucson AZ 85719 Office: U Ariz Dept Ecology & Evol Biology Tucson AZ 85721

VAN WAGENEN, STERLING, film producer, director; b. Provo, Utah, July 2, 1947; s. Clifton Gray and Donna Anna (Johnson) Van W.; m. Marilee Jeppson; children: Sarah, Kristina, Arthur, William, Hugh, Andrew. BA, Brigham Young U., 1972. Exec. dir. U.S. Film Festival, Park City, Utah, 1978-80; exec. dir. Sundance Inst., Salt Lake City, 1980-84, v.p., 1984-86. Dir.: (plays) King Lear, 1974, Othello, 1984, Hamlet, 1972, The Flies, 1970, (film) Christmas Snows, Christmas Winds (2 regional Emmy awards), Alan and Naomi, 1990; producer: (films) Faith of an Observer, 1984, The Trip to Bountiful, 1986, Yosemite: The Fate of Heaven, 1988, The Witching of Ben Wagner, 1989, Convicts, 1989. Office: 2230 East 6014 South Salt Lake City UT 84121

VAN WEST, CARLA REBECCA, archaeologist, consultant; b. Boston, July 23, 1951; d. Joseph Barnes and Selma Natalie (Snider) Van W.; m. Roger Dale Irwin, May 25, 1980. BA in Anthropology cum laude, Elmira (N.Y.) Coll., 1973; MA in Anthropology, U. Ariz., 1976; PhD in Anthropology, Wash. State U., 1990. Cert. C.C. instr., Ariz. Asst. archaeologist Ariz. State Mus., U. Ariz., Tucson, 1973-76; archaeologist S.W. Regional Office, Nat. Park Svc., Santa Fe, 1976-77; archaeologist Midwest Archaeology Ctr., Nat. Park Svc., Lincoln, Nebr., 1977-80; field dir. Predynastic of Egypt Project, Nagada, 1981; instr. Pima C.C., Tucson, 1983, 87-88; archaeologist, dir. survey Crow Canyon Archaeol. Ctr., Cortez, Colo., 1984-86, field seminar leader, 1986—, rsch. assoc., 1987—; project dir., prin. investigator Statis. Rsch., Inc., Tucson, 1992—; archaeol. cons., Tucson, 1990-92; pub. speaker various orgns., 1986—; reviewer Wenner-Gren Found. for Anthrop. Rsch., Washington, 1992—. Author: Modeling Prehistoric Climatic Variability and Agricultural Production inn Southwestern Colorado, A.D. 901-1300: A GIS Approach, 1993; also articles. Rsch. fellow U. Ariz., 1973-76; grantee Wenner-Gren Found. for Anthrop. Rsch., 1987. Mem. Soc. for Am. Archaeology, Am. Anthrop. Assn., Ariz. Archaeol. Coun., Ariz. Archaeol. and Hist. Soc. (v.p. 1974-75, pres. 1975-76, asst. editor 1986-88), Sigma Xi (rsch. grantee 1985). Home: 19 N Silverbell Rd Tucson AZ 85745-2855 Office: Statis Rsch Inc 2500 N Pantano Rd Ste 218 Tucson AZ 85751

VANYO, JAMES PATRICK, engineering educator; b. Wheeling, W.Va., Jan. 29, 1928; s. John Andrew and Thelma Rose (Barrett) V. BSME, W.Va. U., 1952; JD, Chase Law Coll., 1959; MA in Astronomy, UCLA, 1966, PhD in Engring., 1969. Bar: Ohio 1959, U.S. Patent Office 1959, Calif. 1961. Asst. traffic supr. AT&T, N.Y.C., 1952-53; engr./designer Van Industries, Dayton, Ohio, 1953-59; engr. mgr. Remanco, Inc., Santa Monica, Calif., 1959-61; proposal/contracts staff Marquardt Corp., Van Nuys, Calif., 1961-63; researcher UCLA, 1963-69; long range planning specialist Litton Industries, Woodland Hills, Calif., 1969-70; prof. U. Calif., Santa Barbara, 1970—; reviewer grants NSAS, NSF, USN, others, 1972—; cons. Ford Aerospace, 1980—, ERNO Raumfahrttechnik, Bremen, 1991—. Author: Rotating Fluids in Engineering and Science, 1993; editorial bd. Jour. Environ. Systems, 1972—; reviewer articles sci. and engring. jours., 1972—, books tech. book pubs., 1972—; contbr. articles to profl. jours. Mem. Harbor Commn., Santa Barbara, 1980-84; mem. exec. com. Sierra Club, Santa Barbara, 1988-90. Doctoral fellow NASA, 1966-69; grantee NASA, NSF, and others, 1975—. Mem. Calif. Bar Assn., Ohio Bar Assn., Am. Geophysical Union, Am. Phys. Soc., Tau Beta Pi, Sigma Xi. Office: U Calif Mech & Environ Engring Santa Barbara CA 93106

VAN ZANT, DONALD LEE, clinical hypnotherapist; b. Joplin, Mo., Jan. 26, 1934; s. Frances Marion and Cleo Marie (Williams) Van Z.; m. Margarita Pena, Aug. 13, 1955; children: Carol, Ronald, Steven. BA, Western Ill. U., 1990. Cert. clin. hypnotherapist. 1988. Patrol inspector U.S. Border Patrol, Calexico, Calif., 1955-57; customs inspector U.S. Customs Svc., Calexico, 1957-66; instr., course writer U.S. Customs Svc. Hdqrs., Washington, 1966-68; supr. inspector U.S. Customs Svc., Calexico, 1970-83; mgr. D.L. Van Zant Speciality Sales, Calexico, 1972—; supr.-in-charge, contraband enforcement team U.S. Customs Svc., 1983-84, chief inspector, 1984-89; clin. hypnotherapist pvt practice, Calexico, 1988—. Author: (tng. manual) Narcotics; Search, 1966, Guidelines, Public Relations, 1966. With USMC, 1951-54, Korea. Mem. Nat. Assn. Retired Fed. Employees (pres. 1990), Am. Coun. Hypnotherapists, Hypnotis Examining Coun. of Calif. Republican. Roman Catholic. Home and office: 16 Las Flores Dr Calexico CA 92231-1840

VANZI, MAX BRUNO, editor; b. Ferrara, Italy, Sept. 24, 1934; s. Lambert S. Vanzi and Helen (Larimer) Hughes; m. Lynn A. D'Costa; children: Linda, Victor. A.B. in Journalism, U. Calif., Berkeley, 1959. Reporter Oroville (Calif.) Mercury, 1959-60; reporter UPI, Seattle, 1960-62, San Francisco, 1962-64, Japan, India, Pakistan, 1964-67; editor, correspondent UPI, Hong Kong, 1967-68; mgr. Southeast Asia UPI, Singapore, 1969-75; editor for Tex. UPI, Dallas, 1975-77; editor for Calif. UPI, San Francisco, 1977-81, gen. editor for Pacific div., 1981-84; editor L.A. Times, Washington Post News Service, L.A., 1984-86; asst. met. editor L.A. Times, 1986—; news editor Los Angeles Times, Sacramento Bureau, Sacramento, 1990—. Co-author: Revolution in the Philippines: The United States in a Hall of Cracked Mirrors, 1984. Served with USAF, 1953-55. Am. Press Inst. fellow Reston, Va., 1980; recipient cert. excellence Overseas Press Club. Am., N.Y.C., 1983. Office: LA Times Times Mirror Sq Los Angeles CA 90053-3816

VARALLO, FRANCIS VINCENT, security executive, consultant; b. Chgo., June 28, 1935; s. Frank vincent and Winifred Eileen (Durkin) V.; m. Merrilyn Susan Hire, June 26, 1970; children: Valerie, Sean, Cara. Bs in Humanities, Loyola U., Chgo., 1953-58. From second lt. to col. U.S. Army, 1958-74, attache, 1974-75, plans & policy intelligence officer, def. intelligence agy., 1975-78, installation commdr., 1978-79, duty dir. for intelligence, def. intelligence agy., 1979-81; sr. intelligence officer U.S. Army, Japan, 1981-84; dir. intelligence and security, def. nuclear agy. U.S. Army, 1985-88; regional security mgr. Unisys Corp., Salt Lake City, 1988-90; pres. Unicorn Assocs., Bountiful, Utah, 1990—. Col. U.S. Army, 1958-88. Mem. Am. Soc. Indsl. Security, Am. Mgmt. Assn., Nat. Assn. of Chiefs of Police, Assn. of Former Intelligence Officers, Rotary Internat., K. of C., Am. Legion, Retired Officers Assn. Roman Catholic. Home: 826 N Ridge Dr Bountiful UT 84010

VARANESE, MICHELE LYN, lawyer; b. Highland Park, Mich., Sept. 6, 1964; d. Daniel Wayne and Shirlyan (Starks) H.; m. Michael John Varanese, Oct. 5, 1985. Student, L.A. Valley Coll., 1982-83; BA, Calif. State U., Northridge, 1988, JD, 1991. Bar: Calif., 1991. Mem. support staff HealthPace div. of Coroon & Black Ins., Studio City, Calif., 1985; asst. adminstr. For Kids' Sake, Tarzana, Calif., 1985-86; law clk., extern tax div. U.S. Atty.'s Office, L.A., 1990; pvt. practice Santa Monica, Calif., 1992—. Mem. choir North Rim Christian Fellowship, Northridge, 1989—; vol. food preparer Salvation Army, Van Nuys, Calif., 1992—. Mem. L.A. Bar Assn. (real estate, tax and estate planning sect.), Women Lawyers Assn. L.A., Calif. Young Lawyers Assn. Office: 2001 Wilshire Blvd Ste 505 Santa Monica CA 90403

VARDI, MOSHE YA'AKOV, computer science researcher; b. Haifa, Israel, July 4, 1954; came to U.S., 1981; s. Pinchas and Zipporah (Mandel) V.; m. Pamela K. Geyer, Dec. 1986; 1 child, Aaron P. Hertzmann. BSc in Physics, Computer Sci., Bar-Ilan (Israel) U., 1974; MSc, Weizmann Inst., Rehovot, Israel, 1980; PhD, Hebrew U., Jerusalem, 1981. Teaching asst. dept. math. Bar-Ilan U., 1972-73; programmer The Weizmann Inst.Sci., Rehovot, 1978-79; rsch. asst. Inst. Math. and Computer Sci. Hewbrew U., Jerusalem, 1979-80, instr. Inst. Math. and Computer Sci., 1980-81; postdoctoral scholar dept. computer sci. Stanford U., Palo Alto, Calif., 1981-83, rsch. assoc. Ctr. for Study Lang. and Info., 1984-85; vis. scientist dept. computer sci. IBM Rsch. Lab., San Jose, Calif., 1983-84; mem. rsch. staff IBM Almaden Rsch. Ctr., San Jose, 1985—, 2d-level mgr. dept. math and related computer sci., 1989—; cons. assoc. prof. dept. computer sci. Stanford U., 1988-91, cons. prof. dept. computer sci., 1991—; program chair 6th Assn. for Computing Machinery Symposium on Prins. Database Systems, 1987, 2d Conf. on Theoretical Aspects Reasoning About Knowledge, 1988; conf. chair 3d Conf. on Theoretical Aspects Reasoning About Knowledge, 1990, 11th ACM Symposium on Prins. Database Systems, 1992, 7th IEEE Symposium on Logic in Computer Sci., 1993, others; bd. dirs. Theoretical Aspects Reasoning About Knowledge, Inc., 1991—. Editor conf. procs. Theoretical Aspects Reasoning About Knowledge, 1988; assoc. editor Info. and Computation, 1989—; contbr. articles to profl. jours. Mem. Beth Jacob Temple. Lt. Israeli Artillery Corps, 1974-78. Sharpiro fellow Bar-Ilan U., 1971-73, Weizmann postdoctoral fellow, 1981-83; recipient Fulbright award U.S.-Israel Edn. Found., 1981. Office: IBM Rsch Almaden Rsch Ctr K53-802 650 Harry Rd San Jose CA 95120-6099

VARGA, STEVEN CARL, reinsurance company official; b. Columbus, Ohio, Jan. 19, 1952; s. Stephen Thomas and Eva Jeney V.; BA in Psychology and Philosophy magna cum laude, Carthage Coll., 1977, MSA with honors Cen. Mich. U., 1986; m. Michelle L. Auld, Nov. 17, 1973; children: Zachary Steven, Joshua Lewis. Svc. mgr. Chem-Lawn Corp., Columbus, 1972-75; respiratory therapist St. Catherine's Hosp., Kenosha, Wis., 1975-77; policy analyst Nationwide Ins. Cos., Columbus, 1978-79, asst. mgr. Corp. Tng. Ctr., 1979-86; dir. ednl. tng. Sullivan Payne Co., Seattle, 1986-88, asst. v.p. human resource devel., 1989—. Mem. civic action program com., 1979-86, Nat. Mental Health Assn., 1972-79; mem. occupational adv. coun. Bellevue Community Coll., 1989—; v.p. Kenosha County chpt., 1975-77; mem. Franklin County (Ohio) Mental Health Assn., 1978-86. Rhodes scholar, 1976-77. Mem. Am. Soc. Tng. and Devel., Soc. Broadcast Engrs., Ins. Inst. Am. (contbg. author Principles of Reinsurance, vol. I and II, nat. advisory com. assoc. in reinsurance program), Brokers and Reinsurers Markets Assn. (edn. and tng. co-chair), Am. Psychol. Assn., Am. Mgmt. Assn., Soc. of Ins. Trainers and Educators (chmn. regional area planning com.), Carthage Coll. Alumni Assn., Phi Beta Kappa, Psi Chi. Home: 15586 Sandy Hook Rd Poulsbo WA 98370 Office: Sedgwick Payne Co 1501 4th Ave Seattle WA 98101-1662

VARGAS, DONATO TORRES, court interpreter; b. Pangasinan, Philippines, Aug. 7, 1917; s. Alejo Dulay and Augustina (Torres) Vargas; m. Marcela Asuncion, Dec. 24, 1939 (dec. Dec. 1972); children: Donato Jr., Milagros, William, Edith, Virginia, Henry, Violeta, Jessie, Fordeliza, Romeo, Cynthia; m. Sol Maralit, June 12, 1973. Tchr.'s cert. edn. diploma, Philippine Sch. Arts & Trades, Manila, Philippines, 1939; AA, Sto. Tomas U., Quezon City, Philippines, 1951-52; student, U. Sto. Tomas, Manila, 1952-55. Lt. col. Philippine Army, 1941-60; comdr./operator Scouts Commando Sec. and Inv. Detective Agy., Manila, Quezon City, 1961-71; high sch. prin. Bur. of Edn., Quezon City, 1960; resident mgr. Barcelon Mgmt. Corp., Stockton, Calif., 1974-77; farm labor contractor San Joaquin County, Calif., 1974-77; life ins. agt. Equitable Life Ins. Co., San Joaquin County, 1976-82; sr. citizen coord. Dept. of Aging, Stockton, San Joaquin, 1981-82; ct. interpreter Calif. Ct. Inter. Assn., San Joaquin County, 1975—. Pres. Crusade Against Crime, Quezon City, 1962-65; v.p. Filipino Community of Stockton, 1980-85; sr. citizen coord. Dept. of Aging, Stockton, 1982-85; coord. for Dr. Saqueton Councelor Movement-Filipino Community, Stockton, 1989-90; bd. chmn., legal adviser Caoayan Am. Generation of San Joaquin County, Stockton, 1985-92. Decorated Asiatic-Pacific Ribbon with 1 Bronze Star, World War II Victory medal, Philippine Liberation medal, Philippine Def. Ribbon with Bronze Star, Philippine Ind. Ribbon. Mem. Filipino U.S. Vets. Ass. (San Joaquin County chpt.), KC (3rd degree). Republican. Roman Catholic. Home: PO Box 2494 Stockton CA 95210

VARMUS, HAROLD ELIOT, microbiologist, educator; b. Oceanside, N.Y., Dec. 18, 1939; s. Frank and Beatrice (Barasch) V.; m. Constance Louise Casey, Oct. 25, 1969; children: Jacob Carey, Christopher Isaac. AB, Amherst Coll., 1961, DSc (hon.), 1984; MA, Harvard U., 1962; MD, Columbia U., 1966. Lic. physician, Calif. Intern, resident Presbyterian Hosp., N.Y.C ., 1966-68; clin. assoc. NIH, Bethesda, Md., 1968-70; lectr. dept. microbiology U. Calif.-San Francisco, 1970-72; asst. prof. U. Calif., San Francisco, 1972-74; assoc. prof. U. Calif., San Franisco, 1974-79; prof. U. Calif., San Francisco, 1979—, Am. Cancer Soc. research prof., 1984-93; dir. National Institutes of Health, Bethesda, Md., 1993—; chmn. bd. on biology NRC. Editor: Molecular Biology of Tumor Viruses, 1982, 85; Readings in Tumor Virology, 1983; assoc. editor Genes and Development Jour., Cell Jour.; mem. editorial bd. Cancer Surveys. Named Calif. Acad. Sci. Scientist of Yr., 1982; co-recipient Lasker Found. award, 1982, Passano Found. award, 1983, Armand Hammer Cancer prize, 1984, GM Alfred Sloan award 1984, Shubitz Cancer prize, 1985, Nobel Prize in Physiology or Medicine, 1989. Mem. AAAS, NAS, Inst. Medicine of NAS, Am. Soc. Virology, Am. Soc. Microbiology, Am. Acad. Arts and Scis. Democrat. Home: 956 Ashbury St San Francisco CA 94117-4409 Office: National Institutes of Health 9000 Rockville Pike Bethesda MD 20892*

VARNES, DAVID JOSEPH, engineering geologist; b. Howe, Ind., Apr. 5, 1919; s. David Joseph and Florence (Culmer) V.; m. Helen Dowling, Mar. 21, 1943 (dec. Mar. 1964); m. Katharine Lutz Buck, Aug. 30, 1966. BS with honors, Calif. Inst. Tech., Pasadena, 1940; postgrad., Northwestern U., 1941. Registered profl. engr., Colo., geologist, Calif. Geologist U.S. Geol. Survey, various locations, 1941-60; branch chief U.S. Geol. Survey, 1961-64, research geologist, 1965—; lectr., researcher U.S. Geol. Survey-Academia Sinica Coop, Szechuan-Yunnan, People's Republic China, 1984; lectr. advisor, Chinese U. Devel. Project II, Changchun, People's Republic China, 1987. G.K. Gilbert fellow, 1992; named Outstanding Scientist, Denver Fed. Exec. Bd., 1987; recipient Disting. Svc. award Dept. Interior, 1975. Fellow Geol. Soc. Am. (recipient Burwell award 1970, 76), Geol. Soc. London; mem. AAAS, Internat. Assn. Engring. Geology (v.p. N.Am. 1982-86, Hans Cloos medal 1989). Methodist, Episcopalian. Office: US Geol Survey MS 966 Box 25046 Denver CO 80225

VARNEY, BERNARD KEITH, financial executive, consultant; b. Coos Bay, Oreg., Nov. 5, 1919; s. Earnest and Daisy Inez (Lattin) V.; m. Norma Betty Rosick, Aug. 31, 1945; children: Mark Keith, Michael Matthew. B of Econs. and Bus. cum laude, U. Wash., 1950. CPA, Wash. Acctg. mgr. Rainier Nat. Ins. Co., Seattle, 1950-55; v.p. fin. Calif. State Auto Assn. Inter-Ins. Bur., San Francisco, 1955-84; treas. Calif. State Auto Assn., San Francisco, 1955-84, investment and fin. cons., 1984—; bd. dirs. Auto Club Ins. Co., Columbus, Ohio. 2d lt. U.S. Army, 1944-46. Decorated Army Commendation Medal, 1946. Mem. Ins. Acctg. and Statis. Assn. (pres.), Marin Country Club, Phi Beta Kappa, Beta Gamma Sigma, Beta Alpha Psi. Home: 313 Fairway Dr Novato CA 94949

VARNEY, PETER JUSTIN, international geology consultant; b. San Diego, Oct. 26, 1942; s. Newell Foster Varney and Mary Lillian (Norris) Dennis; m. Sara Carol Yaple, Feb. 28, 1967 (div. 1980); children: Darcy Gwen, Jonathan Glenn; m. Patricia Gail Evans, Apr. 1, 1983. BA, U. Colo., 1966; MS, U. Utah, 1972. Cert. profl. geologist, Am. Inst. Profl. Geologists. Exploration mgr. Wise Oil Co., Denver, 1975-78; chief geologist Impel Energy Corp., Denver, 1978-81; v.p. exploration J.M. Resources, Inc., Denver, 1981-84; sr. geologist Tex. Gas Exploration Co., Denver, 1984-86; exec. v.p. TerraSciences, Denver, 1988-90; ind. cons. petroleum and computer geology Denver, 1986-88, 90—; instr. geology Denver Free U., 1975-76, Colo. Women's Coll., Denver, 1982. Contbr. articles on computer geology to sci. publs. Pres. Denver Concert Band, Inc., 1979-81; bd. dirs. Littleton (Colo.) Chamber Orch., 1990-93, Great West Rocky Mountain Brass Band, Silverton, Colo., 1989—. 1st lt. U.S. Army, 1967-69. Named Man of Yr., Mile High Desk and Derrick Club, Denver, 1982. Mem. Am. Assn. Petroleum Geologists (computer applications com. 1990-93), Computer Oriented Geol. Soc., Rocky Mountain Assn. Geologists (editor Mountain Geologist 1986, treas. 1992). Home: 5903 S Fairfield St Littleton CO 80120-2821

VARNEY, ROBERT NATHAN, retired physicist, researcher; b. San Francisco, Nov. 7, 1910; s. Frank Hastings Sr. and Emily Patricia (Rhine) V.; m. Astrid Margareta Riffolt, June 19, 1948; children: Nils Roberts, Natalie Rhine. AB with highest honors in Physics, U. Calif., Berkeley, 1931, MA, 1932, PhD, 1935; DSc (hon.), Leopold Franzens U., Innsbruck, Austria, 1983. Instr. NYU, 1936-38; asst. prof., assoc. prof., prof. Washington U., St. Louis, 1938-64; mem. rsch. lab. Bell Labs, Murray Hill, N.J., 1951-52; sr. mem. rsch. lab., sr. sci cons. Lockheed Missiles & Space Co., Palo Alto, Calif., 1964-75; guest prof. Leopold Franzens U., Innsbruck, 1977-78; mem. Mo. Gov.'s Sci. Adv. Com., St. Louis, 1960-64; mem. tech. staff Bell Telephone Labs., Murray Hill, N.J., 1951-52. Author: Engineering Physics, 1948; (with others) Methods of Experimental Physics, 1968, Introduction to ... Atmospheric Pollution, 1972; contbr. 82 articles to scholarly and profl. jours. Comdr. USNR, 1931-57. Fulbright fellow Leopold Franzens U., Innsbruck, 1971-72, 76-77, NSF sr. postdoctoral fellow Inst. Tech., Stockholm, 1958-59, NRC sr. postdoctoral fellow U.S. Army Ballistic Rsch. Lab., Aberdeen, Md., 1975-76; recipient Cross of Honor 1st Class Austrian Govt., 1981. Fellow Am. Phys. Soc.; mem. Am. Assn. Physics Tchrs., Phi Beta Kappa, Sigma Xi, Tau Beta Pi, Omicron Delta Kappa. Episcopalian. Home: 4156 Maybell Way Palo Alto CA 94306-3820

VASEY, WILLIAM JOSEPH, director college outreach program, state legislator; b. Saratoga, Wyo., Jan. 13, 1939; s. George Oliver and Marjorie Elizabeth (Munz) V.; m. Judith Lesley Bakken, Aug. 21, 1968; children: Susan, Michael, Richard. BS, Valley City State Coll., 1969; MEd, U. Wyo., 1984. Tchr. Zeeland (N.D.) Pub. Schs., 1968-69; salesman 3M Co., Bismark, N.D., 1969-70; tchr. Saratoga Pub. Schs., 1970-73; supr. Peter Kiewit Sons, Sheridan, Wyo., 1973-83; Kellogg Grant coord. Carbon County Libr., Rawlins, Wyo., 1984-89; dir. Carbon County Higher Edn. Ctr., Rawlins, 1989—; state rep. Wyo. State Legislature, Cheyenne, 1989—. Bd. dirs. Spl. Olympics, Casper, Wyo., 1992—, COVE Family Violence Protection, Rawlins, 1991—, devel. disabilities workshop ARK Industries, Laramie, 1989—; mem. Rawlins City Coun., 1988-89; trustee Carbon County Meml. Hosp., Rawlins, 1985-89, Sch. Dist. 2, Saratoga, 1980-84. Mem. Wyo. Assn. Continuing, Community and Adult Edn. (Disting. Svc. award 1993). Democrat. Home: 1106 Date St Rawlins WY 82301 Office: Carbon County Higher Edn Ctr 600 Mahoney PO Box 1114 Rawlins WY 82301

VASILEV, STEVEN ANATOL, gynecologic oncologist, educator; b. San Francisco, July 17, 1954; s. Anatol and Katherina (Welbitzky) V.; m. Kathryn Joanne Shaw, Jan. 13, 1985; children: Alexander, Andrei. BS in Biol. Scis., U. So. Calif., 1979, BA in Slavic Langs. and Lits., 1979, MD, 1984. Diplomate Am. Bd. Ob.-Gyn. and Gynecologic Oncology. Intern/resident L.A. County USC Med. Ctr.; fellow in gynecologic oncology U. So. Calif., L.A., 1988-90; staff surgeon City of Hope Nat. Med. Ctr., Duarte, Calif., 1990—; asst. prof. in residence U. Calif., Irvine, 1991—; dir. dept. gynecology City of Hope Nat. Med. Ctr., 1992—. Contbr. articles and abstracts to profl. jours. and chpts. to books. Chmn. Calif. State Cervical Adv. Coalition Com., 1992; chmn. pub. edn. com. Am. Cancer Soc., Coastal Cities Unit, Calif., 1977-84. Recipient Outstanding Achievement award Am. Cancer Soc., 1980. Fellow Am. Coll. Ob.-Gyn., Am. Coll. Surgeons; mem. Am. Soc. Clin. Oncologists, Soc. Gynecologic Oncologists, AMA, Calif. Med. Assn., Soc. Critical Care Medicine, Sigma Xi, Alpha Omega Alpha. Republican. Russian Orthodox. Office: City of Hope Nat Med Ctr 1500 E Duarte Rd Duarte CA 91010

VASQUEZ, GADDI, county official; b. Carrizo Springs, Tex., Jan. 22, 1955; m. Elaine Vasquez; 1 child, Jason. AA in Criminal Justice, Rancho Santiago C.C., 1972; BA in Pub. Svc. Mgmt., U. Redlands, 1980. Police officer City of Orange, Calif., 1975-79; coord. community rels., mgr.'s office City of Riverside, Calif., 1979-81; exec. asst. Orange County Bd. Supervisors, 3d Dist., Calif., 1981-85; mem. Orange County Bd. Supervisers 3d Dist., Calif., 1987—; area mgr. So. Calif. Edison Co., 1985; hispanic liaison Office of Gov. George Deukmejian, Calif., 1985, from dep. appointments sec. to chief dep. appointments sec., 1985-87; Mem. Transp. Corridor Agys. Bd., 1987—, chmn. 1990-91; local agy. formation commn., 1988-93, chmn. 1990-91; mem. Calif. Film Commn., 1988-91, Calif. Coun. Criminal Justice, 1989—; founder, co-chair, Orange County Health Care Task Force, 1990—; with White House Fellowships Commn., 1990-91; co-chmn. Orange County Congestion Mgmt. Policy Task Force, 1990—; bd. dirs. Orange County Transp. Authority, 1991—, exec. com. 1992—, vice chmn. 1993—; regional advisory and planning coun., 1991—, vice chmn. 1992, chmn. 1993; official observer Armenian Independence elections, 1991. Bd. dirs. Future Leaders Am., Southwest Voter Rsch. Inst., calif. First Amendment Coalition, Orange County Boy Scout Coun., So. Area Foster Care Effort, Orange County Performing Arts Ctr., Opera Pacific; trustee Am. Coun. Young Polit. Leaders; adv. bd. Pediatric Cancer Rsch. Found, Orange County Juvenile Connection Project, Calif. Office Traffic Safety, The Salvation Army Orange County, Project AERO, Constitutional Rights Found. Orange County; community coun. Prentice Day Sch.; hon. adv. bd. Adam Walsh Ctr.; hon. bd. govs. Bower Mus.; leadership coun. Orange County Points Light. Named Officer of Yr., Am. Legion, 1977. Outstanding Young Man of Am. U.S. C.of C., 1985, One of 100 Most Influential Hispanics in U.S. Hispanic Bus. Mag., 1986-87, 88-89, 91-92, 92-93, Govt. Hispanic Bus. Advocate of Yr. U.S. Hispanic Champer Region I, 1991; recipient Alumni Achievement award, Santa Ana Coll., 1988, Alumni of Yr.award U. Redlands, 1989, Humanitarian award Nat. Conf. Christians and Jews, 1989, award State Child Devel. Adv. Com., 1990, Tree of Life award Jewish Nat. Fund, 1991, Ralph E. Hudson Open Space award Landscape Architects Found., 1992. Office: Orange County Bd of Supervisors 10 Civic Center Plaza Santa Ana CA 92701

VASQUEZ, NICK ANTONIO, educator; b. Pittsburg, Calif., June 9, 1951; s. Antonio Joseph and Virginia Marie (Ruiz) V. BA, UCLA, 1976, MEd, 1987. Youth coordinator United Coun. Spanish Speaking Orgns., Pittsburg, 1977; tchr. Pittsburg Unified Sch. Dist., 1977-78, LA Unified Sch. Dist./Union Ave. Sch., 1978-83; broadcast ops. asst. KCET Channel 28, L.A., 1984; coord. partnership program UCLA Undergrad. Admissions and Rels with Schs., 1984-90; pre-coll. program expert, parent programs UCLA, 1990—; tchr. Fernangeles Elem. Sch., 1990—; cons. in field; lectr. in field. Narrator, producer ednl. video: The University Express, 1989. Cons. sci. curriculum Nat. Coun. of La Raza, Washington, 1986—, PBS spl., 1993, ARCO Found., 1993. Inst. Ednl. Leadership fellow, 1986; UCLA Adminstrv. and Profl. Staff Achievement awardee, 1989; named tchr. of yr. Fernangles Sch., 1992. Mem. ASCD, Calif. Assn. Bilingual Educators, UCLA Latino Alumni Assn., UCLA Grad. Sch. Edn. Alumni Assn. Democrat. Office: 22925 White Pine Pl Santa Clarita CA 91350-4120

VASSALLI, SHORTY See COLLINGS, CELESTE LOUISE

VASU, BANGALORE SESHACHALAM, biology educator; b. Bangalore, India. MA, U. Madras, 1959, MS, 1962; PhD, Stanford U., 1965. Rsch. asst./grad. student Stanford (Calif.) U., 1962-65; post-doctoral rsch. assoc. U. Notre Dame, Ind., 1965-67; asst. prof. of zoology Ohio Wesleyan U., Delaware, 1967-68, 74; UNESCO specialist in biology U. Zambia, Lusaka, 1968-73; visiting prof. of Zoology Calif. State U., Chico, 1974-77; prof. of Biology Menlo Coll., Atherton, Calif., 1978—; chmn. Bioscience, Biotechnology Mgmt., Menlo Coll., 1986—. Fulbright fellow U.S. Edn. Founds., Washington, India, 1962. Mem. AAAS, NAAHP, Sigma Xi. Home: 35686 Nuttman Ln Fremont CA 94536-2546 Office: Menlo Coll 1000 El Camino Real Menlo Park CA 94025-4327

VASUDEVAN, RAMASWAMI, engineering consultant; b. Trichi, Tamil Nad, India, Nov. 28, 1947; came to U.S. 1970; s. Rajagopal and Jembakalakshmi; m. Padmini Vasudevan, Mar. 20, 1980 (div. 1992); m. Suryaprabha, June 11, 1993. BE, Madras U., India, 1970; MS, UCLA, 1972. Registered profl. engr., Calif.; cert. plant engr., Calif. Project engr. Anco Engrs., Culver City, Calif., 1971-77; mgr. Wyle Labs., Norco, Calif., 1977-78, EDAC, Palo Alto, Calif., 1978-82; project mgr. Los Alamos (N.Mex.) Tech. Assocs., 1982-85; assoc. EQE Inc., Irvine, Calif., 1985-87; pres. Sidhi Cons., Inc., Santa Ana, Calif., 1987—. Contbr. articles to profl. jours. Mem. ASME, IEEE (stds. com. 1982-84), EERI, NFPA, EPRI-EQAG, Am. Inst. Plant Engrs. Republican. Office: Sidhi Cons Inc 4642 E Chapman #210 Orange CA 92669-4198

VATTER, HAROLD GOODHUE, economics educator; b. Glen Rock, N.J., Dec. 18, 1910; s. George C. and Della Goodhue V.; children: Marguerita, Theresa, Marc. B.A., U. Wis.-Madison, 1936; M.A., Columbia U., 1938; Ph.D., U. Calif.-Berkeley, 1950. Assoc. prof. econs. Oreg. State U., Corvallis, 1948-56, U. Mass., Amherst, 1956-58; assoc. prof. Carleton Coll., Northfield, Minn., 1958-64; prof. econs. Portland State U., Oreg., 1965-79, prof. econs. emeritus, 1980—. Author: U.S. Economy in the 1950s, 1960, Drive to Industrial Maturity, 1975, U.S. Economy in World War II, 1985, (with John Walker) The Inevitability of Government Growth, 1990. Lilly fellow, U. Chgo., 1964. Mem. Am. Econ. Assn., Econ. History Assn., Assn. Evolutionary Econs. Home: 3041 NE 25th Ave Portland OR 97212-3462 Office: Portland State U PO Box 751 Portland OR 97207-0751

VATZ, OLGA, artist; b. Toronto, Ont., Apr. 21, 1954; d. John and Violet (Zaika) Watts; m. David Lee Cramer, May 27, 1989. Student, Pa. State U., 1971-73; BFA in Illustration, Phila. Coll. Art, 1976. Portrait artist Louis Artists Village, Atlantic City, 1974-78; resident & commd. portrait artist Regency Art Gallery, Reese-Palley, Caesar's Hotel, Atlantic City, 1979-80; illustrator Chip Braymes & Assocs., Atlantic City, 1979-81; commd. portrait artist Cashman Photo Enterprises/Caesar's Hotel & Casino, Atlantic City, 1983-84; airbrush painter Smithville (N.J.) Woodcarving Factory, 1984-86; ind. artist oils, pastels & charcoal Phoenix, 1987—. Mem. S.W. Profl. Artists, Women Artists of West, Palo Verde Arts & Crafts Guild (publicity chair 1992—), Pastel Soc. West Coast. Republican. Greek Orthodox. Home: 3132 W Port Royale Ln Phoenix AZ 85023

VAUGHAN, ELIZABETH CROWNHART, management consultant, book editor; b. Madison, Wis., Jan. 9, 1929; d. Jesse George and Hildegarde Lucretia (Wooll) Crownhart; m. Thomas James Vaughan, June 16, 1951; children: Meagan, Margot, Stephen, Cameron. BA, U. Wis., 1950; MA, Portland State U., 1970. Script writer Wis. Pub. Broadcasting, Madison, 1950-52; women's program dir. KEX Westinghouse Broadcasting, Portland, Oreg., 1954-56; sec., treas. Salar Enterprises, Ltd., Portland, 1968-86, pres., 1987—; bd. dirs. First Interstate Bank of Oreg., Portland, mem. exec. com., 1987—, chmn. audit and examining, 1983—; bd. dirs. Nordstrom, Inc., Seattle, chmn. compensation com., 1977—. Translator, editor: Explorations of Kamchatka, 1972, Colonial Russian America, 1976, End of Russian America, 1979, Russia's Conquest of Siberia and the North Pacific, 3 vols., 1984-88; contbr. articles to profl. jours. With Russian desk Oreg. Hist. Soc., Portland, 1972-78, fgn. archives coord., 1978—; bd. dirs. Oreg. Ind. Coll. Found., Portland, 1983—, Chamber Music Northwest, Portland, 1983-85; exec. dir. N. Pacific Studies Ctr., Oreg. Hist. Soc., 1988-90. Recipient Aubrey Watzek award Lewis and Clark Coll., 1975. Fellow Royal Geog. Soc. (London), Royal Asiatic Soc. (London); mem. Capital Funds Com., Oreg. Pub. Broadcasting, Am. Assn. Advancement of Slavic Studies, Western Slavic Assn., No. Am. Falconry Assn., Am. Com. on East-West Accord, Arlington Club, Town Club, Univ. Club, Phi Kappa Phi. Office: 2135 SW Laurel St Portland OR 97201-2367

VAUGHAN, JAMES ARTHUR, JR., surgeon; b. Sherman, Tex., Aug. 16, 1914; s. James Arthur and Nola Beatrice (Lawrence) V.; B.S., East Tex. State Coll., 1947, M.S., 1950; D.O., Chgo. Coll. Osteopathy, 1951; M.D., Calif. Coll. Medicine, 1962; m. Betty Ruth Brecheen, June 19, 1942 (dec.); children: J.A., James A. III; m. 2d, Betty Jo Stewart, Nov. 14, 1958 (div.); 1 dau., Karen. Intern Dallas Osteo. Hosp., 1951-52; pvt. practice, Dallas, 1952-63; assoc. Antelope Valley Med. Clinic, 1963-77; practice medicine, 1977-86; vice chief staff Lancaster Community Hosp., 1968, chief of staff, 1980-86; staff mem. Antelope Valley Hosp.; bd. dirs. Dallas Osteo. Hosp. until 1963; mem. adv. com. LVN Sch. Nursing until 1963. Served from seaman 2d class to lt. comdr. USNR, 1941-46, now lt. comdr. ret. Decorated Air medal with 1 gold star; recipient Disting. Service award CAP. Mem. AMA, Los Angeles County Med. Assn., Ret. Officers Assn. (life), Nat. Aero. Assn., Flying Doctors Soc. Africa (life), D.A.V. (life), Am. Legion (life), VFW (life), Sigma Tau Gamma, Iota Tau Sigma, Sigma Sigma Phi. Mason (32 deg., Shriner); mem. Order Eastern Star, Amaranth. Democrat. Episcopalian. Club: Caterpillar. Office: James A Vaughan Jr M D 45800 Challenger Way Space 98 Lancaster CA 93535

VAUGHAN, MICHAEL B., economist; b. Springdale, Ark., Oct. 30, 1954; s. Bruce C. and Mary F. (Maestri) V.; m. Kathleen M. Lukken, Aug. 15, 1992. BS, U. Ark., 1976, MBA, 1977; PhD, U. Nebr., 1981. Faculty Dept. Econs. Weber State U., Ogden, 1981-89, chair, 1986-89; assoc. dean Coll. Bus. and Econs. Weber State U., Ogden, 1989-90, dean, 1991—; cons. Weber Econ. Devel. Corp., 1989. Contbr. articles to profl. jours. Pew Trust fellowship Princeton U., 1989, Willard L. Eccles fellow Weber State U., 1986-89. Mem. Am. Assembly Collegiate Schs. of Bus. (rep.), Am. Econ. Assn., Rotary Club Odgen, Ogden/Weber C. of C. Home: 2797 Shamrock Ogden UT 84403

VAUGHAN, RICHARD ALARIC, software engineer, consultant; b. Richland, Wash., Mar. 31, 1965; s. Peter David Gross and Joan Roberta Wirth. BA in Math., U. Va., 1986, MS in Computer Sci., 1986; postgrad., Stanford (Calif.) U., 1988. Mem. tech. staff Computer Scis. Corp., Herndon, Va., 1981-86, instr., teaching asst. computer sci. dept., 1987-88; rsch. asst. computer sci. dept. Stanford U., 1987; intern Western Software Lab. Digital Equipment Corp., Palo Alto, Calif., 1988; program mgr. Microsoft Corp., Redmond, Wash., 1988-89, software design engr., 1989—; cons. math. and computer scis. dept. U. Va., 1985-86. Treas. Stanford Women's Ctr., 1986-88; vol. Planned Parenthood, 1991—; bd. dirs. Eastside Domestic Violence Program, 1992—. Echols scholar U. Va., 1983-86; NSF fellow, 1986-89, Stanford U. fellow, 1987. Home: PO Box 6063 Bellevue WA 98008-0063 Office: Microsoft Corp 1 Microsoft Way Redmond WA 98052-6393

VAUGHAN, WARREN TAYLOR, JR., psychiatrist; b. Boston, Aug. 24, 1920; s. Warren Taylor and Emma Elizabeth (Heath) V.; m. Cecil Todd Knight, Dec. 19, 1942 (div. 1958); children: W. Taylor III, Christopher, Todd Jameson; m. Clarice Helm Haylett, Aug. 16, 1960; children: Richard Haylett, Jennifer Anne. BS, Harvard U., 1942, MD, 1943. Diplomate Am. Bd. Psychiatry. Resident Boston U. Sch. Medicine, 1946-48; fellow child psychiatry Judge Baker Guidance Ctr., Boston, 1948-50; from rsch. fellow to asst. prof. Harvard U. Sch. Pub. Health, Boston, 1950-59; asst. clin. prof. U. Colo. Sch. Medicine, Denver, 1959-60; from assoc. clin. prof. to lectr. in psychiatry Stanford U., Palo Alto, Calif., 1966—; chmn. dept. psychiatry Peninsula Hosp., 1968-69; cons. in field. Contbr. articles to profl. jours. Dir. mental hygiene Mass. Dept. Mental Helth, Boston, 1952-59; chmn. com. Futures Planning Council, 1967-74; bd. dirs. Planned Parenthood, 1987-90. Capt. AUS, 1944-46. Recipient Svc. award NIMH, 1976. Fellow Am. Psychiatric Assn., Northern Calif. Psychiatric Assn. (pres. 1970-71), Am. Orthopsychiatric Assn., Am. Acad. Child and Adolescent Psychiatry; mem. Group for Advancement Psychiatry, Am. Coll. Psychiatry (emeritus). Episcopalian. Home: 41 Stonegate Rd Portola Valley CA 94028-7646 Office: PO Box 620458 Woodside CA 94062

VAUGHN, DANNY MACK, physical geography educator; b. Muskegon, Mich., Aug. 19, 1948; s. Louis Emerson and Evelyn Elona (Hamen) V.; m. Mary Kathleen Frisz, July 16, 1978; children: Benjamin Patrick, Emily Elizabeth. BS in Earth Sci., Ind. State U., 1978, PhD, 1984. Asst. prof. geography Lake Superior State U., Sault Ste. Marie, Mich., 1984-85, U. Mo., Kansas City, 1985-87, Jacksonville (Ala.) State U., 1987-90; assoc. prof. geography and dir. remote sensing & GIS lab. Weber State U., Ogden, Utah, 1990—; faculty rsch. assoc. NASA, Huntsville, Ala., 1991—; condr. workshops in digital image processing and Geographic Info. System. Contbr. articles to profl. jours. With USAF, 1967-71. Grantee Weber State U., 1990-92, NSF, 1991, NASA Joint Venture, 1990, Jacksonville State U., 1988, U. Mo., 1985, 86, 87. Mem. Nat. Coun. for Geographic Edn., Assn. Am. Geographers (Great Plains/Rocky Mountain divsn.), Geol. Soc. Am., Nat. Speleological Soc., Am. Soc. for Photogrammetry and Remote Sensing, Sigma Xi, Gamma Theta Upsilon (chpt. pres. 1978-80), Sigma Gamma Epsilon (chpt. v.p. 1977-78). Home: 5178 W 4250 S Hooper UT 84315 Office: Weber State U Dept Geography Sci Lab Ogden UT 84408-2510

VAUGHN, JAMES ENGLISH, JR., neurobiologist; b. Kansas City, Mo., Sept. 17, 1939; s. James English and Sue Katherine (Vaughn); m. Christine Singleton, June 18, 1961; children: Stephanie, Stacey. B.A., Westminster Coll., 1961; Ph.D., UCLA, 1965. Postdoctoral rsch. fellow in brain rsch. U. Edinburgh (Scotland), 1965-66; asst. prof. Boston U. Sch. Medicine, 1966-70; head sect. of molecular neuromorphology Beckman Rsch. Inst. of City of Hope, Duarte, Calif., 1970—, pres. rsch. staff, 1986, chmn. div. neuroscience, 1987—. Fellow Neuroscience Rsch. Program, 1969; Rsch. grantee NIH, 1969—, NSF, 1983-87. Mem. AAAS, Am. Soc. Cell Biology, Am. Assn. Anatomists, Soc. for Neuroscience (chmn. short course 1977), Internat. Brain Rsch. Orgn., N.Y. Acad. Scis., Sigma Xi. Achievements include original immunoelectron microscopic demonstration of a neurotransmitter synthesizing enzyme in brain synaptic terminals; original proposal and evidence of synaptotropic modulation of dendritic development in the central nervous system; discovered that genetically-associated changes in neuronal migration correlate with altered patterns of synaptic connectivity in the brain; discovered that all neurons of a major brain relay station use GABA as their neurotransmitter; discovered previously unknown cholinergic neurons in the brain and spinal cord; discovered unique migratory patterns of preganglionic sympathetic neurons in developing spinal cord; first immunocytochemical evidence of a role gamma aminobutyric acid (GABA) neurons in focal epilepsy; first demonstration of lesion-induced synaptic plasticity of GABA neurons; contbr. articles to profl. jours.; assoc. editor Jour. Neurocytology, 1978-86; mem. editorial bd. Synapse, 1986—; reviewer for Jour. Comparative Neurology, 1974—, Brain Research, 1976—. Office: Beckman Research Inst 1450 E Duarte Rd Dept Neurosci Duarte CA 91010

VAUGHN, NORMAN, land agent, lawyer; b. Alabama City, Ala., June 13, 1932; s. Oscar Nicholas and Dorothy Lorena (Orebaugh) V.; m. Anna Jean Owen, Nov. 27, 1982. BA in Journalism, U. Ga., 1966; JD summa cum laude, John Marshall U., 1973. Bar: Ga. 1973, Calif. 1979. Radio announcer, newsman various stas., 1954-73; solo gen. law practice Cornelia, Ga., 1973-74; sr. right of way agt. Ford, Bacon & Davis Constrn. Co., Monroe, La., 1974-76; sr. land agt. Shell Pipe Line Corp., Anaheim, Calif., 1976—. With USN, 1949-53, 63-64. Mem. Underground Svc. Alert of So. Calif. (dir.), Internat. Right of Way Assn.

VAUGHT-ALEXANDER, KAREN, English language educator; b. Clinton, Iowa, Jan. 10, 1951; d. Wallace Foster and Lamoyne (Mayes) Vaught; m. David Vaught-Alexander. BA, Ind. U., 1970, PhD, 1988; MA, Ind. State U., 1972. Grad. fellow, teaching asst. Ind. State U., Terre Haute, 1970-72, assoc. instr., 1972-73; assoc. instr. Ind. U., Bloomington, 1973-74; instr., writing lab. coord. South Ga. Coll., Douglas, 1975-78; drama/English tchr. Brantley County High Sch., Nahunta, Ga., 1980-81; drama, French & English tchr. Atkinson County High Sch., Pearson, Ga., 1981-86; drama/English tchr. Valdosta (Ga.) High Sch., 1986-88; instr. Valdosta State Coll., 1988-89; asst., then assoc. prof. English, dir. integrated writing program U. Portland, Oreg., 1989—. Contbr. articles to profl. jours. Trainer, vol. tutor N.W. China Coun., Portland, 1991-92; mem., cons. Teaching Other Tchrs. About Literacy, Oreg. Dept. Edn., Salem, 1989—; pvt. univ. rep. Oreg. Adv. Com. on Composition, Oreg. Dept. Higher Edn., 1990—. Named ORA Reading Tchr. of Yr. Okefenokee Reading Assn., 1986, Tchr. of Yr. Valdosta Pub. Schs., 1988. Mem. MLA, Nat. Coun. Tchrs. English (lang. & learning across the curriculum adv. com. 1992—), Nat. Coun. Writing Program Adminstrs., Writing Across the Curriculum Network, Assn. Bus. Communicators, Assn. Tech. Writing Tchrs., Nat. Network for Coop. Learning in Higher Edn., Internat. Soc. for Ednl. Teaching Alternative. Office: U Portland 5000 N Willamette Blvd Portland OR 97203-5798

VAUX, DORA LOUISE, sperm bank official, consultant; b. White Pine, Mont., Aug. 8, 1922; d. Martin Tinus and Edna Ruth (Pyatt) Palmlund; m. Robert Glenn Vaux, Oct. 25, 1941; children: Jacqueline, Cheryl, Richard, Jeanette. Grad. high sch., Bothell, Wash. Photographer Busco-Nestor Studios, San Diego, 1961-68; owner, mgr. Vaux Floors & Interiors, San Diego, 1968-82; cons., mgr. Repository for Germinal Choice, Escondido, Calif., 1983-91; adminstr. Found. for the Continuity of Mankind, Spokane, 1991—. Republican. Home: S 605 Liberty Lake Rd Liberty Lake WA 99019 Office: Found Continuity of Mankind W 1209 1st St Spokane WA 99204

VAUX, HENRY JAMES, forest economist, educator; b. Bryn Mawr, Pa., Nov. 6, 1912; s. George and Mary (James) V.; m. Jean Macduff, Jan. 11, 1937; children: Henry J., Alice J. B.S., Haverford Coll., 1933, D.Sc. (hon.), 1985; M.S., U. Calif., 1935, Ph.D., 1948. Forest engr. Crown Willamete Paper Co., Portland, Oreg., 1936-37; instr. Sch. Forestry, Oreg. State Coll., Corvallis, 1937-42; assoc. economist La. Agrl. Expt. Sta., Baton Rouge, 1942-43; economist U.S. Forest Service, Berkeley, Calif. and Wash., 1946-48; lectr. Sch. Forestry, U. Calif.-Berkeley, 1948-50, assoc. prof., 1950-53, prof., 1953-78, prof. emeritus, 1978—, dean, 1955-65; asst. dir. Agrl. Expt. Sta. U. Calif., 1955-65, dir. Wildland Research Center, 1955-65; chmn. Calif. Bd. Forestry, 1976-83. Author tech. articles, bulls. Served from ensign to lt. (j.g.) USNR, 1943-46. Recipient Berkeley citation U. Calif., 1978, Disting. Service award Forestry Assn., 1986; hon. fellow Calif. Acad. Scis., 1986. Fellow AAAS, Soc. Am. Foresters (Gifford Pinchot medal 1983); mem. Forest History Soc. (dir. 1971-75), Sigma Xi, Xi Sigma Pi. Mem. Soc. of Friends. Home: 622 San Luis Rd Berkeley CA 94707-1726 Office: University of California California Water Resources Ctr Riverside CA 92521

VAWTER, DONALD, personnel management consultant; b. Spokane, Wash., May 19, 1920; s. Edgar F. and Lina M. V.; student polit. sci. Wash. State U., 1946-49; m. Margaret Schroeder, May 5, 1950; children: Charlotte, Sara. Supr. employee svcs. Wash. State Employment Svc., Seattle, 1950-58; employment mgr. Sundstrand Data Control, Redmond, Wash., 1958-72; profl. recruiter DBA Bellevue Employment Agy., Bellevue, Wash., 1972-73; pers. mgr., workers compensation adminstr. Crown Zellerbach, Omak, Wash., 1973-82; bd. dirs. Pacific N.W. Pers. Mgmt. Assn. 1974-78; apptd. Gov's. Svcs. Coun., 1977-83; treas. econ. devel. corp. North Okanogan County, 1984—. Served with USCGR, 1942-46, 50-53, comdr. Res. ret., 1968. Mem. Am. Soc. Pers. Adminstrn. (accredited pers. mgr.). Home: PO Box 296 Tonasket WA 98855-0296

VAX, MICHAEL NORMAN, musician, bandleader, producer; b. Oakland, Calif., Oct. 30, 1942; s. Sydney and Virginia (Greenberg) V.; m. Peggy S. Salmen, July 20, 1975; 1 child, Leslie April. BMus, U. of the Pacific, Stockton, Calif., 1991. Owner Mike Vax Music Prodns., Pitts., 1960—; producer John Ascuaga's Nugget Jazz Festival, Sparks, Nev., 1982—; dir. of jazz studies U. of the Pacific, Stockton, 1985—; clinician Schilkie Music Products, Chgo., 1980—. 1st trumpet, rd. mgr. Stan Kenton Orch., L.A., 1970-72; leader, trumpet Mike Vax Big Band, San Francisco, 1973-74, Dukes of Dixieland, New Orleans, 1975-76, Great Am. Jazz Band, 1980—, TRPTS (Trumpets), 1984—; 1st trumpet Clark Terry Big Bad Band, N.Y.C., 1978; contbr. articles to profl. jours. Music dir. San Francisco Rotary Jazz Festival, San Mateo, Calif., 1982—. Mem. Internat. Assn. of Jazz Educators (Svc. to Jazz 1989), Calif. Music Educators Assn., Internat. Assn. of Classical Jazz Festivals (v.p. 1990-92), Internat. Found. for Jazz (bd. dirs. 1987-92), Internat. Trumpet Guild (Soloist for Conv. 1981). Democrat. Jewish. Office: Mike Vax Music Prodns PO Box 8337 Pittsburg CA 94565

VAZQUEZ CORREA, BERALDO ANTONIO, internist; b. N.Y.C., Sept. 25, 1946; s. Beraldo and Marcelina (Correa) Vazquez; m. Frances Megan Corso, Aug. 23, 1987; children: Michelle, Beraldo Antonio, Ernesto Antonio, Jorge Luis, Javier Orlando, Alejandro Francisco. Student, Cath. U. P.R., Ponce, 1978-80; MD, Ponce Sch. Medicine, 1985. Diplomate Nat. Bd. Med. Examiners, Am. Bd. Internal Medicine; lic. physician, N.Y., Nev. Intern Maimonides Med. Ctr., Bklyn., 1985-86, resident, 1986-88; emergency rm. physician Brunswick Hosp. Ctr., Amityville, N.Y., 1987-88, Kings Hwy. Hosp. Ctr., Bklyn., 1987, The Parkway Hosp., Forest Hills, N.Y., 1987-88; physician The Cumberland Hosp., Cumberland Family Care Ctr., Bklyn., 1987-88, The Bklyn. Med. Group, Empire Health Ins. Plan, 1986-87; med. dir. extended care & respiratory therapy, dir. ICU/CCU NYE Regional Med. Ctr., Tonopah, Nev., 1988-91, chief medicine, attending physician, 1988—; attending physician Battle Mountain (Nev.) Gen. Hosp., 1990—; physician Charter Hosp., Las Vegas, Nev., 1992—, Lake Mead Hosp. Med. Ctr., North Las Vegas, 1992—, Desert Springs Hosp., Las Vegas, 1991—, Humana Hosp.-Sunrise, Las Vegas, 1991—; asst. clin. instr. dept. internal medicine U. Nev. Sch. Medicine, Reno, 1989—, asst. clin. instr. dept. rural and community medicine, 1989—; bd. mem. Rural Healthcare Assocs., Inc., Tonopah, 1989—; physician reviewer Nev. Peer Rev. Orgn., Reno, 1990—; mem. Nat. Health Svc. Corps, Region IX, Tonopah, 1988-91. With USMC, 1966-72. Mem. AMA, ACP, Am. Geriatrics Soc. Office: 2121 E Flamingo Rd Ste 110 Las Vegas NV 89119

VEAL, DONALD LYLE, former university president, aircraft instrumentation executive and researcher, educator; b. Chance, S.D., Apr. 17, 1931; s. Boyd William and Esther Mabel (Iverson) V.; m. Bonita Dale Larson, May 8, 1953; children: Sherrill, Barbara. B.S.C.E., S.D. State U., 1953; M.S.C.E., U. Wyo., 1960, Ph.D. in Civil Engring., 1964. Lic. profl. engr. Wyo. Asst. prof. civil engring. U. Wyo., 1964-66, assoc. prof., 1966-71, prof., 1971—, head dept. atmospheric sci., 1971-76, 77-80, v.p. rsch., 1980-81, acting pres., 1981-82, pres., 1982-87; dir. nat. hail rsch. expt. Nat. Ctr. Atmospheric Rsch., Boulder, Colo., 1976-77, trustee, 1978-90, chmn., 1980-82; commr. Western Interstate Commn. for Higher Edn., Salt Lake City, 1981-87; mem. ROTC adv. com. U.S. Army Command and Gen. Staff Coll., Fort Leavenworth, Kans., 1982-87; dir. Particle Measuring Systems, Inc., Boulder, 1982—, pres., 1987—; dir. First Interstate Bank, Laramie, Wyo., 1974-88; mem. NAS-NRC panel on low-altitude wind variability; mem. NAS-NRC panel on modernization of Nat. Weather Svc. Mem. Brees Field Airport Authority, Laramie, 1962-76; pres. Bress Field Airport Authority, 1964-76; mem. Wyo. Congl. Award Council, 1983; pres. Western Athletic Conf. Found., 1983—. Served to 1st lt. USAF, 1953-57. Recipient Disting. Alumnus award U. S.D., 1983, Medallion Svc. award U. Wyo., 1990. Fellow Am. Meteorol. Soc.; mem. Nat. Soc. Profl. Engrs., Am. Soc. Engring. Edn., ASCE, Weather Modification Assn., N.Y. Acad. Scis., Sigma Xi. Lodge: Rotary (Laramie). Office: Particle Measuring Systems Inc 1855 57th Ct S Boulder CO 80301-2886

VEAL, WILLIAM THOMAS, JR., orthodontist; b. New London, Conn., Mar. 18, 1939; s. William Thomas Sr. and Natalie Whetmore (Borges) V.; m. Cornelia Cron, June 11, 1960 (div. 1964); children: Laird Langhorne, Nancy Lee. BS, U.S. Mil. Acad., 1960; DDS, U. Tenn., 1968; MS in Orthodontics, Loma Linda U., 1971. Artillery officer U.S. Army, 1960-65; orthodontist Oxnard, Calif., 1971—. Lt. col. USAR, 1965—. Mem. ADA, Am. Assn. Orthodontics. Republican. Home: 4181 Ocean Dr Oxnard CA 93035 Office: 951 W 7th St Oxnard CA 93030

VECCI, RAYMOND JOSEPH, airline executive; b. N.Y.C., Jan. 22, 1943; s. Romeo John and Mary (Fabretti) V.; m. Helen Cecelia Clampett, Sept. 3, 1967; children: Brian John, Damon Jay. BBA, CCNY, 1965; MBA, NYU, 1967. Adminstrv. asst. Internat. Air Transport Assn., N.Y.C., 1961-66; econ. analyst United Airlines, Chgo., 1967-74; asst. v.p. planning and regulatory affairs Alaska Airlines Inc., Seattle, 1975-76, staff v.p. planning and regulatory affairs, 1976-79, staff v.p. planning, 1979, v.p. planning, 1979-85, exec. v.p., chief operating officer, 1986-90, pres., chief exec. officer, 1990—; chmn. Alaska Airlines Inc., 1991—; also chmn., pres., chief exec. officer Alaska Air Group Inc. Served with U.S. Army, 1968-69, Vietnam. Decorated Bronze Star. Roman Catholic. Office: Alaska Airlines Inc PO Box 68900 19300 Pacific Hwy S Seattle WA 98188-5303*

VEDVIK, JERRY DONALD, French language educator; b. Madison, Wis., Nov. 4, 1936; s. Andrew and Nellie (Jensen) V.; m. Julie Mia Westerlund, June 14, 1969; children: Kristianna, Erik. BA, U. Wis., 1958; MA, U. Mo., 1962, PhD, 1965. Lectr. U. Mo., Columbia, 1961-65; asst. prof. Ind. U., Bloomington, 1965-69; assoc. prof. George Washington U., Washington, 1969-72; assoc. prof. French Colo. State U., Ft. Collins, 1972—, interim chair Dept. Fgn. Langs. and Cultures, 1992; fgn. campus dir. U.S. Internat. U., San Diego, 1976. Editor: French 17, 1967—. Mem. Poudre R-1 Bd. Edn., Ft. Collins, 1983-92. With U.S. Army, 1959-61. NEH fellow Haverford Coll., 1978. Mem. MLA, Am. Assn. Tchrs. French, Colo. Congress Fgn. Lang. Tchrs. Republican. Lutheran. Office: Colo State U Dept Fgn Langs and Lit Fort Collins CO 80523

VEESART, JANET LYLE, military career officer, engineer; b. Kansas City, Mo., Nov. 10, 1961; d. Ray Malcolm and Emma Lou (Burbank) Lyle; m. Michael Raymond Veesart, Mar. 10, 1985. BSME, Wash. State U., Pullman, 1985; MS in Aero. Engring., Air Force Inst. Tech., 1989; disting. grad., USAF Squadron Officers Sch., 1990. Commd. 2d lt. USAF, 1985—, advanced through grades to capt.; asst. project engr. Advanced Tactical Fighter Engine Program, Wright-Patterson AFB, Ohio, 1985-86; project mgr. Expendable Turbine Engine Concept Program, 1986-87; space launch project engr., project mgr. Advanced Turbine Engine Gas Generator Program, 1987-88; project engr. Titan-Centaur Launch Complex Program, Vandenberg AFB, Calif., 1989-90; project mgr. Centaur Processing Facility Project, Cape Canaveral AFS, Fla., 1990-92; aero. engring. instr. USAF Acad., Colo., 1992—. ROTC scholar USAF, 1982-85, Boeing Co. scholar Wash. State U., 1983, 84. Mem. ASME, Phi Kappa Phi, Tau Beta Pi. Office: DFAN USAF Acad Colorado Springs CO 80840

VEGA, BENJAMIN URBIZO, retired judge; b. La Ceiba, Honduras, Jan. 18, 1916; m. Janie Lou Smith, Oct. 12, 1989; AB, U. So. Calif., 1938, postgrad., 1939-40; LLB, Pacific Coast U. Law, 1941. Bar: Calif. 1947, U.S. Dist. Ct. (so. dist.) Calif. 1947, U.S. Supreme Ct. 1958. Assoc. Anderson, McPharlin & Connors, L.A., 1947-48, Newman & Newman, L.A., 1948-51; dep. dist. atty. County of L.A., 1951-66; judge L.A., County Mcpl. Ct., East L.A. Jud. Dist., 1966-86, retired, 1986; leader faculty seminar Calif. Jud. Coll. at Earl Warren Legal Inst., U. Calif-Berkeley, 1978. Mem. Calif. Gov.'s Adv. Com. on Children and Youth, 1968; del. Commn. of the Califs., 1978; bd. dirs. Los Angeles-Mexico City Sister City Com.; pres. Argentine Cultural Found., 1983. Recipient award for outstanding services from Mayor of L.A., 1973, City of Commerce, City of Montebello, Calif. Assembly, Southwestern Sch. Law, Disting. Pub. Service award Dist. Atty. L.A. Mem. Conf. Calif. Judges, Mcpl. Ct. Judges' Assn. (award for Outstanding Services), Beverly Hills Bar Assn., Navy League, L.A. County, Am. Judicature Soc., World Affairs Council, Pi Sigma Alpha. Home: 101 California Ave Apt 1207 Santa Monica CA 90403-3525

VEGA, JOSE GUADALUPE, psychologist, clinical director; b. San Benito, Tex., June 4, 1953; s. Jose Guadalupe and Bertha (Saenz) V.; m. Beth Susan Brimmer, Aug. 20, 1979 (div. 1986); children: Lilian Anna, Jose Guadalupe III; m. Andrea M. Arnold, Mar. 23, 1988 (div. 1989); m. Alberta L. Valdez,

Oct. 5, 1990. BA, Pan. Am. U., Edinburg, Tex., 1975; MA, U. Denver, 1976, PhD, 1979. Lic. psychologist, Colo., 1983, profl. counselor, Tex., 1982; diplomate Am. Bd. Med. Psychotherapists, Am. Bd. Vocat. Neuropsychology, Am. Bd. Profl. Disability Cons.; cert. adminstrn. Halstead-Reitan Neuropsychology test batteries. With Oasis of Chandala, Denver, 1978-79, Maytag-Emrick Clinic, Aurora, Colo., 1979; psychologist Spanish Peaks Mental Health Ctr., Pueblo, Colo., 1980-85; pvt. practice Assocs. for Psychotherapy and Edn., Inc., 1985-86; co-owner Affiliates in Counseling, Psychol. Assessment and Consultation, Inc., Pueblo, 1986-87; psychologist Parkview Psychol. Testing Clinic, Pueblo, 1987-93; pvt. practice, Pueblo, 1993—; mem. state grievance bd. Psychology Augment Panel, 1988—. Active Colo. Inst. Chicano Mental Health Community Youth Orgn., Boys Club Pueblo. Mem. Am. Psychol. Assn., Nat. Acad. Neuropsychology, Internat. Neuropsychol. Soc., Colo. Neuropsychol. Soc., Am. Assn. for Counseling and Devel., Health and Human Services Com. City of Pueblo, Colo. Psychol. Assn., Nat. Hispanic Psychol. Assn., Phi Delta Kappa, Kappa Delta Pi. Democrat. Roman Catholic. Office: 1624 Bonforte Pueblo CO 81001

VEHAR, GORDON ALLEN, biochemist, researcher; b. Cleve., Apr. 26, 1948; s. Victor Andy and Georgian Marie (Krause) V.; m. Janet Cox, Dec. 30, 1977; 1 child, Kevin Cox. BA, Bowling Green State U., 1970; PhD, U. Cinn., 1976. Postdoctoral fellow U. Wash., Seattle, 1976-80; sr. scientist Genentech Inc., San Francisco, 1980-87, staff scientist, 1987—, dir. cardiovascular rsch. dept., 1986-90. Editor: Thrombosis Rsch., 1986-91; contbr. articles to profl. jours.; patentee in field. Named Inventor of Yr., Intellectual Property Owners, Inc., 1989; recipient Disting. Alumnus award Bowling Green State U., 1987, Murray Thelin award for outstanding rsch. Nat. Hemophilia Found., 1989, Disting. Alumnus award Bowling Green State U., 1987. Mem. Am. Soc. Biochemistry and Molecular Biology. Home: 110 Leslie Dr San Carlos CA 94070-3461 Office: Genentech Inc 460 Point San Bruno Blvd South San Francisco CA 94080-4918

VEIT, WILLIAM ARTHUR, financial planner; b. Altadena, Calif., July 10, 1947; s. Richard Earl and Sally Nell (Brown) V.; m. Maureen Alice Connors, Sept. 13, 1969; children: Stephen, Shereen. BS, Ariz. State U., 1969. Cert. fin. planner. Assoc. v.p. Prudential-Bache, Phoenix, 1983-88; asst. v.p. Kidder, Peabody & Co., Phoenix, 1988-90; v.p. fin. planner Cushman Ramras Cornelius & Crowe, Scottsdale, Ariz., 1990-91; dir., sr. cons. Anasazi Investment Group Inc., Phoenix, 1991—. Coach Little League, Scottsdale, 1979-83, Pop Warner Football, Scottsdale, 1979-82. Mem. Internat. Bd. Cert. Fin. Planners (Phoenix chpt.). Republican. Roman Catholic. Office: Anasazi Investment Group Inc 11801 N Tatum Blvd # 240 Phoenix AZ 85028

VELASCO, JULIO HUMBERTO CRUZ, construction executive; b. Sinaxtla, Oax, Mex., Dec. 22, 1950; came to U.S., 1958; s. Guadalupe Velasco and Guadalupe (Cruz) Lozano; m. Guadalupe Vidal, Sept. 16, 1973 (div. Dec. 1990); children: Isabel, Julio Jr., Gabriel. Owner Creative Interiors, Santa Ana, Calif., 1982-83, Voz Constrn., Santa Ana, Calif., 1984-90, Fiesta Constrn., Santa Ana, Calif., 1990—. Democrat. Roman Catholic. Home: PO Box 178 Santa Ana CA 92702 Office: Fiesta Constrn 110 B E 4th St # 107 Santa Ana CA 92701

VELASQUEZ, THOMAS AQUINAS, English language educator; b. Trinidad, Colo., June 23, 1935; s. Thomas Aquinas and Josephine (Sandoval) V.; m. Ruth Laura Lind, Aug. 14, 1957; children: Laura Lind Velasquez-Murray, Donna Lind Velasquez-Lee. BA, San Francisco State U., 1969, MA, 1970. Hwy. engr.-technician State of Calif. Div. of Hwys., San Francisco, 1954-60, materials engr., surveyor, 1960-68; dir. SB164 program City Coll. San Francisco, 1970-71, prof. English, 1970-91, prof. emeritus, 1992—; staff devel. dir. City Coll. San Francisco, 1986-87; dir. First Stage Reading Co., Daly City, Calif. Author: (reading program) 1st Stage Reading, 1974-91; editor: (monthly mag.) Scootourist, 1964-68. Bd. dirs. Com. for Better Informed Citizens, San Mateo County, Calif., 1974-78. Mem. Internat. Reading Assn., Internat. Soc. of Semantics, Am. Fedn. Tchrs. (exec. v.p. City Coll. San Francisco 1981-83), Bay Area Epson Salts (pres., editor 1988-93). Home: 703 Higate Dr Daly City CA 94015

VELDE, THOMAS JAMES, health facility administrator; b. Pekin, Ill., May 14, 1957; s. Richard Henry and Yvonne Therese (Minnert) V. Student, U. Phoenix, 1992—. Technician U. Ariz. Hosp., Tucson, 1974-77, supr., 1977-80; mgr. Kino Community Hosp., Tucson, 1980-82, dir. materials mgmt., 1982-85, asst. adminstr. materials mgmt., 1985-89, asst. adminstr. support svcs., 1989—. Mem. Health Care Material Mgmt. Soc. (Greater Ariz. chpt., pres. 1986-87, Best Published Article 1988). Democrat. Roman Catholic. Home: 3425 W Greer Rd Tucson AZ 85745-9468 Office: Kino Community Hosp 2800 E Ajo Way Tucson AZ 85713-6204

VELISARIS, CHRIS NICHOLAS, research executive; b. Berwyn, Ill., June 2, 1961; s. Nicholas Chris and Panagiota Nicholas (Georgiou) v. BS, U. Ill., 1983; MS, U. Wash., 1985; MBA, Dartmouth Coll., 1990; postgrad., U. Naples, Italy, 1991-93. Rsch. engr. Amoco Chem. Co., Naperville, Ill., 1983, 85—; cons. Orco Ltd., Athens, 1989; rsch. mgr. U. Wash., Seattle, 1990—; cons. in field. Author: Proc. 31st Ann. Nat. Sampe Symp., 1986, Polymer Engring. and Sci., 1986, 88, Proc. of the 5th European Conf. on Comp. Materials, 1992. Counselor Valleyview Correctional Ctr., Ill. Benedictine Coll., St. Charles, 1988; advisor Jr. Achievement of Chgo., Naperville, 1987-88. Mem. Tri-Orgn. of Amoco Corp. (bd. dirs. 1987-88). Greek Orthodox. Home: 3805 Raymond Ave Brookfield IL 60513 Office: U Wash Dept Chem Engring BF-10 Seattle WA 98195

VELK, ROBERT JAMES, psychologist; b. Chgo., Feb. 27, 1938; s. Jerry E. and Sylvia B. (Wladar) Vlk; m. Vera A. Kraml, Nov. 25, 1961; children—Robert Frank, Cheryl Anne. B.B.A., Northwestern U., 1963, M.B.A., 1968; M.A., Rutgers U., 1980, Ph.D., 1983. Asst. mgr. product decorations Meyercord Co., Carol Stream, Ill., 1959-65, nat. account mgr., 1965-68; assoc. Kepner Tregoe, Inc., Princeton, N.J., 1968-70, Western region mgr., 1970-72, dir. mktg. N.Am. ops., 1972-73; pres. Creative Leadership Inc., Princeton, 1973-83; pres. Cognitive Sci. Corp., Ft. Collins, Colo., 1983—; dir. mgmt. Devel. Ctr. Anderson Sch. Mgmt. U. N.Mex., 1991—. Author: Information and Imagination, 1978; Thinking About Thinking, 1978. Mem. Am. Psychol. Assn., Am. Soc. Tng. and Devel., Nat. Soc. Performance and Instrn., Cognitive Sci. Soc. Clubs: Christian Businessmen's Com. of Central Jersey (chmn. 1974-75), Gideon's. Office: U NM Anderson Grad Sch Mgmt 9440 Callaway Cir NE # NE Univ Of New Mexico NM 87131-1221

VENEKLASEN, LEE HARRIS, physicist; b. Santa Monica, Calif., Oct. 24, 1942; s. Paul Schulke and Louise (Harris) V.; m. Mary Elizabeth Bradley, June 17, 1967; children: Ethan, Noah. BS, MIT, 1964, MS, 1966; PhD, Cornell U., 1970. Physicist Siemens AG, Berlin, 1970-76; sr. scientist ETEC Inst. Co., Hayward, Calif., 1976-87; vis. scientist Tech. U. Clausthal, Clausthal-Zellerfeld, Fed. Republic Germany, 1988-90; sr. scientist KLA Inst. Co., Santa Clara, Calif., 1990-92, Etec Systems Inc., 1992—. Designer numerous electron optical systems; contbr. 25 articles to profl. jours., 2 chpts. to books; patentee in field. Home: 3445 Badding Rd Castro Valley CA 94546 Office: Etec Systems Inc 26460 Corporate Ave Hayward CA 94545

VENEMA, JON ROGER, pastor, educator; b. Modesto, Calif., Apr. 11, 1953; s. Roger Edwin and Marilyn Ailene (Johnson) V.; m. Shelley Elizabeth, Mar. 29, 1974; children: Jordan Christopher Wilder, Susanna Lee. AA, Modesto (Calif.) Jr. Coll., 1974; BA magna cum laude, Simpson Coll., 1976; MDiv, Mennonite Brethren Bibl. Sem., 1980; postgrad., Golden Gate Bapt. Theol. Sem., 1990—. Instr. bibl. and religious studies Fresno Pacific Coll., Modesto, 1980-84; pastor 1st Bapt. Ch., So. San Francisco, 1984—; adj. faculty Fresno Pacific Coll., 1984-87, Simpson Coll., San Francisco, 1987-88; instr. St. James Coll., Pacifica, Calif., 1987-90; adj. prof. Golden Gate Bapt. Theol. Sem., Marin, Calif., 1992, mem. faculty Highland Christian Coll. San Bruno, Calif., 1992-93. Mem. So. San Francisco Ministerium, 1984—. Mem. Soc. Bibl. Lit., Delta Epsilon Chi. Republican. Home: 307 Magnolia South San Francisco CA 94080 Office: 1st Bapt Ch 600 Grand Ave South San Francisco CA 94080

VENKATA, PADMA SUBRAHMANYAM, technical editor, writer; b. Coimbatore, Madras, India, Feb. 5, 1948; came to U.S., 1971; d. Coimbatore Anantanarayan and Sundari (Iyer) Mahadevan; m. Subrahmanyam S. Venkata, Sept. 3, 1971; children: Sridevi S., Harish S. BA in English, Nirmala Coll., Madras, 1969; MA in English, U. Madras, 1971, U. Wash., 1991. Lectr. in English U. Madras, 1971; author, editor Boeing Computer Svcs., Bellevue, Wash., 1989-90; sr. tech. writer, editor, quality assurance engr. Tandem Computers, Inc., Kirkland, Wash., 1991—; editor U. Wash. Elec. Engring., Seattle, 1979—. Editor: Electric Energy and Power Systems, 1985. Mem. Hindu Temple and Cultural Ctr. of the Pacific N.W., Seattle, 1986—. Rhodes scholar, 1971. Mem. Soc. for Tech. Communication. Democrat. Hindu. Home: 14520 183d Ave NE Woodinville WA 98072 Office: Tandem Computers Inc 10210 NE Points Dr Kirkland WA 98033

VENKATESAN, VAIDYANATHAN, finance executive; b. Madras, India, Jan. 30, 1944; came to U.S., 1967; s. Ramaswamy and Swarnam (Subramaniam) V.; m. Sushila Ramadurai, Sept. 15, 1971; children: Priya, Aruna. BS, Indian Inst. Tech., 1966; MS, U. Calif., 1968. Sr. systems analyst Weyerhaeuser Co., Tacoma, 1968-73; mgr. planning, analysis Bendix Forest Products, Martell, Calif., 1973-77; dir. palnning Bendix Forest Products, San Francisco, 1977-80; mgr. econ. planning Potlatch Corp., Spokane, 1980-84; mgr. mktg. Potlatch Corp., Walnut Creek, Calif., 1985-86; pres. Eastern Systems Tech., Campbell, Calif., 1986-87; cons. Pleasanton, Calif., 1987—; bd. dirs. Eastern Systems Tech., 1986-87. Mem. ASME, Rotary. Home and office: 4950 Dolores Dr Pleasanton CA 94566-7666

VENKATESH, ALAGIRISWAMI, cardiologist; b. Madras, Tamilnadu, India, July 4, 1946; came to U.S., 1972; s. Alwar Naicker and Hamsa (Alagarsingari) Alagiriswami; m. Nagammal Sampath, July 15, 1970; 1 child, Sujatha. P.U.C., Madras U., 1962. Intern Jewish Hosp. Bklyn., 1972-73, resident, 1973-75; cardiology fellow U. Wis. Hosps., Madison, 1975-77, U. Iowa Hosps., Iowa City, 1977-78; asst. prof. medicine U. Okla., Oklahoma City, 1978-79; pvt. practice cardiology Encino, Calif., 1979—; asst. clin. prof. medicine UCLA, 1980—. Fellow Am. Coll. Cardiology, Coun. on Geriatric Cardiology (founder). Office: 16133 Ventura Blvd Ste 1015 Encino CA 91436-2085

VENKATRAMANAN, SATHYAMANGALAM RAMASWAMY, computer engineer; b. Dharmapuri, India, Apr. 12, 1952; came to U.S., 1984; s. Sathyamangalam Srinivasan and Seethalakshmi (Mukambeeswara) Ramaswamy; m. Usha Ramachandra Iyers, July 9, 1982; children: Maya, Sahaja, Akshar. BS, Madras U., Tiruchirapalli, India, 1972; B of Engring., Indian Inst. of Sci., Bangalore, 1975, M of Technology, 1977; MS, U. Alberta, 1985. Computer engr./scientist Indian Space Rsch. Orgn., Bangalore, 1977-81; mem. tech. staff Lachman Assocs., Inc., Naperville, Ill., 1984-88; sr. systems engr. Amdahl Corp., Sunnyvale, Calif., 1988-89, staff systems engr., 1989-90, sr. staff systems engr., 1990-92, staff software engr., 1992—; mem. tech. staff-resident visitor AT&T Bell Labs., Naperville, 1986-87. Treas. Alberta Tamil Assn., Edmonton., 1982-83. Mem. IEEE, Assn. Computing Machinery. Office: Amdahl Corp 1250 E Arques Ave Ste 214 Sunnyvale CA 94088-3470

VENNESLAND, BIRGIT, biochemistry educator; b. Kristiansand, Norway, Nov. 17, 1913; came to U.S, 1917; d. Gunnuf Olav and Sigrid Kristine (Brandsborg) V. BS in Biochemistry, U. Chgo., 1934, PhD in Biochemistry, 1938; D.Sc. (hon.), Mt. Holyoke Coll., 1960. Asst. biochemistry U. Chgo., 1938-39; fellow biochemistry Harvard Med. Sch., Boston, 1939-41; instr. biochemistry U. Chgo., 1941-44, asst. prof. biochemistry, 1944-48, assoc. prof. biochemistry, 1948-57, prof. biochemistry, 1957-68; dir. Max-Planck Inst. for Cell Physiology, Berlin, 1968-70; leader Forschungsstelle Vennesland, Berlin, 1970-81; adj. prof. biochemistry and biophysics U. Hawaii, Honolulu, 1986—. Editor: Cyanide in Biology, 1981; contbr. rsch. papers and rev. articles to sci. jours. Study sec. mem. NSF, USPHS, Washington, 1954-63; mem. Wooldridge Com., Washington, 1964. kRecipient Hales award Am. Soc. Plant Physiology, 1950. Fellow AAAS, N.Y. Acad. Scis.; mem. Am. Chem. Soc. (Garvan medal 1964), Am. Soc. Biol. Chemistry, Am. Soc. Plant Physiology. Home: 1206 Mokapu Blvd Kailua HI 96734-1847

VENOSA, ROBERT RENALDO, artist, author; b. N.Y.C., Jan. 21, 1936; s. Joseph E. and Rose A. (Mariconda) V.; m. Edith Strofield (div. 1963); children: Laura, Stephen; m. Jutta S. Cwik, Mar. 21, 1974 (div. Mar. 1990); children: Marcus, Celene, Christan; m. Martina Hoffmann, Nov. 8, 1990. BA, NYU, 1965. Creative dir. CBS, N.Y.C., 1963-65; co-owner, v.p. Forlenza-Venosa Assocs., N.Y.C., 1965-68; owner, pres. Havona Assocs., N.Y.C., 1968-70; design cons. Celestial Seasonings Tea Co., Boulder, Colo., 1971—, Albion Films, Hollywood, Calif., 1992; conceptual designer Paramount Pictures, Hollywood, 1992. One-man shows include Gallery-64, N.Y.C., 1972, Galerie Pietner-Lichtenfels, Vienna, 1973, Kunstmesse, Basel, Switzerland, 1973, 75, Galerie Eichinger, Munich, 1974, Galerie Gerard, Schreiner, Geneve/Basel, 1975, Galerie D'hiver, Monte Carlo, 1976, Galeria Alembic, Cadaques, Spain, 1976, Gallery Husstege, Amsterdam, 1976, Galeria Luna, Cadaques, 1977, Mirandy Gallery, London, 1978, Galeria Sirena, Cadaques, 1979, Castillo de Perelada, Spain, 1981, Galerie Hofstee, Frankfurt, 1982, Angel Art Internat., L.A., 1983, Art Expo, L.A., 1985, Gallery Jessen, Oslo, Norway, 1987, S.F. Art Internat., 1992, Paolo Gallery, San Paolo, Brazil, 1993, Peticov Gallery, Rio de Janiero, 1993, numerous others; represented in permanent collections Ludwig Mus., Cadaques Mus., Galerie Gerard Schreiner, Celestial Seasonings Tea Co., Govinda Gallery, Markus Galleries, Price Gallery, Isis Gallery, Galerie Hofstee, Galerie Eichinger, Galerie De Sacy, numerous other pub. and pvt. collections; numerous reproductions in art books and mags. and prints and posters; numerous TV interviews; more than 50 album cover designs and graphics; author: Manas Manna, 1978, Noospheres, 1992. Recipient Design award N.Y. Art Dirs. Club, N.Y.C., 1968, design/graphics awards, 1970. Fellow Urantia Found. Democrat. Home: 1430 High St Boulder CO 80304

VENTURINI, DONALD JOSEPH, special education educator; b. San Francisco, Feb. 7, 1930; s. Mansueto Giuseppe and Josephine (Ingrassia) V. BA, U. San Francisco, 1954; cert., San Francisco State Coll., 1960, San Francisco State Coll., 1965. Tchr. orthpaedically handicapped Sonoma (Calif.) State Hosp., 1965-83, ret., 1983. Author: Poems of Love and the Sea, 1989, Alexander Glazounov, 1992; freelance sleeve writer for compact discs. Mem. Glazounov Soc. (pres.). Home: 17320 Park Ave Sonoma CA 95476-3447

VERA, RONALD THOMAS, lawyer; b. Pomona, Calif., Oct. 16, 1946; s. Marcelino and Mary (Regaldo) V.; m. Christina Vega, June 10, 1972; children: Noah, Luis, Adam, Paul. BS, Mich. State U., 1970; JD, UCLA, 1973. Bar: Calif., 1974. Atty. Calif. Rural Legal Assistance, El Centro, Calif., 1973-77; dep. dir. Calif. Rural Legal Assistance, San Francisco, 1977-79; staff atty. Mex.-Am. Legal Defense & Ednl. Fund, San Francisco, 1979-85; assoc. scholar Tomas Rivera Ctr. for Policy Studies, Claremont, Calif., 1985-86; ptnr. Barbosa & Vera, L.A., 1986-90; of counsel Best, Best & Krieger, Riverside, Calif., 1990-92. Contbr. articles to Ednl. Jours. Bd. dirs. Contra Costa Pers. Commn., Contra Costa County, Calif., 1984-86, Nat. Ctr. for Fair and Open Testing, Cambridge, Mass., 1986—, Damien Prep. High Sch., La Verne, Calif., 1990—, Pub. Counsel, 1989-92, Pomona Valley Med. Ctr., 1992—. Recipient fellowship NEH, Cambridge, Mass., 1980, Tomas Rivera Ctr. for Policy Studies, Clarement, Calif., 1985-86. Mem.. ABA, L.A. County Bar Assn. Office: Loyola Law School 1441 W Olympic Blvd Los Angeles CA

VERDUGO, JANE M. See ROMJUE, JANE MURPHY

VERHEY, JOSEPH WILLIAM, psychiatrist, educator; b. Oakland, Calif., Sept. 28, 1928; s. Joseph Bernard and Anne (Hanken) V.; BS summa cum laude, Seattle U., 1954; MD, U. Wash., 1958; m. Darlene Helen Seiler, July 21, 1956. Intern, King County Hosp., Seattle, 1958-59; resident Payne Whitney Psychiatric Clinic, N.Y. Hosp., Cornell Med. Center, N.Y.C., 1959-62, U. Wash. Hosp., Seattle, 1962-63; pvt. practice, Seattle, 1963-78; mem. staff U. Providence Hosp., 1963-78, Fairfax Hosp., 1963-78, VA Med. Center, Tacoma, 1978-83, chief inpatient psychiatry sect., 1983—; clin. instr. psychiatry U. Wash. Med. Sch., 1963-68, clin. asst. prof. psychiatry, 1968-82, clin. assoc. prof., 1982—; cons. psychiatry U.S. Dept. Def., Wash. State Bur. Juvenile Rehab.; examiner Am. Bd. Psychiatry and Neurology. Diplomate Am. Bd. Psychiatry and Neurology. Fellow N. Pacific Soc. Psychiatry and Neurology, Am. Psychiat. Assn.; mem. AMA, Am. Fedn. Clin. Rsch., World Fedn. Mental Health, Soc. Mil. Surgeons of U.S., Wash. Athletic Club, Swedish Club (life). Home: 1100 University St Seattle WA 98101-2844 Office: VA Med Ctr Tacoma WA 98493

VERKAMP, JOHN, lawyer, state legislator; b. Grand Canyon, Ariz., July 31, 1940; s. Jack and Mary (O'Leary) V.; m. Linda L. Meline, Sept. 14, 1965; children—Melanie, Jay, Gregory. B.S. in Bus. Adminstrn., U. Ariz., 1962, J.D., 1965. Bar: Ariz. 1965, U.S. Ct. Mil. Appeals 1965, U.S. Supreme Ct. 1973. Dep. county atty. Coconino County, Flagstaff, Ariz., 1970-71, county atty., 1981-92; assoc. Mangum, Wall & Stoops, Flagstaff, 1972-74; ptnr. Verkamp & Verkamp, Flagstaff, 1974-80; assoc. Morgan, Wall, Stoops & Warden, 1993—; mem. governing bd. Ariz. Pros. Attys. Adv. Council, Phoenix, 1981-92, chmn. 1985—. Chmn. Coconino County Republican Com., Flagstaff, 1974-76, Coconino County Legal Aid, 1976-78; vice chmn. Cath. Social Services, 1982-83. Served as capt. JAGC, U.S. Army, 1965-70, Europe. Mem. Nat. Dist. Attys. Assn., Ariz. County Attys. and Sheriffs Assn. (pres. 1985-86), Ariz. Alliance Police Chiefs, Sheriffs and County Attys. (Ariz. County Atty. of Yr. 1985, 87), Ariz. Assn. Counties (pres. 1989), Flagstaff C. of C., Am. Legion. Home: 2620 N Fremont Blvd Flagstaff AZ 86001-1021 Office: Ariz Ho Reps 2620 N Fremont Flagstaff AZ 86001

VERMAAS, SUSAN KIM, casino professional; b. Bossier City, La., Aug. 3, 1964; d. John and Maria Luisa (Uresti) V. BS, Tex. Women's U., 1988. Store activities rep. Haljohn, Inc./McDonald's, Austin, Tex., 1985-87; advt. mgr. Daily Lasso, Denton, Tex., 1987-88; dealer Casino Concepts, Inc., San Padre Island, Tex., 1988-89; customer svc. rep. Desert Inn Hotel and Casino, Las Vegas, Nev., 1990—. Pro-choice adv. Choices, Inc., Las Vegas. Mem. NOW, NAFE, Amnesty Internat. Democrat. Methodist. Office: Desert Inn Hotel and Casino Casino Mktg/Spl Events 3145 Las Vegas Blvd S Las Vegas NV 89109-1916

VERMAAS, WILLEM FREDERIK JOHAN, molecular biologist; b. Rhoon, The Netherlands, June 3, 1959; came to U.S., 1980; s. Arie and Wilhelmina Frederika Johanna (Traas) V.; m. Meintje Klasina Baudina van der Heide, Apr. 10, 1985; 1 child, Joshua Vincent. BS, Agrl. U., Wageningen, Netherlands, 1980, MS, 1982, Doctorate, 1984. Rsch. assoc. U. Ill., Urbana, 1980-81, Mich. State U., East Lansing, 1981-82, T.U., Berlin, 1982-83; scientist Agrl. U., Wageningen, 1983-84; vis. scientist E.I. du Pont de Nemours & Co., Inc., Wilmington, Del., 1984-86; asst. prof. Ariz. State U., Tempe, 1986-90, assoc. prof., 1990—; vis. prof. Stockholm U., 1992-93; lectr. in field. Contbr. articles to profl. jours. Recipient Unilever Chemistry award, 1980, Presdl. Young Investigator award NSF, 1990; DAAD fellowship Deutsche Akademische Austauschdienst, 1982; numerous grants. Mem. AAAS, Internat. Soc. for Plant Molecular Biology (travel grant 1988). Office: Ariz State U Dept of Botany Tempe AZ 85287-1601

VERNA, DONNA JOYCE, paralegal; b. Bend, Oreg., July 16, 1951; d. Donald Ralph Nelson and Esther Isabel (Goff) Kynaston; m. Thomas James Verna, July 17, 1977; children: Jonathan Steele, Kimberly Caroline. AA, Phoenix Coll., 1976; legal asst. cert., Canada Coll., 1983. Legal asst. Arcata Corp., Menlo Park, Calif., 1977-82, Sequoia Assocs., Menlo Park, 1982—. Dir. Schola Cantorum, Mountain View, Calif., 1991. Home: 1449 Ben Roe Ave Los Altos CA 94024 Office: Sequoia Assocs 3000 Sand Hill Rd #2 140 Menlo Park CA 94025

VERNIERO, JOAN EVANS, special education educator; b. Wilkes-Barre, Pa., Nov. 30, 1937; d. Raymond Roth and Cary Hazel (Casano) Evans; m. Daniel Eugene Verniero Jr., Jan. 7, 1956; children: Daniel Eugene III, Raymond Evans. BA, Kean Coll., 1971; MS in Edn. Adminstrn., Monmouth Coll., West Long Branch, N.J., 1974; postgrad., Calif. Coast U., 1986-92. Cert. elem. sch. tchr., cert. spl. edn. tchr.; cert. sch. adminstr., N.J., N.Mex., Colo. Tchr. Children's Psychiat. Ctr., Eatontown, N.J., 1965-69; tchr. Arthur Brisbane Child Treatment Ctr., Farmingdale, N.J., 1969-71, prin., 1971-75; prin. S.A. Wilson Ctr., Colorado Springs, Colo., 1976-82; tchr. pub. schs. Aurora, Colo., 1982-93; retired, 1993; edn. rep. Aurora Pub. Schs. Crew leader Black Forest (Colo.) Rescue Squad, 1979-85, treas., bd. dirs. Fire Protection Dist., 1980-85. Mem. Phi Delta Kappa. Republican. Presbyterian. Home: 671 S Paris St Aurora CO 80012

VERNON, DAVID PAUL, systems engineer; b. N.Y.C., July 31, 1948; s. Chester Millman and Lillian (Rosenfeld) V.; m. Joan Phyllis Satow, Oct. 22, 1988. BS, Pa. State U., 1969; MA, Calif. State U., L.A., 1975; MS, Ind. State U., 1983, PhD, 1984. Tech. writer DPAI, Inc., Beachwood, Ohio, 1985; instr. Sawyer Coll. Bus., Cleveland Heights, Ohio, 1986; sr. analyst Bell Tech. Ops., Tucson, 1987-88; systems analyst Comcon, Inc., Sierra Vista, Ariz., 1989; systems engr. Telos Corp., Sierra Vista, Ariz., 1990—. Author: The Guide to Natural Area Inventory, 1982. Mem. choir Temple Emanuel, Cleve., 1985-86, Temple Emanu-El, Tucson, 1987-90. Ind. State U. fellow, 1979-84. Mem. Sigma Xi. Office: Telos Corp 1865 Paseo San Luis Sierra Vista AZ 85632

VERNON, ROBERT BRIAN, cell biologist; b. Wichita, Kans., Jan. 29, 1954; s. William Burke Sr. and Viola Constance (Forrester) V. AA, Highline Community Coll., 1974; BS magna cum laude, U. Wash., 1977, PhD, 1985. Sr. fellow dept. Biol. Structure Sch. of Medicine U. Wash., Seattle, 1985-89, rsch. asst. prof. cell biology, 1990—. Contbr. articles to profl. jours. Home: 14450 24th Ave S Seattle WA 98168-4202 Office: U Wash Dept Biol Structure Seattle WA 98195

VERONDA, RAYMOND JOSEPH, II, protective services professional; b. Alameda, Calif., May 19, 1946; s. Raymond Joseph and Helen (Cheshier) V. AA, Santa Rosa (Calif.) Jr. Coll., 1989; BA, Sonoma State U., 1992; postrad., Calif. Sch. Profl. Psychology, 1992—. Cert. mgmt. and supervisory devel., cert. EMT-1A, cert. chem. dependency counseling. Firefighter Calif. Dept. Forestry & Fire Protection, Napa County, Yountville, 1970-71, firefighter II, 1971-72, fire apparatus engr., 1972-77, fire capt., 1977—. CPR instr. ARC, Napa, St. Helena; bd. dirs. student union Sonoma State U., Rohnert Park, Calif., 1990-92, bd. dirs. children's sch. governing bd., 1990-92, com. mem. student grievance com. 1990-91, com. mem., student rep. grade appeals com., 1990-91, bd. dirs. inter cultural ctr. adv. bd., 1991-92; adminstrv. v.p., bd. mem. pers. bd. Associated Students-Sonoma State U., Rohnert Park, 1990-91, com. mem. student equity com., 1989-91; co-chair student assn., student rep. campus exec. com., Calif. Sch. Profl. Psychology, 1992—. Recipient Spl. recognition Alpha Gamma Sigma, 1988. Mem. APA (student affiliate), Western Psychol. Assn. (student affiliate), Calif. Dept. Forestry and Firefighters Assn., Internat. Assn. Firefighters, Acad. Mgmt., Amnesty Internat., Sierra Club, Psi Chi (pres. 1989-92, Svc. award 1989, Chpt. Pres. cert. appreciation 1989-92). Democrat. Home: 2447 Jamaica Way San Leandro CA 94577 Office: Napa County Fire 6589 Jefferson St Yountville CA 94599

VEROSUB, KENNETH LEE, geology educator, researcher; b. N.Y.C., July 10, 1944; s. Bernard B. and Vera (Lipman) V.; m. Evelyn Kay Falkenstein, June 15, 1967; children: Abra Laurie, Ellis Marshall. BA, U. Mich., 1966; MS, Stanford U., 1971, PhD, 1973. Asst. prof. Amherst (Mass.) Coll., 1972-75; asst. prof. U. Calif., Davis, 1975-79, assoc. prof., 1979-84, prof., 1984—, chmn. grad. group in earth scis. and resources, 1980-87, faculty asst. to provost, 1992-93; vis. researcher Centre des Faibles Radioactivities, Gif-Sur-Yvette, France, 1982-83; vis. researcher Centre de Geologie et Geophysique, Montpellier, France, 1989-90; vis. prof. Universite des Science et Technique du Languedoc, Montpellier, France, 1989-90. Contbr. articles, abstracts to profl. jours. Bd. dirs. Davis Sci. Ctr., 1983-85. Fellow NSF, 1966, Danforth Found., 1966, Woodrow Wilson Found., 1966; recipient Disting. Teaching award U. Calif.-Davis, 1988; Fulbright fellow, France, 1989-90. Mem. Am. Geophys. Union, Geol. Soc. Am., AAAS, Earthquake Engring. Research Inst. Office: Univ of Calif Davis Dept of Geology Davis CA 95616

VERRONE, PATRIC MILLER, lawyer, writer; b. Glendale, N.Y.C., Sept. 29, 1959; s. Pat and Edna (Miller) V.; m. Margaret Maiya Williams, 1989. BA, Harvard U., 1981; JD, Boston Coll., 1984. Bar: Fla. 1984, U.S. Dist. Ct. (mid. dist.) Fla. 1984, Calif. 1988. Assoc. Allen, Knudsen, Swartz, DeBoest, Rhoads & Edwards, Ft. Myers, Fla., 1984-86; writer The Tonight Show, Burbank, Calif., 1987-90, The Critic, 1993—. Dir., producer, writer The Civil War-The Lost Episode, 1991; writer Basketball, 1992, The Larry Sanders Show, 1992-93, The Critic, 1993—; editor Harvard Lampoon, 1978-

84, Boston Coll. Law Rev., 1983-84, Fla. Bar Jour., 1987-88; contbr. articles to profl. jours. Mem. ABA, Calif. Bar, Calif. Lawyers for Arts, L.A. County Bar Assn. (sec. exec. com., barristers homeless shelter com., chmn. artists and the law com.), Fla. Bar Assn., Writers Guild of Am. West, Harvard Club Lee County (v.p. 1985-86), Harvard Club of So. Calif. Republican. Roman Catholic. Home and Office: 6466 Odin St Los Angeles CA 90068-2730

VERRY, WILLIAM ROBERT, mathematics researcher; b. Portland, Oreg., July 11, 1933; s. William Richard and Maurine Houser (Braden) V.; m. Bette Lee Ronspiess, Nov. 20, 1955 (div. 1981); children: William David, Sandra Kay Verry Londregan, Steven Bruce, Kenneth Scott; m. Jean Elizabeth Morrison, Oct. 16, 1982; step-children: Lucinda Jean Hale, Christine Carol Hale Fortner, Martha Jean Johnson, Brian Kenneth Lackey, Robert Morrison Lackey. BA, Reed Coll., 1955; BS, Portland State U., 1957; MA, Fresno State U., 1960; PhD, Ohio State U.-Columbus, 1972. Instr. chemistry Reedley (Calif.) Coll., 1957-60; ops. research analyst Naval Weapons Center, China Lake, Calif., 1960-63; ordnance engr. Honeywell Ordnance, Hopkins, Minn., 1963-64; sr. scientist Litton Industries, St. Paul., 1964-67; project mgr. Tech. Ops., Inc., Alexandria, Va., 1967-70; research assoc. Ohio State U., Columbus, 1970-72; prin. engr. Computer Sci. Corp., Falls Church, Va., 1972-77; mem. tech. staff MITRE Corp., Albuquerque, 1977-85; C3 program dir., assoc. prof. math. sci. Clemson U., S.C., 1985-87; mgr. simulation and modeling Riverside Research Inst., Rosslyn, Va., 1987-91; mgr. Hillcrest Gardens, Livermore, Calif., 1992—. Founder, minister Christian Love Ctr. Mem. Ops. Research Soc. Am. Home and Office: 550 Hillcrest Ave Livermore CA 94550-3771

VER STEEG, DONNA LORRAINE FRANK, nurse, sociologist, educator; b. Minot, N.D., Sept. 23, 1929; d. John Jonas and Pearl H. (Denlinger) Frank; m. Richard W. Ver Steeg, Nov. 22, 1950; children: Juliana, Anne, Richard B. BS in Nursing, Stanford, 1951; MS in Nursing, U. Calif. at San Francisco, 1967; MA in Sociology, UCLA, 1969, PhD in Sociology, 1973. Clin. instr. U. N.D. Sch. Nursing, 1962-63; USPHS nurse rsch. fellow UCLA, 1969-72; spl. cons., adv. com. on physicians' assts. and nurse practitioner programs Calif. State Bd. Med. Examiners, 1972-73; asst. prof. UCLA Sch. Nursing, 1973-79, assoc. prof., 1979—, asst. dean, 1981-83, chmn. primary ambulatory care, 1976-87, assoc. dean, 1983-86; co-prin. investigator PRIMEX Project, Family Nurse Practitioners, UCLA Extension, 1974-76; assoc. cons. Calif. Postsecondary Edn. Commn., 1975-76; spl. cons. Calif. Dept. Consumer Affairs, 1978; accredited visitor Western Assn. Schs. and Colls., 1985; mem. Calif. State Legis. Health Policy Forum, 1980-81. Contbr. chpts. to profl. books. Recipient Leadership award Calif. Area Health Edn. Ctr. System, 1989; named Outstanding Faculty Mem. UCLA Sch. Nursing, 1982. Fellow Am. Acad. Nursing; mem. AAAS, Am. Pub. Health Assn., Am. Soc. Law and Medicine, Gerontol. Soc. Am., Nat League Nursing, Calif. League Nursing, N.Am. Nursing Diagnosis Assn., Am. Assn. History Nursing, Assn. Health Svcs. Rsch., Am. Nurse Assn., Calif. Nurse Assn. (pres. 1979-81, Jean Sullivan award 1992), Am. Sociol. Assn., Stanford Nurses Club, Sigma Theta Tau, Sigma Xi. Home: 708 Swarthmore Ave Pacific Palisades CA 90272-4353 Office: UCLA Sch Nursing 10833 Le Conte Ave Los Angeles CA 90024-6919

VERTS, LITA JEANNE, university administrator; b. Jonesboro, Ark., Apr. 13, 1935; d. William Gus and Lolita Josephine (Peeler) Nash; m. B. J. Verts, Aug. 29, 1954 (div. 1975); 1 child, William Trigg. BA, Oreg. State U., 1973; MA in Lingustics, U. Oreg., 1974; postgrad., U. Hawaii, 1977. Librarian Forest Research Lab., Corvallis, Oreg., 1966-69; instr. English Lang. Inst., Corvallis, 1974-80; dir. spl. svcs. Oreg. State U., Corvallis, 1980—, faculty senator, 1988—. Editor ann. book: Trio Achievers, 1986, 87, 88; contbr. articles to profl. jours. Precinct com. Rep. Party, Corvallis, 1977-80; adminstrv. bd. 1st United Meth. Ch., Corvallis, 1987-89, mem. fin. com., 1987-93, tchr. Bible, 1978—; adv. coun. Disabilities Svc., Linn, Benton, Lincoln Counties, 1990—, vice chair, 1992-93, chair, 1993—. Mem. N.W. Assn. Spl. Programs (pres. 1985-86), Nat. Coun. Ednl. Opportunities Assn. (bd. dirs. 1984-87), Nat. Gardening Assn., Alpha Phi (mem. corp. bd. Beta Upsilon chpt. 1990—). Republican. Methodist. Home: 530 SE Mayberry Ave Corvallis OR 97333-1866 Office: Spl Svcs Project Waldo 337 OSU Corvallis OR 97331

VERWOLF, WILLIAM JOSEPH, municipal government official; b. Bozeman, Mont., Jan. 28, 1943; s. Joe P. and Elizabeth (Cummings) V.; m. Helen Marie Hendon, Sept. 25, 1971; children: Angela, Curtis, Shelly, Brian. BS in Acctg., Mont. State U., 1966. Fin. dir. City of Bozeman, 1971-74; fin. dir., mgr. Ketchikan (Ala.) Gateway Borough, 1974-77; dir. fin. and adminstrv. services City of Helena, Mont., 1977-85; city mgr. City of Helena, 1985—. Bd. dirs. United Way of Helena, Mont. League of Cities and Towns, Helena Rotary. Served with U.S. Army, 1966-70, Vietnam. Mem. Govt. Fin. Officers Assn., Internat. City Mgrs. Assn. Roman Catholic. Home: 318 Harrison Ave Helena MT 59601-6240 Office: City of Helena 316 N Park Ave Helena MT 59623-0002

VESELY, CHARLES STEVEN, technical safety administrator; b. Bad Connstadt, Germany, July 29, 1953; came to U.S., 1954; s. Carl Dan and Ann Mary (Kish) V.; m. Margaret Arlene Crooks, Nov. 19, 1982. BSChemE, U. Ariz., 1975; MBA, Calif. Luth. U., 1985. Operating team mgr. Procter & Gamble, Oxnard, Calif., 1975-78, project mgr., 1978-88, tech. safety mgr., 1991—; process engr. Procter & Gamble, Iowa City, 1989-91. Republican. Home: 543 Otero Ct Camarillo CA 93010 Office: Procter & Gamble Paper Prod 800 N Rice Ave Oxnard CA 93030

VETTE, DAVID EDWARD, sales executive; b. Grand Rapids, Mich., Mar. 18, 1946; s. Edward F. and Jeannette (Berry) Vette; m. Janet Marie Blank, July 17, 1970. BS, Calif. State Poly. U., 1969. Sales/mgmt. exec. George T. Schmidt Inc., L.A., 1970-80, McMullen Oil Co., Santa Fe Springs, Calif., 1983-88; sales exec. Team Sales, Whittier, Calif., 1980-83; owner, pres. Ettev Enterprises, Inc., Downey, Calif., 1989—. Lt. L.A. County Sheriff Res., 1974—. Mem. Santa Fe Springs C. of C. (past chmn., ambassador), Lincoln Club of L.A. County, Kiwanis (past pres.). Republican. Mem. Ch. of Religious Science. Home: PO Box 3186 Whittier CA 90605-0186 Office: Ettev Enterprises Inc 8645 Florence Ave Downey CA 90240-4032

VETTERLI, DORIS ARLENE, construction company executive; b. Montrose, Colo., July 25, 1941; d. Thalmer Peter and Jina Elizabeth (Coker) Johnson; m. Peter Miles Standish, May 15, 1957 (div.); children: Mary Candace, Janine Sue, Steffani Arlene, Peter Miles Jr.; m. Byron Godfrey Vetterli, June 10, 1979. Cert., Bryman Schs., San Jose, Calif., 1975. Office mgr. Dr. Orhan Oral, Los Gatos, Calif., 1979-81, Dr. Henry Kung, Walnut Creek, Calif., 1981-83; owner, operator Contempo Exec. Computers, Bethel Island, Calif., 1980-84, Seville Enterprises, Palm Desert, Calif., 1978—, R&B Lathing & Plastering, Phoenix, 1983-85, Revelation Beauty Salon, Inc., Phoenix, 1983-85, Vetterli Constrn. Co., Palm Desert, 1985—, Vetterli Plastering Co., Palm Desert, 1985—. Mem. Nat. Assn. Women in Constrn. (sec. 1987—, bd. dirs. 1987—), Scaffold Industry Assn., Desert Contractors Assn., Western Lath, Plaster and Drywall Industries Assn. Republican.

VEZOLLES, JANET LEE, newspaper publisher; b. Evansville, Ind., June 13, 1953. BA in English, Fresno State U., 1990. Commd. USMC, 1977, electronic calibrator, 1977-81; with air ops. USAF, Fresno, Calif., 1982-85; pub., contbr. Sunnyside News, Fresno, 1986—; pres. Sunnyside Bus. Assn., Fresno, 1991-92; owner Cross Country Equestrian Acad. Pres. Patrons for Cultural Arts, Fresno, 1988-90. Mem. MENSA (internat.), U.S. Trotting Assn., Jr. League Fresno. Office: Sunnyside News PO Box 8031 Fresno CA 93747

VIA, CLARENCE WILSON, management consultant; b. Denison, Tex., Sept. 29, 1914; s. Andrew Jackson and Mattie Jewel (Pike) V.; m. Hazelbel Hutchins, June 20, 1942 (div. Oct. 1966); m. Mary Parker, Nov. 1967; children: Lawrence Michael, Melinda Ilene. Grad. high sch., Old Glory, Tex. V.p. Gen. Air Conditioning Corp., Kansas City, Mo., 1936-41; mech. engr. various engring firms, Mo. and N.Mex., 1941-46; pres. Via Devel. Corp., Santa Fe, 1946-66; pvt. practice mgmt. cons. Albuquerque and Mesa, Ariz., 1966—. Chmn. legis. com. Engrs. Wildlife, Santa Fe, 1956-60; candidate gov. N.Mex. State, 1962. With USMM, 1944-45. Mem. NSPE (life), Masons, Elks, Loyal Order of Moose. Republican. Methodist.

VIALLE, KAREN, mayor; b. Tacoma. B in Polit. Sci., U. Puget Sound; postgrad., Wash. State U. Prof. U. Puget Sound Sch. Bus. and Pub. Adminstrn.; adminstrv. asst. dept. city planning City of Tacoma, now mayor; program analyst, asst. dir. Office of Fin. Mgmt., Office of Dep. Commr. and Office of State Ins. Commr. Gov. of Wash. Office: City of Tacoma Office of Mayor 747 Market St Ste 1200 Tacoma WA 98402-3701

VIAR-HOLT, DIXIE FAE, psychotherapist; b. Topeka, Mar. 9, 1936; d. George Raymond and Agnes Fern (Anderson) Viar; m. Wendell Dean Holt, June 1, 1957; children: Steven Dean, Holly Diane. BS in Elem. Ed. with highest honors, Kans. State U., 1957; MA in Psychology Counseling with honors, U. No. Colo., 1971; postgrad., Menninger Sch. of Psychiatry and Mental Health Scis. in Psychotherapy, 1986-88. Tchr. homebound pupils Dist. 50 Schs., Westminster, Colo.; treas., fundraiser, bd. dirs. Adams County Community Ctr for Retarded Citizens, Denver; pvt. practice psychotherapist Westminster; adj. prof., coord. counseling dept internships Denver Sem. Patron Menninger Found. Mem. Am. Counseling Assn., Christian Assn. for Psychol. Studies, Phi Kappa Phi. Home: 900 W 79th Pl Denver CO 80221-3751

VICE, CHARLES LOREN, electro-mechanical engineer; b. LaVerne, Okla., Jan. 2, 1921; s. Cyrus Christopher and Ethel Segwitch (Hoy) V.; m. Katherine Margaret Maxwell, July 14, 1949; children: Katherine Lorene, Charles Clark, Ann Marie. Cert., Oreg. State U., 1944, BSME, 1947; postgrad., U. So. Calif., 1948-55. Registered profl. engr., Calif. Mgr. magnetic head div. Gen. Instrument Corp., Hawthorne, Calif., 1959-62; sr. staff engr. magnetic head div. Ampex Corp., Redwood City, Calif., 1962-66; chief mech. engr. Collins Radio Corp., Newport Beach, Calif., 1967-69; pres. FerraFlux Corp., Santa Ana, Calif., 1970-78; sr. staff engr. McDonnell Douglas Computer Systems Co., Irvine, Calif., 1979-89, Santa Ana, Calif., 1989; ret. McDonnell Douglas Computer Systems Co., 1989; cons. Teac Corp. Japan, 1974-78, Otari Corp. Japan, 1975-77, Univac Corp., Salt Lake City, 1975-76, Crown Radio Corp. Japan, 1979-80, Sabor Corp. Japan, 1982, Empire Corp., Tokyo, 1987-89, DIGI SYS Corp., Fullerton, Calif., 1988-89, Puritan Bennett Aerosystems, El Segundo, Calif., 1989—. Patentee in field. Served with U.S. Army Engrs., 1943-46. Decorated Bronze Star. Mem. NSPE. Republican. Club: Toastmasters. Home: 5902 E Bryce Ave Orange CA 92667-3305 Office: Precision Cons Inc 5902 E Bryce Ave Orange CA 92667-3305

VICINO, FRANK LEO, experimental psychologist; b. N.Y.C., Jan. 20, 1935; s. Gene and Lena (Buda) V.; m. Esta Skelly, June 17, 1958 (div.); children: Gene, Mitchell; m. E. Byars Mathewson, Aug. 13, 1971; children: F. Scott, Dawn Lena, Gregory Anderson. BA, Hunter Coll., 1958; MS, U. Md., 1962; postgrad., George Washington U., 1962-63; EdD, Western Colo. U., 1977. Rsch. asst. U. Md., 1958-62; exptl. psychologist VA Hosp., Martinsburg, W.Va., 1958-61; project dir. U.S. Army Pers. Rsch. Office, Washington, 1962-66; project chief psychologist Litton Sci. Support Lab., Ft. Ord, Calif., 1966-68, mgr. project scis. sect., 1968-71; evaluation specialist, site team Ohio State U., Mesa, Ariz., 1971-72; dir. rsch. and evaluation Mesa Pub. Schs., 1972-81; exec. dir., cons. for rsch. and explt. design Info. Analysis Assocs., Mesa, 1975-81; dir. div. applied testing USN Pers. R & D Ctr., San Diego, 1989—; prof. Nat. Acad. Sch. Execs.; instr. Hist. Perspectives Inst., San Diego, 1985—, North County Arts Coun., San Diego, 1991—. Contbr. chpt. to book, numerous articles to profl. jours. Vice chmn. bd. dirs. Interfaith Counseling Svcs., Scottsdale, Ariz., 1977-78; founder, exec. dir. Argosy Fine Arts, San Diego, 1979—. Mem. AAAS, APA, Am. Ednl. Rsch. Assn. (program chmn. Div. H. 1979, 81, editor PrePost Press 1979—), New England Appraiser's Assn., D.C. Psychol. Assn., Washington D.C. Print Soc., San Diego Mus. Art Prints and Drawings Soc., Albany Print Club, N.W. Print Coun., Western Psychol. Assn., Human Factors Soc., Nat. Acad. Sch. Adminstrs., Adminstrs. Curriculum and Tech. Svc. (chpt. pres.), Psi Chi. Home: 1045 Novara St San Diego CA 92107 Office: USN Pers R & D Ctr San Diego CA 92152

VICK, GINA MARIE, environmental communications consultant; b. Colorado Springs, Colo., June 14, 1968; d. Edward Eugene and Shirley Maxine (Scarafiotti) V. BA, U. Denver, 1990, postgrad, 1990—; cert. in pub. rels., 1992. From reporter to mng. editor The Clarion, Denver, 1987-90; adminstrv. asst. Poulson, Odell & Peterson, Denver, 1990—; intern State of Colo. Internat. Trade Office, Denver, 1990. Contbg. author: (poetry anthology) The American Muse, 1986. Chmn. Residence Hall Jud. Coun. U. Denver, 1987; co-founder Symposium Group, Denver, 1988; active LWV, Colo., 1992; mem. environ. health com. Colo. Environ. Coalition, Denver, 1992—. Mem. Sierra Club.

VICKER, RAY, writer; b. Wis., Aug. 27, 1917; s. Joseph John and Mary (Young) V.; m. Margaret Ella Leach, Feb. 23, 1944. Student, Wis. State U., Stevens Point, 1934, Los Angeles City Coll., 1940-41, U.S. Mcht. Marine Officers' Sch., 1944, Northwestern U., 1947-49. With Chgo. Jour. Commerce, 1946-50, automobile editor, 1947-50; mem. staff Wall St. Jour., 1950-83; European editor Wall St. Jour., London, Eng., 1960-75. Author: How an Election Was Won, 1962, Those Swiss Money Men, 1973, Kingdom of Oil, 1974, Realms of Gold, 1975, This Hungry World, 1976, Dow Jones Guide to Retirement Planning, 1985, The Informed Investor, 1990; also numerous articles. Served with U.S. Merchant Marine, 1942-46. Recipient Outstanding Reporting Abroad award Chgo. Newspaper Guild, 1959; Best Bus. Reporting Abroad award E. W. Fairchild, 1963, 67; hon. mention, 1965; Bob Considine award, 1979; ICMA Journalism award, 1983. Mem. Soc. Profl. Journalists, Authors Guild. Roman Catholic. Clubs: Overseas Press (Reporting award 1963, 67) (N.Y.C.); Press (Chgo.). Home and Office: 4131 E Pontatoc Canyon Dr Tucson AZ 85718-5227

VICKERMAN, SARA ELIZABETH, ecology organization executive; b. Aspen, Colo., Sept. 20, 1949; d. Harry Edwin and Sarah Elizabeth (Forbes) V.; m. Charles Polenick, Feb. 5, 1972 (div. Feb. 1982). AA, Fullerton (Calif.) Jr. Coll., 1969; BS in Anthropology, Calif. State U., Fullerton, 1972; MS in Biology Geography Edn., So. Oreg. State Coll., 1974. Tchr. Medford (Oreg.) Sch. Dist., 1974-78; N.W. field rep. Defenders of Wildlife, Salem, Oreg., 1978-82; legis. dir. Defenders of Wildlife, Washington, 1982-84; dir. state conservation programs Defenders of Wildlife, Washington, Portland (Oreg.), 1984—; mem. adv. coun. Bur. Land Mgmt., Medford, 1978-80; chairperson adv. coun. Oreg. Dept. Fish and Wildlife; mem. Oreg. State Parks and Recreation Commn., 1992—. Bd. dirs. Oreg. League Conservation Voters. Mem. Soc. for Conservation Biology, Nat. Audubon Soc., The Nature Conservancy. Democrat. Office: Defenders of Wildlife 0434 SW Iowa St Portland OR 97201-3626

VICKERS, BILLY JACK, automotive industry executive; b. Mt. Pleasant, Tex., July 11, 1957; s. T. O. and Norma Vickers; m. Anita Clare Green, Aug. 8, 1980. BS in Automotive Engring., Weber State Coll., 1982. Zone mgr. Ford Motor Co., Milpitas, Calif., 1982-85; dist. mgr. Chrysler Corp., Pleasanton, Calif., 1985, 89-91; customer satisfaction mgr. Chrysler Corp., Pleasanton, 1985-89; dist. mgr. Chrysler Corp., Salt Lake City, 1991—. Scouting coord. LDS Ch./Boy Scouts Am., San Jose, Calif., 1989-91, varsity team coach, Salt Lake City, 1992—. Recipient Duty to God award LDS Ch., Denver, 1973, Eagle scout Boy Scouts Am., Denver, 1974, On My Honor award LDS Ch., San Jose, 1990. Mem. Soc. Automotive Engrs. (assoc.), Inst. for Automotive Svc. Excellence (master technician). Home: 90 W Rosewood Circle Centerville UT 84014-1168 Office: Chrysler Corp Phoenix Zone Ste 4025 11811 N Tatum Blvd Phoenix AZ 85028-1627

VICKERS, ROBERT ARTHUR, chemist, consultant; b. Hardin, Mont., Aug. 9, 1918; s. Robert Arthur and Myrla (Hogoboom) V.; m. Catherine Anne Fay, Aug. 22, 1942; children: Leo Robert, Catherine Anne Brown. BA in Chemistry, U. Mont., 1947. Rsch. chemist Nat. Bur. Standards, Washington, 1947-49; rsch. assoc. U. Cin., 1949-51; materials engr. Gates Rubber Co., Denver, 1951-55, Boeing Airplane Co., Seattle, 1955-77; tech. dir. Scougal Rubber Corp., Seattle, 1977-83; cons., 1984—. Contbr. articles to profl. jours. Lt. (j.g.) USN, 1941-45, MTO, PTO. Mem. Am. Chemical Soc. (mem. rubber divsn., emeritis), Explosive Ordinance Disposal Assn. (hon.), VFW (life). Home: 11838-77th Ave S Seattle WA 98178-3808

VICKERY, BYRDEAN EYVONNE HUGHES (MRS. CHARLES EVERETT VICKERY, JR.), library services administrator; b. Belleview, Mo., Apr. 18, 1928; d. Roy Franklin and Margaret Cordelia (Wood) Hughes; m. Charles Everett Vickery, Jr., Nov. 5, 1948; 1 dau., Camille. Student, Flat River (Mo.) Jr. Coll., 1946-48; B.S. in Edn., S.E. Mo. State Coll., 1954; M.L.S., U. Wash., 1964; postgrad. Wash. State U., 1969-70. Tchr. Ironton (Mo.) Pub. Schs., 1948-56; elem. tchr. Pasco (Wash.) Sch. Dist. 1, 1956-61, jr. high sch. libr., 1961-68, coord. librs., 1968-69; asst. libr. Columbia Basin Community Coll., Pasco, 1969-70, head libr., dir. Instructional Resources Ctr., 1970-78, dir. libr. svcs., 1979-87, assoc. dean libr. svcs., 1987-90, retired, 1990; owner Vickery Search & Research, 1990—; chmn. S.E. Wash. Libr. Svc. Area, 1977-78, 88-90. Bd. dirs. Pasco-Kennewick Community Concerts, 1977-88, pres., 1980-81, 87-88, Pasco-Kennewick Community Concerts, treas., 1991—; bd. dirs. Mid-Columbia Symphony Orch., 1983-89; trustee Wash. Commn. Humanities, 1982-85; bd. mem. Arts Coun. Mid-Columbia Region, 1991-93. Author, editor: Library and Research Skills Curriculum Guides for the Pasco School District, 1967; author (with Jean Thompson), also editor Learning Resources Handbook for Teachers, 1969. Recipient Woman of Achievement award Pasco Bus. and Profl. Women's Club, 1976. Mem. ALA, AAUW (2d v.p. 1966-68, corr. sec. 1969), Wash. Dept. Audio-Visual Instrn., Wash. Libr. Assn., Am. Assn. Higher Edn., Wash. Assn. Higher Edn., Wash. State Assn. Sch. Librs. (state conf. chmn. 1971-72), Tri-Cities Librs. Assn., Wash. Libr. Media Assn. (community coll. levels chmn. 1986-87), Am. Assn. Rsch. Libr., Soroptimist Internat. Assn. (rec. sec. Pasco-Kennewick chpt. 1971-72, treas. 1973-74, pres. 1978-80, v.p. 1989-90, treas. 1991), Columbia Basin Coll. Adminstrs. Assn. (sec.-treas. 1973-74), Pacific N.W. Assn. Ch. Libr., Women in Communications, Pasco Bus. and Profl. Women's Club, PEO, Beta Sigma Phi, Delta Kappa Gamma, Phi Delta Kappa (sec. 1981-82, Outstanding Educator award 1983). Home: 4016 W Park St Pasco WA 99301-2936

VICKERY, MELBA, retired nurse anesthetist, nursing consultant; b. Granite City, Ill., Jan. 28, 1925; d. George Abert and Eulah Edna (Hunt) Reis; m. Walter C. Kawelaske, Oct. 25, 1969 (dec. Mar. 1975); m. Earl Clark Vickery, June 13, 1979. Diploma summa cum laude, St. Elizabeth Hosp. Sch. Nursing, Granite City, 1949; BS in Nursing Edn. cum laude, St. Louis U., 1951; diploma summa cum laude, Barnes Hosp. Anesthesia Sch., 1958. RN., Mo., Ill.; cert. RN Anesthetist Am. Assn. Nurse Anesthetists. Dir. nursing edn., research and service St. Elizabeth Hosp., Granite City, 1951-55; instr. clin. anesthesia Barnes Hosp. Group, St. Louis, 1958, 65-68; anesthetist Greater St. Louis Hosps., 1965-79; cons. patient care Hope Clinic Women, Granite City, 1975—; writer, portait artist free lance, Sierra Vista, Ariz., 1983—; speaker meetings Nurse Anesthetists, Iowa, Ill., Mo., 1965-79, Am. Soc. Clin. Hypnosis, 1963-75, speaker continuing med. edn. program (video) U. Pitts., 1992. Author: Introducing Patients to Med. Procedures, 1950's; author hosp. cartoon book, 1950's; contbr. articles to profl. jours.; inventor in field. Vol. Civil Def. Nursing, Granite City, 1940's; vol. Jane Goodall Inst. for Wildlife Rsch., Edn. and Conservation; pioneered Inservice Nursing Edn. Svcs., Gianite City, 1950. Home and Office: PO Box 872 Sierra Vista AZ 85636-0872

VICTOR, JAMES, actor; b. Santiago, Dominican Republic, July 27, 1939; came to U.S., 1945; s. Rafael and Julia (Diaz) Peralta. Grad. high sch., N.Y.C.; student, Actors Studio West. Appeared on stage in Bullfight, Ceremony for and Assassinated Blackman, Latina (L.A. Drama-Logue Critics award 1980), The Man in the Glass Booth, The M.C. (Drama-Logue Critics & Cesar best actor awards 1985), I Gave You a Calendar (Drama-Logue Critics award 1983), I Don't Have to Show You No Stinking Badges (Drama-Logue Critics award 1986); appeared in films Fuzz, Rolling Thunder, Boulevard Nights, Defiance, Losin' It, Borderline, Stand and Deliver; TV appearances include (series) Viva Valdez, Condo, I Married Dora, Angelica Mi Vida, The New Zorro, Mug Shot (Cleo award 1975), (movies for TV) Robert Kennedy and His Times, Twin Detectives, The Hound of Hell, Remington Steel, The Streets of L.A., I, Desire, Second Serve, Grand Slam, also numerous specials. Recipient Golden Eagle award for consistent outstanding performances in motion pictures, Nosotros Orgn., 1981. Mem. AFTRA, SAG, Acad. Motion Picture Arts & Scis. (actors br.), Actors Equity Assn.

VICTORS, ALEXIS PETER, real estate executive; b. San Francisco, Sept. 13, 1937; s. Peter and Alexandra Victors; m. Joan Diane Whitham, June 12, 1960; children: Gregory, Mark, Charissa, Katherine. BS in Engring. and Physics, U. Calif., Berkeley, 1960; MSME, Stanford U., 1966. Lic. broker, Calif. Engring. trainee Boeing Co., Seattle, 1959; design engr. United Techs., Sunnyvale, Calif., 1962-66; engr. project mgr. Gen. Motors Corp., Santa Barbara, Calif., 1966-72; from market mgr. to sr. v.p. Western Pacific R.R. Co., San Francisco, 1972-82; pres. Standared Realty and Devel. Co., 1973-82; from exec. v.p. to pres. Upland Industries Corp., Omaha, 1982-87; prin. Victors & Assocs., Portola Valley, Calif., 1987—; cons. in field. Contbr. articles to profl. jours. Served with USNR, 1960-62. Mem. Am. Soc. Real Estate Counselors, Soc. Ind. Realtors, Nat. Assn. Indsl. and Office Pks., Urban Land Inst. (exec. chmn. edn. com., ex-trustee). Clubs: Bankers (San Francisco); Happy Hollow (Omaha). Office: 5 Applewood Ln Portola Valley CA 94028

VIDOLI, VIVIAN ANN, biology educator, university dean; b. Bridgeport, Conn., Nov. 2, 1941; d. Walter and Ann (Carnicky) V. BA in Biology, So. Conn. State Coll., New Haven, 1963; MS in Zoology, Ariz. State U., 1966, PhD in Zoology, 1969. Asst. prof. biology Calif. State U., Fresno, 1970-74, assoc. prof., 1974-78, asst. dir. div. health professions, 1975-76, dean div. grad. studies, 1976—; vis. prof. biology Ariz. State U., Tempe, 1970-74; chair svcs. com. Grad. Record Exam., Princeton, N.J., 1991, chair bd. dirs. Coun. Grad. Schs., Washington, 1987-88, chair exec. com., 1988-89; chair bd. Grad. Record Examinations, 1993. Mem. nat. pub. affairs com. YWCA, Fresno, 1990-91; bd. dirs. Vol. Bur., Fresno, 1992-93; mem. Calif. Student Aid Commn. Sacramento, 1988-92. Mem. AAAS, AAUW, LWV, Am. Assn. for Higher Edn., Women's Coun. of the State U., Calif. Elected Women's Assn. for Edn. and Rsch. Office: Calif State U Fresno 5241 N Maple Ave Fresno CA 93740-0051

VIDT, KARL JOHN, architect; b. Pitts., June 11, 1955; s. John Robert and Lois Ruth (Baum) V. BS in Architecture with honors, Calif. Polytechnic State U., 1978. Registered architect, Calif. Mgr. Yosemite Park (Calif.) and Curry Co., 1975-78; architect MBA Architects (Marvin Bamburg Assocs.), San Jose, Calif., 1979—. Bd. dirs., v.p. San Jose Symphonic Choir, 1989-92; bd. dirs., clk. Met. Community Ch., 1985—. Named Vol. of Yr. Met. Community Ch., San Jose, 1991. Mem. AIA, Silicon Valley Bus. Assn. (founding mem., sec. 1991—). Democrat. Home: 251 N 14th St San Jose CA 95112 Office: MBA Architects 1176 Lincoln Ave San Jose CA 95125

VIERHELLER, TODD, software engineering consultant; b. Winter Park, Fla., June 22, 1958; s. Irvin Theodore and Jeanne Marie (Zeller) V.; m. Susan Lindhe Watts, Dec. 22, 1984; children: Renate Jeanne, Clark, Lindhe Marie. BS in Computer Sci., U. Mo., Rolla, 1980; MA in Bibl. Studies, Multnomah Sch. Bible, Portland, Oreg., 1986. Tech. writer, software engr. Tektronix, Beaverton, Oreg., 1981-86, software engring. mgr., 1988-89; software engr., supr. Intel Corp., Hillsboro, Oreg., 1986-88; software engring. mgr. Summation, 1989-90; software cons. Quality First, Lynnwood, Wash., 1990—; software engring. cons. Digital Equipment Corp., Bellevue, Wash., 1990-91, GTE, Bothell, Wash., 1990-91, Frank Russell Co., Tacoma, Wash., 1992-93; software engring. mgmt. cons. Weyerhauser, Federal Way, Wash., 1991-92. Mem. IEEE, Profl. Photographers Am., Nat. Assn. Realtors, Upsilon Pi Epsilon, Kappa Mu Epsilon. Republican. Mem. Evang. Christian Ch. Home: 22810 25th Ave W Lynnwood WA 98036 Office: Quality First PO Box 6212 Lynnwood WA 98036

VIERLING, JOHN MOORE, physician; b. Bellflower, Calif., Nov. 20, 1945; s. Lester Howard and Ruth Ann (Moore) V.; m. Gayle Aileen Vandermast, June 30, 1968 (div. 1984); children: Jeffrey M., Janet A; m. Donna Marie Sheps, May 4, 1985; children: Matthew R., Mark L. AB in Biology with great distinction, Stanford U., 1967, MD, 1972. Intern then resident Strong Meml. Hosp. U. Rochester, N.Y., 1972-74; clin. assoc. liver unit NIH, Bethesda, Md., 1974-77; gastroenterology fellow U. Calif., San Francisco, 1977-78, instr. medicine, 1978-79; from asst. to assoc. U. Colo. Sch. Medicine, Denver, 1979-90; dir. hepatology, med dir. liver transplantation Cedars-Sinai Med. Ctr., L.A., 1990—; assoc. prof. medicine UCLA, 1990—; lectr. Schering Corp., Kenilworth, N.J., 1990—. Assoc. editor: Prinicples and Practice of Gastroenterology and Hepatology, 1992; editorial bd. Hepatology, 1985-90, Gastroenterology, 1993—; co-patentee in hybridization assay for hepatitis virus, 1992. With USPHS, 1974-77. Fellow ACP; mem. Am. Assn. Study Liver Diseases, Am. Gastoenterological Assn., Internat. Asn. for Study Liver, European Assn. for Study Liver. Office: Cedars-Sinai Med Ctr Hepatology Dept 8700 Beverly Blvd Los Angeles CA 90048

VIG, BALDEV KRISHAN, genetics educator, researcher; b. Lyalpur, Punjab, India, Oct. 1, 1935; came to U.S., 1964; s. Behari Lal and Sheela Wanti (Watta) V.; m. Gargi Dilawari, Dec. 13, 1964; children: Anjana, Pamela. BS, Khalsa Coll., Amritsar, India, 1957; MS, Punjab U., 1961; PhD, Ohio State U., 1967. Diplomate Am. Bd. Med. Genetics. Cytogeneticist Children's Hosp., Columbus, Ohio, 1967-68; asst. prof. U. Nev., Reno, 1968-72, assoc. prof., 1972-78, prof. genetics, 1978—, chmn. biology dept., 1985-88; pvt. practice med. genetics Reno, 1982-87; Dir. genetics program State of Nev., Reno, 1975-81; panel mem. environ. biology EPA, Washington, 1983-93; chmn. Somatic Cell Genetics, 1982, internat. conf. Aneuploidy, 1989; dir. NATO, ARW on Chromosome Segregation and Aneuploidy, 1992. Recipient Outstanding Researcher award Grad. Sch. U. Nev., 1979; D.F. Jones fellow, 1974-75, 91, 92, Alexander von Humboldt Found. fellow, 1975, 92, Deutscher Akademischer Austauschdienst fellow, 1985, German Cancer Rsch. Ctr. fellow, 1987, 88, 89, 91, 93, U. Wurzburg fellow, 1990, 91, 92; named U. Nev. Found. Prof., Reno, 1986-89. Mem. Genetics Soc. Am., Am. Soc. Human Genetics, Genetics Soc. Can., Sigma Xi, Phi Kappa Phi. Democrat. Hindu. Office: U Nev Dept Biology Reno NV 89557

VIGIL, CHARLES S., lawyer; b. Trinidad, Colo., June 9, 1912; s. J.U. and Andreita (Maes) V.; m. Kathleen A. Liebert, Jan. 2, 1943; children: David Charles Edward, Marcia Kathleen. LL.B., U. Colo., 1936. Bar: Colo. 1936. Dep. dist. atty. 3d Jud. Dist. Colo., 1937-42, asst. dist. atty., 1946-51; U.S. atty. Dist. Colo., 1951-53; pvt. practice law Denver.; Dir., sec. Las Animas Co. (Colo); ARC. Author: Saga of Casimiro Barela. Bd. dirs. Family and Children's Svc. Denver, Colo. Humane Soc., Animal Rescue Soc., Auraria Community Ctr.; mem. Bishop's com. on housing; Dem. candidate for U.S. Congress, 1988. Lt. USCG, 1942-46. Recipient award of civil merit Spain, 1960, award of civil merit Colo. Centennial Expn. Bd., 1976; award Colo. Chicano Bar Assn., 1979. Mem. Internat. Law Assn., ABA, Fed. Bar Assn., Colo. Bar Assn. (bd. govs.), So. Colo. Bar Assn., Hispanic Bar Colo. (bd. dirs.), Am. Judicature Soc., Internat. Bar Assn., Inter-Am. Bar, V.F.W. (comdr.), Am. Legion (comdr.), Nat. Assn. Def. Lawyers, Assn. Trial Lawyers Am., Lambda Chi Alpha, Elks, Eagles, Cootie. Home: 1085 Sherman St Denver CO 80203-2880 Office: 1715 Colo State Bank 1600 Broadway Denver CO 80202

VIGIL, DANIEL AGUSTIN, assistant dean; b. Denver, Feb. 13, 1947; s. Agustin and Rachel (Naranjo) V.; m. Claudia Cartier. BA in History, U. Colo., Denver, 1978, JD, 1982. Bar: Colo. 1982, U.S. Dist. Ct. Colo. 1983. Project mgr. Mathematics Policy Rsch., Denver, 1978; law clk. Denver Dist. Ct., 1982-83; ptnr. Vigil and Bley, Denver, 1983-85; asst. dean sch. law U. Colo., Boulder, 1983-89; assoc. dean sch. law U. Colo., 1989—; apptd. by chief justice of Colo. Supreme Ct. to serve on Colo. Supreme Ct. Ad Hoc Com. on miniority participation in legal profession; adj. prof. U. Colo. Sch. Law; bd. dirs. Continuing Legal Edn. in Colo., Inc.; mem. Gov. Colo. Lottery Commn. Editor (newsletter) Class Action, 1987-88; co-editor (ethics com. column) Colo. Lawyer. Bd. dirs. Legal Aid Soc. Met. Denver, 1986—; past v.p. Colo. Minority Scholarship Consortium, pres., 1990-91; mem. Task Force on Community Race Rels., Boulder, 1989—; past mem. jud. nomination rev. com. U.S. Senator Tim Wirth. Mem. Colo. Bar Assn. (mem. legal edn. and admissions com. 1989—, chmn. 1989-91, bd. govs. 1991), Hispanic Nat. Bar Assn. (chmn. scholarship com. 1990—), Colo. Hispanic Bar Assn. (bd. dirs. 1985-89, pres. 1990), Denver Bar Assn. (joint com. on minorities in the legal profession), Boulder County Bar Assn. (ex-officio mem., trustee), Phi Delta Phi (faculty sponsor). Roman Catholic. Home: 4415 Laguna Pl Apt 209 Boulder CO 80303-3784 Office: U Colo Sch Law Campus Box 401 Boulder CO 80309-0401

VIGIL, DAVID CHARLES, lawyer; b. Bklyn., Jan. 29, 1944; s. Charles S. and Kathleen A. (Liebert) V. B.A., U. Colo., 1966; J.D., U. N.Mex., 1969. Bar: Colo. 1969, U.S. Dist. Ct. Colo. 1969, U.S. Ct. Appeals (10th cir.) 1969, U.S. Supreme Ct. 1974. Sole practice, Denver, 1969-80; ptnr. Vigil & Vigil, Denver, 1980—. Nat. Inst for Trial Advocacy grantee, 1983. Mem. ABA, Colo. Bar Assn. (ethics com. 1973-79, legal fee arbitration com. 1980—), Denver Bar Assn. (jud. selection and benefits com. 1975—, chmn. 1988-90), Assn. Trial Lawyers Am., Assn. Trial Lawyers Colo., Colo. Hispanic Bar Assn. (bd. dirs. 1986-89, treas. 1988), Cath. Lawyers Guild, NITA Advocates Assn. Democrat. Roman Catholic. Clubs: Columbine County (Littleton, Colo.). Lodge: Elks. Office: Vigil & Vigil Colo State Bank Bldg Suite 1715 Denver CO 80202

VIGIL, EDWARD FRANCIS, finance company executive; b. Raton, N.Mex., Aug. 9, 1964; s. Frank Cecilio and Veronica Catherine (Tafoya) V. Student, UCLA, 1984-87. Analyst The Adrogan Group, L.A., 1982-86, jr. ptnr., 1986-88; ptnr. The Adrogan Group, Albuquerque and L.A., 1988—. Mem. Rep. Nat. Com., Washington, 1984—; bd. dirs. Norman Topping Scholarship Fund U. So. Calif., L.A., 1982-83. Baptist. Office: The Adrogan Group 632 Burma Dr NE Albuquerque NM 87123-1409

VIGIL, MAURILIO EUTIMIO, political science educator; b. Las Vegas, N.Mex., Aug. 30, 1941; s. Melecio and Juanita (Lopez) V.; m. Alberta Gonzales, July 3, 1965; children: David, Teresa, Daniel. BA, N.Mex. Highlands, 1964, MA, 1966; PhD, U. N.Mex., 1974. Prof. polit. sci. N.Mex. Highlands U., Las Vegas, 1972—. Author: Chicano Politics, 1978; The Hispanics of New Mexico, 1984, Hispanics in American Politics, 1987, Los Patrones: Profiles of Hispanic Leaders, 1980, New Mexico Government and Politics, 1990—; contbr. articles to profl. jours. 1st lt. U.S. Army, 1966-69. Mem. Western Polit. Sci. Assn., Western Social Sci. Assn., Nat. Assn. Chicano Studies, Phi Kappa Phi, Pi Gamma Mu. Democrat. Roman Catholic. Home: 702 Kay Lynn Dr Las Vegas NM 87701-5118 Office: NMex Highlands U University Ave Las Vegas NM 87701-4347

VIGLIONE, EUGENE LAWRENCE, automotive executive; b. Paterson, N.J., Nov. 23, 1931; s. Fred and Caroline (Cantilina) V.; m. Vera Yonkens, June 12, 1954 (div. June 1976), m. Evila (Billie) Larez Viglione, Sept. 19, 1976; children: Victoria, David, Valerie, Vanessa, Francine, Margaret, Robert. Student, Cooper Union, N.Y., 1950-51. Sales mgr. Village Ford, Ridgewood, N.J., 1953-66, Carlton Motors, Frankfurt, Germany, 1966-67, Jones Minto Ford, Burlingame, Calif., 1967-72, Terry Ford, Pompano Beach, Fla., 1974-75; gen. mgr. Kohlenberg Ford, Burlingame, 1975-76; v.p. Morris Landy Ford, Alameda, Calif., 1976-80, Burlingame Ford, 1980-85; emeritus chmn. bd. Valley Isle Motors, Wailuku, Hawaii, 1985—; pres. Marriott Luau, Lahaina, Hawaii; pres. Maui Auto Dealers Assn., Wailuku, 1986-87. Del. Rep. State Conv., Honolulu, 1988, State House of Rep.'s, 1992; v.p. Rep. Party Precinct, Lahaina, Hawaii, 1988, trustee Rep. Presdl. Task Force, Washington, 1983-88, pres. Maui County Rep. Party, 1993; pres. Big Bros./Big Sisters, 1993; exec. dir.'s Light Bringers. Sgt. USMC, 1950-52. Named Top 250 Exec. Hawaii Bus. Mag., 1986-92. Mem. Nat. Auto Dealers Assn., Internat. Auto Dealers Assn., Nat. Fed. of Ind. Bus., Maui Rotary, Lahaina Yacht Club, Maui Country Club, Gideons, Maui C. of C. Home: 2481 Kaanapali Pky Lahaina HI 96761-1994 Office: Valley Isle Motors 2026 Main St Wailuku HI 96793-1647

VIGNOLES, MARK, business owner; b. London, Apr. 5, 1957; s. Sean F. and Nuala V. BA, St. Mary's Coll, 1979. Serviceman Hoge and Assocs., Calif., 1979-81; owner Service West, Oakland, Calif., 1981—. Office: Svc West 2121 E 12th St Oakland CA 94606

VIHSTADT, ROBERT FRANCIS, real estate broker; b. Rochester, Minn., Oct. 6, 1941; s. Francis A. and Catherine P. (Condon) V.; m. Kathleen A. McGuire, Sept. 14, 1963 (div. Oct. 1976); children: Maureen T., Michael R., Mark T.; m. Leslie P. Teutsch, Mar. 16, 1979 (div. Jan. 1988). BA, Mankato State Coll., 1962. Employment counselor Minn. Dept. Employment Security, St. Paul, 1963-64; mktg. adminstr. IBM Corp., St. Paul, 1964-65; dir. mktg. adminstrn. Control Data Corp., Albuquerque, Los Angeles, and Bloomington, Minn., 1965-70; mgr. Ackerman-Grant, Inc., Realtors, Albuquerque, 1970-74; pres. Key Realty, Albuquerque, 1974—; dir. mktg. Stewart Title Co., Albuquerque, 1984-86; exec. v.p. Am. Property Tax Co., 1988—. Active Ronald McDonald House, John Baker PTA, Mile-High Little League. Mem. Nat. Assn. Realtors, Realtors Assn. N.Mex., Albuquerque Bd. Realtors (cert. residential specialist, bd. dirs., com. chmn.). Democratic. Roman Catholic. Lodge: Lions. Office: Key Realty PO Box 11771 Albuquerque NM 87192-0771

VILARDI, AGNES FRANCINE, real estate broker; b. Monson, Mass., Sept. 29, 1918; d. Paul and Adelina (Mastrioanni) Vetti; m. Frank S. Vilardi, Dec. 2, 1939; children: Valerie, Paul. Cert. of dental assisting Pasadena Jr. Coll., 1954. Lic. real estate broker. Real estate broker, owner Vilardi Realty, Yorba Linda, Calif., Placentia, Calif., Fullerton, Calif., 1968—; cons. in property mgmt. Mem. Am. Dental Asst. Assn., North Orange County Bd. Realtors (sec./treas. 1972), Yorba Linda Country Club, Desert Princess Country Club. Home and Office: 18982 Villa Ter Yorba Linda CA 92686-2611

VILGALYS, PATRICIA WELZEL, marketing consultant; b. Verdun, France, Nov. 22, 1957; came to U.S. 1958; d. Rainer and Karin Erika (Kruegel) Welzel; m. Aidas Justas Vilgalys, Sept. 10, 1988; 1 child, Tauras Patrick. BS in BA, SUNY, Albany, 1979; MBA, N.Y. Inst. Tech., 1985. Supr. mktg. Amdax Corp., Bohemia, N.Y., 1979-82; sales planning supr. Databit - A Siemens Co., Hauppauge, N.Y., 1983-84; mgr. mktg. svc. Eaton Corp., L.A., 1984-88; mktg. mgr. Crystalite Corp., L.A., 1988; dir. Laurch Systems, Torrance, Calif., 1988-91; pres. Vilgalys & Assocs., Long Beach, Calif., 1991—. Tutor Project Read, Long Beach, 1987-92; lector coord. St. Barnabas Ch., Long Beach, 1989—, mem. choir, 1991—. Democrat. Roman Catholic. Office: Vilgalys & Assocs 3249 Maine Ave Long Beach CA 90806-1235

VILKITIS, JAMES RICHARD, natural resources management educator; b. Rush, Pa., Oct. 31; s. Joseph Edgar and Kathryn Ann (Fetchkowsky) V. BS, Mich. State U., 1965; MS, U. Idaho, 1968; PhD, U. Mass., 1970, postdoctoral, 1971-72. Big game project leader Maine Dept. Inland Fisheries, Augusta, 1970-71; prin. Carlozzi, Sinton Vilkitis Inc., Amherst, Mass., 1970-80; professor Calif. Poly. State U., San Luis Obispo, 1980—; cons. Watkins-Johnson Co., 1986-89; assoc. R.L. Stollar & Assocs., 1986-91; statistician Regional Planning and Design Assn., Amherst, 1969-70; lectr. U. Mass., Amherst, 1971-80; owner TLC Leather Works, Shutesbury, Mass., 1974-80; staff officer USFS, 1987-88. Author: Management Model for Terrestrial Systems, 1973, Fish Cookery, 1974. Dir. Coastal Resources Inst. Calif. Poly. State U., San Luis Obispo, 1989—. Taoist. Office: Calif Poly State U San Luis Obispo CA 93407

VILLANI, JOSEPH TRIGG, communications company executive; b. Greenwich, Conn., Oct. 20, 1961; s. Joseph Louis and Lolita Deloris (Rodier) V.; m. Deidre Ann Smith, Apr. 22, 1989; 1 child, Joseph Dante. BA in Bus., Gonzaga U., 1985. Account exec. NBI, Seattle, 1985-87, AT&T, Spokane, Wash., 1987—. Roman Catholic. Office: AT&T N 9 Post 300 Spokane WA 99201

VILLAVICENCIO, ANA, psychotherapist, psychologist; b. San Francisco, Aug. 11, 1962. BA, San Francisco State U., 1985, MA, 1987; PhD, Calif. Sch. Profl. Psychology, 1992. Adminstrv. aide Helen Keller Nat. Ctr. Deaf-Blind Youth and Adults, San Francisco, 1983; psychology intern dept. psychiatry Comprehensive Child Crisis Svc. Children's Hosp., San Francisco, 1987-88; psychology intern infant parent program San Francisco Gen. Hosp., 1988-89; therapist Mt. Zion Outpatient Psychotherapy Clinic, San Francisco, 1989-91, Family Svc Agy., San Mateo, Calif., 1991-92; psychologist Inst. for Art of Living, San Francisco, 1993—. Contbr. profl. jours.; editor, book reviewer Jour. Homosexuality, 1986. Mem. APA (div. psychotherapy), No. Calif. Soc. Psychoanalytic Psychotherapy, Menninger Found., Extended Edn. Faculty San Francisco State U. (hon.), San Francisco Psychoanalytic Inst. (friend). Democrat. Office: 2299 Post St # 308 San Francisco CA 94115-3443

VILLEGAS, RICHARD JUNIPERO, artist; b. Santa Monica, Calif., Apr. 19, 1938; s. Robert Narciso and Jessie (Rodrigues) V. Student, Art Students League, N.Y.C., 1965-66. Artist Joseph Sarosi Inc., N.Y.C., 1961-62, Vozzo & Binetti, N.Y.C., 1962-64, Siegman-Ambro, N.Y.C., 1964-77; chief artist Greenbaum Bros., Paterson, N.J., 1978-89; owner The Villegas Art Studio, Thousand Oaks, Calif., 1989—. Mem. Westlake Village (Calif.) C. of C., C.G. Jung Found., Am. Mus. Natural History, Nat. Geog. Soc., Nat. Trust for Hist. Preservation, Gold Coast Bus. and Profl. Alliance. Home and Studio: 980 Camino Flores Thousand Oaks CA 91360-2367

VILLELLA, GARY ALLEN, human resources professional; b. St. Mary's, Pa., Aug. 10, 1947; s. Frank Anthony and Velma (Kopchick) V.; m. Kathy Beling (div. 1990). BSBA, Boston U., 1971; MBA, St. Mary's Coll., 1991. Mgr. employment and labor rels. RCA Avionics Systems, Van Nuys, Calif., 1971-75; mgr. wage and salary adminstrn. RCA Svc. Co., Cherry Hill, N.J., 1975-76; v.p. human resources Pertec Peripherals Corp., Chatsworth, Calif., 1976-86, Allergan Humphrey, San Leandro, Calif., 1987-91; dir. human resources Bard Access Systems, Salt Lake City, 1992—; search cons. Hergenrather & Co., L.A., 1986-87. Mem. No. Calif. Human Resource Coun., Salt Lake C. of C., Human Resource Exec. Roundtable Salt Lake. Republican. Home: 3012 E Danish Ridge Way Salt Lake City UT 84121 Office: Bard Access Systems 5425 W Amelia Earhart Dr Salt Lake City UT 84111

VILLENEUVE, DONALD AVILA, biology educator; b. Ventura, Calif., Oct. 25, 1930; s. Victor Fredrick V.; and Florence Ann (Pelletier) Goodin; m. Marylyn Yvonne Peoples, Jan. 7, 1950; children: Debra Lynn, Theresa Dianne, Karen Elaine, Kathryn Anne. BS, U. Idaho, 1958; MS, Univ. of Pacific, 1960; MA, U. Colo., 1967; PhD, UCLA, 1976. Cert. tchr., Calif., cert. community coll. tchr., adminstr. Biology tchr. Glendora (Calif.) High Sch., 1960-61; prof. biology and environ. sci. Ventura Coll., 1961-76; dir. div. math. and sci. Moorpark (Calif.) Coll., 1976-78; asst. prof. biol. sci. Calif. Poly. U., San Luis Obispo, Calif., 1978; prof. biology and environ. sci. Ventura Coll., 1978-92 (ret.); pres. acad. senate Ventura Coll., 1985-87; bd. dirs. Calif. Acad. Partnership Program, Long Beach, 1985-88; mem. sci. tchr. preparatory panel Calif. Commn. on Tchr. Credentialing, Sacramento, 1988—; curriculum cons. Calif. State Dept. Edn., Sacramento, 1986-87. Mem. City Coun., City of San Buenaventura, Ventura, 1987-91; mem. Calif. Coastal Commn., Santa Barbara, 1977-81; mem. planning commn. City of San Buenaventura, 1975-77, parks and recreation commn., 1974-75; v.p. Ventura County Symphony Assn., 1969-71; bd. dirs. Beach Erosion Authority, 1987-91, League for Coastal Protection, League Calif. Cities, 19896; mem. Ventura County Ctr. Planned Parenthood Adv. Coun., 1991—. Sgt. U.S. Army, 1950-53. NIMH grantee, 1971-72. Mem. Faculty Assn. Calif. Community Colls., Calif. Fedn. Tchrs. (bd. dirs. 1985-87), Lincoln Continental Owners Club, Volvo Sports Am. Democrat. Home: 239 Brevard Ave Ventura CA 93003-2319

VILLHARD, VICTOR JOSEPH, military career officer, aerospace engineer; b. St. Louis, Sept. 26, 1957; s. Vincent Leo and Anna B. (Ackerman) V.; m. Diane L. Reitz, July 10, 1982. BS in Aerospace Engring., Parks Coll., 1979; MS in Aerospace Engring., Air Force Inst. Tech., 1980. Commd. 2d lt. USAF, 1979, advanced through grades to maj.; researcher Frank J. Seiler Rsch. Lab. USAF Acad., 1981-84; systems engr. Space Shuttle Orbiter 6595th Shuttle Test Group, Kennedy Space Center, Fla., 1984-86; mgr. advanced space systems requirements Vandenberg AFB, Calif., 1986-91; br. chief, comml. space launch support Air Force Space Command Hdqrs., Peterson AFB, Colo., 1991—. Co-inventor air augmented core engine. Mem. Planetary Soc. Republican. Roman Catholic.

VILNROTTER, VICTOR ALPÁR, research engineer; b. Kunhegyes, Hungary, Nov. 8, 1944; came to U.S., 1957; s. Nicholas and Aranka (Vidovits) V.; m. Felicia D'Auria, Jan. 20, 1974; children: Katherine, Brian. BSEE, NYU, 1971; MS, MIT, 1974; PhD in EE, U. So. Calif., L.A., 1978. Teaching asst. MIT, Cambridge, Mass., 1972-74; rsch. engr. Jet Propulsion Lab., Pasadena, Calif., 1979—. Contbr. articles to profl. jours.; patentee in field. Mem. IEEE (referee in communications soc. 1980—), N.Y. Acad. Scis., Sigma Xi, Eta Kappa Nu. Home: 1334 Greenbriar Rd Glendale CA 91207-1254

VINCENT, DAVID RIDGELY, management consulting executive; b. Detroit, Aug. 9, 1941; s. Charles Ridgely and Charlotte Jane (McCarroll) V.; m. Margaret Helen Anderson, Aug. 25, 1962 (div. 1973); children: Sandra Lee, Cheryl Ann; m. Judith Ann Gomez, July 2, 1978; 1 child, Amber; stepchildren: Michael Jr., Jesse Joseph Flores. BS, BA, Calif. State U.-Sacramento, 1964; MBA, Calif. State U.-Hayward, 1971; PhD Somerset U, 1991. Sr. ops. analyst Aerojet Gen. Corp., Sacramento, 1960-66; contr. Hexcel Corp., Dublin, Calif., 1966-70; mng. dir. Memorex, Austria, 1970-74; sales mgr. Ampex World Ops., Switzerland, 1974-76; dir. product mgmt. NCR, Sunnyvale, Calif., 1976-79; v.p. Boole & Babbage Inc., gen. mgr. Inst. Info. Mgmt., Sunnyvale, Calif., 1979-85; pres. The Info. Group, Inc., Santa Clara, Calif., 1985—. Trustee Republican Nat. Task Force; deacon Union Ch., Cupertino, Calif.; USSF soccer referee. Author: Perspectives in Information Management, Information Economics, 1983, Handbook of Information Resource Management, 1987, The Information-Based Corporation: stakeholder economics and the technology investment, 1990; contbr. monographs and papers to profl. jours. Home: 2803 Kalliam Dr Santa Clara CA 95051-6838 Office: PO Box Q Santa Clara CA 95055-3756

VINCENT, EDWARD, mayor; b. Steubenvill, Ohio, 1934. Student, State U. Iowa; BA in Corrections and Social Welfare, Calif. State U. With L.A. County Probation Dept. Mcpl. and Superior Cts.; mayor City of Inglewood, Calif., 1983—. Bd. dirs. Inglewood Neighbors, Inglewood Neighborhood Housing Svcs., Inc.; mem. Urban League, New Frontier Dem. Club, Inglewood Dem. Club, Morningside High Sch. PTA, Monroe Jr. High Sch. PTA, Kew-Bennett PTA; pres. Morningside High Sch. Dad's Club. With U.A. Army, 1957-1959. Mem. NAACP, Calif. Probation Parole Corrections Assn., Black Probation Officers Assn., Calif. Narcotic Officers Assn., Mexican-Am. Corrections Assn., S.W, Horeseman, Assn., Imperial Village Blck Club, Inglewood Block Club (chmn. human affairs). Office: Office of Mayor 1 W Manchester Blvd Inglewood CA 90301-1750*

VINCENT, MARCUS ALAN, art gallery director, artist; b. San Francisco, Mar. 23, 1956; Ronald Glen and Lenore (Bennion) V.; m. Janice Broomhead, June 20, 1981; children: Justin Marcus, Jasmine Claire, Ian Chase, Trevor Dane, Camille Dominique. BFA, Brigham Young U., 1981, MFA, 1986. Registrar Mus. Fine Arts Brigham Young U., Provo, Utah, 1986-90; gallery dir. dept. art Brigham Young U., Provo, 1990—; chair search com., registrar's com. RCWR, 1989. Mem. Am. Assn. Mus. (state rep., registrar's com. 1986-90), Western Mus. Conf. Office: Brigham Young U Art Gallery F-303 HFAC Provo UT 84602

VINCENT, MARK KENT, lawyer; b. Murray, Utah, May 10, 1959; s. Kent Bryan and Edith Theone (Paxton) V. BA, Brigham Young U., 1984; JD, Pepperdine U., 1987. Corp. sec. Vincent Drug Co. Inc., Midvale, Utah, 1980-87; dep. dist. atty. Office of Dist. Atty. County of Ventura, Calif., 1987-89; asst. U.S. atty. U.S. Dept. of Justice, Salt Lake City, 1989—; law clk. Utah State Supreme Ct., Salt Lake City, 1986; v.p. Barrister's Bar Orgn., Ventura, 1988-89. Margaret Martin Brock scholar Pepperdine U., 1986-87. Mem. Calif. Bar Assn., Utah Bar Assn. Mormon. Office: US Attys Office 350 S Main St # 476 Salt Lake City UT 84101-2106

VINCENTI, SHELDON ARNOLD, legal educator, lawyer; b. Ogden, Utah, Sept. 4, 1938; s. Arnold Joseph and Mae (Burch) V.; m. Elaine Cathryn Wacker, June 18, 1964; children—Matthew Lewis, Amanda Jo. A.B., Harvard U., 1960, J.D., 1963. Bar: Utah 1963. Sole practice law, Ogden, 1966-67; ptnr. Lowe and Vincenti, Ogden, 1968-70; legis. asst. to U.S. Rep. Gunn McKay, Washington, 1971-72, adminstrv. asst., 1973; prof., assoc. dean U. of Idaho Coll. of Law, Moscow, Idaho, 1973-83, dean, prof. law, 1983—. Home: 2480 W Twin Rd Moscow ID 83843-9114 Office: U Idaho Coll Law 6th & Rayburn St Moscow ID 83843

VINES, DOYLE RAY, municipal official; b. Anna, Ill., Sept. 16, 1947; s. William Raymond and Lova Maldetta (Karraker) V.; m. Patricia Ruthann Sprague, Aug. 22, 1987. BA, So. Ill. U., 1969; CPM, Ariz. State U., 1993. Underwriter USF&G, Chgo., 1969-70; reimbursement officer Maricopa Community Health Network, Phoenix, 1972-74; cons. various orgns. including Maricopa County Health Dept. Phoenix, 1974-75; owner, mgr. Desert Flower, Tempe, Ariz., 1976-80; mgr. Town of Jerome, Ariz., 1980-86; adminstr. City of Bisbee, Ariz., 1986-89; mgr. Town of Superior (Ariz.), 1990-91. Bd. dirs. Copper Basin Behavioral Health, Kearny; candidate Ariz. Corp. Commr., 1992; state vice chmn. Ariz. Libertarian Party, 1993-94; dir. speakers bur. Advocates for Self Govt., Ariz. chpt. Mem. Internat. Inst. of Mcpl. Clks., Govt. Fin. Officers' Assn., Ariz. City Mgmt. Assn., Ariz. Mcpl. Clks. Assn. Libertarian.

VINEY, JOHN ALVIN, systems engineer; b. San Francisco, Dec. 7, 1932; s. Alvin Galt and Allene (Strubel) V.; m. Marlowe Elizabeth Delphey, Apr. 1, 1958; children: Patricia M., Jacquallene E., Diane Y. BS in Engring., U.S. Military Acad., West Point, 1955; MS in Systems Engring., U. So. Calif., 1972. Officer U.S. Army, 1955-68; engr. North Am. Rockwell, L.A., 1968-76; gen. mgr. PDA Assoc., Costa Mesa, Calif., 1976-78; engr. analyst Ford Aerospace, Costa Mesa, Calif., 1978-81, Aero and Gen., Azusa, Calif., 1981-83; sr. systems engr. Hughes Aircraft, Fullerton, Calif., 1984—. Col. U.S. Army, 1955-87. Home: 1160 Ginger Ln Corona CA 91719 Office: Hughes Aircraft Co Box 3310 Fullerton CA

VINSON, JOHN WILLIAM, aerospace engineer; b. Champaign, Ill., Feb. 3, 1955; s. William Glenn and Virginia Grace (Marsh) V.; m. Connie Sue Messer, Jan 24, 1987; 1 child, Richard Glenn. BS in Aero. and Astronautical Engring., U. Ill., 1977; MS in Aerospace Engring., U. Cin., 1982. Engr. GE Aircraft Engines, Cin., 1977-84; mgr. combustor design GE Aircraft Engines, Lynn, Mass., 1984-86, mgr. augmentor design, 1986-87; mgr. NASP propulsion module design GE Aircraft Engines, Cin., 1987-88, mgr. demonstrator engine cycle design, 1988-89; mem. tech. staff hypersonic and combined cycle Rocketdyne div. Rockwell Internat., Canoga Park, Calif., 1989—. Co-patentee gas turbine engine carburetor, bimodal swirler injector for gas turbine carburetor. Mem. AIAA, Nat. Mgmt. Assn. Home: 2666 N Velarde Dr Thousand Oaks CA 91360 Office: Rocketdyne Div Rockwell Internat 6633 Canoga Ave IB45 Canoga Park CA 91303

VINT, MURIEL MOSCONI, retired music educator; b. San Francisco; d. James and Adeline (Hovious) Mosconi. AB, San Jose State U., 1939; MA, San Francisco State U., 1952; postgrad., Stanford U., 1952-55, 66. Cert. in elem. and jr. high sch. music, secondary music, music supervision, gen. elem. credential, secondary credential, gen. adminstrv. credential. Music supr. Jefferson Elem. Sch. Dist., Daly City, Calif., 1927-71; lectr. music San Francisco State U., 1968-69; music supr. 9 parochial schs. Coll. Notre Dame, San Mateo County, Calif., 1971-75; tchr. music. edn. Coll. Notre Dame, Belmont, Calif., 1971-75; lectr. music edn. San Francisco State U., 1975, 77, 79-81; musician, leader M. Mosconi Dance Band, and small ensembles, Burlingame, Calif., 1924-39. Composer, arranger (song) California, 1928, (piano composition) Soft Shoe Teddy Bear, 1930, (band composition) March Orientale, 1935; arranger secular and holiday songs for elem. sch. chorus and choir, band, orch. and ensemble for elem. sch. musicians. Mem. Half Moon Bay Community Band, 1920-23; dir. Jefferson Elem. Sch. Dist. Choruses with Daly City Community Band Recreation Dept. (ann. festival), 1958-62; musician lodges, bus. orgns., rallies, Burlingame, 1924-39; mem. com. San Francisco Opera for Children, 1965-81, Young Peoples Symphony, 1960-79. Mem. Music Educators Nat. Conf., Calif. Music Educators Assn., Spanishtown Hist. Soc. (Half Moon Bay), Hist. Guild Daly City-Colma, Order Ea. Star, Kappa Delta Pi. Republican.

VINT, ROBERT JAMES, construction company executive; b. Washington, Jan. 30, 1934; s. Thomas Chalmers and Mary Alice (Waring) V.; m. Katherine Lois Brown, Aug. 18, 1956; children—Thomas Arthur, Robert Walter, Mary Katherine, James Michael, William Waring. A.B. in Psychology, Colgate U., 1956; postgrad. U. Ariz., 1961-65. Computer programmer Hughes Aircraft Co., Tucson, 1959-61; sr. computer programmer Pan Am. World Airways, Tucson, 1961-62; programmer-analyst Bunker-Ramo Corp., Ft. Huachuca, Ariz., 1962-65; mgr. computer services Bell Aerospace Co., Tucson, 1965-76; v.p. data processing M.M.Sundt Construction Co., Tucson, 1976-83; v.p. systems and data processing Sundt Corp., Tucson, 1983—; dir. M.M.Sundt Construction Co., 1980-83. Vestryman St. Michaels Episcopal Ch., Tucson, 1965-76. Served with U.S.

Army, 1957-59. Republican. Home: 7409 E Calle Antigua Tucson AZ 85710-3707 Office: Sundt Corp 4101 E Irvington Rd Tucson AZ 85714

VINTON, ALICE HELEN, real estate company executive; b. McMinnville, Oreg., Jan. 10, 1942; d. Gale B. and Saima Helen (Pekkola) V. Student, Portland State Coll., Northwestern Sch. Commerce. Lic. real estate broker, Hawaii. Owner, prin. broker Vinton Realty, Honolulu, 1918—. Founder, bd. dirs. Kekuaanaui, Hawaii Big Sisters, 1972-76; former vol. Child and Family Svc., women's div. Halawa Prison; bd. dirs. Kindergarten and Children's Aid Assn., 1977-88, advisor, mem. long range planning com., 1988—; former mem. tuition aid com., chmn. nominating com. and capital improvements com. Laura Morgan Pre-Sch.; bd. dirs. Hawaii Theatre Ctr., 1985-86. Recipient proclamation Hawaii Ho. of Reps., cert. of merit for disting. svc. to community, Dictionary of Internat. Biography, Vol. XXI, 1990. Mem. Nat. Assn. Realtors, Hawaii Assn. Realtors, Honolulu Bd. Realtors, Honolulu C. of C., Downtown Improvement Assn., Acad. Arts, Bishop Mus. Assn., Wildlife Fedn., Neighborhood Justice Ctr. Honolulu, Friends of Iolani Palace, Smithsonian Inst., Hawaii Polo Club, Honolulu Press Club (membership chmn. 1988-90), Rainbow Girls Club (life), Hawaii Humane Soc., Sierra Club, Hist. Hawaii, Cen. Bus. Club Honolulu, Nature Conservancy Hawaii, Women's Healthsource, YWCA, Coustea Soc., Wolf Haven, Honolulu Polo Club, Orchid Soc. Manoa, North Shore Animal League, Nat. Pks. and Conservation Assn., Wilderness Soc. Republican. Episcopalian. Office: 650 Ala Moana Blvd Ste 211 Honolulu HI 96813

VINZANT, JANET COBLE, political science educator; b. Kirkland, Wash., Aug. 21, 1954; d. Howard Melvin and Marilyn Jean (Ness) Coble; m. Douglas Hunt Vinzant Jr., June 7, 1980; children: Benjamin, Mary. BA, Wash. State U., 1976; MPA, U. So. Calif., 1979, DPA, 1991. Mgmt. cons. Miller & Assocs. Inc., Olympia, Wash., 1976-78; mgmt. analyst office of the sec. U.S. Dept. of HHS, Washington, 1979; spl. asst. to dir. Human Devel. Svcs., HHS, Washington, 1979-81; sr. mgmt. analyst U.S. Dept. of HHS, Washington, 1981-82; mgmt. cons. office of fin. mgmt. State of Wash., Olympia, 1985; asst. prof. polit. sci. Ea. Wash. U., Cheney, 1988-91, assoc. prof. polit. sci., 1992—. Mem. ASPA, Western Pol. Sci. Assn., Pi Sigma Alpha.

VIOLANTE, LAWRENCE JOSEPH, life underwriter; b. Jersey City, Dec. 8, 1924; s. Joseph A. and Victoria (Triano) V.; m. Mildred M. Burak, Dec. 15, 1945; children: Dana, Mark, Luke, Paul. CLU, ChFC. Spl. agt. N.Y. Life Ins. Co., Santa Cruz, Calif., 1946—; registered rep. NYLIFE Securities Inc., Santa Cruz, 1986—; agt. N.Y. Life Ins. and Annuity Corp., Santa Cruz, 1975—; mem. agt.'s adv. coun. N.Y. Life Ins. Co., 1970-71, life mem. couns.; moderator Life Underwriter Tng. Coun., Santa Cruz, 1972—. Pres. Holy Cross High Sch. Parents' Club, Santa Cruz, 1969; chmn. Santa Cruz County Civil Svc. Commn., 1971-73; past pres. Santa Cruz County Grand Jury Assn.; dir. Santa Cruz Pony-Colt Boys Baseball Tournament, 1967; commentator-lectran Holy Cross Ch. Lt. USN, 1943-46. Mem. Nat. Assn. Life Underwriters (nat. committeeman 1986-87, Nat. Quality award, Nat. Sales Achievement award), Calif. Assn. Life Underwriters (state legislation 1986-87), Santa Cruz County Life Underwriters Assn. (past pres. 1984-85), Am. Soc. CLU and ChFC, Santa Cruz County Estate Planning Coun. (chartered mem.), Elks (past exalted ruler Santa Cruz lodge # 824). Roman Catholic. Home: 200 Sheldon Ave Santa Cruz CA 95060 Office: 331 Soquel Ave Santa Cruz CA 95062

VIOLET, WOODROW WILSON, JR., retired chiropractor; b. Columbus, Ohio, Sept. 19, 1937; s. Woodrow Wilson and Alice Katherine (Woods) V.; student Ventura Coll., 1961-62; grad. L.A. Coll. Chiropractic, 1966; m. Judith Jane Thatcher, June 15, 1963; children: Woodina Lonize, Leslie Alice. Pvt. practice chiropractic medicine, Santa Barbara, Calif., 1966-73, London, 1973-74, Carpinteria, Calif., 1974-84; past mem. coun. roentgenology Am. Chiropractic Assn. Former mem. Parker Chiropractic Rsch. Found., Ft. Worth; mem. Scripps Clinic Rsch. Coun. Served with USAF, 1955-63. Recipient award merit Calif. Chiropractic Colls., Inc., 1975, cert. of appreciation Nat. Chiropractic Antitrust Com., 1977. Mem. Nat. Geog. Soc., L.A. Coll. Chiropractic Alumni Assn., Delta Sigma. Patentee surg. instrument.

VIOLETTE, GLENN PHILLIP, construction engineer; b. Hartford, Conn., Nov. 15, 1950; s. Reginald Joseph and Marielle Theresa (Bernier) B.; m. Susan Linda Begam, May 15, 1988. BSCE, Colo. State U., 1982. Registered profl. engr., Colo. Engring. aide Colo. State Hwy. Dept., Glenwood Springs, Colo., 1974-79, hwy. engr., 1980-82; hwy. engr. Colo. State Hwy. Dept., Loveland, Colo., 1979-80; project engr. Colo. State Hwy. Dept., Glenwood Canyon, Colo., 1983—; guest speaker in field. Contbg. editor, photographer publs. in field. Recipient scholarship Fed. Hwy. Adminstrn., 1978. Mem. ASCE, Amnesty Internat., Nat. Rifle Assn., Siera Club, Audubon Soc., Nature Conservancy, World Wildlife Fund, Cousteau Soc., Chi Epsilon. Office: Colorado Dept Transp 202 Centennial St Box 1430 Glenwood Springs CO 81602

VIREN, JOHN JOSEPH, multimedia engineer, computer graphics developer; b. Rock Island, Ill., Apr. 25, 1949; s. Richard O'Connell and Phyllis Ruby (Goodman) V.; m. Catherine Marie Lievens, Oct. 24, 1970. AA in Art, Blackhawk Coll., 1971; BS in Computer Graphics, Teikyo Marycrest U., 1984, MS in Computer Sci., 1986; postgrad., Nova U., 1992—. Facilities mgr. St. Mary's, East Moline, Ill., 1975-88; cons., owner Compix, Moline, Ill., 1985-88; engr. Interstate Electronics Corp., Anaheim, 1989—; interactive videodisc presenter Naval Warfare Assessment Ctr., North Corona, Calif., 1991; guest panelist Artiste: Symposium, Davenport, Iowa, 1985. Computer graphic works exhibited at Davenport Mcpl. Art Gallery, 1984; developer interactive videodisc. Friend KOCE-TV, Huntington Beach, Calif., 1990-91; planning com. Michalski for Congress, Moline, 1988. Mem. IEEE, Nat. Computer Graphics Assn., Soc. for Applied Learning Tech. (speaker 1990), Royal Order of Vikings, Toastmasters. Office: Interstate Electronics Corp 1001 E Ball Rd Anaheim CA 92803

VIRTUE, THOMAS GOODWIN, video producer, photographer; b. Houston, Dec. 27, 1948; s. Ralph T. and Jane (Goodwin) V.; m. Patricia Stirling, May 26, 1971; 1 child, Theron. Student, U. Colo., 1967-70. Audio engr. Audicom Corp., Denver, 1972-74, Applewood Studio, Golden, Colo., 1974-79; profl. musician Denver, 1979-81; audio producer Communicreations, Inc., Denver, 1981-87, video producer, 1987—. One-man show Auraria Libr. Gallery, U. Colo., Denver, 1993; editor ESPN TV Show, 1988, cable TV series Ski the Rockies, 1988-92. Judge regional broadcast Clio Awards, Denver, 1988. Recipient Photography award Gilpin Co. Arts Assn., 1985, Top award Camera Obsura Gallery, 1987; finalist Best of Photography Ann., 1984, 85, Clio awards for advt., 1989. Mem. Denver Musicians Assn. Home: 4151 S Verbena St Denver CO 80237-1747

VISHER, EMILY B., psychologist. BA in Chemistry with honors, Wellesley Coll., 1940; PhD in Psychology, U. Calif., Berkeley, 1958. Rsch. chemist Nutrition Clinic, Birmingham, Ala., Cin., 1940-41; postdoctoral clin. psychology trainee VA Clinic, San Francisco, 1958-59; pvt. practice, 1958-86; diagnostic evaluator Calif. Vocat. Rehab. Svc., Almeda County Welfare Dept., Children's Home Soc. Calif., 1960-66; staff psychologist VA Hosp., Menlo Park, Calif., 1966-68; cons., evaluator Portola Valley (Calif.) Sch. Dist., 1967-71; staff psychologist Kaiser Found. Hosp., Redwood City, Calif., 1970-77; instr. stepfamily classes U. Calif., 1983-91; stepfamily workshop leader, 1979—; mem. adv. panel on divorce, single parenting and remarriage Am. Inst. Rsch., 1979; fellowship chmn. AAUW, Marin County, 1947-48, pres., 1948-50, recent grad. chmn. Calif., 1949-50; mem. adj. faculty Calif. Sch. Profl. Psychology, 1992—; lectr. psychiatry Harvard U., 1992-93; speaker, lectr. in field. Co-author (with John S. Visher) three books on stepfamily issues; contbr. articles to profl. jours. Co-founder, dir. Stepfamily Assn. Am., Inc., 1979—, pres., 1979-83. Anne Louise Barrett fellow Wellesley Coll., 1953-54, nat. fellow AAUW, 1956-57. Mem. Am. Psychol. Assn., Am. Orthopsychiatric Assn. (mem. planning coms. 1978-87), Am. Assn. Marriage and Family Therapists (disting. profl. contbn. to family therapy award, 1993), Am. Family Therapy Assn., Nat. Coun. Family Rels., Wellesley Coll. Alumnae Assn. (pres. No. Calif. Club 1948-49, pres. West Bay Club, 1970-71, v.p. Class of 1940 1980-85, alumnae achievement award 1986), Sigma Xi , Phi Beta Kappa. Home and Office: 599 Sky-Hy Circle Lafayette CA 94549-5225

VISINTAINER, CARL LOUIS, insurance company executive; b. Parlett, Ohio, Dec. 7, 1939; s. Joseph L. and Louise E. (Salamon) V.; m. Linda M. Yott, Sept. 2, 1961; children: Eva, Michelle, Laurie, Lindy, Joseph. PhB, U. Detroit, 1962. CLU; CPCU. Agt. State Farm Ins. Cos., Allen Park, Mich., 1963-68; agy. mgr. State Farm Ins. Cos., Rochester, Mich., 1968-72, Albuquerque, 1980-84; agy. dir. State Farm Ins. Cos., Marshall, Mich., 1972-75; exec. asst. State Farm Ins. Cos., Bloomington, Ill., 1975-77, v.p. agy. svcs., 1977-80; agy. dir. State Farm Ins. Cos., Phoenix, 1984—. Mem. Nat. Republican Com., 1980-87. Mem. ACLU, Soc. CLU, Soc. CPCU, Coun. Dem. and Secular Humanism, Mensa. Office: State Farm Ins Cos 1665 W Alameda Tempe AZ 85289

VITALE, VINCENT PAUL, lawyer; b. L.A., Oct. 14, 1947; s. Vincent and Alice Louise (Withrow) V.; divorced; children: Matthew, Christine; m. Judith M. Rich. BA in Govt., U. Calif., Santa Cruz, 1969; JD, U. Calif., Davis, 1972. Cert. civil trial specialist. Atty. Alaska Legal Svcs. Corp., Anchorage, 1972-73; asst. city atty. City of Anchorage, 1973-74; assoc. Johnson, Christensen & Shambers, Anchorage, 1974-75; sole practice Anchorage, 1975—. Chmn. Alaska Commn. on Jud. Conduct, Anchorage, 1987. Mem. ABA, Nat. Bd. Trial Advocacy. Home: 2830 E 88th Ave Anchorage AK 99507-3906 Office: 725 Christensen Dr Anchorage AK 99501-2101

VITE, MARK STEVEN, educational administrator; b. Elkhart, Ind., Oct. 18, 1956; s. Frank Anthony and Barbara Ann (Decio) V. BS, Miami U., Oxford, Ohio, 1978. Tchr. Elkhart Community Schs., 1979-81; asst. high sch. swim coach Elkhart Cen. Sch., 1980-81; tchr. Judson Sch., Scottsdale, Ariz., 1981-82; supr. Marriott's Mountain Shadows, Scottsdale, Ariz., 1982-83; tchr. Camelback Desert Sch., Scottsdale, 1983-85; pres. Marc III Inc., Tempe, Ariz., 1985-88; treas. B&F Realty, Inc., Elkhart, 1988—; prin. Kachina Country Day Sch., Paradise Valley, Ariz. Water safety instr. ARC, Elkhart, 1973-81, Phoenix, 1981—; bd. dirs. United Food Bank, Mesa, Ariz., 1988-90, Friends of the Suite Mus., 1990—. Mem. Tempe C. of C. (amb.'s com.). Democrat. Roman Catholic. Home: 5904 E Oak St Scottsdale AZ 85257-1936

VITULLI, MARIE ANGELA, mathematician; b. Mineola, N.Y., Nov. 19, 1949; d. Vito Nunzio and Marie Georgiana (Mangoni) V. BA, U. Rochester, N.Y., 1971; MA, U. Pa., 1973, PhD, 1976. Asst. prof. math. U. Oreg., Eugene, 1976-82; assoc. prof. math. U. Oreg., 1982-91, prof. math, 1991—. Contbr. articles to profl. jours. Mem., chmn. Com. on Status of Women, Eugene, 1989-92; prin. violist Emerald Chamber Orch., 1988—. NSF traineeship, 1972-73; U. Pa. fellow, 1975; Stoddard Prize in Math., U. Rochester, 1969. Mem. Am. Math. Soc., Am. Assn. U. Profs., Math. Assn. Am., Assn. for Women in Math., Phi Beta Kappa. Home: 4427 Fox Hollow Rd Apt 16 Eugene OR 97405-4575 Office: Dept Math Univ of Oregon Eugene OR 97403

VIVIAN, LINDA BRADT, sales and public relations executive; b. Elmira, N.Y., Nov. 22, 1945; d. Lorenz Claude and Muriel (Dolan) Bradt; m. Robert W. Vivian, Apr. 5, 1968 (div. Sept. 1977). Student, Andrews U., 1966. Adminstrv. asst. Star-Gazette, Elmira, 1966-68; editor Guide, staff writer Palm Springs (Calif.) Life mag., 1970-75; dir. sales and pub. rels. Palm Springs Aerial Tramway, 1975—; sec. Hospitality and Bus. Industry Coun. Palm Springs Desert Resorts, 1989-91, vice-chmn., 1991—. Mem. Hotel Sales and Mktg. Assn. (allied nominating chmn. Palm Springs chpt. 1986-88), Am. Soc. Assn. Execs., Travel Industry Assn., Hospitality Industry and Bus. Coun. of Palm Springs Resorts (sec. 1989-91, vice-chmn. 1991—), Nat. Tour Assn., Calif. Travel Industry Assn., Palm Springs C. of C. (bd. dirs. 1984-85). Republican. Office: Palm Springs Aerial Tramway One Tramway Rd Palm Springs CA 92262

VIZENOR, GERALD ROBERT, literature educator, writer; b. Mpls., Oct. 22, 1934; s. Clement William and LaVerne Lydia Vizenor; m. Judith Horns, Sept. 1960 (div. 1969); 1 child, Robert Thomas; m. Laura Jane Hall, May 1981. BA, U. Minn., 1960. Staff writer Mpls. Tribune, 1968-70; prof. Am. studies U. Minn., Mpls., 1980-83; prof. ethnic studies U. Calif., Berkeley, 1986; prof. lit. U. Calif., Santa Cruz, 1987-89; provost Kresge Coll., 1989-90; prof. lit. U. Okla., 1990-91; prof. Native Am. Studies U. Calif., Berkeley, 1991—. Author: Word Arrows: Indians and Whites in the New Fur Trade, 1976, The People Named the Chippewa: Narrative Histories, 1984, (novels) Darkness In Saint Louis Bearheart, 1978, Griever: An American Monkey King in China, 1987 (award Fiction Collective 1987, Am. Book award Before Columbus Found. 1988), The Trickster of Liberty, 1988, Narrative Chance, 1989, The Heirs of Columbus, 1991, Dead Voices, 1992, (autobiography) Interior Landscapes, 1990, (essays) Crossbloods, 1990, Manifest Manners: Postindian Survivance, 1993, (short stories) Landfill Meditation, 1991, Summer in the Spring: Anishinaabe Lyric Poems and Stories, 1993; series editor Am. Indian Lit. and Critical Studies, U. Okla. Press. Office: Univ of Calif NAS 3415 Dwinelle Hall Berkeley CA 94720

VLACHOS, EVAN CONSTANTINE, sociology and civil engineering educator; b. Athens, Greece, Nov. 15, 1935; came to U.S., 1960; s. Constantine and Irene Vlachos; m. Virginia Helen Pakes, Sept. 7, 1962; children: Irene Diana, Dean Evan. MA, Ind. U., 1962, PhD, cert. Russian studies, 1964. Asst. prof. Pierce Coll., Athens, 1964-66, U. Colo., Boulder, 1966-67; prof. Colo. State U., Ft. Collins, 1976—; assoc. dir. Internat. Sch. for Water Resources, Colo. State U., Ft. Collins, 1989—. Author: Coping with Droughts, 1983, Water Resources of Southern Portugal, 1988; assoc. editor Water Internat., 1989—. Rsch. grantee NSF, Ford Found., U.S. Army Corps of Engrs.; recipient Outstanding Civilian Svc. medal U.S. Army Corps of Engrs., 1987. Mem. Population Assn. Am., World Future Soc., AAAS,. Greek Orthodox. Office: Colo State U Dept of Sociology Fort Collins CO 80523

VLASAK, WALTER RAYMOND, state official, management development consultant; b. Hartsgrove, Ohio, Aug. 31, 1938; s. Raymond Frank and Ethel (Chilan) V.; m. Julia Andrews, Feb. 25, 1966; children: Marc Andrew, Tanya Ethel. BSBA, Kent State U., 1963; MA, U. Akron, 1975. Commd. 2d lt. U.S. Army, 1963; platoon leader, anti-tank platoon leader and battalion adjutant 82d Airborne Div., 1963-65; combat duty Viet Nam, 1965-66, 68-69; exec. officer, co. comdr. and hdqrs. commandant of the cadre and troops U.S. Army Sch. Europe, Oberammergau, Fed. Republic Germany, 1966-68; asst. prof. Mil. Sci. Kent (Ohio) State U., 1970-74; infantry battalion exec. officer 9th Infantry Div., Ft. Lewis, Wash., 1976-77, orgnl. effectiveness cons. to commanding gen., 1977-79, brigade exec. officer, 1980-82; orgnl. effectiveness cons. to commanding gen. 8th U.S. Army, U.S. Forces, Korea, 1979-80; advanced through ranks to lt. col. U.S. Army, 1980, ret., 1984; pres. Comsult, Inc., Tacoma, 1984—; mgr. employee devel. tng. dept. social and health svcs. State of Wash., Tacoma, 1985—. Decorated Legion of Merit, Bronze Star with V device and two oak leaf clusters, Air medal, Purple Heart, Vietnamese Cross of Gallantry with Silver Star. Mem. Am. Soc. for Tng. and Devel., Assn. U.S. Army (bd. dirs. Tacoma 1984—). Home: 10602 Hill Terrace Rd SW Tacoma WA 98498-4337 Office: State of Wash Dept Social and Health Svcs 8425 27th St W Tacoma WA 98466-2722

VO, HUU DINH, pediatrician, educator; b. Hue, Vietnam, Apr. 29, 1950; came to U.S., 1975; s. Chanh Dinh and Dong Thi (Pham) V.; m. Que Phuong Tonnu, Mar. 22, 1984; children: Katherine Hoa-An, Karyn Bao-An. MD, U. Saigon, 1975. Diplomate Am. Bd. Pediatrics. Adminstr. bilingual vocat. tng. Community Care and Devel. Svc., L.A., 1976-77; resident in pediatrics Univ. Hosp., Jacksonville, Fla., 1977-80; physician, surgeon, chief med. officer Lanterman Devel. Ctr., Pomona, Calif., 1980-92, chief med. staff, 1984-88, coord. med. ancillary svc., 1984-88, 91—; physician Pomona Valley Community Hosp., 1988-90; asst. clin. prof. Loma Linda (Calif.) Med. Sch., 1985-92; chief med. officer So. Reception Ctr.and Clinic., Norwalk, Calif., 1992—; bd. dirs. Pomona Med. Clinic Inc. Pres. Vietnamese Community Pomona Valley, 1983-85, 87—; bd. dirs. YMCA, Pomona, 1988—, Sch.-Community Partnership, Pomona, 1988—. Mem. AMA (Physician recognition award 1989, 1992), L.A. Pediatrics Soc., Vietnamese-Am. Physicians Assn. La. and Orange County (founding mem., sec. 1982-84, bd. dirs. 1987-90). Republican. Buddhist. Home: 654 E Lennox Ct Brea CA 92621-7302 Office: So Reception Ctr and Clinic 13200 S Bloomfield Ave Norwalk CA 90650

VOAKE, RICHARD CHARLES, banker; b. Albuquerque, July 21, 1940; s. Charles Frederick and Irene Adelaide (Simms) V.; m. Karen Anderson, Sept. 24, 1966. AB in Econ., Stanford U., 1962; MBA in Fin., UCLA, 1965. With Security Pacific Nat. Bank, L.A., 1965-87, sr. v.p., 1984-87; sr. v.p. Security Pacific Corp., L.A., 1987—. Trustee U. LaVerne, Calif., 1988—. Mem. Assocs. Calif. Inst. TEch. (chair investment com., fin. com.), Jonathan Club. Republican. Lutheran. Office: Security Pacific Corp 333 S Beaudry Ave Ste 2830W Los Angeles CA 90017-1466

VOBEJDA, WILLIAM FRANK, aerospace engineer; b. Lodgepole, S.D., Dec. 5, 1918; s. Robert and Lydia (Stefek) V.; m. Virginia Parker, Oct. 24, 1942; children—William N., Margaret, Mary Joan, Barbara, Lori. B.C.E., S.D. Sch. Mines and Tech., 1942. Registered profl. engr., Colo. Stress analyst Curtiss Wright Corp., Columbus, Ohio, 1942-45; civil/hydraulic engr. Bur. Reclamation, Denver, 1945-54; mech. supr. Stearns Roger Corp., Denver, 1954-62; mgr. Martin Marietta Corp., Denver, 1962-86, mgr. engring. M-X Program, 1978-86; pres. BV Engring., Inc., Englewood, Colo., 1986-89. Active Boy Scouts Am. Recipient Silver Beaver award. Mem. Englewood City Council 1984-87, Englewood Water and Sewer Bd., 1990—. Mem. AIAA. Democrat. Roman Catholic. Clubs: St. Louis Men's, K.C., Martin Marietta Chess, Lions (sec.).

VODA, ISADORE LEON, dentist; b. Clinton, Ind., Mar. 12, 1913; s. Harold and Tillie (Bass) V.; m. Tillie Balch, Dec. 28, 1939; children: Hal M., Lynne, Alan M. DDS, Washington U., St. Louis, 1937. Pvt. practice Las Vegas, N.Mex., 1937-83, Albuquerque, 1983—. V.p. N.Mex. unit Am. Cancer Soc., 1963-66, pres., 1966-68. 1st lt. U.S. Army, 1942-46. Recipient Disting. Alumnus award Sch. Dental Medicine Wash. U., 1976. Fellow Internat. Coll. Dentists (dep. regent 1987-80, life), Am. Coll. Dentists (life), Acad. Gen. Dentistry; mem. ADA (life, del. N.Mex. chpt. 1952-63), N.Mex. Dental Assn. (life, v.p. 1959-60, pres. 1961-62, Disting. Svc. award 1984, 50-Yr. cert. 1987, Gold medal of Distinction 1989), Am. Soc. Geriatric Dentistry, Am. Assn. Pub. Health Dentists (life), Am. Prosthodontic Soc., Santa Fe Dist. Dental Soc. (life, v.p. 1953, pres. 1954), N.Mex. Acad. Gen. Dentistry. Office: 6800 Montgomery Blvd NE # K Albuquerque NM 87109-1425

VOELKER, MARGARET IRENE (MEG VOELKER), gerontology, medical/surgical nurse; b. Bitburg, Fed. Republic Germany, Dec. 31, 1955; d. Lewis R. and Patricia Irene (Schaffner) Miller; 1 child, Christopher Douglas. Diploma, Clover Park Vocat.-Tech., Tacoma, 1975, diploma in practical nursing, 1984; AS in Nursing, Tacoma Community Coll., 1988. Cert. ACLS. Nursing aide Jackson County Hosp., Okla., 1976; nursing asst. Jackson County Hosp., Altus, Okla., 1976-77; receptionist Western Clinic, Tacoma, 1983; lic. practical nurse Tacoma Gen. Hosp., 1984-88, clin. geriatric nurse, 1988-90, clin. nurse post anesthesia care unit, 1990—.

VOGEL, ERIC LESLIE, software research and development project manager; b. L.A., May 22, 1955; s. Jack Morris and Harriett (Wheeler) V.; m. Carole Lea Holmquist, Oct. 11, 1980; children: Stuart Lawrence, Kathryn Lorraine, Frederic Lloyd. BSME, Oreg. State U., 1978. Support engr. Hewlett-Packard, Corvallis, Oreg., 1976-78; tech. writer Alpha-Omega Computer Systems, Corvallis, Oreg., 1979; applications engr. Hewlett-Packard, Corvallis, Oreg., 1980-81, R&D software engr., 1982-84, R&D project leader, 1985-89, R&D project mgr., 1990—; cons. PennWell Books, Tulsa, 1983; editorial cons. Armstrong Pub. Co., Corvallis, 1989—. Author: Mental Meals, 1978; co-author: HP-41 Reservoir Engineering Manual, 1982; author owners and reference manuals, 1979-86; co-inventor patented multiple equation solver, unit mgmt. system. Nat. ednl. dir. Acacia Fraternity, Boulder, Colo., 1979; vol. Vol. Income Tax Assistance, Albany, Oreg., 1984. Recipient Walter Davis scholarship Acacia Fraternity, 1975, William M. Porter Meml. scholarship Oreg. State U., 1976, undergrad. scholarship Boeing, 1977, student award Am. Soc. for Testing and Materials, 1977. Mem. Tau Beta Pi, Pi Tau Sigma. Republican. Home: 1720 NW 13th St Corvallis OR 97330 Office: Hewlett-Packard 1000 NE Circle Blvd Corvallis OR 97330

VOGEL, JOHN ARNOLD, physician; b. Hollywood, Calif., Jan. 14, 1962; s. John Charles and Shirley Ann (Perdew) V.; m. Gaylen Marie Johnson. AA, L.A. Valley Coll., 1983; BS, D in Chiropractic, Cleve. Chiropractics, 1986. Lic. chiropractor, Calif. Physician Sylmar (Calif.) Chiropractic, 1986-87, Lancaster (Calif.) Chiropractic, 1987—. Mem. APHA, Am. Chiropractic Assn., Calif. Chiropractic Soc., Parker Chiropractic Rsch. Found. (Cert. 1985), The Network (v.p. 1988-90), Optimists (pres. 1987—, Cert. of Appreciation 1990), High Desert Chiropractic Soc. (v.p. 1989-90), Lancaster C. of C. (amb. 1989—). Republican. Mem. Christian Ch. Office: Lancaster Chiropractic 720 W Milling St Lancaster CA 93534-3142

VOGEL, RANDY CHARLES, state legislator, police officer; b. Feb. 3, 1953; s. Ruben and Dorothy (Hilderman) V.; m. Christy Lynn Henry, Feb. 10, 1973; children: Matthew, Jeremy, Katie. Student, Rocky Mountain Coll. With uniform divsn., 1974-76, 79-80, 85-90, dispatcher, 1976-77, foot patrol, 1977-78, pub. rels., crime prevention, 1978-79, with detective divsn., 1980-85, with Selective Traffic Enforcement Program, 1990—; mem. dist. 86 Mont. Ho. Reps., vice chmn. judiciary com.; pres. Rimrock Credit Union.; mem. Law Enforcement Adv. Coun. to Atty. Gen. Trustee Faith Ch., past mem. missions com.; mem. adv. bd. Crises Pregnancy Ctr.; active Billings Urban Fire Svc. Area Bd; past chmn. Yellowstone County Gambling Commn.; past coach Canyon Creek Elem. Sch.; youth leader AWANA. Mem. State Bd. Pvt. Security and Investigators, Mont. Police Protective Assn. (legis. com.), Billings Police Protective Assn., Billings Police Union, Police Marksman Assn. (charter). Home: 5953 Lazy Ln Billings MT 59106 Office: Billings Police Dept City Hall Billings MT 59101

VOGELAAR, CARL BENGEMIN, chaplain; b. Pella, Iowa, Mar. 16, 1925; s. Ben and Gertrude (Van Omen) V.; m. Joan Ruth Ver Meer, June 10, 1948; children: Marla Vogelaar Snider, Paulette Vogelaar Wagner, Ted. AB, Ctrl. Coll., 1948; BD, New Brunswick Theol. Sem., 1963; MDiv, Ashland Theol. Sem., 1971. Owner hardware store, Pella, 1950-60; pastor Philmont (N.Y.) Reformed Ch., 1963-67, Parkview Community Ch., Fairview Park, Ohio, 1967-74; sr. pastor Ch. of the Chimes, San Jose, Calif., 1974-89; chaplain Holland Am. Line Cruise Ships, Seattle, 1988—; moderator gen. program coun. Ref. Ch. in Am., N.Y.C., 1982-88; pres. Classis of Ctrl. Calif., Sonoma, 1979-80, 91-92. 1st lt. U.S. Army, 1943-45. Mem. Ch. of the Chimes. 1st lt. U.S. Army, 1943-45. Mem. Mountain Retreat, Quality Resorts. Republican. Home and Office: 1455 Church Dr San Jose CA 95118

VOGLER, JAMES WAYLAN, physicist, consultant; b. Barrington, Ill., June 4, 1948; s. Richard D. and Shirlee (Gardner) V. BS in Physics, MIT, 1971; MA in Physics, U. Ill., Chgo., 1978; PhD in Physics, U. Calif., Berkeley, 1988. Engr. Hewlett-Packard, Palo Alto, Calif., 1971-76; staff engr. Motorola, Schaumburg, Ill., 1976-83; staff engr., cons. Omni Spectra div. M/A Co., Tempe, Ariz., 1983-86; sr. ptnr. Mirage/KLM Communs., Morgan HIll, Calif., 1989—; ptnr., v.p. R&D, sr. scientist Atlantis Fiberoptics, Scottsdale, Ariz., 1988—; pwner, sr. cons. JV Assocs., Phoenix, 1986—; cons. Rockwell Internat., Cedar Rapids, Iowa, 1987-89, Teledyne, Culver City, Calif., 1989—, Hughes Aircraft Co., L.A., 1987—. Contbr. articles to profl. jours.; patentee in field. NSF fellow U. Cambridge, Eng., 1970; recipient John T. Chambers Meml. award Ctrl. States VHF Soc., 1991. Mem. IEEE, Am. Inst. Physics. Office: JV Assocs 2540 E Heatherbrae Dr Phoenix AZ 85016

VOGLER, KEVIN PAUL, systems engineer; b. Detroit, Aug. 17, 1957; s. Roger James and Vera Mae (Streng) V.; m. Michelle Marie Bensch, May 5, 1984; children: Brian William, Allison Marie. BSChemE, Mich. Technol. U., 1980; MBA, U. Santa Clara, 1987. Registered profl. engr., Calif. Program mgr. nuclear power systems div. GE Co., San Jose, Calif., 1980-81, project engr. domestic projects dept., 1981-86; systems safety engr. space systems div. Lockheed Missiles and Space Co., Sunnyvale, Calif., 1986-88, sr. rsch. engr. space systems div., 1988—. Active Big Brothers/Sisters Santa Clara (Calif.), 1980-81; instr. econs. Jr. Achievement, Santa Clara, 1987. Mem. Mensa, Beta Gamma Sigma, Sigma Tau Gamma. Republican. Roman Catholic. Home: 271 Mimosa Way Portola Valley CA 94028-7431 Office: Lockheed Missiles and Space Co 74-02 Bldg 159 1111 Lockheed Way # 3504 Sunnyvale CA 94089-1212

VOGNILD, LARRY L., state senator; b. Spokane, Jan. 21, 1932; s. James Howard and Helen Mildred (Pinkerton) V.; m. Dorothy L. Vognild; children—Valerie Ann, Margo Elaine. Mem. City of Everett (Wash.) Fire Dept., 1954-78, bn. chief, 1976-78; mem. Wash. Senate, 1979—, now majority whip. Served with USN, 1951-54. Democrat. Lutheran.

VOGT, EVON ZARTMAN, III, merchant banker; b. Chgo., Aug. 29, 1946; s. Evon Zartman Jr. and Catherine C. (Hiller) V.; m. Mary Hewit Anschuetz, Sept. 26, 1970; 1 child, Elizabeth Christine. AB, Harvard U., 1968; MBA, U. Colo., 1976. Vol., then staff mem. U.S. Peace Corps., Brazil, 1968-72; asst. dir. Stanford Program Indian Demography, Mex., 1973; v.p. Wells Fargo Bank, Sao Paulo, Brazil, 1977-81; mng. dir. Wells Fargo Internat. Ltd., Grand Cayman, 1982-84; mgr. global funding Wells Fargo Bank, San Francisco, 1984-86; mng. dir. Arbi Transnational, Inc., San Francisco, 1986—, also bd. dirs.; bd. dirs. Magtech Recreational Products, Inc., Las Vegas, 1990—. Bd. dirs. Internat. Visitors Ctr., San Francisco, 1990—. Mem. Brazil Soc. No. Calif. (pres. 1989—), Pan Am. Soc. Calif. (bd. dirs. 1990—, pres. 1991—). Office: Arbi Transnational Inc 600 Montgomery St Ste 350 San Francisco CA 94111

VOGT, ROCHUS EUGEN, physicist; b. Neckarelz, Germany, Dec. 21, 1929; came to U.S., 1953; s. Heinrich and Paula (Schaefer) V.; m. Micheline Alice Yvonne Bauduin, Sept. 6, 1958; children: Michele, Nicole. Student, U. Karlsruhe, Germany, 1950-52, U. Heidelberg, Germany, 1952-53; S.M., U. Chgo., 1957, Ph.D., 1961. Asst. prof. physics Calif. Inst. Tech., Pasadena, 1962-65, assoc. prof., 1965-70, prof., 1970—, R. Stanton Avery Disting. Service prof., 1982—, chmn. faculty, 1975-77, chief scientist Jet Propulsion Lab., 1977-78, chmn. div. physics, math. and astronomy, 1978-83; acting dir. Owens Valley Radio Obs., 1980-81; v.p. and provost Calif. Inst. Tech., Pasadena, 1983-87; vis. prof. physics MIT, 1988—; dir. Caltech/MIT Laser Interferometer Gravitational Wave Observatory Project, 1987—. Author: Cosmic Rays (in World Book Ency.), 1978, (with R.B. Leighton) Exercises in Introductory Physics, 1969; contbr. articles to profl. jours. Fulbright fellow, 1953-54; recipient Exceptional Sci. Achievement medal NASA, 1981, Profl. Achievement award U. Chgo. Alumni Assn., 1981. Fellow AAAS, A. Phys. Soc. Office: Calif Inst Tech 102-33 Pasadena CA 91125

VOICE, JACK WILSON, JR., foundation administrator; b. N.Y.C., June 25, 1945; s. Jack Wilson and Dorothy Eileen (O'Connor) V.; m. Kelsey Kay Holler, 1967 (div. 1977); m. Lynne Adelle Van Cleave, Sept. 21, 1986; children: Andrea Keifer, Douglas Keifer. Student, Fresno State Coll., 1963-66; AA in Liberal Arts, De Anza Coll., Cupertino, Calif., 1971; BS in Fin., San Jose State U., 1972. Loan officer Bank of Am., Visalia, Calif., 1973-74; rental mgr. The Hertz Corp., Sacramento, Calif., 1974-78; licensee Thrifty Rent-a-Car, Fresno and Visalia, 1978-82; v.p. Easter Seal Soc. Cen. Calif., Fresno, 1982-90; pres., chief exec. officer Cen. Valley VMC Found., Fresno, 1990—. Author, editor: (newsletter) Easter Seal News, 1985-90. Founder Calif. Balloon Festival, Fresno, 1986-90, Bucks for Books, Fresno County Library, 1989; v.p., tickets Calif. Bowl, Fresno, 1987, v.p., mdse., 1988, dir., 1985-90; 1st v.p. Friends of the Fresno County Library, 1987-88, sec., 1986-87; dir. Central Valley Hospice, 1990—. With USN, 1967-70. Mem. Mensa, Dugout Club (dir. 1985-90). Republican. Roman Catholic. Home: 5921 E Saginaw Way Fresno CA 93727-7963 Office: Cen Valley VMC Found PO Box 15189 Fresno CA 93702-5189

VOIGT, DONALD BERNARD, tool designer; b. St. Cloud, Minn., Jan. 24, 1947; s. Roman Edward and Alma Mary (Weber) V.; m. Delphine B. (Schmitz) Kliber, Aug. 25, 1990; stepchildren: Ross Louis Kliber, Jason Gilbert Kliber, Shawn Eugene Kliber, Kurt Gerald Kliber, Karl Raphael Kliber. Student, St. Cloud Area Voc. Tech. Inst. Machinist Nat. Bushing and Parts, St. Cloud, 1966-67, Am. Machine and Tool, Mpls., 1967-72; tool maker, designer Columbia Gear, Avon, Minn., 1972-89; machinist U.S. Mint, Denver, 1989—; cons. Joseph Kenning, St. Cloud, 1985-90. Author: Effects of Electromagnetic Fields on Biological Systems, Magnets in Your Future, Vol. 3, No. 4, April, 1988. Mem. AAAS, N.Y. Acad. Scis. Roman Catholic. Home: 7611 Shrine Rd Larkspur CO 80118-8701 Office: US Mint 320 W Colfax Ave Denver CO 80204-2693

VOIGT, MILTON, English language educator; b. Milw., Mar. 19, 1924; s. Arthur and Esther Johanna (Bartelt) V.; m. Leta Jean Slack, July 27, 1947 (div. 1969); children: John Gregory, James Lewis, Andrew Charles. Ph.B., U. Wis., 1948; MA, U. Calif., Berkeley, 1950; PhD, u. Minn., Mpls., 1960. Assoc. U. Calif., Berkeley, 1949-50; instr. English U. Idaho, Moscow, 1952-55, U. Ky., Lexington, 1956-60; asst. prof. U. Utah, Salt Lake City, 1960-64, assoc. prof., 1964-68, prof., 1968-92, assoc. dean Coll. of Letters and Sci., 1965-66, acting dean, 1966-67, dean, 1967-70, chair English dept., 1971-75, prof. emeritus, 1992—. Author: Swift & the 20th Century, 1964; contbr. articles to profl. jours. Sec. ACLU, Salt Lake City, 1979-83, Chamber Music Soc., Salt Lake City, 1982-86. 2d lt. USAAF, 1943-45. John R. Park fellow U. Utah, 1970. Mem. MLA, Am. Soc. 18th Century Studies. Episcopalian. Home: 1376 Princeton Ave Salt Lake City UT 84105-1921 Office: U Utah Dept English Salt Lake City UT 84112

VOIGT, SCOTT KENNETH, electrical, computer engineer; b. Milw., June 16, 1964; s. Kenneth August and Carol Jean (Schramm) V.; m. Donna Marie Jones, Aug. 12, 1989. BSEE, U. Calif., Santa Barbara, 1986. Project engr. Delco Sys. Ops., Goleta, Calif., 1985—. Team mem. Los Padres Search & Rescue, Santa Barbara, 1987—. Republican. Lutheran. Office: Delco Systems Ops 6767 Hollister Ave Santa Barbara CA 93117-3086

VOIGT, WALTER C., bottled water company executive; b. Alameda, Calif., Aug. 14, 1939; s. Ralph C. and Marion Voigt; m. Charlotte Pauline Voigt, Feb. 22, 1958; children: Michael Paul, Kristine Lee Graham. Grad. high sch., Oakland, Calif. Grocery clk. and dept. mgr. Emby Foods, Oakland, 1958-67; svc. technician Culligan Water Conditioning, Santa Maria, Calif., 1967-77; salesman Culligan San Paso, Santa Maria, 1972-73; sales mgr. Culligan Santa Barbara, Santa Maria, 1973-74; v.p. Growth Systems, Monterey and Los Gatos, Calif.; owner Culligan Softwater Svc., Dinuba, Calif., 1974-80; pres. Walter C. Voigt Inc., Dinuba, 1980—. Adminstrv. team Christian Marriage Comm., Fresno, Calif., 1975—; chmn. bd. dirs. BOD Christian Marriage and Family Ministries, 1990-91. Recipient Regional Budget Buster award, 1982-83, Circle of Excellence award, 1991. Republican. Office: Culligan 228 North L St Dinuba CA 93618

VOJTA, PAUL ALAN, mathematics educator; b. Mpls., Sept. 30, 1957; s. Francis J. and Margaret L. V. B in Math., U. Minn., 1978; MA, Harvard U., 1980, PhD, 1983. Instr. Yale U., New Haven, 1983-86; postdoctoral fellow Math. Scis. Rsch. Inst., Berkeley, Calif., 1986-87; fellow Miller Inst. for Basic Rsch., Berkeley, 1987-89; assoc. prof. U. Calif., Berkeley, 1989-92, prof., 1992—; mem. Inst. for Advanced Study, Princeton, 1989-90. Author: Diophantine Approximations and Value Distribution Theory, 1987. Recipient perfect score Internat. Math. Olympiad, 1975, Cole prize in Number Theory, 1992. Mem. Am. Math. Soc., Math. Assn. Am., Phi Beta Kappa, Tau Beta Pi. Office: Univ Calif Dept of Math Berkeley CA 94720

VOLBERG, HERMAN WILLIAM, electronic engineer, consultant; b. Hilo, Hawaii, Apr. 6, 1925; s. Fred Joseph and Kathryn Thelma (Ludloff) V.; m. Louise Ethel Potter, Apr. 26, 1968; children: Michael, Lori. BSEE, U. Calif., Berkeley, 1949. Project engr. Naval Electronics Lab., San Diego, 1950-56; head solid state rsch. S.C. div. Gen. Dynamics, San Diego, 1956-60; founder Solidyne Solid State Instruments, La Jolla, Calif., 1958-60; founder, v.p. electronics div. Ametek/Straza, El Cajon, Calif., 1960-66; founder, cons. H.V. Cons., San Diego, 1966-69; sr. scientist Naval Ocean Systems Ctr., Oahu, Hawaii, 1970-77; chief scientist Integrated Scis. Corp., Santa Monica, Calif., 1978-80; founder, pres. Acoustic Systems Inc., Goleta, Calif., 1980-84; founder, pres. Invotron, Inc., Lafayette, Calif., Murray, Utah, 1984—; tech. dir. Reson, Inc., Santa Barbara, Calif., 1992—; lectr. solid state course UCLA and IBM, 1956-62; instr. Applied Tech. Inst., Columbia, Md., 1988—. Contbr. articles to IRE Bull., IEEE Ocean Electronics Symposium. Mem. adv. panels for advanced sonar systems and for high resolution sonars, USN, 1970-77. 1st lt. U.S. Army, 1944-47, ETO. Recipient award of merit Dept. Navy, 1973. Mem. IEEE, NRA, Planetary Soc., Assn. Old Crows, Masons, Elks. Home and Office: 41 W 6830 S Salt Lake City UT 84107-7124

VOLBORTH, ALEXIS, geochemistry and geological engineering educator; b. Viipuri, Finland, July 11, 1924; came to U.S., naturalized; married 1947 (div.); 7 children. PhC, U. Helsinki, 1950, PhLic and PhD in Geology-Mineralogy, 1954. Mineralogist, rsch. assoc., assoc. prof., prof. U. Nev., Reno, 1956-68; Killam vis. prof. geology, Killam rsch. prof. Dalhousie U., Can., 1968-72; vis. prof. NASA Lunar Sci. Inst., U. Houston, 1972-73; vis. rsch. chemist U. Calif., Irvine, 1973-76; prof. geology and chemistry N.D. State U., 1975-78; prof. geology, scientist Nucleaar Radiation Ctr., Wash. State U., Pullman, 1978-79; prof. geochemistry and chemistry Mont. Coll. Mineral Sci. and Tech., Butte, 1979—, prof. geol. engring., 1987-92, dir. accelerator lab., 1983-86, sr. radiation safety officer, 1983-86; prin. investigator Stoichiometry Study Lunar Rocks, NASA, 1972-73; cons. AEC, 1961-63, NASA, 1965-73, Anaconda Co., 1968, Atomic Energy Orgn. Iran, 1975, Johns Manville Corp., Chevron, 1980-83, Pegasus Gold Inc., 1987, Placer Dome Inc., Echo Bay, Inc., 1990; U.S. rep., del. 2d Conf. on Natural Reactors, IAEC, Paris, 1977; U.S. rep. Internat. Geol. Correlation Program, 1990—; interpreter, Russian translator in Soviet Siberia for major U.S. and Can. mining cos., 1990—. Contbr. articles to profl. jours. Traveling rsch. fellow Outokumpu Found., U. Vienna, U. Heidelberg, 1954-55, Hoover fellow Calif. Inst. Tech., 1955-56, sr. fellow Australian Acad. Sci., 1965, fellow Guggenheim Found., 1965-66. Fellow Mineral. Soc. Am., Am. Inst. Chemists; mem. Am. Chem. Soc., Am. Nuclear Soc., Soc. Econ. Geologists, Internat. Precious Metals Inst. Home: PO Box 80 Dayton MT 59914 Office: Mont Coll Mineral Sci-Tech Dept Chemistry-Geochem Butte MT 59701

VOLCKMANN, DAVID BOYD, psychology educator; b. Kingston, N.Y., Jan. 19, 1942; s. Frederick William and Norma (Hill) V.; m. Jean Pierce, July 26, 1967 (div. May 1987); m. Barbara Currier Green, June 6, 1987; children: Matthew, Nicholas, Hannah. AB, Hamilton Coll., 1964; PhD, Ind. U., 1970. Asst. prof. Whittier (Calif.) Coll., 1970-78, assoc. prof., 1978-89, prof., 1989—, dir. instnl. rsch., 1983—. Author: Instructors' Resource, 1980, 83, 84, Working with Psychology, 1975. Recipient Title VI award HEW, 1975; vis. scholar Lily Found., 1975. Mem. Calif. Assn. Instnl. Rschrs. Office: Whittier Coll Whittier CA 90608

VOLCKMANN, PETER TERREL, investor; b. E. Orange, N.J., June 13, 1941; s. Herbert Richard and Solveig (Kolstad) V.; m. Rosemary Esther True, June 30, 1973. BS, U. N.H., 1968. Program adminstr. Sanders Assocs., Inc., Nashua, N.H., 1961-70; pres., chief exec. officer Troll House, Inc., Nashua, 1973-80; gen. mng. ptnr. P. Volckmann & Assocs., Inc., Sedona, Ariz., 1981—; pres., dir. Foothills North Assocs., Sedona, 1982-88; dir., v.p. Am. Heart Assn., Sedona-Verde Valley, 1988-89. Vice mayor City of Sedona, Ariz., 1988; bd. dirs. Bd. Adjustment & Appeal, Yavapai County, Ariz., 1988, Sedona Fire Dept. Pension Bd., 1982-89; vol. paramedic, 1982-89. Capt. CAP, 1993—. Republican. Home and Office: 160 Camino Del Caballo Sedona AZ 86336-3016

VOLGY, THOMAS JOHN, mayor, political science educator; b. Budapest, Hungary, Mar. 19, 1946; m. Susan Dubow, Feb. 1987. BA magna cum laude, Oakland U., 1967; MA, U. Minn., 1969, PhD, 1972. Assoc. prof. polit. sci. U. Ariz., Tucson; dir. Univ. Teaching Ctr.; mayor City of Tucson, 1987-91; chmn. telecommunications com. U. Conf. Mayors, 1988—; cons. high sch. curriculum project Ind. U.; bd. dirs. Nat. League Cities, 1989-91. Co-author: The Forgotten Americans, 1992; editor: Exploring Relationships Between Mass Media and Political Culture: The Impact of Television and Music on American Society, 1976; contbr. numerous articles to profl. jours.; producer two TV documentaries for PBS affiliate. Mem. Nat. Women's Polit. Caucus Conv., 1983, U.S. Senate Fin. Com., 1985, U.S. Ho. of Reps. Telecommunications Com., 1988—, Polit. Sci. Adminstrn. Com., 1986, Gov.'s Task Force on Women and Poverty, 1986, United Way, 1985-87; bd. dirs. Honors Program, 1981—, U. Teaching Ctr., 1988—, Tucson Urban League, 1981, Ododo Theatre, 1984, So. Ariz. Mental Health Care Ctr., 1987, Nat. Fedn. Local Cable TV Programmers; chmn. Internat. Rels. Caucus, 1981, 86—, Transp. and Telecommunications Com. Nat. League Cities, 1986, 88, 89-91. Recipient NDEA scholarship, 1964-76, NDEA fellowship, 1967-70, Oasis award for oustanding prodn. of local affairs TV programming; named Outstanding Young Am., 1981, Outstanding Naturalized Citizen of Yr., 1980; faculty research grantee U. Ariz., 1972-73, 73-74, 74-75, 77-78. Mem. Pima Assn. Govts., Nat. Fedn. Local Cable Programmers. Democrat. Jewish. Office: U Ariz Polit Dept Sci Tucson AZ 85721

VOLK, ROBERT HARKINS, aviations company executive; b. East Orange, N.J., Nov. 27, 1932; s. Harry Joseph and Marion (Waters) V.; m. Barbara June Klint, Sept. 10, 1954; children: Christopher G., William W., Laura L., Elisabeth M. BA, Stanford U., 1954, LLB, 1958. Bar: Calif. 1959. Assoc. Adams Duque & Hazeltine, L.A., 1959-62; ptnr. Adams Duque & Hazelyine, L.A., 1962-67; commr. of corps. State of Calif., Sacramento, 1967-69; pres. Union Bancorp, L.A., 1969-73; pres., chmn. Union Am., L.A., 1973-79; owner, chief exec. officer Martin Aviation Inc., Santa Ana, Calif., 1980-90, Media Aviation L.P. Burbank, 1984—. Sgt. USAF, 1955-57. Mem. Calif. Bar Assn. Republican. Episcopalian. Home: 332 Conway Ave Los Angeles CA 90024-2604 Office: Media Aviation LP 3000 N Clybourn Ave Burbank CA 91505-1012

VOLKAN, KEVIN, psychologist; b. Chapel Hill, N.C., Dec. 5, 1958; s. Vamik Djemal and Esther (Boger) V.; m. Panda Lynn Kroll, Dec. 20, 1987. EdD, No. Ill. U., 1987; PhD, Ctr. for Psych. Studies, Albany, Calif., 1991. lic. Psychol., Calif. Asst. to the Dean of Edn., Dept. of Edn. No. Ill. Univ., 1984-85, rsch. assoc., Health Promotion Rsch. Project, 1985-87, asst. prof., dir. rsch., Dept. of Edn., 1987-88; rsch. assoc. ETR Assocs., Scotts Valley, Calif., 1988-89; asst. to the Dean, Grad. Divsn. Univ. Calif., Sant Cruz, 1989-91; clin. psychol. Agnews State Hosp., San Jose, Calif., 1991—; pres. Oz Projects, Santa Cruz, 1990—. Author: Dancing Among the Maenads: The Psychology of Compulsive Drug Use; contbr. articles to profl. jours. Mem. Am. Psychol. Soc., Western Psychol. Assn., Mid-Coast Psychol. Assn., Calif. Psychol. Assn. Democrat. Buddhist. Home: 104 Errett Circle Santa Cruz CA 95060 Office: Agnews State Hosp 3500 Zanker Road San Jose CA 95134

VOLLACK, ANTHONY F., state supreme court justice; b. Cheyenne, Wyo., Aug. 7, 1929; s. Luke and Opal Vollack; m. D. Imojean; children: Leah, Kirk. Bar: Colo. 1956. Pvt. practice law Colo., from 1956; formerly state senator; judge Colo. Dist. Ct. (1st jud. dist.), 1977-85; justice Colo. Supreme Ct., 1986—. Office: Colo Supreme Ct 2 E 14th Ave Denver CO 80203-2116*

VOLLHARDT, KURT PETER CHRISTIAN, chemistry educator; b. Madrid, Mar. 7, 1946; came to U.S., 1972; Vordiplom, U. Munich, 1967; PhD, U. Coll., London, 1972. Postdoctoral fellow Calif. Inst. Tech., Pasadena, 1972-74; asst. prof. chemistry U. Calif., Berkeley, 1974-78, assoc. prof., 1978-82, prof., 1982—; prin. investigator Lawrence Berkeley Lab., 1975—; cons. Monsanto Corp., St. Louis, Exxon Corp., Annandale, N.J., Maruzen Corp., Tokyo; vis. prof. U. Paris-Orsay, 1979, U. Bordeaux, 1985, U. Lyon, 1987, U. Rennes, 1991, U. Paris VI, 1992. Author: Organic Chrmistry, 1987, 2nd edit., 1993; co-author: Aromatizität, 1972; assoc. editor: Synthesis, 1984-89, Editor Synlett, 1989; contbr. articles to profl. jours.; patentee in field. Sloan fellow, 1976-90; Camille and Henry Dreyfus scholar, 1978-83; recipient Adolf Windaus medal, 1983, Humboldt Sr. Scientist award, 1985, 92, Otto Bayer prize, 1990, A.C. Cope Schoalr award, 1991; named of one Am.'s 100 Brightest Scientist Under 40, Sci. Digest, 1984. Mem. Am. Chem. Soc. (Organometallic Chemistry award 1987), German Chem. Soc., Chem. Soc. of London, Internat. Union Pure & Applied Chemistry (organic chemistry div. com.). Office: U Calif Berkeley Dept of Chemistry Berkeley CA 94720

VOLMER, NANCY KAY, cultural organization administrator, writer; b. Salt Lake City, May 10, 1960; d. Jack L. and Marilyn (Southam) V. BS in Recreation and Leisure, U. Utah, 1983, BS in Journalism, 1984. Asst. mgr. Pier I Imports, Murray, Utah, 1981-85; tourism mgr. Salt Lake Conv. and Visitors Bur., Salt Lake City, 1985-86; freelance writer Salt Lake City, 1984—; communications dir. Park City (Utah) Chamber Bur., 1986—. Contbr. articles to profl. jours. Mem. Women in Communications (membership chair elect Salt Lake City chpt. 1986-87, membership chair 1987-88, v.p. 1988-89, pres. 1989-90), Internat. Assn. Bus. Communications (v.p. student rels. 1990-91, v.p. programs 1991-92, v.p. comm. 1992-93, pres. 1993—), Am. C. of C. (communications coun.). Democrat. Roman Catholic. Office: Park City Chamber Bur 1910 Prospector Ave Park City UT 84060-7319

VOLPE, RICHARD GERARD, insurance accounts executive, consultant; b. Swickley, Pa., Apr. 10, 1950; s. Ralph Carl and Louise P. (Cosentino) V.; m. Janet Lynn Henne, May 10, 1986; 1 child, John Ralph. BA, Vanderbilt U., 1972. CPCU. Trainee, asst. mgr. Hartford (Conn.) Ins. Group, 1973-74; v.p. sales Roy E. Barker Co., Franklin, Tenn., 1975-80; asst. v.p., product mgr. comml. ins. Nat. Farmers Union Ins., Denver, 1980-82; prin. R.G. Volpe & Assocs, Denver, 1982-85; account exec. Millers Mut. Ins., Aurora, Colo., 1985-89; pres, chief exec. officer AccuSure, Inc., Arvada, Colo., 1989—; account exec. J.R. Misken, Inc., Denver, 1990-92, The Prudential, Colorado Springs, 1992—; edn. chmn. Insurors Tenn., Nashville, 1978-79; new candidate chmn. Mid-Tenn. chpt. CPCU, Nashville, 1979-80; cons. Bennett Nat. Bank Colo., mktg. mgr., 1989-90; cons. Plains Ins., Inc., 1987-90. Contbr. articles to profl. jours. Dem. chmn. Williamson County, Tenn., 1979; campaign mgr. legis., Franklin, 1979. Named Hon. Col. Gov. Tenn., 1979. Mem. Soc. Property and Casualty Underwriters, Aurora C. of C., Sierra Club. Roman Catholic. Home: 10908 W Snow Cloud Trl Littleton CO 80125-9211 Office: The Prudential 5225 N Academy Blvd Ste 310 Colorado Springs CO 80918

VOLPERT, RICHARD SIDNEY, lawyer; b. Cambridge, Mass., Feb. 16, 1935; s. Samuel Abbot and Julia (Fogel) V.; m. Marcia Flaster, June 11, 1958; children: Barry, Sandy, Linda, Nancy. B.A., Amherst Coll., 1956; LL.B. (Stone scholar), Columbia U., 1959. Bar: Calif. bar 1960. Atty. firm O'Melveny & Myers, Los Angeles, 1959-86; ptnr. O'Melveny & Myers, 1967-86, Skadden, Arps, Slate, Meagher & Flom, Los Angeles, 1986—; pub. Jewish Jour. of Los Angeles, 1985-87 . Editor, chmn.: Los Angeles Bar Jour, 1965, 66, 67, Calif. State Bar Jour, 1972-73. Chmn. community relations com. Jewish Fedn.-Council Los Angeles, 1977-80; bd. dirs. Jewish Fedn.-Council Greater Los Angeles, 1976—, v.p., 1978-81; pres. Los Angeles County Natural History Mus. Found., 1978-84, trustee, 1974—, chair bd. dirs., 1992—; chmn. bd. councilors U. So. Calif. Law Center, 1979-85; vice chmn. Nat. Jewish Community Relations Adv. Council, 1981-84, mem. exec. com., 1978-85; bd. dirs. U. Judaism, 1973-89, bd. govs., 1973-89; bd. dirs. Valley Beth Shalom, Encino, Calif., 1964-88; mem. capital program major gifts com. Amherst Coll., 1978-86; bd. dirs., mem. exec. com. Los Angeles Wholesale Produce Market Devel. Corp., 1978—, v.p., 1981-93, pres. 1993—; mem. exec. bd. Los Angeles chpt. Am. Jewish Com., 1967—; vice-chmn. Los Angeles County Econ. Devel. Council, 1978-81; bd. dirs. Jewish Community Found., 1981—; mem. Pacific S.W. regional bd. Anti Defamation League B'nai B'rith, 1964—. Named Man of Year, 1978. Fellow Am. Bar Found.; mem. ABA, Am. Soc. Planning Ofcls., Urban Land Inst., Los Angeles County Bar Assn. (trustee 1968-70, chmn. real property sect. 1974-75), Los Angeles County Bar Found. (trustee 1977-80), Calif. Bar Assn. (com. on adminstrn. justice 1973-76), Am. Coll. Real Estate Lawyers, Anglo-Am. Real Property Inst., Amherst Club of So. Calif. (dir. 1968-85, pres. 1972-73), City Club (L.A.). Jewish. Home: 4001 Stansbury Ave Sherman Oaks CA 91423-4619 Office: Skadden Arps Slate Meagher& Flom 300 S Grand Ave Los Angeles CA 90071-3144

VOLTURA, GERALD ANTHONY, philosophy educator, substitute teacher; b. Passaic, N.J., Apr. 2, 1965; s. Orazio Anthony and Mary (Riccio) V.; m. Tracy Lynn Castoe, Oct. 30, 1992; 1 child, Steven. BA, U. Nev., Las Vegas, 1989, MA in Ethics and Policy Studies, 1993. Clk. data processing Barnes & Noble Bookstore, Las Vegas, 1986-90; paralegal Apple and Bunitsky, Las Vegas, 1990-91; instr. philosophy U. Nev., Las Vegas, 1987—; notary pub., Las Vegas, 1990-94. Co-author essay Legal Rights and Personal Injury, 1990. Instr. CPR ARC, Las Vegas, 1990. Recipient Louis Armstrong Jazz award Jazz Com. Las Vegas, 1982. Mem. Nat. Assn. Legal Assts., Nat. Anti-Vivisection Soc. Home: PO Box 81771 Las Vegas NV 89121

VOLZ, JIM, management consultant, writer; b. Dayton, Ohio, Aug. 1, 1953; s. John Louis and Betty Jean (Lauber) V.; m. Evelyn Carol Case, May 22, 1982; children: Nicholas, Caitlin. BA in English Lit., BA in Theatre, Wright State U., 1975; MA in Coll. Student Personnel, Bowling Green (Ohio) State U., 1976; PhD in Theatre, U. Colo., 1984. Reporter, writer, photographer Wright State U., Dayton, 1973-75, acting chmn. theatre dept., 1980, bus. mgr. theatre dept., 1979-81; activities programmer Bowling Green State U., 1975-76; asst. to the dean Colo. Coll., Colorado Springs, 1976-78; tchr., adminstr. U. Colo., Boulder, 1981-82; mng. dir. Ala. Shakespeare Festival, Montgomery, Ala., 1982-91; prof. theatre Calif. State U., Fullerton, 1991—; sec. Southeastern Theatre Conf., Greensboro, N.C., 1989-90. Author: Shakespeare Never Slept Here, 1986, (with others) Words for Lovers, 1990. Chmn. Auburn (Ala.) Fine Arts Coun., 1987-91. U. Colo. fellow, 1982. Mem. Nat. Theatre Conf., Dramatists Guild, Am. Theatre in Higher Edn., Theatre Comm. Group. Office: Calif State U Dept Theatre & Dance Fullerton CA 92634-9480

VOMHOF, DANIEL WILLIAM, chemist; b. Grant, Nebr., Apr. 19, 1938; s. Milton W. and Viola H. (Louis) V.; m. Joan Elizabeth Lienemann, July 16, 1960 (div. 1975); children: Daniel William III, Tanya Sue, Lysia Ann. BS in Chem., Augsburg Coll., Mpls., 1962; MS, U. Ariz., 1966, PhD, 1967; BS, MS, Nat. U., 1986. Research assoc. corn industry rsch. found. Nat. Bur. Standards, Washington, 1967-69; dir. lab. div. U.S. Customs Service, Chgo., 1969-72; forensic scientist U.S. Customs Service, San Diego, 1972-74; pres. Expert Witness Services, Inc., La Mesa, Calif., 1974—; mng. ptnr. 4N6XPRT Systems, La Mesa, 1988—; adj. prof. Nat. U., San Diego, 1984—, Coleman Coll., 1989—; instr., chmn. dept. gen. edn. Coleman Coll., La Mesa, Calif., 1986-89. Recipient Cert. Appreciation Evidence Photographers Internat. Council, U. So. Calif., 1984, Cert. Appreciation San Diego Trial Lawyers Assn., 1983. Fellow Am. Inst. Chemists; mem. AAAS, ASTM, IEEE Computer Soc., Forensic Cons. Assn. (founder, first pres.), Inst. Indsl. Engrs., Am. Chem. Soc., Sigma Xi. Office: Expert Witness Svcs Inc 8387 University Ave La Mesa CA 91941-3889

VONDERHEID, ARDA ELIZABETH, nursing administrator; b. Pitts., June 19, 1925; d. Louis Adolf and Hilda Barbara (Gerstacker) V.; diploma Allegheny Gen. Hosp. Sch. Nursing, 1946; B.S. in Nursing Edn., Coll. Holy Names, Oakland, Calif., 1956; M.S. in Nursing Adminstrn., UCLA, 1960. Head nurse Allegheny Gen. Hosp., Pitts., 1946-48; staff nurse Highland-Alameda County Hosp., Oakland, Calif., 1948-51, staff nurse poliomyelitis units, 1953-55; pvt. duty nurse Directory Registered Nurses Alameda County, Oakland, 1951-53; adminstrv. supervising nurse Poliomyelitis Respiratory and Rehab. Center, Fairmont, Alameda County Hosp., Oakland, 1955-58; night supr., relief asst. dir. nursing Peninsula Hosp., Burlingame, Calif., 1960, adminstrv. supr., 1961-62, inservice educator, 1963-69; staff nurse San Francisco Gen. Hosp., 1969, asst. dir. nurses, 1969-72; mem. faculty continuing edn. U. Calif., San Francisco, 1969-71; dir. nursing services Kaiser Permanente Med. Center, South San Francisco, 1973-1982, asst. adminstr. Med. Center Nursing Services, 1982-85; asst. adminstr. Kaiser Hosp., San Francisco, 1985-87; ret. 1987. Chmn. edn. com. San Mateo County (Calif.) Cancer Soc., 1962-69; bd. dirs. San Mateo County Heart Assn., 1968-71; mem., foreman pro tem San Mateo County Civil Grand Jury, 1982-83; mem. San Mateo County Health Council, 1982-85, vice chmn., 1984; mem. all ch. coms., lay leader Honolua United Meth. Ch. Cert. advanced nursing adminstrn. Mem. San Mateo County (dir. 1964-69, pres. elect 1967-68, pres. 1968-70), Golden Gate (1st v.p. 1974-78, dir. 1974-78), Calif., Am. nurses assns., Nat. League Nursing, Soc. for Nursing Service Adminstrs., State Practice and Edn. Council, AAUW, Maui Hospice Assn. (vol.), San Mateo County Grand Jury Assn., Calif. Grand Jury Assn., Sigma Theta Tau. Republican. Club: Kai-Perm. Contbr. articles in field to profl. jours. Home: 150 Puukolii Rd Apt 47 Lahaina HI 96761-1961

VON DESTINON, MARK ALAN, academic administrator; b. Muskegon, Mich., Oct. 30, 1956; s. Irvin Andrew and Rose Mary (Spicklemire) von D. BA, U. Ariz., 1978, MEd, 1985, PhD, 1989. Page U.S. Congress, Washington, 1973-74; polit. cons. Foudy, Zimmerman and Assocs., Tucson, 1975-76; asst. mgr. Cliff Manor Inn Resort Hotel, Tucson, 1976-78; admissions supr. U. Ariz., Tucson, 1978-80; registrar Cochise Coll., Douglas, Ariz., 1980-84; asst. dir. admissions Glendale (Ariz.) Community Coll., 1984-85; fin. aid counselor U. Ariz., Tucson, 1985-86, rsch. assoc., 1986-89, asst. to v.p. student affairs, 1989-92; dean of students Cochise Coll., Sierra Vista, Ariz., 1992—. Co-chair Lambda Dem. Caucus, Tucson, 1989-91. Mem. Nat. Assn. Student Pers. Adminstrs. (at-large mem. rsch. and program com. 1989-90, newsletter editor 1988-90, chair gay and lesbian network 1990-92), Am. Coll. Pers. Assn. (gay and lesbian standing com.). Lutheran. Home:

4009 Paseo Grande Tucson AZ 85711 Office: Cochise Coll Sierra Vista AZ 85635

VONDRAK, ROBERT RICHARD, environmental engineer; b. Chgo., Jan. 4, 1949; s. Henry Francis and Mary Ann Vondrak. BS in Chemistry, Loyola U., Chgo., 1972; MS in Chemistry, Ariz. State U., Tempe, 1977. Grad. teaching assoc. chemistry dept. Ariz. State U., Tempe, 1972-77; chemist Ariz. Dept. Health Svcs., Phoenix, 1978-79; environ. engring. specialist Ariz. Dept. Environ. Quality, Phoenix, 1979-87, environ. program supr., 1987-88; utilities cons. Ariz. Corp. Commn., Phoenix, 1988-90. Mem. Soc. Applied Spectroscopy. Republican. Roman Catholic. Home: 343 E Garfield St Tempe AZ 85281-1014

VON HIPPEL, PETER HANS, chemistry educator; b. Goettingen, Germany, Mar. 13, 1931; came to U.S., 1937, naturalized, 1942; s. Arthur Robert and Dagmar (franck) von H.; m. Josephine Baron Raskind, June 20, 1954; children: David F., James A., Benjamin J. B.S., MIT, 1952, M.S., 1953, Ph.D., 1955. Phys. biochemist Naval Med. Research Inst., Bethesda, Md., 1956-59; from asst. prof. to assoc. prof. biochemistry Dartmouth Coll., 1959-67; prof. chemistry, mem. Inst. Molecular Biology U. Oreg., 1967-79, dir. Inst. Moledular Biology, 1969-80, chmn. dept. chemistry, 1980-87; rsch. prof. chemistry Am. Cancer Soc., 1989—; mem. study sect. USPHS, 1963-67; chmn. biopolymers Grodon Conf., 1968; mem. trustees' vis. com. biology dept. MIT, 1973-76; mem. bd. sci. counsellors Nat. Inst. Arthritis, Metabolic and Digestive Diseases, NIH, 1974-78; mem. coun. Nat. Inst. Gen. Med. Scis., NIH, 1982-86, mem. dir.'s adv. com. NIH, 1987-92; mem. Sci. and Tech. Ctrs. Adv. Com., NSF, 1987-89. Mem. editorial bd. Jour. Biol. Chemistry, 1967-73, 76-82, Biochem. Biophys. Acta, 1965-70, Physiol. Revs., 1972-77, Biochemistry, 1977-80, Trends in Biochem. Sci., 1986—, Protein Sci., 1990—; editor: Jour. Molecular Biology, 1986—; contbr. articles to profl. jours., chpts. to books. Lt. M.S.C. USNR, 1956-59. NSF predoctoral fellow, 1953-55; NIH postdoctoral fellow, 1955-56; NIH sr. fellow, 1959-67; Guggenheim fellow, 1973-74. Fellow Am. Acad. Arts and Scis.; mem. AAAS, Am. Chem. Soc., Am. Soc. Biol. Chemists, Biophys. Soc. (mem. council 1970-73, pres. 1973-74), Nat. Acad. Scis., Fedn. Am. Scientists, Sigma Xi. Home: 1900 Crest Dr Eugene OR 97405-1753

VON KALINOWSKI, JULIAN ONESIME, lawyer; b. St. Louis, May 19, 1916; s. Walter E. and Maybelle (Michaud) von K.; m. Penelope Jayne Dyer, June 29, 1980; children by previous marriage: Julian Onesime, Wendy Jean von Kalinowski. BA, Miss. Coll., 1937; JD with honors, U. Va., 1940. Bar: Va. 1940, Calif. 1946. Assoc. Gibson, Dunn and Crutcher, L.A., 1946-52, ptnr., 1953-62, mem. exec. com., 1962-82, adv. ptnr., 1985—; CEO Litigation Scis., Inc., Culver City, Calif., 1991—, also chmn. bd. dirs.; bd. dirs., mem. exec. com. W.M. Keck Found.; mem. faculty Practising Law Inst., 1971, 76, 78, 79, 80; instr. in spl. course on antitrust litigation Columbia U. Law Sch., N.Y.C., 1981; mem. lawyers dels. com. to 9th Cir. Jud. Conf., 1953-73; UN expert Mission to People's Republic China, 1982. Contbr. articles to legal jours.; author: Antitrust Laws and Trade Regulation, 1969, desk edit., 1981; gen. editor: World Law of Competition, 1978, Antitrust Counseling and Litigation Techniques, 1984. With USN, 1941-46, capt. Res. ret. Fellow Am. Bar Found., Am. Coll. Trial Lawyers (chmn. complex litigation com. 1984-87); mem. ABA (mem. ho. dels. 1970, chmn. antitrust law sect. 1972-73), State Bar of Calif., L.A. Bar Assn., U. Va. Law Sch. Alumni Assn., Calif. Club, L.A. Country Club, La Jolla Beach and Tennis Club, N.Y. Athletic Club, Regency Club, The Sky Club (N.Y.C.), Phi Kappa Psi, Phi Alpha Delta. Republican. Episcopalian. Home: 12320 Ridge Cir Los Angeles CA 90049-1151 Office: Litigation Scis Inc 200 Corporate Pointe Ste 300 Culver City CA 90230

VON KAMINSKY, ELAINE ISABELLE, financier, congresswoman; b. Geneva, Switzerland, Nov. 26, 1963; came to U.S., 1964; d. Peter Johannes and Juliette Isabelle (Bourbon et Bourbon) Von K.; m. Laurenz DiMedici, June 11, 1974; 1 child, Alfonso Sebastian Von Kaminski DiMedici deBourbon. Student, Oberlin Coll., 1984, Fullerton (Calif.) Coll., 1983-86, U. So. Calif., 1986-88, U. Geneva, 1988-90; JD, Harvard U., 1988, BA, MM, BS. Pres. Sapho & Co., L.A., 1990—; CEO Sapho Bank Corp., San Francisco, 1991—; researcher Presdl. Adv. Com., Washington, 1992—; mem. Ho. of Reps., Washington, 1991—; CEO Sapho Bank Corp, S.F., Royal Bank of Russa, NBR., N.A.; del.-at-large Rep. Platform Com., 1991—; mem. nat. Rep. senatorial com., 1992—. Columnist for Washington Post/ABC-TV. Republican. Roman Catholic. Address: 9951 Platanal Dr Villa Park CA 92667-6773

VON KRENNER, WALTHER G., artist, writer, art consultant and appraiser; b. W. Ger., June 26, 1940; s. Frederick and Anna-Marie (von Wolfrath) von K.; m. Hana Renate Geue, 1960; children—Michael P., Karen P. Privately educated by Swiss and English tutors; student Asian studies, Japan, 1965-68; student of Southeast Asia studies, Buddhist U., Bankok, Thailand, Cambodia. Curator, v.p. Gallery Lahaina, Maui, Hawaii; pres. Internat. Valuation Honolulu, 1980—; owner Al Hilal Arabians; instr. aikido, 1962—. Mem. Am. Soc. Appraisers (sr. mem.; pres., dir.). Author books on Oriental art. Home: PO Box 1338 Kalispell MT 59903-1338

VON MINDEN, MILTON CHARLES, JR., internist; b. La Grange, Tex., Nov. 29, 1936; s. Milton and Lillian (Falke) Von M.; m. Catherine Brawner, July 5, 1963; children: Milton III, Susan, Mark. BS, Tex. A&M U., 1958; MD, Baylor Med. Schl, 1962. Diplomate Am. Bd. Internal Medicine. Intern Ben Taub Hosp., Houston, 1962-63; resident in internal medicine Baylor U. affiliated hosps., Houston, 1967-69, nephrology fellow, 1969-70; practice medicine specializing in internal medicine and nephrology Colorado Springs, Colo., 1970—. Mem. ACP, Am. Soc. Nephrology, Colo. Med. Soc., El Paso Med. Soc., Pikes Peak Nephrology Assn. (pres. 1977—). Office: 2130 E LaSalle Colorado Springs CO 80906

VON PAGENHARDT, ROBERT, political science educator, diplomat; b. St. Louis, Aug. 21, 1923; s. Maximilian Hugo and Marie Dupuy (Adams) von P.; m. Hope Allen, 1946 (div. 1954); m. Heidi Elizabeth Schwitzer, June 25, 1962; children: Alexandra, Tania, stepchildren: Christian Fischbacher, Chasper Fischbacher, Joy Fischbacher Law. BA summa cum laude, Stanford U., 1948, MA in Internat. Rels., 1954, PhD, 1970. Teaching asst., Polit. Sci. Stanford Univ., 1948-49, 51-54; staff asst., Office Sec. Gen. UN, N.Y., 1949; fulbright scholar Univ. Paris, 1949-51; dep. exec. dir. World Affairs Coun. of No. Calif., San Francisco, 1951-52; instr. Univ. of Santa Clara, Calif., 1953-54; foreign svc. officer, Bur. Internat. Affairs Dept. of State, 1957-59, U.S. Embassy to Pakistan, 1959-61, U.S. Mission to UNESCO, NATO, Paris, 1962-67; prof. Policy Scis., diplomatic advisor supt. Naval Postgrad. Sch. & Defense Resources Mgmt. Inst., Monterey, Calif., 1967—; commodor Monterey Peninsula Yacht Club, 1972; pres. Monterey Inst. of Internat. Studies, 1977; chmn. advisory bd. Salvation Army, 1980-82; v. chmn. U.S. Assn. for Club of Rome, 1990-92. Author: (with others) To Unite Our Strength, 1992. pres. No. Calif. Divsn. UN Assn., 1977-79, Monterey Bay Chpt. UNA-USA, 1975-77, Sons of the Am. Revolution, 1980-90; v.p. Calif. Soc. Sons of the Am. Revolution, 1990—. Recipient Silver Citizenship Medal Sons of the Am. Revolution, 1992, Meritorious Svc. Medal, 1991. Mem. UN Assn. of the U.S., Internat. Studies Assn., Salvation Army (Monterey Peninsula fin. chair 1978—), Old Capital Club. Democrat. Episcopalian. Office: Defense Resources Mgmt Inst Naval Postgrad Sch Monterey CA 93943

VON PASSENHEIM, JOHN BURR, lawyer; b. Riverside, Calif., Nov. 25, 1964; s. Burr Charles and Kathryn E. (Kirkland) Passenheim. BA in English with honors, U. Calif.-Santa Barbara, 1986; JD, U. Calif., Hastings, 1989. Bar: Calif. 1989. Pvt. practice law San Diego, 1990—; organizer Rock the Vote, San Diego, 1992; primary atty. Calif. Lawyers for the Arts, San Diego; panel atty. Independent Music Seminar, 1992. Contbg. staff DICTA mag.; editor (legal column) It's the Law, 1990-93. Bd. dirs. Surfrider Found., San Diego chpt; vol. atty. San Diego Vol. Lawyer Program. Mem. San Diego County Bar Assn. Civil Libertarian. Office: 4425 Bayard St Ste 240 San Diego CA 92109

VON REICHBAUER, PETER GRAVES, senator; b. Seattle, Dec. 30, 1944; s. Ludwig and Marian VonR.; m. Martha Ann Lindberg, June 26, 1983; children: Jeff, Jeremy, Katherine. BA, U. Ala., 1971. Senator State of Wash., Olympia, 1986—; Rep. whip Senate Rep. Caucus, Olympia, 1985—. Treas. St. Francis Community Hosp., Federal Way, Wash., 1986; vice chmn. U.S. Olympics Com., 1986; bd. dirs. Federal Way Boys and Girls Club, 1986. Served to capt. inf. U.S. Army. Roman Catholic. Lodge: Kiwanis (pres. Federal Way club 1986). Home: 3417 St Andrews Court Tacoma WA 98422 Office: Senate Rep Caucus 113 Institutions Bldg Olympia WA 98504

VON RIESEMANN, WALTER ARTHUR, research engineer; b. Bklyn., Feb. 12, 1930; s. Carl Von Riesemann and Clara (Ammann) Hansen; children: James D., Paul D. BS, Poly. Inst. Bklyn., 1958; MS, U. Ill., 1959; PhD, Stanford U., 1968. Registered profl. engr., N.Mex. Rsch. engr. Alcoa Rsch. Labs, New Kensington, Pa., 1959-60; staff mem. Sandia Nat. Labs, Albuquerque, 1960-65, 68-77, supr., 1977-91, mgr. 1991—; mem. Pressure Vessel Research Com. N.Y.C., 1978—. Contbr. articles to profl. jours. Served with U.S. Army, 1948-52. NASA trainee Stanford U., 1965; fellow U. Ill., 1958. Fellow ASCE (pres. N.Mex. sect. 1975-76, tech. council 1980—), ASME (chmn. N.Mex. sect. 1980-81, PV and P Paper award 1975), Am. Nuclear Soc. Republican. Office: Org 6403 Sandia Nat Labs Albuquerque NM 87185-5800

VON STUDNITZ, GILBERT ALFRED, state official; b. Hamburg, Germany, Nov. 24, 1950; came to U.S., 1954.; s. Helfrid and Rosemarie Sofie (Kreiten) von S.; m. Erica Lynn Hoot, May 26, 1990. BA, Calif. State U., L.A., 1972. Adminstrv. hearing officer State of Calif., Montebello, 1987-91; mgr. III driver control policy unit Dept. Motor Vehicles State of Calif., Sacramento, 1991-93; ops. mgr. Driver Safety Review, 1993—. Author: Aristocracy in America, 1989; editor publs. on German nobility in U.S., 1986—. Active L.A. Conservancy, West Adams Heritage Assn., dir., 1989-91. Mem. Calif. State Mgrs. Assn., Assn. German Nobility in N.Am. (pres. 1985—), Driver Improvement Assn. Calif. (v.p. 1992—), Benicia Hist. Soc., Sierra Club, Intertel Club, Phi Sigma Kappa (v.p. chpt. 1978). Roman Catholic. Home: 1101 W 2d St Benicia CA 94510

VON TILSIT, HEIDEMARIE, information management specialist; b. Heinrichswalde, Germany, Sept. 26, 1944; came to U.S., 1967; d. Heinz and Kaethe Krink; m. Leonard Wierzba, May 14, 1969 (div. 1980). Buchhandel, Dt. Buchh. Schule, Kiel, Germany, 1965; profl. cert., Coll. of Further Edn., Oxford, Eng., 1966; BA, Calif. State U., Fullerton, 1979. Library asst. Allergan, Inc., Irvine, Calif., 1975-76; info. analyst Allergan Pharms., Irvine, Calif., 1976-79, library supr., 1979-81, mgr. corp. info. ctr., 1982—; cons. in field, Irvine, 1980—; owner, pres. Unitran, Corona, Calif., 1980—; mem. adv. bd. CB&S Career Cons., Orange, Calif., 1987—; mem. adv. bd. for univ.-industry rsch. and tech. U. Calif., Irvine, 1992—. Editor/writer articles sci. and information mgmt. Bd. dirs. Nat. Woman's Polit. Caucus, Irvine, 1984-85. Mem. Indsl. Tech. Info. Mgmt. Group (steering com. 1984-86, acting pres. 1986), Am. Soc. Info. Sci., Spl. Librs. Assn., Pharm. Mfg. Assn. (com. info. mgmt. sect. 1985—), Monterey Village Homeowners Assn. (pres. 1992—). Democrat. Home: 1543 San Rafael Dr Corona CA 91720-3795 Office: Allergan Inc 2525 Dupont Dr Irvine CA 92715-1599

VONTVER, LOUIS ANDREW, physician, educator; b. Billings, Mont., May 10, 1936; s. Simon A. and May (Anderson) V.; m. Yvonne Lorree Courteau, Mar. 21, 1960; children: Kirsten, Ross, Jason. BA, U. Minn., 1957, BS, MD, 1960; MEd, U. Wash., 1970. Diplomate Am. Bd. Ob-Gyn. (examiner); bd. cert. ob-gyn. Intern Harbor Gen. Hosp., Torrance, Calif., 1960-61; fellow in reproductive endocrinology U. Wash., Seattle, 1964-65, resident in ob-gyn., 1965-69, jr. faculty ob-gyn., 1969-75, assoc. prof., 1975-83, prof., 1983—, dir. divsn. edn. ob-gyn., 1977—; mem. Coun. Resident Edn. in Ob-Gyn. Com. in Tng. Exam, Chgo., 1979-85. Author: Obstetrics and Gynecology Review, Edition 1-4, 1975-89, Differential Diagnosis Gynecology, Edition 1, 1978, Edition 2, 1984, Comprehensive Gynecology Review Edition 1-2, 1989-92; contbr. articles to profl. jours. Chief gynecology, USPHS, Seattle, 1975-77. Capt. USAF, 1961-64. Recipient Excellence in Teaching award Assn. Profs. Gynecology & Obstetrics Found., 1992. Mem. AMA, Am. Coll. Obstetricians and Gynecologists (chmn. PROLOG unit 5 1985-86), Assn. Profs. Gynecology and Obstetrics (coun. 1988-91, undergrad. med. edn. com. 1991—), Pacific Coast Obstet. and Gynecol. Soc., Seattle Gynecol. Soc. (pres. 1985). Office: Univ Wash Med Ctr Dept Ob-Gyn RH-20 Seattle WA 98195

VOORHEES, LORRAINE ISOBEL, college dean; b. Pitts., Sept. 23, 1947; d. Glenn and Helen L. (Urban) V. OD, So. Calif. Coll. Optometry, Fullerton, 1971; MS, Calif. State U., Fullerton, 1986. Asst. prof. So. Calif. Coll. Optometry, 1972-80, dir. admissions and records, 1980-86, dir. student affairs, 1986-90, dean student affairs, 1990—. Office: So Calif Coll Optometry 2575 E Yorba Linda Blvd Fullerton CA 92631-1699

VORE, RONALD EUGENE, rancher; b. Lead, S.D., July 28, 1950; s. Robert E. and Clara Lee (Smith) V.; m. Terry S. Denzin, Feb. 9, 1974; children: Kari E., Radona R. BS, U. Wyo., 1978, MS, 1980, PhD, 1982. Supr. Crook County Weed & Pest Bd., Sundance, Wyo., 1976-77; rsch. assoc. U. Wyo., Laramie, 1977-80, rsch. scientist, 1980-82; owner, mgr. Six-T-Nine Ranch, Beulah, Wyo., 1982—. Contbr. numerous articles to profl. and trade jours. Chmn. Cook County Fair Bd., 1984-89; sec. Crook County Weed and Pest Bd., 1985-89; chmn. Devils Tower Conservation Dist., Sundance, 1990—; mem. Wyo. State Bd. of Agr. With U.S. Army, 1972-73. Mem. Wyo. Stockgrowers Assn., Bear Lodge Livestock Assn. (treas. 1990—), Sundance Rod and Gun Club. Home and Office: Box 306 Beulah WY 82712

VORENBERG, ALAN R., real estate broker; b. Carlsbad, N.Mex., Dec. 10, 1951; s. Morris and Adele (Rich) V. Grad. high sch., Carlsbad, 1969. Cert. Residential Specialist; lic. real estate sales assoc. Head waiter La Tertulia Restaurant, Santa Fe, N.Mex., 1973-89; real estate broker Coldwell Banker Trails West Realty, Santa Fe, 1989—. Home: 103 Rio Vista Pl Santa Fe NM 87501 Office: Coldwell Banker 2000 Old Pecos Trail Santa Fe NM 87501

VORHEES, FRANCINE BARBARA, accountant; b. Gilroy, Calif., Nov. 12, 1956; d. Mario Charlie and Ines Barbara (Valbusa) Fiorio; m. Jon Purn Vorhees, Sept. 13, 1980; children: Joshua, Justin. BA in Bus., Calif. State U., Sacramento, 1979. CPA, Calif. CPA Donoho, Cohn & Co., Sacramento, Calif., 1979-87; pvt. practice Roseville, Calif., 1987-91; CPA, owner Zimrick Vorhees, Sacramento, 1991—. Vice pres., treas. Sacramento Women's Network, 1981-83, mem. scholarship com., 1985-90; bd. dirs. Placer Youth Soccer League, Roseville, 1992—, Linking Edn. and Econ. Devel. (Sacramento task force mem. 1993—). Office: Zimrick Vorhees 1616 29th St Sacramento CA 95661

VORHIES, CARL BRAD, dentist; b. Indpls., Jan. 21, 1949; s. Jack Mckim and Georgia Thelma (Reese) V.; m. Catherine Isabel Leitch, Aug. 30, 1975; children: Michael, Colin, Jeffrey. BA, Ind. U., 1971, DDS, 1975. Practice dentistry Beaverton, Oreg., 1975—; team dentist Portland Winterhawks Hockey Team, 1979—. Vol. Dental Aid for Children, Washington County, Oreg. Named Dentist of Yr. Oreg. Acad. Gen. Dentistry, 1990; Paul Harris fellow, 1985. Fellow Am. Coll. Dentists, Internat. Coll. Dentists; mem. ADA, Acad. Gen. Dentistry (master 1986, bd. dirs. 1987-91, bd. trustees 1991-93, treas. 1992—), Oreg. Acad. Gen. Dentistry (pres. 1985-86), Oreg. Dental Assn. (sec.-treas. 1980-82), Rotary Club. Home: 5240 SW Humphrey Blvd Portland OR 97221-2315 Office: 12755 SW 2nd St Beaverton OR 97005-2765

VORIES, DENNIS LYNN, consulting electrical engineer; b. Walla Walla, Wash., July 5, 1952; s. Eldon Lynn and Barbara Lou (Merklin) V.; m. Beverly B. Boyle, Mar. 19, 1989. BS in Elec. Engring., Walla Walla Coll., 1974. Registered profl. engr., Nev., Calif. Electronics engr. Naval Weapons Ctr., China Lake, Calif., 1974-79; pvt. practice Valley Center, Calif., 1979—. Author: Solar Savers, 1977; patentee in field. Mem. IEEE, Nat. Soc. Profl. Engrs., Calif. Soc. Profl. Engrs., Forensic Cons. Assn. Seventh-Day Adventist.

VORIS, WILLIAM, educational administrator; b. Neoga, Ill., Mar. 20, 1924; s. Louis K. and Faye (Hancock) V.; m. Mavis Marie Myre, Mar. 20, 1949; children: Charles William II, Michael K. BS, U. So. Calif., 1947, MBA, 1948; PhD, Ohio State U., 1951; LLD, Sung Kyun Kwan U. (Korea), 1972, Eastern Ill. U., 1976. Teaching asst. Ohio State U., Columbus, 1948-50; prof. mgmt. Wash. State U., Pullman, 1950-52; prof., head dept. mgmt. Los Angeles State Coll., 1952-58, 60-63; dean Coll. Bus. and Pub. Adminstrn., U. Ariz., Tucson, 1963-71; pres. Am. Grad. Sch. Internat. Mgmt., Glendale, Ariz., 1971—. Ford Found. research grantee Los Angeles State Coll., 1956; prof. U. Tehran (Iran), 1958-59; Ford Found. fellow Carnegie Inst. Tech., Pitts., 1961; prof. Am. U., Beirut, Lebanon, 1961, 62; cons. Hughes Aircraft Co., Los Angeles, Rheem Mfg. Co., Los Angeles, Northrop Aircraft Co., Palmdale, Calif., Harwood Co., Alhambra, Calif., ICA, Govt. Iran. Served with USNR, 1942-45. Fellow Acad. Mgmt.; mem. Ariz. Acad., Beta Gamma Sigma, Alpha Kappa Psi, Phi Delta Theta. Author: Production Control, Text and Cases, 1956, 3d edit., 1966; Management of Production, 1960. Research in indsl. future of Iran, mgmt. devel. in Middle East. Home: Thunderbird Campus Glendale AZ 85306

VORPAGEL, WILBUR CHARLES, historical consultant; b. Milw., Feb. 26, 1926; s. Arthur Fred and Emma (Hintz) V.; Betty J. Hoch, June 19, 1952; stepchildren: Jerry L., Sharon Belveal Sullenberger. Student Army specialized tng. program, U. Ill., 1943-44; BBA, U. Wis., 1949; MBA, U. Denver, 1953. Cert. tchr., Colo. Instr. Montezuma County High Sch., Cortez, Colo., 1949-51; coord. bus. edn. Pueblo (Colo.) Pub. Schs., 1951-56; pvt. practice bus. cons. Pueblo and Denver, 1956—; tchr. bus. edn. Emily Griffith Opportunity Sch., Denver, 1959-69; various positions with Denver & Rio Grande Western R.R. Co., Denver, 1959-88; cons. in field. Bd. dirs. Colo. Ret. Sch. Employees Assn., Denver, 1988—; rep. Custer Battlefield Hist. & Mus. Assn. Sgt. U.S. Army, 1944-46, ETO. Mem. Augustan Soc., St. John Vol. Corp., S.E. Colo. Geneal. Soc., Rio Grande Vets. Club (bd. dirs. Pueblo chpt.), Biblical Archaeol. Soc. (contbg. writer), Nat. Huguenot Soc., Colo. Huguenot Soc. (organizing pres. 1979-89), 70th Inf. Div. Assn., Shriners, Masons. Republican. Mem. Christian Ch. Home and Office: 335 Davis Ave Pueblo CO 81004-1019

VOTH, ALDEN H., political science educator; b. Goessel, Kans., May 4, 1926; s. John F. and Helena (Hildebrandt) V.; m. Norma E. Jost, Aug. 18, 1956; children: Susan, Thomas. BA, Bethel Coll., 1950; MS in Econs., Iowa State U., Ames, 1953; PhD in Internat. Rels., U. Chgo., 1959. Assoc. prof. polit. sci. Upland (Calif.) Coll., 1960-63; prof. polit. sci. San Jose (Calif.) State U., 1963-65, 67-91, prof. emeritus, 1991—; vis. prof. polit. sci. Am. U. in Cairo, 1965-67. Author: Moscow Abandons Israel, 1980, (with others) The Kissinger Legacy, 1984. Trustee Pomona (Calif.) Valley Am. Assn. UN, 1963. Am. U. in Cairo Rsch. grantee, 1966; Nat. Coun. on U.S.-Arab Rels. fellow, 1990—. Home: 1385 Kimberly Dr San Jose CA 95118-1426 Office: San Jose State U One Washington Sq San Jose CA 95192

VOTH, ANDREW C., museum director; b. Akron, Ohio, Aug. 4, 1947; s. Roland L. and Dorothy (Fynn) V. BA, Ambassador Coll., 1970. Chmn. art Amb. Coll., Pasadena, Calif., 1976-78; dir. galleries and fine arts Amb. Coll., Pasadena, 1979; dir. Pasadena Festival of Art, 1980, Carnegie Art Mus., Oxnard, Calif., 1981—; cultural arts supr. City of Oxnard, 1981—; dir. Art in Pub. Places, City of Oxnard, 1988—; pres. Pacific Art Svcs., Santa Barbara, 1987—; reveiwer Inst. Mus. Svcs., Washington, 1985—. Author: (catalog) Mcpl. Art Collection, 1984; editor: Sacha Moldovan - Painter, 1990, The Pastel Landscapes of Theodore Lukits, 1991; producer Dialogs in Creativity for the 1990's. Pres. Pasadena Inst. Arts, 1978-80; v.p. Pasadena Arts Coun., 1979-80; tech. adv. Ventury County Arts Commn., 1981—; treas. Patrons of Cultural Arts, 1985—; trustee Inst. Human Devel., Ojai, Calif., 1990—. Recipient numerous awards for paintings, 1960—. Mem. Calif. Assn. Mus. (trustee 1987-92), Am. Assn. Mus., Tower (com. mem. 1987-92). Office: Carnegie Art Mus 424 S C St Oxnard CA 93030-5944

VOULKOS, PETER, artist; b. Bozeman, Mont., Jan. 29, 1924. B.S., Mont. State U., hon. doctorate, 1968; M.F.A., Calif. Coll. Arts and Crafts, hon. doctorate, 1972; hon. doctorate, Otis Inst. of Parsons Sch. Design, 1980, San Francisco Art Inst., 1982. Tchr. Archie Bray Found., Helena, Mont., Black Mountain Coll., Los Angeles County Art Inst., Mont. State U., Greenwich House Pottery, N.Y.C., Columbia U. Tchrs. Coll., U. Calif.-Berkeley, ret. 1985. One man shows include Gump's Gallery, San Francisco, U. Fla., Hist. Soc. Mont., Felix Landau Gallery, Chgo. Art Inst., Bonniers, Inc., N.Y.C., Fresno State Coll., Scripps Coll., U. So. Calif., Pasadena Art Mus. (purchase prize), Scripps Coll., Nat. Ceramic Exhbn., U. Tenn., Brussels World's Fair, 1958, de Young Mus., Seattle World's Fair, 1962, Whitney Mus. Art, Denver Art Mus. (purchase prize), Smithsonian Instn. (purchase prize), Los Angeles County Mus. Art (purchase prize), Okun-Thomas Gallery, St. Louis, 1980, Morgan Gallery, Kansas City, Kans., 1980, Exhibit A, Chgo., 1976, 79, 81, Braunstein Gallery, San Francisco, 1968, 75, 78, 82, 86, 87, 91, 93, Cowles Gallery, N.Y.C., 1981, 83, 90, Thomas Segal Gallery, Boston, 1981, 88, Twining Gallery, N.Y.C., 1988, 89, Point View, Tokyo, 1983, Hordaland Kunstnersentrum, Bergan, Norway, 1993, travelling retrospective show, San Francisco Mus. Modern Art, 1978-79, Contemporary Arts Mus., Houston, Mus. Contemporary Craft, N.Y.C., Milw. Art Ctr.; exhibited in group shows, including Whitney Mus., N.Y.C., 1981, San Francisco Mus. Modern Art, 1981, Los Angeles County Mus. Art, Kunst Industri Museet, Oslo, Norway, 1993; represented in permanent collections Balt. Mus. Art, Denver Art Mus., Univs. Calif., Colo., Fla., Ill., Mich., Utah, Wis., Ind., Mont. State U., Ariz. State U., Bemidji State U., Fresno State U., Iowa State U., Tokyo Folk Art Mus., Los Angeles County Art Mus., Mus. Contemporary Crafts, N.Y.C., Oakland Art Mus., Pasadena Mus. Art, San Francisco Mus. Modern Art, Smithsonian Instn., Boston Mus. Fine Arts, Corcoran Gallery, Washington, Den Permanente, Copenhagen, Fed. Bldg., Honolulu, Everson Mus., Syracuse, N.Y., Long Beach (Calif.) Mus. Art, Milw. Art Mus., Minn. Mus. Art, Mus. Boymans van Beuningen, Netherlands, Mus. Modern Art, N.Y.C., Portland Art Mus., Whitney Mus., N.Y.C., Stedelijk Mus., Amsterdam and Eindhoven, Netherlands, Nelson Atkins Mus., Kansas City. Recipient first prize RAC, Nat. Decorative Art Show, Wichita, award N.W. Craft Show, award Pacific Coast Ceramic Show, purchase prize Cranbrook Art Mus., award Los Angeles County Fair, Ford. Found., Silver medal Internat. Ceramic Exhbn., Ostend, Belgium, 1954, Gold medal Cannes, France, award I Paris Biennial, 1959, Rodin Mus. prize in sculpture, citation for disting. contbns. to visual arts Nat. Assn. Schs. Art, 1980, award of honor San Francisco Art Commn., 1981, Creative Arts Awards medal for sculpture Brandeis U., 1982, Gold medal Am. Craft Council, 1986; Nat. Endowment for Arts sr. fellow, 1976 and grantee, 1986; Guggenheim fellow, 1984. Mem. Soc. Centennial Alumni Mont. State U. Address: 951 62d St Oakland CA 94608

VOUTILAINEN, ERKKI JUHANI, land development company executive; b. Kuopio, Finland, Aug. 3, 1946; came to U.S., 1968; s. Otto Elmar and Saga Hellin (Tiilikainen) V.; m. Kathleen Sue Duran, Dec. 27, 1986; children: Erika Kristine, Heather Lee, Tiffany Dawn. BA, Brigham Young U., 1972. Mktg. mgr. AT&T, L.A., 1974-85; pres., CEO Florentine Engerprises Inc., Florence, Oreg., 1986—. Mem. Rotary Internat. Mem. Ch. of LDS. Home: PO Box 2419 Florence OR 97439

VREELAND, ROBERT WILDER, electronics engineer; b. Glen Ridge, N.J., Mar. 4, 1923; s. Frederick King and Elizabeth Lenora (Wilder) V.; m. Jean Gay Fullerton, Jan. 21, 1967; 1 son, Robert Wilder. BS, U. Calif., Berkeley, 1947. Electronics engr. Litton Industries, San Carlos, Calif., 1948-55; sr. devel. electronics engr. U. Calif. Med. Ctr., San Francisco, 1955-89; ret.; cons. electrical engring; speaker 8th Internat. Symposium Biotelemetry, Dubrovnik, Yugoslavia, 1984, RF Expo, Anaheim, Calif., 1985, 86, 87. Contbr. articles to profl. jours., also to internat. meetings and symposiums; patentee in field. Recipient Chancellor's award U. Calif., San Francisco, 1979; cert. appreciation for 25 years' service U. Calif., San Francisco, 1980. Mem. Nat. Bd. Examiners Clin. Engring. (cert. clin. engr.), IEEE, Assn. Advancement Med. Instrumentation (bd. examiner), Am. Radio Relay League (pub. service award 1962). Home: 45 Maywood Dr San Francisco CA 94127-2007 Office: U Calif Med Ctr 4th and Parnassus Sts San Francisco CA 94143

VRIESMAN, ROBERT JOHN, mathematics educator; b. Muskegon, Mich., May 19, 1953; s. Robert John Vriesman and Gloria Ruth (Bultema) Fowler. B of Music Edn., Ea. Mich. U., 1975; MMus, U. Mich., 1990. Orch. dir. Tuscaloosa (Ala.) County Schs., 1976-78; band dir. Grossmont Union Sch. Dist., El Cajon, Calif., 1983-84; algebra tchr. San Dieguito Union Sch. Dist., Encinitas, Calif., 1985-87; tchr. Muskegon Pub. Schs., 1987-88; algebra tchr. L.A. Unified Sch. Dist., 1990—; TV tchr. KLCS TV, L.A., 1991—. Founder, conductor Coastal Communities Civic Band, Encinitas, 1983-87. Mem. Nat. Coun. of Tchrs. of Math., Calif. Tchrs. of Math. Home: 2810 Base Line Trail Hollywood CA 90068

VUCANOVICH, BARBARA FARRELL, congresswoman; b. Fort Dix, N.J., June 22, 1921; d. Thomas F. and Ynez (White) Farrell; m. Ken Dillon, Mar. 8, 1950 (div. 1964); children: Patty Dillon Cafferata, Mike, Ken, Tom, Susan Dillon Stoddard; m. George Vucanovich, June 19, 1965. Student, Manhattanville Coll. of Sacred Heart, 1938-39. Owner, operator Welcome Aboard Travel, Reno, 1968-74; Nev. rep. for Senator Paul Laxalt, 1974-82; mem. 98th-103rd Congresses from 2d Nev. dist., 1983—; mem. coms. interior and insular affairs, appropriations com., subcom. agrl., military construction, mining and natural resources com., Nat. Parks, Forests, Pub. Lands. Pres. Nev. Fedn. Republican Women, Reno, 1955-56; former pres. St. Mary's Hosp. Guild, Lawyer's Wives. Roman Catholic. Club: Hidden Valley Country (Reno). Office: 2202 Rayburn House of Representatives Washington DC 20515-2802*

VUKASIN, JOHN PETER, JR., federal judge; b. Oakland, Calif., May 25, 1928; s. John P. and Natalie Vukasin; m. Sue D. Vukasin, July 1, 1956; children: John P. III, Kirk E., Alexander G., Kim V. Greer, Karen V. Zeff. AB, U. Calif., 1950, JD, 1956. Bar: Calif. 1956. Commr. Calif. Pub. Utilities Commn., 1969-74, chmn., 1971, 72; judge Superior Ct. of Calif., 1974-83, U.S. Dist. Ct. (no. dist.) Calif., San Francisco, 1983—; mem. Adminstrv. Conf. of U.S., 1972-75. Contbr. articles to legal jours. With U.S. Army, 1951-53. Mem. ABA (chmn. pub. utility law sect. 1981-82). Republican.

VUKSTA, MICHAEL JOSEPH, surgeon; b. Pitts., Apr. 25, 1926; s. Michael and Mary Sarah (Hanulya) V.; m. Dorothy Ann Bosak, Sept. 12, 1953; children: Patricia, Michael, Carol, Janet. BA, Youngstown State U., 1949; MD, Ohio State U., 1957. Diplomate Am. Bd. Surgery. Enlisted USN, advanced through grades to capt., 1974; intern St. Elizabeth Hosp., Youngstown, Ohio, resident in gen. surgery, 1958-62; pvt. practice gen. surgery Youngstown, 1962-89; head blue team surgery Oak Knoll U.S. Naval Hosp., Oakland, Calif., 1989—. Capt. USN. Fellow ACS, Am. Coll. Sports Medicine, Southwestern Surg. Congress; mem. Nat. Athletic Trainers Assn. (advisor). Byzantine Catholic. Home: 1 Williams St # A Oakland CA 94605-4556 Office: US Naval Hosp 8750 Mountain Blvd Oakland CA 94627-0001

VURICH, JOHN DAVID, electronics company executive, engineer; b. Detroit, Mar. 13, 1946; s. Joseph Peter and Elisebeth (Vahlberg) V.; m. Sandra Ann Burris, July 12, 1968 (div. Aug. 1975); 1 child, Daniel John; m. Mary Sharman Summers, Sept. 8, 1985. BSEE, Ariz. State U., 1968. Engr. Motorola Inc., Tempe, Ariz., 1968-75; chief engr. Mirco Inc., Phoenix, 1975-76; mgr. product mktg. Nat. Semicondr., Santa Clara, Calif., 1976-77; mgr. product planning Atari Inc., Sunnyvale, Calif., 1977-79; pres., founder Axlon Inc., Sunnyvale, Calif., 1980-85; mgr. advanced products Plantronics Inc., Santa Cruz, Calif., 1986-87; v.p. Advanced Transducer Devices, Sunnyvale, 1987-89; pres., founder BFM Products, Los Gatos, Calif., 1989—; cons. ACS Inc., Scotts Valley, Calif., 1988-89. Inventor 1st computer pinball Spirit of '76 (best design award 1975), smallest computer terminal Datalink 1000, cordless headset telephone (best design award 1987). Pres. Lunar Landowners Assn., Los Gatos, 1989. Home: 876 Brookside Dr Felton CA 95018-9109 Office: BFM Products 876 Brookside Dr Felton CA 95018-9109

WAANDERS, GERALD L., consulting palynologist; b. Grand Rapids, Mich., July 6, 1944; s. J. William and Alice Mae (Oostenbrug) W.; m. Harriet Avner, Aug. 18, 1969; 1 child, Jason. BA, Hope Coll., 1966; MS, U. Okla., 1968; PhD, Mich. State U., 1974. Rsch. paleontologist Amoco Prodn. Co., Tulsa, 1971-74; sr. paleontologist Amoco Prodn. Co., New Orleans, 1974-78; cons. palynologist Anderson, Warren & Assoc., San Diego, 1978-80; prin. Waanders Palynology Cons., San Marcos, Calif., 1980—. Contbr. articles to profl. jours. Musician Jewish Community Ctr. Civic Orch., San Diego, 1985—. Mem. Am. Assn. Strategic Palynologists, So. Calif. Assn. Palynologists (pres. 1990—), Soc. Econ. Paleontologists and Mineralogists, Soc. for Organic Petrologists. Office: Waanders Palynology Cons Inc 1611 S Rancho Santa Fe Rd Ste C San Marcos CA 92069-5157

WACHBRIT, JILL BARRETT, accountant, tax specialist; b. Ventura, Calif., May 27, 1955; d. Preston Everett Barrett and Lois JoAnne (Fondersmith) Batchelder; m. Michael Ian Wachbrit, June 21, 1981; children: Michelle, Tracy. AA, Santa Monica City Coll., 1975; BS, Calif. State U., Northridge, 1979; M in Bus. Taxation, U. So. Calif., 1985. CPA. Supervising sr. tax acct. Peat, Marwick, Mitchell & Co., Century City, Calif., 1979-82; sr. tax analyst Avery Internat., Pasadena, Calif., 1982-83; tax mgr., asst. v.p. First Interstate Leasing, Pasadena, 1983-88, Gibraltar Savs., 1988, Security Pacific Corp., L.A., 1988-92; tax mgr., acct. El Camino Resources Ltd., Woodland Hills, Calif., 1992—. Republican. Jewish.

WACHNER, LINDA JOY, apparel marketing and manufacturing executive; b. N.Y.C., Feb. 3, 1946; d. Herman and Shirley W.; m. Seymour Applebaum, Dec. 21, 1973 (dec., 1983). BS in Econs. and Bus., U. Buffalo, 1966. Buyer Foley's Federated Dept. Store, Houston, 1968-69; sr. buyer R.H. Macy's, N.Y.C., 1969-74; v.p. Warner div. Warnaco, Bridgeport, Conn., 1974-77; v.p. corp. mktg. Caron Internat., N.Y.C., 1977-79; chief exec. officer U.S. div. Max Factor & Co., Hollywood, Calif., 1979-82, pres., chief exec. officer, 1982-83; pres., chief exec. officer Max Factor & Co. Worldwide, 1983-84; mng. dir. Adler & Shaykin, N.Y.C., 1984-86; owner, pres., chmn., chief exec. officer Warnaco Inc., N.Y.C., 1991—; chmn., CEO Authentic Fitness Corp., 1990—; bd. dirs. Primerica Corp., Castle & Cooke Homes, Inc.; mem. Cooperation Ireland. Presdl. appointee Adv. Com. for Trade, Policy, Negotiations; trustee U. Buffalo Found., Carnegie Hall, Aspen Inst. Recipient Silver Achievement award L.A. YWCA; named Outstanding Woman in Bus. Women's Equity Action League, 1980, Woman of Yr., MS. Mag., 1986, one of the Yr.'s Most Fascinating Bus. People, Fortune Mag., 1986, one of 10 Most Powerful Women in Corp. Am., Savvy Woman Mag., 1989, 90, Am.'s Most Successful Bus. Woman, Fortune Mag., 1992. Mem. Young Pres.'s Orgn., Com. of 200, Am. Mgmt. Assn., Am. Apparel Mktg. Assn. (bd. dirs.), Bus. Roundtable. Republican. Jewish. Office: Warnaco Inc 90 Park Ave New York NY 10016-1302 also: Warnaco Inc 11111 Santa Monica Blvd Los Angeles CA 90025

WACHTEL, ALAN LARRY, writer, transportation consultant; b. Cin., Aug. 14, 1947; s. Jacques Louis and Rose (Edlin) W.; m. Cathleen Clarice Moran, Sept. 12, 1984; children: Elizabeth Jean, Anna Rebecca. BA, Yale U., 1968; postgrad., Stanford U., 1970-77. Vol. Peace Corps, Kenya, 1969; tchr. Lawrence Acad., Groton, Mass., 1969-70; teaching asst. Dept. of Physics, Stanford U., 1970-77; instr. Dept. Physics, San Francisco State U., 1977-78; instr. vacuum tech. tng. program Stanford Mid-Peninsula Urban Coalition, 1978-81; engring. trainer Racal-Vadic, Milpitas, Calif., 1981-85; ind. tech. writer/cons. Palo Alto, Calif., 1985—; cons. 3Com Corp., Santa Clara, Calif., 1986-88, 91-92, County of Santa Clara (Calif.), 1986-87, SynOptics Comm., Santa Clara, 1988-91, Alantec Internetworking Systems, San Jose, Calif., 1992-93, City of Berkeley (Calif.), 1992—, County of Marin (Calif.), 1993—. Author computer user and adminstr. manuals; contbr. articles to profl. jours. Mem. Am. Nat. Standards Inst. Inst. Z90 Com. on Vehicular Head Protection, 1982—; mem. Palo Alto Bicycle Adv. Com., 1978—, chmn., 1983-86; chmn. Mountain View (Calif.) Bikeway Com., 1985; mem. Proposition 116 Bicycle Program Tech. Adv. Com., 1992; vice chair State of Calif. Bicycle Adv. Com., 1992-93; mem. Regional Bicycle Adv. Com. of San Francisco Bay Area. Mem. Nat. Writers Union, Soc. for Tech. Comm., Calif. Assn. of Bicycling Orgns. (govt. rels. dir. 1986—, pres. 1982-84, 85-86), League of Am. Wheelmen (state legis. rep. 1987—, Effective Cycling Instr. cert. 1983, regional dir.'s Disting. Svc. award 1991), Cycling Rsch. Assn., Western Wheelers Bicycle Club (pres. 1980), Bikecentennial, Silicon Valley Bicycle Coalition. Home and Office: 3446 Janice Way Palo Alto CA 94303-4212

WACHTELL, ROGER BRUCE, merchant banker; b. N.Y.C., May 5, 1959; s. Thomas and Esther (Pickard) W. BA in Econs., Polit. Sci., UCLA, 1981; MBA, Harvard U., 1985. Analyst Salomon Bros. Inc., San Francisco, 1981-83; assoc. Salomon Bros. Inc., N.Y.C., 1985-87; ltd. ptnr. Gibbons, Green, Van Amerongen, L.A., 1987-89; ptnr. Leonard Green & Ptnrs., L.A., 1989-90; pres. Alpine Equity Ptnrs., Inc., L.A., 1991—; bd. dirs. Quantitative Data Svcs., Inc., Irvine, Calif. Mem. unified fund cabinet Music Ctr. of L.A. County, L.A., 1990—; mem. letters and sci. fund UCLA, L.A., 1991—. Office: Alpine Equity Ptnrs Ste 301 9560 Wilshire Blvd Beverly Hills CA 90212

WACHTELL, THOMAS, petroleum company executive, lawyer; b. Crestwood, N.Y., Mar. 27, 1928; s. Theodore and Carolyn (Satz) W.; grad. Choate Sch., 1946; BS, Syracuse U., 1950; LLB., Cornell U., 1958; m. Esther Carole Pickard, Jan. 27, 1957; children: Roger Bruce, Wendy Ann, Peter James. Bar: N.Y. 1958. Assoc. Livingston, Wachtell & Co., C.P.A.s, N.Y.C., 1958-60; pres. Allied Homeowners Assn., Inc., White Plains, N.Y., 1960-63, pres. Gen. Factoring Co., White Plains, N.Y., 1960-63; exec. asst. to pres. Occidental Petroleum Corp., L.A., 1963-65, v.p., exec. asst., chmn. bd., 1965-72, exec. v.p., 1972-73, officer, dir. numerous subs.; pres. Hydrocarbon Resources Corp., 1973-81; chmn. Oriental Petroleum Corp., 1982-86; pres. Petroleum Power Corp., 1989-91; chmn., pres. MSR Exploration, Ltd., 1990-91; exec. v.p. Frontier Oil and Refining Co., Denver, 1985-87, also bd. dirs.; chmn. bd. Frontier Oil Internat., 1985-87; pres., chief exec. officer, dir. NMR Ctrs., Inc., 1982-83; pres., dir. Cayman Petroleum Corp., 1974-75, Ridgecrest Energy Corp., 1979; dir. Tanglewood Consol. Resources, 1982-84; bd. dirs. Paramount Petroleum Corp., L.A., 1989—, chmn., CEO 1990—; bd. dirs. World Trade Bank, Beverly Hills, Calif., 1985—. Panelist, lectr. Nat. Indsl. Conf. Bd.; bd. govs. The L.A. Music Ctr., 1973-88; chmn., chief exec. officer, bd. dirs. Los Angeles Music Center Opera Assn., 1972—, chmn., chief exec. officer, 1981-86; trustee Good Hope Med. Found., Los Angeles, 1974—. Served to lt. Office Naval Intelligence, USNR, 1952-56. Mem. Am. Mgmt. Assn., Los Angeles World Affairs Council, Choate Alumni Assn. So. Cal. (chmn. 1969—), Confrerie des Chevaliers du Tastevin, Beta Theta Pi, Phi Delta Phi.

WACKER, JOHN FREDERICK, geochemist, planetary scientist; b. Boston, Dec. 10, 1954; s. Warren Ernest Clyde and Ann Romeyn (MacMillan) W.; m. Nancy Joann Becker, June 20, 1981; children: Margaret Ann, Alexandra Romeyn. BS, MIT, 1976; PhD, U. Ariz., 1982. Rsch. assoc. U. Chgo., 1982-86; asst. rsch. physicist Scripps Inst. Oceanography, LaJolla, Calif., 1986-87; sr. rsch. scientist Battelle, Pacific N.W. Lab., Richland, Wash., 1987-93, tech. group leader, 1993—. Contbr. articles to profl. jours. Howard Hughes Med. Found. fellow, 1973; recipient U. Ariz. State scholar, 1977. Mem. AAAS, Am. Astron. Soc., Am. Geophys. Union, Am. Soc. Mass Spectrom, Meteoritical Soc., Sigma Xi. Democrat. Episcopalian. Home: 1967 Mc Pherson Ave Richland WA 99352-2420 Office: Battelle Pacific NW Labs PO Box 999 Richland WA 99352-0999

WADA, HENRY GARRETT, biochemist; b. San Mateo, Calif., May 13, 1948; s. Henry Hideo and Mary Nobuko (Ono) W.; m. Donna Jean Fong, June 20, 1971; children: Jarod James, Lisa Emiko. AB, U. Calif., Berkeley, 1970; PhD, U. Oreg., 1974. Postdoctoral fellow Stanford (Calif.) U. Sch. Medicine, 1974-76, rsch. assoc., 1977-79; product support specialist Calbrochem.-Behring Corp., La Jolla, Calif., 1979-81; mgr. product devel. Monoclonal Antibodies Inc., Mountain View, Calif., 1981-84; scientist, assoc. dir. Cetus Corp., Emeryville, Calif., 1984-86; scientist, mgr. Molecular Devices Corp., Menlo Park, Calif., 1986—. Contbr. articles to profl. publs.; patentee in field. NCI fellow, 1974-76. Mem. Am. Soc. Microbiologists, Am. Soc. Cell Biologists, N.Y. Acad. Sci. Democrat. Presbyterian. Office: Molecular Devices Corp 4700 Bohannon Dr Menlo Park CA 94025

WADDELL, PERRY, public defender; b. Sept. 5, 1964. Student, U. New Eng., Armidale, NSW, Australia, 1985; BA in Polit. Sci., Boise State U., 1988; JD, U. Idaho, 1993. Campaign mgr. for candidate Idaho Senate, Emmett, 1988; video photographer CBS TV, Boise, Idaho, 1988-90; pub. defender Nez Perce Tribal Ct., Lapwai, Idaho, 1992—. Vol. various polit. campaigns, 1974—; candidate for Idaho Senate, 1986. Scholar U. Idaho Law Sch., 1990-93. Mem. ABA, Environ. Law Soc., Idaho Trial Lawyers Assn.

WADDINGHAM, JOHN ALFRED, artist, journalist; b. London, Eng., July 9, 1915; came to U.S., 1927, naturalized, 1943; s. Charles Alfred and Mary Elizabeth (Coles) W.; m. Joan Lee Larson, May 3, 1952; children: Mary Kathryn, Thomas Richard. Student, Coronado (Calif.) Sch. Fine Arts, 1953-54, Portland Art Mus., 1940-65, U. Portland, 1946-47; pupil, Rex Brandt, Eliot Ohara, George Post. Promotion art dir. Oreg. Jour., Portland, 1946-59; with The Oregonian, Portland, 1959-81; editorial art dir. The Oregonian, 1959-81; tchr. watercolor Ore. Soc. Artists, 1954-56; tchr. art Oreg. Sch. Arts and Crafts, 1981—, Portland Community Coll. One man show includes Art in the Gov.'s Office Ore State Capitol, 1991; rep. mus. rental collections, Portland Art Mus., Bush House, Salem, Ore., U. Oreg. Mus., Vincent Price collection, Ford Times collection, also Am. Watercolor Soc. Travelling Show; judge art events, 1946—, over 50 one-man shows; ofcl. artist, Kiwanis Internat. Conv., 1966; designed, dir. constrn. cast: concrete mural Genesis, St. Barnabas Episcopal Ch., Portland, 1960; spl. work drawings old Portland landmarks and houses; propr. John Waddingham Hand Prints, fine arts serigraphs and silk screen drawings, 1965—; featured artist: Am. Artist mag., May 1967, June 1990, published in numerous mags. Served with USAAF, 1942-46. Recipient gold medal Salone Internazionale dell' Umorismo, Italy, 1974, 76, 80; honored with a 45 yr. retrospective Assignment: The Artist as Journalist Oreg. Hist. Soc., 1991. Artist mem. Portland Art Mus.; mem. Portland Art Dirs. Club (past pres.), N.W. Watercolor Soc., Watercolor Soc. Oreg., Oreg. Soc. Artists (watercolor tchr.), Multnomah Athletic Club, Jewish Community Ctr., Univ. Oreg. Med. Sch., Art in the Mounts., Oreg. Old Time Fiddlers, Clan Macleay Bigpipe Band. Home: 955 SW Westwood Dr Portland OR 97201-2744

WADDINGTON, GARY LEE, physician; b. Grand Island, Nebr., Feb. 6, 1944; s. C. Earl and Edna E. Waddington; m. Mary Jane Boden, Dec. 16, 1968; children: Erin Michael, Sara Nicole, Ryan Matthew. BS, U. Nebr., 1968, MD, 1972. Commd. 2d lt. U.S. Army, 1972, advanced through grades to lt. col., 1981; intern U.S. Army M. C., San Francisco, 1972-73; chief U.S. Army M. C., Buffalo, 1973-74; resident in tng. U.S. Army M. C., San Francisco, 1974-77; chief dept. medicine and dermatology U.S. Army M. C., Nuremberg, Fed. Republic of Germany, 1977-80; physician U.S. Army M. C., Colorado Springs, 1980-81; ret. U.S. Army M. C., 1981; ptnr. Allergy & Dermatology Specialists, Phoenix, 1981—; chief dermatology Maricopa County Med. Ctr., Phoenix, 1981-84, St. Joseph's Hosp. & Med. Ctr., Phoenix, 1984—; mem. adv. counsel Biltmore Nat. Bank, Phoenix, 1988—. Fellow Am. Acad. Dermatology. Republican. Lutheran. Office: Allergy & Dermatology Specialists Inc 5040 N 15th Ave Ste 307 Phoenix AZ 85015-3376

WADDINGTON, RAYMOND BRUCE, JR., English language educator; b. Santa Barbara, Calif., Sept. 27, 1935; s. Raymond Bruce and Marjorie Gladys (Waddell) W.; m. Linda Gayle Jones, Sept. 7, 1957 (div.); children: Raymond Bruce, Edward Jackson; m. Kathleen Martha Ward, Oct. 11, 1985. B.A., Stanford U., 1957; Ph.D., Rice U., 1963; postdoctoral (Univ. fellow in Humanities), Johns Hopkins U., 1965-66. Instr. English U. Houston, 1961-62; instr. U. Kans., 1962-63; asst. prof., 1963-65; asst. prof. English lit. U. Wis., Madison, 1966-68; asso. prof. U. Wis., 1968-74, prof., 1974-82; prof. English lit. U. Calif., Davis, 1982—. Author: The Mind's Empire, 1974; co-editor: The Rhetoric of Renaissance Poetry, 1974, The Age of Milton, 1980; mem. editorial bd. Sixteenth Century Jour, 1975, The Medal, 1991; editor: Garland Studies in the Renaissance. Huntington Library fellow, 1967, 75; Inst. Research in Humanities fellow, 1971-72; Guggenheim fellow, 1972-73; NEH fellow, 1977, 83; Newberry Library fellow, 1978; Am. Philos. Soc. grantee, 1965. Mem. Renaissance Soc. Am., Milton Soc. Am., 16th Century Studies Conf. (pres. 1985). Club: Logos. Home: 39 Pershing Ave Woodland CA 95695-2845 Office: U Calif Dept English Davis CA 95616

WADE, GERALD JAMES, electrical and biomedical engineer; b. Calgary, Alta., Can., May 10, 1942; came to U.S., 1966; s. Roy Henry James and Vida Gladys (Lawrence) W.; m. Patricia Anne Miller, Dec. 28, 1969; children: Peter James, Adam Henry. BASc, U. B.C., Vancouver, Can., 1964; MASc, U. Sask., Saskatoon, Can., 1966. Staff engr. Hoffman LaRoche, Nutley, N.J., 1966-68; sr. staff engr. Canberra Electronics, Meriden, Conn., 1968-69, Picker Nuclear, Hamden, Conn., 1969-70; pres. Wade Assocs., Wallingford, Conn., 1970-77; engring. fellow Honeywell, Denver, 1977-90, Metrum Info. Storage, Denver, 1990—. Inventor patient monitor, 1976, specimen bottle, 1984, blood culture device, 1985, recording head, 1985. Coach Littleton Youth Hockey, Denver. Recipient IR 100, Denver/Chgo., 1985. Home: 7196 S Franklin Way Littleton CO 80122 Office: Metrum Info Storage 4800 E Dry Crk Rd Littleton CO 80122

WADE, JOHN H., II, basketball coach; b. San Francisco, Nov. 24, 1959; s. John H. Sr. and Marie (Garrison) W. BA in Urban and Regional Planning, Ea. Wash. U., 1982; M in Sports Coaching, U.S. Sports Acad., Daphne, Ala., 1991. Asst. Ea. Wash. U., Cheney, 1980-81, grad. asst., 1981-82, asst. coach, 1982-88, head coach, 1990—; asst. coach U. Pacific, Stockton, Calif., 1988-90. Mem. Nat. Assn. Basketball Coaches, Black Coaches Assn., African Am. Forum. Office: Ea Wash U Cheney WA 99004

WADE, JUDY LEE, journalist; b. St. Cloud, Minn., Mar. 12, 1939; d. Howard Walter and Mildred Mary (Jung) Wittmayer; m. Gerald H. Wade, Mar. 3, 1969 (div. Apr. 1988); m. William S. Baker Jr., June 22, 1991. BA, U. Minn., 1960. Free-lance mag. writer, 1960—. Author: Disneyland and Beyond: the Ultimate Guide, 1992. Mem. Soc. Am. Travel Writers. Republican. Home and Office: 15025-B Sherman Way Van Nuys CA 91405

WADE, MARK LLOYD, mortician; b. Pocatello, Idaho, Sept. 15, 9157; s. David R. and Virla Sharlene (Nalder) W.; m. Sheryl Searle, Oct. 25, 1978; children: Camilla, Travis, Jason, Bryan, Joshua. AS, Fullerton (Calif.) Coll., 1981. Apprentice Nalder Mortuary, Shelley, Idaho, 1978, Chapel of the Desert, Indio, Calif., 1978-79, McAulay & Wallace Funeral Home, Fullerton, 1979-82; embalmer Lucero-Carlson Funeral Home, Susanville, Calif., 1982-85, Henderson Funeral Home, Pocatello, Idaho, 1985-87; owner, operator Wade Funeral Home, Driggs, Idaho, 1987—, Ashton, Idaho, 1987—; owner, operator Valley Mortuary, Jackson Hole, Wyo., 1990—; adv. coun. Ea. Idaho Regional Med. Ctr., Idaho Falls, 1990—; coun. mem. Pvt. Industry Coun., Southeast Idaho Region, 1989—. Coroner Teton County Idaho, Driggs, Idaho, 1988—; councilman Driggs City Coun., 1990—; bishop LDS Ch., 1991—. Mem. Rotary Club (pres. 1988-89), Lions Club (pres. 1987-88). Republican. Home: 290 N Main PO Box 429 Driggs ID 83422 Office: Valley Mortuary 170 E Broadway PO Box 9059 Jackson WY 83001

WADE, MARTHA GEORGIE, university administrator; b. Memphis, May 27, 1939; d. William Edward and Martha Wade. AB, U. Tenn., 1961; MEd, Ind. U., 1965; PhD, Vanderbilt U., 1989. Asst. dean students for freshmen Stephens Coll., Columbia, Mo., 1965-68, asst. dean students, dir. student activities, 1968-71, v.p., dean student life, 1971-77, v.p., dean of admissions and fin. aid, 1977-79, v.p., dean adminstrn. and fin. aid, 1979-82, v.p. instl. and enrollment planning, 1982-83; asst. dir. Inst. Pub. Policy Studies Vanderbilt U., Nashville, 1984-86; dir. admissions and records U. So. Colo., Pueblo, 1986-90, dean admissions and enrollment svcs., 1990—; mem. transfer adv. com. Colo. Commn. on Higher Edn., Denver, 1988—. V.p. Columbia chpt. Altrusa, Columbia, 1977-79; mem. Mayor's Adv. Com. on Labor Rels., Columbia, 1979. Mem. AAUW, Am. Assn. Higher Edn., U. So. Colo. Faculty Women, Alpha Lambda Delta (v.p. fin. 1990—). Office: U So Colorado 2200 Bonforte Blvd Pueblo CO 81001-4990

WADE, MICHAEL STEPHEN, management consultant; b. Mesa, Ariz., Sept. 13, 1948; s. William Conrad and Geraldine (Pomeroy) W.; m. Mary Ann Kraynick, Aug. 30, 1971; children: Jonathan, Hilary. BA, U. Ariz., 1970, JD, 1973. Command equal opportunity officer U.S. Army Criminal Investigation Command, Washington, 1974-76; EEO investigative specialist City of Phoenix, 1977-79, EEO adminstr., 1979-84; cons. Phoenix, 1984—; instr. Ariz. Govtl. Tng. Service. Author: The Bitter Issue: The Right to Work Law in Arizona, 1976. Active Ch. of the Beatitudes, Ariz. Rep. Caucus. With U.S. Army, 1974-76. Recipient Phoenix Mayor's Com. on Employment of Handicapped award, 1984, Cert. Appreciation award Phoenix Fire Dept. Mem. Nat. Assn. Pub. Sector EEO Officers (founding pres. 1984-85, Pres.'s award 1989), Am. Soc. Equal Opportunity Profls. (bd. dirs.), North Cen. Phoenix Homeowners Assn. Home: 7032 N 3rd Ave Phoenix AZ 85021-8704 Office: PO Box 34598 Phoenix AZ 85067-4598

WADE, PATRICK JOHN, neurosurgeon; b. Glendale, Calif., Dec. 27, 1941; s. William John and Yvonne Van (Phoenix) W.; m. Christina Theresa Gonzales, Apr. 30, 1966; children: Matthew Patrick, Theresa Anne, Thomas Edward. BS, Loyola U., 1963; MD, U. So. Calif., 1967. Intern L.A. U. So. Calif. Med. Ctr., 1967-68, resident, 1970-75; neurol. surgeon Glendale Neurosurgical Group, 1975—. Lt. cmdr. USN Med. Corp. Mem. Glendale C. of C., Jonathan Club, Verdugo Club. Republican. Roman Catholic. Office: Glendale Neurosurg Group 940 N Brand Blvd Glendale CA 91202-2905

WADE, RODGER GRANT, financial systems analyst; b. Littlefield, Tex., June 25, 1945; s. George and Jimmie Frank (Grant) W.; m. Karla Kay Morrison, Dec. 18, 1966 (div. 1974); children: Eric Shawn, Shannon Annelle, Shelby Elaine; m. Carol Ruth Manning, Mar. 28, 1981. BA in Sociology, Tex. Tech. U., 1971. Programmer First Nat. Bank, Lubbock, Tex., 1971-73, Nat. Sharedata Corp., Odessa, Tex., 1973; asst. dir. computing ctr. Odessa Community Coll., 1973-74; programmer/analyst Med. Sci. Ctr., Tex. Tech. U., Lubbock, 1974-76; sys. mgr. Hosp. Info. Sys., Addison, Tex., 1976-78; programmer, analyst Harris Corp., Grapevine, Tex., 1978-80, Joy Petroleum, Waxahachie, Tex., 1980-82; owner R&C Bus. Sys./Requerdos de Santa Fe, N.Mex., 1982-84; fin. sys. analyst Los Alamos (N.Mex.) Tech. Assocs., 1984—; owner El Rancho Herbs, Santa Fe, 1988-91, Wade Gallery, Santa Fe, 1990-91, Wade Systems, Santa Fe, 1992—. Vol. programmer Los Alamos Arts Coun., 1987-88; mem. regulations task force N.Mex. Gov.'s Health Policy Adv. Com.; vol. systems support Amigos Unidos of Taos, 1990—. Republican. Home: RR 5 Box 271H Santa Fe NM 87501-9805 Office: Los Alamos Tech Assocs 1650 Trinity Dr Los Alamos NM 87544-3065

WADIA, MANECK SORABJI, management consultant, writer; b. Bombay, Oct. 22, 1931; came to U.S., 1953.; s. Sorabji Rattanji and Manijeh M. (Pocha) W.; m. Harriet F. Schilit, Nov. 22, 1962; children: Sara Jean, Mark Sorab. MBA, Ind. U., 1958, PhD, 1957. Mem. faculty Ind. U., Bloomington, 1958-60; Ford Found. fellow U. Pitts., 1960-61; prof. Stanford U., Palo Alto, Calif., 1961-65; mgmt. and personal cons., pres. Wadia Assoc., Inc., Del Mar, Calif., 1965—; cons., lectr. presenter in field. Author: The Nature and Scope of Management, 1966, Management and the Behavioral Sciences, 1968, Cases in International Business, 1970, Holistic Management: A Behavioral Philosophy of Successful Leadership, 1990; co-author: (with Harper W. Boyd, Jr.) Cases from Emerging Countries, 1977; contbr. articles to profl. publs. Fellow Soc. Applied Anthropology; mem. Soc. Advancement Mgmt., Acad. Mgmt., Ind. Acad. Sci. (pres. anthropology sect.), Sigma Xi (assoc.), Sigma Iota Epsilon. Home and Office: 1660 Luneta Dr Del Mar CA 92014-2435

WADLEY, M. RICHARD, consumer products executive; b. Lehi, Utah; s. Merlyn R. and Verla Ann (Ball); m. Nancy Zwiers; children: Lisa Kathleen, Staci Lin, Eric Richard. BS, Brigham Young U., 1967; MBA, Northwestern U., 1968. Brand asst. packaged soap and detergent div. Procter & Gamble Co., Cin., 1968-69, asst. brand mgr. packaged soap and detergent div., 1970-71, brand mgr. Dawn detergent, 1972-73, copy supr. packaged soap and detergent div., 1974-75, brand mgr. Tide detergent, 1975-77, assoc. advt. mgr. packaged soap and detergent div., 1977-81; corp. product dir. Hallmark Cards, Inc., Kansas City, Mo., 1982-83, corp. product dir. Ambassador Cards div., 1983-85; v.p., gen. mgr. feminine protection div. Tambrands Inc., Lake Success, N.Y., 1986-88; sr. v.p. Bongrain, Inc., N.Y.C., 1988-89; pres., chief exec. officer Alta-Dena Inc. div. Bongrain, N.A., L.A., 1989-91; pres. The Summit Group, 1991—; mgmt. bd. Bongrain N.A., 1988-91; mgmt. bd. Bongrain N.A., 1988-91; bd. dirs. Calif. Dairy Inst., 1989-90, Nat. Milk Assn., 1990-91, Alta Dena, Inc., 1989-91, Creative Nail Design, 1992—. Bd. dirs. Long Beach Opera, 1991—, L.I. Friends of the Arts, 1986-88; mem. adv. bd. Bus. Sch. Calif. State U., Long Beach, 1991—. Recipient scholarship Northwestern U., 1967-68; named An Outstanding Sr. Grad. Coll. Bus. Brigham Young U., 1967. Mem. Beta Gamma Sigma. Republican.

WADLINGTON, W. M., tool company executive; b. Madisonville, Ky., Oct. 28, 1944; s. W. Milton and Ellen Christine (Bryan) W.; m. Anne R. Lewis, Apr. 29, 1979; children: Andrew Stephen, Michael Edward, Thomas Scott. BA, Vanderbilt U., 1967. Commd. 2d lt. U.S. Army, 1967, advanced through grades to capt., 1970, field artillery officer, 1967-78, resigned, 1978; chief fin. officer Tech. Tools Inc., San Diego, 1992—; CFO Tech. Tools, 1992—. Trustee The Child's Primary Sch., San Diego, 1988—; vestryman Good Samaritan Epis. Ch., San Diego, 1988; bd. dirs. Chantemar HDA Bd., 1985—; pres. club Rep. Party, San Diego, 1984—. Decorated Silver Star. Mem. Nat. Soc. Pub. Accts., Am. Numismatic Assn. Republican.

WADLOW, JOAN KRUEGER, university official; b. LeMars, Iowa, Aug. 21, 1932; d. R. John and Norma I. (IhLe) Krueger; m. Richard R. Wadlow, July 27, 1958; children: Dawn, Kit. B.A., U. Nebr., Lincoln, 1953; M.A. (Seacrest Journalism fellow 1953-54), Fletcher Sch. Law and Diplomacy, 1956; Ph.D. (Rotary fellow 1956-57), U. Nebr., Lincoln, 1963; cert., Grad. Inst. Internat. Studies, Geneva, 1957. Mem. faculty U. Nebr., Lincoln, 1966-79; prof. polit. scis. U. Nebr., 1964-79, assoc. dean Coll. Arts and Scis., 1972-79; prof. polit. scis., dean Coll. Arts and Scis., U. Wyo., Laramie, 1979-84, v.p. acad. affairs, 1984-86; prof. polit. sci., provost U. Okla., Norman, 1986-91; chancellor U. Alaska, Fairbanks, 1991—; cons. fed. grants. Author articles in field. Bd. dirs. Nat. Merit Scholarship Corp., Lincoln United Way, 1976-77, Bryan Hosp., Lincoln, 1978-79, Washington Ctr., 1986—; v.p., exec. commr. North Cen. Assn., pres., 1991; pres. adv. bd. Lincoln YWCA, 1970-71; mem. def. adv. com. Women in the Svcs., 1987-89; mem. community adv. bd. Alaska Airlines. Recipient Mortar Board Teaching award, 1976, Disting. Teaching award U. Nebr., Lincoln, 1979; fellow Conf. Coop. Man, Lund, Sweden, 1956. Mem. Internat. Studies Assn. (co-editor Internat. Studies Notes 1978-91), Nat. Assn. State Univs. and Land-Grant Colls. (exec. com. coun. acad. affairs 1989-91), Western Assn. Africanists (pres. 1980-82), Assn. Western Univs. (pres.-elect 1993—), Coun. Colls. Arts and Scis. (pres. 1983-84), Greater Fairbanks C. of C., Gamma Phi Beta. Republican. Congregationalist. Home and Office: PO Box 900147 Fairbanks AK 99775-1060

WADMAN, WILLIAM WOOD, III, health physicist, consulting company executive, consultant; b. Oakland, Calif., Nov. 13, 1936; s. William Wood, Jr., and Lula Fay (Raisner) W.; children: Roxanne Alyce Wadman Hubbing, Raymond Alan (dec.), Theresa Hope Wadman Beaudreaux; m. Barbara Jean Wadman; stepchildren: Denise Ellen Varine Skrypkar, Brian Ronald Varine Skrypkar. M.A., U. Calif., Irvine, 1978. Radiation safety specialist, accelerator health physicist U. Calif. Lawrence Berkeley Lab., 1957-68; campus radiation safety officer U. Calif., Irvine, 1968-79; dir. ops., radiation safety officer Radiation Sterilizers, Inc., Tustin, Calif., 1979-80; prin., pres. Wm. Wadman & Assocs. Inc., 1980-87; pres. Intracoastal Marine Enterprises Ltd., Martinez, Calif., 1981-86; mem. team No. 1, health physics appraisal program NRC, 1980-81; cons. health physicist to industry; lectr. sch. social ecology, 1974-79, dept. community and environ. medicine U. Calif., Irvine, 1979-80, instr. in environ. health and safety, 1968-79,Orange Coast Coll., in radiation exposure reduction design engring. Iowa Electric Light & Power; trainer Mason & Hanger-Silas Mason Co., Los Alamos Nat. Lab.; instr. in medium energy cyclotron radiation safety UCLBL, lectr. in accelerator health physics, 1966, 67; curriculum developer in field. Active Cub Scouts; chief umpire Mission Viejo Little League, 1973. Served with USNR, 1955-63. Recipient award for profl. achievement U. Calif. Alumni Assn., 1972, Outstanding Performance award U. Calif., Irvine, 1973. Mem. Health Physics Soc. (treas. 1979-81, edittor proc. 11th symposium, pres. So. Calif. chpt. 1977, Professionalism award 1975), Internat. Radiation Protection Assn. (U.S. del. 4th Congress 1977, 8th Congress 1992), Am. Nuclear Soc., Am. Public Health Assn. (chmn. program 1978, chmn. radiol. health sect. 1979-80), Campus Radiation Safety Officers (chmn. 1975, editor proc. 5th conf. 1975), ASTM. Club: UCI Univ. (dir. 1976, sec. 1977, treas. 1978). Contbr. articles to tech. jours. Avocation: achievement include research in radiation protection and environmental sciences. Home: 3687 Red Cedar Way Lake Oswego OR 97035-3525 Office: 675 Fairview Dr Ste 246 Carson City NV 89701-5436

WAETJEN, HERMAN CHARLES, theologian, educator; b. Bremen, Germany, June 16, 1929; Arrived in U.S., Sept., 1931.; s. Henry and Anna (Ruschmeyer) W.; m. Mary Suzanne Struyk, July 15, 1960; children: Thomas (dec.), Thembisa, Lois, David. BA, Concordia Sem., St. Louis, 1950, BD, 1953; Dr. Theol., Tuebingen U., Fed. Republic Germany, 1958; postgrad., Hebrew U., Jerusalem, 1955. Instr. Concordia Sem., 1957; asst. prof. U. So. Calif., L.A., 1959-62; assoc. prof. San Francisco Theol. Sem., San Anselmo, Calif., 1962-70, prof., 1970-74, Robert S. Dollar prof. of New Testament, 1974—; vis. prof. U. Nairobi, Kenya, 1973-74, Fed. Theol. Sem., Republic South Africa, 1979-80, U. Zimbabwe, 1986-87. Author: Origin and Destiny of Humanness, 1976, 78, A Reordering of Power, 1989, (with others) Reading from this Place: Social Location and Biblical Interpretation; contbr. chpts. to texts. mem. Soc. Biblical Lit., Pacific Coast Theol. Soc., Pacific Coast Theol. Soc. Democrat. Presbyterian. Home: 83 Jordan Ave San Anselmo CA 94960-2351 Office: San Francisco Theol Sem 2 Kensington Rd San Anselmo CA 94960-2997

WAGAR, KENNETH EUGENE, underwriter; b. Slayton, Minn., Feb. 3, 1956; s. Cecil Irven and Helena Mae (Kortlever) W.; m. Carol Lee Spiegelberg, Dec. 27, 1980; children: Eric Thomas, Timothy Andrew, Steven Merrill. BA, Wash. State U., 1979. CLU; ChFC. Coll. agt. Northwestern Mutual Life Ins. Co., Pullman, Wash., 1978-80; spl. agt. Northwestern Mutual Life Ins. Co., Yakima, Wash., 1980-92, dist. agt., 1992—. Pres. Sacred Messengers Inc., Yakima, 1990-91. Mem. Am. Soc. of CLU and ChFC, Yakima Fly Fishers Assn., Inc., U.S. Tennis Assn., Yakima Valley Assn. of Life Underwriters (v.p. 1988-89, bd. dirs. 1986-88). Office: Northwestern Mutual Life 307 N 3rd St Ste 2 Yakima WA 98901

WAGEMAN, THOMAS J., bank executive. BA, Notre Dame, 1956; MBA, Univ. of Chgo., 1962. Formerly pres., chief exec. officer NCNB Tex. Nat. Bank, Midland; now pres., chief exec. officer, HomeFed, San Diego, Calif., 1991—. Office: HomeFed Corp 625 Broadway San Diego CA 92101

WAGENHALS, WALTER LINCOLN, lawyer; b. Dayton, Ohio, June 29, 1934; s. Howard Blaine and Frances (Durning) W.; m. Patricia Aura Garver, Apr. 24, 1959; 1 child, Ann. BA, U. Washington, 1956; LLB, U. Colo., 1962. Bar: Colo. 1962. Asst. city atty. City of Boulder, Colo., 1963-68, city atty., 1968-78; legal counsel Oxford Properties, Inc., Denver, 1978-81; assoc. atty. Bailey Law Assocs., P.C., Lakewood, Colo., 1981—. Served to 1st lt. USMC, 1956-59. Mem. Colo. Bar Assn. (forms standardisation com. 1985-87). Office: Bailey Law Assocs PC Ste 301 215 Union Blvd Lakewood CO 80228

WAGER, JERRY WILLIAM, probation officer; b. Toledo, Ohio, Mar. 14, 1937; s. Montcalm Arnold and Elizabeth (Wagner) W.; married; children: Marc Anthony, Jerry Lance. BEd, U. Toledo, 1959; postgrad., U. Mich., Flint, 1961. Tchr., coach various schs., Ohio and Mich., 1959-61; west coast dir. Hickory Farms of Ohio, Las Vegas, Nev., 1961-63; dir. advt. and publicity Diamond Jim's Nev. Club, Las Vegas, 1963-66, adminstrv. asst., 1967-68; dir. advertising, publicity and entertainment El Dorado Club, Henderson, Nev., 1966-67; owner, dir. Promotion In Motion Advt. Agy., Las Vegas, 1968-70; supr. Clark County Road Dept., Las Vegas, 1970-80; probation officer Juvenile Ct., Clark County, Las Vegas, 1980—. Ofcl., coach, tour dir. Nat. Amateur Athletic Union, 1959—, U.S.A. Wrestling, 1984—, Jr. World Championships, 1977; head ofcl. World Police and Fire Games, 1979—, Nat. Law Enforcement Olympics, 1988—, World Firefighter Games, 1991—; coach Las Vegas YMCA, 1967-80; pres. So. Nev. Amateur Athletic Union, Las Vegas, 1977-87. Coached 7 straight World Championship wrestling teams, 1975, 76, 77, 87. Mem. Fedn. Internat. Lutte Amateur (ofcl. 1962—, Gold medal 1977, Bronze medal 1988, USA Wrestling Gold Coaches award 1991). Home: 1805 S 14th St Las Vegas NV 89104 Office: Clark County Juvenile Ct 3401 E Bonanza Rd Las Vegas NV 89101-2499

WAGGENER, SUSAN LEE, lawyer; b. Riverside, Calif., Oct. 21, 1951; d. Lee Richard and Alice Lillian (Fritch) W.; m. Steven Carl McCracken, July 29, 1979; children: Casey James McCracken, Scott Kevin McCracken. BA magna cum laude, U. So. Calif., 1973; JD magna cum laude, U. San Diego, 1976. Bar: Calif. 1977, Hawaii 1977. Law clk. to hon. Samuel P. King, Jr. U.S. Dist. Ct. Hawaii, Honolulu, 1976-77; assoc. Gibson, Dunn & Crutcher, Newport Beach, Calif., 1978-86; ptnr. Gibson, Dunn & Crutcher, Newport Beach, 1986—. Exec. editor U. San Diego Law Rev., 1975-76. V.p. 552 Club Hoag Hosp., Newport Beach, 1982-85. Mem. ABA, Orange County Bar Assn. Office: Gibson Dunn & Crutcher Jamboree Ctr 4 Park Plz Irvine CA 92714

WAGGENER, THERYN LEE, law enforcement professional; b. Cedar Rapids, Iowa, Sept. 7, 1941; s. Hollis Angisa (Fowler) Hogan; m. Zoetta Jean Hamilton, May 30, 1967; 1 child, Drugh Kincade. BBA, Nat. U., 1977, MBA, 1979. Traffic officer Calif. Hwy. Patrol, San Diego, 1966-72; owner, operator Am. Nat. Chem., San Diego, 1972-82; chief investigator N.Mex. Real Estate Commn., Albuquerque, 1983-86, Nev. Real Estate Div., Carson City, 1986-89; Nev. Dept. Prisons, Ely, 1989—; prof., Sierra Nev. Coll., Incline Village, 1988-89, Western Nev. Community Coll., Carson City, 1987-89; No. Nev. C.C., 1992—. Mem. Washoe County (Nev.) Rep. Cen. Com., 1989. With USN, 1960-65. Mem. Nat. Assn. Real Estate Lic. Law Ofcls. (enforcement and investigative com. 1987-89), Toastmasters, Rotary, Lions, Masons, Shriners, Nu Beta Epsilon.

WAGGONER, DAVID CARL, college administrator; b. Boise, Idaho, Jan. 17, 1953; s. J. Earl and Pauline Ann (Vocu) W.; m. Lorette Diane Koenig, June 18, 1977; 1 child, Bethany. BA, Northwest Christian Coll., 1976; MDiv, Tex. Christian U., 1979; MA, U. Oreg., 1981. Ordained to ministry Disciples of Christ Ch., 1979. Minister of youth Rosemont Christian Ch., Dallas, 1977-79; assoc. minister First Christian Ch., Eugene, Oreg., 1980-82; v.,p., dean student affairs Northwest Christian Coll., Eugene, 1982—; coord. Willamette Valley Collegiate Drug and Alcohol Consortium, 1991-93; chair Oreg. Higher Edn. Alcohol and Drug Coordinating Com., 1993—; mem. Commn. on Ministry, Christian Ch. Oreg. Recipient 1st Pl. Speech Contest Toastmasters Internat. Oreg. Cen. Div., 1985, 89; Consortium grantee Fund for the Improvement Post-Secondary Edn., 1991. Mem. Assn. Christians in Student Devel. (N.W. regional dir. 1989-93), Nat. Assn. Student Pers. Adminstrs., Western Assn. Student Employment Adminstrs., N.W. Coll. Pers. Assn., Eugene Lunch Bunch Toastmasters (pres. 1991). Republican. Office: Northwest Christian Coll 828 E 11th Ave Eugene OR 97401-3727

WAGGONER, JAMES CLYDE, lawyer; b. Nashville, May 7, 1946; s. Charles Franklin and Alpha (Noah) W.; m. Diane Dusenbery, Aug. 17, 1968; children: Benjamin, Elizabeth. BA, Reed Coll., 1968; JD, U. Oreg., 1974. Bar: Oreg. 1974, U.S. Dist. Ct. Oreg. 1975, U.S. Ct. Appeals (9th cir.) 1980, U.S. Tax Ct. 1979, U.S. Supreme Ct. 1979. Clerk to presiding justice Oreg. Supreme Ct., Salem, 1974-75; assoc. Martin, Bischoff & Templeton, Salem, 1975-78; ptnr. Martin, Bischoff & Templeton, Portland, 1978-82, Waggoner, Farleigh, Wada, Georgeff & Witt, Portland, 1982-89, Davis Wright Tremaine, Portland, 1990—. Contbr. articles to profl. jours. Mem. ABA, Oreg. Bar Assn., Multnomah Bar Assn., Reed Coll. Alumni Assn. (v.p. 1988, pres. 1989, bd. mgmt.), Order Coif, Phi Beta Kappa. Democrat. Office: Davis Wright Tremaine 1300 SW 5th Ave Ste 2300 Portland OR 97201-5630

WAGGONER, LAINE MORAIS, public relations consultant; b. N.Y.C., Nov. 19, 1933; d. S. Balfour and Cathryn (Smith) Morais; m. Rex Robert Waggoner, Apr. 8, 1966. BA, Hunter Coll., N.Y.C., 1956; MA, NYU, 1957. Owner, dir. Waggoner Pub. Rels., L.A. County, Calif., 1967-74; communications dir. CamaCal Corp., 1987-92; dir. pub. rels. Dept. Adoptions, L.A., 1974-81; pub. affairs mgr. Calif. State U., L.A., 1981-84; pub. rels. cons., Camarillo, Calif., 1984—; exec. dir. Community Assns. Inst., 1985-89. Mem. Pub. Rels. Soc. Am. (accredited; Prisms award 1977), Nat. Assn. Pub. Info. Officers, Nat. Assn. Govt. Communicators (Excellence award 1979), Pub. Info. Radio & TV Edn. Soc. (Bucaneer award 1981, 82), Pub. Info. Communicators Assn., Ventura County Profl. Women's Network, Ventura County Coun. Promote Self Esteem, Nat. Soc. Fund Raising Execs., Phi Beta Kappa. Home and Office: 838 Piropo Ct Camarillo CA 93010-1040

WAGGONER, LINDA SUZETTE, office administrator, auditor; b. Dallas, Apr. 13, 1947; d. Robert L. and Dolores G. (Kramer) W.; married, July 19, 1969 (div. Dec. 1980); children: Jennifer L., David R., Lisa S., Melinda S. Student, El Camino Coll., 1968, Westchester Adult Sch., 1969, Dibble Mgmt. Devel., 1983. Procurement mgr. Internat. Customs Svc., Inc., L.A., 1964-73; office mgr., sec. Our Lady of Refuge Sch., Long Beach, Calif., 1983-88; office mgr., adminstrv. asst., cert. auditor Unisys Corp., Mission Viejo, Calif., 1988—; independent travel agent World View Internat., La Jolla, Calif., 1993—; part time adminstr. CPC Laguna Hills (Calif.) Hosp., 1988; part time purchasing agt. Toshiba Corp., Irvine, Calif., 1989. Sec., bd. dirs. St. Catherines Mil. Sch., Anaheim, Calif., 1989-90, Our Lady of Refuge Sch., 1987-88, Internat. Customs Svc., Inc., 1975-80, Unisys Corp., 1989—; asst. sec. Nat. Customs Brokers/Freight Forwarders Assn., N.Y., 1978-80, 90-91. Mem. NAFE, Unisys Corp. Quality Mgmt. Assn. Republican. Roman Catholic.

WAGNER, C. PETER, theology educator, author; b. N.Y.C., Aug. 15, 1930; s. C. Graham Wagner and Mary Lewis; m. Doris Mueller, Oct. 15, 1950; children: Karen Potter, Ruth Irons, Rebecca. BS, Rutgers U., 1952; MDiv, Fuller Theol. Sem., 1955, MA in Missiology, 1968; ThM, Princeton (N.J.) Theol. Sem., 1963; PhD, U. So. Calif., 1977. Ordained to minstry Conservative Congl. Christian Ch., 1955. Missionary South Am. Mission, San Jose, Bolivia, 1956-61, SIM Internat., Cochabamba, Bolivia, 1963-71; sr. cons. Charles E. Fuller Inst., Pasadena, Calif., 1971-92; prof. ch. growth Fuller Theol. Sem., Pasadena, 1971—; charter mem. Lausanne Com. for World Evangelization, London, 1974-89; coord. Spiritual Warfare Network, Pasadena, 1990—. Author over 30 books including: Your Church Can Grow, 1976, 84, Your Spiritual Gifts, 1979, Leading Your Church to Growth, 1984, Engaging the Enemy, 1991, Warfare Prayer, 1992, Prayer Shield, 1992; contbr. articles to profl. jours. Mem. Evang. Missiological Soc., Am. Soc. Missiology, N.Am. Soc. for Ch. Growth, Soc. for the Sci. Study of Religion. Office: Fuller Theol Sem 135 N Oakland Ave Pasadena CA 91182-0001

WAGNER, CARRUTH JOHN, physician; b. Omaha, Sept. 4, 1916; s. Emil Conrad and Mabel May (Knapp) W. A.B., Omaha U., 1938; B.Sc., U. Nebr., 1938, M.D., 1941, D.Sc., 1966. Diplomate: Am. Bd. Sugery, Am. Bd. Orthopaedic Surgery. Intern U.S. Marine Hosp., Seattle, 1941-42; resident gen. surgery and orthopaedic surgery USPHS hosps., Shriners Hosp., Phila., 1943-46; med. dir. USPHS, 1952-62; chief orthopaedic service USPHS Hosp., San Francisco, 1946-51, S.I., N.Y., 1951-55; health mblzn. USPHS Hosp., 1959-62; asst. surgeon gen. dep. chief div. hosps. UPHS, 1957-59; chief div. USPHS, 1962-65, USPHS (Indian Health), 1962-65; dir. Bur. Health Services, 1965-68; Washington rep. AMA, 1968-72; health services cons., 1972-79; dept. health services State of Calif., 1979—. Contbr. articles to med. jours. Served with USCGR, World War II. Recipient Pfizer award, 1962; Meritorious award Am. Acad. Gen. Practice, 1965; Distinguished Service medal, 1968. Fellow A.C.S. (bd. govs.), Am. Soc. Surgery Hand, Am. Assn. Surgery Trauma, Am. Geriatrics Soc., Am. Acad. Orthopaedic Surgeons; mem. Nat. Assn. Sanitarians, Am. Pub. Health Assn. Sanitarians, Am. Pub. Health Assn., Washington Orthopaedic Club, Am. Legion, Alpha Omega Alpha. Lutheran. Club: Mason (Shriner). Home: 6234 Silverton Way Carmichael CA 95608-0757 Office: PO Box 638 Carmichael CA 95609-0638

WAGNER, CHRISTIAN JOERGEN, business educator; b. Hamburg, Fed. Republic of Germany, Apr. 2, 1960; came to U.S., 1988; s. Helmuth Ludwig Hugo and Iris Karin (Schalcher) W.; m. Rano Jacqueline Sihota, Mar. 21, 1990. BS, Tech. U., Berlin, 1981, MS, 1984; PhD, U. B.C., 1989. Rsch. assoc. Daimler-Benz AG, Berlin, 1981; lectr. U. B.C., Vancouver, 1985-88; asst. prof. U. So. Calif., L.A., 1989—; dir. VCS Rsch., Inc., Vancouver; adv. bd. Internat. Circle, L.A., 1991—. Contbr. articles to profl. jours. Panelist Aspen Inst. Berlin, 1983; speaker VWI Congress, Berlin, 1983; keynote speaker Acad. for Mgmt. Info. Conf., Tokyo, 1991, various confs., 1988-90. Fellow Deutscher Akademischer Austauschdienst, 1984, World U. Svc. Can., 1986, 87; Rsch. grantee NSF, 1991—. Mem. Arbeitsgruppe Wirtschaftsingenieure (bd. dirs. 1983-84), Verband Deutscher Wirtschaftsingenieure, Inst. Mgmt. Sci., Decision Scis. Inst., Internat. Circle L.A. (adv. bd. 1991). Home: 15641 Hortense Dr Westminster CA 92683-7519 Office: U So Calif Sch Bus Bridge Hall 401S Los Angeles CA 90089-1421

WAGNER, CHRISTIAN NIKOLAUS JOHANN, engineer, educator; b. Saarbrucken-Dudweiler, Germany, Mar. 6, 1927; came to U.S., 1959, naturalized, 1969; s. Christian Jakob and Regina (Bungert) W.; m. Rosemarie Anna Mayer, Apr. 5, 1952; children—Thomas Martin, Karla Regine, Petra Susanne. Student, U. Poitiers, France, 1948-49; Licence es Sci., U. Saar, Ger., 1951, Diplom-Ingenieur, 1954, Dr.rer.nat., 1957. Research asst. Inst. fur Metallforschung, Saarbrucken, 1953-54; vis. fellow M.I.T., 1955-56; research asso. Inst. fur Metallforschung, 1957-58; teaching, research asst. U. Saarbrucken, 1959; asst. prof. Yale U., New Haven, Conn., 1959-62; assoc. prof. Yale U., 1962-70; prof. dept. materials engring. UCLA, 1970-91, prof. emeritus, 1991—, chmn. dept., 1974-79, asst. dean undergrad. studies Sch. Engring. and Applied Sci., 1982-85, acting chmn., 1990-91; vis. prof. Tech. U., Berlin, 1969, U. Saarbrücken, 1979-80. Contbr. articles to profl. jours. Recipient U.S. Sci. Humboldt award U. Saarbrucken, 1989-90, 92. Fellow Am. Soc. Metals Internat.; mem. Am. Phys. Soc., Am. Crystallographic Assn., Minerals, Metals and Materials Soc., Materials Rsch. Soc., Sigma Xi. Home: 20407 Seaboard Rd Malibu CA 90265-5349 Office: UCLA 5731 Boelter Hall Los Angeles CA 90024-1595

WAGNER, DAVID J., art center director; b. Fort Knox, Ky., Mar. 4, 1952; s. Walter W. and Elsie G. (Zillner) W.; m. Kaye M. Kronenburg, June 21, 1975. BMA, U. Wis., Stevens Point, 1974; MA, Ind. U., 1976; PhD, U. Minn., 1992. Grad. asst. Univ. Mus., Bloomington, Ind., 1975-76; intern Children's Mus., Indpls., 1976; dir. Leigh Yawkey Woodson Art Mus., Wausau, Wis., 1977-87; exec. dir. Colorado Springs (Colo.) Fine Arts Ctr., 1987—; scholar-in-residence Sitka Ctr. Art and Ecology, Newskowin Found., Otis, Oreg., 1990; mem. adv. bd. Nat. Park Art Acad., Jackson Hole, Wyo., 1988-90; assoc. bd. Nat. Art Mus. of Sport, Indpls.; bd. dirs. Arts Commn. Pikes Peak Region, Colorado Springs; mem. adv. com. U. Colo., Colorado Springs, 1987—. Contbr.: (exhbn. catalogs) Americans in Glass, 1984, Rembrandt's Etchings, 1985, Wildlife in Art, 1987, Pikes Peak Vision: The Broadmoor Art Academy, 1919-1945; contbr. Wis. Acad. Rev., 1986, Arts for the Parks, 1988-90. Chmn. non-profit orgn. com. United Way, Wausau, 1981, 84; bd. dirs. Wis. Citizens for the Arts, Madison, 1984-86; negotiator Budapest Mus. Old Masters Am. Tour, 1986, Birds in Art China Exhbn. Tour, 1987; bd. dirs. Wis. Humanities Com., Madison, 1984-87; treas. Persons for Arts and Scis., Colorado Springs, Colo., 1991-92. Winterthur Summer Ins. scholar, 1979, Victorian Soc. scholar, 1981, Inst. European Studies scholar, 1982; U. Minn. fellow, 1987, 90. Mem. Am. Assn. Mus., Am. Studies Assn., Assn. Art Mus. Dirs. Office: Colo Springs Fine Arts Ctr 30 W Dale St Colorado Springs CO 80903-3249

WAGNER, DAVID JAMES, lawyer; b. Cleve., Feb. 7, 1946; m. Martha Wilson, June 22, 1979; 1 child, Diana Jane. BS, USAF Acad., 1969; JD, Georgetown U., 1973. Bar: Colo. 1973, U.S. Supreme Ct. 1975, U.S. Dist. Ct. of Colo. 1973, U.S. Tax Ct. 1974. Asst. assoc. gen. counsel Presdl. Clemency Bd., Washington, 1974-75; sec., gen. counsel Cablecomm-Gen. Inc., Denver, 1975-77; adj. prof. law Metro. State Coll., Denver, 1975-80; atty., mng. prin. Wagner & Waller, P.C., Denver, 1977-84; chmn. bd. GILA Comm., Inc., Denver, 1987; pvt. practice David Wagner & Assocs., P.C., Englewood, Colo., 1984—. Editor Am. Criminal Law Rev., Georgetown U. Law Sch., 1972-73. Trustee Kent Denver Sch., Cherry Hills Village, Colo., 1990—, treas., 1992, pres. 1992—; treas., dir. Denver Chamber Orch., 1979-81; dir. Leadership Denver Assn., 1978-80, World Music Found., Denver, 1991—. Capt. USAF, 1973-75. Republican. Episcopalian. Office: David Wagner & Assocs PC Penthouse 8400 E Prentice Ave Englewood CO 80111

WAGNER, DOUGLAS T., state legislator, millwright; b. Whitefish, Mont., Sept. 6, 1954; s. Harry Franklin Wagner and Roslynn Dorothy (Stevens) Kristopherson; m. Peggy Ann Stipe, July 10, 1977; 1 foster child, Laura Jean; children: Jonathan David, Jennilee Lindsay. Grad. high sch., Col. Falls, Mont. Cert. water system operator. Millwright plywood plant Plum Creek Timber Co.; mem. Mont. Ho. of Reps., Helena. Asst. chief Hungry Horse (Mont.) Vol. Fire Dept., 1982-88; pres. Hungry Horse Water Dist., 1986-91, Montanans for Multiple Use, 1991-92. Republican. Home: PO Box 21 Hungry Horse MT 59919-0021

WAGNER, JOHN KYLE, corporate professional; b. Detroit; s. Robert Alexander Wagner and Gladys Riding; m. Janet Marie Juback, July 14, 1984; childrne: Elizabeth Colleen, Olivia Kyle. MBA, Regis Coll., Gainesville, 1990. Sr. v.p. mktg. Qual-Med, Inc., Colorado Sprgs; dir. mktg. Fairlane Health Svcs. Corp., Detroit, Mich., 1985; nat. accounts rep. Cigna Healthplan, Tampa, Fla.; account exec. Cigna Healthplan, Tampa, Fla., account mgr., 1983; dir. R&D Health Net, Woodland Hills, Calif. Mem. El Paso County Young Republicans, 1987. Mem. Am. Mktg. Assoc., Group Health Assn. Am. (voting del.). Republican. Catholic. Home: 3154 N Old Coach Dr Camarillo CA 93010-1634

WAGNER, JUDITH BUCK, investment firm executive; b. Altoona, Pa. Sept. 25, 1943; d. Harry Bud and Mary Elizabeth (Rhodes) B.; m. Joseph E. Wagner, Mar. 15, 1980; 1 child, Elizabeth. BA in History, U. Wash., 1965; grad. N.Y. Inst. Fin., 1968. Registered Am. Stock Exchange; registered N.Y. Stock Exchange; registered investment advisor. Security analyst Morgan, Olmstead, Kennedy & Gardner, L.A., 1968-71; rsch. cons., St. Louis, 1971-72; security analyst Boettcher & Co., Denver, 1972-75; pres. Wagner Investment Mgmt., 1975—; chmn., bd. dirs. The Women's Bank, N.A., Denver, 1977—, organizational group pres., 1975-77; chmn. Equitable Bankshares Colo., Inc., Denver, 1980—; bd. dirs. Equitable Bank of Littleton, 1983-88, pres., 1985; bd. dirs. Colo. Growth Capital, 1979-82; lectr. Denver U., Metro State, 1975-80. Author: Woman and Money series Colo. Woman Mag., 1976; moderator 'Catch 2' Sta. KWGN-TV, 1978-79. Pres. Big Sisters Colo., Denver, 1977-82, bd. dirs., 1973—; bd. fellows U. Denver, 1985—; bd. dirs. Red Cross, 1980, Assn. Children's Hosp., 1985, Colo. Health Facilities Authority, 1978-84, Jr. League Community Adv. Com., 1979—, Brother's Redevel., Inc., 1979-80; mem. Hist. Paramount Found., 1984, Denver Pub. Sch. Career Edn. Project, 1972; mem. investment com. YWCA, 1976-88; mem. adv. com. Girl Scouts U.S.; mem. agy. rels. com. Mile High United Way, 1978-81, chmn. United Way Venture Grant com., 1980-81; fin. chmn. Schoettler for State Treas., 1986; bd. dirs. Downtown Denver Inc., 1988—; bd. dirs., v.p., treas. The Women's Found. Colo., 1987-91; treas., trustee, v.p., Graland Country Day Sch., 1990—; trustee Denver Rotary Found., 1990—. Recipient Making It award Cosmopolitan Mag., 1977, Women on the Go award, Savvy mag., 1983, Minouri Yasoui award, 1986, Salute Spl. Honoree award, Big Sisters, 1987; named one of the Outstanding Young Women in Am., 1979; recipient Woman Who Makes A Difference award Internat. Women's Forum, 1987. Fellow Assn. Investment Mgmt. and Rsch.; mem. Women's Forum of Colo. (pres. 1979), Women's Found. Colo., Inc. (bd. dirs. 1986-91), Denver Soc. Security Analysts (bd. dirs. 1976-83, v.p. 1980-81, pres. 1981-82), Rotary (treas. Denver chpt. found., pres. 1993—), Leadership Denver (Outstanding Alumna award 1987), Pi Beta Phi (pres. U. Wash. chpt. 1964-65). Office: Wagner Investment Mgmt Inc Ste 840 410 17th St Denver CO 80202-4418

WAGNER, NORMAN ERNEST, energy company executive, formerly university president; b. Edenwold, Sask., Can., Mar. 29, 1935; s. Robert Eric and Gertrude Margaret (Brandt) W.; m. Catherine Hack, May 16, 1957; children: Marjorie Dianne, Richard Roger, Janet Marie. B.A., U. Sask., 1958, M.Div., 1958; M.A., U. Toronto, Ont., Can., 1960, Ph.D. in Near Eastern Studies, 1965; LL.D. (hon.), Wilfrid Laurier U., 1984. Asst. prof. Near Eastern studies Wilfrid Laurier U., Waterloo, Ont., 1962-65, assoc. prof., 1965-69, prof., 1970-78, dean grad. studies and rsch., 1974-78; pres. U. Calgary, Alta., Can., 1978-88; chmn. bd. Alta. Natural Gas Co., Ltd., 1988—; pres. emeritus U. Calgary, Can.; officer Order of Can., 1989; bd. dirs. CFCN Comm. Ltd., Alta., Terry Fox Humanitarian award Program. Author: (with others) The Moyer Site: A Prehistoric Village in Waterloo County, 1974. Mem. Adv. Coun. on Adjustment, OCO '88, Alta. Heritage Found. for Med. Rsch., Nat. Adv. Bd. Sci. and Tech., Internat. Trade Adv. Com.; chmn. Can. Mus. Nature; chmn. Terry Fox Humanitarian Award program Can. Mus. Nature. Mem. Can. Soc. Bibl. Studies. Lutheran. Home: Box 5 Site 33 RR # 12, Calgary, AB Canada T3E 6W3 Office: Alta Natural Gas Co Ltd, 2900 240 Fourth Ave SW, Calgary, AB Canada T2P 4L7

WAGNER, ORVIN EDSON, physicist, research facility administrator; b. L.A., Jan. 23, 1930; s. Edward Benjamin and Mary Esther (May) W.; m. Doris Joan Byram, Aug. 23, 1953 (div. Aug. 1976); children: Dianne, Darrell, Susan, Sharon; m. Claudia May Eells, Aug. 12, 1977; children: Raymond, Michael, Kimberly. BA, Walla Walla Coll., 1953, BS, 1959; MS, Ariz. State U., 1963; PhD, U. Tenn., 1968. Registered profl. engr., Calif. Scientist Lockheed Rsch. Labs., Palo Alto, Calif., 1961-62; physics instr. Walla Walla Coll., College Pl., Wash., 1962-64; asst. prof. Calif. State Poly. U., San Luis Obispo, 1969-74; pres. Wagner Rsch. Lab., Rogue River, Oreg., 1976—; cons. Wagner Electronic Products, Rogue River, 1969—. Author: W-Waves and A Wave Universe; contbr. articles to profl. jours.; patentee in field. With U.S. Army, 1955-57. Fellow NIH, 1964-68, AEC, 1968-69. Mem. Am. Physical Soc., Sigma Xi, Sigma Pi Sigma. Republican. Home: 2500 Sykes Creek Rd Rogue River OR 97537-9703 Office: Wagner Rsch Lab 2645 Sykes Creek Rd Rogue River OR 97537-9703

WAGNER, RAY DAVID, historian, educator, consultant; b. Phila., Feb. 29, 1924; s. James D. and Ethel S. (Schreiber) W.; m. Beatrice Walsh, Apr. 1952 (div. Nov. 1965); 1 child, Roger Ray; m. Mary Kathleen Davidson, Nov. 17, 1967; children: Wendy Lynne, David Frederick. BS, U. Pa., 1953, MS in Edn., 1955; postgrad., San Diego State U., 1958-65. Tchr. Crawford High Sch., San Diego, 1957-84; instr. City Colls. USN/PACE, 1985; archivist San Diego Aerospace Mus., 1985—. Author: American Combat Planes, 1960, 68, 82, North American Sabre, 1963, German Combat Planes, 1970, Mustang Designer, 1990; editor: The Soviet Air Force in World War II, 1973, Guide for Teaching World History, 1974. Air Force Hist. Ctr. grantee, 1988. Mem. Am. Aviation Hist. Soc. (v.p. 1973-76), Air Force Hist. Found. Home: 5865 Estelle St San Diego CA 92115-5432 Office: San Diego Aerospace Mus 2001 Pan American Plz San Diego CA 92101-1636

WAGNER, RICHARD, baseball club executive; b. Central City, Nebr., Oct. 19, 1927; s. John Howard and Esther Marie (Wolken) W.; m. Gloria Jean Larsen, May 10, 1950; children—Randolph G., Cynthia Kaye. Student, pub. schs., Central City. Gen. mgr. Lincoln (Nebr.) Baseball Club, 1955-58; mgr. Pershing Mcpl. Auditorium, Lincoln, 1958-61; exec. staff Ice Capades, Inc., Hollywood, Calif., 1961-63; gen. mgr. Sta. KSAL, Salina, Kans., 1963-65; dir. promotion and sales St. Louis Nat. Baseball Club, 1965-66; gen. mgr. Forum, Inglewood, Calif., 1966-67; asst. to exec. v.p. Cin. Reds, 1967-70, asst. to pres., 1970-74, v.p. adminstrn., 1975, exec. v.p., 1975-78, gen. mgr., 1977-83, pres., 1978-83; pres. Houston Astros Baseball Club, 1985-87; spl. asst. Office of Baseball Commr., 1988-93; asst. to chmn. Major League Exec. Coun., Phoenix, 1993—; pres. RGW Enterprises, Inc., Phoenix, 1978—. Served with USNR, 1945-47, 50-52. Named Exec. of Yr., Minor League Baseball, Sporting News, 1958. Mem. Internat. Assn. Auditorium Mgrs. Republican. Methodist.

WAGNER, RICHARD ELLIOTT, museum director; b. Newark, N.J., June 4, 1932; s. Harry and Sylvia (Spevack) W.; m. Colleen V. Luebke, Aug. 27, 1964; children: Michael R., David R. BArch, Yale U., 1957. Pvt. practice architecture, 1957-80; exec. dir. Ctr. for Wooden Boats, Seattle, 1980—; maritime preservationist State of Wash., 1990. Designer Neighborhood Designs That Work, Seattle, 1989. Mem. Mayor's Small Bus. Task Force, Seattle, 1991—, Assn. of King County Hist. Orgns., 1992—; bd. dirs. Lifetime Learning Ctr., 1991—. Columbia U. scholar, 1951-53, Goodrich fellow Yale U., 1956-57. Mem. Mus. Small Craft Assn. (bd. dirs. 1989—), Nat. Maritime Alliance (bd. dirs. 1991—), Alexandria Seaport Found. (bd. dirs. 1992—). Office: Ctr for Wooden Boats 1010 Valley St Seattle WA 98109-4332

WAGNER, SHELDON LEON, clinical toxicologist, agricultural chemistry educator; b. Merrill, Wis., Apr. 4, 1929; s. Louis and Frieda (Charne) W.; m. Linda Wessel, May 28, 1960; children: Diane, Deborah. BS, U. Wis., 1954, MD, 1957. Intern Wayne County Hosp., Detroit, 1957-58; resident VA Rsch. Hosp., Chgo., 1958-61; fellow Northwestern U., Chgo., 1961-63; pvt. practice physician Corvallis, Oreg., 1963-70; prof. in agrl. chemistry Oreg. State U., Corvallis, 1970—; cons. Oreg. Dept. Agrl., Salem, 1970—, Oreg. Health Scis. U., Portland, 1978—, EPA, Washington, 1986—; adminstr. Nat. Pesticide Med. Monitoring Program, 1986—. Author: Clinical Toxicology of Agricultural Chemicals, 1981, Toxicologic Emergencies, 1984, Acute Health Hazards of Pesticides, 1985; contbr. articles to profl. publs. Mem. curriculum com. Corvallis Sch. Dist., 1968; committeeman Benton County Hospice Program, Corvallis, 1990; chmn. ethics com. Good Samaritan Hosp., Corvallis, 1989. Sgt. USAF, 1946-49. Mem. Am. Coll. Occupational Medicine, Soc. Toxicology, Am. Soc. Internal Medicine, Oreg. Med. Assn., Rotary. Home: 1684 NW Crest Pl Corvallis OR 97330-1812 Office: Oreg State U Dept Agrl Chemistry Agrl and Life Scis 1007 Corvallis OR 97331-7301

WAGNER, STEVE, social service program director; b. Colfax, Wash., Feb. 20, 1949; s. George David and Trudy Adella (Vowell) W.; m. Catherine Huhndorf, Feb. 24, 1970 (div. Dec. 1971); m. Beth Golladay, Oct. 21, 1978; 1 child, Heather. Paralegal cert., City Coll., 1987. Coord. Echo Landlord/Tenant Program, Hayward, Calif., 1987-90; program dir. Echo Housing, Inc., Oakland, Calif., 1990—; bd. dirs. Emergency Svc. Network, Oakland. Editor (newsletter) S.E.T. Free the Newsletter Against Television. Organizer Lake Merritt Neighbors Organized for Peace, Oakland, 1991. Recipient Vol. Mediator Cert. Victim-Offender Reconciliation Program, 1990. Mem. Soc. for the Eradication of TV (bd. dirs. 1986—). Democrat. Home: Box 10491 Oakland CA 94610-0491

WAGNER, SUE ELLEN, state official; b. Portland, Maine, Jan. 6, 1940; d. Raymond A. and Kathryn (Hooper) Pooler; m. Peter B. Wagner, 1964 (dec.); children: Kirk, Kristina. B.A. in Polit. Sci., U. Ariz., 1962; M.A. in History, Northwestern U., 1964. Asst. dean women Ohio State U., 1963-64; tchr. history and Am. govt. Catalina High Sch., Tucson, 1964-65; reporter Tucson Daily Citizen, 1965-68; mem. Nev. Assembly, 1975-83; mem. Nev. Senate from 3d dist.; elected lt. gov. of Nev., 1990. Author: Diary of a Candidate, On People and Things, 1974. Mem. Reno Mayor's Adv. Com., 1973-84; chmn. Blue Ribbon Task Force on Housing, 1974-75; mem. Washoe County Republican Central Com., 1974-84, Nev. State Rep. Central Com., 1975-84; mem. Nev. Legis. Commn., 1976-77; del. social service com. Council State Govts.; v.p. Am. Field Service, 1973, family liaison, 1974, mem.-at-large, 1975. Kappa Alpha Theta Nat. Grad. scholar, also Phelps-Dodge postgrad. fellow, 1962; named Outstanding Legislator, Nev. Young Republicans, 1976. Mem. AAUW (legis. chmn. 1974), Bus. and Profl. Women, Kappa Alpha Theta. Episcopalian. Home: 845 Tamarack Dr Reno NV 89509-3640 Office: Office of Lt Governor Capitol Complex Carson City NV 89710*

WAGNER, WILLIAM GERARD, university dean, physicist, consultant, information scientist, investment manager; b. St. Cloud, Minn., Aug. 22, 1936; s. Gerard C. and Mary V. (Cloone) W.; m. Janet Agatha Rowe, Jan. 30, 1968 (div. 1978); children: Mary, Robert, David, Anne; m. Christiane LeGuen, Feb. 21, 1985 (div. 1989). B.S., Calif. Inst. Tech., 1958, Ph.D. (NSF fellow, Howard Hughes fellow), 1962. Cons. Rand Corp., Santa Monica, Calif., 1960-65; sr. staff physicist Hughes Research Lab., Malibu, Calif., 1960-69; lectr. physics Calif. Inst. Tech., Pasadena, 1963-65; asst. prof. physics U. Calif. at Irvine, 1965-66; assoc. prof. physics and elec. engring. U. So. Calif., L.A., 1966-69, prof. depts. physics and elec. engring., 1969—, dean div. natural scis. and math. Coll. Letters, Arts and Scis., 1973-87, dean interdisciplinary studies and developmental activities, 1987-89, spl. asst. automated record services, 1975-81; founder program in neural, informational & behavioral scis., 1982—; chmn. bd. Malibu Securities Corp., L.A., 1971—; cons. Janus Mgmt. Corp., L.A., 1970-71, Croesus Capital Corp., L.A., 1971-74, Fin. Horizons Inc., Beverly Hills, Calif., 1974—; allied mem. Pacific Stock Exch., 1974-82; fin. and computer cons. Hollywood Reporter, 1979-81; mem. adv. coun. for emerging engring. techs. NSF, 1987—. Contbr. articles on physics to sci. publs. Richard Chase Tolman postdoctoral fellow, 1962-65. Mem. Am. Phys. Soc., Nat. Assn. Security Dealers, Sigma Xi. Home: 2828 Patricia Ave Los Angeles CA 90064-4425 Office: U So Calif Hedco Neurosci Bldg Los Angeles CA 90089-2520

WAGONER, DAVID EVERETT, lawyer; b. Pottstown, Pa., May 16, 1928; s. Claude Brower and Mary Kathryn (Groff) W.; children: Paul R., Colin H., Elon D., Peter B.; m. Jean Morton Saunders; children: Dana F., Constance A., Jennifer L., Melissa J. B.A., Yale U., 1950; LL.B., U. Pa., 1953. Bar: D.C. 1953, Pa. 1953, Wash. 1953. Law clk. U.S. Ct. Appeals (3d cir.), Pa., 1955-56; law clk. U.S. Supreme Ct., Washington, 1956-57; ptnr. Perkins & Coie, Seattle, 1957—. Mem. sch. com. Mcpl. League Seattle and King County, 1958—, chmn., 1962-65; mem. Seattle schs. citizens coms. on equal ednl. opportunity and adult vocat. edn., 1963-64; mem. Nat. Com. Support Pub. Schs.; mem. adv. com. on community colls., to 1965, legislature interim com. on edn., 1964-65; mem. community coll. adv. com. to state supt. pub. instrn., 1965; chmn. edn. com. Forward Thrust, 1968; mem. Univ. Congl. Ch. Council Seattle, 1968-70; bd. dirs. Met. YMCA Seattle, 1968; bd. dirs. Seattle Pub. Schs., 1965-73, v.p., 1966-67, 72-73, pres., 1968, 73; trustee Evergreen State Coll. Found., chmn. 1986-87, capitol campaign planning chmn.; trustee Pacific NW Ballet, v.p. 1986. Served to 1st lt. M.C., AUS, 1953-55. Fellow Am. Coll. Trial Lawyers (mem. ethics com., legal ethics com.); mem. ABA (mem. standing com. fed. judicial imprisionment, chmn. appellate advocacy com.), Wash. State Bar Assn., Seattle-King County Bar Assn., Nat. Sch. Bds. Assn. (bd. dirs., chmn. coun. Big City bds. edn. 1971-72), English Speaking Union (v.p. Seattle chpt. 1961-62), Chi Phi. Office: Perkins Coie 1201 3rd Ave Fl 40 Seattle WA 98101-3000

WAGONER, THOMAS FRANK, protective services official; b. St. Paul, June 15, 1952; s. Jack Homer and Wanda Marie (Wakeland) W.; m. Brenda Colleen Newman, Nov. 6, 1971; children: Jamie Noel, Joshua Thomas. AS in Police Sci., Danville (Ill.) Jr. Coll., 1978; AA in Liberal Arts, Aims Community Coll., Greeley, Colo., 1980; BA in Criminal Justice, U. No. Colo., 1983; MA in Mgmt., U. Phoenix, Denver, 1986. Cert. police officer, Wis., Ill., Colo., Tenn. Police officer Village Thiensville, Wis., 1974-75, City of Hoopeston, Ill., 1976-79; police officer, sgt. City of Greeley, 1979-87; chief police City of Tullahoma, Tenn., 1987-89, City of Loveland, Colo., 1989—; instr. Aims Community Coll., 1986—; assessor Commn. Law Enforcement Accreditation, Fairfax, Va., 1986—, Pers. Performance, Inc., Chesapeake Beach, Md., 1990—. Contbr. articles to profl. jours. Mem. exec. bd. Drug Abuse Rsch. and Edn., Loveland, 1989—, Ptnrs., Inc., Ft. Collins, Colo., 1989-90, Berthond Loveland Team, 1992—; vice chmn., exec. bd. Larimer County E911 Bd., Ft. Collins, 1990—; vol. instr., exec. bd. Loveland Ctr. for Bus. Devel.; elder, tchr. Grace Community Ch. With U.S. Army, 1972-74. Mem. Colo. Assn. Chiefs Police (assessor 1989—, com. mem. 1989—), Internat. Assn. Chiefs Police, Police Exec. Rsch. Forum, Tri-County Law Enforcement Assn., IACA (investigative orgn. com.). Mem. Evangelical Ch. Office: Loveland Police Dept 410 E 5th St Loveland CO 80537-5641

WAGSCHAL, KATHLEEN, education educator; b. Woburn, Mass., May 30, 1947; d. John Kenneth and Elizabeth (Ginivan) Lanpher; m. Peter Henry Wagschal, July 17, 1971; 1 child, Adam Colin. MEd, U. Mass., 1972, U. Mass., 1975. Cert. secondary tchr., Calif. Adminstrv. dir. lab. sch. Greenfield (Mass.) Community Coll., 1978-83; adj. faculty mem. Sch. Edn. Nat. U., San Diego, 1985-87, dir. student tchr. program, 1987-88, chair tchr. edn. program, 1987—, dean Sch. Edn., 1988—; cons., co-dir. Futures Unltd., N.Y. and Mass., 1972-85. Grantee Mass. Dept. Social Svcs., Mass. Dept. Edn., Bur. Nutrition and Edn., 1981-84. Mem. Calif. Assn. Colls Tchr. Edn., Calif. Coun. Edn. of Tchrs. Office: Nat U 4141 Camino Del Rio S San Diego CA 92108-4103

WAGSTAFF, LEE STILLMAN, advertising executive; b. Salt Lake City, Feb. 29, 1944; s. Albert Stillman and Fay (Shelton) W.; m. Paula Miles, Aug. 11, 1967; children: Skye, Sloane. BS, U. Utah, 1966. Prodn. mgr. Ross Jurney & Assocs., Salt Lake City, 1967-71, account exec., 1971-78; exec. v.p. Ross Jurney, 1978-84; ptnr. First Mktg. Group, Salt Lake City, 1984-90, owner, 1990—; cons. Utah Advt. Fedn., Salt Lake City, 1972-93. Com. mem. Stiener Pool Com., Salt Lake City, 1990; bd. dirs. Vols. of Am., Utah. With U.S. Army N.G., 1966-72. Mem. Utah Advt. Fedn. (27 gold awards, 50 silver awards, 16 bronze awards). Home: 2005 Herbert Ave Salt Lake City UT 84108 Office: First Mktg Group PO Box 581021 Salt Lake City UT 84158-1021

WAHL, FLOYD MICHAEL, geologist; b. Hebron, Ind., July 7, 1931; s. Floyd Milford and Ann Pearl (DeCook) W.; m. Dorothy W. Daniel, July 4, 1953; children: Timothy, David, Jeffrey, Kathryn. A.B., DePauw U., 1953; M.S., U. Ill., 1957, Ph.D., 1958. Cert. profl. geologist. Prof. geology U. Fla., Gainesville, 1969-82, assoc. dean Grad. Sch., 1974-80, acting dean, 1980-81; exec. dir. Geol Soc Am., Boulder, Colo., 1982—. Contbr. articles to profl. jours. Served to cpl. U.S. Army, 1953-55. Recipient Outstanding Tchr. award U. Ill., 1967. Fellow Geol. Soc. Am.; mem. Mineral Soc. Am., Am. Inst. Profl. Geologists (chpt. pres.), Sigma Xi. Office: Geol Soc Am PO Box 9140 3300 Penrose Pl Boulder CO 80301

WAHLEN, BRUCE EDWARD, mathematical statistician; b. Chgo., Dec. 5, 1947; s. Ralph Edward and Jeanne Elizabeth (Buchanan) W.; m. Margaret Ruth Craig, July18, 1975; children: Sarah, Rebekah. BA in Math., U. Calif. San Diego, La Jolla, 1969, PhD in Math., 1991; MS, San Diego State U., 1978. Lifetime Calif. secondary teaching credential. Statistician Nat. Marine Fisheries Svc., NOAA, S.W. Fisheries Sci. Ctr., La Jolla, 1976-91; mathematician Naval Command, Control, and Ocean Surveillance Ctr., San Diego, 1991—. Contbr. articles to profl. jours. With U.S. Army, 1970-72. Am. Soc. Engring. Edn. fellow, 1991. Mem. Soc. for Indsl. and Applied Math., Inst. Math. Stats. Baptist. Office: Naval Comand Control and Ocean Surveillance Ctr RDT&E Divsn Code 732 San Diego CA 92152

WAHLER, HARRY JOE, psychologist, researcher; b. Pueblo, Colo., Oct. 5, 1919; s. August Harry and Marjory (Ragle) W.; m. Doris Elizabeth Ogden, Apr. 1, 1948; children: Heidi, Terry, Anita, Betsy. MusB, U. Rochester, 1947, MusM, 1948; BS, U. Ind., 1950; PhD, U. Iowa, 1954. Clin. rsch. psychologist VA Mental Hygiene Clinic, Iowa City, Iowa, 1954-56, VA Hosp., Knoxville, Iowa, 1956-58; dir. psychol. svcs. and rsch. Ohio State U., Columbus, 1958-66; dir. psychol. rsch. Mental Health Rsch. Inst., Fort Steilacom, Wash., 1966-67; sr. rsch. investigator rsch. div. Dept. of Instns., Fort Steilacom, 1967-71; part-time cons. psychologist Good Samaritan Mental Health, Puyallup, Wash., 1971—; dir. RECOVER, Tacoma, Wash., 1969-72, CMH Expediter Project, Tacoma, 1969-72. Author: Breaking Vicious Circles, 1990. Bd. dirs. Tacoma-Pierce County Narcotics Ctr., 1968-69, Greater Lakes Mental Health Found., Tacoma, 1969-70, Model Cities Coord. Coun., Tacoma, 1969-70; panel mem. Tacoma Community Mental Health Ctr., 1967-72. Cpl. USAAF, 1941-44. Mem. Phi Beta Kappa, Sigma Xi. Home: 12513 44th St Ct E Sumner WA 98390

WAHLKE, JOHN CHARLES, political science educator; b. Cin., Oct. 29, 1917; s. Albert B.C. and Clara J. (Ernst) W.; m. Virginia Joan Higgins, Dec. 1, 1943; children: Janet Parmely, Dale. A.B., Harvard U., 1939, M.A., 1947, Ph.D., 1952. Instr., asst. prof. polit. sci. Amherst (Mass.) Coll., 1949-53; prof. polit. sci. Vanderbilt U., Nashville, Tenn., 1953-63, SUNY, Buffalo, 1963-66, U. Iowa, 1966-71, SUNY, Stony Brook, 1971-72, U. Iowa, Iowa City, 1972-79; prof. polit. sci. U. Ariz., Tucson, 1979-87, prof. emeritus, 1987—. Author: (with others) The Legislative System, 1962, Government and Politics, 1966, The Politics of Representation, 1978; editor: Causes of the American Revolution, 1950, Loyalty in a Democratic State, 1952; co-editor: Legislative Behavior, 1959, The American Political System, 1967, Comparative Legislative Behavior, 1973. Served to capt., F.A. AUS, 1942-46. Decorated Air medal with 2 oak leaf clusters. Mem. AAAS, Am. Polit. Sci. Assn. (past pres.), Internat. Polit. Sci. Assn., So. Polit. Sci. Assn., Midwest Polit. Sci. Assn. (past pres.), Western Polit. Sci. Assn., Southwestern Polit. Sci. Assn., Assn. Politics and the Life Scis. Home: 5462 N Entrada Catorce Tucson AZ 85718-4851 Office: U Ariz Dept Polit Sci Tucson AZ 85721

WAHLSTROM, HAROLD EUGENE, service executive; b. Chgo., Nov. 15, 1947; s. Winston Arthur Wahlstrom and Billie Louise (Cox) Day; m. Linda Marguarite Bezy, Apr. 20, 1968; children: Mary Ann, Rebecca Lynn, Veronica Sue, Von Christopher. Student, Phoenix Coll., 1966-67. Gen. mgr. Western World Foods, Inc., Phoenix, 1971-74, Sizzler, Phoenix, 1974-75; dist. mgr. Denny's Restaurants, Inc., Denver, 1975-80, Arlington, Tex., 1981-83, Phoenix, 1986—; pres. Net Line Living Assocs., Lubbock, 1979-81; v.p., gen. mgr. Lubbock's Big Apple Restaurants, 1980-81; div. mgr. Pizza Time Theatre, Inc., Euless, Tex., 1983-85; regional mgr. Sea Galley Stores East, Falls Church, Va., 1985-86; cons. LRG Internat., Inc., Scottsdale, Ariz., 1986, Showbiz Pizza, Irving, Tex., 1984; dist. mgr., safety and loss control rep., franchise dist. leader Denny's Restaurants, 1986—. Bd. dirs. The Bridge Assn., Ft. Worth, Tex., 1982-83; officer Phoenix Police Dept. Res., 1968-69; dep. Coconino County Sheriff's Res., 1976-77. Mem. Ariz. Restaurant Assn., Nat. Restaurant Assn., Tau Omega (pres. 1966-67). Republican. Mem. Disciples of Christ. Home: 5244 W Cortez St Glendale AZ 85304-3418 Office: Dennys Restaurants Inc 203 E Main St Spartanburg SC 29319

WAIDE, JACQUELINE ANN, aeronautical educator; b. Petersburg, Va., Sept. 18, 1938; d. William Edward and Elizabeth L. (Hunt) Tench; 1 child from previous marriage: Catherine Elizabeth; m. Jeffery William Hanson, Feb. 14, 1989. B of Aeronautics, Embry-Riddle, 1982-84; EdD, Calif. Coast U., 1983-85. Cert. tchr, airline transport pilot, FAA flight and ground instr, FAA flight examiner. Ground and flight instr. Nystrom Aviation, Palo Alto, Calif., 1966-68; prof. Ohlone Coll., Fremont, Calif., 1968—; pres. Ho. of Hanson, San Carlos, Calif.; cons. to adminstrn., FAA, Washington, 1963-70. Author: (with others) An Invitation to Fly Viewer Guide, 1985-86, 88-89. Recipient Unique Accomplishments in Am. Aviation, FAA, Washington, 1964, Outstanding Contribution to Transport Industry, Airport Execs., San Jose, Calif., 1974, Flight Instr. of the Year, FAA, Oakland, Calif., 1976. Mem. No. Calif. Examiner Assn. (pres.). Lodge: Order of Eastern Star. Office: Ohlone Coll 43600 Mission Blvd Fremont CA 94539-5884

WAIHEE, JOHN DAVID, III, governor, lawyer; b. Honokaa, Hawaii, May 19, 1946; m. Lynne Kobashigawa; children: John David, Jennifer. B.A. in History and Bus., Andrews U., 1968; postgrad., Central Mich. U., 1973; J.D., U. Hawaii, 1976. Bar: Hawaii 1976. Community edn. coordinator Benton Harbor (Mich.) Area Schs., 1968-70, asst. dir. community edn., 1970-71; program evaluator, adminstrv. asst. to dirs., planner Honolulu Model Cities Program, 1971-73; sr. planner Office Human Resources City and County of Honolulu, 1973-74, program mgr. Office Human Resources, 1974-75; assoc. Shim, Sigal, Tam & Naito, Honolulu, 1975-79; ptnr. Waihee, Manuia, Yap, Pablo & Hoe, Honolulu, 1979-82; mem. Hawaiian Ho. of Reps., 1980-82; lt. gov. State of Hawaii, Honolulu, 1982-86, gov., 1986—. Del. 1978 Constnl. Conv.; del. Hawaii Dem. State Conv., 1972,74, 76, 78, 82; dir. and past pres. Kalihi-Palama Community Council; mem. steering com. Goals for Hawaii Orgn., past chmn. land use goals com., past co-chmn. outreach com.; past bd. dirs. Hawaii Sr. Citizens Travel Bd.; past mem. State Council on Housing and Constrn. Industry; mem. Kalihi-Palama Hawaiian Civic Club; past bd. dirs. Legal Aid Soc. of Hawaii, Alu Like. Mem. Hawaii Bar Assn. (chmn. unauthorized practice of law com. 1979, chmn. legis com. 1980), ABA, U. Hawaii Law Sch. Alumni, Filipino C. of C. Lodge: Kalakaua Lions. Office: Office of Gov State Capital 5th Fl Honolulu HI 96813

WAILES, RODNEY DUANE, banker; b. Oceanside, Calif., Jan. 24, 1956; s. Franklin Delano and Dolores Genevieve (Swenson) W.; m. Donna Lisa Cromwell, Aug. 7, 1982. BS in Animal Sci. cum laude, Colo. State U., 1984; MBA in Agribus., Santa Clara U., 1987. Mng. gen. ptnr. Wailes Custom Harvesting, Loveland, Colo., 1975-77; mktg./sales analyst Agriproducts, Internat. Inc., Loveland, 1977-87; bus. analyst Tri/Valley Growers, Inc., San Francisco, 1987-88; prin., owner Wailes & Assocs., Ft. Collins, Colo., 1988-90; chief fin. officer Agriproducts Internat., Inc., Ft. Collins, 1988—; loan officer Farm Credit Bank of Wichita, Kans., 1990-92; with OBD, Denver, 1992—; advisor, speaker dept. agr. Colo. State U., Ft. Collins, 1989—. Vol. Poudre R1 Sch. Dist., Ft. Collins, 1988—, Nightwalker Enterprises, Ft. Collins, 1992; bd. dirs. Small Bus. Fin. Corp. Santa Clara U. acad. fellow, 1985-87; recipient Marianni award Inst. Agribus. Santa Clara U., 1987. Mem. Nat. Agri-Mktg. Assn. (careers chmn. 1984-85), Western Stock Show Assn., Phi Kappa Phi, Gamma Sigma Delta. Presbyterian. Office: OBD 1625 Broadway Ste 1710 Denver CO 80201

WAIN, CHRISTOPHER HENRY, JR., marketing executive; b. L.A., Dec. 3, 1951; s. Christopher and Jeane (Thomas) W.; m. Katrina Sumner, Feb. 6, 1986. BA, Lafayette Coll., 1973; postgrad., Harvard U., 1973; MBA, UCLA, 1981. Cert. bus. communicator. Copywriter Prentice Hall, Englewood Cliffs, N.J., 1973-76; advt. prodn. mgr. Goodyear Pub., Santa Monica, Calif., 1976-80; advt. specialist Hewlett Packard, Corvallis, Oreg., 1981-83; mgr. mktg. channel support Hewlett Packard, Cupertino, Calif., 1983-84; mktg. communications mgr. Intel Corp., Hillsboro, Oreg., 1984—. Mem. Oreg. Direct Mktg. Assn., Portland Advt. Fedn., Bus. and Profl. Advt. Assn., Beta Gamma Sigma. Office: Intel Corp 5200 NE Elam Young Pky Hillsboro OR 97124-6497

WAINA, RICHARD BAIRD, software engineer; b. Greensburg, Pa., Apr. 13, 1939; s. William Frank and Averista (Baird) W.; m. Carole Jane Segars, Sept. 11, 1964; children: Laura Lynn, Philip Richard. BSEE, Carnegie Mellon U., 1960; MSME, N.Mex. State U., 1966; PhD in Indsl. Engring., Ariz. State U., 1968. Registered profl. engr., N.Mex. Engr. Bethelem Steel Co., Johnstown, Pa., 1960-61; gen. engr. White Sands Missile Range, Las Cruces, 1961-66; systems rsch. engr. Rand Corp., Santa Monica, Calif., 1968-71; mem. tech. staff Hughes Aircraft Co. (now Hughes Missile Systems Co.), Canoga Park, Calif., 1971-73, sect. head, 1974-78, sr. staff engr., 1979-80; sr. staff engr. Hughes Aircraft Co. (now Hughes Missile Systems Co.), Tucson, 1980-85, sr. scientist, 1985-89, chief scientist, 1989—. 1st lt. U.S. Army, 1961-64. Mem. Am. Inst. Indsl. Engrs., Nat. Soc. Profl. Engrs., Nat. Security Indsl. Assn. (chmn. software quality com. 1988—), Soc. Logistics Engrs. (editor annals 1977-79). Republican. Baptist. Office: Hughes Missile Systems Co 807/G3 PO Box 11337 Tucson AZ 85734-1337

WAINER, STANLEY ALLEN, electronics industry executive; b. L.A., May 10, 1926; s. Calman and Katherine (Copeland) W.; m. Shirlene Joy Goldberg, Feb. 3, 1949; 1 child, William Edward. B.S. with honors, UCLA, 1950, postgrad., 1958. Acct. Price Waterhouse & Co., L.A., 1950-55; chief fin. and adminstrv. officer Paramount Pictures Corp., and subsidiaries, 1955-60; v.p., sec.-treas. Royal Industries, Pasadena, Calif., 1960-61; with Wyle Labs., El Segundo, Calif., 1962—; pres. Wyle Labs., 1970-85, chief exec. officer, 1979-88, chmn., 1984-91, chmn. exec. com., 1991—, also dir.; dir. City Nat. Corp./City Nat. Bank, Liberty Mut. Ins. Co., Liberty Mut. Fire Ins., 1990—, Liberty Life Assurance Co. Boston, Liberty Fin. Cos., Inc., 1991—, Centinela Valley Health Svcs., Inc., Centinela Health Found., 1992—; Pres., dir. UCLA Bus. Sch. Alumni Assn., 1968-69; chmn. bd. dirs. Calif. C. of C., 1990-91. Trustee, mem. exec. com. UCLA Found., 1972-93; bd. visitors UCLA Grad. Sch. Mgmt., 1983-92, UCLA, 1990— ; bd. dirs. NCCJ, 1974-80, bd. govs., 1980—; bd. dirs. Los Angeles Urban League, 1978-80; regent U. Calif., 1980-82; trustee Orthopaedic Hosp., Los Angeles, 1974-81, adv. council, 1980—; dir. Four A's Found., 1988—; bd. dirs. Coro Found., 1982-85 , El Segundo Ednl. Found., 1984-87 . Served with USNR, 1944-46. Named Man of Yr. City of Hope Aids, 1979; honoree NCCJ, 1981. Mem. Financial Execs. Inst., Technion Soc. (past dir.), Am. Inst. CPAs, C. of C. of U.S., Calif. C. of C. (dir.), L.A. C. of C. (dir. 1980—, chmn. fed. affairs com.), UCLA Alumni Assn. (dir. 1979—, pres. 1980-82), Soc. Order Blue Shield, Beta Gamma Sigma. Clubs: Riviera Tennis, Hillcrest Country. Home: 1151 Hilary Ln Beverly Hills CA 90210-2712 Office: Wyle Labs 128 Maryland St El Segundo CA 90245-4115

WAINESS, MARCIA WATSON, legal administrator; b. Bklyn., Dec. 17, 1949; d. Stanley and Seena (Klein) Watson; m. Steven Richard Wainess, Aug. 7, 1975. Student, UCLA, 1967-71, 80-81, Grad. Sch. Mgmt. Exec. Program, 1987-88, grad. Grad. Sch. Mgmt. Exec. Program, 1988. Office mgr., paralegal Lewis, Marenstein & Kadar, L.A., 1977-81; office mgr. Rosenfeld, Meyer & Susman, Beverly Hills, Calif., 1981-83; adminstr. Rudin, Richman & Appel, Beverly Hills, 1983; dir. adminstrn. Kadison, Pfaelzer, L.A., 1983-87; exec. dir. Richards, Watson and Gershon, L.A., 1987—; faculty mem. UCLA Legal Mgmt. & Adminstrn. Program, 1983, U. So. Calif. Paralegal Program, L.A., 1985; mem. adv. bd. atty. asst. tng. program, UCLA, 1984-88. Mem. ABA (chmn. Displaywrite Users Group 1986, legal tech. adv. coun. litigation support working group 1986-87), State Bar Calif., L.A. County Bar Assn. (exec. com. law office mgmt. sect. 1986-90), Assn. Profl. Law Firm Mgrs., Assn. Legal Adminstrs. (bd. dirs. 1990-92, asst. regional v.p. Calif. 1987-88, regional v.p. 1988-89, pres. Beverly Hills chpt. 1985-86, membership chmn. 1984-85, chmn. new adminstrn. sect. 1982-84, mktg. mgmt. sect. com. 1989-90, internat conf com), Internat Platform Assn. Office: Richards Watson & Gershon 333 S Hope St Bldg 38 Los Angeles CA 90071-3003

WAINIO, MARK ERNEST, insurance company consultant; b. Virginia, Minn., Apr. 18, 1953. BA, Gustavus Adolphus Coll., 1975. Cert. safety profl., assoc. loss control mgmt., assoc. risk mgmt., assoc. claims, CPCU. Carpenter ABI Contracting Inc., Virginia, 1975-77; co-owner Mesabi Builders, Albuquerque and Eveleth, Minn., 1977-79; sr. engring. rep. Aetna Life & Casualty, Albuquerque, 1979-86; loss control specialist CNA Ins. Cos., Albuquerque, 1986-91, loss control cons., 1991—; owner MEW Safety and Risk Mgmt., 1989—; pres. MW Enterprises, 1990—. Mem. Am. Soc. Safety Engrs., CPCU. Office: CNA Ins Cos 8500 Menaul Blvd NE Albuquerque NM 87112-2298

WAINIONPAA, JOHN WILLIAM, systems engineer; b. Quincy, Mass., July 13, 1946; s. Frank Jacob and Jennie Sofia (Kaukola) W.; m. S. Linda Rapo, Oct. 18, 1969; children: Heidi Liisa, Erik David, Sinikka Lin. BSEE, U. N.Mex., 1972; MS in Aero. Engring., Naval Postgrad. Sch., 1981. Engr.-in-tng., Colo. Enlisted USN, 1968, commd. ens., 1972, advanced through grades to lt. comdr., 1982; flight instr. Tng. Squadron 27, Corpus Christi, Tex., 1973-75; aircraft, mission comdr. Patrol Squadron 49, Jacksonville, Fla., 1976-79; ops. officer Anti-Submarine Warfare Ops. Ctr., Kadena,

Okinawa, Japan, 1982-84; launch and control systems officer Naval Space Command, Dahlgren, Va., 1984-86; naval space systems ops. officer U.S. Space Command, Colorado Springs, 1986-88; ret. USN, 1988; systems engr. CTA Inc., Colorado Springs, 1988-93, tng. coord., 1993—. Merit badge counselor Boy Scouts Am., Colorado Springs, 1986—. Mem. AIAA (sr.), IEEE, U.S. Naval Inst., Sigma Tau, Eta Kappa Nu. Office: CTA Inc 7150 Campus Dr Ste 100 Colorado Springs CO 80920-6592

WAIT, MARK W., dean; b. Wichita, Kans., Nov. 16, 1947; s. Roger W. and Icel (Smotherman) W.; m. Deborah Nelson, Sept. 22, 1978; 1 child, Mia. MusB, Wichita State U., 1971; MusM, Kans. State U., 1973; D Mus. Arts, Peabody Conservatory, Balt., 1976. Prof. music U. Colo., Boulder, 1975-93, asst. to pres., 1985-92, exec. officer to chancellor, 1992-93; dean Blair sch. music Vanderbilt U., Nashville, 1993—; mem. artistic adv. com. Gilmore Internat. Keyboard Festival, 1989—. Pianist on recs. Works of Morris Cotel, 1980, Works of Frederico de Freitas, 1984, Stravinsky the Composer, Vol. 2, 1992. Mem. Am. Liszt Soc. (bd. dirs. 1992—, editor jour. 1992—), Presdl. Assts. in Higher Edn. (steering com. 1989-93).

WAKE, DAVID BURTON, biology educator, researcher; b. Webster, S.D., June 8, 1936; s. Thomas B. and Ina H. (Solem) W.; m. Marvalee Hendricks, June 23, 1962; 1 child, Thomas Andrew. B.A., Pacific Luth. U., 1958; M.S., U. So. Calif., 1960, Ph.D., 1964. Instr. anatomy and biology U. Chgo., 1964-66, asst. prof. anatomy and biology, 1966-69; assoc. prof. zoology U. Calif., Berkeley, 1969-72, prof., 1972-89, prof. integrative biology, 1989-91, John and Margaret Gompertz prof., 1991—; dir. Mus. Vertebrate Zoology U. Calif., Berkeley, 1971—. Author: Biology, 1979; co-editor: Functional Vertebrate Morphology, 1985, Complex Organismal Functions: Integration and Evolution in the Vertebrates, 1989. Mem. nat. bd. Nat. Mus. Natural History. Recipient Quantrell Teaching award U. Chgo., 1967, Outstanding Alumnus award Pacific Luth. U., 1979; grantee NSF, 1965—; Guggenheim fellow, 1982. Fellow AAAS, NRC (bd. biology 1986-92); mem. Internat. Union for Conservation of Nature and Natural Resources (chair task force on declining amphibian populations 1990-92), Am. Soc. Zoologists (pres. 1992), Am. Soc. Naturalists (pres. 1989), Am. Soc. Ichthyologists and Herpetologists (bd. govs.), Soc. Study Evolution (pres. 1983, editor 1979-81), Soc. Systematic Biology (coun. 1980-84), Herpetologist's League (Disting. Herpetologist 1984). Home: 999 Middlefield Rd Berkeley CA 94708-1509

WAKE, MARVALEE HENDRICKS, biology educator; b. Orange, Calif., July 31, 1939; d. Marvin Carlton and Velvalee (Borter) H.; m. David B. Wake, June 23, 1962; 1 child, Thomas A. BA, U. So. Calif., 1961, MS, 1964, PhD, 1968. Teaching asst./instr. U. Ill., Chgo., 1964-68, asst. prof., 1968-69; lectr. U. Calif., Berkeley, 1969-73, asst. prof., 1973-76, assoc. prof., 1976-80, prof. zoology, 1980-89, chmn. dept. zoology, 1985-89, chmn. dept. integrative biology, 1989-91, assoc. dean Coll. Letters and Sci., 1975-78, prof. integrative biology, 1989—. Editor, co-author: Hyman's Comparative Vertebrate Anatomy, 1979; co-author: Biology, 1978; contbr. articles to profl. jours. NSF grantee, 1978—; Guggenheim fellow, 1988-89. Fellow AAAS, Calif. Acad. Scis.; mem. Am. Soc. Ichthyology and Herpetology (pres. 1984, bd. govs. 1978—), Internat. Union Biol. Scis. (U.S. Nat. Com. 1986-94, chair 1992—). Home: 999 Middlefield Rd Berkeley CA 94708-1509 Office: U Calif Dept Integrative Biology Berkeley CA 94720

WAKEFIELD, HOWARD, medical representative; b. Chgo., Dec. 19, 1936; s. Howard and Thelma Elizabeth (Roach) W.; m. Laura Collier, Jan. 1, 1957 (div. June 1976); children: Kimberly, Howard III, Anthony. BA in Econs., U. Ariz., 1959. Sales rep. N.Y. Life, Tucson, 1959-63; sr. med. rep. Pfizer Pharm., Ventura County, Calif., 1963—. Fund raiser Am. Heart Assn., Ventura, Calif., 1983—; mgr. Pleasant Valley Boys Baseball, Camarillo, Calif., 1968-82; vol. Arthritis Found. Mem. Ventura County Pharm. Assn. (v.p.). Republican. Home: PO Box 626 Somis CA 93066-0626 Office: Pfizer Pharm 16700 Red Hill Ave Irvine CA 92714-4800

WAKHAM, BERNARD BROCK, electrical engineer; b. Atlanta, Dec. 4, 1964; s. Ernest C. and Francis Dianne (Mitchell) W.; m. Terri Ann Shea, Nov. 4, 1989. BSEE/Computer Sci., U. Colo., 1986. Intern in software devel. Nat. Ctr. for Atmospheric Rsch., Boulder, Colo., 1985-86; design engr. NCR Corp., San Diego, 1986—. Advisor Jr. Achievement Co., San Diego, 1986; cons. Project Bus., San Diego, 1987, Applied Econs., Escondido, Calif., 1988. Mem. IEEE (Engr. in Tng. award 1986). Home: 803 Sumac Pl Escondido CA 92027

WAKIN, MALHAM M., philosophy educator, air force officer; b. Oneonta, N.Y., Mar. 31, 1931; s. Chickery A. and Hattie (Nauseef) W.; m. Marion Margaret Beni, Dec. 26, 1954 (dec. 1974); children: Pamela, Mary, Margaret, Susan, Mala; m. Linda Mack Nelson, June 21, 1976; children: Kelly, Keith, Karen. AB, U. Notre Dame, 1952; AM, SUNY, Albany, 1953; PhD, U. So. Calif., L.A., 1959; HDL, Ill. Benedictine Coll., 1991. Commd. 2d lt. USAF, 1953, advanced through grades to col., 1967; mem. faculty USAF Acad. USAF, Colorado Springs, Colo., 1959—, prof. philosophy, 1964—, asst. dean, then assoc. dean, 1964-67, 77-91, head dept. philosophy, 1967—; nat. chmn. Joint Svcs. Conf. Profl. Ethics, Colorado Springs, 1979—; mem. ethics oversight com. U.S. Olympic Com., Colorado Springs, 1991—; mem. ethics vis. com. U.S. Naval Acad., Annapolis, 1991—. Author: Viet Cong Political Infrastructure, 1968; author, editor: War, Morality and the Military Professional, 1979, 2d edit., 1986; co-author: Introduction to Symbolic Logic, 1976, 2d edit., 1991; contbr. articles to profl. publs. Mem. acquisitions com. Colorado Springs Fine Arts Ctr., 1986—. Mudd Meml. fellow U. So. Calif., 1958-59; recipient Cardinal Cooke award U.S. Mil. Ordinariate, Washington, 1982, Rev. William Corby award U. Notre Dame, 1986; named Scholar of Univ., St. Mary's U., San Antonio, 1970. Mem. Am. Cath. Philos. Assn., Phi Beta Kappa. Roman Catholic. Home: 135 Desert Inn Way Colorado Springs CO 80921 Office: Dept Philosophy, Fine Arts USAF Acad Colorado Springs CO 80840

WALASEK, OTTO FRANK, chemical engineer, biochemist, photographer; b. Park Falls, Wis., Mar. 11, 1919; s. Frank Otto and Mary (Swoboda) W.; m. Annie May Stockton (div. Nov. 1959); 1 child, Richard A.; m. Joan Constance Ashton, Sept. 18, 1965; children: Arthur, Carl. BS in Chem. Engring., U. Wis., 1946; MS in Biochemistry, U. Ill., 1968; postgrad., Loyola U., 1968-72. Penicillin processing product engr. I Abbott Labs., North Chgo., Ill., 1946-49; antibiotic process rsch. and devel. Abbott Labs., North Chgo., 1950-55, biochemical rsch., 1956-68, sr. biochemist, 1968-77, staff Leukemia project, 1978-80; pvt. photographer Sonora, Calif., 1981—. Patentee in field; contbr. articles to profl. jours. Recipient Excellence award Fedn. Internat. of Art Photographic, Switzerland, 1972; named Hon. Master of Profl. Photography, Profl. Photographic Assns., Taiwan, 1990. Mem. Photographic Soc. Am., Royal Photographic Soc., Nat. Stereoscopic Soc., Internat. Stereoscopic Union. Democrat. Office: 10165 Hwy 49 Sonora CA 95370

WALBA, DAVID MARK, chemistry educator; b. Oakland, Calif., June 29, 1949; s. Harold and Beatrice (Alpert) W.; m. Cassandra Geneson, Oct. 30, 1981; 1 child, Paul Geneson. BS, U. Calif., Berkeley, 1971; PhD, Calif. Inst. Tech., 1975; postdoctoral, UCLA, 1977. Asst. prof. chemistry U. Colo., Boulder, 1977-83, assoc. prof., 1983-87, prof., 1987—; cons. Displaytech Inc., Boulder, 1986—. Contbr. articles to profl. jours.; patentee in field. Sloan Found. fellow 1982-84; Dreyfus Tchr. scholar 1984-86. Mem. Am. Chem. Soc., Materials Rsch. Soc., Sigma Xi. Office: U Colo Dept Chemistry PO Box 215 Boulder CO 80309-0001

WALCH, PETER SANBORN, museum director, publisher; b. Portland, Maine, Oct. 10, 1940; s. J. Weston and Ruth Dyer (Sanborn) W.; m. Margaret S. Segal, June 29, 1962 (div. 1983); children: Maximilian F.S., Abigail M.; m. Linda P. Tyler, Aug. 3, 1990. BA, Swarthmore Coll., 1962; MFA, Princeton U., 1964, PhD, 1968. Asst. prof. fine arts Pomona Coll., Claremont, Calif., 1966-68, Vassar Coll., Poughkeepsie, N.Y., 1968-69, Yale U., New Haven, 1969-71; assoc. prof. U. N.Mex., Albuquerque, 1971-85, dir. Art Mus., 1985—; chmn., bd. dirs. J. Weston Walch, Pub., Portland, 1990—. Author: (exhbn. catalog) French Eighteenth-Century Oil Sketches, 1980; editor New Mexico Studies in the Fine Arts jour., 1978-86. Mem. Contemporary Art Soc. Home: 1520 Columbia Dr NE Albuquerque NM 87106-2635 Office: Univ NMex Art Mus Fine Arts Ctr Albuquerque NM 87131

WALD, ROBERT GRAY, electro-optical engineer; b. Kansas City, Mo., Nov. 9, 1963; s. Robert Irwin and Helen Jane (Gray) W. BS in Elec. Engring., Kans. State U., 1986; MS in Optical and Elec. Engring., U. Colo., Boulder, 1990. Power engr. Burns & McDonnel Engring., Kansas City, Mo., 1984; control engr. Black & Veatch Engring., Overland Park, Kans., 1985, Kansas City, 1986; artificial intelligence researcher Boeing/Kans. State U., Manhattan, 1986-87; optical artificial intelligence computing researcher NSF, Boulder, 1987-88; laser power energy engr. Nat. Inst. Standards and Tech., U.S. Dept. Commerce, Boulder, 1988-90; cons. in photonics, electronics and software applications Boulder, 1991—; telcom. project mgr. U. Colo., Boulder, 1993. Contbr. articles to profl. jours. Mem. IEEE, Nat. Soc. Profl. Engrs. (v.p. 1985-86), Lasers and Electro-Optical Soc. of IEEE, Am. Assn. Artificial Intelligence, Soc. for Photo-Instrumentation Engrs. Roman Catholic. Home: 437 University Ave Boulder CO 80302-5805

WALDECK, GARY CRANSTON, communications executive; b. Hanford, Calif., Apr. 19, 1943; s. Ralph A. and Dorothy L. (Cranston) W.; m. Lee S. Waldeck; children: Karen Ann, Kathryn Louise, Kenneth March. BSEE, U. Calif., Davis, 1971; MBA, Santa Clara (Calif.) U., 1989. Sr. technician U. Calif., Davis, 1971; engr. GTE Lenkurt, San Carlos, Calif., 1972-74; sr. engr. Fluid Ionic Systems, Phoenix, 1974-75; prin. engr. Gulton DSD, Albuquerque, 1975-76; program mgr. Sperry Corp., Phoenix, 1976-85; supr. Ford Aerospace Corp., San Jose, Calif., 1985-90; v.p. Calif. Microwave, Inc., 1990—. With USN, 1960-65. Office: Calif Microwave Inc 985 Almanor Ave Sunnyvale CA 94086-2903

WALDEN, BEN PARRISH, thoroughbred horseman, breeding consultant; b. Greensboro, N.C., July 21, 1931; s. W. Julian and Lily (Parrish) W.; m. Margaret Elliott, Apr. 26, 1954 (div. 1985); children: Hallie Gay Bagley, Ben P. Jr., W. Elliott. BA, Washington & Lee U., 1953. Owner, sole proprietor Dearborn Farm, Midway, Ky., 1965-90; gen. mgr. Calif. Thoroughbred Sales, Del Mar, Calif., 1990-92; pres. Thoroughbred Breeders of Ky., Lexington, 1975-78, Thoroughbred Club Am., Lexington, 1988. With U.S. Army, 1954-55. Mem. Thoroughbred Club of Am., Thoroughbred Owners and Breeders Assn., Ky. Thoroughbred Assn., Idle Hour Country Club.

WALDEN, JAMES LEE, telecommunications specialist, consultant; b. Pitts., Sept. 2, 1955; s. James Edwin and Marilyn Lee (Wolf) W.; m. Kathleen Dyck, June 24, 1983. AA in Pre-Medicine, Coll. of San Mateo, Calif., 1975; diploma, Squadron Officers Sch., 1978; BA in Phys. Scis., U. Calif., Berkeley, 1977; Diploma, Air Command & Staff Coll., 1984. Commd. 2d lt. USAF, 1977, advanced through grades to capt., 1981; communications requirements officer AFFTC Edwards AFB, Rosamond, Calif., 1978-81; communications staff officer Hdqrs. Space Command/ADCOM/NORAD, Colorado Springs, Colo., 1981-84; resource analyst 1836 EIG Lindsey AS, Wesbaden, Fed. Republic of Germany, 1984-87; communications staff officer Hdqrs. TAC Langley AFB, Hampton, Va., 1987-89; mgr. trainee Radio Shack, Hampton, 1989; sr. communications engr. Input Output Computer Svcs., L.A. AFB, 1989-90; telecommunications systems specialist East Bay Mcpl. Utility Dist., Oakland, Calif., 1990—; vol. examiner Amateur Radio Relay League, Pleasant Hill, Calif., 1989—. Contbr. articles to profl. jours. Participant Contra Costa (Calif.) Radio Amateur Emergency Svc., 1991—. Named Eagle Scout. Mem. Am. Radio Relay League (life, vol. examiner 1989—), Northern Calif. and Nat. CENTREX Users Group. Republican. Baptist. Home: 2512 Norwalk Ct Martinez CA 94553

WALDHAUER, FRED DONALD, health care executive; b. Bklyn., Dec. 6, 1927; s. Fred G. and Elsie L. (Haybach) W.; B.E.E., Cornell U., 1948; M.S.E.E., Columbia U., 1960; m. Ruth Irene Waina, Feb. 12, 1955; children—Neil, Amy, Ann, Alice, Kim. Engr. RCA, Camden, N.J., 1948-55, patent agt., Princeton, N.J., 1953-55; mem. tech. staff Bell Telephone Labs., Holmdel, N.J., 1956-87, supr. transmission tech. lab., 1963-87; with venture start-up in hearing health care Resound Corp., Redwood City, Calif., 1987—; sec., dir. Expts. in Art and Tech., Inc. Fellow IEEE (mem. solid state circuits council 1974-78, mem. steering com. on lightwave tech. 1982); mem. Audio Engring. Soc. Author: Feedback, 1982. Patentee in field; contbr. articles to profl. jours. Home: 22296 Skyline Blvd La Honda CA 94020-9728

WALDMAN, JERALD PAUL, orthopedic surgeon; b. Newark, N.J., Apr. 9, 1946; s. Samuel and Estelle (Lefkowitz); m. Patricia Maite, Sept. 8, 1973; children: Genevieve, Dawn, Jacqueline, Aimee, Olivia. BA in Biology, U. Rochester, 1968; MD, U. Md., 1972. Diplomate Am. Bd. Surgeons. Surg. intern Harbor Cen./UCLA, Torrance, Calif., 1973, orthopedic resident, 1977; orthopedic surgeon Community Orthopedic Med. Group, Mission Viejo, Calif., 1977—; bd. dirs. Mission Quality IPA, Mission Viejo; clin. faculty UCI Med. Sch., Orange, Calif., 1978—; chmn. interdisciplinary coms. Mission Hosp. Regional Med. Ctr., Mission Viejo, 1992-93, mem. vis. com., 1988—, others. Bd. dirs. Laguna Beach (Calif.) School Power, 1990-92. Fellow Am. Acad. Orthopedic Surgeons, Am. Coll. Surgeons, Internat. Coll. Surgeons; mem. Calif. Med. Assn., Orange County Med. Assn., Undersea Med. Soc. Office: Community Orthopedic Med 27800 Medical Center Rd Mission Viejo CA 92691

WALDO, BURTON CORLETT, lawyer; b. Seattle, Aug. 11, 1920; s. William Earl and Ruth Ernestine (Corlett) W.; m. Margaret Jane Hoar, Aug. 24, 1946; children: James Chandler, Bruce Corlett. BA, U. Wash., 1941, JD, 1948. Bar: Wash. 1949. Assoc. Vedova, Horswill & Yeomans, Seattle, 1949-50, Kahin, Carmody & Horswill, Seattle, 1950-54; ptnr. Keller Rohrback & predecessor firms, Seattle, 1954-86; mng. ptnr. Keller Rohrback & predecessor firms, 1978-83, sr. ptnr., 1983—. Mem. Seattle Bd. Theater Suprs., 1958-61, Mcpl. League of Seattle/King County, 1949—. Capt. U.S. Army, 1942-46; ETO. Mem. ABA, Internat. Assn. Def. Counsel, Fedn. of Ins. and Corp. Counsel., Wash. Bar Assn., Wash. Def. Trial Lawyers Assn., Seattle-King County Bar Assn. (trustee 1965-68), Rainier Club, Wash. Athletic Club, The Steamboaters, Fedn. of Fly Fishers (life), Flyfisher's Club of Oreg., Delta Tau Delta, Phi Delta Phi, Alpha Kappa Psi.

WALDRAM, SCOTT G., financial planner; b. Pocatello, Idaho, May 11, 1951; s. Hal Garner and Barbara (Heaton) W.; m. Carla J. Merrill, July 18, 1974; children: Melissa, Michelle, Aaron, Michael. Student, Idaho State U., 1970-72, Brigham Young U., 1973-74. Sales rep. Blocks Inc., Pocatello, 1972-75; prodn. analyst Bucyrus-Erie, Pocatello, 1975-77; fin. planner IDS Am. Express, Mpls., 1977—; Bd. dirs. Simplot Games, Pocatello. Master track officer Idaho State U., 1978—; bishop LDS Ch., 1978, high coun., 1980. Mem. LDS Ch. Home: 560 Canyon Dr Pocatello ID 83204 Office: IDS Fin Svcs PO Box 6 Pocatello ID 83204

WALDSCHMIDT, PAUL EDWARD, clergyman; b. Evansville, Ind., Jan. 7, 1920; s. Edward Benjamin and Olga Marie (Moers) W. B.A., U. Notre Dame, 1942; student, Holy Cross Coll., Washington, 1942-45; S.T.L., Laval U., Que., Can., 1947; S.T.D., Angelicum U., Rome, Italy, 1948. Ordained priest Roman Catholic Ch., 1946; prof. apologetics and dogmatic theology Holy Cross Coll., 1949-55; v.p. U. Portland, 1955-62, dean faculties, 1956-60, pres., 1962-78; aux. bishop of Portland, 1978-90. Mem. Cath. Theol. Soc. Am. (v.p. 1954-55), NEA, Delta Epsilon Sigma. Club: K.C. (4 deg.). Address: 5826 N Williamette Blvd Portland OR 97203

WALEN, JAMES ROBERT, project engineer, artist; b. N.Y.C., Nov. 23, 1947; s. John Nicholas and Carol Susan (Rannbury) W.; m. Donna Kay Whitely, June 23, 1967 (div. 1992); children: Heather Renee, Aaron James. Grad., Citrus Coll., 1966, Orange Coast Coll., 1970. Assoc. engr. Hughes Aircraft Co., Irvine, Calif., 1966-78; ptnr., chief engr. D&L Engring., Irvine, 1978-80; design supr. Interconics, Irvine, 1980-85; sr. project engr. Hughes Interconnect Systems, Irvine, 1985—; instr. Inst. for Interconnecting & Pkg. Electronic Circuits, 1979, 82. Inventor, patentee in field. Mem. Rep. Nat. Com., 1981—, Nat. Rep. Congl. Com., 1988—, Ronald Reagan Presdl. Found., 1989—; vol. Friendship Home of Laguna Beach, Calif., 1992—. With U.S. Army, 1968. Mem. San Onofre Surfing Club (bd. dirs. 1985-88). Office: Hughes Interconnect Systems 17150 Von Karman Ave Irvine CA 92713

WALES, HUGH GREGORY, marketing educator, business executive; b. Topeka, Feb. 28, 1910; s. Raymond Otis and Nola V. (Chestnut) W.; m. Alice Fulkerson, June 11, 1938. A.B., Washburn Coll., 1932; M.B.A., Harvard U., 1934; Ph.D., Northwestern U., 1944; D.Sc., Washburn Municipal U., 1968. Dean men N.W. Mo. State Tchrs. Coll., 1935-38, dean students, head dept. econs., 1938-39; dean students, dir. summer sch., vets. bur., head dept. econs. Washburn U., 1939-46; assoc. prof. marketing U. Ill., 1946-53, prof., 1953-70, prof. emeritus, dir. micro-precision projects, 1970—; prof. marketing and mgmt., head dept. Roosevelt U., 1970-75; pres. Decisions, Evaluations & Learning, Internat. Assocs.; vis. prof. marketing U. South Africa, Pretoria, 1962; lectr. U. Stellenbosch, South Africa, 1973, 75, 76; cons. South African Govt., Pretoria, 1974; participant internat. confs.; bus., marketing research cons.; internat. pres. Micro-precision Miniaturization Inst., 1970—, dir., program chmn., Chgo., 1970—. Author: Changing Perspectives in Marketing, 1951, Marketing Research, 1952, 4th edit., 1974, Marketing Research-Selected Literature, 1952, Cases and Problems in Marketing Research, 1953, (with Robert Ferber) Basic Bibliography in Marketing Research, 1956, 3d edit., 1974, Motivation and Market Behavior, (with Ferber), 1958, Advertising Copy, Layout, and Typography, (with Gentry and M. Wales), 1958, (with R. Ferber) The Champaign-Urbana Metropolitan Area, (with Engel and Warshaw) Promotional Strategy, 1967, 3d edit., 1975, (with Dik Twedt and Lyndon Dawson) Personality Theory in Marketing Research: A Basic Bibliography, 1976, (with Sharon Abrams) English as a Second Language in Business, 1978, (with Luck, Taylor and Rubin) Marketing Research, 1978; numerous others, works transl. several langs.; Contbr. (with Luck, Taylor and Rubin) articles to profl. jours. Pres. Civic Symphony Soc., 1964-65. Mem. Am. Econ. Assn., Am. Marketing Assn. (sec., acad. v.p.), Am. Watchmakers Inst. (dir. research and edn. 1963-66), Nat. Assn. Watch and Clock Collectors (chpt. pres. 1981, 83), Arizonans for Nat. Security (chmn. visual aids com. 1979—), Internat. Alliance Theatrical Stage Employees and Moving Picture Machine Operators, Internat. Platform Assn., Internat. TV Assn., Assn. Edn. Internat. Bus., Soc. Internat. Devel., Am. Statis. Assn., Nat. Assn. for Mgmt. Educators., Acad. Mgmt., We the People United (treas.), Tempe Republican Men's Club, Tempe Bus. and Profl. Men's Club. Clubs: Ariz. Breakfast. Lodge: Rotary. Home: 2625 E Southern Ave Apt 244C Tempe AZ 85282-7634

WALES, RICHARD BERT, computer systems programmer, computer analyst; b. San Francisco, Mar. 30, 1952; s. Richard B. and Mary Evangeline (Lofthus) W.; m. Jenifer Lynn Broderick, Dec. 19, 1989; 1 child, Marie Louise. AB in Music, BS in Math., Stanford U., 1975; MA in Music, UCLA, 1977, MS in Computer Sci., 1979, Engr. in Computer Sci., 1992. Programmer housing office Stanford (Calif.) U., 1974-75; teaching asst. computer sci. dept. UCLA, 1977-80, programmer, analyst computer sci. dept., 1980—. Democrat. Mem. LDS Ch. Office: UCLA Computer Sci Dept 3531 Boelter Hall Los Angeles CA 90024

WALIZE, REUBEN THOMPSON, III, health research administrator; b. Williamsport, Pa., May 28, 1950; s. Reuben Thompson Jr. and Marion Marie (Smith) W.; m. Kathleen Anne Smith, Aug. 13, 1979; children: Heather, Amanda, Reuben IV. BS, Pa. State U., 1972; MPH magna cum laude, U. Tenn., 1975. Manpower planner Northcentral Pa. Area Health Edn. System, Danville, 1975-76, asst. dir., 1976, exec. dir., 1976-78; health mgr. Seda-Cog, Timberhaven, Pa., 1978; exec. asst. VA Med. Ctr., Erie, Pa., 1978-81; trainee VA Med. Ctr., Little Rock, 1981; adminstrv. officer rsch. svc. VA Med. Ctr., White River Junction, Vt., 1981-88; mgmt. analyst Dept. Vets. Affairs Med. Ctr., Roseburg, Oreg., 1988-90, health systems specialist, 1990-92; adminstrv. officer rsch. Vets. Affairs Med. Ctr. Am. Lake, Tacoma, 1992—; Mem. Pa. Coun. Health Profls., 1975-77, Ctrl. Pa. Health System Agy. Manpower Com., 1975-77; mem. Interagy. Coun. Geisinger Med. Ctr., Danville, 1976-78; liaison for rsch. Dartmouth Med. Sch., Hanover, N.H., 1981-88; cons. in field. Recipient Man of Achievement award Queens Coll., Eng., 1978, Student Am. Med. Assn. Found. award, 1975; 1st pl. Douglas County Lamb Cooking Contest, 1992. Mem. APHA, AAAS, N.Y. Acad. Scis., Soc. Rsch. Adminstrs., Pa. State Alumni Assn., Nat. Audubon Soc., Steamboaters, Nat. Wildlife Fedn., Record Catch Club, VIP Club. Home: 1103 25th Ave SE Puyallup WA 98374-1362

WALKER, BRUCE HOWARD, drilling research company executive; b. Salt Lake City, Sept. 22, 1946; s. William S. and Beverly M. (Christensen) W.; m. Janice Romick Mayhew, July 9, 1970; children—Nicole, Paige, Valerie. B.A., Whitman Coll., 1970; B.S., Columbia U., 1970. Operating research engr. Christensen Diamond Products, Salt Lake City, 1970-74, group leader, 1974-76, mgr. research, 1976-81, product mgr., 1981-83; pres. Terra Tek-Drilling Research Lab., Salt Lake City, 1983—. Contbr. articles to profl. jours.; patentee in field. Mem. ASME, Soc. Petroleum Engrs.-AIME (Cedric K. Fergusén medalist 1974, disting. mem.). Office: 400 Wakara Way Salt Lake City UT 84108-1292

WALKER, BURTON LEITH, engineering writer, psychotherapist; b. Mt. Morris Twp., Mich., Oct. 23, 1927; s. Dalton Hugh and Muriel Joyce (Black) W.; m. Norva Jean Trochman, June 28, 1949; children: Paul, Cynthia Halverson, Mark; m. Carol Jean D'Andrea, July 31, 1981. Cert. psychology. tchr., lic. psychotherapist, hypnotherapist, Calif. A.A., Allan Hancock Coll., 1971; B.A., Chapman Coll., 1974, M.A., 1975. Contract estimator Ryan Aeronaut., San Diego, 1949-59; logistics rep. GD/A, San Diego, 1960-62; systems engr., cons. fgn. svc. Ralph M. Parsons, L.A., 1962-68; lead engring. writer, sr. analyst Fed. Electric, Vandenberg AFB, Calif., 1969-86; psychotherapist Access, Vandenberg Village, Family Guidance Svc., Santa Ynez, Calif.; ret.; part time prof. Allan Hancock Coll., Santa Maria, Calif., 1974-93, small bus. owner 1974-86. Active Santa Ynez Valley Presbyn. Ch.; mem. Republican Nat. Com. Served with USN, 1946-48. Mem. Am. Assn. Christian Counselors, Nat. Mgmt. Assn. (Outstanding Svc. award 1982), Calif. Assn. Marriage and Family Therapists, Assn. Advancement Ret. People. Republican. Home: 3149 E Hwy 246 Santa Ynez CA 93460-9634

WALKER, CAROLYN LOUISE, nursing researcher, educator; b. Ft. George, Wash., Apr. 4, 1947; d. Marvin John and Louise Olive (Billings) W.; m. Simon I. Zemel, Apr. 6, 1968 (div. 1981); children: Michelle, Brent Zemel. AA, Fullerton (Calif.) Coll., 1968; BSN, Calif. State U., Fullerton, 1976; MSN, Calif. State U., L.A., 1979; PhD in Nursing, U. Utah, 1986. RN, Calif. Staff nurse Children's Hosp. Orange (Calif.) County, 1969-71; instr. nursing Cypress (Calif.) Coll., 1978-81, 81-82, Saddleback Coll., Mission Viejo, Calif., 1979-80; nurse oncology Children's Hosp. Orange County, 1980-81; asst. prof. U. Utah, Salt Lake City, 1984-85; asst. prof. San Diego State U., 1986-90, assoc. prof., 1990—. Mem. editorial rev. bd. Am. Jour. Continuing Edn. in Nursing, 1987-90, Oncology Nursing Forum, 1988-91, Jour. Pediatric Oncology Nursing, 1991—. Mem. children's com. Am. Cancer Soc., San Diego, 1988—. Mem. ANA, Assn. Pediatric Oncology Nurses (chair rsch. 1988-91, exec. bd. dirs. 1992—), Oncology Nursing Soc. Democrat. Episcopalian. Office: San Diego State U Sch Nursing San Diego CA 92182-0254

WALKER, DAVID T., artist, musician; b. Tulsa, June 25, 1941; s. Julius McClendon and Ruth Roland (Virginia) W.; children: Davette Michelle, Denise, Maya Segirah. Musician 14 solo albums; contbr. over 2,000 albums with various artists; studio musician films, TV soundtracks and commls. Recipient L.A. Resolution Achievement awards LA City Coun. Community, 1968, 69, 71, 76, 84, Over 300 Platinum and Gold Records; named Best Guitarist Ebony Music Awards, 1975. Mem. NARAS, Recording Musicians Assn., Internat. Assn. of Jazz Appreciation.

WALKER, DEWARD EDGAR, JR., anthropologist, educator; b. Johnson City, Tenn., Aug. 3, 1935; s. Deward Edgar and Matilda Jane (Clark) W.; m. Candace A. Walker; children: Alice, Deward Edgar III, Mary Jane, Sarah, Daniel, Joseph Benjamin. Student, Ea. Oreg. Coll., 1953-54, 56-58, Mexico City Coll., 1958; BA in Anthropology with honors, U. Oreg., 1960-61, PhD in Anthropology, 1964; postgrad., Wash. State U., 1962. Asst. prof. anthropology George Washington U., Washington, 1964-65; asst. prof. anthropology Wash. State U., Pullman, 1965-67, research collaborator, 1967-69; assoc. prof., chmn. dept. Sociology/Anthropology, lab. dir. U. Idaho, Moscow, 1967-69; prof. U. Colo., Boulder, 1969—, research assoc. in population processes program of inst. behavioral sci., 1969-73, assoc. dean Grad. Sch., 1973-76; affiliate faculty U. Idaho, 1971—. Founder, co-editor Northwest Anthropol. Rsch. Notes, 1966—, editor, Plateau Vol.: Handbook of North American Indians, 1971—; contbr. articles to profl. jours.; author, co-author of twelve books on tribes of Idaho and the Northwest. Mem. tech/ steering panel Hanford Environ. Dose Reconstrn. Project; advisor on Native Am. affairs Smithsonian Inst. With U.S. Army, 1954-62. Fellow NSF, 1961, NDEA, 1961-64. Fellow Am. Anthropol. Assn. (assoc. editor

Am. Anthropologist 1973-74), Soc. Applied Anthropology (hon. life, exec. com. 1970-79, treas. 1976-79, chmn. High Plains Regional sect. 1980-82, cons., expert witness tribes of N.W., editor Human Orgn. 1970-76, rsch. with twenty separate tribes); mem. AAAS, Am. Acad. Polit. Social Scis., Northwest Anthropol. Conf. Home: PO Box 4147 Boulder CO 80306-4147 Office: U Colo Dept Anthropology Box 233 Boulder CO 80309

WALKER, DUNCAN EDWARD, military officer; b. Washington, Aug. 2, 1942; s. Edward John and Katherine Edith (Duncan) W. BA in Indsl. Psychology, N.Mex. State U., 1965; MS in Systems Mgmt., U. So. Calif., 1978; MPA, Golden Gate U., 1980. Commd. 2d lt. USAF, 1965, advanced through grades to lt. col., 1981; grad. Squadron Officers Sch., 1973, Air Command and Staff Coll., 1974, Indsl. Coll. Armed Forces, 1977; chief devel. and deployment br. ICBM requirements SAC, Offutt AFB, Nebr., 1981-84; dep. for ICBM ops. and evaluation Air Force Operational Test and Evaluation Ctr., Vandenberg AFB, Calif., 1984-88; program engr. Fed. Svcs. Corp., Western Space and Missile Ctr., Vandenberg AFB, Calif., 1988-92. Mission coun. exec. Boy Scouts of Am. Decorated Bronze Star, Meritorious Service medal with two oak leaf cluster, Air Force Commendation medal with three oak leaf clusters. Mem. AIAA, Order Pour Le Merite, Internat. Test and Evaluation Assn., Air Force Assn., Mil. Order of World Wars, Am. Legion, Elks (past exalted ruler). Republican. Methodist. Home: 113 N Y St Lompoc CA 93436-5514

WALKER, E. JERRY, clergyman; b. Seattle, May 31, 1918; s. Septimus and Mae Ruth (Roys) W.; m. Holly Rae Harding, Nov. 10, 1941; children: Jerrianne, Dale Harding, Barbara Rae. AB, Seattle Pacific U., 1940; MDiv, Garrett Theol. Sch., 1945; DD, Wiley Coll., 1958, Northland Coll., 1971. Ordained to ministry United Meth. Ch. Teaching fellow State Coll. Wash., 1940-41; dir. edn. Prairie Farmer Sta. WLS, Chgo., 1942-45; dir. radio Internat. Coun. Religious Edn., 1945-48; freelance writer, dir. radio and TV Sta. WBKB-TV, Chgo., 1948-53; pastor St. James Meth. Ch., Chgo., 1953-62, First United Meth. Ch., Duluth, 1962-74; freelance daily commentary Sta. KDAL-TV, Duluth, Minn., 1964—; exec. dir. Ctr. for Family Studies, Duluth, 1972-82; ptnr. SoundVideo Prodns., Tahuya, Wash., 1987—; cons. environ. grants, 1987—; project dir. Hood Canal Wetlands Interp Ctr., 1988—; bd. dirs. Pacific Northwest Writers Conf., Wash., 1983-88. Author: Five Minute Stories from the Bible, 1948, Stories from the Bible, 1955, Seeking a Faith of Your Own, 1961, Sinner's Parish, 1963, (plays) Checkerboard, Kyrie, The Unpainted Wall; also numerous articles. Bd. dirs. Chgo. chpt. Nat. Conf. Christians and Jews, 1955-62, nat. bd. trustees, 1974-76; mem. Kenwood-Ellis Community Renewal Commn., 1957-62, Gov. Ill. Adv. Commn. on Aged, 1958-62, S.E. Chgo. Commn., 1958-62, United Fund Survey Com., 1968-70; co-chmn. Duluth Citizens Com. Secondary Edn., 1963-64; bd. dirs. Mary E. Theler Community Ctr., Belfair, Wash., 1988-91; cons. Mason County United Way, 1990—, co-chair needs assessment com., 1992—; cons. Olympic Coll. Expansion Program, Shelton and. Recipient Human Rels. award Chgo. Commn. Human Rels., 1954, Friend of Youth award Southside Community Com., 1955, Disting. Citizen award Com. of One Hundred, 1962, Achievement award Freedom Found., 1963-65, Broadcast Journalism award Minn. Coun. Chs., 1971, Appreciation award North Mason Sch. Dist., 1990, Environ. Pride award Pacific Northwest Mag., 1992; named Chicagoan of Yr. Chgo. Jaycees, 1962. Mem. Internat. Platform Assn., Kiwanis. Democrat. Home: E 18341 Hwy 106 Belfair WA 98528 Office: North Mason Sch Dist Box 167 Belfair WA 98528

WALKER, ELIZABETH VIRGINIA, food service administrator; b. Youngstown, Ohio, Nov. 11, 1947; d. Floyd D. and Elizabeth V. (Linge) Perry; children: Sean, Distin; m. Dan Walker, Jan. 24, 1991. AS, U. Wyo., 1987. With day care ctr. Jackson (Wyo.) Pub. Schs. System, 1972-79; concessions mgr. Jackson Hole Rodeo Assn., 1979-80; food svc. dir. Residential Sch. for Handicapped, Jackson, 1980—; coord. food svc. program for handicapped, Wilson, Wyo., 1983—. Author: mag. Am. Sch. Food Svc., 1987. Coord. Muscular Dystrophy Assn., Jackson, 1986-88; sec. Babe Ruth Assn., Jackson, 1986-88. Named Woman of the Yr., Bus. & Profl. Women, 1979. Mem. Am. Sch. Food Svc. Assn., Wyo. Sch. Food Svc. Assn. (regional rep. 1978—, Louise Sublette award 1988). Democrat. Episcopalian. Office: Residential Sch Handicapped PO Box 240 Wilson WY 83014-0240

WALKER, ELJANA M. DU VALL, civic worker; b. France, Jan. 18, 1924; came to U.S., 1948; naturalized, 1954; student Med. Inst., U. Paris, 1942-47; m. John S. Walker, Jr., Dec. 31, 1947; children—John, Peter, Barbara. Pres., Loyola Sch. PTA, 1958-59; bd. dirs. Santa Claus shop, 1959-73; treas. Archdiocese Denver Catholic Women, 1962-64; rep. Cath. Parent-Tchr League, 1962-65; pres. Aux. Denver Gen. Hosp., 1966-69; precinct committeewoman Arapahoe County Republican Women's Com., 1973-74; mem. re-election com. Arapahoe County Rep. Party, 1973-78, Reagan election com., 1980; block worker Arapahoe County March of Dimes, Heart Assn., Hemophilia Drive, Muscular Dystrophy and Multiple Sclerosis Drive, 1978-81; cen. city asst. Guild Debutante Charities, Inc. Recipient Distinguished Service award Am.-by-choice, 1966; named to Honor Roll, ARC, 1971. Mem. Cherry Hills Symphony, Lyric Opera Guild, Alliance Franciase (life mem.), ARC, Civic Ballet Guild (life mem.), Needlework Guild Am. (v.p. 1980-82), Kidney Found. (life), Denver Art Mus., U. Denver Art and Conservation Assns. (chmn. 1980-82), U. Denver Women's Library Assn., Chancellors Soc, Passage Inc. Roman Catholic. Clubs: Union (Chgo.); Denver Athletic, 26 (Denver); Welcome to Colo. Internat. Address: 2301 Green Oaks Dr Greenwood Village CO 80121

WALKER, FRANCIS JOSEPH, lawyer; b. Tacoma, Aug. 5, 1922; s. John McSweeney and Sarah Veronica (Meechan) W.; m. Julia Corinne O'Brien, Jan. 27, 1951; children: Vincent Paul, Monica Irene Hylton, Jill Marie Nudell, John Michael, Michael Joseph, Thomas More. B.A., St. Martin's Coll., 1947; J.D., U. Wash., 1950. Bar: Wash. Asst. atty. gen. State of Wash., 1950-51; pvt. practice law, Olympia, Wash., 1951—; gen. counsel Wash. Cath. Conf., 1967-76. Lt. (j.g.) USNR, 1943-46; PTO. Home and Office: 2723 Hillside Dr SE Olympia WA 98501-3460

WALKER, HOMER FRANKLIN, mathematics educator; b. Beaumont, Tex., Sept. 7, 1943; s. John Harrell and Esther Orlou (Hooks) W.; m. Elizabeth Mary Thompson, July 28, 1984; children: Benjamin Thompson, John Harrell. BA, Rice U., 1966; MS, NYU, 1968, PhD, 1970. Asst. prof., assoc. prof. Tex. Tech U., Lubbock, 1970-74; vis. assoc. prof. U. Houston, 1974-75, assoc. prof., 1975-80, prof., 1980-85; prof. math. Utah State U., Logan, 1985—; vis. assoc. prof. U. Denver, 1973-74, Cornell U., Ithaca, N.Y., 1978; vis. prof. U. N.Mex., Albuquerque, 1981-82, Yale U., New Haven, 1989. Contbr. articles to profl. jours. Recipient Gov.'s medal for sci. and tech. State of Utah, 1987. Office: Utah State U Math and Stats Dept Logan UT 84322-3900

WALKER, JAMES RODERICK, academic administrator; b. San Diego, Sept. 20, 1946; s. Roderick Colin and Sofia Dolores (Ruiz) W.; m. Margaret Denise Rush, Dec. 17, 1967; children: Richard W., Robert C. Student, San Diego State U., 1965-69. Apprentice Despie's Music, San Diego, 1966-69; instrument repair technician Reese's Music, Escondido, Calif., 1969-72; with DoAll Corp., Escondido, 1972-74; restoration metalsmith Escondido, 1974-85; dir. Inst. Metal Repair, Escondido, 1985—. Author: Replacing Knife Blades, 1988, Protecting Your Valuables, 1988, IMR Sourcebook, 1989, how-to instrnl. videos on metal care, restoration, repair; editor, pub. newsletter Repairing Metalware, 1985—, Fine Metal Gazette, 1991—. Choir dir. World Wide Ch. of God, Escondido, 1970—. Home and Office: 1558 S Redwood St Escondido CA 92025-5643

WALKER, JERRY QUENTEN, professional sports team executive; b. Anacortes, Wash., Aug. 8, 1953; s. Ivan Millard and Janet Jean (Holeman) W.; m. Patricia Rae Duncan, Aug. 3, 1973 (div. Jan. 1984); children: Tracey, Brittany. AA in Bus., Everett Community Coll., 1973; BA in Mktg., U. Wash., 1976. Mktg. supr. Everett (Wash.) Herald, 1970-79; owner, operator Ruedi's Record Ctr., Everett, 1980-81; owner, broker Century 21 Champion Real Estate, Everett, 1981-82; sales mgr. Century 21 North Homes Realty, Everett, 1983-84; owner, broker Walker-Wells & Assoc., Inc., Everett, 1984-89; chief exec. officer, pres. Bellingham (Wash.) Mariners, 1989—; Bd. dirs. N.W. League Profl. Baseball, Portland, Oreg, 1989—. Bd. dirs., mem. Bellingham Cen. Lions Club, 1989—. Home: 2421 Vista Dr Bellingham WA 98226-4512 Office: Bellingham Mariners 1316 King St Bellingham WA 98226-6263

WALKER, JILL MARIE, writer, consultant; b. Olympia, Wash., June 4, 1955; d. Francis Joseph and Julia Corrine (O'Brien) W.; m. Franklin Dean Hobbs, June 21, 1975 (div. Dec. 1982); m. Bruce Mitchell Nudell, Sept. 15, 1985; children: Matthew Phillip, Jamie Alexandra. Student, Scripps Coll., Claremont, Calif., 1973-75; grad. gemologist, Gemological Inst. Am., Santa Monica, Calif., 1977; BA, UCLA, 1980. Continuing edn. course designer/internat. instr., alumni dir. Gemological Inst. Am., Santa Monica, Calif., 1983-85; course designer, instr. Safeco Ins. Cos., Seattle, 1986-89, tng. needs cons., 1990; co-author bilingual children's video Boulder, Colo., 1991—; keynote gemology speaker Am. Gemology Soc. Nat. Conv., Washington, 1979; TV gemology guest Hour Mag. and News on Channel 9, L.A., 1984; resident instr. colored stones and gem identification Gemological Inst. Am., Santa Monica, Calif., 1977-81, asst. mgr. home study dept., 1981-83. Author: (book chpt. with others) Jade 1991; contbr. Gems and Gemology mag. (article of the year award 1981, 82, Gems and Gemology mag.). Community dir. Jr. League of L.A. Bd., 1982-85; mgr. trainer nonprofit bds. United Way of L.A., 1982-84, United Way of Seattle, 1986-87; commr. Planning Policy Commn., Issaquah, Wash., 1987-91. Mem. ASTD, Nat. Soc. Performance and Instrn. Home: 1052 Meadow Ct Louisville CO 80027

WALKER, JOHN SUMPTER, JR., lawyer; b. Richmond, Ark., Oct. 13, 1921; s. John Sumpter, Martha (Wilson) W.; m. Eljana M. duVall, Dec. 31, 1947; children: John Stephen, Barbara Monika Ann, Peter Mark Gregory. BA, Tulane U., 1942; MS, U. Denver, 1955, JD, 1960; diploma Nat. Def. U., 1981. Bar: Colo. 1960, U.S. Dist. Ct. Colo. 1960, U.S. Supreme Ct., 1968, U.S. Ct. Appeals (10th cir.) 1960, U.S. Tax. Ct., 1981. With Denver & Rio Grande Western R.R. Co., 1951-61, gen. solicitor, 1961-89 ; pres. Denver Union Terminal Ry. Co. Apptd. gen. counsel Moffat Tunnel Commn., 1991. With U.S. Army, 1942-46. Decorated Bronze Star. Mem. Colo. Bar Assn., Arapahoe County Bar Assn., Alliance Francaise (life), Order of St. Ives, U. Denver Chancellors' Soc., Cath. Lawyers Guild. Republican. Roman Catholic. Club: Denver Athletic. Office: 6185 S Columbine Way Littleton CO 80121-2637

WALKER, J(OHN) WILLIAM, film/video producer; b. Terre Haute, Ind., Jan. 5, 1938; s. Warren E. and Iva L. (Tryon) W.; m. Janet Y. Modesitt, June 27, 1959; children: Jill Ann, Drew C. BS, Ind. State U., 1959; MS, U. Kans., 1961. Producer-dir. Coronet Film and Video, Chgo., 1961-72, v.p., exec. producer, 1973-84; pres. Bill Walker Prodns., Inc., Scottsdale, Ariz., 1984—. Film producer ednl. films. Mem. adv. bd. film, radio, TV, U. Kans., Lawrence, 1982-85; mem. comm. adv. bd. Ch. Fedn. Greater Chgo., 1980-84; producer SW Leadership Found., Phoenix, 1988—. Mem. Assn. for Ednl. Communications and Tech. (pres. media design div. 1984-85, pres.-elect, pres. and past pres. 1983-86). Home and office: Bill Walker Prodns Inc 6476 N 79th St Scottsdale AZ 85250

WALKER, JOSEPH ROBERT, neurosurgeon; b. Atlantic City, N.J., Mar. 2, 1942; s. Joseph West and Helen (Mendte) W.; m. Mary Cynthia Long, Aug. 23, 1968; children: Joseph West II, Scott Robert, Heather Elizabeth. BS, St. Josephs Coll., 1964; MD, Creighton U., 1968. Diplomate Am. Bd. Neurol. Surgery. Intern Atlantic City (N.J.) Hosp., 1968-69; resident surgery Jefferson Med. Coll. Hosp., Phila, 1969-70; resident neurosurgery U. N.C., Chapel Hill, 1972-76, fellow, instr. neurosurgery, 1976-77; chief neurosurgery Washoe Med. Ctr., Reno, Nev., 1982, St. Mary's Hosp., Reno, 1982; vice-chief neurosurgery Washoe Med. Ctr., Reno, 1989, St. Mary's Hosp., Reno, 1989; asst. prof. U. Nev. Med. Sch., Reno, 1979—. Served as lt. comdr. USN, 1970-72. Office: 850 Mill St 3d flr Reno NV 89502-1338

WALKER, JOYCE MARIE, secondary school educator; b. Kansas City, Kans., Jan. 24, 1948; d. Frank Cornelius and Inez (Pennington) W.; divorced; 1 child, Kevin Cornelius. BS, U. Ark., Pine Bluff, 1972. Bus. tchr. U.S. Trade Sch., Kansas City, 1972-74; exec. sec. Kansas City Mo. Sch. Dist., 1974-77; tchr. vocat. bus. Aurora (Colo.) Pub. Sch., 1977—; vocat. bus. tchr. Pioneer Community Coll., 1975-77. Mem. Aurora Human Rels. Martin Luther King Jr. Com., 1986—; asst. sec. Sunday sch. Macedonia Bapt. Ch., 1985—, 2d v.p. E.L. Witchfield Missionary Soc., 1989; chmn. We. States Fgn. Mission, 1990. Mem. Nat. Coun. Negro Women, Nat. Assn. Bus. Educators, Delta Sigma Theta. Home: 12948 E 48th Ave Denver CO 80239 Office: Aurora Pub Schs 11700 E 11th Ave Aurora CO 80010-3758

WALKER, KEITH ALLEN, plant genetics company executive; b. Cleve., Oct. 17, 1948; s. Joseph Fordun and Audrey Marie (Brindley) W.; m. Marguerite Joyce Ming, Aug. 29, 1970; children: Kenneth Alec, Andrew Fordun. BA, Coll. of Wooster, 1970; PhD, Yale U., 1974. Sr. rsch. biologist Monsanto Chem. Co., St. Louis, 1974-76, rsch. group leader, 1976-79, sr. rsch. group leader, 1979-81; dir. product devel. Plant Genetics, Inc., Davis, Calif., 1981-82, v.p. rsch., dir., 1982-89; dir. devel. and licensing Agrigenetics Co., Davis, Calif., 1989-93; dir. planning and licensing Mycogen Corp., San Diego, 1993—; vice chair Gordon Rsch. Conf. in Plant Cell and Tissue Culture, 1985, chair, 1987. Assoc. editor: Plant Cell, Tissue & Organ Culture, 1988; contbr. articles to tech. jours., chpts. to books. Mem. Am. Soc. Plant Physiologists, Am. Soc. Agronomy, Crop Sci. Soc. Am., Am. Oil Chem. Soc., Sigma Xi. Office: Mycogen Corp 4980 Carroll Canyon Rd San Diego CA 92121

WALKER, KENT ARTHUR, business executive; b. Springfield, Ohio, Mar. 12, 1954; s. Roger Wellington and Julie Marie (Zeller) W.; m. Jill Kathleen Teskey, June 4, 1983; children: Ryan, Alyssa. BA, Colgate U., 1976; MBA, Coll. William and Mary, 1978. Sr. cons. Arthur Andersen & Co., Washington, 1978-82; mgr. MCI Telecommunications, Washington, 1982-85; treas. Teskey Enterprises, Inc., Huntington Beach, Calif., 1985-90, pres., 1991; v.p., bd. dirs. Ryadon, Inc., Los Alamitos, Calif., 1992—. Mem. bd. stewards Bayshore Congl. Ch., Long Beach, Calif., 1992. Mem. Phi Delta Theta.

WALKER, KERRY L., insurance executive; b. Cozad, Nebr., Apr. 12, 1955; s. William Newell and Myra Cordella (Franzen) W.; m. Peggy Lynn Welliver, Mar. 21, 1979; 1 child, Ashleigh N. Student, U. Nebr., 1973-74. Asst. mgr. Mead Lumber Co., Cozad, 1975-81; mgr. Logan County Lumber, Sterling, Colo., 1981-86; agt., registered rep. N.Y. Life Ins. Co., Sterling, 1986-89; sales mgr. N.Y. Life Ins. Co., Denver, 1989—. Mem. Nat. Assn. Life Underwriters (Million Dollar Round Table 1987, 88). Republican. Evangelical Christian. Home: 5957 S Clarkson Littleton CO 80121 Office: NY Life Ins Co Penthouse Ste 3200 Cherry Creek S Dr Denver CO 80209

WALKER, KEVIN PATRICK, journalist; b. San Francisco, Oct. 26, 1966; s. Robert Louis and Madeline Marie (Brusca) W. Student, Acad. Art Coll, San Francisco, 1986-87, Chabot Coll., Hayward, Calif., 1988-90; AB in Anthropology and Mass Comm., U. Calif., Berkeley, 1992. Assoc. editor Adland Advt., San Francisco, 1988-89; reporter Sta. KPFA-FM.

WALKER, LEILA STEPHANIE, actress, dancer; b. Seattle, Dec. 14, 1979; d. Stephen Jonathan Walker and Jennifer Leila Carroll. Dancer Nightingale Dance Team, Seattle, 1984-90; actress Seattle Repertory Theatre, 1990; artist pvt. practice, Seattle, 1991—. Home: 1140 Eastlake Ave E Seattle WA 98109

WALKER, LELAND JASPER, civil engineer; b. Fallon, Nev., Apr. 18, 1923; s. Albert Willard and Grayce (Wilkinson) W.; m. Margaret Frances Noble, Jan. 21, 1946; children: Thomas, Margaret, Timothy. B.S. in Civil Engring, Iowa State U., 1944; D. Eng. (hon.), Mont. State U., 1983. Engr. with various govtl. depts., 1946-51, 53-55; v.p. Wenzel & Co. (cons. engrs.), Great Falls, Mont., 1955-58; pres., chmn. bd. No. Engring. and Testing, Inc., Great Falls, 1958-88; pres. Ind. Labs. Assurance Co., 1977-79; bd. dirs. Mont. Power Co., Entech Inc., 1982-92, Lewis and Clark Biologicals, Inc., 1989-92, Applied Tech., Inc. Pres., trustee Endowment and Rsch. Found. Mont. State U., 1969-82, Mont. Deaconess Hosp., Great Falls, 1959-67, McLaughlin Rsch. Inst. Biol. Scis., 1989-92, Mont. Sch. Deaf and Blind Found., 1984—; trustee Rocky Mountain Coll., 1977-80, Dufresne Found., 1979-87; chmn., bd. dirs. Mont. Tech. Svcs. Adv. Coun. adv. coun. Engring. Coll. Mont. State U.; bd. dirs. Mont. State Fair, Engring. Socs. Commn. on Energy, 1977-79, Mont. Bd. Sci. and Tech., 1983-88, Great Falls Chamber Found., 1989-91. Fellow ASCE (pres. 1976-77), AAAS, Cons. Engrs. Coun. (pres. Mont. 1971), Accrediting Bd. Engring. and Tech. (v.p. 1978-79, pres. 1980-83); mem. Nat. Acad. Engring., Am. Coun. Ind. Labs. (hon. sec. 1973-76), Meadowlark Country Club, Pachyderm Club (bd. dirs., v.p. 1992—), Chi Epsilon (nat. hon.), Tau Beta Pi (hon.). Republican. Methodist. Home: 2819 8th Ave S Great Falls MT 59405-3219 Office: PO Box 7425 Great Falls MT 59406-7425

WALKER, LINDA ANN, financial planner; b. Denver, May 10, 1956; d. Ruth (Rogers) M.; m. Sidney C. Walker III, Feb. 9, 1992. BA, U. Colo., 1978; CFP, Coll. Fin. Planning, Denver, 1985. Account exec. EF Hutton, Boulder, Colo., 1980-84, Fin. Planning and Mgmt., Boulder, 1984-91, Premier Planning Assocs., Boulder, 1991—. Performer Shadow of a Gunman, 1991, Who's There?, 1991, La Ronde, 1992. Bd. dirs. Nancy Spanier Dance Theatre. Mem. Internat. Assn. Fin. Planners, Inst. Cert. Fin. Planners, Registry Fin. Planners. Office: Premier Planning Assn 4730 Walnut Ste 208 Boulder CO 80301

WALKER, MICHAEL JOHN, life insurance company executive; b. Schenectady, N.Y., Nov. 16, 1946; s. Chapman Johnston and Mathea Cornelia (Copeland) W.; m. Janet Marie Gray, Sept. 29, 1973; children: Matthew Chapman, Rachel Lynn. BA in History, Fairfield U., 1969; M Urban and Reg. Planning, Va. Poly. Inst. and State U., 1972. Planner Fairfax County, Va., 1973-74, adminstrv. asst. planning commn., 1974-76; sr. planner State of Colo., Grand Junction, 1976-78; planning cons. Paragon Engring., Inc., Grand Junction, 1978-79; asst. appraiser Met. Life Ins. Co., N.Y.C., 1980-81, appraiser, 1982-85, sr. appraiser, 1985-87, portfolio mgr., 1987-88, asst. v.p., 1988—. Chmn. planning City of Naperville (Ill.), 1982-85; mem. parish coun. Immaculate Heart of Mary Ch., Grand Junction, 1976-79. Lt. col. USAR, 1971—. Mem. Assn. Investment Mgmt. Sales Execs., Am. Planning Assn. (exec. com. Colo. chpt. 1978-79), Pension Real Estate Assn., Nat. Coun. Real Estate Investment Fiduciaries, Res. Officers Assn., Assn. U.S. Army, Air Force Assn.

WALKER, MOIRA KAYE, sales executive; b. Riverside, Calif., Aug. 2, 1940; d. Frank Leroy and Arline Rufina (Roach) Porter; m. Timothy P. Walker, Aug. 30, 1958 (div. 1964); children: Brian A., Benjamin D., Blair K., Beth E. Student, Riverside City Coll., 1973. With Bank of Am., Riverside, 1965-68, Abitibi Corp., Cucamonga, Calif., 1968-70; with Lily div. Owens-Illinois, Riverside, 1970-73; salesperson Lily div. Owens-Illinois, Houston, 1973-77; salesperson Kent H. Landsberg div. Sunclipse, Montebello, Calif., 1977-83, sales mgr., 1983-85; v.p., sales mgr. Kent H. Landsberg div. Sunclipse, Riverside, 1985—. Mem. Nat. Assn. Female Execs., Women in Paper (treas. 1978-84). Lutheran. Office: Kent H Landsberg Div Sunclipse 1180 W Spring St Riverside CA 92507-1300

WALKER, OLENE S., lieutenant governor; b. Ogden, Utah, Nov. 15, 1930; d. Thomas Ole and Nina Hadley (Smith) W.; m. J. Myron Walker, 1957; children: Stephen Brett, David Walden, Bryan Jesse, Lori, Mylene, Nina, Thomas Myron. BA, Brigham Young U., 1954; MA, Stanford U., 1954; PhD, U. Utah, 1986. V.p. Country Crisp Foods; mem. Utah Ho. of Reps. Dist. 24; lt. gov. State of Utah, 1993—. Mem. Salt Lake Edn. Found. bd. dirs. 1983-90; dir. community econ. devel.; mem. Ballet West, Sch. Vol., United Way, Commn. on Youth, Girls Village, Salt Lake Conv. and Tourism Bd. Mormon. Office: 210 State Capitol Salt Lake City UT 84114

WALKER, PRISCILLA BOWMAN, marketing and communications administrator; b. Palisade, Colo., May 2, 1949; d. Marion George and Helen Elizabeth (Maher) Bowman; m. Bruce Alan Walker, Dec. 20, 1970; 1 child, William Matthew. BA in Mass Comm., U. Denver, 1970. Rush hour traffic reporter AAA Auto Club, Denver, 1970-71; account exec. Piper & Assocs., Denver, 1971-75; mktg. mgr. Am. TV & Comm. Corp., Denver, 1975-78; dir. Am. TV & Comm. Corp., Englewood, Colo., 1979-87; dir. mktg. Am. Cablevision, Thornton, Colo., 1987-89; cons. Priscilla Walker Comm., Palisade, Colo., 1989—. Named Women of Achievement Honoree YWCA, 1985. Mem. Colo. Cable TV Assn. (conv. com.), Women in Cable (charter exec. mem., pres. Rocky Mountain chpt. 1983-84, nat. bd. dirs., sec. 1985-88). Home and Office: PO Box 363 Palisade CO 81526

WALKER, RAYMOND FRANCIS, business and financial consulting company executive; b. Medicine Lake, Mont., Nov. 9, 1914; s. Dennis Owen and Rose (Long) W.; m. Patricia K. Blakey, May 15, 1951; children: Richard A., Mark D., Maxie R. Forest, Victoria L. Le Huray, Suzanne J. Buhl, Tracy Walker Stampanoni. Grad. pub. schs.; student, Edison Vocat. Sch., 1935-39. Truck mgr. Pacific Food Products, Seattle, 1939-42; machinist Todd Shipyard, Seattle, 1943-45; owner Delbridge Auto Sales, Seattle, 1945-48; pres. Pacific Coast Acceptance Corp., 1949-60; v.p. West Coast Mortgage, Seattle, 1960-67, United Equities Corp., Seattle, 1965-69; pres. Income Mgmt. Corp., Seattle, 1970-90; v.p. Internat. Mint and Foundry, Redmond, Wash., 1983-87; pvt. practice bus. and fin. cons. Sequim, Wash., 1987—; cons. Life Ins. Co. Am., Bellevue, Wash., 1982-87, Consumer Loan Svc., Lynwood, Wash., 1980-92; dir., cons., v.p. fin. Am. Campgrounds, Bellevue, 1971-79; cons., bd. dirs. Straits Forest Products, Inc., Port Angeles, Wash.; dir., cons. Synergy Techs., Inc., Sequim, 1990—, Syntec Electronics Corp., 1993. Mem. Nat. Assn. Security Dealers. Methodist. Lodge: Elks. Home: 777 W Sequim Bay Rd Sequim WA 98382-9056

WALKER, RICHARD ALLEN, data processing executive, consultant; b. Flushing, N.Y., Sept. 24, 1935; s. John Randall and Estella Viola (Stephenson) W.; m. Jauhree Ann Sparks, July 14, 1973. BA in Econs. and History, U.S. Internat. U., 1963, MS in Mgmt. Sci., 1968; PhD in Instructional Sci., Brigham Young U., 1978. Commd. ensign USN, 1958, advanced through grades to comdr., ret., 1976; sr. instructional psychologist Courseware, Inc., 1978-82, mgr. electronics pub. group, 1982-83; founder, pres., acting v.p. instrnl. devel. Interactive Tech. Corp., 1983-86, chmn., 1986; pvt. practice, 1986-87; dir. tng. svcs. WICAT Systems, Inc., 1987-90; group dir. Jostens Learning Corp., 1990-92; pres. Multimedia Group, Coronado, Calif., 1992—. Mem. Soc. for Applied Learning Tech. (sr.), Am. Ednl. Rsch. Assn., Assn. Aviation Psychologists, Eagle Scout Assn., Arlberg Ski Club (silver medal), Crown Club (v.p. 1985). Republican. Presbyterian. Home: 740 Olive Ave Coronado CA 92118-2136 Office: Multimedia Group 740 Olive Ave Coronado CA 92118

WALKER, SALLY C., fundraising executive. BA cum laude with honors, Stetson U., Deland, Fla., 1971; grad., Grantsmanship Ctr. Tng. Program, 1980, Mgmt. Fund Raisers Program, 1987. Devel. dir. Direct Relief Found., Santa Barbara, Calif., 1977-82; prin., cons. Walker & Assocs., Santa Barbara, 1982—; endowment dir. United Way Santa Barbara, 1982—, devel. cons., 1982—; devel. cons., trainer United Way of Am., Alexandria, Va., 1984, 87; devel. cons. Santa Barbara Symphony, 1984-85, Child Abuse Listening Meditation, Santa Barbara, 1987-88, Community Environ. Coun., Santa Barbara, Calif., 1990—; mem. steering com., del. Nat. Conf. Planned Giving, 1987-88, Nat. Editorial Bur. chief, 1989; faculty mem. Nat. Acad. Voluntarism, Washington. Contbg. editor: The Endowment Builder. Co-founder, pres. Planned Giving Roundtable Santa Barbara County, Calif., 1986-88, v.p., 1984-86. Mem. Nat. Soc. Fund-Raising Execs. (chair endowment com. 1989-90), Santa Barbara Audubon Soc. (bd. dirs. 1989—, pres. 1992—). Office: 1423 W Valerio St Santa Barbara CA 93101-4954

WALKER, SHARON LESLIE, oceanographer; b. Orange, N.J., May 7, 1958; d. Richard Alden and Jacquelyn (Sovulewski) Walker; m. Edward Walker; d. Cora Marie. BS, U. Wash., 1981. Oceanographer NOAA/Pacific Marine Environ. Lab., Seattle, 1979—. Mem. City Coun., City of Brier, Wash., 1991—. Mem. Am. Geophys. Union. Office: NOAA/Pacific Marine Environ Lab Bldg 3 7600 Sandpoint Way NE Seattle WA 98115

WALKER, STEVEN ANDERSON, computer scientist, executive; b. Manila, Philippines, May 29, 1957; s. Henry L. and K. (Jane) W.; m. Lori L. Walker, Dec. 29, 1984. BS in Forestry, No. Ariz. U., 1979; MS in Forest Biometrics, Va. Tech., 1981. Chmn. Animation Tech., Castle Rock, Colo., 1988—; dir. DCSI, Englewood, Colo., 1984-86; program mgr. Relational Tech., Alameda, Calif., 1986-87; dir. programs Geodynamics, Englewood, Colo., 1988-90, mem. profl. staff, 1990-92; site mgr. Autometric, Inc., Flagstaff, Ariz., 1992—. Contbr. articles to profl. jours. Pres. Homeowners Assn., Castle Rock, 1989. Mem. IEEE, Assn. for Computing Machinery, Spl. Interest Group on Graphics, Spl. Interest Group on Simulation, Phi Kappa Phi.

WALKER, VAUGHN R., judge; b. Watseka, Ill., Feb. 27, 1944; s. Vaughn Rosenworth and Catharine (Miles) W. AB, U. Mich., 1966; JD, Stanford U., 1970. Intern economist SEC, Washington, 1966, 68; law clk. to the Hon. Robert J. Kelleher U.S. Dist. Ct. Calif., L.A., 1971-72; assoc. atty. Pillsbury Madison & Sutro, San Francisco, 1972-77, ptnr., 1978-90; judge U.S. Dist. Ct. (no. dist.) Calif., San Francisco, 1990—; mem. Calif. Law Revision Commn., Palo Alto, 1986-89. Dir. Jr. Achievement of Bay Area, San Francisco, 1979-83, St. Francis Found., San Francisco, 1991—. Woodrow Wilson Found. fellow U. Calif., Berkeley, 1966-67. Fellow Am. Bar Found.; mem. ABA (jud. rep., antitrust sect. 1991—), Lawyers' Club (pres. 1985-86), Commonwealth Club, City Club, Am. Law Inst., Am. Saddlebred Horse Assn., San Francisco Mus. Modern Art. Office: US Dist Ct 450 Golden Gate Ave San Francisco CA 94102-3400

WALKOV, PERRY, data processing executive; b. Phila., Apr. 30, 1951; s. Samuel Walkov and Esther Trachtman. Grad., L.A. Valley Coll., 1974. Programmer/analyst Acctg. Corp. Am., L.A., 1973-76, Swett & Crawford, L.A., 1976-77; pres. Applications for Bus. Computers, L.A., 1977-79; support mgr. Wang Labs., L.A., 1980-81; MIS dir. VHD Programs, Irvine, Calif., 1981-82; pres. Application Systems Knowhow, Inc., Van Nuys, Calif., 1982—. Mem. IEEE. Office: Application Systems Knowhow 6650 Aqueduct Ave Van Nuys CA 91406

WALKWITZ, JON JEFFREY, lawyer; b. Kansas City, Mo., Nov. 11, 1949; s. Marvin Leroy and June Lavonne (Brown) W. BA, U. Colo., 1971, JD, 1978; MA, U. Colo., Denver, 1980; postgrad., Nat. Def. U., 1987. Bar: Colo. 1978. Atty. Towey and Zak, Westminster, Colo., 1979-80, Wagner and Waller, Denver, 1980-83, McNally and Bain, Boulder, 1983-84; law clerk to Judge D.P. Smith Colo. Ct. Appeals, Denver, 1978-79, dep. chief staff atty., 1984—. Mem. alumni adv. bd. U. Colo. Denver Coll., Liberal Arts an Scis., 1987-91. Served to lt. (j.g.) USN, 1971-75; comdr. USNR, 1980—. Mem. Naval Res. Assn., U.S. Naval Inst., State Corr. Selden Soc., Army Navy Club Washington, Mt. Vernon COuntry Club. Office: Colo State Jud Bldg 2 E 14th Ave Denver CO 80203-2116

WALL, BRIAN RAYMOND, forest economist, policy analyst, consultant; b. Tacoma, Wash., Jan. 26, 1940; s. Raymond Perry and Mildred Beryl (Pickert) W.; m. Joan Marie Nero, Sept. 1, 1962 (div. Aug. 1990) children: Torden Erik, Kirsten Noel. BS, U. Wash., 1962; MF, Yale U., 1964. Forestry asst. Weyerhaeuser Timber Co., Klamath Falls, Oreg., 1960; inventory forester West Tacoma Newsprint, 1961-62; timber sale compliance forester Dept. Nat. Resources, Kelso, Wash., 1963; rsch. forest economist Pacific N.W. Rsch. Sta., USDA Forest Svc., Portland, Oreg., 1964-88, cons. 1989—; co-founder, bd. dirs. Cordero Youth Care Ctr., 1970-81; owner Brian R. Wall Images and Communications; cons. to govt. agys., Congress univs., industry; freelance photographer. Co-author: An Analysis of the Timber Situation in the United States, 1982; contbr. articles, reports to profl. publs., newspapers. Interviewed and cited by nat. and regional news media. Recipient Cert. of Merit U.S. Dept. Agr. Forest Service, 1982. Mem. Soc. Am. Foresters (chmn. Portland chpt. 1973, Forester of Yr. 1975), Conf. of Western Forest Economists Inc. (founder, bd. dirs. 1988-91, treas. 1982-87), Portland Photographic Forum, Common Cause, Nat. Audubon Soc., Zeta Psi. Home and Office: 16810 S Creekside Ct Oregon City OR 97045-9206

WALL, FRANCIS JOSEPH, statistical consultant; b. Moss Point, Miss., Mar. 22, 1927; s. Thomas J. and Nina B. (Brewer) W.; m. B. Jean, Apr. 15, 1950; children: David W., Karen S., Leslie J. BS, Sul Ross State U., 1947; MS, U. Colo., 1956; PhD, U. Minn., 1961. Statistician Dow Chem. Co., Boulder, Colo., 1952-57, Sperry Univac, St. Paul, 1957-61, Dikewood Corp., Albuquerque, 1961-69, Lovelace Found., Albuquerque, 1969-71; pvt. practice cons. Albuquerque, 1972—. Author: Statistical Data Analysis Handbook, 1986. Mem. Am. Statis. Assn., Biometric Soc., Sigma Xi. Republican. Mem. United Ch. of Christ. Home: 634 E Harvard Rd Apt E Burbank CA 91501 Office: PO Box 427 Burbank CA 91503-0427

WALL, LLOYD L., geological engineer; b. Jerome, Idaho, Feb. 2, 1936; s. Lloyd and Ola (Buck) W.; m. Myrna Bradshaw, Aug. 25, 1954; children: Jeffrey B., Julie, Neil S., Charlene, Gail, Matthew W., Suzzane, Michael L., Connie. AS, Coll. Eastern Utah, 1956; BS in Geology, Brigham Young U., 1958. Pres., owner Cons. Geologist, Salt Lake City and Brigham City, 1958—; plant mgr. Thiokol, Brigham City, Utah, 1958-66; mgr. ops. Sealcraft, Salt Lake City, 1966-68; mgr. programs Eaton-Kenway, Bountiful, Utah, 1968-76; pres., owner HydraPak, Inc., Salt Lake City, 1976-86; pres. Kolt Mining Co., Salt Lake City, 1979—; owner Lloyd L. Wall & Assocs., Salt Lake City, 1986—. Author: Seal Technology, 1993; developer largest rocket motor vacuum casting system in free world, only high pressure water reclaimation system for solid propellant rocket motors in free world, only acceptable seal mfg. process for NASA Space Shuttle rocket motor. Vol. tchr. Alta Acad., Salt Lake City, 1983—. Served as sgt. N.G., 1954-62. Mem. Geol. Soc. Am., Utah Geol. Assn. Republican. Mormon. Home: 2180 Claybourne Ave Salt Lake City UT 84109-1727

WALL, MARK HENRY, surgeon; b. Superior, Wis., June 2, 1932; s. Mark Henry and Anna Stephana (Sokolnikoff) W.; m. Mary Thomasine Micetich, Dec. 26, 1954; children: Yvonne, Linda, Mark Jr., Stephen, Scott, Thomasine Ann. BS, U. Wis., 1954; MD, U. So. Calif., 1958. Diplomate Am. Bd. Surgery, Am. Bd. Thoracic Surgery. Intern L.A. County Hosp., 1958-59; resident in gen. surgery Harbor Gen. Hosp., Torrance, Calif., 1959-63; resident in thoracic surgery City of Hope Med. Ctr., Duarte, Calif., 1965-67; pvt. practice as thoracic surgeon Santa Barbara, Calif., 1967-73, Santa Fe, N.Mex., 1973-79, Auburn, N.Y., 1979-87, Cleve., 1989-91. Contbr. articles to profl. jours. Fellow ACS, Am. Coll. Chest Physicians; mem. Soc. Thoracic Surgeons, Soc. Clin. Vascular Surgery. Home and Office: 31614 Ponserosa Way Evergreen CO 80439

WALL, ROBERT SETH, physician; b. Athens, Greece, Jan. 20, 1958; came to U.S., 1958; s. Ralph and Joyce Millicent (Brines) W. BS in Chemistry summa cum laude, U. Denver, 1980; MD, U. Colo., 1984. Diplomate Nat. Bd. Med. Examiners. Commd. ensign USN, 1980, advanced through grades to lt. comdr., 1989, resigned, 1990; lt. comdr. USNR, 1990—; intern Mercy Hosp., Denver, 1985; resident in neurology U. Colo., Denver, 1990—; med. officer USMC, Camp Lejeune, N.C., 1985-87, USN, Key West, Fla., 1988-90; emergency physician Profl. Emergency Svc., Key West, 1988-90; emergency physician Nat. Emergency Svcs. Fitzsimmons Army Med. Ctr., Aurora, Colo., 1991—; med. faculty Fla. Keys Community Coll., Key West, 1988-90; med. dir. Offshore Power Boat Race Assn., Key West, 1988-90; med. dir. advanced cardiac life support U. Colo. Health Scis. Ctr., Denver, 1991—. Bd. dirs. Key West unit Am. Heart Assn., 1989-90; active Key West Founder's Soc., 1988-90, Art and Hist. Soc., 1988-90. Scholar USN Neurology Resident Program, 1991. Mem. AMA, Am. Acad. Neurology, Assn. Mil. Surgeons of U.S., Conch Republic Offshore Power Boat Race Assn., Key West Skeet Club, Tri-Svc. Skeet Club, Am. Chem. Soc., Denver Polo Club, Denver Athletic Club, Phi Beta Kappa, Phi Delta Epsilon. Office: U Colo Health Sci Ctr Dept Neurology 4200 E 9th Ave Denver CO 80220-3700

WALL, SONJA ELOISE, nurse, administrator; b. Santa Cruz, Calif., Mar. 28, 1938; d. Ray Theothornton and Reva Mattie (Wingo) W.; m. Edward Gleason Holmes, Aug. 1959 (div. Jan. 1968); children: Deborah Lynn, Lance Edward; m. John Aspesi, Sept. 1969 (div. 1977); children: Sabrina Jean, Daniel John; m. Kenneth Talbot LaBoube, Nov. 1, 1978 (div. 1989); 1 child, Tiffany Amber. BA, San Jose Jr. Coll., 1959; BS, Madonna Coll., 1967; student, U. Mich., 1968-70. RN, Calif., Mich., Colo. Staff nurse Santa Clara Valley Med. Ctr., San Jose, Calif., 1959-67, U. Mich. Hosp., Ann Arbor, 1967-73, Porter and Swedish Med. Hosp., Denver, 1973-77, Laurel Grove Hosp., Castro Valley, Calif., 1977-79, Advent Hosp., Ukiah, Calif., 1984-86; motel owner LaBoube Enterprises, Fairfield, Point Arena, Willits, Calif., 1979—; staff nurse Northridge Hosp., L.A., 1986-87, Folsom State Prison, Calif., 1987; co-owner, mgr. nursing registry Around the Clock Nursing Svc., Ukiah, 1985—; staff nurse Kaiser Permanente Hosp., Sacramento, 1986-89, hospice nurse, 1990-93; home care nurse HSSI-Care Point, 1993—; owner Royal Plantation Petites Miniature Horse Farm. Contbr. articles to various publs. Leader Coloma 4-H, 1987-91; mem. mounted divsn. El Dorado County Search and Rescue, 1991-93; docent Calif. Marshall Gold Discovery State Hist. Park, Coloma, Calif. Mem. AACN, NAFE, Soc. Critical Care Medicine, Am. Heart Assn. (CPR trainer, recipient awards), Calif. Bd. RNs, Calif. Nursing Rev., Calif. Critical Care Nurses, Soc. Critical Care Nurses, Am. Motel Assn. (beautification and remodeling award 1985), Nat. Hospice Nurses Assn., Soroptimist Internat. Calif., Am. Miniature Horse Assn. (winner nat. grand championship 1981-82, 83, 85, 89), DAR (Jobs Daus. hon. mem.), Cameron Park Country Club. Republican. Episcopalian. Home and Office: Around the Clock Nursing Svc PO Box 559 Coloma CA 95613-0559

WALL, THOMAS ULRICH, real estate development executive; b. Washington, Nov. 20, 1944; s. Herbert and Doris (Hazel) W.; m. Elizabeth Ann Hallin, May 31, 1980. BA, Pa. State U., 1966; MA, U. Minn., 1977; MS, U. So. Calif., 1979; MBA with honors, Pepperdine U., 1985. Lic. real estate broker, Calif. Commd. 2nd lt. USMC, 1966, advanced through grades to lt. col., 1981, ret., 1986; dir. USN/USMC Helicopter Test Pilot Sch., 1970-71; asst. prof. naval sci. U. Minn., 1974-77; sr. instr. Dept. Def. Planning, Programming and Budgeting Sch., 1977-78; program mgr. USN, 1977-79; dir. facilities USMC Air Sta., Tustin, Calif., 1983-85; v.p. comml. devel. Polygon Group, 1986-87; pres., chief exec. officer Pacifica West Properties, Newport Beach, Calif., 1987-88; mgr. Transwestern Property Co., Newport Beach, 1988-90; sr. v.p. The Wolff Co., Irvine, Calif., 1990—; pres. Seeley/Wolff Property Mgmt. Co., Irvine, Calif., 1991—. Commr. Orange County Airport Land Use Commn.; bd. govs. Irvine Valley Coll. Found.; bd. dirs. The Nat. Chamber Found. Decorated Purple Heart, 2 D.F.C. with bronze oak leaf cluster, 52 Air medals. Mem. Comml. Indsl. Devel. Assn. (bd. dirs. local chpt.), Irvine C. of C. (bd. dirs.), Exch. Club. Republican. Office: The Wolff Co 7700 Irvine Center Dr Ste 710 Irvine CA 92718-2929

WALL, WILLIAM E., lawyer, former utility executive; b. 1928. BS, U. Wash., 1951, LLB, 1954. Asst. atty. gen. State of Wash., 1956-59; chief examiner Pub. Svc. Commn., 1959; sec., house counsel Cascade Natural Gas Corp., 1959-64; pres. United Cities Gas Co., 1964-65; exec. v.p. Cascade Natural Gas Corp., 1965-67; spl. asst. to chmn. bd. Consol. Edison Co., N.Y.C., 1967-68, v.p., 1968-70, sr. v.p. gas ops., 1970-71, exec. v.p. div. ops., 1971-73; gen. mgr. pub. affairs Standard Oil Co., 1973-74; exec. v.p. Kans. Power and Light Co., Topeka, 1974-75, pres., 1975-85, chief exec. officer, 1976-88, chmn., 1979-88; of counsel Siderius, Lonergan & Crowley, Seattle, 1988—. Served with AUS, 1954-56. Office: Siderius Lonergan & Crowley 847 Logan Bldg Seattle WA 98101

WALLACE, GEORGE KARREN, lawyer; b. Salt Lake City, Nov. 3, 1958; s. Earl M. and Esther (Jackson) W.; m. Deborah Lee Bateman; 1 child, Kira Lee Kealohilani. BA in Fin., U. Utah, 1982; JD, Taft U., 1989. Bar: Calif. 1990. Staff acct. Huntsman Christensen, Inc., Salt Lake City, 1980-81; contr. Healthtram Industries, Orem, Utah, 1981-82; v.p. Landeck Resources Inc., Salt Lake City, 1982-84; asst. v.p. Western Savs. and Loan, Salt Lake City, 1984-86; mng. officer FSLIC, L.A., 1986-89; dept. head FDIC, Irvine, Calif., 1989-91; assoc. Lorance & Thompson, Phoenix, 1991-92; ptnr. Dominguez & Martinez, San Diego, Calif., 1992—; bd. dirs. Am. Diversified Capital Corp., Costa Mesa, Calif., Sun Devel. Corp., L.A. Author: Insiders. Missionary Ch. of Jesus Christ of Latter-day Saints, Milan, 1977-79; chmn., bd. dirs. Mountain Am. Credit Union, Salt Lake City, 1984-86; trustee Sun Charitable Found., San Diego, 1986-88. Mem. ABA, Calif. Bar Assn. Republican. Office: Dominguez & Martinez 11440 W Bernardo Ct Ste 300 San Diego CA 92127

WALLACE, HELEN MARGARET, physician, educator; b. Hoosick Falls, N.Y., Feb. 18, 1913; d. Jonas and Ray (Schweizer) W. A.B., Wellesley Coll., 1933; M.D., Columbia U., 1937; M.P.H. cum laude, Harvard U., 1943. Diplomate: Am. Bd. Pediatrics, Am. Bd. Preventive Medicine. Intern Bellevue Hosp., N.Y.C., 1938-40; child hygiene physician Conn. Health Dept., 1941-42; successively jr. health officer, health officer, chief maternity and new born div., dir. bur. for handicapped children N.Y.C. Health Dept., 1943-55; prof., dir. dept. pub. health N.Y. Med. Coll., 1955-56; prof. maternal and child health U. Minn. Sch. Pub. Health, 1956-59; chief profl. tng. U.S. Children's Bur., 1959-60, chief child health studies, 1961-62; prof. maternal and child health U. Calif. Sch. Pub. Health, Berkeley, 1962-80; prof., head div. maternal and child health Sch. Pub. Health San Diego State U., 1980—; Univ. Research lectr. San Diego State U., 1985—; cons. WHO, Uganda, 1961, Philippines, 1966, 68, 75, Turkey, 1968, India, Geneva, 1970, Iran, 1972, Burma, India, Thailand, Sri Lanka, 1975, East Africa, 1976, Australia, 1976, Burma, 1977, India, Indonesia, Thailand, Burma, 1978, 79, India, 1981, Burma, 1985, Peoples Republic of China, 1988; Cons. Ford Found., Colombia, 1971; Traveling fellow WHO, cons., 1989—; U.N. cons. to Health Bur., Beijing, China, 1987; WHO cons. to China, 1988, Taiwan, 1992; dir. Family Planning Project, Zimbabwe, 1984-87. Author, editor 10 textbooks; contbr. 325 articles to profl. jours. Mem. coun. on Disabled Children to Media, 1991; dir. San Diego County Infant Mortality Study, 1989—, San Diego Study of Prenatal Care, 1991. Recipient Alumnae Achievement award Wellesley Coll., 1982, Outstanding Faculty award San Diego State U., 1983, Martha Eliot award Am. Pub. Health Assn., 1978, Job Smith award Am. Acad. Pediatrics, 1980, U. Minn. award 1985, Ford Found. study grants 1986, 87, 88; World Rehab. Fund fellow, India, 1991-92; Fulbright fellow, 1992—. Fellow Am. Acad. Pediatrics (Job Smith award 1980, award 1989), Am. Pub. Health Assn. (officer sect., Martha May Eliot award 1978); mem. AMA, Assn. Tchrs. Maternal and Child Health, Am. Acad. Cerebral Palsy, Ambulatory Pediatric Assn., Am. Sch. Preventive Medicine. Home: 850 State St San Diego CA 92101-6046 Office: San Diego State U San Diego CA 92182

WALLACE, J. CLIFFORD, federal judge; b. San Diego, Dec. 11, 1928; s. John Franklin and Lillie Isabel (Overing) W.; m. Virginia Lee Schlosser, Apr. 8, 1957; children: Paige, Laurie, Teri, John. B.A., San Diego State U., 1952; LL.B., U. Calif., Berkeley, 1955. Bar: Calif. 1955. With firm Gray, Cary, Ames & Frye, San Diego, 1955-70; judge U.S. Dist. Ct. (so. dist.) Calif., 1970-72; judge U.S. Ct. Appeals (9th cir.), 1972-91, chief judge, 1991—. Contrbr. articles to profl. jours. Served with USN, 1946-49. Mem. Am. Bd. Trial Advocates, Inst. Jud. Adminstrn. Mem. LDS Ch. (stake pres. San Diego East 1962-67, regional rep. 1967-74, 77-79). Office: US Ct Appeals 9th Cir 940 Front St Rm 4192 San Diego CA 92101-8918

WALLACE, JAMES WENDELL, lawyer; b. Clinton, Tenn., July 13, 1930; s. John Nelson and Rose Ella (Carden) W.; m. Jeanne Mary Ellen Newlin; children: Karen Wallace Young, Michael James. Student, Syracuse U., 1952-53; BS, U. Tenn., Knoxville, 1959, JD, 1958. Bar: Calif. 1959, U.S. Dist. Ct. (cen. dist.) Calif. 1959, U.S. Ct. Appeals (9th cir.) 1977, U.S. Supreme Ct. 1964. Sec., legal counsel Guidance Tech., Inc., Santa Monica, Calif., 1958-65; sr. atty., asst. sec. Varian Assocs., Palo Alto, Calif., 1965-67; gen. counsel, asst. sec. Electronic Splty. Co., Pasadena, Calif., 1967-69; asst. gen. counsel, asst. sec. The Times Mirror Co., L.A., 1969-75, assoc. gen. counsel, asst. sec., 1976-85, assoc. gen. counsel, sec., 1985-89; dir., v.p. and sec. Flintridge Asset Mgmt. Co., San Marino, Calif., 1990—. Mem. editorial bd. Tenn. Law Rev., 1956-58. Mem. Town Hall of Calif. World Affairs Coun., L.A. Served with USAF, 1951-55. Mem. ABA, L.A. County Bar Assn., Am. Soc. Corp. Secs. (bd. dirs. 1979-82), Jonathan Club, Phi Delta Phi, Phi Kappa Phi. Home: 5822 Briartree Dr La Canada Flintridge CA 91011-1825

WALLACE, JEANNETTE OWENS, state legislator; b. Scottsdale, Ariz., Jan. 16, 1934; d. Albert and Velma (Whinery) Owens; m. Terry Charles Wallace Sr., May 21, 1955; children: Terry C. Jr., Randall J., Timothy A., Sheryl L., Janice M. BS, Ariz. State U., 1955. Mem. Los Alamos (N.Mex.) County Coun., 1981-82; cons. County of Los Alamos, 1983-84; chmn., vice chmn. Los Alamos County Coun., 1985-88; cons. County of Los Alamos, Los Alamos Schs., 1989-90; rep. N.Mex. State Legislature, 1991—; mem. Appropriations & Fin. Govt. and Urban Affairs, N.Mex., 1991—; co-chmn. Los Alamos County's Dept. Energy Negotiating Com., 1987-88; mem. legis. policy com. Mcpl. League, N.Mex., 1986-88. Bd. dirs. Tri-Area Econ. Devel., Pojoaque, N.Mex., 1987-92, Los Alamos Econ. Devel., 1988-93, Crime Stoppers, Los Alamos, 1988-92, Los Alamos Citizens Against Substance Abuse, 1989-93; mem. N.Mex. First, Albuquerque, 1989-93, LWV, legis. chmn., 1990; mem. Los Alamos Rep. Women, pres., 1989-90. Mem. Los Alamos Bus. & Profl. Women (legis. chmn. 1990), Los Alamos C. of C., Mana del Norte, Kiwanis. Methodist. Home: 146 Monte Rey S Los Alamos NM 87544

WALLACE, JOEL KEITH, hospital chaplain; b. San Bernardino, Calif., Nov. 3, 1933; s. Perry A. and Margaret S. (McCuen) W.; m. Winifred Lynne Capps, June 17, 1961; children: David Mark, Susanne Lynne Wallace Trumble, Jason Glenn. BA, Bob Jones U., 1958; BD, Talbot Theol. Sem., 1961, MDiv, 1970; DMin, Luther Rice Sem., 1977. Ordained to ministry Ind. Fundamental Chs. Am., 1961. Commd. 2d lt. U.S. Army, 1962, advanced through grades to lt. col., 1985, chaplain, various locations including Vietnam, 1962-72; ret. USAR, 1986; pastor Amarillo (Tex.) Bible Ch., 1972-76; ins. agt. Prudential Ins. Co., Amarillo, 1976-80; intermittent chaplain VA Med. Ctr., Amarillo, 1975-80; staff chaplain VA Med. Ctr., Dayton, Ohio, 1980-87; chief chaplain svc. VA Med. Ctr., Boise, Idaho, 1987—; instr., Regional Med. Edn. Ctr., Salt Lake City, 1988—. Police dept. chaplain, City of West Carrollton, Ohio, 1986-87; mem. City Beautiful Commn., 1987; loaned exec. United Way/Combined Fed. Campaign, 1989. Decorated Bronze Star from Vietnam. Mem. Ind. Fundamental Chs. Am. (regional pres. 1989-93), Idaho Assn. Pastoral Care (pres., treas. Valley chpt. 1990-91), Coll. Chaplains (state rep. 1989-92), Res. Officers Assn. (pres. Idaho 1989-92, editor newsletter 1989—, sec. 1992—), VFW (chaplain), Mil. Order World Wars (chaplain 1989-92, sr. vice comdr. 1991-92, commdr. 1993—), Mini Le Bois, Dayton Miniature Soc., Kiwanis. Democrat. Office: VA Med Ctr 500 W Fort St Boise ID 83702-4598

WALLACE, JOHN JOSEPH, real estate consultant, economist; b. San Francisco, Feb. 15, 1947; s. Charles Arthur and Grace Catherine (King) W.; m. Gloria Ann Robles, July 19, 1974; children: Robert, Michelle, Johanna. AA, San Francisco City Coll., 1968; BA, San Francisco State Coll., 1972; MBA, San Francisco State U., 1975. Analyst Larry Smith & Co., San Francisco, 1972-75; sr. economist Stanford Rsch. Inst., Menlo Park, Calif., 1976-77; pres. Database Software Corp., Palo Alto, Calif., 1983-86; pres., prin. Wallace & Steichen, Inc., Palo Alto, 1980—. Bd. dirs. Caminar, San Mateo County, 1990-93; adult leader Boy Scouts Am., Menlo Park; coach Little League, Menlo Park. With USN, 1968-70. Mem. Am. Soc. Real Estate Counselors, Urban Land Inst. (assoc.), Internat. Coun. Shopping Ctrs., Nat. Assn. Corp. Real Estate Execs. (assoc.), Nat. Assn. Realtors (assoc.), Urban Ecology. Democrat. Roman Catholic. Office: 261 Hamilton Ave Ste 420 Palo Alto CA 94301-2536

WALLACE, KENNETH ALAN, investor; b. Gallup, N.Mex., Feb. 23, 1938; s. Charles Garrett and Elizabeth Eleanor (Jones) W. A.B. in Philosophy, Cornell U., 1960; postgrad. U. N.Mex., 1960-61; m. Rebecca Marie Odell, July 11, 1980; children: Andrew McMillan, Aaron Blue, Susanna Garrett, Megan Elizabeth, Glen Eric. Comml. loan officer Bank of N.Mex., Albuquerque, 1961-64; asst. cashier Ariz. Bank, Phoenix, 1964-67; comml. loan officer Valley Nat. Bank, Phoenix, 1967-70; pres. WWW, Inc., Houston, 1970-72; v.p. fin. Hometels of Am., Phoenix, 1972-77, Precision Mech. Co., Inc., 1972-77; ptnr. Schroeder-Wallace, 1977—; chmn. Shalako Corp., Phoenix; mng. ptnr. , pres. Blackhawk, Inc., Phoenix, 1977—; also, bd. dirs. ; pres., chmn. bd. AlphaSat Corp., Phoenix, 1990—; pres. chmn. bd. dirs. AlphaVision, Inc., Las Vegas; gen. ptnr. Wallco Enterprises, Ltd., Mobile, Ala.; mng. gen. ptnr. The Village at University Heights, Flagstaff. Loaned exec. Phoenix United Way, 1966, Tucson United Way, 1967; mem. Valley Big Bros., 1970—; bd. dirs. Phoenix Big Sisters, 1985-87; mem. Alhambra Village Planning Com.; fin. dir. Ret. Sr. Vol. Program, 1973-76; mem. Phoenix Men's Arts Coun., 1968—, dir., 1974-75; mem. Phoenix Symphony Coun. Campaign committeeman Rep. gubernatorial race, N.Mex., 1964; treas. Phoenix Young Reps., 1966; bd. dirs. Devel. Authority for Tucson, 1967. Mem. Soaring Soc. Am. (Silver badge), Am. Rifle Assn. (life), Nat. Mktg. Assn. (Mktg. Performance of Year award 1966), Nat. Assn. Skin Diving Schs., Pima County Jr. C. of C. (bd. dir. 1967), Phoenix Little Theatre, Phoenix Musical Theatre, S.W. Ensemble Theatre (bd. dir.), Wheelmen of Am., Masons, Shriners, Kona Kai Club (San Diego), Paradise Valley Country Club, Alpha Tau Omega. Office: Schroeder-Wallace PO Box 7703 Phoenix AZ 85011-7703

WALLACE, LEIGH ALLEN, JR., bishop; b. Norman, Okla., Feb. 5, 1927; s. Leigh Allen Sr. and Nellie Elizabeth (Whittemore) W.; m. Alvira Kinney, Sept. 2, 1949; children: Jenny Leigh, Richard Kinney, William Paul. BA, U. Mont., 1950; M in Divinity, Va. Theol. Sem., 1962, DD, 1979. Ordained priest Episcopal Ch.; vicar chs., Sheridan, Virginia City, Jeffers, Mont., 1962-65; rector St. Luke's Ch., Billings, Mont., 1965-71, Holy Spirit Parish, Missoula, Mont., 1971-78; bishop of Spokane, 1979-90, retired bishop, 1990—. Served with USNR, 1945-46. Address: 245 E 13th Ave Spokane WA 99202

WALLACE, MARC CHARLES, dentist; b. Portland, Oreg., Aug. 8, 1957; s. Francis Ronald and Donna Mae (Schulz) W. BS, U. Wash., 1979, DDS, 1983. Pvt. practice Woodinville, Wash., 1983-84, Beverly Hills, Calif., 1985-93, Bellevue, Wash., 1986-88, Costa Mesa, Calif., 1989—. Actor Poor Little Rich Girl Prodns., L.A., 1986, appeared in commls., L.A., 1986—. Mem. ADA, AFTRA, Acad. Gen. Dentistry, Screen Actors Guild, Flying Club (pvt. pilot). Republican. Roman Catholic. Home: 3400 Avenue Of The Arts Costa Mesa CA 92626-1927 Office: 1503 S Coast Dr # 201 Costa Mesa CA 92626

WALLACE, MATTHEW WALKER, entrepreneur; b. Salt Lake City, Jan. 7, 1924; s. John McChrystal and Glenn (Walker) W.; m. Constance Cone, June 22, 1954 (dec. May 1980); children—Matthew, Anne; m. Susan Struggles, July 11, 1981. B.A., Stanford U., 1947; M.C.P., MIT, 1950. Prin. planner Boston City Planning Bd., 1950-53; v.p. Nat. Planning and Research, Inc., Boston, 1953-55; pres. Wallace-McConaughy Corp., Salt Lake City, 1955-69; pres. Ariz. Ranch & Metals Co., Salt Lake City, 1969-84; chmn. Wallace Assocs., Inc., Salt Lake City, 1969—; dir. 1st Interstate Bank, Salt Lake City, 1956—, dir. Arnold Machinery Co., 1988—, dir. Roosevelt Hot Springs Corp., 1978—; mem. adv. bd. Mountain Bell Telephone Co., Salt Lake City, 1975-85. Pres., Downtown Planning Assn., Salt Lake City, 1970; chmn. Utah State Arts Coun., Salt Lake City, 1977; mem. Humanities and Scis. Coun., Stanford U., also mem. athletic bd., bd. vis. sch. law; mem. nat. adv. bd. Coll. Bus., U. Utah; lifetime dir. Utah Symphony Orch.; chmn. arts adv. coun. Westminster Coll. Lt. (j.g.) USN, 1944-46; PTO. Recipient Contbn. award Downtown Planning Assn., 1977, Govs. Award in the Arts, 1991. Mem. Am. Inst. Cert. Planners (charter), Am. Arts Alliance (bd. dirs. 1991), Alta Club (dir.), Cottonwood Club (pres. 1959-63), Salt Lake Country Club (dir.) Club, Masons, Phi Kappa Phi. Home: 2510 Walker Ln Salt Lake City UT 84117-7729 Office: Wallace Assocs Inc 165 S Main St Salt Lake City UT 84111-1918

WALLACE, NANCY DIANE, industrial engineer; b. Artesia, Calif., Dec. 22, 1958; d. George and Juanita Reba (Gilliland) W.; 1 child, Toy Lynn. BS in Indsl. Engring., U. Okla., 1982. Indsl. engr. II Digital Equipment Corp., Phoenix, 1982-85, sr. indsl. engr., 1985-87; customer program mgr. Digital Equipment Corp., Santa Clara, Calif., 1990—; mgr. indsl. engring. Digital Equipment Corp., Phoenix, 1987-89, mgr. mfg. engring., 1989-90; mem. indsl. engring. adv. bd. U. Okla. Chmn. Nat. Am. Week, Phoenix Indian Ctr., 1986. Mem. Inst. Indsl. Engrs., Am. Indian Sci. and Engring. Soc. (sec. bd. 1984-88), Nat. Assn. Minority Engring. Program Adminstrs., U. Okla. Am. Indian Alumni Soc. Democrat. Baptist. Office: Digital Equip Corp 2525 Augustine Dr Santa Clara CA 95054-3097

WALLACE, PATRICIA JEAN, artist, educator, writer; b. Sacramento, Jan. 3, 1945; d. Millard Edward Rogers and Katherine Lottie (Crabtree) Briggs; m. Feb. 23, 1964 (div. July 1992); children: Raabe, Brian, Marni. Student, Calif. Bapt. Coll., 1962-63, Am. River Coll., 1976-77, Tahoe Community Coll., 1991-92. Art, music tchr. Sunrise Elem. Sch., Citrus Heights, Calif., 1977-80; art restorer Arcade Antiques, North Sacramento, 1977-79; artist P.J.'s Illustration, North Sacramento, 1982—; instr. adult arts and crafts Community of Fair Oaks, Calif., 1982-84; instr., artist Laughing Cir. Gallery, Colo., Tex., N.Mex., 1984-92; writer On the Wing mag., No. Calif., 1988-90; artist ArtWorks Gallery, Fair Oaks, 1989—, Sacramento, 1988-91; artist S.W. Gallery, Fair Oaks and San Antonio, 1988—; set artist Fair Oaks Shakespeare Theatre, 1990. Illustrator numerous books, 1982—; contbr. articles to profl. mags. Pres. Sacramento Women's Club, 1984-85; city coun. rep. South Lake Tahoe Women's Ctr., 1978-79; amb. C. of C., Citrus Heights, 1985-89; rep. Historic Assn., Citrus Heights, 1987-88; adv. Bus. and the Arts, Sacramento County, 1987-89, C. of C., Sacramento, 1987-89; mem., guest artist KVIE-Channel 6, Sacramento, 1986-88; contbr. AIDS Found., Sacramento, 1990. Recipient award Citrus Heights C. of C., 1989, U. Nev., 1990, Process Theatre Prodns., 1988. Mem. Tallac Historic Assn., Citrus

Heights Art Assn. (pres., bd. dirs. 1985-89), Crocker Art Mus. Address: c/o M. Gates 3313 Eisenhower Dr Sacramento CA 95826

WALLACE, PAUL HARVEY, lawyer, educator; b. Fresno, Calif., Oct. 27, 1944; s. Samuel Dunn and Naomi (Hickman) W.; m. Randa Fay Steckler, Mar. 20, 1987; children: Tim, Laura, Christy. BS in Criminology, Calif. State U., Fresno, 1966; JD, U.S. Internat. U., 1974; MPA, Golden Gate U., 1989. Bar: Calif. 1974, U.S. Dist. Ct. (so. dist.) Calif. 1974, U.S. Dist. Ct. (no. dist.) Calif. 1982, U.S. Ct. Appeals (9th cir.) 1985. Dep. dist. atty. San Diego Dist. Atty.'s Office, 1975-79; assoc. Harrison and Watson, San Diego, 1979-81; dep. county counsel Butte County Counsel's Office, Oroville, Calif., 1981-85; county counsel Butte County Counsel's Office, Oroville, 1985-87; city atty. City of Fresno, 1987-92; assoc. prof. Calif. State U., Fresno, 1992—; adj. prof. Nat. U., Fresno, 1987—; bd. dirs. Ctrl. Calif. Legal Svcs. Corp., 1993—. Asst. coord. San Diego County for U.S. Senator Alan Cranston, 1974. Lt. USMCR, 1967-70, col. Res. Decorated Silver Star, Purple Heart with oak leaf cluster. Mem. State Bar Assn. Calif., Butte County Bar Assn., San Diego Dep. Dist. Attys. Assn. (sec.-treas. 1976-77, v.p. 1977-78, pres. 1978-79), Am. Legion, VFW, Masons, Shriners. Office: Calif State U Fresno CA 93740

WALLACE, ROBERT ARDELL, writer, educator; b. Detroit, Aug. 18, 1938; s. Elmer Ardell and Gladys Sarah (Simmons) W.; m. Bonni Symington, Feb. 2, 1976 (div. Sept. 1982); m. Jayne Talley Austin. BA, Harding U., 1960; MA, Vanderbilt U., 1965; PhD, U. Tex., 1969. Author Wallace Writing Enterprises, Gainesville, Fla., 1968—; adj. assoc. prof. zoology U. Fla., Gainesville, 1982-92; vis. scholar Duke U., Chapel Hill, N.C., 1980-82; dir. Steamboat Springs (Colo.) Ednl. Inst., 1991—; explorer Search for Medicines in the Amazon, 1982-93. Author: (textbook) Biology, The Realm of Life, 1989, Biology, The Science of Life, 1991, Biology, The World of Life, 1992 (design award 1992), Perspectives in Animal Behavior, 1993, (trade) How They Do It, 1980. Fellow The Explorers Club. Home and Office: PO Box 775067 1165 Overlook Dr C4 Steamboat Springs CO 80477

WALLACE, ROBERT EARL, geologist; b. N.Y.C., July 16, 1916; s. Clarence Earl and Harriet (Wheeler) W.; m. Gertrude Kivela, Mar. 19, 1945; 1 child: Alan R. BS, Northwestern U., 1938; MS, Calif. Inst. Tech., 1940, PhD, 1946. Registered geologist, Calif., engring. geologist, Calif. Geologist U.S. Geol. Survey, various locations, 1942—; regional geologist U.S. Geol. Survey, Menlo Park, Calif., 1970-74; chief scientist Office of Earthquakes, Volcanoes and Engring. U.S. Geol. Survey, Menlo Park, 1974-87; asst. and assoc. prof. Wash. State Coll., Pullman, 1946-51; mem. adv. panel Nat. Earthquake Prediction Evaluation Coun., 1980-90, Stanford U. Sch. Earth Sci., 1972-82; mem. engring. criteria rev. bd. San Francisco Bay Conservation and Devel. Commn. Contbr. articles to profl. jours. Recipient Meritorious Service award U.S. Dept. Interior, 1978, Disting. Service award U.S. Dept. Interior, 1978; Japanese Indsl. Tech. Assn. fellow, 1984. Fellow AAAS, Geol. Soc. Am. (chair cordillidan sect. 1967-68), Earthquake Engring. Research Inst., mem. Seismol. Soc. Am. (medalist 1989). Office: US Geol Survey MS-977 345 Middlefield Rd Menlo Park CA 94025-3591

WALLACE, WILLIAM ARTHUR, JR., environmental engineering executive; b. N.Y.C., Dec. 6, 1942; s. William Arthur and Helene Marie (Hoene) W.; m. Diane Marie Guillot, July 11, 1964; children: Kathleen Marie, Jane Coventry. BSChemE, Clarkson U., 1964; MS in Mgmt., Rensselaer Poly. Inst., 1971; advanced mgmt. program course, Harvard U., 1989. Chief plans and programs U.S. Naval Ammunition Depot, Hawthorne, Nev., 1973-75; chief hazardous waste enforcement EPA, Washington, 1975-78; chief enforcement br. U.S. Dept. Interior, Washington, 1978-79; v.p. Fred C. Hart Assocs., N.Y.C., 1979-81; engring. exec. strategic planning CH2M Hill, Bellevue, Wash., 1981—; testified Overview of Superfund Cleanup Techs. U.S. Ho. Reps., Washington, 1985, Overview of Superfund, 1988, 91, Soil Contaminants: PCB, 1988, U.S. Senate inquirey into environ. tech., 1993. Bd. dirs. Hazardous Waste Action Coalition, 1986—, treas., 1990-91; invited panel mem. Office of Tech. Assesment Nuclear Waste Remediation Workshop, Washington, 1990; mem. sci. adv. com. Western Regional Hazardous Substance Rsch. Ctr. Stanford U., 1989—; mem. panel ad hoc criteria group environ. tech., We. Govs.' Assn., 1993. Recipient George A. Hogaboom award Am. Electroplaters Soc., 1968, Bronze Medal award EPA, 1978, Outstanding Citizenship award Met. Law Enforcement Assn., Denver, 1980. Mem. Assn. Wash. Bus., Water Pollution Control Fedn., Water Sci. and Tech. Com., Hazardous Materials Control Rsch. Inst., Air and Waste Mgmt. Assn., Bellevue Athletic Club, Lakes Club. Office: CH2M Hill 777 108th Ave NE PO Box 91500 Bellevue WA 98009-2050

WALLACE, WILLIAM WALES, bank executive; b. Salt Lake City, Jan. 10, 1959; s. Ashley Harper and Ellen (Wales) W.; m. Jennifer Lloyd, May 20, 1982; children: Elen Suzanne, Whitney Elizabeth, Lydia Lute. BS in Econs. cum laude, U. Utah, 1983, cert. internat. rels., 1983, MS in Econs., 1987. Mgmt. intern Key Bank of Utah, Salt Lake City, 1983-84, loan officer, 1984-85, investment officer, 1985-89, asst. v.p. investment dept., mgr., 1989-91, v.p., investment dept. mgr., 1991—; adj. prof. Westminster Coll., Salt Lake City, 1988-91, U. Utah, Salt Lake City, 1988-90; sec. Wasatch Front Econ. Forum, Salt Lake City, 1986-88; mcpl. securities rep. Mcpl. Securities Rule Making Bd., Washington, 1988-93, prin., 1993—. Mem. Assn. for Investment Mgmt. and Rsch., Omicron Delta Epsilon. Republican. Mormon. Office: Key Bank Utah PO Box 30815 Salt Lake City UT 84130-0815

WALLACH, PAUL, publishing executive, author; b. L.A., May 23, 1925; s. Charles Wallach and Carolyn (Agate) Bak; m. Merle Wallach, Apr. 19, 1945 (div. 1974); children: Stuart Lane, Brad Paul. Student, Calif. State U., Long Beach, 1977. Freelance writer, 1960—; pres., chief exec. officer Wallach Co., Anaheim, Calif., 1960-74, Paul Wallach Inc., Glendale, Calif., 1974—; author Travel Guides Inc., Burbank, Calif., 1971—; columnist Westways mag., L.A., 1972—, Guide Publs., L.A., 1974-90. With USNR, 1942-45, PTO. Named Man of the Yr., Pub. Rels Inst., 1970; recipient Lifetime Achievement award City of Hope, Commendation, City of L.A., 1984, County of L.A., 1985; knighted Chevalier L'Oure des Coteaux de Champagne Govt. France, 1988; named Conferie de Vignorons da St. Vincent, 1988. Home: 712 E Angeleno Ave Burbank CA 91501-2213

WALLER, CHERYL LYNN GARY, aerospace company professional; b. Monterey Park, Calif., May 8, 1955; d. Gerald Howard and Betty Lou (Carrick) Frost. AA, Chaffey Coll., 1988. Enlisted USAF, 1973, advanced to staff sgt., served in various assignments, 1973-81, resigned, 1981; sec. Weyerhaeuser Corp., Fontana, Calif., 1981-82; sec. TRW Corp., San Bernardino, Calif., 1982-84, adminstr., 1984-89, mgr. computer graphics, 1989—; mem. Air Force speakers bur. Mem. NAFE, Vietnam Vets. Am., Calif. Air Force Assn., Air Force Assn. (nat. dir. 1988-91, state pres. 1992—), Airlifters Assn., Beta Sigma Phi. Republican. Home: 10449 Shore Crest Terr Moreno Valley CA 92557-2928 Office: TRW PO Box 1310 San Bernardino CA 92402-1310

WALLER, JOHN JAMES, lawyer; b. Red Cloud, Nebr., May 14, 1924; s. James Emery and Gail Fern (Perry) W.; m. Norma Louise Kunz, June 19, 1949; children: Diane Leslie, John James Jr, William Scott. Student, Rhode Island State Coll., Kingston, 1943-44, Biarritz Am. U., France, 1945-46; BA magna cum laude, Harvard U., 1947, JD, 1950. Bar: Calif. 1951, U.S. Dist. Ct. (cen. dist.), 1951, U.S. Ct. Appeals (9th cir.) 1959, U.S. Tax Ct. 1959, U.S. Supreme Ct. 1976. Assoc. Gibson, Dunn & Crutcher, L.A., 1950-62; ptnr. Flint & MacKay, L.A., 1962-67; with Law Offices of Max Fink, Beverly Hills, Calif., 1968-73; pvt. practice Santa Ana, Tustin, Calif., 1973-83, Buena Park, Calif., 1984—; spl. counsel Fluor Corp., Irvine, Calif., 1983-84; judge pro-tem Orange County (Calif.) Superior Ct., 1992—. Chmn. unification com. Buena Park Sch. Dist., 1969-70; pres., sec., dir. Bellehurst Community Assn., 1970; chmn., mem. City of Buena Park Airport Commn., 1969-74, City Buena Park Transp. Com., 1975-77; dist. vice chmn. Boy Scouts Am., 1970. Sgt. U.S. Army, 1943-46, ETO. Recipient Merit award Boy Scouts Am.. Mem. ABA, State Bar Calif., L.A. County Bar Assn., Orange County Bar Assn. (del. 1984), Am. Judicature Soc., Banyard Am. Inn of Ct. Democrat. Office: 5591 Monticello Ave Buena Park CA 90621-1543

WALLER, LARRY GENE, mortgage banking executive; b. Corpus Christi, Tex., Nov. 18, 1948; s. Paul Hobson and Marie (Armellini) W.; m. Mary Sandra Cupp, Dec. 27, 1969 (div. 1987); children: Stacey Ann, Jaime Lynn; m. Sharon Elizabeth Falls, Jan. 28, 1988; 1 child, Lisa Suzanne Cantello. AA, Bakersfield Jr. Coll., 1970. Lic. real estate broker, Calif. Asst. v.p. Bank of Am., Stockton, Calif., 1970-78, Wells Fargo Mortgage Co., Sacramento, 1978-81; regional v.p. Weyerhauser Mortgage Co., Sacramento, 1981-89; sr. v.p. Koll Realty Advisors, Sacramento, 1989-91; pres. L. G. Waller Co., 1991—; pres., CFO Waller, Kaufman & Sutter, Sacramento, 1991—. Mem. Com. to Help Attract Maj. Profl. Sports, Sacramento. Mem. Nat. Assn. Indsl. and Office Parks (bd. dirs. Sacramento chpt.), Mortgage Bankers Assn. (income property com.), Calif. Mortgage Bankers Assn. Home: 180 Dawn River Way Folsom CA 95630-5046 Office: Ste 400 2277 Fair Oaks Blvd Sacramento CA 95825

WALLER, PETER WILLIAM, public affairs executive; b. Kewanee, Ill., Oct. 1, 1926; s. Ellis Julian and Barodel (Gould) W.; m. Anne-Marie Appelius van Hoboken, Nov. 10, 1950; children: Catherine, Hans. BA with hons., Princeton U., 1949; MA with hons., San Jose State U., 1978. Bur. chief Fairchild Publs., San Francisco, 1953-55; freelance writer Mountain View, Calif., 1956-57; pub. relations coord. Lockheed Missiles and Space, Sunnyvale, Calif., 1957-64; pioneer info. mgr. for 1st mission to Jupiter, Saturn and beyond and 1st mapping and photo mission to Venus NASA Ames Rsch. Ctr., Mountain View, 1964-83, mgr. pub. info., 1983—; speechwriter for pres. Lockheed Missiles and Space, 1960-64. Producer (documentary) Jupiter Odyssey, 1974 (Golden Eagle, 1974); producer, writer NASA Aero. program, 1984; contbr. articles to profl. jours, encyclopedias. Cons. on preservation of Lake Tahoe, Calif. Resources Agy., Sacramento, 1984. Mem. No. Calif. Sci. Writers Assn., Sierra Club. Democrat. Congregationalist. Home: 3655 La Calle Ct Palo Alto CA 94306-2619 Office: NASA Ames Rsch Ctr Moffett Field CA 94035

WALLER, RAY ALBERT, statistician; b. Grenola, Kans., Mar. 4, 1937; s. Clarence Freeman and Dorothea Mae (Wilson) W.; m. Carolyn Ann McCoy, July 23, 1960; children: Lance Allyn, Jay Andrew. BA, Southwestern Coll., 1959; MS, Kans. State U., 1963; PhD, The Johns Hopkins U., 1967. Tchr. St. John's Sch., Santurce, P.R., 1960-61; grad. teaching asst. Kans. State U., Manhattan, 1961-63, from asst. to assoc. prof., 1967-74; NDEA fellow The Johns Hopkins U., Balt., 1963-66; asst.prof. Towson (Md.) State Coll., 1966-67; mem. staff, from asst. to group leader Los Alamos (N.Mex.) Nat. Lab., 1974-80, dep. div. leader, 1980-87, staff asst., 1987-92, directorate office leader, 1992—. Author: Statistics: An Introduction to Numerical Reasoning, 1979; co-author: Bayesian Reliability Analysis, 1982. With USAR, 1959-65. Mem. Am. Statis. Assn., Soc. for Risk Analysis. Methodist. Office: Los Alamos Nat Lab Univ Rsch & Sci Edn PO Box 1663 P313 Los Alamos NM 87545

WALLERSTEIN, BRUCE LEE, psychologist; b. Boston, May 23, 1943; s. Michael and Mildred (Cohen) W. AB, Boston U., 1965; MS, PhD, U. Pa., 1968. Cons. Met. State Hosp., Norwalk, Calif., 1968-70; assoc. prof. U. So. Calif., L.A., 1970-72; pvt. practice Long Beach, Calif., 1969—. Author: A Place to Live Not to Die: A Practical Guide to Nursing Homes, 1975. Fellow Am. Orthopsychiat. Assn., Group Psychotherapy Assn. So. Calif. (pres. 1975-77), Calif. Assn. Health Facilities (assoc.), Long Beach Yacht Club, Naples Bus. Assn., Long Beach C. of C. Office: Naples Counseling Ctr 5855 E Naples Plz Ste 308 Long Beach CA 90803-5068

WALLERSTEIN, RALPH OLIVER, physician; b. Dusseldorf, Germany, Mar. 7, 1922; came to U.S., 1938, naturalized, 1944; s. Otto R. and Ilse (Hollander) W.; m. Betty Ane Christensen, June 21, 1952; children: Ralph Jr., Richard, Ann. A.B., U. Calif., Berkeley, 1943; M.D., U. Calif., San Francisco, 1945. Diplomate: Am. Bd. Internal Medicine. Intern San Francisco Hosp., 1945-46, resident, 1948-49; resident U. Calif. Hosp., San Francisco, 1949-50; research fellow Thorndike Meml. Lab., Boston City Hosp., 1950-52; chief clin. hematology San Francisco Gen. Hosp., 1953-87; faculty U. Calif., San Francisco, 1952—; clin. prof. medicine U. Calif., 1969—. Served to capt. M.C. AUS, 1946-48. Mem. AMA, ACP (gov. 1977-87, chmn. bd. govs. 1980-81, regent 1981-87, pres. 1988-89), Am. Soc. Hematology (pres. 1978), San Francisco Med. Soc., Am. Clin. and Climatol. Assn., Am. Fedn. Clin. Rsch., Am. Soc. Internal Medicine, Am. Bd. Internal Medicine (bd. govs. 1975-83, chmn. 1982-83), Am. Assn. Blood Banks, Inst. Medicine, Calif. Acad. Medicine, Internat. Soc. Hematology, Western Soc. Clin. Rsch., Western Assn. Physicians, Gold Headed Cane Soc. Republican. Home: 3447 Clay St San Francisco CA 94118-2008 Office: Ste 707 3838 California St San Francisco CA 94118

WALLERSTEIN, ROBERT SOLOMON, psychiatrist; b. Berlin, Jan. 28, 1921; s. Lazar and Sarah (Guensberg) W.; m. Judith Hannah Saretsky, Jan. 26, 1947; children—Michael Jonathan, Nina Beth, Amy Lisa. B.A., Columbia, 1941, M.D., 1944; postgrad., Topeka Inst. Psychoanalysis, 1951-58. Assoc. dir., then dir. rsch. Menninger Found., Topeka, 1954-66; chief psychiatry Mt. Zion Hosp., San Francisco, 1966-78; tng. and supervising analyst San Francisco Psychoanalytic Inst., 1966—; clin. prof. U. Calif. Sch. Medicine, Langley-Porter Neuropsychiat. Inst., 1967-75, prof., chmn. dept. psychiatry, also dir. inst., 1975-85, prof. dept. psychiatry, 1985-91, prof. emeritus, 1991—; vis. prof. psychiatry La. State U. Sch. Medicine, also New Orleans Psychoanalytic Inst., 1972-73, Pahlavi U., Shiraz, Iran, 1977, Fed. U. Rio Grande do Sul, Porto Alegre, Brasil, 1980; mem., chmn. rsch. scientist career devel. com. NIMH, 1966-70; fellow Ctr. Advanced Study Behavioral Scis., Stanford, Calif., 1964-65, 81-82, Rockefeller Found. Study Ctr., Bellagio, Italy, 1992. Author 11 books and monographs; mem. editorial bd. 12 profl. jours.; contbr. articles to profl. jours. Served with AUS, 1946-48. Recipient Heinz Hartmann award N.Y. Psychoanalytic Inst., 1968, Disting. Alumnus award Menninger Sch. Psychiatry, 1972, J. Elliott Royer award U. Calif., San Francisco, 1973, Outstanding Achievement award No. Calif. Psychiat. Soc., 1987, Mt. Airy gold medal, 1990, Mary Singleton Sigourney award, 1991. Fellow ACP, Am. Psychiat. Assn., Am. Orthopsychiat. Assn.; mem. Am. Psychoanlytic Assn. (pres. 1971-72), Internat. Psychoanalytic Assn. (v.p. 1977-85, pres. 1985-89), Group for Advancement Psychiatry, Brit. Psycho-Analytical Soc. (hon.), Phi Beta Kappa, Alpha Omega Alpha. Home: 290 Beach Rd Belvedere Tiburon CA 94920-2472 Office: 655 Redwood Hwy Ste 261 Mill Valley CA 94941-3011

WALLIN, ANGIE, public relations consultant; b. L.A., Nov. 15; d. Francisco Antonio and Juventina (Garcia) Grippo; m. Donald Gilday, Apr. 1951 (div. 1976); children: Julie Gilday Shaffer, Grace Gilday Brackett, Kara Gilday Tucker; m. Charles Cromwell Wallin, Dec. 23, 1981 (dec. Mar. 1989). Student, L.A. City Coll., 1949-51, U. Nev., 1984, Clark County C.C. of So. Nev., 1983. Owner Tropicana Tennis Shop, Las Vegas, 1967-77, Cambridge Tennis Shop, Las Vegas, 1962-65, The Red Apple, Las Vegas, 1978-89; with mktg., pub. rels. dept. Lake Mead Hosp., North Las Vegas, 1983-84; pres. Cons., Ltd., Las Vegas, 1984—; pres. Wallin Internat., 1992. Goodwill amb. City of Las Vegas, 1991; commr. Las Vegas Arts Commn., 1987-91; mem. Nev. State Coun. on Arts, Las Vegas, 1984-93; exec. dir. Nev. Alliance for the Arts, 1991—. Recipient Art Patron award, Nev. Opera Theatre, 1987, Humanitarian award Nat. Jewish Ctr. Immunology & Respiratory, 1989; named hon. citizen Republic of Korea, 1970, Dame of Grace, Grand Cross, Soverign Order Oak, 1990, Woman of Achievement award in Arts, Las Vegas C. of C., 1992. Mem. Pub. Rels. Soc. Am. Democrat. Roman Catholic. Office: Cons Ltd 7555 Spanish Bay Dr Las Vegas NV 89113-1308

WALLINS, ROGER PEYTON, English language educator, university administrator; b. N.Y.C., Oct. 24, 1941; s. Albert J. and Beatrice Wallins; m. Judith Beach, Mar. 19, 1967; children: Rachel, Beatrice. Student, Rensselaer Poly. Inst., 1958-60; AB in English with honors, CCNY, 1962; MA in English, Ohio State U., 1964, PhD in English, 1972. Asst. prof. U. Idaho, Moscow, 1970-75, assoc. prof., 1975-84, prof., 1984—, asst. dean, 1983-88, assoc. dean, 1988—; dir. writing U. Idaho, Moscow, 1970-73, chmn. faculty coun., 1979-80. Contbr. articles to profl. jours. and scholarly presses. Pres. local chpt. AAUP, Moscow, 1977-79; state coord. Nat. Coun. Tchrs. English, Achievement Awards in Writing, 1975-79; bd. dirs. U. Idaho Fed. Credit Union, Moscow, 1973-77, pres., 1976-77; chmn. Moscow Fair Housing Commn., 1976, 77; bd. trustees Sch. Dist. 281, Moscow, 1982-88, chmn. bd. trustees, 1986-87; trustee Sta. KUID Pub. Broadcasting Sta., Moscow, 1988-94, pres., 1991—; mem. Moscow human rels. com., 1992—. Penrose Fund grantee Am. Philos. Soc., Phila., 1977, Lectr. grantee Assn. for the Humanities in Idaho, 1983, GTE Found., 1992, Abbott Labs, 1992; recipient Excellence in Teaching award Alumni Assn., U. Idaho, Moscow, 1983. Mem. Rsch. Soc. for Victorian Periodicals. Office: U Idaho Coll Grad Studies Moscow ID 83843

WALLIS, CATHERINE LOUISE (KITTY WALLIS), artist; b. Sellersville, Pa., July 13, 1938; d. Edwin Harold and Edna Anglemoyer (Ziegler) W.; m. David Forrest Stephens, Jan. 26, 1930 (div. 1970); 1 child, Bryn Stephens. Student, Cooper Union, 1956-61. art instr. De Young Mus. Art Sch., San Francisco, 1976-78; pvt. art instr., Santa Cruz, Calif., 1969—, Santa Fe, N.Mex., 1980-83. One-woman shows include Nimbus Gallery, Dallas, 1976, 79, 81, 82, 86, Dancing Man Gallery, Santa Cruz, 1977, 81, 82, 87, 88, 92, Scott Gallery, Orinda, Calif., 1981, 84, Stremmel Gallery, Reno, 1983, Harris Gallery, Houston, 1987, 91; exhibited in group shows at Santa Cruz County Hist. Mus., 1985, Dancing Man Gallery, 1987, Harris Gallery, Houston, 1991, Ruth Volid Gallery Ltd., Chgo., C. G. Rein Galleries, Scottsdale, Ariz., Santa Fe., Edina, Minn. Singer, mem. steering com. Cabrillo Chorus, Santa Cruz, 1986—; mem. open studio com. Cultural Coun., Santa Cruz, 1988—; organizer Double Vision, Santa Cruz, 1984-85. Office: PO Box 7626 Santa Cruz CA 95061

WALLMANN, JEFFREY MINER, author; b. Seattle, Dec. 5, 1941; s. George Rudolph and Elizabeth (Biggs) W.; B.S., Portland State U., 1962. Pvt. investigator Dale Systems, N.Y.C., 1962-63; asst. buyer, mgr. pub. money bidder Dohrmann Co., San Francisco, 1964-66; mfrs. rep. electronics industry, San Francisco, 1966-69; dir. pub. rels. London Films, Cinelux-Universal and Trans-European Publs., 1970-75; editor-in-chief Riviera Life mag., 1975-77; cons. Mktg. Svcs. Internat., 1978—; instr. U. Nev., Reno, 1990—; books include: The Spiral Web, 1969, Judas Cross, 1974, Clean Sweep, 1976, Jamaica, 1977, Deathtrek, 1980, Blood and Passion, 1980; Brand of the Damned, 1981; The Manipulator, 1982; Return to Conta Lupe, 1983; The Celluloid Kid, 1984; Business Basic for Bunglers, 1984, Guide to Applications Basic, 1984; (under pseudonym Leon DaSilva) Green Hell, 1976, Breakout in Angola, 1977; (pseudonym Nick Carter) Hour of the Wolf, 1973, Ice Trap Terror, 1974; (pseudonym Peter Jensen) The Virgin Couple, 1970, Ravished, 1971; (pseudonmy Jackson Robard) Gang Initiation, 1971, Present for Teacher, 1972, Teacher's Lounge, 1972; (pseudonym Grant Roberts) The Reluctant Couple, 1969, Wayward Wives, 1970; (pseudonym Gregory St. Germain) Resistance #1: Night and Fog, 1982, Resistance #2: Maygar Massacre, 1983; (pseudonym Wesley Ellis) Lonestar on the Treachery Trail, 1982, numerous others in the Lonestar series; (pseudonym Tabor Evans) Longarm and the Lonestar Showdown, 1986; (psyeudonym Jon Sharpe) Trailsman 58: Slaughter Express, 1986, numerous others in Trailsman series; also many other pseudonyms and titles; contbr. articles and short stories to Argosy, Ellery Queen's Mystery Mag., Alfred Hitchcock's Mystery Mag., Mike Shayne's Mystery Mag., Zane Grey Western, Venture, Oui, TV Guide; also (under pseudonym William Jeffrey in collaboration with Bill Pronzini) Dual at Gold Buttes, 1980, Border Fever, 1982, Day of the Moon, 1983. Mem. Mystery Writers of Am., Sci. Fiction Writers Am., Western Writers Am., Crime Writers Assn., Nevada World Trade Commn.

WALLOP, MALCOLM, senator, rancher; b. N.Y.C., Feb. 27, 1933; s. Oliver M. and Jean (Moore) W.; m. French Carter, May 26, 1984; children: Malcolm, Amy, Paul, Matthew. BA English, Yale U., 1954. Owner, operator Canyon Ranch, Big Horn, Wyo.; mem. Wyo. Ho. of Reps., 1969-73, Wyo. Senate, 1973-77; mem. U.S. Senate from Wyo., 1976—, mem. coms. on energy and natural resources, armed svcs., small bus.; ofcl. observer from Senate on arms control negotiations; mem. Commn. on Security and Cooperation in Europe. Served to lt. U.S. Army, 1955-57. Mem. Wyo. Stockgrowers Assn., Am. Nat. Cattleman's Assn., Am. Legion. Republican. Episcopalian. Office: US Senate 237 Russell Senate Bldg Washington DC 20510-5001*

WALLS, DAVID STUART, college administrator; b. Chgo., Oct. 21, 1941; s. John Archer and Elizabeth (Smith) W.; m. Lucia V. Gattone, Nov. 25, 1971; 1 child, Jesse Michael. BA, U. Calif., Berkeley, 1964; MA, U. Ky., 1972, PhD, 1978. Mgmt. intern U.S. Dept. Health, Edn. and Welfare, Washington, 1964-65; adminstrv. asst. Office Econ. Opportunity, Washington, 1965-66; field coord., dir. Appalachian Vol. Inc., Prestonsburg, Ky., 1966-70; asst. prof. Coll. Social Professions U. Ky., Lexington, 1974-81; dir. sponsored programs Sonoma State U., Rohnert Park, Calif., 1982-90; gen. mgr. Sonoma State U. Found., Rohnert Park, 1982-93, dean extended edn., 1984—. Author: The Activist's Almanac, 1993; editor: Appalachia in the Sixties, 1972; mem. editorial bd. Appalachian Jour., Boone, N.C., 1979—; contbr. ency. entry and articles to profl. jours. Office: Sonoma State U 1801 E Cotati Ave Rohnert Park CA 94928

WALLSTRÖM, WESLEY DONALD, bank executive; b. Turlock, Calif., Oct. 4, 1929; s. Emil Reinhold and Edith Katherine (Lindberg) W.; student Modesto Jr. Coll., 1955-64; certificate Pacific Coast Banking Sch., U. Wash., 1974; m. Marilyn Irene Hallmark, May 12, 1951; children: Marc Gordon, Wendy Diane. Bookkeeper, teller First Nat. Bank, Turlock, 1947-50; v.p. Gordon Hallmark, Inc., Turlock, 1950-53; asst. cashier United Calif. Bank, Turlock, 1953-68, regional v.p., Fresno, 1968-72, v.p., mgr., Turlock, 1972-76; founding pres., dir. Golden Valley Bank, Turlock, 1976-84; pres. Wallström & Co., 1985—. Campaign chmn. United Crusade, Turlock, 1971; chmn., founding dir. Covenant Village, retirement home, Turlock, 1973—, treas. Covenant Retirement Communities West; founding pres. Turlock Regional Arts Coun., 1974, dir., 1975-76. Served with U.S. N.G., 1948-56. Mem. Nat. Soc. Accts. for Coops., Ind. Bankers No. Calif., Am. Bankers Assn., U.S. Yacht Racing Union, No. Calif. Golf Assn., Turlock C. of C. (dir. 1973-75), Stanislaus Sailing Soc. (commodore 1980-81), Turlock Golf and Country Club (pres. 1975-76, v.p., 1977, dir. 1977, 83), Stockton Sailing Club, Masons, Rotary. Republican. Mem. Covenant Ch. Home: 1720 Hammond Dr Turlock CA 95380-2850 Office: Wallstrom & Co 2925 Niagara St Turlock CA 95380-1056

WALLYN, ROBERT HENRY, ophthalmologist; b. Chgo., 1945; m. Carol Kay Stallard, 1972. AB in Philosophy cum laude, Coll. of Holy Cross, 1967; MD, Harvard U., 1971. Diplomate Am. Bd. Ophthalmology. Intern U. Mich. Affiliated Hosps., Ann Arbor, 1971-72; resident in ophthalmology Manhattan Eye, Ear and Throat Hosp., N.Y.C., 1972-75, chief resident, 1975; fellow in retinal ophthalmology U. Calif. Med. Ctr., San Francisco, 1975-76; pvt. practice Monterey, Calif., 1976—. Contbr. to profl. publs. Recipient award for ophthalmic rsch. N.Y. Acad. Medicine, 1975, Heed fellow in diseases of retina and vitreous, 1975. Fellow ACS, Am. Acad. Ophthalmology. Office: 1001 Pacific St Monterey CA 93940

WALRAD, CHARLENE CHUCK, software and total quality management consultant; b. Palm Beach, Fla., Feb. 21, 1946; d. Jack Maynard and Marian (Davenport) W.; m. Larry Starr, Oct. 1, 1972 (div. 1980). BA, Ariz. State U., 1967, MA, 1969; MA, U. Calif., San Diego, 1971. Linguist LATSEC, Inc., La Jolla, Calif., 1971-75, sr. linguist, 1975-84; v.p. World Translation Ctr., La Jolla, 1981-84; dir. mktg. Automated Lang. Processing Systems, Provo, Utah, 1984-85; dir. R & D, WICAT Systems, Orem, Utah, 1985-86; dir. quality mgmt. Relational Tech., Alameda, Calif., 1986-87; machine translation software cons. San Francisco, 1987—; co-founder North Beach Software, 1993; cons. Xerox Corp., Webster, N.Y., 1983-84, Sci. Applications, Inc., La Jolla, 1984, Dept. Commerce, 1988, CIA, 1989, NAS, 1989, Control Data Corp., 1989, Word Star, 1990, Ford Motor Co., 1990-91, Dialog/Knight-Ridder, 1991, IBM, 1991—, Esprit de Corps, 1992-93; presenter in field. Co-author: Introduction to Luiseno, 1972. Bd. dirs. Shelter Ridge Assn., Mill Valley, Calif., 1988-90, v.p. 1989-90, pres. 1990; mem. Mill Valley Bus. Task Force, 1990-91; bd. dirs. Marin Mus. of the Am. Indian.; chmn. Bus. Advocacy Ctr., Mill Valley, 1992-93. Mem. Ariz. State U. Alumni Assn. (pres. San Diego chpt. 1982-83, Utah chpt. 1985-86), Mensa. Home: 12 Brooke Cir Mill Valley CA 94941

WALRATH, HARRY RIENZI, minister; b. Alameda, Calif., Mar. 7, 1926; s. Frank Rienzi and Cathren (Michlar) W.; A.A., City Coll. San Francisco, 1950; B.A., U. Calif. at Berkeley, 1952; M.Div., Ch. Div. Sch. of Pacific, 1959; m. Dorothy M. Baxter, June 24, 1961; 1 son, Gregory Rienzi. Dist. exec. San Mateo area council Boy Scouts Am., 1952-55; ordained deacon Episcopal Ch., 1959, priest, 1960; curate All Souls Parish, Berkeley, Calif., 1959-61; vicar St. Luke's, Atascadero, Calif., 1961-63, St. Andrew's, Garberville, Calif., 1963-64; asso. rector St. Luke's Ch., Los Gatos, 1964-65, Holy Spirit Parish, Missoula, Mont., 1965-67; vicar St. Peter's Ch., also headmaster St. Peter's Schs., Litchfield Park, Ariz., 1967-69; chaplain U.

Mont., 1965-67; asst. rector Trinity Parish, Reno, 1969-72; coordinator counciling services Washoe County Council Alcoholism, Reno, 1972-74; adminstr. Cons. Assistance Services, Inc., Reno, 1974-76; pastoral counselor, contract chaplain Nev. Mental Health Inst., 1976-78; contract mental health chaplain VA Hosp., Reno, 1976-78; mental health chaplain VA Med. Ctr., 1978-83, staff chaplain, 1983-85, chief, chaplain service, 1985-91, also triage coord. for mental health, ret., 1991; dir. youth Paso Robles Presbytery; chmn. Diocesan Commn. on Alcoholism; cons. teen-age problems Berkeley Presbytery; mem. clergy team Episcopal Marriage Encounter, 1979-85, also Episc. Engaged Encounter. Mem. at large Washoe dist. Nev. area council Boy Scouts Am., scoutmaster troop 73, 1976, troop 585, 1979-82, asst. scoutmaster troop 35, 1982-92, assoc. adviser area 3 Western region, 1987-89, regional com. Western Region, 1989-90; lodge adviser Tannu Lodge 346, Order of Arrow, 1982-87; docent coun. Nev. Hist. Soc., 1992; South Humboldt County chmn. Am. Cancer Soc. Trustee Community Youth Ctr., Reno. Served with USNR, 1944-46. Decorated Pacific Theater medal with star, Am. Theater medal, Victory medal, Fleet Unit Commendation medal; recipient dist. award of merit Boy Scouts Am., St. George award Episc. Ch.-Boy Scouts Am., Silver Beaver award Boy Scouts Am., 1986, Founders' award Order of the Arrow, Boy Scouts Am., 1985; performance awards VA-VA Med. Ctr., 1983, 84; named Arrowman of Yr., Order of Arrow, Boy Scouts Am. Cert. substance abuse counselor, Nev. Mem. Ch. Hist. Soc., U. Calif. Alumni Assn., Nat. Model R.R. Assn. (life), Sierra Club Calif., Missoula Council Chs. (pres.), Alpha Phi Omega. Democrat. Club: Rotary. Home: 580 E Huffaker Ln Reno NV 89511-1203

WALRAVENS, PHILIP ALFRED, physician, researcher; b. St. Jean de Luz, Basses-Pyrenees, France, Oct. 30, 1939; came to U.S., 1967; s. Gerard and Maria (Cabrera) W.; m. Nicole Marcelle Spaey, Apr. 10, 1965; children: Patrick Didier, Christine Françoise, Sylvia Ann. MD, U. Louvain (Belgium), 1965. Diplomate Am. Bd. Pediatrics, Am. Bd. Nutrition. Intern and resident in pediatrics Univ. Hosps., Louvain, 1965-67; research fellow U. Colo. Med. Ctr., Denver, 1967-69, successively resident, fellow, asst. clin. prof., assoc. clin. prof. pediatrics, assoc. prof. 1972—. Contbr. sci. articles to med. jours., chpts. to pediatric textbooks; reviewer articles. Served to maj. U.S. Army, 1969-72. Mem. Am. Soc. Clin. Nutrition, Am. Inst. Nutrition, Am. Diabetes Assn., Western Soc. Pediatric Research. Democrat. Roman Catholic. Office: U Colo Health Sci Ctr 4200 E 9th Ave Denver CO 80262

WALSER, RANDAL LOUIS, computer scientist; b. Decatur, Ill., Feb. 20, 1949; s. Bernard Louis and Virginia Selene (Osborne) W.; m. Judith Lynn Walser, Oct. 30, 1982; 1 child, Nicholas. MS in Computer Sci., U. Ill., 1975. Rschr. U. Ill., Chgo., 1974-78; rsch. systems mgr. Knowledge Systems Lab., U. Ill., Chgo., 1977-78; cons. Envisioneering, Inc., Chgo., 1978-82; videogame designer Bally Midway, Chgo., 1982-84; software developer various cos., Chgo., 1984-86; sr. computer scientist Advanced Decision Systems, Mountain View, Calif., 1986-88; Cyberspace architect Autodesk, Inc., Sausalito, Calif., 1988-90, mgr. Cyberspace devel., 1990-92, mgr. spacemaking, 1992—; speaker in field. Contbr. articles to profl. jours. Home: 2 Willow Ln Sausalito CA 94965 Office: Spacetime Arts Sausalito CA 94965

WALSH, BERNARD LAWRENCE, JR., physicist; b. Detroit, Jan. 11, 1932; s. Bernard Lawrence Sr. and Catherine Bridget (McCarthy) W.; m. Margaret Barbara Milko, Feb. 16, 1957; children: Bernard Lawrence III, Catherine Teresa. AB, U. Detroit, 1954. With Hughes Aircraft Co., L.A., 1954--, sr. scientist, 1968-75, chief scientist, 1975--. Contbr. articles to profl. jours.; patentee in field. Mem. IEEE, Am. Phys. Soc., ASM Internat., Profl. Group Electron Devices, Profl. Group Microwave Theory and Techniques. Home: 9609 Wystone Ave Northridge CA 91324-1858 Office: Hughes Aircraft Co PO Box 92919 Los Angeles CA 90009-2919

WALSH, DANIEL FRANCIS, bishop; b. San Francisco, Oct. 2, 1937. Grad., St. Joseph Sem., St. Patrick Sem., Catholic U. Am. Ordained priest, Roman Catholic Ch., 1963. Ordained titular bishop of Tigia, 1981; aux. bishop of San Francisco, 1981-87, bishop of Reno-Las Vegas, 1987—. Home: 2809 Cameo Circle Reno NV 89107 also: Diocese of Reno-Las Vegas Office of Bishop PO Box 18316 Las Vegas NV 89114*

WALSH, DENNY JAY, newspaperman; b. Omaha, Nov. 23, 1935; s. Gerald Jerome and Muriel (Morton) W.; m. Peggy Marie Moore, Feb. 12, 1966; children by previous marriage—Catherine Camille, Colleen Cecile; 1 son, Sean Joseph. B.J., U. Mo., 1962. Staff writer St. Louis Globe-Democrat, 1961-68; asst. editor Life mag., N.Y.C., 1968-70; assoc. editor Life mag., 1970-73; reporter N.Y. Times, 1973-74, Sacramento Bee, 1974—. Served with USMCR, 1954-58. Recipient Con Lee Kelliher award St. Louis chpt. Sigma Delta Chi, 1962; award Am. Polit. Sci. Assn., 1963; award Sigma Delta Chi, 1968; Pulitzer prize spl. local reporting, 1969; 1st prize San Francisco Press Club, 1977. Office: Sacramento Bee 21st and Q Sts Sacramento CA 95813

WALSH, EDWARD JOSEPH, toiletries and food company executive; b. Mt. Vernon, N.Y., Mar. 18, 1932; s. Edward Aloysius and Charlotte Cecilia (Borup) W.; m. Patricia Ann Farrell, Sept. 16, 1961; children: Edward Joseph, Megan Simpson, John, Robert. BBA, Iona Coll., 1953; MBA, NYU, 1958. Sales rep. M & R Dietetic Labs., Columbus, Ohio, 1955-60; with Armour & Co., 1961-71, Greyhound Corp., 1971-87; v.p. toiletries div. Armour Dial Co., Phoenix, 1973-74; exec. v.p. Armour Dial Co., 1975-77; pres. Armour Internat. Co., Phoenix, 1978-84; pres. The Dial Corp. (formerly Armour-Dial Co.), Phoenix, 1984-87, chief exec. officer, 1984-87; pres., chief exec. officer Purex Corp., 1985; chmn., chief exec. officer The Sparta Group Ltd., Scottsdale, Ariz., 1988—; bd. dirs. Phillips Ramsey Advt., San Diego, Phoenix, Guest Supply Inc., New Brunswick, N.J., WD-40 Co., San Diego, Nortrust Ariz. Holding Corp., Phoenix, Ariz., No. Trust Bank of Ariz., N.A., Executive Services Corps. of Ariz., Inc. Pres. Mt. Vernon Fire Dept. Mems. Assn., 1960-61. Served with U.S. Army, 1953-55, Germany. Mem. Am. Mgmt. Assn., Nat. Meat Canner Assn. (pres. 1971-72), Cosmetic, Toiletries and Fragrance Assn. (bd. dirs. 1985—), Nat. Food Processors Assn. (bd. dirs.). Republican. Roman Catholic. Office: The Sparta Group Ltd 6623 N Scottsdale Rd Scottsdale AZ 85250-4421

WALSH, KENNETH ANDREW, biochemist; b. Sherbrooke, Que., Can., Aug. 7, 1931; s. George Stanley and Dorothy Maud (Sangster) W.; m. Deirdre Anne Clarke, Aug. 22, 1953; children: Andrew, Michael, Erin. BSc in Agr., McGill U., 1951; MS, Purdue U., 1953; PhD, U. Toronto, 1959. Postdoctoral fellow U. Wash., Seattle, 1959-62, from asst. prof. to assoc. prof. Biochemistry, 1962-69, prof. Biochemistry, 1969—, chair, 1990—. Author (book) Methods in Protein Sequence Analysis, 1986. Mem. The Protein Soc. (sec.-treas. 1987-90), Am. So. Biochemistry/Molecular Biology. Office: U Wash Dept Biochem SJ-70 Seattle WA 98195

WALSH, LARRY DONALD, construction executive; b. Mason City, Iowa, June 14, 1956; s. Dan Anthony and Evelyn Ann (Carmany) W.; m. Melissa Kay Stout, Mar. 7, 1981; 1 child, Garrett. BS in Constrn. Enging., Iowa State U., 1979; MBA in Bus., U. Colo., 1992. Mgr. constrn. Civil Construction, Grand Junction, Colo., 1979-83; project mgr. Flatiron Structures, Longmont, Colo., 1983—. Planning commr., advisor constrn. bd. City of Loveland, Colo. Home: 2331 Bismarck Ave Loveland CO 80538 Office: Flatiron Structures Co PO Box 2239 Longmont CO 80502

WALSH, MASON, retired newspaperman; b. Dallas, Nov. 27, 1912; s. Herbert C. and Margaret (Hayes) W.; m. Margaret Anne Calhoun, Mar. 7, 1947; children—Margaret Anne, Timothy Mason, Kevin Calhoun. B.A. in Polit. Sci., So. Meth. U., 1934. Staff Dallas Evening Jour., 1929-37; staff Dallas Dispatch-Jour. (later Dallas Jour.), 1938-42; editor Austin (Tex.) Tribune, 1942; dir. employee relations N.Am. Aviation, Dallas, 1942-45; with Dallas Times-Herald, 1945-60, mng. editor, 1952-60; mng. editor Phoenix Gazette, 1960-66; gen. mgr. Phoenix Newspapers, Inc., 1966-75, asst. pub., 1975-78; pub. Ariz. Republic and Phoenix Gazette, 1978-80, pub. emeritus, 1980—. Profl. musician, 1929-35. Chmn. Ariz. Dept. Econ. Planning and Devel. Bd., 1968-71; bd. dirs., v.p. Goodwill Industries Central Ariz., 1978-84, v.p., 1982-83; bd. dirs. Western Newspaper Found., 1974-81; trustee Desert Found., Scottsdale, 1982-85; mem. Nat. Def. Exec. Res., 1964-80. Mem. A.P. Mng. Editors Assn. (dir. 1956-63, pres. 1963), A.P. Assn. Calif., Ariz., Hawaii and Nev. (pres. 1976-77), Ariz. Acad. (dir. 1973-81, v.p. 1980-81), Valley Forward Assn. (dir. 1970-87), Newcomen Soc., Phoenix 40, Sigma Delta Chi. Episcopalian. Clubs: University, Arizona. Home: 4102 N 64th Pl Scottsdale AZ 85251-3110

WALSH, MICHAEL FRANCIS, education consultant, marketing research executive; b. Bell Harbor, N.Y., Dec. 5, 1947; s. Michael Francis and Patricia (Bratz) W.; m. Julia Ann Finn, Apr. 17, 1983; 1 child, Kelly Michelle . Student, U. Tex., Arlington, 1966-67, Coll. San Mateo, 1967-69; BA in Psychology, U. Calif., Santa Barbara, 1971; MS in Psychology, U. Wis., 1976. Cert. instr. community colls., Calif. Instr. Berlitz Sprachenschule, Munich, 1971-72; research asst. U. Wis., Madison, 1972-75; project dir. Ednl. Testing Service, Berkeley, Calif., 1976-82, dir. representation of western states, 1980-82; founder, pres. Walsh and Assocs., El Sobrante, Calif., 1982—; mem. adv. bd. Internat. Trade Inst., Berkeley, 1983-88, chmn. funding com., 1986-88; cons. World Bank. Editor, contbg. author: Handbook for Proficiency Assessment, 1979; author: (state agy. reports) Evaluation of Artists in Social Institutions for California Arts Council, 1981, Evaluation of Creative Arts Computer Course, 1985, Humanists-in-Schools: Eight Years Later, 1986 (Joint Dissemination and Rev. Panel Nat. Dissemination Program award 1986), Conversations with Teacher Leaders: Their Reflections on Leadership, Equity, Mathematics Instruction, and other Topics, 1989, Feasibility Study of Assessment Approaches for Credentialing School Administrators in California, 1990, Teacher Leadership Development in Mathematics: An Evaluation of the California Mathematics Leadership Program, 1992, Evaluation of a Regional Partnership Training and Internship Program for School-site Counseling Teams, 1992. Commr. Richmond (Calif.) Arts Commn., 1988-91; rep. Sch. Site Council, Valley View Sch., El Sobrante, Calif. Pres.'s Research grantee U. Calif., 1970. Mem. Am. Mktg. Assn. (exec.), Am. Coun. Arts, Am. Ednl. Rsch. Assn., Am. Evaluation Assn., Nat. Coun. Measurement Edn. Democrat. Roman Catholic. Office: Walsh & Assocs 3817 San Pablo Dam Rd Ste 127 El Sobrante CA 94803-2803

WALSH, MICHAEL PATRICK, securities analyst; b. N.Y.C., Dec. 3, 1961; s. John Francis and Anne Theresa (Murtha) W. AB, Harvard Coll., 1983; MBA, Harvard U., 1987. Fin. analyst Drexel Burnham Lambert Inc., N.Y.C., 1983-85; dir. corp. devel. Dionex Corp., Sunnyvale, Calif., 1987-90; pres. Biotech Bus. Devel., San Francisco, 1990-91; v.p. Robertson, Stephens & Co., San Francisco, 1991—. Mem. Commonwealth Club Calif., Harvard Club San Francisco. Office: Robertson Stephens & Co 5555 California St San Francisco CA 94104

WALSH, ROBERT ANTHONY, lawyer; b. Boston, Aug. 26, 1938; s. Frank and Emily Angelica (Bissitt) W.; m. Angela Rosalie Barile, Aug. 3, 1966; children: Maria, Robert II, Amy. SB, MIT, 1960; MS, Fla. Inst. Tech., 1967; JD, Suffolk U., 1971. Bar: Mass. 1971, Ill. 1976, U.S. Dist. Ct. Mass. 1972, U.S. Patent Office 1972, Can. Patent Office 1973, U.S. Supreme Ct. 1976, U.S. Ct. Appeals (Fed. cir.) 1982, U.S. Ct. Mil. Appeals 1983; registered profl. engr., Mass. Engr. Saturn Boeing, Michaud, La., 1964-65; program analyst RCA, Cape Canaveral, Fla., 1965-68; patent trainee, engr. Avco Research Lab., Everett, Mass., 1968-72; patent atty. GTE Labs., Waltham, Mass., 1972-73; group patent counsel Bell & Howell Co., Chgo., 1973-78; patent counsel ITT E. Coast Patents, Nutley, N.J., 1978-80, patent counsel internat., 1980-82, sr. patent counsel internat., 1982-86; dir. internat. patents ITT Corp., N.Y.C., 1986-87; gen. patent counsel ITT Def. Tech. Corp., Nutley, 1987-89; chief patent counsel Allied-Signal Aerospace Co., Phoenix, 1989—; ednl. counselor admissions MIT, No. N.J., 1978-89, Ariz., 1989—; with Office of Judge Adv. Gen., Washington. Col. USAR, 1960-92. Mem. ABA (co-chmn. subcom. PTC sect. 105), Tri-State USAFR Lawyers Assn. (meritorious achievement award 1980), Internat. Patent Club (pres. 1988-89), Am. Intellectual Property Law Assn., Aerospace Industry Assn. (chmn. Intellectual Property com.), Chgo. Patent Law Assn. (chmn. intellectual property com.), N.J. Patent Law Assn., KC Coun. (fin. sec. 1993—), Sigma Xi. Roman Catholic. Lodge: K.C. (fin. sec. coun. 11007 Scottsdale, Ariz.). Home: 5716 N Monte Vista Dr Paradise Vly AZ 85253-5921 Office: Allied Signal Aerospace Co Patent Dept 111 S 34th St Phoenix AZ 85034-2892

WALSH, ROBERTA ANNETTE, conservation biologist; b. Bellingham, Wash., Dec. 11, 1938; d. Robert Davis and Freida Caroline (Hirschkorn) Blake; m. James Anthony Walsh, Sept. 17, 1957; children: Jennifer Margaret, Robert Adam. Student, Stanford U., 1956-57; BS, U. Wash., 1960; post-grad., Iowa State U., 1968-70; MS, U. Mont., 1992. Sr. ptnr. Evaluation Rsch. Assocs., Missoula, Mont., 1964—; cons. Casey Family Program, Seattle, 1981-88, Gov.'s Office of Budget and Program Planning, Helena, Mont., 1980-81. Co-author: Quality Care for Tough Kids, 1990; contbr. articles to profl. jours. Scholar Nat. Merit Scholarship Corp., 1956-60. Mem. Soc. Conservation Biology, Sigma Xi (nat. sci. hon.). Democrat. Home: 2340 55th St # 15 Missoula MT 59803 Office: Evaluation Rsch Assocs 2340 55th St # 15 Missoula MT 59803

WALSH, TIMOTHY JOHN, geologist; b. L.A., Aug. 9, 1952; s. Edward Francis and Lenore (Beerli) W.; m. Pamela Jeanne Shaffer, Sept. 10, 1977; children: Maureen Elizabeth, Brigid Eileen. BS, UCLA, 1976, MS, 1979. Staff geologist Dept. Natural Resources, Divsn. Geology and Earth Resources, Olympia, Wash., 1980-88; chief geologist, environ. sect. Dept. Natural Resources, Divsn. Geology and Earth Resources, 1988—. Contbr. numerous articles to profl. jours. Recipient Honor by Resolution, Wash. State Ho. of Reps., 1988, Disting. Lectr., N.W. Petroleum Assn., 1990. Mem. Am. Geophysical Union (sec. Pacific N.W. Br. 1986-87, pres. 1987-88), Am. Assn. Petroleum Geologists, Soc. Econ. Paleontologists and Mineralogists (Pacific sect.). Office: Wash Dept Natural Resources PO Box 47007 Olympia WA 98504-7007

WALSH, WILLIAM, football coach; b. Los Angeles, Nov. 30, 1931. Student, San Mateo Jr. Coll.; BA, San Jose State U., 1954, MA in Edn., 1959. Asst. coach Monterey Peninsula Coll., 1955, San Jose State U., 1956; head coach Washington Union High Sch., Fremont, Calif., 1957-59; asst. coach U. Calif., Berkeley, 1960-62, Stanford U., 1963-65, Oakland Raiders, Am. Football League, 1966-67, Cin. Bengals, 1968-75, San Diego Chargers, Nat. Football League, 1976; head coach Stanford U., 1977-78; head coach, gen. mgr. San Francisco 49ers, NFL, 1979-89, exec. v.p., 1989; broadcaster NBC Sports, 1989-91; head coach Stanford U., 1992—. Named NFL Coach of Yr., Sporting News, 1981; coached Stanford U. winning team Sun Bowl, 1977, Bluebonnet Bowl, 1978, Blockbuster Bowl, 1993, San Francisco 49ers to Super Bowl championships, 1981, 84, 88; elected to Pro Football Hall of Fame, 1993. Office: Stanford U Gary Migdol Sports Info Office Dept Athletics Stanford CA 94305-1684

WALSKE, M(AX) CARL, JR., physicist; b. Seattle, June 2, 1922; s. Max Carl and Margaret Ella (Fowler) W.; m. Elsa Marjorie Nelson, Dec. 28, 1946; children: C. Susan, Steven C., Carol A. B.S. in Math. cum laude, U. Wash., 1944; Ph.D. in Theoretical Physics, Cornell U., 1951. Staff mem., then asst. theoretical div. leader Los Alamos Sci. Lab., 1951-56; dep. research dir. Atomics Internat., Canoga Park, Calif., 1956-59; sci. rep. AEC in U.K., London, Eng., 1961-62; theoretical physicist RAND Corp., 1962-63; sci. attache U.S. missions to NATO and OECD, Paris, France, 1963-65; staff mem. Los Alamos Sci. Lab., 1965-66; asst. to sec. def. (atomic energy), 1966-73; pres., chief operating officer Atomic Indsl. Forum, Inc., Washington, 1973-87; Chmn. Dept. Def. Mil. Liason Com. to U.S. AEC, 1966-73; Mem. U.S. del. Conf. Suspension Nuclear Tests, Geneva, Switzerland, 1959-61. Served to lt. (j.g.) USNR, 1943-46. Recipient Disting. Civilian Service medal Dept. Def. Fellow Explorers Club, Am. Phys. Soc.; mem. Am. Nuclear Soc., U.S. Power Squadrons, Poulsbo Yacht Club, Phi Beta Kappa, Sigma Xi. Home: PO Box 370 Silverdale WA 98383-0370

WALSMITH, CHARLES RODGER, psychologist, educator; b. Denver, May 19, 1926; s. Joseph Francis and Florence Ophelia (Brown-Smith) W.; children: Karen Frances, Cynthia Ann, Erik Konrad. BA (Chancellor's Ednl. scholar), U. Denver, 1956, MA, 1962; postgrad. U. Wash., 1986-76; PhD, Stanton U., 1976. Rsch. psychologist Personnel Tng. and Rsch. Ctr., Maintenance Lab., USAF Lowery AFB, Denver, 1956; rsch. asst. U. Colo. Med. Ctr., Denver, 1956-57, rsch. assoc., 1957-64; assoc. prof. psychology North Park Coll., Chgo., 1965-66; sr. human enging. analyst, psychoacoustics Boeing Co., Seattle, 1965-68; instr. psychology dept. behavioral scis. Bellevue (Wash.) Community Coll., 1968-87, chmn. dept., 1968-75, 79-82, Phi Theta Kappa adviser, 1981-87, instr., chmn. dept. emeritus, 1987—. Resident trainer Gestalt Inst. of Can., Lake Cowichan, B.C., summers 1969-71, assoc., 1969—; dir. Gestalt Inst. of Wash., Bellevue, 1970—. Dem. precinct chmn., Renton, Wash., 1966-68. With USNR, 1944-46. Mem. NEA, Phi Beta Kappa, Psi Chi. Home: Gestalt House 14909 SE 44th Pl Bellevue WA 98006-2421

WALSTON, RICK LYLE JOSH, educator, clergyman; b. Longview, Wash., Sept. 3, 1954; s. Lyle Basil and Harriet Marion (Salhus) W.; m. Susan Elizabeth Insel, Oct. 29, 1988. AS in Practical Theology, Christ for the Nations Inst., 1980; BA, Warner Pacific Coll., 1982, MREL magna cum laude, 1987; STD summa cum laude, Bethany Theol. Sem., 1988; PhD, Greenwich U., 1991. Ordained minster. Assoc. pastor Christian Life Ctr. Assemblies of God Ch., Longview, 1977-82; tchr., registrar Berean Coll. Extension Sch., Longview, 1980-82; sr. pastor Praise Song Assemblies of God Ch., Longview, 1982-86; registrars asst. Warner Pacific Coll., Portland, Oreg., 1986-87; sr. pastor Home Fellowship Assembly Ch., Longview, 1988; ednl. cons., owner Coll. Degree Cons. Svcs., Longview, 1989-92; sr. pastor Christian Assembly, Longview, 1992—; pres. Faraston Theol. Sem., Longview, 1990—; co-founder Clackamas (Oreg.) Bible Inst., Clackamas Christian Ctr., 1987; co-dir. edn. dept. Kelso (Wash.) First Assembly of God Ch., 1989-92. Author: Divorce and Remarriage, 1991, (with John Bear) Walston & Bear's Guide to Earning Religious Degrees Non-Traditionally, 1993; contbr. articles to profl. jours. Coord. religious events Christian Life Ministerial Assn., Longview, 1979-82; retirement home minister Praise Song Assembly of God Ch., 1982-86, hosp. minister, 1982-86. Recipient Cert. of Recognition, Christ for the Nations Inst., 1980, Full Gospel Fellowship Internat., 1980. Fellow Faraston Theol. Rsch. Fellowship (pres. 1990-92, Rsch. Fellow of Yr. 1990); mem. Oreg. Assn. for Psychol. Type, Evang. Theol. Soc., Evang. Philos. Soc., Assn. Christian Continuing Edn. Schs. and Sems. Republican. Office: Faraston Theol Sem PO Box 847 Longview WA 98632-7521

WALSTON, RODERICK EUGENE, attorney general; b. Gooding, Idaho, Dec. 15, 1935; s. Loren R. and Iva M. (Boyer) W.; m. Margaret D. Grandey; children: Gregory Scott W., Valerie Lynne W. A.A., Boise Jr. Coll., 1956; B.A. cum laude, Columbia Coll., 1958; LL.B. scholar, Stanford U., 1961. Bar: Calif. 1961, U.S. Supreme Ct. 1973. Law clk to judge U.S. Ct. Appeals 9th Cir., 1961-62; dep. atty. gen State of Calif., San Francisco, 1963-91, head natural resources sect, 1969-91, chief asst. atty. gen. pub. rights div., 1991—; spl. dep counsel Kings County, Calif., 1975-76; mem. environ. and natural resources adv. coun. Stanford (Calif.) Law Sch. Contbr. articles to profl. jours.; bd. editors: Stanford Law Rev., 1959-61, Western Natural Resources Litigation Digest, Calif. Water Law and Policy Reporter; spl. editor Jour. of the West. Co-chmn. Idaho campaign against Right-to-Work initiative, 1958; Calif. rep. Western States Water Coun., 1986—; environ. and natural resources adv. coun., Stanford Law Sch. Nat. Essay Contest winner Nat. Assn. Internat. Rels. Clubs, 1956, Stanford Law Rev. prize, 1961; Astor Found. scholar, 1956-58. Mem. ABA (chmn. water resources com., 1988-90, vice chmn. and conf. chmn., 1985-88, 90—), Contra Costa County Bar Assn., U.S. Supreme Ct. Hist. Soc., World Affairs Coun. No. Calif. Office: Calif Atty Gen's Office 1515 K St Fl 6 Sacramento CA 95814-4089

WALTER, BERT MATHEW, federal mediation commissioner; b. Devils Lake, N.D., July 11, 1915; s. Alois and Margaret (Bauer) W.; m. Phyllis Traynor, July 3, 1950. AA, U. Minn., 1936; BBA, U. Balt., 1938. Shop employee GE Co., Pittsfield, Mass., 1938-41; dir. indsl. relations Consol. Vultee Aircraft Co., Tucson, 1941-49, Bendix Aviation Corp., Kansas City, Mo., 1949-55; v.p. indsl. relations Clark Equipment Co., Buchanan, Mich., 1955-64, Chesebrough Pond's, N.Y.C., 1964-66; pres. Leasing Internat. Corp., Madrid, 1966-68; commr. Fed. Mediation and Conciliation Svc., L.A., 1968—; pres. Buchannan (Mich.) United Funds, 1956-57. Contbr. articles to profl. publs. Mem. Conseil Internat. Orgn. Scientifique (bd. dirs. 1967), Coun. Internat. Progress Mgmt. (bd. dirs. 1967), Nat. Metal Trades Assn. (pres. 1962-63), Soc. Human Resource Mgmt. (founder, chmn. 1958-59), Indssl. Rels. Rsch. Assn., Soc. Profls. in Dispute Resolution, Rotary (pres. Niles, Mich. 1959), Elks. Republican. Roman Catholic. Home: 2598 Ayala Dr 92 Rialto CA 92376-8819

WALTER, BRUCE ALEXANDER, physician; b. Seattle, Apr. 15, 1922; s. Ernest R. and Marion (Alexander) W.; BA, U. Wash., 1944, BS, 1948, MD, 1951; MPH, UCLA, 1962; m. Gloria Helen Parry, Feb. 4, 1956; children: Maia Marion, Wendy Diane, Shelley Kathleen, Allison Ann. Cert. Am. Bd. Preventative Medicine. Intern Los Angeles County Gen. Hosp., 1951-52; resident internal medicine Wadsworth Hosp., U. Calif., 1952-54; dir. grad. program hosp., health facilities adminstrn. UCLA, 1965-68; attending staff Salt Lake County Hosp., 1954-55; fellow medicine U. Utah, 1954-55; fellow medicine U. So. Calif., 1955-56, mem. faculty, 1956-65; attending staff Los Angeles County Hosp., 1956-65; physician internal medicine, Palm Springs, Calif., 1956-61; chief staff Desert Hosp., 1960-61; dir. med. care studies Calif. Dept. Pub. Health, Berkeley, 1962-65; dir. Med. Care Services, State of Utah, 1969-71, dep. dir. health, 1971-79, acting dir. health, 1979; cons. Newport Med. Group and Advanced Health Systems, Inc., Newport Beach, Calif., 1979-84; practice medicine specializing in internal medicine, Costa Mesa, Calif., 1984—; asst. prof. community and family medicine U. Utah Sch. Medicine, Salt Lake City, 1969-79; mem. Utah State Bd. Aging; bd. dirs. South Coast Inst. Applied Gerontology, Blue Shield of Utah, Utah Profl. Standards Rev. Orgn. 1st lt. Signal Corps, AUS, 1943-46. Fellow Am. Coll. Preventative Medicine; mem. Am. Coll. Hosp. Health Administrs., Nat. Assn. Health Facility Licensing and Certification Dirs. (pres. 1975-76), Alpha Delta Phi, Alpha Kappa Kappa, Alpha Delta Sigma. Home: 2821 Blue Water Ln Corona Del Mar CA 92625-1304

WALTER, FREDERICK JOHN, motel executive; b. East Orange, N.J., Jan. 26, 1944; s. Fred Gottlieb and Emily (Mast) W.; m. Jane Elizabeth Schackner, Aug. 20, 1966; children: Emily Jane, Meredith Waite. BA, N.C. State U., 1966; MBA, Ga. State U., 1968. Exec. Intercontinental Diversified Corp., Freeport, Bahamas, 1969-76; mng. ptnr. Best Western-Nellis Motor Inn, Las Vegas, Nev., 1977-87, Best Western-Lake Mead Motel, Henderson, Nev., 1984-87, Best Western-McCarran Inn, Las Vegas, 1986—; hotel-motel cons., sales rep. Helen Naugle & Assocs., Las Vegas, 1982—; regional gov. Best Western Internat., Inc., Phoenix, 1977-91, bd. dirs., 1991—. Bd. dirs. Boys and Girls Clubs, Las Vegas, 1982—, Las Vegas Conv. and Visitors Authority, 1988-91; chmn. Taxicab Authority of Nev., 1989-93, So. Nev. Civilian Mil. Coun., Las Vegas, 1983—. With USMC, 1963-65. Mem. Nev. Hotel and Motel Assn. (bd. dirs., pres. 1981—), Greater Las Vegas C. of C. (bd. dirs. 1990-91), Am. Hotel and Motel Assn. (cert. hotel adminstr.), Air Force Assn., Rotary. Lutheran. Office: Best Western McCarran Inn 4970 Paradise Rd Las Vegas NV 89119-1206

WALTER, JAMES LLOYD, hotel manager; b. Compton, Calif., Aug. 11, 1946; s. Lew Cauffer and Nyla Arleen (Childers) W.; m. Karen Jungk, Aug. 8, 1969 (div. May 1976). BA, Ctrl. Wash. U., 1969; M in Internat. Mgmt., Am. Grad. Sch. for Mgmt., 1970. Tribunal adminstr. Am. Arbitration Assn., Phoenix, 1970-78; v.p., adminstr. Unity House Inc., Honolulu, 1978-89; pres., treas., gen. mgr. Waikiki Marina Hotel, Honolulu, 1981-89; v.p., gen. mgr. Pk. Plz. Waikiki Hotel, Honolulu, 1989—; bd. dirs. Unity House, Inc., Honolulu. Exec. com. mem. Hawaii Conv. Pk. Coun., Honolulu, 1990—; mem. Hawaii Visitors Bur., 1987, Waikiki-Oahu Visitors Orgn., 1990. Mem. Am. Arbitration Assn. (tribunal adminstr. 1970-78, arbitrator 1988—), Japan-Am. Soc., Hawaii Pacific Cinema Found. (sec. 1982—), Hawaii Hotel Assn., Honolulu C. of C. Office: Pk Plz Waikiki Hotel 1956 Ala Moana Blvd Honolulu HI 96815-1897

WALTER, MICHAEL CHARLES, lawyer; b. Oklahoma City, Nov. 25, 1956; s. Donald Wayne and Viola Helen (Heffelfinger) W. BA in Polit. Sci., BJ, U. Wash., 1980; JD, Univ. Puget Sound, 1983. Bar: Wash. 1985, U.S. Dist. Ct. (9th cir. 1985). Shareholder Keating, Bucklin & McCormack, Seattle, 1985—; instr. Bellevue (Wash.) C.C., 1983—. Mem. ABA, ACLU, Internat. Assn. Bus. Communicators, Wash. State Bar Assn., Reporters Com. for Freedom of Press, Seattle-King County Bar Assn., Wash. Assn. Def. Counsel, Seattle Claims Adjustors Assn., Wash. Assn. Mcpl. Attys. Home: 256 NE 43d St Seattle WA 98105 Office: Keating Bucklin & McCormack 4141 SeaFirst 5th Ave Pla Seattle WA 98104

WALTER-ROBINSON, CAROL SUE, investment executive; b. Joliet, Ill., Dec. 24, 1942; d. Loren John Sr. and Myrtle F. (Sistler) Walter; m. Patrick

Allen Robinson, Apr. 17, 1991; adopted children: Teresa, Christopher, Ellen, Melissa, Catrina, Elizabeth, Sherlene. Student, Waubonsee Jr. Coll., Aurora, Ill., 1963-65, Aurora Coll., 1967-71, Hypnosis Motivation Inst., 1992, U. Metaphysics, 1992. Lic.. cosmetologist, paralegal; cert. hypnotherapist. Office mgr., bookkeeper Edward M. Kyser Appraiser, Aurora, 1961-66; legal sec., aide Hon. Paul Schnake, Aurora, 1961-66; pers. mgr. H.W. Gossard Co., Batavia, Ill., 1966-68; pers. recruiter Dresser Industries, Franklin Park, Ill., 1968-71; exec. sec., pres. Am. Picture Co., Anaheim, Calif., 1972-75; contract mgr. Mobile Oil Corp., Soi Divsn., Orange County, Calif., 1975-81; owner Inland Tele-Sec., Riverside, Calif., 1982-84; pvt. practice investment mgr. Riverside, 1984—; sec. Legal Sec.-Fox Valley, Aurora, 1964-66. Author: Capital Punishment—Pro and Con, 1970; editor (newsletter) Humane News, 1964-68. Pres./founder The Fosterkids Alliance, Riverside, 1988-91; exec. sec. Fox Valley Animal Welfare, Aurora, 1963-68; historian Am. Cancer Soc., Aurora, 1964; exec. sec. pub. rels. Humane Soc. U.S., Garden Grove, Calif., 1972; community liaison El Centro Hispano Americano, Aurora, 1970; coord. No. Ill. Pers. Assn., Chgo., 1966-68; com. chair-advisor Employee Personnel Testing, Melrose Park, Ill., 1965; arbitration moderator I.G.W.U., Chgo., 1969. Democrat. Unity. Home: 845 Spruce St Riverside CA 92507 Office: TFA PO Box 52092 Riverside CA 92517-3092

WALTERS, ERIC, real estate advisor; b. London, United Kingdom, Feb. 4, 1937; came to U.S., 1980; s. Sidney S. and Marie W.; m. Shirley Simove, June 30, 1963; children: Michelle, Tina, Mark. Student, U. Reading, 1958. Prin. Eric Walters & Co., Cardiff, United Kingdom, 1960-70; project mgr./devel. dir./asst. gen. mgr. devel. group The Hong Kong Land Co. Ltd., Hong Kong, 1970-80; pres. Heron Properties Inc., Phoenix, 1980-85, Inland Village Realty, Phoenix, 1985—; mgr. U.S. Behco Investments N V, Phoenix, 1989, Driffield Corp. N V, Phoenix, 1989. Fellow Royal Inst. Chartered Surveyors; mem. Internat. Real Estate Fedn, Urban Land Inst. Office: Inland Village Realty 7313 E Valley Vista Dr Scottsdale AZ 85253

WALTERS, JESSE RAYMOND, JR., judge; b. Rexburg, Idaho, Dec. 26, 1938; s. Jesse Raymond and Thelma Rachael (Hodgson) W.; m. Harriet Payne, May 11, 1959; children—Craig T., Robyn, J. Scott. Student Ricks Coll., 1957-58; B.A. in Polit. Sci., U. Idaho, 1961, J.D., 1963; postgrad. U. Washington, 1962; LLM U. Va., 1990. Bar: Idaho 1963, U.S. Dist. Ct. Idaho 1964, U.S. Ct. Appeals (9th cir.) 1970. Law clk. to chief justice Idaho Supreme Ct., 1963-64; sole practice, Boise, Idaho, 1964-77; atty. Idaho senate, Boise, 1965; dist. judge 4th Jud. Dist., Idaho, Boise, 1977-82, adminstrv. dist. judge, 1981-82; chief judge Idaho Ct. Appeals, Boise, 1982—; chmn. magistrate's commn. 4th jud. dist.; chmn. Supreme Ct. mem. services; chmn. Criminal Pattern Jury Instrn. Com.; mem. Civil Pattern Jury Instrn. Com; Republican committeeman, Boise, 1975-77; mem. Ada County Rep. Central Com., 1975-77. Mem. Idaho Bar Assn. (bankruptcy com.), Idaho Adminstrv. Judges Assn., ABA, Am. Judicature Soc., Assn. Trial Lawyers Am. Idaho Trial Lawyers Assn., Council Chief Judges Ct. Appeals, Boise Estate Planning Council, Jaycees (nat. dir. 1969-70, pres. Boise chpt. 1966-67). Mormon. Lodges: Lions, Elks, Eagles. Office: State Idaho Ct Appeals 537 W Bannock St Boise ID 83720-0001

WALTERS, LINDA JANE, marine biologist, researcher; b. Easton, Pa., Aug. 2, 1961; d. Lee Rudyard and Evelyn (Hood) W.; m. Paul Eric Sacks, Aug. 1, 1992. BS, Bates Coll., 1983; MS, U. S.C., 1986, PhD, 1991. Technician Bristol Shellfish Farms, Walpole, Maine, 1983; project leader Operation Raleigh, Chile, Australia, N.Z., Alaska, 1985-87; rschr. U. Hawaii-Manoa, Honolulu, 1992—; judge various sci. fairs, S.C. and Hawaii, 1990—. Contbr. articles to profl. jours. Sci. by mail scientist Boston Mus. Sci., 1988-91; adult literacy tutor, Honolulu, 1992—. NATO fellow NSF, 1991, Fulbright Indo-Am. fellow, 1993; recipient Lerner-Gray award Am. Mus. Natural History, 1986, 90. Mem. AAUW (America fellowship 1990-91), Assn. for Women in Sci. (mentor 1992—), Am. Soc. Zoologists, Ecol. Soc. Am., Internat. Bryozoan Assn., Western Soc. Naturalists, Sigma Xi (outstanding grad. award 1992). Office: U Hawaii Kewalo Marine Lab 41 Ahui St Honolulu HI 98613

WALTERS, RAYMOND L., private investigator, association executive; b. Highland Park, Mich., June 6, 1943; s. Raymond E. and Peggy J. W.; m. Linda L. Hochwalt, Jan. 29, 1964; children: Amy L., Wendy L., Heather L., Summer L. BS, Mich. State U., 1970, MS, 1977; EdS, Temple U., 1986. Lic. pvt. investigator, Mont. Instr. Lansing Community Coll., East Lansing, Mich., 1973-74; supr. jail tng. Mich. Dept. Corrections, East Lansing, 1972-74; prison warden Detroit House Corrections, Plymouth, Mich., 1974; supr. advanced police tng. Mich. State Police, East Lansing, 1974-77; asst. prof. West Chester (Pa.) State U., 1977-82; assoc. prof. Coll. Gt. Falls, Mont., 1982-86; instr. Park Coll., Gt. Falls, 1988—; pres. Mont. Security Works/Walters' Investigative Svcs., Gt. Falls, 1986—, USA-Korean Karate Assn., Gt. Falls, 1981—; owner Jade Dragon Martial Arts Acad., Gt. Falls, 1988—; pub. info. officer Cascade County Sheriff Dept., Gt. Falls, 1989—. Contbr. articles to edn. and martial arts publs. Bd. dirs. Pre-Release Ctr., Gt. Falls, 1983-84, Demolay Youth Ctr., Gt. Falls, 1985. With USNR, 1961-65. Recipient Spl. award Am. Soc. Tng. and Devel., 1973; named Outstanding Instr. Martial Arts Hall of Fame, 1989. Mem. Mont. Assn. Pvt. Investigators, Mont. Assn. Law Enforcement Profls. (pres. 1983-84). Democrat. Office: USA Korean Karate Assn PO Box 1401 Great Falls MT 59403-1401

WALTERS, RONALD ARLEN, research biological scientist; b. Greeley, Colo., Apr. 25, 1940; s. Reuben and Esther Marie (Anderson) W.; m. Geraldine Jane Huck, 1969; children: Christian Grant, Colin Jeremy. BS with high distinction, Colo. State U., 1962, MS, 1964, PhD, 1967. Engr. GE, Richland, Wash., 1962-63; staff mem. U. Calif.-Los Alamos Nat. Lab., 1967-93, group leader for genetics, 1980-84, asst. to assoc. dir., 1984-88, program dir. biol. and environ. rsch., 1988-92; dir. lab. quality and policy office Batelle Pacific N.W. Lab., Richland, Wash., 1992-93; mgr. life sci. ctr. Batelle Pacific N.W. Lab., Richland, 1993—; mem. NRC-NAS, Washington, 1987-88; bd. dirs. John K. Frost Ctr., Johns Hopkins U., 1990—. Contbr. over 100 articles to sci. jours., chpts. to books. Mem. exec. com. Boy Scouts Am., Los Alamos, 1984-89; pres. United Ch., Los Alamos, 1989, Boosters of Naval Jr. ROTC, Los Alamos, 1990. Recipient Disting. Performance award Los Alamos Nat. Lab., 1981, Outstanding Young Scientist GE Co., 1963; fellow USPHS, 1963-65, Assoc. Western Univs., 1965-67. Fellow AAAS, Am. Soc. Biochemistry and Molecular Biology; mem. Biophys. Soc., Radiation Rsch. Soc., Am. Chem. Soc., Sigma Xi, Phi Kappa Phi, Kappa Mu Epsilon, Beta Beta Beta. Republican. Presbyterian. Home: # G141 2455 George Washington Way Richland WA 99352 Office: Battelle Pacific N W Labs KI-50 PO Box 999 Richland WA 99352

WALTERS, STACEY ANN, reporter; b. Spokane, Wash., Nov. 11, 1957; d. Robert James and Roberta Joyce (Woods) W. Student, Univ. Coll., Cardiff, Gt. Britain, 1978-79; BA, Wash. State U., 1980. Intern BBC, 1978-79; anchor, writer and reporter KWSU-TV, Pullman, Wash., 1979-80; fl. dir. KING-TV, Seattle, 1980-81, assoc. producer, 1981-83; anchor, producer, reporter KCPQ-TV, Tacoma, Seattle, 1983-86; reporter KCRA-TV, Sacramento, 1986-87, KXTV-TV, Sacramento, 1988—. Grantee Haas Found. 1978. Mem. Phi Beta Kappa.

WALTERS, SYLVIA SOLOCHEK, art educator; b. Milw., Aug. 24, 1938; d. Bernard and Becky (Perlstein) Solochek; m. James H. Walters, Aug. 26, 1963. BS, U. Wis., 1960, MS, 1961, MFA, 1962. Prof. painting Keuka (N.Y.) Coll., 1962-63; prof. printmaking Layton Sch. of Art, Milw., 1963-64; book designer U. Wis. Press, Madison, 1964-67; prof. art St. Louis U., 1968-69; prof. art, art dept. chair, gallery dir. U. Mo., St. Louis, 1969-84; prof., art dept. chair San Francisco State U., 1984—. Bd. dirs. Art Coordinating Coun. for the Area, St. Louis, 1976-79, Bay Area Consortium for the Visual Arts, San Francisco, 1984-91, Calif. Printmakers Soc., no. Calif., 1985-86, 1989—; mem. nat. bd. Women's Caucus Art, 1978-80. Office: San Francisco State U Art Dept 1600 Holloway Ave San Francisco CA 94132-1722

WALTERS, TIMOTHY CARL, telecommunications executive; b. Independence, Mo., Sept. 27, 1955; s. Samuel R. and Marian (Mullins) W.; m. Beth E. Greene, Apr. 4, 1981; children: Jeffrey K., Courtney L. BS in Pub. Adminstrn. magna cum laude, U. MO., 1976; MBA in Strategic Planning Systems, U. Pa., 1980. Researcher, field worker King for U.S. Congress campaign, Independence, 1976; ops. supr. Roadway Express, Kansas City, Mo., 1976-78; mgr. mktg. and sales Assoc. Truck Lines, Grand Rapids, Mich., 1980-82; sr. planning analyst ANR Freight System, Detroit, 1982-85; dir. mktg., fin. and planning ANR Freight System, Denver, 1985-90, dir. corp. logistics, 1990-92; mgr. mktg. U.S. West, Inc., Denver, 1992—. Author: Market-Oriented Strategic Management for Motor Carriers (Best in the Industry award, Regulated Common Carrier Conf. 1985). Precinct com. capt. Rep. Party, Jefferson County, Colo., 1986-90; chmn. Jefferson Community Action Com., 1984-85. Mem. Southwest Jefferson County Rep. Club, Beta Gamma Sigma, Omicron Delta Kappa. Home: 9104 W Prentice Ave Littleton CO 80123-2137 Office: US West Enhanced Svcs Inc 1999 Broadway 10th Fl Denver CO 80202

WALTHALL, DANIEL EUGENE, nurse, retired air force officer; b. Provo, Utah, Jan. 14, 1956; s. Glen Arthur and Rosalie June (Guild) W.; m. Donna Naomi Furukawa, Nov. 12, 1977; 1 child, Kimiko Akiko June. Student, Southwestern Coll., Chula Vista, Calif., 1974-75, C.C. Air Force, Montgomery, Ga., 1976-90, U. Md., Balt., 1990; AA in nursing mgmt., CC Air Force, 1992. RN. Enlisted USAF, 1978, advanced through grades master sgt., 1992, ret., 1992; staff technician, then adminstrv. asst. to chief nurse Keesler Med. Ctr., Biloxi, Miss., 1979-82; instr. Combat Casualty Care Course, San Antonio, 1982-85; asst. noncommd. officer-in-charge orthopedic unit USAF Acad. Hosp., Colorado Springs, Colo., 1985-86, noncommd. officer-in-charge nursing staff devel., 1986-89; ind. duty med. technician 6717th Air Base Squadron, Kwang Ju, Republic of Korea, 1989-90; noncommd. officer-in-charge nursing staff devel. 22d Med. Group, March AFB, Calif., 1990-91, supt. hosp. svcs., 1992; ctr. mgr. M.D. Labs., San Diego, 1992—. Counselor Boy Scouts Am., Biloxi, 1980-81; pres. Sunday sch. LDS Ch., Colorado Springs, 1987-89; pres. March Hosp. Booster Club, 1991. Named Noncommd. Officer of Quarter, USAF Acad. Hosp., 1985, Noncommd. Officer of Yr., 1988; Mil. Mem. of Yr., Colorado Springs C. of C., 1989. Mem. Non Commd. Officers Assn., Air Force Sgts. Assn. (pres. Colorado Springs 1986-87, Mem. of Yr. award 1987). Republican. Home: 11525 Kiwi Ct Moreno Valley CA 92557

WALTI, RANDAL FRED, management consultant; b. Chgo., Apr. 10, 1939; s. Fred Henry and Alice Ann (Steger) W.; m. Judith Ann Hodson, Jan. 31, 1960; children: Lee, Rod, Lynn. BSME, Purdue U., 1961. Program mgr. Aerojet Gen., El Monte, Calif., 1961-66; applications mgr. TRW Systems, Redondo Beach, Calif., 1966-70; br. mgr. A.B. Dick Co., Long Beach, Calif., 1970-71; pres. Randal Data Systems, Inc., Torrance, Calif., 1971-79, The Oaktree Consulting Group, Torrance, Calif., 1980—; founder, bd. dirs. Software Coun. So. Calif., Torrance; bd. dirs. Silver Cloud Travel, Inc., Torrance; chmn. The Exec. Com., La Jolla, Calif., 1986-88. Chmn. So. Calif. Leadership Coun., Christian Businessmen's Com., Santa Ana, Calif., 1991-92. Republican. Mem. Covenant Ch. Home: 1806 Mount Shasta San Pedro CA 90732 Office: Oaktree Consulting Group 21041 Western Ave #160 Torrance CA 90501

WALTNER, RICHARD HEGE, sociology educator; b. Freeman, S.D., July 27, 1931; s. Richard L. and Hilda M. (Hege) W.; m. Bonnie Fay Leisy, July 11, 1954; children: Richard L., Scott W. BA, U. S.D., 1956, MA, 1957; PhD, U. Utah, 1979. Faculty sociology Freeman (S.D.) Jr. Coll., 1957-65; prof. sociology Ea. Mont. Coll., Billings, 1965—; marital therapist in pvt. practice, Billings, 1970-76. With U.S. Army, 1952-54. Diplomate Am. Bd. Sexology; mem. Am. Assn. Marriage and Family Therapists, Am. Assn. Sex Educators, Counselors and Therapists, Western Social Sci. Assn., Midwest Sociol. Assn., Mont. Acad. Scis., Lions (pres. 1968-69, 72-73). Home: RR 1 Park City MT 59063-9801 Office: Eastern Montana Coll 1500 N 30th St Billings MT 59101-0298

WALTON, BRIAN, lawyer, union administrator; b. London, Dec. 24, 1947; came to U.S., 1966; s. Frank William and Irene Mary (Thornton) W.; m. Pamela Abegg Nemelka (div.); children: Robert, Sarah. BA with honors, Brigham Young U., 1969, MA in Polit. Sci., 1971; JD, U. Utah, 1974. Bar: Calif. 1974, U.S. Dist. Ct. (ctrl., so. and no. dists.) Calif. 1974. Law clk. to Hon. J. Allan Crockett Utah Supreme Ct., 1974; assoc. Reavis & McGrath and predecessor firms, L.A., 1974-82; ptnr. Selvin and Weiner, L.A., 1982-85; exec. dir. Writers Guild Am., West, Inc., L.A., 1985—; teaching asst. Coll. Law, Utah U., 1973, asst. to v.p. of spl. projects, 1971-73, rsch. asst. Coll. Law, 1972-74, tchr., dir. legal skills seminar Coll. Law, 1974. Contbr. articles to law jours. Edwin S. Hinckley scholar. Mem. ABA (antitrust sect.), L.A. County Bar Assn. (antitrust sect., intellectual property and unfair competition sect.), Assn. Bus. Trial Lawyers, Internation Assn. des Avocats du Droits d'Auteur. Office: Writers Guild Am West Inc 8955 Beverly Blvd West Hollywood CA 90048

WALTON, CLYDE FRANCIS, educator; b. Des Moines, Feb. 6, 1946; s. Clyde F. Sr. and Gladys (Wray) W.; m. Jacque Hair; children: Pam, Christopher, Cody, Emily. BA, U. Mass., 1980; MA, N.Mex. State U., 1982. Cert. adminstrv. Dir. Head Start Program, Las Cruces, N.Mex., 1983-85; tchr. Las Cruces Sch. Dist., 1985—; cons. Los Alamos Nat. Labs., Las Cruces, 1989—, Migrant Program, Las Cruces, 1989—. Contbr. articles to profl. jours. Bd. dirs. Las Cruces Mus. for Children, 1992—; tech. mem. Las Cruces Schs. Tech. Com., 1991-92. With U.S. Army, 1965-68. Head Start grantee U.S. Govt., 1983. Democrat. Roman Catholic.

WALTON, (DELVY) CRAIG, philosopher, educator; b. L.A., Dec. 6, 1934; s. Delvy Thomas and Florence (Higgins) W.; m. Nancy Young, June 6, 1965 (div. May 1977); children: Richard, Kerry; m. Vera Allerton, Aug. 30, 1980; children: Matthew, Ruth, Peter, Benjamin. BA, Pomona Coll., 1961; PhD, Claremont Grad. Sch., 1965. Asst. prof. U. So. Calif., L.A., 1964-68; asst. prof. No. Ill. U., DeKalb, 1968-71, assoc. prof., 1971-72; assoc. prof. U. Nev., Las Vegas, 1972-75, prof., 1975—, chmn. dept. philosophy, 1986-89, dir. Inst. for Ethics and Policy Studies, 1986—; bd. dirs. Jour. History of Philosophy. Author: De la recherche du Bien, 1972, Philosophy & the Civilizing Arts, 1975, Hobbe's Science of Natural Justice, 1987; translator: (intro.) Treatise on Ethics (Malebranche), 1992; mem. editorial bd. Studies in Early Modern Philosophy, 1986—; contbr. articles to profl. jours. V.p. Nev. Faculty Alliance, 1984-86; mem. Clark County Sch. Dist. Task Force on Ethics in schs., 1987. 1st lt. USAF, 1956-59. Recipient NDEA Title IV fellowship Claremont Grad. Sch., 1961-64, rsch. sabbaticals U. Nev., 1978, 85, 92; named Barrick Disting. scholar U. Nev., 1988. Mem. AAUP (pres. Nev. chpt. 1983-84), Internat. Hume Soc. (exec. com. 1979-81), Am. Philos. Assn., Soc. for Study History of Philosophy (exec. com. 1974-91), Internat. Hobbes Soc., Phi Beta Kappa. Democrat. Home: 6140 Eisner Dr Las Vegas NV 89131-2303 Office: U Nev Inst Ethics Policy Studies 4505 S Maryland Pky Las Vegas NV 89154-5049

WALTON, DEBORAH GAIL, advertising agency executive; b. L.A., June 22, 1950; d. Philip Hall and Virginia Mary (Schreiber) W.; m. Timothy Alan Schaible, Sept. 12, 1987; children: Adam, Melissa, Amanda, Jennifer (dec.). BA in English, Russell Sage Coll., 1972. Copywriter STA-Power Industries, San Rafael, Calif., 1972-73; asst. advt. mgr. Albany (N.Y.) Pub. Markets, 1973-75; dir. pub. relations Sta. WMHT-TV, Schenectady, N.Y., 1975-78; creative dir. LUYK Advt., Albany, 1978-81; freelance pub. relations cons. Albany, 1981-85; creative dir. H. Linn Cushing Co., Albany, 1985-87; pres. Genus Group, Inc., Santa Rosa, Calif., 1987—. Bd. dirs. Sonoma County Pvt. Industry Coun., 1988-89, Sonoma County World Affairs Coun., 1988-89; grad. Leadership Santa Rosa, 1990. Recipient cert. excellence No. Calif. Addy awards, 1989. Mem. Am. Mktg. Assn., Am. Assn. Advt. Agys., San Francisco Ad Club, Sonoma County Ad Club, Saanta Rosa C. of C. Office: Genus Group Inc 375 E St # 200 Santa Rosa CA 95404-4427

WALTON, FRANK EMULOUS, writer; b. Vincennes, Ind., Feb. 13, 1909; s. Frank E. and Emma Bell (Miller) W.; m. Carol King Shaw, Aug. 17, 1932 (dec. 1989); m. Virginia Anne Conradt, Jan. 5, 1993. Student, U. Oreg., Northwestern U., U. So. Calif., Calif. State U.-Los Angeles; M.S. in Govt., Calif. State U.-Los Angeles, 1958. Life guard Los Angeles County, 1931-36, dep. sheriff, 1936-38; with Los Angeles Police Dept., 1938-59, sgt., 1941-46, lt., 1946, capt., 1947-50, inspector, 1950-55, dep. chief, 1955-59; fgn. service officer U.S. Dept. State, 1959-71; chief pub. safety advisor U.S. Ops. Mission U.S. Dept. State, Saigon, 1959-64, 69-71; chief Far East div. office pub. safety U.S. Dept. State, Washington, 1964-69; pres. bd. dirs. Colony Surf Ltd., Honolulu. Author: The Sea is My Workshop, 1935, Once They Were Eagles, 1986; contbr. articles on police adminstrn. and mil. to profl. jours. Served with USMCR, 1943-46, 50-51, PTO; col. ret. Mem. Internat. Assn. Chiefs Police (life), Marine Corps Aviation Assn. (life), Ret. Officers Assn. (life), Am. Legion, Mensa. Clubs: Los Angeles Athletic; Outrigger Canoe (Honolulu); Marines Meml. (San Francisco); Army-Navy (Manila); Nat. Writers. Home: Colony Surf 2895 Kalakaua Ave Honolulu HI 96815-4040

WALTON, JAMES MEADE, director fish technology, educator; b. Ypsilanti, Mich., Feb. 9, 1947; s. Francis James and Jessie Ruth (Meade) W.; m. Pamela Jean Nelson, Mar. 24, 1970; children: James Kyle, Robert Nelson. BS, U. Mich., 1972, MS, 1974; PhD, U. Wash., Seattle, 1979. Fish biologist Wash. Dept. Fisheries, Olympia, 1977-80; dir. fish tech. program, prof. Peninsula Coll., Port Angeles, Wash., 1980—; pres. faculty assn. Peninsula Coll., 1986-87, chmn. tech. div., 1987-88, 90-92; adv. com. U. Wash. Sch. Fisheries. Editor: Olympic Wild Fish Conference Proceedings, 1984; contbr. articles to profl. jours. Appointed commr. Wash. Wildlife Commn., Olympia, 1985, re-appointed, 1990-95, chmn., 1986-89, vice chmn., 1992—, appointed to Old Growth Alternatives Commn., 1988-89, adv. panel, 1989—; bd. dirs. Ctr. for Streamside Studies U. Wash. With USN, 1967-71. Coun. for Vocat. Edn. grantee, 1981, 82, 84. Mem. Am. Inst. Fisheries Rsch. Biologists, Am. Fisheries Soc., North Pacific Internat. chpt. Am. Fisheries Soc. (pres. 1985-86), Rotary (bd. dirs. 1985-86). Home: 251 E Simmons Rd Port Angeles WA 98362-6954 Office: Peninsula Coll 1502 E Lauridsen Blvd Port Angeles WA 98362-6698

WALTON, RALPH ERVIN, community mental health services administrator; b. Council Bluffs, Iowa, Aug. 9, 1903; s. Willard Ervin and Maude Jesse (Crow) W.; m. Norma Ruth Needham, Mar. 4, 1944 (dec. Apr. 1980); children: Lawrence, Dennis, Patrick, Carol. LLB, U. Omaha, 1927, AB in Psychology, 1933, MA in Psychology, 1935; MA in Edn., U. Chgo., 1941. Bar: Nebr. 1927. Asst. to dean of men U. Omaha, Nebr., 1935-37; counselor Huron (S.D.) Coll., 1939-40; part time stats. worker U. Chgo., Ill., 1940-42; counselor N.Y. State Tng. Sch. for Boys, Warwick, 1943-45; psychologist Mich. Dept. Mental Health, Detroit, 1945-47; adminstr. div. mental hygiene Mich. Dept. Mental Health, Lansing, 1947-73; ret., 1973; adminstr. State Mental Health Statutes Rev. Commn.; dept. rep. State Commn. on Aging. Adult leader 4-H Youth Movement, Mason, Mich., 1960's; bd. mem. State Employee Retirees Assn., 1974-78, Sr. Ctr., Florence, Oreg., 1983-85; bd. mem., pres. Unitarian Ch., Lansing, 1976-78; pres. Neighborhood Assn., Florence, 1979-80, Tenant's Assn., Willamette Oaks Retirement Community, Eugene, Oreg., 1991—. Democrat. Unitarian. Home: 455 Alexander Loop 443 Eugene OR 97401

WALTON, ROGER ALAN, public relations executive, writer; b. Denver, June 25, 1941; s. Lyle R. and Velda V. (Nicholson) W.; m. Helen Anderson. Attended, U. Colo., 1960-63. Govt. rep. Continental Airlines, Denver, 1964-72; dir. pub. affairs Regional Transp. Dist., Denver, 1972-77; pub. affairs cons. Denver, 1977—; pres. Colo. Times Pub. Co. Author: Colorado-A Practical Guide to its Government and Politics, 1973, 6th rev. edit., 1990, Colorado Gambling - A Guide, 1991; columnist The Denver Post newspaper, 1983—, The Rocky Mountain Jour., 1977-81. Mem. U.S. Presdl. Electoral Coll., Washington, 1968; commr. U.S. Bicentennial Revolution Commn., Colo., 1972-76, U.S. Commn. on the Bicentennial of the U.S. Constitution, Denver, 1985-90, pres.; trustee Arapahoe County (Colo.) Library Bd., 1982-86; chmn. lobbyist ethics com. Colo. Gen. Assembly. Republican. Home and Office: 12550 W 2d Dr Lakewood CO 80228

WALTON, RONALD LINN, hospital administrator; b. Vallejo, Calif., Jan. 18, 1955; s. Frank J. and Joyce (Ellis) W.; m. Holly Ann Humpert, Apr. 29, 1978; children: Ronald Jr., Tyler, Janalee, Danielle. BS in Health Adminstrn., Idaho State U., 1982; MBA in Health Adminstrn., Golden Gate U., 1988. Adminstr. Care Enterprises, St. Helena, Calif., 1982-84, Casa Serena Nursing & Rehab. Hosp., Salinas, Calif., 1984-91, Sutter Midtown & Transitional Care Ctr., Sacramennto, Calif., 1991—; preceptor Bd. Examiners of Nursing Home Adminstrs., Calif. 1985—. Patentee children's game. Missionary LDS Ch., 1974-76; soccer coach; asst. scoutmaster Boy Scouts Am., Roseville, 1991—. Mem. Am. Health Care Assn., Calif. Assn. Health Facilities (treas. 1986, v.p. 1987, pres. 1988-90), Am. Coll. Health Care Adminstrs., Calif. Assn. Hosps. and Health Systems, Midtown Bus. Assn. (bd. dirs., treas. 1993—). Republican. Home: Apt 1611 8800 Sierra College Blvd Roseville CA 95661-6421 Office: Sutter Midtown Transitional Care Ctr 2801 L St Sacramento CA 95816-5693

WALTON, S. ROBSON, discount department store chain executive; b. 1945; s. Sam Moore W.; married. Grad., Columbia U., 1969. Formerly with Conner, Winters, Ballaine, Barry & McGowen; with Wal-Mart Stores Inc., Bentonville, Ark., 1969—, sr. v.p., 1978-82, also bd. dirs., vice chmn. bd., 1982-92, chmn., 1992—. Office: Wal-Mart Stores Inc 702 SW 8th St Bentonville AR 72712-6299

WALTON, STEVEN L., electric utility executive, electrical engineer; b. Afton, Wyo., July 25, 1945; s. Wayne A. and A. June (Lindberge) W.; m. Karen Marie Williams, Aug. 22, 1968; children: David, Terri, Heather, Ellen, Melinda, Kirk. BSEE, Brigham Young U., 1970, MSEE, 1970; M Engring. Adminstrn., U. Utah, 1979. Registered profl. engr., Utah. Jr. relaying engring. Utah Power & Light Co., Salt Lake City, 1974-75, transmission planning engr., 1975-83, supr. rate planning, 1983-86, mgr. pricing, 1987—; chmn. rate rsch. com. NELPA, Portland, Oreg., 1987-88; chmn. subsychronous working group WSCC, Salt Lake City, 1979-81. 1st lt. U.S. Army, 1970-74. Mem. Power Engring. Soc. of IEEE (chmn. Utah sect. 1977), Tau Beta Pi. Republican. Mem. LDS Ch. Office: Utah Power & Light Co 1407 W North Temple Rm 1108 Salt Lake City UT 84140

WALTRIP, MATHER K., nuclear and mechanical engineer; b. Houston, Sept. 2, 1960; s. Mather Lee and Mary Frances (Moore) W.; m. Ellen Sara Graff, June 2, 1990. BSME, U. Tex., 1982; MS in Nuclear Engring, MSME, MIT, 1989. Registered profl. engr., Calif.; qualified surface warfare officer, engring. duty officer, in submarines. Commd. ensign USN, 1982, advanced through grades to lt., 1987; nuclear power trainee Nuclear Power Sch., Orlando, Fla., 1983, Nuclear Power Tng. Unit, Idaho Falls, Idaho, 1984; div. officer USS Holland (AS-32), Charleston, S.C., 1984-87, USS Henry M. Jackson (SSBN-730), Bangor, Wash., 1989-90; project supt. Mare Island Naval Shipyard, Vallejo, Calif., 1990-93; with fuel svcs. group Pacific Nuclear, San Jose, Calif., 1993—. Contbr. articles to profl. jours. Dow Chem. Co. scholar U. Tex., 1982. Mem. ASME (assoc.), Am. Nuclear Soc., U. Tex. Ex-Students Assn., MIT Alumni Assn., MIT Club No. Calif., Delta Sigma Phi. Republican. Office: Pacific Nuclear Fuel Svcs Group 6203 San Ignacio Ste 100 San Jose CA 95119

WALTS, LOU EUGENE, retired business and management consultant; b. San Francisco, May 31, 1932; m. Diane Mann, Dec. 7, 1958; children: Elisabeth Louise, Jackie Lynne. BS, San Francisco State U., 1958. CPCU; assoc. risk mgmt. Various underwriting and sales positions Fireman's Fund Ins. Co., Novato, Calif., 1958-65, mgr., 1965-70, asst. v.p., 1970-78, v.p., 1978-85, v.p. systems, 1985-90. Dir. Diablo Scholarships Inc., Concord, Calif., 1968—, pres., 1985; nat. chmn./commodore Sea Exploring/Sea Scouts, Boy Scouts Am., 1990-93. With USN, 1956-58. Mem. Commonwealth Club. Republican. Espiscopalian. Home: 90 Normandy Ln Walnut Creek CA 94598-1249

WALTZ, MARCUS ERNEST, prosthodontist; b. Brownsville, Oreg., July 29, 1921; s. Roswell Starr and Eva Ione (Cherrington) W.; m. Constance Jean Elwood, May 31, 1952 (div. Nov. 1973); children: Melody Ann, Martha Louise, Kathryn Jean, Holly Jay, Joy Evalyn, Ross Elwood; m. Shelby Annette Schwab, June 10, 1975. AB, Willamette U., 1942; DMD, U. Oreg., 1945. Practice dentistry specializing in prosthodontics Forest Grove, Oreg., 1946-52, Reno, 1954—; councillor Pacific Coast Dental Conf.; pres. Pacific Coast Soc. of Prosthodontics, 1983. Served to lt. USN, 1945-46, 52-54, Korea. Decorated Combat Medics award, Battle Stars (oak leaf cluster). Fellow Internat. Coll. Dentistry, Acad. Dentistry Internat.; mem. ADA, Northern Nev. Dental Soc. (pres. 1959), Nev. Dental Assn., Nev. Acad. Gen. Dentistry (pres. 1974), Sigma Chi, Omicron Kappa Upsilon. Democrat. Methodist. Club: Reno Exec. (dir. 1960-66, pres. 1964-65). Lodges: Sigma Tau (pres. 1941-42), Masons (32 degree), Shriners. Home: 715 Manor Dr Reno NV 89509-1944

WALZER, EDWARD JULIUS, special education educator; b. San Francisco, Dec. 23, 1943; s. Moses and Helen Grace (Gross) W.; m. Encarnacion Panadero, Dec. 16, 1967 (div. June 1985); children: Mark, David; m. Bonnie Thoma; children: Matt, Gina. BA, U. San Francisco, 1966, cert. in teaching, 1967; cert. in teaching, San Jose State U., 1972. Tchr. spl. edn. Eastside Union High Sch. Dist., San Jose, Calif., 1967-68, Fremont Union High Sch. Dist., Sunnyvale, Calif., 1968—. Paul Harris fellow Rotary Internat., 1988. Mem. Calif. Tchrs. Assn. (del. state coun. 1979-84). Republican. Jewish. Home: 3297 Walton Way San Jose CA 95117 Office: Fremont Union High Sch Dist PO Box F Sunnyvale CA 94087

WAMBOLT, THOMAS EUGENE, financial consultant; b. Scottsbluff, Nebr., Aug. 9, 1938; s. Andrew, Jr. and Anne (Altergott) W.; B.S., Met. State Coll., Denver, 1976; cert. Total Quality Mgmt. m. Linda E. Shifflett, Oct. 31, 1967; 1 son, Richard Duane King. Pres. Universal Imports Co., Westminster, Colo., 1967-71; printer Rocky Mountain News, Denver, 1967-78; propr., accountant Thomas E. Wambolt Co., Arvada, Colo., 1974-77, fin. cons., 1977—. Baptist. Address: 6035 Garrison St Arvada CO 80004

WAMPLER, FRED BENNY, chemist; b. Kingsport, Tenn., Apr. 2, 1943; s. Fred D. and Jeanette (Broadwater) W.; m. Beverly K. Wolfe, Sept. 1, 1963 (div. July 1983); children: Valerie K., Kevin B., Susan M.; m. Elvira L. Martinez, Nov. 23, 1984. BS, U. Tenn., 1965; PhD, U. Mo., 1970. Postdoctoral fellow Ohio State U., Columbus, 1970-72; sr. scientist Allison div. GM, Indpls., 1972-74; staff mem. Los Alamos (N.Mex.) Nat. Lab., 1974-79, asst. group leader, 1979-80, dep. group leader, 1980-82, group leader, 1982—; lectr. Butler U., Indpls., 1973-74. Contbr. articles to profl. jours. Postdoctoral fellow Ohio State U., Columbus, 1970-72. Mem. Am. Chem. Soc. Home: 708 Avenida Castellano Santa Fe NM 87501 Office: Los Alamos Nat Lab PO Box 1663 Los Alamos NM 87545

WAMPLER, W(ILLIAM) NORMAN, retired small business owner; b. Morristown, Tenn., Feb. 27, 1907; s. W. Rieves and Lydia C. (Grizzle) W.; m. Lois E. Morse, Feb. 14, 1932 (dec. 1965); 1 child, Leland N.; m. Martha M. Maybury, June 30, 1967. BA, Rocky Mt. Coll., 1929; MA, U. Wash., 1933; PhD, U. So. Calif., 1947. Cert. sch. adminstr., Calif. Tchr. Mont. Pub. Schs., Hobson, Big Sandy, 1929-32; prin. Shelby (Mont.) Pub. Schs., 1932-33, supt., 1933-43; prin. Mt. Baldy Boys Sch., Los Angeles, 1943-46; supt. Bellflower (Calif.) Unified Sch. Dist., 1946-72; ednl. cons. Los Angeles County Schs., Downey, Calif., 1972-90; owner, operator Gem Roots Internat., Santa Monica, Calif., 1978-90. Chmn. Bellflower Community Chest, 1958. Mem. Calif. Assn. Sch. Adminstrs. (pres. 1970-71), Los Angeles County Supts. Assn. (pres. 1956-58), NEA, Am. Assn. Sch. Adminstrs. Republican. Presbyterian. Lodge: Rotary (pres. Bellflower chpt. 1950-51). Home: 804 Princeton St Santa Monica CA 90403-2218 Office: Inst Press 2210 Wilshire Blvd Ste 171 Santa Monica CA 90403-5784

WAMSER, CARL CHRISTIAN, chemistry educator; b. N.Y.C., Aug. 10, 1944; s. Christian A. and Madeline G. (Miller) W.; m. Laurie A. Schmidt, Aug. 12, 1984; children: Scott C., Kimberly Joy, Zoe E. ScB, Brown U., 1966; PhD, Calif. Inst. Tech., 1970. Research fellow Harvard U., Cambridge, Mass., 1969-70; prof. chemistry Calif. State U.-Fullerton, 1970-83, Portland (Oreg.) State U., 1983-; vis. prof. U. So. Calif., 1975-76, U. Hawaii, 1981, Reed Coll., 1989-90; rsch. assoc. U. Calif.-Berkeley, 1980; prof. invité Ecole Polytechnique Fédérale de Lausanne, 1992; adj. prof. Oreg. Grad. Inst., Beaverton, 1987—. Author: (with J.M. Harris) Fundamentals of Organic Reaction Mechanisms, 1976, (with G. W. Stacy) Organic Chemistry: A Background for the Life Sciences, 1985. Recipient Outstanding Prof. award, Calif. State U.-Fullerton, 1983, Alumni Disting. Faculty award, 1983. Mem. Am. Chem. Soc., Inter-Am. Photochem. Soc. Home: 19440 Wilderness Dr West Linn OR 97068-2024 Office: Portland State U Dept Chemistry Portland OR 97207-0751

WAMSLEY, WILLIS HARRY, JR., metallurgical industry executive, consultant; b. Washington, Mo., Dec. 30, 1935; s. Willis H. and Virginia (Cunio) W.; m. Eleanor Jane Riles, June 20, 1962 (div. Nov. 1986); children: Annelise Riles, Elisabeth Marguerite. BS in Mining Engring., Stanford U., 1958, MS in Mining Engring., 1963. Mining engr. ALCOA (Suralco), Suriname, 1963-64, mine supt., 1964-66; sales rep. Westinghouse Air Brake Co., Peoria, Ill., 1966-68; mktg. mgr. ESCO Corp., Portland, Oreg., 1968-69; div. mgr. ESCO Corp., Danville, Ill., 1969-71; pres. ESCO S.A., Lyon, France, 1971-78, ESCO Internat., Portland, 1978-83; exev. v.p., CEO, Aimpoint, Herndon, Va., 1983-86; pres. Schmitt Forge Inc., Portland, 1986—; cons. Fire Arms Acccessories, Mehopaney, Pa., 1985—, Computers Plus, Lake Oswego, Oreg., 1991—. Author: Yesterday, Tomorrow, 1987; patentee electronic gun sight. Capt. USMC, 1958-62. Episcopalian. Home: 5225 N Emerson Dr Portland OR 97217 Office: Schmitt Forge Inc PO Box 10246 Portland OR 97210

WAN, FREDERIC YUI-MING, mathematician; b. Shanghai, China, Jan. 7, 1936; s. Wai-Nam and Olga Pearl (Jung) W.; m. Julia Y.S. Chang, Sept. 10, 1960. SB, MIT, 1959, SM, 1963, PhD, 1965. Mem. staff MIT Lincoln Lab., Lexington, 1959-65; instr. math. MIT, Cambridge, 1965-67, asst. prof., 1967-69, assoc. prof., 1969-74; prof. math., dir. Inst. Applied Math. and Stats. U. B.C., Vancouver, 1974-83; prof. applied math. and math. U. Wash., Seattle, 1983—, chmn. Dept. Applied Math., 1984-88, assoc. dean scis. coll. arts and scis., 1988-93; program dir. Div. Math. Sci. NSF, 1986-87, divsn. dir. 1993—; cons. indsl. firms and govt. agys. Mem. M.I.T. Ednl. Coun. for B.C. Area of Can., 1974-83. Assoc. editor Jour. Applied Mechanics, Can. Applied Math. Quar., Studies in Applied Math.; contbr. articles to profl. jours. Sloan Found. award, 1973, Killam sr. fellow, 1979. Fellow ASME, Am. Acad. Mechanics (sec. fellows 1984-90, pres.-elect 1992-93, pres. 1992-93, past pres. 1993-94), Soc. Indsl. and Applied Math., Can. Applied Math. Soc. (coun. 1980-83, pres. 1983-84, Arthur Beaumont Disting. Svc. award 1991), Am. Math. Soc., Math. Assn. Am., Sigma Xi. Office: Nat Sci Found Div Math Scis 1800 G St NW Washington DC 20550

WANCHOW, SUSAN BETH, marketing consultant; b. East Orange, N.J., Aug. 28, 1965; d. John Joseph and Trudie (Haddon) W. BBA magna cum laude, U. Notre Dame, Ind., 1986; MBA summa cum laude, U. So. Calif., L.A., 1989. Tech. account specialist TRW Target Mktg. Svcs., Orange, Calif., 1987-89; mktg. cons. Nat. Decision Sys., San Diego, 1989—. GSBA fellow, U. So. Calif., 1986; Wesley C. Bender awardee, 1986. Mem. Direct Mktg. Assn., Am. Mktg. Assn., Beta Gamma Sigma, Alpha Mu Alpha. Home: 1815 Glasgow Ave Cardiff By The Sea CA 92007-1624 Office: National Decision Systems 5375 Mira Sorrento Pl Ste 400 San Diego CA 92121

WANDS, JOHN MILLAR, English language educator, researcher; b. Buffalo, Jan. 18, 1946; s. John and Mildred Carmella (Denall) W.; m. Frances Terpak, June 22, 1974; 1 child, Ann. BA, Canisius Coll., 1968; MA, U. Chgo., 1970; PhD, Pa. State U., 1976. Instr. English Pa. State U., University Park, 1974, European divsn. U. Md., Heidelberg, Germany, 1974-75; asst. prof. Yale U., New Haven, 1976-78, Carnegie-Mellon U., Pitts., 1978-84; head English dept. Marlborough Sch., L.A., 1984—; fellow Calhoun Coll., Yale U., 1977-78; test cons. Ednl. Testing Svc., Princeton, N.J., 1979-80; reader Advanced Placement Ednl. Testing Svc., Princeton, 1987-91, table leader, 1992—. Contbr. articles to profl. jours. Mem. Friends of UCLA Libr. NEH grantee, 1981, A. Whitney Griswold grantee Yale U., 1977-78, Falk Found. grantee, 1979, Elizabethan Club grantee, 1981; Exxon Found. fellow Newberry Libr., 1982, Coun. Basic Edn./NEH fellow, 1987. Mem. MLA, Nat. Coun. Tchrs. of English, Renaissance Soc. Am. Democrat. Home: 11817 Bellagio Rd Los Angeles CA 90049-2116 Office: Marlborough Sch 250 S Rossmore Ave Los Angeles CA 90004

WANG, ARTHUR C., state legislator, lawyer, educator; b. Boston, Feb. 4, 1949; s. Kung Shou and Lucy (Chow) W.; m. Wendy F. Hamai, May 22, 1976 (div. 1981); m. Nancy J. Norton, Sept. 1, 1985; children: Alexander Xinglin, Sierra Xinan. BA, Franconia Coll., 1970; JD, U. Puget Sound, 1984. Bar: Wash. 1984. Printer Carmel Valley (Calif.) Outlook, 1970-73; project coord. Tacoma (Wash.) Community House, 1973-76; rsch. analyst Wash. Ho. of Reps., Olympia, Wash., 1977-80, mem., 1981—; assoc. Davies Pearson, P.C., Tacoma, 1984—; adj. prof. U. Puget Sound Law Sch., Tacoma, 1987—. Assoc. editor U. Puget Sound Law Review, 1983-84. Vista vol. Tacoma Urban League, 1973-74; del. Dem. Nat. Conv., 1976. Named Chinese Am. Man of Yr., Seattle Chinese Post, 1991, Legislator of Yr., Wash. Health Care Assn., 1992. Democrat. Home: 3319 N Union Tacoma WA 98407 Office: Wash Ho of Reps John L O'Brien Bldg Olympia WA 98504

WANG, CHEN CHI, electronics company executive, real estate executive, finance company executive, food products executive, international trade executive; b. Taipei, Taiwan, China, Aug. 10, 1932; came to U.S., 1959, naturalized, 1970; s. Chin-Ting and Chen-Kim Wang; m. Victoria Rebisoff, Mar. 5, 1965; children: Katherine Kim, Gregory Chen, John Christopher, Michael Edward. B.A. in Econs., Nat. Taiwan U., 1955; B.S.E.E., San Jose State U., 1965; M.B.A., U. Calif., Berkeley, 1961. With IBM Corp., San Jose, Calif., 1965-72; founder, chief exec. officer Electronics Internat. Co., Santa Clara, Calif., 1968-72, owner, gen. mgr., 1972-81, reorganized as EIC Group, 1982, now chmn. bd., chief exec. officer; dir. Systek Electronics Corp., Santa Clara, 1970-73; founder, sr. ptnr. Wang Enterprises (name changed to Chen Kim Entrprises 1982), Santa Clara, 1974—; founder, sr. ptnr. Hanson & Wang Devel. Co., Woodside, Calif., 1977-85; chmn. bd. Golden Alpha Enterprises, San Mateo, Calif., 1979—; mng. ptnr. Woodside Acres-Las Pulgas Estate, Woodside, 1980-85; founder, sr. ptnr. DeVine & Wang, Oakland, Calif., 1977-83; Van Heal & Wang, West Village, Calif., 1981-82; founder, chmn. bd. EIC Fin. Corp., Redwood City, Calif., 1985—; chmn. bd. Maritek Corp., Corpus Christi, Tex., 1988-89; chmn. EIC Internat. Trade Corp., Lancaster, Calif., 1989—, EIC Capital Corp., Redwood City, 1990—. Served to 2d lt., Nationalist Chinese Army, 1955-56. Mem. Internat. Platform Assn., Tau Beta Pi. Mem. Christian Ch. Author: Monetary and Banking System of Taiwan, 1955, The Small Car Market in the U.S., 1961. Home: 195 Brookwood Rd Woodside CA 94062 Office: EIC Group Head Office Bldg 2055-2075 Woodside Rd Redwood City CA 94061

WANG, CHIHPING, computer science educator, electrical engineer; b. Taipei, Taiwan, May 30, 1961; came to U.S., 1983; s. Te-Yin and Lu-Ning (Ti) W.; m. Shiow-Chen (Shyu) Wang, Dec. 27, 1987. BSEE, Nat. Taiwan U., 1983; PhD, U. So. Calif., L.A., 1988. Registered profl. engr., Taiwan. Softare engr. Multi-Tech Computer Inc., Taiwan, 1984-85; rsch. asst. U. So. Calif., L.A., 1985-88; asst. prof. computer sci. U. Calif., Riverside, 1988—. Contbr. articles to profl. jours. Vice-chair Chinese Student Assn., U. So. Calif., 1985-86. Mem. IEEE (reviewer), Assn. Computing Machinery. Home: 16402 Monte Cristo Dr Hacienda Heights CA 91745 Office: U Calif Dept Computer Sci 900 University Ave Riverside CA 92521-0002

WANG, HUAI-LIANG WILLIAM, mechanical engineer; b. Hsinchu, Taiwan, Republic of China, Apr. 4, 1959; came to U.S., 1984; s. Feng-Chi and Hu-Mei (Chou) W.; m. Wen-Pei Chen, June 28, 1986; 1 child, James. BSME, Tatung Inst. of Tech., Taipei, Taiwan, 1981; MSME, Okla. State U., 1985. Asst. engr. Teco Electric and Machinery Corp., Taipei, Taiwan, 1984; electro-mech. engr. Microsci. Internat. Corp., Sunnyvale, Calif., 1987-89; engr. Lockheed Engring. and Scis. Co., Houston, 1989-91, sr. engr., 1991-92; mgr. mech. engring. Orbiter Tech. Co., Fremont, Calif., 1992; sr. engr. Avatar Systems Corp., Milpitas, Calif., 1993—. Mem. IEEE. Office: Avatar Systems Corp 1455 McCarthy Blvd Milpitas CA 95035

WANG, I-TUNG, atmospheric scientist; b. Peking, People's Republic of China, Feb. 16, 1933; came to U.S., 1958; s. Shen and Wei-Yun (Wen) W.; m. Amy Hung Kong; children: Cynthia P., Clifford T. BS in Physics, Nat. Taiwan U., 1955; MA in Physics, U. Toronto, 1957; PhD in Physics, Columbia U., 1965. Rsch. physicist Carnegie-Mellon U., Pitts., 1965-67, asst. prof., 1967-70; environ. systems engr. Argonne (Ill.) Nat. Lab., 1970-76; mem. tech. staff Environ. Monitoring and Svcs. Ctr. Rockwell Internat., Creve Coeur, Mo., 1976-80, Newbury Park, Calif., 1980-84; sr. scientist, combustion engr. Environ. Monitoring and Svcs. Inc., Newbury Park, Camarillo, 1984-88; sr. scientist ENSR Corp (formerly ERT), 1988; pres. EMA Co., Thosand Oaks, Calif., 1989—; tech. advisor Bur. of Environ. Protection, Republic of China, 1985; environ. cons. ABB Environ., 1989-92, ARCO, 1990-91, Du Pont (SAFER Systems Divsn.), 1992—. Contbr. papers to profl jours. First violin Conejo Symphony Orch., Thousand Oaks, Calif., 1981-83. Grantee Bureau of Environ. Protection, Taiwan, 1985. Mem. N.Y. Acad. of Scis., Air and Waste Mgmt. Assn., Sigma Xi. Office: EMA Co Ste 435 2219 E Thousand Oaks Blvd Thousand Oaks CA 91362-2921

WANG, JAMES CHIA-FANG, political science educator; b. Nanling, China, Apr. 4, 1926; came to U.S., 1946, naturalized, 1962; s. Chien-Yu and Lilian W.; m. Sarah Cutter, May 7, 1960; children—Sarah, Eric. BA in Polit. Sci., Oberlin Coll., 1950; postgrad., N.Y. U., 1951; PhD in Polit. Sci, U. Hawaii, 1971. Rsch. asst., internat. study group Brookings Instn., 1951-53; adminstrv. and tng. officer UN Secretariat, N.Y.C., 1953-57; editor-in-charge UN Documents Edit., Readex Corp., N.Y.C., 1957-60; lectr. far eastern politics NYU, N.Y.C., 1957-60; instr. Asian history and econs. Punahou Sch., Honolulu, 1960-64; program officer Inst. Student Interchange, East-West Ctr., Honolulu, 1964-69, acting dir. participant svcs., 1970, adminstrv. officer admissions, 1969-71; dir. freshmen integrated program Hilo (Hawaii) Coll., 1971-72; asst. prof. polit. sci. and internat. studies U. Hawaii, Hilo, 1971-72, assoc. prof., 1973-76, prof., 1976—; mem. U. Hawaii Contemporary China Study Group), Hilo, 1971—; chmn. dept. polit. sci. U. Hawaii, Hilo, 1973-75, 84—; profl. assoc. East-West Communications Inst., Honolulu, 1978, East-West Communications Inst. (Resource System Inst.), 1980-81; adviser to AAUW, Hawaii, 1978-79; cons. World Polit. Risk Forecast, Frost & Sullivan, Inc., N.Y.C., 1980-81. Author: The Cultural Revolution in China: An Annotated Bibliography, 1976, Contemporary Chinese Politics: An Introduction, 1980, 85, 89, 91, Hawaii State and Local Politics, 1982, Study Guide for Power in Hawaii, 1982, Ocean Law and Politics, 1992 (selected One of 1993 Outstanding Academic Books, ALA); contbr. articles to scholarly jours. Mem. Hawaii County Bicentennial Commn., 1975-76, Chinese Bicentennial Com., 1988-89; vice chmn. Democratic Party, County of Hawaii, 1972-76, chmn. 1982-84; mem. Dem. State Central Com., 1982-84; chmn. univ. adv. com. to Hawaii county council; mem. coordinating com. Hawaii Polit. Studies Assn., 1986—; mem. Hawaii State Campaign Spending Commn., 1990—. U. Hawaii Rsch. Found. grantee, 1972-78. Mem. Assn. Asian Studies, Internat. Studies Assn., Coun. Ocean Law and the Law of the Sea Inst., Big Island Press Club. Home: PO Box 13 Hilo HI 96721-0013 Office: U Hawaii Dept Polit Sci Hilo HI 96720-4091

WANG, JAMES QI, system design engineer, consultant; b. Shanghai, China, July 12, 1953; came to U.S., 1981; s. Yi-Ling and Jane (Zhu) W.; m. Jane Wei Jin, Aug. 28, 1988. BS, Inst. Power Engring., Shanghai, 1981; MS, Claremont Grad. Sch., 1986. Test engr. Metra Instrument, San Jose, Calif., 1986-90; sr. software engr. Pyramid Tech., San Jose, 1990-92; sr. system design engr. Amdahl Co., Fremont, Calif., 1992—; diagnostic-test cons. Metra Instruments, San Jose, 1990—. Mem. IEEE. Home: 15143 Rosemar Ave San Jose CA 95127 Office: Amdahl Co 46525 Landing Pky Fremont CA 94538

WANG, JAW-KAI, agricultural engineering educator; b. Nanjing, Jiangsu, People's Republic of China, Mar. 4, 1932; came to U.S., 1955; s. Shuling and Hsi-Ying (Lo) W.; m. Kwang Mei Chow, Sept. 7, 1957 (div. Oct. 1989); children: Angela C.C., Dora C.C., Lawrence C.Y. BS, Nat. Taiwan U., 1953; MS in Agrl. Engring., Mich. State U., 1956, PhD, 1958. Registered profl. engr., Hawaii. Faculty agrl. engring. dept. U. Hawaii, Honolulu, 1959—; assoc. prof., chmn. dept. U. Hawaii, 1964-68, prof., 1968—, chmn. dept. agrl. engring., 1968-75, dir. Aquaculture Program, 1990—; pres. Wang & Assocs., 1979—; spl. asst., Internat. Rsch. Dept., Office of Internat. Cooperation and Devel. U.S. Dept. Agr., 1988; pres. Aquaculture Tech., Inc., 1990—; co-dir. internat. sci. and ednl. coun. U.S. Dept. Agr.; vis. assoc. dir. internat. programs and studies office Nat. Assn. State Univs. and Land-Grant Colls., 1979; vis. prof. Nat. Taiwan U., 1965, U. Calif., Davis, 1980; cons. U.S. Army Civilian Adminstrn., Ryukus, Okinawa, 1966, Internat. Rice Rsch. Inst., Philippines, 1971, Pacific Concrete and Rock Co. Ltd., 1974, AID, 1974, Universe Tankships, Del., 1980-81, World Bank, 1981, 82, ABA Internat., 1981-85, Internat. Found. for Agrl. Devel./World Bank, 1981, Rockefeller Found., 1980, Orizaba, Inc., 1983, Agrisystems/FAO, 1983, Info. Processing Assocs., 1984, County of Maui, 1984, 85, Alexander and Baldwin, 1986; mem. expert panel on agrl. mechanization FAO/UN, 1984—; sr. fellow East-West Center Food Inst., 1973-74; dir. Info. Systems and Svcs. Internat., Inc., 1986—; mem. Am. Soc. Agrl. Cons. Internat. Dept. of State, 1985. Author: Irrigated Rice Production Systems, 1980; editor: Taro—A Review of Colocasia Esculenta and its Potentials, 1983; mem. editorial bd. Aquacultural Engring., 1982—; assoc. editor Am. Soc. of Aquacultural Engrs., 1988—. Recipient Exemplary State Employee award State of Hawaii, 1986, State of Hawaii Employee of Yr. award Office of the Gov., 1990, Kishida Internat. award Am. Soc. Agrl. Engrs., 1991. Fellow Am. Soc. Agrl. Engrs. (chmn. Hawaii sect. 1962-63, chmn. grad. instrn. com. 1971-73, chmn. aquacultural engring. com. 1977-79, chmn. Pacific region 1975-76, emerging tech. task force, engr. of yr. 1976, Tech. Paper award 1978, assoc. editor aquac engring. com.); mem. Chinese Soc. Agrl. Engrs., Sigma Xi, Gamma Sigma Delta (pres. Hawaii chpt. 1974-75), Pi Mu Epsilon. Office: U Hawaii Dept of Agrl Engring 3050 Maile Way Honolulu HI 96822-2271

WANG, LIN, physicist, computer science educator, computer software consultant; b. Dandong, China, June 11, 1929; came to U.S., 1961, naturalized, 1972; s. Lu-Ting and Shou-Jean (Sun) W.; m. Ingrid Ling-Fen Tsow, July 8 1961; children: W. Larry, Ben. BS in Physics, Taiwan U., 1956; MS in Physics, Okla. State U., 1965, PhD in Physics, 1972. Mem. physics faculty Cheng Kung U., Tainan, China, 1957-61; asst. prof. physics Southwestern Okla. State U., Weatherford, 1965-72; prof., chmn. physics dept. N.E. Coll. Arts and Sci., Maiduguri, Nigeria, 1973-75; mem. tech. staff Pacific Engring. Corp., Bellevue, Wash., 1976-78; sr. software engr., Far East cons. Electro-Sci. Industries, Inc., Portland, Oreg., 1979-82; mem. sr. computer sci. faculty South Seattle C.C., 1983—. Mem. Assn. for Computing Machinery, Am. Phys. Soc., AAUP. Home: 9322 168th Pl NE Redmond WA 98052

WANG, PONG-SHENG, computer software development professional; b. Taipei, Taiwan, Republic of China, Sept. 13, 1950; s. Man-Po and Ching-Fang (Yin) W.; m. Ai-Chu Yeh, Aug. 6, 1974; children; Annie A., Charles Li-cheng. BS, Nat. Taiwan U., 1972; MS, Ind. U., 1976; PhD, Ohio State U., 1980. Assoc. instr. Ind. U., 1974-76; programmer/analyst Shoe Corp. Am., Columbus, Ohio, 1976-78; grad. assoc. Ohio State U., Columbus, 1976-80; prin. rsch. scientist Honeywell, Inc., Bloomington, Minn., 1980-83; staff and adv. programmer IBM, San Jose, Calif., 1983-89, devel. program mgr., 1989—. Author conf. papers. Mem. IEEE, Assn. Computing Machinery,. Home: 955 Hampswood Way San Jose CA 95120-3367 Office: IBM 5600 Cottle Rd San Jose CA 95193-0001

WANG, RAN-HONG RAYMOND, optical engineer, scientist; b. Tai Chung, Taiwan, Republic of China, May 31, 1957; came to U.S., 1986; s. Tsing-Thu and Mi (Chaug) W.; m. Min-Shine Chow, Jan. 6, 1985; children: Patrick, Allen. BS, Soo Chow U., Taipei, Taiwan, 1979; MS, Tsing Hwa U., Hsingchu, Taiwan, 1981, U. Ariz., 1988; PhD, U. Ariz., 1990. 2d lt. Chinese Army, Taiwan, Republic of China, 1981-83; supr., asst. Melles Griot Ky., Hsingchu, Taiwan, Republic of China, 1983-86; grad. student U. Ariz., Tucson, 1986-90; sr. devel. scientist Melles Griot Inc., Irvine, Calif., 1990—. V.p. Chinese Student Assn., Tucson, 1988-89. Recipient Phi Tau Phi Honors award, 1981. Mem. Optical Soc. Am., Am. Mgmt. Assn., Internat. Soc. Optical Engring., Optical Engring. Soc. of Rep. of China, Photonics Soc. Chinese-Ams. Office: Melles Griot 1770 Kettering Irvine CA 92714-5670

WANG, RICHARD RUEY-CHYI, plant geneticist, researcher; b. China, Sept. 1, 1943; came to U.S., 1969; s. Tze-Ching and Tin-Shi (Liao) W.; m. Yee-Lan Ma, Oct. 16, 1971; children: Aaron En-Yu, Brian En-Lin. BS, Nat. Taiwan U., Taipei, Republic of China, 1967; MS, Rutgers U., 1971, PhD, 1974. Postdoctoral fellow Kans. State U., Manhattan, 1975-77; cytopathologist DeKalb Hybrid Wheat, Inc., Wichita, Kans., 1977-82; rsch. scientist Internat. Plant Rsch. Inst., San Carlos, Calif., 1982-83; rsch. geneticist forage and range rsch. USDA-ARS, Logan, Utah, 1983—. Contbr. articles to profl. jours. USDA-ARS grantee, 1987-88, fellow, 1989. Mem. Am. Soc. Agronomy, Crop Sci. Soc. of Am., Genetics Soc. Can., Assn. Chinese Soil and Plant Scientists in N. Am. (sec., treas. 1990-91, v.p. 1991-92, pres. 1992-93), Sigma Xi. Office: USDA-ARS FRRL Utah State U Logan UT 84322-6300

WANG, ROBERT CHING-HUEI, engineer; b. Taipei, Taiwan, Aug. 6, 1957; s. Ping-Huang and Chin-Chih (Lo) W.; m. Glori Chu-shu Lee, Dec. 28, 1981; children: Terrence, Edward. BS in Indsl. Engring., Tsing Hwa U., Hsin-Chu, Taiwan, 1979; ME in Indsl. Engring., Rochester Inst. of Tech., 1983; MS in Computer Sci., SUNY, Buffalo, 1985, PhD in Computer Sci., 1988. Engr. Boeing, Seattle, 1988—. Patentee in field. Mem. Soc. of Chinese Engrs. of Seattle (chmn. bd. dirs. 1992—, pres. 1991, v.p. 1990), Am. Assn. of Computing Machinery. Home: 4207 170th Ct NE Redmond WA 98052 Office: Boeing PO Box 3999 MS 9F-61 Seattle WA 98124-2499

WANG, TONY KAR-HUNG, automotive and aerospace company executive; b. Shanghai, People's Republic of China, Apr. 28, 1952; came to U.S., 1970; s. Kuo-Tung and Chien-Wen (Chu) W.; m. Vivian Wei-Bie, May 25, 1980; children: Stephen, Jason. BSE in Materials and Metall. Engring., U. Mich., 1973, MSE in Materials, 1975. Materials engr. Burroughs Corp., Detroit, 1976-78; sr. project engr. Gen. Motors Corp., Warren, Mich., 1978-85; staff engr. Hughes Aircraft Co., El Segundo, Calif., 1985; staff engr. Gen. Motors-Hughes Electronics Corp., El Segundo, 1986-87, mgr. program, staff engr., 1987-89, sr. staff engr., 1989-93; exec. v.p. Xenon Group USA, 1993—. Contbr. articles to profl. jours. Goodrich scholar, U. Mich., Ann Arbor, 1974. Mem. Soc. Advanced Materials and Process Engring. Republican.

WANG, WILLIAM CHUNG-GEN, computer software engineer; b. Hsinchu, Taiwan, June 28, 1960; came to U.S., 1988; s. Hsiao-Shih and Huei-Chun (Hu) W. BS, Cheng-Kung U., Tainan, Taiwan, 1982; MS in Engring., U. Mich., 1990. Software engr. ITT-Taiwan, Taipei, 1984-86, Neotech Devel. Corp., Taipei, 1986-88, Link Techs., Inc., Fremont, Calif., 1991—. 2d lt. Taiwan Army, 1982-84. Mem. Assn. for Computing Machinery. Office: Link Techs Inc 46595 Landing Pky Fremont CA 94538

WANGER, OLIVER WINSTON, judge, educator; b. L.A., Nov. 27, 1940; m. Lorrie A. Reinhart; children: Guy A., Christopher L., Andrew G. Student, Colo. Sch. Mines, 1958-60; BS, U. So. Calif., 1963; JD, U. Calif., Berkeley, 1966. Bar: Calif. 1967, U.S. Dist. Ct. (ea. dist.) Calif. 1969, U.S. Tax Ct. 1969, U.S. Dist. Ct. (cen. dist.) Calif. 1975, U.S. Dist. Ct. (so. dist.) Calif. 1977, U.S. Dist. Ct. (no. dist.) Calif. 1989, U.S. Ct. Appeals (9th cir.) 1989. Dep. dist. atty. Fresno (Calif.) County Dist. Atty., 1967-69; ptnr. Gallagher, Baker & Manock, Fresno, 1969-74; sr. ptnr. McCormick, Barstow, Sheppard, Wayte & Carruth, Fresno, 1974-91; judge U.S. Dist. Ct. (ea. dist.) Calif., Fresno, 1991—; adj. prof. law Humphreys Coll. Law, Fresno, 1968-70, San Joaquin Coll. Law, Fresno, 1970—, dean law sch. 1980-82, pres. chmn. bd. dirs., 1982—. Fellow Am. Coll. Trial Lawyers, Internat. Acad. Trial Lawyers; mem. Am. Bd. Trial Advs. (pres. San Joaquin Valley chpt. 1987-89, nat. bd. dirs. 1989-91), Am. Bd. Profl. Liability Attys. (founder, diplomate), Calif. State Bar (mem. exec. com. litigation sect. 1989-92, mem. com. on fed. cts. 1989-90), San Joaquin Valley Am. Inn of Ct. (pres. 1992—), Beta Gamma Sigma. Office: US Dist Ct 5104 US Courthouse 1130 O St Fresno CA 93721

WANK, NEIL N., accountant, financial executive; b. N.Y.C., Sept. 9, 1944; s. Hyman and Mae (Perlberg) W.; m. Reneé Laddin, Nov. 1, 1969; children: Kenneth Bradley, Danielle Eden, Jeffrey Ross. BS in Acctg., CUNY, 1965. CPA, N.Y., Calif. Prin. Neil N. Wank & Co., N.Y.C., 1965-76; ptnr. Touche, Ross & Co., L.A., 1976-88; pres. Wank Fin. Group, L.A., 1989—; ptnr. Wank, Berss & Co., L.A., 1990—. Mem. Jewish Fedn. Coun. Mem. AICPA, Calif. Soc. CPAs, N.Y. State Soc. CPAs, Calif. Soc. Real Estate Coms., Calif. Soc. Sports and Entertainment Coms., Variety Club. Republican. Home: 6244 Warner Dr Los Angeles CA 90048-5310 Office: 5900 Wilshire Blvd Los Angeles CA 90036-5013

WAPLES, ERIC SNOWDEN, headmaster; b. Lafayette, Ind., Oct. 16, 1944; s. Eliot Otto and Margaret (Miller) W.; m. Carolyn M., June 11, 1968; children: Jacob Snowden, Megan Elizabeth. AB in History, Dartmouth Coll., 1966; MAT in History, Colo. Coll., 1972; postgrad., Trinity Coll., 1967. History tchr. The Loomis Sch., Windsor, Conn., 1966-68; staff trust dept. First Nat. Bank & Trust, Evanston, Ill., 1970-71; tchr. history Fountain Valley Sch., Colorado Springs, Colo., 1972-80, acad. dean, 1980-83, asst. headmaster, 1983-87, headmaster, 1987—. Bd. dirs. Found. for Dist. #11, Colorado Springs, 1991—; co-pres. Pikes Peak Squash Assn., Colorado Springs, 1982-86; del. Colo. State Dem. Conv., 1976. Ballantine fellow Fountain Valley Sch., 1978. Mem. Assn. of Colo. Ind. Schs. (sec. 1988-89, treas. 1989—), Nat. Assn. of Exptl. Edn., VFW, Am. Hist. Assn., U.S. Squash Racquets Assn., Wilderness Soc., Outward Bound, Sierra Club. Methodist. Office: Fountain Valley Sch 6155 Fountain Valley Sch Rd Colorado Springs CO 80911

WARAN, DAVID ANTHONY, naval officer; b. Chgo., July 18, 1957; s. Adam Joseph and Lorraine Marie (Chess) W. BS, U. So. Calif., 1979; MS, Salve Regina Coll., Newport, R.I., 1991; MA, U.S. Naval War Coll., Newport, 1991. Commd. ensign USN, 1979, advanced through grades to lt. comdr., 1989; officer aviation arm div. VS33, San Diego, 1982-86; asst. ops. officer VS35, San Diego, 1986-87; model mgr. USN and Lockheed Corp., San Diego, 1987-89; instr. pilot VS41, San Diego, 1987-89; safety and adminstrv. ops. officer VS37, San Diego, 1990—; dir. Auto Submarine Warfare Ops. Center, San Diego, 1993—. Mem. Inst. Indsl. Engrs., Tailhook Assn., U. So. Calif. Alumni Assn., U.S. Naval Inst., Classic TBird Club Internat., Inland Empire Classic TBird Club. Republican. Roman Catholic. Home: 8916 Corte Quezada Spring Valley CA 91977

WARD, ALBERT EUGENE, research center executive, archeologist, ethnohistorian; b. Carlinville, Ill., Aug. 20, 1940; s. Albert Alan and Eileen (Boston) W.; m. Gladys Anena Lea, Apr. 26, 1961 (div. Apr. 4, 1974); children—Scott Bradley, Brian Todd; m. Stefanie Helen Tschaikowsky, Apr. 24, 1982. A.A., Bethany Luth. Jr. Coll., Mankato, Minn., 1961; B.S., No. Ariz. U., 1968; M.A., U. Ariz., 1972. Lab. asst., asst. archeologist Mus. No. Ariz., Flagstaff, 1965-67; research archeologist Desert Research Inst., U. Nev., Las Vegas, 1968; research archeologist Archeol. Survey, Prescott Coll., Ariz., 1969-71, research assoc., 1971-73; research archeologist Ariz. Archeol. Ctr., Nat. Park Service, Tucson, 1972-73, research collaborator Chaco Ctr., Albuquerque, 1975; founder, dir. archeol. research program Mus. Albuquerque, 1975-76; founder, dir., 1976-79 pres. bd. dirs. Ctr. Anthrop. Studies, Albuquerque, 1976—; lectr. U. N.Mex. Community Coll., 1974-77, others; contract archeol. salvage and research projects in N.Mex. and Ariz. Editorial adv. bd. Hist. Archeology, 1978-80; editor publs. Ctr. Anthrop. Studies, 1978—. Contbr. articles to scholarly jours. Grantee Mus. No. Ariz., 1972, S.W. Monuments Assn., 1973, CETA, 1975-79, Nat. Park Service, 1978-79. Mem. Soc. Am. Archeology, Soc. Hist. Archeology, No. Ariz. Soc. Sci. and Art, Ariz. Archeol. and Hist. Soc., Archeol. Soc. N.Mex., Albuquerque Archeol. Soc., Am. Anthrop. Assn., S.W. Mission Research Ctr., Am. Soc. Conservation Archeology, Soc. Archeol. Scis., Southwestern Anthrop. Assn., N.Mex. Archeol. Council, Living Hist. Farms and Agrl. Mus. Assn. Republican. Lutheran.

WARD, ANN DEVOE, educational administrator; b. Worcester, Mass., July 11, 1930; d. Robert Valentine and Anna Rose (St. Martin) DeVoe; m. Edward Kemp Jr., June 20, 1952; children: Edith M. Willis, Susan A. Stegall; m. Paul Arnold Ward, May 15, 1972 (div. 1978). BS, Simmons Coll., 1952; postgrad., U. Oreg., 1970-72, 1970—. Rsch. asst. U. Oreg., Eugene, 1969-72; office mgr. Ward Decorating, Eugene, 1972-78; field advisor, editor Western Rivers Girl Scout Coun., Eugene, 1973-76; trainer, fin. devel. dir. Frontier Girl Scout Coun., Las Vegas, Nev., 1976-79; exec. dir. Winema Girl Scout Coun., Medford, Oreg., 1979-81; employment counselor Valley Employment, Las Vegas, 1982; adj. instr. Continuing Edn. U. Nev., Las Vegas, 1982-83; dir. student and grad. svcs. Edn. Dynamics Inst., Las Vegas, 1983-85; asst. dir. community edn. Community Coll. So. Nev., Las Vegas, 1986—. Author, editor (edn. resource) Govt. in Oreg., 1971, (rsch. publ.) Oreg. Tax/Sch. Fin. Study, 1969, Your Lane County Govt., 1968. Instr. of trainers Girls Scouts U.S.A. 1990—, nat. operational vol., 1992—; lay mem. Lane County Bd. Equalization, Eugene, 1969-70; bd. dirs. LWV of Oreg., Portland, 1969, LWV of Eugene, 1967-68. Mem. ASTD (bd. dirs. 1986, 91), U.S. Senate Productivity Awards (com. 1990—, examiner 1991—, govt. conference on Women sub com. chmn. 1990).

WARD, BONNIE JEAN, interior designer; b. Jeffersonville, Ind., Mar. 31, 1947; d. Lloyd Russell and Wilma Jane (McKim) Hill; m. James Daniel Ware, Jan. 24, 1969 (div. 1984); m. Donald Devereux Ward, Nov. 16, 1985. BA, Purdue U., 1969. Sec., treas. Empire Designs Inc., Denver, 1969-74; pvt. practice interior design Denver, 1974-76; interior designer Victor Huff & Assoc., Denver, 1976-77; pres. ADR: The Design Group, Denver, 1977-88; co-owner Designward Inc., Orcas Island, Wash., 1988—. Mem. Am. Soc. Interior Designers (profl., Colo. chpt. bd. dirs. 1983-84), Inst. Bus. Designers (profl.). Home: PO Box 1267 Eastsound WA 98245-1267 Office: Designward Inc PO Box 1267 Eastsound WA 98245-1267

WARD, CARL EDWARD, research chemist; b. Albuquerque, Oct. 16, 1948; s. Joe E. and Loris E. (Wenk) W.; m. Bertha R. Schloer, June 9, 1970. BS in Chemistry, N.Mex. Inst. Mining and Tech., 1970; MS in Chemistry, Oreg. Grad. Ctr., 1972; PhD in Chemistry, Stanford U., 1977. Research chemist Union Carbide Corp., Charleston, W.Va., 1977-79, Dynapol Corp., Palo Alto, Calif., 1979-80; research chemist Chevron Chem. Co., Richmond, Calif., 1980-85, sr. research chemist, 1986-88; apptd. supr. chemical synthesis Chevron Chem. Co., Richmond, 1988-90; sr. rsch. assoc. Chevron Rsch. & Tech. Co., Richmond, 1990-91, staff scientist, 1991—. Referee Jour. Organic Chemistry, 1983—; patentee in field; contbr. articles to profl. jours. Recipient NSF traineeship, Stanford U., 1972-73; Upjohn fellow, Stanford U., 1976-77. Mem. AAAS, Am. Chem. Soc., Stanford Alumni Assn, Planetary Soc., Calif. Acad. Sci. Democrat. Club: N.Mex. Inst. Mining and Tech. Pres.'s (Socorro). Home: 1355 Bagely Way San Jose CA 95122-3002 Office: Chevron Rsch & Tech Co PO Box 1627 Richmond CA 94802-1796

WARD, DIANE KOROSY, lawyer; b. Cleve., Oct. 17, 1939; d. Theodore Louis and Edith (Bogar) Korosy; m. S. Mortimer Ward IV, July 2, 1960 (div. 1978); children: Christopher LaBruce, Samantha Martha; m. R. Michael Walters, June 30, 1979. AB, Heidelberg Coll., 1961; JD, U. San Diego, 1975. Bar: Calif. 1977, U.S. Dist. Ct. (so. dist.) Calif. 1977. Ptnr. Ward & Howell, San Diego, 1978-79, Walters, Ward & Howell, A.P.C., San Diego, 1979-81; mng. ptnr. Walters & Ward, A.P.C., San Diego, 1981—; dir., v.p. Oak Broadcasting Systems, Inc., 1982-83; dir. Elisabeth Kubler-Ross Ctr., Inc., 1983-85; sheriff Ranchos del Norte Corral of Westerners, 1985-87; trustee San Diego Community Defenders, Inc., 1986-88; dir. Calif. State U. Found., San Marcos, 1990—. Pres. bd. dirs. Green Valley Civic Assn., 1979-80; dir. Poway Ctr. for the Performing Arts, 1990-93; trustee Palomar-Pomerado Hosp. Found., 1985-89; v.p. Endowment Devel., 1989-91; bd. dirs. Clean Found.; trustee Episc. Diocese of San Diego. Recipient Dove award Assn. Retarded Citizens, 1992. Mem. ABA, Rancho Bernardo Bar Assn. (chmn. 1982-83), Lawyers Club San Diego, Profl. and Exec. Women of the Ranch (founder, pres. 1982—), San Diego Golden Eagle Club, Soroptimist Internat. (pres. chpt. 1979-80, Woman of Distinction 1992), Phi Delta Phi. Republican. Episcopalian. Home: 16503 Avenida Florencia Poway CA 92064-1807 Office: Walters & Ward 11665 Avena Pl Ste 203 San Diego CA 92128-2498

WARD, JAMES DAVID, lawyer; b. Sioux Falls, S.D., Sept. 8, 1935; s. Charles David Jr. and Juanita Marion (Senecal) W.; m. Carole J. Sander, Aug. 4, 1956; children: Kelly, Bruce, Mark. BA, U. S.D., 1957; JD, U. San Francisco, 1959. Bar: Calif. 1960, U.S. Dist. Ct. (cen. dist.) Calif. 1964, U.S. Supreme Ct. 1979. Dep. dist. atty. Dist. Atty.'s Office County of Riverside, Calif., 1960-61; ptnr. Badger, Schulte & Ward, Riverside, 1961-64, Thompson & Colegate, Riverside, 1964—; adj. prof. U. Calif., Riverside, 1983-89, LaVerne (Calif.) U., 1988-89. Mem. Calif. Bar Assn. (exec. com. conf. dels. 1979-81, bd. govs. 1981-84, v.p. 1984, chair discovery commn. 1984-87, chair jud. nominees evaluation com. 1984-87), Am. Judicature Soc. (bd. dirs. 1984-87), Am. Bd. Trial Advs., Riverside County Bar Assn. (pres. 1973-74), So. Calif. Def. Counsel. Republican. Home: 2649 Anna St Riverside CA 92506-4504 Office: Thompson & Colegate PO Box 1299 Riverside CA 92502-1299

WARD, JAMES HUBERT, social work educator, university dean, researcher, consultant; b. Lawndale, N.C., Apr. 8, 1937; s. Frank A. and Helen (Wray) W.; m. Jacqueline Ferman Ward, Dec. 29, 1966; children—Dawn Alese, Audran Maria, James H., Christopher F. B.S., N.C. A&T State U., 1960; M.S.W., U. Md., 1968; Ph.D., Ohio State U., 1974. Tchr., counselor Ohio Youth Commn., Columbus, 1962-66, dep. dir., 1971-73; adj. instr. social work dept. sociology and anthropology, U. Dayton (Ohio), 1968-69; exec. dir. Montgomery County Community Action Agy., Dayton, 1969-71; asst. prof. sociology and anthropology, Central State U., Wilberforce, Ohio, 1973; asst. prof., sr. research assoc. Sch. Applied Social Scis., Case Western Res. U., Cleve., 1975-76, asst. prof., assoc. dean, 1976-79, assoc. prof., assoc. dean, 1979-81; dean, prof. Sch. Social Work, U. Ala., Tuscaloosa, 1981-88; prof., dean, Grad. Sch. Social Work, Portland State U., Portland, Oreg., 1988—; cons. in field; mem. Ala. Juvenile Justice Adv. Com., 1983—; mem. adv. council on social work edn. Ala. Commn. on Higher Edn., 1982—; mem. ho. of dels. Council on Social Work Edn., 1981-87; mem. Coun. Social Work Edn. Accreditation Commn., 1987—; mem. annual program planning com. Council on Social Work Edn., 1984-85; bd. dirs. United Way of Columbia-Willamette, 1988—, mem. exec. com., mem. community orgn. and planning com., chair agency rels. com., mem. strategic planning com.; bd. dirs. Urban League, Portland, 1988-89; bd. dirs. Mt. Hood Community Mental Health Ctr., 1988-91; mem. govs. panel on ecclesia, 1988-89; mem adv. coun. mental health edn. planning Dept. Human Resources, Mental Health Divsn., Salem, Oreg., 1988-91; mem. Portland City Club, 1988—; mem. task force on licensing for social work practice, Ala. State Bd. Social Work Examiners, 1985; mem.local human resources bd. Tuscaloosa County Dept. Pensions and Security, 1982-87, mem. external central adminstrv. rev. panel, 1985. Bd. dirs. Greater Tuscaloosa chpt. ARC, 1982-87; pres. Eastwood Middle Sch. PTA, Tuscaloosa Bd. Edn., 1983-84; hon. mem. bd. Parents Anonymous of Ala. State Bd., 1982; mem. W. Ala. Nat. Issues Forum, 1984-86; bd. dirs., chmn. fin. com. Tuscaloosa County Mental Health Assn., 1984-87. Served to capt. U.S. Army, 1960-68. Recipient Pace Setters award for disting. achievement Coll. Adminstrv. Sci., Ohio State U., 1974; named Outstanding Profl. in Human Services, Acad. Human Services, 1974. Mem. Acad. Cert. Social Workers (cert), Council on Social Work Edn., Internat. Assn. Schs. Social Work, Internat. Council on Social Welfare, Nat. Assn. Social Workers (mem.-at-large, bd. dirs. Ala. Chpt. 1985, v.p. Oreg. chpt. 1991—, edit. bd. jour. Social Work 1990—), Am. Assn. Deans and Dirs. of Grad. Schs. of Social Work (chair deans group S.E. region 1985-87), Ala. Conf. of Social Work (chmn. program com.), Greater Tuscaloosa C. of C. Contbr. numerous articles to various profl. jours., also chpts. to books. Office: Portland State Univ Grad Sch Social Work PO Box 751 Portland OR 97207-0751

WARD, JAMES VERNON, biologist, educator; b. Mpls., Mar. 27, 1940; s. Vernon G. and Nela J. (Kemmer) W.; m. Janice Ann Walstrom, June 14, 1963. BS, U. Minn., 1963; MA, U. Denver, 1967; PhD, U. Colo., 1973. Biology tchr. Denver Pub. Schs., 1963-70; asst. prof. Colo. State U., Fort Collins, Colo., 1974-79, assoc. prof., 1979-83, prof., 1983—; lectr. in field. Editor: The Ecology of Regulated Streams, 1979; author: Aquatic Insect Ecology, 1992, Illustrated Guide to the Mountain Stream Insects of Colorado, 1992; contbr. over 100 sci. papers to profl. jours.; editor Regulated Rivers, 1987—. Mem. North Am. Benthological Soc. (pres. 1987-88), Ecol. Soc. of Am., Sigma Xi. Office: Colorado State U Department of Biology Fort Collins CO 80523

WARD, JOHN J., bishop; b. Los Angeles, 1920. Student, St. John's Sem., Camarillo, Calif., Catholic U. Am. Ordained priest, Roman Catholic Ch., 1946. Apptd. titular bishop of Bria, aux. bishop Diocese of Los Angeles Roman Cath. Ch., 1963—; vicar gen. Roman Cath. Ch., Los Angeles., 1963—. Office: 10425 W Pico Blvd Los Angeles CA 90064-2307*

WARD, JOHN ROBERT, physician, educator; b. Salt Lake City, Nov. 23, 1923; s. John I. and Clara (Elzi) W.; m. Norma Harris, Nov. 5, 1948; children: John Harris, Pamela Lyn, Robert Scott, James Alan. BS, U. Utah, 1944, MD, 1946; MPH, U. Calif., Berkeley, 1967; Masters, Am. Coll. of Rheumatology, 1990. Diplomate Am. Bd. Internal Medicine. Intern Salt Lake County Gen. Hosp., 1947-48, asst. resident, 1949-50, resident physician internal medicine, 1950-51, asst. physician, 1957-58, assoc. physician, 1958-69; instr. medicine Med. Sch. U. Utah, Salt Lake City, 1954-58, asst. prof., 1958-63; assoc. prof. U. Utah Med. Sch., Salt Lake City, 1963, prof., chmn. dept. preventive medicine, 1966-70, prof., 1969—, chief div. rheumatology, 1957-88; clin. fellow medicine Harvard, 1955-57; attending physician internal medicine Salt Lake City VA Hosp., 1957—; Nora Eccles Harrison prof. medicine, Am. Coll. Rheumatology. Served as capt. M.C. AUS, 1951-53. Master Am. Coll. Rheumatology; fellow ACP; mem. Am. Coll. Rheumatology, Salt Lake County, Utah Med. Assns., Western Soc. Clin. Res., Western Assn. Phys. Home: 1249 E 3770 S Salt Lake City UT 84106-2446 Office: U Utah Health Scis Ctr 50 N Medical Dr Salt Lake City UT 84132-0002

WARD, JOHN WILLIAM, physical chemist; b. Moline, Ill., Oct. 16, 1929; s. William Ewald and Violet Xenia (Nordquist) W.; m. Nima Diane Copeland, June 4, 1955; children: William, David, Daniel, Michael. BA, Augustana Coll., 1952; MS, Washington U., St. Louis, 1956; PhD, U. N.Mex., 1966. Staff mem. Los Alamos (N.Mex.) Nat. Lab., 1956-87, sect. leader, 1987—; guest scientist European Inst. for Transuranium Elements, Karlsruhe, Fed. Republic Germany, 1972-73, 81-82. Author: (with others) Handbook on the Physics and Chemistry of the Actinides, Vol. III, 1985 Vol. IV, 1985; contbr. articles to profl. jours. Bd. dirs. Los Alamos Choral Soc., 1966—. Named U.S. Preisträger, Alexander von Humboldt Found., Fed. Republic Germany, 1972; lab. fellow Los Alamos Nat. Lab., 1983. Fellow Am. Inst. Chemists; mem. Am. Chem. Soc., Am. Vacuum Soc., Catgut Acoustical Soc. Democrat. Lutheran. Home: 2501 Calle Melecio Santa Fe NM 87505-6497

WARD, LAURA SUZANNE, director university program; b. Cheyenne, Wyo., July 7, 1956; d. Ernest Edward Maese and Dorothea Patricia (Miller) Ward. AS, Laramie County Community Coll., 1984, AA, 1992; BS, Regis Coll., 1991. Bookkeeper Clark Co., Cheyenne, 1980; data specialist Southeast Wyo. Mental Health Ctr., Cheyenne, 1980-87; advisor vet. benefits Laramie County Community Coll., Cheyenne, 1987—; cons. Dept. Vets. Affairs, 1991, Frontier Bank, 1992—. Chair Adopt-A-Hwy. Dept. Trans., pub. rels. Girl Scouts Am., 1990-91; vol. Dept. Vets. Affairs, 1993—. With U.S. Army, 1976-80. Named Outstanding Young Woman Am., 1988, Sr. Marshall Regis Coll., 1991. Mem. Am. Bus. Women's Assn. (treas. 1984-85, v.p. 1985-86, pres. 1986-87, sec. 1991-92), Nat. Assn. Vets. Program Adminstrs. Democrat. Roman Catholic. Home: 1601 Big Horn Ave # 4 Cheyenne WY 82001 Office: Laramie County Community Coll 1400 E College Dr Cheyenne WY 82007

WARD, LESTER LOWE, JR., lawyer, arts executive; b. Pueblo, Colo., Dec. 21, 1930; s. Lester Lowe and Alysmai (Pfeffer) W.; m. Rosalind H. Felps, Apr. 18, 1964; children: Ann Marie, Alison, Lester Lowe. AB cum laude, Harvard U., 1952, LLB, 1955. Bar: Colo. 1955. Pvt. practice Pueblo, 1957-89; ptnr. Predovich, Ward & Banner, Pueblo, 1974-89; pres., chief oper. officer Denver Ctr. for the Performing Arts, 1989—. Trustee, Thatcher Found., Frank I. Lamb Found., Helen G. Bonfils Found.; pres. bd. trustees Pueblo Pub. Library, 1960-66; trustee St. Mary-Corwin Hosp., 1972-80, pres., 1979-80. With U.S. Army, 1955-57. Named Outstanding Young Man of Yr., Pueblo Jaycees, 1964. Fellow Am. Coll. Trust and Estate Counsel; mem. ABA (house of dels. 1986-88), Colo. Bar Assn. (bd. govs. 1977-79, 82-88, pres. 1983-84), Pueblo County Bar Assn. (Outstanding Young Lawyer award 1965, 67, pres. 1976-77), Harvard Law Sch. Assn. Colo. (pres. 1972), Kiwanis (pres. 1969). Democrat. Roman Catholic. Home: 1551 Larimer St Apt 2601 Denver CO 80202-1638 Office: Denver Ctr Performing Arts 1050 13th St Denver CO 80204-2157

WARD, LEWIS EDES, mathematician; b. Arlington, Mass., July 20, 1925; s. Lewis E. Sr. and Mary C. (Ball) W.; m. Grace J. Ward, Jan. 31, 1949; children: Lawrence, Dinah, Michael. AB, U. Calif., Berkeley, 1949; MS, Tulane U., 1951, PhD, 1953. Instr. U. Nev., Reno, 1953-54; asst. prof. U. Utah, Salt Lake City, 1954-56; rsch. mathematician USN, China Lake, Calif., 1956-59; lectr. UCLA, 1957-59; assoc. prof. U. Oreg., Eugene, 1959-65, assoc. dean, 1966-69, prof., 1965-91, prof. emeritus, 1991—. Author: Topology, 1972; contbr. articles to profl. jours. Mem. Math. Assn. Am. (vis. mathematician, 1960-64), Am. Math. Soc. (organizer spl. sessions, 1980, 82), Oregon Acad. Sci. (vis. scientist, 1962-64). Office: U Oreg Dept Math Eugene OR 97403

WARD, LOWELL SANFORD, state official; b. L.A., Nov. 21, 1949; s. Jimmy Lee and Artis Eleane (Nelson) W. AS, BA, U. Nev., Reno, 1974, postgrad., 1977-78; postgrad., U. Pacific, 1982-84, Portland State U., 1986. Detective organized crime City of Reno Police Dept., 1975-81; in-depth investigator State of Oreg. Liquor Control Commn., Portland, 1985-86; auto theft investigator Motor Vehicles div. State of Oreg., Medford, 1986-88; sr. fraud investigator Dept. Justice, State of Oreg., Salem, 1989—. Contbg. reporter Oreg. State Police Officer's Assn. Trooper News, 1987—, Northwest Law Enforcement Jour., 1989—. Mem. Internat. Assn. Auto Theft Investigators, Western States Auto Theft Investigators, NW Fraud Investigators Assn. Republican. Methodist. Office: Dept Justice Fraud Sect Justice Bldg Salem OR 97310

WARD, MICHAEL GEORGE, mechanical engineering educator, consultant; b. San Francisco, Aug. 22, 1951; s. Peter Joseph and Lillian Hazel (Baker) W.; m. Teresa Marie Roche, Mar. 23, 1974; children: Eric John, Allan Jacob, Brian Thomas. BSME, U. Calif., Davis, 1973, MS in Mech. Engring., 1975; PhD in ME, Stanford U., 1983. Registered profl. engr., Calif. Engr. Gen. Electric Co., San Jose, 1975-78; sr. rsch. engr. Lockheed Missiles & Space Co., Sunnyvale, Calif., 1978-82; asst. prof. mech. engring. U. Pacific, Stockton, Calif., 1982-85, assoc. prof., 1985-88; assoc. prof. mech. engring. Calif. State U., Chico, 1988-90, prof. mech. engring., 1990-92, dean Coll. Engring., Computer Sci. & Tech., 1992—. Mem. ASME, Am. Soc. for Engring. Edn., Soc. for Computer Simulation, Sigma Xi (Sci. Rsch. Soc.). Home: 1034 Sir William Ct Chico CA 95926-2096 Office: Calif State U Coll Engring Computer Sci & Tech Chico CA 95929-0003

WARD, MILTON HAWKINS, mining company executive; b. Bessemer, Ala., Aug. 1, 1932; s. William Howard and Mae Ivy (Smith) W.; m. Sylvia Adele Randle, June 30, 1952; children: Jeffrey Randle, Lisa Adele. BS in Mining Engring., U. Ala., 1955, MS in Engring., 1981; MBA, U. N.Mex., 1974. Registered profl. engr., Tex., Ala. Supr., engr. San Manuel (Ariz.) Copper Corp., 1955-60; mine supt., divsn. supt., gen. supt. of mines, divsn. engr. Kerr-McGee Corp., Oklahoma City and Grants, N.Mex., 1960-66; gen. mgr. Homestake Mining Co., Grants, 1966-70; v.p. ops. Ranchers Exploration & Devel. Corp., Albuquerque, 1970-74; pres., bd. dirs. Freeport Minerals Co., N.Y.C., 1974-85; pres., COO Freeport-McMoRan, Inc., New Orleans, 1985-92, also bd. dirs.; chmn., pres., CEO Cyprus Minerals Co., Englewood, Colo., 1992—; bd. dirs. Mineral Info. Inst., Inc., Am. Found. for Phosphate Prodn., Internat. Copper Assn., Adv. Coun. Internat. Investments; bd. dirs., mem. exec. com. Sulfer Inst. Contbr. articles to profl. jours. Former bd. trustees New Orleans Mus. Art, former pres.; bd. trustees Children's Hosp., New Orleans, Tulane U. Bd. Adminstrs.; bd. dirs. Smithsonian Nat. Mus. Natural History, Nat. Mining Hall of Fame and Mus.; former mem. pres. coun. Contemporary Arts Ctr.; mem. corp. adv. com. World Wildlife Fund; former adv. com. chmn. Tulane U. Bioenviron. Rsch. Ctr.; former adv. bd. bus. coun. Tulane U. Sch. Bus.; disting. engring. fellow U. Ala., also mem. mining engring. adv. coun., mem. pres. cabinet. Fellow Inst. Mining & Metallurgy (London); mem. Am. Mining Congress (chmn., dir. 1989-92, vice chmn., dir.), AIME (former sect. chmn., Disting. Mem. award, Saunders Gold medal), Am. Found. Phosphate Prodn. (bd. dirs.), Am. Australian Assn., Mining and Metall. Soc. Am. (pres. 1981-83, mem. exec. com.), Can. Inst. Mining and Mettal., Soc. Mining. Engrs. (Jackling award 1993), NAM (mem. natural resource com.), N.Mex. Mining Assn. (former chmn., dir.), Internat. Copper Assn. (bd. dirs.), Adv. Coun. Internat. Investments, Internat. Coun. Metals and Environ. (bd. dirs.), New Orleans City Club (bd. govs.), Met. Club Denver, Sky Club, Copper Club, Univ. Club, Mining Club (v.p., gov. 1979—), Petroleum Club (New Orleans), Sierra Club. Republican. Presbyterian. Clubs: City, New Orleans Country; Univ. (N.Y.C.). Office: Cyprus Minerals Co 9100 E Mineral Circle Englewood CO 80155

WARD, PAUL HUTCHINS, otolaryngologist, educator; b. Lawrence, Ind., Apr. 24, 1928; s. Howard Hutchins and Lillian (Anderson) W.; m. Suzanne Fowler, Feb. 7, 1976; children: Walter, Judith. AB, Anderson Coll., 1953; MD, John Hopkins U., 1957. Diplomate Am. Bd. Otolaryngology (chmn. exam. com. 1988—, mem. exec. com.). Intern Henry Ford Hosp., Detroit, 1957-58; resident U. Chgo. Hosps., 1958-61, spl. fellow, 1962-64; asst. prof. surgery, chief head and neck svc. U. Chgo. Sch. Medicine, 1962-64; assoc. prof., chmn. div. otolaryngology Vanderbilt U. Sch. Medicine, Nashville, 1964-68; prof. surgery, chief div. head and neck surgery UCLA Sch. Medicine, 1968-92, prof. emeritus, 1992—; cons. Wadsworth VA Hosp., L.A., 1968-92, U.S. Naval Hosp., 1969-92, emeritus, 1992—; staff UCLA Hosps. and Clinic, 1968-92, L.A. County-Harbor Gen. Hosp., Torrance, Calif., 1968-92, Cedars-Sinai Med. Ctr., L.A., 1977-92, L.A. County-Olive View Hosp., Van Nuys, Calif., 1978-92; lectr. in field. Author 9 books, including: Deafness in Childhood, 1978; cons. editor Western Jour. Medicine, 1970-80, Annals Ototoly, Rhinolaryngology, 1968—; sr. editor Laryngoscope, 1979-92, Acta Otolaryngolica Scandinavia, 1980—; contbr. over 320 articles to profl. jours. Bd. dirs., v.p. Hope for Hearing Found., 1969—, UCLA Hosp. Chaplaincy Svc., 1975-82, pres. 1977-81; trustee Blalock Found., 1979-92. Staff sgt. Med. Svc. Corps, U.S. Army, 1946-49. Recipient Gold medal Ill. Med. Soc., 1963, Ethicon Spectacular Problems in Surgery Cine award, 1963, Ignacio Barraquer award. Mem. ACS (sr. advisor com. on med. motion pictures, 1984-89, sr. advisor 1988-89, regent 1990—), Am. Acad. Ophthalmology and Otolaryngology (1st v.p. 1979-80, coord. continuing edn. 1983-89, Gold medal 1974-75), AMA (Billings Silver medal 1975), Calif. Med. Assn., L.A. County Med. Soc., Am. Acad. Facial Plastic and Reconstructive Surgery (com. on rsch. 1973-80), Am. Coun. of Otolaryngology, Am. Laryngological Assn (editor Historian 1989—), Am. Soc. Head and Neck Surgery (coun. 1979—, pres. 1983-84), Triological Soc. (coun. mem. 1988—, pres.-elect 1990, pres. 1990-91), Pan Pacific Surg. Soc. (v.p. 1982-92, program chmn. otolaryngology 1988, 90), Am. Broncho-Esophogological Assn. (pres. 1977-78), Collegium Otorhinolaryngologicum Sacrum, PAcific Caost Oto-Ophthal. Soc. (v.p. 1975-76), Otological Soc., Barany Soc., Cleve. Otolaryngology Soc. (hon.), Acoustical Soc. Am., Internat. Soc. Lymphology, Soc. Univ. Otolaryngologists (pres. 1976), Sigma Xi. Office: UCLA Sch Medicine 10833 Le Conte Ave Los Angeles CA 90024-1602

WARD, PAUL JERALD, lawyer; b. Chgo., Sept. 1, 1949; m. Cynthia Ann Blair, 1973; children: Meredyth, Emerson. BS in History, Ea. Ill. U., 1971, MA in Polit. Sci., 1974; JD, So. Meth. U., 1975; cert., Harvard U., 1982. Bar: Tex. 1976, Ind., 1976, D.C. 1977, S.C. 1980, Ariz. 1992. Program assoc. Lilly Endowment, Inc., Indpls., 1976-77; assoc. Casey, Lane and Mittendorf, Washington, 1977-79; sr. v.p., gen. counsel U. S.C., Columbia, 1979-91; gen. counsel Ariz. State U., 1991—. Contbr. articles to profl. jours. Mem. Leadership S.C., 1980-81, Columbia, 1984-85; mem. residential design rev. com. Harbison Community Assn., 1986-90; bd. patrons Koger Ctr. for Performing Arts, 1985-91; loaned exec. United Way, Midlands; bd. dirs. Meadowfield Neighborhood Assn., 1982-84, Am. Heart Assn. of Richard County, 1987-90. Mem. ABA, Nat. Assn. Coll. and Univ. Attys. (chmn. electronic networking com. 1988-90, bd. dirs. 1988-92), Am. Corp. Counsel Assn., Pi Sigma Alpha, Phi Alpha Theta, Phi Alpha Delta, Sigma Chi. Methodist. Home: 1606 E Glenhaven Dr Phoenix AZ 85044-9431 Office: Ariz State U Office Gen Counsel Tempe AZ 85287-2003

WARD, ROBERT EDWARD, retired political science educator and university administrator; b. San Francisco, Jan. 29, 1916; s. Edward Butler and Claire Catherine (Unger) W.; m. Constance Regina Barnett, Oct. 31, 1942; children: Erica Anne, Katherine Elizabeth. B.A., Stanford U., 1936; M.A., U. Calif.-Berkeley, 1938, Ph.D., 1948. Instr. in polit. sci. U. Mich., 1948-50, asst. prof. polit. sci., 1950-54, assoc. prof., 1954-58, prof., 1958-73; prof. Stanford U., 1973-87, dir. Center for Research in Internat. Studies, 1973-87; cons. in field; advisor Center for Strategic and Internat. Studies, Washington, 1968-87. Author: Modern Political Systems: Asia, 1963, Political Modernization in Japan and Turkey, 1964. Mem. nat. council Nat. Endowment for Humanities, Washington, 1968-73; mem. Pres.'s Commn. on Fgn. Lang.-Internat. Studies, 1978-79; chmn. Japan-U.S. Friendship Commn., 1980-83; mem. Dept. Def. Univ. Forum, 1982-87. Served to lt. (j.g.) USN, 1942-45. Recipient Japan Found. award Tokyo, 1976; recipient Order of Sacred Treasure 2d class (Japan), 1983. Fellow Am. Acad. Arts and Scis.; mem. Am. Polit. Sci. Assn. (pres. 1972-73), Assn. Asian Studies (pres. 1972-73), Social Sci. Research Council (chmn. 1969-71), Am. Philos. Soc. Home: Box 8129 501 Portola Rd Portola Valley CA 94028

WARD, ROGER WILSON, corporate executive, physicist; b. Paris, Tex., Dec. 2, 1944; s. Alvin Lavell Ward and Anna Muriel (Miller) Anderson; m. Patricia Ann Lambright, Aug. 20, 1967 (div. 1979); m. Kimberley Elaine Lohman, May 4, 1979; children: Tara D., Eric N.D. BA in Physics, McMurry Coll., 1967; MS in Physics, Purdue U., 1969. With Hewlett Packard Co., Palo Alto, Calif., 1969-75; product mgr. Litronix, Cupertino,

Calif., 1975-77; design engr. Statek, Orange, Calif., 1977-79; v.p. Colo. Crystal Corp, Loveland, 1979-81; engring mgr. Motorola Corp., Ft. Lauderdale, Fla., 1981-83; v.p., co-owner Quartztronics, Inc., Salt Lake City, 1983-90; pres., co-owner QuartzDyne, Inc., Salt Lake City, 1990—; chmn. bd. QuartzDyne. Inventee in field; contbr. articles to profl. jours. Mem. IEEE (sr.), Instrument Soc. of Am. (sr.), Sigma Pi Sigma. Office: QuartzDyne Inc 1020 Atherton Dr Bldg C Salt Lake City UT 84123-3402

WARD, STEPHEN BEECHER, investment company executive, economist; b. Arlington, Va., Apr. 5, 1955; s. Henry Beecher and Frances Wright (Galvin) W.; m. Elizabeth Sarah Hirsch, July 5, 1981. BA in Econs., Va. Poly. Inst. and State U., 1977; MBA, U. Pa., 1982. Economist EPA, Washington, 1977-80; investment analyst Federated Investors Inc., Pitts., 1982-84, asst. v.p., 1984-88, v.p., 1988-91; v.p. Charles Schwab Investment Mgmt, San Francisco, 1991-92, chief investment officer fixed income portfoios, 1992—. Mem. Assn. for Investment Mgmt. and Rsch., Nat. Fedn. Mcpl. Analysts, Security Analysts San Francisco. Republican. Office: Charles Schwab Investment Mgmt 101 Market St San Francisco CA 94105

WARDEN, JOHN PETER, vocational school educator; b. Marion, Ind., Apr. 7, 1942; s. John Lavonne Biddle and Marjorie Louise (Pitts) Wyncoop; m. Dolly Padageorgiou, Sept. 26, 1961 (div. 1979); m. Millie Calcagny Paollela, Oct. 20, 1984; children: Jim, Cheryl, Rocco. AS, Chaffey Coll., 1985; BS in Edn. and History, Indiana U., 1969, MS in Social Studies, 1972. Insp. Chrysler Corp., Kokomo, Ind., 1965-67; tchr. Martinville (Ind.) Sch. Dist., 1969-81; substitute tchr. Chino (Calif.) Unified Sch. Dist., 1982-84; GED tchr. Inland Empire Job Corps Ctr., San Bernardino, Calif., 1984-86, academic supr., 1986-91, vocat. supr., 1992—; owner Warden's Tax Svc.; cons. San Bernardino (Calif.) Schs./Multi Media, 1988-90. Home: 1610 N El Dorado Ave Ontario CA 91764 Office: Inland Empire Job Corp Ctr 3173 Keny St San Bernardino CA 92405

WARDEN, ROBERT MARTIN, design engineer; b. Madelia, Minn., May 20, 1953; s. Harry L. and Lois (Martin) W.; m. Janet Elaine Maddox, June 25, 1978; children: Patrick, Ronda. BSME, U. Calif. Santa Barbara, 1977. Design engr. Astro Rsch. Corp., Carpinteria, Calif., 1977-83; engr. Anarad, Santa Barbara, 1983-85; sr. engr. Able Engring. Co., Goleta, Calif., 1985—; session chmn. NASA Mechanisms Symposium, Jet Propulsion Lab., Pasadena, Calif., 1991; author, presenter various confs. Patentee in field. Office: Able Engring Co Inc 93 Castilian Dr Goleta CA 93117

WARD-HAGEN, STACEY LEA, nurse; b. San Antonio, Jan. 20, 1959; d. William Tate and Dorothy Ward; m. Lonnie Lee Hagen, Feb. 20, 1988. BSN, U. San Antonio, 1981. RN, Tex., Calif.; cert. ACLS; CCRN. Nurse Med. Ctr. Hosp., San Antonio, 1981-85, Nurse Focus, Napa, Calif., 1989—. Vol. Am. Diabetes Assn., Napa, 1990—. 1st lt. USAF, 1986-89. Mem. AACN, U. Tex. Health Sci. Ctr. Sch. Nursing Alumni Assn., Peanuts Collector Club. Lutheran.

WARD-SHAW, SHEILA THERESA, nurse; b. N.Y.C., June 20, 1951; d. Arthur and Cynthia Melba (Mapp) Jenkins; m. Howard V. Ward, Nov. 1977 (div. 1981); m. Thomas N. Shaw, Sept. 1988; children: Tanyatta, Barbara, Thomas. Student, Rockland Community Coll., 1973, U. Nev., Las Vegas, 1984. Charge nurse Hillcrest (N.Y.) Nursing Home, 1973-74; infirmary nurse St. Agatha's Home for Children, Nanuet, N.Y., 1974-75; temp. bldg. charge nurse Letchworth Village, Thiells, N.Y., 1976; charge nurse New Paltz (N.Y.) Nursing Home, 1977; non secure detention, foster bdg. parent St. Agatha's Home for Children, Nanuet, 1977-79; asst. nursing supr., inservice coord., infection control nurse So Nev. Mental Retardation, Las Vegas, 1979-84; psychiat. nurse II evening duty officer Harbor View Devel. Ctr., Valdez, Alaska, 1987-89; infection control, employee health nurse, unit coord. North Star Hosp., Anchorage, 1989-92; psychiat. nurse, infection control Oak Creek Hosp., San Jose, Calif., 1992—; psychiat. nurse VA Hosp. Menlo Park Divsn., Palo Alto, 1992—. Campaign worker Nev. Gov. Bryan Dem. Candidate, Las Vegas, 1983-84, Pearson for County Commn. Race, Las Vegas, 1984; pres. Clark County Health Educators, 1983; mem. APIC., 1980-85. Mem. Assn. for Practioners of Infection Control. Roman Catholic. Office: VA Hosp Palo Alto MPD 3801 Miranda Palo Alto CA 94304

WARD-STEINMAN, DAVID, composer, music educator; b. Alexandria, La., Nov. 6, 1936; s. Irving Steinman and Daisy Leila (Ward) W.-S.; m. Susan Diana Lucas, Dec. 28, 1956; children: Jenna, Matthew. MusB cum laude, Fla. State U., 1957; MusM, U. Ill., 1958, DMA, 1961; studies with, Nadia Boulanger, Paris, 1958-59; postdoctoral vis. fellow, Princeton U., 1970. Grad. instr. U. Ill., 1957-58; mem. faculty San Diego State U., 1961—, prof. music, 1968—, dir. comprehensive musicianship program, 1972—, composer in residence, 1961—, univ. research lectr., 1986-87; mem. summer faculty Eastman Sch. Music Workshop, 1969; Ford Found. composer in residence Tampa Bay (Fla.) Area, 1970-72; acad. cons. U. North Sumatra (Indonesia), 1982; concert and lecture tour U.S. Info. Agy., Indonesia, 1982; mem. faculty Coll. Music Soc. Nat. Inst. for Music in Gen. Studies, U. Colo., 1983, 84, Calif. State Summer Sch. for the Arts, Loyola Marymount U., 1988; composer-in-residence Brevard Music Ctr., N.C., summer 1986. Composer: Symphony, 1959, Prelude & Toccata for orch., 1962, Concerto No. 2 for chamber orch., 1962, ballet Western Orpheus, 1964, Cello Concerto, 1966, These Three ballet, 1966, The Tale of Issoumbochi chamber opera, 1968, Rituals for Dancers and Musicians, 1971, Antares, 1971, Arcturus, 1972, The Tracker, 1976, Brancusi's Brass Beds, 1977; oratorio Song of Moses, 1964; Jazz Tangents, 1967, Childs Play, 1968; 3-act opera Tamar, 1977; Golden Apples, 1981; choral suite Of Wind and Water, 1982; Christmas cantata And In These Times, 1982; Moiré for piano and chamber ensemble, 1983, And Waken Green, song cycle on poems by Douglas Worth, 1983, Olympics Overture for orchestra, 1984, Children's Corner Revisited, song cycle, 1984, Summer Suite for oboe and piano, 1984, Quintessence for double quintet and percussion, 1985, Chroma concerto for multiple keyboards, percussion and chamber orch., 1985, Winging It for chamber orchestra, 1986, Elegy for Astronauts, for orchestra, 1986, What's Left for piano, 1987, Gemini for 2 guitars, 1988, Intersections II: Borobudur, Under Capricorn, 1989, 1989 Voices from the Gallery, 1990, Cinnabar for viola and piano, 1991, Seasons Fantastic for chorus and harp, 1992, Cinnabar Concerto for Viola and Chamber Orchestra, 1993; recs. include Fragments from Sappho, 1969; Duo for cello and piano, 1974, Childs Play for bassoon and piano, 1974, The Tracker, 1989, Brancusi's Brass Beds, 1984, concert suite from Western Orpheus, 1987, Sonata for Piano Fortified, 1987, Moiré, 1987, 3 Songs for Clarinet and Piano, 1987, Concerto #2 for Chamber Orchestra, 1990; commd. by Chgo. Symphony, Joffrey Ballet, numerous others; author: (with Susan L. Ward-Steinman) Comparative Anthology of Musical Forms, 2 vols, 1976, Toward a Comparative Structural Theory of the Arts, 1989. Recipient Joseph H. Bearns Prize in Music Columbia U., 1961, SAI Am. Music award, 1962, Dohnanyi award, 1965, ann. BMI awards, 1970—, Broadcast Music prize, 1954, 55, 60, 61; named Outstanding Prof., Calif. State Univs. and Colls., 1968; Fulbright sr. scholar La Trobe U. and Victorian Coll. Arts, Victorian Arts Ctr., Melbourne, Australia, 1989-90. Mem. Broadcast Music, Inc., Soc. Composers, Inc., Coll. Music Soc. (nat. bd. dirs. composition 1992-93), Am. Music Center. Presbyterian. Club: Golden State Flying. Office: San Diego State U Dept Music San Diego CA 92182

WARE, CLYDE, film director, writer, producer; b. Clarksburg, W.Va., 1934; s. C. C. Ware and M. Dorothy Scott; m. Kay Doubleday, 1960; m. Davey Davison, 1962; m. Charlie Young, 1977; children: Jud Scott, Lee Ashby. Student, W.Va. U., Lee Strasberg Inst., 1955-61. Writer, dir. (feature films) The Spy with My Face, 1967, No Bugles, 1972, Human Error, 1989, Bad Jim, 1990, Another Time, Another Place, 1991, (TV movies) Pretty Boy Floyd, 1975, Hatfields and McCoys, 1976, 300 Miles for Stephanie, 1981, Coward of the County, 1985, The Alamo, 1987, Mojave, 1993, The Silent Gun, All the Kind Strangers, (TV episodes) Gunsmoke, Rawhide, Bonanza, Airwolf, Knots Landing, McGiver, Dynasty; author: The Innocents, The Eden Tree. Recipient Spur award, 1970, Emmy award, 1975. Home: 1252 N Laurel Ave B Los Angeles CA 90046 Office: 7510 Sunset Blvd # 552 Los Angeles CA 90046

WARE, JAMES EDMAN, human resources consultant; b. Nampa, Idaho, Jan. 19, 1937; s. Alden Edman and Ruby Lillian (Bachman) Ware.; m. Judith Lee Druxman, July 17, 1959; children: Bradford James, Heather Lee. BBA, U. Wash., 1959. Mgr. employee tng. Transamerican Ins. Co., Los Angeles, 1959-66; regional personnel mgr. Allstate Ins. Co., Pasadena, Calif., 1966-69, Salem, Oreg., 1969-70, Seattle, 1970-72; v.p. adminstrv. services Intermountain Gas Co., Boise, Idaho, 1972-92. bd. dirs. Stemilt Growers, Idaho St. Personnel Com., Boise, 1988, Ada County Civil Service Com., Boise, 1978-88. Named Profl. of the Year 1985, Human Resources Assn. of Treasure Valley, Boise, ID. Mem. Am. Soc. Personnel Adminstrn., Soc. Human Resource Mgmt. (past nat. chmn.). Office: IEC Mgmt Resource Group PO Box 7186 Boise ID 83707

WARE, JAMES W., federal judge; b. 1946. BA, Calif. Luth. U., 1969; JD, Stanford U., 1972. Assoc. Blase, Valentine & Klein, Palo Alto, Calif., 1972-77, ptnr., 1977; judge Santa Clara County Superior Ct., U.S. Dist. Ct. (no. dist.) Calif., 1990—; pro bono East Palo Alto Law Project. Active Am. Leadership Forum; mem. bd. visitors Stanford Law Sch.; active Martin Luther King Papers Project. 2nd lt. USAR, 1969-86. Office: US Dist Cts 280 S First St Rm 2112 San Jose CA 95113*

WARE, WILLIS HOWARD, computer scientist; b. Atlantic City, Aug. 31, 1920; s. Willis and Ethel (Rosswork) W.; m. Floy Hoffer, Oct. 10, 1943; children—Deborah Susanne Ware Pinson, David Willis, Alison Floy Ware Manoli. B.S.E.E., U. Pa., 1941; M.S.E.E., MIT, 1942; Ph.D. in Elec. Engring, Princeton U., 1951. Research engr. Hazeltine Electronics Corp., Little Neck, N.Y., 1942-46; mem. research staff Inst. Advanced Study, Princeton, N.J., 1946-51, North Am. Aviation, Downey, Calif., 1951-52; mem. corp. research staff Rand Corp., Santa Monica, Calif., 1952—; adj. prof. UCLA Extension Service, 1955-68; first chmn. Am. Fedn. Info. Processing Socs., 1961, 62; chmn. HEW sec.'s Adv. Com. on Automated Personal Data Systems, 1971-73; mem. Privacy Protection Study Commn., 1975-77, vice chmn., 1975-77; mem. numerous other adv. groups, spl. coms. for fed. govt., 1959—. Author: Digital Computer Technology and Design, vols. I and II, 1963. Recipient Computer Scis. Man of Yr. award Data Processing Mgmt. Assn., 1975, Exceptional Civilian Svc. medal USAF, 1979, Disting. Svc. award Am. Fedn. Info. Processing Socs., 1986, Nat. Computer System Security award Nat. Computer Systems Lab./Nat. Computer Security Ctr., 1989. Fellow IEEE (Centennial medal 1984), AAAS; mem. Assn. Computing Machinery, NAE, AIAA, Sigma Xi, Eta Kappa Nu, Pi Mu Epsilon, Tau Beta Pi. Office: The Rand Corp 1700 Main St Santa Monica CA 90407-2138

WAREHALL, WILLIAM DONALD, art educator; b. Detroit, July 12, 1942; s. John P. and Helen (Szymanski) W.; 1 child, Eric Ryder; m. Kathryn Coolbaugh, Dec. 21, 1985; 1 child, Elle Lauren. BFA, Wayne State U., 1968; MFA, U. Wis., 1971. Instr. of art U. Minn., Mpls., 1971-73; artist in residence L.I. U., 1972-73; asst. prof. of art Calif. State U., San Bernardino, 1973-77; artist in residence U. So. Calif., 1974-75; asst. prof. of art La. State U., Baton Rouge, 1977-78; assoc. prof. art Calif. State U., San Bernardino, 1978-82, prof., 1982—; exchange prof. Va. Commonwealth U., Richmond, Va., 1986; chair Calif. State U., San Bernardino, 1988-90; artist in residence Buckingham Coll. Art & Design, High Wycomb, England, 1993—. Executed reproduction of 1000 A.D. shipping bottles Inst. of Nautical Archaeology, 1990. Mem. Coll. Art Assn., Am. Crafts Coun. Home: 1340 S Center St Redlands CA 92373 Office: Calif State U 5500 University Pky San Bernardino CA 92407-2318

WARK, JOHN CHARLES, broadcasting executive, consultant; b. Pueblo, Colo., Apr. 15, 1959; s. James Gordon and Judith Carol (Springer) W. BS in Journalism, U. Colo., 1986. Radio talk show host Sta. KBPI/KNUS-FM, Denver, 1984-87; freelance reporter Denver, 1986-87; cons. U.S. AID, Washington, 1987-88; gen. mgr. Sta. KNUS-KBXG, Denver, 1989-90; pres. Boulder (Colo.) Broadcasting Corp., 1988-90; owner Juhu Wark Comml. Photography, Pueblo, Colo., 1990—; bd. dirs. KAIR, Boulder, 1985-86. Office: 706 S Main St Pueblo CO 81004

WARNAS, JOSEPH JOHN, municipal official; b. Boston, Aug. 31, 1933; s. Augustas and Nellie (Pipiras) W.; m. Bernice Gearlene Sarver (dec. July 1983); children: Robert John, Kimberly Joanne; m. Ruth Ellen Haaker, Jan. 12, 1985. BS in Mgmt., Boston Coll., 1955; MBA in Mgmt., Ariz. State U., 1971. Adminstr. subcontract Gen. Motors, Oak Creek, Wis., 1958-65; mgr. purchasing Sperry Rand Corp., Phoenix, 1965-70; dir. material mgmt. dept. Maricopa County, Phoenix, 1970—; Mem. Joint Fed., State and local Govt. Adv. Bd GSA, Washington, 1974; mem. exptl. tech. adv. com. Nat. Inst. Govt. Purchasing & GSA, Washington, 1975; guest lectr. Ariz. State U., Tempe, Glendale Community Coll.; instr. seminars Nat. Inst. Govt. Purchasing, Washington. Assoc. editor Aljian's Purchasers Handbook, 4th rev. edit., 1982; contbr. articles to profl. jours. Mem. State Ariz. Purchasing Rev. Bd., Phoenix, 1980, Men's Zoo Aux., Phoenix, 1976—. Served as 1st lt. U.S. Army, 1956-58. Mem. Nat. Inst. Govtl. Purchasing (pres. 1971, bd. dirs. 1972—, sr. del. to Internat. Fedn. Purchasing and Mgmt. 1983), Ariz. State Capitol Chpt. Nat. Inst. Govtl. Purchasing Inc. (founder, pres. 1977), Purchasing Mgmt. Assn. Ariz. (pres. 1973), Sigma Iota Epsilon. Republican. Roman Catholic. Home: 12511 N 76th Pl Scottsdale AZ 85260-4839 Office: Maricopa County Material Mgmt Ctr 320 W Lincoln St Phoenix AZ 85003-2438

WARNATH, MAXINE AMMER, organizational psychologist, educator; b. N.Y.C., Dec. 3, 1928; d. Philip and Jeanette Ammer; m. Charles Frederick Warnath, Aug. 20, 1952; children: Stephen Charles, Cindy Ruth. B.A., Bklyn. Coll., 1949; M.A., Columbia U., 1951, Ed.D., 1982. Lic. psychologist, Oreg. Various profl. positions Hunter Coll., U. Minn., U. Nebr., U. Oreg., 1951-62; asst. prof. psychology Oreg. Coll. Edn., Monmouth, 1962-77; assoc. prof. psychology, chmn. dept. psychology and spl. edn. Western Oreg. St. Coll., Monmouth, 1978-83, prof. 1986—, dir. organizational psychology program 1983—; pres. Profl. Perspectives Internat., Salem, Oreg., 1987—; cons., dir. Orgn. Rsch. and Devel., Salem, Oreg., 1982—, seminar leader Endeavors for Excellence program. Author: Power Dynamism, 1987. Mem. APA (com. pre-coll. psychology 1970-74), ASTD, N.Y. Acad. Sci., Oreg. Acad. Sci., Oreg. Psychol. Assn. (pres. 1980-81, pres.-elect 1979-80, legis. liaison 1977-78), Western Psychol. Assn. Office: Profl Perspectives Internat PO Box 2265 Salem OR 97308-2265

WARNE, WILLIAM ELMO, irrigationist; b. nr. Seafield, Ind., Sept. 2, 1905; s. William Rufus and Nettie Jane (Williams) W.; m. Edith Margaret Peterson, July 9, 1929; children: Jane Ingrid (Mrs. David C. Beeder), William Robert, Margaret Edith (Mrs. John W. Monroe). AB, U. Calif., 1927; DEcons (hon.), Yonsei U., Seoul, 1959; LLD, Seoul Nat. U., 1959. Reporter San Francisco Bull. and Oakland (Calif.) Post-Enquirer, 1925-27; news editor Brawley (Calif.) News, 1927, Calexico (Calif.) Chronicle, 1927-28; editor, night mgr. L.A. bur. AP, 1928-31, corr. San Diego bur., 1931-33, Washington corr., 1933-35; editor, bur. reclamation Dept. Interior, 1935-37; on staff Third World Power Conf., 1936; assoc. to reviewing com. Nat. Resources Com. on preparation Drainage Basin Problems and Programs, 1936, mem. editorial com. for revision, 1937; chief of information Bur. Reclamation, 1937-42; co-dir. (with Harlan H. Barrows) Columbia Basin Joint Investigations, 1939-42; chief of staff, war prodn. drive WPB, 1942; asst. dir. div. power Dept. Interior, 1942-43, dept. dir. information, 1943; asst. commr. Bur. Reclamation, 1943-47; apptd. asst. sec. Dept. Interior, 1947, asst. sec. Water and Power Devel., 1950-51; U.S. minister charge tech. cooperation Iran, 1951-55, Brazil, 1955-56; U.S. minister and econ. coord. for Korea, 1956-59; dir. Cal. Dept. Fish and Game, 1959-60, Dept. Agr., 1960-61, Dept. Water Resources, 1961-67; v.p. water resources Devel. and Resources Corp., 1967-69; resources cons., 1969—; pres. Warne & Blanton Pubs. Inc., 1985-90, Warne Walnut Wrancho, Inc., 1979—; Disting. Practitioner in Residence Sch. Pub. Adminstrn., U. So. Calif. at Sacramento, 1976-78; adminstr. Resources Agy. of Calif., 1961-63; Chmn. Pres.'s Com. on San Diego Water Supply, 1944-46; chmn. Fed. Inter-Agy. River Basin Com., 1948, Fed. Com. on Alaskan Devel., 1948; pres. Group Health Assn., Inc., 1947-51; chmn. U.S. delegation 2d Inter-Am. Conf. Indian Life, Cuzco, Peru, 1949; U.S. del. 4th World Power Conf., London, Eng., 1950; mem. Calif. Water Pollution Control Bd., 1959-67; vice chmn. 1960-62; mem. water pollution control adv. bd. Dept. Health, Edn. and Welfare, 1962-65, cons., 1966-67; chmn. Calif. delegation Western States Water Council, 1965-67. Author: Mission for Peace-Point 4 in Iran, 1956, The Bureau of Reclamation, 1973, How the Colorado River Was Spent, 1975, The Need to Institutionalize Desalting, 1978; prin. author: The California Experience with Mass Transfers of Water over Long Distances, 1978; editor Geothermal Report, 1985-90. Served as 2d lt. O.R.C., 1927-37. Recipient Disting. Svc. award Dept. Interior, 1951, Disting. Pub. Svc. Honor award FOA, 1955, Order of Crown Shah of Iran, 1955, Outstanding Svc. citation UN Command Korea, 1959, Order of Indsl. Sv. Merit Bronze Star, Korea, 1991. Fellow Nat. Acad. Pub. Adminstrn. (sr., chmn. standing com. on environ. and resources mgmt. 1971-78); mem. Nat. Water Supply Improvement Assn. (pres. 1978-80, Lifetime Achievement award 1984), Internat. Desalination Assn. (founding mem., Lifetime Disting. Service award 1991), Soc. Profl. Journalists, Sutter Club, Nat. Press Club (Washington), Lambda Chi Alpha. Home and Office: 1570 Madrono Ave Palo Alto CA 94306-1015

WARNER, FRANK SHRAKE, lawyer; b. Ogden, Utah, Dec. 14, 1940; s. Frank D. and Emma (Sorensen) W.; m. Sherry Lynn Clary; 1 child, Sheri. JD U. Utah 1964. Bar: Utah 1964. Assoc. Young, Thatcher, Glasmann & Warner, and predecessor, Ogden, 1964-67, ptnr., 1967-72; chmn. Pub. Svc. Commn. Utah, Salt Lake City, 1972-76; ptnr Warner & Wikstrom, Ogden, 1976-79, Warner, Marquardt & Hasenyager, Ogden, 1979-82; pvt. practice, Ogden, 1982-89; ptnr. Warner & Phillips, 1989—. Mem. Utah Gov.'s Com. on Exec. Reorgn., 1978-80. Mem. ABA, Utah Bar Assn. (ethics and discipline com. 1981—), Ogden Gun Club (pres.), Wolf Creek Country (Eden, Utah). Office: 505 27th St Ogden UT 84403-0101

WARNER, JOHN NORTHRUP, tropical agriculture consultant; b. Los Angeles, May 19, 1919; s. Howry Haskell and Mary Stoddard (Roof) W.; m. Dorothy Ann Buese, Nov. 28, 1942 (div. 1979); children—Sherman F., John H., Richard L.; m. Martha Sylvia Dennis, May 12, 1979. B.S., U. Hawaii, 1941; Ph.D., U. Minn.-St. Paul, 1950. Commd. 2d lt. USAR, 1940, advanced through grades to col.; ret. 1968; staff dept. genetics and pathology Exptl. Sta. Hawaiian Sugar Planters' Assn., Honolulu, 1946-61, then head, 1961-66; dir. agrl. svcs., Hawaiian Agronomics, Honolulu, 1966-72, v.p., Iran, Tehran, 1972-75, v.p., dir. agrl. services, Honolulu, 1976-84, ret., 1984; dir. rsch. Sugar Ind. Jamaica, 1988-90; pvt. practice cons. tropical agr. Recipient Gen. John J. Pershing award U.S. Army Command and Gen. Staff Coll., 1962. Mem. Hawaiian Acad. Sci. (pres. Honolulu 1962-63), Hawaiian Sugar Technologists, Internat. Soc. Sugar Cane Technologists, Am. Soc. Agronomy, Crop Sci. Soc. Am., Sigma Xi. Republican. Episcopalian. Home: 79 Ocean Pines Ln Pebble Beach CA 93953

WARNER, LEE MICHAEL, food products executive; b. Cleve., Oct. 10, 1917; s. Ray I. and Ann (Goldber) W.; m. Janet Hoffman, Aug. 3, 1941 (dec. 1961); m. Hope Landis, Mar. 1, 1963; 1 child, Christopher Arthur. BSc, Ohio State U., 1939. Pres., chief executive officer Laurbank Sales Corp., L.A., 1947-53, Pacific Fruit Processing, Beverly Hills, Calif., 1960-78, CENSA, Beverly Hills, 1967-78, Santa Fe Driscoll, Beverly Hills, 1952-78; chmn. Pacific Fruit Processing Inc., South Gate, Calif., 1978—; chmn. State of Calif. Strawberry Adv. Bd., Sacramento, 1963-65; pres. Warner Investment Co., Santa Monica. Bd. mem. Andrus Sch. Gerentology, L.A., 1987—. Capt. U.S. Army, 1942-46. Office: Warner Investment Co 2850 Ocean Park Blvd Ste 292 Santa Monica CA 90405-6200

WARNER, ROLLIN MILES, JR., economics educator, financial planner, real estate broker; b. Evanston, Ill., Dec. 25, 1930; s. Rollin Miles Warner Sr. and Julia Herndon (Polk) Clarkson. BA, Yale U., 1953; cert. in law, Harvard U., 1956; MBA, Stanford U., 1960; cert. in edn. adminstrn., U. San Francisco, 1974. Asst. to v.p. fin. Stanford U., 1960-63; instr. history Town Sch., San Francisco, 1963-70; instr. econs. and math., dean Town Sch., 1975—; prin. Mt. Tamalpais, Ross, Calif., 1972-74; dir. devel. Katharine Branson Sch., Ross, 1974-75, instr. in econs. and math., computer-aided design and Mathematica; cons. Educators Collaborative, San Anselmo, Calif., 1983—, Nat. Ctr. for Fin. Edn., San Francisco, 1986—. Author: America, 1986, Europe, 1986, Africa, Asia, Russia, 1986, Greece, Rome, 1981, Free Enterprise at Work, 1986. Scoutmaster to dist. commr. Boy Scouts Am., San Francisco, 1956—. Recipient Silver Beaver award Boy Scouts Am., 1986. Mem. Am. Econs. Assn., Am. Mgmt. Assn., Inst. Cert. Fin. Planners, Manteca Bd. Realtors, Boston Computer Soc., Berkeley Macintosh User's Group, Real Estate Cert. Inst., Grolier Club N.Y., Univ. Club San Francisco, San Francisco Yacht Club (Belvedere, Calif.), Old Oundelian Club London. Office: Town Sch 2750 Jackson St San Francisco CA 94115-1195

WARNER, VINCENT W., bishop. Bishop Diocese of Olympia, Seattle, 1990—. Office: Diocese of Olympia PO Box 12126 1551 10th Ave E Seattle WA 98102*

WARNER, WALTER DUKE, corporate executive; b. Davenport, Iowa, Feb. 26, 1952; s. Robert Martin and Opal Louise (Gibbons) W.; m. Susan Dee Hafferkamp, Nov. 15, 1975 (div. 1982); 1 child, Natalie. BS, Drake U., 1975. Ops. officer Iowa-Des Moines Nat. Bank, 1975-78; from asst. v.p. to v.p. ops., to v.p. corp. rsch. and devel., to v.p. and dir. mktg. and pub. rels. Cen. Savs. and Loan Assn., San Diego, Calif., 1978-84; pres. The Lomas Santa Fe Cos., Solana Beach, Calif., 1985-91; pres. Ebert Composites Corp., San Diego, 1991—, also bd. dirs.; bd. dirs. Torrey Pines Bank, Solana Beach, Lomas Group Inc., Del Mar, Calif., Madison Valley Properties, Inc., La Jolla, Calif., Nature Preserved of Am. Inc., San Clemente, Calif.; pres., bd. dirs. Regents Pk. Comml. Assns., La Jolla. Bd. dirs. Inst. of the Ams., La Jolla, 1986—, mem. internat. council, 1986—; chmn. bd. dirs., pres. San Diego chpt. Arthritis Found., 1985-87; dir., pres. Gildred Found., Solana Beach, 1986—; founding dir., treas. Golden Triangle Arts Found. Mem. The Exec. Com., Calif. League of Savs. and Loans (mem. mktg. and ops. com. 1982-84), Internat. Forum for Corp. Dirs., Iowa Club of San Diego (founding dir. 1984-85). Republican. Protestant. Office: Ste 1300 701 B St San Diego CA 92101

WARNICK, CLARK ANDREW, financial executive; b. Logan, Utah, Jan. 26, 1959; s. Robert Eldredge and Carol (Porter) W.; m. Lisa Ann Steck, Nov. 15, 1980; children: Amy, Lindsey, Chase. BS, Utah State U., 1984. CPA, Utah. Audit sr. Arthur Young & Co., Salt Lake City, 1984-89; asst. dir. fin. Nu Skin Internat., Inc., Provo, Utah, 1989—. Zone commr. Boy Scouts Am., Orem, 1991—. Mem. AICPA, Utah Assn. of CPA. Mem. LDS. Home: 954 E 1100 North Orem UT 84057 Office: Nu Skin Internat Inc 75 West Center Provo UT 84601

WARNICK, KENNETH L., mining company executive; b. Provo, Utah, June 2, 1944; s. Fred W. and Mary E. (Daly) W.; m. Julie Searle, Sept. 9, 1976; children: Shannon, Jeff, Brett, Kim. BS in Acctg., Brigham Young U., 1968; MA in Econs., U. Okla., 1974. Fin. analyst Ford Motor Co., Dearborn, Mich., 1972-73; bus. analyst Great Salt Lake Minerals & Chems. Corp., Ogden, Utah, 1973-75, corp. planner, 1975-79, v.p. adminstrn., sec., treas., 1979—. Lt. col. USAFR, 1968—. Recipient Nat. Leadership award Jr. Achievement, 1988. Mem. Rotary (pres. Mt. Ogden chpt. 1986-87). Office: PO Box 1190 Ogden UT 84402-1190

WARNKE, ROGER ALLEN, pathology educator; b. Peoria, Ill., Feb. 22, 1945; s. Delmar Carl and Ruth Armanelle (Peard) W.; m. Joan Marie Gebhart, Nov. 18, 1972; children: Kirsten Marie, Lisa Marie. BS, U. Ill., 1967; MD, Washington U., St. Louis, 1971. Diplomate Am. Bd. Pathology. Intern in pathology Stanford (Calif.) U. Med. Sch., 1971-72, resident in pathology, 1972-73, postdoctoral fellow in pathology, 1973-75, postdoctoral fellow in immunology, 1975-76, asst. prof. pathology, 1976-82, assoc. prof., 1983-90; prof., 1991—; cons. Becton Dickinson Monoclonal Ctr., Mountain View, Calif., 1982-88, IDEC, Mountain View, 1985-90; sci. advisor Ventana Med. Systems, Inc., Tucson, 1986—. Contbr. over 150 articles to med. jours., chpts. to books. Recipient Benjamin Castleman award Mass. Gen. Hosp., 1981; Agnes Axtel Moule faculty scholar Stanford U., 1979-82; Nat. Cancer Inst. and NIH rsch. grantee, 1978—. Mem. So. Bay Pathology Soc., Calif. Soc. Pathologists, U.S. Can. Acad. Path., Am. Assn. Pathologists, Soc. for Hematopathology, European Assn. for Haematopathology. Home: 845 Tolman Dr Palo Alto CA 94305-1025 Office: Stanford U Dept Pathology Stanford CA 94305

WARNKEN, DOUGLAS RICHARD, publishing consultant; b. N.Y.C., Apr. 17, 1930; s. Richard William and Juliette (Lindsay) W.; m. Virginia M. Thompson, Sept. 16, 1957; 1 child, William Monroe. A.B., Norwich U., 1952. Sales rep. Prentice-Hall, Inc., Nashville, 1954-56; regional sales mgr. Wadsworth Pub. Co., Inc., Chgo., 1957-59; nat. sales mgr. Wadsworth Pub. Co., Inc., Belmont, Calif., 1960-64; v.p., marketing mgr. Wadsworth Pub. Co., Inc., Belmont, 1964-68; exec. v.p. Wadsworth Pub. Co., Inc., 1968-77, pres., 1977-78, dir., 1971-78; pres., dir. Wadsworth, Inc., 1978-85, chief exec. officer, 1980-84, vice chmn., 1985-86; chmn. bd. Wadsworth Pubs. of Can., Ltd., 1975-80; chmn. bd. Van Nostrand Reinhold Co. Inc., 1981-83, dir., 1983-85; chmn. bd. Anaheim Pub. Co., Inc., 1982-85; dir. Van Nostrand Reinhold Co., Inc., Lange Med. Pubs., Inc., Internat. Thomson Orgn., Inc., 1982-85; chmn. HDL Communications, Inc., 1988—. Active Boy Scouts Am. Served to 1st lt. AUS, 1952-54. Named hon. Ky. col., 1978. Mem. Vols. for Internat. Tech. Assistance, Belmont C. of C. (dir. 1970-80, pres. 1972-73), Western Book Pubs. Assn. (dir. 1971-78), Press Club of San Francisco. Republican. Presbyterian. Clubs: Carmel Valley Golf and Country, Monterey Country, Peninsula Golf and Country. Lodge: Knights of the Vine.

WARNKEN, VIRGINIA MURIEL THOMPSON, social worker; b. Anadarko, Okla., Aug. 13, 1927; d. Sam Monroe and Ruth L. (McAllister) Thompson; A.B., Okla. U., 1946; M.S.W., Washington U., 1949; m. Douglas Richard Warnken, Sept. 16, 1957; 1 son, William Monroe. Med. social cons. Crippled Children's Svcs., Little Rock, 1950-54; supr. VA Hosp., 1954-55; asst. prof. U. Tenn. Sch. Social Work, Nashville, 1955-57; dir. social svcs. N.Y. State Rehab. Hosp., Rockland County, 1957-58; asst. prof. U. Chgo. Sch. Social Svc. Adminstrn., 1958-59; free lance editor, 1960—; instr. evening div. Coll. of Notre Dame, Belmont, Calif., 1967-68; assoc. Mills Hosp., San Mateo, Calif., 1978—; med. aux. Community Hosp., Pacific Grove, Calif., 1980—. Com. mem. C. of C. Miss Belmont Pageant, 1971-84, co-chmn., 1975-78; mem. Monterey Bay Aquarium, 1987—. U.S. Children's Bur. scholar, 1947-49. Mem. Assn. Crippled Children and Adults (dir. 1952-55), Assn. Mentally Retarded (dir. 1953-55), Am. Assn. Med. Social Workers (practice chmn. 1954-55), Nat. Assn. Social Workers (dir. 1962-66), Acad. Cert. Social Workers, Am. Assn. Med. Social Workers, Nat. Rehab. Assn., Am. Psychol. Assn., Am. Orthopsychiat. Assn., Coun. Social Work Edn. Democrat. Presbyterian. Clubs: Carmel Valley Golf and Country, Peninsula Golf and Country, Monterey Golf and Country (Palm Desert, Calif.). Author: Annotated Bibliography of Medical Information and Terminology, 1956. Address: 1399 Bel Aire Rd San Mateo CA 94402

WARNOCK, HAROLD CHARLES, lawyer; b. N.Y.C., Jan. 6, 1912; s. Harry G. and Madge O. (Leunig) W.; m. Mary Louise Phelps, Aug. 29, 1937; children: John Phelps, Martha Ann. LLB, U. Ariz., 1935. Bar: Ariz. 1935, U.S. Supreme Ct. 1952; cert. real estate specialist. Profl. baseball player St. Louis Browns, 1935-36; spl. agt. U.S. Govt., various cities, 1936-38; atty., to pres. Bilby Shoenhair Warnock and Dolph, P.C., Tucson, 1938-88; sr. ptnr. Lesher and Williams, P.C., Tucson, 1988—. Contbr. articles to profl. jours. Active, Republican Party, 1938—; mem. Ariz. Commn. on Uniform Laws, 1955-61, Employment Security Commn., Ariz., 1970-76. Lt. commdr. USNR, 1942-46, Pacific. Fellow Am. Coll. Trial Lawyers, Am. Coll. Trust and Estate Counsel; mem. Am. Bd. Trial Advocates (pres. Tucson chpt. 1973), Nat. Assn. Railroad Trial Counsel (v.p. Pacific chpt. 1974), Tucson Country Club (dir. 1971-75), Old Pueblo Club (dir. 1976-79). Office: 3773 E Broadway Tucson AZ 85716

WARNOCK, PATRIC FRANCIS, executive recruiter; b. Cin., May 5, 1951; s. Francis Michael and Ruth Jane (Benz) W.; m. Anna Elizabeth Vugrinecz, May 18, 1985. BA in Journalism and Math, Syracuse U., 1973, MLS, 1976; MBA, Pace U., 1986. Market researcher Find/SVP, N.Y.C., 1977-79, AT&T, Bedminister, N.J., 1979-86, Newton Evans Research Co., Sunnyvale, Calif., 1986-87, Internat. Tech. Group, Los Altos, Calif., 1987-88, Ernst & Young, San Francisco, 1990-91; owner, mgr. Warnock Rsch., Redwood City, Calif., 1988-90; exec. recruiter Domann Orgn., San Francisco, 1992—. Mem. Am. Mktg. Assn., Spl. Librs. Assn., Soc. Competitive Intelligence Profls. Roman Catholic.

WARREN, BARBARA KATHLEEN (SUE WARREN), wildlife biologist; b. Appleton, Wis., Oct. 3, 1943; d. Richard Grant and Beatrice Marie (Kath) Henika. Diploma, St. Luke's Sch. Nursing, San Francisco, 1965; AS in Forest Tech., Green River Community Coll., Auburn, Wash., 1976; BS in Wildlife Biology, U. Calif., Davis, 1990. RN, Calif.; cert. merit wildlife program devel. Nurse ICU, Ross (Calif.) Gen. Hosp., 1965-66; nurse emergency room CCU, St. Luke's Hosp., 1966-68; head nurse ICU and CCU, Valley Gen. Hosp., Auburn, 1971-76; forest technician Wash. Dept. Natural Resources, Husum, 1976-77; nurse emergency room ICU, Marshall Hosp., Placerville, Calif., 1977-78; forestry and wildlife biology technician U.S. Forest Svc., Pioneer, Calif., 1978-89, trainer for critical incident stress, Region 5, 1987—, dist. wildlife biologist, 1989-90, career advisor, 1990—; asst. forest wildlife biologist U.S. Forest Svc., 1990-91, asst. dist. ranger, 1991-92. Chmn. outdoor program com. Girl Scouts U.S.A., Sacramento, 1981-85, master planning cons., 1984-86; vol. ARC, Sacramento, 1985—, vol. disaster nurse, 1986—. With Nurse Corps, U.S. Army, 1968-71. Recipient award for outstanding svc. Girl Scouts U.S.A., 1987, Role Model of Yr. award, 1989; Sustained Superior Performance and Host of Yr. award Eldorado Nat. Forest, 1988, Regional Affirmative Action award U.S. Forest Svc., 1990, Outstanding Woman award YWCA, 1991. Mem. Wildlife Soc. Democrat. Office: Dist Ranger Pineridge Rd PO Box 300 Shaver Lake CA 93664

WARREN, CHRISTOPHER CHARLES, electronics executive; b. Helena, Mont., July 27, 1949; s. William Louis and Myrtle Estelle (Moren) W.; m. Danette Marie Geordge, Apr. 21, 1972; 1 child, Jeffrey Scott. Grad. high sch., Helena, 1967. Electrician Supreme Electronics, Helena, 1972-81; v.p., svc. technician Capital Music Inc., Helena, 1981—; state exec. Amusement & Music Operators Assn. Coun. of Affiliated States, Chgo., 1990-92, bd. dirs., 1992—. Sgt. USAF, 1968-72, Vietnam. Mem. Internat. Flipper Pinball Assn. (sec., treas. 1992—), Mont. Coin Machine Operators State 8-Ball (chmn.), Valley Nat. 8 Ball Assn. (charter), Amusement and Music Operators Assn. (bd. dirs. 1992—), Ducks Unltd., Eagles, Moose, Rocky Mountain Elk Found. Home: 8473 Green Meadow Dr Helena MT 59601-9379 Office: Capital Music Inc 3108 Broadwater Ave Helena MT 59601-9201

WARREN, DWIGHT WILLIAM, III, physiology educator; b. L.A., Dec. 21, 1942; s. Dwight William Jr. and Edna (Rainen) W.; m. Grace Anita Sturm, Nov. 24, 1965; 1 child, Jennifer Anne. AB, U. Calif., Berkeley, 1964; PhD, U. So. Calif., L.A., 1972. Asst. prof. U. So. Calif., L.A., 1972-78, assoc. prof., 1978-88, prof. dept. physiology and biophysics, 1988—, prof. and acting chmn., dept. Pharmacology and Nutrition, 1992—. Editorial bd. Reproductive Scis., 1989—, Biology of Reproduction, 1990—; contbr. articles to sci. jours. Nat. rsch. svc. sr. fellow USPHS, 1980-81; Fulbright scholar USIA, Finland, 1990. Mem. AAAS, Endocrine Soc., Soc. Study Reproduction, Am. Soc. Andrology, N.Y. Acad. Scis., Assn. Rsch. in Vision and Ophthalmology. Office: Univ So Calif 1333 San Pablo St Los Angeles CA 90033-1026

WARREN, GEORGE EDWARD, television news anchor, reporter; b. Palo Alto, Calif., Dec. 27, 1956; s. James Wilbur and Janet Adelle (Williams) W. Student, U. Mass., 1977-78; BA in Comm., Calif. State U., Chico, 1979. News anchor/reporter KTVL Channel 10, Medford, Oreg., 1979-81, KXTV Channel 10, Sacramento, 1981—. Host March of Dimes "Bid for Bachelors," Sacramento. Recipient Calif. State Fair media awards for best news reporting in large markets, 1984, Best Live News Coverage in Large Markets award Ratio-TV News Dirs. Assn., 1991, Best Live/Spot News Coverage statewide AP, 1991, Best Live/Spot News Coverage, Sacramento Soc. Profl. Journalists, 1991. Office: KXTV PO Box 10 Sacramento CA 95812

WARREN, GERALD LEE, newspaper editor; b. Hastings, Nebr., Aug. 17, 1930; s. Hie Elias and Linnie (Williamson) W.; m. Euphemia Florence Brownell, Nov. 20, 1965 (div.); children: Gerald Benjamin, Euphemia Brownell; m. Viviane M. Pratt, Apr. 27, 1986. A.B., U. Nebr., 1952. Reporter Lincoln Star, Nebr., 1951-52; reporter, asst. city editor San Diego Union, 1956-61; bus. rep. Copley News Service, 1961-63; city editor San Diego Union, 1963-68, asst. mng. editor, 1968-69, editor, 1975-92; editor San Diego Union-Tribune, 1992—; dep. press sec. to Pres. Richard Nixon, 1969-74, Pres. Gerald Ford, 1974-75. Served to lt. (j.g.) USNR, 1952-56. Mem. Am. Soc. Newspaper Editors, Coun. Fgn. Rels., Sigma Delta Chi, Sigma Nu. Republican. Episcopalian. Office: Copley Press Inc 350 Camino De La Reina San Diego CA 92108-3003

WARREN, JAMES DAVID, JR., management consultant, musician; b. Ann Arbor, Mich., Jan. 1, 1951; s. James David and L. Eleanor (Newman) W. BSE in Indls., Ops. Engring. cum laude, U. Mich., 1974, BA in Music cum laude, 1974, MBA, 1976. Cert. mgmt. cons. Systems analyst, project leader, and fin. analyst The Gap Stores, Inc., San Bruno, Calif., 1976-79; sr. cons., mgr., and sr. mgr. Price Waterhouse, San Francisco, 1979-86; mgmt. dir. BDO/Seidman, San Francisco, 1986-88, ptnr., 1988-90; mgmt. cons. Arthur Andersen & Co., 1990—. Organist Park Blvd. Presbyn. Ch., Oakland, Calif., 1977—. Mem. Inst. Mgmt. Cons. v.p. San Francisco chpt. 1985-88), Bohemian Club (organist 1983—). Presbyterian. Home: 1770 Pacific Ave Apt 303 San Francisco CA 94109-2411 Office: Arthur Andersen & Co 1 Market Plz Ste 3500 San Francisco CA 94105-1119

WARREN, LARRY MICHAEL, clergyman; b. Bonne Terre, Mo., Nov. 25, 1946; s. Orson Wesley and Ruth Margaret (Stine) W.; m. Bonnie Jean Monk Chandler, Apr. 9, 1983; children: Samantha Chandler, John, Abigail Chandler, Anne, Meredith. BA cum laude, Lincoln U., 1969; MDiv with honors, St. Paul Sch. Theology, Kansas City, Mo., 1976; D of Ministry, San Francisco Theol. Sem., 1987. Ordained elder United Meth. Ch., 1978. Pastor Cainsville (Mo.) United Meth. Ch., 1975-76, Lakelands Parish, Rathdrum, Idaho, 1976-78; assoc. pastor Audubon Park United Meth. Ch., Spokane, Wash., 1978-83; pastor Faith United Meth. Ch., Everett, Wash., 1983-90, Tacoma First United Meth. Ch., 1990—; adviser Kairos Prison Ministry Wash., Monroe, 1984—; conf. rep. grad. bd. St. Paul Sch. Theology, Kansas City, 1984. Contbr. to col. Dialogue Everett Herald, 1984-88. Adviser DeMolay, Spokane, 1979-81; team mem. Night-Walk, inner-city ministry, Spokane, 1979-82; coord. Ch. Relief Overseas Project Hunger Walk, Spokane and Everett, 1981, 85; vol. chaplain Gen. Hosp. Everett, 1983-90; trustee Deaconess Children's Svcs., Everett, 1983-88. Recipient Legion of Honor DeMolay Internat., 1982. Mem. Fellowship of Reconciliation, North Snohomish County Assn. Chs. (v.p. 1985-89), Pacific N.W. Ann. Conf. Bd. Global Ministries (sec. 1988-92, pres. 1993—). Democrat. Home: 3312 N 19th St Tacoma WA 98406-6007 Office: Tacoma 1st United Meth Ch 423 S K St Tacoma WA 98405-4294

WARREN, NICHOLAS WALTER, synergetics educator; b. Champaign, Ill., Apr. 12, 1941; s. William Joseph and Annette (Chemielewski) W.; m. Sally Lappen, Aug. 2, 1980; children: Adria, Caitrina, Kaitlin. BA in Physics, U. Calif., Berkeley, 1964; MA in Astronomy, Columbia U., 1966, PhD in Geophysics, 1971. Research geophysicist UCLA, 1971-80, assoc. research geophysicist, 1980-83; faculty Otis-Parsons Art Inst., Los Angeles, 1980-90, Internat. Coll., Los Angeles, 1984-86; dean dept. natural sci. Sierra U., Santa Monica, Calif., 1986-87; cons. in art and sci., 1984—. Editor IS Jour., 1989-90; contbr. articles to profl. jours. Mem. AAAS, Internat. Soc. for the Arts Scis and Technology, Nat. Sci. Tchrs. Assn., N.Y. Acad. Sci., Union Concerned Scientists, Wilderness Soc., Amnesty Internat., Sigma Xi. Home: 1016 Spruce St Berkeley CA 94707 Office: Art/Sci Cons 1016 Spruce St Berkeley CA 94707-2628

WARREN, PATRICIA J., museum director; b. Seattle, Dec. 12, 1950; d. Vernon Sidney and Ernestine Abernathy (Bilan) W. BA, U. Wash., 1972, BS, 1975, JD, 1978, MA, 1990. Atty. City Kirkland, Wash., 1978-80, City Bellevue, Wash., 1980-86; mus. dir. Jefferson County Hist. Soc., Port Townsend, Wash., 1990—. Precinct chair 46th Dist., Seattle, 1985-88; mem. Jefferson County AIDS Task Force, Port Townsend, 1991—. U. Wash. fellow, 1988-89. Mem. AAUW, Wash. State Bar Assn., Wash. Mus. Assn. (trustee 1991-93, v.p. 1993—), Rotary Club. Democrat. Office: Jefferson County Hist Soc City Hall 210 Madison St Port Townsend WA 98368

WARREN, PETER WHITSON, art educator; b. Concord, Mass., Sept. 7, 1941; s. Richard and Dorothy Esther (Brown) W.; m. Sandra Twomey, July 1972 (div. 1973); m. Dawn Lee Cannon, Apr. 23, 1975; 1 child, Jonathan Mark Whitson. BA, U. N.H., 1963; MA, U. Iowa, 1967, MFA, 1967. Teaching asst. U. Iowa, Iowa City, 1965-67; instr. to prof. art Ea. Mont. Coll., Billings, Mont., 1967—; chmn. dept. Art Ea. Mont. Coll., 1986-87, 92—. Author: Al's Ham-'n'-Egger & Body Shop Again, 1974; editor/contbr. book: The SLUJ Book, 1976; editorial bd. Alkali Flats, 1982, 85, 90; art exhibited in U.S., Can., N.Z., Australia, Japan, Eng., Italy, Uruguay, Netherlands, Sweden, Argentina, Poland, Ger., Belgium, Spain, France, Brazil, Yugoslavia, Pero, Colombia, Korea. Title III Faculty Devel. grantee, 1979, 84, 85, 90, others. Mem. AAUP, Yellowstone Art Ctr., Photographic Hist. Soc. N. Eng., Kodak Hist. Soc., Photographic Inst. Billings (bd. dirs. 1984-86). Home: 902 24th St W Billings MT 59102-3806 Office: Eastern Montana Coll 1500 N 30th St Billings MT 59101

WARREN, RICHARD WAYNE, obstetrician and gynecologist; b. Puxico, Mo., Nov. 26, 1935; s. Martin R. and Sarah E. (Crump) W.; m. Rosalie J. Franzola, Aug. 16, 1959; children: Lani Marie, Richard W., Paul D. BA, U. Calif., Berkeley, 1957; MD, Stanford U., 1961. Intern, Oakland (Calif.) Naval Hosp., 1961-62; resident in ob-gyn Stanford (Calif.) Med. Ctr., 1964-67; practice medicine specializing in ob-gyn, Mountain View, Calif., 1967—; mem. staff Stanford and El Camino hosps.; pres. Richard W. Warren M.D., Inc.; assoc. clin. prof. ob-gyn Stanford Sch. Medicine. Served with USN, 1961-64. Diplomate Am. Bd. Ob-Gyn. Fellow Am. Coll. Ob-Gyn; mem. AMA, Am. Fertility Soc., Am. Assn. Gynecologic Laparoscopists, Calif. Med. Assn., San Francisco Gynecol. Soc., Peninsula Gynecol. Soc., Assn. Profs. Gynecology and Obstetrics, Royal Soc. Medicine, Shufelt Gynecol. Soc. Santa Clara Valley. Contbr. articles to profl. jours. Home: 102 Atherton Ave Menlo Park CA 94027-4021 Office: 2500 Hospital Dr Mountain View CA 94040-4106

WARREN, WALTER RAYMOND, JR., fluid dynamics and chemical laser company executive; b. N.Y.C., Nov. 25, 1929; s. Walter Raymond and Helen Veronica (McNally) W.; m. Austine Rose Warren, Apr. 24, 1954; children: Michael, Christopher, Walter, Austine, Susan, Richard, Jennifer, John, David, James. B of Aero. Engring., NYU, 1950; MS in Aero. Engring., Princeton U., 1952, PhD in Aero. Engring., 1957. Lab. leader Lockheed Missile and Space Co., Van Nuys, Calif., 1955-56; mgr. exptl. fluid physics Missile and Space div. GE, Valley Forge, Pa., 1956-68; mgr. Aeromechanics and Materials Lab., Valley Forge, 1968; dir Aerophysics Lab. Aerospace Corp., El Segundo, Calif., 1968-81; pres. Pacific Applied Rsch., Palos Verdes, Calif., 1981—; grad. tchr. hypersonics U. Pa., 1962-68; mem. fluid dynamics adv. com. NASA, 1970; mem. laser subcom. USAF Sci. Adv. Bd., 1970-75; mem. device com. High Energy Laser Rev. Group, 1975-78. Contbr. articles to profl. jours. Convair scholar NYU, 1949-50; Guggenheim fellow Princeton U., 1952-53; recipient Sci. award Aerospace Corp., 1979. Fellow AIAA (chmn. plasmadynamics tech. com., assoc. editor). Republican. Roman Catholic. Home and Office: 6 Crestwind Dr Palos Verdes Peninsula CA 90274-5028

WARREN, WILLIAM W., retired academic administrator; b. St. Louis, Mar. 23, 1924; s. Maximillian and Elizabeth (Frahm) W.; m. Norma E. Walk, Nov. 9, 1946; children: Margot E., Renee B. Student, Acme Inst. South Bend, Ind., 1948-50, Ill. Inst. Tech., 1950-52. Registered profl. engr., Wis.; cert. mfg. engr., Wis. Tool and die maker Western Electric Co., Chgo., 1942-48; tool designer Acme Steel Co., Chgo., 1948-50; tool and die design engr. A.B. Dick Co., Chgo., 1950-54; chief prodn. and tooling engr. Am. Hosp. Supply, Two Rivers, Wis., 1954-56; pres. Acme Inst. Tech., Manitowoc, Milw., Wis., 1955-88; sales and cons. engr. Bellows Internat., Akron, Ohio, 1956-78; pres. Cons. and Design Co., Inc., Manitowoc, 1976-88, Scottsdale, Ariz., 1989-92, Tech. Publs., Ltd., Manitowoc, 1976-88, Scottsdale, 1989-92. With U.S. Army, 1944-46. Mem. Soc. Mfg. Engrs. (sec., vice chmn., chmn. Fond du Lac, Wis. chpt. 1955-60, editor monthly bull. 1957-88), Soc. Plastics Engrs. Lutheran. Home: 8027 E La Junta Rd Scottsdale AZ 85255

WARRICK, MARY LELANE, chemicals executive; b. St. Louis, July 21, 1940; d. Marion Lester and Mary Louise Maroney; m. Theodore D. Warrick, Sept. 19, 1977; 1 child, Chrys Noel Wilkinson. BS magna cum laude, So. Oreg. State Coll., 1979. Escrow officer Great Western Fin. Corp., L.A., 1959-65; customer svc. rep. Trans World Airlines, L.A., 1967-77; co-owner Warrick Vineyard & Wooldridge Creek Vineyard, Applegate, Oreg., 1977—; v.p. Sattex Corp., White City, Oreg., 1984-87, pres., chief exec. officer, 1987—. Contbg. author: Three Communities Under Ash. Bd. dirs. North Applegate Watershed Protection Assn., 1989—. Mem. Winegrape Growers Assn., Medford-Jackson County C. of C., Rotary. Office: Sattex Corp PO Box 2593 7932 Pacific Ave White City OR 97503

WARRICK, MILDRED LORINE, librarian, civic worker; b. Kellerton, Iowa, June 21, 1917; d. Webie Arthur and Bonnie Lorine (Hyatt) DeVries; m. Carl Wesley Warrick, Feb. 11, 1937; children: Carl Dwayne, Arthur Will. BS in Edn., Drake U., 1959; M of Librarianship, Kans. State Tchrs. Coll., 1970. Cert. tchr., libr., Iowa. Elem. tchr. Monroe Ctr. Rural Sch., Kellerton, Iowa, 1935-37, Denham Rural Sch., Grand River, Iowa, 1945-48, Grand River Ind. Sch., 1948-52, Woodmansee Rural Sch., Decatur, Iowa, 1952-55, Centennial Rural Sch., Decatur, 1955-56; elem. tchr., acting libr. Cen. Decatur Sch., Leon, Iowa, 1956-71, media libr. jr. and sr. high sch., 1971-79; libr. Northminster Presbyn. Ch., Tucson, 1985—; media resource instr. Graceland Coll., Lamoni, Iowa, 1971-72; lit. dir. S.W. Iowa Assn. Classroom Tchrs., 1965-69. Editor (media packet) Mini History and Quilt Blocks, 1976, Grandma Lori's Nourishing Nuggets for Body and Soul, 1985, As I Recall (Loren Drake), 1989, Foland Family Supplement III, 1983; author: (with Quentin Oiler) Van Der Vlugt Family Record, 1976; compiler, editor Abigail Specials, 1991; compiler Tribute to Ferm Mills 1911-1992, 1992; co-editor: (with Dorothy Heitlinger) Milestones and Touchstones, 1993; contbr. articles to publs. Leader Grand River 4-H Club for Girls, 1954-58; sec. South Ctrl. Iowa Quarter Horse Assn., Chariton, 1967-68; chmn. Decatur County Dems., 1981-83, del., 1970-83; pianist Salvation Army Amphi League of Mercy Rhythm Noters, 1984-90; pianist, dir. Joymakers, 1990—; Sunday Sch. tchr. Decatur United Meth. Ch., 1945-54, 80-83, lay speaker, 1981-83, dir. vacation Bible sch., 1982, 83. Named Classroom Tchr. of Iowa Classroom Tchrs. Assn., 1962, Woman of Yr., Leon Bus. and Profl. Women, 1978, Northminster Presbyn. Ch. Women, 1990; English and reading grantee Nat. Dept. Edn., 1966. Mem. NEA (life), AAUW (chmn. Tucson creative writing/cultural interests 1986-87, 89-93, Honoree award for ednl. found. programs Tucson br., Svc. award 1991), Internat. Reading Assn. (pres. Clarke-Ringgold Decatur chpts. 1967-68), Cen. Community Tchrs. Assn. (pres. 1961-62), Pima County Ret. Tchrs. Assn. (pres. 1989-90), Tucson Bus. and Profl. Women, Decatur County Assn. (pres. 1961-63), Decatur County Ret. Tchrs. Assn. (historian 1980-83), Iowa Edn. Assn. (life), Presbyn. Women (hon. life 1990—), Luth. Ch. Libr. Assn. (historian Tucson area chpt. 1991-92, v.p. 1993-94), Delta Kappa Gamma (pres. Iowa Beta XI chpt. 1974-76, historian Ariz. Alpha Gamma chpt. 1986-89). Democrat. Presbyterian. Home: 2879 E Presidio Rd Tucson AZ 85716-1539

WARSHAUER, JACQUES, financial executive; b. N.Y.C., Apr. 30, 1915; s. Harry and Anna (Chartoff) W.; m. Violet Gilmore, Feb. 12, 1939; children: John Steven, Priscilla, Alan, Victoria. BA, UCLA, 1936; MS, U. Santo Tomas, 1938; teaching credential, Claremont Grad. Sch., 1939; cert. in data processing, Orange Coast Coll., 1964. Founder, dir. Computer Rsch. Corp. (then Electronic Computer div. NCR Co.), 1951-55; exec. Atlas Corp., 1955-58; v.p. long range planning Whittaker Corp., 1958-61; v.p. fin. cons. United Indsl. Corp., 1961-66; adminstr., cons. Guam Econ. Devel. Authority, 1966-67; v.p., mng. dir. Litton Greece, 1967-71; dir. mgmt. advisory svcs. Fox and Co., L.A., 1971-75; pres. Belmont Gen. Corp., 1974-76, Dolphin Equities, 1976-, Alaska Rural Investments, Inc., 1982-84; lectr. U. So. Calif., UCLA, U. Calif., Irvine; prof. bus. U. Ala.; speaker, seminar leader in field; chmn. bd. dirs. Irvine Indsl. Devel. Authority. Columnist weekly newspaper Grunion Gazette, 1978—. Mem. citizens advisory com. Orange County Transp. Commn.; chmn. spl. to study adminstrv. problems of state ednl. system, Ala.; campaign chmn. So. Calif. Arthritis Found. With USAF, 1942. Republican. Methodist. Home: 5 Redwood Tree Ln Irvine CA 92715 Office: Belmont Fin Corp 4032 E Broadway Long Beach CA 90803

WARSHAWSKY, ARNOLD STEPHEN, military analyst; b. Bronx, N.Y., Apr. 18, 1946; s. Nathan and Lillian Warshawsky; m. Gale Ellen Solotar, Sept. 10, 1967; children: Jay David, Barbara Lynn. BS in Chemistry, Poly. Inst. Bklyn., 1967; MS in Physics, Naval Postgrad. Sch., 1973. Commd. 2d lt. U.S. Army, 1966, advanced through grades to lt. col., 1982; intelligence officer 1st Calvalry Div., South Vietnam, 1970-71; weapon effects officer Army Nuclear Agy., Ft. Bliss, Tex., 1973-76; mil. rsch. assoc. Lawrence Livermore (Calif.) Nat. Lab., 1976-79, staff scientist, 1986-88, application project mgr., 1988—; staff analyst OSD/Program Analysis and Evaluation, Washington, 1979-83; intelligence analyst Joint Intelligence Coord. Staff, Washington, 1983-86; ret. U.S. Army, 1986. Scoutmaster, trainer Boy Scouts Am., Danville, Calif., 1967—; bd. dirs. Congregation B'nai Shalom, Walnut Creek, Calif., 1990-91. Decorated Bronze Star with oak leaf cluster, Air medal with silver oak leaf cluster; recipient Dist. award of merit Boy Scouts Am., 1981, Silver Beaver award Boy Scouts Am., 1982. Mem. Mil. Ops. Rsch. Soc. (chmn. composite group 1992—), Am. Philatelic Soc. Jewish. Home: 377 Borica Dr Danville CA 94526

WARTER, CARLOS, psychiatrist; b. Santiago, Chile, May 23, 1947; came to U.S., 1973; s. S. Warter-Tanner and Lotty Goldhaker; m. Carolina Penna Arruabarena, May 25, 1985; children: S. Alexandra, Charles Elliot. MD, U. Chile, Mo., 1971; PhD, Advanced Inst. Social Studies, Mo., 1984. Diplomate Am. Bd. Family Practice, Am. and Internat. Assn. Group Psychotherapy, Internat. Acad. Behavioral Medicine. Intern U. Chile Med. Ctr., 1970, resident in psychiatry, 1971-73; tchr. dept. psychiatry U. Chile, 1971-77; dir. Inst. Health Awareness, Denver, 1974-78; pres. Found. Warter Salud Edn. Paz, 1986—, Found. Gota de Miel, Chile, Colombia, Venezuela, 1978—, World Health Found. for Devel. of Peace, Berkeley, Calif., 1985—; keynote speaker various meetings. Author: Global Vision, Soul Remembers, Despertar, 11 others. Mem., advisor, bd. dirs. Forum Internat. Ctr. Integrative Studies N.Y., Centro Di Studi de l'evoluzione Umana Roma Italy, Environ. Liason Ctr. Nairobi, Kenya; senator Internat. Parliament for Safety and Peace; roving ambassador The Trialogue. Recipient Knight Grand Cross of Order of St. John of Jerusalem, Knight of Malta; Peace Messenger award UN Sec. Gen., 1987, Golden Dolphin award Iberoam. Radio and TV Network, 1987, Pax Mundi award Dag Hamerskjold Diplomatic Acad. in Holland, 1989, medal of Illustrious Messenger of Peace, Ecumenical Confederacy in Argentina and Comdr. in Chief of Air Force, 1990; Knighted in Russia, Ancient Assyrian Chivalric Order, Internat. Congress for Alternative Medicine. Fellow Internat. Acad. Behavioral Medicine; mem. Am. Coll. Preventive Medicine, Internat. Assn. Educators World Peace, Soc. Cientifique du Chile, Inst. Cultural Rsch. U.K. Home: 35 Shadow Circle Sedona AZ 86336 Office: World Health Found, CC 615, Buenos Aires Argentina also: 1400 Shattuck Ave Berkeley CA 94709

WASBAUER, MARIUS SHERIDAN, insect biosystematist; b. Rockford, Ill., Sept. 29, 1928; s. Alfred Marius and Elizabeth (Reed) W.; m. Ruth Kattenberg, June 1951 (div. 1957); children: Carol, David; m. Joanne Elisabeth Slansky, Apr. 12, 1969; 1 child, Kevin Michael. BS, U. Calif., Berkeley, 1951, PhD, 1962. Systematic entomologist Calif. Dept. Food and Agr., Sacramento, 1959-80, sr. insect biosystematist, 1980-92 (ret.); asst. prof. Calif. State U., Sacramento, 1965; dir. Biol. Inst. Tropical Am., San Mateo, Calif. and Quito, Ecuador, 1985-91, pres., 1991—; rsch. assoc. U. Calif., 1979-89; collaborator U.S. Nat. Mus., Washington, 1970—. Author: North American Wasps-Brachystis, 1968, Host Catalog of North American Fruit Flies, 1972, Pompiline Spider Wasps of California, 1986; also articles. With U.S. Army, 1951-53. Fellow Calif. Acad. Scis.; mem. Am. Philos. Soc., Pacific Coast Entomol. Soc., Kans. Entomol. Soc., Sacramento Orchid Soc. (bd. dirs. 1965), Sacramento Recorder Soc. (bd. dirs., treas. 1987-89), Sigma Xi. Home: 6596 Gloria Dr Sacramento CA 95831

WASDEN, WINIFRED SAWAYA, English language educator, writer; b. Kemmerer, Wyo., Apr. 15, 1938; d. George Sabeh and Letta Louise (Gerken) Sawaya; m. John Frederic Wasden, Dec. 20, 1960; children: Frederic Keith, Carol Elizabeth. BA with honors, U. Wyo., 1960, MA, 1961. Emergency instr. U. Wyo., Laramie, 1960-61; tchr. English Worland (Wyo.) High Sch., 1963; instr. NW Community Coll., Powell, Wyo., 1964-91, prof., 1991—, English coord., 1990—. Contbr. articles to pubs.; author numerous poems. Mem. Powell Bd. Adjustments, 1974-86; chmn., bd. dirs. Civic Orch. and Chorus, Powell, 1981-88; mem. Wyo. Coun. for the Humanities, 1978-79, coord. Big Horn Basin Project, 1980-85. Mem. Wyo. Oral History and Folklore Assn. (v.p. 1984-85, bd. dirs. 1985-86), Wyo. Assn. Tchrs. English, N.W. Community Coll. Faculty Assn. (pres. 1977-78), AAAUW, Oral History Assn., Am. Folklore Soc., Northwest Oral History Assn., Delta Kappa Gamma (pres. Powell chpt. 1978-80), Phi Rho Pi (hon.). Republican. Roman Catholic. Office: NW Community Coll Powell WY 82435

WASHBURN, FRANK MURRAY, management consultant; b. Portland, Oreg., Feb. 28, 1926; s. Fred Lucian and Dorothy (Murray) W.; m. Buena

Stewart, Sept. 3, 1950; children: Bonnie Belle, Mary Ann, Terri Lee, Scott Stewart, Nancy Ellen. BA, Willamette U., 1950; MS, Springfield (Mass.) Coll., 1952. Camp dir. YMCA, Portland, 1950; youth work dir. YMCA, Salem, Oreg., 1952-57; adult program dir. YMCA, Seattle, 1957-59, asst. met. dir., 1959-63, assoc. met. dir., 1963-68; exec. dir. YMCA Blue Ridge Assembly, Black Mountain, N.C., 1968-85; pres. Frank M. Washburn and Assocs., Salem, 1985—. Contbr. articles to profl. jours. Bd. dirs. Salem Family YMCA, 1989—; pres. Highland Farms Retirement Ctr., Black Mountain, 1980-82. Sgt. USAF, 1944-46. Named Jr. 1st Citizen Jaycees, Salem, 1956; recipient Distinguished Alumni award Willamette U., Salem, 1973. Mem. Am. Camping Assn. (pres. 1968-70, Disting. Service award 1974), Internat. Assn. Conf. Ctr. Adminstrs. (pres. 1976-80), Ret. YMCA Dirs. (pres. Allen Stone chpt.). Republican. Presbyterian. Home and Office: 398 Jerris Ave SE Salem OR 97302-5278

WASHBURN, LAWRENCE ROBERT, manufacturing executive; b. Jackson, Mich., Aug. 5, 1941; s. Lawrence Merton and Elvina Marie (Morgan) W.; m. Kay France Wieczerzak, Nov. 21, 1970; children: Lawrence Robert II, Alexa Kay. BA in History, Govt., So. Calif. Coll., 1974. Supr., engr. Tool Rsch. & Engring., Inc., Santa Ana, Calif., 1968-77; ops. mgr. Knudsen Systems, Inc., Anaheim, Calif., 1977-86; plant mgr. Flourcarbon, Anaheim, Calif., 1986-88; dir. engring. Ricoh Electronics, Inc., Tustin, Calif., 1988-92; chmn., CEO Teqcom Industries, Santa Ana, 1992—. Dist. commr. Boy Scouts Am., Orange County, Calif., 1982-90; exec. dir. Immanuel Luth. Ch. & Sch., 1987-92; bd. dirs. Luth. High Sch. Orange County, 1991-93. With USN, 1966-68. Decorated Navy Achievement medal; recipient Scouter medal Boy Scouts Am., 1986, Award of Merit, 1988. Mem. Am. Soc. Mech. Engrs., Soc. Mfg. Engrs., Air Traffic Control Assn., Ridgeline Country Club. Republican. Office: Teqcom Industries 1712 Newport Circle Ste O Santa Ana CA 92705-5118

WASHBURN, PETER LLOYD, internist; b. Niagara Falls, N.Y., Mar. 3, 1943; s. Lloyd Jerome and Bonnie (Fenska) W. BA, U. Pa., 1965, MD, 1969. Diplomate Am. Bd. Internal Medicine. Lt. USN, 1971, advanced through grades to comdr., 1983; intern U. Conn., 1969-71; resident Portsmouth (Va.) Naval Hosp., 1973-75; chief alcohol rehab. svc. Naval Hosp., Newport, R.I., 1978-83; chief drug dependence treatment clinic VA, Boston, 1985; fellow in substance abuse VA, San Francisco, 1985-87; med. dir. Merritt Peralta Chem. Dependency Recovery Hosp., Oakland, Calif., 1987—. Mem. Am. Soc. of Addiction Medicine, Calif. Soc. for Treatment Alcoholism and Other Drug Dependencies. Office: Merritt Peralta Inst 435 Hawthorne Ave Oakland CA 94609-3081

WASHINGTON, CHARLES EDWARD, educator, insurance executive; b. Little Rock, Nov. 27, 1933; s. David D. and Hzel M. Washington; BA, Philander Smith Coll., Little Rock, 1958; MEd, U. Okla., 1962; postgrad. U. So. Calif., umpire Internat. Fedn. Amateur Softball Assn. Umpires, 1961-63; m. Ruby N. Jones, Sept. 4, 1956 (div. 1965); 1 dau., Toni Regail. Tchr. public schs., Ft. Smith, Ark., 1958-60, Oklahoma City, 1960-69, L.A., 1969—; registered rep. ITT Hamilton Mgmt. Corp., 1963-70; fin. counselor Fin. Congeneric Corp., 1971-74, Am. Inst. Property and Liability Underwriters; spl. agt. Welsh & Assos., Ins. Svcs., Walnut, Calif., 1979—; sales mgr. Sun Belt Ins. Svcs., Walnut, 1982—; gen. agt. Alvo Ins. and Fin. Svcs., 1984—. Mem. Crenshaw Christian Center. Served with USMC, 1951-54; Korea. Mem. NEA, Calif. Tchrs. Assn., United Tchrs. L.A., Ind. Ins. Assn. Calif., U. Okla. Alumni Assn. (class rep. 1964-67), Nat. Dunbar High Sch. Alumni Assn., Philander Smith Coll. Alumni Assn., Nat. Notary Assn. Omega Psi Phi. Democrat. Home and Office: 20023 Alvo Ave Carson CA 90746-2576

WASHINGTON, CHARLES JOSEPH, manufacturing company executive; b. Indiana, Pa., Oct. 30, 1938; s. Harry J. and Elizabeth D. (Buckley) W.; m. Ruth Elizabeth Popp, June 11, 1960; children—Paul C., Susan M., Mark B. B.S., Loyola U., 1961; M.B.A., U. Chgo., 1969. Corp. staff Timex, Waterbury, Conn., 1974-75, gen. mgr., 1975-76; mgr. ops. Optical div. Bell & Howell Co., Chgo., 1976-78; plant mgr. E Z Por div. Ekco, Wheeling, Ill., 1978-79, Hon Industries, Muscatine, Iowa, 1979-80, plant mgr. 1980-87, v.p., gen. mgr. 1987-88, pres. BPI (Divsn. of Hon.); Stanton Industries Tualatin, Oreg., 1989-90, v.p. Ops.; Innovative Co. Ft. Collins Co., 1991 Gen. mgr., COO, pres. Advantage Cons. Enterprises, Fort Collins, Colo., 1991—. V.p. ops. Illowa council Boy Scouts Am., Davenport, Iowa, 1982-84, pres., 1985-86; bd. dirs. Sheltered Workshop, Muscatine, 1985-87. Mem. Am. Inst. Indsl. Engrs.; Lodge: Elks. Home: 1601 Brentford Ln Fort Collins CO 80525

WASHINGTON, EARL STANLEY, electronics company executive; b. L.A., Dec. 28, 1944; s. George Ernest and Violete Nadine (Hamilton) W.; m. Brenda Joyce Foreman, Feb. 6, 1965; children: Shaune, Stacey, Miles. BA, Calif. State U., L.A., 1968; Diploma, UCLA Grad. Sch. Mgmt., 1982. Asst. mgr., internat. Autonetics Group, Anaheim, Calif., 1972-73; mgr., strategic planning Collins Govt. Telecom, Newport Beach, Calif., and, Dallas, 1973-76; dir. mktg. svcs. Collins Radio Can., Toronto, 1976-78; prog. mgr. missile C-3 systems Collins Govt. Telecom, Dallas, 1978-79; dir. strategy devel. Rockwell Internat., Anaheim, 1979-81, v.p. bus. devel., 1981-85, v.p. strategic mgmt., internat., 1985-88, v.p., gen. mgr. autonetics marine systesm, 1988-90, v.p. strategic mgmt., 1990—. Editorial adv. bd. Def. Electronics mag. Bd. dirs., pres. Exec. Leadership Coun., Washington; active Boy Scouts Am. Mem. Armed Forces Communications and Electronics Assn., Am. Def. Preparedness Assn. (bd. dirs.). Office: Rockwell Internat 3370 E Miraloma Ave Anaheim CA 92803-3105

WASHINGTON, JAMES WINSTON, JR., artist, sculptor; b. Gloster, Miss., Nov. 10, 1909; s. James and Lizie (Howard) W.; m. Janie R. Miller, Mar. 29, 1943. Student, Nat. Landscape Inst., 1944-47; D.F.A., Center Urban-Black Studies, 1975. tchr. summer class N.W. Theol. Union Seattle U., 1988. One man shows U.S.O. Gallery, Little Rock, 1943, Foster-White Gallery, Seattle, 1974, 78, 80, 83, 89 (also at Bellevue Art Mus., 89), Charles and Emma Frye Art Mus., Seattle, 1980, Mus. History and Industry, Seattle, 1981; exhibited in group shows Willard Gallery, N.Y.C., 1960-64, Feingarten Galleries, San Francisco, 1958-59, Grosvenor Gallery, London, Eng., 1964, Lee Nordness Gallery, N.Y.C., 1962, Woodside Gallery, Seattle, 1962-65, Foster-White Gallery, Seattle, 1974, 76, 89, Smithsonian Instn., 1974, San Diego, 1977, Foster/White Gallery, Seattle, 1992, others; retrospective exhbn. Bellevue Art Mus., Washington, 1989; represented in permanent collections Seattle, San Francisco, Oakland art museums, Seattle First Nat. Bank, Seattle Pub. Library YWCA, Seattle, Meany Jr. High Sch., Seattle World's Fair, Expo 70 Osaka, Japan., Whitney Mus. Am. Art, N.Y.C.; commd. sculpture: Bird With Covey, Wash. State Capitol Mus., Olympia, 1983, Obelisk with Phoenix and Esoteric Symbols of Nature in granite, Sheraton Hotel Seattle, 1982, Life Surrounding the Astral Alter, In Matrix, owner T.M. Rosenblume, Charles Z. Smith & Assocs., Seattle, 1986, The Oracle of Truth (6 1/2 ton sculpture at M. Zion Bapt. Ch., Seattle, 1987, commd. sculptures King County Arts Commn., 1989, Bailey Gatzent Elem. Sch., Seattle, 1991, Twin Eaglets of the Cosmic Cycle for Quincy Jones, 1993, Fountain of Triumph for Bangasser Assocs. Inc., 1992-3; subject of essay The Spirit in the Stone by Paul Karlstrom, Smithsonian Instn. Passover leader Mt. Zion Baptist Ch., Seattle, 1974-87. Recipient Spl. Commendation award for many contbns. to artistic heritage of state Gov., 1973, plaque City of Seattle, 1973, plaque Benefit Guild, Inc., 1973, arts service award King County Arts Commn., 1984, cert. of recognition Gov. of Wash., 1984, Editor's Choice award Outstanding Achievement in Poetry Nat. Libr. Poetry, 1993; named to Wash. State Centennial Hall of Honor, Wash. State Hist. Soc., 1984; home and studio designated historic landmark (city and state), 1991. Mem. Internat. Platform Assn., Profl. Artists Phila., Masons (33 degree Prince Hall Lodge #67). Home: 1816 26th Ave Seattle WA 98122-3110

WASHINGTON, NAPOLEON, JR., insurance agent, clergyman; b. Ft. Baker, Calif., Apr. 12, 1948; s. Napoleon and Annie D. (Carter) W.; m. Nadine Reed, Nov. 6, 1968; children: Gregory D., Kimberlee N., Geoffrey N. AA, Merced Coll., 1976; student Stanislaus State Coll., 1976-77; grad. Billy Graham Sch. Evangelism, 1987. Ordained Baptist Gospel minister, 1989. Agt., Met. Life Ins. Co., Merced, Calif., 1970-72, sr. sales rep., 1972-83; broker Gen. Ins. Brokers, Merced, 1973—; owner Washington Assocs. Fin. Services; tchr. salesmanship Merced Coll., 1979—; assoc. pastor Christian Life Ctr., Merced, Calif., 1993. Chmn. bd. trustees St. Matthew Baptist Ch., 1978-84, ordained deacon, lic. minister, assoc. minister, 1982-91; pastor New Canaan Bapt. Ch., Los Banos, Calif., 1991-92; vice-chmn. Merced County Pvt. Industries Coun., 1981-83; mem. ins. adv. coun. City of Merced Schs.; vocat. mgr. New Hope Found., Dos Palos, Calif., 1984-85; trustee Matthew Bapt. Ch., 1978-84; pastor New Canaan Bapt. Ch., 1991-92. Served with U.S. Army, 1968-70. Recipient Nat. Quality award Nat. Assn. Life Underwriters, 1979, Nat. Sales Achievement award, 1979, Health Ins. Quality award, 1977; mem. Million Dollar Round Table, 1973-78; teaching cert. Calif. community colls.; Life Underwriting Coun. fellow, 1987. Mem. Nat. Assn. Life Underwriters, Calif. Assn. Life Underwriters (dir. 1975-76), Merced County Assn. Life Underwriters (pres. 1976-77), Merced County Estate Planning Council (dir.), Merced County Pvt. Industries Council, NAACP, Rotary (dir. 1974-76), Phi Beta Lambda. Democrat. Home: 1960 Cedar Crest Dr Merced CA 95340-2729 Office: 935 W 18th St Merced CA 95340-4502

WASHINGTON, REGINALD LOUIS, pediatric cardiologist; b. Colorado Springs, Colo., Dec. 31, 1949; s. Lucius Louis and Brenette Y. (Wheeler) W.; m. Billye Faye Ned, Aug. 18, 1973; children: Danielle Larae, Reginald Quinn. BS in Zoology, Colo. State U., 1971; MD, U. Colo., 1975. Diplomate Nat. Bd. Med. Examiners, Am. Bd. Pediatrics, Pediatric Cardiology. Intern in pediatrics U. Colo. Med. Ctr., Denver, 1975-76, resident in pediatrics, 1976-78, chief resident, instr., 1978-79, fellow in pediatric cardiology, 1979-81, asst. prof. pediatrics, 1982-1988, assoc. prof. pediatrics, 1988-90, assoc. clin. prof. pediatrics, 1990—; staff cardiologist Children's Hosp., Denver, 1981-90; v.p. Rocky Mountain Pediatric Cardiology, Denver, 1990—; mem. admissions com. U. Colo. Sch. Medicine, Denver, 1985-89; bd. dirs. Children's Health Care Assn.. Cons. editor Your Patient and Fitness, 1989—. Adv. bd. dirs. Equitable Bank of Littleton, Colo., 1984-86; bd. dirs. Cen. City Opera, 1989—, Cleo Parker Robinson Dance Co., 1992—, Rocky Mountain Heart Fund for Children, 1984-89, Raindo Ironkids, 1989—; nat. bd. dirs. Am. Heart Assn., 1992—; bd. dirs. Nat. Coun. Patient Info. and Edn., 1992—, Children's Heart Alliance, 1993—. Named Salute Vol. of Yr. Big Sisters of Colo., 1990. Fellow Am. Acad. Pediatrics (cardiology subsect.), Am. Coll. Cardiology, Am. Heart Assn. (coun. on cardiovascular disease in the young, exec. com. 1988-91, nat. devel. program com. 1990-94, vol. of yr. 1989, pres. Colo. chpt. 1989-90, Torch of Hope 1987, Gold Heart award Colo. chpt. 1990, bd. dirs. Colo. chpt., exec. com. Colo. chpt. 1987—, grantee Colo. chpt. 1983-84, mem. editorial bd. Pediatric Exercise Scis. 1988—), Soc. Critical Care Medicine; mem. Am. Acad. Pediatrics/Perinatology, N.Am. Soc. Pediatric Exercise Medicine (pres.), Denver C. of C. (gov.'s coun. for phys. fitness 1990-91, Leadership Denver 1990), Denver Athletic Club, Met. Club, Glenmoor Golf Club. Democrat. Roman Catholic. Home: 7423 Berkeley Cir Castle Rock CO 80104-9278 Office: Rocky Mountain Pediatric Cardiology 1601 E 19th Ave Ste 5600 Denver CO 80218-1022

WASILEWSKA, EWA, anthropologist, educator, international consultant; b. Gdansk, Poland, Feb. 12, 1958; came to U.S., 1983; d. Czeslaw and Izabela (Dziedzic) W. MA in Archeology and History, U. Warsaw, Poland, 1982; MA in Middle Ea. Studies, U. Utah, 1989, PhD in Anthropology, 1991. Assoc. instr. Dept. of Anthropology, U. Utah, Salt Lake City, 1986-90; acting dir. of Turkish program, asst. instr. Middle East Ctr., U. Utah, Salt Lake City, 1989-90; cons. Salt Lake City, 1991—; adj. asst. prof. Dept. Anthropology, U. Utah, 1990—; instr. social scis. dept. and history dept. Calif. State Poly. U., Pomona, 1991—; lectr. in field. Contbr. articles to profl. jours. Fellowship Am. Rsch. Inst. in Turkey, 1986, U. Utah, 1988-89, Inst. of Turkish Studies, 1988-89, 90. Mem. Am. Antropol. Assn., Am. Oriental Soc., Am. Rsch. Inst. in Turkey, Am. Sch. of Oriental Res., British Inst. of ARchaeology in Ankara, Soc. for Am. Archaeology, Phi Kappa Phi. Roman Catholic. Office: Dept Anthropology U Utah Salt Lake City UT 84112

WASKELL, LUCY ANN, anesthesiologist, researcher; b. Radford, Va., Feb. 1, 1942; d. Ernest and Suzanne (Hosage) W. B.S., Pa. State U., 1963; M.D., Columbia U., 1967; Ph.D., U. Calif.-Berkeley, 1974. Diplomate Am. Bd. Anesthesiology. Intern San Francisco Gen. Hosp., 1967-68; resident Stanford U. Hosp., Palo Alto, Calif., 1973-74; assoc. prof. U. Calif.-San Francisco, 1979—. Office: VA Hosp 43d and Clement St San Francisco CA 94121

WASSERBURG, GERALD JOSEPH, geology and geophysics educator; b. New Brunswick, N.J., Mar. 25, 1927; s. Charles and Sarah (Levine) W.; m. Naomi Z. Orlick, Dec. 21, 1951; children: Charles David, Daniel Morris. Student, Rutgers U.; BS in Physics, U. Chgo., 1951, MSc in Geology, 1952, PhD, 1954, DSc (hon.), 1992; Dr. Hon. Causa, Brussels U., 1985, U. Paris, 1986; DSc (hon.), Ariz. State U., 1987. Research assoc. Inst. Nuclear Studies, U. Chgo., 1954-55; asst. prof. Calif. Inst. Tech., Pasadena, 1955-59, assoc. prof., 1959-62, prof. geology and geophysics, 1962-82, John D. MacArthur prof. geology and geophysics, 1982—; served on Juneau Ice Field Research Project, 1950; cons. Argonne Nat. Lab., Lamont, Ill., 1952-55; former mem. U.S. Nat. Com. for Geochem., com. for Planetary Exploration Study, NRC, adv. council Petroleum Research Fund, Am. Chem. Soc.; mem. lunar sample analysis planning team (LSAPT) Manned Spacecraft Ctr., NASA, Houston , 1968-71, chmn.,1970; lunar sample rev. bd. 1970-72; mem. Facilities Working Group LSAPT, Johnson Space Ctr., 1972-82; mem. sci. working panel for Apollo missions, Johnson Space Ctr., 1971-73; advisor NASA, 1968-88, physical scis. com., 1971-75, mem. lunar base steering com., 1984; chmn. com. for planetary and lunar exploration, mem. space sci. bd. NAS, 1975-78; chmn. div. Geol. and Planetary Scis., Calif. Inst. Tech., 1987-89; vis. prof. U. Kiel, Fed. Republic of Germany, 1960, Harvard U., 1962, U. Bern, Switzerland, 1966, Swiss Fed. Tech. Inst., 1967, Max Planck Inst., Mainz and Heidelberg, Fed. Republic of Germany, 1985; invited lectr., Vinton Hayes Sr. Fellow, Harvard U., 1980, Jaeger-Hales lectr., Australian Nat. U., 1980, Harold Jeffreys lectr. Royal Astron. Soc., 1981, Ernst Cloos lectr., Johns Hopkins U., 1984, H.L. Welsh Disting. lectr. U. Toronto, Can. 1986., Danz lectr. U. Washington, 1989. Green vis. prof. U. B.C. 1982; 60th Anniversary Symposium speaker, Hebrew U., Jerusalem, 1985. Recipient Group Achievement award, NASA, 1969, Exceptional Sci. Achievement award, NASA, 1970, Disting. Pub. Service medal, NASA, 1973, J.F. Kemp medal Columbia U., 1973, Profl. Achievement award U. Chgo. Alumni Assn., 1978, Disting. Pub. Service medal with cluster, NASA, 1978, Wollaston medal Geol. Soc. London, 1985, Sr. Scientist award, Alexander von Humboldt-Stiftung, 1985, Crafoord prize Royal Swedish Acad. Scis., 1986. Gold medal Royal Astron. Soc., 1991; named Hon. Fgn. Fellow European Union Geoscis., 1983, recipient Holmes medal 1987; Rgents fellow Smithsonian Inst. Fellow AAAS, Am. Geophysical Union (planetology sect., Harry H. Hess medal 1985), Geol. Soc. Am. (life, Arthur L. Day medal 1970), Meteoritical Soc. (pres. 1987-88, Leonard medal 1975); mem. Geochem. Soc. (Goldschmidt medal 1978), Nat. Acad. Scis. (Arthur L. Day prize and lectureship 1981, J. Lawrence Smith medal 1985), Norwegian Acad. Sci. and Letters, Am. Phil. Soc. Office: Calif Inst of Tech Divsn Geol & Planetary Scis Pasadena CA 91125

WASSERMAN, BRUCE ARLEN, dentist, mail order company executive; b. San Mateo, Calif., June 7, 1954; s. Albert and Dunia (Frydman) W.; m. Pamela Carole Ward, June 8, 1972; children:Rachael, Rebecca, Meir, Keren. BA in Mass Communications, Winona State U., 198l; DDS, U. Pacific, 1985. Apprentice blacksmith Reuben Syhre Blacksmith Shop, Pine River, Minn., 1973-74; blacksmith Walden Forge, Pine River, 1974-79; founding dir. Team Redeemed, San Mateo, 1984-92; pvt. practice dentistry San Mateo, 1985—; pres. Manx USA, San Mateo, 1987-92. Editor: (quar. jour.) Cycle Lines, 1983-85, Good News, 1984-92, No. Calif. Reporter, 1987-90; assoc. editor: Internat. Communicator, 1988-89, editor, 1990; editor: (mo. jour.) The Mouthpiece, 1986-89; author: A Manual of Uniforming. Cubmaster Boy Scouts Am., San Mateo, 1986-87; fund raiser Am. Lung Assn., San Mateo County, 1986-90, bd. dirs., 1989—, chmn. Bike Trek, 1989, fund devel. com., 1989-90, membership com., 1991; chmn. Sofitel Bastille Tour, 1992—. Recipient Disting. Young Alumni award Winona State U., 1988; Mosby scholar Tau Kappa Omega, 1985. Fellow Am. Acad. Dentistry Internat. (editor 1990, mem. bylaws com. 1990), Am. Coll. Dentists, Royal Soc. Health, Pierre Fauchard Acad. (chmn. No. Calif. sect. 1992—); mem. ADA (cert. recognition 1987, 89, 90), Calif. Dental Assn. (Disting. Svc. award 1987), San Mateo County Dental Soc. (exec. bd. 1986-89, editor 1986-89, Pres. award 1989, Bd. Dirs. award 1987, bd. dirs. 1991-92), Acad. Gen. Dentistry, Christian Classic Bikers Assn. (Calif. rep. 1983—), Order Ky. Cols., 78th Fraser's Highlanders Regiment (lt./capt., recruiting officer 1993—), Pacific Road Riders (pres., editor 1983-85). Office: 410 N San Mateo Dr San Mateo CA 94401-2418

WASSERMAN, IRVING N., management consultant; b. N.Y.C., Nov. 26, 1921; s. Samuel and Anna (Barkan) W.; m. Mollie Scher, June 7, 1942 (dec. Oct. 1988); children: Jerry Steven, Glenn Fredric, Paul Stuart. Cert. of completion, CCNY, 1948. V.p. sales Longines-Wittnauer Watch Co., Inc., N.Y.C., 1949-68; pres. Capitol Record and Tape Clubs, Newbury Park, Calif., 1968-73, Concept Mktg. Internat., Sherman Oaks, Calif., 1974-81, Irving Wasserman Mgmt. Cons., Westlake Village, Calif., 1986—; area mgr. Volt Tech., Woodland Hills, Calif., 1981-86; instr. customer svc. Learning Tree U., Thousand Oaks, Calif., 1986-87. Mem. planning commn. City of Thousand Oaks, 1990—, vice chmn., 1993—; chmn. Coun. on Aging, Thousand Oaks, 1985-90; mem. Thousand Oaks Franchise Adv. Bd., 1987-89. Tech. sgt. USAAC, 1942-46. Recipient award for svc. to franchise adv. bd. City of Thousand Oaks, 1989. Mem. Bnai Brith (pres. Haverim chpt. 1984-85, Svc. award 1985). Republican.

WASSERMAN, JAMES DONALD, columnist; b. Tiffin, Ohio, June 8, 1952; s. Donald Hugo and Margaret Mary (Koerper) W.; m. Laura Jo Bartels, Nov. 10, 1980; 1 child, Dillon James. BJ, Bowling Green State U., 1974. Reporter Lake County Record-Bee, Lakeport, Calif., 1981-83, Upland (Calif) Today, 1983; city editor Palm Springs (Calif.) Desert Sun, 1984-86; capitol reporter Anchorage Times, 1986-87; metro columnist Fresno (Calif.) Bee, 1987—. Author: Fabulously Fresno, 1990; commentator KFSN-TV Channel 30, Fresno. Named Best Local Columnist Calif. Newspaper Pubs. Assn., 1990. Mem. Nat. Soc. Newspaper Columnists. Home: 3917 E Huntington Blvd Fresno CA 93702 Office: The Fresno Bee 1626 E St Fresno CA 93786

WASSERMAN, LEW R., film, recording, publishing company executive; b. Cleve., Mar. 15, 1913; m. Edith T. Beckerman, July 5, 1936; 1 dau., Lynne Kay. D (hon.), Brandeis U., NYU. Nat. dir. advt. and publicity Music Corp. Am., 1936-38, v.p., 1938-39, became v.p. charge motion picture div., 1940; now chmn., chief exec. officer, dir., mem. exec. com. MCA, Inc., also chmn. bd., chief exec. officer, dir. subsidiary corps.; dir. Am. Airlines; chmn. emeritus Assn. Motion Picture and TV Producers. Trustee John F. Kennedy Library, John F. Kennedy Center Performing Arts, Calif. Inst. Tech., Jules Stein Eye Inst., Carter Presdl. Ctr., Lyndon Baines Johnson Found.; pres. pres. Hollywood Canteen Found.; chmn. Research to Prevent Blindness Found.; hon. chmn. bd. Center Theatre Group Los Angeles Music Center; bd. dirs. Amateur Athletic Found. of Los Angeles (chmn. fin. com.), Los Angeles Music Ctr. Found.; bd. gov.'s Ronald Reagan Presdl. Found. Recipient Jean Hersholt Humanitarian award Acad. Motion Picture Arts and Scis., 1973. Democrat. Office: MCA Inc 100 Universal City Plz Universal City CA 91608-1002

WASSERMAN, MARK DANIEL, marketing professional; b. Boston, Sept. 7, 1964; s. Gerald S. and Louise (Mund) W. BS in Biology with high honors, Ind. U., 1986. Mktg. mgr. ICN Biomedicals/Cell Biology Div., Costa Mesa, Calif., 1990—. Office: ICN Biomeds Rsch Product Div PO Box 5023 Costa Mesa CA 92628-5023

WASSERMAN, ROBERT ZACHARY, lawyer; b. Hollywood, Calif., June 25, 1947; s. Jess Lloyd and Ruth (Russell) W.; m. June 14, 1970; children: Jacob, Misha. BA, U. Calif., Santa Cruz, 1969; JD, Stanford U., 1972. Bar: Calif., 1972; U.S. Dist. Ct. (no. dist.) Calif., 1973. Assoc. White, Cruickshank & White, Oakland, Calif., 1972-75; ptnr. Wasserman & Gordon, Oakland, 1975-78; prin. R. Zachary Wasserman, Oakland, 1978-79; ptnr. Goldfard & Lipman, Oakland, 1979-84, Kennedy & Wasserman, Oakland, 1984—. Commr. Port of Oakland, 1987-90; chair Oakland City Charter Rev. Com., 1979-80, Bay Area Ptnrs., Oakland, 1983-88, City Assets Com., Oakland, 1988—. Mem. Urban Land Inst., Calif. Community Redevel. Agys. Assn., Calif. Bar Assn., Alameda County Bar Assn., Contra Costa County Bar Assn. Office: Kennedy and Wasserman 1970 Broadway Fl 12 Oakland CA 94612-2212

WASSON, (ARNOLD) DOUGLAS, retired clergyman; b. Minot, N.D., Aug. 21, 1927; s. Robert Lawrence and Jenny Marguarite (Clark) W.; m. Mary Jo Peacock, June 2, 1958. BA, Case Western Res. U., 1950; M in Divinity, Oberlin (Ohio) Grad. Sch. of Theology, 1953; M in Edn., Auburn (Ala.) U., 1961. Ordained to ministry United Ch. of Christ, 1953. Adminstrv. asst. Pittman Community Ctr., Sevierville, Tenn., 1954-55; instr., pub. relations dir. So. Union Coll., Wadley, Ala., 1955-56, acting pres., 1956-58; asst. to pres. Snead Jr. Coll., Boaz, Ala., 1958-60; pastor First Congl. Ch., Rock Springs, Wyo., 1961-68, Colorado Springs, Colo., 1968-72; coordinator religious activities Woodmoor Corp., Monument, Colo., 1972-74; pastor The Ch. at Woodmoor, Monument, Colo., 1972-90, pastor emeritus, 1990—; moderator Wyo. Assn. United Ch. Christ, 1963, Southeastern United Ch. Christ, 1970; mem. mission and stewardship com. Rocky Mountain Conf. United Ch. of Christ, 1991—, coord. hunger action, 1991—. Chmn. Sweetwater County Outdoor Recreation Bd., Rock Springs, 1966-68, Pikes Peak Area Com. for Heifer Project Internat., 1989—; adv. mem. Wyo. Land and Water Conservation Com., Cheyenne, 1966-68; founder, coord. Pikes Peak Advocates for San Luis Valley, 1990—; coord. Pikes Peak Area 10K Hunger Hike, 1990—; coord. Fast for the Hungry of the World, 1975—; bd. dirs. Franciscan Family Wellness Program 1990-92, chmn. 1992—, Cath. Community Svcs. Diocese of Colorado Springs, 1992—; exec. dir. The Fellowship of the Second Mile, 1991—. Recipient Citation for Service award Circle K Internat., 1979, Citation for Leadership award Heifer Project Internat., 1986, Citation for Fund Raising award Ch. World Svc., 1985; named Young Men of Yr. Rock Springs Jaycees, 1963. Mem. San Luis Valley Christian Community Services (Alamosa, Colo. bd. dirs. 1975—), Christian Ministry in Nat. Parks (nat. bd. dirs. 1965—), Kiwanis (pres. 1958, 61, lt. gov. 1963, gov. Rocky Mountain dist. 1968, internat. trustee 1974-78). Democrat. Mem. United Ch. of Christ. Home: 1677 Shrider Rd Colorado Springs CO 80920-3375

WASSON, JAMES WALTER, aircraft manufacturing company executive; b. Pitts., Dec. 9, 1951; s. George Fredrick and Dolores Helen (Weurl) W.; m. Evelyn Fay Gonzales, Dec. 28, 1974; children: Robert, Brian. AST, Pitts. Inst. Aeronautics, 1972; BSET, Northrop U., Inglewood, Calif., 1981; MBA, U. Phoenix, 1988, govt. contracts mgmt. cert., 1989. Avionics technician various cos., 1972-74; electronics prodn. mgr. Ostgaard Industries, Gardena, Calif., 1974-75; sr. avionics design engr. Airesearch Aviation Co., L.A., 1975-81; v.p. engring. Avionics Engring. Svcs., Inc., Tucson, 1980-81; sr. tech. specialist Northrop Aircraft Div., Hawthorne, Calif., 1981-84; prog. mgr. McDonnell Douglas Helicopter Co., Mesa, Ariz., 1984-86; research mgr. McDonnell Douglas Helicopter Co., 1986—; exec. v.p. Leading Edge Technologies, Inc., Mesa, 1991—; adj. prof. govt. contract mgmt., program mgmt., proposal devel., strategic planning, rsch. projects U. Phoenix, 1990—; cons. in field. Author: Avionics Technology, 1983, Business Opportunities in Artificial Intelligence, 1988; inventor in field; contbr. articles to profl. jours. Com. chmn. Northrop U. Industry Adv. Bd., 1981; chmn. bd. dirs. Alta Mesa Community Assn., 1989; organizer Boys Scouts Am., Mesa, 1988. Named Engr. of Yr., Northrup U., 1980; recipient Disting. Alumnus award Pitts. Inst. Aeronautics, 1981; named to Hall of Fame, Career Colls. Assn., 1991. Mem. IEEE, NSPE, Soc. Automotive Engrs. (aerospace div.), Army Aviation Assn. (chpt. sr. v.p. 1988-91), Am. Def. Preparedness Assn., Am. Helicopter Soc. (chmn. avionics com. 1990). Republican. Roman Catholic. Home: 5213 E Fairfield Cir Mesa AZ 85205-5423 Office: McDonnell Douglas Helicoptr # 530/B338 5000 E McDowell Rd Mesa AZ 85205-9707

WAT, JAMES KAM-CHOI, retail executive; b. Hong Kong, Sept. 9, 1949; came to U.S., 1977; s. Biu Wat and Yuk (Ping) Tank; m. Miranda Kwai-Fong Leong, Oct. 6, 1974; children: Bryan, Vincent, Tiffany. Cert. edn., U. London, Hong Kong, 1969. Bus. mgr., asst. mgr., then sales mgr. Texwood Ltd., Hong Kong, 1970-77; gen. mgr. Texwood, Inc. (USA), N.Y.C., 1977-80, exec. v.p., dir., 1980-81; v.p. Jive Sportswear, Inc., N.Y.C., 1980-81; exec. v.p. Drager Industries, Inc., N.Y.C., 1980-81; pres. Am. Jeaneration Apparel, Inc., L.A., 1982-83; asst. import mgr. Millers Outpost Hub Distbg., Inc., Ontario, Calif., 1983-86; import mgr. Millers Outpost Hub Distbg., Inc., 1986-88, import dir. men's dept., 1988-91; pres. Mdse. Devel. & Sourcing Group, Inc., 1991—. Office: MDSG Inc 21660 E Copley Dr Ste 390 Diamond Bar CA 91765

WATANABE, CORINNE KAORU AMEMIYA, lawyer, judge, state official; b. Wahiawa, Hawaii, Aug. 1, 1950; d. Keiji and Setsuko (Matsumiya)

Amemiya; m. Edwin Tsugio Watanabe, Mar. 8, 1975; children: Traciann Keiko, Brad Natsuo, Lance Yoneo. BA, U. Hawaii, 1971; JD, Baylor U., 1974. Bar: Hawaii 1974. Dep. atty. gen. State of Hawaii, Honolulu, 1974-84, 1st dep. atty. gen., 1984-85, 87-92, atty. gen., 1985-87; assoc. judge Hawaii Intermediate Ct. Appeals, Honolulu, 1992—. Mem. ABA, Hawaii Bar Assn. Democrat. Office: Hawaii Intermediate Ct Appeals PO Box 2560 Honolulu HI 96804

WATANABE, ERIC KATSUJI, accountant, financial executive; b. Honolulu, Sept. 23, 1951; s. Fred K. and Clara N. (Nakama) W. BBA, U. Hawaii, 1975. CPA, Hawaii. Acct. Kida Nursing Home, Inc., Honolulu, 1974-75, Nagaue and Nagaue CPAs, Inc., Honolulu, 1975-79; contr., dir. MIS Hawaii Loa Coll., Kaneohe, 1979-85; chief fin. officer Honolulu Acad. Arts, 1985—; lectr. in acctg. Hawaii Loa Coll., 1980-87. Mem. AICPA, Am. Asn. Mus., Hawaii Assn. Pub. Accts., Hawaii Soc. CPAs. Home: 45-719 Lanipola Pl Kaneohe HI 96744 Office: Honolulu Acad Arts 900 S Beretania St Honolulu HI 96814-1495

WATANABE, HIROSHI, film production company executive; b. Sappro, Hokkaido, Japan, Jan. 12, 1951; came to U.S., 1976; s. Tetsuo and Sachiko (Kotani) W.; m. Ellen G. McLaughlin, Feb. 15, 1977 (div. Dec. 31, 1988); children: Aya Nicole, Mika Linette; m. Eiko Fukuhara, Sept. 2, 1989. BA, Nihon U., Tokyo, 1976; postgrad. in Bus. Adminstrn., UCLA, 1991—. Prodn. mgr. Creative Enterprises Internat., L.A., 1976-80; producer Chapman & Olson Film Co., L.A., 1980-82; pres. Sunny Side Up, Inc., L.A., 1983—. Mem. Japan-US Producers Assn. (chmn. 1991). Office: Sunny Side Up Inc 8810 Melrose Ave West Hollywood CA 90069

WATANABE, JEFFREY NOBORU, lawyer; b. Wailuku, Hawaii, Jan. 30, 1943; s. Robert Wataru and Mildred Shizue (Shiramizu) W.; m. Lynn Shelley Manildi, Dec. 28, 1969; children: Michael, Molly, Katherine, Robert. BA, U. Calif., 1965; JD, George Washington U., 1968. Bar: Hawaii 1968. Dep. atty. gen. State of Hawaii, Honolulu, 1968-70; ptnr. Watanabe, Ing & Kawashima, Honolulu, 1970—; bd. dirs. Am. Savs. Bank, Grace Pacific Corp., Hawaiian Electric Industries. Trustee Children's TV Workshop, N.Y.C., 1982—, Queen's Health Systems, Queen's Med. Ctr., 1990—, Blood Bank Hawaii, 1983—, Bishop Mus., 1987—, Nature Conservancy of Hawaii, 1988—, Smithsonian Instn. Nat. Bd., 1992—, U. Hawaii Found., 1985—. Mem. ABA, Hawaii State Bar Assn., Waialae Country Club, Pacific Club, Honolulu Club, Plaza Club, Oahu Country Club. Democrat. Office: Watanabe Ing& Kawashima 745 Fort Street Mall Fl 5 Honolulu HI 96813-3889

WATANABE, LARRY GEO, biomaterials scientist; b. Fresno, Calif., May 7, 1950; s. George and Hanayo (Yokota) W.; m. Janice Elaine Lee, Nov. 1, 1980; 1 child, Lauren Elisabeth. AA, Fresno City Coll., 1970; BA in Indsl. Arts, Fresno State U., 1972; cert., San Francisco City Coll., 1974. Mgr. crown and bridge dept. McLaughlin Dental Lab., Oakland, Calif., 1975-76; sr. rsch. technician USPHS Hosp., San Francisco, 1976-83; coord. biomaterials rsch. testing, mgr. U. Calif., San Francisco, 1983—; presenter in field. Contbr. articles and abstracts to profl. jours. Bd. dirs. Wah Mei Presch. Mem. Internat. Assn. Dental Rsch., Am. Assn. Dental Rsch., ASTM, Acad. Dental Materials, San Francisco Amateur Golf Assn., U. Calif. Golf Sports Club, Epsilon Pi Tau. Buddhist. Home: 1963 12th Ave San Francisco CA 94116-1305

WATANABE, RICHARD MEGUMI, medical research assistant; b. San Fernando, Calif., Sept. 7, 1962; s. Takashi and Toshiko (Yamane) W. BS, U. So. Calif., L.A., 1986; MS, U. So. Calif., 1989, postgrad., 1989—. Lab. asst. U. So. Calif. Sch. Medicine, L.A., 1985-87; data entry clk. L.A. County/U. So. Calif. Med. Ctr. Women's Hosp., 1985-89; rsch. asst. U. So. Calif. Sch. Medicine, L.A., 1987—; statis. cons. U. So. Calif. Sch. Medicine, 1988, dir. kinetic core, 1992—. Recipient Pacific Coast Fertility Soc. 1st prize in-tng. award, 1990; NIH fellow, 1990. Mem. AAAS, Am. Diabetes Assn., Am. Physiol. Soc., European Assn. Study of Diabetes. Office: 2025 Zonal Ave # 110 Los Angeles CA 90033-4526

WATANABE, WALTER YUKIAKI, service company executive; b. Nagoya, Japan, June 14, 1924; came to U.S., 1960; s. Teiichi and Tsu (Kakimi) W.; m. Setsuko Torii, Nov. 16, 1952; children: Yoshiya, Atsushi. BA in Econs., Doshisha U., Kyoto, Japan, 1948. Salesman, clk. fgn. trade dept. S. Kamei & Co., Ltd., Yokohama, Japan, 1948-50, mgr. fgn. trade dept., 1965-69; gen. mgr. KAMEI USA Corp., N.Y.C., 1960-65; regional mgr. for Far East Asia Interject Cargo Systems Inc., Tokyo, 1969-72; v.p. WITS Airfreight Inc., Seattle, 1972-75, Enterprise Shipping Corp., San Francisco, 1975-83; founder, pres. SEINO Am. Inc., Inglewood, Calif., 1983-89, chmn., 1989—; owner SYW Assocs. Inc., doing bus. as Pac Rim Developing. Recipient Best Employee award Yokohama C. of C., 1959, Outstanding Contbr. award Yokohama Fgn. Trade Assn., 1965. Mem. Doshisha U. Alumni Assn. (chmn. Western chpt. 1989-90), Wash. Athletic Club (Saettle), Palos Verdes Golf Club, Manhattan Country Club (Manhattan Beach Calif.). Home: 2204 Rocky Point Pl Palos Verdes Estates CA 90274 Office: SEINO Am Inc 8728 Aviation Blvd Inglewood CA 90301

WATERER, LOUIS PHILLIPP, aerospace engineer; b. Berger, Mo., Mar. 12, 1939; s. Frederick and Lillie Louise (Diederich) W.; m. Bonnie Clausing, June 18, 1961; children: Ryan, Reid. BS in Physics, Ohio State U., 1961; MS in Physics, San Jose State U., 1965; MBA, Santa Clara U., 1972. Test engr. Lockheed Missile and Space, Sunnyvale, Calif., 1961-67; design engr. Lockheed Missile and Space, Sunnyvale, 1967-73, system integration engr., 1973-85, group engr., 1985—. Council pres. Piedmont Sch., San Jose, Calif., 1984-85; com. chmn. troop 165 Boy Scouts Am., 1980-85. Mem. Internat. Interconnect Tech. Study Group. Republican. Methodist. Home: 3836 Suncrest Ave San Jose CA 95132-3204

WATERMAN, EMMA CAROLINE, artist, piano instructor; b. Torrington, Wyo., Jan. 19, 1931; d. Walter Martin and Eliza Ruth (Whitfield) Schumacher; m. Merle Aldon Waterman, Nov. 1, 1958; children: Marian Louise, Melody Joy, Merle Aldon II. Student, U. Wyo., 1948-50; grad. in music, Cen. Bible Coll., Springfield, Mo., 1954; postgrad., Linn-Benton C.C., Albany, Oreg., 1986-90. Pvt. tchr. Pendleton, Oreg., 1960-72, Corvallis, Oreg., 1988—. Watercolor paintings represented in pvt. and corp. collections. Sec. Corvallis Art Guild, 1988—. Home: 2822 NE Sherwood Pl Corvallis OR 97330

WATERMAN, LORI, artist; b. Eagle Lake, Tex., Mar. 3, 1914; d. Robert E. and Loretta (Dinkelspiel) Walker; m. Alan Tower Waterman Jr., Oct. 12, 1946; children: Linda Schrader, Donna, Alan Dane, Bruce Earl. AA, Foothill Coll., Los Altos, Calif., 1967; BA, San Jose (Calif.) State U., 1969. Cert. tchr., Calif. Tchr. Los Altos-Mountain View Sch. Dist., 1970-80; artist Stanford, Calif., 1980—. One-woman shows include Triton Mus., Santa Clara, 1975, El Gatito Gallery, Los Gatos, Calif., 1976, 78, 80, Artists Coop. Gallery, San Francisco, 1979, 81, 83, 85, Rosicrucian Mus., Santa Clara, 1984, Spanish Town Gallery, Half Moon Bay, Calif., 1985, Viewpoints Gallery, Los Altos, Gallery Saratoga, Calif., 1992; represented in permanent collection Triton Mus., Monterey Peninsula Mus. Art and numerous pvt. collections. Active League Women Voters. Recipient numerous awards in juried shows. Mem. Nat. League Am. Pen Women, Allied Artists West, Soc. Western Artists (signature), Pacific Art League, Pastel Soc. West Coast, San Francisco Women Artists, Artists Equity League.,. Studio: 562 Gerona Rd Stanford CA 94305-8449

WATERS, GEORGE GARY, financial service executive; b. Garyville, La., June 3, 1928; s. Elisha McCLendon and Lena Mae (Anderson) W.; m. Genevieve Corley, Aug. 15, 1952; children: Gary, George D., Gina, Glenda, Genevieve J., Grant. BA, U. Nebr., 1963; MBA, Nat. U., San Diego, 1979. Lic. inst. agt., securities aft., tax. advisor, enrolled agent lic. to practice before IRS. Enlisted USAF, 1951, advanced through grades to lt. col.; stationed at Keesler AFB Biloxi, Miss., 1958-59; detachment comdr. Encampment, Wyo, 1959-61, AFTAC 415, Chiengmai, Thailand, 1962-65, AFTAC Det 333, Teheran, Iran, 1970-72; plans officer HQ USAF, Washington, 1966-69; sr. air force advisor 162 Mobile Command, Sacramento, Calif., 1976-78; systems analyst Planning Rsch. Corp., Camp Pendleton, Calif., 1979-80; tax practitioner, pres. Palomar Tax. Svc. Inc., San Marcos, Calif., 1979—; speaker in field. Pub. Palomar Tax Svc. newsletter. Alt. del. Calif. Reps., 1992. Fellow Nat. Tax Practice Inst.; mem. Inland Soc. Tax Cons. (founding pres. No. San Diego 1985-86, past pres. 1987), Calif. Assn. Enrolled Agts. (pres.-elect, pres. 1993—), Nat. Soc. Pub. Accts. (del. to conv. 1990-93), Nat. Soc. Enrolled Agts., San Marcos C. of C. Republican. Roman Catholic. Home: 326 Sunrise Circle Vista CA 92084 Office: Palomar Tax Svc Inc 470 S Rancho Santa Fe Rd San Marcos CA 92069

WATERS, J. KEVIN, university administrator, educator; b. Seattle, June 24, 1933; s. Thomas and Eleanor (Hynes) W. BA in Classics, Gonzaga U., Spokane, Wash., 1957; MA in Philosophy, Gonzaga U., 1958; MA Theology, Santa Clara (Calif.) U., 1963; BA in Music, U. Wash., 1964, D of Music Arts, 1970. Asst. prof. Seattle U., 1969-74; vis. prof. Gonzaga-in-Florence, Italy, 1971; assoc. prof. Seattle U., 1974-81, prof. fine arts, 1981-83; prof. music Gonzaga, 1983—, dean arts and scis., 1983—; sec., trustee Seattle U., 1971-73, presiding officer, bd. dirs., 1975-77; pres. Seattle Archdiocesan Music Com., 1978-80; chmn. Jesuit Inst. For Arts, Washington, 1980—; panelist Nat. Endowment Arts, 1991—. Composer various musical compositions; commn. work Hearst Found. The Mask of Hiroshima, 1970, Job: A Play with Music, 1971, Solemn Liturgy, 1973, Dear Ignatius, Dear Isabel, 1978, Edith Stein, 1987, Psalm 150, 1991. Mem. Am. Guild Organists. Home: 502E E Boone Ave Spokane WA 99258-0001 Office: Gonzaga U Sch Arts & Scis Spokane WA 99258

WATERS, KATHLEEN FRANCES, automotive company executive; b. L.A., Aug. 24, 1940; d. Maurice Martin Haskell and Virginia Louise (Bennett) Rubin; m. Marcus Mertsching (dec. Feb. 1964); 1 child, Marcus C. Mertsching; m. Irving Waters, Mar. 17, 1965; 1 child, David Bennett Waters. Student, U. Calif., Berkeley, 1958-63. Exec. sec. Eastman Kodak Co., San Francisco, 1960-66; gen. mgr. Oakland (Calif.) Symphony, 1976-78; pres. Siena Corp., Berkeley, 1990—. Mem. exec. com. Oakland Symphony, 1974-78; pres. Oakland Symphony Guild, 1974-76, San Antonio Area Youth Project, Oakland, 1980-84; mem. Exec. Sec.'s, San Francisco, 1962-66; chmn. Acacia br. Children's Hosp., Oakland, 1985-86; bd. dirs., v.p. Dominican Grad. Sch. Philosophy and Theology, Berkeley, 1990—. Mem. Berkeley C. of C., East Bay Autobody Assn. (Bd. dirs. 1991-92), Calif. State Automobile Assn., Commonwealth Club of Calif., Bellevue Club of Oakland (bd. dirs. 1990-91), Berkeley Rotary. Republican. Office: Siena Corp Shattuck Auto Ctr 3207 Shattuck Ave Berkeley CA 94611

WATERS, LAUGHLIN EDWARD, judge; b. L.A., Aug. 16, 1914; s. Frank J. and Ida (Bauman) W.; m. Voula Davanis, Aug. 22, 1953; children: Laughlin Edward, Maura Kathleen, Deirdre Mary, Megan Ann, Eileen Brigid. A.B., UCLA, 1939; J.D., U. So. Calif., 1946. Bar: Calif. 1946. Dep. atty. gen. Calif., Los Angeles, 1946; individual practice law Los Angeles, 1947-53; sr. ptnr. Nossaman, Krueger & Marsh, 1961-76; U.S. atty. So. Dist. Calif., 1953-61; judge U.S. Dist. Ct. (cen. dist.) Calif., 1976—; cons. U.S. Dept. State in London, 1970; mem. U.S. Del. to Conf. Environ. Problems in Prague, 1971, White House Conf. on Aging, 1970-71; chmn. ABA Com. Housing and Urban Devel., 1977-79. Mem. Calif. Legislature, 1946-53; bd. dirs. Legal Aid Found., 1954-60; active Cath. Big Brother. Served as capt. U.S. Army, 1942-46. Decorated Bronze Star, Purple Heart with oak leaf cluster, Combat Inf. badge. Fellow Am. Bar Found., Am. Coll. Trial Lawyers; mem. Am. Judicature Soc., U. So. Calif., UCLA Law Assn., Am. Legion, U. So. Calif. Legion Lex, Order Blue Shield, Town Hall, Polish Order Merit with Swords, Hon. Citizen of Chambois, Trun, France, 10th Polish Dragons (hon.), Soc. Friendly Sons St. Patrick. Republican. Roman Catholic. Clubs: Knights of Malta, Anchor, Calif. Office: US Dist Ct 255 E Temple St Los Angeles CA 90012-4701

WATERS, LINDA JULENE, printing company executive; b. Bell, Calif., Jan. 21, 1941; d. Grant Jay Gunderson and Norma Brower Schutz; m. Gary L. Waters, June 30, 1940; children: Brett Waters, Jana Bolland, Travis. Student, Glen & Clark Bus. Coll., Idaho Falls, Idaho, 1962. Loan officer Seaboard Fin., Idaho Falls, 1963-65; acctg. supr. GMAC, Idaho Falls, 1965-85; pres., owner Print Craft Press, Idaho Falls, 1985—; dir. Westmark Credit Line, Idaho Falls. Bd. dirs. ISU Graphic Arts, Pocatello, Idaho, 1988—; dir. Econ. Chamber Affairs Coun., Idaho Falls, 1992—. Recipient award for outstanding svc. Melaleuca, Inc., Idaho Falls, 1991. Mem. Idaho Falls C. of C. (bd. dirs. 1990—, Svc. award 1992), Rotary (pres. 1990-91, Svc. award), YMCA. Republican. LDS. Office: Printcraft Press 319 Constitution Way Idaho Falls ID 83405

WATERS, M. BRUCE, engineering technician, small business owner; b. Houston, Apr. 17, 1950; s. Wayland O. and Snellah G. (Holt) W.; m. Jean H. Sudduth, June 26, 1971; 1 child, Tegan Joy. Student, La. State U., 1968-69, '70-74, U. Houston, 1969, San Jacinto Jr. Coll., Deer Park, Tex., 1969. Engring. aide I La. Dept. Highways, Baton Rouge, 1971-73, engring. aide II, 1973-74; sta. mgr. Cliff Brice Gas Stas., Boulder, Colo., 1975; mill worker Red Dale Coach, Longmont, Colo., 1975; engring. aide B Colo. Dept. Highways, Boulder, 1975-76, engring. aide C, 1976-91, engring. tech. I, 1991—. Blood donor Belle Bonfils, Boulder, Colo., 1975—; mem. and crew leader Vols. for Outdoor Colo.; sec. Boulder County Libertarian Party, 1991-93. Mem. Nat. Inst. Cert. Engring. Techs., Chpt. C Freewheelers, Am. Motorcyclist Assn., Soc. for Preservation and Encouragement of Barbershop Quartet Singing in Am. Office: Colo Dept Transp 1100 Lee Hill Rd Boulder CO 80302

WATERS, MAXINE, congresswoman; b. St. Louis, Aug. 15, 1938; d. Remus and Velma (Moore) Carr; m. Sidney Williams, July 23, 1977; children: Edward, Karen. Grad. in sociology Calif. State U., L.A.; hon. doctorates, Spelman Coll., N.C. Agrl. & Tech. State U., MOrgan State U. Former tchr. Head Start; mem. Calif. Assembly from dist. 48, 1976-91, Dem. caucus chair, 1984; mem. 102nd-103rd Congresses from Dist. 35, Calif., 1991—; mem. Banking, Fin., Urban Affairs com., subcom. Consumer Credit and Ins., Housing and Community devel., internat. devel., trade and minetary policy, fin. instns. supervision, regulations and deposit ins., veterans affairs com., subcom. oversight and investigations. Mem. Dem. Nat. Com., Dem. Congrl. Campaign com.; del. Dem. Nat. Conv., 1972, 76, 80, 84, 88, 92, mem. rules com. 1984; mem. Nat. Adv. Com. for Women, 1978—; bd. dirs. Essence mga., TransAfrica Found., Nat. Women's Polit. Caucus, Ctr. Nat. Policy, Clara Elizabeth Jackson Carter Found. Spellman Coll., Nat. Minority AIDS Project, Women for a Meaningful Summit, Nat. Coun. Negro Women, Black Women's Agenda; founder Black Women's Forum. Office: US Ho Reps 1207 Longworth Washington DC 20515-0535

WATFORD, GLEN ALAN, nuclear engineer; b. Ft. Pierce, Fla., Apr. 11, 1957; s. John Bryan and Ruth Madeline (Fulford) W.; m. Judith Gail Shannon, June 6, 1981; children: Christopher A., Taylor Zachary, Kelsey Rae, Jackson Colt. BS in Nuclear Engring., U. Fla., 1979; MME, U. Calif., 1982. Registered profl. engr., mech. engr., Calif. Engr. GE Nuclear Energy, San Jose, Calif., 1979-85, sr. engr., 1985-89, prin. engr., 1989-92, nuclear svcs. mgr., 1992—. Inventor in field; contbr. articles to profl. jours. Mem. Am. Nuclear Soc., GE Elfun Soc. Republican. Office: GE Nuclear Energy 8499 Darrow Rd Twinsburg OH 44087

WATIA, TARMO, artist; b. Detroit, May 11, 1938; s. Oiva and Mildred (Saari) W.; divorced; 1 child, Talvi Oiva. BS inDesign, U. Mich., 1960, MFA, 1962. Prof. Minot (N.D.) State Coll., 1964, Montana State U., Bozeman, 1965, So. Oreg. Coll., Ashland, 1965-69, Boise (Idaho) State U., 1969-86; artist Boise, Idaho, 1986—. One-man exhibitions include Raven Gallery, Detroit, AAA Gallery, Detroit, Rackham Galleries, Ann Arbor, Mich., White Chapel Gallery, Bozeman, Rogue Valley Art Assn., Medford, Oreg.; exhibited in numerous group shows including The Art Studio Gallery, Birmingham, Mich., U. Oreg. Art Mus., Eugene, Am. Relief Prints, Pitts., Image Gallery, Portland, Oreg., Redwood Show, Eureka, Calif.; selected juried exhibitions at Art Mus. Show, Coos Bay, Oreg., Rock Springs (Wyo.) Nat. Art Exhibit, 5th Annual Nat. Art Exhibition Soumi Coll., Hancock, Mich., 15th Annual Watercolor Exhibition Wayne State U., Detroit, Graphics 71 Nat. Print and Drawing Exhibition, Silver City, N.Mex., among others. Home: 1015 N 10th St Boise ID 83702-4132

WATKINS, ANN ESTHER, mathematics educator; b. L.A., Jan. 10, 1949; d. Rex Devere and Burnice Gordine (Duckworth) Hamilton; m. William Earl Watkins, Oct. 5, 1973; children: Mary Ann, Barbara Lee. BA, Calif. State U., Northridge, 1970, MS, 1972; PhD, UCLA, 1977. Instr. math. Los Angeles Pierce Coll., Woodland Hills, Calif., 1975-90; prof. math. Calif. State U., Northridge, 1990—. Editor: (with Albers, Rodi) New Directions in Two Year College Mathematics, 1985; co-author: (with Landwehr) Exploring Data, 1986, (with Landwehr, Swift) Exploring Surveys, 1987, (with Albers, Loftsgaarden, Rung) Statistical Abstract of Undergraduate Programs in the Mathematical Sciences and Computer Science, 1992; editor Coll. Math. Jour., 1989—. Grantee NSF, 1987-90, 92-93. Mem. Math. Assn. Am. (2d v.p. 1987-88, chair So. Calif. sect. 1988-89), Am. Statis. Assn. Office: Calif State U Northridge CA 91330

WATKINS, CHARLES REYNOLDS, medical equipment company executive; b. San Diego, Oct. 28, 1951; s. Charles R. and Edith A. (Muff) W.; children: Charles Devin, Gregory Michael. BS, Lewis and Clark Coll., 1974; postgrad., U. Portland, 1976. Internat. salesman Hyster Co., Portland, Oreg., 1975-80, Hinds Internat. Corp., Portland, 1980-83; mgr. internat. sales Wade Mfg. Co., Tualatin, Oreg., 1983-84; regional sales mgr. U.S. Surg., Inc., Norwalk, Conn., 1984-86; nat. sales mgr. NeuroCom Internat., Inc., Clackamas, Oreg., 1986-87; pres. Wave Form Systems, Inc., Portland, 1987—; bd. dirs. U.S. Internat., Inc., Portland, Clearfield Med., Minorax, Inc. Bd. dirs. Portland World Affairs Coun., 1980. Mem. Am. Soc. Laser Medicine and Surgery, Am. Fertility Soc., Am. Assn. Gynecol. Laparoscopists, Portland City Club. Republican. Office: Wave Form Systems Inc PO Box 3195 Portland OR 97208-3195

WATKINS, EVAN PAUL, English educator; b. Wichita, Kans., Oct. 25, 1946; s. Evan Edward and Aileen Josephine (Elgin) W.; m. Diane Candace Logan, July 8, 1968; 1 child, Christopher Morgan. BA, U. Kans., 1968; PhD, U. Iowa, 1972. Asst. prof. English Mich. State U., 1972-77, assoc. prof. English, 1977-83; assoc. prof. English U. Wash., Seattle, 1983-90, prof. English, 1990—; reader for numerous U. jours. and presses., 1972—. Author: The Critical Act, 1978, Work Time, 1989, Throwaways, 1993; contbr. essays on contemporary lit. and theory in profl jours. Recipient summer rsch. grant Mich. State U., 1973, '76, course devel. grant Mich. State U., 1977, U. Wash., 1986, Fulbright-Hays Rsch. grant, Rome, 1978-79. Mem. Modern Lang. Assn. Office: Dept of English GN-30 Univ Wash Seattle WA 98195

WATKINS, JOHN GOODRICH, educator, psychologist; b. Salmon, Idaho, Mar. 17, 1913; s. John Thomas and Ethel (Goodrich) W.; m. Evelyn Elizabeth Browne, Aug. 21, 1932; m. Doris Wade Tomlinson, June 8, 1946; m. Helen Verner Huth, Dec. 28, 1971; children: John Dean, Jonette Alison, Richard Douglas, Gregory Keith, Rodney Philip, Karen Stroobonts, Marvin R. Huth. Student, Coll. Idaho, 1929-30, 31-32; BS, U. Idaho, 1933, MS, 1936; PhD, Columbia U., 1941. Instr. high sch. Idaho, 1933-39; faculty Ithaca Coll., 1940-41, Auburn U., 1941-43; assoc. prof. Wash. State Coll., 1946-49; chief clin. psychologist U.S. Army Welch Hosp., 1945-46; clin. psychologist VA Hosp., American Lake, Wash., 1949-50; chief clin. psychologist VA Mental Hygiene Clinic, Chgo., 1950-53, VA Hosp., Portland, Oreg., 1953-64; prof. psychology U. Mont., Missoula, 1964-84; prof. emeritus U. Mont., 1984—, dir. clin. tng., 1964-80; lectr. numerous univs.; clin. asso. U. Oreg. Med. Sch., 1957; pres. Am. Bd. Examiners in Psychol. Hypnosis, 1960-62. Author: Objective Measurement of Instrumental Performance, 1942, Hypnotherapy of War Neuroses, 1949, General Psychotherapy, 1960, The Therapeutic Self, 1978, (with others) We, The Divided Self, 1982, Hypnotherapeutic Techniques, 1987, Hypnoanalytic Techniques, 1992; contbr. articles to profl. jours. Mem. Internat. Soc. Clin. and Exptl. Hypnosis (co-founder, pres. 1965-67, recipient awards 1960-65), Soc. Clin. and Exptl. Hypnosis (pres. 1969-71, Morton Prince award), Am. Psychol. Assn. (pres. div. 30 1975-76), Sigma Xi, Phi Delta Kappa. Home and Office: 413 Evans Ave Missoula MT 59801-5827

WATKINS, JUDITH ANN, nurse; b. Chgo., Mar. 11, 1942; d. Russell and Louise Bernadine (Aloy) Keim; m. Thomas H. Watkins III, Dec. 24, 1961; children: Tamara Sue, Randall Scott. Grad. in nursing, Knapp Coll. Nursing, Santa Barbara, Calif., 1963; BSN, Pacific Union Coll., 1991, PHN cert., 1991. Cert. CPR instr., vocat. edn. instr. Obstetrics supr. Bowling Green (Ky.) Warren County Hosp., 1963-67; clin. staff nurse Chula Vista (Calif.) Med. Clinic, 1967-69; nurse aide instr. Sawyers Coll., Ventura, Calif., 1972; ob-gyn. supr. Westlake (Calif.) Community Hosp., 1972-77; RN acute patient care Medical Personnel Pool, Bakersfield, Calif., 1984; med. asst. instr., dir. of allied health San Joaquin Valley Coll., Bakersfield, 1984-88; dir. nurses Bakersfield Family Med. Ctr., 1988-92, dir. client svcs., 1992—. Named Mother of the Yr., Frazier Pk. (Calif.) Community Ch., 1979, Instr. of the Yr., 1986. Mem. Kern County RN Soc., Kern County Trade Club, Pine Mt. Golf Club (founder Lilac Festival 1982, Lady of the Yr. 1983) Sundale Country Club, Toastmasters Internat. Home: 9513 Steinbeck Ln Bakersfield CA 93311-1445 Office: Bakersfield Family Med Ctr 4580 California Ave Bakersfield CA 93309-1152

WATKINS, KAY ORVILLE, college dean, chemistry educator; b. Nunn, Colo., Apr. 28, 1932; s. Paul Edmond and Freda May (Orndorff) W.; m. Janice Annette Rogers, June 24, 1961; children: Susan, Melissa, Laura. BA, Adams State Coll., 1955; PhD, Vanderbilt U., 1961. Prof. chemistry Adams State Coll., Alamosa, Colo., 1961—, dean Sch. Sci., 1977—; rsch. chemist Brandeis U., Waltham, Mass., 1961-62; vis. scientist Brookhaven Nat. Lab., Upton, N.Y., 1968, Argonne (Ill.) Nat. Lab., 1973, U. Utah, Salt Lake City, 1981; vis. prof. U. Hawaii, Honolulu, 1987. Contbr. articles to profl. jours. Advisor Colo. Minority Engring. Assn., San Luis Valley, 1983—; bd. dirs. San Luis Valley Regional Sci. Fair, Alamosa, 1975—. Named one of Outstanding Young Men Am., Alamosa Jaycees, 1967; grantee NSF, 1978, rsch. fellow, 1978. Mem. Am. Chem. Soc., Colo. Alliance for Sci., Sigma Xi. Republican. Home: 74 El Rio Dr Alamosa CO 81101-2117 Office: Adams State Coll Sch of Sci Math & Tech Alamosa CO 81102

WATKINS, RUFUS NATHANIEL, editorial assistant; b. Laurel, Miss., Sept. 27, 1963; s. Rufus Sr. and Mary Helen (Washington) W. AA, City Coll. of San Francisco, 1983; BA in Speech Communications, Baylor U., 1987. Sr. copy clk., editorial asst. San Francisco Chronicle, 1988—. Mem. Mayor Frank Jordan Transition Team, San Francisco, 1992, mem. Housing and Econ. Devel. Team, 1992, mem. Citizens Com. on Community Devel. Adv. Bd., 1993—, mem. subcoms. community facilities, pub. open space, 1993—, mem. community budget forum panel, 1993; mem. election panel Robert F. Kennedy Bus. Dem. Club, 1992. Named to Outstanding Young Men of Am., 1989. Mem. World Affairs Coun. (internat. forum steering com. mem. 1993—), San Francisco Jaycees (dir. pub. rels. 1989-90, chair ana. Halloween party youths 1990-93, v.p. membership devel. 1990-91, chmn. bd. 1991—, Officer of Yr. 1989, Presdl. award 1990, 91, Calif. Presdl. award 1992-93), No. Calif. Baylor U. Alumni, Toastmasters Internat. (treas. Pacific Heights chpt. 1993—, v.p. membership devel. 1993—). Home: 2060 O'Farrell St # 102 San Francisco CA 94115 Office: San Francisco Chronicle 901 Mission St San Francisco CA 94103

WATKINS, WILLIAM SHEPARD See SIVADAS, IRAJA

WATKINSON, PATRICIA GRIEVE, museum director; b. Merton, Surrey, Eng., Mar. 28, 1946; came to U.S., 1972; d. Thomas Wardle and Kathleen (Bredl) Grieve. BA in Art History and Langs. with honors, Bristol U., Eng., 1968. Sec. Mayfair Fine Arts and The Mayfair Gallery, London, 1969-71; adminstr. Bernard Jacobson, Print Pub., London, 1971-73; freelance exhbn. work, writer Kilkenny Design Ctr., Davis Gallery, Irish Arts Council in Dublin, Ireland, 1975-76; curator of art Mus. Art, Wash. State U., Pullman, 1978-83, dir., 1984—; asst. prof. art history Wash. State U., Pullman, 1978. Co-author, co-editor: Gaylen Hansen: The Paintings of a Decade, 1985. Mem. Assn. Coll. & Univ. Museums and Galleries (western regional rep. 1987-89), Art. Mus. Assn. Am. (Wash. state rep. 1986-87), Internat. Council Museums (modern art com. 1986-89), Wash. Mus. Assn. (bd. dirs. 1984-87), Am. Fedn. Arts (western region rep. 1987-89). Office: Wash State U Mus Art Pullman WA 99164-7460

WATKINSON, W. GRANT, distribution company executive; b. Seattle, Oct. 17, 1941; s. Percy John and Betty Lou (Grant) W.; m. Diane Weiblen, June 25, 1966; children: Brett, Tara. BS, Oreg. State U., 1964; MBA, U. Oreg., 1966, PhD, 1971. Asst. prof. Pacific Luth. U., Tacoma, 1970-72; v.p. fin. Stiles Enterprises, Portland, Oreg., 1972-76, Discount Fabrics, Portland, 1976; pres. Paulsen & Roles Labs., Portland, 1977—; bd. dirs. Internat. Sanitary Supply Assn., Chgo.; pres. Preferred Distbrs., Inc., San Antonio,

1988-89. Office: Paulsen & Roles Labs 1836 NE 7th Ave Portland OR 97212

WATRING, WATSON GLENN, gynecologic oncologist, educator; b. St. Albans, W.Va., June 2, 1936; m. Roberta Tawell. BS, Washington & Lee U., 1958; MD, W.Va. U., 1962. Diplomate Am. Bd. Ob-Gyn, Am. Bd. Gynecol. Oncology. Intern The Toledo Hosp., 1963; resident in ob-gyn Ind. U., Indpls., 1964-66, Tripler Gen. Hosp., Honolulu, 1968-70; resident in gen. and oncologic surgery City of Hope Nat. Med. Ctr., Duarte, Calif., 1970-71, assoc. dir. gynecol. oncology, sr. surgeon, 1973-77; fellow in gynecol. oncology City of Hope Nat. Med. Ctr. and UCLA Med. Ctr., 1972-74; asst. prof. ob-gyn UCLA Med. Ctr., 1972-77; assoc. prof., sr. gynecologist, sr. surgeon Tufts New Eng. Med. Ctr. Hosp., Boston, 1977-80, asst. prof. radiation therapy, 1978-80; practice medicine specializing in ob-gyn Boston, 1980-82; assoc. prof. ob-gyn U. Mass., Worcester, 1982; regional dir. gynecol. oncology So. Calif. Permanente Med. Group, Los Angeles, 1982—, asst. dir. residency tng., 1985—; dir. gynecol. oncology St. Margarets Hosp. for Women, Dorchester, Mass., 1977-80; clin. prof. ob-gyn U. Calif., Irvine, 1982—. Contbr. articles to profl. jours. Mem. ch. council Luth. Ch. of the Foothills, 1973-75. Served to lt. col. M.C., U.S. Army, 1965-71. Fellow Am. Coll. Ob-Gyn, Los Angeles Obstet. and Gynecol. Soc.; mem. AAAS, ACS (Calif. and Mass. chpts.), Boston Surg. Soc., AMA, Mass. Med. Soc., Mass. Suffolk Dist. Med. Soc., Internat. Soc. Gynecol. Pathologists, Western Soc. Gynecologists and Obstetricians, Am. Soc. Clin. Oncology, Soc. Gynecol. Oncologists, Western Assn. Gynecol. Oncologists (sec.-treas. 1976-81, program chmn. 1984, pres. 1985—), New Eng. Assn. Gynecol. Oncologists (chmn. charter com.), New Eng. Obstet. and Gynecol. Soc., Obstet. Soc. Boston, Am. Radium Soc., Soc. Study Breast Disease, New Eng. Cancer Soc., Internat. Gynecol. Cancer Soc., Daniel Morton Soc., Sigma Xi. Republican. Office: So Calif Permanente Med Group 4950 W Sunset Blvd Los Angeles CA 90027-5821

WATSON, BRIAN HOYT, software engineer, computer programmer; b. Ft. Bragg, N.C., Apr. 30, 1962; s. Gerald Evan and Margaret Ellen (Abel) W.; m. Theresa JoAnn Robinson, Feb. 6, 1982 (div. Aug. 1984); 1 child, Jason B. BS in Applied Math, Computer Sci., U. Idaho, 1990. Programmer Agrl. Coll. U. Idaho, Moscow, 1990-91; programmer Tribune Pub. Co., Lewiston, Idaho, 1991; software test engr. Micorsoft Corp., Redmond, Wash., 1991—. Mem. Computer Soc. of IEEE, Soc. for Indsl. and Applied Math., Assn. for Computing Machinery. Home: 1721 161st Ave NE Bellevue WA 98008

WATSON, DAVID COLQUITT, electrical engineer, educator b. Linden, Tex., Feb. 9, 1936; s. Colvin Colquitt and Nelena Gertrude (Keasler) W.; m. Flora Janet Thayn, Nov. 10, 1959; children: Flora Janeen, Melanie Beth, Lorrie Gaylene, Cheralyn Gail, Nathan David, Amy Melissa, Brian Colvin. BSEE, U. Utah, 1964, PhD in Elec. Engring. (NASA fellow), 1968. Electronic technician Hercules Powder Co., Magna, Utah, 1961-62; rsch. fellow U. Utah, 1964-65, rsch. asst. microwave devices and phys. electronics lab., 1964-68; sr. mem. tech. staff ESL, Inc., Sunnyvale, Calif., 1968-78, head dept. Communications, 1969-70; sr. engring. specialist Probe Systems, Inc., Sunnyvale, 1978-79; sr. mem. tech. staff ARGO Systems, Inc., Sunnyvale, 1979-90; sr. mem. tech. staff GTE Govt. Systems Corp., Mountain View, Calif., 1990-91; sr. cons. Watson Cons. Svcs., 1991-92; sr. staff engr. ESL, Inc., 1992— ; mem. faculty U. Santa Clara, 1978-81, 1992—, San Jose State U., 1981—, Coll. Notre Dame, 1992—, Chapman U., 1993—. Contbr. articles to IEEE Transactions, 1965-78; co-inventor cyclotron-wave rectifier; inventor gradient descrambler. Served with USAF, 1956-60. Mem. IEEE, Phi Kappa Phi, Tau Beta Pi, Eta Kappa Nu. Mem. LDS Ch. Office: GTE Govt Systems Corp 100 Ferguson Dr Mountain View CA 94043-5294

WATSON, DIANE EDITH, state legislator; b. L.A., Nov. 12, 1933; d. William Allen Louis and Dorothy Elizabeth (O'Neal) Watson. A.A., L.A. City Coll., 1954, B.A., UCLA, 1956; M.S., Calif. State U., Los Angeles, PhD Claremont Grad. Sch., 1987. Tchr., sch. psychologist L.A. Unified Sch. Dist., 1960-69, 73-74; assoc. prof. Calif. State U., L.A., 1969-71; health occupations specialist Bur. Indsl. Edn., Calif. Dept. Edn., 1971-73; mem. L.A. Unified Sch. Bd., 1975-78; mem. Calif. Senate from dist. 28, 1978—, chairperson health and human svcs. com.; Legis. Black Caucus, mem. edn. com., judiciary com., ins. com., budget and fiscal review com.; del. Calif. Democratic Party; mem. exec. com. Nat. Conf. State Legislators. Author: Health Occupations Instructional Units-Secondary Schools, 1975; Planning Guide for Health Occupations, 1975; co-author; Introduction to Health Care, 1976. Del. Democratic Nat. Conv., 1980. Recipient Mary Church Terrell award, 1976, Brotherhood Crusade award, 1981, Black Woman of Achievement award NAACP Legal Def. Fund, 1988; named Alumnus of Yr., UCLA, 1980, 82. Mem. Calif. Assn. Sch. Psychologists, Los Angeles Urban League, Calif. Tchrs. Assn., Calif. Commn. on Status Women. Roman Catholic. Office: 4401 Crenshaw Blvd #300 Los Angeles CA 90043

WATSON, HAROLD GEORGE, ordnance company executive, mechanical engineer; b. Phoenix, Oct. 19, 1931; s. Clarence Elmer and Eunice A. (Record) W.; m. Ruth May Thomas, Aug. 30, 1951 (dec.); children: Patricia Ruth, Linda Darlene, Harold George; m. Katherina Anna Kish, Sept. 22, 1990. B.S., U. Ariz., 1954. Engr. Shell Oil Co., L.A., 1954; project engr. Talco Engring. Co., Hamden Conn., 1956, area mgr., Mesa, Ariz., 1956-57, chief engr. Rocket Power, 1958-61, dir. engring., 1961-64; dir. engring. Space Ordnance Systems, El Segundo, Calif., 1964-68; dir. engring. Universal Propulsion Co., Riverside, Calif., 1968-70, gen. mgr., v.p. engring., Tempe, Ariz., 1970-76, v.p., mgr., 1976-77, pres., gen. mgr., Phoenix, 1977—. Patentee in field. 1st lt. USAR, 1954-56. Mem. Am. Mgmt. Assn., SAFE Assn. (past pres.), AIAA, Air Force Assn., Internat. Pyronetics Soc., Am. Def. Preparedness Assn. Office: Universal Propulsion Co Inc 25401 N Central Ave Phoenix AZ 85027

WATSON, JEANETTE MARIE, councilwoman, historian; b. San Jose, Calif., Mar. 12, 1931; d. Joseph Vincent and Jennie Isabel (Yerkovich) Gomes; m. Courtland Leroy Watson, May 29, 1954; children: Kathleen Marie Johnson, Teresa Lynn Fine, Courtland Joseph. BA in Edn., San Jose State U., 1953. Councilman City of Campbell, Calif., 1985—, mayor, 1988-89. Author: Campbell the Orchard City, 1990. Vice chmn. Santa Clara Cities Assn., 1990-91; bd. dirs. West Valley Coll./Mission Colls. Found.; del. Santa Clara County Water Commn., San Jose, 1989-90. Mem. Campbell C. of C. (pres. 1978, Citizen of the Yr. 1968), Country Women's Club of Campbell (pres. 1964-65), Kiwanis (hon.). Home: 61 Catalpa Ln Campbell CA 95008-3405 Office: City of Campbell 70 N 1st St Campbell CA 95008-1423

WATSON, JOHN EDWARD, mining company executive; b. Galveston, Tex., Apr. 9, 1949; s. Paul and Evelyn (LaKaff) W.; m. Sara Ann Ramsey, June 15, 1973 (div. 1978); m. Linda Kay, Sept. 26, 1982. BA, U. Tex., 1972; MS, Colo. Sch. of Mines, Golden, 1976. Geologist Union Carbide, Hot Springs, Ark., 1970, 73; geologic field asst. U.S. Geol. Survey, Golden, 1974-76; mineral analyst Gulf Mineral Resources, Denver, 1976-78; mineral economist Exxon Minerals, Houston, 1978-79; founder, pres., CEO, chmn. bd. dirs. Resources Corp., Golden, 1980-93. Mem. Nev. Mining Assn., Colo. Mining Assn. Office: Horizon and Resources Corp 1536 Cole Blvd Ste 140 Golden CO 80401-3413

WATSON, JOHN FRANCIS, software engineer, consultant; b. Glendive, Mont., Jan. 23, 1962; s. Harry Lawrence and Marian Francis (McNulty) W.; m. Crystal Lee Flanders, May 1, 1986; children: Chester Lawrence, Quinton John. BSEE, U. Utah, 1985. Software engr. Dept. Air Force, Hill AFB, Utah, 1985—; cons. in field. Mem. Golden Key, Tau Beta Pi, Eta Kappa Nu.

WATSON, KENNETH FREDERICK, molecular biologist, consultant; b. Pasco, Wash., Feb. 17, 1942; s. Walter Irvin and Isabel Danforth (Frost) W.; m. Janice Pauline Wilson, June 6, 1964; children: Heidi Michelle, Julie Monique. A.B., N.W. Nazarene Coll., 1964; Ph.D., Oreg. State U., 1969. Postdoctoral fellow Columbia U., N.Y.C., 1969-71, instr. human genetics, 1971-72; research fellow Internat. Agy. for Cancer Research, Berlin, 1972-73; from asst. prof. to prof. U. Mont., Missoula, 1973-83; head Lab. Viral Genetics, Abbott Labs, Abbott Park, Ill., 1983-85; v.p. academic affairs Northwest Nazarene Coll., 1985-87; asst. to pres. and prof. biochemistry, 1989—; cons. Abbott Labs., North Chicago, 1981-83; cons. Life Scis. Inc., St. Petersburg, Fla., 1976-83, Molecular Genetic Resources, Tampa, Fla., 1983—. Achievements include patent in Transferase Enzymes which Modify the 3'-Termini of Ribonucleic Acids and Methods. Bd. regents N.W. Nazarene Coll., 1980-83. Faculty research award Am. Cancer Soc., 1976-81; research grantee USPHS, 1973-83, Am. Cancer Soc., 1976-82. Mem. Am. Soc. Microbiology, N.W. Nazarene Coll. Alumni Assn. (bd. dirs. 1973-83, pres. 1980-83), Sigma Xi. Avocations: fly fishing, skiing, jogging. Home: 3600 S Midland Blvd Nampa ID 83686-8215 Office: NW Nazarene Coll 623 Holly St Nampa ID 83686-5855

WATSON, KENNETH MARSHALL, physics educator; b. Des Moines, Sept. 7, 1921; s. Louis Erwin and Irene Nellie (Marshall) W.; m. Elaine Carol Miller, Mar. 30, 1946; children: Ronald M., Mark Louis. B.S., Iowa State U., 1943; Ph.D., U. Iowa, 1948; Sc.D. (hon.), U. Ind., 1976. Rsch. engr. Naval Rsch. Lab., Washington, 1943-46; mem. staff Inst. Advanced Study Princeton (N.J.) U., 1948-49; rsch. fellow Lawrence Berkeley (Calif.) Lab., 1949-52, mem. staff, 1957-81; asst. prof. physics U. Ind., Bloomington, 1952-54; asso. prof. physics U. Wis., Madison, 1954-57; prof. physics U. Calif., Berkeley, 1957-81; prof. oceanography, dir. marine physics lab. U. Calif., San Diego, 1981—; cons. Mitre Corp., Sci. Application Corp.; mem. U.S. Pres's. Sci. Adv. Com. Panels, 1962-71; adviser Nat. Security Coun., 1972-75; bd. dirs. Ctr. for Studies of Dynamics, 1979-88; mem. JASON Adv. Panel. Author: (with M.L. Goldberger) Collision Theory, 1964, (with J. Welch and J. Bond) Atomic Theory of Gas Dynamics, 1966, (with J. Nutall) Topics in Several Particle Dynamics, 1970, (with Flatté, Munk, Dashen) Sound Transmission Through a Fluctuating Ocean, 1979. Mem. Nat. Acad. Scis. Home: PO Box 9726 Rancho Santa Fe CA 92067-4726 Office: U Calif Marine Physics Lab La Jolla CA 92093-0213

WATSON, LYNDON LEE, bank officer; b. Roswell, N.Mex., May 8, 1960; s. Donald Wayne and Marilyn Fern (Rounds) W. BBA, Ea. N.Mex. U., 1983, MBA, 1986. Teller 1st Fed. Savs. Bank, Roswell, 1987, exec. loan asst., 1987-92, comml. loan officer, 1992—. Profl. freelance photographer N.Mex. Mag., N.Mex. Bus. Jour., 1987—. Mem. Hist. Soc. for S.E. N.Mex. (bd. dirs. 1990—, v.p. 1991—), Sun Country Coop. (bd. dirs. 1989), Wilderness Hikers (editor newsletter 1987—). Democrat. Methodist. Home: 15 Cedar Dr Roswell NM 88201 Office: 1st Fed Savs Bank 300 N Pennsylvania Roswell NM 88201

WATSON, MARY ANN, psychologist, educator; b. St. Clairsville, Ohio, Jan. 27, 1944; d. William Glenn and Jeanette (Shannon) W.; m. Robert Montgomery (div. 1974); m. Dennis A. Whitlock, Oct. 6, 1978; children: Suzanne, Matthew Montgomery. BA, Grove City (Pa.) Coll., 1966; PhD, U. Pitts., 1969; postgrad., Johns Hopkins U., Balt., 1972-73. Lic. psychologist, Colo. Rsch. assoc. dept. biophysics and genetics/psychiatry U. Colo. Med. Ctr., Denver, 1973-77; prof. psychology Met. State Coll., Denver, 1974—, U. Colo., Denver, 1979-82; pvt. practice clin. psychology, 1975—; clin. psychologist Pub. Health Svc., Navajo and Hopi Reservations, Ariz., 1970-72; asst. prof. psychology Community Coll. of Phila., 1969-70; lectr. in field; cons. in field; mem. State Bd. Psychologist Examiners, 1979-85, chmn., 1981-83. Contbr. articles to profl. jours.; author: Breaking the Bonds, 1981; editor: Reading in Sexology, 1986, 2d edit. 1991. Home: 6840 Richthofen Pky Denver CO 80220-4848 Office: Met State Coll Denver Dept Psychology Campus Box 54 PO Box 173362 Denver CO 80217-3362

WATSON, MARY ELLEN, ophthalmic technologist; b. San Jose, Calif., Oct. 29, 1931; d. Fred Sidney and Emma Grace (Capps) Doney; m. Joseph Garrett Watson, May 11, 1950; children: Ted Joseph, Tom Fred, Pamela Kay Watson Niles. Cert. ophthalmic med. technologist and surg. asst. Ophthalmic technician Kent W. Christoferson, M.D., Eugene, 1965-80; ophthalmic technologist, surg. asst., adminstr. I. Howard Fine, M.D., Eugene, 1980—; course dir. Joint Commn. Allied Health Pers. in Ophthalmolgy, 1976-, lectr., mem. faculty, 1983--, skill evaluator and site coord., Eugene, 1988--; interant. instr. advanced surgical techniques. Contbr. articles to profl. jours. Recipient 5-Yr. Faculty award Joint Commn. for Allied Health Pers. in Ophthalmology, 1989. Mem. Allied Tech. Pers. in Ophthalmology, Internat. Women's Pilots Assn. Home: 2560 Chaucer Ct Eugene OR 97405-1217 Office: I Howard Fine MD 1550 Oak St Eugene OR 97401-7701

WATSON, MILTON RUSSELL, surgeon; b. Silverton, Oreg., July 14, 1934; s. Milton R. and Alice Violet (Sommers) W.; m. Shirley Ilene Kiel, June 20, 1958; children: Mark R., Tamara Faye. BA in Biology, Whitman Coll., Walla Walla, 1956; MD, U. Wash., 1960. Intern, then resident Santa Clara County Medical Ctr., San Jose, Calif., 1960-65; pvt. practice Walla Walla Clinic, 1969--. Contbr. articles to profl. jours. Capt. U.S. Army, 1965-69. Paul Harris fellow Rotary, 1980. Fellow ACS; mem. AMA, North Pacific Surg. Soc., Soc. Clin. Vascular Surgery, Internat. Cardiovascular Soc., Christian Med. Soc. (del. 1989). Presbyterian. Home: 545 Edgewood Dr Silverton OR 97381 Office: 324 Fairview Silverton OR 97381

WATSON, OLIVER LEE, III, aerospace engineering manager; b. Lubbock, Tex., Sept. 18, 1938; s. Oliver Lee Jr. and Sallie Gertrude (Hale) W.; m. Judith Valeria Horvath, June 13, 1964; 1 child, Clarke Stanford. BSEE, U. Tex., 1961; MSEE, Stanford U., 1963; MBA, Calif. State U., Fullerton, 1972; cert., U. So. Calif., 1980. Mgr. ballistic analysis Rockwell Internat. Autonetics Div., Anaheim, Calif., 1973-78, mgr. minuteman systems, 1978-83, mgr. preliminary engring., 1983-84, mgr. analysis group, 1984-85; mgr. aircraft systems Rockwell Internat. Autonetics Dept., Anaheim, Calif., 1985—; lectr. engring. Calif. State U., Fullerton, 1981-90. Co-author Digital Computing Using Fortran IV, 1982; Fortran 77, A Complete Primer, 1986. Bd. dirs. Olive Little League, Orange, 1980; vol. Stanford U. Engring. Fund, Orange County, Calif., 1983, regional chmn., 1984-86, So. Calif. chmn. 1986-88; mem. Stanford Assocs., 1988—. N.Am. Aviation Sci.-Engring. fellow, L.A., 1962, 63, Inst. Advancement Engring. fellow, L.A., 1976. Mem. IEEE (sr.; sect. v.p. 1974-75, sect. chmn. 1975-76), Am. Assn. Artificial Intelligence, Inst. Navigation (corp.), Jaycees (v.p. Orange chpt. 1973-74), Rockwell-Calif. State Univ. Alumni Club (v.p. 1993). Republican. Club: Lido Sailing. Office: Rockwell Internat 3370 E Miraloma Ave # 031-DF62 Anaheim CA 92806-1911

WATSON, RICHARD H., state official; b. Elmhurst, Ill., July 12, 1941; s. Richard O. and Helen (Haines) W.; m. Marilyn Overgaard, June 9, 1963; children: Richard, Karen. BS in Aero. and Astronautical Engring., U. Ill., Chgo., 1963, MS in Aero. and Astronautical Engring., 1966; postgrad., Harvard U., 1988. Rsch. engr. Boeing Co., Seattle, 1966-74; rsch. asst. prof. U. Wash., Seattle, 1974-78; sr. rsch. analyst energy and utilities com. Wash. State Senate, Olympia, 1978-81; dir. Wash. State Energy Office, Olympia, 1981—; chmn. Western Interstate Energy Bd., Denver, 1988-90. Recipient Exemplary Mgmt. of State Agy. award Assn. Wash. Cities, 1985, Conservation Eagle award N.W. Conservation Act Coalition, 1988, Exceptional Pub. Svc. award Bonneville Power Adminstrn., 1990. Mem. Nat. Assn. State Energy Ofcls. (bd. dirs. 1986—, chmn. 1990-91). Office: Wash State Energy Office M/S FA-11 809 Legion Way Olympia WA 98504-1211

WATSON, SHARON GITIN, psychologist, executive; b. N.Y.C., Oct. 21, 1943; d. Louis Leonard and Miriam (Myers) Gitin; m. Eric Watson, Oct. 31, 1969; 1 child, Carrie Dunbar. B.A. cum laude, Cornell U., 1965; M.A., U. Ill., 1968, Ph.D., 1971. Psychologist City N.Y. Prison Mental Health, Riker's Island, 1973-74; psychologist Youth Services Ctr., Los Angeles County Dept. Pub. Social Services, Los Angeles, 1975-77, dir. clin. services, 1978, dir. Youth Services Ctr., 1978-80; exec. dir. Crittenton Ctr. for Young Women and Infants, Los Angeles, 1980-89, Assn. Children's Svcs. Agys. of So. Calif., L.A., 1989-92, L.A. County Children's Planning Coun., 1992—. Contbr. articles to profl. jours. Mem. Rebuild L.A. Human Svcs. Com., The 2000 Partnership Human Svcs. Task Force , L.A. Learning Ctrs. Design Team, Interagency Coun. Child Abuse and Neglect Policy Com.; bd. dirs. L.A. Roundtable Children, Adolescent Pregnancy Childwatch, 1985-89; trustee L.A. Ednl. Alliance for Restructuring Now; co-chmn. Los Angeles County Drug and Alcohol Abuse Task Force, 1990, Dept. Children's Svcs. Planning Coun., 1986-88; mem. steering com. western region Child Welfare League Am., 1985-87. Mem. APA, Calif. Assn. Svcs. for Children (sec.-treas. 1983-84, pres. elect 1985-86, pres. 1986-87), Assn. Children's Svcs. Agys. So. Calif. (sec. 1981-83, pres. elect 1983-84, pres. 1984-85), Town Hall Calif., U.S. Figure Skating Assn. (bd. dirs.), Inter-Club Assn. Figure Skating Clubs (chmn.), Pasadena Figure Skating Club (bd. dirs.). Home: 4056 Camino Real Los Angeles CA 90065-3928 Office: LA County Children's Planning Coun 500 W Temple St Rm B-26 Los Angeles CA 90012

WATSON, WILLIAM RANDY, marketing executive; b. Roswell, N.Mex., July 13, 1950; s. William Floyd and Billie Dean (Mathews) W.; m. Dorothy Elinor Connole, Feb. 28, 1987; children: Matthew Scott, Amy Suzanne, Chadd William, Tyler William; 1 stepdaughter, Nicole Maloney. AAS, N.Mex. Jr. Coll., 1970; BBA, Ea. N.Mex. U., 1972. Telecommunications specialist Electronic Data Systems, Dallas, 1973-78; regional product specialist Storage Tek, Dallas, 1978-82; hdqr. product specialist Storage Tek, Louisville, Colo., 1982-84, disk mktg. product mgr., 1984-85; dir. tech mktg. Aweida Systems, Boulder, Colo., 1985-86; owner, pres. Tech. Mktg. Cons., Boulder, 1986—; pres. Midrange Performance Group, Boulder, 1989—. Election judge Boulder County, 1988. Home: 445 Poplar Ave Boulder CO 80304-1059 Office: Tech Mktg Cons 445 Poplar Ave Boulder CO 80304-1059

WATSON-BRODNAX, SHIRLEY JEAN, industrial hygienist; b. Norfolk, Va.; d. John B. and Louise (Booker) Holloway; m. Jack Leon Brodnax, July 31, 1976; children: Melodie, Tracey, Maisha. AA, Contra Costa Coll., 1978; BS in Cell and Molecular Biology, San Francisco State U., 1985. Jr. accountant Philco Corp., Phila.; sec., supr. U.S. Govt., Phila. and San Francisco, 1968-76; research asst., microbiologist Kelly Tech. Services, Oakland, Calif., 1986; microbiologist Nabisco Brands, Inc., Oakland, 1986-89; indsl. hygienist Naval Hosp., NSC Med. Command, Oakland, Calif., 1989—; supr. divsn. indsl. hygiene Naval Hosp., NSC Med. Command, Oakland. Kennedy King scholar Contra Costa Coll., 1978-80. Mem. AAAS, Internat. Platform Assn., Am. Microbiology Soc., Am. Chem. Soc., Inst. of Food Technologists, Am. Biog. Inst. Rsch. Assn. (dep. gov. bd. of govs. 1988—). Roman Catholic. Home: 1537 Hellings Ave Richmond CA 94801-2435 Office: Naval Hosp San Francisco Indsl Hygiene Div Bldg S90 Oakland Army Base Oakland CA 94630

WATT, DIANA LYNN, social worker; b. Leon, Iowa, Mar. 21, 1956; d. Charles Edward and Nora Eunice (Dickerson) W. BSW, Graceland Coll., 1980; postgrad., U. Kans., 1981-83. Social work intern St. Michael's (Ariz.) Sch., 1979, Father Benedict Justice Sch. and Seton Ctr., Kansas City, Mo., 1980, Mattie Rhodes Ctr., Kansas City, Mo., 1982-83; child care worker Gillis Home for Boys, Kansas City, 1980-84; community work experience program worker Social and Rehab. Svcs. State of Kans., Kansas City, 1983-84; contractual assignee Reorganized Ch. of Jesus Christ of Latter-day Saints, San Jose, Calif., 1984-87; counselor II summer youth NOVA/Summer Youth Employment Program, 1987; tchr. ESL Wilson Adult Edn. Ctr., 1987-88, Overfelt Adult Edn. Ctr., 1987—; eligibility worker II East Valley Social Svcs., 1992—; Occupational Tng. Inst. Job Tng. Partnership Act Intake specialist for GAIN, JTPA, NOVA, 1987—; instr. DTAC Serra Residential Ctr., Fremont, Calif., ESL instr. Overfelt Adult Edn. Program, 1990—. Counselor in tng. for camps and bible schs. Reorganized Ch. Jesus Christ Latter-day Saints, Iowa, 1969-73, counselor children's camp, San Jose, 1985, mem. ethnic community program com., East San Jose, 1984-87. Honored for Community Outreach in Ethnic Ministries, Reorganized Ch. Jesus Christ Latter-day Saints, 1985-87. Mem. Nat. Assn. Soc. Workers (cert.). Club: Intercultural (Lamoni, Iowa) (activity chmn. 1977-79).

WATTERS, ROBERT JAMES, geology educator; b. Glasgow, Scotland, July 22, 1946; came to U.S., 1974; s. Robert James and Catherine (Gordon) W.; m. Colleen Ida Murray, Dec. 10, 1988; children: Colin, Alexander. BS, U. Strathclyde, Scotland, 1969; MS, Diploma Imperial Coll., U. London (Eng.), 1970, PhD, 1972. Registered profl. geol. engr., Nev. Site engring. geologist Sir Alexander Gibbsptns, London, 1972-74; geol. engr. Dames and Moore, L.A., 1974-78; prof. Geology U. Nev., Reno, 1978—. Editor (book) Engineering Geology, 1989. Fellow Geol. Soc. London; mem. Inst. of Civic Engrs., Am. Soc. Civic Engrs., Assn. Engring. Geologists, Internat. Assn. Engring. Geologists, Internat. Assn. Rock Mechanics. Office: U Nev Mackay Sch of Mines Reno NV 89557

WATTS, BARBARA KAREN, non-profit social services administrator; b. Jellico, Tenn., Dec. 3, 1954; d. Jack Hyland and Ethel Minnie (Malicoat) Heywood; m. Gary L. Wilkens, Nov. 24, 1973 (dec. Oct. 1975); 1 child, Cain Earl Jackson; m. Kenneth R. Watts, Feb. 18, 1989. Student, C.C. Denver. Caseworker Denver Dept. Social Svcs., 1989-90, dir. statis. advocacy and mediation project, 1990—; cons. Ctrl. Denver Community Svcs., 1990—. Vol. St. Francis Day Shelter, Denver, 1990—; pres. Episcopal Churchwomen, 1991-92. Republican. Office: Denver Dept Social Svcs 2200 W Alameda Ave Denver CO 80223

WATTS, BARRY ALLEN, mental health counselor, administrator; b. Payette, Idaho, Nov. 15, 1943; s. Dale E. and Juanita Ruth (Amick) W.; m. Bonnie Lee McKean, Dec. 28, 1965; children: Kelly Dale Watts Harvey, Robert Allen. BA in Religion, Pepperdine U., 1968; MS in Psychology, Ea. Wash. U., 1972; PhD in Counseling Psychology, Columbia Pacific U., 1988. Lic. profl. counselor, Idaho; nat. cert. counselor. Psychologist Warm Springs Ctr., Boise, 1971-74; exec. dir. Warm Springs Counseling Ctr., Boise, 1974—; spl. lectr. Boise State U., 1978-83; adj. faculty Coll. Idaho, 1984—; bd. dirs. Idaho Network for Children, 1982-86, Hays Shelter Home, 1985-92, Idaho Counselor Licensing Bd., 1986—, Guidance Adv.-Boise Schs., 1988—, all Boise. Bd. dirs. Eagle (Idaho) Citizens Assn., 1979-81; cubmaster Eagle area Boy Scouts Am., 1980-82. With U.S. Army, 1963-65. Mem. ACA, Am. Mental Health Counselors Assn., Idaho Counseling Assn. (pres. 1986-87), Idaho Mental Health Counselors Assn., Christian Assn. Psychol. Studies (area coord. 1982-83), Play Therapy Assn., Soc. Exploration Psychotherapy Integration. Office: Warm Springs Counseling Ctr 740 Warm Springs Ave Boise ID 83712-6420

WATTS, CYNTHIA GAY, lawyer; b. Indpls., Aug. 20, 1962; d. Leslie J. and Nell (Jackson) W. BA magna cum laude, Yale U., 1984; JD cum laude, Harvard U., 1988. Bar: Calif. 1988. Assoc. Paul, Hastings, Jahofsky & Walker, L.A., 1988-93; v.p., gen. counsel, sec. Leslie's Poolmart, Chatsworth, Calif., 1993—. Mem. ABA, Calif. State Bar Assn., L.A. County Bar Assn. Episcopalian. Home: 1032 2nd St # 303 Santa Monica CA 90403 Office: Leslie's Poolmart 20222 Plummer St Chatsworth CA 91311

WATTS, JAMES HARRISON, architect; b. Cleve., Apr. 28, 1951; s. Gregory Dean and Bubbles Joan (Browning) W.; m. Janice Fahey, Aug. 28, 1976; children: Jane, Molly. BArch, R.I. Sch. Design, 1974. Registered architect, Calif. Urban designer, film maker State of R.I., Providence, 1976-77; project mgr. Thomas Williamson Architect, San Diego, 1979-82; prin. Williamson & Watts Architects, San Diego, 1982-88, Fahey-Watts Architects, San Diego, 1988—; asst. architect San Diego Unified Sch. Dist., 1989—. Vol. architect U.S. Peace Corps, Nuku Alofa Tonga, 1977-79; chmn. San Diego Noise Abatement and Control Bd., 1988—. Mem. AIA, Am. Arbitration Assn., San Diego Yacht Club. Home: 3619 Front St San Diego CA 92103-4005

WATTS, JAMES LAWRENCE, investment banker; b. Minot, N.D., June 3, 1949; s. Lawrence Robert and Deloris Marie (Anderson) W. BA in Econs., U. Wis., Green Bay, 1972; MA in Econs., Am. U., 1975, JD, 1981. Bar: D.C., U.S. Supreme Ct. Legis. asst. U.S. Ho. Reps., Washington, 1975-76; assoc. dir. Nat. Assn. Small Bus. Investment Cos., Washington, 1976-81; fin. cons. Leighton, Lemov, Jacobs & Buckley, Washington, 1981-85; ptnr. Venture Internat., Alexandria, Va., 1985-86; v.p. corp. fin. McKewon & Timmins, San Diego, 1986-87; sr. v.p. Cruttenden & Co., Newport Beach, Calif., 1987-92; mng. dir. CFI Ltd., Irvine, Calif., 1992—; bd. dirs. IRSC, Inc., Anaheim, Calif., Candy's Tortilla Factory, Inc., Pueblo, Colo, Graftek, Inc., Boulder, Colo. Chmn. fin. com. Canal Way Homeowners Assn., Alexandria, 1981-83. Recipient Presdl. cert. White Ho. Conf. on Small Bus., 1980, Cert. Achievement, Nat. Assn. Small Bus. Investment Cos., 1981. Mem. ABA. Republican. Office: CFI Ltd 19800 MacArthur Blvd Irvine CA 92715

WATTS, JEFFREY ALAN, investment officer; b. Pontiac, Mich., Sept. 28, 1950; s. Harold Maurice and Jeanne Lucille (Helgeson) W.; m. Linda Ginsburg, Sept. 2, 1978; children: Robert, Kelly. BS in Cellular Biology, U. Mich., 1972, MBA in Fin. and Acctg., 1975. CPA, Calif., Ill., chartered fin. analyst. Acct., sr. cons. Arthur Andersen & Co., Chgo., 1975-78; loan officer No. Trust & Co., Chgo., 1978-82; sr. investment officer Union Venture Corp., L.A., 1982-86, v.p., 1986-87, pres., 1987-91, Watts Group, 1992,

Wash. State Investment Bd., 1993—. Mem. AICPA, Nat. Assn. Small Bus. Investment Cos. (bd. govs. 1986-91, mem. exec. com. 1987-88), Western Regional Assn. Small Bus. Investment Cos. (pres. 1986), Fin. Analysts Fedn., Calif. Soc. CPA's, Ill. Assn. CPA's, L.A. Soc. Fin. Analysts. Avocations: skiing, scuba diving, swimming, golf. Office: Washington State Investment Bd PO Box 40916 2424 Heritage Court SW Olympia WA 98504-0916

WATTS, OLIVER EDWARD, engineering consultancy company executive; b. Hayden, Colo., Sept. 22, 1939; s. Oliver Easton and Vera Irene (Hockett) W.; m. Charla Ann French, Aug. 12, 1962; children—Erik Sean, Oliver Eron, Sherilyn. B.S., Colo. State U., 1962. Registered profl. engr., Colo., Calif. Crew chief Colo. State U. Research Found., Ft. Collins, 1962; with Calif. Dept. Water Resources, Gustine and Castaic, 1964-70; land and water engr. CF&I Steel Corp., Pueblo, Colo., 1970-71; engring. dir. United Western Engrs., Colorado Springs., Colo., 1971-76; ptnr. United Planning and Engring Co., Colorado Springs., Colo., 1976-79; owner Oliver E. Watts, cons. engr., Colorado Springs., Colo., 1979—. Dir. edn. local Ch. of Christ, 1969-71, deacon, 1977-87, elder, 1987— . Served to 1st lt. C.E., AUS, 1962-64. Recipient Individual Achievement award Colo. State U. Coll. Engring., 1981. Fellow ASCE (v.p. Colorado Springs br. 1975, pres. 1978); mem. Nat. Soc. Profl. Engrs. (pres. Pikes Peak chpt. 1975, sec. Colo. sect. 1976, v.p. 1977, pres. 1978-79, Young Engr. award 1976, Pres.'s award 1979), Cons. Engrs. Coun. Colo. (bd. dirs. 1981-83), Am. Cons. Engrs. Coun., Profl. Land Surveyors Colo., Colorado Springs Homebuilders Assn., Colo. Engrs. Coun. (del. 1980—), Colo. State U. Alumni Assn. (v.p., dir. Pike's Peak chpt. 1972-76), Lancers, Lambda Chi Alpha. Home: 7195 Dark Horse Pl Colorado Springs CO 80919-1442 Office: 614 Elkton Dr Colorado Springs CO 80907-3514

WATTS, PATSY JEANNE, management company executive; b. Portland, Oreg., Oct. 19, 1943; d. Eugene Estelle and Maxine (Muldoon) Nicks; m. James Lowell Watts, June 5, 1964 (div. Aug. 1974); 1 child, Douglas James. Hon. cert. in realty, Grossmont Coll., 1978; paralegal cert., U. San Diego, 1980. Realtor assoc. Schwab Realty, La Mesa, Calif., 1976-78; office mgr. Office of Dist. Atty., Fallon, Nev., 1978-81; cons., adminstr. Calif. and Fla., 1981-85; real estate and legal exec. adminstr. Keegan Mgmt. Co., San Jose, Calif., 1985-91. Co-Author: Real Estate Marketing, 1977. Fund-raiser Citizens for Pete Wilson, San Diego, William Cleator for San Diego City Coun., 1981-82; staff reporter Citizens vs. Pub. Funds for Pvt. Contracting of San Diego Conv. Ctr., 1983. Named Miss Water Festival City of Portland, 1961. Mem. NAFE, San Francisco Assn. Legal Assts., Internat. Council Shopping Ctrs., Ams. For Legal Reform. Republican.

WAUTERS, SHIRLEY STAPLETON, retired real estate executive; b. Boise, Idaho, June 17, 1936; d. Charles Edward Lee and Eleanor L. (Swiggart) Noble; m. Bruce F. Wauters, May 23, 1986. AA in Liberal Arts summa cum laude, DeAnza Coll., Cupertino, Calif., 1975; BS in Bus. Mgmt., Ariz. State U., 1979. Lic. realtor assoc. Founder, dir. Women's Opportunity Ctr., Cupertino, 1970-73; owner, pub. Ariz. Women's Yellow Pages, Inc., Scottsdale, Ariz., 1973-80; pvt. practice cons. Cupertino, 1967-73, Scottsdale, Ariz., 1983-83; ptnr. The Weigelt Co., Inc., Phoenix, 1973-87; br. mgr. B. Rich, Inc., Tempe, Ariz., 1987, R. Richard Vick, Inc., Scottsdale, 1987-88; v.p. real estate sales TransWestern Consol. Realty, Inc., Phoenix, 1988-89; assoc. Internat. Ariz. Investments, Inc., Scottsdale, 1989-91; sec. Ariz. State U. Ctr. Environ. Studies, Tempe, 1992—; comml. real estate cons., Scottsdale. Mem. Ariz. State U. Alumni.

WAXMAN, HENRY ARNOLD, congressman; b. Los Angeles, Sept. 12, 1939; s. Louis and Esther (Silverman) W.; m. Janet Kessler, Oct. 17, 1971; children: Carol Lynn, Michael David. B.A. in Polit. Sci, UCLA, 1961, J.D., 1964. Bar: Calif. 1965. Mem. Calif. State Assembly, 1969-74, chmn. com. on health, until 1974; mem. 94th-103rd Congresses from 24th (now 29th) Calif. dist., 1975—, chmn. house subcom. on health and environment, 1979—. Pres. Calif. Fedn. Young Democrats, 1965-67. Mem. Calif. Bar Assn., Guardians Jewish Home for Aged, Am. Jewish Congress, Sierra Club, B'nai B'rith, Phi Sigma Alpha. Office: House of Representatives 2408 Rayburn House Office Washington DC 20515

WAY, E(DWARD) LEONG, pharmacologist, toxicologist, educator; b. Watsonville, Calif., July 10, 1916; s. Leong Man and Lai Har (Shew) W.; m. Madeline Li, Aug. 11, 1944; children: Eric, Linette. BS, U. Calif., Berkeley, 1938, MS, 1940; PhD, U. Calif., San Francisco, 1942. Pharm. chemist Merck & Co., Rahway, N.J., 1942; instr. pharmacology George Washington U., 1943-46, asst. prof., 1946-48; asst. prof. pharmacology U. Calif., San Francisco, 1949-52; assoc. prof. U. Calif., 1952-57, prof., 1957-87, prof. emeritus, 1987—, chmn. dept. pharmacology, 1973-78; USPHS spl. rsch. fellow U. Berne, Switzerland, 1955-56, China Med. Bd.; rsch. fellow, vis. prof. U. Hong Kong, 1962-63; Sterling Sullivan disting. vis. prof. Martin Luther King U., 1982; hon. prof. pharmacology and neurosci. Guangzhou Med. Coll., 1987; mem. adv. com. Pharm. Mfrs. Assn. Found., 1968—; mem. coun. Am. Bur. for Med. Advancement in China, 1982—; bd. dirs. Li Found., pres., 1985—; Tsumura prof. neuropsychopharmacology med. sch. Gunma U., Maebashi, Japan, 1989-90; sr. staff fellow Nat. Inst. on Drug Abuse, 1990-91; researcher on drug metabolism, analgetics, devel. pharmacology, drug tolerance, drug dependence and Chinese materia medica. Contbr. numerous articles and revs. to profl. publs.; editor: New Concepts in Pain, 1967, (with others) Fundamentals of Drug Metabolism and Drug Disposition, 1971, Endogenous and Exogenous Opiate Agonists and Antagonists, 1979; mem. editorial bd. Clin. Pharmacology, Therapeutics, 1975-87, Drug, Alcohol Dependence, 1976-87, Progress in Neuro-Psychopharmacology, 1977-91, Research Communications in Chem. Pathology and Pharmacology, 1978-91, Alcohol and Drug Dependence, 1986-91, Asian Pacific Jour. Pharm., 1985—. Recipient Faculty Rsch. Lectr. award U. Calif., San Francisco, 1974, San Francisco Chinese Hosp. award, 1976, Cultural citation and Gold medal Ministry of Edn., Republic of China, 1978, Nathan B. Eddy award Coll. on Problems in Drug Dependence, 1979; Chancellor's award for pub. svc. U. Calif., 1986, Disting. Alumnus award U. Calif. San Francisco, 1990. Fellow AAAS, Am. Coll. Neuropsychopharmacology, Am. Coll. Clin. Pharmacology (hon.); mem. Am. Soc. Pharmacology, Exptl. Therapeutics (bd. editors 1957-65, pres. 1976-77, Torald Sollman award 1992), Fedn. Am. Socs. Exptl. Biology (exec. bd. 1975-79, pres. 1977-78), Am. Pharm. Assn. (life, co-recipient Ebert prize certificate 1962), AMA (affiliate), Soc. Aid and Rehab. Drug Addicts (Hong Kong, life), Western Pharmacology Soc. (pres. 1963-64), Japanese Pharm. Soc. (hon.), Coun. Sci. Soc. Pres.' (exec. com. 1979-84, treas. 1980-84), Coll. on Problems of Drug Dependence (bd. dirs. 1978-92, chmn. 1978-82), Chinese Pharmacology Soc. (hon.), Academia Sinica. Office: U Calif Dept of Pharmacology 1210 S San Francisco CA 94143-0450

WAY, GREG, business owner, consultant, writer; b. Seattle, Oct. 7, 1950; s. George Dean and Josephine Catherine (De Matis) W. BA in Sociology, U. Wash., Seattle, 1973. Owner Way Enterprises, Seattle, 1962—; newsroom aide Seattle Times, 1968-76, AP, Seattle, 1978. Author: (stage plays) How Does Your Father Dance?, 1979, Kiss Me or Bless Me!, 1981, The Queets, 1991, One Axe, 1993, (screenplay) The Queets, 1989, (one-act play) Musical Memories, 1993; contbr. numerous articles to profl. jours. Mem. NRA, Mensa, Seattle Film Soc. (charter), Am. Cryonics Soc., Planetary Soc. Office: PO Box 1182 Seattle WA 98111-1182

WAY, JACOB EDSON, III, museum director; b. Chgo., May 18, 1947; s. Jacob Edson Jr. and Amelia (Evans) W.; m. Jean Ellwood Chappell, Sept. 6, 1969; children: Sarah Chappell, Rebecca Stoddard, Jacob Edson IV. BA, Beloit Coll., 1968; MA, U. Toronto, 1971, PhD, 1978. Instr. Beloit (Wis.) Coll., 1972-73, asst. prof., 1973-80, assoc. prof., 1980-85; dir. Logan Mus. Anthropology, Beloit, 1980-85, Wheelwright Mus. Am. Indian, Santa Fe, 1985-89; acting dir. New Mex. Mus. Natural History, Albuquerque, 1990-91; exec. dir. Space Ctr. Internat. Space Hall of Fame, Alamogordo, N.Mex., 1991—; evaluator Nat. Park Service, Denver, 1986. Contbr. articles to profl. jours. Mem. Nuke Watch, Beloit, 1983-84. Research grants Wis. Humanities Com., 1984, NSF, 1981; grantee Cullister Found., 1978-84; fellow U. Toronto, 1971. Mem. Am. Assn. Mus., Am. Assn. Phys. Anthropology, Can. Assn. for Phys. Anthropology, N.Mex. Assn. Mus., Soc. Am. Archaeology, Wis. Fedn. Mus. (adv. bd. 1982-85). Mem. Soc. Friends. Office: Space Ctr Hwy 2001 PO Box 533 Alamogordo NM 88310

WAY, STEVEN H., insurance company executive; b. San Francisco, July 3, 1950; s. Greville L. and Lois (Coombs) W.; m. Sandra Lee Fultz, Sept. 7, 1974; children: Brian, Kelley, Shannon. BA in Econs., U. Calif., Berkeley, 1973. CLU, chartered fin. cons. Sales spl. agt. Northwestern Mut. Life, Milw., 1973—; pres., CEO Way Fin., Walnut Creek, Calif., 1986—; mem. Contra Costa Estate Planning Coun., Walnut Creek, 1986—. Mem. Million Dollar Round Table. Liberterian. Office: Way Fin 3075 Citrus Circle Ste 204 Walnut Creek CA 94598

WAYBURN, EDGAR, internist, environmentalist; b. Macon, Ga., Sept. 17, 1906; s. Emanuel and Marian (Voorsanger) W.; m. Cornelia Elliott, Sept. 12, 1947; children: Cynthia, William, Diana, Laurie. AB magna cum laude, U. Ga., 1926; MD cum laude, Harvard U., 1930. Hosp. tng. Columbia-Presbyn. Hosp., N.Y.C., 1931-33; assoc. clin. prof. Stanford (Calif.) U., 1933-65, U. Calif., San Francisco, 1960-76; practice medicine specializing in internal medicine San Francisco, 1933-1985; mem. staff Pacific Presbyn. Med. Ctr., San Francisco, 1959-86, chief endocrine clinic, 1959-72, vice chief staff, 1961-63, hon. staff, 1986—. Editor: Man Medicine and Ecology, 1970; contbr. articles to profl. and environ. jours. Mem. Sec. of Interior's Adv. Bd. on Nat. Park System, 1979-83, commn. on nat. parks and protected areas Internat. Union for Conservation Nature and Natural Resources; leader nat. campaigns Alaska Nat. Interest Lands Conservation Act; trustee Pacific Presbyn. Med. Ctr., 1978-86; mem. citizens' adv. commn. Golden Gate Nat. Recreation Area, San Francisco, 1974—, leader nat. campaigns, 1978-86; prin. citizen advocate Redwood Nat. Park; dir. The Antarctica Project; mem. adv. bd. Pacific Forest Trust; hon. chmn. Tuolumne River Preservation Trust; bd. dirs. Garden Sullivan Hosp., 1965-78. Maj. USAF, 1942-46. Recipient Douglas award Nat. Pks. and Conservation Assn., 1987, Leopold award Calif. Nature Conservancy, 1988. Fellow ACP; mem. AMA, Am. Soc. Internal Medicine, Calif. Med. Assn. (del. 1958-83, Recognition award 1986, Leadership and Quality awards 1986), San Francisco Med. Soc. (pres. 1965, Resolution of Congratulations 1986), Sierra Club (pres. 1961-64, 67-69, John Muir award 1972), Fedn. Western Outdoor Clubs (pres. 1953-55). Home: 314 30th Ave San Francisco CA 94121-1705

WAYBURN, PEGGY (CORNELIA E. WAYBURN), author, editor; b. N.Y.C., Sept. 2, 1917; d. Thomas Ketchin and Cornelia (Ligon) E.; m. Edgar Wayburn Sept. 12, 1947; children: Cynthia, William, Diana, Laurie. BA, Barnard, 1942. Copywriter Vogue Mag., N.Y.C., 1943-45, J. Walter Thompson, San Francisco, 1945-47; self employed freelance writer, San Francisco, 1948—; Author: Adventuring in the San Francisco Bay Area, Adventuring in Alaska; (audio visual series) Circle of Life; contbr. articles to profl. jours. Mem. bd. advisors Am. Youth Hostels; trustee Sierra Club Found. Recipient annual award Calif. Conservation Assn., 1966. Mem. Sierra Club (special svc. award 1967, women's award 1989). Home: 314 30th Ave San Francisco CA 94121

WAYLAND, J(AMES) HAROLD, biomedical scientist, educator; b. Boise, Idaho, July 2, 1909; s. Charles William and Daisy (McConnell) W.; m. Virginia Jane Kartzke, June 24, 1933; children—Ann Marie Peters, Elizabeth Jane (Mrs. Paul T. Barber). B.S., U. Idaho, 1931, D.Sc. (hon.), 1977; M.S., Calif. Inst. Tech., 1935, Ph.D., 1937. Am. Scandinavian Found. fellow U. Copenhagen, 1937; asst. prof. physics U. Redlands, 1938-41; mil. research in mine warfare and torpedo devel., 1941-48; assoc. prof. applied mechanics Calif. Inst. Tech., Pasadena, 1949-57; prof. Calif. Inst. Tech., 1957-63, prof. engring. sci., 1963-79, prof. emeritus, 1979—; U.S. coordinator U.S.-Japan Coop. Seminars on Peripheral Circulation, 1967, 70; mem. cardiovascular and renal study sect. NIH, 1973-77; vis. prof. Shinshu U., Matsumoto, Japan, 1973, U. Limburg, Maastricht, The Netherlands, 1979, U. New South Wales, Australia, 1980, U. Heidelberg, 1982, U. of Tsukuba, Japan, 1987; Disting. vis. prof. U. Del., 1985. Contbr. articles to profl. publs., also books and articles on history of playing cards. Recipient Ordnance Devel. award U.S. Navy, 1945, Cert. of Recognition, NASA, 1975, Humboldt Sr. Scientist Rsch. award U. Heidelberg, 1982, 91, Malpighi prize, 1988; named to Alumni Hall of Fame, U. Idaho, 1990; Guggenheim fellow, 1953-54; rsch. grantee NIH, NSF, John A. Hartford Found., Kroc Found. Fellow AAAS (chmn. med. scis. sect. 1976); founding fellow Am. Inst. Med. and Biol. Engring.; mem. AAUP, Microcirculatory Soc. (pres. 1971-72, Landis award 1981), Am. Phys. Soc., Am. Physiol. Soc., European Microcirculatory Soc. (hon.), German Microcirculatory Soc. (hon.), Internat. Soc. Biorheology, Am. Heart Assn., Am. Inst. Archeology, Am. Soc. Enologists, Playing Card Soc., Sigma Xi, Phi Beta Kappa, Sigma Tau. Democrat. Unitarian. Club: Athenaeum. Home: Apt B-21 900 E Harrison Ave Pomona CA 91767-2053 Office: Calif Inst Tech Mail Code 104 44 Pasadena CA 91125

WAYNE, DAVID ALAN, organizational psychologist; b. Toronto, Ontario, Can., Mar. 23, 1946; came to U.S., 1986; s. Irving and Margaret Naomi (Ginsburg) W.; m. Judy Gail Fisher, Jan. 3, 1967 (div. 1992); children: Jonathan David, Daniel Joshua, Michael Jacob. AB, Shimer Coll., 1967; MEd, U. Toronto, 1974; MSEd, Niagra U., 1976; PhD, Walden U., 1981. Dept. chmn. Langdon Park Comprehensive, London, Eng., 1969-70; cons. staff devel. Hamilton (Ontario) Bd. Edn., Can., 1970-87; assoc. clin. prof. psychiatry McMaster U., Hamilton, 1978-87; course dir. counseling York U., Toronto, 1980-89; dir. Ariz. Leadership Academies Ariz. Dept. Edn., Phoenix, 1987—; co-pres. Med. Communications Consortium, Tucson, 1991—; v.p. Med. TV Network, Tucson, 1988—; dir staff devel. J.C. Lincoln Hosp., Phoenix, 1993—; pres. CANUSA Internat. Cons., Scottsdale, Ariz., 1977—; facilitator Bur. Indian Affairs, Washington, 1986-92; adj. prof. edn. Ariz. State U., Phoenix, 1987—; trainer Inst. for Ednl. Leadership, Washington, 1989-91; lead trainer, cons. Ariz. Prevention Resource Ctr. Author Not Alone, 1981, Lead Time, 1982, Peer Action, 1987. Chmn. edn. Coun. on Road Trauma, Hamilton, 1982-86, Statewide Chem. Abuse Prevention Interagy. Com., Phoenix, 1987-91; mem. Valley Leadership, Inc., Phoenix, 1991—. Recipient R.W.B. Jackson Rsch. award, Ontario Edn. Rsch. Coun., Toronto, 1981, Beattie Profl. Contbn. award Ontario Sch. Counselors Assn., Toronto, 1983, Hilroy fellowship Canadian Tchrs. Fedn., 1984, Community Leadership award Hamilton-Wentworth Police Dept., Hamilton, 1985. Mem. ASCD, Nat. Peer Helpers Assn., Valley Citizens League, Ariz. Road Racers. Jewish. Home: 9620 E Cinnabar Ave Scottsdale AZ 85258 Office: John C. Lincoln Hosp 250 E Dunlap Phoenix AZ 85020-2871

WAYNE, KYRA PETROVSKAYA, writer; b. Crimea, USSR, Dec. 31, 1918; came to U.S., 1948, naturalized, 1951; d. Prince Vasily Sergeyevich and Baroness Zinaida Fedorovna (Fon-Haffenberg) Obolensky; m. George J. Wayne, Apr. 21, 1961; 1 child, Ronald George. B.A., Leningrad Inst. Theatre Arts, 1939, M.A., 1940. Actress, concert singer, USSR, 1939-46; actress, U.S., 1948-51; enrichment lectr. Royal Viking Line cruises, Alaska-Can., Greek Islands-Black Sea, Russia/Europe, 1978-79, 81-82, 83-84, 86-87, 88. Author: Kyra, 1959; Kyra's Secrets of Russian Cooking, 1960, 93; The Quest for the Golden Fleece, 1962; Shurik, 1971; The Awakening, 1972; The Witches of Barguzin, 1975; Max, The Dog That Refused to Die, 1979 (Best Fiction award Dog Writers Assn. Am. 1980); Rekindle the Dreams, 1979, Quest for Empire, 1986, Li'l Ol' Charlie, 1989. Founder, pres. Clean Air Program, Los Angeles County, 1971-72; mem. women's council KCET-Ednl. TV; mem. Monterey County Symphony Guild, 1989-91, Monterey Bay Aquarium, Monterey Peninsula Mus. Art, Friends of La Mirada. Served to lt. Russian Army, 1941-43. Decorated Red Star, numerous other decorations USSR; recipient award Crusade for Freedom, 1955-56; award Los Angeles County, 1972, Merit award Am. Lung Assn. L.A. County, 1988. Mem. Soc. Children's Book Writers, Authors Guild, P.E.N., UCLA Med. Faculty Wives (pres. 1970-71, dir. 1971-75) UCLA Affiliates (life), Los Angeles Lung Assn. (life), Friends of the Lung Assn. (pres. 1988), Carmel Music Soc. (bd. dirs. 1992—), Idyllwild Sch. Music, Art and Theatre Assn. (trustee 1987), Los Angelenos Club (life). Home: 25031 Hidden Mesa Ct Monterey CA 93940-6633

WAYNE, LOWELL GRANT, air pollution scientist, consultant; b. Washington, Nov. 27, 1918; s. Glenn Lytten and Bonnie Jean (Leming) W.; m. Martha Lee Dolson, June 21, 1942; children: Garth Lee, Randall Rush. BS, U. Calif., Berkeley, 1937; student, U. Calif., Davis, 1939-41, Harvard U., 1942; PhD, Calif. Inst. Technology, 1948. Diplomate Am. Bd. Indsl. Hygiene. Fellow Mellon Inst. for Indsl. Rsch., Pitts., 1949-52; phys. chemist Stanford Rsch. Inst., Menlo Park, Calif., 1953-54; occupational health engr. U. Calif., L.A., 1954-56; rsch. photochemist Air Pollution Control Dist., L.A., 1956-62; rsch. analyst Hancock Found. U. So. Calif., L.A., 1962-72, section head Air Pollution Control Inst., 1966-72; v.p., sr. scientist Pacific Environ. Svcs., Inc., Santa Monica, Calif., 1972-85; cons. L.A., 1985—; sr. scientist Valley Rsch. Corp., Van Nuys, Calif., 1987—. Lt. comdr. USNR, 1942-46. Fellow AAAS; mem. So. Calif. Fedn. Scientists, Air and Waste Mgmt. Assn., Sigma Xi. Unitarian. Home: 285 Bayside Rd Arcata CA 95521-6463

WAYNE, M. HOWARD, deputy attorney general; b. Fresno, Calif., Nov. 2, 1948; s. William W. and Blanche F. W.; m. Mary C. Lundberg, July 8, 1988. BA, San Diego State U., 1969; JD cum laude, U. San Diego, 1972. Bar: Calif. 1972, U.S. Dist. Ct. (so. dist.) Calif. 1972, U.S. Dist. Ct. (ctrl. dist.) Calif. 1992, U.S. Ct. Appeals (D.C. cir.) 1975, U.S. Supreme Ct. 1976. Rsch. atty. Calif. Ct. Appeals, San Diego, 1972-73; dep. atty. gen. Calif. Dept. Justice, San Diego, 1973—; adj. prof. Nat. U., San Diego, 1979-83. Author: (handbook) Dept. of Justice Family Support Manual, 1987. Dir. Mid City Devel. Corp., 1992—; chmn., San Diegans for Good Govt., 1986—; comptroller Neighborhoods for Dist. Elections, San Diego, 1987-88; chmn., rep. 78th Assembly Dist., 1987-93, candidate, 1990. Mem. Assn. of Calif. State Attys. (bd. dirs. 1978—), San Diego County Bar Assn. (chmn. law week 1989-92, Outstanding Pub. Atty. 1989), Uptown Dem. Club (Dem. of Yr. 1990), U. San Diego Law Alumni Assn. (pres., bd. dirs. 1975-78). Office: Atty Gens Office 110 W A Ste 700 San Diego CA 92101

WAYNE, MARVIN ALAN, emergency medicine physician; b. Detroit, Dec. 11, 1943; s. Jack I. and Marian M. (Berk) W.; m. Joan A. Tobin, Dec. 30, 1971; children: Michelle, Dana. MD, U. Mich., 1968. Diplomate Am. Bd. Emergency Medicine. Fellow St. Bartholomew's Hosp., London, 1968, Virginia Mason Hosp., Seattle, 1973-74; resident in surgery U. Colo. Med. Ctr., Denver, 1968-71; pvt. practice Bellingham, Wash., 1974—; staff emergency dept. St. Joseph's Hosp. (merger St. Joseph's Hosp. and St. Luke's Hosp.), Bellingham, Wash., 1974—, vice chmn. dept. emergency medicine, 1980-83, chmn., 1984-86; med. dir. Emergency Med. Svcs., Bellingham, Wash., 1975—; assoc. clin. prof. health scis. U. Wash., Seattle, 1986—; vice chmn. emergency med. svcs. com. State of Wash., 1982-83, chmn., 1983-86; med. dir. Med-Flight Helicopter, 1980--, Inst. for Pre-Hosp. Medicine, 1980--; pres. Whatcom County Emergency Med. Svcs. Coun., 1979; med. advisor Mt. Baker Ski Patrol; speaker nat. and internat. edn. programs; founder, owner Dr. Cookie Inc., Bothell, Wash., 1985--. Contbr. articles to med. jours. Bd. dirs. YMCA, Bellingham, 1980-84. Maj. M.C., U.S. Army, 1971-73, Vietnam. Recipient Outstanding Achievement award Whatcom County Emergency Med. Svcs. Coun., 1980, Outstanding Ednl. Achievement award Abbott Labs., 1982, Outstanding Advanced Life Support System award State of Wash., 1983, Emergency Med. Svc. rsch. award Wash. Assn. Emergency Med. Technicians and Paramedics, 1983. Fellow Am. Coll. Emergency Physicians (bd. dirs. Wash. chpt. 1977-84, pres. 1978, sci. meetings com. 1984, Outstanding Ednl. Achievement award 1982), Royal Soc. Medicine (Eng.); mem. Wash. State Med. Soc. (emergency med. svc. adv. com. 1978--), Whatcom County Med. Soc., Univ. Assn. for Emergency Medicine, Soc. Critical Care Medicine, Am. Trauma Soc. (founding), Nat. Assn. Emergency Med. Svc. Physicians, Am. Soc. Automotive Medicine, Nat. Assn. Emergency Med. Technicians. Office: Emergency Med Svcs 1200 Dupont Ste 1A 1800 Broadway Bellingham WA 98225

WAYT, MICHAEL ALLEN, military officer; b. Scott AFB, Ill., Apr. 23, 1963; s. Ronald Dale and Nobuko (Wako) W.; m. Lara Anne Rupley, June 21, 1985; children: Stephanie Marie, Emily Danyel. Commd. tech. sgt. USAF, 1983, advanced through grades to sgt., 1986; field survival instr. 3612 CCTS USAF, Fairchild AFB, Wash., 1983-84, parachute survival instr., 1985-86; pararescue instr. 1550th CCTW USAF, Kirkland AFB, N.Mex., 1987-90; pararescueman 210th ARS Alaska ANG, Kulis ANGB Anchorage, 1990—. Protestant. Home: 2824 E 88th Anchorage AK 99507 Office: 210th ARS DOJ Kulis ANGB 6000 Air Guard Rd Anchorage AK 99502

WEARLY, WILLIAM LEVI, business executive; b. Warren, Ind., Dec. 5, 1915; s. Purvis Gardner and Ethel Ada (Jones) W.; m. Mary Jane Riddle, Mar. 8, 1941; children: Patricia Ann, Susan, William Levi, Elizabeth. B.S., Purdue U., 1937, Dr. Engring. (hon.), 1959. Student career engr. C.A. Dunham Co., Michigan City, Ind., 1936; mem. elec. design staff Joy Mfg. Co., Franklin, Pa., 1937-39; v.p., gen. sales mgr. Joy Mfg. Co., 1952-56, exec. v.p., 1956-57, pres., dir., 1957-62; v.p., dir. Ingersoll-Rand Co., 1964-66, exec. v.p., 1966-67, chmn., chief exec. officer, 1967-80, chmn. exec. com., 1981-85; dir. ASA Ltd., Med. Care Am.; trustee LMI; speaker engring. groups. Author tech. publs. relating to mining. Bd. dirs. Boys Clubs Am. Mem. NAE, IEEE, AIME, Nat. Acad. of Engring., C. of C., Sky Club N.Y.C., Blind Brook Golf Club, Desert Forest Golf Club, Ariz. Club, Masons, Shriners, Eta Kappa Nu, Tau Beta Pi, Beta Theta Pi. Republican. Methodist. Home: One Milbank IIF Greenwich CT 06830 also: PO Box 1072 Carefree AZ 85377

WEATHERFORD, ALAN MANN, business educator; b. Lake Charles, La., Feb. 6, 1947; s. Clester Mann and Nell (Birdsong) W.; m. Elizabeth A. Weatherford (div. Dec. 1991); children: William B., Victoria L. BA, La. State U., 1969; MBA, U. Dallas, 1981; PhD, U. Tex., Richardson, 1986. Claims adjuster Royal Globe Ins. Cos., San Antonio, 1969-71; staff nurse Univ. Hosp., Augusta, Ga., 1977, Garland (Tex.) Community Hosp., 1978-79; mem. staff Baylor Med. Ctr., Grapevine, Tex., 1982-85; rsch. asst. U. Tex., 1983-85; assoc. prof. bus. Calif. Poly. State U., San Luis Obispo, 1986—. Editor Econ. Rev., 1991—; contbr. articles to profl. jours. Assoc. dir. Small Bus. Inst., San Luis Obispo, 1991—. 1st lt. USAF, 1973-76. Mem. Fin. Mgmt. Assn., Am. Fin. Assn., S.W. Fin. Assn., Mensa. Office: Calif Poly State U Sch Bus San Luis Obispo CA 93407

WEATHERHEAD, ANDREW KINGSLEY, educator; b. Manchester, Eng., Oct. 8, 1923; came to U.S., 1951; s. Leslie Dixon and Evelyn (Triggs) W.; m. Ingrid Antonie Lien, Aug. 28, 1952; children: Lyn Kristin, Leslie Richard, Andrea Kathryn. BA, U. Cambridge, Eng., 1944, MA, 1947; MA, U. Edinburgh, Scotland, 1950; PhD, U. Wash., Seattle, 1958. Assoc. prof. La. State U., New Orleans, 1958-60; with U. Oreg., Eugene, 1960—, assoc. prof., 1962-68, prof., 1968-89, prof. emeritus, 1990—. Author: A Reading of Henry Green, 1961, The Edge of the Image, 1967, Stephen Spender and the Thirties, 1975, Leslie Weatherhead: A Personal Potrait, 1975, The British Dissonance, 1983; contbr. articles to profl. jours. Home: 2698 Fairmount Blvd Eugene OR 97403-1758 Office: U Oreg English Dept 118 PLC Eugene OR 97403

WEATHERHEAD, LESLIE R., lawyer; b. Tacoma, Sept. 28, 1956; s. A. Kingsley and Ingrid A. (Lien) W.; m. Anali C. Torrado, June 24, 1985; children: Spencer, Madeleine. BA, U. Oreg., 1977; JD, U. Wash., 1980. Bar: Wash. 1980, U.S. Ct. Appeals (9th cir.) 1981, U.S. Dist. Ct. (ea. dist.) Wash. 1984, U.S. Ct. Internat. Trade 1984, Hawaii 1987, U.S. Dist. Ct. (we. dist.) Wash. 1989, Idaho 1989, U.S. Dist. Ct. Idaho 1989. Asst. terr. prosecutor Territory of Guam, Agana, 1980-83; spl. asst. U.S. Atty. Dist. of Guam and No. Marianas, Agana, 1982-83; atty. Witherspoon, Kelley, Davenport & Toole, Spokane, 1984—; lawyer-rep. 9th cir. jud. conf., 1990-92, exec. com. 9th cir. jud. conf., 1992—. Contbr. articles on Indian law and administrv. investigations to profl. jours. Bd. dirs. Spokane Uptown Opera, 1989—, pres. 1992—. Mem. ABA, Hawaii Bar Assn., Idaho Bar Assn., Wash. State Bar Assn. Office: Witherspoon Kelley Davenport & Toole W 428 Riverside Spokane WA 99201

WEATHERS, WARREN RUSSELL, forester, appraiser, consultant; b. La Jolla, Calif., Feb. 17, 1947; s. Warren Obert and Cicely Joanne (Hawken) W.; m. Terri Ruth Pillette, May 5, 1988; children: Nathan, Stuart, Erik. BS in Forestry, Oreg. State U., 1970; MBA, U. Oreg., 1985. Chief forester Pacific Timber Products, Haines, Alaska, 1972-75; exec. v.p. Shee Atika, Inc., Sitka, Alaska, 1975-82; cons. forester, 1982—; commr. Alaska State Bd. Forestry, Juneau, 1979-80. Mem., pres. Lowell (Oreg.) City Coun., 1987-91, chmn. budget com., 1987-88; mayor City of Lowell, 1991—. 1st lt. U.S. Army Res., 1971-80. Mem. Nat. Trappers Assn., Worldwide Outfitter and Guides Assn., Forest Products Soc., Soc. Am. Foresters (chpt. chair 1979-80), Assn. Consulting Foresters. Office: 29 1/2 S Alder St PO Box 39 Lowell OR 97452

WEATHERUP, ROY GARFIELD, lawyer; b. Annapolis, Md., Apr. 20, 1947; s. Robert Alexander and Kathryn Crites (Hesser) W.; m. Wendy Gaines, Sept. 10, 1977; children: Jennifer, Christine. AB in Polit. Sci., Stanford U., 1968, JD, 1972. Bar: Calif. 1972, U.S. Dist. Ct. 1973, U.S. Ct.

Appeals (9th cir.) 1975, U.S. Supreme Ct. 1980. Assoc. Haight, Brown & Bonesteel, L.A., Santa Monica and Santa Ana, Calif., 1972-78, ptnr., 1979—; mem. Book Approved Jury Selections com. L.A. Superior Ct; Moot Ct. judge UCLA, Loyola U., Pepperdine U.; arbitrator Am. Arbitration Assn.; mem. com. Book Approved Jury Instructions. Mem. ABA, Calif. Acad. Appellate Lawyers, Town Hall Calif., L.A. County Bar Assn. Republican. Methodist. Home: 17260 Rayen St Northridge CA 91325-2919 Office: Haight Brown & Bonesteel 1620 26th St Santa Monica CA 90404

WEATHERWAX, MICHAEL DWAINE, accountant; b. Austin, Minn., June 3, 1945; s. Dwaine Laverne and Ruby Joan (Teff) W.; m. Linda Dianne Penn, Aug. 3, 1968; children: Kristin Laine, Justin Michael. BS with distinction, U. So. Colo., 1967; MSBA, U. Denver, 1974. CPA, Colo.; cert. fin. planner. Grad. teaching asst. U. Denver, 1967-68; tax staff, mgr. Arthur Young & Co., Denver, 1968-76; tax ptnr. Rhode, Scripter & Assocs., Boulder, Colo., 1977-82; pres. Weatherwax & Assocs., P.C., Boulder, 1982—; dir. Denver Paralegal Inst., 1982-89. Author: Real Estate Taxation and Planning, 1980-93, Passive Activity Taxation and Management, 1987-93, Ethical Responsibilites in Tax Practice, 1990-93. Pres. Community Action Devel. Corp., Boulder, 1985; trustee Boulder County United Way, 1985-88, Boulder Community Hosp. Found., 1991—, treas. 1993. Fellow Colo. Soc. CPAs (pres. 1989-90, continuing edn. faculty 1973—, Golden Key award 1967); mem. Boulder County Pvt. Industry Coun., AICPA, Nat. Accreditation Bd. for CPA Specialties, Inc. (pres. 1986), Denver Tax Assn., Boulder C. of C. (chmn. bd. 1988), Flatirons Ctr. for the Arts (trustee 1992—, treas. 1992—), Rotary Club. Democrat. Roman Catholic. Home: 5161 Ellsworth Pl Boulder CO 80303-1209 Office: Weatherwax & Assocs PC 5350 Manhattan Cir Boulder CO 80303-4272

WEAVER, GRACE MARGARET, minister; b. Phila., Sept. 4, 1909; d. James Henry and Beulah Grace (Davis) W. BA, Morningside Coll., 1947; ThM, Iliff Sch. Theology, 1955. Tchr. elem. West Berlin, N.J., 1929-44, Clementon, N.J., 1944-45; missionary worker United Meth. Ch., Utah, 1948-51; min. Emmett, Glenns Ferry, Fruitland and Am. Falls, Idaho, and Ketchikan, Alaska, 1954-76; ret., 1976. Recipient 4 Golden Poet awards, 1989. Home: 1551 Center St NE Salem OR 97301-4201

WEAVER, HOWARD CECIL, newspaper editor; b. Anchorage, Oct. 15, 1950; s. Howard Gilbert and Lurlene Eloise (Gamble) W.; m. Alice Laprele Gauchay, July 16, 1970 (div. 1974); m. Barbara Lynn Hodgin, Sept. 16, 1978. BA, Johns Hopkins U., 1972; MPhil, Cambridge U., 1993. Reporter, staff writer Anchorage Daily News, 1972-76, columnist, 1979-80, mng. editor, 1980-83, editor, 1983—; editor, owner Alaska Advocate, Anchorage, 1976-79; internat. co-chair Northern News Svc., 1989—; disting. lectr. journalism U. Alaska, Fairbanks, 1991. Pulitzer Prize juror, 1988, 89. Recipient Pulitzer prize, 1976, 89, Pub. Svc. award AP Mng. Editor's Assn., 1976, 89, Headliner award Press Club of Atlantic City, 1976, 89, Gold medal Investigative Reporters and Editors, 1989. Mem. Am. Soc. Newspaper Editors, Investigative Reporters and Editors, Sigma Delta Chi (Nat. award 1989), Alaska Press Club (bd. dirs. 1972-84), Upper Yukon River Press Club (pres. 1972). Avocations: ice hockey, foreign travel.

WEAVER, JOHN CARRIER, university president emeritus; b. Evanston, Ill., May 21, 1915; s. Andrew Thomas and Cornelia Myrta (Carrier) W.; m. Ruberta Louise Harwell, Aug. 8, 1940; children: Andrew Bennett, Thomas Harwell. A.B., U. Wis., 1936, A.M., 1937, Ph.D., 1942; LL.D., Mercer U., 1972; L.H.D., Coll. St. Scholastica, 1973; Litt.D., Drury Coll., 1973. Mem. editorial and research staff Am. Geog. Soc. of N.Y., 1940-42; mem. research staff Office of Geographer, U.S. Dept. State, 1942-44; asst. prof. dept. geography U. Minn., 1946-47, assoc. prof., 1947-48, prof., 1948-55; prof. geography, dean Sch. Arts and Sci., Kans. State U., 1955-57; prof. geography, dean grad. coll. U. Nebr., 1957-61; v.p. research, dean grad. coll., prof. geography State U. Iowa, 1961-64; v.p. academic affairs, dean faculties, prof. geography Ohio State U., Columbus, 1964-66; pres., prof. geography U. Mo., 1966-70, U. Wis., 1971; pres. U. Wis. System, 1971-77, emeritus, 1977—; prof. geography U. Wis. Milw., Madison, Green Bay, 1971-78; hon. prof. geography U. Wis. at Oshkosh; Disting. prof. U. So. Calif., 1977-85, emeritus, 1985—; exec. dir. Center for Study of Am. Experience, 1978-81, Annenberg Disting. scholar, 1981-82; research cons. Midwest Barley Improvement Assn., Milw., 1946-50; expert cons. to Com. on Geophysics and Geography, Research and Devel. Bd., Washington, 1947-53; mem. adv. com. on geography Office Naval Research, NRC, 1949-52, chmn., 1951-52; vis. prof. U. Oreg., summer 1951, Harvard U., summer 1954; cons. editor McGraw-Hill series in geography, 1951-67; mem. adv. com. to sec. HEW, 1958-62; mem. Mid-Am. State U. Assn., 1959-70, chmn., 1959-61, 70-71; chmn. Council Grad. Schs. U.S., 1961-62; mem. Woodrow Wilson fellow selection com., 1961-70; mem. com. instl. coop. Univs. Western Conf. and Chgo., 1962-66, chmn., 1964-66; pres. Assn. Grad. Schs. in Assn. Am. Univs., 1963-64; Wilton Park fellow Brit. Fgn. Office, 1965, 67, 70, 74, 76; chmn. Nat. Task Force on Future of Pharmacy Edn., 1981-84. Author: Ice Atlas of the Northern Hemisphere, 1946, American Barley Production, A Study in Agricultural Geography, 1950, A Statistical World Survey of Commercial Production, (with Fred E. Lukerman) A Geographical Source book, 1953, The American Railroads, 1958, Minnesota and Wisconsin, 1961; illustrator: Quiet Thoughts, 1971; contbr. articles to books and profl. periodicals; contbg. editor: Geog. Rev, 1955-70. Mem. Mo. Commn. of Higher Edn., 1966-70; mem. White House Task Force on Priorities in Higher Edn., 1969-70, Edn. Commn. of States, 1971-77; Bd. dirs. Harry S. Truman Library Inst. Nat. and Internat. Affairs, 1967-70; trustee Nat. Com. on Accreditation, 1966-76, Johnson Found., Racine, Wis., 1971-77, 81-82, Am. Univs. Field Service, 1971-75, Nat. Merit Scholarship Corp., 1971-77, 80-82; trustee Chadwick Sch., Palos Verdes Peninsula, 1987-93, mem. exec. com., 1989-93; mem. citizens' stamp adv. com. to Postmaster Gen., 1981-85. Served as lt. (j.g.) USNR, 1944-46; assigned specialist Hydrographic Office, Office of Chief of Naval Ops. Washington. Recipient Vilas medal U. Wis., 1936, Letter Commendation from Chief of Naval Ops., 1946; Carnegie Found. adminstrv. fellow, 1957-58. Fellow Am. Geog. Soc. (governing council 1974—, John Finley Breeze Morse medal 1986), AAAS; mem Assn. Am. Geographers (council 1949-51, Nat. Research award 1955), Am. Geophys. Union, Arctic Inst. N.Am. (charter assoc.), Am. Polar Soc., Internat. Geog. Union, Am. Pharm. Assn. (hon.), Am. Friends of Wilton Park (pres. 1980-81), Phi Beta Kappa, Sigma Xi, Phi Kappa Phi, Delta Sigma Rho, Phi Eta Sigma, Alpha Kappa Psi, Beta Kappa Sigma, Chi Phi. Home: 2978 Crownview Dr Rancho Palos Verdes Peninsula CA 90274-6483

WEAVER, MARK ARTHUR, international trade specialist, educator, interpreter, translator; b. Visalia, Calif., Feb. 14, 1952; s. Arthur Roy and Dorothy Jean (Sawyer) W. Student, U. Wash., 1972-73; BA in Polit. Sci. with hons., San Francisco State U., 1981, MA in Romance Langs., Lit., 1984; MA in Internat. Bus. with distinction, George Washington U., 1986; postgrad., U. Geneva, 1993—. Cert. consecutive interpretation. Free-lance writer, tchr. Europe, North Africa and Latin America, 1973-79; asst. to chief editor corr., editor, copy editor Bancroft-Whitney Pub., San Francisco, 1981-82; asst. to dep. asst. sec. trade adjustment assistance U.S. Department of Commerce, Washington, 1985, internat. market analyst office product devel., 1985-86, editor, trade specialist Caribbean Basin Ctr., 1986-87, dir. mktg. Caribbean Basin Ctr., 1987-88; internat. trade specialist U.S. Fgn. Comml. Svc. U.S. Department of Commerce, L.A., 1988-89, sr. internat. trade specialist U.S. Fgn. Comml. Svc., 1990-93; dir., eastern Washington br., U.S. Fgn. Comml. Svc. U.S. Department of Commerce, Kennewick, Wash., 1993—; dir. internat. sales Am. Bur. Collections, Santa Ana, Calif., 1989-90; bd. dirs. Greater L.A. World Ctr. Com., 1990—; prof. internat. bus. West Coast U., L.A., Long Beach City (Calif.) Coll., 1990-93. Editor jurisprudence law books, 1982—, Caribbean Bus. Bull., 1986-88, L.A.-So. Calif. World Trade Week, 1988-89. Capt. Volvo Amateur Tennis Teams, Washington, 1987, L.A., 1989. Wolcott Pub. Svc. fellow Masonic Lodge, 1984. Mem. French-Am. C. of C. L.A. (bd. dirs. 1988-89), Coun. European C. of C., Calif.-Chile C. of C., Calif.-Columbia C. of C., Torrance C. of C. (founder, chmn. internat. bus. com. 1990—), Long Beach C. of C. (bd. dirs. internat. bus. assn. 1990—). Republican. Lutheran. Office: US Dept Commerce US Fgn Comml Svc 320 N Johnson Ste 350 Kennewick WA 99336

WEAVER, MAX KIMBALL, social worker, consultant; b. Price, Utah, Apr. 4, 1941; s. Max Dickson and Ruth (Kimball) W.; m. Janet Hofheins, Sept. 13, 1963; children: Kim, Cleve, Chris, Wendy, Michael, Amyanne, Heather. Student, So. Utah State Coll., 1959-60; BS, Brigham Young U., 1965; MSW, U. Utah, 1967. Lic. clin. social worker and marriage counselor, Utah. Cons. Utah State Tng. Sch., American Fork, 1966; dir. Dept. Pub. Welfare, Cedar City, Utah, 1967-70; social worker Latter Day St. Social Services, Cedar City, 1970-75; with Mental Retardation Devel. Disabled Adult Services Dept. Social Services, Cedar City, 1975—; cons. nursing homes, Utah, 1974—; tchr. So. Utah State Coll., Cedar City, 1972, 77. Contbr. articles to mags. Pres. Am. Little League Baseball, 1977-84, 86, Cedar High Booster Club, 1984—; chmn. Rep. Precinct #1, 1984; v.p. Big League Baseball, 1986—. Mem. Nat. Assn. Social Work (nominating com., licensing com.), Am. Pub. Welfare Assn., Utah Pub. Employees Assn. Mormon. Lodge: Rotary. Home: 116 N 200 E Cedar City UT 84720-2617 Office: Dept Social Svcs 106 N 100 E Cedar City UT 84720-2608

WEAVER, MICHAEL JAMES, lawyer; b. Bakersfield, Calif., Feb. 11, 1946; s. Kenneth James and Elsa Hope (Rogers) W.; m. Valerie Scott, Sept. 2, 1966; children: Christopher James, Brett Michael, Karen Ashley. AB, Calif. State U., Long Beach, 1968; JD magna cum laude, U. San Diego, 1973. Bar: Calif., 1973, U.S. Dist. Ct. (so. dist.) Calif. 1973, U.S. Ct. Appeals (9th cir.) 1975, U.S. Supreme Ct. 1977. Law clk. to chief judge U.S. Dist. Ct. (so. dist.) Calif., San Diego, 1973-75; assoc. Luce, Forward, Hamilton & Scripps, San Diego, 1975-80, ptnr., 1980-86; ptnr. Sheppard, Mullin, Richter & Hampton, San Diego, 1986—; judge pro tem San Diego Superior Ct.; master of the Bench of the Inn, Am. Inns of Ct., Louis M. Welch chpt.; lectr. Inn of Ct., San Diego, 1981—, Continuing Edn. of Bar, Calif., 1983—, Workshop for Judges U.S. Ct. Appeals (9th cir.) 1990. Editor-in-chief: San Diego Law Rev., 1973; contbr. articles to profl. jours. Bd. dirs., pres. San Diego Kidney Found., 1985—; bd. dirs. San Diego Aerospace Mus., 1985—; trustee La Jolla (Calif.) Playhouse, 1990—. Served to lt., USNR, 1968-74. Fellow Am. Coll. of Trial Lawyers; mem. San Diego Trial Lawyers Assn., San Diego Assn. Bus. Trial Lawyers (founding mem., bd. govs.), Am. Arbitration Assn., Standing Com. on Discipline, Ninth Cir. Jud. Conf. (del. 1987-90). Republican. Presbyterian. Office: Sheppard Mullin Richter & Hampton 501 W Broadway Fl 19 San Diego CA 92101-3536

WEAVER, VELATHER EDWARDS (VAL WEAVER), small business owner; b. Union Hall, Va., Feb. 20, 1944; d. Willie Henry and Ethel (Smith) Edwards; m. Ellersn Fitzpatrick Weaver; children: Frankie Lawrence Mattox Jr., Terence Leon Mattox, Christopher Lamar Williams, Sharon, Shelley, Stephanie. Student, Sonoma State Coll., 1972, U. Calif., Berkeley, 1972; BA, Calif. State U., Hayward, 1973; MBA, St. Mary's Coll., Moraga, Calif., 1989. Coach, counselor Opportunities Industrialization Ctr., Oakland, Calif., 1967-69; tchr. Berkeley Headstart, 1969-70; instr., cons. external degree program Antioch Coll.-West, San Francisco, 1971-74; market analyst World Airways, Inc., Oakland, 1972-75, affirmative action adminstr., 1975-78; cons. A.C. Transit, Oakland, 1982; owner, mgr. Val's Designs and Profl. Svcs., Lafayette, Calif., 1980—; mgr. adminstrn., tng. supr. North Oakland Pharmacy, Inc., 1970—, also bd. dirs.; adv. bd. The Tribune, Oakland, 1982-88. Program coord., publicity Lafayette Arts and Sci. Found., 1982-83; admission bd. grad. bus. sch. St. Mary's Coll., 1990; bd. mem. Acalanes High Sch., Lafayette, 1980-82, Lafayette Elem. Sch., 1975-80. Mem. Calif. State Pharmacists Assn. Aux. (pres. Contra Costa Aux. 1980, pres. state aux. 1986-88, recognition award 1987), Calif. Pharmacists Polit. Action Com. (appreciation award 1988), Diablo Valley Bus. and Profl. Women (pub. rels. com. 1986-87, best local orgn. award 1987, author yearbook 1987), No. Calif. Med., Dental and Pharm. Assn. Aux. (bd. dirs., com. chair 1975—, pres. elect 1991, pres. 1991—), Links, Inc. Home: PO Box 1954 Lafayette CA 94549-9054 Office: North Oakland Pharmacy Inc 5705 Market St Emeryville CA 94608-2892

WEBB, BETSY JOHNSTON, human resources administrator; b. Phila., May 1, 1958; d. Frank Bremond and Jean Sarah (Caton) Johnston; m. William Bradford Webb, June 23, 1984; 1 child, Sarah Elizabeth. BS, Dickinson Coll., 1980; MS, Western Ill. U., 1984; MSW, U. Denver, 1989. Program adminstr. Chaddock Sch., Quincy, Ill., 1984-85; social worker, mental health worker Cedar Springs Psychiat. Hosp., Colorado Springs, Colo., 1985-89; program dir. Colo. Outward Bound Sch., Denver, 1989-92, dir. human resources, 1992—. Contbr. chpt. to book. Vol. instr. ARC, Colo., 1982-92; vol. counselor Colo. AIDS Project, 1989-90. Charles P. Dana scholar Dickinson Coll., 1979-80; named to Outstanding Young Women in Am., 1983. Mem. Assn. for Experiential Edn., Nat. Assn. Social Workers, Phi Beta Kappa, Omicron Delta Kappa. Home: Box 892 Palmer Lake CO 80133

WEBB, DAVID RITCHIE, immunologist, science administrator; b. Taft, Calif., Nov. 10, 1944; s. David R. and Maude (Glynn) W.; m. Lila Lee Schupbach, June 18, 1966; children: Scott, Linly. BA, Calif. State U., Fullerton, 1966, MA, 1968; PhD, Rutgers U., 1971. Teaching asst. Calif. State U., Fullerton, 1966-68; pre-doctoral fellow Rutgers U., New Brunswick, N.J., 1968-71; Dernham fellow U. Calif. Med. Ctr., San Francisco, 1971-73; asst. mem. Roche Inst. Molecular Biology, Nutley, N.J., 1973-79, assoc. mem., 1979-87; disting. scientist Syntex Rsch., Palo Alto, Calif., 1987; dir. IBS Syntex Rsch., Palo Alto, Calif., 1990—; mem. study sect. NSF, 1981-83, Am. Cancer Soc., 1985-87. Contbr. over 100 articles to profl. jours.; editor 4 books on immunology; editorial bd. 6 sci. jours. Bd. dirs. Foothill Bobby Sox League, Cupertino, Calif., 1989-91. Am. Cancer Soc. fellow, 1972; recipient Calif. State U. Disting. Alumni award, 1988. Fellow N.Y. Acad. Sci.; mem. AAAS, Am. Soc. Microbiology, Am. Assn. Immunologists, Sigma Xi. Office: Syntex Rsch Dept Molecular Immunology S3-6 3401 Hillview Ave Palo Alto CA 94304

WEBB, LELAND FREDERICK, education and mathematics educator; b. Hollywood, Calif., July 27, 1941; s. Robert Wallace and Evelyn Elaine (Gourley) W.; m. Janie Rae Yoder, Jan. 26, 1963; children: Robert Leland, Tamara Lynn Elaine. BA with high honors, U. Calif.-Santa Barbara, 1963; MA, Calif. State Poly. U., 1968; PhD, U. Tex.-Austin, 1971. Lectr. dept. edn. Calif. State Poly. U., 1967-68; teaching asst. dept. math. U. Tex.-Austin, 1970-71, curriculum writer and staff devel. specialist, Southwest Educational Devel. Ctr., Austin, summer 1990; rsch. assoc. IV R & D Ctr. for Tchr. Edn., 1971; asst. prof. Calif. State Coll., Bakersfield, 1971-73, assoc. prof., 1973-78, prof. math. and edn., 1978-85, chmn. dept. math. and computer sci., 1982-85; prof. math, 1985—; chair dept. math, 1990—; mem. math assessment adv. com. Calif. State Dept. Edn., 1985-88, math framework com., 1983-85, math test 12th grade writing com. assement program, 1986-87; cons. NSF workshops, 1972-76, Tokyo, 1975, various sch. dists. and county offices of edn., Calif.; sabbatical leave Agder Regional Coll., Kristiansand, Norway, 1980. Author: K-8 Math. Texts, Houghton Mifflin Co., 1985—; contbr. numerous articles to profl. jours. Served to capt. U.S. Army, 1963-67. Grantee NSF, 1972-76, Calif. State U. Chancellor's Office, 1981-83; U.S. Office Edn. fellow, 1968-71. Mem. Math. Assn. Am., Nat. Council Tchrs. Math., Nat. Math Counts Question Writing Com., 1987-89, Calif. Math Council (v.p. cen. sect. 1982-84, nat. council rep. 1982-90, state rep. 1986-90), Bakersfield Math. Council (pres. 1976-78), Sch. Sci. and Math. Assn., Sigma Xi, Phi Kappa Phi, Phi Delta Kappa. Unitarian. Home: 7300 Dos Rios Way Bakersfield CA 93309-2712 Office: Calif State U Math Dept Bakersfield CA 93311

WEBB, PAUL STEPHEN, physicist; b. Peacock, Tex., Oct. 24, 1943; s. Stephen Josira and Pauline Lucille (Veach) W.; m. Nina Jeanette Hodges, Aug. 23, 1962; children: Mark Stephen, Paul Shannon. BS, Tex. Tech. U., 1967; MS, Tex. A&M U., 1970. Cert. secondary tchr., Tex. Tchr. math., biology Lubbock (Tex.) Ind. Sch. Dist., 1966-67; environ. sanitarian Tex. Tech. U., Lubbock, 1967-69; mgr. and radiol. engr. GE, Pleasanton, Calif., 1971-84; physicist Lawrence Livermore Nat. Lab., Livermore, Calif., 1984-91; sr. health physicist, consulting health physicist M.H. Chew & Assocs., Inc., Livermore, 1991—. Lubbock Classroom Tchrs. Assn. scholar, 1965. Mem. Internat. Soc. for Respiratory Protection, Am. Nuclear Soc., Health Physics Soc. Republican. Office: M H Chew & Assocs Inc 1424 Concannon Blvd Livermore CA 94550

WEBB, STANLEY MAXWELL, lawyer; b. Independence, Kans., Apr. 18, 1956; s. Gerald Lee and Gwendolyn Jane (Graves) W. BS in Biology, U. Kans., 1978, JD, 1982; MPA, Harvard U., 1993. Cert. Comml.-Investment Real Estate Inst. Realty officer Bur. of Indian Affairs, Ashland, Wis., 1983-85; rights protection specialist Bur. of Indian Affairs, Washington, 1985-87; white earth project dir. Bur. of Indian Affairs, Cass Lake, Minn., 1987-88; realty specialist Bur. of Indian Affairs, Washington, 1988-89, Phoenix, 1989—. Active Assn. for Retarded Citizens, Phoenix, Heard Mus., Phoenix, Ariz. Hist. Soc., Phoenix. Mem. ABA, State Bar Ariz., State Bar Colo., Fed. Bar Assn., Nat. Assn. Realtors, Nat. Assn. Real Estate Appraisers, Rocky Mountain Mineral Law Found. Democrat. Methodist. Home: 8749 E Starlight Way Scottsdale AZ 85250 Office: Bur of Indian Affairs 1 N 1st St Phoenix AZ 85001

WEBB, WELLINGTON E., mayor; elected auditor City of Denver, 1987-91, mayor, 1991—. Address: Office of Mayor City & County Bldg Rm 350 1437 Bannock St Denver CO 80202

WEBBER, CATHERINE CARNEY, state legislator, lawyer, social worker, state official; b. New Bedford, Mass., Aug. 11, 1942; d. Henry D. Carney and Catherine (Breault) Richetson; m. William B. Webber, May 21, 1971 (div. 1981); 1 child, Carney. BA in Edn., U. Fla., 1964; MSW, U. Hawaii, 1971; M in Mgmt., Willamette U., 1985, JD, 1985. Bar: Oreg. Supr. social svcs. Dept. Pub. Welfare, Cambridge, Mass., 1966-73; program exec. Children's Svcs. Divsn., 1974-79; program mgr. Oreg. Advocacy Project, 1979-82; law clk.to Hon. Kurt Rossman Oreg. Ct. Appeals, 1985; adminstr./counsel joint interim task force liability ins. Oreg. State Legislature, Salem, 1986; assoc. William, Troutwine & Bowersox, Portland, Oreg., 1987-88; mem. parole bd. Oreg. Bd. Parole and Post Prison Supervision, 1989-91; sr. policy advisor, adminstr. Gov.'s Office, Criminal Justice Svcs. Divsn., 1991-93; mem. Oreg. Senate, 1993—, chair senate edn. com., co-chair joint legis. com. data processing, mem. various coms.; sr. counsel, adminstr. ho. judiciary com. Oreg. Legislature, 1987, sr. counsel, adminstr. senate judiciary com., 1989; mem. exec. bd. Oreg. Coun. Crime and Delinquency. Mem. citizens' budget com. Salem-Keizer Sch. Bd.; mem. citizens budget adv. com., cable regulatory commn. Marion County/City of Salem; mem. Marion County Juvenile Svc. Commn., Oreg. Commn. Hispanic Affairs; bd. dirs. Cath. Community Svcs. Found. Recipient Women of Achievement award YWCA, 1993. Mem. Ladies Aux. VFW. Democrat. Roman Catholic. Office: Oregon Senate State Capital Senate 215 Salem OR 97310

WEBBER, EBBERT TRUE, photojournalist; b. Edgewood, Md., Oct. 22, 1921; s. Matthew Ebbert and Mary Kathryn (True) W.; m. Marjorie Jean Renfroe, July 9, 1944; children: Richard Ebbert, Mary Merle, Dale Brien, Lauren Thomas. Graduate, Nat. Sales Training Inst., Fishers Island, 1956; BA in Journalism, Whitworth Coll., 1965; MLS, U. Portland, 1968. Owner, gen. mgr. Webber Photo Supply Co., Sedro-Woolley, Wash., 1946-55; free-lance comml. photographer Sedro-Woolley, 1945-55; acct. rep. typewriter div. Remington Rand, Seattle, 1955-58; resident rep. for no. Idaho and ea. Wash. Sperry-Rand Bus. Machines, Spokane, 1958-61; chief photo svcs. Whitworth Coll., Spokane, 1961-65; head libr. Waluga Jr. High Sch., Lake Oswego, Oreg., 1965-69; dir. librs. Medford (Oreg.) Sr. High Sch., 1969-70; freelance rsch. photojournalist Medford, 1970-73; owner, gen. mgr. Pacific N.W. Books Co., Medford, 1973—; pub., editor-in-chief Webb Rsch. Group, Medford, 1979—. Author numerous books, including: Oregon Covered Bridges: An Oregon Documentary in Pictures, 1991, Indians Along the Oregon Trail: The Tribes of Nebraska, Wyoming, Idaho, Oregon and Washington Identified, 1992, Bayocean, The Oregon Town That Fell Into the Sea, 2d printing, 1992, Battle Rock, The Hero's Story, 1992, Ezra Meeker, Champion of the Oregon Trail, 1992, Terrible Tilly, The Biography of a Lighthouse, 1992, Silent Siege III, Japanese Attacks on North America in WWII, 1992, I'd Rather Be Beachcombing, 1993; contbr. articles to profl. publs. Ruling elder Lidgerwood Presbyn. Ch., Spokane, 1962-65, 1st Presbyn. Ch., Central Point, Oreg., 1992; mem. So. Oreg. Symphonic Band. Cpl. U.S. Army, 1940-45. Oreg. Assn. Sch. Librs. scholar, 1966, Library Sci. fellowship Tangley Oaks Graduate, 1968. Mem. Clackamas County Hist. Soc. (bd. dirs. 1967-69), Am. Legion (historian 1946-55). Prebyterian. Office: Webb Rsch Group Pubs PO Box 314 Medford OR 97501

WEBBER, JUDD LORY, marketing professional; b. Medford, Oreg., Sept. 23, 1951; s. A. Weldon and Dorothy T. (Harris) W.; m. Deborah Lynn Burres, Aug. 15, 1981; children: Kelly Christine, Tyler Burres Webber. BS in Internat. Affairs, Oreg. State U., 1973; Cert., Oreg. Real Estate Ctr., Eugene, 1985. Lic. real estate agt., Oreg. Outside sales rep. Oregon Pacific Industries/Sequoia Supply, Fairfield, Calif., 1973-76; sales mgr., trader Oreg.-McKenzie Lbr., Eugene, 1976-81; internat. trader Olympic Cascade Corp., Eugene, 1981-82; pres. Blue Heron Products, Ltd., Eugene, 1982-85; comml. property mgr. Income Property Mgmt. Co., Eugene, 1985-86; econ. devel. mgr. Emerald Peoples Utility, Eugene, 1986-88; internat. mktg. dir. Western Wood Products Assn., Portland, Oreg., 1988—; owner J. Webber Japanese Armor, Lake Oswego, Oreg., 1990—; chmn. Willamette Valley World Trade Ctr., Eugene, 1985-86; mem. Oreg. Internat. Trade Dept. Adv. Com., Portland, 1984-90, U.S. Dist. Export Coun., Portland, 1984—; exec. com. Willamette World Affairs Coun., Eugene, 1985-86. Contbr. articles to trade publs. Bd. dirs. Eugene-Springfield Met. Partnership, 1987-88, Fern Ridge Devel. Corp., Veneta, Oreg., 1987-88. Recipient Presdl. E award U.S. Dept. Commerce, 1986, Outstanding Scholar-Leader/Finalist, 1970. Mem. Pacific Lumber Exporters Assn., Pacific Northwest Internat. Trade Assn., Oreg. Village (Japan), Northwestern Hist. Mil. Collectors Assn., Oreg. Knife Collectors, Inc., Rubicon Soc. (v.p. 1985-87), Phi Eta Sigma. Office: Western Wood Products Assn 522 SW 5th Ave Portland OR 97204-2117

WEBBER, MILO MELVIN, radiologist, educator; b. L.A., Sept. 27, 1930; s. George Clifford and Sophia (Binkowski) W.; m. Vivienne Marie Larson, Dec. 18, 1955 (div. Dec. 1987); children: Sonja Elizabeth, Linda Marie. Student, Calif. Inst. Tech., 1948-51; AB, UCLA, 1952, MD, 1955; LLB, La Salle Extension U., Chgo., 1973. Bar: Calif. 1974. From instr. to assoc. prof. radiology UCLA Sch. Medicine, 1960-74, prof., 1974—; bd. dirs. Omnimedical, Inc., Northbrook, Ill.; examiner Am. Bd. Radiology, 1975-78. Contbr. articles to profl. jours., chpts. to books in field. Chmn. L.A. County Dist. Med. Quality Rev. Com. of Med. Bd. Calif., 1978-87. Recipient rsch. grants NIH, Bethesda, Md., 1976-79, 1977-79, 1988—. Mem. Am. Coll. Radiology, Soc. Nuclear Medicine (pres. So. Calif. chpt. 1971), Radiol. Soc. N.Am., Calif. Med. Assn., L.A. County Med. Assn., Calif. Bar Assn. Office: UCLA Sch Medicine Rm BL 428 CHS 405 Hilgard Ave Los Angeles CA 90024-1721

WEBBER, WILLIAM ALEXANDER, university administrator, physician; b. Nfld., Can., Apr. 8, 1934; s. William Grant and Hester Mary (Constable) W.; m. Marilyn Joan Robson, May 17, 1958; children—Susan Joyce, Eric Michael, George David. M.D., U. B.C., Can., Vancouver, 1958. Intern Vancouver Gen. Hosp., 1958-59; postdoctoral fellow Cornell U. Med. Coll., N.Y.C., 1959-61; asst. prof. medicine U. B.C., 1961-66, assoc. prof., 1966-69, prof., 1969—, dean faculty medicine, 1977-90, assoc. v.p. acad., 1990—. Mem. B.C. Med. Assn., Can. Assn. Anatomists, Am. Assn. Anatomists, Can. Nephrological Soc. Home: 2478 Crown St, Vancouver, BC Canada V6R 3V8 Office: U BC, Old Administration Bldg, 6328 Memorial Rd Rm 132, Vancouver, BC Canada V6T 1Z2

WEBER, ALOIS HUGHES, principal; b. Clay County, Mo., Dec. 19, 1910; d. William Swan and Nora Mildred (Elam) Hughes; m. Frank Thomas Ewing Weber, May 28, 1934 (dec. 1980); children: Patricia Katherine Weber Brusuelas, Susan Weber Mills. BA, William Jewell Coll., Liberty, Mo., 1955; MA, U. Mo., Kansas City, 1971. Elem. prin. Linden (Mo.) Sch. Dist. #72, 1931-34; elem. tchr. Eugene (Mo.) Sch. Dist., 1935-38, Sycamore Sch., Boone County, Mo., 1938-41; reserve tchr. Kansas City (Mo.) Schs., 1941-55, contract tchr., 1955-63; head tchr. Allen Sch., Kansas City, 1963-67; remedial reading tchr. Benjamin Franklin Sch., Kansas City, 1967-69; reading cons. Div. Urban Edn., Kansas City, 1969-73; coord. Title I Elem. Reading and Compensatory Edn., Kansas City, 1974-79; ret.; instr., trainer Staying Healthy After Fifty, State of N.Mex., 1987-89, 91—, Growing Old with Health and Wisdom, 1991—; tutor Literacy Vols. of Am., Inc., Corrales, N.Mex., 1989-91; tutor, trainer Rio Rancho, N.Mex., 1990—; speaker AARP Health Care Reform, Health Care Am., 1992—; Lovelace sr. adv. group, 1993—. Instr. AARP, Staying Healthy After Fifty, Albuquerque, 1987-88; vol. Corrales Libr., 1980-88; bd. dirs. Read West Literacy Vols., Rio Rancho, 1989—; bd. dirs. Adobe Community Theatre, Corrales, 1989-90; lectr. in field; mem. Bernalillo County steering com. Growing Old with Health and Wisdom, 1988—, instr. trainer, 1992. NSF grantee, 1973; recipient Area Community Svc. award AARP, State of N.Mex., 1988, Cert. of Appreciation, ARC, 1988, others. Mem. AAUW, N.Mex. Assn. Edn.

Retirees (exec. com. 1987-89), Albuquerque Assn. Edn. Retirees (exec. sec., bd. dirs. 1990—), PEO (chpt. BD chaplain, 1990—), West Mesa Assn. Ednl. Retirees (membership chmn. 1991—, v.p. 1993), Grad. Club Albuquerque. Democrat. Baptist. Home: 3321 Esplanade Cir SE Rio Rancho NM 87124-2156

WEBER, CHARLENE LYDIA, social worker; b. Phila., Mar. 2, 1943; d. Walter Gotlieb and Dorothy (Peart) W.; m. Billy Mack Carroll, Oct. 3, 1959 (div. Sept. 1974); children: Dorothy Patricia, Robert Walter, Lydia Baker, Billy Bob, Elizabeth Louise; m. John Edward Thomaston, Sept. 26, 1974 (div. July 1986). BSW with honors, Coll. Santa Fe, 1983; MSW, N.Mex. Highlands U., 1988. Client service agt. I Social Svcs. div. Dept. Human Svcs., Albuquerque, 1975-78, client service agt. IV, 1978-83; social worker II Social Svcs. div. Dept. Human Svcs., Bernalillo, N.Mex., 1983, social worker III, 1983—. Mem. Nat. Assn. Social Workers, N.Mex. Council on Crime and Deliquency, Albuquerque Retarded Assn., Child Welfare League. Democrat. Home: 72 Umber Ct NE Albuquerque NM 87124-2454 Office: Dept Human Svcs Div Social Svcs PO Box 820 Bernalillo NM 87004-0820

WEBER, DARRELL JACK, plant biochemistry educator; b. Thornton, Idaho, Nov. 16, 1933; s. John and Norma (Severson) W.; m. Carolyn Foremaster, Aug. 24, 1962; children:Becky, Brian, Todd, Kelly, Jason, Trent. BS, U. Idaho, 1958, MS, 1959; PhD, U. Calif., Davis, 1963. Postdoctoral fellow U. Wis., Madison, 1963-65; from assist. to assoc. prof. biology U. Houston, 1965-69; assoc. prof. botany Brigham Young U., Provo, Utah, 1969-74, prof. botany, 1976—; postdoctoral fellow Mich. State U., East Lansing, 1975-76. Author: (with others) Introductory Plant Biology Manual, 1973, Mechanisms of Pesticide Resistance in Non-Target Organisms, 1981; Principals and Application of Instrumentation in the Biological Sciences, 1976; contbr. numerous articles to profl. jours. Recipient Rsch. award Karl G. Maeser, Provo, 1974; Utah Acad. Sci. fellow, Salt Lake City, 1972. Mem. Am. Mycol. Soc. (editor), Sigma Xi (sec. Brigham Young U. chpt. 1982-85). Republican. Mormon. Office: Brigham Young U. 285 Widtsoe Provo UT 84602

WEBER, DENNIS PAUL, social studies educator; b. Longview, Wash., Jan. 21, 1952; s. John L. and Emelia E. (Klein) W.; m. Kristine A. McElroy-Weber, March 26, 1977; children: Kathryn, Sarah, Juliana. BA in Polit. Sci., U. Wash., 1974. Cert. tchr., Wash. Social studies tchr. R.A. Long High Sch., Longview, Wash., 1975-78, social studies tchr. and dept. chmn., 1984—; alternative edn. tchr. Natural High Sch., Longview, Wash., 1978-84; mayor City of Longview, 1984-91; mem. Rotary Internat. Group Study Exchange, Surrey, Eng., 1984. Violinist S.W. Wash. Symphony Orch., 1968—; mem. planning commn. Cowlitz County, Kelso, Wash., 1978-84, chmn. 1982-84; coun. mem. Longview City Coun., 1979-91, mayor pro tempore 1982-84; bd. dirs. Community Urban Bus. Systems Bd., Kelso, 1984-89, chmn., 1988; bd. dirs. S.W. Wash. Air Pollution Control Authority, Vancouver, 1984-90, chmn. air pollution control authority, 1988-90; bd. dirs. Cowlitz Transit Authority, 1990-91; mem. governing bd. St. John's Med. Ctr., Longview, 1991—; bd. dirs. Longview Community Ch., 1992—; mem. mgmt. coun. R.A. Long High Sch., 1992—. Recipient Outstanding Young Men in Am. award N.J. C. of C., 1978; named Am. Govt. and Politics fellow Taft Inst. for Teaching, 1988, 91, Sr. fellow James Madison Found., 1993. Mem. NEA (nat. del. 1980-82), LWV (sec. Cowlitz County chpt. 1993—), Wash. Edn. Assn. (state del. 1979), Longview Edn. Assn. (bd. dirs. 1978-84, 92—), Wash. State Coun. for Social Studies, A Presdl. Classroom for Young Ams. Alumni Assn. (life), U. Wash. Alumni Assn. (life), Ripon Soc., Nation Conservancy, Nat. Audubon Soc. Republican. Lodge: Rotary (Paul Harris fellow 1987). Office: PO Box 1042 Longview WA 98632-7623

WEBER, DOROTHY JO, management and trade show consultant; b. Denver, Nov. 3, 1951; d. Herbert Eugene and Marian Rose (Walsh) F.; m. Paul L. Weber, Aug. 21, 1971 (div. Nov. 1978); 1 child, Dawn Michelle; m. Jim Shadrick, 1989. BBA, U. Denver, 1985. Cert. exposition mgr. Sec. Jet-X-Corp., Denver, 1969-71, State of Colo., Denver, 1971-76; with meetings dept. AWWA, Denver, 1977-78; pres. ACE Mgmt., Denver, 1988—; asst. dir. meeting services AORN, Denver, 1978-87; v.p. Price & Assocs., Denver, 1987-88. Contbr. articles to profl. jours. Mem. Nat. Assn. Exhbn. Mgrs. Rocky Mountain Assn. (v.p. 1981-82, pres. 1983), RMAMPI (bd. dirs. 1981-82, sec. 1982-83), Am. Soc. Assn. Execs. Republican. Office: ACE Mgmt 2108 S Telluride Ct Aurora CO 80013-4234

WEBER, EICKE RICHARD, physicist; b. Muennerstadt, Fed. Republic Germany, Oct. 28, 1949; s. Martin and Irene (Kistner) W.; m. Magdalene Graff (div. 1983); m. Zuzanna Liliental , June 10, 1985. BS, U. Koeln, Fed. Republic of Germany, 1970, MS, 1973, PhD, 1976, Dr.Habil., 1983. Sci. asst. U. Koeln, 1976-82; rsch. asst. U. Lund, Sweden, 1982-83; asst. prof. Dept. Material Sci. U. Calif., Berkeley, 1983-87, assoc. prof., 1987-91, prof. materials sci., 1991—; prin. investigator Lawrence Berkeley Lab., 1984—; vis. prof. Tohoku U., Sendai, Japan, 1990; cons. in field; internat. fellow Inst. for Study of Defects in Solids, SUNY, Albany, 1978-79; chmn. numerous confs.; lectr. in field. Contbr. more than 180 articles to profl. jours.; editor: Defect Recognition and Image Processing in III-V Compounds, 1987, Imperfections in III-V Compounds, 1993; co-editor: Chemistry and Defects in Semiconductor Structures, 1989, others; series co-editor: Semiconductors and Semimetals, 1991—, Growth and Characterization of Semiconductor Materials, 1992—. Recipient IBM Faculty award, 1984; rsch. grantee Dept. of Energy, 1984—, Office Naval Rsch., 1985—, Air Force Office Sci. Rsch., 1988—, NASA, 1988-90, Nat. Renewable Energy Lab., 1992—. Mem. Am. Phys. Soc., Matls. Rsch. Soc. Office: U Calif Dept Materials Sci 272 Hearst Mining Bldg Berkeley CA 94720

WEBER, EUGEN, historian, educator, author; b. Bucharest, Romania, Apr. 24, 1925; came to U.S., 1955; s. Emanuel and Sonia (Garrett) W.; m. Jacqueline Brument-Roth, June 12, 1950. Student, Institut d'etudes politiques, Paris, 1948-49, 51-52; M.A., Emmanuel Coll., Cambridge U., 1954, M.Litt., 1956. History supr. Emmanuel Coll., 1953-54; lectr. U. Alta., 1954-55; asst. prof. U. Iowa, 1955-56; asst. prof. history UCLA, 1956, assoc. prof., 1959-63, prof., 1963—, Joan Palevsky prof. modern European history, 1984—, chmn. dept., 1965-68; dir. study center UCLA, France, 1968-70; dean social scis. UCLA, 1976-77, dean Coll. Letters and Scis., 1977-82; Ford faculty lectr. Stanford U., 1965; Patten lectr. Ind. U., 1981; vis. prof. Collège de France, Paris, 1983; directeur d'études Ecole des hautes études, Paris, 1984-85; Christian Gauss lectr., Princeton U., 1990. Author: Nationalist Revival in France, 1959, The Western Tradition, 1959, Paths to the Present, 1960, Action Française, 1962, Satan Franc-Maçon, 1964, Varieties of Fascism, 1964, (with H. Rogger) The European Right, 1965, A Modern History of Europe, 1970, Europe Since 1715, 1972, Peasants into Frenchmen, 1976 (Commonwealth prize Calif. 1977), La Fin des terroirs, 1983 (Prix de la Société des gens de lettres 1984), France Fin-de-siècle, 1986 (Commonwealth prize Calif. 1987), My France, 1990, Movements, Currents, Trends, 1991; adv. editor Jour. Contemporary History, 1966—, French History, 1985—, French Cultural Studies, 1990—, Am. Scholar, 1992—. Served as capt. inf. Brit. Army, 1943-47. Recipient Luckman Disting. Teaching award UCLA, 1992; decorated Ordre Nat. des Palmes Academiques, France; Fulbright fellow, 1952, 82-83; research fellow Am. Philos. Soc., 1959, Social Sci. Research Council, 1959-61, Am. Council Learned Socs., 1962; Guggenheim fellow, 1963-64; NEH sr. fellow, 1973-74, 82-83. Fellow Netherlands Inst. Advanced Studies, Assn. française de science politique, Am. Acad. Arts and Scis.; mem. Am. Hist. Assn., Soc. d'histoire moderne, Soc. French Hist. Studies, Phi Beta Kappa (hon., Ralph Waldo Emerson prize 1977, senator 1988—).

WEBER, FRED J., state supreme court justice; b. Deer Lodge, Mont., Oct. 6, 1919; s. Victor N. and Dorothy A. (Roberts) W.; m. Phyllis M. Schell, June 2, 1951; children: Anna Marie, Donald J., Mark W., Paul V. B.A., U. Mont., 1943, J.D., 1947. Bar: Mont. 1947. Atty. Kuhr & Weber, Havre, Mont., 1947-55, Weber, Bosch & Kuhr, and successors, 1956-80; justice Supreme Ct. Mont., Helena, 1981—. Served to capt. inf. U.S. Army, 1943-46. Fellow Am. Bar Found., Am. Coll. Probate Counsel; mem. ABA, Am. Judicature Soc. Office: Mont Supreme Ct Justice Bldg 215 N Sanders St Helena MT 59620

WEBER, GEORGE RICHARD, financial consultant, writer; b. The Dalles, Oreg., Feb. 7, 1929; s. Richard Merle and Maud (Winchell) W.; m. Nadine Hanson, Oct. 12, 1957; children: Elizabeth Ann Weber Katooli, Karen Louise Weber Zaro, Linda Marie. BS, Oreg. State U., 1950; MBA, U. Oreg., 1962. CPA, Oreg. Sr. trainee U.S. Nat. Bank of Portland (Oreg.), 1950-51; jr. acct. Ben Musa, CPA, The Dalles, 1954; tax and audit asst. Price Waterhouse, Portland, 1955-59; sr. acct. Burton M. Smith, C.P.A., Portland, 1959-62; pvt. practice, Portland, 1962—; lectr. acctg. Portland State Coll.; expert witness fin. and tax matters. Sec.-treas. Mt. Hood Kiwanis Camp, Inc., 1965. Exec. counselor SBA; mem. fin. com., powerlifting team U.S. Powerlifting Fedn., 1984, amb. People to People, China, 1987. With AUS, 1951-53. Decorated Bronze Star. Mem. AICPA, Internat. Platform Assn., Oreg. Hist. Soc.,Oreg. City Traditional Jazz Soc., Order of the Holy Cross Jerusalem, Order St. Stephen the Martyr, Order St. Gregory the Illuminator, Knightly Assn. St. George the Martyr., World Literary Acad., Portland C.S. Lewis Soc., Beta Alpha Psi, Pi Kappa Alpha. Republican. Lutheran. Clubs: Kiwanis, Portland Track, City (Portland); Multnomah Athletic; Sunrise Toastmasters. Author: Small Business Long-term Finance, 1962, A History of the Coroner and Medical Examiner Offices, 1963, CPA Litigation Service References, 1991; contbr. to profl. publs. and poetry jours. Home: 2603 NE 32d Ave Portland OR 97212 Office: 4380 SW Macadam Ste 100 Portland OR 97201

WEBER, JOSEPH JAMES, management consultant; b. Lorain, Ohio, Aug. 12, 1942; s. Joseph Sylvester and Loyola Ruth (Oberst) W.; m. Joanne Carol Kenagy, Oct. 18, 1975. BS, Bowling Green U., 1964, MA, 1966. Registered psychologist, Ill. Asst. supt. Ill. Dept. Corrections, Decatur, 1971-75, supt., chief officer, 1975-80; sr. assoc. Contact, Inc., Tucson, Ariz., 1981-84, regional dir., 1984-86; pres. J. Weber & Assocs., Tucson, 1986—. Mem. Wellness Coun. Tucson, 1987-91. 1st lt. U.S. Army, 1966-68. Mem. Employee Assistance Soc. N.Am., Wellness Coun. Tucson. Office: J Weber & Assocs 7700 N Lundberg Dr Tucson AZ 85741-1749

WEBER, M(ARY) SUZANNE, private school educator; b. Casper, Wyo., Aug. 23, 1953; d. James Ira Jr. and Myrtle Marie Michael; m. James Forrest Weber; children: Clarissa Rose Marie, Forrest James. BS in Secondary Edn., Baylor U., 1975; postgrad., various schs., Colo., 1979-85; MA in Edn., U. Colo., 1993. Cert. tchr. reading and writing, K-12. Tchr. Sch. Dist. 1, Powell, Wyo., 1971-81; instr. N.W. C.C., 1981-82; learning disabilities instrs. asst. Allan Hancock Coll., 1984; 1st and 2d grade tchr. Children's House Montessori Sch., Santa Maria, Calif., 1984—; ESL, Spanish instr. Allan Hancock Coll., 1983—; 2d grade migrant edn. tchr. Lompoc Sch. Dist., summer, 1984; tutor Lindamood Lang and Literacy Ctr., 1983-84, Baylor U. Adult Edn., 1974-75; translator, researcher NBC News Documentaries, 1983; adult edn. instr. Santa Maria High Sch., 1982-83; area rep. L.A. Fgn. Student Exchange Program, 1981-82; tchr. N.W. Comm. Act Program Wyo., 1978-79, Peace Corps, Nicaragua, 1976-78; reading instr. Arapahoe C.C., Littleton, Colo., 1992—; presenter in field. Author Link ednl. materials, Sand Cake activity packet. Tchr. arts and crafts Laity Lodge Christian Youth Camp Coun., 1973; vol. tutor Better Jobs for ESL Students, 1979—; bd. dirs. LWV, 1981-82; sec. Farmworkers Assn., 1980-82; home-schooling mother, 1992—. Mem. Internat. Reading Assn., Christian Women's Club, Sigma Tau Delta, Alpha Lambda Delta, Kappa Delta Pi. Home: 826 Mercury Cir Littleton CO 80124

WEBER, THOMAS ALAN, deputy state conservationist; b. Portage, Wis., Aug. 19, 1949; s. John Martin and Phyllis (Lunde) W.; m. Anita Lucile Thomas, June 6, 1970; children: Matthew Kyle, Timothy John. BS, U. Wis., Stevens Point, 1971; MS, No. Ariz. U., 1972; MS in Mgmt., Stanford U., 1989. Soil scientist USDA, Sterling, Colo., 1972-74; adminstrv. asst. USDA, Raleigh, N.C., 1974-75; budget officer, contract specialist USDA, Spokane, Wash., 1975-78; asst. state adminstrv. officer, state adminstrv. officer USDA, St. Paul, 1978-89; asst. state conservationist USDA, Davis, Calif., 1989-90; dep. state conservationist USDA, Davis, 1990—. V.p. U.S. Employees Fed. Credit Union, St. Paul, 1987; elder Presbyn. Ch., Stillwater, Minn., 1988. Mem. Nat. Assn. Conservation Dists., Soil and Water Conservation Soc., Calif. Soil Conservation Svc. Employees Assn., No. Ariz. U. Alumni Assn., Assn. Profl. Hispanic Employees, Assn. Profl. Black Employees, Stanford U. Alumni Assn., Phi Kappa Phi. Office: USDA Soil Conservation Svc 2121C 2nd St Davis CA 95616-5472

WEBER, WILHELM K., language professional; b. Cologne, Germany, Dec. 13, 1939; came to U.S., 1978; naturalized, 1985; s. Matthias and Maria (Eck) W.; m. Maria Angela Gradenigo, Nov. 30, 1968; children: Armelle, Philippe. MA, U. Geneva, 1964. Freelance conf. interpreter German, English, Spanish, Italian, Dutch langs. Geneva, 1964-78; adj. prof. U. Geneva, 1964-78; program head Monterey (Calif.) Inst. Internat. Studies, 1978-80, dept. chair, 1980-85, dean grad. div. translation and interpretation, 1985-91; pres. Lang. Svcs. Internat., Inc., Carmel, Calif., 1991—; cons. Govt. of Hong Kong, Govt. of Province of Ont., Govt. of France in Guadalupe, U.S. Dept. State; presenter program Moscow Sch. Translation and Interpretation, Hankuk U. Fgn. Studies, Seoul, Korea; speaker at internat. confs. and seminars. Contbr. articles to profl. publs. Vol., trained shelter mgr. ARC. Mem. No. Calif. Translators Assn., Am. Translators Assn., Internat. Assn. Conf. Interpreters (past. exec. sec.), UN Assn. of USA (past pres. Monterey Bay chpt., past treas. No. Calif. div.), Sons of Italy in Am. Republican. Roman Catholic. Office: Lang Svcs Internat Inc 26555 Carmel Rancho Blvd Carmel CA 93923

WEBER, WILLIAM PALMER, chemistry educator; b. Washington, Nov. 7, 1940; s. Frederick Palmer and Lillian (Dropkin) W.; m. Heather Ross Wilson, Oct. 10, 1963; children: Edward Palmer, Robert Owen, Justin Sprague, Nathaniel Pittman. BS in Chemistry, U. Chgo., 1963; MS in Chemistry, Harvard U., 1965, PhD in Chemistry, 1968. Rsch. chemist Dow Chem. Co., Wayland, Mass., 1967-68; asst. prof. of chemistry U. So. Calif., L.A., 1968-72, assoc. prof. of chemistry, 1972-78, prof. of chemistry, 1978—; chair Univ. admissions com. U. So. Calif., L.A., 1980-84; pres. faculty senate U. So. Calif., L.A., 1985-86; chmn. Dept. of Chemistry U. So. Calif., L.A., 1986-89. Author: Phase Transfer Catalysis in Organic Synthesis, 1977, Silicon Reagents for Organic Synthesis, 1983. Mem. Phi Beta Kappa (U. Chgo. chpt.), Phi Kappa Phi (recipient award for scholarly work 1983). Home: 3341 Country Club Dr Los Angeles CA 90019-3535 Office: Univ So Calif Loker Hydrocarbon Rsch Inst Los Angeles CA 90089-1661

WEBSTER, DONALD EVERETT, history educator, retired; b. Bennington, Vt., Mar. 10, 1901; s. Homer Harris and Fannie (Everett) W.; m. Mabel Ruth Whaley, 1925. AB, Oberlin Coll., 1923; MA, U. Wis., 1935. Asst. prof. social scis. Internat. Coll., Izmir, Turkey, 1931-35; adj. lectr. Am. U. of Beirut, 1934-35; James-Rowe fellow Am. Acad. Polit. and Social Sci., Turkey, 1936-37; asst. prof. sociology Beloit (Wis.) Coll., 1938-42; mgr. Near East sect. Office of Strategic Svcs., Div. Rsch. and Analysis, 1941-43; cultural attache Am. Embassy, Ankara, 1943-50; prin. officer U.S. Consulate, Mashhad, Iran, 1952-54; dep. examiner Fgn. Svc., 1954-55; first sec. of embassy Taipei, 1955-57; rsch. writer history office Dept. State, Washington, 1957-59; tchr. Am. Acad. for Girls, Üsküdar, Istanbul, 1961-65; field researcher, Turkey, 1960, 68, 72, 73, 77, 80, 81; speaker internat. confs., 1980, 81, Am. Hist. Assn., 1980; rsch. assoc. Blaisdell Inst. for Advanced Studies in World Cultures and Religions, Claremont, 1960—; program planner Fulbright Programs, Dept. State, 1950-52; counselor U. Wis., 1927-31, Ohio State, 1935-36. Author: The Turkey of Ataturk, 1939, reprinted 1972. Hon. mem. Turk Tarin Kurumu/Turkish History Soc., 1988. Home: 627 Leyden Ln Claremont CA 91711

WEBSTER, GARY DEAN, geology educator; b. Hutchinson, Kans., Feb. 15, 1934; s. John Raymond and Mable Fae (Randles) W.; m. Beverly Eileen Wilson, Aug. 30, 1964; children—Dean, Karissa. Student Hutchinson Jr. Coll., 1951-53; B.S. in Geol. Engring., U. Okla., 1956; M.S. in Geology, U. Kans., 1959; Ph.D. in Geology, UCLA, 1966. Geologist, Amerada Petroleum Corp., Williston, N.D., 1956-57, Belco Petroleum Corp., Big Piney, Wyo., 1960; lectr. Calif. Luth. Coll., Thousand Oaks, 1963-64; curator UCLA, 1964-65; asst. prof. San Diego State U., 1965-68, prof. geology Wash. State U., Pullman, 1968—, chmn. dept., 1980-85 . Contbr. numerous articles to profl. jours. Fellow Geol. Soc. Am.; mem. Am. Inst. Profl. Geologists, Paleontol. Soc. Am. (Western regional chmn. 1979-80), Soc. Econ. Paleontologists and Mineralogists, Paleontol. Assn. Office: Wash State U Dept Geology Pullman WA 99164-2812

WEBSTER, JOHN CHAS, human resources management consultant; b. L.A., May 5, 1944; s. Leo Paul and Agnes (Melavic) W.; m. Bonnie L. Lloyd, Apr. 18, 1971 (div. Sept. 1978); children: Miriam, Mark. BA in Sociology, German, Benedictine Coll., 1973; cert., Johns Hopkins U., 1974; MA in Social Psychology, U. No. Colo., 1975. Cert. alcohol, drug therapist. Staff psychologist, alcohol and drug programs U.S. Army, Ft. Carson, Colo., 1965-76; dir. alcohol and drug program Coconino County, Flagstaff, Ariz., 1976-78; dir. univ. rels. Intel Corp., Phoenix, Ariz., 1978-80; dir. employment G.T.E. Microcircuits, Phoenix, 1980-81; v.p. Monarch Computer Corp., Phoenix, 1981-83; dir. Found. for Human Resources, Santa Cruz, Calif., 1982—, v.p., 1983—; lectr. No. Ariz. U., Flagstaff, 1977-78, Regis Coll., Colorado Springs, Colo., 1985-88, U. Colo., Colorado Springs, 1985-88, Calif. State Employment Com., Sunnyvale, 1991-92; cons. Seagate Tech., Scotts Valley, Calif., 1991—. Designed Navajo Tribal Mental Health Program, Window Rock, Ariz., 1978. With U.S. Army, 1965-75. Recipient Outstanding Contbn. award Mental Health Dept., Colo., 1974, Ariz. Hwy. Patrol, 1978, Ariz. Adult Probation, 1978, Navajo tribe, Window Rock, Ariz., 1978. Mem. U. No. Colo. Alumni Assn. (Recognition award 1978), Benedictine Coll. Alumni Assn. (Svc. award 1991). Republican. Home and Office: Found for Human Resources 140 Wissahickon Ave Los Gatos CA 95030

WEBSTER, JOHN KINGSLEY OHL, II, health administrator, rehabilitation manager; b. L.A., July 27, 1950; s. John Kingsley Ohl and Inez (Gilbert) W.; m. Marcia Lanier McKnight, June 16, 1977; children: David Lilly, Jason Kingsley McKnight. AA, Pasadena (Calif.) City Coll., 1973; BS, San Jose (Calif.) State U., 1975; MS, Calif. State U., L.A., 1989. Registered occupational therapist, Calif. Supervising occupational therapy cons. San Gabriel Valley Regional Ctr., 1976-79; supr. II occupational therapy cons. San Diego Regional Ctr., 1979-83; sr. occupational therapist Mesa Vista Hosp., 1983-84; pvt. practice Vista, Calif., 1983-85; occupational therapy cons. Calif. Children Svcs., State Dept. Health Svcs., L.A., 1985-86, regional adminstrv. cons., 1986-90; dir. occupational therapy Eureka Gen. Hosp., 1990; dir. ops. and mktg. Life Dimensions Inc., Newport Beach, Calif., 1990; occupational therapy cons., licensing and cert. Calif. Dept. Health Svcs., 1990-93; program dir. rehab. svcs. Scripps Meml. Hosp., Encinitas, Calif., 1993—; cons. Hopi and Navajo Tribes, Winslow, Ariz., 1978; dir. Imperial County SPRANS grant, El Centro, Calif., 1986-88; pres., owner Kingsley Constrn., Vista, 1988—. Artist (sculpture) Free Form (3d pl. award 1973), (oil painting) Jamaican Woman (3d pl. award 1979). Recipient Esquire title Lady Elliott of STOBS, Edinburough, Scotland, 1973, spl. dept. recognition Calif. State U., 1989. Mem. Am. Occupational Therapy Assn., Inst. Profl. Health Svc. Adminstrs., Student Assn. of Am. Coll. Health Care Execs.

WEBSTER, JOHN M., biologist, educator; b. Wakefield, Yorkshire, England, May 5, 1936; s. Colin Ernest and Marion Webster; m. Carolyn Ann McGillivray, May 15, 1970; children: Gordon John, Sandra Jane. BSc, Imperial Coll. London U., 1958, PhD, 1962, DSc, 1988. Scientific officer Rothamsted Experimental Sta., Harpenden, England, 1961-66; rsch. scientist Agrl. Can. Rsch. Inst., Belleville, Can., 1966-67; assoc. prof. dept. biol. scis. Simon Fraser U., Burnaby, B.C., Can., 1967-71, prof., 1971—, chmn. dept. biol. scis., 1974-76, dean sci., 1976-80, assoc. v.p. acad., 1980-85, dean grad. studies, 1982-85, rsch. prof., 1987; pres. Sci. World, Vancouver, 1980-82, Vancouver Pub. Aquarium, 1990-92; mem. Sci. Coun. Can., 1982-89, Premier's Adv. Coun. on Sci. and Tech., 1991—; v.p. Tynehead Zool. Soc., Vancouver, 1984-88. Editor: Economic Nematology, 1972; contbr. numerous articles to profl. jours. Fellow Linnean Soc. London, Soc. Nematologists (pres. 1982-83); mem. Can. Soc. Zoologists, Can. Phytopathol. Soc., European Soc. Nematologists, British Soc. Parasitology, Am. Soc. Parasitology. Office: Simon Fraser U, Dept Biol Scis, Burnaby, BC Canada V5A 1S6

WEBSTER, MERLYN HUGH, JR., manufacturing engineer, information systems consultant; b. Beaver Falls, Pa., Nov. 7, 1946; s. Merlyn Hugh and Helen Ruth (Dillon) W.; m. Linda Jeanne Gundlach, June 14, 1969; children: Matthew Jason, Nathaniel Kevin. AA, Palomar Coll., San Marcos, Calif., 1975; BA, Chapman Coll., 1978. Registered profl. engr., Calif. Sr. cons., pres. WEB Internat. Corp., 1992—; mfg. analyst NCR Corp., Rancho Bernardo, Calif., 1968-72, indsl. engr., 1972-76, sr. indsl. engr., 1976-78; sr. project mgr. Tektronix, Beaverton, Oreg., 1978-83, corp. distbn. I.E. mgr., 1983-86; sr. info. systems cons. Intel Corp., Hillsboro, Oreg., 1986—; pres. WEB Internat. Corp., Tualatin, Oreg., 1992—; cons. material handling Intel Mfg., Puerto rico and Ireland, 1989-92; cons. info. systems M.I.S.I., N.Y.C., 1992-93. Chmn. United Way Hillsboro, Oreg., 1986. With USMC, 1964-68, Vietnam. Mem. NSPE, Inst. Indsl. Engrs. (cert.), Shelby Car Club Am. Republican. Home: 5200 SW Joshua St Tualatin OR 97062-9792 Office: WEB Internat Corp 5200 SW Joshua Tualatin OR 97062-9792

WEBSTER, RALPH TERRENCE, metallurgical engineer; b. Crookston, Minn., Nov. 24, 1922; s. Clifford and Elmira Kathleen (Johnson) W.; m. Eileen Mathilde Carrow, Aug. 9, 1947; children: Paul David, Kathleen Mary, Keith Clifford, Richard Terrence. BS, U. Nev., 1949. Registered profl. engr., Calif., Oreg. Metall. engr. U.S. Steel, Pitts., 1949-51; group leader U. Calif. Radiation Lab., Livermore, Calif., 1951-52; asst. chief metallurgist Rockwell Nordston Valve Co., Oakland, Calif., 1953-54; sr. engr. Westinghouse Atomic Power, Pitts., 1954-59; supr. engr. Aerojet Nucleonics, San Ramon, Calif., 1959-62; plant mgr. metals div. Stauffer Corp., Richmond, Calif., 1962-64; prin. metall. engr. Teledyne Wah Chang, Albany, Oreg., 1964-91; metall. cons., 1991—; part time tchr. Linn Benton Community Coll., Albany, 1964—. Contbr. articles to profl. publs. Active Episc. Ch., Lebanon, Oreg., 1975-92. Sgt. U.S. Army, 1942-48; 1st lt. USAF, 1949-64. Fellow ASTM (award of merit 1981, 1st vice chmn. 1979—); mem. Am. Soc. Metals (chmn. com.), Am. Welding Soc. (chmn. com.), Nat. Assn. Corrosion Engring., ASME (chmn. com.). Democrat. Office: Metallurgical Cons 36088 Tree Farm Rd Scio OR 97374

WEBSTER, ROBIN WELANDER, interior designer; b. Bethesda, Md., Sept. 24, 1956; d. Robert Oscar and Patricia (Benson) W.; m. Bryan Douglas Webster, Oct. 9, 1982. BA, Mary Washington Coll., Fredericksburg, Va., 1978. Design asst. Del Mar (Calif.) Designs, 1983-84; ptnr., interior designer Corp. Design, Solana Beach, Calif., 1984-86; owner, mgr. R Designs, San Diego, 1986—. Bd. dirs. Save Our Heritage Orgn., San Diego, 1986-92, pres., 1988-89; vol. San Diego Mus. Art, 1986—; bd. dirs. Contemporaries San Diego Mus. Art, 1989—; del. Calif. Legis. Conf. on Interior Design. Lt. USN, 1978-83. Mem. Internat. Soc. Interior Designers (com. chmn. San Diego 1989—), Color Mktg. Group.

WECHSLER, MARY HEYRMAN, lawyer; b. Green Bay, Wis., Jan. 8, 1948; d. Donald Hubert and Helen (Polcyn) Heyrman; m. Roger Wechsler, Aug. 1971 (div. 1977); 1 child, Risa Heyrman; m. David Jay Sellinger, Aug. 15, 1981; 1 stepchild, Kirk Benjamin; 1 child, Michael Paul. Student, U. Chgo., 1966-67, 68-69; BA, U. Wash., 1971; JD, U. Puget Sound, 1979. Bar: Wash. 1979. Assoc. Law Offices Ann Johnson, Seattle, 1979-81; ptnr. Johnson, Wechsler, Thompson, Seattle, 1981-83, Musshel, Rosenbert et al, Seattle, 1987-88; pvt. practice, Seattle, 1984-87; ptnr. Weschler, Besk, Erickson, Ross & Rubik, Seattle, 1988—; presenter in field. Author: Family Law in Washington, 1987, rev. edit., 1988; contbr. articles to legal pubs. Mem. Wash. State Ethics Adv. Com., 1992-93. Fellow Am. Acad. Matrimonial Lawyers; mem. ABA (membership chmn. Wash. state 1987-88), Wash. State Bar Assn. (exec. com. family law sect. 1985-91, chair 1988-89, legis. com. 1991—, Outstanding Atty. of Yr. award family law sect. 1988, rep. Wash. State Judicial Ethics adv. com.), Wash. Women Lawyers, Seattle-King County Bar Assn. (legis. com. 1985—, vice chmn. 1990-91, chmn. family law sect. 1986-87, chair domestic violence com. 1986-87, trustee 1988-90, policy planning com. 1991-92, 2d v.p. 1992-93, 1st v.p. 1993-94), LWV (bd dirs. Seattle 1991-92). Office: 5700 Columbia Ctr 701 5th Ave Seattle WA 98104

WECHTER, WILLIAM JULIUS, medical researcher; b. Louisville, Feb. 13, 1932; s. Louis and Elsie (Strauss) W.; m. Roselyn Ann Greenman, May 22, 1956 (div. 1974); children: Laurie Jo, Diane Joy, Julie Lynn; m. Kathryn Elaine Edwards, Apr. 16, 1982. AB, U. Ill., 1953, MS, 1954; PhD, UCLA, 1957. Rsch. mgr. The Upjohn Co., Kalamazoo, Mich., 1957-84; dir. long-range planning Boehringer-Ingelhein Zetralle, Ingelheim, Fed. Republic Germany, 1984; dir. clin. and pharm. rsch. Boots Pharms., Inc., Shreveport, La., 1985-88; rsch. prof. medicine Loma Linda (Calif.) U., 1988—; cons. Sepracor, Inc., Marlborough, Mass., 1988—. Editorial bds. J. Clin. Pharm., Jour. of Clinical Trials and Meta-Analysis; patentee over 30 pharm. patents;

contbr. to profl. publs. Fellow Am. Coll. Clin. Pharmacology; mem. AAAS, Am. Soc. Pharmacology and Exptl. Therapeutics, Transplantation Soc., Am. Chem. Soc. (sect. pres. 1967), Am. Assn. Immunologists, Am. Rheumatology Assn., Royal Soc. Medicine, Nephrology Soc., Hypertension Soc. Democrat. Jewish. Home: 12876 Highview Dr Redlands CA 92373-7567 Office: Loma Linda U Med Ctr Dept Medicine 1516 Loma Linda CA 92350

WECKER, (ANN) DENESE, political science educator; b. Wellington, Utah, Mar. 9, 1931; d. George B. and Clara (Oman) Milner; m. Donald W. Wecker, Jan. 22, 1950; children: Gyorge Ann Wecker Yawn, Katherine LaDeanne Wecker Evans, Karen Celeste. Grad., Henager Bus. Coll., Salt Lake City, 1948; AA in Edn., San Bernardion C.C., 1969; BA in Polit. Sci., UCLA, 1971; MA in Polit. Sci., Calif. State U., Long Beach, 1982. Cert. life coll. instr. Calif. C.C.s. Realtor L.A. and Orange Counties, 1981—; C.C. instr. Coast and North Orange C.C. dists., Orange County, Calif., 1984—; producer LWV TV show on current campaign issues, Pub. TV, Orange County, Calif.;TV lectr. on polit. issues; organizer candidate debates, forums. Lobbyist LWV, Mobile, Ala., Phoenix, Orange County, Calif., 1973—; instr. ARC, 1973, sec. coord. coun. 1978-80, 1991—; mem. steering com. State of Ala. Alliance for Human Needs, 1974-75, Ariz. Coalition for Juv. Justice, 1975-77, L.A. County Contract Svcs. Com., 1982-83, Stringfellow Adv. Com., Glen Avon, Calif., 1986—; with Affordable Housing Task Force, 1990—; dir. pub. affairs LDS Ch., 1988—. Mem. LWV (pres. Cen. Orange County Area 1984-87, 1991—), Daughters of Utah Pioneers (sec., parliamentarian 1956—, pres.). Democrat.

WEDDLE, JUDITH ANN, social services administrator; b. Burlington, Iowa, Aug. 28, 1944; d. Kenneth Ivan and Betty Ruth (Neiswanger) Shipley; 1 child, Brian Douglas. BA, Midland Coll., 1966. Social worker Dodge County Welfare Dept., Fremont, Nebr., 1967-68; social worker L.A. County Dept. Pub. Social Svcs., 1969-71, appeals hearing specialist, 1971-78; supr., appeals hearing specialist L.A. Welfare Dept., 1978-86; human svcs. adminstr. Los Angeles Welfare Dept., 1986—. Pres. Gardena (Calif.) Hotline, 1971-72, Gardena Swimteam Parents, 1978-79; elder Presbyn. Ch., Gardena, 1987—; active Torrance (Calif.) Civic Chorale, 1989—. Republican.

WEDEL, MILLIE REDMOND, educator; b. Harrisburg, Pa., Aug. 18, 1939; d. Clair L. and Florence (Heiges) Aungst; BA, Alaska Meth. U., 1966; MEd, U. Alaska, Anchorage, 1972; postgrad. in comm. Stanford U., 1975-76; m. T.S. Redmond, 1956 (div. 1967); 1 child, T.S. Redmond II; m. Frederick L. Wedel, Jr., 1974 (div. 1986). Profl. model Charming Models & Models Guild of Phila., 1954-61; public rels. staff Haverford (Pa.) Sch., 1959-61; asst. dir. devel. in charge public rels. Alaska Meth. U., Anchorage, 1966, part-time lectr., 1966-73; comm. tchr. Anchorage Sch. Dist., 1967—; owner Wedel Prodns., Anchorage, 1976-86; pub. rels. staff Alaska Purchase Centennial Exhibit, U.S. Dept. Commerce, 1967; writer gubernatorial campaign, 1971; part-time instr. Chapman Coll., 1990-93; adj. prof. U. Alaska, Anchorage, 1972, 77-79, 89—; cons. Cook Inlet Native Assn., 1978, No. Inst., 1979; judge Ark. Press Women's Writing Contest, 1990-91. Bd. dirs. Sta. KAKM, Alaska Pub. TV, membership chmn., 1978-80, nat. lay rep. to Pub. Broadcasting Svc. and Nat. Assn. Pub. TV Stas., 1979; bd. dirs. Ednl. Telecom. Consortium for Alaska, 1979, Mid-Hillside Community Coun., Municipality of Anchorage, 1979-80, 83-88, Hillside East Community Coun., 1984-88, pres. 1984-85; rsch. writer, legal asst. Vinson & Elkins, Houston, 1981; mem. Valley Forge Freedoms Found., Murdoch Scholarships, Valley Forge; bd. dirs. Rev. Richard Gay Trust, Alaska and Pa., 1992—. Recipient awards for newspapers, lit. mags.; award Nat. Scholastic Press Assn., 1968, 74, 77, Am. Scholastic Press Assn., 1981, 82, 83, 84; Alaska Coun. Econs., 1982, Merits award Alaska Dept. Edn.; lic. third class broadcasting, FCC, legis. commendation State of Alaska. Mem. NEA (state del.), Nat. Assn. Secondary Sch. Prins., Assn. Pub. Broadcasting (charter mem., nat. lay del. 1980), Indsl. TV Assn. (San Francisco and Houston 1975-81), Alaska Press Club (chmn. high sch. journalism workshops, 1968, 69, 73, awards for sch. newspapers, 1972, 74, 77), Alaska Fedn. Press Women (dir. 1978-86, youth projects dir., award for brochures, 1978), World Affairs Coun., Alaska Coun. Tchrs. of English, Chugach Electric (chair 1990, nomination com. for bd. dirs. 1988-90), Stanford Alumni Club (pres. 1982-84, 90-92), Capt. Cook Athletic Club, Alaska (Anchorage), Edgewater Beach Club, Glades Country Club (Naples, Fla.), Delta Kappa Gamma. Presbyterian. Office: PO Box 730 Girdwood AK 99587-0730

WEDEMEIER, ROBERT GORHAM, government official; b. Fairbanks, Alaska, Feb. 10, 1942; s. Robert Gorham Wedemeier Sr. and Virginia (Rivers) Proffitt; m. Caroline Ann Gregor, May 8, 1970; children: Anna Mae, Aimee Maureen. BA, U. Alaska, 1981; MS, U. LaVerne (Calif.), 1987. Sr. customs inspector U.S. Customs Svc., Anchorage, 1975-83; orgn. specialist Bur. Land Mgmt., Anchorage, 1983-87, mgr. tng., 1986-87; mgr. OE br. FAA, Anchorage, 1987—; 1st vice chmn. U. Alaska, Anchorage Adv. Coun., 1989-90, 90-91, chmn. 1991-93; bd. dirs. Alaska Common Ground, 1991. Bd. dirs. Alaska Common Ground, 1991-93. With USAFR, 1963—. Recipient Univ. Svc. award, 1992-93. Mem. Pioneers of Alaska, U. Alaska-Anchorage Alumni (chmn. scholarship com. 1986-90, 1st recipient Alumni Recognition medal 1987-88), Phi Alpha Theta. Home: 2612 Lord Baranof Dr Anchorage AK 99517-1262 Office: FAA 222 W 7th Ave # 14 Anchorage AK 99513-7587

WEED, FREDERIC AUGUSTUS, retired political science educator; b. Potsdam, N.Y., Sept. 9, 1918; s. Frederic Barker and Marion Grace (Sisson) W.; m. Ruth Marjorie Head, Mar. 26, 1944; children: Mary Alison, Joseph Barker, Katherine Jane, Frederic Augustus. B.A., N.Y. State Coll. for Tchrs., 1940; M.A., Columbia U., 1941, J.D., 1948, Ph.D., 1949. Bar: Calif. 1978. Tutor CCNY, 1946-48; instr., supr. social studies N.Y. State Coll. Tchrs., 1948-50; asst., then asso. prof. polit. sci. No. Ill. U., 1950-56; asst., asso. prof. polit. sci. San Jose State U., 1956-60, head dept. polit. sci. and pub. adminstrn., 1960-65, prof. polit. sci., 1965-88, ret., 1988, interim chmn. dept. polit. sci., 1970-71, coord. internat. programs, 1971-73; Fulbright lectr. polit. sci. and Am. law, Lima, Peru, 1966-67. Author: (with Dorothy B. Robins) The UN Story, 1947; Contbr. articles and book reviews to profl. publs. Mem. DeKalb City Council, 1954-56. Served with AUS, 1942-45; lt. col. (ret.). Mem. ABA, Am., Western, No. Calif. polit. sci. assns., NEA, Am. Soc. Internat. Law, Calif. Tchrs. Assn. Home: 4225 Bloomfield Dr San Jose CA 95124-4741

WEED, RONALD DE VERN, engineering consulting company executive; b. Indian Valley, Idaho, Sept. 1, 1931; s. David Clinton and Grace Elizabeth (Lavendar) W.; m. Doris Jean Hohener, Nov. 15, 1953; children: Geraldine Gayle, Thomas De Vern, Cheryl Ann. BSChemE, U. So. Calif., 1957; MS in Chem. Engring., U. Wash., 1962; LLB, La Salle U., Chgo., 1975; postgrad., Century U., Beverly Hills, Calif., 1979—. Registered profl. engr., Washington, Calif. Devel. engr. GE Co., Richland, Washington, 1957-65, Battelle N.W. Labs., Richland, 1965-68; oper. plant engr. NIPAK, Inc., Kerens, Tex., 1968-72; aux. systems task engr. Babcock & Wilcox Co., Lynchburg, Va., 1972-74; materials and welding engr. Bechtel Group Cos., San Francisco, 1974-85; cons. engr. Cygna Energy Svcs., Walnut Creek, Calif., 1985-91; with inter city fund Cygna Energy Svcs., Oakland, Calif., 1991—. Contbr. rsch. reports, papers and chpts. in books; patentee in field. With U.S. Army, 1951-53. Mem. Am. Inst. Chem. Engrs., Am. Welding Soc., Nat. Assn. Corrosion Engrs. (cert., sect. vice chmn. and chmn. 1962-68). Home and Office: 74 Sharon St Pittsburg CA 94565-1527

WEEKS, DENNIS ALAN, computer programmer; b. Brainerd, Minn., May 29, 1943; s. Dale Harvey and A. Irene (Jacobs) W.; m. Shana Blaford, June 10, 1968; 1 child, Kerensa Alayne. BA with honors, U. Ill., 1967. Sr. programmer, analyst Decision, Inc., Oakland, Calif., 1970-72, Calma Co., Sunnyvale, Calif., 1972-73; mem. tech. staff SCM Corp., Palo Alto, Calif., 1973-74; programmer, analyst Spectra Med. Systems, Inc., Palo Alto, 1976-77; systems engr. Data Gen. Corp., Bellevue, Wash., 1977-83; proprietor, cons. Matrix Assocs., Anchorage, 1983-87; systems engr. Convex Computer Co., San Jose, Calif., 1987-89; sr. applications specialist MasPar Computer Corp., Sunnyvale, 1989-92; software engr. Convex Computer Corp., Richardson, Tex., 1992-. Translator/editor: Edward Waring's Meditatines Algebraicae, 1992; contbr. articles to profl. jours. Mem. Assn. for Computing Machinery. Democrat. Mem. Soc. of Friends.

WEEKS, DOROTHY MAE, publishing executive; b. Shanghai, China, Jan. 18, 1924; d. Herbert Clarence and Anna Louise (Johnson) White; m. Howard Benjamin Weeks, Dec. 12, 1946; children: John Howard, Douglas Alan, Carolyn M., Donna Louise. RN, Glendale Adventist Med. ctr., 1946; BA, Columbia Union Coll., 1961; MA, Loma Linda U., 1964. Assoc. prof. nursing Loma Linda (Calif.) U. Sch. of Nursing, 1964-73; instr., inservice tng. Cottage Hosp., Santa Barbara, Calif., 1973-74; sec., bd. mgr. Woodbridge Press Pub. Co., Santa Barbara, Calif., 1974-84, pres., 1984-91, chmn. bd., 1991—. Mem. Santa Barbara Seventh-day Adventist Ch. Office: Woodbridge Press 815 De La Vina St Santa Barbara CA 93101

WEEKS, WILFORD FRANK, geophysics educator, glaciologist; b. Champaign, Ill., Jan. 8, 1929; married; 2 children. BS, U. Ill., 1951, MS, 1953; PhD in Geology, U. Chgo., 1956. Geologist mineral deposits br. U.S. Geol. Survey, 1952-55; glaciologist USAF Cambridge Research Ctr., 1955-57; asst. prof. Washington U., St. Louis, 1957-62; adj. prof. earth scis. Dartmouth Coll., Hanover, N.H., 1962-85; glaciologist Cold Regions Rsch. and Engring. Lab., Hanover, 1962-89; chief scientist Alaska Synthetic Aperture Radar Facility, Fairbanks, 1986-93; prof. geophysics Geophys. Inst. U. Alaska, Fairbanks, 1986—; vis. prof. Inst. Low Temperature Sci. Hokkaido U., Sapporo, Japan, 1973; chair Arctic marine sci. USN Postgrad. Sch., Monterey, Calif., 1978-79; mem. earth system sci. com. NASA, Washington, 1984-87; advisor U.S. Arctic Rsch. Commn., div. polar programs NSF, Washington, 1987-88; chmn. NAS Com. on Cooperation with Russia in Ice Mechanics, 1991-92. Capt. USAF, 1955-57. Fellow Arctic Inst. N.Am., Am. Geophys. Union; mem. NAE, Internat. Glaciological Soc. (v.p. 1969-72, pres. 1973-75, Seligman Crystal award 1989). Office: U Alaska Fairbanks Geophys Inst Fairbanks AK 99775-0800

WEESE, NORRIS KEITH, accountant, real estate agent; b. Montgomery, W.Va., Jan. 15, 1939; s. Norman Earl and Bertha Oakland (Jackson) W.; m. Velma Watson, Aug. 15, 1961 (div. Sept. 1968); m. M. Judith Rutherford, May 2, 1970; children: Sharron, Lenard, Ravena, Scott, Chet, Danita, David. AA in Mgmt., Olympic Coll., 1975; BA in Acctg., U. Puget Sound, 1983, JD, 1989. Commd. ensign USN, 1957; budget dir., cost acct. Lock Heed Ship Repair, Seattle, 1980-83; acct. Weese's Acctg., Port Orchard, Wash., 1983—; cons. J.R.W., Inc., Olympia, Wash., 1990—, Bethel Evergrefry, Port Orchard, 1988—, KBP Fabrications, Inc., Kent, Wash., 1984—. Decorated Vietnam Cross of Gallentry; recipient Joint Svcs. award USN and USAF, 1976. Mem. Nat. Assn. Enrolled Agts., Nat. Bd. Realtors, State Bd. Realtors, Wash. Assn. Accts., Wash. State Tax Cons. Republican. Baptist. Home and Office: 2530 Woods Rd E Port Orchard WA 98366

WEESNER, LOWELL MICHAEL, retail executive; b. Marion, Ind., May 15, 1949; s. Lowell Max and Ruth Evangeline (Riley) W.; m. Hilary Fiona Goodson, Dec. 9, 1967; children: Catriona Ann, David Michael. AA in Data Processing, Fullerton (Calif.) Coll., 1970; student, Calif. State U., Fullerton, 1970-73. Quality control mgr. Essex Wire and Cable, Anaheim, Calif., 1966-74; mdse. control mgr. Thrifty Corp., L.A., 1974—. Mem. Diamond Bar (Calif.) High Sch. Booster Club, 1991-92. Recipient 1st Pl. amateur gun dog western field classic, Am. Kennel Club, 1985, Sullivan award Am. Weimaraner Club, 1985. Mem. Orange Coast Weimaraner Club (treas. 1984-85, field trial chmn. 1985-86). Mem. Soc. of Friends. Home: 1704 Autumnglow Dr Diamond Bar CA 91765 Office: Thrifty Corp 3424 Wilshire Blvd Los Angeles CA 90010

WEGEMAN, ALVIN PAUL, JR., paramedic, business executive; b. L.A., Jan. 24, 1964; s. Alvin Paul Sr. and Nancy Mae (Stevens) W.; m. Joan Marcia McQuaid, Dec. 2, 1989; stepchildren: Jennefer, Jeffrey. Cert. med. technician, Pikes Peak Community Coll., 1982; cert. paramedic, U. Ark., 1984; student, U. Colo. Coll. Bus., Colorado Springs, 1989—. Emergency med. technician A-1 Paramedics, Colorado Springs, 1982-83, paramedic, 1984—; paramedic Arapahoe Basin Ski Area, Summit County, Colo., 1986-90; med. gases supr. A-1 Paramedics, Colorado Springs, 1986-89; ACLS instr. Meml. Hosp., Colorado Springs, 1988-90; pres. C.M.E. Internat., 1992—. Jr. high counselor Bel-Air Presbyn. Ch., L.A., 1981; vol. emergency med. technician Tri-Lakes VFD, Monument, Colo., 1982; vol. paramedic Bicycling World Championships, Colorado Springs, 1986; vol. medic, stadium med. team U. Ark., Little Rock, 1983, Colo. State Games, 1990, KRDO Garden of the Gods 15k race, 1991; mem. planning com. Mountain Bike Fun Ride Mar. Dimes, 1992. Recipient merit award San Fernando Valley Flyers R.C. Club, 1981; named to Outstanding Young Men of Am., 1986. Mem. U. Colo.-Colorado Springs bus. Club, Internat. Platform Assn. Republican. Office: A-1 Paramedics 305 Auburn Dr Colorado Springs CO 80909-6424

WEGGE, LEON LOUIS FRANÇOIS, economics educator; b. Breendonk, Antwerp, Belgium, June 9, 1933; came to U.S., 1959; s. Petrus Maria and Alberta (De Maeyer) W.; m. Beate Maria Teipel, Nov. 22, 1962; children: Simone, Robert, Elizabeth. B in Thomistical Philosophy, Cath. U. Louvain, Belgium, 1957, Licentiate in Econ. Sci., 1958; PhD in Indsl. Econs., MIT, 1963. Assoc. lectr. U. New S. Wales, Kensington, Australia, 1963-66; prof. econs. U. Calif., Davis, 1966—; vis. prof. U. Bonn, Fed. Republic Germany, 1980-81. Assoc. editor Jour. Internat. Econs., 1971-84; contbr. articles to profl. jours. Rsch. fellow Ctr. for Ops. Rsch. and Econometrics, 1972-73, fellow The Netherlands Inst. for Advanced Study, 1987-88. Mem. Econometric Soc., Am. Statistical Assn. Roman Catholic. Home: 26320 County Rd # 98 Davis CA 95616-9406 Office: Univ of Calif Davis Dept of Economics Davis CA 95616

WEGHER, PEARL ELLA, retired special education educator; b. Newcastle, Wyo., Jan. 7, 1911; d. Solon Henry and Nina Ethel (Furman) Dewey; m. Arthur Florian Wegher, May 17, 1936; children: Carol, Roland, Rosemary, A. Gene, Marise, Joanne. BA, U. Wyo., 1931; MA, U. No. Colo., 1966. Cert. tchr., remedial reading tchr., spl. edn. tchr. Tchr. Sch. Dist. One, Newcastle, 1928-29, 31-36, 1945-49; remedial reading tchr. Sch. Dist. Seven, Kersey, Colo., 1957-62; spl. edn. tchr. Weld Bd. Coop. Ednl. Svcs., Weld County, Colo., 1962-76; vol. tchr. Right to Read, Greeley, 1978-93. Frequent election judge Weld County and City of Greeley, 1980-92; active Ch. Women United, 1982-93; vol. tax aid. Recipient Honor scholarship U. Wyo., 1926. Republican. Roman Catholic. Home: 1051 6th St #310 Greeley CO 80631

WEGST, WALTER FREDERICK, JR., company executive; b. Phila., Dec. 26, 1934; s. Walter F. and Marion (Scott) W.; m. Audrey Smith, Sept. 1958 (div.); children: Gregory Scott, Andrew Walter; m. Kathleen S. McCoy, Apr. 22, 1984. BS in Electronics, U. Mich., 1956, MSE (Nuclear), 1957, PhD in Environ. Health, 1963. Cert. health physicist; cert. safety profl.; cert. hazardous materials mgr.; registered profl. engr. Inst. health physicist Calif. Inst. Tech., Pasadena, 1963-69, mgr. safety, 1969-79; radiation safety officer Jet Propulsion Lab., Pasadena, 1963-69; mgr. environ. safety and health UCLA, 1979-88; cons. Sierra Madre, Calif., 1988-89; radiol. safety dir. ICN Biomeds., Irvine, Calif., 1989-90; mgr. environ. safety and health Raytheon Svc. Nev., Las Vegas, 1990—. Chmn. Calif. Radiol. Materials Mgmt. Forum, 1987. Mem. Health Physics Soc. (So. Calif. chpt. chair 1974, 90, Disting. Achievement award, dir. 1982-84), Am. Indsl. Hygiene Assn. Home: 7620 Cruz Bay Ct Las Vegas NV 89128 Office: Raytheon Svcs Nev 1551 Hillshire Dr Las Vegas NV 89134

WEH, ALLEN EDWARD, airline executive; b. Salem, Oreg., Nov. 17, 1942; s. Edward and Harriet Ann (Hicklin) W.; m. Rebecca Ann Roberton, July 5, 1968; children: Deborah Susan, Ashley Elizabeth, Brian Roberton. BS, U. N.Mex., 1966, MA, 1973. Asst. to chief adminstrv. officer Bank N.Mex., Albuquerque, 1973; pres., owner N.Mex. Airways, Inc., Albuquerque, 1974; dep. dir. N.Mex. Indochina Refugee Program, Santa Fe, 1975-76; dir. pub. affairs UNC Mining & Milling Co., Albuquerque, 1977-79; pres., chief exec. officer Charter Svcs., Inc., Albuquerque, 1979—, Falls Church, Va., 1984-90. Mem. steering com. Colin McMillan for lt. gov., Albuquerque, 1982; bd. dirs. N.Mex. Symphony Orgh., Albuquerque Conv. and Visitors Bur., 1982; mem. Albuquerque Police Adv. Bd., 1977-78; treas., bd. dirs. Polit. Action Com., Albuquerque, 1982. Capt. USMC, 1966-71, Vietnam; col. USMCR, 1971-90, 92-93, Col. USMC, 1990-91, Persian Gulf. Decorated Bronze Star, Purple Heart with gold star, Air medal, Merit Svc. medal. Mem. Marine Corps. Res. Officers Assn. (life, bd. dirs. 1973, 86), Res. Officers Assn. U.S. (life), SCV (life), Mil. Order Stars and Bars (life), N.Mex. Amigos. Republican. Episcopalian. Home: 6722 Rio Grande Blvd NW Albuquerque NM 87107-6330 Office: Charter Svcs Inc 3700 Rio Grande NW Albuquerque NM 87107

WEHLING, FRED LOWELL, political scientist, consultant; b. Burbank, Calif., Jan. 7, 1963; s. Robert and Anna Clara (Chiodo) W. AB in Internat. Rels., U. So. Calif., 1985; MA in Polit. Sci., UCLA, 1987, PhD in Polit. Sci., 1992. Cons. Rand/UCLA Ctr. Soviet Studies, Santa Monica, Calif., 1985—. Contbr. articles, papers to profl. publs. Graham fellow UCLA, 1990. Mem. Am. Assn. Advancement of Slavic Studies, Am. Polit. Sci. Assn., Internat. Studies Assn., Sierra Club, Phi Beta Kappa. Office: Rand UCLA Ctr Soviet Studies 1700 Main St Santa Monica CA 90406-2138

WEHMHOEFER, RICHARD ALLEN, lawyer, educator; b. Minot, N.D., Mar. 15, 1951; s. Leo W. and Myrtle C. (Wickman) W.; m. Gail M. Prostrollo, July 9, 1983. BA, U. Colo., 1973, MA, 1974, PhD, 1979, M in Urban Adminstrn., 1977, MPA, 1978; JD, U. Denver, 1982. Bar: Colo. 1983, U.S. Dist. Ct. Colo., 1983. Rsch. assoc. Denver Urban Obs., 1974-78; exec. asst. to regional adminstr. HUD, Denver, 1978-81; pvt. practice Denver, 1982—; asst. prof. mgmt. U. Denver, 1985-88, Disting. prof. of ethics, 1988-89; exec. dir., gen. counsel Colo. Commn. on Jud. Discipline, Denver, 1986—; cons. in ethics Pub. Svc. Co. Colo., Denver, 1987—; mem. core curriculum com. U. Denver, 1987-89. Author: Statistics in Litigation, 1985, Agriculture's Legal Rights Under the Bankruptcy Laws, 1987. Com. Colo. Dem. Party, Denver, 1980—; mem. Mayor's Com. on Keeping Denver a Great City, 1974—. Henderson fellow Fed. Exec. Inst., Charlottesville, Va., 1977. Mem. ABA (bd. dirs. jud. performance and conduct com., 1987—), Am. Judicature Soc., Assn. Jud. Disciplinary Counsel, Colo. Bar Assn., Colo. State Mgrs., Assn., Denver Bar Assn. Home: 2277 Holly St Denver CO 80207 Office: Colo Commn Jud Discipline 1301 Pennsylvania St Ste 260 Denver CO 80203-5012

WEHNER, ALFRED PETER, inhalation toxicologist, biomedical scientist; b. Wiesbaden, Germany, Oct. 23, 1926; came to U.S., 1953, naturalized, 1958; s. Paul Heinrich and Irma (Schulze) Wl; m. Ingeborg Hella Miller, Aug. 30, 1955; children: Patricia Ingeborg, Alfred Peter, Jr., Jackie Diane, Peter Hermann. Cand. med., Johannes Gutenberg U., 1949, Zahnarzt DDS, 1951, D.M.D. cum laude, 1953. Diplomate Acad. Toxicol. Scis., 1988. Individual practice dentistry Wiesbaden, 1951-53; fellow clin. pedodontia Guggenheim Dental Clinic, N.Y.C., 1953-54; dentist 7100th Hosp., USAF, 1954-56; rsch. asst. Mobil Oil Co., Dallas, 1957-62; sr. rsch. scientist Biometrics Instrument Corp., Plano, Tex., 1962-64; pres. Electro-Aerosol Inst., Plano, Tex.; dir. Electro-Aerosol Therapy Centers, 1964-67; prof., chmn. dept. sci. U. Plano, 1966-67; sr. rsch. scientist biology dept. Battelle Pacific Northwest Labs., Richland, Wash., 1967-78; mgr. environ. and indsl. toxicology Battelle Pacific Northwest Labs., 1978-80, project dir., task leader indsl. toxicology, 1980-89; founder, pres. Biomed. & Environ. Cons., Inc., 1989—; cons. VA Hosp., McKinney, Tex., 1963-65; chmn., guest speaker 16 internat. sci. congresses and symposia. Author: From Hitler Youth to U.S. Citizenship, 1972; more than 120 sci. publs., including chpts. to books.; editor-in-chief: Am. Inst. Biomed. Climatology Bull.; editor: MEDICEF Direct Information (Federal Republic of Germany); reviewer various sci. jours.; patentee in field. Fellow Internat. Soc. Med. Hydrology, Tex. Acad. Sci.; mem. AAAS, Am. Inst. Biomed. Climatology (bd. dirs. 1972-90, sec. 1972-83, pres. 1984-90), Academia degli Abruzzi per le Scienze e le Arti, Italy (hon. academician, v.p.), Pacific NW Assn. Toxicologists, Internat. Soc. Biometeorology (U.S. rep. 1972-80), Soc. Exptl. Biology and Medicine, Internat. Soc. Aerosols in Medicine (exec. bd. 1970-80), Dallas County Dental Soc. (hon.), Internat. Assn. Aerobiology, Sigma Xi. Home and Office: 312 Saint St Richland WA 99352-2033

WEHRLY, JOSEPH MALACHI, industrial relations executive b. County Armagh, Ireland, Oct. 2, 1915; s. Albert and Mary Josephine (Gribbon) W.; came to U.S., 1931, naturalized, 1938; student Los Angeles City Coll., evenings 1947-49; certificate indsl. relations U. Calif. at Berkeley Extension, 1957; m. Margaret Elizabeth Banks, July 3, 1946; children—Joseph Michael, Kathleen Margaret, Stephen Patrick. Mgr. interplant relations Goodyear Tire & Rubber Co., Los Angeles, 1935-42; dir. indsl. relations Whittaker Corp., Los Angeles, 1946-60, Meletron Corp., Los Angeles, 1960-61; asst. indsl. relations mgr. Pacific Airmotive Corp., Burbank, Calif., 1961-63; personnel mgr. Menasco Mfg. Co., Burbank, 1963-66; indsl. relations adminstr. Internat. Electronic Research, Burbank, 1966; dir. indsl. relations Adams Rite Industries, Inc., Glendale, Calif., 1966-75, cons., 1975-76; personnel mgr. TOTCO div. Baker Internat. Corp., Glendale, 1975-80; instr. indsl. relations and supervision Los Angeles Pierce Coll., 1949-76. Served with U.S. Army, 1942-46. Mem. Personnel and Indsl. Relations Assn., Mchts. and Mfrs. Assn. Republican. Roman Catholic. Home: 90 Shorebreaker Dr Laguna Niguel CA 92677

WEI, JEN YU, physiologist, educator; b. Fukien, China, Jan. 26, 1938; came to U.S., 1979; s. Soen Yu Wei and Soen Sang Hoeng; m. Lian Shen, Jan. 19, 1966; 1 child, Ching Wei. BS, Fu-Dan U., Shanghai, China, 1962; PhD, Inst. Physiology, Shanghai, China, 1966, U. Utah, 1987. Researcher Inst. of Physiology, Shanghai, 1966-77, rsch. assoc., 1977-78; rsch. assoc. dept. Physiology U. Hong Kong, China, 1979; rsch. assoc. dept. Physiology U. Utah, Salt Lake City, 1979-81, rsch. instr. dept. Physiology, 1981-87, rsch. asst. prof. Physiology, 1987-89; asst. rsch. neurophysiologist dept. Medicine UCLA, 1989-91, assoc. rsch. neurophysiologist dept. Medicine, 1991—. NIH Individual Investigator Rsch. grantee, 1990—. Mem. AAAS, The Chinese Physiology Soc., Soc. for Neurosci., Internat. Brain Rsch. Orgn., Sigma Xi. Office: UCLA Rsch Inst Dept Medicine & Brain Los Angeles CA 90024-1761

WEIBELL, FRED JOHN, biomedical engineer; b. Murray, Utah, Oct. 18, 1927; s. John Christian and Agnes Anna (Kielgass) W.; m. Carol K. Finch, Mar. 18, 1949; children: Mark J., Carol Lee, Marci Ann Olsen, John Christian. BSEE, U. Utah, 1953; MS, UCLA, 1967, PhD, 1977. Staff engr. Sandia Corp., Albuquerque, 1953-62; chief med. instrumentation sect. VA Western Rsch. Support Ctr., Sepulveda, Calif., 1962-67; asst. chief VA Western Rsch. Support Ctr., Sepulveda, 1967-72; chief VA Biomed. Engring. and Computing Ctr., Sepulveda, 1972-93. Author: (with others) Biomedical Instrumentation and Measurements, 1973, 80, Medical Instrumentation for Health Care, 1976. With USN, 1945-48. Mem. Biomed. Engring. Soc. (sec., treas. 1980—), Assn. for Advancement of Med. Instrumentation. Home: 18914 Kinzie St Northridge CA 91324-1831 Office: VA Med Ctr 16111 Plummer St Sepulveda CA 91343-2036

WEIDA, GEORGE ALBERT F., human resources executive; b. Pangkatan, Sumatra, Indonesia, Aug. 16, 1936; came to U.S., 1940; s. Frederick Shepherd and Flora (Miller) W.; m. Marilee Horton, Oct. 31, 1962 (div. 1974); children: Frederick Edmund, David James, George Bradley, Craig Miller; m. Julie Ann McGrain, Oct. 4, 1974. AB in Psychology, Kenyon Coll., 1958. Group personnel mgr. Kaiser Aluminum and Chem. Corp., Oakland, Calif., 1963-69; v.p. indsl. rels. Republic Corp., L.A., 1969-78; corp. dir. employee rels. AM Internat., Inc., L.A., 1978-81; prin. Employers' Labor Rels. Coun., L.A., 1981-83; v.p. human resources Loral Electro/Optical Systems, Pasadena, Calif., 1983, San Diego Gas & Electric Co., 1983—. chair corp. adv. bd. Chicano Fedn., San Diego, 1988—; bd. dirs. Police Athletic League, San Diego, 1988—, Calif. Employment Law Coun., 1985—, Found. on Employment and Disability, 1985—; mem. industry adv. bd. Math. Engring. Sci. Achievement, 1985—. Mem. Orgn. Resources Counselors. Episcopalian. Home and Office: PO Box 61 Rancho Santa Fe CA 92067-0061 Office: San Diego Gas & Electric Co 101 Ash St San Diego CA 92101

WEIDE, WILLIAM WOLFE, housing and recreational vehicles manufacturer; b. Toledo, Aug. 19, 1923; s. Samuel and Pearl Celia (Weide) W.; m. Beatrice Lieberman, June 4, 1950; children: Brian Samuel, Bruce Michael, Robert Benjamin. Student, U. Toledo, 1942, Marquette U., 1943-44; B.S., U. So. Calif., 1949. Asst. controller Eldon Mfg., 1950; mem. Calif. Franchise Tax Bd., 1951; controller Sutone Corp., 1951-53; contr., treas. Pacific Concessions Corp., 1953; treas. Descoware Corp., 1953-58; sr. v.p., dir. Fleetwood Enterprises, Inc., Riverside, Calif., 1958-73, pres., chief oper. officer, 1973-82, vice chmn., 1982—, dir.; treas. So. Eastern Manufactured Housing Inst., Atlanta., 1972-74; vice chmn. bd. dirs. Fleetwood Enterprises, Inc.. Mem. City of Riverside Housing Com.; mem. exec. com. of policy adv. bd. Joint Ctr. for Urban Studies, Harvard-MIT, Cambridge; trustee City of Hope Hosp., Duarte, Calif.; Orange County chmn. United Jewish Welfare Fund, 1982-83; mem. Pres.'s Circle of U. So. Calif.; pres. Orange County Jewish Community Found., 1986-88; chmn. Calif. Mfrs. Housing Inst. Polit Action Com., 1986-92; vice chmn., chmn. devel. Wellness Community of

Orange County. With USNR, 1942-46. Recipient Jack E. Wells Meml. award for service to manufactured housing industry, 1976; named to Recreational Vehicle/Manufactured Housing Industry Hall of Fame Elkhart, Ind., 1981; named Man of Yr., City of Hope, 1986. Mem. Nat. Assn. Accts. (past v.p., dir. Los Angeles and Orange County chpt.), Manufactured Housing Inst. (chmn., founding com. Calif. chpt. 1986), Western Manufactured Housing Inst. (vice-chmn.), Trailer Coach Assn., NAM (public affairs com.), Riverside C. of C. Office: Fleetwood Enterprises Inc 3125 Myers StPO Box 7638 Riverside CA 92513

WEIDENHOFER, NEAL, systems programer, computer company executive; b. Chgo., June 18, 1940; s. William Joseph and Pearl Martha (Miller) W.; m. Joan Foster, June 17, 1962 (div. 1974); children: Mark Raymond, Lisa Marie; m. Dennise Marie Harrington, June 18, 1988. BS, U. N.Mex., 1964, MA, 1965; MA, Dartmouth Coll., 1967, PhD, 1968. Grad. asst. Dartmouth Coll., Hanover, N.H., 1965-68; asst. prof. U. Ill., Urbana, 1968-69; systems programmer United Computing Systems, Kans. City, Mo., 1969-80; researcher United Telecommunications, Mission, Kans., 1981-83; asst. to v.p. software lang. Denelcor, Aurora, Colo., 1983-85; systems programmer Amdahl, Sunnyvale, Calif., 1985—. Mem. Am. Nat. Standards Inst. (X3J11 and X3J16 lang. standards coms.). Libertarian.

WEIGAND, WILLIAM KEITH, bishop; b. Bend, Oreg., May 23, 1937. Ed., Mt. Angel Sem., St. Benedict, Oreg., St. Edward's Sem. and St. Thomas Sem., Kenmore, Wash. Bishop Diocese Salt Lake City, 1980—; Ordained priest Roman Cath. Ch., 1963. Office: Pastoral Ctr 27 C St Salt Lake City UT 84103-2397*

WEIGEL, STANLEY ALEXANDER, judge; b. Helena, Mont., Dec. 9, 1905; s. Louis and Jennie (Hepner) W.; m. Anne Kauffman, Apr. 21, 1940; children: Jane Anne, Susan Mary. AB, Stanford U., 1926, JD, 1928. Bar: Calif. 1928. Pvt. practice law San Francisco, 1928-62; judge U.S. Dist. Ct. (no. dist.) Calif., from 1962, now sr. judge; non-resident lectr. Stanford Law Sch., 1952—; mem. Jud. Panel on Multidist. Litigation, 1968-79; mem. temporary emergency Ct. Appeals of U.S., 1980—; pres. Internat. Hospitality Ctr. Bay Area, 1959-68, Nat. Council for Community Services to Internat. Visitors, 1972-73; adv. gov. Calif. on Automobile Accident Commn., 1959; chmn. bd. visitors Stanford Law Sch., 1958-63; trustee World Affairs Council No. Calif., 1960—, pres., 1973-74; chmn. Ford Found. vis. com. to study behavioral sci. depts. Stanford U., 1956-57; mem. jud. conf. com. on jud. ethics, 1982-87. Served to lt. USNR, 1943-45. Decorated chevalier Order Leopold II (Belgium). Mem. Delta Sigma Rho, Phi Alpha Delta, Sigma Delta Chi. Office: US Ct Appeals PO Box 36060 450 Golden Gate Ave San Francisco CA 94102

WEIGEND, GUIDO GUSTAV, geographer, educator; b. Zeltweg, Austria, Jan. 2, 1920; came to U.S., 1939, naturalized, 1943; s. Gustav F. and Paula (Sorgo) W.; m. Areta Kelble, June 26, 1947; children: Nina, Cynthia, Kenneth. B.S., U. Chgo., 1942, M.S., 1946, Ph.D., 1949. With OSS, 1943-45; with mil. intelligence U.S. War Dept., 1946; instr. geography U. Ill., Chgo., 1946-47; instr. then asst. prof. geography Beloit Coll., 1947-49; asst. prof. geography Rutgers U., 1949-51, assoc. prof., 1951-57, prof., 1957-76, acting dept. chmn., 1951-52, chmn. dept., 1953-67, assoc. dean, 1972-76; dean Coll. Liberal Arts, Prof. geography Ariz. State U., Tempe, 1976-84, prof. geography, 1976-89; ret., 1989; Fulbright lectr. U. Barcelona, 1960-61; vis. prof. geography Columbia U., 1963-67, NYU, 1967, U. Colo., summer 1968, U. Hawaii, summer 1969; liaison rep. Rutgers U. to UN, 1950-52; invited by Chinese Acad. Scis. to visit minority areas in Chinese Cent. Asia, 1988; mem. U.S. nat. com. Internat. Geog. Union, 1951-58, 61-65; chmn. Conf. on Polit. and Social Geography, 1968-69. Author articles, monographs, bulls. for profl. jours.; contbr.: (4th edit.) A Geography of Europe, 1977; geog. editor-in-chief: Odyssey World Atlas, 1966. Bd. adjustment Franklin Twp., N.J., 1959; mem. Highland Park (N.J.) Bd. Edn., 1973-75, v.p., 1975; mem. Ariz. Coun. on Humanities and Pub. Policy, 1976-80; vice chmn. Phoenix Com. on Fgn. Rels., 1976-79, chmn., 1979-81; mem. exec. com. Fedn. Pub. Programs in Humanities, 1977-82; bd. dirs. Coun. Colls. Arts and Scis., 1980-83; commr. N. Cen. Assn. Colls. and Schs., 1976-80, bd. dirs. commn. on instns. of higher edn., 1980-83. Research fellow Office Naval Research, 1952-55, Rutgers Research Council, 1970-71; grantee Social Sci. Research Council, 1956, Ford Found., 1966, Am. Philos. Soc., 1970-71, German Acad. Exchange Service, 1984; Fulbright travel grantee Netherlands, 1970-71. Mem. Assn. Am. Geographers (chmn. N.Y. Met. div. 1955-56, editorial bd. 1955-59, mem. coun. 1965-66, chmn. N.Y.-N.J. div. 1965-66), Am. Geog. Soc., Sigma Xi (pres. Ariz. State U. chpt. 1989-91). Home: 2094 E Golf Ave Tempe AZ 85282-4046 Office: Ariz State U Dept Geography Tempe AZ 85287-0104

WEIGHT, GEORGE DALE, banker, educator; b. Salt Lake City, Mar. 25, 1934; s. Sheldon J. and Florence (Noe) W.; m. Carilee Kesler, June 16, 1959; children: Camille, Kristene, Denise, Marcie, Nancy. BS, U. Utah, 1961; MS, U. Oreg., 1965, PhD, 1968. Instr. U. Oreg., Eugene, 1963-68; economist Fed. Res. Bank, Cleve., 1968-69; asst. v.p. fiscal ops. Fed. Res. Bank, Pitts., 1969-71; v.p. bank ops. Fed. Home Loan Bank Bd., Pitts., 1971-73; exec. v.p. Syracuse Savs. Bank, N.Y., 1972-73, pres., chief exec. officer, 1973-83; chmn., chief exec. officer Ben Franklin Fed. Savs. and Loan Assn., Portland, Oreg., 1983-90; dean Atkinson Grad. Sch. Mgmt. Willamette U., Salem, Oreg., 1990—; adj. prof. Syracuse U., 1974; chmn. bd. Savs. Banks Life Ins. Fund, N.Y.C.; bd. dirs. Onondaga County Indsl. Devel. Agy., Fed. Res. Bank of San Francisco, Portland Br., State Accident Ins. Fund, Fed. Home Loan Bank Seattle; chmn. Oreg. State Bd. Edn., 1991. Pres. Hiawatha coun. Boy Scouts Am., Syracuse, 1974-77; chmn. bd. Crouse-Irving Meml. Hosp., 1978-83; pres. Canal Mus.; bd. dirs. Oreg. Bus. Coun.; mem. Gov.'s Commn. Edn. Reforms, 1988, Oreg. State Bd. Edn., 1989—, chmn., 1991-92. Recipient Silver Beaver award Boy Scouts Am., 1978; recipient Vol. of Yr. award Am. Heart Assn., 1980, Community Service award Rotary, Syracuse, 1982. Mem. Am. Fin. Assn., Arlington Club, Beta Gamma Sigma. Republican. Home: 14235 Harvest Ln Portland OR 97229-3672 Office: Willamette U Atkinson Grad Sch Mgmt 900 State St Salem OR 97301-3922

WEIGHTMAN, JUDY MAE, lawyer; b. New Eagle, Pa., May 22, 1941; d. Morris and Ruth (Gutstadt) Epstein; children: Wayne, Randall, Darrell. BS in English, California U. of Pa., 1970; MA in Am. Studies, U. Hawaii, 1975; JD, U. Hawaii, 1981. Bar: Hawaii 1981. Tchr. Fairfax County Sch. (Va.), 1968-72, Hawaii Pub. Schs., Honolulu, 1973-75; lectr. Kapiolani Community Coll., Honolulu, 1975-76; instr. Olympic Community Coll., Pearl Harbor, Hawaii, 1975-77; lectr. Hawaii Pacific Coll., Honolulu, 1977-78; law clk. to atty. gen. Hawaii & Case, Kay & Lynch, Davis & Levin, 1979-81, to chief judge Intermediate Ct. Appeals State of Hawaii, 1981-82; dep. pub. defender Office of Pub. Defender, 1982-84; staff atty. Dept. Commerce & Consumer Affairs, State of Hawaii 1984-86; pres., bd. dirs. Am. Beltwrap Corp., 1986—; asst. prof. law, dir. pre-admission program, asst. prof. Richardson Sch. Law, U. Hawaii, 1987—, faculty senator. Author: Days of Remembrance: Hawaii Witnesses to the Holocaust; producer (documentary) The Panel: The First Exchange, Profile of An Aja Soldier, Profile of a Holocaust Survivor; patentee in field; mem. Richardson Law Rev., 1979-81. Mem. neighborhood bd. No. 25 City and County Honolulu, 1976-77; vol. Legal Aid Soc., Honolulu, 1977-78; bd. dirs. Jewish Fedn., Protection and Advocacy Agy.; parent rep. Wheeler Intermediate Adv. Coun., Honolulu, 1975-77; trustee Carl K. Mirikitani Meml. Scholarship Fund, Arts Coun. Hawaii; membership dir. ACLU, 1977-78, bd. dirs., Hawaii, 1988—, treas. Amicus; founder Hawaii Holocaust Project; trustee Jewish Fedn. Hawaii. Community scholar, Honolulu, 1980; grantee in internat. rels. Chaminade U., 1976. Mem. ABA, Afro-Am. Lawyers Assn. (bd. trustee), Hawaii Women Lawyers, Assn. Trial Lawyers Am., Hawaii State Bar Assn., Am. Judicature Soc., Richardson Sch. Law Alumni Assn. (alumni rep. 1981-82), Advocates for Pub. Interest Law, U. Hawaii Senate Faculty (senator), Phi Delta Phi (v.p. 1980-81), Hadassah Club, Women's Guild Club. Democrat. Jewish. Office: U Hawaii William S Richardson Sch Law 2515 Dole St Honolulu HI 96822-2386

WEIGLE, WILLIAM OLIVER, immunologist, educator; b. Monaca, Pa., Apr. 28, 1927; s. Oliver James and Caroline Ellen (Alsing) W.; m. Kathryn May Lotz, Sept. 4, 1948 (div. 1980); children—William James, Cynthia Kay; m. Carole G. Romball, Sept. 24, 1983. B.S., U. Pitts., 1950, M.S., 1951, Ph.D., 1956. Research assoc. pathology U. Pitts., 1955-58, asst. prof. immunochemistry, 1959-61; assoc. div. exptl. pathology Scripps Rsch. Inst., La Jolla, Calif., 1961-62, assoc. mem. div., 1962-63; mem. dept. exptl. pathology Scripps Rsch. Inst., La Jolla, 1963-74, mem. dept. immunopathology, 1974-82, chmn. dept. immunopathology, 1980-82, mem., vice chmn. dept. immunology, 1982-85, mem. dept. immunology, 1982—, chmn. dept. immunology, 1985-87; adj. prof. biology U. Calif., San Diego; McLaughlin vis. prof. U. Tex., 1977; mem. adv. bd. Immunetech Pharms., San Diego, 1988—; cons. in field. Author: Natural and Acquired Immunologic Unresponsiveness, 1967; assoc. editor: Clin. and Exptl. Immunology, 1972-79; Jour. Exptl. Medicine, 1974-84; Immunochemistry 1964-71; Procs. Soc. Exptl. Biology and Medicine, 1967-72; Jour. Immunology, 1967-71; Infection and Immunity, 1969-86, Aging: Immunology and Infectious Disease, 1987—; sect. editor: Jour. Immunology, 1971-75; editorial bd.: Contemporary Topics in Immunobiology, 1971—; Cellular Immunology, 1984—; contbr. articles to profl. jours. Trustee Lovelace Med. Found., Albuquerque. With USNR, 1945-46. Pub. Health Research fellow, Nat. Inst. Neurol. Diseases and Blindness, 1956-59; NIH sr. research fellow, 1959-61, Research Career award, 1962. Mem. Am. Assn. Immunologists, Am. Soc. Exptl. Pathology (Parke Davis award 1967), Am. Soc. Microbiology, N.Y. Acad. Scis., Am. Acad. Allergy, Am. Assn. Pathologists, Soc. Exptl. Biology and Medicine. Home: 688 Via De La Vly Solana Beach CA 92075-2461 Office: Scripps Rsch Inst Dept Immunology IMM9 10666 N Torrey Pines Rd La Jolla CA 92037-1027

WEIGNER, BRENT JAMES, educator; b. Pratt, Kans., Aug. 19, 1949; s. Doyle Dean and Elizabeth (Hanger) W.; m. Sue Ellen Weber Hume, Mar. 30, 1985; children: Russell John Hume, Scott William Hume. BA, U. No. Colo., 1972; MEd, U. Wyo., 1977, PhD, 1984. Counselor, coach Olympia Sport Village, Upson, Wyo., summer 1968; dir. youth sports F.E. Warren AFB, Cheyenne, summers 1973, 74; instr. geography Laramie County Community Coll., Cheyenne, 1974-75; tchr. social sci. McCormick Jr. High Sch., Cheyenne, 1975—, Laramie County Sch. Dist. 1, Cheyenne, 1975—; head social studies dept. McCormick Jr. High Sch., 1987—; curriculum adv. coun. chmn. Laramie County Sch. Dist. No. 1, 1988-89; lectr. ednl. methods U. Wyo., 1989, mem. clin. faculty, 1992—; nat. chmn. Jr. Olympic cross-country com. AAU, Indpls., 1980-81; pres. Wyo. Athletic Congress, 1981-87; tchr. cons. Nat. Geog. Soc. Geography Inst., summer 1991; bd. dirs. Shadow Mountain Lodge, Aspen, Colo. Fgn. exch. student U. Munich, 1971-72; head coach Cheyenne Track Club, 1976—, pres. 1980-80; deacon 1st Christian Ch., Cheyenne, 1987-90, elder, 1991—; rep. candidate general election Wyo. Legis., 1991. Named Wyo. U.S. West Outstanding Tchr., 1989; fellow Taft Found., summer 1976, Earthwatch-Hearst fellow, Punta Allen, Mex., summer 1987, Christa McAuliffe fellow, 1991-92; Fulbright grantee, Jerusalem, summer 1984; cross country finalist NCAA, 1971. Mem. ASCD, NEA, Nat. Network for Ednl. Renewal, Nat. Coun. Social Studies, Nat. Coun. Geog. Edn., Dominican Republic Nat. Coun. for Geog. Edn. (Cram scholarship 1992), Wyo. Geog. Alliance (steering com.), Cheyenne Tchrs. Edn. Assn. (govtl. rels. com., instrn. and profl. devel. com.), U. No. Colo. Alumni Assn., Cheyenne C. of C., Wyo. Heritage Soc., Wyo. Edn. Assn. (accountability task force 1989-90), Fulbright Alumni Assn., U. Wyo. Alumni Assn. (life), Lions (bd. dirs. Cheyenne 1987-90, 1st v.p. 1993-94), Phi Delta Kappa (bd. dirs. Cheyenne 1989—, v.p., edn. award for rsch. 1990, pres. 1992-93, ednl. found. rep. 1993—). Home: 3204 Reed Ave Cheyenne WY 82001-2558 Office: McCormick Jr High Sch 3204 Reed Ave Cheyenne WY 82001-3999

WEIHAUPT, JOHN GEORGE, geosciences educator, scientist, university administrator; b. La Crosse, Wis., Mar. 5, 1930; s. John George and Gladys Mae (Ash) W.; m. Audrey Mae Reis, Jan. 28, 1961. Student, St. Norbert Coll., De Pere, Wis., 1948-49; B.S., U. Wis., 1952, M.S., 1953; M.S., U. Wis.-Milw., 1971; Ph.D., U. Wis., 1973. Exploration geologist Am. Smelting & Refining Co., Nfld., 1953, Anaconda Co., Chile, S.Am., 1956-57; seismologist United Geophys. Corp., 1958; geophysicist Arctic Inst. N.Am., Antarctica, 1958-60, Geophys. and Polar Research Center, U. Wis., Antarctica, 1960-63; dir. participating Coll. and Univ. program, chmn. dept. phys. and biol. sci. U.S. Armed Forces Inst., Dept. Def., 1963-73; assoc. dean for acad. affairs Sch. Sci., Ind. U.-Purdue U., Indpls., 1973-78; prof. geology Sch. Sci., Ind. U.-Purdue U., 1973-78; asst. dean (Grad. Sch., prof. geoscis. Purdue U.), 1975-78; prof. geology, assoc. acad. v.p., dean grad. studies and research, v.p. Univ. Research Found., San Jose (Calif.) State U., 1978-82; vice chancellor for acad. affairs U. Colo., Denver, 1982-86, prof. geoscis., 1987—; Sci. cons., mem. sci. adv. bd. Holt Reinhart and Winston, Inc., 1967—; sci. editor, cons. McGraw-Hill Co., 1966—; hon. lectr. U. Wis., 1963-73; geol. cons., 1968—; editorial cons. John Wiley & Sons, 1968; editorial adv. bd. Dushkin Pub. Group, 1971—. Author: Exploration of the Oceans: An Introduction to Oceanography; mem. editorial bd. Internat. Jour. Interdisciplinary Cycle Research, Leiden; co-discoverer USARP Mountain Range (Arctic Inst. Mountain Range), in Victoria Land, Antarctica, 1960; discoverer Wilkes Land Meteorite Crater, Antarctic. Mem. Capital Community Citizens Assn.; mem. Madison Transp. Study Com., Found. for Internat. Energy Research and Tng.; U.S. com. for UN Univ.; mem. sci. council Internat. Center for Interdisciplinary Cycle Research; mem. Internat. Awareness and Leadership Council; mem. governing bd. Moss Landing Marine Labs.; bd. dirs. San Jose State U. Found. Served as 1st lt. AUS, 1953-55, Korea. Mt. Weihaupt in Antarctica named for him, 1966; recipient Madisonian medal for outstanding community service, 1973; Outstanding Cote Meml. award, 1974; Antarctic medal, 1968. Fellow Geol. Soc. Am., Explorers Club; mem. Antarctican Soc., Nat. Sci. Tchrs. Assn., Am. Geophys. Union, Internat. Council Corr. Edu., Soc. Am. Mil. Engrs., Wis. Alumni Assn., Soc. Study Biol. Rhythms, Internat. Soc. for Chronobiology, Marine Tech. Soc., AAAS, Univ. Indsl. Adv. Council, Am. Council on Edn., Expdn. Polaire France (hon.), Found. for Study Cycles, Assn. Am. Geographers, Nat. Council Univ. Research Adminstrs., Soc. Research Adminstrs., Man-Environ. Communication Center, Internat. Union Geol. Scis., Internat. Geog. Union, Internat. Soc. Study Time, Community Council Pub. TV, Internat. Platform Assn., Ind., Midwest assns. grad. schs., Western Assn. Grad. Schs., Council Grad. Schs. in U.S., Wis. Alumni Assn. of San Francisco, Kiwanis, Carmel Racquet Club (Rinconada), The Ridge at Hiwan (Evergreen, Colo., pres. 1991-93). Home: 23906 Currant Dr Golden CO 80401-9214 Office: U Colo Campus Box 172 1200 Larimer Denver CO 80217-3364

WEIHE, CLIFTON MEYER, clergyman; b. Postville, Iowa, Oct. 21, 1916; s. John Christian and Caroline (Meyer) W. BA, Luther Coll., Decorah, Iowa, 1938; MDiv, Luth. Theol. Sem., Phila., 1944. Ordained to ministry Luth. Ch., 1944. Assoc. pastor St. John's Luth. Ch., Allentown, Pa., 1944-48; assoc. dir. evangelism United Luth. Ch. Am., N.Y.C., 1949-62; dir. San Fernando Valley Project Luth. Ch. Am., L.A., 1962-66; assoc. pastor Messiah Luth. Ch., Redwood City, Calif., 1967-72; pastor Gloria Dei Luth. Ch., Santa Maria, Calif., 1972-84; chmn. Luth. Evangelism Coun., Chgo., 1960, editor, 1952-62. Editor: (sound film strip) Share Christ Today, 1952, (book of sermons) Share Christ Today, 1952; co-editor: Evangelism Handbooks, 1961-62. Hon. life mem. United Way Ctrl. Coast, Santa Maria, 1984—, sec., 1980. Democrat. Home: 1210 Jackie Ln Santa Maria CA 93454

WEIL, ROBERT IRVING, mediator, retired judge; b. N.Y.C., Apr. 6, 1922; s. Irving Julius and Esther (Aisenstein) W.; m. Carol Ethel Tannenbaum, Nov. 6, 1946 (div. 1953); children: David Irving, Timothy Robert; m. Dorothy Granet Kornhandler, Sept. 12, 1958. AB, UCLA, 1943; MS in Journalism, Columbia U., 1944; JD, U. So. Calif., L.A., 1951. Bar: Calif. 1951, U.S. Dist. Ct. (cen. dist.) Calif. 1951, U.S. Supreme Ct. 1961. Assoc. Pacht, Tannenbaum & Ross, L.A., 1951-54; ptnr. Tannenbaum, Steinberg & Shearer, Beverly Hills, Calif., 1954-58, Aaronson, Weil & Friedman, L.A., 1958-75; judge Calif. County Superior Ct., L.A., 1975-90; pvt. practice L.A., 1990—; v.p. L.A. Police Commn., 1973-75; chmn. Calif. Ctr. for Jud. Edn. and Rsch., Emoryville, 1989-90; lectr., seminar leader Calif. Jud. Coll., Berkeley, 1981—, The Rutter Group, L.A., 1981—. Co-author: California Practice Guide: Civil Procedure Before Trial, 1983; contbr. articles to profl. jours. Mem. ABA, Am. Judges Assn., Calif. Judges Assn. (pres. 1985-86, Pres.'s award 1987, v.p. 1993—), L.A. County Bar Assn., L.A. Copyright Soc., Beverly Hills Bar Assn. Home and Office: 2686 Claray Dr Los Angeles CA 98077-2017

WEIL, STEVEN MARK, high risk alternative educator, science educator; b. Chgo., Feb. 28, 1949; s. Ronald Leo and Leona Ann (Fein) W.; m. Mary Arlene Bartelheim, Aug. 1970 (div. 1977); 1 child, Meredith; m. Mary Clare Klaus, May 11, 1979 (div. Aug. 1990); children: Nethaniel, Rachael. Student, Chgo. City Coll.-Loop Coll., 1966-68, Chgo. State Coll., 1968-69; BS in Psychology and Physical Sci. Edn., Roosevelt U., 1980; MS in Edn./Phys. Sci., U. Nebr., 1982, MS in Vocat. Needs, 1982, MS in Vocat. Adminstrn., 1983. Tchr. DuSable High Sch., Chgo., 1980, Millard Pub. Schs., 1980-81; tchr. Fremont Learning Ctr. Fremont (Nebr.) Pub. Schs., 1981-86; tchr. Webster Mid. Sch., 1986-88; software educator Calif. State U., Stockton, Calif., 1993—; fellow Leadership Inst. for Environ. Edn., 1992—; curriculum evaluator Calif. State Integrated Waste Mgmt., 1993. Contbr. articles to profl. jours. mem. dist. computer com. Stockton Unified Sch. Dist.; instr. CPR and first aid ARC, Fremont and Stockton, 1985-88; mem. mcpl. rels. commn. Village of Wheeling, Ill., 1976-77; grant proposal reader NSF, 1987, 89. Grantee Fremont Alternative Learning Ctr., 1982-83, grantee Stockton Enrichment Found., 1986. Mem. NEA (v. chair Jewish Affairs Caucus 1991-93), Am. Vocat. Assn. (ops./policy com. 1984-85), Fremont Edn. Assn. (rep. bldg. 1981-82, 84-86, negotiations team 1985-86), Millard Edn. Assn. (rep. bldg. 1980-81, negotiations com. 1980-81), Mo. Valley Alternative Edn. Coun. (pres. 1983-85), Nat. Sci. Tchrs. Assn. (life, spl. edn. adv. bd. 1984-87, chmn. spl. edn. adv. bd. 1986-87, adv. bd. jour. 1987-91, mem. NSTA Reports adv. bd. 1991—), Nebr. Assn. Vocat. Spl. Needs Pers. (pres. 1983-84), Nebr. Vocat. Assn., Sci. Handicapped Assn., Stockton Tchrs. Assn., Phi Delta Kappa. Home: 7100 Shore Line Dr # 113 Stockton CA 95219-5458 Office: Franklin High Sch Discovery Sch 300 N Gertrude Ave Stockton CA 95215-4897

WEIL, SUZANNE S. FERN, producer; b. Mpls., June 22, 1933; d. Maurice and Esther (Sperling) Swiller; m. Fred Weil, Jr., Sept. 14, 1952 (dec. Apr. 1983); 1 dau., Peggy. Student, U. Minn.-Mpls. Coordinator performing arts Walker Art Center, Mpls., 1969-76; dir. dance program Nat. Endowment for Arts, Washington, 1968-78; sr. v.p., mng. dir. Pub. Broadcasting Service, Washington, 1980-81; sr. v.p. programming Pub. Broadcasting Service, 1981-90; exec. dir. The Sundance Inst., 1990-91; cons. Nat. Cultural Alliance, 1991—. Bd. dirs. Cunningham Dance Found., N.Y.C., 1982—; bd. dirs.Guthrie Theater, Mpls., 1982—; mem. panel Nat. Sci. Found., 1989—. Bush fellow Harvard U. Inst. for Arts Adminstrn., 1973. Club: Mpls. Home: 1033 Ocean Ave Santa Monica CA 90403-3543

WEILER, CAROLINE SUSAN, association executive; b. Fairbanks, Alaska, Jan. 29, 1949; d. Frederick Jacob and Caroline Hunter (Willis) Weiler; m. Paul Herbert Yancey, Sept. 14, 1978; 1 child, Ross Weiler Yancey. Student, U. Nairobi, 1968-69; BA, U. Calif., San Diego, 1972; postgrad., U. Mich., 1972-73; PhD, U. Calif., San Diego, 1978. Postdoctoral fellow U. B.C., Vancouver, 1978-79, U. Oslo, Norway, 1980-81; lectr. Whitman Coll., Walla Walla, Wash., 1981-82, rsch. assoc., 1983—, vis. asst. prof., 1983-87; program officer Polar Biology & Medicine Program, NSF, Washington, 1987-88; exec. dir. Am. Soc. Limnology and Oceanography, Walla Walla, 1990—. Assoc. editor Oceanography Mag., 1989-91; contbr. articles to profl. jours. Tchr. Harambee Sch., Migori, Kenya, 1969. Mem. AAAS, Am. Geophys. Union, Am. Soc. Limnology and Oceanography, Ecol. Soc. Am., Oceanography Soc., Sigma Xi (N.W. regional dir. 1991—, bd. dirs. 1991—). Office: Whitman Coll Dept Biology Walla Walla WA 99362

WEILER, DENNIS EDWARD, surgeon; b. Salt Lake City, Sept. 4, 1952; s. James Leo and Elizabeth Ann (Schlegel) W.; widowed, 1984; m. Dawn Marie Fitch, Jan. 28, 1989. BA, U. Minn., 1973, MD, 1978. Diplomate Am. Bd. Surgery. Mem. med. staff Mercy Med. Ctr., Nampa, Idaho, 1983—. Co-editor: Colossus, 1989. Mem. ACS (cancer liaison physician 1989-92, mem. trauma com. Idaho chpt. 1990—); mem. Soc. Am. Gastrointestinal Endoscopic Surgeons. Home: 3918 S Chicago St Nampa ID 83686

WEILER, DOROTHY ESSER, librarian; b. Hartford, Wis., Feb. 21, 1914; d. Henry Hugo and Agatha Christina (Dopp) Esser; A.B. in Fgn. Langs., Wash. State U., 1935; B.A.L., Grad. Library Sch., U. Wash., 1936; postgrad. U. Ariz., 1956-57, Ariz. State U., 1957-58, Grad. Sch. Librarianship, U. Denver, 1971; m. Henry C. Weiler, Aug. 30, 1937; children—Robert William, Kurt Walter. Tchr.-librarian Roosevelt Elem. Schs., Dist. #66, Phoenix, 1956-59; extension librarian Ariz. Dept. Library and Archives, Phoenix, 1959-67; library dir. City of Tempe (Ariz.), 1967-79; assoc. prof., dept. library sci. Ariz. State U., 1968; vis. faculty Mesa Community Coll., 1980-84. Mem. public relations com. United Fund; treas. Desert Samaritan Hosp. and Health Center Aux., 1981, v.p. community relations Hosp., 1982, vol. asst. chaplain, 1988—, pastoral care vol. Named Ariz. Librarian of Yr., 1971; recipient Silver Book award Library Binding Inst., 1963. Mem. Tempe Hist. Soc., Ariz. Pioneers Hist. Soc., Am. Radio Relay League, Am. Bus. Women's Assn., ALA, Southwestern Library Assn., Ariz. State Libr. Assn. (pres. 1973-74), Ariz. Libr. Pioneer. Roman Catholic. Clubs: Our Lady of Mt. Carmel Ladies' Sodality, Soroptimist Internat. Founder, editor Roadrunner, Tumbling Tumbleweed; contbr. articles to mags. Home: PO Box 26018 Tempe AZ 85285-6018

WEILERT, MATTHEW EDWARD, quality engineer, researcher; b. Topeka, Oct. 10, 1961; s. Otto Samuel and Evelyn Agnes (Paramore) W.; m. Donna Sheilah McCoy, Dec. 5, 1992; children: Heather Ann Hudon-McCoy. BS in Safety Engring., Tex. A & M U., 1985. Materials coord. Sharp Industries, Bastrop, Tex., 1978-90; with Weilert Info. Svc., Vallejo, Calif., 1988-90, Tri Cities, Wash., 1990-91; with Weilert Mktg., Tri Cities, 1991—; quality tng. engr. Battelle Pacific N.W. Labs., Richland, Wash., 1990—; cons. San Mateo County Contractor Bldg. Info. System, Redwood City, Calif., 1989. Author: The Echo, 1983, Sean's Quest, 1984, How Two What 4, Win Six, 1986. With USN, 1985-90. Recipient Bronze medal for paper competition ASME, 1984. Mem. KC (chair youth activities). Republican. Roman Catholic. Home: PO Box 3057 Richland WA 99352 Office: Batelle Pacific NW Labs PO Box 999 Mailstop P7-72 Richland WA 99352

WEILL, SAMUEL, JR., automobile company executive; b. Rochester, N.Y., Dec. 22, 1916; s. Samuel and Bertha (Stein) W.; student U. Buffalo, 1934-35; m. Mercedes Weil, May 20, 1939 (div. Aug. 1943); children: Rita and Eric (twins); m. Cléanthe Kimball Carr, Aug. 12, 1960 (div. 1982); m. Jacqueline Natalie Bateman, Jan. 5, 1983. Co-owner, Brayton Air Coll., St. Louis, 1937-42; assoc. editor, advt. mgr., bus. mgr. Road and Track Mag., Los Angeles, 1951-53; pres. Volkswagen Pacific, Inc., Culver City, Calif., 1953-73, Porsche Audi Pacific, Culver City, 1953-73; chmn. bd. Minto International, Inc., London; v.p. fin. Chieftain Oil Co., Ojai, Calif. Recipient Tom May award Jewish Hosp. and Research Center, 1971. Served with USAAF, 1943-45. Home: 305 Palomar Rd Ojai CA 93023-2432 Office: Chieftain Oil Co 214 W Aliso St Ojai CA 93023-2599

WEILLER, DAVID BARRY, music educator; b. Carlsbad, N.Mex., July 30, 1957. BA, Occidental Coll., 1979; MusM, U. Ill., 1982. Asst. prof. music U. Nev., Las Vegas, 1984—; dir. choral studies U. Nev., 1984—; prin. conductor Coll. Light Opera Co., Falmouth, Mass., 1980—. conductor of 3 univ. choral ensembles and numerous musical theatre prodns. Recipient William Morris award for excellence in teaching, U. Nevada, 1987. Mem. Am. Choral Dirs. Assn., Music Educators Nat. Conf., Nat. Assn. Tchrs. of Singing. Office: Music Dept U Nev Las Vegas 4505 S Maryland Pky Las Vegas NV 89154-0002

WEIMAN, MARK BERNARD, publisher, graphic designer; b. Phila., Oct. 18, 1950; s. Jerome Saul and Hassie Isabel (Lasensky) W. BA, U. Pa., 1972. Mng. editor Norwood Editions, Phila., 1972-78; owner, pub. Regent Press, Berkeley, Calif., 1978—. Bd. dirs. Arts and Edn. Media, Inc., Berkeley, 1990-92. Home: 2747 Regent St Berkeley CA 94608 Office: Regent Press 6020-A Adeline Oakland CA 94608

WEIMERS, LEIGH ALBERT, newspaper columnist; b. Napa, Calif., Nov. 11, 1935; s. Leigh and Stella Marie (Heflin) W.; m. Geraldine Louise Stone, Aug. 25, 1962; children: Kristin Louise, Karin Leigh. BA in Journalism, San Jose State Coll., 1958. Sports editor Napa Jour., 1952-53, Napa Register, 1954-55; reporter San Jose Mercury News, 1960-62, asst. city editor, 1962-65, columnist, 1965—; pres. Edgecombe Corp., Los Gatos, Calif., 1984-89. Author: Insider's Guide to Silicon Valley, 1986, 2d rev. edit., 1993, (with Gael Douglass) The Ghosts of Sarah Winchester, 1987. Bd. dirs. Redwood Mut. Water Co., Redwood Estates, Calif., 1965-66, Ctr. Living with Dying, San Jose, 1979-82, San Jose Trolley Corp., 1988, Villa Montalo Ctr. for Arts, 1988—, O'Connor Hosp. Found., 1991—. Served with U.S. Army, 1958-60. Mem. Newspaper Guild, San Jose State Alumni Assn. (bd. dirs. 1984-89), Rotary (bd. dirs. San Jose chpt. 1988-91), Sigma Chi. Home: 21661 Woolaroc Dr Los Gatos CA 95030-8940 Office: San Jose Mercury News 750 Ridder Park Dr San Jose CA 95190-0001

WEINBERG, D. MARK, health insurance company executive; b. Aug. 4, 1952; s. Melvin Weinberg; m. Allyson Weinberg; children: Amanda, Sarah, Tiffany, Sean. BS in Elec. Engring., U. Mo., 1975. Gen. mgr. CTX Products div. Pet, Inc., St. Louis, 1975-81; prin. Touche-Ross and Co., Chgo., 1981-87; exec. v.p. Blue Cross of Calif., Thousand Oaks, 1987—. Contbr. articles to profl. jours. Mem. exec. bd. United Way; pres. Sr. Alliance, Inc.; vice-chmn. Calif. Ins. Mktg. Svc., Inc. Mem. Conejo Valley C. of C. (bd. dirs.). Office: Blue Cross Calif 4553 Latienda Dr Thousand Oaks CA 93012

WEINBERG, HORST D., pediatrician; b. Halle, Germany, Feb. 28, 1928; came to U.S., 1946; s. Max H. and Kathe (Benjamin) W.; m. Carol M. DeSandre, 1956; children: David, Susan, Carla. BS, U. Mich., 1949; MD, U. Chgo., 1953. Diplomate Am. Bd. Pediatrics. Pediatrician Valley Children's Hosp., 1959-72, chief med. staff, 1970-72, med. dir. Intensive Care Unit, 1980-84, med. dir. acute care areas, 1993—; asst. clin. prof. U. Calif., San Francisco, 1981-88, assoc. clin. prof., 1988—; pvt. practice Fresno, 1959—. Contbr. articles to profl. jours. Flight surgeon USAF, 1955-57. Recipient Disting. Achievement award Am. Heart Assn., 1970. Mem. AMA, Am. Acad. Pediatrics, Calif. Med. Assn., Fresno Madera Med. Soc. Jewish.

WEINBERG, IRA JAY, interior designer; b. Los Angeles, Apr. 18, 1959; s. Jack and Roz (Candler) W.; m. Wendy Gates, Aug. 10, 1985. BS, Art Ctr. Coll. of Design, Pasadena, Calif., 1982. Jr. staff Milton Swimmer Planning and Design, Beverly Hills, Calif., 1977-79; space planner, designer Swimmer Cole Martinez & Curtis, Marina Del Rey, Calif., 1982-84, sr. designer, 1985-87; space planner, designer Robinson Mills & Williams, San Francisco, 1984-85; prin. Weinberg Design, West Hollywood, Calif., 1987—. Office: 516 N Harper Ave West Hollywood CA 90048-2223

WEINBERG, JOHN LEE, judge; b. Chgo., Apr. 24, 1941; s. Louis Jr. and Jane Kitz (Goldstein) W.; m. Sarah Kibbee, July 6, 1963; children: Ruth, Leo. BA, Swarthmore Coll., 1962; JD, U. Chgo., 1965. Bar: Ill. 1966, Wash. 1967, U.S. Dist. Ct. (we. dist.) Wash. 1967, U.S. Ct. Appeals (9th cir.) 1967. Law clk. to Hon. Henry L. Burman Ill. Appellate Ct., Chgo., 1965-66; law clk. to Hom. Walter V. Schaefer Ill. Supreme Ct., Chgo., 1966; law clk. to Hon. William T. Beeks U.S. Dist. Ct. Wash., Seattle, 1967-68; atty. Perkins Coie Law Firm, Seattle, 1968-73; judge U.S Magistrate Ct., Seattle, 1973—. Author: Federal Bail and Detention Handbook, 1988. Mem. ABA, Am. Judicature Soc., Wash. State Bar Assn., Seattle-King County Bar Assn., Fed. Magistrate Judges Assn. (nat. pres. 1982-83). Office: US Magistrate Judge 407 US Courthouse 1010 5th Ave Seattle WA 98104

WEINBERG, WILLIAM HENRY, chemical engineer, chemical physicist, educator; b. Columbia, S.C., Dec. 5, 1944; s. Ulrich Vivian and Ruth Ann (Duncan) W. BS, U. S.C., 1966; PhD in Chem. Engring, U. Calif., Berkeley, 1970; NATO postdoctoral fellow in phys. chemistry, Cambridge U., Eng., 1971. Asst. prof. chem. engring. Calif. Inst. Tech., 1972-74, asso. prof., 1974-77, prof. chem. engring. and chem. physics, 1977-89, Chevron disting. prof. chem. engring. and chem. physics, 1981-86; prof. chem. engring. and chemistry U. Calif., Santa Barbara, 1989—, assoc. dean Coll. Engring., 1992—; vis. prof. chemistry Harvard U., 1980, U. Pitts., 1987-88, Oxford U., 1991; Alexander von Humboldt Found. fellow U. Munich, 1982; cons. E.I. DuPont Co. Author: (with Van Hove and Chan) Low-Energy Electron Diffraction, 1986; editor 4 books in field; mem. editorial bd. Jour. Applications Surface Sci., 1977-85, Handbook Surfaces and Interfaces, 1978-80, Surface Sci. Reports, 1980—, gen. editor, 1992—, Applied Surface Sci., 1991—, Langmuir, 1990—, Surface Sci., 1992—; contbr. articles to profl. jours., chpts. to books. Recipient Giuseppe Parravano award Mich. Catalysis Soc., 1989; fellow NSF, 1966-69, Alfred P. Sloan Found., 1976-78, Camille and Henry Dreyfus Found. fellow 1976-81. Fellow Am. Phys. Soc. (Nottingham prize 1973); mem. AAAS, Am. Chem. Soc. (LaMer award 1973, Kendall award 1991), Am. Inst. Chem. Engrs. (Colburn award 1981), Am. Vacuum Soc., N.Am. Catalysis Soc., Phi Beta Kappa, Sigma Xi. Home: 877 Summit Rd Santa Barbara CA 93108-2321 Office: U Calif Dept Chem & Nuclear Engring Santa Barbara CA 93106

WEINBERGER, FRANK, information systems advisor; b. Chgo., Sept. 18, 1926; s. Rudolph and Elaine (Kellner) W.; m. Beatrice Natalie Fixler, June 27, 1953; children: Alan J., Bruce I. BSEE, Ill. Inst. of Tech., 1951; MBA, Northwestern U., Evanston, 1959. Registered profl. engr., Ill, Calif. Engr. Admiral Corp., Chgo., 1951-53; sr. engr. Cook Rsch., Chgo., 1953-59; mem. tech. staff Rockwell Internat., Downey, Calif., 1959-80, info. systems advisor, 1980—. Pres. Temple Israel, Long Beach, Calif., 1985-87, bd. dirs. 1973-85. With USN, 1944-46. Mem. Assn. for Computer Machinery. Democrat. Jewish. Home: 3231 Yellowtail Dr Los Alamitos CA 90720 Office: Rockwell Internat 12214 Lakewood Blvd Downey CA 90241

WEINER, DORA B., medical humanities educator; b. Furth, Germany, 1924; d. Ernest and Emma (Metzger) Bierer; m. Herbert Weiner, 1953; children—Timothy, Richard, Antony. Baccalaureat, U. Paris, 1941; B.A. magna cum laude, Smith Coll., 1945; M.A., Columbia U., 1946, Ph.D., 1951. Lectr. gen. studies Columbia U., N.Y.C., 1949-50, instr., 1950-52, vis. lectr. Tchrs. Coll., 1962-63; instr. Barnard Coll., 1952-56; fellow in history of medicine Johns Hopkins U., Balt., 1956-57; mem. faculty dept. social sci. Sarah Lawrence Coll., 1958-62; asst. prof. history Manhattanville Coll., 1964-65, assoc. prof., 1966-78, prof., 1978-82; adj. prof. med. humanities UCLA Sch. Medicine, Los Angeles, 1982—, prof., 1987—; cons. and lectr. in field. Author: Raspail: Scientist and Reformer, 1968; The Clinical Training of Doctors: An Essay of 1793, 1980, The Citizen-Patient in Revolutionary and Imperial Paris, 1993; co-editor: From Parnassus; Essays in Honor of Jacques Barzun, 1976; contbr. chpts. to books, articles to profl. jours. Grantee numerous profl. and ednl. instns. Mem. Am. Hist. Assn. (nominating com. 1979-82, Leo Gershoy award com. 1985-88), AAUP, Am. Assn. History Medicine (past mem. numerous coms.), Soc. 18th Century Studies, Soc. for French Hist. Studies (exec. com. 1978-81), History of Sci. Soc. Office: UCLA 12-138 Ctr Health Scis Los Angeles CA 90024

WEINER, NORMAN, pharmacology educator; b. Rochester, N.Y., July 13, 1928; m. Diana Elaine Weiner, 1955; children: Steven, David, Jeffrey, Gareth, Eric. BS, U. Mich., 1949; MD, Harvard U., 1953. Diplomate Am. Bd. Med. Examiners. Intern 2d and 4th Harvard Med. Svc., Boston City Hosp., 1953-54; rsch. med. officer USAF, 1954-56; instr. dept. pharmacology-biochemistry Sch. of Aviation Medicine, San Antonio, 1954-56; instr. dept. pharmacology, biochemistry Sch. Aviation Medicine, San Antonio, 1954-56; from instr. to asst. prof. Harvard Med. Sch., Boston, 1956-67; prof. pharmacology U. Colo. Health Sci. Ctr., Denver, 1967—; chmn. dept. pharmacology U. Colo. Health Sci., Denver, 1967-87; interim dean U. Colo. Sch. Medicine, 1983-84; vis. prof. U. Calif., Berkeley, 1973-76; div. v.p. Abbott Labs., Abbott Park, Ill., 1985-87, disting. Volwiler rsch. fellow, 1988; Allan D. Bass lectr. Vanderbilt U. Sch. Medicine, Nashville, 1983; Pfizer lectr. Tex. Coll. Osteo. Medicine, Ft. Worth, 1985; disting. prof. U. Colo., 1989. ecipient rsch. career devel. award USPHS, 1963, award Kaiser Permanente, 1974, 81; spl. fellow USPHS, London, 1961-62. . Recipient rsch. career devel. award USPHS, 1963, award Kaiser Permanente, 1974, 81; spl. fellow USPHS, London, 1961-62. Mem. AAAS, Am. Soc. for Pharmacology and Exptl. Therapeutics (Otto Krayer award 1985), N.Y. Acad. Scis., Assn. Med. Sch. Pharmacology, Am. Soc. Neurochemistry, Western Pharmacology Soc., Am. Coll. Neuropsychopharmacology, Soc. Neurosci., Biochem. Soc., Internat. Brain Rsch. Orgn., Internat. Soc. Neurochemistry, Rsch. Soc. on Alcoholism, Phi Beta Kappa, Sigma Xi, Alpha Omega Alpha, Phi Eta Sigma, Phi Lambda Upsilon, Phi Kappa Phi. Office: U Colo Health Sci Ctr 4200 E 9th Ave Rm C236 Denver CO 80262-0001

WEINER, RICHARD S., healthcare administrator; b. Yonkers, N.Y., July 14, 1951; s. Joseph and Muriel (Zucker) W.; m. Kathryn, Aug. 25, 1985; children: Jason C., Rebecca E. BA, U. Del., 1976, MC, 1978, PhD, 1981. Nat. cert. counselor, crt. behavioral medicine, mediator; diplomate med. psychotherapy, profl. counseling; diplomate in pain mgmt. Exec. dir. Inst. Pain Mgmt., Ceres, 1983-90; assoc. dir. planning Meml. Hosp., Ceres, Calif., 1987-90; exec. dir. Am. Acad. Pain Mgmt., 1988—. Contbr. articles to profl. jours. Hon. citizen ambassador Med. Exch. Program to People's Republic China, coleader to Russia, Czechoslovakia, Hungary, Vietnam, Singapore, Thailand. Mem. Am. Pain Soc. (profl. edn. com.), Am. Mental Health Counseling (editorial rev. bd.). Home: 2601 Pinot Ln Modesto CA 95356-0616

WEINHEIMER, ANDREW JOHN, scientist; b. Richmond, Va., Aug. 29, 1953; s. Alfred J. and Kathryn (Westrick) W.; m. Sue Lynn Eyler, Sept. 16, 1989. BS, Duke U., 1975; MS, Rice U., 1979, PhD, 1980. Rsch. assoc. Rice U., Houston, 1980-83; scientist Nat. Ctr. for Atmospheric Rsch., Boulder, Colo., 1983—. Mem. Am. Meterol. Soc., Am. Geophys. Union, Phi Beta Kappa, Sigma Xi. Office: Nat Ctr Atmospheric Rsch PO Box 3000 Boulder CO 80307-3000

WEINHOLD, ALBERT RAYMOND, plant pathologist; b. Evans, Colo., Feb. 14, 1931; s. Albert Raymond and Ruth Evelyn (Stocks) W.; m. Connie Marie Seastrand, Mar. 15, 1952; children: Albert Raymond, Kathryn Beth. BS, Colo. State U., 1953, MS, 1955; PhD, U. Calif., Davis, 1958. Asst. prof. to prof. plant pathology U. Calif., Berkeley, 1960-93; prof. emeritus U. Calif., 1993—, chmn. dept. plant pathology, 1976-84, acting dean Coll. Natural Resources, 1984-86. Contbr. articles to profl. jours., chpts. to books; editor-in-chief Phytopathology, 1973-76. 1st Lt. USAF, 1958-60. Mem. AAAS, Am. Phytopathol. Soc. (pres. 1987-88); mem. Mira Vista Golf and Country Club (dir. 1989-92, pres. 1991-92). Republican. Presbyterian. Home: 213 Arlington Ave Kensington CA 94707-1401 Office: University of California Dept Plant Pathology Berkeley CA 94720

WEINMANN, ROBERT LEWIS, neurologist; b. Newark, Aug. 21, 1935; s. Isadore and Etta (Silverman) W.; m. Diana Weinmann, Dec. 13, 1980 (dec. Dec. 1989); children: Paul, Chris, Dana, Paige. BA, Yale U., 1957; MD, Stanford U., 1962. Diplomate Am. Bd. of EEG and Neurophysiology, v.p.; diplomate Am. Acad. Pain Mgmt. Intern Pacific Presbyn. Med. Ctr., San Francisco, 1962-63; resident in neurology Stanford U. Hosp., 1963-66, chief resident, 1965-66; pvt. practice San Jose, Calif., 1969—. Chmn. editorial bd. Clin. EEG Jour.; mem. editorial bd. Jour. Am. Acad. Pain Mgmt.; formerly mem. editorial bd. Clin. Evoked Potentials Jour.; contbr. articles to various publs. Capt. M.C., U.S. Army, 1966-68, Japan. Award recipient State of R.I., Santa Clara County Med. Soc., Epilepsy Soc., other orgns.; fellow Univ. Paris, 1957-58. Union of Am. Physicians and Dentists (pres. 1990—, bd. dirs. 1972—, pres. Calif. fedn. 1990—). Office: Union Am Physicians & Dentists 1330 Broadway Ste 730 Oakland CA 94612-2506

WEINREB, BRADLEY ALLEN, deputy attorney general; b. Great Neck, N.Y., Sept. 29, 1966; s. Marshall Alan and Marcia Lee (Saltsburg) W.; m. Lisa Beth Selbst, Aug. 13, 1989. MA in Govt., U. Tex., 1988; JD, U. San Diego, 1991. Bar: Calif. 1991. Dep. atty. gen. Office of Atty. Gen., San Diego, 1992—. Assoc. editor Journal of Contemporary Legal Issues, 1991. Assoc. mem. San Diego County Rep., 1992. Mem. Nat. Trial Team, 1991, Nat. App. Moot Ct. Bd., 1991. Mem. State Bar Calif., Federalist Soc. (San Diego chpt. lawyers rep. 1992—, v.p. 1992—). Office: Office of Atty Gen 110 West A St Ste 700 San Diego CA 92101

WEINRICH, JAMES DONALD, psychobiologist, educator; b. Cleve., July 2, 1950; s. Albert James and Helen (Lautz) W. AB, Princeton U., 1972; PhD, Harvard U., 1976. Postdoctoral fellow, then instr. Johns Hopkins U., Balt., 1980-82; rsch. assoc., then asst. rsch. prof. psychiatry Boston U., 1983-87; asst. rsch. psychobiologist, project mgr. U. Calif., San Diego, 1987-89, asst. rsch. psychobiologist, ctr. mgr., 1989-91, sr. investigator sexology, 1991—; bd. dirs. Found. Sci. Study of Sexuality, Mt. Vernon, Iowa. Author: Sexual Landscapes, 1987; co-editor: Homosexuality: Social, Psychological and Biological Issues, 1982, Homosexuality: Research Implications for Public Policy, 1991. Mem. Internat. Acad. Sex Rsch., Soc. for Sci. Study of Sex (Hugo Beigel award 1987), Am. Coll. Sexologists (cert.), Phi Beta Kappa. Office: Univ Calif San Diego 2760 5th Ave Rm 200 San Diego CA 92103-6325

WEINSHIENK, ZITA LEESON, federal judge; b. St. Paul, Apr. 3, 1933; d. Louis and Ada (Dubov) Leeson; m. Hubert Troy Weinshienk, July 8, 1956 (dec. 1983); children: Edith Blair, Kay Anne, Darcy Jill; m. James N. Schaffner, Nov. 15, 1986. Student, U. Colo., 1952-53; BA magna cum laude, U. Ariz., 1955; JD cum laude, Harvard U., 1958; Fulbright grantee, U. Copenhagen, Denmark, 1959; LHD (hon.), Loretto Heights Coll., 1985; LLD (hon.), U. Denver, 1990. Bar: Colo. 1959. Probation counselor, legal adviser, referee Denver Juvenile Ct., 1959-64; judge Denver County Ct., 1964-71; Denver dist. judge, 1972-79, U.S. dist. judge for dist. Colo., 1979—. Precinct committeewoman Denver Democratic Com., 1963-64; bd. dirs. Crime Stoppers. Named one of 100 Women in Touch with Our Time Harper's Bazaar Mag., 1971, Woman of Yr., Denver Bus. and Profl. Women, 1969; recipient Women Helping Women award Soroptimist Internat. of Denver, 1983, Hanna G. Solomon award Nat. Coun. Jewish Women, Denver, 1986. Fellow Colo. Bar Found., Am. Bar Found.; mem. ABA, Denver Bar Assn., Colo. Bar Assn., Nat. Conf. Fed. Trial Judges (exec. com.), Dist. Judges' Assn. of 10th Cir. (past pres.), Colo. Women's Bar Assn., Fed. Judges Assn., Denver Crime Stoppers Inc. (bd.dirs.), Devner LWV, Women's Forum Colo., Harvard Law Sch. Assn., Phi Beta Kappa, Phi Kappa Phi, Order of Coif (hon. Colo. chpt.). Office: US Dist Ct 1929 Stout St Denver CO 80294-2900*

WEINSTEIN, ALLAN M., medical device company executive; b. Bklyn., June 25, 1945; s. Henry I. Weinstein and Hannah L. (Broidy) Glasser; m. Phyllis Fishman, Aug. 28, 1965; children: Craig, Brett, Danielle. BS, Poly. Inst., Bklyn., 1965, MS, 1966, PhD, 1972. Registered profl. engr. Postdoctoral fellow U. Pa., Phila., 1971-72; asst. prof. Clemson U., 1972-75; prof., dir. biomaterials Tulane U., New Orleans, 1975-81; v.p. tech. affairs Intermedics Orthopaedics, Dublin, Calif., 1981-83, also bd. dirs.; pres., chief exec. officer Harrington Arthritis Rsch. Ctr., Phoenix, 1983-87; co-founder, chmn., pres., chief exec. officer OrthoLogic Corp., Phoenix, 1987—. Editor: spl. publs. 472, 601, Nat. Bur. Standards, 1977, 81; contbr. numerous articles to profl. jours. Patentee (3) in field. Rsch. grantee NIH, 1973-93. Mem. Soc. for Biomaterials (charter mem., pres. 1985-86), Orthopaedic Rsch. Soc., Am. Soc. Metals, N.Y. Acad. Scis., Sigma Xi. Republican. Jewish. Home: 6019 E Indian Bend Rd Paradise Valley AZ 85253-3437 Office: OrthoLogic Corp 2850 S 36th St Phoenix AZ 85034

WEINSTOCK, GEORGE A., security alarm manufacturing company; b. Cleve., Oct. 4, 1937; s. Morris Fred and Anne (Orner) W.; m. Linda Jane Katz, Mar. 13, 1960; children: David, Jennifer, Amy. With Morse Signal Devices of Calif. Inc., Los Angeles, 1955-81, pres., dir., 1969-81; pres., dir. Morse Signal Devices, Oxnard, Calif., 1970-81, Morse Signal Devices of Ohio, Cleve., 1969-74; exec. v.p., dir. Morse Security Group, Sylmar, Calif., 1969-92; ptnr. Ans-R-Tel Answering Service, San Diego, 1957-83; v.p., dir. Am. Home Security, Van Nuys, Calif., 1983-84, pres., chief exec. officer, 1984—; ptnr. Weinstock Co. I, 1967—, Weinstock Co. II, 1978—, The Grill Restaurant, Beverly Hills, Calif., 1983—; mem. Blue Ribbon com. Los Angeles Police Commn., 1969, liaison com. alarm industry and Law Enforcement Administrv. Agy., 1972-73; participant industry adv. conf. Burglary Protection Systems and Services of Underwriters' Labs., Inc., 1969-76; bd. dirs., mktg. com., audit com., mem. exec. com. Charter Nat. Bank. Bd. dirs., mem. budget/fin. com., planning com. Rancho Encino Hosp., 1985-88, chmn. search com., 1985; bd. dirs. Temple Shir Chadash Bldg./Land Planning Corp., 1986-87, chmn. project coord. com., 1988-90; mem. Found. for the Jr. Blind, Jr. Diabetes Assn., The Guardians of the Jewish Home for the Aged. Sgt. USAF, 1958-63. Recipient Certifications of Appreciation Internat. Security Conf., 1967, Nat. Police Officers Assn., 1971; named Hon. Citizen City New Orleans, 1974. Mem. Nat. Burglar and Fire Alarm Assn. (chmn. industry regulations com. 1969-71, grievance com. 1971-72, govt. liaison com. 1974-75, nominating com. 1976-77, pres. 1973-74, Western v.p. 1971-72, executor Morris F. Weinstock Meml. Man-of-the-Yr. award 1970—, award of appreciation 1974), Western Burglar and Fire Alarm Assn. (chmn. pub. relations com. 1971-72, industry regulations com. 1972-73, by-lawd com. 1984—, dir. exec. com. 1978-84, mem. govt. leaison com. 1973-74, pres. 1976-77, v.p. so. region 1973-74, Disting. Services award 1977), Cen. Sta. Electrical Protection Assn. (chmn. city and state ordinance com. 1971-72, bd. dirs. 1972-73), Nat. Assn. Pvt. Security Vaults (bd. dirs. 1982-84), Am. Soc. Indsl. Security, Calif. Automatic Fire Alarm Assn., Nat. Safety Council, Hollywood C. of C., Stanford Alumni Assn., Brandeis Inst. Alumni Assn., Am. Philatelic Soc., Porsche Club Am., Sunrise Alejo Property Owners Assn. (bd. dirs. 1984-86). Office: Am Home Security 7650 Gloria Ave Van Nuys CA 91406-1805

WEINSTOCK, RONALD JAY, research and development company executive; b. L.A., Mar. 14, 1960; s. Howard Frank and Anne Carol (Schneider) W.; m. Sigrid Lipsett, June 11, 1988; children: Rachel, Brent. Student, U. Calif., San Diego, 1978-80, U. Calif., Santa Barbara, 1980-81. CEO Magnetic Resonance Diagnostics Corp., Thousand Oaks, Calif., 1989—; vice chmn. Magnetic Resonance Rsch. Soc., Tokyo, 1991—; lectr. in field. Co-developer Magnetic Resonance Analyzer; contbr. articles to profl. jours. CPR instr. Am. Heart Assn., Beverly Hills, 1981; EMT, UCLA, 1980.

WEINTRAUB, ARDEN LOREN, psychiatrist; b. L.A., Dec. 22, 1949; s. Henry Herbert and Mildred M. (Meyerson) W.; m. Margarita Elvira Plummer, Jan. 31, 1971 (div. Aug. 1975); 1 child, Kim Pascha; m. Becky Ann Tolley, June 18, 1977. BS Biology, Idaho State U., 1976; MD, U. Utah Sch. Medicine, 1981. Diplomate Am. Bd. Med. Examiners. Internship U. Utah, Salt Lake City, 1982, gen. psychiatry, 1983-85, child psychiatry fellow, 1982-83,85-86; child psychiatrist Valley Mental Health, Salt Lake City, 1986—; clin. dir. Tooele County (Utah) Mental Health Ctr., 1986-89, cons. Human Affairs Internat., Salt Lake City, 1990—. Bd. dirs. Oquirrh Hills Found., Tooele, Utah. Recipient rsch. grant, U. Utah Sch. Medicine, 1978. Mem. Intermountain Acad. Child and Adolescent Psychiatry (pres. 1989-91), Am. Acad. Child and Adolescent Psychiatry, Am. Psychiatric Assn., Utah Psychiatric Assn. Office: 501 Chipeta Way Ste 1670 Salt Lake City UT 84108

WEINY, GEORGE AZEM, physical education educator, consultant; b. Keokuk, Iowa, July 24, 1930; s. George Dunn and Emma Vivian (Kraushaar) W.; m. Jane Louise Eland, Sept. 29, 1956 (div. 1985); children: Tami L., Tomas A., Aaron A., Arden G.; m. Lori Arlene Rowe, Aug. 6, 1985; children: Austin George, Breck Philip. BA, Iowa Wesleyan Coll., 1957; MA, State U. Iowa, 1962; PhD, U. Beverly Hills, 1980. Phys. dir. YMCA, Keokuk, 1956-57; asst. dir. pub. relations Iowa Wesleyan Coll., Mt. Pleasant, Iowa, 1957-58; prin., tchr., coach Hillsboro (Iowa) High Sch., 1958-59; tchr., coach Burlington (Iowa) High Sch. and Jr. Coll., 1959-62, Pacific High Sch., San Bernardino, Calif., 1962-67; prof. phys. edn. Calif. State U., San Bernardino, 1967—; ednl. cons. Belau Modekngei Sch., West Caroline Islands, 1984-85; swim meet dir. Nat. Collegiate Athletic Assn., 1982-84, 86-94; tng. dir. for ofcls. So. Calif. Aquatics Fedn., 1967-78; asst. swim coach Calif. State U., Chico, 1979, guest lectr. summer program water safety & mainstreaming spl. populations Calif. State U., San Bernardino, 1990-93; scuba tour guide Dive Maui Resort, Hawaii, 1982-83; salvage diver U.S. Trust Territories, 1973; coach YMCA swim team, San Bernardino, 1962-77, 84-94. Editor: Swimming Rules and Case Studies, 1970-73; author: Snorkeling Fun for Everyone, 1982; contbr. articles to profl. jours. Mem. county water safety com. ARC, San Bernardino, 1968-80, 88-90, 91-93; bd. dirs. YMCA, San Bernardino, 1970-77; mem. Bicentennial Commn., San Bernardino, 1975-76. Sgt. 1st class U.S. Army, 1953-55, Iowa NG, 1955-58. Decorated Combat Infantryman's badge, Good Conduct medal, Nat. Def. Svc. medal, Korean Svc. medal, UN Svc. medal, Presdl. Unit citation; recipient Outstanding Svc. award So. Calif. Aquatics Fedn., 1978. Mem. ARC Water Safety (40-yr. Outstanding Svc. award 1990), Profl. Assn. Diving Instrs. (cert.), Nat. Assn. Underwater Instrs. (cert.), Am. Assn. Health Phys. Edn. Recreation and Dance, Coll. Swim Coaches Assn. Am. (25 Yr. Svc. award 1987), Nat. Fedn. Interscholastic Ofcls. Assn. (25 yr. award 1991), Am. Swim Coaches Assn. (cert.), Nat. Interscholastic Swim Coaches Assn. (25yr. Svc. award 1985), Sea Sons Dive Club (Rialto Calif., pres. 1982-83, sec. 1983-92, Diver of Yr. award 1983, 87, 91). Home: PO Box 30393 San Bernardino CA 92413-0393 Office: Calif State U 5500 University Pky San Bernardino CA 92407-2318

WEIR, ALEXANDER, JR., utility consultant, inventor; b. Crossett, Ark., Dec. 19, 1922; s. Alexander and Mary Eloise (Field) W.; m. Florence Forschner, Dec. 28, 1946; children: Alexander III, Carol Jean, Bruce Richard. BSChemE, U. Ark., 1943; MChemE, Poly Inst. Bklyn., 1946; PhD, U. Mich., 1954; cert., U. So. Calif. Grad. Sch. Bus. Adminstrn., 1968. Chem. engr. Am. Cyanamid Co., Stamford Rsch. Labs., 1943-47; with U. Mich., 1948-58; rsch. assoc., project supr. Engring. Research Inst., U. Mich., 1948-57; lectr. chem. and metall. engring. dept. U. Mich., 1954-56, asst. prof., 1956-58; cons. Ramo-Wooldridge Corp., Los Angeles, 1956-57, mem. tech. staff, sect. head, asst. mgr., 1957-60, incharge Atlas Missile Captive test program, 1956-60; tech. adv. to pres. Northrop Corp., Beverly Hills, Calif., 1960-70; prin. scientist for air quality So. Calif. Edison Co., Los Angeles, 1970-76, mgr. chem. systems research and devel., 1976-86, chief research scientist, 1986-88; utility cons. Playa Del Rey, Calif., 1988—; rep. Am. Rocket Soc. to Detroit Nuclear Council, 1954-57; chmn. session on chem. reactions Nuclear Sci. and Engring. Congress, Cleve., 1955; U.S. del. AGARD (NATO) Combustion Colloquium, Liege, Belgium, 1955; Western U.S. rep. task force on environ. research and devel. goals Electric Research Council, 1971; electric utility advisor Electric Power Research Inst., 1974-78, 84-87; industry advisor Dept. Chemistry and Biochemistry Calif. State U., Los Angeles, 1981-88. Author: Two and Three Dimensional Flow of Air through Square-Edged Sonic Orifices, 1954; (with R.B. Morrison and T.C. Anderson) Notes on Combustion, 1955, also tech. papers; inventor acid rain prevention device used in 5 states. Bd. govs., past pres. Civic Union Playa del Rey, chmn. sch., police and fire, nominating, civil def., army liaison coms; mem. Senate, Westchester YMCA, chmn. Dads sponsoring com., active fundraising; chmn. nominating com. Paseco del Rey Sch. PTA, 1961; mem. Los Angeles Mayors Community Adv. Com.; asst. chmn. advancement com., merit badge dean Cantinella dist. Los Angeles Area council Boy Scouts Am. Recipient Nat. Rsch. Coun. Flue Gas Desulfurization Industrials Scale Reliability award NAS, 1975, Power Environ. Achievement award EPA, 1980, Excellence in Sulfur Dioxide Control award EPA, 1985. Mem. Am. Geophys. Union, Navy League U.S. (v.p. Palos Verdes Peninsula council 1961-62), N.Y. Acad. Scis., Sci. Research Soc. Am., Am. Chem. Soc., Am. Inst. Chem. Engrs., U.S. Power Squadron, Sigma Xi, Phi Kappa Phi, Phi Lambda Upsilon, Alpha Chi Sigma, Lambda Chi Alpha. Club: Santa Monica Yacht. Office: 8229 Billowvista Dr Playa Del Rey CA 90293-7807

WEIR, JIM DALE, small business owner; b. Phoenix, Feb. 2, 1956; s. Jim Earl and Laverne Alice (Mahan) W.; m. Myra Yvonne Anglin, July 19, 1980; children: Justin, Kevin, Amanda, Jordan. Student, Phoenix Coll., 1978; BS, Grand Canyon Coll., 1980. Owner Quality S Mfg., Phoenix, 1980—. Vol. Tempe (Ariz.) Ch. of the Nazarene, 1987-89, Latin Am. Ch. of the Nazarene, Phoenix, 1988-89. Recipient Key of City award Phoenix, 1987, Fast Growth award Inc. mag., 1988. Republican. Home: PO Box 23910 Phoenix AZ 85063-3910

WEIR, MAURICE DEAN, mathematics educator; b. Seattle, June 6, 1939; s. William Deo and Flora Ann (Beaudin) W.; m. Mary Gale Hempstead, Dec. 26, 1961; children: Maia Deborah, Renee Elizabeth. BA, Whitman Coll., 1961; MS, Carnegie Inst. Tech., 1963; ArtsD, Carnegie-Mellon U., 1970. Instr. Whitman Coll., Walla Walla, Wash., 1963-66; from asst. prof. to prof. math., assoc. dean instrn. Naval Postgrad. Sch., Monterey, Calif., 1969—; vis. prof. math. U.S. Mil. Acad., West Point, N.Y., 1985-86. Author: Differential Equations, 1991, Calculus Student Guide, 4th edit., 1992, Mathematical Modeling with Minitab, 1987, A First Course in Math Modeling, 1985. Recipient Outstanding Civilian Svc. U.S. Mil. Acad., West Point, N.Y., 1986, John Jay Schieffelin for Excellence in Teaching Naval Postgrad. Sch., Monterey, Calif., 1983. Mem. Math. Assn. Am. (vice chmn. no. Calif. sect.), Soc. Sigma Xi. Mem. Unitarian. Office: Naval Postgrad Sch Dept Math Monterey CA 93943

WEIR, MICHAEL ROSS, pediatrician; b. Austin, Tex., Dec. 30, 1942. BA, Harvard U., 1965; MD, U. Tex., 1969. Diplomate Am. Bd. Pediatrics. Commnd. 2d lt. U.S. Army, 1968, advanced through grades to col., 1983; intern Letterman Army Med. Ctr., San Francisco, 1969-70, resident in pediatrics, 1970-72; chief pediatrics U.S. Army Hosp., Vicenza, Italy, 1972-76, chief outpatient clinic, 1973-74, staff pediatric nephrologist, 1976-87; chief pediatric outpatient svc. William Beaumont Army Med. Ctr., El Paso, 1978-82, asst. chief dept. pediatrics, 1982-84, chief. dept. clin. investigation, 1984-87, dir. pediatric/medicine residency program, 1984-87; chief dept. pediatrics, pediatric program dir. Madigan Army Med. Ctr., Tacoma, Wash., 1987-91, dep. comdr. for clin. svcs., dir. med. edn., 1991-92, dir. grad. med. edn., 1992—; affiliated asst. prof. Uniformed Svcs. U Health

Scis., 1980-86, assoc. clin. prof., 1986-91, clin. prof., 1991—; assoc. clin. prof. U. Wash., 1987—, U. N.Mex., 1980-87, Tex. Tech U., 1976-77; adj. assoc. prof. biol. scis. U. Tex., El Paso, 1985-87; speaker, presenter in field. Contbr. numerous articles to profl. jours. Nephrology fellow U. Tex., 1979; recipient Robert Skelton award, 1972. Fellow Am. Acad. Pediatrics; mem. Alpha Omega Alpha, Mu Delta, Sigma Xi.

WEISBAUM, RICHARD BRUCE, business owner; b. Chgo., Jan. 20, 1936; s. Norman Lewis and Vera Francis (Gubricky) W.; m. Joanne Margret Hahn, May 23, 1959; children: Karen Anne, Richard Bruce II. BS, U. Ill., 1958. Sales rep. CPC Internat., Chgo., 1958-68; mktg. specialist Anheuser-Busch, St. Louis, 1968-72; sales mgr. Boise Cascade, Portland, Oreg., 1972-81; owner The Lamp Gallery, Beaverton, Oreg., 1979—, RBW & Assocs., Portland, 1981—. Mem. exec. coun. Mazamas, Portland, 1990. With USAF, 1960-61. 0em. Inst. Food Technologists (emeritus), Am. Assn. Cereal Chemists, Rotary (local treas. 1992—, Paul Harris fellow), Pi Kappa Alpha Found. Home: 3483 SW Patton Rd Portland OR 97201 Office: RBW & Assocs PO Box 698 Portland OR 97207

WEISBROD, KEN (JOSEPH LOUIS WEISBROD), marketing professional; b. Los Angeles, July 31, 1957; s. Louis Isadore and Dolores Joan (Adamczyk) W.; m. Kary Lin Shirley, Jan. 25, 1992; 1 child, Katherine Irene. Cert., Gemological Inst. Am, 1988. Jewelry designer House of Time Jewelers, Granada Hills, Calif., 1968-79; pres. Ken Weisbrod Prodns., Inc., Chatsworth, Calif., 1979-85; v.p. The Ramolap Co., Chatsworth, 1985—; dir. prodn. Katherine's of Broadway Market, Chatsworth, 1987—. Designer jewelry for numerous art exhibits, 1969-75. Mem. Greater L.A. Zoo Assn., Publ. Prodn. Club So. Calif. Democrat. Roman Catholic. Office: Ramolap Co PO Box 5359 Chatsworth CA 91313-5359

WEISBROD, MARK EDWARD, communications inspector, consultant; b. Washington, Oct. 1, 1954; s. Fred Edgar and Ann Marie (Rossiter) W.; m. Marie Terry Steelmon, Aug. 25, 1984 (div. June 1986). Student, U. So. Colo., 1976. Constrn. supr. Kentron Internat., Jubail, Saudi Arabia, 1981-83, Ford Aerospace & Comms., Cairo, 1983-85; contract inspector Butler Telecommunications, various, 1985-88; contract coord. Butler Telecommunications, L.A., 1989-91, cons., 1992—; BICS engr. Carrol Engring., Wichita, Kans., 1988; project engr. Lightwave Spectrum, Point Pleasant, N.J., 1989; contract instpector Bentheimer Engring., Anchorage, 1992; cons. Sub Sub, Inc., L.A., 1989-91. Artist: (water color) Ship At Bay, 1969 (Hon. mention award 1969). With U.S. Army, 1972-75. Republican. Roman Catholic. Home: 505 Starlite Dr Pueblo CO 81005 Office: Butler Telecom 9212 W Royal Ln Irving TX 75063

WEISENBURGER, THEODORE MAURICE, judge, poet; b. Tuttle, N.D., May 12, 1930; s. John and Emily (Rosenau) W.; children: Sam, Jennifer, Emily, Todd, Daniel, Dwight, Holly, Michael, Paul, Peter; m. Maylyne Chu, Sept. 19, 1985; 1 child, Irene. BA, U. N.D., 1952, LLB, 1956, JD, 1969; BFT, Am. Grad. Sch. Internat. Mgmt., Phoenix, 1957. Bar: N.D. 1963, U.S. Dist. Ct. N.D. 1963. County judge Benson County, Minnewaukan, N.D., 1968-75, Walsh County, Grafton, N.D., 1975-87; tribal judge Devils Lake Sioux, Ft. Totten, N.D., 1968-84, Turtle Mountain Chippewa, Belcourt, N.D., 1974—; U.S. magistrate U.S. Dist. Ct., Minnewaukan, 1972-75; Justice of the Peace pro tem Maricopa County, Ariz., 1988—; instr. Rio Salado C.C., 1992—; tchr. in Ethiopia, 1958-59. 1st lt. U.S. Army, 1952-54. Author: Poetry and Other Poems, 1991. Recipient Humanitarian award U.S. Cath. Conf., 1978, 82, Right to Know award Sigma Delta Chi, 1980, Spirit of Am. award U.S. Conf. Bishops, 1982. Home: 17801 N 35th Pl Phoenix AZ 85032-1308

WEISER, FRANK ALAN, lawyer; b. L.A., Dec. 12, 1953; s. Carl and Rose (Klein) W.; m. Susan Koenig, Aug. 12, 1983. BA, UCLA, 1976; JD, Southwestern U., L.A., 1979; LLM in Taxation, U. San Diego, 1986. Bar: Calif. 1979, U.S. Dist. Ct. (cen. dist.) Calif. 1981, U.S. Tax Ct. 1982, U.S. Ct. Appeals (9th cir.) 1982, U.S. Supreme Ct. 1987, U.S. Ct. Claims 1987, U.S. Ct. Mil. Appeals 1988, U.S. Ct. Appeals (fed. cir.) 1989, U.S. Ct. Internat. Trade 1989, U.S. Ct. Appeals Temporary Emergency Ct., 1989, U.S. Ct. Vets. Appeals 1990, U.S. Dist. Ct. (no. and so. dists.) Calif. 1993. Tax cons., advanced underwriter Transam. Occidental Life Ins. Co., L.A., 1979-80; assoc. Law Offices Herman English, 1980-81; atty., owner Frank A. Weiser-A Law Corp., L.A., 1981—; judge pro tem L.A. County Mcpl. Ct., 1987—. Editor So. Calif. mag., 1987—; contbr. articles to profl. jours. Bd. suprs. Michael Antonovich Election Com., 1988; mem. World Affairs Coun., L.A.; mem. U.S. Ct. of Vets. Appeals, 1990; assoc. mem. Calif. Rep. Cen. Com. Recipient official resolutions from Calif. State Legislature, 1989, joint rules com. resolution for state assembly and sate senate, 1990, Calif. State Assembly and Senate, 1989, L.A. County Bd. of Suprs., 1989, City Coun. of L.A., 1987, Congressional Cert. of Appreciation; tribute to him placed into official Congl. record, 1989; Nat. Merit scholar, 1971. Mem. ABA (internat. labor com., arts control and disarmament com., internat. employment practices com., editorial advisor internat. law and practive sect. publs. com., internat. property, estate and trust com., fgn. investment in U.S. com.), Fed. Bar Assn. (internat. law com.), Inter-Am. Bar Assn., Am. Judicature Soc., Assn. Trial Lawyers Am., Calif. Trial Lawyers Assn., L.A. Trial Lawyers Assn., Internat. Bar Assn., World Affairs Coun. L.A., World Inst. Achievement, L.A. Athletic Club. Office: 3460 Wilshire Blvd Bldg 903 Los Angeles CA 90010-2229

WEISER, MARK DAVID, computer scientist, researcher; b. Chgo., July 23, 1952; s. David Warren and Audra Laverne (Hunsaker) W.; m. Victoria Ann Reich, Dec. 16, 1976; children: Nicole Reich-Weiser, Corinne Reich-Weiser. Student, New Coll., Sarasota, Fla., 1969-71; MS, U. Mich., 1976, PhD, 1979. V.p. Cerberus Video, Ann Arbor, Mich., 1972-75; programmer Omnitext, Ann Arbor, Mich., 1971-76; project leader MIS, Internat., Romulus, Mich., 1975-76; from asst. to assoc. prof. computer sci. U. Md., College Park, 1979-87; prin. scientist Xerox Palo Alto (Calif.) Rsch. Ctr., 1987—, lab. mgr., 1988—; founder Cerberus Video, Ann Arbor, 1972-75. Contbr. over 70 articles to profl. jours. Mem. IEEE, AAAS, Assn. for Computing Machinery. Office: Xerox PARC Computer Sci Lab 3333 Coyote Hill Rd Palo Alto CA 94304-1314

WEISGERBER, JOHN SYLVESTER, provincial legislator; b. Barrhead, Alta., Can., June 12, 1940; s. Sylvester and Eva (Kilshaw) Harrison; m. Judith Muriel Janke, June 30, 1961; children: Joanne, Pamela. BBA, N. Alta. Inst. Tech., 1962. Owner Carland Ltd., 1975-81; econ. devel. commr. Peace River-Liard Regional Dist., Dawson Creek, 1982-84; sales mgr. Timberline Pontiac Buick GMC Ltd., Dawson Creek, 1984-86; mem. legis. assembly Govt. of B.C. (Can.), Victoria, 1986—, parliamentary sec. to minister of state, 1987-88, minister of state for Nechako and N.E., 1988-89, minister native affairs, 1989—; chmn. Cabinet Com. on Native Affairs, Victoria, 1988-90; mem. Cabinet Com. on Sustainable Devel., Victoria, 1988-90; mem. Select Standing Com. of Forests and Lands, Victoria, 1988-90; mem. Select Standing Com. on Agr. and Fisheries, Victoria, 1988-90; interim leader B.C. Social Credit Party, 1992—. Bd. dirs., pres. Dawson Creek and Dist. Fall Fair, 1980-86. Mem. Rotary (past pres.), Mile O Riding Club (bd. dirs., pres. 1976-81). Office: Parliament Bldgs, Room 102, Victoria, BC Canada V8V 1X4

WEISKOPF, WILLIAM HARVARD, accountant; b. Chgo., Feb. 18, 1938; s. William Herman and Josephine (Marron) W.; m. Carol Ruth Soderstrom, June 14, 1958; children: Cheryl Ruth, William Helge, Richard Harvard. BSBA, Northwestern U., 1960, MBA, 1967. CPA, Colo., Ill. Controller Clare Ceramics, Cary, Ill., 1960-63; chief fin. officer S.C. Lawlor Co., Melrose Park, Ill., 1964-65; staff acct. Ernst & Young, Chgo., 1967-69; staff acct. Ernst & Young, Denver, 1970-71, mgr., 1972-75, sr. mgr., 1976-78, ptnr., 1979-91; exec. dir. Colo. Sch. Mines Found., Inc., Golden, Colo., 1992—. Mem. exec. bd. Denver Coun. Boy Scouts Am., 1981—. Mem. AICPA (coun. mem. 1989-92), Colo. Soc. CPAs (pres. 1988-89), Leadership Denver Assn., Colo. Alliance of Bus. (dir., treas. 1986-91). Republican. Lutheran. Office: Colo Sch Mines Found Inc 19th and Elm St Golden CO 80401-0005

WEISMAN, MARTIN JEROME, manufacturing company executive; b. N.Y.C., Aug. 22, 1930; s. Lewis E. and Estelle (Scherer) W.; m. Sherrie Cohen, Jan. 27, 1952; children: Jane Dory, Andrea Sue, Amy Ellen. B in Chem. Engring., N.Y.U., 1951. Sr. chem. engr. Ideal Toy Corp., Hollis, N.Y., 1951-57; research chemist Chesebrough-Ponds, Stamford, Conn., 1957-62; mgr. nail products lab. Max Factor and Co., Hollywood, Calif., 1962-81; v.p., tech. dir. Sher-Mar Cosmetics div. Weisman Industries, Inc., Canoga Park, Calif., 1981—. Patentee in field. Mem. Soc. Cosmetic Chemists, Los Angeles Soc. Coatings Tech., Am. Chem. Soc. Office: Sher-Mar Cosmetics 8755 Remmet Ave Canoga Park CA 91304-1519

WEISMAN, ROBERT EVANS, caterer; b. N.Y.C., Feb. 11, 1950; s. Arnold and Selma (Leinow) W.; m. Margaret Lavin, July 3, 1983; 1 child, Sarah Miriam. BA, U. Wis., 1972. Gen. mgr. Medieval Manor, Boston, 1976-80, Ruppert's Restaurant, N.Y.C., 1980-82; owner Bobby Weisman Caterers, Los Angeles, 1983—. Office: Bobby Weisman 1105 S La Brea Ave Los Angeles CA 90019-6908

WEISMEYER, RICHARD WAYNE, academic administrator; b. Loma Linda, Calif., Oct. 15, 1943; s. Norman Glenn and Nedra Aileen (McGinniss) W.; m. Carol Mae Siebenlist, Aug. 16, 1970; children: Michael Brett, Marci Diann. BA in English, Loma Linda U., Riverside, Calif., 1966. Editorial asst. Loma Linda U., Loma Linda, 1966-70, editor new publs., 1970-75, dir. pub. rels., 1975—; mem. panel Heart Transplantation and Pub. Rels. sponsored by USA Today and fellows of ACS; bd. dirs. Sta. KSGN-FM, Riverside, Loma Linda Acad. Press; mem. group on pub. rels. Am. Med. Colls. Bd. dirs. Loma Linda Acad., Adventist Editors Internat. Mem. Pub. Rels. Assn. So. Calif., Coun. for Advancement and Support of Edn. Adventist. Home: 143 Browning St Riverside CA 92507-1204 Office: Loma Linda U Dept Pub Rels Loma Linda CA 92350

WEISS, BERNARD, advertising executive; b. N.Y.C., Jan. 14, 1943; s. David G. and Sylvia (Micklin) W.; divorced, 1986; children: Meredith J., Andrew J., Owen N. BA, Am. U., Washington, 1964. CLU. Various mktg., underwriting and communications positions The Travelers Ins. Co., Hartford, Conn., 1964-78; asst. dir. sales promotion The Travelers Ins. Co., 1978-86, asst. dir. communication and promotions, 1986-89; dir. advt. Nat. Music Svc., Spokane, Wash., 1989—; pres. Communication for Mktg., Spokane, 1989—; prin. Dexter, Scarpato & Weiss, Spokane, 1989—; lectr. profl. seminars and convs. Contbg. editor Ins. Conf. Planner Mag., 1976-86; contbr. articles to profl. publs. Mem. Life Communicators Assn. (past mem. bd. dirs., chmn. various meetings, com. and seminars, Spl. Recognition award 1988). Home: S 2811 Fiske Spokane WA 99223

WEISS, DONALD RICHARD, civil engineer; b. Omaha, June 16, 1943; s. Richard Ernest Frederick and Lucille Marie (Cordes) W.; m. Lucille Lynnette Shore, Sept. 21, 1968 (div. Apr. 1977); 1 child, Sherry Lynn. BS, U. Nebr., 1966; postgrad., Ariz. State U., 1983-85. Registered profl. engr., Tenn., Ariz., Nev., Calif. Design trainee U.S. Corps Engrs., Omaha, 1965-66; engr. field inspection Swift & Gregg, Augusta, Ga., 1968-70; design engr. Concrete Materials, Inc., Atlanta, 1970-73; chief engr. Featherlite Prestress, Memphis, 1973-78; engring. supr. Prestress div. Tanner Co., Phoenix, 1978—. Mem. Germantown (Tenn.) Planning Commn., 1975. 1st lt. U.S. Army, 1966-69. Mem. Prestressed Concrete Inst. (TAC com. 1988-90, chmn. quality control com. 1992—), Structural Engring. Assn. Ariz. (assoc.), Structural Engring. Assn. Calif. (assoc.), Am. Concrete Inst. Home: 1221 E Claire Dr Phoenix AZ 85022 Office: Tanner Co Prestress Div 3052 S 19th Ave Phoenix AZ 85009

WEISS, HERBERT KLEMM, aeronautical engineer; b. Lawrence, Mass., June 22, 1917; s. Herbert Julius and Louise (Klemm) W.; m. Ethel Celesta Giltner, May 14, 1945 (dec.); children: Janet Elaine, Jack Klemm (dec.). B.S., MIT, 1937, M.S., 1938. Engr. U.S. Army Arty. Bds., Ft. Monroe, Va. 1938-42, Camp Davis, N.C., 1942-44, Ft. Bliss, Tex., 1944-46; chief WPN Systems Lab., Ballistic Research Labs., Aberdeen Proving Grounds, Md, 1946-53; chief WPN systems analysis dept. Northrop Aircraft Corp., 1953-58; mgr. advanced systems devel. mil. systems planning aeronutronic div. Ford Motor Co., Newport Beach, Calif., 1958-61; group dir., plans devel. and analysis Aerospace Corp., El Segundo, Calif., 1961-65; sr. scientist Litton Industries, Van Nuys, Calif., 1965-82; cons. mil. systems analysis, 1982—; Mem. Sci. Adv. Bd. USAF, 1959-63, sci. adv. panel U.S. Army, 1965-74, sci. adv. commn. Army Ball Research Labs., 1973-77; advisor Pres.'s Commn. Law Enforcement and Adminstrn. Justice, 1966; cons. Office Dir. Def., Research and Engring., 1954-64. Contbr. articles to profl. jours. Patentee in field. Recipient Commendation for meritorious civilian service USAF, 1964, cert. appreciation U.S. Army, 1976. Fellow AAAS, AIAA (assoc.); mem. IEEE, Ops. Research Soc. Am. Republican. Presbyterian. Club: Cosmos. Home: PO Box 2668 Palos Verdes Peninsula CA 90274-8668

WEISS, LOREN ELLIOT, lawyer, educator; b. Cleve., Sept. 28, 1947; s. Harry and Gertrude (Rapport) W. BA with honors, UCLA, 1969; JD cum laude, U. San Diego, 1972. Bar: Calif. 1972, U.S. Dist. Ct. (so. dist.) Calif. 1972, Utah 1983, U.S. Dist. Ct. (cen. dist.) Calif. 1983, U.S. Dist. Ct. Utah 1983, U.S. Ct. Appeals (9th cir.) 1972, U.S. Ct. Appeals (10th cir.) 1986. With various law firms, San Diego, 1972-80; owner, gen. mgr. Mid-Mountain Lodge, Park City, Utah, 1980-83; pvt. practice, Salt Lake City, 1983-89; of counsel Purser, Okazaki & Berrett, Salt Lake City, 1989-93; mem. Utah Com. Bar Examiners, Salt Lake City, 1986-90; adj. prof. Brigham Young U. J. Reuben Clark Law Sch., Provo, Utah, 1990—; tng. coord. Criminal Justice Act Atty. Panel, U.S. Dist. Ct. for Utah, 1990—; mem. adv. com. U.S. Jud. Conf. Defender Svc. Com., Washington, 1991—. Contbr. articles to legal jours. Trustee Utah Trout Found., Salt Lake City, 1988—. Mem. Fed. Bar Assn., Calif. Bar Assn., Utah Bar Assn., Nat. Assn. Criminal Def. Lawyers (co-chmn. continuing legal edn. com. 1992-93), Utah Assn. Criminal Def. Lawyers (pres.-elect 1992-93). Office: Purser & Edwards P C Ste 300 39 Market St Salt Lake City UT 84101

WEISS, MARTIN HARVEY, neurosurgeon, educator; b. Newark, Feb. 2, 1939; s. Max and Rae W.; m. R. Debora Rosenthal, Aug. 20, 1961; children: Brad, Jessica, Elisabeth. A.B. magna cum laude, Dartmouth Coll., 1960, B.M.S., 1961; M.D., Cornell U., 1963. Diplomate Am. Bd. Neurol. Surgery (bd. dirs. 1983-89, vice chmn. 1987-88, chmn. 1988-89). Intern Univ. Hosps., Cleve., 1963-64; resident in neurosurgery Univ. Hosps., 1966-70; sr. instr. to asst. prof. neurosurgery Case Western Res. U., 1970-73; asso. prof. neurosurgery U. So. Calif., 1973-76, prof., 1976-78, prof., chmn. dept., 1978—; chmn. neurology B study sect. NIH; mem. residency rev. com. for neurosurgery Accreditation Commn. for Grad. Med. Edn., 1989—, vice chmn., 1991-93, chmn., 1993—; Courville lectr. Sch. Medicine, Loma Linda U., 1989; W. James Gardner lectr. Cleve. Clinic, 1993. Author: Pituitary Diseases, 1980; editorial bd.: Neurosurgery, 1979-84, Neurol. Research, 1980—; editor in chief: Clin. Neurosurgery, 1980-83; assoc. editor: Bull. Los Angeles Neurol. Socs, 1976-81, Jour. Clin. Neurosci., 1981—; mem. editorial bd. Jour. Neurosurgery, 1987—; contbr. articles sci. jours. Served to capt. USAR, 1964-66. NIH spl. fellow in neurosurgery, 1969-70; Edgar Kahn prof. neurosurgery, U. Mich., 1987; Arthur A. Ward Jr. prof. neurosurgery, U. Wash., 1989; Loyal Davis lectr., Northwestern U., 1990; honored guest Neurol. Soc. of Virginias, 1990; Afrox prof., XII S. African Neurosurg. Congress, 1990. Mem. ACS (adv. coun. neurosurgery 1985-88), Soc. Neurol. Surgeons, Neurosurg. Soc. Am., Am. Acad. Neurol. Surgery (exec. com. 1988-89, v.p. 1992-93), Rsch. Soc. Neurol. Surgeons, Am. Assn. Neurol. Surgeons (bd. dirs. 1988-91), Congress Neurol. Surgeons (v.p. 1982-83), Western Neurosurg. Soc., Neurosurg. Forum, So. Calif. Neurosurg. Soc. (pres. 1983-84), Phi Beta Kappa, Alpha Omega Alpha. Home: 357 Georgian Rd La Canada Flintridge CA 91011-3520 Office: 1200 N State St Box 1931 Los Angeles CA 90033

WEISS, MURRAY JOHN, physician; b. L.A., Mar. 24, 1922; s. Nathan John and Lillian Esther (Turner) W.; m. Twyla Yorkshire, May 19, 1946; children: Robert Mark, Nancy Weiss Lampert. AB, U. So. Calif., L.A., 1943, MD, 1947. Intern L.A. County Hosp., 1946-47, resident, internal medicine, 1948-51; pvt. practice medicine Sherman Oaks, Calif., 1951—; chief of staff St. Joseph Med. Ctr., Burbank, Calif., 1973; clin. prof. medicine U. So. Calif. Sch. Medicine, L.A., 1980—. Contbr. med. articles on diabetes, pancreatic diseases to profl. jours. Pres. Diabetes Assn. So. Calif., L.A., 1965. Fellow ACP, Alpha Omega Alpha. Jewish.

WEISS, NORM A., Canadian provincial government official; b. Edmonton, Alta., Can., Dec. 23, 1935; m. Carol Dittberner; 1 child, Jill. Grad. high sch., Edmonton. Zone mgr. Internat. Harvester; market devel. specialist Shell Can., Ltd.; then co-owner restaurant, real estate co., car wash-service station, sporting goods retail store; Minister of Parks and Recreation Province of Alta., Edmonton, 1986-89; assoc. minister Family and Social Svcs. Province of Alta, Edmonton, 1989; minister of career devel. and employment Province of Alta., Edmonton, 1989-92; with Alta. Legislature, 1979—, bd. dirs. Syncrude Can. Ltd., Northern Alta. Devel. Council, 1979-82, chmn., 1982-86. Past pres. Lac La Biche/Ft. McMurray Polit. Constituency Assn.; past v.p. Edmonton Jaycees; former mem. Alta. Oil Sands Tech. and Rsch. Authority; past adv. com. Northeastern Alta. Regional Commn.; bd. dirs. Ft. McMurray Oil Barons Hockey Club, Alta. '85 Summer Games, Can.-Chinese Cultural Assn., Mt. McMurray Interpretive Centre, Keyano Coll. Found. Mem. Ft. McMurray Businessmen's Assn. (past bus. mgr.), Ft. McMurray C. of C., Kinsmen, Rotary (bd. dirs.), Muffaloose Trailblazers (hon.). Office: Alta Legislature, 503 Legislature Bldg, Edmonton, AB Canada T5K 2B6

WEISS, NORMAN LOUIS, environmental consultant; b. Phoenix, Jan. 21, 1951; s. Hyman and Hattie (Merlinsky) W.; m. Robin Byram, Aug. 16, 1985; children: Samuel, Dale. AA, Phoenix Coll., 1972; BS, Ariz. State U., 1974, MA, 1977, postgrad., 1978-81. Registered hazardous substance profl.; cert. environ. mgr., Nev.; cert. C.C. instr., Ariz. Environ. cons. Bioconn Environ. Studies, Phoenix, 1973-74; environ. planner Ariz. Dept. Health Svcs., Phoenix, 1978-80, dir. waste planning, 1980-83, bur. chief, 1983-84, program mgr., 1984-86, dir. environ. planning, 1986-88; asst. dir. Ariz. Dept. Environ. Quality, Phoenix, 1988-91; environ. cons. Emcon Assocs., Phoenix, 1991—; mem. Hazardous Waste Enforcement Investigation Project, Ariz., 1984-86; mem. task force on hazardous waste capacity assurance Nat. Govs. Assn., 1987-88; participant Pub. Policy Forum on Incineration, MIT, 1988; mem. Western States Hazardous Waste Enforcement Project, 1988-91; presenter in field. Contbr. articles to profl. jours. Invited participant Siting Hazardous Waste Facilities, Nat. Gov.'s Assn., 1992. Recipient cert. of achievement Ariz. Adminstrs. Assn., 1987. Mem. Nat. Hazardous Waste Siting Consortium (bd. dirs. 1988-89), Ariz. Pub. Health Assn. ((bd. dirs. 1981-83), Ariz. Environ. Health Assn. (bd. dirs. 1981-82, 85), Western Waste Exch. (exec. bd. 1986-87), Ariz. Hazardous Waste Soc. (bd. dirs. 1986-87), Gamma Theta Upsilon. Jewish. Office: Emcon Assocs 3922 E University Dr Ste 7 Phoenix AZ 85034

WEISS, PETER H., business consultant; b. N.Y.C., Oct. 12, 1956; s. Edward and Janis (Silbert) W. AB cum laude, Princeton U., 1979; MBA, Harvard U., 1984. Gen. mgr. Paprikas Weiss Importer, N.Y.C., 1979-80; fin. analyst Warburg Paribas Becker, N.Y.C., 1980-82; asst. to pres. Barnes Drill Co., Rockford, Ill., 1983-84; v.p. Trump Group, N.Y.C., 1984-86; pres. P. Weiss & Co., Inc., Seattle, 1986—, Call Carpet, Inc., Seattle, 1987—; bd. dirs. Gerbeaud, Inc., N.Y.C. Mem. regional adv. bd. AntiDefamation League Pacific N.W. Mem. Am. Floor Covering Assn. (bd. dirs.). Office: Call Carpet Inc PO Box 3771 Seattle WA 98124-9999

WEISS, REGIS JOHN, gynecologic oncologist; b. Cleve., Mar. 24, 1949; s. Regis L. and Eleanor Mary (Deptowicz) W.; m. Marianne Elizabeth Rennie, Juen 22, 1972; children: Stephanie, David. BS in Biology, Georgetown U., 1970; MD, McGill U., 1974. Diplomate Am. Bd. Ob/Gyn. Intern Bethesda (Md.) Naval Hosp., 1974-75; resident in ob/gyn. San Diego Naval Hosp., 1975-78, gynecologic oncologist, 1981-84, obstetrician, gynecologist, 1978-79; fellow U. Calif., San Diego, 1979-81, gynecologic oncologist, 1984-87; gynecologic oncologist Oncology Assocs. San Diego, 1987—. Comdr. USN, 1971-84. USN scholar, 1971. Fellow Am. Coll. Ob/Gyn.; mem. Am. Soc. Clin. Oncologists, Phi Beta Kappa. Office: Oncology Assocs San Diego 3930 4th Ave # 301 San Diego CA 92103

WEISS, RICHARD LOUIS, biochemistry educator; b. Evanston, Ill., June 24, 1944; s. Louis Christian and Patty Jean (Campbell) W.; m. Marjorie Ann Bates, Dec. 30, 1984. BS in Chemistry, Stanford U., 1966; PhD in Biochemistry, U. Wash., 1971. NIH postdoctoral fellow U. Mich., Ann Arbor, 1971-72, Am. Cancer Soc. postdoctoral fellow, 1972-73; asst. prof. UCLA, 1974-80, assoc. prof., 1980-85, prof. biochemistry, 1985—. NIH sr. postdoctoral fellow Stanford U., 1989. Mem. Am. Chem. Soc., Am. Soc. Microbiology, Genetics Soc. Am., Am. Soc. Biochemistry and Molecular Biology, Am. Soc. Cell Biology. Office: UCLA Dept Chemistry & Biochemistry 405 Hilgard Ave Los Angeles CA 90024-1569

WEISS, ROBERT STEPHEN, medical manufacturing and services company financial executive; b. Honesdale, Pa., Oct. 25, 1946; s. Stephen John and Anna Blanche (Lescinski) W.; BS in Acctg. cum laude, U. Scranton, 1968; m. Marilyn Annette Chesick, Oct. 29, 1970; children: Christopher Robert, Kim Marie, Douglas Paul. CPA, N.Y. Supr., Peat, Marwick, Mitchell & Co., N.Y.C., 1971-76; asst. corp. contr. Cooper Labs., Inc., Parsippany, N.J., 1977-78, v.p., corp. contr. Palo Alto, Calif., 1981-83; v.p., corp. contr. The Cooper Cos., Inc. (formerly CooperVision, Inc.), Palo Alto, Calif., 1984-89; v.p., treas., chief fin. officer The Cooper Cos., Inc., Pleasanton, Calif., 1989—, sr. v.p., 1992—; v.p. fin., contr. CooperVision Pharms., Mountain View, Calif., 1979, v.p. fin., group contr., 1980; bd. dirs. The Cooper Cos., Inc., N.Y.C., 1992—. With U.S. Army, 1969-70. Decorated Bronze Star with oak leaf cluster, Army Commendation medal. Mem. AICPA, N.Y. State Soc. CPAs. Home: 446 Arlington Ct Pleasanton CA 94566-7708 Office: The Cooper Cos Inc 6140 Stoneridge Mall Rd Pleasanton CA 94588-3232

WEISS, SANFORD RONALD, neurosurgeon; b. Cleve., Jan. 22, 1931; s. Morris Fenmore and Rose Mary (Tomsick) W.; m. Oct. 1962 (div. 1966); 1 child, Leah Beth. BA, Case Western Res. U., 1955, MD, 1958. Diplomate Am. Bd. Neurosurgery. Surg. internship Columbia-Presbyn. Med. Ctr., N.Y.C., 1958-59, surg. residency, 1959-60, neurosurg. residency, 1960-64; neurosurgeon pvt. practice L.I., N.Y., 1964-66; neurosurgeon Kaiser Hosp., Oakland, Calif., 1966-70; neurosurgeon pvt. practice San Leandro, Calif., 1970-81; asst. prof. neurosurgery U. Calif., San Francisco, 1966-81; hon. staff mem. Eden Hosp., Castro Valley, 1981—, Humana Hosp., Calif. 1981—. Contbr. numerous articles to profl. jours. Fellow Am. Coll. Angiology, Am. Geriatric Soc., Am. Coll. Surgeons, Internat. Coll. Surgeons; mem. Calif. Med. Assn., Am. Assn. Neurol. Surgeons, Calif. Assn. Neurol. Surgeons, Congress Neurol. Surgeons, Pan Pacific Surg. Assn. Republican. Jewish. Home: 739 Estudillo Ave San Leandro CA 94577-5109

WEISS, WILLIAM HANS, small business owner; b. Spokane, Wash., Feb. 25, 1952. BA in Human Svcs., Western Wash. U., 1977; MA in Psychology, Goddard Coll., 1980. Prin. Vocat. Mgmt. Resources, Redmond, Wash., 1980—; vocat. cons. various cities Social Security Adminstrn.; instr. Western Wash. U., 1990; adj. faculty mem. Seattle Pacific U., 1991; cons. U.S. Dept. Edn. Rehab. Svcs. Adminstrn. Roman Catholic. Office: Vocat Mgmt Resources PO Box 381 Redmond WA 98073-0381

WEISS BIZZOCO, RICHARD LAWRENCE, biology educator; b. N.Y.C., Dec. 28, 1940; s. Louis Lawrence Weiss and Annette Bizzoco; divorced; children: Shaynon Andrew, Wendy Alicia. BA, U. Conn., 1964; MS in Microbiology, Calif. State U., 1970; PhD in Microbiology/Biophysics, Ind. U., 1972. Am. Cancer Soc. rsch. fellow U. Calif., Berkeley, 1973; EM lab. dir. Harvard U., Cambridge, Mass., 1973-74, NIH fellow, 1975; assoc. med. microbiologist U. Calif. Med. Sch., Irvine, 1976-77; prof. San Diego State U., 1977—. NSF Instrumentation award, 1986. Mem. Phycological Soc. Am., Sigma Xi. Roman Catholic. Office: San Diego State U Dept Biology 5300 Campanile Dr San Diego CA 92182-0057

WEISSER, HENRY GEORGE, history educator, writer; b. N.Y.C., May 21, 1935; s. Reginald Jacob and Katherine Caroline (Oetter) W.; m. Marian Cadman, July 4, 1957 (div. May 1976); children: Steven, Jeanette, Tim, Elizabeth. BA, Hartwick Coll., 1957; MA, Columbia U., N.Y.C., 1958, PhD, 1965. Tchr. Robert Louis Stevenson Sch., N.Y.C., 1960-61, East Brunswick (N.J.) High Sch., 1961-62; instr. in history Luther Coll., Decorah, Iowa, 1962-64; asst. prof. history Colo. State U., Ft. Collins, 1965-70, assoc. prof. history, 1970-75, prof. history, 1975—; vis. fellow Warwick U., Eng., 1980-81; vis. prof. hist. U. Colo. 1992-93; cons. in field. Author: British Working Class Movements and Europe, 1815-1848, 1975, April 10: Challenge and Response in England in 1848, 1983, Understanding th U.K., 1987, Hippocrene Companion Guide to Ireland, 1990, Hippocrene USA Guide to Rocky Mountain States, 1992. Social Sci. Found. grantee U. Denver, 1968, Colo. State U. grantee Africa, 1979, NEH Rsch. grantee, 1980-81. Mem.

Am. Hist. Assn., Western Conf. on Brit. Studies (pres. 1979-80), Am. Conf. for Irish Studies. Democrat. Home: 504 Brown Ave Fort Collins CO 80525-1802 Office: Colo State U Dept History Fort Collins CO 80525

WEISSMAN, JERROLD, metal products executive; b. Great Falls, Mont., June 25, 1936; m. Nadyne B. Weissman; children: Aaron, Leila. Student, Denver U., 1953, U. Mont., 1954-55; AB in History and Econs., U. Miami (Fla.), 1958, postgrad. in history, 1958-61. Chmn. bd. dirs., chief operating officer, chief exec.officer N.W. Steel, Inc., 1962-81; chief exec. officer N.W. Steel of Idaho, Inc., 1973-81; sales mgr., asst. v.p., exec. v.p., pres., chief exec. ofcr. Carl Weissman & Sons, Inc., Great Falls, 1987—; pres., bd. dirs. Mont. Compressed Steel, Inc., N.W. Fence Products Co., Nat. Gen. Supply, Inc.; v.p., bd. dirs. N. Warehouse Distbrs. Bd. dirs. Great Falls Children's Receiving Home, 1971-75; active United Way, 1961—; mem. City Trade Commn., 1983-85; fundraiser ARC; chmn. univ. com. Forward Great Falls, 1984; asst. scout master Boy Scouts Am., 1985-86; pres. Great Falls Hebrew Assn., 1984-86, v.p. 1987, bd. dirs., 1990—; mem. Mont. Assn. Jewish Communities, 1986—; founding mem. N.W. Assn. Against Malicious Harassment; mem. Mont. Hist. Soc., various mus.; campaign worker, del. Rep. Party. Mem. INst. Scrap Iron and Steel (chpt. officer, bd. dirs. 1963-86), Nat. Assn. Recycling Industries (mem. nat. legis. com. 1967-86), Inst. Crasp Recycling Industries, Nat. Assn. Steel Pipe Distbrs. (bd. dirs.1976-80, mem. standards com. 1976-80, convention dir. 1976-80), Masons (master 1969-70, mem. jr. exec. com. 1964-67, pres. jr. exec. com. 1966-67), Shriners, Meadowlark Country Club. Home: 2777 Greenbrier Dr Great Falls MT 59404-3639 Office: Carl Weissman & Sons Inc 420 3d St S Great Falls MT 59405

WEISSMANN, PAUL MARTIN, state legislator; b. Denver, Colo., June 9, 1964; s. Max Ludwig and Arlene Frances (Bloom) W. BA in Polit. Sci., U. Colo., 1986. Bartender Blue Parrot Restaurant, Louisville, Colo., 1989—; mem. Colo. State Senate, Denver, 1992—. Democrat. Jewish. Home: 822 LaFarge Ave Louisville CO 80027 Office: Colo State Senate State Capitol Denver CO 80203

WEISSMANN, PAUL THOMAS, software engineer; b. Little Rock, Apr. 19, 1948; s. Franz Paul and Margaret Elizabeth (Hammon) W.; m. Ellen Laverne Lowers, June 21, 1980. BS, U. Tex., 1970, MS, 1972. Systems programmer U. Tex., El Paso, 1975-77; systems analyst Tex. A&M U., College Station, 1977-78; mgr. systems programs Tex. Tech. U., Lubbock, 1978-79; mgr. lang. devel. Datapoint Corp., San Antonio, 1979-83; systems analyst U. Tex. Health Sci. Ctr., San Antonio, 1983-84; systems programmer North Tex. State U., Denton, 1984; sr. MIS systems cons. Intelogic Trace, Inc., San Antonio, 1984-91; sr. software engr. Storage Tech. Corp., Louisville, Colo., 1991—; mem. faculty math. dept., Palo Alto Coll., San Antonio, 1988-90. Mem. IEEE Computer Soc., Assn. Computing Machinery, Nat. Systems Programmers Assn. Office: Storage Tech Corp 2270 South 88th St Louisville CO 80028-4232

WEITKAMP, FREDRICK JOHN, lawyer; b. L.A., Nov. 14, 1927; s. Robert M. and Joanna (Fox) W.; m. Betty Sue Stiller, June 9, 1972; children: John F., Robert D., Melinda S., Valerie A. AB, Occidental Coll., 1950; LLB, U. So. Calif., 1952. Bar: Calif. 1953. Practice law, L.A., 1953-92; exec. dir. Phi Alpha Delta Law Frat. Internat., L.A., 1953-92; sr. ptnr. Weitkamp & Weitkamp, Granada Hills, Calif., 1953—; judge pro tem L.A. Mcpl. Ct., 1965—; arbitrator L.A. Superior Ct., 1980—; chmn. bd. dirs. Bank Granada Hills, 1983—. With U.S. Army, 1946-47. Fellow Am. Coll. Trust & Estate Counsel; mem. ABA, Am. Judicature Soc., Calif. Bar Assn., Los Angeles County Bar Assn., San Fernando Valley Bar Assn., Granada Hills C. of C. (pres. 1956-57, Man of Yr. 1956), Toastmasters, Masons, Optimists (pres. 1964). Republican. Lutheran. Lodges: Masons, Optimists. Office: Weitkamp & Weitkamp 10724 White Oak Ave Granada Hills CA 91344-4690

WEITZ, SUE DEE, academic administrator; b. Coeur D'Alene, Idaho, Oct. 16, 1948; d. Donald and Larraine (Kiefer) W.; m. Greg Intinarelli, Nov. 25, 1984; children: Derek, Lauran, Marcus. BA cum laude, Coll. Idaho, 1971, MEd, 1975; postgrad., Ind. U., 1979-81; EdD, Gonzaga U., 1990. Coord. student activities, then asst. dean students Coll. Idaho, Caldwell, 1971-73, dean student life, 1974-76; assoc. dean students U. Cen. Ark., 1976-78; v.p. student affairs St. Mary-of-the-Woods (Ind.) Coll., 1978-81; dean of students Gonzaga U., Spokane, Wash., 1981-87, v.p. student life, 1987—; cons. Seattle U., 1989; evaluator Commn. on Colls., Seattle, 1990. Contbr. to profl. publs. Mem. Nat. Assn. Student Pers. Adminstrs., N.W. Assn. Coll. and Univ. Housing Officers, Nat. Assn. Coll. Activities, N.W. Coll. Pers. Assn. Office: Gonzaga Univ E 502 Boone Spokane WA 99258

WEITZE, WILLIAM FREDERICK, mechanical engineer; b. Westwood, N.J., May 4, 1960; s. Joseph Harry and May Elizabeth (Donnelly) W.; m. Sylvia Bankston Garcia, June 1, 1985 (div. Nov. 1991). BS in Mech. Engring., Rutgers U., 1982; MS in Mech. Engring., U. Calif., Berkeley, 1985. Lic. profl. engr., Calif. Program engr. nuclear energy GE, San Jose, Calif., 1982-85, engr., 1985-91, sr. engr., 1991—; cons. Engring. Cons. Svcs., San Jose, 1990—. Editor newsletter Silicon Valley Engring. Coun., 1991-92; contbr. articles to popular publs. Mem. ASME (treas. Santa Clara Valley 1990-91, sec. 1991-92, vice chmn. 1992-93, editor newsletter Santa Clara Valley 1988-90). Office: GE Nuclear Energy 175 Curtner Ave M/C 775 San Jose CA 95125

WEITZEL, JOHN QUINN, bishop; b. Chgo., May 10, 1928; s. Carl Joseph and Patricia (Quinn) W. BA, Maryknoll (N.Y.) Sem., 1951, M of Religious Edn., 1953; PMD, Harvard U. Ordained priest Roman Cath. Ch., 1955. With ednl. devel. Cath. Fgn. Mission Soc. of Am., Maryknoll, 1955-63, nat. dir. vocations for Maryknoll, dir. devel. dept. and info. services, 1963-72, mem. gen. council, 1972-78; asst. parish priest Cath. Ch., Western Samoa, 1979-81, pastor, vicar gen., 1981-86; consecrated bishop, 1986; bishop Cath. Ch., Am. Samoa, 1986—. Office: Diocese of Samoa-Pago Pago Fatuoaiga PO Box 596 Pago Pago AS 96799-0596

WEITZMAN, MARC HERSCHEL, lawyer; b. Milw., Feb. 1, 1950; s. J. Leonard and Esther (Charne) W.; m. Natalyn Ann Gipstein, Oct. 5, 1980; children: Benjamin, Marissa, Laura, Emily. BA, U. Calif., Santa Barbara, 1972; JD, Western State U., 1976. Bar: Calif. 1978, U.S. Dist. Ct. (cen. dist.) Calif. 1979, U.S. Ct. Appeals (9th cir.) 1981, U.S. Supreme Ct. 1987. Atty. State Compensation Ins. Fund, Long Beach, Calif., 1979-82, State Farm Ins. Co., Costa Mesa, Calif., 1982-85; assoc. Grancell, Grancell & Marshall, Santa Ana, Calif., 1985-88; ptnr. Hertz & Weitzman, Huntington Beach, Calif., 1988—; pvt. practice Seal Beach, Calif., 1989—. Judge pro tem State of Calif. Div. Indsl. Rels.-Div. Indsl. Accidents, Norwalk, 1986—, Long Beach, 1984—; cert. worker's compensation specialist Calif. Bd. Legal Specialization-State Bar Calif., 1988—; arbitrator State of Calif. Divs. of Indsl. Rels. and Indsl. Accident, 1991. Mem. L.A. County Bar Assn., Orange County Bar Assn., Orange County Workers' Compensation Def. Assn., So. Calif. Rehab. Exch., Long Beach Bar Assn. Office: 3010 Old Ranch Pky Ste 200 Seal Beach CA 90740-2750

WEKEZER, JERZY WLADYSLAW, civil engineering educator; b. Czestochowa, Poland, June 27, 1946; came to U.S., 1982; s. Kazimierz and Janina (Rosikon) W.; m. Mariola Nowak, July 15, 1969 (div. July 1980); 1 child, Michal; m. Henryka Debska, Dec. 27, 1983; 1 child, Joanna Amy. BS in Civil Engring., Gdansk Tech. U., Poland, 1969, PhD in Applied Mechanics, 1974. Cert. prof. engr., Alaska. Lectr., asst. prof. Gdansk Tech. U., Poland, 1969-81; rsch. assoc. Inst. Fluid-Flow Machinery, Gdansk, 1973-74; lectr. U. Basrah, Iraq; vis. asst. prof. U. So. Calif., L.A., 1983-85; assoc. prof. U. Alaska, Anchorage, 1985-87, prof., 1987—, head, civil engring. dept., 1990—; cons. Autogenesis, Anchorage, 1990, Fed. Hwy. Adminstrn., 1991-92, ARCO Alaska, Inc., 1992-93. Co-author two books, monographs; reviewed jour. articles. Mem. ASCE. Office: U Alaska Sch Engring 3211 Providence Dr Anchorage AK 99508-4614

WELBORN, HELEN, former association executive, consultant; b. Kansas City, Mo., Jan. 12, 1956; d. Wiley Raymond Jr. and Patricia Ann (White) W. Student, S.W. Mo. State U., Springfield, 1975-78; BA in Bus. and Communicatons, U. Wash., 1988, postgrad. Technician various hosps., Kansas City and Seattle, 1975-87; exec. coord. Vols. for Outdoor Wash., Seattle, 1982-89; assoc. dir. Wash. Trails Assn., Seattle, 1987-88; interim editor Signpost Mag., 1991-92; program adminstr. Student Conservation Assn., Charlestown, N.H., 1989; regional adminstr. Student Conservation Assn., Seattle, 1989-91; cons. Student Conservation Assn., Seattle, 1991—, Wash. Trails Assn., Seattle, 1991—, budget analyst City of Seattle, 1993, King County Gov., 1993. Mem. Nat. Com. for Responsive Philanthropy, Washington, 1991—; v.p. bd. dirs. Earth Share of Wash., Seattle, 1989—; mem. Wash. Environ. Coun., Seattle, 1989—. Recipient Take Pride in Am. award U.S. Dept. Interior, 1990, Presdl. Point of Light Environ. Achievement award Nat. Environ. Awards Coun., others. Mem. N.W. Devel. Officers Assn., Quartertomes, NOW, Phi Beta Kappa. Democrat. Home: PO Box 85295 Seattle WA 98145

WELCH, BETTY LEONORA, accountant; b. Missoula, Mont., July 18, 1961; d. George Oliver and Betty June (Dolton) W. BBA, U. Mont., 1983. CPA, Mont. Staff acct. Ellis & Assocs., Boise, Idaho, 1984; acct. Glacier Electric Coop., Cut Bank, Mont., 1984-86, office mgr., 1986—; income tax cons. Mem. AICPA, Beta Gamma Sigma. Democrat. Roman Catholic. Avocations: skiing, sewing, reading, hunting. Office: Glacier Electric Coop Inc 410 E Main St Cut Bank MT 59427-3012

WELCH, BOB (ROBERT LYNN WELCH), baseball player; b. Detroit, Nov. 3, 1956. Student, Ea. Mich. U. Pitcher L.A. Dodgers, 1978-87, Oakland Athletics, 1988—. Recipient Cy Young award, 1990; named to Sporting News All-Star team, 1990, Sporting News Am. League Pitcher of Yr., 1990. Office: Oakland A's Oakland Coliseum Oakland CA 94621

WELCH, BRENT BALLINGER, computer scientist; b. Albuquerque, Apr. 28, 1960; s. Jasper Arthur Jr. and Carroll (Wright) W.; m. Jolene Marie Badger, June 24, 1988. BS, U. Colo., 1982; MS, U. Calif., Berkeley, 1986, PhD, 1990. Mem. rsch. staff Xerox Parc, Palo Alto, Calif., 1990—. Contbr. articles to profl. jours. Mem. IEEE Computer Soc., Assn. of Computing Machinery. Home: 2540 Dell Mountain View CA 94043 Office: Xerox Parc 3333 Coyote Hill Rd Palo Alto CA 94304

WELCH, CLAUDE (RAYMOND), theology educator; b. Genoa City, Wis., Mar. 10, 1922; s. Virgil Cleon and Deone West (Grenelle) W.; m. Eloise Janette Turner, May 31, 1942 (div. 1970); children—Eric, Thomas, Claudia; m. Theodosia Montigel Blewett, Oct. 5, 1970 (dec. 1978); m. Joy Neuman, Oct. 30, 1982. BA summa cum laude, Upper Iowa U., 1942; postgrad., Garrett Theol. Sem., 1942-43; BD cum laude, Yale U., 1945, PhD, 1950; DD (hon.), Ch. Div. Sch. of Pacific, 1972, Jesuit Sch. Theology, 1982; LHD (hon.), U. Judaism, 1976. Ordained to ministry Meth. Ch., 1947. Instr. religion Princeton (N.J.) U., 1947-50, asst. prof., 1950-51, vis. prof., 1962; asst. prof. theology Yale U. Div. Sch., New Haven, 1951-54, assoc. prof., 1954-60; Berg prof. religious thought, chmn. dept. U. Pa., Phila., 1960-71, assoc. dean Coll. Arts and Scis., 1964-68, acting chmn. dept. philosophy, 1965-66; prof. hist. theology Grad. Theol. Union, Berkeley, Calif., 1971—, dean, 1971-87, pres., 1972-82; vis. prof. Garrett Theol. Sem., 1951, Pacific Sch. Religion, 1958, Hartford Sem. Found., 1958-59, Princeton Theol. Sem., 1962-63, U. Va., 1987; Fulbright sr. lectr. U. Mainz, Germany, 1968; Sprunt lectr. Union Theol. Sem., Richmond, Va., 1958; dir. study of grad. edn. in religion Am. Council Learned Socs., 1969-71; del. World Conf. on Faith and Order, 1963. Author: In This Name: the Doctrine of the Trinity in Contemporary Theology, 1952, (with John Dillenberger) Protestant Christianity, interpreted through its Development, 1954, 2d rev. edit., 1988, The Reality of the Church, 1958, Graduate Education in Religion: A Critical Appraisal, 1971, Religion in the Undergraduate Curriculum, 1972, Protestant Thought in the 19th Century, vol. 1, 1799-1870, 1972, vol. 2, 1870-1914, 1985; Editor, translator: God and Incarnation in Mid-19th Century German Theology (Thomasius, Dorner and Biedermann), 1965; Contbr. to publs. in field. Recipient decennial prize Bross Found., 1970; Guggenheim fellow, 1976; NEH research fellow, 1984, Fulbright research fellow, 1956-57. Mem. Am. Acad. Religion (pres. 1969-70), Coun. of Socs. for Study of Religion (chmn. 1969-74, 85-90), Soc. for Values in Higher Edn. (pres. 1967-710, Am. Soc. Ch. History, Am. Theol. Soc., Phi Beta Kappa. Home: 123 Fairlawn Dr Berkeley CA 94708-2107

WELCH, GARRY LEE, communications company executive; b. Winner, S.D., Aug. 12, 1948; s. Lewis Martin and Vraina May (Leech) W.; m. Donna G. Wright, May 23, 1969; children—Kelly Ann, Sean Michael. B.S. in Math. and Indsl. Tech., Southwest Mo. State U., 1970, M.B.A., 1975; postgrad. Santa Clara U., 1976. With ops. research Gen. Electric, Springfield, Mo., 1972-75, with mfg., engring., Louisville, Ky., San Jose, Calif., 1976-78; acctg. supr. AT&T Long Lines, Kansas City, Mo., 1978-79, cons., 1979-82, dist. nat. acct. mgr., 1982-83; divsn. mgr. AT&T Communications, Seattle, 1983—. Producer, advisor safety film: When You Are a Stranger, 1980. Deacon Presbyn. Ch., Kansas City, 1980-81; ruling elder Presbyn. Ch., Dash Point, Wash., 1983—; trustee Corp. Coun. for the Arts, Seattle, 1985—, chmn. 1992; coach Little League, Kansas City, 1978-81. Served with U.S. Army, 1970-72. Mem. IEEE, Epsilon Pi Tau. Republican. Clubs: Pacific West (Federal Way, Wash.), Twin Lakes Country (Federal Way, Wash.). Home: 716 S Marine Hills Way Federal Way WA 98003 Office: AT&T Communications 700 Fifth Ave Ste 2200 Seattle WA 98104

WELCH, GARTH LARRY, chemistry educator; b. Brigham City, Utah, Feb. 14, 1937; s. Samuel and Minnie Jane (Hughes) W.; m. Melba Lael Coombs, Sept. 9, 1960; children: Larry Kent, Kathryn Louise, Richard Samuel, Garth Edward, Robert Irvine, David Jonathan. B.S., U. Utah, 1959, Ph.D., 1963. Teaching asst. U. Utah, 1959-62; postdoctoral research fellow UCLA, 1962-64; asst. prof. Weber State U., Ogden, Utah, 1964-68; assoc. prof. Weber State U., 1968-72; prof. Weber State U., Ogden, 1972—, dean Sch. Natural Sci., 1974-83, exec. dir. bus. affairs, 1983-89, assoc. v.p. phys. facilities, 1990-91; mem. Utah State Council on Sci. and Tech., 1980-84. Mem. Mormon Tabernacle Choir, Salt Lake City, 1958-62, Jay Welch Chorale, 1983—, Pleasant View Planning Commn., 1988-91, chmn., 1990-91. Mem. Am. Chem. Soc., Sigma Xi, Phi Kappa Phi. Mem. LDS Ch. (bishop 1966-74). Home: 3910 N 800 W Ogden UT 84414-1066

WELCH, GARY LEE, credit union executive; b. Idaho Falls, May 18, 1946; s. Golden Marchant and WyNona (Waddel) W. BA in Edn., Idaho State U., 1969, BA in English, 1969; cert. of grad., Nat. Credit Union Adminstn., San Diego, 1988, Nat. Credit Union Adminstn., San Antonio, 1990. Cert. tchr., Idaho, Utah. Pub. sch. tchr. Idaho Sch. Dist. #291, Pocatello, 1969-71; mgr. Wells Distbg. Co., Salt Lake City, 1971-75; corp. mgr. Utah State Credit Union, Salt Lake City, 1976-86; exec. v.p., COO L.A. Tchrs. Credit Union, 1986—, pres., CEO, 1990-91; cons. Calif. Credit Union League, Pomona, 1986—, Credit Union Times, West Palm Beach, 1990—, Nat. Credit Union Assn., Madison, Wis., 1991—. Author: Evergreen, 1969, West World, 1988; editor (newsletter) News and Views, 1991. Vol. L.A. Mission, 1988—; assoc. AIDS Project L.A., 1990—; advocate PAC Calif. Credit Union League, Pomona, 1992—; mem. YMCA; sponser Celebration Theatre, 1990—. Mem. L.A. County Art Mus., Credit Union Soc. (Moebs award 1991), Idaho State U. Alumni Assn. (Profl. Achievement 1986). Office: LA Tchrs Credit Union 420 N Rosenell Terr Los Angeles CA 90026

WELCH, LLOYD RICHARD, engineering educator, communications consultant; b. Detroit, Sept. 28, 1927; s. Richard C. and Helen (Felt) W.; m. Irene Althea Main, Sept. 12, 1953; children—Pamela Irene Welch Towery, Melinda Ann, Diana Lia Welch Worthington. B.S. in Math., U. Ill., 1951; Ph.D. in Math., Calif. Inst. Tech., 1958. Mathematician NASA-Jet Propulsion Lab., Pasadena, Calif., 1956-59; staff mathematician Inst. Def. Analyses, Princeton, N.J., 1959-65; prof. elec. engring. U. So. Calif., L.A., 1965—; cons. in field. Contbr. articles to profl. jours. Served with USN, 1945-49, 51-52. Fellow IEEE; mem. Nat. Acad. Engring., Am. Math. Soc., Math. Assn. Am., Soc. for Indsl. and Applied Math., Phi Beta Kappa, Sigma Xi, Phi Kappa Phi, Pi Mu Epsilon, Eta Kappa Nu. Office: U So Calif Elec Engring Bldg 506 Los Angeles CA 90089-2565

WELCH, TIMOTHY LEROY, real estate developer; b. Yuba City, Calif., Dec. 25, 1935; s. Roy L. and Estelle J. (Brockman) W.; m. Jacalea D. Wood, Aug. 29, 1960; children: Timothy II, Nicole, Dominie, Susan. BA in History, Stanford U., 1958, MA in Speech and Drama, 1961; PhD in Community Coll. Mgmt., U. Calif., Berkeley, 1973. Reporter Los Gatos (Calif.) Times-Observer, 1961-62; instr. journalism, pub. info. officer Fresno (Calif.) City Coll., 1963-67; dean community svcs. Cabrillo (Calif.) Coll., 1967-81; mgr. Hare, Brewer & Kelley, Inc., Santa Cruz, Calif., 1981-91; mng. ptnr. Aptos Ptnrs., 1986—. Author: The Tennis Murders, 1976, The Pro-Am Murders, 1979, Tape It Off!, 1983. Acting exec. Wingspread Arts Found., 1983-88; bd. dirs. Miss Calif. Pageant, 1967-71, Community Action Bd., 1968-69, Fats Waller Jazz Festival, 1992—; active Santa Cruz County Arts Commn., 1971-73, personal gifts campaign Stanford U., 1972—, Santa Cruz County Planning Commn., 1973-75; treas. Dawson for Supr., 1976, Santa Cruz Actors Theater, 1988-89, Petersen for Assessor, 1978; major gifts com. Dominican Hosp. Found., 1977-81; resource com. Santa Cruz Cultural Action Plan, 1979-80. Mem. Coll. Assn. for Pub. Events and Svcs. (pres. 1970-71), Calif. Community Svcs. Assn. (founding pres. 1971-73), Calif. Community and Jr. Coll. Assn. (chmn. com. community svcs. 1971-75, 78-80), Nat. Coun. for Community Svcs. (v.p. 1971-73, editor nat. quarterly 1971-74), Rio del Mar Tennis Club (pres. 1988-90, bd. dirs. 1973-74), Aptos C. of C. (pres. 1985-86, chmn. econ. concerns com. 1986—).

WELCH, WILLIAM JOHN, astronomer; b. Chester, Pa., Jan. 17, 1934; s. William Taylor and Ruth (van Leuven) W.; m. Jill C. Tartar, July 4, 1980; children by previous marriage—Eric, Leslie, Jeanette. B.S., Stanford U., 1955; M.S., U. Calif., Berkeley, 1958, Ph.D., 1960; Hon. Dr., Universite de Bordeaux, 1979. Asst. prof. elec. engring. U. Calif., Berkeley, 1960-65; asso. prof. U. Calif., 1965-69, prof. astronomy and elec. engring., 1969—; dir. Radio Astronomy Lab., 1972. Contbr. numerous articles on radio astronomy and related fields to profl. jours. Bd. trustees Asso. Univs., Inc.; mem. Arecibo Adv. Bd. Grantee in radio astronomy NSF; Grantee in radio astronomy NASA. Mem. Internat. Astron. Union, Internat. Union Radio Sci., AAAS, Am. Astron. Soc. Home: 2727 Shasta Rd Berkeley CA 94708-1923 Office: U Calif-Berkeley Radio Astronomy Lab 601 Campbell Hall Berkeley CA 94720

WELCHERT, STEVEN JOSEPH, public affairs consultant; b. Davenport, Iowa, June 16, 1956; s. Richard Marshall and Norma Jean (Waters) W.; m. Kathleen Ann Agnitsch, June 13, 1981; children: Sarah Elizabeth, Matthew Joseph. BGS, U. Iowa, 1979. Nat. field staff Ted Kennedy for President, 1979-80; polit. dir. Lucero for U.S. Senate, Denver, 1984; legis. dir. for Gov. Richard Lamm, Denver, 1984-87, sr. edn. advisor for, 1985-87; issues dir. for Mayor Federico Peña, Denver, 1987; v.p. Bonham/Shlenker & Assocs., Denver, 1988-90; pres. The Welchert Co., Denver, 1990—; staff chmn. Nat. Govs. Assn., Washington and Denver, 1986; on-air analyst Sta. KMGH-TV, Denver, 1987—; Wis. dir. Gore for Pres., Milw., 1988; floor whip Dem. Nat. Platform Com., 1988. Writer radio series Ind. Thinking, 1987-88. Advisor Cultural Facilities Dist., Denver, 1988; mem. Denver Baseball Commn., 1986-89, chmn. govt. com.; dir. Citizens for Denver's Future, 1989-90. Named Rising Leader for 90's Colo. Bus. Mag., 1990. Democrat. Roman Catholic. Office: The Welchert Co 50 S Steele Ste 270 Denver CO 80209

WELD, ROGER BOWEN, clergyman; b. Greenfield, Mass., Dec. 1, 1953; s. Wayland Mauney and Luvycie (Bowen) W.; m. Patricia Ann Kaminski, June 7, 1978 (div. 1979). Grad., Sacred Acad. Jamilian U. of the Ordained, Reno, 1976-77, Seminary, 1978-82; student, U. Nev., 1983-85; postgrad., Sacred Coll. Jamilian Theology, 1988-90. Ordained to ministry, Internat. Community of Christ Ch. of Second Advent, 1977. Adminstrv. staff Internat. Community of Christ Ch. of Second Advent, Reno, 1977—, exec. officer dept. canon law, 1985—, exec. officer advocates for religious rights and freedoms, 1985—, exec. officer speakers bur., 1985—, exec. officer office pub. info., 1986—, mgr. Jamilian Univ. Press, 1987—, dir. advt. prodns., 1988—; founder, pres. Crown Rsch. Found., 1992—. Author: Twelve Generations of the Family of Weld: Edmund to Wayland Mauney, 1986. Staff sgt. USAF, 1971-75. Named Life Mem., Sacred Oversee, 1991. Mem. Nev. Clergyman's Assn., Andean Explorers Found. (Explorer's medal 1990), Ocean Sailing Club (exec. sec. 1988—, Participant's Silver Medallion 1989). Republican. Office: Internat Community Christ 643 Ralston St Reno NV 89503-4436

WELDON, BARBARA MALTBY, artist, painter; b. Yuma, Ariz., Aug. 29, 1931; d. John and Johnnie (Gammon) Maltby; m. James Bryce Weldon, Jr., June 21, 1952 (div. Dec. 1972); children: Laura Weldon Thomas, Scott Matthew. Student, San Diego U., 1949-52, U. Calif.-San Diego, 1973. Artist-in-residence, San Diego; juror for paintings So. Calif. Exposition, 1982, 92; speaker Women's Opportunity Week, 1982, 83; hostess art auction Sta. KPBS-TV, San Diego, 1983, commemorative artist 25th Anniversary Poster, 1992. One-woman shows include San Diego Mus. Art, 1976, Laguna Art Mus., 1984, Thomas Babeor Gallery, La Jolla, Calif., 1980, 81, 82, 83, 84, 86, 88, 90, Ivory/Kimpton Gallery, San Francisco, 1982, 83, 84, 85, 89, Clark Gallery, Boston, 1979, 80, 82. Various offices Childrens Home Soc., 1965—; represented in numerous pub. & pvt. collections. Active Pub. Arts Adv. Bd. City San Diego, 1986-87. Recipient William Paton prize for watercolor Nat. Acad. Design, 1979, 1st award Southern Calif. Exposition, 1974. Mem. Rsch. Coun. Scripps Clin., Old Globe Theatre, LaJolla Playsouse, Nat. Watercolor Soc. (1st prize drawing 1974), San Diego Watercolor Soc. (1st prize 1974), San Diego Mus. Art (artist guild bd. 1977, mus. coordinating com. 1968—), San Diego Mus. Contemporary Art., Balboa Tennis Club, Lake Murray Tennis Club, Makua, Aux. to Childrens Home Soc., Kappa Alpha Theta. Avocations. tennis, music, skiing, travel. Home and Office: 6131 Romany Dr San Diego CA 92120-4609

WELLER, DONALD DOUGLAS, software quality assurance professional; b. Caldwell, Idaho, Oct. 4, 1945; s. Edward P. and Emelie M. (Nackard) W.; m. Yvonne N. Wood, Jan. 4, 1992; children: Douglas, Charles, Phillip, Joel, Sandra, David. Student, Okla. Bapt. U., 1972-74, Boise (Idaho) State U., 1974-76; BS in Computer Sci., Nat. U., 1991. Enlisted USN, 1965; nuclear power instr. USS Long Beach, USS Enterprise, USS Ark., others, 1968-86; ret. USN, 1990; sr. quality mgmt. analyst Mitchell Internat., San Diego, 1990—. Mem. Assn. for Computing Machinery. Office: Mitchell Internat 9889 Willow Creek Rd San Diego CA 92131

WELLER, GUNTER ERNST, geophysics educator; b. Haifa, June 14, 1934; came to U.S., 1968; s. Erich and Nella (Lange) W.; m. Sigrid Beilharz, Apr. 11, 1963; children: Yvette, Kara, Britta. BS, U. Melbourne, Australia, 1962, MS, 1964, PhD, 1968. Meteorologist Bur. Meteorology, Melbourne, 1959-61; glaciologist Australian Antarctic Exps., 1964-67; from asst. prof. to assoc. prof. geophysics Geophys. Inst., U. Alaska, Fairbanks, 1968-72, prof., 1973—, dep. dir., 1984-86, 90—; project dir. NASA-UAF Alaska SAR Facility, Fairbanks, 1986—; program mgr. NSF, Washington, 1972-74; pres. Internat. Commn. Polar Meteorology, 1980-83; chmn. polar rsch. bd. NAS, 1985-90, Global Change Steering Com. Sci. Com. on Antarctic Rsch., 1988-92; chmn. Global Change Working Group Internat. Sci. Com., 1990—; dir. Ctr. for Global Change and Arctic System Rsch., U. Alaska, 1990—. Contbr. numerous articles to profl. jours. Recipient Polar medal Govt. Australia, 1969; Mt. Weller named in his honor by Govt. Australia, Antarctica; Weller Bank named in his honor by U.S. Govt., Arctic. Fellow Arctic Inst. N.Am.; mem. AAAS (exec. sec. arctic divsn. 1982—), Internat. Glaciological Soc., Am. Meteorol. Soc. (chmn. polar meteorology com. 1980-83), Am. Geophys. Union. Home: PO Box 81024 Fairbanks AK 99708-1024 Office: U Alaska Geophys Inst Fairbanks AK 99775-0800

WELLER, HAROLD LEIGHTON, conductor; b. Dayton, Ohio, July 6, 1941; s. Eugene Lommell and Rita May (Glaser) W.; m. Elizabeth Ann Welch; children: Kurt Eugene, Christopher Howard. Student, Interlochen Music Camp, 1957-58, Oberlin Conservatory of Music, 1959-61, Cin. Conservatory of Music, 1962-63; MusB, Miami U., 1969; MA, Ohio State U., 1976. Asst. opera dir. Cin. Conservatory, 1962-64; mus. dir. Hamilton Symphony, Ohio, 1963-70, Ashland Symphony, Ohio, 1970-78; instr. music Ashland Coll., 1970-77; asst. prof. music Old Dominion U., Norfolk, Va., 1977-79; mus. dir. Old Dominion U. Symphony, Va., 1977-79; dir. orch. and opera U. N.Mex., 1979-82; asst. prof. music U. New Mexico, Albuquerque, 1979-82; mus. dir., gen. mgr. Flagstaff Symphony Orch., 1982—; adj. prof. music Northern Ariz. U., Flagstaff, 1982—; guest condr. Phoenix Symphony Orch., 1985, 86, 87; mus. dir. Phoenix Ballet Co., 1985-86, Youngstown (Ohio) Symphony, Dubuque (Iowa) Symphony, York (Pa.) Symphony; staff announcer Sta. KH-FM, Albuquerque, 1977-79; mus. advisor Sta. KNME-TV, Albuquerque, 1977-79; chmn. ALL State Orch. Ohio Music Edn. Assn., 1972-77. Contbr. articles to profl. jours., producer, host The Music Makers on Sta. KNAU-FM, Flagstaff, 1982—. Treas. Flagstaff Twenty-Five, 1987-88; mem. Exchange Club of Flagstaff, 1982—, Tourist Tax Com., 1986-87, The Ariz. Acad., Flagstaff Economic Council; steering com. Flagstaff Town Hall, 1986-88; chmn. Flagstaff Crime Prevention Week; delegate 50th Ariz. Town Hall, 1987; mem. tourism commn. City of Flagstaff, 1988—, chmn.,

1990—; chmn. Flagstaff Arts Council, 1980-86; bd. dirs. Main St. Flagstaff Found., 1988-90, Sedona Cultural Park, Inc., Flagstaff Leadership Program, 1992—; screening com. supt. Flagstaff Unified Sch., 1993. Named Flagstaff's Citizen of Yr. Ariz. Daily Sun, 1990. Mem. Am. Symphony Orch. League, Arizonans for Cultural Devel., Ariz. Orch. Assn.(pres.), Ariz. Commn. on the Arts (cons. Panel mem. 1983—), Conductors Guild, 1990—. Home: 1741 Columbia Cir Flagstaff AZ 86004-7387 Office: Flagstaff Symphony Orch PO Box 122 Flagstaff AZ 86002-0122

WELLER, LOUIS STEVAN, lawyer; b. L.A., May 31, 1949. BA, Yale U., 1970; JD, U. Calif., Berkeley, 1975, M in Pub. Policy, 1975. Bar: Calif. 1975. Pvt. practice law San Francisco, 1975—; ptnr. Weller & Drucker, San Francisco, 1988; adj. prof. Golden Gate U., San Francisco, 1982—; cons. Calif. Continuing Edn. Bar, Berkeley, 1981—. Editor: Real Estate Tax Digest; contbr. articles to profl. jours. Trustee World Affairs Coun., San Francisco. Mem. ABA (com. chmn.), Bar Assn. San Francisco (sec. chmn.), Calif. Bar Assn. Office: 425 California St Ste 1800 San Francisco CA 94104-2203

WELLES, JOHN GALT, museum director; b. Orange, N.J., Aug. 24, 1925; s. Paul and Elizabeth Ash (Galt) W.; m. Barbara Lee Chrisman, Sept. 15, 1951; children: Virginia Chrisman, Deborah Galt, Barton Jeffery, Holly Page. BE, Yale U., 1946; MBA, U. Pa., 1949. Test engr. Gen. Electric Co., Lynn, Mass., 1947; labor relations staff New Departure div. Gen Motors Corp., Bristol, Conn., 1949-51; mem. staff Mountain States Employers Council, Denver, 1952-55; head indsl. econs. div. U. Denver Research Inst., Denver, 1956-74; v.p. planning and devel. Colo. Sch. Mines, Golden, 1974-83; regional adminstr. EPA, Denver, 1983-87; exec. dir. Denver Mus. Natural History, 1987—; adv. bd. ADA Techs., Inc., 1989—. Sr. cons. Secretariat, UN Conf. Human Environment, Geneva, 1971-72; cons. Bus. Internat., S.A., Geneva, 1972; trustee Tax Free Fund of Colo., N.Y., 1987—; exec. com. Denver Com. on Fgn. Rels., 1987—; chmn. Colo. Front Range Project, Denver, 1979-80. Contbr. articles to profl. jours., newspapers. Recipient Disting. Service award Denver Regional Council Govts., 1980, Barnes award EPA, 1987. Mem. AAAS, Am. Assn. Museums (ethics commn. 1991—, v.p. 1992—), Assn. Sci. Mus. Dirs., World Future Soc., Tau Beta Pi, Blue Key. Republican. Episcopalian. Clubs: Arapahoe Tennis (pres. 1964-65); University (Denver), Denver Athletic. Office: Denver Mus Natural History City Park Denver CO 80205

WELLES, MELINDA FASSETT, artist, educator; b. Palo Alto, Calif., Jan. 4, 1943; d. George Edward and Barbara Helena (Todd) W. Student, San Francisco Inst. Art, 1959-60, U. Oreg., 1960-62; BA in Fine Arts, UCLA, 1964, MA in Spl. Edn., 1971, PhD in Ednl. Psychology, 1976; student fine arts and illustration Art Ctr. Coll. Design, 1977-80. Cert. ednl. psychologist, Calif. Asst. prof. Calif. State U., Northridge, 1979-82, Pepperdine U., L.A., 1979-82; assoc. prof. curriculum, teaching and spl. edn. U. So. Calif., L.A., 1980-89; mem. acad. faculty Pasadena City Coll., 1973-79, Art Ctr. Coll. Design, 1978—, Otis Parsons Sch. Art and Design, L.A., 1986—, UCLA Extension, 1980-84, Coll. Devel. Studies, L.A., 1978-87, El Camino C.C., Redondo Beach, Calif., 1982-86; cons. spl. edn.; pub. adminstrn. analyst UCLA Spl. Edn. Rsch. Program, 1973-76; exec. dir. Atwater Park Ctr. Disabled Children, L.A., 1976-78; coord. Pacific Oaks Coll. in svc. programs for L.A. Unified Schs., Pasadena, 1978-81; mem. Southwest Blue Book, Freedom's Found. at Valley Forge, Friends of French Art, Costume Coun. L.A. County Mus. of Art. Author: Calif. Dept. Edn. Tech. Reports, 1972-76; editor: Teaching Special Students in the Mainstream, 1981, Educating Special Learners, 1986, 88, Teaching Students with Learning Problems, 1988, Exceptional Children and Youth, 1989; group shows include: San Francisco Inst. Art, 1960, U. Hawaii, 1978, Barnsdall Gallery, L.A., 1979, 80; represented in various pvt. collections. HEW fellow, 1971-72; grantee Calif. Dept. Edn., 1975-76, Calif. Dept. Health, 1978. Mem. Calif. Learning Disabilities Assn., Am. Council Learning Disabilities, Calif. Scholarship Fedn. (life), Alpha Chi Omega. Office: 700 Levering Ave Apt 1 Los Angeles CA 90024-2795

WELLINGTON, ROBERT JOHN, systems engineer; b. Mio, Mich., Oct. 7, 1954; s. Robert Jay W.; m. Holley Helen Kushman, June 22, 1975. MS in Math., U. Chgo., 1974, PhD in Math., 1977; MS in Computer Sci., U. Wash., 1982. Asst. prof. dept. math. Loyola U., Chgo., 1977-78; acting asst. prof. dept. math. U. Wash., Seattle, 1978-82; mem. tech. staff TRW Inc., Redondo Beach, Calif., 1982-83; engring. specialist Gen. Dynamics, San Diego, 1983-86; engring. chief Gen. Dynamics, 1986-89; lead engr. MITRE Corp., San Diego, 1989—. Author: Memoir of Am. Math. Soc., 1982: The Unstable Adams Spectral Sequence for Free Iterated Loop Spaces. Mem. IEEE, Am. Math. Soc., Soc. Indsl. and Applied Math. Office: MITRE Corporation 271 Catalina Blvd San Diego CA 92152-5000

WELLISCH, WILLIAM JEREMIAH, social psychology educator; b. Vienna, Austria, July 3, 1938; came to U.S., 1940; s. Max and Zelda (Schanser) W.; m. Geraldine Eve Miller (dec. Feb. 1970); children: Garth Kevin, Miriam Rhoda; m. Claudine Abbey Truman, Sept. 5, 1971; children: Rebecca Colleen, Marcus Joshua, Gabriel Jason. MA in Sociology, U. Mo., 1965, PhD in Sociology, 1968. Researcher urbanization Hemispheric Consultants, Columbia, Mo., 1968-69; cons. to local govt. ofcl. on L.Am. Bi-cultural Consultants, Inc., Denver, 1969-70; prof. Red Rocks Coll., Lakewood, Colo., 1970-76, 77—. Author: Bi-Cultural Development, 1971, Honduras: A Study in Sub-Development, 1978. Mem. citizen's adv. bd. Sta. KCFR Pub. Radio, Denver, 1989—. Republican. Mem. Unification Ch. Home: 2325 Clay St Denver CO 80211 Office: Red Rocks CC 13300 W 6th Ave Lakewood CO 80401

WELLS, CAROL MENTHE, educational and management consultant. BS cum laude, U. Bridgeport, 1963; MA, Rutgers U., 1964; Diploma in Ednl. Adminstrn., U. Conn., 1981, PhD in Curriculum and Instrn. Bus., 1984. Cert. C.C. supr. and instr. bus. and indsl. mgmt., Calif., cert. psychology, sch. psychologist, counseling, kindergarten, elem. and secondary supt. Mem. faculty Valley Coll., C.C. System Conn., Greater Hartford, Manchester, 1977-79, San Bernardino Valley Coll., Calif.; tchr. ind. study Skidmore Coll., N.Y. and Conn., 1977; dir. accounts and pub. rels. Windsor (Conn.) Communications, 1977-79; tchr. ind. study Trinity Coll., Hartford, Conn., 1978; with mktg., sales and pub. rels. depts. LTC div. U.S. Express, Hartford, 1979-80; cen. office adminstr. Grand Canyon Schs., Ariz., 1983-84; v.p. Am. Mgmt. Inst., Hartford, 1984-85; principles of learning instructional specialist Ariz. State Dept. Edn., 1985-86; co-dir. corp. staff tng. div., dir. R & D Jobwatch, Inc., Ariz., 1986-87; dir. sch. system, corp. specialist, indsl. cons. program mgmt., specialist in tng., devel. and grantsmanship Acad. Assocs., Beverly Hills, Calif., 1986—, dir. div. acad. intervention; devel. cons. United Technologies Corp., 1987-88, Guardianships of So. Ariz., AOT Learning Disabilities, Tucson Art Inst., numerous others; cons. pub. health, mental health San Bernardino County Schs., 1990; lectr. staff devel., workshop dir. Wadsworth Atheneum Mus., So. Conn. State Coll., Hartford Sem. Found., St. Joseph's Coll., West Hartford Art League, West Hartford Pub. Schs., Windsor Pub. Schs., Enfield Pub. Schs. Child's Interaction Analysis Learning Survey Instrument (CIALS). Author: Hemispheric Functioning for Administrators, 1986, (manuals), Decision Making and Hemispheric Functioning, 1986, Success Skills for Professional Women, 1986, (workbook) Specific Accountability Guardianship Instrument for Task Structuring Problems, 1988; contbr. articles to profl. jours. Home: PO Box 3854 Fullerton CA 92634-3854

WELLS, DONNA FRANCES, distribution company executive; b. Lima, Ohio, Dec. 19, 1948; d. Arthur Robert and Frances Lucille (Knudtson) W.; m. Darrell Donald Erickson, Nov. 26, 1980. Cert., Parks Bus. Sch., 1972; student, Sheridan Coll., 1984—. Dir. purchasing Wolff Distbg., Gillette, Wyo., 1973—. Mem. Nat. Assn. Purchasing Mgmt., Nat. Assn. of Female Execs., Gillette Racing Assn. (aux. v.p. 1986—), VFW Aux., Am. Legion Aux. Home: 105 Sequoia Dr Gillette WY 82716-6308

WELLS, FRANK G., entertainment company executive, lawyer; b. Mar. 4, 1932. BA summa cum laude, Pomona Coll., 1953; MA in Law, Oxford (Eng.) U., 1955; LLB, Stanford U., 1959. Former vice chmn. Warner Bros. Inc.; ptnr. Gang Tyre & Brown, 1962-69; pres., chief operating officer Walt Disney Co., Burbank, Calif., 1984—. Co-author: Seven Summits. Trustee Pomona Coll., Nat. History Mus., Sundance Inst., S. Paul Getty Trust, Calif. Inst. Tech.; mem. bd. overseers for RAND/UCLA Ctr. Study of Soviet Behavior; mem. svcs. policy adv. com. U.S. Trade Regulation. 1st lt. U.S. Army, 1955-57. Rhodes scholar, 1955. Mem. ABA, State Bar Calif., L.A. County Bar Assn., Explorers Club, Phi Beta Kappa. Office: Walt Disney Co 500 S Buena Vista St Burbank CA 91521-0001*

WELLS, JAMES WAYNE, educator; b. Birmingham, Ala., Feb. 13, 1941; s. William Edward and Margaret Louise (Wainwright) W.; m. Jan. 30, 1965; children: Erin Elizabeth,Risa Kathryne. BS, U. Ala., 1963; postgrad., No. Ariz. U., 1975, U. Ala., 1987, Calif. State U., San Bernadino, 1992. Sci. tchr. Rockdale County High Sch., Conyers, Ga., 1964-67; Spanish tchr. Charlotte (N.C.) Country Day Sch., 1967-69; tchr. mat. Charles Hard Sch., Bessemer, Ala., 1970-72; sci. tchr. Hayes High Sch., Birmingham, Ala., 1973-74; biology tchr. Chinle (Ariz.) High Sch., 1974-87, Jess Lahier High Sch., Bessemer, 1987-88; dir. Scouting Report of Ariz., Phoenix, 1988-89; English as a second lang. tchr. Calif. Dept. Corrections, Blythe, Calif., 1990—. Mem. Calif. Prof. Educator Assn., Scottsdale C. of C. (com. mem. pub. affairs 1988). Democrat. Lutheran. Home: 9510 E Hobson Way Apt 52 Blythe CA 92225-1967 Office: Chuckawalla Valley State Prison PO Box 2289 Blythe CA 92226-2289

WELLS, JON BARRETT, engineer; b. Sewickley, Pa., Oct. 21, 1937; s. Calvin and Martha Barrett (Byrnes) W.; m. Nancy Lou LaFrance, Nov. 18, 1967; children: James Jonathan, Tiffany Lynn. BSEE, Calif. Poly U., 1961. Various positions Bell & Howell Co. Datatape Div., Pasadena, Calif., 1961-73; chief engr. Bell & Howell Co. Datatape Div., 1973-75; engring. mgr. Bell & Howell Co. Datatape Div., Baldwin Park, Calif., 1975-87, Lundy Fin. Systems, Rancho Cucamonga, Calif., 1987—; pres. Datatape Fed. Credit Union, Pasadena, 1978-93; v.p. Recognition Tech. Users Assn., Boston, 1987—; sec. Am. Nat. Standard Inst. X9B6, Washington, 1989-92. Patentee in field; contbr. articles to publs. Sec., founder Pasadena Neighborhood Housing Svcs., Pasadena, 1976-80. Mem. IEEE, Pasadena IBM Personal Computer Users Group, U.S. Power Squadrons, Aircraft Owners and Pilots Assn., Internat. Underwater Explorers Soc. Republican. Home: 2058 E Maverick La Verne CA 91750-2211 Office: Lundy Fin Systems 9431 Hyssop Dr Rancho Cucamonga CA 91730-6107

WELLS, LU, artist; b. Althouse, Oreg., May 10, 1915; d. Joseph Lee and Emma (Hervey) Sowell; m. Charles Keith Wells, May 4, 1933; children: Tommy Lee, Donald Eugene. Comml. Art Design and Illus., Oreg. Inst. Tech., 1955. instr. pvt. classes and local galleries, Tri-Hue Watercolor, Klamath Falls, 1989-92. Exhibited in group shows at Crater Lake Nat. Park, Oreg. Caves Chateau, first tri-hue show Maui, Hawaii. With USAF, 1945-58. Recipient Spl. Svc. award The Favell Mus., Klamath Falls, 1991. Mem. Watercolor Soc. Oreg. (recipient awards), Daus. Am. Colonists (regent 1962-64), Daus. Am. Revolution (registrar). Home: 256 1/2 N Laguna Klamath Falls OR 97601

WELLS, MARK ALAN, production and development executive; b. Burlington, Vt., Jan. 16, 1960; s. Charles H. and Sally (Temple) Whitson; m. Michelle M. Murphy, Feb. 23, 1985; children: Benjamin Mark, Richard Alan, Kendall Colby. Grad., Boulder Vo-Tech, 1977. Screen dept. mgr. Centerline Cirs., Longmont, Colo., 1978-87; prodn. mgr. GTE Corp., Printed Cir. Bd. Operation, Muncy, Pa., 1987-88; card store mgr. Heinrich Mktg., Denver, 1988—, mgr. prodn., MIS; bus. owner Reflective Images, Longmont, Colo., 1984-87; cons. MW Svcs., Arvada, Colo., 1990-91. With U.S. Army, 1977. Home: 10363 W 68th Way Arvada CO 80004-1512 Office: Heinrich Mktg Inc 830 Kipling St Lakewood CO 80215-5867

WELLS, MERLE WILLIAM, historian, state archivist; b. Lethbridge, Alta., Can., Dec. 1, 1918; s. Norman Danby and Minnie Muir (Huckett) W.; student Boise Jr. Coll., 1937-39; A.B., Coll. Idaho, 1941, L.H.D. (hon.), 1981; M.A., U. Calif., 1947, Ph.D., 1950; L.H.D., U. Idaho, 1990. Instr. history Coll. Idaho, Caldwell, 1942-46; assoc. prof. history Alliance Coll., Cambridge Springs, Pa., 1950-56, 58, dean students, 1955-56; cons. historian Idaho Hist. Soc., Boise, 1956-58, historian and archivist, 1959—; hist. preservation officer, archivist State of Idaho, Boise, 1968-86. Treas., So. Idaho Migrant Ministry, 1960-64, chmn., 1964-67; nat. migrant adv. com. Nat. Council Chs., 1964-67, gen. bd. Idaho council, 1967-75; bd. dirs. Idaho State Employees Credit Union, 1964-67, treas., 1966-67; mem. Idaho Commn. Arts and Humanities, 1966-67; mem. Idaho Lewis and Clark Trail Commn., 1968-70, 84-88; mem. Idaho Bicentennial Commn., 1971-76; bd. dirs. Sawtooth Interpretive Assn., 1972—, dept. history United Presbyn. Ch., 1978-84; v.p. Idaho Zool. Soc., 1982-84, bd. dirs., 1984—, treas., 1988-90, historian, 1990—. State Hist. Preservation Officers (dir. 1976-81, chmn. Western states council on geog. names 1982-83), Am. Hist. Assn., Western History Assn. (council 1973-76), AAUP, Am. Assn. State and Local History (council 1973-77), Soc. Am. Archivists, others. Author: Anti-Mormonism in Idaho, 1978, Boise: An Illustrated History, 1982, Gold Camps and Silver Cities, 1984, Idaho: Gem of the Mountains, 1985. Office: Idaho Hist Soc 610 Julia Davis Dr Boise ID 83702-7695

WELLS, PATRICIA BENNETT, business administration educator; b. Park River, N.D., Mar. 25, 1935; d. Benjamin Beekman Bennett and Alice Catherine (Peerboom) Bennett Breckinridge; AA, Allan Hancok Coll., Santa Maria, Calif., 1964; BS magna cum laude, Coll. Great Falls, 1966; MS, U. N.D., 1967, PhD, 1971; children: Bruce Bennett, Barbara Lea Ragland. Fiscal acct. USIA, Washington, 1954-56; pub. acct., Bremerton, Wash., 1956; statistician USN, Bremerton, 1957-59; med. svcs. accounts officer U.S. Air Force, Vandenberg AFB, Calif., 1962-64; instr. bus. adminstrn. Western New Eng. Coll., 1967-69; vis. prof. econs. Chapman Coll., 1970; vis. prof. U. So. Calif. systems Griffith AFB, N.Y., 1971-72; assoc. prof., dir. adminstrv. mgmt. program Va. State U., 1973-74; assoc. prof. bus. adminstrn. Oreg. State U., Corvallis, 1974-81, prof. mgmt., 1982-90, emeritus prof. mgmt., 1990—, univ. curriculum coord., 1984-86, dir. adminstrv. mgmt. program, 1974-81, pres. Faculty Senate, 1981, Interinstl. Faculty Senate, 1986-90, pres., 1989-90; cons. process tech. devel. Digital Equipment Corp., 1982. Pres., chmn. bd. dirs. Adminstrv. Orgnl. Svcs.,Inc., Corvallis, 1976-83, Dynamic Achievement, Inc., 1983—; bd. dirs. Oreg. State U. Bookstores, Inc., 1987-90; exec. dir. Bus. Enterprises Ctr., Inc., 1990-92; dir., cons. Oregonians in Action, 1990-91; Cert. adminstrv. mgr. Pres. TYEE Mobil Home Park, Inc., 1987-92; Fellow Assn. Bus. Communication (mem. internat. bd. 1980-83, v.p. Northwest 1981, 2d v.p. 1982-83, 1st v.p. 1983-84, pres. 1984-85); mem. Am. Bus. Women's Assn. (chpt. v.p. 1979, pres. 1980, named Top Businesswoman in Nation 1980, Bus. Assoc. Yr. 1986), Assn. Info. Systems Profls., Adminstrv. Mgmt. Soc., AAUP (chpt. sec. 1973, chpt. bd. dirs. 1982, 84-89, pres. Oreg. conf. 1983-85), Am. Vocat. Assn. (nominating com. 1976), Associated Oreg. Faculties, Nat. Bus. Edn. Assn., Nat. Assn. Tchr. Edn. for Bus. Office Edn. (pres. 1976-77, chmn. public relations com. 1978-81), Corvallis Area C. of C. (v.p. chamber devel. 1987-88, pres. 1988-89, chmn. bd. 1989-90, Pres.' award 1986), Boys and Girls Club of Corvallis (pres. 1991-92), Sigma Kappa. Roman Catholic. Lodge: Rotary (pres.-elect 1992). Contbr. numerous articles to profl. jours. Office: Enterprise Ctr of La Inc PO Box 43732 SBDC USL Lafayette LA 70504

WELLS, PATRICK HARRINGTON, biology educator; b. Palo Alto, Calif., June 19, 1926; s. Harrington and Doris Virginia (Lacsten) W.; m. Pearl Marie Pernich, July 27, 1951; children: Harrington, Patricia Ann, John Thomas. BA, U. Calif., Santa Barbara, 1948; PhD, Stanford U., 1951. Asst prof. biology U. Mo., Columbia, 1951-57; from asst. prof. to prof. biology Occidental Coll., L.A., 1957—, prof. emeritus, 1991. Co-author (book) Anatomy of a Controversy: the Question of a Language Among Bees, 1990; contbr. articles to profl. jours. Fellow AAAS, So. Calif. Acad. Sci. (dir. 1972-78, mem. adv. bd. 1977—); mem. Am. Zoologists Soc., Zool. Soc. Japan, History of Sci. Soc., Internat. Bee Rsch. Assn., Western Soc. of Naturalists. Office: Occidental Coll Dept Biology 1600 Campus Rd Los Angeles CA 90041-3314

WELLS, ROBERT LEWIS, radiation biologist, educator; b. Denver, Oct. 3, 1952; s. Lewis Gillespie and Jeanne Adelaide (Carter) W.; m. Peggy Jo Brown, Apr. 11, 1981; children: Amanda Jo, Andrew Lewis. BS, Colo. State U., 1975, PhD, 1982. Postdoctoral fellow Argonne (Ill.) Nat. Lab., 1982-84; asst. prof. radiation biology Colo. State U., Ft. Collins, 1984—. Contbr. articles to profl. publs. Mem. Radiation Rsch. Soc., Health Physics Soc., Phi Beta Kappa, Phi Kappa Phi. Home: 1507 Freedom Ln Fort Collins CO 80526 Office: Colo State U Dept Radiol Health Scis Fort Collins CO 80523

WELLS, ROGER STANLEY, software analyst; b. Seattle, Apr. 13, 1949; s. Stanley A. and Margaret W. BA, Whitman Coll., 1971; postgrad., U. Tex., Austin, 1973-74; BS, Oreg. State U., 1977. Software evaluation engr. Tektronix, Beaverton, Oreg., 1979-83; computer engr. Aramco, Dhahran, Saudi Arabia, 1983-84; software engr. Conrac Corp., Clackamas, Oreg., 1984-85, Duarte, Calif., 1985; software analyst Lundy Fin. Systems, San Dimas, Calif., 1986-89; contract software analyst for various orgns. Seattle, 1989-92; software analyst U.S. Intelco, Olympia, Wash., 1993—. Sgt. USAF, 1971-75. Mem. Am. Philatelic Soc., Oxford Club, Portland Sci. Fiction Soc., N.W. Sci. Fiction Assn., L.A. Sci. Fantasy Soc., Oreg. Sci. Fiction Convs. (pres., co-founder 1979-81), Seattle Westercon Organizing Com. (sec., bd. dirs. 1991-93), Toastmasters Internat. (club pres. 1980). Home: 3430 Pacific Ave SE Apt A6-353 Olympia WA 98501

WELLS-MAMLET, DAPHNE, travel consultant; b. London, Sept. 22, 1934; came to U.S., 1956; d. John Arthur and Nancy (Rogers) Wells; m. Howard L. Mamlet, Feb. 14, 1963; 1 stepchild. MSW, London U., 1951; internat. registered meeting planner, Pvt. Bus. Coll., Phoenix, 1991. With Rank Pictures, London, 1951-56; social worker Valley Childrens Hosp., Fresno, Calif., 1956-59; dir. CBS Discount Shopping Mall, Sacramento, Calif., 1959-61; office mgr. Dental Clinic, L.A., 1962-75; owner DA Well Cruise & Tours, Glendale, Calif., 1975—; instr. bus. ethics A Travel Centre, Studio City, Calif., 1987-91, Internat. Registered Meeting Planners, Phoenix, 1992. Creator knitting patterns. Pres., cons. Sisterhood Temple Sinai, Glendale, 1985-86; ombudsman Long Term Care, Glendale, 1989—. Named Woman of Yr. San Fernando Women, 1989; Woman of Decade Sisterhood Temple Sinai, 1990. Mem. B'nai B'rith Women (pres. 1985-86, Woman of Yr. 1985), Brit. Am. C. of C., St. James Club. Office: DA Well Cruise and Tours 571 South St Glendale CA 91202

WELSCH, JAMES LESTER, municipal judge; b. Catskill, N.Y., Oct. 2, 1917; s. Wolfgang Frederick and Hazel Juene (Lester) W.; m. Grace Warner, Oct. 23, 1963. BS, Purdue U., 1942; MA, L.A. State Coll., 1954; grad., Nat. Jud. Coll., 1985. Lic. ednl. adminstr., N. Mex., Ariz., Colo. real estate broker, N.Mex. Pers. mgr., safety dir. Nat. Cash Register Co. electronics div., Hawthorne, Calif., 1952-55; dir. indsl. rels., safety dir. Mercast Mfg. Corp., LaVerne, Calif., 1955-57; asst. prof. mgmt. Eastern N.Mex. U., Portales, 1957-58; asst. prof. indsl. mgmt. Calif. Western U., San Diego, 1958-63; dir. Montelores Multicultural Ctr., Cortez, Colo., 1967-68; chmn. Assn. Dirs. Colo. Bds. Cooperative Svcs., 1968; guidance counselor Dzilth-Na-o-dith-hle Sch., Bur. Indian Affairs, Bloomfield, N.Mex., 1974-76, supervisory guidance counselor, Huerfano, N.Mex., 1976-80, realty specialist, rights protection Bur. Indian. Affairs, Juneau, Alaska, 1980, supervisory realty specialist, safety mgr. Alaska Native Claims Settlement Act, Anchorage, 1981-83; ret., 1983; mcpl. judge, Bloomfield, N.Mex., 1983-84. Chmn. San Juan County (N.Mex.) planning and zoning commn., 1973; bd. dirs. San Juan County Mus. Assn., 1978-79, San Juan County chpt. ARC, 1980, dir. of bd., 1987-88; bd. dirs. Salvation Army Bd., 1987-88, Anasazi Pageant Found., 1988—; chmn. Bloomfield Pride Commn., 1988—; mem. House Arrest and Intensive Supervision, 1987-88; del. N.Mex., State Republican Conv., 1974, 76; sustaining mem. Rep. Nat. Com.; bd. dirs. Farmington Conv. and Visitors Bur., 1988—, N.Mex. Supreme Ct. Jud. Edn. and Tng. Adv. Com., 1991—; mem. World Safety Orgn., 1990—. Served to lt. USN, 1942-46, WWII; Korean War, 1951-52; ret. USNR, 1960. Recipient Cert. of Award, U.S. Coast Guard, 1971, Outstanding Achievement and Exceptional Accomplishment award N.Mex. Legislature, 1990; named adm. Tex. Navy, Citizen of Yr., 1990. Mem. Am. Judges Assn., Nat. Judges Assn. (chaplain 1987—, named Outstanding Non-Atty. Judge of the U.S., Kenneth L. MacEachern Meml. award, 1993), Am. Soc. Safety Engrs., N.Mex. Mcpl. Judges Assn. (pres. 1988—),, Bloomfield C. of c. (pres. 1987-88), Phi Delta Kappa (pres. Mesa Verde, Colo. chpt., 1979), Am. Legion, VFW, Disabled Am. Vets., Elks, Masons, Red Cross Constantine, Nat. Sojourners, Lambda Chi Alpha. Home: 707 N Frontier St Bloomfield NM 87413-5535 Office: 915 N 1st St Bloomfield NM 87413-5221

WELSH, MARY MCANAW, educator, family mediator; b. Cameron, Mo., Dec. 7, 1920; d. Francis Louis and Mary Matilda (Moore) McA.; m. Alvin F. Welsh, Feb. 10, 1944 (dec.); children: Mary Celia, Clinton F., M. Ann. AB, U. Kans., 1942; MA, Seton Hall U., 1960; EdD, Columbia U., 1971. Reporter, Hutchinson (Kans.) News Herald, 1942-43; house editor Worthington Pump & Machine Corp., Harrison, N.J., 1943-44; tchr., housemaster, coordinator Summit (N.J.) Pub. Schs., 1960-68; prof. family studies N.Mex. State U., Las Cruces, 1972-85; adj. faculty dept. family practice Tex. Tech. Regional Acad. Health Ctr., El Paso, 1978-82, Family Mediation Practice, Las Cruces, 1986—. Mem. AAUW (pres. N.Mex. 1981-83), AAUP, N.Mex. Council Women's Orgn. (founder, chmn. 1982-83), Theta Sigma Phi, Delta Kappa Gamma, Kappa Alpha Theta. Democrat. Roman Catholic. Author: A Good Family is Hard to Found, 1972; Parent, Child and Sex, 1970; contbr. articles to profl. jours.; writer, presenter home econs. and family study series KRWG-TV, 1974; moderator TV series The Changing Family in N.Mex./LWV, 1976. Home and Office: PO Box 3483 University Park Las Cruces NM 88003

WELTON, CHARLES EPHRAIM, lawyer; b. Cloquet, Minn., June 23, 1947; s. Eugene Frances and Evelyn Esther (Koski) W.; m. Nancy Jean Sanda, July 19, 1969; children: Spencer Sanda, Marshall Eugene. BA, Macalester Coll., 1969; postgrad., U. Minn., 1969-70; JD, U. Denver, 1974. Bar: Colo. 1974, U.S. Dist. Ct. Coio. 1974, U.S. Supreme Ct. 1979, U.S. Ct. Appeals (10th cir.) 1980. Assoc. Davidovich & Assocs., and predecessor firm, Denver, 1974-77, Charles Welton and Assocs., Denver, 1978-80, 1984-88; ptnr. Davidovich & Welton, Denver, 1981-84, OSM Properties, Denver, 1982—; prin. Charles Welton, P.C., 1988—; faculty Inst. Advanced Legal Studies U. Denver, 1991—; lectr. in field. Contbr. articles to profl. jours. Sch. pres. PTSA, Denver, 1983-84; coach Colo. Jr. Soccer League, 1980-85; coach Odessey of the Mind (formerly Olympics of the Mind), 1986-88; bd. dirs. Virginia Vale Swim Club, officer, 1989-91, Pioneer Jr. Hockey Assn., 1990-92. Served alt. mil. duty Denver Gen. Hosp., 1970-72. Mem. Denver Bar Assn. (law week case mediator, legal fee arbitration com.), Colo. Bar Assn. (legal fee arbitration com.), Assn. Trial Lawyers Am., Colo. Trial Lawyers Assn. (bd. dirs. 1985-90, chmn. seminar com. 1986-88, exec. com. 1987-88, legis. com. 1988—), Am. Bldg. a Lasting Earth (founder), Exec. Ventures Group of Am. Leadership Forum (adv. bd. 1987-90). Democrat. Lutheran. Home: 5020 Montview Blvd Denver CO 80207-3825 Office: Old Smith Mansion 1751 Gilpin St Denver CO 80218-1205

WELTON, MICHAEL PETER, dentist; b. Milw., Apr. 19, 1957; s. Lloyd Peter and Allegra (Nimmer) W.; m. Etsuko Suehiro, Nov. 21, 1986. BS in Biology, Carroll Coll., 1979; DDS, U. Minn., 1983. Commd. lt. USN, 1983; resident Naval Hosp. Camp Pendleton, Oceanside, Calif., 1983-84; with periodontics dept. Naval Dental Clinic, Yokosuka, Japan, 1984-85; clinic dir. Negishi Dental Annex, Yokohama, Japan, 1985-87; gen. dentistry Br. Dental Clinic Mare Island Naval Sta., Vallejo, Calif., 1987-90; with Paul R. Thomassen and Assocs., Stockton, Calif.; legis. extern Am. Student Dental Assn., Washington, 1982; student rep. Minn. Dental Assn., Mpls., 1980. Active Rep. Presdl. Task Force, Washington, 1981—, Nat. Rep. Congl. Com., Washington, 1982—. Mem. ADA, Calif. Dental Assn., Napa-Solano Dental Soc., World Affairs Coun. No. Calif., Art Deco Soc. Calif., Commonwealth Club, No. Calif. Golf Assn., Tilden Park Golf Club, Delta Sigma Delta (treas. Mpls. chpt. 1982-83, Outstanding Mem. award 1982-83). Home: 480 Evelyn Cir Vallejo CA 94589-3259 Office: Paul R Thomassen and Assocs 9409 Thornton Rd Stockton CA 95209

WENAAS, ERIC PAUL, electrical engineering executive; b. Chgo., Jan. 9, 1942; s. Paul E. and Esther P. (Pierson) W.; m. Heather A. Anderson, Aug. 15, 1964 (div. 1974); 1 child, Christopher; m. Karen M. Dawson, Oct. 24, 1987. BSEE, Purdue U., 1963, MSEE, 1964; PhD, SUNY, Buffalo, 1969. Scientist Bell Aerospace Corp., Buffalo, 1968-69, Gulf Gen. Atomic, San Diego, 1969-72; scientist, v.p. IRT Corp., San Diego, 1972-76; sr. v.p. Jaycor, San Diego, 1976-91, pres., ceo, 1991—; lectr. SUNY-Buffalo, 1969. Contbr. articles to profl. publs. Republican. Office: Jaycor 9775 Towne Centre Dr San Diego CA 92121

WENDER, PAUL HERBERT, psychiatrist, researcher; b. N.Y.C., May 12, 1934; m. Frances Burger. AB, Harvard U., 1955; MD, Columbia U., 1959. Intern Barnes Hosp., St. Louis, 1959-60; resident psychiatry Mass. Mental Health Ctr., Boston, 1960-62, St. Elizabeth's Hosp., Balt., 1962-63; fellow child psychiatry Johns Hopkins Hosp., Balt., 1964-67; prof. psychiatry, dir. psychiat. rsch. U. Utah Med. Ctr., Salt Lake City, 1973—; Cert. psychiatry and neurology, child psychiatry. Author: The Hyperactive Child Adolescent-Adult, 1987, (with others) Do You Have A Depressive Illness, 1988. Fellow Am. Acad. Child Psychology, Am. Psychiat. Assn., Am. Coll. Neuropsychopharmacology; mem. Am. Psychopathol. Assn., Nat. Depressive and Manic Depressive Assn., Nat. Found. for Depressive Illness (chmn. bd.), Soc. for Psychiat. Rsch. (pres. 1978-79). Office: U Utah Med Ctr 50 N Medical Dr Salt Lake City UT 84132-0002

WENDLANDT, JOHN CHARLES, lawyer; b. Spencer, Iowa, May 3, 1960; s. William Charles and Anita Marie (Wendland) W.; m. Diane Lynne Hinderliter, Sept. 2, 1989. BA, U. Iowa, 1984; JD, U. Mich., 1988. Bar: Alaska 1989, Oreg. 1989. Jud. clk. Hon. Peter A. Michalski Alaska Superior Ct., Anchorage, 1987-88; assoc. Davis, Wright, Tremaine, Portland, 1988-90, Hughes, Thorsness, Gantz, Powell & Brundin, Anchorage, 1990—. Author: (column student newspaper) U. Mich. Law Sch.-The Res Gestae, 1985-86, features editor, 1986-87. Dir. Anchorage (Alaska) Festival Music, 1990—, v.p., 1992—. Recipient Found. Honors award U. Iowa Found., Iowa City, 1984. Mem. ABA, Alaska Bar Assn., Oreg. Bar Assn., Anchorage Bar Assn., Sigma Pi, Phi Alpha Theta. Methodist. Home: 19825 Fairmount Cir Eagle River AK 99577 Office: Hughes Thorsness Gantz Powell & Brundin 509 W Third Ave Anchorage AK 99501

WENDT, MICHAEL JAMES, production potter; b. Bemidji, Minn., Jan. 7, 1948; s. George Rudolph and Isabel Mary (Zimmermann) W.; m. Rosemary Ann Pittenger, Nov. 10, 1972; children: Natalie Kathleen, Elizabeth Mary. BA, U. Idaho, 1971. Cert. secondary edn. tchr. Idaho. Tchr. German, English Lewiston (Idaho) High Sch., 1971-73; tchr. art Culdesac (Idaho) Sch. Dist., 1974; research asst. U. Idaho, 1976; instr. Walla Walla Community Coll., Clarkston, Wash., 1979, Lewis Clark State Coll., Lewiston, 1985; owner Wendt Pottery, Lewiston, 1973—. Mem. Phi Beta Kappa, Phi Kappa Phi, Am. Field Service Club (pres. 1978), Computer Literacy Support Soc. Home: 1510 9th Ave Lewiston ID 83501-3108 Office: Wendt Pottery 2729 Clearwater Ave Lewiston ID 83501-3234

WENDT, STEVEN WILLIAM, business educator; b. Rockford, Ill., Sept. 18, 1948; s. Roy W. Wendt and Betty Lou (Phillips) Wendt Oser. AAS, Clark County Community Coll., North Las Vegas, Nev., 1982; BS, U. Nev., 1985, MBA, 1987. Cert. vocat. adult educator, Nev. Electronics tech. engr. Rockford Automation, Inc., 1972-74; owner, operator S.W. Ltd., Rockford, 1972-76, S.W. Enterprises, Henderson, Nev., 1977—; instr. electronics Nev. Gaming Sch., Las Vegas, 1977-83; gen. mgr., corp. sec. treas. Customs by Peter Schell, Las Vegas, 1977-83; field engr. Bell & Howell Mailmobile Ops. div., Zeeland, Mich., 1982-90; instr. bus. U. Nev., Las Vegas, 1985—; dir. Wing Fong & Family Microcomputer Labs. Coll. Bus. and Econs. U. Nev., 1990—; bus. cons. Small Bus. Devel. Ctr., Las Vegas, 1985—; incorporator, v.p. Info. Systems, Warren, Mich., 1990-91; fin. officer, gen. ptnr. Obsidian Pub. Press, Henderson, Nev., 1991—; sr. arbitrator Better Bus. Bur., Las Vegas, 1982—; mem. faculty senate U. Nev., 1993; bd. dirs. Gem Crafters Inc., Warren. Author: Intro to Microcomputers, For Future PC Experts, 1992. Treas. U. Nev. Grad. Student Assn, 1986-87. Served with USN, 1967-71. Recipient Cert. Appreciation UNICEF, 1984. Mem. Strategic Gaming Soc., U. Neb. Alumni Assn., Fin. Mgmt. Assn. (Nat. Honor Soc., 1985), U. Nev. Computer User Group (exec. com., chair standards com.), Am. Legion, Phi Lambda Alpha. Home: 1325 Chestnut St Henderson NV 89015-4208 Office: U Nev 4505 S Maryland Pky Las Vegas NV 89154-6034

WENER, MARK HOWARD, rheumatologist, medical educator; b. Chgo., Mar. 14, 1949; s. Leon E. and Sadie (Freeland) W.; m, Corinne L. Fligner, Aug. 8, 1982; children: Leah, Zachary. AB in Chemistry, U. Chgo., 1970; MD, Washington U., St. Louis, 1974. Diplomate Am. Bd. Internal Medicine, Am. Bd. Rheumatology, Am. Bd. Diagnostic Lab. Immunology. Resident in medicine U. Iowa Hosp., Iowa City, 1974-78, fellow in rheumatology, 1978-79, assoc. in rheumatology and internal medicine, 1979-80; fellow in rheumatology and immunology U. Wash., Seattle, 1980-82, dir. immunology divsn. dept. lab. medicine, 1983—, asst. prof., 1983-89, assoc. prof. depts. lab. medicine and medicine, 1989—. Contbr. articles to profl. jours., chpt. to book. Fellow Am. Coll. Rheumatology; mem. ACP, Acad. Clin. Lab. Physicians and Scientists, Am. Assn. Clin. Chemists, Assn. Med. Lab. Immunologists. Office: U Wash Dept Lab Medicine SB-10 Seattle WA 98195

WENGERD, SHERMAN ALEXANDER, geologist, educator; b. Millersburg, Ohio, Feb. 17, 1915; s. Allen Stephen and Elizabeth (Miller) W.; m. Florence Margaret Mather, June 12, 1940; children: Anne Marie Wengerd Riffey, Timothy Mather (dec.), Diana Elizabeth Wengerd Roach, Stephanie Katherine Wengerd Allen. AB, Coll. Wooster, 1936; MA, Harvard U., 1938, PhD, 1947. Registered profl. engr., N.Mex.; profl. geologist; lic. pilot, FAA. Geophysicist, Shell Oil Co., 1937; mining geologist, Ramshorn, Idaho, 1938; Austin teaching fellow Harvard U., 1938-40; rsch. petroleum geologist Shell, Mid-continent, 1940-42, 45-47; prof. geology U. N.Mex., 1947-76; ret., 1976; disting. prof. petroleum geology, 1982; rsch. geologist, 1947—, Petroleum Ind., 1976—; past co-owner Pub. Lands Exploration, Inc., Corona and Capitan Oil Cos.; ltd. ptnr. Rio Petro Oil Co., Dallas. Col. aide-de-camp staff Gov. State N.Mex., 1992. Served to lt. comdr. USNR, 1942-45; capt. Res., ret. Recipient Disting. Alumnus citation Coll. Wooster, 1979. Author chpts. in textbooks and encys., articles in geol. bulls., newsletters. Fellow Geol. Soc. Am., Explorers Club of N.Y., Ret. Officers Assn.; mem. Four Corners Geol. Soc. (hon. life mem., pres. 1953), N.Mex. Geol. Soc. (hon. life mem. 1972—), Albuquerque Geol. Soc. (hon. life mem. 1989—), Am. Assn. Petroleum Geologists (hon. life, nat. editor 1957-59, pres. 1971-72, chmn. adv. council 1972-73, Presdl. award 1948, Sydney Powers Gold medal 1992), Am. Petroleum Inst. (acad. mem., exploration com. 1970-72), Am. Inst. Profl. Geologists (state sect. pres. 1970, nat. editor 1965-66), Soc. Econ. Paleontologists and Mineralogists (dir. found. 1982-86), Aircraft Owners and Pilots Assn., Nat. Aero. Assn. (life), OX5 Aviation Pioneers (life), Silver Wings Flying Fraternity (life), Thomas L. Popejoy Soc., Naval Res. Assn. (life), Assn. Naval Aviation, Am. Legion (life), VFW (life), U. N.Mex. 21 Club, Sigma Xi, Sigma Gamma Epsilon, Phi Kappa Phi. Home: 1040 Stanford Dr NE Albuquerque NM 87106-3720

WENKERT, DANIEL, instrument scientist, atmospheric scientist; b. Ames, Iowa, July 1, 1956; s. Ernest and Ann (Davis) W. BA, Rice U., 1978; PhD, Calif. Inst. Tech., Pasadena, 1986. NRC resident rsch. assoc. Jet Propulsion Lab., Pasadena, 1985-87, mem. tech. staff, 1987—; detailee, program advisor NASA Hdqrs., Washington, 1990-92. Contbr. articles to profl. jours. Nat. Merit scholar, 1974-77; NSF fellow, 1978-81. Mem. Am. Geophys. Union.

WENNER, PAUL FRANCIS, food products executive; b. San Francisco, June 5, 1947; s. Richard Paul and Frances Delores (Hutchings) W. AA in Gen. Studies and TV Prodn., Mount Hood Coll., 1973. With TV prodn. dept. various TV stas. and pvt. prodn. facilities, Portland, Oreg., 1973-77; food instr. various colls., Portland, 1977-85; CEO, founder Wholesome & Hearty Foods, Portland, 1985—; gourmet chef Garden House Restaurant, Portland, 1980-85. With USAF, 1965-69. Mem. Social Venture Network. Home: 1237 SE 36th Portland OR 97214 Office: Wholesome & Hearty Foods In 2422 SW Hawthorne Blvd Portland OR 97214

WENRICH, KAREN JANE, geologist; b. Lebanon, Pa., Apr. 9, 1947; d. George Luther and Joyce Olivia (Eberly) W.; m. Earl Raymond Verbeek, June 21, 1969 (div. Dec. 1981); m. Miles Louis Silberman, June 25, 1983. BS, Pa. State U., 1969, MS, 1971, PhD, 1975. Geologist Molybdenum Corp. Am., Questa, N.Mex., 1969; instr. Bucknell U., Lewisburg, Pa., 1973; geologist U.S. Geol. Survey, Denver, 1974—. Contbr. 130 articles to profl. jours. Recipient Energy Minerals Div. Best Paper award Am. Assn. Petroleum Geologists, 1985, 86. Mem. Geol. Soc. Am., Assn. Exploration Geochemists (v.p.), Friends of Mineralogy, Am. Geophys. Union, Sigma Xi. Home: 63 S Devinney St Golden CO 80401-5314 Office: US Geol Survey MS939 Federal Ctr Denver CO 80225

WENTWORTH, THEODORE SUMNER, lawyer; b. Bklyn., July 18, 1938; s. Theodore Sumner and Alice Ruth (Wortmann) W.; AA, Am. River Coll., 1958; JD, U. Calif., Hastings, 1962; m. Sharon Linelle Arkush, 1965 (dec. 1987); children: Christina Linn, Kathryn Allison; m. Diana Webb Welanetz, 1989; 1 stepchild, Lisa Welanetz. Bar: Calif. 1963; cert. civil trial specialist; diplomate Nat. Bd. Trial Advocacy. Assoc. Adams, Hunt & Martin, Santa Ana, Calif., 1963-66; ptnr. Hunt, Liljestrom & Wentworth, Santa Ana, 1967-77; pres. Solabs Corp.; chmn. bd., exec. v.p. Plant Warehouse, Inc., Hawaii, 1974-82; prin. Law Offices of Theodore S. Wentworth, specializing in personal injury, product liability and profl. malpractice litigation, Irvine, Calif.; judge pro tem Superior Ct. Attys. Panel, Harbor Mcpl. Ct.; owner Eagles Ridge Ranch, Temecula, Calif. Pres., bd. dirs. Santa Ana-Tustin Community Chest, 1972; v.p., trustee South Orange County United Way, 1973-75; pres. Orange County Fedn. Funds, 1972-73; bd. dirs. Orange County Mental Health Assn. Mem. ABA, State Bar Calif., Orange County Bar Assn. (dir. 1972-76), Am. Trial Lawyers Assn., Calif. Trial Lawyers Assn. (bd. govs. 1968-70), Orange County Trial Lawyers Assn. (pres. 1967-68), Lawyer-Pilots Bar Assn., Aircraft Owners and Pilots Assn., Am. Bd. of Trial Advs. (assoc.), Bahia Corinthian Yacht Club, Balboa Bay Club, Fourth of July Yacht Club, Corsair Yacht Club, The Center Club, Pacific Club, Newport, Fourth of July Yacht Club (Catalina Island). Research in vedic prins., natural law, metaphysics. Office: 2112 Business Center Dr Ste 220 Irvine CA 92715-1083

WENTZ, JEFFREY LEE, information systems consultant; b. Philippi, W.Va., Nov. 29, 1956; s. William Henry and Edith Marie (McBee) W. AS in Data Processing, BS in Acctg., Fairmont (W.Va.) State Coll., 1978. Programmer/analyst U.S. Dept. Energy, Morgantown, W.Va., 1978-79, Middle South Svcs., New Orleans, 1979-81; sr. analyst Bank of Am., San Francisco, 1981-83; pres., cons. Wentz Cons. Inc., San Francisco, 1983—. Mem. ACLU, Nature Conservancy, Planned Parenthood. Office: Wentz Cons Inc 1378 34th Ave San Francisco CA 94122

WENZEL, CAROL MARION NAGLER, family therapist; b. Chgo., Nov. 17, 1936; d. Philip L. and Grace (Hindley) Nagler; m. Gene H. Wenzel, July 25, 1954; children: Scott, Jamie, Philip, Sue Ellen. BA in Communication and Social Scis., Marylhurst Coll., 1982; MSW, Portland State U., 1984. Lic. clin. social worker. Pvt. practice counseling Child Within, Oreg., 1986—; trainer alcoholic family systems, various agys., Portland, 1982-86. Mem. Nat. Assn. Social Workers (cert.), Acad. Clin. Social Workers. Democrat. Lutheran. Home: 8325 SE Carnation St Portland OR 97267-2426 Office: Child Within 12608 SE Stark St Portland OR 97233-1058

WENZEL, ELIZABETH MARIE, research psychologist; b. Phoenix, Sept. 24, 1954; d. Robert Henry and Loraine (Hagerty) W.; m. Gary Lee Payne, Sept. 2, 1984; 1 child, Connor Tomás Payne. BA in Psychology, U. Ariz., 1976; PhD in Cognitive Psychology, U. Calif., Berkeley, 1984. Rsch. technician NASA-Ames Life Scis. Div., Moffett Field, Calif., 1977; rsch. asst. NASA-Ames Human Factors Rsch. Div., Moffett Field, Calif., 1977-78; postdoctoral rsch. asst. aerospace human factors rsch. div. NRC/NASA-Ames, Moffett Field, Calif., 1984-86; rsch. psychologist NASA-Ames Aerospace Human Factors Rsch. Div., Moffett Field, Calif., 1986—; dir. auditory spatial displays lab. NASA-Ames, Moffett Field. Contbr. articles to jours. on virtual acoustic displays. Mem. Assn. for Computing Machinery, Acoustical Soc. Am. (assoc.), Audio Engring. Soc., IEEE, Human Factors Soc. Office: NASA-Ames Rsch Ctr Mail Stop 262-2 Moffett Field CA 94035-1000

WERBACH, MELVYN ROY, physician, writer; b. Tarzana, Calif., Nov. 11, 1940; s. Samuel and Martha (Robbins) W.; m. Gail Beth Leibsohn, June 20, 1967; children: Kevin, Adam. BA, Columbia Coll., N.Y.C., 1962; MD, Tufts U., Boston, 1966. Diplomate Am. Bd. Psychiatry and Neurology. Intern VA Hosp., Bklyn., 1966-67; resident in psychiatry Cedars-Sinai Med. Ctr., L.A., 1969-71; chmn. dept. mental health Ross-Loos Med. Group, L.A., 1972-75; dir. psychol. svcs., clin. biofeedback UCLA Hosp. and Clinics, 1976-80; pres. Third Line Press, 1986—; asst. clin. prof. Sch. Medicine, UCLA, 1978—; mem. nutritional adv. bd. Cancer Treatment Ctrs. Am., 1989—. Author: Third Line Medicine, 1986, Nutritional Influences on Illness, 1987, 2d edit., 1993, Nutritional Influences on Mental Illness, 1991, Healing Through Nutrition, 1993; Nutritional Medicine,, Eng., 1990—; mem. editorial bd. Jour. of Nutritional Medicine, 1993—; mem. med. adv. bd. Let's Live Mag., 1989—; contbr. articles to med. jours. Mem. Biofeedback Soc. Calif. (life, pres. 1977, Cert. Honor 1985).

WERKHEISER, STEVEN LAWRENCE, financial specialist; b. Mankato, Minn., Oct. 6, 1945; s. Laverne Eugene and Dorothy M. W.; m. Michelle Sue Phelan; student L.A. Pierce Coll., 1964-66, Oreg. State U., 1963-64; BA, UCLA, 1970, MS, 1971; children: Steven Lawrence, Kirsten Elizabeth. Mcpl. bond trader/underwriter Blyth & Co., Los Angeles, 1971-72, Blyth Eastman Dillon, 1972-73, mgr. mcpl. bond dept., 1974; fin. analyst Northrop Corp., Hawthorne, Calif., 1974-75, fin. planning analyst, 1976-80; v.p. trading R.H. Moulton & Co., Los Angeles, from 1980; div. fin. specialist, mgr. planning and adminstrn. Northrop Corp., Hawthorne, corp. fin. cons., L.A., 1975-92; bus. devel., treas., CFO Ticom Corp., Warren, Mich., 1992—. Served with AUS, 1966-68. Mem. Los Angeles Bond Club, In the Wings, Assn. MBA's, UCLA Alumni Assn. Republican. Methodist. Home: 25102 Avenida Ignacio Santa Clarita CA 91355-3033

WERMERS, MARY ANN, nursing executive, educator; b. St. Louis, Nov. 19, 1946; d. Anthony Gaylord and Cecilia Agnes (Tewes) Minnick; m. Joseph J. Wermers, July ll, l970; children: Patricia, Alyssa, Aaron. BSN, St. Louis U., 1968, MSN, 1970. RN, Colo.; vocat. credential, Colo. Staff nurse, nurse aide John Cochran VA Hosp., St. Louis, 1967-69; staff nurse, head nurse Incranate Word Hosp., St. Louis, 1969-70; staff nurse Rush-Presbyn. Hosp., Chgo., summer 1970, St. Benedict's Hosp., Ogden, Utah, 1972-73; instr. nursing U. Ill., Chgo., 1970-72; asst. prof. nursing, coord. U. Nebr., Omaha, 1974-75; instr. nursing, coord. Pikes Peak Community Coll., Colorado Springs, Colo., 1976-82, mem. nursing adv. bd., 1987--; asst. prof. nursing, coord. U. So. Colo., 1985-90; chmn. dept. Pueblo (Colo.) Community Coll., 1985-90; asst. v.p. patient svcs. Parkview Hosp., Pueblo, 1990-91, v.p. patient svcs., 1991—; mem. nursing adv. bd. U. So. Colo., 1987—, Pueblo C.C. Nursing Program; staff nurse Fantus Clinic, Cook County Hosp., Chgo., part-time 1971-72; workshop speaker; adminstrv. cons. Parkview Hosp., Pueblo, summer 1987. Mem. coun. Divine Redeemer Parish, Colorado Springs, 1983-85; participant Career Days, Pueblo, 1985--; mem. adv. bd. Divine Redeemer Sch., 1987--. Recipient Outstanding Women's award U. So. Colo., 1985, Nightingale award U. Colo., 1986, 93; edn. grantee St. Louis U., 1964-65, President's honor scholar, 1968; Pueblo Community Coll. faculty grantee, 1987-88. Mem. AACN, Am. Soc. Quality Control (pres. 1987-88), Colo. Orgn. Nurse Execs., Sigma Theta Tau. Republican. Roman Catholic. Office: Parkview Hosp 400 W 16th St Pueblo CO 81003-2745

WERNER, BARRY LEONARD, radiation physicist; b. Bklyn., Feb. 15, 1944; s. Herman Philip and Anna (Akronowitz) W.; m. Helene Esther March (div.). BS in Physics, CCNY, 1965; MA in Physics, Brandeis U., 1967, PhD in Physics, 1972. Sr. physicist N.E. Ctr. for Radiol. Physics Meml. Sloan-Kettering Cancer Ctr., N.Y.C., 1975-79; asst. prof. dept. therapeutic radiology U. Minn., Mpls., 1979-89, assoc. prof. dept. therapeutic radiology, 1989-92; co-dir., Med. Physics Divsn. Inst. Applied Physiology and Medicine, Seattle, 1992—; assoc. dir. Lawrence H. Lanzl Inst. Med. Physics, Seattle, 1993—. Mem. Am. Assn. Physicists in Medicine (Farrington Daniels award 1988, cons. task group 25 clin. electron dosimetry, internat. affairs com.). Jewish. Home: 3225 Benton Pl SW # 404 Seattle WA 98116 Office: Inst Med Physics 134 N 81st St Seattle WA 98103

WERNER, E. LOUIS, JR., lawyer, insurance company executive; m. Sandra M. Johnston; children: E. Louis III, Eric R., Matthew J. BA, Princeton U., 1949; BS, Washington U., St. Louis, 1950, LLB, 1952, JD, 1952. Bar: Mo. 1952, U.S. Ct. Mil. Appeals 1963, U.S. Supreme Ct. 1963; CPCU 1957; lic. pilot single, multi-engine and instrument ratings. Exec. v.p. TOR Mgmt., Shawnee Mission, Kans.; mng. ptnr. Dukes Deux Leasing Co., Scottsdale, Ariz.; dir. ABC Moving and Storage Co., Inc., Phoenix; v.p. devel. Phoenix (Ariz.) Country Day Sch.; chmn. emeritus, dir. Insurers Svc. Corp., Briarcliff Manor, N.Y.; magistrate judge Town of Paradise Valley, Ariz.; v.p., bd. dirs. Butch Baird Enterprises, Inc., Hialeah, Fla., Pacific Tooling Corp.; exec. v.p. Frank B. Hall Svcs., Briarcliff Manor; chmn., chief exec. officer Insurers Svc. Corp., St. Louis; exec. v.p., bd. dirs. Safety Mutual Casualty Corp., St. Louis; v.p., bd. dirs. St. Louis Indoor Soccer Club; bd. dirs., past pres. Nat. Assn. Safety and Claims Orgn.; v.p., bd. dirs. Chester Broadcasting Corp., St. Louis. Trustee Scottsdale Meml. Health Found., Valley Presbyn. Found.; bd. dirs. Playgoers of St. Louis, Inc., Rossman Sch., St. Louis; deacon, trustee, ruling elder Ladue Chapel, St. Louis; ruling elder Valley Presbyn. Ch., Paradise Valley, Ariz.. Served to col. USAR. Mem. Fed. Bar Assn., Mo. Bar Assn., St. Louis Bar Assn., Mo. Athletic Club, USPGA (assoc.), Assn. Corp. Growth (Ariz. chpt.), Am. Soc. CPCU, Aircraft Owners and Pilots Assn., Econ. Club of Phoenix, Paradise Valley Country Club, Forest Highlands Golf Club, Desert Mtn. Golf Club, Desert Highland Golf Club. Home: 5715 N Cameldale Way Paradise Vly AZ 85253-5207 Office: 6900 E Camelback Rd Ste 700 Scottsdale AZ 85251-2472

WERNER, GLORIA S., librarian; b. Seattle, Dec. 12, 1940; d. Irving L. and Eva H. Stolzoff; m. Newton Davis Werner, June 30, 1963; 1 son, Adam Davis. BA, Oberlin Coll., 1961; ML, U. Wash., 1962; postgrad. UCLA, 1962-63. Reference librarian UCLA Biomed Library, 1963-64, asst. head pub. services dept., 1964-66, head pub. services dept., head reference div., 1966-72, asst. biomed. librarian public services, 1972-77, asso. biomed. librarian, 1977-78, biomed. librarian, assoc. univ. librarian, dir. Pacific S.W. regional Med. Library Service, 1979-83; asst. dean library services UCLA Sch. Medicine, 1980-83; assoc. univ. librarian for tech. services, 1983-89, dir. libraries, acting univ. librarian, 1989-90, univ. librarian, 1990—; adj. lectr. UCLA Grad. Sch. Library and Info. Sci., 1977-83. Mem. ALA . Editor, Bull. Med. Library Assn., 1979-82, asso. editor, 1974-79; mem. editorial bd. Ann. Stats. Med. Sch. Libraries U.S. and Can., 1980-83; mem. accrediting commn. Western Assn. Schs. and Colls.; mem. Northwest Assn. Schs. and Colls. Office: UCLA Rsch Libr Libr Adminstrv Office 405 Hilgard Ave Los Angeles CA 90024-1575

WERNER, MARLIN SPIKE, speech pathologist and audiologist; b. Portland, Maine, Aug. 15, 1927; s. Leonard Matthews and Margaret (Steele) W.; m. Caroline Emma Paul, Dec. 23, 1985; children: Leo Hart, Joseph Hart. BA in Sociology and Social Work, U. Mo., 1950; ScM in Audiology and Speech Pathology, Johns Hopkins U., 1957; PhD in Speech and Hearing Sci., Ohio State U., 1966. Lic. in audiology, hearing aid dispensing, speech pathology, Hawaii; lic. in audiology and speech pathology, Calif. Audiologist/speech pathologist, dir. Speech and Hearing Ctr. Asheville (N.C.) Orthopedic Hosp., 1960-64; assoc. prof. speech pathology and audiology We. Carolina U., Cullowhee, N.C., 1965-69; assoc. prof. speech pathology, audiology and speech sci. Fed. City Coll. (now U. D.C.), Washington, 1969-73; pres. Friends of Nepal's Hearing Handicapped, Oakland, Calif., 1979-84; hearing aid dispenser, audiologist, speech pathologist pvt. practice, Oakland and Lafayette, Calif., 1973-85; pvt. practice Lafayette, 1985-87; pvt. practice speech pathology and audiology Hilo, Hawaii, 1987—; speech and hearing cons. VA Hosp., Oteen, N.C., 1960-64; clin. cons. Speech and Hearing Clinic, Asheville Orthopedic Hosp., 1966-67; lectr., presenter in field. Contbr. articles to profl. jours.; contbr. to Ency. Brit., Am. Heritage Book of Natural Wonders, others. Mem. hearing impaired svcs. task force State of Hawaii Dept. Health; mem. Hawaii County Mayor's Com. for Persons with Disabilities; chmn. adv. bd. Salvation Army; bd. dirs. Hawaii chpt. Am. Arthritis Found.; past pres. Big Island Safety Assn.; mem. Hawaii Gov's. bd. Hearing Aid Dealers And Fitters; mem. adv. com., pres. Older Adult Resource Ctr., Laney Coll., Oakland, others. MCH fellow Johns Hopkins U., 1954, Pub. Health fellow Ohio State U., 1964. Fellow Nat. Speleological Soc.; mem. AAAS, Am. Speech and Hearing Assn., Acoustical Soc. Am., Calif. Speach and Hearing Assn., Calif. Writers Club (bd. dirs., past pres.), Hawaii Speech/Lang. Hearing Assn. Home: 15-2680 Opelu St Pahoa HI 96778-8712 Office: 1292 Waianuenue Ave Hilo HI 96720

WERNER, RICHARD ALLEN, entomologist; b. Reading, Pa., Feb. 20, 1936; s. Roy M. and Hazel (Rightmeyer) W.; m. Patricia Thomas, Aug. 25, 1973; children: Sarah T., Luke O. BS in Forestry, Pa. State U., 1958, BS in Entomology, 1960; MS in Entomology, U. Md., 1966; PhD in Entomology, N.C. State U., 1971. Forester Forest Svc., USDA, Roseberg, Oreg., 1957-60; rsch. entomologist Forest Svc., USDA, Juneau, Alaska, 1960-64; insect toxicologist Forest Svc., USDA, Research Triangle Park, N.C., 1965-74; rsch. entomologist Forest Svc., USDA, Fairbanks, Alaska, 1974-85, project leader, 1985-91, chief rsch. entomologist, 1991—; adj. prof. U. Alaska, Fairbanks, 1980—; prin. rsch. assoc. Inst. Arctic Biology, U. Alaska, 1985—. Author: Insects and Diseases of Alaskan Forests, 1980, 2d edit. 1985. Counselor Boy Scouts Am., Fairbanks, 1989—. Mem. Entomol. Soc. Am., Soc. Am. Foresters, Ga. Entomol. Soc., Entomol. Soc. Can., Chem. Ecology Soc. Am., Western Forest Insect Wk. Conf. (sec.-treas. 1980-82), N. Am. Forest Insect Wk. Conf. (steering com. 1989-91). Office: Inst of No Forestry USDA 308 Tanana Dr Fairbanks AK 99775-5500

WERNER, ROGER HARRY, archaeologist; b. N.Y.C., Nov. 11, 1950; s. Harry Emile and Rena (Roode) W.; m. Kathleen Diane Engdahl, Feb. 20, 1982; children: Meryl Lauren, Sarah Melise, Jeremy Marshall; 1 stepchild, Amber Fawn. BA, Belknap Coll., 1973; MA, Sonoma State U., Rohnert Park, Calif., 1982. Curatorial aide Anthro. Lab. Sonoma State Coll., 1975-76, curatorial asst., 1976-77, staff archaeologist, 1977-80; staff archaeologist Planning Dept., Lake County, Calif., 1977; cir. riding archaeologist western region Nat. Park Service, Tucson, Ariz., 1978; prin. investigator Archaeol. Services, Inc., Stockton, Calif., 1979—; cons. Calif. Indian Legal Services, Ukiah, 1977, Geothermal Research Impact Projection Study, Lakeport, Calif., 1977; instr. Ya-Ka-Ama Indian Ednl. Ctr., Santa Rosa, Calif., 1978-79; lead archaeologist No. Calif., WESTEC Services, Inc., San Diego, 1979-81. Sec. Colonial Hts. PTA, 1983-84, 2d v.p., 1985-86, historian, 1986-87, v.p., 1987-88; cons., instr. Clovis Adult Sch., 1984-85; instr. U. Pacific Lifelong Learning Ctr., 1987—, San Joaquin Delta Coll., 1990—, Calif. State U., Fresno, 1992—; bd. dirs. Valley Mountain Regional Ctr., 1987-88, treas., 1988-89, v.p., 1989-90, pres.-elect, 1990-91, pres., 1991—; active Spl. Olympics, Stockton, Calif.; bd. dirs., treas. Stockton Chorale 1992-93. Anthropology dept. research grantee, Sonoma State U., 1980. Mem. Geol. Soc. Am., Soc. for Am. Archaeologists, Great Basin Anthropol. Conf., Soc. for Calif. Archaeology, Soc. Profl. Archaeologists, Soc. for Hist. Archeology, Assn. for Retarded Citizens, Am. Soc. Photogrammetry and Remote Sensing, Urban Regional Info. Systems Assn., Bay Automated Mapping Assn., Kiwanis. Democrat. Lodge: Kiwanis (Stockton). Home: 1117 Aberdeen Ave Stockton CA 95209-2625 Office: Archaeol Svcs Inc 8110 Lorraine Ave Ste 408 Stockton CA 95210-4241

WERNER, ROY ANTHONY, aerospace executive; b. Alexandria, Va., June 30, 1944; s. William Frederick and Mary Audrey (Barksdale) W.; m. Paula Ann Privett, June 8, 1969; children: Kelly Rene, Brent Alastair. BA, U. Cen. Fla., 1970; MPhil, Oxford U., 1973; MBA, Claremont (Calif.) Grad. Sch., 1986. Reporter St. Petersburg (Fla.) Times, 1968-69; assoc. dir. White House Conf. on Youth, 1970-71; exec. sec. Oxford Strategic Studies Group, 1971-73; internat. officer Fed. Energy Adminstrn., 1973-74; mem. legis. staff U.S. Senate, Washington, 1974-79; prin. dept. asst. Sec. of The Army, Washington, 1979-81; dir. policy rsch. Northrop Corp., L.A., 1982-83, spl. asst. to sr. v.p., mktg. to mgr. program planning and analysis electronics system divsn., 1989; chmn. U.S. Delegation/polit. com. Atlantic Treaty Assn. Mtg., Brussels, 1989, mem. U.S. delegation, Paris, 1990, others; staff dir. East Asian and Pacific Affairs Subcom., U.S. Senate Fgn. Rels. Com., 1977-79; councilor Atlantic Coun. of the U.S., 1985—; speaker Pacific Parliamentary Caucus, numerous acad. confs. in U.S. and East Africa. Editorial bd. Global Affairs, 1982-86; contbr. numerous articles to profl. jours./publs. Pres. Irvine (Calif.) Boys and Girls Club, 1990-92, v.p., 1989-90, bd. dirs., 1987—; treas. Irvine Temporary Housing, 1988-91, bd. dirs., 1986-91; chmn. fin. com. Outreach Univ. United Meth. Ch., Irvine, 1989-90, others; corp. sec. Irvine Housing Opportunities, 1988-89, bd. dirs. Harbor Area Boys and Girls Clubs, 1991-94. Maj. USAR, 1963-81. Recipient Disting. Alumnus award U. Ctrl. Fla. Alumni Assn., Orlando, 1982, Outstanding Civilican Svc. medal Dept. of the Army, 1981, Atlantic Coun. of the U.S. Sr. Rsch. Fellow, 1988-89. Mem. Am. Fgn. Svc. Assn., Am. Def. Preparedness Com. Democrat. Methodist. Home: 28 Fox Hill Irvine CA 92714-5493

WERNER, TOM, television producer, professional baseball team executive; m. Jill Werner; 3 children, Teddy, Carolyn, Amanda. BA, Harvard Univ., 1971. With ABC Television, Inc., 1972-82; co-owner Carsey-Werner Co., Studio City, Calif., 1982—; chmn. San Diego Padres, 1991—; mem. bd. dirs.: Old Globe Theatre; Sharp Hospital. Co-exec. producer TV series: Oh, Madeline, 1983; exec. producer: The Cosby Show, (Emmy awd. Outstanding Comedy Series-1985), 1984-92, A Different World, 1987-93, Roseanne, 1988—, Chicken Soup, 1989-90, Grand, 1990, Davis Rules, 1991, You Bet Your Life, 1992-93, Frannie's Turn, 1992. Office: Carsey Werner Co A

Differen World Bldg 3 Studio City CA 91604 also: San Diego Padres PO Box 2000 San Diego CA 92112*

WERTZ, HARVEY JOE, computer scientist; b. Muskogee, Okla., May 1, 1936; s. Bradley Leo and Beulah (Snider) W.; m. Joan Margaret Orson, July 20, 1968. BSEE, U. Kans., 1958, MSEE, 1959; PhD, U. Wis., 1962. Asst. prof. U. Wis., Madison, 1962-66, assoc. prof., 1968-69; mem. tech. staff Aerospace Corp., L.A., 1966-68, dept. head, 1969-79, prin. dir., 1979—. Fellow NSF, 1959. Mem. IEEE, Sigma Xi. Office: Aerospace Corp PO Box 92957 Los Angeles CA 90009-2957

WESLEY, VIRGINIA ANNE, real estate property manager; b. Seattle, Apr. 29, 1951; d. Albert William and Mary Louise (Heusser) W. BA in Speech, U. Hawaii, Hilo, 1978. Cert. property mgr. Mgr. office, traffic Sta. KIPA-Radio, Hilo, 1972-74; reporter West Hawaii Today, Kailua-Kona, Hawaii, 1974; mgr. office U. Hawaii, Hilo, 1975-78; dir. property mgmt. First City Equities, Seattle, 1978-88, Winvest Devel. Corp., Seattle, 1988-89; with Quadrant Corp, Bellevue, Wash., 1992—; instr. Bellevue (Wash.) Community Coll., 1982-85. Bd. dirs. Mayor's Small Bus. Task Force, Seattle, 1981-83, 1st Hill Improvement Assn., Seattle, 1982—; active Goodwill Games, Seattle, 1990, Kauri Investments, Ltd., Seattle, 1991-92. Mem. Inst. Real Estate Mgmt., Internat. Coun. Shopping Ctrs., Comml. Real Estate Women, Women's Bus. Exch., Seattle-King County Bd. Realtors, Big Island Press Club, Phi Kappa Phi. Home: 4841 S Raymond St Seattle WA 98118-2854

WESNICK, RICHARD JAMES, newspaper editor; b. Racine, Wis., Oct. 14, 1938; s. John and Julia (Kassa) W.; m. Elaine Apoline Smith, Sept. 30, 1967; children: Catherine Elaine, Julia Ann. BA, U. Houston, 1961. Reporter Jour. Times, Racine, 1965-76; mng. editor Ind. Record, Helena, Mont., 1976-80; editor Billings Gazette, Mont., 1980—; mem. Pulitzer Prize Jury, 1989, 90, 91. Editor: Death Sentences, Best of Bragg, Yellowstone on Fire, The Big Drive, Montana From the Big Sky, Wagons Across Wyoming, Yellowstone in the Eagle's Eye. Served with USMC, 1961-64. Mem. Mont. AP (chmn., bd. dirs. 1985-88, freedom of info. com., legis. rev. com.), Soc. Newspaper Designers, Am. Soc. Newspaper Editors. Roman Catholic. Lodges: Kiwanis, Rotary. Home: 2214 22nd St W Billings MT 59102-2236 Office: Billings Gazette 401 N Broadway Billings MT 59101-1243

WESSEL, WILLIAM ROY, mathematician; b. Louisville, Nov. 20, 1937; s. William LeRoy and Florence (Aubrey) W. BS in Physics magna cum laude, U. Notre Dame, 1959; MS in Physics, U. Mich., 1961, PhD in Physics, 1965. Rsch. scientist Argonne (Ill.) Nat. Lab., 1966-72; rsch. assoc. Fla. State U., Tallahassee, 1972-74; vis. scientist Nat. Ctr. Atmospheric Rsch., Boulder, Colo., 1974-79; sr. cons. Control Data Corp., Mpls., 1979-87; scientific cons. W. Roy Wessel & Assocs., Boulder, 1987—. NSF scholar, 1960, 61. Mem. Am. Math. Soc. Soc. Ind. Applied Math. Home and Office: 3545 Arthur Ct Apt 3 Boulder CO 80304-2031

WESSELS, IZAK FREDERICK, ophthalmologist; b. Johannesburg, South Africa, Oct. 2, 1948; came to U.S., 1986; s. Hans Jacob and Anna Elizabeth (Van Heerden) W.; m. Elza Elaine Blake, Dec. 10, 1972; children: Gunter F., Delia A., Rhoda N. BSc, U. Witwaterstrand, Johannesburg, 1970, MD, 1973, M of Medicine Ophthalmology, 1985. Diplomate Am. Bd. Ophthalmology. Intern J.G. Strijdom Hosp., Johannesburg, 1974; resident in pathology U. Cape Town, 1975; supt. Maluti Adventist Hosp., Mapoteng, Lesotho, 1977-79; resident ophthalmology U. Witwaterstrand, 1979-83; pvt. practice Roodepoort, South Africa, 1983-86; asst. prof. Loma Linda (Calif.) U., 1989-91, assoc. prof., 1991—; adj. clin. faculty So. Coll. Optometry, Memphis, 1992—; vis. prof. Kasturba Med. Coll., Manipal, India, 1990—. Contbr. articles to profl. jours. Fellow ACS, Royal Coll. Surgeons, Am. Acad. Ophthalmology, Coll. of Ophthalmology of United Kingdom; mem. AMA, APHA, Calif. Med. Assn., San Bernardino County Med. Assn. (disaster com.), Calif. Cornea Club, Am. Assn. for Lab. Animal Sci., Am. Soc. of Cataract and Refractive Surgery, Assn. for Rsch. in Vision and Optics, Calif. Cornea Club (Max Fine Soc.), San Bernardino County Med. Soc., Tri-County Soc. Ophthalmology, Loma Linda U. Sch. Medicine Alumni Assn., Adventist Internat. Eye Soc., Adventist Internat. Med. Soc., Lions, Sigma Xi. Home: 12825 Amber Ln Yucaipa CA 92399 Office: Loma Linda U Dept Opthalmology 11370 Anderson St 1800 Loma Linda CA 92399

WESSLER, MELVIN DEAN, farmer, rancher; b. Dodge City, Kan., Feb. 11, 1932; s. Oscar Lewis and Clara (Reiss) W.; grad. high sch.; m. Laura Ethel Arbuthnot, Aug. 23, 1951; children: Monty Dean, Charla Cay, Virgil Lewis. Farmer-rancher, Springfield, Colo., 1950—; dir., sec. bd. Springfield Co-op. Sales Co., 1964-80, pres. bd., 1980—. Pres., Arkansas Valley Co-op. Council, SE Colo. Area, 1965-87, Colo. Co-op. Council, 1969-72, v.p. 1974, sec. 1980-86; community com. chmn. Baca County, Agr. Stablzn. and Conservation Svc., Springfield, 1961-73, 79—, vice chmn. Baca County Com., 1980-90; mem. spl. com. on grain mktg. Far-Mar-Co.; mem. adv. bd. Denver Bapt. Bible Coll., 1984-89; chmn., bd. dirs. Springfield Cemetery Bd., 1985—; apptd. spl. com. Farmland Industries spl. project Tomorrow, 1987—. Recipient The Colo. Cooperator award The Colo. Coop Coun., 1990. Mem. Colo. Cattlemen's Assn., Colo. Wheat Growers Assn., Southeast Farm Bus. Assn. (bd. dirs. 1991—), Big Rock Grange (treas. 1964-76, master 1976-82). Address: 18363 County Rd PP Springfield CO 81073

WEST, BILLY GENE, public relations executive; b. Richmond, Ind., Nov. 22, 1946; s. Billy D. and Jean C. (Cox) W. AA, Cerritos Coll., 1966; BA, U. So. Calif., 1969; MA, U. Minn., 1971. Salesman, Marina Art Products, L.A., 1967-73; v.p. Am. Telecon Network, Dallas, 1974-77; gen. mgr. Phoenix Publs., Houston, 1977-78; pres. San Dark, Inc., San Francisco, 1978-82; gen. ptnr. Billy West & Assocs., 1982—; pres. V.G. Prodns., 1983—; chief exec. officer Westmarking, San Francisco, 1989— ; exec. dir. Young Ams. for Freedom, Minn. and Wis., 1970-72; pres. S.F.P.A., San Francisco, 1982-83. Mem. Assn. MBA Execs. Mem. Am. Ref. Ch.

WEST, CHRISTOPHER WAYNE, small business manager; b. Pueblo, Colo., June 11, 1961; s. Billy W. and Josie L. W. Grad. high sch., Delta, Colo. Salesman Gambles, Delta, 1978-80; office mgr. West's Home Ctr., Delta, 1982—; mil. advisor U.S. Army Res., Mid-States region, 1982—. Mem. Republican Nat. Com., 1986—. Served to 2d lt. U.S. Army, 1980-82. Mem. Am. Fedn. Police (cert. appreciation 1988), Council Inter-Am. Security, Delta Jaycees (officer 1988). Office: West's Home Ctr 327 Main St Delta CO 81416-1885

WEST, DALE REED, accountant; b. Ogden, Utah, May 23, 1954; s. Reed Z. and DeLoris (Petersen) W.; m. Deborah Kay Lunt, June 9, 1978; children: Reed, Shannell, Krista, Aaron, Jaime. AAS, Weber State U., 1973, BS in Acctg., Econs. and Comm., 1979. Mem. staff Shamrock Svc., Layton, Utah, 1971-73, mgr. ops., 1976-80; pub. acct. West & West Acctg., Layton, 1978—; staff acct. Sipple & Assocs., Salt Lake City, 1979-83; office mgr., contr. Wayne T. Smedley & Assocs., Inc., Layton, 1979-83; contr. Electro Tech. Corp., Salt Lake City, 1983-86, Trans-West Electric, Salt Lake City, 1986-89; sec., treas. bd. dirs. Wayne T. Smedley & Assocs., Inc.; bd. dirs. Profl. Seminars, Provo, Utah; lectr. in field. State del. Utah Dem. Party, Salt Lake City, 1978; mem. coun. staff com. Boy Scouts Am., Layton, 1980—. Mem. Utah Assn. Pub. Accts., Am. Tax Profl. Soc. Mem. LDS Ch. Home and Office: 3101 E 1830 N Layton UT 84040

WEST, DELNO CLOYDE, JR., writer, educator; b. Skyler County, Mo., Apr. 8, 1936; s. Delno C. Sr. and Elsie (Cornett) W.; m. Jean Donald, Aug. 31, 1958; children: Douglas, Delisa, Dawn. BS, N.E. Mo. StateU., 1961; MA, U. Denver, 1962; PhD, UCLA, 1970. Prof. history No. Ariz. U., Flagstaff, 1969—. Author: Joachim in Christian Thought, 1975, Joachim of Fiore, 1983, Christopher Columbus, 1991, The Libro de las Profecías of Christopher Columbus, 1991. Mem. Ariz.-Mex. Commn., Phoenix, 1975-79; chmn. Milligan House Hist. Trust Commn., Flagstaff, 1983-85, Flagstaff-Coconino County Libr., 1987—. Recipient Bronze medal, Congresso Internazionale Studi Gioachimiti, Italy, 1984, 1989, Scholar of Year award, Phi Kappa Phi, 1984. Fellow Ariz. Ctr. for Medieval and Renaissance Studies, Ctr. Theol. Inquiry; mem. Am. Hist. Assn., Medieval Acad. Am., Cath. Hist. Assn., Soc. for History of Discoveries, UCLA Ctr. for Medieval and Renaissance Studies (corr.), Rocky Mountain Medieval and Renaissance Assn. (pres. 1975, 1979). Home: 3120 Walkup Dr Flagstaff AZ 86001-8978 Office: No Ariz U Box 6023 Flagstaff AZ 86011

WEST, EDWARD ALAN, graphics communications executive; b. Los Angeles, Dec. 25, 1928; s. Albert Reginald and Gladys Delia (White) W.; m. Sonya Lea Smith, Jan. 2, 1983; children: Troy A., Tamara L. A.A., Fullerton Coll., 1966; student, Cerrotos Coll., 1957, UCLA, 1966-67. Circulation mgr. Huntington Park (Calif.) Signal Newspaper, 1946-52; newspaper web pressman Long Beach (Calif.) Press Telegram, 1955-62; gravure web pressman Gravure West, Los Angeles, 1966-67; sales engr. Halm Jet Press, Glen Head, N.Y., 1968-70; salesman Polychrome Corp., Glen Head, 1970-74; supr. reprographics Fluor Engring & Construction, Irvine, Calif., 1974-81; dir. reprographics Fluor Arabia, Dhahran, Saudi Arabia, 1981-85, Press Telegram, Long Beach, 1986—. Author: How to Paste up For Graphic Reproduction, 1967. Sgt. USMC, 1952-55. Decorated with three battle stars, Korea. Mem. In-Plant Printing Assn. (cert. graphics comm. mgr. 1977, editor newsletter 1977—, pres. Orange County chpt. 1979—, Internat. Mem. of Yr. 1980), 1st Marine Div. Assn. (life), VFW (life), Masons, Shriners (pres. South Coast 1991, editor Blue and Gold Legion of Honor unit El Bekal Temple 1989—, comdr. Legion of Honor 1992, life mem.), Knight Templar Calif. (life mem. # 9 L.A.), Am. Legion. Presbyterian. Home: 198 Monarch Bay Dr Dana Point CA 92629-3437 Office: 604 Pine Ave Long Beach CA 90844-0001

WEST, HUGH STERLING, aircraft leasing company executive; b. Kansas City, Kans., Apr. 5, 1930; s. Gilbert Eugene and Dorothy (Johnson) W.; BS, U. Va., 1952; BS in Aero., U. Md., 1959; grad. U.S. Naval Test Pilot Sch., 1959; m. Willa Alden Reed, Jan. 16, 1954; children: Karen, Phillip, Susan. Commd. 2d lt. U.S. Marine Corps., 1948, advanced through grades to maj., 1961; exptl. flight test pilot, U.S. Naval Air Test Center, Patuxent River, Md.; resigned, 1961; program mgr. Boeing Aircraft Co., Seattle and Phila., 1961-66, dir. airworthiness, comml. airplane div., 1969-71; dir. aircraft sales Am. Airlines, Tulsa, 1971-76; v.p. equipment mgmt. GATX Leasing Corp., San Francisco, 1976-80; v.p. tech., partner Polaris Aircraft Leasing Corp., San Francisco, 1980-85; v.p., co-founder U.S. Airlease, Inc., 1986—; aircraft cons. Mem. Soc. Exptl. Test Pilots, Army Navy Country Club. Republican. Episcopalian. Home: 387 Darrell Rd Hillsborough CA 94010 Office: US Airlease Inc 615 Battery St San Francisco CA 94111-1808

WEST, JACK HENRY, petroleum geologist; b. Washington, Apr. 7, 1934; s. John Henry and Zola Faye (West) Pigg; m. Bonnie Lou Ruger, Apr. 1, 1961; children: Trent John, Todd Kenneth. BS in Geology, U. Oreg., 1957, MS, 1961. Cert. petroleum geologist. Geologist Texaco Inc., L.A and Bakersfield, Calif., 1961-72; asst. dir. devel. geologist Texaco Inc., L.A., 1972-78; geologist Oxy Petroleum Inc., Bakersfield, 1978-80, div. geologist, 1980-83; exploitation mgr. Oxy U.S.A. Inc./Cities Svc. Oil and Gas, Bakersfield, 1983-89; sr. petroleum advisor WZI Inc., Bakersfield, 1990—. Active Beyond War, Bakersfield, 1983-90. Mem. Am. Assn. Petroleum Geologists (pres. Pacific sect. 1988-89, adv. coun. 1992—), Soc. Petroleum Engrs., San Joaquin Geol. Soc. (pres. 1984-85), Alfa Romeo Owners Club. Republican. Methodist.

WEST, JAMES JOE, real estate sales agent, organization executive; b. Sacramento, Nov. 10, 1936; s. James Clifford and Zella Sada (Craft) W.; m. Barbara Ann Hutson, May 19, 1965; children: Tamara Lynn West Conn, Andrea Dawn West Millage. Radio communications analyst USAF Security Service, Far East Asia, 1956-60; staff bridge and hwys. dept. Sacramento County, 1960-62; photolog coord. State Bus., Transp. and Housing Agy., Sacramento, 1962-91; real estate sales agt. Century 21 Nolan Realty, Sacramento, 1992—. Contbr. articles to profl. jours. on disaster preparedness, emergency communications, rescue. Mem. community devel. Block Grant Com., 1982-84. Mem. Sacramento Assn. Realtors, Sacramento County C. of C. (pres. 1984-91). Democrat. Club: Sacramento Amateur Radio (pres. 1982-83). Home: 6110 Mateo Ct Rio Linda CA 95673-4320 Office: Chamber of Commerce 6110 Mateo Ct Rio Linda CA 95673

WEST, JERRY ALAN, professional basketball team executive; b. Chelyan, W.Va., May 28, 1938; s. Howard Stewart and Cecil Sue (Creasey) W.; m. Martha Jane Kane, May, 1960 (div. 1977); children: David, Michael, Mark; m. Karen Christine Bua, May 28, 1978; 1 son, Ryan. BS, W.Va. Coll.; LHD (hon.), W.Va. Wesleyan Coll. Mem. Los Angeles Lakers, Nat. Basketball Assn., 1960-74, coach, 1976-79, spl. cons., 1979-82, gen. mgr., 1982—; mem. first team Nat. Basketball Assn. All-Star Team, 1962-67, 70-73, mem. second team, 1968, 69. Author: (with William Libby) Mr. Clutch: The Jerry West Story, 1969. Capt. U.S. Olympic Basketball Team, 1960; named Most Valuable Player NBA Playoff, 1969, Allstar Game Most Valuable Player, 1972; named to Naismith Meml. Basketball Hall of Fame, 1979, NBA Hall of Fame, 1980; mem. NBA 35th Anniversary All-Time Team, 1980. Office: LA Lakers 3900 W Manchester Blvd PO Box 10 Inglewood CA 90306*

WEST, JOHN BURNARD, physiologist, educator; b. Adelaide, Australia, Dec. 27, 1928; came to U.S., 1969; s. Esmond Frank and Meta Pauline (Spehr) W.; m. Penelope Hall Banks, Oct. 28, 1967; children: Robert Burnard, Joanna Ruth. M.B.B.S., Adelaide U., 1952, M.D., 1958, D.Sc., 1980; Ph.D., London U., 1960; Dr. honoris causa, U. Barcelona, Spain, 1987. Resident Royal Adelaide Hosp., 1952, Hammersmith Hosp., London, 1953-55; physiologist Sir Edmund Hillary's Himalayan Expdn., 1960-61; dir. respiratory research group Postgrad. Med. Sch., London, 1962-67; reader medicine Postgrad. Med. Sch., 1968; prof. medicine and physiology U. Calif. at San Diego, 1969—; leader Am. Med. Rsch. Expdn. to Mt. Everest, 1981; mem. life scis. adv. com. NASA, 1985-88, mem. task force sci. uses of space sta., 1984-87, chmn. sci. verification com. Spacelab SLS-1; prin. investigator, experiment E198, Spacelab SLS 1 and 2, 1983—; co-investigator European Spacelab D2, 1987—; mem. commn. on respiratory physiol., 1985—; mem. commn. on clin. physiol., 1991—, mem. commn. gravitation physiol., 1986—; mem. U.S. nat. com. Internat. Union Physiol. Scis.; mem. study sect. NIH, chmn., 1973-75; Hermann Rahn lectr. SUNY Buffalo, 1992, H. Menkes lectr. Johns Hopkins, 1992. Author: Ventilation/Blood Flow and Gas Exchange, 1965, Respiratory Physiology-The Essentials, 1974, Translations in Respiratory Physiology, 1975, Pulmonary Pathophysiology-The Essentials, 1977, Bioengineering Aspects of the Lung, 1977, Regional Differences in the Lung, 1977, Pulmonary Gas Exchange (2 vols.), 1980, High Altitude Physiology, 1981, High Altitude and Man, 1984, Everest-The Testing Place, 1985, Best and Taylor's Physiological Basis of Medical Practice, 1985, 91, High Altitude Medicine and Physiology, 1989, The Lung: Scientific Foundations, 1991, Lung Injury, 1992. Recipient Ernest Jung prize for medicine, Hamburg, 1977, Reynolds Prize for history Am. Physiol. Soc., 1987; I.J. Flance lectr. Washington U., 1978; G.C. Griffith lectr. Am. Heart Assn., 1978; Kaiser teaching award 1980; W.A. Smith lectr. Med. Coll. S.C., 1982; S. Kronheim lect. Undersea Med. Soc., 1984; D.W. Richards lectr. Am. Heart Assn., 1980, E.M. Papper lectr. Columbia U., 1981, I.S. Ravdin lectr. ACS, 1982, Burns Amberson lectr. Am. Thoracic Soc., 1984, Harry G. Armstrong lectr. Aerospace Med. Assn., 1984, Annual Space Life Scis. lectr. Federation Associated Socs. of Experimental Biology, 1991, Hermann Rahn lectr. SUNY Buffalo, 1992, Jeffries Med. Rsch. award Am. Inst. Aeronautics and Astronautics, 1992. Fellow Royal Coll. Physicians (London), Royal Australasian Coll. Physicians, Royal Geog. Soc. (London), AAAS (med. sci. nominating com. 1987), Am. Inst. for Med. and Biol. Engring., Internat. Soc. for Mountain Medicine (pres. 1991); mem. NAS (com. space biology and medicine 1986-90, subcom. on space biology 1984-85, com. advanced space tech. 1992-93), Nat. Bd. Med. Examiners (physiology com. 1973-76), Am. Physiol. Soc. (pres. 1984-85, chmn. sect. on history of physiology 1984—), Am. Soc. Clin. Investigation, Brit. Physiol. Soc., Am., Thoracic Soc., Assn. Am. Physicians, Western Assn. Physicians, Explorers Club, Am. Alpine Club, Brit. Alpine Club, Fleischner Soc. (pres. 1985), Harveian Soc. (London), Royal Instn. Gt. Britain, Hurlingham Club (London), La Jolla Beach & Tennis Club. Home: 9626 Blackgold Rd La Jolla CA 92037-1110 Office: U Calif San Diego Sch Medicine 0623 Dept Medicine La Jolla CA 92093-0623

WEST, LLOYD ALBERT, science administrator; b. Washington, Dec. 10, 1944; s. Lloyd Albert and E. Arlene (Casady) W.; m. Carol J. Neal, Mar. 31, 1973. BA, U. Oreg., 1967; MS, U. Calif., Berkeley, 1969, PhD, 1971. Mem. tech. staff Sandia Nat. Labs., Livermore, Calif., 1971-77, supr., 1977-91, dept. mgr., 1991-92, dir., 1992—. Mem. Am. Chem. Soc., Am. Phys. Soc., Phi Beta Kappa. Office: Sandia Nat Labs ORG 8600 PO Box 969 Livermore CA 94551-0969

WEST, LOUIS JOLYON, psychiatrist; b. Bklyn., Oct. 6, 1924; s. Albert Jerome and Anna (Rosenberg) W.; m. Kathryn Louise Hopkirk, Apr. 29, 1944; children—Anne Kathryn, Mary Elizabeth, John Stuart. B.S., U. Minn., 1946, M.B., 1948, M.D., 1949; LHD (hon.), Hebrew Union Coll., 1990. Diplomate: Nat. Bd. Med. Examiners, Am. Bd. Psychiatry and Neurology. Chief psychiatry service USAF Hosp., Lackland AFB, San Antonio, 1952-56; prof. psychiatry, head dept. psychiatry, neurology and behavioral scis. U. Okla. Sch. Medicine, 1954-69; chief mental health sect. Okla. Med. Research Found., 1956-69; cons. psychiatry Oklahoma City VA Hosp., Tinker AFB Hosp., 1956-69; fellow Center for Advanced Study in Behavioral Scis., Stanford U., 1966-67; prof. psychiatry UCLA, 1969—, chmn. dept. psychiatry and biobehavioral sci., 1969-89; dir. Neuropsychiat. Inst. at UCLA Center for Health Scis., 1969-89; psychiatrist-in-chief UCLA Med. Ctr., 1969-89; nat. cons. psychiatry Surgeon Gen. USAF, 1957-62; cons. psychiatry Brentwood and Sepulveda VA hosps., 1969—; nat. adv. mental health coun. (past) NIMH, profl. adv. coun. NAMH, USAF Office Sci. Rsch., USPHS, Va., HEW, Nat. Acad. Scis., NRC, Nat. Inst. Medicine, U.S. Army Med. Rsch. and Devel. Panel, AMA, Am. Family Found. (adv. bd.) Nat. Depressive and Manic Depressive Assn. (adv. bd.), White House Conf. Civil Rights, internat. adv. bd. Israel Ctr. for Psychobiology, Jerusalem Mental Health Ctr. Author: Hallucinations, 1962, editor: Explorations in the Physiology of Emotions, 1960, Hallucinations: Behavior, Experience, and Theory, 1975, Treatment of Schizophrenia: Progress and Prospects, 1976, Research on Smoking Behavior, 1977, Critical Issues in Behavioral Medicine, 1982, Alcoholism and Related Problems: Issues for the American Public, 1984, Drug Testing: Issues and Options, 1991; mem. editorial bd. Directions in Psychiatry, Medical Update, Cultic Studies Jour., others; contbr. articles to profl. jours. Past trustee UCLA Found.; bd. dirs. Caring For Children, Alcoholism Coun. Calif. Fellow AAAS, Am. Coll. Neuropsychopharmacology (founding), Am. Coll. Psychiatrists, Am. Psychiat. Assn. (life), Soc. Behavioral Medicine; mem. AMA, Am. Acad. Psychiatry and Law, Soc. Biol. Psychiatry, Am. Orthopsychiat Assn., Am. Acad. Psychoanalysis, Assn. Psychophysiol. Study Sleep, Am. Psychosomatic Soc., Am. Psychopath. Assn., Am. Psychol. Assn., Assn. Rsch. in Nervous and Mental Disease, Nat. Acad. Religion and Mental Health (founding), Nat. Coun. on Alcoholism, Pavlovian Soc. (pres. 1975), Soc. Biol. Psychiatry, Soc. Psychophysiol. Rsch., Soc. Profs. Psychiatry (pres. 1963), Soc. Clin. and Exptl. Hypnosis, Alpha Omega Alpha, Sigma Xi. Office: UCLA Neuropsychiat Inst 760 Westwood Pla Los Angeles CA 90024

WEST, RALPH W., JR., academic administrator. Supt. Naval Postgrad. Sch., Monterey, Calif., 1989—. Office: Naval Postgrad Sch Monterey CA 93943-5000

WEST, RICHARD PAUL, academic program administrator; b. Carlsbad, Calif., June 19, 1947; s. O. Kenneth and Mildred S. (Ponstler) W.; m. Catherine Held, June 28, 1969. BA in Econs., U. Calif., Santa Cruz, 1969; MBA, U. Calif., Berkeley, 1971. Sr. adminstrv. analyst U. Calif., Berkeley, 1969-72, coordinator student info. systems office of pres., 1972-75, mgr. student fin. aid, 1975-76, dir. info. mgmt., 1976-79, asst. v.p. info. systems and adminstrv. svcs., 1979-89, assoc. v.p. info. systems and adminstrv. svcs., 1989—; lectr. Sch. Bus., U. Calif., Berkeley, 1984—, corp. edn., 1988—; bd. dirs. Advanced Network Svcs., Inc.; chmn. libr. resources bd. commn. on info. tech. Nat. Assn. Univs. and Land Grant Colls. Contbr. articles to profl. jours. Chmn. Am. Assn. Univs. Task Force on Sci. and Tech. Info., 1992—. Mem. Nat. Coalition Networked Info. Resources (chair steering com. 1990—). Republican. Home: 1600 Mountain Blvd Oakland CA 94611 Office: 300 Lakeside Dr Oakland CA 94612-3524

WEST, ROBERT SUMNER, surgeon; b. Bowman, N.D., Nov. 20, 1935; s. Elmer and Minnie (DeBode) W.; m. Martha W. Hopkins, Mar. 23, 1957; children: Stephen, Christopher, Anna Marie, Catherine, Sarah. BA, U. N.D., 1957, BS in Medicine, 1959; MD, Harvard U., 1961. Diplomate Am. Bd. Surgery. Intern U.S. Naval Hosp., Chelsea, Mass., 1961-62; resident in surgery U. Vt. Med. Ctr. Hosp., 1965-69; pvt. practice Coeur d'Alene, Idaho, 1969—; coroner Kootenai County, Coeur d'Alene, 1984—. Trustee, pres. Coeur d'Alene Sch. Dist. 271 Bd. Edn., 1973-77. Lt. M.C., USN, 1960-65. Fellow ACS (pres. Idaho chpt. 1985, gov. at large); mem. Idaho Med. Assn. (pres. 1989-90, trustee), Kiwanis. Republican. Lutheran. Office: 920 W Ironwood Dr Coeur D Alene ID 83814-2643

WEST, SHELBY JAY, insurance agent; b. Salt Lake City, Feb. 21, 1938; s. Shelby J. and Grace (Hunsaker) W.; m. Judene Casper, Apr. 14, 1961; children: Shauri Lynne, Pamela Joy, Christopher J., Troy Jay. Student, U. Utah, 1956-57, Utah State U., 1961-62. CLU, Utah, chartered fin. cons., Utah. Ins. agt. State Farm Ins. Cos., Salt Lake City, 1961—. Rep. dist. chmn., Midvale, Utah, 1984. Mem. Valley Assn. Life Underwriters (sec. 1983-84, v.p. 1984-85, pres. 1985-86, mem. nat. com. 1986-87), Rotary (Ft. Union, Midvale, sec. 1971-73, v.p. 1973-74, pres. 1974-75, sec. 1977-79, bd. dirs. 1990-92, pres. 1993—). Mormon. Home: 635 Marquette Dr Midvale UT 84047-3617 Office: Jay West Ins Agy 114 E 7200 S Midvale UT 84047-1587

WEST, THOMAS MOORE, engineering educator, consultant; b. Weston, W.Va., Nov. 10, 1940; s. Stanley Rymer and Dorothy (Moore) W.; m. Carmen Wessner West, Aug. 31, 1967. BS in Engring., U. Tenn., 1963, MS in Indsl. Engring., 1965; PhD, Oreg. State U., 1976. Registered profl. engr., Tenn., Oreg. Engrs. analyst Monsanto, Greeneville, S.C., 1964-66; instr. engring. Ga. Inst. Tech., Atlanta, 1966-67; systems engr. IBM, Essex Junction, Vt., 1967; asst. prof. U. Tenn., Knoxville, 1968-72; asst. prof. Oreg. State U., Corvallis, 1976-80, assoc. prof., 1980-88, head dept. indsl. and mfg. engring., 1988-91, assoc. dean of engring., 1992—; engring. cons. Union Carbide, Oak Ridge, Tenn., 1975-76, U.S. govt. agys., Pacific Northwest, 1976-87. Co-author: Engineering in Economy, 1986, Essentials of Engineering, 1986; author: Review of 1986 Tax Act, 1988; author numerous articles in field. Mem. Inst. Indsl. Engrs. (sr., v.p., pres. Portland, Oreg. chpt., mem. nat. bd. trustees, div. dir., honors chmn., Oreg. State U. acad. advisor), Soc. Mfg. Engrs. (sr., Oreg. State U. chpt. advisor, regional meeting chairperson, com. mem.), Am. Soc. Engring. Edn. (sr., div. dir., regional meeting chairperson, Oreg. State U. campus chmn.), Ops. Rsch. Soc. Am. (sr.). Office: Oregon State Univ Coll of Engring 101 Covell Hall Corvallis OR 97331-2409

WEST, TONY, state official; b. Phoenix, Ariz., Oct. 29, 1937; m. Margaret O'Malley, 1962; 3 children: William A., III, John Patrick, Stephen Michael. BS, Ariz. State Univ., 1961. Formerly pres., chief exec. officer Shenendoah Ranches; Ariz. state rep., 1973-82, former Ariz. state senator, dist. 18, now Ariz. state treas. Mem. Ariz. Club (formerly pres.), Ariz. Found. for Handicapped (pres.), John C. Lincoln Hosp. Found. Republican. Office: Office of the State Treas 1700 W Washington St Phoenix AZ 85007-2812*

WEST, VIKKI LYNN, healthcare executive recruiter; b. Oklahoma City, Dec. 16, 1948; d. Stanley Richard and Lynn (Shelton) Kaplan; m. John Michael Black, Aug. 31, 1967; children: Michael Scott Black, Christopher Lee Black, Jennifer Michelle Black; m. Kenneth William West, June 2, 1984. Student, U. Tex., 1966-67; student, N. Tex. State U., 1967-68, Rio Salado Coll., Phoenix, 1988-90, Ariz. State U., 1990—. Bookkeeper, mktg. asst. Paradynamics, Inc., Scottsdale, Ariz., 1975-77; ins. agt. Lincoln Nat., Phoenix, 1977-78; sales mgr. Plymouth Tube Co., Chandler, Ariz., 1978-81; v.p. Robert Half Ariz., Inc., Phoenix, 1981-90; exec. recruiter Pearson & Assocs., Phoenix, 1990-93, exec. recruiter, acctg. bookkeeping personnel, 1993—. Mem. Ariz. Assn. Temp. Svcs. (treas. 1987—), Phoenix Personnel Mgmt. Assn., Ariz. Small Bus. Assn., United Methodist Women. Republican. Office: Pearson & Assocs 11811 N Tatum Blvd # 1015 Phoenix AZ 85028

WEST, WELDON WALLACE, vascular surgeon; b. Modesto, Calif., May 17, 1921; s. Wirt Mercer and Ada May (McCoy) W.; m. Pearl Steiner, June 15, 1945; children: Donald, William, James, Robert. AA, Stockton (Calif.) Jr. Coll., 1941; BA, Coll. Pacific, 1943; MD, Harvard U., 1947. Am. Bd. Surgery. Surg. resident Mass. Gen. Hosp., Boston, 1947-54; med. staff St. Joseph's Hosp., Stockton, 1954-87, chief surgery, 1972-78, chief of staff, 1969; med. staff Dameron Hosp., Stockton, 1954-87, San Joaquin Gen. Hosp., French Camp, Calif., 1954-87; monitoring com. mem. Calif. Med. Rev. Inc., San Francisco, 1988-89. With USN, 1943-46; Lt. U.S. Army,

1951-52. Fellow Am. Coll. Surgeons; mem. Am. Med. Informatics Assn. Democrat. Home: 3731 Portsmouth Cir N Stockton CA 95219-3842

WEST, WILLIAM M., accountant; b. L.A., Mar. 31, 1948; s. William West and Barbara A. McClure MacDonald. BA, Claremont Men's Coll., 1969; MBA, U. Chgo., 1971. CPA, Calif. V.p. fin. Nat. Auto Ins. Group, L.A., 1971-72, pres., 1972; COO Estate Ins. Co./Maricopa Life Group, L.A., 1973-78; CFO Veedercrest Vineyards, Emeryville, Calif., 1978-81; pvt. practice San Jose, Calif., 1981—. Contbr. aricles to profl. jours. Mem. LWV, 1992. Lt. U.S. Army, 1972. Mem. Exch. Club of San Jose (pres.), Calif. Soc. of CPA's (bd. dirs. San Jose chpt. 1991-93),. Office: 1290 W Hedding St San Jose CA 95126

WESTBO, LEONARD ARCHIBALD, JR., electronics engineer; b. Tacoma, Wash., Dec. 4, 1931; s. Leonard Archibald and Agnes (Martinson) W.; B.A. in Gen. Studies, U. Wash., 1958. Electronics engr. FAA, Seattle Air Route Traffic Control Center, Auburn, Wash., 1961-72; asst. br. chief electronics engring. br. 13th Coast Guard Dist., Seattle, 1972-87. Served with USCG, 1951-54, 1958-61. Registered profl. engr., Wash. Mem. Aircraft Owners and Pilots Assn., IEEE, Am. Radio Relay League. Home and Office: 10528 SE 323d St Auburn WA 98002

WESTCOTT, BRIAN JOHN, manufacturing executive; b. Rexford, N.Y., June 19, 1957; s. John Campbell and Norma (Cornell) W.; m. Andrea Belrose, Apr. 23, 1988; 1 child, Sarah Katharine. BS, Lehigh U., 1979; MS, Stanford U., 1980, PhD, 1987. Engr. Combustion Engring., Windsor, Conn., 1980-81; rsch. engr. Gen. Electric Corp. Rsch., Niskayuna, N.Y., 1981-83; rsch. fellow Stanford (Calif.) Grad. Sch. Bus., 1987-88; mgr. Gen. Electric Corp. Mgmt., Bridgeport, Conn., 1988-89; prin. A.T. Kearney Tech. Inc., Redwood City, Calif., 1989—; chief exec. officer Westt, Inc., Menlo Park, Calif., 1990—; cons. GE, Bridgeport, 1989-90, 3M, Baxter, Medtronics, Snap-on Tool, Ciba-Geigy. Author: (with others) Paradox and Transformation, 1988; contbr. articles to profl. jours.; inventor, patentee in field. Campaign com. James Buckley Senate Campaign, Conn., 1980; mem. Dean's Panel Campus Housing, Stanford, 1987-88. Postdoctoral rsch. fellow Stanford U. Grad. Sch. Bus., 1987; rsch. fellow Electric Power Rsch., Stanford, 1983-87. Mem. ASME, Soc. Mfg. Engrs. Office: Westt Inc 980 O'Brien Dr Menlo Park CA 94025

WESTENFELDER, CHRISTOF, physician; b. Stuttgart, Germany, July 1, 1942; came to U.S., 1970; s. Wilhelm and Elisabeth (Floerke) W. BS, Wilhem's Coll., Stuttgart, 1962; MD, U. Kiel-Luebeck, Fed. Republic of Germany, 1968. Diplomate Am. Bd. Internal Medicine, Am. Bd. Nephrology. Intern in medicine Univ. Hosp., Berlin, 1969-70; intern medicine Cook County Hosp., Chgo., 1970-71; resident medicine U. Ill., Chgo., 1971-73, fellow in nephrology, 1973-75, asst. prof. medicine, 1975-82, dir. Dialysis Ctr., 1982-83; assoc. prof. medicine U. Utah, Salt Lake City, 1983-89, prof. medicine, 1989—; chief sect. of Nephrology VA Med. Ctr., Salt Lake City, 1983—. Contbr. articles to profl. publs. Mem. Nat. Kidney Foun. Rsch. grantee NIH, VA, Am. Heart Assn., Nat. Kidney Found., 1975—. Fellow Am. Coll. of Physicians; mem. WAP, AFCR, WSCI, Am. Soc. Nephrology, Internat. Soc. of Nephrology. Office: VA Med Ctr 500 Foothill Dr Salt Lake City UT 84148-0002

WESTER, KEITH ALBERT, film and television recording engineer; b. Seattle, Feb. 21, 1940; s. Albert John and Evelyn Grayce (Nettell) W., m. Judith Elizabeth Jones, 1968 (div. Mar. 1974); 1 child, Wendy Elizabeth. AA, Am. River Coll., Sacramento, 1959; BA, Calif. State U., L.A., 1962; MA, UCLA, 1965. Lic. multi-engine rated pilot. Prodn. asst. KCRA-TV, Sacramento, 1956; announcer KSFM, Sacramento, 1960; film editor, sound rec. technician Urie & Assocs., Hollywood, Calif., 1963-66; co-owner Steckler-Wester Film Prodns., Hollywood, 1966-70; owner Profl. Sound Recorders, Studio City, Calif., 1970—, Aerocharter, Studio City, 1974—, Wester Devel., Sun Valley (Idaho) and Studio City, 1989—. Mem. NATAS (Emmy award An Early Frost 1986, Emmy nominations: Further Adventures of Tom Sawyer and Huck Finn 1982, Gambler II 1984, Malice in Wonderland 1985, Amerika 1987), Acad. Motion Picture Arts Scis. (sound br. exec. bd., Acad. award nomination for best sound Black Rain 1990), Cinema Audio Soc. (sec. 1985-91, Sound award 1987), Soc. Motion Picture and TV Engrs., Internat. Sound Technicians, Local 695, Assn. Film Craftsmen (sec. 1967-73, treas. 1973-76), Screen Actors Guild, Aircraft Owners & Pilots Assn. (Confederate Air Force col.), Am. Radio Relay League. Home: 4146 Bellingham Ave Studio City CA 91604-1601 Office: Profl Sound Recorders 22440 Clarendon St Woodland Hills CA 91367-4467

WESTERDAHL, JOHN BRIAN, nutritionist, health educator; b. Tucson, Dec. 3, 1954; s. Jay E. and Margaret (Meyer) W.; m. Doris Mui Lian Tan, Nov. 18, 1989. AA, Orange Coast Coll., 1977; BS, Pacific Union Coll., 1979; MPH, Loma Linda U., 1981. Registered dietitian. Chartered herbalist. Nutritionist, health educator Castle Med. Ctr., Kailua, Hawaii, 1981-84, health promotion coord., 1984-87, asst. dir. health promotion, 1987-88, dir. health promotion, 1988-89; dir. nutrition and health rsch. Health Sci., Santa Barbara, Calif., 1989-90; sr. nutritionist Shaklee Corp., San Francisco, 1990—; talk show host Nutrition and You, Sta. KGU Radio, Honolulu, 1983-89; nutrition com. mem. Hawaii div. Am. Heart Assn., Honolulu, 1984-87; mem. nutrition study group Govs. Conf. Health Promotion and Disease Prevention for Hawaii, 1985. Mem. AAAS, Am. Coll. Sports Medicine, Am. Dietetic Assn., Am. Nutritionists Assn., Am. Coll. Nutrition, Soc. for Nutrition Edn., Nat. Wellness Assn., Nutrition Today Soc., Am. Soc. Pharmacognosy, Inst. Food Technologists, Hawaii Nutrition Coun. (v.p. 1983-86,m pres.-elect 1988-89, pres. 1989), Hawaii Dietetic Assn., Calif. Dietetic Assn., N.Y. Acad. Scis., Seventh-day Adventist Dietetic Assn., several other profl. assns. Republican. Seventh-Day Adventist. Office: Shaklee Corp 444 Market St San Francisco CA 94111-5325

WESTFALL, JOHN EDWARD, geography educator; b. San Francisco, Aug. 16, 1938; s. Jesse Barry and Borghild Marie (Johnson) W.; m. Elizabeth Watkins, Sept. 2, 1965; children: Edward, Erik. BA, U. Calif., Berkeley, 1960; MA, George Washington U., 1964, PhD, 1969. Cartographer U.S. Coast & Geodetic Survey, Washington, 1960-64; teaching fellow George Washington U., 1964-66, NSF fellow, 1966-68; geography faculty mem. San Francisco State U., 1968—; bd. dirs. Corp for Rsch. Amateur Astronomy, San Francisco, 1989—; exec. dir. Assn. Lunar and Planetary Observers, San Francisco, 1985—. Editor: Assn. Lunar and Planetary Observers Jour., 1985—, Solar System Ephemeris, 1986—. Recipient Walter H. Haas Observing award, 1988; named Amateur of the Yr., Astronomical Assn. No. Calif., 1989; recipient G. Bruce Blair Achievement for Amateur Astronomy award Western Amateur Astronomers, 1991. Mem. Assn. Lunar and Planetary Observers, Brit. Astronomical Assn., Div. for Planetary Scis. Office: Lunar Planetary Observers PO Box 16131 San Francisco CA 94116-0131

WESTFALL, RICHARD MERRILL, chemist, research administrator; b. Denver, Dec. 17, 1956; s. Robert Raymond and Madelyn Evastine (Cornwell) W. Student, U. Colo., 1976-80. Mem. lab. staff NOAA, Boulder, Colo., 1978-79, Solar Energy Rsch. Inst., Golden, Colo., 1979-80; dir. rsch. Galactic Products, Denver, 1981-82; pres., dir. rsch. CEL Systems Corp., Arvada, Colo. and Schertz, Tex., 1982—; process chemist, optical detector fabrication engr. Tex. Med. Instruments, Schertz, 1986-87; dir. rsch., chief exec. officer Galactic Mining Industries Inc., Denver, 1988—; founder, exec. dir. Galactic Ednl. Devel. Inst., Denver, 1989—. Inventor electrolytic growth tin and other metals, and process, 1980-82; patentee in field. Mem. AIAA, Air Force Assn. Home: 4838 Stuart St Denver CO 80212-2922

WESTHEIMER, GERALD, optometrist, educator; b. Berlin, Germany, May 13, 1924; naturalized, 1944, came to U.S., 1951; s. Isaak and Ilse (Cohn) W. Optometry diploma, Sydney (Australia) Tech. Coll., 1943, fellowship diploma, 1950; BSc, U. Sydney, 1947; PhD, Ohio State U., 1953; DSc (hon.), U. NSW, Australia, 1988; ScD (hon.), SUNY, 1990. Practice optometry Sydney, 1945-51; research fellow Ohio State U., 1951-53; prof. physiol. optics U. Houston, 1953-54; asst. prof., then assoc. prof. physiol. optics Ohio State U., 1954-60; postdoctoral fellow neurophysiology Marine Biol. Lab., Woods Hole, Mass., 1957; vis. researcher Physiol. Lab., U. Cambridge, Eng., 1958-59; mem. faculty U. Calif. at Berkeley, 1960—, prof. physiol. optics, 1963-68, chmn. group physiol. optics, 1964-67, prof. physiology, 1968-89, prof. neurobiology, 1989—, head div. neurobiology, 1987-92; adj. prof. Rockefeller U., N.Y., 1992—; Sackler lectr. Tel Aviv U. Med. Sch., 1988, D.O. Hebb lectr. McGill U., 1991, Grass Found. lectr. U. Ill., 1991; mem. com. vision NRC, 1957-72; mem. visual scis. study sect. NIH, 1966-70, chmn. visual scis. B study sect., 1977-79; mem. vision, research and tng. com. Nat. Eye Inst., NIH, 1970-74, chmn. bd. sci. counselors, 1981-83; mem. exec. council com. vision NAS-NRC, 1969-72; mem. communicative scis. cluster Pres.'s Biomed. Rsch. Panel, 1975. Author rsch. papers; editor: Vision Rsch., 1972-79; editorial bd.: Investigative Ophthalmology, 1973-77, Exptl. Brain Rsch., 1973-89, Optics Letters, 1977-78, Spatial Vision, 1985—, Ophthalmic and Physiological Optics, 1985—, Vision Rsch., 1985-92, Jour. of Physiology, 1987—; corr. editor Procs. of Royal Soc. London, 1990—. Recipient Von Sallman Prize Columbia U., 1986; Prentice Medal Am. Acad. Optometry, 1986. Fellow Royal Soc. London (Ferrier lectr. 1992), AAAS, Optical Soc. Am. (Tillyer medal 1978, assoc. editor jour. 1980-83), Am. Acad. Optometry; mem. Royal Soc. New So. Wales, Soc. Neurosci., Assn. Rsch. in Vision and Ophthalmology (Proctor medal 1979), Internat. Brain Rsch. Orgn., Physiol. Soc. Gt. Britain, Sigma Xi. Home: 582 Santa Barbara Rd Berkeley CA 94707

WESTIN, ROBERT LEE, management consultant; b. Center, Colo., Nov. 5, 1932; s. Henri Charles and Catherine Lucile (Head) W.; m. Leontine Mae Eckhardt, Jan. 11, 1953; children: Patricia, Robert, Theresa, Susan, Richard, Katherine. BSBA, U. Denver, 1956. CPCU. Gen. mgr. Home Ins. Co., L.A., 1956-65; sr. v.p. Penn Gen. Agys. Inc., L.A., 1965-78; pres. Physicians and Surgeons Exch., L.A., 1978-83, Victus, Inc., Pasadena, Calif., 1983—; chmn., founder Brookside Savs. & Loan, Pasadena, 1982-85; pres. Flying V Ranch, Lompoc, Calif., 1985—; bd. dirs. M.H. Ross Co., Inc., Sepulveda, Calif., Medex Internat. Corp., Balt. Author: Management by Objectives for Insurance Agents and Brokers, 1978; contbr. over 70 articles to profl. jours. Bd. dirs. Am. Heart Assn., L.A., 1982-84; chmn. ins. com. AAU, L.A., 1988-90. With USN, 1951-53. Mem. Am. Inst. Property and Casualty Underwriters. Republican. Roman Catholic.

WESTINE, LEZLEE HIEGEL, lawyer; b. Chgo., Aug. 28, 1960; d. John Roland and Diane Lynn (Rosacker) W.; m. Scott Alan Hiegel, May 21, 1988. Student, Sweet Briar Coll., 1978-80; BS, U. Fla., 1982; MBA, UCLA, 1985; JD, Georgetown U., 1988. Bar: Calif. 1989. Govt. rels. liaison Comm. Satellite Corp., Washington, 1983; assoc. Nielsen, Merksamer, Parrinello, Mueller & Naylor, San Francisco, 1988—. Bd. dirs. Hunters Point Boys and Girls Club, San Francisco, 1990—; mem. Calif. Commn. on Status of Women, 1991—; election observer Freedom House Project, El Salvador, 1991. Recipient Key to City, City of Delray Beach, Fla., 1978. Mem. State Bar Calif., D.C. Bar Assn. Republican. Roman Catholic. Office: Nielsen Merksamer Parrinello Mueller & Naylor 650 California St Ste 2650 San Francisco CA 94910

WESTLING, LOUISE HUTCHINGS, English language educator; b. Jacksonville, Fla., Feb. 13, 1942; d. William Evelyn and Louise Dillon (Van Winkle) Hutchings; m. George Attout Wickes, Nov. 8, 1975. AB, Randolph-Macon Woman's Coll., 1964; MA, U. Iowa, 1965; PhD, U. Oreg., 1974. Instr. English Centre Coll., Danville, Ky., 1965-67; research assoc. N.W. Regional Ednl. Lab., Portland, Oreg., 1968-71; instr. English Oreg. State U., Corvallis, 1974-77; grad. teaching fellow U. Oreg., Eugene, 1971-74, asst. prof. Honors Coll., 1977-81, instr. Eng. dept., 1981-85, asst. prof., 1985-88, assoc. prof., 1988. Author: Sacred Groves and Ravaged Gardens, 1985, Eudora Welty, 1989; editor: He Included Me: The Autobiography of Sarah Rice, 1989. Mem. MLA, Soc. for the Study So. Lit., Philol. Assn. Pacific Coast (exec. dir. 1985-88). Democrat. Office: U Oreg Dept English Eugene OR 97403

WESTLY, STEVEN PAUL, economic development deputy; b. L.A., Aug. 27, 1956; s. Roy Messell and Sylvia (Snow) Westly Elliott. BA, Stanford U., 1978, MBA, 1983. Program mgr. GTE Sprint, Burlingame, Calif., 1982-85; mng. dir. Bridgemere Capital, San Francisco, 1986-88; pres. Codd & Date Internat., San Jose, Calif., 1988-91; deputy dir. econ. devel. San Jose, Calif., 1991—; bd. dirs. Am. Data Mgmt., Mountain View, 1988—, Lane Bros., Menlo Park, Calif. Editor: Energy Efficiency & The Utilities, 1980. Controller Calif. dem. com., 1983-85, no. chair, 1985-87, vice-chmn., 1987-89; mem. Dem. Nat. Com., 1988—; adv. bd. U. San Francisco. Democrat. Presbyterian. Home: 2120 Camino Del Los Robles Menlo Park CA 94025 Office: Ste 900 50 W San Francisco St San Jose CA 95113

WESTON, DEIRDRE DENISE, actress; b. Phila., July 7, 1964; d. Nanci Carol Nixon. BFA, Wright State U., 1986. Instr., dir. Freedom Theatre, Phila.; instr. Marla Gibbs Theatre CrossRoads Arts Acad.; owner, founder Faith Acting Studios, L.A. Plays include South of Where We Live, Simply Heavenly, One Acre at a Time; television programs include Crimestoppers NBC affiliate, Aerobics Channel 4, Dayton, Don't Do Drugs PBS series, General Hospital; films include Lady Bugs; dir., writer play Romyo and Julie Mae. Mem. Black Women in Theatre (Best Actress award N.Y., 1989. Home: 6520 Selma Ave PO Box 355 Los Angeles CA 90028

WESTON, EDWARD, art dealer, consultant; b. N.Y.C., Feb. 25, 1925; s. Joseph and Mona Weston; m. Ann Jean Gould, May 4, 1974; children: Jon Marc, Cari Alyn Rene. News editor Sta. WMCA, N.Y.C., 1940-41; announcer news dept. Sta. WSAV, Savannah, Ga., 1941-43; newscaster, disc jockey Sta. WNOX, Knoxville, Tenn., 1943-45; program dir. Sta. WXLH, Okinawa, Japan, 1945-47; newscaster, announcer Sta. WAVZ, New Haven, 1947-48; program dir. Sta. WCCC, Hartford, Conn., 1948-49; asst. gen. mgr. Sta. WCPO AM-FM-TV, Cin., 1949-59; pres., gen. mgr. Sta. WZIP, Cin., 1959-61; pres. Weston Entertainment, Northridge, Calif., 1961—, Edward Weston Fine Art; chmn. bd. Fulton J. Sheen Communications; pres. Inspirational Programs, Inc., 1983—, Weston Editions, 1970—, Marilyn Monroe Editions, 1975—. Producer TV/video cassettes Life Is Worth Living; PBS TV series How to Paint with Elke Sommer, 1984. Founder Cin. Summer Playhouse, 1950. Served with U.S. Army, 1945-46. Recipient Outstanding News Coverage award Variety mag., 1949, Outstanding Sta. Ops. award Variety mag., 1950, Best Programming award Nat. Assn. Radio TV Broadcasters, 1951. Mem. Nat. Franchise Assn. (founder). Home: 10511 Andora Ave Chatsworth CA 91311-2004 Office: Weston Entertainment 19355 Business Center Dr Northridge CA 91324-3503

WESTON, KATH, anthropology educator; b. Ill., Nov. 2, 1958. AB, U. Chgo., 1978, AM, 1981; AM, Stanford U., 1984, PhD, 1988. Rsch. and teaching asst. dept. anthropology Stanford (Calif.) U., 1982, teaching asst. dept. feminist studies, 1987; asst. prof. anthropology Ariz. State U. West, Phoenix, 1990—; speaker various nat. confs., colloquia and workshops, 1988—. Author: Families We Choose: Lesbians, Gays, Kinship, 1991 (Ruth Benedict prize); co-editor: The Lesbian Issue: Essays from SIGNS, 1985; also articles. Fellow NSF, 1980-83, 85-87, Rockefeller Found., U. Miinn. Ctr. for Advanced Feminist Studies, 1989-90. Mem. MLA, AAUW (fellow 1985-86), Am. Anthrop. Assn., Soc. for Cultural Anthropology, Soc. Lesbian and Gay Anthropologists, Assn. for Feminist Anthropology. Office: Ariz State U West PO Box 37100 4701 W Thunderbird Rd Phoenix AZ 85069-5100

WESTON, THEODORE BRETT, photographer; b. Los Angeles, Dec. 16, 1911; s. Edward and Flora (Chandler) W.; divorced; 1 dau. Freelance photographer Calif. One-man shows include: U. Ariz. Ctr. for Creative Photography, Tucson, 1983, San Francisco Mus. Modern Art, 1983; represented in permanent collections: Mus. Modern Art, N.Y.C., Library of Congress, Washington, Art Inst. Chgo.; photography books: Brett Weston Photographs, Brett Weston Voyage of the Eye; Photographs from Five Decades. Recipient Guggenheim award, 1946. Address: PO Box 694 Carmel Valley CA 93924

WESTOVER, SAMUEL LEE, insurance company executive; b. Soap Lake, Wash., May 30, 1955; s. Gordon Kent Westover and Janice Lelia (Matlock) Jensen; m. Susan Kern, July 13, 1977; children: Michael, S. Fielding, Austin, Clinton, Cassandra. BS in Acctg., Brigham Young U., 1978. Acct. Price Waterhouse, L.A., 1978-80; chief fin. officer, sr. v.p. Maxicare Health Plans, Inc., L.A., 1981-88; chief exec. officer and chief operating officer Western Health Plans, Inc., San Diego, 1988-90; chief fin. officer, sr. v.p. Blue Cross of Calif., Woodland Hills, 1990-93; CFO, sr. v.p. WellPoint Health Networks, Inc., Woodland Hills, 1993—. Office: WellPoint Health Networks 21555 Oxnard St Woodland Hills CA 91367-4999

WESTPHAL, PAUL, professional basketball coach; b. Torrance, Calif., Nov. 30, 1950; m. Cindy Westphal; children: Victoria, Michael Paul. Degree in phys. edn., U. So. Calif., 1972. Player Boston Celtics, 1972-75, Phoenix Suns, 1975-80, 83-84, Seattle Supersonics, 1980-81, N.Y. Knicks, 1981-83; coach S.W. Coll., Phoenix, 1985-86, Grand Canyon Coll., 1986-88; asst. coach. Phoenix Suns, 1988-92, head coach, 1992—. Named All-Star 5 times, Comeback Player of Yr.; uniform number retired by Suns, 1989. Office: Phoenix Suns 2910 N Central Ave Phoenix AZ 85012

WESTWATER, HEATHER, marketing executive; b. Zurich, Switzerland, May 23, 1968; came to U.S., 1968; d. Michael John and Jan (Justice) W. BA in Urban Studies, Stanford U., 1990. Project mgr. The Westwater Group, Boulder, 1990-92; mktg. program mgr. Raima Corp., Issaquah, Wash., 1992—. Organizer, vol. div. City of Louisville, 1991-92. Mem. Washington Software Assn. Home: 2306 N 77th St Seattle WA 98103 Office: Raima Corp 1605 NW Sammamish Rd Issaquah WA 98027

WETHERELL, CLAIRE, state legislator; b. Flandreau, S.D., Feb. 18, 1919; d. Thomas James and Margaret (Hefron) H.; m. Robert Miles Wotherell (dec. 1943); children: Michael Edward, Dennis Hart, Ellen Ann Hermann, Robert Thomas. Student, U. Calif., Berkeley, 1937-39; RN, Mercy Hosp. Sch. Nursing, 1942. City councilwoman Mountain Home, Idaho, 1971-78; mem. Idaho State Senate. Dem. committeewoman Elmore County, 1955—; vice chmn. Idaho State Dem. Party, 1962-72. Served as ensign, Navy Nurse Corps, 1942-43. Named Disting. Citizen Idaho Daily Statesman, Boise, 1978. Mem. Mountain Home Com. of Fifty, Bus. and Profl. Women (named Woman of Progress, S.W. Idaho, 1976), C. of C. (pres. 1971-72), Idaho Land Title Assn. (pres. 1977-78). Roman Catholic. Home: 360 E 15th N Mountain Home ID 83647-1702

WETHERELL, MICHAEL E., lawyer; b. Redding, Calif., Mar. 2, 1945; s. Robert Miles and Rose Clair (Hart) W.; m. Karen Lansdowne Mackenzie, Aug. 16, 1969; children: Kelly Mackenzie, Kristen Michelle, Katherine Marie. BS in Edn., U. Idaho, 1967; JD, George Washington U., 1972. Bar: Idaho 1972, U.S. Dist. Ct. Idaho 1972, U.S. Ct. Appeals (9th cir.) 1984. Copywriter KBOI-AM-FM-TV, Boise, Idaho, 1965-67; legis. asst. Senator Frank Church, Washington, 1967-72, chief legal counsel, 1972-74, adminstrv. asst., 1975-76; sole practice Boise, 1977-78; assoc. Martin, Chapman & Hyde, Boise, 1978-82; ptnr. Hyde & Wetherell, Boise, 1982-85, Hyde, Wetherell, Bray & Haff, Boise, 1985-93, Hyde, Wetherell, Bray, Haff & French Ltd., Boise, 1993—. Author: The Worker's Compensation Law of Idaho, 1989, 2d ed. 1991; contbr. articles to profl. jours. Dem. candidate for Idaho atty. gen., 1976; pres. Boise City Coun., 1986-92; mem. human welfare com. Mountain States Tumor Inst., Boise, 1985—; bd. dirs. Epilepsy Found. Am., 1980-87, United Way of Ada County, Boise, 1982-88, Idaho Epilepsy League, Boise, 1977—; chmn. Idaho State Dem. Party, 1991-93, exec. com., 1993—. Recipient Outstanding Personal Achievement award Epilepsy Found. Am., 1987. Mem. Idaho State Bar Assn. (Outstanding Service to Handicapped award 1981), Assn. Trial Lawyers Am., Idaho Trial Lawyers Assn. (editor Idaho Trial Lawyers Mag. 1978-85, bd. govs. 1979-85, Outstanding Svc. award 1990). Roman Catholic. Lodge: Kiwanis (Boise) (pres. 1985-86). Home: 1292 Candleridge Dr Boise ID 83712-6504 Office: Hyde Wetherell Bray Haff & French Ltd 1109 Main St Ste 500 Boise ID 83702-5641

WETSCH, PEGGY A., nursing administrator, educator; b. San Diego; d. Harvey William Henry and Helen Catherine (Thorpe) Brink; m. Gearald M. Wetsch, June 26, 1971; children: Brian Gearald, Lynette Kirstiann Nicole. Diploma, Calif. Hosp. Sch. Nursing, 1971; BSN cum laude, Pepperdine U., 1980; MS in Nursing, Calif. State U., L.A., 1985. Cert. in nursing adminstrn., human resource devel. Clin. nurse Orange County Med. Ctr./U. Calif. Irvine Med. Ctr., Orange, Calif., 1971-75; pediatric head nurse U. Calif. Irvine Med. Ctr., 1975-79; clin. nurse educator Palm Harbor Gen./Med. Ctr. Garden Grove, Calif., 1980-81; dir. ednl. svcs. Med. Ctr. of Garden Grove, 1981-85; dir. edn. Mission Hosp. Regional Med. Ctr., Mission Viejo, Calif., 1986-92; coord. computer and learning resources L.A. Med. Ctr. Sch. Nursing, 1992—; assoc. part time faculty Saddleback Coll., 1990—; lectr. statewide nursing program Calif. State U., Dominguez Hills, 1986-92; ednl. cons. Author: (with others) Nursing Diagnosis Guidelines to Planning Care; contbr. articles to profl. jours. Treas. Orange County Nursing Edn. Coun., 1986-87, 88-90, pres., 1987-88. Mem. ANA, Am. Nursing Informatics Assn. (So. Calif. chpt.)Calif. Nurses Assn. (regional mem.-at-large 1990-92), Am. Soc. for Health Edn. and Tng., N.Am. Nursing Diagnosis Assn. (secondary reviewer Diagnostic Rev. 1989-90, expert adv. panel 1990—, mem. diagnostic review com. 1992-94), So. Calif. Nursing Diagnosis Assn. (membership chmn. 1984-92, pres. 1992-93), Nat. Am. Mgmt. Assn. (charter L.A. County, U. So. Calif. Med. Ctr. chpt.), Spina Bifida Assn. Am., Sigma Theta Tau (pres. chpt. 1991-93), Phi Kappa Phi. Home: 1520 San Clemente Ln Corona CA 91720-7949

WETTACH, GEORGE EDWARD, physician; b. San Jose, Calif., June 11, 1940; s. George Angevine and Glodine Lillian (Wilks) W.; m. Rosanne Nemeth, Nov. 24, 1966 (div. Mar. 1988); children: George R., Shannon Elizabeth, Robin Scot; m. Linda Kay Ridgley, June 10, 1989. Degree in premed, San Jose State Coll., 1962; MD, St. Louis (Mo.) U., 1966. Intern St. Louis City Hosp., 1966-67; medical resident Highland Gen. Hosp., Oakland, Calif., 1970-71; cardiac fellow Huntington Meml. Hosp., Pasadena, Calif., 1971-72, Stanford U., 1972-73; chief med. resident St. Louis U., 1973-74; emergency room physician St. Louis City Hosp., 1974-75, St. John's Med. Ctr., Creve Coeur, Mo., 1975-77; emergency med. services med. dir. City of St. Louis, 1977-85; emergency room physician Nat. Emergency Svcs., Inc., Tiburon, Calif., 1985-90; sr. flight surgeon Naval Air Res., Alameda, Calif., 1990—; attending physician San Francisco Gen. Hosp., 1988—; clin. instr. medicine U. Calif., San Francisco, 1989—; pres. Health Edn. Found. for TV, 1978—. Producer (TV show): Pulse (Aerospace Med. Assn. conv. award 1984), 1983-85. Mem. Pasadena Community Symphonic Orch., 1971-72; commr. Arts Coun. Menlo Park, Calif., 1987—. Capt. USNR, 1986—. Recipient Nat. Polaroid Photo Contest award 1985, Univ. City Photo Contest award, 1987, U.S. Naval Inst. Maritime Photo Contest award, 1989. Fellow Aerospace Med. Assn. (assoc.); mem. Naval Res. Assn., Res. Officers Assn., Assn. Mil. Surgeons U.S., Aerospace Med. Assn., Nat. Geography Soc., Monterrey Bay Aquarium. Republican. Home: 193 Willow Rd Menlo Park CA 94025-2709 Office: Naval Air Reserve Med Dept Alameda CA 94501

WETTER, JACK, psychologist, educator; b. Brussels, Apr. 26, 1943; came to U.S., 1950; s. Irving and Blanche (Zuchachovitz) W.; m. Helen R. Slotow, Mar. 23, 1968; children: Michael G., Karin M. BA, UCLA, 1967, MA, 1969, EdD, 1970. Diplomate Am. Bd. Profl. Psychology; lic. clin. psychologist, Calif. Chief psychologist UCLA Med. Ctr., 1970-72, dir. psychol. svcs. dept. pediatrics, 1972-83; assoc. prof. dept. pediatrics UCLA Sch. Medicine, 1971-83, assoc. clin. prof. dept. family medicine, 1985—; pvt. practice L.A., 1971—. Mem. APA, Calif. Psychol. Assn., Nat. Coun. Mental Health Providers. Office: 1100 Glendon Ave Bldg 2046 Los Angeles CA 90024-3519

WETZEL, KARL JOSEPH, dean, physics educator; b. Waynesboro, Va., May 29, 1937; s. Mark Ernest and Margaret K. (Jungbluth) W.; m. Barbara Carol Damutz, Aug. 3, 1968; children: Sebastian P., Christopher M. BS in Physics, Georgetown U., 1959; MS in Physics, Yale U., 1960, PhD in Physics, 1965. Physicist Nat. Bur. Standards, Washington, 1959; postdoctoral fellow Inst. Nuclear Physics, Darmstadt, Fed. Republic Germany, 1965-67, Argonne (Ill.) Nat. Lab., 1967-69; asst. prof. U. Portland (Oreg.), 1969-72, assoc. prof., 1972-80, prof. of physics, 1980—, chair sci. dept., 1980-86, dean grad. sch., 1987—; cons. in field; adj. prof. State of Oreg. Dept. Continuing Edn., Portland, 1976—. Contbr. articles to profl. publs. Bd. dirs. Friendly House Ctr., Portland, 1979-82, Choral Arts Ensemble, Portland, 1988—. NSF fellow, 1965, 76-77; recipient Pres.' award Oreg. Mus. Sci. and Industry, 1972, Outstanding Advisor award Am. Coll. Test/Nat. Academic Advising Assn., 1984. Mem. Am. Phys. Soc., AAUP. Office: U Portland 5000 N Willamette Blvd Portland OR 97203

WEXLER, JUDIE GAFFIN, sociology educator, researcher; b. N.Y.C., Apr. 15, 1945; d. Isaac and Sara (Widensky) Pearlman; m. Howard M. Wexler, Mar. 11, 1973; children—Robyn, Matthew. B.A. in Sociology, Russell Sage U., Troy, N.Y., 1965; M.A. in Demography, U. Pa., 1966; Ph.D. in

Sociology, U. Calif.-Berkeley, 1975. Researcher N.Y. Mental Health Dept., Albany, 1966-67; demographer City Planning Dept., San Francisco, 1967-68; prof. Holy Names Coll., Oakland, Calif., 1974—, dean of acad. affairs, 1992—; cons. in field. Contbr. articles to profl. jours. Fellow Ford Found., NDEA. Mem. Am. Sociol. Assn., Am. Psychol. Assn. Home: 23 Cresta Vista Dr San Francisco CA 94127-1632 Office: Holy Names Coll 3500 Mountain Blvd Oakland CA 94619-1699

WEYAND, FREDERICK CARLTON, retired military officer; b. Arbuckle, Calif., Sept. 15, 1916; s. Frederick C. W. and Velma Semans (Weyand); m. Lora Arline Langhart, Sept. 20, 1940; children: Carolyn Ann, Robert Carlton, Nancy Diane. A.B., U. Calif.-Berkeley, 1939; LL.D. (hon), U. Akron, 1975. Officer U.S. Army, advanced to gen. chief of staff, 1940-76; sr. v.p. First Hawaiian Bank, Honolulu, 1976-82; trustee Estate of S.M. Damon, Honolulu, 1982—; bd. dirs. First Hawaiian, Inc., Ltd., First Hawaiian Bank, First Hawaiian Credit Corp. Chmn. ARC, Honolulu, 1982, Hawaiian Open golf Tourney, 1981-82. Decorated D.S.C. U.S. Army, 1967, D.S.M. Army (3), Dept. Def. (1), 1966-76, other U.S. and fgn. mil. decorations. Mem. Am. Def. Preparedness Assn., Assn. U.S. Army, U.S. Strategic Inst. (v.p. 1976—), USAF Assn. Lutheran. Clubs: Waialae Country. Lodge: Masons. Home: 2121 Ala Wai Blvd Ph 1 Honolulu HI 96815-2216 Office: SM Damon Estate Ste 1520 1132 Bishop St Honolulu HI 96813-3598

WEYERHAEUSER, GEORGE HUNT, forest products company executive; b. Seattle, July 8, 1926; s. John Philip and Helen (Walker) W.; m. Wendy Wagner, July 10, 1948; children: Virginia Lee, George Hunt, Susan W., Phyllis A., David M., Merrill W. BS with honors in Indsl. Engring., Yale U., 1949. With Weyerhaeuser Co., Tacoma, 1949—, successively mill foreman, br. mgr., 1949-56, v.p., 1957-66, exec. v.p., 1966-88, pres., chief exec. officer, 1988, chmn. bd., chief exec. officer, 1988—; bd. dirs. Boeing Co., SAFECO Corp., Chevron Corp.; mem. Bus. Coun., Bus. Roundtable, Wash. State Bus. Roundtable. Office: Weyerhaeuser Co Office Chmn Tacoma WA 98477*

WEYGAND, LEROY CHARLES, service executive; b. Webster Park, Ill., May 17, 1926; s. Xaver William and Marie Caroline (Hoffert) W.; BA in Sociology cum laude, U. Md., 1964; m. Helen V. Bishop, Aug. 28, 1977; children: Linda M. Weygand Vance (dec.), Leroy Charles, Cynthia R., Janine P. Enlisted in U.S. Army, 1944, commd. 2d lt., 1950, advanced through grades to lt. col., 1966; service in Korea, 1950; chief phys. security U.S. Army, 1965-70; ret., 1970; pres. Weygand Security Cons. Srvcs., Anaheim, Calif., 1970—, W & W Devel. Corp., 1979—; security dir. Jefferies Banknote Co., 1972-78; pres. Kern County Taxpayers Assn., 1986—; dir. Mind Psi-Biotics, Inc. Bd. dirs. Nat. Assn. Control Narcotics and Dangerous Drugs. Decorated Legion of Merit. Mem. Am. Soc. Indsl. Security. Contbr. articles profl. jours. Patentee office equipment locking device. Home: 12110 Backdrop Ct Bakersfield CA 93306-9707 Office: Kern County Taxpayers Assn 1415 18th St Ste 407 Bakersfield CA 93301-4442

WEYMAN, MARK, real estate executive; b. Berkeley, Calif., Apr. 8, 1947; s. Walter Edgar and Ruth Caroline (Stromquist) W.; m. Gail A. Damskey, Sept. 15, 1973 (div. 1988); 1 child, Alyse Marika; m. Jeanie Ann Walker, Apr. 2, 1989; 1 stepchild, Korie Alison Rekers. BA in Journalism, Humboldt State U., 1985. Lic. realtor, Calif. Sea capt. various seafood processing cos., Alaska, 1970-82; realtor assoc. Coldwell Banker Grass Roots Realty, Grass Valley, Calif., 1980-90, gen. mgr., 1990—; with Commonwealth Land Title Co., Redwood City, Calif. Vice chmn. Nevada City (Calif.) Planning Commn., 1985-88, Nevada County Fish and Wildlife Commn., 1983-88. Mem. Sierra Club. Home: 100 Beach Way Moss Beach CA 94038 Office: Commonwealth Land Title Co 805 Veterans Blvd Ste 100 Redwood City CA 94063

WHALEN, MARGARET CAVANAGH, civic worker, former educator; b. Des Moines, Iowa, Mar. 9, 1913; d. Thomas J. and Ann Lenore (Paul) Cavanagh; m. George Hubert Whalen, Aug. 3, 1946; children: Michael T., Ann Whalen Carrillo, George Patrick (dec.), Cheryl. BS in Commerce, St. Teresa Coll., Winona, Minn., 1935. Head bus. dept. St. Augustine High Sch., Austin, Minn., 1935-36, Parochial High Sch., Caledonia, Minn., 1936-37; clk., typist U.S. Govt., Dept. Socicl Security, Des Moines, 1937-38; county investigator for old age asst., aid to blind Marion County, Knoxville, Iowa, 1938; hydro dept. U.S. Weather Bur. Regional Office, Iowa City, Kansas City, Mo., 1939-42; head bills/warrants dept. IRS, Des Moines, 1942-46; substitute tchr. Los Gatos High Sch., Calif., 1961-65, Saratoga High Sch., Calif., 1961-65. Vol. Girl Scouts U.S.A., Boy Scouts Am., Saratoga, 1957-62; poll insp. Santa Clara County Regional Voters, Saratoga; precinct insp. Saratoga for Santa Clara County Registrar of Voters; organizer, vol. Saratoga Area Sr. Coordinate Coun., 1979—; Eucharistic minister, lector, commentator, v.p. coun. Sacred Heart Ch., Saratoga, 1986-87; charter pres. Oz chpt. Children's Home Soc., Saratoga; active Sacred Heart Women's Club, Our Lady of Los Gatos #197 Young Ladies Inst. Recipient Papal Bronze medal for Pub. Rels. Nat. Coun. Cath. Women, Saratoga, 1958, Merit award Friends of Saratoga Librs., 1975—, Merit award Saratoga Area Sr. Coord. Coun., 1980; AAUW fellow, Los Gatos, 1980. Mem. AAUW (corr. sec., chmn. social arts, bridge, hospitality Los Gatos Saratoga br., Friday matinee sect., book review sect.), Saratoga Hist. Found., Alumnae Assn. St. Teresa Coll., Montalvo Assn., Saratoga Foothill Club (Calif. 1978—). Democrat. Roman Catholic. Home: 14140 Victor Pl Saratoga CA 95070-5425

WHALEN, MICHELLE O., workers' compensation underwriter; b. Bloomington, Ill., Jan. 14, 1964; d. Michael Bernard and Dorothy (Juanita) W. BS, No. Ariz. U., 1986; MBA, U. Redlands, 1991. Display artist Levitz Furniture, San Diego, 1987-88; underwriter Indsl. Indemnity, San Diego, 1988-91; sr. underwriter Transamerica Ins. Group, San Diego, 1991-93, Fremont Compensation, San Diego, 1993—. Named one of Outstanding Young Women in Am., 1991. Roman Catholic.

WHALEN, THOMAS EARL, psychology educator; b. Toledo, June 26, 1938; s. T. Mylo and Alice E. (Tallman) W.; m. Carolyn Margaret Lapham, Dec. 24, 1960; children: Jennifer Susan, Holly Elizabeth. BA, UCLA, 1960; MA, San Diego State U., 1967; PhD, U. Conn., 1970. Cert. secondary tchr., Calif. Secondary tchr. San Diego City Schs., 1964-68; rsch. assoc. Southwest Regional Lab., Inglewood, Calif., 1969; prof. Calif. State U., Hayward, Calif., 1970—; ednl. psychology dept. chair 1977-79, assoc. dean sch. edn. 1987-89, Calif. State U. Hayward; rsch. cons. Evaluation Assocs. San Francisco Bay Area Schs., 1971-88, Lawrence Livermore Nat. Lab., Livermore, Calif., 1982-83. Author: (text book) Ten Steps to Behavioral Research, 1989; contbr. articles to profl. jours. Lt. USN, 1960-63. Recipient U.S. Office of Edn. fellowship, U. Conn., 1968-70, post doctoral scholarship Am. Edn. Rsch. Assn., U. Iowa, 1972. Mem. Am. Ednl. Rsch. Assn., APA, Calif. Ednl. Rsch. Assn. (bd. dirs. 1982-84), Bay Area Coun. on Measurement and Evaluation in Edn. (pres. 1976-77), United Profs. of Calif. (exec. bd. Calif. State U. Hayward 1975-76). Home: 325 Conway Dr Danville CA 94526-5511 Office: Calif State U 25800 Carlos Bee Blvd Hayward CA 94542-3001

WHALEY, CHARLES EDWARD, health agency executive; b. Williamstown, Ky., Feb. 29, 1928; s. Charles Fred and Mary Kathleen (Neal) W.; m. Carol Sutton, Nov. 23, 1957 (dec. 1985); children: Carrie Elizabeth Whaley Orman, Kate Wallace Whaley Archer. AB in Journalism, U. Ky., 1949; MS, Columbia U., 1950; MA, U. Manchester, Eng., 1957; postgrad., U. Louisville, 1965. Asst. to rsch. dir. Sch. Exec. Mag., N.Y.C., summer 1949; reporter The Courier-Jour., Louisville, 1950-60, edn. editor, 1960-64; dir. rsch. and info. Ky. Edn. Assn., Louisville, 1964-72, dir. pub. rels. and rsch., 1972-82, dir. communications, 1982-85; exec. dir. Am. Lung Assn. of San Francisco, 1985—. Co-author: Beyond the Minimum: A New Dimension for Kentucky's Foundation Program for Education, 1967; columnist, reviewer STAGES mag., 1986—. President bd. trustees First Unitarian Ch., Louisville, 1980; chmn. Quito com. Sister Cities of Louisville, 1982-84; bd. dirs. Louisville and Jefferson County Youth Orch., Louisville, 1980-81, Louisville Art Gallery, 1982-85, Louisville Theatrical Assn., 1982-83. With U.S. Army, 1950-52. Marshall scholar U. Manchester. Mem. Pub. Rels. Soc. Am. (pres. Louisville chpt. 1978, San Francisco Bay area 1991), Bay Area Theatre Critics Circle (sec., treas. 1990-92). Home: 443 Prentiss St San Francisco CA 94110-6142 Office: Am Lung Assn San Francisco 562 Mission St Ste 203 San Francisco CA 94105-2991

WHALLEY, LAWRENCE ROBERT, computer engineer, consultant; b. L.A., Dec. 13, 1943; s. Robert George Whalley and Victoria (Campiglia) Grier; m. E.M. Keremitsis, Apr. 1, 1985. BS in Physics, U. So. Calif., 1966, MS in Physics, 1970; PhD in Physics, U. Ill., 1974. Postdoctoral fellow, asst. prof. U. Maine, Orono, 1975-79; founder, chief technologist Maine Sci. Assocs., Orono, 1979-84; sr. design engr. Digital Sound Corp., Santa Barbara, Calif., 1984-87; mgr. prodn. cert. Telebit Corp., Mountain View, Calif., 1987-89; founder, prin. Rhinoceros Cons., San Francisco, 1989—. Contbr. articles to profl. jours. Mem. IEEE, Am. Phys. Soc., Assn. for Computing Machinery. Home: 46 Grand View Terr San Francisco CA 94114

WHAM, DOROTHY STONECIPHER, state legislator; b. Centralia, Ill., Jan. 5, 1925; d. Ernest Joseph and Vera Thelma (Shafer) Stonecipher; m. Robert S. Wham, Jan. 26, 1947; children: Nancy S. Wham Mitchell, Jeanne Wham Ryan, Robert S. II. BA, MacMurray Coll., 1946; MA, U. Ill., 1949; D of Pub. Adminstrn. (hon.), MacMurray Coll., 1992. Counsellor Student Counselling Bur. U. Ill., Urbana, 1946-49; state dir. ACTION program, Colo./Wyo. U.S. Govt., Denver, 1972-82; mem. Colo. Ho. of Reps., 1986-87; mem. Colo. Senate, 1987—, chair jud. com., 1988—, chmn. capital devel. com., health, environ, welfare, instns. Mem. LWV, Civil Rights Commn. Denver, 1972-80; bd. dirs. Denver Com. on Mental Health, 1985-88, Denver Symphony, 1985-88. Mem. Am. Psychol. Assn., Colo. Mental Health Assn. (bd. dirs. 1986-88), Colo. Hemophilia Soc. Republican. Methodist. Lodge: Civitan. Home: 2790 S High St Denver CO 80210-6352 Office: State Capitor Rm 338 Denver CO 80203

WHARTON, BLAZE DOUGLAS, county official; b. Pueblo, Colo., Sept. 1, 1956. Student, St. Patrick's Coll. Polit. advisor AFL-CIO, Salt Lake City; exec. dir. Utah State Dem. Party, Salt Lake City; exec. asst. Salt Lake County Commn.; mem. Utah State Ho. Reps., Salt Lake City, 1981-92, Utah State Senate, Salt Lake City, 1992—. Named Legislator of Yr. Utah State Sch. Employees, Salt Lake City, 1990, Utah Assn. Health Officers, Salt Lake City, 1991. s. Norman Stuart and Maxine Elenor (Atchinson) W.; m. Lisa Marie Adkisson; children: Matthew Blaze, Nathan Douglas, Cole William, Kennedy Marie. Roman Catholic. Home: 153 E Kensington Salt Lake City UT 84115

WHARTON, CHARLES ELLIS, legal administrator; b. Shelbyville, Tenn., Apr. 5, 1943; s. Frank Mears and Myra (Green) W.; m. Julie Anne Kitchen, Dec. 23, 1967. BS in Indsl. Engring., U. Tenn., 1965; MBA, U. Chgo., 1970. Systems engr. Chrysler Corp., Huntsville, Ala., 1966-68, Gen. Electric, Houston, 1968-69; sr. assoc. McKinsey & Co., Chgo., 1971-73; asst. to pres. North Am. Royalties, Inc., Chattanooga, 1973-77; v.p., chief fin. officer Glover, Inc., Roswell, N.Mex., 1977-79; exec. v.p. Carbon Co. Internat., Houston, 1980; chief adminstrv. officer Fulbright & Jaworski, Houston, 1980-85; exec. dir. O'Melveny & Myers, L.A., 1985—; bd. govs. U. Tenn., 1987-89. With USAF, 1965. Mem. L.A. Soc. Prevention of Cruelty to Animals (bd. dirs., exec. com.), L.A. Athletic Club. Office: O'Melveny & Myers 400 S Hope St Los Angeles CA 90071-2899

WHARTON, DAVID W., artist, educator; b. Wichita Falls, Tex., Nov. 19, 1951; s. Raymond Earl Wharton and Jane (Neely) Rudd; m. Sarah Emily Phillips, Jan. 22, 1993; 1 child, Caroline Lafferty. BFA, U. Okla., 1973; MFA, Cranbook Acad., Bloomfield Hills, Mich., 1977. Civil engr. U.S. Forest Service, Montgomery, Ala., 1977-86; dir. fine arts Sun Valley Ctr. for the Arts and Humanities, 1978-85; employed by artist Harvy K. Littleton to develop and publish fine art prints from glass, 1986—; artist in residence Windsor Printmaking Forum Windsor Art Mus., Univ. Windsor, Ontario, Can.; lectr. U. Wash., Seattle, 1981, Humboldt State Coll., 1982, Hartford Art Sch., 1986, Kent (Ohio) State U., 1988; vis. lectr. Lethbridge U., Alta., Can., 1982, Banff Sch. Art, Alta., 1982, Calgary U., Alta., 1982; vis. artist Pilchuk Sch., Seattle, 1986, Penland Sch., N.C., 1986. Author (art book) Suite Southern Prints, 1977, Rain Baby, 1981, (Dade Book award); (portfolio) Indian Self Rule, 1983, Potters and Prints, 1984. Recipient Ten Western Paintmakers award Western States Arts Found., Santa Fe, 1979. Mem. Coll. Art Assn. Address: PO Box 84 Ketchum ID 83340

WHARTON, THOMAS WILLIAM, health administration executive; b. St. Louis, Nov. 20, 1943; s. Thomas William and Elaine Margaret (Bassett) w.; divorced; children: Thomas William, Christopher John. BSc in Econs., U. Mo., 1967; M in Health Adminstrn., U. Ottawa, Ont., Can., 1978. Asst. to exec. dir. Ottawa Civic Hosp., 1978-80; exec. dir. Caribou Meml. Hosp., Williams Lake, B.C., Can., 1980-83; dir. clinic and rehab. services Workers' Compensation Bd., Vancouver, B.C., 1983-89; pres. Gold Canyon, Lansdowne & Bradner Resources Corps., 1989—, Diagnostic and Health Cons., Vancouver, 1989—; ptnr., dir. Lynn Valley Med. Ctr., North Vancouver, B.C., 1993. Recipient Founder award Cariboo Musical Soc., 1983; named Lord of the Manors of Wharton and Kirkby Stephen (Eng.), 1991. Mem. Can. Coll. Health Service Execs., Am. Coll. Health Execs., Am. Acad. Med. Adminstrs., Health Adminstrs. Assn. B.C., U. Ottawa Health Service Alumni Assn. (pres. 1983-84).

WHARTON, TOM MICHAEL, newspaper editor; b. Salt Lake City, Nov. 9, 1950; s. John R. and Violet M. (Ruga) W.; m. Gayen Lee Bennett, June 17, 1972; children: Emma, Rawl, Jacob, Bryer. BS, U. Utah, 1973. Sports writer Deseret News, Salt Lake City, 1969-70; sports writer, outdoor editor Salt Lake Tribune, 1970-92, asst. sports editor, 1992—. Author: Utah! A Family Travel Guide, 1987, Utah!, 1992. Bd. dirs. Utah Friendship Force, Salt Lake City, 1981. Recipient award Utah Football Coaches Assn., 1987, Media Support award Utah Div. Parks and Recreation, 1987, lst ann. media award Utah Marine Dealers Assn., 1988. Mem. Outdoor Writers Assn. Am. (com. 1988, 3 third place awards, bd. dirs. 1992), Utah N.G. Assn. (pub. affairs officer 1970—). Roman Catholic. Home: 1024 Ramona Ave Salt Lake City UT 84105 Office: Salt Lake Tribune l43 S Main St Salt Lake City UT 84110

WHATLEY, ALFRED THIELEN, retired nuclear engineer; b. Denver, Apr. 20, 1922; s. Barney Lee and Gertrude (Thielen) W.; m. Margaret Tovani, Apr. 6, 1944 (div. Sept. 1970); children: Christine Whatley Difani, Trudy Whatley Havener, Barney Lee II, Kathrin Whatley Gunnels. BA, Princeton U., 1948, MA, 1950, PhD, 1952. Scientist GE, Richland, Wash., 1952-55; engring. specialist GE, Idaho Falls, Idaho, 1955-57; sr. scientist GE, Pleasanton, Calif., 1957-61; propulsion engr. Martin-Marietta Co., Littleton, Colo., 1961-62; program mgr. Lawrence Livermore Nat. Lab. EG&G, Inc., Las Vegas, Nev., 1962-70; exec. dir. Western Interstate Nuclear Bd., Denver, 1970-76; ret., 1976; mem. adv. com. on power plant siting AEC, 1974-76; mem. adv. com. on solar energy NSF, 1975-76; mem. gov.'s adv. com. on project Rio Blanco, State of Colo., 1974. Contbr. articles to profl. jours. Mem. Colo. Air Pollution Control Commn., Denver, 1973-76, chmn., 1976; chmn. Summit County Citizens Assn., Breckenridge, Colo., 1975-78; mem. Regional Planning Commn., Summit County, 1980-84; bd. dirs. Breckenridge Sanitation Dist., 1990—. Mem. Am. Nuclear Soc. (chmn. Idaho sect. 1956), Sigma Xi. Democrat. Home: PO Box 540 Breckenridge CO 80424-0540

WHEATLEY, FORD HARRY, IV, lawyer, financial consultant, former elected official, judge; b. Detroit, Oct. 26, 1953; s. F. Harry and Theresa (Mabarak) W. BA in Communications with honors, Mich. State U., 1976; JD cum laude, U. Mich., 1979; cert. fin. planner, Coll. for Fin. Planning, Denver, 1988. Colo. 1979, U.S. Dist. Ct. Colo. 1979, U.S. Ct. Appeals (10th cir.) 1980; lic. real estate broker, Colo. Ptnr. Porterfield, Richtsmeier & Wheatley, Denver, 1979-82, Porterfield & Wheatley, Denver, 1982-86; councilman City of Glendale, Colo., 1984-86, 1987-88, mayor, 1988-92, assoc. mcpl. judge, 1992—; sec., treas. Registered Agts., Inc., Denver 1980-86, also bd. dirs. Mem. Colo. Bar Assn., Arapahoe County Bar Assn., Phi Kappa Phi. Home and Office: 4866 E East Kentucky Ave Glendale CO 80222

WHEATLEY, JEAN GEORGE, physical education educator, administrator; b. Tarkio, Mo., June 20, 1936; d. Robert Wilfred and Mildred Margaret (Davis) George; m. Stan H. Wheatley, June 5, 1958; children: Georgia, Greg, Jennifer. BA, Tarkio Coll., 1958; MEd, U. Wyo., 1965. Tchr. elem. schs. Sch. Dist. #1, Casper, Wyo., 1958-64, elem. phys. edn. supr., 1964-65; instr. phys. edn., intramural dir. Casper Coll., 1965-87, assoc. athletic dir., dept. head, 1972-87, athletic dir., dept. head, 1987—; instr. tennis clinics. Elder Presbyn. Ch., Casper, 1972—, deacon, 1987-90; bd. dirs. Fitness-Wellness Ctr., Casper, 1985—. Named Outstanding Phys. Educator State of Wyo., 1984. Mem. Nat. Jr. Coll. Athletic Assn. (regional tournament dir.), U.S. Tennis Assn., Cen. Dist. Assn. Health Phys. Edn. Recreation and Dance (hon. award 1989), Wyo. Assn. Health Phys. Edn. Recreation and Dance (pres. 1978-79), PEO (pres. 1985), Wyo. Community Coll. Athletic Conf. (coach, Tennis Coach of Yr. 1979, 80, 82, 84, 85). Republican. Home: 4990 Chinook St Casper WY 82601 Office: Casper Coll 125 College Dr Casper WY 82601-4699

WHEATLEY, STANLEY HAROLD, school system administrator; b. Anita, Iowa, July 21, 1934; s. Harold Archie Wheatley and Leila Christensen; m. Jean George, June 5, 1958; children: Georgia Lynn, Gregory Lee, Jennifer Sue. BS, Tarkio Coll., 1956; MEd, U. Wyo., 1960, EdD, 1969. Tchr. Tarkio (Mo.) Pub. Schs., 1956-58; tchr. Natrona County Sch. Dist., Casper, Wyo., 1958-61, elem. prin., 1961-71, assoc. supt., 1971—. Vol. United Fund, Casper. Mem. Am. Assn. Sch. Adminstrs., Phi Delta Kappan. Home: 4990 Chinook Trl Casper WY 82601 Office: Natrona County Sch Dist 970 North Glen Rd Casper WY 82601

WHEATON, ALICE ALSHULER, real estate loan secretary; b. Burbank, Calif., Mar. 20, 1920; d. Elmore and Anzy Jeanette (Richards) Wheaton; m. Robert Edward Alshuler, Sept. 19, 1942 (div. 1972); children: John Robert, Katherine Dennis. BA in Edn., UCLA, 1942. Owner, dir. The Fitness Studio, Washington, 1974-85; staff asst. Pres. Coun. Phys. Fitness and Sports, Washington, 1980-89; coord. Fed. Inter Agy. Health Fitness Coun., Washington, 1980-89; expert advisor U.S. Office Pers. Mgmt., Washington, 1986-89; loan sec. North County Bank, Escondido, Calif., 1990—; cons. Pres. Coun. Phys. Fitness and Sports, Gov.'s Coun. Phys. Fitness, Health, Welfare, Wash., 1989-90. Editor: The Federal FitKit-Guidelines for Federal Agencies, 1988. Recipient Gold Key award L.A. Area United Way, 1966. Mem. Profl. Secs. Internat. (pres. Palomar chpt. 1993—), UCLA Gold Shield Hon. (pres.), UCLA Alumni Assn. (v.p., Disting. Com. Svc. award 1968), San Diego Hist. Soc., Kappa Kappa Gamma. Republican. Episcopalian.

WHEATON, HARRY JAMES, corporate executive; b. Alliance, Ohio, May 11, 1941; s. Harry E. and Eila F. (Cowles) W.; m. Margo Ann Stubblefield, Oct. 2, 1975. BSBA, Franklin U., 1975. Salesman Texaco, Chgo., 1971-75; v.p. sales Cushion Foam Corp., Haverhill, Mass., 1975-81; gen mgr. Voltek, Inc., Lawrence, Mass., 1981-83; pres., CEO, bd. dirs. Cantrick Corp Corp., Lexington, Mich., 1983-87; v.p., gen. mgr., bd. dirs. Hartech USA Ltd., Scottsdale, Ariz., 1987-91; pres., EOO, bd. dirs. Impressive Labels, Inc., Safford, Ariz., 1991—; bd. dirs. U.S. Tool, Chgo., Tarva Industries, Detroit. With USN, 1967-71, Vietnam. Buddhist. Home: 322 E Quail Trail Rd Safford AZ 85546-9124 Office: Impressive Labels Inc PO Box J 300 E 4th St Safford AZ 85548

WHEELER, BENITA LOUISE, artist; b. St. Ignatius, Mont., Sept. 25, 1939; d. Thomas B. and Lucille (Brush) Williamson; m. Camille D. Bisson, Mar. 17, 1963 (div. Aug. 1970); m. Walter L. Wheeler; children: Daniel, James, Marshall (dec.). BA, Coll. Great Falls, 1976. Logging acct. Champion Internat., Polson, Mont., 1962-67; rep. patient accounts Columbus Hosp., Great Falls, Mont., 1970-73, Mont. Deaconess Med. Ctr., Great Falls, 1977-86; artist Great Falls, 1986—. Represented in permanent collection CM Russell Mus., Great Falls. Recipient 1st place watercolor award, St. Fair, Great Falls, 1985, juried whow, West Side Meth. Ch., Great Falls, 1986. Mem. NOW (pres. Mont. chpt. 1992—), Great Falls Art Assn., Western Heritage Artists (v.p. 1987-88, show chair 1988-90), Bus. and Profl. Women (pres. 1985-86). Democrat. Unitarian. Home: 1804 16th Ave S Great Falls MT 59405-4827

WHEELER, DONALD CRAIG, diagnostic radiologist; b. Fresno, Calif., Feb. 15, 1959; s. Norman Orion Wheeler and Susan Carol (Wristen) Flynn; m. Grace Don-Wheeler, June 14, 1986. BS in Physics, U. Calif., Davis, 1980; MD, U. So. Calif., L.A., 1986. Diplomate Nat. Bd. Med. Examiners, Am. Bd. Radiology. Rsch. asst. Genentech, Inc., San Francisco, 1981-82; intern L.A.C./U. So. Calif. Med. Ctr., 1986-87; resident Cedars-Sinai Med. Ctr., L.A., 1987-90, chief resident, 1990-91; fellow Harbor-UCLA, Torrance, Calif., 1991-92; staff radiologist Hollywood Community Hosp. and Westside Hosp., L.A., 1992—. Co-author: Lymphokine Actions, 1982; contbr. articles to profl. jours. Mem. AMA, Am. Roentgen Ray Soc., Radiologic Soc. N.Am., Japanese Am. Nat.Mus. Home: 11010 Rose Ave # 104 Los Angeles CA 90034

WHEELER, HELEN RIPPIER, writer, educator, consultant. BA, Barnard Coll., 1950; MS, Columbia U., 1951; MA, U. Chgo., 1954; PhD, Columbia U., 1964. Media adminstr. Chgo. City Colls., 1958-62; Latin Am. coord. Columbia U. Librs., N.Y.C., 1962-64; assoc. prof. La. State U., Baton Rouge, 1971-73; cons. Womanhood Media, Berkeley, Calif., 1973—; vis. lectr. U. Calif., Berkeley, 1978-87; cons. U. Hawaii Community Coll. System. Author: Womanhood Media, 1972, The Bibliographic Instruction Course Handbook, 1988, Getting Published in Women's Studies, 1989, others; contbr. chpts. to books, articles to profl. jours, scripting for instructional media. Presdl. appointee Comm. on Status of Women, Internat. Rels. Com.; subcom. mem. Sexist Subject-Heads; caucus mem. Nat. Women's Studies Assn. Mem. ALA, NOW (chpt. founder), Josei to Toshokan No Tameno Network, Women's Inst. for Freedom of Press. Democrat. Address: Womanhood Media PO Box 9373 Berkeley CA 94709-0373

WHEELER, JAMES RICHARD, retired surgeon; b. Red Oak, Iowa, Aug. 26, 1925; s. Paul LeRoy and Laura (Jones) W.; m. Shirley Ann Miller, June 21, 1952; children: Gail, Scott, Karen, Kent, Ann. BS in Zoology, Iowa State U., 1949; MD, Northwestern U., 1952. Diplomate Am. Bd. Surgery. Intern Wesley Meml. Hosp., Chgo., 1952-53; resident in gen. surgery VAH, Hines, Ill., 1953-57; gen. surgeon Med. Group Greeley, Colo., 1957-85; clin. fac. U. Colo. Med. Sch., 1958-92; gen. surgeon Greeley Med. Clinic, 1985-92; med. dir. North Colo. Regional Burn Unit, Greeley, 1984-92; med. dir. emeritus North Colo. Regional Burn Unit, 1993—. Contbr. articles to profl. jours. Vice-pres. bd. Colo. Blue Shield, Denver, 1972-74; pres. sch. bd. Greeley Pub. Sch., 1970. Staff sgt. U.S. Army, 1943-46, ETO. Fellow ACS (pres., bd. dirs. Colo. chpt. 1980); mem. AMA, Am. Burn Assn., Denver Acad. Surgery (pres. 1992, bd. dirs.), S.W. Surgical Congress, Rotary (Rotarian of Yr. 1978-79). Home: 1730 Glen Meadows Dr Greeley CO 80631-6832

WHEELER, JOS RIDLEY, consumer products executive, retired; b. Springfield, Mo., Oct. 3, 1927; s. Joe R. and Thelma (Ridley) W.; m. Barbara Guthrie, Sept. 27, 1947; children: Kathleen, Nancy. BA in Econs., Drury Coll., 1949. Sales mgr. Procter & Gamble, various, 1949-71; v.p. mktg., exec. v.p. Kingsford Co., Louisville, 1971-73; v.p., gen. mgr. Kingsford Div. Clorox Co., Oakland, Calif., 1973-77; v.p. sales, group v.p. Clorox Co., Oakland, 1977-85; owner, operator Pleasant Hill Ranch, Sebastopol, Ky., 1979-89; chmn. bd. Oakland (Calif.) City Center Hotel Corp., Oakland, 1985-87. Dir. Santa Rosa Symphony Orchestra (chmn. investment com. 1983), Oakland (Calif.) Symphony Orchestra, 1980-85. With U.S. Army, 1946-48. Republican. Episcopalian. Home: 6419 Timber Springs Ct Santa Rosa CA 95409-5934

WHEELER, LARRY RICHARD, accountant; b. Greybull, Wyo., Nov. 30, 1940; s. Richard F. and Olive B. (Fredrickson) W.; m. Marjorie A. Frady, Dec. 20, 1961; m. Patricia C. Marturano, Dec. 3, 1977; children: Anthony, Richard, Teresa, Kara. BS, U. Wyo., 1965. CPA, Colo. Staff acct. H. Greger CPA, Ft. Collins, Colo., 1965-66, sr. acct. Lester Draney & Wickham, Colorado Springs, Colo., 1966-67; acct., controller/treas., J.D. Adams Co., Colorado Springs, 1967-74; ptnr. Wheeler Pierce & Hurd, Inc., Colorado Springs, 1974-80; gen. mgr., v.p. Schneebeck's, Inc., Colorado Springs, 1980-81; prin. L.R. Wheeler & Co., P.C., Colorado Springs, 1981—; dir. Schneebeck's Industries, Williams Printing, Inc. Mem. U.S. Taekwondo Union; bd. dirs. Domestic Violence Prevention Ctr. Paul Stock Found. grantee, 1962. Mem. Internat. Assn. Fin. Planners, Am. Inst. CPA's, Nat. Contract Mgmt. Assn., Colo. Soc. CPA's (map. com.), Colo. Litigation Support Group. Office: 317 E San Rafael Colorado Springs CO 80903

WHEELER, WAYNE CABLE, society administrator; b. Buffalo, N.Y., May 3, 1938; s. Albert Henry and Glenda Marie (Bixby) W.; m. Sally Ann Hales, June 6, 1976; 1 child, Scott Hales. BFA, Syracuse U., 1962. Commd. 2d lt. USCG, 1963, advanced through grades to lt., 1966, resigned, 1975, ops.

officer, navigator SWEETBRIER, 1963-65; assigned aids to navigation br. USCG, Cleve., 1965-67; exec. officer IRONWOOD, 1967-69, hdqtrs. staff mem., 1969-72; vessels svc. staff mem. San Francisco, 1972-75; asst. chief aids to navigation br. 12th Coast Guard Dist., San Francisco, 1976-87; pres., founder U.S. Lighthouse Soc., San Francisco, 1984—. Editor: (jour.) The Keeper's Log; contbr. articles to profl. jours. Bd. govs. Navy-Marine Corps-Coast Guard Mus., Treasure Island, San Francisco, 1979—; bd. dirs. Am. Youth Hostels, San Francisco, 1989-90. Recipient Outstanding Pub. Svc. award, Sec. of Transp., 1986. Republican. Office: US Lighthouse Soc 244 Kearny St Fl 5 San Francisco CA 94108-4507

WHEELON, ALBERT DEWELL, physicist; b. Moline, Ill., Jan. 18, 1929; s. Orville Albert and Alice Geltz (Dewell) W.; m. Nancy Helen Hermanson, Feb. 28, 1953 (dec. May 1980); children—Elizabeth Anne, Cynthia Helen; m. Cicely J. Evans, Feb. 4, 1984. B.Sc., Stanford U., 1949; Ph.D., Mass. Inst. Tech., 1952. Teaching fellow, then rsch. assoc. physics MIT, Boston, 1949-52; with Douglas Aircraft Co., 1952-53, Ramo-Wooldridge Corp., 1953-62; dep. dir. sci. and tech. CIA, Washington, 1962-66; with Hughes Aircraft Co., L.A., 1966-88, chmn., chief exec. officer, 1987-88; vis. prof. MIT, 1989; mem. Def. Sci. Bd., 1968-76, Pres.'s Fgn. Intelligence, 1983-88, presdl. commn. on space shuttle Challenger accident, 1986; trustee Calif. Inst. Tech., Aerospace Corp., Rand Corp. Author 30 papers on radiowave propagation and guidance systems. Fellow IEEE, AIAA (Von Karman medal 1986); mem. NAE, Am. Phys. Soc., Coun. on Fgn. Rels., Sigma Chi. Republican. Episcopalian. Address: 181 Sheffield Dr Montecito CA 93108

WHELAN, JAMES MICHAEL, consultant; b. Joliet, Ill., Feb. 15, 1925; s. James M. and Ellena (Johnson) W.; m. Mary Rockett, June 14, 1952; 1 child, Deirdre (dec.). BS, U. Ill., 1948; PhD, U. Calif., Berkeley, 1952. Mem. tech. staff Calif. Rsch. Corp., Richmond, Calif., 1951-53; supr. Bell Telephone Labs., Inc., Murray Hill, N.J., 1953-64; prof. materials sci., elec. engring., chem. engring. U. So. Calif., L.A., 1964-87; pres. Fugacity, Inc., Wilmington, Calif., 1987—; cons. Hughes Aircraft Co., Torrence, Carlsbad, Calif., 1970—. Contbr. articles to profl. jours.; patentee in field. With U.S. Army, 1944-46. Democrat. Roman Catholic. Home: PO Box 2129 Wilmington CA 90748

WHELAN, ROBERT LOUIS, bishop; b. Wallace, Idaho, Apr. 16, 1912. Ed., St. Michael's Coll., Spokane, Wash., Alma (Calif.) Coll. Mem. S.J.; ordained priest Roman Catholic Ch., 1944; titular bishop of Sicilibba and coadjutor bishop, Fairbanks, Alaska, 1967-68; bishop of Fairbanks, 1968-85; retired bishop Diocese of Fairbanks, Alaska, 1985—. Address: 1316 Peger Rd Fairbanks AK 99709

WHELAN, WILLIAM ANTHONY, forest products company executive; b. Bklyn., Aug. 18, 1921; s. Daniel and Catherine (Pugh) W.; m. Marcia M. McCorkle, Nov. 14, 1948; children—Michael, Greer, Daniel, Ann. B.S.M.E., U. Calif.-Berkeley. Vice pres. Klamath Machine & Locomotive Works, 1948-58; plant and dist. mgr. U.S. Plywood, 1959-68; v.p. West Coast ops. Champion Internat., 1968-74; exec. v.p. Roseburg Lumber Co., 1975-77; exec. v.p. Pope & Talbot Inc., Portland, Oreg., 1978, pres., 1979-84, vice chmn., 1984-86, cons., also bd. dirs. Served with U.S. Army. Mem. Western Wood Products Assn. (bd. dirs.), Nat. Forest Products Assn. (bd. dirs.). Club: Arlington. Office: Roseburg Forest Products PO Box 1088 Roseburg OR 97470

WHELCHEL, SANDRA JANE, writer; b. Denver, May 31, 1944; d. Ralph Earl and Janette Isabelle (March) Everitt; m. Andrew Jackson Whelchel, June 27, 1965; children: Andrew Jackson, Anita Earlyn. BA in Elem. Edn., U. No. Colo., 1966; postgrad. Pepperdine Coll., 1971, UCLA, 1971. Elem. tchr. Douglas County Schs., Castle Rock, Colo., 1966-68, El Monte (Calif.) schs., 1968-72; br. librarian Douglas County Libraries, Parker, Colo., 1973-78; zone writer Denver Post, 1979-81; reporter The Express newspapers, Castle Rock, 1979-81; history columnist Parker Trail newspapers, 1985—; columnist Gothic Jour. 1993; writing tchr. Aurora Parks and Recreation, 1985-91; writing instr. Arapahoe Community Coll., 1991; editor Authorship mag., 1992—; contbr. short stories and articles to various publs. including: Writer's World, Writer's Open Forum, Writer's Jour., Reunions, Ancestry Newsletter, Empire mag., Calif. Horse Rev., Host mag., Jack and Jill, Child Life, Children's Digest, Peak to Peak mag.; author (non-fiction books): Your Air Force Academy, 1982, A Guide to the U.S. Air Force Acad., 1990, Parker, Colorado: A Folk History, 1990; (coloring books): A Day at the Cave, 1985, A Day in Blue, 1984, Pro Rodeo Hall of Champions and Museum of the American Cowboy, 1985, Pikes Peak Country, 1986, Mile High Denver, 1987; co-author: The Register, 1989; lectr. on writing. Mem. Internat. Platform Assn., Nat. Writers Club (treas. Denver Metro chpt. 1985-86, v.p. membership 1987, sec. 1990, bd. dirs. 1990-91, pres. 1990-91, nat. exec. dir. 1991—, v.p. programs 1992), Parker Area Hist. Soc. (pres. 1987, 88, 89).

WHELLOCK, JOHN GRAHAM, technology company executive; b. Croydon, Surrey, England, Aug. 26, 1947; came to U.S., 1980; s. Reginald Baldwin and Doreen Joan (Kitching) W.; m. Jennifer Ann Hill, Aug. 12, 1975 (div. 1981); m. Ginger Gray, May 15, 1992. BS with honors, Birmingham U. Chem. Engring., 1969, PhD, 1972. Chartered engr., England. Chief systems engr. Redman Heenan Internat., Worcester, England, 1972-74; tech. dir. Tolltreck Ltd., Droitwich, England, 1974-80; v.p. process engring. Tolltreck Internat. Ltd., Denver, 1980-90; v.p. tech. Minproc Engrs. Inc., Denver, 1990-91; pres. Minproc Tech., Inc., Denver, 1991—; dir. Minproc Corp., Denver, 1991—, Minproc Resources Inc., Denver, 1991—, Minproc Engrs. Inc., Denver, 1991—. Contbr. articles to profl. jours. Mem. AICE, AIME, Nat. Soc. Prof. Engrs., Am. Soc. Metals, Inst. Chem. Engrs. U.K. Office: Minproc Tech Inc 5600 S Quebec St STe B300 Englewood CO 80111

WHETTEN, JOHN THEODORE, geologist; b. Willimantic, Conn., Mar. 16, 1935; s. Nathan Laselle and Theora Lucille (Johnson) W.; m. Carol Annette Jacobsen, July 14, 1960; children—Andrea, Krista, Michelle. A.B. with high honors, Princeton U., 1957; Ph.D., 1962; M.S., U. Calif.-Berkeley, 1959. Mem. faculty U. Wash., Seattle, 1963-81; research instr. oceanography U. Wash., 1963-64, asst. prof., 1964-68, assoc. prof., 1968-72, prof. geol. scis. and oceanography, 1972-81, chmn. dept. geol. scis., 1969-74; assoc. dean Grad. Sch., 1968-69; geologist U.S. Geol. Survey, Seattle, 1975-80; asst. div. leader geoscis. div. Los Alamos Nat. Lab., 1980-81, dep. div. leader earth and space scis. div., 1981-84, div. leader earth and space scis. div., 1984-86, assoc. dir. energy and tech., 1986-92, assoc. dir. quality, policy and performance, 1992—. Contbr. articles to profl. jours. Fulbright fellow, 1962-63. Home: 154 Piedra Loop Los Alamos NM 87544-3837 Office: Los Alamos Nat Lab MS A-108 Los Alamos NM 87545

WHIDDON, CAROL PRICE, writer, editor, consultant; b. Gadsden, Ala., Nov. 18, 1947; d. Curtis Ray and Vivian (Dooly) Price; m. John Earl Caulking, Jan. 18, 1969 (div. July 1987); m. Ronald Alton Whiddon, Apr. 13, 1988. Student, McNeese State U., 1966-68; BA in English, George Mason U., 1984. Flute instr. Lake Charles, La., 1966-68; flutist Lake Charles Civic Symphony, 1966-69, Beaumont (Tex.) Symphony, 1967-68; freelance editor The Washington Lit. Rev., 1983-84, ARC Hdqrs., Washington, 1984; writer, editor Jaycor, Vienna, Va., 1985-87; writer, editor Jaycor, Albuquerque, 1987-90, publs. mgr., 1990-91; writer, editor Proteus Corp., Albuquerque, 1991-92; owner Whiddon Editorial Svcs., Albuquerque, 1989—; mem. S.W. Writer's Workshop, 1991—. Co-author: The Spirit That Wants Me: A New Mexico Anthology, 1991; contbr. various articles to Albuquerque Woman and mil. dependent pubs. in Fed. Rpublic Germany. Bd. dirs. Channel 27-Pub. Access TV, 1991—, exec. bd. sec. 1992, v.p., 1993; dep. mgr. Fed. Women's Program, Ansbach, Fed. Republic Germany, 1980-81; pres. Ansbach German-Am. Club, 1980-82; sec. Am. Women's Activities, Fed. Republic Germany, 1980-81, chairwoman, 1981-82. Recipient cert. of appreciation from Am. amb. to Germany Arthur T. Burns, 1982, medal of appreciation from comdr. 1st Armored Div., Ansbach, Germany, 1982. Mem. NAFE, Women in Comm. (newsletter editor 1989-90, 91-92, v.p. 1990-91, pres.-elect 1992-93, pres. 1992—, chair programs com. Nat. Profl. Conf. 1994), Soc. Tech. Comm. (membership dir. 1993—), Nat Assn. Desktop Pubs., Am. Mktg. Assn., Greater Albuquerque C. of C., N.Mex. Cactus Soc. (historian 1989—, sec. 1991, newsletter editor 1992—, various show ribbons 1989-91). Republican. Home: 1129 Turner Dr NE Albuquerque NM 87123-1917

WHINNERY, JOHN ROY, electrical engineering educator; b. Read, Colo., July 26, 1916; s. Ralph V. and Edith Mable (Bent) W.; m. Patricia Barry, Sept. 17, 1944; children—Carol Joanne, Catherine, Barbara. B.S. in Elec. Engring, U. Calif. at Berkeley, 1937, Ph.D., 1948. With GE, 1937-46; part-time lectr. Union Coll., Schenectady, 1945-46; asso. prof. elec. engring. U. Calif., Berkeley, 1946-52, prof., vice chmn. div. elec. engring., 1952-56, chmn., 1956-59, dean Coll. Engring., 1959-63, prof. elec. engring., 1963-80, Univ. prof. Coll. Engring., 1980—; vis. mem. tech. staff. Bell Telephone Labs., 1963-64; research sci. electron tubes Hughes Aircraft Co., Culver City, 1951-52; disting. lectr. IEEE Microwave Theory and Technique Soc., 1989-92. Author: (with Simon Ramo) Fields and Waves in Modern Radio, 1944, 2d edit. (with Ramo and Van Duzer), 1985, (with D. O. Pederson and J. J. Studer) Introduction to Electronic Systems, Circuits and Devices; also tech. articles. Chmn. Commn. Engring. Edn., 1966-68; mem. sci. and tech. com. Manned Space Flight, NASA, 1963-69; mem. Pres.'s Com. on Nat. Sci. Medal, 1970-73, 79-80; standing com. controlled thermonuclear research AEC, 1970-73. Recipient Lamme medal Am. Soc. Engring. Edn., 1975, Centennial medal, 1993, Engring. Alumni award U. Calif.-Berkeley, 1980, Nat. Medal of Sci., 1992; named to Hall of Fame Modesto High Sch. (Calif.), 1983, ASEE Hall of Fame, 1993.; Guggenheim fellow, 1959. Fellow IRE (bd. dirs. 1956-59), IEEE (life, bd. dirs. 1969-71, sec. 1971, Edn. medal 1967, Centennial medal 1984, Medal of Honor 1985), Optical Soc. Am., Am. Acad. Arts and Scis.; mem. NAS, NAE (Founders award 1986), IEEE Microwave Theory and Techniques Soc. (Microwave Career award 1977), Phi Beta Kappa, Sigma Xi, Tau Beta Pi, Eta Kappa Nu. Congregationalist. Home: One Daphne Ct Orinda CA 94563 Office: U Calif Dept Electrical Engineering Berkeley CA 94720

WHIPPLE, DOUGLAS R., lawyer; b. Camp LeJeune, N.C., May 11, 1953; s. Dale E. and Marilyn (Jensen) W.; m. Z. Christine Trimble, Aug. 6, 1976; children: Benjamin, Stephan, Jacob, Rebekah, Philip, Thomas. BS, Utah State U., 1977; JD, Pepperdine U., 1980. Missionary Ch. Jesus Christ Latter-day Saints, Chgo., 1972-74; law clk. State Bar Calif., L.A., 1979-80; ptnr. Bedke & Whipple, Burley, Idaho, 1980-84; pres. Whipple & Byington, Burley, Idaho, 1984-87, Whipples Law Office, Burley, Idaho, 1987-89, Byington, Holloway, Whipple & Jones, Burley, Idaho, 1989—; pub. defender Cassia County, Burley, Idaho, 1984—; dist. atty. Joint Sch. Dist. No. 151, Burley, Idaho, 1984—; adjunct instr. Coll. So. Idaho, Lewis Clark State Coll. County pres. Am. Cancer Soc., Cassia County, Idaho, 1988; dir. Magic Valley Rehab. Svcs., Idaho, 1990-91; trustee Elizabeth Burton Scholarship Fund, Burley, Idaho, 1992—. Mem. Idaho State Bar, Idaho Supreme Court Adv. Com. for Criminal Rules, Nat. Sch. Bds. Assn. Coun. Sch. Attys. Mem. LDS Ch. Office: Byington Holloway et al 111 W 15th St Burley ID 83318

WHIPPLE, GEORGE STEPHENSON, architect; b. Evanston, Ill., Sept. 21, 1950; s. Taggart and Katharine (Brewster) W.; m. Lydia Buckley, May 30, 1981; children: Katherine Elizabeth, John Taggart. B.A., Harvard U., 1974; student Boston Architectural Ctr., 1975-76. Vice-pres., Call Us Inc., Edgartown, Mass., 1970-74; pres. Cattle Creek Assocs., Carbondale, Colo., 1976—, Earthworks Constrn., Carbondale, 1978-87; pres., Whipple and Brewster Corp., Aspen, 1988—. Chmn., Redstone Hist. Preservation Commn., Colo. Mem. Pitkin County Planning and Zoning Commn., 1989—. Mem. Rocky Mountain Harvard Club. Office: 121 S Galena St Ste 203 Aspen CO 81611-1960

WHIPPLE, V. THAYNE, II, financial firm executive; b. Glendale, Calif., Nov. 6, 1964; s. Verland Thayne and Mary Lou (Parkes) W.; m. Sheryl Brimhall, Nov. 25, 1988; children: Graham Thayne, Haven. BS, U. So. Calif., L.A., 1983. Sr. assoc. Imperial Securities Corp., San Ramon, Calif., 1985-88; pres. Pub. Funding Grp., Santa Monica, Calif., 1988—. Author: A Year of Verse, 1989, Witness to History: A Coversation with Will Rogers, 1992; composer (song) Easter Hymn, 1979. Republican. Mem. LDS Church. Office: Public Funding Group 9911 W Pico Blvd Ste 1440 Los Angeles CA 90035-2703

WHIPPLE, WALTER LEIGHTON, electrical engineer; b. Washington, June 23, 1940; s. Walter Jones and Marian Katharine (Leighton) W.; m. Jean Anne Ewer, Sept. 11, 1965; children: Kathryn Whipple Mulligan, Sara Marie. BS in Engring. Sci., Harvey Mudd Coll., 1962; MS in Computer, Info. and Control Engring., U. Mich., 1974, PhD in Computer, Info. and Control Engring., 1988. Registered profl. engr., Calif., Mich. Field svc. rep. ordnance dept. GE, Pittsfield, Mass., 1962-65; insp. Welker & Assocs., Marietta, Ga., 1966-67; engr. space and info. systems div. Raytheon Co., Sudbury, Mass., 1967-69; sr. elec. engr. profl. svc. div. Control Data Corp., Waltham, Mass., 1969-73; sr. programmer-analyst Control Data Corp., Southfield, Mich., 1973-78; design specialist Gen. Dynamics Corp., Pomona, Calif., 1978-83; prin. engr. electromagnetic systems div. Raytheon Co., Santa Barbara, Calif., 1983-91, sr. engr., electromagnetic systems div., 1992—; propr. Wingineering, Goleta, Calif., 1992—. Contbr. articles to profl. publs. Mem. loaned exec. Santa Barbara (Calif.) United Way, 1988-89; bd. dirs. Tres Condados coun. Girl Scouts U.S., 1985-86. Gen. Electric Found. fellow, 1973. Fellow AIAA (assoc.); mem. IEEE (sr., sec. Santa Barbara chpt. 1992, pace chair 1992—, L.A. Coun. legis. liaison, 1992—), AAUP, NSPE (treas. Ventura, Santa Barbara chpt., 1991-93), Assn. Old Crows. Office: Raytheon Co Software Design Engring Dept 9283 6380 Hollister Ave Goleta CA 93117-3197

WHISENHUNT, DONALD WAYNE, history educator; b. Meadow, Tex., May 16, 1938; s. William Alexander Whisenhunt and Beulah (Johnson) King; m. Betsy Ann Baker, Aug. 27, 1960; children: Donald Wayne Jr., William Benton. BA, McMurry Coll., 1960; MA, Tex. Tech U., 1962, PhD, 1966. Tchr. Elida (N.Mex.) High Sch., 1961-63; from asst. to assoc. prof. history Murray (Ky.) State U., 1966-69; assoc. prof., chmn. dept. Thiel Coll., Greenville, Pa., 1969-73; Dean Sch. Liberal Arts and Scis., Ea. N.Mex. U., Portales, 1973-77; v.p. acad. affairs U. Tex., Tyler, 1977-83; v.p., provost Wayne (Nebr.) State Coll., 1983-91, interim pres., 1985; prof. history, chmn. dept. Western Wash. U., Bellingham, 1991—. Author: Environment and American Experience, 1974, Depression in the Southwest, 1979, Chronological History of Texas, Vol. 1, 1982, Vol.2, 1987, Texas: Sesquicentennial Celebration, 1984; editor: Encyclopedia USA, 1988—. Democrat. Methodist. Office: Western Wash U Dept History Bellingham WA 98225

WHISLER, KIRK, publishing executive; b. Omaha, Calif., June 7, 1951; s. Donald Dee and Biddy Louise (Covert) W.; m. Magdalena Gonzalez, June 15, 1985; children: Spencer Diego, Tito Andres, Zeke Emilio. Student, U. Calif., Santa Barbara, 1969-72, Escuela de Artes Plasticas, Guadalajara, Mex., 1972; BA in History and Politics, U. Calif., Riverside, 1973. Pub. Somos Mag., San Bernardino, Calif., 1977-79, Caminos Mag., Los Angeles, 1979-86; dir. mktg. Embassy Pictures-Gregorio Cortez, Los Angeles, 1983-84; pres. Am. Internat. Hispanic Communications, Los Angeles, 1983-89; with Travel Mex. Mag. Group, Carlsbad, Calif., 1992—; pres. Nat. Assn. Hispanic Publs., L.A., 1984-86. Editor: National Hispanic Conventioneer, 3d rev. edit., 1985, National Hispanic Media Directory, 1985; author: National Hispanic Readership Study, 1985, Familia Latina Hispanic Market Fact Book, 1984; pub. Nev. Mag., 1986-92, New Events, 1987-92, Nev. Golf, 1990-92, Nev. Travel Update, 1992, Mex. Events and Destination Mag., 1992—, Mex. Update Mag., 1992—, Mex. Tourism News, 1992—. Del. Commn. of the Califs., Sacramento and Mex., 1977—; mem. L.A. Olympic Organizing Com., 1981-84, San Bernardino (Calif.) City Community Devel. Commn., 1979-83, San Bernardino City Econ. Devel. Coun., 1981-83. Recipient Golden Eagle award Nosotros, 1979, Leadership award San Bernardino Unified Sch. Dist. Bilingual Dist. Adv. Com., 1981, Contributor award Children's Mus., Los Angeles, 1985; Kirk Whisler Day proclaimed by Nev. Gov. Miller, 1992. Mem. U.S. Hispanic C. of C., Western Pubs. Assn. Democrat. Methodist. Office: Travel Mex Mag Group PO Box 188037 Carlsbad CA 92009

WHITACRE, JOHN, apparel executive; b. 1953. Student, U. Wash. With Nordstrom Inc., 1976—; co-pres. Nordstrom Inc., Seattle, 1991—. Office: Nordstrom Inc 1501 5th Ave Seattle WA 98101*

WHITACRE, WENDELL BRITT, plastic surgeon; b. Columbus, Ohio, Oct. 6, 1927; s. Asia Harold and Lena May (Sams) W.; m. Pierette Jeanine Pechmajou, Aug. 4, 1952 (div. 1982); children: Marc Michel, Eric Bruce, Anne Laura, Alice Lena; m. Sandy Marie Vigil, June 3, 1982 (div. 1988). AB, Ohio U., 1951; MD, Ohio State U., 1955. Diplomate Am. Bd. Plastic and Reconstructive Surgery. Rotating intern Phila. Gen. Hosp., 1955-56; resident in gen. surgery Hosp. U. Pa., Phila., 1956-60, resident in plastic and reconstructive surgery, 1960-62; pvt. practice Tucson, 1962--; assoc. in plastic surgery Coll. Medicine, U. Ariz., 1974-87; clin. lectr. in surgery U. Ariz., 1987—, part-time lectr. Coll. Medicine, 1990—, acting chief sect. plastic surgery, 1990-91, clin. asst. prof. surgery, 1992. Contbr. articles to profl. jours. Bd. dirs. Found. for St. Joseph's Hosp., Tucson, 1976-86; mem. profl. com. BCBS of Ariz., 1979-88. Fellow ACS; mem. Am. Soc. Plastic and Reconstructive Surgeons, AMA, Phi Beta Kappa, Alpha Omega Alpha. Republican. Methodist. Home: 5133 E River Rd Tucson AZ 85718-7250 Office: 310 N Wilmot Rd # 104 Tucson AZ 85711-2695

WHITAKER, BRUCE D., interior designer; b. Pocatello, Idaho, June 1, 1948; s. Donald C. Whitaker and Lois R. (Wilson) Wright; m. Juliana Stockman, Sept. 7, 1969; children: Jennifer Elizabeth, Laura Melissa. BA in Interior Design, Bus. Adminstrn., Wash. State U., 1971. Designer Lloyds Interiors, Portland, Oreg., 1971-73; prin. Bruce Whitaker Design Co., Portland, 1973-76, 77-78; sr. project designer Howard Hermanson & Assocs. Inc., Portland, 1976-77; v.p. for design Petter Moe & Assocs. Inc., Portland, 1978-87; prin. Whitaker Assocs., Portland, 1987—. Mem. Am. Soc. Interior Designers (profl., various offices Portland chpt. 1973—, Presdl. citation 1979, 87, 88, pres.-elect 1993), Inst. Bus. Designers. Home: 3654 SW Patton Rd Portland OR 97221-4127 Office: Whitaker Assocs 606 NW Front Ave Apt A3 Portland OR 97209-3718

WHITAKER, FRED MAYNARD, insurance agent; b. Cambridge, Mass., July 29, 1925; s. Sidney and Alva G. (Maynard) W.; m. Jane Manning, Dec. 31, 1960; children: Fred Manning, Charles Sidney. AB, Stanford U., 1953. Group rep. The Travelers, L.A., 1953-62; agt., broker W. M. Eastus & Assocs., L.A., 1962-68; exec. cons. Johnson & Higgins, L.A., 1968-72; agt., broker Prin. Fin. Group, L.A., 1972—. Vestryman Episcopal Ch., 1968-91, diocesan commns., nat. ch. posts, nat. chmn., 1958-61; chmn. Rep. Com., 1985-87; mem. L.A. County Rep. Ctrl. Com., 1977-93; chmn. 41st A.D. Ctrl. Com., 1985-87, 88; pres. Pres. Adv. Coun. of Glendale, 1991, 92. With U.S. Army, 1943-46, ETO. Decorated Bronze Star, Purple Heart, 3 Battle Stars, Combat Inf. Badge. Mem. Calif. Assn. Life Underwriters, Nat. Assn. Life Underwriters, Assn. Health Ins. Agts., Life Underwriters L.A., Am. Legion. Republican. Episcopalian. Home: 863 Matilija Rd Glendale CA 91202 Office: Prin Fin Group 3731 Wilshire Blvd Ste 610 Los Angeles CA 90010

WHITAKER, MORRIS DUANE, university administrator; b. Pocatello, Idaho, Apr. 4, 1940; s. Mirl William and Ada Belle (Bruesch) W.; m. Marguerite Fae Benson, Sept. 3, 1963; children: Jacqueline, Cynthia, Angela, Carolyn, Melinda, James, William, Christina. BS in Econs., Utah State U., 1965, MS in Econs., 1966; PhD in Agrl. Econs., Purdue U., 1970. Asst. prof. econs. Utah State U., Logan, 1970-75, assoc. prof. econs., 1976-83, prof. econs., 1983—; co-dir. planning Bolivian Ministry of Agr., La Paz, 1973-76; dep. exec. dir. Bd. for Internat. Food and Agrl. Devel., Washington, 1978-82; sr. advisor, adminstr. U.S. AID, Washington, 1981-82, policy advisor agr. programs, Quito, Ecuador, 1987-90, cons. on Asia, Near East, Latin Am., 1971-90; dir. internat. programs Utah State U., Logan, 1982-87, 90—. Author: Status of Bolivian Agriculture, 1975, Agricultural Development in Bangladesh, 1984, Agriculture and Economic Survival/Ecuador, 1990; contbr. articles to profl. jours. Com. mem. sch. bd. Cotopaxi Acad., Quito, 1987-90; asst. scoutmaster troop 240 Boy Scouts Am., Quito, 1987-90; mem. U.S. Presidential Task Force in Agr. to Ecuador, 1984. Mem. Am. Agrl. Econs. Assn., Consortium for Internat. Devel. (bd. trustees). Republican. LDS. Office: Utah State U Internat Programs Logan UT 84322-9500

WHITAKER, RUPERT EDWARD DAVID, neuroimmunologist and behavioral scientist, consultant; b. London, May 6, 1963; came to U.S., 1985; BSc in Psychology with honors, London U., 1984; PhD, Boston U., 1990. Instr. in medicine New Eng. Med. Ctr., Boston, 1989-90; rsch. fellow Dept. Psychiatry U. Mich., 1990-91, Immunology Rsch. Lab. Dept. Lab. Medicine U. Calif., San Francisco, 1992—. Author: (with others) AIDS Care, 1991, Hospital Formulary, 1991, (with Edwards R.K.) AIDS and Public Policy Jour., 1991, Am. Jour. Pub. Health, 1990. Co-founder, trustee Terrence Higgins Trust, London, 1984-88; mem. AIDS Action Com., Boston, 1986-88; active Internat. AIDS Soc. Mem. Internat. Soc. Neuroimmunomodulation, N.Y. Acad. Scis. Buddhist. Home: 4618 18th St San Francisco CA 94114 Office: U Calif Immunology Rsch Lab Box 0100 HSE 590 500 Parnassus San Francisco CA 94143-0100

WHITAKER, WAYNE ORSON, finance manager; b. Provo, Utah, Aug. 31, 1960; s. William Orson and Marilyn Blanche (Hug) W.; m. Rebecca Kay Beckstrand, Aug. 20, 1982; children: Weston, David, Bradley, Jeffrey, Steven. BS in Fin., Mktg. and Internat. Bus., Brigham Young U., 1984; MBA, Utah State U., 1991. Credit and collections specialist Iomega Corp., Roy, Utah, 1984-86, credit mgr., 1986-87, mgr. fin. resources, 1987—. Brigham Young U. scholar, 1978. Mem. Treasury Mgrs. Assn. Utah (v.p. 1990). Republican. LDS. Home: 8098 S 2350 E South Weber UT 84405 Office: Iomega Corp 1821 W 4000 S Roy UT 84067-3149

WHITCOMB, HAROLD CRAIG, educator; b. Walla Walla, Wash., May 21, 1939; s. Harold Charles and Virginia Mable (Schütte) W.; m. Stephanie Helen Chod, Dec. 14, 1968; children: Laurie Anne, Geoffrey Richard. BA in Polit. Sci., Wash. State U., 1961; BS in Social Sci., Lewis-Clark State Coll., Lewiston, Idaho, 1983; MEd in Secondary Edn. and English, U. Idaho, 1989, postgrad., 1989—. Cert. tchr., Wash., Idaho, N.H., Oreg. Commd. 2d lt. USAF, 1961, advanced through grades to maj., 1972; staff intelligence officer, asst. chief staff intelligence The Pentagon, 1968-71; staff intelligence officer Joint Strategic Target Planning Staff, Offutt AFB, Neb., 1971-72; sr. intelligence officer, palace sentinel, hdqrs. Mil. Pers. Ctr., Randolph AFB, Tex., 1973-75; chief intelligence 92 Bomb Wing SAC, Fairchild AFB, Wash., 1980-81; ret., 1981; instr. Walla Walla Community Coll., Clarkston, Wash., 1985—; grad. asst. U. Idaho Coll. Edn., Moscow, 1988-89; tchr. Shiloh Schs., Lewiston, 1986-88, 89—; head tchr. Shiloh High Sch., 1989—; mem. teaching staff U.S. ESL summer tng. course Pace Group, Internat. Culture Pub. Corp., Beijing and Shanghai, P.R.C. Ministry of Edn., 1993. Pres., bd. dirs. Regional and City Librs., Lewiston, 1984—; treas. Community Concerts Assn., Lewiston, 1985—. Decorated Bronze Star, Meritorious Svc. medal; fellow Idaho Dept. End. and Whittenberger Found., 1986-90, 91, Idaho Scottish Rite Found., 1988-89; grantee Grace Nixon Found., 1987, 88, 90, 92, 93, NEH, 1990, 91. Home: 712 9th Ave Lewiston ID 83501-2651

WHITCOMB, STANLEY R., supermarket executive; b. Wisner, Nebr., Aug. 18, 1944; s. W. Theodore and Helen M. (Jensen) W.; m. Gladys M. Means, Sept. 12, 1964; children: Christine R. (Whitcomb) Jenkins, Jean L. Whitcomb. BS in Math., U. Nebr., 1966; MBA with honors, Fordham U., 1975. Programmer GM Pontiac Motor Divsn., Pontiac, Mich., 1967-71; sr. systems analyst GMAC, N.Y.C., 1971-72; data processing mgr. GM Stock Transfer/Treas. office, N.Y.C., 1972-81; sr. systems assurance cons. McGraw-Hill, Hightstown, N.J., 1981; data processing mgr. Checker Auto Parts, Phoenix, 1981-84; dir. Phoenix Data Ctr. Lucky Stores, Inc., 1985-87; v.p. info. systems Lucky Stores, Inc., Dublin, Calif., 1987-89; sr. v.p. info. systems Am. Stores Co. (formerly Lucky Stores, Inc.), Salt Lake City, 1989—. Named Employer of the Year, Phoenix Urban League, 1985. Mem. Food Mktg. Inst. (mem. Advanced Mgmt. Info. Systems Com. 1988—). Methodist. Home: 2987 E Sunset Ridge Dr Sandy UT 84092 Office: American Stores Co 709 E South Temple Salt Lake City UT 84102

WHITE, ALLEN MARK, network engineer; b. Logan, Utah, Sept. 22, 1959; s. Larrie Dale and Jean (Marcusen) W. BA in Fin., Utah State U., 1984, MBA, 1990. Network engr. Thiokol, Brigham, Utah, 1984-92; mgr. 21st Century, Honolulu, 1993—; cons. Taki Casuals, Logan, Utah, 1988-90. Contbr. articles to profl. jours. Vol. Hansen for Gov., Salt Lake City, 1992, Fjeldsteel for mayor, Logan, 1990. Mem. Associated Students Utah Staet U. (advisor 1982-84), Body Fitness Ctr. Home: 1778 Ala Moana Blvd # 4020 Honolulu HI 96815

WHITE, BARBARA ANN, trade association executive; b. Phila., Oct. 24, 1942; d. Novia James and Ida Nannette (Von Siebenthal) W.; children: Dana E. Hartley, Robyn L. Davis. Student, Agnes Scott Coll., Atlanta, 1960-63; BA, San Jose State U., 1964; postgrad., U. Phoenix, 1986; grad., Inst. Organizational Mgmt., 1989. Exec. dir. Livermore (Calif.) C. of C., 1983-87, Palo Alto (Calif.) C. of C., 1987-89; exec. v.p. Rotary Internat., 1987-92, Mountain View (Calif.) C. of C., 1989-92; mem. adv. coun. Palo Alto Sister City, 1987-89; bd. dirs. Greenhouse Condos., Palo Alto, 1990—, pres., 1992, Mountain View Redevel. Com., 1989-92; mem. capitol campaign steering com. Community Svc. Agy., 1991. Editor Livermore Guidebook Association of Printing House Craftsmen, 1985 (3d pl. internat. award 1985), Livermore Jour., 1986 (1st pl. award in Calif. 1986), Palo Alto Bus., 1988 (3d pl. in Calif. 1988). Co-chair Downtown Redevel. Project, Livermore, 1983-87; founder Livermore Main St. Project, 1985-87, Valley Econ. Devel. Coun., Livermore, 1986-87; mem. study team Bay Area Coun. Growth Strategy Study, San Francisco, 1986-87. Named Outstanding Citizen of Livermore Eagles, 1985. Mem. Calif. Assn. C. of C. Execs. (bd. dirs. 1985-92), Santa Clara County C. of C. (bd. dirs., exec. com. 1987-92, pres. 1992). Presbyterian. Address: PO Box 391540 Mountain View CA 94039-1540

WHITE, BEATRICE LOCKHART, retired English language educator; b. Garfield, Wash., July 19, 1906; d. Edwin Bayard and Jennette (Meredith) Lockhart; m. Jackson A. Bliss, June 16, 1936 (dec. Dec. 1978); children: William (dec.), Meredith; m. Ivan Bertis White, Sept. 16, 1982. BA, Willamette U., 1929; MA, U. So. Calif., L.A., 1939. Chair Eng. dept. Ashland (Oreg.) High Sch., 1929-37, Forest Grove (Oreg.) High Sch., 1944, 51-69; ret., 1971; instr. Pacific U., Forest Grove, 1947-51. Author: Reluctant Pioneer, 1972, 3rd edit., 1992, Not On a Silver Platter, 1989. Apptd. mem. City Planning Comm., Forest Grove, 1947. Mem. AAUW (v.p.), LWV (sec.), Oreg. Hist. Soc., Symphony Auxiliary, Pi Beta Phi, Delta Kappa Gamma. Republican. Methodist.

WHITE, BONNIE YVONNE, management consultant, educator; b. Long Beach, Calif., Sept. 4, 1940; d. William Albert and Helen Iris (Harbaugh) W. BS, Brigham Young U., 1962, MS, 1965, EdD in Ednl. Adminstrn., 1976. Tchr., Wilson High Sch., Long Beach, Calif., 1962-63; grad. asst. Brigham Young U., Provo, Utah, 1963-65; instr., dir. West Valley Coll., Saratoga, Calif., 1965-76; instr., evening adminstr. Mission Coll., Santa Clara, Calif., 1976-80; dean gen. edn. Mendocino Coll., Ukiah, Calif., 1980-85; dean instrn. Porterville (Calif.) Coll., 1985-89, dean adminstrv. svc., 1989-93; rsch. assoc. SAGE Rsch. Internat., Orem, Utah, 1975—. Delegate Tulare County Ctrl. Com. Rep. Party, 1993—; pres. community adv. bd. Calif. Conservation Corps, 1989-93; v.p. Porterville Community Concerts, 1990—; bd. dirs. United Way North Bay, Santa Rosa, Calif., 1980-85; mem. Calif. Commn. on Basic Skills, 1987-89, Calif. Commn. on Athletics, 1987-90. Mem. AAUW, Faculty Assn. Calif. Community Colls., Calif., Coun. Fine Arts Deans, Assn. Calif. Community Coll. Adminstrs. Assn. Calif. Community Coll. Adminstrs. Liberal Arts, Zonta (intern), Soroptimists (intern). Republican. Mormon.

WHITE, BRIAN GEORGE, geologist, researcher; b. Sault Ste. Marie, Mich., Sept. 5, 1944; s. Byron Merrill and Ila Helen (Mikkola) W. BS, Mich. Tech. U., 1966; MS, U. Mont., 1970, PhD, 1978. Asst. prof. earth sci. Bloomsburg (Pa.) State Coll., 1970-73; geologist Mont. Dept. Natural Resources, Helena, 1974; rsch. geologist Bunker Hill Mining Co., Kellogg, Idaho, 1975-77; project geologist WGM, Anchorage, 1978; exploration geologist Asarco, Spokane, 1979; mining engr. U.S. Forest Svc., Libby, Mont., 1980-83; sr. exploration geologist Hecla Mining Co., Coeur d'Alene, Idaho, 1983-90; head of rsch. Revett Resources, Coeur d'Alene, 1990—, field trip leader, 1990-92; rschr. U.S. Bur. of Mines. Contbr. articles to profl. jours. Mem. Soc. Econ. Geologist, N.W. Mining Assn. Home: 101 Theresa Dr Coeur D Alene ID 83814 Office: Revett Resources 101 Theresa Dr Coeur d'Alene ID 83814

WHITE, BRIAN WILLIAM, investment company executive; b. Seattle, Sept. 5, 1934; s. George Carlos and Mary Mae (McCann) W.; m. Christine C. Nelson, Oct. 21, 1955 (div. 1970); children: Catherine, Teresa, Patrick, Melissa, Christopher; m. B. Maureen Scott, June 21, 1972; children: Meghan Mary, Erin Maureen. Acctg. mgr. Pacific Northwest Bell, Seattle, 1960-68; rep. Dominick and Dominick, Inc., Seattle, 1968-74; dir. Western Search Assn., San Diego, 1974-80; acct. exec. Bateman Eichler Hill Richards, San Diego, 1982-90; pres. White Securities, La Mesa, Calif., 1990—. Republican. Roman Catholic. Office: White Securities Inc 8363 Center Dr # 600 La Mesa CA 91942

WHITE, BRITTAN ROMEO, manufacturing company executive; b. N.Y.C., Feb. 13, 1936; s. Brittan R. and Matilda H. (Baumann) W.; m. Esther D. Friederich, Aug. 25, 1958 (dec. May 1981); children: Cynthia E., Brittan R. VII; m. Peggy A. Lee, Aug. 30, 1990. BSChemE, Drexel U., 1958; MBA, Lehigh U., 1967; JD, Loyola U., Los Angeles, 1974; MA, Pepperdine U., 1985. Bar: Calif., U.S. Dist. Ct. Calif.; registered profl. engr., Calif. Process engr. Air Reduction Co., Bound Brook, N.J., 1958-64; area supr. J.T. Baker Chem. Co., Phillipsburg, N.J., 1964-66; asst. plant mgr. Gamma Chem. Co., Great Meadows, N.J., 1966-69; plant mgr. Maquite Corp., Elizabeth, N.J., 1969-70; purchasing mgr. Atlantic Richfield Co., Los Angeles, 1970-79; dir. mfg. Imperial Oil, Los Angeles, 1979-82; mgr. chem. mgmt. program Hughes Aircraft Co., Los Angeles, 1982—; bd. dirs. Diversified Resource Devel. Inc., Los Angeles, 1979—; seminar moderator and speaker Energy Conservation Seminars, 1979-83. Editor Rottweiler Rev., 1979-81; chief award judge Chem. Processing mag., 1976, 78, 80; contbr. articles to profl. jours. Vice chmn. Bd. Zoning and Adjustment, Flemington, N.J., 1970-72; pres. bd. dirs. Homeowners' Assn., Palm Springs, Calif., 1983-90. Capt. C.E., U.S. Army, 1958-60, res., 1960-68. Mem. ABA, Am. Inst. Chem. Engrs., Am. Chem. Soc., Mensa, Psi Chi. Republican. Lodge: Elks. Home: 3664 Vigilance Dr Rancho Palos Verdes CA 90274-6126 Office: Hughes Aircraft Co 7200 Hughes Terr Los Angeles CA 90045

WHITE, CECIL RAY, librarian, consultant; b. Hammond, Ind., Oct. 15, 1937; s. Cecil Valentine and Vesta Ivern (Bradley) W.; m. Frances Ann Gee, Dec. 23, 1960 (div. 1987); children—Timothy Wayne, Stephen Patrick. B.S. in Edn., So. Ill. U., 1959; cert. in Czech., Syracuse, U., 1961; M. Div., Southwestern Bapt. Sem., 1969; M.L.S., N. Tex. State U., 1970, Ph.D., 1984. Librarian, Herrin High Sch. (Ill.), 1964-66; acting reference librarian Southwestern Sem., Ft. Worth, 1968-70, asst. librarian, 1970-80; head librarian Golden Gate Bapt. Sem., Mill Valley, Calif., 1980-88; head librarian West Oahu Coll., Pearl City, Hawaii, 1988-89; dir. spl. projects North State Coop. Library System, Yreka, Calif., 1989-90; dir. library St. Patrick's Sem., Menlo Park, Calif., 1990—; library cons. Hist. Commn., So. Bapt. Conv., Nashville, 1983-84, mem. Thesaurus Com., 1974-84. Bd. dirs. Hope and Help Ctr., 1986-88, vice chmn. 1987-88. With USAF, 1960-64. Lilly Found. grantee Am. Theol. Library Assn., 1969. Mem. Am. Theol. Library Assn. (coord. consultation svc. 1973-78, program planning com. 1985-88, chmn., 1986-88), Nat. Assn. Profs. Hebrew (archivist 1985—), ALA, Assn. Coll. and Rsch. Librarians, Phi Kappa Phi, Beta Phi Mu. Democrat. Baptist. Home: 186 Palisades Dr Daly City CA 94015 Office: St Patricks Sem 320 Middlefield Rd Menlo Park CA 94025-3596

WHITE, CLARICE MARY, art educator; b. Bath, Maine, June 21, 1947; d. John Clifton Sr. and Mary Roberta (Hyde) Little; m. Leith Duane Hagen, Dec. 17, 1966 (div.); children: Angela Gai Garner, Chad Cameron; m. Leonard Robert Barnes, Apr. 10, 1981 (div. Jan. 1988); m. Theodore Edward White, Dec. 13, 1990. BA, Ea. Wash. U., 1973, Portland State U., 1991. Dir. pub. info. Inland Empire Goodwill Ind., Spokane, 1975-76; news anchorwoman Sta. KSPO Radio, Spokane, 1976-77; pub. rels. specialist Battelle N.W. Lab., Richland, Wash., 1977-81; feature writer, reporter Evening Sun, Norwich, N.Y., 1981-83; editor, writer Miccosukee-Everglades News, Miami, Fla., 1982-83; reporter East Oregonian/Agri-Times, Pendleton, Oreg., 1984-85; pub. info. officer Confederated Tribes, Umatilla, Pendleton, Oreg., 1986; media rep. No on 14 Com., Portland, Oreg., 1986; rep. nuclear issues Trojan Nuclear Plant, Rainier, Oreg., 1986-88; comm. dir. N.W. Forestry Assn., Portland, 1989. Writer (TV pub. svc. announcement) Ripples, 1975 (Spokane Advt. Assn. award). Sec., mem. Comprehensive Health Planning Commn., Spokane, 1974-76; chair Citizens to Retain North Precinct, Portland, 1991, North Portland Multi-Svcs. Planning Commn., 1992.

WHITE, CONSTANCE BURNHAM, state official; b. Ogden, Utah, July 2, 1954; d. Owen W. and Colleen (Redd) Burnham; m. Wesley Robert White, Mar. 18, 1977. BA in English magna cum laude, U. Utah, 1976, postgrad., 1977; postgrad., Boston Coll., 1979; JD, Loyola U., 1981. Law clerk Kruse, Landa, Zimmerman & Maycock, Salt Lake City, 1979; law clerk legal dept. Bell & Howell, Lincolnwood, Ill., 1980; clerk, assoc. Parsons, Behle & Latimer, Salt Lake City, 1981-82; assoc. Reynolds, Vance, Deason & Smith, Salt Lake City, 1982-83; chief enforcement sect. Utah Securities Divsn., Salt Lake City, 1984-87, chief licensing sect., 1988, asst. dir., 1989-90; legal counsel Utah Dept. Commerce, Salt Lake City, 1990-92, exec. dir., 1993—; mem. Gov.'s Securities Fraud Task Force, 1984; spl. asst. atty. gen., 1986-88; spl. asst. U.S. atty., 1986—. Mem. North Am. Securities Adminstrs. Assn. (vice chair market manipulation com. 1988-89, penny stock/telecom. fraud com. 1989-90, chair uniform examinations com. 1990-92, chair forms revision com. 1992), Utah State Bar (securities adv. com. 1991—, task force on community-based mediation 1991—, chair securities sect. 1992-93). Office: PO Box 45802 Salt Lake City UT 84145-0802

WHITE, DANNY LEVIUS, counselor, consultant, educator; b. Temple, Tex., Oct. 9, 1956; s. Chester Allen and Elizabeth (Jimmerson) W.; m. Phemonia Lyvette Miller, July 23, 1988. AA, Mesa (Ariz.) Community Coll., 1976; BA, Ottawa (Kans.) U., 1982; postgrad., Chapman Coll., 1989-90; MEd magna cum laude, No. Ariz. U., 1993. Cert. lifetime jr. coll. instr., Ariz. Clinician V Phoenix South Mental Health, 1982-85; therapist I Ariz. Dept. of Correction, Tucson, 1985-87; cons. Tucson Urban League, 1987-88; counselor, assessment specialist Pima County Atty.'s Office, Tucson, 1988—; adj. faculty Pima Community Coll.; mem. com. So. Ariz. Task Force Against Domestic Violence, Tucson, 1989—, outreach coord., 1992—; cons. Inmate Family Assistance Program, Tucson, 1988. Dem. precinct committeeman, Tucson, 1988-92; del. 1988 Nat. Dem. Conv.; dep. registrar Pima & Maricopa County Recorders Office, Phoenix and Tucson, 1983-90; mem. citizens adv. coun. Phoenix Elem. Sch. Dist. 1, 1983-85; chair radiothon membership drive com. Tucson chpt. NAACP, 1990-93, chair health fair drive, 1992-93; pres. bd. dirs. P.A.S.A.R., Tucson, 1989-91; booster Spl. Olympics, 1980-90; spl. friend Ariz. Children's Home Foster Care, 1990; implemented Will to Win and Stay In Sch. drive programs, 1987-91; vol., blooddrive coord. United Blood Svcs., Phoenix, 1983-87. Mem. AFSCME (union com. 1989-91), United Parent and Youth League Inc. (pres. bd. dirs. 1984-85), Gov.'s Alliance Against Drugs (bd. dirs. 1989-91), Omega Psi Phi (named Man of Yr. Ariz. chpts. 1983, 85, pres. Tucson grad. chpt. 1991—), Delta Alpha Alpha. Home: PO Box 1135 Tucson AZ 85702-1135

WHITE, DAVID OLDS, education researcher; b. Fenton, Mich., Dec. 18, 1921; s. Harold Bancroft and Doris Caroline (Olds) W.; m. Janice Ethyl Russell, Sept. 17, 1923; children: John Russell, David Olds Jr., Benjamin Hill. BA, Amherst Coll., 1943; MS, U. Mass., 1950; PhD, U. Oreg., 1970. Tchr. human physiology Defiance (Ohio) Coll., summer 1950; sci. tchr. Roosevelt Jr. High Sch., Eugene, Oreg., 1951-52; prin. Glide (Oreg.) High Sch., 1952-56; tchr. Munich Am. Elem. Sch., 1957-69; prin. Wurzburg (Fed. Republic Germany) Am. High Sch., 1959-60, Wertheim (Fed. Republic Germany) Am. Elem. Sch., 1960-61; tchr. Dash Point Elem. Sch., Tacoma, 1961-63, Eugene (Oreg.) Pub. Schs., 1963-81; researcher in field. Contbr. articles to profl. publs.; patentee electronic model airplane. Staff sgt. U.S. Army, 1942-45, PTO. Fulbright grantee, 1956-57, 72-73. Mem. NEA, Fulbright Alumni Assn., Phi Delta Kappa. Home: 4544 Fox Hollow Rd Eugene OR 97405-4577

WHITE, DEANNA H., social worker; b. Pocatello, Idaho, Jan. 13, 1959; d. Willard Lloyd and Norma Margaret (Hall) W.; m. Jesse Reece, Aug. 5, 1977 (div. Aug. 1979); m. Danny Sylvester Smith, June 29, 1985 (div. May 1991). B in Social Work, Idaho State U., 1988. Lic. social worker, Idaho. Program mgr. Easter Seal, Goodwill, Idaho Falls, 1988-89; case mgr. RehabCare, Idaho Falls, 1989—; Cons. in field. Chairperson Mayor's Com. Employment of Disabled and Older Workers, Blackfoot, Idaho, 1988-90; presenter Head and Spinal Cord Prevention Project, Idaho State U., Pocatello, 1988—. Named Rehab. of Yr. Gov.'s Com. Idaho, 1982, Disabled Employee of Yr., 1989. Mem. NASW, Coop. Wilderness Handicapped Outdoors Group, Soroptimists Internat. (community svc. 1989-90), Southeastern Idaho Brain Injury Assn. (co-chair 1992—).

WHITE, DON WILLIAM, banker; b. Santa Rita, N.Mex., June 27, 1942; s. Thomas Melvin and Barbara (Smith) W.; m. Jacqueline Diane Bufkin, June 12, 1965; children: Don William Jr., David Wayne. BBA, Western N.Mex. U., 1974, MBA, 1977. Field acct. Stearns Roger Corp., Denver, 1967-70; controller, adminstrv. mgr. USNR Mining and Minerals Inc., Silver City, N.Mex., 1970-72; devel. specialist County of Grant, Silver City, 1973-77; divisional controller Molycorp. Inc., Taos, N.Mex., 1977-78; mgr. project adminstrn. Kennecott Minerals Co., Hurley, N.Mex., 1978-83; sr. v.p. Sunwest Bank Grant County, Silver City, N.Mex., 1983-84, exec. v.p., 1984-85, pres., chief exec. officer, 1985—; bd. dirs. Bank of Grant County. Bd. dirs. Sunwest Bank of Grant County, Silver City/Grant County Econ. Devel., 1983—; councilman Town of Silver City, 1977; chmn. Dems. for Senator Pete Domenici, 1986; pres. Gila Regional Med. Found., 1989-92; pres. SWNM Econ. Devel. Corp., 1984—; trustee Indian Hills Bapt. Ch., 1988-89; mem. State of N.Mex. Small Bus. Adv. Coun.; mem. vocat. edn. adv. com. We. N.Mex. U., 1989; mem. Silver Schs.-Sch./Bus. Partnership Coun. Named Outstanding Vol., Silver City/Grant County Econ. Devel., 1987, FFA, 1985. Mem. Am. Bankers Assn., N.Mex. Bankers Assn., Bank Adminstrn. Inst., Assn. Commerce and Industry (bd. dirs. 1988-91), N.Mex. Mining Assn. (assoc.), Rotary (past pres., dist. gov. rep.). Office: Sunwest Bank of Grant County 1203 N Hudson PO Box 1449 Silver City NM 88062

WHITE, DONALD HARVEY, physicist, educator; b. Berkeley, Calif., Apr. 30, 1931; s. Harvey Elliott and Adeline White; m. Beverly Evalina Jones, Aug. 8, 1953; children: Jeri, Brett, Holly, Scott, Erin. AB, U. Calif., Berkeley, 1953; PhD, Cornell U., 1960. Rsch. physicist Lawrence Livermore (Calif.) Nat. Lab., 1960-71, cons., 1971-90; prof. physics Western Oreg. State Coll., Monmouth, 1971—; vis. rsch. scientist Inst. Lave-Langevin, Grenoble, France, 1977-78, 84-85, 91-92. Author (with others): Physics, an Experimental Science, 1968, Physics and Music, 1980; contbr. numerous articles to profl. jours. Pres. Monmouth-Independence Community Arts, 1983; pres. E. Smith Fine Arts Series, Monmouth, 1987. DuPont scholar, 1958; Minna-Heineman Found. fellow, Hannover, Fed. Republic Germany, 1977. Mem. Am. Phys. Soc., Am. Assn. Physics Tchrs. (pres. Oreg. sect. 1974-75), Oreg. Acad. Sci. (pres. 1979-80), Phi Kappa Phi (pres. West Oreg. chpt. 1989-90). Democrat. Presbyterian. Home: 411 S Walnut Dr Monmouth OR 97361-1948 Office: Western Oreg State Coll Dept Phys & Earth Scis Monmouth OR 97361

WHITE, DOUGLAS R., anthropology educator; b. Mpls., Mar. 13, 1942; s. Asher Abbott and Margaret McQuestin (Richie) W.; m. Jayne Chamberlain (div. Feb. 1971); m. Lilyan Amdur Brudner, Mar. 21, 1971; 1 child, Scott Douglas. BA, U. Minn., 1964, MA, 1967, PhD, 1969. Asst. prof. U. Pitts., 1967-72, assoc. prof., 1972-76; assoc. prof. U. Calif., Irvine, 1976-79, prof., 1979—; dep. dir. Lang. Attitudes Rsch. Project, Dublin, Ireland, 1971-73; vis. prof. U. Tex., Austin, 1974-75; chmn. Linkages: World Devel. Res. Coun., Md., 1986—, pres. 1986-90. Co-editor: Research Methods in Social Networks, 1972, Anthropology of Urban Environments; founder, gen. editor World Cultures Jour., 1985-90; author sci. software packages; contbr. articles to prof. jours. Fellow Ctr. for Advanced Studies, Western Behavioral Sci. Inst., La Jolla, Calif., 1981-84; recipient Sr. Scientist award Alexander von Humboldt Stiftung, Bonn, Germany, 1989-91, Bourse de Haute Niveau award Ministry of Rsch. and Tech., Paris, 1992. Mem. Social Sci. Computing Assn. (pres. elect 1991, pres. 1992.). Democrat. Home: 8888 La Jolla Scenic Dr N La Jolla CA 92037 Office: U Calif Irvine School of Social Sci Irvine CA 92717

WHITE, EDWARD ALLEN, electronics company executive; b. Cambridge, Jan. 1, 1928; s. Joseph and Bessie (Allen) W.; m. Joan Dixon, Dec. 22, 1949 (div. Aug. 1978); children: Dixon Richard, Leslie Ann White Lollar; m. Nancy Rhoads, Oct. 6, 1979. B.S., Tufts U., 1947. Chmn. Bowmar Instrument Corp., Phoenix, Mass., 1951—, White Technology Inc., Phoenix, 1980-86; pres. Ariz. Digital Corp., Phoenix, 1975-91; chmn., chief exec. officer AHI, Inc., Ft. Wayne, Ind., 1970-88; mem. World Pres's. Orgn., Washington D.C., 1978—. Patentee in field. Bd. dirs. Gov.'s Council Children, Youth and Families, Phoenix, 1982-84, Planned Parenthood Fedn. Am., 1984-88; pres., bd. dirs. Planned Parenthood Central and No. Ariz., 1984-88; trustee Internat House, N.Y.C., 1973-75, Tufts U., 1973-83. Mem. Tau Beta Pi. Club: Paradise Valley Country. Home: 5786 N Echo Canyon Cir Phoenix AZ 85018-1209 Office: Bowmar Instrument Corp 5080 N 40th St Ste 475 Phoenix AZ 85018-2158

WHITE, ELIZABETH FLAD, financial executive; b. Kenosha, Wis., Oct. 22, 1954; d. Gilbert George and Laura Antoinette (Johnson) Flad. BS, U. Wis., Oshkosh, 1977. Account exec. Kenosha Broadcasting, Wis., 1977-80; assoc. editor Bender Pubs., Dallas, 1980-83; sales rep. NCR Corp., Dallas, 1983-85; account mgr. NCR Corp., 1985-88; account exec. Fin. Info. Trust, L.A., 1988-91; sr. acct. mgr. NCR Corp., L.A., 1991—; lectr. in field. Mem. AAUW. Roman Catholic. Office: NCR Corp 1940 Century Park E Los Angeles CA 90067

WHITE, GARY CONNER, small business owner; b. Sutherland, Nebr., Dec. 8, 1937; s. Charles Conner and Frances Elizabeth (Stringfield) W.; m. Mary Anne Salfrank, Dec. 30, 1967 (div. July 19991); children: Zane Conner, Benjamin William; m. Diane Lynn Sander, Apr. 25, 1992. BS in Biol. Sci., Colo. State U., 1961. Terminal mgr. Ward Transport, Inc., Commerce City, Colo., 1967-69; sec., treas, co-owner Kamp Moving and Storage, Inc., Denver, 1970-75; pres., owner White Moving and Storage, Inc., Denver, 1977—; pres. Colo. Transfer and Warehousemen's Assn., Denver, 1987-89; chmn. adv. coun. Bekins SDS agt., Chgo., 1990. Republican. Methodist. Office: White Moving & Storage Inc 4760 Holly St Denver CO 80216

WHITE, GAYLE CLAY, aerospace company executive; b. Wyandotte, Mich., Sept. 28, 1944; d. John Leonard and Irene Francis (Clay) W.; m. Sharon Wong, June 8, 1968; children: Lai Jean, Quinn Yee. BBA, Ea. Mich. U., 1967; MBA, Utah State U., 1971; MPA, Auburn U., 1976; postgrad., Nova U., 1985—. Computer system analyst USAF Logistics Command, Odgen, Utah, 1967-71, U.S.-Can. Mil. Officer Exec., Ottawa, Ont., 1971-73; mgr. software devel. USAF Data System Design Ctr., Montgomery, Ala., 1973-77; data base adminstr. Supreme Hdqrs. Allied Powers Europe, Casteau, Belgium, 1977-81; mgr. software configuration System Integration Office, Colorado Springs, Colo., 1981-83; mgr. computer ops. N.Am. Aerospace Def. Command, Colorado Springs, 1983-84; dir. ops. 6 Missile Warning Squadron, Space Command, Cape Cod, Mass., 1984-86, comdr., 1986-87; mgr. program devel. Rockwell Internat., Colorado Springs, 1987—; mem. faculty computer sci. Regis U., Colorado Springs, 1981—. Treas. Christian Ctr. Ch., Colorado Springs, 1989—; v.p. European Parents, Tchrs. and Students Assn., 1979-81. Recipient Mil.-Civilian Rels. award Otis Civilian Adv. Coun., 1987, awarded cert. Data Processing Mgmt. Assn., 1973. Mem. Am. Mgmt. Assn., Armed Forces Communications Electronics Assn., U.S. Space Found., Nat. Security Indsl. Assn. (bd. dirs. Rocky Mountain chpt. 1990—), Christian Businessmen's Assn., Am. Amateur Racquetball Assn., Colorado Springs C. of C., Air Force Assn., Lynmar Racquet Club, Toastmasters (pres. 1975-76), Alpha Kappa Psi. Republican. Home: PO Box 17184 Colorado Springs CO 80935-7184 Office: Rockwell Internat 1250 Academy Park Loop Colorado Springs CO 80910-3708

WHITE, HARLOW F., real estate management company executive; b. Middletown, Del., Nov. 10, 1941; s. Carl F. and Lulubelle (Manwaring) W.; m. Nancy Darling, June 15, 1963; children—Tracey, Brian, Kelsey, Rachel. B.S., Cornell U., 1963. Recruiter, Pfizer, Inc., N.Y.C., 1965-67, personnel mgr., Terre Haute, Ind., 1967-68, nat. personnel dir., San Francisco and N.Y.C., 1968-72; v.p. Victorial Station, Inc., San Francisco, 1972-77; pres., chief exec. officer SHR Internat., Mill Valley, Calif., 1977-81; pres., chief exec. officer Condotech's Hawaiiana Resorts, Honolulu, 1981—, chmn. Condotech, Inc. Author industry study: Employee Attitudes and Behavior, 1979, Industry Study of Buyers-Supermarkets, 1981. Alt. del. Republican Party Conv., Hawaii, 1984. Served to lt. USN, 1963-65. Mem. Hawaii Visitors Bur., Hawaii Hotel Assn., Hawaii Resort Condominium Assn. Republican. Club: Palo Alto Hills Golf and Country (Calif.). Office: Hawaiiana Resorts 1270 Ala Moana Blvd Honolulu HI 96814

WHITE, JAMES EDWARD, geophysicist; b. Cherokee, Tex., May 10, 1918; s. William Cleburne and Willie (Carter) W.; m. Courtenay Brumby, Feb. 1, 1941; children: Rebecca White Vanderslice, Peter McDuffie, Margaret Marie White Jamleson, Courtenay White Forte. B.A., U. Tex., 1941, M.A., 1946; Ph.D., MIT, 1949. Dir. Underwater Sound Lab., MIT, Cambridge, 1941-45; scientist Def. Research Lab., Austin, Tex., 1945-46; research assoc. MIT, 1946-49; group leader, field research lab. Mobil Oil Co., Dallas, 1949-55; mgr. physics dept. Denver Research Center, Marathon Oil Co., 1955-69; v.p. Globe Universal Scis., Midland, Tex., 1969-71; adj. prof. dept. geophysics Colo. Sch. Mines, Golden, 1972-73, C.H. Green prof., 1976-87, prof. emeritus, 1986—; L.A. Nelson prof. U. Tex., El Paso, 1973-76; Esso vis. prof. U. Sydney, Australia, 1975; vis. prof. MIT, 1982, U. Tex.-Austin, 1985, Macquarie U., Sydney, 1988; del. U.S.-USSR geophysics exchange Dept. State, 1965; mem. bd. Am. Geol. Inst., 1972; mem. space applications bd. Nat. Acad. Engring., 1972-77; exchange scientist Nat. Acad. Sci., 1973-74; del. conf. on oil exploration China Geophys. Soc.-Soc. Exploration Geophysicists, 1981; cons. world bank Chinese U. Devel. Project II, 1987. Author: Seismic Waves: Radiation, Transmission, Attenuation, 1965, Underground Sound: Application of Seismic Waves, 1983, (with R.L. Sengbush) Production Seismology, 1987; editor: Vertical Seismic Profiling (E.I. Galperin), 1974; contbr. articles to profl. jours.; patentee in field. Fellow Acoustical Soc. Am.; mem. Soc. Exploration Geophysicists (hon., Maurice Ewing medal 1986, Halliburton award 1987), Nat. Acad. Engring., Sigma Xi. Unitarian. Club: Cosmos. Office: Colo Sch Mines Dept Geophysics Golden CO 80401

WHITE, JANE SEE, journalist; b. St. Louis, Aug. 26, 1950; d. Robert Mitchell and Barbara Whitney (Spurgeon) White; children: Laura, Mitchell. BA in History and Am. Studies, Hollins Coll., 1972. Reporter Roanoke (Va.) Times, 1972-73, Kansas City (Mo.) City Star, 1973-76, AP, N.Y.C., Hartford, 1976-78; spl. writer AP, N.Y.C., 1978-81; sr. writer, chief news and bur., chief profl. div. Med. Econs. Mag., Oradell, N.J., 1981-87; dep. city editor, city editor Roanoke Times World News, 1987-91; asst. metro. editor Phoenix Gazette, 1991-93; asst. city editor Ariz. Rep., 1993—. Editor: Medical Practice Management, 1985; contbr. articles to profl. jurs. Home: 1617 N 11th Ave Phoenix AZ 85007 Office: Phoenix Gazette 120 E Van Buren Phoenix AZ 85004

WHITE, JEANNE ANN, preschool owner, educator; b. Vermillion, S.D., Apr. 15, 1931; d. John Walse and Frances (Davis) Malone; m. Lee Roland White, Mar. 12, 1950 (dec. Jan. 27, 1992); children: Kathleen, Bradley, Andrew, Mitchell, James. AA, Merced Coll., 1984. Early Childhood Center permit. Supr. Maple Sch., Tulare, Calif., 1969-70; tchrs. aide Weaver Sch., Merced, Calif., 1975-80; tchr. Head Start, Merced, Calif., 1984-85; tchr., owner pvt. learning ctr., Merced, Calif., 1985—; Author: I'm A Rainbow, 1989, Tiny, 1990, (songs) To Plo' the Mountain, 1983. Named Golden Poet, World of Poetry, 1985-88. Republican. Home and Office: 3013 Nottingham Merced CA 95340-2515

WHITE, JOHN ABIATHAR, pilot, consultant; b. Chgo., May 29, 1948; s. Abiathar Jr. and Gretchen Elizabeth (Zuber) W.; m. Therese Ann Denz, June 21, 1980; children: Kathryn Ann, Laura Ellen. Student, Art Ctr. Coll. of Design, 1969-70, Calif. Inst. Tech., 1966-67; BArch, U. Ill., 1972. Archtl. apprentice Farner Und Gründer Industriearchitekten, Zürich, Switzerland, 1972; archtl. draftsman Walter Carlson Assocs., Elk Grove, Ill., 1973; archtl. designer Unteed Assocs., Palatine, Ill., 1974-75; flight instr. Planemasters, Inc., West Chicago, Ill., 1976; pilot Aero Am. Aviation, West Chicago, 1977, Beckett Aviation, Cleve., 1978; pilot Am. Airlines, Chgo. and L.A., 1979—, capt., 1988—; archtl. cons. Nat. Accelerator Lab., Batavia, Ill., 1980, Constrn. Collaborative, Park Ridge, Ill., 1982, L.K. White Assocs., San Diego, 1988—. Nat. Coun. Tchrs. of English scholar, 1966. Mem. Nat. Assn. Flight Instrs., Planetary Soc. Unitarian. Home: 6429 La Garza Ct Carlsbad CA 92009-4332 Office: Am Airlines World Way Los Angeles CA 90045-5804

WHITE, JOHN C., accountant manager; b. Lourdes, Can., Oct. 5, 1945; s. Gilbert C. and Dorothy A. (Duffenais) W.; m. Lorraine J. Nyby, Jan. 3, 1966; children: Angela, John, Cami. Student, So. Colo. State U., 1967, Bellevue Coll., 1974. Soldier, student, sgt. U.S. Army, 1965-68; mgr. acctg. Lakeside Industries, Redmond, Wash., 1968—; trustee Lakeside Pension Plan, Redmond, 1980—; chmn. audit com. Lakeside Credit Union, Bellevue, 1975. Author: (manual) Lakesive Cont. Administration Policy, 1975. Coach Lake Wash. Soccer Assn., Kirkland, Wash., 1980-87. Sgt. U.S. Army, 1965-

68. Recipient 15-Yr. Longevity award Lakeside Industries, 1983, 20 Yr. Longevity award, 1988. Republican. Roman Catholic. Office: Lakeside Industries 7735 178th Pl NE Redmond WA 98052-4954

WHITE, JOHN WYTHE, freelance writer, advertising consultant; b. N.Y.C., May 3, 1945; s. David Wythe and Janet (Cartwright) W.; m. Debra Aki, Feb. 29, 1984 (div. June 1989); m. Victoria Gail, Oct. 3, 1992. BA, Stanford U., 1966; MA in English, UCLA, 1967. Cert. jr. coll. tchr., Calif. Copywriter BBDO, N.Y.C., 1965-66; instr. English U. Hawaii, Honolulu, 1974-76; copy chief Peck Sims Mueller, Honolulu, 1978-80; assoc. creative dir. Fawcett-McDermott Cavanagh, Honolulu, 1980-82; journalist for various publs. Honolulu, 1972—; creative dir. Hill and Knowlton/Communications Pacific, Honolulu, 1990-91; freelance writer/cons., Honolulu, 1991—; cons. VeriFone, Inc., Honolulu, 1984-85. Theater reviewer Honolulu Star-Bull., 1985-91; author: (play) Biff Finds Himself In Hawii, 1988; contbr. numerous articles to mags. Recipient Cert. of Recognition, Hawaiian State Theatre Coun., 1991. Mem. Honolulu Commun. Media Coun. Home and Office: 3835 Sierra Dr Honolulu HI 96816-3853

WHITE, JULIAN EUGENE, JR., modern and classical languages educator; b. Hanover County, Va., Dec. 21, 1932; s. Julian Eugene and Mary Washington (Lowry) W.; m. Ellen Elizabeth Hockaday, Sept. 4, 1953; children: Susan Dianne, Laura Ellen, Geoffrey Douglas. AB, Randolph-Macon Coll., 1952; MA, U. N.C., 1954, PhD, 1962. Asst. prof. Mary Baldwin Coll., Staunton, Va., 1960-64; asst. prof., assoc. prof. modern and classical langs. U. N.Mex., Albuquerque, 1964-71, prof., 1971—, assoc. dean Coll. Arts and Scis., 1976-88, vice dean, 1988-91. Author: Nicolas Boileau, 1969; editor: Three Philosophical Voyages, 1964;' contbr. articles to 17th century and medieval French lit. to profl. jours. Lt. (j.g.) USN, 1956-60. Fulbright fellow, Paris, 1955, also other scholarships and fellowships. Mem. Phi Beta Kappa. Republican. Anglican. Home: 8303 Connecticut St NE Albuquerque NM 87110-2409 Office: U NMex Coll Arts & Scis Dept Fgn Langs & Lits Albuquerque NM 87131

WHITE, KARL RAYMOND, psychology educator, researcher; b. Cedar City, Utah, July 21, 1950; s. Raymond Hamilton and Marietta (Nyman) W.; m. Amy Jane Howells, Jan. 8, 1975; children: Rebecca, Ruth, Carolyn, Katherine, Allyson, Brigham, Geoffrey, Jenkin. BS summa cum laude, Brigham Young U., 1973; MA, U. Colo., 1976, PhD, 1976. Grad. fellow U. Colo., Boulder, 1973-76; asst. prof. Nat. Tech. Inst. for Deaf, Rochester, N.Y., 1976-78, head dept., 1977-78; asst. prof. psychology Utah State U., Logan, 1978-81, assoc. prof., 1981-87, prof., 1987—, dir. Early Intervention Rsch. Inst., 1987-89, 7th ann. faculty honor lectr., 1990; rsch. asst. NW Regional Ednl. Lab., Portland, Oreg., 1974; cons. U.S. Dept. Edn., Washington, 1988-90, Utah Office Edn., Salt Lake City, 1980—; Ellemann lectr. U. Bern, Switzerland, 1990. Author: Evaluating Educational and Psychological Programs, 1987, Measurement and Evaluation in the Schools, 1993; also articles. Rsch. grantee fed. govt., 1978—; Congl. Sci. fellow U.S. Senate, 1984-85. Fulbright award U. Münster, 1993—. Mem. LDS Ch. Home: PO Box 686 Hyde Park UT 84318-0686 Office: Utah State U Dept Psychology UMC 2810 Logan UT 84322

WHITE, KATHLEEN MERRITT, geologist; b. Long Beach, Calif., Nov. 19, 1921; d. Edward Clendenning and Gladys Alice (Merritt) White; m. Alexander Kennedy Baird IV, Oct. 1, 1965 (dec. 1985); children: Pamela Roberts, Peter Madlem, Stephen Madlem, Mari Madlem. BS, Pomona Coll., 1962; MS, Claremont Grad. Sch., 1964. Rsch. asst. geology Pomona Coll., Claremont, Calif., 1962-66, rsch. assoc. geology, 1966-75; cons. geology Claremont, Calif., 1975-77; sr. scientist Jet Propulsion Lab./NASA, Pasadena, 1977-79, mem. tech. staff, 1979-86; ind. rschr. Claremont, 1986—; cons. Pangaea Inc., Santa Barbara, Calif., 1991-92; vol. U.S. Geol. Survey, Riverside, Calif., 1991-92. Contbr. Geosat Report, 1986; contbr. articles to profl. jours. Grantee NASA, 1984, 85; Pomona Coll. scholar, 1963. Mem. Geol. Soc. Am., Am. Geophys. Union, Pomona Coll. Alumni Assn. Democrat. Home: 265 W 11th St Claremont CA 91711

WHITE, LAURENS PARK, physician; b. St. Louis, Dec. 21, 1925; s. Park Jerauld and Maria (Bain) W.; m. Sylvia Wisotzky, 1950 (div. 1972); m. Annette Jeanne Marie Campbell, May 19, 1983; children: Sonia Pearson, Maria Southworth. Student, Westminster Coll., 1945; MD, Washington U., 1949. Diplomate Am. Bd. Internal Medicine, Am. Bd. Med. Oncology. Intern then resident Mass Gen. Hosp., Boston, 1949-51; resident U. Calif., San Francisco, 1951-53; fellow U. London, Bethesda, 1953-55; instr. Stanford Med. Sch., San Francisco, 1955-59; rschr. Children's Cancer Rsch. Found., Boston Mass., 1959-63; pvt. practice San Francisco, 1963—; clin. prof. medicine U. Calif. Med. Sch., San Francisco, 1975—. Editor: Enzymes in Blood, 1958, Care of Patients With Fatal Illness, 1969; contbr. articles to profl. jours. Mem. State of Calif. AIDS Adv. Com., Sacramento, 1988-90; co-chair AIDS Testing Sub Com., 1989-90. With USPHS, 1951-55. Recipient Leadership award San Francisco AIDS Found., 1989. Mem. Calif. Med. Assn. (pres. 1988, chmn. bd. trustees 1983-87), San Francisco Med. Soc. (pres. 1979), Internat. Work Group Death and Dying (sec. 1980-83), Health Outreach Team (bd. dirs. 1990—). Office: 1580 Valencia Rm 707 San Francisco CA 94110

WHITE, LORAY BETTY, writer, actress, producer; b. Houston, Nov. 27, 1934; d. Harold White and Joyce MAe (Jenkins) Mills; m. Sammy Davis Jr.; 1 child, Deborah R. DeHart. Student, UCLA, 1948-50, 90-91; AA in Bus., Sayer Bus. Sch., 1970; student, Nichiren Shoshu Acad., 1968-92; study div. mem. dept. L.A., Soka U., Japan, 1970-86. Editor entertainment writer L.A. Community New, 1970-81; exec. sec. guest rels. KNBC Prodns., Burbank, Calif., 1972-75; security specialist Xerox X10 Think Tank, L.A., 1975-80; exec. asst. Ralph Powell & Assocs., L.A., 1980-82; pres., owner, producer LBW & Assocs. Pub. Rels., L.A., 1980—; owner, producer, writer, host TV prodn. co. Pub. Pub. Rels., L.A., 1987—; dir., producer L.B.W. Prodn. "Yesterday, Today, Tomorrow, L.A., 1981—. Actress (film) Ten Commandments, 1956, (Broadway) Joy Ride; appeared in the following endorsements including Budweiser Beer, Old Gold Cigarettes, Salem Cigarettes, TV commls. including Cheer, Puffs Tissue, Coca Cola, Buffern, others; writer (column) Balance News, 1980-82. Mem. Soka Gakkai Internat. Youth Div., ARC, Urban League, Nat. Audubon Found., Nat. Parks Assn., Smithsonian Inst., World Peace Cultural Festival '72, Bicentennial Celebration '76, United High Blood Pressure Telethon, Com. for Sr. Citizens, Beverly Hills-Westwood Sr. Citizen Community Ctr. Recipient award ARC, 1955, Cert. of Honor Internat. Orgn. Soka Gakkai Internat. of Japan; named Performer of Yr. Cardella Demillo, 1976-77. Mem. UCLA Alumni Assn. Buddhist. Home and Office: 1958 Apex Ave Silver Lake CA 90039

WHITE, LYNETTE MICHELE, health facility supervisor; b. Lebanon, Oreg., Feb. 16, 1950; d. Chester Lyle and Mable Olive (Wyatt) Smith; m. Ward Russell White, May 12, 1972; 1 child, Lee Edward. Grad. high sch., Lebanon, 1968. Lab asst. Oreg. Health Scis. U., Portland, Oreg., 1969-71; lab asst. Good Samaritan Hosp., Corvallis, Oreg., 1971-73, histotechnologist, 1973-74, histotechnologist supr., 1974—. Den leader, unit commr. Boy Scouts Am., 1986-88, dir. day camp Cascade Area coun., Salem, Oreg., 1988, 89, 92, chairperson tng. Calapooia Dist. Cascade Area coun., 1993. Mem. Oreg. Soc. for Histotechnology (sec./treas. 1978, v.p. 1985), Am. Legion Aux. (sec. Santiam unit 51 1989, pres. 1990, 91). Home: 380 7th St Lebanon OR 97355-2278

WHITE, MATTHEW, family practice physician; b. Phila., May 21, 1941; s. Frank and Minerva (Shiffmann) W.; m. Kristina J. Johnson, Aug. 15, 1978. AB in Chemistry, Temple U., 1963; MD, Jefferson Med. Coll., 1967. Diplomate Am. Bd. Family Practice. Commd. lt. USN, 1967, advanced through grades to comdr., 1975; intern U.S. Naval Hosp., Newport, R.I., 1967-68; resident U.S. Naval Hosp., Jacksonville, Fla., 1968-70; family practice medicine USN, Japan, 1970-73, Bremerton, Wash., 1973-77; family practice medicine Sand Pt. Naval Air Sta., Seattle, 1977-78; resigned USN, 1978; family practice medicine Tacoma, 1978—; mem. active staff, bd. dirs., exec. com. St. Claire Hosp.; mem. courtesy staff Humana Hosp., Multicare Hosp., St. Joseph's Hosp.; pres. med. staff Lakewood Hosp., 1989-90. Mem. utilization rev. com. Sherwood Terr. Nursing Home, Georgian House Nursing Home, Meadow Park Nursing Home, Lakewood Health Care N.H. Fellow Am. Acad. Family Practice; mem. AMA, Nat. Assn. Family Practice, Wash. State Assn. Family Practice, Wash. State Med. Assn., Tacoma Med. Assn., Tacoma Assn. Family Practice. Republican. Jewish. Office: 11311 Bridgeport Way SW #304 Tacoma WA 98467

WHITE, MAUDE ADAMS, retired educator; b. Danielsville, Ga., Jan. 15, 1916; d. Clarence E. and Tula E. (Smith) Adams; children: Percy Daniel Jr., Maude Adams Wilkinson, Elizabeth Brownstein. BSN, Duke U., Durham, N.C., 1939; MEd, George Mason U., 1975; grad., Young Harris Coll., Ga., 1935. Staff nurse Norfolk (Va.) Gen. Hosp., 1939-41, Med. Coll. Va. Hosp., Richmond, 1955-56; sch. nurse Richmond Pub. Schs., 1957-60; coord., instr. sch. nursing Riverside Hosp., Newport News, Va., 1962-65; tchr. Portsmouth (Va.) City Pub. Schs., 1967-69, Fairfax County Pub. Schs., Centreville, Va., 1969-81; cons. U.S. Agy. for Internat. Devel./Egyptian Ministry Edn., Cairo, 1977, 79. Editor: Low-Cost Teaching Materials for Egyptian Teachers, 1977. Vol. local hospice, Yolo County, Calif., 1987-89, Loaves and Fishes, Sacramento, Calif., 1988-89. Recipient Wm. C. Lowry Outstanding Math. Tchr. award Va. Coun. Tchr. Math., 1981' named Artist of Month Davis (Calif.) Sr. Ctr., 1989. Democrat. Quaker. Home: 2550 Sycamore Ln Apt 5D Davis CA 95616-5905

WHITE, MORGAN WILSON, investment executive; b. L.A., May 10, 1945; s. Robert Jenkins and Lorraine (Keck) W.; m. Nancy Macdonald, June 22, 1969 (div. Dec. 1981); children: Marshall Garrett, Stephanie Lynn; m. Joyce Donovan Nash, Feb. 6, 1983. BSEE, Stanford U., 1967, MSEE, 1968, MBA, 1974. V.p. Bailard, Biehl & Kaiser, Inc., San Mateo, Calif., 1974-79, The Portola Group, Inc., Menlo Park., Calif., 1979-87; prin. Woodside Asset Mgmt., Inc., Menlo Park, 1987—. Bd. dirs. The Catalyst Found., Palo Alto, Calif., 1987—, St. Francis High Sch., Mountain View, Calif., 1992—. Lt. USNR, 1969-71. Mem. Security Analysts of San Francisco. Republican. Home: 55 Skywood Way Woodside CA 94062 Office: Woodside Asset Mgmt Inc 3000 Sand Hill Rd # 160 Menlo Park CA 94025-7116

WHITE, NATHANIEL MILLER, astronomer; b. Providence, Feb. 28, 1941; s. Russell Harkness and Anna Alila (Tuthill) W.; m. Jean Evelyn Moore, June 10, 1967; children: Grace, Andrew, Charles. AB, Earlham Coll., 1964; MSc, Ohio State U., 1967, PhD, 1971; BSEE, No. Ariz. U., 1985. Researcher Lowell Obs., Flagstaff, Ariz., 1969-71, staff astronomer, 1972-78, sr. staff astronomer, 1978—, dir. engring., 1979-92, project mgr. navy prototype optical interferameter, 1992—; instr. Yavapai Community Coll., Prescott, Ariz., 1977-78. Contbr. articles to profl. jours. Elected mem. Flagstaff City Coun., 1988-92, vice-mayor City of Flagstaff, 1990-92; active City Planning and Zoning, City Councils, Flagstaff, 1970—; dir. Local Foot Races, Flagstaff, 1975—; Cub Scout leader Boy Scouts Am., Flagstaff, 1979—. Mem. AAAS, Am. Astron. Soc., Internat. Astron. Union, IEEE, Sigma Xi. Mem. Soc. of Friends. Home and Office: Lowell Obs Mars Hill Rd Flagstaff AZ 86001-4470

WHITE, PERRY JAMES, environmental planner, consultant; b. Orange, Calif., June 25, 1944; s. Arthur Joy White and Jean Beebe (Johnson) Chung-Hoon; m. Joan Mary Prindiville, Oct. 18, 1968; children: Logan Paiea, Makena Barrett. BA, Stanford U., 1965; teaching cert. secondary edn., U. Hawaii, 1967; M in Regional Planning, U Pa., 1972. Analyst Burroughs Corp., Honolulu, 1966; supr. Pacific S.W. Airlines, San Francisco, 1966-67; teacher Iolani Sch., Honolulu, 1968-69; instr., rschr. U. Hawaii, Honolulu, 1968-70; planner H. Mogi Planning & Rsch., Honolulu, 1973-76; planner Belt Collins & Assocs., Honolulu, 1976-80, sr. planner, 1980-90, dir. planning, 1990—. V.p. St. Louis Heights Community Assn., Honolulu, 1976-80; bd. dirs. Tantalus Community Assn., Honolulu, 1986—; coach Am. Youth Soccer Orgn., Honolulu, 1983-88. Recipient Nat. Merit scholarship, 1961-65, NDEA fellowship, 1967; grantee NEA, 1972. Mem. Am. Assn. Environ. Profls., Am. Planning Assn., Nature Conservancy, Sierra Club. Office: Belt Collins & Assocs 680 Ala Moana Blvd Ste 200 Honolulu HI 96813

WHITE, RAYMOND EDWIN, JR., astronomer, educator, researcher; b. Freeport, Ill., May 6, 1933; s. Raymond Edwin White and Beatrice Ellen (Rahn) Stone; m. Ruby Elaine Fisk, Oct. 16, 1956; children: Raymond Edwin III, Kathleen M., Kevin D. BS, U. Ill., 1955, PhD in Astronomy, 1967. Instr. astronomy U. Ariz., Tucson, 1964-65, asst. prof. astronomy, 1965-71; program officer astronomy NSF, Washington, 1971-72; lectr. astronomy U. Ariz., Tucson, 1972-81, assoc. prof. astronomy, 1981-93, prof. astronomy, 1993—. Editor: Observational Astrophysics, 1992; editor Astronomy Quar. jour., 1989-91; North Am. editor Vistas in Astronomy jour., 1992—. 1st lt. U.S. Army, 1955-58. Fellow AAAS, Royal Astron. Soc.; mem. Am. Astron. Soc., Am. Assn. Physics Tchrs., Math Assn. Am., Internat. Astron. Union, Sigma Xi. Office: Univ Ariz Steward Observatory Tucson AZ 85721

WHITE, ROBERT GORDON, educator, researcher; b. Lithgow, NSW, Australia, Jan. 17, 1938; s. Richard Robert and Francis Elsie (Schubert) W.; m. Sandra Elizabeth Ferrier, Dec. 9, 1961; children: Robert Ian, Andrew Douglas. B. in Agrl. Sci., Melbourne U., Australia, 1962; M in Rural Sci./Physiology, U. New Eng., Australia, 1968, PhD, 1974. Rsch. asst. Melbourne U., 1962-63; demonstrator U. New Eng., Armidale, Australia, 1963-66, teaching fellow, 1966-69; asst. prof. zoophysiology and nutrition Inst. Arctic Biology, U. Alaska, Fairbanks, 1970-75; assoc. prof. U. Alaska, Fairbanks, 1975-81, prof., 1981—; acting dir. Inst. Arctic Biology, U. Alaska, Fairbanks, 1985, 92, dir., 1993—; dir. Large Animal Rsch. Sta., 1979—. Co-editor: (with Hudson) Bioenergetics of Wild Herbivores, 1985; editor: (proceedings, with Klein, Keller) First International Muskox Symposium, 1984 (proceedings, with Luick, Lent, Klein) First International Reindeer and Caribou Symposium, 1975; editorial bd.: Rangifer/Biol. Papers U. Alaska; contbr. over 100 papers to profl. jours. Pipe major Fairbanks Red Hackle Pipe Band, 1975-90; pres. Fairbanks Nordic Ski Club, 1973-75. NATO Rsch. fellow, Trondheim, Norway, 1975-76. Fellow Arctic Inst. N.Am.; mem. AAAS (Alaska chmn. 1985), Am. Physiol. Soc., Wildlife Soc., Am. Soc. Mammologists, The Wildlife Mgmt. Soc., Australasian Soc. Wildlife Mgmt., Australian Soc. of Animal Prodn., Australian Soc. Biochemistry and Molecular Biology, Sigma Xi. Office: U Alaska Inst Arctic Biology Fairbanks AK 99775

WHITE, ROBERT LEE, electrical engineer, educator; b. Plainfield, N.J., Feb. 14, 1927; s. Claude and Ruby Hemsworth Emerson (Levick) W.; m. Phyllis Lillian Arlt, June 14, 1952; children: Lauren A., Kimberly A., Christopher L., Matthew P. B.A. in Physics, Columbia U., 1949, M.A., 1951, Ph.D., 1954. Assoc. head atomic physics dept. Hughes Rsch. Labs., Malibu, Calif., 1954-61; head magnetics dept. Gen. Tel. and Electronics Rsch. Lab., Palo Alto, Calif., 1961-63; prof. elec. engring. Stanford U., Palo Alto, 1963, chmn. elec. engring. dept., 1981-86; William E. Ayer prof. elec. engring. Stanford U., 1985-88; exec. dir. The Exploratorium, San Francisco, 1987-89; dir. Inst. for Electronics in Medicine, 1973-87, Stanford Ctr. for Rsch. on Info. Storage Materials, 1991—; initial ltd. ptnr. Mayfield Fund, Mayfield II and Alpha II Fund, Rainbow Co-Investment Ptnrs., Halo Ptnrs.; vis. prof. Tokyo U., 1975; cons. in field. Author: (with K.A. Wickersheim) Magnetism and Magnetic Materials, 1965, Basic Quantum Mechanics, 1967; Contbr. numerous articles to profl. jours. With USN, 1945-46. Fellow Guggenheim, Oxford U., 1969-70, Kantonsspital Zurich, 1977-78, Christensen fellow Oxford, 1986. Fellow Am. Phys. Soc., IEEE; mem. Sigma Xi, Phi Beta Kappa. Home: 450 El Escarpado Stanford CA 94305 Office: Stanford U Dept Material Sci & Engring Stanford CA 94305

WHITE, ROBERT MILTON, lawyer; b. Tachikawa AFB, Japan, Oct. 10, 1948; came to U.S., 1948; s. Triggs Reeves and Josephine (Fowler) W. BA, U. N.Mex., 1970; JD, U. Houston, 1973. Bar: N.Mex. 1973, U.S. Dist. Ct. 1973. Ptnr. Levy, White, Ferguson and Grady, Albuquerque, N.Mex., 1973-80, Lastrapes and White, Albuquerque, 1980-83; deputy dir. Dept. of Corrections City of Albuquerque, 1983-86; asst. city atty. City of Albuquerque, 1986-92; pvt. practice Albuquerque, 1992—; bd. dirs. Quote-Unquote, Inc., 1984-89, New Art Connections, 1990—; pres. Hogares, Inc.; mem. Med. Review Commn. State Bar of N.Mex., 1987—. Mem. Albuquerque City Coun., 1979-83, pres. 1983, Nat. League of Cities, Wilmington, Del. (steering com. on transp. and communications), 1981-83, Arthritis Found. 1983-85. Mem. State Bar N.Mex., Order of Barons, Phi Delta Phi. Democrat. Home: 236 Solano Dr NE Albuquerque NM 87108-1042 Office: 4101 Silver SE Albuquerque NM 87108

WHITE, ROBERT RANKIN, writer and historian, hydrologist; b. Houston, Feb. 8, 1942; s. Rankin Jones and Eleanor Margaret (White) W. BA in Geology, U. Tex., 1964; MS in Hydrology, U. Ariz., 1971; PhD in Am. studies, U. N.Mex., 1993. Hydrologist Tex. Water Devel. Bd., Austin, 1972-74; hydrologist U.S. Geol. Survey, Las Cruces, N.Mex., 1974-78, Santa Fe, 1978-80, Albuquerque, 1980-89; writer, historian Albuquerque, 1989—; mem. planning bd. N.Mex. Art History Conf., Taos, N.Mex., 1987—. Author: The Lithographs and Etchings of E. Martin Hennings, 1978, The Taos Society of Artists, 1983, (with others) Pioneer Artists of Taos, 1983; contbr. articles to profl. jours. Bd. dirs. Friends of U. N.Mex. Librs., Albuquerque, 1984-90. With U.S. Army, 1965-68. Mem. Western History Assn., Hist. Soc. N.Mex. (pres. 1991-93), N.Mex. Book League (v.p. 1993), Taos County Hist. Soc., Santa Fe Trail Assn., NRA (life mem.). Episcopalian. Home and Office: 1409 Las Lomas Rd NE Albuquerque NM 87106-4529

WHITE, ROBERT STEPHEN, physics educator; b. Ellsworth, Kans., Dec. 28, 1920; s. Byron F. and Sebina (Leighty) W.; m. Freda Marie Bridgewater, Aug. 30, 1942; children: Nancy Lynn, Margaret Diane, John Stephen, David Bruce. AB, Southwestern Coll., 1942, DSc hon., 1971; MS, U. Ill., 1943; PhD, U. Calif., Berkeley, 1951. Physicist Lawrence Radiation Lab., Berkeley, Livermore, Calif., 1948-61; head dept. particles and fields Space Physics Lab. Aerospace Corp., El Segundo, Calif., 1962-67; physics prof. U. Calif., Riverside, 1967-92, dir. Inst. Geophysics and Planetary Physics, 1967-92, chmn. dept. physics, 1970-73; prof. physics emeritus Rsch. Physicist Inst. Geophysics and Planetary Physics, Riverside, 1992—; lectr. U. Calif., Berkeley, 1953-54, 57-59. Author: Space Physics, 1970; contbr. articles to profl. jours. Officer USNR, 1944-46. Sr. Postdoctoral fellow NSF, 1961-62; grantee NASA, NSF, USAF, numerous others. Fellow Am. Phys. Soc. (exec. com. 1972-74); mem. AAAS, AAUP, Am. Geophys. Union, Am. Astron. Soc. Republican. Methodist. Home: 5225 Austin Rd Santa Barbara CA 93111 Office: U Calif Inst Geophysics & Planetary Physics Riverside CA 92521

WHITE, ROBIN SHEPARD, geologist; b. Oak Ridge, Tenn., July 30, 1950; s. George Shepard and Maida Linn (Robinson) W. BA, Alfred U., 1972; MS, U. Ariz., 1976. Lic. geologist, N.C.; cert. geologist, Ind. Geologist Century Geophys. Corp., Tulsa, 1977-79; supr. Century Geophys. Corp., Grants, N.Mex., 1979-80; area mgr. Century Geophys. Corp., Moab (Utah) and Kenedy (Tex.), 1980-81; phys. sci. technician U.S. Dept. Army, Yuma, Ariz., 1983-84; trainee geologist Soil Conservation Svc., USDA, Davis, Calif., 1984-85; state geologist Soil Conservation Svc., USDA, Speedway, Ind., 1985-87; watershed planning and river basin staff geologist Soil Conservation Svc., USDA, Davis, 1987-88, river basin staff geologist, 1988-89, staff geologist water resources planning, 1989-92; state geologist Hawaii and Pacific Basin, Soil Conservation Svc., USDA, Honolulu, 1992—. Copyright electronic spreadsheet template computer program on sediment routing. Mem. Computer-Oriented Geol. Soc., Am. Assn. Individual Investors, Assn. Engring. Geologists, Health Physics Soc. (plenary). Office: USDA-SCS PO Box 50004 Honolulu HI 96850-0001

WHITE, ROGER BRUCE, architect; b. Granhaven, Mich., Nov. 16, 1947; s. John Cecil and Helen Ilona W.; children: Scott, Nicole. Student, Victor Valley Coll., Victorville, Calif., 1965-66, Merrit Coll., Oakland, Calif., 1966-67, Chabot Coll., Hayward, Calif., 1967-68, Diablo Valley Coll., Pleasant Hill, Calif., 1970-71, Los Medonas Coll., Pittsburg, Calif., 1979. Lic. architect, Calif. Designer, assoc. ptnr. J. Cruit, Incline Village, Nev., 1971; designer Mullen-Morris-Alexander, Hayward, Calif., 1971-74, Kinney E. Griffin & Assocs., Fremont, Calif., 1974, E.G. Craig Architect, Lafayette, Calif., 1974-75; prin., owner Roger B. White-Architect, Walnut Creek and Concord, Calif., 1975-82; architect Laser Facilities Laser Facilities, Architecture, Engring. Divsn./Plant Engring., 1982-87; project mgr. AED/Plant Engring. Lawrence Livermore (Calif.) Nat. Lab., 1987-89, UDS/SDF Conf. Facility Engring. Mgr., 1989-91, assoc. div. leader, 1991—; designer, draftsman Kitchen & Hunt Architects, San Francisco, 1967-68, Oakland Redevel. Agy., Oakland, 1968-69, William A. Lane, Architect, Oakland, 1969-74, Morgan D. Howell & Assocs., Hayward, 1969-70, Lundberg/Klein Assocs., South Lake Tahoe, Calif., 1970-71; engring. mgr. U-Avlis Uranium Demonstration Systems, 1991; lead architect NOVA Laser Fusion Facility, 1985, Pin Wheel Multifamily Complex, Fairfield, 1981. Mem. Lake Tahoe Jaycees (state dir. 1971), Greater Hayward Kiwanis (officer 1971-74). Office: Lawrence Livermore Nat Lab PO Box 808 L-541 Livermore CA 94550

WHITE, RUSSELL LYNN, fashion designer; b. Omaha, May 8, 1950; s. Russell Alfred White and Jo Ann (Steepy) Blotti. AA, Modesto Jr. Coll., 1970; BA in Art, Calif. State U., San Francisco, 1971; student, Coll. of Alameda, 1971-72, Laney Coll., 1976-78, Pierce Coll., 1981-82, Otis Art Inst. of Parsons Sch. Design, 1984-85. Designer Levi Strauss & Co., San Francisco, 1976-79, Jantzen Inc., L.A., 1979-80; head designer Keepers Industries, Woodland Hills, Calif., 1981-83; merchandiser, designer Domino/Victory Mens Wear, L.A., 1983-85; merchandiser, designer Joel/Cal-Made, Ltd., L.A., 1985-86, mdse. mgr., 1986; dir. design Balboa Sportswear Co., L.A., 1986—; prin. BRW & Assocs., L.A., 1986-89; designer Catalina Swimwear, L.A., 1989-91; assoc. prof. fashion design Woodbury U., Burbank, Calif., 1992—; merchandiser, designer Lavon Sportswear, LaVerne, Calif., 1992—; tchr. fashion design Learning Tree U., L.A., 1989-91. Music dir. Holy Trinity Community Ch., L.A., 1981-85, v.p., sec., 1981-83, social dir., 1984-85, treas., 1987-90; buddy vol. AIDS Project, L.A., 1987, facilitator, 1990—; facilitator Being Alive Support Group, L.A., 1989-91. Frank S. Ione Mancini scholar 1968. Mem. Am. Designer Guild (treas. Los Angeles steering com. 1987), Textile Assn. Los Angeles. Republican. Club: Mcpl. Election Com. of Los Angeles (election com. 1982, mem. adv. council) Lodge: Masons (De Molay of Yr. 1968, chevalier 1971). Home and Office: 20300 Valerio St Canoga Park CA 91306-2846

WHITE, RUSSELL NEIL, export management executive; b. Burlingame, Calif., Mar. 17, 1958; s. L. Neil and Judith (Lucas) W. BA, Western Wash. U., 1980, MA, 1982; PhD, U. Calif., Riverside, 1987. Mgr. AT&T, Seattle, 1985-86; pres. Latin Am. Cons., Kent, Wash., 1988-92, SPEC de Mexico, Mexico City, 1992-93; also dir. SPEC de Mexico. Author: State, Class and Nationalization of the Mexican Banks, 1992; assoc. editor Latin. Am. Perspectives, 1988—. Active Amnesty Internat., Kent, 1988—. U. Calif. fellow, Mexico City, 1984, 85. Mem. Confrerie des Vignerons de Saint Vincent Macan, World Trade Club (v.p. 1992-93, pres. 1993-94). Office: Latin Am Cons 29422 192nd Ave SE Kent WA 98042

WHITE, RUTH MARGARET, health education educator, nurse; b. Battle Creek, Mich., Apr. 8, 1922; d. Samuel Lee and Cora Beatrice (Whisenant) W. DrPH, UCLA, 1973; BS in Nursing Edn., Wash. Missionary Coll., 1946; MS in Community Nursing, UCLA, 1958; MPH, Johns Hopkins U., 1964. RN, Calif. Staff nurse Detroit Vis. Nurse Assn., 1944-45; instr. nursing/health svc. dir. Columbia Union Coll., Takoma Park, Md., 1946-48; supr. outpatient dept. Washington Sanitarium/Hosp., Takoma Park, 1948-51; nurse midwife, supt. nurses Surat (India) Mission Hosp., 1951-55; instr. pub. health nursing Coll. Med. Evangelists, L.A., 1955-57; intern supr. Los Angeles County Health Dept., L.A., 1958-59; assoc. prof. pub. health nursing Loma Linda U., L.A., 1959-63, prof. grad. program Sch. Nursing, 1965-77, dir. DPH program, prof., 1981-87, coord. DPH program, prof. Sch. Pub. Health, 1987-90; prof. health promotion/edn. Sch. Pub. Health, Loma Linda U., 1981-92, short term internat. cons., 1992—; cons. East Africa Loma Linda U. Sch. Pub. Health, 1957, 67, Balt. City Health Dept., 1964-65, Jhns Hopkins U. Sch. Hygiene and Pub. Health, Nigeria and India, 1968-73, Loma Linda U. Sch. Pub. Health, Tanzania, 1974-77; cons. Adventist Devel. and Relief Agy., Nepal, 1991—, Indonesia, 1992; world nursing cons. Seventh Day Adventist Ch., 1977-81. Contbr. numerous articles to med. jours. Named to Assn. Seventh-day Adventist Nurses Hall of Fame, 1980. Mem. Am. Pub. Health Assn., Am. Coll. Nurse Midwives, Assn. Seventh-day Adventist Nurses, Am. Coll. Nurse Midwifery, Sigma Xi, Sigma Theta Tau, Delta Omega. Republican. Home: 25652 Mead St Loma Linda CA 92354-2421

WHITE, STANLEY ARCHIBALD, research electrical engineer; b. Providence, Sept. 25, 1931; s. Clarence Archibald White and Lou Ella (Givens) Arford; m. Edda María Castaño-Benítez, June 6, 1956; children: Dianne, Stanley Jr., Paul, John. BSEE, Purdue U., 1957, MSEE, 1959, PhD, 1965. Registered profl. engr., Ind., Calif. Engr. Rockwell Internat., Anaheim, Calif., 1959-68, mgr., 1968-84, sr. scientist, 1984-90; pres. Signal Processing and Controls Engring. Corp., 1990—; adj. prof. elec. engring. U. Calif.,

1984—; cons. and lectr. in field; bd. dirs. Asilomar Signals, Systems and Computers Conf. Corp. Publisher, composer music; contbr. chpts. to books; articles to profl. jours.; patentee in field. Fellow N.Am. Aviation Sci. Engring., 1963-65; recipient Disting. Lectr. award Nat. Electronics Conf., Chgo., 1973, Engr. of Yr. award Orange County (Calif.) Engring. Coun., 1984, Engr. of Yr. award Rockwell Internat., 1985, Leonardo Da Vinci Medallion, 1986, Sci. Achievement award, 1987, Disting. Engring. Alumnus award Purdue U., 1988, Meritorious Inventor's award Rockwell Internat. Corp., 1989, Outstanding Elec. Engr. award Purdue U., 1992. Fellow AAAS, IEEE (founding chmn. Orange chpt.), Acoustics, Speech and Signal Processing Soc. (vice chmn. 1983, gen. chmn. Internat. Symposium on Cirs. and Systems 1992, gen. chmn. Internat. Conf. Acoustics, Speech and Signal Process 1984, Centennial medal 1984), IEEE Signal Processing Soc. (disting. lectr. 1991-92), Inst. Advancement Engring., N.Y. Acad. Scis.; mem. Sci. Rsch. Soc., Sigma XI (founding pres. Orange County chpt.), Tau Beta Pi, Eta Kappa Nu (internat. dir. emeritus). Home: 433 E Avenida Cordoba San Clemente CA 92672-2350

WHITEHEAD, CHRISTOPHER CLEO, computer company executive, researcher; b. Fort Carson, Colo., Dec. 9, 1954; s. Robert Joseph and Iris Ellen (Thomason) W.; m. Susie Manuelita Gallegos, Dec. 29, 1972; children: Christopher Michael, Charles Alexander, Stephanie Michell, Steven Andrew, Sean Michael. BSEE, U. Tex., 1978; MS in Ops. Rsch., Naval Postgrad. Sch., Monterey, Calif., 1986. Cert. naval aviator. Enlisted USMC, 1972; commd. 2d lt. USN, 1978; advanced through grades to lt. comdr., 1988; aviation radar technician U.S. Marine Corps., Denver, 1972-75; naval aviator Patrol Squadron Fifty, Moffett Field, Calif., 1980-84, pilot-in-command, mission comdr., 1982-84; staff comm. officer Carrier Group Seven, San Diego, 1986-89; asst. prof. math. scis. USAF Acad., Colo., 1989-92; exec. dir. Computers With A Smile, Pueblo, Colo., 1992—; aviation safety officer Patrol Squadron Fifty, 1982-84; sci. analyst math dept. USAF Acad., 1989-92, sci. rschr. UN AIDS model, 1989-91, Coast Guard drug interdiction program, 1990; dir. computer resources, 1990-92; lectr. U. So. Colo., Pueblo, 1992;. Contbr. articles to profl. jours. Assoc. mem. Smithsonian Inst. Mem. Ops. Rsch. Soc. Am., Am. Soc. Quality Control, So. Colo. Amiga Network, Am. Bowling Congress, VFW, Moose, Pi Mu Epsilon. Home: 2 Baybridge Ct Pueblo CO 81001-1301 Office: Computers With A Smile 140 W 29th St Ste 195 Pueblo CO 81008

WHITEHEAD, DAVID BARRY, lawyer; b. San Francisco, Oct. 14, 1946; s. Barry and Fritzi-Beth (Bowman) W.; m. René Dayan, May 26, 1990. AB in History, Stanford U., 1968, JD, 1971. Bar: Calif. 1972, U.S. Dist. Ct. (no. dist.) Calif. 1972, U.S. Ct. Appeals (9th cir.) 1972, U.S. Dist. Ct. (cen. dist.) Calif. 1974. Assoc. Cullinan Hancock Rothert & Burns, San Francisco, 1972-74; assoc. Cullinan Burns & Helmer, San Francisco, 1975-77, ptnr., 1977-78; ptnr. Burns & Whitehead, San Francisco, 1979-85, Whitehead & Porter, San Francisco, 1986—; bd. dirs. Rainbow Music, Inc., San Francisco, ITP, Inc., Sunnyvale, Calif.; founding dir. A. Lincoln High Sch. San Fancisco, 1989—. Mem. San Francisco Rep. Steering Com., 1984—; bd. dirs. Enterprise for High Sch. Students, San Francisco, 1982-86, San Francisco chpt. Easter Seal Soc., 1986—, Opera West Found., San Francisco, 1986—, Traveler's Aid Soc., San Francisco, 1989—. 1st lt. USAR, 1968-71. Mem. ABA, Calif. Bar Assn., San Francisco Bar Assn., Calif. Scholarship Fedn. (life) Family Club San Francisco (bd. dirs. 1986-89), Abraham Lincoln High Sch. San Francisco Alumni Assn. (founding dir.). Roman Catholic. Home: 1896 Pacific Ave Apt 502 San Francisco CA 94109-2302 Office: Whitehead & Porter 100 Bush St Fl 11 San Francisco CA 94104-3902

WHITEHILL, JAMES ARTHUR, lawyer; b. Tucson, Aug. 27, 1959; s. Charles Henry and Lorraine (Levy) W.; m. Jane Leslie Rodda, June 27, 1987. BA cum laude, Knox Coll., 1981; JD, U. Ariz., 1985. Bar: Ariz. 1986, U.S. Dist. Ct. Ariz. 1987. Assoc. Whitehill, West, Rowland, Christoffel & Zickerman, P.C., Tucson, 1989—. Bd. dirs., v.p., treas., Jewish Family and Children's Svc., Tucson, 1987—. Mem. ABA (young lawyers div., Affiliate Outreach Project Leadership Skills presenter, real property com., vice chair Bar Leadership Devel. Project), Pima County Bar Assn. (pres. young lawyers div. 1988-89), State Bar Ariz. (bd. govs. 1992, pres. young lawyers div. 1988—), Cardozo Soc. Jewish Attys. (steering com. 1987), Knox Coll. Alumni Club (pres. 1982-83), Wildcat Club. Democrat. Jewish. Home: 5010 N Siesta Dr Tucson AZ 85715-9652 Office: Whitehill West et al 335 N Wilmot Ste 500 Tucson AZ 85711

WHITEHOUSE, JACK PENDLETON, public relations executive; b. Los Angeles, Aug. 18, 1924; s. Marvin and Lola Katherine (Gerber) W.; m. Phyllis Jeanne Stockhausen, Mar. 6, 1964 (div. 1983); 1 child, Mark Philip. Student, The Principia Coll., 1942-43, UCLA, 1945-49. Editor L.A. Ind. Pub. Co., 1946-48; writer UCLA Office Pub. Info., 1948-51; mng. editor Yuma (Ariz.) Daily Sun, 1951-53; assoc. editor Desert Mag., 1953-54; owner Whitehouse & Assocs., L.A., 1954-55; dir. West Coast press rels. Shell Oil Co., L.A., 1955-56; pub. rels. dir. Welton Becket & Assocs., L.A., 1956-58; owner, pres. Whitehouse Assocs. Inc., L.A., 1958—, Internat. Pub. Rels. Co. Ltd., L.A., 1959—; exec. dir. Japan Steel Info. Ctr., L.A., 1966—; U.S. Justice Dept. fgn. agt. Consulate-Gen. Japan, L.A., 1971—; frequent guest lectr. to colls., univs. Author: International Public Relations, 1978. Mem. Los Angeles World Affairs Council; advisor Japanese Philharmonic Soc., 1975—. With AC, U.S. Army, 1943-45. Mem. Pub. Rels. Soc. Am., Japan-Am. Soc. (exec. council 1968—), Fgn. Trade Assn. (bd. dirs. 1978-80), Japan-West Coast Assn., Greater L.A. Press Club, L.A. Athletic Club. Office: Internat Pub Rels Co Ltd 523 W 6th St Los Angeles CA 90014-1001

WHITE-HUNT, KEITH, business executive; b. Rowlands Gill, Eng., Sept. 6, 1950; s. Thomas William and Louisa (Robson) W-H.; m. Brenda Liddle, Jan. 1, 1970; children: Keith Brendan, John Roland, Daniel Thomas, Broooke Arran, Edward James, Ross Andrew. BA in Econ. Studies with honors, U. Exeter, United Kingdom, 1973; MS in Indsl. Mgmt., U. Bradford, Eng., 1975; cert. in edn., U. Leeds, 1976; DSc in Bus. Econs., U. Lodz, Poland, 1982; postgrad., Cornell U., 1986, Stanford U., 1987. Registered cons. in info. tech., registered cons. in export sales. Asst. prof. U. Bradford, 1973-77; assoc. prof. U. Sokoto, Nigeria, 1977-78, U. Stirling, Scotland, 1978-80; v.p. corp. devel. Lithgows Ltd., Scotland, 1980-83; deputy chief exec.. & pres. N. Am. Yorkshire & Humberside Devel. Assn., Eng., 1983-90; dir. Internat. Devel. Regent Pacific Mgmt. Corp., Cupertino, Calif., 1990—; vis. prof. U. R.I., 1980-88, Tech. U. of Lodz, 1985-90, adj. prof. internat. bus. San Francisco State U., 1991; bd. dirs. White-Hunt Industries Ltd., Eng., GKWH Inc. and British Market Inc., Calif., Tex. contbr. numerous articles to profl. jours. Recipient David Forsyth award U. Leeds, 1976, Amicus Poloniae award for Contbn. to Coop. Acad. Research in Poland, 1981. Fellow British Inst. Mgmt., Inst. Sales and Mktg. Mgmt., Inst. Petroleum, Internat. Inst. Social Econs., Chartered Inst. Mktg.; mem. Inst. Info. Scientists, Inst. of Wastes Mgmt. Home: 141 Pepper Ct Los Altos CA 94022-3754 Office: 10600 N De Anza Blvd Cupertino CA 95014-2059

WHITEHURST, HARRY BERNARD, chemistry educator; b. Dallas, Sept. 13, 1922; s. Clement Monroe and Grace Annette (Walton) W.; m. Audry Lucile Hale, June 12, 1948; children: Jonathan Monroe, Katherine Annette Whitehurst Hilburn. BA, Rice U., 1944, MA, 1948, PhD, 1950. Rsch. chemist Manhattan Project, Oak Ridge, Tenn., 1944-46, U.S. Naval Radiol. Def. Lab., San Francisco, 1959; postdoctoral fellow U. Minn., Mpls., 1950-51; rsch. chemist Owens-Corning Fiberglas Corp., Newark, Ohio, 1951-55, rsch. dept. head, 1955-59; assoc. prof. chemistry Ariz. State U., Tempe, 1959-70, prof., 1970-92. Contbr. articles on oxides to profl. jours.; patentee glass fibers field. With C.E., AUS, 1944-46. Fellow Am. Inst. Chemists, AAAS, Ariz. Acad. Sci. (pres. 1960-61); mem. Am. Chem. Soc., Phi Lambda Upsilon. Democrat. Baptist. Home: 630 E Concorda Dr Tempe AZ 85282-2319 Office: Ariz State U Dept Chemistry Tempe AZ 85287-1604

WHITELAW, DAVID PETER, religion educator; b. Johannesburg, Rep. of South Africa, June 4, 1935; came to U.S., 1988; s. George and Gertrude E. (Marais) W.; m. A. Myrna Roux, Oct. 3, 1959; children: Beverley, Ruth, Andrew, Paul. BSc in Chem. Engring., U. of the Witwatersrand, Johannesburg, 1957; BA, U. South Africa, Pretoria, 1974, M.Th., 1979, D.Th., 1985. Ordained to ministry, Ch. of the Nazarene, 1963. With Johannesburg City Coun., 1957-60; chem. engr. Chem. Divsn., Johannesburg, 1962-72; rector, pres. Nazarene Theol. Coll., Florida, Rep. of South Africa, 1972-75; dist. supt. Ch. of the Nazarene South Africa Dist., Florida, 1975-80; sr. lectr. ch. history U. South Africa, Pretoria, 1980-88; chair divsn. religion, assoc. prof. dept. theology Olivet Nazarene U., Kankakee, Ill., 1988-92; assoc. prof. dept. of religion and philosophy Point Loma Nazarene Coll., San Diego, 1992—. Author: A History of the Church of the Nazarene in Southern Africa, 1979, Channels for Change--The Role of God's Pople in South Africa, 1981; co-author: God, Youth and Women--The YWCAs of South Africa, 1886-1986, 1986; co-editor: Windows on Origins, Festschrift J.A.A.A. Stoop, 1985. Mem. think tank Nat. Initiative for Reconciliation, Pietermaritzburg, Rep. of South Africa, 1985-88; bd. reference inst. Africa Enterprize, Calif., 1991—. With Rep. of South Africa mil., 1952-58. Sr. overseas researcher's grantee U. South Africa and Human Scis. Rsch. Coun.-Pretoria, 1987-88. Mem. South African Missiological Soc., Ch. History Soc. So. Africa (international bd. Studia Historiae Ecclesiasticae 1988—), Am. Acad. Religion, Am. Ch. History Soc., Wesleyan Theol. Soc. Home: 4191 McAlifan Dr San Diego CA 92111 Office: Point Loma NAzarene Coll Dept Religion/Philosophy 3900 Lomeland Dr San Diego CA 92106-9984

WHITELEY, BENJAMIN ROBERT, insurance company executive; b. Des Moines, July 13, 1929; s. Hiram Everett and Martha Jane (Walker) W.; m. Elaine Marie Yunker, June 14, 1953; children—Stephen Robert, Benjamin Walker. B.S., Oreg. State U., 1951; M.S., U. Mich., 1952; postgrad. advanced mgmt. program, Harvard U. Clk. group dept. Standard Ins. Co., Portland, Oreg., 1956-69, asst. actuary group dept. then asst. actuary acturial dept., 1959-63, asst. v.p., asst. actuary, 1963-64, asst. v.p., assoc. actuary, 1964-70, v.p. group ins. adminstrn., 1970-72, v.p. group ins. div., 1972-80, exec. v.p. group ins., 1980-81, exec. v.p., 1981-83, pres., chief exec. officer, 1983-92, chmn. bd. dirs., CEO, 1993—; bd. dirs. Gunderson, Inc., Portland, U.S. Bank of Oreg., N.W. Natural Gas Co., Willamette Industries, Inc., Oreg. Natural Gas Devel. Corp. and Canor Energy Ltd. Past pres. Columbia Pacific coun. Boy Scouts Am.; past chmn. bd., trustee Pacific U., Forest Grove, Oreg.; bd. dirs. St. Vincent Med. Found., Portland, Oreg. Served to 1st lt. USAF, 1952-55. Recipient Silver Beaver award Boy Scouts Am., 1983, Harvey and Emiline Clark medal Pacific U., 1991, Oreg. State U. Alumni Fellow award 1991. Fellow Soc. Actuaries; mem. Am. Acad. Actuaries (bd. dirs. 1984-86), Am. Council of Life Ins. (bd. dirs. 1986-89), Internat. Congress Actuaries, Portland C. of C. (bd. dirs. 1983-89). Republican. Methodist. Clubs: Arlington, Waverley Country, Multnomah Athletic (Portland, Oreg.). Office: Standard Ins Co PO Box 711 Portland OR 97207-0711

WHITENER, PHILIP CHARLES, aeronautical engineer, consultant; b. Keokuk, Iowa, July 9, 1920; s. Henry Carroll and Katherine Ethel (Graham) W.; m. Joy Carrie Page, Oct. 9, 1943; children: David A., Barbara C., Wendy R., Dixie K. BSME, U. N.Mex., Albuquerque, 1941. Ordained to elder Presbyn. Ch., 1956. Engr. Boeing Airplane Co., Seattle, 1941-47, supr. wind tunnel model design, 1947-57, project engr. B-52 flight test, 1957-62, engring. mgr. Fresh I hydrofoil, 1962-65, configurator supersonic transport, 1965-70, with preliminary design advanced concepts, 1970-83, ret., 1983; pres., chief engr. Alpha-Dyne Corp., Bainbridge Island, Wash., 1983—. Inventee in field. Organizer Trinity Ch., Burien, Wash., 1962, Highline Reformed Presbyn., Burien, 1970, Liberty Bay Presbyn., Poulsbo, Wash., 1978; pres. Whitener Family Found., Bainbridge Island, 1979; dir. Mcpl. League of Bainbridge, 1993—. Republican. Home: 5955 Battle Point Dr NE Bainbridge Is WA 98110-3407

WHITESCARVER, OLIN DRAVO, oil company executive; b. Pasadena, Jan. 4, 1936; s. Loren and Hannah O. (Beatty) W.; m. Jacqueline George, June 24, 1961; children: Laura Lea Whitescarver Mohun, William Loren. Petroleum Engr., Colo. Sch. Mines, Golden, 1958. Petroleum engr. Pur Oil Co., Van, Tex., 1959-60, Midland, Tex., 1960-63; area petroleum engr. Pur Oil Co., Lafayette, La., 1963-65; area prodn. engr. Unocal, Houma, La., 1966-73; sr. engr. Unocal, Lafayette, 1973; dist. prodn. supt. Unocal, Santa Rosa, Calif., 1973-79; dist. ops. mgr. Unocal, Indio, Calif., 1979-92; v.p., gen. mgr. Unocal Geothermal of Indonesia Ltd., Jakarta, 1992—. Patentee in field. Chmn. bd. trustees FUMC, Indio, 1988. 1st lt. U.S. Army Res., 1958-59. Mem. Soc. Petroleum Engrs. (sect. chmn. 1971-72), Am. Petroleum Inst., Geothermal Resource Coun., Colo. Sch. Mines Alumni Assn. Republican. Methodist. Home: Unocal Geothermal PO Box 7600 Rm M-20A Los Angeles CA 90051 Office: Unocal Ratu Plz Office Tower, PO Box 1264/JKT, Jakarta 10012, Indonesia

WHITESIDE, CAROL GORDON, state official, former mayor; b. Chgo., Dec. 15, 1942; d. Paul George and Helen Louise (Barre) G.; m. John Gregory Whiteside, Aug. 15, 1964; children: Brian Paul, Derek James. BA, U. Calif., Davis, 1964. Pers. mgr. Emporium Capwell Co., Santa Rosa, 1964-67; pers. asst. Levi Strauss & Co., San Francisco, 1967-69; project leader Interdatum, San Francisco, 1983-88; with City Coun. Modesto, 1983-87; mayor City of Modesto, 1987-91; asst. sec. for intergovtl. rels. The Resources Agy., State of Calif., Sacramento, 1991—. Trustee Modesto City Schs., 1979-83; nat. pres. Rep. Mayors and Local Ofcls., 1990. Named Outstanding Woman of Yr. Women's Commn., Stanislaus County, Calif., 1988, Woman of Yr., 27th Assembly Dist., 1991. Republican. Lutheran. Office: The Resources Agy 1416 9th St Ste 1311 Sacramento CA 95814-5569

WHITESIDE, LOWELL STANLEY, seismologist; b. Trinidad, Colo., Jan. 7, 1946; s. Paul Edward and Carrie Belle (Burgess) W. BS, Hamline U., 1968; postgrad., Oswego State U. of N.Y., 1970-72; MS, U. Nebr., 1985; postgrad., Ga. Inst. of Tech., 1986-88. Instr. U.S. Peace Corps, Mhulume, Swaziland, 1968-71; rsch. assoc. CIRES, U. Colo., Boulder, 1988-90; seismologist, geophysicist NOAA, Nat. Geophys. Data Ctr., Boulder, 1990—. Scoutmaster Boy Scouts Am., St. Paul, Lincoln, Nebr., 1968-80, camp counselor, 1968-76. Recipient Eagle Scout award Boy Scouts Am., 1968. Mem. AAAS (chmn. 1986-87, vice chmn. 1985-86, Geology-Geography, Rocky Mountain sect., Outstanding Articles Referee 1992, Best Student Paper Award 1984, 85), Seismol. Soc. of Am., Am. Geophys. Union, Sierra Club, Planetary Soc. Presbyterian. Home: PO Box 3141 El Dorado Springs CO 80025 Office: NOAA/NGDC/NESOIS 325 Broadway Boulder CO 80303

WHITE-THOMSON, IAN LEONARD, chemical company executive; b. Halstead, Eng., May 3, 1936; came to U.S., 1969; s. Walter Norman and Leonore (Turney) W-T.; m. Barbara Montgomery, Nov. 24, 1971. B.A. with 1st class honors, New Coll., Oxford U., 1960, M.A., 1969. Mgmt. trainee Borax Consol. Ltd., London, 1960-61; asst. to sales mgr. Borax Consol. Ltd., 1961-64, asst. to sales dir., 1964; comml. dir. Hardman & Holden Ltd., Manchester, Eng., 1965-67; joint mng. dir. Hardman & Holden Ltd., 1967-69; v.p. mktg. dept. U.S. Borax & Chem. Corp., Los Angeles, 1969-73; exec. v.p. mktg. U.S. Borax & Chem. Corp., 1973-88, pres., 1988—, also dir.; group exec. Pa. Glass Sand Corp., Ottawa Silica Co., U.S. Silica Co., 1985-87; bd. dirs. Canpotex Ltd.; chmn. bd., 1974-76; bd. dirs. KCET, Oryx Energy Co. Served with Brit. Army, 1954-56. Mem. Canadian Potash Producers Assn. (v.p. 1976-77, dir. 1972-77), Chem. Industry Coun. of Calif. (dir. 1982-85, chmn. 1984), Calif. Club, Am. Mining Congress (bd. dirs. 1989), RTZ Borax and Minerals (bd. of dirs. 1992), Oryx Energy Co. (bd. dirs. 1993). Home: 851 Lyndon St South Pasadena CA 91030-3712

WHITE-VONDRAN, MARY ELLEN, retired stockbroker; b. East Cleveland, Ohio, Aug. 21, 1938; d. Thomas Patrick and Rita Ellen (Langdon) White; m. Gary L. Vondran, Nov. 25, 1961; children: Patrick Michael, Gary Lee Jr. BA, Notre Dame Coll., South Euclid, Ohio, 1960; postgrad., John Carroll U., 1960, U. Mass., 1961, U. S.C., 1969, San Jose State U., 1971-75, U. Santa Clara, Calif., 1972, Stanford U., 1989. Cert. life secondary tchr., Calif. Tchr. Cleve. Sch. Dist., 1960-61, East Hartford (Conn.) Sch. Dist., 1961-62, San Francisco Bay Area Sch. Dist., 1970-75; life and disability agt. Travelers Ins. Co. and BMA Ins. Co., San Jose, Calif., 1975-77; stockbroker Reynolds, Bache, Shearson, Palo Alto, Calif., 1977-78, Schwab & Co., San Francisco, 1980; adminstr. pension and profit Crocker Nat. Bank, San Francisco, 1980-82; stockbroker Calif. Fed./Invest Co., San Francisco, 1982-83; head trader, br. mgr. Rose & Co., San Francisco, 1983-84; ret. Peninsula Law U., Mountain View, Calif., 1990—; tchr. citizenship for fgn. born adult community edn. Fremont Union High Sch. Dist., Sunnyvale, Calif., 1988—. Author: Jo Mora-Renaissance Man, 1973, Visit of Imperial Russian Navy to San Francisco, 1974, John Franklin Miller, 1974, 1905 Quail Meadow Road. Sec. Quota Internat., Los Altos, Calif., 1987; constn. chairperson LWV, Los Altos, 1985—, lectr. speakers bur. 1987, co-producer TV programs; precinct capt. 1988 & 90 Elections, Los Altos; appointee ad hoc com. for transp. of mibility impaired Santa Clara County, 1988; vol. tchr. English in Action; usher lively arts Stanford U.; active Internat. Vis. Com., Palo Alto, People for Accessible Health Care, Women in History Mus., Calif. History Ctr., Cupertino, Palo Alto Neighbors Abroad, Peninsula Dem. Coalition. Recipient Valley Cable Recognition award, 1988. Mem. AAUW, ACLU, NOW (speakers bur. coord.), World Affairs Forum, Women in History Assn., The Great War Soc., Am. Assn. Retired Persons, Older Women's League, Los Altos Women in Bus., Women's Internat. League for Peace & Freedom, Commonwealth Club (steering com., program com. Palo Alto/Midpeninsula chpt.), Kenna Club. Democrat. Roman Catholic.

WHITFIELD, GLEN SMITH, real estate broker; b. Bellingham, Wash., Dec. 11, 1947; s. George Whitfield and Hazel Helen (Speirs) Smith; m. Katharine Merry Mermin, Oct. 23, 1986; children: Alisa Rose, Evan George. Student, U. Wash., 1975. Realtor Northland Sales, Bellingham, 1977-79, Greenlake Realty, Seattle, 1986-88; assoc. broker Windermere Real Estate, Seattle, 1988-90; broker, owner Help-U-Sell, Spokane, 1990-92; owner Direct Realty Svc., Spokane, 1992—. Mem. Spokane Apt. Owners Assn. Office: Direct Realty Svc 1104 W Wellesley Spokane WA 99205

WHITING, ALLEN SUESS, political science educator, writer, consultant; b. Perth Amboy, N.J., Oct. 27, 1926; s. Leo Robert and Viola Allen (Suess) W.; m. Alice Marie Conroy, May 29, 1950; children: Deborah Jean, David Neal, Jeffrey Michael, Jennifer Hollister. B.A., Cornell U., 1948; M.A., Columbia U., 1950, cert. Russian Inst., 1950, Ph.D., 1952. Instr. polit. sci. Northwestern U., 1951-53; asst. prof. Mich. State U., East Lansing, 1955-57; social scientist The Rand Corp., Santa Monica, Calif., 1957-61; dir. Office Research and Analysis Far East U.S. Dept. State, Washington, 1962-66; dep. consul gen. Am. Consulate Gen., Hong Kong, 1966-68; prof. polit. sci. U. Mich., Ann Arbor, 1968-82; prof. U. Ariz., Tucson, 1982—, dir. Ctr. for East Asian Studies, 1982-93; cons. U.S. Dept. State, 1968-88; dir. Nat. Com. on U.S.-China Relations, N.Y.C., 1977—; assoc. The China Council, 1978—; pres. So. Ariz. China Coun., Tucson, 1983—. Author: Soviet Policies in China: 1917-1924, 1954, China Crosses the Yalu, 1968, Chinese Calculus of Deterrence, 1975, Siberian Development and East Asia, 1981, China Eyes Japan, 1989, others; contbr. articles to profl. jours.; spl. commentator McNeill-Lehrer Program; CBS and NBC Spls. on China. Served with U.S. Army, 1945. Social Sci. Research Council fellow, 1950, 74-75; Ford Found. fellow, 1953-55; Rockefeller Found. fellow, 1978. Mem. Assn. Asian Studies. Home: 125 E Canyon View Dr Tucson AZ 85704-5901 Office: U Ariz Dept Polit Sci Tucson AZ 85721

WHITING, ARTHUR MILTON, diversified company executive; b. St. Johns, Ariz., 1928. With Kaibab Industries, chmn., chief exec. officer; formerly bd. dir. Western Savs. & Loan, Western Fin. Corp. Office: Kaibab Industries 4602 E Thomas Rd Phoenix AZ 85018-7789*

WHITING, JAMES VINCENT, cartoonist; b. Canton, Pa., May 19, 1926; s. George Edward and Grace Electa (Dann) W.; m. Bernita Mae Blanchard, Nov. 20, 1945; children: James, Donna, John, Andrea, David. Student, Chgo. Acad. of Fine Arts, 1948, Sch. Visual Arts, 1949-51. Radio sales, air work Sta. WFLR-AM & FM, Dundee, N.Y., 1956-84; free-lance cartoonist Solana Beach, Calif., 1984—. Mem. team producing Ad Libs for syndicated newspaper panel; produced panels Wee Women, Li'l Ones, Gen. Features Corp., L.A. Times Syndicate, 1957-72. With USN, 1944-46. Mem. Southern Calif. Cartoonists Soc. (pres. 1986—, co-founder), Upstate Cartoonists League Am. (co-founder). Home and Office: 773 S Nardo Ave Apt 10 Solana Beach CA 92075-2338

WHITING, LYNN GARY, dentist; b. Spokane, Wash., July 17, 1944; s. George William and Norine Dorothy (Doran) W.; m. Janie Marie, July 31, 1966; children: Shawna, Brent. Student, Gonzaga U., Spokane, Wash.; DDS, Creighton U., Omaha, 1969. Newsletter editor Spokane (Wash.) Dist. Dental Soc., 1975, exec. coun., 1976, treas., 1978-79, sec., 1979-80, v.p., 1980-81, pres., 1981-82; dentist. Lt. USN, 1969-72. Presbyterian. Office: E 12122 Cataldo Spokane WA 99206-6724

WHITING, PAMELA JANE, industrial electronics firm administrator; b. Santa Monica, Calif., June 22, 1958; d. William Irving and Dorothy Anne (Abernathy) McAuliffe. BS in Mktg., Calif. State U., Long Beach, 1992. Med. asst. D. Wayne Perry, M.D., Torrance, Calif., 1980-81, South Bay Gastroenterology, Torrance, Calif., 1981-85; security adminstr. Hughes Aircraft Co., Torrance, Calif., 1985-93, workers' compensation adminstr., 1993—; mktg. com. Jr. C. of C. L.A. Open Golf Tournament, 1992-93; canvasser U.S. Dept. of Treas. Hughes Aircraft Co., Torrance, 1990—. Recipient Patriotic Svc. award, U.S. Dept. of Treas., Washington, 1992. Mem. Am. Mktg. Assn. (mem. mktg. com. 1992, mem. program com. 1992—, assoc. dir. advt. 1992, elected v.p. programs So. Calif. chpt. 1994-95, Dedicated Svc. award 1992, Ford Sammis Excellence award 1993), Calif. State U. Alumni Assn., Forum for Profl. Businesswomen. Office: Hughes Aircraft Co 3100 W Lomita Blvd Torrance CA 90509

WHITING, VAN ROBERT, JR., political science educator; b. Balt., Jan. 26, 1950; s. Van Robert Sr. and Sara Frances (Hollister) W.; m. Christine Mary Lux, June 5, 1971; 1 child, Van Michael. BA magna cum laude, Yale U., 1973; MA, Harvard U., 1978, PhD in Polit. Sci., 1981. Mellon fellow/vis. lectr. U. Calif., Berkeley, 1981-82; asst. prof. Brown U., Providence, R.I., 1982-89; sr. rsch. fellow U. Calif., San Diego, 1990—; vis. scholar Ctr. for Internat. Affairs, Harvard U., Cambridge, Mass., 1984; bd. dirs. Brown/Mexico program, Providence, 1986-89; cons. Internat. Inst. of R.I., 1983, 89; project dir. Liberalization and Competitiveness. Author: The Political Economy of Foreign Investment in Mexico, 1992; author: (with others) The Dynamics of Regional Integration; contbr. articles to profl. jours. and books. Recipient Distinction in Polit. Sci. award, Charles Washburn Clark prize Yale U., 1973, grad. fellowship NSF, 1974-79, Fulbright fellowship to Mexico, 1978-79, Wriston fellowship Brown U., 1984, Indo-Am. fellowship, 1990. Mem. Am. Polit. Sci. Assn., Latin Am. Studies Assn., Internat. Studies Assn., Yale Club. Home: 4240 Porte De Palmas # 52 San Diego CA 92122 Office: Univ of Calif San Diego D-010 La Jolla CA 92093

WHITLEY, DAVID SCOTT, archeologist; b. Williams AFB, Ariz., Mar. 5, 1953; s. Edgar Duer and Yvonne Roca (Wightman) W.; m. Tamara Katherine Koteles, Feb. 13, 1987; 1 child, Carmen. AB in Anthrop. & Geog. (magna cum laude), U. Calif., 1976, MA in Geography, 1979, PhD in Anthropology, 1982. Soc. Profl. Archeology. Chief archeologist Inst. Archeology UCLA, L.A., 1983-87; rsch. fellow Archeology Dept. U. Witwatersrand, Johannesburg, S. Africa, 1987-89; pres. W&S Cons., Canoga Park, Calif., 1989—; U.S. rep. internat. com. rock art Internat. Com. Monuments and Sites, 1992—. Author: Rock Art of Ancient America, 1983; editor: archeological monographs; contbr. articles to profl. jours. Prehistoric Archeologist, State of Calif. Hist. Resources Commn., 1986-87. Recipient post doctoral fellowship, Assn. for Field Archeology, 1983, tech. specialist grant, U.S. Aid, 1986. Fellow Am. Anthrop. Assn.; mem. Soc. Am. Archeology, SAR, Sons of the Indian Wars. Home: 447 3rd St Fillmore CA 93015-1413 Office: W&S Consultants 21822 Sherman Way Ste 201 Canoga Park CA 91303-1942

WHITLOCK, GAYLORD PURCELL, nutrition educator; b. Mt. Vernon, Ill., July 7, 1917; s. Walter Patton and Ferne Iola (Purcell) W.; m. Margaret Elizabeth Baumbach, Aug. 14, 1941; children: Margay Jo, Pamela Kay Nicholson. BEd, So. Ill. U., 1939; MS, Pa. State U., 1941, PhD, 1942; Profl. Deg. in Meteorology, UCLA, 1944. Asst. prof. Iowa State U., Ames, 1943-47; tech. sales advisor Merck & Co., Inc., Rahway, N.J., 1947-56; dir. health edn. Nat. Dairy Coun., Chgo., 1956-61; program leader agr. ext. svc. U. Calif., Berkeley, 1961-74; nutrition specialist U. Calif., Davis, 1974-79; prof. emeritus U. Calif., Berkeley, 1979—; fieldman Solano County Farm Bur., Fairfield, Calif., 1980—. Advisor Solano County Bd. Suprs., Fairfield, 1980—. Lt. USN, 1943-46. Mem. Rotary (pres. 1983-84), Masons (chaplain). Republican. Lutheran. Home: 1641 Rockville Rd Suisun City CA 94585-1373

WHITMAN, JAMES THOMAS, healthcare system executive, accountant; b. Portland, Oreg., Aug. 9, 1940; s. Orval Melvin and Ruth Thorbjorg (Rodley) W.; m. Anne Aleatha Sjoboen, Aug. 12, 1961; children: Stephen Dwight, Elizabeth Anne, Daniel Robert. BS cum laude, Lewis & Clark Coll., 1962. CPA, Oreg., Wash. Acct. Arthur Young & Co., Portland, 1962-66; adminstrv. asst. Blue Cross of Oreg., Portland, 1966-67; dir. fin.

Sacred Heart Gen. Hosp., Eugene, Oreg., 1967-75; v.p. fin. Sisters of St. Joseph of Peace Health and Hosp. Svcs., Bellevue, Wash., 1975-78; pres. Healthcare Fin. Mgmt. Assn., Chgo. and Oak Brook, Ill., 1978-82; v.p. corp. affairs Sisters of St. Joseph Peace Health and Hosp. Svcs., Bellevue, Wash., 1982-89; pres. Whitman Garvey Inc., Seattle, 1989—; advisor Health Mgmt. Ctr., Case Western Res. U., Cleve., 1980-84; mem. Fin. Acctg. Standards Adv. Coun., Stamford, Conn., 1981-82, Govtl. Acctg. Standards Adv. Coun., Norwalk, Conn., 1986-90. Contbr. articles to profl. jours. Elder Westminster Chapel, Bellevue, 1977-78, 83-84, Crossroads Bapt. Ch., Bellevue, 1988-91; mem. governing bd. Snoqualmie (Wash.) Valley Hosp., 1984-87, Marianwood Extended Healthcare of Issaquah, Wash., 1986-92; bd. dirs. Fred Lind Manor, Seattle, 1992—. Fellow Healthcare Fin. Mgmt. Assn. (life, Frederick C. Morgan award 1984); mem. Am. Coll. Healthcare Execs., AICPA, AHA, Cath. Health Assn., Oreg. Soc. CPAs, Gen. Soc. Mayflower Descendants. Republican. Office: Whitman Garvey Inc 1191 Second Ave 18th Fl Seattle WA 98101

WHITMAN, KENNETH JAY, advertising executive; b. N.Y.C., May 4, 1947; s. Howard Jay and Suzanne Marcia (Desberg) W.; m. Linda Loy Meisnest, Nov. 25, 1968; 1 child, Tyler Ondine. Student, Berklee Sch. Mus., 1965-66, Hubbard Acad., 1968-70. Nat. dep. dir. Pub. Relations Bur., Los Angeles, 1970-75; pres. Creative Cons., Los Angeles, 1975-82; pres., creative dir. Whitman & Green Advt., Toluca Lake, Calif., 1982-86, Whitman-Olson, Toluca Lake, 1986-92; v.p. mktg. Maxa Corp., 1992—; ptnr. Hesse, McMahon, Whittman, Toluca Lake, Calif., 1992—. Co-author: Strategic Advertising, 1986; editor Freedom news jour., 1971-79; contbr. newspaper column Shape of Things, 1971-79. Pres. Los Angeles Citizens Commn. Human Rights, 1971-75. Recipient Cert. of Design Excellence Print Regional Design Ann., 1985, 87, Award of Excellence Consolidated Papers, 1985, Award of Excellence Print Mag., 1985, 87, 1st place award Sunny Creative Radio, 2 Telly awards, 1988, Belding award Advt. Club Los Angeles, Excellence award Bus. and Profl. Advt. Assn., 1987, Internat. Gold Medallion award Broadcast Promotion and Mktg. Execs. Mem. Art Dirs. Club of Los Angeles, VSC (pres. 1964-65), CEOs Circle. Office: Hesse McMahon Whittman 10200 Riverside Dr Toluca Lake CA 91602-2539

WHITMONT, ANDREW DOUGLAS, clinical psychologist; b. N.Y.C., June 21, 1947; s. Edward C. and Gretchen W.; m. Ulla Helga Glejsted, Nov. 22, 1975; children: Nicholas Lawrence, Maya Elizabeth. BA, Reed Coll., 1968; MA, New Sch., N.Y.C., 1971; PhD, U. Wash., 1975. Psychologist Mid Columbia Mental Health Ctr., Richland, Wash., 1975-78; pvt. practice Yakima (Wash.) Psychol. Svcs., 1978—. Com. chair Unitarian Ch., Yakima, 1985. Mem. Wash. State Psychol. Assn. (chpt. pres. 1991-92). Office: Yakima Psychol Svcs 307 S 12th Ave Yakima WA 98902

WHITMORE, DONALD CLARK, retired engineer; b. Seattle, Sept. 15, 1932; s. Floyd Robinson and Lois Mildred (Clark) W.; m. Alice Elinor Winter, Jan. 8, 1955; children: Catherine Ruth, William Owen, Matthew Clark, Nancy Lynn, Peggy Ann, Stuart John. BS, U. Wash., 1955. Prin. engr. The Boeing Co., Seattle, 1955-87, ret., 1987; developer, owner mobile home pk., Auburn, Wash., 1979—. Author: Towards Security, 1983, (monograph) SDI Software Feasibility, 1990, Characterization of the Nuclear Proliferation Threat, 1993. Activist for arms control, Auburn, Wash., 1962—; chmn. Seattle Coun. Orgns. for Internat. Affairs, 1973, Auburn Citizens for Schs., 1975; v.p. Boeing Employees Good Neighbor Fund, Seattle, 1977, Spl. Svc. award, 1977; bd. dirs. 8th Congl. Dist. Sane/Freeze, 1992—. Home and Office: 16202 SE Lake Moneysmith Rd Auburn WA 98002

WHITMORE, WILLIAM FRANCIS, physicist, retired missile scientist; b. Boston, Jan. 6, 1917; s. Charles Edward and Elizabeth Manning (Gardiner) W.; m. Elizabeth Sherman Arnold, Nov. 1, 1946; children: Charles, Edward, Thomas, Peter. SB, MIT, 1938; PhD (Univ. fellow), U. Calif., Berkeley, 1941. Math. physicist Naval Ordnance Lab., 1941-42; instr. physics MIT, 1942-46; sr. staff mem. ops. evaluation group USN, 1946-57, chief scientist spl. projects office, 1957-59; mem. chief scientist's staff missiles and space divsn. Lockheed Aircraft Corp., 1959-62; dep. chief scientist Lockheed Missiles & Space Co., Sunnyvale, Calif., 1962-64, asst. to pres., 1964-69, chief scientist (ocean systems), 1969-83, cons., 1984-88; ret., 1988; cons. evaluation bd. of USAAF, ETO, 1945; sci. analyst to comdg. gen. 1st Marine Wing, Korea, 1953; sci. analyst to asst. chief naval ops. for guided missiles, 1950-56; cons. adv. panel ordnance, transport and supply Dir. Def. Rsch. and Engring., 1958-62; mem. adv. bd. Naval Ordnance Labs., 1968-75, chmn., 1968-73; cons. mem. bd. NRC, 1973-80. Mem. vis. com. math. dept. MIT, 1971-78. Recipient Navy Meritorious Pub. Svc. citation, 1961, Sec. of Navy cert. of commendations (3), 1960-66. Fellow AIAA (assoc.); mem. NRA (life), Am. Math. Soc., Math. Assn. Am., Optical Soc. Am., Ops. Rsch. Soc. Am., Cosmos Club, Phi Beta Kappa, Sigma Xi. Home: 555 Glenwood Ave # B-108 Menlo Park CA 94025

WHITNER, JANE MARVIN, scientific applications programmer; b. Oakland, Calif., Aug. 29, 1935; d. Chauncey Hill and Alice Belle (Cromwell) Whitner. BA in Biol. Sci., San Jose State U., 1958; MA in Biostatistics, U. Calif., Berkeley, 1960. EDP programmer San Mateo County EDP Ctr., Redwood City, Calif., 1962-65; sci. programmer Lockheed Missiles & Space Co., Sunnyvale, Calif., 1967-68, Stanford U. Med. Ctr., 1969-73; sci. sys. programmer Physics Internat. Co., San Leandro, Calif., 1980-84; bioanalyst Syntex Rsch. Corp., Palo Alto, Calif., 1985—. Mem. ACM, Astron. Soc. Pacific, Smithsonian Instn., U. Calif. Alumni Assn., Commonwealth Club of Calif.

WHITNEY, CONSTANCE CLEIN, psychologist, educator, consultant; b. Seattle; BA, Stanford U.; MA; PhD, Washington U., St. Louis; children: Mark Wittcoff, Caroline Wittcoff. instr. U. Mo., St. Louis, 1976-78; rsch. assoc., Wash. U. Med. Sch., 1977-78; dir. Motivation Rsch. Inst. U. Wash., 1979-83; post doctoral fellow Grad. Sch. Bus. and Pub. Adminstrn. Wash. U., 1983-86; dir., exec. edn. Town Hall Calif., 1989-92. Bd. dirs. UCLA Arts Coun., Club 100 Music Ctr., Leadership So. Calif., Stanford Alumni So. Calif., Nat. Commn. for UN Conv. to eliminate discrimination; mem. Pres.' Circle L.A. County Mus. Art. Mem. Robinson Garden, Friends of French Art, Am. Psychol. Assn., Calif. Psychol. Assn., AAUP, ASTD, Acad. Mgmt., Orgn. Behavior and Teaching Soc. Author, producer, dir.: (film) Women and Money: Myths and Realities. Home: # 1202 10601 Wilshire Blvd Los Angeles CA 90024-4518

WHITNEY, DANIEL DEWAYNE, anthropology educator; b. Alma, Mich., July 25, 1937; s. Frank J. Whitney and Irene E. (Duffy) Morey; m. Hiroko Saito, Jan. 7, 1959 (div. 1982); children: Teresa, Wendi; m. Phyllis A. Tubbs, May 7,1983. BA in Journalism, Mich. State U., 1962, MA in Anthropology, 1963, PhD in Anthropology, 1968; JD with honors, Western State U., 1976. Asst. dir. Asian Studies Mich. State U., 1965-66; asst., assoc., prof. San Diego State U., 1966—, assoc. dean, 1969-72; ptnr. Gallatin & Whitney, San Diego, 1976-83; program dir. Am. Anthropol. Assn., Washington, 1983-85; Fulbright lectr. U. Ryukyus, Naha, Okinawa, 1986-87; dir. Ctr. Asian Studies. San Diego State U., 1987-89, prof., chmn. Anthropology dept., 1989—; rsch. prof. Am. U., Washington, 1984-85. Author book; contbr. articles to profl. jours. with USAF, 1955-59. Mem. Am. Anthropol. Assn. (program dir. annual meeting, 1970), Calif. Faculty Assn. (grievance officer 1987—). Democrat. Home: 5352 W Falls View Dr San Diego CA 92115-1426

WHITNEY, DAVID CLAY, educator, consultant, writer; b. Astoria, Oreg., May 30, 1937; s. Rolla Vernon and Barbara (Clay) W.; m. Kathleen Donnelley, 1956 (div. 1963); children: David Jr., Gordon, Sara; m. Zelda Gifford, 1967 (div. 1973); m. Emily Jane Williams, 1992. BS in Chemistry, San Diego State U., 1959; PhD in Chemistry, U. Calif., Berkeley, 1963. Cert. data processor, cert. data educator. Acting asst. prof. U. Calif., Davis, 1962-63; chemist, mathematician Shell Devel. Corp., Emeryville, Calif., 1963-72; dir. computer services Systems Applications, Inc., San Rafael, Calif., 1973-77; prof. Sch. Bus. San Francisco State U., 1977—; info. systems cons. numerous cos., 1977—; textbook reviewer numerous pubs., 1979—. Author: Instructors' Guides to Understanding Fortran 77, 1983, 87, Understanding Fortran, 1984, 88, Basic, 1988, 89. Mem. Assn. Computing Machinery, Data Processing Mgmt. Assn., Soc. Data Educators, Mensa. Home: 1501 S Norfolk St San Mateo CA 94401-3605 Office: San Francisco State U Sch of Bus San Francisco CA 94132

WHITNEY, JANE, foreign service officer; b. Champaign, Ill., July 15, 1941; d. Robert F. and Mussette (Cary) W. BA, Beloit Coll., 1963; CD, U. Aix, Marseille, France, 1962. Joined Fgn. Service, U.S. Dept. State, 1965, vice consul, Saigon, Vietnam, 1966-68, career counselor, 1968-70, spl. asst. Office of Dir. Gen., 1970-72, consul, Stuttgart, Fed. Republic Germany, 1972-74, Ankara, Turkey, 1974-76, spl. asst. Office of Asst. Sec. for Consular Affairs, 1976-77, mem. Bd. Examiners Fgn. Service, 1977-78, 79-81, consul, Munich, Germany, 1978-79, Buenos Aires, 1981-82, Argentina, ethics officer Office of Legal Adviser, 1982-85, advisor Office of Asst. Sec. for Diplomatic Security, 1985-86, dep. prin. officer, consul, Stuttgart, 1986-90, prin. officer, consul gen., Perth, Australia, 1990-91. Recipient awards U.S. Dept. State, 1968, 70, 81, 85, 87, 90. Democrat. Roman Catholic.

WHITNEY, JON R., gas company executive; b. 1944; married. BS, Colo. State U. Sr. acct. Alvin J. Krutchen CAA, 1966-68; acct. Colo. Interstate Gas Co., Colorado Springs, 1968-69, supr. acct., then rate analyst, 1969-71, sr. rate analyst, 1971-73, mgr. rates, 1973-75, contr., 1975—, v.p., 1980-84, sr. v.p., from 1984, now exec. v.p., dir. Office: Colo Interstate Gas Co 2 N Nevada Ave Colorado Springs CO 80903-1715

WHITSEL, RICHARD HARRY, biologist; b. Denver, Feb. 23, 1931; s. Richard Elstun and Edith Muriel (Harry) W.; children by previous marriages: Russell David, Robert Alan, Michael Dale, Steven Deane. BA, U. Calif., Berkeley, 1954; MA, San Jose State Coll., 1962. Sr. rsch. biologist San Mateo County Mosquito Abatement Dist., Burlingame, Calif., 1959-72; environ. program mgr., chief of watershed mgmt. Calif. Regional Water Quality Control Bd., Oakland, 1972—; mem. grad. faculty water resource mgmt. U. San Francisco, 1987-89. Served with Med. Service Corps, U.S. Army, 1954-56. Mem. Entomol. Soc. Am., Entomol. Soc. Wash., Am. Mosquito Control Assn., Calif. Alumni Assn., The Benjamin Ide Wheeler Soc., Nat. Parks and Conservation Assn. (life), Sierra Club. Democrat. Episcopalian. Contbr. articles to profl. jours. Home: 4331 Blenheim Way Concord CA 94521-4258 Office: Calif Regional Water Quality Control Bd 2101 Webster St Oakland CA 94612-3027

WHITSITT, ROBERT JAMES, professional sports executive; b. Madison, Wis., Jan. 10, 1956; s. Raymond Earl and Dolores June (Smith) W.; m. Jan Leslie Sundberg; children: Lillian Ashley, Sean James. BS, U. Wis., Stevens Point, 1977; MA, Ohio State U., 1978. Intern Indiana Pacers, Inpls., 1978, bus. tickets mgr., 1979, dir. bus. affairs and promotions, 1980, asst. gen. mgr., 1981-82; v.p. mktg. Kansas City (Mo.) Kings, 1982-84, v.p., asst. gen. mgr., 1984-85; v.p., asst. gen. mgr. Sacramento Kings, 1985-86; pres. Seattle Supersonics, 1986—. Mem. Nat. Basketball Assn. (alternate gov., mem. competition and rules com.). Republican. Lutheran. Lodge: Rotary. Office: Seattle Supersonics 190 Queen Anne Ave N Seattle WA 98109-4926*

WHITTAKER, ALUN HOWARD, geologist, educator, writer; b. Crewe, Great Britain, Mar. 28, 1946; came to U.S., 1974; s. Joseph and Gladys Jane (Prince) W.; m. Jennifer Lynn Cartlidge, May 25, 1970 (div. 1977); m. Jane Angela Sanders, Nov. 14, 1978. BS with combined honors, U. Exeter, Great Britain, 1967; diploma, Tex. A&M U., 1972. Registered geologist, Calif. Geologist Exploration Logging Div., Windsor, Great Britain, 1967-74; dir. rsch. Baker-Hughes Corp., Inc., Houston, 1974-78, Sacramento, Calif., 1978-88; writer, cons. Sanders Whittaker and Assocs., Sacramento, London, 1988—. Author: Modern Mud Logging, 1990; editor Petroleum Technology Series, 1982-87; patentee computer controlled model; contbr. numerous articles to profl. jours.; writer television documentaries medicine, agriculture, social issues, 1990-92. Mem. neighborhood adv. com. City Transp. Study, Sacramento, 1989-90. Fellow Geol. Soc.; mem. AAAS, Am. Assn. Petroleum Geologists (sr.), Am. Film Inst., Planetary Soc., Royal Inst. Chemists (lic.), Soc. Petroleum Engrs., Soc. Profl. Well Log Analysts (pres. No. Calif. chpt. 1984-86). Office: Sanders-Whittaker 244 Ohio St Vallejo CA 94590-5051

WHITTAKER, DAVID MICHAEL, sales executive; b. Boise, Idaho, Nov. 13, 1959; s. Donald Lee and Virginia (Chapman) W.; m. Jean Marie Royston, May 3, 1982; children: Matthew, Jacob, Jenna Lyn. BS in Bus. Mgmt., Brigham Young U., 1984. Sales rep. TSI, Salt Lake City, 1984-85; account mgr. NCR Corp., Salt Lake City, 1985-87; sales rep. Harris/3M, Salt Lake City, 1987-88; systems specialist Superior Bus. Comms., Reno, 1988-92, v.p. sales, 1992—. Mem. exec. sec. LDS Ch., Sparks, Nev., 1991-93; mem. VDI Adv. Coun., 1990—. Mem. Mgmt. Soc. Marriot Sch. Mgmt. Republican. Office: Superior Bus Comms 2001 E Flamingo Rd Ste 107 Las Vegas NV 89119

WHITTINGTON, H(ORACE) G(REELEY), health care administrator, psychiatrist; b. Galveston, Tex., Jan. 5, 1929; s. Thomas Monroe and Hallie Marie (Hobbs) W.; m. Cynthia J. Reed, Mar. 17, 1979; 1 child, Alexander Earle Lee. BA, Rice U., 1948; MD, Baylor U., 1952. Dir. mental health clinic Student Health Svcs. U. Kans., Lawrence, 1958-61; dir. community mental health svcs. State of Kans., Topeka, 1961-65; dir. psychiatry Denver Dept. Health and Hosps., 1965-73; pvt. practice Denver, 1973-83, Lubbock, Tex., 1983-87; dir. med. svcs. Prudential Ins. Co., Houston, 1987-91; v.p., med. dir. Managed Health Network, Inc., L.A., 1991—. Author: Psychiatry on College Campus, 1963, Psychiatry in American Community, 1966, Handbook of Community Mental Health, 1972; editor: Development of Urban Mental Health Center, 1971. Capt. USAF, 1952-55, Korea. Fellow Am. Psychiat. Assn. (life). Office: Managed Health Network Inc 5100 W Goldleaf Circle # 300 Los Angeles CA 90056

WHITTINGTON, JEREMIAH, physician; b. Eagle Mills, Ark., Jan. 25, 1946; s. George Washington Jr. and Lula (Brooks) W.; m. Mary Ellen Branch, July 1, 1972 (div. July 1976); 1 child, Carrie Kenyatta; m. Kaye Francis Atkinson, June 18, 1977; 1 child, Christopher Jerome. Student, Calvin Coll., 1969; MA, U. Mich., 1970, postgrad., 1971-72; MD, Mich. State U., 1979. Diplomate Am. Bd. Ob./Gyn. Intern, resident ob/gyn intern, resident ob-gyn, Youngstown, Ohio, 1979-83; physician Planned Parenthood of Mahoning County, Youngstown, 1980-83, Ashtabula (Ohio) County Commn. Action Agy., 1981-83; practice medicine specializing in ob-gyn Grand Rapids, Mich., 1984-89; attending physician City of Faith Med. and Research Ctr., Tulsa, 1985-89; clin. asst. prof. UCLA, Sylmar; physician specialist dept. ob-gyn L.A. County Hosp., Olive Med. Ctr., Sylmar, 1989-90; ob-gyn physician So. Calif. Permanente Med. Group, Panorama City, Calif., 1990-93, Providence Hosp. Med. Ctrs., Southfield, Mich., 1993—; physician Ambulatory Gynecology, Infertility and Obstetrics, Claremore, Okla., 1983-86; staff physician USPHS and Claremore Indian Hosp., 1983-86; asst. prof. dept. ob.-gyn. Oral Roberts U. Sch. Medicine, Tulsa, 1985-89; cons., physician Rogers County Health Dept., Claremore, 1983-86; mem. People to People delegation Citizens Amb. Program to Finland, 1987; tchr., speaker Sch. Medicine U. Zambia, Lusaka, 1990; speaker Victory Celebrations, Zambia, 1988, 90. Contbr. articles to hosp. jour. Mem. Okla. Med. Polit. Action Com., Oklahoma City, 1986. Pub. health service scholar U.S. Pub. Health Service, 1976. Fellow Am. Coll. Ob-Gyn.; mem. AMA, Calif. Med. Assn., L.A. County Med. Assn., L.A. Ob-Gyn. Soc. Democrat. Home: 45196 Courtview Trl Novi MI 48375 Office: 2575 North Woodward Ave Ste 120 Panorama City CA 48702 also: Providence Hosp Med Ctrs 16001 West 9 Mile Rd Southfield MI 48037

WHITWORTH, PEGGY W., association official, statistician; b. Kosse, Tex., Sept. 25, 1939; d. Elmer Wilmer and Annie Lee (Ray) Lewis; m. Carl Nelson Whitworth, Feb. 15, 1958; children: Beth Whitworth McClary, Carl Nelson Jr., Veronica, Robert. Student, U. So. Colo., 1980-85. Data entry supr. Assn. Am. R.R.'s, Pueblo, Colo., 1982-88, purchasing agt., 1988—. Fundraiser March of Dimes, Pueblo, 1987—, Women's Pregnancy Ctr., Pueblo, 1990—, Am. Heart Assn., Pueblo, 1990—. Office: Assn Am RRs PO Box 11130 Pueblo CO 81001

WHYTE, HELENA MARY, chemist, educator; b. Albuquerque, Dec. 19, 1948; d. Alexander Peter and Helen (Mriz) Mozden.; m. Kent Neil Whyte, July 6, 1973; children: Stacey Helene, Kurt Neil. BS in Chemistry with honors, N.Mex. Inst. Mining Tech., 1970; MA in Sci. Teaching, U. N.Mex., 1971. Lab. asst. N.Mex. Bur. Mines, Socorro, 1966-70; rsch. asst. Los Alamos (N.Mex.) Sci. Lab., 1970-71; tchr. chemistry Los Alamos High Sch., 1971-79; instr. chemistry U. N.Mex., Los Alamos, 1981-84; staff mem. Los Alamos Nat. Lab., 1979—; appointed to women's com. Los Alamos Nat. Lab., 1986-88, sect. leader, 1988-90, appointed div. affirmative action rep., 1992. Mem. manuscript rev. panel Sci. Tchr. mag., 1987-89; contbr. articles to profl. pubs. Fellow Am Inst. Chemists (cert.; adv. bd. Nat. Certification for Chemistry and Chem. Engring. 1991); mem. AAUW (div. liaison legal advocacy fund 1988-92), Am. Chem. Soc., Nat. Sci. Tchrs. Assn., Nat. Environ. Trainers Assn., Women in Sci., Alpha Delta Kappa (local pres. 1979-80). Democrat. Roman Catholic. Office: Los Alamos Nat Lab K494 HS-5 Los Alamos NM 87545

WHYTE, RONALD M., federal judge; b. 1942. BA in Math., Wesleyan U., 1964; JD, U. So. Calif., 1967. Bar: Calif. 1967, U.S. Dist. Ct. (no. dist.) Calif. 1967, U.S. Dist. Ct. (ctrl. dist.) Calif. 1968, U.S. Ct. Appeals (9th cir.) 1968. Assoc. Hoge, Fenton Jones & Appel, Inc., San Jose, Calif., 1971-77, atty., 1977-89; judge Superior Ct. State of Calif., 1989-92, U.S. Dist. Ct. (no. dist.) Calif., San Jose, 1992—; judge pro-tempore Superior Ct. Calif., 1977-89; lectr. Calif. Continuing Edn. of Bar, Rutter Group, Santa Clara Bar Assn., State Bar Calif.; legal counsel Santa CLara County Bar Assn., 1986-89; mem. county select com. Criminal Conflicts Program, 1988. Bd. trustees Santa Clara County Bar Assn., 1978-79, 84-85. Lt. Judge Advocate Gen.'s Corps, USNR, 1968-71. Recipient Judge of Yr. award Santa Clara County Trial Lawyers Assn., 1992, Am. Jurisprudence award. Mem. Calif. Judges Assn., Assn. Bus. Trial Lawyers (bd. govs. 1991—). Office: US Courthouse 280 South First St San Jose CA 95113*

WHYTE-BANKS, HILA JANE, communication technician; b. St. Joseph, Mo., Oct. 21, 1949; d. Everett Louis and Janet Lee (Biggerstaff) Whyte; m. Henry Lee Clark, Feb. 19, 1980 (div. Mar. 1984); children: Haléa Lanay Clark, Heather Lynn Clark; m. Robert Banks Jr., Jan. 2, 1985; 1 child, Robert Banks III. Student, Tarkio Coll., 1967-69; BA, Calif. State U., San Diego, 1972. Mail aide U.S. Post Office, San Diego, 1970-72; order typist Pacific Bell, San Diego, 1972-74, staff clk., 1974-78, frame attendant, 1978-80, communication technician, 1980—; factory worker Whittaker Cable Corp., St. Joseph, summer 1969; illustrator, comedy writer, dramatic writer Reflections of Real Life, San Diego, 1990—. Author musical play, song. Min. music Antioch Ch. of God in Christ, San Diego, 1976-86, Christian Compassion Ctr., San Diego, 1987—; singer Patrick Whyte Singers, San Diego, 1982—, Cox Cable TV, Christian Compassion Ctr., San Diego, 1988—, corp. officer, sec.-treas., 1993—. Scholar Tarkio Coll., 1967. Mem. Word of Faith Ch. Office: Reflections of Real Life PO Box 740422 San Diego CA 92174

WIBORG, JAMES HOOKER, chemicals distribution company executive; b. Seattle, Aug. 26, 1924; s. John R. and Hazel (Hooker) W.; m. Ann Rogers, July 1948; children: Katherine Ann, Mary Ellen, Caroline Joan, John Stewart. B.A., U. Wash., 1946. Owner, Wiborg Mfg. Co., Tacoma, 1946-50; securities analyst Pacific N.W. Co., Seattle, 1950-53; founder Western Plastics Corp., Tacoma, 1953; pres. Western Plastics Corp., 1953-55, chmn. bd., dir., ret.; exec. v.p. Wash. Steel Products Co., Tacoma, 1955-58; mgmt. cons. Tacoma, 1958-60; v.p. United Pacific Corp., Seattle, 1960; pres. Pacific Small Bus. Investment Corp., Seattle, 1961-63; sr. v.p. indsl. div. United Pacific Corp., Seattle, 1963-65; pres., chief exec. officer, dir. United Pacific Corp., 1965; past pres., chief exec. officer, dir. Univar Corp. (formerly VWR United Corp.), Seattle, from 1966; chmn., chief exec. officer Univar Corp. (formerly VWR United Corp.), 1983-86, chief strategist, 1986-91, chmn., 1991—; dir., chmn., chief strategist VWR Corp., 1986—; dir. Seattle, Seafirst Corp., PACCAR Inc., Seattle-First Nat. Bank, Gensco Inc., Tacoma, Penwest Ltd., Momentum Distbn., Inc., vice chmn., chief strategist. Trustee U. Puget Sound. Clubs: Tacoma Country and Golf, Tacoma, Tacoma Yacht; Rainier (Seattle), Columbia Tower (Seattle). Office: Univar Corp PO Box 34325 Seattle WA 98104-1509*

WICK, JAMES EUGENE, physician, pulmonologist; b. Dayton, Ohio, Dec. 15, 1947; s. Glenn Austin and Marjorie Maxine (McAfee) W.; m. Doris Elaine Reed. MS in Elec. Engring., U. Colo., 1971; BME, Gen. Motors Inst., 1972; MD, Med. Coll. of Ohio, 1976. Diplomate Am. Bd. Internal Medicine; bd. cert. internal medicine and pulmonary disease. Intern Presbyn. Med. Ctr., Denver, 1976-77, resident, 1977-80; fellow Ind. U. Med. Ctr., Indpls., 1980-82; pvt. practice specializing in pulmonary disease Aurora, Colo., 1983—. Fellow Am. Coll. Chest Physicians. Office: James E Wick MD PC 750 Potomac St Ste 227 Aurora CO 80011

WICK, JAMES JOSEPH, computer graphics software professional; b. Racine, Wis., Sept. 9, 1960; s. Raymond Matthew and Irene Marie (Eigner) W.; m. Roberta Ann Kellogg, Apr. 11, 1987; 1 child, Alexandra Anna. BS, U. Wis., 1985. Specialist U. Wis. Parkside, Kenosha, 1985-86; scientist Naval Rsch. Lab., Washington, 1986; systems engr. Datalogics Inc., Chgo., 1986-87; sr. software engr. Polygen Corp., Waltham, Mass., 1987-88, mgr. graphics, 1988-89; mgr. software Spatial Systems Inc., Concord, Mass., 1989-90; dir. software Spaceball Technologies, Sunnyvale, Calif., 1991-92, v.p. software devel., 1992—. Mem. IEEE, Special Interest Groups on Computer Graphics, Bay Computer and Human Interaction, Assn. for Computing Machinery, Software Entrepreneurs' Forum.

WICK, RAYMOND VICTOR, physicist, chief scientist; b. Pitts., Mar. 17, 1940; s. Charles Victor and Sara Ruby (Calhoun) W.; m. Kathy Greenfield, Aug. 15, 1942; children: David Victor, Michael Wesley, Matthew James. BA in Physics, Thiel Coll., 1962; MS in Physics, Pa. State U., 1964, PhD in Laser Physics, 1966. Project officer effects br. Air Force Weapons Lab., Kirtland AFB, N.Mex., 1966-72, sci. advisor tech. br., 1972-74; tech. advisor optics br. Air Force Weapons Lab., Kirtland AFB, 1976-84, laser div., 1976-84, tech. dir. program office, 1984-88, tech. rsch. dir. laser optics div., 1988-91; chief scientist for space and missiles tech. Phillips Lab., Albuquerque, 1991—; chmn. sensors, laser and optics com. Office of Under Sec. of Def., Washington, 1982—; chmn. directed energy com. Office of Under Sec. of Def./ Analysis, Washington, 1984—; dept. def. tech. rep. to coord. com. NATO, Paris, 1987—; cons. Inst. for Def. Analyses, Washington, 1984—. Contbr. articles on lasers and optics to profl. jours.; patentee in field. Mentor Nat. Rsch. Coun. and the Palace Knight, Air Force Office. NASA fellow, 1964-66, NRC fellow, 1966-67. Mem. ASTM, AIAA, Optical Soc. Am., Soc. Photog. Instrumentation Engrs. (conf. chmn. 1978-89), Am. Inst. Physics, Internat. Sci. Soc. Home: 10421 Karen NE Albuquerque NM 87111 Office: Phillips Lab PL/VT Kirkland AFB Albuquerque NM 87117

WICKER, ALLAN WERT, psychology educator; b. Elk Falls, Kans., Aug. 10, 1941; s. Lester Allen and Hazel Katherine (Clum) W.; m. Kathleen O'Brien, Feb. 5, 1973; 1 child, David Allan. BA, U. Kans., 1963, MA, 1965, PhD, 1967. Asst. prof. psychology U. Wis., Milw., 1967-69, U. Ill., Urbana, 1969-71; assoc. then prof. psychology Claremont (Calif.) Grad. Sch., 1971—. Author: Introduction to Ecological Psychology, 1979; contbr. articles to profl.jours., chpts. to books. Rsch. grantee NIMH, 1968-72, NSF, 1972-76, Haynes Found., 1985-87; Fulbright sr. lectr. Coun. for Internat. Exchange of Scholars, Zimbabwe, 1989, Ghana, 1993. Fellow Am. Psychol. Soc.; mem. Am. Sociol. Assn., Acad. Mgmt., Internat. Assn. Applied Psychology. Office: Claremont Grad Sch Ctr Orgnl and Behavioral Sci 130 E 9th St Claremont CA 91711-6190

WICKES, GEORGE, educator, writer; b. Antwerp, Belgium, Jan. 6, 1923; came to U.S., 1923; s. Francis Cogswell and Germaine (Attout) W.; m. Louise Westling, Nov. 8, 1975; children by previous marriage: Gregory, Geoffrey, Madeleine (dec.), Thomas, Jonathan. BA, U. Toronto, Ont., Can., 1944; MA, Columbia U., 1949; PhD, U. Calif., Berkeley, 1954. Asst. sec. Belgian Am. Ednl. Found., N.Y.C., 1947-49; exec. dir. U.S. Ednl. Found. in Belgium, 1952-54; instr. Duke U., Durham, N.C., 1954-57; from asst. prof. to prof. Harvey Mudd Coll. and Claremont Grad. Sch., Calif., 1957-70; prof. English and comparative lit. U. Oreg., Eugene, 1970—; dir. comparative lit. U. Oreg., 1974-77, head English dept., 1976-83; lectr. U.S. Info. Service, Europe, 1969, Africa, 1978, 79; vis. prof. U. Rouen, France, 1970, U. Tubingen, W. Ger., 1981. Editor: Lawrence Durrell and Henry Miller Correspondence, 1963, Henry Miller, Letters to Emil, 1989; author: Henry Miller, 1966, Americans in Paris, 1969, The Amazon of Letters, 1976; adv. editor: Northwest Rev., 1972—; translator: The Memoirs of Frédéric Mistral, 1986. Served with U.S. Army, 1943-46. Fulbright lectr. France, 1962-63, 66, 78; sr. fellow Ctr. for Twentieth Century Studies, U. Wis.-Milw., Milwaukee, 1971, Creative Writing fellow Nat. Endowment Arts, 1973, Camargo fellow, 1991. Mem. PEN. Office: U Oreg English Dept Eugene OR 97403

WICKES, MARY, actress; b. St. Louis, June 13; d. Frank A. and Mary Isabella (Shannon) Wickenhauser. A.B., D.Arts (hon.), Washington U., St. Louis; postgrad., UCLA, 1972—. Lectr. seminars on acting in comedy Coll. William and Mary, Williamsburg, Va., Washington U. at St. Louis, Am. Conservatory Theatre, San Francisco. Debut at Berkshire Playhouse, Stockbridge, Mass.; appeared in: Broadway plays Stage Door, 1936, Father Malachy's Miracle, 1937, The Man Who Came to Dinner, 1939, Jackpot (musical), 1944, Hollywood Pinafore (musical), 1945, Town House, 1948, Park Avenue (musical), 1946, Oklahoma (revival), 1979, others; numerous appearances in dramatic and musical stock, including St. Louis Mcpl. Opera, Cape Playhouse, Dennis, Mass., Bucks County Playhouse, Pa., Alliance Theater, Atlanta, The Coconut Grove Playhouse, Miami, Fla., Burt Reynolds Theatre, Jupiter, Fla., Fox Theatre, St. Louis, Mark Taper Forum, Anson Theater and Chandler Pavilion, Los Angeles, Am. Shakespeare Festival, Stratford, Conn., Am. Conservatory Theater, San Francisco, Berkshire Playhouse, Mass., 1937-78; film debut in The Man Who Came to Dinner, 1941; other film appearances include Now Voyager, 1942, Higher and Higher, 1943, June Bride, 1948, Anna Lucasta, 1949, On Moonlight Bay, 1951, By the Light of the Silvery Moon, 1952, The Actress, 1953, White Christmas, 1959, The Music Man, 1962, The Trouble with Angels, 1966, Where Angels Go, Trouble Follows, 1968, Touched by Love, 1979, Postcards from the Edge, 1990, Sister Act, 1992, Sister Act II, 1993; TV debut as Mary Poppins: other TV appearances include Studio One, 1946; regular: TV series Doc, Halls of Ivy, Lucy shows, Dennis the Menace, The Canterville Ghost, Murder, She Wrote, Wonderworks (PBS), Twigs, Highway to Heaven, others; co-star ABC series Father Dowling Mysteries, 1989-91. Mem. aux. Hosp. Good Samaritan, Los Angeles; chmn. Nat. Crippled Children's Soc., Mo., 1969; bd. dirs. Med. Aux. Center for Health Scis., UCLA, 1977—, Los Angeles Oncologic Inst., 1987—. Recipient numerous awards including Outstanding Actress award Variety Clubs, 1967; awards for vol. work UCLA; Humanitarian award Masons; elected to St. Louis Mcpl. Opera Hall of Fame, 1987; 1st annual Starbiird lectr. Washington U., St. Louis, 1988; nominated best comedy supporting-actress for Sister Act Am. Comedy awards, 1993. Mem. AFTRA, NATAS (Emmy award nomination), SAG, Actors Equity Assn., Acad. Motion Picture Arts and Scis., Phi Mu. Republican. Episcopalian. Office: care Artists Agy 10000 Santa Monica Blvd Los Angeles CA 90067-7007

WICKES, WILLIAM CASTLES, computer research and development section manager; b. Lynwood, Calif., Nov. 25, 1946; s. William Hopkins Wickes and Nancy Rose (Castles) Pantley; m. Susan Jane Monroe, Feb. 17, 1971; children: Kenneth, Lara. BS, UCLA, 1967; MA, Princeton U., 1969, PhD, 1972. Asst. prof. physics Princeton (N.J.) U., 1972-77, U. Md., College Park, 1978-81; rsch. and devel. project mgr. Hewlett Packard, Corvallis, Oreg., 1981—. Author: Synthetic Programming on the HP41, 1980, HP28 Insights, 1988, HP48 Insights, 1991, HP 48 Insights II, 1992; patentee computer designs; contbr. articles on astronomy and astrophysics. Scoutmaster Boy Scouts Am., Corvallis, 1988-90. Mem. Am. Math. Soc., Am. Astron. Soc., Math. Assn. Am. Office: Hewlett Packard Corvallis Divsn 1000 NE Circle Blvd Corvallis OR 97330-4239

WICKIZER, CINDY LOUISE, elementary school educator; b. Pitts., Dec. 12, 1946; d. Charles Sr. and Gloria Geraldine (Cassidy) Zimmerman; m. Leon Leonard Wickizer, Mar. 21, 1971; 1 child, Charlyn Michelle. BS, Oreg. State U., 1968. Tchr. Enumclaw (Wash.) Sch. Dist., 1968—. Mem. NEA, Wash. Edn. Assn., Enumclaw Edn. Assn., Buckley Ednl. Agrl. Coun., Buckley C. of C., Wash. Contract Loggers Assn., Am. Rabbit Breeders Assn. (judge, chmn. scholarship found. 1986-87, pres. 1988—, Disting. Svc. award 1987), Wash. State Rabbit Breeders Assn. (life, President's award 1983), Vancouver Island Rabbit Breeders Assn. (life), Fla. White Rabbit Breeders Assn. (pres. 1984-88), Wash. State Evergreen Rabbit Assn. (sec., v.p. pres.), Alpha Gamma Delta. Home: 26513 112th St E Buckley WA 98321-9720

WICKIZER, MARY ALICE See BURGESS, MARY ALICE

WICKMAN, PAUL EVERETT, public relations executive; b. Bisbee, Ariz., Aug. 21, 1912; s. Julius and Hilda Wilhelmina (Soderholm) W.; m. Evelyn Gorman, Nov. 22, 1969; children by previous marriage: Robert Bruce, Bette Jane, Marilyn Faye. Student, LaSierra U., Arlington, Calif., 1928-30, Pacific Union Coll., Angwin, Cal., 1931-32; spl. student, Am. U., 1946. Min., 1931-53, Internat. traveler, lectr., writer, 1937-44; assoc. sec Internat. Religious Liberty Assn., 1944-46; travel lectr. Nat. Lecture Bur., 1944-55; exec. sec., dir. internat. radio and TV prodns. Voice of Prophecy Corp., Faith for Today Corp., 1946-53; v.p. Western Advt. Agy., Los Angeles, 1953-55; dir. devel. Nat. Soc. Crippled Children and Adults, Inc., Chgo., 1955-56; exec. dir. Pub. Relations Soc. Am., Inc., N.Y.C., 1956-57; dir. corp. pub. relations Schering Corps., Bloomfield, N.J., 1957-58; pres. Wickman Pharm. Co., Inc., Calif., 1959-83, Paul Wickman Co., 1984—. Mem. Newport Beach CSC, mem. Orange County Children's Hosp. Fund; trustee Walla Walla (Wash.) Coll., 1989-91. Mem. Newcomen Soc., Pub. Rels. Soc. Am. (accredited), Internat. Platform Assn., Swedish Club (L.A., past pres.), Newport Beach Country Club, Vikings, 552 Hoag Hosp. Club, Elks, Masons, Shriners, Royal Order Jesters, Kiwanis (past pres. Newport Beach club, lt. gov. Div. 41 Cal-Neva Hi 1990-91). Home and Office: 28 Point Loma Dr Corona Del Mar CA 92625-1026

WICKSTRAND, OWEN CONRAD, real estate developer, consultant; b. Kenosha, Wis., Aug. 5, 1936; s. Roger Richard and Grace Bede (Laudane) W.; m. Patricia Ellen Phillips, Sept. 6, 1958; children: Shan Patricia, Susan Elizabeth. Student, Occidental Coll., 1955, Pasadena City Coll., 1955-56; BS in Mech. Engring., U. Calif., Berkeley, 1961; postgrad., Calif. State U., L.A., 1964-66. Engr. in tng. Continental Can Co., L.A., San Jose, 1955-61; project engr. Continental Can Co., L.A., Chgo., 1963-68; regional v.p. Ind. Securities Corp., La Jolla, Calif., 1968-70; pres. Multi-Lateral Fin. Group, La Jolla, 1970; controller Gibbs Flying Svcs. & Affiliates, San Diego, 1970-73; pres. Univ. Fin., San Diego, 1973-82, Wickstrand Devel. Co., La Jolla, Del Mar, Calif., 1982—; real estate cons. Univ. Fin. Corp., 1982—, La Jolla Bank & Trust Co. (now Bank of Am.), 1986-88, Univ. Redmond Corp., 1987—, Union Fed. Bank, Brea, Calif., 1991-92. Chmn., editor Mission Study of La Jolla Presbyn. Ch., 1972, Mission Study of Chula Vista Presbyn. Ch., 1973, Mission Study of Presbytery of San Diego, 1973; bd. dirs. Airport Planning Com., City of San Diego, 1974-75; treas. Ardis Heiss Election Com., San Diego, 1976. Capt. U.S. Army, 1961-68. Recipient Golden Nugget award Builders and Contractors Assn. Western States, 1982. Mem. Internat. Coun. Shopping Ctrs., Bldg. Owners and Mgrs. Assn., Torrey Pines Mens' Club. Republican. Presbyterian.

WICKWIRE, PATRICIA JOANNE NELLOR, psychologist, educator; b. Sioux City, Iowa; d. William McKinley and Clara Rose (Pautsch) Nellor; BA cum laude, U. No. Iowa, 1951; MA, U. Iowa, 1959; PhD, U. Tex., Austin, 1971; postgrad. U. So. Calif., UCLA, Calif. State U., Long Beach, 1951-66; m. Robert James Wickwire, Sept. 7, 1957; 1 son, William James. Tchr., Ricketts Ind. Schs., Iowa, 1946-48; tchr., counselor Waverly-Shell Rock Ind. Schs., Iowa, 1951-55; reading cons., head dormitory counselor U. Iowa, Iowa City, 1955-57; tchr., sch. psychologist, adminstr. S. Bay Union High Sch. Dist., Redondo Beach, Calif., 1962-82, dir. student svcs. and spl. edn.; cons. mgmt. and edn.; pres. Nellor Wickwire Group, 1981—; mem. exec. bd. Calif. Interagency Mental Health Coun., 1968-72, Beach Cities Symphony Assn., 1970-82; chmn. Friends of Dominguez Hills (Calif.), 1981-85. Lic. ednl. psychologist, marriage, family and child counselor, Calif. Mem. AAUW (exec. bd., chpt. pres. 1962-72), L.A. County Dirs. Pupil Svcs. (chmn. 1974-79), L.A. County Personnel and Guidance Assn. (pres. 1977-78), Assn. Calif. Sch. Adminstrs. (dir. 1977-81), L.A. County SW Bd. Dist. Adminstrs. for Spl. Edn. (chmn. 1976-81), Calif. Assn. Sch. Psychologists (bd. dirs. 1981-83), Am. Psychol. Assn., Am. Assn. Sch. Adminstrs., Calif. Assn. for Measurement and Evaluation in Guidance (dir. 1981, pres. 1984-85), Am. Assn. Counseling and Devel. (chmn. Coun. Newsletter Editors 1989-91, mem. com. on women 1989-92), Assn. Measurement and Eval. in Guidance (Western regional editor 1985-87, conv. chair 1986, editor 1987-90, exec. bd. dirs. 1987-91), Calif. Assn. Counseling and Devel. (exec. bd. 1984—, pres. 1988-89, jour. editor 1990—), Internat. Career Assn. Network (chair 1985—), Pi Lambda Theta, Alpha Phi Gamma, Psi Chi, Kappa Delta Pi, Sigma Alpha Iota. Contbr. articles in field to profl. jours. Home and Office: 2900 Amby Pl Hermosa Beach CA 90254

WIDAMAN, GREGORY ALAN, financial executive, accountant; b. St. Louis, Oct. 4, 1955; s. Raymond Paul Sr. and Louise Agnes (Urschler) W. BS in Bus. Econs. cum laude, Trinity U., 1978. CPA, Tex. Sr. auditor Arthur Andersen & Co., Houston, 1978-82; sr. cons. Price Waterhouse, Houston, 1983-85; fin. advisor to segment pres. Teledyne, Inc., Century City, Calif., 1985—; cons. Arthur Andersen & Co., Price Waterhouse, Teledyne, Inc. Mem. AICPAs, Calif. Soc. CPAs, Christian Bus. Mens com. of U.S.A., World Affairs Coun., MIT/Calif. Tech. Enterprise Forum. Republican. Home: 1416 S Barrington Ave # 4 Los Angeles CA 90025-2363 Office: Teledyne Inc 1901 Avenue Of The Stars Ste 1800 Los Angeles CA 90067-6040

WIDDER, PATRICIA A., helicopter company research and engineering technical specialist; b. Lorain, Ohio, Jan. 30, 1953; d. James Russell and Sallie Grace (Fox) W. BS, John Carroll U., Cleve., 1975; postgrad., Ariz. State U., 1978-86, Keller Grad. Sch. Mgmt., 1992—. Programmer Gould/Sel, Williams AFB, Ariz., 1978-81; programmer, analyst USAF, Williams AFB, 1981-84; R & E specialist McDonnell Douglas Helicopter Co., Mesa, Ariz., 1984—. Contbr. articles to profl. jours. Mem. IEEE Computer Soc., AIAA, Assn. Computing Machinery, Image Soc., Am. Def. Preparedness Assn., Am. Helicopter Soc., Nat. Computer Graphics Assn. Office: McDonnell Douglas Helicopter Combat Simulation & Systems Evaluation 5000 E Mcdowell Rd # 531/C240 Mesa AZ 85205-9707

WIDMAN, JOSEPH JAMES (JAKE WIDMAN), magazine editor; b. Washington, Dec. 6, 1952; s. Joseph William and Marguerite Marie (Phelan) W.; m. Caryn Louise Leschen, June 9, 1985. BA in Anthropology, Brown U., 1974. Sr. editor Oceans, San Francisco, 1983-85, Calif. Waterfront Age, Oakland, 1985-86; editor in chief Publish, San Francisco, 1986—. Editor: Public Beaches, 1987, The Whales of Hawaii, 1988. Democrat. Office: Publish Mag 501 2d St San Francisco CA 94107

WIDMANN, GLENN ROGER, electrical engineer; b. Newark, Jan. 8, 1957; s. Elmer and Ellen (Eccles) W. BSEE, Rutgers U., 1979; MSEE, Purdue U., 1981, PhDEE, 1988. Engr. N.J. Bell Telephone Co., Hopelawn, 1979; instr. Purdue U., West Lafayette, Ind., 1979-81, 83-88; prof. elec. engring. Colo. State U., Ft. Collins, 1989-91; engr. Hughes Aircraft Co., Canoga Park, Calif., 1980-83, scientist, project mgr., 1991—; cons. Bur. Reclamation, Denver, 1989, Benjamin Cummings Pub. Co., Ft. Collins, 1989; mem. program com. Internat. Symposium Robotics and Mfg., Santa Fe, N.Mex., 1991—. Contbr. articles to tech. jours.; patentee in robotics field. Recipient presentation award Am. Controls Conf., 1990. Mem. IEEE, Soc. Automotive Engrs., Tau Beta Pi, Eta Kappa Nu. Office: Hughes Aircraft Co MS N54 8433 Fallbrook Ave Canoga Park CA 91309-7928

WIDMER, KINGSLEY, educator, writer; b. Mpls., July 17, 1925; s. Vera Estes (Bingham) W.; children: Matthew, Jonah. Student, U. Wis., 1942-43; BA magna cum laude, U. Minn., 1949, MA, 1951; PhD, U. Wash., 1957. Instr. Reed Coll., 1955-56; prof. English San Diego State U., 1956-91, prof. emeritus, 1991—; vis. prof. English U. Calif., Berkeley, 1960-61, Tel Aviv, U., 1963-64, Simon Fraser U., Vancouver, Can., 1967, SUNY, Buffalo, 1974, U. Tulsa, 1975, 76, 78. Author: Art of Perversity: D.H. Lawrence, 1962, Henry Miller, 1963, 70, 90, The Literary Rebel, 1965, Ways of Nihlism: Melville's Short Novels, 1970, The End of Culture, 1975, Paul Goodman, 1980, Edges of Extremity: Problems of Literary Modernism, 1980, Nathaneal West, 1982, Counterings: Utopian Dialectics, 1988, Defiant Desire, 1992; editor: Literary Censorship, 1960, Freedom & Culture, 1970; contbr. poems, social criticism, personal essays in profl. jours. editor, contbr. anarchist jours. With U.S. Army, 1943-46, PTO and ETO. Ford Found. fellow, 1955, Fulbright fellow, 1963, Nat. Endowment for the Humanities fellow, 1979, 82, 85, Inst. for Humane Studies fellow, 1980. Home: 1743 Haydn Dr Cardiff By The Sea CA 92007-2305

WIDMER, RICHARD WILLIAM, computer system manager; b. Twin Falls, Idaho, Jan. 5, 1957; s. Eugene Carrol and Edythe (Nielsen) W. Student, Computer Sci. Inst. Mechanic Widmer's Texaco, Kimberly, Idaho, 1970-73; electronic tech. Raytheon Svc. Co., Virginia Beach, Va., 1980, Heathkit Electronic Ctr., Louisville, 1980-81; stereo installer Sound Co., Twin Falls, 1982-84, Audio Warehouse, Twin Falls, 1986-87; computer programmer Coll. So. Idaho, Twin Falls, 1987-93; owner CR Technology, Twin Falls, 1993—. With USN, 1974-80. Mem. Assn. of Computing Machines (voting mem. 1993). Office: CR Tech 141 Shoshone Ave N Ste 203A Twin Falls ID 83301

WIEBE, JACQUELINE CATHERINE, clinical research associate; b. Neustadt an der Weinstrasse, West Germany, Mar. 24, 1957; came to U.S., 1958; d. Franklin Edward and Frieda (Minder) W. BA in Music, San Jose State U., 1980. Music dir. San Jose City Coll. Shakespeare Festival, 1976-77; guest conductor San Jose State U. Faculty Artist Series, 1978-79; music dir. San Jose Civic Light Opera, 1981; asst. conductor San Jose Symphony Orch., 1978-86; staff conductor San Jose Symphony/Opera, 1979-84; clin. data specialist Syntex Rsch., Palo Alto, Calif., 1981-83; bioanalyst Syntex Rsch., Palo Alto, 1983-88, clin. rsch. assoc., 1988—; violist Willow String Quartet, No. Calif., 1985—, Palo Alto Philharm., 1989—. Mem. Assocs. Clin. Pharmacology, No. Calif. Pharm. Discussion Group, Assocs. Clin. Pharmacology, Am. Fedn. Musicians. Democrat. Office: Syntex Rsch 3401 Hillview Ave Palo Alto CA 94304-1397

WIEBE, LEONARD IRVING, radiopharmacist, educator; b. Swift Current, Sask., Can., Oct. 14, 1941; s. Cornelius C. and Margaret (Teichroeb) W.; m. Grace E. McIntyre, Sept. 5, 1964; children: Glenis, Kirsten, Megan. BSP, U. Sask., 1963, MS, 1966; PhD, U. Sydney, Australia, 1970. Pharmacist Swift Current Union Hosp., 1963-64; sessional lectr. U. Sask., Can., 1965-66; asst. prof. U. Alta., Can., 1970-73, assoc. prof., 1973-78, prof., 1978—, dir. Slowpoke Reactor Facility, 1975-89, asst. dean rsch., 1984-87; assoc. dean U. Alta., 1990—; sessional lectr. U. Sydney, Australia, 1973; pres. Internat. Bionucleonics Cons. Lts., 1991—; dir. BMH, Australian Nuclear Sci. Tech. Orgn., 1990; rsch. assoc. Cross Cancer Inst., Edmonton, 1978—, med. Rsch. Coun. Can.; vis. prof. Royal P.A. Hosp., Sydney, 1983-84, Searle vis. profl., 1986; MRC vis. prof., Toronto, 1987; PMAC vis. prof., 1988; McCalla prof. U. Alt., 1993-94; radiopharmacy cons. Australian Atomic Energy Commn., Sydney, 1983-84. Editor: Liquid Scintillation: Science and Technology, 1976; Advanced in Scintillation Counting, 1983; guest editor Jour. of Radioanalytical Chemistry, 1981; editor Internat. Jour. Applied Radiation Instrumentation Sect. A, 1988-90; regional editor Internat. Jour. Nuclear Biology and Medicine, 1992—. Commonwealth Univs. Exchange grantee, 1966; Alexander von Humboldt fellow, 1976-79, 82. Mem. Pharm. Bd. of New South Wales, Sask. Pharm. Assn., Soc. Nuclear Medicine, Assn. Faculties of Pharmacy of Can. (McNeil Rsch. award 1988), Can. Radiation Protection Assn., Can. Assn. Radiopharm. Scientists, Am. Pharm. Assn., Am. Assn. Pharm. Sci., Australian Nuclear Sci. Tech. Orgn. (bd. dirs. biomedicine and health 1990), Internat. Assn. Radiopharmacy (exec. sec. 1991—), University Club (Edmonton). Mem. Mennonite Ch.

WIEBE, MICHAEL EUGENE, microbiologist, cell biologist; b. Newton, Kans., Oct. 1, 1942; s. Austin Roy and Ruth Fern (Stucky) W.; m. Rebecca Ann Doak, June 12, 1965; children: Brandon Clark, Thomas Huntington. BS, Sterling Coll., 1965; PhD, U. Kansas, 1971. Rsch. assoc. Duke U. Med. Ctr., Durham, N.C., 1971-73; asst. prof. Cornell U. Med. Coll., N.Y.C., 1973-81, assoc. prof., 1981-85; assoc. dir. rsch. and devel. N.Y. Blood Ctr., N.Y.C., 1980-83, dir. Leukocyte products, 1983-84; sr. scientist Genentech Inc., South San Francisco, Calif., 1984-88, assoc. dir. medicinal and analytical chemistry, 1988-90, dir. quality control, 1990—. Contbr. articles to profl. jours. Mem. Sterling Coll. Bd. of Trustees, 1990—. Postdoctoral fellow NIH, 1971-73. Mem. AAAS, Am. Soc. for Microbiology, Am. Soc. Virology, Soc. Exptl. Biology and Medicine, Parenteral Drug Assn. Presbyterian. Home: 44 Woodhill Dr Redwood City CA 94061-1827 Office: Genentech Inc 460 Point San Bruno Blvd South San Francisco CA 94080-4918

WIEBELHAUS, PAMELA SUE, educator; b. Stanley, Wis., May 28, 1952; d. Wilbur Leroy and Marjorie Jean (Bernse) Thorne; m. Mark Robert Wiebelhaus, Apr. 27, 1985; 1 child, Sarah Jean. AS in Nursing, No. Ariz. U., 1973, BS in Gen. Home Econs., 1974. R.N. Ariz., Colo; cert. post secondary voct. tchr., Colo. Nurse Flagstaff (Ariz.) Community Hosp., 1973-75, Children's Hosp., Denver, 1975, St. Joseph's Hosp., Denver, 1980; office nurse, surg. asst. OB-Gyn Assocs., P.C., Aurora, Colo., 1975-78; nursing coordinator perinatal services Community Hosp. Smaritan Health, Phoenix, 1978-79; nurse, mem. personnel pool Good Samaritan Hosp., Phoenix, 1979-80, J. Bains, MD, Phoenix, 1979-80; file clk. Pharm. Card Systems, Inc., Phoenix, 1979-80; office nurse S. Eisenbaum, MD, Aurora, Colo., 1980; instr., coordinator mem. office program T.H. Pickens Tech. Ctr., Aurora (Colo.) Pub. Schs., 1980—; med. supr. healthfair sites, Denver, 1982-85; mem. adv. com. Emily Griffith Opportunity Sch., Denver, 1984-90; mem. survey team North Cen. Bd. Edn., 1985, Colo. Bd. Edn., Denver, 1987. Acad. scholar No. Ariz. U., 1970, nat. def. grantee, 1970-74; PTA and Elks Club scholar, 1970. Mem. Am. Assn. Med. Assts. (cert.; membership chmn. Capitol chpt. Colo. Soc. 1981). Lutheran.

WIEDERHOLD, BRENDA KAY, financial analyst, consultant; b. Falfurrias, Tex., July 27, 1960; d. Melvin Joseph and Ona Lee (Raglin) Wishard; m. Mark Dale Wiederhold, Aug. 15, 1992. BBA, Tex. A&M U., 1982; MBA, Chapman U., 1992. Cert. govt. auditor. Acct. King Ranch, Inc., Kingsville, Tex., 1982-85; internal bank auditor MCorp Bank Mgmt. Co., Corpus Christi, 1985-86; head of internal audit U.S. Naval Mag., Subic Bay, Philippines, 1987-89; sr. fin. analyst Dyna-Plex Venture Capital Corp., San Diego, 1989-92; pres. The Brynmar Fin. Group, San Diego, 1992—; CFO Med. Techs. Applications, San Diego, 1992—. Mem. S.D. Rep. Bus. Women, San Diego, 1991-92; mem. fund-raising com. Am. Cancer Soc., Corpus Christi, 1985-86; mem. election com. Reagan Presdl. Campaign, Kingsville, 1980, 84. ZTA Merit scholar, 1980-82. Mem. NAFE, Women's Inst. for Fin. Edn. (Profl. Forum), Rancho Santa Fe Bus. and Profl. Women, Zeta Tau Alpha, Alpha Lambda Delta, Delta Mu Delta. Republican. Office: The Brynmar Fin Group 10896 Terraza Floracion San Diego CA 92127

WIEDERHOLT, WIGBERT C., neurologist, educator; b. Germany, Apr. 22, 1931; came to U.S., 1956, naturalized, 1966; m. Carl and Anna-Maria (Hoffmann) W.; student (Med. Sch. scholar), U. Berlin, 1952-53; M.D., U. Freiburg, 1955; M.S., U. Minn., 1965; children—Sven, Karen, Kristin. Intern in Ob-Gyn, Schleswig (W. Ger.) City Hosp., 1955-56; rotating intern Sacred Heart Hosp., Spokane, Wash., 1956-57; resident in medicine Cleve. Clinic, 1957-58, 60-62, U.S. Army Hosp., Frankfurt, W. Ger., 1958-59; resident in neurology Mayo Clinic, Rochester, Minn., 1962-65; assoc. prof. medicine, dir. clin. neurophysiology Ohio State U. Med. Sch., Columbus, 1966-72; prof. neuroscis. U. Calif. Med. Sch., San Diego, 1972—, neurologist-in-chief, 1973-83, chmn. dept. and group in neuroscis. 1990-93; chief neurology VA Hosp., San Diego, 1972-79. Fulbright scholar, 1956-58. Diplomate Am. Bd. Psychiatry and Neurology. Fellow Am. Acad. Neurology (S. Weir Mitchell award 1956); mem. Internat. Brain Research Orgn., Am. Assn. EEG and Electrodiagnosis (sec.-treas. 1971-76, pres. 1977-78), AAAS, Soc. for Neurosci., Am. Neurol. Assn., Am. EGG Soc., Western EEG Soc., Calif. Neurol. Soc., San Diego Neurol. Soc., N.Y. Acad. Scis., AMA, Calif. Med. Assn., San Diego County Med. Soc. Club: La Jolla Tennis. Contbr. numerous articles to med. jours. Home: 6683 S La Jolla Scenic Dr La Jolla CA 92037-5735 Office: Univ Calif at San Diego Dept Neuroscis 0624 La Jolla CA 92093-0624

WIEDERSPAHN, ALVIN LEE, lawyer, former state senator; b. Cheyenne, Wyo., Jan. 18, 1949; s. John Arling and Edvina (Fahrenbruch) W.; m. Cynthia Marie Lummis, May 30, 1983; 1 child, Annaliese. BS, U. Wyo., 1971; JD, U. Denver, 1976. Bar: Wyo. 1978, U.S. Dist. Ct. Wyo. 1978, U.S. Ct. Appeals (10th cir.) 1985. Assoc. Guy, Williams & White, Cheyenne, 1977-79, Kline & Swainson, Cheyenne, 1979-81, Holland & Hart, Cheyenne, 1981-85; ptnr. Wiederspahn, Lummis & Liepas, P.C., Cheyenne, 1985-89; senator State of Wyo., Cheyenne, 1984-88; chmn. Rocky Mountain Bank F.S.B., Cheyenne, 1988—, Rocky Mountain Fin. Corp., 1990—. Mem. Wyo. Ho. of Reps., Cheyenne, 1979-84; chmn. Devel. Disabilities Protection and Advocacy System, Cheyenne, 1980-84, S.E. Wyo. Mental Health Ctrs., Cheyenne, 1982-85, Wyo. Gov.'s Task Force on Chronically Mentally Ill, 1984-87, Wyo. Energy Conservation Office, 1980-83, Cheyenne Downtown Devel. Authority, 1984-88; pres. Assn. for Retarded Citizens, Cheyenne, 1979-81, 90-92; bd. dirs. Symphony and Choral Soc., Cheyenne, 1984-86, COMEA Homeless Shelter, 1992—, chmn. bldg. com.; pres. Wyo. Taxpayers Assn., 1990-92; bd. dirs. Trinity Luth. Sch., 1991—, sec. 1992—. Named Outstanding Vol., Youth Alternatives, 1982; recipient Disting. Svc. award Rocky Mountain Conf. Community Mental Health Ctrs., Outstanding Svc. award Assn. for Retarded Citizens, 1986, Downtown Devel. Authority Mayors award, 1987. Mem. ABA (pub. utility sect.), Wyo. State Bar. Democrat. Lutheran. Home: 3905 Bent Ave Cheyenne WY 82001-1132 Office: 2020 Carey Ave Cheyenne WY 82001-3639

WIEDLE, GARY EUGENE, real estate management company executive; b. San Antonio, July 28, 1944; s. Eugene Wiley and Melba Frances (Keeney) W.; m. Regena Zokosky, July 7, 1977 (div. June 1983); children: Ana Lauren, Aric Brandt. AA, Coll. of the Desert, Palm Desert, Calif., 1975; BA, Calif. State U., Long Beach, 1967; MA, U. So. Calif., 1973. Lic. real estate broker, Calif.; cert. profl. community assn. mgr. Adminstrv. asst. City of Inglewood, Calif., 1967-68, asst. city mgr., 1970-74; exec. dir. Coachella Valley Assn. of Govts., Palm Desert, 1974-84; mgr. The Springs Country Club, Rancho Mirage, Calif., 1984-87; prof. polit. sci. Coll of the Desert, Palm Desert, 1987-90; owner Fortune West Mgmt., Palm Desert, 1990—; cons. polit. orgns., bus. and community groups, Riverside County, Calif., 1984—. Dept. comdr. DAV, Dept. Calif., 1982. 1st lt. U.S. Army, 1968-70, Vietnam. Decorated Bronze Star for valor, Purple Heart, Commendation of valor. Mem. Am. Inst. Cert. Planners (cert. planner), Community Assns. Inst. (pres. 1986-89), Calif. Assn. Community Mgrs., Real Estate Educators Cert. Inst., Bd. Realtors Palm Desert, Am. Planning Assn., Western Govtl. Rsch. Assn. Republican. Lutheran. Home: 82-362 Gable Dr Indio CA 92201-7439 Office: Fortune West Mgmt GE Wiedle Co 73-900 El Paseo Ste 3 (rear) Palm Desert CA 92260

WIEL, STEPHEN, state official; b. San Francisco, Jan. 9, 1939; s. Alan S. and Jane (Davis) W.; m. Karen Thompson, Sept. 30, 1961; children: Devon Elizabeth, Colin Thompson. BSChemE, Stanford U., 1960, MSChemE, 1961; PhD, U. Pitts., 1972. Registered profl. engr., Nev. Engr. McDonnell Douglas Corp., Santa Monica, Calif., 1961-68; cons. S. Wiel & Assocs., Washington, 1969-72; exec. v.p. Airways Engring. Corp., Washington, 1973-76; pres. S. Wiel & Assocs., Reno, 1976-81, Xenarcz Inc., Reno, 1981-84; mem. Nev. Pub. Svc. Commn., Carson City, 1984—; profl. lectr., 1972-76; instr. solar bldg. design and energy conservation Truckee Meadows C.C., 1978-80; asst. prof. mech. engring. U. Nev., Reno, 1980-84; bd. dirs. Alliance To Save Energy, 1987—, Am. Coun. for Energy Efficient Economy, 1988—; presenter on energy and environ. issues, 1959—; mem. Keystone Project on Global Warming, Keystone Project on State/Fed. Regulatory Jurisdictional Issues Affecting Electricity. Contbr. numerous articles to profl. jours. Co-founder, pres. Nev. Solar Energy Advs., Reno, 1979-84; mem. Truckee Meadows Air Quality Task Force, 1978—, Sparks (Nev.) Energy Adv. Com., 1982-83. Mem. ASCE, ASHRAE, NSPE, AICE, AIAA, Nat. Assn. Regional Utility Commrs. (chmn. conservation com. 1986-89, mem. exec. com.), Western Conf. Pub. Svc. Commrs. (pres. 1987-88), Soc. Automotive Engrs. (nat. com. SC-9), Am. Planning Assn., Air Pollution Control Assn., Passive Solar Industries Coun. (nat. bd. dirs.). Democrat. Home: 2071 Mountain Vista Way Reno NV 89509 Office: Nev Pub Svc Commn 727 Fairview Dr Carson City NV 89710

WIEMANN, JOHN MORITZ, communications educator, consultant; b. New Orleans, July 11, 1947; s. John M. and Mockie (Oosthuizen) W.; m. Mary Eileen O'Loghlin, June 7, 1969; children: Molly E., John M. BA, Loyola U., New Orleans, 1969; postgrad., NYU, 1970-71; MS, Purdue U., 1973, PhD, 1975. With employee communications dept. IBM, East Fishkill, N.Y., 1969-71; asst. prof. Rutgers U., New Brunswick, N.J., 1975-77; from asst. prof. to prof. communication U. Calif., Santa Barbara, 1977—. Editor: Nonverbal Interaction, 1983, Advancing Communication Science, 1988, Communication, Health and the Elderly, 1990, Miscommunication and Problematic Talk, 1991, Strategic Interpersonal Communication, 1993; series editor Sage Ann. Rev. Communication Rsch., 1988—. Bd. dirs. Goleta Youth Basketball Assn., 1987-92; mem. sch. site coun. Foothill Elem. Sch., 1987-88, budget adv. com. Goleta Union Sch. Dist., 1982-84. David Ross fellow Purdue U., 1975, W.K. Kellogg Found. fellow, 1980-83; Fulbright-Hayes sr. research scholar U. Bristol, U.K., 1985. Mem. Internat. Communication Assn. (bd. dirs. 1988-90), Speech Communication Assn. (bd. dirs. 1984-86), Am. Psychol. Assn., Western States Communication Assn., Internat. Network on Personal Rels., Internat. Pragmatics Assn., Sigma Xi, Phi Kappa Phi. Democrat. Roman Catholic. Office: U Calif Dept Comm Santa Barbara CA 93106-4020

WIEMER, ROBERT ERNEST, film and television producer, writer, director; b. Highland Park, Mich., Jan. 30, 1938; s. Carl Ernest and Marion (Israelian) W.; m. Rhea Dale McGeath, June 14, 1958; children: Robert Marshall, Rhea Whitney. BA, Ohio Wesleyan U., 1959. Ind. producer, 1956-60; dir. documentary ops. WCBS-TV, N.Y.C., 1964-67; ind. producer of television, theatrical and bus. films N.Y.C., 1967-72; exec. producer motion pictures and TV, ITT, N.Y.C., 1973-84; pres. subs. Blue Marble Co., Inc., Telemontage, Inc., Alphaventure Music, Inc., Betaventure Music, Inc. ITT, 1973-84; founder, chmn., chief exec. officer Tigerfilm, Inc., 1984—; chmn., bd. dirs. Golden Tiger Pictures, Hollywood, Calif., 1988—; pres, CEO Tuxedo Pictures Corp., Hollywood, Calif., 1993—; bd. dirs. Princeton-Am. Communications, Inc., 1986-87. Writer, producer, dir. feature films: My Seventeenth Summer, Witch's Sister, Do Me a Favor, Anna to the Infinite Power, Somewhere, Tomorrow, Night Train to Kathmandu; exec. producer Emmy and Peabody award winning children's TV series Big Blue Marble; dir. TV episodes Star Trek: The Next Generation, The Adventures of Superboy; composer (country-western ballad) Tell Me What To Do; child actor Jam Handy Orgn., Detroit, 1946-48. Deacon Dutch Reform Ch. in Am. Served to capt. USAF, 1960-64. Recipient CINE award, 1974, 76, 77, 79, 81, Emmy award, 1978. Mem. NATAS, ASCAP, Info. Film Producers Assn. (Outstanding Producer award), Nat. Assn. TV Programming Execs., Am. Women in Radio and TV, N.J. Broadcasters Assn., Dirs. Guild Am. Office: Golden Tiger Pictures 205 S Beverly Dr Ste 200 Beverly Hills CA 90212

WIENER, DAVID JON, author, editor; b. Milw., Feb. 7, 1957; s. Robert and Marilyn (Kagan) W.; m. Susan Youngdale, Jan. 11, 1986. BA in Comm. cum laude, U. Calif., San Diego, 1978. Assoc. editor, book reviewer POV Mag., Beverly Hills, Calif., 1990—; conductor seminars U. Calif., San Diego State U., U. San Diego, others. Assoc. editor Producers Guild of Am. Jour.; Voice of Am. corres. L.A. Bur.; PBS radio documentary producer; exec. producer: The Secret History of the Atomic Bomb; contbr. numerous articles to profl. jours. Founder, mgr. LaJolla (Calif.) Playreader/Play Discover Group, 1992. SIP grantee for film, 1974. Mem. Authors Guild, Inc. Address: PO Box 12193 La Jolla CA 92039

WIENER, JON, history educator; b. St. Paul, May 16, 1944; s. Daniel N. and Gladys (Aronsohn) Spratt. BA, Princeton U., 1966; PhD, Harvard U., 1971. Vis. prof. U. Calif.-Santa Cruz, 1973; acting asst. prof. UCLA, 1973-74; asst. prof. history U. Calif.-Irvine, 1974-83, prof., 1984—; plaintiff Freedom of Info. Lawsuit against FBI for John Lennon Files, 1983—. Author: Social Origins of the New South, 1979; Come Together: John Lennon in his Time, 1984, Professors, Politics, and Pop, 1991; contbg. editor The Nation mag.; contbr. articles to profl. jours. including The New Republic and New York Times Book Review. Rockefeller Found. fellow, 1979, Am. Council Learned Socs.-Ford Found. fellow, 1985. Mem. Am. Hist. Assn., Nat. Book Critics Circle, Orgn. Am. Historians, Nat. Writers' Union, The Authors' Guild, So. Hist. Assn. Office: U Calif Dept History Irvine CA 92717

WIENER, MICHAEL CHARLES, biophysicist; b. Long Branch, N.J., May 24, 1962; s. Albert Wiener and Arlene (Kraft) Fox; m. Anne Elizabeth Schwartz, July 12, 1987; 1 child, Simon Albert. BS in Physics, U. Rochester, 1983; MS in Physics, Carnegie Mellon U., 1985, PhD in Physics and Biophysics, 1988. Postgrad. researcher dept. physiology and biophysics U. Calif., Irvine, 1988-91; postgrad researcher dept. biochemistry and biophysics U. Calif., San Francisco, 1991—. Contbr. articles to profl. jours. Mem. Am. Phys. Soc. (Biol. Physics div.), Biophys. Soc. Office: U Calif Dept Biochemistry & Biophysics San Francisco CA 94143-0448

WIENER, SYDNEY PAUL, mortgage broker; b. N.Y.C., Aug. 18, 1918; s. Nathan and Lillian (Fortunoff) W.; m. Charlotte Rosen, Jan. 28, 1945; children: Laura Jane Mills, Barbara Hanawalt. DMD, U. Louisville, 1943. Gen. practice dentistry Flushing, N.Y., 1947-68; pvt. investor El Cajon, Calif., 1968—; mortgage sales rep. El Cajon, 1972—; dentist Booth Meml. Hosp., Flushing, 1963-68; researcher Anti-Coronary Club N.Y.C. Dept. Health, 1962-67. Contbr. articles on coronary disease, remedial edn., intergovt. rels. to profl. jours. Past bd. dirs. Calif. Community and Jr. Colls.; bd. dirs. Calif. Community Coll. Trustees, Sacramento, 1975-89; chmn. bd. trustees Grossmont-Cuyamaca Community Coll. Dist., El Cajon, 1973-90; dep. sheriff San Diego Sheriff Aero-squadron, 1971-82; pres. El Cajon San Diego County Civic Ctr. Authority, 1973-77; fundraiser East County Performing Arts Ctr, El Cajon, cons. to bd. dirs. Capt. U.S. Army, 1941-47. Recipient Commendation, Sheriff Maricopa County, Phoenix, 1981, Sheriff San Diego County, 1981; award, City El Cajon, 1973-74, Associated Students Grossmont Coll., El Cajon, 1975, 91, Grossmont Coll. Learning Skills, 1983, Calif. Community Coll. Trustees award, 1987, Trustee Emeritus award, 1990, Cuyamaca Coll., 1990, Grossmont/Cuyamaca Community Coll. Dist., 1991. Democrat. Jewish.

WIENER, VALERIE, communications company executive; b. Las Vegas, Nev., Oct. 30, 1948; d. Louis Isaac and Tui Ava (Knight) W. BJ, U. Mo., 1971, MA, 1972; MA, Sangamon State U., 1974; postgrad., McGeorge Sch. Law, 1976-79. Producer TV show "Checkpoint" Sta. KOMU-TV, Columbia, Mo., 1972-73; v.p., owner Broadcast Assocs., Inc., Las Vegas, 1972-86; pub. affairs dir. First Ill. Cable TV, Springfield, 1973-74; editor Ill. State Register, Springfield, 1973-74; producer and talent "Nevada Realities" Sta. KLVX-TV, Las Vegas, 1974-75; account exec. Sta. KBMI (now KFMS), Las Vegas, 1975-79; nat. traffic dir. six radio stas., Las Vegas, Albuquerque and El Paso, Tex., 1979-80; exec. v.p., gen. mgr. Stas. KXKS and KKJY, Albuquerque, 1980-81; exec. adminstr. Stas. KSET AM/FM, KVEG, KFMS and KKJY, 1981-83; press sec. U.S. Congressman Harry Reid, Washington, 1983-86; adminstrv. asst Friends for Harry Reid, Nev., 1986; press sec. U.S. Senator Harry Reid, Washington, 1987-88; owner Wiener Communications Group, Las Vegas, 1988—. Author: Power Communications: Positioning for High Visibility; contbg. writer The Pacesetter. Sponsor Futures for Children, Las Vegas, Albuquerque and El Paso, 1979-83; mem. Exec. Women's Coun., El Paso, 1981-83; mem. VIP bd. Easter Seals, El Paso, 1982; appointee, media chair Gov.'s Coun. Small Bus., 1989-93, Clark Coun. Sch. Dist. and Bus. Community PAYBAC Speaker's and Partnership Programs, 1989-93; media dir. 1990 Conf. on women Gov. of Nev.; media chair Congl. Awards Coun., 1989-93; media chair, nat. rep. Nat. Assn. Women Bus. Owners, So. Nev., 1990-91; appointee Gov.'s Commn. Postsecondary Edn. Named Outstanding Vol. United Way, El Paso, 1983, finalist Women of Achievement in Media, 1990, 91, winner Women of Achievement in Media, 1992, SBA Nev. Sml. Bus. Media Advocate of Yr., 1992; recipient 35 1st pl. Nev. Press Women Media awards, 1990-93, Outstanding Achievement award Nat. Fedn. Press Women, 1991, numerous other awards. Mem. NAFE, Nev. Press Assn., Nat. Speakers Assn., Internat. Speakers Network, Nat. Assn. Women Bus. Owners (Nev. Advocate of Yr. 1992), Dem. Pres. Secs. Assn., El Paso Assn. Radio Stas., U.S. Senate Staff Club, L.V. C. of C., Soc. Profl. Journalists. Democrat. Christian Scientist. Office: 1500 Foremaster Ln Ste 2 Las Vegas NV 89101-1103

WIENS, DUANE DATON, matrix-graphic design firm owner; b. Inman, Jan. 13, 1935; s. Jacob D. and Anna Marie (Dirks) W.; m. Barbara A. Hege, Nov. 5, 1959 (div. Nov. 1984); children: Brian V., David K.; m. Paula M. Streiff, Aug. 18, 1990; stepson, Luke Ouellette. Art sch. diploma, Colo. Inst. of Art, 1964. Graphic designer Hesdorfer Comml. Art, Denver, 1964-65, McCormick-Armstrong Printing, Wichita, Kans., 1965-67; co-founder, ptnr. Unit 1/ Graphic Design, Denver, 1967-78; founder, owner Matrix Internat. Assocs., Denver, 1978—. Works published in profl. jours. Inductee Hall of Fame, Colo. Inst. of Art, 1989, Nat. Hall of Fame, Nat. Assn. Trade and Tech. Schs., 1990. Mem. Art Dirs. Club of Denver. Home: 7269 S Cook Cir Littleton CO 80122 Office: Matrix Internat Assocs 50 S Steele Ste 875 Denver CO 80209

WIESE, WAYNE WALTER, geologist, consultant, computer scientist; b. Milw., May 23, 1953; s. Marcella Hulda (Buob) W.; m. Sandra Sue Potter; children: Brian Matthew, Melissa Ann. BS in Geology, U. Wis., 1975, MS in Oceanography and Limnology, 1977. Rsch. asst. Marine Rsch. Lab., Madison, Wis., 1975-77; from prodn. geologist to coord. computer applications Gulf Oil Exploration and Prodn. Co., Houston, 1977-85; coord. computer applications, info. systems advisor Chevron Overseas Petroleum, Inc., San Ramon, Calif., 1985-89; coord. upstream info. systems Chevron Overseas Petroleum, Inc., San Ramon, 1993—; computer and support svcs. cons. Chevron Nigeria Ltd., Lagos, 1989-92, mgr. exploration, production computer svcs., 1992-93. Author: (instrn. manual) EDBINDEX Users Guide, 1984, Exploration Software Usage I, II, III, 1983, Production Software Usage I, II, 1982, Overview Course, 1983. Recipient Outstanding Contbn. award Houston Geol. Soc. 1985, Svc. award 1984. Mem. Am. Assn. Petroleum Geologists, Soc. Petroleum Engrs., Delta Upsilon (pres. Wis. chpt. 1975). Office: Chevron Overseas Petroleum PO Box 5046 San Ramon CA 94583-0946

WIESENTHAL, ANDREW MICHAEL, pediatrician; b. N.Y.C., Mar. 5, 1950; s. Jerome Mitchell and Gladys (Heilig) W.; m. Billie Gunkel, July 1, 1978. BA, Yale U., 1971; MD, SUNY, Bklyn., 1975. Diplomate, Am. bd. Pediatrics. Intern U. Colo. Health Scis. Ctr., Denver, 1975-76; resident in pediatrics U. Colo. Health Scis. Ctr., 1976-78, fellow in pediatric infectious disease, 1980-83, instr. pediatrics, 1982-84, clin. asst. prof. pediatrics, 1984—; epidemic intelligence svc. officer Ctrs. Disease Control/USPHS, Atlanta, 1978-80; pediatrician Colo. Permanente Med. Group, Denver, 1983—, chief pediatrics Arapahoe facility, 1987-89, dir. quality assurance, 1988—; clin. assoc. dept. pediatrics So. Ill. U., Springfield, 1979-80; bd. dirs. Colo. Permanente Med. Group, Denver, 1988—, chmn. bd. dirs., 1991—. Contbr. numerous articles to profl. jours. Mem. Am. Acad. Pediatrics, Epidemic Intelligence Svc. Alumni Assn., Denver Med. Soc. Jewish. Home: 6 Ivy Ln Denver CO 80220-5314 Office: Colo Permanente Med Group 2045 Franklin St Denver CO 80205-5409

WIESER, SIEGFRIED, planetarium executive director; b. Linz, Austria, Oct. 30, 1933; came to Can., 1955; s. Florian Wieser and Michaela Josepha (Kaufmann) Wieser-Burgstaller; m. Joan Xaven Quick, Sept. 8, 1962; children: Leonard Franz, Bernard Sidney. BS in Physics, U. Calgary, Alta., Can., 1966. Lead chorus singer, dancer Landes Theatre, Linz, 1949-53; project engr. EBG, Linz, 1952-54; with Griffith Farms Ltd., Eng., 1954-55; seismic computer operator Shell Can., Calgary, 1956-61; GTA systems analyst U. Calgary, 1961-66; planetarium dir. Centennial Planetarium, Calgary, 1966-84, exec. dir., 1984-91; exec. dir. emeritus Alberta Sci. Ctr., 1991—; cons. Electro Controls, Salt Lake City, 1978-79. Contbr. articles to profl. publs. Recipient Violet Taylor award U. Calgary, 1964; Queen Elizabeth scholar Province Alta., 1961; Paul Marris fellow Rotary Internat. Mem. AAAS, Royal Astron. Soc. Can., Internat. Planetarium Soc., Can. Planetarium Soc., Can. Mus. Assn., Alberta Coll. of Art Alumni Assn. (pres. 1991-92). Anglican. Club: Magic Circle (Calgary).

WIGGINS, CHARLES EDWARD, federal judge; b. El Monte, Calif., Dec. 3, 1927; s. Louis J. and Margaret E. (Fanning) W.; m. Yvonne L. Boots, Dec. 30, 1946 (dec. Sept. 1971); children: Steven L., Scott D.; m. Betty J. Koontz, July 12, 1972. B.S., U. So. Calif., 1953, LL.B., 1956; LL.B. (hon.) Ohio Wesleyan, 1975, Han Yang. U., Seoul, Korea, 1976. Bar: Calif. 1957, D.C. 1978. Lawyer, Woods & Wiggins, El Monte, Calif., 1956-66, Musick, Peeler & Garrett, Los Angeles, 1979-81, Pierson, Ball & Dowd, Washington, 1982-84, Pillsbury, Madison & Sutro, San Francisco, 1984; mem. 90-95th congresses from 25th and 39th Calif. Dists.; judge U.S. Ct. Appeals 9th Circuit, 1984—. Mayor City of El Monte, Calif., 1964-66; mem. Planning Commn. City of El Monte, 1956-60; mem. Commn. on Bicentennial of U.S. Constitution, 1985—, mem. standing com. on rules of practice and procedure, 1987—. Served to 1st lt. U.S. Army, 1945-48, 50-52, Korea. Mem. ABA, State Bar Calif., D.C. Bar Assn. Republican. Lodge: Lions. Office: US Ct Appeals 9th Cir 50 W Liberty St Ste 950 Reno NV 89501-1949

WIGGLESWORTH, DAVID CUNNINGHAM, business and management consultant; b. Passaic, N.J., Sept. 23, 1927; s. Walter Frederick and Janet (Cunningham) W.; m. Rita Domínguez, Mar. 15, 1956 (dec.); children: Mitchell Murray, Marc David, Miles Frederick, Janet Rose; m. Gayle Coates, Aug. 1, 1981; 1 child, Danielle. BA, Occidental Coll., 1950, MA, 1953; postgrad. U. de las Ams., 1954-56; PhD, U. East Fla., 1957; LHD (hon.), Arubaanse Handels Academie, 1969. Dir., Spoken English Inst., Mexico City, also lectr. Mexico City Coll., 1954-56; headmaster Harding Acad., Glendale, Calif., also lectr. Citrus Jr. Coll., 1956-58; dir. Burma-Am. Inst., Rangoon, 1958-60; project dir. Washington Ednl. Rsch. Assocs., Washington, Conakry, Guinea, Benghazi, Libya, Carbondale, Ill., 1960-64; mng. editor linguistics div. T. Y. Crowell Pub. Co., N.Y.C., 1964-66; dir. linguistic studies Behavioral Rsch. Labs., Palo Alto, Calif., 1966-67; pres. D.C.W. Rsch. Assocs. Internat., Foster City, Calif., 1967—. Author: PI/LT-Programmed Instruction/Language Teaching, 1967, Career Education, 1976, ASTD in China, 1981; contbr. articles to profl. publs.; mem. editorial bd. Vision/Action. Trustee, City U. L.A.; mem. adv. bd. Martin Luther King Reading Acad., L.A., Internat. Ctr. Cultural Ergonomics, 1990—; mem. tng. systems design and prodn. program adv. bd. U. Calif.-Santa Cruz; U.S. rep. Internat. Com. Human Resources Devel., Kuwait, 1990—; ordained minister Universal Life Ch., 1969. Served with U.S. Army, 1945-46, 52-54. Mem. Am. Mgmt. Assn., Orgn. Devel. Network, Am. Soc. Tng. and Devel. (bd. dirs. internat. div., named Practitioner of Yr. 1988), Internat. Fedn. Tng. and Devel. Organs. (task force), Soc. Internat. Edn. Tng. and Rsch., 1st World Congress Internat. Orgn. Devel., Orgn. Devel. Forum, Peninsula Orgn. Devel. Support, Mideast Am. Bus. Conf., World Future Soc., Peninsula Exec. Club (Los Altos), SEDUMEX (Mexico City), Benghazi Sailing Club, Orient Club (Rangoon). Office: DCW Rsch Assocs Internat PO Box 4400 San Mateo CA 94404-0400

WIGGS, P. DAVID, real estate executive; b. Alva, Okla., Dec. 6, 1942; s. Conrad Lee and Wanda B. (Kreie) W.; B.S., Ariz. State U., 1964, 77; postgrad. Chapman Coll., 1967; M.B.A., Ariz. State U., 1974; grad. Realtors Inst.; m. Saundre Eugenia Young, June 6, 1964. Cashier, A.J. Bayless Markets, Phoenix, 1960-64; staff accountant Peat, Marwick, Mitchell & Co., C.P.A.'s, Dallas, 1964-66, sr. auditor, Phoenix, 1970-72; commd. 2d lt. USAF, 1967, advanced through grades to capt., 1970; Officer Tng. Sch., 1966-67, logistics officer Vandenberg AFB, Cal., 1967-68, dir. logistics plans, 1968-70; staff accountant Diehl, Evans & Co., C.P.A.'s Santa Maria, Calif., 1967-70; gen. partner Satellite Investment Co., Ltd., Tempe Ariz., 1968—, DPI Assoc., Tempe, 1977-85, Homevest Assoc., Tempe, 1978-91; controller Valley Enterprises, Inc., Phoenix, 1972-73, Diversified Properties, Inc., Tempe, 1973-76, v.p., treas., 1976-88; treas. Freeway Lumber and Materials, Inc., Phoenix, 1972-73; Realtor, 1980—; pres. Wiggs Co., Tempe, Ariz., 1980—; div. controller Pulte Home Corp., Tempe, 1981-82; v.p., treas. Hunsinger Homes, Inc., Tempe, 1982-83; controller Val Vista Lakes, Gilbert, Ariz., 1983-88; contr. Osselaer Co., Phoenix, 1988-89, Leisure World Community Assn., Mesa, Ariz., 1990-93. Sec., supervisory com. Vandenberg Fed. Employees Credit Union, Vandenberg AFB, Calif., 1969-70. Bd. dirs., treas. Lakes Community Assn., Tempe, 1974-77, treas. Val Vista Lakes Community Assn., Gilbert, Ariz., 1985-88. CPA, Tex., Ariz. Mem. AICPA, Ariz. Soc. CPA's, Tex. Soc. CPA's, Nat. Assn. Realtors, Beta Gamma Sigma, Beta Alpha Psi, Delta Sigma Pi. Republican. Baptist (deacon). Home: 1902 E Julie Dr Tempe AZ 85283-3212

WIGHT, NANCY ELIZABETH, neonatologist; b. N.Y.C., Aug. 27, 1947; d. John Joseph and Gisela (Landers) Probst; m. Robert C.S. Wight, Oct. 1, 1988; 1 child, Robert C.S. II. Student, Cornell U., 1965-67; AB in Psychology, U. Calif., Berkeley, 1968; postgrad., George Washington U., 1971-72; MD, U. N.C., 1976. Diplomate Am. Bd. Pediatrics. Resident in pediatrics U. N.C., Chapel Hill, 1976-79; fellow in neonatal/perinatal medicine U. Calif., San Diego, 1979-81; clin. instr. Dept. of Pediatrics La. State U. Sch. of Medicine, Baton Rouge, 1982-86; neonatologist The Baton Rouge Neonatology Group, 1981-86; co-dir. neonatology, med. dir. respiratory therapy Woman's Hosp., Baton Rouge, 1981-85; med. dir. newborn svcs., neonatal respiratory therapy HCA West Side Hosp. Centennial Med. Ctr., Nashville, 1986-88; staff pediatrician, neonatologist Balboa Naval Hosp., San Diego, 1988-89; attending neonatologist Sharp Meml. Hosp., San Diego, 1990—, Children's Hosp.-San Diego, 1990—; asst. clin. prof. U. Calif. San Diego, 1991—; physician assoc. La Leche League. Contbr. articles to profl. jours. mem. exec. bd. Capital Area Plantation chpt. March of Dimes, Baton Rouge, 1981-86, chmn. health adv. com., 1982-86; mem. health com. Capital Area United Way, Baton Rouge, 1982-86; bd. mem. Baton Rouge Coun. for Child Protection, 1983-86, NICU Parents, Baton Rouge, 1981-86; mem. health adv. com. Nashville Area March of Dime, 1987-88. Recipeint Am. Med. Women's Assn. award. Mem. AMA, Am. Acad. Pediatrics, Calif. Med. Assn., So. Med. Assn., San Diego County Med. Assn., Calif. Perinatal Assn., So. Perinatal Assn., Nat. Perinatal Assn., La. Perinatal Assn. (past 1st v.p. and pres.), Internat. Lactation Cons. Assn. (cert.), Hastings Soc. Home: 3226 Newell St San Diego CA 92106 Office: Children's Assoc Med Group 8001 Frost St San Diego CA 92123

WIGHT, RANDY LEE, military officer; b. Seattle, Sept. 8, 1951; s. Guy Eugene and Jeraline Mae (Green) W.; m. Linda Ann Ruark, June 8, 1973; chidren: Kathryn Ann, David Michael. BS, U.S. Naval Acad., 1973; student, Naval Aviation Schs. Command, Pensacola, Fla., 1973-74; MSEE, Naval Postgrad. Sch., Monterey, Calif., 1990. Commd. ensign USN, 1973; advanced through grades to comdr., 1988; VAQ-129 Naval Air Sta , Whidby Island, Oak Harbor, Wash., 1974-75; from legal to div. officer VAQ-136, Oak Harbor, 1975-78; flight instr. VAQ-129, Oak Harbor, 1978-81; asst. maintenance and tng. officer VAQ-137, Oak Harbor, 1981-83; flight instr. VAQ-129, Oak Harbor, 1983-85; maintenance officer VAQ-135, Oak Harbor, 1985-88; mil. prof. U.S. Naval Postgrad. Sch., Monterey, Calif., 1991—; comdg. officer golden intruder squadron U.S. Naval Sea Cadet Corps., Oak Harbor, 1979-81. Mem. NSPE, IEEE, U.S. Naval Acad. Alumni Assn., U.S. Naval Inst. Office: CDR R L Wight USN Code SP/WT Naval Postgrad Sch Monterey CA 93943

WIGHTMAN, THOMAS VALENTINE, rancher, researcher; b. Sacramento, Oct. 7, 1921; s. Thomas Valentine and Pearl Mae (Cutbirth) W.; m. Lan Do Wightman. Student, U. Calif., Berkeley, 1945-46; B of Animal Husbandry, U. Calif., Davis, 1949; student, Cal. Poly. Inst., 1949-50. Jr. aircraft mechanic SAD (War Dept.), Sacramento, Calif., 1940-42; rancher Wightman Ranch, Elk Grove, Calif., 1950-59; machinest Craig Ship-Bldg. Co., Long Beach, Calif., 1959-70; rancher Wightman Ranch, Austin, Nev., 1970-88; dir. Wightman Found., Sacramento, 1988—. Dir. med. rsch. Staff sgt. U.S. Army, 1942-45. Recipient scholarship U.S. Fed. Govt., 1945-50. Fellow NRA, VFW, U. Calif. Alumni Assn., U. Calif. Davis Alumni Assn., Bowles Hall Assn.; mem. Confederate Air Force. Republican. Home and Office: Wightman Found PO Box 278016 Sacramento CA 95827

WIGNARAJAH, KANAPATHIPILLAI, plant physiologist, researcher, educator; b. Batticaloa, Sri Lanka, Dec. 26, 1944; came to U.S., 1988; s. Sinnathoamby and Nagaratnam (Nallathamby) K.; m. Asha Vasanti Ramcharan, Aug. 2, 1984; children: Avisha Nia, Amira Tari. BS in Botany, U. Ceylon, Colombo, Sri Lanka, 1969; PhD in Plant Physiology, U. Liverpool, Eng., 1974. Asst. lectr. in botany U. Ceylon, Sri Lanka, 1969-71; rsch. assoc. agronomy dept. U. Western Australia, 1974-75; lectr. U. Malawi, Africa, 1975-76, U. West Indies, Trinidad, 1976-84; sr. lectr. U. Guyana, S. Am., 1985-86; rsch assoc. U. Wales, Bangor, United Kingdom, 1986-87; rsch. assoc. Ctr. Nat. de la Recherche Sci., Montpellier, France, 1987-88, U. Okla., Norman, 1988-89, U. Calif., Santa Cruz, 1989-90; plant scientist The Bionetics Corp., Moffett Field, Calif., 1990—; cons. Nat. Inst. for Sci. and Tech., Georgetwon, Guyana, 1985-86; Inter-Am. Inst. for Coop. in Agrl., 1985-86; reviewer for Tropical Agrl., 1980-86, Oecologia Plantarium, 1986-87, Environ. and Exptl. Botany, 1990—, Grant Proposals to NASA, 1991—. Contbr. articles to profl. jours. Sec. Ceylon Nat. Hist. Soc., Sri Lanka, 1969-71. Recipient Wheat Bd. Rsch. grant, Australian Reserve Bank, Nedlands, 1974, Swedish Guest scholarship The Swedish Inst., Stockholm, 1980, King Gustav Lectr. medal, U. Stockholm, 1980, Yamani Found. U. fellowship, U. Wales, 1986, European Econ. Commn., Centre Nat. de la Recherche Scientifique fellowship Montpelier, France, 1987. Fellow Indian Chem. Soc.; mem. Scandinavian Soc. Plant Physiologists, Physiotochem. Soc. of Europe. Hindu. Office: The Bionetics Corp NASA Ames Rsch Ctr Moffett Field CA 94035-1000

WIIG, HOWARD CALVERT, state official; b. Honolulu, Nov. 7, 1940; s. Howard Egerton Wiig and Jean Carolyn Calvert. BA, U. Calif., Berkeley, 1962; diploma, U. Heidelberg, Germany, 1962; MA, U. Hawaii, 1968, postgrad., 1969-72. Instr. Am. studies dept. U. Hawaii, Honolulu, 1969-72; pres. Charger Hawaii, Honolulu, 1975-76; energy analyst Hawaii Dept. Bus. and Econ. Devel., Honolulu, 1976—; freelance writer various publs., 1963-75; state rep. Nat. Conf. States on Bldg. Codes and Standards, Inc., Honolulu, 1982, 85. Author: Freedom or Jail for Imogene Cole, 1974. Bd. dirs. Young Dems. Honolulu, 1970; pres. Zero Population Growth, Honolulu, 1968-70; statute revisor State of Hawaii, Honolulu, 1984. Recipient Disting. Svc. award Internat. Planned Parenthood Fedn., 1968, cert. of recognition Bldg. Owners and Mgrs. Assn., 1982, cert. of svc. State of Hawaii, 1988. Mem. Illuminating Engring. Soc. (chmn. lighting design awards Honolulu 1986—, pres. 1987, 89—, svc. award 1988), Audubon Soc., Wilderness Soc., World Wildlife Fund, Dances We Dance, Sierra Club, Mid Pacific Road Runners Club (race dir. 1987). Mem. Unity Ch. Home: 3593-A Alani Dr Honolulu HI 96822 Office: Hawaii Energy Div 335 Merchant St Rm 110 Honolulu HI 96813

WIKER, STEVEN FORRESTER, industrial engineering educator; b. Alhambra, Calif., Sept. 29, 1952; s. Bruce Forrester and Joan (Centers) W.; m. Jody Louise Wiker, Jan. 24, 1976; children: Douglas Forrester, James McCallum. BS in Physiology, U. Calif., Davis, 1975; MS in Biol. Scis., Washington U., 1981; MS in Indsl. Engring., U. Mich., 1982, PhD in Indsl. Engring., 1986. Rsch. project officer USCG, Washington, 1976-79; rsch. asst. U. Mich., Ann Arbor, 1979-86; rsch. engr. Naval Ocean Systems Ctr. Lab., Kailua, Hawaii, 1986-87, Naval Ocean Systems Ctr., San Diego, 1987-88; asst. prof. indsl. engring. U. Wis., Madison, 1988-93, head indsl. ergonomics rsch. lab., 1989-93; assoc. prof.dept. environ. health U. Wash., Seattle, 1993; faculty indsl. engring. Dept. Environ. Health, U. Wash., Seattle, 1993—; sr. rsch. engr. James Miller Engring., Inc., Ann Arbor, 1981-88; dirs. telerobotics lab. Wis. Ctr. for Space Automation and Robotics, 1991-93. Contbr. articles to profl. jours. Comdr. USCGR, 1976—. Recipient Achievement medal USCG, 1988, 92, Humanitarian Svc. medal, 1993; fellow Ford Motor Co., Detroit, 1983-86; grantee Nat. Inst. Occupational Safety and Health, Washington, 1979-84, NASA, Ctrs. for Disease Control. Mem. Am. Soc. Safety Engrs., Inst. Indsl. Engrs., Internat. Soc. Biomechs., Aerospace Med. Soc., Human Factors Soc., Res. Officers Assn., N.Y. Acad. Scis., Sigma Xi, Alpha Pi Mu. Office: Univ of Wash SC-84 Dept Environ Health Seattle WA 98195

WILBARGER, EDWARD STANLEY, engineer, software developer; b. Billings, Mont., Feb. 21, 1931; s. Edward Stanley and Elizabeth Ingaborg (Hansen) W.; m. Patricia Lee Williams, June 20, 1959 (div. June 1977); m. Lila Sears, July 9, 1977. BS in Civil Engring., Va. Mil. Inst., 1952; MS in Physics, U.S. Naval Postgrad. Sch., 1956; PhD in Mech. Engring., U. Calif., Santa Barbara, 1980. Registered profl. engr., Va. Head biotech. sect., biol. scis. dept., Def. Systems div. Gen. Motors Corp., Birmingham, Mich., 1960-62; tech. specialist, Def. Rsch. Labs. Gen. Motors Corp., Santa Barbara, Calif., 1962-67; head design & devel., aerophysics dept., Delco Systems Ops. Gen. Motors Corp., Santa Barbara, 1967-84; mgr. aerophysics range facility, Delco Electronics div. Delco Electronics Corp., Gen. Motors Corp., Santa Barbara, 1984-89; software developer DYNEQN, Santa Barbara, 1989—; com. mem. Nat. Rsch. Coun. Bd. on Army Sci. and Tech., Washington, 1987-89. Author: A Computer Simulation of The Two Stage Light Gas Gun, 1989. Capt. U.S. Army, 1952-60, Korea. Recipient Commendation medal, U.S. Army, Korea, 1954. Mem. Am. Acad. Mechanics. Office: DYNEQN 3830 Center Ave Santa Barbara CA 93110-1221

WILBER, CHARLES GRADY, forensic science educator, consultant; b. Waukesha, Wis., June 18, 1916; s. Charles Bernard and Charlotte Agnes (Grady) W.; m. Ruth Mary Bodden, July 12, 1944 (dec. 1950); children: Maureen, Charles Bodden, Michael; m. Clare Marie O'Keefe, June 14, 1952; children: Thomas Grady (dec.), Kathleen, Aileen, John Joseph. B.Sc., Marquette U., 1938; M.A., Johns Hopkins U., 1941; Ph.D., Johns Hopkins, 1942. Asst. prof. physiology Fordham U., 1945-49; assoc. prof. physiology, dir. biol. labs. St. Louis U., 1949-52; leader Arctic expdns., 1943-44, 48, 50, 51; physiologist Chem. Corps, U.S. Army, 1952-61; assoc. physiology and pharmacology U. Pa., 1953-61, chief comparative physiology, 1956-61; profl. lectr. biol. scis. Loyola Coll., Balt., 1957-61; dir. Loyola Coll. (In-Service Inst. Sci. Tchrs.), 1958-61; prof. biol. scis., univ. research coordinator, dean Grad. Sch., Kent State U., 1961-64; dir. marine laboratories U. Del., 1964-67; chmn., prof. dept. zoology Colo. State U., 1967-73, prof., 1967-87, emeritus prof. and chmn., 1987—, dir. forensic sci. lab., 1965—; dep. coroner, Larimer County, Colo., 1968-78; pres. Manresa Co., 1978—; mem. Center for Human Identification; expert witness fed. and state cts. on poisons, firearms, others. mem. Marine Biol. Lab., Woods Hole, Mass., 1947—; mem. U.S. Army Panel Environ. Physiology, 1952-61; mem. study group Nat. Acad. Scis.-USAF, 1958-61; Wellcome vis. prof. basic med. scis. Ohio U. Med. Sch., 1983-84. Author: Biological Aspects of Water Pollution, 2d edit, 1971, Japanese edit., 1970, Forensic Biology for the Law Enforcement Officer, 1975, Contemporary Violence, 1975, Ballistic Science for the Law Enforcement Officer, 1977, Medicolegal Investigation of The President John F. Kennedy Murder, 1978, Chemical Trauma from Pesticides, 1979, Forensic Toxicology, 1980, Beryllium, 1980, Agent Orange, 1980; Author: Turbidity, 1983, Selenium, 1983; contbr. articles to profl. jours.; exec. editor: Adaption to the Environment, vol. in series, 1962; editor: Am. Lecture Series in Environ. Studies; mem. editorial bd.: Am. Jour. Forensic Medicine and Pathology; contbr.: Harper Ency. Nat; vis. lectr.: Am. Inst. Biol. Scis, 1957—. Served to capt. USAAF, 1942-46; col., ret. USAF. Disting. scholar in criminal justice Albany State Coll., 1993. Fellow N.Y. Acad. Scis., Am. Acad. Forensic Sci.; mem. Am. Physiol. Soc., Phi Beta Kappa, Sigma Xi, Phi Sigma, Gamma Alpha. Republican. Catholic. Club: Cosmos (Washington). Home: 900 Edwards St Fort Collins CO 80524-3824 Office: Colo State U Dept Biology Fort Collins CO 80523

WILBER, CLARE MARIE, musician, educator; b. Denver, Mar. 21, 1928; d. Thomas A. and Kathleen M. (Brennan) O'Keefe; m. Charles Grady Wilber, June 14, 1952; children: Maureen, Charles, Michael, Thomas (dec.), Kathleen, Aileen, John Joseph. AB, Loretto Heights Coll., 1948; MS, Fordham U., 1950; MM, Colo. State U., 1972. Instr. of music various colls. and univs., 1951-83; mgr. Ft. Collins (Colo.) Symphony, 1969-81, exec. dir., 1981-85, exec. dir. emerita, 1985—; pvt. music instr. Ft. Collins, 1973—; trustee Ft. Collins Symphony, 1986—; v.p., bd. dirs. Elite Music Co., Ft. Collins. Composer Fantasie Romantique, 1972, Mass in D, 1980, Seasons for Suzanne, 1988, Panoramas for Polly, 1990. Mem. adv. coun. Ft. Collins High Sch., Ft. Collins, 1972-74, adv. bd. Children's Sch. of Sci., Woods Hole, Mass., 1965—. Recipient AT&T Crystal Clef award, 1982, Clare Wilber award, Ft, Collins Symphony, 1992. Mem. Ft. Collins Music Tchrs. Assn. (treas. 1984-90), Colo. State Music Tchrs. Assn., Music Tchrs. Nat. Assn. (cert. tchr. pieano 1978—), Marine Biol. Lab. Assocs., Sigma Xi (assoc.), Delta Omicron (local chpt. pres. 1970-72, sec. 1988—, Spl. Svc. award 1974). Republican. Roman Catholic. Home and Office: 900 Edwards St Fort Collins CO 80524-3824

WILBER, JOHN JAMES, computer consultant, software engineer; b. Kassel, Germany, Apr. 3, 1967; came to U.S., 1967; s. Glenn Edmond and Edelgard Ursula (Manthey) W. BSEE, U. So. Calif., 1990. Cons. Symantec Corp., Santa Monica, Calif., 1990-92; software engr. Western Technologies, Culver City, Calif., 1992; pres. Pacific Computing Solutions, L.A., 1993—. Mem. IEEE, Assn. Computing Machinery. Republican. Office: Pacific Computing Solutions 12021 Wilshire Blvd Ste 182 Los Angeles CA 90025

WILBUR, CLAUDE GLENN, software engineer, musician; b. Denver, Mar. 5, 1956; s. William Bryson and Joan Frances (Ritter) W.; m. Debra K. Tuntavitch, May 4, 1991; 1 child, Michael Fetzer. MusB, Chapman Coll., 1978; MusM, Mich. State U., 1980. Programmer Zipco Mailing, Denver, 1983-86, CM Robbins Co., Aurora, Colo., 1986-87, United Software Industries, Aurora, Colo., 1987-89; quality control tester CM Robbins Co., Aurora, 1989; software engr. Formation Tech., Denver, 1990—. Mem. IEEE, Assn. for Computing Machinery, Front Range Com. on Software Quality, Am. Soc. for Quality Control, Denver Musicians Assn., Internat. Clarinet Soc. Republican. Methodist. Office: Formation Tech 1873 S Bellaire Denver CO 80222

WILBUR, LESLIE EUGENE, education educator; b. Modesto, Calif., Jan. 11, 1924; s. Horace Gilbert and Grace (King) W.; m. Norma June Lash, June 14, 1946; children: Stuart Alan, Lesley Lynn. AA, Modesto Jr. Coll., 1943; BA, U. Ill., 1948; MA, U. Calif., Berkeley, 1951; PhD, U. So. Calif., 1962. Instr. Bakersfield (Calif.) Coll, 1950-58, assoc. dean, 1958-62; pres. Barstow (Calif.) Coll., 1962-65; prof. edn. U. So. Calif., L.A., 1965-89, chmn. higher edn. dept., 1968-85, pres. faculty senate, 1972-73; cons. L.A. County Office Schs., 1966-79; dir. Pullias Lecture Programs, L.A., 1978—; v.p. So. Calif. TV Consortium, Cypress, 1976-90. Co-author: Improving English Skills, 19650, Teaching in the Community Junior College, 1972, Principles and Values for College and University Administration, 1984. With AUS, 1943-46, ETO. Recipient We Honor Ours award Calif. Tchrs. Assn., 1972; Faculty Rsch. grantee U. S.C. Sch. Edn., 1986, 87, 88. Mem. Am. Assn. for Higher Edn., Assn. for Study Higher Edn., Community Coll. Rsch. Assn. (bd. dirs. 1975—), Calif. Coll. and Univ. Faculty Assn. (pres. U. So. Calif. chpt. 1965-68). Democrat. Mem. United Ch. of Christ. Home: 1434 Punahou St # 1031 Honolulu HI 96822

WILBUR, PAUL JAMES, mechanical engineering educator; b. Ogden, Utah, Nov. 8, 1937; s. Earl Burton and Ada (James) W.; m. Twyla Beck Wilbur, June 8, 1960; children: Wendy Lee, Dagny Ann. BS, U. Utah, 1960; PhD, Princeton U., 1968. Registered profl. engr., Colo. Nuclear power engr. U.S. Atomic Energy Commn., Washington, 1960-64; prof. of mech. engring. Colo. State U., Fort Collins, 1968—; bd. dirs., sec. Ion Tech Inc., Fort Collins; cons., researcher NASA, Washington, 1970—. Author: Solar Cooling, 1977; contbr. numerous articles to profl. jours. Lt. USN, 1960-64. Mem. ASME (pres. local sect.), AIAA (tech. com., jour. editor). Home: 1500 Teakwood Ct Fort Collins CO 80525-1954 Office: Colo State U Mech Engring Dept Fort Collins CO 80523

WILCK, CARL THOMAS, public relations executive; b. Quantico, Va., May 26, 1933; s. Carl and Glennie Alma (Jones) W.; m. Tommie England, June 16, 1961 (dec. Sept. 1985); m. Nadine Bagley Henry, May 21, 1989; 1 child, Jacqueline Leigh Henry. AA, Santa Monica Coll., 1955; BA in Polit. Sci., UCLA, 1957. Pres. Thomas Wilck Assocs., L.A., 1960-70, chmn., pres.; asst. adminstr. SBA, Washington, 1971; dep. chmn. Rep. Nat. Com., Washington, 1972-73; v.p. pub. affairs Irvine Co., Newport Beach, Calif., 1973-85; pres. Thomas Wilck Assocs., Orange County, 1985—. Bd. chmn. Coro Found., L.A., 1982-83. Sgt. USMC, 1950-52, PTO. Fellow Pub. Rels. Soc. Am. (Silver Anvil award 1964, 77); mem., bd. dirs. Cord Found., Orange County C. of C. Republican. Presbyterian. Office: Thomas Wilck Assocs 2600 Michelson Dr Irvine CA 92715-1311

WILCOX, BRETT E., aluminum company executive; b. Denver, Apr. 30, 1953; s. Blakely F. Wilcox and Betty J. (Cosslett) Gilkinson; m. Mary Davis, May 25, 1986; children: Molly, Natalie. AB, Princeton U., 1975; JD, Stanford U., 1978. Atty. Preston, Thorgrimson, Ellis & Holman, Seattle, 1978-81; exec. dir. Direct Svc. Industries, Portland, Oreg., 1981-85; pres. Northwest Aluminum Co., The Dalles, Oreg., 1985—. Chmn. Oreg. Trail Coordinating Coun., Portland, 1990—; vice chmn. Citizens for the Columbia Gorge, The Dalles, 1989—; mem. Oreg. Progress Bd., Salem, 1992—; mem. Gov.'s Task Force on the Structure and Efficiency of Oreg. Govt., Salem, 1991-92; bd. dirs. Reed Coll., Oreg. Bus. Coun. Named The Dalles Businessman of Yr., C. of C., 1986, Productivity award U.S. Senate, 1988, Coun. for Econ. Devel. award State of Oreg., 1988, Gold Schmidty award State of Oreg., 1987. Mem. Nature Conservancy (bd. dirs.).

WILCOX, CALVIN HAYDEN, mathematics educator; b. Cicero, N.Y., Jan. 29, 1924; s. Calvin and Vara (Place) W.; m. Frances I. Rosekrans, May 29, 1947; children: Annette Faye, Victor Hayden, Christopher Grant. Student, Syracuse U., 1947-48; A.B. magna cum laude, Harvard U., 1951, A.M., 1952, Ph.D., 1955. Mem. faculty Calif. Inst. Tech., Pasadena, 1955-61; asst. prof. math. Calif. Inst. Tech., 1957-60, asso. prof., 1960-61; prof. U. Wis.-Madison, 1961-66; prof., head dept. U. Ariz., Tucson, 1966-69; prof. U. Denver, 1969-70, U. Utah, Salt Lake City, 1971—; vis. prof. U. Geneva, 1970-71, U. Liege, Belgium, 1973, U. Stuttgart, Fed. Republic Germany, 1974, 76-77, Kyoto (Japan) U., 1975, Ecole Polytechnique Fédérale, Lausanne, Switzerland, 1979, U. Bonn (W. Ger.), 1980. Author: Lectures on Scattering Theory for the d'Alembert Equation in Exterior Domains, 1975; monograph Scattering Theory for Diffraction Gratings, 1983, Sound Propagation in Stratified Fluids, 1983; Editor: Asymptotic Solutions of Differential Equations and Their Applications, 1964, Perturbation Theory and its Application in Quantum Mechanics, 1966. Served with AUS, 1945-47. NSF predoctoral fellow, 1952-53; Sr. U.S. Scientist award Alexander von Humboldt Found., W. Ger., 1976-77. Mem. AAAS, Soc. Indsl. and Applied Math., Am. Math. Soc., Math. Assn. Am. Office: Univ Utah Dept Math Salt Lake City UT 84112

WILCOX, DAVID ROBERT, archaeologist; b. Albany, N.Y., Mar. 31, 1944; s. Robert Guy and Eleanor Elisabeth (Vann) W.; m. Susan Louise Furer, Sept. 7, 1971. BA, Beloit Coll., 1966; PhD, U. Ariz., 1977. Scholar-in-residence Western Archeol. Ctr., Nat. Pk. Svc., Tucson, 1977-78; vis. asst. prof. anthropology Ariz. State U., Tempe, 1978-79; archaeologist Ariz. State Museum, Tucson, 1980-83; itinerant scholar Tempe, 1983-84; scholar-in-residence Museum of No. Ariz./No. Ariz. U., Flagstaff, 1984-85; assoc. curator anthropology Museum of No. Ariz., Flagstaff, 1985-88, assoc. curator anthropology, dept. head, 1988—. Co-author: (with Lynette O. Shank) The Architecture of the Casa Grande and Its Interpretation, 1977, (with Thomas R. McGuire, Charles Sternberg), Snaketown Revisited, 1981, (with Charles Sternberg) Hohoram Ballcourts and Their Interpretation, 1983; editor: (with W. Bruce Masse) The Protohistoric Period in the North American Southwest, AD 1450-1700, 1981, (with Vernon Scarborough) The Mesoamerican Bellgame, 1991. Fellow Am. Anthrop. Assn., AAAS, Soc. for Am. Archaeology; mem. Soc. Mexicana de Antropologia, N.Y. Acad. Scis., Sigma Xi. Home: 1440 Shullenbarger Dr Flagstaff AZ 86001-8961 Office: Museum of No Ariz RR 4 Box 720 Flagstaff AZ 86001-9302

WILCOX, DENNIS LEE, public relations educator; b. Rapid City, S.D., Mar. 31, 1941; s. Herbert Dennis and Star (Polhemus) W.; m. Marianne Milstead, May 24, 1969; 1 child, Anne-Marie Elizabeth. BA, U. Denver, 1963; MA, U. Iowa, 1967; PhD, U. Mo., 1974. Reporter Daily Sentinel, Grand Junction, Colo., 1963-65; writer U. Iowa, Iowa City, 1965-67; editor, writer Ohio State U., Columbus, 1965-67; pub. rels. dir. Ketchum, Inc., 1967-70; info. officer Chapman (Calif.) Coll. World Campus, 1970; prof. San Jose (Calif.) State U., 1974—. Author: African Press, 1975, Effective Publicity, 1984, Public Relations Writing, 1990, Public Relations Strategy and Tactics, 1992. Fellow East-West Ctr., Pub. Rels. Soc. Am. Coll. Fellows (bd. dirs. 1986-88, Outstanding Educator 1984); mem. Assn. Edn. in Journalism, Internat. Assn. Bus. Communicators, San Francisco Pub. Rels. Roundtable. Republican. Episcopalian.

WILCOX, EVLYN, businesswoman, former city official; children: Wayne, Moire, Marlene. Owner, pres. Manpower, Inc., San Bernardino, Riverside, Upland, San Gabriel Valley and Corona, Calif.; former mayor City of San Bernardino. Pres. Arrowhead United Way, 1983, 92, campaign chmn., 1981, 90; pres. Community Arts Prodns.; treas., bd. dirs. Nat. Orange Show; bd. dirs. YMCA; bd. councilors Calif. State U., San Bernardino. Named Citizen of Yr. Inland Empire mag., 1979. Mem. Exec. Women Internat. (pres. Inland Empire chpt. 1975), Inland Empire Bus. and Profl. Women USA (pres. San Orco dist.), San Bernardino Area C. of C. (pres. 1978, Athena award 1986), Rotary (pres. 1992). Office: ED 998 N D St San Bernardino CA 92410-3520

WILCOX, FRED T., human resource consulting firm executive; b. Portland, Oreg., July 1, 1935; m. Elisa H. Wilcox; children: Traci K., Robert H. BA in Bus./Econs., Lewis & Clark, 1957. Buyer Liberty House, Hawaii, 1961-67; gen. mgr. Liberty House, Waikiki, Hawaii, 1967-69; div. mgr. Liberty House, Hawaii, 1969-71; gen. mgr. Liberty House, Pearl Ridge Kahala, Hawaii, 1971-72, Liberty House, Sunrise Store, Sacramento, 1972-74; v.p., dir. stores Liberty House Dept. Stores, 1974-79; v.p., gen. mgr. Liberty House, Sacramento, Fresno, 1979-82; pres. Wilcox, Bertoux & Miller, Sacramento, 1982—; vice chair Am. River Hosp. Found., Sacramento, 1990—; dir. Eskaton Inc., Sacramento, 1991—. Mem. United Way, Sacramento; dir. Goodwill, Sacramento; mem. Golden Empire Coun. Boy Scouts, Sacramento; advanced mem. Healthcare Fin. Mgmt., Sacramento Coun., 1991. Mem. Healthcare Execs. No. Calif. Office: McCracken Wilcox et al 601 University Ave Ste 236 Sacramento CA 95825

WILCOX, HAROLD EDGAR, procurement management executive; b. Washington, Feb. 15, 1940; s. Harold Edgar and Glenna Maude (Austin) W.; m. Catherine E. Kruger, June 25, 1971. BSBA, Miami U., 1961; MBA, George Washington U., 1972. Commd. ens. USN, 1961, advanced through grade to capt., 1982, supt. purchasing Phila. Naval Shipyard, 1967-69, dep. dir. Aircraft Weapon Systems Purchasing div.; with Naval Air Systems Command Hdqrs. USN, Washington, 1972-76; comptroller, dir. Regional Contracting Dept.; dir. Regional Contracting Dept. USN; dir. Naval Supply Ctr. USN, Pearl Harbor, Hawaii, 1976-79; dir. purchasing Navy Aviation Supply Office USN, Phila., 1979-82; dir. acquisition Joint Cruise Missiles Project USN, Washington, 1982-84; ret. USN, 1984; dir. contracts for aerospace and logistics Cubic Corp., San Diego, 1985-88; v.p. procurement AIRCOA, Denver, 1988-89, AspenCrest Hospitality, Inc., Denver, 1989—. Decorated Def. Superior Svc. medal, Merit svc. medal with gold star recipient Recognition award U.S. Dept. Commerce, 1978, Vietnam Svc. medal with silver and bronze stars. Mem. U.S. Naval Inst., Nat. Contracts Mgmt. Assn. (cert. conract mgr. 1976), Denver Sporting Club. Republican. Methodist. Office: AspenCrest Hospitality Inc 8100 E Arapahoe Rd Ste 301 Englewood CO 80112-9999

WILCOX, LYNN E., psychology educator; b. Huntsville, Ala., Sept. 4, 1935; d. William Francis and Anna Mae (Linthicum) Esslinger; 1 child, Gregory C. Haun. BS cum laude, Southwest Mo. State U., 1959; MEd, U. Mo., 1961, PhD, 1968; postgrad., U. Catolica, Quito, Ecuador, 1976-78. Cert. sch. counselor and sch. psychologist, Calif.; lic. marriage, family and child counselor, Calif. Tchr. high sch. Springfield, Mo., 1958-60; grad., rsch. asst. U. Mo., Columbia, 1960-64; counselor Pub. Schs., Smyrna, Ga., 1965-67; asst. prof. Ga. State U., Atlanta, 1968-69; prof. edn. Calif. State U., Sacramento, 1969—, dept. chair, 1973-75, counselor, edn. coord., 1986-88, mem. women's studies bd., 1972; pvt. practice marriage, family and child counselor Sacramento, 1970—; instr. in Sufi mediation, M.T.O. Shahmaghsoudi, Sacramento and San Francisco, 1984—. Pres. Wayfinders Inc., Sacramento, 1986—; chmn. Am. Personnel & Guidance Assn. Com. for Women, 1972-74; bd. dirs. Community Interaction Program, Sacramento, 1972; prof. adv. com. Suicide Prevention Service, Sacramento, 1970-72; rep. Sacramento Community Commn. for Women, 1971-73. Fellow Gregory 1962, Danforth 1975; recipient Profl. Promise award Calif. State U., Sacramento, 1986, Meritorious Performance award, 1988. Mem. AAUW, NOW, APA, AACD, Western Psychol. Assn., Faculty Womens Assn. (v.p. 1971-73, pres. 1973-74), Sacramento Symphony League. Republican. Muslim. Office: Calif State U Dept Counselor Edn 6000 J St Sacramento CA 95819-2605

WILCOX, RHODA DAVIS, educator; b. Boyero, Colo., Nov. 4, 1918; d. Harold Francis and Louise Wilhelmina (Wilfert) Davis; m. Kenneth Edward Wilcox, Nov. 1945 (div. 1952); 1 child, Michele Ann. BA in Elem. Edn., U. No. Colo., 1941; postgrad., Colo. Coll., 1955-65. Cert. tchr., Colo. Elem. tchr. Fruita (Colo.) Pub. Sch., 1938-40, Boise, Idaho, 1940-42; sec. civil service USAF, Ogden, Utah, 1942-43, Colorado Springs, Colo., 1943-44; sec. civil service hdqtrs. command USAF, Panama Canal Zone; sec. Tech. Libr., Eglin Field, Fla., 1945-46; elem. tchr. Colorado Springs Sch. Dist. 11, 1952-82, mem. curriculum devel. com., 1968-69; lectr. civic, profl. and edn. groups, Colo.; judge for Excellence in Literacy Coldwell Bankers Sch. Dist. 11, Colo. Coun. Internat. Reading. Assn. Author: Man on the Iron Horse, 1959, Colorado Slim and His Spectacklers, 1964, (with Jean Pierpoint) Changing Colorado (Social Studies), 1968-69, Founding Gathers and Their Friends, 1971, The Bells of Manitou, 1973, (with Ben Foisland) In the Footsteps of the Founder, 1993. Mem. Hist. Adv. Bd. State Colo., Denver, 1976; mem. Garden of the Gods Master Plan Rev. Com. City of Colorado Springs, 1987—; mem. cemetery adv. bd. City Colorado Springs, 1988-91; mem. adv. bd. centennial com., 1971; mem. steering com. Spirit of Palmer Festival, 1986; judge Nat. Hist. Day, U.C.C.S. and Colo. Coll., Colorado Springs; hon. trustee Palmer Found., 1986—; mem. Am. the Beautiful Centennial Celebrations, Inc., 1992-93. Named Tchr. of the Yr., Colorado Springs Sch. Dist. 11, 1968. Mem. AAUW (Woman of Yr. 1987), Colo. Ret. Educators Assn., Colorado Springs Ret. Educators Assn., Helen Hunt Jackson Commemorative Coun. Home: 1620 E Cache La Poudre St Colorado Springs CO 80909-4612

WILCOX, TIMOTHY JAMES, media relations, marketing director, writer; b. Taxila, Pakistan, Dec. 24, 1949; s. Frances Earl and Amelia Johanna (Hoeger) W. BA, U. Calif., Irvine, 1974; MA, Luther Northwestern Seminary, 1979. Asst. editor The Lutheran Standard, Mpls., 1979-83; editor Calif. Riveria, Laguna Beach, 1983-91; dir. media and mktg. Festival of Arts, Laguna Beach, 1992—; editorial cons. Sir Speedy, Inc., Laguna Hills, Calif., 1987—, Comprehensive Bus. Svcs., Carlsbad, Calif., 1989—, Calif. Riviera Mag., Laguna Beach, 1992—. Editor: A Funny Thing Happened On The Way To Church, More Funny Things; contbr. articles to mags. Mem. Festivals Coord. Com., Laguna Beach, 1992—. Governor's scholar State of Calif., 1968, Regents' scholar U. Calif., 1974. Democrat. Lutheran. Office: Festival of Arts 650 Laguna Canyon Rd Laguna Beach CA 92651

WILCOX, WINTON WILFRED, JR., computer specialist, consultant; b. Independence, Mo., Aug. 24, 1945; s. Winton Wilfred Wilcox Sr. and LaPreal (Adams) Craig; m. Kathy Pope, July 4, 1990; children: Steven Michael, Jake Anders. BS, U. Nev., 1973. Nat. product dir. Am. Photography Corp., N.Y.C., 1974-77; gen. mgr. Golden Valley (Minn.) Coffee, 1977-80; div. mgr. Cable Data, Sacramento, 1981-84; v.p., chief operating officer Cultch Enterprises, Inc., Sacramento, 1980-86; v.p. mktg. div. Parallex, Winston-Salem, N.C., 1985-88; owner IK & Cons., Sacramento, 1988—; instr. Heald Bus. Coll., 1990—. Author: How to Create Computer Entertainment, 1985; contbg. author: Apple Fun & Games, 1986. With USAF, 1966-70. Mem. Cable TV Adminstrn and Mktg. (pay view com. Washington chpt. 1985-87, SE chpt. formation com. Tampa, Fla. chpt. 1986-87), Crown Rm., Red Carpet. Republican. Home: 9443 Roseburg Ct Sacramento CA 95826-5231 Office: IK & Cons 3009 1/2 C St Sacramento CA 95816

WILCZEK, JOHN FRANKLIN, history educator; b. San Francisco, Jan. 9, 1929; s. Leonard Matthew and Teresa Edith (Silvey) W.; m. Kuniko Akabane, Nov. 14, 1966; 1 child, Mary Theresa Wilczek. BA in History, U. Calif., Berkeley, 1952; MA, U. Calif., 1953; PhD, Pacific Western U., Encino, Calif., 1978. Cert. secondary tchr., Calif. Instr. history City Coll. of San Francisco, 1956—; instr. Kobe (Japan) Women's Coll., 1979-81; instr. Seido Lang. Inst., Kobe, 1979-81; sec.-treas. Tokyo TV Broadcasting Corp., San Francisco, 1975—. Author: The Teaching of Japanese History on the Community College Level, 1978. Sgt. U.S. Army, 1953-55. Mem. U. Calif. Alumni Assn. Republican. Roman Catholic. Home: 5 Windsor Dr Daly City CA 94015 Office: City Coll of San Francisco 50 Phelan Ave San Francisco CA 94112

WILDE, DAVID GEORGE, electrical engineer, consultant; b. Rock Springs, Wyo., Aug. 26, 1928; s. David George and Mayme Elizabeth (Savela) W.; m. Mildred Marie Levar, June 20, 1954; children: David Levar, Diane L. Wilde Duhl, Wade Wallace, Deborah Lynn. BSEE, U. Wyo., 1950. Registered profl. engr., Wyo. Engr. Bur. Reclamation, Rock Springs, 1952-55, supervising engr., 1955-61, chief office engring., 1961-64; chief Dixie project Bur. Reclamation, St. George, Utah, 1964-66; Wyo. rep. Bur. Reclamation, Cheyenne, 1966-78; project mgr. Bur. Reclamation, Grand Island, Nebr., 1978-80, Casper, Wyo., 1980-88; cons. Dept. Justice, Casper, 1988—; pvt. practice cons., Casper, 1988—. Lt. U.S. Army, 1950-52, Korea. Decorated Silver Star, Purple Heart; named Outstanding Engr. Wyo., Wyo. Engring. Soc., 1985. Fellow ASCE (pres. Wyo. sect. 1972); mem. DAV, NSPE (pres. Cheyenne chpt. 1974), Am. Water Resource Assn., Am. Legion, Soil and Water Conservation Soc., Elks. Democrat. Methodist. Home: 4731 S Center Casper WY 82601

WILDE, JAMES DALE, archaeologist, educator; b. Las Vegas, N.Mex., May 9, 1950; s. Ralph M. and Joyce (Anderson) W.; m. Deborah Thompson, Oct. 6, 1973 (div. 1979); 1 child, Colin James Post; m. Deborah E. Newman, June 4, 1983; children: Matthew Catlow, Russell James. BA, U. N.Mex., 1972; MA, U. Oreg., 1978, PhD, 1985. Archaeologist Deerlodge Nat. Forest, U.S. Forest Svc., Butte, Mont., 1977, Earth Tech. Corp., Seattle, 1981-82, Geo-Recon Internat., Ltd., Seattle, 1982-84; asst. dir. office pub. archaeology Brigham Young U., Provo, Utah, 1984-88, dir., 1988—, adj. prof. dept. anthropology, 1985—; mem. com. on archaeology Brigham Young U., 1986-90, mem. mus. adv. com., 1990—; mem. subcom. on antiquities legis. Utah Legislature, Salt Lake City, 1988-90. Author: Utah Avocational Archaeologist Certification Program: Teaching Guide (vols. I-III), 1988, Utah Avocational Archaeologist Certification Program: Student Handbook (vols. I-III), 1988; contbr. articles to profl. pubs., encys. Mem. vestry St. Mary's Episc. Ch., Provo, 1992—. Mem. Am. Anthropol. Assn., Soc. Am. Archaeology, Soc. Profl. Archaeologists, Utah Profl. Archaeol. Coun. (treas. 1986-88, pres. 1988-90), Am. Quaternary Assn., Sigma Xi. Democrat. Home: 1003 E 420 S Provo UT 84606 Office: Brigham Young Univ Office Pub Archaeology 105 Allen Hall Provo UT 84602

WILDER, JAMES D., geology and mining administrator; b. Wheelersburg, Ohio, June 25, 1935; s. Theodore Roosevelt and Gladys (Crabtree) W.; children: Jaymie Deanna, Julie Lynne. Graduated high sch., Wheelersburg. Lic. real estate agt., Ohio. Real estate agt. Portsmouth, Ohio; mgr. comml. pilots, fixed base operator Scioto County Airport, Ohio; mgr. and part owner sporting goods store, Portsmouth; cons. geologist Paradise, Calif., 1973-81; pres. Mining Cons., Inc., Paradise, 1981-84; dir. geology and devel. Para-Butte Mining, Inc., Paradise, 1984-88, pres., 1988-90, pres., chief exec. officer, 1990—. Served with U.S. Army, 1956-57. Home and Office: Para-Butte Mining Inc PO Box 564 Paradise CA 95967

WILDES, DUDLEY JOSEPH, career naval officer; b. Greenville, Maine, Feb. 8, 1935; s. Thomas Roy and Margaret Hilma (Norwood) W.; m. Elinor June Buckelew, Aug. 17, 1957; children: Thomas Roy, Jeffery Wade, Rebecca Noel, Joseph Tyler. BS, George Washington U., 1972, MBA in pers. mgmt., 1978. Enlisted USN, 1954, commd. ensign Med. Svc. Corps, 1967, advanced through grades to capt., 1986; adminstrv. officer 4th Force Dental Co. FMFLANT USN, Camp LeJeune, N.C., 1967-69; adminstrv. officer 3d Dental Co. USN, Okinawa, Japan, 1969-70; student Naval Sch. Health Scis., Bethesda, Md., 1970-72; pers. officer Naval Hosp., Newport, R.I., 1972-75; dir. med. programs recruiting office USN, Arlington, Va., 1975-77; comdg. officer George Washington U., 1977-78; pers. officer Naval Hosp., San Diego, 1978-80; with OIC Br. Hosp., Palms, Calif., 1980-82; comdg. officer Naval Med. Clin., Quantico, Va., 1982-84; dir. health care ops. Naval Med. Command, Washington, 1984-86; comdg. officer Naval Hosp., P.R., 1986-89, Pensacola, Fla., 1989-91, Lemoore, Calif., 1991-93; tchr. grad. and undergrad. courses in bus. mgmt. and health care Coll. of Desert and Redlands U., Calif., No. Va. Community Coll., Park Coll., Va., N.H. Coll., Naval Sta., P.I., 1980—, Pensacola Jr. Coll., U. West Fla. Mil. advisor United Svcs. Orgn., Pensacola, 1989-90. Decorated Legion of Merit, Meritorious Svc. medal, Navy Commendation medal, Navy Achievement medal. Mem. Am. Coll. Health Care Execs., Am. Assn. Med. Adminstrs., Pensacola C. of C, Pensacola Area Hosp. Coun. Republican. Home: Naval Air Sta 111 Dauntless Lemoore CA 93246 Office: Naval Hosp Naval Air Sta Lemoore CA 93246

WILDEY, ROBERT LEROY, astrophysicist educator; b. L.A., Aug. 22, 1934; s. Charles Dickens and Lillian Fern (Houts) W.; m. Diana Herberta Skolfield, June 27, 1959; children: Robert Bismarck, Wendy Carol, Herbert Charles. AA, John Muir Coll., 1954; BS, Calif. Inst. Tech., 1957, MS, 1958, PhD, 1962. Rsch. fellow in space sci. Calif. Inst. Tech., Pasadena, 1962-63, rsch. fellow in astronomy and geology, 1963-64, asst. prof. planetary sci., 1964-65; astrophysicist astrogeology br. U.S. Geol. Survey, Flagstaff, Ariz., 1965—; vis. prof. astronomy U. Calif., Berkeley, 1966; assoc. prof. astrophysics and astronomy No. Ariz. U., Flagstaff, 1971-79, prof. astrophysics and astronomy, 1979-82, prof. math., physics and astonomy, 1982—; cons. United Geophys. Corp., Pasadena, 1962, Aeronautics div. Ford Motor Co., Newport Beach, Calif., 1963-64, World Book Ency. Sci. News, N.Y.C., 1964-65, Nat. Acad. Scis., Washington, 1967-69; pioneer in cyrogenic infrared astronomy; discovered Wildey effect, occasional hot satellite shadows on Jupiter, first detection of far-infrared radiation from a star. Inventor radarclinometry (topography from single radar images); studies in stellar and galactic evolution; contbr. numerous articles to profl. jours. Search pilot CAP, No. Ariz., 1979-81. Van Maanen fellow Carnegie Inst., 1960; recipient Cert. of Appreciation, NASA, 1970, Cert. of merit Internat. Biol. Inst., 1970. Fellow Royal Astron. Soc., Geol. Soc. Am., Explorers Club; mem. NRA, Am. Geophys. Union, Am. Astron. Soc., Internat. Astron. Union (commr. 1970). Democrat. Buddhist. Home: 414 E Cherry Ave Flagstaff AZ 86001-4640 Office: No Ariz U Dept Physics & Astronomy Box 6010 Flagstaff AZ 86011

WILDFOGEL, JEFFREY ALAN, psychologist, educator; b. N.Y.C., July 3, 1950; s. Paul and Sylvia W. BA, CUNY, 1972; PhD, Stanford U., 1978.

Asst. prof. psychology Baruch Coll. CUNY, N.Y.C., 1980-83; cons. prof. psychology Stanford (Calif.) U., 1983—; pres. The Mental Edge, Mountain View, Calif., 1985—; cons. Stanford U. Baseball Team, 1985-88, Women's Basketball Team, 1985-89. Mem. Nat. Speakers Assn. No. Calif. (bd. dirs. 1991-92), Assn. for Advancement of Applied Sports Psychology, Peninsula Executives Assn., Mountain View C. of C., Phi Beta Kappa. Office: The Mental Edge 201 San Antonio Cir Ste 212 Mountain View CA 94040

WILDMAN, WESLEY JOHN, religious studies educator; b. Adelaide, Australia, Feb. 23, 1961; came to U.S. 1987; s. Phillip Charles and Elizabeth Phoebe (Mills) W.; m. Suzanne Gai Roth, Jan. 18, 1986; children: Samuel Grant, Benjamin Lawson. BA, Flinders U., Australia, 1980, BA with 1st class honors, 1981; BD, U. Sydney, 1984; PhD, Grad. Theol. Union, Berkeley, Calif., 1993. Ordained to ministry Uniting Ch. in Australia, 1986. Minister Parramatta Parish Uniting Ch., N.S.W., 1986-87; owner Pricom USA Cons., Oakland, Calif., 1987—; assoc. pastor Piedmont (Calif.) Community Ch., 1988—; acting asst. prof. dept. religious studies Stanford U., 1993; asst. prof. Sch. Theology Boston U., 1993—. Contbr. articles to profl. jours. Grad. Theol. Union scholar, 1987-88; Wesley Coll. fellow U. Sydney, 1983-85; recipient Rachel McKibbon prize, Lambert George Little award U. Sydney, 1984, 85, With Love to the World scholarship, 1987. Mem. Am. Acad. Religion.

WILENSKY, HAROLD L., political science and industrial relations educator; b. New Rochelle, N.Y., Mar. 3, 1923; s. Joseph and Mary Jane (Wainsten) W.; children: Stephen David, Michael Alan, Daniel Lewis. Student, Goddard Coll., 1940-42; AB, Antioch Coll., 1947; MA, U. Chgo., 1949, PhD, 1955. Asst. prof. sociology U. Chgo., 1951-53, asst. prof. indsl. relations, 1953-54; asst. prof. sociology U. Mich., Ann Arbor, 1954-57, assoc. prof., 1957-61, prof., 1961-62; prof. U. Calif., Berkeley, 1963-82, prof. polit. sci., 1982—, research sociologist Inst. Indsl. Relations, 1963—, project dir. Inst. Internat. Studies, 1970—; mem. research career awards com. Nat. Inst. Mental Health, 1964-67; cons. in field. Author: Industrial Relations: A Guide to Reading and Research, 1954, Intellectuals in Labor Unions: Organizational Pressures on Professional Roles, 1956, Organizational Intelligence: Knowledge and Policy in Government and Industry, 1967, The Welfare State and Equality: Structural and Ideological Roots of Public Expenditures, 1975, The New Corporatism, Centralization, and the Welfare State, 1976, (with C.N. Lebeaux) Industrial Society and Social Welfare, 1965, (with others) Comparative Social Policy, 1985, (with L. Turner) Democratic Corporatism and Policy Linkages, 1987; editor: (with C. Arensberg and others) Research in Industrial Human Relations, 1957, (with P.F. Lazarsfeld and W. H. Sewell) The Uses of Sociology, 1967; contbr. articles to profl. jours. Recipient aux. award Social Sci. Research Council, 1962, Book award McKinsey Found., 1967; fellow Ctr. for Advanced Study in Behavorial Scis., 1956-57, German Marshall Fund, 1978-79; Harry A. Millis research awardee U. Chgo., 1950-51. Fellow AAAS; mem. Internat. Sociol. Assn., Internat. Polit. Sci. Assn., Indsl. Relations Research Assn. (exec. com. 1965-68), Soc. for Study Social Problems (chmn. editorial com.), Am. Polit. Sci. Assn., Am. Sociol. Assn. (exec. council 1969-72, chmn. com. on info. tech. and privacy 1970-72), Council European Studies (steering com. 1980-83), AAUP, ACLU. Democrat. Jewish. Office: U Calif Dept Polit Sci 210 Barrows Hall Berkeley CA 94720

WILES, CHERYL B., dental hygienist, artist, trainer; b. Watertown, S.D., Jan. 5, 1951; d. Charles Brooks and Yvonne (Balsiger) W. BS, U. S.D., 1973; MS, Columbia U., 1974; sr. tng. cert., Regis U., 1991. Asst. prof. Sch. Dentistry U. Mo., Kansas City, 1974-80; watercolor artist Wiles Enterprises, Steamboat Springs and Nederland, Colo., 1981—; pvt. practice dental hygienist Boulder, 1981—; asst. prof. U. Colo. Dental Sch., Denver, 1991—; instrnl. designer Storage Tech., Louisville, 1991; cons. Procter & Gamble, Cin., 1989-92, Vipont Labs., Ft. Collins, Colo., 1991-92; trainer/educator Wiles Enterprises, Nederland, Colo., 1990—. Author: Complete Dental Letters Handbook, 1990; co-author: Communication Skills for Dental Hygienist, 1982; contbg. author: Clinical Dental Hygiene, 1992; contbr. articles to profl. jours.; commd. artist Women's World Cup Ski Racing, Steamboat Springs, Colo., 1989-92. Vol. Steamboat Springs Art Coun., 1981—; vol., mem. nat. membership com. AAUW, Washington, 1973—; auctioneer Morning Star Abuse Ctr., Oak Creek, Colo., 1991—. Named for best of show-interpretive landscape Nat. Wildlife Art Show, Kansas City, 1989. Mem. ASTD (internship com.), AAUW (mem.-at-large, membership com.), Am. Dental Hygienist Assn. (rsch. com.). Republican. Home: Wiles Enterprises 129 S Skyview Dr Nederland CO 80466

WILES, THOMAS MILTON, clergyman; b. Louisville, June 10, 1952; s. John Calvin and Esther Ruth (Keating) W.; m. Linda Sheryl Bryant, Aug. 16, 1974; children: Catherine Melissa, John Leonard, April Elizabeth. BA, Okla. Bapt. U., 1974; MA, Baylor U., 1987. Ordained to ministry Bapt. Ch., 1981. Adminstr. First Bapt. Ch., Ardmore, Okla., 1977-79; bus. adminstr. First Bapt. Ch., Waco, Tex., 1979-81; pastor Harris Creek Bapt. Ch., McGregor, Tex., 1981-86, First So. Bapt. Ch., Buckeye, Ariz., 1986—; trustee Ariz. Bapt. Children's Svcs., Phoenix, 1987—, chmn. trustees, 1992-93; Vacation Bible Sch. specialist Ariz. Soc. Bapt. Conv., Phoenix, 1989—, Assn. Sunday Sch. Improvement Support Team specialist, 1991—, chair order of bus., 1991-92; mem. task force for Christian studies Grand Canyon U., Phoenix, 1990-91. Columnist Uplift, 1990. Vol. Am. Cancer Soc., Buckeye, 1991, Buckeye Chem. Abuse Prevention Alliance. Mem. Buckeye Valley Ministerial Fellowship (pres. 1990-92), Buckeye C. of C. Democrat. Home: 717 Eason Ave Buckeye AZ 85326 Office: First So Bapt Ch 3d and Eason Buckeye AZ 85326

WILETS, LAWRENCE, physics educator; b. Oconomowoc, Wis., Jan. 4, 1927; s. Edward and Sophia (Finger) W.; m. Dulcy Elaine Margoles, Dec. 21, 1947; children—Ileen Sue, Edward E., James D.; m. Vivian C. Wolf, Feb. 8, 1976. B.S., U. Wis., 1948; M.A., Princeton, 1950, Ph.D., 1952. Research asso. Project Matterhorn, Princeton, N.J., 1951-53, U. Calif. Radiation Lab., Livermore, 1953; NSF postdoctoral fellow Inst. Theoretical Physics, Copenhagen, Denmark, 1953-55; staff mem. Los Alamos Sci. Lab., 1955-58; mem. Inst. Advanced Study, Princeton, 1957-58; mem. faculty U. Wash., Seattle, 1958—; prof. physics U. Wash., 1962—; cons. to pvt. and govt. labs.; vis. prof. Princeton, 1969, Calif. Inst. Tech., 1971. Author: Theories of Nuclear Fission, 1964, Nontopological Solitons, 1989, also over 165 articles. Del. Dem. Nat. Conv., 1968. NSF sr. fellow Weizmann Inst. Sci., Rehovot, Israel, 1961-62; Nordita prof. and Guggenheim fellow Lund (Sweden) U., also Weizmann Inst., 1976—; Sir Thomas Lyle rsch. fellow U. Melbourne, Australia, 1989; recipient Alexander von Humboldt sr. U.S. scientist award, 1983. Fellow Am. Phys. Soc., AAAS; mem. Fedn. Am. Scientists, AAUP (pres. chpt. 1969-70, 73-75, pres. state conf. 1975-76), Phi Beta Kappa, Sigma Xi. Club: Explorers. Office: U Washington Dept Physics FM 15 Seattle WA 98195

WILEY, MADELINE DOLORES, family nurse practitioner; b. Syracuse, N.Y., May 25, 1955; d. Raymond Aloysius and Elizabeth Mary (Schneider) W.; m. Robert Thomas Smithing, Sept. 9, 1978; 1 child, Alex Wiley. BSN, SUNY, Buffalo, 1977; MS in Nursing, U. Pa., 1980. Cert. in family nursing practice. Family nurse practitioner, adminstr. Vis. Nurse Assoc. of Camden, N.J., 1981-85; coord. geriatric nursing liaison Group Health Coop., Seattle, 1985-87; family nurse practitioner Va. Mason Med. Ctr., Seattle, 1987-88; clin. faculty U. Wash., Seattle, 1986—; pres. Health Connections, Kent, Wash., 1986—. Contbg. editor The Nurse Practitioner Jour., 1991—, editorial bd., 1992—; contbr. articles to profl. jours. Recipient Anne Sengbusch Leadership award SUNY at Buffalo, 1977. Mem. Am. Acad. Nurse Practitioners (state rep. 1988-91, bd. dirs. 1986-88, recording sec. 1985-86, recipient Cert. of Appreciation award 1991), ANA, Sigma Theta Tau. Office: Health Connections 24837 104th Ave SE Ste 100 Kent WA 98031-6800

WILEY, MARIA ELENA (NENA WILEY), writer, author; b. Mexico City, June 2, 1947; came to U.S., 1965; d. Mario Hector and Martha Joy Gottfried; m. Michael Bolin Wiley, Dec. 19, 1967; children: Michael, Marta Elena, Cristiana Joy, Samuel. Student, U. Ariz., 1965-67, U. Americas, Mexico City, 1967, Stanford U., 1967; BFA in Graphics, Ariz. State U., 1969; postgrad., No. Calif. State U., Stanislau, 1972-73. Pres. Canapes, SA, Mexico City, 1975-76, Little Eden, SA, Mexico City, 1976-79; editor, owner Fla. Aviation News, Miami, 1987; freelance photojournalist for major aviation publs. Author: America's Drug Enforcement Air Force, 1992, mil. novels, 1989—; contbr. aviation news articles on air def. to profl. jours. Bd. dirs. Jr. League, Mexico City, 1972-79, Jr. Women's Club, Miami, 1980-86. Squadron comdr. PAO/mission pilot Civil Air Patrol USAF, 1986—. Mem. Nat. Aero. Assn., Aircraft Owners and Pilots Assn., Air Force Assn., Ariz. Author's Assn., Challenger Ctr., Assn. Naval Aviation, Air & Space Assn., Aviation/Space Writers Assn. (award of Excellence in Journalism 1990). Republican. Home and Office: 940 Castillo Dr Litchfield Park AZ 85340-4535

WILEY, MICHAEL DAVID, chemistry educator; b. Long Beach, Calif., Nov. 28, 1939; s. David Michael and Elsa Louise (Magnuson) W.; m. Mary Alice Kuehne, Dec. 16, 1961 (div. July 1986); children—David Michael, Heather Jane. B.S. in Chemistry, U. So. Calif., 1961; Ph.D. in Organic Chemistry, U. Wash., 1969. Asst. prof. chemistry Calif. Luth. U., Thousand Oaks, 1968-74, assoc. prof., 1974-84, prof., 1984—; research assoc. U. Liverpool, Eng., 1981. NSF fellow, 1963-64; State of Calif. scholar, 1957-61. Mem. Am. Chem. Soc., Royal Soc. Chemistry, AAUP. Democrat. Lutheran. Office: Calif Luth U 60 Olsen Rd Thousand Oaks CA 91360-2787

WILEY, RANDY DUANE, electronics engineer; b. Denver, Feb. 6, 1958; s. Gerald Duane and Carol Jean (Hacking) W.; m. Paula Rae Floerchinger, Aug. 25, 1979; children: Megan Rae, Andrew William. A., C.C. of Denver, 1983; BS in Electronics Engring. Tech., Met. State Coll. of Denver, 1991. Fluid technician Beech Aircraft Corp., Boulder, Colo., 1977-81; v.p. Floerchinger Concrete Sawing, Denver, 1981-84; electronics technician Storage Tech. Corp., Louisville, 1984-85, Tallgrass Technologies Corp., Boulder, 1985; test analysis engr. Martin Marietta Astronautics Group, Denver, 1985-91; v.p. Chief Well Logging, Denver, 1980—; design test engr. Martin Marietta Astronautics Group, Denver, 1991—; PC computer cons., Broomfield, Colo., 1990—. Mem. The Planetary Soc. Office: Martin Marietta Astronautics Group 12275 S Hwy 121 Littleton CO 80127

WILEY, WILLIAM RODNEY, microbiologist, administrator; b. Oxford, Miss., Sept. 5, 1931; s. William Russell and Edna Alberta (Threlkeld) W.; m. Myrtle Louise Smith, Nov. 10, 1952; 1 child: Johari. B.S., Tougaloo Coll., Miss., 1954; M.S., U. Ill., Urbana, 1960; Ph.D., Wash. State U., Pullman, 1965. Instr. electronics and radar repair Keesler AFB-U.S. Air Force, 1956-58; Rockefeller Found. fellow U. Ill., 1958-59; research assoc. Wash. State U., Pullman, 1960-65; research scientist dept. biology Battelle-Pacific N.W. Labs., 1965-69, mgr. cellular and molecular biology sect. dept. biology, 1969-72, inst. coordinator, life scis. program, assoc. mgr. dept. biology, 1972-74, mgr. dept. biology, 1974-79, dir. research, 1979-84; sr. v.p., dir. Pacific N.W. div. Battelle Meml. Inst., Richland, Wash., 1984—; adj. assoc. prof. microbiology Wash. State U., Pullman, 1968—; found. assoc. Pacific Sci. Ctr., Seattle, 1989—; bd. dirs. Sta. KCTS Channel 9, Seattle, 1990—; trustee Oreg. Grad. Inst. Sci. and Tech., 1990—; cons. and lectr. in field. Contbr. chpts. to books, articles to profl. jours. Co-author book in microbiology. Bd. dirs. Wash. Tech. Ctr., 1984-88, sci. adv. panel Wash. Tech. Ctr., 1984-88, Fed. Res. Bank of San Francisco (Seattle branch) 1991—; mem. adv. com. U. Wash. Sch. Medicine, 1976-79; trustee Gonzaga U., 1981-89, bd. regents, 1986-81; bd. dirs. MESA program U. Wash., Seattle, 1984-90, United Way of Benton & Franklin Counties, Wash., 1984—, Tri-City Indsl. Devel. Council, 1984-92; mem. Wash. Council Tech. Advancement, 1984-85; bd. dirs. Forward Wash., The Voice for Statewide Econ. Vitality, 1984—, N.W. Coll. and Univ. Assn. for Sci., 1985—; mem. Tri-City Univ. Ctr. Citizens Adv. Council, 1985—; apptd. Wash. State Higher Edn. Coordinating Bd., 1986-89, Wash. State U. Found., 1986-89; mem. Wash. State U. bd. Regents, 1989—; bd. dirs. Washington Roundtable, 1989—, Goodwill Games, 1989-90; mem. adv. coun. Mont. State Sci. and Tech., 1990-91; mem. bd. overseers Whitman Coll., 1990—; mem. external adv. bd. Clark Atlanta U., 1991—; mem. Cen. Wash. U. Inst. for Sci. and Society Bd. of Advisors, 1991—, Engring. exec. com. Southern U., Baton Rouge, La, 1992—; mem. Coun. Govt. Univ. Industry Rsch. Roundtable, 1993—; bd. trustees Fred Hutchinson Cancer Rsch. Ctr., 1992—; engring. exec. com. Southern U., 1992—. With U.S. Army, 1954-56. Mem. Am. Soc. Biol. Chemists, Am. Soc. Microbiology, AAAS, Soc. Exptl. Biology and Medicine, Sigma Xi. Office: Battelle Meml Inst Pacific NW Divsn Battelle Blvd Richland WA 99352

WILFLEY, GEORGE MERRITT, manufacturing company executive; b. Denver, May 23, 1924; s. Elmer R. and Margaret W., B.A. U. Colo., 1950, postgrad., 1977; m. Eleanore Breitenstein; children—George Michael, John Frederick. With A.R. Wilfley & Sons, Inc., Denver, 1950—, pres., 1958—, also dir.; pres., dir. Western Foundries, Inc.; dir. First Interstate Bank of Denver. hon. trustee, chmn. bd. Boys Club of Denver, Inc. Served with F.A., AUS, 1943-46. Mem. AIME, Nat. Assn. Corrosion Engrs., Colo. Mining Assn., NAM (dir.). Denver Country Club (past pres.), University Club (past treas.), Alto Lakes Club, Castle Pines Club (charter). Republican. Episcopalian. Avocations: wine and art collecting, golf, fishing, hunting. Home: 34 Polo Club Cir Denver CO 80209-3308 Office: A R Wilfley and Sons Inc 7350 E Progress Pl Englewood CO 80111-2130

WILHELM, MARY LOU, librarian; b. Custer, S.D., Sept. 27, 1937; d. John Albert and Mary (Koch) W.; Richard Edgar Root, Jan. 14, 1990. BS in Elem. Edn., Concordia Tchrs. Coll., River Forest, Ill., 1960; MS in Library Sci., U. So. Calif., 1966; postgrad., U. Calif., Irvine, 1968-74. Librarian San Marino (Calif.) Pub. Libary, 1964-66; head librarian Orange Coast Coll., Costa Mesa, Calif., 1967-74, assoc. librarian, 1966-67, 74-76; dir. library svcs. Cuesta Coll., San Luis Obispo, Calif., 1976—. Contbr. articles to profl. jours. Mem. AAUW, Calif. Library Assn., Community Coll. Assn. Instrn. and Tech., Faculty Assn. Calif. Community Colls., Sierra Club. Office: Cuesta Coll Libr PO Box 8106 San Luis Obispo CA 93403-8106

WILHELM, ROBERT OSCAR, lawyer, civil engineer, developer; b. Balt., July 7, 1918; s. Clarence Oscar and Agnes Virginia (Grimm) W.; m. Grace Sanborn Luckie, Apr. 4, 1959. B.S. in Civil Engring., Ga. Tech. Inst., 1947, M.S.I.M., 1948; J.D., Stanford U., 1951. Bar: Calif. 1952, U.S. Supreme Ct. Mem. Wilhelm, Thompson, Wentholt and Gibbs, Redwood City, Calif., 1952—; gen. counsel Bay Counties Gen. Contractors; pvt. practice civil engring., Redwood City, 1952—; pres. Bay Counties Builders Escrow, Inc., 1972-88. With C.E., AUS, 1942-46. Mem. Bay Counties Civil Engrs. (pres. 1957), Peninsula Builders Exchange (pres. 1958-71, dir.), Calif. State Builders Exchange (tres. 1971). Clubs: Mason, Odd Fellows, Eagle, Elks. Author: The Manual of Procedures for the Construction Industry, 1971, Manual of Procedures and Form Book for Construction Industry, 8th edit., 1987; columnist Law and You in Daily Pacific Builder, 1955—; author: Construction Law for Contractors, Architects and Engineers. Home: 134 Del Mesa Carmel Carmel CA 93923 Office: 600 Allerton St Redwood City CA 94063-1596

WILHELM, STEPHEN PAUL, business executive; b. Berkeley, Calif., Oct. 28, 1948; s. Stephen and Elizabeth Ruth (Wilson) W.; m. Lila Marie Osborn, Aug. 21, 1971. B.A. in Physiology and Psychology, U. Calif.-Berkeley, 1971. Sr. claim rep., med. cost containment analyst Aetna Life Ins. Co., Oakland, Calif., 1971-81; v.p. Nematode Farm, Inc., Palo Alto, Calif.; founder, pres. NEMATEC-Biol. Control Agts., Lafayette, Calif. Chmn. community adv. council Mt. Diablo Hosp. Med. Ctr., Concord, Calif., 1978-82. Home: 4009 W Lakeshore Dr San Ramon CA 94583-4823 Office: NEMATEC-Bio Control Agts PO Box 93 Lafayette CA 94549-0093

WILHITE, RICHARD JAMES, media company executive; b. Boston, June 5, 1938; s. Richard Dodge and Mary Mildred (Crum) W.; m. Patricia Norris Ahern, Sept. 7, 1971; 1 child, Jennifer Jamie. AA, Worcester Jr. Coll., 1958; BS, Boston U., 1960; postgrad., U. So. Calif., 1960-62. Dir. community relations Orange & Rockland Utilities, Spring Valley, N.Y., 1964-69; comptroller Video Systems, L.A., 1969-71; pres. Wilhite Prodns., Inc., Malibu, Calif., 1971—. Produced Sorry No Vacancy, 1972. With USCG Aux. Mem. Acad. TV Arts and Scis. Republican. Home and Office: 3742 Seahorn Dr Malibu CA 90265-5699

WILHITE, WILSON CECIL, JR., anesthesiology educator; b. Birmingham, Ala., Apr. 19, 1935; s. Wilson Cecil and Lorraine (Gibbs) W.; m. Patricia Sewell, Aug. 13, 1957; children: Jennifer Lee Wilhite Pierce, Tiffany Patrice. BA, Samford U., 1956; MD, U. Ala., 1960. Diplomate Am. Bd. Anesthesiology. Intern U. Miami, Fla., 1960-61; resident in anesthesiology Wilford Hall USAF Med. Ctr., San Antonio, 1962-64; chmn. dept. anesthesiology Carraway Meth. Med. Ctr., Birmingham, 1966-82, pres. med. staff, 1975-77; vice chmn. dept. anesthesiology Bapt. Med. Ctr.-Montclair, Birmingham, 1982-83, chmn. dept., 1983-87; attending anesthesiologist Phenix Med. Park Hosp., Phenix City, Ala., 1987-89; prof. U. Tex. Med. Sch., Houston, 1989-91; prof., vice chmn. dept. anesthesiology UCLA Sch. Medicine, 1991—; nat. lectr. in field. Hon. dep. sheriff Jefferson County (Ala.) Sheriff's Dept., 1971—. Capt. M.C., USAF, 1961-66. Named Outstanding Clin. Instr. Dept. Anesthesiology, U. Tex. Med. Sch., 1990, 91. Fellow Am. Coll. Anesthesiologists; mem. AMA, Am. Soc. Anesthesiologists (bd. dirs. dist. 9 1971-80, nat. treas. 1980-85, 1st v.p. 1991-92, pres.-elect. 1993), Assn. Anesthesiology Clin. Dirs., So. Med. Assn., Internat. Anesthesia Rsch. Soc., Soc. Cardiovascular Anesthesiologists, Calif. Med. Assn., Calif. Soc. Anesthesiologists (ex-officio mem. bd. dirs. and ho. of dels. 1991-92), L.A. County Med. Assn., Am. Soc. Post Anesthesia Nurses (hon. life), Ala. Post Anesthesia Nurses Assn. (hon. life). Republican. Baptist. Home: 207 N Oakhurst Dr Beverly Hills CA 90210 Office: UCLA Sch Medicine 10833 Le Conte Ave Los Angeles CA 90024

WILKE MONTEMAYOR, JOANNE MARIE, patient care coordinator; b. Jerome, Ariz., Sept. 10, 1941; d. Karl Nickolas and Anna Linda (Worgt) Wilke; m. Casimiro L. Montemayor, Oct. 8, 1978. BS in Nursing, U. Colo., 1965; M in Nursing, U. Washington, 1974. Patient care coord. Vesper Hospice, San Leandro, Calif., 1989—. With USNR, 1959-79. Mem. Nat. Hospice Orgn. Democrat. Methodist.

WILKEN, LINDA MARLENE, musician, flight attendant; b. Kankakee, Ill., Dec. 3, 1957; d. Charles Edward and Verena Cecelia (Vogel) W. BMus, Eastern Ill. U., 1979; MMus, U. Colo., 1983. Piano instr. Tarrant County Jr. Coll., Hurst, Tex., 1983-84; summer intern Arvada (Colo.) Ctr. for Arts and Humanities, 1988; kindermusik tchr. Louisville, Colo., 1988-89; flight attendant Am. Airlines, Dallas, 1983—; pianist on tour Two Piano/Four Hand Duo with ptnr. Alex Craig, 1990—; piano soloist and accompanist, 1970—; pvt. piano tchr., 1978—. Author musical workshops; composer piano pieces; practitioner Circles of Life, 1992—.

WILKENING, JANE SHEPARD, secondary school educator; b. Jacksonville, N.C., Jan. 24, 1943; d. Percil Henry and Margaret Susan (King) S.; m. Peter Kohler Wilkening, Feb. 12, 1970; children: Brent Colin, Derek Stefan. BA, Atlantic Christian Coll., 1965. Cert. English, mental retarded educator, learning handicapped educator, resource specialist. English tchr. Perry High Sch., Pitts., 1965-67, Northwoods Park Jr. High, Jacksonville, N.C., 1967-68; tchr. of the educable retarded Sun Valley Jr. High, Los Angeles Unified Sch. Dist., 1968-73, reading coordinator, 1973-80; tchr. of educable retarded Sun Valley Jr. High, Los Angeles, 1980—; lectr. edn. colloquium LAUSD, Calif., 1984, spl. edn. fall conf., LAUSD, Calif., 1985; leader staff devel. programs: needs assessment for spl. edn., Sun Valley, Calif., 1983-85. Contbr. articles to profl. jours. Sec. Laurel Hall Day Sch. Com., North Hollywood, Calif., 1984-87; mem. ch. council Emmanuel Lutheran Ch., 1984-87. Mem. Spl. Educator's Resource Network, Downs Syndrome Parent's Group, Council for Exceptional Children, Computer Using Educators, NEA, United Tchrs. Los Angeles. Home: 14032 Hartsook St Sherman Oaks CA 91423-1212 Office: Sun Valley Jr High Sch 7330 Bakman Ave Sun Valley CA 91352-4999

WILKENING, LAUREL LYNN, university official, planetary scientist; b. Richland, Wash., Nov. 23, 1944; d. Marvin Hubert and Ruby Alma (Barks) W.; m. Godfrey Theodore Sill, May 18, 1974. BA, Reed Coll., 1966; PhD, U. Calif., San Diego, 1970. Asst. prof. to assoc. prof. U. Ariz., Tucson, 1973-80, dir. Lunar and Planetary Lab., head planetary scis., 1981-83, vice provost, prof. planetary scis., 1983-85, v.p. rsch., dean Grad. Coll., 1985-88; div. scientist NASA Hdqrs., Washington, 1980; prof. geol scis., adj. prof. astronomy, provost U. Washington, Seattle, 1988-93; chancellor U. Calif., Irvine, 1993—; vice chmn. Nat. Commn. on Space, Washington, 1984-86, Adv. Com. on the Future of U.S. Space Program, 1990; chair Space Policy Adv. Bd., Nat. Space Coun., 1991-92; co-chmn. primitive bodies mission study team NASA/European Space Agy., 1984-85; chmn. com. rendezvous sci. working group NASA, 1983-85; mem. panel on internat. cooperation and competition in space Congl. Office Tech. Assessment, 1982-83. Author: (monograph) Particle Track Studies and the Origin of Gas-Rich Meteorites, 1971; editor: Comets, 1982. U. Calif. Regents fellow, 1966-67; NASA trainee, 1967-70. Fellow Meteoritical Soc. (councilor 1976-80), Am. Assn. Advanced Sci.; mem. Am. Astron. Soc. (chmn. div. planetary scis. 1984-85), Am. Geophys. Union, AAAS, Internat. Astron. Union (orgn. com. 1979-82), Phi Beta Kappa. Democrat. Office: U Calif Chancellors Office 501 Adminstrn Bldg Irvine CA 92717

WILKES, JENNIFER RUTH, designer; b. St. Louis, Oct. 13, 1960; d. Philip Henry and Sheila Marlene (Meyer) Ilten; m. Evan T. Wilkes, Sept. 7, 1985; 1 child, Carter Christian. BA cum laude, U. Calif., San Diego, 1983. Sales coord. Vidal Sassoon Inc., 1984-85; designer, ptnr. Wilkes Fine Home Bldg., L.A., 1985—. Democrat. Lutheran. Home: 626 Palmera Pacific Palisades CA 90272

WILKES, PENNY FERANCE, writer; b. Pasadena, Calif., Aug. 8, 1946; d. Wesley Innis and Margaret (Lewis) Dumm; m. Michael B. Wilkes, June 29, 1968. BA in Anthropology, U. So. Calif., L.A., 1968. Dir. publs. The Bishop's Sch., La Jolla, Calif., 1973-78; editorial coord. Am. Jour. Orthodontics, La Jolla, 1978-84; writer, cons., owner Creative Communications, La Jolla, 1984—; creative dir. Creative Collaborative, San Diego, 1991—. Author: (short stories) Seven Smooth Stones, 1991; contbr. to numerous publs. Mem. lit. com. Old Globe Theatre. First Place award Nat. League Am. Pen Women, 1993. Mem. San Diego Writers and Editors Guild, Nat. League Am. Pen Women (publicist La Jolla chpt. 1988-89, v.p. 1989-90), Nat. Carousel Assn. (archivist 1986—), LEAD San Diego Inc., Toastmasters (v.p. La Jolla 1990, pres. 1991, Toastmaster of Yr. 1991), Laughmasters (v.p. membership 1991). Home and Office: PO Box 2201 La Jolla CA 92038-2201

WILKES, ROBERT LEE, educator; b. Omaha, Nebr., Oct. 2, 1942; s. Robert Calvin and Mary E. (Jones) W.; m. Joan S. Wexman (div.); children: Erin E., Jason S. (dec.), McKinnon L. BS, Iowa State U., 1965, MS, 1967. Tchr. Casper (Wyo.) Coll., 1971—; sr. scientist Essex Corp., Alexandria, Va., 1984-89. Contbr. articles to profl. jours. Lt. USN, 1968-70. Mem. Am. Psychol. Soc. Office: Casper Coll 125 College Dr Casper WY 82601-4699

WILKIE, DONALD WALTER, biologist, aquarium museum director; b. Vancouver, B.C., Can., June 20, 1931; s. Otway James and Jessie Margaret (McLeod) W.; m. Patricia Ann Archer, May 18, 1980; children: Linda, Douglas, Susanne. B.A., U. B.C., 1960, M.Sc., 1966. Curator Vancouver Pub. Aquarium, 1961-63, Phila. Aquarama, 1963-65; exec. dir. aquarium-mus. Scripps Instn. Oceanography, La Jolla, Calif., 1965—; aquatic cons. Author books on aquaria; contbr. numerous articles to profl. jours. Fellow San Diego Mus. Natural History.; mem. Am. Assn. Zoo Parks and Aquariums, Internat. Assn. Aquatic Animal Medicine, Nat. Marine Edn. Assn., Am. Assn. Mus., Am. Soc. Ichthyologists and Herpetologists, San Diego Zool. Soc. (animal health and conservation com.), Miramar Trap and Skeet Club (bd. dirs.). Home: 4548 Cather Ave San Diego CA 92122-2632 Office: U Calif San Diego Scripps Instn Oceanography Aquarium Mus 8602 La Jolla Shores Dr La Jolla CA 92093-0207 also: U Calif San Diego La Jolla CA 92093

WILKIE, MARGERY MICHELLE, banker; b. Longview, Wash., Mar. 15, 1958; d. Alan B. and Marilyn E. (Carlstrom) W.; m. James P. Miller, Aug. 3, 1985; children: Lucas Alan Miller, Matthew J. Miller. BS in Econs., Whitman Coll., 1979. Lic. assoc. fin. planner. Nat. bank examiner U.S. Treasury Dept., Great Falls, Mont., 1979-83; loan rev. officer 1st Interstate Bank, Great Falls, 1983-84; asst. v.p., mktg. officer 1st Interstate Bank, 1984-85; asst. v.p., comml. loan officer 1st Interstate Bank, Casper, Wyo., 1985-87; v.p., mktg. mgr. 1st Interstate Bank, 1987-90; with spl. projects First Interstate Bank of Ariz., Phoenix, 1991-92; recruiter First Interstate Bank of Ariz., 1992—. Founder Leadership Casper, 1987, chmn. steering com., 1990; head pub. rels and mktg. United Way, Casper, 1988-89, bd. dirs., 1989-90, tng. vol., 1990; vol. Literacy Vols. Am., 1990. Named Young Career Woman of Yr., Casper Bus. and Profl. Women's Club, 1988. Democrat. Presbyterian.

WILKIN, EUGENE WELCH, broadcasting executive; b. North Attleborough, Mass., May 14, 1923; s. Laurence Welch and Ruth Marion (Totten) W.; m. Anita Drake, Sept. 10, 1949; children: Judith Louise, Lawrence Welch 2d, Diana Lewis, William Alexander. A.B., Dartmouth Coll., 1948; postgrad., Grad. Sch. Bus. Adminstrn., Harvard, July 1963. Surety rep. Aetna Casualty Ins. Co., Boston, Providence, 1949-50; asst. to pres., graphic arts salesman J.C. Hall Co., Pawtucket, R.I., 1950-51; copywriter T. Robley Louitt Advt. Agy., Providence, 1951-52; sales rep., local sales mgr. WPRO, Providence, 1952; sales mgr. WPRO-Am-TV, 1953, nat. sales mgr. TV, 1955-61; gen. mgr. WGAN-TV, Portland, Maine, 1961-63; v.p., dir. Guy Gannett Broadcasting Services, Portland, 1963-68; dir. corporate devel. Guy Gannett Broadcasting Services, 1966-68; gen. mgr. King Broadcasting Co., Spokane, 1968-73; pres. Wilkin Broadcast Cons., Inc., 1974-90; with Wilkin Communications, 1990—. Author: Where Does Daddy Go, 1962, Broadcasting Directions, 1965. Chmn. for Maine Radio Free Europe Fund, 1963-65; pres. Northeast Hearing and Speech Center, Portland, 1965-68; mem. Gov.'s Com. on Voluntary Programs, 1973-75; chmn. pub. assistance com., citizens adv. bd. Wash. Dept. Social/Health Service; bd. dirs., chmn. 1973 sustaining fund drive Spokane Symphony Soc.; mem. devel. com. Whitworth Coll.; ex-officio mem. devel. com. Mental Health Center; chmn. pub. relations com. United Fund; vice chmn. pub. relations com. Retail Trade Bd.; mem. Am. Com. on E.W. Accord/Communications sub. com.; sec. ad hoc coalition Spokane County Homeowners Assns.; pres. Los Verdes Homeowners Assn., 1993; vol. comm. United Way San Luis Obispo, 1993—. Served to capt. C.E. U.S. Army, 1942-46, PTO. Mem. Advt. Fedn. Am. (gov. 1960, bd. dirs. 1966-67), San Juan C. of C., Nat. Assn. Broadcasters, Nat. Assn. TV Program Execs., Spokane and Inland Empire Dartmouth Alumni Assn. (pres. 1970-73), Orange County (Calif.) Dartmouth Alumni Assn. (pres. 1979-82, sec. 1982-85), Delta Upsilon (life). Home: 11 Villa Court San Luis Obispo CA 93401

WILKINS, CAROLINE HANKE, consumer agency administrator, political worker; b. Corpus Christi, Tex., May 12, 1937; d. Louis Allen and Jean Guckian Hanke; m. B. Hughel Wilkins, 1957; 1 child, Brian Hughel. Student, Tex. Coll. Arts and Industries, 1956-57, Tex. Tech. U., 1957-58; BA, U. Tex., 1961; MA magna cum laude, U. Ams., 1964. Instr. history Oreg. State U., 1967-68; adminstr. Consumer Services Div., State of Oreg., 1977-80, Wilkins Assoc., 1980—; mem. PFMC Salmon Adv. subpanel, 1982-86. Author: (with B. H. Wilkins) Implications of the U.S.-Mexican Water Treaty for Interregional Water Transfer, 1968. Dem. precinct committeewoman, Benton County, Oreg., 1964-90; publicity chmn. Benton County Gen. Election, 1964; chmn. Get-Out-the-Vote Com., Benton County, 1966; vice chmn. Benton County Dem. Cen. Com., 1966-70; vice chmn. 1st Congl. Dist., Oreg., 1966-68, chmn. 1968; vice chmn. Dem. Party Oreg., 1968-69, chmn. 1969-74; mem. exec. com. Western States Dem. Conf., 1970-72; vice chmn. Dem. Nat. Com., 1972-77, mem. arrangements com., 1972, 76, mem. Dem. charter commn., 1973-74; mem. Dem. Nat. Com., 1972-77, 85-89, mem. size and composition com., 1987-89, rules com. 1988; mem. Oreg. Govt. Ethics Commn., 1974-76; del., mem. rules com. Dem. Nat. Conv., 1988; 1st v.p. Nat. Fedn. Dem. Women, 1983-85, pres., 1985-87, parliamentarian, 1993—; mem. Kerr Libr. bd. Oreg. State U., 1989—, Corvallis-Benton County Libr. Found., 1991—, sec., 1993. Named Outstanding Mem., Nat. Fedn. Dem. Women, 1992. Mem. Nat. Assn. Consumer Agy. Adminstrs., Soc. Consumer Affairs Profls., Oreg. State U. Folk Club (pres. faculty wives 1989-90), Zonta (vice area bd. dirs. dist. 8, 1992—). Office: 3311 NW Roosevelt Dr Corvallis OR 97330-1169

WILKINS, CHARLES L., chemistry educator; b. Los Angeles, Calif., Aug. 14, 1938; s. Richard and Lenore M. (McKean) W.; m. Susan J., Oct. 17, 1966; 1 child, Mark R. BS, Chapman Coll., 1961; PhD, U. Oreg., 1966. Prof. chemistry U. Nebr., Lincoln, 1967-81; prof. U. Calif., Riverside, 1981—. Office: Univ of Calif-Riverside Dept of Chemistry Riverside CA 92521

WILKINS, CHRISTOPHER PUTNAM, conductor; b. Boston, May 28, 1957; s. Herbert Putnam and Angela (Middleton) W. BA, Harvard U., 1978; MusM, Yale U., 1981. Condr.-in-residence SUNY, Purchase, 1981-82; asst. condr. Oreg. Symphony, Portland, 1982-83, Cleve. Orch., 1983-86; assoc. condr. Utah Symphony, Salt Lake City, from 1986; condr. Colo. Springs Symphony Orch., 1989—; condr. Exxon Arts Endowment, 1982-86. Home: 168 Nashawtuc Rd Concord MA 01742-1617 Office: Colo Springs Symphony Orch PO Box 1692 Colorado Springs CO 80901-1692

WILKINS, KAY H., lawyer; b. Eagar, Ariz., June 4, 1940; d. Milford A. and Genevieve (Udall) Hall; m. Phelps W. Wilkins, Sept. 9, 1960; children: Wallace P., Kent. BA, Brigham Young U., 1962; JD, Ariz. State U., 1976. Bar: Ariz. 1976. Corp. counsel Johnson Stewart Johnson, Mesa, Ariz., 1976-81; assoc. Law Offices of Edward Doney, Phoenix, 1981-86; owner Kay H. Wilkins, atty., Mesa, 1986-81; ptnr. Wilkins & Tidd, Mesa, 1986—. Democrat. Office: Wilkins & Tidd 644 E Southern Ave Mesa AZ 85204-4934

WILKINS, MICHAEL GRAY, engineering educator, researcher, consultant; b. Northampton, Eng., Sept. 9, 1938; s. Norman Gray L. and Marian (Williams) W.; m. Ebtisam Seoudi, 1976; 1 child, Peter Ahmed. BSc with honors, U. Manchester, Eng., 1958; PhD, U. Ill., 1969. Trainee English Electric Weapons, Luton, 1966, Atomic Weapons Rsch. Establishment, Aldermaston, Eng., 1967; asst. prof. U. Va., Charlottesville, 1969-75; rsch. assoc. Simon Fraser U., Burnaby, B.C., 1976-78; sr. physicist U. Dayton Rsch. Inst., Albuquerque, 1979-81; sr. analyst Rockwell Internat., Albuquerque, 1981-86; mem. tech. staff Analytic Scis. Corp., McLean & Reston, Va., 1986-88; staff scientist Los Alamos (N.Mex.) Nat. Lab., 1988-90; rsch. prof. elec. engring. & computer engring. U. N.Mex., Albuquerque, 1992—. Researcher in RF systems for cosmic ray rsch., electrostatics, martian dust; patentee in field. Office: U NMex Dept Elec & Computer Engring Albuquerque NM 87131-1356

WILKINS, PHILIP CHARLES, judge; b. Jan. 27, 1913; student Sacramento Jr. Coll.; LL.B., U. Calif., San Francisco, 1939; m. Sue Wilkins, Aug. 9, 1941. Bar: Calif. 1939. Mem. firm A.D. McDougall, Sacramento, 1940-42, Rowland & Craven, Sacramento, 1946-54; individual practice law, Sacramento, 1954-59; ptnr. firm Wilkins, Little & Mix, Sacramento, 1959-65, Wilkins & Mix, Sacramento, 1966-69; judge U.S. Dist. Ct., Eastern Dist. Calif., Sacramento, 1969—, now sr. judge. Served to lt. USNR, 1942-46. Office: US Dist Ct 2028 US Courthouse 650 Capitol Mall Sacramento CA 95814-4708

WILKINS, RICHARD GUNDERSEN, law educator, consultant; b. Salt Lake City, Dec. 12, 1952; s. George R. and Marjorie (Gundersen) W.; m. Melany Moore Wilkins, Sept. 12, 1974; children: Brooke, Brinton, Claire, Rex. BA, Brigham Young U., Provo, Utah, 1976, JD, 1979. Bar: Calif. 1980, D.C. 1981, U.S. Supreme Ct. 1983, Utah 1986. Law clk. U.S. Ct. Appeals (5th cir.), New Orleans, 1979-80; assoc. Vinson & Elkins, Washington, 1980-81; asst. to solicitor gen. U.S. Dept. Justice, Washington, 1981-84; assoc. prof. law J. Reuben Clark Law Sch., Brigham Young U., 1984-89, prof., 1989—; of counsel Holme Roberts & Owen, Denver, 1985-93, Wood, Spendlove & Quinn, Salt Lake City, 1993—. Contbr. articles to legal jours. Advisor on abortion policy Gov. Utah Gov. Norman Bangeter, Salt Lake City, 1989-90. Mem. Order of Coif. Republican. Mormon. Office: Brigham Young U J Reuben Clark Law Sch 436 JRCB Provo UT 84602

WILKINSON, CHARLES MCNULTY, broadcasting executive; b. Pasadena, Calif., July 24, 1962; s. Burton Francis and Mary (Casten) W.; m. Patricia May Dunn, Sept. 15, 1992; 1 child, Alia Mary. BS, San Diego State U., 1988. Controller The Wilkinson Group, San Diego, L.A., 1984-87; controller McNulty Broadcasting, Chico, Calif., 1988-89, chief operating officer, 1989-91, CEO, 1991—. Office: McNulty Broadcasting 312 Otterson Ste F Chico CA 95928

WILKINSON, DAVID LAWRENCE, lawyer; b. Washington, Dec. 6, 1936; s. Ernest LeRoy and Alice Valera (Ludlow) W.; m. Patricia Anne Thomas, Dec. 30, 1976; children: David Andrew, Samuel Thomas, Margaret Alice, Katherine Anne. B.A. cum laude in History, Brigham Young U., 1961; B.A. in Jurisprudence, Oxford U., Eng., 1964, M.A., 1969; J.D., U. Calif.-Berkeley, 1966. Bar: Calif. 1966, Utah 1972. Assoc. Lawler, Felix & Hall, Los Angeles, 1966-71; ptnr. Cook & Wilkinson, Los Angeles, 1971-72; asst. atty. gen. State of Utah, Salt Lake City, 1972-76, 77-79; chief dep. to Salt Lake County Atty., 1979-80; atty. gen. State of Utah, Salt Lake City, 1981-89; inspector gen. Legal Svcs. Corp., Washington, 1989-91; cons., 1991—; spl. instr. Brigham Young U. Sch. Law, 1976-77, bd. visitors Sch. of Law, 1983-85; panelist Robert A. Taft Inst. Of Govt., Salt Lake City, 1974-76, 83-84; founder, mgr. Utah Bar. Rev. Course, 1973-76. Mem. Utah Council Criminal Justice Adminstrn., 1974-76, 77, Council Criminal and Juvenile Justice, 1984-89. Served with U.S. Army, 1961-62. Rhodes scholar, 1961-64. Mem. Utah Bar Assn. (chmn. eminent domain sect. 1979-80). Republican. Mormon.

WILKINSON, EUGENE PARKS, nuclear engineer; b. Long Beach, Calif., Aug. 10, 1918; s. Dennis William and Daisy Amelia (Parks) W.; m. Janice Edith Thuli, Mar. 28, 1942; children: Dennis Eugene, Stephen James, Marian Lynn, Rodney David. AB in Chemistry, San Diego State U., 1938. Instr. chemistry San Diego State U., 1938-39; commd. ensign U.S. Navy, 1940, advanced through grades to vice adm., 1970; served various locations including 1st comdg. officer USS Nautilus (1st nuclear-powered submarine), 1953-57; 1st comdg. officer USS Long Beach, 1959-63, 1st nuclear-powered surface ship; ret., 1974; exec. v.p. Data Design Labs., Cucamonga, Calif., 1977-80; pres., chief exec. officer Inst. Nuclear Power Ops., Atlanta, 1980-84, pres. emeritus, 1984—; bd. dirs. Data Design Labs.; emeritus bd. dirs. Advanced Resource Devel. Corp. Columbia, Md., MDM Engring. Corp., San Clemente, Calif., chmn. bd. Decorated Legion of Merit, Silver Star, D.S.M. with three oak leaf clusters, others, Second Order Sacred Treasure Japan; recipient George Westinghouse Gold medal ASME, 1983, Oliver Townsend medal Atomic Indsl. Forum, 1984, Gold medal Uranium Inst., 1989. Mem. Am. Soc. Naval Engrs., Am. Nuclear Soc., Navy League, Submarine League, Nat. Acad. Engring. Home: 1449 Crest Rd Del Mar CA 92014

WILKINSON, JEFFREY WADE, military officer; b. Greeley, Colo., Jan. 1, 1966; s. Leslie Virgle and Karen Sue (Lendrum) W. BS in Computer Sci., USAF Acad., 1990. Commd. 2d lt. USAF, 1990, advanced through grades to 1st lt., 1992; satellit attitude software analyst 1001 Space Systems Squadron, Denver, 1990-92; lead satellite attitude software analyst 21 Space Systems Squadron, Denver, 1992—, space craft simulator system mgr., 1992—. Mem. Assn. of Computing Machinery. Home: 7500 E Quincy Ave # G208 Denver CO 80237 Office: 21 Space System Squadron Bldg 1534 Lowery AFB Denver CO 80237

WILKINSON, LAURA, radio station owner, management executive; b. Auburn, N.Y., Dec. 11, 1957; d. Burton F. Jr. and Mary Casten Wilkinson; children: Matheson Charles, Cameron James. Student, UCLA, 1975-77; BA, San Diego State U., 1985. With talent div. Sta. WQSR-FM, Tampa, St. Petersburg, Fla., 1977, Sta. WLUP-FM, Chgo., 1978-79, Sta. KPRI-FM, San Diego, 1979-81, Sta. KCBQ-AM/FM, San Diego, 1981-87, Sta. KGTV-10, San Diego, 1985-87; pres., gen. mgr., v.p., prin., dir. Stas. KALF/KZZP, Chico, Calif., 1987—; vice chmn. McNulty Broadcasting Corp., Chico, 1987—; bd. dirs. Coyote Communications Corp., Morgan Hill, Calif., KIXE-TV, Redding, Calif., Chico Econ. Planning Corp., 1991—. Co-prodr.: Sports Week San Diego, 1981-83. Bd. dirs. Tehama County United Way, 1988—; mem. Bus. and Profl. Women, Red Bluff, 1987-89. Recipient Ace award Cable TV, N.Y.C., 1983, 3 Beam awards Chico (Calif.) Ad Club, 1988. Libertarian. Presbyterian. Office: McNulty Broadcasting Corp PO Box 7950 Chico CA 95927-7950

WILKINSON, ROSEMARY REGINA CHALLONER, poet, author; b. New Orleans, Feb. 21, 1924; d. William Lindsay Challoner Jr. and Julia Regina (Sellen) Challoner/Schillo; m. Henry Bertram Wilkinson, Oct. 15, 1949; children: Denis James, Marian Regina, Paul Francis, Richard Challoner. Lifetime credential to teach poetry, San Francisco State U., 1978; LHD (hon.), Livre U., Pakistan, 1975; DLitt (hon.), World Acad. Arts & Culture, Rep. of China, 1981. Author: (poetry books) A Girl's Will, 1973, California Poet, 1976, Earth's Compromise, 1977, It Happened to Me, 1978, I Am Earth Woman, 1979, The Poet and the Painter, 1981, Poetry and Arte, 1982, Gems Within, 1984, Nature's Guest, 1984, In the Pines, 1985, Longing For You, 1986, Purify the Earth, 1988, Sacred in Nature, 1988, Earth's Children, 1990, New Seed, 1991, Angels and Poetry, 1992, Cambrian Zephyr, 1993; (epic) An Historical Epic, 1974. Founder Poetry-Fine Arts Div. of San Mateo (Calif.) County Fair, 1977, for USA World Acad. of Arts & Culture-USA, San Francisco, 1985, Dr. Williams Poetry Workshop, Burlingame High Sch., 1985. Mem. World Congress of Poets (Taipei, Taiwan bd. dirs. 1973—, San Francisco pres. 1981), Nat. League Am. Pen Women Inc. (Washington 4th and 5th v.p. 1986-90, Berkeley, Calif. pres. 1988-90), The Authors Guild, Authors League of Am., P.E.N., Soroptomist Internat. (hon.). Democrat. Roman Catholic. Home and Office: World Congress of Poets and World Acad of Arts Culture 3146 Buckeye Ct Placerville CA 95667-8334

WILL, PETER MILNE, communications research company executive; b. Peterhead, Scotland, Nov. 2, 1935; came to U.S., 1964; s. James and Margaret (Milne) W.; m. Angela Hay Giulianotti, Mar. 21, 1959; children: Christopher, Jonathan, Gabrielle. BS in Engring., Aberdeen U., 1958, PhD, 1960. Mgr., rsch. scientist IBM Rsch., Yorktown Heights, N.Y., 1965-78; industry tech. advisor IBM Advt. Mfg. Systems, Boca Raton, Fla., 1978-80; dir. prodn. systems Schlumberger, Houston, 1980-83; dir. systems sci. Schlumberger, Ridgefield, Conn., 1983-86; dir. Schlumberger/Fairchild Rsch., Palo Alto, Calif., 1986-87; dir. measurement & mfg. rsch. Hewlett-Packard Labs., Palo Alto, 1987-90; dir. design strategy HP Corp., Palo Alto, 1990-92; dir. high performance computing and communication USC/ISI, Marina del Rey, Calif., 1992—; mem. cmputer sci. & tech. bd. Nat. Rsch. Coun., Washington, 1982-85; mem. info. sci. & technology adv. group DARPA, Washington, 1987—; chmn. adv. coms., NSF, Washington, 1978-86; mem. selection com. Sci. Rsch. Ctr. Grants, Canadian Sci. Coun., Ottawa, 1988-89. Contbr. articles to profl. jours.; patentee in field. Recipient Joseph Engelberger award in Robotics, Robotics Inst. of Am., 1989. Mem. IEEE, Assn. for Computing Machinery. Presbyterian. Office: USC/ISI 4676 Admiralty Way Marina Del Rey CA 90292

WILL, TIMOTHY JOSEPH, military officer; b. Poughkeepsie, N.Y., July 18, 1960; s. Joseph John and Patricia Ann (Smith) W.; m. Kelly Kathleen Cooper, June 9, 1989; 1 child, Tiffany Joy. BS in Biology, USAF Acad., 1982. Commd. 2d lt. USAF, 1982, advanced through grades to capt., 1986; biologist Bird/Aircraft Strike Hazard Team, Panama City, Fla., 1982-86; orbital analyst Space Surveillance Ctr., Cheyenne Mountain Complex, Colorado Springs, Colo., 1986-87; orbital analyst instr. Air Force Space Command, 1013th Combat Crew Tng. Squadron, Colorado Springs, 1987-89; chief ops. tng. 13th Missile Warning Squadron, Clear Air Force Sta., Alaska, 1989-90; mech. radar systems program mgr. HQ Air Force Space Command, Peterson AFB, Colorado Springs, Colo., 1990-91, spacetrack program element monitor, 1991—. Republican. Office: HQ AFSPACE COM Peterson AFB CO 80914

WILLARD, H(ARRISON) ROBERT, electrical engineer; b. Seattle, May 31, 1933; s. Harrison Eugene and Florence Linea (Chelquist) W.; B.S.E.E., U. Wash., 1955, M.S.E.E., 1957, Ph.D., 1971. Staff asso. Boeing Sci. Research Labs., Seattle, 1959-64; research asso. U. Wash., 1968-72, sr. engr. and research prof. applied physics lab., 1972-81; sr. engr. Boeing Aerospace Co., Seattle, 1981-84; dir. instrumentation and engring. MetriCor Inc. (previously Tech. Dynamics, Inc.), 1984—. Served with AUS, 1957-59. Lic. profl. engr., Wash. Mem. IEEE, Am. Geophys. Union, Phi Beta Kappa, Sigma Xi, Tau Beta Pi. Contbr. articles to tech. jours. Patentee in field. Office: 18800 142D Ave NE Ste 4 Woodinville WA 98072

WILLARD, NANCY ELLEN, communications director; b. Phila., June 22, 1952; d. Miles Jamison and Alice Mildred (Schreiber) Willard; 1 child, Jordan Jamison. BS in Elem. Edn., U. Utah, 1975; MS in Spl. Edn., U. Oreg., 1977; JD, Willamette U., 1983. Co-counselor Children's Ctr., Salt Lake City, 1974-75; spl. edn. tchr. Medford (Oreg.) Sch. Dist., 1977-80; law clk. Garrett, Seideman et al, Salem, Oreg., 1980-83, Lane County Cir. Ct., Eugene, Oreg., 1983-84; pvt. practice law Eugene, Oreg., 1984-90, edn. and econ. devel. cons., 1990—; dir., community info. communications network Lane On Line, Eugene, Oreg., 1993—; dir. Pacific Rsch. Inst., Eugene, 1991—. Mem. Eugene City Club. Home and Office: 788 W 23d Ave Eugene OR 97405

WILLARD, ROBERT EDGAR, lawyer; b. Bronxville, N.Y., Dec. 13, 1929; s. William Edgar and Ethel Marie (Van Ness) W.; m. Shirley Fay Cooper, May 29, 1954; children: Laura Marie, Linda Ann, John Judson. B.A. in Econs., Wash. State U., 1954; J.D., Harvard U., 1958. Bar: Calif. 1959. Law clk. to U.S. dist. judge, 1958-59; pvt. practice L.A., 1959-82; assoc. firm Flint & Mackay, 1959-61; pvt. practice, 1962-64; mem. firm Willard & Baltaxe, 1964-65, Baird, Holley, Baird & Galen, 1966-69, Baird, Holley, Galen & Willard, 1970-74, Holley, Galen & Willard, 1975-82, Galvin & Willard, Newport Beach, Calif., 1982-86; pvt. practice Newport Beach, 1987-89; mem. firm Davis, Punelli Keathley & Willard, Newport Beach, 1990—; Dir. various corps. Served with AUS, 1946-48, 50-51. Mem. ABA, Los Angeles County Bar Assn., State Bar Calif., Assn. Trial Lawyers Am., Am. Judicature Soc., Acacia Frat. Congregationalist. Club: Calcutta Saddle and Cycle. Home: 1840 Oriole Dr Costa Mesa CA 92626-4758 Office: 610 Newport Center Dr Ste 1010 Newport Beach CA 92660-6462

WILLARD, THOMAS SPAULDING, English language educator; b. Richmond, Va., Nov. 25, 1944; s. DeVoe Holmes and Martha Louise (Daniels) W.; m. Marilyn Eve Sheridan, Aug. 28, 1976; children: Christopher DeVoe, Gregory Benjamin. BA, George Washington U., 1967, MA, 1970; PhD, U. Toronto, Ont., Can., 1978. Assoc. editor Internat. Rev., Toronto, 1972-73; sr. writer Imperial Oil Ltd., Toronto, 1974-75; ptnr. Minds & Resources, Toronto, 1976-78; lectr. U. Ariz., Tucson, 1978-81, asst. prof., 1981-87, assoc. prof., 1987—. Author: (with others) Theorien vom Ursprung der Sprache, 1989, Literature and Medicine During the 18th Century, 1993; co-editor: Visionary Poetics, 1991; rev. editor Cauda Pavonis: Studies in Hermeticism, 1982—. Rsch. grante Embassy of Can., 1983. Mem. MLA, Phi Beta Kappa (pres. Ariz. chpt. 1991). Home: 3718 N Placita Chimenea Tucson AZ 85716-0805 Office: U Ariz Dept English Tucson AZ 85721

WILLBANKS, ROGER PAUL, publishing and book distributing company executive; b. Denver, Nov. 25, 1934; s. Edward James and Ada Gladys (Davis) W.; m. Beverly Rae Masters, June 16, 1957; children: Wendy Lee, Roger Craig. B.S., U. Denver, 1957, M.B.A., 1965. Economist, bus. writer, bus. forecaster Mountain States Tel. Co., Denver, 1959-66; dir. pub. relations Denver Bd. Water Commrs., 1967-70; pres. Royal Publs. Inc., Denver, 1971—, Nutri-Books Corp., Denver, 1971—, Inter-Sports Book and Video, 1986—. Editor Denver Water News, 1967-70, Mountain States Bus., 1962-66. Mem. Gov. of Colo.'s Revenue Forecasting Com., 1963-66. Served with U.S. Army, 1957-58. Recipient Pub. Rels. award Am. Water Works Assn., 1970, Leadership award Nat. Inst. of Nutritional Edn., 1989. Mem. Am. Booksellers Assn., Nat. Nutritional Foods Assn., Pub. Rels. Soc. Am. (charter mem. health sect.), Denver C. of C., SAR. Republican. Lutheran. Clubs: Columbine Country, Denver Press, Auburn Cord Duesenberg, Rolls Royce Owners, Classic Car of Am., Denver U. Chancellor's Soc., Ferrari. Address: Royal Publs Inc PO Box 5793 Denver CO 80217

WILLDEN, GARY DELBERT, recreation and outdoor educator; b. Delta, Utah, Dec. 17, 1946; s. Delbert Verland and LaRue (Bennett) W.; m. Joan Lambert, June 2, 1969; children: Jeffrey, Jeremy, Gregory, Matthew, Michael, Steven, Kelsey. BS, Brigham Young U., 1972, MA, 1973; PhD, U. Utah, 1983. Community edn. dir. Kearns High Sch., Salt Lake City, 1972-75; outdoor adventure program dir. Realms of Inquire Pvt. Sch., Salt Lake City, 1975-77; lectr. health, phys. edn., recreation and dance Weber State Coll., Ogden, Utah, 1977-79, asst. prof. health, phys. edn., recreation and dance, 1979-84, assoc. prof. health, phys. edn., recreation and dance, 1984-89, prof. health, phys. edn., recreation and dance, 1989—; chmn. dept. health, phys. edn., recreation and dance Weber State Coll., 1985-90; dir. Intermtn. Leisure Symposia, Ogden, 1986, 87; cons. in field; lectr. in field. Contbr. articles to various profl. jours. Chmn. varsity scouting Lake Bonneville Coun. Boy Scouts Am., Ogden, 1986; bd. dirs. Ogden Community Nature Ctr., 1984-86. With U.S. Army Res., 1964-68. Mem. Am. Assn. Leisure and Recreation (nat. necrology chmn. 1985—, bd. dirs. southwest dist., intramural v.p. 1988-90), Assn. Exptl. Edn., Utah Assn. Health, Phys. Edn., Recreation and Dance (v.p. recreation 1981-82), Utah Gov.'s Coun. Health and Phys. Fitness (chmn. 1988-89), Utah Recreation Parks Assn. (edn. v.p. 1984-87, editor Leisure Insights jour. 1985-87), Ogden Community Nature Ctr. (bd. dirs. 1984-86), Clowns of Am. Internat., Nat. Speleol. Soc., Internat. Jugglers Assn., Unicycling Soc. Am., Phi Kappa Phi, Phi Eta Sigma. Mormon. Home: 1378 N 75 W Centerville UT 84014-3300 Office: Weber State U Ogden UT 84408-2801

WILLEMS, ARNOLD LEE, curriculum and instruction educator; b. Millersburg, Ohio, Sept. 16, 1942; s. Abraham Lincoln and Ruth (Miller) W; m. Wanda Lucille Mast, June 5, 1964; children: Emily Marie, David Arnold. BA, Goshen Coll., 1964; MA, Western Mich. U., 1968; EdD, Ind. U., 1971. Elem. tchr. Goshen (Ind.) Community Schs., 1964-69; from. asst. prof. to prof. curriculum and instruction U. Wyo., Laramie, 1971—, head dept. curriculum and instruction, 1983-85, asst. dean Coll. Edn., 1984-87; cons. pub. schs. and profl. orgns. Co-author textbook Living Wyoming's Past, 1983; editor (books) Elementary Music Theory: Curriculum Ideas and Guides for Teachers, 1978, Peopling the High Plains-Wyoming's European Heritage: Curriculum Ideas and Guides for Teachers, 1977, India Seminar: Primary Curriculum Unit, 1974, India Seminar: Intermediate Curriculum Unit, 1974. Recipient Merit award for edn. leadership Project Innovation, Chula Vista, Calif., 1985; Sch. Edn. fellow Ind. U., 1970-71. Mem. Assn. for Supervision and Curriculum Devel., Assn. Tchr. Educators, Internat. Reading Assn., Nat. Coun. Tchrs. of English, Phi Delta Kappa (rsch. dir. 1986-88, Rsch. award 1986), Kappa Delta Pi. Democrat. Presbyterian. Home: 5517 Bill Nye Ave Laramie WY 82070-5307 Office: U Wyo McWhinnie Hall Rm 316 Laramie WY 82071

WILLEMS, JOHN JOSEPH, physician; b. N.Y.C., Aug. 6, 1947; s. Hartman John and Mary Margaret (Phillips) W.; m. Christine Ann Batten, Feb. 22, 1975; children: Amy Lynn, Amanda Louise. BS, Manhattan Coll., 1969; MD, N.Y. Med. Coll., 1973. Intern U. Man., Winnipeg, Can., 1973-74; resident in ob-gyn. Health Scis. Ctr., Winnipeg, 1974-76; asst. prof. reproductive medicine U. Calif., San Diego, 1978-82; staff physician in ob-gyn. Scripps Clinic and Rsch. Found. Med. Group, La Jolla, Calif., 1982—; lectr. in field. Contbr. articles to profl. jours. Fellow Am. Coll. Obstetricians and Gynecologists, Soc. Obstetricians and Gynecologists of Can., Internat. Soc. for Study of Vulvar Disease; mem. Royal Soc. Medicine (assoc.), Royal Coll. Physicians and Surgeons of Can., Am. Inst. Ultrasound in Medicine, San Diego County Med. Soc., Calif. Med. Assn., S.W. Ob-Gyn. Soc. Republican. Presbyterian. Office: Scripps Clinic & Rsch Found 10666 N Torrey Pines Rd La Jolla CA 92036

WILLENBERG, JAY MICHAEL, environmental engineer; b. N.Y.C., Jan. 21, 1948; s. Larry E. and Ethel (Horowitz) W.; m. Linda Kay Ward, Nov. 27, 1971; 1 child, Paul. BSME, U. Wash., 1969, BS in Indsl. Engring., 1970. Registered profl. engr., Wash. Environ. engr. Wash. State Dept. Ecology, Redmond, 1971—; instr. Air Pollution Tng. Inst., EPA, Seattle, 1980—. Contbr. articles to profl. jours. Mem. Air and Waste Mgmt. Assn. (sec.-treas. Pacific N.W. internat. sect. 1988-90, pres. 1991, pres. Puget Sound chpt. 1987), Source Evaluation Soc. (pres. 1989). Home: 18635 NE 21st St Redmond WA 98052 Office: Wash State Dept Ecology 4350 150th Ave NE Redmond WA 98052

WILLENBRINK, JOSEPH LAWRENCE, III, environmental industry executive, consultant; b. Louisville, Nov. 4, 1955; s. Joseph L. Jr. and Mary Margaret (Williams) W. BS in Chemistry, U. Louisville, 1985; MBA, UCLA, 1991, cert. hazardous materials mgmt., 1993. Registered environ. assessor, Calif. Mfrs. rep., cons. Jellico Chem. Co., Louisville, 1980-86; hazardous materials cons. Rho-Chem Corp., Inglewood, Calif., 1986-90; exec. v.p., gen. mgr. Summit Environ. Corp., Alhambra, Calif., 1990-91; owner, pres. W.E.S.T. (Willenbrink Environ. Svcs. and Tech.), L.A., 1990—. Tchr./tutor L.A. Libr. Adult Reading Program, 1990—. Mem. Nat. Environ. Health Assn., Calif. Environ. Health Assn., Profl. Environ. Mktg. Assn., Mensa, Intertel. Office: W E S T PO Box 658 Venice CA 90291

WILLEY, DANIEL SCOTT, environmentalist; b. Corpus Christi, Tex., June 2, 1950; s. Donald Scott and Gladys Consuelo (Bernal) W.; m. Mary Elaine Kuchar, Feb. 14, 1983; 1 child, Bray Scott. AA, Centralia (Wash.) Coll., 1982; BS, BA, Evergreen State Coll., Olympia, Wash., 1984. 0regional EPA and state TSCA insp. Wash. State Dept. Ecology, Olympia, 1989-90, sr. water quality insp., 1986-88, nuclear and mixed waste compliance officer,

1990—. With U.S. Army, 1975-78. Recipient Outstanding Svc. award Wash. State Dept. Ecology, 1987. Office: Mailstop PV-11 Wash State Dept Ecology Olympia WA 98504

WILLEY, ELIZABETH LOU, lawyer; b. Salt Lake City, Oct. 7, 1952; d. Walter Wilson and Dorothy Leola (Ryan) W. BSN, U. Utah, 1976; M Nursing in Physiol., U. Wash., 1979; JD, U. Utah, 1989. Lic. nurse clinician, Utah; bar: Utah, U.S. Dist. Ct. Utah 1990, U.S. Ct. Appeals (D.C. cir.) 1992. Staff nurse ICU Holy Cross Hosp., Salt Lake City, 1979; faculty Coll. of Nursing Brigham Young U., Provo, Utah, 1979-89; assoc. law clk. Strong & Hanni, 1987—; mem. State Bd. Nursing, 1981-87, chmn. edn. com., 1983-84, mem. rules and regulations com., edn. com., 1983-87, chmn. state bd., 1984-87; mem. Nursing Leadership Forum, 1984-87; chmn. Utah State Bd. Nursing Entry into Practice Task Force, Nat. Coun. state Bds. Nursin Entry into Practice Com., 1985-86; mem. SBN/UNA Ad Hoc Com., Nurse Practice Act, 1983-84; lectr. in field. Author: (with others) Risk Management in Health Care: An Updated Service, 1990; contbr. articles to profl. jours. NIH Nursing Edn. grantee, 1978; recipient Outstanding Young Women of Am. award 1983, Outstanding Young Women award Bountiful (Utah) Jaycee Aux., 1983, Tchr. of Yr. award Utah Student Nurses Assn., 1985, 86, Nurse Visible in Politics award Utah Nurse Assn., 1987. Mem. ABA, ANA, Salt Lake County Bar Assn., Washington D.C. Bar, Utah Bar Assn., Utah Nurses' Assn., Mortar Bd., Sigma Theta Tau, Phi Kappa Phi. Democrat. Mem. LDS Church. Office: Strong & Hanni 600 Boston Bldg Salt Lake City UT 84111

WILLHIDE, GARY L., educational administrator; b. Chambersburg, Pa., Oct. 6, 1944; s. Leon Seaton and Annabelle (Nye) W. BS in Edn., Shippensburg U., 1966, MS in Communications, 1974. Staff writer, bur. chief Harrisburg (Pa.) Patriot-News, 1966-70; asst. dir., then dir. pub. rels. Shippensburg U. Pa., 1970-88; dir. pub. affairs Oreg. Inst. Tech., Klamath Falls, 1988—; founding bd. dirs., treas., exec. com. Coll. and Univ. Pub. Rels. Assn. Pa., 1976-88; chair pub. info. adv. com. Pa. Assn. Colls. and Univs., 1983-88; chair pub. rels. coun. Pa. State System Higher Edn., Harrisburg, 1985-87. Mem. Cumberland County Bicentennial Commn., Carlisle, Pa., 1970-76; vice chair Cumberland County Drug/Alcohol Commn., Carlisle, 1983-88; mem., treas. Klamath County HIV-AIDS Coun., 1988-90; mem. adv. bd. Stepping Stones Treatment Ctr., Klamath Falls, 1989—, v.p., 1991, pres., 1992—. Recipient Disting. Svc. award Cumberland County Drug/Alcohol Commn., 1987. Mem. Am. Assn. State Colls. and Univs. (pub. info. adv. com. 1990-92), Coun. Advancement and Support of Edn. Home: 2525 Yonna St Klamath Falls OR 97601-1263 Office: Oreg Inst Tech 3201 Campus Dr Klamath Falls OR 97601-8801

WILLIAMS, ALBERT PAINE, economist; b. Elgin, Tex., Mar. 5, 1935; s. Albert Paine and Mary Dempes (Hudler) W.; m. Elizabeth Ann Whitaker, June 22, 1957; children: Albert, Robert, John. B.S., U.S. Naval Acad., 1957; M.A., Fletcher Sch., Tufts U., 1963; M.A.L.D., Tufts U., 1964, Ph.D., 1967. Budget examiner, internat. economist Bur. Budget, Washington, 1965-67; adv. on fgn. assistance strategy and econ. policy White House Staff, Washington, 1967-68; economist RAND Corp., Santa Monica, Calif., 1968-72, sr. economist, 1972—, dir. health scis. program, 1976-90; dir. RAND/UCLA Ctr. for Health Policy Study, 1982—, corp. rsch. mgr., social policy, 1990—; prof. RAND Grad. Sch., 1971—, mem. adv. bd., 1975—. Trustee Santa Monica Hosp. Med. Ctr., 1992—, Ednl. Commn. for Fgn. Med. Grads., 1993—; scoutmaster Great Western coun. Boy Scouts. Am., 1971-78, 82-88. With USN, 1957-62. Recipient Profl. Achievement award Exec. Office of Pres., 1967. Mem. AAAS, Am. Econ. Assn., Assn. Pub. Policy Analysis and Mgmt., Assn. for Health Svcs. Rsch., Sierra Club. Unitarian. Office: 1700 Main St Santa Monica CA 90401-3297

WILLIAMS, ARTHUR COZAD, broadcasting executive; b. Forty Fort, Pa., Feb. 12, 1926; s. John Bedford and Emily Irene (Poyck) W.; m. Ann Cale Bragan, Oct. 1, 1955; children: Emily Williams Van Hoorickx, Douglas, Craig. Student, Wilkes Coll., 1943-44; B.A. cum laude, U. So. Calif., 1949. With Kaiser Aluminum, 1949, Sta. KPMC, 1950-51; v.p., mgr. KFBK and KFBK-FM Radio Stas., Sacramento, 1951-80; with public relations dept. Sacramento Bee, McClatchy Newspapers, 1981—; dir.-treas. Norkal Opportunities, Inc.; pres. Sacramento Bee Credit Union. Served with AUS, 1944-46. Mem. Sigma Delta Chi. Clubs: Rotary, Sutter, Valley Hi Country, Masons, Shriners. Home: 1209 Nevis Ct Sacramento CA 95822-2532 Office: Sacramento Bee PO Box 15779 Sacramento CA 95852-0779

WILLIAMS, BEN ALBERT, state official; b. San Diego, Dec. 14, 1946; s. Ben Albert and Frances Elizabeth (Arnold) W.; m. Gloria Jean Dieken, Sept. 25, 1976; children: Megan Ann, Alec Benjamin. BSBA, San Diego State U., 1969; MPA, Calif. State U., Hayward, 1977. Budget and econ. analyst Calif. Dept. Indsl. Rels., San Francisco, 1973-76; administrv. officer Calif. Coastal Commn., San Francisco, 1976-79; dep. dir. administrn. Calif. Gov.'s Office Planning and Rsch., Sacramento, 1979—, interim dir., 1988; exec. officer Gov.'s Bd. Inquiry of 1989 Loma Prieta Earthquake, 1989-90; mem. Calif. Commn. on State Mandates, 1988; state coord. military base reuse, 1988—; staff coord. Geog. Info. Task Force, 1992-93. Contbr. articles to profl. publs. Mem. facilities reuse com. Sacramento Area Commn. on Mather Conversion, 1989-90. With U.S. Army, 1969-71, Vietnam. Mem. Am. Soc. Pub. Adminstrn. (treas. Sacramento chpt. 1984-86, coun. 1987-88, pres. 1988-89), Calif. Forum on Info. Tech. (exec. com. 1986-88). Baptist. Office: Govs Office Planning & Rsch 1400 10th St Sacramento CA 95814-5502

WILLIAMS, BERNADINE, social worker, music educator; b. Harrisburg, Pa., Aug. 28, 1939; d. Edward Augustus and Ida (Kuhnert) Blumenstine; m. H. Robert Williams, Apr. 12, 1991; children: Karen Rosenkilde, Paul Rosenkilde. BA, Gettysburg (Pa.) Coll., 1961; MA, U. Chgo., 1963; BA, Calif. State U., Hayward, 1986, MA, 1989. Cert. Social Worker. Pvt. practice music tchr. Pleasanton, Calif., 1982—; activity dir. Golden Manor Board and Care Home, Livermore, Calif., 1985-86; social worker VA Hosp., Livermore, 1989, Santa Clara County Social Svcs., San Jose, Calif., 1990-91, VA Med. Ctr. Nursing Home, Livermore, 1990—. Home: 7119 Valley Trails Dr Pleasanton CA 94588-5225

WILLIAMS, BETTY LOURENE, office manager; b. Topeka, Oct. 3, 1934; d. Jim and Catherine (Sears) Lewis; m. Herman Williams, Sept. 21, 1950; children: Herm Jr., Danny Clay, Iris Angela, John Joseph, Steve Arnold. AA, Compton Coll., 1988. Lic. real estate agt., Calif. Lumbleau Real Estate Sch. Kindergarten, music tchr. St. Catherine Cath. Mission Sch., Guthrie, Okla., 1956-57; sales clk. Mantral Drugstore, L.A., 1958; typist clk. med. records U. So. Calif. Med. Ctr., L.A., 1960-61; real estate agt. Diamond Realty, Compton, Calif., 1964-65; office mgr. J & H Clin. Lab., Inglewood, Calif., 1967-71; exam clk. typist Fed. Office of Personnel Mgmt., L.A., 1981, cons. adminstrv. coord., 1983; vol. Harbor Chpt. AAKP, Long Beach, Calif., 1979—; designed systems for office ops. J & H Clin. Lab., Inglewood, 1983; office orgn., cons. Inglewood Chpt., 1989—; kidney peer patient counseling. Author: (book of poems) Expressions, 1988. Mem. NAACP, Compton, Calif. Br., 1992; mem. Congl. hearing com. Nat. Urologic and Kidney Diseases Adv. Bd. for West Coast, L.A., 1988; organizer tng. seminar Calif. State Rehab. Dept. Mem. Am. Assn. Kidney Patients, Normal Bridge Club-Am. Assn. Bridge (sec. 1986-87). Democrat.

WILLIAMS, BEVERLY BEATRICE, retired elementary school educator; b. El Nido, Calif., Mar. 30, 1932; d. James and Beatrice Idaho (Haskins) Buchholz; m. Harvey Donald Williams, Dec. 5, 1953; children: Eileen Celeste, Corinne Beth, Kevin Keoki. BS, U. Calif., 1953. Cert. elem. tchr., Calif., Hawaii. Tchr. TIVY Union Elem. Sch., Sanger, Calif., 1959-61, Armona (Calif.) Union Elem. Sch., 1963-64, Trust Ter. of The Pacific, Tinian and Saipan, 1964-66, Hawaii Dept. of Edn., Wailuka, Paia and Kula, 1966-90; retired, 1990; mem. staff H&R Block, Wailuku, Hawaii, 1988-90, Truckee, Calif., 1991—; grade level chmn. Iao Sch., 1970-71, 73-74, 78-79, 85-87, co-chmn. Accreditation Team, 1988; chmn. Lang. Arts dept. 1980-81. Precinct vice chmn. Dem. Party, Kahului, Hawaii, 1986-88; state del. Dem. party conv., Kahului, 1982, 84, 86; mem. PTA, PTSA, Wailuku, 1977-78, 85-90. Mem. Hawaii State Tchrs. Assn. (faculty rep. 1987-88), Hawaii Fedn. Bus. and Profl. Women, Inc. (state pres. 1985-86, Bus. Woman of Yr. 1988). Democrat. Mem. Christian Sci. Ch. Home: 12075 Bavarian Way Truckee CA 95737

WILLIAMS, BUCK, professional basketball player; b. Rocky Mount, N.C., Mar. 8, 1960; s. Moses and Betty Williams. Forward New Jersey Nets, NBA, 1981-89; with Portland Trail Blazers, 1989—. Mem. U.S. Olympic Team, 1980; player NBA All-Star Games, 1982, 83, 86; named NBA Rookie of Yr., 1982. Office: Portland Trail Blazers Lloyd Bldg Ste 950 700 NE Multnomah St Portland OR 97232

WILLIAMS, CAROLYN DELORES, pharmacist; b. Tallahassee, Feb. 28, 1954; d. Theodore Williams and Ruthie Lee (Allen) Flowers. D of Pharmacy, U. Calif., San Francisco, 1978. Community pharmacist Oakland, Calif., 1978-87, San Francisco, 1987—. Founder, pres., ednl. mentor Exodus Mentorship Program, Richmond, Calif., 1989—. Mem. NAACP, Calif. Pharmacist Assn., Bay Area Minority Women Entrepreneurial Network (publicist 1992), U. Calif. San Francisco Sch. Pharmacy Alumni, Cult Awareness Network. Home: 3318 Parkgate Ct Richmond CA 94806-1989

WILLIAMS, DARLEEN DOROTHY, librarian; b. Bay City, Mich., May 8, 1938; d. Albert Carl and Irene Dorothy (Szafran) Fritz; m. Joe Lee Williams, June 2, 1966; children: Julie Ann, Amy Louise Williams Huggins. Student, Bay City Jr. Coll., 1956-57; BA, Cen. Mich. U., 1959; MALS, U. Mich., 1963; postgrad., Cath. U. Am., Washington, D.C., 1965, U. Ariz., 1989, No. Ariz. U., 1990. Cert. secondary tchr., Ariz., libr., Ariz. Asst. libr. Handy High Sch., Bay City, 1959-63; libr. Gibson Jr. High Sch., Las Vegas, Nev., 1963-66; asst. reference libr. U. Nev., Reno, 1966-70; interlibr. loan libr. Case Western Res. U., Cleve., 1970-71, assoc. libr., 1971-72; libr. Kingman (Ariz.) High Sch., 1972—. Author: American West Magazine Index (1974-1983), 1985. Mem. ALA, Mtn. Plains Libr. Assn., Ariz. State Libr. Assn., Kingman Secondary Edn. Assn. Home: 2540 Crozier Ave Kingman AZ 86401-4712 Office: Kingman High Sch 400 Grandview Ave Kingman AZ 86401-5796

WILLIAMS, DAVID MICHAEL, manufacturing executive; b. Bklyn., Feb. 25, 1936; s. Robert Irving and Patricia Margaret (Flanagan) W.; m. Carol Bultmann, Nov. 13, 1965; children: Mark, Jennifer. Cert., NYU, Ctr. for Safety Engring., Manhattan, N.Y., 1960. Mgr. various mfrs., 1956-79; pres. D.M. Williams, Inc., Livermore, Calif., 1979—; cons. various mfrs., 1979—. Candidate for gov., Calif., 1990; candidate for Congress, Calif., 1986, 88, 89, 92; active Rep. Cen. Com., Calif., 1987-88. Cole grantee NYU, 1960. Mem. Inst. Packaging Profls. (bd. dirs. no. Calif. chpt., 1982-85, chmn. 1985-86), ASTM, Mensa (founder interest group 1983-86). Roman Catholic. Office: 1560 Kingsport Ave Livermore CA 94550-6149

WILLIAMS, DAVID WELFORD, federal judge; b. Atlanta, Mar. 20, 1910; s. William W. and Maude (Lee) W.; m. Ouida Maie White, June 11, 1939; children: David Welford, Vaughn Charles. A.A., Los Angeles Jr. Coll., 1932; A.B., UCLA, 1934; LL.B., U. So. Calif., 1937. Bar: Calif. 1937. Practiced in Los Angeles, 1937-55; judge Mcpl. Ct., Los Angeles, 1956-62, Superior Ct., Los Angeles, 1962-69, U.S. Dist. Ct. (cen. dist.) Calif., Los Angeles, 1969—; now sr. judge U.S. Dist. Ct. (cen. dist.) Calif.; judge Los Angeles County Grand Jury, 1965. Recipient Russwurm award Nat. Assn. Newspapers, 1958; Profl. Achievement award UCLA Alumni Assn., 1966. Mem. ABA, Los Angeles Bar Assn., Am. Judicature Soc. Office: US Dist Ct 255 E Temple St Rm 7100 Los Angeles CA 90012-4701

WILLIAMS, DEREK, JR., pharmaceutical professional; b. Ft. Rucker, Ala., June 25, 1958; s. Derek W. Sr. and Carol E. (Kaufman) W.; m. Penny L. Bradly, Apr. 22, 1991; children: Jason Brian, Courtney Elizabeth. AS, U. Nev., 1981; BA, U. Colo., 1984; MA, U. Nev., 1986. Rsch. asst. U. Nev., Reno, 1984-86; surgical counselor St. Lukes Hosp., Denver, 1987-89; pub. health advisor Ctrs. for Disease Control, Atlanta, 1989-91; clin. rsch. assoc. Amgen, Inc., Thousand Oaks, Calif., 1991-92, regulatory affairs specialist, 1992—. Named Outstanding Young Men of Am., 1989-90. Mem. Assocs. Clin. Pharmacology, Regulatory Affairs Profls. Soc. Internat. Aids Soc., Am. Pub. Health Assn., Drug Info. Assn., Brit. Inst. Regulatory Affairs. Office: Amgen Inc 1840 De Havilland Dr Thousand Oaks CA 91320-1789

WILLIAMS, DONALD SPENCER, scientist; b. Pasadena, Calif., May 28, 1939; s. Charles Gardner and Delia Ruth (Spencer) W. BS, Harvey Mudd Coll., 1961; MS, Carnegie Inst. Tech., 1962; PhD, Carnegie-Mellon U., 1969. Asst. project dir. Learning Rsch. & Devel. Ctr., Pitts., 1965-67; cons. system design, Pitts., 1967-69; mem. tech. staff RCA Corp., Palo Alto, Calif., 1969-72; prin. investigator robot vision Jet Propulsion Lab., Calif. Inst. Tech., Pasadena, 1972-80; chief engr. oper. TRW, Inc., Redondo Beach, 1980—; cons. system design, 1984—. Japan Econ. Found. grantee, 1981. Mem. AAAS, Assn. Computing Machinery, Audio Engring. Soc., Nat. Fire Protection Assn., IEEE, Soc. Motion Picture & TV Engrs., Town Hall Calif. Contbr. articles to profl. jours. Home: PO Box 40700 Pasadena CA 91114-7700 Office: TRW Inc 1 Space Park Dr Redondo Beach CA 90278-1071

WILLIAMS, DONALD VICTOR, office manager, coach; b. Decatur, Ill., May 8, 1936; s. Victor H. and Dorothy M. (Runion) W.; m. Helen Williams (div. 1977); m. Barbara A. Porter, July 4, 1980; children: Kevin, Brian, Michael. Corrections officer State of Oreg., Salem, 1959-69, adminstrv. asst. dept. corrections, 1969-76; spl. dep. Marion County, Salem, 1976-78; job svcs. rep. div. of employment State of Oreg., Gold Beach, 1979; adminstrv. asst. airport mgr. Port of Portland, Oreg., 1980; office mgr. North Opinion Rsch., Portland, 1980. Contbr. numerous articles to profl. jours. Sport tech. officer U.S. Cerebral Palsy Athletic Assn., Mich., 1990—; exec. bd. Multnomah Art Assn., Portland, 1985-89; com. mem. Portland/Sapporo Sister City Assn., 1989-90; dir. Oreg. Jr. Olympic Shooting Program, Portland, 1980-89; coach Region I Daisy Air Gun Program, Portland, 1980-83; head coach U.S.C.P. Shooting Team 1990 World Championships, Assen, Holland; commr. State Games Oreg., 1986-89. With U.S. ARNG, 1954-88. Mem. Internat. Shooting Coaches Assn. (editor 1988—, life), NRA (endowment 1980—), Oreg. State Rifle/Pistol Assn. (life), Oreg. 4-H Shooting Sports Com. (bd. dirs. 1985-91). Home: 17446 SW Granada Dr Beaverton OR 97007-5364

WILLIAMS, DOUGLAS, management consultant; b. Newburgh, N.Y., Oct. 13, 1912; s. Everett Frank and Marjorie Tuthill W.; m. Esther Grant, Sept. 23, 1939; children: Penelope Williams Winters, Grant. AB, Cornell U., 1934; MBA, Harvard U., 1936. With Air Reduction Co., 1936-37, Am. Inst. Pub. Opinion, 1938, Elmo Roper Co., 1939-40; assoc. dir. Nat. Opinion Research Ctr., U. Denver, 1940-42; pres. Douglas Williams Assos., Carefree, Ariz. and N.Y.C., 1948—. Pres. Community Chest, Larchmont, N.Y., 1959; bd. mgrs. West Side YMCA, N.Y.C., 1957-60; dir. Scottsdale Meml. Hosp. Found.; mem. nat. adv. bd. Heard Mus.; mem. Ariz. State U. Council of 100, Ariz. State U. Council of Emeritus Advisers, Foothills Com. Adv. Council; dir. Scottsdale Meml. Hosp. Found. Served to lt. col. U.S. Army, 1942-45. Republican. Episcopalian. Clubs: Larchmont Yacht, Desert Mountain, Garden of the Gods, Harvard, Union League, Cornell, Winged Foot Golf, Desert Forest Golf, Ariz. Home: PO Box 941 7612 E Horizon Dr Carefree AZ 85377 Office: Exec Ctr PO Box 941 Carefree AZ 85377-0941

WILLIAMS, DOUGLAS ALLAN, household products company executive; b. Elgin, Ill., Dec. 17, 1938; s. Robert Orren and Margaret (Perry) W.; m. Barbara Annette Brown,. BA, Beloit Coll., 1960. Mgr. tech. suppport CNA Ins., Chgo., 1969-75; regional mgr. computer audit Coopers & Lybrand, San Francisco, 1976-82; audit mgr. Sohio Petroleum, San Francisco, 1982-83; mgr. fin. systems The Clorox Co., Oakland, Calif., 1983—; cons. in field. Bd. dirs. Berkeley Schs. Computer adv. Council, 1981—. Mem. EDP Auditors Assn. (pres. 1984-85), Assn. for Systems Mgmt. Episcopalian. Home: 470 Rheem Blvd Moraga CA 94556 Office: The Clorox Co 1221 Broadway Oakland CA 94612-1837

WILLIAMS, EDGAR PURELL, aerospace engineer; b. Pierpont, Ohio, Aug. 17, 1918; s. Edgar Ward and Margaret E. (Smith) W.; m. Esther Lowrie Elliott, May 12, 1945 (div. June 1962); children: Katherine Williams Saunders, Ruth Williams Abatzoglou, Carol Williams Robertson, Edna Williams Moore. BA, Oberlin Coll., 1940; MS in Aeronautics, Engr's. Degree in Aeronautics, Calif. Inst. Tech., 1942. Registered mech. engr., Calif. Aerodynamics engr. Douglas Aircraft Co., Santa Monica, Calif., 1942-48; chief aerodynamics Rand Corp., Santa Monica, 1949-63; chief aeromech. br., chief engr. aerodynamics and thermodynamics dept., sr. staff engr. McDonnell Douglas Astronautics Co., Santa Monica and Huntington Beach, Calif., 1963-74; contract aerodynamics engr. CDI/Hughes Aircraft, Canoga Park, Calif., 1977-78; design specialist Pomona (Calif.) div. Gen. Dynamics, 1978-84; engring. specialist Northrop Corp., Pico Rivera, Calif., 1984—; missiles advisor Air Force Office, Washington, 1952-53; lectr. UCLA, 1956-58. Contbr.: Space Handbook, 1959; also articles. Bd. dirs., corr. sec. Westwood Gardens Civic Assn., Inc., L.A., 1950-57. Fellow AIAA (assoc.); mem. Sigma Xi (assoc.). Home: 6721 Cory Dr Huntington Beach CA 92647-5612 Office: Northrop Corp W402/UB W431/UB 8900 Washington Blvd Pico Rivera CA 90660-3783

WILLIAMS, ERNEST CURRAN, academic administrator; b. Alturas, Calif., Feb. 14, 1944; s. J. Post and Margret C. (Curran) W.; m. Susan Jane Peoples, June 11, 1966; children: Kirstin Elizabeth, Deidre Joyce. AA in Biology, Coll. of Sequoias, 1965; BS in Natural Resources Conservation, Calif. Humboldt State U., Arcata, 1967; MA in Adminstrn. in Edn., Calif. State U., Bakersfield, 1976. Cert. elem., secondary, and coll. tchr., adminstr., supr. From tchr. to prin. Burton Sch. Dist., Porterville, Calif., 1969-90; asst. to supt. Burton Sch. Dist., Porterville, 1990—. Supr. com. mem. Tulare County Employees Assn., 1992-93; adminstr. Porterville Women's Shelter/Support Svc. Project, 1992-93. Mem. Assn. Calif. Sch. Adminstrs. (bd. dirs. 1980-82), Calif. Assn. Compensatory Edn., Joint Sch. CPS/Mental Health Com., Safety Com., Porterville Prevention Alliance, Kiwanis Club (pres., 1st v.p., 2nd v.p., bd. dirs.), Monache Band Boosters (bd. dirs.), Monache Athletic Boosters (bd. dirs.), Phi Delta Kappa (pres. 1981-82, 1st v.p. 1980-81, 2nd v.p. 1979-80, adv. bd. mem. 1982-84). Republican. Episcopalian. Home: 322 W Mulberry Ave Porterville CA 93257-1653 Office: Burton Sch Dist 264 N Westwood St Porterville CA 93257-2542

WILLIAMS, FORMAN ARTHUR, combustion theorist and engineering science educator; b. New Brunswick, N.J., Jan. 12, 1934; s. Forman J. and Alice (Pooley) W.; m. Elsie Vivian Kara, June 15, 1955 (div. 1978); children: F. Gary, Glen A., Nancy L., Susan D., Michael S., Michelle K.; m. Elizabeth Acevedo, Aug. 19, 1978. BSE, Princeton U., 1955; PhD, Calif. Inst. Tech., 1958. Asst. prof. Harvard U., Cambridge, Mass., 1958-64; prof. U. Calif.-San Diego, 1964-81; Robert H. Goddard prof. Princeton U., N.J., 1981-88; prof. dept. applied mechs. and engring. scis. U. Calif., San Diego, 1988—. Author: Combustion Theory, 1965, 2d edit., 1985; contbr. articles to profl. jours. Fellow NSF, 1962; fellow Guggenheim Found., 1970; recipient U.S. Sr. Scientist award Alexander von Humboldt Found., 1982, Silver medal Combustion Inst., 1978, Bernard Lewis Gold medal Combustion Inst., 1990. Fellow AIAA; mem. Am. Phys. Soc., Combustion Inst., Soc. for Indsl. and Applied Math., Nat. Acad. Engring., Nat. Acad. Engring. Mex. (fgn. corr. mem.), Sigma Xi. Home: 8002 La Jolla Shores Dr La Jolla CA 92037-3230 Office: U Calif San Diego Ctr Energy & Combustion Rsch 9500 Gilman Dr La Jolla CA 92093

WILLIAMS, HARRY EDWARD, manufacturing, quality and engineering executive, consultant; b. Oak Park, Ill., July 20, 1925; s. Harry E. and Mary E.; m. Jean Horner; 1 child, Jeanne. Student, West Coast U., Los Angeles, 1958-60; BS in Engring., Calif. Coast Coll., Santa Ana, 1975; MA, Calif. Coast Coll., 1975; PhD, Golden State U., Los Angeles, 1981. Registered profl. engr., Calif. Mgr. Parker Aircraft Co., Los Angeles, 1958-60, Leach Corp., Los Angeles, 1968-69, Litton, Data Systems, Van Nuys, Calif., 1969-72; dir. Electronic Memories, Hawthorne, Calif., 1972-78, Magnavox Co., Torrance, Calif., 1978-80; v.p. Stacoswitch Inc., Costa Mesa, Calif., 1981-87; mgmt. cons. Seal Beach, Calif., 1987--; cons. in field. Contbr. articles to profl. jours. With USAF, 1943-46. Named Internat. Man of Yr., Internat. Biographical Ctr., Cambridge, Eng., 1991-92. Fellow Internat. Acad. Edn., Am. Soc. Quality Control; mem. Soc. for Advancement Mgmt. (Mgr. of Yr. 1984, Phil Carrol award 1985). Republican. Methodist. Home: 15111 Bushard St # 93 Westminster CA 92683-6532

WILLIAMS, HENRY STRATTON, radiologist, educator; b. N.Y.C., Aug. 26, 1929; m. Frances S. Williams; children: Mark I, Paul S., Bart H. BS, CCNY, 1950; MD, Howard U., 1955. Diplomate Nat. Bd. Med. Examiners. Intern Brooke Army Hosp., San Antonio, 1956; resident in radiology Letterman Army Hosp., San Francisco, 1957-60; pvt. practice radiology L.A., 1963—; assoc. clin. prof. radiology Charles R. Drew Med. Sch., L.A.; chmn. bd. Charles Drew U. Medicine and Sci. Found.; interim pres. Charles R. Drew U. of Medicine and Sci. Mem. ad hoc adv. com. Joint Commn. Accreditation Hosps. Served to maj. U.S. Army, 1960-63. Fellow Am. Coll. Radiology; mem. Calif. Physicians Service (bd. dirs. 1971-77), Calif. Med. Assn. (counselor, mem. appeals bd., del., chmn. urban health com.), Los Angeles County Med. Assn. Office: 3756 Santa Rosalia Dr Los Angeles CA 90008-3606

WILLIAMS, HERBERT RUSSELL, educator, watercolorist; b. Independence, Mo., Sept. 14, 1945; s. Roy H. and Florence V. (Woodheaed) W.; m. Nancy J. Parker, June 1, 1968 (div. 1973); 1 child, Denis R. Storey. BA, Graceland Coll., Lamoni, Iowa, 1968. Cert. tchr., Calif. Tchr. Park Hill High Sch., Kansas City, Mo., 1972-75; with Hyatt Hotels, Chgo., 1975-79, Berkshire Hotel, N.Y.C., 1979-81; art tchr. Elementary Sch's., Orange, N.J., 1979-81; substitute tchr. L.A. Unified Schs., 1981-85; tchr. L.A. High Sch., 1985—. With U.S. Army, 1968-72. Mem. Nat. Watercolor Soc. (assoc.). Democrat. Mem. Reformed LDS Ch. Home: 8045 Lesner Ave Van Nuys CA 91406 Office: L A High Sch 4650 W Olympic Blvd Los Angeles CA 90019

WILLIAMS, HIBBARD EARL, medical educator, physician; b. Utica, N.Y., Sept. 28, 1932; s. Hibbard G. and Beatrice M. W.; m. Sharon Towne, Sept. 3, 1982; children: Robin, Hans. A.B., Cornell U., 1954, M.D., 1958. Diplomate: Am. Bd. Internal Medicine. Intern Mass. Gen. Hosp., Boston, 1958-59, resident in medicine, 1959-60, 62-64, asst. physician, 1964-65; clin. assoc. Nat. Inst. Arthritis and Metabolic Diseases, NIH, Bethesda, MD, 1960-62; instr. medicine Harvard U., Boston, 1964-65; asst. prof. medicine U. Calif.-San Francisco, 1965-68, assoc. prof., 1968-72, prof., 1972-78, chief div. med. genetics, 1968-70, vice chmn. dept. medicine, 1970-78; prof., chmn. dept. medicine Cornell U. Med. Coll., N.Y.C., 1978-80; physician-in-chief N.Y. Hosp.-Cornell Med. Ctr., N.Y.C., 1978-80; dean Sch. Medicine, U. Calif.-Davis, 1980-92; prof. internal medicine U. Calif.-Davis, 1980—; mem. program project com. NIH, Nat. Inst. Arthritis and Metabolic Diseases, 1971-73. Contbr. articles to med. jours.; editor med. staff confs.: Calif. Medicine, 1966-70; mem. editorial bd.: Clin. Research, 1968-71; assoc. editor: Metabolism, 1970-80; mem. adv. bd. physiology in medicine: New Eng. Jour. Medicine, 1970-75. Served with USPHS, 1960-62. Recipient Career Devel. award USPHS, 1968; recipient award for excellence in teaching Kaiser Found., 1970, Disting. Faculty award U. Calif. Alumni-Faculty Assn., 1978; John and Mary R. Markle scholar in medicine, 1968. Fellow ACP; mem. AAAS, Am. Fedn. Clin. Rsch., Am. Soc. Clin. Investigation (sec.-treas. 1974-77), Assn. Am. Physicians, Assn. Am. Med. Colls. (adminstrv. bd., coun. deans 1989-92, exec. coun. 1990-92), Calif. Acad. Medicine (pres. 1984), San Francisco Diabetes Assn. (bd. dirs. 1971-72), Western Assn. Physicians (v.p. 1977-78), Western Soc. Clin. Rsch., Calif. Med. Assn. (chmn. coun. sci. affairs 1990—, bd. dirs. 1990—), Am. Clin. and Climatol. Soc., St. Francis Yacht Club, Alpha Omega Alpha. Office: U Calif Sch Medicine Davis CA 95616

WILLIAMS, HOWARD RUSSELL, lawyer, educator; b. Evansville, Ind., Sept. 26, 1915; s. Clyde Alfred and Grace (Preston) W.; m. Virginia Merle Thompson, Nov. 3, 1942; 1 son, Frederick S.T. AB, Washington U., St. Louis, 1937; LLB, Columbia U., 1940. Bar: N.Y. 1941. With firm Root, Clark, Buckner & Ballantine, N.Y.C., 1940-41; prof. law, asst. dean U. Tex. Law Sch., Austin, 1946-51; prof. law Columbia U. Law Sch., N.Y.C., 1951-63; Dwight prof. Columbia Law Sch., 1959-63; prof. law Stanford U., 1963-85, Stella W. and Ira S. Lillick prof., 1968-82, prof. emeritus, 1982, Robert E. Paradise prof. natural resources, 1983-85, prof. emeritus, 1985—; Oil and gas cons. President's Materials Policy Commn., 1951; mem. Calif. Law Revision Commn., 1971-79, vice chmn., 1976-77, chmn., 1978-79. Author or co-author: Cases on Property, 1954, Cases on Oil and Gas, 5th edit, 1987, Decedents' Estates and Trusts, 1968, Future Interests, 1970, Oil and Gas Law, 8 vols, 1959-64, abridged edit., 1973, Manual of Oil and Gas Terms, 8th edit., 1991. Bd. regents Berkeley Baptist Div. Sch., 1966-67; trustee Rocky Mountain Mineral Law Found., 1964-66, 68-85. Served to maj. U.S. Army, 1941-46. Mem. Phi Beta Kappa. Democrat. Home: 360 Everett Ave Apt 4B Palo Alto CA 94301-1422 Office: Stanford U Sch Law Nathan Abbott Way Stanford CA 94305

WILLIAMS, HOWARD VERNON, physician; b. N.Y.C., Dec. 23, 1951; s. Sylvester Francis and Faye Marie (Smock) W.; m. Kathy Browder, May 7, 1983; 1 child, Rebecca Faye. BA, Cornell Coll., 1973; MD, U. So. Calif., Los Angeles, 1982. Diplomate Am. Bd. Internal Medicine. Chief resident internal medicine U. Calif. San Francisco-Fresno Med. Edn. Program, Fresno, Calif., 1985-86; chmn. dept. internal medicine Smith-Hanna Med. Group, San Diego, 1986-88; pvt. practice internal medicine San Diego, 1989—; bd. dirs. Mercy Healthcare. Mem. Sierra Club. Office: 4060 4th Ave Ste 420 San Diego CA 92103-2170

WILLIAMS, HOWARD WALTER, aerospace engineer; b. Evansville, Ind., Oct. 18, 1937; s. Walter Charles and Marie Louise (Bollinger) W.; m. Phyllis Ann Scofield, May 4, 1956 (div. Sept. 1970); m. Marilee Sharon Mulvane, Oct. 30, 1970; children: Deborah, Steven, Kevin, Glenn, Lori, Michele. AA, Pasadena City Coll., 1956; BSME, Calif. State U., Los Angeles, 1967; BSBA, U. San Francisco, 1978; PhD (hon.), London Inst. Applied Rsch., 1992. Turbojet, rocket engr. Aerojet-Gen. Corp., Azusa, Calif., 1956-59, infrared sensor engr., 1959-60, rocket, torpedo engr., 1960-66; power, propulsion mgr. propulsion divsn. Aerojet-Gen. Corp., Sacramento, 1967-73, high speed ship systems mgr., 1974-78, combustion, power mgr., rocket engine and energy mktg. mgr., 1979-89, dir. strategic planning, 1989—. Author: (with others) Heat Exchangers, 1980, Industrial Heat Exchangers, 1985; co-inventor Closed Cycle Power System, 1969. Recipient Energy Innovation award U.S. Dept. Energy, 1985. Mem. AIAA (sr.; Best Paper 1966), Am. Soc. Metals (organizing dir. indsl. heat exchange confs. 1985—). Office: Aerojet Propulsion Divsn Aerojet Rd Rancho Cordova CA 95742

WILLIAMS, JEFFREY CLARKE, insurance executive; b. Portland, Oreg., Nov. 4, 1940; s. Grover Cleveland and Elizabeth Clarke (Williams); m. Patricia Ann Dabb, Nov. 11, 1972 (div. 1991). BA, U. Washington, Seattle, 1969. Cert. Safety Profl. Loss Control rep. United Pacific Ins., Boise, Idaho, 1971-76; sr. Loss Control rep. Reliance Ins. Group, Portland, Oreg., 1976-81; Loss Control mgr. Pacific Marine Ins., Seattle, 1981-85; v.p. Loss Control Svcs. Eagle Ins. Group, Seattle, 1985—. Editor: Risky Business, 1988—. Mem. bd. Cert. Safety Profls. Mem. Am. Soc. Safety Engrs. (exec. bd. 1987-90). Office: Eagle Ins Group 4025 Delridge Way SW Ste 300 Seattle WA 98106-1276

WILLIAMS, JEFFREY THOMAS, economist; b. Duluth, Minn., Sept. 30, 1952; s. Bruce Foch Pershing and Kathleen (Griffee) W.; m. Theresa Ann Moore, May 29, 1987; children: Spencer Thomas, Sarah Christine. BS in Finance, U. Utah, 1975, BS in Econs., 1975, MS in Econs., 1981. Research fellow Utah Ctr. for Pub. Affairs, U. Utah, Salt Lake City, 1981; economist Utah Energy Office, State of Utah Dept. of Nat. Resources, Salt Lake City, 1981-85; sr. economist com. consumer svcs. Utah Dept. Commerce, Salt Lake City, 1985-90; econ. cons. Evergreen, Colo., 1990—; mem. Salt Lake Community Coll. Computer Tech. Adv. Com., Salt Lake City, 1985-89; expert witness PacificCorp cost allocation case, 1990, merger case, 1988, fuel procurement cases, 1986, Utah Power and Light Co. Co-author: State Review of the Bonneville Unit Central Utah Project, 1984; author, editor: Study of a Conceptual Nuclear Energy Center at Green River, 1982 and others. Vol. Nat. Ski Patrol System, Park City, Utah, 1980-89. Mem. Internat. Assn. Energy Economists. Roman Catholic. Home and Office: 3077 S Hiwan Dr Evergreen CO 80439-8951

WILLIAMS, JERALD ARTHUR, mechanical engineer; b. Miller, S.D., Dec. 22, 1942; s. Willard Arthur and Mildred Irene Williams; m. Judy Deannia Allsip, May 30, 1966; children: Todd, Monique, Heather. BSME, Wash. State U., 1966; MS in Mech. Engring., U. Wash., 1967. Mech. engr. Mobile Oil Co., Bakersfield, Calif., 1966; assoc. rsch. engr. Boeing Airplane Co., Seattle, 1968; mech. engr. Boeing Airplane Co., Renton, Wash., 1971-72; exec. v.p. Bouillon, Christofferson & Schairer, Seattle, 1972—. Contbr. articles to profl. jours. Cub scout pack leader Boy Scouts Am., Issaquah, Wash., 1979-80. Capt. U.S. Army, 1968-71, Viet Nam. Mem. Cons. Engrs. Coun. Wash. (dir. 1986-90, chair various coms. 1982-92), Am. Cons. Engrs. Coun. (naval fac. engring. command liaison com. 1985-92, chmn. 1989-92), Seattle Rotary, Phi Eta Sigma, Phi Kappa Phi, Sigma Tau, Tau Beta Pi. Home: 16151 SE 42d St Bellevue WA 98006 Office: Bouillon Christofferson & Schairer 1201 3d Ave Ste 800 Seattle WA 98101

WILLIAMS, JOHN BRINDLEY, English language educator, writer; b. N.Y.C., Aug. 4, 1919; s. Elmer Reed and Stella (Brindley) W.; m. Jean Elizabeth Humphrey, Aug. 24, 1951; children: Marilyn, Evelyn, Heather, Laura. BA, U. So. Calif., L.A., 1948; MA, UCLA, 1955; PhD, U. Southern Calif., 1965. Suburban editor San Pedro (Calif.) News-Pilot, 1948-53; instr. in English Glendale (Calif.) Coll., 1955-66; prof. English Calif. State U., Long Beach, 1966-92. Author: Style and Grammar, 1973, White Fire: The Influence of Emerson on Melville, 1990. With U.S. Army, 1943-45, ETO. Recipient Disting. Faculty Teaching, 1987. Mem. Modern Lang. Assn., Melville Soc. Republican. Presbyterian. Home: 9791 El Tulipan Cir Fountain Valley CA 92708-5114

WILLIAMS, JOHN JAMES, JR., architect; b. Denver, July 13, 1949; s. John James and Virginia Lee (Thompson) W.; m. Mary Serene Morck, July 29, 1972. BArch, U. Colo., 1974. Registered architect, Colo., Calif., Idaho. Project architect Gensler Assoc. Architects, Denver, 1976, Heinzman Assoc. Architects, Boulder, Colo., 1977, EZTH Architects, Boulder, 1978-79; prin. Knudson/Williams PC, Boulder, 1980-82, Faber, Williams & Brown, Boulder, 1982-86, John Williams & Assocs., Denver, 1986—; panel chmn. U. Colo. World Affairs Conf.; vis. faculty U. Colo. Sch. Architecture and Planning, Coll. Environ. Design, 1986-91. Author (with others) State of Colorado architect licensing law, 1986. Commr. Downtown Boulder Mall Commn., 1985-88; bd. dirs. U. Colo. Fairway Club, 1986-88; mem. Gov's. Natural Hazard Mitigation Coun., State of Colo., 1990. Recipient Teaching Honorarium, U. Colo. Coll. Architecture and Planning, 1977, 78, 79, 80, 88, Excellence in Design and Planning award City of Boulder, 1981, 82, Citation for Excellence, WOOD Inc., 1982, Disting. Profl. Service award Coll. Environ. Design U. Colo., 1988. Mem. AIA (sec. 1988, bd. dirs. Colo. North chpt. 1985-86, pres. North chpt. 1990, v.p. 1989, sec. 1987, sec. Colo. chpt. 1988, ednl. fund Fisher I traveling scholar 1988, state design conf. chair 1991), Intersoc. Color Coun., Designed Communications Assn., Am. Soc. Archtl. Perspectives, Architects and Planners of Boulder (v.p. 1982), Nat. Coun. Architect Registration Bd., Nat. Golf Found. (sponsor), Kappa Sigma (chpt. pres. 1970). Home: 1031 Turnberry Circle Louisville CO 80027 Office: John Williams & Assocs 1475 Lawrence St Ste 302 Denver CO 80202-2200

WILLIAMS, JOHN LYLE, lawyer; b. Saginaw, Mich., Oct. 2, 1944; s. John Lyle and Jean Elizabeth (Cleary) W.; m. Jane Farmer Edwards, Apr. 19, 1969; children: Jennifer Leigh, Benjamin Winn. BA, Mich. State U., 1965; LLB, Stanford U., 1968. Assoc. Hall, Henry, Oliver & McReary, San Francisco, 1970-72; atty. Santa Clara County Pub. Defender, San Jose, Calif., 1972-79; ptnr. Manchester & Williams, San Jose, 1979—; dir. Advanced Criminal Practitioners Seminar, San Jose, Hawaii, 1980-87; lectr. Calif. Continuing Edn. of Bar, 1985—. Capt. U.S. Army, 1968-70. Mem. Calif. Attys. for Criminal Justice, Santa Clara County Bar Assn., State Bar Calif., Inns. of Ct. Santa Clara U. (bencher 1990—). Office: Manchester & Williams 100 Park Center Plz # 525 San Jose CA 95113

WILLIAMS, JOHN PERSHING, consultant, retired manufacturing and mining company executive; b. Bluefield, W.Va., July 25, 1919; s. Deck Christopher and Zeora Monte (Brocklehurst) W.; m. Ruth Elizabeth Jones, Sept. 10, 1947; 1 child, Jeanne Lynn. BS, U. Mich., 1951. Mem. indsl. rels. staff King-Seeley Thermos Co., Ann Arbor, Mich., 1950-63; personnel mgr., then indsl. rels. mgr. Butler Mfg. Co., Kansas City, Mo., 1963-66; dir. indsl. rels. Mueller Brass Co., Fort Huron, Mich., 1966-69; v.p. indsl. rels. Mueller Brass Co., Port Huron, 1969-78; dir. indsl. rels. U.S. Smelting, Refining & Mining, N.Y.C., 1966-78; indsl. rels. cons. UV Industries, N.Y.C., 1969-78; dir. indsl. rels. Fed. Pacific Electric Co., Newark, 1970-76; dir. labor rels. Anamax Mining Co., Sahuarita, Ariz., 1978-85; pres. Alert Consulting Corp., Tucson, 1985—. Co-author: Collective Bargaining, 1985, Strike Planning, 1985. Pres., Perry Nursery Sch., Ann Arbor, Mich., 1957; rd. commr., Scio Twp., Ann Arbor, 1961; del. State Rep. Conv., Detroit, 1961; mem. parents coun., Adrian (Mich.) Coll., 1973-74; bd. dirs., Blue Cross-Blue Shield Mich., Detroit, 1971-77. Mem. Masons. Methodist. Home and Office: Alert Consulting Corp 775 W Samalayuca Dr Tucson AZ 85704-3233

WILLIAMS, JOHN STEVEN MEURIG, computer company executive; b. North Wales, Mar. 30, 1948; came to U.S., 1983; s. Richard Thomas Meurig and Jean Barbara (Anderson) W.; m. Jane Bevan, Aug. 29, 1975 (div. 1982); 1 child, Joanna Jane; m. Nancy McNamara, July 27, 1985. Student, N. Wales Coll., U.K., 1966-68. Sales rep. IBM U.K. Ltd., London, 1970-79, sales mgr., 1979-83; sr. product mgr. IBM Corp., Boulder, Colo., 1983-86; v.p. sales Digitalmicrowave Corp., San Jose, Calif., 1986-87, Esprit System Inc., San Jose, Calif., 1987-88; pres. Intralink, Sunnyvale, 1989—. Mem. Army & Navy Club. Home: 825 E Evelyn Ave Sunnyvale CA 94086-6533

WILLIAMS, JOHN WALTER OLDING, computer industry executive; b. Nanking, China, Sept. 3, 1936; came to U.S., 1946; s. Walter Henry and Kathryn Elizabeth (Tesack) W.; m. Joan Porter, Jan. 1963 (div. July 1967); m. Linda Lee Duhaime, Mar. 1968 (div. Apr. 1979); 1 child, Erika Anne. BS, Ariz. State U., 1963; MBA, Cen. Mo. State U., 1975. Commd. 2d lt. USAF, 1963, advanced through grades to capt., data info. officer, 1963-77, ret., 1977; computer ops. mgr. Med. Mutual of Cleve., 1977, Case Western Res. U., Cleve., 1978-79; computer ops. supr. Systems Devel. Corp., Slidell, La., 1979-80; mgmt. info. systems mgr. Equitable Shipyards, Inc., New Orleans, 1981-82; computer systems mgr. New Orleans Dist. Atty., 1983-84; computer systems mgr., EDP instr. New Orleans Regional Vo-Tech. Inst., 1984-85; EDP/QA auditor Mason Chamberlain Inc., Stennis Space Ctr., Miss., 1986-90; programmer/analyst Snohomish County D.I.S., Everett, Wash., 1990-91; owner, cons. HWIT-BERA Enterprises, Personal/Computer Solutions, Everett, 1992—. Pres. Silver Plume Samoyed Club, Denver, 1968-69; bd. dirs. Knob Noster (Mo.) Saddle Club, 1972. Decorated Bronze Star. Mem. AARP, Ret. Officer's Assn., Mensa.

WILLIAMS, KEITH EDWARD, software development consulting company executive; b. Hampton, Va., Aug. 2, 1958; s. Frank Edward Jr. and Jannie Ruth (Jones) W.; m. Willa Maria Williams, May 18, 1981; children: Christina, Anthony. BS in Math. Sci., Elizabeth City (N.C.) State U., 1981. MIS software engr. Hughes Aircraft Co. GSG, Fullerton, Calif., 1981-86; system analyst, programmer ADP, Arcadia, Calif., 1986-88; sr. programmer analyst DataLine, Covina, Calif., 1988; software engr. MTSA, Teradata, El Segundo, Calif., 1988—; owner, sr. software developer WMS Cons. Diversified Svcs., Irvine, Calif., 1989—; nat. offensive coord. Minor League Football Alliance, 1990; bd. dirs. Calif. Gen. Pro Football. Mem. Youth Motivation Task Force, 1982 (commendation 1983,84). mem. Nat. Alliance of Bus. Office: WMS Cons Diversified Svcs Jamboree Ctr One Park Plz 6th Fl Irvine CA 92714

WILLIAMS, KENNETH JAMES, retired county official; b. Eureka, Calif., Apr. 28, 1924; s. E. J. and Thelma (Hall) W.; student Humboldt State Coll., 1942-43; B.S., U. Oreg., 1949, M.Ed., 1952; m. Mary Patricia Warring, Sept. 3, 1949; children—James Clayton, Susan May, Christopher Kenneth. Engaged as mountain triangulation observer with U.S. Coast and Geodetic Survey, 1942; instr. bus. and geography Boise (Idaho) Jr. Coll., 1949-51; tchr. Prospect High Sch., 1952-54; prin. Oakland (Oreg.) High Sch., 1954-58; supt. prin. Coburg Public Schs., 1958-64; supt. Yoncalla (Oreg.) Public Schs., 1964-66, Amity (Oreg.) Public Schs., 1966-72; adminstr. Yamhill County, McMinnville, Oreg., 1974-85; cons., 1985—; county liaison officer Land and Water Conservation Fund, 1977-85. Dist. lay leader Oreg.-Idaho ann. conf. United Methodist Ch., 1968-80, bd. dirs. western dist. Ch. Extension Soc., 1976; mem. Mid-Willamette Manpower Council, 1974-85; bd. dirs. Lafayette Noble Homes, 1970-72; mem. adv. com. local budget law sect. State of Oreg. Served with AUS, 1943-46. Decorated Purple Heart. Mem. NEA, Oreg. Edn. Assn., Oreg. Assn. Secondary Prins., Nat. Assn. Secondary Prins., AAUP, Oreg., Am. Assn. Sch. Adminstrs., Assn. Supervision and Curriculum Devel., Nat. Sch. Pub. Relations Assn., Phi Delta Kappa. Mason (Shriner), Lion. Home: 21801 SE Webfoot Rd Dayton OR 97114-8832

WILLIAMS, KNOX, water conditioning company executive; b. Grandfield, Okla., Aug. 9, 1928; s. Knox B. and Clara Mae (Butler) W.; m. Juanita June Wood, Sept. 9, 1951; children—Jodi Ann and Jeri Ruth (twins), Drue Knox. B.A., UCLA, 1951. With Wilson-McMahan Furniture Stores, Santa Barbara, Calif., 1951-61; prin., pres. Rayne of North San Diego County, Vista, Calif., 1961—, Aqua Fresh Drinking Water Systems, Inc., San Diego, 1980—. Mem. bd. counsellors UCLA; chmn. Santh Margarita Br. YMCA, 1991-93. With USNR, 1947-48. Mem. Carlsbad C. of C., Pacific Water Quality Assn. (pres. 1975-76), Water Quality Assn. (bd. dirs. 1980-83). Republican. Presbyterian. Clubs: El Camino Rotary (pres. 1989-90) (Oceanside, Calif.), Masons (Santa Barbara). Office: Rayne of North San Diego County 2011 W Vista Way Vista CA 92083-6013 also: Aqua Fresh Drinking Water Systems 7370 Opportunity Rd Ste I San Diego CA 92111

WILLIAMS, LARRY MCCLEASE, chemical engineer; b. Elizabeth City, N.C., Oct. 23, 1955. BS in Chem. Engring., N.C. State U., 1978; PhD in Chem. Engring., U. Calif., Berkeley, 1982. Rsch. asst. Lawrence Berkeley Lab., 1978-82; mem. tech. staff AT&T Bell Labs., Murray Hill, N.J., 1982-89; prin. investigator ROEX Tech., Santa Rosa, Calif., 1989—. Editor: Chemical Vapor Deposition Patents; contbr. articles to profl. jours.; inventor in field. J.M. Johnston scholar, 1974; IBM fellow, 1981. Mem. Am. Chem. Soc., Am. Vacuum Soc., The Electrochem. Soc., Calif. Alumni Assn. Office: ROEX 1150 Coddingtown Ctr # 252 Santa Rosa CA 95401-3555

WILLIAMS, LARRY RICHARD, commodities trader; b. Miles City, Mont., Oct. 6, 1942; s. Richard Sigwart and Sylva (Brurs) W.; m. Carla Williams, Jan. 19, 1976; children: Kelley, Jason, Sarah, Shelley, Paige. BS, U. Oreg., 1964. Prin. Larry Williams, Commodity Trading Adviser, Solana Beach, Calif., 1967—. Author: The Secret of Selecting Stock, 1970, How I Made Million Dollars Trading Commodities, 1973, How Seasonal Factors Influence Commodity Prices, 1976, How to Prosper in the Coming Good Years, 1982, The Definitive Guide to Futures Trading, vols. I and II, 1988. Republican. Office: PO Box 8162 Rancho Santa Fe CA 92067-8162

WILLIAMS, LEONA RAE, lingerie retailer; b. Fairfield, Nebr., July 1, 1928; d. Melton M. and Helga D. (Sorensen) Brown; m. Eugene F. Williams, June 6, 1946; 1 child, Dennis D. Grad. high sch., Fairfield. Owner Alice Rae Apparel Shop, Tucson, 1953—, second location 1967—, Green Valley, Ariz., 1976-93, Sun City, Ariz., 1993—. Sponsor Distributive Edn. Program, 1978-82; coord. fashion shows Am. Cancer Soc., Tucson, 1987, 88, 89. Mem. Exec. Women's Internat. Assn., Mchts. Assn. (pres., 1987-89), Soroptimists, C. of C. Better Bus. Bureau. Republican. Baptist. Office: Alice Rae Intimate Apparel 2914 N Campbell Ave Tucson AZ 85719-2876

WILLIAMS, LEWIS FREDERICK, lawyer; b. Helena, Ark., Nov. 3, 1938; s. Lewis Maurice and Mabel Irene (Lovelace) W.; m. Adeline Navarra, Sept. 1, 1963; children: Michael Frederick, Carolyn Ann. BS Acctg., San Diego State U., 1964; JD cum laude, San Fernando Valley Coll. Law, 1969. Agt. IRS, L.A., 1964-68, estate tax atty., 1968-72; atty. Miller & Kearney, San Diego, 1972-75, Becea & Williams, San Diego, 1975-77, L. Frederick Williams, Inc., San Diego, 1977-80, Williams & Bregante, San Diego, 1980-82, L. Frederick Williams, Inc., San Diego, 1982-91, Harrigan, Ruff, Ryder & Sbardellati, San Diego, 1991—; instr. San Diego State U., 1981-83, U. Calif., San Diego, 1977-78, The Am. Coll. Bryn Mawr, Pa., 1975-79. Mem. Planned Giving Com., San Diego State U., 1990—, Western Pension Benefits Conf., 1992—, Deferred Gifts Com., Roman Cath. Diocese San Diego, 1978-80. With U.S. Army, 1962-68. With U.S. Army, 1962-68. Mem. ABA, Calif. Bar, San Diego County Bar Assn., Calif. Soc. CPA. Democrat. Office: Harrigan Ruff et al 1855 First Ave Ste 200 San Diego CA 92101

WILLIAMS, LINDA TURNER, social services organization administrator; b. St. Louis, Oct. 28, 1941; d. Lucius Don IV and Louise Patton (Richardson) Turner; m. John Howard Williams, Aug. 17, 1963; children: Don Sheldon, John Rolland. AB, U. Ill., 1963; MA, Santa Clara U., 1976. Lic. marriage, family and child counselor, Calif. Tchr. Community Sch. Music and Art, Mountain View, Calif., 1972-77; therapist intern North County Mental Health, Palo Alto, Calif., 1975-77; dir. social svcs. Palo Alto chpt. ARC, 1977-80, exec. dir., 1982-89; exec. dir. Planned Parenthood Santa Clara and San Benito Counties, San Jose, Calif., 1989—; project dir. Bus. Info. Analysis Corp., Haverford, Pa., 1980-82, mgmt. cons. Western chpts., 1987-89; vice chmn. Pvt. Industry Coun., Sunnyvale, Calif., 1987-92. Bd. dirs. Vol. Exch., San Jose, 1986—, Planned Parenthood Affiliates of Calif., Sacramento, 1989—, Woodside (Calif.) Cons. Group, 1986—, Boys and Girls Club of Santa Clara County, 1991—; vol. Santa Clara (Calif.) United Way, 1983—. Mem. APHA, Assn. United Way Agys. (mem. exec. com., past pres. Santa Clara chpt.), Neighbors Abroad, Nat. Women's Polit. Caucus, Santa Clara County Strategic Vision Roundtable. Republican. Office: Planned Parenthood 1691 The Alameda San Jose CA 95126

WILLIAMS, MARC H., electroencephalography technologist; b. L.A., Mar. 31, 1952; s. Edward S. and Florence R. (Fisher) W.; m. Rebecca L. May, May 29, 1976 (div. 1980); 1 child, James S.; m. Corinne A. Woolley, June 17, 1989; 1 child, Matthew J. B in Vocat. Edn., Calif. State U., Long Beach, 1992. Reg. EEG technologist, 1976. Hosp. corpsman USN, 1969-77; dept. mgr. Mansfield (Ohio) Gen. Hosp., 1977-78; rsch. technologist UCLA-NPI, L.A., 1978-83; EEG technologist Long Beach Meml. Med. Ctr., 1983-88, dept. mgr., 1988—; cons. Electroneuroniagnostics, 1988—; exec. com. Am. Soc. of ELectro-Neurodiagnostic Technologists, 1983—. vol. ARC, 1989; adj. instr. Orange Coast Coll., 1984. Tech. sgt. USN, 1969-77, USNG, 1980-89. Mem. Am. Soc. of Electro-Neurodiagnostic Technologists (bd. trustees 1983-85, v.p. 1987-89, 1991-93), Am. EEG Soc., Western Soc. EEG Technologists (nominating chair, 1972-76, 1985-92). Democrat. Home: 6721 Santa Catalina Garden Grove CA 92645 Office: Long Beach Meml Med Ctr 2801 Atlantic Ave Long Beach CA 90801

WILLIAMS, MARION LESTER, government official; b. Abilene, Tex., Dec. 1, 1933; s. Martin Lester and Eddie Faye (Wilson) W.; m. Johnnie Dell Ellinger, Dec. 14, 1957; children: Tammy Dawn Cole, Pamela DeAnn Ritterbush. BS, Tex. A&M U., 1956; MS, U. N.Mex., 1967; PhD, Okla. State U., 1971. Test engr. Sandia Nat. Labs., Albuquerque, 1959-61; weapons sys. engr. Naval Weapons Evaluation Facility, Albuquerque, 1961-66; ops. rsch. analyst Joint Chiefs of Staff/Joint Task Force II, Albuquerque, 1966-68; chief reliability div. Field Command DNA, Albuquerque, 1969-71; prin. scientist SHAPE Tech. Ctr., The Hague, Netherlands, 1971-74; chief tech. advisor HQ AF Test & Evaluation Ctr., Albuquerque, 1974-81; chief scientist HQ AF Operational Test & Evaluation Ctr., Albuquerque, 1981-89; tech. dir. HQ AF Operational Test & Evaluation Ctr., 1989—; vis. adv. com. Okla. State U., Stillwater, 1988—; adv. com. U. N.Mex., Albuquerque, 1985—. Editor T&E Tech. Jour., 1987—; contbr. articles to profl. jours. Sci. advisor N.Mex. Sci. & Tech. Oversigh Com., Albuquerque, 1988; bd. advisors U. N.Mex. Cancer Ctr., 1987—; bd. dirs. Contact Albuquerque, 1986-87. 1st lt. USAF 1956-59. Recipient Presdl. Rank award, 1987, 92. Fellow Mil. Ops. Rsch. Soc. (pres. 1982-83, bd. dirs. 1976-81, Wanner award 1991), Internat. Test & Evaluation Ctr. (bd. dirs. 1984-86, 88-90, v.p. 1990, pres. 1992-93), Ops. Rsch. Soc. Am., Tau Beta Pi, Phi Eta Sigma, Alpha Pi Mu, Sigma Tau, Kappa Mu Epsilon. Democrat. Baptist. Home: 1416 Stagecoach Ln SE Albuquerque NM 87123-4429 Office: HQ AF Operational Test Ctr Kirtland AFB Albuquerque NM 87117-7001

WILLIAMS, MARK ALVIN, writer, director, producer; b. Chgo., Feb. 12, 1935; s. Joseph and Berdie (Holnitzky) Stein; children: Aimee, Debra, Iris, Amanda; m. Elizabeth Shinoda Williams, Aug. 13, 1989. BA, DePaul U., 1956. Writer, dir., producer (play) JFK, 1970-75 (critically acclaimed), (TV) Dave Del Dotto Infomercials; prodr. documentaries including (with E.G. Marshall) How to Be Successful In America. Mem. BMI, Writers Guild of Am., Dirs. Guild of Am., Masons, Nat. Infomercial Mktg. Assn. Democrat. Jewish. Home: PO Box 4959 Kailua-Kona HI 96745 Office: 2566 Overland Ave Los Angeles CA 90064

WILLIAMS, MARY D(ENNEN), psychologist; b. Cin.; d. Frank Eugene and Katharine Powell (Wiley) D.; children from previous marriage: John Wiley Hartung, Katharine D. Hartung, Denny Hartung. AB, Radcliffe Coll., 1943; MS, U. Vt., 1948; MPA in Pub. Health, U. R.I., 1965; PhD, U. Oreg., 1982. Lic. psychologist, Oreg., Idaho. Instr. zoology U. R.I., Kingston, 1950-51, asst. prof. zoology in Pub. Health, 1957-59; grad. teaching fellow U. Oreg., Eugene, 1978-80; resident psychologist Portland, Oreg., 1982-85; pvt. practice psychologist Portland, 1985—. Mem. Am. Psychol. Assn., Oreg. Psychol. Assn., Portland Psychol. Assn., Am. Assn. Sci., Sigma Xi, Pi Sigma Alpha, Phi Kappa Phi.

WILLIAMS, MATT (MATTHEW DERRICK WILLIAMS), baseball player; b. Bishop, Calif., Nov. 28, 1965. Student, U. Nev., Las Vegas. With San Francisco Giants, 1987—. Recipient Gold Glove award, 1991, Silver Slugger award, 1990; named to All-Star team, 1990, Coll. All-Am. team Sporting News, 1986; Nat. League RBI Leader, 1990. Office: San Francisco Giants Candlestick Park San Francisco CA 94124

WILLIAMS, NANCY ELLEN-WEBB, social services administrator; b. Quincy, Ill., Aug. 1; d. Charles and Garnet Naomi (Davis) Webb; m. Jesse B. Williams, Apr. 11, 1959; children: Cynthia L. Williams Clay, Troy Andrea Williams Redic, Bernard Peter. BA, Quincy Coll., 1957; postgrad., Tenn. A&I U., 1961; M Pub. Adminstrn., U. Nev., Las Vegas, 1977; LHD (hon.), U. Humanistic Studies, 1986. Cert. peace officer, Nev. (chmn. Standards and Tng. Com., 1978-81); cert. social worker. Tchr. Shelby County Tng. Sch., Memphis, 1957-61; dep. probation officer Clark County Juvenile Ct., Las Vegas, 1961-66, supervising probation officer, 1966-74, dir. probation services, 1974-80, dir. intake admissions, 1980-81, dir. Child Haven, 1989—; mem. Nev. Crime Commn., 1970-81. Author: When We Were Colored, 1986, Dinah's Pain and Other Poems of the Black Life Experience, 1988, Them Gospel Songs, 1989; contbr. poetry to various mags. Mem. exec. com. Clark County Econ. Opportunity Bd., Las Vegas, 1963-71; chmn. So. Nev. Task Force on Corrections, 1974-81; mem. Gov.'s Com. on Justice Standards and Goals, 1979-81; bd. dirs. U. Humanistic Studies, Las Vegas, 1984—. Recipient Friend of Golden Gloves award Golden Gloves Regional Bd., 1981, Tribute to Black Women award U. Nev., Las Vegas, 1984, Commr.'s award HHS, 1991, Folklore mini-grant Nev. Coun. of the Arts, 1992. Fellow Am. Acad. Neurol. and Orthopedic Surgeons (assoc.); mem. AAUW, Nat. Council Juvenile Ct. Judges, Nat. Writers Assn. Democrat. Office: Flamingo Pecos Plaza 3430 E Flamingo Rd Ste 210 Las Vegas NV 89121-5018

WILLIAMS, PAT, congressman; b. Helena, Mont., Oct. 30, 1937; m. Carol Griffith, 1965; children: Griff, Erin, Whitney. Student, U. Mont., 1956-57, William Jewell U.; BA, U. Denver, 1961; postgrad., Western Mont. Coll.; LLD (hon.), Carroll Coll., Montana Coll. of Mineral Sci. and Tech. Mem. Mont. Ho. of Reps., 1967, 69; exec. dir. Hubert Humphrey Presdl. campaign, Mont., 1968; exec. asst. to U.S. Rep. John Melcher, 1969-71; mem. Gov.'s Employment and Tng. Council, 1972-78, Mont. Legis. Reapportionment Commn., 1973; co-chmn. Jimmy Carter Presdl. campaign, Mont., 1976; mem. 96th-102nd Congresses from 1st Mont. dist., 1979—; chmn. labor mgmt. rels. subcom. Coordinator Mont. Family Edn. Program, 1971-78. Served with U.S. Army, 1960-61; Served with Army N.G., 1962-69. Mem. Mont. Fedn. Tchrs. Democrat. Lodge: Elks. Office: House of Representatives 2457 Rayburn House Office Washington DC 20515*

WILLIAMS, PHILIP F. C., Chinese literature educator; b. Little Rock, Apr. 5, 1956; s. Franklin Springer and Elizabeth Corbett (Bassett) W. BA, U. Ark., 1978; postgrad., Cornell U., 1978-79; MA, UCLA, 1981, PhD, 1985. Rsch. grantee Com. for Scholarly Communication with China Nat. Acad. Scis., Beijing, 1982-83; lectr. Occidental Coll., L.A., 1984; vis. asst. prof. UCLA, 1986; asst. prof. Ariz. State U., Tempe, 1986-93, assoc. prof., 1993—; escort interpreter U.S. Dept. State, Washington, 1986—; mem. com. Ctr. Asian Studies, Ariz. State U., 1987, chair library com., 1988—; reviewing staff mem. World Literature Today, 1992—. Author: Village Echoes: The Fiction of Wu Zuxiang, 1993; mem. editorial bd. Ctr. Asian Studies, monograph series, Ariz. State U., 1986—, Jour. Asian Culture, 1979-81, 84-86. Fairbank Ctr. for East Asian Rsch. fellow Harvard U., 1990-91; rsch. grantee Pacific Cultural Assns., 1990-91; faculty grantee-in-aid Ariz. State U., 1988; NEH rsch. grantee, summer 1989. Mem. Assn. Asian Studies, Chinese Lang. Tchrs. Assn., Am. Comparative Lit. Assn., UCLA Alumni Assn. (acad. achievement award 1981), Phi Beta Kappa. Democrat. Office: Ariz State U Dept Fgn Langs Tempe AZ 85287-0202

WILLIAMS, PHYLLIS CUTFORTH, retired realtor; b. Moreland, Idaho, June 6, 1917; d. William Claude and Kathleen Jessie (Jenkins) Cutforth; m. Joseph Marsden Williams, Jan. 21, 1938 (dec. 1986); children: Joseph Marlis, Bonnie L. Williams Thompson, Nancy K. Williams Stewart, Marjorie Williams Karren, Douglas Claude, Thomas Marsden, Wendy K. Williams Clark, Shannon I. Williams. Grad., Ricks Coll., 1935. Lic. realtor, Idaho. Tchr. Grace (Idaho) Elem. Sch., 1935-38; realtor Williams Realty, Idaho Falls,

Idaho, 1972-77; mem. Idaho Senate, Boise, 1977; owner, mgr. 100-acre farm, 1980—, also river property. Compiler: Idaho Legisladies Cookbook, Cookin' Together, 1981. With MicroFilm Ctr., LDS Ch. Mission, Salt Lake City, 1989-90; block chmn. Easter Seals Soc.; active Idaho State Legisladies Club, 1966-84, v.p., 1982-84. Republican. Home: 1950 Carmel Dr Idaho Falls ID 83402-3020

WILLIAMS, QUINN PATRICK, lawyer; b. Evergreen Park, Ill., May 6, 1949; s. William Albert and Jeanne Marie (Quinlan) W.; m. Linda Irene Prather, Apr. 21, 1979; children: Michael Ryan, Mark Reed, Kelly Elizabeth. BBA, U. Wis., 1972; JD, U. Ariz., 1974. Bar: Ariz. 1975, N.Y. 1984, U.S. Dist. Ct. Ariz. 1976. Vice pres., sec., gen. counsel Combined Comm. Corp., Phoenix, 1975-80; v.p., sec., gen. counsel Swensen's Ice Cream Co., Phoenix, 1980-83; sr. v.p. legal and adminstrn. Swensen's Inc., Phoenix, 1983-86; of counsel Winston & Strawn, Phoenix, 1985-87, ptnr., 1987-89, ptnr. Snell & Wilmer, Phoenix, 1989—. Vice chmn., treas. Combined Comm. Polit. Action Com., Phoenix, 1976-80; chmn. Ariz. Tech. Inventor, Ariz. Tech. Incubator, Ariz. Venture Capital Conf. Served with USAR, 1967-73. Mem. ABA, Maricopa County Bar Assn., N.Y. Bar Assn., State Bar Ariz., Internat. Franchise Assn., Paradise Valley Country Club, Phi Alpha Delta. Republican. Roman Catholic. Home: 8131 N 75th St Scottsdale AZ 85258-2781 Office: Snell & Wilmer One Arizona Ctr Phoenix AZ 85004

WILLIAMS, RICHARD PASCAL, JR., epidemiologist, military career officer; b. Asheville, N.C., Oct. 5, 1939; s. Richard Pascal Sr. and Rosetta Gloria (Adams) W.; m. Shelvie Roberts, Sept. 6, 1960 (div. 1972); children: Richard Pascal III, Derek Lance; m. Juanita Elizabeth Wheeler, Sept. 11, 1981. BS, U. Tenn., 1962; MD, U. Ky., 1966; MPH, Uniformed Svcs. U. Health Scis, 1990. Diplomate Am. Bd. Emergency Medicine. Gen. med. officer USAF, Tachikawa AB, Japan, 1967-70; pvt. practice family medicine Houston, 1971-77, pvt. practice emergency medicine, 1977-85; asst. 6th fleet surgeon USN, Naples, Italy, 1986-87; asst. head dept. emergency mediicne Nat. Naval Med. Ctr., Bethesda, Md., 1987-88, head dept. mil. medicine, 1989; resident in preventive medicine U. Hawaii, Honolulu, 1990-91; epidemiologist Navy Environ. & Preventive Medicine Unit # 6, Pearl Harbor, Hawaii, 1991—; chmn. Instn. Rev. Bd., Bethesda, 1988-89; mem. cons. staff Nat. Naval Med. Ctr., 1989-91; v.p. New Age Hospice, 1978-80. Contbr. articles to profl. jours. Mem. Assn. Mil. Surgeons of U.S. Roman Catholic. Home: 175 Mcgrew Loop Aiea HI 96701-4216 Office: Navy Environ & Preventive Medicine Unit # 6 Naval Sta Pearl Harbor HI 96860

WILLIAMS, ROBB, athletic trainer; b. Cin., July 4, 1962; s. Carol J. Metz. BS in Edn., Ohio State U., 1983; MEd, U. Cin., 1984. Head trianer Liberty U., Lynchburg, Va., 1984-86; dir. sports medicine Strand Orthopedics, S.C., 1986-88; assoc. head athletic trainer U. Wyo., Laramie, 1988—; cons. in field. Mem. Nat. Athletic Trainers Assn. Republican. Home: 2123 Hancock Laramie WY 82070

WILLIAMS, ROBERT STONE, protective services official; b. Mathews, Va., Jan. 22, 1952; s. Charles H. and Anne (Stone) W.; m. Danielle Williams, July 1987. AAS, Rowan Tech. Inst., 1972; BS in Fire Protection and Safety Engring., Okla. State U., 1975, MBA, 1976. Adminstrv. specialist Oklahoma City Fire Dept., 1977-79; dep. fire chief Clovis Fire Dept., N.Mex., 1979-82; fire chief Billings Fire Dept., Mont., 1982-88; fire chief City of Spokane, Wash., 1988—. Mem. Wash. State Bldg. Code Coun., 1989—; bd. dirs. Salvation Army, Billings, 1984-85, Am. Heart Assn., Clovis, N.Mex., 1980-82, Internat. Fire Code Inst., 1990—. Named Fireperson Yr. Billings Downtown Exchange Club, 1988. Mem. Western Fire Chiefs Assn. (1st v.p. 1984-85, pres. 1985-86), Internat. Assn. Fire Chiefs, Nat. Fire Protection Assn., Curry County Jaycees (v.p. 1981-82, Jaycee of Yr. 1982), Billings Jaycees (bd. dirs. 1983-87, v.p. community devel. 1985, Outstanding Jaycee 1983, Disting. Service award 1985), Mont. Jaycees (treas. 1986-87, speak-up program mgr. 1986-87, Outstanding Young Montanan award 1985-86). Roman Catholic. Office: Spokane Fire Dept 44 W Riverside Ave Spokane WA 99201-0189

WILLIAMS, ROBERT WILMOT, actuary; b. N.Y.C., Sept. 6, 1943; s. Roger and Odessa Roane (Lastrapes) W.; m. Arleen Rolling, Aug. 13, 1965 (div.); children: Laura Roane, Keith Clayon; m. Margaret Carol Slyter, May 13, 1989. BA, La. State U., 1965; postgrad., Am. U., Washington, 1966-67, Ariz. State U., Tempe, 1975-78. Statistician USPHS, Washington, 1965-68; chief statistician V.I. Health Dept., St. Thomas, 1968-71; actuary Ariz. State Compensation Fund, Phoenix, 1972—; cons. Ariz. State Personnel Com., Phoenix, 1975-82; chmn. stats. com. Am. Assn. State Funds, 1983. Contbr. articles to profl. jours. Mem. Villa Montessori Sch. Bd. Dirs., Phoenix, 1978-82. Mem. Ariz. Statis. Assn. (pres. 1979), Mensa, 20-30 Internat. Office: State Compensation Fund 3031 N 2d St Phoenix AZ 85012

WILLIAMS, ROBIN PATRICIA, writer; b. Berkeley, Calif., Oct. 9, 1953; d. Gerald Wilford and Patricia May (Weber) W.; children: Ryan, Jimmy Thomas, Scarlett. AA, Santa Rosa Coll., 1981. Designer The Double Image Design Assoc., Santa Rosa, Calif., 1980-82; designer, prodn. Selwyn Assocs. Advt., Santa Rosa, Calif., 1982-83; designer Now Showing Video Prodns., Santa Rosa, Calif., 1981-83; instr. graphic design Santa Rosa Jr. Coll., 1982—; writer, trainer self-employed Santa Rosa, 1989—; columnist Desktop Comms. Mag., N.Y.C., 1991—, Boston Computer Soc. Mag., 1992—; editor-at-large Mac Home Jour. Mag., San Francisco, 1992—. Author: The Little Mac Book, 1990 (Ben Franklin award 1990), The Mac is not a Typewriter, 1990 (Ben Franklin award 1990), The PC is not a Typewriter, 1991, PageMaker 4: An Easy Desk Reference, 1991 (Best Computer Book on Any Subject 1992), Jargon, An informal dictionary of computer terms, 1993. Mem. North Coast Macintosh User Group (leader 1991—), Santa Rosa Jr. Coll. Applied Graphics Adv. Bd. (chmn. 1985-88), Sonoma County Ad Club. Democrat.

WILLIAMS, RONALD DAVID, electronics materials executive; b. Marshall, Ark., Mar. 15, 1944; s. Noble Kentucky and Elizabeth (Karns) W.; m. Beth L. Williams, Nov. 1977; children: Stephanie Noble, Keith Michael. BA, Columbia U., 1966, BS, 1967, MBA, 1973. Process engr. DuPont, Deepwater, N.J., 1966; design engr. Combustion Engring. Co., Hartford, 1971; cons. Arthur Andersen & Co., N.Y.C., 1973-76; corp. planner Amax Inc., Greenwich, Conn., 1976-77, group planning adminstr., 1978-80, mgr. corp. planning and analysis, 1980-84, dir. fin. analysis, 1984-86; project mgr. Olin Corp., Stamford, Conn., 1977-78; mgr. ops planning, analysis Savin Corp., Stamford, 1986-88; dir. fin., Bandgap Tech. Corp., Broomfield, Colo., 1988-90; v.p. fin. and adminstrn., 1990-93; dir., 1991—; v.p. and gen. mgr. Bandgap Chem. Corp., 1992—. Served with USN, 1967-70, Vietnam. NASA traineeship, 1971; S.W. Mudd scholar, 1971. Mem. AAAS, Am. Chem. Soc., Am. Mgmt. Assn. Democrat. Club: Appalachian Mountain, Boulder Road Runners. Home: 7361 S Meadow Ct Boulder CO 80301-3951 Office: Bandgap Tech Corp 325 Interlocken Pky Broomfield CO 80021-3437 also: Bandgap Chem Corp 1861 Lefthand Circle Longmont CO 80501

WILLIAMS, RONALD LEE, pharmacologist; b. Koleen, Ind., June 26, 1936; s. Marion Raymond and Doris May (Lynch) W.; m. Sondra Sue Cobb, June 7, 1957; children: Robin Lee, Christopher P., David R., Jonathon V. BS, Butler U., 1959, MS, 1961; PhD, Tulane U., 1964. Registered pharmacist, Colo. From instr. to assoc. prof. pharmacology La. State U., New Orleans, 1964-84, assoc. prof. medicine, 1978-84, ret., 1984; asst. dir. Dept. of Corrections Hosp. Pharmacy, Canon City, Colo., 1986—; expert adv. panel renal drugs U.S. Pharmacopeia Drug Info., 1981-85; cons. in field. Editorial bd. jour. Pharmacology, 1979; reviewer jour. Pharmaceutical Sci., 1976; contbr. articles to profl. jours. La. Heart Assn. grantee, 1964, 66. Mem. Am. Soc. Pharmacology, N.Y. Acad. Sci., Fedn. Am. Soc. Exptl. Biology, So. Colo. Soc. Hosp. Pharm. Assn., Sigma Xi. Republican. Baptist. Home: 1004 Greenwood Ave Canon City CO 81212-3440 Office: D O C Pharmacy W Hwy 50 Box 1010 Canon City CO 81212

WILLIAMS, RONALD OSCAR, systems engineer; b. Denver, May 10, 1940; s. Oscar H. and Evelyn (Johnson) W. BS in Applied Math., U. Colo. Coll. Engring., 1964, postgrad. U. Colo., U. Denver, George Washington U. Computer programmer Apollo Systems dept., missile and space divsn. Gen. Electric Co., Kennedy Space Ctr., Fla., 1965-67, Manned Spacecraft Ctr., Houston, 1967-68; computer programmer U. Colo., Boulder, 1968-73; computer programmer analyst def. systems divsn. System Devel. Corp. for NORAD, Colorado Springs, 1974-75; engr. def. systems and command-and-info. systems Martin Marietta Aerospace, Denver, 1976-80; systems engr. space and comm. group, def. info. systems divsn. Hughes Aircraft Co., Aurora, Colo., 1980-89. Vol. fireman Clear Lake City (Tex.) Fire Dept., 1968; officer Boulder Emergency Squad, 1969-76, rescue squadman, 1969-76, liaison to cadets, 1971, pers. officer, 1971-76, exec. bd., 1971-76, award of merit, 1971, 72, emergency med. technician 1973—; spl. police officer Boulder Police Dept., 1970-75; spl. dep. sheriff Boulder County Sheriff's Dept., 1970-71; nat. adv. bd. Am. Security Coun., 1979-91, Coalition of Peace through Strength, 1979-91. Served with USMCR, 1958-66. Decorated Organized Res. medal; recipient Cost Improvement Program award Hughes Aircraft Co., 1982, Systems Improvement award, 1982, Top Cost Improvement Program award, 1983. Mem. AAAS, Math. Assn. Am., Am. Math. Soc., Soc. Indsl. and Applied Math., AIAA, Armed Forces Comm. and Electronics Assn., Assn. Old Crows, Am. Def. Preparedness Assn., Marine Corps Assn., Air Force Assn., U.S. Naval Inst., Nat. Geog. Soc., Smithsonian Instn., Met. Opera Guild, Colo. Hist. Soc., Hist. Denver, Inc., Historic Boulder, Inc., Hawaiian Hist. Soc., Denver Art Mus., Denver Botanic Gardens, Denver Mus. Natural History, Denver Zool. Found., Inc., Mensa, Hour of Power Eagles Club. Lutheran.

WILLIAMS, RUBY ORA, English language educator; b. Lakewood, N.J., Feb. 18, 1926; d. Charles and Ida (Bolles) W. BA, Va. Union U., Richmond, 1950; MA, Howard U., Washington, 1953; PhD, U. Calif., Irvine, 1974. Instr. English, So. U., Baton Rouge, 1953-55, Tuskegee (Ala.) Inst., 1955-57, Morgan State U., Balt., 1957-65; program advisor Camp Fire Girls Inc., N.Y.C., 1965-68; prof. English, Calif. State U., Long Beach, 1968-88, prof. emeritus, 1988—; vis. prof. Va. Union U., Richmond, 1990-91. Author: American Black Women in the Arts and Social Sciences: A Bibliographic Survey, 1973, 2d edit., 1978; contbr. articles to profl. jours. Bd. dirs. Inner City Ctr., L.A., 1970—, Beem Found. for Advancement of Music, L.A., 1972—. Recipient Pillar of the Community award, Long Beach Improvement Assn., 1988, Edn. Community Svc. award, Mayor Ernie Kell, Long Beach, 1988, The Consortium of Doctors award, Savannah, Ga., 1993; Patent Found. grantee, 1972. Mem. Coll. Lang. Assn., Va. Union U. Alumni Assn. So. Calif. (Ann. Achievement award 1983).

WILLIAMS, RUTH J., mathematics researcher and educator; b. Melbourne, Australia. BS with honors, U. Melbourne, 1976, MS, 1978; PhD, Stanford U., 1983. Postdoctoral mem. Courant Inst., N.Y.C., 1983-84; asst. prof. U. Calif., San Diego, 1984-88, assoc. prof., 1988-91, prof., 1991—. Assoc. editor jour. Annals of Probability, 1988-93. Co-author: Introduction to Stochastic Integration, 1983, 2d edit. 1990. Alfred P. Sloan Found. fellow, 1988-92; recipient Presdl. Young Investigator award NSF, 1987-92. Fellow Inst. Math. Stats.; mem. AAAS, Am. Math. Soc., Am. Math. Soc. Coun. Office: Univ Calif Dept Math 0112 La Jolla CA 92093-0112

WILLIAMS, RUTH LEE, clinical social worker; b. Dallas, June 24, 1944; d. Carl Woodley and Nancy Ruth (Gardner) W. BA, So. Meth. U., 1966; M Sci.in Social Work, U. Tex., Austin, 1969. Milieu coordinator Starr Commonwealth, Albion, Mich., 1969-73; clin. social worker Katherine Hamilton Mental Health Care, Terre Haute, Ind., 1973-74; clin. social worker, supr. Pikes Peak Mental Health Ctr., Colorado Springs, Colo., 1974-78; pvt. practice social work Colorado Springs, 1978—; pres. Hearthstone Inn, Inc., Colorado Springs, 1978—; practitioner Jin Shin Jyutsu, Colorado Springs, 1978—; pres., v.p. bd. dirs. Premier Care (formerly Colorado Springs Mental Health Care Providers Inc.), 1986-87, chmn. quality assurance com., 1987-89, v.p. bd. dirs., 1992-93. Author, editor: From the Kitchen of The Hearthstone Inn, 1981, 2d rev. edit., 1986, 3d rev. edit., 1992. Mem. Am. Bd. Examiners in Clin. Social Work (charter mem., cert.), Colo. Soc. Clin. Social Work (editor 1976), Nat. Assn. Soc. Workers (diplomate), Nat. Bd. Social Work Examiners (cert.), Nat. Assn. Ind. Innkeepers, So. Meth. U. Alumni Assn. (life). Home: 11555 Howells Rd Colorado Springs CO 80908-3735 Office: 536 E Uintah St Colorado Springs CO 80903-2515

WILLIAMS, SPENCER M., federal judge; b. Reading, Mass., Feb. 24, 1922; s. Theodore Ryder and Anabel (Hutchison) W.; m. Kathryn Bramlage, Aug. 20, 1943; children: Carol Marcia (Mrs. James B. Garvey), Peter, Spencer, Clark, Janice, Diane (Mrs. Sean Quinn). A.B., U. Calif. at Los Angeles, 1943; postgrad., Hastings Coll. Law, 1946; J.D., U. Calif. at Berkeley, 1948. Bar: Calif. bar 1949, U.S. Supreme Ct. bar 1952. Assoc. Beresford & Adams, San Jose, Calif., 1949, Rankin, O'Neal, Center, Luckhardt, Bonney, Marlais & Lund, San Jose, Evans, Jackson & Kennedy, Sacramento; county counsel Santa Clara County, 1955-67; adminstr. Calif. Health and Welfare Agy., Sacramento, 1967-69; judge U.S. Dist. Ct. (no. dist.) Calif., San Francisco, from 1971, now sr. judge; County exec. pro tem, Santa Clara County; adminstr. Calif. Youth and Adult Corrections Agy., Sacramento; sec. Calif. Human Relations Agy., Sacramento, 1967-70. Chmn. San Jose Christmas Seals Drive, 1953, San Jose Muscular Dystrophy Drive, 1953, 54; team capt. fund raising drive San Jose YMCA, 1960; co-chmn. indsl. sect. fund raising drive Alexian Bros. Hosp., San Jose, 1964; team capt. fund raising drive San Jose Hosp.; mem. com. on youth and govt. YMCA, 1967-68; Candidate for Calif. Assembly, 1954, Calif. Atty. Gen., 1966, 70; Bd. dirs. San Jose Better Bus. Bur., 1955-66, Boys City Boys' Club, San Jose, 1965-67; pres. trustees Santa Clara County Law Library, 1955-66. Served with USNR, 1943-46; to lt. comdr. JAG Corps USNR, 1950-52, PTO. Named San Jose Man of Year, 1954. Mem. ABA, Calif. Bar Assn. (vice chmn. com. on publicly employed attys. 1962-63), Santa Clara County Bar Assn., Sacramento Bar Assn., Calif. Dist. Attys. Assn. (pres. 1963-64), Nat. Assn. County Civil Attys. (pres. 1963-64), Ninth Circuit Dist. Judges Assn. (pres. 1981-83), Fed. Judges Assn. (pres. 1982-87), Theta Delta Chi. Club: Kiwanian. Office: US Dist Ct 280 S 1st St San Jose CA 95113-3002

WILLIAMS, STANLEY CLARK, medical entomologist, educator; b. Long Beach, Calif., Aug. 24, 1939; s. Thomas and Sadie Elenore (Anderson) W.; m. Charlene E. Fernald; children: Lisa M., Thomas S.; m. Roxanna Berlin, Aug. 30, 1981; 1 child, Erin B. AB, San Diego State Coll., 1961, MA, 1963; postgrad., U. Kans., 1963-64; PhD, Ariz. State U., 1968. Cert. secondary tchr., Calif. Instr. San Diego Mus. Nat. History, 1957-59, asst. curator herpetology, 1957-61; park naturalist U.S. Nat. Park Svc., San Diego, 1960-62; instr. Grossmont (Calif.) High Sch. Dist., 1962-63, Ariz. State U., Tempe, 1964-66; prof. biology San Francisco State U., 1967—; bd. dirs. West Point Acad. Sci., Calif.; mem. adv. bd. San Francisco Insect Zoo; vis. prof. biology USAF Acad., 1992-93. Contbr. over 60 articles to profl. jours. Grantee NSF, 1968-72; recipient Travel grant T.P. Hearne Co. Fellow Calif. Acad. Sci.; mem. Am. Arachnological Soc., Ecol. Soc. Am., San Francisco Beekeepers Assn. (pres. 1984-85), Pacific Coast Entomol. Soc. (pres. elect 1986, pres. 1987), Assn. Biologists for Computing (pres. 1986-88), Soc. Vector Ecologists (edit. bd. 1986—), Western Apicultural Soc. (v.p. 1987-88, pres. 1988-89), Soc. Systematic Biologists, Willi Hennig Soc., Brit. Arachnological Soc., Sigma Xi. Office: San Francisco State U Dept Biology San Francisco CA 94132

WILLIAMS, STEPHEN JOSEPH, education educator, researcher; b. Washington, Dec. 14, 1948; s. David and Nettie (Robbins) W.; m. Sandra J. Guerra, Jan. 19, 1980; children: Jeffrey, Daniel. BS, Carnegie Mellon U., 1970; MS, MIT, 1971; SM, Harvard U., 1972, ScD, 1974. Assoc. prof. health adminstrn. program Sch. of Pub. Health U. Wash., Seattle, 1975-80; prof., dept. head div. health svcs. adminstrn. Grad. Sch. Pub. Health San Diego State U., 1980—. Adv. editor Internat. Dictionary of Medicine and Biology, 1981-87; series editor, cons.: Wiley Series in Health Services, 1978-89, Delmar Series in Health Services, 1989—; mem. editorial bd. Jour. of Practice in Mgmt., 1989—; contbr. numerous articles to profl. jours. Office: San Diego State U Coll Health & Human Svcs San Diego CA 92182-0405

WILLIAMS, STUART KONRADD, biomedical educator, researcher; b. Wilmington, Del., Apr. 3, 1952; s. Stuart Konradd and Ann Lee (Mammele) W.; m. Carol Lynn Mraz, July 16, 1976; children—Kyle Clifford, Ross Stuart. B.A., U. Del., 1974, M.S., 1976, Ph.D., 1979. Postdoctoral fellow Yale U. Sch. Med. Pathology, New Haven, 1979-81; asst. prof. Jefferson Med. Coll., Phila., 1981-85, assoc. prof. surgery and dir. research, 1986-91; prof. surgery and physiology, chief sect. surg. biol. dept. surgery, U. Ariz. Health Scis. Ctr., Tucson, 1991—. Mem. Am. Heart Assn. Postdoctoral fellow NSF, 1979; recipient Lamport award Am. Microcirculatory Soc., 1981; Searle scholar Chgo. Community Trust, 1983; Research Career Devel. awardee NIH, 1985. Mem. Am. Soc. Cell Biologists, Microcirculatory Soc., Am. Physiol. Soc. Democrat. Achievements include numerous patents on cell transplantation. Home: 5181 N Circulo Sobrio Tucson AZ 85718-6037 Office: U Ariz Health Sci Ctr 1501 N Campbell Ave Rm 5334 Tucson AZ 85724

WILLIAMS, STUART MENDENHALL, independent photojournalist, consultant; b. Charleston, W. Va., July 27, 1936; s. John Sharf and Virginia Gold (Clendening) W. BA, Yale U., 1958; MA, U. Calif., 1959. Asst. prof. English Am. U. of Beirut, Lebanon, 1963-65, U. Md., Heidelberg, Fed. Republic Germany, 1965-68; asst. dir. Winchester Adventures, N.Y.C., 1968-71; shooting editor Field & Stream Mag., N.Y.C., 1971-74; photojournalist pvt. practice Seattle, 1974—; internat. editor Hunting Report Newsletter, Miami, Fla., 1987—, Sporting Clays Mag., Hilton Bend, S.C., 1989—; travel editor Sporting Classics Mag., Camden, S.C., 1989—; cons. Aerolineas Argentinas, Buenos Aires, 1986—. Author: Birds on the Horizon, 1992; contbr. over 500 articles to various mags., 1971—. With U.S. Army, 1960-62,. Recipient Hon. Mention Canon Nat. Photo Competition, N.Y.C., 1984. Mem. Seattle Photographic Soc. (bd. dirs. 1988-90), Photographic Soc. Am., Safari Club Internat., Internat. Order St. Hubert. Home and Office: 532 Belmont Ave E Seattle WA 98102

WILLIAMS, SUE M., corporate communications specialist, writer; b. Sumter, S.C., Aug. 20, 1942; d. Perry Harrington and Ida (Sumter) Taylor; m. Elwood E. Williams, Mar. 9, 1963 (div. 1969); 2 children. Diploma, cert., Communications Inst. of Am., 1968; BA, U. Colo., 1974; R. Sc. F., Ernest Holmes Coll. Ch. of Religious Sci., 1979. Ordained to ministry. Long distance operator Mountain Bell/Penn Bell, Phila. & Colorado Springs, Colo., 1964-69; comml. teller Exch. Nat. Bank, Colorado Springs, 1969-74; ops. trainee Cen. Bank of Denver, 1974-75; legal specialist USAFR, Lowry AFB, Colo., 1975-77; asst. mgr. Western Airlines, L.A., 1974-87; supr. reservation sales Delta Air Lines, L.A., 1987-88; sr. sec., office mgr. U. Colo., Denver, 1988-89; sales coord. Hewlett Packard Co., Englewood, Colo., 1989-90; supr. U.S. Sprint (United Telecom), Denver, 1990—. Contbr. articles to profl. jours. Mem. Vets. Club, Colorado Springs, 1973-74; various offices L.A. Election Dept., 1983-85; appointed vet. com. Calif. Reps., L.a., 1985; participant Hands Across Am., L.A., 1985, The Bolder Boulder, various walking races for local charity; charter mem. Women in Mil. Meml. Found., Washington, 1990. With USAF, 1961-63. Mem. Am. Legion, Coll. Devine Metaphysics Alumni Assn. (area v.p. 1982—). Office: US Sprint 1099 18th St Ste 1200 Denver CO 80202-1912

WILLIAMS, SUSAN EILEEN, urban planner; b. Chgo., Dec. 13, 1952; d. Joseph Andrew and Alice (Regnier) W.; 1 child, Ryan Joseph. AA in Polit. Sci., Coll. of Desert, Palm Desert, Calif., 1971; BA in Polit. Sci., U. Calif., Riverside, 1973; M of Pub. Adminstrn., Consortium Calif. State Colls. and Univs., 1982. Planning trainee City of Indio, Calif., 1975-79, assoc. planner, 1979-80, prin. planner, 1980-90, prin. planner redevel. agy., 1983-90; supervising planner J.F. Davidson Assocs., Inc., Palm Desert, Calif., 1990—. Mem. Am. Planning Assn., Assn. Environ Profls., Ill. Geneal. Soc., Geneal. Club Am. Roman Catholic. Office: JF Davidson Assocs Inc 77-564 Country Club Dr Ste 400B Palm Desert CA 92260

WILLIAMS, THEODORE EARLE, industrial distribution company executive; b. Cleve., May 9, 1920; s. Stanley S. and Blanche (Albaum) W.; m. Rita Cohen, Aug. 28, 1952; children: Lezlie, Richard Atlas, Shelley, William Atlas, Wayne, Marsha, Patti Blake, Jeff Blake. Student, Wayne U., 1937-38; BS in Engring, U. Mich., 1942, postgrad. in bus. adminstrn, 1942. Pres. Wayne Products Co., Detroit, 1942-43, L.A., 1947-49; pres. Williams Metal Products Co., Inglewood, Calif., 1950-69; chmn. bd., pres., chief exec. officer Bell Industries, L.A., 1970—; instr. U. Mich., 1942. Patentee in field. Served to 1st lt. AUS, 1943-46. Recipient Humanitarian award City of L.A., 1977. Democrat. Home: 435 N Layton Way Los Angeles CA 90049-2022 Office: Bell Industries Inc 11812 San Vicente Blvd Los Angeles CA 90049

WILLIAMS, THOMAS JAMES, bank examiner; b. Faribault, Minn., Feb. 12, 1963; s. Vance Oran and Joan Gertrude (Yahna) W.; m. Lynne Joanne Christiansen, Aug. 17, 1991. BSBA in Econs., U. S.D., 1985. Cert. nat. bank examiner. Nat. bank examiner Compt. of Currency, Iowa City, 1985-90; chmn. microcomputer users group midwestern dist. Compt. of Currency, Kansas City, Mo., 1988-89; nat. bank examiner Compt. of Currency, L.A., 1990—; mortgage banking and capital markets expert. Author various computer programs. Recipient nat. creativity award Compt. of Currency, 1990. Mem. U.S. Chess Fedn., Friends Pub. TV, Amnesty Internat.

WILLIAMS, THOMAS JOSEPH, realtor, property manager; b. L.A., Sept. 26, 1951; s. Donald Joseph and Virginia Loretta (Guesetas) W.; m. Delora Rosselle Campbell, Apr. 24, 1976; children: Paul, Mike. Student, L.A. Pierce Jr. Coll., 1970. Store mgr. Southland Corp., Northridge, Calif., 1968-73; outside salesman BASF, L.A., 1973-75; hardware salesman Curtis Industries, L.A., 1975-77; outside salesman C.R. Daniels, L.A., 11977-85; real estate agt. ERA Hoover Realty, Simi Valley, Calif., 1982-90, Valley Homes Realtors, Simi Valley, 1990—. Mem. Police, Fire, Pub. Safety Commn. L.A. 12th Dist., Northridge, 1988—; past pres. LAPD Devonshire Area PALS, 1988, Citizens Emergency Mobile Patrol, 1980-84; ops. chmn. Tri Chamber Com., 1978—; parade chmn. Granada Hills Youth Parade, 1977-82, Chatsworth Chamber Holiday, 1992; bd. dirs. Simi Valley Little League; cubmaster Boy Scouts Am., Simi Valley. With USN, 1971. Named Citizen of Yr. Granada Hills C. of C., 1977; recipient R. Bradley Trafton award Calif. Jaycees, 1992. Mem. Simi Valley/Moorpark Assn. Realtors (bd. dirs. 1990—), North Hills Jaycees (past pres., Jaycee of Yr. 1985). Republican. Roman Catholic. Office: Valley Homes Realtors 1777 Los Angeles Ave Simi Valley CA 93065

WILLIAMS, TYRELL CLAY, computer science and math educator, small business owner; b. St. Helena, Calif., Mar. 16, 1949; s. William Ollie and Lois Irene (Gribble) W.; m. Patricia Kathlene McDonald, May 1, 1970; children: Robin Tracy, Courtney Elizabeth. AA, Cabrillo Coll., Aptos, Calif., 1968; BA, U. Calif., San Cruz, 1970. Cert. secondary tchr., Calif. Tchr. jr. high sch. math. North Monterey County Unified Sch. Dist., Moss Landing, Calif., 1970-83; tchr. computer sci. North Monterey County Unified Sch. Dist., Castroville, Calif., 1983-92, Watsonville (Calif.) High Sch., 1992—; owner Dataphile, Watsonville, 1983-91; seasonal ranger Dept. Pks. and REcreation, State of Calif., Felton, 1967-70; faculty advisor Computer Catz. With USCG, Aux. Mem. Calif. Fedn. Tchrs., F.I.A.S.C.O. Club (sgt.-at-arms 1987-90, advisor to computer catz 1992—). Democrat. Home: 215 Ponderosa Ave Watsonville CA 95076-0937

WILLIAMS, WALTER, public affairs educator; b. Houston, Dec. 13, 1932; s. Walter and Rosalie (Lazarus) W.; m. Jacqueline Block, Jan. 30, 1958; children: Stuart, David. BBA, U. Tex., 1955, MBA, 1956; PhD, Ind. U., 1960. Asst. prof. Ind. U., Bloomington, 1960-64; assoc. prof. U. Ky., Lexington, 1964-65; chief research and plans div. OEO, Washington, 1967-69; dir. Inst. Pub. Policy and Mgmt., Seattle, 1980-84; prof. pub. affairs U. Wash., Seattle, 1970—; vis. scholar London Sch. Econs., 1983, U. Bergen, 1988. Author: Social Policy Research and Analysis, 1971, Implementation Perspective, 1980, Government By Agency, 1980, Disaster Policy Implementation, 1986, Washington, Westminister and Whitehall, 1988, Mismanaging America, 1990. Served to 1st lt. U.S. Army, 1955-57. Postdoctoral fellow Ford Found., 1962-63; grantee NSF, 1974-84, German Marshall Fund, 1980-82. Mem. Assn. Pub. Policy Analysis and Mgmt. (policy coun. 1987-89), Am. Polit. Sci. Assn. Democrat. Jewish. Home: 1235 22d Ave E Seattle WA 98112 Office: U Wash Grad Sch Pub Affairs DC-13 Seattle WA 98195

WILLIAMS, WALTER BAKER, mortgage banker; b. Seattle, May 12, 1921; s. William Walter and Anna Leland (Baker) W.; m. Marie Davis Wilson, July 6, 1945; children: Kathryn Williams-Mullins, Marcia Frances Williams Swanson, Bruce Wilson, Wendy Susan. BA, U. Wash., 1943; JD, Harvard U., 1948. With Bogle & Gates, Seattle, 1948-63, ptnr., 1960-63; pres. Continental Inc., Seattle, 1963-91, chmn., 1991—; bd. dirs. United Graphics Inc., Seattle, 1973-86, Fed. Nat. Mortgage Assn., 1976-77; chmn. Continental Savings Bank, 1991—. Rep. Wash. State Ho. of Reps., Olympia, 1961-63; sen. Wash. State Senate, Olympia, 1963-71; chmn. Econ. Devel. Council of Puget Sound, Seattle, 1981-82; pres. Japan-Am. Soc. of Seattle, 1971-72; chmn. Woodland Park Zoo Commn., Seattle, 1984-85. Served to capt. USMC, 1942-46, PTO. Recipient Brotherhood Citation,

NCCJ, Seattle, 1980. Mem. Mortgage Bankers Assn. Am. (pres. 1973-74), Wash. Mortgage Bankers Assn., Fed. Home Loan Mortgage Corp. (adv. com.), Wash. Savs. League, bd. dirs., chmn. 1991-92), Rotary (pres. local club 1984-85), Rainier Club Seattle (pres. 1987-88). Republican. Congregationalist.

WILLIAMS, WALTER HARRISON, nuclear medicine physician, educator; b. Topeka, Mar. 28, 1941; s. Walter Harrison Williams and Marjorie L. (McCord) Spearman; m. Patricia Ann Edwards, Aug. 18, 1968; children: Steven H., David A. BS, U. Mo., Kansas City, 1963; PhD, Purdue U., 1969; MD, Yale U., 1980. Diplomate Am. Bd. Nuclear Medicine, Nat. Bd. Med. Examiners. Sr. scientist Jet Propulsion Lab., Calif. Inst. Tech., Pasadena, 1968-74, staff scientist, 1974-79; asst. prof. chemistry Calif. State U., L.A., 1970-71; intern Good Samaritan Hosp., Portland, Oreg., 1981; resident in nuclear medicine U. Oreg. VA Med. Ctr., Portland, 1982-84; clin. instr. nuclear medicine U. Oreg. Med. Sch., Portland, 1984-85, Harvard U., Boston, 1985-87; staff physician Portland VA Hosp., 1984-85; attending physician Tucson VA Hosp., 1987—; asst. prof. radiology U. Ariz., Tucson, 1987-92, assoc. prof. radiology, 1992—; radiation safety officer, clin. instr. Brockton-West Roxbury (Mass.) VA Hosp., 1985-87. Contbr. numerous articles on atomic physics and nuclear medicine to sci. jours.; reviewer J. Lymphology, 1990—, Jour. Investigative Radiology, 1990—. Grantee NASA, 1970-77, Queen's U., No. Ireland, 1977, U. Ariz., 1988, NIH, 1989-90. Mem. Am. Coll. Nuclear Physicians, Soc. Nuclear Medicine, Ariz. Nuclear Physicians Assn. (sec.-treas. 1991). Democrat. Methodist. Home: 1541 W Canyon Shadows Ln Tucson AZ 85737-7717 Office: U Ariz Sch Medicine Divsn Nuclear Medicine Tucson AZ 85724

WILLIAMS, WARREN GAMIEL, secondary educator, writing-literature consultant; b. San Francisco, Apr. 23, 1948; s. Warren G. and Dolores F. (Davanis) W.; m. Susan M. Du Bois, Aug. 21, 1970; children: Joshua Aaron, Jessica Marie, JoHanna Lee, Jeremiah Gabriel. AA, Mira Costa Coll., Oceanside, Calif., 1968; BA, San Diego State Coll., 1970; MA, San Diego State U., 1987. Life standard secondary teaching credential, Calif. Tchr. San Diego County Ct. Schs., Campo, Calif., 1974-76; program dir. Survival III-Youth for Christ, San Diego, 1976-77; shipyard worker, book editor, car salesman, 1977; tchr. studies program Navy High Sch., San Diego, 1978-79; tchr. lang. arts and social studies Hilltop Jr. High Sch., Chula Vista, Calif., 1979, Palomar High Sch., Chula Vista, 1980, Gateway Jr. High Sch., Imperial Beach, Calif., 1980-81, Castle Park Jr. High Sch., Chula Vista, 1981-83, Chula Vista Jr. High Sch., 1983—; tchr. leader, Calif. Lit. Project, 1992; reader Calif. Reading Assesment, 1992; adj. prof. lit. The Union Inst., 1993—. Asst. editor, writer Fire & Movement, 1974-76 (Charles Roberts award 1978). Fellow San Diego Writing Project, 1984, Calif. Lit. Project, 1988; recipient Mentor Tchr. award State of Calif., 1990-92. Mem. Nat. Coun. Tchrs. English, Calif. Assn. Tchrs. English, Calif. Humanities Assn., Bread for World, Nature Conservancy, Cousteau Soc. Democrat. Office: Chula Vista Jr High Sch 415 5th Ave Chula Vista CA 91910

WILLIAMS, WILLIAM ARNOLD, agronomy educator; b. Johnson City, N.Y., Aug. 2, 1922; s. William Truesdall and Nellie Viola (Tompkins) W.; m. Madeline Patricia Moore, Nov. 27, 1943; children—David, Kathleen, Andrew. B.S., Cornell U., 1947, M.S., 1948, Ph.D., 1951. Prof. agronomy U. Calif., Davis, 1965—. Editor agr. sect. McGraw-Hill Ency. Sci. & Tech.; contbr. articles to profl. jours. Mem. Nat. Alliance for Mentally Ill. Served to lt. U.S. Army, 1943-46. Grantee NSF, 1965-82, Kellogg Found., 1963-67; Fulbright scholar, Australia, 1960, Rockefeller Found. scholar, Costa Rica, 1966. Fellow Am. Assn. Advance Sci., Am. Soc. Agronomy, Crop Sci. Soc. Am.; mem. Soil Sci. Soc. Am., Soc. Range Mgmt., Am. Soc. Plant Physiology, Ecol. Soc. Am., Am. Statis. Assn., Brit. Ecol. Soc., Assn. for Tropical Biology, AAAS, Fedn. Am. Scientists, Am. Math. Soc., Math. Assn. Am. Democrat. Home: 718 Oeste Dr Davis CA 95616-3531 Office: Univ California Dept Agronomy and Range Sci Davis CA 95616

WILLIAMS, WILLIAM COREY, Old Testament educator, consultant; b. Wilkes-Barre, Pa., July 12, 1937; s. Edward Douglas and Elizabeth Irene (Schooley) W.; m. Alma Simmenroth Williams, June 27, 1959; 1 child, Linda. Diploma in Ministerial Studies, NE Bible Inst., 1962; BA in Bibl. Studies, Cen. Bible Coll., 1963, MA in Religion, 1964; MA in Hebrew and Near Ea. Studies, NYU, 1966, PhD in Hebrew Lang. and Lit., 1975. Ref. libr. Hebraic section Libr. of Congress, Washington, 1967-69; prof. Old Testament So. Calif. Coll., Costa Mesa, 1969—; adj. prof. Old Testament Melodyland Sch. Theology, Anaheim, Calif., 1975-77; vis. prof. Old Testament Fuller Theol. Sem., Pasadena, Calif., 1978-81, 84, Asian Theol. Ctr. for Evangelism and Missions, Singapore and Sabah, E. Malaysia, 1985, Continental Bible Coll., Saint Pieters-Leeuw, Belgium, 1985, Mattersey Bible Coll., Eng., 1985, Inst. Holy Land Studies, Jerusalem, 1986; transl. cons. and reviser New Am. Standard Bible, 1969—; transl. cons. The New Internat. Version; transl. cons. and editor Internat. Children's Version, 1985-86. Author: (books, tapes) Hebrew I: A Study Guide, 1986, Hebrew II: A Study Guide, 1986; translation editor: Everyday Bible, 1990; contbr. articles to profl. jours; contbr. notes to Spirit Filled Life Study Bible, NAS Study Bible. Nat. Def. Fgn. Lang. fellow NYU, 1964-67; Alumni scholar N.E. Bible Inst., 1960-61; NEH fellow, summer 1992. Mem. Soc. Bibl. Lit., Am. Oriental Soc., Evang. Theol. Soc. (exec. office 1974-77), Am. Acad. Religion, Nat. Assn. Profs. of Hebrew, Inst. Bibl. Rsch., The Lockman Found. (editorial bd. 1974—). Home: 1817 Peninsula Pl Costa Mesa CA 92627-4591 Office: So Calif Coll 55 Fair Dr Costa Mesa CA 92626-6597

WILLIAMS, WILLIE, protective services official; b. 1943; m. Evelina; children: Lisa, Willie Jr., Eric. AS, Phila. Coll. Textiles and Sci., 1982; postgrad., St. Joseph U., 1991. Police officer City of Phila., 1964-72, police detective, 1972-74, police sgt., 1974-76, police lt. juvenile aid div., 1976-84, police capt. 22nd and 23rd dists., 1984-86, police inspector, head tng. bur., civil affairs div., North police div., 1986-88, dep. commr. adminstrn., 1988, police commr., 1988-92; chief of police L.A. Police Dept., 1992—; lecture, instr. Temple U., Univ. Pa., Univ. Del. Former scout master Boy Scouts of Am.; mem. West Oak Lane Youth Assn., Pa. Juvenile Officer's Assn., Southeastern Pa. Chiefs of Police, James Meml. Meth. Ch. Mem. Nat. Orgn. Black Law Enforcement Execs. (nat. pres.), Internat. Assn. Chiefs of Police, Alpha Sigma Lambda. Office: Office of Police Chief 150 S Los Angeles St Los Angeles CA 90012

WILLIAMS, WILLIS RAY, paint manufacturing company executive; b. Iaeger, W. Va., Mar. 8, 1937; s. Hobart Virgil and Thelma Belle (Blankenship) W.; m. Gale Jacqueline Scott, Aug. 27, 1956; children: Ray, Scott, Michael, Mark. B.S. in Chemistry, Marshall U., 1963. Chemist, Columbia Paint Co., Huntington, W.Va., 1957-63, tech. dir., 1963-66, v.p., 1966-71, pres., 1971-79; pres., owner Wiltech Corp., Wash., 1979—. Mem. Nat. Paint and Coatings Assn., Portland Paint and Coatings Assn. (pres. 1984-85). Huntington Kiwanis (pres. 1978). Methodist. Home: 4400 Sunset Way Longview WA 98632-9528 Office: Wiltech Corp PO Box 517 Longview WA 98632-0050

WILLIAMSON, DON, newspaper columnist; b. St. Louis. Attended, Wichita State U. Editor, pub. 67214 Mag., Wichita, Kans., 1973-74; prodr., cons. As We See It Series Chgo. Pub. TV, 1974-76; gen. assigment reporter Wichita (Kans.) Eagle-Beacon, 1977-78, news, pub. affairs dir., 1978-79, editorial writer, columnist, 1979-83; edn. writer San Diego Union, 1983-85; assoc. editor, columnist, editorial pages Phila. Daily News, 1985-89; columnist, editorial bd. Seattle Times, 1989—; instr. Inst. Journalism Edn.; dir. Urban Newspaper Workshop High Sch. Students; minority profl. in-residence program Am. Soc. Newspaper Editors. Recipient William Allen White Found. Kans. News Enterprise award, AP Sports Editors Investigative Reporting award, Outstanding Reporting award Nat. Headliners, Washington Gov.'s Child Abuse Prevention award, Outstanding Govtl. News Reporting award Seattle Mcpl. League, Journalism award Kans. NAACP, Investigative Reporting award Kans. Press Women, Proficiency in Eng. Program Vol. award, Seattle Pub. Schs. Vol. award, Community Svc. award Royal Esquire Club Seattle, Community Svc. award Atlantic St. Ctr., Benefit Guild Seattle Children's Svc. award; John S. Knight Stanford U. fellow. Mem. Nat. Conf. Editorial Writers, Nat. Assn. Black Journalists (Leadership award, Region 10 Mem. of Yr. award), Soc. Profl. Journalists, Sigma Delta Chi. Office: The Seattle Times PO Box 70 Fairview Ave N & John St Seattle WA 98111

WILLIAMSON, EDWIN LEE, wardrobe and costume consultant; b. Downey, Calif., Dec. 2, 1947; s. Cecil Earnest and Edwina Louise (Tedie) W. AA, L.A. City Coll., 1967-70; BA in Theater and Music Edn., 1971, MA in Theater and Music Edn., 1973; student, U. So. Calif., 1971-73. Wardrobe master Ice Capades, 1973-76; mem. wardrobe dept. Paramount Studios, 1976-78, Disney Studios, 1978-81; freelance wardrobe and costume cons., L.A., 1981—. Appeared as Michael in original mus. Peter Pan. Mem. adv. bd. Halfway House and AIDS Hospsice, Valley Presbyn. Hosp.; founder West Coast Singers L.A., Inner City Athletic Union L.A.; founding mem. Gay Mens Chorus, Gt. Am. Yankee Freedom Band L.A., L.A. Gay and Lesbian Community Ctr.; hon. mem. bd. dirs. U. So. Calif. Idylwild Sch. Music and Arts.; bd. dirs. One Christopher St. West; founding vol. Gay Community Svc. Ctr.; emperor Imperial Ct. of San Fernando Valley. Scholar U. So. Calif., 1971-73. Mem. SAG, AFTRA, Wardrobe Union, Masons. Lutheran. Home and Office: 4741 Elmwood Apt 4 Los Angeles CA 90004

WILLIAMSON, JACK (JOHN STEWART WILLIAMSON), writer; b. Bisbee, Ariz., Apr. 29, 1908; s. Asa Lee and Lucy Betty (Hunt) W.; m. Blanche Slaten Harp, Aug. 15, 1947 (dec. Jan. 1985); stepchildren: Keign Harp (dec.), Adele Harp Lovorn. BA, MA, Eastern N.Mex. U., 1957, LHD (hon.), 1981; PhD, U. Colo., 1964. Prof. English Eastern N.Mex. U., Portales, 1960-77. Author numerous sci. fiction books including The Legion of Space, 1947, Darker Than You Think, 1948, The Humanoids, 1949, The Green Girl, 1950, The Cometeers, 1950, One Against the Legion, 1950, Seetee Shock, 1950, Seetee Ship, 1950, Dragon's Island, 1951, The Legion of Time, 1952, (with Frederik Phhl) Star Bridge, 1955, Dome Around America, 1955, The Trial of Terra, 1962, Golden Blood, 1964, The Reign of Wizardry, 1965, Bright New Universe, 1967, Trapped in Space, 1968, The Pandora Effect, 1969, People Machines, 1971, The Moon Children, 1972, H.G. Wells: Critic of Progress, 1973, Teaching SF, 1975, The Early Williamson, 1975, The Power of Blackness, 1976, The Best of Jack Williamson, 1978 Brother to Demons, Brother to Gods, 1979, Teaching Science Fiction: Education for Tomorrow, 1980, The Alien Intelligence, 1980, The Humanoid Touch, 1980, Manseed, 1982, The Queen of a Legion, 1983, Wonder's Child: My Life in Science Fiction, 1984 (Hugo award 1985), Lifeburst, 1984, Firechild, 1986, Mazeway, 1990; (with Frederik Pohl) Undersea Quest, 1954, Undersea Fleet, 1955, Undersea City, 1956, The Reefs of Space, 1964, Starchild, 1965, Rogue Star, 1969, The Farthest Star, 1975, Wall Around a Star, 1983, Land's End, 1988, Mazeway, 1990, (with Frederik Pohl) The Singers of Time, 1991, Beachhead, 1992; (with Miles J. Breuer) The Birth of an New Republic, 1981. Served as staff sgt. USAAF, 1942-45. Mem. Sci. Fiction Writers Am. (pres. 1978-80, Grand Master Nebula award 1976), Sci. Fiction Research Assn. (Pilgrim award 1968), World Sci. Fiction, Planetary Soc. Home: PO Box 761 Portales NM 88130-0761 Office: Ea NMex U Golden Libr Portales NM 88130

WILLIAMSON, J(OHN) CRAIG, professional golfer; b. Evanston, Ill., Feb. 26, 1935; s. John Paul and Marbry Thurber (Henning) W.; m. Susan Rodman Lamberth, Aug. 10, 1957 (div. 1972); children: Kristi Anne, John Craig Jr.; m. Sharon Lee Neet, Sept. 13, 1980. Grad. high sch., Berkeley, Calif. Asst. profl. Tilden Park Golf Club, Berkeley, 1956-57, Castlewood Country Club, Pleasanton, Calif., 1957-62; dir. gold, head pro Silverado Country Club, Napa, Calif., 1962-75, Kapalua Golf Club, Maui, Hawaii, 1975-86; dir. golf Blackhawk Country Club, Danville, Calif., 1986-87, Chardonnay Club, Napa, 1987-89, Ko Olina Golf Club, Ewa Beach, Hawaii, 1989—; cons. Pro Craft Interior/Fixtures, Bend, Oreg., 1990—; adv. bd. Lynx Golf, City of Industry, Calif., 1992—, Maxfli Golf, Greenville, S.C., 1987—. With U.S. Army, 1954-56. Mem. PGA (v.p., treas., Pro of Yr. 1983, Horton Smith award 1990, Merchandiser of Yr. local 1985, 91, nat. 1985), Assn. of Golf Merchandisers (bd. dirs. 1991—), PGA of Am. (bd. dirs. Aloha sect. 1991, mem. comm./pub. awarenss 1987—), Hawaii State Golf Assn. (bd. dirs. 1992). Home: 94-1029 Ahahui Pl Mililani HI 96789 Office: Ko Olina Golf Club 92-1220 Aliinui Dr Ewa Beach HI 96707

WILLIAMSON, JOHN PRITCHARD, utility executive; b. Cleve., Feb. 22, 1922; s. John and Jane (Pritchard) W.; m. Helen Morgan, Aug. 3, 1945; children: John Morgan, James Russell, Wayne Arthur. BBA, Kent State U., 1945; postgrad., U. Toledo, 1953-56, U. Mich., 1956. CPA, Ohio. Sr. acct. Arthur Andersen & Co., Detroit and Cleve., 1945-51; dir. methods and procs. Toledo Edison Co., 1951-59, asst. treas., 1959-60, sec., 1960-62, sec.-treas., 1962-65, v.p. finance, 1965-68, sr. v.p., 1968-72, pres., chief exec. officer, 1972-79, chmn., chief exec. officer, 1979-86; chmn. emeritus Toledo Edison Co., Centerior Energy Corp., 1986—; chmn. N.Am. Reliability Coun., 1984-87. Pres. Ohio Electric Utility Inst., 1972; chmn. East Cen. Area Power Coordination Pool, 1971-72, mem. exec. com. Edison Electric Inst., 1981-85; trustee Assn. Edison Illuminating Cos., 1982-84; trustee Toledo Symphony Orch., pres., 1985-86; trustee Toledo Mus. Art, Toledo Hosp., Kent State U. Found.; vice chmn. Greater Toledo Corp., 1984-86; trustee, treas. Rio Verde Community Ch., 1989-92; elder Presbyn. Ch.; mem. Toledo Comm. Chest (pres. 1972), Area United Way (chmn. 1971). Named Toledo Outstanding Citizen, 1976; recipient Kent State U. medallion, 1992;Williamson Alumni Ctr. named in his honor, 1991. Mem. Fin. Analysts Soc. Toledo (pres. 1968-69), Systems and Procs. Assn. (internat. treas. 1960), Inst. Pub. Utilities (chmn. exec. com. 1969-70), Toledo C. of C. (pres. 1970), Ohio C. of C. (chmn. 1979-81, life dir.), Toledo Boys Club (Echo award 1974), Kent State U. Alumni Assn. (pres. 1971-72, outstanding alumnus 1974), Belmont Country Club, Rio Verde Country Club, Rio Verde Saddle Club (past pres.), Kiwanis (past pres. Toledo, Disting. Svc. award 1977), Blue Key, Delta Sigma Pi, Beta Alpha Psi, Delta Upsilon. Republican. Home: 10661 Cardiff Rd Perrysburg OH 43551-3404 also: 18524 Poco Vista Dr Rio Verde AZ 85253

WILLIAMSON, KENNETH ROBERT, retired oil company executive, geologist; b. Scottsbluff, Nebr., Oct. 18, 1929; s. Edward James and Nellie May (Campbell) W.; m. Jeanine Elaine Philippi, June 12, 1954; children: Leigh, Sandra, Susan, Roger. BS, U. Nebr., 1956. Cert. petroleum geologist. Devel. geologist STD Oil Co. of Tex., various, 1956-60; exploration geologist STD Oil Co. of Tex., Midland, Tex., 1960-66; exploration geophysicist Chevron Overseas Petroleum Inc., various, 1966-78; exploration cons. Chevron Overseas Petroleum Inc., San Ramon, Calif., 1988; exploration coord. Chevron Overseas Petroleum Inc., San Francisco, 1978-80, mgr. China project, 1980-81; exploration coord. Chevron North Sea Ltd., London, 1981-84; exploration mgr. Chevron Spain, Madrid, 1984-88; exploration cons. Walnut Creek, Calif., 1988—. With USN, 1947-52. Mem. Soc. of Exploration Geophysicist, Am. Assn. Petroleum Geologists (dist. rep. 1967-68), Contra Costa Mineral and Gem Soc. (pres. 1992-94), Nat. Watch and Clock Collectors (Diablo chpt.). Republican. Presbyterian.

WILLIAMSON, LOWELL JAMES, oil industry executive; b. Canton, Ohio, July 19, 1923; s. Daryl and Catherine (Hayes) W.; m. Dorothy McGuire, Dec. 6, 1958; children: Eric Dean, Rhonda Lynn, Rex Edward, David James. BA, Anderson U., 1950; postgrad, Ind. U., 1950-52; LLD (hon.), Warner Pacific Coll., 1973. Pres., chief exec. officer Williamson Oil & Gas Ltd., Denver and Russell, Kans., 1952-57, Calgary, Alta., Can., 1955-74; pres., chief exec. officer Glenex Petroleum, Ltd., Calgary, 1963-88, MGF Mgmt., Inc., Calgary, 1964-73, Glenex Petroleum, Inc., Scottsdale, Ariz., 1974—, Williamson Group, Inc., Scottsdale, 1984—. Served as tech. sgt. USAAF, 1943-45, prisoner of war, ETO. Decorated Purple Heart, Air medal with three oak leaf clusters, Ex-Prisoner of War medal. CLubs: Paradise Valley Country, Calgary Golf and Country. Home: 5635 E Lincoln Dr # 20 Paradise Vly AZ 85253-4192 Office: The Williamson Group Inc 7001 N Scottsdale Rd Ste 1027 Scottsdale AZ 85253

WILLIAMSON, MAURICE ALAN, consulting forester; b. Louisiana, Mo., Dec. 28, 1946; s. J.D. and Mary (Ayrom) W.; m. Donna Jo Duvall, June 11, 1965; children: Denise M. Williamson Jording, Darla M. BS in Forest Mgmt., U. Mo., 1970. Pre-sales forester Wash. State Dept. Natural Resources, Omak, 1970-72; asst. supt. honor camp Wash. State Dept. Natural Resources, Vancouver, 1972-74; dist. forester State of Wyo., Newcastle, 1974-75; woods supt. Cambria Forest Industries, Newcastle, 1975-76; procurement forester Ga.-Pacific Corp., Stamps, Ark., 1976-78, prodn. mgr., 1978-79; procurement forester, sales rep. San Poil Lumber Co., Republic, Wash., 1979-81; cons. forester Ferry, Stevens, Pend Oreille County Conservation Dists., Colville, Wash., 1981—; assoc. supr. Ferry County Conservation Dist., Republic, 1981—. Contbr. articles to profl. publs. Mem. Pub. Land Users Coalaition, 1989—, Environ. 2000, Seattle, 1988—, Upper Columbia Timber, Fish and Wildlife Com., 1988—; chmn. Clarence Pump Scholarship Com., 1985—; speaker Wash. Bus. Week, 1986—. Recipient Disting. Svc. award for forest mgmt. Ferry County Conservation Dist., 1983, Outstanding Achievement award for practical conservation Wash. Assn. Conservation Dists., 1988. Mem. Soc. Am. Foresters, Assn. Cons. Foresters, Internat. Soc. Tropical Foresters, Wash. Forest Protection Assn. (trustee 1987—), Wash. State Farm Forestry Assn. (pres. 1993—), N.E. Wash. Farm Forestry Assn. (pres. 1985-90), Colville C. of C., KP. Republican. Office: 270 S Main Colville WA 99114

WILLIAMSON, NEIL ROBERT, psychiatrist; b. LaGrande, Oreg., Oct. 14, 1940; s. Robert Elton and Lorene Adeline (Johnson) W. BS, U. Oreg., Eugene, 1962; MD, U. Oreg., Portland, 1967; postgrad. in Advanced Studies Social Welfare, Heller Sch., Brandeis U., 1973-77. Intern Balt. City Hosps., 1967-68; fellow in medicine Johns Hopkins U. Hosps., Balt., 1967-68; staff physician Hall Health U. Wash., Seattle, 1970-72; resident in psychiatry Worcester (Mass.) State Hosp., 1973-77, assoc. outpatient treatment clin., 1977-78; instr. U. Mass. Med. Sch., Worcester, 1978-82; cons. Josephine County Mental Health Program, Grants Pass, Oreg., 1982-88; pvt. practice in psychiatry Grants Pass, Oreg., 1982—; med. dir. Southern Oreg. Adolescent Study and Treatment Ctr., Grants Pass, Oreg., 1986—; med. dir. Josephine County Coun. on Alcohol and Drug Abuse, 1987—; cons.-supr. Basics, Inc. Substance Abuse Treatment Program, 1989-92; cons. Western Med. Cons., 1989—, applicant appeals & hearings Social Security System, 1991—; supr. to pvt. practice counselors, 1987—; supr. treatment planning decisions ALC program, 1992—. Donor Ashland Shakespearean Festival. Served to capt. U.S. Army, 1968-70. Mem. Oreg. Med. Assn., Josephine County Med. Soc., Grants Pass C. of C. Democrat. Office: Williamson MD PC 243 NE C St Grants Pass OR 97526-2191

WILLIAMSON, NEIL SEYMOUR, III, aircraft company executive, retired Army officer; b. Dumont, N.J., Jan. 5, 1935; s. Neil Seymour and Mary Louise (Bittenbender) W.; m. Sue Carrole Cooper, Dec. 15, 1985; children: Deborah D., Leisa L., Neil S. IV, Dirk A., Wendy L. BS, U.S. Mil. Acad., 1958; MSME, U. Mich., 1963. Commd. 2d lt. U.S. Army, 1958, advanced through grades to col., 1976; assoc. prof. dept. earth, space and graphic scis. U.S. Mil. Acad., West Point, N.Y., 1965-68; chief edn. sect. U.S. Army, Ft. McNair, D.C., 1970-71; analyst armor infantry systems group Pentagon U.S. Army, Washington, 1972-73, systems analyst requirements office Pentagon, 1974-75, program analyst, 1975-76; chief advanced systems concept office U.S. Army, Redstone Arsenal, Ala., 1976-77; comdr., dir. fire control & small caliber weapon systems lab. U.S. Army, Dover, N.J., 1977-78; project mgr. Tube-Launched, Optically-Tracked, Wire-Command-Link, US Army, Redstone Arsenal, 1978-81; ret. U.S. Army, 1981; program mgr. Hughes Aircraft Co., El Segundo, Calif., 1981—. Decorated Bronze Star with bronze oak leaf cluster, Legion of Merit with bronze oak leaf cluster, Air medal with silver oak leaf cluster and two bronze oak leaf clusters, Purple Heart. Mem. DAV, Soc. Automotive Engrs., Am. Def. Preparedness Assn., Army Aviation Assn. (pres. Tenn. Valley chpt. 1980), Am. Helicopter Soc., U.S. Armor Assn. Office: Hughes Aircraft Co PO Box 902 El Segundo CA 90245-0902

WILLIAMSON, OLIVER EATON, economics and law educator; b. Superior, Wis., Sept. 27, 1932; s. Scott Gilbert and Lucille S. (Dunn) W.; m. Dolores Jean Celeni, Sept. 28, 1957; children: Scott, Tamara, Karen, Oliver, Dean. SB, MIT, 1955; MBA, Stanford U., 1960; PhD, Carnegie-Mellon U., 1963; PhD (hon.), Norwegian Sch. Econs. and Bus. Adminstrn., 1986; PhD in Econ. Sci. (hon.), Hochschule St. Gallen, Switzerland, 1987, Groningen U., 1989. Project. engr. U.S. Govt., 1955-58; asst. prof. econs. U. Calif., Berkeley, 1963-65; assoc. prof. U. Pa., Phila., 1965-68, prof., 1968-83, Charles and William L. Day prof. econs. and social sci., 1977-83; Gordon B. Tweedy prof. econs. law and orgn. Yale U., 1983-88; Transam. prof. of bus., econs. and law U. Calif., Berkeley, 1988—; spl. econ. asst. to asst. atty. gen. for antitrust Dept. Justice, 1966-67; dir. Ctr. for Study of Organizational Innovation, U. Pa., 1976-83; transam. prof. of bus., econs. and law U. Calif., Berkeley, 1988—; cons. in field. Author: The Economics of Discretionary Behavior, 1964, Corporate Control and Business Behavior, 1970, Markets and Hierarchies, 1975, The Economic Institutions of Capitalism, 1985, Economic Organization, 1986, Antitrust Economics, 1987; assoc. editor: Bell Jour. Econs., 1973-74, editor, 1975-82; co-editor: Jour. Law, Econs., and Orgn., 1983—. Fellow Ctr. for Advanced Study in Behavioral Scis., 1977-78; Guggenheim fellow, 1977-78; Am. Acad. Arts and Scis. fellow, 1983; recipient Alexander Henderson award Carnegie-Mellon U., 1962, Alexander von Humboldt Rsch. prize, 1987, Irwin award Acad. of Mgmt. Fellow Econometric Soc.; mem. Am. Econ. Assn. Office: U Calif Dept Econs Berkeley CA 94720

WILLIAMSON, RICHARD ARTHUR, English language and film educator, writer; b. San Francisco, Oct. 16, 1930; s. Arthur Louis and Edith Lillian (Partridge) W. AA, City Coll. San Francisco, 1950; BA, San Francisco State U., 1953, MA with honors, 1958; postgrad., Ctr. Advanced Film Studies, 1971; intern, Dirs. Guild Am., 1978-82. Cert. tchr. English and film, Calif. Teaching asst. San Francisco State U., 1957, instr. lang. arts, 1957-58, lectr. education, 1966; instr. English Santa Barbara (Calif.) City Coll., 1958-63, chmn. English, 1961-63; coord. film and composition U. Calif. Edn. Extension, San Francisco, 1971; prof. English and film Coll. San Mateo, Calif., 1963—; cons. Coll. Entrance Exam. Bd., San Francisco, 1966-67; juror Nat. Endowment Humanities, San Francisco, 1973-74, San Francisco Internat. Film Festival, 1979-80; judge Calif. State Student Film Festival, L.A., 1974, 75, 79; writer, cons. Aspen Inst. Humanistic Studies, Palo Alto, Calif., 1974-79. Author: (with Laura Hackett) Anatomy of Reading, 1965, Design for a Composition, 1966, Anatomy of Reading 2d Edit., 1970; contbr. articles to profl. jours. With USN, 1953-55. Mem. Conf. Coll. Composition and Communication (exec. com. 1969-76, chmn. 2-yr. coll. com. 1972-74), Nat. Coun. Tchrs. English, Film Arts Found., Bay Area Film/Tape Coun. Democrat. Buddhist. Office: Coll San Mateo (17-149) 1700 W Hillsdale Blvd San Mateo CA 94402-3757

WILLIAMSON, ROBERT EMMETT, mathematics educator; b. Ashland, Kans., June 9, 1937; s. Robert Emmett and Andre P. (Viguier) W.; m. Diana R. Colladay, 1958 (div. 1978); children: Brian, David, Joan; m. Kathleen Marie Davis, June 19, 1982. BA, U. Ariz., 1959; PhD, U. Calif., Berkeley, 1963. Visitor Inst. for Advanced Study, Princeton, N.J., 1963-65; vis. prof. U. Warwick, Eng., 1965-66; asst. prof. Yale U., New Haven, 1966-69; assoc. prof. Claremont (Calif.) Grad. Sch., 1969—. Contbr. articles to profl. jours. Mem. Am. Math. Soc. Home: 353 W 7th St Claremont CA 91711-4312 Office: Claremont Grad Sch 143 E 10th St Claremont CA 91711-3988

WILLIG, KARL VICTOR, computer firm executive; b. Idaho Falls, Idaho, June 4, 1944; s. Louis Victor and Ethel (McCarty) W.; m. Julianne Erickson, June 10, 1972; 1 son, Ray. BA magna cum laude, Coll. of Idaho, 1968; MBA (Dean Donald Kirk David fellow), Harvard U., 1970. Pres. Ariz. Beef, Inc., Phoenix, 1971-73; group v.p. Ariz.-Colo. Land & Cattle Co., Phoenix, 1973-76; v.p. Rufenacht, Bromagen & Hertz, Inc., Chgo., 1976-77; pres. Sambo's Restaurants, Inc., Santa Barbara, Calif., 1977-79; ptnr. Santa Barbara Capital, 1979-85; pres. EURUSA Equities Corp., 1985-86; pres., chief exec. officer InfoGenesis, 1986—; trustee Am. Bapt. Sem. of West, 1977-85. Named one of Outstanding Young Men of Am., 1972; recipient Assn. of U.S. Army award, 1964.

WILLING, JAMES RICHARD, computer technician; b. Portland, Oreg., Apr. 1, 1958; s. James Albert and Venita Faye (Fishburn) W.; m. Carole Marguerite Babbitt, Feb. 10, 1979; children: Robert James, Paul David. G-rad. Beaverton High Sch., Oreg. Shop technician Byte N.W. Inc., Beaverton, 1976-79; field service technician N.W. Computer Support, Beaverton, 1979-81; systems programmer Johnson-Laird Inc., Portland, 1982; project dir. CB CBBS/NW, Beaverton, 1979—; lead technician Computerland, Tigard, Oreg., 1982-86; field engr., tech. Compu-Shop, 1986-88, Portland Computer Arts Resource Ctr., 1986-88; field svc. rep. Sears Computer and Peripheral Svc., Tigard, Oreg., 1988-90; offline customer support engr. Intel Corp., Hillsboro, Oreg., 1991—; mem. steering com. Portland Computer Arts Resource Ctr., 1986-89. Writer, co-host ChipChat, 1991-92. Mem. computer edn. task force Oreg. Mus. Sci. and Industry, Portland, 1984. Mem. Control Program for Microcomputers User's Group NW (founder 1979), pres. 1979-82). Republican. Methodist. Home: 14120 SW 20th St Beaverton OR 97005-

4971 Office: Intel PC Enhancements C03-13 5200 NE Elam Young Pky Hillsboro OR 97124-6497

WILLIS, CLIFFORD LEON, geologist; b. Chanute, Kans., Feb. 20, 1913; s. Arthur Edward and Flossie Duckworth (Fouts) W.; m. Serreta Margaret Thiel, Aug. 21, 1947 (dec.); 1 child, David Gerard. BS in Mining Engring., U. Kans., 1939; PhD, U. Wash., 1950. Geophysicist The Carter Oil Co. (Exxon), Tulsa, 1939-42; instr. U. Wash., Seattle, 1946-50, asst. prof., 1950-54; cons. geologist Harza Engring. Co., Chgo., 1952-54, 80-82, chief geologist, 1954-57, assoc. and chief geologist, 1957-67, v.p., chief geologist, 1967-80; pvt. practice cons. geologist Tucson, Ariz., 1982—; cons. on major dam projects in Iran, Iraq, Pakistan, Greece, Turkey, Ethiopia, Argentina, Venezuela, Colombia, Honduras, El Salvador, Iceland, U.S. Lt. USCG, 1942-46. Recipient Haworth Disting. Alumnus award U. Kans., 1963. Fellow Geol. Soc. Am., Geol. Soc. London; mem. Am. Assn. Petroleum Geologists, Soc. Mining, Metallurgy and Exploration Inc., Assn. Engring. Geologists, Sigma Xi, Tau Beta Pi, Sigma Tau. Republican. Roman Catholic. Home: 4795 E Quail Creek Dr Tucson AZ 85718-2630

WILLIS, DAWN LOUISE, paralegal, small business owner; b. Johnstown, Pa., Sept. 11, 1959; d. Kenneth William and Dawn Louise (Joseph) Hagins; m. Marc Anthony Ross, Nov. 30, 1984 (div.); m. Jerry Wayne Willis, Dec. 16, 1989. Grad. high sch., Sacramento, Calif. Legal sec. Wilcoxen & Callahan, Sacramento, 1979-87, paralegal asst., 1987-88; legal adminstr. Law Office Jack Vetter, Sacramento, 1989—; owner, mgr. Your Girl Friday Secretarial and Legal Support Svcs., Sacramento, 1991—; with Amway Distbr., 1992—. Vol. ARC, 1985. Mem. NAFE, Assn. Legal Adminstrs., Calif. Trial Lawyers Assn., Sacramento Legal Secs. Assn. Republican. Lutheran. Home: 3672 Sun Maiden Way North Highlands CA 95660-5925

WILLIS, GEORGE CLARK, dance educator; b. L.A., Nov. 29, 1938. BA in Phys. Edn., Calif. State U., L.A., 1962; MA in Phys. Edn., Calif. State U., 1967; MFA in Dance, Ariz. State U., 1983; postgrad., Calif. Inst. of the Arts, 1973. performer/dancer Charles Weidman Dance Theatre; dancer with San Diego Dance Theatre, San Diego Ballet, Harry Partch Ensemble, Starlight Opera, 3's Co.; choreographer for San Diego Area Dance Alliance for Festivals III, IV, Grossmont Coll., Southwestern Coll., San Diego Ballet, Brooks Athletic Sportswear; performer/choreographer: Face Dancing, Introductions, Scratch, Low Impact Boxing, Kill Them with Comedy. Mem. Congl. Arts adv. bd., Congressman Jim Bates, 44th Dist., 1985-90. Mem. San Diego Dance Theatre (pres. 1978—), San Diego Area Dance Alliance (founding mem.), Nat. Dance Assn., AAHPERD. Office: San Diego State Univ PE121 Dept Music and Dance San Diego CA 92182

WILLIS, HAROLD WENDT, SR., real estate developer; b. Marion, Ala., Oct. 7, 1927; s. Robert James and Della (Wendt) W.; student Loma Linda U., 1950, various courses San Bernardino Valley Coll.; m. Patsy Gay Bacon, Aug. 2, 1947 (div. Jan. 1975); children: Harold Wendt II, Timothy Gay, April Ann, Brian Tad, Suzanne Gail; m. Vernette Jacobson Osborne, Mar. 30, 1980 (div. 1984); m. Ofelia Alvarez, Sept. 23, 1984; children: Ryran Robert, Samantha Ofelia. Ptnr., Victoria Guernsey, San Bernardino, Calif., 1950-63, co-pres., 1963-74, pres., 1974—; owner Quik-Save, 1966—, K-Mart Shopping Ctr., San Bernardino, 1969—; pres. Energy Delivery Systems, Food and Fuel, Inc. San Bernardino City water commr., 1965—. Bd. councillors Loma Linda (Calif.) U., 1968-85, pres., 1971-74; mem. So. Calif. Strider's Relay Team (set indoor Am. record in 4x800 1992, set distance medley relay U.S. and World record for 60 yr. old 1992). Served as officer U.S. Mcht. Marine, 1945-46. Mem. Calif. Dairy Industries Assn. (pres. 1963, 64), Liga Internat. (2d v.p. 1978, pres. 1982, 83). Seventh-day Adventist (deacon 1950-67). Lic. pvt. pilot; rated twin engr. Office: PO Box 5607 San Bernardino CA 92412-5607

WILLIS, JIMMY ROY, accountant; b. Hunsville, Ala., July 21, 1942; s. Roy P. and Estelle E. (Callas) W.; m. Linda Elizabeth Shoemaker, June. BS, Pepperdine U., 1964; MBA, Oregon State U., 1970. CPA. Asst. acct. Swinerton & Walberg Co., Honolulu, 1964; acctg. supr. Coopers & Lybrand, Eugene, Oreg., 1970-76; acctg. mgr. Lee, Coleman & Allen, Eugene, Oreg., 1977-78; CPA, ptnr. Young, Willis & Co., Eugene, Oreg., 1978-80; CPA ptnr. Molatore Gerbert, Eugene, Oreg., 1981-88, Isler & Co., Eugene, Oreg., 1988--; Instr. Lane Community Coll., Eugene, 1976-81, Ore. State U., 1984; cons. treas. SW Ore. Mus. of Sci. & Industry, Eugene, 1974, Lane Regional Arts. Recipient: 3rd place, Nat. Masters, Eugene, 1985. mem. Nat Assn. Accts. (pres., 1980-81), Oregon Soc. of CPAs (pres.,. Republican. Home: 2172 Elysium Ave Eugene OR 97401-7467 Office: Isler and Co 1976 Garden Ave Eugene OR 97403-1989

WILLIS, NELL ELAINE, small business owner; b. Anderson, S.C., June 19, 1940; d. Howard Sidney and Nell (Foster) Behr; m. Norman E. Willis, Jan. 9, 1989. BA, Western Wash. U., 1962. Stewardess Pan Am. Airways, Seattle, 1962-63; clk. Sea-First Bank, Seattle, 1963-65; customer contact Wash. Natural Gas, Seattle, 1965-66; programmer NCR, Seattle, 1966-72; rsch. analyst Boeing Computer Systems, Seattle, 1972-82; owner Nelco Ent., Seattle, 1982—. Mem. N.W. Bead Soc. Home and Office: 7811 SE 27th St # 246 Mercer Island WA 98040

WILLIS, SELENE LOWE, electrical engineer; b. Birmingham, Ala., Mar. 4, 1958; d. Lewis Russell and Bernice (Wilson) Lowe; m. André Maurice Willis, June 12, 1987. BSEE, Tuskegee (Ala.) U., 1980; postgrad. in Computer Programing, UCLA, 1993. Component engr. Hughes Aircraft Corp., El Segundo, Calif., 1980-82; reliability and lead engr. Aero Jet Electro Systems Corp., Azusa, Calif., 1982-84; sr. component engr. Rockwell Internat. Corp., Anaheim, Calif., 1984; design engr. Lockheed Missile & Space Co., Sunnyvale, Calif., 1985-86; property mgr. Penmar Mgmt. Co., L.A., 1987-88; aircraft mechanic McDonnell Douglas Corp., Long Beach, 1989-93; sr. component engr. Gen. Data Communications Corp., Danbury, Conn., 1984-85. Vol. Mercy Hosp. & Children's Hosp., Birmingham, 1972-74; mem. L.A. Gospel Messengers, 1982-84, West Angeles Ch. of God & Christ, L.A., 1990. Bell Labs. scholar, 1976-80; named one of Outstanding Young Women in Am., 1983, 87. Mem. IEEE, ASME, Aerospace and Aircraft Engrs., So. Calif. Profl. Engring. Assn., Tuskegee U. Alumni Assn., Eta Kappa Nu. Mem. Christian Ch.

WILLITS, LON KEDRIC, business owner; b. Tacoma, Wash., Feb. 16, 1939; s. Leonard Homer and Gunneld (Bjarke) W.; m. Doris A. Glasgow, Oct. 14, 1960 (div. Aug. 1980); children: Kendal, Cindy. BS, 1965; postgrad., Wash. State U., 1971-72, Wash. State U., 1977-78. Owner Willits Enterprises, Tacoma, 1958—; bus. mgr. IBEW, Tacoma, 1989—; cons. Pacific N.W. Bell, Seattle, 1963-64, Dept. Pub. Utilities, Tacoma, 1964-89;. Author: (computer programs) Toxic Waste Disposal, 1988, Asset Allocation, 1989. Organizer United Way of Pierce County, Tacoma, 1979; bd. dirs. ARC, Tacoma, 1989—. Mem. Lyons Mens Club (ruler 1988-89), Elks (ruler 1975-76). Home: 2408 Day Island Blvd Tacoma WA 98466-1812 Office: IBEW Local # 483 2811 S Mullen St Tacoma WA 98409-2322

WILLMARTH, MARY SUE, public information executive; b. Pocatello, Idaho, Jan. 2, 1963; d. Jack R. and Donna Mae (Sponheim) Polanchek; m. Mark Stephen Willmarth, June 23, 1990. BA, Coll. of Great Falls, Mont., 1987. Dir., camera operator Sta. KRTV-3, Great Falls, 1985; pub. rels. adminstr., intern City of Great Falls, 1985-86; account coord. Wendt Advt., 1987-88; pub. info dir. Coll. of Great Falls, 1988—; chairperson Spl. Events Adv. Com., Great Falls, 1988—. Mem. Leadership Great Falls, 1989; advisor Leadership High Sch., Great Falls, 1990-91; campaign v.i.p. Easter Seals Soc., Great Falls, 1990-92; bd. dirs. Mental Health Assn. of Great Falls, 1990-93, chmn. pub. edn./media com., 1992; mem. mktg. com. Great Falls Ams. Hockey Team; publicity dir. C.M. Russell We. Art Auction, 1993—. Scripps-Howard scholar, 1986. Mem. Women in Communications (job chair 1988-89, 91-92, nat. del. 1989), Coun. for Advancement and Support of Edn., Mont. Devel. Officers Assn., Great Falls Advt. Fedn. Home: 4409 3d Ave N Great Falls MT 59405 Office: Coll of Great Falls 1301 20th St S Great Falls MT 59405-4996

WILLMS, RICHARD SCOTT, chemical engineer; b. San Bernadino, Calif., Feb. 26, 1957; s. Richard Kenneth and Wilda Jane (Foushee) W.; m. Mary Patricia Hurstell, Aug. 5, 1983; children: Richard Benjamin, Joshua Owen, Molly Jean. BS, La. State U., 1980, MS, 1983, PhD, 1985. With Los Alamos (N.Mex.) Nat. Lab., 1985—. Mem. Am. Inst. Chem. Engrs., Am. Chem. Soc. Republican. Mem. Evangelical Free Ch. Office: Los Alamos Nat Lab Mail Stop C-348 Los Alamos NM 87545

WILLOUGHBY, JAMES RUSSELL, artist; b. Toronto, Ohio, Apr. 22, 1928; s. Russell Lee and Edna Gertrude (McKeown) W.; m. Dorothy M. Ponder, Sept. 12, 1952 (div. 1958); children: Jim Jr., David; m. Susan N. Boettjer, Nov. 28, 1980. AA, Pasadena City Coll., 1951; postgrad., Art Ctr. Sch. Mem. staff Chrysler Corp., Maywood, Calif., 1951-57; adminstrv. asst., tech. artist Ramo-Woolridge Corp., El Segundo, Calif., 1957-59; adminstr. asst. Space Tech. Labs., El Segundo, 1959-61; intelligence analyst Aerospace Corp., El Segundo, 1961-65; freelancer Calif., 1965-72, Filmation Studios, Reseda, Calif., 1972-82, various orgns., 1982—; storyboard designer Hanna-Barbera, Disney Studios, 1987-90. Illustrator Cowboy Country Cartoons, 1988; co-author, illustrator Cowboy Cartoon Cookbook, 1990, Cactus County, 1992. Mem. Nat. Cartoonist Soc., Westerners Internat., Prescott Corral. Home: 1407 Sierra Vista Dr Prescott AZ 86303-4545

WILLOUGHBY, STUART CARROLL, contractor; b. Tucson, Mar. 19, 1951; s. Stuart Carroll and Margeret Ann (Thornton) W.; children: Julie Ann, Aimee Sue, Scott Tyler. Student, U. Ariz., 1970-74, U. Ariz., 1973. Owner Willcox (Ariz.) Realty and Constrn. Co., 1974-75, Willoughby Constrn. and Devel. Corp., Tucson, 1975—; owner, broker Red Baron Realtors, Inc., Tucson, 1978—; owner Willoughby Plumbing Corp., Tucson, 1985—, Sunshine Solar Co., Tucson, 1980—. Leader 4H Club. Mem. So. Ariz. Home Builders Assn. (bd. dirs. 1978—, life dir., Bd. Mem. of Yr. award 1981, honored PAC com. 1985, 86, 87), Tucson Bd. Realtors, Nat. Assn. of Home Builders (Life Spike award 1980). Republican. Home: 7979 S Camino Loma Alta Tucson AZ 85747-9735

WILLS, J. ROBERT, academic administrator, drama educator, writer; b. Akron, Ohio, May 5, 1940; s. J. Robert and Helen Elizabeth (Lapham) W.; m. Barbara T. Salisbury, Aug. 4, 1984. B.A., Coll. of Wooster, 1962; M.A., U. Ill., 1963; Ph.D., Case-Western Res. U., 1971; cert. in arts adminstrn, Harvard U., 1976. Instr. to asst. prof., dir. theatre Wittenberg U., Springfield, Ohio, 1963-72; assoc. prof., dir. grad. studies, chmn. dept. theatre U. Ky., Lexington, 1972-77; prof. theatre, dean U. Ky. (Coll. Fine Arts), 1977-81; prof. drama, dean Coll. Fine Arts, U. Tex., Austin, 1981-89, Effie Marie Cain Regents chair in Fine Arts, 1986-89; provost, prof. theatre Pacific Luth. U., Tacoma, Wash., 1989—; cons. colls., univs., arts orgns., govt. agencies. Author: The Director in a Changing Theatre, 1976, Directing in the Theatre: A Casebook, 1980, rev. edit., 1993; dir. 90 plays; contbr. articles to profl. jours. Bd. dirs. various art orgns., Ky. Tex. and Wash. Recipient grants public and pvt. agencies. Mem. Nat. Assn. State Univs. and Land-Grant Colls.(chmn. commn. on arts 1981-83), Coun. Fine Arts Deans (exec. com. 1984-89, sec./treas. 1986-89), Univ. and Coll. Theatre Assn. (pres. 1981-82), Assn. for Communication Adminstrn. (pres. 1986-87), Ky. Theatre Assn. (pres. 1976). Office: Pacific Luth U Office of Provost Tacoma WA 98447

WILLS, PENELOPE HORNSCHEMEIER, college dean; b. Cin., Sept. 8, 1952; d. Frank Charles and Constance (Collier) Hornschemeier; m. Ronald F. Wills, May 29, 1981. BS, U. Cin., 1974; MS, Miami U., Oxford, Ohio, 1975; PhD, Mich. State U., 1982. Freshman advisor Miami U., 1974-77; head resident Mich. State U., East Lansing, 1977-79, fin. aid advisor, 1979, acad. advisor Coll. Engring., 1980; assoc. dir. student devel. N.Mex. State U., Las Cruces, 1980-82; dir. resident programs Reed Coll., Portland, Oreg., 1983-88; dean student devel. Portland C.C., 1988—; mem. faculty Union Inst., Cin., 1992—; dir. Cascade Project, Portland, 1992-93. Contbr. articles to profl. jours. Mem. bd. project network Emanuel Hosp., Portland; mem. North/Northeast Bus. Assn., Portland. Mem. Nat. Assn. Student Pers. Adminstrs. (regional v.p. 1991-93), Am. Assn. C.C.'s, Nat. Coun. for Instrnl. Adminstrs. (state membership chmn. 1991-93), Oreg. Coun. Student Svc. Adminstrs. (chmn. 1992-93). Office: Portland CC PO Box 19000 Portland OR 97280

WILLSON, JOHN HARRISON, III, firefighter; b. Port Angeles, Wash., Aug. 12, 1959; s. John Harrison Jr. and Doris Kay (Atwood) W. B of Gen. Studies, U. Idaho, 1985; AAS in Fire Sci., Colo. Mountain Coll., Vail, 1988. Cert. emergency technician, firefighter/driver operator, fire instr., Colo. Forest firefighter Dept. Natural Resources, Forks, Wash., 1979; various positions Potlatch and Moscow, Idaho, 1980-86; resident firefighter Moscow Vol. Fire Dept., 1981-85, fire capt., 1985-86; emergency med. technician Eagle County Ambulance Dist., Vail, 1989-92; pub. safety officer Beaver Creek (Colo.) Security, 1986—; firefighter Avon (Colo.) Fire Dept., 1986-91, fire capt., 1991—; tchr. Colo. Mountain Coll., 1991-92; bd. dirs. Moscow Fire Dept., 1984-86. Named to Outstanding Young Men of Am., 1986; recipient firefighting awards. Presbyterian. Home: PO Box 590 Avon CO 81620 Office: Avon Fire Dept 0351 Benchmark Rd Avon CO 81620

WILLSTATTER, ALFRED, diplomat; b. Landsberg, Germany, Oct. 17, 1925; came to the U.S., 1938; s. Louis M. and Lucia (Cahn) W.; m. Edith R. Klabunde, Dec. 24, 1955; children: Kurt, Karl, Steve. BA, U. Minn., 1951. Commd. 2d lt. U.S. Army, 1944, advanced through grades to lt. col., 1966, ret., 1979; owner, operator Twin Plunges, Ashland, Oreg., 1966-77; fraud investigator L.A. County Charities, 1957-66. Coun. mem., City of Ashland, 1969-72, chmn. 1971; bd. dirs. Rogue Valley Transit Dist., Medford, Oreg., 1975—, vice chmn.; vol. probation officer Project Misdemeanant, Medford, 1969—; vol., arbitrator Better Bus. Bur., Portland, Oreg., 1985—. Recipient Cert. of Svc. Project Misdemeanant, 1992; named Outstanding Bd. Mem. Spl. Dists., 1991. Mem. Nat. Counter Intelligence Corps Assn. Home: 128 Central Ave Ashland OR 97520

WILMARTH, MARY ANN, physical therapist; b. Wilmington, Del., Apr. 14, 1960; d. Chester John and Patricia Ada (Cassidy) Petkiewicz; m. Roger Joseph Wilmarth, May 23, 1986; two children. BA, Middlebury Coll., 1982; MS in Phys. Therapy, Duke U., 1984. Cert. phys. therapist. Staff phys. therapist Lahey Clinic Med. Ctr., Burlington, Mass., 1984-85; phys. therapist N.H. Ctr. of Orthopedic Rehab. and Sports Medicine, Manchester, 1985-86; phys. therapy cons. Northmeadow Racquet and Health Club, Tewksbury, Mass., 1986; staff phys. therapist Palo Alto (Calif.) Phys. Therapy and Sports Injury Ctr., 1986-87; clin. supr. Assoc. Phys. Therapy and Sports Rehab. Ctr., Sunnyvale, Calif., 1987-89; co-owner, chief exec. officer Shoreline Phys. Therapy and Sports Rehab. Ctr., Mountain View, Calif., 1989—; aerobics instr. Aerobics and Fitness Assn. Am., 1986-88. Contbr. articles to profl. jours. Mem. Am. Phys. Therapy Assn., Calif. Chpt. Am. Phys. Therapy Assn., Mountain View C. of C. Home: 862 Somerset Dr Sunnyvale CA 94087-2223 Office: Shoreline Physical Therapy & Sports Rehab Ctr 278 Hope St # E Mountain View CA 94041-1308

WILSON, ALAN FENN, systems engineer; b. San Rafael, Calif., July 13, 1919; s. William Jerome and Clyde Emeretta (Turner) W.; m. Marie Ann Azpeitia, Dec. 27, 1956; 1 child, Cynthia Nell Wilson Kennedy. BSE, West Coast U., 1957, MSE, 1960. Systems analyst Atlantic Rsch. Corp., Costa Mesa, Calif., 1962-66; sr. dynamics engr. Gen. Dynamics Corp., Pomona, Calif., 1966-67; systems engr. Douglas Aircraft Co., Long Beach, Calif., 1967-70, Grumman Aerospace Corp., Point Mugu Naval Air Sta., Calif., 1972-73, Fed. Electric Corp., Vandenberg AFB, Calif., 1973-76, Interstate Electronics Corp., Anaheim, Calif., 1977-80, Boeing Co., Seattle, 1980-88; ind. researcher Everett, Wash., 1988—. Author: Message to the Stars, 1981; researcher empirical explorations in mathematical physics, exploration of regular polygons. Sgt. U.S. Army, 1943-46, CBI. Home: 4932 Glenwood Ave Everett WA 98203

WILSON, ALLYN, lawyer, arbitrator; b. Idaho Falls, Idaho, Jan. 25, 1943; s. George Arthur and April W.; m. Alma Lynn Wilson, Oct. 29, 1968; children: George, Roger, Alma, Richard. AA, Foothill Coll., 1965; BA in Mktg., Advt., Brigham Young U., 1967, MBA, 1969; LLB, Stanford U., 1972. Inspector Counsel Wall Covering, 1981—; arbitrator Arbitration Bur., L.A., 1978—. Actor: (movies) Measure of Man, 1976 (award 1979), Bombing of St. Jude, 1977. Capt. USAF, 1961-65. Mem. Am. Arbitrators Assn. (pres. Calif. 1978-80), Arbitrators BBB (v.p. Calif. 1980-82). Republican. Home: PO Box 3871 Citrus Hills CA 95611-3871

WILSON, ANDREW JAMES (AYJAY), environmental engineer, speaker, lecturer; b. N.Y.C., Oct. 23, 1926; s. James and Rose (James) W.; m. Nancy Young, Sept. 27, 1952; children: Claire Ann Wilson Gaval, Deborah Jayne Wilson Hulet. B Chem. Engring., CCNY, 1948; M Chem. Engring., NYU, 1949. Registered profl. engr., Calif. Instr. U. Hawaii, Honolulu, 1949-50; technologist Hawaiian Sugar Planters' Assn., Honolulu, 1951-52; supr. Kekaha (Hawaii) Sugar Co., 52-56; mem. tech. staff Rocketdyne div. Rockwell, Canoga Park, Calif., 1956-68; supervising engr. South Coast Air Quality Mgmt. Dist., Diamond Bar, Calif., 1968-92; lectr. U. Calif., Berkeley, 1988—, UCLA, 1974-78; cons. air pollution engring., 1992—. Contbr. articles to profl. jours. Lt. col. U.S. Army, 1950-51, mem. Res. ret. Home: 6162 Huntdale St Long Beach CA 90808-2936 Home: 91 1002 Kaihuopalaai St Ewa Beach HI 96706-3516

WILSON, ANN DUSTIN, singer, recording artist; b. 1950; d. John and Lou Wilson. Ed., Cornish Allied Inst. Fine Arts, Seattle. Lead singer rock group Heart, 1975—. Albums include: Dreamboat Annie, 1975, Magazine, 1975, Little Queen, 1977, Dog and Butterfly, 1978, Bebe le Strange, 1980, Heart Live-Gr, Private Audition, 1982, Passionworks, 1983, Heart, 1985, Bad Animals, 1987, Brigade, 1990, Rock the House--Live; single recs. include: Magic Man, 1976, Barracuda, 1977, Crazy on You, 1976, Straight On, 1978, Even It Up, 1980, Sweet Darlin', 1980, Tell It Like It Is, 1981, Unchained Melody, 1981, This Man is Mine, 1982, City's Burning, 1982, Bright Light Girl, 1982, How Can I Refuse, 1983, Sleep Alone, 1983, Almost Paradise, 1984, The Heat, 1984, What About Love, 1985, Never, 1985, These Dreams, 1986, Nothin' at All, 1986, Alone, 1987, Who Will Run to You, 1987, There's The Girl, 1987, I Want You So Bad, 1988, Surrender to Me, 1988, All I Wanna Do Is Make Love To You, 1990, I Didn't Want to Need You, 1990, Stranded, 1990, You're the Voice, 1991. Office: 1202 E Pike St Ste 767 Seattle WA 98122

WILSON, A(RNOLD) J(ESSE), city manager, consultant, communications executive; b. St. Louis, Oct. 18, 1941; s. Arnold Jesse and Eleanor (Zinn) W.; m. Patricia Ann Wilson, Mar., 7, 1961 (div. Aug. 1970); children: Mark, Mary Beth; m. Sara Roscoe, Aug. 29, 1970; children: Kristin, Jesse. AA, S.W. Bapt. Coll., 1961; BA in Psychology, William Jewell Coll., 1963; BD, Yale U., 1966, ThM, 1967. Assoc. minister, community cons. United Ch. on the Green, New Haven, 1964-67; salesperson Clark Peeper Co., St. Louis, 1967-68; dir. human resources City of University City, Mo., 1968-69; exec. dir. St. Louis County Mcpl. League, Clayton, Mo., 1969-70; exec. asst. to mayor City of St. Louis, 1971-76; mgr. City of Portland, Maine, 1976-80, City of Santa Ana, Calif., 1980-83, City of Kansas City, Mo., 1983-85; pres. Wilson Communications, Kansas City and Fallbrook, Calif., 1985-88; city adminstr. City of Pomona, Calif., 1988-90; exec. dir. Western Riverside (Calif.) Coun. Govts., 1990—; cons. U.S. Dept. HUD, Washington, 1975-76, U.S. Dept. HHS, Washington, 1978, 1st Nat. Bank of Boston, 1979-80, Nat. League of Cities, Washington, 1988—. Contbr. articles to profl. jours. Mem. human devel. com. Nat. League of Cities, Washington, 1978-84, 88; mem. resolutions com. Mo. Mcpl. League, 1978-79; mem. com. on revenue and fin. Calif. League of Cities, 1980-83; chmn. exec. adv. com. St. Louis Regional Coun., 1975. Recipient Golden City award City of Santa Ana, 1983, Community Svc. award Orange County (Calif.) Bd. of Suprs., 1983, Life Svc. award S.W. Bapt. Coll., 1984. Mem. Internat. City Mgmt. Assn., Am. Soc. Pub. Adminstrn., Govt. Fin. Officers Assn., Internat. Assn. Human Rights Orgn., Nat. Assn. Housing Redevel. Officers, Calif. Community Renewal Assn., Women and Minorities in Mgmt., City Mgrs. Assn. (social action com. 1987-88). Home: 1523 Green Canyon Rd Fallbrook CA 92028-4329 Office: Western Riverside Coun Govt 3544 University Ave Riverside CA 92501-3329

WILSON, BARBARA LOUISE, communications executive; b. Bremerton, Wash., Aug. 3, 1952; d. Algernon Frances and Dorothy Virginia (Martin) W.; m. Ashby A. Riley III, Feb. 7, 1979 (div. Dec. 1983). BA in Fin. and Econs., U. Puget Sound, 1974; MBA, U. Wash., Seattle, 1985. With Pacific N.W. Bell, Seattle and Portland, Oreg., 1974-86, dir. pub. communications, 1983-85, dir. number svcs. mktg., 1985-86; v.p. implementation planning US West, Inc., Englewood, Colo., 1986-87; pres. US West Info. Systems, Englewood, 1987-89; v.p. govt. and edn. svcs. US West Comm., Englewood, 1989; v.p. human resources U.S. West Comm., Denver, 1989-92; v.p., chief exec. officer Idaho state U.S. West Communications, Boise, 1992—; bd. dirs. U.S. West New Vector Group, Bellevue, Wash., 1988-90; chair nat. adv. com. Tel. Pioneers Am., N.Y.C., 1989. Bd. dirs., mem. exec. com. Wash. Coun. for Edn. Edn., Seattle, 1985-86; team capt. major gifts com. Boys and Girls Club, Seattle, 1986; chairperson co. campaign United Way, Seattle, 1985; bd. dirs Denver Arts Ctr. Found., 1989-91; bd. advisors U. Wash. Exec. MBA Program, 1991-93; mem. adv. bd. Boise State U. Sch. Bus.; active Boise State U. Found. Mem. Idaho Bus. Coun. (bd. dirs.), Idaho Assn. Commerce and Industry (vice chmn. bd. dirs. 1992—), Boise C. of C. (bd. dirs. 1992—), Arid Club Boise. Roman Catholic. Office: US West Communications 999 Main St 11th Fl Boise ID 83702

WILSON, BLENDA JACQUELINE, university chancellor; b. Woodbridge, N.J., Jan. 28, 1941; d. Horace and Margaret (Brogsdale) Wilson; m. Louis Fair Jr. AB, Cedar Crest Coll., 1962; AM, Seton Hall U., 1965; PhD, Boston Coll., 1979; DHL (hon.), Cedar Crest Coll., 1987, Loretto Heights Coll., 1988, Colo. Tech. Coll., 1988, U. Detroit, 1989; LLD (hon.), Rutgers U., 1989, Ea. Mich. U., 1990, Cambridge Coll., 1991, Schoolcraft Coll., 1992. Tchr. Woodbridge Twp. Pub. Schs., 1962-66; exec. dir. Middlesex County Econ. Opportunity Corp., New Brunswick, N.J., 1966-69; exec. asst. to pres. Rutgers U., New Brunswick, N.J., 1969-72; sr. assoc. dean Grad. Sch. Edn. Harvard U., Cambridge, Mass., 1972-82; v.p. effective sector mgmt. Ind. Sector, Washington, 1982-84; exec. dir. Colo. Commn. Higher Edn., Denver, 1984-88; chancellor and prof. pub. adminstrn. & edn. U. Mich., Dearborn, 1988-92; pres. Calif. State U., Northridge, 1992—; dir. Internat. Found. Edn. and Self-Help; Am del. U.S./U.K. Dialogue About Quality Judgments in Higher Edn.; adv. bd. Mich. Consolidated Gas Co., Stanford Inst. Higher Edn. Rsch., U. So. Col. Dist. 60 Nat. Alliance, Nat. Ctr. for Rsch. to Improve Postsecondary Teaching and Learning, 1988-90; bd. dirs. Alpha Capital Mgmt.; mem. higher edn. colloquium Am. Coun. Edn., vis. com. Divsn. Continuing Edn. in Faculty of Arts & Scis., Harvard Coll., Pew Forum on K-12 Edn. Reform in U.S.; trustee Children's TV Workshop. Dir. U. Detroit Jesuit High School, Northridge Hosp. Med. Ctr., Arab Community Ctr. for Econ. & Social Svcs.; dir., vice-chair Met. Affairs Corp.; exec. bd. Detroit area coun. Boy Scouts Am.; bd. dirs. Commonwealth Fund, Henry Ford Hosp.-Fairlane Ctr., Henry Ford Health System, Met. Ctr. for High Tech., United Way for Southeastern Mich.; mem. Nat. Coalition 100 Black Women, Detroit, Race Rels. Coun. Met. Detroit, Women & Founds. (corp. philanthropy), Greater Detroit Interfaith Round Table NCCJ; trustee assoc. Boston Coll., trustee emeritus Cambridge Coll., trustee emeritus/bd. dirs. Found. Ctr.; trustee Henry Ford Mus. & Greenfield Village, Sammmy Davis Jr. Nat. Liver Inst. Mem. AAUW, Assn. Governing Bds. (adv. coun. of pres.'s), Edn. Commn. of the States (student minority task force), Am. Assn. Higher Edn. (chair-elect), Am. Assn. State Colls. & Univs. (com. on policies & purposes, acad. leadership fellows selection com.), Assn. Black Profls. and Adminstrs., Assn. Black Women in Higher Edn., Women Execs. State Govt., Internat. Women's Forum, Mich. Women's Forum, Women's Econ. Club Detroit, Econ. Club, Rotary. Office: Calif State U Northridge Office of President 18111 Nordhoff St Northridge CA 91330

WILSON, BRANDON LAINE, writer, advertising and public relations consultant, photographer; b. Sewickley, Pa., Oct. 2, 1953; s. Edgar C. and Mary Beth (Tuttle) W.; m. Kathryn Langton Ward, Oct. 3, 1974 (div. 1977); m. Cheryl Ann Keefe, June 23, 1989. BA, U. N.C., 1973; Cert. Am. Acad. Dramatic Arts, 1974. Asst. acct. exec. Hill & Knowlton Pub. Rels., Pitts., 1973; dir. video Seattle Repertory Co., 1975-76; asst. dir., cameraman Pub. Broadcasting Network, Chapel Hill, 1976-77; dir. advt. and TV Prodn. N.Am. Films, Eugene, Oreg., 1977-79; gen. mgr. Boulder Community Coops., 1980-81; pub. info. officer, asst. to mayor City of Barrow, Alaska, 1981-82; dir. advt. and promotion Anchorage Conv. and Visitors Bur., Anchorage, 1983-85; mgr. mktg. communications GTE, Honolulu, 1986-87; v.p., sr. copywriter, producer Peck, Sims, Mueller Advt., Honolulu, 1987-89; pres., creative dir. Wilson & Assoc., Honolulu, 1987-90, pres., Vail, Colo., 1991-92, Wilson Brandon Wilson Lit. Svcs., 1991—. Author: Pole! Pole! A Couple's Trans-African Odyssey, Yak Butter Blues; prin. works (TV) include The General Assembly Today, 1976-77, (films) Sasquatch, Mystery of the Sacred Shroud, Buffalo Rider; contbr. articles to nat. mags. and newspapers.

Named Eagle Scout Boy Scouts Am., one of Exceptionally Able Youth, 1970, one of Outstanding Young Men in Am., 1986, Men of Achievement award U.K., 1987; recipient Order of the Arrow, two Iki Pono Gold awards Internat. TV Assn., 6 creative advt. awards. Mem. Am. Advt. Fedn. (accredited), Pub. Rels. Soc. Am., Cousteau Soc., Soc. of Friends, Mensa, Amnesty Internat. Journeyed length of Africa overland (Ceuta to Capt Town); half of fisrt western couple to cross Himalayas form Lhasa, Tibet to Kathamandu, Nepal, 1992; climbed Mt. Nyragongo, Mt. Kilimanjaro, Mt. Olympus, Mt. Everest Base Camp, Mt Miyajima, Crough Patrick, Te Rua Manga; rafted down the Zambezi River; tracked mountain gorillas in Zaire; journeyed overland across C.Am.; explored Eastern Europe. Home and Office: care KEEFE 1200 Sandra Cir Vista CA 92084

WILSON, BRUCE EVERETT, electronics engineer; b. Havre, Mont., Mar. 1, 1955; s. Kenneth Everette and Stella Marie (Twedt) W.; m. Jane Piller, Jan. 1987; children: Isaac Buchanan, Benjamin Alexander Black. BA, Rice U., 1977, MSEE, 1978. Systems engr. ESL, Inc., Sunnyvale, Calif., 1978—; cons. U.S. Ctr. for World Mission, Pasadena, Calif. 1982. Mem. IEEE, Am. Radio Relay League. Office: ESL Inc 495 Java Dr Sunnyvale CA 94086

WILSON, CARL ARTHUR, real estate broker; b. Manhasset, N.Y., Sept. 29, 1947; s. Archie and Florence (Hefner) W.; divorced; children: Melissa Starr, Clay Alan. Student UCLA, 1966-68, 70-71. Tournament bridge dir. North Hollywood (Calif.) Bridge Club, 1967-68, 70-71; computer operator IBM, L.A., 1967-68, 70-71; bus. devel. mgr. Walker & Lee Real Estate, Anaheim, Calif., 1972-76; v.p. sales and mktg. The Estes Co., Phoenix, 1976-82, Continental Homes Inc., 1982-84; pres. Roadrunner Homes Corp., Phoenix, 1984-86, Lexington Homes, Inc., 1986, Barrington Homes, 1986-90; gen. mgr. Starr Homes, 1991—; pres. Offsite Utilities, Inc., 1992—; adv. dir. Liberty Bank. Mem. Glendale (Ariz.) Citizens Bond Coun., 1986-87, Ariz. Housing Study Commn., 1988-89, Valley Leadership, 1988—; pres.'s coun. Am. Grad. Sch. Internat. Mgmt., 1985-89; vice-chmn. Glendale Planning and Zoning Commn., 1986-87, chmn., 1987-91; mem. bd. trustees Valley of Sun United Way, 1987-92, chmn. com. Community Problem Solving and Fund Distbn., 1988-89; mem. City of Glendale RTC Task Force, 1990, Maricopa County Citizens Jud. Refprm Com., 1990-92, Maricopa County Citizens Jud. Adv. Coun., 1990-91. Mem. Nat. Assn. Homebuilders (bd. dirs. 1985-93, nat. rep. Ariz. 1990-92), Cen. Ariz. Homebuilders Assn. (adv. com. 1979-82, treas. 1986, sec. 1987, v.p. 1987-89, pres. 1989—, bd. dirs. 1985—); mem. bd. adjustments City of Glendale, 1976-81, chmn., 1980-81, mem. bond coun., 1981-82; mem. real estate edn. adv. coun. State Bd. Community Coll., 1981-82; precinct committeeman, dep. registrar, 1980-81. With U.S. Army, 1968-70. Mem. Glendale C. of C. (dir. 1980-83, 89-91), Sales and Mktg. Coun. (chmn. edn. com. 1980, chmn. coun. 1981-82, Mame grand award 1981). Home: PO Box 39985 Phoenix AZ 85069-0985 Office: Starr Homes Inc Offsite Utilities Inc 2432 W Peoria Ave Ste 1190 Phoenix AZ 85029

WILSON, CARLOS GUILLERMO (CUBENA), Spanish language educator, writer; b. Panama City, Panama, Apr. 1, 1941; came to U.S., 1959; s. Henrieta (Wilson) Williams; m. Colombina Chiru, Feb. 14, 1980; children: Jaime Jose Wilson-Chiru, Carlos Jose Wilson-Chiru. BA in Spanish, Loyola U., L.A., 1968; MA in Spanish, UCLA, 1970, PhD in Hispanic Langs., 1975; MEd in Urban Edn., Loyola Marymount U., L.A., 1982, MA in Counseling, 1983. Cert. Spanish educator, Calif. Tchr. Verbum Dei High Sch., L.A., 1964-68; prof. dept. Modern Langs. Loyola Marymount U., 1971-91; prof. dept. Spanish and Portuguese San Diego State U., 1992—; adj. instr. El Camino Coll., Torrance, Calif., 1987-91; co-founder Afro-Hispanic Rev., Washington, 1982—; co-dir Cuernavaca (Mex.) Program, Loyola Marymount U., 1990-91; bd. dirs. Hispanic Pastoral Summer Inst., L.A., 1989, Latin Am. Studies, L.A., 1977-79; vis. prof. U. Calif., San Diego, 1993. Author: (novels) Chombo, 1981, Los Nietos de Felicidad Dolores, 1990; (short stories) Cuentos del Negro Cubena, 1977; (poetry) Pensamientos del Negro Cubena, 1977; contbr. articles to profl. jours. Mem. Am. Assn. Tchrs. Spanish and Portuguese, Latin Am. Studies Assn., Latin Am. Writers Inst. Home: 10884 Calle Verde Apt 106 La Mesa CA 91941-7356 Office: San Diego State U Dept Spanish and Portuguese San Diego CA 92182-0440

WILSON, CHARLES ZACHARY, JR., newspaper publisher; b. Greenwood, Miss., Apr. 21, 1929; s. Charles Zachary and Ora Lee (Means) W.; m. Doris J. Wilson, Aug. 18, 1951 (dec. Nov. 1974); children: Charles III, Joyce Lynne, Joanne Catherine, Gary Thomas, Jonathan Keith; m. Kelly Freeman, Apr. 21, 1986; children: Amanda Fox, Walter Bremond. BS in Econs., U. Ill., 1952, PhD in Econs. and Stats., 1956. Asst. to v.p. Commonwealth Edison Co., Chgo., 1956-59; asst. prof. econs. De Paul U., Chgo., 1959-61; assoc. prof. bus. SUNY, Binghamton, 1961-67, prof. econs. and bus., 1967-68; prof. mgmt. and edn. UCLA, 1968-84, vice chancellor acad. programs, 1985-87; chief exec. officer, pub./pres. Cen. News-Wave Publs., Los Angeles, 1987—, chmn., bd. dirs., publisher, 1987—; mem. adv. council Fed. Res. Bank, San Francisco, 1986-88, 2001 com. Office of Mayor of Los Angeles, 1986-89. Author: Organizational Decision-Making, 1967; contbr. articles on bus. to jours. Bd. dirs. Los Angeles County Mus. Art, 1972-84; com. on Los Angeles City Revenue, 1975-76, United Nations Assn. panel for advancement of U. and Japan Relations, N.Y.C. 1972-74; chmn. Mayor's task force on Africa, 1979-82. Fellow John Hay Whitney, U. Ill., 1955-56, Ford Found., 1960-61, 81-82, 84, Am. Council of Edn., UCLA, 1967-68, Aspen Inst. for Human Studies; named one of Young Men of Yr., Jaycees, 1965. Mem. AAAS, Am. Econ. Assn., Nat. Newspaper Pub. Assn., Am. Mgmt. Assn., Alpha Phi Alpha (pres., pledgemaster 1952-54), Phi Kappa Phi, Order of Artus (pres.). Home: 1053 Tellem Dr Pacific Palisades CA 90272-2243 Office: Cen Newspaper Publs 2621 W 54th St Los Angeles CA 90043-2698

WILSON, CHRISTIAN PAUL, computer programmer; b. L.A., Aug. 2, 1958; s. Paul Mauritz and Lois (Christensen) W.; m. Patricia Pairu Hutihuti, Oct. 2, 1982; 1 child, Lucie. AA, Ricks Coll., Rexburg, Idaho, 1980; BS, Brigham Young U., Laie, Hawaii, 1984. Sr. programmer analyst Polynesian Cultural Ctr., Laie, 1982—; pres. Pareo Paradise Polynesian Cultural Ctr., 1986—; dir. fin. Heipua o Hawaii, 1991—; dir. fin. Moemoea Prodns., Laie, 1988—. Asst. dir. pub. communications LDS Ch., Laie, 1990—; adminstrv. dir. Kauai-Tahiti Fete Com., Lihue, Hawaii, 1991—; sec.-treas. Tahitian Cultural and Community Assn., Laie, 1992—. Named to Outstanding Young Men of Am., 1987. Republican. Home: PO Box 311 Laie HI 96762 Office: Polynesian Cultural Ctr 55-370 Kamehameha Hwy Laie HI 96762

WILSON, DALE OWEN, JR., physiology educator; b. Euclid, Ohio, Jan. 7, 1955; s. Dale Owen and Lois (Cyr) W.; m. Polly Meg Wilson, Aug. 17, 1974; children: Gregg, Susan, Kathrine. BS, U. Wis., 1977; MS, Ohio State U., 1983, PhD, 1986. Asst. prof., S.W. Idaho Rsch. and Extension Ctr. U. Idaho, Parma, 1986—. Contbr. articles profl. jours. Mem. AAAS, Am. Soc. Agronomy, Nat. Sweet Corn Breeders Assn., Sigma Xi. Mem. Evang. Christian Ch. Office: Parma Rsch Ext Ctr 29603 U of I Ln Parma ID 83660

WILSON, DAVID ALLEN, political scientist, science policy consultant; b. Rockford, Ill., May 1, 1926; s. Allen C. and Margaret (McKay) W.; m. Marie Wilson; children: Elizabeth, Stephen; m. Belle Lifson Cole, Jan. 1, 1989. BA, U. Toledo, 1948; PhD, Cornell U., 1960. Prof. UCLA, 1959—; pres. The PMR Group, Northridge, Calif., 1988—; cons. The Rand Corp., Santa Monica, Calif., 1963-68, Aid U.S. Ops. Mission Thailand, Bangkok, 1968-71, Dept. Def./Office Sec. Def., Washington, 1982-86. Author: Politics In Thailand, 1961, United States and Future of Thailand, 1970; editor: Universities And Military, 1988; co-editor: Future of State University, 1986. Ford Found. fellow, 1955-58. Fellow AAAS; mem. Am. Pol. Sci. Assn. Office: UCLA Dept Polit Sci Los Angeles CA 90024

WILSON, DAVID EUGENE, magistrate judge; b. Columbia, S.C., Jan. 12, 1940; s. David W. and Emma (Moseley) W.; m. Nancy Ireland, Sept. 5, 1964; children: Amy R., Cara S. BA, U. S.C., 1963, JD, 1966; MA, Boston U., 1971. Bar: Vt. 1972, D.C. 1973, Wash. 1980, U.S. Dist. Ct. Vt. 1972, U.S. Dist. Ct. (we. dist.) Wash. 1976. Asst. atty. gen. State of Vt., Montpelier, 1972-73; asst. U.S. atty. U.S. Dist. Ct. D.C., Washington, 1973-76; asst. U.S. atty. U.S. Dist. Ct. (we. dist.) Wash., Seattle, 1976-89, U.S. atty., 1989, asst. U.S. atty., chief criminal div., 1989-92; U.S. magistrate judge Seattle, 1992—; mem. faculty Atty. Gen.'s Advocacy Inst., Washington, 1979—, Nat. Inst. Trial Advocacy, Seattle, 1987-89. Capt. U.S. Army, 1960-71, col. res. Recipient Disting. Community Svc. award B'nai Brith, 1987. Fellow Am. Coll. Trial Lawyers; mem. Fed. Bar Assn., Wash. State Bar, Seattle-King County Bar. Office: 103 US Courthouse Seattle WA 98104

WILSON, DAVID LEE, clinical psychologist; b. Mooresville, N.C., July 5, 1941; s. William John Mack and Joyce Evelyn (Evans) W.; m. Barbara Ann Klepfer, Apr. 22, 1960 (div. Jan. 1982); children: Cheryl, Lisa, David; m. Cheryl Jean Andersen, May 22, 1983 (div. Jan. 1992). Student, Auburn U., 1959-60; AB in Psychology, Davidson Coll., 1963; PhD in Clin. Psychology, U. N.C., 1967. Teaching fellow U. N.C., Chapel Hill, 1964; psychology intern Letterman Hosp., San Francisco, 1966-67, supr., 1967-70; sr. psychologist Kaiser Hosp., Hayward, Calif., 1970-72; pvt. practice psychology San Francisco, 1970-72; mem. staff Far No. Regional Ctr., Redding, Calif., 1970-74; dir. Redding Psychotherapy Group, 1974--, Vietnam Vets. Readjustment Program, Shasta and Tehama, 1984--; cons. in field. Author: play The Moon Cannot Be Stolen, 1985; contbr. articles to profl. jours. Chmn. Shasta Dam P.U.D. Com., Shasta County, 1981-82, Shasta County Headstart Bd., 1982-85, Criminal Justice Adv. Bd. Shasta County, 1982-87, Youth and Family Counseling Ctr., Shasta County, 1986—. Capt. U.S. Army, 1965-70. Recipient Danforth award Danforth Found., 1963; Woodrow Wilson Found. fellow, 1963; Smith Fund grantee, 1966. Fellow Am. Bd. Med. Psychotherapy; mem. Am. Psychol. Assn., Calif. State Psychol. Assn.(chpt. rep. 1990-93, bd. dirs. 1990-93, exec. com. 1993), Shasta County Psychol. Assn.(pres. 1990—). Democrat. Office: Redding Psychotherapy Group 616 Azalea Ave Redding CA 96002-0217

WILSON, DEBORAH THROOP, artist; b. Miami Beach, Fla., July 22, 1951; d. Gaines Roberts and Cordelia Throop (Cole) W.; m. Farouk M. Aqeel, Aug. 10, 1978 (div. Dec. 1982); m. Manuel B. Lopez, Sept. 22, 1984; 1 child, Alexander Throop Lopez-Wilson. BA in Art, U. Calif., Berkeley, 1974; MFA in Painting, Lone Mountain Coll., 1977. instr. in drawing, painting and watercolor Cen. Wyo. Coll., 1988—; gallery mgr. Artwest Gallery, Jackson, 1984; art instr. Jackson Hole Art Assn.; teaching asst. for undergrad. painting Lone Mountain Coll., San Francisco, 1975-76; teaching asst. community children's art program U. Calif. Art Mus., Berkeley, 1974. One-woman shows include Wyo. State Mus., Cyeyenne, 1986-88, 91, Wyo. Coun. on Arts, Cheyenne, 1985, Spaso House Gallery, Moscow, 1990, Far-Eastern State U., Vladivostok, USSR, 1990, Siberian Regional Mus., USSR, 1990, River Rock Gallery, Jackson, Wyo., 1990, 92, Western Wyo. Coll. Gallery, Wyo., 1992, numerous others; exhibited in groups shows at Chaminade Convention Ctr., Santa Cruz, Calif., 1991, Ward-Nasse Gallery, N.Y.C., 1991, Artwest Gallery, Jackson, Wyo., Wyo. Arts Coun., 1993, 6th Annual Coastal Nat., St. Simons Island, Ga., 1993, Galesburg (Ill.) Civic Art Ctr., 1993, numerous others. Mem. arts edn. com. Wildlife of Am. West Mus., Jackson, 1990-91. Visual arts fellow Wyo. Coun. on Arts, 1990; recipient award Hills Country Art Found., 1991. Mem Community Visual Art Assn. (pres., v.p. 1989-91, creator Christmas children's project 1989-91). Home: PO Box 928 Jackson WY 83001

WILSON, EDWARD DOTSON, state assembly clerk; b. Berkeley, Calif., Dec. 11, 1954; s. Sheila Frances (Younge) W.; m. Jacqueline R. Silas, Apr. 3, 1993. BA in Polit. Sci., UCLA, 1976; JD, U. Calif., San Francisco, 1979. Legis. aide Calif. State Assembly, Sacramento, 1979-92, dep. chief staff to Assembly Speaker Willie L. Brown, Jr., 1988-92, chief clerk, parliamentarian, 1992—. Assembly fellow Assembly Fellowship program, 1979. Mem. NAACP (Sacramento chpt.), Am. Soc. Legis. Clerks and Secs., Women's Civic Improvement Club (bd. dirs. 1984—). Office: State Capitol Rm 3196 Sacramento CA 95814

WILSON, EMILY MARIE, sales executive; b. Aberdeen, Wash., Mar. 24, 1951; d. Charles Robert and Alice Adele (Robinson) W.; m. Michael A. Rich, July 1, 1976. Student, U. Puget Sound, 1969-71, Austro-Am. Inst., Vienna, 1971; BA in Polit. Sci., U. Wash., 1973. U.S. sales mgr. Adventures Abroad, Seattle, 1990-92; U.S. sales mgr. Clairol, Inc., Seattle, 1975-81, sales rep. N.W. Wash., drug-mass mdse. div., 1975-77, sales rep. Met. Seattle, 1977-78, dist. mgr. sales western Wash., 1978-81; trainer territorial sales reps., mgr. dist. dollar sales, and dist. sales mgr. of Wash., Oreg., Idaho and Mont., Clorox, Inc., Seattle, 1981-82, assoc. regional mgr. Western div. spl. markets, 1982-83; regional mgr. Olympic Stain Co., Bellevue, Wash., 1983-86; dir. sales Inscape Products The Weyerhauser Co., Tacoma, 1986-88; dir. ops. Wildland Journeys, Seattle, 1988-89; Traveller World Wide Explorations, 1989—; owner Emily Unlimited, 1992—. Mem. Transcendental Meditation Soc., Oreg. Hist. Soc., Sons and Daus. of Oreg. Pioneers, Pioneer Assn. Wash., Seattle Hist. Soc., Sidha of the Age of Enlightenment World Govt. Assn., Grad. Sci. of Creative Intelligence, Women's Profl. Managerial Network. Office: 4417 54th Ave NE Seattle WA 98105-4942

WILSON, ERIC RANDALL, human resource manager; b. Santa Barbara, Calif., July 9, 1964; s. Clyde Clarence and Andrea Kay (Ridenour) W. Student, Drury Coll., 1982-84; BS in Psychology and Human Resource Mgmt., S.W. Mo. State U., 1986; postgrad., Portland State U., 1990-91, Oreg. State U., 1993—. Cert. sr. profl. in human resources. Legal investigator Lowther, Johnson, Lowther, Cully, Springfield, Mo., 1983-84; pvt. investigator Bill Lloyd Investigations, Springfield, 1983-86; steward, store clk. Dillon's Grocery Store, Springfield, 1985-87; mgr. human resources Platt Electric Supply, Inc., Beaverton, Oreg., 1987—; lectr. Portland State U. and Portland Community Coll., 1987—. chair human resource com. Am. Lung Assn. Oreg., Portland, 1990—, Assn. Retarded Citizens/Kidney Assn. Oreg. Benefit Fundraiser Bingo, Portland, 1988-89; caucus leader Dem. Party Mo., Willard, 1984; active Big Bros. and Big Sisters, Springfield, 1984. Mem. Northwest Human Resource Mgmt. Assn. (treas. Portland chpt.), Human Resource System Profls. (bd. dirs. 1989-92), Soc. Human Resource Mgmt. (chmn. bd. 1988—), Repertoire User Group (founding mem., bd. dirs. 1990-92). Office: Platt Electric Supply Inc PO Box 3167 Portland OR 97208-3167

WILSON, ERVIN MCDONALD, music consultant; b. Pacheco, Mex., June 11, 1928; came to U.S., 1944; s. Marion Lyman and Luisa (McDonald) W. Student, Brigham Young U., 1949-52. Draftsman Douglas Aircraft, Santa Monica, Calif., 1953-57; microtonal music cons. L.A. Editorial bd. XenHarmonikon, 1974—; inventor keyboard musical instruments; contbr. articles on speculative music theory to XenHarmonikon. Cpl. USAF, 1946-49. Home: 844 N Ave 65 Los Angeles CA 90042

WILSON, F(RANK) DOUGLAS, geneticist; b. Salt Lake City, Dec. 17, 1928; s. Frank LeRoy and Nellie Mae (Roach) W.; m. Beverly Ann Urry, Nov. 27, 1950; children: Kerry, Leslie, Eileen, John, Greg, Cynthia, Angela, David. BS, U. Utah, 1950, MS, 1953; PhD, Wash. State U., 1957. Rsch. geneticist agrl. rsch. svcs. U.S. Dept. Agr., Belle Glade, Fla., 1957-65; geneticist agrl. rsch. svcs. U.S. Dept. Agr., College Station, Tex., 1965-71, Phoenix, 1971—. Bd. dirs., tng. chmn. Boy Scouts Am., Phoenix, 1977-88. Recipient Silver Beaver award Boy Scouts Am., 1984. Mem. Agronomy Soc. Am. (assoc. editor 1978-80), AAAS, Ariz-Nev. Acad. Sci. Mormon. Office: USDA Western Cotton Rsch 4135 E Broadway Rd Phoenix AZ 85040-8803

WILSON, GERALD ALAN, retail executive; b. Portland, Oreg., Jan. 30, 1951; s. Stanley Edward and Frances (O'Brien) McBarron; m. Francee Lee Davies, Aug. 21, 1972 (div. Nov. 1980); 1 child, Joel Alan. BS in Biology, U. Oreg., 1973, MS in Curriculum and Instrn., 1975. Cert. tchr., Oreg. Tchr. biology Molalla (Oreg.) Union High Sch., 1974-75; instr. biology Lane Community Coll., Eugene, Oreg., 1975; with sci. curriculum, design and implementation dept. Oaklea Mid. Sch., Junction City, Oreg., 1975-78; ptnr. Wilson Music House, Eugene, 1978-83, prin., 1983—; adviser small bus. mgmt. com. Lane Community Coll., Eugene, 1983-93. Mem. budget com. City of Eugene, 1978-80; chairperson Westside Neighborhood Orgn., 1977-78; mem. bachelor auction Lane County March of Dimes, 1987-91; trustee Wilson Trusts. Mem. U. Oreg. Alumni Assn. (dir. Lane County chpt. 1987-92). Republican. Methodist. Club: Downtown Athletic (Eugene) (charter). Office: Wilson Music House 943 Olive St Eugene OR 97401-3006

WILSON, GORDON RUSSEL, art educator; b. Portland, Oreg., Jan. 6, 1947; s. Leo Barney Wilson and Evelyn Elizabeth (Craig) Wilson Ramus; children: Anthony, Christine. BS, Portland State U., 1970; MFA, Ft. Wright Coll., 1972. Art instr. Spokane (Wash.) Studio Sch., 1972-74, artist in residence, 1974-76; assoc. prof. in art Whitworth Coll., Spokane, 1976—; art program coord. Whitworth Coll., 1982-86; juror paper selection for Intercollegiate Ctr. for Nursing, Spokane, 1981, 5th Congl. Dist. Art, Spokane, 1990, 2nd Ann. Wash. Art Instrs. of Higher Learning Invitational, Polack Gallery, Seattle; dir. Koehler Gallery, Whitworth Coll., 1991—. One man shows include Cheney Cowles Mus. Spotlight Series, 1979, Spokane Art Sch., 1987, Whitworth Coll., Spokane, 1992; artist whose paintings, drawings, mixed media have been exhibited in a wide range of exhibits including Spokane Painters '75 Invitational, Carnegie Art Ctr. Ann. Regional Juried Art, 1979, 84 (1st pl. drawing 1983), Berkeley Nat. 1983, 84, N.W. Juried Art 1983, 88, A Spokane Sampler 1981, 82, 84, 85, 87, 89, 90, 92, Hockaday Ctr. for the Arts, Kalispell Montana, 1984, NIC Coll., Coeur d'Alene, Idaho, 1988, 89; art at work program Cheney Cowles Mus., Spokane, 1987-92. Invited participant in Goodwill Games Exhibit, Spokane, 1990. Mem. Cheney Cowles Mus. Home: 11814 N Anna J Dr Spokane WA 99218-2708 Office: Whitworth Coll Hawthorne Rd Spokane WA 99251-0001

WILSON, HELEN MARIE, real estate executive; b. San Francisco, Jan. 27, 1930; d. Ross Holcomb Rich and Helen Catherine (Squire) Thomas; m. Dale L. Wilson, Sept. 1, 1951 (dec.); children: Dale P., Paul C., Cynthia M. BS, U. Calif., Berkeley, 1952. Med. lab. technician various hosps., Calif., Minn., 1952-60; buyer-mgr. Fine Jewelry, Sacramento, Calif., 1975-80; sr. exec. assoc. Lyon Real Estate, Sacramento, 1982—; bd. govs. Lyon & Assocs. Realtors. Mem. Sacramento Traditional Jazz Soc. Mem. Sacramento Assn. Realtors (life mem. Masters Club), Sacramento Comml. Realtors, Comstock Club, Phi Mu. Republican. Presbyterian. Home: PO Box 255763 Sacramento CA 95865-5763 Office: Lyon & Assocs 2580 Fair Oaks Blvd Sacramento CA 95825-7692

WILSON, HERSCHEL MANUEL (PETE WILSON), retired journalism educator; b. Candler, N.C., July 17, 1930; s. Shuford Arnold and Ida Camilla (Landreth) W.; m. Ruby Jean Herring, Aug. 10, 1952. AB in Journalism, San Diego State U., 1956; MS in Journalism, Ohio U., Athens, 1959; postgrad., U. So. Calif., 1966-70. Reporter, copy editor, picture editor The San Diego Union, 1955-58; reporter, wire editor Long Beach (Calif.) Ind., 1959-65; prof. journalism Calif. State U., Northridge, 1965-71; fgn. desk copy editor L.A. Times, 1966-71; prof. and former chmn. journalism Humboldt State U., Arcata, Calif., 1971-91; ret., 1991; cons. KVIQ-TV News Dept., Eureka, Calif., 1985-87. Contbr. articles to profl. jours. Publicity dir. Simi Valley (Calif.) Fair Housing Coun., 1967; bd. dirs., publicity dir. NAACP, Eureka, Calif., 1978-80. With USN, 1948-52, Korea. Named Nat. Outstanding Advisor, Theta Sigma Phi, 1970. Mem. Soc. Profl. Journalists. (named Disting. Campus Advisor 1982), San Fernando Valley Press Club (v.p. 1969-70), Beau Pre Men's Golf Club (McKinleyville, Calif., pub. rels. dir., treas. 1978). Democrat. Methodist. Home: 115 Bent Creek Ranch Rd Asheville NC 28806

WILSON, JAMES ERNEST, petroleum consultant, writer; b. McKinney, Tex., Apr. 19, 1915; s. James Ernest and Agnes (Neill) W.; m. Elloie Barkely, Apr. 4, 1940; children: Judith Wilson Grant, Elizabeth Wilson. BS, Tex. A&M U., 1937. Surface geologist Shell Oil Co., Tex., 1938-41, various positions, 1945-59, v.p., Houston, New Orleans and Denver, 1959-73; cons., Denver, 1973—. Trustee and chmn. Am. Assn. Petroleum Geologists Found., 1975-79; trustee Children's Hosp. Denver, 1970-83, Denver Symphony, 1968-82, Inst. Internat. Edn., Denver, 1968-82; mem. bd. University Park Meth. Ch., 1968—. Maj. U.S. Army, 1941-45; ETO. Recipient Geosciences and Earth Resources medal Tex. A&M, 1986, Disting. Alumnus, 1991. Fellow Geol. Soc. Am., Soc. Petroleum Engrs., Am. Assn. Petroleum Geologists (hon., recipient Sidney Powers Meml. medal, 1988). Republican. Methodist. Clubs: Cherry Hill Country (Denver); Confrerie des Chevaliers du Tastevin (pres. 1983). Home: 4248 S Hudson Pky Englewood CO 80110-5015

WILSON, JAMES ROBERT, lawyer; b. Meade, Kans., Dec. 3, 1927; s. Robert J. and Bess O. (Osborne) W.; m. Marguerite Jean Reiter, Nov. 27, 1960; 1 son, John Ramsey. B.A., Kans. U., 1950, LL.B., 1953. Bar: Kans. 1953, Nebr. 1961, Colo. 1981. Pvt. practice Meade, Kans., 1953-57, Lakewood, Colo., 1989-93; county atty. Meade County, 1954-57; city atty. Meade, 1954-57; asst. gen. counsel Kans. Corp. Commn., 1957-59, gen. counsel, 1959-61, mem., 1961; atty. KN Energy, Inc., 1961-75, personnel dir., 1964-67, v.p., treas., 1968-75, exec. v.p., 1975-78, pres., chief operating officer, 1978-82, pres., chief exec. officer, 1982-85, chmn., pres., chief exec. officer, 1985-88, chmn., 1988-89; bd. dirs. Alliance Ins. Cos. With USNR, 1945-46. Mem. Phi Kappa Sigma. Democrat. Home: 1725 Foothills Dr S Golden CO 80401-9167

WILSON, JAMES ROBERT, nuclear engineer, educator; b. Lindsay, Calif., July 7, 1948; s. Woodrow Jennings and Betty (Abercrombie) W.; m. Colleen Peterson, July 26, 1980; children: Rick, Andrew, Danielle. BSME, U. Calif., Berkeley, 1970, MS in Nuclear Engring., 1971, postgrad., 1973-74. Rsch. engr. EG&G, Idaho Falls, Idaho, 1974-79; pres. New Creation, Idaho Falls, 1979-80; sr. engr. in probabilistic risk assessment Idaho Chem. Processing Plant, Idaho Falls, 1981—; lectr. Idaho Nat. Engring. Lab., Idaho Falls, 1975—, Idaho State U., Pocatello, 1985—. Contbr. articles to profl. jours. Lt. comdr. Royal Rangers, Idaho Falls, 1979—; coach co-ednl. softball, Idaho Falls, 1986—. With USN, 1971-73. Republican. Mem. Assembly of God Ch. Home: 511 N Ridge Idaho Falls ID 83402 Office: Idaho Chem Processing Plant Box 4000 MS-5304 Idaho Falls ID 83403-4000

WILSON, JAY D., tapestry weaver; b. Clarksburg, W.Va., May 21, 1947; s. William Hall and Elizabeth (Wamsley) W. BArch, Auburn U., 1971. Archtl. designer Architects Hawaii, Honolulu, 1972-75; pvt. practice Honolulu, Hawaii, 1976—; juror numerous art exhbns., 1989—. Represented in pvt., corp. and pub. collections in Hawaii, on U.S. mainland and Can.; exhibited in numerous juried & invitational art exhbns., 1972—, including solo exhbn. at Contemporary Arts Ctr., Honolulu, 1980, 3 tapestries with juried exhibit Artists of Hawaii, Honolulu Acad. Arts, 1987, 1 tapestry at 25th Anniversary of Hawaii State Found. on Culture & the Arts Exhbn., Contemporary Mus., Honolulu, 1990, 1 tapestry 30 yrs. of Honolulu Advertiser Gallery, 1991. Named Master Artist Hawaii State Found. on Culture and Arts; featured in art and craft publs. Mem. Hawaii Craftsmen (annual exhbn., cash award 1972, jurors spl. mention 1980), Am. Tapestry Alliance, Internat. Tapestry Network, Handweavers Guild Am. (award of merit 1989, juror's spl. mention 1980). Home and Office: 3155 Nahenahe Pl Kihei HI 96753-9314

WILSON, JEANETTE KURTZ, elementary and middle school educator, behavior specialist; b. Albion, Mich., July 15, 1929; d. Ivory Lee and Nora (Coates) Kurtz; m. Lucius Wilson, Nov. 21, 1953 (div. 1987); children: Michael, Debra, Karen. Grad., Cleary Coll., Ypsilanti, Mich., 1949; BS, W.Va. State Coll., Institute, 1952; MA, Newark State Tchrs. Coll., Union, N.J., 1966; EdD, Calif. Coast U., Santa Ana, 1991. Cert. elem. tchr., Calif.; clear adminstrv. svcs. credential, 1991. Receptionist Am. Cancer Soc., Newark, 1953-54; sec. Muscular Dystrophy, Newark, 1954-57; tchr. pub. schs. Linden and Elizabeth, N.J., 1957-73; ins. rep. Anaconda Telecommunications, Anaheim, Calif., 1974-79; tchr. Moreno Valley (Calif.) Unified Sch. Dist., 1980—; researcher Delta Sigma Theta Rsch. and Ednl. Found., Washington, 1990. Author: (autobiography) Every Knock a Boost, 1983; contbr. poetry to New Voices in Am. Poetry, 1972, 75, 82. Chmn., co-chmn. Social Action Legis., Riverside, 1989-90. Mem. NEA, Calif. Tchrs. Assn., Associated Tchrs Met. Riverside, Arco Civic Action Program. Home: 8374 Magnolia Ave Riverside CA 92504-3241

WILSON, JOHN FRANCIS, religion educator; b. Springfield, Mo., Nov. 4, 1937; s. Frederick Marion and Jesse Ferrel (Latimer) W.; m. L. Claudette Faulk, June 9, 1961; children: Laura, Amy, Emily. BA, Harding U., Searcy, Ark., 1959; MA, Harding Grad. Sch., Memphis, 1961; PhD, U. Iowa, 1967. Dir. Christian Student Ctr., Springfield, 1959-73; prof. religious studies S.W. Mo. State U., Springfield, 1961-83; prof. of religion, dean Seaver Coll. Arts, Letters and Scis. Pepperdine U., Malibu, Calif., 1983—. Author: Religion: A Preface, 1982, 2d edit., 1989; co-author: Discovering the Bible, 1986, Excavations at Capernaum, 1989; contbr. articles, revs. to profl. publs. Mem. Am. Schs. of Oriental Rsch., Soc. Biblical Lit., Am. Numismatic Soc., Am. Coun. Acad. Deans. Mem. Ch. of Christ. Office: Pepperdine U Seaver Coll 24255 Pacific Coast Hwy Malibu CA 90263-9999

WILSON, JOHN JAMES, federal judge; b. Boston, Dec. 23, 1927; s. John J. and Margaret (Thomas) W.; m. Joan Ellen Bostwick, Sept. 1, 1951 (div. Sept. 1975); children: Jeffrey, John, Julie; m. Elizabeth Brower, Dec. 4, 1975; 1 child, Stephane. AB, Tufts U., 1951; LLB, Stanford U., 1954. Bar: Calif.

1954, Mass. 1954, Oreg. 1982, U.S. Dist. Ct. (no., cen., ea. and so. dists.) Calif., U.S. Dist. Ct. Oreg. Asst. U.S. atty. L.A., 1958-60; ptnr. Hill, Farrer & Burrill, L.A., 1960-85; bankruptcy judge U.S. Dist. Ct. Calif., San Bernardino, 1985-88, Santa Ana, Calif., 1989—. Lt. (j.g.) USN, 1945-50. Seventh Day Adventist. Office: US Bankruptcy Ct 506 Fed Bldg PO Box 12600 34 Civic Center Plz Santa Ana CA 92712-9998

WILSON, JOHN LEWIS, academic administrator; b. Columbus, Ohio, Mar. 18, 1943; s. John Robert and Betty Marie (Barker) W.; m. Linda Patricia Kiernan, Apr. 23, 1966; 1 child, Heidi Annette. BA in Internat. Rels., Am. U., 1963, MA in Econs., 1973, PhD, 1977. Staff asst. Congressman Paul N. McCloskey, Washington, 1968-72; sr. assoc. Govt. Affairs Inst., Washington, 1973-77; pres. Experience Devel., Inc., Tucson, 1978-85; asst. dean U. Ariz., Tucson, 1985-90, assoc. dean, 1990—, acting asst. to sr. v.p. adminstrn. and fin., 1988-89; instr. U. Phoenix, Tucson, 1980-83. Author: (with others) Managing Planned Agricultural Development, 1976. 1st lt. U.S. Army, Vietnam, 1964-68. Decorated Bronze Star with oak leaf cluster and V device. Mem. ASTD (pres. local chpt. 1984), Am. Econ. Assn., Tucson Met. C. of C., Toastmasters (v.p. edn. 1987-88, pres. 1988-89). Democrat. Home: 8030 E Garland Rd Tucson AZ 85715-2830 Office: U Ariz Gould-Simpson 1025 Tucson AZ 85721

WILSON, JOHN PASLEY, law educator; b. Newark, Apr. 7, 1933; s. Richard Henry and Susan Agnes (Pasley) W.; m. Elizabeth Ann Reed, Sept 10, 1955; children: David Cables, John, Jr., Cicely Reed. AB, Princeton U., 1955; LLB, Harvard U., 1962. Bar: N.J. 1963, U.S. Dist. Ct. N.J. 1963, Mass. 1963, U.S. Dist. Ct. Mass. 1963. Budget examiner Exec. Office of Pres., Bur. of Budget, Washington, 1955-56; assoc. Riker, Danzig, Scherer & Brown, Newark, 1962-63; asst. dean Harvard U. Law Sch., Cambridge, Mass., 1963-67; assoc. dean Boston U. Law Sch., 1968-82; dean Golden Gate U. Sch. Law, San Francisco, 1982-88, prof., 1988—; vis. prof. dept. health policy and mgmt. Harvard U., 1988; cons. Nat. Commn. for the Protection of Human Subjects of Biomed. and Behavioral Rsch.; mem. Mass. Gov's. Commn. on Civil and Legal Rights of Developmentally Disabled; chmn. adv. com. Ctr for Community Legal Edn., San Francisco. Author: The Rights of Adolescents in the Mental Health System. Contbr. chpts. to books, articles to profl. jours. Bd. dirs. Greater Boston Legal Svcs., Chewonki Found.; mem. Health Facilities Appeals Bd., Commonwealth of Mass.; assoc. mem. Democratic Town Com., Concord; chmn. Bd. Assessors, Concord; bd. overseers Boston Hosp. for Women, past chmn. med. affairs com.; mem. instl. rev. bd. Calif. Pacific Hosp., San Francisco. Served to lt. (j.g.) USNR, 1956-59. NIMH grantee, 1973. Mem. Am. Arbitration Assn., Alameda/Contra Costa Med. Assn. (bioethics com.), Nat. Assn. Securities Dealers (arbitrator). Office: Golden Gate U Sch Law 536 Mission St San Francisco CA 94105-2967

WILSON, JOHN RICHARD MEREDITH, history educator, author, editor; b. Vancouver, B.C., Can., Feb. 16, 1944; came to US., 1951; s. John Abraham Ross and Nora Margaret (Mains) W.; m. Mary Ann Ahlberg, Aug. 5, 1967; children: Amy Annee Ahlberg, Christine Allison Ahlberg. BA, U. Calif., Santa Barbara, 1964; PhD, Northwestern U., 1971. Asst. prof. history Minot (N.D.) State Coll., 1966-74, assoc. prof., 1974; contract historian FAA, Washington, 1974-76; assoc. prof. MidAm. Nazarene Coll., Olathe, Kans., 1976-79, prof., 1979-89; prof. So. Calif. Coll., Costa Mesa, 1989—; chairperson social sci. divsn. So. Calif. Coll., 1992—. Author: Turbulence Aloft: The Civil Aeronautics Administration, 1938-53, 1979, A New Research Guide in History, 1986, Herbert Hoover and The Armed Forces, 1993; editor: Shaping the American Character, 1980, Forging the American Character, 1990. Active Kans. Speakers Bur., 1988-89, Cultural Arts Com., Costa Mesa, 1990—; Dem. candidate N.D. Ho. Reps., Minot, 1972; pres. So. Johnson County Dem. Club, Olathe, 1980; del. Witness for Peace, Nicaragua, 1986. Fellow NEH/Woodrow Wilson Found., Princeton, 1980, NEH/Christian Coll. Coalition, Gordon Coll., 1984, Joseph Malone fellow Nat. Coun. on Arab-U.S. Rels. Am. U., Cairo, 1986; Danforth assoc. Danforth Found., 1980-86. Mem. Orgn. Am. Historians, Am. Hist. Assn., Conf. on Faith and History. Democrat. Mem. Assemblies of God Ch. Home: 924 Tanana Pl Costa Mesa CA 92626-2918 Office: So Calif Coll 55 Fair Dr Costa Mesa CA 92626-6597

WILSON, JON STEPHEN, instrumentation consultant; b. Chickasha, Okla., June 10, 1935; s. Marion A. and Zella Mae (Eisfelder) W.; m. Nancy Lee Trostle, May 31, 1958; children: Marion Howard, Stephenie Lee Nagle. BSME, Okla. U., 1958; B Automotive Engring., Chrysler Inst. Engring., 1960; MS in Engring. in Indsl. Engring., Ariz. State U., 1969. Test engr. Chrysler Corp., Detroit, 1958-61, ITT Cannon Electric Co., Phoenix, 1961-65; sr. test engr., environ. lab. mgr. Motorola, Phoenix, 1965-74; applications engring. and mktg. mgr. Endevco Corp., San Juan Capistrano, Calif., 1974-85; owner, cons. The Dynamic Cons. and Master Mind Assocs., San Juan Capistrano, 1985—. Editor: (books) Shock and Vibration Measurement Technology, 1986, Dynamic Pressure Measurement Technology, 1991; contbr. 20 tech. articles to profl. jours. Mem. Inst. Environ. Scis. (sr., nat. dir., many local chpt. offices 1965-91), Instrument Soc. Am. (sr.), Soc. Automotive Engrs., Toastmasters (chpt. offices 1990). Home: 32871 Via Del Amo San Juan Capistrano CA 92675-4400 Office: The Dynamic Cons 32871 Via Del Amo San Juan Capistrano CA 92675-4400

WILSON, JOSEPH CHARLES, communications executive; b. Tucson, June 19, 1952; s. Charles Wesley and Anna (Toby) W.; m. Robyn Iaggi, July 19, 1975; children: Melinda J., Craig Joseph. BSBA, No. Ariz. U., 1974; MBA, Ariz. State U., 1978. Cert. purchasing mgr. Subcontract adminstr. Battelle N.W. Labs., Richland, Wash., 1978-80; sr. subcontract adminstr. Solar Energy Rsch. Inst., Golden, Colo., 1980-83; purchasing agt. Stearns-Roger, Denver, 1983-85; dir. contracts Motorola Satellite Communications, Chandler, Ariz., 1985—; cons. Clevlab, Denver, 1981-85. Contbr. articles to profl. jours. Mem. leadership program City of Chandler, 1991. Mem. Nat. Contract Mgmt. Assn. Republican. Presbyterian. Home: 2156 E Gemini Dr Tempe AZ 85283

WILSON, JOSEPHINE FRANCES, health care facility administrator, audiologist; b. Dayton, Ohio, Oct. 13, 1937; d. Edmund Francis and Leona Esther (Noffsinger) Clark; m. Robert E. Wilson, Jan. 13, 1961 (div.); children: DeAnn Marie, Kimberly Jo. BA in Edn., U. Ariz., 1959; MA, Stanford (Calif.) U., 1960; postgrad., U. San Francisco, 1984-86. Audiologist VA Hosp., San Francisco, 1960-64; lectr., audiologist U. Ariz., Tucson, 1964-66; audiologist San Diego Speech-Hearing and Neurosensory Ctr., 1967-77, HEAR Ctr., Pasadena, Calif., 1977-82; exec. dir. Hear Ctr., Pasadena, Calif., 1982—; mem. adv. bd. Pasadena Head Start, 1989-90; bd. dirs. Consortium Children with Spl. Needs, Pasadena, 1990—. Mem. Am. Speech and Hearing Assn., Calif. Speech and Hearing Assn., Alexander Graham Bell Assn. for the Deaf, Calif. chpt. Alexander Graham Bell Assn. for the Deaf, Auditory/Verbal Internat. Republican. Home: 4228 Walnut Grove Ave Rosemead CA 91770-1311 Office: HEAR Ctr 301 E Del Mar Blvd Pasadena CA 91101-2714

WILSON, J.R., editor; b. Oklahoma City, Oct. 5, 1949; s. Ralph Clayton and Wilma (Melton) W. B of Journalism, U. Mo., 1971; postgrad., Calif. State U., Long Beach, 1981-83. Reporter Springfield (Mo.) Daily News, 1970, Okla. Jour., Oklahoma City, 1971; bur. mgr. UPI, Tulsa, 1972-75; regional staff editor UPI, Atlanta, 1976-79; mgr. external rels. McDonnell Douglas Astronautics Co., Huntington Beach, Calif., 1980-83; mgr. pub. rels. Cubic Corp., San Diego, 1983-85; pres. Calif. Sun Stoppers Inc., El Cajon, Calif., 1986-87; contbg. editor ComputorEdge Mag., San Diego, 1987—; North Am. Aerospace editor Jane's Info. Group, Irvine, Calif., 1988-92; mng. editor Today's Officer, L.A., 1992—; owner Computor Aide, Santa Ana, Calif., 1993—; freelance writer Monch Media, Washington, 1986, Interavia Aerospace Bus. and Tech., Asian Aerospace, Mil. and Aerospace Electronics, Flight Internat., 1992—, Revista Aerea, Air Letter; mem. organizing bd. Aviation/Space Writers Assn. convs., San Diego, 1987; pub. rels. chmn. Winter Conv. of Industry/Govt. on Nat. Defense, Costa Mesa, Calif., 1984; nat. rep., Atlanta chmn. contract drafting com. Wire Svc. Guild, Atlanta, N.Y.C., 1978-79. Author: position paper Requirements for a Manned Space Station, 1983 (AIAA L.A. Section Svc. award). Bd. dirs. Clairemont Town Coun., San Diego, 1986-87; adv. bd. Orange County Community Airport Coun., 1981-83; pub. rels com. Orange County chpt. ARC, 1980-83; adv. coun. Orange County Transit Dist., 1981-83. Mem. Aviation/Space Writers Assn., Soc. Profl. Journalists, Am. Mensa (Atlanta v.p. 1978-79). Republican. Office: 118 W MacArthur Blvd Ste 275 Santa Ana CA 92707

WILSON, KIRK GEORGE, medical service executive; b. Great Falls, Mont., Apr. 1, 1951; s. Floyd Daniel and Lorna (Stark) W.; m. Monica Jane Moline, Aug. 17, 1975; 1 child, Bret Michael. BABS, Concordia Coll., Moorhead, Minn., 1972; MA in Hosp. Adminstrn., U. Iowa, 1975. Adminstrv. asst. Columbus Hosp., Great Falls, 1975-78, asst. adminstr., 1978-80; asst. adminstr., profl. services St. Anthony Hosp., Oklahoma City, Okla., 1981-83, St. Vincent Med. Ctr., Portland, Oreg., 1983-86; adminstr. Meml. Women's/Childrens Hosp., Meml. Med. Ctr., Long Beach, Calif., 1987-88; pres., chief exec. officer Mont. Deaconess Med. Ctr., Great Falls, 1988—; Bd. dirs. Mountain States VHA Regional Bd., Denver, Bank of Mont. Co-author: (monograph) Mental Health Care Systems, 1975. Bd. dirs. Symphony Assn. Bd., Great Falls, 1988—; mem. pres.'s coun. Coll. Great of Falls. Fellow Am. Coll. Healthcare Execs., Mont. Hosp. Assn. (bd. dirs. Dist. II), Mont. Amb., Great Falls C. of C. (bd. dirs., Leadership award 1981), Rotary. Republican. Congregationalist. Home: 520 Fox Ct Great Falls MT 59404-3874 Office: Mont Deaconess Med Ct 1101 26th St S Great Falls MT 59405-5193

WILSON, KRISTIN MARIE, computer scientist; b. Phila., Sept. 9, 1947; d. Raymond Hiram Jr. and Irene Gladys Louise (Hansing) W.; m. Frank Nelson Young III, Dec. 4, 1967 (div. May 1990); children: Marnin Ehrling, Nicolas Leon. Student, Swarthmore Coll., 1965-67; BA in Studio Art, Ind. U., 1973; BS in Computer Sci., U. Oreg., 1985; postgrad., U. Calif., Berkeley, 1986. Programmer Commerce Clearing House, San Rafael, Calif., 1986-88, programmer, analyst, 1988-90, systems analyst, 1990-91; product specialist Medicus Systems, Alameda, Calif., 1991-93; instr., cons. Interactive Devel. Environments, San Francisco, 1993—. Mem. Spl. Interest Group on Graphics, Spl. Interest Group on Computer Human Interface, Spl. Interest Group on Software, Bay Area Computer Human Interface, Assn. for Computing Machinery. Home: 6057 Claremont Ave Oakland CA 94618 Office: Interactive Devel Environments 595 Market St 10th Fl San Francisco CA 94105

WILSON, LOIS MAYFIELD, English language educator; b. Berea, Ky., Jan. 28, 1924; d. Samuel Martin and Flora Terrill (Sweeney) Mayfield; m. Graham Cunningham Wilson, July 9, 1948; 1 child, Erin Cressida. BS, Bowling Green State U., 1943; MA, U. Mich., 1944; PhD, Stanford U., 1954. Reporter Toledo Morning Times, summer 1944; instr. English, U. Ill., Urbana, 1944-46, Stanford (Calif.) U., 1946-48; from instr. to prof. San Francisco State U., 1949—; research fellow U. Chile, Santiago, 1947; Fulbright prof. linguistics U. Rome, 1956-57. Co-author: Inglese Parlato, 1958. Mem. selection com. for Fulbright scholars, Inst. Internat. Edn., Washington, 1979; Transpacific orientation dir. & lectr. Inst. Internat. Edn./Asia Found., 1956, 61. Mem. Tchrs. English to Speakers of Other Langs., Calif. Assn. Tchrs. English to Speakers of Other Langs., Nat. Assn. Fgn. Student Advisors. Democrat. Unitarian. Office: San Francisco State U Dept English 1600 Holloway Ave San Francisco CA 94132-1722

WILSON, MATTHEW FREDERICK, newspaper editor; b. San Francisco, May 10, 1956; s. Kenneth E. and Verna Lee (Hunter) W. BA in Philosophy, U. Calif., Berkeley, 1978. Copy person San Francisco Chronicle, summers 1975, 76, 77, copy editor, 1978-82, editorial systems coord., 1982-84; budget analyst San Francisco Newspaper Agy., 1984085; asst. news editor San Francisco Chronicle, 1985-87, asst. to exec. editor, 1987-88, mng. editor, 1988—. Mem. Am. Soc. Newspaper Editors, AP Mng. Editors, Calif. Soc. Newspaper Editors. Office: San Francisco Chronicle 901 Mission St San Francisco CA 94103-2988

WILSON, MICHAEL B(RUCE), lawyer; b. Boise, Idaho, Aug. 5, 1943; s. George E. and Helen E. (Hughes) W.; m. Sarah J. Copeland, June 18, 1966; children: David B., Janet L. BS in Math., Oreg. State U., 1965, MS in Gen. Sci., 1966; JD, Lewis and Clark Coll., 1978. Bar: Oreg. 1978, U.S. Ct. Mil. Appeals 1978. Commd. 2d lt. USAF, 1966, advanced through grades to maj., 1978, served in Vietnam, 1968; chief of logistics 3d Weather Wing, Offut AFB, Nebr., 1969-71; chief maintenance 2d Weather Wing, Wiesbaden AFB, Fed. Republic Germany, 1971-75; chief civil law HQ Chanute TTC, Chanute AFB, Ill., 1978-80; chief civil and mil. affairs HQ 17th Air Force, Sembach AFB, Fed. Republic Germany, 1980-83; dir. telecommunications and contract law Air Force Communications Command, Scott AFB, Ill., 1983-87; counsel U.S. West Communications, Englewood, Colo., 1988—; chmn. Joint Svcs. Telecommunications Working Group, 1983-87, Air Force Comml. Communications Working Group, Scott AFB, 1985-87, AFCC Comml. Communications Working Group, Scott AFB, 1985-87, DOD Comml. Telecommunications Com. Liason Officer Boy Scouts Am., Sembach AFB, 1981-83; mem. U.S. West Coun. of Leaders. Recipient Mgmt./Adminstrv. Excellence award Interagy. Com. on Info. Resources Mgmt., 1987. Mem. ABA, Fed. Communications Bar Assn., Armed Forces Communications Electronics Assn., Nat. Contract Mgmt. Assn.

WILSON, MICHAEL GREGG, film producer, writer; b. N.Y.C., Jan. 21, 1942; s. Lewis Gilbert Wilson and Dorothy (Natol) Broccoli; m. Coila Jane Hurley; children: David, Gregg. BS, Harvey Mudd Coll., 1963; JD, Stanford U., 1966. Bar: D.C., Calif., N.Y. Legal advisor FAA-DOT, Washington, 1966-67; assoc. Surrey, Karasik, Gould, Green, Washington, 1967-71; ptnr. Surrey and Morse, Washington and N.Y.C., 1971-74; legal advisor Eon Prodns., London, 1974-78, producer, mng. dir., 1978—. Writer/producer For Your Eyes Only, 1981, Octopussy, 1983, View to a Kill, 1985, The Living Daylights, 1987, Licence to Kill, 1989.

WILSON, MYRON ROBERT, JR., former psychiatrist; b. Helena, Mont., Sept. 21, 1932; s. Myron Robert Sr. and Constance Ernestine (Bultman) W. BA, Stanford U., 1954, MD, 1957. Diplomate Am. Bd. Psychiatry and Neurology. Dir. adolescent psychiatry Mayo Clinc, Rochester, Minn., 1965-71; pres. and psychiatrist in chief Wilson Ctr., Faribault, Minn., 1971-86; ret., 1986; chmn. Wilson Ctr., 1986-90; ret., 1990; assoc. clin. prof. psychiatry UCLA, 1985—. Contbr. articles to profl. jours. Chmn., chief exec. officer C.B. Wilson Found., L.A., 1986—; mem. bd. dirs. Pasadena Symphony Orchestra Assn., Calif., 1987. Served to lt. comdr., 1958-60. Fellow Mayo Grad. Sch. Medicine, Rochester, 1960-65. Fellow Am. Psychiat. Assn., Am. Soc. for Adolescent Psychiatry, Internat. Soc. for Adolescent Psychiatry (founder, treas. 1985-88, sec. 1985-88, treas. 1988-92); mem. Soc. Sigma Xi (Mayo Found. chpt.). Episcopalian. Office: Wilson Found 8439 W Sunset Blvd Ste 104 West Hollywood CA 90069-1947

WILSON, PETE, governor; b. Lake Forest, Ill., Aug. 23, 1933; s. James Boone and Margaret (Callaghan) W.; m. Betty Robertson (div.); m. Gayle Edlund, May 29, 1983. B.A. in English Lit., Yale U., 1955; J.D., U. Calif., Berkeley, 1962; LL.D., Grove City Coll., 1983, U. Calif., San Diego, 1983, U. San Diego, 1984. Bar: Calif. 1962. Mem. Calif. Legislature, Sacramento, 1966-71; mayor City of San Diego, 1971-83; U.S. Senator from Calif., 1983-91; gov. State of Calif., 1991—. Trustee Conservation Found.; mem. exec. bd. San Diego County council Boy Scouts Am.; hon. trustee So. Calif. Council Soviet Jews; adv. mem. Urban Land Inst., 1985-86; founding dir. Retinitis Pigmentosa Internat.; hon. dir. Alzheimer's Family Ctr., Inc., 1985; hon. bd. dirs. Shakespeare-San Francisco, 1985. Recipient Golden Bulldog award, 1984, 85, 86, Guardian of Small Bus. award, 1984; ROTC scholar Yale U., 1951-55; named Legislator of Yr., League Calif. Cities, 1985; Man of Yr. award Nat. Guard Assn. Calif., 1986, Man of Yr. citation U. Calif. Boalt Hall, 1986. Mem. Nat. Mil. Family Assn. (adv. bd.), Phi Delta Phi, Zeta Psi. Republican. Episcopalian. Office: State Capitol Office of Governor Sacramento CA 95814*

WILSON, RICHARD RANDOLPH, lawyer; b. Pasadena, Calif., Apr. 14, 1950; s. Robert James and Phyllis Jean (Blackman) W.; m. Catherine Goodhugh Stevens, Oct. 11, 1980; children: Thomas Randolph, Charles Stevens. BA cum laude, Yale U., 1971; JD, U. Wash., 1976. Bar: Wash. 1976, U.S. Dist. Ct. (we. dist.) Wash. 1976, U.S. Ct. Appeals (9th cir.) 1977. Assoc. Hillis, Phillips, Cairncross, Clark & Martin, Seattle, 1976-81, ptnr., 1981-84; ptnr. Hillis, Cairncross, Clark & Martin, Seattle, 1984-87, Hillis, Clark, Martin & Peterson, Seattle, 1987—; bd. dirs. Quality Child Care Svcs., Inc., Seattle, Bldg. Industry Legal Trust Fund, Bellevue; mem. land use com. Downtown Human Svcs. Coun.; lectr. various bar assns., 1980—. Contbr. articles to profl. jours. Active Mayor's Kidsplace Adv. Task Force, Seatle, 1985; chmn. class agts. Yale Alumni Fund, New Haven, 1985-87, class agt., 1971—; mem. Yale Class Coun., New Haven, 1991—, Western Wash. Exec. Com., Yale Capital Campaign; mem., vice chair City of Medina Planning Commn., 1990-92; bd. dirs. Gilbert and Sullivan Soc., Seattle. Mem. ABA, Wash. State Bar Assn. (dir. environ. and land use law sect. 1985-88), Seattle-King County Bar Assn., Kingsley Trust Assn., Yale Assn. of Western Wash., Overlake Golf and Country Club. Congregationalist. Home: 2305 86th Ave NE Bellevue WA 98004-2416 Office: Hillis Clark Martin & Peterson 1221 2d Ave Ste 500 Seattle WA 98101-2925

WILSON, ROBERT LEE, geological consultant; b. Peoria, Ill., Dec. 16, 1918; s. Harry James and Alta May (Matthews) W.; m. Annabell June Tullis, May 25, 1941; children: Cheryl D., Sandra J., David L. Geol. Engr., Colo. Sch. Mines, 1941; PhD, U. Ariz., 1956. Registered geologist, Calif.; cert. engring. geologist, Calif. Asst. regional geologist Bur. Reclamation, Colo., Nev., Ariz., 1946-51; dist. geologist Corps of Engrs., Ga., Fla., S.C., 1951-53; pvt. practice geol. cons. Ariz., 1953-55, Calif., 1984—; raw materials geologist Kaiser Steel Corp., Calif., Utah, N.Mex., 1956-66; chief geologist Kaiser Steel Corp., Calif., Utah, N.Mex., also Can., 1967-70; exploration mgr. Kaiser Steel Corp., U.S. and 25 other countries, 1970-84. Contbg. author and editor articles to profl. jours. Maj. Corps of Engrs., U.S. Army, 1941-46. Fellow Navajo Indian Svc., 1953-55. Mem. AIME, Am. Inst. Profl. Geologists, Geol. Soc. Am., Soc. Econ. Geologists, Sigma Xi, Community Club (Walnut Creek chpt.). Home and Office: 2646 Saklan Indian Dr # 3 Walnut Creek CA 94595-3014

WILSON, ROBIN SCOTT, university president, writer; b. Columbus, Ohio, Sept. 19, 1928; s. John Harold and Helen Louise (Walker) W.; m. Patricia Ann Van Kirk, Jan. 20, 1951; children: Kelpie, Leslie, Kari, Andrew. B.A., Ohio State U., 1950; M.A., U. Ill., 1951, Ph.D., 1959. Fgn. intelligence officer CIA, Washington, 1959-67; prof. English Clarion State Coll., (Pa.), 1967-70; assoc. dir. Com. Instnl. Cooperation, Evanston, Ill., 1970-77; assoc. provost instrn. Ohio State U., Columbus, 1977-80; pres. Calif. State U., Chico, 1980—. Author: Those Who Can, 1973; short stories, criticism, articles on edn. Lt. USN, 1953-57. Mem. AAAS, Phi Kappa Phi. Office: Calif State U 105 Kendall Hall Chico CA 95929

WILSON, SONJA MARY, business and computer educator, consultant; b. Lake Charles, La., Mar. 28, 1938; d. Albert Ronald and Annelia (DeVille) Molless; m. Willie McKinley Williams, Apr. 28, 1956 (div. May 1969); children: William P. Williams, Dwayne L. Williams, Rachelle A. Smith, Devon A. Williams, Lisa M. Lewis, Ricardo Soto Williams; m. Howard Brooks Wilson, Nov. 12, 1982; stepchildren: Howard N. Wilson, Yvonne Wilson. AA in Behavioral Scis., Mt. St. Jacinto Jr. Coll., 1992; student, U. Calif., San Bernardino, 1983, Calif. State Poly. U., 1986, Laverne U., 1984-85, So. Ill. U., 1985-86, 93, Riverside (Calif.) City Coll., 1988-89. Prin.'s sec. Elsinore (Calif.) High Sch., 1974-83, tchr. adult vocat. edn., 1979-84, notary pub., 1981-85, coord. vocat. edn., 1983-84, tchr. bus. and vocat. edn., class adviser, 1983-88. Pres. Lake Elsinore Unified Sch. Dist. Bd., 1979-88; pres. Lake Elsinore Elem. Sch. Bd., 1981-83, v.p., 1988-89; pres. Riverside County Sch. Bds. Assn., 1979—; assoc. sponsor, advisor Black Student Union/Future Leaders of Am., 1984-90; leader Girl Scouts U.S.A.; den mother Boy Scouts Am.; mem. Cen. Dem. Com., 1989-91; del. PTSA, 1991-93. Tribute in her honor Black Student Union/Future Leaders Am., 1989; recipient Excellence in Edn. award Hilltop Community Ctr. Club, 1989, Leadership award Black Art and Social Club, 1989, Svc. award Sojourner Truth Media Network, 1989, Proclamation award City of Elsinore, 1989, County of Riverside, 1984. Mem. NAACP (Lake Elsinore affiliate, plaque), Calif. Sch. Bds. Assn. (regional dir. 1988-92, mem. conf. planning com. 1989, mem. legis. com. 1981—, mem. nominations com. 1988, mem. media com.), Calif. Elected Women Ofcls. Assn., Calif. Sch. Employees Assn. (pres., treas., regional rep. asst., mem. state negotiation com., del. to conf.), Internat. Soc. Poets, Lake Elsinore C. of C., Calif. Coalition Black Sch. Bd. Members (v.p. 1989, pres. 1990, program liaison 1989), Nat. Coun. Negro Women (charter, Willa Mae Taylor sect.), Black Art and Social Club, Hilltop Community Club (plaque), Sojourner Truth Media Network (plaque), Eta Phi Beta (treas. Gamma Alpha chpt., plaque, pres. 1992—). Democrat. Home: 21330 Waite St Lake Elsinore CA 92530-9503

WILSON, STEPHEN HARTH, art educator; b. St. Louis, Mar. 15, 1944; s. Julius and Sally W. BA, Antioch Coll., 1967; MEd, Boston Coll., 1968; MFA, Sch. of Art Inst., Chgo., 1980; PhD, U. Chgo., 1972. Rsch. dir. Ctr. for New Schs., Chgo., 1973-77; psychology prof. Forrest Inst., Des Plaines, Ill., 1978-80; art prof. Art Inst. Chgo., 1980-81, San Francisco State U., 1981—; cons. Interactive Arts, San Francisco, 1981—, Exploring System Earth Project, San Francisco, 1988—. Author: Multimedia Design With Hypercard, 1991, Using Computers to Create Art, 1986; inventor interactive print media. Office: San Francisco State U Dept Art 1600 Holloway Ave San Francisco CA 94132-1722

WILSON, STEPHEN VICTOR, federal judge; b. N.Y.C., Mar. 26, 1942; s. Harry and Rae (Ross) W. B.A. in Econs., Lehigh U., 1963; J.D., Bklyn. Law Sch., 1967; LL.M., George Washington U., 1973. Bars: N.Y. 1967, D.C. 1971, Calif. 1972, U.S. Ct. Appeals (9th cir.) U.S. Dist. Ct. (so., cen. and no. dists.) Calif. Trial atty. Tax div. U.S. Dept. Justice, 1968-71; asst. U.S. atty., L.A., 1971-77, chief spl. prosecutions, 1973-77; ptnr. Hochman, Salkin & Deroy, Beverly Hills, Calif., from 1977; judge U.S. Dist. Ct. (cen. dist.) Calif., L.A,, 1985—; adj. prof. law Loyola U. Law Sch., 1976-79; U.S. Dept. State rep. to govt. W.Ger. on 20th anniversary of Marshall Plan, 1967; del. jud. conf. U.S. Ct. Appeals (9th cir.), 1982-86. Recipient Spl. Commendation award U.S. Dept. Justice, 1977. Mem. ABA, L.A. County Bar Assn., Beverly Hills Bar Assn. (chmn. criminal law com.), Fed. Bar Assn. Jewish. Contbr. articles to profl. jours. Home: 9100 Wilshire Blvd Beverly Hills CA 90212-3403 Office: US Dist Ct 312 N Spring St Los Angeles CA 90012-4701

WILSON, STEVEN BRIAN, accountant, auditor, financial consultant; b. Honolulu, Jan. 13, 1963; s. Harvey Andrew and Beverly (Brown) W.; m. Sarah Frances Adams, July 6, 1991. BS in Acctg. cum laude, Brigham Young U., 1988. CPA, Calif.; lic. real estate salesman, Hawaii. Mgr. Orient Express Restaurant, Provo, Utah, 1984-86; real estate agt. The Realty Group, Honolulu, 1985, 86; staff acct. Price Waterhouse, West Los Angeles, Calif., 1988-90, sr. acct., 1991—. Missionary LDS Ch., Sapporo, Japan, 1982-84. Mem. Wilderness Fly Fishing Club, Golden Key, Beta Gamma Sigma, Beta Alpha Psi. Office: Price Waterhouse 1880 Century Park E West Los Angeles CA 90067

WILSON, TED LEWIS, educator, former mayor; b. Salt Lake City, May 18, 1939; s. Robert L. and Eva (Simpson) W.; m. Kathryn Carling, June 10, 1963; children—Benjamin, Jennifer, Melissa, Jessica, Joseph. B.S., U. Utah, 1964; M.Ed. (NSF fellow), U. Wash., 1969. Tchr. Granite Sch. Dist., Salt Lake City, 1966-73; adminstrv. asst. to a congressman, 1973-75; social services dir. Salt Lake County, Utah, 1975-76; mayor of Salt Lake City, from 1976; now dir. Hinckley Inst. Politics, U. Utah. Contbr. articles to profl. jours. Bd. dirs. Intermountain Health Care, Inc.; bd. advs. Mountain Bell. Served with Army NG, 1957-62. Recipient Valor award Dept. Interior, 1968. Mem. U.S. Conf. of Mayors (dir.), Nat. League Cities and Towns, Am. Soc. Pub. Adminstrs., Common Cause. Democrat. Mormon. Office: Univ Utah Hinckley Inst Pol 253 Orson Spencer Hall Salt Lake City UT 84112-1103

WILSON, THEODORE HENRY, retired electronics company executive, aerospace engineer; b. Eufaula, Okla., Apr. 23, 1940; s. Theodore V. and Maggie E. (Buie) W.; m. Barbara Ann Tassara, May 16, 1958 (div. 1982); children: Debbie Marie, Nita Leigh, Wilson Axten, Pamela Ann, Brenda Louise, Theodore Henry II, Thomas John; m. Colleen Fagan, Jan. 1, 1983 (div. 1987); m. Karen L. Lerohl, Sept. 26, 1987. BSME, U. Calif., Berkeley, 1962; MSME, U. So. Calif., 1964, MBA, 1970, MSBA, 1971. Sr. rsch. engr. N.Am. Aviation Co. div. Rockwell Internat., Downey, Calif., 1962-65; propulsion analyst, supr. div. applied tech. TRW, Redondo Beach, Calif., 1965-67, mem. devel. staff systems group, 1967-71; sr. fin. analyst worldwide automotive dept. TRW, Cleve., 1971-72; contr. systems and energy group TRW, Redondo Beach, 1972-79; dir. fin. control equipment group TRW, Cleve., 1979-82, v.p. fin. control indsl. and energy group, 1982-85; mem. space and def. group TRW, Redondo Beach, 1985-93, ret., 1993; lectr., mem. com. acctg. curriculum UCLA Extension, 1974-79. Mem. Fin. Execs. Inst. (com. govt. bus.), Machinery and Allied Products Inst. (govt. contracts coun.), Nat. Contract Mgmt. Assn. (bd. advisors), Aerospace Industries Assn. (procurement and fin. coun.), UCLA Chancellors Assocs., Tau Beta Pi, Beta Gamma Sigma, Pi Tau Sigma. Republican. Home: 3617 Via La Selva Palos Verdes Peninsula CA 90274-1115

WILSON, THOMAS CHARLES, secondary education educator; b. Klamath Falls, Oreg., Feb. 3, 1950; s. Charles Edward and Eleanore Mae (Kandra) W.; m. Susan Lee Wright, Feb. 12, 1983 (div. Dec. 1989); 1 child, Julie; m. Melissa McConnell Foster, Aug. 3, 1991; children: Christine, Lucinda. FCC Lic., Ogden Radio Engrng. Sch., Huntington Beach, Calif., 1971; student, Diablo Valley Coll., 1979-85; BBA, U. Phoenix, 1986; post-grad., Calif. State U., Hayward, 1990-91. Disc jockey, ops. mgr. KWUN Radio, Concord, Calif., 1971-80; electronics instr. Diablo Valley Coll., Pleasant Hill, Calif., 1986-88; radio instr. KVHS Radio, Concord, Calif., 1978—; dir. student activities Clayton Valley High Sch., Concord, Calif., 1989—; chmn. Clayton Valley High Site Coun., Concord, 1990-91. Recipient Outstanding Contbn. to Edn. award Mt. Diablo Sch. Bd., 1985. Republican. Office: KVHS Radio 1101 Alberta Way Concord CA 94521-3747

WILSON, THOMAS DALE, university administrator, fundraising consultant; b. Lincoln, Nebr., June 2, 1952; s. Richard Barr and Charlotte Adele (Brown) W.; m. Susette Adele Eddinger, Mar. 9, 1973; children: Christine, Richard, Charles, Kathryn. B in Music Edn., U. Nebr., 1974; MusM, Northwestern U., 1976. Dir. corp. found. rels. Field Mus. Natural History, Chgo., 1984-85; dir. devel. Phoenix Symphony, 1985-86; sr. campaign dir. Devel. Mgmt. Assn., Portland, Oreg., 1986-89; v.p. devel. Oreg. Grad. Inst. Sci. & Tech., Portland, 1989—. Trustee Valley Community Presbyn. Ch., Found., 1989—, music dir. English Handbell Choir, 1989—. Mem. Nat. Soc. Fund Raising Execs. (Oreg. pres. 1990). Office: Oreg Grad Inst Sci & Tech 20000 NW Walker Rd Portland OR 97291-1000

WILSON, WARREN BINGHAM, artist, art educator; b. Farmington, Utah, Nov. 4, 1920; s. Alma L. and Pearl E. (Bingham) W.; B.S. in Edn., Utah State U., 1943; M.F.A., U Iowa, 1949; m. Donna Myrle VanWagenen, Dec. 22, 1948; children—Vaughn Warren, Michael Alma, Annette, Pauline, Douglas George, Craig Aaron, Robert Kevin. Asst. prof. art Utah State U., Logan, 1949-54; vis. instr. Salt Lake Art Center, Utah, 1952-53; prof. art and edn. Brigham Young U., Provo, Utah, 1954-83; ret., 1983 vis. lectr. ceramics U. Calif., Davis, 1968; fellow in residence Huntington Hartford Found., Pacific Palisades, Calif., 1960-61; vis. instr. Pioneer Crafthouse, Salt Lake City, 1969-70; one-man shows of paintings and/or sculpture include: Salt Lake Art Center, 1951, Yakima Valley Coll., 1962, UCLA, 1962, Mont. State U., Bozeman, 1963, Stanford U., 1963, Wash. State U., Pullman, 1964, Central Wash. State Coll., Ellensburg, 1964, Nev. So. U., Las Vegas, 1967, Ricks Coll., Rexburg, Idaho, 1976, 80, Brigham Young U., Provo, Utah, 1970, 75, 79, 82, retrospective retirement exhbn. of sculpture, ceramics and paintings, 1983; group shows include: Denver Art Mus., 1951, Colorado Springs (Colo.) Fine Arts Center, 1951, Santa Fe Art Mus., 1953, Madison Sq. Gardens, N.Y.C., 1958, Wichita Art Center, 1960, Ceramic Conjunction Invitational, Glendale, Calif., 1973; represented in permanent collections: Utah State Inst. Fine Arts Salt Lake City, Utah State U., Logan, Utah State Fair Assn., Utah Dixie Coll., St. George, Coll. So. Utah, Cedar City, Brigham Young U., also numerous pvt. collections. Asst. dist. commr. Boy Scouts Am., 1975-80; counselor in Ward Bishopric, Ch. of Jesus Christ of Latter-day Saints, 1981-83. Served with USAAF, 1943-46. Recipient Am. Craftsman Council merit award, 1964; Silver Beaver award Boy Scouts Am. Republican. Home: 1000 Briar Ave Provo UT 84604-2868

WILSON, WESLEY ALVIN, accountant, minister; b. Waterloo, Iowa, July 13, 1928; s. Ralph Horton and Margie Leota (Owen) H.; m. Golda Ruth Orr, Aug. 16, 1952; children: Ruth Esther, Paul Wesley, David Mark. BA in Bus. Adminstrn., Lewis & Clark Coll., 1952; MDiv, Western Bapt. Sem., Portland, Oreg., 1955. CPA, Oreg., Wash. Staff acct. George Black & Co., Portland, 1949-56; chief auditor Evang. Alliance Mission, Tokyo, 1956-72; staff acct. Ronald S. Berg, CPA, Portland, 1972-74, 86-88; sr. internal auditor City of Portland, 1974-76; sr. ptnr. Wilson, Steffen & Assocs., Silverton, Oreg., 1976-86; pvt. practice Vancouver, Wash., 1988—. Mem. Nat. Fedn. Ind. Bus. (guardian), C. of C. (pres. 1981, bd. dirs. 1977-82), Silverton Area Rotary. Republican. Baptist. Home and Office: 12116 SE Riveridge Dr Vancouver WA 98684

WILSON, WILLIAM C., microbiologist, researcher; b. St. Albans, Vt., Aug. 8, 1957; s. Amos P. and Margaret (Smith) W.; m. Cynthia N. Choy, May 25, 1984. BSc, U. Ill., 1979, PhD, 1985. Rsch. asst. U. Ill., Urbana, 1979-84; rsch. assoc. Eppley Cancer Inst., Omaha, 1984-86; microbiologist USDA Agrl. Rsch. Svc., Laramie, Wyo., 1986—; adj. faculty U. Wyo., Laramie, 1987—; affiliate faculty Colo. State U., Ft. Collins, 1989—. Contbr. chpts. to books, articles to profl. jours. NIH grantee, 1979; Norman Cromwell fellow, 1984; Agrl. Rsch. fellow, 1986. Mem. AAAS, Am. Soc. for Virology, Am. Soc. for Microbiology, Am. Soc. for Tropical Medicine, Am. Soc. for Tropical Vet. Medicine, U.S. Animal Health Assn., Sigma Xi (chpt. pres. 1992-93). Office: USDA Agrl Rsch Svc Laramie WY 82071-3965

WILSON, WILLIAM HARWELL, psychiatry educator, researcher; b. Memphis, Feb. 6, 1951; s. Joseph Harwell Wilson and Helen Wilson (Cobb) Carruthers; m. Paula Rea, Oct. 18, 1986; children: Rea Xan, Sanford Shepherd. BA, Brown U., 1973; MD, U. Pa., 1981. Diplomate Am. Bd. Psychiatry and Neurology, Nat. Bd. Med. Examiners. Resident in psychiatry U. Wis., Madison, 1981-85; asst. prof. psychiatry U. Pitts. Sch. Medicine, 1985-86, Med. Coll. Pa., Phila., 1986-89; asst. prof. psychiatry Oreg. Health Scis. U., Portland, 1989—, asst. dir. pub. psychiatry tng. program, 1989—, assoc. prof. psychiatry, 1993—; dir. prof. edn. unit Dammasch State Hosp., Wilsonville, Oreg., 1989—. Contbr. numerous articles on treatment of schizophrenia to sci. jours. Grantee NIMH, 1989-93. Mem. Am. Psychiat. Assn., Am. Assn. Community Psychiatrists, Soc. for Biol. Psychiatry, West Coast Coll. Biol. Psychiatry, World Fedn. Mental Health, Nat. Alliance for Mentally Ill (Exemplary Psychiatrist award 1992). Office: Oreg Health Scis U Mail Code OP02 3181 SW Sam Jackson Park Rd Portland OR 97201

WILTBANK, JOSEPH KELLEY, university counsel, lawyer; b. Albuquerque, June 5, 1950; s. William J. and Joyce I. (Jones) W.; m. Antonia Louise Urquidi, Aug. 5, 1978; children: Mitch, Drew, Jay, Neeley. BA in History, U. Fla., 1972; JD, Gonzaga U., 1977; BA in French with high honors, Idaho State U., 1990. Bar: Idaho 1977, U.S. Dist. Ct. Idaho 1977, U.S. Ct. Appeals (9th cir.) 1979. Adminstrv. asst. to mayor Mountain Home, Idaho, 1977-79; dep. prosecuting atty. Ada County, Boise, Idaho, 1979-83; univ. counsel, counsel to pres. Idaho State U., Pocatello, 1983—; interim dir. athletics Idaho State U., 1989-90. Editor: The Practical Aspects of Technology Transfer, 1990. Ex officio bd. dirs. Idaho State U. Found., 1983—; bd. dirs. First Security Games of Idaho, 1991—, pres. 1992—, Bannock Boys Baseball, Pocatello, 1989-91, Real Dairy Bowl (formerly Centennial Bowl), 1987—, exec. dir., 1991—; advisor Mortar Bd. Idaho State U., 1988-91. Mem. Nat. Assn. Coll. and Univ. Attys. (bd. dirs. 1990—), Rotary.

WILTSE, CHLORYCE JERENE, home economics and computer science educator, electronics executive; b. Arnolds Park, Iowa, Nov. 25, 1933; d. Carl J. and Leila L. (Gibbs) Ode; m. Gary L. Wiltse, June 9, 1957; children—Mark, Lynn Wiltse Braswell. B.S., U. Nebr., 1955; postgrad. Iowa State, 1982, Mont. State U., 1968-81, U. Mont., 1967-72, Eastern Mont. Coll., 1965. Tchr. home econs. Osceola (Nebr.) High Sch., 1955-57; rural tchr. Billup Sch., Powder River County, Mont., 1957-58; tchr. home econs., computer sci. Powder River High Sch., Broadus, Mont., 1964-83; lectr. computers in home econs. edn., rural family fin. mgmt. telecomputing. Named Mont. Home Econs. Tchr. of Yr., Mont. Home Econs. Assn. and Family Circle mag., 1976, Mont. Outstanding Home Economist, Mont. Home Econs. Assn., 1989. Mem. Mortar Bd., Delta Kappa Gamma, Phi Upsilon Omicron, Omicron Nu, Gamma Alpha Chi, Alpha Lambda Delta, Phi Sigma Chi, Kappa Delta. Republican. Lutheran. Order of Eastern Star. Author publs. in field. Home: PO Box 72 Volborg MT 59351-9998

WIMER, BRUCE MEADE, hematologist, researcher; b. Tuckerton, N.J., Aug. 31, 1922; s. John Wade and Margaret Ellen (Brugh) W.; m. Polly Reynolds Wheaton, Nov. 18, 1950; children: Susan Wheaton Wimer Chapman, Bruce Woodruff, Katherine Wade Wimer Tawney. BS, Franklin and Marshall Coll., 1943; MD, Jefferson Med. Coll., 1946. Diplomate Am. Bd. Internal Medicine and Hematology. Intern Jefferson Med. Coll. Hosp., Phila., 1946-47, resident in internal medicine and hematology, 1948-51; gen. resident Williamsport (Pa.) Hosp., 1947-48; internist, hematologist Guthrie Clinic, Sayre, Pa., 1953-59, Overlook Hosp., Summit, N.J., 1959-60; asst. med. dir. Squibb Inst. Med. Rsch., New Brunswick, N.J., 1960-62; chief sect. hematology-oncology Lovelace Med. Ctr., Albuquerque, 1962-81; assoc. prof. hematology Tex. Tech. U., Lubbock, 1982-89; ind. researcher JBMW Immunotherapeutics, Albuquerque, 1990—. Editorial bd. Molecular Biotherapy, 1991—, Cancer Biotherapy, 1992—; contbr. articles to profl. publs. Capt. U.S. Army, 1951-53. Fellow ACP; mem. AMA., Am. Soc. Hematology, Internat. Soc. Hematology. Republican. Episcopalian. Home and Office: 1609 Catron Ave SE Albuquerque NM 87123-4255

WIMMERS, STEVEN HARRY, accountant; b. Hamilton, Ohio, Aug. 18, 1951; s. Maurice Eugene and Dorothy Ann (Herbers) W.; m. Marille Luree Belshe, Aug. 16, 1974; children: Eric, Brett, Kurt. BS, Ohio State U., 1973. CPA, Calif. Staff acct. Deloitte Haskins & Sells, Columbus, Ohio, 1973, Touche Ross & Co., San Diego, 1973-74; controller H&M Landing, San Diego, 1975-76, Calif. Minicomputer, San Diego and L.A., 1976-80; prin. Steven H. Wimmers, CPA, San Diego, 1977—; treas. Samaritan Ctr., San Diego, 1989-90; treas., chief fin. officer Ocean Frontier Corp., Seattle, 1990—; bd. dirs. YMCA, San Diego. Mem. Mayor's Neighborhood Adv. Com., San Diego, 1983, Western Area Citizen's Adv. Com., San Diego, 1986; chairperson Ocean Beach Planning Bd., San Diego, 1982-84; pres. Ocean Beach Mchts. Assn., San Diego, 1984-86. recipient Svc. to Youth award Ocean Beach Child Care Devel. Ctr., 1985, Community Contbn. award Ocean Beach Town Coun., 1986. Mem. AICPAs, Calif. Soc. CPAs (tax com., mgmt. acctg. com.). Home: 1542 Guizot St San Diego CA 92107-3621 Office: 4870 Santa Monica Ave Ste 2B San Diego CA 92107-4802

WIN, KHIN SWE, anesthesiologist; b. Rangoon, Burma, Sept. 27, 1934; came to U.S., 1962; d. U Mg and Daw Aye (Kyin) Maung; m. M. Shein Win, May 28, 1959; children: Tha Shein, Thwe Shein, Maw Shein, Thet Shein, Htoo Shein. Intermediate of Sci. Degree, U. Rangoon, 1954, MB, BS, 1962. Intern Waltham (Mass.) Hosp., 1962-63; resident anesthesiology Boston City Hosp., 1963-65; fellow pediatric anesthesiology New Eng. Med. Ctr. Hosps., Boston, 1965-66; fellow anesthesiology Martin Luther King Jr. Gen. Hosp., L.A., 1978-79; pvt. practice anesthesiology Apple Valley, Calif., 1984—; asst. prof. anesthesiology Martin Luther King Jr./Charles R. Drew Med. Ctr., L.A., 1979-84. Republican. Buddhist. Home: 13850 Pamlico Rd Apple Valley CA 92307-5400

WINANS, EDGAR VINCENT, academic administrator, consultant, educator; b. Salt Lake City, Apr. 23, 1930; s. Edgar McKinley and Marye (Vincent) W.; m. Patricia Ann Boyce, June 20, 1952; children: Gretchen C., John B. BA in Anthropology, UCLA, 1952, MA in Sociology, 1954, PhD in Anthropology, 1959. Asst. prof. U. Calif., Riverside, 1959-63, assoc. prof., 1963-65; prof. U. Wash., Seattle, 1966—, chair anthropology dept., 1973-75, 93—, chair African studies dept., 1986-92; cons. adviser Ministry of Planning, Nairobi, Kenya, 1972-74; program officer Ford Found. Internat. Div., Nairobi, 1975-78; vis. scholar U. Bergen, Norway, 1990; mem. vis. mission Internat. Labor Orgn., Kenya. Author: Shambala: Constitution of a Traditional State, 1962, (with others) Development Plan, Kenya, 1974; contbr. articles to profl. jours. Bd. dirs. Overlake Sch., Redmond, Wash., 1974-90. Social Sci. Rsch. Coun. fellow, 1956-58, Haines Found. fellow, 1958; NSF grantee, 1962-69, NIH grantee, 1964-66, Rockefeller Found. grantee, 1975-76. Fellow Am. Anthropologist Assn., Am. Ethnological Soc., Royal Anthropological Inst. of Great Britain, Sigma Xi; mem. Tanzania Soc. Office: U Wash Dept of Anthropology DH-05 Seattle WA 98195

WINARSKI, DANIEL JAMES, mechanical engineer; b. Toledo, Dec. 16, 1948; s. Daniel Edward and Marguerite (Pietersien) W.; BS in Engring., U. Mich., 1970, PhD (NSF fellow), 1976; MS, U. Colo., 1973; m. Donna Ilene Robinson, Oct. 10, 1970; 1 son, Tyson York. Mech. engr. Libbey Owens Ford Co., Toledo, summers 1968, 69, 72; petroleum engr. Exxon Production Research, Houston, 1976-77; staff engr. mech. engring. sect. IBM Adstar, Tucson, 1977-84, adv. engr., 1984-86, systems engr., performance evaluator, 1986—; assoc. prof. dept. civil/mech. engring. U.S. Mil. Acad., 1980—; instr. minority computer edn. No. Ariz. U., 1983-85. Served to 1st lt. U.S. Army, 1970-72; lt. col., Res., 1991. Recipient 10 IBM Invention Achievement award, 1981-93, IBM Mfg. award, 1986; registered profl. engr., Ariz., Colo. Mem. ASME (pub. chmn. U. Mich. 1974), Phi Eta Sigma, Pi Tau Sigma, Tau Beta Pi. Republican. Methodist. Designer adjustable artificial leg; patentee tape reel hub, tape loose-wrap check, tape reel sizing, tape reel-cartridge, calibrating optical disk drives, automated storage library. Office: IBM Adstar 67E/060-1 Tucson AZ 85744

WINCHELL, ROBERT ALLEN, government agency administrator, accountant; b. Ft. Monmouth, N.J., Oct. 28, 1945; s. Robert Winslow Winchell; B.A., U. Calif., Santa Barbara, 1967; M.B.A., U. Pa., 1969. CPA, Calif. Air Force Audit Agy., El Segundo, Calif., 1972-73; accountant Scholefield, Bellanca & Co., W. Los Angeles, 1974-75, So. Calif. Gas Co., Los Angeles, 1975-76; auditor Def. Contract Audit Agy., Dept. Def., Los Angeles, 1976-86, supervisory auditor, 1986—. Served with AUS, 1969-71; Vietnam. Decorated Bronze Star. Mem. Assn. Govt. Accountants, Am. Inst. C.P.A.'s, Alpha Kappa Psi. Republican. Presbyterian. Club: Los Angeles Country. Home: 2008 California Ave Santa Monica CA 90403-4506

WINCOR, MICHAEL Z., psychopharmacology educator, clinician, researcher; b. Chgo., Feb. 9, 1946; s. Emanuel and Rose (Kershner) W.; m. Emily E.M. Smythe; children: Meghan Heather, Katherine Rose. SB in Zoology, U. Chgo., 1966; PharmD, U. So. Calif., 1978. Rsch. project specialist U. Chgo. Sleep Lab., 1968-75; psychiat. pharmacist Brotman Med. Ctr., Culver City, Calif., 1979-83; asst. prof. U. So. Calif., L.A., 1983—; cons. Fed. Bur. Prisons Drug Abuse Program, Terminal Island, Calif., 1978-81, Nat. Inst. Drug Abuse, Bethesda, Md., 1981, The Upjohn Co., Kalamazoo, 1982-87, 91-92, Area XXIV Profl. Standards Rev. Orgn., L.A., 1983, Brotman Med. Ctr., Culver City, Calif., 1983-88, SmithKline Beecham Pharms., Phila., 1990—, Tokyo Coll. of Pharmacy, 1991. Contbr. over 30 articles to profl. jours., chpts. to books, papers presented at nat. and internat. meetings and reviewer. Mem. adv. coun. Franklin Ave. Sch., 1986-89; bd. dirs. K.I. Children's Ctr., 1988-89; trustee the Sequoyah Sch., 1992-93. Recipient Cert. Appreciation, Mayor of L.A., 1981, Bristol Labs Award, 1978; Faculty scholar U. So. Calif. Sch. Pharmacy, 1978. Mem. Am. Coll. Clin. Pharmacy (chmn. constn. and bylaws com. 1983-84, mem. credentials com. 1991-93), Am. Assn. Colls. Pharmacy (focus group on liberalization of the profl. curriculum), Am. Soc. Hosp. Pharmacists (chmn. edn. and tng. adv. working group 1985-88), Am. Pharm. Assn. (del. ann. meeting ho. dels. 1989), Sleep Rsch. Soc., Am. Sleep Disorders Assn., U. So. Calif. Sch. Pharmacy Alumni Assn. (bd. dirs. 1979—), Rho Chi. Office: U So Calif 1985 Zonal Ave Los Angeles CA 90033-1086

WINDER, DAVID KENT, federal judge; b. Salt Lake City, June 8, 1932; s. Edwin Kent and Alma Eliza (Cannon) W.; m. Pamela Martin, June 24, 1955; children: Ann, Kay, James. BA, U. Utah, 1955; LLB, Stanford U., 1958. Bar: Utah 1958, Calif. 1958. Assoc. firm Clyde, Mecham & Pratt Salt Lake City, 1958-66; law clk. to chief justice Utah Supreme Ct., 1958-59; dep. county atty. Salt Lake County, 1959-63; chief dep. dist. atty., 1965-66; asst. U.S. atty. Salt Lake City, 1963-65; partner firm Strong & Hanni, Salt Lake City, 1966-77; judge U.S. Dist. Ct., Dist. Utah, Salt Lake City, 1979—; examiner Utah Bar Examiners, 1975-79, chmn., 1977-79. Served with USAF, 1951-52. Mem. Am. Bd. Trial Advocates, Utah State Bar (Judge of Yr. award 1978), Salt Lake County Bar Assn., Calif. State Bar. Democrat. Office: US Dist Ct 235 US Courthouse 324 S State St Ste 105 Salt Lake City UT 84111-2321

WINDHAM, EDWARD JAMES, bank executive, leasing company executive; b. Salt Lake City, Dec. 13, 1950; s. James Rudolph and Margaret Ann (Griffith) W.; m. Marilyn Ann Kenyon, Mar. 27, 1973; children: Ian James (dec.), Kendra Ann. Student, U. Calif., San Diego, 1969-70, 72-74, U. Calif., Santa Barbara, 1970-72. Cert. mortgage credit examiner HUD. Salesman Bonanza Properties, Tustin, Calif., 1976; loan officer Medallion Mortgage, Santa Cruz, Calif., 1976-80; sr. loan officer Cen. Pacific Mortgage, Santa Cruz, 1980-83, v.p., 1983-86; ptnr. Winn Leasing Co., Santa Cruz, 1983-90; v.p. Community West Mortgage, 1986-89, Central Pacific Mortgage, Citrus Heights, Calif., 1989—; cons. Contour Inc., San Jose, Calif., 1983-85. Pres. Evergreen Estates Homeowners Assn., Soquel, Calif., 1983-85. No. Calif. State champion #3 Nat. Age Group award Am. Bicycle Assn., 1991. Mem. Nat. Assn. Rev. Appraisers and Rev. Underwriters (sr., cert.), Mortgage Bankers Assn., Calif. Mortgage Bankers Assn., Mensa, Intertel. Republican. Lodge: Masons (master Santa Cruz 1987). Home: 1610 Dana Way Roseville CA 95661-4728 Office: Central Pacific Mortgage 5620 Birdcage St Ste 230 Citrus Heights CA 95610

WINDOM, ROBERT NEAL, JR., contractor, consultant, planner; b. Birmingham, Ala., Sept. 23, 1947; s. Robert Neal Sr. and Frances Elizabeth (Winn) W. AA, Young Harris Coll., 1967; BA, Birmingham So. Coll., 1969; MDiv, Emory U., 1973. Lic. gen. contractor, Hawaii; ordained deacon United Meth. Ch., 1970-75. Rsch. asst. Anesthesia Rsch. Woodruff Ctr. Emory U., Atlanta, 1970-71; inner city min. Bd. Inner City Ministries North Ga. Conf. of United Meth. Ch., Atlanta, 1970-75; with emergency claims Crawford & Co. Ins. Adjusters, Atlanta, 1971-72; owner Windom Woodwork, Atlanta, 1976-87; pres. Windom Constrn. Co., Honolulu, 1989—; asst. planner and rsch. asst. State of Ga. Merit System, 1976. Chmn. parks and environment com. Area Planning Unit, Atlanta, 1976-78; staff corr. Nat. Dem. Campaign Com., Atlanta, 1976; project supr. Lower East Side Habitat for Humanity, N.Y.C., 1984. Mem. Building Industries Assn. Hawaii (bd. dirs. 1993), Constrn. Specifications Inst., Associated Builders and Contractors Hawaii, Hawaii Remodelers Coun., Comml. Builders Coun., Hawaii C. of C. Office: Windom Constrn Co 1200 College Walk Ste 202 Honolulu HI 96817

WINEBERG, HOWARD, director research; b. N.Y.C., Aug. 30, 1955; s. Moe and Ruth (Blinder) W. BA, Bowling Green (Ohio) State U., 1977, MA, 1980; PhD, Johns Hopkins U., 1985. Demographer Indian Nations Coun. of Govts., Tulsa, 1985; asst. dir. Population Rsch. Ctr., assoc. prof. urban studies and planning Portland (Oreg.) State U., 1986—; co-founder Oreg. Demographic Group, Portland, 1990; Oreg. rep. to Fed.-State Coop. Program for Population Estimates, 1986—. Author: Population Estimates for Oregon 1980-90, 91, 92; contbr. articles to profl. jours. Johns Hopkins U. fellow, 1980-82; Children's Svcs. Commn., grantee, 1989. Mem. APHA, Population Assn. Am., Population Reference Bur., Soc. for the Study of Social Biology, Internat. Soc. for Philos. Enquiry, So. Demographic Assn., Oreg. Acad. Sci. Office: Portland State U Population Rsch Ctr 632 SW Hall St Portland OR 97201-5215

WINECOFF, DAVID FLEMING, real estate broker; b. Shanghai, Peoples Republic China, Aug. 12, 1939; s. Joseph L. and Catherane Ann (Challacombe) W.; m. Wanda Julie Carlson, June 15, 1963 (div. May 1990); children: Mary, Mark, Steven, Scott. BA, U. Wash., 1962; MA, Pepperdine U., 1977. Lic. real estate broker. Commd. 2d lt. USMC, 1962, advanced through ranks to lt. col., 1979, retired, 1983; profl. writer, speaker, 1983-84; sales rep. Chuck Olsen, 1985; assoc. realtor D.A. Duryee, 1985-87; assoc. broker Coldwell Banker, 1987-88; mktg. rep. City U., Bellevue, Wash., 1988; assoc. broker Prudential Richard James Realtors, Everett, Wash., 1989-92; dir. Mill Creek (Wash.) Wellness Ctr., 1992—. Contbr. articles to profl. jours. City councilman Mill Creek, 1988—; precinct capt. 44th dist. Rep. Cen. Com., Wash., 1991-92, candidate U.S Ho. of Reps., 1988; mem. Pointman Ministries. Lt. col. USMCR, 1983-92. Decorated Silver Star USN, 1969; named Rookie Yr. Am. Heart Assn., 1987-88; recipient Armed Forces Vets. Community Svc. Award Snohomish County Coun., 1989. Roman Catholic. Home: 15212 Bothell Way SE # F-332 Bothell WA 98012 Office: Mill Creek Wellness Ctr 17707 15th Ave SE Ste C Mill Creek WA 98012

WING, G(EORGE) MILTON, educator, mathematician; b. Rochester, N.Y., Jan. 21, 1923; s. George O. and Louise (Weiss) W.; m. Nina A. John, June 7, 1958 (div. Nov. 1970); m. Janet Sweedyk Bendt, Aug. 26, 1972 (div. Jan. 1987). B.A., U. Rochester, 1944, M.S., 1947; Ph.D., Cornell U., 1949. Staff mem. Los Alamos Nat. Lab., 1945-46, 51-58, 81-87, Sandia Lab., Albuquerque, 1959-64; faculty UCLA, 1949-52, U. N.Mex., 1958-59; prof. applied math. U. Colo., Boulder, 1964-66; prof. math. U. N.Mex., Albuquerque., 1966-73; chmn. dept. math. So. Meth. U., Dallas, 1977-78; prof. So. Meth. U., 1978-80; cons. Rand Corp., 1958-65, Sandia Corp., 1958-59, E.H. Plesset & Assos., 1958-59, 64-67, Los Alamos Sci. Lab., 1958-59, 64-81, 87—, U. So. Calif. Project on Applications Math. to Medicine, 1970-73; vis. prof. Tex. Tech. U., Lubbock, 1975-76. Author: An Introduction to Transport Theory, 1962, (with R.C. Allen, Jr.) Problems for a Computer-Oriented Calculus Course, 1973, (with Richard Bellman) An Introduction to Invariant Imbedding, 1975; Assoc. editor: (with Richard Bellman) Jour. Math. Analysis and Applications, 1969-86, (with P. Nelson) Transport Theory and Statistical Physics, 1983. Mem. Am. Math. Soc., Math. Assn. Am., Soc. Indsl. and Applied Math. (vis. lectr. 1961-62, 64-66), Phi Beta Kappa, Sigma Xi. Home: 262 Camino De La Sierra Santa Fe NM 87501-1175

WING, ROGER, management consultant; b. N.Y.C., May 26, 1945; s. John A. and Norma M. (LeBlanc) W.; m. Judith A. King, June 7, 1963 (div. 1980); m. Peggy J. McFall, Aug. 27, 1983; children: Roger, Karin, Nicole, Sean, Nathan. BBA, Cleve. State U., 1972, MBA, 1975. Supr. Am. Greetings Co., Brooklyn, Ohio, 1969-74; dir. Revco D.S. Inc., Twinsburg, Ohio, 1974-78; mgr. Hughes Aircraft Co., Los Angeles, 1978-79; sr. dir. Continental Airlines, Los Angeles, 1979-81; dir. Coopers & LyBrand, Los Angeles, 1981-83; pres. Huntington Cons. Group, Huntington Beach, Calif., 1983—; prof. Cleve. State U., 1977-78. Named Systems Man of Yr., Assn. Systems Mgmt., 1978. Office: The Huntington Cons Group 8531 Topside Cir Huntington Beach CA 92646-2117

WINGATE, MARCEL EDWARD, speech educator; b. New Castle, Pa., Feb. 27, 1923; s. Morton Harvey and Elizabeth (Martin) Wingett; m. Elaine C. Kayser, June 8, 1948 (div. July 1968); children: Nancy, Amy, Jennifer; m. Cicely Anne Johnston, June 7, 1969; children: Marcel Richard, Cicely Anna Marie. BA, Grinnell (Iowa) Coll., 1948; MA, U. Wash., 1952, PhD, 1956. Lic. psychologist, Wash., N.Y. Psychologist Childrens Hosp., Seattle, 1953-57, Wash. State C.P. Ctr., Seattle, 1954-57; asst. prof. U. Wash., Seattle, 1957-65, assoc. prof., 1965-68; prof. SUNY, Buffalo, 1968-73, U. Ariz., Tucson, 1973-75; prof. speech, hearing sci. Wash. State U., Pullman, 1975—; cons. psychologist St. Mary's Hosp., Lewiston, N.Y., 1969-73. Author: Stuttering: Theory and Treatment, 1976, Structure of Stuttering, 1988; assoc. editor Jour. Speech/Hearing Disorders, 1966-73; editorial cons. Jour. Speech/Hearing Rsch., 1974-80; editorial bd. Jour. Fluency Disorders, 1974—; contbr. articles to profl. jours., chpts. to books. With U.S. Army, 1942-45, ETO. Fellow Am. Speech and Hearing Assn. Home: RR 2 Box 102 Pullman WA 99163-9605 Office: Wash State U Speech and Hearing Sci Pullman WA 99164

WINGER, MARC ALLAN, school district administrator; b. Cleve., Oct. 1, 1951; s. Robert Jack and Ruth (Felder) W.; m. Eileen S. Mann, Dec. 24, 1982; children: Seth, Evan. BA, U. Calif., Berkeley, 1973; MEd, UCLA, 1980, EdD, 1992. Cert. sch. adminstr., Calif. Tchr. Newhall (Calif.) Sch. Dist., 1974-83; prin. Burbank (Calif.) Unified Sch. Dist., 1983-86; asst. supt. Sulphur Springs Sch. Dist., Canyon Country, Calif., 1986—. Contbr. articles to profl. jours. Mem. Drug/Alcohol Prevention Edn. Com., Santa Clarita, Calif.; bd. dirs. Santa Clarita Repertory Theatre. Recipient Who award Calif. Tchrs. Assn., 1979. Mem. Assn. Calif. Sch. Adminstrs., Santa Clarita Valley Adminstrs. Assn. (v.p. 1990, Outstanding award 1988, Svc. award 1989). Home: 23308 Cedartown St Newhall CA 91321

WINGET, CHARLES MERLIN, comparative physiologist; b. Garden City, Kans., Dec. 26, 1925; s. Charles Ansel and Ruth May (Coburn) W.; m. Katherin H. Barkas, Oct. 31, 1976; children: Jean Ann, JoAnne, Steven Charles, Eleni Ruth. AA in Bus. Adminstrn., San Francisco City Coll., 1948; BA in Biol. Sci., San Francisco State Coll., 1951; PHD in Comparative Physiology, U. Calif., Berkeley/Davis, 1957. Chemist U. Calif., Davis, 1951-53, fellow in physiology, 1953-59; assoc. prof. Ont. Agrl. Coll., Guelph, 1959-63; rsch. scientist NASA/Ames Rsch. Ctr., Moffett Field, Calif., 1963-87, sci. mgr. Space Sta., 1985-86, IML-1 payload scientist, 1985—; assoc. clin. prof. Wright State U., Dayton, Ohio, 1982—; prof. pharmacology Fla. A&M U., Tallahassee, 1975—; lectr. U. Calif., Davis, 1964—. Editor: Chronopharmacology, 1981, Microgravity at College Level, 1989; author book chpt. Sports medicine advisor U.S. Olympic Com., 1982-84, 88-91; mem. aero. systems com. USAF, San Antonio, 1982-84. With USN, 1944-46, PTO. NIH rsch. fellow, 1957. Mem. Aerospace Med. Assn. (Arnould D. Tuttle award 1982), Endocrine Soc., Am. Physiol. Soc., Biophys. Soc., Poultry Scis. Assn., Sigma Xi. Office: NASA/Ames Rsch Ctr 236-5 Moffett Field CA 94035-1000

WINGET, RODNER REED, marine biologist, biochemist; b. Mpls., Aug. 1, 1936; s. Earl Tallman and Dee (Rodner) W.; children: Laura Anne, Carol Anne. BS, Fla. State U., 1962; MS, San Diego State U., 1968; PhD, U. Minn., 1976. Resident biologist Coll. Marine Studies U. Del., Lewes, 1969-71; postdoctoral fellow Sch. Medicine U. Minn., Mpls., 1976-77, U. Wash., 1977-78; dir. natural resources Small Tribes Orgn. Western Wash., Sumner, 1978-82; mng. ptnr. Fisheries Devel. Assn., Redmond, Wash., 1982-86; founder, dir. rsch. BioMarine Techs., Inc., Seattle, 1987—, also bd. dirs. Editor: Integration: Problems and Promises in Northwest Seafood Industry, 1981; contbr. articles to profl. publs.; program producer KBCS-FM, Bellevue, 1989-90. Bd. dirs. Seattle Storytelling Guild, 1990-91; mem. fellowship com. Univ. Congl. Ch., Seattle, 1990—. With USN, 1956-58. Recipient Pub. Health Rsch. awards NIH, 1977-78, Small Bus. Innovation Rsch. awards, 1988, 90, 91, 92, 93. Home: 13265 89th Ave S Renton WA 98055 Office: 4459 S 134th Pl Seattle WA 98168

WINGO, MICHAEL, artist, educator; b. L.A.; s. W.R. and Katie Lois (Hall) Mahan. BA, Claremont McKenna Coll., 1964; BFA, MFA, Otis Art Inst., L.A., 1967; 1985. Instr. Pasadena (Calif.) Art Mus., 1968-72, Otis Art Inst./Parsons Sch. Design, L.A., 1984-92; instr. Calif. State Summer Sch. Arts Calarts, Loyola Marymount U., L.A., 1987, 88; vis. artist San Francisco Art Inst., 1987, guest lectr., 1984. Prin. works exhibited in numerous one-man shows including Terry DeLapp Gallery, L.A., 1985, Janet Steinberg Gallery, San Francisco, 1984, Turnbull Lutjeans Kogan Gallery, Costa Mesa, Calif., 1983, Newport Harbor Art Mus., Newport Beach, Calif., 1976, Santa Barbara Mus. Art, 1970, others; works represented in numerous pub. and pvt. collections; contbr. works to profl. publs. NEA Visual Artists fellow in painting, 1989-90; Adolph and Esther Gottlieb Found. grantee in painting, 1992. Office: 7051 N Figueroa St Los Angeles CA 90042-1276

WINGO, ROBERT DEAN, motion picture set decorator; b. Phila., Aug. 19, 1949; s. Robert Dean Wingo Sr. and Philomena (Ciardelli) Chaffin. BS in Interior Design summa cum laude, Woodbury U., 1978. Art dir. No. Communications, Los Angeles, 1976; set decorator Universal City (Calif.) Studios, 1978—. Nominated Emmy awards Acad. TV Arts and Scis., Burbank, 1984, 85, 86, 88, 89, 90. Mem. Acad. TV. Arts and Scis. (Nominated Emmy award 1984, 85, 86, 88, 89, 90), Am. Film Inst., Internat. Alliance Theatrical and Stage Employees, Amnesty Internat. Democrat. Office: Universal City Studios 100 Universal City Plz Universal City CA 91608-1002

WINKLER, AGNIESZKA M., advertising agency executive; b. Rome, Italy, Feb. 22, 1946; came to U.S., 1953, naturalized, 1959; d. Wojciech A. and Halina Z. (Owsiany) W.; children from previous marriage: children: Renata G. Sworakowski, Dana C Sworakowski.; m. Arthur K. Lund. BA, Coll. Holy Name, 1967; MA, San Jose State U., 1971; MBA, U. Santa Clara, 1981. Teaching asst., San Jose State U., 1968-70; cons. to ea. European bus., Palo Alto, Calif., 1970-72; pres./founder Commart Communications, Palo Alto, 1973-84; pres./founder, chmn. bd. Winkler McManus, Santa Clara, Calif., 1984—; bd. dirs. Supercuts, Inc. Trustee Tech. Mus. Innovation, 1991—, Santa Clara U., 1991—; trustee O'Connor Found., 1987—, mem. exec. com., 1988—, mem. Capital Campaign steering com., 1989; mem. nat. adv. bd. Comprehensive Health Enhancement Support System, 1991; mem. mgmt. west com. A.A.A.A. Agy., 1991; project dir. Poland Free Enterprise Plan, 1989—; mem. adv. bd. Normandy France Bus. Devel., 1989—; mem. bd. regents Holy Names Coll., 1987—; mem. adv. bd. Nat. Assn Bus. Deans Jesuit Insts.; chair emeritus, mem. adv. bd. Leavey Sch. Bus. and Adminstrn. Univ. Santa Clara, 1989—; bd. dirs. San Jose Mus. Art, 1987; mem. San Jose Symphony, Gold Baton, 1986; mem. nat. adv. com. CHESS, 1991—. Recipient CLIO award in Advt., Addy award and numerous others. Mem. Family Svc. Assn. (trustee 1980-82), Am. Assn. Advt. Agys. (agy. mgmt. west com. 1991), Bus. Profl. Advt. Assn., Polish Am. Congress, San Jose Advt. Club, San Francisco Ad Club, Beta Gamma Sigma (hon.), Pi Gamma Mu, Pi Delta Phi (Lester-Tinneman award 1966, Bill Raskob Found. grantee 1965). Office: Winkler McManus 150 Spear St 16th Fl San Francisco CA 94105-1535

WINKLER, DAVID ARTHUR, army officer; b. Joliet, Ill., Aug. 6, 1952; s. Lester George Winkler and Doris Rosaline (Jones) Winkler Gabel; m. Rachelle Louise Werme, Feb. 12, 1979. BA, Southern Ill. U., 1974; MA, Boston U., 1989. Enlisted U.S. Army, 1974; intelligence ops. officer U.S. Army, Ft. Lewis, Wash., 1990—. Decorated Commendation medal, Achievement medal, Nat. Def. medal, SW Asia Campaign medal, Kuwait Liberation medal. Mem. Am. Assn. Advancement Slavic Studies, Am. Mil. Inst., Am. Acad. Polit. and Social Scis., Acad. Polit. Sci., U.S. Strategic Inst., Fgn. Policy Rsch. Inst., Air Force Assn., U.S. Naval Inst. Home: 13313 119th Avenue Ct E Puyallup WA 98374-4616 Office: PO Box 33176 Tacoma WA 98433-0176

WINKLER, HOWARD LESLIE, investment banker, stockbroker, business consultant; b. N.Y.C., N.Y., Aug. 16, 1950; s. Martin and Magda (Stark) W.; m. Robin Lynn Richards, Sept. 12, 1976; 1 child, David Menachem. AA in Mktg., Los Angeles City Coll., 1973, AA in Bus. Data Processing, 1977, AA in Bus. Mgmt., 1981. Sr. cons. Fin. Cons. Inc., Los Angeles, 1972-81; asst. v.p. Merrill Lynch, Inc., Los Angeles, 1981-83; v.p. Drexel, Burnham, Lambert, Inc., Beverly Hills, Calif., 1983-84; pres. Howard Winkler Investments, Beverly Hills, Calif., 1984—; ptnr. N.W.B. Assocs., L.A., 1988-91; chmn. bd. United Community and Housing Devel. Corp., L.A.; bd. dirs. Earth Products Internat., Inc., Kansas City, Kans., 1992, Fed. Home Loan Bank of San Francisco, 1991—. Nat. polit. editor B'nai Brith Messenger, 1986—. Mem. Calif. Rep. Cent. Com., 1985-93; mem. L.A. County Rep. Cent. Com., 1985-92, chmn. 45th Assembly Dist., 1985-90; mem. Rep. Senatorial Inner Circle, 1986—, Rep. Presdl. Task Force, 1985— (Legion of Merit award 1992); mem. Rep. Eagles, 1988-92; Nat. Rep. Senatorial Com., 1986—, Golden Circle Calif., 1986—, Sen. Inner Circle, 1986—, GOP Platform Planning Com. at Large del., 1992; del.to GOP nat conv., Houston, 1992; chmn. Jack Kemp for Pres., Calif., 1988, mem. nat. steering com. Bush-Quayle '88, 1987, nat. exec. com. Bush-Quayle '92, 1991; mil. adminstrv. supr. CID US Army, 1969-72, SE Asia; legis. and civic action Agudath Israel Calif., 1985—; mem. L.A. County Narcotics and Dangerous Drugs Commn., 1988—; trustee, sec.-treas. Minority Health Professions Edn. Found., 1989—; program chmn. Calif. Lincoln Clubs Polit. Action Com., 1987-88; state chmn. Pete Wilson for Gov. Campaign, 1989, John Seymour for Lt. Gov. Campaign, 1989-90; chpt. pres. Calif. Congress of Reps., 1989—; chmn. Claude Parrish for Bd. of Equalization, 1989-90; founder, dir. Community Rsch. & Info. Ctr.; mem. fin. com. John Seymour for Senate '92, 1991; mem. Rep. Presdl. Task Force 1985—, Legion of Merit award 1992; state chmn. Kemp for Pres. '88, 1987. Recipient Community Service award Agudath Israel Calif., 1986, President's Community Leadership award, 1986, Disting. Community Service US. Senator Pete Wilson, 1986, Calif. Gov.'s Leadership award, 1986, Community Service award U.S. Congresswoman Bobbi Fiedler, 1986, Resolution of Commendation Calif. State Assembly, 1986, Outstanding Community Service Commendation Los Angeles County Bd. Suprs., 1986, 90, Outstanding Citizenship award City of Los Angeles, 1986, 90. Mem. Calif. Young Reps., Calif. Rep. Assembly, VFW, Jewish War Veterans. Jewish. Office: Howard Winkler Investments PO Box 480454 Los Angeles CA 90048

WINKLER, JOSEPH MARK, aeronautical engineer; b. Brooklyn, N.Y., Nov. 15, 1952; s. Leonard Charles and Ann (Zucker) W.; m. Debra Jo Staub, May 21, 1983; children: Jamie Suzanne, Brandon Edward. AAS in Aerospace Design, Acad. Aeronautics, 1973; BSCE, U. New Orleans, 1979; M in Mech. Engring., U. Colo., 1991. Reg. profl. engr., Ohio, Colo. Sr. engr. Martin Marietta, New Orleans, 1973-82; task mgr. structures Perkin Elmer, Danbury, Conn., 1982-84; engr., CAE rep. Gen. Electric, Cin., 1984—; pvt. practice engring. Denver, 1984-88; sr. staff engr. Martin Marietta Astronautics, Denver, 1988—. Mem. Am. Inst. Aero. Astronautics (officer student chpt. 1971-73, photographer New Orleans chpt. 1980-82), Acad. Aeronautics Alumni Assn. (founders award 1973), U. Colo. Alumni Assn., Bklyn. Tech. High Sch. Alumni Assn. Democrat. Jewish. Home: 13722 Tradition St San Diego CA 92128

WINKLER, MARJORIE EVERETT, protein chemist, researcher; b. Suffern, N.Y., July 19, 1954; d. Lucius Theodore and Marian Florence (Greenwood) E.; m. James Roy Winkler, Aug. 23, 1975 (div. 1985); m. Paul Frank Hohenschuh, May 31, 1987; children: William Everett, Charles Theodore. BS, SUNY, Buffalo, 1975, PhD, 1980. Postdoctoral researcher MIT, Cambridge, 1980-82; scientist Genentech Inc., South San Francisco, Calif., 1982-89, sr. scientist, 1989—. Contbr. to profl. publs. NIH fellow, 1980-82. Mem. Am. Chem. Soc., Phi Beta Kappa, Sigma Xi. Home: 2884 Canyon Rd Burlingame CA 94010 Office: Genentech Inc 460 Point San Bruno Blvd South San Francisco CA 94080

WINKLER, RALPH EUGENE, real estate investor; b. Elkville, Ill., Feb. 3, 1927; s. Hugh Stelle and Vesta M. (Schimpf) W.; m. Margaret Mae Novaria, Dec. 30, 1981; 1 child by previous marriage: Esther Marie Milligan. BS in Mgmt., U. Ill., 1950; postgrad., DePaul U., Chgo., 1957-58. Lic. real estate broker, Calif. Commd. U.S. Air Force, 1950, advanced through grades to maj., 1970; comdr. Office of Spl. Investigations, Edwards AFB, Calif., 1963-66; agt.-in-charge OSI Investigations Unit, N.Y.C., 1967; comdr. OSI, Greenland, 1968; staff responsibility, counterintelligence in 5-state Midwestern area USAF, 1969-70; ret.; real estate investor, 1956—. Author numerous genealogical papers on ancestry of Winkler and related families. Nat. chmn. N.O.S.I. (orgn. to oppose Panama Canal Treaties), 1977-79; mem. Rep. Cen. Com., Orange County, Calif., 1977-83; mem. San Diego County Rep. Cen. Com., 1988-89, Lakeside Community Planning Group, 1987-88; Rep. Party chmn. City of Los Alamitos, Calif., 1982-83; Rep. candidate Calif. Sec. of State 1986 primary; dep. senatorial dist. dir. Calif. Rep. Assy., 1978-79; camp program dir., asst. dist. commr. Far East Coun. Japan Boys Scouts Am., 1954-55. Awarded Commendatory Resolution by Calif. State Senate Rules Com., 1979; recipient Air Force Meritorious Svc. medal. Mem. Am. Legion (post historian 1976-77), VFW (del. to Calif. state, nat. convs. 1982), SAR. Methodist. Home and Office: 10332 Escadera Dr Lakeside CA 92040

WINKLESS, NELSON BROCK, III, communications company executive; b. Milw., July 2, 1934; s. Nelson Brock Jr. and Ethel Lucille (Withrow) W.; m. Madge Harvey, Nov. 23, 1955; children: Chantal, Nelson Brock IV, Danielle, Garth. BA in Russian, East European studies, U. Calif., Berkeley, 1956. Writer, dir. Pilot Prodns., Inc., Evanston, Ill., 1958-60; ind. cons. San francisco, 1960; prodn. coord. FilmFair, Inc., Hollywood, Calif., 1961-63; founder, pres. Communications Contact, Inc., various locations, Calif., 1963-68; v.p. Thomas Bede Found., Albuquerque, 1968-77; pres. Farm Info. Machinery, Ltd., Albuquerque, 1978-79, ABQ Communications Corp., Albuquerque, 1978—; founder, cons. Excalibur Technologies Corp., Albuquerque, 1980-85; cons. Microbics Corp., Carlsbad, Calif., 1986—, Interlearn Corp., West Linn, Oreg., 1990—. Co-author: Climate and The Affairs of Men, 1975, Robots on Your Doorstep, 1978; author: If I Had A Robot, 1984, (as A.B. Quist): Excuse Me, What Was That?, 1980; founding editor Personal Computing Mag., Albuquerque, 1976-77; patentee dynamic game bd.; contbr. articles to various publs. Mem. Nat. Personal Robot Assn. (founding bd. dirs. 1986-89). Office: ABQ Communications Corp PO Box 1432 Corrales NM 87048-1432

WINN, ALFRED VERNON, chemistry educator; b. Galt, Calif., Mar. 15, 1915; s. Henry August and Luella Irene (Moon) W.; m. Helen Margaret Corey, June 3, 1940; children: Alfred Vernon Jr., Kenneth Gerald. BS, Pacific Union Coll., 1938; MS, U. Wash., 1950; PhD, Stanford U., 1959. Prin. El Centro (Calif.) Jr. Acad., 1938-41; tchr. Auburn (Wash.) Acad., 1941-49; tchr. Can. Union Coll., College Heights, Alberta, Can., 1950-54, adminstr., 1953-54; tchr. Pacific Union Coll., Angwin, Calif., 1954-80, dept. chmn., 1960-86, acad. dean, 1983-84, assoc. acad. dean, 1985-90; tchr. Antillian Coll., Mayaguez, P.R., 1980-82. Mem. Am. Chem. Soc., Sigma Xi. mem. Seventh-Day Adventist Ch. Home: 235 Cold Springs Rd Angwin CA 94508

WINN, DARYL NORMAN, business educator; b. Eugene, Oreg., Dec. 20, 1941; s. Thomas and Leola (Snyder) W.; m. Elizabeth Lytton Cox, Nov. 4, 1965; children: David Scott, Thomas Gordon. BS, Ariz. State U., 1964; MBA, U. Mich., 1964-68, PhD, 1970. Chair div. bus. environ. and polity U. Colo., Boulder, 1980-84; asst. prof. Coll. Bus. U. Colo, Boulder, 1970-76, assoc. prof., 1976—. Author: Industrial Market, 1971. Mem. Boulder Country Club (pres. 1993, bd. dirs. 1990—).

WINN, IRA JAY, education and urban studies educator, consultant; b. Boston, Feb. 15, 1929; m. Arlene Winn; 1 child, Ian Muir. BA, U. Ill., 1950, MA, 1952; EdD, U. Calif., L.A., 1966. Prof. Calif. State U., Northridge, 1966—; project dir., asst. Peace Corps tng. U. Calif., San Diego, 1966; edn. planner U.S. AID/Brazilian Ministry, Rio de Janeiro, 1967-70; tchr. L.A. City Schs., 1955-62; mem. tng. staff Teach for Am., 1992, 93; environ. impact cons. Laramie Energy Tech. Ctr., Wyo., 1980; cons. EPA, Jerusalem, 1977; presenter at numerous confs. on edn., environment and pub. policy. Author: Basic Issues in Environment, 1972; contbr. numerous articles and photo. essays to profl. jours., mags. Fulbright grantee Germany, 1974, Zimbabwe, Botswana, Malawi, 1991; NEH fellow Middlebury (Vt.) Coll., 1986. Office: Calif State U Monterey Hall 230 Northridge CA 91330

WINN, ROBERT CHARLES, retired military officer, aeronautical engineer, consultant; b. Chgo., Sept. 4, 1945; s. Bart James and Dorothy Eleanor (Smith) W.; m. Kathleen Nowak, Aug. 3, 1968; children: Eric Michael, Kara Michelle. BSME, U. Ill., 1968, MSME, 1969; PhD in Mech. Engring., Colo. State U., 1982. Registered profl. engr., Colo. Enlisted USAF, 1969, advanced through grades to lt. col., 1991; instr. pilot 14 student squad USAF, Columbus AFB, Mo., 1970-74; instr. pilot 61 Tactical Airlift Squad USAF, Little Rock AFB, 1974-76; asst. prof. dept. aeronautics USAF Acad., Colorado Springs, Colo., 1976-79, assoc. prof., 1982-90; chief scientist USAF European Office of Aerospace R&D, London, 1986-88; prof. USAF Acad., 1988-91; adj. prof. Colo. Tech. Coll., 1991—; cons. Colorado Springs, 1991—. Contbr. articles to profl. jours. Mem. AIAA (assoc. fellow, vice chmn. Rocky Mountain sect. 1985, sec. 1984, mem. terrestrial energy systems nat. tech. com. 1984-91, dep. dir. energy conversion 1989—); mem. Am. Soc. Engring. Edn. Roman Catholic. Office: 410 Silver Spring Cir Colorado Springs CO 80919

WINN, SUZANNE BARBARA, marketing professional; b. Passaic, N.J., Feb. 11, 1957; d. Roger Emmett and Claire Louise (Nicholson) Behre; m. Mitchell D. Winn, May 13, 1978; children: Casey Anne, Amanda Christine. BS in Communications, U. Idaho, 1992. Asst. mgr. Jay Jacobs Clothing, Moscow, Idaho, 1980, Small World Toys and Pets, Moscow, 1980-81; mgr. Fitness Unlimited, Moscow, 1983-87; office mgr., exec. asst. Moscow C. of C., 1987-89; sales mgr. Creative Workshops, Moscow, 1992—. Bd. dirs. Moscow Mardi Gras, 1989. Mem. Moscow C. of C. (tourism com. 1988-89, retail com. 1988-89, chair awards banquet 1989), Am. Advt. Fedn.

WINNINGHOFF, MARY ELLEN (ELLIE), writer; b. Norwalk, Conn., Jan. 25, 1953; d. John Dawson and Louise (Debevoise) W. BA n Econs., Williams Coll., 1975. Equity merchandiser syndicate Dan Bosworth Inc., Mpls., 1976-78; internat. trade rep. Minn. Dept. Econ. Devel., St. Paul, 1979-80; corp. fin. assoc. Craig-Hallum Inc., Mpls., 1981-83; freelance writer, 1983—. Columnist Mpls. City Bus., 1983-87 (Best Column 1987), contbr. to publs. including Working Woman, Savvy, Venture, Corp. Fin., Independent Bus. Entrepreneur, Entrepreneurial Woman and many others. Mem. World Future Soc., Inst. Noetic Scis., Seattle Women's Bus. Exch.

WINOGRADSKY, STEVEN, lawyer; b. N.Y.C., Sept. 22, 1949; s. Harry J. and Hazel (Sadoff) W.; m. Rosemary K. West, Dec. 8, 1985. BA in Polit. Sci., Calif. State U., Northridge, 1971; JD, U. San Fernando, 1977. Bar: Calif., 1977. V.p. bus. affairs Clearing House, Ltd., Hollywood, Calif., 1980-86; mng. dir. music, bus. and legal affairs MCA Home Entertainment and Universal Pictures and TV, Universal City, Calif., 1986-89; dir. music, bus. affairs Hanna-Barbera Prodns., Inc., L.A., 1989-91; pres. Winogradsky Co., Granada Hills, Calif., 1992—. Mem. Calif. State Bar, Calif. Copyright Conf. (bd. dirs. 1986-92), Assn. Ind. Music Pubs. (bd. dirs. 1989-90, pres. 1991-93). Home and Office: Winogradsky Co 12408 Jolette Ave Granada Hills CA 91344

WINSKILL, ROBERT WALLACE, manufacturing executive; b. Tacoma, Oct. 30, 1925; s. Edward Francis William and Margaret Eyre (Myers) W. BA, Coll. Puget Sound, Tacoma, 1947. Field rep. Ray Burner Co., San Francisco, 1954-57, nat. sales mgr., 1960-69; v.p. sales Western Boiler Co., L.A., 1957-60; gen. sales mgr. Ray Burner Co., San Francisco, 1973-82; v.p., chief exec. officer Orr & Sembower, Inc., Middletown, Pa., 1969-73; pres. Combustion Systems Assocs., Inc., Mill Valley, Calif., 1982—; bd. dirs. Sino-Am. Boiler Engring. Co., Shaghai, China. Contbr. articles to profl. jours.; columnist Scope Pub. Mill Valley Harold, 1991—. With U.S. Army, 1943-44. Mem. ASME, Am. Boiler Mfrs. Assn., Olympic Club (San Francisco), Rotary. Office: Combustion Systems Assocs Inc PO Box 749 Mill Valley CA 94942-0749

WINSLOW, DAVID ALLEN, chaplain, naval officer; b. Dexter, Iowa, July 12, 1944; s. Franklin E. and Inez Maude (McPherson) W.; m. Frances Lavinia Edwards, June 6, 1970; children: Frances, David. BA, Bethany Nazarene Coll., 1968; MDiv, Drew U., 1971, STM, 1974. Ordained to ministry United Meth. Ch., 1969. Assoc. minister All Sts. Episcopal. Ch., Millington, N.J., 1969-70; asst. minister Marble Collegiate Ch., N.Y.C., 1970-71; min. No. N.J. Conf., 1971-75; joined chaplain corps USN, 1974, advanced through grades to lt. comdr., 1980. Contbr. articles to profl. jours. Bd. dirs. disaster svcs. and family svcs. ARC, Santa Ana, Calif., 1988-91, Child Abuse Prevention Ctr., Orange, Calif., 1990-91; bd. dirs. Santa Clara County Coun. Chs., 1993. Mem. ACA, Am. Mental Health Counselors Assn., Internat. Soc. Traumatic Stress Studies, Mil. Chaplain Assn. USA, Commonwealth Club Calif., Rep. Assocs. Orange County, USN League (hon.), Sunrise Exch. Club (chaplain 1989-91), Dick Richards Breakfast Club (chaplain 1988-91), Masons (charter, 32 degree), Shriners, Scottish Rite. Home: 757 Inverness Way Sunnyvale CA 94087-4730

WINSLOW, KENELM CRAWFORD, mining engineer; b. Albany, N.Y., Jan. 24, 1921; s. Leon Loyal and Lois Esther (Crawford) W.; m. Bette Jean Killingsworth, Sept. 5, 1947; children: Katherine, Jeanette, Kenelm, Elizabeth, Priscilla. BS in Liberal Arts, Bowling Green State U., 1941; diploma in Mil. Meteorology, N.Y.U., 1943; BS in Mining Engring., Mich. Tech. U., 1948, BS in Geol. Engring., 1948. Registered profl. engr. and land surveyor, N.Mex. Mining engr. Hanna Coal and Ore Corp., DeGrasse, N.Y., 1948-50, Warren Foundry & Pipe Corp., Dover, N.J., 1950-53, Cleve.-Cliffs Iron Co., Ishpeming, Mich., 1953-64, Molybdenum Corp. Am., Questa, N.Mex., 1964-66; pvt. practice cons. engr. El Prado, N.Mex., 1966—. Cpt. Air Corps U.S. Army, 1943-46; lt. col. USAFR, ret. 1981. Mem. Soc. Mining Engrs. of AIME, Soc. Am. Mil. Engrs., Tau Beta Pi. Republican. Presbyterian. Home and Office: Box 927 El Prado NM 87529

WINSLOW, LILLIAN RUTH, nurse; b. Laconia, N.H., Oct. 23, 1930; d. James Edwin and Clemency (Anstey) Burbank; m. John Herrick Winslow, Apr. 25, 1964; children: Alice Faith Winslow Gay, Ruth Ellen Tenpenny. Diploma, Laconia (N.H.) Hosp. Sch. Nursing, 1951; BA, Providence Barrington Bible Coll., 1956; postgrad., Escuela de Idiomas, San Jose, Costa Rica, 1959. Sch. RN emotionally disturbed and handicapped Bedell Sch., Apache Junction, Ariz.; sch. RN East Mesa (Ariz.) Christian Acad.; nurse Mesa (Ariz.) Gen. Hosp. Med. Ctr. Missionary RN, World Radio Missionary Fellowship, Inc., Quito, Ecuador, 1959-63; camp RN, Camp Good News, Camp Pinnacle, N.H.; mem., choir RN the Acapella Choir, Providence Barrington Bible Coll. Recipient Cert. of Appreciation for Devoted and Invaluable Svcs., Maranatha Christian Acad.. Home: 1981 W 10th Ave Apache Junction AZ 85220-6933

WINSLOW, NORMAN ELDON, business executive; b. Oakland, Calif., Apr. 4, 1938; s. Merton Conrad and Roberta Eilene (Drennen) W.; m. Betty June Cady, Jan. 14, 1962 (div. Aug. 1971); 1 child, Todd Kenelm; m. Ilene Ruth Jackson, Feb. 3, 1979. BS, Fresno (Calif.) State U., 1959. Asst. mgr. Proctors Jewelers, Fresno, 1959-62; from agt. to dist. mgr. Allstate Ins. Co., Fresno, 1962-69; ins. agt. Fidelity Union Life Ins., Dallas, 1969-71; dist. and zone mgr. The Southland Corp., Dallas, 1971-78; owner Ser-Vis-Etc., Goleta, Calif., 1978—; bd. dirs. United Retailers, Inc. Pub./editor Franchiser-viceNews; author: Hands in Your Pockets, 1992; contbr. numerous articles to profl. jours. With USAFNG, 1961-67. Mem. Nat. Coalition of Assn. of 7-11 Franchises (affiliate, mem. adv. bd. Glendale, Calif. chpt. 1984-90), Am. Arbitration Assn. (expert witness/cons. Calif. superior cts.). Republican. Methodist. Home: 1179 N Patterson Ave Santa Barbara CA 93117-1813 Office: Ser-Vis-Etc PO Box 2276 Goleta CA 93118-2276

WINSLOW, PHILIP CHARLES, agriculturist, marketing consultant; b. Carthage, Ind., Jan. 13, 1924; s. William Howard and Ione (Morris) W.; m. Arlis Brown, Oct. 6, 1951; children: Mark, Jay, Julie. BS, Purdue U., 1948. Successively dist. mgr., regional product mgr., asst. div. sales mgr., div. sales mgr., nat. product mgr., nat. mktg. mgr. Ralston Purina Co., 1950-1970; v.p. mktg. Namolco, Inc., Willow Grove, Pa., 1971-84; dir. mktg. molasses div. Cargill, Inc., Willow Grove, 1984-85; nat. mktg. cons. Cargill, Inc., Mpls., 1986-88; v.p. Walt Montgomery Assoc., Indpls., 1989—; pres., dir. Winslow Farms, Inc., Carthage, 1982—. Sgt. U.S. Army, 1948-50. Mem. Am. Feed Industry Assn. (com. chmn. 1975-76, com. sec. 1982-83), Big 10 Club Phila. (pres. 1981), Shadowridge Golf Club (sec.-treas. 1992, pres. 1993, bd. govs. 1993—), Purdue Club Phila. (v.p. 1982-83, pres. 1983-86), Masons. Republican. Lutheran. Home: 1305 La Salle Ct Vista CA 92083-8945

WINSOR, DAVID JOHN, cost consultant; b. Duluth, Minn., May 27, 1947; s. Alphonse Joseph and Sylvia Mae (Petrich) W.; m. Linda Kay Sanders, Dec. 22, 1968 (div. Mar. 1974). BA in Bus., U. Puget Sound, 1978; M of Mech. Engring., Pacific Western U., 1979. Jr. engr. J.P. Head Mech., Inc., Richland, Wash., 1965-67; estimator, project engr. Subs. of Howard S. Wright Co., Seattle, 1972-75; sr. estimator Massart Co., Seattle, 1975-76; project mgr. Univ. Mechanical, Portland, Oreg., 1976; cons. Kent, Wash., 1976-79; owner Leasair, Federal Way, Wash., 1978-83; pres., owner Expertise Engring. & Cons., Inc., Bellevue, Wash., 1979-82, 90—; cons. Winsor & Co., Walnut Creek, Calif., 1983—; cons. NASA, Mountain View, Calif., 1986, Lockheed Missile & Space, Sunnyvale, Calif., 1984-87, The Boeing Co., Seattle, 1979-82. Author: (with others) Current Construction Costs, 1987, 88, 89, Construction Materials Inventory Systems, 1973, 74, Construction Inflation Trends, 1975, 76, 77, 78, 79, 80, 81, Construction Claims and Prevention, 1981, 82. Served to sgt. USAF, 1967-71. Mem. Jaycees (state dir. 1972-73, state chmn. 1973-74). Republican. Roman Catholic. Office: Winsor & Co PO Box 6788 Concord CA 94524-1788

WINSTON, MORTON MANUEL, equipment executive; b. N.Y.C., Dec. 9, 1930; s. Myron Hugh and Minna (Schneller) W.; m. Katherine Tupper Winn, Feb. 3, 1979; 1 child, Kate Winston; children by previous marriages: Gregory Winston, Livia Winston; stepchildren—Wesley Hudson, Laura Hudson. A.B., U. Vt., 1951; M.A., U. Conn., 1953; LL.B. magna cum laude, Harvard U., 1958. Bar: D.C. 1961. Law clk. to Justice Frankfurter, Supreme Ct. U.S., 1959-60; asso. firm Cleary, Gottlieb, Steen & Hamilton, N.Y.C., Washington, 1960-67; v.p. Tosco Corp., N.Y.C., 1964-67; exec. v.p. Tosco Corp., 1967-71, pres., 1971-83, chief exec. officer, 1976-83, chmn., 1983-84, dir., 1984-86; pres., chmn. Stamet, Inc., Gardena, Calif., 1987—; chmn. Norad Corp., 1986—; dir. Stamet, Inc. and Norad Corp, 1986—; bd. dir. Baker Hughes Corp. trustee George C. Marshall Research Found., Lexington, Va., Mus. Contemporary Art, L.A.; chmn. Station KLON-FM, Long Beach, Calif.; trustee Calif. State Summer Sch. for the Arts Found. Served to lt. (j.g.) USCGR, 1953-55. Office: Stamet Inc 17244 South Main St Gardena CA 90248

WINTER, CARYL ELYSE, communications specialist, educator; b. N.Y.C., Feb. 14, 1944; d. Irving and Eva (Berger) Yellin. BA, Am. U., 1965; MA, NYU, 1968; JD, UCLA, 1993. Cert. tchr., N.Y., Calif. Tchr. English, N.Y.C. Sch. System, 1965-69; communications specialist TIAA-CREF, N.Y.C., 1969-72; editorial mgr. Boone, Young & Assocs., mgmt. cons., N.Y.C., 1972-73; mgr. communications Pierce Nat. Life Ins. Co., L.A., 1973-75; mgmt. analyst Cedars-Sinai Med. Ctr., L.A., 1976-79; asst. v.p. communications City Nat. Bank, Beverly Hills, Calif., 1979-80; pres., seminar leader Presentations with Impact, Beverly Hills, 1980—; instr. writing skills UCLA Sch. Mgmt., 1976—. Author: Present Yourself with Impact, 1983; also articles on bus. communications. Bd. dirs. support group Kennedy

Med. Ctr., L.A., 1985-88, organizer book affairs, 1985-88; bd. dirs. Moot Ct. U. West L.A. Sch. Law, 1991-93. Mem. Authors Guild, Women in Bus. (retreat organizer 1986, 87). Office: Presentations with Impact 400 S Beverly Dr Ste 214 Beverly Hills CA 90212-4482

WINTER, DENNIS WAYNE, corporate treasurer; b. Milw.; s. Jerome J. and Emma (Shaffer) W.; m. Susan Gerathy, 1964 (div. 1984); children: Anette, James. BA, U. Wis., Milw., 1962, MBA, 1966. Internat. fin. rep. Allis-Chalmers Mfg. Co., Milw., 1962-66; vice dir. Internat. Harvester Finanz AG, Zürich, Switzerland, 1966-70; treas. Planning Rsch. Corp., L.A., 1970-78, Hydril Co., L.A., 1978—. Mem. Risk and Ins. Mgmt. Soc., Tax Exec. Inst., L.A. Treas.'s Club, L.A. Athletic Club, Braemar Country Club. Office: Hydril Co 714 W Olympic Blvd Los Angeles CA 90015

WINTER, MICHAEL ALEX, executive director; b. Chgo., Sept. 7, 1951; s. Stephen Ray and Caroline Betty (Terzian) W.; m. Atsuko Kuwana, Aug. 19, 1984; 1 child, Takayoshi Michael. BA in Philosophy, So. Ill. U., 1974. Evaluator, counselor Evaluation & Devel. Ctr., Carbondale, Ill., 1976-77; intern Comprehensive Health Planning Ctr., Carbondale, 1977; dep. dir. Ctr. for Ind. Living, Berkeley, Calif., 1977-81; exec. dir. Hawaii Ctrs. for Ind. Living, Honolulu, 1981-82, Ctr. for Ind. Living, Berkeley, 1982—. Bd. dirs. Alameda County Transit County, 1988—; del. Dem. Nat. Conv., Atlanta, 1988, N.Y.C., 1992. Named to The Best of the New Generation Men and Women Under Forty Who Are Changing Am., Esquire Mag., 1984. Mem. Nat. Coun. on Ind. Living (bd. dirs. 1983-86, internal v.p. 1988-89, pres. 1989-91, past pres. 1991—). Office: Ctr for Ind Living 2539 Telegraph Ave Berkeley CA 94704

WINTER, RICHARD SAMUEL, JR., computer training company owner, writer; b. Denver, Mar. 17, 1958; s. Richard Samuel and Jerryl Dene (Gano) W.; m. Karen Annette Hansen, May 27, 1989. Student, Griffith U., Brisbane, Australia, 1979; BA in Internat. Environment, Colo. Coll., 1981; MA in Pub. Adminstrn., U. Colo., Denver, 1989. Range aide U.S. Forest Svc., Desert Exptl. Station, Utah, 1976-77; pub. health investigator, lab. technician Denver Health Dept., 1982-84; projects mgr. Colo. Statesman, Denver, 1984-85; editor Mile Hi Prep, Denver, 1985; fin. analyst Pan Am. World Airways, N.Y.C., 1985-88; sr. ptnr., owner PRW, Denver, 1988—; v.p. info. systems Trainers, Denver, 1993. Co-author, revisor: MicroRef Quick Reference Gd. Lotus 1-2-3 Rel. 3.0, 1990, MicroRef Quick Reference Gd. Lotus 1-2-3 Rel. 2.2, 1990, Que Q&A QueCards, 1991, Que 123 Release 2.3 QuickStart, 1991, Que 123 Release 3.1 QuickStart, 1991, Que 123 Release 2.4 QuickStart, 1992, Que Look Your Best with Excel, 1992, Que 123 Release 3.4 QuickStart, 1992, Que Excel for Windows Sure Steps, 1993. Chmn. N.Y. Victims for Victims, N.Y.C., 1986-87; bd. dirs. Colo. Common Cause, Denver, 1984-85; steering com. Voter Registration "Motor Voter" Amendment, Denver, 1983-84; pres. Broadway Commons Homeowners Assn., Denver, 1982-84. Recipient Vigil Honor, Order of the Arrow, 1976. Mem. Phi Beta Kappa, Alpha Lambda Delta.

WINTER, STEWART MEYER, retired real estate broker; b. Steubenville, Ohio, May 4, 1914; s. Stewart and Nancy Jane (Winesburg) W.; m. Karolyn M. Reynolds, Sept. 11, 1939 (dec. 1971); children: Karen L. Lassell, Gary R.; m. Dorothy Perletta McRoberts, Sept. 13, 1972. Grad., Wells High Sch., Steubenville, 1931. Acct. Weirton (W.Va.) Steel Co., 1931-46; real estate salesman Voight Realty Co., Tucson, 1946-49, Hodges Realty Co., Tucson, 1949-52; real estate broker Winter Realty Co., Tucson, 1952-55; pres., broker Winter-Loety Realty, Tucson, 1955-72, Winter Co., Tucson, 1972-90; ret. Author: A Salesman's Introduction to Real Estate, 1958; co-author and assoc. editor: Farm and Ranch Brokers Manual, 1959. Mem., chmn. Ariz. Real Estate Commn., 1969-75; active in past various charitable orgns. Mem. Nat. Assn. Real Estate Bds. (dir. 1964-66), Tucson Bd. Realtors (life, pres. 1959-60, Realtor of the Yr. 1958, 61, 62), Ariz. Assn. Realtors (life, pres. 1961-62, State Realtor of the Yr. 1961, 62), Nat. Assn. Realtors (life, dir. 1964-66), Nat. Assn. Ind. Fee Appraisers (pres. 1976-78, State Man of the Yr.), Elks, Old Pueblo Lapidary Club (dir. 1980). Republican. Roman Catholic. Home: 9755 E Shiloh Tucson AZ 85748

WINTER, WILLIAM, news analyst, correspondent, editor, publisher; b. Newark, May 6, 1907; s. Louis and Theresa (Morawetz) W.; m. Celia Cobin, Dec. 4, 1930 (dec. Mar. 1956); m. Sandra Johnston, Feb. 22, 1959 (div. Dec. 1963); m. Peggy Riddle Bennett, July 16, 1968; children: Dita Wolanow, Diane Durkin. LLB, Asheville U., 1928. Bar: N.C. 1928. Pvt. practice law Asheville, N.C., 1928-30; atty. Consol. Indemnity & Ins. Co., N.Y.C., 1930-34; pvt. practice Charlotte, N.C., 1934-41; news commentator, editor Sta. WBT, Charlotte, 1935-41; news analyst, fgn. correspondent CBS-Radio/TV, San Francisco, 1941-45, ABC-Radio/TV, San Francisco and L.A., 1950-63; editor, pub. William Winter Comments, Woodland Hills, Calif., 1960—; lectr. on world affairs UCLA-Extension, L.A., 1958—. Co-author: (with Myron Prinzmetal) Heart Attack, 1958; author: White Shadow on Black Africa, 1979, Voice of an American, 1991. Recipient Ouissam Alouite Govt. of Morocco, Rabat, 1955, Legion of Honor Govt. of Philippines, Manila, 1956; cited for Excellence in Commentary Calif. AP, Radio-TV News Assn., 1950, for Best News Program NATAS, San Francisco, 1951. Democrat. Office: 6025 El Escorpion Rd Woodland Hills CA 91367-1199

WINTERLIN, WRAY LAVERN, environmental chemist emeritus, educator; b. Sioux City, Iowa, July 20, 1930; s. William and Nettie (Larson) W.; m. Arlene Fay Harper, Nov. 15, 1929; children: Jerry and Larry (twins), Dwight. Student, Morningside Coll., 1948-50, Iowa State U., 1950-51; BS, U. Nebr., 1955, MS, 1956. Jr. chemist Calif. Dept. Water Resources, Sacramento, 1958-59; staff rsch. assoc., exptl. sta. specialist U. Calif., Davis, 1959-79, lectr., environ. chemist, 1979—, dir. pesticide residue and trace analysis lab., 1965-84, acting chmn. dept. environ. toxicology, 1972; instr. workshops Nat. Inst. Environ. Health Scis., Cairo, Egypt, 1982. Contbr. to numerous profl. publs. With U.S. Army, 1951-53, Korea. Grantee numerous fed. and state agys., indsl. orgns. Mem. AAAS, Am. Chem. Soc., Sigma Xi, Gamma Sigma Delta. Republican.

WINTERROND, WILLIAM J., bishop. Bishop Diocese of Colo., Denver, 1991—. Office: Diocese of Colo 1300 Washington Denver CO 80203*

WINTERS, BARBARA JO, musician; b. Salt Lake City; d. Louis McClain and Gwendolyn (Bradley) W. AB cum laude, UCLA, 1960, postgrad., 1961; postgrad., Yale, 1960. Mem. oboe sect. L.A. Philharm., 1961—, now prin. oboist.; clinician oboe, English horn, Oboe d'amore. Recs. movie, TV sound tracks. Home: 3529 Coldwater Canyon Ave Studio City CA 91604-4060 Office: 135 N Grand Ave Los Angeles CA 90012-3013

WINTERS, LISA GANTT, gallery owner, public relations executive; b. Bradenton, Fla., Apr. 18, 1963; d. John Greenville III and Jacqueline Ann (Treadway) Stone; m. Todd Abbott Winters, July 1, 1989. BA, S.W. Tex. State U., 1986. Intern reporter Sta. KTVV, Austin, Tex., 1985-86; adminstrv. asst. Davis Kinard & Co., Austin, 1986-87; dir. mktg. Page Southerland Page, Austin, 1987-88; mgr. pub. rels. Tex. Mcpl. League, Austin, 1988-90; owner, dir., mgr. pub. rels. Winters Gallery and Studio, Taos, N.Mex., 1991—. Mem. citizens police acad. Austin Police Force, 1990. Mem. Taos Arts Assn., St. Francis Plz. Mchts. Assn. (founder, cons.). Republican. Baptist. Office: Winters Gallery PO Box 485 Ranchos De Taos NM 87557

WINTERS, RICHARD ALLEN, mineral economist; b. Butte, Mont., Feb. 19, 1963; s. Allen S. and Doris Ellen (Taylor) W.; m. Laura Therese Donahue, July 5, 1987 (div. Mar., 1991). BS in Fin., Econs., U. Mont., 1986; MS in Mineral Econs., Colo. Sch. Mines, 1990, postgrad. mineral econs. dept., 1991—. Office engr. Morrison Knudsen Engrs., Richland, Wash., 1986-88; project acct. Morrison Knudsen Engrs., Richland, 1987-88; ops. analyst Echo Bay Mines, Denver, 1989; instr. Colo. Sch. Mines, Golden, Colo., 1991—; cons. Coors Brewing Co., Golden, 1991—; sr. rsch. engr. Phelps Dodge Mining Co., Morenci, Ariz., 1992—. Pres. Mineral Econ. Grad. Student Assn., 1989-90. Mem. Soc. Mining, Metallurgy and Exploration, Assn. Environ. Resource Economists, Mineral, Econs. and Mgmt. Soc. Home: 148 Yucca Ave Morenci AZ 85540 Office: Phelps Yucca Dodge Mining Co Rsch Bus & Devel Morenci AZ 85540

WINTHROP, KENNETH RAY, insurance executive; b. N.Y.C., Dec. 29, 1950; s. Ralph and Lore (Bruck) W.; m. Sharon Swinnich, 1976 (div. 1978); m. Diane Louise Denney, June 27, 1981; children: Alyssa Louise, Matthew Lawrence, Andrew Lee. BA in English, SUNY, Buffalo, 1972. Agt. Northwestern Mut. Life Ins., Woodland Hills, Calif., 1975-78, Nat. Life of Vermont, L.A., 1978—. Mem. Nat. Life of Vt. Pres. Club, Million Dollar Round Table. Democrat. Home: 7609 W 83d St Playa Del Rey CA 90293 Office: 1900 Avenue Of The Stars Los Angeles CA 90067-4317

WIPIOR, KURT VICTOR, aeronautical engineer; b. Miami, Fla., Aug. 1, 1960; s. Henry George and Marjorie Alva (Johnson) W. BS in Aero. Sci., Embry-Riddle Aero. U., Daytona Beach, Fla., 1982; M. Aviation Mgmt., Embry-Riddle Aero. U., 1984. Design asst. Julian Designs, Miami, Fla., 1976-78; sr. tech. writer The Dee Howard Co., San Antonio, 1984-87; pubs. supr. The Dee Howard Co., 1987-90; engr. Boeing Comml. Airplane Group, Seattle, 1990—; cons. Kurt Wipior Assocs., 1982-89. Mem. Seattle Profl. Engring. Assn. Home: 10709 Glen Acres Dr S Seattle WA 98168-1554

WIRBEL, LORING DOUGLAS, journalist; b. Grand Ledge, Mich., May 31, 1957; s. Louis Edward and Louise Jane (Fox) W.; m. Carol Ledesa Rumsey, Aug. 30, 1986; 1 child, Abigail. BA in Journalism, U. Ariz., 1982. Sci. editor Albuquerque Tribune, 1982-84; bay area tech. editor Electronic News, San Jose, Calif., 1984-87; San Jose news editor Elec. Engring. Times, San Jose, Calif., 1987-90; western states news editor Elec. Engring. Times, Colorado Springs, 1990—. Contbr. articles to profl. jours.; author: (series) Star Wars, 1983. Writer Colo. Peace and Justice Commn. Colorado Springs, 1990-92; mem. ACLU, Colo., 1986—; mem. facilitator Citizen Trade, Colo., 1992. Home and Office: 1310 Stella Dr Colorado Springs CO 80921

WIRE, DENNIS CHARLES, nurse; b. Upland, Calif., Jan. 20, 1949; s. Donald Edgar and June Ethel (Orr) W.; m. Sheril Ann Green, July 25, 1981; 1 child, Donna June. BA, Westmont Coll., 1971; MA, Azusa Pacific U., 1972; postgrad., Los Angeles Valley Coll., 1988-89; AS, Coll. of the Canyons, 1991. RN, Calif. Tchr. Progress Sch., Long Beach, Calif., 1978-79; actor SAG, Hollywood, Calif., 1979-81; sales rep. Pepsi-Cola Bottlers, Inc., San Fernando, Calif., 1981-83; mktg. rep. Profl. Info. Network, Sherman Oaks, Calif., 1983-84; mktg. dir., cons. Sr. Referral Svcs., Sherman Oaks, 1984-87; mktg. dir., nursing cons. Trimar Hollywood, Reseda, Calif., 1986—; nurse Henry Mayo Newhall Meml. Hosp., Valencia, Calif., 1990-92, Holy Cross Med. Ctr., Mission Hills, Calif., 1993—, Ahimsa Care Ctr., Van Nuys, Calif., 1993—, Estelle Doheny Eye Hosp., 1992—; prof. Coll. of the Desert, 1972-73. Vol. Calif. Rep. Assn., Newhall, 1984, Burbank, 1988. Mem. ANA, Calif. Nurse's Assn., Westmont Coll. Alumni Assn., Coll. of Canyons Alumni Assn., Azusa Pacific U. Alumni Assn., Coachell Valley High Sch. Alumni Assn. Baptist. Office: Trimar Hollywood 19234 Vanowen St Reseda CA 91335

WIRT, MICHAEL JAMES, library director; b. Sault Ste. Marie, Mich., May 21, 1947; s. Arthur James and Blanche Marian (Carruth) W.; m. Barbara Ann Hallesy, Aug. 12, 1972; 1 child, Brendan. BA, Mich. State U., 1969; MLS, U. Mich., 1971. Cert. librarian, Wash. Acting librarian Univ. Mich., Ctr. for Research on Econ. Devel., Ann Arbor, 1971-72; instnl. services librarian Spokane County Library Dist., Wash., 1972-76, asst. dir., 1976-79, acting dir., 1979, dir., 1980—. Mem. Adv. com. Partnership for Rural Improvement, Spokane, 1982-85, Wash. State Libr. Planning and Devel. Com., 1984-85, Ea. Wash. U. Young Writers Project Adv. Bd., 1988-89; mem. issues selection com. Citizens League of Greater Spokane, 1991—. Mem. Wash. Libr. Assn. (2d v.p. 1984-86, Merit award 1984, dir. 1989-91, legis. planning com., 1991—), Wash. Libr. Network (rep. Computer Svc. Coun. 1983-86, v.p., treas. State Users Group 1986-87), Am. Libr. Assn. (Pub. Libr. Affiliates Network 1990—, PLA Bus. Coun. 1990—, chmn. 1991—), Spokane Valley C. of C. (local govt. affairs com. 1987—), Spokane Area C. of C. (local govt. com. 1990—, human svcs. com. 1990-92, chmn. 1991-92), Momentum (local govt. strategy com. 1992—.

WISCOTT, RICHARD ANDREW, banker; b. Youngstown, Ohio, Mar. 2, 1966; s. Peter Anthony Jr. and Caroline Ann (Keenan) W. Student, Youngstown State U., 1983-85. Teller, note asst. City Nat. Bank, Beverly Hills, Calif., 1986-87; note mgr. Lincoln Nat. Bank, Encino, Calif., 1987-91; v.p. ctrl. svcs. Silicon Valley Bank, San Jose, Calif., 1991—. Mem. Contact Bankers Assn. Democrat. Office: Silicon Valley Bank 2240 N First St San Jose CA 95131

WISE, JANET ANN, college official; b. Detroit, Aug. 8, 1953; d. Donald Price and Phyllis (Licht) W.; m. Peter Anthony Eisenklam, Oct. 16, 1976 (div. Aug. 1982); m. Edward Henry Moreno, Mar. 31, 1984; 1 child, Talia. Student, U. N.Mex., 1971-73; BA in English, Coll. of Santa Fe, 1989. Editorial asst., writer The New Mexican, Santa Fe, 1975-77; press asst., press sec. Office of Gov. N.Mex., Santa Fe, 1979-82; dir. pub. relations City of Santa Fe, 1983-84, Coll. of Santa Fe, 1984—. Bd. dirs. Santa Fe Bus. Bur., 1984-87, Santa Fe Girl's Club, 1986-89. Recipient Exemplary Performance award Office Gov. of N.Mex., Santa Fe, 1981, Outstanding Service award United Way of Santa Fe, 1982. Mem. Pub. Rels. Soc. Am., N.Mex. Press Women, Santa Fe Media Assn. (pres. 1989-91). Democrat. Unitarian. Home: # 7 Conchas Ct Santa Fe NM 87505 Office: Coll of Santa Fe 1600 St Michael's Dr Santa Fe NM 87501

WISE, WILLIAM NESBITT, agricultural commission administrator; b. Traverse City, Mich., June 2, 1959; s. William Lytle and Jeanne (Nesbitt) W. BS, Oreg. State U., 1982, MAgr, 1985. Co-foreman Murray Farms, Inc., Traverse City, Mich., 1976-79; field rep. Oreg. Onions, Inc., Brooks, Oreg., 1981-82; mktg. rep. Bostsford and Goodfellow, Inc., Portland, Oreg., 1985; rsch. assoc. agr. econs. dept. Oreg. State U., Corvallis, 1985; admistr., chief exec. officer Oreg. Potato Commn., Portland, 1986—; chmn. Nat. Potato Coun. Mgrs. Com., Denver, 1990-91, Ore. Agrl. Trade and Mktg. Program adv. com., 1992—; sec. NW Potato Varietal Devel. Com., Aberdeen, Idaho, 1989-91; advisor fgn. mktg. com. U.S. Potato Bd., 1986—; lectr. gov.'s trade mission, Taiwan, Korea, Japan, 1987; guest lectr. Agrl. and Resource Econs. dept. Oreg. State U., 1991; mem. Northwest China Council, 1988-91. Asst. coach Wilson High Sch. Ski Team, Portland, 1987-91; higher edn. advocate Oreg. State U. Alumni Assn., Corvallis; mem. Beaverton Birobizhan (Russia) Sister Cities Com. Recipient Award of Excellence, Oreg. Agri-business Coun., 1988, 89; Gen. Dillingham scholar Gen. Dillingham Scholarship Fund, L.A., 1980-81, 81-82. Mem. Alpha Zeta, Gamma Sigma Delta, The Nature Conservancy. Buddhist. Home: 11114 SW 65th Ave Portland OR 97219-6704 Office: Oreg Potato Commn 700 NE Multnomah St Ste 460 Portland OR 97232-4104

WISE, WOODROW WILSON, JR., small business owner; b. Alexandria, Va., Mar. 9, 1938; s. Woodrow Wilson Sr. and Helen (Peverill) W.; m. Barbara Jean Hatton, Oct. 6, 1956 (div. 1975); m. Sandra Kay Habitz, Dec. 17, 1983; children: Anthony P., Laura J. Gen. mgr. Alexandria (Va.) Amusement Corp., 1956-73; curator Harold Lloyd Estate, Beverly Hills, Calif., 1973-75; pres. Discount Video Tapes, Inc., Burbank, Calif., 1975—. Office: Discount Video Tapes Inc PO Box 7122 833 "A" N Hollywood Way Burbank CA 91510

WISEMAN, ARTHUR FRANCIS, JR., software engineer, graphic designer; b. Bklyn., July 14, 1950; s. Arthur F. Sr. and Opal (Pugh) W.; m. Donna Lee Fusco, May 29, 1980; children: Kathleen Candice, Bryan Mathew. OCS, Ft. Benning, Ga., 1970; student, flight sch., Ft. Walters, Tex., 1970-71. With U.S. Postal Svc., Bklyn., 1980-83; owner, CEO Green Diamond Group, Las Vegas, Nev., 1990—. Author computer software; inventor toys. 1st lt. U.S. Army, 1969-72. Republican. Roman Catholic. Home: 5801 W Lake Meade Blvd Las Vegas NV 89108 Office: Green Diamond Group 5801 W Lake Meade Blvd Las Vegas NV 89108

WISEMAN, JAY DONALD, photographer, mechanical designer and contractor; b. Salt Lake City, Dec. 23, 1952; s. Donald Thomas and Reva (Stewart) W.; m. Barbara Helen Taylor, June 25, 1977; children: Jill Reva, Steve Jay. Ed. Utah State U., Logan, U. Utah. Cert. profl. photographer. Pvt. practice photography; owner, pres. JB&W Corp. Recipient Grand prize Utah State Fair, 1986, Kodak Crystal for Photographic Excellence, 1986, 87, Master of Photography degree, 1989, Best of Show award, 1991-92; cover photo, 1988; numerous photos inducted for permanent collection Internat. Photographic Hall of Fame, 1989; photo named one of World's Greatest, Kodak, 1987-88; 2 photos named among World's Best, Walt Disney World and Profl. Photographers Assn., 1988, 2 prints tied for Best of Show award RMPPA Regional contest, 1991; recipient Gold Medallion award Am. Soc. Photographers. Mem. Profl. Photographers Assn. Am. (one of top 10 scores internat. photo contest), Rocky Mountain Profl. Photographers (Best of Show, highest score ever 1987, Master Photographer of Yr. 1991, Ct. of Honour), Inter-Mountain Profl. Photographers Assn. (Master's Trophy Best of Show 1982, 86, 88, Photographer of Yr. award 1986, Ct. of Honour), Photographers Soc. Am (Best of Show award Utah chpt. 1986). Latter Day Saints. Represented in Salt Lake City Internat. Airport permanent photo exhibit, various traveling loan collections, U.S. and Europe, 1988, loan collection Epcot Ctr., 1988-91; photographs published numerous profl. jours.

WISHNIEWSKY, GARY, international educator, university volunteer program director; b. Cedar Rapids, Iowa, Nov. 4, 1946; s. Bolek Bernard and Arvada Mae (Buresh) W. BA in Philosophy and Media, Antioch Coll., 1969; MBA in Fin., Golden Gate U., 1984, MBA in Mktg., 1985, postgrad., 1986—. Tchr. English U.S. Peace Corps., Istanbul, Turkey, 1969-70; supr. mkt. rsch. Wade West Assocs., Inc., San Francisco, 1973-75; regional rep. Expt. in Internat. Living, San Francisco, 1976-78, vol. mgr., 1978-80; asst. dir. Western Regional Office CARE, San Francisco, 1981-82; alumni dir. Golden Gate U., San Francisco, 1982-90, dir. instnl. rsch., 1989-90, professorial lectr., 1987—, dir. S.E. Asian programs, 1990—. French Ministry Edn. fellow, Antibes, France, 1977. Mem. Nat. Soc. Fund Raising Execs. (bd. dirs. Golden Gate chpt. 1988-90, sec. 1988-90, fin. chair 1990), Nat. Assn. Fgn. Student Affairs: Assn. Internat. Educators (region XII, no. Calif. dist. various chairmanships 1976-92), Coun. for Advancement and Support Edn., No. Calif. Consultative Group World Affairs, No. Calif. Coun. Returned Peace Corps Vols. (founding bd. 1978), Pacific Asia Travel Assn. (adv. coun. 1991—). Office: Golden Gate U 536 Mission St San Francisco CA 94105-2968

WISNIEWSKI, STEPHEN ADAM, professional football player; b. Rutland, Vt., Apr. 7, 1967. Student, Pa. State U. Offensive guard L.A. Raiders, 1989—. Office: L A Raiders 332 Center St El Segundo CA 90245

WISNOSKY, JOHN G., artist, educator; b. Springfield, Ill., Mar. 21, 1940; s. August Peter and Ann Alice (Tisckos) W.; m. Merium Norma Corl, June 22, 1966; 1 child, Merium Evelyn. BFA, U. Ill., 1962, MFA, 1964. Instr. Va. Poly. Inst., Blacksburg, Va., 1964-66; chmn. art dept. U. Hawaii, Honolulu, 1976-85; acting chmn. George Mason U., Fairfax, Va., 1987-88; prof. U. Hawaii, Honolulu, 1966—, chmn. grad. field in art, 1990—. Co-designer: (permanent exhbn.) Onizuka Ctr. for Internat. Astronomy, 1985; numerous one man shows; represented in permanent collections The Honolulu Acad. of Art, The Contemporary Arts Ctr. Hawaii, Bank of Hawaii and numerous private collections. Recipient Purchase award State Found. on Culture and the Arts, 1990, Dept. of Edn. Hawaii, 1990, Commns. award Toyota Corp., Beta West, Inc., 1992. Office: U Hawaii Dept Art 2535 The Mall Honolulu HI 96822-2233

WISOTSKY, JERRY JOSEPH, graphic arts company executive; b. N.Y.C., Oct. 22, 1928; s. Abraham I. and Anna P. (Slipoy) W.; student CCNY, 1946-48; m. Helen E. Lerner, Nov. 12, 1949; children: Pearle Eve Wisotsky Marr, Ronald Ian. Apprentice, Triplex Lithographic Corp., N.Y.C., 1949-51; pres. Kwik Offset Plate Inc., N.Y.C., 1952-59; chmn. bd. Imperial Litho/Graphics Inc., Phoenix, 1959—; bd. dirs. Am. West Airlines. Mem. bd. Appeals, Phoenix, 1974-76; pres. Ariz. Found. for Handicapped, 1976—; campaign chmn. corp. div. United Way, 1975, gen. campaign chmn., 1977; trustee St. Luke's Hosp. Med. Ctr.; pres. Phoenix Jewish Community Ctr., 1970-71; v.p. bd. dirs. United Way; pres. United Way Phoenix-Scottsdale, 1981; chmn. Valley of Sun United Way, 1981; chmn. Ariz. bd. dirs. Anti-Defamation League, also nat. commr.; bd. dirs. NCCJ; charter pres. Metro-Phoenix Citizens Coun., 1986-87; chmn. Boys'& Girls' Clubs Met. Phoenix, 1989—; bd. dirs. Ariz.-Weizmann Inst., 1984, Ariz. Mus. Sci. and Tech., 1984, Golden Gate Settlement Devel. Coun., Phoenix Community Alliance, 1984; pres. Dean's Coun. of 100 Coll. Bus. Ariz. State U., 1989; chmn. Combined Health Resources, 1984; mem. 1986 Nat. UN Day Program, state exec. bd. U.S. West Communications, 1984—; hon. bd. dirs. Valley of the Sun United Way; past chmn. bd. dirs. St. Luke's Hosp., Phoenix; bd. dirs. Combined Health Resources, 1982-83; mem. NCCJ, 1989. Recipient Disting. Svc. award Rotary Internat., Phoenix, 1985, Humanitarian award Nat. Asthma Ctr. Nat. Jewish Hosp., Torch of Liberty award Anti-Defamation League, 1977, 12 Who Care Hon Kachina award, 1980, Tom Chauncey award, 1984, Volunteerism award Valley of the Sun United Way, Gates of Jerusalem award State of Israel Bonds, 1987, Human Rels award NCCJ, 1989, Master Entrepreneur of th Yr. Ernst and Young, 1990; named Phoenix Man of Yr., 1985, Exec. of Yr., Exec. Women Internat, 1991. Mem. Am. Greyhound Found. (bd. dirs.), Nat. Jewish Hosp. Immunology & Respiratory Medicine (bd. dir. 1986—), Met. C. of C. (intercity com.), Ariz. Jewish Hist. Soc. (bd. dirs. 1984), Valley Forward Assn., Econ. Club Phoenix (founding bd. dirs. 1984), Phoenix 40 Club. Home: 7520 N 1st St Phoenix AZ 85020-4001 Office: 210 S 4th Ave Phoenix AZ 85003-2173

WISSMAN, LAWRENCE YARNELL, medical device company executive; b. Oneida, N.Y., Sept. 19, 1947; s. Joseph Arthur and Julia Elizabeth (Yarnell) W.; m. Diana Beatriz Di Menna, June 6, 1986; children: Stephanie, Alexander, Matthew, Camille. BS, Union Coll., Schenectady, 1969. Program mgr. internat. div. Bausch & Lomb, Rochester, N.Y., 1974-86; cons. Buenos Aires, 1986-89; head R&D engring. Mentor Corp., Santa Barbara, Calif., 1989-91; v.p. R&D Coast Vision, Inc., Huntington Beach, Calif., 1991—. Patentee in field. With U.S. Army, 1970-72. Mem. Am. Chem. Soc. Republican.

WITHAM, CLYDE LESTER, chemical engineer, researcher; b. L.A., Jan. 15, 1948; s. Robert O. and Dora H. (Elsher) W.; m. Julia N. Bettilyon, Aug. 27, 1971; children: Amy, Jason, Trevor, Alyssa. BSChemE, Brigham Young U., 1973; MS in Civil Engring., Stanford U., 1977. From chem. engr. to sr. chem. engr. to program mgr. fine particle tech. SRI Internat., Menlo Park, Calif., 1973—. Inventor in field; contbr. articles to profl. jours. Advisor Sewer Bd., San Jose, Calif., 1979; leader Boy Scouts Am., San Jose and Half Moon Bay, Calif., 1982, 85; mem. LDS Ch., Half Moon Bay, 1983-90. Mem. Am. Inst. Chem. Engrs., Am. Chem. Soc., Am. Assn. for Aerosol Rsch., Gesellschaft fur Aerosolforschung, Soc. Plastic Engrs., Tau Beta Pi. Republican. Office: SRI Internat 333 Ravenswood Ave Menlo Park CA 94025-3493

WITHERSPOON, GREGORY JAY, financial services company executive; b. Quantico, Va., Sept. 30, 1946; s. Thomas Sydenham and Dorothy M. (Jordan) W.; m. Judith A. Klein, Feb. 11, 1966 (dec. Oct. 1984); children: Lisa Marie, Michelle, Rene. BS, Calif. State U., Long Beach, 1970. CPA, Calif. Sr. acct. Peat, Marwick & Main, L.A., 1969-72; sr. mgr. Deloitte & Touche & Co., L.A., 1972-79; v.p. fin. Nanco Enterprises, Santa Barbara, Calif., 1979-84; pres. Pea Soup Andersen's, Buellton, Calif., 1984-86, VWB & P Cons., Santa Barbara, 1986-87; sr. v.p. fin. and adminstrn. Aames Fin. Svcs., L.A., 1987—; owner, founder Witherspoon Properties Ltd., L.A., 1976—; owner, mgr. Witherspoon Leasing, L.A., 1976—. Mem. Calif. Rep. Com., 1978—, Nat. Rep. Com., 1978—. Mem. AICPA, Calif. Inst. CPA's, Tennis Club, Ski Clubs. Office: Aames Fin Svcs 3731 Wilshire Blvd Fl 10 Los Angeles CA 90010-2830

WITKIN, JOEL-PETER, photographer; b. Bklyn., Sept. 13, 1939; s. Max and Mary (Pellegrino) W.; m. Cynthia Jean Bency, June 30, 1978; one child, Kersen Ahanu. B.F.A., Cooper Union, 1974; M.F.A., U. N.Mex., 1986; student (fellow), Columbia U., 1973-74. Exhibited in Projects Studio One, N.Y.C., 1980, Galerie Texbraun, Paris, 1982, Kansas City Art Inst., 1983, Stedelijk Mus., Amsterdam, 1983, Fraenkel Gallery, 1983, 84, 87, 91, 93, Pace/MacGill Gallery, N.Y.C., 1983, 84, 87, 89, 91, 93, San Francisco Mus. Modern Art, 1985, Bklyn. Mus., 1986, Centro de Arte Reina Sofia Mus., Madrid, 1988, Palais de Tokyo, Paris, 1989, Gahey/Klein Gallery, L.A., 1989, 92, 93, Mus. Modern Art, Haifa, Israel, 1991, Museo Pignatelli, Naples, 1993; group shows: Mus. Modern Art, N.Y.C., 1959, San Francisco Mus. Modern Art, 1981, Whitney Biennial, 1985, Palais de Tokyo, Paris, 1986; represented in permanent collections, Mus. Modern Art, N.Y.C., San Francisco Mus. Modern Art, 1980, Nat. Gallery Art, Washington, Victoria and Albert Mus., London, George Eastman House, N.Y., The Getty Collection, Modern Museet, Stockholm, Sweden, Whitney Mus., N.Y.C.; represented by Pace/MacGill, N.Y.C., Fraenkel Gallery, San Francisco, Baudoin Lebon Gallery, Paris, Hamilton Gallery, London, Fay Gold Gallery, Atlanta; subject of monographs: Joel-Peter Witkin, 1985, 88, 89, 91, 93. Served with U.S. Army, 1961-64. Decorated Chevalier Des Arts et de Letters (France), 1990; recipient Disting. Alumni award The Cooper Union, 1986, Internat. Ctr. Photography award, 1988; Ford Found. grantee, 1977, 78, Nat. Endowment in Photography grantee, 1980, 81, 86, 92. Address: 1707 Five Points Rd SW Albuquerque NM 87105

WITKIN, SUSAN BETH, broadcast journalist, reporter; b. Denver, June 10, 1959; d. Bernard Theodore and Sharon Elaine (Ginsberg) W. BA in Communications Arts, Fort Lewis Coll., 1982. Anchor, gen. assignment reporter Sta. KBCO-FM/KADE-AM, Boulder, Colo., 1982-83; asst. news dir. Sta. KSPN-FM/TV, Aspen, Colo., 1983-84, Sta. KIUP/KRSJ-FM, Durango, Colo., 1984-85; anchor, gen. assignment reporter Sta. KOA, Denver, 1985-90; anchor, reporter Sta. KGO ABC/Capital Cities, San Francisco, 1990—. Producer, reporter series on st. gangs Nothing To Do, No Place To Go, 1986 (1st place gen. reporting category Soc. Profl. Journalists, 2nd place feature category AP). Bd. dirs. Allied Jewish Fedn. Women's Div., Denver, 1987-89, March of Dimes, San Francisco, 1991—. Named one of Outstanding Young Women of Am., 1987; recipient 2d Pl. award Spl. Report Saudi Arabia AP, 1990, 1st Place award L.A. Riot Coverage, 1992, 1st Place award RTNDA, 1992. Mem. AFTRA, AP, Bus. Profl. Women's Orgn., Soc. Profl. Jours. Democrat. Office: Sta KGO 900 Front St San Francisco CA 94111-1427

WITT, HERBERT, federal auditor; b. Stockton, Calif., May 9, 1923; s. Arnold and Sarah (Peletz) W.; m. Hiala Einhorn, Nov. 17, 1957; children: Heidi, Julie, Amy. AB, Coll. Pacific, Stockton, 1943; MBA, U. Calif., 1949. CPA, Calif. Staff auditor Price Waterhouse, San Francisco, 1953-55; asst. dist. mgr. U.S. Army Audit Agy., 1951-53, 55-65; chief spl. projects Def. Contract Audit Agy., 1965-66; regional insp. gen. audit HHS, 1966—; instr. auditing U. Calif., Berkeley, 1960—; adj. faculty U. San Franciso, 1983—. Author: (V. Brink) Modern Internal Auditing, 1982, (with R. Atkisson and V. Brink) Modern Internal Auditing, 1986. Lt. USNR, 1943-48. Recipient Presdl. award Assn. Govt. Accts., 1975, Gen. Profl. Devel. award Office Insp. Gen., 1987, Thomas Morris Leadership award Office Inspector Gen., 1988, Exceptional Achievement award 1990. Mem. AICPA, Inst. Internal Auditors (past pres. San Francisco chpt., Disting. Svc. award 1992), Calif. Soc. CPAs, Am. Acctg. Assn., Western Intergovtl. Audit Forum (Jack Birkholtz Leadership award 1989, past chair), Calif. Bd. Accts. (positive enforcement com. 1989—). Democrat. Jewish. Home: 105 La Verne Ave Mill Valley CA 94941-3429 Office: HHS 50 United Nations Plz San Francisco CA 94102-4912

WITTE, NANCY MARIE, special education educator, occupational therapist; b. Richardton, N.D., Mar. 31, 1946; d. Victor Earl and Agnes Catherine (Koller) W. BA in Edn., We. Wash. State Coll., Bellingham, 1968; MS in Spl. Edn., U. Oreg., 1973; M in Occupational Therapy, Tex. Woman's U., 1983. Cert. tchr.; registered/lic. therapist. Tchr. Manson (Wash.) Pub. Schs., 1968-71; vol. tchr. Children's Hosp. Sch., Eugene, Wash., 1972-73; master tchr. Busy Bee Presch., Anchorage, 1973-74; program dir., itinerant spl. edn. tchr. State Operated Schs. of Anchorage, Ft. Yukon, Alaska, 1974-76; program devel. careers and continuing edn. U. Alaska, Faribanks, 1976-78; staff developer, ednl. mgr. A Sch. For Me, Inc., Tohatchi, N.Mex., 1978-81; spl. edn. tchr., therapist for severe-profoundly retarded Fairbanks Sch. Dist., 1983-90, occupational therapist, 1990—; cons. to spl. edn. presch. programs, Ft. Yukon, Delta, and Dillingham, Alaska, 1974-76. Founding mem., v.p. Assn. for Children with Learning Disabilities, Fairbanks, 1975; mem. St. Raphael's Parish Coun., Fairbanks, 1984-90, also pres.; mem. Interior Alaska Peace with Justice Coun., Fairbanks, 1985-89. Named to Outstanding Young Women of Am., 1981. Mem. Am. Occupational Therapy Assn., Peace with Justice Orgn., N.W. Directory of Occupational Therapists for Rural Consultation. Home: 1990 Milky Way Box 10642 Fairbanks AK 99710

WITTE, WREATHA ANN, museum curator; b. Great Bend, Kans., Oct. 14, 1947; d. Edwin William and Helen Louise (Edmondson) W. BA in French, U. Utah, 1970, MA in Linguistics, 1975. Mus. edn. curator Utah State Hist. Soc., Salt Lake City, 1979—. Trustee, sec. Utah Citizens for the Arts, Salt Lake City, 1980-86, others in past. Mem. AAUW, Utah Mus. Assn. (dir., treas. 1985-90, 2d Mile award 1989), Utah Mus. Vols. Assn. (adv. bd., co-founder), Am. Assn. Mus. Vols. (adv. bd. 1986-90, 2d v.p. 1990—, edn. com.), Mus. Edn. Roundtable, Folklore Soc. Utah. Office: Utah State Hist Soc 300 Rio Grande St Salt Lake City UT 84101-1182

WITTENSTEIN, GEORGE JUERGEN, surgeon, educator; b. Tubingen, Germany, Apr. 26, 1919; s. Oskar Juergen and Elisabeth (Vollmoeller) W.; m. Elisabeth Hartert, Apr. 26, 147 (dec. Jan. 1966); m. Christel J. Bejenke, July 1, 1966; children: E. Deirdre, Nemone E., W. Andreas, Catharina J. MD, U. Munich, 1944; MSc in Surgery, U. Colo., 1956, MD, 1956. Diplomate Am. Bd. Surgery and Thoracic Surgery. Instr. U. Colo. Sch. Medicine, Denver, 1953-60; instr., clin. asst., then prof. UCLA Sch. Medicine, 1964-73, prof. surgery, 1974-90, prof. surgery emeritus, 1990—; chmn. dept. surgery Olive View Med. Ctr., Sylmar, Calif., 1974-89; pvt. practice surgery Santa Barbara, Calif., 1989—; vis. prof. at various European med. sch., 1958—. Contbr. sci. articles to profl. publs. Bd. dirs. Friends of U. Calif.-Santa Barbara Libr., 1965-75; trustee Santa Barbara Mus. Art, 1968-75. Boettcher Found. scholar, 1955. Home: 4004 Cuervo Ave Santa Barbara CA 93110 Office: 2410 Fletcher Ave # 204 Santa Barbara CA 93105

WITTER, WENDELL WINSHIP, financial executive, retired; b. Berkeley, Calif., Oct. 16, 1910; s. George Franklin Jr. and Mary Ann (Carter) W.; m. Florence Corder, Oct. 18, 1935 (div. Oct. 1973); 1 child, Wendelyn; m. Janet Hutchinson Alexander, Dec. 12, 1973 (dec. 1977); m. Evelyn Grinter Harkins Gooding, Mar. 26, 1978. BA, U. Calif., Berkeley, 1932; Diploma, Investment Bankers Inst., Wharton Bus. Sch., 1955. Salesman Dean Witter & Co., San Francisco, 1933-50, ptnr., 1950-68, exec. v.p., 1968-76; cons. Dean Witter, Reynolds, Inc., San Francisco, 1976-82, retired cons., 1982—. Past Regent U. Calif., 1969-70; mem. Coordinating Coun. Higher Edn., Calif., 1970-71; trustee State Univs., Long Beach, Calif., 1971-79. Lt. col. Army Air Force, 1941-46. Mem. San Francisco Bond Club (pres. 1955), Assn. of Stock Exch. Firms (pres. 1962), Investment Bankers Assn. Am. (pres. 1965), U. Calif. Alumni Assn. (pres. 1969-70), Berkeley Fellows, Pacific Union Club, San Francisco Golf Club, Bohemian Club, Zeta Psi. Republican. Episcopalian. Home: 1400 Geary Blvd Apt 2109 San Francisco CA 94109-6572 Office: 101 California St PO Box 7597 San Francisco CA 94120

WITTICH, WILLIAM VINCENT, academic administrator, educator; b. N.Y.C., Jan. 17, 1941; s. Fred W. and Gertrude L. (Pildegard) W.; 1 child, Tami Lynn; m. Ann Argo, May 18, 1991. BA, Calif. State U., L.A., 1965; MA, Calif. State U., Long Beach, 1969; EdD, U. So. Calif., L.A., 1975. Tchr. Bellflower Unified Sch. Dist., Lakewood, Calif., 1963-66; prof. Calif. State U., Long Beach, 1967—, dept. chair, 1988—; cons. Del Mar Pubs., Albany, N.Y., 1987—, Glencoe Mc-Graw Hill, Mission Hills, Calif., 1988—; reviewer Nat. Ctr. for Rsch., Berkeley, 1988—, U.S. Dept. Edn., Washington, 1989—. Recipient Orange award Advt. Fedn., 1986. Mem. Nat. Assn. Vocat. Leadership Devel. (pres. 1988-90), Internat. Tech. Edn. Assn., Nat. Photo Instrs. Assn. (pres. 1972-74), U. So. Calif. Alumni Assn. (pres. 1988-90). Home: 3932 N Cielo Pl Fullerton CA 92635-1102 Office: Calif State U 1250 N Bellflower Blvd Long Beach CA 90840-0001

WITTIG, ERLAND PAUL, research chemist; b. Fairbury, Ill., July 2, 1955; s. William M. and Isabelle F. (Nelson) W.; m. Pamela S. Schaefer, June 23, 1984; children: Anne E., Katherine N. AB, Wartburg Coll., 1976; PhD in Analytical Chemistry, Ind. U., 1981. Rsch. chemist Chevron Rsch. Co., Richmond, Calif., 1981-88; sr. rsch. chemist Chevron Rsch. and Tech. Co. (formerly Chevron Rsch. Co.), Richmond, 1988-91; sr. chemist Chevron USA Products Co., El Segundo, Calif., 1991—; adj. prof. So. Oreg. State Coll., Ashland, 1988-91. V.p. Richmond Unified Edn. Fund, 1988-89, pres., 1989-90, bd. dirs., 1986-91, Young Human Resources Devel. Corp., Richmond, 1986-91. Mem. Soc. for Applied Spectroscopy. Office: Chevron USA Products Co Lab Divsn 324 W El Segundo Blvd El Segundo CA 90245

WITTMAN, STEPHEN CHARLES, market research professional; b. San Francisco, Mar. 26, 1953; s. Arthur Miedling and Margaret (Cullen) W. Student, Westminster Choir Coll., 1971-75; BA, Webster U., 1992. Gen. sales mgr. Baldwin Piano and Organ Co., Chgo., 1976-80; regional sales mgr. Baldwin Piano and Organ Co., Cin., 1980-82, Allen Organ Co., Macungie, Pa., 1982-85; regional mktg. mgr. Yamaha Corp. Am., Buena Park, Calif., 1985-92, nat. rsch. & mktg. mgr., 1992—. Mem. Am. Mktg. Assn. Republican. Presbyterian. Home: Ste 1108 4550 Warwick Blvd Kansas City MO 64111-1830 Office: Yamaha Corp Am 6600 Orangethorpe Ave Buena Park CA 90620

WITTROCK, MERLIN CARL, educational psychologist; b. Twin Falls, Idaho, Jan. 3, 1931; s. Herman C. and Mary Ellen (Baumann) W.; m. Nancy McNulty, Apr. 3, 1953; children: Steven, Catherine, Rebecca. BS in Biology, U. Mo., Columbia, 1953, MS in Ednl. Psychology, 1956; PhD in Ednl. Psychology, U. Ill., Urbana, 1960. Prof. grad. sch. edn. UCLA, 1960—, founder Ctr. Study Evaluation, 1966, chmn. div. ednl. psychology, chmn. faculty, 1991—; fellow Ctr. for Advanced Study in Behavioral Scis., 1967-68; vis. prof. U. Wis., U. Ill., Ind. U., Monash U., Australia; bd. dirs. Far West Labs., San Francisco, 1989—; chmn. com. on evaluation and assessment L.A. Unified Sch. Dist., 1988—; mem. nat. adv. panel for math. scis. NRC of NAS, 1988-89; chmn. nat. bd. Nat. Ctr. for Rsch. in Math. Scis. Edn., 1991—. Author, editor: The Evaluation of Instruction, 1970, Changing Education, 1973, Learning and Instruction, 1977, The Human Brain, 1977, Danish transl., 1980, Spanish transl., 1982, The Brain and Psychology, 1980, Instructional Psychology: Education and Cognitive Processes of the Brain, Neuropsychological and Cognitive Processes of Reading, 1981, Handbook of Research on Teaching, 3d edit., 1986, The Future of Educational Psychology, 1989, Research in Learning and Teaching, 1990, Testing and Cognition, 1991. Capt. USAF. Recipient Thorndike award for outstanding psychol. rsch., 1987, Disting. Tchr. of Univ. award UCLA, 1990; Ford Found. grantee. Fellow AAAS, APA (pres. divsn. ednl. pscyholgy 1984-85, assn. coun. 1988-91, Award for Outstanding Svc. to Ednl. Psychology 1991), Am. Psychol. Soc. (charter), Am. Ednl. Rsch. Assn. (chmn. ann. conv., chmn. publs. 1980-83, assn. coun. 1986-89, bd. dirs. 1987-89, chmn. com. on ednl. TV 1989—, Outstanding Contbns. award 1986, Outstanding Svc. award 1989); mem. Phi Delta Kappa. Office: UCLA 321 Moore Hall Los Angeles CA 90024

WIZARD, BRIAN, publisher, author; b. Newburyport, Mass., June 24, 1949; s. Russell and Ruth (Hidden) Willard. BA, Sonoma (Calif.) State U., 1976. Pvt. practice jeweler, sculptor, craftsman Sebastopol, Calif., 1974-79; prin. The Starquill Pub., Port Douglas, Queensland, Australia, 1981—; with Starquill Internat., Santa Rosa, Calif., 1986—; singer, songwriter, 1988—. Author: Permission to Kill, 1985, Tropical Pair, 1986, Shindara, 1987, Metempsychosis, 1988, Heaven On Earth, 1990, Coming of Age, 1990, Permission to Live, 1992; contbr. to SpaceArc; producer video documentary Thunderhawks, 1987; songwriter, producer cassette Brian Wizard Sings for His Supper, 1989. Renovator historic landmark the Tope Creek Lookout (Skyship). Served with U.S. Army, 1967-70. Decorated Air medals (26). Mem. Vietnam Helicopter Crewmember Assn., 145th Combat Aviation Bn. Assn., Vietnam Combat Vets. Assn., Vietnam Vets. Am., Vietnam Vets. Australia Assn. Office: PO Box 42 Wallowa OR 97885-0042

WLODKOWSKI, RAYMOND JOHN, psychology educator; b. Detroit, Aug. 7, 1943; s. Joseph John and Josephine (Wincek) W.; children: Phillip, Katherine, Claire. BS, Wayne State U., 1965, PhD, 1970. Lic. psychologist. Tchr. Detroit Pub. Schs., 1965-67, sch. psychologist, 1967-68; prof. U. Wis., Milw., 1970-88; human rels. specialist Milw. Pub. Schs., 1977; mem. core faculty Antioch U., Seattle, 1989-92; field adv. Fielding Inst., Santa Barbara, Calif., 1989-92; cons. AT&T Communications, Newark, N.J., 1987-90, ASCD, 1983-92. Author: Enhancing Adult Motivation to Learn, 1985, Motivation and Teaching, 1978; co-author: Eager to Learn, 1990. Recipient Teaching award U. Wis., Milw., 1974. Mem. APA, Nat. Soc. of Performance and Instruction, ASCD, Am. Ednl. Rsch. Assn. Home and Office: 6033 Jay Rd Boulder CO 80301

WOBBEKIND, RICHARD LOUIS, business research director, economics educator; b. N.Y.C., Mar. 16, 1953; s. William Joseph and Florence (Rasulo) W.; m. Carol Ann Hoops, June 4, 1977; children: Daniel, Amber, Kate. BA, Bucknell U., Lewisburg, Pa., 1975; MA, U. Colo., 1979, PhD in Econs., 1984. Rsch. assoc. Inst. for Regional Affairs, Lewisburg, 1975-76; teaching asst. dept. econs. U. Colo., Boulder, 1976-79, instr. Econs. Inst., 1979-84, rsch. assoc. Ctr. for Econ. Analysis, 1984-85, asst. prof. Coll. Bus., 1985-88, assoc. dir., asst. prof. Bus. Rsch Div., 1988-91, dir., asst. prof. Bus. Rsch. Div., 1991—. Contbr. chpt. to book, articles to profl. jours. Coach, South Boulder Little League, 1988-89, bd. dirs., 1991—; coach Boulder Valley Girls Softball, 1992—. Mem. Nat. Assn. Bus. Ecoomists, Am. Econs. Assn., Fin. Mgmt. Assn., Colo. Planning Forum, Denver Assn. Bus. Economists, Travel and Tourism Rsch. Assn. (Mountain States chpt.), Denver Assn. Bus. Economists (sec.-treas. 1991-92, v.p. 1992-93), Assn. for Univ. Bus. and Econs. Rsch. (bd. dirs. 1991-93). Home: 873 Columbia Pl Boulder CO 80303 Office: U Colo Campus Box 419 Boulder CO 80309

WOCHOK, ZACHARY STEPHEN, biotechnology company executive; b. Phila., Dec. 29, 1942; s. Andrew and Mary (Tomaszewsky) W.; m. Barbara Nadya Wylder, Apr. 3, 1949; children: Adria, Alexis, Zachary, Larys-sa. BA, LaSalle U., 1964; MS, Villanova U., 1967; PhD, U. Conn., 1970. Postdoctoral fellow Yale U., New Haven, 1971; assoc. prof. U. Ala., Tuscaloosa, 1971-76; group leader Weyerhaeuser, Centralia, Wash., 1976-78; dir. rsch. and devel. Native Plants, Inc., Salt Lake City, 1978-80; mgr. bus. devel. Monsanto, St. Louis, 1980-83; v.p. Plant Genetics, Inc., Davis, Calif., 1983-84, pres., CEO, 1984-89; pres., COO Calgene, Inc., Davis, 1989-91; chmn., CEO Nurture, Inc., Missoula, Mont., 1992—; pres. Seren Agricorp, Davis, 1992—. Patentee in field; contbr. more than 80 articles to profl. jours. Mem. Am. Soc. Plant Physiology, Calif. Indsl. Biotechnology Assn. (bd. dirs. 1988-92, chmn. 1991-92). Ukrainian Catholic. Home: 39816 Morning Dove Pl Davis CA 95616

WODELL, GEOFFREY ROBERT, management consultant; b. Madison, Wis., June 15, 1949; s. Robert Holland and Juanita Jacqueline (Francisco) W.; m. Lynn Johnson, Aug. 2, 1975; 1 child, Haaland Johnson. BA, U. Wis., 1971; postgrad., Met. State U., 1987, U. Oslo, Norway, 1987, Loretto Heights U., 1987-88; MA, Webster U., 1990. Mgr. Contact Electronics, Madison, 1972-74; buyer, mgr. Cecil's Boot Ranch, Madison, 1974-76; salesman Miller Stockman div. Miller Internat., Denver, 1976-77, asst. mgr., 1977-78; mgr. Miller Internat., Inc., Denver, 1978-79; buyer Miller Internat., Inc., 1979-80, real estate exec., 1980-89; human resource devel. cons. Nyveg Cons., Mpls., 1989—. Mem. Econ. Devel. and Revitalization Commn. of Wheat Ridge. Mem. Internat. Transactional Analysis Assn., Nat. Assn. Neuro-Linguistic Programmers, Sons of Norway (mgmt. trainer 1980—, pres. 6th dist. 1988, internat. dir. 1988—), Nordmanns Forbundet, Nat. Wildlife Fedn., World Wildlife Fedn., Better World Soc., Nature Conservancy, Eagles Soccer Club, Kicker Sports, Masons. Lutheran. Home: 3935 Garland St Wheat Ridge CO 80033-4210 Office: 7500 W 29th Ave Wheat Ridge CO 80033

WOELLMER, RALPH, hotel executive; b. White Plains, N.Y., Nov. 13, 1958; s. Helmut Erich and Christa (Hurrle) W.; m. Shelley Lynn Godown, July 1, 1989. BS, No. Ariz. U., 1984. Cert. hotel adminstr. Owner, operator Matterhorn Motor Lodge, Sedona, Ariz., 1980-85; front office mgr. Boars Head Inn, Charlottesville, Va., 1985-86; gen. mgr. Archbishops Mansion Inn, San Francisco, 1987-88, Kensington Park Hotel, San Francisco, 1988-90; v.p., gen. mgr. Bodega Bay (Calif.) Lodge, 1990—; v.p. Matterhorn Shoppes Inc., Sedona, 1984—. Bd. dirs. Sonoma County Conv. and Visitors Bur., Santa Rosa, 1992—. Mem. Bodega Bay Area C. of C. (bd. dirs. 1991—). Republican. Roman Catholic. Home: 230 Apple Ave Sedona AZ 86336 Office: Bodega Bay Lodge 103 Coast Hwy 1 Bodega Bay CA 94923

WOESSNER, FREDERICK T., composer, pianist; b. Teaneck, N.J., July 23, 1935; s. Fred and Bertha W.; m. Lise, Feb. 14, 1960 (div. 1973); children: Betty, Allison. Student, Peabody Conservatory of Music, Balt., 1960-61; MBA, NYU, 1968; MA, Calif. State U., Los Angeles, 1975; pvt. study with, David Diamond, Charles Haubiel, Albert Harris. Pres., chmn. Music and the Arts Found. of Am., Inc., Los Angeles, 1971—; owner Al-Fre-Bett Music, Los Angeles, 1980—. Composer (for orch.) Nursery Song, Variations on an Irish Air, Reflections for Strings, Fanfare for Winds, String Quartet, Concerto for piano improvisations and orch., Secret Gospels (Cantata), Sonic studies for Piano I, (music for films) Sky Bandits, Pale Horse, Pale Rider, The Curb Your Appetite Diet, Centerfold, (title music for TV) Actors Forum, (for stage) From Berlin to Broadway, Oh Atlantis, Kurt, Lil Nell, Another Town, Victorian Atmospheres; composer and pianist, album-film/video, Vincent Moreaux, His Finest HourIn My Forest Cathedral; rec. artist Sonic Arts and Repertoire Records. V.p., bd. dirs. U. Hollywood; mem. bd. gov's. L.A. Songwriters Showcase-Songwriters Expo. With U.S. Army, 1960-61. Mem. ASCAP, Nat. Acad. Recording Arts and Scis., Dramatists Guild, Soc. Composers and Lyricists, Am. Fedn. Musicians, Am. Soc. Music Arrangers and Composers (treas. 1978—), Composers and Arrangers Found. Am. (sec.). Democrat. Office: Al-Fre-Bett Music PO Box 45 Los Angeles CA 90078-0045

WOFSY, DAVID, medical educator; b. N.Y.C., Dec. 26, 1946; s. Leon and Rosalind (Taub) W.; m. Constance Bell, July 16, 1970; children: Kevin, Susan. AB, Harvard U., 1968; MD, U. Calif., 1974. Diplomate Am. Bd. Internal Medicine, Am. Bd. Rheumatology. Intern/resident in internal medicine U. Calif., San Francisco, 1974-77, asst. prof., 1982-87, assoc. prof., 1987-93, prof., 1993—. Contbr. articles to profl. jours.

WOGAN, TERRI KAY, volunteer administrator; b. Honolulu, May 22, 1953; d. William Neil and Barbara Rose (Faus) Walton; m. W. Mark Wogan, Oct. 26, 1974; children: Lindsay Ann, Meghan Lynn, Jennifer Kay. BA in Elem. Edn., Ariz. State U., 1975, Libr. Endorsement, 1975. Libr., media specialist Paradise Valley Schs., Phoenix, 1976-80; vol. adminstr. State of Ariz. Dept. of Econ. Security, Phoenix, 1990—. Campaign worker Bill Walton, City Coun. Election, Scottsdale, Ariz., 1984-88. Named Clubwoman of Yr., Scottsdale Jr. Woman's Club, 1987, Outstanding Young Women of Am., 1988. Mem. Dirs. of Vols. in Agencies, GFWC Scottsdale Woman's Club (pres. 1989-90), Gen. Fedn. Woman's Clubs Jr. (2d v.p. 1992-94). Lutheran. Home: 4817 E Marconi Ave Scottsdale AZ 85254

WOHL, ARMAND JEFFREY, cardiologist; b. Phila., Dec. 11, 1946; s. Herman Lewis and Selma (Paul) W.; m. Marylouise Katherine Giangrossi, Sept. 4, 1977; children: Michael Adam, Todd David. Student, Temple U., 1967; MD, Hahnemann U., 1971. Intern Bexar County Hosp., San Antonio, 1971-72; resident in internal medicine Parkland Hosp., Dallas, 1972-74; fellow in cardiology U. Tex. Southwestern Med. Ctr., Dallas, 1974-76; chief of cardiology USAF Hosp. Elmendorf, Anchorage, 1976-78; chief cardiologist Riverside (Calif.) Med. Clin., 1978-79; cardiologist Grossmont Cardiology Med. Group, La Mesa, Calif., 1980-84; pvt. practice, La Mesa, 1985—; chief of cardiology Grossmont Hosp., La Mesa, 1988-90; asst. clin. prof. Sch. Medicine. U. Calif., San Diego, 1990—. Contbr. articles to profl. jours. Bd. dirs. San Diego County chpt. Am. Heart Assn., 1981-87. Maj. USAF, 1976-78. Fellow Am. Coll. Cardiology (councilor Calif. chpt. 1991—), Am. Coll. Physicians, Coun. on Clin. Cardiology. Office: 5565 Grossmont Center Dr La Mesa CA 91942-3021

WOHLER, JEFFERY WILSON, newspaper editor; b. Eugene, Oreg., Dec. 30, 1947; s. Benjamin Otto and Mildred Martha (Wilson) W.; m. Kandis Brewer, May 4, 1974 (div. 1985); m. Mary Lou Fletcher, Aug. 30, 1986; 1 child, Kennedy Read. BS in Journalism, U. Oreg., 1970. Staff writer Oreg. Jour., Portland, 1970-76, suburban editor, 1976-78, asst. city editor, 1978-80, city editor, 1980-82; dep. metro. editor The Oregonian, Portland, 1982-84, sports editor, 1984-92, editor, voice info. svcs., 1992—. Mem. Assoc. Press Sports Editors (v.p. 1989-91, pres. 1991-92), City Club of Portland (com. chair). Home: 7610 NE Sacramento Portland OR 97213 Office: Oregonian 1320 SW Broadway Portland OR 97201-3469

WOHLETZ, KENNETH HAROLD, volcanologist; b. Chico, Calif., Jan. 19, 1952; s. Norbert Harlod and Martha Deborah (Focht) W.; m. Ann Grayson Barker. BA, U. Calif., Santa Barbara, 1974; MS, Ariz. State U., 1976, PhD, 1980. Grad. rsch. asst. Ariz. State U., Tempe, 1974-79, postdoctoral rsch. asst., 1980-81; vis. scientist Consiglio Nationale della Ricerche, Pisa, Italy, 1980; postdoctoral rsch. asst. Ariz. State U., Tempe, 1980-81; geology instr. U. N.Mex., Los Alamos, 1982-83; vis. staff mem. Los Alamos (N.Mex.) Nat. Lab., 1975-80, postdoctoral fellow, 1981-83, staff mem., 1983—; volcanology prof. U. N.Mex., Albuquerque, 1991—; Ariz. coord. Internat. Kimberlite Conf., Tempe, 1977-78; vis. prof. U. Naples Federico II, Italy, 1992—. Author: Explosive Volcanism, 1984, Volcanic Ash, 1985 (award of excellence 1986), Volcanology and Geothermal Energy, 1992; contbr. articles to profl. jours. Mem. Internat. Assn. Volcanology and Chemistry of the Earth's Interior (organizer gen. assembly 1989), Am. Geophys. Union, Geol. Soc. Am., Sigma Xi. Roman Catholic. Home: 4 Karen Cir Los Alamos NM 87544-3797 Office: Los Alamos Nat Lab EES -1 MS D462 Los Alamos NM 87545

WOHLETZ, LEONARD RALPH, soil scientist, consultant; b. Nekoma, N.D., Oct. 22, 1909; s. Frank and Anna (Keifer) W.; m. Jane Geisendorfer, Sept. 1, 1935; children: Mary Jane, Leonard Ralph Jr., Elizabeth Ann, Catherine Ellen, Margaret Lee. BS, U. Calif., Berkeley, 1931, MS, 1933. Jr. soil expert USDA Soil Erosion Svc., Santa Paula, Calif., 1934; asst. regional chief soil surveys USDA Soil Conservation Svc., Santa Paula, 1935; asst. regional chief soil surveys USDA Soil Conservation Svc., Berkeley, 1939-42, soil survey supr., 1942-45, state soil scientist, 1945-68, asst. to state conservationist, 1969-71; cons. soil scientist Berkeley, 1973—. Author: Survey Guide, 1948; contbr. articles to profl. publs. including Know Calif. Land, Soils and Land Use Planning, Planning by Foresight and Hindsight. Mem. Waste Mgmt. Commn., Berkeley, 1981; chmn. com. Rep. for Congress, 8th Dist. Calif., 1980; pres. State and Berkeley Rep. Assembly, 1985—. Recipient Soil Conservationist of Yr., Calif. Wildlife Fedn., 1967. Mem. AAAS, Soil and Water Conservation Soc. (chmn. organic waste mgmt. com. 1973—, sect. pres., Dist. Svc. award, charter and life mem., Disting. Svc. award 1971, Outstanding Svc. award 1983), Soil Sci. Soc. Am. (emeritus), Internat. Soc. Soil Sci., Profl. Soil Sci. Assn. Calif., Commonwealth Club Calif., San Francisco Farmers Club. Roman Catholic. Home: 510 Vincente Ave Berkeley CA 94707-1522

WOHLFORTH, CARL CURTI, software engineer; b. N.Y.C., Nov. 19, 1956; s. Timothy and Martha (Curti) W. BS in Computer Sci., Rutgers U., 1982. Software engr. Symantec, Cupertino, Calif., 1983-84, KLA, San Jose, Calif., 1984-85, Cadtrak, Santa Clara, Calif., 1985-87, Quadrex, Campbell, Calif., 1987-88, Novell, San Jose, 1988-91; mgr. Norell, San Jose, 1991—. Designer (software) Lantern Svcs. Mgr., 1991. Mem. Assn. for Computing Machinery. Home: 15812 Alta Vista Way San Jose CA 95127 Office: Novell 2180 Fortune Dr San Jose CA 95131

WOJAHN, R. LORRAINE, state legislator; b. Tacoma, Wash. M. Gilbert Wojahn (dec.); 1 child. Mem. Wash. State Ho. of Reps., 1969-76; mem. Wash. State Senate from dist. 27, 1977—, pres. pro tempore; mem. rules, labor and commerce, health and human svcs., ways and means coms. Democrat. Office: State Senate State Capitol Olympia WA 98504 Other: 2515 S Cedar Tacoma WA 98405

WOJCIK, RICHARD FRANK, pharmaceutical company executive; b. Chgo., Apr. 1, 1936; s. Francis Joseph and Marie Cora (Szalecki) W.;m. Kathleen Mary Janousek, Nov. 18, 1961; children: Richard, Margaret, Christopher. BS, S.D. State U., 1958; cert., Columbia U., Harrison, N.Y., 1976. Registered pharmacist, Ill. Various sales positions Eli Lilly & Co., Chgo., 1960-67; market rsch. analyst Eli Lilly & Co., Indpls., 1967-68; dist. mgr. Eli Lilly & Co., Buffalo, 1968-71; mktg. plans mgr. Eli Lilly & Co., Indpls., 1971-72; regional mgr. southern region Dista Products, Atlanta, 1972-75; dir. sales eastern region Eli Lilly & Co., Boston, 1975-76; U.K. dir. mktg. Eli Lilly Internat., Basingstoke, Eng., 1976-79; European dir. mktg. Eli Lilly Internat., London, 1979; v.p. sales pharm. div. Eli Lilly & Co., Indpls., 1979-92; sr. v.p. sales and customer svc. McKesson Drug Co., San Francisco, 1992—. Fund raiser Indpls. Ballet Co., 1989, Indpls. Art Mus., 1990; adv. bd. U. Tex. Pharmacy Sch., Austin, 1986—. Capt. U.S. Army, 1958-59; capt. USAR, 1959-67. Mem. Meridian Hills Country Club, Hawthorne Golf and Country Club (bd. dirs. Noble Ctrs., adv. bd. govs.). Office: McKesson Drug Co One Post St San Francisco CA 94104-5296

WOLANER, ROBIN PEGGY, magazine publisher; b. Queens, N.Y., May 6, 1954; d. David H. and Harriet (Radlow) W.; m. Steven J. Castleman, 1992. B.S. in Indsl. and Labor Relations, Cornell U., 1975. Sr. editor Viva Mag., N.Y.C., 1975-76; editor Impact Mag., N.Y.C., 1976-77; circulation mgr. Runner's World Mag., Mountain View, Calif., 1977-79; cons. Ladd Assocs., San Francisco, 1979-80; gen. mgr. Mother Jones Mag., San Francisco, 1980-81, pub., 1981-85; founder, pub. Parenting Mag., San Francisco, 1985-91, pres., 1991-92; v.p. Time Pub. Ventures, 1990—; pres., chief exec. officer Sunset Pub. Corp., 1992—; trustee Muir Investment Fund, 1991—. Mem. bd. advisors Grad. Sch. Journalism, U. Calif., Berkeley, 1991—; bd. dirs. Bay Area Coun., 1992—. Jewish. Office: Sunset Pub 80 Willow Rd Menlo Park CA 94025

WOLAS, HERBERT, lawyer; b. Bronx, N.Y., June 27, 1933; s. Irving and Mary (Kessner) W.; m. Annette Rudolph, Aug. 20, 1957; children: Cherise, Collette, Claudine. AA, UCLA, 1953, BA, 1954, JD, 1960. Bar: Calif. 1961. Since practiced in L.A. Served with F.A. AUS, 1955-56. Office: 1875 Century Pk E Ste 2000 Los Angeles CA 90067

WOLBERS, HARRY LAWRENCE, engineering psychologist; b. L.A., Jan. 29, 1926; s. Harry Lawrence and Edith Christine (Nordeen) W.; m. Mary Lou Jordan Call, Feb. 18, 1972; children: Harry L., Richard C., Leslie A., Suzanne M. BS, Calif. Inst. Tech., 1946; MA, U. So. Calif., L.A., 1949, PhD, 1955. Lic. psychologist Calif. V.p. Psychol. Svcs., Inc., L.A., 1948-54; chief systems rsch. Douglas Aircraft Co., El Segundo, Calif., 1954-63; chief program engr. space systems Douglas Aircraft Co., Santa Monica/Huntington, 1963-74; chief systems engr. advanced space systems McDonnell Douglas Astronautics Co., Huntington Beach, Calif., 1974-85; adj. prof. dept. indsl. and systems engring. U. So. Calif., L.A., 1954-85; dep. dir. flight crew systems McDonnell Douglas Space Systems Co., Huntington Beach, 1985-91; ret.; mem. USAF Sci. Adv. Bd., Washington, 1991—; cons. NASA, Washington, 1988—. Contbr. articles to profl. jours. Lt. (j.g.) USN, 1943-47; ATO; PTO. Recipient Engring. Merit award San Fernando Valley Engrs. Coun., Calif., 1988. Fellow Human Factors Soc. (Orange County chpt. pres. 1989); mem. APA, Soc. Indsl. and Orgnl. Psychologists, Sigma Xi, Psi Chi.

WOLCOTT, OLIVER, psychiatrist, educator; b. Barneveld, N.Y., Feb. 25, 1930; s. George N. and Magdalen (Ames) W.; m. Helen Louise Mag, Aug. 29, 1950; children: Steven, Betsy, Peter, Andrew, Jennifer. BA, Western Res. U., 1951; MD, U. Rochester, 1955. Diplomate Am. Bd. Psychiatry and Neurology. Intern USPHS Hosp., San Francisco, 1955-56; resident in psychiatry U. Colo. Sch. Medicine, Denver, 1958-61, instr., then asst. prof., 1961-65, clin. asst. prof., 1965—; pvt. practice, Denver, 1965—; staff psychiatrist Mental Health Corp. Denver, 1982—; mem. staff State Hosp., Mental Health Ctr. Med. dir. USPHS, 1955-58, mem. Res. Fellow Am. Psychiat. Assn.; mem. Colo. Psychiat. Soc., Am. Soc. Hispanic Psychiatrists. Democrat. Unitarian. Office: 1514 Fairfax St Denver CO 80220

WOLD, ALEXANDER AUD, JR., lawyer; b. Phoenix, Mar. 15, 1946; s. Odd Alexander and Anne (Soucek) W.; m. Suzanne Marie Tessar, Dec. 20, 1968 (div. Apr. 1976); 1 chld, Rebecca E.; m. Rosemary Ann Shaw, Aug. 4, 1979; children: Kirsten A., Alexis M. BA in Latin Am. Studies, U. Wash., 1969, BS in Forestry, 1969, JD, 1977. Bar: Oreg. 1977, U.S. Ct. Appeals (9th cir.) 1983, U.S. Supreme Ct. 1989, N.Mex. 1990, Ariz. 1990, U.S. Dist. Ct. Ariz. 1991, U.S. Ct. Appeals (10th cir.) 1991, Calif. 1993; cert. civil trial lawyer Nat. Bd. Trial Advocacy. Asst. dist. atty. Lane County Dist. Atty., Eugene, Oreg., 1977-81; trial atty., ptnr. Dwyer, Simpson & Wold, Eugene, 1981-90; pvt. practice trial law Albuquerque, 1990-92; ptnr., trial atty. Flinn Wold Attys., Albuquerque, 1992—; Bar: Oreg. 1977, N.Mex. 1990, Ariz., 1990, Calif. 1993, U.S. Ct. Appeals (9th and 10th cirs.), U.S. Dist. Ct. Oreg., 1978, U.S. Dist. Ct. N.Mex., 1991, U.S. Dist. Ct. Ariz., 1991, U.S. Supreme Ct., 1989; cert. civil trial lawyer Nat. Bd. Trial Advocacy. V.p. Bethesda Luth. Ch., 1983-85. Capt. U.S. Army, 1969-74, Vietnam; lt. col. USAR, 1977—. Mem. ABA, Assn. Trial Lawyers Am., Oreg. State Bar, State Bar Calif., State Bar Calif., State Bar Ariz., Ariz. Trial Lawyers Assn., N.Mex. Trial Lawyers Assn., Wash. Trial Lawyers Assn. Democrat. Home: 1040 Red Oaks Lp NE Albuquerque NM 87122 Office: Flinn Wold Attys 302 Silver Ave SE Albuquerque NM 87102

WOLD, JOHN SCHILLER, geologist, former congressman; b. East Orange, N.J., Aug. 31, 1916; s. Peter Irving and Mary (Helff) W.; m. Jane Adele Pearson, Sept. 28, 1946; children: Peter Irving, Priscilla Adele, John Pearson. AB, St. Andrews U., Scotland and Union Coll., Schenectady, 1938; MS, Cornell U., 1939; LLD (hon.), U. Wyo., 1991. Dir. Fedn. Rocky Mountain States, 1966-68; v.p. Rocky Mountain Oil and Gas Assn., 1967, 68; mem. Wyo. Ho. of Reps., 1957-59; Republican candidate for U.S. Senate, 1964, 70; mem. 91st Congress at large from, Wyo.; pres. BTU, Inc., Wold Oil & Gas Co., Wold Nuclear Co., Wold Mineral Exploration Co., Casper, Wyo.; founding pres. Wyo. Heritage Soc.; founder Central Wyo. Ski Corp.; chmn. Wyo. Nat. Gas Pipeline Authority, 1987-91; bd. dirs. Plains Petroleum Co., Coca Mines, Inc.; chmn. bd. dirs. Nuclear Exploration and Devel. Corp., Mineral Engring. Co. Contbr. articles to profl. jours. Chmn. Wyo. Rep. Com., 1960-64, Western State Rep. Chmns. Assn., 1963-64; mem. exec. com. Rep. Nat. Com., 1962-64; chmn. Wyo. Rep. State Fin. Com.; Active Little League Baseball, Boy Scouts Am., United Fund, YMCA, Boys Clubs Am.; former pres. bd. trustees Casper Coll.; trustee Union Coll. Served to lt. USNR, World War II. Named Wyo. Man of Yr. AP-UPI, 1968; Wyo. Mineral Man of Yr., 1979, Wyo. Heritage award, 1992. Mem. Wyo. Geol. Assn. (hon. life, pres. 1956), Am. Assn. Petroleum Geologists, Ind. Petroleum Assn. Am., AAAS, Wyo. Mining Assn., Sigma Xi, Alpha Delta Phi. Episcopalian (past vestryman, warden). Home: 1231 W 30th St Casper WY 82604-4738 Office: Mineral Resource Ctr 139 W 2d St Casper WY 82601

WOLF, CHARLES, JR., economist, educator; b. N.Y.C., Aug. 1, 1924; s. Charles and Rosalie W.; m. Theresa van de Wint, Mar. 1, 1947; children: Charles Theodore, Timothy van de Wint. B.S., Harvard U., 1943, M.P.A., 1948, Ph.D. in Econs., 1949. Economist, fgn. service officer U.S. Dept. State, 1945-47, 49-53; mem. faculty Cornell U., 1953-54, U. Calif., Berkeley, 1954-55; sr. economist The Rand Corp., Santa Monica, Calif., 1955-67; head econs. dept. The Rand Corp., 1967-81; dean The Rand Grad. Sch., 1970—, dir. internat. econ. rsch., 1981—; sr. fellow Hoover Inst., 1988—; bd. dirs. Fundamental Investors Fund, Capital Income Builder Fund, Am. Capital Fund, Capital World Growth Fund; mem. exec. com. Rand-UCLA Health Policy Ctr.; mem. adv. com. UCLA Clin. Scholars Program; lectr. econs. UCLA, 1960-72; mem. exec. com. Rand Ctr. for Russian and Eurasian Studies. Author: The Costs and Benefits of the Soviet Empire, 1986, Markets or Governments: Choosing Between Imperfect Alternatives, 1988, 93, (with others) The Impoverished Superpower: Perestroika and the Soviet Military Burden, 1990, Linking Economic Policy and Foreign Policy, 1991, Promoting Democracy and Free Markets in Eastern Europe, 1992; contbr. articles to profl. jours. Mem. Assn. for Public Policy Analysis and Mgmt. (pres. 1980-81), Am. Econs. Assn., Econometric Soc., Coun. on Fgn. Rels., Internat. Inst. Strategic Studies London. Clubs: Cosmos (Washington); Riviera Tennis (Los Angeles); Harvard (N.Y.). Office: RAND Grad Sch Policy Studies 1700 Main St Santa Monica CA 90401-3297

WOLF, CYNTHIA TRIBELHORN, librarian, library educator; b. Denver, Dec. 12, 1945; d. John Baltazar and Margaret (Kern) Tribelhorn; m. H.Y. Rassam, Mar. 21, 1969 (div. Jan. 1988); children: Najma C., Yousuf J. BA, Colo. State U., 1970; MLS, U. Denver, 1985. Cert. permanent profl. librarian, N.Mex. Elem. tchr. Sacred Heart Sch., Farmington, N.Mex., 1973-78; asst. prof. library sci. edn. U. N.Mex., Albuquerque, 1985-90, dir. libr. sci. edn. divsn., 1989-90; pres. Info. Acquisitions, Albuquerque, 1990—; libr. dir. Southwestern Coll., Santa Fe, 1992—; fine arts resource person for gifted edn. Farmington Pub. Schs., 1979-83. Mem. Farmington Planning and Zoning Commn., 1980-81; bd. dirs. Farmington Mus. Assn., 1983-84; pres. Farmington Symphony League, 1978. Mem. ALA, N.Mex. Library Assn., LWV (bd. dirs. Farmington, 1972-74, 75, pres.). Office: Southwestern Coll PO Box 4788 Santa Fe NM 87502

WOLF, DOUGLAS JEFFREY, lawyer; b. Merced, Calif., June 19, 1953; s. Stanley William and Phyllis (Donner) W.; m. Vicki Lynn Fields, July 8, 1979; children: Joshua Michael, Carly Suzanne, Jordan Matthew. AB, U. Calif., Davis, 1974; JD, Southwestern U., Los Angeles, 1977. Bar: U.S. Dist. Ct. (cen. dist.), U.S. Ct. of Appeals (9th cir.). Criminal justice planner San Mateo County Criminal Justice Council, Burlingame, Calif., 1972-74; law clk. Friedman and Cone, Los Angeles, 1974-79; pvt. practice Los Angeles, 1979-82, Woodland Hills, Calif., 1982—. Pres. The Cheryl Fields Found. for Victims, L.A., 1984; bd. dirs. Adam Walsh Child Resource Ctr., Orange, Calif., 1986; bd. dirs. Mothers Against Sexual Abuse; adv. Visiting Nurses Assn., Van Nuys, Calif. Mem. Calif. State Bar, San Fernando Valley Bar Assn., Los Angeles County Bar Assn. Democrat. Jewish. Office: 6355 Topanga Canyon Blvd Woodland Hills CA 91367-2107

WOLF, G. VAN VELSOR, JR., lawyer; b. Balt., Feb. 19, 1944; s. G. Van Velsor and Alice Roberts (Kimberly) W.; m. Ann Holmes Kavanagh, May 19, 1984; children: George Van Velsor III, Christopher Kavanagh, Elisabeth Huxley. BA, Yale U., 1966; JD, Vanderbilt U., 1973. Bar: N.Y. 1974, Ariz. 1982, U.S. Dist. Ct. (so. dist.) N.Y. 1974, U.S. Dist. Ct. Ariz. 1982, U.S. Ct. Appeals (2d cir.) 1974, U.S. Ct. Appeals (9th cir.) 1982. Agrl. advisor U.S. Peace Corps, Tanzania and Kenya, 1966-70; assoc. Milbank, Tweed, Hadley & McCloy, N.Y.C., 1973-75; vis. lectr. law Airlangga U., Surabaya, Indonesia, 1975-76, U. Ariz. 1990, Vanderbilt U., 1991; editor in chief Environ. Law Reporter, Washington, 1976-81; cons. Nat. Trust for Historic Preservation, Washington, 1981; assoc. Lewis & Roca, Phoenix, 1981-84, ptnr., 1984-91; ptnr. Snell & Wilmer, Phoenix, 1991—. Bd. dirs. Ariz. div. Am. Cancer Soc., 1985—. Editor: Toxic Substances Control, 1980; contbr. articles to profl. jours. Bd. dirs. Phoenix Little Theater, 1983-90, chmn., 1986-88. Mem. ABA, Assn. Bar City N.Y., Ariz. State Bar Assn. (coun. environ. & nat. res. law sect. 1988—, chmn. 1991-92), Maricopa County Bar Assn., Ariz. Acad., Union Club (N.Y.C.), Univ. Club (Phoenix). Office: Snell & Wilmer One Arizona Ctr Phoenix AZ 85004-0001

WOLF, JACK KEIL, electrical engineer, educator; b. Newark, Mar. 14, 1935; s. Joseph and Rosaline Miriam (Keil) W.; m. Toby Katz, Sept. 10, 1955; children—Joseph Martin, Jay Steven, Sarah Keil. B.S., U. Pa., 1956; M.S.E., Princeton, 1957, M.A., 1958, Ph.D., 1960. With R.C.A., Princeton, N.J., 1959-60; asso. prof. N.Y. U., 1963-65; from asso. prof. to prof. elec. engring. Poly. Inst. Bklyn., 1965-73; prof. dept. elec. and computer engring. U. Mass., Amherst, 1973-85; chmn. dept. U. Mass., 1973-75; chaired prof. Ctr. Magnetic Rec. Research, dept. elec. engring. and computer sci. U. Calif.-San Diego, La Jolla, 1985-92, Stephen O. Rice Prof., 1992—; Mem. tech. staff Bell Telephone Labs., Murray Hill, N.J., 1968-69; engring. assoc. Qualcomm Inc., San Diego, 1985—. Editor for: coding I.E.E.E. Transactions on Information Theory, 1969-72. Served with USAF, 1960-63. NSF sr. postdoctoral fellow, 1971-72; Guggenheim fellow, 1979-80. Fellow IEEE (pres. info. theory group 1974, co-recipient info. theory group prize paper award 1975, co-recipient Comm. Soc. prize paper award 1993), Nat. Acad. Engring.; mem. AAAS, Sigma Xi, Sigma Tau, Eta Kappa Nu, Pi Mu Epsilon, Tau Beta Pi. Home: 197 Desert Lakes Dr Rancho Mirage CA 92270-4053

WOLF, JOHN CHARLES, construction executive; b. Duluth, Minn., Mar. 10, 1947; s, William Chester and Adeline (Loughlin) W.; m. Mary Beth Stokes, Nov. 8, 1980; children: Peter, Marisa. Student, U. Minn., 1965-67. Supr. Leo Burnett Advt., Chgo., 1968-71; prin. Wolf Constrn., Chgo., 1972-75; pres. Wolf Corp., Santa Fe, N.Mex., 1976—; cons. Coldwell Banker, Santa Fe, 1986-89, Bert Pro Agy., Santa Fe, 1987-89, Allene LaPides Galleries, Santa Fe, 1988-89; developer and builder of various residential and comml. properties, 1979—. Mem. Better Bus. Bur., Nat. Assn. Home Builders, Assn. Gen. Contractors Am. Office: Wolf Corp 984 Acequia Madre Santa Fe NM 87501-2873

WOLF, JOSEPH ALBERT, mathematician, educator; b. Chgo., Oct. 18, 1936; s. Albert M. and Goldie (Wykoff) W. BS, U. Chgo., 1956, MS, 1957, PhD, 1959. Mem. Inst. for Advanced Study, Princeton, 1960-62, 65-66; asst. prof. U. Calif., Berkeley, 1962-64, assoc. prof., 1964-66, prof., 1966—, Miller research prof., 1972-73, 83-84; prof. honorario Universidad Nacional de Cordoba, Argentina, 1989; vis. prof. Rutgers U., 1969-70, Hebrew U., Jerusalem, 1974-76, Tel Aviv U., 1974-76, Harvard U., 1979-80, 86. Author: Spaces of Constant Curvature, 1967, 72, 74, 77, 84, Unitary Representations on Partially Holomorphic Cohomology Spaces, 1974, Unitary Representations of Maximal Parabolic Subgroups of the Classical Groups, 1976, Classification and Fourier Inversion for Parabolic Subgroups with Square Integrable Nilradical, 1979; co-editor, author: Harmonic Analysis and Representations of Semisimple Lie Groups, 1980; editor Geometriae Dedicata, Math Reports, Journal of Mathematical Systems, Estimation and Control, Nova Journal of Algebra and Geometry, Letters in Mathematical Physics, Journal of Group Theory in Physics; contbr. articles to profl. jours. Alfred P. Sloan rsch. fellow, 1965-67, NSF fellow, 1959-62; recipient Médaille de l'Université de Liège, 1977. Mem. Am., Swiss math. socs. Office: Dept Math U Calif Berkeley CA 94720

WOLF, KENNETH ERWIN, audiologist; b. Los Angeles, Dec. 24, 1948; s. Max B. and Sarah (Segal) W.; m. Laurel Adrianne Weinstein, June 20, 1970; children: Allison, Wendy. BA, U. Calif., 1970, MA, 1972; PhD, U. Wis., 1977. Asst. dir. Cin. Ctr. Developmental Disorders, 1977-78; dir. audiology Pulec Ear Clinic, Los Angeles, 1978-79; chief communicative sci. & disorders, assoc. prof. otoloaryngology King/Drew Med. Ctr., Los Angeles, 1980—; adj. prof. Calif. State U., Northridge, 1985—. Contbr. articles to profl. jours., chpts. to books. Bd. dirs. Inst. Human Svcs., Van Nuys, Calif., 1987, Van Gogh St. Sch., Granada Hills, Calif., 1984-87, San Fernando Valley Child Guidance Ctr., 1988—; mem. profl. adv. bd. TRIPOD, L.A., 1988. Fellow Soc. Ear, Nose & Throat Advances Children, Am. Speech Lang. Hearing Assn. (cert. 1979, councilor 1988—), Calif. Speech Lang. Hearing Assn. (commn. legis. 1985-89, pres. 1991-92), Am. Acad. Audiology; mem. Am. Auditory Soc., Am. Acad. Otolaryngology. Democrat. Jewish. Office: King/Drew Med Ctr 12021 Wilmington Ave Los Angeles CA 90059-3099

WOLF, LAWRENCE JOSEPH, engineering educator; b. St. Louis, Aug. 10, 1938; s. Vincent F. and Clara A. (Holtkamp) W.; m. Barbara Ann Bieber, Aug. 12, 1961; children: Theresa, Carl, Lawrence V. AA, Harris Tchrs. Coll., 1959; BSME, Washington U., St. Louis, 1961, MS, 1962, DSc, 1971. Registered profl. engr., Tex., Mo., Ind., Ill. Engr. Monsanto Corp., St. Louis, 1962-63; design engr. McDonnell Douglas, St. Louis, 1963-64; from instr. to assoc. prof. to prof. to dept. head St. Louis Community Coll.-Florissnat Valley, 1964-72, assoc. dean, 1975-78; assoc. prof. U. Petroleum and Minerals, Dhahran, Saudi Arabia, 1972-74; dean instrn. Wentworth Inst., Boston, 1974-75; dept. head Purdue U.-Calumet, Hammond, Ind., 1978-80; dean tech. U. Houston, from 1980; pres. Oreg. Inst. of Tech., Klamath Falls, 1991—; cons. engr. Nooter Corp., St. Louis, 1965-72; guest scientist Brookhaven Nat. Lab. and Superconducting Supercollider Lab., 1989—; bd. dirs. United Way of Klamath Falls, Cascades East Area Health Edn. Ctr. Author: Understanding Structures...A Parallel Approach to Statics and Strength of Materials; editor Jour. Engring. Tech., 1983-87; contbr. 40 articles to profl. jours. Leader Webelos Boy Scouts Am., Houston; chmn. Sesquicentennial Cannon Com., Houston, 1986. Served with U.S. Army, 1956-57. Mem. Am. Soc. Engring. Edn. (div. chmn., James H. McGraw award 1987), Soc. Mfg. Engrs., ASME, Accrediting Bd. Engring. and Tech. (chmn. commn.). Office: Oreg Inst Tech Office of Pres 3201 Campus Dr Klamath Falls OR 97601-8801

WOLF, MONICA THERESIA, procedures analyst; b. Germany, Apr. 26, 1943; came to U.S., 1953, naturalized, 1959; d. Otto and Hildegard Maria (Heim) Bellemann; children: Clinton, Danielle. BBA, U. Albuquerque, 1986. Developer Word Processing Ctr., Pub. Service of N.Mex., Albuquerque, 1971-74, word processing supr., 1974-78, budget coordinator, 1978-80, lead procedures analyst, 1980-88; owner Monica's Woodworks, 1988—; mem. adv. bd., student trainer APS Career Enrichment Ctr. Instr. firearm safety and pistol marksmanship. Mem. Internat. Word Processing Assn. (founder N.Mex. chpt.), Nat. Assn. Female Execs., Nat. Rifle Assn., N.Mex. Shooting Sports Assn. Democrat. Club: Sandia Gun (adv. bd., coach). Home and Office: 305 Alamosa Rd NW Albuquerque NM 87107-5312

WOLF, NORMAN SANFORD, cell biologist; b. Kansas City, Mo., July 22, 1927; s. Edward J. and Sadie H. Wolf; m. Joanne Cisneros, Dec. 1967 (div. Jan. 1975); 1 child, Jeremy R. BS, Kansas State U., 1953, DVM, 1953; PhD, Northwestern U., 1960. Diplomate Am. Coll. Lab. Animal Medicine. Dir. vivarium Northwestern U. Med. Sch., Chgo., 1953-58, postdoctoral fellow, 1953-60; NSF postdoctoral fellow Pasteur Inst., Paris, 1960-61; cons. Biology div. Oak Ridge (Tenn.) Nat. Lab., 1962-63; rsch. asst. prof. Div. Experimental Cell Biology Baylor Coll. Medicine, Houston, 1963-68; assoc. prof. Dept. Experimental Animal Medicine U. Wash. Med. Sch., Seattle, 1968-72; assoc. prof. Dept. Pathology U. Wash. Med. Sch., Seattle, 1968-90, prof., 1990—; adj. prof. dept. comparative medicine U. Wash., Seattle, 1990—; vis. scientist Cell Biology, Peter MacCallum Cancer Inst., Melbourne, Australia, 1988; chmn. animal care com. U. Wash., Seattle, 1987, 90-91. Contbr. articles to profl. jours. With U.S. Army, 1945-47. Postdoctoral Rsch. grant Nat. Inst. Scis., 1960-61; grantee NIH, 1969—. Mem. AAUP (exec. com. 1989—), Internat. Soc. for Exptl. Hematology, Soc. for Investigative Pathology, Am. Coll. Lab. Animal Medicine, ACLU, Common Cause, Amnesty Internat. Office: U Wash Dept Pathology SM-30 Seattle WA 98195

WOLFE, ALAN RHOADS, biochemist, researcher; b. Midland, Mich., Aug. 14, 1953; s. Richard Allen and Ellen Marie (Lane) W. BS, Mich. State U., 1979. Rsch. asst. Mich. Molecular Inst., Midland, 1980-84; postgrad. rschr. U. Calif., San Francisco, 1985—. Contbr. articles to profl. jours. Alumni scholar Mich. State U., 1972. Mem. AAAS, Am. Chem. Soc., Phi Beta Kappa. Home: 2525 Balboa St Apt 205 San Francisco CA 94121 Office: U Calif Dept Pharmacy San Francisco CA 94143-0446

WOLFE, BRENDA L., psychologist; b. Montreal, Can., Oct. 5, 1956; came to U.S., 1980.; d. Joseph and Mania (Tisch) Lichtenstein; m. Kenneth E. Wolfe; children: Alissa Jennifer, Emily Jeanne. BA, McGill U., 1980; MA, U. Calif., Santa Barbara, 1982, PhD, 1985. Teaching assoc. U. Calif., Santa Barbara, 1980-85; mgr. project and curriculum prodn. Edn. Systems Corp., San Diego, 1985-86; sr. project mgr. Jostens Learning Corp., San Diego, 1986-89; dir. rsch. Jenny Craig, Inc., San Diego, 1989—. Co-author: Jenny Craig's What Have You Got to Lose?, 1992; contbr. numerous articles to profl. jours. Scholar Western Psychol. Assn., 1982, 83, McGill U. faculty scholar, 1979; First Class Honors, 1980. Mem. APA, Assn. Advancement Behavior Therapy, Western Psychol. Assn., Sci. Rsch. Soc., Soc. of Behavioral Medicine, Sigma Xi.

WOLFE, BRIAN AUGUSTUS, sales executive; b. Mexico City, Nov. 23, 1946; came to U.S., 1947; s. Steward Augustus and Vivia Idalene (Fouts) W.; m. Holly Joyce Gilhart, Dec. 29, 1981; 1 child, Derek Augustus. BSME, Tex. A&M U., 1968. Project engr. Tex. Power & Light Co., Dallas, 1968-72; service engr. Babcock & Wilcox, Chgo., 1972-74; sales engr., New Eng. dist. Babcock & Wilcox, Boston, 1974-79; area mgr., Far East, internat. bus. Babcock & Wilcox, Barberton, Ohio, 1979-81; dist. sales mgr. Babcock & Wilcox, Lakewood, Colo., 1981—. Mem. Rocky Mountain Elec. League (bd. dirs. 1988—, v.p. 1990-91, pres.-elect 1991-92, pres. 1992-93). Home: 7285 W Vassar Ave Denver CO 80227-3303 Office: Babcock & Wilcox 7401 W Mansfield Ave Ste 410 Denver CO 80235-2224

WOLFE, CLIFFORD EUGENE, architect, writer; b. Harrington, Wash., Mar. 26, 1906; s. Delwin Lindsley and Luella Grace (Cox) W.; m. Frances Lillian Parkes, Sept. 12, 1936 (dec.); children: Gretchen Yvonne Wolfe Mason, Eric Von; m. Mary Theye Worthen. A.B. in Architecture, U. Calif.-Berkeley, 1933. Registered architect, Calif. Assoc. architect John Knox Ballantine, Architect, San Francisco, 1933-42; supervising architect, prodn. engr. G.W. Williams Co. Contractors, Burlingame, Calif., 1942-44; state-wide coord. med. schs. and health ctrs. office archs. and engrs. U. Calif.-Berkeley, San Francisco and Los Angeles, 1944-52; sec. council on hosp. planning Am. Hosp. Assn., Chgo., 1952-59; dir. planning dept. Office of York & Sawyer, Architects, N.Y.C., 1959-74; prin. Clifford E. Wolfe, AIA-E, Oakland, Calif., 1974-88; ret.; assoc. designer State of Calif. Commn. for Golden Gate International. Exposition, San Francisco, 1938-39; cons. Fed. Hosp. Council, Washington, 1954-60; mem. Pres.'s Conf. on Occupational Safety, Washington, 1955; rsch. architect Hosp Rsch. and Ednl. Trust, Chgo., 1957-59; instr. hosp. planning Columbia U., N.Y.C., 1961-73. Author, editor manuals on hosp. planning, engring. and safety, 1954-58. Author: Ballad of Humphrey The Humpback Whale, 1985; contbr. poetry to Tecolote Anthology, 1983, The Ina Coolbrith Circle, 1985, 87, 89, 91 (Grand prize Ina Coolbrith award 1986, Cleone Montgomery award 1990), Islandia, 1986, Tidings, 1989, Calif. Fedn. Chaparral Poets (pres. Tecolote chpt. 1982-86, 91—). Hosp. planning research grantee USPHS, 1956. Mem. AIA (chmn. honor awards com. Chgo. chpt. 1958-59, chmn. activities com. N.Y. chpt. 1972-74, mem. emeritus East Bay chpt. 1974—). Address: 3900 Harrison St Apt 306 Oakland CA 94611

WOLFE, KARL ROBERT, communications company executive, creative consultant; b. Sherwood, N.Y., Apr. 19, 1944; s. William Arron Mattis and Hazel Marie (Riey) W. Student, Coll. William and Mary, 1967-68; BSEE, U. Buffalo, 1973. Supt. Anaconda Am. Brass, Buffalo, 1973-74; mgr. engring. Arco Metals, Buffalo, 1974-81; dir. design and mktg. Tak Automation, Burlingame, Calif., 1981-82; pres., founder Creative Personal Comm., San Francisco and L.A., 1982—, Ctr. Excellence, San Francisco, 1986-88; assoc. John F. Kennedy U, Orida, Calif., 1983-89, Ctr. for Applied Instn., San Francisco, 1988-90. Active fundraising bd. Project Angel Food., 1993. With USAF, 1965-68. Mem. Assn. Transoprtational Psych., Assn. Past Life Rsch. and Therapy (assoc.), L.A. Ctr. for Living (assoc.). Office: Creative Personal Comm PO Box 691751 West Hollywood CA 90069

WOLFE, NICOLA, neuropsychologist; b. London, Nov. 26, 1956; came to U.S., 1956; d. Raymond and Ursula (Kaufmann) W.; m. Matthew Noah Tuchow, June 30, 1991. AB, Cornell U., 1978; MA, Harvard U., 1984, PhD, 1986. Lic. psychologist, Mass., Calif. Postdoctoral fellow Boston U. Sch. Medicine and Boston VA Med. Ctr., 1986-89; lectr. psychology Harvard U., Cambridge, Mass., 1986-89; faculty scholar rsch. Fulbright Found., Tokyo, 1989-90; staff neuropsychologist U. Calif.-Davis Sch. Medicine-Neurology, Berkeley, 1991—; cons. neuropsychology NIH Study of Guam-Parkinsonism-Dementia-Complex, 1986-91. Contbr. articles to profl. jours. Vol. English tchr. Community Edn. Svc., San Francisco, 1991—, Little Bros., Friends of the Elderly, Boston, 1988-89. NSF grad. fellow, Washington, 1982-85. Mem. Internat. Neuropsychol. Soc., Gerontologic Soc. Am., Internat. Psychogeriatric Assn. Democrat. Jewish. Office: U Calif Davis No Calif Alzheimers Disease Ctr 2001 Dwight Way Berkeley CA 94704

WOLFE, WILLIAM DOWNING, public utility administrator; b. Zanesville, Ohio, Nov. 14, 1947; s. William Jr. and Wava Benetta (Downing) W.; m. Laura Olivia Soza, July 29, 1972; children: Lisa Anne, Erin Nicole. BBA, U. Ariz., 1969. Instr. RTV Internat., N.Y.C., 1969-70; mgr. prodn. Sta. KUAT-TV/AM/FM, Tucson, 1969-76; lectr. U. Ariz., Tucson, 1970-78; mgr. prodn. Sta. KGUN-TV, Tucson, 1976-79; exec. producer Sta. KTVK-TV, Phoenix, 1979-82; writer, producer Ariz. Pub. Svc. Co., Phoenix, 1982-83, supr. pub. info., 1983-86; coord. emergency planning Palo Verde Nuclear Generating Sta., Phoenix, 1986—; cons. Nat. Student Films, Hollywood, Calif., 1975, Warner for Gov., Phoenix, 1986, various advt. agys., Tucson, Phoenix, various U.S. locations, 1974-83. writer, producer, dir. over 800 TV and multi-media programming and comml. advertisements for PM Mag., Wide World Sports, Good Morning Am., local, others, 1969—. Advisor Jr. Achievement, Tucson, 1976; chmn. com. Ariz. Citizens for Edn., Phoenix, 1988—; mem. budget adv. com., long-range planning com., supt. search profile com., supt. search com., bond election com., curriculum exit outcomes planning com., campus improvement team Deer Valley Sch. Dist.; bd. dirs. So. Ariz. chpt. Muscular Dystrophy Assn., 1976-79. Grantee Ford Found., 1969; recipient Golden Sch. Bell award Ariz. Dept. Edn., 1974-79, Emmy nomination Nat. Acad. TV Arts and Scis., 1979, Bronze Anvil nat. award Pub. Rels. Soc. Am., 1983, award Excellence Internat. Assn. Bus. Communicators. Mem. Nat. Emergency Mgmt. Assn., Nat. Radiol. Emergency Preparedness Conf. (Intercom 190, presdl. adv. com. on EBS system 1992—). Democrat. Roman Catholic. Office: Palo Verde Nuclear Generating Sta PO Box 52034 Phoenix AZ 85072-2034

WOLFE, WILLIAM JEROME, librarian, English language educator; b. Chgo., Feb. 24, 1927; s. Fred Wiley and Helen Dorothea (Lovaas) W.; m. ViviAnn Lundin, June 25, 1960 (div. 1962); 1 child, Lund. AB, U. Chgo., 1948; BA, Roosevelt U., Chgo., 1953; MEd, Chgo. State U., 1963; AA, Pima C.C., 1992. Tchr. English John Marshall High Sch., Chgo., 1956-60; libr. Safford Jr. High Sch., Tucson, Ariz., 1961-71, Santa Rita High Sch., Tucson, 1971-75, Tucson High Sch., 1975-87; tutor Eastside Ctr., Tucson Adult Lit. Vols., 1988-92, supr., 1993. Co-founder Tucson Classic Guitar Soc., 1969-72; docent U. Ariz. Mus. Art, Tucson, 1989-92; singer U. Ariz. Collegium

Musicum, Sons of Orpheus Male Chorus. With U.S. Army, 1945-46, ETO. Mem. Sons of Norway, Am. Legion, U. Chgo. Century Club, Roosevelt U. Sparling Soc., U. Ariz. Pres. Club, U. Ariz. Hon. Fellows Soc., Tuscon Post Card Exch. Club, U. Ariz. Assocs. of Art History. Republican. Mem. Ch. of Christ Scientist. Home: 8460 E Rosewood Tucson AZ 85710

WOLFE, WILLIAM LOUIS, optics educator; b. Yonkers, N.Y., Apr. 5, 1931; s. William Louis and Louise Helene (Becker) W.; m. Mary Lou Bongort; children: Carol, Barbara, Douglas. BS in Physics, Bucknell U., 1953; MS in Physics, U. Mich., 1956, MSEE, 1966. Research engr., lectr. U. Mich., Ann Arbor, 1953-66; dept. mgr., chief engr. Honeywell Radiation Ctr., 1966-69; prof. Optical Sci. Ctr., U. Ariz., Tucson, 1969—. Author (with others) Fundamentals of Infrared Technology, 1962; (with George J. Zissis) The Infrared Handbook, 1979; series editor: Optical Physics and Engineering; editor: Handbook of Military Infrared Technology; Am. editor Infrared Physics; contbr. numerous articles to profl. jours. Fellow Optical Soc. Am. (many bds. and coms.), Soc. Photo-optical Instrumentation Engrs. (pres., bd. govs., chmn. symposia, exec. com.); mem. IEEE (sr. mem.), Nat. Acad. Sci. (many coms.), Infrared Info. Symposia, Naval Intelligence Adv. Bd. (sci. adv. bd.), Air Force Ad Hoc Electro-Optics Com., Army Research Office Adv. Com., Army Scientific Adv. Bd., Am. Men of Sci., Leaders in Am. Sci., Phi Beta Kappa, Sigma Xi, Omicron Delta Kappa, Pi Mu Epsilon, Sigma Pi Sigma, Phi Eta Sigma. Office: U Ariz Tucson AZ 85721

WOLFF, DONALD GEORGE, theatrical agent, business owner; b. N.Y.C., Jan. 30, 1934; s. Milton Bernard and Gertrude (Levy) W. BS, Lehigh U., 1955. Agt. Baum-Newborn Agy., N.Y.C., 1955-60; v.p. Gen. Artists Corp., N.Y.C., 1960-68; v.p. Creative Mgmt. Assocs., N.Y.C., 1968-69, L.A., 1969-72; co-owner Bresler Wolff Cota and Livingston, L.A., 1972-79, The Artists Agy., L.A., 1979—. Office: Artists Agy 10000 Santa Monica Blvd Los Angeles CA 90067-7007

WOLFF, HOWARD KEITH, computer science educator, consultant; b. Los Angeles, Mar. 28, 1948; s. Fred and Yvonne (Primock) W.; m. Anna Bornino, Dec. 6, 1966 (div. June 1971); children: Francesea, Jeffrey; m. Cindy Brattan, June 4, 1981; children: Jeffrey, Mariya. BA, Calif. State U., Dominguez Hill, 1969; MPA, U. So. Calif., 1971, PhD, 1973; MS, Calif. State U., Chico, 1992. Prin. investigator U. Simon Fraser, Vancouver, B.C., Can., 1970-71; prof. U. So. Calif., L.A., 1971-73, Tribhuvan (Nepal) U., 1974-75, Calif. State U., Chico, 1976-85, 87—, Colo. State U., Ft. Collins, 1985-87; evaluation cons. Nat. Planning Commn., Kathmandu, Nepal, 1973-75; statis. cons. Nat. Population Commn., Kathmandu, 1983-87; cons. Butte Canyon Rsch. Assocs., Chico, Calif., 1979—, evaluation for Calif. State Dept. Edn. migrant edn. program, 1992—. Author: Social Science and Thesis Handbook, 1974; contbr. articles to profl. jours. Research grantee Can. Govt., Vancouver, 1970. Mem. IEEE, Am. Assn. Computing Machinery, Am. Soc. Pub. Adminstrn., Soc. Computer Simulations. Democrat. Club: Gears (Chico). Home: 1966 Honey Run Rd Chico CA 95928-8835 Office: Calif State U Dept Computer Sci/Dept Polit Sci Chico CA 95929

WOLFF, LOUIS ARTHUR, computer information systems educator; b. Altamont, Ill., Nov. 26, 1933; s. Louis August and Eileen Alice (Koberlein) W.; m. Norma Jean Weaver, June 21, 1952; children: Larry Alan, Cathy Ann Wolff Gustafson, Susan Eileen Wolff Beck. BS in Bus. Mgmt., U. La Verne, 1984, MS in Bus. Orgnl. Mgmt., 1986. Field engr. IBM, Madison, Wis., 1957-59; computer instr. IBM, Kingston, N.Y., 1959-63, program analyst, 1963-64; program rev. analyst IBM, Huntsville, Ala., 1964-71; program control mgr. IBM, Westlake Village, Calif., 1971-78, program adminstr., 1978-82; instr. computer software Moorpark (Calif.) Coll., 1974-82, prof. computer info. systems, 1982—; cons. The Other Office, Thousand Oaks, Calif., 1982—. Co-author: Fundamentals of Structured COBOL Programming, 6th edit., 1991. With USN, 1952-56. Mem. Assn. for Computing Machinery, Data Processing Mgmt. Assn. Democrat. Mem. Christian Ch. Home: 1443 Warwick Ave Thousand Oaks CA 91360-3548 Office: Moorpark Coll 7075 Campus Rd Moorpark CA 93021-1600

WOLFF, NELS CHRISTIAN, contracting officer; b. Cedar Falls, Iowa, Mar. 26, 1936; s. Jens Christian and Anna Marie (Sorensen) W. AA, Long Beach (Calif.) City Coll., 1982; JD, Pacific Coast U., 1984. Bar: Guam 1985. Remedial instr. Long Beach (Calif.) Sch. Dist., 1976-77; acct. Bethlehem Steel, 1977-80; supply tech. U.S. Army, 1980-81; contracting officer U.S. Coast Guard, 1981—; referee State Bar Ct., State of Calif., 1992—. Vol. Long Beach Unified Sch. Dist., 1975-76, 76-77, 77. Mem. USCG Auxiliary 1974, Assn. Trial Lawyers Am., Am. Soc. Mil. Comptrs., Nat. Contract Mgrs. Assn., Calif. Trial Lawyers Assn., L.A. Trial Lawyers Assn., Air Force Assn., NAVY League, Am. Legion, Sigma Delta Kappa. Office: 11th Coast Guard Dist 501 W Ocean Blvd Ste 7170 Long Beach CA 90822-5399

WOLFF, SIDNEY CARNE, astronomer, observatory administrator; b. Sioux City, Iowa, June 6, 1941; d. George Albert and Ethel (Smith) Carne; m. Richard J. Wolff, Aug. 29, 1962. BA, Carleton Coll., 1962, DSc (hon.), 1985; PhD, U. Calif., Berkeley, 1966. Postgrad. research fellow Lick Obs, Santa Cruz, Calif., 1969; asst. astronomer U. Hawaii, Honolulu, 1967-71, assoc. astronomer, 1971-76; astronomer, assoc. dir. Inst. Astronomy, Honolulu, 1976-83, acting dir., 1983-84; dir. Kitt Peak Nat. Obs., Tucson, 1984-87, Nat. Optical Astronomy Observatories, 1987—; dir. Gemini Project Gemini 8-Meter Telescopes Project, 1992—. Author: The A-Type Stars--Problems and Perspectives, 1983, (with others) Exploration of the Universe, 1987, Realm of the Universe, 1988, Frontiers of Astronomy, 1990; contbr. articles to profl. jours. Trustee Carleton Coll., 1989—. Research fellow Lick Obs. Santa Cruz, Calif., 1967. Mem. Astron. Soc. Pacific (pres. 1984-86, bd. dirs. 1979-85), Am. Astron. Soc. (coun. 1983-86, pres.-elect 1991, pres. 1992-94). Office: Nat Optical Astronomy Obs PO Box 26732 950 N Cherry Ave Tucson AZ 85726

WOLFGANG, BONNIE ARLENE, musician, bassoonist; b. Caribou, Maine, Sept. 29, 1944; d. Ralph Edison and Arlene Alta (Obetz) W.; m. Eugene Alexander Pridonoff, July 3, 1965 (div. Sept. 1977); children: George Randall, Anton Alexander, Stephan Eugene. MusB, Curtis Inst. Music, Phila., 1967. Soloist Phila. Orch., 1966; soloist with various orchs. U.S., Cen. Am., 1966-75; prin. bassoonist Phoenix Symphony, 1977—, with Woodwind Quintet, 1986—. Home: 10475 N 105th Way Scottsdale AZ 85258

WOLFINGER, BARBARA KAYE, film company executive; b. N.Y.C.; d. Louis and Margaret (Goodman) Klatzkie; m. Raymond E. Wolfinger, Aug. 8, 1960; 1 child, Nicholas Holm. AB, U. Mich., 1951. Dir. design rsch. McCann-Erickson Advt., N.Y.C., 1954-58; research assoc. Calif. Dept. Pub. Health, Berkeley, 1961-64, Stanford (Calif.) U., 1968-70, Inst. Research in Social Behavior, Berkeley, 1971-73; producer Berkeley Stage Co., 1973-78; pres. Berkeley Prodns., Inc., 1978—. Producer: (ednl. films) Black Girl, Sister of the Bride, Poetry Playhouse, Chile Pequin, Nine Months, Almost Home, Your Move, 1980-87; author: (with others) Values Under Pressure, AIDS and Civil Liberties in Reasoning and Choice: Explorations in Political Psychology, 1991 (Woodrow Wilson award 1992). Bd. dirs. Planned Parenthood, San Francisco, 1985-91, v.p., 1988-89; bd. dirs. Suicide Prevention Alameda County, 1991—, v.p., 1992—. Recipient Noble Hancock Found. award, 1973, NEH award, 1975, Golden Eagle award Coun. Internat. Nontheatrical Events, 1978, Creative Excellence award U.S. Industry Film Festival, 1979, Essa award U.S. Dept. Edn., 1979, 80, 81, 82, red ribbon Am. Film Festival, 1983, Learning award Nat. Coun. Human Rels., 1983, 84. Democrat. Jewish. Office: Berkeley Prodns 2288 Fulton St Berkeley CA 94704-1449

WOLFLE, DAEL LEE, public affairs educator; b. Puyallup, Wash., Mar. 5, 1906; s. David H. and Elizabeth (Pauly) W.; m. Helen Morrill, Dec. 28, 1929 (dec. July 1988); children: Janet Helen (Mrs. Wilhelm G. Christophersen), Lee Morrill, John Morrill. B.S., U. Wash., 1927, M.S., 1928; postgrad., U. Chgo., summers 1929, 30; Ph.D., Ohio State U., 1931, D.Sc., 1957; D.Sc., Drexel U., 1956, Western Mich. U., 1960. Instr. psychology Ohio State U., 1929-32; prof. psychology U. Miss., 1932-36; examiner in biol. scis. U. Chgo., 1936-39, asst. prof. psychology, 1938-43, assoc. prof., 1943-45; on leave for war work with Signal Corps, 1941-43; with OSRD, 1944-45; exec. sec. Am. Psychol. Assn., 1946-50; dir. commn. on human resources and advanced tng. Assoc. Research Councils, 1950-54; exec. officer AAAS, 1954-70; editor Sci., 1955, pub., 1955-70; prof. pub. affairs U. Wash., Seattle, 1970-76; prof. emeritus U. Wash., 1976—; mem. sci. adv. bd. USAF, 1953-57; mem. def. sci. bd. Dept. Def., 1957-61; mem. adv. council on mental health NIMH, 1960-64; mem. nat. adv. health council USPHS, 1965-66; mem. commn. on human resources NRC, 1974-78; mem. adv. bd. Geophys. Inst., Fairbanks, Alaska., 1970-93, chmn. adv. bd., 1972-81. Author: Factor Analysis to 1940, 1941, Science and Public Policy 1959, The Uses of Talent, 1971, The Home of Science, 1972, Renewing a Scientific Society, 1989; editor: America's Resources of Specialized Talent, 1954. Trustee Russell Sage Found., 1961-78, Pacific Sci. Cent. Found., 1962-80, Biol. Scis. Curriculum Study, 1980-85; chmn. bd. J. McK. Cattell Fund, 1962-82. Named Alumnus Summa Laude Dignatus, U. Wash., 1979. Mem. AAAS (pres. Pacific div. 1991-92), AAUP, Am. Psychol. Assn., Am. Acad. Arts and Scis. (exec. com. western sect. 1985-92), Sigma Xi. Home: 4545 Sand Point Way NE Seattle WA 98105-3926 Office: U Wash Grad Sch Public Affairs Seattle WA 98195

WOLFLEY, VERN ALVIN, dentist; b. Etna, Wyo., Aug. 4, 1912; s. Rudolf E. and Eliza (Neuenschwander) W.; m. Bernice Michaelson, June 12, 1936; children: Norda Beth Wolfley Brimley, Vern A. Jr., Paul R., Carol Jo Wolfley Bennett. BS, U. Wyo., 1934; BS in Dentistry and DDS, U. Nebr., 1947. Farm mgmt. specialist USDA, 1934-43; placement officer War Relocation Authority, 1943; pvt. practice, Idaho Falls, Idaho, 1947-57, Phoenix, 1957—. Pres. Ariz. Children's Soc., Phoenix, 1960-61. With AUS, 1943; 1st lt. USAF, 1954. Mem. ADA (life), Ariz. Dental Assn. (life), Idaho Falls Dental Soc. (pres. 1949-50), Upper Snake River Dental Soc. (pres. 1955-56), Am. Soc. Dentistry for Children (life), Acad. Gen. Dentistry, Internat. Assn. Orthodontics (life), Am. Assn. Functional Orthodontists (charter), Fedn. Dentaire Internat., Cen. Ariz. Dist. Dental Soc. (life), Am. Legion, Lions (v.p. 1956), Omicron Kappa Upsilon, Alpha Zeta. Republican. Mem. LDS Ch. Office: 2837 W Northern Ave Phoenix AZ 85051-6646

WOLFSBERG, MAX, chemist, educator; b. Hamburg, Germany, May 28, 1928; came to U.S., 1939, naturalized, 1945; s. Gustav and Ida (Engelmann) W.; m. Marilyn Lorraine Fleischer, June 23, 1957; 1 dau., Tyra Gwendolen. A.B., Washington U., St. Louis, 1948, Ph.D., 1951. Asso. chemist Brookhaven Nat. Lab., Upton, N.Y., 1951-54; chemist Brookhaven Nat. Lab., 1954-63, sr. chemist, 1963-69; prof. chemistry SUNY, Stony Brook, 1966-69; vis. prof. chemistry Ind. U., Bloomington, 1965, Cornell U., Ithaca, N.Y., 1963; prof. chemistry U. Calif., Irvine, 1969—, chmn. dept., 1974-80; Deutsche Forschungs Gemeinschaft guest prof. U. Ulm, Fed. Republic Germany, 1986; Forchheimer vis. prof. Hebrew U., 1993. Assoc. editor: Jour. Chem. Physics, 1968-70; editor: Comments on Chemical Physics, 1986-89; mem. editorial bd. Isotopenpraxis, 1987—; contbr. articles to profl. jours. AEC fellow, 1950-51; NSF sr. postdoctoral fellow, 1958-59; Alexander von Humboldt awardee, 1977, reinvitations 1982, 93. Mem. Am. Chem. Soc., Phi Beta Kappa, Sigma Xi. Jewish. Home: 4533 Gorham Dr Corona Del Mar CA 92625-3111 Office: U Calif Dept Chemistry Irvine CA 92717

WOLFSON, MARSHA, internist, nephrologist; b. Bklyn., Feb. 14, 1944; d. Murray and Rose (Cohen) W. Student, Boston U., 1961-63; BS, Fairleigh Dickinson U., 1965; MD, Med. Coll. Pa., 1970. Diplomate Am. Bd. Internal Medicine, Am. Bd. Nephrology. Staff physician NIH, Bethesda, Md., 1975-77; clinic instr. Georgetown U. Sch. Medicine, Washington, 1975-77; asst. prof. medicine Oreg. Health Scis. U., Portland, 1977-82; attending physician VA Hosp., Portland, 1983-87, chief nephrology, 1977—; assoc. prof. medicine Oreg. Health Scis. U., Portland, 1982—; med. dir. nutrition support svc. VA Hosp., Portland, 1987—; cons. in field. Co-author: The Science and Practice of Clinical Medicine, 1980, Clinical Dialysis, 1984, 90, Current Nephrology, 1984, Progress in Clinical Kidney Disease and Hypertension, 1985, Dialysis Therapy Handbook, 1986, Clinical and Physiological Applications of Vitamin B6, 1988, Acute Renal Failure: Diagnosis, Treatment, and Prevention, 1989; contbr. numerous articles to profl. jours. Bd. dirs. Kidney Assn. Oreg., Portland. Lt. comdr. USPHS, 1975-77. Mem. ACP, Women in Nephrology (pres. 1988), Multnomah County Med. Soc., Oreg. Med. Assn., Am. Soc. Parenteral and Enteral Nutrition, Am. Soc. Artificial Internal Organs, Am. Soc. Clin. Nutrition, Am. Inst. Nutrition, Am. Fedn. for Clin. Rsch., Internat. Soc. Nephrology, Am. Soc. Nephrology, Alpha Omega Alpha. Office: VA Med Center 3710 SW US Vet Hosp Rd Portland OR 97207

WOLFSON, MURRAY, economics educator; b. N.Y.C., Sept. 14, 1927; s. William and Bertha (Finkelstein) W.; m. Betty Ann Goessel, July 21, 1950; children: Paul G., Susan D., Deborah R. BS, CCNY, 1948; MS, U. Wis., 1951, PhD, 1964; postgrad., Marquette U., 1958-59. Cert. secondary tchr., Wis., Mich. Tchr. math. Montrose (Mich.) High Sch., 1959-61; instr. econs. Thornton Jr. Coll., Harvey, Ill., 1961-63; prof. Oreg. State U., Corvallis, 1963-86, Calif. State U., Fullerton, 1986—; vis. prof. numerous univs., including Ahamdu Bello U., Zaria, Nigeria, U. Canterbury, Christchurch, New Zealand, U. Wis., Milw., Marquette U., Milw., U. Durham, Eng., U. Oreg., U. So. Calif., Haifa (Israel) U., U. Adelaide, Australia; Fulbright specialist lectr., Japan, 1976-77, Tokyo U., Hitotsubashi U., Waseda U., Keio U.; docent Groningen U., The Netherlands; vis. fellow history of ideas unit Australian Nat. U.; adj. prof. U. Calif., Irvine, 1986—; others. Author: A Reappraisal of Marxian Economics, 1968, (transl. into Japanese and Portuguese), Karl Marx, 1971, Spanish transl., 1977, A Textbook of Economics: Structure, Activities, Issues, 1978, Marx: Economist, Philosopher, Jew, 1982, Japanese transl., 1987, Economic Activities: Microeconomics, 1989, rev. edit., 1991, Essays on the Cold War, 1992, (with Vincent Buranelli) In the Long Run We Are All Dead, A Macroeconomics Murder Mystery, 1983, 2d edit., 1989; also numerous articles. Adv. bd. Yale U. Civic Edn. Project. With USN, 1945-46. Recipient 1st nat. prize of excellence in teaching coll. econs. Joint Coun. on Econ. Edn., 1970; scholar N.Y. Bd. Regents, 1943; staff devel. fellow Oreg. State U., 1976; travel grantee Am. Coun. Learned Socs., 1979. Mem. AAUP (chpt. pres. 1983-84), Am. Econ. Assn., Hist. of Econs. Soc., Peace Sci. Soc., Def. Econs. Assn., Western Econs. Assn., Peace Sci. Soc. (pres.-elect). Home: 2022-D Via Mariposa E Laguna Hills CA 92653

WOLIN, MERLE LINDA, journalist, consultant; b. Cheyenne, Wyo., Jan. 1, 1948; d. Morris Aaron and Helen (Sobol) W. AA, Pine Manor Coll., 1968; BA, U. Calif., Berkeley, 1970. Co-founder, philanthropic cons. Pacific Change, San Francisco, 1971-73; mem editorial staff City Mag., San Francisco, 1974-75; co-founder, assoc. pub. Mother Jones mag., San Francisco, 1973-74; freelance writer N.Y Times, L.A. Times, People, 1976-79; Latin affairs writer L.A. Herald Examiner, 1979-82; nat. Latin affairs writer Wall Street Journal, L.A., 1982-83; correspondent Latin Am. L.A. Herald Examiner, Mexico City, 1983-86; freelance journalist Life, L.A. Times, The New Republic, 1986—; tv. news feature producer BBC Fox TV., 1991—. Recipient Mark Twain prize, regional prize AP, 1981, Journalism Atrium award U. Ga. 1981, econ. understanding award Dartmouth Coll., 1981, disting. writing award Hearst Newspapers, 1981, Paul Tobenkin Meml. award Columbia U., 1982, Robert F. Kennedy award, 1982, best investigative reporting award, L.A. Press Club, 1982, best fgn. press writing award, 1985, Clarence Darrow award ACLU, 1982, Unity award Lincoln U. Mo., 1982. Mem. Writers Guild Am., PEN Internat. (award for meritorious achievement, 1982). Office: 170 S Beverly Dr Ste 300 Beverly Hills CA 90212

WOLIVER, ROBERT, psychologist; b. Cin., May 29, 1947; s. Edward Charles and Esther (Cottingham) W.; m. Akiko Ito (div. 1985), 1 child, Keiko; m. Gail Muranaka, Sept. 19, 1985. BS, Georgetown U., 1969; MA, U. Hawaii, 1976, PhD, 1979. Lic. psychologist, Hawaii. Pvt. practice Kaneohe, HI, 1980—; cons. Queen's Med. Ctr., Honolulu, 1980-83, Hawaii Job Corps, Honolulu, 1986-93, Leahi Hosp. Children's Unit, Honolulu, 1985-86, Windward Children's team, Kaneohe, 1991-92; pres. Hawaii Sch. Profl. Psychologists, Honolulu, 1980-87; dean Forest Inst. Profl. Psychologists, Honolulu, 1987-89; lectr. U. Hawaii, Kaneohe, 1976-93. Author (chpts. in text) Functional Psychological Testing, 1986, Understanding the Gifted Adolescent, 1991; contbr. articles to profl. jours. Mem. APA, Hawaii Yacht Club.

WOLK, MARTIN, electronic engineer, physicist; b. Long Branch, N.J., Jan. 13, 1930; s. Michael and Tillie (Barron) W.; 1 child, Brett Martin. BS, George Washington U., 1957, MS, 1968; PhD, U. N.Mex., 1973. Physicist Naval Ordnance Lab., White Oak, Md., 1957-59, Nat. Oceanic and Atmospheric Adminstrn., Suitland, Md., 1959-66; solid state physicist Night Vision Lab., Fort Belvoir, Va., 1967-69; rsch. asst. U. N.Mex., Albuquerque, 1969-73; electronics engr. Washington Navy Yard, 1976-83, TRW, Inc., Redondo Beach, Calif., 1983-84; physicist Metrology Engring. Ctr., Pomona, Calif., 1984-85; electronics engr. Naval Aviation Depot North Island, San Diego, 1985—; cons. Marine Corps Logistics Base, Barstow, Calif., 1985—, Naval Weapons Station, Fallbrook, Calif., 1987-89, Naval Weapons Support Ctr., Crane, Ind., 1989—. Contbr. articles to Jour. Quantitative Spectroscopy and Radiative Transfer, Monthly Weather Rev., Proceedings of SPIE. Cpl. U.S. Army, 1946-49, Japan. Mem. IEEE, Soc. Photo-Optical Instrumentation Engring., Sigma Pi Sigma, Sigma Tau. Home: 740-91 Eastshore Ter Chula Vista CA 91913-2421

WOLLENBERG, DAVID ARTHUR, real estate developer; b. Longview, Wash., Aug. 6, 1947; s. Richard Peter and Leone (Bonney) W.; m. Katrina Moulton, Aug. 30, 1975; children: Andrew Richard, Blake Endicott. BA, Brown U., 1969; MBA, Stanford U., 1973. Front office mgr. Caneel Bay Plantation, St. John, V.I., 1969-71; adminstrn. asst. AMFAC Communities-Hawaii, Honolulu, 1973-77; exec. v.p. The Cortana Corp., Palo Alto, Calif., 1977-83, pres., 1983—; dir. Longview Fibre Co., Wash. 1979—. Dir. Peninsula Ctr. for the Blind, Palo Alto, Calif., 1984-90, Christmas in April, Mid-Peninsula, 1992. Mem. Outrigger Canoe Club Honolulu, Menlo Circus Club. Republican. Office: The Cortana Corp 800 El Camino Real Ste 175 Menlo Park CA 94025

WOLLENBERG, RICHARD PETER, paper manufacturing company executive; b. Juneau, Alaska, Aug. 1, 1915; s. Harry L. and Gertrude (Arnstein) W.; m. Leone Bonney, Dec. 22, 1940; children: Kenneth Roger, David Arthur, Keith Kermit, Richard Harry, Carol Lynne. BSME, U. Calif., Berkeley, 1936; MBA, Harvard U., 1938; grad., Army Indsl. Coll., 1941; D in Pub. Affairs (hon.), U. Puget Sound, 1977. Prodn. control Bethlehem Ship, Quincy, Mass., 1938-39; with Longview (Wash.) Fibre Co., 1939—, safety engr., asst. chief engr., chief engr., mgr. container operations, 1951-57, v.p., 1953-57, v.p. ops., 1957-60, exec. v.p., 1960-69, pres., 1969-78, pres., chief exec. officer, 1978-85, pres., chief exec. officer, chmn. bd., 1985—, also bd. dirs.; mem. Wash. State Council for Postsecondary Edn., 1969-79, chmn., 1970-73; mem. western adv. bd. Allendale Ins. Bassoonist SW Washington Symphony. Trustee Reed Coll., Portland, 1962—, chmn. bd. 1982-90. Served to lt. col. USAAF, 1941-45. Mem. NAM (bd. dirs. 1981-86), Pacific Assn. Pulp and Paper Mfrs. (pres. 1981-92), Inst. Paper Sci. and Tech. (trustee), Wash. State Roundtable, Crabbe Huson (bd. dirs.). Home: 1632 Kessler Blvd Longview WA 98632-3633 Office: Longview Fibre Co PO Box 639 Longview WA 98632-0053

WOLLERT, GERALD DALE, retired food company executive, investor; b. LaPorte, Ind., Jan. 21, 1935; s. Delmar Everette and Esther Mae W.; m. Carol Jean Burchby, Jan. 26, 1957; children—Karen Lynn, Edwin Del. B.S., Purdue U., 1957. With Gen. Foods Corp., 1959-89; dir. consumer affairs Gen. Foods Corp., White Plains, N.Y., 1973-74; mng. dir. Cottee Foods div. Gen. Foods Corp., Sydney, Australia, 1974-76; gen. mgr. Mexico div. Gen. Foods Corp., Mexico City, 1978-79; pres. Asia/Pacific ops. Gen. Foods Corp., Honolulu, corp. v.p. worldwide coffee and internat. div., 1979-89; ret., 1989; dir. Gen. Foods cos., Japan, Peoples Republic China, Korea, India, Taiwan, Singapore, Philippines. Webelos leader Boy Scouts Am., Mexico City, 1978-79; co. gen. chmn. United Fund campaign, Battle Creek, Mich., 1964-65, White Plains, N.Y., 1972-73. Served with U.S. Army, 1958. Mem. Asian-U.S. Bus. Coun., Oahu Country Club (Hawaii), Beacon Hills and Beechwood (Ind.) Club.

WOLLMAN, ARTHUR LEE, urologist; b. Bklyn., Apr. 30, 1943; s. Leo and Eleanor (Rakow) W.; m. Maxine Marsha Mandel, Aug. 23, 1964; 1 child, D. Bruce. AB, Middleburg Coll., 1963; PhD, Downstate Med. Ctr., Bklyn., 1967, MD, 1969. Diplomate Nat. Bd. Med. Examiners, Am. Bd. Urology. Intern U.S. Pub. Health Svc. Hosp., Staten Island, N.Y., 1969-70; resident in gen. surgery U.S. Pub. Health Svc. Hosp., Staten Island, 1970-71, resident in urology, 1971-74; fellowship in nephrology Meml. Sloan Kettering Inst., N.Y.C., Jan.-Mar. 1972; fellowship in pediatric urology Presbyn. Hosp., Columbia U., N.Y.C., July-Dec., 1972; ptnr., urologist So. Calif. Permanente Med. Group, San Diego, 1974—; mem. active surg. staff Kaiser Permanente Med. Ctr., San Diego, 1974—. Cmmdr. PHS, 1969-74. Mem. Phi Beta Kappa, Sigma Xi, Alpha Omega Alpha. Republican. Jewish. Office: So Calif Permanente Med Group 4647 Zion Ave San Diego CA 92120

WOLLMER, RICHARD DIETRICH, statistics and operations research educator; b. L.A., July 27, 1938; s. Herman Dietrich and Alice Myrtle (Roberts) W. BA in Math., Pomona Coll., 1960; MA in Applied Math., Columbia U., 1962; MS in Engring. Sci., U. Calif., Berkeley, 1963, PhD Engring. Sci., 1965. Scientist Rand Corp., Santa Monica, Calif., 1965-70; prof. ops. rsch. and stats. Calif. State U., Long Beach, 1970—; vis. prof. Calif. State U., Northridge, 1981-82; cons. McDonnell Douglas, Long Beach, Calif., 1978-80, 82, 85-91, Logicon, San Pedro, Calif., 1979-81; vis. assoc. prof. Stanford U., 1976; rsch. asst. Electric Power Rsch. Inst., Palo Alto, Calif., 1977; rsch. engr. Jet Propulsion Lab., Pasadena, Calif., 1971. Contbr. articles to profl. jours. Deacon Bel Air Presbyn. Ch., L.A., 1982-84, treas. 1983. Mem. So. Calif. Inst. Mgmt. Sci.-Ops. Rsch. Soc. (chmn. 1981, 89, vice chmn., 1980, 88, treas. 1979), Ops. Rsch. Soc. Am., Inst. Mgmt. Sci. Republican. Home: 6132 Fernwood Dr Huntington Beach CA 92648-5574 Office: Calif State U 1250 N Bellflower Blvd Long Beach CA 90840-0001

WOLLUM, OWEN LEE, newsletter publisher; b. Yakima, Wash., July 27, 1959; s. Leo and Dolores Lucille (Ringer) W.; m. Sandra Ellen Larsen, Nov. 26, 1988. AAS, Yakima Valley Coll., 1981; BA in Psychology, Pacific Luth. U., Tacoma, 1983. Software designer Pacific Luth. U., 1983-84; prin. Johnson & Wollum, Tacoma, 1984-87; pres., dir. Pinnacle Pub., Inc., Federal Way, Wash., 1987-91; pres., chmn. Palisade Press, Inc., Auburn, Wash., 1991—. Democrat. Lutheran.

WOLTERS, GALE LEON, range science professional; b. Portis, Kans., Apr. 25, 1939; s. Lester Orin and Dalice Marie (Smith) W.; m. Justine Louise Beatty, May 29, 1960; children: Ty, Amy. BS, Ft. Hays State U., 1961, MS, 1962; PhD, N.D. State U., 1968. Instr. N.D. State U., Fargo, 1965-66; range scientist Southern Forest Experiment Sta. USDA, Alexandria, La., 1966-75; project leader Pacific Southwest Forest and Range Experiment Sta. USDA, Fresno, Calif., 1975-80; range rsch. br. chief U.S. Forest Svc., Washington, 1980-87; range scientist Rocky Mountain Forest and Range Experiment Sta., Albuquerque, 1987—; del. 2d Internat. Rangeland Congress, Adelaide, Australia, 1984, 4th Internat. Rangeland Congress, Montpellier, France, 1991, Agr. Goodwill Tour, People-to-People program, People's Republic of China, 1986. Contbr. to Jour. Range Mgmt. Mem. Soc. Range Mgmt. (pres. regional sects., 1972, 82), Wildlife Soc., Soc. Am. Foresters, Sigma Xi, Beta Beta Beta. Home: 801 Navarra Way SE Albuquerque NM 87123-4522 Office: Rocky Mountain Exptl Sta 2205 Columbia Dr SE Albuquerque NM 87106-3222

WOLVERTON, JAMES NEWTON, JR., general sales manager, educator, consultant; b. Clarksburg, W.Va., May 23, 1943; s. James Newton and Ruth Marie (Nixon) W.; m. Marita Rae Meyers, June 14, 1972; children: James, William, Mary, Daniel. B in Edn., U. Alaska, 1966, MAT in Music, 1971. Acting dir. Upward Bound Project, Mt. Edgecumbe, Alaska, 1966; tchr. Harrison County Schs., Clarksburg, W.Va., 1968-69, Yakutat (Alaska) City Schs., 1971-73, Kenai Peninsula Borough Schs., Soldotna, Alaska, 1973-74; WW treatment plant operator City of Soldotna, Alaska, 1974-76; WWT plant operator level III City of Kenai, Alaska, 1976-82; account exec. Sta. KSRM Inc., Soldotna, Alaska, 1982-92, sales mgr., 1992—. Emergency mgr. Fed. Emergency Mgmt. Agy., Kenai, Alaska, 1989—; capt., oper. and tng. officer Alaska State Def. Force, Kenai, 1987—; mem. Water Pollution Control Fedn., Washington, 1976-82; mem. exec. bd. Tustamena Baptist Assn., 1973—, Alaska Baptist Conv., 1980-83; conf. leader Tustamena Baptist Assn. Assisteam Dir., 1987—, Alaska Baptist Conv. Assisteam, 1992-93; mem. Gideons Internat., 1980—, pres. 1983-84; cons. Alaska Baptist Conv. Ch. Growth, 1992—. 1st Lt., U.S. Army, 1966-78. Mem. Alaska Broadcasters Assn., Assn. U.S. Army, Sons of Am. Revolution. Republican. So. Baptist. Home: PO Box 7492 Nikiski AK 99635 Office: Sta KSRM Inc HC 02 PO Box 852 Soldotna AK 99669

WOMACK, JAMES ERROL, college president; b. Eugene, Oreg., June 27, 1940; s. John Leon and Dorothy Laverne (Yarbrough) W.; m. Sharron Kay McCullough, June 8, 1963; children: Timothy, Steven, Joseph, Marilee. BS, N.W. Christian Coll., 1963; M Teaching, Cen. Okla. State U., 1968; postgrad., Pacific Luth. U., 1958-60, U. Oreg., 1960-63, Phillips U., 1966-68; HHD (hon.), Phillips U., 1987. Cert. tchr., Okla., Calif.; cert. fund raising exec.; ordained to ministry Christian Ch. (Disciples of Christ, 1963. Youth min. Lowell (Oreg.) Christian Ch., 1962-63, First Christian Ch., The Dalles, Oreg., 1963-65; youth and edn. min. Putnam City Christian Ch., Oklahoma City, 1965-68; tchr. English and social studies, coach basketball Patterson (Calif.) High Sch., 1968-71; min. youth and edn. Maze Blvd. Christian Ch., Modesto, Calif., 1968-71; dir. devel. Nat. Benevolent Assn. (Colo. Christian Home), Denver, 1976-86; coord. campus activities, coach basketball N.W. Christian Coll., Eugene, 1971-73, dir. planned giving, 1973-76, pres., 1986—; cons. Luth. Social Svcs. Colo., Denver, 1984-85, Dayton, Ohio, 1986-89, Florence Crittenton Home Svcs., Little Rock, 1985—; presenter in field. Mem. devel. coun. Woodhaven Learning Ctr.; mem. fin. com. and nurture commn. Cen. Rocky Mountain Region Christian Ch.; chmn. N.W. Oklahoma City Youth Week Activities; trustee N.W. Christian Coll.; active Denver Planned Giving Roundtable; regional bd. dirs. N.W. Regional Ch., Christian Ch. in Kans. Recipient Book Award for Acad. Excellence Christian Bd. of Pub. Mem. Nat. Soc. Fund Raising Execs., Nat. Benevolent Assn. (trustee best of caring fund), Oreg. Ind. Coll. Assn. (mem. exec. com.), Colo. Assn. Fund Raisers (past sec., bd. dirs.), Emerald Empire Fellowship of Christian Athletes (charter mem., sec., bd. dirs.), Ministerial Alliance (chmn. migrant ministries), Rotary (mem. program com. Eugene chpt. 1990), Optimists (bd. dirs. Highland Park chpt.), Civitan, Denver City Club. Home: 250 N Adams St Eugene OR 97402-4206 Office: NW Christian Coll 828 E 11th Ave Eugene OR 97401-3727

WOMACK, THOMAS HOUSTON, manufacturing company executive; b. Gallatin, Tenn., June 22, 1940; s. Thomas Houston and Jessie (Eckel) W.; Linda Walker Womack, July 20, 1963 (div. Dec. 1989); children: Britton Ryan, Kelley Elizabeth; m. Pamela Ann Reed, Apr. 20, 1991. BSME, Tenn. Tech. U., Cookeville, 1963. Project engr. U.S. Gypsum Co., Jacksonville, Fla., 1963-65; project mgr. Maxwell House Div. Gen. Foods Corp., Jacksonville, 1965-68; mfg. mgr. Maxwell House Div. Gen. Foods Corp., Hoboken, N.J., 1968-71, div. ops. planning mgr., 1971-73; industry sales mgr. J.R. Schneider Co., Tiburon, Calif., 1973-79; pres. Womack Internat., Inc., Novato, Calif., 1979—. Mem. Soc. Tribologists and Lubrication Engrs., Am. Filtration Soc., Soc. Mfg. Engrs., Am. Soc. Chem. Engrs. Office: Womack Internat Inc One Digital Dr Novato CA 94949

WON, KYUNG-SOO, symphony conductor, director; b. Korea, Dec. 4, 1928; m. Hae-Ja (Won). Jan. 9, 1944; children: Alisa, Justin. Mus.M., Cin. Conservatory, 1957; diploma Mozarteum, Salzburg, Austria, protege of Pierre Monteux; postgrad. Ind. U. Cert. tchr., Calif. Formerly prof. Seoul (Korea) Nat. U., music dir. Modesto (Calif.) Symphony, Seoul Philharm. Orch.; music dir., condr. Stockton (Calif.) Symphony; now spl. prof. Kyung-Won U.; violin soloist Cin. Symphony. Soul Philharm., Manila Symphony, Korean Broadcasting System Orch., Korea; guest condr. orchs., London, Berlin, Paris, Vienna, Austria, Ireland, Mexico City, S. Am. cities, Orient. Served with Korean Navy. Recipient Bartok award, Emeel Hermann award, Star award. Mem. Am. Symphony League. Office: Stockton Symphony 37 W Yokuts Ave Ste 4C Stockton CA 95207-5725

WONDER, JOHN PAUL, educator; b. Long Beach, Calif., July 29, 1921; s. John Paul and Etta (Jones) W.; m. Jane Josephine Walder, Dec. 22, 1946; children: John Walder, Peter Charles. A.B., Stanford U., 1943, A.M., 1948, Ph.D., 1952; Exchange scholar, Universidad Central, Madrid, 1950-51. Grad. fellow Stanford, 1946-50; instr., asst. prof. Spanish U. Ariz., 1951-56; dir. Binational Center, Belo Horizonte, Brazil; with USIA, also Rio de Janeiro and Port-au-Prince, Haiti, 1956-62; asst. prof. Los Angeles State Coll., 1962-63; prof. Spanish U. Pacific, Stockton, Calif., 1963-91; chmn. dept. modern langs. U. Pacific, 1964-75; dir. Center for Internat. Programs, 1979-82. Author: (with Aurelio M. Espinosa, Jr.) Gramática Analítica, 1976; assoc. editor: (theoretical linguistics) Hispania, 1979-89. Served as 1st lt., arty. M.I. AUS, 1943-46, ETO. Mem. Alpha Tau Omega. Home: 660 W Euclid Ave Stockton CA 95204-1819

WONDERS, WILLIAM CLARE, geography educator; b. Toronto, Ont., Can., Apr. 22, 1924; s. George Clarence and Ann Mary (Bell) W.; m. Lillian Paradise Johnson, June 2, 1951; children—Karen Elizabeth, Jennifer Anne, Glen William. B.A. with honors, Victoria Coll., U. Toronto, 1946; M.A., Syracuse U., 1948; Ph.D., U. Toronto, 1951; Fil. Dr. h.c., Uppsala U., 1981. Teaching asst. dept. geography Syracuse U., 1946-48; lectr. dept. geography U. Toronto, 1948-53; asst. prof. geography dept. polit. economy U. Alta., 1953-55, assoc. prof. geography, 1955-57, prof., head dept. geography, 1957-67, prof. dept. geography, 1967-87, Univ. prof., 1983—, prof. emeritus, 1987—; vis. prof. geography U. B.C., 1954, U. Okla., 1965-66, St. Mary's U., 1977, U. Victoria, 1989, J.F. Kennedy Inst., Free U. Berlin, 1990; guest prof. Inst. Geography, Uppsala (Sweden) U., 1962-63; rsch. fellow in Geography U. Aberdeen, Scotland, 1970-71, 78; vis. fellow in Can. Studies, U. Edinburgh, Scotland, 1987. Author: Looking at Maps, 1960, The Sawdust Fusiliers, 1991, Norden and Canada-A Geographer's Perspective, 1992; co-author: (with T. Drinkwater et al.) Atlas of Alberta, 1969, (with J. C. Muller et al.) Junior Atlas of Alberta, 1979; contbr., editor: Canada's Changing North, 1971, The North, 1972, The Arctic Circle, 1976, Knowing the North, 1988; contbr. articles to jours., encys., chpts. to books. Mem. Nat. Adv. Com. on Geog. Rsch., 1965-69; mem. Can. Permanent Com. on Geog. Names, 1981—, Alta. Historic Sites Bd., 1978-83; mem. policy bd. Can. Plains Rsch. Centre, U. Regina (Sask.), 1975-86; mem. adv. bd. Tyrrell Mus. Paleontology, 1984-89; bd. dirs. The Muttart Found., 1986-93, v.p. 1991-93, mem. 1991—. NSF sr. fgn. scientist fellow, 1965-66; Canada Council leave fellow, 1969-70, 77-78; Nuffield Found. fellow, 1970-71. Fellow Arctic Inst. N.Am., Royal Soc. Can.; mem. Canadian Assn. Geographers (past. pres.), Royal Scottish Geog. Soc., Canadian Assn. Scottish Studies (councillor 1974-77), Scottish Soc. Northern Studies, Champlain Soc. (councillor 1981-86), Sigma Xi, Gamma Theta Upsilon.

WONG, ANDRES RUBEN, educator; b. Manila, Dec. 23, 1958; came to U.S., 1989; s. Pedro Erasquin and Rosa (Galvez) W. BS cum laude, U. Philippines, Quezon City, 1980. Metall. engr. II, Marcopper Mining Corp., Makati, Rizal, Philippines, 1980-83; metall. engr. Surigao Consol. Mining Corp., Makati, 1983-86; tchr. Southridge High Sch., Manila, 1986-89, Ribet Acad., La Canada, Calif., 1990-91, St. Anthony High Sch., Long Beach, 5, 1991—. Scholar Nat. Sci. Devel. Bd., 1975. Mem. Holy Name Soc. (vol. award 1992), Nat. Right to Life, Caths. United for Life. Republican.

WONG, ASTRIA WOR, cosmetic business consultant; b. Hong Kong, Oct. 23, 1949; came to U.S., 1970; B in Vocat. Edn., Calif. State U., Long Beach, 1976. Cert. coll. tchr. (life), Calif. West coast sales trainer Revlon Inc., N.Y.C, 1975-82; nat. tng. dir. diReniel Internat., Palm Springs, Calif., 1982; dir. Beauty Cons. Service Agy., Long Beach, Calif., 1983—. Author: The Art of Femininity, 1971; editor (newsletter) So. Calif. Cosmetic, 1983-86. Named Salesperson of Yr., Revlon, Inc., N.Y.C., 1978. Mem. So. Calif. Cosmetic Assn. (correspondence sec. 1982—), Women's Council, Cosmetologist Tchr. Assn., Bus. and Profl. Women. Republican. Office: Beauty Cons Service Agy 7121 E 1st Ave Scottsdale AZ 85251-4305

WONG, BERNARD P., anthropology educator; b. China, Feb. 12, 1941; came to U.S., 1969; s. Maurice S. and Theresa S. (Chau) W.; m. Rosemarie Deist, Apr. 14, 1973; children: Veronica, Alexandra. BA, Berchmans Coll., Quezon City, Philippines, 1966; post grad., Ateneo de Manila, Philippines, 1968; MA, U. Wis., 1971, PhD, 1974. Asst. prof. U. Wis., Anthropology Dept., Janesville, 1974-81, assoc. prof., 1981-86; assoc prof. San Francisco State U., Anthropology Dept., 1986-88, prof., 1988—; dir. San Francisco State U., Ctr. Urban Anthropology, 1988—, chair anthropology dept., 1990. Author: A Chinese American Community, 1979, Chinatown, 1982, Patronage Brokerage, 1988; editor: Bridge: An Asian American Perspective, 1978-80; contbr. articles to profl. jours. Coun. mem. Gov's. Asian Adv. Coun. Wis., 1983-86. Fellow; Am. Anthrop. Assn., Soc. Applied Anthropology; mem. Am. Ethnological Soc., Soc. Urban Anthropology, Soc. Anthropology Work, Chinese Hist. Soc. Am. (bd. dirs.). Office: San Francisco State Univ Dept of Anthropology 1600 Holloway Ave San Francisco CA 94132-1722

WONG, BONNIE LEE, systems analyst; b. L.A., Nov. 30, 1957; d. Robert Lee and Betty Rose (Woo) W. Student, Cambridge (Eng.) U., 1979; BS, U. So. Calif., L.A., 1979, MPA, 1981. Resident, adminstrv. asst. Olive View Med. Ctr., Sylmar, Calif., 1980-81; quality assurance coord. Lincoln Hosp. Med. Ctr., L.A., 1982; cons. Ernst & Whinney, L.A., 1983-85; systems coord., analyst, then cons. Am. Med. Internat., L.A., 1985-87; client svcs. rep. McDonnell Douglas Health Systems, L.A., 1987-89; mktg. support rep. Sci. Dynamics Corp., Torrance, Calif., 1989—; bus. analyst The Hosp. of the Good Samaritan, L.A., 1990—. Mem. Healthcare Fin. Mgmt. Assn. (mem. roster com. 1985, info. systems com. 1988), U. So. Calif. Healthcare Alumni. Office: The Hosp of Good Samaritan 616 Witmer St Los Angeles CA 90017-2395

WONG, CHUN WA, physics educator; b. Hong Kong, Jan. 22, 1938; came to U.S., 1957; s. Joo Fong and Kit Cheng (Fan) W.; m. Ah Cheng Wee, Aug. 12, 1967; children: Jennifer Mun-Ling, Angelina Mun-Cheng. BS, U. Calif., L.A., 1959; AM, Harvard U., 1960, PhD, 1965. Rsch. assoc. Princeton (N.J.) U., 1965-66; rsch. officer Oxford (Eng.) U., 1966-67; rsch. scientist Saclay, Gif-Sur-Yvette, France, 1967-68; rsch. officer Oxford, Eng., 1968-69; asst. prof. physics U. Calif., L.A., 1969-70, acting assoc. prof. physics, 1970-71, assoc. prof. physics, 1971-75, prof. physics, 1975—. Author: Introduction to Mathematical Physics, 1991; contbr. numerous articles to profl. jours. Alfred P. Sloan Found. fellow, 1970-72. Fellow Am. Phys. Soc. Democrat. Office: U Calif Dept of Physics Los Angeles CA 90024

WONG, DONALD GUY, retired civil engineer; b. San Francisco, July 24, 1934; s. Edward Gim and Alice G. (Owyoung) W.; m. Jeanette C. Cheu, Aug. 16, 1959; children: Randy Scott, Jerry Guy, Brent Edward. BS in CE, U. Calif., Berkeley, 1956, MS in CE, 1960; MDiv, Western Sem., Los Gatos, Calif., 1993. Registered profl. engr., Calif. Rsch. specialist loads and structural dynamics Lockheed Missiles and Space Co., Sunnyvale, Calif., 1965-68, group engr. loads and structural dynamics, 1968-74, mgr. structures, 1974-86, mgr. Trident I operational systems engring., 1986, mgr. Trident II systems engring., 1986-89; pastor in tng., 1989—; instr. Merritt Coll., Oakland, Calif., 1965-66. Contbr. articles to profl. jours. Commencement speaker MDiv recipients. Recipient Robert E. Gross award Lockheed Horizons, 1981. Mem. Young Life for Silicon Valley (chmn. 1979-80), Chi Epsilon. Republican. Evangelical Christian. Home: 1649 Eagle Dr Sunnyvale CA 94087

WONG, HARRY CHOW, anesthesiologist, educator; b. Beloit, Wis., June 26, 1933; s. Charles T. and Yee S. W.; m. Jean A. Nagahiro, June 21, 1958; children: Jeffrey, Stacey, Daphne, Steven. BS, U. Wis., 1955, MD, 1958. Diplomate, Am. Bd. Anesthesiology. Intern Providence Hosp., Portland, Oreg., 1958-59; resident in anesthesiology U. Wis., Madison, 1959-61; pvt. practice Salt Lake City, 1961-88; chmn. dept. anesthesiology, Latter-day Saints Hosp., 1966-67, 74-76, chmn. ICU com., 1971-75; pres. med. staff, Salt Lake Surg. Ctr., 1976-88; mem. Joint Commn. Accreditation Health Orgns., 1983—, cons. surveyor, 1985—; prof. anesthesiology, U. Utah, Salt Lake City, 1988—. Mem. AMA, Am. Soc. Anesthesiologists (chmn. com. ambulatory surgical care 1983-85, patient safety 1986-88, com peer review 1986—, chmn. 1993—), Internat. Anesthesia Rsch. Soc., Am. Heart Assn., Federated Ambulatory Surg. Assn. (bd. dirs. 1976—), Soc. Ambulatory Anesthesia (bd. dirs. 1985—, pres. 1990), Utah Med. Ins. Assn. (bd. govs. 1980-90), Utah State Soc. Anesthesiologists (pres. 1966). Home: 1060 Oak Hills Way Salt Lake City UT 84108-2073 Office: Dept Anesthesiology 50 N Medical Dr Salt Lake City UT 84132-0002

WONG, HENRY LI-NAN, bank executive, economist; b. Rangoon, Burma, Nov. 3, 1940; s. Chew King and Jenny (Yu) W.; came to U.S., 1946. m. Laurie Yap, Apr. 11, 1968; children: Rachael S.Y., Remle S.W. BS, Waynesburg Coll., 1965; MS, U. Hawaii, 1968, PhD, 1969. Economist, Econ. Research Service U.S. Dept. Agr., Washington, 1969-70; economist Hawaii Dept. Budget and Fin., Honolulu, 1970-73; dir. Hawaii film office Hawaii Dept. Planning and Econ. Devel., Honolulu, 1973-84; exec. v.p. and chief adminstr., office of chmn. CB Bancshares Inc., Honolulu, 1984—; vice chmn., dir. Hawaii Strategic Devel. Corp., Honolulu, 1991—; v.p., bd. dirs. Friends of East West Ctr., Honolulu, 1983-84. NDEA fellow, 1965-69. Mem. Assn. Film Commrs. (pres. 1980), Am. Econ. Assn., Am. Agrl. Econs. Assn., Hawaii Internat. Film Festival, Chinese C. of C., Hawaii Soc. Corp. Planners, Lanakila Rehab. Ctr. (trustee), Alpha Kappa Psi, Theta Chi. Democrat. Presbyterian. Lodges: Elks, Masons (trustee), Shriners. Office: City Bank City Fin Tower 201 Merchant St Honolulu HI 96813-2929

WONG, JAMES BOK, economist, engineer, technologist; b. Canton, China, Dec. 9, 1922; came to U.S., 1938, naturalized, 1962; s. Gen Ham and Chen (Yee) W.; m. Wai Ping Lim, Aug. 3, 1946; children: John, Jane Doris, Julia Ann. BS in Agr., U. Md., 1949, BS in Chem. Engring., 1950; MS, U. Ill., 1951, PhD, 1954. Rsch. asst. U. Ill., Champaign-Urbana, 1950-53; chem. engr. Standard Oil of Ind., Whiting, 1953-55; process design engr., rsch. engr. Shell Devel. Co., Emeryville, Calif., 1955-61; sr. planning engr., prin. planning engr. Chem. Plastics Group, Dart Industries, Inc. (formerly Rexall Drug & Chem. Co.), L.A., 1961-66, supr. planning and econs., 1966-67, mgr. long range planning and econs., 1967, chief economist, 1967-72, dir. econs. and ops. analysis, 1972-78, dir. internat. techs., 1978-81; pres. James B. Wong Assocs., L.A., 1981—; chmn. bd. dirs. United Pacific Bank, 1988—; tech. cons. various corps. Contbr. articles to profl. jours. Bd. dirs., pres. Chinese Am. Citizens Alliance Found.; mem. Asian Am. Edn. Commn., 1971-81. Served with USAAF, 1943-46. Recipient Los Angeles Outstanding Vol. Service award, 1977. Mem. Am. Inst. Chem. Engrs., Am. Chem. Soc., VFW (vice comdr. 1959), Commodores (named to exec. order 1982), Sigma Xi, Tau Beta Pi, Phi Kappa Phi, Pi Mu Epsilon, Phi Lambda Upsilon, Phi Eta Sigma. Home: 2460 Venus Dr Los Angeles CA 90046

WONG, JAN H., surgical oncologist; b. Honolulu, Aug. 17, 1953. BA, Stanford U., 1974; MD, Rush Medical Coll. Diplomate Am. Bd. Surgery, Nat. Bd. Med. Examiners. Intern Oreg. Health Scis. U., Portland, 1978-79, resident, 1979-84, chief resident in surgery, 1984-85; fellow U. Calif. Sch. Medicine, L.A., 1985-87; staff surgeon Sepulveda (Calif.) Vets. Med. Ctr., 1987—, chief sect. surg. oncology, 1988—; asst. prof. UCLA Sch. Medicine, 1985-91, assoc. prof., 1991-93, prof. 1993—. Author of over 105 presentations, abstracts, and articles in profl. jours.; ad hoc reviewer profl. jours. Grantee Plastic Surgery Edn. Found., Calif. Inst. for Cancer Rsch.; clin. fellow Am. Cancer Soc., 1981-83, 86-87, recipient Career Devel. award. Fellow AMS; mem. Assn. Acad. Surgery, Am. Soc. Clin. Oncology, Am. Assn. Cancer Rsch., Soc. Surg. Oncology, Am. Radium Soc., Pacific Coast Surg. Assn. Office: Univ Hawaii John A Burns Sch of Medicine 1356 Lusitana St 6th Flr Honolulu HI 96813

WONG, KENNETH LEE, software engineer, consultant; b. L.A., Aug. 15, 1947; s. George Yut and Yue Sam (Lee) W.; m. Betty (Louie) Wong, June 29, 1975; children: Bradford Keith, Karen Beth. BS in Engring., UCLA, 1969, MS in Engring., 1972, postgrad., 1972-73, 76-78. Cert. community coll. instr., Calif. Engring. aide Singer Librascope, Glendale, Calif., 1972-73; computer system design engr. Air Force Avionics Lab., Wright-Patterson AFB, Ohio, 1973-75; mem. tech. staff Hughes Aircraft Co., various cities, Calif., 1976-78, 79-81, TRW Def. and Space Systems Group, Redondo Beach, Calif., 1975-76, 78-79; engring. specialist Northrop Corp., Hawthorne, Calif., 1981-84; mem. tech. staff Jet Propulsion Lab., Pasadena, Calif., 1984-87; software cons. EG&G Spl. Projects, Las Vegas, Nev., 1987, AT&T Bell Labs., Warren, N.J., 1987-88, Westinghouse Electric Corp., Linthicom, Md., 1988, E Systems, Inc., Greenville, Tex., 1988-89; prin. Wong Soft Works, L.A., 1989—. Author tech. reports. Coach, Tigers Youth Club, L.A. 1st lt. USAF, 1973-75. Mem. AIAA, IEEE, Assn. Computing Machinery, Upsilon Pi Epsilon. Republican. Home and Office: Wong Soft Works 3385 Mclaughlin Ave Los Angeles CA 90066-2004

WONG, KIN-PING, university dean, biotechnology researcher, company executive, educator, science administrator; b. Guangzhou, China, Aug. 14, 1941; s. Kwok-Keung and Yuan-Kwan (Loo) W.; m. Anna S.K. Koo, Sept. 16, 1968; children: Voon-Chung Wong, Ming-Chung Wong. BS, U. Calif., Berkeley, 1964; PhD, Purdue U., 1968. Postdoctoral fellow Duke U., Durham, N.C., 1968-70; asst. and assoc. prof. chemistry U. South Fla., Tampa, 1970-75; vis. scientist Max Planck Inst. Molecular Genetics, Berlin, 1972; vis. prof. U. Uppsala, Sweden, 1975; assoc. and prof. biochemistry U. Kans., Kansas City, 1975-83, dean grad. studies, 1980-83; vis. prof. biochemistry U. Tokyo, 1979; program dir. of biophysics NSF, Washington, 1982-83; sci. dean, prof. Calif. State U., Fresno, 1983—; founder, chmn., pres. RiboGene Inc., Menlo Pk., Calif., 1989-91; vis. prof. biochemistry Stanford U. Med. Ctr., summer 1985; adj. prof. medicine U. Calif. San Francisco Med. Sch., 1986—; adj. prof. biochemistry and biophysics, U. Calif., San Francisco, 1987—; mem. U.S. Govt. Interagency Com. on Radiation, Washington, 1982-83; gov. Moss Landing (Calif.) Marine Labs., 1983—; cons. HHS, Washington, 1985—; trustee U. Calif., San Francisco, Fresno 1986—; mem. rev. panel NSF; mem. sci. expert panel Calif. Commn. Tchr. Credentialing. Contbr. over 50 research articles to prof. jours.; 32 pub. research abstracts; author various keynote speeches, convocation lectures. Chmn. sci. com. Fresno Met. Mus., 1983-85; co-chmn. planning com. Cen. Calif. Biomed. Rsch. Inst., Fresno, 1987—; co-chmn. multicultural coun. Clovis Unified Sch. Dist., 1988-90. Recipient cancer research grants and awards, Damon Runyan Fund, Milheim Found., Am. Cancer Soc., Eli Lilly Corp., Research Corps., Am. Heart Assn., 1980-81; grantee HHS, 1986-89, Nat. Inst. Heart Lung and Blood, 1972-87, Nat. Inst. Gen. Med. Scis., 1972-80; research career devel. awardee NIH, 1972-75; sr. research fellow European Molecular Biology Orgn., 1975; NSF summer rsch. professorship Stanford U., 1985; Laval Research award in innovative scis. and tech. Calif. State U., Fresno, 1985; scholarship Pepperdine U. presdl. and key exec. program, 1986-88; Calif. Sea grant Dept. Commerce, 1987-90. Fellow Royal Soc. Chemistry, Am. Inst. Chemists; mem. Am. Soc. Biol. Chemistry (membership com. 1983-86), AAAS, Biophys. Soc., Am. Chem. Soc., Sigma Xi. Office: Calif State U Sch of Natural Sci Fresno CA 93740-0090

WONG, NANCY L., dermatologist; b. Chung King, China, Aug. 23, 1943; came to U.S., 1947; d. Alice (Lee) Wong; m. Robert Lipshutz; children: Seth, Alison, David. BS, Pa. State U., 1963; MS in Physics magna cum laude, Columbia U., 1965; MD, Jefferson Med. Coll., Phila., 1971. Diplomate Am. Bd. Dermatology. Intern Wilmington Med. Ctr., 1992; resident Jackson Meml. Hosp., Miami, Mount Sinai Med. Ctr., Miami, 1977; physician Kaiser Med. Ctr., Hayward, Calif., 1987—. Fellow NSF. Fellow Am. Acad. Dermatology. Office: 3690 Point Eden Way Hayward CA 94545

WONG, OTTO, epidemiologist; b. Canton, China, Nov. 14, 1947; came to U.S., 1967, naturalized, 1976; s. Kui and Foon (Chow) W.; m. Betty Yeung, Feb. 14, 1970; children: Elaine, Jonathan. BS, U. Ariz., 1970; MS, Carnegie Mellon U., 1972; MS, U. Pitts., 1973, ScD, 1975. Cert. epidemiologist, Am. Coll. Epidemiology, 1982. USPHS fellow U. Pitts., 1972-75; asst. prof. epidemiology Georgetown U. Med. Sch., 1975-78; mgr. epidemiology Equitable Environ. Health Inc., Rockville, Md., 1977-78; dir. epidemiology Tabershaw Occupational Med. Assocs., Rockville, 1978-80; dir. occupational rsch. Biometric Rsch. Inst., Washington, 1980-81; exec. v.p., chief epidemiologist, ENSR Health Scis., Alameda, Calif., 1981-90; chief epidemologist, pres. Applied Health Scis., San Mateo, Calif., 1991—; cons. Nat. Cancer Inst., Nat. Inst. Occupational Safety and Health, Occupational Safety and Health Adminstrn., Nat. Heart, Lung and Blood Inst., Ford Motors Co., Gen. Electric, Mobil, Chevron, Union Carbide, Fairfax Hosp., Va. U. Ariz. scholar, 1967-68. Fellow Am. Coll. Epidemiology, Human Biology Council; mem. Am. Pub. Health Assn., Biometric Soc., Soc. Epidemiologic Rsch., Phi Beta Kappa, Pi Mu Epsilon. Republican. Contbr. articles to profl. jours. Office: Applied Health Scis PO Box 2078 181 Second Ave Ste 628 San Mateo CA 94401

WONG, PAMELA LYNN, computer training consultant; b. Berkeley, Calif., May 14, 1947; d. John Foo and Dorothea Marie (Quan) W. BA, Whitman Coll., 1969. Owner Sew Biz, San Francisco, 1977-81; exec. asst. MicroPro Internat., San Rafael, Ga., 1981-83; office mgr. Bay Area Teleguide, San Francisco, 1983-86; adminstrv. dir. Internat. Devel. Environs., San Francisco, 1986-88; cons. Pamela L. Wong Macintosh Consulting Svcs., Mill Valley, Calif., 1989—; mem. Apple Tng. Alliance and Apple Cons. Rels. Program, Cupertino, Calif., 1991—. Alumni admissions rep. Whitman Coll., Walla Walla, Wash., 1985—. Named Alumni Admissions Vol. of Yr., Whitman Coll., 1991. Mem. Assn. for Women in Computing (v.p. publs. 1992—), No. Bay Systems Profls. Office: Macintosh Consulting Svcs 116 Carlotta Cir Ste 9 Mill Valley CA 94941

WONG, PETER K., newspaper reporter; b. Fall River, Mass., Mar. 20, 1952; s. Tung Sam and Mae Ling (Joe) W. BA, U. So. Calif., 1974. Press aide, rschr. to Senator Lee Metcalf U.S. Senate, Washington, 1973; copy editor Evening Bulletin, Providence, 1973; reporter, copy editor The Daily Report, Ontario, Can., 1975-79; reporter The News Review, Roseburg, Oreg., 1979-89, Mail Tribune, Medford, Oreg., 1989—. Recipient awards Press Club So. Calif., 1976, 77, 78, Calif. Newspaper Pubs. Assn., 1977, Oreg. Newspaper Pub. Assn., 1986, 90. Mem. Soc. Profl. Journalists (Willamette Valley chpt., awards 1982, 84, 86, 87, pres. 1985-88, dep. dir. Northwest region, 1985-87), Asian-Am. Journalists Assn., Investigative Reporters and Editors, Inc. Office: Mail Tribune 33 N Fir St Medford OR 97501

WONG, ROBERTA JEAN, pharmacist, educator; b. Cleve., Nov. 23, 1957; d. Robert Y. and Ellen J. (Woo) W. Student, U. Calif., Davis, 1976-79; PharmD, U. Calif., San Francisco, 1983, clin. residency cert., 1984. Lic. pharmacist, Calif. Pharmacist intern Good Samaritan Hosp., San Jose, Calif., 1980-82, Kaiser Found. Hosp., South San Francisco, Calif., 1982-83; pharmacist Kaiser Found. Hosp., South San Francisco, 1983-87; clin. pharmacist AIDS activities div. San Francisco Gen. Hosp., 1984-89; investigational drug specialist UCLA Med. Ctr., 1989—; asst. clin. prof. pharmacy div. clin. pharmacy U. Calif., San Francisco, 1985-89; instr. UCLA Sch. Medicine, 1989-91; reviewer Am. Hosp. Formulary Svc., Bethesda, Md., 1987—; mem. Asian AIDS Task Force, 1987-89; instr. UCLA Sch. Medicine, 1989-91; lectr. and presenter in field. Mem. editorial bd. Clin. Pharmacy, 1990—. Recipient Asst. Sec. of Health's award for outstanding contbrn. to the AIDS epidemic in clin. and rsch. pharmacy svcs. Fellow Am. soc. Hosp. Pharmacists (practice adv. panel 1990-92); mem. Calif. Soc. HOps. Pharmacists (ho. of dels. 1985-86, clin. affairs coun. 1989-90, chmn. logistics seminar 1990, ednl. affairs coun. 1992-93), Golden Gate Soc. Hosp. Phamacists (chmn. programs com. 1986-87), Am. Pharm. Assn., Internat. AIDS Soc. Office: UCLA Med Ctr Drug Info 16-131CHS 10833 Le Conte Ave Los Angeles CA 90024

WONG, ROSALIA PING, software engineer; b. Fresno, Calif., Sept. 18, 1962; d. Harold C. and Cecilia (Yau) W. BS in Computer Sci. and Math., U. Calif., Davis, 1985. Programmer imaging graphics div. Gould, Fremont, Calif., 1985-87; software engr. Loma Park Assocs., Campbell, Calif., 1987-88, Cemax, Santa Clara, 1988-90; applications project mgr. Digital F/X, Mountain View, 1990—. Mem. Assn. for Computing Machinery (special interest group on graphics), Soc. Motion Picture TV for Entertainment. Home: 395 Ano Nuevo Ave # 908 Sunnyvale CA 94086 Office: Digital F/X 755 Ravendale Dr Mountain View CA 94043

WONG, SUE SIU-WAN, health educator; b. Hong Kong, Apr. 6, 1959; came to U.S., 1966; d. Tin Ho and Yuet Kum (Chan) E. BS, UCLA, 1981; MPH, Loma Linda (Calif.) U., 1990; postgrad., Loma Linda U., 1991—. Cert. health edn. specialist. Asst. to the dir. Project Asia Campus Crusade for Christ, San Bernardino, Calif., 1982-83, Campus Crusade for Christ-Internat. Pers., San Bernardino, 1983-90; health educator San Bernardino County Pub. Health, 1990-92; community lab. instr., rsch. asst. dept. health promotion and edn. Loma Linda (Calif.) U. Sch. Pub. Health, 1992—; rsch. asst., community lab. instr. Sch. Pub. Health Loma Linda U., 1992—. Mem. Minority Health Coalition, San Bernardino, 1990—, Com. for the Culturally Diverse, San Bernardino, 1990—; vol. Am. Cancer Soc.; chair Gt. Am. Smokeout, Inland Empire, 1991. Hulda Crooke scholar Loma Linda U., 1989; named Outstanding Young Woman of Yr., 1983; recipient Am. Cancer Soc. (Calif.) Rose award, 1991, Am. Cancer Soc. (nat.) Gaspar award, 1991. Mem. APHA, Nat. Coun. for Internat. Health, Soc. Pub. Health Edn., Loma Linda U. Alumni Assn.

WONG, THEODORE YAU SING, insurance agent; b. Honolulu, Apr. 24, 1940; s. Robert B. and Lucille (Young) W.; m. Myrna O.G. Wong, Sept. 6, 1964; children: Christine, Jennifer, Michael. BSEE, Oreg. State U., 1963; MBA, Santa Clara U., 1973. Agy. mgr. Conn. Gen. Life, Honolulu, 1973-84; pres. Sovereign Pacific Ltd., Honolulu, 1984-86; resident ins. specialist Merrill Lynch Life Agy. Inc., Honolulu, 1986-91, estate planning and bus. ins. specialist, 1992—. Sec. Wong Kong Har Tong, Honolulu, 1979-80;

chmn. profl. div. Aloha United Way, Honolulu, 1982. Capt. U.S. Army, 1963-67. Mem. Nat. Assn. Life Underwriters (state rep. 1979), Hawaii Estate Planning Coun. (dir. 1980-81), Hawaii Gen. Agts. and Mgrs. Assn. (pres. 1982), Hawaii CLU/Chartered Fin. Cons. (dir. 1980), Million Dollar Round Table (Top of Table, Ct. of Table). Office: Merrill Lynch Life Agy 1001 Bishop St Honolulu HI 96813-3429

WONG, WALLACE, medical supplies company executive, real estate investor; b. Honolulu, July 13, 1941; s. Jack Yung Hung and Theresa (Goo) W.; m. Amy Ju, June 17, 1963; children: Chris, Bradley, Jeffery. Student, UCLA, 1960-63. Chmn., pres. South Bay Coll., Hawthorne, Calif., 1965-86; chmn. Santa Barbara (Calif.) Bus. Coll., 1975—; gen. ptnr. W B Co., Redondo Beach, Calif., 1982—; CEO Cal Am. Med. Supplies, Redondo Beach, 1986—, Cal Am. Exports, Inc., Redondo Beach, 1986—, Pacific Am. Group, Redondo Beach, 1991—, Cal Am. Technics, Redondo Beach, 1991—; chmn, CEO Alpine, Inc., El Monte, 1993—; CEO Alpine, Inc., Rancho Santa Margarita, Calif., 1993—; bd. dirs. Metrobank, L.A., 1981—, Correia Art Glass, Santa Monica, Calif., 1984—. Acting sec. of state State of Calif., Sacramento, 1982; founding mem. Opera Pacific, Orange County, Calif., 1985; mem. Hist. and Cultural Found., Orange County, 1986; v.p. Orange County Chinese Cultural Club, Orange County, 1985. Named for Spirit of Enterprise Resolution, Hist. & Cultural Found., Orange Country, 1987; recipient resolution City of Hawthorne, 1973. Mem. Westren Accred Schs. & Colls. (v.p. 1978-79), Magic Castle (life), Singapore Club. Office: Alpine Inc 23042 Arroyo Vista Rancho Santa Margarita CA 92688

WONG, WALTER FOO, county official; b. San Francisco, Apr. 11, 1930; s. Harry Yee and Grace (Won) W. AA, Hartnell Coll., 1952; BS, U. Calif., Berkeley, 1955; MPH, U. Hawaii, 1968. Registered sanitarian, Calif. Sanitarian Stanislaus County Health Dept., Modesto, Calif., 1955-56; sanitarian Monterey County Health Dept., Salinas, Calif., 1956-67, sr. sanitarian, 1968-69, supervising sanitarian, 1969-70, dir. environ. health, 1971—; sec. Monterey County Solid Waste Mgmt. Com., 1976—, Monterey County Hazardous Wast Mgmt. Com., 1987—; coord. Monterey County Genetic Engring. Rev. Com., 1987—; mem. Monterey County Hazardous Materials Response Task Force, 1988—; mem. tech. adv. com. Monterey Peninsula Water Mgmt. Dist., 1985—, Monterey Regional Water Pollution Control Agy., 1985—; chmn. task force Monterey Regional Wastewater Reclamation Study for Agr., EPA and State of Calif. Chmn. Salinas Bicentennial Internat. Day Celebration, 1974, Pollution Clean-up Com. of Fort Ord Task Force, 1992; mem. Calif. Bare Closure Environ. adv. com., 1993. Mem. Calif. Conf. Dirs. Environ. Health (pres. 1982-83), Assn. Environ. Health Adminstrs. (pres. 1982-83), Salinas C. of C. (Mem. of Yr. award 1971), U. Calif. Berkeley Alumni Assn., U. Hawaii Alumni Assn. (Disting. Alumni award 1992). Republican. Presbyterian. Home: 234 Cherry Dr Salinas CA 93901-2807 Office: Monterey County Health Dept 1270 Natividad Rd Rm 301 Salinas CA 93906

WONG, WAYNE D., nutritionist; b. San Francisco, May 13, 1950; s. Chaney Noon and La Dean Maryan (Mah) W. m. Betty Lee, Oct. 16, 1977; children: Michael Gabriel, Elizabeth Catherine, Whitney Forbes, Ellesse Florence. BS in Dietetic Adminstrn., U. Calif., Berkeley, 1972; MS in Sch. Bus. Mgmt., Pepperdine U., 1976; student, Nikon Sch. Photography, San Francisco, 1969. Cert. Food Svc. Dir., Calif. Community Coll. tchr.; Registered Dietitian, Sch. Bus. Official, Benefit specialist. Food svc. worker, lab. asst. U. Calif., Berkeley, 1968-69, 70-71; mgmt. intern Mich. State U., East Lansing, 1970; dietetic intern Milw. Pub. Schs., 1972-73; food svc. cons. Trader Vic's, San Francisco, 1973; dir. food svcs. Bakersfield (Calif.) City Sch. Dist., 1973—; instr. Bakersfield Coll., 1978—; cons. Wong, R.D., Bakersfield, 1978—; registered Benefit Specialist Investors Retirement Mgmt., Carpenteria, Calif., 1988—; Nat. Child Nutrition Adv. Coun. USDA, Washington, 1977-79; first v.p. Partners in Nutrition Coop., Lancaster, Calif., 1988-90; food svc. edn. task force Calif. Dept. Edn., Sacramento, 1979—; project coord. nutrition edn. and tng. exemplary program adoption grant Bakersfield City Sch. Dist., 1982; project dir. basic skills, basic foods course, curriculum and recipe devel. grant Calif. Dept. Edn., 1985, cons. teaching course, 1985-88; mem. adv. coun. Calif. State U. Long Beach Child Nutrition Program Mgmt. Tng. Ctr., 1991; mem. Sch. Nutrition Adv. Coun., Bakersfield, 1990—. Author: Food Service Equipment-How Long Should It Last?, 1985; co-author (videotape) Bettermade Plastics, 1991, Recycle: Save Earth's Resources Now; programmer Food Svc. Pers. Database, 1988, Dishmachine Labor and Energy Matrix, 1991; contbr. articles to profl. jours. BBQ fund-raiser co-chmn. Citizens for Yes on Measure B, Bakersfield, 1989; legis. com. Child Nutrition Facilities Act 1975, Sacramento, 1973-76; expert witness State Senate Select Subcom. on Nutrition and Human Needs, Sacramento, 1973; asst. troop leader Boy Scouts Am., Troop 219, San Francisco, 1965-67; participant Chinese Family Life Study U. Calif., Berkeley; dir. polystyrene recycling project Bakersfield City Sch. Dist., 1990; team leader Healthy Kids, Healthy Calif. program Calif. Dept. Edn., 1985-87; sponsor Christian Broadcasting Network Satellite Communications Ctr., 1978; world vision sponsor India Community Devel. Program, 1974-92. Recipient Leadership award Calif. State Dept. Edn., 1987, Outstanding Sch. Lunch Program award USDA, 1989; 1st pl. Calif. Sch. Food Svc. Assn. Country Cook-off, 1983, 84; Toto Wizard nominee Sabatasso Foods, 1985, Best Practice award USDA, 1992. Mem. Am. Dietetic Assn. (Young Dietitian of Yr. 1976), Am. Sch. Food Svc. Assn. (child nutrition mktg. bike ride 1991, Cycle Across Am. for Child Nutrition an dFitness 1993), Am. Running and Fitness Assn., Calif. Assn. Sch. Bus. Ofcls. (photographer 1985, food svc. R&D chmn. 1985-87, recognition 1987, food and nutrition R&D com. 1984), Calif. Sch. Food Svc. Assn. (edn. tng. chmn. 1975-76, wellness awareness bike ride 1990-91, child nutrition bike ride 1991, 1st pl. photo contest 1993, cover photographer assn. jour. Poppyseeds 1992, 1st place photo contest, 1993), Sports and Cardiovascular Nutritionists, Kern County Sch. Food Svc. Assn. (pres. 1987-90, recipient Golden Poppy award 1990), Kern Wheelmen (v.p. 1992), Pi Alpha Phi, Omicron Nu. Republican. Baptist. Home: 4901 University Ave Bakersfield CA 93306-1773

WONG, WILLIAM SHEH, librarian; s. Po and Te-i (Liao) W.; m. Eugenia J.K. Shih, June 27, 1964; 1 child, Alexander. BA, Taiwan Normal U., 1956; MA, Meiji U., 1960, George Peabody Coll., 1963; PhD, Northwestern U., 1971. Cataloger U. N.H., Durham, 1963-64; asst. East Asian libr. U. Kans., Lawrence, 1964-67; curator East Asian collection Northwestern U., Evanston, Ill., 1967-70; chief bibliographer Loyola U. Libr., Chgo., 1970-71; East Asian libr., assoc. prof. U. Minn., Mpls., 1971-78; Asian libr., prof. libr. adminstrn. U. Ill., Urbana, 1978-90; East Asian libr. U. Calif., Irvine, 1990—. Mem. ALA, Am. Assn. Chinese Studies, Internat. Assn. Orientalist Librs. (sec., treas. 1983-86, 86-90), Assn. Asian Studies. Home: 23 Zola Ct Irvine CA 92715-4061 Office: U Calif Libr PO Box 19557 Irvine CA 92713-9557

WONG, Y(ING) WOOD, real estate investment company executive, venture capital investment company executive; b. Hong Kong, Apr. 28, 1950; came to U.S., 1969; s. Loyee K.H. and Margaret M.C.L. Wong; m. Leslie K. P. Chan, Dec. 18, 1977; children: Joshua H., Jonathan H. AA in Biology, Menlo Coll., 1971, BSBA, 1974; BA in Zoology, U. Calif., Berkeley, 1972; M in Mgmt., Northwestern U., 1976. Auditor, Touche Ross & Co., CPA's, San Francisco, 1976-78; founder, mng. dir. Wong Properties, Palo Alto, Calif., 1976—; founder, gen. ptnr. Wongfratris Co., Palo Alto, 1986—; instr. Golden Gate U., 1977. Trustee Crystal Springs Uplands Sch., Hillsborough, Calif. Mem. Internat. Platform Assn., Commonwealth Club Calif., Beta Alpha Psi. Office: 51 Jordan Pl Palo Alto CA 94303-2903

WONG-DIAZ, FRANCISCO RAIMUNDO, lawyer; b. Havana, Cuba, Oct. 29, 1944; came to U.S., Nov. 1961; s. Juan and Teresa (Diaz de Villegas) Wong; 1 child, Richard Alan. BA with honors, No. Mich. U., 1963; MA with highest honors, U. Detroit, 1967; PhD, MA, U. Mich., 1974; JD, U. Calif.-Berkeley, 1976. Bar: Calif. 1980, U.S. Dist. Ct. (no. dist.) Calif. 1990, Fla. 1987. Asst. prof. San Francisco State U., 1977; vis. scholar U. Calif. Berkeley Sch. Bus., Berkeley, 1983-84; prof. City Coll. San Francisco, 1975—, dept. chmn., 1978-85; rsch. atty. Marin Superior Ct., 1980-81; ct. arbitrator Marin Mcpl. Ct., 1985; sole practice, Kentfield, Calif., 1980—; assoc. dean Miami-Dade Coll., 1986; dir. Cutcliffe Consulting, Inc., Hawthorne, LaFamila Ctr., Inc., San Rafael, Calif., 1980-85, Small Bus. Inst., Kentfield, 1982-86; cons. ICC Internat., San Francisco, 1980-82. Bd. editors Indsl. Relations Law Jour., 1975-76; mem. editorial bd. California Lawyer, 1991-93; lector St. Sebastian's Ch., 1984—. Diplomat-scholar U.S. Dept. State, Washington, 1976; Horace C. Rackham fellow U. Mich., 1970. Mem. Am. Polit. Sci. Assn., Latino Ednl. Assn. (treas. 1985), Cuban Am. Nat. Council, World Affairs Council (seminar leader San Francisco 1980). Roman Catholic. Club: Commonwealth.

WONNACOTT, ELIZABETH SAGONA, software marketing consultant; b. Bklyn., Feb. 3, 1951; d. Stuart H. and Grace (Goie) Sagona; m. Roger Warren, Jan. 27, 1978 (div. Feb. 1987); 1 child, Lindsay; m. Larry R. Wonnacott, Mar. 10, 1990; 1 child, Stefan. BA in English Lit., Fla. Atlantic U., 1973. Mktg. dir. Wind-2 Rsch., Inc., Ft. Collins, Colo., 1985-89, Anatel Corp., Boulder, Colo., 1988-89; pres. Esprit Mktg., Inc., Boulder, Colo., 1989—. Editor, First Class Object Mgmt. Group Newsletter, 1992. Office: Esprit Mktg Inc 4730 Walnut Ste 206 Boulder CO 80301

WOO, CHRISTOPHER ALLEN, pharmacist; b. El Centro, Calif., Nov. 21, 1963; s. John Yum and May (Quan) W. PharmD, U. Pacific, 1988. Registered lic. pharmacist, Calif., Nev. Cashier Food Palace Grocery Store, El Centro, Calif., 1977-85; intern pharmacist Community Pharmacy, Imperial, Calif., 1985-86, Imperial Drugs, El Centro, Calif., 1986; teaching asst. U. Pacific, Stockton, Calif., 1986-87; staff pharmacist Payless Drugs, San Marcos, Calif., 1988-90; relief pharmacist Plaza Sorrento Pharmacy, San Diego, 1990—; pharmacy mgr. Payless Drugs, San Diego, 1990—; adj. faculty mem., U. Pacific, Stockton, Calif., 1991—. Contbr. articles to profl. jours. Active Am. Polit. Action Com., Calif. Polit. Action Com. Mem. Am. Pharm. Assn., Nat. Assn. Retail Druggists (com. mem. 1989-90), Calif. Pharmacists Assn. (vice speaker 1991-92, trustee Dist. 11 1993—, Disting. Young Pharmacist 1992), San Diego County Pharmacists Assn. (pres. 1992, Pharmacist of Yr. 1990), Kappa Psi (Grand Ritualist 1991-93), Pacific Assocs. Alumni Assn., Phi Lambda Sigma Pharmacy Leadership Soc., Order of Omega Greek Leadership Soc. Office: Payless Drugs 13167 Black Mountain Rd San Diego CA 92129

WOO, DAVID SONNY, programmer analyst; b. Taipei, Taiwan, Mar. 9, 1954; came to U.S., 1977; s. John Timothy and Delphine (Sun) W.; m. Jean W. M. Lee, July 11, 1978; children: Daniel, Dean. AAS, Truckee Meadow C.C., Reno, Nev., 1987; BS, U. Nev., 1988. Stacks clk. U. Nev., Reno, 1979-84; floor mechanic Harrah's Hotel Casino, Reno, 1981-85, sr. operator, 1985-88; software engr. Internat. Game Tech., Reno, 1988-89; tech. support Truckee Meadow C.C., Reno, 1988—; sr. programmer analyst Eldorado Hotel Casino, Reno, 1989—. Former instr. Chinese Assn. of Nev.-Reno. Home: 908 Lester Ave Reno NV 89502 Office: Eldorado Hotel Casino 345 N Virginia St Reno NV 89501

WOO, VERNON YING-TSAI, lawyer, real estate developer; b. Honolulu, Aug. 7, 1942; s. William Shu-Bin and Hilda Woo; m. Arlene Gay Ischar, Feb. 14, 1971; children: Christopher Shu-Bin, Lia Gay. BA, U. Hawaii, 1964, MA, 1966; JD, Harvard U., 1969. Pres. Woo Kessner Duca & Maki, Honolulu, 1972-87; pvt. practice law Honolulu, 1987—; judge per diem Honolulu Dist. Ct., 1978-84. Bd. dirs. Boys and Girls Club of Honolulu, 1985—, pres., 1990-92; counsel Hawii Med. Assn., 1988—. Mem. ABA, Hawaii Bar Assn., Honolulu Bd. Realtors, Waikiki Yacht Club (judge advocate 1987—), Pacific Club. Home: 2070 Kalawahine Pl Honolulu HI 96822-2518 Office: 1019 Waimanu St Ste 205 Honolulu HI 96814-3409

WOO, WILBERT YUK CHEONG, contracting officer, college instructor; b. Honolulu, Feb. 7, 1942; s. Jabob Yue Tak and Beatrice Yuet Laan (Wong) W. BS, Calif. State U., L.A., 1970, MBA, 1977. CPA, cert. cost analyst. Acct. So. Calif. Gas Co., L.A., 1971-73; auditor Def. Contract Audit Agy., Pasadena, Calif., 1973-74; sr. auditor Def. Contract Audit Agy., Gardena, Calif., 1986-88; sr. auditor Office of Insp. Gen. HHS, Beverly Hills, Calif., 1974-86; cost mgr. USAF Space Systen Div., L.A., 1988—; instr. S.W. Coll., L.A., 1980—, El Camino Coll., 1984-87. With U.S. Army, 1965-67, Korea. Mem. AICPAs, Calif. Inst. CPAs (govt. contracts com.), Assn. Govt. Accts., Soc. of Cost Estimating and Analysis, Chinese Am. Soc. So. Calif. (bd. dirs.). Office: USAF Space Missile Ctr PO Box 92960 Los Angeles CA 90009-2960

WOOD, ALAN KEITH, wildlife biologist; b. Downey, Calif., Mar. 20, 1956; s. Myron Jonathon and Mary El Jean (Rathbun) W.; m. Sylvie Corbeil, June 14, 1989; 1 child, Andrea Marie. BS in Biology, Utah State U., 1978; MS in Wildlife Resources, Brigham Young U., 1980; PhD in Biol. Scis., Mont. State U., 1987. Cert. wildlife biologist. Teaching/rsch. asst. Brigham Young U., Provo, Utah, 1978-80; soil conservationist Bur. of Land Mgmt., Vernal, Utah, 1980-82; rsch. asst. Mont. State U., Bozeman, 1982-86, teaching asst./postdoctoral fellow, 1986-88; project biologist Wyo. Game and Fish Dept., Casper, 1988-89; wildlife program specialist Mont. Dept. of State Lands, Missoula, 1989—; lchmn. Interagy. Granite Butte Elk Project, Missoula, 1991-92. Contbr. articles to profl. jours. Recipient Commendation for Dedication and Professionalism Mont. Dept. Fish, Wildlife, 1989, Cert. of Appreciation Mont. Dept. State Lands, 1992. Mem. The Wildlife Soc., Sigma Xi, Phi Kappa Phi. Office: Mont Dept State Lands 2705 Spurgin Rd Missoula MT 59801

WOOD, CHARLES CRESSON, information systems security consultant, software firm executive, educator; b. Phila., Feb. 22, 1955; s. Charles Wistar and Margaret Davis (Ansley) W. BSE with honors in Acctg., U. Pa., 1976, MSE in Computer and Info. Sci., 1979, MBA in Fin., 1979. CPA, Calif. Teaching fellow computer sci. U. Pa., Phila., 1976-79; system performance engr. Booz-Allen & Hamilton, Washington, 1976; systems designer Am. Mgmt. Systems, Washington, 1977; acct. Richard Eisner & Co., N.Y.C., 1978; cons. in computer systems security Stanford Rsch. Inst., Menlo Park, Calif., 1979-83; sr. info. security cons. Bank of Am., San Francisco, 1984-85; mem. faculty Golden Gate U., 1984-88; founder, prin. cons. Info. Integrity Investments, 1984—; pres. Baseline Software, 1989—; security cons., analyst specializing in fin. info. system, computer security and privacy, cryptography. Cert. info. systems security profl., info systems auditor. Sr. N.Am. editor: Computers and Security mag., 1983—, Computer Fraud and Security Bulletin. Author 3 books on computer security; co-author 3 computer security software packages; columnist Computer Security Alert; contbr. 90 tech. articles on info. security to profl. jours.; speaker over 100 confs. and seminars in field. Founder and former pres. Found. for Alternative Research; past bd. dirs. Mid-Peninsula Peace Ctr. EDP Auditors' Assn., World Future Soc., Info. Systems Security Assn. Quaker. Office: PO Box 1219 Sausalito CA 94966-1219

WOOD, DARRELL EUGENE, English language educator, councilman; b. Louisville, Nov. 26, 1929; s. Charles Wood and Flossie (Boggs) Harlan; m. Virgenne Jurgens, May 27, 1956; children: Marcus L., Melissa L., Jon E., Jyl E. BA, Nebr. State Coll., Chadron, 1957; MA, Nebr. State U., 1960; EdS, Kans. State U., 1969. Cert. tchr., Nebr. Tchr. English and social sci. Lorenzo Consol. Schs., Sidney, Nebr., 1957-61; supt. Center (Nebr.) Pub. Schs., 1961-62; chmn. communications dept. Norfolk (Nebr.) Jr. Coll., 1962-63; prof. English, history and photography Northeastern Jr. Coll., Sterling, Colo., 1963—, prof. Emeritus, 1993—; coun. mem. City of Sterling, 1989-91; mem. exec. bd. faculty adv. com. Colo. Commn. of Higher Edn., Denver, 1978-86. Precinct committeeman City of Sterling, 1967-69, 75-76; trustee Logan County Hist. Soc.; mem. adv. bd. Parks-Recreation-Museum. With USN, 1950-54, Korea. Regents scholar U. Nebr., 1949, Aksarben scholar, 1960. Mem. NEA, Nat. Coun. Tchrs. English, Northeastern Faculty Assn. (pres. 1975-76), VFW, Am. Legion (comdr. 1991-92), Colo. Edn. Assn. Democrat. Home: 504 Holly Dr Sterling CO 80751-4646 Office: Northeastern Jr Coll Sterling CO 80751

WOOD, DAVID BRUCE, naturopathic physician; b. Fayetteville, N.C., Jan. 21, 1954; s. Marvin James and Rachel Elenor (Thom) W.; m. Wendy Ann McKiernan, Aug. 1974 (div. Aug. 1976); m. Cheryl Lynn Garbarino, Aug. 17, 1980. BS in Microbiology, U. Wash., 1977; D in Naturopathic Medicine, John Bastyr Coll., Seattle, 1983. Pres., co-founder Trinity Family Health Clinic, Inc., P.S., Edmonds, Wash., 1984—. Singer Sound of Praise Choir, Overlake Christian Ch., Kirkland, Wash., 1987—; narrator Easter Pagent, 1989. Mem. Am. Assn. Nutritional Cons., Nat. Health Fedn., Am. Assn. Naturopathic Physicians, Wash. Assn. Naturopathic Physicians (trustee, exec. bd. 1989-92). Home: 13721 Cascadian Way Everett WA 98208 Office: Trinity Family Health Clinic Inc PS 7614 195th St SW Edmonds WA 98026

WOOD, DONALD FRANK, transportation educator, consultant; b. Waukesha, Wis., Feb. 22, 1935; s. Frank Blaine and Uilah (Mathson) W.; m. Doreen Johnson, July 5, 1968; children: Frank, Tamara. BA, U. Wis., 1957, MA, 1958; PhD, Harvard U., 1970. Transp. planner State of Wis., Madison, 1960-70; prof. San Francisco State U., 1970—. Author: El Camino, 1982, (with others) Motorized Fire Apparatus of The West, 1991, Contemporary Transportation, 1993, Contemporary Logistics, 1993, American Volunteer Fire Trucks, 1993; contbr. Encyc. Britannica, 1993. 2d lt. U.S. Army, 1958. Mem. Coun. of Logistics Mgmt. (chpt. pres. 1975-76), Transp. Rsch. Forum (chpt. pres. 1974), Am. Truck Hist. Soc. Presbyterian. Home: 321 Riviera Cir Larkspur CA 94939-1508 Office: San Francisco State Univ Sch Bus San Francisco CA 94132

WOOD, EDWARD NEWTON, civil and mechanical engineer; b. Smethwick, Eng., Aug. 3, 1928; came to U.S., 1930; s. Harold Arthur and Maud (Newton) W.; m. Eileen Magginis, May 5, 1952 (div. 1962); children: Mary, Wendy; m. Mary Rose Daniels, Feb. 25, 1965; children: Dennis, Gary, Pamela. Student, Columbia U., 1948-50; BS, UCLA, 1957. Lic. profl. engr., Calif., Oreg. Engr. Nat. Presto Industries, Eau Claire, Wis., 1958-59; engr. Aerojet Gen., Downey, Calif., 1958-60, Rohr Corp., Riverside, Calif., 1960-62, Atlantic Rsch. Corp., Costa Mesa, Calif., 1962-69; city engr. City of Seal Beach, Calif., 1970-73, City of Roseburg, Oreg., 1973-75; pres. Wood Engring. Inc., Umpqua, Oreg., 1975—; asst. bldg. official Douglas County Oreg., 1984-86; mem. Nat. Defense Exec. Res., 1982—. Mem. and chmn. Douglas County Planning Commn., 1978-87, mem. and chmn. Douglas County Traffic Safety Commn., 1976—. Mem. ASCE, ASME, Profl. Engrs. Oreg. (pres. Umpqua chpt. 1983-84, 88-94), Masons, Elks. Home and Office: 311 Smethwick Dr Umpqua OR 97486-9731

WOOD, F. RUSSELL, broadcast executive; b. Farmington, N.Mex., Aug. 21, 1947; s. William R. and Lorna Mae (Richey) W.; m. Ilene Elfors, Jan. 29, 1971; children: Jonathon, Jeremy, Thelissa, Tamilisa. BA in Broadcasting, Brigham Young U., 1971; MA in Communications, U. Mo., Kansas City, 1982. Announcer KRGO Radio, Salt Lake City, 1971-72, KLAK Radio, Denver, 1972-73; agy. acct. exec., announcer Intermark Inc./KSL Radio, Salt Lake City, 1973-74; acct. exec. KSL Radio, Salt Lake City, 1974-75, sales mgr., 1975-80, announcer, 1980-84, gen. mgr. 1987—; gen. mgr. KMBZ/KMBR Radio, Kansas City, Mo., 1980-84; mktg. devel. dir. KSL Radio/TV, Salt Lake City, 1986-87. Bd. dirs. City Repertory Theatre, Salt Lake City, 1989—. Mem. Utah Broadcasters Assn (legis. liaison 1987—), Nat. Assn. Broadcasters (bd. dirs. 1988—), CBS Racio Affiliates Assn. (bd. dirs. 1989). Mormon. Office: Sta KSL(AM) KSL Broadcasting House Salt Lake City UT 84110-1160

WOOD, FERGUS JAMES, geophysicist, consultant; b. London, Ont., Can., May 13, 1917; came to U.S., 1924, naturalized, 1932; s. Louis Aubrey and Dora Isabel (Elson) W.; student U. Oreg., 1934-36; AB, U. Calif., Berkeley, 1938, postgrad., 1938-39; postgrad. U. Chgo., 1939-40, U. Mich., 1940-42, Calif. Inst. Tech., 1946; m. Doris M. Hack, Sept. 14, 1946; children: Kathryn Celeste Wood Madden, Bonnie Patricia Wood Ward. Teaching asst. U. Mich., 1940-42; instr. in physics and astronomy Pasadena City Coll., 1946-48, John Muir Coll., 1948-49; asst. prof. physics U. Md., 1949-50; assoc. physicist Johns Hopkins U. Applied Physics Lab., 1950-55; sci. editor Ency. Americana, N.Y.C., 1955-60; aero. and space rsch. scientist, sci. asst. to dir. Office Space Flight Programs, Hdqrs., NASA, Washington, 1960-61; program dir. fgn. sci. info. NSF, Washington, 1961-62; phys. scientist, chief sci. and tech. info. staff U.S. Coast and Geodetic Survey, Rockville, Md., 1962-66, phys. scientist Office of Dir., 1967-73, rsch. assoc. Office of Dir., 1973-77, Nat. Ocean Svc.; cons. tidal dynamics, Bonita, Calif., 1978—; mem. Am. Geophys. Union, ICSU-UNESCO Internat. Geol. Correlation Project 274, Working Group #1-Crescendo Events in Coastal Environments, Past and Future (The Millennium Project), 1988—. Capt. USAAF, 1942-46. Recipient Spl. Achievement award Dept. Commerce, NOAA, 1970, 74, 76, 77. Mem. Sigma Pi Sigma, Pi Mu Epsilon, Delta Phi Alpha. Democrat. Presbyterian. Author: The Strategic Role of Perigean Spring Tides in Nautical History and North American Coastal Flooding, 1635-1976, 1978; Tidal Dynamics; Coastal Flooding, and Cycles of Gravitational Force, 1986; contbr. numerous articles to encys., reference sources, profl. jours.; writer, tech. dir. documentary film: Pathfinders from the Stars, 1967; editor-in-chief: The Prince William Sound, Alaska, Earthquake of 1964 and Aftershocks, vols. 1-2A and sci. coordinator vols. 2B, 2C and 3, 1966-69. Home: 3103 Casa Bonita Dr Bonita CA 91902-1735

WOOD, GEORGE DOUGLAS, insurance agent, writer; b. Ogden, Utah, Aug. 1, 1919; s. George Douglas and Lena Marie (Mouritsen) W.; m. Viola Stucki, Sept. 22; children: Steven, Alan, Sydney, Donald, Sheri, Teresa. BS in Edn., Idaho State Coll., 1948. Tchr. Sch. Dist. 25, Pocatello, Idaho, 1948-52, 54-55; ins. agt. Farmers Ins. Group, Pocatello, 1955-93. Contbr. articles to profl. jours. With USN, 1941-46, PTO; lt. comdr. USNR, ret. Decorated D.F.C., Air Medal. Mem. Am. Nuclear Soc. (chair Idaho sect.-Pocatello br. 1989-91). Republican. Mem. LDS Ch. Home: 1680 N Mink Creek Rd Pocatello ID 83204

WOOD, GLADYS BLANCHE, retired educator and journalist; b. Sanborn, N.D., Aug. 12, 1921; d. Charles Kershaw and Mina Blanche (Kee) Crowther; m. Newell Edwin Wood, June 13, 1943; children: Terry N., Lani, Brian R., Kevin C. BA in Journalism, U. Minn., 1943; MS in Mass Communication, San Jose State U., 1972. Cert. secondary tchr., Calif. Reporter St. Paul Pioneer-Dispatch, 1943-45; editor J.C. Penney Co., N.Y.C., 1945-46; tchr. English and journalism Willow Glen High Sch., San Jose, Calif., 1968-87; freelance writer, photographer, 1947—; cons. in field. Named Secondary Journalism Tchr. of Yr. Calif. Newpaper Pubs. Assn., 1977. Mem. AAUW, Soc. Profl. Journalists, Journalism Edn. Assn., Calif. Tchrs. English, Calif. Ret. Tchrs. Assn., Women in Communications, Santa Clara County Med. Assn. Aux., Montalvo Assn., LWV, Friends of Libr., Delta Kappa Gamma, Alpha Omicron Pi. Republican. Methodist. Home: 14161 Douglass Ln Saratoga CA 95070-5535

WOOD, HAROLD SAMUEL, educator; b. Long Beach, Calif., Mar. 8, 1913; s. Samuel Bury and Helen Imogene (Hawkins) W. BA, U. Redlands, 1942; MBA, U. So. Calif., 1947; AM, Columbia U., 1954; LLD (hon.), St. Louis U., 1985. With cargo ops. Trans World Airlines, L.A., 1946-49; prof. St. Louis U., 1949-80, prof. emeritus, 1980; cons. Air Afrique, 1970-75, Air Nippon Airways, 1975-85, S.A.S. Airline, Copenhagen, 1975-77, TWA, 1972-79. Author: Organization and Management of College Flying Clubs, 1965. With U.S. Army, 1941-46. Recipient Brewer Trophy Nat. Aeronautic Assn., 1971, Disting. Svc. award Dept. of Transp., 1982. Fellow U. Aviation Assn. (pres. 1961-63, sr. advisor 1964-80, emeritus 1980—), Nat. Intercollegiate Flying Assn. (exec. dir. 1978-83, emeritus 1983—), Aviation-Space Edn. Assn., Flying Assn. Exec. (dir. 1967-83, emeritus 1983—), Phi Delta Kappa, Delta Nu Alpha. Republican. Baptist. Home: 1325 Las Villas Way #302 Escondido CA 92026 Office: Alpha Eta Rho Palamar Coll San Marcos CA 92069

WOOD, HARRY GEORGE, packaging engineering and electrostatic discharge control consultant; b. Orchard Park, N.Y., Jan. 22, 1915; s. William A. and Marie E. (Schmidt) W.; m. Ruth Farber, Oct. 20, 1939; children—Keith F., Eugene F. B.S. in Edn., SUNY-Buffalo, 1936. Planning supr. Morrison Steel Products, Buffalo, 1944-51; sr. methods engr., materials handling supr. Schlage Lock Co., San Francisco, 1953-57; prodn. mgr. M. Greenberg's Sons Foundry & Machine Shop, San Francisco, 1957-58; packaging mgr. Hewlett-Packard Co., Santa Clara, Calif., 1959-83, introduced first electrostatic discharge control program, 1981-83; cons. on packaging engring. and electrostatic discharge. H.G. Wood & Assocs., Palo Alto, 1983—; instr. factory planning and plant layout Foothill Jr. Coll., Los Altos, 1959-60; mem. nat. packaging industry adv. council U. Calif.-Davis, 1971-73; chmn. Internat. Air Cargo Forum, 1968-71; designed and built Ruth Wood Nursery Sch., 1962, ptnr. and bus. mgr., 1962—. Contbr. articles to profl. jours. Patentee in field. Recipient Grayson Lynn award for package design Lockheed Missile and Space Div., 1964, Ann. Achievement award Nat. Inst. Packaging Handling and Logistics Engrs., 1974. Fellow Soc. Packaging and Handling Engrs. (hon. life mem., cert. profl. in packaging, 5 Nat. Design awards, exec. v.p., program chmn. Golden Gate chpt. 1955, 63, pres. chpt. of yr. 1964-65, chmn. bd. dirs. 1966), Internat. Materials Mgmt. Soc. (nat. bd.

dirs. 1956-57, pres. No. Calif. chpt. 1956-57); mem. Internat. Platform Assn. Home and Office: 849 Mesa Ave Palo Alto CA 94306-3710

WOOD, HUGH BERNARD, retired educator; b. Angola, Ind., Feb. 18, 1909; s. Weir and Merle (Saylor) W.; m. Helen Launa Croyle, Oct. 19, 1928 (dec. June 1984); children: Wayne Bernard, Pamela Lynn. BA, U. Toledo, 1931; MA, U. Colo., 1935; EdD, Columbia U., 1937. Cert. elem. and secondary tchr., curriculum design specialist. Prof. of edn. U. Oreg., Eugene, 1939-74, prof. emeritus, 1974—; co-founder, exec. dir., pres. Am. Nepal Edn. Found., 1955—; Fulbright lectr., India, 1953-54; ednl. advisor, Govt. of Nepal, chief Edn. Div. of US Ops. Mission in Nepal, 1953-59; dir. for curriculum devel. Tongue Point Job Corps Ctr., Astoria, Oreg., 1965-66; convocation speaker Tribhuvan U., Nepal, 1983, others. Author 300 publs. including Curriculum Planning and Development, 1940, revised edit. 1960, Evaluation of Pupil Growth and Development, 1940, Manual for Educational Research, 1950, Nepal Diary, others; contbr. articles to profl. jours. and books. Lt. comdr. USN, 1942-45. Recipient Svc. awards, Nepal, 1959-62, 81, Outstanding Adminstrv. Svc. medal Souh Vietnam, 1968, Birendra Prajnalankar award Nepal, 1988, others. Home: 2790 Cape Meares Loop Tillamook OR 97141-9328

WOOD, JAMES LESLIE, sociology educator; b. Aug. 30, 1941. BA in Sociology, U. Calif., Berkeley, 1963, postgrad.; MA in Sociology, 1966, PhD in Sociology, 1973. Asst. prof. San Francisco State U., summer 1972; instr. in sociology Holy Names Coll., 1971-73; lectr. in sociology U. Calif., Riverside, 1973-75; lectr. in sociology San Diego State U., 1975-76, asst. prof. sociology, 1976-78, assoc. prof. sociology, 1978-81, prof. sociology, 1981—, chmn. sociology, 1991—; SDSU mem. Promotions com., Executive com., Curriculum Com., Methodology com., Syposium com., Post-Tenure review com. (chair), San Diego Poll com., Personnel com., Rsch. Human Subjects com., Applied Social Rsch. Group com., Reappointment Tenure com. (chair), Master's essay com., Graduate com., Master's Degree theory and Methodology Exam com., Colloquium com., Teaching Eval. com.; lectr. in field; resident scholar U. London, Goldsmiths' Coll., 1984. Author: The Sources of American Student Activism, 1974, (co-author) Sociology: Traditional and Radical Perspectives, Adapted for the United Kingdom, 1982, Social Movements: Development, Participation and Dynamics, 1982, 3d printing, 1985, Sociology: Traditional and Radical Perspectives, 2d edit., 1990; author: (monographs) Political Consciousness and Student Activism, New Left Ideology: Its Dimensions and Development, 1975, Aging in America; works presented at profl. organizations; contbr. articles to profl. jours. U. Calif. grantee, 1969, 73-74, 75, San Diego State U. grantee, 1976, 79, 81, 82, 88, 83, 85, 90. Mem. Am. Sociol. Assn. (collective behavior and social movements sect., polit. sociology sect.), Internat. Soc. Polit. Psychology, Pacific Sociol. Assn., Soc. for the Study of Social Problems, Calif. Sociol. Assn., Phi Beta Delta, Alpha Kappa Delta. Office: San Diego State U Dept of Sociology 5300 Campanile Dr San Diego CA 92182-0383

WOOD, JEFFREY BULLARD, career counselor, educator; b. New Haven, June 30, 1948; s. Robert Kenneth and Constance Wilson (Rice) W.; m. Katherine Frances Burrows, Aug. 28, 1971; children: Marjory Megan, Tyler Ellis. BA in History, Lake Forest Coll., 1971; MEd in Orgn. and Mgmt., Antioch New Eng. Grad. Sch Edn, 1975. Exec dir. Trement Rehab. and Info. Programs, Inc., New Britain, Conn., 1971-72; student liaison Vt. Pub. Interest Rsch. Group, Montpelier, 1972-73; admissions intern Bennington (Vt.) Coll., 1974-75, acting co-dir. student svcs., 1975-76; asst. dir. office career devel. Williams Coll., Williamstown, Mass., 1976-79; dir. career ctr. Occidental Coll., L.A., 1979-85; dir. career devel./alumni Monterey (Calif.) Inst. Internat. Studies, 1985—; job search instr. UCLA Extension, 1980-83; co-founder, co-chmn. No. Calif. Internat. Careers Consortium, 1991—; co-founder, coord. Common Knowledge (Community Free Sch.), Williamstown, 1977-79. Author: Student Dreams and the Real International Job Market, 1992; co-author: Head South Young Graduate, 1992; contbr. articles to profl. jours. and Mag. Den leader, asst. den leader Webelos Cub Scouts, Carmel/Carmel Valley, Calif., 1991-93; bd. dirs. Carmel Valley Little League, 1993—. Mem. Coll. Placement Coun. (global issues task force 1992-93), Western Coll. Placement Assn. Democrat. Home: 15 Lilac Ln Carmel Valley CA 93924 Office: Monterey Inst Internat Studies 425 Van Buren St Monterey CA 93940

WOOD, JOHN DENISON, utility company executive; b. Calgary, Alta., Can., Sept. 28, 1931; s. Ernest William and Ellen Gartshore (Pender) W.; m. Christena Isabel; 1 dau., Donna M. BSCE, U. B.C., 1953; MSCE, Stanford U., 1954, PhDCE and Engring. Mechs., 1956. Research asst. in civil engring. and engring. mechs. Stanford U., Palo Alto, Calif., 1953-56; assoc. mgr. dynamics dept. Engring. Mechs. Lab. Space Tech. Labs., Inc., Redondo Beach, Calif., 1956-63; pres., dir. Mechs. Research, Inc., El Segundo, Calif., 1963-66; sr. v.p. engring. and research ATCO Ind., Ltd., Calgary, Alta., 1966-68, sr. v.p. eastern region, 1968-75, sr. v.p. planning, 1975-77; pres., chief exec. officer ATCO Industries N.A., Ltd., Calgary, Alta., 1977-82, ATCOR Resources Ltd., Calgary, 1982-84; pres., chief operating officer Can. Utilities, Ltd., Edmonton, Alta., 1984-88, pres., chief exec. officer, 1988—; bd. dirs. ATCO Ltd., Can. Utilities Ltd., ATCOR Ltd., ATCO Enterprises Inc., Thames Power Ltd., Barking Power Ltd., Vencap Equities Alta. Ltd.; chmn. bd., CEO Can. Western Natural Gas Co. Ltd., Northwestern Utilities Ltd., Alta. Power Ltd., Northland Utilities Enterprises Ltd.; chmn. bd. Frontec Logistics Corp. Co-author: Ballistic Missile and Space Vehicle Systems, 1961. Mem. Pres.'s Club adv. com. U. Alta.; bd. dirs. Jr. Achievement Can., Western Orthopaedic and Arthritis Rsch. Found., Coun. for Can. Unity; bd. govs. Jr. Achievement No. Alta.; mem. adv. coun. Calgary Econ. Devel. Authority, Econ. Devel. Edmonton Bus. Adv. Coun. Athlone fellow, Can. Acad. Engring. fellow. Mem. Engring. Inst. of Can., Sci. Rsch. Soc. Am., Assn. Profl. Engrs. Alta., Sigma Xi, Tau Beta Pi. Baptist. Clubs: Glencoe, Earl Grey, Calgary Petroleum, Mayfair Golf and Country. Office: Can Utilities Ltd, 10035 105th St, Edmonton, AB Canada T5J 2V6 also: Can Western Natural Gas Co Ltd, 909-11 Ave S W, Calgary, AB Canada T2R 1L8

WOOD, JOHN MORTIMER, aerospace executive, aeronautical engineer; b. New Orleans, July 7, 1934; s. John Mortimer Sr. and Annie Jeff (Gates) W.; m. Bonnie Ann Blanchette, June 6, 1958 (div. Oct. 1977); m. Barbara Lee Butler, Aug. 12, 1978; 1 child, Mark Douglas. BA in Aero. Engring., U. Tex., 1957. Project engr. Gen. Dynamics/Convair, San Diego, 1957-58, Rocket Power, Inc., Mesa, Ariz., 1961-64; sales mgr. S.E. region Rocket Power, Inc., Huntsville, Ala., 1964-67; dir. mktg. Quantic Industries, San Carlos, Calif., 1967-70; sr. mktg. mgr. Talley Industries of Ariz., Mesa, 1970-77; dir. mktg. Universal Propulsion Co., Inc., Phoenix, 1977-85, v.p. mktg., 1985-91, v.p. contract mgmt., 1992—. 1st lt. USAF, 1958-61. Mem. Am. Def. Preparedness Assn., Assn. for Unmanned Vehicle Sytsems, Tech. Mktg. Soc. of Am., Survival and Flight Equipment Assn. Republican. Home: 111 W Canterbury Ln Phoenix AZ 85023-6252 Office: Universal Propulsion Co Inc 25401 N Central Ave Phoenix AZ 85027-7837

WOOD, KENNETH ARTHUR, newspaper editor emeritus, writer; b. Hastings, Sussex, Eng., Feb. 25, 1926; came to U.S., 1965; s. Arthur Charles and Ellen Mary (Cox) W.; m. Hilda Muriel Harloe, Sept. 13, 1952. Educated in Eng. Editor Stamp Collector newspaper Van Dahl Publs., Albany, Oreg., 1968-80, editor emeritus, 1980—. Author (ency.) This Is Philately, 1982, (atlas) Where in the World, 1983, Basic Philately, 1984, Post Dates, 1985, Modern World, 1987; author several hundred articles and columns published in the U.K. and U.S.A., 1960—. Served with Brit. Army WW II. Recipient Disting. Philatelist award Northwest Fedn. Stamp Clubs, 1974, Phoenix award Ariz. State Philatelic Hall of Fame, 1979, Disting. Philatelist award Am. Topical Assn., 1979. Fellow Royal Philatelic Soc. (London); mem. Am. Philatelic Soc. (Luff award 1987, Hall of Fame Writers Unit, 1984). Office: Van Dahl Publications PO Box 10 520 E First Albany OR 97321-0006

WOOD, LARRY (MARY LAIRD), journalist, author, university educator, public relations executive, environmental consultant; b. Sandpoint, Idaho; d. Edward Hayes and Alice (McNeel) Small; children: Mary, Marcia, Barry. BA summa cum laude, U. Wash., 1939, MA summa cum laude, with highest honors, 1940; postgrad., Stanford U., 1941-42, U. Calif., Berkeley, 1946-47; cert. in photography, U. Calif., Berkeley, 1971; postgrad. journalism, U. Wis., 1971-72, U. Minn., 1971-72, U. Ga., 1972-73; postgrad. in art, architecture and marine biology, U. Calif., Santa Cruz, 1974-76, Stanford Hopkins Marine Sta., Santa Cruz, 1977-80. Feature writer and columnist Oakland Tribune and San Francisco Chronicle, Calif., 1939—; archtl. and environ. feature writer and columnist San Jose (Calif.) Mercury News (Knight Ridder), 1972-90; teaching fellow Stanford U., 1940-43; pub. rels. dir. 12-county East Bay Regional Park Dist., No. Calif., 1948-68; pres. Larry Wood Pub. Rels., 1946—; prof. (tenure) pub. rels., journalism and investigative reporting, San Diego State U., 1974, 75; disting. vis. prof. journalism San Jose State U., 1976; assoc. prof. journalism Calif. State U., Hayward, 1978; prof. sci. and environ. journalism U. Calif. Berkeley Extension grad. div., 1979—; press del. nat. convs. Am. Geophys. Union Internat. Conf., 1986—, AAAS, 1989—, Nat. Park Svc. VIP Press Tour, Yellowstone after the fire Nat. Pk. Svc. VIP Press Tour, 1989, Nat. Assn. Sci. Writers, 1989, George Washington U./Am. Assn. Neurol. Surgeons Sci. Writers Conf., 1990, Am. Inst. Biol. Scis. Conf., 1990; EPA del. to USSR and Ea. Europe; expert witness on edn., affirmative action, pub. rels., journalism and copyright; cons. sci. writers interne project, Stanford U., 1989—; spl. media guest Sigma Xi, 1990—; mem. numerous spl. press corps; appeared in TV documentary Larry Wood Covers Visit of Queen Elizabeth II. Contbr. over 5,000 articles on various topics for newspapers, nat. mags., nat. and internat. newspaper syndicates including L.A. Times, Washington Post, Phila. Inquirer, Chgo. Tribune, Miami Herald, Oakland Tribune, Seattle Times, San Francisco Chronicle, Parade, San Jose Mercury News (Nat. Headliner award), Christian Sci. Monitor, L.A.Times/Christian Monitor Syndicate News Syndicate, MonitoRadio, Sports Illus., Mechanix Illus., Popular Mechanics, Parents, House Beautiful, Am. Home (awards 1988, 89), National Geographic World, Travel & Leisure, Chevron USA/Odyssey (Calif. Pub.'s award 1984), Xerox Edn. Publs., Europe's Linguapress, PSA Mag., Off Duty, Oceans, Sea Frontiers, AAA Westways, AAA Motorland, Travelin', others. Significant works include home and garden columnist and editor, 5-part series Pacific Coast Ports, 5-part series Railroads of the West; author: Wonderful U.S.A.: A State-by-State Guide to Its Natural Resources, 1989; co-author over 21 books including: McGraw-Hill English for Social Living, 1944, Fawcett Boating Books, 1956-66, Fodor's San Francisco, Fodor's California, 1982-89, Charles Merrill Focus on Life Science, Focus on Physical Science, 1983, 87, Focus on Earth Science; 8 works selected for use by Europe's Woltors-Nordoff-Longman English Language Texts, U.K., Netherlands, 1988; author: (with others) anthology West Winds, 1989; reviewer Charles Merrill texts, 1983-84; book reviewer Profl. Communicator, 1987—; selected writings in permanent collections Oakland Pub. Libr., U. Wash. Main Libr.; environ. works included in Dept. Edn. State of Md. textbook; contbr., author Journalism Quar. Nat. chmn. travel writing contest for U.S. univ. journalism students Assn. for Edn. in Journalism/Soc. Am. Travel Writers, 1979-83; judge writing contest for Nat. Assn. Real Estate Editors, 1982—; Italy; press del. 1st Internat. Symposium Volcanism and Aviation Safety, 1991, Coun. for the Advancement of Science Writing 1977—, Sigma Xi nat. conf., 1988-90, Rockefeller Media Seminar Feeding the World-Protecting the Earth, 1992, Global Conf. on Mercury as Pollutant, 1992, Earth Summit Global Foe Janeiro, 1992; invited Postmaster Gen.'s 1992 Stamps, 1991, Internat. Geophysical Union 27th Cong., 1992, EPA and Dept. Energy Tech. Conf., 1992, Am. Soc. Photogammetry and Remote Sensing Internat. Conv. Mapping Global Change, 1992, N.Y. Mus. Mod. Art Matisse Retrospective Press Rev., 1992 (celebration 150th anniversary Oreg. Trail 1993, coun. advancement sci. writing 1993, Sigma Xi Nat. Conf. 1988—, PRSA Travel and Tourism Conf. 1993); press guest State of Conn., 1993. Numerous awards, honors, citations, speaking engagements including induction into Broadway Hall of Fame U. Wash., Seattle, 1984, citations for environ. writing from Nat. Park Service, U.S. Forest Service, Bur. Land Mgmt., Oakland Mus. Assn., Oakland C. of C., Chevron USA, USN plaque and citation, Best Mag. Articles citation Calif. Pubs. Assn., 1984; co-recipient Nat. Headliner award for Best Sunday Newspaper Mag.; co-recipient citation Oakland Mus. for archtl. features, 1983; honoree Nat. Mortar Bd. for Achievements in Journalism, 1988, 89; selected as one of ten V.I.P. press for Yellowstone Nat. Park field trip on "Let Burn" rsch., 1989; named one of Calif.'s top 40 contemporary authors for 1989; invited V.I.P. press, spl. press guest numerous events worldwide. Mem. Calif. Acad. Scis., San Francisco Press Club, Nat. Press Club, Pub. Rels. Soc. Am. (charter mem. travel, tourism, environment and edn. divs.), Nat. Sch. Pub. Rels. Assn., Environ. Cons. N.Am., Am. Assn. Edn. in Journalism and Communications (exec. bd. nat. mag. div. 1978, panel chmn. 1979, 80, author Journalism Quar. jour.), Women in Communications (nat. bd. officer 1975-77, book reviewer Prof. Communicator), Soc. Profl. Journalists (nat. bd. for hist. sites 1980—, charter mem. investigative reporters and editors), Nat. Press Photographers Assn. (cons. Bay Area interne project 1989—), Investigative Reporters and Editors (charter), Bay Area Advt. and Mktg. Assn., Nat. Assn. Sci. Writers, Calif. Writers Club (state bd., Berkeley bd. 1989—, honoree ann. conv. Asilomar, Calif. 1990), Am. Assn. Med. Writers, Internat. Assn. Bus. Communicators, Am. Film Inst., Am. Heritage Found. (citation 1986, 87, 88), Soc. Am. Travel Writers, Internat. Oceanographic Found., Oceanic Soc., Calif. Acad. Environ. News Writers, Seattle Advt. and Sales Club (former officer), Nature Conservancy, Smithsonian Audubon Soc., Nat. Wildlife Fedn., Nat. Parks and Conservation Assn., Calif. State Parks Found., Fine Arts Mus., San Francisco, Seattle Jr. Advt. Club (charter), U. Wash. Comm. Alumni (Sch. Comm. alumni, life, charter mem. ocean scis. alumni, Disting. Alumni 1987), U. Calif., Berkeley Alumni (life, v.p., scholarship chmn. 1975-81), Stanford Alumni (life), Mortar Board Alumnae Assn. (life, honoree 1988, 89), Am. Mgmt. Assn., Nat. Soc. Environ. Journalists (charter), Phi Beta Kappa (v.p., bd. dirs. Calif. Alumni Assn., statewide chmn. scholarship awards 1975-81), Pi Lambda Theta, Theta Sigma Phi. Home: Piedmont Pines 6161 Castle Dr Oakland CA 94611-2737

WOOD, LINCOLN JACKSON, aerospace engineer; b. Lyons, N.Y., Sept. 30, 1947; s. William Hulbert and Sarah Brock (Strumsky) W. BS with distinction, Cornell U., 1968; MS in Aeronautics and Astronautics, Stanford U., 1969, PhD, 1972. Staff engr. Hughes Aircraft Co., El Segundo, Calif., 1974-77; mem. tech. staff Jet Propulsion Lab. Calif. Inst. Tech., Pasadena, 1977-81, tech. group supr. Jet Propulsion Lab., 1981-89, tech. mgr., 1989-91, dep. tech. section mgr., 1991—; Bechtel instr. engring. Calif. Inst. Tech., Pasadena, 1972-74, lectr. in systems engring., 1975-76, vis. asst. prof., 1976-78, vis. assoc. prof., 1978-84; coord. case studies Project Galileo, 1987, 89; cons. in field. Contbr. articles on space navigation and optimal control theory to profl. jours. Bd. dirs. Boys Republic, Chino, Calif., 1991. Assoc. fellow AIAA (Tech. com. on astrodynamics 1985-86, chmn. 1986-88, assoc. editor Jour. Guidance, Control and Dynamics 1983-89); mem. Am. Astro. Soc. (st., space flight mechanics com. 1980—, assoc. editor Jour. of Astro. Scis. 1980-83, gen. chmn. AAS/AIAA Space Flight Mechanics Meeting 1993), IEEE, AAAS, Los Solteros (pres. 1991), Sigma Xi. Office: Jet Propulsion Lab 4800 Oak Grove Drive Mail Stop 301-125L Pasadena CA 91109

WOOD, LINDA MAY, librarian; b. Fort Dodge, Iowa, Nov. 6, 1942; d. John Albert and Beth Ida (Riggs) Wiley; m. C. James Wood, Sept. 15, 1964 (div. 1984). BA, Portland State U., 1964; M in Librarianship, U. Wash., 1965. Reference libr. Multnomah County Libr., Portland (Oreg.), 1965-67, br. libr., 1967-72, adminstrv. asst. to libr., 1972-73, asst. libr., 1973-77; asst. city libr. L.A. Pub. Libr., 1977-80; library dir. Riverside (Calif.) City and County Pub. Libr., 1980-91; county libr. Alameda County Libr., Fremont, Calif., 1991—. Chmn. bd. dirs. Inland Libr. System, 1983-84; League of Calif. Cities Community Svcs. Com., 1985-89; mem. users coun. Online Computer Libr. Ctr., 1986-89. Mem. AAUW, ALA (councilor Calif. chpt. 1992—), Pub. Libr. Assn., Libr. Adminstrn. and Mgmt. Assn., Calif. Libr. Assn. (pres. 1985), Calif. County Librs. Assn. (pres. 1984), LWV. Democrat. Office: Alameda County Libr 2450 Stevenson Blvd Fremont CA 94538-2326

WOOD, MICHAEL NEALL, surgeon; b. Temple, Tex., Feb. 15, 1956; s. Harold Lee and Betty Jane (Bottomley) W.; m. Sandra Jean Quinn, Aug. 6, 1988. BA in Chemistry, Southern Coll., 1977; Dr.med., Loma Linda U., 1981. Diplomate Am. Bd. Surgery. Resident Med. Ctr. Loma Linda (Calif.) U., 1981-86, cardiothoracic resident Med. Ctr., 1986-89, cardiothoracic surgeon Med. Ctr., 1989-90, instr. surgery Med. Sch., 1985-89; asst. prof. surgery Loma Linda U. Med. Ctr., 1989—. Mem. ACS (assoc.), Calif. Med. Assn., Am. Coll. Cardiology, Am. Coll. Chest Physicians. Republican. Office: 1060 E Foothill Blvd # 201 Upland CA 91786

WOOD, NATHANIEL FAY, editor, writer, public relations consultant; b. Worcester, Mass., June 23, 1919; s. Henry Fletcher and Edith (Fay) W.; m. Eleanor Norton, Dec. 19, 1945; children: Gary Nathaniel, Janet Ann. BS in Journalism, Bus. Adminstrn., Syracuse U., 1946. Editor, writer various publs., various cities, 1946-51; mng. editor Butane-Propane News, L.A., 1951-52; editor Western Metalworking Mag., L.A., 1952-62; western editorial mgr. Penton Pub. Co. Cleve., L.A., 1962-71; editor Orange County Illustrated, Orange County Bus., Newport Beach, Calif., 1971-72; western editor Hitchcock Pub., L.A., 1972-75; co-owner, mgr. Norton-Wood Pub. Rels. Svcs., Pasadena, Calif., 1975—; editorial dir. Security World, SDM and SCA Mags., Culver City, Calif., 1975-80; mgr. trade show Cahners Pub. and Expo Group, L.A., 1979-82; sr. editor Alarm Installer Dealer Mag., L.A., 1982-89; editor CNC West Mag., Long Beach, Pasadena, Calif., 1982—. Freelance indsl. writer miscellaneous bus. pubs. Organizer Wilkie Presdl. Campaign, Syracuse, N.Y., 1940; advisor various GOP campaigns, L.A., Washington, 1940-92; donor L.A. Civic Light Opera; mem., donor L.A. Mus. Art, 1989—; founding mem. Western Heritage Mus., L.A., 1989—; active Met. Opera Guild, Colonial Williamsburg Found., Mus. Natural History L.A. 2d lt. U.S. Army, 1943-45, PTO. Decorated Purple Heart; recipient Silver, Bronze and Gold medals for Editorial Excellence Gov. of Calif., 1959, 60, 62. Mem. Am. Legion. Scabbard and Blade, L.A. World Affairs Coun., Smithsonian Instn., Alpha Epsilon Rho, Sigma Delta Chi. Home: 1430 Tropical Ave Pasadena CA 91107-1623 Office: Norton-Wood Pub Rels Svcs 1430 Tropical Ave Pasadena CA 91107-1623

WOOD, RAYMUND FRANCIS, retired librarian; b. London, Nov. 9, 1911; came to U.S., 1924; s. George S. and Ida A. (Lawes) W.; m. Margaret Ann Peed, Feb. 26, 1943; children: Paul George, Gregory Leo, David Joseph. AB, St. Mary's U., Balt., 1931; MA, Gonzaga U., 1939; PhD, UCLA, 1949; MS in Libr. Sci., U. So. Calif., L.A., 1950. Instr. English U. Santa Clara (Calif.), 1939-41; rehab. officer VA, L.A., 1946-48; prin. libr. Fresno (Calif.) State Coll., 1950-66; prof. libr. sci. UCLA, L.A., 1966-77, prof. emeritus, 1977—, from asst. dean to assoc. dean Grad. Sch. Libr. & Info. Sci., 1970-77. Author: California's Augua Fria, 1952, Life and Death of Peter Lebec, 1954, The Saints of the California Landscape, 1987; co-author: Librarian and Laureate: Ina Coolbrith of California, 1973, many others. Vol. driver ARC, Van Nuys, Calif., 1977—; pres. Friends of the Encino/Tarzana Br. Libr., Tarzana, Calif., 1977-80, Jedediah Smith Soc., Stockton, Calif., 1987-90. With U.S. Army, 1942-46, ETO. Travel grantee Am. Book Found., 1964, Del Amo Found., 1974. Mem. ALA (book reviewer 1974—), Calif. Libr. Assn. (many offices), Mariposa County Hist. Assn. (life), Oral History Assn. (life), Fresno County Hist. Soc. (editor 1959-66), Westerners L.A. Corral (editor of Brand Book 1982). Democrat. Byzantine Catholic. Home: 18052 Rosita St Encino CA 91316-4217

WOOD, ROBERT WARREN, lawyer; b. Des Moines, July 5, 1955; s. Merle Warren and Cecily Ann (Sherk) W.; m. Beatrice Wood, Aug. 4, 1979; 1 child, Bryce Mercedes. Student, U. Sheffield, Eng., 1975-76; AB, Humboldt State U., 1976; JD, U. Chgo., 1979. Bar: Ariz. 1979, Calif. 1980, U.S. Tax Ct. 1980, N.Y. 1989, D.C. 1993. Assoc. Jennings, Strouss, Phoenix, 1979-80, McCutchen, Doyle, San Francisco, 1980-82, Broad, Khourie, San Francisco, 1982-85; assoc. Steefel, Levitt & Weiss, San Francisco, 1985-87, ptnr., 1987-91; ptnr. Bancroft & McAlister, San Francisco, 1991-93; prin. Robert W. Wood, P.C., San Francisco, 1993—; instr. in law U. Calif. San Francisco, 1981-82. Author: Taxation of Corporate Liquidations: A Complete Planning Guide, 1987, The Executive's Complete Guide to Business Taxes, 1989, Corporate Taxation: Complete Planning and Practice Guide, 1989, S Corporations, 1990, The Ultimate Tax Planning Guide for Growing Companies, 1991, Taxation of Damage Awards and Settlement Payments, 1991, Tax Strategies in Hiring, Retaining and Terminating Employees, 1991, The Home Office Tax Guide, 1992; (with others) California Closely Held Corporations: Tax Planning and Practice Guide, 1987, Legal Guide to Independent Contractor Status, 1992, Home Office Money & Tax Guide, 1992, Tax Aspects of Settlements and Judgements, 1993; editor-in-chief The M & A Tax Report; mem. editorial bd. Corporate Taxation, Taxation for Lawyers, Jour. Real Estate Taxation. Mem. Calif. Bd. Legal Specialization (cert. specialist taxation), Internat. Platform Assn., Bohemian Club, Internat. Order of St. Hubert. Republican. Office: 235 Montgomery St Ste 972 San Francisco CA 94104

WOOD, ROGER HOLMES, financial planner, educator; b. Corning, N.Y., Apr. 26, 1920; s. James Orville and Helen Lucille (Winemiller) W.; m. Phyllis Elizabeth Anderson, Dec. 26, 1947; children: Stephen, David, Elizabeth. AB, U. Pitts., 1944; MS, Columbia U., 1945; MA, San Francisco State U., 1951; PhD, Internat. Coll., 1978. CLU, Calif.; CFP, Calif., ChFC, Calif. Tchr. Oakdale (Calif.) High Sch., 1947-49, Galileo High Sch., San Francisco, 1949-54; instr. Coll. San Mateo, Calif., 1960-70; mem. nat. faculty Am. Coll., Bryn Mawr, Pa., 1960-70; lectr. Golden Gate U., San Francisco, 1983-84; agt. N.Y. Life Ins. Co., San Francisco, 1954—; tchr. Jefferson High Sch. Dist., Daly City, Calif., 1965—; pres. Leading Life Ins. Producers, San Francisco, 1960-62. Contbg. editor Western Underwriter, 1959-63. Mem. bd. dirs. San Francisco Coun. Chs., 1954-60. With U.S. Army, 1940-42. Mem. Internat. Assn. Fin. Planning, Am. Risk and Ins. Assn., San Francisco Estate Planning Coun., Peninsula Estate Planning Coun., Am. Soc. CLU and Chartered Fin. Cons., Interant. Transactional Analysis Assn., San Francisco Life Underwriters Assn. (v.p. 1960-62), Soc. Genealogists (London), SAR, Phi Delta Kappa, Phi Gamma Delta. Republican. Presbyterian. Home: 65 Capay Cir South San Francisco CA 94080-4117

WOOD, STUART KEE, engineering administrator; b. Dallas, Mar. 8, 1925; s. William Henry and Harriet (Kee) Wood; m. Loris V. Poock, May 17, 1951 (dec. June 1990); children: Linda S. Kuehl, Thomas N., Richard D. BS in Aero. Engring., Tex. A&M U., 1949. Aircraft sheet metal worker USAF SAC, Kelly Field, San Antonio, Tex., 1942-45; structural design engr. B-52, 367-80, KC-135, 707 Airplanes Boeing, Seattle and Renton, Wash., 1949-55; thrust reverser design engr. 707 and 747 Airplanes Boeing, Renton, 1955-66; supr. thrust reverser group 747 Airplane Boeing, Everett, Wash., 1966-69; supr. rsch. basic engine noise 727 airplane FAA, NASA, 1969-74; supr. jetfoil propulsion Jetfoil Hydrofoil Boeing, Renton, 1974-75; supr. rsch. basic engine performance loss JT9D Pratt & Whitney, 1975-79; supr. propulsion systems 757 Airplane Boeing, Renton, 1979-90; supr., propulsion systems thrust reverser 737, 747, 757, 767 Boeing, Kent, Wash., 1990—. Patentee in field. Recipient Ed Wells award AIAA, N.W. chpt., Bellevue, Wash., 1992. Republican. Presbyterian. Home: 3831 46th St SW Seattle WA 98116

WOOD, WILLIS BOWNE, JR., utility holding company executive; b. Kansas City, Mo., Sept. 15, 1934; s. Willis Bowne Sr. and Mina (Henderson) W.; m. Dixie Gravel, Aug. 31, 1955; children: Bradley, William, Josh. BS in Petroleum Engring., U. Tulsa, 1957; grad. advanced mgmt. program, Harvard U., 1983. Various positions So. Calif. Gas Co., Los Angeles, 1960-74, v.p. then sr. v.p., 1975-80, exec. v.p., 1983-84; pres., chief exec. officer Pacific Lighting Gas Supply Co., Los Angeles, 1981-83; sr. v.p. Pacific Enterprises, Los Angeles, 1984-85; exec. v.p. Pacific Enterprises, L.A., 1985-89, pres., 1989-91, pres., CEO, 1991-92, chmn., pres., CEO, 1992--; bd. dirs. Gt. Western Fin. Corp., Gt. Western Bank, L.A.; dir. Automobile Club of So. Calif. Trustee harvey Mudd Coll. Claremont, Calif., S.W. Mus, L.A.; vice chmn., trustee Calif. Med. Ctr. Found., L.A.. Mem. Soc. Petroleum Engrs., Am. Gas Assn., Pacific Coast Gas Assn. (past bd. dirs.), Pacific Energy Assn., Calif. Bus. Roundtable, Calif. State C. of C., Automobile Club So. Calif. (dir.), Ctr. Club, Calif. Club. Republican. Office: Pacific Enterprises PO Box 60043 633 W 5th St Los Angeles CA 90071

WOODALL, JAMES BARRY, information systems specialist; b. San Diego, Aug. 15, 1945; s. Jame Franklin and Mildred Lorenia (Nielsen) W.; m. Bonnie Erharda Gloth (div. 1973); m. Kathleen Dee Smith; children: Robert, Mathew, Diane. BA, Randolph-Macon Coll., 1966; MS, Am. U., 1972; MBA, George Washington U., 1978. Systems engr. RCA, Washington, 1969-72; MIS analyst FNMA, Washington, 1972; spl. project mgr. GTE, Washington and San Carlos, Calif., 1973-83; LOA project mgr. Comsat, Washington, 1978-80; cons. Southcoast Cons., San Diego, 1984-90; mem. sr. tech. staff Litton Co., 1990-91; sr. bus. analyst CEC-Lear Astronics, 1991—; head MIS Royal Saudi Navy and Ministry of Def., 1984-85; dep. program mgr. MIS NASA, Washington, 1986—, Citicorp, H/SOA, GFB, 1988-90. Author: NASA-Strategy on Technology, 1986, Information Analysis & Design, 1989. Precinct capt. Rep. Party; trustee fin. com. United Meth. Ch., Woodland Hills, 1986—, Odyssey Found., L.A., 1988—. Capt. USMCR, 1963-69. Whitehouse fellow, 1972; recipient Letter of Appreciation, White House, 1979, 87. Mem. U.S. Jaycees (chpt. pres. 1975-77, state v.p. community devel. com. 1977-79, nat. v.p. community devel. 1979, 27 awards). Home: 24438 Watt Rd Ramona CA 92065-4157 also: 7109 Farralone Ave # 10 Canoga Park CA 91303

WOODARD, ALVA ABE, business consultant; b. Roy, N.Mex., June 28, 1928; s. Joseph Benjamin and Emma Lurania (Watkins) W.; m. Esther Josepha Kaufmann, Apr. 5, 1947; children: Nannette, Gregory, Loreen, Arne, Mark, Kevin, Steven, Curtis, Marlee, Julie, Michelle. Student, Kinman Bus. U., 1948-49, Whitworth Coll., 1956, Wash. State U., 1953-54. Sec.-treas., dir. Green Top Dairy Farms, Inc., Clarkston, Wash., 1948-52; v.p., treas., sec., dir. ASC Industries, Inc., Spokane, Wash., 1953-75; dir. Guenther Irrigation, Inc., Pasco, Wash., 1966-71; mng. dir. Irrigation Rental, Inc., Pasco, 1968-75, Rain Chief Irrigation Co., Grand Island, Nebr., 1968-75; sec., dir. Keeling Supply Co., Little Rock, 1969-72; pres., dir. Renters, Inc., Salt Lake City, 1971-75, Woodard Western Corp., Spokane, 1976-86, Woodard Industries, Inc., Auburn, Wash., 1987-90; cons. Woodard Assocs., Spokane, Wash., 1985—; pres., dir. TFI Industries, inc., Post Falls, Idaho, 1989-90; v.p., sec., treas., dir. Trans-Force, Inc., Post Falls, 1989-90, TFI Computer Scis., Inc., Post Falls, 1989-90. Newman Lake (Wash.) Rep. precinct committeeman, 1964-80; Spokane County del. Wash. Rep. Conv., 1968-80. Mem. Adminstrv. Mgmt. Soc. (bd. dirs. 1966-68), Optimists. Home and Office: PO Box 4673 Spokane WA 99202-0673

WOODARD, DOROTHY MARIE, insurance broker; b. Houston, Feb. 7, 1932; d. Gerald Edgar and Bessie Katherine (Crain) Floeck; student N.Mex. State U., 1950; m. Jack W. Woodard; June 19, 1950 (dec.); m. Norman W. Libby, July 19, 1982 (dec. Dec. 1991). Ptnr. Western Oil Co., Tucumcari, N.Mex., 1950—; owner, mgr. Woodard & Co., Las Cruces, N.Mex., 1959-67; agt., dist. mgr. United Nations Ins. Co., Denver, 1968-74; agt. Western Nat. Life Ins. Co., Amarillo, Tex., 1976—. Exec. dir. Tucumcari Indsl. Commn., 1979—; dir. Bravo Dome Study Com., 1979—; owner Libby Cattle Co., Libby Ranch Co.; regional bd. dirs. N.Mex., Eastern Plains Council Govts., 1979—. Mem. NAFE, Tucumcari C. of C., Mesa Country Club. Home: PO Box 823 Tucumcari NM 88401-0823

WOODARD, LARRY L., academic program director; b. Lebanon, Oreg., Apr. 16, 1936; s. Hugh Frank and Ima Ellen (Bilyeu) W.; m. Bette Jeanette Brown, Aug. 10, 1956; children: Perry, Craig, Stacy. BS in Forestry, Oreg. State U., 1957. Forester Bur. of Land Mgmt., Oreg., 1957-69, Washington, 1969-72; dist. mgr. Bur. of Land Mgmt., Coeur d'Alene, Idaho, 1972-76; assoc. state dir. Bur. of Land Mgmt., Boise, Idaho, 1976-78, Santa Fe, 1978-82, Boise, 1982-86; state dir. Bur. of Land Mgmt., Santa Fe, 1987-93; dir. devel. Boise Bible Coll., 1993—. Author: A to Z, The Biography of Arthur Zimmerman, 1988. Bd. dirs. Boise Bible Coll., 1977-87; trustee N.Mex. Nature Conservancy, 1987-90. Recipient Disting. Svc. award U.S. Dept. Interior, 1986, Sec.'s Stewardship award U.S. Dept. Interior, 1989, Pres.'s Meritorious Exec. award, 1991. Republican. Home: 1701 Almaden Meridian ID 83642 Office: Boise Bible Coll 8695 Marigold Boise ID 83714

WOODARD, SCOTT ALAN, public policy consultant; b. Fort Belvoir, Va., Aug. 16, 1951; s. Carleton Robertson and Charlotte Georgette (Verdoodt) W.; m. Leslie Margaret Bayliff, Sept. 18, 1982; children: Christopher Reed, David Patrick. BA, Old Dominion U., 1974; MPA, George Mason U., 1984. Cons. U.S. Dept. Energy, Washington, 1974-82; staff researcher Denver Mayor Campaign, Denver, 1982-83; issues dir. Colo. U.S. Senate Campaign, Denver, 1983-84; sr. staff Colo. State Govt., Denver, 1984-91; pres. Woodard Consulting, Inc., Denver, 1991—. Author, prin. investigator: Series of Public Policy Reports on Economic Development, Education, and Training, 1985-92. Democrat. Office: Woodard Consulting Inc 1323 Forest St Denver CO 80220

WOODBURY, LAEL JAY, theatre educator; b. Fairview, Idaho, July 3, 1927; s. Raymond A. and Wanda (Dawson) W.; m. Margaret Lillian Swenson, Dec. 19, 1949; children: Carolyn Inez (Mrs. Donald Hancock), Shannon Margaret (Mrs. Michael J. Busenbark), Jordan Ray, Lexon Dan. BS, Utah State U., 1952; MA, Brigham Young U., 1953; PhD (Univ. fellow), U. Ill., 1954. Teaching asst. U. Ill., 1953; assoc. prof. Brigham Young U., 1954-61; guest prof. Colo. State Coll., 1962; asst. prof. Bowling Green State U., 1961-62; asso. prof. U. Iowa, 1962-65; producer Ledges Playhouse, Lansing, Mich., 1963-65; prof. speech and dramatics, chmn. dept. Brigham Young U., 1966-70, assoc. dean Coll. Fine Arts and Communications, 1969-73, dean Coll. Fine Arts and Communications, 1973-82; vis. lectr. abroad; bd. dirs. Eagle Systems Internat.; bd. dir. workshop Fedn. for Asian Cultural Promotion, Republic of China; dir. European study tour. Author: Play Production Handbook, 1959, Mormon Arts, vol. 1, 1972, Mosaic Theatre, 1976, also articles, original dramas; profl. actor PBS and feature films. Chmn. gen. bd. drama com. Young Men's Mut. Improvement Assn., 1958-61; bd. dirs. Repertory Dance Theatre; chmn. Utah Alliance for Arts Edn.; mem. advisory council Utah Arts Festival. With USNR, 1942-46. Recipient Creative Arts award Brigham Young U., 1971, Disting. Alumni award, 1975, Tchr. of Yr. award, 1988, Excellence in Rsch. award, 1992, Disting. Svc. award, 1992. Mem. Rocky Mountain Theatre Conf. (past pres.), Am. Theatre Assn. (chmn. nat. com. royalties 1972—, mem. fin. com. 1982—), NW Assn. Univs. and Colls. (accrediting officer), Am. Theatre Assn. (v.p. Univ. and Coll. Theatre Assn.), Theta Alpha Phi, Phi Kappa Phi. Home: 1303 Locust Ln Provo UT 84604-3651

WOODBURY, RICHARD COULAM, electrical engineer, educator, researcher; b. Salt Lake City, Apr. 19, 1931; s. Harvey Charles and Lucille (Coulam) W.; m. Patricia Anne Johnson, Sept. 9, 1954; children: Pamela Woodbury Platt, David, Marie Woodbury LeFevre, Ann Woodbury Heiner, Karen Woodbury Patchett, Sandra. BSEE, U. Utah, 1956; MS, Stanford U., 1958, PhD, 1965. With Hewlett Packard Corp., Palo Alto, Calif., 1956-59; rsch. asst. Stanford (Calif.) Electronics Labs., 1962-65; asst. prof. dept. elec. engring. Brigham Young U., Provo, Utah, 1959-62, prof., 1965—; memory designer Advance Memory Systems, Sunnyvale, Calif, 1974-75; cons. Trans Era Corp., Provo, 1980—, R-Con Internat., Salt Lake City, 1987-89. Contbr. articles to profl. jours.; patentee Analog Memory Device; co-patentee 2 micro-machined devices. Recipient rsch. grants NSF, 1968-70, 70-72, Eyring Rsch. Inst., 1975-77, Moxtek Inc., 1985-86. Mem. IEEE (sr., area chmn. 1980-82), Sigma Xi (chpt. pres. elect. 1990—), Phi Kappa Phi, Eta Kappa Nu, Tau Beta Pi. Mormon. Office: Brigham Young U Bldg 459 CB Provo UT 84602

WOODBURY, VERL ANGUS, software company executive, software designer; b. Burley, Idaho, June 3, 1953; s. Leland Rogers and Luella Myrlene (Snow) W.; m. Jean Susan Thorpe, May 1975 (div. Dec. 1975); 1 child, Jennifer; m. Hilda Terrazas, Aug. 25, 1977; children: Ryan, Tami, Jarom, Erik, Daniel. AA, Ricks Coll., 1976; BA, Brigham Young U., 1980, MA, 1986. Cert. tchr. of English as 2d lang. Lang. cons. TDK Electronics, Tokyo, 1982-84, Toho Life Ins. Co., Tokyo, 1984-85; English instr. Brigham Young U., Provo, Utah, 1985-87; pres. ICD Corp., Provo, Utah, 1987—; chmn. CD-ROM SIG, Computer-Assisted Lang. Instrn. Consortium, Provo, 1986-90. Author: (textbook) Focused on Listening, 1983; co-designer software application, 1989-92. Recipient scholarship Brigham Young U., 1976. Mem. Provo/Bran C. of C., Utah Valley Choral Soc. Mem. LDS Ch. Home: 253 N 2250 W Provo UT 84601 Office: ICD Corp 319 N Freedom Blvd Provo UT 84601

WOODCOCK, GEORGE, author; b. Winnipeg, Man., Can., May 8, 1912; s. Samuel Arthur and Margaret Gertrude (Lewis) W.; m. Ingeborg Hedwig Elisabeth Linzer, Feb. 10, 1949. Student, Morley Coll., London; LLD, U. Victoria, U. Winnipeg; DLitt, Sir George Williams U., U. Ottawa, U. B.C. Broadcaster contbg. several hundred talks and scripts of plays and documentaries to CBC programs; editor of Now, 1940-47; profl. writer, 1946—; first in Eng. to 1949 and afterwards in Can.; faculty U. Wash., 1954-55; asso. prof. English U. B.C., Vancouver, 1956-63; lectr. Asian studies U. B.C., 1963—; editor Canadian Lit., 1959-77. Author: The White Island, 1940, The Centre Cannot Hold, 1943, William Godwin, A Biography, 1946, The Incomparable Aphra: A Life of Mrs. Aphra Behn, 1948, The Writer and Politics, 1948, Imagine the South, 1947, The Paradox of Oscar Wilde, 1950, A Hundred Years of Revolution: 1848 and After, 1948, The Letters of Charles Lamb, 1950, The Anarchist Prince, 1950 (later trans. into French), Ravens and Prophets: Travels in Western Canada, 1952, Pierre-Joseph Proudhon, 1956, To the City of the Dead: Travels in Mexico, 1956, Incas and Other Men: Travels in Peru, 1959, Anarchism, 1962, Faces of India, 1964, Asia, Gods and Cities, 1966, The Greeks in India, 1966, A Choice of Critics, 1966, The Crystal Spirit, 1966 (Gov. Gen. award for Eng. Non-fiction), Kerala, 1967, Selected Poems, 1967, The Doukhobors, 1968, Canada and the Canadians, 1969, The Hudson's Bay Company, 1970, Odysseus Ever Returning, 1970, Gandhi, 1971 (U. B.C. medal), Dawn and the Darkest Hour: A Study of Aldous Huxley, 1972, Herbert Read, The Stream and the Source, 1972, The Rejection of Politics, 1972, Who Killed the British Empire?, 1974, Amor de Cosmos, 1975, Gabriel Dumont, 1975 (U. B.C. medal), Notes on Visitations, 1976, South Sea Journey, 1976, Peoples of the Coast, 1977, Thomas Merton, Monk and Poet, 1978, Faces from History, 1978, The Kestrel and Other Poems, 1978, The Canadians, 1979, The World of Canadian Writing, 1980, The George Woodcock Reader, 1980, The Mountain Road, 1981, Taking it to the Letter, 1981, Confederation Betrayed, 1981, Ivan Eyre, 1981, The Benefactor, 1982, Letter to the Past, 1982, Collected Poems, 1983; British Columbia, a Celebration, 1983, Orwell's Message: 1984 and the Present, 1984, Strange Bedfellows: The State and the Arts in Canada, 1985, The Walls of India, 1985, The University of British Columbia, 1986, Northern Spring, 1987, Beyond the Blue Mountain, 1987, The Social History of Canada, 1988, Caves in the Desert, 1988, The Marvelous Century, 1988, Powers of Observation, 1989: The Century That Made Us, 1989, British Columbia: A History of the Province, 1990, Tolstoy at Yasnaya Polyana and other poems, 1991, The Monk and his Message, 1992, Anarchism and Anarchists, 1992, Power To Us All!, 1992, Letter from the Khyber Pass, 1993, George Woodcock's Introduction to Canadian Poetry, 1993, George Woodcock's Introduction to Canadian Fiction, 1993. Recipient Gov. Gen.'s award, 1966, Molson prize, 1973, Can. Authors' award, 1989; Can. Coun. Travel grantee, 1961, 63, 65; Guggenheim fellow, 1951-52, Can. Govt. Overseas fellow, 1957-58, Can. Coun. Killam fellow, 1970-71, Can. Coun. Sr. Arts fellow, 1975, 78. Home: 6429 McCleery St, Vancouver, BC Canada V6N 1G5

WOODCOCK, RICHARD WESLEY, educational psychologist; b. Portland, Oreg., Jan. 29, 1928; s. Carol Wesley and Captola Winifred (Catterlin) W.; m. Annie Lee Plant, Aug. 16, 1951; children: Donna, Dianne, Judy, Wayne; m. Ana Felicia Muñoz-Sandoval, June 14, 1991. BS, U. Oreg., 1949, MEd, 1953, EdD, 1956. Diplomate of Am. Bd. of Profl. Psychol. Lt. USN, 1945-46, 50-51; elem. tchr. Arago Schs., Oreg., 1951-52; dir. spl. edn. Coos County Sch., Coquille, Oreg., 1952-54, Corvallis Pub. Schs., Coquille, 1955-57; asst. prof. psychol. Western Oreg. State Coll., 1957-61; assoc. prof. spl. edn. Univ. No. Colo., Greeley, 1961-63; prof. spl. edn., Peabody Coll. Vanderbilt Univ., 1963-68; editor, dir. rsch. Am. Guidance Svc., 1968-72; dir. Measurement Learning Cons., Tenn., Oreg., 1972—; vis. scholar Univ. of Ariz., 1985-88, Univ. So. Calif., L.A., 1988-91; cons. NCAA, 1989—. Author: (battery tests) W-J Psycho-Edn. Battery, 1977, 89, Woodcock Reading Mastery Tests, 1973, 87, Scales of Independent Behavior, 1984, G-F-W Auditory Skills Battery, 1976, The Peabody Reading Program, 1967, The Colo. Braille Battery, 1966; contbr. numerous articles to profl. jours. Office: Measurement Learning Cons PO Box 22786 Nashville TN 37202

WOODEN, JOHN ROBERT, former basketball coach; b. Martinsville, Ind., Oct. 14, 1910; s. Joshua Hugh and Roxie (Rothrock) W.; m. Nellie C. Riley, Aug. 8, 1932; children: Nancy Anne, James Hugh. B.S., Purdue U., 1932; M.S., Ind. State U., 1947. Athletic dir., basketball and baseball coach Ind. State Tchrs. Coll., 1946-48; head basketball coach UCLA, 1948-75; lectr. to colls., coaches, business. Author: Practical Modern Basketball, 1966, They Call Me Coach, 1972; Contbr. articles to profl. jours. Served to lt. USNR, 1943-46. Named All-Am. basketball player Purdue U., 1930-32, Coll. Basketball Player of Yr., 1932, to All-Time All-Am. Team Helms Athletic Found., 1943, Nat. Basketball Hall of Fame, Springfield (Mass.) Coll., as player 1960, as coach, 1970, Ind. State Basketball Hall of Fame, 1962, Calif. Father of Yr., 1964, 75, Coach of Yr. U.S. Basketball Writers Assn., 1964, 67, 69, 70, 72, 73, Sportsman of Yr. Sports Illustrated, 1973; recipient Whitney Young award Urban League, 1973, 1st ann. Velvet Covered Brick award Layman's Leadership Inst., 1974, 1st ann. Dr. James Naismith Peachbasket award, 1974, medal of excellence Bellarmine Coll., 1987.

WOODHALL, WILLIAM FULTON, minister, religious organization administrator; b. Peoria, Ill., Jan. 27, 1944; s. William Rozell and Elsie Lucille (Fulton) W.; m. Gayle Marie Phillips, May 11, 1964; children: Heather Suzanne Dominguez, Matthew Charles, Blake Jarrod. BA, Sacramento Bapt. Coll., 1972; ThB, Sacramento Bapt. Theol. Sem., 1973, MA, 1973, MDiv, 1977, ThM, 1979; BA, Bapt. Christian Coll., 1984; PhD, Bapt. Christian U., 1981, ThD, 1983; DD (hon.), Calif. Christian Coll., 1973; LLD (hon.), John Wesley Coll., 1980. Lic. minister, 1968; ordained to ministry, 1970. Pastor E. Belmont Community Bible Ch., Fresno, Calif., 1970-71, Sierra Hills Bapt. Ch., Auberry, Calif., 1972-74; sr. pastor Fountain Ave. Bapt. Ch., Hollywood, Calif., 1975-76, Mountain View Presbyn., Grand Terrace, Calif., 1976-85; pvt. practice as ch. cons. Eugene, Oreg., 1986; pres. Bible Analysis Cons., Inc., Grand Terrace, 1987—; vis. lectr. Calif. Christian Coll., Fresno, 1973-74; prof. Bible Thomas Road Bible Inst., Fresno, 1973-74; chaplain, reserve officer Los Angeles Police Dept. Hollywood div., 1975-76; prof. hermeneutics San Bernardino (Calif.) Bible Coll., 1979. Mem. Pacific Presbytery-Presbyn. Ch. Am. (stated clk. 1977-82), Fellowship Christian Peace Officers (assoc.), Christian Edn. Fellowship (hon.), Christian Legal Soc. Ctr. Law and Religious Studies (assoc.). Republican. Home: 5745 Via Dos Caminos Riverside CA 92504-1359 Office: Bible Analysis Cons Inc 22797 Barton Rd Ste 171 Colton CA 92324-5207

WOODHOUSE, STEPHEN KENT, college president; b. Payson, Utah, June 17, 1940; s. William Howard and Marie (Cloward) W.; m. Sytske Saskia VanZyverden, June 1966; children: Stephen Troy, Christiaan Cory, Cameron Tyler, Jayme Parker, Sytske Sjoukje, Kirsten Helena (dec.). BA in Math., U. Utah, 1965, MBA, 1966. Ordained bishop LDS Ch., 1991. Systems engr. IBM Corp., 1966-69, mktg. rep., 1969-72; co-founder Telesystems Corp., Salt Lake City, Denver, 1972; exec. v.p. Jeremiah Corp., Denver; pres. Eagle Info. Systems Corp., Salt Lake City, 1981-89; instr. computer info. systems dept. LDS Bus. Coll., Salt Lake City, 1989-92, pres., 1992—. Mem. Utah State Office Rehab. Ind. Living Coun., Salt Lake Conv. and Visitors Bur.; missionary dist. leader, traveling elder, br. pres. LDS Ch., West German Mission, bishopric counselor bishop, mem. high coun., mem. Young Men's presidency; scoutmaster, Blazer Scout leader A.P. Hill, Va., 1985, scouting dist. commr. Lone Peak dist., 1990. Mem. Salt Lake City C. of C., Salt Lake Oratorio Soc. Office: LDS Bus Coll 411 E South Temple St Salt Lake City UT 84111-1392

WOODHOUSE, THOMAS EDWIN, lawyer; b. Cedar Rapids, Iowa, Apr. 30, 1940; s. Keith Wallace and Elinor Julia (Cherny) W.; m. Kiyoko Fujiie, May 29, 1965; children: Miya, Keith, Leighton. AB cum laude, Amherst Coll., 1962; JD, Harvard U., 1965. Bar: N.Y. 1966, U.S. Supreme Ct. 1969, Calif. 1975. Assoc. Chadbourne, Parke, Whiteside & Wolff, N.Y.C., 1965-68; atty./adviser AID, Washington, 1968-69; counsel Pvt. Investment Co. for Asia S.A., Tokyo, 1969-72; ptnr. Woodhouse Lee & Davis, Singapore, 1972-74; assoc. Graham & James, San Francisco, 1974-75; asst. gen. counsel Natomas Co., San Francisco, 1975-81; mem. Lasky, Haas, Cohler & Munter, San Francisco, 1982-90; trust adminstr. Ronald Family Trust A, 1989—; sole practice, Berkeley, 1990—; of counsel Wilson, Sonsini, Goodrich & Rosati, Palo Alto, Calif., 1992—; instr. law faculty U. Singapore, 1972-74. chmn. Police Rev. Com. of Berkeley (Calif.), 1980-84; mem. Berkeley Police Res., 1986—; bd. dirs. Friends Assn. of Svcs. for Elderly, 1979-84; clk. fin. com. Am. Friends Svc. Com. of No. Calif., 1979-83; pres. Zyzzyva Inc., lit. quar., 1985-87. Trustee Freedom from Hunger, 1989—. With U.S. Army, 1958. Fellow Am. Bar Found.; mem. ABA, Internat. Bar Assn., Calif. Bar Assn., Assn. Internat. de Bibliophilie, Harvard Club, Univ. Club, Tanglin Club, Cricket Club, Book Club Calif., Roxburghe Club. Democrat. Roman Catholic. Home and Office: 1800 San Antonio Ave Berkeley CA 94707-1618

WOODING, WALTER HARRISON, metallurgical engineer; b. Phila., Mar. 12, 1910; s. Walter and Kathryn (Reynolds) W.; m. Mildred Armstrong, Oct. 31, 1931 (dec. 1939); m. Dorothy Cloud Worrilow, Apr. 26, 1941. Student, U.S. Naval Acad., 1928-29; Cert. Mech. Engring., Drexel Inst., Phila., 1941-44. Registered profl. engr., Pa. Jr. physicist USN Engring. Experiment Sta., Annapolis, Md., 1929-39; metallurgist I.T.L. Phila. Naval Shipyard, Phila., 1940-56, phys. sci. adminstr., 1956-60; mgr. welding equip. Arcos Corp., Phila., 1960-64; cons. Phila., 1964-65; mgr. welding engring. Baldwin-Lima-Hamilton Corp., Eddystone, Pa., 1966-72; mgr. materials-welding-quality assurance Gilbert Assocs., Reading, Pa., 1972-76; cons. in metall. engring. Reading, Pa., 1976-82; ret. Contbr. articles to profl. jours. Mem. ASM, Am. Welding Soc. (adv. mem. D-14 Machinery & Equip. Com. 1982—, Lincoln Gold medal 1953, Meritorious award 1958), U.S. Naval Acad. Alumni Assn. Home: 3078 S Camino Kino Green Valley AZ 85614

WOODLAND, IRWIN FRANCIS, lawyer; b. New York, Sept. 2, 1922; s. John James and Mary (Hynes) W.; m. Sally Duffy, Sept. 23, 1954; children: Connie, J. Patrick, Stephen, Joseph, William, David, Duffy. BA, Columbia U., 1948; JD, Ohio State U., 1959. Bar: Calif. 1960, Wash., 1991, U.S. Dist. Ct. (cen. dist.) Calif. 1960, U.S. Dist. Ct. (no. dist.) Calif. 1962, U.S. Dist. Ct. (so. dist.) Calif. From assoc. to ptnr. Gibson, Dunn & Crutcher, L.A., 1959-88; ptnr. Gibson, Dunn & Crutcher, Seattle, 1988—; Bd. dirs. Sunlaw Energy Corp., Vernon, Calif. With USAF, 1942-45, ETO. Mem. ABA, Calif. Bar Assn., L.A. Bar Assn., Wash. State Bar Assn., Fed. Energy Bar Assn., Am. Mgmt. Assn., Phi Delta Phi, Jonathan Club, Bel Air Bay Club. Roman Catholic. Office: Gibson Dunn & Crutcher 999 3d Ave Ste 2500 Seattle WA 98104

WOODLAND, STEVEN DEE, lawyer; b. Logan, Utah, Aug. 27, 1951; s. Daniel Platt and Althea (Rawlins) W.; m. Darlene Anderson, Apr. 19, 1974; children: Jonathan, Natalie, Camille, Ryan, Jeffrey. BS, Brigham Young U., 1974, JD magna cum laude, 1977. Bar: Ariz. 1978, Utah 1979, U.S. Dist. Ct. Utah, U.S. Ct. Appeals (10th cir.), U.S. Tax Ct., U.S. Supreme Ct. Jud. law clk. to Hon. Richard H. Chambers, U.S. Ct. Appeals (9th cir.), San Francisco, 1977-78; assoc. Van Cott, Bagley, Cornwall & McCarthy, Salt Lake City, 1978-83, ptnr., 1983—, chmn. employee benefits group, 1990—; lectr. Utah Fed. Tax Inst. Salt Lake City, 1981; bd. adv. CPA Forum, 1992-93; lectr. Utah Info. Tech. Assn. Seminar, 1992. Mem. dist. com. Boy Scouts Am., 1989—. J. Reuben Clark scholar Brigham Young U., Provo, 1977. Mem. ABA (tax sect.), Utah Bar Assn. (tax sect., lectr. ann meeting 1982, lectr. probate sect. 1984), Ariz. Bar, We. Pension & Benefit Conf. (program com. 1987, lectr. 1986), Salt Lake Area C. of C. (govt. affairs com. 1989—). Mem. LDS Church. Office: Van Cott Bagley Cornwall & McCarthy 50 S Main St Ste 1600 Salt Lake City UT 84144-0402

WOODNUTT, THOMAS LLOYD, college director; b. Oakland, Calif., May 24, 1943; s. William L. and Phyllis (Reeves) W.; m. Anita D. Ferris, Feb. 1, 1969; children: Dawn Marie, Dale Anne. BBA, Golden Gate U., 1965, MBA, 1967. Dir. sch. and community rels. Golden Gate U., San Francisco, 1967-69, dir. coop. edn., 1969-73; dir. coop. edn. Chemeketa C.C., Salem, Oreg., 1973-78, dir. placement, 1978-83; dir. coop. edn. South Puget Sound C.C., Olympia, Wash., 1983-86, dir. admissions and records, 1986—. Pres. Vol. Bd. Salem, 1980-83. Mem. WAACRO (sec.-treas. 1990), PACCRO. Office: South Puget Sound CC 2011 Mottman Rd SW Olympia WA 98502

WOODROW, JAMES IRVIN, university administrator, consultant; b. Somerset, Pa., May 3, 1953; s. Paul A. and Dorothy L. (Brougher) W. BA, David Lipscomb U., 1975; MS, Vanderbilt U., 1977, EdD, 1985; MS, U. So. Calif., 1981. Asst. to dean students Pepperdine U., Malibu, Calif., 1977-78, dir. career planning and alumni rels. Law Sch., 1978-81, asst. to exec. v.p., 1983-84; rsch. coord. Vanderbilt U., Nashville, 1981-83; asst. dean Grad. Sch. Pepperdine U., Culver City, Calif., 1984-93, assoc. dean adminstrn. Grad. Sch., 1993—; pres., sr. cons. Inst. for Advancement Pvt. Higher Edn., Thousand Oaks, Calif., 1991—. Author: The Christian College Advantage, 1992. Mem. Ch. of Christ. Home: 50-8 Maegan Pl Thousand Oaks CA 91362

WOODROW, KENNETH M., psychiatrist; b. Yonkers, N.Y., Mar. 20, 1942; s. Jack H. and Grace (Lewis) W.; m. Mary Mack, June 9, 1968 (div. 1985); 1 child, Laura; m. Patricia Robin Stokes, July 1, 1989. BA, Wesleyan U., 1964; postgrad., U. Calif., Davis, 1964; MD, U. Md., 1968. Diplomate Am. Bd. Psychiatry and Neurology. Intern Kaiser Found. Hosp., Oakland, Calif., 1968-69; resident psychiatry Stanford (Calif.) U. Med. Ctr., 1969-72; clin. assoc. NIMH Lab. Clin. Pschopharmacology, USPHS, 1972-74; pvt. practice psychiatry Menlo Park, Calif., 1977—; clin. assoc. prof. dept. psychiatry Stanford U. Sch. Medicine, 1975—; staff psychiatrist, chmn. pharmacy and therapeutics com. Stanford U. Hosp.; staff psychiatrist Sequoia Hosp., Redwood City, Calif.; examiner Am. Bd. Psychiatry and Neurology; rsch. assoc. NIH, Lab. Socioenviron. Studies, 1963-65; rsch. fellow U. Md. Psychiat. Inst., Balt., 1966; cons. Kaiser Permanente Med. Group, 1969; grant rev. cons. nSF, 1970; psychiat. emergency svc. and med. cons. Highland Alameda Hosp., 1970-72; clin. assoc. NIMH, 1972-74; exec. com. Com. for Concerned Psychiatrists, 1972-74; staff psychiatrist Palo Alto VA Hosp., 1974-76; psychiat. cons. Job Corps, San Jose, 1975-82; lectr. San Jose Hosp., 1976-83. Cons. editor Drug Info. Svc. Newsletter, Stanford U. Hosp.; referee Am. Jour. Psychiatry, 1976-77, Jour. Nervous and Mental Disease, 1978; book reviewer Am. Jour. Psychiatry, 1977, Contemporary Psychology, 1978; contbr. articles to profl. jours. Mem. Am. Psychiat. Assn. Office: 1225 Crane St Ste 106 Menlo Park CA 94025-4253

WOODRUFF, FAY, paleoceanographer, geological researcher; b. Boston, Jan. 23, 1944; d. Lorande Mitchell and Anne (Fay) W.; m. Alexander Whitehill Clowes, May 20, 1972 (div. Oct. 1974); m. Robert G. Douglas, Jan. 27, 1980; 1 child, Ellen. RN, Mass. Gen. Hosp. Sch. Nursing, Boston, 1965; BA, Boston U., 1971; MS, U. So. Calif., 1979. Rsch. assoc. U. So. Calif., L.A., 1978-81, rsch. faculty, 1981—. Contbg. author: Geological Society of America Memoir, 1985; contbr. articles to profl. jours. Life mem. The Nature Conservancy, Washington, 1992. NSF grantee, 1986-88, 88-91, 91-93. Mem. Am. Geophys. Union, Geol. Soc. Am., Internat. Union Geol. Scis. (internat. commn. on stratigraphy, subcommn. on neogene stratigraphy 1991-92), Soc. Women Geographers (sec. So. Calif. chpt. 1990-92), Soc. Econ. Paleontologists and Minerologists (sec., editor North Am. Micropaleontology sect. 1988-90), Oceanography Soc. (chpt. mem.), Sigma Xi. Episcopalian. Office: Dept Geol Scis U So Calif Los Angeles CA 90089-0740

WOODRUFF, JOHN DOUGLAS, career officer; b. Bonham, Tex., Feb. 12, 1944; s. Alexander Campbell and Lois Kathryn (Turner) W.; m. Carol Lynne Thompson, June 11, 1966; children: Keith Byron, Jill Marie, David Kent. BS in Sociology/Psychology, East Tex. State U., 1966; grad. with distinction, AFROTC, 1966; MS in Edn., U. So. Calif., 1970; grad. with distinction, Air Command and Staff Coll., 1977; USAF exch. student, U.S. Army War Coll., 1980-81. Commd. 2d lt. USAF, 1966; advanced through grades to col., commdr. USAF Air Rescue Svc., 1990—; adj. instr. psychology Golden Gate U., Pope AFB, N.C., 1975-76; com. chmn. Sec. of Air Force's Blue Ribbon Panel on Space, Maxwell AFB, Ala., 1988. Contbr. articles to USAF mag. Mil. sponsor for civic leader program Mil. Affairs Com., Abilene, Tex., 1982-83, Logstar Civilian Hon. Comdr. Program, Sacramento, Calif., 1990—. Decorated Legion of Merit, Meritorious Svc. medal with 3 oak leaf clusters. Mem. Air Force Assn. (Citation of Honor 1989), Airlift Assn., Air Rescue Assn., Jolly Green Pilots Assn., Order of Daedalians. Episcoaplian. Home: 105 Arizona Ave Jacksonville AR 72099 Office: USAF Hdqs Air Rescue Svc McClellan AFB CA 95652

WOODS, BERT RUSSELL, protective services official, consultant; b. Kansas City, Mo., Mar. 9, 1946; s. Russell McDonald and Sadie Maxine (Peatling) W.; m. Linda Ann Pahlow, June 14, 1970; children: Derek Russell, Nathan William, Jeramy Morgan. BA, Chaminade U., Honolulu, 1971. Cert. protection profl. Forestry technician Bur. of Land Mgmt., Canon City, Colo., 1977-80; air quality technician Automotive Testing Labs., Aurora, Colo., 1980-81; prodn. specialist Benedict Nuclear Pharms., Golden, Colo., 1981-83; v.p. Met. Security Svcs. Inc., Denver, 1983-89; div. mgr. Arko Exec. Svcs. West, Denver, 1989-90; dep. sheriff Arapahoe County Sheriff's Dept., Englewood, Colo., 1990—. Author: Security Officers Handbook, 1985, Security Officers Training Program. Scoutmaster Boy Scouts Am., 1984-90. Staff sgt. USAF, 1964-68, 71-77, Vietnam. Mem. NRA, Am. Soc. Indsl. Security (vice chmn. 1989-90), Nat. Eagle Scout Assn., Order of the Arrow. Lutheran. Home: 2265 Jamaica St Aurora CO 80010-1250 Office: Arapahoe County Sheriff's Dept 7375 S Potomac St Englewood CO 80112-4030

WOODS, BOBBY JOE (BOB WOODS), transportation executive; b. Frederick, Okla., June 20, 1935; s. Vivin Richard and Mattie Marie (Malone) W.; m. O. Dell Smith, July 21, 1957 (div.); children: Donald B., Kathryn M., David R., Lynda J. Student, U. Calif., Berkeley, 1955-56; AA, Phoenix Coll., 1955; student, Glendale (Ariz.) Coll., 1968, 75. Pres. Southwest Prorate Inc., Phoenix, 1967—; office mgr. Menke Transp., Albuquerque, 1967-68; dist. exec. Boy Scouts Am., Phoenix, 1968-76; owner S.W. Vehicle Title Svc., Phoenix, 1985—, S.W. Bus. Svcs., Yarnell, Ariz., 1988—,

Southwest Land Quail, Yarnell, Ariz., 1991—; pres. Facing E's Enterprises, Inc., Yarnell, Ariz., 1991—. Commr. Boy Scouts Am., Ariz., N.Mex. Mem. Profl. Trucking Svcs. Assn. (pres. 1989-90), Lions Club (dist. gov. 1992-93, zone chmn. 1983-84, dep. dist. gov. 1984-85, lt. gov. 1991-92, dist. sight and hearing chmn. 1985-91, Sight and Hearing Found. state hearing chmn. 1985-89). Republican. Home: 918 W Cochise Dr Phoenix AZ 85021 Office: Southwest Prorate Inc 6819 N 21st Ave Ste L Phoenix AZ 85015

WOODS, DONALD PETER, real estate executive, marketing professional; b. Seneca Falls, N.Y., Oct. 14, 1911; s. James Henry and Isabell Teresa (McDonald) W.; m. June 17, 1935; children: Donald Peter Jr., Richard, Terrence, Lynn, Thomas. PhB, Niagara U., Niagara Falls, N.Y., 1933; postgrad., Bklyn. Law Sch., 1933-36. Law clk. N.Y. State Ins. Dept., N.Y.C., 1933-36; title examiner Abstract Title and Mortgage, Rochester, N.Y., 1936-38; title officer Monroe Abstract & Title, Rochester, 1938-43; pres., chief exec. officer D.P. Woods, Inc., Rochester, 1945-54, Don Woods Realty, Phoenix, 1954-82; assoc. v.p. Iliff Thorn & Co., Phoenix, 1982—. Lt. USNR, 1943-45, PTO. Mem. Cert. Real Estate Appraisal, Internat. Coun. of Shopping Ctrs., Ariz. Club, Camelback Racquet Club (pres. Phoenix chpt. 1959—), Phi Delta Phi. Republican. Roman Catholic. Home: 5301 E Palomino Rd Phoenix AZ 85018 Office: Iliff Thorn & Co 3636 N Central Ave Ste 600 Phoenix AZ 85012-1984

WOODS, GRANT, state official; m. Marlene Galán; children: Austin, Lauren, Cole. Grad., Occidental Coll., Ariz. State Coll., 1979. Atty. gen. Ariz., 1990—. Founder Mesa Boys and Girls Club. Office: Atty General's Office 1275 W Washington St Phoenix AZ 85007-2997

WOODS, GURDON GRANT, sculptor; b. Savannah, Ga., Apr. 15, 1915; s. Frederick L. and Marion (Skinner) W. Student, Art Student's League N.Y.C., 1936-39, Bklyn. Mus. Sch., 1945-46; Ph.D. (hon.), Coll. San Francisco Art Inst., 1966. exec. dir. San Francisco Art Inst., 1955-64; dir. Calif. Sch. Fine Arts, 1955-65; prof. Adlai E. Stevenson Coll., U. Calif. at Santa Cruz, 1966-74; dir. Otis Art Inst., Los Angeles, 1974-77; asst. dir. Los Angeles County Mus. Natural History, 1977-80; Sculptor mem. San Francisco Art Commn., 1954-56; mem. Santa Cruz County Art Commn., Regional Arts Council of Bay Area. Exhibited: N.A.D., 1948, 49, San Francisco Art Assn. anns., 1952-54, Denver Mus. Anns., 1952, 53, Whitney Mus. Ann., 1953, Sao Paulo Biennial, 1955, Bolles Gallery San Francisco, 1969, 70, 72, Los Angeles Mcpl. Gallery, 1977, San Jose Inst. Contemporary Art (Calif.), Washington Project for the Arts retrospective, 1968-1985, Washington, 1985, Retrospective Art Mus. Santa Cruz County, Calif., 1987, d.p. Fong Gallery, 1993; commns. include: cast concrete reliefs and steel fountain, IBM Center, San Jose, Calif., fountain, Paul Masson Winery, Saratoga, Calif., McGraw Hill Pubs., Novato, Calif.; work in permanent collection Oakland (Calif.) Mus.; papers in Archives of Am. Art, Smithsonian Instn., Washington. Recipient citation N.Y.C., 1948; prize N.A.D., 1949; Chapelbrook Found. research grantee, 1965-66; Sequoia Fund grantee, 1967; Research grantee Creative Arts Inst., U. Calif., 1968; grantee Carnegie Corp., 1968-69. Mem. Artists Equity Assn (pres. No. Calif. chpt. 1950-52, nat. dir. 1952-55). Address: 133 Seascape Dr Aptos CA 95003

WOODS, JOE ELDON, general contractor; b. Hammon, Okla., Apr. 24, 1933; s. Joseph W. and Gertrude E. (Martin) W.; student Ariz. State U., 1955-61; O.P.M. Program Harvard U.., 1984-87; m. Nina Jo Shackelford, July 5, 1952; 1 son, J. Grant. Vice-pres. Kitchell Corp., Phoenix, 1965-69; v.p. devel. Doubletree, Inc., Phoenix, 1969-78; pres., owner Joe E. Woods, Inc., Mesa, Ariz., 1977—; bd. dirs. Price-Woods, Inc., Mesa, 1985—; chmn., bd. dirs. Joe Woods Devel., Mesa, 1986—. Bd. dirs. Mesa United Way, 1983-84; v.p., bd. dirs. East Valley Partnership, Mesa, 1985. With U.S. Army, 1953-55, Korea. Mem. Associated Gen. Contractors, Mesa C. of C. (bd. dirs. 1983-87, chmn. 1985-86, v.p. 1984-85, pres. 1985-86), Harvard Bus. Sch. Republican. Presbyterian. Clubs: Mesa Country, White Mountain Country (Pinetop, Ariz.). Lodge: Rotary. Avocations: golf, fishing, skiing. Office: Joe E Woods Inc 63 E Main St Ste 401 Mesa AZ 85201-7417

WOODS, LAWRENCE MILTON, airline company executive; b. Manderson, Wyo., Apr. 14, 1932; s. Ben Ray and Katherine (Youngman) W.; m. Joan Frances Van Patten, June 10, 1952; 1 dau., Laurie. B.Sc. with honors, U. Wyo., 1953; M.A., N.Y. U., 1973, Ph.D., 1975; LL.D., Wagner Coll., 1973. Bar: Mont. 1957; C.P.A., Colo., Mont. Accountant firm Peat, Marwick, Mitchell & Co. (C.P.A.'s), Billings, Mont., 1953; supervisory auditor Army Audit Agy., Denver, 1954-56; accountant Mobil Producing Co., Billings, Mont., 1956-59; planning analyst Socony Mobil Oil Co., N.Y.C., 1959-63; planning mgr. Socony Mobil Oil Co., 1963-65; v.p. North Am. div. Mobil Oil Corp., N.Y.C., 1966-67; gen. mgr. planning and econs. North Am. div. Mobil Oil Corp., 1967-69, v.p., 1969-77, exec. v.p., 1977-85, also dir.; pres., chief exec. officer, dir. Centennial Airlines, Inc., 1985-87; pres., dir. Woshakie Travel Corp., 1988—, High Plains Pub. Co. Inc., 1988—; bd. dirs. Handy & Harman, The Aid Assn. for Lutherans Mutual Funds. Author: Accounting for Capital, Construction and Maintenance Expenditures, 1967, The Wyoming Country Before Statehood, 1971, Sometimes the Books Froze, 1985, Moreton Frewen's Western Adventures, 1986, British Gentlemen in the Wild West, 1989; editor: Wyoming Biographies, 1991; co-author: Takeover, 1980; editor: Wyoming Biographies, 1991; contbr.: Accountants' Encyclopedia, 1962. Bd. dirs. U. Wyo. Research Corp. Served with AUS, 1953-55. Mem. ABA, Mont. Bar Assn., Am. Inst. CPA's, Chgo. Club. Republican. Lutheran. Office: High Plains Pub Co PO Box 1860 Worland WY 82401-1860

WOODS, MELANIE ANN, sales professional; b. Oakley, Kans., Oct. 24, 1957; d. Richard L. and Myrle E. (Arie) Stanfield; m. George K. Woods Jr., Oct. 16, 1982. BSBA, Kans. State U., 1979. Sales rep. George A. Hormel & Co., Kansas City, Mo., 1980-82; sales rep. Hershey Chocolate USA, Phoenix, 1985-86, key account rep., 1987-88, dist. account supr., 1988—. Mem. Kans. State U. Alumni Assn., Kappa Kappa Gamma Alumni Assn. Republican. Home: 3838 E Mountain Sky Ave Phoenix AZ 85044-6618

WOODS, RAYMOND DUVAL, record company executive, music producer; b. N.Y.C., July 7, 1960; m. Elizabeth Weil, Sept. 21, 1986. BS in Engring., W.Va. U., 1982. Promotion asst. Enigma Entertainment, L.A., 1988; engr./analyst Tecolote Rsch. Inc., L.A., 1989; chief exec. officer Rainforest Records, Inc., Portland, Oreg., 1990—. Journalist various music publs., 1987—. Commr. crime prevention City of Redondo Beach (Calif.), 1987-89. Capt. USAF, 1983-87. Decorated Air Force Commendation medal. Mem. NARAS, Portland Music Assn., NW Area Music Assn., Recording Industry Assn. Am., Broadcast Music Internat. Office: Rainforest Records Inc 8855 SW Holly Ln Ste 110 Wilsonville OR 97070-8792

WOODS, RICHARD IRVIN, forester; b. Omak, Wash., Oct. 9, 1932; s. Irvin Robert and Vesta Virginia (Stone) W.; m. Leslie Elsie Hlushko, Sept. 29, 1962; children: John Richard, Steven Robert. BS in Forestry, Wash. State U., 1958; postgrad., Oreg. State U., 1966, U. Wash., 1983, 85, U. Nev., 1987, 92. Forester, appraiser Fed. Land Bank Spokane, Wash., 1965-70; cons. forester Woodland Mgmt., Inc., Portland, Oreg., 1971-80; pres. 4S TREE/NW, Inc., Kelso, Wash., 1981—; Mem. Wash. State Forest Practices Bd., 1974-77, 84-87; mem. steering com. on energy, environ. and natural resources, Nat. League Cities, 1988. Mem. Cowlitz Wahkiakum Health Dist. Bd., chmn., 1987-88; past mem. Kelso City Coun.; mayor City of Kelso, 1982-90; bd. dirs. Kelso-Longview Salvation Army, 1981—, chmn., 1983-85. Sgt. U.S. Army, 1953-55, Korea. Mem. Assn. Cons. Foresters Am. (pres. 1990-92), Soc. Am. Foresters, Wash. Farm Forestry Assn. (pres. 1973-74), Wash. Resources Coun. (bd. dirs. 1982-87), Assn. Wash. Cities (past bd. dirs.), Kiwanis. Republican. Episcopalian. Home and Office: 1606 Cowlitz Way Kelso WA 98626

WOODS, WILLIAM EVERETT, public health administrator, newspaper publisher; b. Decatur, Ill., Oct. 9, 1949; s. Wendell Phillip and Mary Blanche (Fitzjarrald) W. B in Psychology, U. Hawaii, 1971, M in Pub. Health Adminstrn. and Planning, 1980. Psychiat. aide Ill. Adolp Meyer Zone Ctr. State Dept. of Mental Health, Decatur, 1968-70; paramed. asst. mental health div. State Dept. of Health, Kaneohe, Hawaii, 1970-72, rsch. asst. mental health div., 1972-78, adminstr., planner Hansen's Disease Outpatient Program, 1985; exec. asst. to bd. Citizen Against Noise, Kaneohe, 1981-82, pres., 1983-85; coord. equal opportunity/affirmative action, CETA program City and County of Honolulu, 1982-83; exec. dir. Hawaii's Gay Community Ctr., Honolulu, 1973-91; gen. mgr. Hawaii's Gay Community News, Honolulu, 1973—; mgr. Hawaii's Health and Safety Svcs., 1993—; pres. U. Hawaii Sch. Pub. Health and Human Assn., 1985-86. Founder, exec. dir. GLEA Found., 1991—; pres. Pride Parade Rally Coun., Honolulu, 1989—; v.p., vol. Info. and Referral Svc., Honolulu, 1982-84; pres. Gay Community Ctr., 1973-78, 83-86; precinct pres. Dem. Party of Hawaii, Honolulu, 1988—; spokesperson, coord. Gay Rights Task Force State of Hawaii, 1978—; bd. dirs. Hawaii Dem. Movement, 1986—. Named Outstanding Young Man of Am. U.S. Jaycee, 1984. Mem. NOW, Nat. Gay and Lesbian Press Assn. (nat. bd. dirs. 1990—), State Fedn. of Bus. and Profl. Women, Waikiki Bus. and Profl. Women's Club (pres. 1991). Democrat. Office: Hawaii's Gay Community News PO Box 37083 Honolulu HI 96837-0083

WOODSON, MARK WINTER, city engineer; b. Madison, Wis., Apr. 21, 1953; s. William Arther and Ruth Maxine (Ellefson) W.; m. Guadalupe Elizabeth Beck, Mar. 17, 1979; children: John William, Robert Michael, Anna Elizabeth, Katherine Ruth. AS in Civil Engring., Pima Community Coll., Tucson, 1977; BS in Civl Engring., U. Ariz., 1979, MBA, 1985. Profl. civil engr., registered land surveyor. Pvt. practice consulting engr. Tucson, 1979-84; pub. works dir. Town of Eagar, Ariz., 1984-85; capital improvement engr. City of Flagstaff, Ariz., 1985-86, city engr., 1986-93; project mgr. Ariz. Engring. Co., 1993—; adj. faculty Coll. of Engring No. Ariz. U., 1992—. Contbr. articles to profl. jours. Participant Flagstaff Leadership Program, 1990-91, Flagstaff Little League (pres. 1993); com. mem. Boy Scout Troop 33, Flagstaff, 1990—. Mem. ASCE (pres. Ariz. sect. 1990-91), Am. Pub. Works Assn. (awards com. 1987—, no. Ariz. v.p. 1993), Ariz. Profl. Land Surveyors, Mgmt. Orgn. Level, Am. Soc. Civil Engrs. Republican. Lutheran. Office: Ariz Engring Co 419 N San Francisco Flagstaff AZ 86001

WOOD-TROST, LUCILLE MARIE, educator, writer, psychotherapist; b. Candor, N.Y., Nov. 4, 1938; d. Stiles and Alice E. (Keim) Wood; m. Charles Trost, June 18, 1960 (div. 1981); 1 child, Scott. BS in Zoology, Pa. State U., 1960; MS in Biology, U. Fla., 1964; PhD in Human Behavior, Union Grad. Sch., Cin., 1975. Dir. Tamarack Learning Coop., Pocatello, Idaho, 1969-74; freelance writer, 1960-75, 82—; asst. prof. Westminster Coll., Salt Lake City, 1975-80; therapist, planner, writer Garden of Peace Healing Ctr., Stanwell Tops, NSW, Australia, 1980-81; pvt. practice psychotherapy Bellingham, Wash., 1982-84; assoc. prof. Northwest Indian Coll. (formerly Lummi Community Coll.), Bellingham, 1984—; dir. student svcs. N.W. Indian Coll., Bellingham, 1989-92, dir. individualized studies, 1992—. Author: Lives and Deaths in a Meadow, 1973 (award, Am. Assn. Sci. Tchrs.-Children's Book Coun. 1976), others. Mem. Sigma Xi, Phi Sigma. Mem. Science of Mind Church. Home: 2611 MacKenzie Rd Bellingham WA 98226 Office: Northwest Indian Coll 2522 Kwina Rd Bellingham WA 98226-9217

WOODWARD, ALBERT BRUCE, JR., radio broadcaster, investment advisor, arbitrator, expert witness; b. Los Angeles, May 25, 1941; s. Albert Bruce and Virginia Hannah (Lacey) W.; m. Marilyn Ann Werner, June 23, 1962, children: Albert Bruce III, William Garth, Michelle Ann. Student, U. So. Calif., 1960-62; BS in Polit. Sci., U. Nebr., Omaha, 1974; MA in Internat. Mgmt., Monterey (Calif.) Inst. Internat. Studies, 1976. Cert. fin. planner. Pres. Tex. Internat. Cons. Inc., Dallas, 1965-79; div. mgr. Waddell & Reed Inc., Kansas City, Kans., 1983—; chmn. Woodward Fon. Group, Inc., Denver and Naples, Fla., 1983-84, Newport Beach, Calif., 1983-84; bd. dirs. Associated Planners Securities Corp., Los Angeles; mem. securities commr. adv. com. State of Colo., 1988—. Author: How To Be A Financial Planner, 1980, What to Do With Serious Money, 1991, Wealth Management for the 1990s, 1992; editor Planning & Computing, 1979-86; host (radio program) The Money Corner, KNUS Radio, Denver, 1986-88, Bus. Radio Network, 1988-89, Sta. KYBG, 1990—. Chmn. parents div. Kent Denver Fund, 1985-87. Served to maj. U.S. Army, 1962-65, Vietnam. Decorated D.F.C., Bronze Star with 4 bronze oak leaf clusters, Purple Heart with 2 bronze oak leaf clusters. Mem. Inst. Cert. Fin. Planners (ethics com. 1986-87), Internat. Assn. for Fin. Planning (local pres. 1984-86, local chmn. bd. dirs. 1985-86), Internat. Bd. Standards and Practice Cert. Fin. Planners, Am. Arbitration Assn., Registry Fin. Planning Practitioners, Am. Legion, Masons, Shriners, Elks, Denver Athletic Club, Denver Met. Club, Collier Athletic Club (Naples, Fla.). Republican. Episcopalian. Home: 3561 S Dawson St Aurora CO 80014-4402 Office: The Woodward Fin Group Inc 3033 E 1st Ave Ste 410 Denver CO 80206-5619

WOODWARD, GEORGE FREDERICK, III, priest; b. Greensburg, Pa., June 24, 1955; s. George Frederick Jr. and Louise Adele (Frum) W.; m. Shelly Kathleen Pease, Aug. 14, 1982 (div. Aug. 1993). BA, Ohio U., 1978; MA, Ashland Theol. Sem., 1981; MDiv, Seabury-Western Theol. Sem., 1983. Ordained deacon Episcopal Ch., 1983, ordained priest, 1984. Assoc. rector All Saints by the Sea Episcopal Ch., Montecito, Calif., 1983-88; asst. to archdeacon for the Aegean Anglican Diocese of Gibraltar, Turkey, 1989-91; rector, headmaster St. Timothy's Episcopal Ch., Apple Valley, Calif., 1991—; mem. ch. architecture commn. Diocese of L.A., 1984-88, chair World and Domestic Hunger Commn., 1984-88, mem. Commn. on Schs., 1991—; headmaster St. Timothy's Episcopal Sch., Apple Valley, Calif., 1991—; mem. com. structure of the diocese, 1993—. Contbr. to profl. publs. Bd. dirs. Villa Majella, Santa Barbara, Calif., 1983-88. Recipient Resolution of Commendation County Bd. Suprs., Santa Barbara County, Calif., 1988. Mem. Rotary Internat. Republican. Episcopalian. Office: St Timothys Episcopal Ch 15757 St Timothy Rd Apple Valley CA 92307

WOODWARD, JOHN RUSSELL, motion picture production executive; b. San Diego, July 10, 1951; s. Melvin C. and Dora M. (Rorabaugh) W. BA in Visual Arts, U. Calif., San Diego, 1973; MA in Cinema Prodn., U. So. Calif., 1978. V.p. prodn. World Wide Motion Pictures Corp., 1982—. Prodn. asst. various commls., 1977; asst. producer The Manitou, 1977; 1st asst. dir. Mortuary, 1981, They're Playing with Fire, 1983, Prime Risk, 1984, Winners Take All, 1986, Kidnapped, 1986, Slam Dance, 1986, Honor Betrayed, 1986, Hidden, 1987, New Monkees, 1987, Bad Dreams, 1987, Night Angel, 1988, Disorganized Crime, 1988, UHF, 1988, The Horror Show, 1988, Fear, 1989, Tremors, 1989, Young Guns II, 1990, Shattered, 1990, Tales from the Crypt, 1990, Two-Fisted Tales, 1990, Buried Alive, 1990, Dream On, 1991, Strays, 1991, Universal Soldier, 1991, Joshua Tree, 1992, The Vanishing, 1992, Ghost in the Machine, 1992; location mgr. Star Chamber, 1982, To Be or Not to Be, 1983, Flashdance, 1983, Two of a Kind, 1983, Touch and Go, 1984, Explorers, 1984, Sweet Dreams, 1985, The Long Shot, 1985, The Running Man, 1985, A Different Affair, 1985, Walk Like a Man, 1986.

WOODWARD, STEPHEN RICHARD, newspaper editor; b. Fukuoka City, Japan, July 27, 1953; came to U.S., 1954; s. Leonard Edwin and Etsuko (Okumura) W.; m. Sandra Elizabeth Richardson, Dec. 31, 1979; children: Daniel Joseph, Elizabeth Etsuko. BA in English, Wright State U., 1975; MA in Journalism, U. Mo., 1979. Advt. coordinator Wright State U., Dayton, Ohio, 1976-77; reporter Kansas City (Mo.) Star, 1979-82; assoc. editor then editor Kansas City Bus. Jour., 1982-83; editor then gen. mgr. Portland (Oreg.) Bus. Jour., 1984-86; exec. bus. editor The Hartford (Conn.) Courant, 1986-87; editor San Francisco Bus. Times, 1987-88; bus. editor The Oregonian, Portland, 1989—. Recipient 1st Place Investigative Reporting award Assn. Area Bus. Publs., 1983, 1st Place Column Writing award Assn. Area Bus. Publs., 1985. Mem. Investigative Reporters and Editors Inc. Home: 3309 NE Irving St Portland OR 97232-2538 Office: The Oregonian 1320 SW Broadway Portland OR 97201-3469

WOODWARD, WILLIAM EDWARD, marketing consultant; b. Cleve., Aug. 21, 1954; s. Vasyl and Rita Lillian (Dombrowsky) Wodoslawsky. BA, Marietta (Ohio) Coll., 1976. News dir. Sta. WMOA/WMOA-FM, Marietta, 1976-78, Sta. KPWR-TV, Bakersfield, Calif., 1978-79; anchor/talk-show host Sta. KNTB/KLYD-FM, Bakersfield, 1979-80; dir. pub. info. Kern View Hosp., Bakersfield, 1980-84; dir. pub. info. and comms. Camelback Hosps., Inc., Scottsdale, Ariz., 1984-90; mktg. cons. Woodward and Co., Phoenix, 1990—; cons. Ronald McDonald Ho., Phoenix, 1991—; Black Family and Child Svcs. of Ariz., 1990—, St. Luke's Health System, Phoenix, 1991—. Author: (booklet) The 12 Pitfalls of Christmas, 1983 (1st pl. nat. pub. rels. project 1984). Tenor saxophone player New Bros. Rhythm and Blues Band. Recipient Best Hosp. TV Comml. Nat. Assn. of Pvt. Psychiat. Hosps., 1988, Best Mktg. Project, 1988, Best Newscast Calif. Associated Press TV and Radio Assn., 1979. Mem. Am. Soc. for Hosp. Mktg. and Pub. Rels. (treas. Ariz. chpt. 1985-86). Office: Woodward and Co 3104 E Camelback Rd Phoenix AZ 85016

WOODWARD, WILLIAM HERBERT, industrial engineer; b. Springfield, Mass., July 31, 1941; s. Herbert William and Catherine Louise (Carney) W.; m. Mary Martha Schukoske, July 4, 1964; children: Brian William, Mitchell Todd. BS in Mgmt. Engring., Rensselaer Polytechnic Inst., 1964; MS in Indsl. Adminstrn., Union Coll., 1972. Indsl. engr. IBM, East Fishkill, N.Y., 1967-77; prodn. control mgr. IBM, East Fishkill, 1977-79; indsl. engring. mgr. IBM, Tucson, 1979-81, project mgr., 1981-85, adv. engr., 1985-91, sr. adv. engr., 1992—. Firearms instr. NRA, 1985—; mem. steering com. Nat. Tech. U., Ft. Collins, Colo., 1992—, chmn., 1993—. Lt. USNR, 1964-67, Vietnam. Mem. Ariz. Consortium for Edn. and Tng. (exec. com. 1992—), Inst. Indsl. Engrs. (pres. chmn. 1986-87, 1st chpt. achievement award 1987, chpt. dir. 1982), U.S. Naval Inst., Rensselaer Alumni Assn. (so. Ariz. dir. alumni recruiting 1985—, alumni scholarship chair), Chatham Yacht Club (race patrol capt.). Republican. Roman Catholic. Home: 6452 E Calle De Amigos Tucson AZ 85715-2005 Office: IBM 9000 S Rita Rd Tucson AZ 85744-0001

WOODWARD, WILLIAM WALTER, journalism educator; b. Marlin, Tex., Dec. 15, 1943; s. Clarence Walter and Marie Margaret (Frick) W.; m. Gloria Jean Fredericks, Dec. 31, 1965 (div. Dec. 1969); m. Marilyn June Davis, June 26, 1971; children: Arlene Marie, Frederick Walter, Jonathan Walter. AD in Gen. Studies, Arapahoe Community Coll., Littleton, Colo., 1988, AA, 1989; MA, U. No. Colo., Greeley, 1991. News dir. KTVS-TV, Sterling, Colo., 1973-78; news editor, anchor KLZ/KAZY Radio, Denver, 1979-85; news dir. KCOL AM/FM, Ft. Collins, Colo., 1985-89; news stringer KUNC FM, Greeley, 1989-90; news anchor KYGO AM, Denver, 1989—; instr. Resource Tng. Inst., Ft. Collins, 1989; teaching asst. U. No. Colo., 1990-91, instr., 1991—; broadcast coord. Colo. State U., Ft. Collins, 1991-92; cons. Colo. State Alumni Assn., 1991-92, Sterling Kiwanis Club, 1977-78, Sterling Jaycees, 1967-70. Contbr. articles to profl. jours. Bd. dirs. Four Season Homeowners Assn., Ft. Collins, 1989-91, pres., 1991-92; bd. dirs. RE-1 Sch. Bd., Sterling, 1977-78. With U.S. Army, 1962-64. Recipient Best Investigative Report award AP, 1988; recipient scholarships. Mem. Radio-TV News Dirs. Assn., Soc. Profl. Journalists, No. Colo. Media Profls., Elks. Democrat. Lutheran. Home: 713 Arbor Ave Fort Collins CO 80526-3101 Office: U No Colo Candelaria 123 Greeley CO 80639

WOODWORTH, JAMES VICKERS, internist; b. Dover, N.H., Aug. 27, 1921; s. Hazlett A. Vickers and Sarah Louise (Nelson) Woodworth; m. Cara Elisabeth Davis, Sept. 22, 1945; children: Gail L. Woodworth, Vicki S. Terhorst, Linda C. Becker. AB, Whitman Coll., 1943; MD, U. Oreg., 1946. Diplomate Am. Bd. Internal Medicine; lic. MD Oreg., Calif. Intern French Hosp., San Francisco, 1946-47; resident USPHS, San Francisco, 1947-52; pvt. practice in internal medicine Portland, Oreg., 1952-76; founder Suburban Med. Clinic, Portland, 1956; instr. medicine Sch. Dentistry Oreg. Health Scis. U., Portland, 1952-82, prof. emeritus, 1982—, clin. assoc. medicine, 1953-76, assoc. prof., chmn. dept. medicine, 1976-79, prof., chmn. dept. medicine, 1979-82; affiliate faculty advanced cardiac life support Am. Heart Assn., Portland, 1983-88; cons. indsl. medicine So. Pacific Transpn. Co. and Burlington No. RR, Portland, 1977-92, Portland, 1982—; cons. Cardiac Resuscitator Corp., Portland, 1983-87; active staff Providence Med. Ctr., Portland, 1952-77, Portland Adventist Hosp., 1952-76. Contbr. articles to profl. jours. Fellow Am. Coll. Physicians; mem. Am. Soc. Internal Medicine, AMA, Oreg. State Med. Assn. (bd. trustees, house dels.), Multnomah County Med. Soc., Oreg. Heart Assn. (chmn. life support procedures com. 1978-80), Am. Occupational Med. Assn. Republican. Presbyterian. Home: 999 NE 169th Dr Portland OR 97230-6125

WOODWORTH, STEPHEN DAVIS, business and financial consultant, investment banker; b. Stillwater, Okla., Nov. 4, 1945; s. Stanley Davis and Elizabeth (Webb) W.; m. Robin Woodworth; children: Lisa Alexander, Ashley Ives. BA, Claremont McKenna Coll., 1967; MBA, Calif. Lutheran U., 1975; grad. Mgmt. Policy Inst., U. So. Calif., 1981. Div. mgr. Security Pacific Bank, L.A., 1970-86; pres. Channel Island Equities, Oxnard, Calif., 1988—; prin. Woodworth Assocs., Westlake Village, Calif., 1987-88; bd. dirs. Westlake Village, Calif.; advisor to bd. Pacific InterTrade Corp., Hanson Lab Furniture Ind., Inc., Newbury Park, Calif., 1992-93; trustee Calif. Luth. Edn. Found., Thousand Oaks, Calif., 1983-93; chmn. Cen. Coast MIT Enterprise Forum, Santa Barbara, Calif., 1992-93; instr. fin. and banking Calif. Luth. U., 1978-79. Contbr. articles to profl. jours. Chmn. Alliance for the Arts, Thousand Oaks, Calif., 1982-93; vice chmn. Conejo Symphony Orch., Thousand Oaks, 1986-90. 1st Lt. U.S. Army, 1968-70, Korea. Recipient Outstanding Alumnus Calif. Lutheran U., 1986. Mem. Res. Officers Assn. of the U.S., Ventura County Economic Devel. Assn., Am. Mgmt. Assn., Conejo Future Found., Marine Meml. Club, Tower Club. Republican. Roman Catholic. Home: 2384 McCrea Rd Thousand Oaks CA 91362 Office: Channel Island Equities 300 Esplanade Dr Ste 900 Oxnard CA 93030

WOOLARD, HENRY WALDO, aerospace engineer; b. Clarksburg, W.Va., June 2, 1917; s. Herbert William and Elsie Marie (Byers) W.; m. Helen Stone Waldron, Aug. 16, 1941; children: Shirley Ann, Robert Waldron. BS in Aero. Engring., U. Mich., 1941; MSME, U. Buffalo, 1954. Aero. engr. NACA, 1941-46; assoc. prof., acting dept. head, aero. engr. W. Va. U., Morgantown, W.Va., 1946-48; rsch. aerodynamicist Cornell Aero. Lab., Buffalo, 1948-57; sr. staff engr. applied physics lab. Johns Hopkins U., Silver Spring, Md., 1957-63; sr. rsch. specialist Lockheed Calif. Co., Burbank, Calif., 1963-67; mem. tech. staff TRW Systems Group, Redondo Beach, Calif., 1967-70; pres. Beta Tech. Co., Palos Verdes, Calif., 1970-71; aero. engr. Air Force Flight Dynamics Lab., Wright-Patterson AFB, Ohio, 1971-85; aero. cons. Dayton, Ohio, 1985-87, Fresno, Calif., 1987—. Contbr. articles to profl. jours. Recipient Scientific Achievement award Air Force Systems Command, 1982. Assoc. fellow AIAA; mem. ASME, Sigma Xi, Sigma Pi Sigma. Office: Consultant Aerospace 1249 W Magill Ave Fresno CA 93711

WOOLF, LAWRENCE DONALD, physicist; b. Harvey, Ill., Sept. 6, 1953; s. Milton Fuld and Betty (Hocky) W.; m. Wendelin Welsh, Dec. 28, 1977; children: Rebecca, David, Rachel. BS in Physics with highest honors, Rutgers Coll., 1975; MS in Physics, U. Calif., San Diego, 1976, PhD in Physics, 1980. Physicist Gen. Atomics, San Diego, 1982-86, mgr., 1986—. Contbr. numerous articles to profl. jours; patentee in field. Mem. Superconductor Applications Assn. (adv. bd. mem. 1987-90), Am. Phys. Soc., Materials Rsch. Soc., Phi Beta Kappa. Home: 7920 Corte Cardo Carlsbad CA 92009-8924 Office: Gen Atomics 3550 General Atomics Ct San Diego CA 92121-1194

WOOLF, ROBERT HANSEN, periodontist; b. Salt Lake City, Jan. 29, 1945; s. Robert McCarthy and Dorthy (Hansen) W.; m. Linda Gail Maddux, Aug. 18, 1967; children: Robert David, Laura Elizabeth. BS in Molecular and Genetic Biology, U. Utah, 1967; DDS, U. of the Pacific, 1971; cert. in periodontics, U. Oreg., 1976. Lic. dentist, Calif., periodontist, Oreg. Commd. 2d lt USAR, 1963, advanced through grades to capt., 1978; dental intern U.S. Army Hosp., Ft. Jackson, S.C., 1972; clin. instr. depts. geriodontology, periodontology Sch. Dentistry U. Oreg., Portland, 1974-76; asst. prof. dept. periodontology Sch. Dentistry Oreg. Health Scis. U., Portland, 1976—; mem. dental staff Meridian Pk. Hosp., Tualatin, Oreg., 1976—; pvt. practice Lake Oswego, Oreg., 1976—. Mem. YMCA. Fellow Am. Coll. Dentists; mem. ADA, Am. Acad. Periodontology, Am. Acad. Gen. Dentistry, Am. Acad. Dental Anesthesiology, Am. Acad. Dentistry for Children, Oreg. Dental Assn., Oreg. Soc. Periodontists, Oreg. Acad. Gen. Dentistry, Oreg. Acad. Dental Anesthesiology, Oreg. Acad. Dentistry for Children, Oreg. Soc. Craniomandibular Disfunction, Clackamus County Dental Assn., Western Soc. Periodontology, Rotary Internat. (Paul Harris fellow), Xi Xsi Phi (pres. local chpt. 1971), Pi Kappa (chpt. v.p. 1966). Republican. Home: 17346 Canal Cir Lake Oswego OR 97035 Office: 320 A Ave Lake Oswego OR 97034

WOOLF-SCOTT, HELENE LYDA, real estate developer; b. N.Y.C., Apr. 2, 1938; d. Harry and Eleanor (Wolfson) Burke; m. William Woolf, Aug. 17, 1958 (div. 1982); 1 child, Gina Karen; m. Walter Scott Jr., May 1, 1987. BA, NYU, 1959. Lic. real estate agt. Calif. Realtor Wright & Co., Los Altos, Calif., 1974-80; v.p. Munsey Devel. Corp., Los Altos, Calif., 1978—; v.p. McKeon, Scott, Woolf & Assocs., 1982-84; pres. GKW Enterprises, Inc. 1978—, Scott, Woolf & Assocs., 1984—; bd. dirs. Mulford, Moreland, Scott & Assocs., San Jose. Mem. Los Altos Bd. Realtors, Am. Mgmt. Assn., Nat. Trust for Historic Preservation, Nat. Assn. Realtors, Calif. Assn. Realtors. Democrat. Home: 564 Santa Rita Ave Palo Alto CA 94301-4035 Office: Scott Woolf & Assocs 701 Welch Rd Ste 323 Palo Alto CA 94304-1796

WOOLLEY, J(ONATHAN) MICHAEL, public administration educator, economic consultant; b. Norfolk, Va., Mar. 2, 1958; s. Herbert Thomas Woolley and Jane Kennedy (Dodson) Genet; m. Diana Elaine Gorrie, Aug. 1, 1987; children: Christian David, Thomas Michael. BA in Econs., U. Calif., San Diego, 1981; MA in Econs., U. Calif., Santa Barbara, 1983, PhD in Econs., 1987. Economist Fed. Res. Bd., Washington, 1987-89; asst. prof. Sch. Pub. Adminstrn. U. So. Calif., L.A., 1989—; econ. cons. Econ. Analysis Corp., L.A., 1990—. Co-author: (book) Handbook for Microeconomic Principles, 1983; contbr. articles to profl. jours. Regents fellow U. Calif., Santa Barbara, 1981-82, Earhart Found. fellow, 1985-86, Haynes Found. fellow, 1990-91. Mem. Am. Econ. Assn., Am. Fin. Assn., Western Econ. Assn., Health Econ. Rsch. Orgn. Home: 122 N Berkeley Ave Pasadena CA 91107 Office: U So Calif Sch Pub Adminstrn Los Angeles CA 90089-0041

WOOLLIAMS, KEITH RICHARD, arboretum and botanical garden director; b. Chester, Eng., July 17, 1940; s. Gordon Frank and Margaret Caroline W.; m. Akiko Narita, Apr. 11, 1969; children: Frank Hiromi, Angela Misako. Grad., Celyn Agrl. & Hort. Inst., N. Wales, 1955; student, U. Liverpool, various horticultural insts., 1956-59; Kew certificate, Royal Botanic Gardens, 1963. Cert. Horticulture Union Cheshire & Lancashire, 1955, Royal Horticulture Soc., 1956, 57, 58, Nat. Cert. Horticulture, 1958, Cert. Arboriculture 1962. Supt. field sta. U. London Queen Mary Coll., Brentwood, Essex, Eng., 1963-65; horticulturist Horizons Ltd., Bermuda, 1965-67; dept. forests, supt. botanic gardens Papua, New Guinea, 1967-68; instr. Eng. staff indsl. cos., Japan, 1968-71; supt., horticulturist Pacific Tropical Botanical Garden, Kauai, Hawaii, 1971-74; horticulturist Waimea Arboretum and Botanical Garden, Haleiwa, Hawaii, 1974-80, dir., 1980—; Contbr. articles to profl. jours., New Royal Horticultural Society's Dictionary of Gardening, 1992. Contbr. articles to profl. jours., dictionary. field assoc. botany Bishop Mus., Honolulu, 1981—; bd. dirs. Friends of Foster Garden, Honolulu Botanic Gardens, 1980—; v.p., founder Waimea Arboretum Found., 1977—. Mem. Am. Assn. Botanical Gardens and Arboreta, Am. Hort. Soc., Hawaii Audubon Soc., Hawaiian Botanical Soc. (pres. 1979), Internat. Assn. Plant Taxonomists, Royal Hort. Soc., Kew Guild. Office: Waimea Arboretum & Bot Garden 59-864 Kamehameha Hwy Haleiwa HI 96712

WOOLMAN, BRUCE ALAN, family practice physician; b. Watonga, Okla., June 16, 1955; s. William Werner and Gwendolyn (DuPree) W.; m. Debra May Smith, Aug. 24, 1985; children: Brittany, David, Christopher. BS in Biology, Southwestern Okla. State U., 1977; DO, Okla. Coll. Osteopathic Med., Tulsa, 1980. Diplomate Am. Bd. Family Physicians. Intern William Beaumont Army Med. Ctr., El Paso, Tex., 1980-81; family practice resident Madigan Army Med. Ctr., Tacoma, 1983-85; commd. U.S. Army, 1980—, advnced through grades to lt. col., 1992; family physician Reynolds Army Community Hosp., Ft. Sill, Okla., 1985-89, Evans Army Community Hosp., Ft. Carson, Colo., 1990—. Fellow Am. Acad. Family Physicians; mem. Am. Osteopathic Assn., Uniformed Svcs. Acad. Family Practice, Aerospace Med. Assn., Soc. of U.S. Army Flight Surgeons, Assn. Mil. Osteopathic Physicians and Surgeons. Methodist. Home: 5021 Broadmoor Bluff Dr Colorado Springs CO 80906-7913 Office: Dept of Family Practice Evans County Community Hosp Fort Carson CO 80913

WOOLSEY, LYNN, congresswoman. Mem. 103rd Congress from 6th Calif. dist., 1993—. Office: US House of Reps 439 Cannon Washington DC 20515-0506

WOOLSEY, ROY BLAKENEY, electronics company executive; b. Norfolk, Va., June 12, 1945; s. Roy B. and Louise Stookey (Jones) W.; m. Patricia Bernadine Elkins, Apr. 17, 1988. Student, Calif. Inst. Tech., 1962-64; BS with distinction, Stanford U., 1966, MS, 1967, PhD, 1970. Sr. physicist Tech. for Communications Internat., Mountain View, Calif., 1970-75; mgr. radio direction finding systems Tech. for Communications Internat., Mountain View, 1975-80, program mgr., 1980-83, dir. strategic systems, 1983-88, dir. research and devel., 1988-91, v.p. engring., 1991-92; v.p. programs Tech. for Communications Internat., Sunnyvale, Calif., 1992—; bd. dirs. Merit Software Corp., Menlo Park, 1990—. Author: (with others) Applications of Artificial Intelligence to Command and Control Systems, 1988, Antenna Engineering Handbook, 1993; contbr. articles to profl. jours. Active YMCA, Palo Alto, Calif. Fellow NSF, 1966-70. Mem. AFCEA, Stanford Club, Sequoia Yacht Club, Sigma Xi, Phi Beta Kappa. Republican. Presbyterian. Home: 26649 Snell Ln Los Altos Hills CA 94022-2039 Office: Tech for Communications Internat 222 Caspian Dr Sunnyvale CA 94089

WOOSLEY, PATRICK GLENN, tax executive; b. Dallas, Nov. 12, 1938; s. Pat and Florrie (Smith) W.; m. Valerie White, Oct. 19, 1974 (div. 1980); children: Trina, Jeff; m. Kazuko Ando, Dec. 29, 1984; children: Christine, Katherine. BBA, North Tex. State U., 1960; MBA, So. Meth. U., 1965, JD, 1968; LLM in Tax, NYU, 1969. Bar: Tex. 1968, Calif. 1973. Tax mgr. Latin Am. Gulf Oil Co., London and Miami, Fla., 1969-73; assoc. Lawler, Felix and Hall, L.A., 1973-75; 1st v.p., sr. tax counsel Security Pacific Nat. Bank, L.A., 1983-84; v.p. tax Parsons Corp., Pasadena, Calif., 1975-83, 84—. Mem. Tax Execs. Inst., Tex. Bar Assn., Calif. Bar Assn., Nation Constrn. Assn. (chmn. tax com. 1980-82, 86-87, 90-91).

WOOTEN, FREDERICK (OLIVER), applied science educator; b. Linwood, Pa., May 16, 1928; s. Frederick Alexander and Martha Emma (Guild) W.; m. Jane Watson MacPherson, Aug. 30, 1952; children: Donald, Bartley. BS in Chemistry, MIT, 1950; PhD in Chemistry, U. Del., 1955. Sr. scientist Lawrence Livermore (Calif.) Lab., 1957-72; prof. applied sci. U. Calif., Davis, 1972—, chmn. dept. applied sci., 1973—; vis. prof. physics Drexel U., Phila, 1964, Chalmers Tekniska Högskola, Göteborg, Sweden, 1967-68, Heriot-Watt U., Edinburgh, Scotland, 1979, Trinity Coll., Dublin, Ireland, 1986; staff physicist All-Am. Engring. Co., Wilmington Del., 1955-57; cons. in field. Author: Optical Properties of Solids, 1972. Mem. AAAS, AM. Phys. Soc., N.Y. Acad. Sci., Materials Rsch. Soc., Sigma Xi. Home: 2328 Alameda Diablo Diablo CA 94528-9999 Office: Univ Calif Dept Applied Sci Davis CA 95616

WORCESTER, THOMAS KINNEY, writer; b. Boulder, Colo., Feb. 12, 1929; s. Philip George and Mollie (Brown) W.; m. Lois Eloise Nichols, July 28, 1951; children: Kenneth Lee, Laura Jane Worcester Law, Mollie Anne Worcester McBride, Andrew Thomas. BA, U. Colo., 1950, MA, 1955. Pub. info. dir. Pueblo (Colo.) Coll., 1954-57, The Colo. Coll., Colorado Springs, 1957-59; dir. info. svcs. Reed Coll., Portland, Oreg., 1959-70; editor Touchstone Press, Beaverton, Oreg., 1970-85; bd. dirs. exec. com. Am. Alumni Coun., Washington, 1966-68, dist. chmn. N.W., 1966-67; advisor Willamette Writers, Portland, 1982—. Co-author: NORJAK: Investigation of D.B. Cooper, 1986; author: Gnomenclature, 1989, A Portrait of Oregon, 1973; author, photographer: A Portrait of Colorado, 1975, and others; contbr. articles to profl. jours. Pres. Clackamas County Mental Health Assn., Marylhurst, Oreg., 1986-88, Multnomah County Friends of the Libr., Portland, 1982; bd. dirs. Sisters Habitat for Humanity, 1991—. Lt. comdr. USN, 1950-53, 61-62. Mem. Western Writers Am., N.W. Assn. Book Pubs. (treas. 1989), Nat. Writers Club, Sisters Kiwanis (pres. 1992-93). Democrat. Home and Office: 6059 Tollgate Sisters OR 97759-3006

WORDELL, EDWIN HOWLAND, artist; b. Phila., Aug. 27, 1927; s. Edwin Howland W. and Cathryn (Williams) Burns; m. Laveta Rose Stehr, May 21, 1948 (div.); children: Cathryn L., Thomas A.; m. Marie Cunningham, Oct. 8, 1977; 1 stepchild, Christopher D. Fillius. BS with honors, San Diego State Coll., 1961; student, San Diego Sch. Arts and Crafts, 1951-53, Coronado (Calif.) Sch. Arts, 1954-56. Meatcutter various retail supermarkets, San Diego, 1949-61; spl. agt. U.S. Dept. Treasury, San Diego, 1961-82; artist San Diego, 1956—. With USN, 1945-49. Recipient Morse Graphics award North Coast Collage Soc., 1990, two George Gray awards USCG, 1986, 90. Mem. Nat. Watercolor Soc. (Experimental Painting award 1990), Watercolor West, Rocky Mountain Watermedia Soc., Nat. Soc. Painters in Casein and Acrylic (Elizabeth Erlanger Meml. award 1990), Am. Soc. Marine Artists, Pastel Soc. San Diego, San Diego Mus. Art (trustee), San Diego Mus. Art Artists Guild (pres. 1990-91), San Diego Watercolor Soc. (pres. 1975-76). Home: 6251 Lorca Dr San Diego CA 92115-5507

WORK, STEPHEN WALTER, engineer; b. Pueblo, Colo., Sept. 19, 1944; s. Walter Douglas and Frances (McInnes) W.; m. Carol R. Gaskill, Oct. 6, 1969; children: Jeanne F., Lori K. BSCE, U. Colo., 1968, MSCE, 1969. Asst. hydraulic engr. Denver Water Dept., 1968-70, reclamation engr., 1973-76, mgr. treated water planning and control, 1977-80, mgr. quality control, 1981-83, coordinator spl. projects, 1984-87, chief of water quality and research, 1988-89, dep. dir. water prodn., 1989-91, dir. oper., 1991—; mgr. two forks EIS Denver Water Dept., 1981—, potable water reuse project, 1976-81, Metro Water Study State Legislature, 1974-75. Contbr. articles to profl. jours. Bd. dirs., chmn., Littleton (Colo.) United Meth. Ch., 1985-89. Served to lt. USNR, 1969-73. Mem. Am. Water Works Assn. (chmn. Rocky Mountain sect. 1984-85, Fuller award 1986). Office: Denver Water Dept Denver CO 80254

WORKMAN, ROGER, academic administrator. Pres. Otis/Parsons Sch. Art and Design, L.A. Office: Otis/Parsons Sch Art and Design Office of the President 2401 Wilshire Blvd Los Angeles CA 90057

WORKMAN, WILLIAM GLENN, economics educator, consultant; b. Sheridan, Wyo., Mar. 19, 1947; s. Glenn Chapman and Selma Dale (Peabody) W.; m. Jolene Jorgensen, Jan. 29, 1972; children: Ben, Emily. AA, Sheridan Coll., 1967; BS, U. Wyo., 1969; MA, Utah State U., 1972, PhD, 1978. Asst. prof. econs. U. Alaska, Fairbanks, 1973-79, assoc. prof. econs., 1979-90; vis. prof. econs. Ea. Oreg. State Coll., 1990—, vis. assoc. prof. agrl. and resource econs. U. Md., College Park, 1985-86, Oreg. State U., 1991-92; cons. in field, 1990—, Frank Orth & Assocs., Kirkland, Wash., 1981-82. Contbr. articles to profl. jours. Mem. Western Agrl. Econ. Assn., Am. Econ. Assn., Assn. Environ. & Resource Economists.

WORLEY, KATHRYN ANN, secondary school educator; b. Vallejo, Calif., July 23, 1960; d. Terry Baldridge and Wilma Anita (Wilson) W. BA Applied Arts and Scis., San Diego State U., 1982, MA Liberal Arts, 1991. Cert. secondary sch. tchr., Calif., tech. writing. cert. Adminstrv. asst. athletic dept. San Diego State U., 1984-86, asst. athletic dir., 1986-87; substitute math. tchr. Lakeside Middle Sch., Lakeside (Calif.) Sch. Dist., 1988; indsl. tech. tchr., dept. chmn., softball team coach Mt. MIguel High Sch., Spring Valley, Calif., 1988—; vocat. site specialist Grossmont Union High Sch. Dist., La Mesa, Calif., 1991-92. Mem. Nat. Assn. Sports Ofcls., Soc. for Tech. Communication, Epsilon Pi Tau. Office: Mount Miguel High Sch 1800 Sweetwater Rd Spring Valley CA 91977

WORLEY KATZ, JOYCE MARIE, computer consultant, journalist, game designer, critic; b. Poplar Bluff, Mo., Jan. 9, 1939; d. Cleburn James and Elizabeth (Randles) Worley; m. Raymond Duggie Fisher, July 21, 1956 (div. 1970); m. Arnie Katz, Apr. 25, 1971. Founder, sr. editor Electronic Games mag., 1981-84; ptnr. Katz Kunkel Worley, Las Vegas, Nev., 1984—; mem. judging com. Electronic Games Design Awards; judge Software Pubs. Assn. Critics' Choice Awards, Parents' Choice Video Games; lectr. in field; referee numerous pubs. Author: How to Win at Video Games, 1981; founder, editor: Hot Line, 1982-84; news editor Video Games and Computer Entertainment Mag., 1988-92; co-editor, pub. Megagaming, 1990—; news editor Electronic Games Mag., 1992—; contbr. articles to profl. jours. and popular mags. including Cosmopolitan, Essence, Women's Wear Daily, Games; newspaper columnist; designer: (with Arnie Katz and Bill Kunkel) (computer games) Borrowed Time, 1986, Microleague Baseball II, 1987, Microleague WWF Wrestling, 1987, Omnicron Conspiracy, 1988, Star Trek First Contact, 1988, Circus Games, 1988, First Person Pinball, 1988, Mayday Squad, 1988, Beverly Hills Cop, 1988, Superstars of Wrestling I & II, 1989, Superman: Man of Steel, 1989, Buffalo Bill's Wild West Show & Rodeo, 1989, Roller Coaster Rumbler, 1989, MicroLeague Wrestling II, 1989, MicroLeague Wrestling II Match Disk I, 1990, Championship MicroLeague Baseball, 1990, MicroLeague Football, 1990, Batman Returns, 1992.

WOROBEC, BRUCE WILLIAM, computer systems analyst; b. Montreal, Que., Can., Jan. 9, 1963; came to U.S., 1971; s. William and Marie (Gancer) W. BS magna cum laude, Gonzaga U., 1985; MS, Wash. State U., 1986. Teaching asst. Wash. State U., Pullman, 1985-87; sr. mem. tech. staff, computer systems analyst U S West, Bellevue, 1987-93; pres. Worobec Cons., Renton, Wash., 1993—; bd. dirs. Vis. Nurse Svcs. of Northwest, 1992—. Mem. Assn. for Computing Machinery, Data Resource Mgmt. Assn. Office: 1904 Monterey Ave NE Renton WA 98056

WORRELL, JIMMIE D., insurance executive; b. Clovis, N.Mex., Aug. 9, 1950; s. Raymond W. and Gladys B. (Casey) W.; m. Pamela S. Johnson, Sept. 11, 1969; children: Damon W., Daron W., Amanda J. Grad. pub. schs., Lovington, N.Mex., 1968. CLU. Area mgr. Stell's Sales & Svc., Hobbs, N.Mex., 1972-79; v.p. McNutt-Worrell Agy., Inc., Lovington, N.Mex., 1979-85; dist. agt. Prudential Ins., Lovington, N.Mex., 1985—. Coach Girls Softball/Basketball, Lovington, 1972—; vice chmn. Lovington Housing Authority, 1987. With U.S. Army N.G., 1970-76. Mem. N.Mex. Assn. Life Underwriters (state pres.-elect 1992), Nat. Assn. Life Underwriters (Nat. Achievement award 1990), Lovington C. of C. (ambassador 1989—), Am. Legion. Office: Prudential Ins PO Box 1445 201 E Washington Lovington NM 88260

WORRELL, RICHARD VERNON, orthopedic surgeon, college dean; b. Bklyn., June 4, 1931; s. John Elmer and Elaine (Callender) W.; BA, NYU, 1952; MD, Meharry Med. Coll., 1958; m. Audrey Frances Martiny, June 14, 1958; children: Philip Vernon, Amy Elizabeth. Intern Meharry Med. Coll., Nashville, 1958-59; resident gen. surgery Mercy-Douglass Hosp., Phila., 1960-61; resident orthopaedic surgery State U. N.Y. Buffalo Sch. Medicine Affiliated Hosps., 1961-64; resident in orthopaedic pathology Temple U. Med. Ctr., Phila., 1966-67; pvt. practice orthopaedic surgery, Phila., 1964-68; asst. prof. acting head div. orthopaedic surgery U. Conn. Sch. Medicine 1968-70; attending orthopaedic surgeon E.J. Meyer Meml. Hosp., Buffalo, Millard Fillmore Hosp., Buffalo, VA Hosp., Buffalo, Buffalo State Hosp.; clin. instr. orthopaedic surgery SUNY, Buffalo, 1970-74; chief orthopedic surgery VA Hosp., Newington, Conn., 1974-80; asst. prof. surgery (orthopaedics) U. Conn. Sch. Medicine, 1974-77, assoc. prof., 1977-83, asst. dean student affairs, 1980-83; prof. clin. surgery SUNY Downstate Med. Ctr., Bklyn., 1983-86; dir. orthopedic surgery Brookdale Hosp. Med. Ctr., Bklyn., 1983-86; prof. of orthopaedics U. N.Mex. Sch. of Medicine, 1986—; dir. orthopedic oncology U. N.Mex. Med. Ctr., 1987—; mem. med. staff U. N.Mex. Cancer Ctr., 1987—; chief orthopaedic surgery VA Med. Ctr., Albuquerque, 1987—; cons. in orthopaedic surgery Newington (Conn.) Children's Hosp., 1968-70; mem. sickle cell disease adv. com. NIH, 1982-86. Bd. dirs. Big Bros. Greater Hartford. Served to capt. M.C., U.S. Army Res., 1962-69. Diplomate Am. Bd. Orthopaedic Surgery, Nat. Bd. Med. Examiners. Fellow ACS, Am. Acad. Orthopaedic Surgeons,Royal Soc. Medicine, London; mem. Am. Orthopaedic Assn., Orthopaedic Rsch. Soc., Internat. Soc. Orthopaedic Surgery and Traumatology, AMA, Alpha Omega Alpha.

WORRILOW, RICHARD CHARLES, small business owner; b. L.A., Feb. 28, 1944; s. Richard Morris and Helen Elizabeth (Charleston) W.; m. Janice Joanne Ludwick, Mar. 9, 1944 (div. Dec. 1977); 1 child, Lisa Anne. BA in Polit. Sci., Calif. State U., Northridge, 1971; MS in Recreation Mgmt., Calif. State U., L.A., 1978. Profl. model Robert Black Agy., Tempe, Ariz., 1958—; sr. account rep. Travelers Ins. Co., L.A., Hartford, Conn., 1971-85; owner Villa Maria Pasta Products, Mesa, Ariz., 1987-88; ptnr. Rickman Assocs., Scottsdale, 1987-88; owner Gourmet Imports, Phoenix, 1982—, Scottsdale Cookie Co., 1985-89, Vis a'Vis, Phoenix, 1984—. Pres. Men's League of Scottsdale, 1986-87. With U.S. Army, 1966-69, Vietnam. Mem. Scottsdale C. of C., Phoenix C. of C. Republican. Office: Gourmet Imports 128 E Wood Dr Phoenix AZ 85022-5236

WORTH, CATHERINE ANNE, audiologist; b. Grand Rapids, Mich., Feb. 13, 1952; d. Harold E. and Phyllis C. W. BA, U. No. Colo., 1974; MSc, Colo. State U., 1977. Clin. audiologist Lovelace Med. Ctr., Albuquerque, 1978-83, dir. audiology, 1983-92; audiologist in pvt. practice Family Hearing Ctr., Albuquerque, 1992—. Contbr. articles to profl. jours. Treas. N.Mex. Assn. of People Living with AIDS, Albuquerque, 1989-90. Lovelace Med. Ctr. grantee, 1981-82; recipient Nat. Disting. Svcs. Registry award, 1990. Fellow N.Mex. Speech-Lang.-Hearing Assn. (pres.-elect 1991-93, treas. 1986-89), Am. Speech & Hearing Assn. (site visitor 1985-92). Office: Family Hearing Ctr 8400 Menaul NE Albuquerque NM 87112

WORTHEY, CAROL, composer; b. Worcester, Mass., Mar. 1, 1943; d. Bernard Krieger and Edith Lilian (Cramer) Symonds; m. Eugene Worthey III, June 1969 (div. 1980); 1 child, Megan; m. Raymond Edward Korns, Sept. 21, 1980. BA in Music Composition, Columbia U., 1965; grad., Dick Grove Sch. Music., L.A., 1979; grad. filmscoring prog., UCLA, 1978; music studies with Darius Milhaud, Walter Piston, Elliot Carter, Vincent Persichetti, Grant Beglarian, Karl Korte, Otto Luening, Eddy Lawrence Manson, Dick Grove. Sr. composer, arranger Celebrity Ctr. Internat. Choir, Hollywood, Calif., 1985—. Composer, arranger The Hollywood Chorale; composer ballets Athena, 1963, The Barren, 1965; composer, lyricist, librettist full-length musical The Envelope Please, 1988; composer piano works performed in France, Italy, Germany, Can., U.S. and Eng. by Mario Feninger, 1982; composer filmscore The Special Visitor, 1992; compositions performed at Aspen Music Festival, 1963, Carnegie Hall, 1954, Dorothy Chandler Pavilion, 1986-89; appeared as singer-songwriter on L.A. Songwriter's Showcase, 1977; arranger Merv Griffin Show, 1981, The Night Before Christmas, L.A. Children's Theatre, 1988-91. Vol. performer various childcare ctrs., old folks homes, etc. Recipient Silver Poet award World of Poetry, 1987, 2nd place winner, 1st BarComposers and Songwriters Competition for "Fanfare for Joy & Wedding March", 1990, Golden Poet award World of Poetry, 1992. Mem. Nat. Assn. Composers, USA, Broadcast Music Inc., Nat. Acad. Songwriters, Songwriters and Composers Assn. Jewish.

WORTHINGTON, ELLIOTT ROBERT, nonfiction writer, journalism educator; b. New Milford, Conn., May 5, 1937; s. Elmer Harry and Mildred (Knight) W.; m. Anita Elliott, Sept. 3, 1959; children: Susan W. Bontly, Julie W. Coley, Karen L. BA in Art, Dartmouth Coll., 1961; MA in Counseling, No. Ariz. U., 1970; MA in Bus. Adminstrn., Webster U., 1978; PhD in Ednl. Psychology, U. Utah, 1973. Cpl. USMC, 1957-59; comd. 2d lt. U.S. Army, 1961, advanced through grades to maj., left active duty, 1969; returned to active duty as clin. psychologist U.S. Army Med. Dept., 1971, ret. as lt. col., 1981; mgmt. prof. Sch. of Bus. West Tex. State U., Canyon, 1981-87; prof. dept. of journalism N.Mex. State U., Las Cruces, 1989—; nonfiction writer, 1967—; vis. prof. mgmt. Coll. of Bus., N.Mex. State U., Las Cruces, 1987-88; owner, cons. Worthington & Worthington mgmt. Cons., San Antonio and Canyon, Tex., 1974-87; dir., cons. WTSU Sml. Bus. Devel. Ctr., Canyon, 1983-87. Co-author: (books) Staffing a Small Business, 1985, 87, People Investment, 1993; contbr. 600 articles on aviation, bus., travel and journalism to profl. publs. Pub. rels. chair N.Mex. Coun. Vietnam Vets. of Am., 1989-92. Decorated Combat Infantry badge, Legion of Merit, 7 awards for valor, Purple Heart, Air medal; recipient 2 teaching awards West Tex. State U., 1984-86; Gannett Teaching grantee Freedom Forum, U. N.C., 1992. Mem. Aviation and Space Writers Assn. (dir. 1990—), U.S. Pilots Assn. (v.p., pres. 1985—, dir., Mem. of Yr. 1985), N.Mex. Pilots Assn. (dir. 1987—), Assn. Edn. in Journalism and Mass Communication, Southwestern Small Bus. Inst. Assn. (v.p. 1987-88), Am. Advt. Fedn. (faculty advisor 1989—), Phi Kappa Phi. Home: 1840 Las Tunas Cas Cruces NM 88001 Office: NMex State U Dept Journalism Las Cruces NM 88003

WORTHY, JAMES, professional basketball player; b. Gastonia, N.C., Feb. 27, 1961; m. Angela Worthy. Grad., U. N.C., 1985. Forward L.A. Lakers, 1982—; mem. NBA championship team, 1985, 87, 88. Named MVP, NBA playoffs, 1988, mem. All-Star team, 1986-92. Office: LA Lakers PO Box 10 Inglewood CA 90306-0010

WOSKOW, ROBERT MARSHALL, management consultant; b. N.Y.C., Aug. 1, 1951; s. Martin and Marion (Kloder) W.; m. Gail Berrin, Apr. 1, 1979; children: Belle Ilysa, Benjamin Hale. BSEE, UCLA, 1973; MSEE, Calif. State U., Northridge, 1976; MBA, Pepperdine U., 1982. Elec. engr. various orgns., L.A., 1973-84; engring. dir. Arts and Sci. Tech., L.A., 1984-85; programs mgr. Pacesetter Systems, Sylmar, Calif., 1985-87; chief exec. officer Robert Marshall and Assocs., Encino, Calif., 1982—. Patentee in field. Home and Office: Robert Marshall and Assocs 16801 Severo Pl Encino CA 91436-4033

WOTT, JOHN ARTHUR, horticulture educator; b. Fremont, Ohio, Apr. 10, 1939; s. Arthur Otto Louis and Esther Wilhelmina (Werth) W.; children: Christopher, Timothy, Holly. BS, Ohio State U., 1961; MS, Cornell U., 1966, PhD, 1968. Mem. staff Ohio State Coop. Extension Svc., Bowling Green, 1961-64; rsch. asst. Cornel U., Ithaca, N.Y., 1964-68; prof. Purdue U., West Lafayette, Ind., 1968-81; prof. Ctr. Urban Horticulture U. Wash., Seattle, 1981—; assoc. dir. Ctr. Urban Horticulture U. Wash., Seattle, 1990—; dir. arboreta Washington Park Arboretum, Seattle, 1993—. Contbr. numerous papers to profl. jours. Mem. Am. Soc. Horticultural Sci. (com. chmn. 1967-82), Am. Assn. Botanic Gardens and Arboreta, Internat. Plant Propagators Soc. (pres. 1984, sec.-treas. 1985—). Office: U Wash Washington Park Arboretum XD-10 Seattle WA 98195

WOUDENBERG, PAUL RICHARD, chaplain; b. Highland Park, Ill., Sept. 1, 1927; s. John Anton and Rosina Wilhelmina (Maechtle) W.; m. Emily Wiltse, June 5, 1967; children: Mary C., Elizabeth L. BA, Occidental Coll., 1949; MDiv, Boston U., 1952, PhD, 1959. Ordained to ministry Meth. Ch., 1952. Minister Echo Park United Meth. Ch., L.A., 1954-61, Calif. Heights United Meth. Ch., Long Beach, Calif., 1961-67, 1st United Meth. Ch., Santa Monica, Calif., 1968-76, Ch. of the Wayfarer, Carmel, Calif., 1975-86; chaplain Robert Louis Stevenson Sch., Pebble Beach, Calif., 1986—. Author: Ford in the Thirties, 1976, Lincoln--The Postwar Years, 1980, Buyer's Guide to Rolls Royce, 1984, Buyer's Guide to Fords, 1987, Buyer's Guide to Lincolns, 1990. Served with USN, 1945-46. Republican. Home: PO Box 1583 Pebble Beach CA 93953-1583

WOWK, VICTOR, mechanical engineer; b. Auschaffenburg, Fed. Republic Germany, Mar. 29, 1948; came to U.S., 1949; s. Wasyl and Maria (Chmil) W.; m. Rose Mary Mello, May 10, 1975; children: Roman M., Nicholas E., Andrew W., Paul V. BS in Mech. Engring., U. Mich., 1975. Registered profl. engr., New Mex. Prodn. engr. Hewlett Packard, Loveland, Colo., 1979-86; sr. engr. Honeywell, Albuquerque, New Mex., 1987-88; owner, prin. Machine Dynamics, Albuquerque, 1987—; cons. engr. Sandia Nat. Labs., Albuquerque, 1989—, Los Alamos (N.Mex.) Nat. Lab., 1991—. Author: Machinery Vibration: Measurement and Analysis, 1991. Capt. USAF, 1975-79. Mem. Vibration Inst., Tau Beta Pi. Republican. Home and Office: Machine Dynamics 10117 Trevino Loop NW Albuquerque NM 87114

WOYCHIK, ERIC CHARLES, energy and resources consultant; b. Portsmouth, Ohio, May 3, 1953; s. Robert Alexander and Janice (Acomb) W.; m. Deborah Davidson, Oct. 23, 1983; 1 child, David. AA in Biology, Diablo Valley Coll., Pleasant Hill, Calif., 1977; BS in Environ. Planning-Policy Analysis, U. Calif., Davis, 1980; MS in Econs., N.Mex. State U., 1991. Policy analyst Lawrence Berkeley (Calif.) Labs., 1978-79, D.A.T.A., Davis, 1979-81, Calif. Energy Commn., Sacramento, 1981-83; regulatory specialist Calif. Pub. Utilities Commn., San Francisco, 1983-85, advisor to commr., 1985-90; mgr. utility econs. Synergic Resources Corp., Oakland, Calif., 1990—. Contbr. articles to various publs. Chmn. Davis Electricity Load Mgmt. Com., 1980, vice chmn., 1981-82. Recipient award for one of top 10 environ. law jour. articles in U.S., Case Western Res. Sch. Law, 1981. Mem. Internat. Energy Econs. Assn. (referee IAEE: The Energy Jour. 1989—). Democrat. Baptist. Office: Synergic Resources Corp 1300 Clay St Ste 600 Oakland CA 94612

WOYSKI, MARGARET SKILLMAN, retired geology educator; b. West Chester, Pa., July 26, 1921; d. Willis Rowland and Clara Louise (Howson) Skillman; m. Mark M. Woyski, June 19, 1948; children: Nancy Elizabeth, William Bruno, Ronald David, Wendelin Jane. BA in Chemistry, Wellesley (Mass.) Coll., 1943; MS in Geology, U. Minn., 1945, PhD in Geology, 1946. Geologist Mo. Geol. Survey and Water Resources, Rolla, 1946-48; instr. U. Wis., Madison, 1948-52; lectr. Calif. State U., Long Beach, 1963-67; lectr. to prof. Calif. State U., Fullerton, 1966-91, assoc. dean Sch. Natural Sci. and Math., 1981-91, emeritus prof., 1991—. Contbr. articles to profl. jours.; author lab. manuals; editor 4 guidebooks. Fellow Geol. Soc. Am. (program chmn. 1982); mem. South Coast Geol. Soc. (hon. pres. 1974), Mineral Soc. Am. Home: 1843 Kashlan Rd La Habra CA 90631-8423

WOYTEK, STEVE EDWARD, secondary education educator, coach; b. Denver, July 25, 1949; s. Steve John and Mary Jean (Bernard) W.; m. Ruth Irene Reece, June 16, 1973; children: Jeff, Justin, Jimmy. AA, Trinidad (Colo.) Jr. Coll., 1969; BA in Bus., Western State Coll., Gunnison, Colo., 1971, MA in Edn., 1980. Tchr. bus. Denver Pub. Schs., 1971-78, Gunnison Pub. Schs., 1978-86; prin. Gunnison High Sch., 1986-87, tchr. bus., 1987—; football coach asst. Denver West High Sch., 1971-78; baseball coach asst. Denver Pub. Schs., 1971-78; football coach asst. Gunnison High Sch., 1978—, head and asst. baseball coach, 1978—, sponsor DECA, 1978—. Dir. Old Timers Baseball, City of Gunnison, 17 yrs., Babe Ruth Summer Baseball, City of Gunnison, 10 yrs. Named Coach of Yr., Gunnison Valley Conf. Baseball Coaches; named to Outstanding Young Men in Am., 1986. Mem. Colo. High Sch. Coaches Assn., Am. Baseball Coaches Assn., Colo. Baseball Assn., Colo. High Sch. Activities Assn. (mem. com. 1992—), Fellowship of Christian Athletes (sponsor various club activities). Democrat. Roman Catholic. Home: 315 S Teller Gunnison CO 81230 Office: Gunnison Pub Schs 215 W Georgia Gunnison CO 81230

WOZNIAK, JOYCE MARIE, sales executive; b. Detroit, Aug. 3, 1955; d. Edmund Frank and Bernice (Liske) W. BA, Mich. State U., 1976; MA, Nat. U., San Diego, 1988; postgrad., U.S. Internat. U., 1989—. Probation officer San Diego County Probation, 1979-81; prodn. engr. Tuesday Prodns., Inc., San Diego, 1981-85; nat. sales mgr. Advance Rec. Products, San Diego, 1986-88; owner Joyce Enterprises, San Diego, 1986—; sales exec. Audio-Video Supply Inc., San Diego, 1988—. Producer (video) Loving Yourself, 1987, southwest cable access program, 1986—, Registered Marriage, Family, and Child Counselor-Intern, California, 1989. Active Zool. Soc. San Diego. Mem. Art Glass Assn. So. calif., Calif. assn. Marriage and Family Therapists, Internat. TV Assn. (treas. San Diego chpt. 1990-91).

WRAGG, LAURENCE EDWARD, university administrator; b. Toronto, Ont., Can., Aug. 12, 1921; s. Thomas Wragg and Mary Jane Houseman; children: Debrah, Cathey, Trent, Darinda, Martin, Sandford. BA, McMaster U., 1946; MA, U. Toronto, 1951; PhD, U. Wis., 1955; MD, Northwestern U., 1962. Diplomate Am. Bd. Family Practice. Asst. prof. U. Tex. Dental Br., Houston, 1955-58; asst. prof. Northwestern U., Chgo., 1958-61, assoc. prof., 1963-67; resident Contra Costa County Hosp., Martinez, Calif., 1971-72; pvt. practice Colusa, Calif., 1972-86; chief staff Colusa County Hosp., 1975-77; med. dir. Valley West Convalescent Hosp., Williams, Calif., 1984-86; dir. Student Health Ctr. Calif. State U.-Stanislaus, Turlock, 1986—. Author 20 teaching films in anatomy, 1968. Office: Calif State U 801 W Monte Vista Turlock CA 95380

WRALSTAD, PHILLIP EVANS, electronic engineer; b. Grand Forks, N.D., Nov. 11, 1932; s. Carl Manvil and Ellen Amanda (Evens) W.; m. Mickie L. Thornton; children: Mark Evans, Beth Ellen Wralstad Voltmann, Laurie Ann Wralstad Lacy. BSEE, U. N.D., 1956; postgrad., U. Denver, 1961, U. Ariz., 1964-65; MPA, U. Okla., 1974. Chief engr. test div. U.S. Army Security Agy. Test and Evaluation Ctr., Ft. Huachuca, Ariz., 1967-77, U.S. Army Electronic Proving Ground, Ft. Huachuca, Ariz., 1977-78; tech. dir. U.S. Army Intelligence and Security Bd., Ft. Huachuca, Ariz., 1978-89; tech dir. Intelligence Electronic Warfare Test Directorate, Ft. Huachuca, Ariz., 1989—. Mem. Sierra Vista (Ariz.) Sch. Bd., 1972-76, clk., 1974, pres., 1975. Capt. U.S. Army, 1957-63. Mem. IEEE (sr., sect. pres. 1970), Armed Forces Communications and Electronics Assn., Assn. Old Crows (bd. dirs. Ft. Huachuca chpt. 1980-83, 88-91, Tau Kappa Epsilon, Huachucans Club, Rotary Internat. (pres. Sierra Vista chpt. 1971, v.p. 1972). Republican. Lutheran. Home: 1264 Yucca Dr Sierra Vista AZ 85635-4220 Office: Intelligence Electronic Warfare Test Dir Fort Huachuca AZ 85613

WRAY, KARL, newspaper broker, former newspaper owner and publisher; b. Bishop, Tex., June 8, 1913; s. Ernest Paul and Gertrude (Garvin) W.; m. Flora-Lee Koepp, Aug. 11, 1951; children: Diana, Mark, Kenneth, Norman, Thomas. A.B., Columbia U., 1935. Auditor U.S. Dept. Agr., Washington, also Little Rock, 1935-37; salesman O'Mara & Ormsbee, Inc., N.Y.C., 1937-42; advt. mgr. Lompoc (Calif.) Record, 1947-54; owner, pub. San Clemente (Calif.) Daily Sun-Post, 1954-67, Coastline Dispatch, San Juan Capistrano, Calif., 1956-67, Dana Point (Calif.) Lamplighter, 1966-67; cons. Lear Siegler, Inc., Washington, 1967-68; pub. Daily Star-Progress, La Habra, Calif., 1969-74, Anaheim (Calif.) Bulletin, 1974-86. Mem. Calif. State Park Commn., 1960-64, vice chmn., 1961-62; mem. exec. bd. Orange County coun. Boy Scouts Am., 1961-64, 76-87; mem. citizens adv. com. Orange Coast Coll., 1963-66; bd. dirs. Calif. Newspaper Youth Found., 1974-84; founder, first pres. Freedom Bowl, Inc., Anaheim, Calif., 1981-84, chmn. bd., 1984-86, bd. dirs., 1986—; authenticated, registered, established Calif. State Hist. Landmarks La Cristianita 1st baptism and Las Flores Asistencia. Mem. Calif. Newspaper Advt. Execs. Assn. (pres. 1952-53), Calif. Newspaper Pubs. Assn. (dir. 1960-64), Am. Theatre Critics Assn., Baseball Writers Assn. Am., Football Writers Assn. Am., Calif. Press Assn., San Juan Capistrano C. of C. (pres. 1966), San Clemente C. of C. (pres. 1956-57), La Habra C. of C. (dir. 1970-74), Anaheim C. of C. (dir. 1974-86). Presbyterian (elder). Address: 2420 S Ola Vista San Clemente CA 92672-4360

WRAY, LARRY RANDALL, economics educator; b. Eureka, Calif., June 19, 1953; s. Allen Leroy and Irene (Culver) W.; m. Shona Kelly, Aug. 11, 1990. BA in Social Scis., U. Pacific, Stockton, Calif., 1976; postgrad., Calif. State U., Sacramento; MA, Washington U., St. Louis, 1985; PhD, Washington U., 1988. Asst. adminstrv. analyst Sacramento County, 1977-82; grad. rsch. asst. Energy Resources Commn., Sacramento, 1982-83; econs. instr. Washington U., St. Louis, 1985-86, St. Louis Community Coll., St. Louis, 1986; asst. prof. econs. U. Denver, 1987—; lectr. in field; conductor seminars in field; nat. referee Nat. Social Sci. Jour., Jour. Econ. Issues, Am. Economist, Jour. of Post Keynesian Econs., The Social Sci. Jour.; resident scholar The Jerome Levy Econs. Inst., Annandale-on-Hudson, N.Y., 1992-93. Author: Money and Credit in Capitalist Economies: The Endogenous Money Approach, 1990; contbr. articles to profl. jours. Fulbright prog. advisor U. Denver. John Stuart Mill fellow, 1983-84, fellow Washington U., 1984-85, Fulbright fellow, Bologna, Italy, 1986-87. Mem. Missouri Valley Econ. Assn., Midwest Econ. Assn., Ea. Econ. Assn., Assn. for Evolutionary Thought, Western Social Sci. Assn., Phi Beta Delta. Office: Econs Dept Univ Denver Denver CO 80208

WRAY, TOM CHARLES, state senator, electrical engineering consultant; b. Converse, La., Feb. 4, 1949; s. Joe O. Wray and Joyce (Tyler) Griffin; 1 child, Tyler Mark Manning-Wray. BSEE, La. State U., 1971; MBA, U. N.Mex., 1984; MSEE, Colo. U., 1988. Cert. profl. engr., N.Mex. Div. engr. Pub. Svc. Commn. of N.Mex., Santa Fe, 1972-75; sr. distbn. standards engr. Pub. Svc. Commn. of N.Mex., Albuquerque, 1975-77; supervising engr. Albuquerque div. Pub. Svc. Commn. of N.Mex., 1977-78, mgr. div. svcs., 1978-84, mgr. strategic planning, 1988; exec. v.p., sec., treas. Dineh Power Project, Albuquerque, 1984-88; cons. Mgmt. Analysis Co., San Diego, 1988-90; ptnr. Groves, Wray & Assoc., Albuquerque, 1991—; mem. N.Mex. State Senate, Albuquerque, 1993—. Exec. v.p. N.Mex. Cystic Fibrosis Found., Albuquerque, 1987—; bd. dirs. U.S. Selective Svc. System Region IV, 1988—; legis. asst. Sen. Les Houston, Albuquerque, 1989. Mem. IEEE, Am. Mgmt. Assn., Nat. Soc. Profl. Engrs. Republican. Home: 1835 Tramway Terrace Loop NE Albuquerque NM 87122-1325

WREDEN, WILLIAM PAUL, rancher, book seller, book publisher; b. Petaluma, Calif., May 2, 1910; s. William P. and Elizabeth E. (Prien) W.; m. Byra J. Smith, Aug. 1, 1936; children : William P. Jr., Paula J. Wreden Campbell, Douglas V., Phillip R., Denise V.B. AB, Stanford U., 1934. Statistician Anglo-Calif. Nat. Bank, San Francisco, 1935-37; owner Wm. P. Wreden Books & Manuscripts, Burlingame, Calif., 1937-53, Wm. P. Wreden Books & Mss., Palo Alto, Calif., 1953—, Pinole Land & Cattle Co., Santa Margarita, Calif., 1941—. Author: Antonio Maglibechi Bibliomaniac Extraordinaire, 1984. Fellow Gleeson Libr. Assocs. Univ. San Francisco; mem. Antiquarian Booksellers Assn. Am., Book Club Calif., Grolier Club, Roxburghe Club, Bibliographical Soc., History of Sci. Soc. Republican.

WRIGHT, ALDEN HALBERT, computer science educator; b. Missoula, Mont., Apr. 23, 1942; s. Philip Lincoln and Margaret (Halbert) W.; m. Sally Weber Fant, Mar. 23, 1967; children: Eric, Kevin. AB, Dartmouth Coll., 1964; PhD, U. Wis., 1969. Asst. prof., assoc. prof., prof. Western Mich. U., Kalamazoo, 1970-83; prof. U. Mont., Missoula, 1983—. Grad. fellow NSF, 1964. Mem. Phi Beta Kappa. Office: U Mont Computer Sci Dept Missoula MT 59812

WRIGHT, BARTON ALLEN, ethnologist, author; b. Bisbee, Ariz., Dec. 21, 1920; s. Roy Joline and Anna Sophronia (Harris) W.; m. Margaret Anna Nickelson, Apr. 16, 1949; children: Frances Elena, Matthew Allen. BA, U. Ariz., 1952, MA, 1954. Tech. illustrator Ariz. State Mus., 1946-53; archaeologist N.C. State U., 1949-41; archaeologist, artist Amerind Found., Dragoon, Ariz., 1953-55; curator exhibits Mus. No. Ariz., Flagstaff, 1955-56, curator mus., 1956-76; asst. dir. mus. Mus. of No. Ariz., Flagstaff, 1976-77; sci. dir. San Diego Mus. of Man, 1978-82; rsch. anthropologist Heard Mus., Phoenix, 1983—; contractor Nat. Park Svc., 1955-82; cons. Nat. Geographic Soc., Washington, 1965-85; bd. dirs. Indian Arts & Crafts Assn., Albuquerque. Author: Kachinas, Hopi Artist, 1973, (Wolfe award 1984), Hopi Kachinas, 1977, Zuni Kachinas, 1986 (S.W. Librs. award), Mythic World of the Zuni, 1988, Hallmarks of the Southwest, 1989; author, artist: Unchanging Hopi, 1975 (Rounce award 1975). Committeman Bicentennial/Centennial, Flagstaff, 1976, Hopi Cultural Values, Hopi Reservation, Ariz., 1976—; rep. Western Mus. League, Flagstaff, 1977—; judge Intertribal Ceremonial, Gallup, N.Mex., 1964-90. With U.S. Army, 1943-46, PTO. Harvey Found. fellow, 1965-77; NEA grantee, 1974, NEH grantee, 1975, NSF grantee, 1978; Inst. Mus. Svcs. scholar, 1979. Mem. Am. Assn. Mus. (accreditor 1970-80), Ariz. Nev. Acad. Sci. (charter), Western Regional History Assn. Home: 4143 W Gelding Dr Phoenix AZ 85023-5327

WRIGHT, BERNARD, artist; b. Pitts., Feb. 23, 1938; s. Garfield and Emma (Jefferson) W.; m. Corrine Westley, Mar. 7, 1964; 1 son, Jeffrey. Student Otis Art Inst., Los Angeles, 1969-70, Los Angeles Trade Tech. Coll., 1971-73. Exhibited traveling art show Moscow, Baku, Leningrad, Alma Alta, USSR, European capitals, 1966, Los Angeles City Hall Rotunda Gallery, 1967, Calif. Lutheran Coll., Thousand Oaks, 1967, Alley Gallery, Beverly Hills, 1968, Florenz Art Gallery, Los Angeles, 1969, San Diego Mus., 1969, Phillip E. Freed Gallery of Fine Arts, Chgo., 1969, Art West Gallery, Los Angeles, 1973, N.J. State Mus., Trenton, Detroit Inst. Arts, Mich., 1974, U. So. Calif., Calif. Mus. Sci. and Industry, 1974, City Art Mus., St. Louis, 1976, N.Y.C. Pub. Library, 1977, Pitts. City Hall Rotunda, 1982, The Mus. of African Am. Art, Los Angeles, 1982, Main Bridge Art Gallery, Los Angeles City Hall, 1983; represented in pvt. and pub. collections including Howard U., Library of Congress. collections past pres. co-founder Wright's & Westley Prodns., furniture and garment designers. Cited by U.S. Rep. Cardiss Collins, Ill., 1978, state senator Bill Greene, Calif, 1981, Mayor Richard S. Callguiri, Pitts., 1981, Mayor Coleman A. Young, Detroit, 1981, Mayor Tom Bradley, Los Angeles. bd. supr. Kenneth Hahn, Los Angeles, 1981; active community involvement Sta. KHJ-TV, 1982. Mem. Art West Assn. (bd. dirs.). Contbr. articles to profl. jours. Home: PO Box 76169 Los Angeles CA 90076-0169

WRIGHT, CAROLE YVONNE, chiropractor; b. Long Beach, Calif., July 12, 1932; d. Paul Burt and Mary Leoan (Staley) Fickes; 1 child, Morgan Michelle. D. Chiropractic, Palmer Coll., Davenport, Iowa, 1976. Instr. Palmer Coll., 1975-76; dir., owner Wright Chiropractic Clinic, Rocklin, Calif., 1978-88, Woodland, Calif., 1980-81; co-owner Ft. Sutter Chiropractic Clinic, Sacramento, 1985-89; owner Wright Chiropractic Health Ctr., Sacramento, 1989—, Capitol Chiropractic, Sacramento, 1993—; practice mgmt. cons. Fortune Practice Mgmt; cons. in field; lectr., speaker on radio and TV programs, at seminars. Contbr. articles to profl. jours. Co-chmn. Harold Michaels for Congress campaign, Alameda, Calif., 1972; dist. dir. 14th Congl. Dist., 1983—. Mem. Internat. Chiropractic Assn. Calif. (bd. dirs. 1978-81, pres. 1983-85), Palmer Coll. Alumni Assn. (Calif. state pres. 1981-83), Rocklin C. of C. (bd. dirs. 1979-81). Republican. Avocations: reading, travel. Home: 1404 Stonebridge Way Roseville CA 95661-5456 Office: Capitol Chiropractic 1972 Stockton Blvd Sacramento CA 95816

WRIGHT, CHARLES LEE, information systems consultant; b. Dalton, Ga., Dec. 18, 1949; s. Charlie William and Catherine Christine (Quarles) W.; children: Charles Lee, Christina. AA in Bus., Dalton Jr. Coll., 1971; BS in Bus., U. Tenn., Chattanooga, 1977; also numerous IBM classes on various machines and systems;. Trainee Ludlow Carpets, Dalton, 1971, EDP supr., 1971-73, EDP mgr., 1973-77; ops. mgr. Walter Carpet Mills, Industry, Calif., 1977-80; ptnr., cons. TCT Systems, San Dimas, Calif., 1978-81; ptnr., CEO Williams, Wright and Assocs., Upland, Calif., 1981—; dir. MIS Roland Corp., U.S., 1993—. Served as sgt. U.S. Army, 1969-71; Vietnam, Cambodia. Decorated Bronze Star, Army Commendation medal with oak leaf and oak leaf cluster, Air medal. Mem. Data Processing Mgmt. Assn., Am. Mgmt. Assn., Small Systems User Group, COMMON. Home and Office: 1401 San Bernadino Rd # M Upland CA 91786 Office: 400 N Mountain Ave Upland CA 91786-5176

WRIGHT, CHARLEYE TAZE, broadcast executive; b. Inglewood, Calif., Mar. 24, 1937; s. C.T. Wright and Marie Elizabeth (Coen) Burton; m. Rebecca Anne Borgert, Nov. 23, 1973; children: April Clarisse, Justin Wallace, Amber Marie. BA in English and Greek, Baylor U., 1962, MA in English, 1964; PhD in English, UCLA, 1967. English tchr. Richfield High Sch., Waco, Tex., 1962-64; newscaster KIIS, KNX, KLAC radio, L.A., 1965-76, KRLD, KLIF radio, Dallas, 1976-81; dir. news and sports KIIS radio, L.A., 1982-90; computer programmer self-employed, L.A., 1986—; dir. news and sports KKBT radio, L.A., 1990—. Author: Genes Are Just a Pair of Pants, 1980, Coachcap Handicapper, 1988; programmer Coachcap data base, 1989. Hon. mayor Long Beach,1986, parade grand marshall Corona, Calif., 1985, 1987; bd. dirs. Athletes and Entertainers for Kids, L.A., 1985-90, So. Calif. Organ Procurement, 1988—, pub. speaker, L.A., 1982—, fund raiser L.A. Transplant Inst., 1986—. With USAF, 1957-58. Named Sportscaster of the Yr. Golden Mike awards, L.A., 1974, 1976, 1983; Man of the Yr. Nat. Kidney Found., 1987. Office: Evergreen Broadcasting Corp 6735 Yucca St Los Angeles CA 90028

WRIGHT, CHATT GRANDISON, academic administrator; b. San Mateo, Calif., Sept. 17, 1941; s. Virgil Tandy and Louise (Jeschien) W.; m. Charlotte Elaine Foster, June 8, 1967; children: Stephen Brook, Jon David, Shelley Adams. Student, U. Calif., Berkeley, 1960-62; BA in Polit. Sci., U. Calif., Davis, 1964; MA in Econs., U. Hawaii, 1968. Instr. econs. U. Hawaii, Honolulu, 1968-70; mgr. corp. planning Telecheck Internat., Inc., Honolulu, 1969-70; economist State of Hawaii, Honolulu, 1970-71; adminstr. manpower City & County of Honolulu, 1971-72; bus. adminstr., dean. Hawaii Pacific U., Honolulu, 1972-74, v.p., 1974-76, pres., 1976—. Commr. City and County of Honolulu Manpower Area Planning Commn., 1976-82; Mayor's Salary Commn. City and County of Honolulu, 1977-80; ethics commr. Honolulu City Ethics Commn., 1978-84; coun. mem. City and County of Honolulu Labor Market Adv. Coun., 1982-84; bd. dirs. Hawaii Econ. Devel. Corp., 1980-84; trustee Queen's Med. Ctr., Honolulu, 1986-92, Honolulu Armed Svcs. YMCA, 1984-86, Hist. Hawaii Found., 1990—, Hawaii Maritime Ctr., 1990-92; mem. adv. bd. Cancer Rsch. Ctr. Hawaii, 1987; bd. dirs. Downtown Improvement Assn., 1988—; bd. govs. Hawaii Med. Libr., 1989-92; mem. adv. bd. Aloha coun. Boy Scouts Am., 1991—; trustee Molokai Gen. Hosp., 1991-92; bd. govs. Plaza Club, 1992—. Served with USN, 1967-80. Mem. Am. Assn. Higher Edn., Coun. of Pres. for Nat. Assn. Intercollegiate Athletics (bd. dirs. 1985-90), Hawaii Joint Coun. on Econ. Edn. (bd. dirs. 1982-88), Western Coll. Assn. (exec. com. 1989-92), Hawaii Assn. Ind. Colls. and Univs. (chmn. 1986), Hawaii C. of C., Sales and Mktg. Execs. Club of Honolulu, Outrigger Canoe Club, Pacific Club. Plaza Club, Oahu Country Club, Rotary (Paul Harris fellow 1986). Mem. Hawaii C. of C., Am. Assn. Higher Edn., Sales and Mktg. Execs. Club of Honolulu, Hawaii Assn. Ind. Colls. and Univs. (chmn. 1986), Coun. of Pres. for Nat. Assn. Intercollegiate Athletics (bd. dirs. 1985-90), Hawaii Joint Coun. on Econ. Edn. (bd. dirs. 1982-88), Western Coll. Assn. (exec. com. 1989-92), Outrigger Canoe Club, Pacific Club (Honolulu), Plaza Club (bd. govs. 1992—), Dahu Country Club, Rotary (Paul Harris fellow 1986). Republican. Episcopalian. Office: Hawaii Pacific U Office Pres 1166 Fort Street Mall Honolulu HI 96813-2717

WRIGHT, DAVID LEE, special events producer, design consultant; b. Peoria, Ill., Nov. 8, 1946; s. Lowell Grandon Wright and Helen Joann (Snyder) Hohstadt; m. Barbara Jane Wick, 1971 (div. 1974); 1 child, Rachael Elizabeth. BA in English, Ill. State U., 1975; MA in English, U. Ill., 1977. Mgr. Studio Instrument Rentals, Chgo., 1980-81; prodn. mgr. Chip Monck Industries, Redondo Beach, Calif., 1981-83; ops. mgr. Greek Theatre, L.A., 1983-84; exec. producer Simas & Assocs., Ventura, 1984—; prodn. mgr. Del Mar (Calif.) Fair, 1983—; pres. Stage Wright Prodns., Inc., Rancho La Costa, Calif., 1980—; prodn. mgr. 22d Dist. Agrl. Assn., Del Mar, 1984—, Southland Concerts, San Diego, 1985-87; dept. supr. Del Mar Satellite Wagering, 1987—; tech. dir. Western Fairs Assn., Sacramento, 1988—; prodn. cons. Hard Rock Cafe, San Diego, 1988—. Campaign worker Hunter S. Thompson, Aspen, Colo., 1980; event coord. Missing Children's Found., San Diego, 1988. With U.S. Army, 1966-68. Mem. Am. Mus. Natural History, Nat. Geog. Soc., San Diego Mus. Fine Art, Audubon Soc., Smithsonian Instn., Am. Legion. Home: 2564 Navarra Apt 206 Rancho La Costa CA 92009 Office: Del Mar Fair 2260 Jimmy Durante Blvd Del Mar CA 92014-2290

WRIGHT, DONALD FRANKLIN, newspaper executive; b. St. Paul, July 10, 1934; s. Floyd Franklin and Helen Marie (Hansen) W.; m. Sharon Kathleen Fisher, Dec. 30, 1960; children: John, Dana, Kara, Patrick. BME, U. Minn., 1957, MBA, 1958. With Mpls. Star & Tribune Co., 1958-77, research planning dir., then ops. dir., 1971-75, exec. editor, 1975-77; exec. v.p., gen. mgr. Newsday, Inc., L.I., 1977-78, pres., chief operating officer, 1978-81; pres., chief operating officer Los Angeles Times, 1981-87; sr. v.p. Times Mirror Co., Los Angeles, 1988—. Mem. exec. com., bd. fellows Claremont Grad. Sch. and Univ. Ctr.; former chmn. Los Angeles area council Boy Scouts Am., dir. Western region area pres. Boy Scouts Am.; vice chmn., 1989— ; dirs. Assocs. of Calif. Inst. Tech.; former chmn. telecommunications com. and prodn. mgmt. com. Am. Newspaper Pubs. Assn.; former mem. Am. Soc. Newspaper Editors; former dir. United Way Long Island, Calif.; bd. dirs. U. Minn. Found. Mem. U. Minn. Alumni Club (bd. dirs.), City Club Bunker Hill. Presbyterian. Office: Times Mirror Co Times Mirror Sq Los Angeles CA 90012-3816

WRIGHT, ERNEST MARSHALL, physiologist, consultant; b. Belfast, Ireland, June 8, 1940; came to U.S., 1965; BSc, U. London, 1961, DSc, 1978; PhD, U. Sheffield, Eng., 1964. Research fellow Harvard U., Boston, 1965-66; from asst. prof. to full prof. physiology UCLA Med. Sch., 1967—, chmn. dept. physiology, 1987—; cons. NIH, Bethesda, Md., 1982—, Senator Jacob K. Javits neurosci. investigator, 1985. Office: UCLA Sch Med Dept Physiology 10833 Le Conte Ave Los Angeles CA 90024-1602

WRIGHT, EUGENE ALLEN, federal judge; b. Seattle, Feb. 23, 1913; s. Elias Allen and Mary (Bailey) W.; m. Esther Ruth Ladley, Mar. 19, 1938; children: Gerald Allen, Meredith Ann Wright Morton. AB, U. Wash., 1935, JD, 1937; LLD, U. Puget Sound, 1984. Bar: Wash. 1937. Assoc. Wright & Wright, Seattle, 1937-54; judge Superior Ct. King County, Wash., 1954-66; v.p., sr. trust officer Pacific Nat. Bank Seattle, 1966-69; judge U.S. Ct. Appeals (9th cir.), Seattle, 1969—; acting municipal judge, Seattle, 1948-52; mem. faculty Nat. Jud. Coll., 1964-72; lectr. Sch. Communications, U. Wash., 1965-66, U. Wash. Law Sch., 1952-74; lectr. appellate judges' seminars, 1973-76, Nat. Law Clks. Inst., La. State U., 1973; chmn. Wash. State Com. on Law and Justice, 1968-69; mem. com. on appellate rules Jud. Conf., 1978-85, mem. com. on courtroom photography, 1983-85, com. jud. ethics, 1984-92, com. Bicentennial of Constn., 1985-87. Author: (with others) The State Trial Judges Book, 1966; also articles; editor: Trial Judges Jour., 1963-66; contbr. articles to profl. jours. Chmn. bd. visitors U. Puget Sound Sch. Law, 1979-84; mem. bd. visitors U. Wash. Sch. Law, 1989—; bd. dirs. Met. YMCA, Seattle, 1955-72; lay reader Episc Ch. Served to lt. col. USAR, 1941-46, col. Res., ret. Decorated Bronze Star, Combat Inf. badge; recipient Army Commendation medal, Disting. Service award U.S. Jr. C. of C., 1948, Disting. Service medal Am. Legion. Fellow Am. Bar Found.; mem. ABA (council div. jud. adminstrn. 1971-76), Fed. Bar Assn. (Disting. Jud. Service award 1984), Wash. Bar Assn. (award of merit 1983), Seattle-King County Bar Assn. (Spl. Disting. Service award 1984), Appellate Judges Conf., Ret. Officers Assn., Order of Coif, Delta Upsilon (Disting. Alumni Achievement award 1989), Phi Delta Phi. Clubs: Wash. Athletic, Rainier. Lodges: Masons (33 degree), Shriners. Office: US Ct Appeals9th Circuit 902 US Courthouse 1010 5th Ave Seattle WA 98104-1179

WRIGHT, FRANCES JANE, educational psychologist; b. Los Angeles, Dec. 22, 1943; d. step-father John David and Evelyn Jane (Dale) Brinegar. BA, Long Beach State U., 1965, secondary tchr. cert., 1966; MA, Brigham Young U., 1968, EdD, 1980; postgrad. U. Nev., 1970, U. Utah, 1972-73; postdoctoral Utah State U., 1985-86. Cert. tchr., adminstr. Utah. Asst. dir. Teenpost Project, San Pedro, Calif., 1966; caseworker Los Angeles County, 1966-67; self-care inservice dir. Utah State Tng. Sch., American Fork, Utah, 1968, vocat. project designer, 1968; tchr. mentally handicapped Santa Ana Unified Schs., Calif., 1968-69; state specialist intellectually handicapped State Office Edn., Salt Lake City, 1969-70; vocat. counselor Manpower, Salt Lake City, 1970-71; tchr. severely handicapped Davis County Schs., Farmington, Utah, 1971-73, diagnostician, 1973-74, resource elem. tchr., 1974-78; instr. Brigham Young U., Salt Lake City, 1976-83; resource tchr. jr. high Davis County Schs., Farmington, 1978-90; ednl. cons., Murray, Utah, 1973-90; chief ednl. diagnostician Ctr. for Evaluation of Learning and Devel., Layton, Utah, 1989-90; clin. dir. assessment and observation program Idaho Youth Ranch, 1990—, clin. dir. intake program, 1992—; cons. and lectr. in field. Author curriculums in spl. edn.; contbr. articles to profl. jours. Named Profl. of Yr., Utah Assn. for Children with Learning Disabilities, 1985. Mem. Assn. Children/Adults with Learning Disabilities (del. 1979-85, 87, nat. nominating com. 1985-86, nat. bd. dirs. 1988-91), Utah Assn. Children/Adults with Learning Disabilities (exec. bd. 1978-84, profl. adv. bd. 1985-90, coord. LDA orgn. Idaho 1991—), Coun. Exceptional Children (div. learning disabilities, ednl. diagnostics, behavioral disorders), Council Learning Disabilities, Assn. Supervisors and Curriculum Devel. (regional adv.), Windstar Found., Smithsonian Found., Cousteau Soc., Am. Biographical Inst. (life, hon. advisor rsch. bd. advisors nat. div.), Nat. Assn. Sch. Adminstrs. Democrat. Mormon. Lodge: Job's Daughters. Avocations: geneology research, horseback riding, sketching, crafts, reading. Home and Office: Idaho Youth Ranch Rupert ID 83350

WRIGHT, FREDERICK FENNING, oceanographic consultant, freelance writer; b. Princeton, N.J., Mar. 16, 1934; s. Walter Livingston Jr. and Katharine Hine (Fenning) W.; m. Wanda Merrell Mead, Mar. 16, 1984. BS, Columbia U., 1959, MA, 1961; PhD, U. So. Calif., 1967. Asst. prof. Inst. Marine Sci., U. Alaska, Fairbanks, 1966-72; assoc. prof. Marine Adv. program U. Alaska, Anchorage, 1972-74; oceanographic cons. Anchorage, 1974-75; dir. Alaska Coastal Mgmt. program Gov.'s Office, Juneau, Alaska, 1975-76, rsch. mgmt. officer, 1976-81; cruised in small sailboat Alaska to Britain and back, 1981-87; oceanographic cons., freelance writer Juneau, 1987—; cons. Standard Oil of Calif., Anchorage, 1973-74, Alaska Dept. Fish and Game, Anchorage, 1974-75. Contbr. articles to profl. jours. Pres. Bonnie Brae Highlander, Fairbanks, 1971-72, Taku Conservation Soc., Juneau, 1977-78; drum sgt. Anchorage Scottish Pipe Band, 1973-75; bd. dirs., sec. Alaska Maritime Heritage Found., Juneau, 1992—. With U.S. Army, 1955-57. Recipient Far Cruising award Juneau Cruising Club, 1982. Mem. Am. Geophys. Union, Arctic Inst. N.Am., Explorers Club, Juneau Sailing Club (sec. 1988—). Home: Box 240537 Douglas AK 99824

WRIGHT, FREDERICK HAMILTON, physicist, consultant; b. Washington, Dec. 2, 1912; s. Frederick Eugene and Kathleen Ethel (Finley) W.; m. May Ann Marmorek, 1946 (div.); m. Marguerite Jane Walker, Sept. 5, 1970; 4 stepchildren. BA, Haverford Coll., 1934; PhD, Calif. Inst. Tech., 1948. Teaching fellow Calif. Inst. Tech., Pasadena, 1937-40; aerodynamicist Douglas Aircraft Co., Santa Monica, Calif., 1940-46; engring. specialist Jet Propulsion Lab., Pasadena, 1946-59; physicist and mgr. Aerojet Gen. Corp., Azusa, Calif., 1959-78; cons. Pasadena, 1978—. Co-author: To the Moon, 1968; contbr. articles to profl. jours. and chpts. to books. Bd. dirs. Mut. Housing Assn., L.A., 1948-50. Fellow AIAA; mem. Am. Phys. Soc., IEEE, Long Beach Yacht Club, Sigma Xi, Phi Beta Kappa. Home: 515 Palmetto Dr Pasadena CA 91105

WRIGHT, FREDERICK HERMAN GREENE, II, computer systems engineer; b. Quincy, Mass., Feb. 23, 1952; s. Frederick Herman Greene and Dorothy Louise (Harrold) W. Student, MIT, 1968-69. Test and measurement technician The Foxboro (Mass.) Co., 1968; hardware and software designer MIT Project MAC, Cambridge, Mass., 1969, Info. Internat., Brookline, Mass., 1969, Stanford Artificial Intelligence Lab, Palo Alto,

Calif., 1971-73, Systems Concepts, San Francisco, 1970, 73-74, 1976-90; hardware and software designer, then pres. Resource One, San Francisco, 1974-76; pvt. cons. San Rafael, Calif., 1991—; computer cons. Langley-Porter Neuropsychiatric Inst., San Francisco, 1976. membership chmn. Pacific Soaring Council, San Francisco, 1983-85, bd. dirs., 1984-85. Recipient Gold Soaring Badge Fed. Aeronautique Internat., 1983. Mem. Digital Equipment Corp. Users Soc., Bay Area Soaring Assn. Republican. Home and Office: 251 C St San Rafael CA 94901-4916

WRIGHT, GARY ALBERT, marketing professional; b. Portland, Oreg., Nov. 26, 1948; s. George Harlan and Thelma Louise (Palmer) W.; m. Patricia Jane Roth, Aug. 4, 1984; children: John Stanton, Robert Conner. BS, U.S. Mil. Acad., 1971. Pres. Action Sports of Denver, Inc., 1976-81, G.A. Wright, Inc., Denver, 1981—; treas. Denver Mobility Inc., 1992—. Chmn. adv. bd. Children's Hosp. Cardiac Care Ctr., 1992—; mem. corp. com. Children's Hosp., Denver, 1992—. Mem. West Point Soc. of Denver, Metro Denver Exec. Club, Denver Athletic Club, Denver Advt. Fedn., Direct Mktg. Assn., Nat. Retail Fedn., Elephant Club. Republican. Office: 1099 18th St Ste 2090 Denver CO 80202-1908

WRIGHT, GARY DONALD, real estate agent; b. Oamk, Wash., June 1, 1944; s. Donald William and Zella Ida (Wehmeyer) W.; m. Donna Marie Doud, June 26, 1962; children: Donald, Pamela, Penny, Gregory, Theodore. Lic. real estate broker, Wash. Pres., gen. mgr. Coldwell Banker Gary Wright Realty, Marysville, Wash., 1968—. Treas. Woodside Assembly Ch., Marysville, 1971—; real estate commr. State of Wash., 1977-83; mem. bus. adv. com. Marysville High Sch., 1988—; precinct com. officer Rep. Cen. Com., Marysville, 1988—. With U.S. Army, 1962-65. Recipient Disting. Svc. award Jaycees, 1973. Mem. Marysville C. of C., Nat. Assn. Realtors (dir. 1991—), Puget Sound Multiple Listing Assn. (founding dir. 1984—), Wash. Assn. Realtors (Achievement award 1990), Snohomish County Assn. Realtors (Realtor of Yr. 1976, 80, 88), Nat. Fedn. Ind. Bus. (Guardian of Freedom). Home: 5533 Parkside Dr Marysville WA 98270 Office: Coldwell Banker Realty 9323 State Ave Marysville WA 98270

WRIGHT, GORDON BROOKS, musician, conductor, educator; b. Bklyn., Dec. 31, 1934; s. Harry Wesley and Helen Philomena (Brooks) W.; m. Inga-Lisa Myrin Wright, June 13, 1958 (div. 1979); children: Karin-Ellen Blindenbacher, Charles-Eric, Daniel Brooks. MusB, Coll. Wooster, 1957; MA, U. Wis., 1961; postgrad., Salzburg Mozarteum, 1972, Loma Linda U., 1979. Founder, music dir. Wis. Chamber Orch. (formerly Madison Summer Symphony), 1960-69; music dir. Fairbanks (Alaska) Symphony Orch., 1969-89; prof. music Univ. Alaska, Fairbanks, 1969-89, prof. emeritus, 1989—; founder, music dir. Arctic Chamber Orch., Fairbanks, 1970-89; exec. dir. The Reznicek Soc., Indian, Alaska, 1982—. Guest condr. Philharmonia Hungarica, Philomusica London, Norwegian Radio Orch., Orch. St. Luke's, Anchorage Symphony Orch.; composer: Suite of Netherlands Dances, 1965, Six Alaskan Tone Poems, 1974, Symphony in Ursa Major, 1979 (Legis. award 1979), 1984 Overture, Scott Joplin Suite, 1987, Toccata Festiva, 1992; columnist Alaska Advocate, Fairbanks Daily News-Miner. Founder, bd. dirs. No. Alaska Environ. Ctr., Fairbanks, 1971-78. Served as pvt. AUS, 1957-59. Mem. Am. Musicol. Soc., Royal Musical Assn., Am. Symphony Orch. League, Condr.'s Guild, Arturo Toscanini Soc., Am. Fedn. Musicians, Royal Mus. Assn., Sierra Club (lchmn. Fairbanks Group 1969-71), Friends of Earth-Alaska (bd. dirs. 1978—), Wilderness Soc., Audubon Soc., Alaska Conservation Soc. (editor Rev. 1971-78), Ctr. for Alaskan Coastal Studies (bd. dirs. 1982—). Home: HC 52 Box 8899 Indian AK 99540-9604

WRIGHT, HAVILAND, software company executive; b. Phila., July 21, 1948; s. Frederick G. and Sara (McCracken) W.; m. Margaret Sterhardt, Feb. 16, 1984. BA, U. Pa., 1972, MBA, 1975, PhD, 1981. CPA, Pa. Asst. prof. U. Denver, 1981-83; cons. Coopers & Lybrand, N.Y.C., 1983-84; adj. prof. U. Colo., Boulder, 1984—; pres. Avalanche Devel. Co., Boulder, 1985—; bd. dirs. Graphic Communications Assn. Rsch. Inst., Arlington, Va. Office: Avalanche Devel Co 947 Walnut St Boulder CO 80302

WRIGHT, HELENE SEGAL, editor; b. L.A., Jan. 31, 1955; d. Alan and Lila E. (Hambro) Segal; m. David Scott Wright, May 6, 1979. Student, Calif. State U., Fullerton, 1973-75; BA in English, U. Calif., Santa Barbara, 1978. Library asst. ABC-CLIO, Santa Barbara, 1979-80, editorial asst., 1980-81, asst. editor, 1981-83, mng. editor, 1983—. Mem. Am. Polit. Sci. Assn., Current World Leaders (adv. bd. 1989—). Home: 142 La Vista Grande Santa Barbara CA 93103 Office: ABC-CLIO 130 Cremona Dr Santa Barbara CA 93117-3075

WRIGHT, JAMES BRYAN, lawyer; b. Olympia, Wash., Apr. 12, 1955; s. James Carol and Charlotte Elizabeth (Guffey) W.; m. Debra Jean Webster, June 16, 1990. BA in Philosophy with honors, U. Puget Sound, 1978; JD, Coll. William and Mary in Va., 1982. Bar: Alaska 1983. Law clk. Third Judicial Dist. State of Alaska, Anchorage, 1982-83; assoc. Lynch, Crosby and Sisson, Anchorage, 1983-89, ptnr., 1989-90; mng. ptnr. Law Office of Timothy M. Lynch, P.C., Anchorage, 1991-92; shareholder, mng. ptnr. Lynch, Wright & Blum, PC, Anchorage, 1993—. Author: Alaska Tort Insurance Law Update, 1993. Mem. ABA (litigation sect., tort and ins. practice sect.), Alaska Bar Assn., Anchorage Bar Assn., Def. Research Inst. (com. ins. law), Def. Counsel Alaska, Phi Delta Phi. Presbyterian. Home: 2903 Doris Pl # 2 Anchorage AK 99517-1964 Office: Lynch Wright & Blum PC 550 W 7th Ave Fl 11 Anchorage AK 99501-3510

WRIGHT, JANET SCRITSMIER, investment consultant; b. Pomona, Calif., May 21, 1960; d. Jerome Lorenzo and Mildred Joan (Lloyd) Scritsmier; m. James Calvin Wright, Mar. 26, 1983; children—Justin Michael, Corey Gray. Student Calif. State Poly. U., 1978-79. Vice pres. sales E.L.A. Co., Industry, Calif., 1979-84; investment cons. Cameron Properties Inc., Covina, Calif., 1980—. Asst. instr. Dale Carnegie Sales Course, 1981-82, Human Relations, 1983. Republican. Mormon. Avocation: snow skiing. Home: 2454 E Cameron Ave Covina CA 91724-3921

WRIGHT, JEAN SUTTON, writer; b. Inglewood, Calif., Nov. 11, 1922; d. Albert Hargrave Sutton and Veronica (Irwin) Sommer; m. Stanton Macdonald Wright (dec. Aug. 1973). BA, UCLA, 1945. Home: 15173 Encanto Dr Sherman Oaks CA 91403-4411

WRIGHT, JOHN GEORGE, JR., manufacturing company executive; b. Cleve., June 5, 1947; s. John George and Margaret Josephine (Laumer) W.; m. Isabelle H. Pasquier, Dec. 21, 1976; children: Daniel William, Marie-Christine, Nicholas Fernand. BS, U. Pa., 1969; MS summa cum laude, U. Minn., 1970; MBA, MAM, Claremont Grad. Sch., 1982, PhD, 1984. corp. gen. mgr., 1973-80, v.p., 1980-87; pres. Columbia France, S.A., 1987-89; pres., chmn. bd. dirs. Columbia Cintas de Impresiones S.A., 1987-89, CGL Holding, 1987-89; chmn., merchant banker Rosman, Wright and Assocs., Bel Air, Calif., 1989-92; mng. dir., Berkshire Venture Ptnrs., Ltd., 1993—; assoc. trustee, mem. pres.'s circle U. Pa., Rotary (bd. dirs. Northridge club), Beta Gamma Sigma (life), Delta Upsilon (life), Delta Sigma Pi (life). Office: Berkshire Ventures Ptnrs 31225 La Baya Ste 110 Westlake Village CA 91362

WRIGHT, JOHN MACNAIR, JR., retired army officer; b. L.A., Apr. 14, 1916; s. John MacNair and Ella (Stradley) W.; m. Helene Tribit, June 28, 1940; children: John MacNair III, Richard Kenneth. B.S., U.S. Mil. Acad., 1940; grad., Airborne Sch., 1947, Strategic Intelligence Sch., 1948; advanced course, Inf. Sch., 1951, Command and Gen. Staff Coll., 1953; M.B.A., U. So. Calif., 1956; grad., Army Logistics Mgmt. Sch., 1957, Advanced Mgmt. Program, U. Pitts., 1959, Nat. War Coll., 1961, Army Aviation Sch., 1965; M.S. in Internat. Affairs, George Washington U., 1973. Enlisted U.S. Army, 1935, comd. 2d. lt., 1940, advanced through grades to lt. gen., 1970; comdr. Battery Wright Corregidor, P.I., 1942; with intelligence div. War Dept. Gen. Staff, 1946-48; mil. attache Am. embassy, Paraguay, 1948-50; bn. comdr. 508th Airborne Regtl. Combat Team, 1951-52; asst. chief of staff for pers. 7th Inf. Div., Korea, 1953, asst. chief staff logistics, 1954; assigned office U.S. Army Chief of Staff, 1956-60; chief staff 8th Inf. Div., 1961-62, asst. chief staff plans and ops. 7th Corps, 1962-63, asst. chief staff plans and ops. 7th Army, 1963-64, asst. div. comdr. 11th Air Assault Div., 1964-65; asst. div. comdr. 1st Cav. Div. (Airmobile) Vietnam, 1965-66; assigned office asst. Chief Staff Force Devel., 1966-67; comdg. gen. U.S. Army Inf. Ctr., 1967-69; comdt. U.S. Army Inf. Sch., 1967-69; comdg. gen. 101st Airborne Div. (Airmobile), Vietnam, 1969-70; controller of the Army Washington, 1970-72; ret., 1973. Dir. research and devel. Boy Scouts Am., 1973, nat. dir. program, 1974-77, nat. dir. program support, 1977-78; nat. dir. exploring 1978-81, mem. nat. exploring com., 1981—; pres. Chattahoochee (Ga.) council Boy Scouts Am., 1968-69, mem. exec. bd. region 5, 1967-69; mem. Nat. council, 1964-73; tech. adviser Vietnamese Boy Scout Assn., 1965-66; Regent for Life Nat. Eagle Scout Assn., 1988—. Decorated D.S.M. with 2 oak leaf clusters, Silver Star with oak leaf cluster, Legion of Merit with oak leaf cluster, D.F.C., Bronze Star with oak leaf cluster, Air medal with 59 oak leaf clusters, Army Commendation medal, Prisoner of War medal, Purple Heart with oak leaf cluster, Combat Inf. badge, Master Parachutist, Sr. Army Aviator, numerous area and campaign ribbons, fgn. decorations; recipient Silver Beaver award Boy Scouts Am., 1961, Silver Antelope award, 1969, Distinguished Eagle Scout award, 1971, Disting. Svc. award Founders and Patriots Am., 1988, Freedoms Found. at Valley Forge Hon. medal, 1992; elected Army Aviation Hall of Fame, 1986. Mem. Assn. U.S. Army, Army Aviation Assn. Am. (pres. 1974-76), 101st Airborne Div. Assn., 1st Cavalry Div. Assn., SAR (pres. Tex. Soc. 1987-88, Silver Good Citizenship medal 1984, 87, Meritorious Svc. medal 1986, Patriot, Liberty and Gold Good Citizenship medals 1988), Ret. Officers Assn., West Point Soc., Mil. Order World Wars (Patrick Henry award 1986, 90, comdr. Dalls chpt. 1985-86 (vice comdr. dept. ctrl. Calif., 1992), Inland Empire chpt. 1992-93), Nat. Order Founders and Patriots of Am. (sec.-gen. 1986-88, gov. gen. 1986-90), Soc. Descendants of Colonial Clergy, Flagon and Tchr. Soc., Soc. Colonial Wars (lt. gov. Calif. soc. 1992—), Sons of the Revolution in state of Calif. (pres. 1993—) Soc. War of 1812 (dist. dep. pres. gen. 1991—, v.p. Calif. Soc. 1993—), Nat. Huguenot Soc., Soc. Sons and Daughters of Pilgrims, Order Ams. Armorial Ancestry, Soc. Descendants Founders of Hartford, Old Plymouth Colony Desendants, Mil. Order of the Loyal Legion of the U.S., Mil. Order Fgn. Wars of the U.S., Hereditary Order of First Families of Mass., Masons, Shriners, Sojourner, Phi Kappa Phi, Beta Gamma Sigma, Alpha Kappa Psi. Home: 21227 George Brown Ave Riverside CA 92518-2881

WRIGHT, JOHN PATRICK, organization executive; b. Clayton, Mo., July 27, 1968; s. James Edward and Patricia Anne (Toohey) W.; m. Lori Jean Ross, Jan. 25, 1992. BA in Humanities, Seattle U., 1990. Founder, pres. The Inquisitive Mind, Redmond, Wash., 1990—. Democrat. Methodist. Home: 15209 NE 16th Pl # 42 Bellevue WA 98007 Office: The Inquisitive Mind 15127 NE 24th St Ste 407 Redmond WA 98052

WRIGHT, KATHRYN MICHELE, grocery retail chain coordinator; b. Boise, Idaho, Apr. 10, 1959; d. Richard William and Helga Marie (Stipa) Madland; m. Robert C. Wright, June 14, 1981; 1 child, Robert William. BBA, Boise State U., 1981. Checker Albertsons Inc., Boise, 1978-84, mgr. ge. mdse., 1984-86, scan coord., 1986-88, pricing clk., 1988-92, dir. store delivery coord., 1992—. Mem. Alpha Kappa Psi. Republican. Office: Albertsons Inc 1404 S Phillipps Boise ID 83705

WRIGHT, LIN MARY, theater educator; b. Mpls., Jan. 19, 1933; d. Nathanial F. and Mary F. (Hargarten) Sommers; m. James L. Wright, Aug. 5, 1963; 1 child, Miriam Sommers. BS, U. Minn., 1954, MA, 1960, PhD, 1973. Cert. secondary tchr., Minn. Tchr. Gilbert (Minn.) High Sch., 1954-55, Mounds View High Sch., New Brighton, Minn., 1957-63; instr. theatre U. Minn., Mpls., 1965-72, asst. prof., 1972-73; prof. theatre Ariz. State U., Tempe, 1973-84, chmn. theatre dept., 1984—; prin. investigator curriculum project Internat. Ctr. Studies in Theatre Edn.; chair Nat. K-12 Theatre Edn. Standards com. Recipient Outstanding Contbns. award So. Calif. Edn. Theatre Assn., 1984. Mem. Coll. of Fellows of Am. Theatre, Am. Assn. Theatre for Youth (chair, founding bd. dirs., rsch. citation 1986), Children's Theatre Assn. Am. (pres. 1981-83, v.p. rsch. 1977-79, Human Awareness award 1976), East Valley Art Assn. (Outstanding Tchr. award 1988). Office: Ariz State U Dept Theater Tempe AZ 85287

WRIGHT, LORIN RODERICK, physical therapist; b. Billings, Mont., May 17, 1948; s. Roderick Roy and Bessie Helen (Steele) W.; m. Barbara Ann Leiper, Jan 13, 1973; children: Danielle, Heather. BA in Phys. Edn., U. Mont., 1971; cert. phys. therapy, U. Pa., 1972. Phys. therapist Gottsche Rehab. Ctr., Thermopolis, Wyo., 1972-73, 74-76, St. Vincent's Hosp., Billings, 1973-74; outreach phys. therapist Mont. Ctr. for Handicapped Children, Ea. Mont. Coll., Billings, 1976-80; founding ptnr., v.p. 1st Phys. Therapy, P.C., 1979—; bd. visitors phys. therapy dept. U. Mont., 1990-91, chmn. bd. visitors, 1992-93. Co-author: (book tape series) Stress and Burnout Reasons and Remedies, 1988, rev. 1991. Bd. dirs. Spl. Tng. for Exceptional People, Billings, Mont., 1978-81; pres. parish counsel Messiah Luth. Ch., Red Lodge, Mont., 1990. Mem.. Am. Phys. Therapy Assn. (past v.p. Mont. chpt., pres. 1990-92, lectr. combined sect. meeting 1987, Nora Staael-Evert award 1991, del. to ho. of dels. 1993), Mont. Assn. Pvt. Practice Phys. Therapists (chmn. 1986-88), Bd. Phys. Therapy Examiners (chmn. bd. dirs. 1988-89, mem. bd. phys. therapy exec. 1988-89), Rotary (pres. 1987-88), Inquiry Club (program cir. 1987-88, sec. 1991, v.p. 1991-92, pres. 1992). Office: Phys Therapy PC 1 S Oaks PO Box 430 Red Lodge MT 59068-0430

WRIGHT, ROSALIE MULLER, newspaper and magazine editor; b. Newark, June 20, 1942; d. Charles and Angela (Fortunata) Muller; m. Lynn Wright, Jan. 13, 1962; children: James Anthony Meador, Geoffrey Shepard. BA in English, Temple U., 1965. Mng. editor Suburban Life mag., Orange, N.J., 1960-62; assoc. editor Phila. mag., 1962-64, mng. editor, 1969-73; founding editor Womensports mag., San Mateo, Calif., 1973-75; editor scene sect. San Francisco Examiner, 1975-77; exec. editor New West mag., San Francisco and Beverly Hills, Calif., 1977-81; features and Sunday editor San Francisco Chronicle, 1981-87, asst. mng. editor features, 1987—; tchr. mag. writing U. Calif.-Berkeley, 1975-76; participant pub. procedure's course Stanford U., 1977-79; chmn. mag. judges Council Advancement and Support Edn. Conf., 1980, judge, 1984. Contbr. numerous mag. articles, critiques, revs., Compton's Ency. Mem. Am. Assn. Sun. and Feature Editors (treas. 1984, sec. 1985, 1st v.p. 1986, pres. 1987), Am. Newspaper Pub. Assn. (pub. task force on minorities in newspaper bus. 1988-89, Chronicle minority recruiter 1987—), Calif. Soc. Newspaper Editors, Internat. Women's Forum, Women's Forum West (bd. dirs. 1993—). Office: Chronicle Pub Co 901 Mission St San Francisco CA 94103-2988

WRIGHT, THEODORE OTIS, forensic engineer; b. Gillette, Wyo., Jan. 17, 1921; s. James Otis and Gladys Mary (Marquiss) W.; m. Phyllis Mae Reeves, June 21, 1942 (div. 1968); children: Mary Suzanne, Theodore Otis Jr., Barbara Joan; m. Edith Marjorie Jewett, May 22, 1968; children: Marjorie Jane, Elizabeth Carter. BSEE, U. Ill., 1951, MS in Engring., 1952; postgrad., Air Command and Staff Coll., 1956-57, UCLA, 1958. Registered profl. engr. Wash. 2d lt. U.S. Air Force, 1942-65, advanced through grades to lt. col., 1957, ret., 1965; dep. for engring. Titon SPO, USAF Sys. Command, L.A., 1957-65; rsch. engr. The Boeing Co., Seattle, 1965-81; pres. The Pretzelwich, Inc., Seattle, 1981—; cons., forensic engr. in pvt. practice Bellevue, Wash., 1988—; adj. prof. U. Wash., Greenriver Jr. Coll., both 1967-68. Contbr. articles to profl. jours. Decorated Purple Heart, Air medal. Mem. Air Force Assn. (life, state pres. 1974-76, 90-91), Jimmy Doolittle fellow 1975), Order Daedalians (life mem.), Nat. Soc. Profl. Engrs. (Western region v.p. 1985-87), Wash. Soc. Profl. Engrs. (cert. advanced metrication specialist 1981, state pres. 1981-82, Disting. Svc. award 1980), Sigma Tau, Eta Kappa Nu, Pi Mu Epsilon, Tau Beta Pi. Democrat. Presbyterian. Home: 9644 Hilltop Rd Bellevue WA 98004-4006

WRIGHT, THOMAS LLEWELLYN, geologist; b. Chgo., July 26, 1935; s. Robert Llewellyn and Elizabeth Bryan (Kehler) W.; m. Mary Saint John Bachman, Sept. 1958 (div. 1975); children: John, Rebecca. AB, Pomona Coll., 1957; PhD, Johns Hopkins U., 1961. Geologist U.S. Geol. Survey, Washington, 1961-63, 69-84; geologist Hawaii Volcano Observatory, U.S. Geol. Survey, 1964-69, scientist-in-charge, 1984-91; geologist Hawaii Nat. Pk., U.S. Geol. Survey, 1992—. Author: Hawaiian Volcanism and Seismicity, 1779-1955: An Annotated Bibiliography and Subject Index, 1989, Hawaii Volcano Watch: A Pictorial History 1779-1991, 1992. Mem. Hawaii Natural History Assn. (bd. mem. 1984-91). Office: US Geol Survey PO Box 51 Hawaii National Park HI 96718

WRIGHT, TIM EUGENE, packaging development executive; b. Weed, N.Mex., Oct. 13, 1943; s. Clyde Everett and Juanita Delores (Barrett) W.; m. Nancy Ann Ausenbaugh, Oct. 2, 1965 (div. 1975); 1 child, Ramsey Jordan. Diploma, Dayton Art Inst., 1967, M.F.A., U. Idaho, 1969. Designer, Lawson Mfg. Co., Troy, Idaho, 1968-70, Boise Cascade, Burley, Idaho, 1970-72; project coord. Boise Cascade, Golden, Colo., 1972-76, product devel. mgr., Wallula, Wash., 1976-84; mng. ptnr. Matrix Applications Co., Pasco, Wash., 1984—. Patentee folding carton, spacer for rolls, collapsible pallet. Recipient Silver award for packaging, 1978. Mem. Inst. Packaging Profls., Western Packaging Assn. (bd. dirs., past pres. Columbia chpt.), Soc. Plastics Engrs., TAPPI. Office: Matrix Applications Co PO Box 1407 Pasco WA 99301-1407

WRIGHT, WADELL, engineer; b. Greenville, S.C., Aug. 29, 1944; s. Thomas C. and Marie (Tate) W.; m. Ines Rosario Teran, Sept. 1, 1977; children: Andre Tyrone, Anthony Wadell, Fionna Michelle, Aljonn Jerome. Diploma, Control Data Inst., Burlington, Mass., 1970. With RCA, Marlboro, Mass., 1971, Honeywell Info. Systems, Waltham, Mass., 1971-74, Bendix Field Engring. Corp., Columbia, Md., 1975-79, Ford Aerospace & Communications Corp., Palo Alto, Calif., 1979-80, Kentron Internat., Pasadena, Calif., 1980-82, Rockwell Internat., Anaheim, Calif., 1983-84; sr. computer engr. Al-Johi Internat., Dhahran, Saudi Arabia, 1984-85; sr. test engr. Gen. Dynamics, San Diego, 1985-87; sr. standards lab. engr. Gen. Dynamics, Rancho Cucamonga, Calif., 1987-88; owner, mgr. WRIGHT Vending Svc., Colton, Calif., 1988—; CEO Wright's Adolescent Devel. Ctr. Inc., San Bernardino, Calif., 1990—; performed work related duties Ascension Island, Atlantic Ocean, Quito, Ecuador, S.Am., Kauai, Hawaii, Seychelles Island, Indian Ocean, Dharan, Saudi Arabia. Author: Its Up to You in America, 1987-88; inventor in field. With U.S. Army, 1962-65. Home: 1397 N Topsail Ave Colton CA 92324-6211 Office: WRIGHT Vending Svc PO Box 1107 Colton CA 92324-0818

WRIGHT-QUASTLER, REBA, urban planner; b. Glendale, Calif., Dec. 11, 1946; d. Glenn Holiday and Nellie Fern (Brandon) Wright; m. Cornelis Daniel Touw, May 17, 1968 (div. Aug. 1987); 1 child, Thomas; m. Imre Ernest Quastler, Aug. 24, 1988. BA, Chapman Coll., 1967; Doctor, U. Utrecht, Utrecht, The Netherlands, 1983. Project mgr. The Nowland Orgn., Greenwich, Conn., 1969-70; translator Dun & Bradstreet, Rotterdam, The Netherlands, 1971-73; asst. mgr. P-E Consulting Group, Staines, Middlesex, Eng., 1973; assoc. planner City of Costa Mesa, Calif., 1978-86; dir. planning City of Poway, Calif., 1986—; adj. prof. San Diego State U., 1992—. Contbr. articles to profl. jours. Mem. Am. Inst. Cert. Planners (cert.), Am. Planning Assn. (San Diego sect. chair various coms., San Diego sect. Contribution to Women in Planning award 1991, Calif. chpt. v.p. adminstrn.). Office: City of Poway 13325 Civic Center Dr Poway CA 92064

WRIGLEY, ELIZABETH SPRINGER (MRS. OLIVER K. WRIGLEY), foundation executive; b. Pitts., Oct. 4, 1915; d. Charles Woodward and Sarah Maria (Roberts) Springer; BA U. Pitts., 1935; BS, Carnegie Inst. Tech., 1936; m. Oliver Kenneth Wrigley, June 16, 1936 (dec. July 1978). Procedure analyst U.S. Steel Corp., Pitts., 1941-43; rsch. asst. The Francis Bacon Found., Inc., Los Angeles, 1944, exec., 1945-50, trustee, 1950—, dir. rsch., 1951-53, pres., 1954—, dir. Francis Bacon Libr.; mem. adv. coun. Shakespeare Authorship Roundtable, Santa Monica, Calif.; mem. regional Fine Arts adv. coun. Calif. State Poly. U., Pomona. Mem. ALA, Calif. Libr. Assn., Renaissance Soc. Am., Modern Humanities Rsch. Assn., Cryptogram Assn., Alpha Delta Pi. Presbyn. Mem. Order Eastern Star, Damascus Shrine. Editor: The Skeleton Text of the Shakespeare Folio L.A. (by W.C. Arensberg), 1952. Compiler: Short Title Catalogue Numbers in the Library of the Francis Bacon Foundation, 1958; Wing Numbers in the Library of the Francis Bacon Foundation, 1959; Supplement To Francis Bacon Library Holdings in the STC of English Books, 1967; (with David W. Davies) A Concordance to the Essays of Francis Bacon, 1973. Home: 4805 N Pal Mal Ave Temple City CA 91780-4129 Office: Francis Bacon Libr 655 N Dartmouth Ave Claremont CA 91711-3979

WROBLEWSKI, KENNETH ANDREW, engineering executive; b. Hammond, Ind., Nov. 10, 1945; s. Medard and Edwina (Scott) W.;m. Kathleen Louise Schubert, Feb. 19, 1966; children: Kenneth Jr., Christine, David, Julie, Laurie. BS, U. Ill., 1972; MBA, Ariz. State U., 1989. Electronics engr. Sperry Flight Systems, Phoenix, 1972-79; systems engr. King Radio Corp., Olathe, Kans., 1979-86; chief div. engr. McDonnell Douglas, Mesa, Ariz., 1986—. Pres. parish coun. Prince of Peace Ch., Olathe, 1985; precinct com. Ariz. Rep. Party, Phoenix, 1975-79, dist. sect., Mesa, 1990—; dep. registrar Ariz. Elections Dept., Phoenix, 1976-79, 87—. Sgt. USAF, 1963-67. Mem. Am. Helicopter Soc. (com. dep. chmn. 1991—), Army Aviation Assn. Am. Roman Catholic. Home: 5647 E Grandview Mesa AZ 85205 Office: McDonnell Douglas Helicopter 5000 E McDowell Mesa AZ 85205

WRONA, PETER ALEXANDER, structural engineer; b. Cracow, Poland, Feb. 19, 1955; came to U.S., 1970; s. Wlodzimierz Stefan and Anna Maria (Czech) W.; m. Bernadette Maria Waskowska, Oct. 9, 1984; 1 child, Marie. BS in Civil Engring., U. Calif., Berkeley, 1976, MS in Structural Engring., 1980. Registered profl. engr., Calif.; lic. pvt. pilot. Staff engr. Bechtel Power Corp., San Francisco, 1977-79; project engr. S. Medwadowski Cons. Engrs., San Francisco, 1980-82, 85-87; cons. Bechtel Power Corp., San Francisco, 1982-83; sr. engr. Forell and Elsesser Engrs., San Francisco, 1983-85; project engr. C.H. Wells & Assocs., San Mateo, Calif., 1987-88; assoc. Dasse Design Inc., San Francisco, 1988—; v.p., bd. dirs. Polam Fed. Credit Union, Redwood City, Calif., 1986—; cert. vol. engr. Office of Emergency Svcs., State of Calif., 1986—. Bd. dirs., treas. Skyview Homeowners Assn., Hayward, Calif., 1986-89. Mem. ASCE, Structural Engrs. Assn. No. Calif. (mem. continuing edn. com. 1984-86), Internat. Assn. for Shell and Spatial Structures, Chi Epsilon. Roman Catholic. Home: 28091 Ziele Creek Dr Hayward CA 94542 Office: Dasse Design Inc 33 New Montgomery St San Francisco CA 94105

WRYE, RICHARD FRED, educator, musician; b. San Francisco, June 10, 1944; s. Fred E. and Alice D. (Westermann) W.; m. Karen A. Sasser, July 1, 1967; children: Timothy P., Matthew S. BA, Concordia U., 1967, MA in Edn., 1968; MusM, U. Portland, 1983. Cert. tchr., Oreg. Tchr. Redeemer Luth. Sch., South Gate, Calif., 1966-67; instr. Concordia Coll., River Forest, Ill., 1967-68; instr. Luth. High Sch., Mayer, Minn., 1968-72, Portland, Oreg., 1972—. Mem. Oreg. Repertory Singers, Portland, 1979-86; mem. worship com. Luth. Ch. (N.W. Dist. Mo. Synod.), Portland, 1981—; cantor St. Michael's Lutheran Ch., Portland. Mem. Am. Guild Organists (dean 1989-91, Svc. Playing Cert. award 1990), Am. Choral Dirs. Assn. (life), Assn. Luth. Ch. Musicians. Home: 6306 NE 26th Ave Portland OR 97211-6049 Office: Portland Luth High Sch 740 SE 182d Ave Portland OR 97233

WU, JAMES BI-CHENG, metallurgical engineer, researcher; b. Chendu, China, Nov. 29, 1943; came to U.S., 1968, naturalized, 1980; s. Cheng-Bi and Yen-Yu (Zhou) W.; m. Lee Nan Jan, June 19, 1971; 1 child, Eva. BS, Cheng Kung U., Taiwan, 1965; MS, Stevens Inst. Tech., 1970; PhD, U. Rochester, 1975. Postdoctoral fellow U. Pa., Phila., 1975-76; research metallurgist Republic Steel Corp. Rsch. Ctr., Independence, Ohio, 1976-81; rsch. engr. tech. dept. cabot Corp., Kokomo, Ind., 1981-83, group leader corrosion, 1983-85, mgr. Asian Ventures, 1985-86, dir. Asian ops. Stoody Deloro Stellite, Inc., 1986-88; mem. tech. adv. com. Materials Tech. Inst., Columbus, Ohio, 1983-86; dir. tech. ops. Stoody Co., 1988-91; div. v.p. Stoody Co., 1991-92, v.p. tech., Deloro Stellite, Inc., 1992—. Contbr. (with others) articles to profl. jours. Fellow Am. Electroplaters Soc.; mem. AIME, Am. Soc. Metals, Nat. Assn. Corrosion Engrs. (vice chmn. T 5K com. 1984-86), Am. Welding Soc. Unitarian. Avocations: golf, tennis, fishing, photography. Office: 16425 E Gale Ave City Of Industry CA 91715-0426

WU, JOHN MING CHEUNG, process control engineer; b. Hong Kong, Feb. 17, 1953; came to U.S., 1968; s. S. Gu and G. Fang (Hel) W.; m. Ying L. Wu, June 30, 1979; 1 child, Heather. BSChemE, Mont. State U., 1974; MSChemE, Washington U., St. Louis, 1976. Registered profl. engr., Mo. Engr. Monsanto Co., St. Louis, 1974-81; engr. B.P. Alaska, San Francisco, 1981-84, Anchorage, 1984—. Mem. Instrument Soc. Am. Home: 2831 Legacy Dr Anchorage AK 99516-2733

WU, JONATHAN CHARNGHAU, accountant, consultant; b. Chungli, Republic of China, Feb. 12, 1953; came to U.S., 1980; s. Fupei and Lianmei (Liu) W.; m. Liming Han, Mar. 25, 1979. BS, Fujen U., Taipei, Republic of China, 1975; M in Mgmt., Northwestern U., 1982; MA, U. Ill., Chgo., 1985. CPA, Tex. Asst. to v.p. Shus Found., Taipei, 1977-78; ptnr. Bianko Co.,

Taipei, 1978-80; adj. lectr. Roosevelt U., Chgo., 1983-84; sr. fin. systems analyst Tex. Dept. Community Affairs, Austin, 1984-86, asst. dir. acctg. system, 1986-87, dir. data services, 1987; chief fin. officer Full Employment Council, Kansas City, Mo., 1987-89; v.p. MC2 Internat., Pullman, Wash., 1989-92, pres., 1992—; mng. dir. The Changao Group (China), Nanjing, 1993—; acctg. and tax systems cons., Austin, 1984-89. Author, editor: Job Tng. Ptnrship. Act Fin. Mgmt. Manual, 1986, Food Science, 1978; also articles. Served to 2d lt. Chinese Air Force, 1975-77. Mem. Am. Inst. CPA's, Tex. Soc. CPA's, Inst. Mgmt. Accts. (cert.), Inst. Internal Auditors (cert.), Northwestern Mgmt. Assn. Home: SW 360 State Pullman WA 99163 Office: MC2 Internat PO Box 246 Pullman WA 99163-0246

WU, SENG-CHAI, financial planner, life insurance agency official; b. Amoy, Fuchian, China, Oct. 19, 1930; came to U.S., 1954; s. Eng-Hwa and Lian-Hoe (Iu) W.; m. Evelyn M. Mangaser, Sept. 9, 1975; children: Patrick O., Michael L., Andrew J. BA, Union Coll., Lincoln, Nebr. CLU; ChFC. Sales rep., also regional sales mgr. Home Health Edn. Svc., Richardson, Tex., 1959-68; sales rep., mgr. Met. Life Ins. Co., N.Y.C., 1968-85; sales mgr. Met. Life Ins. Co., Arcadia, Claremont, Calif., 1982-85; fin. cons. Fin. Design, Rancho Cucamonga, Calif., 1985—; gen. agy. mgr. Franklin Fin. Svcs. Corp., Springfield, Calif., 1988—, Am. Mut. Life Ins. Co., Des Moines, 1991—. Active Philippines and Chinese Assn., Dallas, 1969-75. Mem. Pomona Valley Life Underwriter Assn., Arrowhead CLU Assn. Republican. Adventist. Home: 10988 Wilson Ave Alta Loma CA 91737-2438

WU, SHU-YAU, electrical engineer; b. Changhua, Taiwan, Republic of China, Nov. 6, 1936; came to the U.S., 1961; m. Chih-Ing Lee, Feb., 1969; children: Lillian, Benjamin. PhD, U. Ill., 1966. Engr. Westinghouse Rsch. Ctr., Pitts., 1967-89; sr. tech. specialist McDonnell Douglas Aerospace Co., Huntington Beach, Calif., 1989—. Contbr. articles to profl. jours.; patentee in field. Recipient Engrng. Achievement award for infrared detector arrays devel., 1985, Award of Recognition Internat. Symposium on Integrated Ferroelectrics, 1991. Mem. IEEE, Sigma Xi. Office: McDonnell Douglas Aerospace Co 5301 Bolsa Ave Huntington Beach CA 92647

WU, WILLIAM LUNG-SHEN (YOU-MING WU), aerospace medical engineering design specialist; b. Hangchow, Chekiang Province, China, Sept. 1, 1921; came to U.S., 1941, naturalized, 1955; s. Sing-Chih and Mary (Ju-Mei) Wu. AB in Biochemistry, Stanford U., 1943, MD, 1946; MS in Chemistry and Internal Medicine, Tulane U., 1955; diploma, U.S. Naval Sch. Aviation Medicine, Pensacola, Fla., 1956, USAF Sch. Aviation Medicine, USAF Aerospace Med. Ctr., 1961; cert. of tng. in aviation medicine, UCLA, 1964. Gen. rotating intern U. Iowa Hosps., Iowa City, 1945-46; resident Lincoln (Nebr.) Gen. Hosp., 1946-47, resident in pathology, 1947-48; resident in pathology Bryan Meml. Hosp., Lincoln, 1947-48; fellow, instr. in internal medicine Tulane U., New Orleans, 1948-54; asst. vis. physician Charity Hosp. and Hutchinson Meml. Teaching and Diagnostic and Cancer Detection Clinics, New Orleans, 1948-54; vis. physician Charity Hosp. and Hutchinson Meml. Teaching and Diagnostic Clinics, New Orleans, 1948-54; staff physician Yountville VA Hosp., Napa, Calif., 1958; staff physician Aviation Space and Radiation Med. Group Gen. Dynamics/Convair, San Diego, 1958-61; aerospace med. specialist, med. monitor for Life Sciences Sect. Gen. Dynamics/Astronautics, San Diego, 1961-65; aerospace med. and bioastronautic specialist Lovelace Found. for Med. Edn. and Rsch., Albuquerque, 1965—; staff physician Laguna Honda Hosp., San Francisco, 1968-74; bioastronautics specialist USN, Albuquerque, 1965—; staff physician Kaiser-Permanente Hosp. all-night med. clinic, San Francisco, 1971-73; safety rep. and med. examiner U.S. Civil Aeronaut. Adminstrn., 1959; med. examiner Fed. Aviation Adminstrn., 1961. Author 8 books and 100 tech. papers in field. Comdr., flight surgeon M.C., USNR, 1954-57. Recipient J. Edgar Hoover Gold Disting. Pub. Svc. award Am. Police Hall of Fame, 1991. Fellow San Diego Biomed. Rsch. Inst. (bd. dirs. 1961-65, sec. of fellows 1961-62, chmn. of fellows 1963); mem. AIAA (nom. com. San Diego sect., plant rep. life sci. sect. 1963-65), IEEE (vice chmn. San Diego chpt., profl. tech. group on biomed. electronics 1962-65), N.Y. Acad. Scis., Inst. Environ. Scis., Internat. Univ. Found. (hon. pres.), Internat. Acad. Found. (hon. registrar-sec.), Sigma Xi. Home: 250 Budd Ave Campbell CA 95008-4063

WUEBBLES, DONALD JAMES, atmospheric scientist; b. Breese, Ill., Jan. 28, 1948; s. James Edward and Helen (Isaac) W.; m. Barbara J. Yaley, June 12, 1970; children: Ryan, Kevin, Alan. BS, U. Ill., 1970, MS, 1972; PhD, U. Calif. Davis, 1983. Atmospheric scientist Nat. Oceanic and Atmospheric Adminstrn., Boulder, Colo., 1972-73; atmospheric scientist Lawrence Livermore (Calif.) Nat. Lab., 1973—, group leader, 1987—. Author: Primer on Greenhouse Gases, 1991 (Spl. Achievement Ill. 1991); contbr. articles to profl. jours. Chairperson, mem. sch. site coun., Livermore, 1985-90. Mem. Am. Geophysical Union, Am. Meteorological Soc. Home: 2894 Superior Dr Livermore CA 94550 Office: Lawrence Livermore Nat Lab 7000 East Ave L-262 Livermore CA 94550

WULBERT, DANIEL ELIOT, mathematician, educator; b. Chgo., Dec. 17, 1941; s. Morris and Anna (Greenberg) W.; children: Kera, Noah. BA, Knox U., 1963; MA, U. Tex., Austin, 1964, PhD, 1966. Research assoc. U. Lund (Sweden), 1966-67; asst. prof. U. Wash., Seattle, 1967-73; prof. U. Calif.-San Diego, La Jolla, 1973—; vis. prof. Northwestern U., Evanston, Ill., 1977. Contbr. articles in field. World champion cyclist Masters World Cup Track Points Race, 1990. Office: U Calif San Diego Dept Math0112 La Jolla CA 92038-0109

WULFF, SHARON BEHL, psychotherapist; b. Long Beach, N.Y., Sept. 9, 1956; d. Malcolm Sidney and Joan Gail (Solomon) Behl; m. Stephen A. Wulff, Nov. 16, 1980 (div. Mar. 1988); 1 child, Caitlin Suzanne. AA Mental Health/Creative Arts Therapy, U. Bridgeport, Conn., 1977, BES in Psychology, 1978; MA in Psychology, U. Colo., 1983. Cert. in child life therapy, L.P.C. Therapist Princeton (N.J.) Child Devel. Inst., 1978-79; advocate Nat. Soc. for Autistic Children, Washington, 1979-80; rschr. JFK Child Devel. Ctr., Denver, 1983-84; program coord. Chestor House, Littleton, Colo., 1983; psychol. cons. Head Start, Denver, 1983-84; therapist Mental Health Corp. Denver, 1985-87, clin. supr., 1987-89, program mgr., 1989-91; psychotherapist in pvt. practice Denver, 1991—; psychotherapist assault survivors assistance program Luth. Med. Ctr., Wheat Ridge, Colo., 1991—; cons. Adams County Mental Health, Commerce City, Colo., 1992. Contbr. articles to profl. jours. Vol. Art Reach, Denver, 1989, Jewish Family Svcs., Denver, 1991—; mem. exec. bd. Nat. Soc. for Children and Adults with Autism, Littleton, 1981-84; vol. coord. Colo. Easter Seals Summer Camp, 1981, 82; charter bd. dirs. Colo. Child and Adolescent Mental Health Coalition, sec., 1989-91, bd. dirs., 1992—. Recipient Civic Responsiblitiy award U.S. Postal Svc., 1984; named to Outstanding Young Women of Am., 1988. Mem. Colo. Holistic Health Care Practitioners. Office: 2055 S Oneida St Ste 270 Denver CO 80224

WUN, KAI-LAM WILLIAM, physical chemist; b. Saigon, Vietnam, Aug. 18, 1940; came to U.S., 1960; s. Sing-Hing and Suk-Han (Chan) W.; m. Ching-Man Jennie Yeung, June 23, 1978; children: Aetna, Cary. BSc, U. Calif., Berkeley, 1964; MA, U. Oreg., 1969; PhD, Syracuse (N.Y.) U., 1974. NIH postdoctoral fellow Johns Hopkin's U., Balt., 1974-76, U. Calif., Irvine, 1976-78; asst. prof. U. Louisville, 1978-80; engrng. supr. Hewlett Packard Co., San Jose, Calif., 1981-87; mem. tech. staff Hewlett Packard Co., Palo Alto, Calif., 1987—; tech. mem. ionic contamination subcom., chlorofluro-carbon replacement task force Inst. for Interconnecting and Packaging Electronic Cirs., Lincolnwood, Ill., 1990—. Contbr. articles to profl. jours. Panel cons. elem. sch. math. curriculum Cupertino (Calif.) Union Sch. Dist., 1988, mem. mid. sch. planning com., 1992-93. Mem. IEEE (sr., chmn. SCV/CHMT 1992-93, CHMT/TC-3 1992-93, profl. activities com. of engrs. 1989-91). Roman Catholic. Office: Hewlett Packard Co 1501 Page Mill Rd # 4V Palo Alto CA 94304

WUNDER, BRUCE ARNOLD, zoologist, educator; b. Monterey Park, Calif., Feb. 10, 1942; s. Edwin Claude and Phyllis Viviene (Lehman) W.; children: Michael Brent, Kristin Kathleen. B.A., Whittier Coll., 1963; Ph.D., UCLA, 1968. Teaching asst. in zoology UCLA, 1963-65, assoc. in zoology, 1965-66, USPHS trainee in cardiovascular zoophysiology, 1966-68; postdoctoral fellow NIH, 1968-69; asst. prof. zoology Colo. State U., Ft. Collins, 1969-76, assoc. prof. zoology and entomology, 1976-84, prof., 1984—, asst. chmn. zoology and entomology, 1978-79, 83-84, interim chmn. zoology, 1984-85, chmn., 1985-87, interim chmn. biology, 1987-88, chmn. 1988—; small mammal and physiol. ecologist Ecology Cons., Inc., Biol. Research Assocs., Inc., Fort Collins, Thorne Ecol. Inst., Boulder, U.S. Army C.E., U.S. Fish and Wildlife Service; vis. investigator at biotron U. Wis., Madison, 1971; summer faculty Nat. Wildlife Fedn. Conservation Summit, Estes Park, Colo., 1972-77; summer faculty U. Mich. Biol. Sta., Douglas Lake, 1976, 78; Alexander von Humboldt Research fellow J.W. Goethe U., Frankfort, W.Ger., 1979-80; vis. prof. zoology U. Mont. Biol. Sta., Flathead Lake, 1981, 83, 85, vis. prof. biology, Rocky Mtn. Lab., Gothic, Colo., 1987, 90. Mem. AAAS, Am. Soc. Zoologists, Am. Soc. Mammalogists, Ecol. Soc. Am., Sigma Xi, Omicron Delta Kappa. Contbr. numerous articles to profl. jours. Home: 1315 Kirkwood Dr # 806 Fort Collins CO 80525 Office: Colo State U Dept Biology Fort Collins CO 80523

WUNDER, HAROLDENE FOWLER, accounting educator; b. Greenville, S.C., Nov. 16, 1944; d. Harold Eugene Fowler and Sarah Ann (Chaffin) Crooks. BS, U. Md., 1971; M Acctg., U. S.C., 1975, PhD, 1978. CPA, Ohio. Vis. asst. prof. U. S.C., Columbia, 1977-78; asst. prof. U. Pa., Phila., 1978-81; vis. asst. prof. U. N.C., Chapel Hill, 1981-82; asst. prof. U. Mass., Boston, 1982-86; vis. assoc. prof. Suffolk U., Boston, 1986-87; assoc. prof. U. Toledo, 1987-93; prof. acctg. Calif. State U., Sacramento, 1993—. Contbr. articles to acad. and profl. publs. George Olson fellow, 1975. Mem. AICPA, Ohio Soc. CPAs, Am. Acctg. Assn., Am. Taxation Assn., Nat. Tax Assn.-Tax Inst. Am., NAFE, Beta Gamma Sigma. Office: Calif State U Sch of Bus Adminstrn Sacramento CA 95819

WUNDERLICH, J. ALAN, disability speciality equipment manufacturer, company executive; b. L.A., Feb. 26, 1945; s. Glenn Anthony and Norma Margret (Peglau) W.; m. Constance Jean Fasulo, Oct. 9, 1983 (div. June 1991); stepchildren: Russ John, Jeanine Marie, Jill Ann. AS, AS, Moorpark (Calif.) Coll., 1989. Cert. laser technologist and technician. Engrng. draftsman Rockeydyne, Canoga Park, Calif., 1963-65; co-owner Aztec Redi-Mix Concrete, Glendale, Calif., 1965-70; resl estate speculator, B.C., Can., 1970-75; real estate speculator, Camarillo, Calif., 1984-89; salesman Block Bros. Realty, B.C., 1975-77; v.p. Chanual Holdings Co., B.C., 1977-80; sec.-treas. Verodo Industries Ltd., B.C., 1978-80; bullion broker Coneo Valley Samp and Coin, Thousand Oaks, Calif., 1980-84; pres., CEO, Raptor Inc., Laughlin, Nev., 1990—. Author: (tech. manuals) Fiber Optic Applications, 1985, 590 Dye Laser Operation, 1986. Grantee Optical Soc. Am., 1986. Mem. Laser Inst. Am. (bd. dirs. Moorpark 1985-86, v.p. 1986-87), NRA, Planetary Soc., Amnesty Internat., Smithsonian Assocs. Office: Raptor Inc Box 32021 Laughlin NV 89028

WUNDERMAN, RICHARD LLOYD, earth scientist, educator; b. N.Y.C., Jan. 14, 1952; s. Irwin and Gilda (Margules) W. AB, U. Calif., Berkeley, 1976; MS, Mich. Tech. U., 1983, PhD, 1988. Rsch. libr. J.A. Blume Engrs. and Cons., San Francisco, 1975-76; U.S. ranger Isle Royale Nat. Park Svc., Mich., 1977-78; teaching asst., rschr. Mich. Tech. U., Houghton, 1980-88; volcanologist Cascades Volcano Obs., Vancouver, Wash., 1981; geophysicist Phoenix Geophysics, Denver, 1988-90; pvt. practice cons. Denver, 1989—; geophysicist Interpex Geoscience Software, Ltd., Golden, Colo., 1991; prof. physics Front Range C.C., Westminster, Colo., 1992—; adj. advisor Mich. Tech. U., 1988—; advisor geophysical rsch. The Duluth Complex, 1989. Grantee Geol. Survey, 1987. Mem. Geol. Soc. Am., Soc. Engrng. and Mining Exploration, Am. Geophysical Union, Colo. Mountain Club., Sigma Xi (life). Office: Front Range CC 11611 E 112th St Westminster CO 80030

WUNSCH, KATHRYN SUTHERLAND, lawyer; b. Tipton, Mo., Jan. 30, 1935; d. Lewis Benjamin and Norene Marie (Wolf) Sutherland; m. Charles Martin Wunsch, Dec. 22, 1956 (div. May 1988); children: Debra Kay, Laura Ellen. AB, Ind. U., 1958, JD summa cum laude, 1977; postgrad., Stanford (Calif.) U., 1977. Bar: Calif. 1977, U.S. Dist. Ct. (no. dist.) Calif. 1977. Assoc. Hunt and Hunt, San Francisco, 1977-89; ptnr. Wunsch and George, San Francisco, 1989—. Articles editor Ind. U. Law Rev., 1975-76. Sec., treas. Internat. Visitors Com., Palo Alto, Calif., 1987-90; bd. dirs. Neighbors Abroad, Palo Alto, 1988—. Mem. ABA (com. on small bus.), Calif. Bar Assn. (bus. law com.), Bar Assn. San Francisco (alternative dispute resolution com.), Calif. Acad. Scis., Nat. Assn. Women Bus. Owners (pres. San Francisco chpt. 1992-93, bd. dirs. 1990—), San Francisco Opera Guild, Commonwealth Club, City Club, Phi Beta Kappa, Psi Chi. Republican. Office: Wunsch and George 100 Pine St Fl 21 San Francisco CA 94111-5102

WURSTER, JOHN FREDERICK, management consultant; b. Clinton, Iowa, Apr. 6, 1947; s. Frederick Frehse and Rachel Ann (Shaffer) W.; m. Marjorie Louise Mitzel, May 2, 1970; children: Eric Michael, David John. BS in Chemistry, U. Pitts., 1969, MBA, 1974. Field sales rep. Calgon Corp.-Water Mgmt. Div., Pitts., 1970-74; dist. sales mgr. Calgon Corp.-Water Mgmt. Div., Cin., 1975-76; nat. sales mgr. Calgon Corp. div. Water Mgmt., Pitts., 1976-81; dir. product mgmt. and tech. Calgon Crop.-Water Mgmt. Div., Pitts., 1981-85; v.p. mktg., founder Waste Tech. Svcs. Inc., Golden, Colo., 1985-90, chief ops. officer, 1990-91; pres. Orion Issues Mgmt. Inc., Evergreen, Colo., 1991—, RW2, Inc., Evergreen, Colo., 1991—. Contbr. articles to profl. jours. Com. chmn. Boy Scouts Am., Evergreen, 1987, 88, 89. Mem. Tech. Assn. Pulp and Paper Industry, Assn. Iron and Steel Engrs., Hiwan Golf Club (com. mem. 1991, 92), Sigma Alpha Epsilon. Republican. Home: 3815 Spring Valley Trail Evergreen CO 80439 Office: Orion Issues Mgmt 27985 Meadow Dr Ste 300 Evergreen CO 80439

WURZ, MAX EDWARD, marketing professional; b. Richland, Wash., July 7, 1962; s. Jerry J. and Shirley Ann (Segrest) W.; m. Kristin Kyle Riley, Aug. 5, 1984. BA in Communications, Wash. State U., 1984. Account exec. Met. Graphics, Lynnwood, Wash., 1985, Blakely Burris Loehfelm, Seattle, 1985-87; account mgr. AdWorks/Elgin Syferd, Seattle, 1987; dir. mktg. Egghead Discount Software, Issaquah, Wash., 1987-89; founder, pres. Levy & Wurz Channel Mktg., Seattle, 1989—. Office: Levy & Wurz Channel Mktg 1809 7th Ave Ste 1008 Seattle WA 98101-1313

WURZBERGER, WILLIAM CLARK, executive recruitment company executive; b. Balt., June 2, 1951; s. William Donald Wurzberger and Nancy (Clark) Reynolds; m. Karen Rae Ohl, Oct. 5, 1991; stepchildren: Dan Sullivan, Nancy Sullivan, Sean Sullivan. BA in English, San Diego State U., 1985. Dir. scheduling Calif. Rep. Party, L.A., 1978; dist. rep. Calif. State Assemblyman Bill Lancaster, Covina, 1979-81; legis. asst. Calif. Mfrs. Assn., Sacramento, 1981-82; spl. asst. AID, Washington, 1982-83, congl. liaison officer, 1983-86; spl. asst. for congl. affairs U.S. Dept. State, Washington, 1986-87, legis. mgmt. officer, 1987, White House liaison, 1987-89; dep. asst. to sec. Dept. Def., Washington, 1989-90, asst. to sec., 1990-91; pres. The Clark Co., Burlingame, Calif., 1991—; mgmt. cons.; mem. Sr. Exec. Svc., U.S. Govt., Washington, 1990-91. Chmn. Bush-Quayle Campaign, San Mateo County, Calif., 1992. Recipient medal for disting. pub. svc. Dept. Def., 1991. Mem. Calif. Exec. Recruiters Assn., Am. Astron. Soc. Republican. Office: 1818 Gilbreth Rd Ste 102 Burlingame CA 94010

WUSSLER, ROBERT JOSEPH, broadcasting executive, media consultant; b. Newark, Sept. 8, 1936; s. William and Anna (MacDonald) W.; children: Robert Joseph, Rosemary, Sally, Stefanie, Christopher, Jeanne. BA in Communication Arts, Seton Hall U., 1957, LLD (hon.), 1976; LLD (hon.), Emerson Coll., 1976. With Merlin Cons. Worldwide, CBS News, N.Y.C., 1957-72; v.p., gen. mgr. Sta. WBBM-TV, Chgo., 1972-74; v.p. CBS Sports, N.Y.C., 1974-76, pres., 1977-78; pres. Sta. CBS-TV, N.Y.C., 1976-77, Pyramid Enterprises Ltd., N.Y.C., 1978-80; exec. v.p. Turner Broadcasting System Inc., Atlanta, 1980-87, sr. exec. v.p., from 1987, bd. dirs.; pres. Atlanta Sports Teams, Inc., 1981-87; pres., chief exec. officer COMSAT Video Enterprises, Inc., Washington, 1989-92, ret., 1992; pres. Wussler Group, 1992—; chmn. bd. dirs. Nat. Acad. TV Arts and Scis., 1986-90; bd. dirs. Atlanta Hawks Ltd., Atlanta Braves Nat. League Baseball Club, Inc.; co-owner Denver Nuggets, NBA, 1989-92. Bd. regents Seton Hall U., 1978-84; trustee Marymount Manhattan Coll., 1977-81. Recipient Emmy awards, numerous other nat. and internat. news and sports awards. Mem. Dirs. Guild Am., Internat. Radio and TV Soc., Ariz. Heart Inst., Cable Advt. Bur., Nat. Cable TV Assn. (satellite network com.), European Broadcasting Union. Roman Catholic.

WUSTRACK, KARL OTTO, plastic surgeon; b. Rochester, N.Y., Mar. 6, 1944; s. Otto Henry and Dorothy (Haversack) W.; m. Diane Harris Maurel, July 9, 1966; children: Gretchen, Sonja, Rosanna. BS, Stanford U., 1966; MD, Yale U., 1970. Diplomate Am. Bd. Plastic Surgery. Resident in gen. surgery Oreg. Hosp. State U., Portland, 1970-76; resident in plastic surgery UCLA, 1976-78; pvt. practice Oregon City, Oreg., 1976—. Bd. dirs. Willamette Falls Hosp., Oregon City, 1988—. Named Most Valuable Player Masters Basketball 45 Over Tournament, Ft. Lauderdale, Fla., 1989; Oreg. State 3 on 3 over 40 champion, 1991. Fellow ACS; mem. Am. Soc. Plastic and Reconstructive Surgeons, Am. Soc. for Aesthetic Plastic Surgery. Republican. Office: 605 High St Oregon City OR 97045-2202

WYANT, JAMES CLAIR, engineering company executive, educator; b. Morenci, Mich., July 31, 1943; s. Clair William and Idah May (Burroughs) W.; m. Louise Doherty, Nov. 20, 1971; 1 child, Clair Frederick. BS, Case Western Reserve, 1965; MS, U. Rochester, 1967, PhD, 1968. Engr. Itek Corp., Lexington, Mass., 1968-74; instr. Lowell (Mass.) Tech. Inst., 1969-74; prof. U. Ariz., Tucson, 1974—; vis. prof. U. Rochester, N.Y., 1983; pres. WYKO Corp., Tucson, 1984—; chmn. Gordon Conf. on Holography Plymouth (N.H.) State Coll., 1984. Editor: Applied Optics and Optical Engineering, vols. VII-X, 1979, 80, 83, 87. Mem. Optical Soc. Am. (bd. dirs. 1979-81), Soc. Photo-Optical Instrumentation Engrng. (pres. 1986). Home: 1881 N King St Tucson AZ 85749-9367 Office: U Ariz Optical Scis Ctr Tucson AZ 85721

WYANT, THEODORE, flooring contractor; b. N.Y.C., Dec. 20, 1954; s. Edward Howard and Gloria (Esposito) W.; m. Paul Jean Woodward; children: Margaret, Edward, Amy. Engr. asst. 146 CES, Van Nuys, Calif., 1981-86, 142 CES, Portland IAP, Oreg., 1981-86; contract constrn. insp. 939 CES, Portland IAP, 1986-88; mobility NCO 936 CES, McCellan A.F.B., 1988-89; prodn. contr. 114 ENG, K-Fall, Oreg., 1989-91; flooring contr. Tapem Constrn., Grants Pass, Oreg., 1991—. Bd. dirs., coach Little League Majors, 1989—. Master sgt. USAF/Air Res./Air Guard, 1981—. Mem. Sgt. Assn. Mil. Assn., T. Wyant Builder Assn. Republican. Home and Office: Tapem Constrn 1125 SW Spruce Grants Pass OR 97526

WYATT, EDITH ELIZABETH, educator; b. San Diego, Aug. 13, 1914; d. Jesse Wellington and Elizabeth (Fultz) Carne; m. Lee Ora Wyatt, Mar. 30, 1947 (dec. Jan. 1966); children: Glenn Stanley (dec.), David Allen. BA, San Diego State Coll., 1936. Elem. tchr. Nat. Sch. Dist., National City, Calif., 1938-76. Sec. San Diego County Parks Soc., 1986—; librarian Congl. Ch. Women's Fellowship, Chula Vista, Calif., 1980—; active Boy Scouts Am, 1959—. Recipient Who award San Diego County Tchrs. Assn., 1968, Silver Fawn award Boy Scouts Am. Mem. AAUW (sec. 1978-80, pub. rels. 1985—), Calif. Retired Tchrs. Assn. (scholarhsip com. 1985-90, 1992—), Starlite Hiking Club (sec.-treas. 1979—). Home: 165 E Millan St Chula Vista CA 91910-6255

WYATT, JOSEPH LUCIAN, JR., lawyer, educator; b. Chgo., Feb. 21, 1924; s. Joseph Lucian and Cecile Gertrude (Zadico) W.; m. Marjorie Kathryn Simmons, Apr. 9, 1954; children: Daniel, Linn, Jonathan. AB in English Lit. with honors, Northwestern U., 1947; LLB, Harvard U., 1949. Bar: Calif. 1950, U.S. Dist. Ct. (cen. dist.) Calif. 1950, U.S. Ct. Appeals (9th cir.) 1950, U.S. Tax Ct., U.S. Supreme Ct. 1965. Assoc. firm Brady, Nossaman & Walker, Los Angeles, 1950-58; ptnr. Brady, Nossaman & Walker, L.A., 1958-61; pvt. practice L.A., 1961-71; sr. mem. Cooper, Wyatt, Tepper & Plant, P.C., L.A., 1971-79; of counsel Beardsley, Hufstedler & Kemble, L.A., 1979-81; ptnr. Hufstedler, Kaus & Ettinger, L.A., 1981—; mem. faculty Pacific Coast Banking Sch., Seattle, 1963-92, Southwestern Grad. Sch. Banking, 1988-89; adviser Am. Law Inst. Prudent Investor Rule Restatement, Trusts 3d. Author: Trust Administration and Taxation, 4 vols., 1964—; editor: Trusts and Estates, 1962-74. Lectr. continuing legal edn. programs, Calif. and Tex.; trustee Pacific Oaks Coll. and Children's Sch., 1969—; counsel, parliamentarian Calif. Democratic party and presdl. conv. dels., 1971—; mem. Calif. State Personnel Bd., 1961-71, v.p., 1963-65, pres., 1965-67; bd dirs. Calif. Pub. Employees Retirement System, 1963-71. Served with USAAF, 1943-45. Fellow Am. Coll. of Trust and Estate Counsel; mem. ABA, Internat. Acad. Estate and Trust Law (treas.), Am. Law Inst., Calif. Bar Assn. (del. state conf. 1956, 62-67), L.A. Bar Assn. (trustee 1956). Democrat. Christian Scientist. Home: 1119 Armada Dr Pasadena CA 91103-2805 Office: Hufstedler Kaus & Ettinger 355 S Grand Ave Fl 39 Los Angeles CA 90071-3101

WYCKOFF, MARGO GAIL, psychologist; b. Omaha, Jan. 30, 1941; d. Winfield Jennings and Gail Claudia (Leach) Hartland; m. Tom Lawrence Wyckoff, Mar. 17, 1971; children: Ted, Elizabeth. BA, U. Wash., 1973, MSW, 1975; PhD, Union Grad. Sch., Seattle, 1978; cer. Licensed psychologist. Clin. lectr. U. Wash. Med. Sch., Seattle, 1976-78, asst. prof. univ. Pain Ctr., 1980-87; assoc. dir. pain ctr. Swedish Med. Ctr., Seattle, 1979-83, dir. behavioral svcs., 1979-83; pvt. practice Seattle, 1983—; psychology cons. Providence Med. Ctr., Seattle, 1979-87. Contbr. articles to jours., chpts. to books. Mem. Wash. Psychol. Assn. (bd. dirs. 1986-87), Nat. Orgn. Soc. Workers, Internat. Assn. for the Study of Pain, Psychoanalytic Assn. (bd. dirs. 1982-84), Wash. Environ. Council. Democrat. Office: Springbrook Psychol Group 4540 Sand Point Way NE Seattle WA 98105-3941

WYCOFF, CHARLES COLEMAN, retired anesthesiologist; b. Glazier, Tex., Sept. 2, 1918; s. James Garfield and Ada Sharpe (Braden) W.; m. Gene Marie Henry, May 16, 1942; children: Michelle, Geoffrey, Brian, Roger, Daniel, Norman, Irene, Teresa. AB, U. Calif., Berkeley, 1941; MD, U. Calif., San Francisco, 1943. Diplomate Am. Bd. Anesthesiology. Founder The Wycoff Group of Anesthesiology, San Francisco, 1947-53; chief of anesthesia St. Joseph's Hosp., San Francisco, 1947-52, creator residency tng. programs in anesthesiology, 1950; chief anesthesia San Francisco County Hosp., 1953-54; practice anesthesiology, tchr. Presbyn. Med. Ctr., N.Y.C., 1955-63; asst. prof. anesthesiology Columbia U., N.Y.C., 1955-63; clin. practice anesthesiology St. Francis Meml. Hosp., San Francisco, 1963-84; creator residency tng. programs in anesthesiology San Francisco County Hosp., 1954. Producer, dir. films on regional anesthesia; contbr. articles to sci. jours. Scoutmaster Boy Scouts Am., San Francisco, 1953-55. Capt. M.C., U.S. Army, 1945-47. Mem. Alumni Faculty Assn. Sch. Medicine U. Calif.-San Francisco (councilor-at-large 1979-80). Democrat. Home: 394 Cross St Napa CA 94559

WYCOFF, ROBERT E., petroleum company executive; b. Tulsa, 1930; married. B.S.M.E., Stanford U., 1952, M.S.M.E., 1953. With Atlantic Richfield Co., L.A., 1953—, various engrng. and mgmt. positions, 1957-70, mgr. western region Internat. div., 1971-73, v.p., resident mgr. Alaska region N.Am. Producing div., 1973-74, corp. planning v.p., 1974-77, sr. v.p. planning and fin., 1977-80, exec. v.p., 1980-84, chief corp. officer, 1984, vice chmn., 1985, pres., chief operating officer, 1986—, also dir.; chmn. Lyondell Petrochem. Co., Houston. Mem. ASME, Am. Petroleum Inst. Office: Atlantic Richfield Co PO Box 2579 515 S Flower St Los Angeles CA 90071-2200 also: Lyondell Petrochem 1221 McKinney St Houston TX 77010*

WYDEN, RONALD LEE, congressman; b. Wichita, Kans., May 3, 1949; s. Peter and Edith W.; m. Laurie Oseran, Sept. 5, 1978; 1 child, Adam David. Student, U. Santa Barbara, 1967-69; A.B. with distinction, Stanford U., 1971; J.D., U. Oreg., 1974. Campaign aide Senator Wayne Morse, 1972, 74; co-founder, co-dir. Oreg. Gray Panthers, 1974-80; dir. Oreg. Legal Services for Elderly, 1977-79; instr. gerontology U. Oreg., 1976, U. Portland, 1980, Portland State U., 1979; mem. 97th-103rd Congresses from 3d Oreg. dist., Washington, D.C., 1981—; mem. Energy and Commerce com., subcom. telecom. and fin., health and environment, oversight and investigations, small bus. com., subcom. regulation, bus. opportunities, tech. Recipient Service to Oreg. Consumers award Oreg. Consumers League, 1978, Citizen of Yr. award Oreg. Assn. Social Workers, 1979, Significant Service award Multnomah County Area Agy. on Aging, 1980; named Young Man of Yr. Oreg. Jr. C. of C., 1980. Mem. Am. Bar Assn., Iowa Bar Assn. Democrat. Jewish. Office: 1111 Longworth House of Representatives Washington DC 20515-3703*

WYLE, EWART HERBERT, clergyman; b. London, Sept. 12, 1904; s. Edwin and Alice Louise (Durman) W.; B.A., U. Louisville, 1930; B.D., Lexington Theol. Sem., 1933; postgrad. Louisville Presbyn. Theol. Sem., Temple U., 1933-35; D.D., Tex. Christian U., 1953; m. Prudence Harper, June 12, 1959; 1 son, Ewart Herbert. Ordained to ministry Christian Ch., 1935; pastor First Ch., Palestine, Tex., 1935-37, First Ch., Birmingham, Ala., 1937-41, First Ch., Tyler, Tex., 1944-54, Country Club Ch., Kansas City, Mo., 1954-59; minister Torrey Pines Ch., La Jolla, Calif., 1959-79, minister emeritus, 1979—. Bd. dirs. Scripps Meml. Hosp., pres., 1980-81. Served as chaplain, maj., AUS, 1941-44. Mem. Mil. Order World Wars, Am. Legion, Tau Kappa Epsilon, Pi Kappa Delta. Clubs: Masons (32 deg.), Shriners, Rotary, LaJolla Beach and Tennis. Home: 8850 N La Jolla Scenic Dr La Jolla CA 92037-1608

WYLE, FREDERICK S., lawyer; b. Berlin, Germany, May 9, 1928; came to U.S., 1939, naturalized, 1944; s. Norbert and Malwina (Mauer) W.; m. Katinka Franz, June 29, 1969; children: Susan Kim, Christopher Anthony, Katherine Anne. B.A. magna cum laude, Harvard U., 1951, LL.B., 1954. Bar: Mass. 1954, Calif. 1955, N.Y. 1958. Teaching fellow Harvard Law Sch., 1954-55; law clk. U.S. Dist. Ct., No. Dist. Calif., 1955-57; assoc. firm Paul, Weiss, Rifkind, Wharton & Garrison, N.Y.C., 1957-58; pvt. practice San Francisco, 1958-62; spl. asst. def. rep. U.S. del. to NATO, Paris, 1962-63; mem. Policy Planning Council, Dept. State, Washington, 1963-65; dep. asst. sec. def. for European and NATO affairs Dept. Def., Washington, 1966-69; v.p. devel., gen. counsel Schroders, Inc., N.Y.C., 1969-71; atty., cons. Schroders, Inc., 1971-72; chief exec. officer Saturday Rev. Industries, Inc., San Francisco, 1972-76; individual practice law San Francisco, 1976—; internat. counsel to Fed. States Micronesia, 1974-82; cons. Rand Corp., Dept. of Def., Nuclear Regulatory Commn.; trustee in bankruptcy, receiver various corps since 1974. Contbr. to: Ency. Brit, 1972, also articles in profl. publs. Served with AUS, 1946-47. Mem. World Affairs Coun. (bd. trustees), Am. Council Germany, Internat. Inst. Strategic Studies, Phi Beta Kappa. Office: 2500 Russ Bldg 235 Montgomery St San Francisco CA 94104-2902

WYLIE, JUDITH BABCOCK, writer, educator; b. Balt., Oct. 7, 1943; d. Joseph Brooks and Sara Louise (Morgan) Boynton; m. Frank Winston Wylie, Feb. 19, 1984. BA, U. Akron, 1966; MEd, U. Ky., 1967. Program adviser Baker Student Ctr. Ohio U., Athens, 1968-71; program dir. Student Union U. Ariz., Tucson, 1971-77; program dir. Student Union Calif. State U., L.A., 1977-79, dir. student devel., 1979-80, asst. to v.p. adminstrn., 1980-83; lectr. in writing Pasadena (Calif.) City Coll., 1983-86; owner Judith Babcock Communications, Santa Cruz, 1983—; lectr. in writing NYU, N.Y.C., 1989—; chief travel writer Pasadena Star News, 1986—, San Gabriel (Calif.) Valley Tribune, Whittier Daily News and Star Tribune, 1991—. Author: The Spa Book, 1983, The Romance Emporium, 1986; contbr. numerous articles to newspapers and mags. Mem. PEN, U. Ariz. Friends of Poetry Ctr., Bay Area Travel Writers, Kappa Kappa Gamma. Home: 1900 Smith Grade Pasadena CA 95060

WYLLIE, LORING A., JR., structural engineer; b. Aug. 21, 1938. BS, U. Calif., Berkeley, 1960, MS in Structural Engring., 1962. Registered profl. engr., Oreg., Utah, Nebr., Tex.; registered civil and structural engr., Calif. With H.J. Degenkolh Assoc., San Francisco, 1964—, now chmn., sr. prin. Contbr. artilcle to profl. jours. With U.S. Army. Fellow ASCE (pres. San Francisco sect. 1980-81, chmn. com. on concrete and masonry structures 1980-81, H.J. Brunnier award 1985), Am. Concrete Inst. (mem. com. 318, standard bldg. code 1972—, mem. tech. activities com. 1982-88, bd. dirs. 1985-88, Henry L. Kennedy award 1985); mem. NAE (recognition 1990), Structural Engrs. Assn. Calif. (bd. dirs. 1978-80, 86, 89, pres. 1987-88), Structural Engrs. Assn. No. Calif. (bd. dirs. 1976-78, 84-87, pres. 1985-86), Earthquake Engring. Rsch. Inst. (bd. dirs. 1986-89), Internat. Assn. Bridge and Structural Engrs. (chmn. U.S.A. group 1989—), Phi Beta Kappa, Tau Beta Pi, Chi Epsilon. Office: H J Degenkolb Assocs 2350 Sansome St # 900 San Francisco CA 94104-1304

WYLLIE, PETER JOHN, geologist, educator; b. London, Feb. 8, 1930; came to U.S., 1961; s. George William and Beatrice Gladys (Weaver) W.; m. Frances Rosemary Blair, June 9, 1956; children: Andrew, Elizabeth (dec.), Lisa, John. B.Sc. in Geology and Physics, U. St. Andrews, Scotland, 1952, B.Sc. with 1st class honours in Geology, 1955, Ph.D. in Geology, 1958, D.Sc. (hon.), 1974. Glaciologist Brit. W. Greenland Expdn., 1950; geologist Brit. N. Greenland Expdn., 1952-54; asst. lectr. geology U. St. Andrews, 1955-56; research asst. geochemistry Pa. State U., State College, 1956-58, asst. prof. geochemistry, 1958-59, asso. prof. petrology, 1961-65, acting head, dept. geochemistry mineralogy, 1962-63; research fellow chemistry Leeds (Eng.) U., 1959-60, lectr. exptl. petrology, 1960-61; prof. petrology geochemistry U. Chgo., 1965-77, Homer J. Livingston prof., 1978-83, chmn. dept. geophys. scis., 1979-82, master phys. scis. collegiate div., asso. dean coll., asso. dean phys. scis. div., 1972-73; chmn. div. geol. and planetary scis. Calif. Inst. Tech., Pasadena, 1983-87, prof. geology, 1987—; chmn. commn. exptl. petrology high pressures temperatures Internat. Union Geol. Scis.; mem. adv. panel earth scis. NSF, 1975-78, chmn. adv. com. earth scis. div., 1979-82; mem. U.S. Nat. Com. on Geology, 1978-82; mem. U.S. Nat. Com. Internat. Union Geodesy and Geophysics, 1980-84, U.S. Nat. Com. Geochemistry, 1981-84; chmn. com. on objectives in solid-earth scis. NRC, 1988-93. Author: The Dynamic Earth, 1971, The Way the Earth Works, 1976; editor: Ultramafic and Related Rocks, 1967; chmn. editorial & writing com. Solid-Earth Sciences and Society, 1993; editor Jour. Geology, 1967-83; editor-in-chief Minerals Rocks (monograph series), 1967—. Served with RAF, 1948-49. Recipient Polar medal H.M. Queen Elizabeth, Eng.; Quantrell award, 1979; Wollaston medal Geol. Soc. London, 1982, Abraham-Gottlob-Werner-Medaille German Mineral. Soc., 1987. Fellow Am. Acad. Arts and Sci., Royal Soc. London, Edinburgh Geol. Soc. (corr.), Mineral. Soc. Am. (pres. 1977-78, award 1965), Am. Acad. Scis. (fgn. assoc.), Am. Geophys. Union, Indian Geophys. Union (fgn.), Nat. Acad. Sci. India (fgn.), Russian Acad. Scis. (fgn.), Russian Mineral. Soc. (fgn., hon.), Indian Nat. Sci. Acad. (fgn.), Nat. Acad. Scis. India (fgn.), Geol. Soc. Am.; mem. Mineral. Soc. Gt. Britain and Ireland (hon.), Internat. Mineral. Assn. (2d v.p. 1978-82, 1st v.p. 1982-86, pres. 1986-90), Internat. Union of Geodesy and Geophysics (v.p. 1991—). Office: Calif Inst Tech Geol & Planetary Scis 170-25 Pasadena CA 91125

WYMAN, RICHARD VAUGHN, engineering educator, exploration company executive; b. Painesville, Ohio, Feb. 22, 1927; s. Vaughn Ely and Melinda (Ward) W.; m. Anne Fenton, Dec. 27, 1947; 1 son, William Fenton. B.S., Case Western Res. U., 1948; M.S., U. Mich., 1949; Ph.D., U. Ariz., 1974. Registered profl. engr., Nev.; registered geologist, Ariz., Calif.; lic. water right surveyor, Nev. Geologist N.J. Zinc Co., 1949, 52-53, Cerro de Pasco Corp., 1950-52; chief geologist Western Gold & Uranium, Inc., St. George, Utah, 1953-55, gen. supt., 1955-57, v.p., 1957-59; pres. Intermountain Exploration Co., Boulder City, Nev., 1959—; tunnel supt. Reynolds Electric & Engring. Co., 1961-63, mining engr., 1965-67; asst. mgr. ops. Reynolds Electric and & Engring. Co., 1967-69; constrn. supt. engr. Sunshine Mining Co., 1963-65; lectr. U. Nev., Las Vegas, 1969-73, assoc. prof., 1973-80, dept. chmn., 1976-80, prof., 1980-92, prof. emeritus, 1992—, chmn. dept. civil and mech. engring., 1984-90, chmn. dept. civil and environ. engring., 1990-91; mineral rep. Ariz. Strip Adv. Bd., 1976-80, U.S.B.L.M.; peer rev. com. Nuclear Waste Site, Dept. of Energy, Las Vegas, 1978-82; pres. Ariz. Juno Resources, Boulder City, 1980-83, Wyman Engring. Cons., 1987—; cons. Corp. Andina de Fomento, Caracas, Venezuela, 1977-78; v.p. Comstock Gold, Inc., 1984—. Contbr. articles to profl. jours. Sec. Washington County Republican Party, Utah, 1958-60; del. Utah Rep. Conv., 1958-60; scoutmaster Boy Scouts Am., 1959-69. Served with USN, 1944-46. Fellow ASCE (edn. div. 1990, local rep. nat. conv. Las Vegas 1990), Soc. Econ. Geologists (life); mem. AIME (chmn. So. Nev. sect. 1971-72, dir. 1968—, sec.-treas. 1974—, chmn. Pacific S.W. Minerals Conf. 1972, gen. chmn. nat. conv. 1980, Disting. Mem. award 1989), Assn. Engring. Geologists (dir. South West sect. 1989-91), Nev. Mining Assn. (assoc.), Assn. Ground Water Scientists and Engrs., Arctic Inst. N.Am. (life), Alaska Mining Assn., Geol. Soc. Am., Am. Soc. Engring. Edn., Sigma Xi (pres. Las Vegas sect. 1986-91), Phi Kappa Phi (pres. U. Nev. Las Vegas chpt. 100, 1982-83), Sigma Gamma Epsilon. Congregationalist. Home: 610 Bryant Ct Boulder City NV 89005-3017 Office: U Nev Dept Civil and Environ Engring 4505 S Maryland Pky Las Vegas NV 89154-0002

WYMER, NANCY ELAINE, plant taxonomist, consultant, habitat restorationist, educator; b. Kittanning, Pa., Oct. 5, 1948; d. Ernest and Helen Irene (Rattigan) Ruhland; children: Jason, Shawn. BS in Horticulture, U. Ariz., 1971, MS in Plant Ecology & Physiology, 1979; cert. in hazardous waste mgmt., U. Calif., Davis, 1989. Lab. technician USPA Bee Rsch. Lab., Tucson, 1969; landscape supr. Estes Constrn. Co., Tucson, 1974-76; pub. sch. tchr. Ariz., 1980-82; instr. Calif. State U., Sacramento, 1982-83; environ. intern Aerojet Corp., Sacramento, 1983, mem. sci. real world community rels. program, 1983-90; owner, prin. investigator Wymer and Assocs., Citrus Heights, Calif., 1984—; sr. ecologist Kleinfelder, Sacramento, 1991—; continuing edn. instr. Calif. State U., Sacramento, 1982-83. Author: Planetary Geology, 1988. Mem. Am. Geophys. Union, Calif. Native Plant Soc., Women Geoscience, Soc. Wetland Scientists. Office: 8100 Oak Ave Citrus Heights CA 95610

WYNAR, BOHDAN STEPHEN, librarian, author and editor; b. Lviv, Ukraine, Sept. 7, 1926; came to U.S., 1950, naturalized, 1957; s. John I. and Euphrosina (Doryk) W.; m. Olha Yarema, Nov. 23, 1992; children: Taras, Michael, Roxolana, Yarynka. Diplom-Volkswirt Econs., U. Munich, Germany, 1949, Ph.D., 1950; M.A., U. Denver, 1958. Methods analyst, statistician Tramco Corp., Cleve., 1951-53; freelance journalist Societ Econs., Cleve., 1954-56; adminstrv. asst. U. Denver Librs., 1958-59, head tech. svcs. div., 1959-62; assoc. prof. Sch. Librarianship, U. Denver, 1962-66; dir. div. libr. edn. State U. Coll., Geneseo, N.Y., 1966-67; dean Sch. Libr. Sci. State U. Coll., Geneseo; prof. State U. Coll., 1967-69; pres. Libraries Unlimited Inc., 1969—. Author: Soviet Light Industry, 1956, Economic Colonialism, 1958, Ukrainian Industry, 1964, Introduction to Bibliography and Reference Work, 4th edit, 1967, Introduction to Cataloging and Classification, 8th edit, 1992, Major Writings on Soviet Economy, 1966, Library Acquisitions, 2d edit, 1971, Research Methods in Library Science, 1971, Economic Thought in Kievan Rus', 1974; co-author: Comprehensive Bibliography of Cataloging and Classification, 2 vols., 1973, Ukraine: A Bibliographic Guide to English Language Publications, 1990; editor Ukrainian Quar., 1953-58, Preliminary Checklist of Colorado Bibliography, 1963, Studies in Librarianship, 1963-66, Research Studies in Library Science, 1970—, Best Reference Books, 3d edit., 1985, 4th edit., 1992, Colorado Bibliography, 1980; gen. editor: American Reference Books Ann., 1969—; editor: ARBA Guide to Subject Encyclopedias and Dictionaries, 1985, ARBA Guide To Biographical Dictionaries, Reference Books in Paperback, An Annotated Guide, 2d edit., 1976, 3rd edit., 1991, Dictionary of Am. Library Biography, 1978, Ukraine-A Bibliographic Guide to English-Language Publications, 1990, Recommended Reference Books for Medium-Sized and Small Libraries, 1981—; co-editor, contbr. Ency. Ukraine, 1955—;editor Library Sci. Ann., 1984-90. Bd. dirs., mem. exec. bd. ZAREVO, Inc. Mem. ALA (pres. Ukrainian Congress com. br., Denver 1976), Colo. Library Assn., N.Y. Library Assn., Am. Assn. Advancement Slavic Studies (pres. Ukrainian Research Found. 1976-90), AAUP, Ukrainian Hist. Assn. (exec. bd.), Sevčenko Societe Scientifique (Paris), Ukrainian Acad. Arts and Scis. (N.Y.C.). Office: Librs Unltd Inc 6931 S Yosemite St Englewood CO 80112-1400

WYNIA, JAMES PAUL, software specialist; b. Lincoln, Nebr., Mar. 25, 1964; s. Melvin Eugene and Beverly Loreen (Zinsmaster) W. BS in Computer Sci., Biola U., 1986; MS in Computer Sci., Santa Clara U., 1992. Asst. mgr. McDonald's, San Jose, Calif., 1980-82; summer coop. programmer IBM, San Jose, 1985; computer lab. technician Biola U., LaMirada, Calif., 1984-86; task mgr., software specialist Sterling Software, Moffett Field, Calif., 1982—. Mem. Assn. for Computing Machinery (vis. mem., SIGCOMM, SIGOPS, SIGGRAPH), USENIX Assn. Republican. Office: Sterling Software NASA Ames Rsch Ctr Moffett Field CA 94035-1000

WYNKOOP, DONAL BROOKE, electric power company executive; b. Denver, July 10, 1945; s. Francis Yates and Marylynn Frances (Koogle) W.; m. Sheila Ann Bell, Dec. 17, 1961; children: Donal B. Jr., David Brian, Cheryl Lynn. Grad. high sch., Denver; cert. electric meter course, I.C.S., 1970, cert. electrical distrbn. engr., 1980. Journeyman Pub. Svc. Co. Colo., Denver, 1971-79, sr. meterman, 1979-86, unit mgr., 1986—. Office: Pub Svc Co Colo 1123 W 3rd Ave Denver CO 80223

WYNN, ROBERT RAYMOND, engineer; b. Omaha, Mar. 4, 1929; s. Horace Oscar and Yvonne Cecil (Witters) W.; m. Joann Elizabeth Swicegood, June 28, 1974; children: Kay, William, Frederick, Andrew, Emma, Lawrence, Robert. Diploma in Nuclear Engring., Capitol Radio Engring. Inst., 1964; BSEE, Pacific Internat. Coll. Arts and Scis., 1964; AA in Bus. Adminstrn., Allen Hancock Coll., 1969; MSEE, Pacific Internat. Coll. Arts and Scis., 1971; MSMS, West Coast U., 1975, ASCS, 1985; BSCS, U. State of N.Y., 1985. Registered profl. engr., Calif. Meteorologist United Air Lines, Calif., 1949-53; engring. planner Aircraft Tools Inc., Inglewood, Calif., 1953-55; field service engr. N. Am. Aviation, Inglewood, Calif., 1955-59; R&D engr. Carstedt Research Inc., N. Long Beach, Calif., 1959-60; test engr. Martin Marrietta Corp., Vandenburg AFB, Calif., 1960-64; project engr. Fed. Electric Corp., Vandenburg AFB, Calif., 1965-69; systems engr. Aeronutronic Ford Corp., Pasadena, Calif., 1970-75; MTS Jet Propulsion Lab., Pasadena, Calif., 1975-83; engring. mgr. Space Com., Redondo Beach, Calif., 1983-84; engring. specialist Boeing Service Inc., Pasadena, 1984-86; cons., mem. tech. staff Jet Propulsion Lab., Pasadena, 1986—; instr. computer sci. and CAD, Jet Propulsion Lab., 1980-82. With USAAF, 1946. Mem. Calif. Soc. Profl. Engrs., Exptl. Aircraft Assn. (pres. Lompoc chpt. 1968), W. Coast U. Alumni Assn. Democrat. Home: PO Box 4138 Sunland CA 91041-4138 Office: Jet Propulsion Lab 4800 Oak Grove Dr Pasadena CA 91109-8099

WYNN, STEPHEN A., hotel, entertainment facility executive; b. 1941; married. Pres., chief exec. officer Best Brands, Inc., 1969-72; chmn. bd. dirs. Mirage Resorts Inc. (formerly Golden Nugget Inc.), 1973—. Office: Mirage Resort Inc PO Box 7777 Las Vegas NV 89177-0777

WYRWICKA, WANDA, research anatomist; b. Pabianice, Poland, Sept. 9, 1912; came to U.S., 1966; d. Jacob and Veronica (Rytwinska) W.; m. Leszek Kolodziejczyk, Dec. 26, 1946; 1 child, Joanna. MS, Poznan U., 1937, PhD, 1947. From asst. researcher to prof. extraordinaire Nencki Inst. of Exptl. Biology, Warsaw, Poland, 1947-66; from asst. researcher to full researcher UCLA, 1966-79, rsch. anatomist, 1980—; cons. neuropsychology lab. VA Med. Ctr., Sepulveda, Calif., 1967-72; key investigator Ctr. for Ulcer Rsch. and Edn., VA Med. Ctr., Wadsworth, Calif., 1974-78. Author: The Mechanisms of Conditioned Behavior, 1972, The Development of Food Preferences, 1981, Brain and Feeding Behavior, 1988. Recipient Pavlovian Soc. of N.Am. award, 1977. Office: UCLA Sch Medicine Dept Anatomy Los Angeles CA 90024

WYSE, BONITA W(ENSINK), nutrition educator, researcher; b. Lorain, Ohio, Oct. 2, 1945; d. Norbert B. and Ruth B.(DeChant) Wensink. BS, Notre Dame of Ohio, 1967; MS, Mich. State U., 1970; PhD, Colo. State U., 1977. Registered dietitian. Clin. dietitian St. Lawrence Hosp., Lansing, Mich., 1968-69; instr. nutrition Utah State U., Logan, 1970-73, asst. prof., 1973-77, assoc. prof., dir. coordinated undergrad. med. dietetics program, 1977-81, prof., 1981—, acting dean Coll. Family Life, 1984-86, dean, 1986—; bd. dirs. Gerber Products Co., Fremont, Mich.; cons. Met. Life Found., N.Y.C., 1983-86; mem. adv. bd. Heart, Blood, Lung Inst., NIH, Bethesda, Md., 1984-87. Author: Nutritional Quality Index of Foods, 1979; contbr. articles to profl. jours. Bd. dirs. Citizens Against Phys. and Sexual Abuse, Logan, 1984. Recipient Outstanding Alumna award Dept. Food Sci. and Nutrition, Mich. State U., 1982. Mem. Am. Dietetic Assn. (council on research 1982-87, bd. dirs. 1984-87, Frances E. Fischer Meml. Nutrition Lectr., 1984), Utah Dietetic Assn. (pres. 1976-77), Am. Inst. Nutrition, Am. Home Econs. Assn. (Borden award for research 1981). Republican. Roman Catholic. Office: Utah State Univ Dean's Office Family Life Logan UT 84322-2900

WYSE, HEATHER LEA, public relations specialist; b. Portland, Oreg., Dec. 12, 1966; d. Donald Bruce and Maridel Jane (Warkentin) W. Student, U. Puget Sound, 1985-87; BS, U. Oreg., 1989. Cert. journalism, pub. rels. With pub. rels. U. Puget Sound, Tacoma, 1985-87; campaign asst. Fadely for Supreme Ct., Eugene, Oreg., 1988; with pub. rels. Portland (Oreg.) Rose Festival Assn., 1989; with sales and mktg. The Westgate Hotel, San Diego, 1989-91; pub. rels. coord. Emerald Shapery Ctr./The Pan Pacific Hotel, San Diego, 1991—; owner, pres. Contagion-Creations and Collections, San Diego, 1991—. Author: Patterns!, 1991. Com. chair, vol. March of Dimes, San Diego, 1990-92; fundraiser Casa de Amparo, San Diego, 1991; coord. Toys for Tots, San Diego 1992—. Mem. NAFE, San Diego Travelers Assn., Pub. Rels. Soc. Am., Kappa Alpha Theta. Office: Emerald Shapery Ctr 402 W Broadway San Diego CA 92101

WYSE, WILLIAM WALKER, lawyer; b. Spokane, Wash., July 20, 1919; s. James and Hattie (Walker) W.; m. Janet E. Oswalt, Jan. 30, 1944; children: Wendy L., Scott C., Duncan E. AB, U. Wash., 1941; JD, Harvard U., 1948. Bar: Oreg. 1948. Pvt. practice Portland; ptnr. Stoel, Rives, Boley, Jones & Gray, 1953-88; pres. Wyse Investment Services, 1988—; past dir. Treasureland Savs. and Loan Assn.; past trustee, sec. Pacific Realty Trust; trustee Holladay Park Plaza. Bd. dirs. Community Child Guidance Clinic, 1951-57, pres., 1956-57; chmn. ctrl. budget com. United Fund, 1958-60; 1st v.p. United Good Neighbors; chmn. dir. Portland Sch. Bd., 1959-66; pres. Oreg. Symphony Soc., 1968—; pres. Tri-County Community Coun., 1970-71; bd. dirs. Portland Mental Health Assn.; bd. dirs., sec. Oreg. Parks Found. Lt. USNR, 1942-46. Mem. ABA, Oreg. Bar Assn., Multnomah County Bar Assn., Am. Coll. Real Estate Lawyers, Univ. Club, Arlington Club, Portland City Club (past gov.), Wauna Lake Club, Delta Upsilon. Republican. Presbyterian. Home: 3332 SW Fairmount Ln Portland OR 97201-1446 Office: 319 SW Washington St Portland OR 97204

WYSOCKI, MATTHEW SERGE, minister; b. Detroit, Aug. 4, 1960; s. Anthony Joseph Wysocki and Barbra Xenia (Klotz) Riegler; m. Hye Suk, Aug. 6, 1981; children: Christina Mary, Barbra Julia. BS, San Jose Christian, 1989; MA, Luther Rice Sem., 1991; postgrad., Golden Gate Sem., 1992—. Bus. owner Nicholson Lath & Plastering, Gilroy, Calif., 1984-86; assoc. pastor Monterey (Calif.) Korean Bapt., 1985-86; pastor First Bapt. Ch., Los Lomas, Calif., 1987-89, King City, Calif., 1989-91; community coord. Friends Outside Nat., San Jose, Calif., 1991—; vice moderator Cen. Coast Bapt. Assn., Salinas, Calif., 1989-90; mem. seminary extension com., 1991-92, nominating com., 1991. Mem. law enforcement com. Kings Vision, King City, 1991-92, mem. exec. com., 1991-92. Sgt., 2d lt. chaplain U.S. Army, 1978-84. Recipient Citation People to People, 1983. Office: Friends Outside 2105 Hamilton Ave San Jose CA 95125

YABUTANI, KOICHI MOLE, aerospace executive; b. Brawley, Calif., Jan. 21, 1931; s. Shunzo K. and Toyoko (Kondo) Y.; BS, U. Utah, 1958; Master in Engring., U. Calif. at Los Angeles, 1975; m. Pauline T. Tanabe, Oct. 8, 1960. Equipment engr. RCA, Riverton, N.J., 1959-62; engr. Northrop Corp., Hawthorne, Calif., 1962-63; mem. tech. staff Hughes Aircraft Co., Culver City, 1958-59, group head, 1965-67, staff engr., 1967-68, sr. system engr., 1968-70, section head, 1970-72, asst. dept. mgr., 1972-79, assoc. lab. mgr., 1979-82, lab. mgr., 1982-88, asst. labs. mgr., 1988-89, ret., 1989. With USAF, 1950-54. Mem. IEEE, Eta Kappa Nu, Tau Beta Pi, Phi Kappa Phi. Home: 4665 Guava Ave Seal Beach CA 90740-2941

YACK, PATRICK ASHLEY, editor; b. Little Rock, Oct. 25, 1951; s. Leo Patrick and Sarah Ann (Dew) Y.; m. Susan Marie Courtney, June 7, 1980; children: Alexander Ryan, Kendall Elizabeth. BFA, So. Meth. U., 1974. Staff asst. U.S. Rep. Alan Steelman, Washington, 1975-76; press aide U.S. Senator Charles Percy, Chgo., 1977-78; reporter Fla. Times-Union, Jacksonville, 1979-80; regional reporter Fla. Times-Union, Atlanta, 1981-82; reporter The Denver Post, 1983-85, Washington bur. chief, 1985-87; nat. editor Atlanta Constitution, 1987-89; mng. editor The Register-Guard, Eugene, Oreg., 1989—. Mem. Am. Soc. Newspaper Editors, AP Mng. Editors Assn., Oreg. Newspaper Pubs. Assn. Office: The Register-Guard 975 High St Eugene OR 97401

YAFFE, JAMES, author; b. Chgo., Mar. 31, 1927; s. Samuel and Florence (Scheinman) Y.; m. Elaine Gordon, Mar. 1, 1964; children: Deborah Ann, Rebecca Elizabeth, Gideon Daniel. Grad., Fieldston Sch., 1944; B.A. summa cum laude, Yale U., 1948. Prof. Colo. Coll., Colo. Springs, 1968—; dir. gen. studies Colo. Coll., 1981—. Author: Poor Cousin Evelyn, 1951, The Good-for-Nothing, 1953, What's the Big Hurry?, 1954, Nothing But the Night, 1959, Mister Margolies, 1962, Nobody Does You Any Favors, 1966, The American Jews, 1968, The Voyage of the Franz Joseph, 1970, So Sue Me!, 1972, Saul and Morris, Worlds Apart, 1982, A Nice Murder for Mom, 1988, Mom Meets Her Maker, 1990, Mom Doth Murder Sleep, 1991, Mom Among the Liars, 1992; play The Deadly Game, 1960, (with Jerome Weidman) Ivory Tower, 1967, Cliffhanger, 1985; also TV plays, stories, essays, revs. Served with USNR, 1945-46. Recipient Nat. Arts Found award, 1968. Mem. P.E.N., Authors League, Writers Guild of Am., Dramatists Guild, A.A.U.P., Mystery Writers of Am., Phi Beta Kappa. Jewish. Club: Elizabethan (Yale). Address: 1215 N Cascade Colorado Springs CO 80903 Office: Colo Coll Colorado Springs CO 80903

YAGJIAN, ANITA PALEOLOGOS, lawyer; b. Fresno, Calif., Apr. 5, 1954. BA in Philosophy, Stanford U., 1976, MA in Philosophy, 1977; JD, U. Santa Clara, 1980. Bar: Calif. 1980, U.S. Dist. Ct. (cen. dist.) Calif. 1983, U.S. Tax Ct. 1983. Atty. Sanford, Harmssen & Wilson, San Jose, Calif., 1980-82; assoc. Deering, Walther & Sands, Santa Monica, Calif., 1982-86; assoc. counsel Autoclub of So. Calif., Los Angeles, 1986—. Commr. Santa Monica Fair Election Practice Commn., 1985; appointed by Gov. Deukmejian to Santa Monica Mountains Conservancy Adv. Com., 1986-90; mem. L.A. Opera League; bd. dirs. Santa Monica Rep. Club, 1984-85. Assoc. editor Santa Clara Law Review, 1979-80. Mem. ABA, Calif. Bar Assn., Santa Monica Bar Assn., Westside Women Lawyers, Los Angeles Profl. Rep. Women (v.p., treas. 1984-85), Stanford Profl. Women.

YAGJIAN, MICHAEL ARTHUR, food company executive; b. Lynn, Mass., May 10, 1949; s. John Peter and Cora (Mekalian) Y.; m. Anita Paleologos, May 25, 1987. BA, U. So. Calif., 1970, JD, 1973. Bar: Calif. 1973. Founder, pres. Sub Station Ltd., L.A., 1971—, Gourmet's Fresh Pasta, L.A., 1971—; also bd. dirs. Sub Station Ltd., L.A., 1971—, Gourmet Fresh Pasta, L.A., 1971—; bd. dirs. DMD Food Products, L.A., 1987-89. Bd. dirs. Community Counseling Svcs., L.A., 1986—. Mem. Calif. Bar Assn., Nat. Pasta Assn., Assn. Inst. Food Technologists, Calif. Restaurant Assn., L.A. County Bar Assn., MENSA. Republican. Office: Gourmets Fresh Pasta 2200 S Figueroa St Los Angeles CA 90007-2049

YAKAN, MOHAMAD ZUHDI, political science educator; b. Tripoli, Lebanon, Aug. 28, 1938; came to U.S., 1988; s. Zuhdi Rasheed and Habibah (Shaaban) Y.; m. Sibylle Nickle, Apr. 8, 1988. HS, Internat. Coll., Beirut, Lebanon, 1956; BA, Am. U. Beirut, 1959; MA, A.U.B., Beirut, 1961; PhD, U. Mich., 1965. Asst./acting mgr. Prodeco/Pub. Rels.-Mktg., Beirut, 1965-71; asst. prof. Beirut U. Coll., 1965-71; lectr. law faculty Lebanese U., Beirut, 1966-71; asst. prof., dir. devel. and rel. Beirut U. Coll., 1971-88; lectr. Wayne State U., Detroit, 1988-89, Henry Ford Coll., Dearborn, Mich., 1988-89; v.p., gen. mgr. internat. I.A.S. Group, San Diego, 1989-90; lectr. U. San Diego, 1990-91; adj. prof. U.S. International. U., San Diego, 1991—. Author: Lebanon and Challenges of Future, 1978, Political Authority in Lebanon, 1979, Hijrah Calender, 1981; editor: Lebanese Constitutional Issues, 1975, Roman Law and Muslim Shari'a, 1975, Diwan Al-Mu'atamid Bin Abbad, 1975, Diwan Al-Shafi'e, 1981, Diwan Al-Baghdadi, 1983, Constitutional Law and Political Systems, 1982; co-editor: Documents on Lebanon's Political System, 1975. Founding mem. Salwa Nassar Found., Beirut, 1970, Lebanese Polit. Sci. Assn., Beirut, 1959, Lebanese Assn. for Human Rights, Beirut, 1985, Internat. Coun. for Muslim-Christian Dialogue, Beirut, 1985. Earhart fellow Earhart Found., 1965. Mem. Am. Polit. Sci. Assn., Middle East Inst., Acad. Polit. Sci., Western Polit. Sci. Assn., Acad. Polit. and Social Sci., Middle East Studies Assn. Home: 6359 Caminito Telmo San Diego CA 92111 Office: USIU Coll Arts and Scis 10455 Pomerado Rd San Diego CA 92131

YAKATAN, STAN, biotechnology company executive; b. Phila., Sept. 2, 1942; m. Harriet Schwartz, Oct. 28, 1968; children: Seth, Blake. Student, U. Pa., 1965. Sales rep. Sandoz Pharm., Hanover, N.J., 1965-68; sales mgr., mktg. mgr., biotech planning mgr. New Eng. nuclear divsn. E.I. Dupont, Boston, 1968-82; dir. mktg. ICN BioMedicals, Irvine, Calif., 1982-85; pres. Biosearch, San Rafael, Calif., 1986-88; exec. v.p., chief ops. officer New Brunswick Sci., Edison, N.J., 1985-88; pres., founder, chief exec. officer Unisyn Fiber Tech., San Diego, Calif., 1988—; founder, chmn., CEO Unisyn Techs., Tustin, Calif.; bd. dirs. Techne, Inc., Duxford, Eng., BioMed Mgmt. Corp. Eng., New Brunswick Sci., New Brunswick Sci. U.K., New Brunswick Sci. GMBH, Fed. Republic of Germany, New Brunswick Sci. B.U., The Netherlands, New Brunswick Sci. Denmark, Copenhagen, B.U. GMBH, The Netherlands and Fed. Republic of Germany, New Brunswick Scientific SARL, Paris, San Diego, Gen. Biometrics, San Diego. With U.S. Army, 1964-66. Finalist, Entrepreneur of Yr. award Ernst and Young, 1990, 91. Mem. AAAS, Inst. Dirs. U.K., Tustin Hills Racquet Club. Jewish. Home: 10521 Newport Blvd Santa Ana CA 92705-1579 Office: 12341 Newport Ave Ste 200 Santa Ana CA 92705-3205

YAKICH, DAVID ELI, international sales executive; b. Denver, May 31, 1957; s. Eli and Josephine (Goodnough) Y. Jr.; m. Carrie Elizabeth. BS, Colo. State U., 1979; postgrad., U. Minn., 1980-82; BA, U. Colo., 1984. Geophys. tech. Amoco Prodn. Corp., Denver, 1980-81; cons. geophysicist Lear Petroleum, Denver, 1982-84; computer svc. mgr. Daniel Geophys., Denver, 1984-87; nat. sales mgr. Graphics Info. Inc., Denver, 1987-89; area mgr. Far East Auto-trol Tech., Denver, 1989-91; v.p. sales and support GeoGraphix Inc., Denver, 1991; dir. internat. sales Visual Numerics Inc., 1992—; computer cons. Daniel Geophysical, Denver, 1983. Mem. Soc. Exploration Geophysics, Denver C. of C. Republican. Roman Catholic.

YALAM, ARNOLD ROBERT, allergist, immunologist, consultant; b. N.Y.C., Apr. 1, 1940; s. Herman and Sylvia (Taber) Y.; m. Carol Ann Strocker, June 16, 1964; children: John, Matthew. AB, Johns Hopkins U., 1960; MD, U. Md., Balt., 1964. Diplomate Am. Bd. Internal Medicine, Am. Bd. Allergy and Immunology. Intern Jackson Meml. Hosp., Miami, Fla., 1964-65; resident in internal medicine SUNY Downstate Med. Ctr., Bklyn., 1965-67; fellow Scripps Clinic and Rsch. Found., La Jolla, Calif., 1967-68; cons. allergist and immunologist San Diego, 1970—. Maj. US Army, 1968-70. Fellow Am. Acad. Allergy and Immunoloy; mem. Am. Soc. Addiction Medicine (cert.), San Diego Allergy Soc. Office: 8929 University Center Ln San Diego CA 92122-1006

YALMAN, ANN, lawyer; b. Boston, June 9, 1948; d. Richard George and Joan (Osterman) Y. BA, Antioch Coll., 1970; JD, NYU, 1973. Trial atty. Fla. Rural Legal Svcs., Immokalee, Fla., 1973-74; staff atty. EEO, Atlanta, 1974-76; pvt. practice Santa Fe, N.Mex., 1976—; part time U.S. Magistrate, N.Mex., 1988—. Commr. Met. Water Bd., Santa Fe, 1986-88. Mem. N.Mex. Bar Assn. (commr. Santa Fe chpt. 1983-86). Home: 441 Calle La Paz Santa Fe NM 87501-2821 Office: 304 Catron St Santa Fe NM 87501-1806

YAMAGUCHI, TAMOTSU, bank executive; b. Hokkaido, Japan, Oct. 11, 1930; came to U.S., 1986; s. Chuji and Nami (Inouye) Y.; m. Noriko Yamaguchi; children: Takashi, Masako. BS in Econs., U. Tokyo, 1953. With Bank of Tokyo, 1953-63; dept. mgr. Bank of Tokyo, Dusseldorf, 1963-66; dept. mgr. fgn. exchange and funds ops. Bank of Tokyo, London, 1966-70; acting gen. mgr. Bank of Tokyo, Tokyo, 1970-79; pres., dir. Bank of Tokyo, Sao Paulo, Brazil, 1979-82; gen. mgr., bd. dirs. Bank of Tokyo Ltd., Tokyo, 1982-84, mng. dir. Asian Regions, 1984-87, resident mng. dir. Am.; chmn. bd. Bank Tokyo Trust Co., New York, 1986—; dep. pres. Bank Tokyo, 1988-92; bd. dirs. Bank Tokyo Can., Toronto, Ont.; chmn. bd. Union Bank, L.A., 1992—. Mem. CEO bd. advisors U. So. Calif.; bd. overseers Huntington Libr.; bd. dirs. KCET, L.A. Sports Coun. Served with Japanese Navy, 1945. Mem. Asia Soc. (bd. dirs.), Japan Am. Soc. (bd. dirs.), Calif. Bus. Roundtable, L.A. World Affairs Coun. (bd. dirs.), Mountaingate Country Club, Jonathan Club. Club: Nippon (N.Y.C.). Office: 445 S Figueroa St Los Angeles CA 90071

YAMAKAWA, DAVID KIYOSHI, JR., lawyer; b. San Francisco, Jan. 25, 1936; s. David Kiyoshi and Shizu (Negishi) Y. BS, U. Calif., Berkeley, 1958, JD, 1963. Bar: Calif. 1964, U.S. Supreme Ct. 1970. Prin. Law Offices of David K. Yamakawa Jr., San Francisco, 1964—; bd. dirs. Mt. Zion Ventures Inc.; dep. dir. Community Action Agy., San Francisco, 1968-69; dir. City Demonstration Agy., San Francisco, 1969-70; mem. adv. coun. Calif. Senate Subcom. on the Disabled, 1982-83; chmn. community residential treatment system adv. com. Calif. Dept. Mental Health, 1980-85, San Francisco Human Rights Commn., 1977-80; pres. Legal Assistance to the Elderly, 1981-83; 2d v.p. Nat. Conf. Social Welfare, 1983—; v.p. Region IX, Nat. Mental Health Assn., 1981-83; vice-chmn. Mt. Zion Hosp. and Med. Ctr., 1986-88; bd. dirs. United Neighborhood Ctrs. of Am., 1977-83, ARC Bay Area, 1988-91, Mt. Zion Inst. on Aging, 1993—; bd. trustees Mt. Zion Med. Ctr., U. Calif., San Francisco, 1993—; chmn. bd. trustees United Way Bay Area, 1983-85; chief fin. officer Assisi Nature Coun./USA, 1987—; v.p. Friends of Legal Assistance to the Elderly, 1984—; vice chmn. Friends of the San Francisco Human Rights Commn., 1985—; bd. dirs. Ind. Sector, 1986-92, La Madre de los Pobres, 1982—, Nat. Concilio Am., 1987—, Hispanic Community Fund of Bay Area, 1989—; bd. dirs. Internat. Inst. San Francisco, 1989—, pres., 1990-93; sec. Non-Profit Svcs., Inc., 1987-90, chmn., 1990—; pres. Coun. Internat. Programs, San Francisco, 1987-89; mem. citizens adv. com. San Francisco Hotel Tax Fund Grants for the Arts Program, 1991—. Recipient John B. Williams Outstanding Planning and Agy. Rels. vol. award United Way of the Bay Area, 1980, Mortimer Fleishhacker Jr. Outstanding Vol. award United Way, 1985, Spl. Recognition award Legal Assistance to the Elderly, 1983, Commendation award Bd. Suprs. City and County of San Francisco, 1983, cert. Honor, 1985, San Francisco Found. award, 1985, 1st Mental Health Awareness award Mental Health Assn. San Francisco, 1990; David Yamakawa Day proclaimed in San Francisco, 1985. Mem. ABA (Liberty Bell award 1986). Office: 582 Market St Ste 410 San Francisco CA 94104-5305

YAMAOKA, SEIGEN HARUO, bishop; b. Fresno, Calif., Aug. 21, 1934; s. Haruichi and Rika (Ogawa) Y.; m. Shigeko Masuyama, Apr. 3, 1966; children—Jennifer Sae, Stacy Emi. B.A., Calif. State U.-Fresno, 1956; M.A., Ryukoku U., Kyoto, Japan, 1961; M.R.E., Pacific Sch. Religion, Berkeley, Calif., 1969, D.Min., 1979. Ordained to ministry Buddhist Chs. Am., 1961. Minister Oakland Buddhist Ch., Calif., 1964-71; registrar Inst. Buddhist Studies, Berkeley, 1969-71, lectr., mem. Curriculum com., 1969-81, pres., 1981—; minister Stockton Buddhist Temple, Calif., 1971-81; treas. No. Calif. Radio Ministry, 1975-76; cons. ethnic studies Stockton Unifed Sch. Dist., 1974-76; chmn. Buddhist Chs. Am. Ministers Assn., 1979-81; bishop Buddhist Chs. Am., San Francisco, 1981—, research com., 1970-79; English sec. Ministerial Assn., 1972-75; assoc. in doctrinal studies Hokyo, Kyoto, 1974; mem. Bd. Buddhist Edn., 1975; vice chmn. No. Calif. Ministers Assn., 1976; trustee Numata Ctr. for Buddhist Translation and Research, Buddhist Dharma Kyokai Soc. of Am. Author: Compassion in Encounter, 1970, Teaching and Practice Jodo Shinshu, 1974, Jodo Shinshu: Religion of Human Experience, 1976, Meditation-Gut-Enlightenment... Way of Hara, 1976, Awakening of Gratitude in Dying, 1978; editor, advisor, writer: Dharma School Teachers Guide, 1979. Mem. Japan Karate Fedn., Shinshu Acad. Soc., San Francisco-Japanese Am. Citizens League, Calif. State U.-Fresno Alumni Assn., Pacific Sch. Religion Alumni Assn., Internat. Assn. Shin Buddhist Studies, Internat. Translation Ctr. Kyoto, Hongwanji Bishops Council Kyoto. Home: 37 Waterloo Ct Belmont CA 94002-2936 Office: Buddhist Chs of Am 1710 Octavia St San Francisco CA 94109-4341

YAMASHIRO, LILY HYUN, healthcare administration consultant; b. Wahiawa, Hawaii, July 28, 1931; d. Do Myung and You Sun (Kim) Hyun; m. Isao Yamashiro, Mar. 12, 1960; children: Julie, Kathleen, Lynn. BGS magna cum laude, Chaminade U., 1977; MPH, U. Hawaii, 1978, DPH, 1993. RN, Hawaii. Staff nurse various hosps., Mich., Calif. and Hawaii, 1950's, 60's; sr. nurse Kula Sanitorium, Maui, Hawaii, 1958-63; health and med. svcs. coord. Waikiki Health Ctr., Honolulu, 1978-79; program coord. Office Family Planning, State of Hawaii Dept. of Health, Honolulu, 1979-80; program dir. health screening St. Francis Ctr., Honolulu, 1980-81; v.p. St. Francis Med. Ctr., Honolulu, 1987-91; project dir. LTC channeling demonstration State of Hawaii, Honolulu, 1981-85; pvt. practice health and human svcs. cons. Honolulu, 1991—; bd. dirs. Vol. Info. and Referral Svcs., Honolulu, 1986-89; mem. adv. bd. Straub Gerontology Svcs., Honolulu, 1985—. Chmn. Hawaii LTC Task Force, 1981; mem. adv. bd. Gwenfred Allen Trust Fund, 1988—; bd. dirs. Kukui Gardens Found., Honolulu, 1988-91; mem. Honolulu Sub Area Coun., 1988—. USPHS fellow, 1977-78. Mem. APHA, Hawaii League Nursing (bd. dirs. 1989-91), Hawaii Pacific Gerongol. Soc. (pres. 1987-88). Methodist.

YAMAUCHI, KENT TAKASHI, clinical psychologist. BA, U. So. Calif., 1972, MSW, 1974; MA, Calif. Sch. Profl. Psychology, 1980, PhD, 1981. Lic. psychologist, Calif. Psychology intern Denver Gen. Hosp., 1980-81; psychologist El Dorado County Mental Health Ctr., South Lake Tahoe, Calif., 1981-84, Pasadena (Calif.) City Coll., 1984—. Contbr. articles to profl. jours. Mem. APA. Office: Pasadena City Coll 1570 E Colorado Blvd Pasadena CA 91106-2003

YAMAYEE, ZIA AHMAD, engineering educator, dean; b. Herat, Afghanistan, Feb. 2, 1948; came to U.S., 1974; s. Sayed and Merjan Ahmad; m. Pamela Sue Daisley, May 6, 1989. BSEE, Kabul (Afghanistan) U., 1972; MSEE, Purdue U., 1976, PhD, 1978. Registered profl. engr., Calif., Wash. Mem. faculty of engring. Kabul U., 1978; engr. Systems Control, Inc., Palo Alto, Calif., 1979-81; sr. engr. Pacific N.W. Utilities, Portland, Oreg., 1981-83; assoc. prof. elec. engring. Clarkson U., Potsdam, N.Y., 1983-85; assoc. prof. Gonzaga U., Spokane, 1985-87, dean Sch. Engring., 1988—; prof., chair elec. engring. dept. U. New Orleans, 1987-88; part-time rsch. engr. La. Power and Light Co., New Orleans, 1987-88; sr. cons. Engring. and Cons. Svcs., Spokane, 1989—. Contbr. articles, reports to profl. jours. Bd. dirs. Wash. State Math., Engring. Sci. Achievement, Seattle, 1989—; mem. Spokane Intercollegiate Rsch. and Tech. Inst. Adv. Coun., 1990—. NSF grantee. Mem. Am. Soc. Engring. Edn., IEEE (sr.). Office: Gonzaga U Sch Engring E 502 Boone Spokane WA 99258-0001

YAN, PEI-YANG, electrical engineer; b. Tianjin, People's Republic of China, July 18, 1957; came to U.S., 1981; d. Zhi-Da and De-Qiu (Yu) Y.; m. Xiao-Chun Mu, June 2, 1984; 1 child, Wendy Mu. MS in Physics, Wayne State U., 1983; PhD in Elec. Engring., Pa. State U., 1988. Sr. process engr. Intel Corp., Santa Clara, Calif., 1988—. Contbr. articles on optical bistability on nonlinear thin film, laser induced nonlocal molecular reorientation, beam amplification via four wave mixings, transmission stability and defect printability of I-line and DUV pellicles, lens aberration effect in both off-axis illumination stepper system and excimer laser stepper system. Mem. Soc. Photo-Optical Instrumentation Engrs. Office: Intel Corp PO Box 58119 Santa Clara CA 95052-8119

YANCY, DANIEL JOSEPH, counselor; b. Buffalo, July 26, 1963; s. Donald Robert and Diana Marie (Ryan) Y. BA in Communication and Mass Media, Southwestern Adventist Coll., 1987; M in Marriage, Family & Child Counseling, Profl. Sch. Psychol. Studies, 1991; postgrad, LaJolla U. News editor Southwestern Newspaper, Keene, Tex., 1985-86, dir. photography dept., 1986-87; counselor Odyssey Hander Ind., Keene, 1987-88; counselor, sr. supr. Western Youth Svcs., Fullerton, Calif., 1988-91; case mgr., counselor for 3-5 yr. old abused children Olive Crest, 1991—; counselor Pine Springs Ranch, Idwal, Calif., 1984; weekend supr. Community Living Concepts, Keene, 1986-87; advisor Calif. Police and Probation Depts., Fullerton, 1989—. Republican. Mem. Christian Ch. Home: 1001 W Stevens Ave Apt 260 Santa Ana CA 92707-5037 Office: Olive Crest 1300 N Kellogg Ste D Anaheim CA 92807

YANDELL, GEORGE WILSON, physician, psychiatrist; b. Greenwood, Miss., Mar. 30, 1924; s. George Wilson Sr. and Beatrice (Parsons) Y.; m. Margaret Ann King, Sept. 24, 1950; children: Brian Stuart, Lynn, Paul Reid, George W. III, Bruce Parsons. BA, U. Calif., Berkeley, 1943; MD, U. Rochester, 1947. Diplomate Am. Bd. Psychiatry and Neurology, Am. Bd. Child Psychiatry. Intern Evanston (Ill.) Hosp. Assn., 1947-48; rotating resident Seaside Meml. Hosp., Long Beach, Calif., 1948-49; resident in psychiatry Fairfield State Hosp., Newtown, Conn., 1953-54, Phila. Gen. Hosp., 1953-54; NIMH fellow in child psychiatry Langley Porter Psychiat. Inst., U. Calif. Med. Ctr., San Francisco, 1955-57; asst. clin. prof., supervising psychiatrist children's svc. U. Calif., San Francisco, 1957-68; lectr., asst. rsch. educator U. Calif., Berkeley, 1968-82; sr. psychiatrist Calif. Med. Facility Dept. of Corrections, Vacaville, Calif., 1981-83; pvt. practice psychiatry Orinda, Calif., 1957—. Contbr. articles to profl. jours. Pres., Orinda, Lafayette, Moraga Coun. Civic Unity, Contra Costa County, Calif., 1964-65. With USPHS, 1951-53. Fellow Am. Psychiat. Assn. (life.), Am. Orthopsychiat. Assn. (life), Am. Acad. Child & Adolescent Psychiatry; mem. Calif. Med. Assn., Alameda-Contra Costa Med. Assn., No. Calif. Psychiat. Soc. (chmn. awards com. 1983-88), East Bay Psychiat. Assn. (pres. 1982-83), No. Calif. Regional Orgn. Child and Adolescent Psychiatry. Office: 110 Camino Pablo Orinda CA 94563

YANG, DAVID CHIE-HWA, business administration educator; b. Taiwan, Republic of China, Nov. 7, 1954; came to U.S., 1977; s. Wen-Shen and Chin-Huei (Lee) Y. BA, Nat. Taiwan U., Taipei, 1977; MBA, U. Calif., Berkeley, 1979; PhD, Columbia U., 1985. Assoc. prof., dir. sch. of accountancy U. Hawaii, Honolulu, 1985—; rsch. assoc. Acctg. Rsch. Ctr. Grad. Sch. Bus. Columbia U., N.Y.C., 1981-84; vis. prof. Beijing (People's Republic of China) Inst. Chem. Engring. Mgmt., 1988-89; cons. to China Nat. Chem. Constrn. Corp., 1990, 91, CIEC CPAs, Shanghai Academy Social Scis. CPAs, China. Author: Modern Western Financial Management, 1992, The Association Between SFAS 33 Information and Bond Ratings, 1985; coauthor: FASB Statement 33 Data Bank Users Manual, 1985, FASB Statement 36 Data Bank Users Manual, 1985. Recipient Title VI Grant U.S. Dept. Edn., 1987, curriculum devel. grant Coopers S. Lybrand Found, N.Y.C., 1987, ednl. improvement fund award U. Hawaii, 1987. Mem. Inst. Mgmt. Accts., Am. Acctg. Assn., Inst. of Internal Auditors, EDP Auditors Assn., Beta Gamma Sigma, Beta Alpha Psi (Outstanding Prof. 1989, 91, 92, Dennis Ching 1st Interstate Bank Meml. Teaching award 1993). Office: U Hawaii 2404 Maile Way Coll Bus Adminstrn Honolulu HI 96822

YANG, HSIN-MING, immunologist; b. Taipei, Taiwan, Dec. 2, 1952; came to U.S., 1980; s. Sze Piao and Yun-Huan (Chang) Y.; m. Yeasing Yeh, June 28, 1980; children: Elaine, Albert. BS, Nat. Taiwan U., 1976, MS, 1983; PhD, U. Wash., 1985. Rsch. assoc. Tri-Svc. Gen. Hosp., Taipei, 1979-80; fellow Scripps Clinic and Rsch. Found., La Jolla, Calif., 1986-88, sr. rsch. assoc., 1988-90; asst. prof. U. Nebr. Med. Ctr., Omaha, 1990-91; sr. rsch. scientist Pacific Biotech, Inc., San Diego, 1991—; lectr. Yun-Pei Coll. Med. Tech., Shinchiu, Taiwan, 1979-80. Contbr. articles to profl. jours. and chpt. to book. Joseph Drown Found. fellow, 1986, Nat. Cancer Ctr. fellow, 1987-88. Mem. Am. Assn. Cancer Rsch., N.Y. Acad. Scis. Office: Pacific Biotech Inc 9050 Camino Santa Fe San Diego CA 92121-3235

YANG, JULIE LEE, accountant; b. Hong Kong, Sept. 12, 1952; came to U.S. 1972.; d. Shen Tse and Wai Chen Chu; m. David Yang, Feb. 17, 1972; children: David, Benjamin, Christopher, Andrew. BS, U. Colo., 1975. CPA, Oreg. Staff auditor Affiliated Bankshare of Colo., Greeley, 1975-76; acct./programmer Apollo Info. Sys., Aurora, Colo., 1976; staff acct. Rigsby Lea & Court, Williams Lake, B.C., 1976-77, Reinhardt & Lackman, CPAs, Portland, 1977-79, Wingard Anderson & Adams, Portland, 1979-80, McLeod & Assocs., Portland, 1980-81; sole proprietor Julie L. Yang, CPA, Portland, 1981-85; ptnr. Handy & Yang, CPAs, Lake Oswego, Oreg., 1985-90; pres. Pacific Capital Enterprises, Lake Oswego, Oreg., 1990—; sole proprietor Yang & Co. CPA's, Lake Oswego, 1990-92; pres. Yang Cons. Group, Inc., 1990—, Pacific Capital Enterprises, Inc., 1990—; ptnr. Bennett, Yang, Caplan & Amerine CPAs, Lake Oswego, 1992—. Bd. dirs., treas. Chinese Consolidated Benevolent Assn., Portland, 1981-92; treas. Grove's Cub Scouts, Lake Grove, 1989; bd. dirs. Chinese Lang. Sch., Portland, 1987-92. Mem. AICPAs, Oreg. Soc. CPAs, Chinese C. of C., Taiwan Chinese Assn., Vancouver Chinese Assn., Chinese Scientists and Engrs. (bd. dirs., treas. 1981—), Kiwanis. Presbyterian. Office: Bennett Yang Caplan Amerine CPAs One Center Pointe Dr # 190 Lake Oswego OR 97035

YANG, YENTING, environmentalist; b. Shanghai, Republic of China, Dec. 5, 1933; came to U.S., 1964; s. Peishen and Quen (Chu) Y.; m. Yu-Hsiw Joy Huang, Dec. 25, 1970. BS, Nat. Taiwan U., 1959; MA, U. Calif., Davis, 1967, PhD, 1973. Teaching asst. Nat. Taiwan U., Taipei, 1959-60, 62-64; mgr. Oceanographic Rsch. Inst., Taipei, 1962-64; sci. researcher U. Calif., Davis, 1965-72; environ. specialist State of Calif., L.A., 1973-78; pres. Yang Internat. Co., Arcadia, Calif., 1978—; cons. Puerto Rican Govt., 1974-76. Author: Lake Productivity, 1973, Statistics, 1989. 2d Lt. Republic of China Army, 1960-62.

YANG, ZEREN, obstetrician/gynecologist, researcher; b. Xi Chong, Sichuan, People's Republic of China, July 2, 1958; came to U.S., 1989; s. Di De and Suhua (Zeng) Y.; m. Li Lin Liao, Mar. 30, 1964. MD, West China U. of Med. Scis., Chengdu, Sichuan, 1983, MS, 1986. Intern West China U. of Med. Scis., Chengdu, 1982-83, resident, 1983-88, asst. prof., 1986-88, lectr., 1988—; postdoctoral fellow U. Calif., San Francisco, 1989—. Assoc. editor-in-chief An English-Chinese Dictionary of Ob/Gyn, 1989; contbr. articles to profl. jours. Cheng's scholar U. Calif., 1989; Nat. Com. of Scis. of Beijing, 1987. Mem. Chinese Assn. of Ob./Gyn., Anti-Cancer Assn. of China. Office: Stanford U Sch Medicine CV 194 Falk Cardiovascular Rsch Ctr Stanford CA 94305

YANISH, MICHAEL JOHN, gastroenterologist; b. Yonkers, N.Y., Apr. 14, 1953; s. Casimir V. and Ruth T. (Joyce) Y. BS, U. Pa., 1975; MD, Hahneman U., Phila., 1980. Diplomate Am. Bd. Gastroenterologist. Intern Emory U., Atlanta, 1980-81, resident in internal medicine, 1980-83, res. assoc., 1983-84; fellow in gastroenterology Southwestern Med. Sch., Dallas, 1985-87; pvt. practice Phoenix, 1987—. Mem. Am. Gastroenterological Assn. Office: Ariz Digestive Liver Cons 6036 N 19th Ave Ste 309 Phoenix AZ 85015-2145

YANNONE, MARK JOSEPH, investigating agency executive, data processing executive, computer consultant; b. Hornell, N.Y., Sept. 1, 1949; s. Phillip Michael and Marguerite Joan (Chislett) Y.; m. Toni Cansdale, Jan. 1971 (div. May 1976). BS in Mgmt., Ariz. State U., 1985. Owner, mgr. Auto Svc. Ctr., 1968-76; foreman various constn. projects middle east, 1976-82; owner, founder, mgr. Better Way Systems, Phoenix, 1982—, Prose Perfect, Phoenix, Ariz., 1987—; pres., founder Cert. Credentials, Inc., Phoenix, 1985—; dir. computer svcs. Continental Promotion Group, Inc., Tempe, Ariz., 1989-90; owner, co-founder Perfect Data, Phoenix, 1991—; microcomputer consultant, Phoenix, 1982—. Author, editor: The National Directory of Courts of Law; author: (software) College Majors: A Complete Guide from Accounting to Zoology. Editor Ariz. Libertarian Party, 1988. Scholar, 1967, 82. Mem. Golden Key, Beta Gamma Sigma, Phi Kappa Phi, Sigma Iota Epsilon, Phi Theta Kappa. Home and Office: 2015 W Cactus Rd Ste 215 Phoenix AZ 85029

YANOSHAK, SHARYN, writer, producer; b. Worcester, Mass., Nov. 2, 1945; d. John and Shirley Toner (Bruso) Y. BA, Wilkes Coll., Wilkes-Barre, Pa., 1967; MBA, U. Pitts., 1973. Sys. programmer IBM, Yorktown Heights, N.Y., 1967-69; mgr. customer svcs. Virtual Computer Svcs., N.Y.C., 1969-70; account mgr. ADP Inc., N.Y.C., 1971-72; fin. analyst Xerox Corp., El Segundo, Calif., 1974-75; free lance writer/producer Las Vegas, 1976-90; tchr. National U., Las Vegas, Nev., 1986-87; writer, prodr. Sta. KLVX-TV, Las Vegas, 1989-90; mgr. community rels. and employee comm. Nev. Power Co., Las Vegas, 1990—. Author numerous articles, booklets; writer/producer lifestyle, community affairs, TV stories, electric utility publs. Mem. adv. coun. United Blood Svcs.; mem. Corp. Vol. Coun. Named one of Disting. Women in So. Nev., 1991, 92; Marshall Robinson awardee, U Pitts., 1973; U. Pitts. fellow, 1973; Wilkes Coll. scholar, 1963-67. Mem. Internat. Assn. Bus. Communicators, Nat. League Am. Pen Women (state treas. 1984-86, br. historian 1986-90), Women in Communication, Mensa, Beta Gamma Sigma.

YARCHUN, HYMAN JOSHUA, technical training director; b. Linz, Austria, Oct. 30, 1946; s. Julius and Celia (Schwarcman) Y. BA, Calif. State U., Dominguez Hills, 1976, MS, 1983. Lic. realtor; lic. comml. pilot, multiengine. Advanced through grade to maj. USAF, 1991, fuels tng. instr., 1964-68; aircraft fuels specialist Lockheed, L.A., 1969-71; aircraft aircrew mem. Calif. Air N.G., Van Nuys, 1971-72; communications specialist Dictaphone Corp., L.A., 1973-74; asst. chief air res. mgmt. office USAF Space Systems Div., L.A., 1978-83; mgr. instr. devel. Japan, dir. of U.S./Japan Support Ops. Learning Tree Internat., L.A., 1984—; project mgr. Hughes Space & Communications Group, L.A., 1988-89; prin., tech. tng. cons. Access Tech., Redondo Beach, Calif., 1987—. Bd. dirs. Oceangate Homeowners Assn., Redondo Beach, 1990—; driver, donator Armed Forces Day Parade, Torrance, Calif., 1979—. Life mem. Air Force Assn., Res. Officers Assn. Republican. Jewish. Office: Learning Group Internat 6053 W Century Blvd Los Angeles CA 90045

YARD, SALLY ELIZABETH, art historian; b. Trenton, N.J., Sept. 24, 1951; d. Edward Madison and Mary Emma (Howell) Y. BA, Harvard U., 1973; MFA, Princeton U., 1975, PhD, 1980. Instr., lectr., asst. prof. Mount Holyoke Coll., South Hadley, Mass., 1978-83; vis. asst. prof. Amherst (Mass.) Coll., 1981-83; lectr., cons. La Jolla (Calif.) Mus. Contemporary Art, 1983-89; lectr., vis. asst. prof. U. Calif. San Diego, La Jolla, 1987, 88, 90, 92; asst. prof. U. San Diego, 1989—; guest curator Mount Holyoke Coll. Art Mus., 1984, 85, Mus. Fine Arts, Springfield, Mass., 1981, Hampshire Coll. Gallery, 1979. Author: Christo: Oceanfront, 1975, Willem de Kooning, 1986, Manny Farber, 1991; co-author: Francis Bacon, 1986. Mem. Phi Beta Kappa. Office: U San Diego Alcala Pk San Diego CA 92110

YARIAN, STEPHAN BISHOP, writer, performer, educational administrator; b. Pontiac, Mich., June 23, 1946; s. Henry Herbert and Hazel Augusta (Mickelson) Y. BA, Western Mich. U., 1968; postgrad., Ill. State U., 1969-70, U. Oreg., 1981-83; MFA, U. Conn., 1979. Actor, tchr. various prodns. N.Y.C., 1970-79; asst. prof., dir. of theater Mansfield (Pa.) State U., 1979-81; teaching fellow U. Oreg., Eugene, 1981-83; distbn. coord. Peat, Marwick, N.Y.C., 1984-86; theater dir. various prodn. cos. Sao Paulo, Brazil, 1986-88; exec. asst., researcher Calif. Sch. Profl. Psychology, Alhambra, 1988—; bd. dirs. YAY Prodns., L.A. Democrat. Office: Calif Sch Profl Psychology 1000 S Fremont Ave Alhambra CA 91803-1360

YARIV, AMNON, electrical engineering educator, scientist; b. Tel Aviv, Israel, Apr. 13, 1930; came to U.S., 1951, naturalized, 1964; s. Shraga and Henya (Davidson) Y.; m. Frances Pokras, Apr. 10, 1972; children: Elizabeth, Dana, Gabriela. B.S., U. Calif., Berkeley, 1954, M.S., 1956, Ph.D., 1958. Mem. tech. staff Bell Telephone Labs., 1959-63; dir. laser research Watkins-Johnson Co., 1963-64; mem. faculty Calif. Inst. Tech., 1964—, Thomas G. Myers prof. elec. engring. and applied physics, 1966—; chmn. bd. ORTEL Inc., Accuwave Corp.; cons. in field. Author: Quantum Electronics, 1967, 75, 85, Introduction to Optical Electronics, 1971, 77, 89, Theory and Applications of Quantum Mechanics, Propagation of Light in Crystals. Served with Israeli Army, 1948-50. Recipient Pender award U. Pa. Fellow IEEE (Quantum Electronics award 1980), Am. Optical Soc. (Ives medal 1986, Harvey prize Technion, Israel, 1992), Am. Acad. Arts and Scis.; mem. NAS, NAE, Am. Phys. Soc. Office: 1201 E California Blvd Pasadena CA 91125-0001

YARTER, CLYNTON PAUL, controller; b. Long Beach, Calif., May 29, 1948; s. Robert and Philles (Dekay) Y.; m. Dianne Boyce, July 15, 1978; 1 child, Kimberly. BA in Physics, U. Calif., Irvine, 1974; MBA in Fin., Chapman U., 1982. Devel. tech. U. Calif. Med. Sch., Irvine, 1974-80; engring. mgr. Siemens Corp., Anaheim, Calif., 1980-82; product mgr. Toro Irrigation, Riverside, Calif., 1982-84; v.p. R & D Hochiki Corp., Tokyo, 1984-89; contr. Gibson Assocs., Gardena, Calif., 1989—; lectr. physics U. Calif., Irvine, 1972—. Contbr. articles to profl. jours.; patentee in field. Coach Orange County (Calif.) Soccer Assn., 1992. Sgt. USAF, 1967-72, Vietnam. Mem. IEEE, Mensa. Home: 668 S Chipwood St Orange CA 92669-5305

YASAMI, MASOUD, artist; b. Khoramshar, Iran, Feb. 17, 1949; came to U.S., 1968; s. Nouralah Rais and Effi (Sohani) Y. BFA, Oreg. State U., 1974; MFA, Ariz. State U., 1977. Vis. lectr. U. Utah, Salt Lake City, 1978-79; vis. asst. prof. art Ariz. State U., Tempe, 1979-83; vis. lectr. Farabi U., Tehran, Iran, 1977, U. Oreg., Eugene, 1979, U. Wis., 1980, Kearney (Nebr.) State U., 1981. Exhibited in one-man, group shows from 1979-92 including Utah Mus. Fine Arts, Salt Lake City, Prieb Gallery, U. Wis., Scottsdale (Ariz.) Ctr. for Arts, Kimball Art Ctr., Park City, Utah, Art Inst. of Boston, Tom Luttrell Gallery, San Fransico, Elaine Horwitch Gallery, Scottsdale. Recipient Purchase award Tucson Mus. of Art, 1980, 90, Utah Mus. Fine Arts, 1979, Yuma (Ariz.) Art Ctr., 1980. Democrat. Office: Elaine Horwitch Gallery 4211 N Marshall Way Scottsdale AZ 85251

YASNYI, ALLAN DAVID, communications company executive; b. New Orleans, June 22, 1942; s. Ben Z. and Bertha R. (Michalove) Y.; BBA, Tulane U., 1964; m. Susan K. Manders; children: Benjamin Charles, Evelyn Judith, Brian Mallot. Free-lance exec. producer, producer, writer, actor and designer for TV, motion picture and theatre, 1961-73; producer, performer The Second City; dir. fin. and adminstrn. Quinn Martin Prodns., Hollywood, Calif., 1973-76, v.p. fin., 1976-77, exec. v.p. fin. and corp. planning, 1977; vice chmn., chief exec. officer QM Prodns., Beverly Hills, Calif., 1977-78, chmn. bd., chief exec. officer, 1978-80; pres., chief exec. officer The Synapse Communications Group, Inc., 1981—; participant IC IS Forum, 1990—; exec. prodr. first live broadcast combining Intelsat, Intersputnik, The Voice of Am., and The Moscow World Radio Svc., 1990; resource guest Aspen Inst. Exec. Seminars, 1990; chmn. bd. dirs. Found. of Global Broadcasting, Washington, 1987—. Trustee Hollywood Arts Coun., 1980-83; exec. v.p., trustee Hollywood Hist. Trust, 1981-91; bd. dirs. Internat. Ctr. for Integrative Studies, N.Y.C., 1988-92; bd. dirs. Asthma and Allergy Foun. Am.,

1981-85. Logistical combat officer U.S. Army, 1964-66, Viet Nam. Named to Tulane U. Hall of Fame. Mem. Acad. TV Arts and Scis., Inst. Noetic Scis., Hollywood Radio and TV Soc., Hollywood C. of C. (dir., vice-chmn. 1978—), Screen Actors Guild, Assn. Transpersonal Pyschology (keynote speaker 1988). Office: 4132 Fulton Ave Sherman Oaks CA 91423

YASUDA, MAC, import-export executive; b. Nishinomiya, Hyogo, Japan, Jan. 29, 1949; came to U.S, 1984; s. Osamu and Tamako (Yoshida) Y.; m. Kimiyo Kojima, Dec. 5, 1975; children: Ken, Sotaro. BS, Himeji (Japan) Inst. Tech., 1972; student, Mich. Tech. U., 1970-71. Registered profl. engr., Japan. Asst. mgr. W.T. Grant Co., Osaka, Japan, 1973-76; pres. Macs Internat. Corp., Kobe, Japan, 1976-84, Princeton Acad., Ashiya, Japan, 1979-84; v.p. Yudachi U.S.A. Inc., Torrance, Calif., 1984-85, exec. v.p., 1985-86; pres. Yudachi U.S.A. Inc., Newport Beach, Calif., 1986-88, Tsumura Art & Apparel of the World, Newport Beach, 1988—; pres. Corp. 85, Newport Beach, 1985—. Author: Vintage Guitar Vol. I, 1984, Vintage Guitar Vol. II, 1989. Home: 1429 Keel Dr Corona Del Mar CA 92625-1240 Office: Tsumura Art & Apparel of World 1550 N Bristol St Newport Beach CA 92660-2954

YASUI, BYRON KIYOSHI, musician, music educator; b. Honolulu, Dec. 13, 1940; s. Shigeo and Helen Shizue (Kimura) Y. BE in Music, U. Hawaii, 1965; MusM in Composition, Northwestern U., 1967, D of Mus. Arts in Composition, 1972. Prof. music U. Hawaii, Honolulu, 1972—; double bassist Honolulu Symphony, 1963—. Composer Music for Timpani and Brass, 1974, Four Pieces (double bass quartet), 1984; co-author: Basic Sight Singing, 1988. Served with USAFNG, 1959-65. Named MacDowell Colony fellow, 1979, Nat. Orch. Assn. fellow, 1988. Mem. Am. Soc. Univ. Composers, ASCAP(Std. award ann. 1985—), Internat. Soc. Bassists. Office: U Hawaii Music Dept 2411 Dole St Honolulu HI 96822-2318

YATCHAK, MICHAEL GERARD, electrical engineer; b. Wakefield, Mich., July 3, 1951; s. Roman C. and Mary A. (Zorich) Y.; m. Sachiko Kim, Jan. 29, 1987; 1 child, Rika M. BSEE, Mich. State U., 1974. Assoc. engr. Eagle Signal, Davenport, Iowa, 1974-76; engr. computer lab. Mich. State U., East Lansing, 1977-84; sr. engr. Martin Marietta Corp., Denver, 1984-86; sr. engr. McDonnell Douglas Corp., Huntington Beach, Calif., 1986-92, mgr., 1992—. Mem. IEEE.

YATES, ABBY HARRIS, oil and gas exploration company executive; b. Roswell, N.Mex., June 5, 1952; d. Lawrence C. and Marion V. (Sandrs) Harris; m. George M. Yates, June 12, 1975; children: Lauren S., Lindsey A. BA in Psychology, Okla. State U., 1973. Ptnr. Abby Corp., Roswell, N.Mex., 1973-80; pres. Laurelind Corp., Roswell, 1983—; bd. dirs. Abby Corp.; mem. community adv. coun. Ea. N.Mex. U., Roswell, pres., 1991. Vice pres., chmn. ann. giving com. Ea. N.Mex. Med. Ctr. Found., Roswell, 1985—; membership drive chmn. YMCA, Roswell, 1980-86; elder First Presbyn. Ch., 1985-87; mem. fin. com. Keep Am. Beautiful, 1987—, Chaves County Rep. Party, 1987—; bd. dirs. United Way, 1987—; pres. Mil. Hts. PTA, 1988-89; v.p. Ea. N.Mex. Med. Ctr. Found., 1988-89, pres., 1989-92. Mem. CASA (bd. dirs. Chaves County chpt., nat. corp. bd.), Ind. Petroleum Assn. Am., Ind. Petroleum Assn. Mt. States, Ind. Petroleum Assn. N.Mex., N.Mex. Landmans Assn., Roswell Econ. Forum, Roswell C. of C., Shakespeare Club, PEO. Republican. Presbyterian. Office: Laurelind Corp PO Box 2143 500 N Main St Roswell NM 88202

YATES, ALBERT CARL, university administrator, chemistry educator; b. Memphis, Sept. 29, 1941; s. John Frank and Sadie L. (Shell) Y.; m. Ann Young; children: Steven, Stephanie, Aerin Alessandra. B.S., Memphis State U., 1965; Ph.D., Ind. U., 1968. Research assoc. U. So. Calif., Los Angeles, 1968-69; prof. chemistry Ind. U., Bloomington, 1969-74; v.p. research, grad. dean U. Cin., 1974-81; exec. v.p., provost, prof. chemistry Washington State U., Pullman, 1981-90; pres. Colo. State U., Fort Collins, 1990—; chancellor Colo. State U. System, Fort Collins, 1990—; mem. grad. record exam. bd. Princeton (N.J.) U., 1977-80, undergrad. assessment program council, 1977-81; cons. NRC, 1975-82, Office End., HEW, 1978-80; mem. exec. council acad. affairs NASULGC, 1983-87, ACE, 1983-87,. nat adv. council gen. med. scis. NIH, 1987—. Contbr.: research articles to Jour. Chem. Physics; research articls to Phys. Rev.; research articles to Jour. Physics, Phys. Rev. Letters, Chem. Physics Letters. Served with USN, 1959-62. Recipient univ. and State honors and awards. Mem. Am. Phys. Soc., Am. Chem. Soc., AAAS, Nat. Assn. State Univs. and Land Grant Colls. (mem. exec. council academic affairs), Am. Council Edn. (mem. exec. com. academic affairs), Sigma Xi, Phi Lambda Upsilon. Home: 1744 Hillside Dr Fort Collins CO 80524-1965 Office: Colo State U 102 Administration Bldg Fort Collins CO 80523

YATES, DAVID JOHN C., chemist, researcher; b. Stoke-on-Trent, Staffordshire, Eng., Feb. 13, 1927; came to U.S., 1958; s. Eric John and Beatrice Victoria (Street) Y.; m. Natalie Chmelnitsky, June 22, 1983. B.S. with honors, U. Birmingham, U.K., 1949; Ph.D., U. Cambridge, Eng., 1955, Sc.D., 1968. Rsch. physicist Kodak Labs., Wealdstone, London, 1949-50; rsch. chemist Brit. Ceramic Rsch. Assn., Stoke-on-Trent, 1950-51; rsch. assoc. dept. colloid sci. U. Cambridge, 1951-58; lectr. Sch. Mines and dept. chemistry Columbia U., N.Y.C., 1958-60; sr. rsch. fellow Nat. Phys. Lab., Teddington, U.K., 1960-61; rsch. assoc. corp. labs. Exxon Rsch. and Engring., Annandale, N.J., 1961-86; rsch. prof. dept. of chem. engring. Lafayette Coll., Easton, Pa., 1986-87; rsch. prof. dept. materials sci. Rutgers U., Piscataway, N.J., 1987-88; cons. San Diego, 1988—. Contbr. numerous articles to profl. jours. Fellow Inst. of Physics (U.K.), Royal Soc. Chemistry (U.K.), N.Y. Catalysis Club (chmn. 1966-67). Club: N.Y. Catalysis (chmn. 1965-66).

YATES, KEITH LAMAR, retired insurance company executive; b. Bozeman, Mont., Oct. 29, 1927; s. Thomas Bryan and Altha (Norris) Y.; m. Dolores Hensel, Aug. 30, 1948; children: Thomas A., Molly Yates McIntosh, Richard A., Nancy Yates Sands, Penny Dannielle Yates Clark, Pamela Yates Beeler. BA, Eastern Wash. State U., 1953. Salesman Ancient Order United Workmen, Spokane, Wash., 1952-53, sales mgr., 1953-56, corp. sec., 1956-73; corp. sec. Neighbors of Woodcraft, Portland, Oreg., 1973-89, pres., 1989-92; ret., 1992. Author: Life of Willie Willey, 1966, The Fogarty Years, 1972, History of The Woodcraft Home, 1975, An Enduring Heritage, 1992. Pres. Wash. State Christian Mens Fellowship, Seattle, 1965-67; pres. Met. Area Assn. Christian Chs., 1981-83; mem. regional bd. Christian Chs. Oreg., 1990—. Command sgt.-maj., ret., 1987; served with USN, USANG, 1946-87. Mem. Wash. State Frat. Cong., (cert. Commendation 1969, sec. 1957-68, pres., mem. exec. bd., chmn. conv. program advt. com. 1960-73), Oreg. State Frat. Cong. (Outstanding Frat. 1975-76, Spl. Appreciation award 1984, Frat. Family of Yr. 1986, sec. 1975-87, pres., mem. exec. bd. 1974—), Nat. Fraternal Congress Am. (conv. arrangement com. 1964, 90, publicity com. 1964, 65, 68, 90, credentials com. 1970, 77, 78, pres. press & pub. rels. sec. 1971-72, pub. rels. com. 1971-73, chmn. 1972, co-chmn. press and pub. rels. frat. seminar 1972, frat. monitor com. 1974-75, mem. com. 1975-76, family life com. 1978-80, constitution com. 1980, pres. state frat. congs. sec. 1981-82, historian 1987—, Washington County's Disting. Patriot, 1988), Portland Ins. Acctg. and Statis. Soc. Assn. Records Mgrs. and Adminstrs. (Oreg. chpt.), Portland C. of C., Wash. Ins. Coun., Wash. Claims Assn., Seattle Underwriting Assn. Home: 29860 SW Buckhaven Rd Hillsboro OR 97123-8706 Office: Neighbors of Woodcraft 1410 SW Morrison St Portland OR 97205-1930

YATES, MARGARET MARLENE, educational psychologist; b. Sheridan, Wyo., Feb. 1, 1942; d. James H. and Dorothy H. (Weeks) Guy; m. Alan R. Yates, June 20, 1965 (div. 1978); stpchildren: Elizabeth, Samuel, LaDonna, Susan, Sally. AA, Sheridan Jr. Coll., 1962; BA, U. Wyo, 1964, PhD, 1974; EdS, MA, U. No. Colo., 1968. Lic. clin. psychologist, Wyo.; cert. nat. sch. psychologist, Calif. Caseworker, adminstrv. asst. Wyo. Dept. Health and Social Svcs., Cheyenne, 1964-68; counselor, pschometrist Gradenville Diagnostic Ctr., St. Louis, 1968-70; counselor, instr. Laramie County Community Coll., Cheyenne, 1970-74; psychol. cons. div. mental health Wyo. Bd. Coop. Ednl. Svcs., Rock Springs, 1974-79; guidance counselor Colegio Karl C. Parrish, Barrangvilla, Colombia, 1979-80; sch. psychologist Marin County Office Edn., San Rafael, Calif., 1981—; cons. in field. Founder, pres., Sweetwater County Task Force on Sexual Abuse, Rock Springs, 1974-76; mem. adv. com. Open Day Care Ctr.,Rock Springs, 1974-76, Spl. Edn. Task Force, San Rafael, 1985-87; judge academic decathlon, Marin County Office Edn., 1984-87; mem. adult edn. com., Community Congl. Ch., Tiburon, Calif., 1988—. Mem. Nat. Assn. Sch. Psychologists, Am. Orthopsychiatric Assn., Commonwealth Club San Francisco, Phi Kappa Phi. Republican. Home: 269 Scenic Rd Fairfax CA 94930-1550 Office: Marin County Office Edn 1111 Las Callinas St San Rafael CA 94913

YATES, SONJA L., school system administrator. BA in Psychology/English, U. Calif., Santa Barbara, 1968; MA in Ednl. Supervision, Calif. State Poly. U., 1975; EdD in Policy, Planning and Adminstrn., U. So. Calif., 1990. Cert. in std. elem. K-9, adult, Calif., adminstrv. svcs. pre-sch., K-12, adult, Calif. Clk. dist. libr. Lompoc Unified Sch. Dist., 1960-61, asst. cataloguer, then cataloguer dist. libr., 1961-63, sec. La Cañada Elem. Sch., 1963-65, substitute tchr., 1966-68, tchr. 1st grade La Cañada Elem. Sch., 1968-69, title I tchr. La Cañada, Ruth and Hapgood Elem. Schs., 1969-70, reading specialist Crestview and Ruth Elem. Schs., 1970-74, prin. La Mesa Elem. Sch., 1974-76, prin. Fillmore Elem. Sch., 1976-79, co-prin. Lompoc Valley Mid. Sch., 1979-85; asst. supt. elem. edn. Santa Barbara Sch./High Sch. Dist., 1985-89; supt. Ctrl. Sch. Dist., Rancho Cucamonga, Calif., 1989—; chair Sch. Attendance Rev. Bd., 1974-76; consol. application program reviewer Lompoc Unified Sch. Dist., State Dept. Edn., 1976-79; K-12 users rep. Ctrl. Coast Computing Authority, 1985-89; mem. supt.'s coun. West End Spl. Edn. Local Plan Area, 1989—. Contbr. articles to profl. jours. Active Mental, Emotional, and Social Health Bd., 1986-89, Orton Soc. Bd., 1986-89, Family Svc. Agy. Bd., 1987-89, San Bernardino Dist. Advs. Better Schs., 1991—; mem. family literacy progect bd. VISTA, 1987-89; mem. dean's supts. adv. com. U. So. Calif., 1991—; bd. dirs., flower festival fundraising chair Girls' Club, 1984-85; bd. dirs., v.p. Klein Bottle Social Advs. Youth, 1985-89. Mem. Calif. Assn. Large Suburban Sch. Dists. (curriculum com. 1986-89), Assn. Calif. Sch. Adminstrs., Internat. Reading Assn. (trivalley coun. 1979-85, bd. dirs. south coast coun. 1986—), Bus. Ptnrs. Edn., Industry Edn. Coun. (mem. adopt-a-sch. com. 1986-89), Rancho Cucamonga C. of C., Kiwanis, Phi Beta Kappa. Home: 6143 Orvieto Ct Alta Loma CA 91737 Office: 10601 Church St Ste 112 Rancho Cucamonga CA 91730

YATES, THOMAS EUGENE, broadcasting executive; b. L.A., Dec. 3, 1942; s. William W. and Mary Jane (McCauley) Y.; m. Vicky Sheldon Watts, Dec. 1, 1987. BA in Communications, U. Nebr., 1963. Program dir. KMPX, San Francisco, 1967-71, KLOS, ABC, L.A., 1971-78; talent dir. ABC-FM, L.A., N.Y.C., 1975-78; owner, cons. Nova Broadcast Svcs., L.A., San Francisco, 1978-81; editor, cons. Goodphone Weekly Communications, L.A., San Francisco, 1978-84; program mgr. KSAN Metromedia, San Francisco, 1980; owner Hiatus Prodns., L.A., San Francisco, 1981-86; creator, programmer KKCY, City Broadcasting, San Francisco, 1985-86; program mgr. KLSX, Greater Media Inc., L.A., 1986-89; chief operating officer, gen. ptnr. Calif. Radio Ptnrs., owners/operators Sta. KOZT-FM, Marina Del Rey, Calif., 1990—; bd. mem. Bay Area Music Archives, San Francisco, 1980-86; bd. dirs. L.A. Free Clinic, 1972-78; event coordinator Goodphone Symposiums, L.A., 1979, 80. Bd. dirs. Mus. of Rock, San Francisco, 1985-86. Named Radio Sta. of Yr., Billboard Mag., 1975, Program Dir. of Yr., 1974, 76. Democrat.

YAU, TIMOTHY S., electrical engineer; b. China, June 7, 1946; came to U.S., 1966; s. Ting Hau and Kit Han (Lam) Y.; m. Rosemna C. Yau; children: Jacqueline C., Theodore C.; m. Joan Rheingans, Mar. 18, 1990. BSEE, Calif. State U., Chico, 1969; MSEE, Stanford U., 1973. Project mgr. elec. systems div. Electric Power Rsch. Inst., Palo Alto, Calif., 1974-77, mgr. system studies emergy mgmt. and utilization div., 1977-88, mgr. strategic planning customer systems div., 1988—; lectr. U.S. Dept. State and AID, Brazil, 1981. Contbr. articles to profl. publs. Coord. Western Wheelers Bicycling Club, Palo Alto, 1990. Mem. IEEE. Republican. Office: Electric Power Rsch Inst 3412 Hillview Ave Palo Alto CA 94303

YAW, ROBERT HORTON, atmospheric scientist; b. L.A., Sept. 15, 1921; s. Harold Wheeler and Bessie Evelyn (Horton) Y.; m. Margaret Alice Simonds, Aug.24, 1946; children: Robert Alan, Kenneth Marshall. BA, U. Colo., 1947; MS, Mont. State U., 1968; grad. aircraft navigator, USAF, Ellington Field, Tex., 1943; grad. meteorologist, USAF, Chanute Field, Ill., 1948. Cert. secondary tchr., Mont. Commd 2nd lt. USAF, 1943, advanced through grades to Lt. col., retired, 1966, navigator, atmospheric scientist, 1943-66; tchr. Great Falls (Mont.) High Schs., 1966-67; assoc. prof. Mont. State U., Bozeman, 1967-83; cons. meteorologist, Mont. Dept. Natural Resources and Conservation, Helena, 1972-78. Contbr. articles to profl. jours. Mont. coord 55-alive driver improvement program AARP, Bozeman, 1984-86. Grantee Mont. Dept. Natural Resources and Conservation, 1972-78. Mem. Am. Meteorol. Soc. Home: 2603 Spring Creek Dr Bozeman MT 59715-6040

YAZHE, HERBERT, national monument superintendent; b. Naschitti, N.Mex., Feb. 8, 1938; m. Helena Yazhe, May 26, 1959; children: Lucinda, Herman. Student, Colo. State U., 1966-69. Navajo ranger Navajo Nation, Window Rock, Ariz., 1959-64, asst. chief ranger, 1964-66, asst. dept. head, 1969-72, asst. dir., 1982-85; tng. coordinator Nat. Park Service, Grand Canyon, Ariz., 1972-74; chief interpreter Canyon de Chelly Nat. Monument, Chinle, Ariz., 1974-78, asst. supt., 1985-86, supt., 1986—; program officer Bur. Indian Affairs, Chinle, Ariz., 1978-82. Active Chinle Planning Bd., 1985—, Joint Mgmt. Plan, Chinle, 1985—, Navajo Studies Conf., Tsaile, Ariz., 1987—. Mem. Rotary (spl. recognition, 1973). Democrat. Roman Catholic. Home: PO Box 2191 Chinle AZ 86503-2191 Office: Canyon de Chelly Nat Monument PO Box 588 Chinle AZ 86503-0588

YBARRA, RENALEE TELLEZ, paramedic, educator; b. El Paso, Tex., Aug. 6, 1962; d. Manuel A. Sr. and Ida (Tellez) Y. Student, N.Mex. State U., 1980, 89; cert. emergency med. technician, El Paso C.C., 1984; AA, Dona Ana C.C., 1992. Lic. paramedic, EMT instr., N.Mex. Emergency rm. technician Providence Meml. Hosp., El Paso, 1988-90; CPR instr., coord. Region II Emergency Med. Svc., Las Cruces, N.Mex., 1990—; dep. med. investigator State of N.Mex., 1993—; emergency med. svcs. tng. officer Santa Teresa (N.Mex.) Fire Dept., 1988—; BLS instr. trainer N.Mex. unit Am. Heart Assn., 1990—; mem. FAST team ARC. Vol. ARC, El Paso, 1984-90, Santa Teresa Fire Dept., 1988—; CPR instr. Am. Heart Assn., 1984—. Mem. Nat. Registry EMTs, Tex. Assn. EMTs, Nat. Assn. EMTs (PHTLS instr. 1991), Am. Heart Assn.

YEAGER, CAROLINE HALE, radiologist, consultant; b. Little Rock, Sept. 5, 1946; d. George Glenn and Crenor Burnelle (Hale) Y.; m. William Berg Singer, July 8, 1978; children: Adina Atkinson Singer, Sarah Rose Singer. BA, Ind. U., Bloomington, 1968; MD, Ind. U., Indpls., 1971. Diplomate Am. Bd. Radiology; med. lic. State of Calif. Intern Good Samaritan Hosp., Los Angeles, 1971-72; resident in radiology King Drew Med. Ctr. UCLA, Los Angeles, 1972-76; dir. radiology Hubert Humphrey Health Ctr., Los Angeles, 1976-77; asst. prof. radiology UCLA, Los Angeles, 1977-84; asst. prof. radiology King Drew Med. Ctr. UCLA, Los Angeles, 1977-85, dir. ultrasound, 1977-84; ptnr. pvt. practice Beverly Breast Ctr., Beverly Hills, Calif., 1984-87; cons. Clarity Communications, Pasadena, Calif., 1981—; pvt. practice radiology Claude Hadron Health Ctr., 1991-93; dir. sonograms and mammograms Rancho Los Amigos Med. Ctr., 1993—; trustee Assn. Teaching Physicians, L.A., 1976-81; cons. King Drew Med. Ctr., 1984, Gibraltar Savs., 1987, Cal Fed. Inc., 1986, At Home Professions, 1989—, Mobil Diagnostics, 1991-92, Xerox Corp., 1990-91, Frozen Leopard, Inc., 1990-91. Author: (with others) Infectious Disease, 1978, Anatomy and Physiology for Medical Transcriptionists, 1992; contbr. articles to profl. jours. Trustee U. Synagogue, Los Angeles, 1975-79; mem. Friends of Pasadena Playhouse, 1987-90. Grantee for innovative tng. Nat. Fund for Med. Edn., 1980-81. Mem. Am. Inst. Ultrasound in Medicine, L.A. Radiology Soc. (ultrasound sect.), Nat. Soc. Performance and Instrn. (chmn. conf. Database 1991, publs. L.A. chpt. 1990, info. systems L.A. chpt. 1991, dir. adminstrn. L.A. chpt. 1992, Outstanding Achievement in Performance Improvement award L.A. chpt. 1990, bd. dirs. 1990-93, Pres. award for Outstanding Chpt. 1992, v.p. programs 1993), Stanford Profl. Women L.A. Jewish. Home and Office: 3520 Yorkshire Rd Pasadena CA 91107-5440

YEAGER, CHARLES ELWOOD (CHUCK YEAGER), retired air force officer; b. Myra, W.Va., Feb. 13, 1923; s. Albert Hal and Susie May (Sizemore) Y.; m. Gennis Faye Dickhouse, Feb. 26, 1945; children: Sharon Yeager Flick, Susan F., Donald C., Michael D. Grad., Air Command and Staff Sch., 1952, Air War Coll., 1961; DSc (hon.), W.Va. U., 1948, Marshall U., Huntington, W.Va., 1969; D in Aero. Sci., Salem Coll., W.Va., 1975. Enlisted in USAAF, 1941; advanced through grades to brig. gen. U.S. Air Force, 1969, fighter pilot, ETO, 1943-46, exptl. flight test pilot, 1945-54; various command assignments U.S. Air Force, U.S., Germany, France and Spain, 1954-62; comdr. 405th Fighter Wing, Seymour Johnson AFB, N.C., 1968-69; vice comdr. 17th Air Force, Ramstein Air Base, Fed. Republic Germany, 1969-71; U.S. def. rep. to Pakistan, 1971-73; spl. asst. to comdr. Air Force Inspection and Safety Ctr., Norton AFB, Calif., 1973, dir. aerospace safety, 1973-75; ret., 1975. Author: (with Leo Janos) Yeager: An Autobiography, 1985, (with Charles Leerhsen) Press On!, 1988. Decorated DSM with oak leaf cluster, Silver Star with oak leaf cluster, Legion of merit with oak leaf cluster, DFC with 2 oak leaf clusters, Bronze star with V device, Air medal with 10 oak leaf clusters, Air Force Commendation medal, Purple Heart; recipient Presdl. medal of Freedom, 1985. Home: PO Box 128 Cedar Ridge CA 95924-0128

YEAGER, FREDERICK JOHN, stockbroker; b. Davenport, Iowa, June 22, 1941; s. John Aufderheide and Roselyn Mae (Chapman) Y.; m. Melanie Jane Grant, Aug. 15, 1964; children: John Frederick, Paul Monroe, James Abraham, Penelope Jane. BS in Engring. Scis., U.S. Naval Acad., 1963; MBA, U. Santa Clara, 1976. Acct. exec. Reynolds Securities, San Mateo, Calif., 1969-74; sr. v.p. Dean Witter Reynolds, San Mateo, 1974—; mem. Dean Wittier Pres.'s Club. Ruling elder Burlingame (Calif.) Presbyn. Ch., 1971—; dir. San Mateo Arboretum, 1981-82; mem. Nat Eagle Sout Assn.; pres. Burterian Found., 1987-92. Served to capt. U.S. Army, 1963-68, Vietnam. Mem. Naval Acad. Alumni Assn., Stanford Alumni Assn., Kiwanis (disting. pres. 1983), Commonwealth Club, Rotary, Beta Gamma Sigma. Republican. Home: 200 Occidental Ave Burlingame CA 94010-5221 Office: Dean Witter Reynolds 181 E 2d Ave San Mateo CA 94401-3037

YEAGER, RANDY, pilot; b. Denver, Mar. 2, 1950; s. Harold and Beulah (Fisher) Y. AA in Piloting, U. Alaska, Anchorage, 1983, AA in Social Sci., 1984. Pilot, guide Iliaska Lodge, Iliamna, Alaska, 1980-82; mgr. King Salmon (Alaska) Lodge, 1983-87; pilot, guide Fishing Unltd. Lodges, Port Alsworth, Alaska, 1988—. With U.S. Army N.G., 1983—. Deocrated Purple Heart. Mem. Seaplane Pilots Assn., Aircraft Owners and Pilots Assn., Am. Vets. Assn., Alaska Profl. Sportsmen Assn., Army-Nat. Guard Officers Assn. Home: 12201 Shenandoah Rd Anchorage AK 99516-2204

YEARLEY, DOUGLAS CAIN, mining and manufacturing company executive; b. Oak Park, Ill., Jan. 7, 1936; s. Bernard Cain and Mary Kenny (Howard) Y.; m. Elizabeth Anne Dunbar, Feb. 8, 1958; children: Sandra, Douglas Jr., Peter, Andrew. BMetE, Cornell U., 1958; postgrad., Harvard U., 1968. Engr. welding Gen. Dynamics, Groton, Conn., 1958-60; dir. rsch., project engr. Phelps Dodge Copper Products, Elizabeth, N.J., 1960-68; mgr. ops. Phelps Dodge Internat. Co., N.Y.C., 1968-71; v.p. ops. Phelps Dodge Tube Co., L.A., 1971-73; exec. v.p. Phelps Dodge Cable and Wire Co., Yonkers, N.Y., 1973-75; pres. Phelps Dodge Brass Co., Lyndhurst, N.J., 1975-79, Phelps Dodge Sales Co., N.Y.C., 1979-82; v.p. mktg. Phelps Dodge Corp., N.Y.C., 1979-82, sr. v.p., 1982-87, exec. v.p., 1987-89, chmn., chief exec. officer, 1989—, also bd. dirs.; bd. dirs. USX Corp., J.P. Morgan and Co. Inc. and Morgan Guaranty Trust Co., Phoenix, Lockheed Corp., Calabasas, Calif., Inroads, Inc., So. Peru Copper Co. Mem. Ariz. Econ. Coun., 1989—, Conf. Bd., 1989—; bd. dirs. Am. Grad. Sch. Internat. Mgmt., 1990-92, Phoenix Symphony, 1988—; chmn. Arts Coalition, 1989-90. Mem. Nat. Elec. Mfrs. Assn. (bd. dirs. 1983-92), Internat. Copper Assn. (bd. dirs. 1987—, chmn. 1990—), Am. Mining Congress (vice chmn.), Copper Devel. Assn. (chmn. 1989—), Nat. Assn. Mfrs. (bd. dirs. 1988—), Bus. Roundtable, Business Council Sky Club, Echo Lake Country Club, Paradise Valley Country Club, The Links, Ariz. Club, Blind Brook Country Club. Republican. Congregationalist. Home: 8201 N Via De Lago Scottsdale AZ 85258-4215 Office: Phelps Dodge Corp 2600 N Central Ave Phoenix AZ 85004-3014*

YEATS, ROBERT SHEPPARD, geologist, educator; b. Miami, Fla., Mar. 30, 1931; s. Robert Sheppard and Carolyn Elizabeth (Rountree) V.; m. Lillian Eugenia Bowie, Dec. 30, 1952 (dec. Apr. 1991); children: Robert Bowie, David Claude, Stephen Paul, Kenneth James, Sara Elizabeth; m. Angela M. Hayes, Jan. 7, 1993. B.A., U. Fla., 1952; M.S., U. Wash., 1956, PhD, 1958. Registered geologist, Oreg., Calif. Geologist, petroleum exploration and prodn. Shell Oil Co., Ventura and Los Angeles, Calif., 1958-67; Shell Devel. Co., Houston, 1967; assoc. prof. geology Ohio U., Athens, 1967-70; prof. Ohio U., 1970-77; prof. geology Oreg. State U., Corvallis, 1977—; chmn. dept. Oreg. State U., 1977-85; geologist U.S. Geol. Survey, 1968, 69, 75; Glomar Challenger scientist, 1971, co-chief scientist, 1973-74, 78; mem. Oreg. Bd. Geologist Examiners, 1981-83; vis. scientist N.Z. Geol. Survey, 1983-84, Geol. Survey of Japan, 1992, Inst. de Physique du Globe de Paris, 1993; chmn. Working Group 1 Internat. Lithosphere Program, 1987-90; mem. geophysics study com. NRC, 1987—; chmn. task force group on paleoseismology Internat. Lithosphere Program, 1990—; chmn. subcom. on Himalayan active faults Internat. Geol. Correlation Program, Project 206, 1984-92; researcher on Cenozoic tectonics of So. Calif., Oreg., New Zealand and Pakistan; active faults of Calif. Transverse Ranges, deep-sea drilling in Ea. Pacific; vis. scientist Geol. Survey of Japan, 1992, Inst. de Phys. du Globe de Paris, 1993. Mem. Ojai (Calif.) City Planning Commn., 1961-62, Ojai City Council, 1962-65. 1st lt. U.S. Army, 1952-54. Ohio U. rsch. fellow, 1973-74; grantee NSF, U.S. Geol. Survey. Fellow AAAS, Geol. Soc. Am. (chmn. structural geology and tectonics div. 1984-85, Cordilleran sect. 1988-89, assoc. editor bull. 1987-89); mem. Am. Assn. Petroleum Geologists (Outstanding Educator award Pacific sect. 1991), Am. Geophys. Union, Seismol. Soc. Am., Oreg. Acad. Sci. Home: 1654 NW Crest Pl Corvallis OR 97330-1812 Office: Oreg State U Dept Geoscis Corvallis OR 97331-5506

YEDLICKA, WILLIAM GEORGE, sales professional; b. Apollo, Pa., Dec. 25, 1922; s. Joseph Frank and Katie (Cadena) Y.; m. Theresa Rosamond Unger, July 17, 1970; 1 child, Monte. BS, U. Pitts., 1949, M Letters, 1957. Asst. sales mgr. Bowers Battery & Spark Plug Co. div. Gen. Battery Co., Reading, Pa., 1965-66; regional sales mgr. Gen. Battery Co., Atlanta, 1966-67; spl. products mgr. East Pa. Mfg. Co., Inc., Lyon Station, 1967-74, sales mgr. R.R. and mining, 1974-79, v.p. sales, indsl., R.R. and mining, 1979—; bd. dirs., Molds Corp., Kansas City, Mo. Author tech. papers, procedural manuals. Lt. col. USAF, 1942-46. Decorated, DFC, Air medal with 4 clusters. Mem. Material Handling Inst., Material Handling Equipment Dealers Assn., Nat. Elec. Mfrs. Assn., Ind. Battery Mfrs. Assn., Battery Coun. Internat. (chmn. indsl. battery com.), Indsl. Truck Assn., Indsl. Battery Soc., Pinehurst Country Club, Shriners, Elks. Republican. Presbyterian. Home: 15305 Blue Verde Dr Sun City West AZ 85375-6506

YEE, BEN, import-export business executive; b. Seattle, June 16, 1946; s. Sam and Gertrude (Jue) Y. BA in Mktg. and Bus., Seattle Coll., 1980; BA in Hotel and Restaurant Mgmt., Wash. State U., Pullman, 1982. Importer/exporter, distbr. Internat. Distbr. and Svcs., San Francisco, 1980-86; import/export cons., direct factory contact in China By Enterprises, Inc., Seattle, 1986—, pres., 1986-92, CEO, 1992—; bd. dirs. World Trade Inst., Seattle. Patentee Create-A-Lite; speaker in field. Bd. dirs. Chinese Am. U., Seattle, 1993—. Mem. World Trade Ctr., China Trade Rels. Orgn. Home: 23110 30th Ave S Des Moines WA 98198 Office: By Enterprise Inc PO Box 68305 Seattle WA 98168

YEE, BETTY TING, policy consultant; b. San Francisco, Oct. 19, 1957; d. Ging Chuck and Soo Sum (Lee) Y.; m. Mark W. Houston, Apr. 22, 1989. BA in Sociology, U. Calif., Berkeley, 1979; MPA, Golden Gate U., 1981. Coord. med. residency tng. program, project coord. program U. Calif., San Francisco, 1980-82; dir., agy. assistance coord. Vol. Bur. of Santa Cruz County, Calif., 1983-85; adminstrv. cons. Lifespan: Elder Care Mgmt. Agy., Capitola, Calif., 1986-88; senate fellow Calif. Senate Health and Human Svcs. Com., Sacramento, 1988-89; cons. Calif. Senate Office of Rsch., Sacramento, 1989-91, Assembly Local Govt. Com., Sacramento, 1991—. Pub. health commr. County of Santa Cruz, 1984-88; program chair Asian-Pacific Youth Leadership Project, Sacramento, 1990-91; bd. dirs. Santa Cruz Women's Health Ctr., 1982-86, Women's Crisis Support & Shelter Svcs., Santa Cruz, 1985-87. Mem. Am. Soc. Pub. Adminstrn., AAUW. Office: Assembly Local Govt Com Rm 3120 State Capitol Sacramento CA 95814

YEE, BRUCE JAMES, anesthesiologist; b. San Francisco, Nov. 27, 1950; s. William James and Mildred Ann Y.; m. Pauline J. Tom, July 3, 1977;

children: Catherine, Stephanie, Christopher. BS, Rensellaer Poly. Inst., 1974; MD, Albany Med. Coll., 1974. Diplomate Am. Bd. Anesthesiology, Am. Acad. Pain Mgmt. Intern U. So. Calif. Med. Ctr., 1974-75; resident anesthesiology New England Med. Ctr., 1976-78; anesthesiologist Luth. Care Home, Mesa, Ariz., 1981—; chmn. dept. anesthesiology Mesa Luth. Hosp., 1985-87. Mem. exec. bd. Phoenix House-Chinese Am. Citizen Alliance. Fellow Am. Acad. Anesthesiology; mem. Rotary. Home and Office: Luth Hosp 525 W Brown Rd Mesa AZ 85201-3299

YEE, GEORGE DENNIS, software engineer; b. Tucson, May 20, 1957; s. George Suey and Alice (Lee) Y.; m. Mandelin Li Chan, Apr. 23, 1988: 1 child, Benjamin. BS in Engring. Physics, U. Ariz., 1980, MS in Computer Sci., 1986. Computer programmer Ariz. Drug Control Dist., Tucson, 1980-81; systems analyst Ariz. Criminal Intelligence System Agy., Tucson, 1981-84; software engr. The Singer Co., Tucson, 1984-87; software design engr. United Technologies, Tucson, 1987-90, TechLink Control Systems, Tucson, 1990-92, Envirotest Systems Corp., Tucson, 1992—; cons. Artisoft, Inc., Tucson, 1984, Crawford Assocs., Tucson, 1989. Rep. Traffic Reps. of Ariz., Gov.'s Youth Coun., Eloy, Ariz., 1975; v.p. Soc. Physics Students, Tucson, 1978-80; cons. Crawford for State Treas. Com., Tucson, 1989-90. Mem. Assn. for Computing Machinery (chmn. 1985-86, vice chmn. 1986-89), IEEE Computer Soc. Lutheran. Home: 1847 N Frances Blvd Tucson AZ 85712-3562 Office: Envirotest Systems Corp 2002 N Forbes Blvd Tucson AZ 85745-1446

YEE, RAYMOND KOON SIU, retired structural design engineer; b. Honolulu, July 3, 1926; s. Sheong and Shee (Leong) Y.; m. Alice K. Ho, June 18, 1950 (dec. June 1959); 1 child, Janice Yee Galleher; m. Helene T. Fujiwara, Aug. 17, 1960; children: Randall Allan, Rachel Yee Asman. BA, U. Hawaii, 1950; BS in Engring., U. Mich., 1955. Draftsman Pearl Harbor Naval Shipyard, Honolulu, 1944-46; structural design engr. Douglas Aircraft Co., Santa Monica, Calif., 1955-59; prodn. engr., plant engr. Standard Oil Refinery, Honolulu, 1960-65; sr. design engr. Douglas Aircraft Co. (now McDonnell-Douglas), Huntington Beach, Calif., 1965-87; ret., 1987. Sgt. U.S. Army, 1944-46. Home: 6361 Bellinger Dr Huntington Beach CA 92647

YEEND, WARREN ERNEST, geologist; b. Colfax, Wash., May 14, 1936; s. Kenneth Edward Yeend and Frances Leone (Lynch) Benner; m. Nancy Neal, June 6, 1964 (div. Dec. 1980); 1 child, Erica; m. Elissa Hirsh, Sept. 30, 1985. BS in Geology, Wash. State U., 1958; MS in Geology, U. Colo., 1961; PhD in Geology, U. Wis., 1965. Geologist U.S. Geol. Survey, Menlo Park, Calif., 1966—. Contbr. articles to profl. jours. Mem. History of Earth Scis. Soc., Phi Beta Kappa. Office: US Geol Survey 345 Middlefield Rd Menlo Park CA 94025-3591

YEGGE, ROBERT BERNARD, lawyer, college dean emeritus, educator; b. Denver, June 17, 1934; s. Ronald Van Kirk and Fairy (Hill) Y. A.B. magna cum laude, Princeton U., 1956; M.A. in Sociology, U. Denver, 1958, J.D., 1959. Bar: Colo. 1959, D.C. 1978. Ptnr. Yegge, Hall and Evans, Denver, 1959-78; with Harding & Ogborn successor to Nelson and Harding, 1979—; prof. U. Denver Coll. Law, 1965—, dean, 1965-77, dean emeritus, 1977—; asst. to pres. Denver Post, 1971-75; v.p., exec. dir. Nat. Ctr. Preventive Law, 1986-91. Author: Colorado Negotiable Instruments Law, 1960, Some Goals; Some Tasks, 1965, The American Lawyer: 1976, 1966, New Careers in Law, 1969, The Law Graduate, 1972, Tomorrow's Lawyer: A Shortage and Challenge, 1974, Declaration of Independence for Legal Education, 1976. Mng. trustee Denver Center for Performing Arts, 1972-75; chmn. Colo. Council Arts and Humanities, 1968-80, chmn. emeritus, 1980—; mem. scholar selection com. Henry Luce Found., 1975—; Active nat. and local A.R.C., chmn. Denver region, 1985-88; trustee Denver Symphony Soc., Inst. of Ct. Mgmt., Denver Dumb Friends League, 1992—, Colo. Acad.; trustee, vice chmn. Nat. Assembly State Arts Agys.; vice chmn. Mexican-Am. Legal Edn. and Def. Fund, 1970-76. Recipient Disting. Service award Denver Jr. C. of C., 1965; Harrison Tweed award Am. Assn. Continuing Edn. Adminstrs., 1985. Mem. Law and Soc. Assn. (life, pres. 1965-70), ABA (chmn. lawyers conf. 1987-88, chmn. accreditation commn. for legal assistant programs 1980-90, standing com. legal assts. 1987—, standing com. delivery legal svcs. 1992—, del. to jud. adminstrn. coun. 1989—), Colo. Bar Assn. (bd. govs. 1965-77), Denver Bar Assn., D.C. Bar Assn., Am. Law Inst., Am. Judicature Soc. (bd. dirs. 1968-72, 75-85, Herbert Harley award 1985), Am. Acad. Polit. and Social Sci., Am. Sociol. Soc., Assn. Am. Law Schs., Order St. Ives, Phi Beta Kappa, Beta Theta Pi, Phi Delta Phi, Alpha Kappa Delta, Omicron Delta Kappa. Home: 4209 W 38th Ave Denver CO 80212-1925 Office: Harding & Ogborn 1200 17th St Ste 1000 Denver CO 80202-5810

YEH, PATRICK JEN-HWA, financial executive; b. Kaohsiung, Taiwan, Republic of China, Apr. 26, 1961; came to the U.S., 1986; s. Yen-Lin and Yueh-Hsia (Wu) Y.; m. Shirley Zhaoling, Jan. 28, 1990; 1 child, Jonathan C. BBA, Nat. Taiwan U., 1984; MBA, U. Mich., 1988. Acctg. mgr. Coaster Co. Am., Santa Fe Springs, Calif., 1988-89, controller, 1989-90, v.p. fin., 1990—; adminstr. safety com. Coaster Co. Am., 1991—; cons. The Phantom Royce Co., 1992—. Mem. U. Mich. Alumni Assn. Office: Coaster Co Am 10629 Forest St Santa Fe Springs CA 90670

YEHLE, LAWRENCE C., electric power industry executive; b. Maryville, Mo., May 23, 1938; s. Cleo W. Yehle and Virginia K. (Bennet) Gray; m. Theresa A. Bukaty, May 27, 1961; children: Jeffrey C., Michael D., Catherine M. BA in English, Rockhurst Coll., 1960. Dir. personnel U. N.Mex., Albuquerque, 1966-72, Scottsdale (Ariz.) Pub. Schs., 1972-75; dir. indsl. rels. Lockhead Electronics Co., Las Cruces, N.Mex., 1975-76; dir. personnel U. N.Mex. Hosp., Albuquerque, 1976-80; corp. v.p. human resources, chief adminstrv. officer Bapt. Hosps. and Health Systems, Inc., Phoenix, Ariz., 1980-88; pres. L.C. Yehle & Assocs., Scottsdale, Ariz., 1988-90; exec. dir. Elecric League Ariz., Phoenix, 1990—. Contbr. articles to profl. jours. Dir. Scottsdale Found. for Handicapped, 1981-84. Mem. Am. Arbitration Assn., Am. Mgmt. Assn., Am. Soc. for Assn. Execs., Fed. Mediation and Concilliation Sci. Arbitrators Panels, Soc. for Human Resource Mgmt., Coll. and Univ. Personnel Assn. Republican. Roman Catholic. Office: Electric League Ariz 727 E Bethany Home Rd D-122 Phoenix AZ 85014-2151

YEIN, FREDERICK SHU-CHUNG, analytical biochemist, researcher; b. Pu-Tien, Fu-Jen, Republic of China, Dec. 19, 1942; came to U.S., 1969; s. T.Y. and Yun-Foin (Wang) Y.; m. Alice M. Chen, Nov. 30, 1974; children: Kevin W., James W. MA, U. Mo., 1972; PhD, Western Mich. U., 1987. Rsch. specialist Dalton Rsch. Ctr. U. Mo., Columbia, 1972-78; rsch. biochemist diagnostics div. The Upjohn Co., Kalamazoo, 1978-87, scientist animal health drug metabolism, 1988-91; sr. chemist Syva Div. Syntex Co., Palo Alto, Calif., 1987-88; project scientist DSG Beckman Instrument Inc., Brea, Calif., 1991—. Author: Luminescence Immunoassay and Molecular Applications, 1990; contbr. articles to profl. jours. Fellow Am. Inst. Chemists; mem. Am. Assn. for Clin. Chemistry, N.Y. Acad. Scis. Home: 24198 E Benfield Diamond Bar CA 91765 Office: Beckman Instrument Inc 200 S Kraemer Brea CA 92622

YELENOSKY, PAT See FERNS, PAT AGNES

YELLEN, PAMELA GAY, sales and marketing consultant; b. Buffalo, Nov. 16, 1952; d. Arthur Irwin and Carole (Swartz) Y.; m. James Joseph Donahoe, Dec. 28, 1975 (div. Apr. 1984). BA, Lone Mountain Coll., San Francisco, 1974; postgrad., Calif. Inst. Integral Studies, San Francisco, 1974-76. V.p. sales and mktg. Bench Press, Oakland, Calif., 1974-84; nat. sales mgr. Camp-orama, Sarasota, Fla., 1984-87; speaker, cons. Prospecting and Mktg. Inst., Phoenix, 1987—; cons. Chevron, Phoenix, 1989—, Apple One, Phoenix, 1990—. Author: (video cassette tng. program) Supercharge Your Commissions, 1993; editor: Dream Reality, 1974, Enigma, 1979; author audio cassette album: Simple Selling, 1990, Stay Out of the Cold, 1991, Growing Your Business, 1992, Women In Business, 1992. Pres. Nat. Fedn. Jewish Youth, Buffalo, 1969-70; mem. networking com. Ariz. Coun. Excellence, Phoenix, 1989—; facilitator MMS Self-Esteem Workshops, Phoenix, 1988-90. Mem. Nat. Speakers Assn., Nat. Assn. Life Underwriters (presenter, speaker 1991—). Democrat. Office: PO Box 51657 Phoenix AZ 85076

YEN, DUEN HSI, corporate executive, physicist; b. Nyack, N.Y., Apr. 24, 1949; s. Ernest Chu and Louise (Loo) Y.; m. Linda Leiko Takai, June 22, 1989. BS in Physics, Rensselaer Polytech. Inst., 1971; MA in Biophysics, Johns Hopkins U., 1974; MSEE, U. Vt., 1978. Mem. tech. staff Bell Telephone Labs., Holmdel, N.J., 1978-83; pres. Multipath Systems, Inc., Honolulu, 1984—. Inventor noise detector, electronic travel aids for blind; contbr. articles to profl. jours. Small Bus. Innovation Rsch. grantee, NSF grantee 1984, Nat. Eye Inst. grantee 1988, 89, 91. Mem. Acoustical Soc. Am., Audio Engring. Soc., Sigma Pi Sigma Nat. Physics Honor Soc. Home: 1255 Nuuanu Ave Apt 2315E Honolulu HI 96817-4012

YEN, I-KUEN, chemical engineer, environmental engineer, industrial hygiene consultant; b. Singapore, May 29, 1930; came to U.S., 1955; s. Shang and Juei-hung (Wang) Y.; m. Chen-wan Liu, Feb. 4, 1958; children: Alfred, Albert. BS, Nat. Taiwan U., Taipei, 1954; SM, MIT, 1956, ScD, 1960. Cert. indsl. hygienist; registered environ. assessor. Rsch. asst. Crucible Steel Co., Pitts., 1959-61; rsch. engr. Am. Std. Corp., New Brunswick, N.J., 1961-64; group leader C.F. Braun & Co., Alhambra, Calif., 1964-68; dir. Occidental Rsch. Corp., Irvine, Calif., 1968-83; prin. Ike Yen Assocs., Claremont, Calif., 1983—. Mem. Am. Inst. Chem. Engrs., Am. Chem. Soc., Am. Acad. Indsl. Hygiene, N.Y. Acad. Scis. Office: Ike Yen Assocs 867 Marymount Ln Claremont CA 91711

YEN, TEH FU, civil engineering and environmental educator; b. Kun-Ming, China, Jan. 9, 1927; came to U.S., 1949; s. Kwang Pu and Ren (Liu) Y.; m. Shiao-Ping Siao, May 30, 1959. B.S., Cen. China U., 1947; M.S., W.Va. U., 1953; Ph.D., Va. Poly. Inst. and State U., 1956; hon. doctoral degree, Pepperdine U., 1982. Sr. research chemist Good Yr. Tire & Rubber Co., Akron, 1955-59; fellow Mellon Inst., Pitts., 1959-65; sr. fellow Carnegie-Mellon U., Pitts., 1965-68; assoc. prof. Calif. State U., Los Angeles, 1968-69; assoc. prof. U. So. Calif., 1969-80, prof. civil engring. and environ. engring., 1980—; cons. Universal Oil Products, 1968-76, Chevron Oil Field Rsch. Co., 1968-75, Finnigan Corp., 1976-77, Gen. Electric Co., 1977-80, United Techs., 1978-79, TRW Inc., 1982-83, Exxon, 1981-82, DuPont, 1985-88, Min. Petroleum, Beijing, Peoples Republic China. Author numerous tech. books; contbr. articles to profl. jours. Recipient Disting. Svc. award Tau Beta Pi, 1974, Imperial Crown Gold medal, Iran, 1976, Achievement award Chinese Engring. and Sci. Assocs. So. Calif., 1977, award Phi Kappa Phi, 1982, Outstanding Contbn. honor Pi Epsilon Tau, 1984, Svc. award Republic of Honduras, 1989; named hon. prof. East China U., 1986, U. Petroleum, Beijing, 1987, Daqing Petroleum Inst., 1992. Fellow Royal Chem. Soc., Inst. Petroleum, Am. Inst. Chemists; mem. Am Chem. Soc. (councilor, founder and chmn. geochemistry div. 1979-81). Home: 2378 Morslay Rd Altadena CA 91001-2716 Office: U So Calif University Park KAP 224A Los Angeles CA 90089

YEN, TIEN-SZE BENEDICT, molecular biologist, pathologist; b. Taipei, Republic of China, Oct. 15, 1953; came to U.S., 1965; s. Yen-Chen and Er-Ying (Chi) Y.; m. Maria He, Mar. 26, 1983; children: Cecilia, Brian. BS, Stanford U., 1973; MD, PhD, Duke U., 1982. Diplomate Am. Bd. Pathology. Resident in pathology U. Calif., San Francisco, 1982-85, asst. prof., 1985-91, assoc. prof., 1991—; asst. chief pathology VA Med. Ctr., San Francisco, 1990—. Contbr. numerous articles to med. jours. Fellow Am. Soc. Clin. Pathology; mem. Am. Assn. Pathologists. Office: Anatomic Pathology 113B 4150 Clement St San Francisco CA 94121

YENER, MUZAFFER, civil engineer, educator; b. Iskenderun, Turkey, June 30, 1947; s. Celal and Rahmiye (Koraltan) Y.; m. Barbara Ann Valovage, Dec. 14, 1980; children: Devren Adem, Alden Efrem, Erin Esra, Suzan Nora. BCE, NYU, 1969, MS, 1971; PhD, Cornell U., 1979. Design engr. Herbert Fleisher Assocs., N.Y.C., 1970; teaching asst., rsch. assoc. Cornell U., Ithaca, N.Y., 1974-80; design engr. Turkish Army Engring. Corps., 1976; supervising engr. Dalsar Corp., Turkey, 1977; asst. prof. Purdue U., West Lafayette Ind., 1980-86; assoc. prof. civil engring. Utah State U., 1986—; cons. Served with Turkish Army, 1976. Recipient govt. grants for coll. edn., 1966-72. Mem. ASCE, Am. Concrete Inst., Sigma Xi, Chi Epsilon. Author: Dynamics of Bridge Structures, 1984; contbr. articles to profl. jours. Office: Utah State U Dept Civil Engring Logan UT 84322

YEOMANS, DONALD KEITH, astronomer; b. Rochester, N.Y., May 3, 1942; s. George E. and Jessie (Sutherland) Y.; m. Laurie Robyn Ernst, June 10, 1970; children: Sarah, Keith. BA, Middlebury (Vt.) Coll., 1964; MS, U. Md., 1967, PhD, 1970. Supr. Computer Scis. Corp., Silver Spring, Md., 1973-76; rsch. astronomer Jet Propulsion Lab., Pasadena, Calif., 1976-92, supr., 1993—; discipline specialist Internat. Halley Watch, 1982-89; prin. investigator NASA Comet Mission, 1987-91. Author: Comet Halley: Once in a Lifetime, 1985, The Distant Planets, 1989, Comets: A Chronological History of Observation, Science, Myth, and Folklore, 1991. Recipient Space Achievement award AIAA, 1985, Exceptional Svc. medal NASA, 1986, Achievement award Middlebury Coll. Alumni, 1987. Mem. Internat. Astron. Union, Am. Astron. Soc., Astron. Soc. Pacific. Democrat. Presbyterian. Office: Jet Propulsion Lab 301-150G 4800 Oak Grove Dr Pasadena CA 91109-8099

YEOMANS, RICHARD DOUGLAS, lawyer; b. Arlington, Va., Nov. 22, 1952. BA, Carleton Coll., Northfield, Minn., 1973; JD, Georgetown U., Washington, 1976. Bar: N.Mex. 1976, U.S. Dist. Ct. N.Mex. 1976, U.S. Ct. Appeals (10th cir.) 1978. Mem. firm Poole, Kelly & Ramo, P.C., Albuquerque, 1976—; chmn. N.Mex. Client Security Fund Com., Albuquerque, 1983-84; mem. panel of arbitrators Am. Arbitration Assn., Albuquerque, 1987—. Mem. allocations panel United Way, Albuquerque, 1983-84, Presbyn. Heart Inst., Albuquerque, 1987-88. Recipient Outstanding Contbn. award State Bar Mexico, 1983, 84. Mem. Am. Judicature Soc., State Bar N.Mex., N.Mex. Bar Found., Albuquerque Bar Assn. Office: PO Box 1769 201 3d St NW Albuquerque NM 87103-1769

YEP, LAURENCE MICHAEL, author; b. San Francisco, June 14, 1948; s. Thomas Kim and Franche (Lee) Y. B.A., U. Calif., Santa Cruz, 1970; Ph.D., SUNY, Buffalo, 1975. Tchr. San Jose (Calif.) City Coll., part-time 1975-76, Foothill Coll., Mountain View, Calif., 1975, U. Calif., Berkeley, 1987-89; writer in residence U. Calif., Santa Barbara, 1990; Book-of-the-Month writing fellow, 1970; teaching fellow SUNY, Buffalo, 1970-73, research fellow, 1973-74. Author sci. fiction stories, children's stories, 1968—: Sweetwater, 1973, Dragonwings (Newbery Honor Book award ALA 1976, Children's Book award Internat. Reading Assn. 1976), 1975 (Carter G. Woodson award Nat. Council Social Studies 1976), Child of the Owl, 1977, Seademons, 1977, Sea Glass, 1979 (Commonwealth Club lit. award 1979), Kind Hearts and Gentle Monsters, 1982, The Mark Twain Murders, 1982, Dragon of the Lost Sea, 1982, Liar, Liar, 1983, Tom Sawyer Fires, 1984, Dragon Steel, 1985, Mountain Light, 1985, Shadow Lord, 1985, Monster Makers, Inc., 1986, Curse of the Squirrel, 1987, The Rainbow People, 1989; author one-act plays Pay the Chinaman, 1987, FairyBones, 1987, Dragon Cauldron, 1991, The Lost Garden, 1991, The Star Fisher, 1991 (Christopher award 1992), Tongues of Jade, 1991, theatrical adaption of Dragonwings, 1991, Dragon War, 1992, American Dragons, 1993, Butterfly Boy, 1993, also editor, Dragon's Gate, 1993, The Fox Ghost, 1993, The Man Who Touched a Ghost, 1993, The Shell Woman and the King, 1993. Literature fellow Nat. Endowment for Arts, 1990. Address: 921 Populus Pl Sunnyvale CA 94086

YES, PHYLLIS ANN, artist, video and filmmaker, educator; b. Red Wing, Minn., May 15, 1941; d. Eldon William Dankers and Doris Elaine (Wold) Mendel; m. Paul Stone, May 29, 1987. BA, Luther Coll., Decorah, Iowa, 1963; MA, U. Minn., 1968; PhD, U. Oreg., 1978. Art curriculum coord. Columbia Heights (Minn.) Sch. System, 1968-73; asst. prof. art Oreg. Coll. Edn., Monmouth, Oreg., 1973-76, Oreg. State U., Corvallis, 1976-78; asst. prof. art Lewis & Clark Coll., Portland, Oreg., 1978-88, prof. art, 1988—; juror Puget Sound U., Seattle, 1990; cons. Oreg. Sch. Arts and Crafts, Portland, 1989. Exhibited prin. works in several shows including Nishiazabu Asacloth Gallery, Tokyo, 1991, 93, Charles Allis Mus., 1989, Bklyn. Mus., 1986, Bernice Steinbaum Gallery, 1986, Columbia Mus., 1988. Mem. publicity com. N.Y. Women's Found., 1989-90; contbr. Art AIDS, Portland, 1987-89, OMSI Auction, Portland, 1989; active Beth Israel, Portland, 1989—. NEA fellow, 1987; Barbara Deming grantee, 1987, Oreg. Arts Commn. grantee, 1986; recipient Disting. Alumnus award Luther Coll., 1988, Juror's award Internat. Banners, Flags, Kites Exhibit, 1977. Mem. Japan Soc., Princeton Club, Mus. Modern Art, Artists Equity, Oreg. Alliance for Arts (juror 1990), Portland Ctr. for Visual Arts (exec. bd. dirs. 1980-82), Women's Caucus for Art (bd. dirs. 1979). Home: 5235 SW View Point Ter Portland OR 97201-3909 Office: Lewis & Clark Coll 615 SW Palatine Hill Rd Portland OR 97219-7899

YESKE, DAVID BRENT, financial planner; b. Albany, Calif., May 21, 1957; s. Ronald and JoAnn (Huntsman) Y.; m. Virginia Folwell, Jan. 10, 1987. BS in Applied Econs., U. San Francisco, 1988. CFP. Mng. gen. ptnr. PCM Ltd., Napa, Calif., 1977-83; wire trader Goldberg Securities, San Francisco, 1984-85; brokerage cons. The Paul Revere Cos., San Francisco, 1985-89; pres. Yeske & Co., Inc., San Francisco, 1990—. Mem. Inst. Cert. Fin. Planners, Commonwealth Club of Calif., Hermetic Order of the G.D. Office: Yeske & Co Inc 220 Bush St Ste 1109 San Francisco CA 94104-3513

YETTO, JOHN HENRY, corporation president; b. N.Y.C., Apr. 25, 1928; s. Michael and Josephine (Sofo) Y.; m. Nancy A. Cagliostro, June 9, 1957; children: Sheryl, Kay, Michelle. BSChemE, CCNY, 1950, Bklyn. Poly., 1951; postgrad., Rutgers U., 1952. Devel. engr. Materials Lab. N.Y. Naval Shipyard, Bklyn., 1951-52; process engr. Bakelite Co., Div. UCC, Bound Brook, N.J., 1953-57; asst. plant engr. Revlon, Inc., Passaic, N.J., 1957-59; dept. mgr. Aerojet, Inc., Sacramento, Calif., 1959-71; pres. Systemedics, Sacramento, Calif., 1971-85, Proserv, Inc., Sacramento, Calif., 1975—. Chmn. YMCA Bd. of Mgrs., San Juan, Sacramento, Calif., 1964; pres. C. of C., Fair Oaks, Sacramento, 1984; pres. Rotary Club of Fair Oaks, 1982; pres. Fairway Pines Homeowners Assn., 1989—. 1st lt. USAF, 1952-53.

YGUADO, ALEX ROCCO, economics educator; b. Lackawanna, N.Y., Jan. 17, 1939; s. Manuel and Rose (Barrillio) Y.; m. Patricia Ann Rieker; children: Gary Alexander, Melissa Rose, Charissa Ann. BA, San Fernando State Coll., Northridge, 1968; MA, Calif. State U., Northridge, 1970; MS, U. So. Calif., 1972. Contractor Los Angeles, 1962-69; instr. Calif. Poly. State U., San Luis Obispo, 1969-70, U. So. Calif., Los Angeles, 1970-74; prof. econs. L.A. Mission Coll., San Fernando, Calif., 1975—, acad. senate pres., 1992-93, cluster chair profl. studies, 1993—; cons. Community Service Orgn., Los Angeles, 1969-71. Author: Principles of Economics, 1978; contbr. chpts. to books. Served with U.S. Army, 1957-60. Recipient: Blue Ribbon landscape design City of Albuquerque, 1962, Cert. Appreciation Los Angeles Mission Coll., 1978; Fulbright scholar, 1986-87. Mem. Calif. Small Bus. Assn. Democrat. Roman Catholic. Clubs: Newman (Los Angeles), Sierra Retreat (Malibu) (sponsor). Home: 30960 N Romero Cyn Castaic CA 91384 Office: LA Mission Coll 13356 Eldridge Ave Sylmar CA 91342-3244

YIH, MAE DUNN, state legislator; b. Shanghai, China, May 24, 1928; d. Chung Woo and Fung Wen (Feng) Dunn; m. Stephen W.H. Yih, 1953; children—Donald, Daniel. B.A., Barnard Coll., 1951; postgrad. Columbia U., 1951-52. Asst. to bursar Barnard Coll., N.Y.C., 1952-54; mem. Oreg. Ho. of Reps. from 36th dist., 1977-83, Oreg. Senate from 19th dist., 1983—. Mem. Clover Ridge Elem. Sch. Bd., Albany, Oreg., from 1969-78, Albany Union High Sch. Bd., from 1975-79, Joint Legis. Ways and Means Com., Joint Legis. Audit Com., Redistricting Com., Western States Forestry Task Force, 1992, senate pres. pro-tempore, 1993. Episcopalian. Home: 34465 Yih Ln NE Albany OR 97321-9557 Office: Oreg State Senate 5204 State Capitol Salem OR 97310

YIN, GERALD ZHEYAO, technology and engineering executive; b. Beijing, Jan. 29, 1944; came to U.S., 1980; s. Huaixing and Halumi Yin; m. Junling June Yen, Feb. 28, 1971; 1 child, John Chengjiang. BS in Chem. Physics, U. Sci. & Tech. China, Beijing, 1967; postgrad., Beijing U., 1978-80; PhD in Chemistry, UCLA, 1984. Process engr. Lanzhou Oil Refinery, Lanzhou, People's Republic of China, 1968-73; mgr. research staff Chinese Acad. Sciences, Lanzhou, 1973-78; sr. process engr. Intel Corp. Santa Clara TD, Santa Clara, Calif., 1984-86; mgr., staff engr. Lam Rsch. Corp., Rsch. & Devel., Fremont, Calif., 1986-91; dir. etch tech. and engring., global metal etch product Applied Materials, Inc., Fremont, 1991. Author: Introducing Orthogonal Design to Semiconductor Industry, 1985; inventor multistep power reduction plasma etching, Rainbow oxide etcher, 200mm enhanced ECR reactor. Recipient Nat. Acad. award People's Republic of China, 1979, Nat. Acad. Invention award, People's Republic of China, 1980. Mem. Electrochem. Soc., Am. Chem. Soc., Am. Vacuum Soc., Silicon Valley Chinese Engring. Club (founder, first pres.). Office: Applied Materials Inc 2727 Augustine Dr Santa Clara CA 95054

YINGLING, ROBERT GRANVILLE, JR., accountant; b. Lakewood, Ohio, Nov. 8, 1940; s. Robert Granville and Natalie (Phillips) Y.; m. Linda Kay Patterson, Mar. 30, 1968; 1 child, Michael Philip. AB in Polit. Sci., U. Mo., 1963; postgrad., U. Ariz., 1966-67, Portland State U., 1971-73. CPA, Oreg. Mgmt. trainee Mich. Nat. Bank, Flint, 1963-65; comml. note teller First Nat. Bank Ariz., Tucson, 1965-67; spl. asst. Travelers Ins. Cos., Phoenix, then Portland, Oreg., 1967-70; chief acct. Am. Guaranty Life Ins. Co., Portland, 1970-73; supr. Peat, Marwick, Mitchell & Co., Portland, 1973-79; ptnr. Dietrich, Bye, Griffin & Youel, Portland, 1979-84; prin. Isler, Collins & McAdams, Portland, 1984-85; owner, acct. R.G. Yingling Jr., CPA, Portland, 1985—; adj. asst. prof., U. Portland, 1988. Treas. Portland Amateur Hockey Assn., 1977-78; mem. exec. bd. Columbia Pacific coun. Boy Scouts Am., 1980—, asst. treas., 1986-87, treas. 1988-91, dist. chmn. Mt. View, 1991; bd. dirs. Artist Repertory Theatre, Inc., 1992—,St. Andrew Legal Clinic, Inc., 1992—, treas. Recipient Silver Beaver award, Boy Scouts Am., 1986. Mem. AICPA, Oreg. Soc. CPAs, Nat. Assn. Accts. (nat. dir. 1985-87), Assn. Govt. Accts. (nat. v.p. 1983), Nat. Conf. CPA Practitioners, Rotary. Office: RG Yingling Jr CPA 11409 SE Ash Ct Portland OR 97216-3330

YINGLING, WILLIAM E., III, retail company executive; b. Balt., 1944; married. BS, U. Md., 1971. With Grand Union Stores, 1966-83; with Bi-Lo, Inc., Mauldin, S.C., 1983—, from v.p. store ops. to pres., chief exec. officer, also bd. dirs. Office: Bi-Lo Inc Industrial Blvd Mauldin SC 29662 also: Thrifty Drug Stores 3424 Wilshire Blvd Los Angeles CA 90010

YNDA, MARY LOU, artist, educator; b. Los Angeles, Apr. 4, 1936; d. Ernest Pastor Ynda and Mary Estella (Ruiz) Zapotocky, m. Gary Lynn Coleman, Sept. 1, 1956 (div. Feb. 1983); children: Debra Lynn, Lisa Annette, David Gary; m. Miles Ciletti, May 25, 1991. Student, Immaculate Heart Coll., Los Angeles, 1973-79; AA in Fine Arts, Los Angeles City Coll., 1976; BA, Calif. State U., L.A., 1993. Instr. Fashion Inst. Design, L.A., 1980-81; tchr. art to disabled The Art. Ctr. and First St. Gallery, Claremont, Calif., 1991—. Group shows include Double Rocking G Gallery, L.A., 1983, Improv Theater West, West Hollywood, Calif., 1983, Exposition Gallery Calif. State U., L.A., 1983, L.A. Art Core Gallery, 1985, Poly. Tech. Sch., Pasadena, Calif., 1986, Bad Eye Gallery, L.A., 1987, Art in the Hall VI West Hollywood City Hall, 1989, Echo Park Gallery, L.A., 1991, Art N Barbee Gallery, 1992, A Celebration of City Life, 1993; contbg. author poetry Spoken Word Voices of the Angels, 1982; book rev. Yesterday and Tomorrow: California Women Artists, 1989. Mem. Women's Caucus for Art, Los Angeles Artcore. Democrat. Office: 2118 7th Pl Los Angeles CA 90021-1752

YOCAM, DELBERT WAYNE, communication company executive; b. Long Beach, Calif., Dec. 24, 1943; s. Royal Delbert and Mary Rose (Gross) Y.; m. Janet McVeigh, June 13, 1965; children—Eric Wayne, Christian Jeremy, Elizabeth Janelle. B.A. in Bus. Adminstrn., Calif. State U.-Fullerton, 1966; M.B.A., Calif. State U., Long Beach, 1971. Mktg.-supply changeover coordinator Automotive Assembly div. Ford Motor Co., Dearborn, Mich., 1966-72; prodn. control mgr. Control Data Corp., Hawthorne, Calif., 1972-74; prodn. and material control mgr. Bourns Inc., Riverside, Calif., 1974-76; corp. material mgr. Computer Automation Inc., Irvine, Calif., 1976-78; prodn. planning mgr. central staff Cannon Electric div. ITT, World hdqrs., Santa Ana, Calif., 1978-79; exec. v.p., chief ops. officer Apple Computer Inc., Cupertino, Calif., 1979-89; pres., COO Tektronix Inc., Wilsonville, Oreg., 1992—; mem. faculty Cypress Coll., Calif., 1972-79; bd. dirs. Adobe Systems Inc., Mountain View, Calif., 1991—, Oracle Corp., Redwood Shores, Calif., 1992—, AST Rsch. Inc., Irvine, Calif., 1992—, Textronix Inc., 1992—, Tech. Ctr. of San Jose, Calif., 1987-93, vice chmn., 1989, 90. Mem. Am. Electronics Assn. (bd. dirs. 1988-89), Control Data Corp. Mgmt. Assn. (co-founder 1974), L.A. County Heart Assn. (active 1966). Office: Tektronix Inc PO Box 1000 26600 SW Pkwy Wilsonville OR 97070

YOCHEM, BARBARA JUNE, sales executive, shooting coach, lecturer; b. Knox, Ind., Aug. 22, 1945; d. Harley Albert and Rosie (King) Runyan; m. Donald A. Yochem (div. 1979); 1 child, Morgan Lee; m. Don Heard, Dec. 12, 1987. Grad. high school, Knox, Ind., 1963. Sales rep. Hunter Woodworks, Carson, Calif., 1979-84, sales mgr., 1984-87; sales rep. Comml. Lumber and Pallet, Industry, Calif., 1987-92; owner By By Prodns., Glendora, Calif., 1976—. Author: Barbara Yochem's Inner Shooting; contbr. articles to profl. jours. Head coach NRA Jr. Olympic Shooting Camp, 1992. Recipient U.S. Bronze medal U.S. Olympic Com., 1976, World Bronze Medal U.S. Olympic Com., 1980. Address: By By Prodns PO Box 1676 Glendora CA 91740

YOCOM, JAMES ELVIS, business consultant; b. Quitaques, Tex., Nov. 22, 1936; s. Carl Elvis and Ora Wayne (Maples) Y.; m. Judy Mathews, Dec. 3, 1959 (div. 1982); children: Carey, Michael; m. Barbara Sweat, July 8, 1989. Grad., Tucomcari High Sch., N.Mex., 1955. Regional mgr. Allied Concord Fin. Corp., Lubbock, Tex., 1960-64; pres. First of America Corp., Albuquerque, 1964-78, Synergy Oil Corp., Albuquerque, 1980-83, Synergy Group, Inc., Denver, 1979-87, Marketech Assocs., Inc., Denver, 1988—. Author: Set Yourself Free, 1984, Come Lead with Us, 1985; editor newsletter: Lifetracker, 1990; pubr. ednl. program: The Eagle's Quill, 1986. With USN, 1955-59. Mem. Platform Speakers Assn. Republican. Office: Marketech Assocs Inc 11258 Clermont Dr Denver CO 80233-2711

YODER, JANET SUZANNE, English language educator, academic administrator; b. Lebanon, Oreg., Nov. 17, 1944; d. Paul Emmons and Flossie L. (Lehman) Yoder; m. John Charles Yoder, June 26, 1966; children: Rebecca Suzanne, Luke Edward. BA, Goshen (Ind.) Coll., 1965; MA, U. Ill., 1971. Prof. English Mennonite Cen. Com., Zaire, 1967-69; program dir. YWCA, Evanston, Ill., 1971-72; traffic mgr. Broadcast Communications, Evanston, 1972-74; prof. English Gonzaga U., Spokane, Wash., 1981-83; prof. English Whitworth Coll., Spokane, 1983—, program dir., 1984—; vis. prof. U. Liberia, Monrovia, 1988; del. leader People-to-People, Peoples Republic of China, 1989; cons. Collegiate Press, San Diego, 1990—. Adminstrv. cons. Ch. Related Ednl. Devel. Orgn. Liberia, Monrovia, 1988. Woodrow Wilson Found. fellow, 1965-66. Mem. Nat. Assn. Fgn. Student Affairs, Wash. Assn. Educators of Speakers of Other Langs., Tchrs. English to Speakers of Other Langs. Democrat. Office: Whitworth Coll Dept of English Spokane WA 99251

YOKELL, STANLEY, chemical engineer, consultant; b. Bklyn., May 9, 1922; s. Max Goodman and Rose Beatrice (Diamond) Y.; m. Edith Helen Gersen, Apr. 26, 1944; children: Michael David, June Karen Yokell Scotton, Larry Jay. BChE, NYU, 1947. Registered profl. engr., Colo., Ill., N.J. Plant engr. Kolker Chem. Works, Newark, 1947-49; process engr. Indsl. Process Engrs., Newark, 1949-54; v.p., chief engr. Process Engring. and Machine Co., Inc., Elizabeth, N.J., 1954-71; pres. Process Engring. and Machine Co., Inc., Elizabeth, 1971-76; v.p. Ecolaire, Inc., Malvern, Pa., 1976-79; pres. Pemco subsidiary of Ecolaire, Inc., Elizabeth, N.J., 1976-79; pres. MGT, Inc., Montclair, N.J., 1979-84, Boulder, Colo., 1984—. Author: A Working Guide to Shell and Tube Heat Exchangers, 1990; co-patentee Filter Cake Thickness Indicator, 1973; contbr. articles to profl. jours. Active vol. youth activities, N.J., 1960-80; bd. dirs. Congregational Men's Club. Fellow ASME; mem. Am. Inst. Chem. Engrs., Am. Welding Soc., Nat. Soc. Profl. Engrs., Am. Soc. for Nondestructive Testing.. Office: MGT Inc 1881 9th St Ste 331 Boulder CO 80302

YOKLEY, RICHARD CLARENCE, fire department administrator; b. San Diego, Dec. 29, 1942; s. Clarence Ralph and Dorothy Junese (Sackman) Y.; m. Jean Elizabeth Liddle, July 25, 1964; children: Richard Clarence II, Karin Denise. Student, San Diego City Coll., 1967; AS, Miramar Coll., 1975. Cert. fire officer, fire instr., Calif. Disc jockey Sta. KSDS-FM, San Diego, 1966-67; bldg. engr. Consolidated Systems, Inc., San Diego, 1968-72; with Bonita-Sunnyside Fire Dept., Calif., 1972—; ops. chief Bonita-Sunnyside Fire Dept., 1991—; med. technician Hartson Ambulance, San Deigo, 1978-80, Bay Gen. Hosp. (now Scripps Hosp.), Chula Vista, Calif., 1980-83; chmn. South Bay Emergency Med. Svc., 1988. Contbr. articles to jours., newspapers and mags. Asst. curator Firehouse Mus., San Diego, 1972-89, docent, 1990—; scoutmaster troop 874 Boy Scouts Am., Bonita, Calif., 1978-79. With USAF, 1962-66. Recipient Heroism and Community Svc. award Firehouse Mag., N.Y.C., 1987, Star News Salutes award Chula Vista Star News, 1987, Golden Svc. award San Diego County Credit Union, 1988. Mem. Internat. Assn. Firefighters (pres. local chpt. 1981-82), San Diego County Fire Prevention Officers (v.p. 1984, pres. 1985), San Diego County Fire and Arson Investigators, Calif. Conf. Arson Investigators, Soc. Fire Prevention Engrs., Bonita Bus. and Profl. Assn. (bd. dirs. 1991-93, Historian award 1987), South Bay Commn., Bonita Hist. Mus. (co-founder 1986), Sport Chalet Dive Club (v.p. 1991), Masons. Republican. Methodist. Office: Bonita-Sunnyside Fire Dept 4900 Bonita Rd Bonita CA 91902-1321

YON, JOSEPH LANGHAM, gynecologist, oncologist; b. Charlotesville, Va., Feb. 9, 1936; s. Joseph Langham and Sallie Pugh (Haden) Y.; m. Dagmar Camilla Halmagyi, June 27, 1959 (div. 1979); children: Joseph III, Steven A., Lura C.; m. Edith Jane Maffeo, Nov. 26, 1979. BA in Biology, Va. Mil. Inst., 1957; MD, U. Va., 1961. Diplomate Am. Bd. Ob-Gyn. With med. corps USN, Jacksonville, Fla., 1961-62; med. officer U.S.S. Yellowstone, Jacksonville, 1962-63; resident Ob-Gyn USN, Portmouth, Va., 1962-66; staff Ob-Gyn USN, Quantico, Va., 1967-69, Oakland, Calif., 1970-72; fellow Gyn-Oncology Jackson Meml. Hosp., Miami, 1972-74; staff Gyn-Oncology USN, San Diego, 1974-80; head Ob-Gyn and Gyn-Oncology Va. Mason Clinic, Seattle, 1983—; clin. prof. U. Wash. Sch. Medicine, Seattle, 1983—. Contbr. articles to profl. jours. Fellow Am. Coll. Ob-Gyn (vice chmn. sect. 1971-80), Am. Coll. Surgery, Soc. Gynecology Oncologists (bd. cert. Gyn-Oncology), Am. Soc. Clin. Oncologists, Western Assn. Gynecology Oncologists. Republican. Office: Virginia Mason Clinic 1100 9th Ave Seattle WA 98101-2799

YONAS, GEROLD, research and development director; b. Cleve., Dec. 8, 1939; s. Bernard and Blanch (Simon) Y.; m. Jane E. Papurt, June 11, 1961; children: Jill L., Jodi L. B Engring. Physics, Cornell U., 1962; PhD in Engring. Sci. and Physics, Calif. Inst. Tech., 1966. Sr. scientist Jet Propulsion Lab., Pasadena, Calif., 1962-67; mgr. beam rsch. Physics Internat., San Leandro, Calif., 1967-72; mgr. pulsed power sci. Sandia Nat. Labs., Albuquerque, 1972-84; chief scientist, dep. dir. Strategic Def. Initiative Ofcl., Office Sec. Def., Washington, 1984-86; pres. Titan Technologies, La Jolla, Calif., 1986-89; v.p. systems applications Sandia Nat. Labs., Albuquerque, 1989—; advisor White House, Pentagon, NASA. Mem. editorial bds. Energy, Fusion, Environment, Research: contbr. articles to profl. jours. Recipient medal for outstanding pub. svc. Sec. of Def., 1986. Fellow Am. Phys. Soc.; assoc. fellow AIAA; mem. Fusion Power Assn. (Leadership award), Shaker Heights High Sch. Alumni (Hall of Fame), Sigma Xi, Tau Beta Pi. Republican. Home: 5005 Rio Grande Ln Albuquerque NM 87107 Office: Sandia Nat Labs 9000 Albuquerque NM 87185

YONG, DAVID CHO TAT, public health laboratory director; b. Kaula Lipis, Pahang, Malaysia, Feb. 9, 1943; s. Ban Yien and Shin Yin (Ngaw) Y.; m. Lily Giok Lian Loh, Dec. 21, 1968; children: Celina Mei, Charles Tat. BSc with honors, U. Manitoba, Can., 1968; MSc in Virology, U. Manitoba, 1970, PhD in Med. Microbiology, 1973, postdoc. studies, 1974. Cert. pub. health and clin. microbiologist, Calif. Microbiologist, scientist Pub. Health Lab. Ontario Ministry of Health, Windsor, Ontario, 1975-85; pub. health lab. dir. Sonoma County Health Dept., Santa Rosa, Calif., 1986—; sessional lectr. Sonoma State U., Rohnert Park, Calif., 1986-87, adj. prof. 1992—; adj. asst. prof. U. Windsor, Ontario, 1983-84; sessional instr. St. Clair Coll., Windsor, 1976-84. Contbr. articles profl. jours. Recipient Master of Photographic Arts award, Profl. Photographers of Can., 1986, Craftsman of Photographics Arts award, 1984; Dr. Stanley Reitman Meml. award for Outstanding Achievement in Teaching, Internat. Soc. Clin. Lab. Tech. and Am. Assn. Bioanalysts, 1988. Mem. Am. Soc. Microbiology, Calif. Assn. Pub. Health Lab. Dirs. (pres. 1993—). Methodist. Office: Sonoma County Pub Health Lab 3313 Chanate Rd Santa Rosa CA 95404

YOON, JI-WON, virology, immunology and diabetes educator, research administrator; b. Kang-Jin, Chonnam, Korea, Mar. 28, 1939; came to U.S., 1965; s. Baek-In and Duck-Soon (Lee) Y.; m. Chungja Rhim, Aug. 17, 1968; children: John W., James W. MS, U. Conn., 1971, PhD, 1973. Sr. investigator NIH, Bethesda, Md., 1978-84; prof., chief div. virology U. Calgary, Alta., Can., 1984—, prof., assoc. dir. diabetes rsch. ctr., 1985-90, prof., dir. diabetes rsch. ctr., 1990—; mem. edit. bd. Annual Review Advances Present Rsch. Animal Diabetes, 1990—, Diabetes Rsch. Clin. Practice, 1989—; scientific coord. 10th Internat. Workshop on Immunology Diabetes, Jerusalem, 1989-90; sr. investigator NIH, 1976-84. Contbg. author: Current Topics in Microbiology and Immunology, 1990, Autoimmunity and Pathogenesis of Diabetes, 1990; contbr. articles to New England Jour. Medicine, Jour. Virology, Sci., Nature, The Lancet, Jour. Diabetes. Rsch. fellow Sloan Kettering Cancer Inst., 1973-74, Staff fellow, Sr. Staff fellow NIH, 1974-76, 76-78; recipient NIH Dir. award, 1984, Heritage Med. Scientist award, Alberta Heritage Found. Med. Rsch., 1984, Lectrship. award, 3d Asian Symposium Childhood Diabetes, 1989, 8th Annual Meeting Childhood Diabetes, Osaka, Japan, 1990, 9th Korean/Can. Heritage award, 1989. Mem. Am. Soc. Immunologists, Am. Diabetes Assn., Am. Soc. Microbiology, N.Y. Acad. Sci., Soc. Virology, Internat. Diabetes Fedn. Baptist. Home: 206 Edgeview Dr NW, Calgary, AB Canada T3A 4W9 Office: Julia McFarlane Diabetes, Rsch Ctr, 3330 Hospital Dr NW, Calgary, AB Canada T2N 4N1

YOON, RICK JHIN, glass and ceramics company executive; b. Korea, Oct. 5, 1943; came to U.S. 1969; s. J.R. and J.S. (Kim) Y.; married Nov. 10, 1971; children: Kenneth, Michael. BS, Hanyang U., Seoul, Korea, 1969; MS, Iowa State U., 1972, PhD, 1977. Rsch. assoc. Iowa State U., Ames, 1970-77; material scientist Anchor Hocking Corp., Lancaster, Ohio, 1977-78; rsch. scientist Sybron/Kerr, Romulus, Mich., 1978-81; glass scientist Zenith Corp., Chgo., 1981-82; engring. mgr. SPTC Corp., Van Nuys, Calif., 1982-84; project mgr. Bourns Co., Riverside, Calif., 1984-88; cons. Detoronics Inc., South El Monte, Calif., 1988; pres. IJ Glass & Ceramics Rsch., Santa Ana, Calif., 1988—; cxons. Teltek, Mpls., 1989—. Mem. ASM, Internat. Soc. Hybrid Microelectronics, Internat. Electronics Packaging Soc., Nat. Inst. Ceramic Engrs., Am. Ceramic Soc., IEPS, ISHM, NICE, Keramos, Sigma Xi. Republican. Presbyterian. Office: IJ Rsch 1965 Blair Ave Santa Ana CA 92705

YORK, DOUGLAS ARTHUR, manufacturing, construction company executive; b. Centralia, Ill., June 5, 1940; s. Harry Bernice and Violet Alvera (Johnstone) Y.; student San Diego State Jr. Coll., 1957; m. Linda Kay McIntosh, Sept. 13, 1958; children—Deborah Ann, Darren Anthony. With Meredith & Simpson Constrn. Co./DBA Pressure Cool Co., Indio, Calif., 1958—, v.p., 1968—, sec., gen. mgr., 1976-82, pres., 1982—. Mem. Bldg. and Housing Appeals Bd. City of Indio, City of Coachella, Calif.; bd. dirs. Coachella Valley wild Bird Ctr.; trustee Eisenhower Med. Ctr., Rancho Mirage, Calif. Mem. ASHRAE, Internat. Conf. Bldg. Officials. Republican. Office: 83-801 Ave 45 Indio CA 92201

YORK, EARL DANA, oil company executive, engineering consultant; b. Gary, Ind., July 28, 1928; s. Emil and Irene (Fink) Y.; m. Feb. 12, 1961 (div. June 1988); 1 child, Earl D. II. BS in Chem. Engring., Purdue U., 1950; postgrad., Poly. Inst. Bklyn., 1950-51, U. Tenn., 1951-52, Purdue U.-Calumet, Hammond, Ind., 1959-62. Engr. Otto H. York Co., Inc., East Orange, N.J., 1950-52; devel. engr. Oak Ridge (Tenn.) Nat. Lab., 1952-53; various positions Amoco Oil Co., Whiting, Ind., 1953-64; dir. rsch. assocs. R & D dept. Amoco Oil Co., Naperville, Ill., 1975-79; various positions Amoco Internat., N.Y.C. and Chgo., 1964-69; mgr. tech. svcs. Amoco U.K. Ltd., London and Milford Haven, Wales, 1969-74; spl. engring. assignment Kharg Chem. Co., Tehran, Iran, 1974-75; rsch. assoc., dir. Amoco Oil R&N, Naperville, Ill., 1976-79; v.p. Rio Blanco Oil Shale Co. div. Amoco Corp., Denver, 1979-86, pres., 1986-92; retired Amoco Corp., 1992. Patentee in field. With U.S. Army, 1954-56. Mem. Am. Chem. Soc., Am. Inst. Chem. Engrs., AAAS. Lutheran. Home: 8330 E Quincy Ave Apt H-211 Denver CO 80237

YORK, HARRY LAWRENCE, chamber of commerce executive; b. Grants Pass, Oreg., Aug. 8, 1944; s. Evans H. and Clara A. (Zumstien) Y.; m. Patricia M. Wolfe, Feb. 21, 1964 (div. Oct. 1977); children: John F., David A.; m. Sharon Kay Grisham, Dec. 26, 1977;children: Christina Kay, Ashley Victoria. Student, Diablo Valley Coll.; grad., Inst. Organizational Mgmt.; BA in Mgmt., St. Mary's Coll., 1989. Mgr. Silver Dollar Garden Ctr., Concord, Calif., 1960-72; adminstrv. asst. Calif. Legis., Concord, 1972-80; exec. v.p. Concord C. of C., 1980—; pres. York & Assocs., Concord, 1978-81. Mem. Park and Recreation Commn., Concord, 1970-73; mem. Planning Commn., Concord, 1970-79, chmn., 1973, 76; Mem. Mt. Diablo Unified Sch. Dist. Bd., Concord, 1979-83, 89-91, pres., 1982; mem. Carondelet High Sch. Bd., 1988-92. Mem. Am. Assn. Chamber Execs., Calif. Assn. Chamber Execs. (bd. dirs. 1982-84, v.p. 1992-93), Rotary. Democrat. Roman Catholic. Home: 36 Kirkwood Ct Concord CA 94521-1427 Office: Concord C of C 2151 Salvio St Ste A Concord CA 94520-2458

YORK, HERBERT FRANK, physics educator; b. Rochester, N.Y., Nov. 24, 1921; s. Herbert Frank and Nellie Elizabeth (Lang) Y.; m. Sybil Dunford, Sept. 28, 1947; children: David Winters, Rachel, Cynthia. A.B., U. Rochester, 1942, M.S., 1943; Ph.D., U. Calif.-Berkeley, 1949; D.Sc. (hon.), Case Inst. Tech., 1960; LL.D., U. San Diego, 1964, Claremont Grad. Sch., 1974. Physicst Radiation Lab., U. Calif., Berkeley, 1943-58; assoc. dir. Radiation Lab., U. Calif., 1954-58; asst. prof. physics dept. U. Calif., 1951-54, assoc. prof., 1954-59, prof., 1959-61; dir. Lawrence Radiation Lab., Livermore, 1952-58; chief scientist Advanced Research Project Agy., Dept. Def., 1958; dir. advanced research projects div. Inst. for Def. Analyses, 1958; dir. def. research and engring. Office Sec. Def., 1958-61; chancellor U. Calif.-San Diego, 1961-64, 70-72, prof. physics, 1964—, chmn. dept. physics, 1968-69, dean grad. studies, 1969-70, dir. program on sci., tech. and pub. affairs, 1972-88; dir. Inst. Global Conflict and Cooperation, 1983-88, dir. emeritus, 1988—; amb. Comprehensive Test Ban Negotiations, 1979-81; trustee Aerospace Corp., Inglewood, Calif., 1961-87; mem. Pres.'s Sci. Adv. Com., 1957-58, 64-68, vice chmn., 1965-67; trustee Inst. Def. Analysis, 1963—; gen. adv. com. ACDA, 1962-69; mem. Def. Sci. Bd., 1977-81; spl. rep. of sec. def. at space arms control talks, 1978-79; cons. Stockholm Internat. Peace Research Inst.; researcher in application atomic energy to nat. def., problems of arms control and disarmament, elementary particles. Author: Race to Oblivion, 1970, Arms Control, 1973, The Advisors, 1976, Making Weapons, Talking Peace, 1987, Does Strategic Defense Breed Offense?, 1987, (with S. Lakoff) A Shield in the Sky, 1989; also numerous articles on arms or disarmament.; bd. dirs. Bull Atomic Scientists. Trustee Bishop's Sch., La Jolla, Calif., 1963-65. Recipient E.O. Lawrence award AEC, 1962; Guggenheim fellow, 1972. Fellow Am. Phys. Soc. (Forum on Physics and Society award 1976), Am. Acad. Arts and Scis.; mem. Internat. Acad. Astronautics, Fedn. Am. Scientists (chmn. 1970-71, mem. exec. com. 1969-76, Pub. Svc. award 1992), Phi Beta Kappa, Sigma Xi. Home: 6110 Camino De La Costa La Jolla CA 92037-6520 Office: U Calif-San Diego Mail Code 0518 La Jolla CA 92093

YORK, JESSE LOUIS, chemical engineering and environmental consultant; b. Plains, Tex., May 1, 1918; s. Jesse Lewis and Alma Terrell (Sealy) Y.; m. Eva Jean Woods, Dec. 15, 1945 (div. Sept. 1975); children: Terrell Mae, Kathleen Lenore; m. Ruth Roberta Robinson, Sept. 17, 1975. BS in Engring., U. N.Mex., 1938; MS, U. Mich., 1940, PhD in Chem. Engring., 1950. Registered profl. engr., Mich., Colo., N. Mex. From instr. to prof. dept. chem. and metall. engring. U. Mich., Ann Arbor, 1941-70; chief environ. scientist Stearns-Roger Engring. Corp., Denver, 1970-83; v.p. Sr. Mgmt. Cons., Denver, 1984—; engring. cons., Denver, 1983—. Author: Unit Operations, 1950; contbr. articles to tech. mags.; patentee in field. Exec. dir. Colo. Sch. Mines Found., 1989-92; chmn. planning bd. Scio Twp., Washtenaw County, Dexter, Mich., 1963-70; bd. dirs. Colo. Sch. Mines Found., Golden, 1973—, Denver Symphony Orch., 1982-89; mem. nat. adv. bd. Santa Fe Opera, 1985-92. Mem. ASME, Am. Inst. Chem. Engrs., Am. Chem. Soc., Am. Acad. Environ. Engrs. (diplomate), Air and Waste Mgmt. Assn. Republican. Home and Office: 3557 S Ivanhoe St Denver CO 80237-1122

YORK, RAELENE LEAH, naval officer, fitness instructor; b. Chgo., Apr. 26, 1967; d. Raymond James and Janet Leah (Wytrwal) Ryerson; m. Andrew Lee York, III, June 3, 1989. BS, U.S. Naval Acad., 1989. Commd. ensign U.S. Navy, 1989, advanced through grades to lt., 1992; ops. watch officer Naval Facility Whidbey Island, Oak Harbor, Wash., 1989-92, legal officer, 1992—. Big Sister, YMCA, Oak Harbor, 1990-92; Soroptomist Internation Oak Harbor, 1992—. Decorated Navy Achievement medal. Republican. Baptist. Home: 2154 N Heritage Way Oak Harbor WA 98277

YORK, THEODORE ROBERT, consulting company executive; b. Mitchel Field, N.Y., May 4, 1926; s. Theodore and Helen (Zierak) Y.; m. Clara Kiefer, Jan. 3, 1952; children: Theodore R. II, Sharon L., Scott K., Krista A. BS, U.S. Mil. Acad., 1950; MBA, George Washington U., 1964; MPA, Nat. U., 1984. Commd. 2d lt. USAF, 1950, advanced through grades to col., 1970, ret., 1974; pres. T. R. York Cons., Fairfax, Va., 1974-79, T. R. Cons., San Diego, 1979-85, ULTRAPLECS Intelligent Bldgs., Sandy, Utah, 1991—; dir. Software Productivity Consortium, Herndon, Va., 1985-90. Mem. Loudoun County Rep. Com., Leesburg, Va., 1990-91. Decorated 3 DFC Air medals. Mem. Am. Inst. Plant Engrs., Internat. Facilities Mgmt. Assn., Intelligent Bldgs. Inst., Instituto Mexicana Del Edificios Intelegente (hon.), Shriners, Masons. Office: ULTRAPLECS Intelligent Bldgs 12189 S Bluff View Dr Sandy UT 84092

YOSHIDA, AKIRA, biochemist; b. Okayama, Japan, May 10, 1924; came to U.S., 1961; s. Isao and Etsu (Kagawa) Y.; m. Michiko Suzuki, Nov. 10, 1954; 1 child, Emmy. MSc, U. Tokyo, 1947, DSc, 1954. Assoc. prof. U. Tokyo, 1952-60; sr. rsch. fellow U. Pa., Phila., 1960-63; rsch. scientist NIH, Bethesda, Md., 1963-65; rsch. prof. U. Wash., Seattle, 1965-72; dir. dept. biochem. genetics City of Hope Med. Ctr., Duarte, Calif., 1972—. Contbr. over 250 articles to profl. jours. Rockefeller Found. scholar, 1955-56; recipient Merit award Japanese Soc. Human Genetics, 1980, Achievement award City of Hope, 1981, Merit Grant award NIH, 1988. Mem. AAAS, Am. Soc. Biol. Chemists, Am. Soc. Human Genetics (assoc. editor), Am. Soc. Hematology, N.Y. Acad. Scis. Home: 2140 Pinecrest Dr Altadena CA 91001-2121 Office: City of Hope Beckman Inst 1450 Duarte Rd Duarte CA 91010-3011

YOSHIDA, KAREN KAMIJO CATEEL, public relations professional; b. Honolulu, Sept. 18, 1964; d. William Francis and Masako (Kamijo) Cateel; m. Ken Yutaka Yoshida, Aug. 4, 1990. BSBA in Mktg., Hawaii Pacific Coll., 1989. Jour. editorial asst. Univ. Press, U. Hawaii, Honolulu, 1983; customer svc. rep. GTE Hawaiian Tel, Honolulu, 1988; account coord. Ogilvy & Mather Hawaii, Honolulu, 1989; pub. rels. asst. McCormick Communications, Honolulu, 1989-90; account dir. Joyce Timpson & Assocs., Honolulu, 1989-90; mgr. communications and pub. rels. Hawaii State Bar Assn., Honolulu, 1990—; mng. mag. editor, dir. membership benefits Hawaii State Bar Assn., 1990—; mem. Pub. Radio Community Adv. Bd., 1993; instr. Honolulu C.C., 1993. State contest winner Exec. Women's Internat., 1982. Mem. Sons. and Daus. 442nd RCT (newsletter and membership coms. 1993), Hawaii Pacific U. Alumni Assn. (comm. com. 1993). Home: 60 N Kuakini St Apt 1F Honolulu HI 96817-2468 Office: Hawaii State Bar Assn 1136 Union Mall # 1ph Honolulu HI 96813-2711

YOSHIMOTO, CEDRIC MITSUO, physician; b. Kansas City, Mo., Aug. 22, 1951; s. Mitsuru and Annie Nakami (Koga) Y.; m. Karen Margrethe Bjorn, Apr. 24, 1980 (div. Feb. 1991); 1 child, Walden Emil Bjorn. AB, U. Calif., Berkeley, 1972; MD, U. Hawaii, 1977; DTM&H, London Sch., 1990. Integrated Flexible resident U. Hawaii, Honolulu, 1977-78; staff physician Tumutumu Hosp., Karatina, Kenya, 1979-80; locum tenens physician Kalihi-Palama Clinic, Honolulu, 1982; cons. Hawaii State Dept. of Health, Honolulu, 1983-91; staff physician Waianae Coast Comprehensive Health Ctr., 1983—; lectr. U.S. Fish and Wildlife Svc., Honolulu, 1990—; preceptor Hawaii Dept. of Health, Waianae, 1991—: cons. Ebeye Hosp., Marshall Islands, 1992; asst. clin. prof. Dept. Family Practice and Community Health, John A Burns Sch. Medicine, U. Hawaii, Honolulu, 1992—. Mem. Amnesty Internat., Honolulu, 1983. Fellow Am. Acad. of Family Physicians, Royal Soc. of Tropical Medicine and Hygiene; mem. Am. Soc. of Tropical Medicine and Hygiene, Physicians for Social Responsibility, Wilderness Med. Soc., Sierra Club (instr., cons. 1990—, outing leader, 1990—). Office: Waianae Coast Comprehensive Health Ctr 86-260 Farrington Hwy Waianae HI 96792

YOSHINO, GEORGE, food products executive; b. Kennewick, Wash., June 25, 1928; s. Frank H. and Kazuye (Hada) Y.; m. Frances T. Kaku, Dec. 29, 1951 (div. 1979); children: Jean Frances, Frankie Jo, Michael Stanton, Harry Walter; m. Marguerite Shirley Mosley, Dec. 8, 1990. Grad. high sch., Weiser, Idaho. Owner Yoshino Farms, Quincy, Wash., 1948—; pres. Columbia Growers Inc, Quincy, 1956-62, Yoshino Western, Inc., Quincy, 1962-68, Wyco, Inc., Seattle, 1968-74; asst. sr. v.p. U & I Inc., Pasco, Wash., 1974-79; dir., gen. mgr. Spad Distributing, Inc., Pasco, 1979-86; pres. Century 21 Products, Inc., Pasco, 1987—; bd. dirs. Am. Nat. Bank, Kennewick, 1982—; bd. dirs., pres. Wash. Potato Shippers, Yakima, 1964-84. Mem. City Coun. Quincy, 1964-66; bd. dirs. Columbia Basin Commn., Olympia, Wash., 1964-68. Mem. Produce Mktg. Assn., Associated Wash. Bus. Republican. Office: Century 21 Products Inc 1917 N 2nd Pasco WA 99301

YOSHIOKA, CARLTON FUMIO, education educator; b. Hiroshima, Japan, Nov. 2, 1948; s. Robert Tsuyko and Sawae (Kawate) Y.; m. Audrey Hossbach, June 29, 1975; Zachary, Jami. BS, U. Calif., 1970; MA, Calif State U., 1978; PhD, U. Oreg., 1981. Recreation supr. Ariz. Job Colleges, Casa Grande, Ariz., 1973-75; recreation dir. Kingman Parks and Recreation Dept., 1974-77; instr. Mohave Community Coll., Kingman, Ariz., 1975-77; assoc. prof. Iowa State U., 1981-88, Ariz. State U., 1988—; reviewer Times/Mirror Mosby, St. Louis, 1984-88, W.C. Brown Co., Dubuque, Iowa, 1987-88, Iowa State U. Press, Ames, 1986-88; cons. Cedar Rapids Recreation Commn., 1983-87. Contbr. articles to profl. jours. Bd. mem. Iowa Parks and Recreation Assn., 1984-88; mem. Am. Alliance for Leisure and Recreation, Washington, 1983-88, Ames Boys Club, 1985-88. Mem: Nat. Rec. and Park Assn., Am. Alliance for Health, P.E., Recreation and Dance, Iowa Park and Recreation Assn. (educator chair 1981-88), Resort and Comml. Recreation Assn., Nat. Intramural Recreation Sports Assn. Office: Ariz State U Dixie Gammage Tempe AZ 85287-2302

YOSHIZUMI, DONALD TETSURO, dentist; b. Honolulu, Feb. 18, 1930; s. Richard Kiyoshi and Hatsue (Tanouye) Y.; BS, U. Hawaii, 1952; DDS, U. Mo., 1960, MS, 1963; m. Barbara Fujiko Iwashita, June 25, 1955; children: Beth Ann E., Cara Leigh S., Erin Yuri. Clin. instr. U. Mo. Sch. Dentistry, Kansas City, 1960-63; pvt. practice, Santa Clara, Calif., 1963-70, San Jose, Calif., 1970—. With USAF, 1952-56. Mem. Am. Dental Assn., Calif. Dental Assn., Santa Clara County Dental Soc., Omicron Kappa Upsilon, Delta Sigma Delta. Contbr. articles to profl. jours. Home: 5054 Parkfield Ave San Jose CA 95129-3225 Office: 2011 Forest Ave San Jose CA 95128

YOST, ROGER WILLIAM, advertising and marketing executive; b. Wesson, Miss., Jan. 6, 1936; s. Paul Leslie and Mary Josephine (Hardcastle) Y.; m. Barbara Helen Brown, Aug. 19, 1955 (dec. July 1989); children: Kathryn Elizabeth Anderson, Douglas Roger; m. Patricia Ann Warren, Jan. 1, 1991. BSJ, Northwestern U., 1958. Reporter, columnist, day sports editor Chgo. Sun-Times, 1954-59; v.p., accounts supr. J. Walter Thompson Co., Chgo., 1959-65; producer nationally syndicated TV panel show Investors Forum, Chgo., 1962-65; dir. advt. and pub. rels. Jantzen Inc., Portland, Oreg., 1965-89, v.p. advt. and sales promotions, 1989—; v.p., bd. dirs. Am. Advt. Mus., Portland, 1986—; pres., dir. Ill. Jr. Miss Pageant, Chgo., 1962-65; bd. dirs. Woolknit Assocs., N.Y.C. Author: Raleigh Guide to Boating, 1964; producer (TV film) OPUS 44 Jerry West's Own Story, 1974; dir., narrator (TV Films) On Surfing & Windsurfing, 1979-87; dir., producer (music videos) So Beautiful, Sweet Kona, and others; contbr. numerous articles to profl. jours. Communications cons. United Way, Portland, 1977-80. Recipient 4 Clio awards, 1984-85, 87-89. Mem. Portland Advt. Fedn. (bd. dirs. 1975-81, pres. 1979-80, Advt. Profl. of the Yr. 1982).

YOUKHARIBACHE, PHILIPPE BIJIN, computational chemist, researcher; b. Paris, Sept. 16, 1955; came to U.S., 1986; s. Amedée Mehdi and Alberte Marie (Baldelli) Y. MS in Phys. Chemistry, U. Paris, Orsay, 1976; PhD in Phys. Sci., U. Paris, 1986. Researcher Ecole Poly., Palaiseau, France, 1978-86; postdoctoral fellow Columbia U., N.Y.C., 1986-87; mgr. Polygen (Europe) Ltd., Paris, 1987-88; dir. product planning Biosym Techs. Inc., San Diego, 1988-90, project dir., 1991—. Mem. AAAS, IEEE, Assn. for Computing Machinery, Biophys. Soc., Protein Soc., Molecular Graphics Soc., Am. Chem. Soc. Office: Biosym Techs Inc 9685 Scranton Rd San Diego CA 92121-2777

YOUMANS, CLAIRE, lawyer; b. Seattle; d. Lynn and Margaret Kingsley Youmans; 1 child, Tracie Ann Dates. BA, U. Wash., 1971; JD, U. Oreg., 1975. Bar: Wash. 1975, U.S. Dist. Ct. (we. dist.) 1975, U.S. Tax Ct. 1990. Assoc. gen. counsel IFG Leasing Co., Redmond, Wash., 1982-83; arbitrator

King County Superior Ct.; pvt. practice Seattle, 1975-82, 84—. Contbr. articles on consumer-oriented law and marine topics to gen. publs. Mem. Wash. State Bar Assn. (mem. fee arbitration panel 1991-93, speaker seminar 1991, 92), Seattle-King County Bar Assn. (mem. speakers bur. 1976—, chmn. 1981-82, mem. exec. com. 1977), Wash. Women Lawyers Assn., Seattle Freelances, Mystery Writer Am., Pacific N.W. Writers' Conf. (category chmn. 1990, speaker 1991), Seattle Tennis Club, Wash. Athletic Club.

YOUMANS, WILLIAM BARTON, physiologist; b. Cin., Feb. 3, 1910; s. Charles Trimble and Lucy May (Gardiner) Y.; m. Cynthia McCreary Holbrook, Nov. 24, 1932; children: William Barton, Carol Anne, Charles Gilbert. BS, Western Ky. State Coll., Bowling Green, 1932; MS, Western Ky. State Coll., 1933; PhD, U. Wis., 1938; MD, U. Oreg., 1944. Intern Henry Ford Hosp., Detroit, 1944-45; instr. biology Western Ky. U., Bowling Green, 1932-35; rsch. asst. physiology U. Wis., Madison, 1935-36; instr. physiology U. Wis., 1936-38; instr. physiology to assoc. prof. physiology U. Oreg. Med. Sch., Portland, 1938-42; prof. physiology U. Oreg. Med. Sch., 1942-46, head physiology dept., 1946-52; prof. and chmn. dept. physiology U. Wis., Madison, 1952-71; prof. physiology U. Wis., 1971-76, prof. emeritus, 1976—; mem. physiology study sect. USPHS, 1952-56, mem. tng. grant and fellowship rev. panels, 1956-60, 60-64. Author: Nervous and Neurohumoral Regulation of Intestinal Motility, 1949, Hemodynamics in Failure of the Circulation, 1951, Basic Medical Physiology, 1952, Fundamentals of Human Physiology, 1957, others; contbr. articles to profl. jours. Recipient Meritorious Achievement award, U. Oreg. Med. Sch. Alumni Assn., 1967, Emeritus Faculty award, U. Wis. Med. Alumni Assn., 1985. Fellow AAAS; mem. Am. Physiol. Soc., Am. Soc. Pharmacology and Exptl. Therapeutics, Am. Heart Assn., Alpha Omega Alpha, Phi Sigma, Gamma Alpha. Home: 162 Benson Rd Port Angeles WA 98362-9414

YOUNG, ALAN KEITH, data processing professional; b. Lodi, Calif., Sept. 25, 1950; s. Herbert J. and Valeta M. (Joyner) Y.; divorced; children: Brett A., Carrie E. BS in Computer Sci., Calif. State U., Sacramento, 1981. Software project engr. Lockheed Missiles & Space Co., Sunnyvale, Calif., 1981-84, mgr. program software quality engring., 1984-91; project leader El Dorado County, Placerville, Calif., 1991—. With USAF, 1971-76. Democrat. Home: 672 Allen Ct Placerville CA 95667-3463

YOUNG, ARTHUR WILLIAM, dean, consultant, engineer; b. Rutherfordton, N.C., Sept. 1, 1945; s. Charles Arthur and Elizabeth (Fletcher) Y.; m. Margaret Mary Helling, Sept. 17, 1977; children: Amanda Ruth, Molly Austin. BSChemE, N.C. State U., 1967; MS in Engring., U. Denver, 1974. Staff chem. engr. Procter and Gamble Co., Cin., 1967-68, prodn. mgr., 1968-71; asst. to the dean U. Denver, 1971-73; project engr. McCall, Ellingson & Morrill, Denver, 1973-74; dir. admissions and enrollment mgmt. Colo. Sch. of Mines, Golden, 1974-85, assoc. dean of students, 1985—; co-sponsor Summer Admissions Inst., Colorado Springs, Colo., 1982—; cons. in field; bd. dirs. Denver Edn. Excellence Program. Mem. Nat. Assn. Coll. Admissions Officers, Colo. Coun. on High Sch. and Coll. Rels. (pres. 1976-77, various coms.). Republican. Lutheran. Home: 5398 S Garrison Ct Littleton CO 80123 Office: Colo Sch of Mines Twin Towers 1511 Elm St Golden CO 80401-1873

YOUNG, C. CLIFTON, state supreme court justice; b. Nov. 7, 1922, Lovelock, Nev.; m. Jane Young. BA, U. Nev., 1943; LLB, Harvard U., 1949. Bar: Nev. 1949, U.S. Dist. Ct. Nev. 1950, U.S. Supreme Ct. 1955. Justice Nev. Supreme Ct., Carson City, 1985—, former chief justice, from 1989. Office: Nev Supreme Ct 201 S Carson St Carson City NV 89710-0001

YOUNG, CAPRICE YVONNE, transportation financial executive; b. Palo Alto, Calif., Oct. 11, 1965; d. Michael G. and Nancy (Schwartz) Y. BA in History with Stats., Yale U., 1988; MPA in Pub. Fin., U. So. Calif., 1991. Coro Pub. Policy fellow Coro Found., 1988-89; dir. tng. Liaison Citizen Program, L.A., 1989-90; analyst on contract to dir. fin. and adminstrn. L.A. County Transp. Commn., 1990, analyst to dep. exec. dir./fin. and adminstrn., 1990-92, analyst to exec. dir., 1992-93; chief mgmt. analyst exec. office L.A. County Metro. Transp. Authority, 1993—. Author: Local Youth Group Programs, 1985, Giving Sanctuary, 1986. Grant rev. panel mem. Fund for a Just Soc., 1992—; bd. mem. Liaison Citizen Program, 1990—. Mem. Govt. Fin. Officers' Assn., Am. Soc. Pub. Adminstrn., Yale Club So. Calif. Home: 18307 Burbank Blvd # 207 Tarzana CA 91356 Office: L A County Transp Commn 818 W 7th St # 1100 Los Angeles CA 91356

YOUNG, CEDRIC JAN-YEE, laboratory director, microbiologist; b. Macau, Feb. 23, 1942; came to U.S., 1953; s. Tim-Oy and Sui-On Young; m. Selina Chui-Wah, Sept. 1, 1973; children: Derek Park-Shing, Edmund Park-Wei. BA, Calif. State U., San Francisco, 1970; MS, Calif. State U., Fresno, 1979; postgrad., Loma Linda (Calif.) U., 1981. Pub. health microbiologist Fresno County Pub. Health Dept., 1970-73; dir. pub. health lab. Madera (Calif.) County Pub. Health Dept., 1973-87, Stanislaus County Pub. Health Lab., Modesto, Calif., 1987—; mem. Stanislaus County Tobacco Control Coalition, Modesto, 1990-91. Mem. Am. Cancer Soc., Madera County, 1977-87, Stanislaus and Tuolumne Counties, 1990—, Stanislaus Chinese Assn., Modesto, 1990—. Recipient Cert. San Joaquin (Calif.) Valley Health Consortium, 1985; named to the Order of the Golden Sword Am. Cancer Soc., 1979. Mem. Am. Soc. for Microbiology, Calif. Assn. Pub. Health Lab. Dirs., Calif. Assn. for Med. Lab. Tech. (pres. Stanislaus chpt. 1989-90), Conf. of Pub. Health Laboratorians. Republican. Office: Stanislaus County Public Health Lab 820 Scenic Dr Modesto CA 95350-6194

YOUNG, CHARLES EDWARD, university chancellor; b. San Bernardino, Calif., Dec. 30, 1931; s. Clayton Charles and Eula May (Walters) Y. A.A., San Bernardino Coll., 1954; A.B., U. Calif.-Riverside, 1955; M.A., U. Calif.-Riverside, Los Angeles, 1957, Ph.D., 1960; D.H.L. (hon.), U. Judaism, Los Angeles, 1969. Congl. fellow Washington, 1958-59; adminstrv. analyst Office of the Pres., U. Calif., Berkeley, 1959-60; asst. prof. polit. sci. U. Calif., Davis, 1960; asst. prof. polit. sci. UCLA, 1960-66, assoc. prof., 1966-69, prof., 1969—, asst. to chancellor, 1960-62, asst. chancellor, 1962-63, vice chancellor, adminstrn., 1963-68, now chancellor; bd. dirs. Intel Corp.; cons. Peace Corps., 1961-62, Ford Found. on Latin Am. Activities, 1964-66. Mem. Knight Found. Commn. on Intercollegiate Athletics, Calif. Coun. on Sci. and Tech., NCAA Pres.'s Commn., Coun. for Govt.-Univ.-Industry Rsch. Roundtable and the Nat. Rsch. Coun. Adv. Bd.-Issues in Sci. and Tech., Nat. Com. on U.S.-China Rels., chancellor's assocs. UCLA, coun. trustees L.A. Edni. Alliance for Restructuring Now; past chair. Assn. Am. Univs., Nat. Assn. State Univs. and Land-Grant Colls.; mem. adminstrv. bd. Internat. Assn. Univs.; bd. govs. Found. Internat. Exchange Sci. and Cultural Info. by Telecommunications, The Theatre Group Inc.; v.p. Young Musicians Found.; bd. dirs. Los Angeles Internat. Visitors Council, Greater Los Angeles Energy Coalition, Los Angeles World Affairs Coun.; trustee UCLA Found. With USAF, 1951-52. Named Young Man of Year Westwood Jr. C. of C., 1962. Office: UCLA Office of Chancellor 405 Hilgard Ave Los Angeles CA 90024-1301

YOUNG, CHRISTOPHER MICHAEL, skier; b. San Diego, Dec. 26, 1961; s. Darryl Thomas and Shirley Young; divorced; 1 child, Brandon. Mem. A team U.S. Disabled Ski Team, Park City, Utah, 1988—. Guard Denver Wheelchair Nuggets, 1987—; counselor Rocky Mountain Jr. Wheelchair Sports Camp, Denver, 1987—. Recipient 1st place giant slalom, 2nd place slalom, 3rd place super G, 3rd place combined World Disabled Ski Champs, Winter Park, Colo., 1990, 1st place super G, 2nd place giant slalom, 7th place slalom, U.S. Disabled Alpine Ski Champs, 1991, 1st place downhill, 1st place salom, Subaru U.S. Disabled Apline Ski Championship, 1993, Disabled Am. Vets. Comdrs. trophy, 1990. Mem. Paralyzed Vets. Am., U.S. Ski Assn., Nat. Wheelchair Basketball Assn. Democrat. Home: 4746 Edison Ln Boulder CO 80301-2269

YOUNG, CONNIE SUE, public relations professional; b. Oxnard, Calif.. BS in Psychology, Colo. State U., 1977; MA in Journalism, U. Colo., 1987. Adminstrv. officer Colo. Div. Mental Health, Denver, 1980-86; asst. dir. mktg. Bethesda Hosp., Denver, 1986-87; pub. rels. writer U. Colo., Boulder, 1987-88, cons., 1989-90; pub. info. officer Colo. Div. Wildlife, Denver, 1990—. Contbr. articles to mags. Mem. Colo. Press Women (1st and 2nd pl. awards 1990, 91, 92), Nat. Fedn. Press Women (2nd pl. award 1990). Office: Colo Div of Wildlife 6060 Broadway Denver CO 80216-1000

YOUNG, DAVID CARTER, radio executive; b. Toledo, Jan. 6, 1959; s. Gerald Marlo and Jane Ann (Gockley) Y.; m. Dorothy B. Lang, June 23, 1990; children: Tara Nichole, Jessica Alexis. BS, U. Utah, 1982. Exec. dir. Coalition for 21, Columbus, Ohio, 1982-83; pres. Fairfield, Young & Assocs., Columbus, 1983-84; sr. asst. Babcock and Wilcox Inc., Coply, Ohio, 1984-86; legis. lobbyist Salt Lake County, Salt Lake City, 1987-88; community affairs dir. Cottage Program Internat., Salt Lake City, 1988-89; gen. mgr., pres. Listener's Community Radio, Salt Lake City, 1989—. Prodr. (weekly radio program) Jazz in the Afternoon, 1977-80. Dir. nationwide ballot access Nat. Unity Party, Washington, 1983-84; pres. Ohio Com. to Fight Crime, Columbus, 1983-84. Recipient Gov.'s Folk Arts award Gov. of Utah, 1991. Presbyterian. Office: Listener's Community Radio Sta KRCL-FM 208 W 800 S Salt Lake City UT 84101

YOUNG, DENNIS LEE, statistics educator, consultant; b. St. Louis, Jan. 22, 1944; s. Peter K. and Ella (Loesche) Y.; m. Mary Getz, Jan. 4, 1978; children: Karen, Barbara. BS, St. Louis U., 1965; MS, Purdue U., 1967, PhD, 1970. Asst. prof. N.Mex. State U., Las Cruces, 1970-75; assoc. prof. Ariz. State U., Tempe, 1975-84, prof., 1984—; cons. Motorola, Inc., Mesa, Ariz., 1983—; cons. in field. Contbr. articles to profl. jours. Mem. AAAS, Am. Statis. Assn., Am. Soc. Quality Control, Inst. Math. Statis. Office: Ariz State U Dept Math Tempe AZ 85287-1804

YOUNG, DONALD ALLEN, writer, consultant; b. Columbus, Ohio, June 11, 1931; s. Clyde Allen and Helen Edith (Johnston) Y.; m. Rosemary Buchholz, Feb. 26, 1955 (div. Nov. 1976); children: Kent Allen, Kelly Ann; m. Marjorie Claire Shapiro, Aug. 20, 1977; stepchildren: Jo Alene, Andrea Lynn, Beth Ellen. Student, Ohio State U., 1949-51, Columbia Coll., 1952, North Cen. Coll., Naperville, Ill., 1956, Coll. DuPage, 1978. Editor various newspapers, mags., Detroit, Chgo., Columbus, 1946-63, 1973-74, 1978-79; v.p. Frydenlund Assocs., Chgo., 1963; pub. relations mgr. info. systems div. Gen. Electric Co., Phoenix, 1963-70; publs. dir. Data Processing Mgmt. Assn., Park Ridge, Ill., 1970-72; pub. relations mgr. Addressograph-Multigraph Corp., Arlington Heights, Ill., 1975-76; acct. exec. John Ripley & Assocs., Glenview, Ill., 1977-78; editorial dir. Radiology/Nuclear Medicine mag., Des Plaines, Ill., 1979-81; pres. Young Byrum Inc., Hinsdale, Ill., 1982-83; writer, consultant Tucson, 1983—; cons. various companies, 1973—; sports reporter, Copley newspapers, 1975-83; mem. adv. council Oakton Community Coll., 1970-75. Author: Principles of Automatic Data Processing, 1965, Data Processing, 1967, Rate Yourself as a Manager, 1985, Nobody Gets Rich Working for Somebody Else, 2d edit., 1993, Rate Your Executive Potential, 1988, If They Can...You Can, 1989, The Entrepreneurial Family, 1990, How to Export, 1990, Women in Balance, 1991, Sleep Disorders: America's Hidden Nightmare, 1992. Arbitrator Better Bus. Bur., Tucson, 1987-92; docent Ariz. Sonora Desert Mus., 1988-92. With USAF, 1952-56. Recipient Jesse Neal awards Assn. of Bus. Pub., 1959, 61. Mem. Publicity Club of Chgo. (pres. 1978-79). Soc. Southwestern Authors (pres. 1992), Glen Ellyn (Ill.) Jaycees (bd. dirs., SPOKE award 1959, Outstanding Jaycee 1960), Young Reps. Club (v.p. 1960). Home: 4866 N Territory Loop Tucson AZ 85715-5948

YOUNG, DONALD E., congressman; b. Meridian, Calif., June 9, 1933; m. Lula Fredson; children—Joni, Dawn. Grad., Chico (Calif.) State Coll. Former educator, river boat capt.; mem. Fort Yukon City Council, 6 years, mayor, 4 years; mem. Alaska Ho. of Reps., 1966-70, Alaska Senate, 1970-73, 93rd-103rd Congresses from Alaska, 1973—; mem. natural resources com., subcom. water, power, offshore energy resources, merchant marine and fisheries com., fisheries and wildlife conservation, environment, coastguard navigation, Post Office, Civil svc. com., subcom. compensation and employee benefits, postal ops., svcs. Republican. Office: US House of Representatives 2331 Rayburn House Office Bldg Washington DC 20515-0201*

YOUNG, EDNA ELIZABETH, art gallery director; b. Chgo., July 12, 1936; d. Henry and Josephine (Dunkel) Zimmerman; m. C. Farley Young, Dec. 1, 1972; children: Camella Rainwater, Robin Rainwater. Dir. Young Gallery, Los Gatos, Calif., 1972—. Bd. dirs. San Jose Mus. of Art, 1984-86. Office: Young Gallery 307 N Santa Cruz Ave Los Gatos CA 95030-7229

YOUNG, EDWARD MEDHARD, JR., dermatologist; b. Long Beach, Calif., Apr. 27, 1954. BA in Biology summa cum laude, UCLA, 1976; MD, U. Calif., San Diego, 1980. Diplomate Am. Bd. Dermatology. Intern in gen. surgery U. Calif., San Diego, 1980-81, resident in dermatology, 1981-84; fellow in dermatopathology U. Calif., Irvine; dermatologist, dermatopathologist Sidell, Erickson, McCleary and Young Dermatology Surg. Group, L.A., 1985—. Co-author: Geriatric Dermatology: Color Atlas and Practitioner's Guide, 1991; co-editor: Geriatric Dermatology: Clinical Diagnosis and Practical Therapy, 1989; contbg. author: Problems in Aesthetic Surgery: Biological Causes and Clinical Solutions, 1986, Geriatric Dermatology, 1989; contbr. articles to profl. jours. Mem. UCLA Alumni Band, 1976—. Fellow Am. Acad. Dermatology; mem. Internat. Soc. Dermatopathology, L.A. Met. Dermatol. Soc., Dermatology Radiotherapy Soc., Am. Soc. Dermatologic Surgery, Los Angeles County Med. Assn. (ethics com. 1989), Phi Beta Kappa, Phi Eta Sigma, Kappa Kappa Psi. Office: Sidell Erickson McCleary Young Dermatology Surg Med 4955 Van Nuys Blvd Ste 200 Sherman Oaks CA 91403

YOUNG, EDWIN ALLEN, psychotherapist, consultant; b. Pitts., Jan. 23, 1930. BA, UCLA, 1954; MA, U. So. Calif., 1959, MEd, 1960; EdD, UCLA, 1977. Lic. ednl. psychologist, Calif.; lic. marriage, family and child counselor, Calif. Tchr., counselor L.A. Unified Sch. Dist., 1957-59; dean student affairs L.A. Pierce Coll., Woodland Hills, Calif., 1976-81; v.p. acad. affairs L.A. Valley Coll., Van Nuys, Calif., 1981-89; prof. psychology, counselor L.A. City Coll., 1959-76, pres., 1989-91, psychotherapist and cons., 1991—. Co-author: You, Your Job, and Change, 1968. With USN, 1950-52. Mem. ASTD, Am. Psychol. Asssn., Calif. Psychol. Assn., Calif. Assn. Marriage and Family Therapists, Group Psychotherapy Assn. So. Calif., Acad. Family Mediators, Employee Assistance Profls. Assn.

YOUNG, EDWIN S. W., federal agency official; b. Honolulu, Nov. 13, 1943; s. Hoon Kwan and Clara (Lee) Y.; m. Joan Tay, May 19, 1978. BA, U. Hawaii, 1966; MBA, U. Utah, 1975; MS, U. So. Calif., 1983. Asst. gen. mgr. Royal Men's Shops, Inc., Honolulu, 1973-75; mgmt. analyst U.S. Gen. Acctg. Office, Denver and Honolulu, 1976-83; audit mgr. USAF Audit Agy., L.A., 1983-84, 87-90; fgn. svc. officer Dept. State, 1984-87; with Office of Insp. Gen., Office Policy & Program Rev., Washington, 1984-87; div. dir. and asst. dir. Naval Audit Svc. Western Region, Vallejo, Calif., 1990—; U.S. govt. rep. Pacific and Asian Affairs Coun., Honolulu, 1978-83; USN audit svc. rep. World Affairs Coun. No. Calif., 1990—; officer The Asian-Am. Found., Phoenix, 1990—. Community coord. Kailua Neighborhood Bd., Honolulu, 1978-83; area rep. Urban Mass Transit Authority, Honolulu, 1978-83; active John F. Kennedy Ctr. for Arts, Corcoran Gallery Art, L.A. County Mus. Art. Capt. USAF, 1966-72. Recipient Commendation awards U.S. Gen. Acctg. Office, 1980, USAF Audit Agy., 1983, 88, 90, USAF Acctg. and Fin. Ctr., 1984, U.S. Naval Audit Svc. award, 1992. Mem. Assn. Govt. Accts., Soc. Mil. Compts., Inst. Internal Auditors, Nat. Geog. Soc., Chinese C. of C., World Affairs Council, Smithsonian Inst. Roman Catholic.

YOUNG, FELIX K. C., organization financial executive, consultant; b. Honolulu, Sept. 11, 1960; s. Randolph K.C. and Rose S.J. (Ng) Y. BBA, U. Hawaii, 1982; MBA, U. Wash., 1985. CPA, Hawaii. Auditor Coopers & Lybrand, CPA's, Honolulu, 1985-88, cons., 1988-90; contr. Hawaiian Humane Soc., Honolulu, 1990—. Mem. AICPA, Hawaii Soc. CPA's, John Howard Assn. Hawaii (treas., bd. dirs. 1991—), Honolulu Japanese Jr. C. of C., U. Wash. Alumni Assn.

YOUNG, FLORENCE NELSON, genealogist, researcher; b. Colorado Springs, Colo., Dec. 15, 1921; d. Harold Ferdinand and Edna Lydia (Bertsch) Nelson; m. Virgil Dewey Young, Aug. 26, 1939; children: Jerry Wayne, Sharon Young Strunk, Cindy Young Carpenter. Grad. high sch., Colorado Springs. Owner, mgr. Western Heraldry Orgn., Denver, 1973—. Author, compiler: Mason County, Kentucky Deed Book Abstracts, Vol. I 1789-1810, 1973, Vol. II 1819-1820, 1974, Fleming County, Kentucky Deed Book Abstracts, Vol. I 1797-1818, 1975, Clay County, Kentucky Deed Book Abstracts, Vol. I 1806-1846, 1979. Vol. Rocky Mountain Region br. Nat. Archives, Denver, 1988—. Republican. Presbyterian. Office: Western Heraldry Orgn PO Box 9225 Denver CO 80209-0225

YOUNG, GORDON DOUGLAS, investment company executive; b. Hamilton, Ont., Can., Dec. 18, 1949; came to U.S., 1975; s. William Holton and Frances Joyce (Ferrie) Y.; m. Ellen Lloyd Craver, Nov. 4, 1978; children: Caroline Scott, William Craver. BA, U. Toronto, 1972; MA, Oxford U., 1975; MBA, Harvard U., 1977. Assoc. Lehman Bros. Kuhn Loeb, N.Y.C., 1977-80, v.p., 1980-81, Geddes and Co., Phoenix, 1981-83; exec. v.p. Sunbelt Holdings, Inc., 1984-85, pres., 1985-87; pres. G.D. Young and Co., 1987-91, Young, Warnick, Cunningham & Co., 1991; bd. dirs. Hamilton Group, Ltd., Toronto; mem. local adv. bd. Resolution Trust Corp., Phoenix, 1989-91. Trustee Ariz. Mus. Sci. and Tech.; mem. Phoenix Com. on Fgn. Rels.; Mem. Urban Land Inst., Assn. for Corp. Growth (bd. dirs.), Harvard Bus. Sch. Club Ariz. (dir., treas. Phoenix 1983—, pres. 1986-87), Harvard Bus. Sch. Alumni Assn. (bd. dirs. 1989-92), Paradise Valley Country Club, Osler Bluff Ski Club. Office: Young Warnick Cunningham & Co 2398 E Camelback Rd Ste 910 Phoenix AZ 85016-9002

YOUNG, J. LOWELL, soil chemist, biologist; b. Perry, Utah, Dec. 13, 1925; s. I.A. and Elzada (Nelson) Y.; m. Ruth Ann Jones, Sept. 15, 1950; children: Gordon, LoAnn, Colene, Kathryn. BS, Brigham Young U., 1953; PhD, Ohio State U., 1956. Rsch. asst. Ohio Agrl. Expt. Sta., Columbus, 1953-56, postdoctoral fellow, 1956-57; chemist Agrl. Research Service USDA, Corvallis, Oreg., 1957-64, rsch. chemist, 1964-78; asst. prof. Oreg. State U., Corvallis, 1957-63, assoc. prof., 1963-78, prof. soil sci., 1978-90, Courtesy prof. soil sci., 1990—; rsch. chemist Horticultural Crops Rsch. Unit USDA, Corvallis, 1978-88; collaborator Horticultural Crops Rsch. Unit U.S. Dept. Agrl., Corvallis, 1988-91. Contbr. articles to profl jours. Served with USAAF, 1944-46. Mem. Internat. Soil Sci. Soc., Internat. Humic Substances Soc., Soil Soc. of Am. (officer 1972-75, assoc. editor jour. 1975-80), Am. Soc. Agromony (officer western 1966-72), AAAS, Western Soc. Soil Sci. (officer 1966-71), Inst. for Alternative Agrl. Office: Oreg State U Crops & Soil Sci Dept Corvallis OR 97331

YOUNG, JAY ALAN, clothing manufacturing company; b. Atlantic, Iowa, May 3, 1943; s. Harvey Amos and Florence (Piper) Y.; m. Beth Rosenfeld, July 17, 1976; children: Megan Anne, Daren Jon. BBA, U. Iowa, 1966. V.p. mktg., advt. Salvatori Corp., Altanta, 1963-75; treas. Pants & Duds, Ltd., Englewood, Colo., 1972-84; v.p., nat. mgr. Levis Belts, Chgo., 1985-93; pres. Lewis Accessories, Grand Lake, Colo., 1993—; owner, mgr. Rocky Mountain Apparel Sales, Denver, 1975—; gen. ptnr. Tonahutu Ridge Devel. Group, Denver, 1981—. Home: 4080 S Zephyr Ct Denver CO 80235-1923 Office: PO Box 809 Grand Lake CO 80447-0809

YOUNG, JEFFREY WILLIAM, engineering executive, consultant, engineer; b. Pitts., Jan. 13, 1947; s. William Norman and Wilma (Myers) Y.; m. Karen Lynn Young, Nov. 23, 1973; children: Scott N., Whitney R. BS, U. Calif., Davis, 1969, PhD, 1974; MS, MIT, 1970. Registered profl. engr., Calif. Asst. prof. mech. aerospace engring. U. Mo., Kansas City, 1975-79; dir. engring. Structural Dynamics Rsch. Corp., San Diego, 1979—; cons. engr. SDRC, San Diego, 1979—. NSF grantee, 1969-70, NASA grantee, 1983. Mem. ASME, Phi Kappa Phi, Tau Beta Pi. Office: SDRC 11995 El Camino Real Ste 200 San Diego CA 92130-2566

YOUNG, JOAN CRAWFORD, advertising executive; b. Hobbs, N.Mex., July 30, 1931; d. William Bill and Ora Maydelle (Boone) Crawford; m. Herchelle B. Young, Nov. 23, 1971 (div.). B.A., Hardin Simmons U., 1952; postgrad. Tex. Tech. U., 1953-54. Reporter, Lubbock (Tex.) Avalanche-Jour., 1952-54; promotion dir. KCBD-TV, Lubbock, 1954-62; account exec. Ward Hicks Advt., Albuquerque, 1962-70; v.p. Mellekas & Assocs., Advt., Albuquerque, 1970-78; pres. J. Young Advt., Albuquerque, 1978—. Bd. dirs. N.Mex. Symphony Orch., 1970-73, United Way of Greater Albuquerque, 1985-89. Recipient Silver medal N.Mex. Advt. Fedn., 1977. Mem. N.Mex. Advt. Fedn. (dir. 1975-76), Am. Advt. Fedn., Greater Albuquerque C. of C. (dir. 1984), Albuquerque Petroleum Club (membership chmn. 1992-93, dir. 1993—). Republican. Author: (with Louise Allen and Audre Lipscomb) Radio and TV Continuity Writing, 1962. Home: 3425 Avenida Charada NW Albuquerque NM 87107-2601 also: 303 Roma NW Albuquerque NM 87102

YOUNG, JOHN ALAN, electronics company executive; b. Nampa, Idaho, Apr. 24, 1932; s. Lloyd Arthur and Karen Eliza (Miller) Y.; m. Rosemary Murray, Aug. 1, 1954; children: Gregory, Peter, Diana. B.S. in Elec. Engring, Oreg. State U., 1953; M.B.A., Stanford U., 1958. Various mktg. and finance positions Hewlett Packard Co. Inc., Palo Alto, Calif., 1958-63, gen. mgr. microwave div., 1963-68, v.p. electronic products group, 1968-74, exec. v.p., 1974-77, chief oper. officer, 1977-84, pres., 1977-92, chief exec. officer, 1978-92; ret., 1992; bd. dirs. Wells Fargo Bank, Wells Fargo and Co., Chevron Corp. Chmn. ann. fund Stanford U., 1966-73, nat. chmn. corp. gifts, 1973-77, mem. adv. coun. Grad. Sch. Bus., 1967-73, 75-80, univ. trustee, 1977-87; bd. dirs. Mid-Peninsula Urban Coalition, 1971-80, co-chmn., 1975-80; chmn. President's Commn. on Indsl. Competitiveness, 1983-85, Nat. Jr. Achievement, 1983-84; pres. Found. for Malcolm Baldrige Nat. Quality Award; mem. Adv. Com. on Trade Policy and Negotiations. With USAF, 1954-56. Mem. Am. Electronics Assn., Bus. Roundtable (founder, chmn. coun. on competitiveness 1986), Bus. Coun., Pacific Union Club, Palo Alto Club.

YOUNG, JOHN THOMAS, artist, educator; b. N.Y.C., Apr. 4, 1954; s. Arthur and Barbara (Director) Y.; m. Winifred Chapin, June 17, 1978; children: Hayley Lauren, Eliza Suzanne. BA, Amherst Coll., 1976; MFA, R.I. Sch. Design, 1978. Asst. prof. U. Denver, 1978-82, Stockton State Coll., Pomona, N.J., 1982-84; prof. U. Wash., Seattle, 1984—. Prin. works commd. for pvt. and pub. collections including Wash. State Arts Commn., U. Colo., Colo. Sch. Mines, Met. Arts Commn. Omaha, King County (Wash.) Arts Commn., Rouse Co., Portland, Oreg., Security Pacific Bank, Seattle, Mobil Oil Corp., N.Y.C., Charlotte Mecklenburg, N.C. Arts Commn., 1991, Oreg. Arts Commn., 1992; exhibited in numerous one-man shows including O.K. Harris Gallery, N.Y.C., 1982-91. Louis Comfort Tiffany fellow, 1982, N.J. Counc. Arts fellow, 1983. Home: 7334 Ravenna Ave NE Seattle WA 98115-5842

YOUNG, JON NATHAN, archeologist; b. Hibbing, Minn., May 30, 1938; s. Robert Nathan Young and Mary Elizabeth (Barrows) Roy; m. Karen Sue Johnson, June 5, 1961 (div. May 1980); children: Shawn Nathan, Kevin Leigh; m. Tucker Heitman, June 18, 1988. BA magna cum laude, U. Ariz., 1960, PhD, 1967; MA, U. Ky., 1962. Archeologist Nat. Park Svc. Southwest Archeol. Ctr., Globe and Tucson, Ariz., 1967-76; exec., camp dir. YMCA of Metro. Tucson, 1976-78; asst. dir. Kit Carson Meml. Found., Taos, N.Mex., 1978-79; co-dir. Las Palomas de Taos, 1979-80; archeologist Nat. Forest Svc., Carson Nat. Forest, Taos, 1980—; exec. order cons. U.S. Sec. Interior, 1973-76. Author: The Salado Culture in Southwestern Prehistory, 1967; co-author: Excavation of Mound 7, 1981, First-Day Road Log in Techtonic Development of the Sangre de Cristo Mountains, 1990. Active YMCA (White Rag Soc.). Grantee NEH, 1987; Ariz. Wilson Found., NSF, Ky. Rsch. Found. fellow, 1960-66; Baird Found., Bausch and Lomb, Elks; recipient cert. merit USDA, 1987, 89. Fellow AAAS, Am. Anthrop. Assn., Explorers Club, Royal Anthrop. Inst.; mem. Current Anthropology (assoc.), Ariz. Archaeol. and Hist. Soc., Ariz. Hist. Soc., Coun. on Am.'s Mil. Past, Soc. Hist. Archaeology, Soc. Am. Archaeology, Harwood Found., Millicent Rogers Mus., Taos Archaeol. Soc., Taos County Hist. Soc., Sigma Xi, Phi Beta Kappa, Alpha Kappa Delta, Phi Kappa Phi, Delta Chi. Home: PO Box 2207 Taos NM 87571-2207 Office: Nat Forest Svc Suprs Office PO Box 558 Taos NM 87571-0558

YOUNG, JOSEPH EARNEST, art historian, educator; b. L.A., Sept. 8, 1939; s. Joseph Milo and Henrietta Virginia (Johnson) Y. MA, UCLA, 1978. Asst. curator of prints and drawings L.A. County Mus. of Art, 1965-79; assoc. prof. of art history, dir. Harry Wood Art Gallery Ariz. State U., Tempe, 1979—; art critic Phoenix mag., 1980-81, Scottsdale (Ariz.) Progress, 1983-91. Editor Jour. of the Theory and Criticism of Visual Arts, Tempe, 1980-86; west coast editor Art Internat. mag., Lugano, Switzerland, 1970-71; contbr. articles to profl. jours. Mem. Print Coun. of Am. (bd. dirs. 1976—). Roman Catholic. Home: 8455 E Bonnie Rose Ave Scottsdale AZ 85250-6715 Office: Sch of Art/Ariz State Univ Tempe AZ 85287

YOUNG, JOYCE HENRY, adult education educator, consultant; b. Oak Park, Ill., July 3, 1930; d. Jesse Martin and Adelina Patti (Gillander) H.; m. James Edward Young, Apr. 26, 1958; children: Richard Allen, Patti

Ann. BA, Calif. State U., Fresno, 1951; MA, Northwestern U., 1952; EdD, U. So. Calif., 1986. Tchr. Glencoe (Ill.) Pub. Schs., 1952-53, Hayward (Calif.) Schs., 1953-59, Honolulu Dept. Edn., 1969-83, Kamehameha Schs., Honolulu, 1987; instr. Hawaii Pacific Coll., Honolulu, 1987, Honolulu Community Coll., 1988, Chaminade U., Honolulu, 1990, Kansai Gaidai-Hawaii Coll., 1991—; cons. Computer Lab., Honolulu, 1988. Mem. AAUW, Am. Ednl. Rsch. Assn., Educom, Delta Epsilon, Kappa Delta Pi, Pi Lamda Theta. Democrat. Presbyterian. Office: Charminade U 5257 Kalanianaole Hwy Honolulu HI 96821-1884

YOUNG, KENNETH ROGER, educator; b. L.A., Aug. 25, 1936; s. John Richardson and Jency Florence (Lehman) Y.; m. Lavonne Kurowski, Mar. 17, 1963 (div. June, 1970); m. Suzanne Cecelia Murray, June 20, 1970; children: Christina, Steven, Joseph. AA, Sacramento City Coll., 1956; BA, Sacramento State U., 1958, MA, 1968. Cert. secondary tchr., Calif. Tchr. Roseville (Calif.) High Sch., 1960-65, Oakmont High Sch., Roseville, 1965-70; tchr., resource specialist San Carlos (Calif.) High Sch., 1970-73, tchr., dept. chmn., 1973-82; tchr. Britton Middle sch., Morgan Hill, Calif., 1982-85, Live Oak High Sch., Morgan Hill, 1985—; performer Living Artists' Theater, Calif., 1980—; cons. art history workshop, San Juan Sch. Dist., Sacramento, 1986-87. Performer San Jose Fine Art Mus., 1983-84, Festival of the Arts Week, 1986-88, Fresno Art Mus., 1987. Served with Calif. N.G., 1959-65. Recipient Golden Bell award Calif. Sch. Bds. Assn., 1987. Mem. Am. Fedn. Tchrs., Young Audiences San Jose (bd. dirs. 1985-88), Calif. Art Edn. Assn. (no. area sec. rep. 1988-90). Democrat. Roman Catholic. Home: 1137A Reed Ave Sunnyvale CA 94086-6833 Office: Live Oak High Sch PO Box 927 Morgan Hill CA 95038-0927

YOUNG, LESTER REX, engineering company administrator; b. Marion, Ind., Aug. 26, 1946; s. Harold Leroy and Willow Marie (May) Y.; m. Bonnie Darline Denison, Sept. 5, 1965; children: Tamara Lynn, Kelby Gene, Kadee Lynn. BSEE, Kans. State U., 1969; MBA, Wichita State U., 1979. Reg. engr. Colo., Kans., Ohio, Mont., Utah, La. Plant engr. Beech Aircraft Corp., Wichita, Kans., 1973-75; asst. to v.p. mfg. Beech Aircraft Corp., Wichita, 1975-77; sr. project mgr. Smith & Boucher, Inc., Overland Park, Kans., 1977-80; dir. engring. R.M. Henning, Inc., New Philadelphia, Ohio, 1980-82; mgr. indsl. engring. Williams Internat., Ogden, Utah, 1982-84; mgr. plant engring. Sundstrand Corp., Denver, 1984-86; pres. ECS Engrs. Inc., Arvada, Colo., 1986-90; dir. bus. devel. Morrison Knudsen Corp., Denver, 1990—; cons. Compliance Recycling Industires, Denver, 1984-87. Author: (reference manuals) Selection of Reverse Osmosis for Boiler Applications, 1987, Applications for Enzyme Activated Carbon, 1989, Integrated Refinery Waste Management, 1992. Capt. U.S. Army, 1969-73, Europe. Republican. Nazarene. Office: Morrison Knudsen 7100 E Belleview Ave Ste 300 Englewood CO 80111-1636

YOUNG, LIH-JIUAN SHIAU, energy research and development company manager; b. Taiwan, Republic of China, Mar. 3, 1951; d. Jia-Jen and Yeh-Horn (Shieh) Shiau; m. Masefield J. Young, Apr. 9, 1976; 1 child, Jason S. BS in Nutrition, U. Chinese Culture, Taipei, 1973, MS in Nutrition, 1975; MS in Biochemistry, Duquesne U., 1978, PhD in Phy. Chemistry, 1982. Assoc. rsch. chemist Food Industry R&D Inst., Taiwan, 1975-76; post-doctoral rsch. assoc. Scripps Clinic and Rsch. Found., San Diego, 1984-85, U. Calif., San Diego, 1985-86; R & D lab. mgr. Ahlstrom Pyropower, Inc., San Diego, 1986—. Contbr. articles to profl. jours. Active San Diego Chinese Hist. Soc. Mem. Am. Chem. Soc.

YOUNG, MARILYN RAE, school system administrative secretary, councilman; b. Muskegon, Mich., Dec. 29, 1934; d. Albert Henry Cribley and Mildred Ida (Johnson) Raby; m. Peter John Young, May 21, 1955; children: Pamela Lynn Young-Walker, Lane Allen. Grad. high sch., Calumet City, Ill., 1952. Dep. pub. fiduciary Yuma County, Ariz., 1979-83; adminstrv. sec. Yuma Sch. Dist. One, 1983—; councilman City of Yuma, 1990—. Pres. bd. dirs. Behavioral Health Svcs. of Yuma, 1979-90; vice chmn. Yuma Planning and Zoning Commn., 1985-89; v.p. bd. dirs. Children's Village, Yuma, 1983-89; lay leader Trinity United Meth. Ch., 1986—; grad. Yuma Leadership, Inc., 1985; treas. bd. dirs. Yuma Leadership, Inc., 1986-89; participant Ariz. Women's Town Hall, 1989, various Yuma County Town Halls, 1987-90; chmn Yuma Youth Leadership Com., 1991-92; mem. allocation panel United Way, 1991-93; charter mem. Friends of Roxaboxen; active High Sch. Ad Hoc Com., 1991—;. Mem. Yuma County C. of C. (mem. mil. affairs com. 1988-90). Home: 1288 W 18th St Yuma AZ 85364-5313 Office: City of Yuma 180 W 1st St Yuma AZ 85364-1495

YOUNG, MARTIN DAVID, manufacturing professional; b. Mitchell, S.D., Dec. 26, 1959; s. Robert R. and LaVergne (Rydquist) Y.; m. Jackie Lea Surat, June 26, 1982; children: Rachel Marie, Kristin Nicole, Daniel Martin. BS in Metallur. Engring., S.D. Sch. Mines & Tech., 1982; postgrad., U. Oreg., 1991—. Metallur. engr. Dow Corning Corp., Midland, Mich., 1982-85, assoc. project engr., 1985-89, mfg. engr., 1989-90, prodn. teamleader, 1990—. Vice-chmn., deacon Marcola Christian Ch. Mem. AIME, Am. Soc. Metals (ticket com. Saginaw, Mich. chpt. 1984-89). Republican. Office: Dow Corning Corp 1801 Aster St Springfield OR 97477-5031

YOUNG, MARY JANE, American studies and folklore educator; b. Apollo, Pa., Oct. 25, 1950; d. Floyd Clark and Lillian Grace (Deemer) Y.; m. Robert Henry Leibman, June 12, 1982. BA, St. John's Coll., 1973; MA, U. Pa., 1978, PHD, 1982. Math. tchr. Severn Sch., Severna Park, Md., 1973-75; asst. dir. admissions St. John's Coll., Annapolis, Md., 1975-76; rsch. asst. U. Pa., Phila., 1976-79, teaching fellow dept. folklore, 1979-80, lectr. dept. folklore, 1979-82; asst. prof. folklore ctr. U. Tex., Austin, 1982-87; assoc. prof. Am. studies U. N.Mex., Albuquerque, 1987—; cons. Tribal Mus. Com., Zuni, N.Mex., 1980—. Author: Signs from the Ancestors, 1988; editorial bd. Jour. of the Am. Studies Assn. Tex., 1988—, Archaeoastronomy, bull. for Ctr. for Archaeoastronomy, 1979—; contbr. articles to profl. jours. Fellow Roothbert Found., 1976-79, dissertation fellow AAUW, 1981-82; recipient rsch. assistantship Smithsonian Inst., 1978. Office: U NMex Dept Am Studies 307 Ortega Rd NW Albuquerque NM 87131-0001

YOUNG, NANCY JEANNE PECK, artist; b. Chgo., Nov. 7, 1939; d. Ralph Brazelton and Marjorie Elizabeth (Truby) Peck; m. Charles Allen Young, June 1, 1961; 1 child, Michael Allen. BS, U. Ariz., 1961. represented in permanent collections at U. Ariz., U. N.Mex., U. No. Ariz., Am. Express, IBM Corp., AT&T, Atari Inc., First Interstate Bank, Sun Valley Ctr. for Arts, Idaho, Albuquerque Nat. Bank, Albuquerque pub. schs., Nat. Mus. of Women in the Arts, Washington; commns. include Hallmark Cards, Kansas City, 1989, Burlington No., Houston, 1988, Alaska 1% for Arts, 1986, Albuquerque Tech. Vocat. Inst., 1986, 1991, N.Mex 1% for Arts Program, 1992others; contbr. articles to profl. jours. One man shows at U. Ariz., Tuscon, 1984, 91, U. N.Mex., 1991, 1992, Ea. N.Mex. U., 1990, New Trends Gallery, Santa Fe, 1987, 88, La Fuente Gallery, Ariz., 1988-91, E.S. Lawrence Gallery, Taos, 1987, Andrews Gallery, Albuquerque, 1985-1987, Tarbox Gallery, 1986, La Tienda Gallery, Ariz. 1984-86, others; exhibited in group shows at Santa Fe Festival of Arts, Sun Valley Ctr. for Arts, N.Mex. Gov.'s Gallery, Audubon Artists 39th Exhibition, N.Y., many others. Mem. Artists Equity. Studio: 11416 Brussels Ave NE Albuquerque NM 87111-5212

YOUNG, PATRICIA JANEAN, speech pathologist; b. San Diego, Nov. 30, 1953; d. Bernarr Elbert and Janean Elizabeth (Romig) Y. AA, Palomar Community coll., 1974; BA, Calif. State U., Chico, 1976; MA, Calif. State U., Long Beach, 1981. Mgmt. trainee J.W. Robinson's Dept. Store, Los Angeles, 1977-78; screening coordinator Riverview Hearing, Speech and Lang. Ctr., Long Beach, 1978-81, speech pathologist, 1981-84; speech pathologist, dir. Speech Pathology Svcs., Carlsbad, Calif., 1984—; mem. adv. com. for Developmentally Disabled, San Diego, 1985-91; coord. pub. svc. announcements for Disabilities Awareness Week, ABC-TV, 1986, Inside San Diego program, 1988. Producer (cable TV series), Communicative Disorders, 1983. Active Carlsbad Hist. Soc., 1993. Mem. Am. Speech, Lang. and Hearing Assn. (cert. charter mem. adminstrn. and supervision div. 1990—, augmentative and alternative comm. divsn. 1993), Calif. Speech, Lang. and Hearing Assn. (div. rep. 1985-88, legisl. com. 1992—, Outstanding Achievement award 1987), Calif. and Nat. Speech Pathologists and Audiologists in Pvt. Practice, Nat. Assn. Hearing and Speech Action (chmn. Disney benefit 1983-84), Assn. for Retarded Citizens, Calif. Scholastic Fedn., Zeta Tau Alpha, Phi Delta Gamma (sec. 1982-88, v.p. 1983-84). Republican. Home: 2880 Andover Ave Carlsbad CA 92008-7004 Office: Speech Pathology Svcs PO Box 4355 Carlsbad CA 92018-4355

YOUNG, PATRICK TERRY, retail executive; b. Columbus, Ohio, June 26, 1947; s. Willis Gerald and Frances (Tague) Y.; m. Linda Diane Bollinger, July 26, 1969; 1 child, Amy Melissa. BSBA, Ohio State U., Columbus, 1969. Buyer Wickes Lumber, Saginaw, Mich., 1969-73; v.p. purchasing Erb Lumber Co., Birmingham, Mich., 1973-83; v.p. div. Grossman N.W. GNW Ptnrs., San Carlos, Calif., 1983-90; divisional merchandise mgr. Home Base, Fullerton, Calif., 1990—; mem. adv. coun. Home Ctr. Inst., Chgo., 1991—. Mem. St. Matthias Pastoral Coun., Redwood City, Calif., 1985-90. Republican. Roman Catholic. Home: 6422 Acacia Ln Yorba Linda CA 92686

YOUNG, ROBERT EDWARD, finance company executive; b. L.A., Nov. 28, 1943; s. David and Sue (Wise) Y. Student, E. Los Angeles Coll., 1973, Santa Monica Coll., 1975; BA, UCLA, 1978. Cert. securities analyst N.Y. Inst. Fin., 1972. Computer operator Rocketdyne Corp., Canoga Park, Calif., 1963-65; computer ops. supr. Hughes Aircraft Corp., El Segundo, Calif., 1965-67; with investment securities dept. Smith, Tilton & Co., Inc., Santa Ana, Calif., 1967-70, Morton Seidel & Co., Inc., L.A., 1970-78; sales mgr. comml. interior constrn. NICO Constrn. Co., Inc., L.A., 1978-80; sales mgr. Strauss Constrn. Co., Inc., L.A., 1981-82; v.p., instl. investment officer FCA Asset Mgmt./Am. Savs., Los Angeles, 1982-87; pres., chief exec. officer Avalon Fin. Group, Inc., Los Angeles, 1988-90; prin. Robert Young & Co., 1991—; bd. dirs. RESA Prodns. 1973-80, Edu Care, L.A., 1981-90, ASC Edn. Svcs. Inc., L.A., chmn. fin. com.; mktg. cons. Shehata Enterprises, L.A., 1978-79; sales tng. cons. Versailles Gallery, L.A., Schwartz Constrn., L.A., 1982; cons. PC Etcetera, L.A., 1990-91. Photographer: prin. works include Man at Work or Play UN, Geneva, 1976, Cat of Yr. photo, 1977, Photomontage U. So. Calif. Early Childhood Edn. Ctr., 1977; producer weekly pub. affairs prog. for family fin. planning sta. KPOL Radio, 1974, Stocks and Bonds Show KWHY-TV, 1975-78, MacRadio show, Am. Radio Network, 1989, WinRadio Show, 1990, MacWin Radio, 1991—. Fin. cons. Hofheinz Fund, Houston, 1988. Served with USCGR, 1964-70. Mem. AIA, Cosmopolitan Internat. (pres. 1967-68), Soc. Archtl. Historians, L.A. Conservancy, West L.A. Constitution Observance Day (chmn. 1970), Archtl. Hist. Soc. (life mem. So. Calif. chpt.), Valley MacIntosh User Group, Downtown High Twelve Club (past pres.), Reel Sports Club, Masons, Toastmasters (Outstanding Toastmaster, 1973-74, 76). Home: 2912 Park View Dr Alhambra CA 91803 Office: Robert Young & Co 8306 Wilshire Blvd Ste 499 Beverly Hills CA 90211-2382

YOUNG, ROBYN GAIL, neurologist; b. Danville, Ill., Dec. 24, 1950; d. Martin and Selma (Mervis) Y.; m. David R. Cox, June 12, 1977 (div. Nov. 1985); 1 child, Ian Richard. BS with honors in Chemistry, Stanford U., 1973; MD, Yale U., 1977. Diplomate Nat. Bd. Med. Examiners, Am. Bd. Internal Medicine, Am. Bd. Psychiatry and Neurology. Intern and resident in internal medicine Pacific Presbyn. Hosp., San Francisco, 1977-80; resident in neurology Moffitt Hosp. U. Calif., San Francisco, 1980-83; pvt. practice Oakland, Calif.; mem. staff in neurology Alameda (Calif.) Hosp., Summit Med. Ctr., Oakland, Providence Hosp., Alta Bates Hosp., Berkeley, Calif., Pacific Med. Ctr., San Francisco; clin. instr. dept. neurology U. Calif., San Francisco, 1983—. Profl. adv. bd. No. Calif. chpt. Multiple Sclerosis Soc., 1989—; bd. dirs., profl. adv. bd. Alameda County chpt. Easter Seal Soc., 1990—, med. dir. Oakland Rehab. Ctr., 1993—. Mem. Am. Acad. Neurology, Calif. Med. Assn., Alameda-Contra Costa County Med. Assn., N.Y. Acad. Scis. Office: 947 Marine Village Pkwy Alameda CA 94501

YOUNG, ROGER CARL, computer company executive; b. Clayton, Mo., Mar. 21, 1932; s. Gerald Lee Young and Bertha Augusta (Schlottach) McCulloh; m. Nadine Fay Basch, Apr. 27, 1952; children: Julia Allyn, David Ford. Student, Washington U., St. Louis, 1956-57, U. Calif., Berkeley, 1957-60, Contra Costa Coll., 1970. V.p. and div. mgr. Crocker Nat. Bank, San Francisco, 1967-75; nat. accts. mgr. Wang Labs., San Francisco, 1975-78; industry cons. Fortune 500, 1978-81; pres. ComTrak, Richmond, Calif., 1981-83; dir. mktg. Delphi Systems, Inc., Westlake Village, Calif., 1983-89; regional sales mgr. Applied Systems, Inc., Chgo., 1991-92. Served with USAF, 1951-55. Mem. Data Processing Mgmt. Assn. (cert., bd. dirs., sec. San Francisco chpt. 1965-67), Am. Contract Bridge League (life master 1959), Green Tree Golf Club. Republican. Home and Office: 779 Arbor Oaks Dr Vacaville CA 95687-5252

YOUNG, ROY ALTON, university administrator, educator; b. McAlister, N.Mex., Mar. 1, 1921; s. John Arthur and Etta Julia (Sprinkle) Y.; m. Marilyn Ruth Sandman, May 22, 1950; children: Janet Elizabeth, Randall Owen. BS, N.Mex. A&M Coll., 1941; MS, Iowa State U., 1942, PhD, 1948; LLD (hon.), N.Mex. State U., 1978. Teaching fellow Iowa State U., 1941-42, instr., 1946-47, Indsl. fellow, 1947-48; asst. prof. Oreg. State U., 1948-50, assoc. prof., 1950-53, prof., 1953—, head dept. botany and plant pathology, 1958-66, dean research, 1966-70, acting pres., 1969-70, v.p. for research and grad. studies, 1970-76, dir. Office for Natural Resources Policy, 1986-90; chancellor U. Nebr., Lincoln, 1976-80; mng. dir., pres. Boyce Thompson Inst. Plant Research, Cornell U., Ithaca, N.Y., 1980-86; mem. Commn. on Undergrad. Edn. in Biol. Scis., 1963-68, Gov.'s Sci. Council, 1987-90; cons. State Expt. Stas. div. USDA; chmn. subcom. plant pathogens, agriculture bd. Nat. Acad. Scis.-NRC, 1965-68, mem. exec. com. study on problems of pest control, 1972-75; mem. exec. com. Nat. Govs.' Council on Sci. and Tech., 1970-74; mem. U.S. com. man and biosphere UNESCO, 1973-82; mem. com. to rev. U.S. component Internat. Biol. Program, NAS, 1974-76; mem. adv. panel on post-doctoral fellowships in environ. sci. Rockefeller Found., 1974-78; bd. dirs. Pacific Power & Light Co., 1974-91, PacifiCorp., 1984-91, Boyce Thompson Inst. for Plant Research, 1975—, Boyce Thompson Southwestern Arboretum, 1981-92, Oreg. Grad. Inst., 1987—; mem. adv. com. Directorate for Engring. and Applied Sci., NSF, 1977-81, mem. sea grant adv. panel, 1978-80; mem. policy adv. com. Office of Grants, USDA, 1985-86. Trustee Ithaca Coll., 1982-89. Lt. USNR, 1943-46. Recipient Disting. Svc. award Oreg. State U., 1978. Fellow AAAS (exec. com. Pacific div. 1963-67, pres. div. 1971), Am. Phytopatholgy Soc. (pres. Pacific div. 1957, chmn. spl. com. to develop plans for endowment 1984-86, bd. dirs. 1986-88); mem. Oreg. Acad. Sci., Nat. Assn. State Univs. and Land Grant Colls. (chmn. coun. for rsch. policy and adminstrn. 1970, chmn. standing com. on environment and energy 1974-82, chmn. com. on environment 1984-86), Sigma Xi, Phi Kappa Phi, Phi Sigma, Sigma Alpha Epsilon. Home: 3605 NW Van Buren Ave Corvallis OR 97330-4950

YOUNG, SCOTT THOMAS, business management educator; b. Oak Park, Ill., Dec. 28, 1950; s. Thomas Menzies and Grace (Butler) Y.; m. Teresa M. Foskey, Jan. 2, 1981; children: Reginald, Galen. BA, U. Ga., 1974; MBA, Ga. Coll., 1982; PhD, Ga. State U., 1987. Assoc. prof. U. Utah, Salt Lake City, 1987—; mgmt. cons. to numerous orgns., 1987—. Contbr. numerous articles to profl. jours. With U.S. Army, 1971-73. Decorated Commendation medal; grantee Nat. Assn. Purchasing Mgmt., 1986. Mem. Decision Sci. Inst., Acad. Mgmt., Prodn. and Ops. Mgmt. Soc. Democrat. Methodist. Office: U Utah David Eccles Sch Bus Salt Lake City UT 84112

YOUNG, STEPHEN DEAN, assistive technologist; b. Pasadena, Calif., Apr. 11, 1942; s. Robert T. and Asenath (Kinnear) Y.; m. Sylvia Ruth Tannhauser, June 1, 1963; children: Michael, Melissa. BA, Reed Coll., 1964; MA, UCLA, 1966, PhD, 1969. Postdoctoral fellow U. N.C., Chapel Hill, 1969-71; asst. prof. Ind. U.-Northwest, Gary, 1971-73; rsch. assoc. U. Calif.-San Diego, La Jolla, 1973-75; asst. prof. St. John's U., Jamaica, N.Y., 1975-80; instr. biology Mt. St. Mary's Coll., L.A., 1982-83, L.A. Southwest Coll., 1987-88; instr. biology Calif. State U., Northridge, 1989, assistive technologist, 1988—; ind. software developer Santa Monica, Calif., 1980-87; bd. dirs. Computer Access Ctr., Santa Monica. Cub master Santa Monica area Boy Scouts Am., 1982-84, asst. scoutmaster, 1985—. Pauley Fund fellow, 1967; NIH predoctoral fellow, 1967-69; Nat. Inst. Dental Rsch. postdoctoral fellow, 1969-71. Mem. AAAS, Western Soc. Naturalists, Disabled Children's Computer Group, N.Y. Acad. Scis., Sigma Xi. Unitarian Universalist. Office: DVSS Calif State Univ Northridge 18111 Nordhoff St Northridge CA 91330-0001

YOUNG, STEPHEN JEROME, investment banker; b. Berkeley, Calif., Oct. 20, 1956; s. William Jordan and Marina Solveig (Amdahl) Y.; m. Amy Marie Seminario, Feb. 21, 1987; 1 child, Alden Edward. BA, U. Pa., 1978; MBA, U. Calif., Berkeley, 1983, JD, 1983. Bar: Calif. 1983, Mass. 1986. V.p. real estate investment banking group E.F. Hutton & Co., Inc., San Francisco, 1982-85; assoc. Csaplar & Bok (name changed to Gaston & Snow), Boston and San Francisco, 1986-91; ptnr. Cooper, White & Cooper, San Francisco, 1991-92; v.p. Krambo Corp., San Francisco, 1993—. Mem. Commonwealth Club Calif., Phi Beta Kappa. Office: Krambo Corp 2462 Filbert St San Francisco CA 94123

YOUNG, STEVE, radio station executive; b. Toronto, Ont., Can., Mar. 15, 1953; came to U.S. 1989; s. Benjamin and Toby (Goldberg) Hiltz. BS, York U., Toronto, 1973. Music dir. Sta. CITI-FM, Winnipeg, Man., 1977-80; program dir. Sta. CITI-FM, Winnipeg, 1980-85, Sta. CJAY-FM, Calgary, Alta., 1985-86; program strategist Joint Comm. Corp., Toronto, 1986-89; program dir. Sta. KISW-FM, Seattle, 1989—; group program dir. Nationwide Comm. Inc., 1990—. Named Program Dir. of Yr. Can. Music Industry Assn., 1985. Office: KISW FM 712 Aurora Ave N Seattle WA 98109

YOUNG, STEVEN, professional football player; b. Salt Lake City, Oct. 11, 1961. Student, Brigham Young. With Tampa Bay Buccaneers, 1985-86; quarterback San Francisco 49ers, 1987—. Named NFL's Top-rated quarterback, 1991; named NFL Most Valuable Player, 1992. Office: San Francisco 49ers 4949 Centennial Blvd Santa Clara CA 95054

YOUNG, SUZANNE MARYE, business consultant; b. Kansas City, Mo., Nov. 1, 1946; d. Charles S. and Anne M. (Ceccone) Y. BA, U. Mich., 1968; MS in Organizational Devel., Pepperdine U., 1990. Comml. coord. Sta. WXYZ-TV, Southfield, Mich., 1968; prodn. mgr. Daystar Multi-Media, Ann Arbor, Mich., 1969-74; dir. major events U. Mich., Ann Arbor, 1974-78, dir. spl. programs, 1978-80, exec. dir., 1979-80; adminstr. Tourism Promotion Bur., Jackson Hole, Wyo., 1983-85; exec. dir. Jackson Hole C. of C., 1985-91. Chmn. tourism task force Wyo. Futures Project, 1986-87; bd. dirs. Old West Trail Found., 1988-90, Jackson Hole Land Trust, Nat. Wildlife Art Mus., Community Found. of Jackson Hole; Dem. candidate Wyo. legislature, 1992. Named Promoter of Yr., Billboard mag., 1975, 77, Disting. Service award Jackson Hole C. of C., 1986, Local Woman of Yr. award, Bus. and Profl. Women, 1988. Mem. Wyo. C. of C. Execs. (bd. dirs. 1987-88). Home and Office: PO Box 3351 Jackson WY 83001-3351

YOUNG, THOMAS GERARD, small business owner; b. St. Louis, Aug. 29, 1953; s. William Gerard and Theresa Mary (Friehaut) Y.; m. Wanda Sue Leonhardt, June 20, 1987; 1 child, Robert Lee. Student, St. Louis U., 1979-80. Acct. exec. Southwestern Bell, St. Louis, Tulsa, 1979-82; mgr. Casa Bonita Restaurant, Tulsa, Denver, 1982-85; sales rep. Am. Data Products, Denver, 1985; pres. Automated Info. Svcs., Denver, 1985—. Evangelical. Republican. Office: Automated Info Svcs PO Box 3604 Littleton CO 80161-3604

YOUNG, WALTER KWAI WHUN, otolaryngologist; b. Honolulu, Sept. 24, 1934; s. Leong Quan and Mildred (Chang) Y.; m. Joan Audrey Nichols, Mar. 30, 1963; children: Walter Leong, Adriene Lianne, Curt Yen Pui. Student, Gettysburg Coll., 1954-56, BA, 1956; MD, Jefferson Med. Coll., 1960. Diplomate Am. Bd. Otolaryngology. Intern, then resident in gen. surgery St. Luke's Hosp., Bethlehem, Pa., 1960-62; resident in otolaryngology Grad. Hosp., Phila., 1962-63, Upstate Med. Ctr., Syracuse, N.Y., 1963-65; pvt. practice Honolulu, 1968—; assoc. prof. John A. Burns Sch. Medicine U. Hawaii, past chief of surgery Children's Hosp.; past chief of pediatric surgery Kapiolani Med. Ctr. Women and Children. Capt. USAF, 1965-67. Fellow Am. Acad. Otolaryngology and Head and Neck Surgery, ACS; mem. AMA, Hawaii Med. Assn., Honolulu County Med. Soc., Am. Coll. Surgeons, Pacific Coast Opthlmology and Otolaryngology Assn., State Bd. Hearing Aid Dealers and Fitters, Pan Pacific Surg. Assn. Presbyterian. Office: 1380 Lusitana St Ste 615 Honolulu HI 96813-2449

YOUNG, WILLIAM CHARLES, media production company executive; b. Fond du Lac, Wis., Oct. 5, 1936; s. Warner Roy and Hannah Elizabeth (Nixon) Y.; children: Donovan Charles, Jamison William. BA, Mich. State U., 1958. Reporter, producer Sta. WKZO-TV, Kalamazoo, Mich., 1958-60; writer, producer W.B. Doner Advt. Co., Chgo., 1960-63, Gardner Advt. Co., St. Louis, 1963-68; pres., creative dir. Creative Coalition, Chgo. and L.A., 1968-85; pres., owner Eventures, Beverly Hills, Calif., 1985—; bd. dirs. Internat. Trade Exch., Beverly Hills to Go, Internat. Talent Exch. Writer, producer (film): Good to See You, Alice Cooper, 1974, (play) Let's Party, Suzann, 1988, (TV spl.) Summit Too, 1988, (mixed media show) Man's Oneness, 1989, (classical music concert) Journey Into Night, 1991, (ballet) The Lottery, 1991. Bd. dirs. Young Reps., 1958-64; pres. Kalamazoo County Young Reps., 1958-60; founding dir. Bellini Found., Huntington Beach, Calif., 1988; dir. The Angel Project. Recipient Clio award, 1967. Mem. Alliance of Motion Picture and TV Producers. Republican. Office: Eventures 9903 Santa Monica Blvd Beverly Hills CA 90212-1671

YOUNGBLOOD, ROBERT LINLEY, political science educator; b. Medford, Oreg., Sept. 22, 1938; s. Ross A. and Willena S. Y.; m. Ingrid Gail Brewer, May 9, 1970; children: Erik B., Ingrid A. BA, Willamette U., 1962; MA, U. Hawaii, 1966; PhD, U. Mich., 1972. Asst. prof. Ariz. State U., Tempe, 1973-78, assoc. prof., 1978-88, prof. polit. sci., 1988—; mem. Southeast Asia coun. Assn. Asian Studies, Ann Arbor, Mich., 1987-89. Author: Marcos Against the Church, 1990; contbr. articles to profl. publs. Bd. dirs. Help of Ariz., 1992. Fulbright-Hayes fellow, 1979, Earhart Found. fellow, 1984. Mem. Am. Polit. Sci. Assn., Assn. Asian Studies, Philippine Studies Assn. Democrat. Methodist. Office: Dept Polit Sci Ariz State Univ Tempe AZ 85287-2001

YOUNGBLOOD, RONALD FRED, religious educator; b. Chgo., Aug. 10, 1931; s. William C. and Ethel V. (Arenz) Y.; m. Carolyn J. Johnson, Aug. 16, 1952; children: Glenn, Wendy. BA, Valparaiso U., 1952; BD, Fuller Seminary, Pasadena, Calif., 1955; PhD, Dropsie Coll., Phila., 1961; postgrad., NYU, 1966. Prof. Old Testament Bethel Theol. Seminary, St. Paul, 1961-78; dean, prof. Old Testament Wheaton (Ill.) Coll., 1978-81; prof. Old Testament Trinity Evang. Divinity Sch., Deerfield, Ill., 1981-82, Bethel Seminary West, San Diego, 1982—. Author: Heart of the Old Testament, 1971, Themes From Isaiah, 1983, Exodus, 1983, Book of Genesis: An Introductory Commentary, 1991; editor: The Genesis Debate, 1986, NIV Study Bible, 1985. Owen D. Young fellow Gen. Electric Found., 1959-61, Hebrew Union Coll. fellow, 1967-68. Mem. Evang. Theol. Soc. (editor 1976—), Near East Archaeol. Soc. (sec. 1978—), Inst. for Bibl. Rsch., Internat. Bible Soc. (bd. dirs. 1989—). Office: Bethel Seminary West 6116 Arosa St San Diego CA 92115-3999

YOUNGDAHL, PAUL FREDERICK, mechanical engineer; b. Brockway, Pa., Oct. 8, 1921; s. Harry Ludwig and Esther Marie (Carlson) Y.; m. Elinor Louise Jensen, Nov. 27, 1943; children: Mark Erik, Marcia Linnea, Melinda Louise. Student Pa. State U., 1938-40; BS in Engring., U. Mich., 1942, MS in Engring., 1949, PhD, 1962. Indsl. and devel. engr. duPont, Bridgeport, Conn., 1942-43, Carneys Point, N.J., 1946-48; dir. research Mech. Handling Systems, Detroit, 1953-62; prof. U. Mich., Ann Arbor, 1962-74; cons. mech. engr., Palo Alto, Calif., 1974—; dir. Liquid Drive Corp., Holly, Mich. Contbr. articles to profl. jours. Served with USNR, 1943-46. Mem. Mich. Soc. Profl. Engrs., Nat. Soc. Profl. Engrs., ASME, Am. Soc. Engring. Edn., Mich. Assn. Professions, Sigma Xi, Tau Beta Pi, Phi Kappa Phi, Pi Tau Sigma. Methodist. Address: 501 Forest St PH 4 Palo Alto CA 94301

YOUNGER, JOHN PATRICK, JR., employee benefits director; b. Johnson AFB, Japan, Jan. 29, 1949; came to U.S., 1949; s. John Patrick and Helen Martha (Doka) Y.; m. Karen Lynn Ruse, July 20, 1985; children: Shannon Marie, Traci Elizabeth, Kellie Christine. BA in Econs., Claremont (Calif) Men's Coll., 1971. Asst. group underwriter Occidental Life Ins., Los Angeles, 1972-74; sr. cons. Peat Marwick, Mitchell & Co., Los Angeles, 1974-80; mgr. employee benefits TRW- Space & Def., Redondo Beach, Calif., 1980-86, mgr. Benefits planning & fin. mgmt., 1986-88; dir. employee benefits Pacific Enterprises, Los Angeles, 1988—; bd. dirs. U.S. Corp. Athletic Assn., Los Angeles, So. Calif. Corp. Athletic Assn, Los Angeles. Mem. Am. Gas Assn., Am. Compensation Assn., Nat. Assn. Realtors, Calif. Assn. Realtors, Profl. Coast Bowlers. Republican. Office: Pacific Enterprises 633 W 5th St Ste 5400 Los Angeles CA 90071-2080

YOUNGLOVE, WILLIAM AARON, language arts educator; b. Adrian, Mich., May 23, 1941; s. Leroy Aaron and Rosemond (Barrs) Y. BA in English, Adrian Coll., 1963; MA in English, Western Mich. U., 1966; MA in Am. Studies, U. So. Calif., 1973; EdD, UCLA, 1983. Cert. secondary, jr. coll. tchr., adminstr., Calif., secondary tchr., Mich. Tchr. Kalamazoo (Mich.)-Portage Pub. Schs., 1963-66; tchr. Long Beach (Calif.) Unified Sch. Dist., 1966-84, lang. arts specialist, 1984—; part-time instr. Long Beach C.C., 1967-70, 73-76, 88-90; tchr. Calif. State U. Found. Young Writers' Camp, Long Beach, summers 1990-92; cons. South Basin writing project Calif. State U., Long Beach, 1991—; assoc. Calif. Writing Project/Calif. Tech. Project Alliance, Santa Barbara, 1990—, New Tchr. Project, Long Beach, 1989-90; researcher UCLA, 1981. Author: Without Compromise, 1974. Advisor, mem. curriculum adv. and search coms. ABC Unified Sch. Dist., Cerritos, Calif., 1991—; advisor, mem. jr. coll. transfer scholarship program UCLA, 1990—. Lance cpl. USMCR, 1959-65. Charles F. Kettering II fellow, 1982-83. Mem. NEA, English Coun. Long Beach (ex-officio bd. dirs., scholarship chair, Outstanding English Tchr. 1987), Computing Using Educators, Los Compadres con Libros, Lambda Iota Tau. Unitarian.

YOUNGQUIST, TED NOWAK, mining engineer; b. Stockton, Calif., Sept. 5, 1947; s. Herbert John and May A. (Nowak) Y; student public schs., Stockton; m. Lillie Ellen Younquist, Jan. 16, 1967; children: Philip, Thad, Leif. Lic. state safety instr. Operator own mines, Calif., 1970—; miner El Dorado Limestone, Shingle Springs, Calif., 1970; foreman Alhambra Atlanta Gold Mines, El Dorado County, Calif., 1971, Am. Hill Mine, Placer County, Calif., 1974; cons. engr. French Corral Mine, Nevada County, Calif., 1974; core drilling engr. Mine Rite Corp., El Dorado, Calif., 1974; cons. engr., assayer Manzinita Mine, El Dorado County, 1974; cons. engr. Trail Claim Mine, El Dorado, 1974—; engr. Sergeant Jacobs Placer Mines, Nevada County, 1975; cons. engr. Pease Mining Co., 1976, Horseshoe Bar Mining Co., 1976-77, Glacier King Uranium Mine, Carson City, Nev., 1978, Rolfe Ranches, Coulterville, Calif., 1979, Troy Gold Industries, 1979, Superior Extension Mine, Placerville, Calif., 1980, Relief Silver mine, Asarco County, Nev., 1980; cons. Teritary, Inc., 1977—, Benchmark Mining, Bishop, Calif., 1978—; owner, operator Tungo Mine, El Dorado County, 1977—; cons. Houston Mining & Resources, 1979—, Bentley Internat., Liberia, 1980; owner Youngquist Assaying, Georgetown, Calif., 1980—; operator Wind River Mining Project, 1983—; Calif. safety instr., 1978—. Mem. Dem. Central Com., 1972-73. Mem. AIME, ASME, Constrn. Specifications Inst. Liberian Fellowship of Mining Engrs. Address: 2938 Delta Fair Blvd # 316 Antioch CA 94509

YOUNGS, JACK MARVIN, cost engineer; b. Bklyn., May 2, 1941; s. Jack William and Virginia May (Clark) Y.; BEngring., CCNY, 1964; MBA, San Diego State U., 1973; m. Alexandra Marie Robertson, Oct. 31, 1964; 1 child, Christine Marie. Mass properties engr. Gen. Dynamics Corp., San Diego, 1964-68, rsch. engr., 1968-69, sr. rsch. engr., 1969-80, sr. cost devel. engr., 1980-81, cost devel. engring. specialist, 1981—. Dist. dir. Scripps Ranch Civic Assn., 1976-79; pres. Scripps Ranch Swim Team, 1980-82; dir., 1986-87; judge Greater San Diego Sci. and Engring. Fair, 1981-92. Mem. Princeton U. Parents Assn. Recipient 5th place award World Body Surfing Championships, 1987, 6th place award, 1988. Mem. AIAA, N.Y. Acad. Scis., Alumni Assn, CUNY, Bklyn. Tech. High Sch. Alumni Assn., Inst. Cost Analysis (cert., charter mem., treas. Greater San Diego chpt. 1986-90), Soc. Cost Estimating and Analysis (cert. cost estimator/analyst, pres. San Diego chpt. 1990-91), Internat. Soc. Parametric Analysts (bd. dirs. San Diego chpt. 1987-90), Nat. Mgmt. Assn. (space systems div. charter mem. 1985, award of honor Convair chpt. 1975), Assn. MBA Execs., San Diego State U. Bus. Alumni Assn. (charter mem. 1986), Scripps Ranch Swim and Racquet Club (dir. 1977-80, treas. 1978-79, pres. 1979-80), Beta Gamma Sigma, Chi Epsilon, Sigma Iota Epsilon. Lutheran. Research in life cycle costing and econ. analysis. Home: 11461 Tribuna Ave San Diego CA 92131-1907 Office: PO Box 85990 San Diego CA 92138-5990

YOUNGS, JAMES MURRAY, freelance writer, photographer; b. Abilene, Tex., Apr. 15, 1947; s. William Murray and Mary Nell (Brown) Y.; m. Carolyn Sue Allen, Aug. 14, 1971; children: James Murray Jr., Monica Sue. BA in Journalism, Pepperdine U., 1972. Adminstrv. asst. Los Angeles County Bd. Suprs., 1966-67; photography coord. Pepperdine U., Malibu, Calif., 1971-72; photographer, draftsman Brehler Legal Photos, Los Angeles, 1973; pub. relations, advt. mgr. Griswolds Restuarants, Inc., Claremont, Calif., 1973-74; gen. mgr. Cinemodule, Hollywood, Calif., 1974-77; editor-in-chief Trailer Boats Mag., Carson, Calif., 1977-88; freelance writer Englewood, Colo., 1988—. Contbr. Trailer Boats Mag., Boating Mag., Lakeland Boating, Water Ski, Sports Illustrated, Popular Mechanics, Specialty Car. With USN, 1966-70. Mem. Boating Writers Internat. (dir. 1987-90), Nat. Marine Mfg. Assn., Sigma Delta Chi. Republican. Church of Christ. Home and Office: 34 Sedgwick Dr Englewood CO 80110-4110

YOUNGSTEADT, ROBERT LEE, insurance executive; b. Birmingham, Ala., Oct. 29, 1939; s. Atwood G. G. and Virginia (Lee) Y.; m. Dorothy Jo Fuller, Sept., 1980 (dec. Dec. 1980); m. Paulette C. Mckeown, July 11, 1981; children: Scott, Leslie, Scott P., Sally, Rodney, Patricia. BSBA, Samford U., 1963. Chief risk appraiser State Farm Life Ins. Co., various locations, 1963-70; chief underwriter Life Ins. Co. Calif., San Francisco, 1970-79; regional mgr. Comml. Union Life Ins. Co., Ariz. and Calif., 1979-82; asst. v.p. Exec. Life Ins. Co., Beverly Hills, Calif., 1982-83; dir. mktg. Life Ins. Rx, Sausalito, Calif., 1983-86; v.p. ops. Enumclaw (Wash.) Life Ins. Co., 1986—; speaker in field. Vol. United Fund, Alcohol Recovery Programs; pres. Alpha Kappa Psi Alumni Assn., Atlanta, 1969-70. Fellow Life Mgmt. Inst., CLU Assn. (pres. 1966-67), Home Office Life Underwriters Assn., Inst. Home Office Underwriters, Wash. Underwriters Assn.

YOUNT, DAVID EUGENE, physicist, university official; b. Prescott, Ariz., June 5, 1935; s. Robert Ephram and Jeannette Francis (Judson) Y.; m. Christel Marlene Notz, Feb. 22, 1975; children—Laura Christine, Gregory Gordon, Steffen Jurgen Robert, Sonja Kate Jeannette. B.S. in Physics, Calif. Inst. Tech., 1957; M.S. in Physics, Stanford U., 1959, Ph.D. in Physics, 1963. Instr. Princeton U., 1962-63, asst. prof. physics, 1963-64, Minn. Mining and Mfg. fellow, 1963; NSF postdoctoral fellow U. Paris, Orsay, France, 1964-65; rsch. assoc. Stanford Linear Accelerator Ctr. Stanford U., 1965-69; assoc. prof. U. Hawaii, 1969-73, prof., 1973—, chmn. dept. physics and astronomy, 1979-85, acting asst. v.p. for acad. affairs, 1985-86, v.p. rsch. and grad. edn., 1986—. Mem. Am. Phys. Soc., Undersea and Hyperbaric Med. Soc., Am. Chem. Soc., U.S. Tennis Assn., Sigma Xi. Republican. Lutheran. Home: 5468 Opihi St Honolulu HI 96821-1924 Office: U Hawaii 2505 Correa Rd Honolulu HI 96822-2286

YOUNT, GEORGE STUART, paper company executive; b. Los Angeles, Mar. 4, 1949; s. Stanley George and Agnes (Pratt) Y.; m. Geraldine Marie Silvio, July 18, 1970; children: Trisha Marie, Christopher George. Postgrad., Harvard U., 1983-86. Mgmt. trainee Fortifiber Corp., L.A., 1969-71, asst. to v.p. ops., 1971-75, adminstrv. v.p., treas., sec., 1975-85, exec. v.p., sec., chief fin. officer, 1985-90, chmn., chief exec. officer, 1991—; treas., bd. dirs. Stanwall Corp., L.A., pres., 1989; past pres. Hollister Ranch Cattle Coop., Gaviota, Calif., 1988—; bd. dirs. Consol. Media Corp., Pasadena, Calif. Team leader L.A. United Way, 1981-86; bd. dirs. Big Bros. Greater L.A., 1984-87, L.A. Coun. Boy Scouts Am., 1992—, bd. dirs., 1992—; mem. Young Pres. Orgn., 1991. Mem. Am. Paper Inst. (vice-chmn. splty. coaters and extrusion sect. 1990—), Nat. Assn. Corp. Dirs., Harvard Bus. Club So. Calif., Jonathan Club (L.A.), San Marino City Club (Calif.), Rotary (bd. dirs. L.A. club 1992—). Club Rotary (L.A. bd. dirs. 1992—). Home: 1975 Lombardy Rd San Marino CA 91108-1234 Office: Fortifiber Corp 4489 Bandini Blvd Los Angeles CA 90023-4709

YOUNT, LISA ANN, educational and juvenile writer; b. L.A., July 28, 1944; d. Stanley George and Agnes Sloan (Pratt) Y.; m. Harry Richard Henderson, Sept. 23, 1982. BA in Creative Writing cum laude, Stanford (Calif.) U., 1966. Author: The Telescope, 1983 (Outstanding Sci. Trade Books for Children), Too Hot, Too Cold, Just Right, 1981 (Outstanding Sci. Trade Books for Children), Black Scientists, 1991, Cancer, 1991, True Adventure Readers, 1992. Nature Guide Terwilliger Nature Edn. Ctr., Corte Madera, Calif., 1986—; vol. San Francisco SPCA, 1989—. Home: 2631 Mira Vista Dr El Cerrito CA 94530

YOUNT, PHILIP RICHARD, insurance company executive; b. Hartwick, Iowa, Feb. 7, 1937; s. Fred Austin and Katherine Elizabeth (Gross) Y.; m. Mary Maxine White, June 3, 1956 (div. Jan. 1989); children: Jo Ann Yount Pearson, Mary Beth Yount King, Douglas Alan; m. Donna Mae Eki, Sept. 4, 1989; stepchildren: Maile Hitomi Solis, Gabriella Chiharu Solis, Ayala Masayo Solis. BA magna cum laude, Parsons Coll., 1959. CPCU; cert. in data processing, assoc. in mgmt. Staff acct., instr. Grinnell (Iowa) Coll., 1959-60; from acct. to pres. and chief exec. officer Grinnell Mut. Reins. Co., 1960-91; v.p., sec., treas. Grange Mut. Ins. Co., Tigard, Oreg., 1992—; pres., bd. dirs. Grinnell Realty, Inc., 1985-91, Big M Agy., Inc., Grinnell, 1983-91; bd. dirs. Grinnell Life Ins. Co., 1985-91. Pres. pk. bd. City of Grinnell, 1972-78; pres., founder Grinnell Community Taxpayers Assn., 1974-78; bd. dirs. Grinnell Gen. Hosp., 1989—; pres., bd. dirs. Greater Poweshiek Community Found., Grinnell, 1988-92, GMG Found., Grinnell, 1989-91. Recipient Meritorious Svc. award Nat. Assn. Mut. Insurers, 1989. Mem. CPCU Soc., Ins. Inst. Am., Data Processing Mgmt. Assn., Toastmasters, Chi Beta Chi, Phi Kappa Phi. Office: Grange Mut Ins Co PO Box 230969 7105 SW Varns St Tigard OR 97281-0969

YOUNT, RALPH GRANVILLE, biochemistry and chemistry educator; b. Indpls., Mar. 25, 1932; s. Granville Emery and Edythe Margaret (Bratton) Y.;m. Valerie Ann Piepho, June 22, 1957; children: Jonathan, Andrea, Alison. AB in Chemistry, Wabash Coll., 1954; PhD in Biochemistry, Iowa State U., 1958. Postdoctoral assoc. Brookhaven Nat. Lab., Upton, N.Y., 1958-60; asst. prof. chemistry Wash. State U., Pullman, 1960-67, assoc. prof. chemistry, 1967-72, prof. and chmn. biochemistry, 1972-79, prof. biochemistry and chemistry, 1979—. Editorial bd. Jour. Biol. Chemistry, 1976-81, 86-91. Chmn. fellowship com. Muscular Dystrophy Assn., Tucson, 1986-91, v.p., 1987-92; mem. com. A of Nat. Heart, Lung and Blood Inst., Bethesda, 1986-90; mem. biochem./biophys. panel NSF, 1982-85. Recipient MERIT award NIH, 1986. Fellow AAAS; mem. Biophys. Soc. (nat. coun., pres. elect 1993—), Am. Chem. Soc., Am. Soc. Biochemistry and Molecular Biology (publs. com.). Home: Rte 3 Box 565 Pullman WA 99163 Office: Wash State U Bldg 4660 Pullman WA 99164

YU, KITSON SZEWAI, computer science educator; b. Toishan, Kwangtung, China, Apr. 4, 1950; came to U.S., 1969; s. Ho Yee and Yin Sang (Chan) Y.; m. Mabel Griseldis Wong, July 15, 1972; 1 child, Robin Roberta Emily. BS, Troy State U., 1974, MS, 1977, BS, 1980. Cert. systems profl., data processing educator, Oreg. V.p. Troy (Ala.) Computer Ctr., 1976-81; computer instr. Tory State U., 1980-81, Linn Benton Community Coll., Albany, Oreg., 1981—; dir. real estate program Linn Benton Community Coll., 1985—; mng. broker Kitson Realty, Corvallis, Oreg., 1975—. Vice pres. econ. devel. Daleville C. of C., Ala., 1976; dir. Corvalis Youth Symphony, 1990—. Mem. Data Processing Mgmt. Assn. (bd. dirs. at large 1982—, v.p. 1984-85, pres. 1985-86), Greater Albany Rotary (treas. 1985—), Corvallis Multiple Listing Exch. (bd. dirs. 1990—), Gamma Beta Phi. Home: 2621 NW Lupine Pl Corvallis OR 97330-3537 Office: Linn Benton Community Coll 6500 Pacific Blvd SW Albany OR 97321-3755

YU, ZENG-QI, engineer, researcher; b. Jiansu, China, Nov. 26, 1941; came to U.S., 1980; s. Zu-An Yu and Pin-Yue Yin; m. Hao Jiang, Feb. 4, 1975; 1 child, Hong. BS, Fudan U., Shanghai, Peoples Republic of China, 1965; MS, Colo. State U., 1982, PhD, 1990. Asst. prof., researcher vacuum physics Fudan U., Shanghai, 1965-67, instr. laser physics, 1967-84; vis. scientist Colo. State U., Ft. Collins, 1980-82, rsch. asst., 1985-88, rsch. assoc., 1988-90, rsch. scientist, 1991—; tech. advisor Industry Bur. So. Dist. Shanghai, 1973-77; cons. Applied Electron Corp., Albuquerque, 1986-87, Hewlett Packard Co., Ft. Collins; technique cons. Electronics R&D Nippon Seiko K.K., Kanagawa, Japan, 1990, Quantum Rsch. Corp., 1990—. Coauthor: The Lasers, 1971, Laser Applications on Industry, 1972, Handbook of Thin Film Deposition Processes and Technologies, 1988; contbr. numerous articles to profl. jours.; patentee in field. Recipient ann. rschrs. recognition award Rsch. Found. Bd., Colo. State U., 1987-91. Mem. IEEE (sr.), Optical Soc. Am., Am. Vacuum Soc. Home: 2830 Michener Dr Fort Collins CO 80526 Office: Colo State U Engring Rsch Ctr Fort Collins CO 80523

YUAN, SHAO WEN, aerospace engineer, educator; b. Shanghai, China, Apr. 16, 1914; came to U.S., 1934, naturalized, 1954; s. Ti An and Chieh-huang (Chien) Y.; m. Hui Chih Hu, Nov. 5, 1950. B.S., U. Mich., 1936; M.E., Stanford U., 1939; M.S., Calif. Inst. Tech., 1937, Ph.D., 1941. Rsch. engr. Glenn Martin Co., 1942-43; chief of rsch. Helicopter div. McDonnell Aircraft Corp., 1943-45; instr. Washington U., St. Louis, 1944-45; adj. prof. Poly. Inst. Bklyn., 1946-49, assoc. prof., 1949-54, prof., 1954-57; ptnr. von Kármán, Yuan & Arnold Assocs., 1955-63; prof. aerospace engring. U. Tex., 1958-68; prof., chmn. mech. engring. div. George Washington U., 1968-78, chmn. civil, mech. and environ. dept., 1973-78, 80-81, prof. emeritus, 1984; pres. RISE, Inc., 1977-85; Canadair Chair prof. U. Laval, Can., 1957-58; chmn. adv. com. Joint Inst. for Advancement of Flight Sci., 1970-84; hon. prof. Zhejiang U., 1987—; cons. Edo Aircraft Corp., Aerojet Corp., Cornell Aero. Lab., Dept. of Interior, Oak Ridge Nat. Lab., N.Am., Aviation, Inc., Fairchild-Hiller Corp., McDonnell-Douglas Corp., The World Bank; hon. adviser Nat. Center Research of China, Taiwan, 1958-68; chmn., founder 1st U.S.-China Conf. on Energy, Resources, and Environment, 1982; founder Consortium of Univs. for Promoting Grad. Aerospace Studies, 1984; founder Disting. Lecture Series on Founds. of Aerospace Research and Devel., 1986. Author: Foundations of Fluid Mechanics, 1967; Contbr. to: High Speed Aerodynamics and Jet Propulsion series, 1959, Energy, Resources, and Environment: Procs. at 1st U.S.-China Conf., 1982. Recipient Outstanding Achievements award George Washington U., 1981; named Outstanding Educator of Am., 1970, Outstanding Chinese American, 1983. Fellow AAAS, AIAA; mem. ASME (life), Am. Soc. Engring. Edn., Soc. Engring. Sci. (dir. 1973-78, pres. 1977), Torchbearers of Caltech, Sigma Xi, Phi Kappa Phi, Phi Tau Phi, Sigma Gamma Tau, Pi Tau Sigma, Tau Beta Pi, Tau Xi Sigma. Home: 1700 California St Apt 610 San Francisco CA 94109-4586

YUE, AGNES KAU-WAH, otolaryngologist; b. Shanghai, Peoples Republic China, Dec. 1, 1947; came to U.S., 1967; d. Chen Kia and Nee Yuan (Ying0 ; m. Gerald Kumata, Sept. 25, 1982; children: Julie, Allison Benjamin. BA, Wellesley Coll., 1970; MD, Med. Coll. Pa., 1974; postgrad., Yale U., 1974-78. Intern Yale-New Haven Hosp., 1974-75, resident, 1975-78; fellow U. Tex. M.D. Anderson Cancer Ctr., Houston, 1978-79; asst. prof. U. Wash., Seattle, 1979-82; physician Pacific Med. Ctr., Seattle, 1979-90; pvt. practice Seattle, 1991—. Fellow Am. Acad. Otolaryngology, Am. Coll. Surgeons; mem. Northwest Acad. Otolaryngology. Office: 1801 NW Market St Ste 410 Seattle WA 98107-3909

YUE, ALFRED SHUI-CHOH, metallurgical engineer, educator; b. China, Nov. 12, 1920; s. Choy Noon-woo and Sze Man-hun (Tom) Y.; m. Virginia Chin-wen Tang, May 21, 1944; children: Mary, Raymond Yuan, John, Ling Tsao, David, Nancy Chang. B.S., Chao-tung U., 1942; M.S., Ill. Inst. Tech., 1950; Ph.D., Purdue U., 1956. Assoc. engr. Taiwan Aluminum Co., 1942-47; instr. Purdue U., 1952-56; research engr. Dow Chem. Co., Midland, Mich., 1956-62; sr. mem. Lockheed, Palo Alto Research Lab., 1962-69; now cons.; prof. engring. and applied sci. U. Calif., Los Angeles, 1969—; hon. prof. Xian Jiao-tong U., China, 1980; cons. LTV Aerospace Co., Lockheed Missile & Space Co., Atlantic Richfield Co.; Sec.-gen. Chinese Culture Assn. in U.S.A., 1967, also; bd. dirs. Chinese scholar to U.S.A. Fellow AIAA (assoc.); mem. AAAS, AIME, Am. Soc. Metals, Materials Rsch. Soc., Sigma Xi, Sigma Pi Sigma, Tau Beta Pi, Phi Tau Phi (pres. 1978-82). Office: U of Calif Los Angeles CA 90024

YUEN, ANDY TAK SING, electronics executive; b. Wanchai, Hong Kong, Aug. 26, 1952; came to U.S., 1984; s. Yan Chong and Chi Oi (Tse) Y.; m. Kathy Man Kwan Chan, Jan. 29, 1983; children Lambert Hann Shi, Robin Hann Lang. Higher Cert. in Elec. Engring., Hong Kong Poly., 1975; Diploma in Bus. Mgmt., Hong Kong Bapt. Coll., 1976; Diploma in Exec. Devel., Chinese U., Hong Kong, 1981; MBA, Chui Hai Coll., Hong Kong, 1981; PhD in Bus. Mgmt., Calif. Coast U., 1987. Supervising engr. Teledyne Semiconductor Ltd., Kowloon, Hong Kong, 1976-79; ops. mgr. Microsemi (Hong Kong) Ltd., Kowloon, 1979-81, gen. mgr., 1981-84; corp. mgr. Microsemi Corp., Santa Ana, Calif., 1984-89, corp. v.p., 1989—; corp. dir. Semcon Electronics Pvt. Ltd., Bombay, 1984—. Author (books): Can Quality Circles Bring the Breakthrough to Hong Kong Industrial Management, 1982, Harnessing Japanese Quality Circles in Hong Kong, 1987. Fellow Inst. Sales and Mktg. Mgmt., Brit. Inst. Mgmt., Inst. Elec. and Electronics Inc. Engrs. Office: Microsemi Corp PO Box 26890 Santa Ana CA 92799-6890

YUH, JUNKU, mechanical engineering educator; b. Pusan, Republic of Korea, Feb. 26, 1958; came to U.S., 1981; s. Woon-Sang and Tae-Ok (Kim); m. Jongil Lee, Apr. 5, 1986; children: Jessica W., Jacqueline I. BS in Mechanics and Design, Seoul (Republic of Korea) Nat. U., Seoul, Republic of Korea, 1981; MSME, Oreg. State U., 1982, PhDME, 1986. Registered profl. engr., Oreg. Rsch. engr. Pung San Metal Corp., Bucheon, Republic of Korea, 1979; asst. prof. dept. mech. engring. U. Hawaii, Honolulu, 1986-91, assoc. prof., 1991—; bd. dirs. Robotics Lab., U. Hawaii; chmn. Underwater Mobile Robot session Internat. Conf. on Robotics and Automation, 1990, Advanced Robotics session Internat. Symposium on Robotics and Mfg., 1990, Underwater Robotics session Internat. Symposium on Robotics and Mfg., 1988; condr. numerous workshops in field; lectr. State of Hawaii profl. engrs. rev. course U. Hawaii, 1989-91; presenter internat. profl. meetings. Author: (with others) Robotics and Manufacturing, 1988; guest editor Jour. Robotic Systems, Underwater Robotics, 1991; contbr. articles to profl. publs.; reviewer profl. jours. Recipient Presdl. Young Investigator award NSF, 1991, grantee, 1991—; recipient Boeing Faculty award, 1991; grantee Pacific Internat. Ctr. for High Tech. Rsch., 1987-90, Sea Grant Office, U.S. Dept. Commerce, 1989—. Mem. ASME, IEEE, Soc. Mfg. Engrs. (sr.), Am. Soc. Engring. Educators (Dow Outstanding Young Faculty award 1989), Korean Scientists and Engrs. Assn. in Am. Methodist. Office: Univ Hawaii Dept Mech Engrg Holmes 302 2540 Dole St Honolulu HI 96822-2333

YUKELSON, RONALD ALAN, public relations executive; b. Culver City, Calif., Aug. 30, 1956; s. Joseph N. and Faye (Grossman) Y. AA in Journalism, Los Angeles Valley Coll., 1976; BA in Journalism, San Diego State U., 1978; MBA, U. LaVerne, 1993. Sports editor Madera (Calif.) Tribune, 1978-79; sports writer/columnist Desert Sun, Palm Springs, Calif., 1979-80; dir. sports info. Calif. State U., Northridge, 1980-85; assoc. dir. pub. relations U. So. Calif. Sch. Bus. Adminstrn., Los Angeles, 1985-86; mgr. pub. relations Centinela Hosp. Med. Ctr., Inglewood, Calif., 1987-88; dir. pub. relations and physician rels. Long Beach (Calif.) Meml. Med. Ctr., 1988—; venue press chief/boxing Los Angeles Olympic Organizing Com., 1984. Writer in sports field. Cons. pub. rels./mktg. Santa Monica (Calif.) Family YMCA, 1985-88, rec. sec. phys. edn. com., 1985-88; bd. dirs. Cheviot Hills Baseball League, L.A., 1984-85. Recipient of numerous awards in sports writing field; named Outstanding Young Man Am., Nat. Jaycees, 1977, 78, 82, 83. Mem. Healthcare Pub. Relations Mktg. Assn., AP Sports Editors, Sigma Delta Chi. Club: Publicity Los Angeles.

YURICICH, MATTHEW JOHN, matte artist; b. Lorain, Ohio, Jan. 19, 1923; s. Antone and Anna (Plesivac) Y.; children: Mark, LIsanne, Dirk, Dana, Tanya. BFA, Miami U., Oxford, Ohio, 1949. Asst. matte artist 20th Century Fox, L.A., 1950-54; matte artist MGM Studios, Culver City, Calif., 1954-76, EEG, Culver City, 1977-84, Boss Films, Marina Del Rey, Calif., 1984—. Recipient Acad. award, Motion Picture Acad. Arts. and Scis., 1976. Home and Office: 421 Donner Pass Dr Henderson NV 89014

YURIST, SVETLAN JOSEPH, mechanical engineer; b. Kharkov, USSR, Nov. 20, 1931; came to U.S., 1979, naturalized, 1985; s. Joseph A. and Rosalia S. (Zoilman) Y.; m. Imma Lea Erlikh, Oct. 11, 1960; 1 child, Eugene. M.S. in Mech. Engring. with honors, Poly. Inst., Odessa, USSR, 1954. Engr. designer Welding Equipment Plant, Novaya Utka, USSR, 1954-56; sr. tech. engr. Heavy Duty Automotive Crane Plant, Odessa, 1956-60, asst. chief matallugist, 1971-78; supr. research lab. Inst. Spl. Methods in Foundry Industry, Odessa, 1960-66, project engr. sci. research, 1966-71; engr. designer Teledyne Cast Product, Pomona, Calif., 1979-81; sr. mech. engr. Walt Elliot Disney Enterprises, Glendale, Calif., 1981-83; foundry liaison engr. Pacific Pumps div. Dresser Industries, Inc., Huntington Park, Calif., 1984-86; casting engr. Superior Industries Internat., Inc., Van Nuys, Calif., 1986-89; mech. engr. TAMCO Steel, Rancho Cucamonga, Calif., 1989—. Recipient award for design of automatic lines for casting electric motor parts USSR Ministry Machine Bldg. and Handtools Mfr., 1966, for equipment for permanent mold casting All Union Exhbn. of Nat. Econ. Achievements, 1966-70. Mem. Am. Foundrymen's Soc. Contbr. reports, articles to collections All Union Confs. Spl. Methods in Foundry, USSR; USSR patentee permanent mold casting. Home: 184 W Armstrong Dr Claremont CA 91711-1701 Office: TAMCO Steel 12459 Arrow Hwy Rancho Cucamonga CA 91739-9698

YUWILER, ARTHUR, neurochemist; b. Mansfield, Ohio, Apr. 4, 1927; s. Max and Esther (Schwartz) Y.; m. Alice Lubin, Dec. 16, 1950; children: Janice Anne, Michael Jeffrey, Kenneth Craig. BS, UCLA, 1950, PhD, 1956. Rsch. biochemist U.S. VA, L.A., 1957-58, chief neurobiochemistry rsch., 1962—; mental health trainee dept. anatomy UCLA, 1958-59, asst. rsch. biochemist dept. psychiatry and biochemistry, 1962-64, asst. prof. dept. psychiatry., 1965-70, assoc. prof. dept. psychiatry, 1972-77, prof., 1977—; dir. biochemistry schizophrenia joint rsch. project U. Mich., Ann Arbor, 1959-60, dir. biochemistry, dir. lab., 1960-62, rsch. biochemist Mental Health Rsch. Inst., 1960-62; adj. assoc. prof. dept. psychiatry UCLA, 1970-71; vis. sr. scientist Weizmann Inst. Sci., Israel, 1972-73; vis. prof. Karolinska Inst., Stockholm, 1990; mem. VA basic sci. com., Washington, 1966-69; mem. NIMH career devel. award com., Washington, 1971-76, chmn., 1976. Coauthor: Biochemistry Behaviour, 1964; editorial bd. Jour. of Autism, Neurochem. Rsch.; contbr. articles to profl. jours., publs. Scientific adv. bd. Dystonia Found., 1976-83, 85-88, chmn. 1982-83. Mem. AAAS, Am. Coll. Neuropsychopharmacology, Am. Soc. Biol. Chemistry and Molecular Biology, Am. Soc. Neurochemistry, Internat. Soc. Neurochemistry, Soc. Bio. Psychiatry, Soc. for Neurosci. Jewish. Office: Neurobiochemistry Lab T-85 VAMC Brentwood Wilshire and Sawtelle Blvds Los Angeles CA 90073

ZABINSKY, ZELDA BARBARA, operations research, industrial engineering educator; b. Tonawanda, N.Y., Oct. 31, 1955; d. Joseph Marvin and Helen Phyllis (Kava) Z.; m. John Clinton Palmer, July 15, 1979; children: Rebecca Ann Zabinsky, Aaron Zeff Palmer. BS, U. Puget Sound, Tacoma, 1977; MS, U. Mich., 1984, PhD, 1985. Tutor math. U. Puget Sound, 1975-77; programmer, analyst Nat. Marine Fisheries, Seattle, 1977, Boeing Computer Svcs., Seattle, 1977-78; sr. systems analyst Vector Rsch. Inc., Ann Arbor, Mich., 1980-84; assoc. prof. indsl. engring. U. Wash., Seattle, 1985-93, 1993—; cons. Boeing Corp., Seattle, 1987, Numerical Methods, Inc., Seattle, 1989-90, METRO, Seattle, 1992. Contbr. articles to tech. jours. Mem. faculty adv. bd. Women in Engring., U. Wash., 1990. Recipient E. Goman Math. award, 1977, Rsch. Initiation award NSF, 1992—; Howarth-Thompson scholar, 1973-77; Benton fellow, 1983-84; rsch. grantee NSF, NASA-Langley, Nat. Forest Svc., NATO, Boeing, 1985—. Mem. Ops. Rsch. Soc. Am., Inst. Indsl. Engrs. (sr.), Math. Programming Soc., Mortar Board, Phi Kappa Phi. Jewish. Office: U Wash Dept Indsl Engring FU-20 Seattle WA 98195

ZABOROWSKI, ROY ALLAN, electrical engineer; b. Chgo., Dec. 10, 1946; s. Robert and Julia Louise (Koch) Z.; m. Barbara Lynn Briggs, May 1, 1971; children: Elizabeth M., Christopher R. BSEE, U. Ill., 1973. Staff engr. Sperry Flight Systems subs. Honeywell, Inc., Phoenix, 1973-83, head engring. sect., 1983-88; dept. head Honeywell, Inc., Phoenix, 1988—. Patentee in field. With U.S. Army, 1970-72. Mem. IEEE. Office: Honeywell Inc ATSD PO Box 21111 Phoenix AZ 85036-1111

ZABSKY, JOHN MITCHELL, engineering executive; b. Joplin, Mo., Apr. 18, 1933; s. Joseph Anthony and Joan (Lucas) Z. AS, Joplin Jr. Coll., 1953; BSME, U. Mo., 1956; MSME, U. Kans., 1965. Profl. engr., Mo. System engr. Bendix KCD, Kansas City, Mo., 1958-62; rsch. engr. Rocketdyne, Neosho, Mo., 1962-65, Boeing Co., Huntsville, Ala., 1965-66; prin. rsch. engr., scientist Honeywell Inc., St. Paul, 1966-71; chief engr. Pressure Tank & Pipe Fabrication Co., Nashville, 1971-72, Engring. for Industry, Danville, Va., 1972-73; area mgr. fluid machinery Dresser Adv. Tech. Ctr., Irvine, Calif., 1973-85; v.p. ops. ATI, Laguna Niguel, Calif., 1985-93; pres. Cytoprobe, San Diego, 1993—; cons. Oral Care Products, L.A., 1990-92. Patentee in field. Pres. Mpls.-St. Paul Singletons, 1969-72. Mem. AIAA, ASME, Mo. Profl. Engrs. Home: 3640C S Main St Santa Ana CA 92707

ZACHARATOS, JERRY FRANK, lawyer; b. Chgo., Dec. 25, 1928; s. Jerry A. and Emma C. Zacharatos; m. Jean Affrey, Nov. 20, 1955 (div. Oct. 1963);

m. Ann Marie Zacharatos, Jan. 27, 1964; children: Jerry S., Gary S., Deborah M., Michelle S. AA in Biol. Sci., City Coll., San Francisco, 1960; BA in Social Sci., San Francisco State U., 1969; LLB, LaSalle U., Chgo., 1971; MS in Bus. Adminstrn., PhD in Ins., Pacific Western U., 1979, 81. State ins. examiner State of Calif., San Francisco, 1969-75; ins. officer Improved Risks Mut., San Francisco, 1975-83; account exec. Cigna Ins. Co., San Francisco, 1982-88; ins. officer Argonaut Ins. Co., San Mateo, Calif., 1988-90; pres. JFZ Labs., Walnut Creek, Calif., 1989—; dir., exec. v.p. SBG Ins. Group, San Francisco, 1975-80; dir., pres. Sans Souci H.O.A., Walnut Creek, Calif., 1986—. Author: Federal Goverment U.S. State Insurance Control, 1981. Election officer County of Contra Costa, Walnut Creek Calif., 1992. Maj. U.S. Army, 1953-59, Korea. Recipient Cert. of Honor and Merit San Francisco City and County, 1968. Mem. Livorna Real Estate Assn. (dir., v.p. 1973-80), Walnut Creek Elks Club. Republican. Roman Catholic.

ZACHMAN, JOHN ARTHUR, information planning consultant; b. Toledo, Dec. 16, 1934; s. Arthur S. and Margaret M. (Morrow) Z.; m. Constance L. DeVito, May 14, 1972; children: Sherri L., Zachman Morton, John P. BA, Northwestern U., 1957. Commd. ensign USN, 1957, advanced through grades to lt. comdr., 1964, ret. 1964; food broker Stoler Brokerage Co., South Bend, Ind., 1965; mktg. rep. IBM Corp., Chgo., 1965-70; account mgr. IBM Corp., N.Y.C., 1970-74; cons. IBM Corp., L.A., 1974-91; prin. Zachman Internat., La Canada, Calif., 1991—; bd. councillors Sch. Libr. and Info. Mgmt., U. So. Calif., L.A., 1982-86; bd. advs. info. mgmt. Seattle Pacific U., 1986-89; sch. libr. and info. mgmt. Emporia (Kans.) U., 1991—; sch. libr. and info. mgmt. Rosary Coll., River Forest, Ill., 1991—; bd. dirs. Worship Seminars Internat. Mem. elder council First Foursquare Ch., Van Nuys, Calif., 1978—; mem. Infos. Resource Mgmt. Adv. Coun., Smithsonian Inst., Washington; bd. dirs. Marriage Plus Ministries, 1985—. Mem. Data Adminstrn. Mgmt. Assn. Internat. (bd. advs.), N.Y.C. Data Adminstrn. Mgmt. Assn. (named Man of Yr. 1988), Repository/Architecture Devel. Users Group (bd. dirs., Award for Excellence 1991). Home: 1635 Virden Dr Glendale CA 91208-2721 Office: Zachman Internat 2222 Foothill Blvd Ste 337 La Canada CA 91011

ZACK, JAMES G(ORDON), JR., construction claims executive, consultant; b. Springfield, Mass., Sept. 6, 1946; s. James Gordon and Marione Mildred (Langevin) Z.; m. Yvonne Eileen Beezley, Oct. 26, 1970; children: Jennifer Yvonne, Stacy Rebecca, James William, Trevor David. AB in Polit. Sci., Assumption Coll., 1968; MPA, U. S.C., 1975. Dir. budgets and grants adminstrn. S.C. Dept. Health and Environ. Control, Columbia, 1972-78; mgr. constrn. contracts group CH2M Hill, Inc., Milw., 1978-85; mgr. scheduling and claims dept. CH2M Hill, Inc., L.A., 1986—; cons. EPA, 1977-88; reviewer Engrng. Mgmt. Jour., 1987—; expert witness on constrn. litigation; lectr. profl. devel. seminars. Contbr. articles to profl. jours. Commr. Pacifica dist. Boy Scouts Am., 1987—; mem. Calif. Compact Com., Huntington Beach, 1988—. Capt. U.S. Army, 1968-72, Vietnam. Mem. ASCE, Am. Assn. Cost Engrs., Project Mgmt. Inst. Methodist. Home: 9531 Netherway Dr Huntington Beach CA 92646-6051 Office: CH2M Hill Inc 2510 Red Hill Ave Santa Ana CA 92705-5542

ZACK, NEIL RICHARD, chemist; b. Canton, Ohio, Apr. 26, 1947; s. Joseph Francis and Francis Eleanor (Mansfield) Z.; m. Jean Lucille Harten, Mar. 18, 1978. BS in Chemistry, Rensselaer Poly. Inst., 1969; MS in Chemistry, Marshall U., Huntington, W.Va., 1970; PhD in Chemistry, U. Idaho, 1974. Adj. faculty U. Idaho, Idaho Falls, 1977-87; postdoctoral fellow Utah State U., Logan, 1974-75, U. Idaho, Moscow, 1975-76; sr. scientist Idaho Nat. Engrng. Lab., Idaho Falls, 1976-79, mgr., 1979-87, fellow scientist, 1987-90; sr. staff mem. Los Alamos (N.Mex.) Nat. Lab., 1990—. Contbr. articles to profl. jours. Mem. NRA, Inst. Nuclear Materials Mgmt., Am. Chem. Soc. (chem., health and safety div., fluorine chemistry div.), Sierra Club, Sigma Xi. Baptist. Office: Los Alamos Nat Lab PO Box 1663 MS E541 Los Alamos NM 87545

ZACK, RICHARD STANLEY, JR., museum director, curator, entomologist; b. Cleve., June 8, 1952; s. Richard Stanley and Victoria Ann (Isiros) Z.; m. Victoria Louise Opalecky, June 15, 1977. BS, Ohio State U., 1974; MS, Kent (Ohio) State U., 1976; PhD, Wash. State U., 1982. Curator James Entomol. Coll. Wash. State U., Pullman, 1980-86, dir., curator James Entomol. Coll., 1986—. Mem. Entomol. Soc. Am., Wash. State Entomol. Soc. (past pres.), K.C. (grand knight 1986-88), Sigma Xi. Home: 1511 Pine Cone Rd Moscow ID 83843-9316 Office: Wash State U Dept Entomology Pullman WA 99164-6382

ZACKRISON, EDWIN HARRY, theology educator; b. Hinsdale, Ill.; s. Harry Albin and Esther Virginia (Thorp) Z.; m. Jolene Ann Martinson, June 11, 1963; children: Jill Rochelle, Mark Edwin. BA, Loma Linda U., 1963; MA, Andrews U., 1964, BDiv, 1966, PhD, 1984. Youth pastor So. Calif. Conf. of Seventh-day Adventists, Glendale, 1966-67, pastor, 1967-72; prof. So. Coll. of Seventh-day Adventists, Collegedale, Tenn., 1972-84; tchr. La Sierra Acad., Riverside, 1984-88; prof. LaSierra U., Riverside, 1988—; artistic dir. La Sierra Acad. Performing Arts Soc., Inc., Riverside; dir. Expressions Drama Co., Riverside, Destination Players Drama Co., Riverside; co-dir., writer Scription Drama Co., 1990—; pres. La Sierra Community Performing Arts Assn., Inc., 1990—; editor La Sierra U. Press, 1988—. Cons. editor, writer: These Times mag., 1978-84. Prin. clarinet So. Coll. Symphony Orch., Collegedale, Calif., 1979-84, LaSierra U. Symphony Orch., Riverside, 1984-89. Recipient Community Svc. award La Sierra Acad. Performing Arts Soc., 1988. Mem. Am. Acad. Religion, Religious Edn. Assn., Ednl. Theatre Assn., Evang. Theol. Assn., Assn. Adventist Forums, La Sierra U. Alumni Assn. (pres. 1989-92, editor La Sierra U. press). Republican. Home: 5651 Peacock Ln Riverside CA 92505-3140 Office: LaSierra U Sch Religion Pierce St Riverside CA 92515

ZACKS, ARTHUR, retired radiologist; b. Winnipeg, Manitoba, Can., Mar. 12, 1926; came to U.S., 1946; s. Peter and Elizabeth (Ducan) Z.; m. Betty Lynn Sadis, June 15, 1952; 1 child, Dorothy. Student, U. B.C., Vancouver, Can., 1944-46; BS, U. Wash., 1948, MD, 1952. Diplomate Am. Bd. Radiology. Resident radiology Jewish Hosp., Children's Hosp., Gen. Hosp., Cin., 1953-56; radiologist Kaiser-Permanente Med. Ctr., San Francisco, 1956-58; chief radiology Kaiser-Permanente Med. Ctr., Honolulu, 1958-62; radiologist St. Mary's Hosp., San Francisco, 1962-65; pvt. practice radiology San Francisco, 1962-65; radiologist Kaiser-Permanente Med. Ctr., San Francisco, 1965-71; chief radiology Kaiser-Permanente Med. Ctr., San Rafael, Calif., 1971-80, sr. cons., 1980-86; sr. cons., exec. sec., founding mem. Hawaii Permanente Med. Group, Honolulu, 1958-62; exec. com, Kaiser-Permanente Ctr., San Rafael, 1971-80; mem. radiology chief's com. Kaiser-Permanente Med. Ctrs., no. Calif., 1971-80. Contbr. articles to profl. jours. Mem. World Affairs Coun. of No. Calif., San Francisco, 1989-92; docent San Francisco Mus. of Modern Art, 1987-92: vol. The Friends of Photography, Ansel Adams Ctr., San Francisco, The Calif. Acad. Sci., San Francisco, 1989—, docent, 1993—. Fellow The Royal Soc. Health (U.K.); mem. Soc. Nuclear Medicine, N.Y. Acad. Scis., AAAS, Commonwealth Club Calif. (San Francisco).

ZAFAR, NAEEM, computer industry marketing executive; b. Lahore, Pakistan, Aug. 13, 1957; came to U.S., 1979; s. Zafar Ahmad Khan and Tehmina Zafar; m. Dilek Güven, Mar. 20, 1982; children: Aylin Samina, Sinan Refik. ScB in Engring., Brown U., 1981; MSEE, U. Minn., 1983. Prin. rsch. scientist Honeywell Inc., Mpls., 1981-85; v.p., founder XCAT Inc., Mpls., 1985-88; dir. product mktg. Quickturn Systems, Mountain View, Calif., 1988—; v.p., conf. chair various confs. Contbr. articles to profl. jours.; 4 patents pending. Gold medalist, Nat. Talent scholar Govt. of Pakistan, 1973, 75. Mem. IEEE, Brown U. Alumni Club, Sigma Xi, Tau Beta Pi. Republican. Home: 5769 Dichondra Pl Newark CA 94560 Office: Quickturn Systems 325 E Middlefield Rd Mountain View CA 94043

ZAHARY, WILLIAM (BUD ZAHARY), academic dean, consultant; b. Edmonton, Alta., Sept. 28, 1935; s. John and Mary M. Z.; m. Eleanor Elaine Antaya, Dec. 29, 1965; children: Mary Suzanne, Elizabeth Ann, Christine Monique. MBA, U. Western Ont., London, 1965; BSc, U. Alta., Edmonton, 1970. Devel. engr. Can. Liquid Air, Montreal, Que., 1960-63; dist. engr. Can. Liquid Air, Toronto, Ont., 1963-65; retail mktg. mgr. Can. Liquid Air, Montreal, 1965-68; mktg. and plant mgr. Magadyne Industries, Edmonton, 1968-70; instr. No. Alta. Inst. Tech., Edmonton, 1970-74, asst. dir. advanced edn., 1974-77, dean continuing edn., 1977—; cons. Assn. Can. Community Colls., China, 1988, Ecuador, 1989; dir. Pembina Consortium, Drayton Valley, 1987—, Yellowhead Consortium, Hinton, 1987—. Mem. Alta. Assn. Continuing Edn., Rotary Internat., Derrick Golf & Winter Club (bd. dirs. 1988-93, treas. 1992-93). Home: 11312-35 A Ave, Edmonton, AB Canada T6J 0H8 Office: No Alta Inst Tech, 11762-106 St, Edmonton, AB Canada T6J 0H8

ZAHNISER, RICHARD ALLEN, software engineer; b. Pitts., Sept. 16, 1935; s. Richard Bayard and Mary M. (Kirk) Z.; m. JoAnn Jolley; children: Timothy Scott, Tricia Jolley; m. Charlotte Lenore Thorne, July 11, 1981. BA in Psychology, U. Ariz., 1964; MBA, U. Colo., 1983. Field rep. Kellogg Communications Systems div. ITT, Chgo., 1961-63; systems engr. data processing div. IBM, L.A., Denver, 1964-71; sr. systems analyst, project leader Cibar, Inc., Colorado Springs, 1972-74, 77; computer systems specialist, mgr. system support System Devel. Corp., Colorado Springs, 1974-77; exec. dir. Cibar Systems Inst., Colorado Springs, 1977-81; pres. RIX Software Engrng., Colorado Springs, 1981—; founder, chmn. CASELab, Inc., Colorado Springs, 1989—; founder, v.p. ops. Colo. Software Solutions, Colorado Springs, 1982-84; course author, instr. Learning Tree Internat., Culver City, Calif., 1981-90; mgr. productivity project IMB Users Group, Share, 1978-80; hon. prof. U. Colo., Colorado Springs, 1979. Author, editor software sect. Engrng, Computing Applications Newsletter, 1981-83; contbr. articles to profl. jours; pub. LabNotes, 1991—. Cubmaster, scoutmaster Boy Scouts Am., Denver and Colorado Springs, 1968-74. With U.S. Army, 1953-55. Recipient Outstanding Svc. award Colo. Country Music Assn., 1969. Mem. IEEE, Assn. Computing Machinery (chmn. Pike's Peak chpt. 1975-77), Data Processing Mgmt. Assn. (pres. local chpt. 1984-85), Am. Fedn. Musicians, Internat. Order Rocky Mtn. Goats, Delta Sigma Phi. Republican. Presbyterian.

ZAHOROWSKI, JEFFREY JOHN, computer administrator; b. San Francisco, July 18, 1966; s. John William and Wilma Marguerine (House) Z.; m. Renée Ann Perry, Oct. 14, 1989. Student, San Joaquin Delta Jr. Coll., 1985-88, Calif. State U., Sacramento, 1989-91. Computer adminstr. Law Offices of Brenton A. Bleier, Sacramento, 1988—. Mem. men's ministry com. First Bapt. Ch., Lodi, Calif., 1992—; mem. bd. govs. Delta Coll., Stockton, Calif., 1988, mem. leadership team Intervarsity Christian Fellowship, 1988, v.p. Interclub Coun., 1988. Named to Outstanding Young Men of Am., 1989. Republican. Home: 321 Neplus Ct Apt 14 Lodi CA 95242 Office: Law Offices Brenton Bleier 1001 G St Ste 101 Sacramento CA 95814

ZAIDI, IQBAL MEHDI, biochemist, scientist; b. Bijnor, India, June 30, 1957; s. Iqbal Haider and Habib (Zehra) Z.; m. Nuzhat Shikoh, Jan. 2, 1993. BS in Chemistry with honors, Aligarh M. U., 1976, MS in Biochemistry, 1978, PhD in Biochemistry, 1984. Cert. in radiation; cert. in health and happiness. Rsch. fellow Indsl. Toxicology Rsch. Ctr., Lucknow, India, 1979-83; rsch. affiliate N.Y. State Health Dept., Albany, 1984-91; scientist Applied Biosystems div. Perkin Elmer Corp., Foster City, Calif., 1991—. Contbr. articles to profl. jours. Mem. AAAS, SABA, Am. Chem. Soc. (biochem. tech. div. 1992—), N.Y. Acad. Scis. Office: Applied Biosystems div Perkin Elmer Corp 850 Lincoln Center Dr Foster City CA 94404

ZAIDINS, CLYDE STEWART, physics educator, engineer; b. Cin., Apr. 30, 1939; s. Morris and Thelma M. (Pettay) Z.; m. Florence Brown Merlini, Aug. 5, 1961 (div. Dec. 1979); children: Paul Muir, Sandra Lynn; m. Barbara J. Lambrecht, Dec. 23, 1990. BS in Physics, Calif. Tech. Inst., 1961, MS in Physics, 1963, PhD in Physics, 1967. Registered profl. engr., Colo. Sr. engr. JPL, Pasadena, Calif., 1967; prof. physics U. Colo., Denver, 1967—; vis. rschr. IPN, Universite de Paris-Sud, Orsay, France, 1980-81; vis. prof. IFCTR-Universita degli Studi, Milan, 1988-89, Université Paul, Sabatier, Toulouse, France, 1989; vis. prof. Calif. State U., L.A., 1993. Contbr. numerous articles to profl. jours. Democrat. Office: U Colo Denver 1200 Larimer St # 157 Denver CO 80204-5300

ZAISER, SALLY SOLEMMA VANN, retail book company executive; b. Birmingham, Ala., Jan. 18, 1917; d. Carl Waldo and Einnan (Herndon) Vann; student Birmingham-So. Coll., 1933-36, Akron Coll. Bus., 1937; m. Foster E. Zaiser, Nov. 11, 1939. Acct., A. Simionato, San Francisco, 1958-65; head acctg. dept. Richard T. Clarke Co., San Francisco, 1966; acct. John Howell-Books, San Francisco, 1967-72, sec., treas., 1972-83, 84-85, dir., 1982-85; sec. Great Eastern Mines, Inc., Albuquerque, 1969-81, dir., 1980-85. Braille transcriber for ARC, Kansas City, Mo. 1941-45; vol. worker ARC Hosp. Program, São Paulo, Brazil, 1952. Mem. Book Club Calif., U. Tex. at Austin Libr., Calif. Hist. Soc., Soc. Lit. and Arts, Gleeson Library Assocs. (dir. 1984-87, editor GLA newsletter 1984-87), So. Meth. U. Libr. Assocs., Theta Upsilon. Republican. Episcopalian. Home: 355 Serrano Dr Apt 4C San Francisco CA 94132-2275

ZAISS, CONRAD PENFIELD, financial analyst, consultant; b. Schenectady, N.Y., June 24, 1953; s. Herman Frederick and Barbara Ann (Penfield) Z.; m. Pamela Melissa Heid, June 2, 1984; 1 child, Zachary Robert. BA, U. Calif., Davis, 1978, MBA, 1990. Project/rsch. mgr. U. Calif., Davis, 1979-82; lab. rsch. mgr. Beth Israel Hosp., Boston, 1982-83; mgr. R & D Sontek Industry Inc., Lexington, Mass., 1983-84; chief fin. officer, controller Biologix Inc., Sacramento, 1984-86, project/rsch. mgr. Calif. Primate Rsch. Ctr., 1985-90; fin. cons./acting fin. officer Life Support Systems, Inc., Mountain View, Calif., 1991, CFO, 1991-92; CFO, founder Cardiac Mariners, Inc., 1992; founder, v.p. Fin. & Ops. MediFlex, Inc., 1992—; fin. cons. I-Stat, Sacramento, 1988-89; mgr., fin. cons. PBI Inc., Modesto, Calif., 1989. Author: (chpt.) Cases in Corporate Financial Reports, 1989. Mem. Commonwealth Club of Calif. Home: 8435 Ascolano Ave Fair Oaks CA 95628-5267 Office: MediFlex Inc Cannon Plz S Hwy 52 Cannon Falls MN 55009 also: PO Box 418 Folsom CA 95763-0418

ZAJAC, JOHN, semiconductor equipment company executive; b. N.Y.C., July 21, 1946; s. John Andrew and Catherine (Canepa) Z.; m. Vera Barbagallo, Jan. 13, 1973; children: Jennifer, Michelle. AAS, NYU, 1966; BEE, U. Ky., 1968. Project engr. B.C.D. Computing, N.Y.C., 1968-70; v.p. Beacon Systems, Commack, N.Y., 1970-73, E.T. Systems, Santa Clara, Calif., 1973-77; v.p. research and devel. Eaton Corp., Sunnyvale, Calif., 1977-81; pres. Semitech/Gen. Signal, Los Gatos, Calif., 1981-83; mgr. advanced product div. Tegal/Motorola Inc., Novato, Calif., 1983-86; v.p. research and devel. U.S.A. Inc., San Jose, Calif., 1986—. Author: Delicate Balance, 1988; holder of 19 patents in field. Office: PO Box 21237 San Jose CA 95151-1237

ZAK, MICHELE WENDER, university educator, management communications; b. Beckley, W.Va., Apr. 3, 1940; d. Max Harris and Freda (Lewis) Wender; m. Laurence Michael Zak, Aug. 31, 1963; children: Peter Andrew, Colin Mark. BA in English, Ohio State U., 1962; MA, UCLA, 1966; PhD in English, Ohio State U., 1973. Lectr. dept. English, Ohio State U., Columbus, 1968-71, grad. teaching assoc., 1971-73; exec. dir. Women's Resource and Policy Devel. Ctr., 1974-76; asst. prof. English, dir. Office Human Resource Utilization, Kent (Ohio) State U., 1976-82, coord. women's studies cert. program Coll. Arts and Scis., 1977-82; spl. asst. to the v.p. U. Calif., 1982-83, dir. faculty devel. and affirmative action, 1983-89; prof. John F. Kennedy U. Sch. Mgmt., Walnut Creek, Calif., 1989-92; dir. mgmt. comm., lectr. Stanford (Calif.) U. Grad. Sch. Bus., 1992—; prof. and dir. mgmt. comm. Stanford U. Grad. Sch. Bus.; asst. coord. EEO, chief Office Women's Affairs, State of Ohio, Columbus, 1974-75; speaker in field; pres. Michaels & Assocs. Cons., Oakland, Calif., 1989—. Author: (with Longman) Women and the Politics of Culture, 1983; contbr. articles to profl. jours. and pubs. Edn. com. mem. Ohio Task Force on the Implementation of the Equal Rights Amendment, 1972-73; mem. Govs. Com. on Women in Ohio, 1973-74, Nat. Coalition for Women, 1975-77; bd. of trustees Women's Resource ad Policy Devel. Ctr., 1975—. Mem. MLA, ASTD, Assn. Profl. Writing Cons., Assn. Bus. Comm., Internat. Assn. Bus. Communicators, Mgmt. Comm. Assn.

ZAKIS, MICHAEL WILLIAM, management trainer; b. Chgo., Sept. 10, 1947; s. Edward David and Elsie (Gehrke) Z.; m. Carolyn Marie Dawn, Feb. 9, 1974. Student, Black Hills Sch., 1971, Wright Coll., Chgo., 1971-75, McHenry Coll., 1976-83. Field engr. Univac, Chgo., 1972-74; systems technician Bunker Ramo-ESIS, Rolling Meadows, Ill., 1974-75; br. mgr. Nat. Semi-Conductor, Schaumburg, Ill., 1975-86; dir. Coll. of Strategic Initiatives, Sierra Vista, 1987-88; pres. Clara Vista Mgmt. Devel., Sierra Vista, 1988—; cons., dir. Data Comm., Inc., Casa Grande, Ariz., 1988—; speaker in field. Treas. Jaycees, McHenry, Ill., 1980-82; v.p. Indsl. Devel. Authority, Sierra Vist. With USAF, 1967-71. Mem. Nat. Speakers Assn., Toastmasters (divsn. gov., Able Toastmaster 1992). Office: Clara Vista Mgmt Devel PO Box 3016 Sierra Vista AZ 85636-3016

ZALESKI, BRIAN WILLIAM, chiropractor; b. Trenton, N.J., Oct. 27, 1962; s. Joseph Rudolph and Roseline (Moore) Z.; m. Petra Gertrude Tucker, Apr. 10, 1983; 1 child, Natasha Renee. Student, Def. Lang. Inst., Monterey, Calif., 1980-81; BS, Palmer Coll., 1992, D of Chiropractic, 1992. Grad. researcher Palmer Coll. of Chiropractice, Davenport, Iowa, 1991-92; chiropractor Peninsula Spinal Care, Daly City, Calif., 1992, Creekside Family Chiropractic, Vacaville, Calif., 1992—; prin. investigator, presenter Internat. Conf. on Spinal Manipulation, 1992. Baseball umpire Iowa High Schs., Davenport, 1989-92, Men's Sr. League, Davenport, 1989-91, No. Calif. Umpires Assn., San Mateo, Calif., 1992. Sgt. U.S. Army, 1980-85. Recipient scholarship Internat. Chiropractors Assn., 1989, 90, Cecil M. Grogan scholarship Palmer Internat. Alumni Assn., 1991, Alma Nielsen scholarship Internat. Chiropractors Assn. Aux., 1991, Student Rsch. grant Palmer Coll. Chiropractic, 1992; named to Dean's List, 1991-92. Mem. Internat. Chiropractors Assn., Am. Chiropractors Assn., Calif. Chiropractic Assn., Assn. for the History of Chiropractic, Palmer Internat. Alumni Assn., Roosevelt Lodge #626 A.F. & A.M., Delta Sigma Chi Chiropractic Frat., Chi Rho Theta Chiropractic Rsch. Honors Soc. Republican. Office: Creekside Family Chiropractic 3000 Alamo Dr Ste 104 Vacaville CA 95687

ZALLE, PAUL MARTIN, financial services company executive; b. L.A., Aug. 13, 1945; s. Morris D. and Esther M. (Kahn) Z.; m. Judith Ann Willen, Mar. 31, 1968; children: Melissa Elise, Michael Brandon. BSBA, Calif. State. U., Northridge, 1968; postgrad. in acctg., Calif. State U., L.A., 1969-71. Cert. internal auditor, info. systems auditor. Sr. acct. Cohen & Cohen, CPA's, L.A., 1968-72; mgr. auditing Carte Blanche Corp., L.A., 1973-77; regional audit mgr. Avco. Corp., Newport Beach, Calif., 1978-82; regional dir. auditing Textron Corp., Irvine, Calif., 1983-86; v.p. auditing Avco Fin. Svcs., Inc., Irvine, 1987--; cons. to pres. Bus. Spltys., Inc., Newport Beach, Calif., 1986—; cons. to chmn. Imperial Thrift & Loan Assn., Burbank, Calif., 1987—. Contbr. articles to profl. publs. Family advisor prosthetic program for handicapped UCLA, 1975--. Mem. Am. Fin. Svcs. Assn. (nat. audit com. 1985—, chmn. 1990—), Inst. Internal Auditors (editor, advisor 1980—, hon. svc. award 1983, bd. govs. Orange County chpt. 1990—), EDP Auditors Assn., Orange County Pvt. Investment Club. Democrat. Jewish. Home: 20072 Midland Ln Huntington Beach CA 92646-4915 Office: Avco Fin Svcs Inc 3349 Michelson Dr Irvine CA 92715-1606

ZALLEN, DENNIS MICHAEL, combustion and environmental engineer; b. East Chicago, Ill., Dec. 6, 1943; s. Stanley George and Ann (Kloac) Z.; m. Sallie-White Harvey, May 14, 1977. BSME, Purdue U., 1965, MSME, 1967; postgrad., So. Meth. U., 1968-79; PhD, Purdue U., 1973. Registered profl. engr. Calif. Research engr. Gen. Dynamics Corp., Ft. Worth, 1967-70; asst. project engr. Pratt & Whitney Aircraft, East Hartford, Conn., 1973-75; asst. prof. N.M. State U., Las Cruces, 1975-76; group leader Inst. Mining and Minerals Research Ky. Ctr. Energy Research, Lexington, 1977-78; mgr. energy systems devel. Ultrasystems, Inc. and Energy and Environ. Research Corp., Santa Ana, Calif., 1978-80; sr. engr. analyst, mgr. N.Mex. Engrng. Research Inst. U. N.Mex., Alberquerque, 1980-90; pres. Zallen Internat. Assocs., 1990—; cons. environ, instrumentation Dept. of Energy; tracked vehicle fire survivability Army Safety Ctr. Contbr. articles to profl. jours.; patentee low emissions burner system, automatice fire extinguisher with notification. David Ross fellow Purdue U., 1973. Mem. Combustion Inst., Air Pollution Control Assn., ASME, Am. Phys. Soc., AIAA, Sigma Pi Sigma, Pi Tau Sigma. Home and Office: 14216 Turner Ct NE Albuquerque NM 87123-1836

ZALOKAR, JULIA BALLANTINE, epidemiologist; b. Lincoln, Nebr., Aug. 31, 1926; d. John Perry and Constance (Rummons) Ballantine; m. Marko Zalokar, Dec. 31, 1951; children: Nadja Zalokar Golding, Mira Elizabeth Zalokar Newton. BS, U. Wash., 1946; MA, San Diego State U., 1967; postgrad., Columbia U., 1946-47, U. Calif., La Jolla, 1967-69. Math. stat. Nat. Heart Inst., Bethesda, Md., 1952-54; rsch. asst. Sch. of Pub. Health Yale U., New Haven, 1956-60; lectr. San Diego State U., 1967; rsch. assoc. Inst. Nat. de Sante et de Recherche Medicale, Villejuif, France, 1970-78; attache de recherche Institut National de Sante et de Recherche Medicale, Villejuif, France, 1978-81, charge de recherche, 1981-83; ret. NIH, Villejuif, France, 1983. Contbr. articles to profl. jours. Mem. San Diego LWV (pres. 1985-87, 88-90). Home: 6064 Avenida Chamnez La Jolla CA 92037-7403

ZALTA, EDWARD, otorhinolaryngologist, utilization review physician; b. Houston, Mar. 2, 1930; s. Nouri Louis and Marie Zahde (Lizmi) Z.; m. Carolyn Mary Gordon, Oct. 8, 1971; 1 child, Ryan David; children by previous marriage: Nouri Allan, Lori Ann, Barry Thomas, Marci Louise. BS, Tulane U., 1952, MD, 1956. Diplomate Am. Bd. Quality Assurance and Utilization Rev. Physicians. Intern Brooke Army Hosp., San Antonio, 1956-57; resident in otolaryngology U.S. Army Hosp., Ft. Campbell, Ky., 1957-60; practice medicine specializing in otolaryngology Glendora, West Covina and San Dimas, Calif., 1960-82; ENT cons. City of Hope Med. Ctr., 1961-76; mem. staff Foothill Presbyn.; past pres. L.A. Found. Community Svc., L.A. Poison Info. Ctr., So. Calif. Physicians Coun., Inc.; founder, chief exec. officer, chmn. bd. dirs. CAPP CARE, INC.; chmn. bd. MDM; founder Inter-Hosp. Coun. Continuing Med. Edn. Author: (with others) Medicine and Your Money; mem. editorial staff Managed Care Outlook, AAPPO Jour., Med. Interface; contbr. articles to profl. jours. Pres. bd. govs. Glendora Unified Sch. Dist., 1965-71; mem. Calif. Cancer Adv. Council, 1967-71, Commn. of Californias, Los Angeles County Commn. on Economy and Efficiency, U. Calif. Irvine Chief Exec. Roundtable; bd. dirs. U. Calif. Irvine Found. Served to capt. M.C. AUS, 1957-60. Recipient Award of Merit Order St. Lazarus, 1981. Mem. AMA, Calif. Med. Assn., Am. Acad. Otolaryngology, Am. Coun. Otolaryngology, Am. Assn. Preferred Provider Orgns. (past pres.), Am. Coll. Med. Quality, L.A. County Med. Assn. (pres. 1980-81), Kappa Nu, Phi Delta Epsilon, Glendora CountryClub, Centurion Club, Sea Bluff Beach and Racquet Club; Center Club (Costa Mesa, Calif.), Pacific Golf Club (San Juan, Capistrano). Republican. Jewish. Home: 3 Morning Dove Dr Laguna Niguel CA 92677 Office: West Tower 4000 MacArthur Blvd Ste 10000 Newport Beach CA 92660-2526

ZALUCKY, ALEX DAVID, automation company executive; b. Warsaw, Poland, Mar. 24, 1960; came to U.S., 1967; s. Henry K. and Maria Zalucky. BSME, Purdue U., 1980; MSME, MIT, 1982. Mem. tech. staff IBM, Boca Raton, Fla., 1982-83; mgr. application engrng. Adept Tech., Inc., San Jose, Calif., 1983-86; pres., founder Robotic Development, Mountain View, Calif., 1986—. Patentee in field of active beam bending compensation. Office: Robotic Development 453D Ravendale Dr Mountain View CA 94043

ZALUTSKY, MORTON HERMAN, lawyer; b. Schenectady, Mar. 8, 1935; s. Albert and Gertrude (Daffner) Z.; m. Audrey Englebardt, June 16, 1957; children: Jane, Diane, Samuel. BA, Yale U., 1957; JD, U. Chgo., 1960. Bar: Oreg. 1961. Law clk. to presiding judge Oreg. Supreme Ct., 1960-61; assoc. Hart, Davidson, Veazie & Hanlon, 1961-63, Veatch & Lovett, 1963-64, Morrison, Bailey, Dunn, Cohen & Miller, 1964-69; prin. Morton H. Zalutsky, P.C., 1970-76; ptnr. Dahl, Zalutsky, Nichols & Hinson, 1977-79, Zalutsky & Klarquist, P.C., Portland, Oreg., 1980-85, Zalutsky, Klarquist & Johnson, Inc., Portland, 1985—; instr. Portland State U., 1961-64, Northwestern Sch. of Law, 1969-70; assoc. prof. U. Miami Law Sch.; lectr. Practicing Law Inst., 1971—, Oreg. State Bar Continuing Legal Edn. Program, 1970, Am. Law Inst.-ABA Continuing Legal Edn. Program, 1973—, 34th, 37th NYU ann. insts. fed. taxation, So. Fed. Tax Inst., U. Miami Inst. Estate Planning, Southwestern Legal Found., Internat. Foun. Employee Benefit Plans, numerous other profl. orgns. Author: (with others) The Professional Corporation in Oregon, 1970, 82; contbg. author: The Dentist and the Law, 3d edit.; editor-in-chief (retirement plans) Matthew Bender's Federal Tax Service, 1987—; contbr. to numerous publs. in field. Mem. vis. com. U. Chgo. Law Sch. Mem. ABA (vice chair profl. svcs. 1987-89, mem. coun. tax sect. 1987-89, spl. coord. 1980-85), Am. Law Inst., Am. Bar Retirement Assn. (trustee, bd. dirs., vice chair 1990-92, chair 1991-92), Multnomah County Bar Assn., Am. Coun. Tax Lawyers (charter mem.), Oreg. Estate Planning Coun. Jewish. Home: 3118 SW Fairmount Blvd

Portland OR 97201-1466 Office: 215 SW Washington St Fl 3D Portland OR 97204-2636

ZAMBETTI, DENIS EGAN, product development executive; b. Riverdale, N.Y., Oct. 18, 1953; s. Emil John and Teresa Veronica (McSherry) Z. BS, U.S. Mil. Acad., 1977; MBA, Golden Gate U., 1985. Commd. 2d lt. U.S. Army, 1977, advanced through ranks to capt., 1977-81, resigned, 1985; platoon leader B Co. 2d/22d Inf., Wiesbaden, Fed. Republic Germany, 1977-78, mortar platoon leader, 1978-79, exec. officer, 1979-80; communications and electronics officer HHC Co. 2d/22d Inf., Wiesbaden, 1980-81; morale support fund custodian U.S. Mil. Command Activity Group, Bad Kreuznach, Fed. Republic Germany, 1981-82; equal opportunity staff officer HQ Presidio of San Francisco, 1982-83, chief reserve pay, 1983-85; peninsula area mgr. Beringer Wines/Wineworld, San Francisco, 1985-87; nat. accts. mgr. SW region Beringer Wines/Wineworld, Mission Viejo, Calif., 1987—; v.p. product devel. IQUEST Bus. Devel., Santa Clara, Calif., 1988—; nat. accts. mgr. Sutter Home Winery. Named One of Outstanding Young Men of Am. Jaycees, 1983. Mem. Knights of the Vine, West Point Soc. of Bay Area (bd. govs. 1982-85), West Point Soc. Orange County (admissions rep. 1987—, mil. liaison officer 1991—). Democrat. Roman Catholic. Home: 4843 Kimberly Common Livermore CA 94550-7707

ZAMPARELLI, MARIO ARMOND, designer; b. N.Y.C.; s. Leucio and Giovanina (Ianiri) Z.; divorced; children: Regina, Marisa, Andrea. Student, Pratt Inst., 1946. Exec. personal designer to Howard R. Hughes L.A., 1946-50, exec. designer to Howard R. Hughes, 1950-59; pres. Zamparelli & Co., L.A., 1959-69, 80—; chief exec. designer Summa Corp., L.A., 1969-80; design cons., 1980-90; specialist corp. identity Howard R. Hughes; designer unique Exec. 37' vehicle Kajima Corp., Japan. Contbr. articles to L.A. mag., Esquire mag., L.A. Home, Designers West and Airline Exec. mag. Recipient J.W. Alexander medal Paul Hoffman Sch., Paul Hoffman Gold medal; Haskell Travelling fellow, Pratt Inst.; N.Y. Scholastic scholar Straubenmuller Sch. Office: Zamparelli & Co 1450 Lomita Dr Pasadena CA 91106-4341

ZANETTA, JOSEPH MICHAEL, university administrator, lawyer; b. Jamestown, N.Y., Apr. 26, 1953; s. Joseph A. and Freda (Felanzo) Z.; m. Ellen L. Leggett, June 2, 1979. BS, Cornell U., 1975, JD, 1978. Bar: N.Y. 1980. Mem. Hartley & Fessenden, Attys., Jamestown, 1978-79; devel. officer Cornell U., Ithaca, N.Y., 1979-82; assoc. dir. maj. gifts Tufts U., Medford, Mass., 1982-83; dir. devel. Belmont Hill Sch., Belmont, Mass., 1983-86; exec. dir. external affairs Sch. Bus. Adminstrn. U. So. Calif., L.A., 1986-93; v.p. advancement Whittier (Calif.) Coll., 1993—; bd. dirs. Pasadena Devel. Corp. Sec.-treas. Lord Found. of Calif., L.A., 1988-93. Mem. Coun. for Advancement and Support of Edn. (chair nat. confs. 1990, 92), Univ. Club of L.A. (bd. dirs. 1991—), Phi Kappa Phi (bd. dirs. 1991—). Roman Catholic. Home: 391 S Parkwood Ave Pasadena CA 91107 Office: Whittier College 13406 Philadelphia St Whittier CA 90608

ZAPEL, ARTHUR L., book publishing executive; b. Chgo., 1921; m. Janet Michel (dec.); children: Linda (dec.), Mark, Theodore, Michelle; m. Cynthia Rogers Pisor, 1986; stepchildren: Dawn, Anthony. BA in English, U. Wis., 1946. Writer, prodr. Westinghouse Radio Stas.; film writer Galbreath Studios, Ft. Wayne; creative dir. Kling Studios, Chgo., 1952-54; writer, prodr. TV commls. J. Walter Thompson Advt., Chgo., 1954-61, v.p. TV and radio prodn., 1961-70; founder Arthur Meriwether, Inc., 1970. Created game A Can of Squirms; wrote plays for ednl. use in schs. and chs.; supv. editing and prodn. 1200 plays and musicals from 1970. Past pres. Colo. Springs Symphony Coun. Art Students League Colo. Springs; past bd. dirs., Colo. Springs Festival. Recipient numerous awards Art Dirs. Club N.Y., Art Dirs. Chgo., Hollywood Advt., 1960-67, Gold Records Radio Ad Bur., 1959-60, XV Festival Internat. Du Film Publicitaire Venise, 1968, Gold Camera award U.S. Indsl. Film Fesitval, 1983, Dukane award, 1983, Gold award Houston Internat. Film Festival, 1984. Office: Meriwether Pub Ltd 885 Elkton Dr Colorado Springs CO 80907

ZAPOR, JOHN RANDOLPH, financial consultant; b. Latrobe, Pa., June 26, 1944; s. John Stanley and Esther Mae (Ragan) Z.; m. Rose Mary Barnes, July 11, 1980; children: Miranda Rhea, Jessica Pauline. BA, Elizabethtown Coll., 1981. Claims examiner I Pa. Dept. Labor and Industry, Indiana, 1970-81; mgr. Wewoka (Okla.) C. of C., 1981-84; exec. v.p. Northland C. of C., Kansas City, Mo., 1984-86; mng. dir. Mountain States Hardware and Implement Assn., Lakewood, Colo., 1986-92; with John Hancock Ins. Co., Denver, 1993—. Author: (novel) Code Mobius, 1990; (monographs) Toe To Toe with Wal-Mart, K-Mart, and All The Other Marts, 1990, Mowing Down the Competition, 1991; contbr. articles to trade publs., book revs. to newspapers; playwright, plays produced in Fed. Republic Germany, New Eng. Served with U.S. Army, 1963-67. Recipient Citations, Pa. Senate and Ho. of Reps., 1979. Mem. Am. Soc. Assn. Execs., Colo. Soc. Assn. Execs. Republican. Home: 6630 W 30th Ave Denver CO 80214-8025 Office: Rocky Mountain Lindeman Gen Agy 600 S Cherry St Denver CO 80222

ZAPPE, JOHN PAUL, city editor, educator; b. N.Y.C., July 30, 1952; s. John Paul and Caroline (Pikor) Z.; m. Siobhan Bradshaw, May 30, 1982. AA, Dutchess Community Coll., Poughkeepsie, 1971; BA, Marist Coll., 1973; JD, Syracuse (N.Y.) U., 1978. Reporter Poughkeepsie Jour., 1973-75, Nev. State Jour., Reno, 1979-80; freelance reporter Am. Media Bold, Oakland, Calif., 1981-83; reporter Press-Telegram, Long Beach, Calif., 1983-88, city editor, 1988—; tchr. Syracuse U., 1976-78, Calif. State U., 1985-87; cons. Am. Media Bold, 1981-83. Chmn. Local 69 Newspaper Guild, Long Beach, 1984-87. Mem. Investigative Editors and Reporters. Office: Press-Telegram 604 Pine Ave Long Beach CA 90844-0001

ZAPPIA, CHARLES ANTHONY, history educator; b. DuBois, Pa., Feb. 26, 1947; s. Joseph Carl and Orpha Hortense (Mancuso) Z.; m. Mary Jane Sara Regan, Aug. 15, 1981; children: Angela, Gabriela. BA, U. Pitts., 1969; postgrad., U. Oreg., 1970-72; MA, San Jose State U., 1974; C.Phil., U. Calif., Berkeley, 1982. Community coll. teaching credential, Calif. Instr. West Valley Coll., Saratoga, Calif., 1976-78, Canada Coll., Redwood City, Calif., 1976-81, City Coll. San Francisco, 1980-85, Chabot Coll., Hayward, Calif., 1981-85, Coll. of San Mateo (Calif.), 1984-86; assoc. prof. history San Diego Mesa Coll., 1986—; acting instr. U. Calif., Berkeley, 1981-86; lectr. San Francisco State U., 1983-86, San Diego State U., 1986—; reviewer, cons. Houghton Mifflin Pub. Co., Boston, 1987, Prentice-Hall Pub. Co., Englewood Cliffs, N.J., 1988. McCormack fellow, 1981. Mem. Am. Hist. Assn. (conf. presenter 1986), Orgn. Am. Historians (com. on teaching, focus group 1993—), Am. Italian Hist. Assn. (conf. presenter 1983, 89), Immigration History Soc., S.W. Labor Studies Assn., Am. Fed. Tchrs. (negotiator San Diego Community Coll. Guild 1987—, editor Excellence newsletter 1988—). Democrat. Roman Catholic. Home: 4804 34th St San Diego CA 92116-1816 Office: Mesa Coll History Dept 7250 Mesa College Dr San Diego CA 92111-4902

ZAPRIANOFF, BORIS NICHOLA, geologist; b. Bulgaria, Oct. 25, 1963; s. Nichola Ivanov and Rosalia Petrova (Kodjabasheva) Z. MS, Sofia (Bulgaria) U., 1989. Geologist Oceanography Inst., Varna, Bulgaria, 1988-90. Mem. Assn. Engring. Geologists. Home: 1835 N Kenmore Ave Los Angeles CA 90027

ZARE, RICHARD NEIL, chemistry educator; b. Cleve., Nov. 19, 1939; s. Milton and Dorothy (Amdur) Z.; m. Susan Leigh Shively, Apr. 20, 1963; children: Bethany Jean, Bonnie Sue, Rachel Amdur. BA, Harvard, 1961; postgrad., U. Calif. at Berkeley, 1961-63; PhD (NSF predoctoral fellow), Harvard, 1964; DS (hon.), U. Ariz., 1990, Northwestern U., 1993. Postdoctoral fellow Harvard, 1964; postdoctoral research asso. Joint Inst. for Lab. Astrophysics, 1964-65; asst. prof. chemistry Mass. Inst. Tech., 1965-66; asst. prof. dept. physics and astrophysics U. Colo., 1966-68, assoc. prof. physics and astrophysics, asso. prof. chemistry, 1968-69; prof. chemistry Columbia, 1969-77, Higgins prof. natural sci., 1975-77; prof. Stanford U., 1977—, Shell Disting. prof. chemistry, 1980-85, Marguerite Blake Wilbur prof. chemistry, 1987—, prof. physics, 1992—; cons. Aeronomy Lab., NOAA, 1966-77, radio standards physics div. Nat. Bur. Standards, 1968-77, Lawrence Livermore Lab., U. Calif., 1974—, SRI, Internat., 1974—, Los Alamos Sci. Lab., U. Calif., 1975—; fellow adjoint, Joint Inst. Lab. Astrophysics, U. Colo.; mem. IBM Sci. Adv. Com., 1977-92; chmn. commn. on physical scis., mathematics, and applications Nat. Rsch. Coun., 1992—; researcher and author publs. on laser chemistry and chem. physics. editor Chem. Physics Letters, 1982-85. Recipient Fresenius award Phi Lambda Upsilon, 1974, Michael Polanyi medal, 1979, Nat. Medal Sci., 1983, Soroptimist Internat. Santa Cruz award Spectroscopy Soc. Pitts., 1983, Michelson-Morley award Case Inst. Tech. Case We. Res. U., 1986, ISCO award for Significant Contbns. to Instrumentation for Biochem. Separations, 1990, The Harvey prize, 1993; nonresident fellow Joint Inst. for Lab. Astrophysics, 1970—, Alfred P. Sloan fellow, 1967-69, Christensen fellow St. Catherine's Coll., Oxford U., 1982, Stanford U. fellow, 1984-86. Fellow AAAS, Calif. Acad. Scis. (hon.); mem. Nat. Acad. Sci. (Chem. Scis. award 1991), Nat. Scis. Bd., Am. Acad. Arts and Scis., Am. Phys. Soc. (Earle K. Plyler prize 1981, Irving Langmuir prize 1985), Am. Chem. Soc. (Harrison Howe award Rochester chpt. 1985, Remsen award Md. chpt. 1985, Kirkwood award, Yale U. New Haven chpt. 1986, Willard Gibbs medal Chgo. chpt. 1990, Peter Debye award in phys. chemistry 1991), Am. Philos. Soc., Chem. Soc. London, Phi Beta Kappa. Office: Stanford U Dept Chemistry Stanford CA 94305-5080

ZAREMBA, HUBERT BERNARD, oil company executive; b. Evanston, Ill., Apr. 20, 1923; s. Bernard and Helena (Kawleska) Z.; m. Beverley Mary Smith, Mar. 10, 1949; children: Claudette Ann, Anthony Bernard. B-SChemE, Northwestern U., Evanston, Ill., 1949. Chief petroleum engr. ESSO Intramerica, Venezuela, Peru, 1944-53, Coral Gables, Fla., 1956-62; chief process engr. Black, Sivalls & Bryson, Inc., Oklahoma City, Okla., 1954-55; v.p. Anson Corp., Oklahoma City, 1964-67; ops. mgr. Amoco Internat. Oil Co., 1967-76; regional drilling mgr. Amoco Europe, London, 1976-81; ops. mgr. Amoco Prodn. Co., Houston, 1981-89; v.p. AZ Specialty Svcs., Inc., Durango, Colo., 1989—, also bd. dirs.; cons. AZ Specialty Svcs., Inc., 1989—. Patentee in field. 1st lt. USAF, 1943-45. Decorated 5 Air medals. Mem. Soc. of Petroleum Engrs. Roman Catholic. Office: AZ Specialty Svcs Inc 209 Highland Hill Dr Durango CO 81301

ZARO, BRAD A., research company executive, biologist; b. San Jose, Calif., Dec. 4, 1949; s. Raymond J. and Irene R. (Cunha) Z.; m. Angela M. Greenan, Nov. 20, 1971; children: Amy C., Kristen E. BA in Zoology, San Jose State U., 1974, MA in Biology, 1981. Chemist, Dept. Drug Metabolism Syntex Rsch., Inc., Palo Alto, Calif., 1976-78, chemist II, Dept. Drug Metabolism, 1978-81, chemist III, Dept. Drug Metabolism, 1981-84, clin. rsch. assoc. I, Inst. of Clin. Medicine, 1984-85, clin. rsch. assoc. II, Inst. of Clin. Medicine, 1985-87, sen. clin. rsch. assoc., Inst. of Clin. Medicine, 1985-87; sen. clin. rsch. assoc. Triton Biosciences, Inc., Alameda, Calif., 1988, mgr. clin. trials, 1988; pres. Clinimetrics Rsch. Assoc., Inc., San Jose, 1988—. Contbr. articles to scholarly jours. Mem. Am. Coll. Clin. Pharmacology, Am. Assoc's. for the Advancement of Sci., Assoc's. of Clin. Pharmacology, Prof. Tech. Cons's. Democrat. Roman Catholic. Office: Clinimetrics Rsch Assocs Inc 6531 Crown Blvd Ste 3A San Jose CA 95120

ZASKE, JEANNE ANN, artist, educator; b. Bklyn., Oct. 2, 1930; d. John Morlenko and Maria Basanau; m. Paul E. Sterba (div. 1968); 1 child, Lynn Ann; m. Oscar Conrad Zaske, Mar. 21, 1971. AA, Santa Monica (Calif.) C.C., 1961; student, UCLA, 1962-69; BA, Calif. State U., Dominguez Hills, 1976; MA, Long Beach State U., 1980. Pvt. instr. landscape painting Palos Verdes Estates, Calif., 1977—; artist The Artists Studio Gallery, Palos Verdes Estates, 1990—. Exhibitions include James Chaney collection, Capital Banks, 1993; work represented in numerous permanent pub. and pvt. collections including Long Beach State U.

ZAUNER, CHRISTIAN WALTER, exercise physiologist, exercise science educator, exercise rehabilitation consultant; b. Phila., July 21, 1930; s. Philip Walter and Margaret Helen (Gilmor) Z.; m. Betty Ann Schwenk, Feb. 1, 1957; children: Beth, Ward, Joe. BS, West Chester State, 1956; MS, Syracuse U., 1957; PhD, So. Ill. U., 1963. Asst. prof. Temple U., Phila., 1963-65; prof. phys. edn. and medicine U. Fla., Gainesville, 1965-84; dir. Sports Medicine Inst., Mt. Sinai Med. Ctr., Miami Beach, Fla., 1984-87; chmn. exercise sci. Oreg. State U., Corvallis, 1987—; cons. in exercise rehab. Hosp. Corp. Am.; cons. in sports medicine State of Kuwait, Arab Gulf; cons. sport sci. curriculum Ministry Edn., Thailand. Contbr. numerous articles to various profl. jours. Served with USN, 1951-54. Grantee U. Fla., 1971, Am. Scandinavian Found., 1971, Fla. Blue Key, 1978, Nat. Acad. Sci., 1985-86, 88, 90. Fellow Am. Coll. Sports Medicine; mem. Am. Physiol. Soc., N.Y. Acad. Scis., AAHPERD, Sigma Chi. Democrat. Roman Catholic. Home: 636 NW 2d St Corvallis OR 37330 Office: Oreg State U Dept Exercise and Sport Sci Corvallis OR 97331

ZAVALA, ALBERT, research psychologist; b. Chgo., Mar. 10, 1930; s. Edward and Maria Soledad (Herrejon) Z.; div.; children—Camille, Sally, Elena, Jenifer, Alexis. B.A., Willamette U., Salem, Oreg., 1959; M.A. Mich. State U., 1961; Ph.D., Kans. State U., 1966. Prof., head life scis. Calspan, Buffalo, 1967-73; prof. SUNY Coll. at Buffalo, 1968-78; exec. dir. Corp. IV, Cheektowaga, N.Y., 1973-77; dir. projects Inpsych, Cupertino, Calif., 1978-80; sr. research psychologist SRI Internat., Menlo Park, Calif., 1980-85; sr. staff engr., Lockheed Missiles and Space Co., Sunnyvale, Calif., 1985—. Mem. Erie County (N.Y.) sheriff's sci. staff, 1972-78. Served with U.S. Army, 1955-57. Dunlap fellow, 1964; Greater Kans. City Mental Health Found. fellow, 1962-63. Mem. Am. Psychol. Assn., Human Factors Soc., Sigma Xi, Psi Chi, Phi Kappa Phi. Author: (with J.J. Paley) Personal Appearance Identification, 1972. Contbr. numerous articles to profl. jours. Office: 1111 Lockheed Way Sunnyvale CA 94089-1212

ZAZVRSKEY, MICHAEL EUGENE, secondary education educator; b. Phillipsburg, Pa., May 16, 1947; s. Mike and Mildred (Ribnicar) Z.; m. Judy Kay McCann, Aug. 8, 1970. Student, Central Ohio State U., 1967-69; BS in Math., Cedarville Coll., 1969; postgrad., Fla. Atlantic U., 1983. Cert. tchr., Calif. Tchr. OSSO Home, Xenia, Ohio, 1969-74, Westminster Acad., Ft. Lauderdale, Fla., 1974-87, Brawley (Calif.) High Sch., 1988-89, Christian high Sch., El Cajon, Calif., 1989—.

ZDERIC, JOHN ANTHONY, pharmaceutical company executive; b. San Jose, Calif., Jan. 5, 1924; s. Stephen Anthony and Florence Mathilda (Bush) Z.; m. Marie Alice Lobrovich, Sept. 24, 1949; 1 son, Stephen Anthony. AB, San Jose State Coll., 1950; MS, Stanford U., 1952, PhD, 1955. Research chemist Syntex Corp., Mexico City, 1956-59, asst. dir. chem. research, 1959-61; dir. labs. Syntex Inst. Molecular Biology, Palo Alto, Calif., 1961-62; v.p. comml. devel. Syntex Internat., Mexico City, 1965-70, Syntex Labs., Palo Alto, 1970-72; v.p. research adminstrn. and tech. affairs Syntex U.S.A., Inc., Palo Alto, 1973-93; psl. adv. to chmn. Affymax N.V. Palo Alto, 1992—. Contbr. articles to profl. jours.; patentee in field. Served with USN, 1942-46. Fellow Eidig. Tech. hoch., Zurich, Switzerland, 1963-64; mem. Am. Chem. Soc., Sigma Xi. Home: 2369 Sharon Oak Dr Menlo Park CA 94025-6816 Office: Syntex USA Inc 3401 Hillview Ave Palo Alto CA 94304-1397

ZDUNIAK, GREGORY PETER, record company executive; b. Rockville Centre, N.Y., Feb. 17, 1950; s. Thaddeus Peter and Jane Helen (Hecht) Z.; m. Beverly Jean Grosenheider, Nov. 20, 1976; 1 child, Michael. BME, No. Ariz. U., 1976. Tchr. Cortez High Sch., Glendale, Ariz., 1976-77; process engr. and purchasing mgr. Dolphin, Inc., Phoenix, 1977-83; v.p., dir. purchasing Continental Homes, Inc., Phoenix, 1983-86; v.p., gen. mgr. Sahara Industries, Goodyear, Ariz., 1986-87; v.p., dir. purchasing Crescent Hotel Operating Co., Phoenix, 1987-88; owner, exec. dir. Sound Designs of Ariz., Scottsdale, 1988—. Composer (musical composition) Intimate Voyage, 1990, Streams of Consciousness, 1992. Mem. Phi Mu Alpha. Home and Office: 5321 E Grandview Rd Scottsdale AZ 85254

ZEAMER, RICHARD JERE, engineer; b. Orange, N.J., May 13, 1921; s. Jay and Margery Lilly (Herman) Z.; m. Jean Catherine Hellens, July 8, 1944 (div. 1966); children: Audrie Dagna, Richard Warwick, Geoffrey Hellens; m. Theresa Elizabeth Taborsky, Mar. 27, 1969; children: Emily Elizabeth, Charlotte Anne. BSME, MIT, 1943, MSCE, 1948; PhD in Mech. Engring., U. Utah, 1975. Registered profl. engr., Utah. Civil engr. Morton C. Tuttle, Boston, 1949-53; process design engr. Nekoosa Edwards Paper Co., Port Edwards, Wis., 1953-55; process engr. W.Va. Pulp and Paper Co., Luke, Md., 1955-60; rocket engr., supr. Allegany Ballistics Lab., Rocket Ctr., W.Va., 1960-65; engring. supr. Hercules Powder Co., Magna, Utah, 1965-69; engr. structures, heat flow, combustion & failure analysis Hercules Rocket Plant, Magna, 1969-83; project engring. mgr. Hercules Aerospace Div., Magna, 1983-89; pres., mgr. Applied Sci. Assocs., Salt Lake City, 1989—; chmn. policy studies UN Assn. Utah, 1990—; project leader world problem analyses, 1990—. Contbr. papers, articles, reports to profl. publs. Judge sci. fair, Salt Lake County, Utah, 1985—; chmn. citizens policy panel Utah chpt. UN Assn., U.S.A., N.Y.C., 1990—; mem. Utah State Hist. Soc., Salt Lake City, 1968-91, Mil. History Soc. Utah, Salt Lake City, 1990—. 1st lt. U.S. Army, 1943-46. Recipient commendation for presentation on world population problem Utah's Forum on Global Environ., 1992. Fellow AIAA (astronautics assoc.); mem. Cons. Engrs. Coun. Utah (article award 1992), League Utah Writers, Wasatch Mountain Club (hike leader 1987—). Home and Office: Applied Sci Assocs 843 13th Ave Salt Lake City UT 84103

ZEBAL, KENNETH WALTER, company executive; b. Boston, Sept. 27, 1945; s. Stanley Walter and Catherine Cecille (Shannon) Z.; m. Susan Izzo, Feb. 7, 1967 (div. 1974); children: Beth Ann, James Vincent, Matthew Walter; m. carlane hasty, Sept. 24, 1976 (div. 1977). AA, Palomar Coll., San Marcos, Calif., 1970; BS, U. San Diego, 1977; MBA, U.S. Internat. U., San Diego, 1983. Community coll. teaching credential, Calif. Commd. USMC, 1964, advanced through grades to maj., 1983; ret., 1984; dir. mem. rels. Better Bus. Bur., San Diego, 1985-86; program and mktg. mgr. Perspective, Inc., San Diego, 1986-87; logistics engr., contracts adminstr. JWK Internat., San Diego, 1987-88; program and bus. devel. mgr. Systems Engring. and Mgmt. Co., Carlsbad, Calif., 1988-89; Ils div. mgr. Nat. Steel & Shipbuilding Co. NASSCO, San Diego, 1989-90; logistics cons. Sci. Applications Internat. Corp., Hickam AFB, Hawaii, 1990-92; dep. program mgr. Analytical Systems Engring. Corp., L.A., 1992—; mem. faculty Nat. U., San Diego, 1985-88; cons. Salvation Army, San Diego, 1982-83, San Diego Opera, 1984-85, Vols. Am., San Diego, 1987-88. Co-author: Introduction to SEMS, 1981; author: SEMS Record Linking, 1982, Building a SEMS Database, 1982, Provisioning by the LSAR, 1987. Membership chmn. Park East Guild, San Diego Opera, 1986-89; bd. dirs. Vols. Am., 1987-89; chmn. Adult Rehab. Ctr., Salvation Army, 1987-88; vol. Interfaith Shelter Network, San Diego, 1990. Decorated Meritorious Svc. medal, Navy Commendation medal, Purple Heart; named Vol. of Yr., Vols. Am. ARC, 1989. Mem. Soc. Logistics Engrs., Marine Exec. Assn. (cons. 1987-88), Alpha Gamma Sigma. Republican. Methodist. Office: Analytical Systems Engring Corp AFB Los Angeles CA 90009

ZECHAR, CORWIN STUART, mathematician, mathematics educator; b. Pasadena, Calif., Feb. 5, 1959; s. Robert Dale and Joyce Lorraine (Terrill) Z.; m. Leslie Debra Simmel, Dec. 31, 1980 (div. June 1983); m. Bobbi Harrell, Dec. 14, 1985; children: Katherine Lorraine, Jacqeuline Christine. BS, Loyola Marymount U., L.A., 1982; MS, U. Calif., Riverside, 1987. Tchr. math. Reseda High Sch., L.A., 1984-85; mem. tech. staff Hughes Aircraft Co., Fullerton, Calif., 1985-86; instr. math. San Bernardino (Calif.) Valley Coll., 1986-88; analyst Xontech, Inc., Colorado Springs, Colo., 1988-90; project engr. Xontech Inc., San Bernardino, Calif., 1990—. Mem. Am. Math. Soc. Lutheran. Office: Xontech Inc 720 Carnegie Dr Ste 230 San Bernardino CA 92408-3516

ZECHNICH, DAVID W., accountant, business consultant; b. Syracuse, N.Y., Sept. 16, 1956; m. Karen L. Doane, Aug. 1, 1981; children: Kimberly, Jeffrey. BS, U. Oreg., 1978. CPA, Alaska. Mem. staff Price Waterhouse, Portland, Oreg., 1978-83; mgr. Price Waterhouse, Honolulu, 1983-86; sr. mgr. high tech. svcs. Price Waterhouse, Portland, 1986-89; sr. mgr. Price Waterhouse, Anchorage, 1989-90, mng. ptnr., 1990—; advisor acctg. dept. and dean's couns. U. Alaska, 1990—, co-chair legis. com.; cons. in field. Vol., bd. advisor United Way, Honolulu, 1984-86; bd. dirs. Alaska Festival Theatre. Mem. Alaska Soc. CPAs, Oreg. Soc. CPAs, N.W. Fin. Symposium (pres. 1989), Anchorage C. of C. (Buy Alaska com.), Kappa Sigma (pres. Gamma Alpha chpt. 1988-89). Office: Price Waterhouse 101 W Benson Blvd Anchorage AK 99503-3936

ZEEB, JAMES LAWRENCE, software company executive; b. Ann Arbor, Mich., Sept. 18, 1945; s. Lawrence Edward and Dorothy Ann (Waters) Z.; m. Marcia Morgan Witty, Sept. 30, 1967; children: Eric, Benjamin. BS, Allegheny Coll., 1967. Cert. in data processing. Systems engr. Electronic Data Systems, Dallas, 1972-79; cons., founder Just Tech. Assoc., Inc., Dallas, 1979-87; pres., chmn. Pyramid Computing Inc., Evergreen, Colo., 1987—. Capt. USAF, 1968-72. Mem. Data Processing Mgmt. Assn. Home: 333 Red Lily Pl Evergreen CO 80439-4216 Office: Pyramid Computing Inc PO Box 1119 Evergreen CO 80439-1119

ZEHNER, WILLIAM BRADLEY, II, marketing educator and consultant; b. Albuquerque, May 7, 1944; s. William B. and Mathilda Ida (Metz) Z.; m. Linda C. Trickett, Oct. 12, 1968 (div. 1974); 1 child, Clinton Bradley; m. Tamra Anne Weber, Mar. 26, 1988; children: Christopher Bradley, Jacquelyn Anne. BA in Polit. Sci., U. Calif., Riverside, 1966; MBA in Fin., U. So. Calif., 1968, MS in Mktg., 1970; MA in Psychology, Pepperdine U., 1983. Mng. dir. LEFAR, Hong Kong, 1974-75; v.p. sales Latin Am. and Asia Leesona Corp., Warwick, R.I., 1976-79; v.p. western ops. Leesona Corp., L.A., 1979-82; v.p. strategic planning John Brown PLC, London, 1982-84; pres. worldwide sales John Brown Plastics Machinery, Warwick, R.I., 1984-86; pres., founder Zetec, Westlake Village, Calif., 1987—; mem. MBA faculty, Pepperdine U., 1989—. Mem. Am. Mktg. Assoc., Am. Psychol. Assn. Republican. Roman Catholic. Home: 1665 Berwick Pl Westlake Village CA 91361-1502 Office: Pepperdine U 400 Corporate Pt Culver City CA 90230-7615

ZEHR, NORMAN ROBERT, association administrator; b. Niagara Falls, N.Y., May 19, 1930; s. George Andrew and Ina Kate (Morrell) Z.; Engr. of Mines, Colo. Sch. Mines, 1952, M.S., 1956; m. Janet Hutchinson, Apr. 24, 1976; children—Jeannette Ann, Leslie. Sales trainee Ingersoll-Rand Co., N.Y.C., 1955-56, sales engr., Lima, Peru, 1956-64, regional mgr. mining and constrn. sales, Lima, Peru and N.Y.C., 1964-68, gen. sales mgr. Latin Am., N.Y.C., 1968-69, gen. mgr. Latin Am. ops., N.Y.C., 1969-71, v.p. Ingersoll Rand Internat., Woodcliff Lake, N.J., 1971-72, pres., 1972-83, , v.p. Ingersoll-Rand Co., 1975-83; exec. dir. Colo. Sch. Mines Alumni Assn., 1984—. Served with AUS, 1952-54. Recipient Colo. Sch. Mines Disting. Achievement medal, 1977. Mem. AIME, Scabbard and Blade, Nat. Soc. Pershing Rifles, Mining Club , Sigma Nu. Office: Colo Sch Mines Twin Towers Golden CO 80401

ZEIDMAN, HEYWOOD WILLIAM, physician; b. Bklyn., Jan. 30, 1941; s. Irving and Henrietta (Hertz) Z.; m. Ronni Reider, Nov. 27, 1982; children: Kristee Pauker, Eileen Beres, Jared. BA, Bard Coll., 1963; MS, N.Y. Med. Coll., 1969, MD, 1973. Diplomate Am. Bd. Psychiatry & Neurology, 1978. Fellow Am. Soc. Adolscent Psychiatry, Washington, 1991—; med. dir. adolescent hosp. svcs. Southwood Hosp., Chula Vista, 1992—. Contbr. articles to profl. jours. Mem. Am. Psychiatric Assn., AMA, Am. Soc. Addiction Medicine (cert.), Calif. Psychiatric Soc., San Diego Soc. Psychiatric Physicians, San Diego Soc. Adolscent Psychiatry (pres. 1978-79). Democrat. Jewish. Home: 6248 Via Regla San Diego CA 92122 Office: Psychiatric Ctrs San Diego 6475 Alvarado Rd San Diego CA 92120

ZEIDMAN, ROBERT MARC, engineering consultant; b. Phila., Jan. 18, 1960; s. Morris and Ruth (Mallick) Z. BA in Physics, Cornell U., 1981, BEE, 1981; MEE, Stanford U., 1982. Engr. Signetics Corp., Sunnyvale, Calif., 1983-84, Rolm Corp., San Jose, Calif., 1985, Am. Supercomputers Inc., Sunnyvale, 1985-86, Telestream Corp., Mountain View, Calif., 1986-88; pres. Zeidman Cons., Cupertino, Calif., 1987—; mem. The Tech Mus., San Jose, 1990—. Director, writer: (film) February 20, 1988. Lectr. Discover E Program, Santa Clara Valley, Calif., 1992; sci. fair judge Toyon Sch., San Jose, 1992; alumni ambassador Cornell U., Cupertino, 1990-92; coach Am. Youth Soccer Orgn., Cupertino, 1991-92. Mem. IEEE, Assn. for Computing Machinery, Cornell Alumni Assn., Stanford Alumni Assn., Ind. Feature Project, Film Arts Found. Office: Zeidman Consulting 7599 Squirewood Way Cupertino CA 95014

ZEIG, JEFFREY KENNETH, psychologist; b. N.Y.C., Nov. 6, 1947; s. Martin Joel and Ruth (Epstein) Z.; divorced; 1 child, Nicole Rachel. BS in Zoology, Mich. State U., 1969; MS in Clin. Psychology, San Francisco State U., 1973; PhD, Ga. State U., 1977. Lic. psychologist, Ariz.; lic. and cert. marriage, family and child counselor, Calif., Ariz. Psychologist Ariz. State Hosp., Phoenix, 1978-79; dir. Milton H. Erickson Found., Phoenix, 1979--; lectr. in field. Author: Experiencing Erickson, 1985; editor: The Evolution of Psychotherapy, 1988; editor and/or co-editor numerous books and monographs. Recipient Milton H. Erickson award Netherlands Soc. Clin.

Hypnosis, 1980. Fellow Am. Soc. Clin. Hypnosis (Milton H. Erickson award 1981), Am. Psychol. Assn. Office: Milton H Erickson Found 3606 N 24th St Phoenix AZ 85016-6500

ZEIGER, STEPHEN ALLEN, executive search consultant; b. Joliet, Ill., Mar. 29, 1951; s. Jack and Doris (Barkin) Z.; m. Robin Sellin, Nov. 21, 1979; children: Alexis Barkin, Joshua Edward. BS in Edn., Loyola U., 1972; MS in Edn., No. Ill. U., 1973. Exec. recruiter Purcell Employment Agy., L.A., 1974-79; mgr. recruiting Creative Employment Agy., Encino, Calif., 1978-79; pres., CEO Zeiger Tech. Careers, Woodland Hills, Calif., 1979—. Jewish. Office: ZTC Inc 20969 Ventura Blvd Ste 217 Woodland Hills CA 91364

ZEIHEN, LESTER GREGORY, geology educator; b. Stevensville, Mont., Feb. 8, 1913; s. Gregory Sylvester and Francis M. (Haigh) Z.; m. Jeannette A. McMahon, July 10, 1941; children: Marilyn, Nancy, Donna, Gregory. BS in Geol. Engring., Mont. Sch. Mines, 1935, MS, 1937, profl. degree, 1961. Jr. engr. Anaconda Copper Mining Co., Butte, 1937-38; mine geologist Chile Exploration Co., Chuquicamata, 1938-52; rsch. geologist The Anaconda Co., Butte, 1952-73, cons. mineralogist, 1973-79; adj. assoc. prof. geology, adj. curator mineral mus. Mont. Coll. Mining Sci. and Tech., Butte, 1979—. Author in field. Pres. Silver Bow Humane Soc., Butte, 1971—; bd. dirs. Butte Sheltered Workshop, 1968—, Butte Silver Bow Arts Found., 1979-86, World Mus. Mining, Butte, 1984. Mem. AAAS, AIME (chmn. sect. 1964, Legion of Honor award), Am. Assn. for Advancement Sci., 1990—, Am. Mineral. Assn. (life), Soc. Econ. Geologists, Geochem. Soc., Mineral. Assn. Can., Mont. Tech. Alumni Assn. (sec.-treas. 1977—), Rotary (pres. Butte club 1980-81, Svc. Above Self award 1976, Paul Harris award 1990), Sigma Xi. Republican. Roman Catholic. Home: 834 W Silver St Butte MT 59701-1548 Office: Mont Coll Mineral Sci and Tech W Park St Butte MT 59701-1714

ZEILIG, NANCY MEEKS, magazine editor; b. Nashville, Apr. 28, 1943; d. Edward Harvey and Nancy Evelyn (Self) Meeks; m. Lanny Kenneth Fielder, Aug. 20, 1964 (div. Dec. 1970); m. Charles Elliot Zeilig, Jan. 6, 1974 (div. Dec. 1989); 1 child, Sasha Rebecca. BA, Birmingham-So. Coll., 1964; postgrad., Vanderbilt U., 1971-73. Editorial asst. Reuben H. Donnelley, N.Y.C., 1969-70; asst. editor Vanderbilt U., Nashville, 1970-74; editor U. Minn., St. Paul, 1975; asst. editor McGraw-Hill Inc., Mpls., 1975-76; mng. editor Denver mag., 1976-80; editor Jour. Am. Water Works Assn., Denver, 1981—. Editor, co-pub.: WomanSource, 1982, rev. edit. 1984; editor: 100 Years, 1975; contbr. articles to consumer mags. Office: Jour Am Water Works Assn 6666 W Quincy Ave Denver CO 80235-3098

ZEILINGER, ELNA RAE, educator; b. Tempe, Ariz., Mar. 24, 1937; d. Clayborn Eddie and Ruby Elna (Laird) Simpson; m. Philip Thomas Zeilinger, June 13, 1970; children: Shari, Chris. BA in Edn., Ariz. State U., 1958, MA in Edn., 1966, EdS, 1980. Bookkeeper First Nat. Bank of Tempe, 1955-56; with registrar's office Ariz. State U., 1956-58; piano tchr., recreation dir. City of Tempe; tchr. Thew Sch., Tempe, 1958-61; elem. tchr. Mitchell Sch., Tempe, 1962-74, intern prin., 1976, personnel intern, 1977; specialist gifted edn. Tempe Elem. Schs., Tempe, 1977-86; elem. tchr. Holdeman Sch., Tempe, 1986-89; tchr. Zeilinger Tutoring Svc., 1991—; grad. asst. ednl. adminstrn., Iota Workshop coordinator Ariz. State U., 1978; presenter Ariz. Gifted Conf., 1978-81; condr. survey of gifted programs, 1980; reporter public relations Tempe Sch. Dist., 1978-80, Access com. for gifted programs, 1981-83. Author: Leadership Role of the Principal in Gifted Programs: A Handbook, 1980; Classified Personnel Handbook, 1977, also reports, monographs and paintings. Freedom Train com. Ariz. Bicentennial Commn., 1975-76. Named Outstanding Leader in Elem. and Secondary Schs., 1976' Ariz. Cattle Growers scholar, 1954-55; Elks scholar, 1954-55; recipient Judges award Tempe Art League, 1970, Best of Show, Scottsdale Art League, 1976. Mem. Council Exceptional Children, Ariz. Assn. Gifted and Talented, Ariz. Sch. Adminstrs., Tempe Hist. Assn. (liaison 1975), Scottsdale Artists League, Tempe Art League, Am. Bus. Women's Assn. (Woman of Yr. 1983), Order of Eastern Star, Phi Kappa Phi, Pi Lambda Theta, Kappa Delta Pi, Phi Delta Kappa, Kappa Delta. Democrat. Congregationalist.

ZEITLER, BILL LORENZ, aviation engineer; b. Columbus, Ohio, July 14, 1920; s. Walter Andrew and Naomi Lee (Limes) Z.; BSCE, Calif. State U., Long Beach, 1965; m. Betty Eileen Thomas, Nov. 8, 1942; children: Eddie, Naomi Parker. Cert. vocat. tchr., Calif. Loftsman, Curtiss Wright Corp., Columbus, 1941-43, 44-46; linesman Lockheed Corp., Burbank, Calif., 1943-44; linesman N.Am. Rockwell (and predecessor firms), Inglewood, Calif., 1946-50, airframe designer, 1950-62, supr. engring. coll. unit, 1962-65, project engr. life scis., health care delivery systems, 1965-68, project dir. health care delivery systems, Princeton, W.Va., 1968-69, mem. tech. staff, Downey, Calif., 1956-85; project engr. space shuttle design, 1971-75, shuttle alignment and mating, 1975-77, space shuttle design support extra vehicular stowage and testing, 1978-85; ret., 1985; mem. Space Shuttle Speakers Bur. Instr. 55 Alive-mature driving classes; former pres. Big Bear Valley Sr. Citizens. Mem. AIAA, Nat. Space Inst., Nat. Geog. Soc., Smith Instn. Assocs., Rockwell Mgmt. Club, Toastmasters, Kiwanis.

ZEITLIN, GERALD MARK, electrical engineer; b. Phila., May 7, 1937; s. David Edward and Charlotte (Freedman) Z.; m. Frances Loretta Scherr, May 17, 1983 (div. 1988). BEE, Cornell U., 1960; MSEE, U. Colo., 1969. Electronic engr. Nat. Security Agy., Ft. Meade, Md., 1962-64, Westinghouse Georesearch Lab., Boulder, Colo., 1966-69; owner Sunrise Books, Estes Park, Colo., 1969-71; asst. research computer sci. U. Calif., San Francisco, 1972-78; assoc. devel. engr. U. Calif., Berkeley, 1978-82; sr. systems engr. EEG Systems Lab., San Francisco, 1982-86; computer cons., expert systems design Pacific Bell, San Francisco, 1986-87; mgr. microcomputer security Pacific Bell, San Ramon, Calif., 1987-89; dir. Alliance for Innovation tech. devel. ctr., Scottsdale, Ariz., 1990-91; pres. Centauri Secure Computing, Scottsdale, 1990; computer security cons. Bedford Cons., San Francisco, 1991; owner, operator Mono Communications, Lee Vining, Calif., 1991—, also bd. dirs. Contbr. articles to profl. jours. Served to 1st lt. U.S. Army, 1960-62. Summer Faculty fellow NASA-Am. Soc. Engring. Edn., Ames Research Ctr., 1981. Mem. IEEE, Comm. Soc. IEEE, Civil Air Patrol. Democrat. Jewish.

ZEITLIN, JOEL, mathematics educator; b. L.A., July 9, 1942; s. Jacob Israel and Josephine (Ver Brugge) Z.; m. Emily Ain; m. Ann Louise Fleischer, June 30, 1972; 1 child, Zoe. BA, UCLA, 1963, MA, 1966, PhD, 1969. Systems engr. IBM, L.A., 1963-64; asst. prof. Washington U., St. Louis, 1969-72; vis. prof. Cath. U., Valparaiso, Chile, 1972-73; asst. prof. math. Calif. State U., Northridge, 1973-76, assoc. prof., 1976-80, prof., 1981—. Assoc. editor Coll. Math. Jour., 1989-93; contbr. articles to profl. jours. Rsch. grantee NSF, 1967, 70, 71, R & D grantee Calif. State U.-Northridge Found., 1987, 89-92; Fulbright fellow, Chile, 1972-73. Home: 5011 Odessa Ave Encino CA 91436 Office: Calif State U Math Dept 18111 Nordhoff St Northridge CA 91330

ZEITLIN, MAURICE, sociology educator, author; b. Detroit, Feb. 24, 1935; s. Albert J. and Rose (Goldberg) Z.; m. Marilyn Geller, Mar. 1, 1959; children: Michelle, Carla, Erica. BA cum laude, Wayne State U., 1957; MA, U. Calif., Berkeley, 1960, PhD, 1964. Instr. anthropology and sociology Princeton (N.J.) U., 1961-64, research assoc. Ctr. Internat. Studies, 1962-64; asst. prof. sociology U. Wis.-Madison, 1964-67, assoc. prof., 1967-70, prof., 1970-77, dir. Ctr. Social Orgn., 1974-76; prof. sociology UCLA, 1977—, also research assoc. Inst. Indsl. Relations; vis. prof. polit. sci. and sociology Hebrew U., Jerusalem, 1971-72. Author: (with R. Scheer) Cuba: An American Tragedy, 1963, 1964, Revolutionary Politics and the Cuban Working Class, 1967, 1970, The Civil Wars in Chile, 1984, Landlords and Capitalists, 1988, The Large Corporation and Contemporary Classes, 1989; Latin Am. editor Ramparts mag., 1967-73; editor-in-chief: Political Power and Social Theory, 1980-90; mem. editorial adv. bd. The Progressive mag., 1985—; editor: (with J. Petras) Latin America: Reform or Revolution?, 1968, American Society, Inc., 1970, 1977, Father Camilo Torres: Revolutionary Writings, 1972, Classes, Class Conflict, and the State, 1980, How Mighty a Force?, 1983, Insurgent Workers: The Origins of Industrial Unionism, 1987. Chmn. Madison Citizens for a Vote on Vietnam, 1967-68; chmn. Am. Com. for Chile, 1973-75; mem. exec. bd. U.S. Com. for Justice to Latin Am. Polit. Prisoners, 1977-84; mem. exec. com. Calif. Campaign for Econ. Democracy, 1983-86. Ford Found. fellow, 1965-67, 70-71; Guggenheim fellow, 1981-82; NSF grantee, 1981, 82; recipient Project Censored award Top Censored Story, 1981; named to Ten Best Censored list, 1978. Mem. Am. Sociol. Assn. (governing council 1977-80, Disting. Contbn. Scholarship award in Pol. Sociology 1992), Internat. Sociol. Assn. (editorial bd. 1977-81), Latin Am. Studies Assn., Orgn. Am. Historians. Democrat. Jewish.

ZEKMAN, TERRI MARGARET, graphic designer; b. Chgo., Sept. 13, 1950; d. Theodore Nathan and Lois (Bernstein) Z.; m. Alan Daniels, Apr. 12, 1980; children: Jesse Logan, Dakota Caitlin. BFA, Washington U., St. Louis, 1971; postgrad, Art Inst. Chgo., 1974-75. Graphic designer (on retainer) greeting cards and related products Recycled Paper Products Co., Chgo., 1970—, Jillson Roberts, Inc., Calif.; apprenticed graphic designer Helmuth, Obata & Kassabaum, St. Louis, 1970-71; graphic designer Container Corp., Chgo., 1971; graphic designer, art dir., photographer Cuerden Advt. Design, Denver, 1971-74; art dir. D'Arcy, McManus & Masius Advt., Chgo., 1975-76; freelance graphic designer Chgo., 1976-77; art dir. Garfield Linn Advt., Chgo., 1977-78; graphic designer Keiser Design Group, Van Noy & Co., Los Angeles, 1978-79; owner and operator graphic design studio Los Angeles, 1979—. Recipient cert. of merit St. Louis Outdoor Poster Contest, 1970, Denver Art Dirs. Club, 1973.

ZELDIN, CAMILLE ARTHUR, retired management consultant; b. N.Y.C., Dec. 18, 1918; s. Isidore and Dorothy (Kaufman) Z.; m. Helen Hoffman, Aug. 18, 1940;. BS, Mass. Inst. Technol., Cambridge, 1939; AMP Program, Harvard Bus. Sch., Cambridge, Mass., 1962. Registered profl. metall. engr. Plant metallurgist Kennecott Corp. - Utah Refinery, Magna, 1950-56; project devel. engr. Kennecott Corp. - Research Ctr., Salt Lake City, 1956-59; supt. ops. Kennecott Corp. - Utah Refinery, Magna, 1959-60, plant mgr., 1960-63; gen. mgr. Kennecott Refining Corp., Balt., 1963-69; smelting & refining mgr. Kennecott Corp. - Utah Copper Division, Salt Lake City, 1969-75, spl. project mgr., 1975-79; v.p. Kennecott Minerals Co., Salt Lake City, 1979-82; cons. C.A. Zeldin, Salt Lake City, 1982-90; pres. Utah Chap. Am. Soc. for Metals, S.L.C. 1960-61; bd. dirs. Union Trust Co. of Md. Co-Author: Patent, Continuous Casting 1967. V.p. So. Balt. Gen. Hosp., 1964-69, Anne Arundel County Trade Coun.; chmn. Utah Water Pollution Control Com., 1985-89. Mem. AIME (Metall. Soc., chmn. tech. com. 1963-64, pres. Utah chpt. 1981-82). Home and Office: #904 330 N Leisure World Blvd Silver Spring MO 20906

ZELENY, WILLIAM BARDWELL, physics educator; b. Mpls., Mar. 14, 1934; s. Lawrence and Olive Z.; m. Pimporn Chavasant, 1960 (div. 1983); children: Thomas, Indira; m. Ylda Portillo, 1988. B.S., U. Md.-College Park, 1956; M.S., Syracuse U., 1958, Ph.D., 1960. Lectr. physics U. Sydney, Australia, 1960-62; from asst. prof. to assoc. prof. Naval Postgraduate Sch., Monterey, Calif., 1962—, assoc. chmn. dept. physics, 1980—. Author: (textbook) Introduction to Relativistic Quantum Mechanics, 1975. Contbr. articles to profl. jours. Mem. Am. Physical Soc., Sigma Xi. Home: PO Box 8656 Monterey CA 93943-0656 Office: Dept Physics Naval Postgraduate Sch Monterey CA 93943

ZELEZNY, WILLIAM FRANCIS, retired physical chemist; b. Rollins, Mont., Sept. 5, 1918; s. Joseph Matthew and Birdie Estelle (Loder) Z.; m. Virginia Lee Scarcliff, Sept. 14, 1949. BS in Chemistry, Mont. State Coll., 1940; MS in Metallurgy, Mont. Sch. Mines, 1941; PhD in Phys. Chemistry, State U. Iowa, 1951. Scientist NACA, Cleve., 1951-54; metallurgist div. indsl. research Wash. State Coll., Pullman, 1954-57; scientist atomic energy div. Phillips Petroleum Co., Idaho Falls, Id., 1957-66, Idaho Nuclear Corp., Idaho Falls, 1966-70; mem. staff Los Alamos (N.Mex.) Sci. Lab., 1970-80; instr. metallurgy State U. Iowa, Iowa City, 1948-49; asst. prof. metallurgy Wash. State Coll., 1956-57; instr. U. Idaho, Idaho Falls, 1960-68. Contbr. articles to profl. jours.; patentee in field. Served with AUS, 1944-46. Mem. Am. Chem. Soc. (sec. N.Mex. sect. 1978-79), Microbeam Analysis Soc., Am. Soc. Metals, The Minerals, Metals & Materials Soc., Sigma Xi, Alpha Chi Sigma. Democrat. Methodist. Home: PO Box 37 Rollins MT 59931-0037

ZELLMER, ARLENE, special education educator; b. Audubon, Iowa, Aug. 21, 1920; d. Clyde Lewis and Susan (Law) Hogueisson; m. Neale Albert Zellmer, June 21, 1953; children: Alan Neale, Scott Lewis. BA in Psychology, San Diego State U., 1948, teaching credential, 1951; postgrad., Coll. Notre Dame, Belmont, Calif.; learning handicapped specialist cert., U. Santa Clara, 1978. Cert. learning handicapped specialist, Calif. Tchr. of mentally gifted San Diego Sch. Dist., La Jolla, Calif., 1949-51; tchr. San Diego Sch. Dist., Valencia Park, Calif., 1951-53; tchr. San Carlos (Calif.) Sch. Dist., 1953-57, home tchr. spl. edn. dept., 1967-86; home tchr. spl. edn. dept. Belmont (Calif.) Sch. Dist., 1967-86; ret., 1986; pvt. tutor of learning handicapped, Belmont, 1979—. Contbr. poetry to World of Poetry, 1991. Active Peninsula Symphony Aux., Belmont, 1963-68; cub leader Boy Scouts Am., Belmont, 1966-68; vol. 4-H Clubs Am., Belmont, 1967-73, Am. Heart Assn., Belmont, 1968-78; deacon 1st Presbyn. Ch., San Mateo, 1966, 77; hon. life mem. 1st Presbyn. Ch. Women; mem. bd. Presbyn Women, U.S.A., 1990-91. Mem. AAUW, Calif. Tchrs. Assn., Ind. Order for Foresters, Daughters of Norway, Commonwealth Club (San Francisco), PEO Sisterhood. Republican. Home: 1588 Harbor Blvd Belmont CA 94002-3709

ZEMELMAN, JAMES LOUIS, lawyer; b. Cleve., Sept. 25, 1931; s. Fred J. and Lillian (Bleiweiss) Z.; m. Vicki L. Swier, Dec. 29, 1956 (div.); children—Mark S., Alice Ann, Suzanne I.; m. 2d, Elaine Lois Frankel, Jan. 1, 1982. A.B., Washington U., St. Louis, 1952, J.D., 1957. Bar: Mo. 1957, U.S. Dist. Ct. (ea. dist.) Mo. 1957, U.S. Ct. Appeals (8th cir.) 1968, U.S. Ct. Appeals (9th cir.) 1985, U.S. Supreme Ct. 1969, Nev. 1984, U.S. Dist. Ct. Nev. 1984. Assoc. Blumenfeld, Abrams & Daniel, 1957-62; ptnr. Guilfoil Carruthers, Symington, Montrey and Daniel, 1963-64, Daniel, Raskas, Ruthmeyer & Zemelman, 1964-65; mem. Law Offices of Morris A. Shenker, 1965-83; v.p., gen. counsel Preferred Equities Corp. and Vacation Spa Resorts, Las Vegas, Nev., 1983-86; assoc. Rudin, Richman & Appel, Beverly Hills, Calif., 1986-87; sr. v.p., dir. corp. legal and bus. affairs and human resources New World Entertainment, Ltd., L.A., 1987—; pros. atty. City of Creve Coeur, Mo., 1976-83; dir. Royal Bank of Mid County, St. Louis; dir. various corps. Bd. dirs. Ladue Sch. Dist., v.p., 1977-82; mem. Adult Edn. Council St. Louis, 1960-70, pres., 1968-70. Recipient Svc. award Adult Edn. Coun., 1970, Ladue Sch. Dist., 1983. Served to 1st lt. U.S. Army, 1953-55. Mem. ABA, Bar Assn. Met. St. Louis, Am. Arbitration Assn., Nev State Bd. Med. Examiners (hearing Officer), Am. Film Inst., Acad. TV Arts and Scis., Creve Coeur Racquet Club, Phi Delta Phi. Home: 202 San Vicente Blvd Santa Monica CA 90402-1527 Office: New World Entertainment Ltd 295 Beloit Ave Los Angeles CA 90049-3009

ZEMKE, (E.) JOSEPH, computer company executive. Chief operating officer Auto-Trol Tech., Denver, 1981-84; chief operating officer Amdahl Corp., Sunnyvale, Calif., 1985—, pres., 1987—. Office: Amdahl Corp PO Box 3470 1250 E Arques Ave Sunnyvale CA 94086-4730*

ZEMO-ISRAEL, NINA VERA, marketing professional; b. Stamford, Conn., Sept. 28, 1947; d. Anthony and Francesca (Cashmere) Z.; m. Stephen H. Israel, 1990. BA in Comparative Lit., Anna Maria Coll., Paxton, Mass., 1969; MA in Journalism with highest honors, San Francisco State U., 1973. Asst. buyer I. Magnin & Co., San Francisco, 1971-74; research assoc. Select Police Services Coordination Project, South San Francisco, Calif., 1974-75; dir. prodn., mktg. Inst. Contemporary Studies, San Francisco, 1975-79; dir. pub. relations The Bank of Calif., San Francisco, 1979-80; product mgr. jeanswear div. Levi Strauss & Co., San Francisco, 1980-84; mktg. cons., 1984-88; mktg. dir. U.S. Indsl. Directory/Cahners Pub. Co., Stamford, Conn., 1988-90; novelist Del Mar, Calif., 1990—. Recipient Outstanding Accomplishments award Outstanding Young Women of the Yr. Com., Washington, 1977. Home: 251 Ocean View Del Mar CA 92014

ZENEV, IRENE LOUISE, museum curator; b. Albuquerque, Nov. 18, 1948; d. Stanley D. and Louise Marie (Risler) Z.; 1 child, Carson M. Bell. BA, U. N.Mex., 1971. Dir. Umpqua Valley Arts Assn., Roseburg, Oreg., 1978-82; edn. coord. Douglas County Mus., Roseburg, 1985-86, curator history, 1986—; publs. rschr. Oreg. Mus. Assn., Portland, 1989-92. Reviewer The Roseburg News-Review, 1989—. Chairperson Douglas County Oreg. Trail Sesquicentenial Celebration Com., 1991—. Home: 413 Johnson St Myrtle Creek OR 97457-9501

ZENGER, JOHN HANCOCK, company executive; b. Salt Lake City, Nov. 13, 1931; s. John H. and L. (Hancock) Z.; m. Dixie Robison, June 1, 1955 (div. 1978); children: Mark R., Robin, Todd R., Blake R., Mitchell R., Drew R.; m. Holly Olsen, June 29, 1979; stepchildren: Roger, Kirk, Lori, Michael. BS, Brigham Young U., 1955; MBA, UCLA, 1957; D in Bus. Adminstrn., U. So. Calif., Los Angeles, 1963. Asst. prof. Grad Sch. Bus. U. So. Calif., L.A., 1966-67; exec. v.p. Blanfield-Smith and Co., Pasadena, Calif., 1965-67; v.p. human resources Syntex Corp., Palo Alto, Calif., 1967-77; pres. Zenger-Miller Inc., Cupertino, Calif., 1977-92; v.p. Times Mirror Co., San Jose, 1992—; v.p. Instl. Systems Assn., 1987-88. Chmn. Palo Alto Human Rels. Coun., 1961-66. Ford Found. fellow, 1962-63; recipient Disting. Svc. award Brigham Young U., 1983. Mem. Am. Soc. Tng. and Devel., Brigham Young U. Alumni Assn. (pres. 1981). Republican. Mormon. Home: 27300 Altamont Rd Los Altos CA 94022-4228 Office: 1735 Technology Dr San Jose CA 95110-1313

ZENTMYER, GEORGE AUBREY, plant pathology educator; b. North Platte, Nebr., Aug. 9, 1913; s. George Aubrey and Mary Elizabeth (Strahorn) Z.; m. Dorothy Anne Dudley, May 24, 1941; children: Elizabeth Zentmyer Dossa, Jane Zentmyer Fernald, Susan Dudley. A.B., UCLA, 1935, M.S., U. Calif., 1936, Ph.D., 1938. Asst. forest pathologist U.S. Dept. Agr., San Francisco, 1937-40; asst. pathologist Conn. Agrl. Expt. Sta., New Haven, 1940-44; asst. plant pathologist to plant pathologist U. Calif., Riverside, 1944-62, prof. plant pathology, 1962—, prof. emeritus, 1981—, faculty rsch. lectr., 1964, chmn. dept., 1968-73; cons. NSF, Trust Ty. of Pacific Islands, 1964, 66, Commonwealth of Australia Forest and Timber Bur., 1968, AID, Ghana and Nigeria, 1969, Govt. of South Africa, 1980, Govt. of Israel, 1983, Govt. of Western Australia, 1983, Ministry Agriculture and U. Cordoba, Spain, 1989; mem. NRC panels, 1968-73. Author: Plant Disease Development and Control, 1968, Recent Advances in Pest Control, 1957, Plant Pathology, an Advanced Treatise, 1977, The Soil-Root Interface, 1979, Phytophthora: Its Biology, Taxonomy, Ecology and Pathology, 1983, Ecology and Management of Soilborne Plant Pathogens, 1985; assoc. editor: Ann. Rev. of Phytopathology, 1971—, Jour. Phytopathology, 1951-54; contbr. articles to profl. jours. Bd. dirs. Riverside YMCA, 1949-58, Friends of Mission Inn, 1981—, pres., 1991-93, Calif. Mus. Photography, 1988—; pres. Town and Gown Orgn., Riverside, 1962; bd. dirs. Riverside Hospice, 1982-85, pres., 1984-85; bd. dirs. Friends U. Calif. Riverside Botanic Garden, 1985-89, 91—, pres., 1987-89. Recipient award of honor Calif. Avocado Soc., 1954, spl. award of honor, 1981; recipient Emeritus Faculty award U. Calif., Riverside, 1991; Guggenheim fellow, Australia, 1964-65, NATO sr. sci. fellow, Eng., 1971; NSF rsch. grantee, 1963, 68, 71, 74, 78; Bellagio scholar Rockefeller Found., 1985. Fellow AAAS (pres. Pacific div. 1974-75), Am. Phytopath. Soc. (pres. 1966, pres. Pacific div. 1955, found. bd. dirs. 1987—, v.p. 1991, Award of Distinction 1983, award of Merit Caribbean div. 1972, Lifetime Achievement award Pacific div. 1991), Explorers Club; mem. NAS, Mycol. Soc. Am., Am. Inst. Biol. Scis., Bot. Soc. Am., Brit. Mycol. Soc., Australasian Plant Pathology Soc., Philippine Phytopath. Soc., Indian Phytopath. Soc., Assn. Tropical Biology, Internat. Soc. Plant Pathology (councilor 1973-78), Pacific Assn. Tropical Phytopathology, Sigma Xi, Gamma Sigma Alpha. Home: 708 Via La Paloma Riverside CA 92507-6465

ZEPEDA, SUSAN GHOZEIL, county official; b. N.Y.C., Aug. 8, 1946; d. Harry S. and Anne (Golden) Kantor; m. Isaac Ghozeil, Jan. 29, 1967 (div. Oct. 1979); children: Daniel Jacob, Adam Leo; m. Fernando Zepeda, Jan. 2, 1983; children: Paloma Andrea, Sofia Elisa. BA, Brown U., 1967; MA, U. Ariz., 1971, postgrad., 1971-75; PhD, Internat. Coll., 1985. Rsch. assoc. div. bus. and econ. rsch. U. Ariz., Tucson, 1971-73, rsch. assoc. Coll. Medicine, 1975-76; assoc. dir. Pima Alcoholism Consortium, Tucson, 1976-79, exec. dir., 1979-80; dep. dir. pub. health Orange County Health Care Agy., Santa Ana, Calif., 1980-89; dir. policy, planning Orange County Health Care Agy., Santa Ana, 1989-90; dir. pub. fin. Orange County, 1990-92; dir. San Luis Obispo County Health Agy., 1993—; cons. Tucson Sch. Dist. No. 1, 1973-75, U.S. Dept. Labor, Washington, 1976-79, Indian Health Svc., Rockville, Md., 1984-85; ptnr. Zepeda Assocs., Fullerton, Calif., 1987—; presenter confs. Mem. Fullerton Planning Commn., 1984-91, chmn., 1990-91; mem. Calif. Task Force on Comparable Worth, 1984-85, Calif. Dist. Appeal Bd. No. 510, L.A., 1986—. Recipient Woman of Achievement award Orange County Bd. Suprs., 1988, Disting. Achievement awards Nat. Assn. Counties, 1985, 86, 87, 89. Mem. APHA, Internat. Coun. on Alcohol and Addictions, U.S. Mex. Border Health Assn., County Alcohol Program Adminstrs. Assn. Calif. (v.p. 1983, pres. 1984-85), Rotary Internat. (Santa Ana). Home: 1508 N Moonbeam Pl Fullerton CA 92633-1619 Office: San Luis Obispo County Health Agy 2191 Johnson Ave San Luis Obispo CA 93406

ZERBE, CHARLES JAMES, retail executive; b. Topeka, Kans., Feb. 22, 1951; s. Fred Charles and Lillian Mae (Dieball) Z.; m. Janice Lynne Stephan, May 10, 1980; children: Alana Lynne, Bennett Charles. BA in Psychology, U. Colo., 1974; grad., Gemological Inst. Am., 1975. Cert. gemologist. Treas. Zerbe Jewelers Inc., Colorado Springs, Colo., 1972-80, pres., 1980—. Mem. Am. Gem Soc. (pres. Mountain Area Guild 1979-80, nat. bd. dirs. 1981-85, 93—), Jewelers of Am. (nat. bd. dirs. 1986-89), Colorado Springs Exec. Assn. (pres. 1982, 88), Winter Night Club (v.p. 1989), El Paso Club, Sertoma (pres. Pikes Peak chpt. 1987-88). Office: Zerbe Jewelers Inc 118 N Tejon St Colorado Springs CO 80903-1420

ZERETZKE, FREDERICK FRANK H., artist, educator; b. Milw., July 4, 1919; s. Herman and Hertha Hildegarde (Riebow) Z.; m. Marian Louise Elfers, Dec. 7, 1942; children: Frederick J., David L., Mary J., John E. Student, Milw. Art Inst., 1938-39, Layton Sch. of Art, Milw., 1940-41, Rockford (Ill.) Coll., 1947. Art tchr. Burpee Art Gallery, Rockford, Ill., 1946-48; mural artist People's Real Estate Agy., Rockford, 1958, Grace Luth. Ch., Loves Park, Ill., 1960, Sweden House, Rockford, 1972, Linos, Rockford, 1974; art tchr. pvt. studio, Rockford, Ill., 1968-78; art. tchr. pvt. studio, Burlington, Wash., 1978—; artist and tchr. art in nat. def. Camp Callan, San Diego, 1942-43, Rock Valley Coll., Rockford, Ill., 1970-77, Skagit Valley Coll., Mt. Vernon, Wash., 1978-80. Prin. works include mural in Hadamar, Germany, exhibits in galleries in Wis., Calif., Wash., Ill., sculpture in Mt. Vernon, Wash., 1983, portraits, 1941—. Sec. Loves Park (Ill.) Zoning Bd., 1949-56. With U.S. Army, 1941-45, ETO. Scholar Milw. Art Inst., 1939, Layton Sch. Art, 1940; awarded commission for design for Swedish Tour of Sveas Soner Chorus of Rockford, 1965; named Artist of Yr. Winnebago County, 1974. Mem. Tamaroa Water Color Soc. Rockford (hon. lifetime, founder, pres. 1964), Skagit Art Assn. (pres. 1987-88). Mem. Unitarian Ch. Home: 722 Peterson Rd Burlington WA 98233

ZERLAUT, GENE ARLIS, chemist; b. Bailey, Mich., June 23, 1930; s. George David and Glenna Mae (Palm) Z.; student Western Mich. U., 1948-49; B.S., U. Mich., 1956; m. Cecelia Gail McGukin, Mar. 4, 1961; children—Scott Michael, Christopher Robert. Chemist, U.S. Army Ballistic Missle Agy., Huntsville, Ala., 1958-60; aerospace technologist, chemist NASA, Huntsville, 1960-62; sr. chemist, mgr. polymer chemistry research Ill. Inst. Tech. Research Inst., Chgo., 1962-73; pres., tech. dir. DSET Labs., Inc., Phoenix, 1973-91; pres., mng. dir. SC Internat., Inc., 1991—. Coach, Little League Baseball, 1974-76; bd. dirs., vice chmn. bd. Solar Energy Research and Edn. Found., 1978-79; commr. Ariz. Solar Commn., 1979-83. Served with U.S. Army, 1956-58. Recipient Invention awards NASA, 1968, Innovation award, 1973. Mem. Solar Energy Industries Assn. (bd. govs. 1976, v.p. 1978-79, exec. com. 1979-81, bd. dirs. 1981-86), Am. Inst. Chemists (dir. 1975), ASTM (nat. chmn. solar energy conversion com. 1978-83, award of merit 1987), Am. Council Ind. Labs., Am. Inst. Aeros. and Astronautics, Am. Nat. Standards Inst. (mem. solar energy standards coordinating com. 1979-83, tech. adv. group on plastics, 1974—,), Internat. Solar Energy Soc., Internat. Standards Orgn. (chmn. U.S. tech. adv. com. on solar energy), Soc. Plastics Engrs., Fedn. Paint Socs. Patentee in field. Contbr. articles to profl. jours. Research in spectral solar radiometry and accelerated environ. testing. Home: 346 W Pine Valley Dr Phoenix AZ 85023-5266 Office: Box 1850 Black Canyon Stage I Phoenix AZ 85029

ZERNOW, LOUIS, physicist; b. N.Y.C., Dec. 27, 1916; s. Meyer and Lena (Fradkin) Z.; m. Edith Hazel Weinstein, Nov. 2, 1940; children: Lenore R., Elaine, Melvin R., Richard H. BChemE, Cooper Union Inst. Tech., 1938; PhD in Physics, Johns Hopkins U., 1953. Chief detonation physics br. Ballistic Rsch. Lab., Aberdeen Proving Ground, Md., 1940-55; mgr. ordnance rsch. div. Aerojet Gen. Corp., Downey, Calif., 1955-63; pres. Shock Hydrodynamics Inc., Sherman Oaks, Calif., 1963-67, Shock Hydrodynamics div. Whittaker Corp., N. Hollywood, Calif., 1967-81, Zernow Tech. Svcs. Inc., San Dimas, Calif., 1981—. Contbr. over 200 tech. reports to Dept. Def. agys.; 6 patents in field. Recipient Meritorious Civilian Svc. award U.S. Army Ballistic Rsch. Lab., 1945. Mem. AIME, Am. Phys. Soc., Accoustical Soc. Am., Am. Soc. for Metals, Am. Def. Preparedness Assn. (exec. bd. ballistics div. 1973—, Outstanding Leadership award 1987). Home: 1103 E Mountain View Ave Glendora CA 91740-3165 Office: Zernow Tech Svcs Inc 425 W Bonita Ave San Dimas CA 91773-2541

ZERZAN, CHARLES JOSEPH, JR., gastroenterologist; b. Portland, Oreg., Dec. 1, 1921; s. Charles Joseph and Margaret Cecelia (Mahony) Z.; BA, Wilamette U., 1948; MD, Marquette U., 1951; m. Joan Margaret Kathan, Feb. 7, 1948; children: Charles Joseph, Michael, Kathryn, Paul, Joan, Margaret, Terrance, Phillip, Thomas, Rose, Kevin, Gregory. Commd. 2d. lt., U.S. Army, 1940, advanced through grades to capt., 1945, ret., 1946, re-enlisted, 1951, advanced through grades to lt. col., M.C., 1965; intern Madigan Gen. Hosp., Ft. Lewis, Wash., 1951-52; resident in internal medicine Letterman Gen. Hosp., San Francisco, 1953-56, Walter Reed Gen. Hosp., Washington, 1960-61; chief of medicine Rodriquez Army Hosp., 1957-60, U.S. Army Hosp., Fort Gordon, Calif., 1962-65; chief gastroenterology Fitzsimmons Gen. Hosp., Denver, 1965-66; chief profl. services U.S. Army Hosp., Ft. Carson, Colo., 1967-68; dir. continuing med. edn. U. Oreg., Portland, 1968-73; ptnr. Permanente Clinic, Portland, 1973—; assoc. clin. prof. medicine U. Oreg., 1973—; individual practice medicine, specializing in gastroenterology, Portland, 1968-92; staff Northwest Permanente, P.C.; dir., 1980-83. Mem. Portland Com. Fgn. Rels., 1986—. Decorated Legion of Merit, Army Commendation medal with oak leaf cluster; Meritorious Alumnus award Oreg. Health Scis. U., 1990. Diplomate Am. Bd. Internal Medicine. Fellow A.C.P.; mem. Am. Gastroenterol. Assn., Oreg. Med. Assn. (del. Clackamas County), Ret. Officers Assn. Republican. Roman Catholic. Home and Office: 6364 SE Mcnary Rd Portland OR 97267-5119

ZEWAIL, AHMED HASSAN, chemistry and chemical engineering educator, editor, consultant; b. Damanhour, Egypt, Feb. 26, 1946; came to U.S., 1969, naturalized, 1982; s. Hassan A. Zewail and Rawhia Dar; m. Dema Zewail; children: Maha, Amani, Nabeel. B.S., Alexandria U., Egypt, 1967, M.S., 1969; Ph.D., U. Pa., 1974; MA (hon.), Oxford U., 1991; DS (hon.), Am. U., Cairo, 1993. Teaching asst. U. Pa., Phila., 1969-70; IBM fellow U. Calif., Berkeley, 1974-76; asst. prof. chemistry and chem. engring. Calif. Inst. Tech., Pasadena, 1976-78, assoc. prof., 1978-82, prof., 1982-89, Linus Pauling prof. chem. physics, 1990—; cons. Xerox Corp., Webster, N.Y., 1977-80, ARCO Solar, Inc., Calif., 1978-81. Editor Laser Chemistry jour., 1981-85, Photochemistry and Photobiology, cols. I and II, Advances in Laser Chemistry, Advances in Laser Spectroscopy, Ultrafast Phenomena VII and VIII, The Chemical Bond: Structure and Dynamics; contbr. more than 200 articles in rsch. and devel. in lasers and applications to sci. jour.; patentee solar energy field. Recipient Tchr.-scholar award Dreyfus Found., 1979-85, Alexander von Humboldt Sr. U.S. Scientist award, 1983. John Simon Guggenheim Meml. Found. award, 1987, King Faisal Internat. prize in sci., 1989; Sloan Found. rsch. fellow, 1978-82, Egyptian- Am. Person of Yr., NASA award, Faraday Pub. Discourse, Sir Cyril Hinshelwood chair Lectureship, 1stAMM Achievement award, Nobel Laureate Signature award, Carl Zeiss award, Medal and Shield of Honor. Fellow Am. Phys. Soc.; mem. NAS, Am. Acad. Arts and Scis. (medal of the Royal Netherlands Acad. Arts and Scis.), Third World Acad. Scis., Am. Chem. Soc. (Harrison Howe award 1989, Hochest prize 1990), Sigma Xi (Earle K. Plyler prize 1993, Wolf pioze 1993). Office: Calif Inst Tech Div Chemistry and Chem Engring Mail Code 127 72 Pasadena CA 91125

ZEZZA, MYRNA MAZZOLA, employee relations consultant and trainer; b. Boston, May 28, 1938; d. Michael John and Mary Theresa (Costra) Mazzola; m. Ralph Michael Zezza, June 14, 1958 (div. Aug. 1975); m. William Gerald Chung, Apr. 16, 1988. Student, Tufts U., 1956; BA, U. Hawaii, 1960. Trainee Sun Press Newspapers, Honolulu, 1961-62; asst. buyer, sales mgr. Liberty House, Honolulu, 1962-66; pres., U.S. rep. House of Nora Noh, Inc., Honolulu, 1966-68; customer svc. rep. Paul Revere Cos., San Francisco, 1969-71; v.p., gen. mgr. Wedding Shoppe, Inc., Honolulu, 1972-83; human devel. trainer and cons. Gt. Lovers of World, Honolulu, 1983—; cons., trainer Wåxthuset, Våddo, Sweden, 1987—. Author: How To Be a Great Lover, 1989. Vol. San Francisco Sch. Dept., 1971, Friends of Carol Fukunaga, Honolulu, 1986, 88. Mem. Am. Soc. for Tng. and Devel., Nat. Speakers Assn., Hawaii Speaking Assocs. (v.p. 1986-87), Powerful Women Hawaii (founding com. 1985-86, v.p. 1987-88), Toastmasters Club. Office: Gt Lovers of World PO Box 588 Kaneohe HI 96744-0588

ZGONC, ROBERT JOSEPH, mining company executive; b. Eveleth, Minn., May 22, 1931; s. Frank Edward and Mary Frances (Labernik) Z.; m. Frances Adeline Jasovec, Sept. 10, 1956; children: Frank, Veronica Warden, Valerie Borg, Mark, Michael. AS, Ely (Minn.) Jr. Coll., 1956; BS in Mining Engring., Mich. Tech. U., Houghton, 1958; exec. mgmt. tng., Carnegie Mellon U., 1985. Mining engr. Hanna Mining Co., Iron River, Mich., 1959-66; chief engr. Pilot Knob Pellet Hanna Mining Co., Ironton, Mo., 1966-70, mine supt., 1970-73, gen. supt., 1973-79; v.p., gen. mgr. Am. Borate Co./ Hanna Mining Co., Las Vegas, Nev., 1979-86; mgr. mining Irone Ore Co. Can./Hanna Mining Co., Labrador City, Nfld., Can., 1986-88; cons. engr. mining Las Vegas, 1989—. Author, presenter mining symposium Devel. of Mining Methods, 1971; chmn. symposium on tunnel boring in mining, 1983. With USAF, 1951-55, ETO. Mem. Mo. Mining Assn. (pres. 1979-80). Roman Catholic. Home: 124 Null Ln Las Vegas NV 89128

ZHANG, LIXIA, computer scientist; b. Shanxi, Peoples Republic of China, June 16, 1951; came to U.S., 1979; d. Li and Jie (Liu) Zhang; m. Jiahua Ma, July, 1987; children: Zane Z., Shawn X. BS in Physics, Heilongjiang U., Harbin, Peoples Republic of China, 1976; MEE, Calif. State U., L.A., 1981; PhD, MIT, 1989. Tractor driver Peoples Republic of China, 1969-73; tech. Acheng Relay Factory, Heilongjiang Province, 1976-77; computer operator Harbin Inst. Electronics, 1977-78; rsch. asst. MIT, Cambridge, 1983-89; researcher Xerox, Palo Alto, Calif., 1989—. Contbr. articles to profl. jours. Mem. IEEE (editor IEEE/ACM Transactions on Networking, Jour. High Speed Networks, assoc. editor ACM Computer Comm. Review), Assn. for Computing Machinery. Office: Xerox Palo Alto Rsch Ctr 3333 Coyote Hill Rd Palo Alto CA 94304-1314

ZHELUTKA, MARA, music programmer; b. Whittier, Calif., Sept. 15, 1949; d. Walter Eugene and Wanda Marie (Grimes) Ferrell; m. Ty E. Allison, July 19, 1987. Student, Humboldt State U., Arcata, Calif., 1973. Radio programmer KHSU, Arcata, 1973-75; promotions dir. KCRW, Santa Monica, Calif., 1977-91; radio programmer KCRW, 1977—. Voice over/ narration Long Beach (Calif.) Mus.of Art Video series, 1984; artist, repertory cons. ROM Records, L.A., 1987-90; music dir. KCSN, Northridge, Calif., 1989-90; music programmer radio show Music of the Spheres. Mem. RadioWest (treas. 1984-87). Office: KCRW 1900 Pico Blvd Santa Monica CA 90405-1628

ZHENG, YOULU, computer scientist, educator; b. Hangzhou, Zhejiang, People's Republic of China, Nov. 3, 1942; came to U.S., 1984; s. Fat-Lai and Yi (Tong) Cheng;m. Li Sun, June 20, 1970; 1 child, Nan. BS, Sichuan (People's Republic of China) U., 1967; MS, Zhejiang U., 1981; PhD, Wash. State U., 1987. Engr. Chongqing (People's Republic of China) Automobile Co., 1967-75, Yunnan (People's Republic of China) Electronic Equipment Co., 1975-79, ISC Systems Co., Spokane, Wash., 1986; lectr. Chengdu (People's Republic of China) U. Sci. and Tech., 1981-84; computer scientist, sr. engr. EXP Group, Inc., Fremont, Calif., 1990—; prof. U. Montana, Missoula, 1987—; cons. Meswell Tech., San Leandro, Calif., 1990—; advisor SunLabs, Missoula, Mont., 1991—; dir. computer graphics and visualization lab., U. Mont., 1992—; nat. lectr. IT-China Summer Sch., Chinese Acad. of Scis., Beijing, 1993. Contbr. articles on computer sci. to acad. jours., 1981-93. NSF grantee and prin. investigator. Mem. Math. Assn. Am., Assn. Computer Machinery. Home: 110 Ben Hogan Dr Missoula MT 59803 Office: U Mont Missoula MT 59812

ZHOU, CHIPING, mathematician, educator; b. Shanghai, People's Republic of China, Jan. 21, 1957; s. Xingui Zhou and Qi Zhu; m. Xiaoyu He, June 22, 1986; 1 child, Kevin K. BS, Fudan U., Shanghai, 1983, MS, 1986; PhD, U. Hawaii, 1990. Asst. prof. Fudan U., Shanghai, 1986—; lectr. Chaminade U., Honolulu, 1990; instr. U. Hawaii, Honolulu, 1990--. Author: Some Problems for Elliptic and Hyperbolic Equations, 1986, Maximum Principles and Liouville Theorems for Elliptic Partial Differential Equations, 1991; contbr. articles to profl. jours. Recipient rsch. fellowship Rsch. Corp. of U. Hawaii, 1989. Mem. Am. Math. Soc., Math. Assn. Am. Office: Univ of Hawaii - HCC Math Dept 874 Dillingham Honolulu HI 96817

ZHOU, MING DE, aeronautical scientist, educator; b. Zhejiang, Peoples Republic of China, June 26, 1937; s. Pin Xiang and Ang Din (Xia) Z.; m. Zhuang Yuhua, Aug. 12, 1936; children: Zhengyu, Yan Zhuang. BS, Beijing Aero. Inst., 1962; MS, Northwestern U. Tech., 1967; PhD, Internat. Edn. Rsch. Found., 1992. Tchr. Harbin (China) U. Tech., 1962-64, 67-73; from lectr. to prof. Nanjing (China) Aero. Inst., 1973-86, 86—, dean bd. postgrad. studies, 1985-89; nationally qualified PhD advisor China, 1989—; rsch. scientist U. Ariz., Tucson, 1991-93, rsch. prof., 1993—; vis. scholar Cambridge (England) U., 1980-82; guest scientist Inst. Exptl. Fluid Mechanics, Göttingen, Germany, 1983-84, 85, 87; sr. vis. scientist Tech. U. Berlin, 1988, 90; rsch. assoc. U. So. Calif., L.A., 1989-90. Mem. editorial com. Chinese Jour. Exptl. Mechanics, 1986-89; author: (with others) Viscous Flows and Their Measurements, 1988, (with others) Introduction to Vorticity and Vortex Dynamics, 1992; contbr. articles to Aero. Jour. U.K., Experiments in Fluids, AIAA Jour., Chinese Jour. Aeronautics. Co-recipient Nat. award Progress in Sci. and Tech. first class, Peoples Republic of China, 1985. Mem. AIAA (sr.), Am. Phys. Soc., Chinese Soc. Aeronautics, Chinese Soc. Mechanics (mem. acad. group exptl. fluid mechanics 1986-89), Chinese Soc. Aerodynamic Rsch. (acad. group unsteady flow and vortex control 1985-89).

ZHOU, SIMON ZHENGZHUO, laser scientist; b. Shanghai, China, Jan. 31, 1942; came to U.S., 1987; s. Ming-Qing and Yue-Chun (Hu) Z.; m. Peggy B. Chen, May 16, 1985; children: Shiyun, Stanley. BS, U. Sci. and Tech., Shanghai, 1965, MS, 1967. Engr. Shanghai Metall. Factory, 1968-73; scientist Shanghai Inst. Laser Tech., 1974-87; sr. scientist Florod Corp., Gardena, Calif., 1988—. Contbr. articles to profl. jours. Recipient Invention prize Sci. Com. China, 1991, Sci. Progress prize Sci. Com. Shanghai, China, 1989, Honored Thesis award, 1985, Small Bus. Innovation Rsch. Phase I fund NSF, 1992. Mem. Internat. Soc. Optical Engring., Optical Soc. China, Laser Soc. Shanghai. Office: Florod Corp 17360 Gramercy Pl Gardena CA 90247-5263

ZHOU, TONG, mechanical engineering educator; b. Zhejiang, China, July 30, 1945; came to U.S., 1982; s. Wenqin and Hangxing (Li) Z.; m. Shuling Jiang, Mar. 18, 1976. BA, Zhejiang U., 1968; MS, Mich. State U., 1984, PhD, 1988. Design engr. Kunming Coal Mining Machinery Plant, People's Republic of China, 1968-81; rsch. asst. Mich. State U., East Lansing, 1982-88; assoc. prof. mech. engring. Calif. State U., Sacramento, 1988—. Author: Nomograms for Mechanical Design, 1983. Mem. ASME, Am. Soc. Engring. Edn. Office: Calif State U 6000 J St Sacramento CA 95819-2605

ZHU, JUN, educator; b. Suzhou, Jiangsu, People's Republic of China, June 13, 1957; arrived in Can, 1989; s. Chengyan and Ronghua (Jiang) Z.; m. Yunfang Xu, Jan. 1, 1985; 1 child, Chenchong. Student, Suzhou U., 1982. Tchr. Suzhou (Peoples Republic of China) U., 1982-89; researcher U. B.C., Vancouver, 1989—. Contbr. articles to profl. jours. Office: U British Columbia, Dept Math, 1984 Math Rd, Vancouver, BC Canada V6T 1Z2

ZHU, MINGDE, chemist; b. Shanghia, Peoples Republic of China, Apr. 5, 1940; came to the U.S., 1986; s. Nianci and Naiyun (Du) Z.; m. Yuxin Jin, Apr. 30, 1967; children: Peter, Norman. MS, Beijing U., 1965. Rsch. assoc. Acad. Agriculture, Beijing, 1965-70; chem. engr. Ganjiang Pharm. Factory, Jian, Peoples Republic of China, 1971-79; rsch. chemist Acad. Chinese Traditional Medicine, Beijing, 1980-83; vis. scholar Uppsala (Sweden) U., 1983-86; sr. rsch. chemist Bio-Rad Labs., Richmond, Calif., 1986—. Patentee IEF in capillary, non-gel sieving. Office: Bio-Rad Labs Life Science Group 2000 Alfred Nobel Dr Hercules CA 94547

ZHU, YU, neurologist, neurophysiologist, researcher; b. Shanghai, China, Aug. 10, 1946; came to U.S., 1988; s. Jia Nai Zhu and Yue Rou Sun; m. Ming Tao, May 20, 1975; 1 child, Jay. MD, Zhejiang Med. U., China, 1970; MS, Shanghai Second Med. Coll., 1981. Neurologist Lishui Hosp., Zhejiang, 1971-78, Shanghai Second Med. Coll., Renji Hosp., 1978-82; clin. neurophysiologist U. Montpellier (France) Med. Coll., 1983-88; vis. scientist U. Brussels Brain Rsch. Unit, 1984-85; asst. rschr. U. Calif., Irvine, 1988—. Contbr. articles to profl. jours. Mem. Am. Assn. Electrodiagnostic Medicine, N.Y. Acad. Scis., Soc. d'Eletroencephalographie et de Neurophysiologie Clinique de Lanque Française. Home: 3 Newton Ct Irvine CA 92715 Office: U Calif Irvine Campus Dr Irvine CA 92717

ZHUKOBORSKY, SAVELY L. See **SAVVA, SAVELY L.**

ZIDBECK, WILLIAM EDWARD, educator, consultant; b. Ancon, Canal Zone, Panama, June 7, 1932; came to U.S., 1944; s. George Gustav and Lilly Esmeralda (Gonzalez) Z.; m. Jo Ann Marie Hill, June 13, 1954; children: William Scott, Suzann Marie. BA in Biology, Stanford U., 1954; MA in Internat. Rels., U. So. Calif., 1969; grad. with distinction, Naval War Coll., 1969; grad. (hon.), Nat. Def. U., 1977. Ensign USN, 1954, advanced through grades to capt., 1975; comdg. officer Helicopter ASW Squadron 5, 1968-69, NAS Guantamano Bay, Cuba, 1978-79; comdg. officer Naval Edn., Tng. and Support Pacific Command, 1984, ret., 1984; tchr. biology Castle Park High Sch., Chula Vista, Calif., 1985-91. Mem. Naval Inst. (life), Naval Aviation Mus., Stanford Alumni Assn., U. So. Calif. Alumni Assn., Lighter-Than-Air Assn., Calif. Sci. Educators Assn., Naval Helicopter Assn. (bd. dirs. 1971-91, chmn. 1984-85), Optimists. Republican. Congregationalist. Home: 1107 5th St Imperial Beach CA 91932-3203

ZIEGENBUSCH, TED WAYNE, radio-television personality, actor, screenwriter; b. Lima, Ohio, Mar. 10, 1951; s. Charles Paul and Esther Colleen (Newman) Z.; m. Anne Pearl Cordell, Aug. 21, 1970 (div. Sept. 1977); 1 child, Jeffrey; m. April Ann Lorenz, Dec. 10, 1977; 1 child, Ryan. AA, San Bernardino Valley Coll., 1971. Music dir., radio personality KMEN Radio, San Bernardino, Calif., 1968-73, KCAL Radio, San Bernardino, 1973-80; program dir., radio personality The Mighty 690, San Diego, 1980-81; radio personality KGB Radio, San Diego, 1981, KIFM Radio, San Diego, 1981-82, KOST Radio, Los Angeles, 1982—; actor motion pictures, tv commercials, various, 1982—; cons. KOLA Radio, San Bernardino, 1980-87. Named Best Actor, Nat. Thespian Soc., 1969. Mem. Screen Actors Guild, Am. Fedn. TV and Radio Artists. Republican. Protestant. Office: COX Broadcasting 610 S Ardmore Ave Los Angeles CA 90005-2322

ZIEGLER, R.W., JR., lawyer, consultant; b. Pitts.; children: Caroline, Gretchen, Jeremy, Benjamin, Phoebe, Polly. Student, Carnegie Tech., U. Pitts.; JD, Duquesne U., 1972. Bar: Pa. 1972, Calif. 1981, U.S. Ct. Appeals (3d cir.) 1977, (9th cir.) 1982, U.S. Dist. Ct. (we. dist.) Pa. 1972, Calif., 1982, U.S. Tax Ct. 1978, U.S. Supreme Ct. 1977. Ptnr. Ziegler & Ombres, Pitts., 1973-79; pres. Ziegler Ross Inc., San Francisco, 1979—; lectr. for Bar Assns. Author: Law Management Practice; editor: Law Office Guide in Computing. Mem. ABA, Am. Mgmt. Assn., Pa. State Bar Assn., Calif. State Bar Assn. Office: Ziegler Ross 3772 Sacramento St San Francisco CA 94118-1706

ZIELENZIGER, MICHAEL, journalist; b. N.Y.C., June 28, 1955; s. Eric W. and Ruth (Herrmann) Z.; m. Diane Abt, Nov. 30, 1985. BA in Internat. Affairs, Princeton U., 1977; postgrad. (John S. Knight fellow), Stanford U., 1991. Polit. and urban affairs corres. Chgo. Sun-Times, 1977-81; nat. corres. Kansas City (Mo.) Star-Times, 1982-83; Seattle bur. chief San Jose Mercury News and Knight Ridder Newspapers, 1984-90; Pacific Rim corres. San Jose Mercury News, San Jose, 1992—; regular panelist KCTS-TV, Seattle, 1989-91; mem. adv. bd. Ctr. Pacific Rim U. San Francisco, 1993. Columnist The Weekly, Seattle, 1992. Recipient William S. Miller award U. Fla., 1982, Thomas M. Storke award World Affairs Coun., No. Calif., 1992; named Best in the West, U. Ariz., 1989. Office: San Jose Mercury News 750 Ridder Park Dr San Jose CA 95190

ZIEMANN, G. PATRICK, bishop; b. Pasadena, Calif., Sept. 13, 1941. Attended, St. John's Coll. and St. John's Sem., Camarillo, Calif., Mt. St. Mary's Coll., L.A. Ordained priest Roman Cath., 1967. Titular bishop, aux. bishop Diocese Santa Rosa, Obba, 1986-92; bishop Diocese Santa Rosa, Santa Rosa, Calif., 1992—. Office: Chancery Office PO Box 1297 547 B St Santa Rosa CA 95402*

ZIERNICKI, RICHARD MIECZYSLAW, engineering firm executive; b. Krakow, Poland, Feb. 3, 1950; came to U.S., 1981; m. Mila Kristine Czarnecka, Apr. 1, 1952; children: Maciek, Daniel. BS in Mech. Design, U. Mining and Metallurgy, Krakow, 1973, MS in Mech. Engring., 1975, PhD in Tech. Sci. cum laude, 1979. Registered profl. engr., Colo., Calif., Tex. and Wyo. Asst. prof. engring. Inst. Vibrations and Acoustics, Krakow, 1975-80; mgr. rsch. and devel. Inst. Tech., Krakow, 1980-81; mgr. mech. engring. Over-Lowe Co., Denver, 1981-84; sr. cons., pres. Knott Lab., Denver, 1984—; invited speaker Denver U. Dept. Engring. Contbr. articles to profl. jours.; patentee in field. Mem. ASME, NSPE, Soc. Automotive Engrs., Soc. for Exptl. Stress Analysis, Robotic Internat. Soc. Mfg. Engrs., Profl. Engrs. Colo., Nat. Assn. Profl. Accident Reconstruction Specialists, Nat. Forensic Ctr., Nat. Acad. Forensic Engrs. Home: 8809 S Blue Mountain Pl Highlnds Rnch CO 80126-2802 Office: Knott Lab Inc 2727 W 2d Ave Denver CO 80219

ZIESELMAN, ELLEN, museum curator; b. N.Y.C., Nov. 14, 1965; d. Jerold and Paula (Mack) Z. BA, Brown U., 1987; MA, Williams Coll., 1989. Mus. educator Mus. of N.Mex., Office of Statewide Programs and Edn., Santa Fe, 1989-92; curator of edn. Mus. of Fine Arts, Mus. N.Mex., Santa Fe, 1992—; bd. dirs. Southwest Art Histry Coun., 1992—. Youth group advisor Temple Beth Shalom, Santa Fe, 1990—, religious sch. educator, 1990—. Mem. N.Mex. Jewish Hist. Soc. (bd. dirs. 1991—, v.p. 1993—). Democrat. Jewish. Office: Mus of Fine Arts Po Box 2087 Santa Fe NM 87504

ZIFERSTEIN, ISIDORE, psychoanalyst, educator, consultant; b. Klinkowitz, Bessarabia, Russia, Aug. 10, 1909; came to U.S., 1920; s. Samuel David and Anna (Russler) Z.; m. Barbara Shapiro, June 21, 1935; children: D. Gail, J. Dan. BA, Columbia U., 1931, MD, 1935; PhD, So. Calif. Psychoanalytic Inst. 1977. Intern Jewish Hosp. of Bklyn., N.Y., 1935-37; staff psychiatrist Mt. Pleasant (Iowa) State Hosp., 1937-41; chief resident psychiatrist Psychiat. Inst. of Grasslands Hosp. of Westchester County, Valhalla, N.Y., 1941-44; pvt. practice, psychoanalysis and psychiatry N.Y.C., 1944-47, L.A., 1947—; mem. faculty So. Calif. Psychoanalytic Inst., L.A., 1951-70, mem. bd. trustees, 1953-57, mem. edn. com., 1953-57; cons. L.A. (Calif.) Psychiat. Svcs., 1954-63; researcher The Psychiat. & Psychosomatic Rsch. Inst., Mt. Sinai Hosp., L.A., 1955-65; assoc. clin. prof. of psychiatry Univ. So. Calif., L.A., 1960-64, Univ. Calif., L.A., 1970-77; rsch. cons. Postgrad. Ctr. for Mental Health, N.Y.C., 1962-75; attending staff dept. psychiatry Cedars-Sinai Med. Ctr., L.A., 1975—; psychiat. cons. Iowa State Penitentiary, Ft. Madison; lectr. on transcultural psychiatry, group psychotherapy and group dynamics UCLA, U. Calif., Berkeley, USC, U. Wash., Willamette Coll., Eugene, Oreg., U. Oreg., U. B.C., U. Md., U. Wis., U. Judaism, U. Mex., Wayne State U., U. Pitts., Chgo. Med. Coll., Ctr. for Study of Democratic Instns., U. Leningrad, Bekhterev Psychoneurol. Rsch. Inst., Leningrad, BBC, San Francisco State Coll., others. Contbr. over 65 articles to Am. Jour. Psychiatry, Am. Jour. Orthopsychiatry, Internat. Jour. Group Psychotherapy, Praxis Der Kinderpsychologie Und Kinderpsychiatrie, and others. Bd. dirs. Viewer-Sponsored TV Found., L.A., 1960, Nat. Assn. for Better Broadcasting, L.A., 1962-75, ACLU So. Calif. chpt., L.A., 1962-77; pres. Peace Edn. Coun., Pasadena, Calif., 1960; del. to state conv. Calif. Dem. Coun., Sacramento, 1960; mem. del. to Soviet Union, Promoting Enduring Peace, New Haven, 1959; participant Conf. of Scientists for Peace, Oslo, Norway, 1962; del. to "Pacem in Terris" Convocation, SANE, N.Y.C., 1963, mem. nat. bd., 1970-74, and many others. Recipient Pulitzer scholarship award Pulitzer Found., N.Y.C., 1927, Green Prize for Outstanding scholarship Columbia Coll., N.Y.C., 1930, Peace award Women for Legis. Action, L.A., 1962, grant for rsch. in transcultural psychiatry Founds. Fund for Rsch. in Psychiatry, New Haven, 1963, grant for continuing rsch. in transcultural psychiatry NIMH, Bethesda, Md., 1969, Pawlowski Peace Prize, Pawlowski Peace Found., Inc., Wakefield, Mass., 1974. Fellow Am. Psychiat. Assn. (life, fellowship medal 1970), AAAS (life); mem. AMA (life), Am. Psychoanalytic Assn. (life, cert. in psychoanalysis by bd. profl. standards), Internat. Psychoanalytical Assn., World Fedn. for Mental Health, Westside Jewish Culture Club (lectr.), Physicians for Social Responsibility, Sierra Club, Nat. Wildlife Fedn., Environ. Def. Fund, Common Cause, MADD, Phi Beta Kappa. Democrat. Jewish. Office: 1819 N Curson Ave West Hollywood CA 90046-2205

ZIGMAN, PAUL EDMOND, environmental consultant executive; b. L.A., Mar. 10, 1924; s. Fernand and Rose (Orligan) Z.; children: Andrea, Eric. BS in Chemistry, UCLA, 1948. Supr., applied research U.S. Naval Radiol. Def. Lab., San Francisco, 1949-59, head tech. mgmt. office, 1961-69; supr., analytical chemistry Atomics Internat., Canoga Park, Calif., 1960-61; pres. Environ. Sci. Assocs., San Francisco, 1969—. Contbr. articles to profl. jours. Served as pvt. U.S. Army, 1943. Recipient USN Meritorious Civilian Service award, 1966. Mem. Am. Chem. Soc., Nat. Assn. Environ. Profls. (v.p. 1977), Assn. Environ. Profls. (pres. 1974-76) (Outstanding Service award 1977, Cert. Appreciation 1984). Home: 101 Lombard St Apt 406W San Francisco CA 94111-1149

ZIL, JOHN STEPHEN, psychiatrist, physiologist; b. Chgo., Oct. 8, 1947; s. Stephen Vincent and Marilyn Charlotte (Jackson) Zilius; 1 child, Charlene-Elena. BS magna cum laude, U. Redlands, 1969; MD, U. Calif., San Diego, 1973; MPH, Yale U., 1977; JD with honors, Jefferson Coll., 1985. Intern, resident in psychiatry and neurology U. Ariz., 1973-75; fellow in psychiatry, advanced fellow in social and community psychiatry, Yale community cons. to Conn. State Dept. Corrections, Yale U., 1975-77, instr. psychiatry and physiology, 1976-77; instr. physiology U. Mass., 1976-77; acting unit chief Inpatient and Day Hosp. Conn. Mental Health Ctr., Yale-New Haven Hosp. Inc., 1975-76, unit chief, 1976-77; asst. prof. psychiatry U. Calif., San Francisco, 1977-82, assoc. prof. psychiatry and medicine, 1982-86, vice-chmn. dept. psychiatry, 1983-86; adj. prof. Calif. State U., 1985-87; assoc. prof. bioengring. U. Calif., Berkely and San Francisco, 1982—, clin. faculty, Davis, 1991—; chief psychiatry and neurology VA Med. Ctr., Fresno, Calif., 1977-86, prin. investigator Sleep Rsch. & Physiology Lab., 1980-86; dir. dept. psychiatry and neurology U. Calif.-San Francisco, Fresno-Cen. San Joaquin Valley Med. Edn. Program and Affiliated Hosps. and Clinics, 1983-86; chief psychiatrist State of Calif. Dept. Corrections cen. office, 1986—; chmn. State of Calif. Inter-Agy. Tech. Adv. com. on Mentally Ill Inmates & Parolees, 1986—; mem. med. adv. com. Calif. State Personnel Bd., 1986—; appointed councillor Calif. State Mental Health Plan, 1988—; cons. Nat. Inst. Corrections, 1992—; invited faculty contbr. and editor Am. Coll. Psychiatrist's Resident in Tng. Exam., 1981—. Author: The Case of the Sleepwalking Rapist, 1992, Mentally Disordered Criminal Offenders, 5 vols., 1989, reprinted, 1991; assoc. editor Corrective and Social Psychiatry Jour., 1978—, referee, 1980—, reviewer, 1981—; contbr. articles in field to profl. jours. Nat. Merit scholar, 1965; recipient Nat. Recognition award Bank of Am., 1965, Julian Lee Roberts award U. Redlands, 1969, Kendall award Internat. Symposium in Biochemistry Research, 1970, Campus-Wide Profl. Achievement award U. Calif., 1992. Fellow Royal Soc. Health, Am. Assn. Social Psychiatry; mem. Am. Assn. Mental Health Profls. in Corrections (nat. pres. 1978—), Calif. Scholarship Fedn. (past pres.), AAUP, Am. Psychiat. Assn., Nat. Council on Crime and Delinquency, Am. Pub. Health Assn., Delta Alpha, Alpha Epislon Delta. Office: PO Box 163359 Sacramento CA 95816-9359

ZILER, RAYMOND, accountant. With Arthur Andersen & Co., Albuquerque, 1970-82, ptnr., 1982—. Dir., chmn. United Way, Albuquerque; active Prison Fellowship Ministries, Goodwill Industries. Mem. Albuquerque C. of C. (dir., treas.). address: 6501 Americas Parkway NE Ste 400 Albuquerque NM 87110

ZILLY, THOMAS SAMUEL, judge; b. Detroit, Jan. 1, 1935; s. George Samuel and Bernice M. (McWhinney) Z.; divorced; children: John, Peter, Paul, Luke; m. Jane Greller Noland, Oct. 8, 1988; stepchildren: Allison Noland, Jennifer Noland. BA, U. Mich., 1956; LLD, Cornell U., 1962. Bar: Wash. 1962, U.S. Ct. Appeals (9th cir.) 1962, U.S. Supreme Ct. 1976. Ptnr. Lane, Powell, Moss & Miller, Seattle, 1962-88; judge U.S. Dist. Ct. (we. dist.) Wash., Seattle, 1988—; judge pro tem Seattle Mcpl. Ct., 1972-80. Contbr. articles to profl. jours. Mem. Cen. Area Sch. Council, Seattle, 1969-70; scoutmaster Thunderbird Dist. council Boy Scouts Am. Seattle, 1976-84;

bd. dirs. East Madison YMCA. Served to lt. (j.g.) USN, 1956-59. Recipient Tuahku Dist. Service to Youth award Boy Scouts Am., 1983. Mem. ABA, Wash. State Bar Assn., Seattle-King County Bar Assn. (treas. 1979-80, trustee 1980-83, sec. 1983-84, 2d v.p. 1984-85, 1st v.p. 1985-86, pres. 1986-87). Office: US Dist Ct 410 US Courthouse 1010 5th Ave Seattle WA 98104-1130

ZIMKAS, CHARLES PATRICK, JR., space foundation director; b. Scranton, Pa., Sept. 8, 1940; s. Charles Zimkas Sr. and Margaret (Bakunas) Sullick; m. Ursula Frediel Marten; children: Robert L., Uwe F., Michael P., Brian David. Enlisted USAF, advanced through grades to chief master sgt., 1958; dep. chief of staff, personnel adminstrv. div. Aerospace Def. Command, Colorado Springs, Colo., 1971-74; exec. to dep. chief of staff personnel Aerospace Def. Command, Colorado Springs, 1975-80; chief of adminstrn. Air Forces Iceland, Keflavik, 1974-75; first sr. enlisted advisor USAF Space Command, Colorado Springs, 1980-84; ret., 1984; dir. regional devel. Noncommissioned Officers Assn., San Antonio, 1984-86; dir. ops. U.S. Space Found., Colorado Springs, 1986—. Named Air Force Outstanding Airman of Yr., 1978; recipient Air Force Legion Merit. Mem. Noncommissioned Officers Assn. (bd. dirs. 1978-84, chmn. bd. dirs. 1982-84, Excalibur award 1979, Order of Sword 1978). Home: 729 Drew Dr Colorado Springs CO 80911-2606 Office: US Space Found 2860 S Circle Dr #2301 Colorado Springs CO 80906

ZIMMER, DONALD WILLIAM, former professional baseball manager; b. Cin., Jan. 17, 1931; s. Harold Lesley and Lorraine Bertha (Ernst) Z.; m. Jean Carol Bauerle, Aug. 16, 1951; children: Thomas Jeffrey, Donna Jean. Student pub. schs., Cin. Baseball player Dodger Farm Clubs, 1949-54, Bklyn. Dodgers, 1954-57, Los Angeles Dodgers, 1958-59, Chgo. Cubs, 1960-61, N.Y. Mets, 1962, Cin. Reds, 1962, Los Angeles Dodgers, 1963, Washington Senators, 1963-65, Toei Flyers, Tokyo, 1966; mgr. Cin. Reds Farm Clubs, Knoxville and Buffalo, 1967, Indpls., 1968; mgr. San Diego Padre Farm Clubs, Key West, Fla., 1969, Padre Farm Club, Salt Lake City, 1970; coach Montreal Expos, Que., Can., 1971; mgr. San Diego Padres, 1972-73; coach Boston Red Sox, 1974-76, mgr., 1976-80; mgr. Tex. Rangers, 1981, 82; coach N.Y. Yankees, 1983, fall 1986, Chgo. Cubs, 1984, 85, 86, San Francisco Giants, 1987; mgr. Chgo. Cubs, 1988-91; coach Boston Red Sox, 1992; mgr. Colo. Rockies, Denver, 1993—; mem. minor league All-Star Teams, Hornell, N.Y., 1950, Elmira, N.Y., 1951, Mobile, Ala., 1952, St. Paul, 1953; player World Series teams, 1955, 56, 59, coach, 1975. Recipient Bill Stern award NBC, 1949; named St. Paul Rookie of Yr., 1953; mem. All Star Team, 1961, 78, 81, 90; named Nat. League Mgr. of Yr. 1989. Mem. Profl. Baseball Players Am. (life), Old Time Ball Players Wis.

ZIMMER, MARK VANCE, architect; b. Pitts., June 14, 1960; s. Arnold Arthur and Thelma (Vance) Z. BS in Archtl. Engring., U. Kans., 1983, B in Environ. Design, 1983. Registered architect. Mgr. design dept. Vavrus Assocs., Joliet, Ill., 1983-86; project architect, cadd mgr., sr. assoc. Krommenhoek McKeown Assocs., San Diego, 1986—. Club: So. Calif. Arris Users Group (rep. 1986—). Office: Krommenhoek McKeown Assocs 1515 Morena Blvd San Diego CA 92110-3784

ZIMMERMAN, ADAM HARTLEY, mining and forest industries company executive; b. Toronto, Ont., Can., Feb. 19, 1927; s. Adam Hartley and Mary Ethelwyn (Ballantyne) Z.; m. Janet Lewis, May, 1951; children: Thomas, Barbara, Mary, Kate. Attended, Upper Can. Coll., Toronto, Ridley Coll., St. Catharines, Ont., Royal Can. Naval Coll., U. Toronto; postgrad. in philosophy, 1951. Chartered acct., Ont. With sales dept. Procter & Gamble, 1950; with Clarkson, Gordon & Co., Toronto, 1950-58; asst. comptroller Noranda Mines Group of Cos., from 1958; comptroller Noranda Inc., Toronto, 1961, v.p., 1966-74, exec. v.p., 1974-82, pres., chief oper. officer, 1982-87, vice chmn., 1987-92; chmn. Noranda Forest Inc., Toronto, 1987-93, also bd. dirs.; chmn. MacMillan Bloedel Ltd., 1987-91, vice chmn. 1991-93, bd. dirs.; chmn., Confederation Life Ins. Co., 1992—, vice chmn., 1992-93, bd. dirs.; bd. dirs. Econ. Investment Trust Ltd., The Pittston Co., Toronto-Dominion Bank, Southam Inc., Maple Leaf Foods Inc., Noranda Inc., Northwood Pulp and Timber Ltd., Roy Thomson Hall; mem. adv. bd. Faculty of Foresty U. Toronto. Past chmn. C. D. Howe Inst.; hon. trustee Hosp. for Sick Children; bd. dirs. Hosp. Sick Children Found., World Wildlife Fund Can. Lt. Royal Can. Navy Res., 1946-52. Mem. The York Club, Toronto Golf Club, Mt. Royal Club, Madawaska Club, Craigleigh Ski Club. Office: 1 Toronto St Ste 500, Toronto, ON Canada M5W 2C4

ZIMMERMAN, ARNOLD I., recruiting company executive; b. N.Y.C., Apr. 5, 1946; s. Sydney Harry and Gladys (Chitkin) Z.; m. Jianulla Chapralis, Oct. 20, 1978; children: Kevin, Timothy, Paula, Brian. BS in Chem. Engring., CCNY, 1968; MBA, Iona Coll., 1972. Chem. engr. Gen. Foods, Inc., White Plains, N.Y., 1969-73; group leader Hunt-Wesson, Inc., Fullerton, Calif., 1973-78; exec. search cons. Paul Norsell and Assoc., L.A., 1978-79; pres. Horizon/Arjan Assoc., Redondo Beach, Calif., 1979—. V.p. South Bay L.A. Pvt. Industry Coun., Indlewood, Calif., 1986-90, Beyond War, Torrance, Calif., 1987—. Mem. Inst. Food Technologists, Nat. Assn. Exec. Recruiters (recruitment chmn. 1985-87). Democrat. Jewish. Home: 322 S Broadway Redondo Beach CA 90277-3709 Office: Arjan/Horizon Assoc 1617 Pacific Coast Hwy Redondo Beach CA 90277

ZIMMERMAN, HAROLD SAMUEL, newspaper executive, state senator, state administrator; b. Valley City, N.D., June 1, 1923; s. Samuel Alwin and Lulu (Wylie) Z.; m. Julianne Williams, Sept. 12, 1946; children—Karen, Steven, Judi Jean (dec.). B.A., U. Wash., 1947. News editor Sedro-Woolley (Wash.) Courier-Times, 1947-50; editor, pub. Advocate, Castle Rock, Wash., 1950-57; pub. Post-Record, Camas, Wash., 1957-80; assoc. pub., columnist, 1980; assoc. pub., columnist, dir. Eagle Publs., Camas, 1980-88. Mem. Wash. Ho. of Reps., 1967-80; mem. Wash. Senate, 1981-88, Wash. State Environ. Hearings Bd., Lacey, 1988—. Served with USAAF, 1943-46. Mem. Grange, Sigma Delta Chi, Sigma Chi. Republican. United Methodist. Clubs: Lions, Kiwanis.

ZIMMERMAN, JOHN THOMAS, biological psychologist, sleep disorder specialist; b. Denver, Feb. 27, 1949; s. Richard Gordon Zimmerman and Neva-Jeanne (Bloom) Lavine; m. Marlene Sanae Yamada, Feb. 8, 1970 (div. 1970); m. Lisa Doe Wood, June 21, 1987. BA in Psychology, U. Colo., 1972, MA in Psychology, 1978, PhD in Biol. Psychology, 1981. Diplomate Am. Bd. Sleep Medicine. Rsch. asst. U. Colo. Sch. Medicine, Denver, 1968-72, 79-80, rsch. assoc., 1981-83, asst. prof., 1983-87; profl. cons. Presbyn. Hosp., Denver, 1980-83; pres. Bio-Electro-Magnetics Inst., Reno, Nev., 1986—; lab. dir. Washoe Sleep Disorders Ctr., Reno, Nev., 1989—. Editor: BEMI Currents, 1989—. Fellow Am. Sleep Disorders Assn. Democrat. Home: 2490 W Moana Ln Reno NV 89509-3936 Office: Washoe Sleep Disorder Ctr 75 Pringle Way Ste 701 Reno NV 89502

ZIMMERMAN, KATHLEEN CHERYL, lawyer; b. Kent, Ohio, Mar. 8, 1954; d. Walter Todd and Jane Sophia (Shook) Z. BA, U. Chgo., 1976; JD, Yale Law Sch., 1980. Bar: Washington 1982, Colo. 1991; U.S. Ct. Appeals (D.C. cir.) 1986; U.S. Supreme Ct. 1989. Clk. to Hon. Ann Aldrich U.S. Dist. Ct., Cleve., 1980-81; clk. to Hon. Betty B. Fletcher U.S. Ct. Appeals (9th cir.), Seattle, 1981-82; assoc. Bennett & Bertram, Seattle, 1982-84; counsel Nat. Wildlife Fedn., Washington, 1985-90; sr. atty. Land and Water Fund of the Rockies, Boulder, Colo., 1990—. Contbr. articles to profl. jours. Office: Law Fund 2260 Baseline Boulder CO 80302

ZIMMERMAN, LINDA FRAN, author, periodical publisher, writer; b. Chgo., Sept. 30, 1946; d. Louis Joseph and Sydell Muriel (Lakowitz) Z. Student, Roosevelt U., 1963-65, Santa Monica Coll., 1981-83. Prodn. asst. films, asst. video editor various features, 1970-81; freelance photographer, 1979-86, freelance writer, 1983—; editor, pub. The Food Yellow Pages, L.A., 1987—; contbg. editor Food Arts mag., L.A., 1988-93; creative svcs. dir. El Cholo Restaurants, L.A.; instr. food journalism UCLA and various colls.; speaker radio and TV; specialist food and restaurants L.A. Author: Puddings, Custards and Flans, 1990, (with Peggy Mellody) Cobblers, Crumbles and Crisps, 1991, (with Gerri Gilliland) Grills and Greens, 1993, Chicken Soup, 1993; contbr. articles to mags. and newspapers. Mem. Internat. Assn. Cooking Profls., Women's Culinary Alliance (bd. dirs. 1988-92), So. Calif. Culinary Guild (bd. dirs.), N.Y.C. Authors Guild, Ciao Italia (hon., ednl. bd.). Home: 135 S Harper Ave West Hollywood CA 90048-3505 Office: The Food Yellow Pages PO Box 461449 West Hollywood CA 90046-9449

ZIMMERMAN, MICHAEL DAVID, state supreme court justice; b. Chgo., Oct. 21, 1943; m. Lynne Mariani; children: Evangeline Albright, Alessandra Mariani, Morgan Elisabeth. BS, U. Utah, 1966, JD, 1969. Bar: Calif. 1971, Utah 1978. Law clk. to Chief Justice Warren Earl Burger U.S. Supreme Ct., Washington, 1969-70; assoc. O'Melveny & Myers, L.A., 1970-76; assoc. prof. law U. Utah, 1976-78, adj. prof. law, 1978-84, 89—; of counsel Kruse, Landa, Zimmerman & Maycock, Salt Lake City, 1978-80; spl. counsel Gov. of Utah, Salt Lake City, 1978-80; ptnr. Watkiss & Campbell, Salt Lake City, 1980-84; justice Supreme Ct. of Utah, Salt Lake City, 1984—; co-moderator Just. Soc. Program of Snowbird Inst. for Arts and Humanities, 1991, 92; faculty judging sci. program Duke U., 1992. Editor: Utah Law Rev., 1968-69; contbr. numerous articles to legal publs. Mem. Project 2000, Coalition for Utah's Future. Named Utah State Bar Appellate Ct. Judge of Yr., 1988; recipient fellowship Justice and Soc. Program of Aspen Inst. for Humanistic Studies, 1988, co-moderator, 1989. Mem. ABA (faculty mem. judges' seminar 1993), Am. Law Inst., Utah Bar Assn., Salt Lake County Bar Assn., Jud. Conf. U.S. (adv. com. civil rules 1985-91), Utah Jud. Coun. (supreme ct. rep. 1986-91), Utah Constnl. Revision Commn., Snowbird Inst. for Arts and Humanities (bd. dirs.), Am. Inns of Ct. VIII, Am. Jud. Soc., U. Utah Coll. of Law Alumni Assn. (pres. 1991-92), Order of Coif, Phi Kappa Phi. Office: Utah Supreme Ct 332 State Capitol Salt Lake City UT 84114-1181

ZIMMERMAN, NIEL THOMAS, university administrator; b. Blackduck, Minn., Aug. 27, 1943; s. Roy Arthur and Nielen Carlisle (Lien) Z.; m. Judith Ann Wortman, Mar. 21, 1964; children—Kurt Raymond, Joelle Marie. B.A., U. Calif.-Riverside, 1965, M.A., 1966, Ph.D., 1970. Instr. polit. sci. Mankato State Coll., Minn., 1966-67; asst. prof. govt. Eastern Wash. U., Cheney, 1970-78, prof., 1986—; dir. DSHS Contract, 1973-82, assoc. prof. govt., 1978—, dean Sch. Pub. Affairs, 1978-90, accreditation liaison officer, 1990—, dean Coll. of Letters and Scis., 1990-92, spl. asst. to pres., 1992-93; v.p., legis. rep. Cheney Sch. Bd., 1986—, pres. 1987-93; chmn. com. Boy Scouts Am., Cheney, 1984. Mem. Am. Judicature Soc., Wash. State Sch. Dir.'s Assn. (mem. interscholastic activities com., 1988-90, nomination com.). Democrat. Lutheran. Lodge: Kiwanis (Spokane). Home: 519 S Presley Dr Cheney WA 99004-1338 Office: Ea Wash U Coll Letters and Scis Cheney WA 99004

ZIMMERMAN, RICHARD CLYDE, orthopedic surgeon; b. LaGrande, Oreg., Jan. 17, 1932; s. Doyle Bert and Irma (Lyman) Z.; m. Mary Schouweiler, Dec. 27, 1955 (div. June 1979); children: Robert, Jane, Peter, John; m. Linda Lou Gamblin, Apr. 8, 1984. BS, U. Oreg., 1955, MD, 1957, MBA, 1989. Diplomat Am. Bd. Orthopedic Surgeons. Orthopedic surgeon Portland (Oreg.) Orthopedic Clinic, 1964—, med. dir., 1985—; bd. dirs. Emanuel Hosp., Portland, Managed Care Northwest, Portland. Bd. dirs. Sch. Dist. #48, Beaverton, Oreg., 1970-75, Jesuit High Sch., Portland, 1976-79. Capt. USAF, 1958-60. Fellow Am. Coll. of Surgeons, Am. Acad. of Orthopedic Surgeons, AMA, Western Orthopedic Surgeons, Oreg. Med. Assn.; mem. Phi Beta Kappa, Alpha Omega Alpha. Republican. Roman Catholic. Home: 2936 SW Bennington Dr Portland OR 97201-1805 Office: Portland Orthopedic Clinic 3025 N Vancouver Ave Portland OR 97227-1598

ZIMRING, STUART DAVID, lawyer; b. L.A., Dec. 12, 1946; s. Martin and Sylvia (Robinson) Z.; m. Eve Axelrad, Aug. 24, 1969 (div. 1981); m. Carol Grenert, May 24, 1981; children: Wendy Lynn Grenert, Joseph Noah, Matthew Kevin Grenert, Dov Shimon. BA in U.S. History, UCLA, 1968, JD, 1971. Bar: Calif. 1972, U.S. Dist. Ct. (cen. dist.) Calif. 1972, U.S. Dist. Ct. (no. dist.) Calif. 1984; cert. specialist in estate planning, probate and trust law. Assoc. Law Offices Leonard Smith, Beverly Hills, Calif., 1971-73; ptnr. Law Offices Smith & Zimring, Beverly Hills, Calif., 1973-76; assoc. Levin & Ballin, North Hollywood, Calif., 1976-77; prin. Levin, Ballin, Plotkin, Zimring & Goffin, A.P.C., North Hollywood, 1978-91, Law Offices Stuart D. Zimring, North Hollywood, 1991—; lectr. Los Angeles Valley Coll., Van Nuys, Calif., 1974-82. Bd. dirs. Bet Tzedek, Jewish Legal Svcs., L.A., 1975-88, chmn. legal svcs. com., 1978-82; bd. dirs. Brandeis-Bardin Inst., Simi Valley, Calif., 1976-80; bd. dirs. Bur. Jewish Edn., L.A., 1973-88, chmn. com. on parent and family edn., 1985-87; trustee Adat Ari El Synagogue, L.A., 1982—. Recipient Circle award Juvenile Justice Connection Project, L.A., 1989. Mem. State Bar Calif., San Fernando Valley Bar Assn. (trustee 1979-86), Nat. Acad. Elder Law Attys. Democrat. Office: 12650 Riverside Dr North Hollywood CA 91607

ZINGALE, DONALD PAUL, health and human services educator; b. Bklyn., Aug. 3, 1946; s. Charles and Helen (Puglisi) Z. BS in Health, Phys. Edn., Bklyn. Coll., 1967; MS in Phys. Edn., U. Mass., 1969; PhD in Phys. Edn., Ohio State U., 1973; MSW, Calif. State U., Sacramento, 1984. Lic. clin. social worker, Calif.; lic. marriage and family counselor, Calif.; cert. health and phys. edn. instr. secondary schs., N.Y.C., N.Y.; cert. Alpine ski instr. Teaching asst. Sch. Phys Edn. U. Mass., Amherst, 1967-69; instr. health, phys. edn. NYU, 1969-70; teaching assoc. Sch. Health, Phys. Edn. and Recreation Ohio State U., 1970-72; clin. social work intern Napa County Mental Health Ctr., 1982-83; mental health counselor Sacramento Mental Health Ctr., 1985-86; clin. social work intern U. Calif., Davis, 1983-85; clin. social worker III U. Calif., 1987-88, clin. instr. in psychiatry, 1988—; prof., assoc. dean health, human svcs. and phys. edn. Calif. State U., Sacramento, 1973—; clin. social worker Calif. State U., 1984-85; dir. skiing, Calif. State U., Sacramento, 1973—; ski instr. and educator various orgns., 1967—; pvt. practice psychotherapy, Sacramento, 1985—; lectr. CUNY,1969-70, Bklyn. Coll., 1969-70, Baruch Coll., 1969-70; exec. dir. R.S.V.P., Columbus, 1972-73. Contbr. articles to profl. jours. and publs. Mem. NEA, AAUP, NASW, AAHPERD, Calif. Assn. Health Phys. Edn. Recreation and Dance (pres. no. dist. 1976-77), Congress Faculty Assns., Profl. Ski Instrs. Am. Roman Catholic. Office: Calif State U Sch Health Human Svcs 6000 J St Sacramento CA 95819-2605

ZINGG, PAUL JOSEPH, academic administrator; b. Newark, July 22, 1947; s. Carl William and Dolores (Lucking) Z.; m. Candace Adelaide Slater, Aug. 9, 1980. BA, Belmont Abbey Coll., Charlotte, N.C., 1968; MA, U. Richmond, 1969; PhD, U. Ga., 1974. Instr. Marymont Sch., Richmond, Va., 1969-70; asst. prof. St. Bernard's Coll., Cullman, Ala., 1975-77; exec. dean Williams U., Chgo., 1977-78; vice dean U. Pa., Phila., 1978-83; asst. to pres. U. Pa., 1983-86; dean liberal arts St. Mary's Coll. Calif., Moraga, 1986-93, Calif. Poly. State U., San Luis Obispo, 1993—; bd. dirs. Am. Assn. for Core Curriculum, Denver. Author: Harry Hooper, An American Baseball Life, 1993, Pride of the Palestra, 1987; author, editor: The Sporting Image, 1987; co-author: Through Foreign Eyes, 1982, The Academic Penn, 1986; contbr. over 60 articles and revs. to profl. publs. Fellow Ctr. for Internat. Study/Rsch., 1980-82, Nat. Endowment for Humanities fellow, 1975, grantee, 1989, U. Pa., 1983, 84. Mem. N.Am. Soc. for Sport History, Am. Coun. on Edn. (exec. coun. 1988—, fellow 1983-84), Orgn. Am. Historians, Soc. for Am. Baseball Rsch., Merion Golf Club (Ardmore, Pa.), Sigma Phi Epsilon, Phi Alpha Theta (pres. 1973-74). Home: 47 Northampton Ave Berkeley CA 94707-1714 Office: Calif Poly State U Coll Liberal Arts San Luis Obispo CA 93407

ZINK, RAYMOND OWEN, sales executive; b. Providence, Mar. 30, 1943; s. Albert Noel Zink and Mary Jane (Wilson) Lakenes; m. Janice Noble, June 28, 1980; children: Jennifer Dawn, Raymond II. AA, Peninsula Cll., 1968; postgrad., Southwestern Coll., 1970. Regional mgr. Larwin Home Builders, L.A., 1973-75; loan rep. Home Savs. & Loan, San Bernardino, Calif., 1975-77; nat. exec. Church's Fried Chicken, Calif., Ga., Ala., 1977-79; nat. dir. Primerica Fin. Svcs., Lynnwood, Wash., 1979—. Doner Children's Orthopedic Hosp., Seattle, 1989-90, 91. With USN, 1960-64. Office: Primerica Fin Svcs 6920 220th SW Ste 300 Mountlake Terrace WA 98043

ZINSER, ELISABETH ANN, university president; b. Meadville, Pa., Feb. 20, 1940; d. Merle and Fae Zinser. BS, Stanford U., 1964; MS, U. Calif., San Francisco, 1966, MIT, 1982; PhD, U. Calif., Berkeley, 1972. Nurse VA Hosp., Palo Alto, Calif., 1964-65, San Francisco, 1969-70; instr. Sch. Nursing U. Calif., San Francisco, 1966-69; pre-doctoral fellow Nat. Inst. Health, Edn. and Welfare, 1971-72; adminstr. Sch. Medicine U. Wash., Seattle, 1972-75, Coun. Higher Edn., State of Ky., 1975-77; prof., dean. Coll. Nursing U. N.D., Grand Forks, 1977-83; vice chancellor acad. affairs U. N.C., Greensboro, 1983-89; pres. Gallaudet U., Washington, 1988, U. Idaho, Moscow, 1989—; cons. Ctr. Leadership Devel. Am. Coun. Edn., Washington, Boeing Aircraft Co., Seattle, Nat. Workshop Acad. Deans, Higher Edn. Exec. Assocs., Denver, Bush Found., St. Paul. Author: (with others) Contemporary Issues in Higher Education, 1985, Higher Education Research, 1988; co-author: Nurse: A Changing Word in a Changing World, 1982. Bd. dirs. Humana Hosp., Greensboro, 1986-88; v.p., bd. dirs. Ea. Music Festival, Greensboro, 1987-89; trustee N.C. Coun. Econ. Edn., 1985-89, Greensboro Day Sch., 1987-89. Leadership fellow Bush Found., 1981-82. Mem. Am. Assn. Higher Edn., Assn. Am. Colls. (Coun. Liberal Learning), Am. Assn. Univ. Adminstrs., AAUP, AAUW, Rotary, Pi Lambda Theta, Sigma Theta Tau. Home: 1026 Nez Perce Dr Moscow ID 83843-4138 Office: U Idaho Office of the President Moscow ID 83843*

ZION-SHELTON, OLGA-JEAN, school counselor; b. Omaha, Aug. 10, 1957; d. Howard Kenton and Doris Jean (Harkness) Z. Student, U. Minn., 1975-77; BA, Adams State U., Alamosa, Colo., 1980; MS, Emporia (Kans.) State U., 1987. Cert. in counseling, English, speech and theatre, Kans., Colo. Tchr. speech Upward Bound, Alamosa, 1980; tchr. English Wyandotte High Sch., Kansas City, Kans., 1980-81; tchr. English and speech Bishop Ward High Sch., Kansas City, 1984-86; grad. asst. Emporia State U., 1986-87; counselor Winfield (Kans.) High Sch., 1987-88, Perry (Kans.)-Lecompton High Sch., 1988-91, Clear Creek High Sch., Idaho Springs, Colo., 1991-93; instr. psychology Highland (Kans.) Community Coll., 1989. Editor newsletter for Kans. Sch. Counselors Assn., 1988-91. Grantee in field. Mem. Am. Counselors Assn., Am. Sch. Counselors Assn., Rocky Mountain Soc. Adlerian Psychology (pres. 1993), Kans. Assn. Counseling and Devel. (bd. dirs. 1990-91), Kans. Sch. Counselors Assn. (pub. rels. chmn. 1988-89, pres. 1990-91). Democrat. Roman Catholic. Home: 1489 Hwy 103 Idaho Springs CO 80452-9613

ZIPPER, STUART CHARLES, journalist; b. Bklyn., Mar. 24, 1946; s. Alfred and Annette (Garn) Z.; m. Orah Tovah Friedland, Oct. 12, 1968; children: Michal, Ari, Natan, Avital, Nechama. BA, Queens Coll., 1967; postgrad., U. Miami, Coral Gables, Fla., 1970-72. Staff writer various newspapers N.Y. and Fla., 1967-74; corr. Electronic News, Miami, Fla., 1975-77, Dallas, 1981-84; corr. Electronic News, Denver, 1984-88, regional mgr., 1988-91, sr. bureau mgr., 1991—; corr. Fairchild News Svc., Jerusalem, 1977-81; copy sub-editor Jerusalem Post, 1977-81; writing, research and photography cons. Sec. Hillel Acad., Denver, 1985-87; asst. scoutmaster Boy Scouts Am., 1988-92, scoutmaster, 1992—. With U.S. Army, 1968-70, Vietnam. Decorated. Democrat. Jewish. Home: 351 S Glencoe St Denver CO 80222-1414 Office: Electronic News 3025 S Parker Rd Denver CO 80204

ZIRIN, HAROLD, astronomer, educator; b. Boston, Oct. 7, 1929; s. Jack and Anna (Buchwalter) Z.; m. Mary Noble Fleming, Apr. 20, 1957; children: Daniel Meyer, Dana Mary. A.B., Harvard U., 1950, A.M., 1951, Ph.D., 1952. Asst. phys. scientist RAND Corp., 1952-53; lectr. Harvard, 1953-55; research staff High Altitude Obs., Boulder, Colo., 1955-64; prof. astrophysics Calif. Inst. Tech., 1964—; staff mem. Hale Obs., 1964-80; chief astronomer Big Bear Solar Obs., 1969-80, dir., 1980—; U.S.- USSR exchange scientist, 1960-61; vis. prof. Coll. de France, 1986, Japan Soc. P. Sci., 1992. Author: The Solar Atmosphere, 1966, Astrophysics of the Sun, 1987; co-translator: Five Billion Vodka Bottles to the Moon, 1991; adv. editor: Soviet Astronomy, 1965-69; editor Magnetic and Velocity Fields of Solar Active Regions. Trustee Polique Canyon Assn., 1977-90. Agassiz fellow, 1951-52; Sloan fellow, 1958-60; Guggenheim fellow, 1960-61. Mem. Am. Astron. Soc., Internat. Astron. Union, AURA (dir. 1977-83). Home: 1178 Sonoma Dr Altadena CA 91001-3150 Office: Calif Inst Tech Big Bear Solar Observatory 40386 N Shore Ln Big Bear City CA 92314

ZIRKLE, LEWIS GREER, physician, executive; b. Pittsfield, Mass., July 23, 1940; s. Lewis Greer and Vivian (Shaw) Z.; m. Sara K. Zirkle, Aug. 24, 1963; children: Elizabeth, Molly, Julie. BS, Davidson Coll., 1962; MD, Duke U., 1966. Intern Duke U. Hosp., 1966-67, resident, 1968-73; resident U.S. Army, Shriner's Hosp., 1967-68; pvt. practice Richland, Wash., 1973—; bd. dirs. Orthopedics Overseas, chmn. program in Vietnam, 1992—. Contbr. articles to profl. jours. Maj. U.S. Army, 1968-73. Presbyterian. Home: 2548 Harris Ave Richland WA 99352-1638 Office: NW Orthopedics 875 Swift Blvd Richland WA 99352-3513

ZIRPOLI, ALFONSO JOSEPH, judge; b. Denver, Apr. 12, 1905; s. Vincenzo and Stella (Graziani) Z.; m. Giselda Campagnoli, Sept. 19, 1936; children: Sandra Elena, Jane Amanda. AB, U. Calif., Berkeley, 1926, JD, 1928. Bar: Calif. 1928, U.S. Supreme Ct. 1941. Pvt. practice law, 1928-32, 44-61; asst. dist. atty. City and County San Francisco, 1932-33; asst. U.S. atty. No. Dist. Calif., 1933-44; instr. criminal law Hastings Coll. Law, 1945; sr. judge U.S. Dist. Ct. (no. dist.) Calif., San Francisco, 1961—. Mem. Bd. Suprs. City and County San Francisco, 1958-61. Recipient Star Solidarity, 1953, grand officer Order Merit, 1956; Italy). Fellow Am. Coll. Trial Lawyers; mem. ABA, Fed. Bar Assn., Calif. Bar Assn. Office: US Dist Ct PO Box 36060 450 Golden Gate Ave San Francisco CA 94102

ZISCHKE, JAMES BRADEN, entrepreneur; b. Spokane, Wash., June 4, 1923; s. Herman Albert and Hannah (Harrington) Z.; m. Joan Meert Smith, May 25, 1949 (div. Jan. 1959); children: Gray, Dai, Lance, Jaimee, Starr, Cree; m. Joan Hagey Miller, June 10, 1959; children: Jay, David, Jeffrey, Dana, Bret. BA, Yale U., 1944; MA, Stanford U., 1946, PhD, 1950. V.p. Zischke Orgn. Inc., San Francisco, 1950-59; chmn. bd. Zischke Orgn. Inc., 1959-78; pvt. investor Aptos, Calif., 1978—; instr. bus. adminstrn. extension U. Calif., San Francisco, 1962-78. Contbr. articles to profl. jours. Co-founder Western Pension Conf., San Francisco, 1953, pres., 1960-62. Capt. U.S. Army, 1944-45. Mem. Univ. Club San Francisco. Republican. Home and Office: 550 Bayview Dr Aptos CA 95003-5326

ZISCHKE, MICHAEL HERMAN, lawyer; b. Yokohama, Japan, Dec. 30, 1954; s. Peter H. and Alice Marian (Oliver) Z.; m. Carol Lu Leland, May 23, 1987; 1 child, Julia Carol. BA magna cum laude, Dartmouth Coll., 1977; JD, U. Calif., Berkeley, 1982. Bar: Calif. 1982. Legis. asst. Congressman Bob Carr, Washington, 1977-79; assoc. Miller, Starr & Regalia, Oakland, Calif., 1982-87; assoc. McCutchen, Doyle, Brown & Enersen, Walnut Creek, Calif., 1987-91, counsel, 1991-93; ptnr. Landels, Ripley & Diamond, San Francisco, 1993—; lectr. land use issues U. Calif. Extension, Berkeley, Davis, Santa Barbara, Irvine, 1988—. Co-author: Land Use Initiatives and Referenda in California, 1990, Practice Pursuant to the California Environmental Quality Act, 1993; contbr. articles to profl. jours. Dir. Boys & Girls Clubs Oakland, 1988—. Mem. Calif. State Bar Assn., Contra Costa County Bar Assn., Calif. Bldg. Industry Assn. (select com. on industry litigation), Bar Assn. San Francisco. Democrat. Episcopalian. Office: Landels Ripley & Diamond 350 Steuart St San Francisco CA 94105-1250

ZISK, STANLEY HARRIS, planetary and oceanic scientist, astronomer; b. Boston, July 11, 1931; s. Morris and Edith (Lewenberg) Z.; m. Betty Ann Hershberger, July 3, 1954 (div. Mar. 1977); children: Jonathan, Stephen, Matthew; m. Janet Elaine Clinton, Jun. 26, 1984. BS, MIT, 1953; Phd, Stanford (Calif.) U., 1965. Rsch. assoc. elec. engring. dept. MIT, Cambridge, Mass., 1965-68; staff scientist Lincoln Lab., MIT, Westford, Mass., 1968-88; planetary scientist U. Hawaii Inst. for Geophysics, Honolulu, 1988-90; prof. dept. geology & geophysics U. Hawaii, Honolulu, 1990—; cons. Jet Propulsion Lab., Pasadena, 1988-90. Lt. (j.g.) USN, 1956-59. Mem. Am. Geophys. Union, IEEE, SPIE. Office: U Hawaii Inst Geophysics 2525 Correa Rd Honolulu HI 96822-2285

ZISLIS, PAUL MARTIN, software engineering executive; b. Chgo., Feb. 8, 1948; s. Harold Solomon and Beatrice (Bossen) Z.; m. Sharon Margo Kaufmann, June 8, 1969; children: Daniel, Benjamin, Rachel. BS in Computer Sci., U. Ill., 1969; SM in Info. Sci., U. Chgo., 1971; PhD in Computer Sci., Purdue U., 1974. Mem. tech. staff AT&T Bell Labs., Naperville, Ill., 1969-72, 74-77; supr. data network devel. AT&T Bell Labs., Holmdel, N.J., 1977-81, dept. head data network architecture, 1981-82; dept. head advanced software tech. AT&T Bell Labs., Naperville, 1982-90; dir. software engring. Raynet Corp., Menlo Park, Calif., 1990-92, dir. product validation, 1993—. Contbr. articles to profl. jours. Grad. fellow IBM, 1971-72. Mem. IEEE Computer Soc., Assn. for Computing Machinery, Phi Beta Kappa. Office: Raynet Corp 155 Constitution Dr Menlo Park CA 94025-1106

ZITO, MICHAEL ANTHONY, advertising and graphics design/typesetting company owner; b. San Diego, Feb. 25, 1957; s. Richard and Margaret Jane (Greggs) Z. Student, El Paso Community Coll., 1976-77, Grossmont Coll., 1977-78. Emergency med. technician E&E Ambulance Svc., Colorado Springs, Colo., 1972-73; psychiat. technician Alvarado Hosp., San Diego, 1975-78; surg. technician, orderly Eisenhower Osteopathic Hosp., Colorado Springs, 1973-75; mktg. mgr. Calif. Dept. Forestry Fire Fighters, San Diego, 1978-79; mktg. rep. Mort Fin. Svcs., San Diego, 1980-81, Mil.-Civil Svc. Yellow Pages, San Diego, 1983-84; nuclear technician San Onofre (Calif.) Nuclear Power Plant, 1982-83; mktg. rep. Stas. XPRS, XHRM, KMLO, 1982-84; pres. Discount Yellow Pages, San Diego, 1984-87, 3-D Advt. Graphics and Typesetting Co., San Diego, 1987-92, Anthony Industries and Am. Fin. Svcs., San Diego, 1990—; nat. coord. Robbins Rsch. Internat., La Jolla, Calif., 1993—. Actor TV documentary and movies, San Diego, 1987 (award Nat. Movie Arts Festival and Movies 1988). Instr. YMCA/USO, 1971-72. Recipient award Nat. Movie Arts Festival, 1988. Roman Catholic.

ZITZ, JON THEODORE, freelance writer, retired coffee company executive; b. Hammond, Ind., Sept. 5, 1914; s. John Theodore and Veronica (Nowicki) Z.; m. Mary Virginia Kubicek, Aug. 17, 1939 (dec. 1976); children: Jay, Diane Zitz Scaletta; m. 2d, Geraldine Weber, May 17, 1978; children: Margaret Chumley, Janet Dionne, Sue Duffy. BA cum laude, Yankton Coll., 1937; postgrad. Northwestern U., 1938-39. Sports editor Yankton Press & Dakotan (S.D.), 1935-38; asst. sales mgr. Nat. Stamping & Electric Works, Chgo., 1939-41; v.p. Hill Shaw Co., Chgo., 1941-84. Contbr. articles to industry related trade papers. Colo. Publicity Coord. Tax Aide of AARP; mem. bd. dirs. SET of Colo. Mem. Park Ridge Country Club. Republican. Roman Catholic. Home: 9968 King St Westminster CO 80030-6761

ZITZER, CATHERINE ANN, language and speech pathologist, artist; b. Milw., Feb. 9, 1954; d. James Paul and Margaret Josephine (Nash) Myles; m. Robert Ely Zitzer, July 12, 1981. BS, U. Wisc., Milw., 1977, MS, 1978; PhD, U. Calif., Santa Barbara, 1990. Cert. Speech and Lang. Pathologist, Researcher. Speech clinician Waukesha county, Menomonee Falls, Wisc., 1979; project dir. State of Wisc. Grant, Milw., 1979-80; itinerant speech and hearing specialist Corona-Norco (Calif.) Unified Schs., 1980-83; teaching asst. U. Calif., Santa Barbara, 1983-87; dir. svcs. The Lang. Ctr., Santa Barbara, 1989—; artist CAZ Water Colors, Santa Barbara, 1992—; infant devel. specialist County Schs. Infant Program, Santa Barbara, 1991; infant feeding and disorder specialist in assn. with Marjorie Meyer Palmer U. Calif., San Francisco Med. Ctr., 1992—; ednl. Am. Sign Lang. cons. The Lang. Ctr., 1989—. Contbr. articles to profl. jours.; one woman show at Everything Artistic Art Gallery, 1993; watercolor paintings on exhibit Cabrillo Arts Ctr., Antioch Coll., 1992. Adv. com. mem. Families First, Santa Barbara, 1992—. Spl. Needs Planning grantee State Wisc., 1980, Rsch. grantee U. Calif., Santa Barbara, 1985, Instrnl. grantee, 1986. Mem. Am. Speech Lang. Hearing Assn. (video prodn. dir. 1989), Teaching English to Speakers of Other Langs.

ZLAKET, THOMAS, state judge. State justice Ariz. Supreme Ct. Mem. ABA, State Bar Ariz. (pres.). Office: Office of Supreme Ct 1501 W Washington St Phoenix AZ 85007

ZOBELL, KARL, lawyer; b. La Jolla, Calif., Jan. 9, 1932; s. Claude E. and Margaret (Harding) ZoB.; m. Barbara Arth, Nov. 22, 1968; children: Bonnie, Elizabeth, Karen, Claude, Mary. Student, Utah State U., 1949-51, Columbia U., 1951-52; AB, Columbia U., 1953, student of law, 1952-54; JD, Stanford U., 1958. Bar: Calif., 1959. Assoc., lawyer Gray, Cary, Ames and Frye, San Diego, 1959-64, ptnr., lawyer, 1964—, chmn., 1989-90; bd. dirs., founder La Jolla (Calif.) Bank and Trust Co. Trustee La Jolla Town Coun., 1962-87, chmn. bd. trustees, 1967-68, pres. 1976-77, 80-81, v.p., 1986-87; trustee La Jollans Inc., 1964-80, founder, 1964, pres. 1965-68, 73-76, 78-79, Dr. Seuss Found., 1992—, James C. Copley Charitable Found., 1992—; mem. charter rev. com. City San Diego, 1968, 73; chmn. City of San Diego Planning Commn., 1988-93; trustee La Jolla Mus. Art, 1964-72, San Diego Mus. Contemporary Art, 1990-92; pres. 1967-70, bd. dirs Scripps Meml. Hosp. Found., 1980-84, bd. overseers, Stanford Law Sch., 1977-80, U. Calif., San Diego, 1974-76. Served to lt. USCG, 1954-57. Fellow Am. Coll. Trust and Estate Counsel; mem. ABA, Calif. Bar, La Jolla Beach and Volleyball Club (pres. 1982—), La Jolla Beach and Tennis Club, Lambda Alpha. Republican. Home: Po Box 1 1555 Coast Walk La Jolla CA 92037 Office: Gray Cary Ames & Frye 1200 Prospect St Ste 575 La Jolla CA 92037-3645

ZOCCHI, DONALD ANTHONY, engineering executive, software developer; b. Lorain, Ohio, Oct. 26, 1951; s. Leo David and Rosemary Delores (Schmidt) Z.; m. Karen Vicki Bateman, June 25, 1977; children: David, Michael. BSEE, Akron U., 1975; MS in Computer Sci., George Washington U., 1979. Co-op student Ford Motor Co., Bedford, Ohio, 1973-75; engr. Nat. Security Agy., Ft. Meade, Md., 1975-77; software devel. GE, Rockville, Md., 1977-78, Floating Point Systems, Beaverton, Oreg., 1979, Tektronix, Inc., Beaverton, 1979-89, Microfield Graphics, Inc., Beaverton, 1989-90, Oreg. Health Scis. Univ., Portland, 1991-92; v.p. engring. Health Outcome Techs., Aloha, Oreg., 1991—. Republican. Roman Catholic. Home and Office: 11725 SW Belmont Terr Beaverton OR 97005

ZODL, JOSEPH ARTHUR, international trade executive, consultant; b. Hackensack, N.J., Aug. 13, 1948; s. Joseph Frank and Edna Josephine (Hokanson) Z. BA in Polit. Sci., Fordham Coll., 1970; MA in Polit. Sci., New Sch. for Social Rsch., N.Y.C., 1991. Lic. customhouse broker U.S. Treasury Dept. Export mgr. Savage Universal Corp., Tempe, Ariz., 1984—. Author: Entering Export-Import: Everything You and Your Company Need to Know to Compete in World Markets, 1992; writer syndicated column, Entering Export-Import, 1993; contbr. articles to profl. jours. Vice chmn. Legis. Dist. 20 Dems., 1978-80, chmn., 1980-82; mem. Ariz. State Dem. Com., 1978-89; cand. Ariz. Ho. Reps., 1986. Named Eagle Scout, Boy Scouts Am., 1966. Mem. Am. Polit. Sci. Assn., Ariz. World Trade Ctr., Internat. Transp. Mgmt. Assn. (dir. 1990-91), Phoenix Traffic Club, Phoenix Customs Brokers Assn., Delta Nu Alpha (pres. 1980-81, Ariz. Transp. Man of Yr. 1980), Alpha Phi Omega. Roman Catholic.

ZOELLNER, ROBERT WILLIAM, chemistry educator; b. Marshfield, Wis., May 30, 1956; s. Willard Rudolph and Marie Martha (Prihoda) Z.; m. Barbara Moore, Feb. 5, 1983; children: Joan Moore, Thaddeus Barak. BS, St. Norbert Coll., De Pere, Wis., 1978; PhD, Kans. State U., 1983. Postdoctoral assoc. Cornell U., Ithaca, N.Y., 1983-84; vis. scientist U. Aix-Marseille (France) III, 1984-85; asst. prof. No. Ariz. U., Flagstaff, 1986-92, assoc. prof., 1992—. Mem. AAAS, Am. Chem. Soc., N.Y. Acad. Sci., N.D. Acad. Sci., Wis. Acad. Sci., Arts and Letters, Sigma Xi, Alpha Chi Sigma, Phi Lambda Upsilon. Office: No Ariz U Dept Chemistry PO Box 5698 Flagstaff AZ 86011-5698

ZOHNER, STEVEN K., environmental scientist; b. Driggs, Idaho, June 8, 1953; s. LaVar Orin and Shirley Elizabeth (Kempton) Z.; m. Marivene Amelia List, Apr. 26, 1977; children: Suzanne, Nathan, Julie, Audrey. AS with high honors, Ricks Coll., 1976; BSmagna cum laude, Brigham Young U., 1978, student, 1978-79, MS magna cum laude, 1982; grad., Dept. Energy/Westinghouse Sch. Environ. Excellence, Idaho, 1992. Rsch. chemist Brigham Young U., Provo, Utah, 1978-81; plant chemist Martin Marietta, Lemington, Utah, 1981-82; engr. prodn. dept. Exxon Nuclear Idaho, Idaho Falls, 1982-85; sr. engr. tech. dept. Westinghouse Idaho Nuclear, Idaho Falls, 1985-91, sr. scientist environ. dept., 1991—; cons. EG&G Idaho, Idaho Falls, 1986, Fernald Nuclear Facility, Cin., 1991. Inventor decontamination solution (Recognition award 1990). Lay minister Ch. Jesus Christ Latter Day Sts., Stockholm, 1972-74, ward clerk, 1985—; active Boy Scouts Am., Idaho Falls, 1982—, PTO, Idaho Falls, 1986—. Mem. Phi Kappa Phi. Republican. Home: 1042 Grizzly Ave Idaho Falls ID 83402 Office: Westinghouse Idaho Nuclear Co MS-3202 1955 Fremont Idaho Falls ID 83404

ZOLEZZI, SAMUEL MAURICE, airline pilot; b. San Diego, Oct. 5, 1949; s. Albert and Jo Noveline (Williams) Z.; m. Victoria Brooke Strickler, Mar. 26, 1980. AB in Theater and TV, San Diego State U., 1971. Lic. airline transport pilot; lic. instrument flight instr. Commd. 2d lt. USAF, 1971, advance through grades to capt., 1978; pilot active duty USAF, Southeast Asia, 1971-74; res. pilot USAF, San Bernardino, Calif., 1974-80; resigned USAF, 1980; first officer New World Airways, Chula Vista, Calif., 1974-75; asst. chief pilot 21st Century Aviation, Chula Vista, 1975-76; first officer World Airways, Oakland, Calif., 1978-86, Pacific S.W. Airlines (bought by US Air), San Diego, 1986—. Home: 3012 Colina Verde Ln Jamul CA 91935-3005

ZONGOLOWICZ, HELEN MICHAELINE, retired school principal; b. Kenosha, Wis., July 22, 1936; d. Edmund S. and Helen (Ostrowski) Z.; Ed.B., Dominican Coll., 1966; M.A., Cardinal Stritch Coll., 1973; Ed.D., U. No. Colo., 1977. Tchr. elem. schs. Kenosha, 1956-58, Center Line, Mich., 1958-59, Taft, Calif., 1960-61, Lake Wales, Fla., 1962-63, Albuquerque, 1963-65; tchr., asst. prin. St. Mary's Sch., Taft, 1965-69; asst. sch. supt. Diocese of Fresno, Calif., 1969-70; tchr. primary grades Greasewood Boarding Sch., Ganado, Ariz., 1970-72, coord. spl. projects, 1972-75, liaison to parent adv. coun., 1972-75, tchr. supr., 1972-76; ednl. specialist Ft. Defiance Agy., Navajo Area, Ariz., 1974-75, ednl. diagnostician, 1979-80; vis. asst. prof. U. Colo., 1976; asst. prof. Auburn (Ala.) U., 1977-79, U. N.Mex.-Gallup, 1981—; prin. Chuska Sch., 1980-93. Recipient Spl. Achievement award U.S. Dept. Interior, 1971, 73, Points of Light award, 1990, Superior Performance award, 1982; named Prin. of Yr. Bur. of Indian Affairs, 1990; named Prin. of Yr. Navajo Area Sch. Bd. Assn., 1991. Mem. Am. Assn. Mental Deficiency, Assn. for Supervision and Curriculum Devel., Coun. for Exceptional Children, Coun. for Basic Edn., Am. Ednl. Rsch. Assn., NAFE, Internat. Reading Assn., Assn. for Children with Learning Disabilities Nat. Coun. Tchrs. of English., Assn. Childhood Edn. Internat., Navajo Nation North Cen. Assn. (mem. exec. bd.), Kappa Delta Pi, Phi Delta Kappa. Address: 604 McKee Dr Gallup NM 87301

ZOOK, RONALD Z., school system administrator. Supt. Parkrose Sch. Dist. # 3, Portland, Oreg. Office: Parkrose Sch Dist 3 10636 NE Prescott St Portland OR 97220*

ZOOK, TRACY LYNN, pastor; b. Merriam, Kans., Sept. 7, 1969; d. Lloyd Wayne and Ardith Joan (Harrington) Z. AA, Northwest Coll., 1990, BA, 1992. Children's pastor Redmond Assembly God, Redmond, Wash., 1991-93; youth pastor Vader (Wash.) Assembly God, 1993—. Author of poems and music. Vol. Youth for Christ, Kirkland, Wash., 1992. Mem. Northwest Coll. Alumni Assn. Republican. Home: PO Box 220 Vader WA 98593

ZOOK, WAYNE BOWMAN, physician; b. Cresco, Iowa, Oct. 2, 1927; s. Ray Edward and Mildred Bernice (Bowman) Z.; m. Evelyn Viola Johnson, June 11, 1950; children: Teresa Kay, Kim Wayne, Dale Johnson. BA, Manchester Coll., 1949; MD, Ind. U., 1953. Physician Wenatchee (Wash.) Family Practice, 1956—. Capt. USAF, 1953-56. Fellow Am. Acad. Family Physicians (del.); mem. AMA, Rotary (pres.), Wenatchee Area C. of C. (pres. 1988). Mem. Ch. of the Brethren. Home: 201 Elliott Ave S Apt 16 Wenatchee WA 98801-6325 Office: Wenatchee Family Practice 707 N Emerson Ave Wenatchee WA 98801-2032

ZORNES, MILFORD, artist; b. Camargo, Okla., Jan. 25, 1908; s. James Francis and Clara Delphine (Lindsay) Z.; m. Gloria Codd, 1935; 1 son, Franz Milford; m. Patricia Mary Palmer, Nov. 8, 1942; 1 dau., Maria Patricia. Student, Otis Art Inst., Los Angeles, 1929, Pomona Coll., 1930-34. Instr. art Pomona Coll., 1946-50; art dir. Vortox and Padua Hills Theatre, Claremont, 1954-66. Exhibited, Calif. Water Color Soc., Met. Mus., Am. Watercolor Soc., Corcoran Gallery, Bklyn. Mus., Denver Mus., Cleve. Mus., L.A. Mus., Brooks Gallery, London, Bombay Art Assn., Chgo. Art Inst., Butler Mus., Gallery Modern Masters, Washington, Santa Barbara (Calif.) Museums, Cin. Museums, Laguna (Calif.) Art Gallery, Oklahoma City Mus., Springville (Utah) Mus.; represented in permanent collections at, Galleria Beretich, Claremont, Calif., L.A. Museums, White House Collection, Met. Museums, Pentagon Bldg., Butler Museums, UCLA, Nat. Acad., San Diego Mus., L.A. County Fair, Home Savs. and Loan Assn., L.A., Corcoran Gallery, Washington; mem. art com., Nat. Orange Show, San Bernardino, Calif., 1963-65; author: A Journey to Nicaragua, 1977, The California Style: California Watercolor Artists 1925-1955, 1985. Served with U.S. Army, 1943-45, CBI. Recipient David Pescott Burrows award Pomona Coll. 1991; subject of book by Gordon McClelland, Hillcrest Press, Inc., 1991. Mem. Am. Watercolor Soc., Calif. Watercolor Soc. (past pres.), West Coast Watercolor Soc., Utah Watercolor Soc. Address: PO Box 176 Orderville UT 84758 Gallery: Galleria Beretich 1034 Harvard Claremont CA 91711

ZORZ, RAYMOND BARRY, product support specialist; b. N.Y.C., Jan. 15, 1955; s. Edward and Marion Arlene (Ferro) Z.; m. Pauline Mary Bertucci, children: Kyle Ryan, Taryn Alexandra. BBA, SUNY, Fredonia, 1977. Technician, support analyst Micor, Inc., Phoenix, 1978-81; support analyst, mgr. Informatics Legal Systems, Phoenix, 1981-87; pres. Griffin & Zorz, Inc., Phoenix, 1987-89; cons., analyst Computer Systems Solutions, Inc., Scottsdale, Ariz., 1989-92, Syntellect, Inc., Phoenix, 1992—. Home: 3951 E Waltann Ln Phoenix AZ 85032-4032 Office: Syntellect Inc 15810 N 28th Ave Phoenix AZ 85023

ZUBEK, PHILIP ANTHONY, electronic engineer; b. Gary, Ind., Dec. 7, 1962; s. Carl Andrew and Lucille Annette (Malak) Z.; m. Renee Linda Ivy, June 27, 1987. BSEET, DeVry Inst. Tech., Atlanta, 1986; MBA, Hawaii Pacific U., 1992. Control auditor UPS, Atlanta, 1983-85; computer technician Decision Data Computer Svcs., Atlanta, 1985-86; sr. tech. Singer-Link Flight Sim., Wahiawa, Hawaii, 1986-89; sr. engr. Grumman Tech. Svcs., Wahiawa, 1988-89; site mgr. Grumman Tech. Svcs., 1989—. Home: 2581 Laurelwood Rd Atlanta GA 30360 Office: Grumman Tech Svcs PO Box 250 Wahiawa HI 96786-0250

ZUBRIN, ROBERT MAYNARD, astronautical engineer, educator; b. Bklyn., Apr. 9, 1952; s. Charles and Roslyn (Fallenberg) Z.; m. Maggie Gagnon, 1991; 1 child, Rachel; stepchildren: Eliot, Sarah. BA in Math., U. Rochester, 1974; MS in Nuclear Engring., U. Washington, 1984, MS in Aero. and Astronautics, 1986, PhD in Nuclear Engring., 1992. Cert. math. and sci. tchr., N.Y., N.J., Wash. Tchr. various pub. schs., N.Y., 1974-83; grad. research assoc. Los Alamos (N.Mex.) Nat. Lab., 1985; recording sec. magnetic fusion adv. com. U.S. Dept. of Energy, Washington, 1986-88; health physicist Wash. State Office of Radiation Protection, Seattle, 1987-88; sr. engr. Martin Marietta Astronautics, Denver, 1988—. Inventor Mars Direct Mission Plan, NIMF, magnetic sail, integral power and propulsion stage, nuclear salt water rocket, Mars aerial photography mission, Three Player Chess Game, 1972; author (play) Benedict Arnold, 1983; contbr. articles to profl. jours. Mem. AIAA, AAAS, Am. Nuclear Soc. (v.p. U. Wash. chpt., pub. speaker 1986-88) Am. Phys. Soc., Planetary Soc., Moutaineers Club, Wash. Yacht Club, Tau Beta Pi, Alpha Nu Sigma. Home: PO Box 273 Indian Hills CO 80454-0273

ZUCATI, KATHLEEN D'VAL LOIS, writer; b. Hillsboro, Oreg., May 25, 1953; d. Frederick Daniel and Sharon Doris (Spear) Krauss; m. Paul Edward Zucati, Mar. 3, 1973; 1 child, Hal Daniel Edward. AA, Highline Community Coll., 1985. Mgr. various businesses, Oreg., 1977-87; instr., owner Novelty Ceramic Works, Duvall, Wash., 1980-81; owner Zucati Residential Interiors, SeaTac, Wash., 1987-89; instr. South Seattle Community Coll., 1987-89, Highline Community Coll., Midway, Wash., 1989; freelance writer Seattle, 1989—. Author: Destruction of the Talismen, 1992, Bane, King By His Own Hand, 1991; author short stories, poems, articles. Leader Awana, Seattle, 1986-87; asst. coach Boys' and Girls' Club basketball, Seattle, 1985. Named Hon. Mil. Policewoman, Office of Provost Marshal, Berlin, 1975. Mem. NAAFA, Sierra Club, Greenpeace, One in a Thousand Soc., Triple 9 Soc. Home: 3757 S 172nd St Sea Tac WA 98188-3628

ZUCCARELLI, ANTHONY JOSEPH, microbiology educator, biochemistry educator; b. N.Y.C., Aug. 11, 1944; m. Sharron Adele Ames; children: Cara N., A. Alexandar. BS in Bacteriology, Cornell U., 1966; MS in Microbiology with honors, Loma Linda U., 1968; PhD in Biophysics, Calif. Inst. Tech., 1974; postdoctoral studies in molecular biology, U. Konstanz, Fed. Republic Germany, 1974-76. Asst. prof. grad. sch. biology Loma Linda (Calif.) U., 1976-80, assoc. prof. microbiology sch. medicine, 1980-91; prof. microbiology Sch. Medicine, 1991—; assoc. mem. grad. faculty biology program Loma Linda (Calif.) U., 1982—, mem. grad. faculty microbiology program, 1982-91, asst. prof. biochemistry dept. sch. medicine, 1985—, mem. grad. faculty biochemistry program, 1986—, asst. dir. med. scientist program, grad. coord., 1989-91, dir. med. scientist program, grad. coord., 1991—, prof. microbiology sch. medicine, 1991—; grad. teaching asst. Loma Linda U., 1966-68, grad. student rsch. mentor, chmn., mem. numerous coms. including mem. sch. medicine basic sci. course coords. com., 1987—, sch. medicine basic sci. faculty coun., 1987—, acad. rev. com., 1987—, med. scientist curriculum com., 1989—, microbiology dept. faculty search com., 1988—, grad. sch. coun., 1989—, univ. hazardous materials com. 1982—; rsch. preceptor com. for advanced sci. tng. Calif. Mus. Sci. Industry, 1987; instr. microbial genetics, molecular biology Nat. Med. Sch. Rev., 1987—; outside reviewer grant applications NSF, 1977-78, 81-82. Contbr. articles to profl. jours. Fellow NSF, 1968-71, Am. Cancer Soc., 1974-76; trainee NIH, 1971-74; recipient First Prize for Sci. Exhibit award Macpherson Soc., 1989, Basic Sci. Student-Faculty Rsch. award, 1990, grantee Loma Linda U., 1977, 78, 79, 81, 82, 83, 85, 86, 87, 90. Mem. Am. Soc. Microbiology, Am. Soc. Advancement Sci., Am. Soc. Biotechnology, Am. Chem. Soc., N.Y. Acad. Scis., Sigma Xi. Mem. Seventh Day Adventist Ch. Office: Loma Linda U Microbiology Dept AH115 Loma Linda CA 92350

ZUCKER, ALFRED JOHN, educator, school adminstrator; b. Hartford, Sept. 25, 1940; s. Samuel and Rose (Zucker) Z.; A.A., Los Angeles Valley Coll., 1960; B.A., U. Calif. at Los Angeles, 1962, M.A., 1963, Ph.D., 1966; m. Sallie Lea Friedheim, Dec. 25, 1966; children—Mary Anne, John James, James Patrick, Patrick Jonathan, Anne-Marie Kathleen, Kathleen Mary. Lectr. English, Los Angeles City Coll., 1963-68; prof. English, philosophy, chmn. div. humanities Los Angeles Southwest Coll., 1968-72, chmn. English dept., 1972-74, asst. dean instruction, 1974—; prof. English El Camino Coll., 1985—; prof. English L.A. Valley Coll., 1989—. Mem. Los Angeles Jr. Coll. Dist. Senate, 1969—. Mem. Los Angeles Coll. Tchrs. Assn. (dir.), Calif. Jr. Coll. Assn., Calif. Tchrs. Assn., AAUP, Phi Beta Kappa, Phi Delta Kappa (pres. U. Calif. at Los Angeles chpt. 1966-67, v.p. 1967-68). Lodge: KC. Contbr. articles to profl. jours. Office: 5800 Fulton Ave Van Nuys CA 91401-4062

ZUCKER, ROBERT STEPHEN, neurophysiologist, neurobiology educator; b. Phila., Apr. 18, 1945; s. Irving Aaron and Dorothy Ruth (Pittenturf) Z.; m. Glenda Anita Teal, Sept. 1, 1968 (div. Apr. 1982); 1 child, David Aaron; m. Susan Henrietta Schwartz, Jan. 3, 1983; children: Mark Daniel Isaac, Ariel Dana. SB in Physics, MIT, 1966; PhD in Neurol. Sci., Stanford U., 1971. Asst. prof. physiology U. Calif., Berkeley, 1974-80, assoc. prof., 1980-85, prof., 1985-90, prof. neurobiology, 1990—; vis. investigator Univ. Coll., London, 1971-73, Nat. Ctr. Sci. Rsch., Gif-sur-Yvette, France, 1973-74; corp. mem. Marine Biology Lab., Woods Hole, Mass., 1981—; mem. bd. sci. counselors Nat. Inst. Neurol. and Communicative Disorders and Stroke, Washington, 1982; mem. study sects. NIH, 1983-84, 90; Nachshen meml. lectr. U. Md., 1992. Mem. editorial bd. Jour. Neurobiology, 1982-86, Jour. Neurosci., 1988—; contbr. articles to profl. jours. Recipient Jacob Javits award, 1987—; fellow Helen Hay Whitney Found., NIH, NSF, NATO, Alfred P. Sloan Found.; grantee NIH, NSF, 1976. Mem. AAAS, AAUP, ACLU, Soc. Neurosci., Biophys. Sci., Union Concerned Scientists, Common Cause, Sierra Club, Sigma Xi. Democrat. Jewish. Home: 1236 Oxford St Berkeley CA 94709-1423 Office: U Calif Dept Molecular/Cell Biology Berkeley CA 94720

ZUCKERMAN, MARVIN SIGMAN, English language educator; b. N.Y.C., May 29, 1932; s. Rubin and Manye (Skrczynska) Z.; m. Katherine Klara Kohner, Jan. 19, 1965; children: David Nathan, Philip Joseph. BA, U. So. Calif., 1957, MA, 1960. Sr. project engr. electronics div. Northrop, Hawthorne, Calif., 1960-74; prof. English L.A. Valley Coll., Van Nuys, Calif., 1974-83, chmn. English dept., 1983—; chmn. English coun. L.A. Community Coll. Dist., 1989—; dir. seminars in field. Author: Words, Words, Words, 1974, Yiddish Sayings, 1975, Better College Reading, 1984, Learning Yiddish, 1985, Mendele Moykher-Sforim, 1991. Mem. exec. bd. local chpt. Am. Fedn. Tchrs.-Coll. Guild, L.A., 1980—. Mem. MLA, Workmen's Circle, Jewish Labor Bund, Nat. Coun. Tchrs. of English, Krupnick Found. (bd. dirs.), Am. Assn. Profs. Yiddish (exec. bd. 1990—), Alliance for Advancement of Edn. Found. (bd. dirs.). Democrat. Jewish. Office: L A Valley Coll 5800 Fulton Ave Van Nuys CA 91401-4062

ZUK, JOHN, aerospace engineer; b. Westhampton, N.Y.; s. George and Anna (Stachnik) Z.; m. Maureen Elizabeth Kelly. BSME, Ohio State U., 1961; MS in Aerospace Engring., U. Rochester, 1965; PhD in Engring., Case Western Reserve U., 1972. Registered profl. engr., Ohio. Research engr. NASA Lewis Reseach Ctr., Cleve.; program mgr. NASA Hdqrs., Washington; branch chief NASA Ames Research Ctr., Moffett Field, Calif.; div. chief NASA Ames Research Ctr.; study contributor Ctr. for Strategic & Internat. Studies, Washington, 1984-88, Nat. Research Coun.'s Transp. Research Bd., Washington, 1986-88, Office Sci. & Tech. Policy, Washington, 1981-84, Nat. Acad. Engring., Washington, 1983-84. Author: Fundamentals of Fluid Sealing, 1976. Named for contribution to aviation FAA, 1988; recipient Collier Trophy (Teammember) Nat. Aeronautic Assn., 1987. Home: 2707 Mignon Dr San Jose CA 95132-2120 Office: NASA Ames Rsch Ctr MS 237-11 Moffett Field CA 94035

ZUMBO, JOAN MARIE FRANCES, motel owner; b. Mt. Vernon, N.Y., Dec. 10, 1934; d. William John Fahl Wendlendt and Elizabeth Clancy Fahl; m. Fred Leo Zumbo, Feb. 11, 1956; children: Frederick William, Barbara Ann, Elizabeth Ann. Student, Yavapai Coll., Prescott, Ariz., 1988-89. With N.Y. Telephone Co., Mt. Kisco, N.Y., 1952-53; gen. mgr. Field Club of Greenwich (Conn.), 1968-78; owner Stage Coach Motel, Ash Fork, Ariz., 1978-91, Ash Fork (Ariz.) Electric & Mercantile, 1991—. Sec., bd. dirs. Dist. 1 Bd. Adjustments, Yavapai County, Ariz., 1986—; mng. bd. Yavapai County Free Libr., 1986—, bd. dirs.; county rep. Republican Com., Prescott, 1986-88, state rep., Phoenix, 1988; mem. St. Anns Ch. Coun.; pres. Ash Fork Tourist Ctr.; bd. dirs. Ash Fork Libr. Mem. Ariz. Hotel-Motel Assn., Williams/Grand Canyon c. of C., Ariz. Intra-State Tourism Assn., Ash Fork C. of C. (founder, pres. 1980-82, 88-93), Historic 66 Assn. Roman Catholic. Home: 711 8th St Ash Fork AZ 86320-9999 Office: Ash Fork Electric and Mercantile 805 Park Ave Ash Fork AZ 86320

ZUMETA, WILLIAM MARK, public policy educator; b. Trenton, N.J., Oct. 2, 1947; s. Bertram William and Ruth (Astbury) Z.; m. Terrea Dodge O'Rand, Jan. 4, 1975; children: Rebecca, Benjamin, Brian. BA, Haverford Coll., 1969; MPP, U. Calif., Berkeley, 1973, PhD, 1978. Dir. rsch. Southeastern Pa. Econ. Devel. Corp., Phila., 1971; program review and evaluation analyst Calif. Dept. Fin., Sacramento, 1972-75; vis. asst. prof. faculty commerce U. B.C., Vancouver, 1976-78; asst. prof. Grad. Sch. Mgmt. UCLA, 1978-84, sr. rsch. assoc. Higher Edn. Rsch. Inst., 1979-85; adj. prof. edn. Claremont (Calif.) Grad. Sch., 1983; asst. prof. Grad. Sch. Pub. Affairs U. Wash., Seattle, 1985-87, acting dean Grad. Sch. Pub. Affairs, 1988, assoc. prof. Grad. Sch. Pub. Affairs, 1987—; cons., proposal evaluator NSF, Washington, 1984, 85, 87; cons. Wash. Higher Edn. Coord. Bd., Olympia, 1988-89, 92, Edn. Commn. of States, Denver, 1988-89, N.W. Policy Ctr., 1990-91, Nat. Inst. Ind. Colls. and Univs., Washington, 1990, 92, NRC, 1987, 92, Wash. Office Adult Literacy, 1992, NEA. Co-editor: Washington Policy Choices: 1990s, 1990; author: Extending the Educational Ladder, 1985; mem. editorial bd. Jour. of Pub. Adminstrn. Rsch. and Theory, Rev. of Higher Edn.; contbr. articles, reports to profl. publs. Vol. cons. to various community groups, L.A., 1978-85, Seattle, 1985—. Grantee Spencer Found., Chgo., 1980-81, Lilly Endowment, Indpls., 1981-82, 90-91, Pew Charitable Trusts, 1992-93, NSF, 1981-82. Mem. NEA, Am. Soc. Pub. Adminstrn., Policy Studies Orgn., Assn. Pub. Policy and Mgmt., Assn. Study Higher Edn. Office: Grad Sch Pub Affairs DC 13 Univ Wash Seattle WA 98195

ZUMWALT, ROGER CARL, hospital administrator; b. Eugene, Oreg., Oct. 26, 1943; s. Robert Walter and Jean Elaine (Adams) Z.; m. Sharon Marlene Ryan, Aug. 22, 1970; children: Kathryn Nicole, Timothy Robert. Student, Boise State U., 1963-65; BA, Western Oreg. State Coll., 1969; postgrad., U. Iowa, 1969-71; MA cum laude, Oreg. State U., 1973. Adminstr. Coulee Community Hosp., Grand Coulee, Wash., 1973-75, Eastmoreland Hosp., Portland, Oreg., 1975-81; hosp. surveyor Am. Osteopathic Assn., Chgo., 1977—; exec. dir. Community Hosp., Grand Junction, Colo., 1981—; speaker numerous local and nat. presentations on healthcare, hosp. mktg./success/costs, etc., 1981—; bd. dirs. Healthcare Fin. Mgmt. Assn., Portland, 1978-80; chief exec. officer Community Med. Pla., 1984—, Community Health Care Providers Orgn., 1986—, Community Hosp. Found., 1988—. Newspaper columnist, 1973-75; contbr. articles, presentations to profl. publs.

Commr. Multnomah County Health Care Commn., Portland, 1978-81; health cons. Grant County Housing Authority, Grand Coulee, 1974-75; mem. park bd. City of Tigard, Oreg., 1976-78; caucus rep. Mesa County Rep. Party, Grand Junction, 1988; mem. adv. com., pres.'s office Mesa State Coll., Grand Junction, 1989. With USAF, 1961-65. Fellow Coll. Osteopathic Healthcare Execs. (bd. dirs. 1985-88, pres. 1987, examiner 1989—, Disting. Svc. award 1989); mem. Am. Osteopathic Hosp. Assn. (bd. dirs. 1987—, treas. 1992—), Colo. Hosp. Assn. (bd. dirs. 1987-92), Mountain States Voluntary Hosp. Assn. (bd. dirs. 1984—, exec. com. 1991—, v.p. 1993, vice chmn. bd. 1992—), Western Col. Ind. Practice Assn. (medicine mauls measles com., fin. com. 1991—), Western Colo. Health Care Alliance (bd. dirs. 1989—, v.p. 1992, chmn. bd. 1993), Mesa County Mental Health Assn. (bd. dirs. 1988-89, 1991-92), Grand Junction C. of C. (bd. dirs. 1991—), Rotary, Masons, Shriners (pres. Grand Junction club 1989, bd. dirs. El Jebel 1986-90, 1st v.p. Western Colo. club 1989). Republican. Methodist. Home: 2515 Snowmass Ct Grnd Junction CO 81503-1752 Office: Community Hosp 2021 N 12th St Grand Junction CO 81501-2999

ZUND, JOSEPH DAVID, mathematical sciences educator; b. Ft. Worth, Apr. 27, 1939; s. Emil A. and Lillian A. (Braxton) Z. BS in Math., Tex. A&M U., 1961, MS in Math., 1961; PhD in Math., U. Tex., 1964. From asst. prof. to assoc. prof. N.C. State U., Raleigh, 1965-69; assoc. prof. Va. Poly. Inst. and State U., Blacksburg, 1969-70; assoc. prof. N.Mex. State U., Las Cruces, 1970-72, prof., 1972—. Contbr. rsch. papers to profl. jours. Grantee NSF, 1967-68, USAF Phillips Lab., 1986-88, 89-94. Fellow Royal Astron. Soc.; mem. London Math. Soc., Am. Geophysical Union, Am. Meteorol. Soc., Geol. Soc. Am., Internat. Assn. Geodesy, The Tensor Soc. Office: NMex State U Math Scis Las Cruces NM 88003

ZUNES, J. STEPHEN, political science educator, speaker, consultant; b. Salisbury, N.C., Nov. 5, 1956; s. John Athas and Helen (Karnes) Z.; m. Nanlouise Wolfe, May 23, 1987; children: Shanti, Kalila, Tobin. BA, Oberlin Coll., 1979; MA, Temple U., 1983, Cornell U., 1987; PhD, Cornell U., 1990. Instr. Temple U., Ambler, Pa., 1981; rsch. asst. Inst. Policy Studies, Washington, 1982-83; asst. prof. Ithaca (N.Y.) Coll., 1987-89, Whitman Coll., Walla Walla, Wash., 1989-91; dir. Inst. for a New Middle East Policy, Seattle, 1991—; speaker, cons. on U.S. Middle East rels. Contbr. articles to profl. and gen. publs. Rsch. grantee U.S. Inst. of Peace, 1990-91, Inst. for Global Security Studies, 1993—. Mem. Am. Polit. Sci. Assn., Internat. Studies Assn., Caucus for New Polit. Sci., Consortium on Peace Rsch., Edn. and Devel., Middle East Studies Assn. Home: 353 Wallace Way NE #20 Bainbridge Island WA 98110 Office: Inst for New Middle East Policy PO Box 10898 Bainbridge Island WA 98110

ZUNKER, RICHARD E., insurance company executive; b. 1938. BS, U. Wis., 1964. With Employers Ins. Wausau, Wis., 1964-69, Northwestern Nat. Investors Life, 1969-75; with Safeco Life Ins. Co., Seattle, 1975—, pres., also bd. dirs. With U.S. Army, 1956-58. Office: Safeco Life Ins Co PO Box 34690 Seattle WA 98124-1690*

ZURBRICK, PHILLIP RAYMOND, educator; b. La Grande, Oreg., Nov. 5, 1938; s. Harold Hunter and Emma Lola (Leonard) Z.; m. Shirley Kay Hickox, Aug. 8, 1958 (dec. Sept. 1984); children: Carrie Jo, Joy Elizabeth, Sheri Lyn, Terie Lee (dec.), Kevin Neil; m. Jacquetta Le King, Mar. 25, 1988. BS in Agr., Oreg. State U., Corvallis, 1961; MA in Agr. Edn., U. Ariz., 1965; PhD, Ohio State U., Columbus, 1971. Tchr. agr. Elgin (Oreg.) High Sch., 1961-64, Tempe (Ariz.) High Sch., 1965-68; prof. agr. Mesa (Ariz.) Community Coll., 1968-70; prof. agr. edn. U. Ariz., Tucson, 1971—; acting head dept. agr. edn. U. Ariz., Tucson, 1989-90. Recipient E.B. Knight award NACTA, 1979, Regional Teaching award, 1988, teaching fellow, 1982; recipient Outstanding Svc. award NVATA, 1985, Outstanding Teaching award AATEA, 1986. Mem. Am. Assn. Tchrs. Edn. in Agr. (pres. 1988-89), Agrl. Edn. Mag. (editor 1989-91). Office: U Ariz Dept Agr Forbs Bldg Rm 222 Tucson AZ 85721

ZUSMAN, MARK LEONARD, newspaper editor; b. Hartford, Conn., May 17, 1954; s. Saul and Florence (Gellert) Z.; m. Brenda Elizabeth Bonnell, Sept. 1, 1979; children: Anna, Sam, Madeleine. BA, Hobart Coll., 1976; MA, U. Oreg., 1979. Reporter Finger Lakes Times, Geneva, N.Y., 1979; reporter intern Jack Anderson, Washington, 1979-80; corr. Bus. Week mag., Portland, Oreg., 1980-82; editor Willamette Week newspaper, Portland, Oreg., 1980—; TV host Oreg. Pub. Broadcasting, Portland, Oreg., 1990—; instr. U. Oreg. Sch. Journalism, Eugene, 1989. Recipient Golden Quill award Internat. Soc. Weekly Newspaper Editors, 1986, 88, Gerald Loeb award UCLA Sch. Mgmt., 1986, Bruce Baer award Oreg. Newspaper Pubs. Assn.; Ruhl fellow U. Oreg., 1988. Mem. Assn. Alternative Newsweeklies (bd. dirs. 1989-91), Journalism Advancement Coun. (bd. dirs. 1990—), Inst. Alternative Journalism (bd. dirs. 1990—, pres. 1992—). Office: Willamette Week 2 N W 2nd Ave Portland OR 97209

ZWACK, RAYMOND THEODORE, engineer; b. East Orange, N.J., Nov. 14, 1907; s. Anthony Theodore and Minnie Helena (Weidner) Z.; m. Louise Stark, May 25, 1937 (dec. 1985); children: Robert, David, Donna, Jeffrey. ME, Stevens Inst. Tech., 1930. Registered profl. engr., N.J. Project engr., then sr. project engr. Bendix Corp., Teterboro, N.J.; chief design engr. Walter Kidde and Co., Belleville, N.J.; staff engr. Curtiss-Wright Corp., Caldwell, N.J.; mgr. devel. engring. div. Solar Aircraft Co., Des Moines, Iowa; asst. mgr. devel. engring. div. Thiokol Chem. Corp., Brigham City, Utah; asst. mgr. vehicle systems br. N.Am. Rockwell Corp., Downey, Calif.; staff engr., mgr. polaris propulsion div. Lockheed Missiles & Space Co., Sunnyvale, Calif.; ind. cons. in aerospace field San Jose, Calif., 1968—. Patentee (17) in field. Fellow AIAA (assoc.); mem. ASME, Soc. Automotive Engrs. Home and Office: 3925 Teale Ave San Jose CA 95117-3431

ZWAHLEN, FRED CASPER, JR., journalism educator; b. Portland, Oreg., Nov. 11, 1924; s. Fred and Katherine (Meyer) Z.; m. Grace Eleanor DeMoss, June 24, 1959; children: Molly, Skip. BA, Oreg. State U., 1949; MA, Stanford U., 1952. Reporter San Francisco News, 1949-50; acting editor Stanford Alumni Rev., Palo Alto, Calif., 1950; successively instr. journalism, news bur. asst., prof. journalism, chmn. journalism dept. Oreg. State U., Corvallis, 1950-91, prof. emeritus, 1991—; Swiss tour guide, 1991—; corres. Portland Oregonian, 1950-67. Author: (with others) Handbook of Photography, 1984. Coord. E.E. Wilson Scholarship Fund, 1964—; active budget com. Corvallis Sch. Dist., 1979. Recipient Achievement award Sch. Journalism U. Oregon, 1988. Mem. Assn. for Edn. in Journalism and Mass Communications (conv. chmn. 1983, pres.' award 1988), Oreg. Newspaper Pubs. Assn. (bd. dirs. 1980-85, student loan fund named in his honor 1988), Soc. Profl. Journalists (nat. svc. citation 1988), Corvallis Country Club, Shriners, Masons, Elks, Moose, Eagles, Delta Tau Delta. Republican. Presbyterian. Home: 240 SW 7th St Corvallis OR 97333-4551 Office: Oreg State U Dept Student Activities Corvallis OR 97331

ZWEIFEL, DONALD EDWIN, automobile dealer, civic affairs volunteer; b. L.A., Nov. 30, 1940; s. Robert Fredrick and Eugenia Bedford (White) Z.; m. Donna Jean Croslin; 1 child, Phillip Matthew. Student, Orange Coast Coll., 1963-67, 90-92, U. Calif., Irvine, 1968-70, Western State U. Coll. Law, 1973, Irvine U. Coll. Law, 1974-75, Rancho Santiago Jr. Coll., 1988, Chapman Coll., 1989, 93—. Cert. Student Pilot, 1989. Devel. tech. Hughes Aircraft, Newport Beach, Calif., 1963-64; co-founder Sta. KUCI-FM, Irvine, Calif.; owner, mgr. Zweifel Jaguar Car Sales and Svc., Santa Ana, Calif., 1975-76; pres. Zweifel & Assocs. Inc., Santa Ana, 1977-86, Zweifel South Coast Exotic Cars, Orange, Calif., 1987—. Editor: coll. textbook The Dream Is Alive, Space Flight and Operations In Earth Orbit. Vol. emergency coordinator emergency mgmt. div. Orange County Fire Dept., 1985-87, Navy Relief Soc., 1993, Civil Air Patrol Squadron, 1993, sr. programs officer, 1993—; program coord. Young Astronaut Coun., 1989-90. Cadet CAP, USAF auxiliary, Long Beach, Calif., 1953-60, 62-64. With Army N.G., 1958-59. Recipient 5 Certs. of Achievement Fed. Emergency Mgmt. Agy., 1989-91. Mem. Air Force Assn. (vice-chmn. civilian recruitment Calif. state membership com. 1988-89, 90-91, v.p. membership, Gen. Doolittle chpt. bd. dirs. 1987-89, 90-92, Exceptional Svc. award Gen. Jimmy Doolittle chpt. 1988, 91, Calif. Meritorious Svc. award 1988), Calif. Assn. for Aerospace Edn. (fellow), Marine Corps Hist. Found. (life), Aerospace Edn. Found. (Gen. Jimmy Doolittle fellow 1988, Gen. Ira Eaker fellow 1989, Pres.'s award 1988), U.S. Naval Inst., AIAA (Cert. of Appreciation 1989, L.A. chpt. hist. com. 1989), Marine Corps Assn. (assoc.), Navy League, Gulf & Vietnam Vet. Hist. Assn. (cons., co-founder, trustee 1983—, exec. dir.), Am. Def. Preparedness Assn., Assn. of Old Crows, U.S. Marine Corps Combat Correspondents Assn. (affiliate), Confederate Air Force (col. 1989, adj. 1st Composite Group detachment 1989), Aircraft Owners and Pilots Assn., World Affairs Coun. Orange County.

ZWICK, BARRY STANLEY, newspaper editor, speechwriter; b. Cleve., July 21, 1942; s. Alvin Albert and Selma Davidovna (Makofsky) Z.; m. Roberta Joan Yaffe, Mar. 11, 1972; children: Natasha Yvette, Alexander Anatol. BA in Journalism, Ohio State U., 1963; MS in Journalism, Columbia U., 1965. Copy editor Phila. Inquirer, 1964; night news editor Detroit Free Press, 1965-67; West Coast editor L.A. Times/Washington Post News Svc, 1967-77; makeup editor L.A. Times, 1978—; adj. prof. U. So. Calif., L.A., 1975-77. Author: Hollywood Tanning Secrets, 1980. NEH profl. journalism fellow Stanford U., 1977-78. Jewish. Office: LA Times Times Mirror Sq Los Angeles CA 90012-3816

ZWICK, KEITH ROGER, urban planner, consultant; b. Hutchison, Kans., Aug. 18, 1943; s. Harry and Marjory (Wolf) Z.; children: Brian, Justin. BS, Kans. State U., Manhattan, 1966. Landscape architect, planner Oblinger-Smith Corp., Dallas, 1967-78; dir. downtown devel. City of Loveland, Colo., 1978-85; urban planner EDAW, Inc., Ft. Collins, Colo., 1985-90; sr. urban planner Earth Tech. Corp., San Bernardino, Calif., 1990—. Hon. judge State of Nebr., Lincoln, 1981. Recipient numerous design awards. Mem. Nat. Trust for Hist. Preservation, Calif. Redevel. Assn.

ZWICK, PETER RONALD, political science educator; b. Bklyn., May 28, 1942; s. Jack Nathan and Anne Helen (Lubin) Z.; m. Shelly Kent Crittendon, July 6, 1963; B.A., Grinnell Coll., 1963; M.A., Duke U., 1967, Ph.D., 1971. Asst. prof. polit. sci. La. State U., Baton Rouge, 1968-80, assoc. prof., 1981-88, prof., 1988-90, chmn. dept., 1984-90; prof. Calif. State U., San Marcos, 1990—, coord. internat. edn., 1990—. Author: National Communism, 1983, Soviet Foreign Relations, 1990. Mem. Am. Polit. Sci. Assn., Internat. Studies Assn., We. Polit. Sci. Assn. Office: Calif State U San Marcos Campus San Marcos CA 92096

ZWOYER, EUGENE MILTON, consulting engineer; b. Plainfield, N.J., Sept. 8, 1926; s. Paul Ellsworth and Marie Susan (Britt) Z.; m. Dorothy Lucille Seward, Feb. 23, 1946; children: Gregory, Jeffrey, Douglas. Student, U. Notre Dame, 1944, Mo. Valley Coll., 1944-45; BS, U. N.Mex., 1947; MS, Ill. Inst. Tech., 1949; PhD, U. Ill., 1953. Mem. faculty U. N.Mex., Albuquerque, 1948-71, prof. civil engring., dir. Eric Wang Civil Engring. Rsch. Facility, 1961-70; rsch. assoc. U. Ill., Urbana, 1951-53; owner, cons. engr. Eugene Zwoyer & Assocs., Albuquerque, 1954-72; exec. dir., sec. ASCE, N.Y.C., 1972-82; pres. Am. Assn. Engring. Socs., N.Y.C., 1982-84; exec. v.p. T.Y. Lin Internat., San Francisco, 1984-86, pres., 1986-89; owner Eugene Zwoyer Cons. Engr., 1989—; chief oper. officer, treas. Polar Molecular Corp., Saginaw, Mich., 1990, exec. v.p., 1991-92. Trustee Small Bus. Research Corp., 1976-80; trustee Engring. Info., Inc., 1981-84; internat. trustee People-to-People Internat. 1974-86; v.p. World Fedn. Engring. Orgns., 1982-85. Served to lt. (j.g.) USN, 1944-46. Named Outstanding Engr. of Yr. Albuquerque chpt. N.Mex Soc. Profl. Engrs., 1969, One Who Served the Best Interests of the Constrn. Industry, Engring. News Record, 1980; recipient Disting. Alumnus award the Civil Engring. Alumni Assn. at U. Ill., 1979, Disting. Alumnus award Engring. Coll. Alumni Assn., U. N.Mex., 1982, Can.-Am. Civil Engring. Amity award Am. Soc. Civil Engrs., 1988, Award for Outstanding Profl. Contbns. and Leadership Civil Engring. U. N.Mex., 1989. Mem. AAAS, ASCE (dist. bd. dirs. 1968-71), NSPE, Am. Soc. Engring. Edn., Am. Concrete Inst., Nat. Acad. Code Adminstrn. (trustee, mem. exec. com. 1973-79), Engrs. Joint Coun. (bd. dirs. 1978-79), Engring. Soc. Commn. on Energy (bd. dirs. 1977-82), Sigma Xi, Sigma Tau, Chi Epsilon. Home: 6363 Christie Ave Apt 1326 Emeryville CA 94608-1940 Office: Ste 200C 1172 San Pablo Ave Berkeley CA 94706-2245

ZYGAS, KESTUTIS PAUL, architectural historian, educator; b. Kaunas, Lithuania, June 29, 1942; came to U.S., 1949; s. Kestutis Anthony and Ona (Matulevicius) Z.; m. Nijole Garla,June 6, 1964 (dec. June 1985); children: Jonas, Laura; m. Daiva Ciapaite, Mar. 6, 1992. AB, Harvard U., 1964, MArch, 1968; PhD, Cornell U., 1978. Asst. prof. U. So. Calif., L.A., 1977-84; assoc. prof. Ariz. State U., Tempe, 1984—. Author: Form Follows Form, 1981; contbr. articles on archtl. history to profl. jours. Mem. Soc. Archtl. Historians, Coll. Art Assn. Office: Ariz State U Sch Architecture Tempe AZ 85287

ZYGELMAN, BERNARD, physicist; b. Tirol, Austria, Jan. 6, 1952; came to U.S., 1959; s. Mordecai and Agnes Hinterholzer Z.; m. Judith Ann Villani, Sept. 24, 1983. BS, CCNY, 1975; PhD in Physics, CUNY, 1983. Postdoctoral fellow Harvard Coll. Observatory, Cambridge, Mass., 1983-86; rsch. assoc. Harvard Coll. Observatory, Cambridge, 1986-90; vis. rsch. physicist Inst. for Theoretical Physics, Santa Barbara, Calif., 1988; sci. cons. Spectral Scis., Inc., Burlington, Mass., 1990—; asst. prof. physics U. Nev., Las Vegas, 1990—. Contbr. articles to Physical Review Letters, Am. Inst. Physics Proceedings. Recipient Bernard Baruch scholarship CCNY, 1972. Mem. Am. Physical Soc. Office: U Nev Dept Physics Las Vegas NV 89154

ZYLSTRA, STEVEN GLENN, engineering research executive; b. Grand Rapids, Mich., Mar. 11, 1954; s. Gerrit Glen and Bonnie Marie (Luyk) Z. BS in Automotive Engring., Western Mich. U., 1978. Design engr. Ford Motor Co., Dearborn, Mich., 1978-80, Ford Aerospace & Communications Corp., Newport Beach, Calif., 1980-81; tech. mgr. Bendix Guidance Systems Div., Teterboro, N.J., 1981-82; dir. engring. Gen. Pneumatics Corp., Orange, N.J., 1982-84; gen. mgr. research Gen. Pneumatics Corp., Scottsdale, Ariz., 1984—; v.p., bd. dirs. Botanical Designs, Inc.; founder, chmn. emeritus, dir. Ariz. Innovation Network, Scottsdale, 1986—; spokesman Ariz. Focus on Tech., Scottsdale, 1986—; mem. Enterprise Network Strategic Planning Task Force, Phoenix, 1988—, Ariz. Gov.'s Sci. and Tech. Coun., 1990—, U.S. C. of C., Small Bus. Coun., 1991—; mem. admission com. Ariz. Tech. Incubator, 1992—; vice chmn. Ariz. Environ. Tech. Ind. Cluster, 1992—; bd. dirs. Rsch. Park, Ariz. State U., 1992—. Vol. Valley Big Bros. and Big Sisters Assn., 1990—. Mem. Soc. Automotive Engrs. (assoc.), Ariz. Small Bus. United (v.p., dir., organizer). Republican. Office: Gen Pneumatics Corp Western Rsch Ctr 7662 E Gray Rd Ste 107 Scottsdale AZ 85260-6910

ZYROFF, ELLEN SLOTOROFF, information scientist, classicist; b. Atlantic City, N.J., Aug. 1, 1946; d. Joseph George and Sylvia Beverly (Roth) Slotoroff; m. Jack Zyroff, June 21, 1970; children: Dena Rachel, David Aaron. AB, Barnard Coll., 1968; MA, The Johns Hopkins U., 1969, PhD, 1971; MS, Columbia U., 1973. Instr. The Johns Hopkins U., Balt., 1970-71, Yeshiva U., N.Y.C., 1971-72, Bklyn Coll., 1971-72; libr., instr. U. Calif., 1979, 81, 91, San Diego State U., 1981-85; prof. San Diego Mesa Coll., 1981—; dir. The Reference Desk Rsch. Svcs., La Jolla, Calif., 1983—; prin. libr. San Diego County Libr., 1985—; v.p. Archeol. Soc. Am., Balt., 1970-71; chairperson div. coms., Am. Library Assn., 1981--. Author: The Author's Apostrophe in Epic from Homer Through Lucan, 1971, Cooperative Library Instruction for Maximum Benefit, 1989. Pres. Women's Am. ORT, San Diego, 1979-81. Mem. ALA, Am. Philol. Assn., Calif. Libr. Assn., Am. Soc. Info. Sci., Am. Classical League, Toastmasters, Beta Phi Mu. Office: PO Box 12122 La Jolla CA 92039